40° 80° 120° 160°

ARCTIC OCEAN

ARCTIC OCEAN

SVALBARD (NORWAY)

Laptev Sea

Barents Sea

Bering Strait

FINLAND

Helsinki

Tallinn

ESTONIA

Riga

LATVIA

LITHUANIA

Vilnius

Minsk

BELARUS

Moscow

RUSSIAN FEDERATION

Sea of Okhotsk

Bering Sea

Kyiv

UKRAINE

SLOVAKIA

Bratislava

Budapest

HUNGARY

MOLDOVA

Chişinău

ROMANIA

Bucharest

SERBIA

BULGARIA

Sofia

Skopje

FYRM

GREECE

Athens

Black Sea

GEORGIA

Tbilisi

ARMENIA

Yerevan

AZERBAIJAN

Baku

Astana

KAZAKHSTAN

UZBEKISTAN

Tashkent

TURKMENISTAN

Asgabat

Bishkek

KYRGYZSTAN

Almaty

Dushanbe

TAJIKISTAN

Ulan Bator

MONGOLIA

DEMOCRATIC PEOPLE'S REPUBLIC OF KOREA

Sea of Japan

Beijing

Pyongyang

Seoul

REPUBLIC OF KOREA

JAPAN

Tokyo

40°

Ankara

TURKEY

Nicosia

CYPRUS

SYRIA

Beirut

LEBANON

Damascus

ISRAEL

Amman

JORDAN

Baghdad

IRAQ

Tehran

IRAN

AFGHANISTAN

Kabul

Islamabad

PAKISTAN

PEOPLE'S REPUBLIC OF CHINA

Mediterranean Sea

Sirte

Cairo

PALESTINIAN AUTONOMOUS AREAS

Kuwait City

KUWAIT

BAHRAIN

Manama

QATAR

Doha

Abu Dhabi

UAE

Muscat

OMAN

Riyadh

SAUDI ARABIA

Red Sea

EGYPT

New Delhi

NEPAL

Kathmandu

Thimphu

BHUTAN

BANGLADESH

Dhaka

INDIA

East China Sea

Taipei

TAIWAN

Tropic of Cancer

MACAO (CHINA)

HONG KONG (CHINA)

MYANMAR

Pyinmana

Yangon

Hanoi

Vientiane

LAOS

THAILAND

VIET NAM

Bangkok

CAMBODIA

Phnom-Penh

South China Sea

Manila

PHILIPPINES

Philippine Sea

NORTHERN MARIANA ISLANDS (USA)

GUAM (USA)

PACIFIC OCEAN

CHAD

Khartoum

SUDAN

ERITREA

Asmara

San'a

YEMEN

DJIBOUTI

Addis Ababa

ETHIOPIA

SOMALIA

N'Djamena

CENTRAL AFRICAN REPUBLIC

Bay of Bengal

SRI LANKA

Colombo

Sri Jayawardenepura

MALDIVES

Kuala Lumpur

Putrajaya

MALAYSIA

SINGAPORE

BRUNEI

Bandar Seri Begawan

PALAU

MARSHALL ISLANDS

FEDERATED STATES OF MICRONESIA

NAURU

KIRIBATI

DEMOCRATIC REPUBLIC OF THE CONGO

UGANDA

Kampala

KENYA

Nairobi

Mogadishu

RWANDA

Kigali

BURUNDI

Bujumbura

Kinshasa

Victoria

SEYCHELLES

Dodoma

Dar es Salaam

TANZANIA

BRITISH INDIAN OCEAN TERRITORY (UNITED KINGDOM)

Jakarta

INDONESIA

PAPUA NEW GUINEA

Dili

TIMOR-LESTE

Port Moresby

Honiara

SOLOMON ISLANDS

TUVALU

TOKELAU (NEW ZEALAND)

ANGOLA

Lubumbashi

ZAMBIA

Lusaka

MALAWI

Lilongwe

Moroni

COMOROS

MAYOTTE (FRANCE)

Harare

ZIMBABWE

MOZAMBIQUE

Mozambique Channel

MADAGASCAR

Antananarivo

MAURITIUS

Port Louis

RÉUNION (FRANCE)

INDIAN OCEAN

COCOS ISLANDS (AUSTRALIA)

CHRISTMAS ISLAND (AUSTRALIA)

Coral Sea

VANUATU

Port Vila

WALLIS AND FUTUNA ISLANDS (FRANCE)

SAMOA

FIJI

Suva

AMERICAN SAMOA (USA)

NIUE (NZ)

TONGA

NAMIBIA

BOTSWANA

Gaborone

Pretoria

Maputo

Mbabane

SWAZILAND

LESOTHO

Maseru

SOUTH AFRICA

AUSTRALIA

NEW CALEDONIA (FRANCE)

NORFOLK ISLAND (AUSTRALIA)

Canberra

Tasman Sea

NEW ZEALAND

Wellington

40°

ANTARCTICA

40° 80° 120°

Africa South of the Sahara 2008

Africa South of the Sahara 2008

37th Edition

LONDON AND NEW YORK

First published 1971
Thirty-Seventh Edition 2008

Albert House, 1–4 Singer Street, London EC2A 4BQ, United Kingdom
(Routledge is an imprint of the Taylor & Francis Group, an Informa business)

ISBN13: 978-1-85743-421-7
ISBN10: 1-85743-421-8
ISSN 0065-3896

Library of Congress Catalog Card Number 78-112271

Editor: Iain Frame

Regional Organizations Editors: Catriona Appeatu Holman, Helen Canton

Statistics Editor: Philip McIntyre

Assistant Editors: Kim Chamberlain, Adrian Reynolds, Anna Thomas, Gareth Vaughan

Contributing Editor (Commodities): Simon Chapman

Editorial Clerical Assistant: Charley McCartney

Associate Editor, Directory Research: James Middleton

Series Editor: Joanne Maher

Typeset in New Century Schoolbook

Typeset by Data Standards Limited, Frome, Somerset

Printed and bound in Great Britain by Polestar Wheatons, Exeter

FOREWORD

The 37th edition of AFRICA SOUTH OF THE SAHARA provides coverage of a period of notable developments in the sub-Saharan region. In March 2007 the Ivorian President, Laurent Gbagbo, and the Secretary-General of the Forces nouvelles, Guillaume Soro Kigbafori, agreed upon a detailed timetable for the resolution of the ongoing political crisis that had effectively divided the country in two. Also in March in neighbouring Guinea a period of severe industrial and political unrest was brought to an end, following President Lansana Conté's decision to appoint a new Prime Minister selected from a list supplied by the country's trade unions and political opposition. However, there was continued turbulence in Zimbabwe as the annual rate of inflation reached 7,635% in July. Meanwhile, after the holding of legislative and presidential elections in Mauritania during November 2006–March 2007, the Military Council for Justice and Democracy relinquished power and restored democratically selected institutions to that country. Also during the year under review, multi-party elections were held in the Democratic Republic of the Congo for the first time since independence from Belgium in 1960, while a peace agreement was signed between the Chadian authorities and the rebel Front uni pour le changement démocratique, members of which organization were subsequently incorporated into the Chadian Government. Nevertheless, instability persisted on that country's borders with the Central African Republic and Sudan, and international attention in this last remained predominantly focused on the deteriorating conditions in Darfur, where it was estimated that more than 2m. people had been displaced since 2003. It was, nevertheless, hoped that stability could be brought to the region by the deployment of a 26,000-strong joint African Union-UN peace-keeping mission, which was scheduled to be fully operational there by the end of 2007. Elections held in Nigeria, Africa's most populous nation, where for the first time power was to be transferred between democratically elected civilian leaders, were widely criticized by international observers, but resulted in the installation of a new President, Umara Musa Yar'Adua. Elsewhere on the continent, Yahya Jammeh, Levy Patrick Mwanawasa, Marc Ravalomanana, Abdoulaye Wade and Amadou Toumani Touré secured further presidential terms in The Gambia, Zambia, Madagascar, Senegal and Mali, respectively.

These events, together with the year's main political and economic developments in each of the 52 states that comprise Africa south of the Sahara, are comprehensively narrated and examined. Readers' perspectives are further expanded by the General Survey, which provides an in-depth analysis of current economic trends, an examination of health and medical issues, an assessment of aid and development initiatives over the past 100 years, and an exploration of the phenomenon of failed states and the repercussions of, and responses to, state failure in sub-Saharan Africa. A new essay discusses the People's Republic of China's increasing political and economic interest in the African continent.

In addition to contributions by specialist authors, researchers and commentators, all statistical and directory material in the new edition has been extensively updated, revised and expanded. A calendar of the key political events of 2006–07 provides convenient rapid reference to the year's main developments. Extensive coverage of international organizations and research bodies active in Africa is included, together with detailed background information on the continent's major agricultural and mineral commodities.

The Editors are once again thankful to all the contributors for their articles and advice, and to the numerous governments and organizations that have returned questionnaires and provided statistical and other information.

September 2007

ACKNOWLEDGEMENTS

The Editors gratefully acknowledge the interest and co-operation of the many national statistical and information offices and embassies and high commissions, whose valued assistance in updating the material contained in AFRICA SOUTH OF THE SAHARA is greatly appreciated.

We acknowledge particular indebtedness for permission to reproduce material from the following publications: the United Nations' *Demographic Yearbook, Statistical Yearbook, International Trade Statistics Yearbook* and *Industrial Commodity Statistics Yearbook*; the United Nations Educational, Scientific and Cultural Organization's *Statistical Yearbook*; the International Labour Office's statistical database and *Yearbook of Labour Statistics*; the International Monetary Fund's statistical database, *International Financial Statistics* and *Government Finance Statistics Yearbook*; the World Tourism Organization's *Yearbook of Tourism Statistics*; the Food and Agriculture Organization of the United Nations' statistical database; and *The Military Balance 2007*, a publication of the International Institute for Strategic Studies, Arundel House, 13–15 Arundel Street, London, WC2R 3DX, United Kingdom. We acknowledge *La Zone Franc* and the regular publications of the Banque centrale des états de l'Afrique de l'ouest and of the Banque des états de l'Afrique centrale as the sources of some of our financial information on francophone Africa.

The articles on Saint Helena, Ascension and Tristan da Cunha make use of material from *The Commonwealth Yearbook*, with the kind permission of TSO (The Stationery Office).

HEALTH AND WELFARE STATISTICS: SOURCES AND DEFINITIONS

Total fertility rate Source: WHO Statistical Information System. The number of children that would be born per woman, assuming no female mortality at child-bearing ages and the age-specific fertility rates of a specified country and reference period.

Under-5 mortality rate Source: WHO Statistical Information System. Defined by WHO as the probability of a child born in a specific year or period dying before reaching the age of five, if subject to the age-specific mortality rates of that year or period.

HIV/AIDS Source: UNAIDS. Estimated percentage of adults aged 15 to 49 years living with HIV/AIDS. < indicates 'fewer than'.

Health expenditure Source: WHO Statistical Information System.

US $ per head (PPP)

International dollar estimates, derived by dividing local currency units by an estimate of their purchasing power parity (PPP) compared with the US dollar. PPPs are the rates of currency conversion that equalize the purchasing power of different currencies by eliminating the differences in price levels between countries.

% of GDP

GDP levels for OECD countries follow the most recent UN System of National Accounts. For non-OECD countries a value was estimated by utilizing existing UN, IMF and World Bank data.

Public expenditure

Government health-related outlays plus expenditure by social schemes compulsorily affiliated with a sizeable share of the population, and extrabudgetary funds allocated to health services. Figures include grants or loans provided by international agencies, other national authorities, and sometimes commercial banks.

Access to water and sanitation Source: WHO/UNICEF Joint Monitoring Programme on Water Supply and Sanitation (JMP) (Mid-Term Assessment, 2004). Defined in terms of the percentage of the population using improved facilities in terms of the type of technology and levels of service afforded. For water, this includes house connections, public standpipes, boreholes with handpumps, protected dug wells, protected spring and rainwater collection; allowance is also made for other locally defined technologies. Sanitation is defined to include connection to a sewer or septic tank system, pour-flush latrine, simple pit or ventilated improved pit latrine, again with allowance for acceptable local technologies. Access to water and sanitation does not imply that the level of service or quality of water is 'adequate' or 'safe'.

Human Development Index (HDI) Source: UNDP, *Human Development Report* (2006). A summary of human development measured by three basic dimensions: prospects for a long and healthy life, measured by life expectancy at birth; knowledge, measured by adult literacy rate (two-thirds' weight) and the combined gross enrolment ratio in primary, secondary and tertiary education (one-third weight); and standard of living, measured by GDP per head (PPP US $). The index value obtained lies between zero and one. A value above 0.8 indicates high human development, between 0.5 and 0.8 medium human development, and below 0.5 low human development. A centralized data source for all three dimensions was not available for all countries. In some cases other data sources were used to calculate a substitute value; however, this was excluded from the ranking. Other countries, including non-UNDP members, were excluded from the HDI altogether. In total, 177 countries were ranked for 2004.

CONTENTS

THE CONTRIBUTORS

J. A. Allan. Professor of Geography, School of Oriental and African Studies, University of London.

Ike Anya. Specialist Registrar in Public Health Medicine, Bristol North Primary Care Trust, and Lecturer at the London School of Hygiene and Tropical Medicine.

L. Berry. Former Professor of Geography, University of Dar es Salaam.

E. A. Boateng. Environmental consultant and educationalist.

Richard A. Bradshaw. Professor of History, Centre College, Kentucky.

Sir Mervyn Brown. Former British Ambassador in Madagascar. Member, Académie Malgache.

Richard Brown. Former Dean, School of African and Asian Studies, University of Sussex at Brighton.

Greg Cameron. Assistant Professor of Political Science, University of Asmara.

Marisé Castro. Researcher, Amnesty International, International Secretariat, London.

Christopher Clapham. Professor of Politics and International Relations, University of Lancaster.

Phil Clark. Post-Doctoral Research Fellow, Transitional Justice Institute, University of Ulster.

John I. Clarke. Professor of Geography, University of Durham.

Walter S. Clarke. Senior Advisor for Civil-Military Co-operation, Global Center for Disaster Management and Humanitarian Action, College of Public Health, University of South Florida.

Julian Cooke. Editor of the *Anglo-Malagasy Society Newsletter*.

João Gomes Cravinho. Lecturer in International Relations, University of Coímbra.

Samuel Crowe. Writer specializing in African public health issues.

Pierre Englebert. Assistant Professor of Politics, Pomona College, Claremont, California.

Juan Fandos-Rius. Encyclopaedist and historian of the Central African Republic.

Marek Garztecki. Writer specializing in African political and economic issues.

Edward George. Writer specializing in sub-Saharan African political and economic issues.

Patrick Gilkes. Writer on Africa and the Third World for the BBC External Services.

Pierre Gourou. Professor of Geography, Université Libre de Bruxelles and Collège de France, Paris.

R. J. Harrison Church. Late Professor of Geography, London School of Economics.

David Hilling. Senior Lecturer in Geography, Royal Holloway and Bedford New College, University of London.

Edith Hodgkinson. Writer specializing in the economies of developing countries.

A. MacGregor Hutcheson. Lecturer in Geography, Aberdeen College of Education.

Michael Jennings. Lecturer in International Development and African History, Centre for Development Studies, University of Wales, Swansea.

Zachary D. Kaufman JD candidate, Yale Law School, and Marshall Scholar and DPhil candidate, International Relations, University of Oxford.

George Kay. Head of the Department of Geography and Recreation Studies, Staffordshire University.

B. W. Langlands. Late Professor of Geography, Makerere University College, Kampala.

Bernard Lanne. Late Editor-in-Chief of *La Documentation française*, Paris.

G. C. Last. Former Adviser, Ethiopian Ministry of Education and Fine Arts.

I. M. Lewis. Professor of Anthropology, London School of Economics and Political Science.

Akin L. Mabogunje. Former Professor of Geography, University of Ibadan.

T. C. McCaskie. Lecturer in the Social History of West Africa in the Twentieth Century, Centre of West African Studies, University of Birmingham.

Hugh Macmillan. Former Professor of History, University of Transkei.

François Misser. Writer specializing in the business and economic affairs of developing countries.

Peter K. Mitchell. Honorary Senior Research Fellow, Centre of West African Studies, University of Birmingham.

W. T. W. Morgan. Senior Lecturer, Department of Geography, University of Durham.

Gregory Mthembu-Salter. Writer specializing in the political and economic affairs of African countries.

Katharine Murison. Editor of *Africa South of the Sahara*, 2001–04.

Thomas Ofcansky. Writer specializing in African political and economic issues.

J. D. Omer-Cooper. Late Professor of History, University of Otago.

Quentin Outram. Senior Lecturer in Economics, Leeds University Business School, University of Leeds.

René Pélissier. Author specializing in contemporary Spanish-speaking and Portuguese-speaking Africa.

Luisa Handem Piette. Writer specializing in African political and development issues.

Alan Rake. Former Managing Editor of *African Business* and *New African* magazines, London.

Sarah Rich Dorman. Lecturer in African and International Politics, University of Edinburgh.

Andrew D. Roberts. Former Professor of the History of Africa, School of Oriental and African Studies, University of London.

Christopher Saunders. Department of Historical Studies, University of Cape Town.

Gerhard Seibert. Researcher, Centro de Estudos Africanos e Asiáticos, Lisbon.

Miles Smith-Morris. Writer specializing in developing countries.

Donald L. Sparks. Professor of International Economics, The Citadel, Charleston, South Carolina, and Visiting Professor of Economics, Innsbruck Summer Program.

David Styan. Lecturer in Politics, Birkbeck College, University of London.

Richard Synge. Writer and journalist specializing in African political and economic issues.

Ian Taylor. Professor of International Relations, University of St Andrews.

Nadège Tchotchoe. Researcher, Royal African Society.

António Teixeira. Political and economic analyst of lusophone African countries.

Virginia Thompson. Writer specializing in francophone Africa.

Charlotte Vaillant. Economist specializing in francophone Africa.

Linda Van Buren. Writer specializing in the business and economic affairs of African countries.

Sarah Vaughan. Honorary Fellow, School of Social and Political Studies, University of Edinburgh.

Manickam Venkataraman. Associate Professor of Political Science and International Relations, Addis Ababa University.

Philip Verwimp. Co-director of the Households in Conflict Network and Lecturer in Development Economics, Institute of Social Studies, The Hague.

Geoffrey J. Williams. Former Professor of Geography, University of Zambia.

Paul D. Williams. Associate Professor of International Security, University of Warwick, and Visiting Associate Professor, Elliot School of International Affairs, George Washington University.

John A. Wiseman. Late Senior Lecturer in Politics, University of Newcastle.

Peter Woodward. Professor of Politics, University of Reading.

Ralph Young. Senior Lecturer, Department of Government, University of Manchester.

ABBREVIATIONS

Acad.	Academician; Academy
ACP	African, Caribbean and Pacific (States)
ADB	African Development Bank
ADF	African Development Fund
Adm.	Admiral
Admin.	Administration; Administrative; Administrator
AEC	African Economic Community
AG	Aktiengesellschaft (limited company)
AGOA	African Growth and Opportunity Act
a.i.	ad interim
AIDS	acquired immunodeficiency syndrome
AM	Amplitude Modulation
Apdo	Apartado (Post Box)
Apt	Apartment
ARV	advanced retroviral
Ass.	Assembly
Asscn	Association
Assoc.	Associate
Asst	Assistant
AU	African Union
Aug.	August
auth.	authorized
Av.	Avenida (Avenue)
Ave	Avenue
BCEAO	Banque centrale des états de l'Afrique de l'ouest
Bd	Board
b/d	barrels per day
BEAC	Banque des états de l'Afrique centrale
Bldg(s)	Building(s)
Blvd	Boulevard
BOAD	Banque Ouest-Africaine de développement
BP	Boîte Postale (Post Box)
br.(s)	branch(es)
Brig.	Brigadier
C	Centigrade; Cedi(s) (Ghana currency)
c.	circa
cap.	capital
Capt.	Captain
CEMAC	Communauté économique et monétaire en Afrique centrale
Cen.	Central
CEO	Chief Executive Officer
cf.	confer (compare)
CFA	Communauté financière africaine; Coopération financière en Afrique centrale
Chair.	Chairman/woman
Cie	Compagnie
c.i.f.	cost, insurance and freight
C-in-C	Commander-in-Chief
circ.	circulation
cm	centimetre(s)
cnr	corner
c/o	care of
Co	Company; County
Col	Colonel
Comm.	Commission
Commdr	Commander
Commr	Commissioner
Conf.	Conference
Confed.	Confederation
COO	Chief Operating Officer
Corpn	Corporation
CP	Caixa Postal, Case Postale (Post Box)
Cpl	Corporal
Cttee	Committee
cu	cubic
cwt	hundredweight
Dec.	December
Del.	Delegate
Dem.	Democratic
Dep.	Deputy
dep.	deposits
Dept	Department
Devt	Development
Dir	Director
Div.	Division(al)
Dr	Doctor
Dr.	Drive
Dra	Doctora
dwt	dead weight tons
E	East; Eastern; Emalangeni (Swaziland currency)
€	Euro (currency)
EAC	East African Community
EC	European Community
ECA	Economic Commission for Africa (UN)
ECOWAS	Economic Community of West African States
ECU	European Currency Unit(s)
Ed.(s)	Editor(s)
EDF	European Development Fund
edn	edition
EEZ	Exclusive Economic Zone
e.g.	exempli gratia (for example)
EIB	European Investment Bank
Eng.	Engineer; Engineering
EP	Empresa Pública
EPZ	Export Processing Zone
ESAF	Enhanced Structural Adjustment Facility
est.	established; estimate; estimated
etc.	etcetera
EU	European Union
excl.	excluding
Exec.	Executive
exhbn(s)	exhibition(s)
Ext.	Extension
f.	founded
FAO	Food and Agriculture Organization
f.a.s.	free alongside
Feb.	February
Fed.	Federation; Federal
FG	Guinea Franc
FIDES	Fonds d'investissement et de développement économique et social
Flt	Flight
FMD	foot-and-mouth disease
FMG	Malagasy Franc
fmr(ly)	former(ly)
f.o.b.	free on board
Fr	Father
Fr.	Franc(s)
Fri.	Friday
ft	foot (feet)
FTA	free trade agreement/area
g	gram(s)
GDP	gross domestic product
Gen.	General
GMO(s)	genetically modified organism(s)
GMT	Greenwich Mean Time
GNI	gross national income
GNP	gross national product
Gov.	Governor
Govt	Government
GPO	General Post Office
grt	gross registered ton(s)
GWh	gigawatt hour(s)
ha	hectare(s)
HIPC	heavily indebted poor country
HIV	human immunodeficiency virus
hl	hectolitre(s)
HM	His/Her Majesty
HPAI	highly pathogenic avian influenza
HQ	Headquarters
HYV	high-yielding variety
ibid.	ibidem (from the same source)
IBRD	International Bank for Reconstruction and Development (World Bank)
ICT	information and communication technology
IDA	International Development Association
IDPs	Internally Displaced Persons
i.e.	id est (that is to say)
IGAD	Intergovernmental Authority on Development
ILO	International Labour Organization/Office
IMF	International Monetary Fund
in	inch (inches)
Inc	Incorporated
incl.	include, including

Ind.	Independent
Ing.	Engineer
Insp.	Inspector
Inst.	Institute
Int.	International
Is	Islands
ISIC	International Standard Industrial Classification
ITUC	International Trade Union Confederation
Jan.	January
Jr	Junior
Jt	Joint
K	Kwacha (Malawi and Zambia currencies)
kg	kilogram(s)
km	kilometre(s)
kW	kilowatt(s)
kWh	kilowatt hour(s)
lb	pound(s)
Lda	Limitada (limited company)
LDCs	Least Developed Countries
Le.	Leone (Sierra Leone currency)
LNG	Liquefied natural gas
LPG	Liquefied petroleum gas
Lt	Lieutenant
Ltd	Limited
M	Maloti (Lesotho currency)
m	metre(s)
m.	million
Maj.	Major
Man.	Manager; Managing
MDG	Millennium Development Goal
MDRI	multilateral debt relief initiative
Me	Maître
mem.	member
MFA	Multi-fibre Arrangement
Mfg	Manufacturing
mfrs	manufacturers
mg	milligram(s)
Mgr	Monseigneur, Monsignor
Mil.	Military
Mlle	Mademoiselle
mm	millimetre(s)
Mme	Madame
Mon.	Monday
MP	Member of Parliament
MSS	manuscripts
Mt	Mount
MV	Motor Vessel
MW	megawatt(s); medium wave
MWh	megawatt hour(s)
N	North; Northern
₦	Naira (Nigerian currency)
NA	National Association (banking)
n.a.	not available
Nat.	National
NCO	Non-Commissioned Officer
NEPAD	New Partnership for Africa's Development
n.e.s.	not elsewhere specified
NGO	non-governmental organization
No.	number
Nov.	November
nr	near
nrt	net registered ton(s)
NV	Naamloze Vennootschap (limited company)
OAU	Organization of African Unity
Oct.	October
OECD	Organisation for Economic Co-operation and Development
OIC	Organization of the Islamic Conference
OMVS	Organisation pour la mise en valeur du fleuve Sénégal
OPEC	Organization of the Petroleum Exporting Countries
opp.	opposite
Org.(s)	Organization(s)
oz	ounce(s)
P	Pula (Botswana currency)
p.	page
p.a.	per annum
Parl.	Parliament(ary)
Perm.	Permanent
pl.	place (square)
PLC	Public Limited Company
PMB	Private Mail Bag
PO	Post Office
POB	Post Office Box
Pres.	President
PRGF	Poverty Reduction and Growth Facility
Prin.	Principal
Prof.	Professor
Propr	Proprietor
Prov.	Province; Provincial
Pte	Private
Pty	Proprietary
p.u.	paid up
publ.(s)	publication(s); published
Publr	Publisher
Pvt.	Private
q.v.	quod vide (to which refer)
R	Rand (South African currency)
Rd	Road
regd	registered
reorg.	reorganized
Rep.	Representative
Repub.	Republic
res	reserves
retd	retired
Rev.	Reverend
Rm	Room
RMS	Royal Mail Steamer
RN	Royal Navy
Rs	Rupee(s) (Mauritius currency)
Rt	Right
S	South; Southern
SA	Société Anonyme, Sociedad Anónima (limited company); South Africa
SADC	Southern African Development Community
SARL	Sociedade Anônima de Responsabilidade Limitada (limited company)
Sat.	Saturday
SDR	Special Drawing Right(s)
Sec.	Secretary
Secr.	Secretariat
Sept.	September
Sgt	Sergeant
SITC	Standard International Trade Classification
SME	small and medium-sized enterprises
Soc.	Society
Sq.	Square
sq	square (in measurements)
SR	Seychelles Rupee(s)
Sr	Senior
St	Street; Saint, San, Santo
Sta	Santa
Ste	Sainte
STI(s)	sexually transmitted infection(s)
Stn	Station
Sun.	Sunday
Supt	Superintendent
tech.	technical, technology
trans.	translator, translated
Treas.	Treasurer
TV	Television
UA	Unit(s) of Account
UEE	Unidade Económica Estatal
UEMOA	Union économique et monétaire ouest-africaine
UK	United Kingdom
ul.	ulitsa (street)
UM	Ouguiya(s) (Mauritania currency)
UN	United Nations
UNAIDS	United Nations Joint Programme on HIV/AIDS
UNCTAD	United Nations Conference on Trade and Development
UNDP	United Nations Development Programme
UNESCO	United Nations Educational, Scientific and Cultural Organization
UNHCR	United Nations High Commissioner for Refugees
Univ.	University
UNWTO	World Tourism Organization
US(A)	United States (of America)
USAID	United States Agency for International Development
USSR	Union of Soviet Socialist Republics
Vol.(s)	Volume(s)
W	West; Western
WHO	World Health Organization
WSSD	World Summit on Sustainable Development
WTO	World Trade Organization
yr(s)	year(s)

INTERNATIONAL TELEPHONE CODES

To make international calls to telephone and fax numbers listed in *Africa South of the Sahara*, dial the international code of the country from which you are calling, followed by the appropriate country code for the organization you wish to call (listed below), followed by the area code (if applicable) and telephone or fax number listed in the entry.

	Country code	+ GMT*
Angola	244	+1
Ascension Island	247	0
Benin	229	+1
Botswana	267	+2
British Indian Ocean Territory	246	+5
Burkina Faso	226	0
Burundi	257	+2
Cameroon	237	+1
Cape Verde	238	-1
The Central African Republic	236	+1
Chad	235	+1
The Comoros	269	+3
Congo, Democratic Republic	243	+1
Congo, Republic	242	+1
Côte d'Ivoire	225	0
Djibouti	253	+3
Equatorial Guinea	240	+1
Eritrea	291	+3
Ethiopia	251	+3
Gabon	241	+1
The Gambia	220	0
Ghana	233	0
Guinea	224	0
Guinea-Bissau	245	0
Kenya	254	+3
Lesotho	266	+2
Liberia	231	0
Madagascar	261	+3
Malawi	265	+2
Mali	223	0
Mauritania	222	0
Mauritius	230	+4
Mayotte	262	+3
Mozambique	258	+2
Namibia	264	+2
Niger	227	+1
Nigeria	234	+1
Réunion	262	+4
Rwanda	250	+2
Saint Helena	290	0
São Tomé and Príncipe	239	0
Senegal	221	0
Seychelles	248	+4
Sierra Leone	232	0
Somalia	252	+3
South Africa	27	+2
Sudan	249	+2
Swaziland	268	+2
Tanzania	255	+3
Togo	228	0
Tristan da Cunha	290	0
Uganda	256	+3
Zambia	260	+2
Zimbabwe	263	+2

*Time difference in hours + Greenwich Mean Time (GMT). The times listed compare the standard (winter) times. Some countries may adopt Summer (Daylight Saving) Times—i.e. + 1 hour—for part of the year.

EXPLANATORY NOTE ON THE DIRECTORY SECTION

The Directory section of each chapter is arranged under the following headings, where they apply:

THE CONSTITUTION

THE GOVERNMENT
- HEAD OF STATE
- CABINET/COUNCIL OF MINISTERS
- EXECUTIVE
- MINISTRY ADDRESSES

LEGISLATURE

ELECTION COMMISSION

POLITICAL ORGANIZATIONS

DIPLOMATIC REPRESENTATION

JUDICIAL SYSTEM

RELIGION

THE PRESS

PUBLISHERS

BROADCASTING AND COMMUNICATIONS

FINANCE
- CENTRAL BANK
- NATIONAL BANKS
- COMMERCIAL BANKS
- DEVELOPMENT BANKS
- MERCHANT BANKS
- SAVINGS BANKS
- INVESTMENT BANKS
- FINANCIAL INSTITUTIONS
- STOCK EXCHANGE
- INSURANCE

TRADE AND INDUSTRY
- GOVERNMENT AGENCIES
- DEVELOPMENT ORGANIZATIONS
- CHAMBERS OF COMMERCE
- INDUSTRIAL AND TRADE ASSOCIATIONS
- EMPLOYERS' ORGANIZATIONS
- UTILITIES
- MAJOR COMPANIES
- CO-OPERATIVES
- TRADE UNIONS

TRANSPORT
- RAILWAYS
- ROADS
- INLAND WATERWAYS
- SHIPPING
- CIVIL AVIATION

TOURISM

DEFENCE

EDUCATION

POLITICAL EVENTS IN AFRICA SOUTH OF THE SAHARA, 2006–07

SEPTEMBER 2006

5 **Burundi** Second Vice-President Alice Nzomukunda resigned and was replaced by Marina Barampama. A ministerial reorganization was subsequently effected in which Denise Sinankwa was appointed as Minister of Finance.

6 **Cape Verde** A minor government reshuffle was announced.

7 **Côte d'Ivoire** Prime Minister Charles Konan Banny tendered his resignation and that of his Government, following the death of three people as a result of the illegal unloading of toxic waste from a Panamanian-registered vessel. On 16 September a new Council of Ministers was unveiled; the Minister of Transport and the Minister of the Environment, Water and Forestry were replaced while the remaining portfolios were unaltered.

11 **Ethiopia** A minor governmental reorganization was effected.

16 **Togo** Edem Kodjo was replaced as Prime Minister by Yawovi Madji Agboyibo, the leader of the opposition Comité d'action pour le renouveau.

20 **South Africa** A High Court Judge dismissed charges of fraud and corruption against former Deputy President Jacob Zuma.

22 **Cameroon** A government reshuffle was carried out in which five ministers were dismissed.

The Gambia Incumbent President Col (retd) Alhaji Yahya A. J. J. Jammeh won 67.33% of the votes cast in a presidential election, securing a further five-year term in office.

23 **The Democratic Republic of the Congo** The new Assemblée nationale was inaugurated following the legislative elections of July.

28 **Zambia** At the presidential election Levy Patrick Mwanawasa secured a second term in office winning 42.98% of the votes cast. His nearest opponent was Michael C. Sata, who secured 29.37% of the vote. In concurrently held legislative elections the Movement for Multi-party Democracy secured 75 out of 150 seats in the National Assembly.

OCTOBER 2006

5 **São Tomé and Príncipe** João Paulo Cassandra took office as the President of the Provisional Government of the Autonomous Region of Príncipe.

10 **Zambia** A new Cabinet was unveiled, including George Mpombo, who was appointed as Minister of Defence. Mundia Sikatana assumed the role of Minister of Foreign Affairs, replacing Ronnie Shikapwasha, who was awarded the home affairs portfolio.

11 **The Democratic Republic of the Congo** A reorganization of the Government was carried out, following the resignation of several ministers to assume positions in the newly inaugurated Assemblée nationale; 12 new ministers were appointed.

13 **Somalia** Three members of the Government were dismissed, although the key portfolios remained unchanged.

15 **Tanzania** A cabinet reshuffle took place in which 10 ministers were reassigned to new portfolios, including the Minister of Home Affairs, Capt. John Zefania Chiligati, who was replaced by Joseph James Mungai, hitherto the Minister of Agriculture, Food Security and Co-operatives; Chiligati became the Minister of Labour, Employment and Youth Development, replacing Prof. Jumanne Abdallah Maghembe.

20 **The Gambia** President Jammeh unveiled his new Cabinet, retaining 10 members of the former administration. The most notable appointment was that of Maba Jobe, who replaced Lamin Kaba Bajo as Secretary of State for Foreign Affairs.

29 **The Democratic Republic of the Congo** In the second round of the presidential election Joseph Kabila Kabange received 58.05% of the votes cast, thus defeating his opponent Jean-Pierre Bemba Gombo.

NOVEMBER 2006

1 **Côte d'Ivoire** The UN Security Council adopted Resolution 1721 endorsing the African Union's Peace and Security Council's earlier decision to extend the mandate of the President and the Prime Minister until 31 October 2007.

2 **Nigeria** The Minister of Aviation, Prof. Babalola Borishade, was dismissed after a passenger jet carrying several high-ranking Nigerian officials crashed on 29 October leaving only nine survivors. Borishade was replaced by Femi Fani-Kayode, hitherto the Minister of Culture and Tourism. Among the fatalities in the crash was the Spritual Head of the Muslim community, Alhaji Mohamed Maccido. Col Muhammadu Sa'ad Abubakar was subsequently named as Maccido's successor.

14 **South Africa** The National Assembly approved new civil union legislation that legalized same-sex marriages.

19 **Mauritania** Legislative elections were held, with a second round of voting on 3 December, at which the Rally of Democratic Forces took 15 seats, the Union of Progressive Forces nine and the Republican Party for Democracy and Renewal seven, while the Popular Progressive Alliance and the Centrist Reformists both secured five seats.

23 **Senegal** President Abdoulaye Wade effected a governmental reorganization in which five members of the opposition were appointed to ministerial posts.

26 **Guinea-Bissau** President João Bernardo Vieira dismissed the Minister of the Interior, Ernesto de Carvalho, later appointing Dionísio Cabi to that role.

31 **Zambia** A minor cabinet reshuffle was carried out.

DECEMBER 2006

3 **Madagascar** Incumbent Marc Ravalomanana secured 54.79% of votes cast in the first-round of the presidential election, thus obviating the requirement for a second round of voting. His closest rival was Jean Lahiniriko, who took 11.65% of the votes.

17 **Gabon** At a general election the Parti démocratique gabonais retained power in the Assemblée nationale, securing 82 of the 120 seats available. However, the elections were marred by fraud and logistical problems

and demands were made for a new ballot to be conducted.

22 **Guinea** A government reshuffle was effected in which three ministers were dismissed. A new Minister of the Interior and Security was also appointed following the death of the incumbent, Ibrahima Deing.

29 **Cape Verde** José Brito was appointed Minister of the Economy, Growth and Competitiveness following the resignation of João Pereira Silva.

30 **The Democratic Republic of the Congo** Following his re-election in October, President Kabila appointed Antoine Gizenga as Prime Minister, who was tasked with forming a new Government.

JANUARY 2007

10 **Nigeria** A major government reshuffle took place in which almost one-third of the ministries were dissolved or merged, reportedly to simplify the administration's structure and improve its efficiency ahead of the forthcoming elections. Three new appointments were made during the reorganization, including that of Thomas I. Aguiyi-Ironsi to the defence portfolio.

11 **Tanzania** Several changes to the cabinet were implemented following the death of Juma Akukweti, the Minister of State in the Prime Minister's Office, responsible for Parliamentary Affairs; Dr Batilda Burian was named as his replacement. Bernard Kamillius Membe also assumed the recently vacated foreign affairs and international co-operation portfolio.

18 **Liberia** Speaker Edwin Snowe lost a vote of 'no confidence' in the House of Representatives and was dismissed, having been accused of contravening parliamentary laws.

19 **The Democratic Republic of the Congo** Elections were held to the newly reinstated Sénat, at which the Parti du peuple pour la reconstruction et la démocratie secured 22 of the 108 seats available. The Mouvement de libération du Congo received 14 seats, while the Forces du renouveau and the Rassemblement congolais pour la démocratie each received seven.

Madagascar Ravalomanana was sworn in as President; the following day he appointed Gen. Charles Rabemananjara as Prime Minister, who named his new Council of Ministers later that month. Most notably, Harison Edmond Randriarimanana was appointed to head the newly created Ministry of the Economy, Planning, the Private Sector and Commerce.

25 **The Gambia** The ruling Alliance for Patriotic Reorientation and Construction won 42 of the 48 directly-elected seats at legislative elections, while the United Democratic Party received just four.

27 **Guinea** President Gen. Lansana Conté agreed to nominate a new Prime Minister, ending 18 days of nation-wide industrial action.

FEBRUARY 2007

5 **The Democratic Republic of the Congo** A new administration was unveiled. Among the most notable appointments were Denis Kalume Numbi as Minister of State, in charge of the Interior, Decentralization and Security and Antipas Mbusa Nyamwisi as Minister of State, in charge of Foreign Relations and International Co-operation, while Athanse Matenda Kyelu assumed the post of Minister of Finance.

7 **Somalia** Prime Minister Ali Mohammed Ghedi effected a cabinet reshuffle; four ministers were redesignated, including the Deputy Prime Minister and Minister of Interior and Security, Hussein Mohamed Aidid, who was demoted to the position of Minister of Public Works and Housing.

Zimbabwe President Robert Mugabe appointed a new Government.

9 **Guinea** President Conté announced the selection of Eugène Camara as Prime Minister. The appointment was rejected by the trade unions and the political opposition and violence once again broke out. On 26 February Conté announced that he would select a Prime Minister from a list of candidates supplied by the trade unions and opposition parties.

10 **Burundi** Barampama was dismissed from the post of Second Vice-President. Gabriel Ntiszerana, hitherto the Governor of the central bank, assumed the position. Later that month President Maj. Jean-Pierre Nkurunziza effected a minor reorganization of the Council of Ministers.

17 **Lesotho** Legislative elections took place at which the Lesotho Congress for Democracy retained its parliamentary majority, although the party's total number of seats in the National Assembly was reduced from 77 to 61. The National Independent Party took 21 of the 40 compensatory seats, thus becoming the second largest legislative party.

23 **Chad** Prime Minister Pascal Yoadimnadji died in Paris, France, where he had been receiving emergency medical treatment. It was announced on 26 February that Dr Kassiré Delwa Coumakoye had been appointed as Yoadimnadji's successor.

25 **Senegal** Abdoulaye Wade secured a second term, receiving 55.90% of the votes cast in the presidential election. His nearest opponent, with 14.92%, was former Prime Minister Idrissa Seck.

MARCH 2007

1 **Guinea** Lansana Kouyaté was sworn in as Prime Minister. On 28 March he announced the names of the members of his new administration, which included Abdoul Kabèlè Camara as Minister of Foreign Affairs and the former Deputy Chief of Staff of the Armed Forces, Gen. Arafan Camara, who assumed the national defence portfolio.

Niger President Col (retd) Mamadou Tandja effected a major government reorganization in which the number of ministers was increased to 31.

2 **Lesotho** A new Government was sworn in. Mohlabi Tsekoa became the new Minister of Foreign Affairs and International Relations, while several ministers remained in the Cabinet but assumed new portfolios.

4 **Chad** President Gen. Idriss Deby Itno named a new Government in which, most notably, Capt. Mahamat Nour Abdelkarim was awarded the national defence portfolio.

11 **Mauritania** At the first round of the presidential election Sidi Mohamed Ould Cheikh Abdellahi took 24.79% of votes cast, while Ahmed Ould Daddah won 20.68%, Zeine Ould Zeidane 15.27% and Messaoud Ould Boulkheir 9.80%. Following a second round of voting on 25 March contested by Abdellahi and Ould Daddah, the former was elected President, having secured 52.85% of the valid votes cast.

14 **Togo** Adji Ayassour replaced Payadowa Boukpessi as Minister of Finance, the Budget and Privatization.

19 **Guinea-Bissau** A total of 54 deputies approved a motion of 'no confidence' in Prime Minister Aristides Gomes, who tendered his resignation 10 days later.

22 **The Comoros** President Ahmed Abdallah Sambi carried out a reorganization of the Union Government and created four new portfolios, increasing the number of ministers to 12. Most notably, Mohamed Ali Solihi was appointed Minister of Finance, Budget and Planning, while new departments included a Ministry of Energy and a Ministry of Islamic Affairs, Human Rights and Information.

29 **Côte d'Ivoire** Guillaume Soro Kigbafori was appointed Prime Minister and a new Government was installed on 7 April. Notable appointments included that of the former presidential spokesman, Asségnini Désiré Tagro, who assumed the newly created position of Minister of the Interior; N'Guessan Michel Amani, hitherto Minister of National Education, replaced René Aphing Kouassi as Minister of Defence.

31 **Benin** Legislative elections were held following a delay of one week, owing to organizational difficulties. The Force cauri pour un Bénin émergent (FCBE), a pro-President Boni Yayi coalition of some 20 parties, took 35 of the 83 seats, while the Alliance pour une dynamique démocratique secured 20 seats.

APRIL 2007

10 **Guinea-Bissau** Martinho N'Dafa Cabi was named as the new Prime Minister; he unveiled his new Government on 17 April.

18 **Eritrea** Osman Salih Muhammad was appointed as Minister of Foreign Affairs. The position had remained vacant since the death of Ali Sayyid Abdullah in August 2005.

Somalia Further governmental changes were implemented with Husayn Elabe Fahiye appointed as Minister of Foreign Affairs.

19 **Mauritania** Abdellahi was sworn in as President and named Ould Zeidane as Prime Minister. Of the 28 members of the new Government, 26 were new appointments.

21 **Nigeria** At the presidential election Alhaji Umaru Musa Yar'Adua secured a decisive victory, receiving some 70% of the votes cast. Muhammadu Buhari was his nearest rival with just 19%. International observers cast doubt on the credibility of the polls as reports emerged that no voting took place in some states due to delays in the distribution of ballot papers. Nevertheless, Yar'Adua was sworn in as President on 29 May.

29 **Mali** President Amadou Toumani Touré received 71.20% of the total votes cast in a presidential election, thus securing a second five-year term. His closest rival was Ibrahim Boubacar Kéita, who received 19.15% of the votes cast.

MAY 2007

4 **Benin** Mathurin Nago of the FCBE, hitherto Minister of Higher Education and Professional Training, was elected as President of the Assemblée nationale, defeating Bruno Amoussou by 45 votes to 34.

6 **Burkina Faso** At legislative elections the Congrès pour la démocratie et le progrès (CDP) secured 73 seats to increase its majority in the Assemblée nationale. The Alliance pour la démocratie et la fédération—Rassemblement démocratique africain won 14 seats.

10–12 **Seychelles** The Seychelles People's Progressive Front retained 23 seats and its majority in the National Assembly, securing 56.2% of the votes cast at legislative elections. Prior to the election the Seychelles National Party (SNP) and the Democratic Party (DP) announced that, for the first time since the re-emergence of multi-party politics in 1992, they would form an alliance and nominate common candidates to contest the ballot. The SNP-DP alliance received 43.8% of the votes, and secured the 11 remaining seats.

12 **Guinea** The Minister of National Defence, Gen. Arafan Camara, and the Chief of Staff of the Armed Forces, Gen. Kerfalla Camara, were dismissed following days of rioting by soldiers demanding the reinstatement of military leaders removed from office. Gen. Bailo Diallo was later named as the new Minister of National Defence and Brig.-Gen. Diarra Camara assumed the role of Chief of Staff of the Armed Forces.

14 **Malawi** President Dr Bingu wa Mutharika swore in a new Cabinet, which included Ernest Malenga as Minister of Home Affairs and Internal Security and Tedson Kalebe as Minister of Economic Planning and Development, a portfolio hitherto held by the President.

31 **The Republic of the Congo** Basile Ikouébé was named as Minister of State, Minister of Foreign Affairs and the Francophonie.

Niger Prime Minister Hama Amadou lost a vote of 'no confidence' prompted by allegations of fraud within the education sector dating back to 2005. The result forced the resignation of Amadou and his Government.

JUNE 2007

3 **Burkina Faso** Prime Minister Paramanga Ernest Yonli tendered his resignation and that of his Government following the decisive victory of the CDP, the presidential party, in the June legislative elections. The following day Tertius Zongo was named as Yonli's successor, later announcing the appointment of a new administration, which included Zakaria Koté as Minister of Justice, Keeper of the Seals and Assane Sawadogo as Minister of Security.

Senegal In parliamentary elections President Wade's ruling Sopi Coalition secured victory, receiving 69.21% of the votes cast and winning 131 seats. The Takku Defaraat Sénégal Coalition, the And Defar Sénégal Coalition and the Waar Wi Coalition each took three seats. On 19 June Wade announced the appointment of Cheikh Hadjibou Soumaré as Prime Minister. Soumaré later named his new Government, in which the key portfolios remained unchanged.

Togo Richard Attipoé, Minister of Youth and Sports, died in a helicopter crash in Sierra Leone. Gilbert Kodjo Atsu, Secretary-of-State at the Ministry of Youth and Sports, replaced Attipoé in an acting capacity.

7 **Niger** Seyni Oumarou was sworn in as the new Prime Minister. On 9 June a new Government was approved, comprising 32 ministers. Jidda Hamadou assumed the national defence portfolio while Dagra Mahamadou was appointed Minister of Justice, Attorney-General.

8 **Rwanda** Parliament approved new legislation abolishing capital punishment for all crimes, including genocide. The legislation was formally implemented on 25 July.

10 **Gabon** Following the partial annulment of the results of legislative elections held in December 2006, a new ballot was conducted in 20 of the 120 constituencies.

Nigeria Dr Goodluck Ebele Jonathan was sworn in as Vice-President. On 6 June Patricia Etteh became the first woman to be appointed as Speaker of the House of Representatives.

13 **The Democratic Republic of the Congo** A reshuffle of key defence staff was announced. Lt-Gen. Dieudonne Kayembe Mbandakulu was named as the new Chief of Staff of the Armed Forces, while Vice-Adm. Didier Etumba Longila was appointed as the new Chief of Staff of the Navy and Maj.-Gen. Rigobert Masamba Musungui assumed the role of Chief of Staff of the Air Force.

17 **Benin** President Yayi named his new Government; notable appointments included Lawani Soule Mana, who was appointed as Minister of Finance, and Moussa Okanla, who became Minister of Foreign Affairs, African Integration, Francophone Affairs and Beninois Abroad.

24 **Comoros** Following the second round of island elections, Mohamed Abdouloihabi was named as President of Ngazidja, while Mohamed Ali Said was elected President of Mwali. The first round of elections were held on 10 June; however, in Nzwani voting was postponed until 17 June following incidents of violence and intimidation in the weeks preceding the ballot. Maj. Mohamed Bacar, who had held the presidency since April 2002, defied the decision of the Constitutional Court and proceeded to hold the election on 10 June, later claiming victory with 73.22% of the vote. The decision was not recognized by the Union Government or international observers.

JULY 2007

2 **Seychelles** President James Michel effected a major reorganization of the Government in which several departments were merged, reducing the number of ministries from 10 to eight.

11 **Ghana** A government reshuffle was implemented after the resignation of a number of cabinet ministers intending to contest the presidential election scheduled for December 2007.

18 **Central African Republic** A cabinet reshuffle was announced in which Gen. Raymond Paul Ndougou was appointed Minister of the Interior and Minister of Mines, Energy and Hydraulics and Lt-Col Sylvain N'doutingaï assumed responsibility for the finance portfolio.

22 **Cameroon** Provisional results of legislative elections indicated that President Paul Biya's ruling Rassemblement démocratique du peuple camerounais (RDPC) had increased its majority, winning 152 of the 180 seats available. However, opposition parties denounced the results, citing fraudulent activity and corruption. It was reported that in some areas there were no opposition party ballot papers available and that members of the RDPC had been observed bribing and intimidating voters. The results in five constituencies were subsequently annulled and, in accordance with the Constitution, a rerun was to be held within 60 days.

Mali According to provisional results, the coalition supporting President Touré secured victory after the second round of legislative elections, winning some 128 of the 147 seats available. However, it was reported that 37 seats remained unallocated. Turnout was low at 12%, rising slightly to 33% in rural areas.

24 **Madagascar** President Ravalomanana dissolved the National Assembly, claiming that it was no longer representative, and announced that legislative elections would take place on 23 September. The term of the National Assembly was not due to expire until May 2008.

Kenya David Mwiraria, who had resigned in February 2006 amid allegations of corruption, was reappointed to the Cabinet as Minister of the Environment and Natural Resources.

26 **Nigeria** A new cabinet was sworn in, which included Mahmud Yayale Ahmed as Minister of Defence, Ojo Maduekwe as Minister of Foreign Affairs and Shamsudeen Usman and Minister of Finance.

31 **Sudan/UN** The Security Council adopted Resolution 1769 authorizing the deployment of a 26,000-strong joint AU-UN mission in the Darfur region of Sudan. UNAMID, as it was named, would become the largest peace-keeping force in the world. Initially granted a mandate of 12 months, UNAMID was expected to incorporate the functions of the existing AU Mission in Sudan (AMIS) by the end of 2007. The Resolution demanded that all parties to the conflict in Darfur cease hostilities immediately and UNAMID was authorized to take all necessary action to ensure the safety and security of its personnel and all humanitarian workers, to protect civilians and to prevent armed attacks.

AUGUST 2007

5 **The Republic of the Congo** The delayed second round of the parliamentary elections, which had initially been scheduled for 22 July, was held. Provisional results suggested that the Parti congolais du travail and its allies had secured 124 of the 137 available seats.

11 **Sierra Leone** Presidential and legislative elections were held concurrently, with voter turn-out estimated at 75.8%. Provisional results showed that the All-People's Congress (APC) had secured a parliamentary majority with 59 seats. The Sierra Leone People's Party (SLPP) secured 43 and the People's Movement for Democratic Change took 10. In the presidential election the APC's candidate, party leader Ernest Bai Koroma, secured 44.34% of the vote ahead of the SLPP's Soloman Berewa, who received 38.28%. The two candidates were to contest a second round of balloting in September 2007.

22 **Liberia** President Ellen Johnson-Sirleaf implemented a reorganization of the Government in which Bankie King Akerele replaced George W. Wallace as Minister of Foreign Affairs. Philip Banks became Minister of Justice, replacing Frances Johnson-Morris, who assumed the commerce and industry portfolio.

Zambia President Mwanawasa announced a number of changes to the Cabinet.

PART ONE
General Survey

ECONOMIC TRENDS IN AFRICA SOUTH OF THE SAHARA, 2007

DONALD L. SPARKS

INTRODUCTION

Sub-Saharan Africa has great diversities, yet the 48 countries of the region share many common characteristics. They range significantly in terms of population, size and economic scale. Nigeria had the largest population (135m. in 2005, according to African Development Bank (ADB) estimates), while six other independent countries of the region each contained less than 1m. people. Seychelles had the smallest population, of about 85,000. The region's total population was some 765m. in 2006. Climate and topography vary greatly and include Mediterranean, tropical and semi-tropical, desert, rain forest, savannah, mountains and plains. Some countries are more intensively urbanized than others. Djibouti's urban population, for example, represents some 84% of the country's total, while in Rwanda it accounts for only 6%. Generally, the region has a very low population density, which increases the cost of providing infrastructure and services. Botswana has the lowest density, with three people per sq km, and the Comoros the highest, with 366 per sq km. Gross national income (GNI) per head in 2005 ranged from US $100 in Burundi to $8,180 in Seychelles, while the average for sub-Saharan Africa was $746. Educational levels also vary greatly; for example, 75% of children in the appropriate age-group were enrolled in secondary schools in Mauritius in 2004, while in Niger the proportion was only 7%, the world's lowest. In 2004 Zimbabwe had an adult literacy rate of 92%, while Burkino Faso's was only 21%. In 2004 33% of all adults in the region were illiterate, and only one-quarter of rural females attended primary school. Expenditure on education was low, at an annual average of less than $50 per pupil. Life expectancy at birth also varies, from 31 years in Swaziland to 73 years in Mauritius and Seychelles, averaging 47 years for the region as a whole in 2006, according to the ADB, compared with 49 years in 1990. In many countries, particularly in those most affected by HIV/AIDS, such as Swaziland and Botswana, average life expectancy has been reduced by some 22 years since 1985. Some sub-Saharan countries, including South Africa, the Democratic Republic of the Congo (DRC) and Zimbabwe, are relatively well-endowed with natural resources, while others, for example Niger and Somalia, have few such assets. Sub-Saharan Africa contains some of the world's largest reserves of a number of strategic minerals, including gold, platinum, cobalt and chromium.

The economies of sub-Saharan Africa are, for the most part, small and fragile, and the region is rapidly being left behind in the global economy. The World Bank suggests that the region is caught in a 'poverty trap': low incomes lead to low savings, which lead to low investment and consumer demand; low investment results in lower productivity and lower demand leads to less revenues, both of which lead back to poverty. By 2006 Sub-Saharan Africa accounted for just 2% of world trade and some 1% of global gross domestic product (GDP). Between 1995 and 2000 the region's share of global GDP declined by one-third, and its share of world exports fell by two-thirds, according to the Organisation for Economic Co-operation and Development (OECD). The region is poor: according to the World Bank, its combined GNI was US $554,422m. in 2005, less than that of the Netherlands. If South Africa and Nigeria were excluded from calculations, the combined GNI of $330,871m. would be less than that of Belgium. More than 40% of the population lives on less than $1 per day, the internationally recognized poverty line. Indeed, nearly 75% of all Africans live on less than $2 per day. In addition, the number of poor people increased by one-third during 1990–2005. Moreover, unlike that of all the other developing areas, sub-Saharan Africa's output per head was lower in 2006 than it was 30 years earlier, having declined by 50% in some countries. Indeed, the number of Africa's poor is projected to increase from 313m. in 2001 to 340m. by 2015, according to the World Bank, the only region where there will be an increase (see Table 1). By 2015 sub-Saharan Africa will be home to more very poor people than in the rest of the world combined. It is the only region where child malnutrition is not declining.

Table 1. Population Living on Less Than US $1 per day (%)

	1981	1990	2004
East Asia and Pacific	57.7	29.6	9.1
Europe and Central Asia	0.7	0.5	0.9
Latin America and Caribbean	9.7	11.3	8.6
Middle East and North Africa	5.1	2.4	1.5
South Asia	51.5	41.3	30.1
Sub-Saharan Africa	41.6	44.6	41.1

Source: World Bank, *World Development Indicators 2007*.

Sub-Saharan Africa has the world's second most unequal distribution of income, after Latin America. The supply of food available per person, measured in daily caloric intake, fell from 2,140 calories in 1971 to 2,100 in the mid-1990s, increasing the number of malnourished people from 94m. to 210m., according to FAO; about 32% of the region's children suffered from malnutrition by 2003. By the end of 2003 an estimated 26.6m. people in sub-Saharan Africa were living with HIV/AIDS, with 2.5m. dying in 2004. By 2005 the region accounted for about 65% of the world's HIV-positive adults and 90% of AIDS-infected children. Only about one-half of the region's population has access to safe water and adequate sanitation, and in some nations this is as low as 8%–15%. The constant threat of war and civil conflict poses grave questions about the possibility of economic gain; indeed, one in five Africans currently lives in a country seriously affected by war or strife.

Given this vast diversity, it is, accordingly, difficult to draw general conclusions about the continent's economic performance as a whole during any given year. Nevertheless, some broad comparisons can be made. While improving recently, the region's overall economic growth rate during the 1980s and early 1990s was dismal. Sub-Saharan Africa recorded average annual GDP growth of 3.2% in 1961–2001; this only slightly exceeded the rate of population growth. Taking inflation and population growth into account, the region's real GDP per head actually fell by 42.5% between 1980 and 1990. Growth per head between 1960 and 2000 in sub-Saharan Africa averaged 0.8% per year, compared with an average of 2.3% for all of the world's developing countries. The region's growth rates have also been more volatile than other regions. Between 1960 and 1994 only five countries sustained real per head growth rates above 2% per year: Botswana, Cape Verde, Mauritius, Seychelles and Swaziland. (In fact, Botswana had the world's fastest growing economy during the 1980s and 1990s, recording an average annual increase in GDP of a remarkable 8.1% in 1980–2000 and 13.1% in 1985–89.) In addition, the region's income distribution has become more unequal. By the mid-1990s the region's growth began to improve; during 1998–2006 35 countries persistently recorded real annual growth rates of more than 2%, and the region's average was 4%. OECD estimated that the region's GDP grew by 4.8% in 2006 and projected a rate of 5.7% for 2007. (Equatorial Guinea's 22.9% growth rate, mostly due to petroleum output, was the region's best while Zimbabwe's economy contracted by 4.8%.) The average GDP growth rates varied between regions in 2006, with Southern Africa recording a rate of 5.4% (compared with 5.6% in 2005), followed by 5.1% in Eastern Africa (6.4% in 2005), 4.8% in West Africa (5.6% in 2005) and 3.9% in Central Africa (4.9% in 2005). These positive rates were attributed mostly to oil and non-fuel mineral exports, and generally good growing conditions for agriculture. It should be noted that within these regions, growth varied greatly, especially between the petroleum producers (whose growth was generally much stronger) and other countries.

Table 2. Regional GDP Growth Rates (% change)*

	1984–2004	2005
Central Africa	3.9	4.9
East Africa	4.1	6.4
Southern Africa	3.1	5.6
West Africa	3.6	5.6

* Aggregates exclude Somalia and Liberia.

Source: OECD, *African Economic Outlook 2007*.

As suggested below, by virtually any economic or social indicator, sub-Saharan Africa performs less well than any other developing region. Since 1971 the UN has viewed 'Least Developed Countries' (LDCs) as a category of states which are considered as highly disadvantaged in their development process. Of the 48 countries classified by the UN as 'least developed' in 2006, 33 were in sub-Saharan Africa. In many ways sub-Saharan Africa has found itself retreating economically, while other developing areas of the world are advancing strongly. For example, the region's growth during 1960–73 was virtually indistinguishable from that of South Asia. At independence in 1957, Ghana was more prosperous than the Republic of Korea, but by 2006 Ghana's GDP per head was equal to that of the mid-1960s, and 35 times lower than South Korea's. Between 1965 and 1995 Ghana's exports increased by four times (in current US dollar values), compared with more than 400 times in the Republic of Korea.

Of the world's developing areas, sub-Saharan Africa has the worst record in virtually all of the most important indicators (see Table 3). The region has the lowest level of income per head, the lowest rate of life expectancy, the highest rate of adult HIV infection, the highest number of children not living past five years of age and the lowest rate of access to improved water sources.

None the less, there have also been some improvements: between 1960 and 2004 life expectancy increased from 40 years to 46 years in sub-Saharan Africa, according to WHO (although, as noted above, life expectancy was actually higher in the 1980s); and since the mid-1980s the proportion of the population with access to safe water has more than doubled. During the past two decades adult literacy in the region has advanced from 27% to 50%, while between 1960 and 1997 female enrolment at secondary school level rose from 8% to 23%.

The factors underlying Africa's parlous economic and social condition can be broadly categorized either as 'external' or 'internal'. The major external factors include adverse movements in the terms of trade and declines in foreign aid and foreign investment. The internal factors include small, fragmented economies, high levels of ethnic diversity, poor soils, widely fluctuating and harsh climates, widespread civil strife which often spills over borders, inadequate human and physical infrastructure, the large number of landlocked states, rapid urbanization and population growth, environmental degradation, ineffective government and inappropriate public policies. Unfortunately, African governments have but limited control over many of these factors, particularly the external ones.

EXTERNAL CAUSES OF ECONOMIC DECLINE

The pillars of Africa's external relationship with the Western industrialized countries are trade, aid and investment, and the declines of all three have contributed to the continent's poor economic performance during the past 30 years.

Trade and Regional Co-operation

Sub-Saharan Africa occupies a minor role in global trade, and accounted for only about 2.0% of the world total by 2005 (1.7%, excluding South Africa), compared with about 5.0% in the 1980s. On the positive side, for the past 25 years the region has exported more goods than it has imported (see Table 4). In 2004 merchandise exports totalled US $143,866m. and imports amounted to $141,150m., resulting in a merchandise trade surplus of $2,716m. Exports of services in 2004 were $24,238m., while imports totalled $38,142m., leading to a trade deficit in services of $13,904m. In addition, owing to negative capital flows, the region has run a current-account deficit since the 1980s.

One of the most serious of the external factors underlying this decline has been Africa's worsening terms of trade, with declining traditional exports, both in relation to price and quantity, and increasing imports, also in volume and price. More than one-half of sub-Saharan Africa's exports generally go to OECD countries, from which the region traditionally purchases about 80% of its imports. Europe remains the main trade partner, although its share of trade has declined from 44% of the total in 1995 to 32% in 2005. However, it should be noted that by 2006 the People's Republic of China had taken much of this trade and become a major trading partner, with trade between China and Africa increasing from US $3,000m. in 1995 to more than $39,000m., equivalent to about 10% of Africa's total trade. (This figure is expected to double by 2010.) Furthermore, China is now the major purchaser of the region's petroleum. Nevertheless, African countries typically produce one or two major agricultural or mineral commodities for export to the industrialized countries in the West. Primary products account for approximately 80% of the region's export revenues, about the same level as during the 1960s. The region's exports are not diversified: 29 states have an export mix where five or less products constitute 75% of total exports, and 13 states have one product that contributes 75% of exports. South Africa's exports are the most diverse, with 39 products accounting for more than 75% of total exports. Poor export performances, combined with the range of problems discussed below, have generated increased deficits in most African countries' current accounts.

Table 3. Social and Economic Indicators in the Developing World

	East Asia/ Pacific	Europe/ Central Asia	Latin America/ Caribbean	Middle East/ North Africa	South Asia	Sub-Saharan Africa
GNI per head (US $, 2005)	1,630	2,201	4,045	2,198	692	740
GDP growth (% change, 2005)	8.9	6.0	4.5	4.3	8.7	7.1
HIV prevalence (% of persons aged 15–49, 2005)	0.2	0.7	0.6	0.1	0.7	5.8
Life expectancy (years at birth, 2005)	71	69	72	70	63	47
Under-5 mortality rate (per 1,000 live births, 2005)	33	32	31	53	83	163
Youth literacy rate (% of males aged 15–24, 2003)	98	99	94	92	77	84
Youth literacy rate (% of females aged 15–24, 2003)	98	99	95	82	62	77
Access to improved water sources (% of population, 2003)	81	89	81	87	87	64
External debt (% of GNI, 2005)	20.5	41.2	30.8	27.6	19.1	37.0

Sources: World Bank, *World Development Indicators 2007* and *World Development Indicators* database.

Table 4. Sub-Saharan Africa's Trade and Current-Account Data (US $ '000 million at current prices)

	1980	1993	2004
Merchandise exports	78.7	62.5	143.9
Merchandise imports	60.6	57.0	141.2
Visible trade balance	18.1	5.5	2.7

Source: World Bank, *African Development Indicators 2004* and *World Development Indicators 2006*.

The volumes and price levels for the region's primary exports have been uneven. Table 5 illustrates such fluctuations in 12 major commodities.

Table 5. Exports of Major Commodities from Africa ('000 metric tons)

Commodity	1980	1990	2002*
Copper	1,286	973	316†
Iron	28,215	21,057	19,545‡
Phosphates	4,277	4,995	4,290§
Cocoa	869	1,352	1,695‖
Coffee	819	1,032	647
Cotton	459	700	861
Groundnut	605	674	379
Oil palm	280	233	192
Sisal	109	50	22
Tea	182	267	235
Sugar	2,148	2,441	2,666
Tobacco	1,777	2,259	3,206

* Unless otherwise indicated.

† 1998 figure.

‡ 1996 figure.

§ 1997 figure.

‖ 2001 figure.

Source: World Bank, *African Development Indicators 2004*.

The region's terms of trade declined by 2.8% in 1985–94, but have increased by 0.9% since 1995. Prices for many agricultural commodities have fluctuated greatly. For example, between 1990 and 2005, cocoa declined by 41%, coffee by 69% and tea by 49%. Tobacco prices fell from $3,836 per metric ton in 1970 to $2,535 per ton in 2005, while cotton's prices fell from $2.25 per kg to $1.11 per kg during the same period. Burkina Faso tripled its output of cotton during 1993–97, but its earnings from this export actually fell. The region's petroleum exporters benefited the most, but generally these gains have not been translated into sustained growth.

The purchasing power of the region's exports has fallen since the late 1980s, owing primarily to the general decline in world petroleum prices. The steep decline in sub-Saharan Africa's export revenues was as much attributable to falls in volume as to relative prices. Between 1970 and 1985 Africa's share of the world market for primary (non-petroleum) exports declined from 7% to 4% of the total. The maintenance of Africa's 7% market share would have added US $10,000m. to its overall export income. Economic advance in other areas of the world suggests that increased trade and general integration into the global economy leads to swifter growth. For example, the countries that have integrated most quickly in the past decade experienced growth about 3% in advance of that achieved by the slowest integrating countries. The poorest group of countries are the least able to withstand the side effects of worsening terms of trade.

The import policies of the Western industrialized countries have played a major, and often negative, role in Africa's export performance. The industrialized market economies are Africa's major trading partners. Until recently African exports to the European Union (EU) had preferential access under the successive Lomé Conventions concluded by the EU and the group of African, Caribbean and Pacific (ACP) states. These preferences gave ACP countries' exports to the EU an advantage over other countries. However, in 2000 the Cotonou Agreement replaced Lomé. Under the provisions of the new accord, the EU was to negotiate free trade arrangements with the most developed ACP countries during 2000–08. The preferential treatment currently in force was to be retained initially, but thereafter trade between ACP countries and the EU was to be gradually liberalized over a period of 12–15 years. It was feared that the EU might institute tighter non-tariff barriers (for example, tougher veterinary and safety standards) against African producers. For 34 of the region's poorest countries, duties on beef, rice and sugar exports to the EU were to be eliminated under the 2001 Everything But Arms Initiative. A new generalized system of preferences introduced by the European Commission came into effect in 2005. The scheme offers duty-free access to the EU market for 80% of tariff lines from countries who adhere to international conventions on human rights, labour, good governance and the environment. Meanwhile, in 2004 the USA extended its Africa Growth and Opportunity Act (AGOA) until 2015.

Another major trade policy change in 2004 was the World Trade Organization phase-out of bilateral quotas on textiles and clothing. While China and India are gaining from this development, many African producers are no longer able to compete with them. In fact, in 2005 Mauritius' garment manufacturing industry contracted by 30%, and in Lesotho six textile operations closed, resulting in the loss of some 7,000 jobs. Other badly affected countries were South Africa, Swaziland, Nigeria, Zambia, Madagascar, Tanzania, Malawi, Namibia and Kenya. The International Textile, Garment and Leather Workers' Federation estimates that the region may have lost as many as 250,000 related jobs since 2005.

Notwithstanding the above and the benefits of the Lomé Conventions, protectionism and restrictive agricultural practices, particularly in the EU and (to a lesser extent) the USA, have resulted in an oversupply of some agricultural commodities, and have thus inhibited world-wide demand and weakened world prices. Agricultural subsidies in the USA, Japan and the EU amount to some US $360,000m. annually, more than sub-Saharan Africa's total GDP. Eliminating these supports would benefit sub-Saharan Africa greatly: a recent study suggested that incomes per head would increase by $6. The aid organization Oxfam has estimated that certain countries lose more because of these tariffs than they gain in Western aid. For example, in 2001 Mali received $37.7m. from the USA in aid, but incurred an estimated loss of $43m. owing to US subsidies for cotton farmers. The annual losses for cotton producers in the Third World from US and EU price support policies are estimated at $120m.–$240m. annually. Tariff and non-tariff barriers to trade erected by the Western industrialized countries have discouraged value-added or semi-processed agricultural imports from African states. The World Bank has estimated that high tariffs, anti-'dumping' regulations and other trade barriers cost sub-Saharan Africa $20,000m. annually in lost exports. In 2004 the EU announced it would reduce its sugar production and exports over a four-year period. It also has announced a proposal to change its banana import regime. Besides the decreased demand due to protectionism from the developed nations, as their incomes increase, consumer demand for agricultural products does not advance proportionately (this is termed 'income inelastic demand'). Industry is increasingly turning to substitutes, such as fibre optics for copper wires in telecommunications and beet sugar for cane sugar. Tariffs, which are already high by world comparisons, have yet to show a measurable reduction in the sub-Saharan region. As agricultural prices decline, Western consumers do not increase their consumption (this is known as 'price inelastic demand'). Furthermore, even in countries that have dynamic export sectors such as Kenya (which exports cut flowers) and Lesotho (apparel), benefits for employment and diversification of their respective economies remain low. Finally, many African nations rely on import taxes as major sources of government revenues, and are thus hesitant to reduce such barriers.

Trade between African states is low: in 2002 regional exports within sub-Saharan Africa comprised only 13% of total exports (the EU received the largest share of the region's exports, at 40.5% of the total). Most African states produce similar products for export, generally primary agricultural or mineral commodities, and, as most of the value added is carried out in Western industrialized countries, there is little African demand for these products. African states themselves often discourage trade by their strongly inward-orientated, import-substitution development strategies, including overvalued exchange rates and protectionist trade policies. Their transport infrastructure is geared towards export to the EU, Japan and North America, rather than to nearby countries. Tariffs have been higher than elsewhere in the world because of the limited avenues available for taxation. Owing to the small size of these economies, these barriers to trade are significantly more damaging. Finally, since the land-locked countries' trade is principally with Europe, neighbouring countries are often viewed as competitive obstacles rather than potential markets. In southern Africa, for example, only 4% of the export trade of the 14-member Southern African Development Community (SADC) is transacted among SADC members.

The region could exploit its comparative advantage in commodity exports only if the industrialized countries agreed to support international buffer-stock agreements and implement other arrangements for co-operation. African states have tried various methods of improving their trade performance, and of developing overall regional economic co-operation. Indeed, trade tariffs have been reduced from 30%–40% in the early and mid-1990s to less than 15% in many countries in 2001, and to less than 10% in countries with very open economies, such as Zambia and Uganda. There have been several attempts to form free trade areas or customs unions. Several have failed and have been abandoned, such as the colonially imposed Central African Federation, of Zambia, Zimbabwe and Malawi, and the East African Community (EAC), comprising Kenya, Tanzania and Uganda. It should be noted, however, that in 1996 Kenya, Uganda and Tanzania established the Permanent Tripartite Commission for East African Co-operation, with the aim of eliminating tariffs and co-ordinating members' infrastructure and the development of energy resources. A treaty for the re-establishment of the EAC was ratified by the Kenyan, Tanzanian and Ugandan Heads of State in 1999, and the new EAC was officially inaugurated in January 2001. Thus far the EAC has begun issuing common passports, made its members' currencies convertible, and created a customs union (which came into effect on 1 January 2005). In late June 2007 Burundi and Rwanda were admitted to the EAC. Meanwhile, in early 1997 the Organization of African Unity (OAU) inaugurated the African Economic Community, with the eventual goal of uniting the region's existing economic organizations into a single institution similar to the EU. The OAU was formally replaced by a new African Union (AU) in July 2002. The Constitutive Act of the AU provides for the institution of a central bank. None the less, the results of most regional integration efforts (see below) have been modest.

One of the longest standing, and most successful, regional organizations is the Southern African Customs Union (SACU), founded in 1969 and comprising Botswana, Lesotho, Namibia, South Africa and Swaziland. SACU permits free trade among its members and provides a common external tariff. Customs revenue is generally collected by South Africa and allocated to individual members according to a formula based on members' share of total trade. In 1999 South Africa signed a wide-ranging trade pact with the EU. The Economic Commission for Africa believes that its terms will favour those local businesses that may be able to purchase imported inputs more cheaply; local businesses that may benefit competitively from acquiring new technology; and consumers and businesses for which greater access to European markets will result in lower prices. On the negative side, however, Botswana, Lesotho, Namibia and Swaziland could sustain revenue losses, while some local producers could lose domestic and regional market share to EU businesses. The trade agreement also accords EU producers greater access than neighbouring SACU countries to South African markets.

Two somewhat more recent groupings, commanding good prospects, are SADC and the Economic Community of West African States (ECOWAS). ECOWAS has as its eventual goal the removal of barriers to trade, employment and movement between its 15 member states, as well as the rationalization of currency and financial payments among its members (see Part Three—Regional Information). This membership is drawn from francophone and lusophone as well as anglophone countries, with as much economic diversity as Nigeria and Cape Verde. Owing to the political and economic disparity of its members, it is likely to be many years before the above objectives are fully met. SADC (see Part Three—Regional Information) was established initially as the Southern African Development Co-ordination Conference (SADCC) to provide a counter, during the era of apartheid, to South Africa's economic hegemony over the region. SADCC did not initially seek an economic association or customs union, but rather to function as a sub-regional planning centre to rationalize development planning. Its reconstitution in 1992 as SADC placed binding obligations on member countries with the aim of promoting economic integration towards a fully developed common market.

Another important grouping, the Franc Zone (see Part Three—Regional Information), was formed in 1948 and now comprises, together with France, 13 former French colonies, Equatorial Guinea, a former Spanish colony, and Guinea-Bissau, a former Portuguese possession. It operates with four general principles: fixed parity exchange rates; convertibility guaranteed by the French Treasury; free movement of capital; and a central foreign-exchange reserve. Excluding France, each of the Zone's members are small states, none with a population exceeding 20m., and most are poor. A few, such as Cameroon, the Republic of the Congo, Equatorial Guinea and Gabon, are heavily reliant on petroleum export revenues.

During the early 1990s the French franc appreciated and thus made the CFA countries' exports relatively less competitive on world markets, as they became more expensive. In addition, the Zone's terms of trade declined by about 45%, owing primarily to a fall in world commodity prices (for coffee, cocoa and petroleum in particular). In 1993 real income per head fell by 4.5% and exports declined by 3.9% in volume. As a consequence of these factors, the Zone's attractiveness to potential foreign investment diminished and the outflow of capital from the CFA bloc increased. After prolonged pressure from the IMF and France to remedy the situation, in January 1994 the CFA central banks devalued the CFA franc by 50%. (The Comoros franc, which is aligned with the CFA franc and the French franc exchange rate, was devalued by 33.3%.) This decision forestalled unilateral devaluations by individual member countries, and also set the stage for potentially closer links, eventually leading to a common market in the region. In January 1999 the French franc became one of the 11 EU currencies linked to a single currency unit, the euro, thus effectively pegging the CFA franc to the euro. In 1999 the members of the Union économique et monétaire ouest-africaine (UEMOA), the Zone's West African monetary union, reached agreement on the Convergence, Stability, Growth and Solidarity Pact, which called for increased integration in two stages. In February 2000 UEMOA and ECOWAS, to which UEMOA member countries also belong, adopted an action plan aimed at harmonizing UEMOA's economic programme with that of a planned second West African monetary union (the West African Monetary Zone), scheduled to be established by 2009 by the remaining—mainly anglophone—ECOWAS member states. A merger of the two complementary monetary unions, and the replacement of the CFA franc by a new single West African currency, was envisaged. In addition, a number of other bodies have been established in recent years to facilitate regional integration in such areas as business law, insurance, social affairs and statistics-gathering.

Another noteworthy development in regional co-operation was the initial participation of 13 southern and East African and Indian Ocean states in the Cross Border Initiative (CBI), supported by the World Bank, the ADB and the EU. This initiative is aimed at liberalizing the member countries' foreign-exchange systems, deregulating cross-border investments and facilitating the movement of goods, services and people among the participating countries. The CBI is voluntary, and is still in its formative stages. Most states have joined the WTO and are participating in the Doha Round of trade negotiations, which began in 2002. Most economists agree that a more liberal world-wide trade regime would benefit Africa as much as anywhere.

Foreign Debt, Aid and Investment

Three of the most obvious manifestations of external difficulties are foreign debt, fluctuating levels of international aid and the difficulty of attracting outside investment. In 2005 sub-Saharan Africa's level of official (non-concessional) external debt amounted to US $239,446m. In 1960 the region's total external debt amounted to less than $3,000m., and the average debt-service ratio was only 2% of exports. Since the 1980s indebtedness has advanced rapidly, from $60,661m. in 1980 to $218,405m. in 2004. South Africa became the region's principal debtor in 2005, with $46,209m. of external debt while Nigeria, with a debt of $20,479m. came second. The region's ratio of debt to exports was estimated at 7.9% in 2004, down from 13.5% in 1990. This compared reasonably favourably with the ratio for all developing countries, which was 19.8% in 1990, and 14.5% in 2004. The region's total debt-service payments equalled $15,235m. in 2004. The region's economies are particularly susceptible to external shocks, making it more problematic to service debt.

The majority of the 'most debt-distressed countries' are in sub-Saharan Africa. During the past two decades there has been a continuing debate on how best to reduce poor countries' debt burdens and how to fund such reductions. Several non-governmental organizations (NGOs), led by the Jubilee Debt Campaign, Action Aid and Christian Aid have advocated for complete debt cancellation. Those organizations issued a warning in 2005 that the UN Millenium Development Goals (MDGs, see below) would not be met unless there was complete debt relief. In 1996 the World Bank and IMF launched an initiative for heavily indebted poor countries (HIPCs) to help ensure that the world's poorest countries could reduce their debts to 'sustainable levels'. Of the 38 eligible countries, 32 are from sub-Saharan Africa. The HIPC guide-lines required a candidate country to complete a three-year reform programme. These reforms included economic stabilization programs, restructuring state owned enterprises and targeting public spending toward poverty reduction, health and education. It is then permitted a further three years to carry out further adjustments to obtain the actual debt reductions. In 1998 Uganda became the first country to obtain actual debt reduction under the initiative. Mozambique followed shortly thereafter. In late 1999, following pressure to change the arrangement, the IMF and the World Bank agreed to an enhanced HIPC initiative, which aimed to accelerate the delivery of debt relief. Instead of waiting for up to six years to qualify, new applicants could qualify as soon as they successfully implement policies agreed with the Bank and the IMF and presented in a Poverty Reduction Strategy Paper. By mid-2007 17 states had reached their HIPC completion points or were in the process of doing so. The qualifying nations under HIPC will be challenged to channel those funds which are freed from debt repayment into education and health programs.

In mid-2005 the Ministers of Finance of the Group of Eight leading industrialized nations (G-8) proposed cancelling US $40,000m. worth of debt owed by Benin, Burkina Faso, Ethiopia, Ghana, Madagascar, Mali, Mauritania, Mozambique, Niger, Rwanda, Senegal, Tanzania, Uganda and Zambia (four non-African nations were also included). These countries would still have to meet HIPC criteria to receive the relief. Nine other African countries that have yet to qualify for HIPC (Burundi, Côte d'Ivoire, the Central African Republic, the Comoros, the Republic of the Congo, Liberia, Somalia, Sudan and Togo) will have to make the necessary reforms before becoming eligible for complete relief. This proposal was adopted by the leaders of the G-8 countries at the summit meeting in 2005 in Gleneagles, Scotland, at which they also made significant new aid pledges (see below), and again in mid-2007 at the summit in Heiligendamm, Germany.

It should be noted that many countries in the region have been some of the largest recipients of aid, which has, in many cases, been equivalent to 10%–20% of GDP, and sometimes higher. Indeed, in 1998 official development assistance (ODA) was equivalent to 69% of the GDP of São Tomé and Príncipe, and 46% of Guinea-Bissau's. There is a wide variation of levels of assistance, resulting in 'aid orphans' which receive much less aid than 'aid darlings'. In 1977–84 sub-Saharan Africa's ODA increased, in real terms, at an average annual rate of 7.4%, during 1985–89 it increased by an average of 2.1% per year. However, ODA increased from US $13,108m. in 2000 to $32,673m. in 2005. ODA per head increased from $21 in 1999 to $36 in 2004. In 2005 Nigeria was by far the largest recipient of ODA, with $6,437m. equal to almost 20% of the region's total. Along with Nigeria, seven other states received over one-half of all aid. The composition of ODA has also changed: less is now targeted for long-term economic development and a greater proportion is being devoted to short-term emergency food aid and peace-keeping activities. For example, in 1975–80 just 1% of all aid was allocated to emergency assistance, while in 2003 that figure was some 6%, according to the UN Economic Commission for Africa. Most of the overall decline can be ascribed to increased levels of aid to Eastern Europe and Central Asia.

However, this situation is changing, as demonstrated by the increased levels of aid pledged at the Gleneagles G-8 meeting (see below). In fact, aid (in real terms) to the region is higher in 2005 than it was in the 1990s. By 2007 the sub-Saharan region's major donors were the European Commission, the USA and the United Kingdom, accounting for 51% of the total. This is followed by Germany, Japan and the Netherlands. Under the USA's AGOA, which came into effect in May 2000, African countries satisfying certain 'reforming' criteria are eligible for preferential trade access and increased investment. Eligibility is reviewed on an annual basis, and in December 2003 37 countries were declared eligible to benefit from AGOA during the following year.

It is a widely held view among economists that foreign aid is effective in stimulating growth in countries with sound macroeconomic environments, but is ineffective, and can be detrimental, in countries with weak policy environments. Aid is often given for the construction of physical projects, such as roads and dams, and little is provided for recurrent costs. These projects are generally carried out in an unco-ordinated way, funded by multiple donor agencies. A recent study concluded that when aid was given to governments that were committed to economic reform, it produced growth, while when governments were not so committed, aid had little, if any, positive influence. In 2005 100 partner countries and donors endorsed the Paris Declaration on Aid Effectiveness, an attempt more successfully to co-ordinate aid to ensure more productive results. This programme also forms part of the WTO's Aid for Trade Agenda. That programme recognizes the importance of trade as a part of a country's overall development strategy. Sub-Saharan Africa is the largest recipient of trade-related technical assistance and capacity building, receiving about one-third of the world's total. In 2004 and 2005 the Commission for Africa called for an increase of US $25,000m. from the world's richest countries, representing 0.08% of the 22 richest donors' national income. Meeting the MDGs would require donors to raise their spending from 0.25% of GDP to 0.5% by 2015. For comparison, the USA provided over 1% of its GDP under the Marshall Plan, which helped to rebuild Europe after the Second World War. At the G-8 summit in Gleneagles in July 2005 leaders of those nations pledged to double the amount of aid for Africa to $50,000m. per year by 2010. Although the USA agreed to the pledge, most of those funds represent previous commitments. In June 2007 the G-8 reaffirmed its pledge at the Heiligendamm summit at which leaders agreed to commit $60,000m. to combat disease in Africa. Many anti-poverty activists contended, however, that the rich nations had not kept to their commitments and that the increase in aid had not been as large as promised.

Foreign direct investment (FDI) can bring many benefits to developing countries, and a lack of capital can be, and has been, a major impediment to development. FDI contributes to capital formation, human capital development, technology transfer, increased managerial skills and market expansion. Generally, there is a strong correlation between higher FDI and economic growth. Since the late 1980s increased levels of FDI to developing countries have generated more intense competition for new FDI. Developing countries raised their share of world FDI flows from 21% of the total in 1988 to 42% in 1997. However, sub-Saharan Africa has a poor record of attracting such investment. In 2001 the region attracted only 8% of the total

FDI allocated to all developing countries and the majority of that went to petroleum-producing nations. In 1996 FDI as a percentage of GNI was also low: the region received FDI equivalent to 0.8% of GNI, exactly one-half of the average of all developing countries. In 2004 the region attracted US $12,451m. in FDI, and in 2005 it received $20,118m., led by South Africa's $6,379 (accounting for about 31% of the total, and an increase from only $800m. in 2004). Nigeria was the second largest recipient, receiving $3,403m., primarily in the petroleum sector. A total of 24 states in the region attracted less than $50m. each in 2005. Over one-half of FDI in 2004 to the region came from France, the Netherlands, South Africa, the United Kingdom and the USA. However, in recent years China has become a major investor, with almost $12,000m. invested by 2007 (and the region's major customer, purchasing over 10% of sub-Saharan Africa's exports, equating to $19,000m. in 2007). Most of China's investment has been in oil-producing states. In 2006 China pledged at the Forum on China-Africa Cooperation to double aid to $1,000m. by 2009, provide $3,000m. in preferential loans, cancel debt of $1,400m. for the 31 highly indebted nations, open Chinese markets by increasing from 190 to 440 the number of duty-free products from the region and train 15,000 African professionals.

Virtually all official flows into the region are in the form of bilateral grants or loans on highly concessionary terms from multilateral creditors. Several countries followed a continuing trend in reducing their indebtedness to commercial banks in 1996. Private non-guaranteed financial loans increased from US $5,276m. in 1990 to $14,660m. in 2004. The World Bank has begun to offer guarantees for commercial loans to the private sector. The first of these was obtained by a group of companies in Côte d'Ivoire in 1999. The sub-Saharan region has yet to broaden its investment base beyond energy and mining, which remain its prime attractions. Furthermore, while foreign investors are attracted by the region's vast raw materials and low-wage economies, they are fearful of internal political volatility and the uncertainty of securing the enforcement of commercial contracts. These considerations, combined with the deteriorating human and physical infrastructure, have virtually extinguished investor confidence. Investor perception is of major importance. In 1997 the World Bank conducted a survey to ascertain the level of investor confidence with regard to states ensuring law and order, protection of property, and predictability in applying rules and policies. Sub-Saharan Africa ranked behind Asia, the Middle East, North Africa and Latin America and the Caribbean. A similar study conducted by the World Economic Forum ranked Mauritius as the most competitive country in the sub-Saharan region. The Forum's 'Competitiveness Report' (using an index of several criteria) suggested that those countries that are most serious in reforming their economic policies (such as Uganda, Tanzania and Mozambique) are also those achieving the best rates of economic growth. Countries at the bottom of the list included Angola, Nigeria, Malawi and Zimbabwe. Importantly, optimism appears to be increasing about the region in general. Investors appeared more confident about improvements in tariffs, the rule of law and access to financing (see the section on the private sector business environment, below, for more details). A recent UN report estimated that Africans hold as much as 40% of their financial portfolios outside Africa. If these funds returned, the region would increase its capital stock by about two-thirds.

INTERNAL CAUSES OF ECONOMIC DECLINE

Africa faces a number of 'internal' economic problems, which, in the view of many analysts, outweigh the 'external' factors discussed above. Many countries in sub-Saharan Africa are suffering from a crisis of statehood and a crisis of capability. An urgent priority is to rebuild state effectiveness through an overhaul of public institutions, the resurrection of the rule of law, and credible checks on abuse of state power. Indeed, as far back as 1989 a World Bank study on sub-Saharan Africa's quest for sustainable growth suggested that 'underlying the litany of Africa's problems is a crisis of governance'. This, unfortunately, is still the case.

Governance, Parastatal Organizations and the Private Sector Business Environment

Most sub-Saharan African countries achieved independence in the late 1950s and 1960s and many of the governments quickly became one-party states, with presidents who retained power for life. After independence most newly formed African governments had three fundamental choices for developing their economies and for encouraging industrialization in the broadest sense. They could: (i) nationalize existing entities; (ii) seek to attract private investment from abroad by offering favourable investment incentives (tax 'holidays', for example); or (iii) invest heavily in public enterprises. Most governments adopted combinations of all three, but virtually every national administration south of the Sahara opted for substantial parastatal involvement. At independence the majority of new states had few other options open to them. By and large there was little indigenous involvement in the modern sector, and almost none in the industrial sphere.

Most of the early parastatal organizations operated in natural monopoly areas: large infrastructural projects (highways, railways and dams) and social service facilities (schools, hospitals and medical clinics). Government soon moved into areas that had previously been dominated by the private sector (or, at least, traditionally dominated by the colonial sector in most 'mixed' economies). In the early 1990s public enterprises accounted for as much as 70% of GDP in Malawi and 58% in Tanzania. The share of parastatal bodies in employment was as high as 60% of the labour force in Mozambique in the late 1980s, and accounted for more than one-third of employment in many other countries. In the 1980s Ghana, Mozambique, Nigeria and Tanzania each operated more than 300 parastatal bodies. This expanded use of parastatal operations ideally complemented a range of domestic economic development philosophies, such as 'scientific socialism', 'humanism', 'ujamaa' or whichever term the particular African government applied to its own mode of economic planning. During this period many governments had justifiable concerns that the private sector could not, or would not, help to improve living conditions for the poorest citizens. Most analysts have generally considered parastatal organizations to have failed, at least in terms of economic efficiency criteria. State-owned enterprises accounted for perhaps 13% of the region's GDP in 1993 (compared with almost 15% in the late 1970s), but represented a substantially higher percentage of economic output than in any of the world's other developing regions. After independence most African countries expanded the size of their civil service more rapidly than their economic growth justified. This expansion was designed to provide employment, but civil servants received lower and lower real wages. None the less, African élites looked to the public sector as the avenue of advancement to their careers. The region was generally slow to develop indigenous entrepreneurs. Governments became bloated and corrupt. For most states the need for better governance became critical and many governments have scaled back the role of parastatals in recent years (see Pressures for Economic Policy Reform, below).

The general perception is that the region has not developed an appropriate enabling environment for the private sector to grow and flourish. Indeed, it lags other regions in providing a quality business environment. Of the 20 countries world-wide with the most regulatory obstacles to doing business, 16 are in sub-Saharan Africa, with Angola, Burkina Faso, Chad and the DRC being the worst four ranked. Property transfer is difficult and costly: in 2005 it cost on average 14% of the value of the property and took some 64 days in Africa, compared with 45 days in the Middle East. In some countries it is much worse. In Nigeria, for example, registering property takes 21 separate procedures, 274 days and 27% of the value of the property. The informal sector accounts for more than 70% of non-agricultural employment, and many small firms see no advantage in joining the formal sector. For example, formal employment usually entails rigid employment contracts making the recruitment and dismissal of employees difficult. Many business owners have poor proof of title, and without adequate property rights and contract enforcement, lenders are hesitant to extend credit. According to estimates from the World Bank, countries in the region could boost annual economic growth by 1.6% if they improved their regulatory systems to correspond with those of countries in OECD. In conjunction with the 2005 G-8 meeting (see above), several large multinational corporations (including De Beers, Nestlé and Standard Chartered) formed Business for Africa, a new NGO the mission of which was to help improve overall business conditions in the region. Later in 2005 the Investment Climate Facility for Africa was launched. This facility supports the countries who are undergoing the African Peer Review Mechanism (APRM) of the New Partnership for Africa's Development (NEPAD—see below) by bringing together the government sector and business to improve the investment climate. Many countries in the region rank poorly in Transparency International's corruption perception index. In 2006 Equatorial Guinea, Chad, the DRC, Sudan and Guinea ranked in the bottom 10 countries).

Civil Strife

Social and political stability are generally associated with higher economic growth rates. Since acceding to independence, more than one-half of sub-Saharan African countries have been caught up in civil wars, uprisings, mass migrations and famine. According to the World Bank, between 1965 and 1985 the more unstable countries' average annual GDP growth was 0.5% per head, while the region's 11 most politically stable countries achieved an average rate of 1.4%. The level of strife has, however, increased in the region. A recent study suggests that the typical civil war in the region has lasted about seven years and caused GDP to decline by more than 2% for each year of strife. Furthermore, it typically takes about 14 years after the end of the conflict to recover to its pre-war growth. Many post-conflict governments continue to spend heavily on their military, thus reducing the potential peace dividend. Conflicts can be both a cause and consequence of poverty and some observers have termed this the 'conflict trap'. The office of the UN High Commissioner for Refugees estimated that at the end of 2004 30% of the world's 9.6m. refugees were sub-Saharan Africans. Strife continues to plague many areas of the region, with conflicts sometimes involving neighbouring countries and thus inhibiting economic growth for the entire sub-continent. The UN estimates that there are nearly 50m. landmines buried in 11 countries in the region, mostly in Angola (15m.) and in Mozambique (3m.), where they have so far claimed over 10,000 lives. Food production in Angola has fallen by more than 25% in recent years, and much of that decline is attributable to these mines.

Health, Population, Education, Social Factors and Natural Environment

Virtually all African states face significant problems in providing health services and education. Although both have improved since the mid-1960s, their levels remain the lowest in the world. In 2003 annual government expenditure on health care in sub-Saharan Africa averaged only 6.1% of GDP. This was unevenly distributed among countries, for example in 2003 Eritrea spent less than 2%, while Mali spent more than 9%. Moreover, care was unevenly distributed throughout many countries, with most health facilities concentrated in urban areas. For example, 66% of Ghana's population live in rural areas while only 15% of the country's physicians work there. WHO estimates that for the region to increase its current ratio of less than one health worker per 1,000 people to 2.5 health workers per 1,000 people, it will need to employ 1m. new workers in the health sector between 2005 and 2015. Seychelles leads the region with 151 physicians per 100,000 people, contrasted with Ethiopia's 1.6 per 100,000. According to the UN Children's Fund, a number of countries, including Angola, Ethiopia and Mozambique, spent more over many years on their military requirements than on health and education. While African governments agreed to increase health care funding to 15% of their budgets when signing the 2000 Abuja Declaration, this target has not been met. With declining export receipts and general budget austerity, many African countries have been compelled to decrease their budgetary provisions for health. Indeed, the region's public health spending per head was US $36 in 2003, compared to a developing world average of $294. This reduced spending has resulted, for example, in diminished levels of immunization. Only about 83% of Africa's population living in towns and 45% in the countryside has access to clean, piped water, while access to sanitation facilities is worse: 74% living in urban areas and 43% in rural areas. Importantly, some 80% of illness in Africa's LDCs can be associated with inadequate water supplies or poor sanitation. Between 1990 and 2004 there was an increase of some 60m. in the number of people without access to clean drinking water, and the situation is worse for sanitation. The ADB's assessment in 2007 concluded that the problem is not a lack of water, but a distribution issue. In most cities at least one-half of the water supply is wasted or cannot be accounted for. Urban sanitation access ranges from a high of 90% of the population in Tanzania's cities, to 8% in Rwanda.

HIV/AIDS has become the most threatening health problem in sub-Saharan Africa, with 7.2% of the adult population (aged between 15 and 49 years) being HIV positive in 2003. More than 20m. Africans have already died from the disease and the joint UN programme on HIV/AIDS (UNAIDS) estimated that 24.5m. people in sub-Saharan Africa were living with HIV/AIDS at the end of 2005. This figure represented 63.5% of estimated HIV infection world-wide (more than 85% of the world's HIV-infected children are in Africa). Approximately 6.1% of all adults in the region were living with HIV/AIDS in 2005. Such is the mortality rate among the young that the average life expectancy at birth in eight African countries—Angola, Botswana, Lesotho, Malawi, Sierra Leone, Swaziland, Zambia and Zimbabwe—had fallen to 40 years of age or below by 2005. By the end of 2005 HIV infected 33.4% of the adult population in Swaziland, 24.1% in Botswana and 23.2% in Lesotho, according to estimates by UNAIDS. In 10 of the region's countries HIV had infected at least 10% of the adult population. AIDS in Africa generally affects young adults (aged 20–45 years) in their most economically productive years, and in Africa the educated, urban élite have been hardest hit. In fact, infection rates in urban areas are approximately double those of rural areas. In addition to productivity loss from lost workers, the absentee rates linked to AIDS from sickness and attending funerals is a troubling problem. Owing to the AIDS pandemic there are currently some 12m. orphans in Africa, imposing major strains on individual governments' ability to provide housing, health care and education. Before AIDS one in 50 children in the region were orphans, while in some countries that rate was one in 10 by the late 1990s. The US Agency for International Development (USAID) reported that the number of orphans in Zambia exceeded 1.2m. in 2000, one in every four Zambian children. Given the size of the pandemic in several African states, it is reasonable to expect that AIDS will curtail GDP growth in several countries during the next decade. The World Bank has expressed the view that overall growth in GDP per head is unaffected if a country's overall infection rate remains below 5%. However, when the disease reaches 8% of the adult population, growth per head is 0.4% lower than it would otherwise have been. When the infection rate exceeds 25%, then the cost to growth is close to 1%.

Additionally, incidences of tuberculosis have risen sharply in the recent past, claiming some 2m. deaths world-wide annually. This increase has been linked to the growing AIDS incidence, as about 50% of tuberculosis patients are HIV-infected. The International Partnership Against AIDS in Africa was launched in 1999, with the participation of African governments, the UN, international donors, and the private and community sectors. The Partnership has campaigned for, and 10 states have received, access to lower-cost generic drugs to fight HIV/AIDS and South Africa has successfully negotiated agreements with pharmaceutical companies to produce drugs domestically. In 2000 the USA agreed to allow African states to develop generic AIDS vaccines without regard to US patent protections. In June 2001 Botswana became the first African state to take advantage of lower-priced drugs and hoped to be able to provide therapies for 100,000 infected citizens. Moreover, at WTO meetings held in Doha, Qatar, in November 2001 and Sydney, Australia, in November 2002, delegates agreed to allow some developing nations to manufacture generic drugs previously protected by patents and export the medicines to other needy countries on a case-by-case basis. Of the 4m. Africans requiring antiretroviral treatment, less than 100,000 were receiving it in 2004. However, with the drastic fall in prices mentioned above, treatment expansion is now more likely than at any other time.

The region is also experiencing an increase in malaria. Approximately 11% of disease-induced deaths in Africa are caused by malaria, and approximately 90% of world-wide deaths caused by malaria occur in sub-Saharan Africa. Indeed, malaria's toll is greater than that of all other tropical diseases combined. In early 2000 African leaders met in Nigeria to devise a strategy to combat malaria, which causes 1m.–2m. deaths annually. Some researchers believe that had malaria been eradicated 30 years ago, the region's GDP would now be one-third higher than it is. In 2004 Mozambique was the worst affected country with over 5m. reported cases.

In late 2001 the UN announced a Global AIDS and Health Fund to increase funding for AIDS, malaria and tuberculosis programmes from an annual level of less than US $2,000m. to $7,000m. African trypanosomiasis (sleeping sickness), which had been virtually eradicated in the early 1960s, reappeared in 1970, and is now widespread. WHO has estimated that up to 500,000 Africans are infected with the disease, with a further 60m. at risk. Owing to a lack of screening and treatment, and regional conflict, this disease has become the greatest cause of mortality in areas of southern Sudan, Angola and the DRC. None the less, there have been some successful attempts to combat disease in the region. For example, onchocerciasis (river blindness) has been virtually eliminated in West Africa; WHO estimated that its programme for the control of the disease (concluded in 2002) prevented 600,000 new cases. During the past few years there have been numerous new initiatives to improve health conditions in Africa. The Bill and Melinda Gates Foundation has taken a leading role, and new programmes under the Global Fund to Fight AIDS, Tuberculosis and Malaria, the Global Alliance for Vaccination and Immunization, the US President's Emergency Plan for AIDS Relief, along with some 70 other initiatives, have been launched.

Until relatively recently most African governments did not regard rapid population growth or environmental degradation as matters for concern. Indeed, until quite recently most areas of the region practised what is known as 'slash and burn' agriculture, a technique that can only succeed where land is abundant. During the past decade a succession of countries, realizing that their resources cannot service their population growth, have begun to recognize the necessity for environmental protection.

African countries have some of the highest annual rates of population growth in the world: During 1995–2005 Benin, Chad, The Gambia, Niger, Togo and Uganda all had population growth rates of 3% or greater. During 2004–2020 the World Bank projects annual population growth in the region of 2.2%, with an estimated population growth from 725m. in 2004 to 1,032m. in 2020. Furthermore, Africa's dependency ratio (the ratio of working aged population to dependants) is close to 1:1, compared with East Asia's ratio of 2:1. Of sub-Saharan Africa's total population of 751.3m. in 2005, 43.5% were under 14 years of age, and 3.1% over 65 years old. At current growth rates the region will double its population every 25 years. Indeed, sub-Saharan Africa's population has been forecast to reach 2,000m. by the year 2050, although with continued increases in HIV rates, some demographers are revising this figure significantly downward.

By 2000 about three-quarters of all African countries had family planning programmes, and some have set targets for population growth. Fertility appears to be declining in the small number of states that have established family planning services. Stemming rapid population growth in Africa is difficult because of social as well as economic factors. Most Africans live in rural areas on farms and require large numbers of helpers. The cheapest way of obtaining such assistance is for a farmer to have more children. Owing to the high infant mortality rate (resulting from poor health and nutrition), rural couples tend to want, and have, more babies. Additionally, African countries do not have organized old-age support schemes, and children are often viewed as potential providers of support for the elderly. Furthermore, modern contraceptive methods are used by just 22% of couples in sub-Saharan Africa (and only 8% of the lowest-income population), compared with 78% in East Asia.

Rapid urbanization has also imposed stresses on many African economies. Africa is still very largely rural and agricultural. In 1980 about 75% of the region's population lived in rural areas; by 2004 that figure had declined to around 65%. However, approximately 70% of Africa's poorest live in rural areas. Urbanization has increased at an alarming pace (it is currently growing at an annual rate of 4%, the highest in the world), and it has been forecast that by the year 2025 Africa's urban population will be three times larger than in 2000, with more than one-half of the population living in cities. More than 45% of all urban-dwelling sub-Saharan Africans reside in cities with more than 500,000 inhabitants, compared with only 8% in 1960, when there were only two cities in the region with populations exceeding 500,000. Unemployment and under-employment are rampant in every major city of Africa. Living conditions in virtually every city have worsened over the last two decades. In addition, the cost of living is relatively more expensive in Africa than in many other developing regions. For example, the price of water (per 1,000 litres) is US $1.40 in sub-Saharan Africa, compared to less than $0.60 in Asia, the Middle East and Latin America. Cost of home ownership requires 12.5% of family income in Africa, compared to 11.3% in Asia, 10.9% in the Middle East and 5.4% in Latin America. Africans spend on average 64% of their income on food. Population growth has put additional pressure on good agricultural and grazing lands, and on fuelwood. About 80% of the region's energy needs are supplied by fuelwood gathered by rural dwellers. Furthermore, population pressures add to deforestation, soil degradation and declines in agricultural output. In the early 2000s it was estimated that some 7% of forest cover was being lost annually.

The informal sector has become increasingly important in the region and has been growing at an annual rate of about 6% since the 1980s, according to the International Labour Organization. Perhaps most importantly, the 'hidden economy' absorbs three-quarters of new entrants into the labour market. In any event, productivity is low, owing to a variety of reasons, including limited access to capital (the level of capital per worker is less than one-half that of South Asia).

After initial improvements following independence, education is also declining in many sub-Saharan African countries. There has been a direct link between education and growth—between 1960 and 1980 the African countries that had higher percentages of children enrolled in primary school also had higher economic growth rates. Low primary school enrolments hamper economic development. There are very few examples of countries that have achieved sustained growth with literacy rates below 50%. Additionally, the number of malnourished children increased, from 23m. in 1975 to 53m. in 1995, and to an estimated 70m. in 2002. The percentage of malnourished children rose from 31% in 1992 to 32% in 2003, the only region in the world to witness such an increase. Children who do not have enough to eat perform poorly in school. A further key factor is that of increased education for women, which is clearly associated with lower fertility rates. A recent study by the World Bank found that the three countries with declining fertility—Botswana, Kenya and Zimbabwe—had the highest levels of female schooling and the lowest rates of child mortality. The study also indicated that in the Sahel, where female schooling rates are lowest, both fertility rates and child mortality have remained high. With an average of 5.3 births per female in 2004, sub-Saharan Africa has the highest fertility rate in the world.

Shortly after independence most countries of the sub-Saharan region initiated programmes aimed at establishing universal primary education. In 2004 93% of children in the appropriate age-group were enrolled in primary schools. This compared with an enrolment rate of 91% for all developing countries, and virtually 100% in Western industrialized countries. It should be noted that boys have greater access to education: 94% of boys were enrolled in primary schools in 1998–2000, compared to 81% of girls. About 30% of children in the relevant age-group in the region are enrolled in secondary schools, and only 7% of the poorest rural children. Here again, many governments have found education to be a service for which budgetary allocations may be cut back during times of fiscal crisis. African governments' emphasis on higher education at the expense of primary education has also been a negative factor for economic development. For example, in the late 1990s average expenditure on students at secondary schools per head was some 40 times that of expenditure on students at primary schools, compared with a ratio of 1:16 in Western industrialized countries. Additionally, because courses and textbooks were generally 'imported' direct from the former European colonial powers, much of the education has been inappropriate to the rural settings where most of the students live and will eventually work. Many parents have little or no education—in 2002 adult illiteracy was 35% in sub-Saharan Africa, compared with 13% in Latin America and the Caribbean and 12% in East Asia and the Pacific—and the level of a parent's education is an important indicator of a child's school attendance. Adult illiteracy ranges from lows of 8% and 9% in Zimbabwe and Seychelles, respectively, to rates of 71% in Niger and 81% in Mali.

Africa's environment has been under intense pressure, especially during the past 20 years. With the increases in population discussed above, overcultivation and overgrazing have turned vast areas into virtual wastelands. The UN Environment Programme (UNEP) has estimated that an area twice the size of India is under threat of desertification. During 1990–95, according to UNEP estimates, the region's woodlands were being diminished at an annual rate of 29,400 sq km. During 1990–2005 sub-Saharan Africa had the highest annual average rate of deforestation in the world. According to the World Bank, African forests are believed to contain 45% of the world's bio-diversity, while forest-related activities account for at least 10% of GDP for 17 nations in the region. Civil wars have also contributed to environmental degradation. From the late 1980s civil wars had devastating effects on the environment in such countries as Chad, the DRC, Sudan, Somalia, Mozambique and Angola. In addition, the region's 5m. displaced persons have fled not only repressive political conditions, but also degraded environments unable to support them economically.

Many government leaders in the past suggested that the achievement of economic growth was inconsistent with environmental protection, and that African development could only advance at the expense of its environment. It has only been in the past few years that the two goals have been recognized as not mutually exclusive. Indeed, it is now generally accepted that sustained economic growth is impossible without adequate environmental protection. Specifically, many countries, such as Kenya, Tanzania and South Africa, increasingly depend on tourism based on wildlife and undisturbed natural habitats. According to the UN World Tourism Organization (UNWTO), Africa attracted only 2.9% of the world's tourists in 2005, and absorbed 2.1% of tourism-generated revenue world-wide in that year. South Africa was the only African country among the top 25 world-wide destinations in 2003. None the less, recently Africa has been one of the fastest-growing regions for international tourism; according to the UNWTO, tourist visits to destinations in sub-Saharan Africa totalled an estimated 23.0m. in 2005, with the number of visits increasing at an average annual rate of 5.1% in 2000–05. Total revenue from tourism in the region in 2005 amounted to US $14,500m.

In the late 1980s Lesotho, Madagascar and Mauritius became the first three African countries to develop national environmental action plans (NEAPs). These NEAPs are intended to create a framework for the better integration of environmental concerns into a country's economic development. By 1996 40 African states had begun the NEAP process, with support from a number of UN and bilateral donors. Loss of bio-diversity is also a serious problem, as many of Africa's plant and animal numbers have been extinguished. The long-term success of agriculture, the region's most important economic sector, ultimately will depend on the wise use of the environment. Climate change will affect Africa more seriously than any other area in the world, although the region produces only about 7% of the world's 'greenhouse' gases. Greater rainfall variability will contribute to both more flooding and droughts, and exacerbate the malaria problem. In 2007 the UN's Intergovernmental Panel on Climate Change predicted a minimum increase in temperature of 2.5°C by 2030, suggesting that food security will be severely compromised. Water will become a critical problem. A University of Pretoria study estimates that the region could lose some US $25,000m. as a result of crop failures. The warming trend could affect biodiversity and animal habitats, while rising sea levels could be a problem for low-lying regions. It should be noted, however, that global warming could bring benefits, for example eastern Africa could see increased rainfall in its parched highland areas.

Physical Infrastructure, the Structure of the Economies, Productivity and Employment

For most countries in the region physical infrastructure—including transportation, electricity and communications—has generally deteriorated since the achievement of independence in the early and mid-1960s. Such essential services as electric power, water, roads, railways, ports and communications have been neglected, particularly in rural areas. Businesses in Africa often cite poor infrastructure as one of the major constraints in doing business. Also, as many states are landlocked, additional transportation costs add to the cost of doing business. For many areas it is a lack of sufficient maintenance rather than a lack of infrastructure itself that hinders business growth and, even where the infrastructure exists, it is often of poor quality. The World Bank estimates that the region requires US $17,000m.–$22,000m. annually in 2005–15 for both capital and maintenance expenditures. Given current expenditures of approximately $6,000m. (of which one-half is financed by donors), there will remain a gap of $7,000m.–$12,000m., equivalent to about 4.5% of GDP. Millions of US dollars worth of investment in transportation will be required if Africa is to take advantage of any improvement in agricultural output performances. Transportation costs from and within the region are very high, owing to the vast distances involved, the sparse population, living mostly far from the ocean, and the poor state of the roads. Despite a decline in most other parts of the world, transportation costs have increased in Africa. Poland has more paved roads than sub-Saharan Africa (excluding South Africa). Indeed, only about 16% of all roads in Africa are paved, down from 17% in 1992.

Additional resources will also be needed if Africa's industrial sectors are to advance. Manufacturing has not increased, because of low capacity utilization, limited trained manpower at all levels, small-scale domestic markets, inappropriate technology and poor plant design.

The underlying structure of sub-Saharan Africa's economies has not changed dramatically since independence. In 1965 agriculture accounted for 24% of GDP, industry 30%, and services 46%, according to the World Bank. By 2005 the contribution of agriculture had declined to 17.0% while those of industry and services had increased to 31.8% and 51.2%, respectively. African goals of rapid industrialization were not achieved. Manufacturing advanced rapidly in the early 1960s, but then slowed to about the same average growth rate as overall GDP. While petroleum output expanded more swiftly, only a few states—Angola, Cameroon, the Republic of the Congo, Gabon and Nigeria—benefited. During 2006–07 Nigeria's oil production of 2.5m. barrels per day was cut by 25% due to militant groups attacks demanding a share of the oil revenues. The region's proven oil reserves more than doubled between 1980 and 2005, to 114,300m. barrels, according to British Petroleum. Output increased by 60% during that period, and the region now supplies about 12% of the world's oil. Since 1990 the oil industry has invested more than US $20,000m. in exploration and production activities. It should be noted that with the exception of Nigeria and Angola, none of the other states are members of OPEC, and thus are not subject to output limits. Finally, many economists note that much of the petroleum revenues have not gone toward sustainable development, and in many cases has added to social instability and environmental degradation, resulting in what has been termed 'the oil curse'.

By 2005 manufacturing accounted for only 14.3% of the region's GDP (compared to 17% in 1965). Owing to low productivity and low investment, the growth rate of the region's manufacturing sector declined from 3.8% in 1997 to 0.4% in 1998, before recovering to reach 4.2% in 2005.

The region lacks the technology available in many other parts of the world; for example, only 30 Africans per 1,000 had telephones in 2003. However, the use of mobile cellular telephones was approaching 62 per 1,000 people, making this industry the world's fastest growing and an example of development driven by 'leapfrog technology', i.e. progressing from essentially no telephone to mobile telephone directly. Sub-Saharan Africa has fewer telephones than Brazil, one-half of which are in South Africa. Indeed, in 2002 Africa accounted for only some 2% of the world's total number of telephones and in 2003 had the lowest number of internet hosts (4.2 per 10,000 people) and users (7.5m., of which 3.1m. were in South Africa). In 2005 South Africa led the region in the number of mobile phones, with 71 phones per 100 inhabitants (the lowest adapter was Eritrea with less than one per 100 people. Mauritius had the most land lines, with 29 per 100 people.

As a result of decreased inflationary pressures world-wide, as reflected in the prices of petroleum and many manufactured goods, the average rate of inflation for the sub-Saharan region was 6.1% in 2000, 6.5% in 2003 and 6.0% in 2004. However, inflation rates vary considerably from country to country. Some eight countries had at least double-digit inflation in 2002, and Angola and the DRC experienced high levels of inflation. Zimbabwe's political crisis has also produced extremely high inflation in recent years, reaching 1,200% in 2006. However, food price increases in the region have declined from an average of nearly 14% per year in the 1980s to less than 10% per year in 2002.

Many African countries' currencies appreciated in terms of exchange rate during the mid-1970s. While inflation raised domestic prices, local currencies were not devalued to compensate. Thus, currencies became overvalued, meaning that their purchasing power was stronger for goods from abroad than at home, leading to increased demand for imports. Moreover, their exports became increasingly uncompetitive in price. As their currencies became overvalued, and foreign 'hard' currencies were in short supply, many African governments had to limit or ration foreign exchange. This, in turn, led to 'parallel' or 'black' markets for foreign currencies. Foreign-exchange overvaluation was thus a result of inflation, which was generated, at least in part, by escalations of government budget deficits. In addition, export and import tariff revenue provides a significant portion of African government revenues, as there is little personal or corporate taxation. As trade declines, so does government revenue, thus exacerbating budget deficits. As a result of major policy reforms, most countries have now abandoned these overvalued foreign-exchange policies.

A major problem for the region is the poor level of productivity in general, and of investment productivity in particular, as measured by a capital input-output ratio. This ratio is less than one-half of that recorded in Asia during 1970–97. Thus, even if Africa can attract more foreign investment, it must make that investment more productive.

The region's total labour force in 2004 was 298.5m., of whom 42.2% were women. Estimates for unemployment vary so greatly that it is impossible to provide precise data. It is worth noting, however, that official unemployment estimates are as high as 30% in some countries, while unofficial estimates are higher still. The percentage of children working has declined somewhat in recent years, from 36.2% of all children in 1970 to 29.9% in 2002.

Agriculture and Food Shortages

Unquestionably, the leading factor behind the drastic declines in African economies has been the general neglect of agriculture. This sector basically comprises two components: food production for local consumption, and export commodities. Agriculture accounts for only about one-sixth of GDP for the continent as a whole, two-thirds of employment and 40% of export value. Agricultural labour productivity is quite low, owing to a number of factors discussed below. For virtually all African economies the major agricultural exports consist of one or perhaps two or three primary products (cash crops such as coffee, tea, sugar, sisal, etc.) whose prices fluctuate widely from year to year on the world market. For 44 sub-Saharan African countries their three leading agricultural exports comprise some 82% of their total agricultural exports. Unfortunately, Africa's share of world agricultural exports has declined since the 1970s. For example, its share of the world market for groundnuts has declined by 55%, cocoa by 27% and coffee by 14%. However, there were some increases in Africa's share of the market for bananas, cotton, sugar, tea and tobacco during 1990–97. The value of the region's exports has hardly increased in real terms: in 1980 agricultural exports were valued at US $12,212m. and had increased to only $13,368m. by 1997. A low point of $9,258m. was recorded in 1992. Agricultural output has increased at an average annual rate of 5.5% since 1995.

As suggested by the World Bank, 'if agriculture is in trouble, Africa is in trouble', and agriculture has been in trouble for the past 30 years. The percentage of Africans lacking sufficient food has increased from 38% to 43%; some 41 states in the region are experiencing food deficits. Food imports have increased dramatically, from US $5,433m. in 1980 to $8,352m. in 2000, averaging some $7,000m. during the 1990s.

The region's food production increased at an average annual rate of 0.9% in 1975–85, of 4.1% in 1985–89, and of an estimated 2.6% from 1995–2003, but food production virtually stagnated between 2001 and 2002. Furthermore, these annual growth rates must be balanced by a population growth rate averaging 2.5% per year. In 1996 FAO convened a World Food Summit, where agricultural problems were discussed at the highest international levels. As Africa was the only region where the proportion of people suffering from malnutrition was rising, the summit focused special attention on the problems of the region. The World Bank disclosed that its funding for agriculture and rural development had been reduced from US $6,000m. in 1986 to $2,600m. in 1996, and undertook to ensure that agriculture received priority attention in its agenda in Africa.

In 2006 the UN World Food Programme (WFP) estimated that more than 30m. Africans were in need of food aid. Annual population growth has outpaced food production since 1993, with the result of a 30% increase in the number of hungry people, from 176m. to 210m. Between 1980 and 1990 the region's annual imports of cereals increased from 8.5m. tons to 18.2m. tons. Regional production of cereals has increased steadily since the mid-1990s. In 2002 the region grew 76.1m. tons of cereals, increasing to 82.6m. tons in 2003. Many Africans experience transitory food insecurity owing to fluctuations in prices and production levels attending climatic difficulties and civil unrest. In 1987–2000 there were 116 incidents of severe shortages of rain in 27 countries. Indeed, the drought experienced in southern Africa in mid-2002 was the worst in memory. WFP reported that as many as 20m. people were suffering from hunger and malnutrition. As discussed above, many governments have implemented economic policies that were designed to keep urban wages and living conditions high and farm prices low by maintaining the value of currencies at high, unrealistic rates of exchange. This is understandable and obvious: political power in Africa rests in the city, not in the village or countryside. This 'urban bias' was sometimes a deliberate strategy, at other times more a result of planned rural neglect, and on many occasions was endorsed by the international development community. In addition, producers were often bound by prices fixed by their governments, and at times these 'producer' prices failed to cover input costs. This resulted in farmers reducing their production for sale and reverting to subsistence agriculture. Finally, it should be noted that investment in agriculture has traditionally been low. For example, agriculture typically receives less than 10% of public spending, but can account for up to 80% of GDP. Also, as much as three-quarters of the region's farmlands has become degraded due to erosion and other results of population pressures, resulting, for example, in grain yields stagnating at 1 ton per ha, compared to the world average of about 3 tons.

Fishing has also experienced challenges during the past few years. That sector makes a major contribution to many economies, comprising more than 10% of the value of exports in 11 countries. However, current fishing methods are causing many fisheries to reach their limits.

This bias has resulted in missed opportunities for growth and development, and has contributed to the region's 'brain drain'. The IMF suggested that some 30,000 Africans with doctoral degrees were working in North America and Europe in the early 2000s. The World Bank estimates there are more Nigerian doctors in New York, USA, than in Nigeria, and more Malawian doctors in Manchester, United Kingdom, than in Malawi. Zambia has trained over 600 physicians since its independence but only 50 remain in its health care system. Importantly, the pull from the industrial countries is likely to grow. Nursing shortages in the USA are projected to reach 500,000 by 2015, and already the past decade has seen a dramatic increase in nurses migrating from Africa to the developed nations. Health care is but one illustration of the severe problems caused when the very skilled people trained and needed to develop a country leave for better opportunities.

PRESSURES FOR ECONOMIC POLICY REFORM

African governments have been coming under increasing pressure from a variety of sources to 'liberalize' their public economic policies. During the 1970s and early 1980s the most direct pressure came from the IMF and other donors. They began to insist on 'conditionality' for support, particularly from the IMF; that is, the IMF required specific macroeconomic policy changes, sometimes termed 'structural adjustments', usually in the area of exchange rates (i.e. devaluation), and reductions in government spending before a new loan agreement could be granted. In 1998 35 African countries launched structural adjustment programmes (SAPs) or borrowed from the IMF to support reform policies. Although these programmes (now called Poverty Reduction and Growth Facility arrangements) have many common points, they are actually varied. Additional pressures, now known as the 'Washington consensus', have come from the World Bank and USAID. Specifically, a 1981 World Bank study proposed four major and basic policy changes that it felt were critical: namely, (i) the correction of overvalued exchange rates; (ii) the improvement of price incentives for exports and agriculture; (iii) the protection of industry in a more uniform and less direct way; and (iv) the reduction of direct governmental controls. Other pressures have originated and grown internally, as more people have become increasingly dissatisfied with their declining standard of living and the poor economic performance in their own countries. During the 1990s several countries, most notably Kenya, Madagascar, Malawi, Mauritius, Tanzania, Uganda and Zimbabwe, removed restrictions on external capital transactions. This effectively closed the gap between the official exchange rate and the 'parallel', or 'black market', rate. South Africa abolished its two-tier exchange-rate system in 1995, and Angola, Zambia, Ethiopia and Sierra Leone have also unified their foreign-exchange systems, making foreign trade and investment less cumbersome.

Recognizing their poor past performance, African governments are currently scaling down their involvement in parastatal organizations. The growth of parastatal companies expanded more slowly in the 1980s and early 1990s than in the 1970s. Although the number of parastatal bodies remained fairly constant during 1980–86, at about 3,000, many countries subsequently reduced the number of public enterprises. However, the lack of developed equity markets has posed an obstacle to the progress of privatization. Numerous African countries are now in the course either of reforming the institutional structures of parastatal enterprises, or providing them with greater operating autonomy. In other cases they are being disbanded entirely. None the less, by the mid-1990s less than one-fifth of sub-Saharan Africa's state enterprises had been transferred to the private sector, and few among these were operating in such key sectors as electricity generation, telecommunications, transport and mining. The bulk of the privatization activity—perhaps amounting to as much as two-thirds—had been restricted to only four countries: Kenya, Mozambique, Tanzania and Zambia. Furthermore, in the late 1990s the pace of privatization slowed. The number of public enterprises privatized in 1996 totalled 426, declining to 72 in 2000 and only seven in both 2001 and 2002. According to the World Bank, 3,486 state-owned enterprises in sub-Saharan Africa had been privatized by the end of 2002 (of which 2,777 were privatized prior to 1998), at a value of some US $6,686m.

In addition to the scaling down of parastatal operations, many governments are actively seeking the participation of the private sector, both domestic and foreign. The region has experienced a dramatic growth in stock exchanges, and by the late 1990s new bourses had opened in Zambia, Malawi, Uganda, Sudan, Swaziland and Tanzania. With the continuing dismantlement of nationalized industries, these equity markets should gain in importance.

CURRENT OUTLOOK

Economic reforms have, in general, led to improved economic performance, although certain sectors in most countries have experienced sharp declines, and the gains have not been equally shared. According to an independent report examining the SAP, eight African countries achieved their economic targets in 1992–96. This group performed better than a comparative group that had not undergone the adjustment process. Furthermore, the 31 poor, aid-dependent countries using the SAP reduced their deficits by one-half during this period. None the less, structural adjustment is very controversial. However, some studies have failed to demonstrate a definite linkage between reform and growth. In countries as diverse as Eritrea, Ghana, Namibia and Uganda leaders are developing their own modes of reform. Such reform, however, must include better public administration and good governance. If African governments implement their plans for economic liberalism, encompassing generally higher agricultural producer prices, revised and realistic foreign-exchange rates, together with other publicly unpopular policy measures, they will require increased outside support. By the late 1990s economic assistance to the region was being made increasingly dependent upon economic reform, and the major donor countries of OECD had reallocated most of their economic assistance to countries implementing reform programmes. Additionally, the major multilateral donors were also reallocating their resources on this basis. The region is beginning to show progress in new areas. For example, South Africa's Southern African Large Telescope, located in the Karoo region, is the world's largest. Nigeria has 40% of the world's sickle-cell-anaemia patients, and its pharmaceutical research institute has developed a new medicine to combat that disease. As discussed earlier, the region is also able to take advantage of 'leapfrog technology' in communications, information technology and transportation.

When (and if) peace and stability come to the more strife-ridden parts of the region, economic growth should follow. However, a World Bank report suggests that the 'peace dividend' does not necessarily immediately follow the resolution of civil war. The fact that such conflicts often do not end decisively means that armies are slow to demobilize, and military spending is not quickly reduced. Indeed, military spending actually increased by 40% in Uganda in its early years of peace following the overthrow of Gen. Idi Amin in 1979. Moreover, the resolution of civil conflict does not necessarily lead to increased security. Demobilization often results in former military personnel resorting to banditry to survive, as witnessed in Angola, Chad and Mozambique. Economic output in these countries, according to the UN, may have fallen to only one-half of the levels that would have been achieved in conditions of internal political harmony. None the less, some recent developments may help. For example, in 2002 a new international initiative, known as the Kimberley Process and involving more than 70 countries, introduced a certification scheme for rough diamonds, in an attempt to halt the trade in illicit diamonds (so-called 'conflict diamonds').

Globalization, the accelerated economic integration among nations, has brought benefits in terms of world-wide economic growth. However, these benefits have not been evenly distributed, and income disparities between rich and poor countries, and even within countries, have increased. This is most pronounced in sub-Saharan Africa. None the less, Africa is a resilient continent. It has withstood drastic changes during the past three centuries and especially during the past three decades. The dramatic change that the continent is experiencing is, to a large extent, due to the fact that by 2007 more than 70% of all Africans had been born after the era of colonialism. Recent history elsewhere, particularly in Asia, suggests that the unacceptable economic deterioration of the past 30 years can be reversed. As sub-Saharan Africa moves into the new millennium, its governments have begun to realize that, while many economic problems were inherited, responsibility must be taken for problems that are soluble. Rather than being hostile to foreign entrepreneurs, most African governments are now actively seeking foreign commercial involvement. Certainly by 2007 most African governments were presenting the appearance of reform, and acknowledging the parallel between political pluralism and economic development. The combination of liberalized economic policies, together with more political openness could signal the beginning of sub-Saharan Africa's transformation towards economic recovery and sustained long-term development. Indeed, Freedom House's 2006 ranking of political rights and civil liberties places the region ahead of the Middle East and North Africa as rated 'more free', with 71% of the region classified as free or partially free. After decades of virtual stagnation, and at times decline, sub-Saharan African economies are growing again. However, on average that growth is not high enough, or sustained enough, to reduce the number of people in poverty, which, according to the IMF, has actually increased by 60m. since 1990. The World Bank recently noted that 'it is considerably more difficult to sustain growth than to initiate it'. None the less, many observers view sub-Saharan Africa's economic prospects as more favourable now than at any time during the past 20 years. A 5% rate of economic growth projected through to 2008 represents about double the growth rates of the preceding decade. This projection is based on an improved government policy environment, higher commodity prices, a global economic recovery, favourable weather conditions and an expansion of petroleum production (in Angola, Chad and Equatorial Guinea). However, such estimates have often proved to be unattainable, owing to the region's susceptibility to natural disasters, political turmoil and other shocks. Finally, income per head (adjusted for inflation) is forecast to rise at about 1% annually, which would make it no higher in 2008 than in 1982, and about 4% below the level of 1974. Thus, Africa's growth during the coming decade could place the region in the same state as more than a generation ago.

As noted above, countries that have launched economic policy reforms generally have outperformed those that have not put their programmes into full effect. However, these reforms have not come without costs or criticisms. Many observers believe that 'the medicine is worse than the disease'. More and more countries are 'reforming' in a determined manner. Investors who, only a few years ago, would have overlooked the region, and who might otherwise have focused their attention on Asia or Eastern Europe, may now see Africa as a viable alternative. Perhaps the continent's most ambitious plan for reform, NEPAD, was launched in October 2001. Its founding documents were jointly formulated by the heads of state of Algeria, Egypt, Nigeria, Senegal and South Africa. NEPAD's aim was to develop a 'holistic, comprehensive, integrated, strategic framework for the socio-economic development of Africa'. Specifically, the priorities included: (i) creating peace, security and stability; (ii) investing in people; (iii) promoting industrialization; (iv) increasing information and communications technology; and (v) developing basic infrastructure. In an effort to strengthen NEPAD, the APRM has been developed to monitor the governance of participating countries. Accession to the APRM is voluntary, and the basic areas to be reviewed include political and corporate governance, economic management and respect for human rights. By mid-2006 23 countries (containing some three-quarters of the region's population) had agreed to participate in the programme, with Ghana, Kenya, Rwanda and Mauritius the first countries to commence the peer-review process. The second group will include Mali, Mozambique, Nigeria, Senegal and South Africa.

Africa's path ahead is difficult and uncertain. Perhaps the best way to place sub-Saharan Africa's future in perspective is to examine the progress made towards achieving the MDGs adopted by 189 countries in 2000, and which aim to reduce poverty by one-half and make other important improvements in the developing world by 2015. In mid-2005 the World Bank and the IMF conducted a special study to evaluate progress towards the eight goals. The overall conclusion was not positive, stating that 'in sub-Saharan Africa the momentum has been slower, and most countries are at severe risk of falling short'. In 2007 the ADB reported that only three countries, Botswana, Cape Verde and Ghana were 'on track' (when the actual growth rate of the indicator is at least equal to the required growth rate to meet the target) to reach at least five of the eight goals. The first goal is to reduce extreme poverty by one-half. While three nations (Djibouti, Gabon and Ghana) are making some progress, the rest of the countries in the region are not. However, the poverty rate has declined marginally, to 44% in 2002, down from 44.6% in 1990. The second goal is to achieve universal primary education. In this regard Cape Verde, Lesotho, Madagascar, Malawi, Mauritius, São Tomé and Príncipe, Seychelles and Togo are on track. The elimination of gender disparity is the third goal and five countries—Botswana, Lesotho, Mauritius, Namibia and Seychelles—have achieved greater gender equality in both primary and secondary education. The fourth goal is to reduce child mortality. For the region with 20% of the world's children under the age of five, it accounts for one-half of the world's children deaths. Only three countries, Cape Verde, the Comoros, and Eritrea, are on track to meet this goal. The fifth goal is the improvement of maternal health. No country has met its targets, although nine are on track. The sixth goal relates to the combating of AIDS, malaria and other diseases. As discussed above, in 2006 the region accounted for 64% of the world's HIV-positive adults and 90% of children living with the virus, while the number of tuberculosis cases increased from 148 per 100,000 in 1990 to 281 per 100,000 in 2004. Only four states are on track to meet this goal. Goal seven seeks to ensure environmental sustainability. The region has seen deforestation increasing in recent years due to population pressures. Indeed, the land area covered by forests has decreased from 29% in 1990 to 27% in 2005 and has resulted in more flooding. Malawi, Mauritius and Namibia have achieved their targets to reduce by one-half the number of people without access to clean water and sanitation, although progress in most other countries has been very slow. The eighth goal is to develop a global partnership for development, stressing better trade and aid relations and exchange of new technologies. The ADB did not report on this goal, although many of these issues have been discussed above.

Despite pockets of success, much of the region seems to slip further backward. During the next few years serious questions will be posed by the extent to which the region is truly committed to the principles of NEPAD. Will its leaders insist on better governance, implement the rule of law and generally act in a transparent manner? Will peace come to Sudan, Somalia, and other strife-ridden nations? In addition, will sub-Saharan Africa continue to be marginalized, or can it find ways to integrate more successfully into the global economy? How can the negative effects of globalization be minimized? Will the industrialized countries open their markets to competition from the region? Will the region reduce its own trade barriers and find ways to improve co-operation and integrate its economies? Will the countries begin to invest in an often overlooked resource: their own people, particularly their women? Can the recent, positive signs of economic growth be sustained? At mid-2007 the chances for success remained clouded. It seemed certain, however, that few, if any, countries will be able to achieve most of the important elements of the development agenda as envisaged in the MDGs.

HEALTH AND MEDICAL ISSUES IN SUB-SAHARAN AFRICA

SAMUEL CROWE

Revised by IKE ANYA

The strong influence of socio-economic factors on health outcomes plays a central role in the discussion of health and medical issues in sub-Saharan Africa, making poverty the key focus of many initiatives to improve population health in Africa. In addition to the pervasive poverty at national levels in most sub-Saharan countries, which has led to a steady deterioration in the infrastructure and systems required to deliver health care, poverty at an individual level has, through malnutrition, poor living conditions and the inability to afford treatment, worsened the situation of many individuals and families. The increasing awareness of the links between poverty and ill health perhaps lay at the heart of initiatives in 2007 to hold leaders of the world's largest industrialized nations to the commitments they had made towards tackling poverty and underdevelopment in Africa in the preceding two years. Increasingly, there was also an emphasis on Africans finding their own solutions to the health challenges that faced the continent, with governments being encouraged to channel savings from debt relief into investments in health. While some progress has been made in tackling some of the biggest health problems, the health emergency that faced sub-Saharan Africans at the dawn of the 21st century showed little sign of abating. In 2007 HIV/AIDS, malaria and tuberculosis (TB) remained some of the greatest challenges to the health of sub-Saharan Africans, but maternal and child health and a growing burden of non-communicable diseases were also major challenges.

Much of the burden of disease in sub-Saharan Africa is preventable or treatable, and substantial improvements to health, sanitation and immunization coverage were made during the 1960s and 1970s. However, many of the gains achieved during these decades were lost in the 1980s, as poverty, structural adjustment, bad governance and internal conflicts took their toll.

During the 1990s the emerging HIV/AIDS epidemic, fuelled by poverty, malnutrition and high rates of TB infection, began to reverse many basic health indicators, leading to an average life expectancy in the mid 2000s of just 47 years. The downward spiral of ill health and poverty has since left the region with health problems on an unprecedented scale, many of which have attracted a global response in recognition of their severity. In 2007 it appeared that the political will was beginning to emerge in many African countries to face up to these challenges, although the commitment to devote 15% of national budgets to health remained to be translated into practice.

It is widely accepted that public services in most sub-Saharan countries have failed to deliver even the most basic services required for improving health. To compound this failure, the basic standard of living has fallen for many people, leaving them trapped in a vicious cycle of ill health and poverty. Recent data indicate that while the numbers of people living on less than US $1 per day in other regions of the world have declined, the numbers in sub-Saharan Africa have remained static or risen. According to the World Bank, an estimated 345m. people in the region (more than one-half of the population) were living in poverty in the early 2000s, an increase from 300m. during the 1990s. While the 2006 *World Development Report* suggested that there were grounds for cautious optimism, identifying seven countries in the region which had achieved or were on track to achieve the target of halving poverty rates by 2015, the 2007 report warned that without renewed action, the effects of HIV/AIDS could lead to incomes in sub-Saharan Africa falling to levels not seen since the 1960s. The report also acknowledged that African economies were growing but not at a rate sufficient to meet the UN Millennium Development Goals (MDGs).

Researchers are now beginning to understand more fully the pervasive effect of poverty on health and the fact that ill health hits the poorest hardest. The evidence that the main difference between the poor and the less poor in terms of health was not the likelihood of becoming ill, but that of having access to treatment, was strengthened by a study from Kenya published in 2007, which found similar patterns of illness in all socio-economic groups but different patterns of treatment seeking, largely because of costs. A study conducted in rural Côte d'Ivoire in 2005 found that the poorest children not only had higher parasite burdens, but were also most likely to live the furthest distance away from a health facility.

According to the World Health Organization (WHO) *African Regional Report*, published for the first time in November 2006, a child born in Africa has more than a 50% chance of being malnourished, a high risk of being HIV-positive and was more likely to lose his or her mother in childbirth or as a result of HIV than a child born anywhere else in the world.

The vicious cycle of poverty and ill health evident in the region has meant that many of the development efforts since the early 1990s have focused on poverty reduction strategies. However, it is increasingly accepted that ill health should be tackled in conjunction with poverty, as it directly contributes to poverty itself. Simply relying on economic development to raise standards of living and improve health is not enough. This recognition was evident in the continuing initiatives from the Group of Eight leading industrialized nations (G-8) to improve access to treatment for HIV alongside improving opportunities for African countries to trade globally.

Considering the impact of malaria alone on the economic development of the region, a report in 2000 by researchers from the Center for International Development at Harvard University and the London School of Hygiene and Tropical Medicine estimated that economic growth in African countries with intense malaria was slowed by 1.3% per head per year. If the disease had been eradicated 35 years earlier, the gross domestic product (GDP) of sub-Saharan Africa in 2000 would have been some US $100,000m. more. In other words, the short-term benefit from controlling malaria in the region would amount to an extra $12,000m. per year. The HIV/AIDS epidemic is having a similarly adverse effect on economic development, particularly in the agricultural sector as crop production is hampered by sickness, the time taken to look after sick relatives and loss of income. FAO estimated that by 2003 8m. agricultural workers had died because of AIDS in the 25 worst affected African countries, and that a further 16m. would die before 2020, resulting in the loss of up to one-quarter of the agricultural work-force and a consequent reduction in food production. The impact of fewer farmers is already being felt in sub-Saharan Africa, which continues to experience severe food shortages. In July 2005 the US Agency for International Development-funded Famine Early Warning System estimated the number of people in the region at risk of starvation at over 30m. In 2006 the UN World Food Programme (WFP) revealed that it was feeding twice as many Africans in crisis than a decade ago. The severity of the situation was underlined by the warning from WFP in January 2006 that southern Africa in particular faced a triple threat from HIV/AIDS, food insecurity and weakened government capacity. According to an economic analysis for the World Bank in 2000, growth in GDP per head is up to an estimated 2.6% less among countries with HIV prevalence rates reaching 20%, compared with countries with a lower prevalence of infection. In fact, had the prevalence rate for HIV infection in sub-Saharan Africa not reached 8.6% in 1999, the region's income per head would have grown at a rate of 1.1% per year, compared with the 0.4% growth rate achieved in 1990–97.

Given the completely interdependent relationship between poverty and ill health in sub-Saharan Africa, many experts now argue that the improvement of health should be placed back at the centre of the development agenda, as a way of lifting people out of poverty. The British Government attempted to use its joint chairmanship of both the G-8 and the European Union (EU) in 2005 to renew the response of the international community to tackle poverty and by implication, the health emergency in Sub-Saharan Africa. The report of the Commission for Africa inaugurated by the British Prime Minister, Tony Blair, to produce a blueprint for tackling Africa's problems stressed that new initiatives were not needed to address the health problems of sub-Saharan Africa; rather it stressed the need to implement existing agreements and plans such as the UN General Assembly Declaration on HIV/AIDS. This approach highlighted the problems that have faced the numerous public-private partnerships developed to tackle the most serious diseases. These partnerships include a Global Fund to Fight AIDS, TB and Malaria, a Global Alliance for Vaccines and Immunization, Stop TB and Roll Back Malaria, among others, all of which had struggled to mobilize substantial resources for drugs, treatments and infrastructure improvements.

Following the G-8 leaders meeting in Heiligendamm, Germany, in mid-2007, the world's eight leading industrialized countries reaffirmed their commitment to supporting the economic development of Africa and tackling the problems posed by HIV, TB and malaria. The challenges of persuading donors to fulfil their pledges remained as did debates about how best to deliver health improvement through weak or non-existent health systems. In 2007 there was increasing global focus on strengthening health systems in Africa as it became more obvious that these weaknesses were being exacerbated by the ever increasing depletion of health workers leaving sub-Saharan Africa to work in the West, leading to calls for industrialized countries to commit to providing adequate health workers for their populations without poaching them from the developing world. The increasing recognition that this loss of skilled health workers threatens the success of many of the initiatives aimed at improving health in sub-Saharan Africa suggests that this will be a key issue in the future, highlighting concerns about the capacity to absorb the new resources made available through debt forgiveness and renewed donor support. The scale of this problem was highlighted in the 2006 *World Health Report*, which revealed that 36 of the 57 countries deemed to have a critical shortage of health workers were in sub-Saharan Africa. To tackle this challenge, the new Global Health Workforce Alliance under the aegis of WHO held a conference in Douala, Cameroon, in mid-June 2007. The conference emerged with the Douala Plan of Action which included a framework of action for African countries to develop health workforce plans.

MAIN RISKS TO HEALTH

HIV/AIDS and TB

Although 2006 saw the first indications from WHO that the global HIV/AIDS epidemic appeared to be slowing down, 2007 saw marginal increases in the HIV burden and sub-Saharan Africa remained the region with the greatest burden of infection. Home to just over 10% of the world's population, by the end of 2006 it accounted for 63% of all people living with HIV in the world. Estimates from the Joint United Nations Programme on HIV/AIDS (UNAIDS) at the end of 2006 indicated that there were 24.7m. people living with HIV in sub-Saharan Africa, that 2.1m. deaths in the region in 2006 were attributable to the disease and that in that year there were 2.8m. new infections. These figures were marginally higher than the corresponding figures for the previous year. The pattern of infection varies significantly within the continent, and within individual countries, and to speak of a single African epidemic risks oversimplifying the issue. At the end of 2006 Kenya, Uganda and Zimbabwe continued to see a decline in adult national prevalence of HIV, while most countries in southern Africa (with the exception of Angola) showed little evidence of a decline in the extremely high rates of infection noted there. Apart from Angola where 5% of the population was infected, and Zimbabwe where there was new evidence of a declining trend in national adult HIV prevalence, all other southern African countries had HIV infection rates of more than 10% of their population at the end of 2006. In Namibia, Lesotho and South Africa estimates suggested that more than 20% of the population were infected, while in Botswana and Swaziland nearly 40% of the adult populations were similarly affected. Of particular concern were the expanding epidemics in Mozambique and Swaziland. West and Central Africa which has traditionally had lower prevalence levels than Southern Africa showed little evidence of changes in infection levels with most countries showing a prevalence rate of around 5%, with the exception of Côte d'Ivoire and Cameroon, where prevalence rates appear to have stagnated at the 10% mark over the last few years. At the end of 2006 there appeared to be some evidence emerging of a decline in prevalence in urban parts of Burkina Faso.

HIV and TB have been described as a lethal combination, each accelerating the effects of the other. It is no surprise therefore that TB infection rates are also rising in sub-Saharan Africa, fuelled by the HIV/AIDS epidemic and widespread poverty. The *Global Tuberculosis Control Report*, published by WHO in 2007 and using data from 2005, indicated that for the first time since 1993, global tuberculosis infection rates were levelling off. However, sub-Saharan Africa remained the region with the largest burden of disease and there were concerns around extensively drug resistant tuberculosis and the interaction between HIV and TB. The latest available data demonstrated that in 2005 of the 22 countries identified as high burden countries eight were in Africa. These eight countries, namely Nigeria, South Africa, the Democratic Republic of the Congo (DRC), Ethiopia, Kenya, Tanzania, Uganda and Zimbabwe, had tuberculosis incidence rates between 283 and 640 per 100,000 population per year.

Water, Hygiene and Sanitation

About one in three of the 1.8m. world-wide deaths estimated to be a direct result of unsafe water and sanitation occur in sub-Saharan Africa, according to WHO, and only 36% of the population of the region has access to basic sanitation. Estimating the true impact of these deficiencies on health is difficult, owing to their effect on childhood malnutrition, which in turn contributes to a much higher risk of death from infectious disease.

A recent study by the World Bank in Ethiopia found that while biological factors, such as age and mother's height, and socio-economic factors, such as household wealth and mother's education, were important determinants of children's nutritional status, access to water and sanitation were an important determinant of the probability of a child being underweight. This effect was particularly marked among children living in rural areas. This reinforces earlier suggestions that childhood stunting and poor growth has as much to do with poor hygiene, sanitation and inadequate water supply, as with food availability. Repeated childhood illnesses, and diarrhoea in particular, undermine children's growth and inhibit the absorption of nutrients. More calories are burned up, as the body fights fever and infection, and nutrients are drained through vomiting and diarrhoea.

The effects of a lack of access to sanitation on health are stark. According to WHO estimates, more than 800,000 African children die every year from the 4m. episodes of diarrhoea that occur in the region.

Apart from diarrhoeal diseases and malnutrition, poor access to safe water and sanitation is linked to several infectious diseases in sub-Saharan Africa, including schistosomiasis, malaria, trachoma and hepatitis A. More recently, studies have suggested that handwashing with soap may reduce the risk of childhood pneumonia. Improved hygiene resulting from better sanitation and improved drinking water would do much to reduce the death, disability and illness caused by these preventable diseases. A recent report published in 2006 looking at progress towards achieving the MDGs in the area of water and sanitation found that rural-urban disparities in relation to access to water and sanitation was most marked in Africa. The report also suggested that while countries such as Angola, the Central African Republic, Chad, Malawi and

Tanzania had increased drinking water coverage by 50% or more, poor progress in countries like Niger, Ethiopia and Nigeria meant that sub-Saharan Africa was unlikely to meet the goal of 74% of the population having access to improved drinking water. This meant that in 2006 nearly 300m. Africans still had no access to safe drinking water.

Malaria

Each year, according to WHO, 1m. people die from malaria. Nine out of 10 of these deaths occur in sub-Saharan Africa. In addition, malaria causes 200m.–450m. cases of fever in African children each year. Some 900,000 African children aged under four years die from the disease each year.

Malaria kills one in five children in Africa and accounts for one-third of all clinic visits and between one-quarter and one-half of all hospital admissions. It is also a major cause of anaemia in children and pregnant women and contributes to low birth weight and infant mortality and its apparent synergy with HIV has led to the suggestion that adults infected with HIV should join children and pregnant women as a target group for malaria prevention and treatment. Apart from these direct effects, malaria can reduce school attendance and productivity as well as impair intellectual development in children. The Roll Back Malaria initiative launched at a summit in Abuja, Nigeria, in 2000 was an acknowledgement that malaria prevention and control had worsened in the preceding decade. At that launch, African countries committed to providing prompt and effective treatment and insecticide-treated nets (ITNs) for 60% of the people at highest risk of malaria and intermittent preventive treatment (IPT) for 60% of pregnant women by the end of 2005. The fourth pan-African Malaria Conference held in Yaoundé, Cameroon, in November 2005 acknowledged that the Abuja targets had not been met and called on WHO member countries to support and implement the Roll Back Malaria Global Strategic Plan 2005–2015. By the end of 2005 34 African countries had changed their national drug policy and adopted Artemisinin Combination Therapy (ACT) in place of chloroquine and sulfadoxine-pyrimethamine, which had been made ineffective by rising levels of resistance. As the ACT drugs are priced 10–20 times higher than chloroquine, cost has prohibited use. In 2006 the concern that using artemisinin monotherapy would compromise the long-term effectiveness of the artemisinin derivatives, led WHO to issue new guide-lines for the treatment of malaria which stressed the importance of combination therapy. There was a renewed attempt at reviving the flagging progress in the African malaria sector in 2007 with the launch of the Africa Malaria Elimination Campaign under the auspices of the African Union (AU). The campaign set ambitious targets for the elimination of malaria in countries with low transmission and improved control in countries with high transmission.

WHO has estimated that to provide ACT therapy for 60% of the population who would benefit from it would cost up to US $1,000m. per year, at current prices, with much of the money coming from external donors. However, this has raised questions about the long-term sustainability of the funding. Prevention of malarial episodes with ITNs thus remains a primary objective of initiatives to reduce the impact of the disease on children. While the number of ITNs distributed is said to have increased 10-fold in the last three years, there are still significant variations in uptake and suggestions that the rural poor who need this intervention most were least likely to receive it. A survey showed that on average only 3% of children in sub-Saharan Africa slept under ITNs, although the proportion varied from 2% to 63% in different countries. The question of how best to improve distribution and use of ITNs remains and in 2005 the Roll Back Malaria programme issued a strategic framework to help countries in deciding this process. The framework broadly recommended that to ensure a sustainable distribution programme, nets should be sold and the cost subsidized only for vulnerable groups. The public-private partnerships—the Geneva-based Medicines for Malaria Venture and the Malaria Vaccine Initiative—working in the malaria area continued to hold out hope for the future, with the Medicines for Malaria Venture announcing in 2005 that it had four drugs in phase III clinical trials, including a paediatric version of coartemisinin. Indoor residual spraying with effective insecticides, including dichlorodiphenyltrichloroethane, was adopted as a key measure of control in the AU campaign document of April 2007 reflecting a resolution of controversies that had surrounded the use of the insecticide.

Vaccine-Preventable Childhood Diseases

Sub-Saharan Africa has the lowest coverage rates for childhood immunizations in the world, a situation worsened by conflict in Sudan, Côte d'Ivoire and the DRC. Nevertheless, between 2002 and 2005 immunization rates continued to improve with an estimated 66% of children in the region receiving the full dose of the vaccine that protects against diphtheria, pertussis (whooping cough) and tetanus in 2004. However, in Nigeria only 25% coverage was achieved, while Liberia, Somalia, Gabon Equatorial Guinea had coverage rates below 40%. The effects of the controversy in 2003 over polio vaccination in Nigeria, engendered by claims that the polio vaccine was harmful, continued to linger. In 2006 Nigeria remained one of only six African countries that reported cases of polio, and the only African country where the disease was reported as being endemic. However, the wider epidemics in western and central Africa had been brought under control by the end of 2005. WHO, meeting in October 2005 to review the global target for the eradication of polio, acknowledged that while efforts towards eradication were largely on track, Nigeria would require at least an extra 12 months to achieve the expected goals. In 2007 it was expected that innovations such as the introduction of a new form of the polio vaccine and changes in the delivery of vaccines would lead to improvements in Nigeria. These issues, together with poor progress in India and Pakistan, meant that the target for the global eradication of polio has still not been met by the end of 2006.

WHO and the UN Children's Fund (UNICEF) announced in 2005 that the number of estimated deaths from measles world-wide had decreased by 39% between 1999 and 2003, largely as a result of improved immunization efforts, with vaccination coverage in sub-Saharan Africa increasing from 55% to 65%. Progress was also made with the introduction of new vaccines into national immunization programmes: hepatitis B vaccines were introduced in 24 countries, yellow fever vaccines in 21 countries and haemophilus influenza vaccines in 11 countries by the end of 2004.

Respiratory Disease and Indoor Air Pollution

Of all infectious diseases, acute respiratory infections are the biggest killer of children in sub-Saharan Africa, often striking those who are malnourished, of low birth weight or whose immune systems are weakened. Of a total population of some 75m. children aged under five years, pneumonia kills 1.2m.–1.5m. each year, according to WHO. Pneumonia is not the only cause of respiratory disease in the region, however, and WHO estimates that between 300,000 and 500,000 deaths could be a direct result of indoor pollutants from burning biomass fuels. Sub-Saharan Africa was thought to account for 24% of these deaths and 54% of the morbidity associated with biomass fuels. An assessment by the International Energy Agency in 2004 suggested that the use of biomass fuels such as wood, dung and agricultural residues, for domestic purposes would continue to rise. This increase is likely to be marked in sub-Saharan Africa, owing to population growth and the increasing difficulty of gaining access to alternatives such as kerosene and liquid petroleum gas. Initiatives such as the smoke hoods to reduce indoor air pollution piloted by the Intermediate Technology Development Group in Kenya held potential for tackling this challenge.

Malnutrition in Women and Children

More than perhaps any other indicator, malnutrition is crucial when considering the health of populations, as it underpins many other causes of ill health and is implicated in more than one-half of all child deaths world-wide. Being underweight or malnourished in childhood is a significant risk factor for dying from other diseases, particularly diarrhoea, pneumonia and measles. WHO estimates that 50%–70% of the burden of disease arising from malaria, lower respiratory-tract infections, pneumonia and measles is a result of undernutrition in sub-Saharan Africa. Women who are underweight are at risk of adverse pregnancy outcomes, including death during childbirth.

The prevalence of children classified as severely underweight (more than three standard deviations below the median weight of the reference population) in sub-Saharan Africa ranges from about 6% in Nigeria to 16% and 17% in Eritrea and Ethiopia, respectively. According to UNICEF, 28% of children in Africa who are under the age of five are moderately or severely underweight. The number of underweight children in sub-Saharan Africa in 2006 was estimated at 33m. with 31% of rural children and 20% of urban children underweight, respectively. Projections suggest that the problem of malnutrition in Africa is likely to worsen in the immediate future if current trends continue. WHO estimates that being underweight contributes to the deaths of about 1.8m. people per year in sub-Saharan Africa. Deficiencies in other nutrients, such as iodine, iron, vitamin A and zinc, also contribute to increased rates of death from infectious diseases in the region.

Maternal Health

Nearly one-half of all maternal deaths throughout the world occur in sub-Saharan Africa, with the maternal mortality ratio in the region averaging 920 deaths per 100,000 live births in 2000. Of the 18 countries in the world with maternal mortality ratios greater than 1,000 per 100,000 live births, all but one were in sub-Saharan Africa. Sierra Leone was worst affected with an estimated 2,000 deaths per 100,000 live births, but Malawi, Angola, Niger, Tanzania and Rwanda all had rates greater than 1,400 per 100,000 live births, according to WHO figures. The most effective way of preventing deaths during childbirth is to recognize quickly when complications during birth arise. Ideally, births should be attended by a skilled health professional or birth attendant. However, while 50% of all births in sub-Saharan Africa were carried out in the presence of a skilled attendant in 1990, by 2000 this had declined to 45%. The 2005 estimates from WHO indicated that this figure has increased slightly to 46.5%, but is still far from the target of 90% adopted by the International Conference for Population and Development. More recently there has been increasing acknowledgement of the effects and long term sequelae of poor obstetric care among African women who survive childbirth. It is estimated that 9.5m. women suffer from these effects in sub-Saharan Africa.

Chronic Disease, Accidents and Injuries

Although much emphasis has been on preventable, communicable diseases, as these contribute to some 70% of deaths in sub-Saharan Africa, non-communicable diseases are also emerging as a threat to health and are acknowledged as grossly neglected by both African government and donors. In particular, accidents, injuries and intentional injuries account for more than 1m. deaths per year in the region. There are also increasing numbers of deaths caused by chronic diseases, such as heart disease, chronic obstructive pulmonary disease, cancer, neuropsychiatric disorders and digestive disorders. Some of the cancer burden can be attributed to infectious diseases such as cervical cancer, which is linked to a viral infection, but lifestyle changes including a predicted rise in smoking prevalence is also likely to have an effect. Together, non-communicable chronic diseases account for nearly 2m. deaths in the region and are expected to rise steadily during the next few years.

Disability is a particular problem in sub-Saharan Africa. Not only are there high rates of disability in some rural populations (one in six, according to some estimates), but absolute numbers are also high, with some 60m. disabled people in the region. As the focus of most health interventions in sub-Saharan Africa is on communicable diseases, chronic illness and disability have received rather limited attention, although the HIV/AIDS epidemic has bolstered efforts to redress this imbalance.

THE COST OF ILL HEALTH

Poor health does not just affect individuals, but restricts families and entire societies, and retards the regional development goals of sub-Saharan Africa. In fact, in the countries most affected by the HIV/AIDS epidemic the demographic structure of the country is being changed beyond all recognition.

Ill health in sub-Saharan Africa exerts a toll not just on the individual sufferer, but on families' ability to earn a living, educate their children and save money in order to purchase essential items, such as food and drugs. This, in turn, creates a vicious cycle of ill health and poverty, each fuelling the other and trapping millions of people. The poor describe poverty not as an absence of money, but as powerlessness, alienation, disease, illiteracy and death. Ill health due to poverty directly affects children's ability to go to school, and adults' ability to work and earn a living or grow food to feed the family. For example, according to the African Medical and Research Foundation (AMREF), in Kenya schoolchildren miss 11% of schooldays as a result of malaria, and up to one-half of all medically related absences from school are due to the illness.

Many of the health problems in sub-Saharan Africa affect poorer people disproportionately. Until quite recently it was thought that poorer people in the region faced more ill health purely owing to their low socio-economic and nutritional status. However, recent research has demonstrated how ill health deals the poor a double blow—not only do they suffer more episodes of ill health than wealthier people, but they are much less likely to receive treatment. Results from a survey of rural households conducted in Tanzania in 1999, looking at integrated management of childhood illness, found that wealthier families were more likely than poorer families to have brought their child to a health facility for treatment. Once there, children from wealthier families were much more likely to have been treated with antimalarials and antibiotics for pneumonia compared with children from poorer families. These findings were echoed in a surveys in Côte d'Ivoire in 2005 and in Kenya in 2007 (see above), which found that poorer families had higher parasite burdens, lived further away from health facilities and were less likely to seek treatment than their wealthier counterparts.

On a national scale, diseases like malaria make countries poorer, retard growth and development, and limit countries' GDP. In 1995 average annual GDP per head in malarious countries was US $1,526, compared with $8,268 in non-malarious countries.

Any attempt to assess the economic impact of endemic diseases, such as malaria, must take into account not only the direct and indirect costs borne by those affected, but also wider social costs. For example, malaria changes whole families' behaviours, affecting their ability to work, send children to school, migrate to look for work and save money. However, malaria also affects income on a national level, because of its impact on trade, tourism and direct foreign investment. In the most extreme cases, the health problems in sub-Saharan Africa are not just having macroeconomic effects at regional level, but are changing the demographic structure of entire countries.

In the case of malaria, Sachs and Malaney argue that, because malaria is responsible for about one-quarter of childhood deaths, families compensate by having more children. This higher fertility rate, they maintain, has knock-on effects on future generations of children in poor families. There is less money available to pay for the education of more children, and female children tend to be less likely to be sent to school, as families realize that they are likely to bear the brunt of child-rearing activities. In the long term such factors can have a significant impact on economic growth and productivity.

The most extreme example of long-term demographic change is provided by countries in sub-Saharan Africa with a high prevalence of HIV/AIDS. With HIV/AIDS striking people down when they are at their most productive, the entire population structure of countries such as Botswana is likely to be radically altered by 2020. In turn, fewer adults of working age will contribute less to such countries' economies, further retarding economic and social development in the region.

UNAIDS estimated that in 2004 there were 12m. orphans in sub-Saharan Africa, who had lost one or both parents as a result of AIDS. The organization forecast that by 2010 this figure would increase to some 20m., including 6m. who would have lost both parents. The orphans crisis in sub-Saharan Africa will have far-reaching effects, notably on the long-term economic outlook of the region. One study in Kenya found that only 7% of the farming households headed by orphans knew how to cultivate crops and keep livestock. Rural families are losing their own internal knowledge about how to earn a living, and normal family life is being disrupted irrevocably. A study of HIV orphans in Uganda published in 2005 showed that compared with non-orphans, orphaned children showed higher levels of anger, anxiety and depression and were more likely to have suicidal feelings and hopelessness about the future. The long-term implications of this cohort of traumatized children for Africa's development is unclear.

THE RESPONSE TO THE HEALTH EMERGENCY

Governments in sub-Saharan Africa have failed to provide the most basic health care, and health services have all but collapsed in many countries as a result of the HIV/AIDS epidemic. Such an extreme crisis clearly calls for an appropriate response, and a number of public-private partnerships have been created to manage the funds, resources and expertise required to fight the most deadly diseases. Following the summit of the G-8 at Okinawa, Japan, in 2000, the Global Fund to Fight AIDS, TB and Malaria was established to channel funding to projects tackling the three biggest killers; the initial aim was to raise up to US $10,000m. annually by 2005. However, as at May 2007 the contributions for 2006 stood at $1,839m. with $2.441m. pledged for 2007. As at the same date, the Fund had disbursed $3,700m. to public and private recipients in 132 countries. Fund-raising efforts were continuing on an ongoing basis and yielding results with the G-8, Spain and Thailand all pledging increased contributions to the Fund. The Fund also produced results, helping to increase the number of people receiving antiretrovirals from 130,000 in December 2004 to 770,000 by December 2006. Similar partnerships have been established for malaria (Roll Back Malaria), TB (Stop TB), polio (Global Polio Eradication Initiative) and onchocerciasis (African Programme for the Control of Onchocerciasis) with varying degrees of success. The Global Alliance for Vaccines and Immunization (GAVI) was launched in 2000, while yet another public-private partnership is attempting to improve access to much-needed drugs to treat HIV/AIDS (the Accelerating Access Initiative).

In 2007 under Germany's presidency, the G-8 reiterated the commitment to improving health in Africa earlier made at Gleneagles, Scotland, in July 2005. The communiqué from the Heiligendamm summit committed the G-8 to increasing aid to Africa by US $60,000m. and reiterated the group's commitment to improving access to antiretroviral drugs in Africa by 2010. In addition, the G-8 promised to work with African countries to strengthen health systems, an acknowledgement that progress has been hampered by weak health systems. These announcements were greeted with cautious optimism particularly in the light of a statement that the group aimed to increase access to antiretroviral treatment to 5m. people by 2010, which some observers interpreted as a watering down to the goal of universal access. In 2007 campaigners and civil society groups continued to focus efforts on ensuring that these commitments were met. The US President George W. Bush, in addition to money already committed to the Global Fund to Fight AIDS, TB and Malaria, continued to implement the five-year strategy for the President's Emergency Plan for AIDS Relief (PEPFAR). More than one-half of PEPFAR funding targets increased access to treatment, but more controversial is the caveat that one-third of the available funding for prevention efforts be reserved for abstinence-only programmes. In 2006 President Bush proposed, and the US Congress endorsed, approximately $3,200m. for PEPFAR. In 2007 Congress approved funding of $4,500m., a sum that included $724m. for the Global Fund and was $500m. more than the President had requested. For 2008 President Bush has requested $5,400m. bringing the total spending since 2003 to over $18,000m. WHO's '3 by 5' initiative, which aimed to provide antiretroviral treatment to 3m. people living with HIV/AIDS in developing countries by the end of 2005, failed to meet its target but managed to increase the number of people on antiretroviral treatment world-wide by up to 400% between 2003 and the end of 2005. In sub-Saharan Africa by the end of 2006 an estimated 1.3m. people were on treatment. Building on these successes, WHO announced a new initiative in partnership with the Global Fund, PEPFAR and UNAIDS—the Universal Access Initiative—which aimed to bring prevention, care and treatment for all who need it by 2010. Critics, however, pointed to the absence of specific targets as evidence that efforts were being diluted. Supporters maintained that the new initiative allowed local control of target-setting by local people who understand their context best. The South African Government announced in early August 2003 that it would support the provision of antiretroviral drugs in its public hospitals, and signed a $41m. agreement with the Global Fund on AIDS projects. By April 2005 over 40,000 people were enrolled in the South African Government's treatment programme, although AIDS activists still criticized the Government for the slow pace of the programme and for promoting multivitamins in a way that suggested that they were of similar benefit as antiretrovirals.

Meanwhile the focus of the debate surrounding the pricing of branded antiretroviral drugs, international trade rules and the ability of countries to import cheaper generic copies of drugs changed as India began to implement the World Trade Organization's Agreement on Trade-related Aspects of Intellectual Property Rights in January 2005. This meant that India, one of the two major sources of generic antiretroviral drugs would now have to recognize drug patents on medicines, a move that groups like Médecins sans frontières argued would jeopardize access to newer second-line antiretroviral drugs. At the 2005 conference of the International AIDS Society, humanitarian groups called for more radical approaches to pricing mechanisms for urgent drugs arguing that the current system, which depended on voluntary discounting by pharmaceutical companies, was inadequate to meet the target of universal access to treatment by 2010.

Further progress was made by GAVI, which by the end of 2005 had helped avert an estimated 1.7m. premature deaths through its role in the distribution of vaccines and safe syringes. In this role, GAVI enabled some of the poorest countries in sub-Saharan Africa to administer basic vaccines against diphtheria, tetanus, pertussis, TB, measles and polio to a greater proportion of their child population. As of December 2006 GAVI had secured US $3,600m. in funding pledges from government and private sources, of which $1,900m. had been actually received and $1,300m. had been disbursed. In addition, GAVI had secured long-term commitments by the governments of Brazil, France, Italy, Norway, South Africa, Spain, Sweden, and the United Kingdom through the new International Finance Facility for Immunisation, which was anticipated to prevent 5m. child deaths between 2006 and 2015, and more than 5m. future adult deaths.

There is optimism too that the increased financial support to countries in sub-Saharan Africa from the Global Fund will help reverse previously disappointing progress on TB. While the 2005 WHO target of detecting at least 70% of all infectious cases and curing 85% of these was not reached, it was estimated that about 60% of all cases were detected by the end of 2005 and that 82% of these were cured. There are therefore signs that the detection and cure rates could be improved with greater funding to strengthen the infrastructure and health systems in sub-Saharan Africa. The region has been singled out by WHO as requiring a special focus to reduce the escalating incidence rates fuelled by the HIV epidemic. The Global Tuberculosis Control Report in 2007 found that the rate of growth worldwide had stabilized but that the caseload continued to grow in sub-Saharan Africa.

It must be hoped that a period of sustained investment and co-ordinated effort to improve the health services in each country will result in lasting, sustainable solutions to the health emergency, rather than short-term political gains. Clearly a 'top-down' approach is not enough, yet by 2006 there were some encouraging signs that the decades of underinvestment in health systems and infrastructure in some sub-Saharan African countries was beginning to be reversed, although few countries were meeting the Abuja Commitment of dedicating 15% of their budget to health care. Health-service reform was taking place in some countries in order to provide a more decentralized health service, with the aim of making services more accessible in remote rural areas. In Kenya progress was being made in 2005 towards legislation to ensure universal health and social insurance coverage for the first time and Uganda was preparing to roll out a Social Health Insurance scheme from July 2007. In Tanzania, the success of the Tanzania Essential Health Intervention Project, a collaborative project with the Canadian International Development Research Centre, has led to it being rolled out on a national basis. The project worked by focusing health care spending on cost-effective interventions aimed at the largest contributors to the local burden of disease and was able to achieve a 40% reduction in child mortality in two districts over a period of five years. The structured approach, informed by local needs, is vital if some of the mistakes of the past are to be avoided, when large projects were financed at the behest of donors, with little input from local communities as to what their needs were. In November 2005 the Canadian Government announced that it would be investing C $7m. to build on the success of the project in Tanzania.

There have been some success stories too, where strong government action has been carried out in a climate of openness and honesty. In Uganda, for example, one of the first countries to be seriously affected by the HIV/AIDS epidemic, the early recognition of the severity of the situation by the Government led to a decline in HIV/AIDS prevalence among certain groups from the mid-1990s. This was widely acknowledged to have been a direct result of mass education and prevention campaigns. According to UNAIDS, the percentage of adults (aged 15–49 years) living with HIV/AIDS in Uganda declined from some 14.0% in the early 1990s to 8.3% in 1999 and to 4.1% at the end of 2003.

NGOs perform an important function in facilitating health development in sub-Saharan Africa, but again in the early 2000s there were some signs that the traditional manner of bidding for money from donors for specific projects with limited coverage was changing. Some NGOs, such as Oxfam and Christian Aid, were playing a strong global advocacy role, calling for increased resources from donor countries and organizing specific campaigns aimed at accelerating access to badly needed drugs, a role emphasized by the massive joint collaborative Make Poverty History campaign in 2005. Apart from lobbying governments in industrialized countries for debt relief and fairer trade for Africa, NGOs were also lobbying for trade and patent rules to be relaxed to allow poorer countries to import lower-cost versions of HIV drugs.

Some technical NGOs based in sub-Saharan Africa, such as AMREF, are finding that they are now viewed very much as partners by the governments in the host countries in which they work. This is important, as it allows them to use expertise gained from more than 50 years' experience of health development work in the region to guide and influence national health policies in favour of the poor. In early 2003 AMREF announced that two major donors, the Canadian International Development Agency and the Swedish International Development Agency, had provided it with unrestricted funding, recognizing the organization's role in developing and testing an evidence base of proven interventions to improve the health of the poorest.

Finally, the private sector is also playing an increasingly important role in responding to sub-Saharan Africa's health emergency. In Kenya, for example, employers are being encouraged to work together with NGOs to provide malaria treatment and prevention for local workers, outwith government health services. In South Africa numerous employers have been persuaded of the need to provide antiretroviral drugs to employees and their families, partly in recognition of the devastating effect of HIV/AIDS on the work-force.

None the less, the most visible aspect of private-sector involvement has been the drug-donation programmes of the pharmaceutical industry to combat several diseases in sub-Saharan Africa. By 2006, among others, there were public-private partnerships covering African trypanosomiasis, HIV/AIDS, leprosy, lymphatic filariasis, malaria (including a drug-donation programme for malarone), onchocerciasis, polio, trachoma, TB (Action TB) and vitamin A disorders. There were at least four public-private partnerships aimed at accelerating the development of a vaccine against HIV/AIDS. However, reports of trials for a candidate AIDS vaccine have so far been disappointing, and prevention through education remains at the forefront of efforts to control the spread of infection. The role of public-private partnerships in the development of new drugs for neglected diseases continues to expand. By 2006 there were over 90 of these partnerships, many of them involving major pharmaceutical companies working on a non-commercial basis.

OUTLOOK

After many decades of investment, aid and development, sub-Saharan Africa is at a crossroads. The early health gains made by governments that invested heavily in health services during the 1970s and 1980s have not been sustained, and by 2005 there were more poor people with poorer health in the region than at any time before. As a result, in 2006 there appeared to be a greater willingness on the part of the global community to address these problems. This was helped in part at WHO by the arrival of a new Director-General in July 2003. In his two and a half years in office, Dr Lee Jong-Wook worked to refocus WHO firmly on combating infectious disease and to restore its leadership in the global fight against HIV/AIDS. Following Lee's death in May 2006, Margaret Chan was elected to replace him in November. In her acceptance speech she asked to be judged on the impact her tenure would make on the health of the people of Africa and the health of women. It has become clear that many governments and agencies involved in health and development have realized that relying on economic development alone to improve health is not enough. To defeat poverty, sub-Saharan Africa's health challenges must be tackled in tandem with the economic and social development challenges of the region. To achieve this will require major investment, not only in fighting disease, but also in developing the capacity of health systems. If donor governments were to meet their undertaking to the UN to allocate 0.7% of GDP to international aid and development, a good start could be made towards reversing the decades of underinvestment.

There are other ways that governments in the region could be helped by external action. Debt relief and debt restructuring were one option pursued through the highly indebted poor countries and multilateral debt relief initiatives. None the less, those countries that received debt relief used the savings to invest heavily in social infrastructure projects. Mozambique introduced free immunization for children, while Tanzania, Malawi and Zambia all abolished primary school fees. If the G-8 countries fulfilled their promises on debt, the savings would dwarf the amounts currently being pledged to the Global Fund to Fight AIDS, TB and Malaria. In the latter half of the 21st century, there was cautious optimism that donor countries and African governments were beginning to face up more vigorously to the challenges. The emerging growth trends in the economy of sub-Saharan Africa and a move towards more civil government were yet to be translated into improvement in the health of the population.

For lasting solutions to sub-Saharan Africa's health emergency, health and development workers must turn to proven public health interventions aimed firmly at preventing subsequent generations becoming affected. Most people in the region are not infected with HIV/AIDS, and the challenge during the next decade will be to change behaviours across many diverse societies in order to limit the spread of the virus. Agencies involved in economic development must recognize the critical role of ill health in holding back individuals, families, communities and countries from reaching their potential.

Governments must continue to reform their health sectors and decentralize services, so that they are more accessible to people living in rural areas. They must also make better use of more appropriate technologies in areas such as sanitation and hygiene, if the number of people at risk of environmental health conditions is to be reduced. In addition, African governments will need to identify ways to retain health care workers who will be crucial in any effort to improve health on the continent.

NGOs are likely to continue to play a strong role in health reform, but may move away from project implementation to more strategic work, identifying partners with which to work, including national governments.

Finally, and perhaps most crucially, if the health and poverty problems endemic to sub-Saharan Africa are to be tackled sustainably, top-level political leadership will be required. The problems are multifaceted, and involve addressing the political, economic, social and wider determinants of ill health, poverty and poor socio-economic development, not to mention the problems of environmental degradation that compound the difficulties. Sub-Saharan Africa has the largest share of health and poverty problems in the world today, but it did not reach this situation by accident. Reversing the decades of neglect and underinvestment will require commitment on a global scale never before seen, but the people of the region surely deserve nothing less.

BIBLIOGRAPHY AND REFERENCES

African Medical and Research Foundation. *Better Health for the People of Africa*. Nairobi, 2000.

African Union. 'Fight Malaria: Africa Goes from Control to Elimination by 2010'. *African Union Health Ministers Conference Report*, April 2007.

Asindua, S. *The disabled—Africa's hidden poor*. Paper presented at the African Medical Research Foundation conference, Health Solutions to African Poverty, London, 2003.

Atwine, B., Cantor-Graae, E., and Bajunirwe, F. 'Psychological distress among AIDS orphans in rural Uganda' in *Social Science and Medicine*, Vol. 61, Issue 3, pp. 555–564. London, 2005.

Bonnel, R. *Economic Analysis of HIV/AIDS*. Africa Development Forum 2000, Background Paper. World Bank, September 2000.

Centers for Disease Control and Prevention. 'Progress in Reducing Measles Mortality—Worldwide, 1999–2003' in *Morbidity and Mortality Weekly Report*. Atlanta, GA, 2005.

Chuma J, Gilson L, and Molyneux C. 'Treatment-seeking behaviour, cost burdens and coping strategies among rural and urban households in Coastal Kenya: an equity analysis' in *Tropical Medicine and International Health* Vol. 12, Issue 5, pp. 673–686. Oxford, 2007.

Curtis, V., and Cairncross, S. 'Effect of washing hands with soap on diarrhoea risk in the community: a systematic review' in *The Lancet Infectious Diseases*, Vol. 3, No. 5, pp. 275–281. London, 2003.

Dare, L. 'WHO and the challenges of the next decade' in *The Lancet*, Vol. 361, No. 9352, pp. 170–171. London, 2003.

Famine Early Warning System Network. *Executive Overview Brief, 7 July 2005*. www.fews.net/execbrief.

Filippi, V., Ronsmans, C., Campbell, O. M., Graham, W. J., Mills, A., and Borghi, J., et al. 'Maternal health in poor countries: the broader context and a call for action' in *The Lancet*, Vol. 368, No. 9546, pp. 1535–1541. London, 2006.

Gallup, J. L., and Sachs, J. D. *The Economic Burden of Malaria*. Working Paper No. 52. Cambridge, MA, Center for International Development at Harvard University, July 2000.

Global Polio Eradication Initiative. www.polioeradication.org/content/general/current_monthly_sitrep.asp.

Gwatkin, D. 'How well do health programmes reach the poor?' in *The Lancet*, Vol. 361, No. 9357, pp. 540–541. London, 2003.

Hanson, S. 'AIDS control in sub-Saharan Africa—are more drugs and money the solution?' in *The Lancet Infectious Diseases*, Vol. 2, No. 2, pp. 71–72. London, 2002.

International Development Research Centre *Fixing Health Systems*. www.idrc.ca/tehip.

Luby, Stephen P., et al. 'Effect of handwashing on child health: a randomised controlled trial' in *The Lancet*, Vol. 366, No. 9481, pp. 225–233. London, 2005.

Mahmud Khan, M., Hotchkiss, D. R., Berruti, A. A., and Hutchinson, P. L. 'Geographic aspects of poverty and health in Tanzania: does living in a poor area matter?' in *Health Policy and Planning*, Vol 21, No 2, pp. 110–122. Oxford, 2005.

Médecins sans frontières. *Act now to get malarial treatment that works to Africa*. April 2003.

Moran, M. 'A Breakthrough in R&D for Neglected Diseases: New Ways to Get the Drugs We Need' in *PLoS Medicine*, Vol. 2, Issue 9. San Francisco, CA, 2005.

Murray, C. L., and Lopez, A. D. 'Mortality by cause for eight regions of the world: Global Burden of Disease Study' in *The Lancet*, Vol. 349, No. 9061, pp. 1269–1276. London, 1997.

Raso, G., *et al*. 'Disparities in parasitic infections, perceived ill health and access to health care among poorer and less poor schoolchildren of rural Côte d'Ivoire' in *Tropical Medicine and International Health* Vol. 10, Issue 1, p. 42. Oxford, 2005.

Roll Back Malaria Partnership/WHO. *World Malaria Report* (2005) rbm.who.int/wmr2005/html/exsummary_en.htm.

Rosegrant, M., and Meijer, S. 'Appropriate Food Policies and Investments Could Reduce Child Malnutrition by 43% in 2020' in *The Journal of Nutrition*, Vol. 132. International Food Policy Research Institute. Pennsylvania, PA, 2002.

Sachs, J., and Malaney, P. 'The economic and social burden of malaria' in *Nature*, Vol. 415, No. 6872, pp. 680–685. London, 2002.

Schellenberg, J. A., *et al*. 'Inequities among the very poor: health care for children in rural southern Tanzania' in *The Lancet*, Vol. 361, No. 9357, pp. 561–566. London, 2003.

Sengendo, J., and Nambi, J. 'The psychological effect of orphanhood: a study of orphans in Rakai district' in *Health Transition Review*, Supplement to Vol. 7, pp. 105–124. Canberra, Australian National University, 1997.

Silva, P. *Environmental factors and children's malnutrition in Ethiopia*. Policy Research Working Paper. World Bank, January 2005.

UNAIDS. *AIDS epidemic update* (December 2003).

UNICEF. *Progress for Children No. 5: A Report Card on Water and Sanitation*. (September 2006).

UNICEF, WHO and World Bank. *State of the World's Vaccines and Immunization* (2002).

USAID, UNICEF and UNAIDS. *Children on the Brink 2002: a Joint Report on Orphan Estimates and Program Strategies*.

Wardlaw, T. 'Coverage at country level for child survival interventions' at the UNICEF Tracking Progress in Child Survival Countdown to 2015 Conference held at the University of London on 13–14 December 2005. cs.server2.textor.com/alldocs/6%20-%20Tessa%20Wardlaw%20No%20photos.ppt.

World Bank. *World Development Report* (2004).

World Development Indicators (2006).

WHO. *Global TB Report* (2003).

The World Health Report (2003).

The Health of the People: The African Regional Health Report (2006).

WHO, UNICEF and UNFPA. *Maternal mortality in 2000*.

Yaoundé Call to Action. www.rollbackmalaria.org/forumV/docs/YaoundeCall_to_Action-en.pdf.

A CENTURY OF DEVELOPMENT: POLICY AND PROCESS IN SUB-SAHARAN AFRICA

MICHAEL JENNINGS

The last 100 years have been the century of 'development' in Africa. National governments, external powers, development consultants, policy-makers and analysts have drawn up plans and implemented programmes designed to reduce poverty and improve the socio-economic lives of the continent's inhabitants. Aid policies and structures have emerged and evolved to pay for development activity. Societies have been transformed through the imposition of colonial rule, the birth of nation-states, incorporation into the global capitalist system, and by donor-imposed economic and governmental structures. Vast sums of money have been spent on developing Africa, entire professions have emerged concerned solely with poverty alleviation, and the line of politicians who have declared poverty in Africa to be the world's most pressing issue stretches back through the decades.

Yet, for all the effort, energy and words expended on development in Africa, what has been achieved? Life expectancy for someone living in sub-Saharan Africa was 58 years in 1960. By 1990 it had risen to 70 years, but has since declined to just 46 years (2004). The proportion of undernourished increased from 31% in 1990–92 to 32% in 1999–2001. By 2002 203m. people in sub-Saharan Africa suffered from hunger (33m. more than a decade earlier). By 2000 the proportion of people with sustainable access to clean water had fallen to 53%. Every three seconds a child dies from a preventable disease—30,000 a day—a large proportion of these in Africa. One could be forgiven for assuming that development has achieved little in the continent. Certainly the levels of suffering are almost beyond imagination, reduced to statistics showing in stark numbers the realities of life for millions of people.

Since 2005 the issue of development in Africa has achieved unprecedented prominence on the world stage. The international community has held meeting after meeting to discuss poverty alleviation, aid policy, poor-country debt and related issues. Major reports from the United Kingdom and the UN, amongst others, have sought to highlight the immediateness of the crisis and define new approaches to development, while in the first half of 2006, a potential new major player in African development—the People's Republic of China—appeared to be emerging, raising questions about current policy paradigms.

'Development' has largely been presented as a monolithic, universally understood concept that has stood unchanging across the decades. In reality, the meaning of development, in terms of planned development, and the question of how it should be achieved has shifted during the course of the century of development. In particular, two main questions have exercised those who plan or set policy for, or analyse, development in Africa. First, which agency should be responsible for planning and implementing development? Second, what are the objectives of development, in other words, what does 'development' actually mean? The answers to these questions have changed over the past century of development in Africa, and continue to play central roles in the current debates about aid and support for current and future African development.

This essay will begin with a general survey of how the terms of those debates have shifted over the past century or so, culminating in the development paradigm we have today. It will then look at the current debates and main controversial areas of development and aid policy.

A HISTORY OF DEVELOPMENT IN AFRICA

The Beginnings: Colonial Development to 1939

'Development' in Africa, in the sense of planned interventions in society and economy, began for much of the region with the onset of colonialism. Colonial powers were determined that the newly acquired territories not be a drain on metropolitan treasuries, and that they become sources of income. Early colonial planners regarded Africa as mired in tradition and stagnant economies, lacking in the vital accoutrements of 'civilization': capitalist social and economic structures (in particular a cash economy); modern communications and transport; and a centralized administration. The colonial task, as it liked to present itself at least, was to mould these new societies and 'develop' them, in order to create modern societies operating within a global market. 'Development' was defined by European perceptions of social organization, European economic need, and the requirements of colonial administrations to maintain power and control.

Reflecting the Victorian division of society into rigidly delineated public, private and philanthropic spheres, early colonial development planning relied on the private sector as the engine of change and development. Capitalist investment would create the required modern institutions and structures, with the state providing the rule of law and order. Welfare activities could be left to the charitable sector (in this case the missions) who would provide the bulk of health and education services to the African population. However, the failure of the anticipated private investment to arrive in the new colonies forced the state to accept responsibility for creating the infrastructure—in particular the ports and railways—essential for the colonial development vision.

For most African countries, agriculture was identified as the critical sector which would drive economic growth and expansion. Development planning, by the early 20th century, had thus become a question of how to increase agricultural output. Administrations faced two broad constraints (one real, one contrived by colonial depictions of Africans) in meeting this objective: a poor infrastructure inhibiting the movement of crops from the field to their end destination in Europe; and a belief that traditional land-use practices could not sustain a massive increase in production for the new export market. The first could be met through government investment. Over 90% of British government loans to the colonies, for example, were for the construction of the railways, largely in eastern and central Africa.[1] By the 1930s a network of roads and rail tracks integrated cash-cropping rural hinterlands to the global market. Those areas deemed unproductive were largely ignored and forced to rely on migrant labour as the main opportunity for cash generation.

The second constraint was to be met by encouraging African farmers to change their practices, adopt 'modern' (i.e. European) techniques and new crops. Colonial depictions of African peasantry as inherently conservative and unwilling to change were used to justify compulsion and, in some cases, force. In Uganda in the early 20th century, for example, farmers were forced (often with physical violence) to grow cotton in certain districts. Development was therefore regarded as a fundamentally conflictual process: means were sought to persuade people that the priorities of the colonial state ought to be respected, with such persuasion turning to force where argument alone failed.

Thus over the course of the first two decades of the 20th century, several important characteristics of 'development' had emerged. First, it was defined almost exclusively in economic terms. Welfare services would ultimately expand as national incomes rose, but it was not a priority for development planners. Second, the characterization of African societies as resistant to modernizing demands created a mindset that development implied conflict between planners and target communities. Development was to be a process of encouraging or forcing people to change, regardless of whether they accepted the logic of externally imposed values. Third, development was a process largely set and controlled by the state. However reluctantly, governments had assumed greater responsibility for development planning and financing. Nevertheless, that financing was to be the responsibility of individual territories, not a burden on the taxpayers of the European powers. Until colonial territories had sufficient incomes to pay for their development, European loans, not grants, would provide the necessary funds. Between 1896 and 1923 98% of British government funds for colonial development (across all the British Empire) were in the form of loans. Colonial assistance (or 'aid' as we would now call it) was to be extremely limited.

By the mid-1920s politicians in Europe, especially in France and the United Kingdom, were calling for an interventionist policy, and improved funding mechanisms for the required modernizations. The foundations of modern official development aid were laid at the end of the 1920s: the British Colonial Development Act (CDA) of 1929; and the French Fonds d'Investissement pour le Développement Économique et Social (FIDES) of 1931. For the first time, taxpayers of one country were to support sustained development of those in another, and largely through aid in the form of grants rather than loans. Over 60% of CDA funds were provided in the form of grants, and of the loan element, around 80% was on easy repayment terms (generally with an interest-free period of three or four years and low rates thereafter). The FIDES similarly envisaged grants being made from French national income to support development in its colonial territories.

These acts were of great significance for future development funding. The principle that development should only be funded through internal revenues was broken, and metropolitan regimes accepted they had a responsibility to provide aid. Moreover, the types of intervention that both CDA and FIDES envisaged supporting signalled a new departure in the defining of development. The 'development as economic growth' paradigm was gradually replaced with a model that sought to include welfare concerns. Aid was increasingly understood as a social investment as much as economic. Public health schemes in particular became a significant focus of aid allocations (16% of CDA schemes by 1939, the second highest proportion after communication and transport schemes). Advisory committees reviewing project proposals came to the conclusion that living standards were as important a responsibility of colonial development as increasing productivity and, indeed, could contribute to the latter.

By the end of the 1930s the foundations of the modern development era had been laid. First, the state had gradually accepted responsibility for planning, directing and funding development, abandoning its earlier position that private investment was to be the main driving engine. Second, the definition of what constituted development had widened from almost exclusively economic dimensions to incorporate a social welfare agenda that regarded improving living standards as essential to the developmental mandate.

The Primacy of the State, 1945–70s

Global depression in the 1930s and the onset of war in 1939 impeded the efforts to implement fully the new principles underlying development planning and aid that had emerged by the end of the 1930s. Such efforts were postponed until 1945, from which point colonial and metropolitan governments began to put into effect a more interventionist development policy. Post-war development was characterized by three elements: the absolute primacy of the state in directing, implementing and managing all aspects of development policy; a fuller incorporation of social development/welfarist principles; and the rise of international organizations to prominence in policy-setting and funding of development.

The experiences of central planning at home and in their colonies during the war suggested to the European colonial powers that micro-management of colonial economies was the most efficient means of ensuring development objectives were met. Colonial administrations devised long-term development plans, used marketing boards to set producer prices and purchase entire crops, increased the number of agricultural advisors, and sought to change laws governing land-use, labour migration, urban settlement, pursuing measures designed primarily rapidly to 'modernize' (as they perceived it) colonial societies. The state was able to exert its full authority over development. Following independence from the late 1950s to the mid-1960s for the majority of sub-Saharan African states, this trend was continued.

But the role of the state in development was founded on more than inherited structures and mechanisms for enforcing control. It also rested on a consensus that development was best left to the state. The creation of a large public sphere was not only tolerated, but encouraged by donors. International overseas development assistance (ODA) was directed through government departments and treasuries across Africa. Government ministers were expected to formulate development plans. The World Bank and other Bretton Woods institutions undertook projects with governments for the large part rather than private investors or voluntary agencies.

As the state assumed full control over development processes, the breadth of aims to which its activity was directed continued to expand. The definition of 'development' had fully accepted social welfare principles by this period, culminating in the late 1960s with the emergence of 'social development' as an objective in itself. Social welfare schemes came to dominate colonial aid spending in Africa, a trend continued following independence. The new national governments assumed responsibility for the provision of welfare services. The rise to dominance of social development at the national level reflected broader shifts in the international community: the UN International Development Strategy in 1970 which put social objectives at the heart of the developmental mandate; and the announcement by the President of the World Bank, Robert McNamara, of the 'dethronement of gross national product' as a marker for progress.

Colonial development policy had been geared towards benefiting the metropolitan economy as much as (if not more than) the colonial territories. The independent governments had no such dualistic imperatives to consider in their development policy. However, the departure of colonial administrations left a vacuum into which the emergent international development organizations could enter. While African governments to a large extent could set national policies reflecting their own interpretations of needs and priorities, the IMF, the World Bank, other UN agencies, as well as powerful new donor countries such as the USA, the USSR, non-colonial European powers, etc., were increasingly important partners in the process. African countries had since the onset of colonialism been subject to the policies of those who controlled access to funds. With the massive expansion in aid for development, particularly from the 1960s, they became subject to a broader range of interests. While economies grew, significant power over development remained at the national level in Africa. However, the apparent strength of the state in Africa masked a growing vulnerability. Should economic crisis emerge, the authority of those states could be challenged by the new masters of development.

Rolling Back the State, 1980s–90s

From the mid-1970s a global slump in trade, collapsing commodity prices, and the economic shock of successive oil crises undid the advances made by African governments and led to a fundamental reappraisal of international development policy. The weakening economic position of African governments by the late 1970s and early 1980s left them less able to meet the rising costs of social welfare and development spending. The sudden rise in interest rates led to the African debt crisis with governments now unable to meet the repayments for loans they were encouraged to take out in the more affluent 1960s and early 1970s. Unable to mitigate the effects of economic crisis themselves, African governments could not sustain internal control over development processes, and from the mid-1980s to the early 1990s they saw a gradual transfer of their power to external donors and international organizations.

The state, identified as the driver of development for over 60 years, was now regarded as its chief brake: states were too big, too unwieldy and too inflexible to the demands of the global market. International donors began to call for the public sector to downsize and to undo its network of controls over economy and society. The market was resurgent, and private investment held up as the solution to poverty and new engine of development. The structural adjustment programmes imposed upon African governments called for the state to act as a manager of development and welfare, not the deliverer. The principles of the free market were to be adopted as African regimes were encouraged to sell off parastatals, dramatically cut the number of civil servants and public officials, eliminate subsidies and price-supports and open up their economies.

The 'Washington consensus'—a phrase coined by the economist John Williamson in relation to Latin America—came to characterize the new orthodoxy underlying development policy world-wide. Amongst its key tenets, governments were to impose fiscal discipline, remove controls over interest and exchange rates, liberalize trade, and privatize uncompetitive public assets. Whilst it was never truly a 'consensus' (not all of its policy recommendations were accepted, indeed some were vigorously opposed by the emerging anti-globalization campaigners), its promulgation through organizations such as the World Bank and the IMF and major donors gave it power and authority. Individual countries were forced through economic and political crisis to accept these terms in order to receive continued ODA. In Tanzania, for example, economic crisis and the refusal of its main bilateral donors to consider increasing aid unless it negotiated with the IMF, forced it to accept structural adjustment in the mid-1980s. Almost one-half of World Bank lending in 1986–90 in Tanzania was tied to structural adjustment. The combination of a government crippled by an economic crisis, and Organisation for Economic Co-operation and Development (OECD) member countries prepared to use their aid policies to support the promotion of a new orthodoxy left many African states few options other than to cede to the demands of international donors. Aid had become a tool for control as much as for development.

The State Resurgent: From 'Washington Consensus' to the 'London Agenda'

The hoped for massive inflow of private capital following liberalization and structural adjustment did not occur, and development indicators for much of sub-Saharan Africa during the 1990s seemed to go into reverse. As the HIV/AIDS pandemic swept across eastern, central and southern Africa, in particular, with debt levels increasingly unsustainable, along with a series of crop failures and droughts and famines associated with the El Niño effect, it was becoming increasingly clear that the power of the market alone was not sufficient to break through the development bottleneck. Just as the early colonial development planners had been forced to recognize the limits of private investment, the World Bank acknowledged that it had been overzealous in pursuing the rolling back of the state and had unwittingly undermined the ability of states to pursue development.

Governance became the new watchword of development, with the adoption in the early 1990s of the 'good governance' agenda by the World Bank and national and international donors. A 1989 World Bank report characterized Africa's development failure as the result of a crisis of governance. The 1992 World Development Report coined the phrase 'good governance' and placed it at the heart of international development policy, highlighting four key areas: public sector management; accountability; a sound legal framework for development; and transparency.

During the 1990s the technocratic model of the World Bank was refined by major donors and institutions such as the UN, focusing in particular on the democratic deficit in many African countries, the link between human rights and development and the link between effective and efficient states and the provision of equitable and universal social services. Good governance came to be defined as a democratic system, an independent judiciary, transparent systems, with a strong civil society able to participate fully in public life. Development could be achieved, the new orthodoxy suggested, through the use of aid and international development policy to reinforce good governance across the region. As the 1990s drew to a close international funds that a decade earlier had been channelled through non-official agencies, bypassing government ministries, agencies and treasuries, were now to be directed once more through state institutions. Governments across Africa were required by international donors to draw up Sector-Wide Approaches and Poverty Reduction Strategy Papers (PRSPs) to illustrate a commitment to spending their national income to improve both the developmental prospects of the country and the lives of the most vulnerable. Health ministries were to receive funds earmarked for public health projects; government agencies responsible for water and sanitation projects were once more put in charge of implementing schemes and programmes.

Conditions were still attached to the receipt of aid and donor support, but these conditions were designed to improve the effectiveness of the state rather than seeking to bypass it entirely. Donor aid to Kenya in the late 1990s and 2000s, for example, was tied to the Government addressing human rights issues and tackling corruption. The US Millennium Challenge Fund, for example, as with its free trade-oriented African Growth and Opportunity Act (AGOA) insisted that recipient governments commit to democracy, open markets, and good governance before aid in significant amounts was granted. Increasingly aid has been tied to a raft of measures designed to promote multi-party democracy, transparency and openness in governance, and effective plans for poverty reduction.

Over the past five years, the culmination of this process has emerged in what might tentatively be known as the 'London agenda'. The British Government, in particular, has called for a major restructuring of the way in which aid is delivered, focusing on a twin strategy of significantly expanding total aid flows, and channelling those flows directly to central governments. Central to the 'London agenda' is the restoration of the capacity of the state to manage and implement development by allowing greater direct control over resources, and increasing those resources to which it has access. The approach is at its most advanced stage in Ghana and Tanzania, where the majority of the British funding is channelled through the treasury, which can then choose how to allocate the aid it receives. This 'budget support' is not tied to particular programmes or conditions (other than the Government demonstrating its commitment to good governance principles and poverty alleviation), and is intended to build up local governmental capacity and ensure local ownership of development processes. The result in the early years of the 21st century has been to revive the power of the state to manage development from its moribund state of the late 1980s and early 1990s, but not so completely as seriously to challenge the power of those who hold the purse strings. The state has been resurgent, not victorious

If the period from the late 1990s saw a partial return to earlier notions of the role of the state in promoting and directing development, the scope of what the state was supposed to manage continued to evolve. One of the most significant of these shifts was the rights-based approach. During the 1980s human rights organizations began to consider issues of development as part of their mandate. At the same time, non-governmental organizations and non-official development-sector workers began to consider how the poor and marginalized could best be guaranteed access to particular services and expectations. Gradually the two merged creating an understanding that one central task of development was to ensure that all people had access to a range of services and opportunities to which all had a right under an emerging consensus of universal human rights. Thus the right to a certain level of education, to a particular level of health care, to a sustainable livelihood and security, became not responsibilities of a national government to provide, but the right of all people to expect. By framing development objectives as 'rights', governments which had signed up to the new international treaties that were drafted throughout the 1990s, could be held to account.

To return to the two questions that have formed the basis of development debates over the course of the past century—those of agency and of objective—one can see that the argument has come full circle in the case of the former. In current debates, it is the state which is dominant in managing and implementing development. There is a broad consensus, however, that it must be a particular type of state: one that is transparent and democratic; that pursues sound macroeconomic management; that puts poverty alleviation and eradication at the heart of its agenda; that guarantees the rule of law; and that protects the rights of its citizens. In terms of the objectives towards which this state is oriented, however, the definition of development has continued to widen, incorporating new ideas, notions, priorities and trends. Development no longer means economic growth from which all else will flow: it incorporates broad social objectives; notions of people's right to certain opportunities, services and levels of care; and issues of sustainability and security. Development has come to mean the creation of an entirely different society, where absolute poverty is eradicated, where all people have access to the same opportunities and where all live without fear.

AID AND DEVELOPMENT IN AFRICA TODAY

The current development environment has largely been shaped by the UN Millennium Development Goals (MDGs), and how best to meet the internationally agreed targets by 2015. At the turn of the century, reflecting on four decades of failure following the pronouncement of the 'decade of development', the international community sought to prioritize the development of the world's poorest countries, and the eradication of poverty. A set of eight goals to be achieved by 2015 was agreed by the 191 member-states of the UN:

The eradication of extreme hunger and poverty: reduce by one-half the proportion of people living on less than US $1 per day, and by one-half the number of people suffering from hunger.

Universal primary education.

Promotion of gender equality and female empowerment: eliminate gender disparity in primary and secondary education, and attain a higher proportion of female representation in parliaments.

Reduce child mortality: reduce child mortality rates for under-fives by two-thirds.

Improve maternal health: reduce maternal mortality ratio by three-quarters.

Combat HIV/AIDS, malaria and other preventable diseases: halt and begin to reverse the spread of HIV/AIDS, malaria and other diseases.

Ensure environmental sustainability: reduce by one-half the proportion of people without access to safe water, improve the lives of 100m. slum dwellers, ensure sustainable development.

Develop a partnership for development: ensure fair trade, address the problem of debt, increase access to essential medicines, make new technologies available to poor countries.

In sub-Saharan Africa, at current rates of progress, the targets for universal primary education will not be met until 2130 (some 115 years late); the target of halving poverty until 2150; and that for reducing avoidable child deaths by 2165 (150 years after the MDG deadline). The slow progress towards meeting those targets, indeed the realization that not one of the targets is on course to be met by 2015 in Africa, has provided the backdrop to current concerns about levels of poverty in Africa and international debates on how best to tackle the developmental needs of Africa.

The perception of the scale of the task that lies before development planners and practitioners has led to calls for a radical rethinking over development policy and practice in sub-Saharan Africa, based in particular on three key themes: promoting a fairer trade regime between Africa and the industrialized nations; restructuring aid financing and disbursement; and measures to tackle the massive burden of debt owed by poorer countries, and by African nations in particular. These priorities are linked into the broader good governance agenda promoted by international and national donors.

Fairer Trade

Trade has come to occupy a central place in the development discourse about sub-Saharan Africa. For many, creating a fairer trade regime in which Africa can participate freely without facing restrictions from tariffs and other artificial barriers is regarded as one of the essential and most important catalysts for development. However, the place of trade in development policy has slipped over past decades from its former central position, coinciding with a fall in Africa's share of world trade (down from 6% in 1980 to just 2% in 2002). While it is subject to an array of constraints, international focus has centred on two key factors: the impact of developed world subsidies to its own producers; and the effects of tariffs and artificial barriers in limiting access of African commodities to OECD markets.

Farmers in OECD countries receive more than US $300,000m. in support each year (compared with the $28,000m. in aid to Africa in 2006). The effect of such support is to distort global commodity prices, and leads to the creation of global surpluses (which reduces prices further), both of which impact on the ability of African producers to compete. Cotton subsidies in the USA, for example, amounted to $3,900m. in 2002, and were responsible for a global decline in prices of between 10%–20%. European Union (EU) cotton subsides amounted to around $1,000m. in the same period. The removal of such supports, estimates suggest, could lead to an increase in African cotton production of up to 75%. Food surpluses caused by agricultural subsidies have also undermined local food production in African countries. Rice farming in Ghana, for example, has been severely affected through having to compete with heavily subsidized imported rice. This not only reduces the ability of producers to earn an income, but can increase instability in national food production.

The imposition of barriers on African products (22% tariffs for many agricultural goods in the EU, and 14% in the USA, with higher tariffs for manufactured goods) has made it more difficult for Africa to trade with the developed world. Preferential tariff schemes, such as AGOA, and the EU Everything But Arms (EBA) initiative, have allowed certain countries and commodities to be traded without the imposition of tariffs. However, not all agricultural commodities are included (for example, under the EBA, bananas, rice and sugar are currently excluded). Moreover, crude petroleum accounts for more than one-half of all African exports under AGOA terms to the USA. Agricultural exports under AGOA in 2004 were worth US $265.1m., and apparel just $1,600m. Furthermore, three countries (Nigera, Gabon and South Africa) accounted for 93% of all AGOA exports in the early 2000s.

The removal of protective measures can also impact negatively on Africa's prospects for trade. The ending of the multilateral Multi-fibre Agreement, which imposed quotas on low-cost textile producing countries in Asia, led to Asian investors withdrawing from Africa and returning to their own countries to set up factories. Up to 7,000 textile workers in Lesotho (10% of the industry's workforce) lost their jobs over the Christmas 2004 holidays when six factories failed to reopen. The flight of textile jobs from Africa to Asia continued throughout 2005 and 2006.

The current Doha Round of trade talks, designed to increase developing countries access to industrialized markets, has so far failed to make real progress, and in May 2007 official representatives from the EU, the USA, India and Brazil were once more unable to resolve disagreements over agricultural subsidies, resulting in continued deadlock in the discussions.

Increased Aid

There is an emerging consensus that greater levels of aid need to be provided to Africa if it is to meet the developmental challenge. OECD governments committed themselves to increase aid flows to Africa in 2005, although they failed to reach a consensus on a key demand of the Commission for Africa and that year's Group of Eight industrialized nations (G-8) summit to double aid to Africa to US $50,000m. by 2010, and to increase it to $75,000m. by 2015. In the aftermath of the Gleneagles G-8 Summit, total development aid rose to record levels, reaching $106,800m. in 2005 (representing 0.33% of the gross national income—GNI—of OECD member countries). However, this rise largely reflected the significant increase in debt-relief programmes as part of the 'Paris Club' commitments made in 2005, and masked underlying trends towards a more static picture in terms of non-debt relief aid spending. In 2006 overall aid fell for the first time since 1997, by 5.1% to $103,900m. Aid to sub-Saharan Africa appeared to rise in 2006, despite the overall downward trend, increasing by 23% to $28,000m. However, this figure was distorted by the debt relief of $11,000m. granted to Nigeria in that year. US aid to sub-Saharan Africa in 2006, for example, amounted to $1,400m., of which $600m. (42%) was debt relief for Nigeria. If this figure is excluded from calculations, overall aid to Africa remained relatively static, rising by just 2% in 2006.

While the fall in total aid flows in 2006 was expected, following the substantial increases in 2005 (reflecting 'Paris

Club' commitments to debt relief) the static picture of aid to Africa raised concerns that G-8 commitments to doubling aid to Africa were significantly off target. Whilst the OECD expected a further fall in aid flows in 2007, before beginning to rise again in 2008 with the reallocation of debt-relief funding into more pro-active poverty alleviation programmes, the Africa Progress Panel, headed by the former UN Secretary General, Kofi Annan, and established to monitor donor commitments to Africa, suggested more dramatic increases of US $5,000m. dollars in 2007 and 2008 were required if the 2010 targets were to remain on course.[2]

Furthermore, divisions between donor countries have continued over how to deliver that aid. The 'London agenda' has called for aid to be made in the form of grants (rather than loans), and channelled directly into national budgets (rather than to private non-governmental institutions or through individual government departments). Direct budget support (DBS) has been trialled in Tanzania and Ghana, and is gaining increased (but not universal) acceptance amongst major donors. A key feature of DBS is its links to promoting good governance. Only governments which have proven track records in reform and effective government are eligible for such funding, and they must display their commitment to pro-poor policy and the implementation of continued good governance reforms.

The key instrument for increasing aid levels and for channelling aid under this model is the International Finance Facility (IFF), a frontloaded fund established by borrowing on global capital markets. Donors would pledge to meet the loans from their future aid budgets. The money would be provided to African governments in the form of grants, and the debts incurred by the IFF would be repaid by the developed countries. The proposed establishment of an IFF made little progress in the face of criticism from the US Government in particular, which remained concerned over the lack of conditionality to aid that would result. Nevertheless, a US $4,100m. bond for a global immunization programme for children under the age of five was launched in London, United Kingdom, in November 2006. In a symbolic gesture, the first six bonds were purchased by Pope Benedict XVI and representatives of five British faiths: the Archbishop of Canterbury, the Chief Rabbi of the United Hebrew Congregations of the Commonwealth, the Muslim Council of Britain, the Hindu Forum of Britain, and the Network of Sikh Organisations. In April 2007 the Advance Market Commitment was launched in Rome, Italy, a $1,500m. programme designed to ensure preferential rates for poor countries in securing access to new vaccines for diseases largely affecting developing countries.

The US Administration has increased its aid budget to Africa, but has chosen to disburse grants through its Millennium Challenge Account (MCA). The MCA was established in January 2004 with an initial fund of US $1,000m. and the US Government aims to provide up to $5,000m. per year through the MCA. In order to qualify for funding from the MCA, governments have to sign up to a set of policies covering economic policy and governance.

Ending the Debt Crisis

The issue of debt in the poorest countries saw the most significant movement during 2005, with a major agreement by the G-8 countries in June 2005 immediately to cancel the debt owed to the World Bank, the IMF and the African Development Bank by 18 countries (15 of which are African). The agreement has wiped out US $40,000m. of debt, with the prospect of another 20 countries being eligible to qualify if they meet targets on corruption and good governance, taking the package up to a potential $55,000m. of debt cancellation.

Debt relief continued throughout 2006 and 2007. Debts owed to 'Paris Club' creditors by Cameroon (US $921m.), Malawi ($137m.) and Sierra Leone ($238m.) were cancelled in a series of agreements, and the Central African Republic's debt was restructured, with $9.9m (of the $36.1m. owed to 'Paris Club' creditors) cancelled.[3] In total, debt relief comprised 18% of total ODA. However, criticism continued to be levelled at the initiative for heavily indebted poor countries (HIPCs), under which much debt cancellation has taken place, noting that only 18 African countries have completed the process so far, and too little is being done too slowly to assist other African countries. Moreover, while the 'Paris Club' creditors have made moves in recent years to cancel debts owed to them, commercial creditors in particular have been more reluctant to cancel African debts. Concerns also rose over the emergence of so-called 'vulture funds'—the purchase of developing country debt obligations by commercial companies who then seek to pursue that debt through the courts. In April 2007, following a ruling by the British High Court, US-based Donegal International was awarded $15.5m. (although had claimed $55m.), having purchased Zambia's debt to Romania in 1999 for just $3.2m. Such companies have taken legal action against HIPCs in at least 40 cases, with some cases still outstanding.

As a result of the fall in total aid, slow progress in debt relief within sub-Saharan Africa, and the continued failure to reach agreement in the Doha Round of trade talks, critics of the industrialized countries, especially the G-8, condemned the slow progress in achieving the promised targets, and the impact this was having on levels of poverty in Africa.

CONCLUSION: THE CHALLENGE FOR THE FUTURE

To return to the question posed at the beginning of the essay: has development failed in Africa? It is true that many human development indicators appear to be falling: the proportion of those suffering from hunger has increased since the mid-1990s; life expectancies have fallen across the region; and the daily realities of grinding poverty continue to make their impact on millions of people. The story of development also appears to be one in which voices from Africa have been silenced by successive external powers. But, as ever, external aid and development policy devised in the USA and in Europe is but one aspect of Africa's hope for the future. Ultimately the answers lie, as they always have, within the continent itself. Development policy has too often been implemented with the interests of non-Africans at its heart. Policies have been started and abruptly stopped as trends and debates have shifted. The developed world has forced African countries to accept free markets while continuing to impose restrictions in their own. But through the constantly shifting international policies, the citizens of Africa have sought to improve their daily lives in small, incremental ways.

This essay has focused on the broad debates and shifting agendas in African development. However, it would be wrong to conclude that the sole story of development is located there. Self-help and community groups across Africa, civil society organizations, local faith and secular development groups have undertaken local schemes and projects with little, if any, external assistance. Colonial and international policies have been resisted and refined by those living with the consequences. African governments have in the recent past sought to address in concert some of the problems facing the continent. Through the establishment of the New Partnership for Africa's Development (NEPAD), the African Union, the creation of an African peace-keeping force, through free trade zones and other institutional unions, Africa is gradually restoring a measure of control over its own destiny. Of course, not all is positive. Corruption and violence continue to undermine development efforts. Violent conflict takes its toll in life and human misery. The lack of resources means many states are unable to meet their commitments, even where willing. However, should, as the past tells us is likely, the world avoid its responsibilities and once more push African poverty to the back of the international agenda, the prospects for development and poverty alleviation will continue to lie with Africans themselves.

FOOTNOTES

[1] Havinden M., and Meredith D. *Colonialism and Development: Britain and its Tropical Colonies, 1850–1960*. London and New York, NY, Routledge, 1993.

[2] 'Development aid from OECD countries fell by 5.1% in 2006', 3 April 2007. See www.oecd.org/document/17/0,3343,en_2649_201185_38341265_1_1_1_1,00.html. Accessed 27 June 2007. 'Africa Progress Panel Communiqué', 24 April 2007. See www.africaprogresspanel.org/english/ourworkview.php?id=2&view=6. Accessed 26 June 2007.

[3] See www.clubdeparis.org/sections/services/communiques. Accessed 28 June 2007.

STATE FAILURE IN AFRICA: CAUSES, CONSEQUENCES AND RESPONSES

PAUL D. WILLIAMS

This essay addresses the following four questions: What is meant by state failure? What causes states to fail? What is the scope of this phenomenon in contemporary Africa; and how have insiders and outsiders responded to this process?

Different people find these questions important for different reasons. For the citizens whose states fail the impacts upon their daily lives are rarely uniform: they can range from immense to negligible depending on a wide range of factors, including how much control the state previously exerted over its citizens, or how far the inhabitants happened to live from the capital city and other major urban centres. For Western governments, on the other hand, state failure in Africa is commonly viewed as both a moral catastrophe and, especially after the terrorist attacks on New York and Washington, DC, of 11 September 2001, a security threat. These dual concerns were neatly elucidated by the then British Secretary of State for Foreign and Commonwealth Affairs, Jack Straw, in September 2002. When confronted with state failure, Straw suggested that 'we cannot but be concerned at the implications for the human rights and freedoms of those who are forced to live in such anarchic and chaotic conditions. Yet the events of September 11 devastatingly illustrated a more particular and direct reason for our concern. For it dramatically showed how a state's disintegration can impact on the lives of people many thousands of miles away, even at the heart of the most powerful democracy in the world. In these circumstances turning a blind eye to the breakdown of order in any part of the world, however distant, invites direct threats to our national security and wellbeing. I believe therefore that preventing states from failing and resuscitating those that fail is one of the strategic imperatives of our times.'

Africa is commonly viewed as a particular cause for concern because it is here that the phenomenon of state failure is most widespread and deeply entrenched. In the case of the British Government, this produced a spate of bureaucratic activity culminating in a report in 2005 by the Prime Minister's Strategy Unit entitled *Investing in Prevention*. In a similar vein, after 11 September 2001 the US Government stated it was 'now threatened less by conquering states than...by failing ones.' As a result, the US National Security Strategy published in March 2006 acknowledged that 'our security depends upon partnering with Africans to strengthen fragile and failing states and bring ungoverned areas under the control of effective democracies.' State failure is thus a serious concern for both insiders and outsiders and it is on Africa that the international spotlight has most commonly fallen.

The prominence of such discourses about state failure has also generated a great deal of controversy. One important line of criticism has drawn insights from the post-colonial studies literature and called upon analysts to refrain from using terms such as 'failed states', 'weak states' and 'quasi-states' on the grounds that they are based on ethnocentric assumptions that depict African states as imperfect copies of Western European and North American states and judge them according to external standards in order 'to promote and justify their political and economic domination by Western states and other international actors.'[1] This essay is not intended to refute the post-colonial critique for it raises many sensible questions about the use of terms like 'failure', 'fragility' and 'weakness'. Nor is it intended to advocate the post-colonial critique by refusing to use such terms. Rather, this essay will provide an overview of the dominant discourses on state failure in Africa and will attempt to understand what responses, from both insiders and outsiders, they have helped facilitate.

WHAT IS STATE FAILURE?

Discussions of state failure are essentially about the inter-relationships between patterns of authority, political control and institution-building. Put another way, analysing state failure in Africa requires a keen sense of the shifting configurations of power on the continent and beyond. In most of the literature on the subject, the idea of 'failure' is invoked in two main senses, referred to in this essay as the failure to control and the failure to promote human flourishing.[2]

The Failure to Control

In the first sense, failure is understood in terms of the inability of state institutions to control actors and processes within a given territory. Robert I. Rotberg maintains that 'failed states cannot control their peripheral regions, especially those regions occupied by out-groups...Plausibly, the extent of a state's failure can be measured by the extent of its geographical expanse genuinely controlled (especially after dark) by the official government.' It is important to remember, however, that control and failure should not been seen as absolutes. A 'failed' state in this sense of the term might successfully control some of its territory but not all of it. Sudan, for example, is commonly classified as a failed state yet it continues to exert effective control over large portions of its territory and can wreak havoc and terror on some of those individuals and groups who contest its authority in those areas.

This suggests that viewing the phenomenon of state failure in absolute terms and through solely statist lenses is not always particularly helpful. Rather analysts need to appreciate the degrees of success and failure that can exist within a single state and recognize that so-called 'failed states' are usually made up of numerous (and often interconnected) zones where different sources of authority may dominate the local governance structures. In any given zone the authority in question may vary. Indeed, as Rotberg noted, it may differ considerably within the same zone depending on the time of day or night. The authority structure could be an organ of the state's official government but it may also be, among other things, an insurgency or guerrilla movement, a clan, a militia, an extended family, a spiritual leader, an international peace operation, or even a transnational corporation or a non-govermental organization.

To give one example, the collapse of the Somali central state did not automatically exclude the possibility that zones of alternative forms of governance and authority existed within Somalia's officially recognized international borders. As Kenneth Menkhaus has observed, since 1991 'Somalia has repeatedly shown that in some places and at some times communities, towns, and regions can enjoy relatively high levels of peace, reconciliation, security and lawfulness despite the absence of central authority.' These authority structures have come in various shapes and sizes. They have included local polities comprised of coalitions of businessmen, clan elders and Muslim clergy involved in administering financial services and *Shari'a* courts, and larger-scale structures such as the administrative centres of the 'Republic of Somaliland' (1991–), 'Puntland' (1998–), the Rahanwin Resistance Army's administration of Bay and Bakool regions (1998–2002) and the Banaadir Regional Authority (1996).

When analysing state failure in Africa in this first sense, analysts and practitioners would thus do well to reject a state-centric ontology in favour of a neo-Gramscian frame of reference, wherein the world is not simply seen as being made up of clashing states in an anarchic international system but, instead, is constituted by the complex inter-relationships between states, social forces and ideas within specific world orders.[3] Adopting this ontology is far more useful for analysing state failure because as Timothy Raeymaekers correctly observed, what we are witnessing in several cases of so-called 'state failure' is actually better understood as 'neopatrimonialism without the state'. That is, systems of patron-client relations that may or may not be linked to the official institutions of state power. Arguably the closest Western officialdom has come to adopting such a perspective is the US Government's anxiety about what it terms 'ungoverned spaces', 'defined as geographic areas where governments do not exercise effective control.'[4] Unfortunately, this misses the crucial point that just because official governments do not control these areas it does not necessarily mean that they are completely lacking other structures of governance.

The Failure to Promote Human Flourishing

Failure is also commonly used in a second sense to highlight the ways in which states, either because of a lack of capacity or a lack of political will, fail to provide public goods to their entire population rather than favouring one or other particular segment of it. The idea that states have a responsibility to provide their citizens with certain basic rights has long been an issue of debate within international relations dating back at least as far as notions of popular sovereignty articulated by Jean Bodin in the 16th century. Since the publication in late 2001 of a report by the International Commission on Intervention and State Sovereignty, this line of argument is now commonly known as the 'responsibility to protect'. Although African governments have jealously guarded traditional ideas about sovereignty and non-intervention, the responsibility to protect idea has made significant headway in recent years and with it has come a plethora of literature speaking of 'failure' in these terms. Despite these longstanding reservations, in September 2005 African states, along with the rest of the UN General Assembly, formally accepted the responsibility to protect idea. As defined in the World Summit Outcome document: 'each individual State has the responsibility to protect its populations from genocide, war crimes, ethnic cleansing and crimes against humanity. This responsibility entails the prevention of such crimes, including their incitement, through appropriate and necessary means. We accept that responsibility and will act in accordance with it.' When genocide, war crimes and other atrocities occur states can be said to have failed in their responsibilities to their citizens.

Understood in these two senses, state failure on the African continent is a widespread phenomenon. It is important to note, however, that both these views of failure are based upon a particular conception of statehood: what Rotberg calls 'the fundamental tasks of a nation-state in the modern world' and what William Zartman refers to as 'the basic functions of the state'. The particular idea of statehood that dominates discussions about state failure was born in Europe and is usually associated with the Treaties of Westphalia in 1648. That year is thus commonly understood within mainstream international relations theory as representing the birth of modern interstate relations. Yet while this specific date of origin makes for neat theory, it rests upon a dubious and mythical history. As Benno Teschke has argued, even in its European birthplace the practice of Westphalian statehood as opposed to the ideal of Westphalian statehood did not emerge until well after 1648. Specifically, Teschke has shown how modern international relations based on the Westphalian ideal of statehood only began with the conjunction of the rise of capitalism and modern state formation in England. Thereafter, the English model influenced the restructuring of the old regimes of the European continent, a process that was incremental and highly uneven and was not completed until the First World War.

The relevant point for this discussion is that the nature of statehood itself is contested rather than obviously apparent. Specifically, as Christopher Clapham has argued, the Westphalian ideal rests on 'unsure foundations', not least because in some parts of the world 'the essential conditions for statehood cannot plausibly be met.' The 'fundamental tasks' of statehood envisaged in this Westphalian ideal revolved around the provision of security, welfare and representation. In particular, the defining characteristic of the Westphalian ideal of statehood has been the right of states to exercise five monopoly powers:

the right to monopolize control of the instruments of violence;
the sole right to tax citizens;
the prerogative of ordering the political allegiances of citizens and of enlisting their support in war;
the sovereign right to adjudicate in disputes between citizens;
the exclusive right of representation in international society which has been linked with the authority to bind the whole community in international law.

Even in Europe, as Teschke observed, the practical acquisition of these monopoly powers sometimes took centuries of often violent turmoil and social upheaval. Compared with Europe and viewed from the perspective of the *longue durée*, it is clear that most states in Africa are still mired in the relatively early stages of state formation. Consequently, it should come as little surprise that the practical acquisition of these monopolies has been uneven across the continent.

Although it has been similarly traumatic and drawn out, the process of state-building has unfolded differently in Africa than it did in Europe. Unlike in Europe where state borders were demarcated with reference to their neighbours, in Africa state power tended to radiate from a focal core (usually the capital city) that only rarely came into direct confrontation with its neighbouring governments. As a basic rule of thumb, the further one travelled from this core, the weaker the state's control became. This fact rendered the state borders drawn up by the European colonial powers in Berlin in 1884–85 relatively meaningless, or at least highly porous, for many practical aspects of the local inhabitants' daily existence, including commerce or communicating with individuals who were officially 'foreigners', but who belonged to the same ethnic or tribal groups.

Understood in these terms, the issue of 'failed states' in Africa is largely about the extent to which the Westphalian ideal of statehood has taken root in the rather different and in many ways inhospitable conditions found on the continent. As the Organization of African Unity's (OAU) charter made abundantly clear, the ideal of Westphalian statehood clearly attracted many advocates among Africa's first generation of post-colonial élites. It was also helped by the willingness of the great powers within international society to grant these states international recognition. The practical realization of this ideal, however, has been far more contested and uneven. As a result, from the outside, African states often looked like the Westphalian ideal in that they were recognized members of international society and their representatives sat on the councils of various international organizations. On the inside, however, these governments were often considered illegitimate by much of the local population and wielded the institutions of state to subdue political opponents and benefit their supporters. These were, in Robert Jackson's famous phrase, quasi-states: legal fictions that rarely commanded much in the way of national loyalty or the power to control developments throughout their designated territory.

What this means for an analysis of state failure is simply that depending on the local conditions, 'failure' is far more likely in certain parts of the continent than others. More specifically, as Clapham has argued 'those areas of Africa that maintained reasonably settled and effective state structures during the period prior to colonialism are proving best able to do so as the institutional legacies of colonialism fade.' Where these structures were weak other forms of authority (familial, spiritual, ethnic, etc.) have filled the vacuum.

WHAT CAUSES STATES TO FAIL?

There is no simple or single formula for understanding the causes of state failure in Africa. Nevertheless, the available literature on the subject often makes at least two relevant general distinctions. The first distinction is between states that fail because of a lack of relevant capacities and those that fail to promote the interests of all their inhabitants through political choice, often with the intention of benefiting the incumbent regime and its supporters at the expense of another group within the state. Robert Mugabe's ongoing manipulation of ZANU—PF and state power in Zimbabwe is a paradigmatic example of a regime choosing to deny basic rights to certain segments of its population in an attempt to bolster regime security. The dynamics in this case are somewhat different from instances where a regime may well want to restore order to part of its territory but lacks the relevant capacities to do so. These dynamics are apparent in, for instance, the Ugandan Government's inability to quash the Lord's Resistance Army and Sudan's inability to defeat the Sudan People's Liberation Movement/Army. Such incapacity may sometimes lead to political compromises. At other times the result is simply longstanding stalemates and the de facto partition of a state's territory. Outside of the military sphere, a government might wish to enhance the development prospects of its citizens but lacks the necessary resources and instruments. The incumbent governments in Liberia and Sierra Leone are cases in point.

A second distinction points to the differences between structural and contingent causes of state failure. In the structural category three main arguments are commonly advanced. Firstly, as noted above, the Westphalian ideal of statehood has not successfully taken root across all of Africa because local conditions were inhospitable to state-building and exerting high levels of state control over local societies. Although international society helped the process by granting recognition to Africa's newly independent states—many of which became the archetypal examples of Jackson's quasi-states—it could not ensure that their inhabitants invested a great deal of faith in, or commitment to, them. Not long after independence, however, Cold War politics meant that the superpowers often made genuinely national nation-building even more difficult by stoking the fires of dissent within many African states in the name of either communism or capitalism.

A second structural argument has revolved around the challenges posed by political geography, especially resources and environmental factors. In this case the point is that some African states that were creations of the European colonial powers were not endowed with a physical environment conducive to administering an effective state. In particular, states such as those in the West African savannah suffered from extremely low densities of people, which made administration and social control both costly and difficult. The same was true for much of Africa since large areas of it have ecologies that cannot easily support high densities of population, not least because over 50% of the continent suffers from inadequate rainfall that makes inhospitable environments for both human settlement and agriculture. Indeed, it is arguably only the Great Lakes region and the Ethiopian highlands that have sustained relatively high densities of people.

A third structural argument has applied the concept of the security dilemma to explain how fear of an ungoverned future can propel the actors within states to hasten the collapse of central government once public order begins to erode and a situation of domestic anarchy seems likely to emerge. Here the suggestion is that the Hobbesian fear that lies at the heart of the security dilemma explains why groups begin to think that their potential rivals will not be restrained by state authority once the institutions of state have started to disintegrate. Analytically speaking, the crucial focus becomes understanding the 'tipping point' beyond which actors start to behave as if domestic anarchy exists, even if that is not entirely the case. At that stage, the dynamics of the domestic security dilemma may ensure that their conviction that state collapse and anarchy is imminent becomes a self-fulfilling prophecy.

The contingent causes of state failure in Africa are even more numerous with five main factors commonly cited within the literature. Crudely summarized, these refer to the influence of bad leaders, predatory actors such as warlords and so-called 'spoilers', bad economic policies, bad environments and bad neighbours.

First, much of the blame for state failure has been heaped upon Africa's leaders, not least Maj.-Gen. Mohammed Siad Barre (Somalia), Dr Siaka Stevens (Sierra Leone), Mobutu Sese Seko (Zaire/the Democratic Republic of the Congo—DRC), Gen. Samuel Doe and later Charles Taylor (Liberia) and Robert Mugabe (Zimbabwe). In many African states such leaders and their political élites have been criticized for pursuing patrimonial politics that seek to use external sources of aid and finance to reward their supporters and weaken their opponents rather than to pursue genuinely national development strategies. Second, warlords and other 'spoilers' have been blamed for inflaming ethnic tensions and hastening state failure. The motivations of these predatory actors vary from case to case, but a common claim is that they have pursued violent strategies in order to accumulate wealth through the control of formal and/or informal markets. In this view, weak or failing state institutions provide an environment from which such warlords and 'spoilers' can profit.

The third set of contingent factors concerns the political economy of state failure, especially the adoption by governments of 'bad' macroeconomic policies resulting in fiscal deficits and balance of payments crises, and the paradoxical effects of structural adjustment policies encouraged by a variety of international donors. As Nicolas van de Walle has argued, both of these factors encouraged a 'hollowing out' of the state, which, in turn, increased 'the chances that minor political incidents and disputes could cause the descent into failure.' Such political economies did not, however, automatically produce failed states. Hence, although Zaire/the DRC and Sierra Leone were both 'hollowed out' before failing, states such as the Central African Republic (CAR), Malawi and Niger were also weakened by economic failure but did not suffer a similar fate.

A fourth commonly cited factor relates to the proliferation and availability of armaments, especially small arms and light weapons, in many of Africa's weak and fragile states. An environment awash with arms makes it difficult for governments to control all of their territory or protect all of their citizens because, as Michael Klare suggests, 'antigovernment formations can readily assemble sufficient weaponry to mount a revolution or insurgency.' A fifth contingent cause of state failure concerns the role played by actors within neighbouring states. These have tended to be either incumbent governments hostile to their neighbouring regimes (e.g. Taylor's destabilization of Sierra Leone throughout the 1990s), or insurgent groups which destabilize their target state with or without support from the government of their (temporary) host state (e.g. the Rwandan Patriotic Front's use of Uganda as a base for its operations before it invaded Rwanda in 1990, or Hutu genocidaires using eastern Zaire/the DRC to destabilize Paul Kagame's regime after the 1994 genocide).

All of these factors can play a role in state failure but the current state of knowledge remains far too vague accurately to predict the tipping points in particular cases.

WHAT IS THE SCOPE OF THE PROBLEM?

As noted above, failed states raise challenges both for the great powers concerned about what threats might come out of them and for the locals who have to endure life inside them. Indeed, it has been suggested that since 'the end of the Cold War, weak and failing states have arguably become the single-most important problem for international order.'[5] Although state failure is not confined to Africa the problem is arguably more widespread, deeply rooted and pressing here than in any other continent.

Failed states can spawn a variety of transnational security problems with terrorism, proliferation of weapons of mass destruction (WMD), crime, disease, energy insecurity, and regional instability chief among them. Not all of them, however, are equally prevalent in Africa's cases. With the notable exceptions of actors operating out of Sudan and Somalia, transnational terrorism has been relatively rare in sub-Saharan Africa. The same could also be said for WMD proliferation. In contrast, small arms and light weapons proliferation, transnational crime (especially the illicit trade in drugs, arms, minerals, petroleum, timber, wildlife and human beings), infectious diseases (including HIV/AIDS, malaria, tuberculosis, hepatitis B, Ebola, measles, and the West Nile virus), and political instability in the Horn of Africa and the Gulf of Guinea oil states do pose significant threats and challenges to both the locals and the great powers.

It is important to note, however, that these challenges are unevenly distributed across Africa's failing states. Transnational criminals, for instance, tend not to operate in areas of complete state collapse (such as Somalia), but instead prefer areas where a basic degree of physical and financial infrastructure exists and where bureaucrats and officials are susceptible to bribery (such as Kenya, Nigeria and South Africa). Similarly, cells of transnational terrorist networks are likely to require similar levels of infrastructure and at least a degree of order if they are to use failing states for anything other than transit routes and temporary bases of operations.

The major al-Qa'ida attacks against US embassies in 1998, for instance, took place in Kenya and Tanzania but were allegedly orchestrated from a partially failed state in the form of Sudan and an almost entirely collapsed state in the shape of Somalia. Viewed from a longer-term perspective, however, most terrorism in Africa has been nationally oriented and targeted against white-minority rule or in specific revolutionary settings, notably Ethiopia and Algeria.

During the early stages of the 21st century, Africa has provided many of the usual suspects on the lists of the world's failed states including Chad, the DRC, Liberia, Sierra Leone, Sudan and Zimbabwe. In addition, Somalia is usually classified in a league of its own as having collapsed altogether rather than simply failed. Africa's leading status in these rankings is confirmed by four popular attempts to categorize different types of state failure, namely, the World Bank's Governance Matters data set, the Failed States Index, the UN Development Programme's (UNDP) Human Development Index, and Freedom House's annual surveys of political freedom.

The World Bank's *Governance Matters 2007* data set ranks world-wide governance indicators, covering 212 countries and territories. It defines governance as 'the set of traditions and institutions by which authority in a country is exercised. This includes (1) the process by which governments are selected, monitored and replaced, (2) the capacity of the government to effectively formulate and implement sound policies, and (3) the respect of citizens and the state for the institutions that govern economic and social interactions among them.' The 2007 report measured six dimensions of governance between 1996 and 2006: voice and accountability, political stability and absence of violence, government effectiveness, regulatory quality, rule of law, and control of corruption. The results across these different dimensions confirm Africa's place as the global centre of state failure. In particular, the continent contained 13 of the 30 least accountable states, 12 of the 30 most politically unstable and potentially violent states, 17 of the 30 least effective governments, 15 of the 30 states with the worst regulatory quality, 16 of the 30 states where the rule of law was weakest, and 13 of the 30 states least able to control corruption. On this list, Somalia is, by far, the state with the weakest governance structures, coming top of the global rankings in four of the six dimensions and second and third in the other two. Zimbabwe and the DRC also figure prominently in this ranking system.

A similar picture emerges from the *Failed States Index 2007* compiled by *Foreign Policy* magazine and the Fund for Peace. This measures performance along 12 political, economic, military and social indicators of instability (demographic pressures, refugees and displaced persons, group grievance, human flight, uneven development, economy, delegitimization of the state, public services, human rights, security apparatus, factionalized élites, and external intervention). It concluded that Africa contains eight of the world's 10 most failing states: Sudan (most failing), Somalia (third), Zimbabwe (fourth), Chad (fifth), Cote d'Ivoire (sixth), the DRC (seventh), Guinea (ninth), and the CAR (10th). Continuing down the scale, it suggested that Africa was home to 23 of the world's 40 most failing states.

The third popular ranking system is UNDP's *Human Development Index 2006*. It focuses on indicators of development which provide a reasonable snapshot of the extent to which a particular state is promoting human flourishing. UNDP concluded that Africa contains 35 of the world's 40 most underdeveloped states. In addition, it should be noted that the index did not include Somalia or Liberia, presumably owing to the difficulty of gathering data. The daily realities behind these figures include the uncomfortable facts that one-half of all Africans live on less than one dollar a day, more than one-half of them lack access to hospitals or doctors, one-third suffer from malnutrition, one in six children die before their fifth birthday, and the average African's life expectancy is just 41 years.

The final popular set of indicators is compiled by Freedom House in its annual report, *Freedom in the World*. This measures levels of political freedom, defined as people having 'the opportunity to act spontaneously in a variety of fields outside the control of the government and other centres of potential domination.' It does so by assessing the extent to which citizens enjoy political rights and civil liberties in 193 countries and 15 territories around the world. According to *Freedom in the World 2007*, Africa is currently home to some of the world's most repressive regimes. During 2006, for instance, Freedom House classified 19 African states as 'not free'. Moreover, its analysis suggested that during that year nine African governments became more repressive to the extent that they moved into a new Freedom House category (Burundi, Chad, the Republic of the Congo, Côte d'Ivoire, Guinea-Bissau, Madagascar, Mauritius, Somalia, and South Africa), while only six regimes moved into a less repressive category (the Comoros, the DRC, Liberia, Malawi, Mauritania, and Zambia). In addition, Freedom House's trend indicators suggested that another seven African governments became more repressive but remained within the same category (Egypt, Eritrea, Ethiopia, The Gambia, Kenya, Seychelles, and Zimbabwe), while the trend was towards less repression in only one state, Benin. Overall, Freedom House data suggests that eight of the world's 20 most repressive regimes are on the African continent (Côte d'Ivoire, Equatorial Guinea, Eritrea, Libya, Swaziland, Somalia, Sudan, and Zimbabwe).[6]

These four ranking systems all have significant limitations and have to confront difficult methodological questions but they do have the benefit of highlighting how unwise it is to generalize about the nature or effects of state failure in Africa. Nevertheless, they all make it abundantly clear that the continent is suffering more than most. Thus the pertinent practical question is how locals and outsiders have responded?

HOW HAVE INSIDERS AND OUTSIDERS RESPONDED TO STATE FAILURE IN AFRICA?

It is possible to identify four main types of responses to state failure in Africa. First, there have been external attempts, often led by Western governments, to reassert the failing state's control over its territory. There have also been similar Western-led attempts to encourage Africa's failing governments to provide their citizens with human rights and basic public goods. A third type of response has occurred in relatively rare instances where international society has been willing to permit states to disintegrate and break into separate smaller units. Finally, there have been the responses of local Africans themselves. These have ranged from active participation in the struggle to rebuild and control state power to indifference and sometimes hostility towards the entire process.

Resurrection

Western responses to Africa's failed states have been selective and intermittent. Selectivity is part and parcel of any state's foreign policy and the responses of Western governments to Africa's failing states have concentrated on those which are perceived to pose the greatest threats to Western security concerns. The US Government, for instance, has been criticized for singling out only two African states—Ethiopia and Sudan—for its current Transitional Initiative to encourage democratization in fragile and post-conflict states. (The Initiative allocated US $275m. of its $325m. budget to just four states: Afghanistan, Ethiopia, Haiti and Sudan.) This leaves worthy candidates such as Somalia, the DRC, Liberia, Sierra Leone, Burundi and the CAR with few funds to help democratization and civil society initiatives. However, Western responses to state failure have also been selective in a more geo-strategic sense. Despite suffering from some of the most serious examples of state failure on the planet, the African continent has not attracted a major transitional administration of the kind sponsored by Western states in Bosnia and Herzegovina, Kosovo, Timor-Leste and, to a lesser extent, Afghanistan. In this sense, state failure in Africa remains on the margins of Western concern even after the events of 11 September 2001.

The selective response of Western governments has been mirrored, and to some extent fostered, by the intermittent and transient media coverage given to state failure in Africa. This is usually explained by the fact that failed state stories do not meet enough of the traditional Western news criteria to keep them on the front pages of newspapers or on television screens. The United Kingdom and France appear to have more media coverage of these issues than most Western states but it remains infrequent, concentrated on their former colonies, and often involves stories that score highly in terms of drama, conflict and sensation but provide little in the way of historical background or explanation.

Given this context, when Western states have responded in concrete terms to Africa's failing states, they have usually tried to address the two different types of failure discussed above: the failure to control and the failure to promote human flourishing.

Outsiders have employed several strategies to help failing states reassert control over the actors within their territorial borders. To date, the most resource-intensive have been those designed to disarm, demobilize and reintegrate (DDR) former combatants. These DDR programmes are then usually followed by a process of 'security sector reform', the current pseudonym for building new, usually broad-based security institutions, notably the armed forces, police and intelligence services. Once again, however, and reflecting the powerful influence the Westphalian ideal of statehood exerts over the architects of these programmes, such efforts have been criticized for ignoring the political economy of Africa's failed states and the crucial roles played by private actors in such settings. As part of the reform process, Western powers have been keen to strengthen the capacity of African states to conduct complex peace operations. The most recent framework was announced at the 2004 Group of Eight (G-8) industrialized countries summit where the leaders pledged under the Global Peace Operations Initiative to support the training of some 40,000 African peace-keepers (out of a world-wide total of 75,000) to help make the much vaunted African Standby Force a reality by 2010. Yet, in the USA at least, this laudable programme has been underfunded. In addition to training and helping to equip African peace-keepers, Western states have also deployed small numbers of their own soldiers to so-called 'hybrid' peace operations in some of Africa's failing states, including the United Kingdom in Sierra Leone, France in Côte d'Ivoire, two EU-led operations in the DRC, and the USA in Liberia. In most cases, however, it remains too early to determine whether these efforts to reassert state control have succeeded.

A similar pattern has emerged in relation to external attempts to enhance the provision of public goods in Africa's failing states. Here the primary mechanisms have been increasing levels of foreign aid and development assistance, placing diplomatic pressure on African élites to adopt what the World Bank calls 'good governance', including the strengthening of the African Peer Review Mechanism, and more general attempts to implant the idea that states have a responsibility to protect the human rights of their own citizens.

With few exceptions, aid from most Western states has been concentrated on their traditional friends and allies in Africa. Nevertheless, both the United Kingdom and the USA have made significant increases in certain sectors, notably in funding to stem the prevalence of HIV/AIDS on the continent. On the other hand, the so-called 'global war on terror' has meant that significant amounts of Western development assistance has been allocated to states considered to be in the front line of the fight against terrorism, notably Iraq, Afghanistan and Pakistan. Efforts to encourage 'good governance' have come from a variety of sources, but since its formal adoption by the OAU in July 2001 the New Partnership for Africa's Development (NEPAD) has remained the most comprehensive framework to address this issue. However, NEPAD has suffered from several problems most notably those relating to its élitist and market-driven design, the slow pace of implementation, and perhaps most significantly for both Washington and London, the failure of many African states adequately to criticize Robert Mugabe's regime for plunging Zimbabwe into a crisis from which there will be no quick escape. However, at the same time that many African states were making excuses for the mayhem generated by Mugabe's ZANU—PF regime they were also signing up to a charter for the new African Union (AU) that included a paradigmatic shift in relation to the responsibility to protect idea. Specifically, in stark contrast to its predecessor, Article 4(h) of the AU's new charter permitted the organization 'to intervene in a Member State pursuant to a decision of the Assembly in respect of grave circumstances, namely war crimes, genocide and crimes against humanity'. To date, however, Article 4(h) has not been invoked. This is in spite of clear evidence that 'grave circumstances' have existed in the Darfur region of Sudan since at least mid-2003.

Of course, these two types of response are intimately related to one another. As a result, Western powers have started to pay greater attention to co-ordinating their responses across all the relevant dimensions of state failure. They have also acknowledged that there is an urgent need to prevent state failure rather than just to manage its consequences. One prominent example in this regard is the British Government's *Investing in Prevention* report (see above). This concluded that attempts to resurrect failed states and prevent their (re)occurrence should adopt a 'four S's' strategy:

appropriate scale of political attention and financial resources;
sustaining action over longer time horizons;
developing systematic approaches to action across political, development, economic, security and other dimensions;
achieving greater sophistication of understanding of long run dynamics of instability;

Importantly, the report also emphasized the need to change élite behaviour in fragile and failing states through a series of co-ordinated incentive strategies. Given the importance of contingent causes of state failure discussed above this is an important focus for action.

The State is Dead, Long Live the State

A third type of response has been far less prevalent in Africa. Despite the continuing problems facing attempts to resurrect Africa's failed states, it has been rare for the great powers within international society to countenance their disintegration or what Jeffrey Herbst has called the 'let them fail' approach. Nevertheless, such a response is possible, as indicated by Namibia's independence, Eritrea's secession from Ethiopia, Western Sahara's UN-endorsed (but currently stalled) referendum on secession from Morocco and the referendum on secession in southern Sudan scheduled for 2011 under the terms of the Comprehensive Peace Agreement. These exceptions have occurred when insurgencies have succeeded in gaining and sustaining control over significant areas of territory, usually through a military struggle. The rarity of this outcome suggests two things. First, given the relatively large number of insurgencies in Africa, the small number of secessions suggests that it is difficult for such movements to achieve decisive military victories over incumbent regimes and maintain control of sizeable territories for long periods of time when they do. Second, international society's general reluctance to countenance the 'death' of states and their breaking into smaller units demonstrates the power that the Westphalian ideal of statehood continues to exert even in the face of such implausible candidates for 'successful' state-building as Nigeria and the DRC.

In Herbst's opinion, the crucial issue is not to concentrate on resurrecting the old failed state, but to think through what the alternatives to failed states might look like and 'to increase the congruence between the way that power is actually exercised and the design of units.' As the examples in Somalia noted above suggest, it is clear that alternative units and structures already exist but very few of them are granted official recognition by international society. The first step in this recognition process would be for international society to countenance decertifying states when they fail to meet their sovereign responsibilities (of either control or promoting basic standards of human flourishing). Indeed, the US Administration has previously indulged in this kind of activity by designating certain countries including Iraq, Iran, Libya and the Democratic People's Republic of Korea as rogue, pariah or evil states that are unfit to participate as normal members of international society. The logical next step is to decide the criteria for selecting potential new states. This will be controversial, but a reasonable place to start, as Herbst suggests, is with the question of which actors or institutions are actually providing political order in a given territory. Herbst concludes that 'the long-term aim would be to provide international recognition to the governmental units that are actually providing order to their citizens as opposed to relying on the fictions of the past.'

Local Competition and Local Indifference

Finally, it is important to analyse local responses to state failure in Africa. The first point to note is that these have not been uniform. Some locals have competed to lead the resurrection process and, hopefully, benefit from the material resources that flow from it, including foreign aid and loans from the international financial institutions. Others, however, have tried their best to ignore the collapse of central government institutions and continue to bypass state power in many aspects of their everyday lives. In southern Africa, for instance, states have long failed to meet the needs of the region's peoples. Given the imperial foundations of the region's states this is hardly surprising. As a consequence, as Peter Vale has argued, ordinary southern Africans have lost faith in, and increasingly bypass, a state system that 'neither delivers security nor satisfies a desire for community'. Instead, they have engaged in alternative forms of social intercourse related to, among other things, religious affiliations, trading associations, musicology, and migration patterns, all of which show little respect for the political borders erected by southern Africa's states. In this sense, many ordinary Africans have become adept at forming accommodation strategies in a variety of different arenas to fulfil their needs when their state has failed them.

Over time, this has produced many different attitudes to 'the state' in Africa from squabbling élites desperate to resurrect and then control new state institutions to ordinary people who are often either indifferent or explicitly hostile to state-building projects focused on the urban centres. In Somalia, for example, not only have certain groups carried on their lives in spite of the collapse of the central state but they are extremely suspicious of any attempts to revive it. Whereas the conventional wisdom of Western-dominated institutions such as the World Bank and the G-8 dictates that an effective central state is a prerequisite for national development, many Somalis view the state as 'an instrument of accumulation and domination, enriching and empowering those who control it and exploiting and oppressing the rest.'[7] As a consequence, there have been a variety of groups hostile to international efforts to resuscitate the trappings of central government in Mogadishu. This also raises the important observation made by Menkhaus that state-building and peace-building might at times be 'mutually antagonistic enterprises in Somalia.' Consequently, outsiders should not automatically assume that insiders are united on the need to resurrect failed states. Instead, they should canvass the opinion of insiders and think carefully about when alternatives to failed states should be put into practice.

THE STRANGE CASE OF SOMALIA

As discussed above, the dilemmas and challenges of state-building are exemplified by the case of Somalia, the collapsed state par excellence and the focus of much US counter-terrorism activity. In particular, not only does any potential central government in Somalia face huge incapacity problems, but the process of building central institutions may well exacerbate the likelihood of violent conflict within the country and, ironically, make it a more attractive destination for terrorist organizations.

Contemporary Somalia exemplifies some of the conceptual points raised earlier in this essay. First, just because Somalia was a state without a central government this did not mean it was devoid of various systems of governance and sources of authority. In this sense, it should not be seen as one of the US Government's 'ungoverned spaces'. Although Somalia has lacked a permanent central government since 1991, at the local, municipal and neighbourhood levels coalitions of clan elders, businessmen and Muslim clergy overseeing *Shari'a* courts have provided governance structures and become sources of authority. At the regional/provincial level, power struggles within Somalia have revolved around the capital city, Mogadishu, but also the northern regions of the 'Republic of Somaliland' (which declared itself an independent republic in 1991) and 'Puntland' (which declared itself an autonomous state within Somalia in May 1998). In addition, from 2004, Somalia was in the rare situation of having its recognized Transitional Federal Government (TFG) based outside its territory, in Nairobi, Kenya. The TFG relocated to the Somali town of Baidoa in early 2006.

Second, coalitions of insiders and outsiders have played important roles in both keeping the state fractured and attempts to resurrect a set of central government institutions. Some insiders have asked external actors to provide a variety of peace operations to help the state-building project. In October 2004, for instance, the Somali President, Col Adbullahi Yussuf Ahmed, appealed for 20,000 peace-keepers to secure the country and disarm some 55,000 militiamen. Furthermore, in early 2005 the AU and then the Intergovernmental Authority on Development agreed to authorize the deployment of troops to facilitate the return of Somalia's TFG to Mogadishu. However, neither of these operations were carried out. It was only in late December 2006, after the conflict that expelled the Union of Islamic Courts (UIC) from Mogadishu, that the AU actually deployed approximately 1,600 Ugandan troops as part of its Mission in Somalia (AMISOM). These moves were, of course, criticized by those insiders hostile to the entire state-building project and by those who viewed these external forces as an attempt to install what they perceived to be an illegitimate TFG.

These developments demonstrate Menkhaus's point that there exist competing views of the state in Somalia. For most external actors, the conventional wisdom is that an effective state is a prerequisite for development. This view is supported by those insiders who think they are likely to benefit from the resurrection of a central government. On the other hand, however, for many Somalis, the state is seen as an instrument of accumulation and domination, enriching and empowering those who control it and exploiting and oppressing the rest. For these insiders, state-building is something to be resisted.

Arguably the two main external actors behind the most recent state-building project in Somalia have been Ethiopia and the USA. For Ethiopia, the primary goal has been to avoid a situation where Islamist extremists control a unified Somalia and reawaken nationalist desires to return the Ogaden region of Ethiopia to Somali control. This explains Addis Ababa's strong support for the TFG and its deep suspicion of the UIC. For the USA, on the other hand, the major objective is to avoid a situation where Somalia becomes a safe haven for anti-Western terrorist organizations. From Washington's perspective, the best way to secure this goal is to support a stable, moderate central government and help it build the capacity to police its borders and root out extremists within them. To this end, the US authorities supported the self-styled Alliance for the Restoration of Peace and Counter-Terrorism (ARPCT), which in reality was simply a disorganized collection of warlords and opportunist militia.

The problem with the US position was two-fold. First, Somalia had not become a major safe haven for terrorist organizations in spite of the ascendance of political Islam and the lack of effective government institutions. For example, in 2005 US intelligence gathering in Somalia produced no evidence of al-Qa'ida bases, or that al-Ittihad al-Islam was operating as one of its subsidiaries. Indeed, it was US support for the ARPCT that helped Islamist extremists to gain ascendancy over more moderate Islamic voices in late 2006. Second, Washington's idea that establishing the institutions of a central state would help reduce the threat of transnational terrorists using Somalia as a base was flawed, at least in the short-term.

As Menkhaus has persuasively argued, there are six main reasons that explain why terrorist organizations have not been attracted to Somalia during its period as a collapsed state. First, terrorist cells and bases are much more exposed to international counter-terrorist action in zones of state collapse where US Special Forces could violate state sovereignty regularly and with impunity. The US air strikes in January 2007 against al-Qa'ida suspects in Somalia are a case in point. Second, areas of state collapse tend to be inhospitable and dangerous, particularly for foreigners. Consequently, since few foreigners choose to reside in such environments, foreign terror cells will find it very difficult to blend into the local population and retain the degree of secrecy necessary to conduct their activities. A third factor is the double-edged nature of the lawlessness that accompanies situations of state collapse: while lawlessness reduces the risk of apprehension by law enforcement agencies, it increases the likelihood that terror cells will suffer from more common crimes such as kidnapping, extortion or assassination. As Menkhaus suggests, 'it appears that lawlessness can inhibit rather than facilitate certain types of lawless behavior.'[7] A fourth problem is that any terrorists would be susceptible to betrayal by Somalis looking to ingratiate themselves with the US authorities. Fifth, Somalia represents an environment in which it is very difficult to stay neutral and outside the inter-clan rivalries. Relatively mundane activities such as hiring personnel or renting buildings will inevitably be seen as evidence of taking sides and once this perception has been established the external actor in question becomes a legitimate target of reprisals by rival clans. Finally, the collapse of the Somali state has left it without the usual array of 'soft' Western targets such as embassies and businesses. As a result, Somalia is more likely to be used as a transit point for *materiel* than to act as a more permanent base for cells. Even terrorists, it would seem, require a degree of political order to conduct their activities. The 'security paradox' identified by Menkhaus is that at least in the short-term, attempts to resurrect effective state institutions in Somalia may create an environment that is more, not less, conducive to terrorist cells basing themselves in the country.

On the basis of this analysis, Menkhaus concludes that Somalia poses a uniquely difficult challenge for would-be state-builders. First, the success of local adaptation to state collapse could impede state-building efforts by reducing local incentives to support a revived state. Second, state-building will continue to be a conflict-producing enterprise, due to the zero-sum view that most Somali political actors have of control of the state. Third, a major obstacle to state-building is the lack of revenues that a government can secure from taxes. As a consequence, any project will need major external funding. Menkhaus's solution is for outsiders to support the establishment of a 'mediated state' in which the government co-operates with local intermediaries and rival sources of authority to provide core functions of public security and justice. The process by which such mediation is decided can only emerge from genuine dialogue between insiders.

CONCLUSIONS

What conclusions follow from this analysis of state failure in Africa? In response to the first question, 'what is meant by state failure?', it was suggested that most of the contemporary debate is based upon a particular conception of statehood that invokes an ideal formalized at the Treaties of Westphalia in 1648. For a variety of reasons, this ideal has not successfully taken root in many parts of Africa. As a consequence, not only is state failure widespread on the continent, but significant parts of it should be understood as remaining in the early stages of the state formation process and much more turmoil should therefore be expected. In order to understand the contemporary dynamics of this process, analysts would do well to pay closer attention to the configurations of power on the continent and move beyond state-centric and statist approaches. One plausible alternative would be to utilize the neo-Gramscian approach with its focus on the inter-relationships between states, social forces, ideas and world orders. This would provide a set of conceptual tools to help understand the phenomenon of 'neopatrimonialism without the state'.

In terms of the causes of state failure, contemporary debates distinguish between those states that choose to fail certain segments of their populations, and those which lack the resources effectively to control their territory. In addition, although a wide array of structural and contingent factors continue to generate discussion, collective knowledge about these processes remains limited and unable to predict the tipping points in particular cases. Finally, there is the crucial practical question of responses to state failure in Africa. For outsiders at least, the most common approach has been to resurrect the institutions of state power, usually following Weberian and liberal blueprints. However, as the case of Somalia demonstrates, the processes of state-building and peace-building may sometimes be mutually exclusive enterprises. Moreover, resurrection strategies may, in the short-term at least, make collapsed states a more attractive destination for extremist organizations. In spite of such problems, it is only rarely that international society has agreed to the disintegration of existing states into smaller ones. Sometimes, some insiders have joined the competition to control these new units. In contrast, other insiders have continued to bypass a state system that has consistently failed to meet their basic needs. This suggests that the real solution to state failure in Africa lies in developing political communities that can provide for the needs of their members and gain recognition in wider global politics. How closely these communities will resemble the ideal of Westphalian statehood remains to be seen.

FOOTNOTES

[1] Hill, J. 'Beyond the Other? A postcolonial critique of the failed state thesis' in *African Identities*, Vol. 3, No. 2, pp. 139–140. Abingdon, 2005.

[2] See, for example, Dorff, Robert H. 'Failed States After 9/11: What did we know and what have we learned?' in *International Studies Perspectives*, Vol. 6, No. 1, pp. 20–34. Oxford, 2005. Dorff refers to these two conceptions of failure as 'the ungovernable state' and the 'bad government state'.

[3] The seminal statements of this perspective are R. W. Cox's, 'Social Forces, States and World Orders: Beyond International Relations Theory' in *Millennium*, Vol. 10, No. 2 (1981), pp. 126–55; 'Gramsci, Hegemony and International Relations: An essay in method' in *Millennium*, Vol. 12, No. 2 (1983), pp. 162–75; and *Production, Power, and World Order*. New York, NY, Columbia University Press, 1987. See also Barnett, M. 'Authority, intervention and the outer limits of international relations theory' in Callaghy, T., Kassimir, R. and Latham, R. (Eds). *Intervention and Transnationalism in Africa*. Cambridge, Cambridge University Press, 2001.

[4] See 'Current and Projected National Security Threats to the United States', Vice Adm. Lowell E. Jacoby, US Navy, Director, Defense Intelligence Agency. Statement For the Record Senate Select Committee on Intelligence, 24 February 2004. http://www.dia.mil/publicaffairs/Testimonies/statement12.html.

[5] Fukuyama, F. *State-Building: Governance and World Order in the 21st Century*, p. 92. Ithaca, NY, Cornell University Press, 2004.

[6] The 20 regimes are those that scored the worst rating of 7 for either political rights or civil liberties. This list does not include Morocco's rule over Western Sahara which also falls into this category.

[7] Menkhaus, K. 'State Collapse in Somalia: Second Thoughts', in *Review of African Political Economy*, No. 97 (2003), p. 409.

BIBLIOGRAPHY

Abrahamsen, R., and Williams, M. C. 'Security sector reform: bringing the private in' in *Conflict, Security and Development*, Vol. 6, No. 1, pp. 1–23. Abingdon, 2006.

Ayittey, G. B. N. *Africa Unchained: The Blueprint for Africa's Future*. New York, NY, Palgrave-Macmillan, 2005.

Clapham, C. 'Degrees of Statehood' in *Review of International Studies*, Vol. 24, pp. 143–57. Cambridge, 1998.

'The Challenge to the State in a Globalized World' in *Development and Change*, Vol. 33, No. 5, pp. 775–795. Oxford, 2002.

'Terrorism in Africa: Problems of Definition, History and Development' in *South African Journal of International Affairs*, Vol. 10, No. 2, pp. 13–28. Braamfontein, 2003.

Council on Foreign Relations. *More than Humanitarianism: A Strategic US Approach Toward Africa*. New York, NY, Independent Task Force Report No. 56, pp. 20, 101, 2006.

Freedom House, *Freedom in the World 2007*, available at www.freedomhouse.org.

Fukuyama, F. *State-Building: Governance and World Order in the 21st Century*. Ithaca, NY, Cornell University Press, 2004.

Giddens, A. *The Nation State and Violence*. Berkeley, CA, University of California Press, 1987.

Herbst, J. *States and Power in Africa*. Princeton, NJ, Princeton University Press, 2000.

Hobson, J. M. *The State in International Relations*. Cambridge, Cambridge University Press, 2000.

Holm, H. 'Failing Failed States: Who Forgets the Forgotten?' in *Security Dialogue*, Vol. 33, No. 4, pp. 457–471. London, 2002.

Jackson, R. H. *Quasi-States: Sovereignty, International Relations and the Third World*. Cambridge, Cambridge University Press, 1990.

Jones, B., with Cherif, F. *Evolving Models of Peacekeeping: Policy Implications and Responses*. UN Best Practices Unit, External Study, 2004.

Linklater, A. *The Transformation of Political Community*. Cambridge, Polity, 1998.

Menkhaus, K. 'State Collapse in Somalia: Second Thoughts' in *Review of African Political Economy*, No. 97 (2003), pp. 405–422.

'Somalia and Somaliland' in Robert I. Rotberg (Ed.), *Battling Terrorism in the Horn of Africa*. Washington, DC, Brookings Institution Press, 2005.

'Governance without Government in Somalia: Spoilers, State Building, and the Politics of Coping' in *International Security*, Vol. 31, No. 3 (2006/07), pp. 74–106.

Milliken, J., and Krause, K. 'State Failure, State Collapse, and State Reconstruction: Concepts, Lessons and Strategies' in *Development and Change*, Vol. 33, No. 5, pp. 753–774. Oxford, 2002.

Patrick, S. 'Weak States and Global Threats: Fact or Fiction?' in *The Washington Quarterly*, Vol. 29, No. 2, pp. 27–53. Washington, DC, 2006.

Prime Minister's Strategy Unit (PMSU). *Investing in Prevention: An International Strategy to Manage Risks of Instability and Improve Crisis Response*. London, PMSU, February 2005.

Raeymaekers, T. *Collapse or Order? Questioning State Collapse in Africa*. Conflict Research Group, Working Paper No. 1, p. 6, May 2005.

Reno, W. *Warlord Politics and African States*. Boulder, CO, Lynne Rienner Publishers, 1998.

Reus-Smit, C. 'Human rights and the social construction of sovereignty' in *Review of International Studies*, Vol. 27, No. 4, pp. 519–538. Cambridge, 2001.

Rotberg, R. I. (Ed.). *When States Fail: Causes and Consequences*. Princeton, NJ, Princeton University Press, 2004.

Spear, J. 'From Political Economies of War to Political Economies of Peace: The Contribution of DDR after Wars of Predation' in *Contemporary Security Policy*, Vol. 27, No. 1, pp. 168–189. Abingdon, 2006.

Stedman, S. J. 'Spoiler Problems and Peace Processes' in *International Security*, Vol. 22, No. 2 (1997), pp. 5–53.

Taylor, I. *NEPAD: Towards Africa's Development or Another False Start?* Boulder, CO, Lynne Rienner Publishers, 2005.

'Blind Spots in Analyzing Africa's Place in World Politics' in *Global Governance*, Vol. 10 (2004), pp. 411–417.

Teschke, B. *The Myth of 1648: Class, Geopolitics and the Making of Modern International Relations*. London, Verso, 2003.

The National Security Strategy of the United States of America (September 2002).

The National Security Strategy of the United States of America (March 2006).

UN Development Programme. *Human Development Index 2006*. See http://hdr.undp.org/hdr2006/statistics/. Accessed on 11 July 2007.

Vale, P. *Security and Politics in South Africa: The Regional Dimension*. Boulder, CO, Lynne Rienner Publishers, 2003.

Walter, B. F., and Snyder, J. (Eds). *Civil Wars, Insecurity, and Intervention*. New York, NY, Columbia University Press, 1999.

Williams, P. D. 'Military Responses to Mass Killing: The African Union Mission in Sudan' in *International Peacekeeping*, Vol. 13, No. 2, pp. 168–183. Abingdon, 2006.

Woods, N. 'The Shifting Politics of Foreign Aid' in *International Affairs*, Vol. 81, No. 2, pp. 393–409. Oxford, 2005.

Zartman, W. I. (Ed.). *Collapsed States: The Disintegration and Restoration of Legitimate Authority*. Boulder, CO, Lynne Rienner Publishers, 1995.

2005 World Summit Outcome. UN General Assembly: 60th Session, A/60/L.1, 20 September 2005.

CHINA'S EXPANSION INTO AFRICA

IAN TAYLOR

Beijing's expansion into Africa is increasing at an exponential speed and has become a major topic of interest to observers of both Africa's and the People's Republic of China's international relations. According to the China-Africa Business Council, China is now Africa's third most important trading partner, behind the USA and France, but ahead of the United Kingdom. Published trade figures are indicative of this massive surge in Chinese economic interest in Africa. In 1996 the value of China's trade with Africa was US $4,000m.; by 2004 this had grown to $29,600m., in 2005 reached $39,700m., and in 2006 totalled $55,500m. It is predicted that annual trade volume between China and Africa will increase to more than $100,000m. in the next five years. Much of this expansion is driven by a desire to obtain sources of raw materials and energy for China's ongoing economic growth and for new export markets. This essay seeks to place China's role in Africa into its historical context as well as examine the political and economic implications for Africa of China's growing presence on the continent.

HISTORICAL CONTEXT

The links between China and Africa in the contemporary period traces its essential roots to three things: the crisis in China's international relations after the Tiananmen Square incident in June 1989; the incredible expansion of the Chinese economy in the 1990s and 2000s; and the desire to take advantage of numerical support in the UN granted by, in part, African states, to prevent hostile votes against China *vis-à-vis* its human rights record and to ensure that Taiwan remains an unrecognized international outcast. Prior to this period, Africa's importance in Beijing's foreign policy had declined during the 1980s as China's Socialist Modernization project appealed for massive foreign investment and technology deemed unavailable from Africa.

In addition, Chinese tensions with both the USA and the USSR lessened throughout the 1980s, further marginalizing Africa's importance in China's view. However, post-Tiananmen Square China 'rediscovered' Africa and this renewed interest has been built on every year by the huge growth in Chinese firms and corporations—as well as ordinary Chinese entrepreneurs—who have embarked upon a concerted drive to discover markets and commercial opportunities overseas. The twin motivations of diplomacy and economics now firmly drive China's linkages with the African continent. Both of these impulses help further China's overall political ambition: to be taken seriously as a 'great power' and for China to be restored to its 'rightful place'. The developing world—Africa included—plays a role in this.

Beijing's broader foreign policy essentially stems from the perception held at the élite level that China is actually relatively weak and that it is vulnerable within the international system. However, this assessment clashes with the tangible view in Beijing that China is—or should be—central to the world. Thus, the attainment of great-power aspirations draws upon strong emotions, linked to nationalist sentiments, traditional cultural ethnocentrism and a deeply rooted sense of injustice at the hands of foreign countries.

Inherited from pre-revolutionary China, this feeling of superiority and strong determination to become a great power has compelled the Chinese leadership to attempt to project China's presence and reputation abroad as a means by which Beijing could attempt to make good the gap between the ambitions and aspirations of a reinvigorated China (note Mao's comments in 1949 that 'the Chinese people have stood up'). This desire to possess centrality and autonomy of action in the international system, has been a particular feature of Beijing's foreign policy and China's self-image *vis-à-vis* the rest of the world has influenced China's conceptualization of its relations with the international system. The developing world has long been a particular area where Beijing's foreign policy has been pursued actively, using the development of common interests with the South to raise China's global stature and increase Beijing's bargaining leverage with the USA.

POST-TIANANMEN SQUARE RELATIONS WITH AFRICA

After 4 June 1989 such policy calculations received a major impetus. The events surrounding Tiananmen Square resulted in a severe crisis in China's relations with the West and the depth of Western condemnation surprised the Chinese leadership. Until then, China's human rights record had been basically ignored by the West. Suddenly, foreign—that is Western—criticism of China's human rights abuses became a major issue in the foreign policy formulation of that country. In contrast, while Tiananmen Square ended China's 'honeymoon' relationship with the West, Africa's reaction was far more muted, if not supportive. The events of June 1989 certainly did not affect China's relations with the South as it did with the West. What in fact changed was China's attitude towards the developing world, which switched from one of benign neglect to one of renewed importance. As a result, the developing world was re-elevated in Chinese thinking. The 1970s rhetoric of China and Africa being 'all-weather friends' was reintroduced and deployed with vigour and this has remained the case in the contemporary period. This posture is a reaffirmation of the Five Principles of Peaceful Co-existence, which had been formulated in the 1950s as the basis of Beijing's foreign relations. These Five Principles were namely: mutual respect for each other's territorial integrity; non-aggression; non-interference in each other's internal affairs; equality and mutual benefit; and peaceful coexistence. Thus Chinese policy-makers have returned to their roots in reasserting what is in fact an old theme in Beijing's foreign policy.

The ability to increase efforts to cultivate closer ties with Africa was eased by the response of African élites to the events of 1989. Such reactions and their motives by African leaders might be summarized by three essential points. First, the self-interest of African élites under threat from democratization projects (linked surreptitiously in their eyes to the human rights crusade). Second, solidarity and resentment at perceived 'neo-imperialist' interference in the affairs of a fellow developing country. Third, a pragmatic understanding that overt criticism of Beijing could/would mean an end to Chinese developmental aid and assistance.

The first point is elemental: a large number of African heads of state assumed and maintained office with little reference to (or often, directly against) the popular will. Any mass mobilization of an important segment of the population against an entrenched élite threatened to set a precedent that Africans could well draw from. Combined with the ongoing collapse of the Leninist system in Eastern Europe and the USSR, Tiananmen provided a large number of African heads of state with reason to pause for thought. This fear of the 'domino effect' should not be played down and probably spurred leaders such as Blaise Compaoré of Burkina Faso (who seized power via a coup, executed his predecessor and was himself widely criticized for human rights abuses) to be the first foreign leader to visit Beijing post-Tiananmen. Ironically, Burkina Faso is currently one of the five African nations that maintain official diplomatic relations with Taiwan, not China.

The belief in certain quarters that the developed world's critique of Beijing was a cloak by which the West aimed to retard a rapidly modernizing China was also shared by many African leaders and acted as a powerful spur in rallying them to China's cause. A victim of past and present intrigues by the capitalist West, much of Africa was highly suspicious of the new found 'discovery' that China's record on human rights in Western eyes was suspect. Both China and Africa believed themselves to have experienced and to continue to face common enemies, namely imperialism and neo-imperialism from the developed world. This often translates into a deep suspicion by Chinese and many African leaders of criticism of their regimes on the grounds of the supposedly Western-centric norms of human rights and democracy. Many African governments also continue to view the emphasis by the West on human rights as a pretext to undermine China's development and interfere in its own path to modernization.

Finally, the understanding that China was an important source of external aid and that developmental assistance should not be threatened by involvement in the West's criticism of China no doubt added a further variable to much of Africa's silence on the matter. It must be remembered that from 1956 up to and including 1987, China had provided Africa with nearly US $4,783m. worth of economic aid and assistance. Though the level of aid had stagnated in the 1980s, this aid was a most welcome source of assistance and would not be risked lightly, particularly in the cause of democratization that in any case many African leaders did not share a commitment to. One can say, therefore, that a number of factors meshed together to explain much of Africa's reluctance to join in with the opprobrium heaped on Beijing by the West following Tiananmen Square.

CHINA'S STANCE POST-1989

Although maintaining good links with Washington is central to Chinese foreign policy, Beijing has often expressed concern about the rise of an unchallenged hegemon, namely the USA. China has maintained the position that in the current international system it is imperative that China and the developing world support each other and work together to prevent the over-domination by this new hegemon. Asserting that respect for each other's affairs and non-interference should be the basis of any new international order is fundamental to this stance. Today, Sino-African unity remains as a focal point: '[China and Africa] support each other in international affairs, especially on major issues such as human rights, safeguard the legitimate rights of developing countries and make efforts to promote the establishment of a new just and rational international political and economic order'.[1]

Much of this is tied to the long-held stance by Beijing that it is the leader of the developing world (formerly, the 'Third World'). At the opening of the first Sino-Africa Forum in late 2000, the *People's Daily* cast this posture within the rubric that while 'Africa [is] the continent with the largest number of developing countries', China is 'the largest developing country in the world'. China's audacious ranking of its own Five Principles of Peaceful Coexistence on an equal footing with the Charter of African Union—and even the Charter of the UN—is an example of the way in which Beijing seeks to court Africa within the broader framework of global politics, while at the same time asserting its leadership claims. This, despite Beijing's historic refusal to play any meaningful role in the UN or use its position within the Security Council to assert itself, although this is now slowly changing.

Paradoxically, as China increasingly integrates itself into the global economy and starts tentatively to play by essentially Western rules (as exemplified by its membership of the World Trade Organization), China has sought to strengthen political ties with African countries more as a defensive mechanism, invariably to be deployed against these very same impulses. This irony reflects the overall tension in China's diplomatic policy of pursuing both engagement and a certain distant coolness *vis-à-vis* the global order. This, and the notion that China seeks to 'restore' its 'rightful place' in world politics by being viewed as the leader of the developing world, cannot be overlooked. Such coalition building helps explain the recent diplomatic developments in Chinese links to Africa, so graphically exemplified by the Sino-Africa Forums, held in 2000, 2003 and 2006.

FORUM ON CHINA-AFRICA CO-OPERATION MINISTERIAL CONFERENCE

The first Forum met in October 2000 in Beijing and was attended by nearly 80 ministers from 44 African countries. The meeting essentially had three main objectives. First, the Forum was part of Beijing's overall strategy to at least rhetorically declare its aim of overhauling the global order and advance China's traditional hostility to what it sees as a'hegemony', in this case the domination of the over-weaning power of the USA. This domination, dressed up as 'globalization', is seen as detrimental to the autonomy and sovereignty of China and, by extension, the developing world. As the then Chinese Premier, Zhu Rongji, stated at the Forum, Sino-African ties help 'build up our capacity against possible risks, which will put us in a better position to participate in economic globalization and safeguard our economic interests and economic security'. They also 'improve the standing of the developing countries in North-South dialogue so as to facilitate the establishment of a fair and rational new international political and economic order'.[2]

Such a position is based on the belief that, according to the then Minister of Foreign Trade and Economic Co-operation, Shi Guangsheng, at the 2000 Sino-Africa Forum, 'when the new international economic order has not been established and countries differ considerably in economic development, the benefits of economic globalization are not enjoyed in a balanced way'. Consequently, 'developed countries are benefiting most from economic globalization; but the large number of developing countries are facing more risks and challenges, and some countries are even endangered by marginalization'. As a result, the global community should 'give more considerations to the will and demands of developing countries [including no doubt, China] so as to promote the establishment of a fair and rational new international economic order'. This can be advanced by developing countries building 'a sense of self-protection'.

As mentioned previously, China is intensely suspicious of the West's promotion of human rights and regards such calls as a Trojan horse through which the West might undermine Beijing. Chinese policy in this regard has then been to consistently cast talk of democracy and human rights (and, occasionally, the environment) as a tool of neo-imperialism. This falls on many receptive ears in Africa at the élite level and China is not unaware of this. Indeed, this has been fairly long-standing and China has long managed to take advantage of the developing world's power of numbers to evade international condemnation. As part of this, the Forum was a means by which China could advance a position of moral relativism regarding human rights to a mostly sympathetic audience and thus consolidate its standing within Africa and the developing world as a device to resist American domination and hegemony, understood as Washington's ascendancy in the post-Cold War era. The assertion in the *People's Daily* at the time of the Forum that China and Africa 'should...enhance their co-operation and consultation in multilateral...organizations in order to safeguard the interests of both' is a reflection of this concern. Hence the *Beijing Declaration of the Forum on China-Africa Co-operation*, released at the end of the meeting, asserted that 'countries, that vary from one another in social system, stages of development, historical and cultural background and values, have the right to choose their own approaches and models in promoting and protecting human rights in their own countries'.[3]

Going further, the Declaration made the astounding claim that 'the politicization of human rights and the imposition of human rights conditionalities' themselves 'constitute a violation of human rights' and that conditionalities for development assistance which are based on good governance and respect for human rights 'should be vigorously opposed'. These statements were no doubt well received by many of the African dictators sat in the hall in Beijing, and were all crafted as a means to promote an 'alternative' global order. Of course, such a world order would grant the élites of each country the role of arbiters of what are or what are not 'human rights' and also, how such rights should be protected (or not, as the case may be). This stance is advanced by China even if such sentiments run counter to the prevailing belief today that state élites cannot and should not be allowed to hide behind 'state sovereignty' to abuse their own citizens.

The outcome of the Forum reflected the increased priority China was placing on Africa. As a goodwill gesture, Beijing announced that it would exempt African countries from repaying a total of US $1,200m. worth of debt to China. A cynic might point out that these debts would not have been repaid anyway, but such actions certainly secured Beijing the moral high ground when calling on the West to do the same with much larger quantities of debt owed to them by Africa. At the Forum, the Chinese also put forward a proposal on furthering Sino-African economic ties, proposing the removal of tariff and non-tariff barriers and the creation of better market access to each other. China also promised to establish special funds and incentives to encourage Chinese enterprises to invest in Africa, reflecting the growing economic imperative underpinning Sino-African linkages.

SINO-AFRICAN ECONOMIC INTERACTION

The legitimacy of China's political system is today based upon the Communist Party's ability to sustain economic growth. Intimately linked to this, Beijing is faced with a long-term decline in domestic petroleum production. In contrast to the past heady days of Maoist 'solidarity', China's economic dealings with most African countries are today based on a cool evaluation of their perceived economic potential. Consequently, China is actively and aggressively pursuing petroleum and other natural resources in Africa. China is currently the world's second largest oil importer and the second largest consumer of African resources.[4] The abundance of natural resources in Africa has led China to pursue long-term deals with African governments in order to ensure continued access to all varieties of raw materials and energy in Africa. As China is excluded from the majority of Middle East oil supplies and wishes to limit its vulnerability to the international petroleum market it has invested heavily in Africa, deliberately courting states that the West have overlooked.

Beijing's economic interest in Africa is based on three assumptions. First, Beijing believes that the macroeconomic situation in Africa is taking a favourable turn. This analysis is based on the belief that (as the Chinese would no doubt assert), copying China, African countries have adopted a set of active measures to push forward the pace of privatization and to open up international trade and reform based on bilateral and multilateral trade agreements.

Second, Chinese manufacturers (and shopkeepers) believe that the types of goods (household appliances, garments, and other domestic products) which they produce and sell have immense potential in Africa, where the economy is not yet as developed as in Western nations, and where the consumers are perceived to be more receptive to the type of inexpensive products that China typically produces.

Third, Africa is perceived by both the Chinese Government and by Chinese companies to be rich in natural resources, particularly in crude petroleum, non-ferrous metals and fisheries. Indeed, China's rapidly developing petroleum requirements have helped propel Sino-African trade in recent years. In 1993 China became a net importer of that commodity and petroleum will be the only feasible primary fuel for the foreseeable future that will be in the position to fulfil China's growing needs regarding both transportation and industry. As a result, China has been faithfully developing linkages with oil-rich countries in Africa such as Angola, Nigeria and Sudan. China's approach towards securing access to African resources is what David Zweig and Bi Jianhai have termed a resource-based foreign policy, which by its very nature has 'little room for morality'.[5] In a resource grab in Africa, China has encouraged state-owned oil companies to invest heavily in Africa; in the first 10 months of 2005 alone trade between the continent and China increased 39% largely due to oil exports.[6] In its investment in African states the Chinese Government and state-owned companies firmly emphasize the principle of non-interference in domestic affairs when justifying their involvement with leaders deplored by the West. For example, Chinese oil interest in Sudan is China's premier offshore petroleum source where the China National Petroleum Company (CNPC) is the largest shareholder, owning 40% of the Great Nile Petroleum Operating Company. As a UN Security Council member and a main investor in Sudan's oil fields, China has repeatedly used its influence to render UN drafts ineffective in order to protect its investment. With millions of people displaced and hundreds of thousands killed in Darfur, China has come under international condemnation for blocking international pressure in order to ensure their access to Sudanese oil, thereby allowing the government in Khartoum to continue its bloody conflict in Darfur.

However, China's interest in ensuring its resource security and economic growth through involvement in Africa is by no means restricted to petroleum, and encompasses all natural resources. From investment in copper in Zambia, platinum interests in Zimbabwe and to supporting fishing ventures in Gabon and Namibia, China has vigorously courted and pursued the political and business élite to guarantee its continued access. One of the benefits of Chinese interest in African resources is that it has dramatically increased demand and has revitalized industries such as Zambia's copper sector. However, the influx of capital into weak and authoritarian governments has serious potential for long-term negative consequences in Africa as leaders neglect necessary reforms, bolstered by newly perceived economic security from Chinese receipts.

Returning to oil, in the mid-1990s China began to favour an 'outward-looking oil economy'. This was for primarily economic reasons: the average production cost of Middle Eastern petroleum is still under US $2 per barrel, while the average production cost of Chinese onshore oil is between $9 and $23 per barrel, depending on the oilfield. As a result, the CNPC, the China National Offshore Oil Corporation (CNOOC), and the China Petroleum and Chemical Corporation (Sinopec) were elevated to the status of ministries and located with the State Economic and Trade Commission. The corporations were also granted the task to buy operating rights overseas, and to establish overseas oil exploration contracts. One way by which this policy has been cemented is to use what China refers to as 'special relationships'.

However, with regard to such special relationships, China has repeatedly been active in promoting the idea that Beijing should be given privileged access to African markets on the basis of South-South 'solidarity' and as a concrete manifestation of a broader counter-hegemonic strategy which China is keen to encourage within Africa. The self serving nature of this stance is obvious. When Chinese officials claim that it could not be possible to continuously deepen and develop South-South development without the policy support of governments of developing countries and without preferential treatment, as Shi Guangsheng did at the Sino-Africa Forum, one must remember that with the exception of oil exports to China, Sino-African trade is lopsided in favour of Chinese exporters who are flooding African markets with cheap household products of limited quality. Such imports into Africa most certainly help China's trade development but do little to encourage indigenous African manufacturing. Any 'preferential treatment' for such imports from China would do little to change this milieu. Indeed, the assertion in the *People's Daily* at the Sino-Africa Forum that the Chinese Government would 'encourage' Chinese enterprises to 'give preference to African goods in their imports when all other conditions are the same so as to improve the trade balance between China and African countries' is a caveat of dubious standing and one that commits Beijing to very little indeed.

CHINA'S DEVELOPMENTAL ASSISTANCE

Another core element of China's strategy in Africa is development assistance. As stated in the 2006 governmental White Paper, 'the Chinese Government encourages and supports competent Chinese enterprises to co-operate with African nations...on the principle of mutual benefit and common development'. Chinese development assistance has primarily taken the form of aid packages and investment by state owned corporations. Tremendous debt across the continent and low levels of foreign direct investment (FDI) in Africa mean that Chinese investment and aid packages are both welcomed and needed. Chinese development assistance, however, has had decidedly mixed effects on African states.

In terms of aid packages it is clear that Chinese aid favours countries that are rich in resources and pays little regard to political repercussions. The US $2,000m. aid package that China granted to Angola in 2005, which has the second largest oil resources of any country in Africa, is an example of this resource-driven aid policy. After three decades of civil war, Angolan government officials were on the verge of accepting an IMF loan package that stipulated strict conditions regarding monitoring of the domestic situation and distribution of aid to one of the most corrupt nations on the continent. However, in the face of a $2,000m unconditional aid package from China, the Angolan Government rejected the IMF's offer in favour of China's, of which one of the few stipulations was the right to 10,000 barrels of oil per day. This completely undercut the IMF's efforts at increasing transparency and made it possible for rampant governmental corruption to resume in the war-torn state. The situation in Angola is by no means unique and underscores concerns that China is undermining opportunities for good governance to emerge. Not only does this have negative consequences for the African people, but it also threatens China's legacy in Africa, for if these regimes are removed, China runs a serious risk of being branded as a key partner of the former regime and losing its access to the resources it was trying to secure. Allowing bad governance to continue is to both China and Africa's long-term disadvantage as it sabotages the long-term possibilities of sustained Sino-African economic links and also helps maintain the situation where Africa remains at the bottom of the global hierarchy.

In terms of FDI on the continent unlike other (primarily Western) companies operating in Africa, Chinese corporations are undeterred by risk, as they are state-owned and therefore are not accountable to investors but rather serve political interests. However, as Chinese business dealings progress on the continent the long-term effects on African states are questionable. Although China's connections in Africa can be seen as positive because they bring in a new actor who is eager to invest, they have potentially negative effects for Africa if they allow state leaders to neglect carrying out the necessary political and economic reforms needed to revitalize the continent. While China has forgiven huge sums of debt to African countries, loan packages jeopardize the strongest growth rates since independence and the benefits of having debts forgiven. With regard to trade, China has made much of opening up its markets to Africa and places no tariffs on the 25 poorest African states, as well as encouraging trade between China and Africa as an example of South-South solidarity. However, while there is a huge market for inexpensive Chinese goods in Africa, this pushes domestic African goods out of the market. According to Sanusha Naidu and Martyn Davies, 'African producers have been marginalised and displaced from the market because of the influx of cheap Chinese goods. . .their livelihoods will have been eroded by competition from cheap Chinese goods'.[7] Furthermore, of course, while Chinese rhetoric regarding the opening of its markets to African goods appears as though it is to the continent's economic benefit, the inescapable fact remains that natural resources aside, Africa has very little to sell.

An arguably positive effect of Chinese investment for ordinary Africans is China's focus on building infrastructure, an area that has largely been ignored by the West. This has certainly facilitated the moving of goods and products between states and people. However, a negative side of China's investment and loan packages to African states is that they often stipulate that contracts be awarded to Chinese companies. As Chinese aid often comes in the form of loans, not grants, it allows China the leverage to make this kind of provision. For example, as part of China's US $2,000m. loan to Angola (see above), the terms required that in addition to previously discussed oil rights, 70% of contracts go to Chinese corporations. A further downside of this is that Chinese corporations usually use cheap contract labour from China, as opposed to employing Africans, in order to keep their costs down. This has created resentment in many African states.

CHINESE ARMS SALES TO AFRICA

China's 'non-interference in domestic affairs' stance has not prevented Beijing from involving itself closely in African politics, notably in the support of various highly undemocratic regimes. As part of this, China has been a long-standing exporter of weapons to the developing world. China is the only major arms exporter that has not signed any multilateral agreements prohibiting arms sales that are 'likely to be used for serious human rights violations'.[8] Samuel Kim, furthermore, noted in 1994 that 'China has no principles, only interests, driving its arms sales to the Third World'[9]. Although China stands far behind the leading arms exporters such as the USA, Russia and France, its exporting of Chinese weaponry—either directly or through middlemen—is not inconsequential. In the contemporary period this has not only taken on the guise of providing military supplies and weaponry to Africa, but also an active involvement in actual conflict. Such involvement has passed by with relatively little international attention, yet requires examination.

China is currently the world's fifth largest arms exporter behind the USA, the United Kingdom, France and Russia and exported an estimated US $500m. worth of arms in 2001. It has been apparent for some time that the Chinese Government hoped to turn the country's arms industry into a leading global player by 2020. China reformed its defence industry in mid-1999, dividing its top five defence corporations (space, aviation, shipbuilding, conventional arms and nuclear) into 10 enterprises. This is consistent with the aims of the defence aspect of Socialist Modernization which was, in part, to convert military to civilian production. As part of this transformation of the operational mechanism of military-industrial enterprises, all military-industrial ministries were converted into industrial corporations as economic bodies and industrial groupings. However, concern that the People's Liberation Army (PLA) was becoming too involved in the economy resulted in Premier Jiang Zemin declaring in 1998 that businesses were to be officially delinked from the PLA. Like other state enterprises, China's military-industrial enterprises carried out a 'contract responsibility system', i.e. such enterprises paid the state both taxes and a segment of their profits. Profits that remained from the production of civilian goods were either deployed to develop production and/or went to the military management. However, now that the PLA has been forced to withdraw from openly operating civilian businesses the search for profits is largely concentrated in increased arms sales. While it is true that most major Chinese weapons manufactures are not owned or handled by the PLA, but by one of the civilian ministries, the remuneration from arms sales return to the Chinese state. Either way, there are compelling motives for actors within China to increase arms exports.

The classic contemporary example of Beijing's weapons exporting policy in Africa is China's involvement in Sudan. Through arms sales to the Sudanese Government, China has arguably facilitated the continuation of the situation in the Darfur region. Certainly it is estimated that 80% of the US $500m. the Sudanese Government receives per year for petroleum exports go directly to arms sales to uphold the regime in Khartoum. This underscores the common complaint that China's presence in Africa is motivated by oil supplies and profit and that all other objectives, such as 'South-South co-operation' and 'mutual benefit' are largely rhetorical. Chinese arms sales to Sudan have certainly undermined UN efforts at peace brokering in that country. Apart from the profits accrued from arms sales to Sudan, the policy helps consolidate and protect Chinese shares in the exploitation of Sudan's oil reserves. Reliable reports say that Sudan has obtained 34 new fighter jets from China, and that the Sudanese air force is equipped with $100m. worth of Shenyang fighter planes, including a dozen supersonic F-7 jets.

A CHINESE MODEL FOR AFRICA?

Politically as well as economically, China's presence in Africa has been based on the premise of providing an alternate development model for African states and leaders. According to Naidu, China is seen as 'a refreshing alternative to the traditional engagement models of the West. . .African governments see China's engagement as a point of departure from Western neo-colonialism and political conditions'.[10] Yet the absolute emphasis China places on respect for state sovereignty and non-interference as an article of faith for the Chinese leadership as well as a willingness to deal with states ostracized by the West may appear promising to some African leaders, but it profoundly challenges the Western vision of a flourishing Africa governed by democracies that respect human rights and the rule of law and embrace free markets. A common bond in their desire to overcome and shake off the legacy of colonialism has further united Chinese and African political interests, evinced in a portrayal of the former colonial powers as a common enemy.

In countering the Western promotion of neo-liberal reforms in Africa, China has argued that this imposition of Western ideology on African states is a form of neo-imperialism. Moreover, China's state directed model of development provides an appealing alternative to leaders when neo-liberal economic reforms have not, for a variety of reasons, delivered their promised economic revival. A strong state also of course serves as a shield for authoritarian leaders to maintain tight control over economic policy and continue their patronage networks.

The Chinese leadership has been very politically dextrous in the stylish way China combines its need for resources with diplomacy to court African leaders. Through political and business summits such as the various Sino-African Forums, as well as state visits by high-ranking Chinese political officials, China has accorded Africa equal diplomatic status with the dominant powers. African élites are deeply appreciative of being given a warm reception whenever they visit Beijing. In contrast, they are barely afforded a few minutes in most Western capitals and even then they are more likely to be belaboured for their numerous chronic failures in governance, than they are to be toasted as 'dear friends' and treated as important people. China realizes this and thus expends energy on massaging the egos of Africa's autocrats. And this pays off. China has been successful in gaining African support at institutions such as the UN, where the vote of the African bloc has allowed China to block resolutions on domestic human rights abuses. African support also of course helped Beijing in its campaign to host the 2008 Olympics.

Symbolic diplomacy, defined as the promotion of national representation abroad has become an increasingly important component of Chinese foreign policy in Africa. As a developing nation China is very much aware of the importance of prestige projects in asserting the power of state leaders and as such has been involved in large scale projects of this nature, such as building national stadiums all over Africa. This approach has proven beneficial to both the ruling élites in Africa, who view these as projections of regime legitimacy and power (and suitably impress the local populations) and to China, as it demonstrates China's rising prominence and presence. Through these kinds of project, combined with aid packages and the notion that China may be a 'model' for Africa, Beijing is very much asserting itself as an equal of Western powers as well as appealing to the African élite classes. In fact, it is quite noticeable these days how sensitive African élites are to any criticism of China and/or the suggestion that China is possibly not the saviour of Africa.

CONCLUDING REMARKS

Though Beijing's primary focus is naturally on East Asia and maintaining cordial links with the USA, by advancing the theme of non-interference in domestic affairs and promoting a culturally relativist notion of human rights, China has been able to secure its own position and at the same time, appeal to numerous African leaders. Equally, the Chinese state leadership has been increasingly encouraging Chinese corporations to play a role in Sino-African ties. This emphasis on economic linkages with Africa not only enables Chinese corporations to develop their export capabilities and reach, but also empowers the Chinese state to further project itself on the continent. As a result, the state encourages corporate activity as a means to maintain its commercial and political links with Africa.

In an attempt to offset Washington's position in the international system, Beijing has sought and will continue to seek improved relations with non-Western powers. Africa has not been an exception to this policy and this is likely to continue. Indeed, China's policies are essentially an attempt for the leadership of the developing world. China wishes to play a new international role as a champion of the developing world. Africa is fast emerging as a testing ground for this policy. As part of this strategy, China has over the last decade or so reformed its aid policies, moving away from bilateral economic co-operation schemes and the furnishing of outright aid or low interest loans, to a more focused policy that aims to build up trade, investment and joint ventures in Africa. Whether this linking of aid to the construction of joint ventures with Chinese firms amounts to conditionalities is a moot point. While it is true that China has stated that it will continue to supply aid to Africa, this is couched very much within the confines and limitations of what Beijing terms China's 'capacity'. The stress these days is on improving the overall economic environment in Africa for Chinese trade. This produces a contradiction that China is increasingly coming to understand.

Indeed, in recent months several important developments have taken place indicating a slight moderation in Beijing's Africa policy that shows growing awareness of the fact that 'China's diplomacy towards Africa. . .will have to find new ways to engage the continent, approaches that are not predicated on securing the compliance of African élites alone. Otherwise, it will run the danger of being portrayed—as has been the case of Sudan—as the friend of a military regime set on committing gross violations against the African people in the name of the crudest form of self-interest.'[11] This increased consciousness can be seen in several recent events. In early 2007, on his second tour of Africa in nine months, Chinese President Hu Jintao cancelled millions of dollars worth of debt and made new deals for aid packages in the eight states he visited. What made this visit noteworthy was that Hu conspicuously did not visit Zimbabwe.

Another recent incident when China has shown itself to be slightly more receptive to international pressure regarding its policies in Africa can be seen in regard to China's involvement in Sudan. An American-led civil society movement has been targeting China in recent months for its refusal to use its influence in Sudan to help put an end to the killings in Darfur by referring to the 2008 Beijing Olympic Games as the 'Genocide Olympics'. Due to international pressure and threats of widespread protest at the 2008 Olympics, supposed to be China's coming out party to the world, China has moderated its stance on intervention in Sudan as evidenced when the Chinese Assistant Minister of Foreign Affairs, Zhai Jun, visited Sudan to press the Sudanese Government to accept a UN peace-keeping force, as well as to tour refugee camps. This is a significant event that shows a new concern in Beijing over how its presence in Sudan is hurting its international image and goal of achieving great power status. Such changes in China's policies towards Africa allow a small measure of optimism when looking at the long-term effects on Africa's people of China's presence on the continent.

It can be seen that China's foreign policy in Africa has been based on several key aims. China has focused on ensuring its regime security through access to crucial resources. By portraying itself as an advocate for the developing world and emphasizing the rhetoric of South-South co-operation, China has arguably offered up an alternative model to Western dominance. China has in turn invested substantially in many African states and cancelled millions in debt. However, to achieve its policy goals, Beijing has been prepared to defend autocratic regimes that commit gross human rights abuses. As a repressive government in its own right, the Chinese leadership has implicitly opposed the emergence of civil society in Africa and actively supported authoritarian regimes. The political and economic effects of China's presence in Africa can from one view thus be largely characterized as beneficial to the ruling élite but as being to the long-term disadvantage of Africa's peoples.

However, it must be emphasized that China's policies towards Africa are evolving and maturing and Beijing is experiencing a steep learning curve. Recent developments suggest that China is starting to realize that, like all other actors in Africa, Beijing needs stability and security in order for its investments to flourish and for its connections with the continent to be coherent. Western nations have had to learn the hard way that propping up dictators with no real coherent plan is neither sustainable nor desirable, and China will likewise learn this as its relations unfold. The history and development of Sino-African relations thus far suggest certain patterns, but the relationship is fluid and ever changing. What is certain though is that China's presence in Africa is here to stay and Western actors need to be cognizant of both the opportunities and challenges that this throws up to established players on the continent.

FOOTNOTES

[1] 'Sino-Africa Relations', Embassy of the People's Republic of China in the Republic of Zimbabwe, 2003.

[2] 'Strengthen Solidarity, Enhance Co-operation and Pursue Common Development by Zhu Rongji', Embassy of the People's Republic of China in the Republic of Zimbabwe, 2000.

[3] 'The Beijing Declaration of the Forum on China-Africa Co-operation', Embassy of the People's Republic of China in the Republic of Zimbabwe, 2000.

[4] See Taylor, I. 'China's Oil Diplomacy in Africa' in *International Affairs*, Vol. 82, No. 5, September 2006, pp. 937–960.

[5] Zweig, D., and Jianhai, B. 'China's Global Hunt for Energy' in *Foreign Affairs*, Vol. 84, No.5, September/October 2005, p. 31.

[6] Eisenman, J., and Kurlantzick, J. 'China's Africa Strategy' in *Current History*, May 2006, p. 219.

[7] Naidu, S., and Davies, M. 'China Fuels its Future with Africa's Riches' in *South African Journal of International Affairs*, Vol. 13, No. 2, Winter/Spring 2006, p. 79.

[8] Deen, T. 'How to Curb China's Arms Trade' in *Asia Times*, 14 June 2006.

[9] Kim, S. *China and the World: Chinese Foreign Relations in the Post-Cold War Era*. Boulder, CO, Westview Press, 1994.

[10] Naidu and Davies, op. cit., p. 80.

[11] Alden, C. 'China in Africa' in *Survival*, Vol. 47, No. 43, Autumn 2005, pp. 160–161.

EUROPEAN COLONIAL RULE IN AFRICA

RICHARD BROWN

The colonial era in Africa began with the continent's hectic partition by the European powers in the final quarter of the 19th century. It ended in circumstances of equal haste less than a century later, leaving the present states of Africa as its political legacy. However, Europe had been in direct contact with sub-Saharan Africa from the mid-15th century, following the Portuguese maritime explorations. Commercial contacts gradually became dominated by the massive and destructive trade in slaves carried on by the Portuguese, Dutch, French, British and others. In all, some 14m. Africans are estimated to have been transported to the Caribbean and the Americas or to have lost their lives as a result of the trade. Colonizing efforts were few before the 19th century, but Portugal maintained a token presence in the areas that much later were extended to become Angola and Mozambique, while the Dutch initiated European settlement from Cape Town in 1652. Elsewhere the prolonged trade contacts generated only scattered European footholds along the African coasts.

The United Kingdom was the leading trafficker in slaves in the 18th century, but after 1807, when British subjects were prohibited from further participation in the slave trade, a new era began. The subsequent campaign against the slave trade of other nations; the search for new trade products such as palm oil; the onset of geographical exploration; the outburst of Christian missionary zeal; improved communications (the telegraph and steamships); growing knowledge of tropical medicine; and Europe's new industrial might all combined to make Africa increasingly vulnerable to European colonial encroachment. The discovery of diamonds in southern Africa in 1867, and the opening of the Suez Canal two years later, further focused attention on the continent. Even before the main scramble for colonies began in the 1870s, the United Kingdom and France had been steadily increasing their commercial and political involvement in Africa.

The United Kingdom established a settlement at Freetown (Sierra Leone) as a base for freed slaves from 1808, and subsequently engaged in a series of conflicts with inland Ashanti from its outposts on the Gold Coast (Ghana), while steadily increasing its influence in the Niger delta region, in Zanzibar, and in southern Africa. In the mid-1800s Gen. Louis Faidherbe began France's expansion into the West African interior along the River Senegal from its long-held trading settlements at the river's mouth. Simultaneously, the interests of both countries grew in Madagascar, but it was France that later annexed the island (1896). During this period of colonial expansion France extended its penetration of West Africa from existing bases in the interior, as well as from enclaves on the coast. It created, too, a second colonial fiefdom in Equatorial Africa, with its administrative base in Libreville, on the Gabonese coast. The result of this strategy was the emergence of two large French colonial federations: Afrique occidentale française (AOF, 1895) eventually included Senegal, Upper Volta (Burkina Faso), Soudan (Mali), Dahomey (Benin), Guinea, Niger, Mauritania and Côte d'Ivoire; Afrique equatoriale française (AEF, 1910) comprised Gabon, Middle Congo (Republic of the Congo), Oubangui Chari (Central African Republic) and Chad. Meanwhile, in West Africa, the United Kingdom extended its foothold on the Gambian coast into a protectorate, enlarged its territorial holdings in Sierra Leone, created the Gold Coast Colony (1874, later conquering Ashanti and adding territory to the north as the scramble proceeded), and sanctioned the advance of the Royal Niger Co into the heavily populated region that subsequently, as Nigeria, became the United Kingdom's most important African colony.

The quest for colonies gained momentum as other European powers entered the field. The first of these was Belgium, whose ambitious monarch, Leopold II, created the International Association for the Exploration and Civilization of Central Africa (1876) as a means of establishing and administering a vast personal empire in the Congo basin, which in 1885 was ironically designated the Congo Free State. The Association's infamous regime of exploitation led to international outrage and eventually, in 1908, to the transfer of the territory to the Belgian state. Another late participant in the drive to colonize Africa was Germany, which had newly emerged as a major industrial power. In 1884 its Chancellor, Otto von Bismarck, declared German protectorates over Togoland, Kamerun and South West Africa (Namibia). Bismarck then moved swiftly to organize the Berlin West Africa Conference (1884–85), which created a generally agreed framework for colonial expansion in order to avert any major conflict among the European powers. Shortly afterwards Bismarck added German East Africa (Tanganyika, the mainland of modern Tanzania) to Germany's colonial possessions. (After the German defeat in the First World War, the administration of these territories passed to the victors as League of Nations mandates. South Africa obtained Namibia, Tanganyika was awarded to the United Kingdom, and Ruanda-Urundi to Belgium, while Kamerun and Togoland were each partitioned between the United Kingdom and France.)

Although the United Kingdom, as the leading European economic power, would have preferred to adhere to its traditionally gradual method of empire-building, it emerged from the scramble as the dominant colonial power, both in terms of territory and population. Apart from its West African possessions, the United Kingdom acquired substantial territorial holdings in eastern and southern Africa. The largest of these was the Sudan, a consequence of British involvement in Egypt and the importance attached to the Suez Canal. Egypt had been employing British soldier-administrators in its efforts to gain control of the Sudan, but in 1881 a Muslim cleric proclaimed himself the Mahdi (supreme spiritual leader) and declared a *jihad* (holy war). In 1885 the Mahdi's forces captured Khartoum, killing Gen. Charles Gordon and causing outrage in the United Kingdom. The Mahdist state was destroyed by Anglo-Egyptian forces led by Gen. Horatio Kitchener in 1898, just in time to forestall a parallel French expedition at Fashoda. The Sudan officially became an Anglo-Egyptian condominium, but was in effect administered as a British colony, which became highly valued for its cotton production. Fertile Uganda, supposedly a key to control of the Nile valley, had been made a protectorate in 1894, and neighbouring Kenya (as British East Africa) was added by the United Kingdom the following year in order to secure access to the sea. The offshore island of Zanzibar, long a focus of British interest and commercially significant for its cloves, was formally declared a protectorate in 1890. Further to the south, missionaries played an important part in the British acquisition of the land-locked Nyasaland protectorate (Malawi) in 1891.

In the extreme south the United Kingdom had obtained the Cape Colony by treaty at the end of the Napoleonic Wars (1814), and soon found itself in conflict both with its white settlers of mainly Dutch origin (Afrikaners, or Boers), as well as with the area's many indigenous kingdoms and chieftaincies. In 1843 the British coastal colony of Natal was founded, principally as a means of containing the Afrikaners in the interior, where they established the Orange Free State and Transvaal republics. Fatefully, these developments coincided with the discoveries of immense reserves of diamonds (1867) and gold (1886). The ensuing upheavals and an insatiable demand for 'cheap native labour' brought about the final conquest of the African peoples (most notably in the Zulu War, 1879). Acting on behalf of the United Kingdom, the mining magnate Cecil Rhodes organized from the Cape the further northward conquest and occupation of Southern Rhodesia (Zimbabwe) and Northern Rhodesia (Zambia), beginning in 1890: in 1884 Rhodes had been instrumental in the British acquisition of Bechuanaland (Botswana) as a protectorate, to safeguard the land route from the Cape into the interior, which had been threatened by German activity in South West Africa. The United Kingdom had also obtained Basutoland (Lesotho) in 1868, and formally established a protectorate over Swaziland in 1903. However, British claims to paramountcy throughout southern Africa were challenged by the two Afrikaner republics in the Boer War (1899–1902). The United Kingdom overcame the republics only with great difficulty, and then left the Afrikaners, who formed the main element of the privileged white minority, in political control of a newly fashioned Union of South Africa, which was then granted virtual independence (1910). Known as the high commission territories, Bechuanaland, Basutoland and Swaziland, however, remained under British rule. Subsequent South African ambitions to annex them were thwarted, and they eventually proceeded to independence in the 1960s.

Despite its economic weakness relative to the other European powers, Portugal obtained a major share of the colonial division of southern Africa. British diplomatic support helped Portugal to secure the vast colonies of Angola (including Portuguese Congo, later known as Cabinda) and Mozambique; in West Africa Portugal had long been in control of mainland (Portuguese) Guinea (now Guinea-Bissau), the Cape Verde archipelago and the islands of São Tomé and Príncipe. Spain, meanwhile, acquired the islands of Fernando Póo (Bioko) and Annobón (Pagalu), together with the mainland enclave of Río Muni, which now form the Republic of Equatorial Guinea.

Some African polities themselves participated in the scramble: the kingdoms of Buganda and Ethiopia both seized opportunities to expand. Indeed, Ethiopia successfully defended itself against Italian aggression by winning a famous victory at the battle of Adowa (1896). Italy had to content itself with Eritrea and the major part of Somalia, until Mussolini's armies overran Ethiopia in 1935. (Italian occupation was ended by an Anglo-Ethiopian military expedition in 1941.) Eritrea, however, was not to emerge as an independent state until 1993. Liberia, a US-inspired republic founded in 1847 and politically dominated by descendants of former slaves, remained nominally independent throughout the colonial era, but in practice became an economic dependency of US rubber-growing interests.

COLONIAL RULE

There was much resistance to the European intrusion by many of the Islamized, as well as the indigenous, cultures of West Africa. There were also major rebellions against the Germans in South West Africa and Tanganyika, and against the British in Southern Rhodesia; however, divisions within and between African ethnic groups, superior European weaponry and the widespread use of African troops enabled the colonial powers generally to secure control of their territorial acquisitions without great difficulty (although military operations continued in some areas until the 1920s). Boundaries were, in the main, effectively settled by 1900 or soon afterwards. Most colonies enclosed a varied assortment of societies, but many African groupings found themselves divided by the new frontiers (the Somali, for example, were split among British, French, Italian and Ethiopian administrations). Although in the long run colonialism did much to undermine previous patterns of life, its administrative policies and the development of written languages (mainly by missionaries) fostered ethnic identity, helping to replace pre-colonial cultural and political fluidity by modern tribalism. African reactions to colonialism also contributed to the growing sense of ethnic self-awareness. At the same time, members of the Western-educated indigenous élites were also exploring alternative identities based on the colonial territory (nationalism) or, indeed, on the broader concept of Pan-Africanism.

As military control gave way to civil administration, economic issues came to the fore. In the early decades of colonial rule a considerable amount of railway construction was carried out, and there was a marked development of the export-orientated economy. Colonial taxation was an important stimulus to peasant production and to wage-labour, but in the early period all colonies conscripted labour by force. In the more primitive and undeveloped colonies (as in the Portuguese territories) coercion of labour persisted into the 1960s. In much of West Africa and parts of East Africa export production remained mainly in indigenous hands. Elsewhere, concessionary companies (as in the Belgian Congo and AEF) or white settlers (as in South Africa and Southern Rhodesia) were the major agricultural producers. White settlers, whose interests were almost invariably given priority, were also a significant force in Kenya, as well as in Northern Rhodesia, the Belgian Congo, Angola, Mozambique, Kamerun and Côte d'Ivoire. Mining was a dominant force in a number of areas. In South Africa it provided the main impetus to the development of a strong industrial base by the late 1930s. Southern Rhodesia followed a similar pattern, although on a smaller scale. The important copper mines of the Belgian Congo (subsequently known as Zaire and now the Democratic Republic of the Congo) were later (in the 1920s) joined by those of Northern Rhodesia. Tin in Nigeria, gold in the Gold Coast and, later, diamonds and uranium in Namibia augmented the primary agricultural exports of these territories. Overall, the growth of a money economy did most to change African life, as different areas developed new production, supplied labour, stagnated, or developed the towns that were essential to the conduct of trade and, in the late colonial period, to the growth of manufacturing in some areas additional to that already established in South Africa.

Where settlers monopolized land and resources, colonialism tended to bear harshly on traditional African life. Elsewhere, however, the direct European impact was more muted. The very small number of European colonial officials in non-settler colonies necessitated reliance on African intermediaries to sustain rule. Such administrations had to limit their interventions in African life and rely on traditional and created chiefs to carry out day-to-day administration (often in arbitrary and non-traditional ways), although military power was never far away in the event of any breakdown in control. By the 1920s air power could be used to transport troops quickly to suppress uprisings. The British, in particular, favoured the policy of 'indirect rule', bolstering traditional authorities as subordinate allies, but often with new powers and resources unavailable to their predecessors. The British colonial doctrine emphasized the separateness of its colonies from the imperial power and theoretically envisaged eventual political independence. Some degree of freedom of expression was allowed (many African newspapers flourished in British West Africa), and a limited political outlet for a circumscribed few was eventually provided through the establishment of legislative councils. In contrast, the French doctrine of assimilation theoretically envisaged Africans as citizens of a greater France, but little was done to make this a reality until after the Second World War. These contrasting British and French principles were not without influence on policy, for example in the educational sphere, and they also helped to shape the later patterns of decolonization and post-colonial relationships. Whatever the theory, all colonial regimes were deeply influenced by the racist outlook that had taken hold of the European mind in the 19th century and in practice treated their colonial subjects as inferior beings.

Racial discrimination was deeply resented by the Western-educated élites. In coastal West Africa and in South Africa the existence of these élites actually pre-dated the scramble, and soon lawyers, clergy, teachers and merchants founded moderate protest associations, such as the Aborigines' Protection Society (1897) in the Gold Coast and the Native National Congress (1912), later the African National Congress, in South Africa. By the 1920s clerks and traders in Tanganyika were able to form an African Association on a territory-wide basis. In other social strata religious associations were often the chief vehicles for African assertion. These could be traditional, Christian, Islamic or syncretic in inspiration, and often aroused mass enthusiasm, to the concern of the colonial authorities. Occasionally there were violent clashes. In 1915 Rev. John Chilembwe led an armed uprising, protesting at the recruitment of Africans for service in the First World War and at conditions for tenants on European-owned estates in Nyasaland. Worker protest appeared early in towns, and on the railways and in mines. Rural protest was often about taxation (as in the 1929 riots by women in Eastern Nigeria) or commodity prices (as in the Gold Coast cocoa boycotts of the 1930s). Yet, whatever the level of discontent, prior to the Second World War the colonial grip remained unshaken.

Any complacency about the underlying state of colonial Africa had, however, already been shattered by the world economic depression beginning in 1929–30. The effects of the collapse of prices were so severe that the major European powers, the United Kingdom, France and Belgium, began to perceive the need to provide development funds and to improve social welfare and education in their colonies, if Africa's ability to export tropical products and to import finished goods was to be sustained. These ideas, however, only began to make themselves strongly felt after the Second World War, when they were to add to the ferment of change then gathering force throughout the continent.

DECOLONIZATION

Events inside and outside Africa interacted to produce the surge towards independence after 1945. The Second World War itself provided the immediate context. The war greatly weakened the colonial powers, and brought to the fore the USA, which opposed European colonial control of Africa. African troops were enrolled to fight in Asia and the Mediterranean, returning with a deep resentment at post-war conditions and the continuing colonial subordination. The victory over fascism and the enunciation of the Atlantic Charter also encouraged thoughts of liberation within the continent. Economic change intensified as both the war and its aftermath stimulated demand, and there was a surge of African migration to the towns. Economic and social grievances multiplied, especially in relation to the inadequacy of urban facilities and lack of educational opportunities. Among peasant farmers, prices, marketing arrangements and new levels of bureaucratic interference aroused intense resentment. Owing to labour migration, links between town and country were close and provided opportunities for newly militant nationalist parties in the more developed colonies, such as the Gold Coast and Côte d'Ivoire, to put pressure on the colonial authorities. For the democratic European powers the increasing African discontent raised both the moral and material costs of maintaining colonial rule. In any case, with the exception of Portugal, political control was no longer regarded as essential to the safeguarding of economic interests, particularly as capitalism was becoming increasingly internationalized and the concept of possessing colonies was beginning to appear outmoded.

In French Africa the Second World War helped directly to set in train events that were ultimately to lead to independence. Following the German defeat of France in 1940, AEF repudiated the Vichy Government and declared its support for the 'Free French' under Gen. Charles de Gaulle. The Brazzaville Conference convened by de Gaulle in 1944 spoke in general terms of a new deal for Africans, while the new French Constitution adopted in 1946 provided for direct African elections to the French Assemblée nationale. Political parties established themselves throughout francophone Africa, although their demands were for fuller rights of citizenship within the French state rather than for independence. Attempts by the French Government to thwart African political progress altogether were unsuccessful. The 1956 *loi cadre* (enabling law) introduced universal adult suffrage, but, to the dismay of many nationalist politicians, the franchise was applied individually to the separate states of the two federations, so that the structures of AOF and AEF were allowed to wither away. In 1958 de Gaulle, still attempting to salvage something of the greater France concept, organized a referendum in which only Guinea voted for full independence. By 1960, however, the remaining AOF and AEF territories, as well as Madagascar, had insisted upon receiving *de jure* independence, even if, despite outward appearances, they remained tied economically and militarily to France.

The events that ended the French empire in sub-Saharan Africa were hastened by concurrent developments in neighbouring British colonies, especially the Gold Coast. With no settler communities to placate, decolonization in British West Africa proceeded relatively smoothly, although much more rapidly than had been contemplated. Popular grievances gave a new edge to the political demands of the now sizeable educated middle classes, and the United Kingdom's cautious post-war moves towards granting internal self-government were soon perceived as inadequate even by the British themselves. When police fired on an ex-serviceman's peaceful demonstration in Accra (Gold Coast) in 1948, the resulting unrest, strikes and rural agitation led to major policy changes. Sensing the new mood, the militant nationalist Kwame Nkrumah formed the Convention People's Party (CPP) in 1949 with the slogan 'self-government now'. Its populist appeal enabled it, in 1951, to overcome the more moderate United Gold Coast Convention party (of which Nkrumah had earlier been General Secretary) in an election based on a new and more democratic Constitution. Although in jail for sedition, Nkrumah was released and invited to become head of an independent Government. This dramatic development, followed by the granting of independence in 1957 as Ghana (whose boundaries also took in the former mandated territory of British Togoland), had repercussions throughout black Africa. (In fact, the Sudan had achieved independence in the previous year, when the Anglo-Egyptian condominium was brought to an end, but this had attracted little outside attention.) Nkrumah sought, with some success, to intensify African revolutionary sentiment still further by organizing an African Peoples' Conference in Accra in 1958. Nigeria's progress towards independence, meanwhile, was complicated by its enormous size and colonially imposed regional structure. Rival regional and ethnic nationalisms competed, and no one party could achieve the degree of overall dominance enjoyed by the CPP in the Gold Coast. None the less, a federal Nigeria became independent in 1960, followed by Sierra Leone (1961) and The Gambia (1965).

Belgium initially remained aloof from the movement towards decolonization. It appeared to believe that its relatively advanced provision for social welfare and the rapid post-war economic growth in the Belgian Congo would enable it to avoid making political concessions and to maintain the authoritarian style of government that had characterized its administration of the territory since it took over from the Belgian King. The Belgian Congo, however, could not be insulated—any more than any other part of Africa—from the anti-colonial influences at work throughout the continent. From 1955 onwards nationalist feeling spread rapidly, despite the difficulties in building effective national parties in such a huge country. Urban riots in 1959 led to a precipitate reversal in Belgian policy: at the Brussels Round Table Conference in January 1960 it was abruptly decided that independence was to follow in only six months. Not surprisingly, the disintegration of political unity and order in the country speedily followed the termination of Belgian administration. Belgian rule in the mandated territory of Ruanda-Urundi ended in 1962, and was followed by its division into the separate countries of Rwanda and Burundi.

Meanwhile, in eastern and southern Africa, the United Kingdom was also encountering difficulties in implementing decolonization. In Uganda, where its authority rested to a large extent on an alliance with the kingdom of Buganda, British policies had tended to stratify existing ethnic divisions. The deeply ingrained internal problems that preceded independence in 1962 continued to beset Uganda for the next 25 years. In contrast, however, the nationalist movement led by Julius Nyerere in Tanganyika was exceptionally united, and there was little friction prior to independence in 1961. Three years later Tanganyika united with Zanzibar (which obtained independence in 1963) as Tanzania. In Kenya, as in other colonies with significant settler minorities, the process of decolonization was troubled. In the post-war period the settlers of Kenya sought political domination and worked to suppress emergent African nationalism. African frustrations, particularly about access to land among the Kikuyu, and growing unrest among the urban poor, led in 1952 to the declaration of a state of emergency and the violent revolt the British knew as 'Mau Mau'. This was fiercely suppressed, but only with the help of troops from the United Kingdom, a factor that helped finally to destroy the settlers' political credibility. Kenya eventually achieved independence in 1963 under the leadership of the veteran nationalist Jomo Kenyatta. Vilified by the settlers in the 1950s as a personification of evil, Kenyatta, firstly as Prime Minister and subsequently as President, in fact strove to protect the economic role of the settler population and to maintain good relations with the United Kingdom.

Settler interests were more obstructive further to the south. The whites of Southern Rhodesia had obtained internal self-government as early as 1923, but in 1953 the colony was allowed by the United Kingdom to become the dominant partner in a federation with Northern Rhodesia and Nyasaland. Conflict followed with African nationalists in the two northern territories, and the federation eventually collapsed in 1963, when the United Kingdom had to concede that its policy of decolonization could only effectively apply to the two northern territories whose Governments it still controlled. In 1964 Nyasaland became independent as Malawi and Northern Rhodesia as Zambia. When the United Kingdom then refused white-minority rule independence to Southern Rhodesia, its settler-dominated Government, led by Ian Smith, unilaterally declared independence (1965). This was resisted by the United Kingdom and condemned by the UN, but an ineffectual campaign of economic sanctions was defeated by support for the Smith regime from neighbouring South Africa and Portugal. African nationalists eventually succeeded in organizing the guerrilla war that, in the 1970s, paved the way for a negotiated settlement. With Robert Mugabe as its leader, the country became independent as Zimbabwe (1980), a development that owed much to the collapse of Portuguese rule in Africa after 1974.

During the lengthy dictatorship of Dr António de Oliveira Salazar Portugal regarded its African colonial possessions as inalienable, and in 1951 they were declared to be overseas provinces. However, intense political repression failed to prevent the emergence of armed resistance movements in Angola (1961), Guinea-Bissau (1963) and Mozambique (1964). Most successfully in Guinea-Bissau, under the leadership of Amílcar Cabral, these guerrilla movements succeeded in mobilizing rural support. Eventually, in 1974, following the military overthrow of the Portuguese regime, progress towards internal democratization was accompanied by a determination to implement an accelerated policy of decolonization. In Angola, where the divided nationalist movement provided opportunities for external intervention on opposite sides by South African and Cuban forces, independence proved difficult to consolidate. Mozambique also suffered greatly from South Africa's policy of destabilizing its newly independent neighbours.

During this period South Africa was itself conducting a colonial war in Namibia, which it continued to occupy in defiance of the UN after it had terminated the mandate in 1966. The war against the South West African People's Organisation of Namibia continued until a negotiated settlement finally led to independence in 1990, effectively concluding the colonial era in Africa.

DATES OF INDEPENDENCE OF AFRICAN COUNTRIES

In Chronological Order of Independence—Post-War

Libya	24 Dec. 1951
Sudan	1 Jan. 1956
Morocco	2 March 1956
Tunisia	20 March 1956
Ghana	6 March 1957
Guinea	2 Oct. 1958
Cameroon	1 Jan. 1960
Togo	27 April 1960
Mali	20 June 1960
Senegal	20 June 1960
Madagascar	26 June 1960
The Democratic Republic of the Congo (as the Congo)	30 June 1960
Somalia	1 July 1960
Benin (as Dahomey)	1 Aug. 1960
Niger	3 Aug. 1960
Burkina Faso (as Upper Volta)	5 Aug. 1960
Côte d'Ivoire	7 Aug. 1960
Chad	11 Aug. 1960
The Central African Republic	13 Aug. 1960
The Republic of the Congo (Congo-Brazzaville)	15 Aug. 1960
Gabon	17 Aug. 1960
Nigeria	1 Oct. 1960
Mauritania	28 Nov. 1960
Sierra Leone	27 April 1961
Tanzania (as Tanganyika)	9 Dec. 1961
Rwanda	1 July 1962
Burundi	1 July 1962
Algeria	3 July 1962
Uganda	9 Oct. 1962
Zanzibar (now part of Tanzania)	10 Dec. 1963
Kenya	12 Dec. 1963
Malawi	6 July 1964
Zambia	24 Oct. 1964
The Gambia	18 Feb. 1965
Botswana	30 Sept. 1966
Lesotho	4 Oct. 1966
Mauritius	12 March 1968
Swaziland	6 Sept. 1968
Equatorial Guinea	12 Oct. 1968
Guinea-Bissau	10 Sept. 1974
Mozambique	25 June 1975
Cape Verde	5 July 1975
The Comoros	6 July 1975*
São Tomé and Príncipe	12 July 1975
Angola	11 Nov. 1975
Seychelles	29 June 1976
Djibouti	27 June 1977
Zimbabwe	18 April 1980
Namibia	21 March 1990
Eritrea	24 May 1993

* Date of unilateral declaration of independence, recognized by France (in respect of three of the four islands) in December 1975.

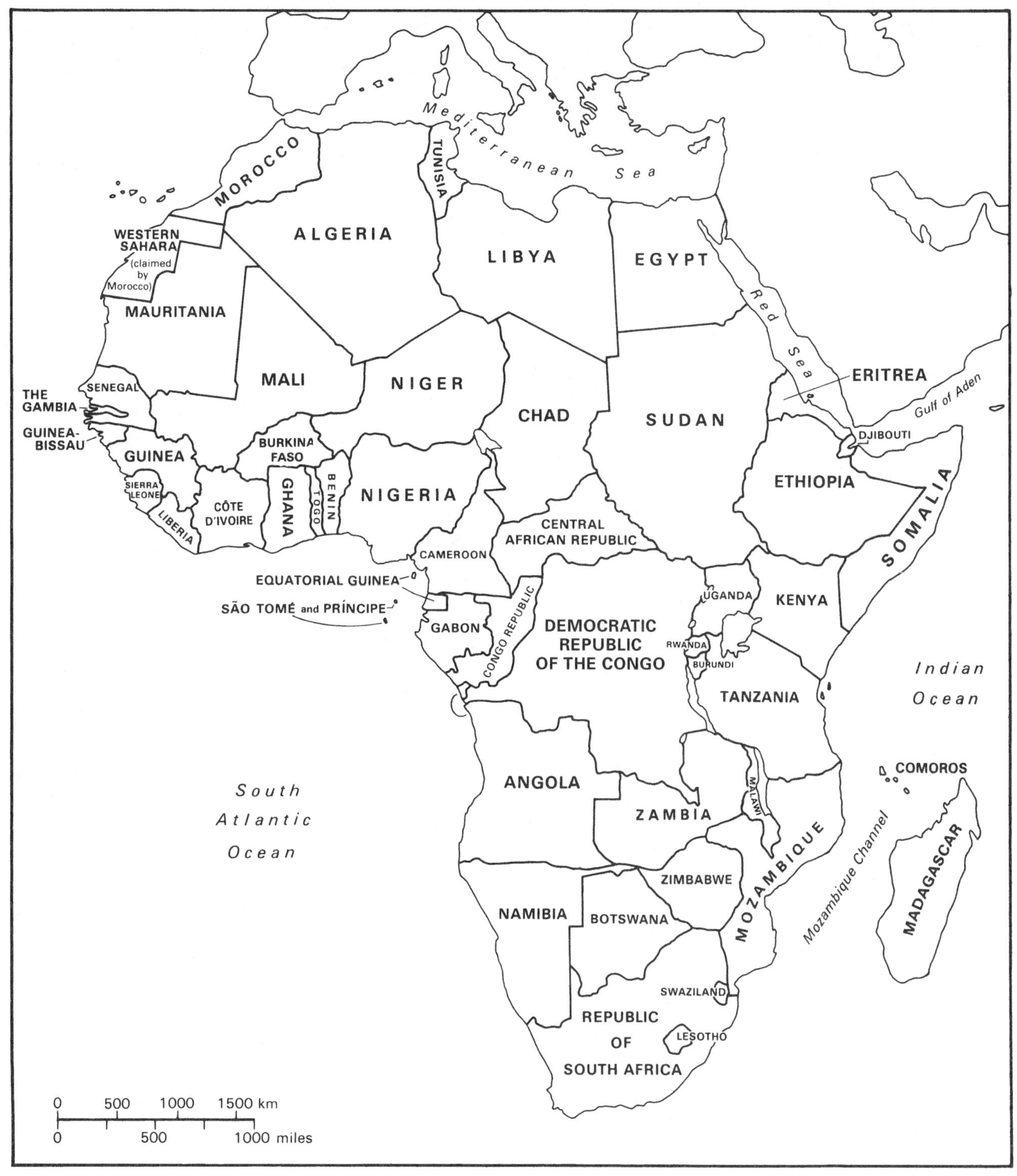

Outline Political Map of Contemporary Africa

PART TWO

Country Surveys

ANGOLA

Physical and Social Geography

RENÉ PÉLISSIER

PHYSICAL FEATURES

The Republic of Angola, covering an area of 1,246,700 sq km (481,354 sq miles), is the largest Portuguese-speaking state in Africa. It is composed of 18 provinces, one of which, Cabinda (formerly known as Portuguese Congo), is separated from the others by the oceanic outlet of the Democratic Republic of the Congo (DRC, formerly Zaire) and the delta of the River Congo. On its landward side Cabinda is surrounded by the DRC and the Republic of the Congo. Greater Angola is bordered to the north and east by the DRC, to the east by Zambia and to the south by Namibia. Excluding the Cabinda enclave, Angola extends 1,277 km from the northern to the southern border, and 1,236 km from the mouth of the Cunene river to the Zambian border.

Two-thirds of Angola is a plateau. The average elevation is 1,050 m–1,350 m above sea-level, with higher ranges and massifs reaching above 2,000 m. The highest point of Angola is Mt Moco (2,620 m) in the Huambo province. Through the central part of the inland plateau runs the watershed of Angola's rivers. The coastal plain on the Atlantic is separated from this plateau by a sub-plateau zone, which varies in breadth from about 160 km in the north to 25 km–40 km in the centre and south. The Namib desert occupies the coastal plain at a considerable height above Namibe. Towards the Cuango (Kwango) basin, in the Zaire province, a sedimentary hollow forms the Cassange depression, in which cotton is cultivated. The north-western section of the Angolan plateau has jungle-covered mountains, which are suitable for the cultivation of coffee. The Mayombe range in Cabinda is covered by equatorial jungle.

Except for the Cuanza (Kwanza) river, which is navigable up to Dondo (193 km upstream), Angolan rivers do not provide easy access to the interior from the coast. On the other hand, they are harnessed for the production of electricity and for irrigation. The main rivers are, above the Cuanza, the Chiloango (Cabinda), the Congo, the M'bridge, the Loge, the Dange and the Bengo. The Cassai (Kasai), Cuilo (Kwilu) and Cuango rivers are known more for their importance to the DRC than for their upper reaches in Angola, although many tributaries of the Kasai intersect the Angolan plateau, exposing rich deposits of alluvial diamonds in the Lunda provinces.

Angola has a tropical climate, locally tempered by altitude. The Benguela current, along the coast, influences and reduces rainfall in that part of the country, which is arid or semi-arid. The interior uplands in the Bié, Huambo and Huíla provinces enjoy an equable climate. On the other hand, along the Cuanza river, in the north-west and north-east, and in the eastern and southern provinces, high temperatures and heavy seasonal rainfall discouraged European colonization wherever there were no economic incentives, such as coffee in the provinces of Zaire and Uíge, and diamonds in Lunda.

POPULATION

Angola is an underpopulated country, with only 5,646,166 inhabitants enumerated at the 1970 census, when the population density was 4.5 persons per sq km. By mid-2006, when the population was estimated at 16,557,000, the density had risen to 13.3 persons per sq km. Angola is overwhelmingly rural and has considerable ethnic diversity, although all indigenous groups, of which the Ovimbundu and Mbundu are the most numerous, are of Bantu stock. An important characteristic of the population is its youth, as 45% are under 15 years old and only 5% are over 60. According to WHO estimates, the average life expectancy at birth in 2004 was 38 years for males and 42 years for females. In 1995–2005 Angola's population increased at an estimated average annual rate of 2.6%.

Since the onset of civil strife in the mid-1970s, Angola has experienced considerable economic dislocation, accompanied by a widespread regrouping of African populations, brought about by insecurity and massacres. The population is predominantly engaged in food-crop farming and, in the south, in cattle-raising. Only in areas where coffee, cotton and maize are cultivated are Angolans engaged to any extent in commercial agriculture. An estimated 70.7% of the economically active population were employed in the agricultural sector in 2004. Since the mid-1980s government-controlled towns and villages have, over large parts of the country, co-existed with groupings of guerrilla-controlled populations sheltered in shifting villages: this has applied mostly to the south-east, east and north-east, and the enclave of Cabinda. Serious food shortages and periods of famine periodically beset central and southern Angola. Despite civil conflict, Angola's substantial petroleum reserves have been developed intensively since the late 1980s, and in 2004 crude petroleum provided 92.4% of export earnings. The war created problems of 'internal' refugees (a total of 4.3m. were believed to have been displaced by the conflict), and in late 2006 it was estimated that there were some 100,000 Angolan refugees in surrounding countries, despite the return of 370,000 since the cease-fire of April 2002. As refugees are repatriated, resettlement is likely to alter the demography of the country significantly.

The population of the capital, Luanda (which was 480,613 at the 1970 census), was estimated to have risen to 2.8m. by mid-2005. Outside the capital, most urban centres are operating at a reduced level, some having been partially destroyed or looted. Benguela and Lobito (the outlet of the Benguela railway, which has been effectively out of operation since 1975, although it was undergoing rehabilitation in the mid-2000s) were among the most seriously damaged by the war, and the port of Lobito suffered from the disruption of traffic with the DRC and Zambia. Plans for the rehabilitation of the Lobito corridor were being developed, under the New Partnership for Africa's Development (NEPAD). Huambo, formerly an important centre for rail traffic to the eastern regions and to the DRC and Zambia, and for road traffic to Luanda and Namibia, should also again become a focal point of economic activity. Other centres, such as Namibe, Lubango, Kuito and Luena, also suffered from the war and local disorder. The city of Cabinda has benefited from the exploitation of offshore petroleum resources, while pioneer towns such as Menongue and Saurimo may eventually assume new importance as regional centres.

Recent History

MAREK GARZTECKI

Revised by EDWARD GEORGE

INDEPENDENCE AND CIVIL WAR

The period preceding its independence in 1975 bestowed the former Portuguese colony of Angola with four competing nationalist movements, none of which was able to assert its supremacy over the others. They comprised the Movimento Popular de Libertação de Angola (MPLA), the Frente Nacional de Libertação de Angola (FNLA), the União Nacional para a Independência Total de Angola (UNITA) and the Frente para a Libertação do Enclave de Cabinda (FLEC). The divisions between the groups stemmed from a combination of factors, including the ethnic and social origins of their respective leaderships, their ideologies and the concomitant international patronage that they received.

The MPLA, a successor to the oldest Angolan anti-colonialist movement, the Partido da Luta Unida dos Africanos de Angola, was considered to be dominated by the Mbundu people, who inhabit the area around the capital, Luanda. Although it aimed to represent all Angolans, the MPLA's programme primarily reflected the views of urban intellectuals, mostly *assimilados* (the Europeanized Africans granted Portuguese citizenship) and *mestiços* (people of mixed African and European descent), as personified by its first leader, Mário de Andrade. From its inception in 1956, the MPLA displayed a strong leftist orientation as well as links with the Portuguese Communist Party. These proclivities led to substantial material support from the countries of the Soviet bloc. Being most exposed, because of its urban base, to Portuguese anti-nationalist repression, the MPLA was significantly bolstered by the appointment, as President of the movement, in 1962, of Dr Agostinho Neto, an *assimilado* Mbundu and former political prisoner.

As the name of the FNLA's predecessor, the União das Populações do Norte de Angola, indicates, the movement was established in 1962 initially to represent the interests of the Bakongo people living in the north of Angola. Although it later abandoned the phrase 'do Norte', the organization continued to retain strong links with the Bakongo of Zaire (now the Democratic Republic of the Congo—DRC), which were cemented by family ties between its leader, Holden Roberto, and the Zairean leader, Mobutu Sese Seko. Largely as a result of Mobutu's high standing among Western powers, the FNLA was able to secure US assistance, which increased as the days of the Portuguese colonial empire were coming to an end. Following an anti-Portuguese uprising, the FNLA formed an Angolan government-in-exile, the Governo Revolucionário de Angola no Exílio (GRAE).

The third major nationalist movement, UNITA, was formed in 1966, following the defection from the FNLA/GRAE of representatives of the Ovimbundu people, led by Jonas Savimbi. The most numerous among the Angolan tribes, the Ovimbundu populate mainly the rural areas of the country's central Bié plateau. With the two superpowers of the USSR and the USA already committed to other Angolan nationalist movements, UNITA turned for support to the People's Republic of China. As well as the receipt of arms deliveries and direct military training from China, UNITA also embraced the Maoist military doctrine and party-political structure.

The smallest of the Angolan nationalist movements, FLEC, never actually aspired to broaden its appeal beyond its regional base in the Cabinda enclave. Its secessionist programme precluded alliances with any of the other movements, as they all supported, at least in theory, Angola's territorial integrity. FLEC's key personalities included António Eduardo Sozinho and N'zita Henriques Tiago.

Each organization had a military wing, in the case of the MPLA entitled the Forças Armadas Populares de Libertação de Angola (FAPLA) and in the FNLA's case the Exército de Libertação Nacional de Angola (ELNA), all of which engaged in armed struggle against Portuguese colonial rule.

Angola's progress towards independence was substantially bolstered by the *coup d'état* in Portugal in April 1974, itself a product of popular dissatisfaction with colonial wars in Africa. Fighting between the nationalists and the Portuguese army ceased and all nationalist organizations were permitted to operate legally. In January 1975, at a meeting in Alvor, Portugal, an agreement was reached between the representatives of the MPLA, UNITA, the FNLA and the Portuguese Government, establishing the date for Angola's independence as 11 November 1975, and allowing for the formation of a transitional Angolan Government. Headed by a Portuguese High Commissioner, the 'Government of National Unity' consisted principally of representatives of the MPLA, UNITA and the FNLA, but excluded FLEC and other smaller groups. The new administration also disregarded the interests of Angola's significant white population. By mid-1975 the fragile governing coalition had started to disintegrate, falling victim to serious internal differences as well as to the growing superpower rivalry in which the Angolans played the role of proxies. The pro-Western FNLA, perceived, at the time, as being the strongest of the three nationalist movements, benefited from a covert mercenary recruitment campaign directed by the US Central Intelligence Agency. In response, the USSR provided the MPLA forces with substantial military aid, which was followed by the clandestine arrival of Cuban military instructors in Angola.

In June 1975 heavy fighting broke out between MPLA and FNLA forces in Luanda, and rapidly spread to other major towns. By the end of that month the FNLA had been ejected from the capital, while the MPLA had been forced out of the northern provinces of Uíge and Zaire, with UNITA drawn into the conflict on the side of the FNLA. The pro-MPLA stance of the Portuguese administration helped to tilt the balance further between the movements. When the transitional Government in Luanda collapsed in August, the positions vacated by the FNLA and UNITA were allocated to MPLA nominees. By early October more Cuban military personnel had arrived, helping the MPLA to gain control of 12 of the country's 16 provincial capitals. Meanwhile, in August South African forces entered Angola, in support of the FNLA-UNITA alliance, and occupied the Ruacana hydroelectric complex on the boundary Cunene river. This was followed, on 23 October, by an invasion of South African-led troops, which rapidly advanced to within 100 km of Luanda. The South African intervention prompted an immediate massive inflow of Soviet arms and Cuban troops. It also resulted in a significant decline in international support for the FNLA and UNITA, especially among their former African backers.

Angolan independence was declared, as originally planned, on 11 November 1975. However, the country found itself divided by two competing administrations. While the MPLA declared the creation of the People's Republic of Angola in Luanda, with Neto as President of the newly independent state, the FNLA and UNITA proclaimed the establishment of the Democratic People's Republic of Angola in Huambo (formerly Nova Lisboa), the country's second largest city. By early 1976 the MPLA had gained the upper hand, bolstered by the support of some 36,000 Cuban troops and an estimated US $200m. worth of Soviet arms. By the end of February the forces of the FNLA and its mercenaries in northern Angola had been decisively defeated, and in the following month South African troops, under international pressure, withdrew into Namibia, while UNITA was forced out of Huambo.

Despite its military success, the MPLA Government faced considerable difficulties. Angola's infrastructure had been damaged by the war, the administration had ceased to function and the economy had collapsed. The exodus of the Portuguese population, which represented a significant proportion of the skilled work-force, as well as the massive internal displacement of the remaining population, served only to worsen the situation. The MPLA itself had come under severe strain from factionalism and internal dissension, exacerbated by an increasingly orthodox communist stance adopted by the dominant grouping led by Neto. At a plenum of its central committee in October 1976 the MPLA formally adopted Marxism-Leninism. The internal opposition to the Neto group included the so-called *Nitistas* faction, led by the Minister of the Interior, Nito Alves, and a central committee member, Fernando José França van-Dúnem.

A bloody power struggle developed in May 1977, during which *Nitistas* were responsible for the deaths of a number of senior government leaders. The *Nitistas* were, however, defeated, following the intervention in support of Neto's faction of Cuban troops stationed in Angola. A thorough purge of the MPLA followed, during which the party lost more than two-thirds of its membership. In December 1977 the first party congress expanded the name of the movement to MPLA—Partido do Trabalho (MPLA—PT), and proclaimed it a vanguard party of the working classes. Substantial political changes, starting in December 1978, cemented the ascendancy of Neto and those loyal to him. The posts of Prime Minister and Deputy Prime Minister were abolished in that month, giving Neto direct control over the Government, while the ethnic composition of the MPLA—PT political bureau was significantly altered by the appointment of several non-Mbundu members. Improved party cohesion allowed the transfer of power (as leader of the MPLA—PT and state President) to José Eduardo dos Santos following Neto's death in September 1979.

The cornerstone of Angolan foreign policy after 1976 was a close relationship with the Soviet bloc countries, although the MPLA—PT regime consistently denied that it was a communist client state. In October 1976 the Angolan Government signed a Treaty of Friendship and Co-operation with the USSR, which gave the latter the right to use Angolan airports and harbours for military purposes. The Government also attempted to improve its relations with Angola's immediate neighbours; however, relations with Zaire deteriorated during 1977, following incursions from Angola into Zaire's Shaba (now Katanga) province by forces of the Zairean anti-Mobutu Front national pour la libération du Congo. As a result of Western pressure, the Mobutu and MPLA—PT Governments agreed in 1978 not to support each other's opponents. The expulsion from Zaire in 1979 of the leaders of the FNLA and FLEC strengthened the international position of the MPLA—PT regime. The overall economic position of the MPLA—PT regime also improved following discoveries of petroleum reserves in the area under its control. The interests of multinational petroleum companies had started increasingly to influence the attitudes of Western Governments towards Luanda.

CONFLICT WITH SOUTH AFRICA

Relations between Angola and Portugal remained under strain until 1978, when the two countries resolved most of their remaining differences. Angola also became an active member of the alliance of the 'front-line states', which opposed the apartheid regime in South Africa. The African National Congress of South Africa (ANC) and the South West Africa People's Organisation of Namibia (SWAPO) both opened offices in Luanda. SWAPO, fighting for the independence of South African-occupied Namibia, was allowed to establish bases on territory controlled by the MPLA—PT. These factors, combined with increasingly open South African support for UNITA, led to increasing confrontation between the MPLA—PT and South Africa.

A key element in UNITA's survival was the South African military and logistical support that it received. The South African Government felt threatened by the continuing presence of a large number of Cuban forces in Angola and resented the MPLA—PT's support for SWAPO. The South African Defence Forces (SADF) established support bases for UNITA in Cuando-Cubango province, while the South African air force provided air cover for Savimbi's headquarters in Jamba. From the late 1970s the SADF regularly launched incursions into Angola in pursuit of SWAPO guerrillas.

The advent of a new Republican Administration in the USA in 1981, led by Ronald Reagan, resulted in a change in US policy towards Africa. The US Administration adopted 'Constructive Engagement' with the South African Government, at the time an international pariah, in an effort to persuade it to accept Namibian independence. Simultaneously, the linking of Namibian independence and the withdrawal of SADF forces from Angola to the withdrawal of Cuban forces from the region was proposed. The new US Administration also reversed its policy towards UNITA. Believing that the Angolan Government needed to be weakened in order to force the Cubans' departure, the USA steadily increased military support for UNITA, although it had to wait until the Clark Amendment (forbidding US involvement in Angola) was repealed in 1985 to offer its full backing.

Armed incursions by South Africa were accompanied by an escalation in the activities of UNITA, which assumed a more prominent military role, expanding its operations in eastern Angola while the Government deployed its main forces in the west against the SADF. Throughout 1982 and 1983 the SADF and UNITA together intensified their activities in Angola, with the South Africans occupying large sections of Cunene province, while UNITA launched attacks on a wide variety of targets. In August 1983 the conflict sharply escalated when a large UNITA force attacked and destroyed the strategic town of Cangamba, in Moxico province, with the aid of intense aerial bombardment by the South African Air Force. In July 1983 regional military councils were established in all areas affected by the fighting, concentrating all state power in the hands of military officers, directly responsible to the President. This increased the efficiency of the FAPLA, which now constituted the country's official armed forces.

In December 1983 the SADF launched Operation Askari, an invasion of southern Angola with 2,000 troops, and following heavy clashes around Cuvelai the US Administration arranged a cease-fire and convened peace talks in Lusaka, Zambia. In February 1984 South Africa and Angola signed the Lusaka Accord, under which South Africa pledged to withdraw its troops from Angola in exchange for Angola restraining SWAPO's activities. The SADF officially withdrew from Angola in April 1985. In the following month, however, a unit of its special forces was captured while engaged in operations against petroleum installations in Cabinda. The SADF's 'hot-pursuit' incursions into Angola were resumed in June. In October 1987 South Africa admitted, for the first time, that it was maintaining a 'limited presence' inside Angola, and in the following month it confirmed that it was providing military support to UNITA, and had engaged in direct military action against Soviet and Cuban forces stationed there. South Africa's intensification of aggression against Angola was widely condemned and in late November the UN Security Council demanded the unconditional withdrawal of South African troops from Angola. Despite agreeing to comply with this demand, South Africa nevertheless continued its military incursions into Angola. These were matched by a massive escalation of UNITA operations in the countryside, which led to the displacement of hundreds of thousands of peasants.

TOWARDS A REGIONAL ACCORD

In April 1987 representatives of the MPLA—PT administration and the US Government resumed efforts to solve the interlinked issues of Namibian independence and the withdrawal of third-party forces from Angola. While negotiations continued, the FAPLA, backed by Cuban artillery and air power, launched an offensive in south-eastern Angola against UNITA's forward base at Mavinga. Facing defeat, UNITA turned to South Africa for support, and in August the SADF dispatched 2,000 troops to push back the MPLA offensive, defeating FAPLA-Cuban forces at the Lomba river. Withdrawing in disorder to Cuito Cuanavale, the FAPLA dug in and, with the support of 15,000–20,000 Cuban reinforcements, they repeatedly repelled the South African attacks, bringing the fighting in Angola to a stalemate.

Negotiations between representatives of Angola, Cuba and the USA continued throughout early 1988, as did separate negotiations between South Africa and UNITA, and the USA and the USSR. UNITA, which was excluded from the consultations, initiated a diplomatic campaign in major Western capitals to advance its terms for an Angolan settlement. On 22 December the participants in the negotiations met in New York, USA, where a bilateral agreement was signed by Angola and Cuba, and a tripartite accord by Angola, Cuba and South Africa. Under these agreements, 1 April 1989 was designated as the date of the implementation of the Namibian independence process, which was to culminate in elections to a constituent assembly. In addition, Cuba undertook to complete a phased withdrawal of its estimated 65,000 troops from Angola by July 1991. Angola, Cuba and South Africa were to establish a joint commission, in which the USA and the USSR would be present as observers. All prisoners of war were to be exchanged and the signatories of the tripartite accord were to refrain from supporting forces intent on undermining each other's Governments. The latter clause necessitated both the curtailment of South African aid to UNITA and the departure from Angola of an estimated 6,000 members of the ANC's military wing, MK. In accordance with the agreements, the UN Security Council authorized the creation of a UN Angola Verification Mission (UNAVEM) to monitor the redeployment and withdrawal of Cuban troops. UNAVEM commenced operations in January 1989.

The New York accords ended South African involvement in Angolan affairs, but failed to resolve the internal conflict in Angola. The MPLA—PT Government continued to reject UNITA's appeals for a cease-fire, instead offering the rebel organization, in early February 1989, a 12-month amnesty. However, UNITA, reiterating its own aim of negotiating a settlement with the Government that would lay the foundations for a multi-party democracy in Angola, responded by launching a major offensive against FAPLA targets. In March, however, following a statement by President dos Santos declaring his willingness to find a resolution to the conflict, Savimbi announced UNITA's intention to honour a unilateral moratorium on offensive military operations until mid-July to facilitate outside mediation. In June 1989 both Savimbi and dos Santos attended a conference in Gbadolite, Zaire, organized by President Mobutu, where they agreed to hold direct negotiations and eventually signed a cease-fire accord. A commission to monitor the implementation of the peace agreement was established, including the Presidents of the People's Republic of the Congo, Gabon and Zaire. The full terms of the accord were interpreted differently by each party, and in August Savimbi announced a resumption of hostilities.

THE ESTORIL PEACE AGREEMENT

Talks between UNITA and the MPLA—PT Government resumed in October 1989. In May 1990 UNITA recognized dos Santos as Head of State, and in October it accepted the MPLA—PT Government as an interim administration, pending elections. At a meeting of the MPLA—PT central committee in July, the country's evolution towards a multi-party political system was finally accepted. Further reforms, including the replacement of the party's Marxist-Leninist ideology with a commitment to 'democratic socialism', the introduction of a market economy, the legalization of political parties, the transformation of the army from a party to a state institution, and a revision of the Constitution, were formally approved at the MPLA—PT congress in December. The legalization of political parties, which was passed by the People's Assembly in March 1991, paved the way for the final round of talks between UNITA and the Government. The legislation, however, stipulated that political parties must enjoy support in at least 14 of Angola's 18 provinces, thereby effectively excluding the Cabinda-based FLEC from the democratic process.

On 1 May 1991 a peace agreement was signed by the two sides in Estoril, Portugal. The agreement provided for a cease-fire from midnight on 15 May, which was to be monitored by a joint political and military committee comprising representatives from the MPLA—PT, UNITA, the UN, Portugal, the USA and the USSR. Immediately following the cease-fire, the provision of aid from abroad to the warring parties was to cease and a new national army was to be established, composed of equal numbers of FAPLA and UNITA soldiers. Free and democratic elections were to be held by the end of 1992, and refugees and exiles were to be allowed to return to Angola.

In September 1991 Savimbi returned to Luanda for the first time since the civil war began in 1975, and UNITA headquarters were transferred to the capital in October 1991. At an extraordinary congress of the MPLA—PT, held in May 1992, delegates voted to readmit a number of prominent ex-dissidents, and removed the suffix 'Partido do Trabalho' from the party's official name. In August a constitutional revision took effect, removing the remnants of the country's former Marxist ideology, and deleting the words 'People's' and 'Popular' from the Constitution and from the names of official institutions. The name of the country was changed from the People's Republic of Angola to the Republic of Angola. In September 1992 FAPLA and UNITA forces were formally disbanded, and the new 50,000-strong national army, the Forças Armadas de Angola (FAA), was officially established.

THE 1992 ELECTIONS

Despite the appointment of Gen. João Baptista de Matos, Commander of FAPLA's ground troops, and Gen. Abilo Kamalata 'Numa', Commander of UNITA's northern front, as joint Supreme Commanders of the FAA in January 1992, concerns were expressed at the declining number of government and UNITA troops in the confinement areas and the reoccupation of territory by rebel forces. Evidence of serious divisions within UNITA became apparent in early March 1992, with the announcement that two leading members, Gen. Miguel N'Zau Puna and Gen. Tony da Costa Fernandes, had resigned. This added to persistent reports of bloody purges and 'disappearances' of Savimbi's opponents or rivals within UNITA. At the same time it became apparent that UNITA had deliberately slowed the process of demobilizing its soldiers, in protest at the formation of a new government paramilitary unit, the 'emergency police', recruited from the MPLA's own special forces.

Presidential and legislative elections took place, as scheduled, on 29–30 September 1992, with dos Santos, Savimbi, and the FNLA President, Holden Roberto, among the 12 registered presidential candidates. Despite fears of violence and intimidation, the level of participation was high, averaging almost 90% of the electorate and international observers judged the conduct of the elections to have been free and fair. This assessment was, however, questioned by Savimbi, when the preliminary results indicated that the MPLA had obtained a majority of seats in the new Assembléia Nacional. He demanded the suspension of the official announcement of the results and an inquiry into the alleged electoral irregularities. On 5 October UNITA withdrew from the FAA. According to the official election results, published on 17 October, dos Santos received 49.6% of the total votes cast in the presidential election, just short of the 50% required to avoid a second round against Savimbi, who secured 40.1%. In the legislative elections the MPLA won 53.7% of the vote and 129 of the 220 seats in the Assembléia Nacional, compared with 34.1% of the vote and 70 seats for UNITA.

RESUMPTION OF THE CIVIL WAR

Following the announcement of the official election results, violence erupted between MPLA and UNITA supporters in various cities, including Luanda and Huambo, and by October 1992 hostilities had spread throughout the country. While the MPLA accused UNITA of renewing the hostilities and rearming the majority of its soldiers, government supporters conducted an effective hunt for opposition supporters in towns under its control. As a result, several thousand people were killed, including a number of senior UNITA officials. While the second round of the presidential election was postponed indefinitely, the newly elected Assembléia Nacional convened in November. It elected as its President an MPLA veteran and former Prime Minister, Fernando José França van-Dúnem. The 70 elected UNITA parliamentarians refused to take their seats, claiming that to convene the assembly in the absence of an elected state President was illegal. This, however, did not prevent dos Santos from nominating the Secretary-General of the MPLA, Marcolino José Carlos Moco, as the new Prime

Minister. The majority of the posts in Moco's Council of Ministers were assigned to members of the MPLA, with four smaller parties also represented. UNITA was allocated one ministerial and four deputy ministerial posts, despite the fact that outside the capital Savimbi's forces were again engaged in full combat with government troops.

Already in control of most of the Angolan countryside, UNITA laid siege to and captured a number of major cities, including Huambo and Kuito. Eventually the FAA repulsed the UNITA forces and retook most of the towns, but at the cost of heavy casualties. Vast tracts of the country were made uninhabitable, displacing millions of Angolans, while thousands more were seriously injured as a result of the large-scale laying of landmines. Lengthy negotiations to end the conflict commenced in October in Lusaka, but gradually a view was formed among international observers that the principal reason for the failure of negotiations lay with Savimbi, who was accused of continuously raising new conditions and objections to procedures that had already been agreed upon. In May 1993 the USA announced its decision to recognize the Angolan Government.

THE LUSAKA ACCORD

In an attempt to apply pressure on UNITA, the UN threatened to impose a number of sanctions on the rebels, including an embargo on the sales of arms and petroleum, the 'freezing' of UNITA's foreign assets, and the expulsion of its representatives from Western capitals. To monitor compliance with the agreed peace measures, UNAVEM II was established by the UN in 1993. However, a lack of adequate co-operation from the Angolan Government, as well as from UNITA, severely limited its effectiveness. A peace accord, which had been agreed upon by the combatants in October 1994, during the talks in Lusaka, was formally signed on 20 November by UNITA's Secretary-General, Eugénio António N'Golo 'Manuvakola', and the Government's Minister of Foreign Affairs, Dr Venâncio da Silva Moura. The Chief of General Staff of the FAA, Gen. João Baptista de Matos, and his UNITA counterpart, Gen. Arlindo Chenda Isaac Pena 'Ben-Ben', agreed, in January 1995, to the immediate cessation of hostilities and the disengagement of troops. Despite these undertakings, hostilities persisted.

In February 1995 the UN Security Council established UNAVEM III, which was to comprise a military peace-keeping force of some 7,000 troops. Its deployment, however, was conditional on the cessation of hostilities and the disengagement of government and UNITA forces. As a result of UN mediation, Savimbi and dos Santos met in May in Lusaka for direct talks. Addressing dos Santos as President of Angola, Savimbi officially accepted dos Santos' election as Head of State and pledged his full co-operation in national reconstruction. Dos Santos requested that Savimbi nominate the UNITA appointees to a new government of national unity. Savimbi was also offered one of two vice-presidential posts that were to be created. In late September 1995 the Government also signed a four-month cease-fire agreement with FLEC—Renovada (FLEC—R), a breakaway faction of the main FLEC separatist movement in Cabinda province.

In March 1996, at discussions held in Libreville, Gabon, dos Santos and Savimbi agreed on terms for the establishment of a government of national unity and reconciliation, in accordance with the provisions of the Lusaka Accord. Savimbi, however, made the participation of UNITA's governmental nominees conditional on the inclusion of other opposition parties in the Government, most notably the President of the FNLA, Holden Roberto. In May Savimbi introduced further conditions, such as the retention under UNITA control of the country's diamond-producing areas in north-eastern Angola. Meanwhile, public protest at deteriorating economic conditions led dos Santos, in June, to replace Moco as Prime Minister with the President of the Assembléia Nacional, van-Dúnem.

In mid-May 1996 the Government and one of the Cabinda secessionist factions, FLEC—Forças Armadas Cabindesas (FLEC—FAC), signed an agreement outlining the terms of a cease-fire. However, following renewed fighting later that month between government troops and the secessionists, the leader of FLEC—FAC, N'zita Henriques Tiago, declared that a definitive cease-fire would only follow the withdrawal of the FAA from Cabinda.

In March 1997 UNITA, which relied on Zaire as a conduit for exporting diamonds and importing arms, was reported to have sent some 2,000 troops to support its ally and maintain supply lines, while the Angolan Government supported the rebels of Laurent-Désiré Kabila. The subsequent capture of Kamina (a military base in southern Zaire, which was of considerable strategic importance to UNITA) by Kabila's forces was believed to have ended any possibility of Savimbi resuming military action against the Angolan Government and consequently appeared to remove any remaining obstacles to UNITA fully implementing the Lusaka Accord.

In April 1997 an agreement was reached to confer on Savimbi the special status of official 'leader of the opposition', following his earlier rejection of the vice-presidency. Following the arrival of the full contingent of UNITA deputies and government nominees in Luanda, on 11 April the new Government of National Unity and Reconciliation was inaugurated. UNITA received four ministerial posts, including that of geology and mines, and seven deputy ministerial posts. A further 10 minor political parties were represented in the 87-member Government.

THE COLLAPSE OF THE LUSAKA ACCORD

In May 1997, however, following the recognition by Luanda of the Democratic Republic of the Congo (DRC, as Zaire was renamed) and its new Government, the FAA launched an offensive against the UNITA-controlled diamond-producing provinces of Lunda-Sul and Lunda-Norte. In June the UN Security Council voted unanimously to approve the Secretary-General's recommendations that UNAVEM III be disbanded and replaced by a scaled-down operation, the UN Observer Mission in Angola (MONUA), to oversee the implementation of the remaining provisions of the Lusaka Accord.

In October 1997 the Angolan Government provided military support to the former President of the Republic of the Congo, Gen. Denis Sassou-Nguesso, in his military coup against the elected Government of President Pascal Lissouba. Angola's involvement was reported to have been prompted by Lissouba's support for FLEC and UNITA forces. Shortly after the installation of the Sassou-Nguesso Government, the Angolan administration's continuing efforts to isolate UNITA were furthered by dos Santos at a summit meeting, held in Angola, attended by the Presidents of the Republic of the Congo, the DRC, Angola and Gabon. The Angolan Government subsequently issued a warning to Zambia that it would not tolerate the use of its territory as a conduit for arms to UNITA, and threatened military intervention. In the same month the UN Security Council finally ordered the implementation of additional sanctions against UNITA, on the grounds that the movement had failed to meet its obligations by the October deadline, as set out under the terms of the peace process. In January 1998 UNITA formally transferred the important Cuango valley diamond mines in Lunda-Norte province to government control. In that month a new schedule was agreed for the implementation of the Lusaka protocol. However, Savimbi remained in the UNITA stronghold of Andulo in central Angola. In August the Government suspended UNITA's government and parliamentary representatives from office.

In September 1998 a group of five UNITA moderates issued a manifesto announcing the suspension of Savimbi and the introduction of an interim UNITA leadership, pending a general congress of the party. However, the group, which styled itself UNITA—Renovada (UNITA—R), commanded very limited support among UNITA's leaders in Luanda. Conversely, the Government quickly recognized the faction as the sole and legitimate representative of UNITA in negotiations concerning the implementation of the Lusaka peace process, prompting several senior UNITA figures, among them Isaías Samakuva, to leave Luanda. While UNITA—R pledged to implement the Lusaka Peace Accord, observers questioned its ability to influence UNITA members outside the capital. In late September the Government revoked the suspension of UNITA's representatives in the Government and legislature. In October the Assembléia Nacional revoked

Savimbi's special status. In that month UNITA—R failed to impose its candidate to lead the UNITA parliamentary group when Abel Chivukuvuku was overwhelmingly re-elected as its Chairman. While no longer claiming allegiance to Savimbi, Chivukuvuku also opposed UNITA—R, and emerged as the informal leader of another faction of UNITA. In January 1999 UNITA—R held its first congress, in Luanda, at which Eugénio 'Manuvakola' was elected leader.

The ruling MPLA also succumbed to increasing factional divisions. At its congress in December 1998 dos Santos strengthened his continuing tenure of the party presidency by having his close ally João Manuel Gonçalves Lourenço elected as Secretary-General of the MPLA. At the end of January 1999 dos Santos reorganized the Council of Ministers, assuming the responsibilities of Prime Minister, a post he had abolished, in line with the Constitution, for an 'exceptional period' in order to conduct the war.

Following an uprising against Kabila's regime in the DRC in the latter half of 1998, the Angolan Government dispatched some 5,000 troops to support its ally in Kinshasa. In early December, at the onset of the dry season, the FAA began its annual offensive against UNITA positions. This followed the established pattern whereby UNITA would gain the upper hand in the wet season, which favoured guerrilla tactics, while the FAA, relying more on heavy armoury and set-piece battles, would try to reverse the situation in the dry season.

In February 1999 the UN Security Council voted unanimously to end MONUA's mandate and withdraw its operatives from Angola by March, on the grounds that conditions had deteriorated to such an extent that UN personnel were no longer able to function. The UN also decided to tighten further its sanctions regime against UNITA. A report prepared by the UN Angola Sanctions Committee, published in June 1999, disclosed the contravention of UN sanctions by a number of African Heads of State, listing, amongst others, the Presidents of Togo and Burkina Faso as allegedly being involved in the trading of arms for UNITA-mined diamonds.

The ensuing furore forced the South African company De Beers, which controls the majority of international trade in diamonds, to announce a policy of purchasing only legitimately mined gems. The Angolan Government also attempted to stem the flow of illegal diamonds by introducing a strict regime of stone certification. A further UN report, published in March 2000, criticized, among others, the leaders of a number of African countries for allegedly violating sanctions that had been imposed on UNITA following the discovery of the trade in illegally mined diamonds. In response, the Angolan Government announced the creation of a new state diamond company, the Sociedade de Comercialização de Diamantes (SODIAM), which was to centralize and regulate the country's diamond trade. All marketing was transferred to the newly created Angolan Selling Corporation, in which SODIAM held a 51% interest. In December the UN Angola Sanctions Committee issued a further report on the smuggling of UNITA diamonds, which confirmed that sanctions had failed to prevent the movement's involvement in the diamond trade.

Meanwhile, in the second half of 1999, backed by superior air power and intelligence, the FAA made considerable military gains against UNITA. By October the UNITA headquarters in Bailundo and the military base in Andulo had fallen to government forces. The FAA's tactics seemed to be based on attempts to split UNITA into small, isolated units and to negotiate their surrender individually, rather than engaging in yet further peace talks with Savimbi.

The fall of Bailundo, which is the traditional seat of the principal Ovimbundu *regulos* (tribal kings), significantly weakened Savimbi's claim to represent Angola's largest ethnic group. It also boosted the position of Luanda-based Chivukuvuku, himself a scion of an Ovimbundu *regulo*. Chivukuvuku's appeal across party-political lines and his skills as a politician marked him out as a credible challenger, not only to Savimbi but also to dos Santos. By July 2000 the Angolan Government claimed that the conventional war against Savimbi was over. However, it was widely believed that without a workable final accord between dos Santos and Savimbi there was little chance of concluding Angola's civil war.

Dos Santos hinted, in June 2000, at the possibility of a reconciliation with Savimbi, underpinned by the view that UNITA, weakened militarily and split into three factions, would not pose a serious political threat, even if allowed to operate unhampered as a purely political party. As part of this strategy, the Government announced that it would hold a long-delayed general election by November 2001, hoping to repeat its earlier victory at the ballot box. However, the MPLA subsequently stated that peace would be a precondition for the holding of elections. The creation of a 'Front for Change', incorporating 17 minor political parties, as well as the formation of a growing church-based peace movement, appeared to indicate the presence of an increasingly vociferous opposition, which was committed to ending the war and holding free and fair elections. However, in December 2000 the elections were postponed until late 2002 by the Government, as a result of significant disagreements over the future Constitution, as well as the unstable military situation.

In October 2000 the mandate for the UN Office in Angola (UNOA) was extended until April 2001, although it was to remain restricted to the monitoring of human rights, capacity building and humanitarian support; the mandate was further extended in April 2001. Also in October UNITA put forward a 12-point peace plan, proposing the formation of a 'broad consensus government', as well as the depoliticization of the armed forces, the police and public administration. However, the proposal was rejected by the Government. A further amnesty against all perpetrators of war crimes, which was proposed by dos Santos in November, was again rejected by UNITA. In December, nevertheless, the Assembléia Nacional approved draft amnesty legislation put forward by the MPLA. However, the principal opposition parties argued that it was unlikely to bring an end to the civil war.

Meanwhile, the opposition organized hunger strikes in protest at the alleged implication of dos Santos in an arms-trafficking scandal involving a French company, Brenco International, and a French businessman, Pierre Falcone. It was alleged that the company, as well as a number of French politicians, had become involved in the unauthorized sales of arms, worth some US $600m., to the Angolan Government in 1993–94. Dos Santos later defended Falcone's actions, stating that they had assisted the Government following the resumption of the civil war, and that France had been rewarded with a substantial expansion of its interests in Angola. Nevertheless, investigations into the dealings, as well as the controversial restructuring of Angola's $5,000m. debt to Russia in 1996, in which Falcone was also involved, continued in France. The Angolan Government expressed its disappointment at the inquiry, and relations with France deteriorated considerably thereafter.

In January 2001 de Matos was replaced as Chief of Staff of the FAA by Armando da Cruz Neto. De Matos' dismissal was thought to indicate a decision by dos Santos to pursue a more aggressive policy against UNITA. In March Savimbi called for a resumption of negotiations between the Government, UNITA and the UN; Savimbi further stated that he was prepared to abide by the Lusaka Accord. However, the Government responded by declaring that it was not willing to resume talks with Savimbi, although it would agree to negotiate the terms of the Lusaka Accord with the pro-Government UNITA—R. In early May, however, dos Santos renewed his appeal for a cease-fire at an international conference on peace and democracy, held in Luanda. Dos Santos further requested that Savimbi indicate when he intended to cease hostilities. UNITA troops subsequently agreed to abide by a cease-fire, on condition that it were called by dos Santos.

Meanwhile, fighting between UNITA and MPLA forces continued throughout early and mid-2001. The conflict also spread to neighbouring countries, with the Zambian army becoming involved in skirmishes with the FAA along the border, while UNITA launched several attacks into Namibian territory.

THE DEATH OF JONAS SAVIMBI

Despite these attacks by UNITA, it became clear that the movement was losing its momentum. Not only was UNITA isolated internationally, but its access to revenue from diamonds was increasingly restricted, while government forces benefited from unlimited access to revenue from petroleum. By early 2002 a substantial portion of Angola's territory had been brought under government control; the Government's apparent objective was either to capture or to kill Savimbi. However, few expected the announcement by the Government that the rebel leader had been killed on 22 February in an army operation, after he and his bodyguards had been ambushed in a remote area in Moxico province, close to the Zambian border. The Government stated that hostilities would continue until UNITA complied with the Lusaka protocol.

Dos Santos embarked on a scheduled visit to the USA to meet President George W. Bush at the end of February 2002, when he rejected a unilateral cease-fire. Nevertheless, US and other Western officials pressed for a dignified surrender of UNITA troops, given that the FAA had effectively defeated the rebel movement. In addition, in early March Savimbi's successor, António Dembo, was either killed by the FAA or died as a result of a shortage of medical supplies. (In April UNITA released a statement claiming that Dembo had died of acute diabetes.) On 13 March the FAA announced that it had halted all military operations against UNITA and had entered into negotiations with the remaining UNITA forces, led by their Chief-of-Staff, Gen. Abreu 'Kamorteiro' Muengo. There were indications that this was part of a strategy to divide the different UNITA elements, as Dembo's successor was likely to have been UNITA's Secretary-General, Gen. Paulo Lukamba 'Gato', who was under house arrest in Luanda.

UNITA finally agreed to a cease-fire on 30 March 2002, and an official agreement was ratified on 4 April in Luanda. The terms of the cease-fire reflected the military victory achieved by the FAA over UNITA. The rebel movement formally accepted the terms of the Lusaka protocol, although considerable changes were made to the cease-fire agreement. Significantly, the UN and Russian, US and Portuguese representatives were excluded from the negotiations, highlighting the Government's distrust of international intervention, and especially of the UN, the presence of which was blamed for facilitating the rearmament of UNITA following the 1994 Lusaka Accord. According to the terms of the cease-fire, within nine months an estimated 50,000 UNITA fighters and 250,000 family members were to be cantoned; only some 5,000 UNITA fighters were to be integrated into the FAA; all UNITA weapons were to be handed over to the FAA; and UNITA officials were to take up the four ministerial positions and other government positions allocated under the Lusaka Accord (posts currently occupied by UNITA—R members). The demobilization process was to be supervised by a Joint Military Commission (JMC), established under the 1994 Lusaka Accord, with a minor role for the UN and Russian, Portuguese and US observers.

In August 2002 UNOA was replaced by the UN Mission in Angola (UNMA). By the end of the year all UN Security Council sanctions against UNITA had been lifted. UNMA's mandate expired in February 2003 and the focus of the remaining UN presence in Angola subsequently shifted to humanitarian issues.

Following the April 2002 cease-fire, UNITA officials were gradually appointed to a number of government, diplomatic and military positions allocated to the party under the 1994 Lusaka Accord. By mid-2003 the party had four ministers, six ambassadors and three provincial governors. The JMC was finally disbanded in November 2002, stating that it had completed its tasks. A total of 400,000 UNITA soldiers and their dependants had been moved to Family Reception Areas (FRAs) established by the Government, where conditions were dire. By July 2003 81,000 UNITA soldiers and 387,000 dependants had been demobilized. By that time the Government had closed the 35 FRAs and moved the remaining UNITA combatants and their families to smaller quartering areas, which were easier to control, and where humanitarian assistance was provided by non-governmental organizations (NGOs) through a US $180m. programme supported by the World Bank's Emergency Demobilization and Reintegration Project. The full demobilization process was completed by the end of 2004. The slow integration of UNITA soldiers has contributed to the precarious security situation in the country, which has been plagued by acts of banditry and landmine incidents since the cease-fire. An estimated 4m. guns remained in circulation in mid-2005, despite repeated government requests for Angolans to turn in their weapons, especially in urban areas, where arms were supplied by the Government to residents during the civil war.

POST-WAR DEVELOPMENTS

A parliamentary commission, comprising members of both UNITA and the MPLA, was established, following the cease-fire, to discuss the terms of a new constitution. An agreement was finally reached in December 2002. The MPLA-controlled commission determined that the President should be both Head of State and Head of Government, with the powers to appoint provincial governors, as well as supreme commander of the armed forces, leaving the Prime Minister with an advisory role. There was to be only one legislative chamber. In addition, a new flag was to be adopted. The proposed constitution was to be submitted to a national referendum by the end of 2003. However, it was not until late January 2004 that the draft constitution was finally presented to the cross-party parliamentary constitutional commission, and there were further delays when, in May, opposition parties on the commission walked out in protest at the President's failure to establish an election timetable. The commission's work resumed in late August after the MPLA published a draft timetable, proposing legislative and presidential elections in September 2006. However, in December 2004 President dos Santos hinted that the presidential election might be delayed until 2007, after the new constitution had been ratified by national referendum. The opposition parties strongly objected to this delay, having envisaged a presidential election in September 2005, but had little choice other than to accept the President's timetable.

Following the death of Savimbi in February 2002, UNITA struggled to make the transformation from a guerrilla movement into a national political party. The organization formed a 'management commission' in an attempt to unite the different components of the movement, namely UNITA's military forces, led by Gen. Gato, UNITA members in exile, led by Samakuva, and the parliamentary UNITA, led by Chivukuvuku. UNITA—R was not included in the commission, reflecting its discredited role within the organization. A UNITA congress was held in June 2003, and Samakuva was elected as the new UNITA President. An Ovimbundu from the central highlands, Samakuva had spent much of his life abroad as UNITA's unofficial representative in the United Kingdom and France, and had headed UNITA's negotiating team at Lusaka in 1994. The appointment of Ernesto Mulato, a non-Ovimbundu from Uíge province, as party Vice-President was seen as an attempt by Samakuva to broaden UNITA's appeal beyond its Ovimbundu base of support. During September–October 2003 Samakuva visited Portugal, Germany, France, Belgium, the USA and the United Kingdom in an attempt to secure support for UNITA, and also to remove UNITA's associations with its former President, Savimbi. In early 2005 Samakuva was presented as UNITA's candidate in the forthcoming presidential election. However, by early 2006 UNITA had failed to make an impact nationally, and its leadership complained of widespread intimidation (including an alleged assassination attempt against Samakuva while speaking at a rally in Huambo in February 2005), attempts by government officials to bribe them to agree to political concessions and the failure of the Government to deliver the administrative posts promised to UNITA under the April 2002 peace accord.

Consequently, from late 2002 the Government was in a stronger position than ever before, bolstered by crucial support from the USA, which was importing an increasing amount of petroleum from Angola. In December 2002 dos Santos took advantage of the MPLA's consolidation of power to reshuffle the Government, appointing a Prime Minister for the first time since January 1999. The new Prime Minister was Fernando (Nando) da Piedade Dias dos Santos, hitherto Minister of the Interior. While some of the changes may have indicated a drive for reform (see Economy), many officials were merely appointed to strengthen the MPLA's network of patronage and rent-seeking. In that respect, in January 2003 an independent newspaper, *Angolense*, published a list of 59 Angolans with personal fortunes of more than US $50m., which included many existing and former government officials. This unwelcome publicity came at a time when the end of the war had placed the Government under increasing scrutiny for having failed to uplift the majority of ordinary Angolans from extreme poverty, despite the country's considerable petroleum resources.

In June 2003 the Angolan Government controversially appointed Pierre Falcone as its ambassador to UNESCO in Paris, France, prompting outcry from opposition groups. Falcone had been under investigation by French courts since 1998 for allegedly violating French law by supplying the Angolan Government with armaments to the value of some US $500m. in the early 1990s. In early December 2003 the MPLA held its fifth party congress, the first to be held in peacetime since the party's foundation in 1956. Expectations in some quarters that President dos Santos would step down as Chairman of the party were frustrated when he was unanimously re-elected to the post, although he refrained from making a formal decision on whether to stand as the MPLA's presidential candidate at the next elections, scheduled for 2007. The Minister of Labour, Public Administration and Social Security, Dr António Domingos Pitra da Costa Neto, a little-known technocrat and loyal supporter of the President, was appointed party Vice-President, while Julião Mateus Paulo, another dos Santos loyalist, replaced Lourenço as the MPLA's Secretary-General. Lourenço had been regarded as a possible successor to dos Santos, and his demotion was viewed as an attempt by the President to thwart his ambitions. As a result of the congress, party hardliners and presidential supporters were firmly entrenched in power, causing great disappointment to moderates and reformists within the MPLA, who had hoped to increase party democracy and continue with reforms.

Meanwhile, controversy continued to surround the management of government petroleum accounts. In January 2004 the US-based Human Rights Watch published a report revealing that US $4,200m. had disappeared from government accounts between 1997 and 2002—approximately equivalent to Angola's total expenditure on the social sectors, or to the amount received in international humanitarian aid, during this period. The Angolan Government dismissed the report's findings, claiming that the actual amount was $673.5m., which resulted from weak accounting and the depreciation of the kwanza. Nevertheless, the allegations made by Human Rights Watch were reaffirmed in a further report published by the NGO Global Witness in March 2004. The Angolan Government suffered further embarrassment when Swiss authorities, investigating the financial operations conducted by members of the Angolan élite through Swiss bank accounts, blocked access to $726m. in funds held in the personal accounts of senior Angolan officials. The Angolan authorities insisted that the funds were 'strategic' rather than personal, and requested that the money be unblocked and used by Swiss charities for humanitarian and de-mining projects in Angola. Following lengthy investigations, in December 2004 the Swiss authorities finally unblocked the funds, accepting the Angolan Government's view that they were 'secret strategic funds', which were necessary to strengthen public order during a time of civil war, and noting that none of the parties involved—Russia, Angola or the private account holders—had complained of irregularities. The move elicited strong criticism, however, from humanitarian groups and NGOs in Switzerland, the United Kingdom and Angola, all of whom claimed it had further undermined the credibility of the Swiss banking system. In October 2005 Angola and Switzerland signed an agreement to repatriate $21m. of other funds blocked during the investigation to fund a humanitarian programme, which was to be monitored by Swiss and Angolan officials.

In October 2003 the World Bank began the third phase of its post-war reconstruction programme for Angola, the Social Action Fund, which was established to provide assistance with the rehabilitation of the country's social and economic infrastructure. The four-year programme brought together US $55m. of funding from the International Development Association, a grant of €45m. from the European Union, $20m. from the Norwegian Government, $10m. from the US Agency for International Development and $10m. from the oil company ChevronTexaco. The World Bank had been attempting to develop a post-war reconstruction and assistance programme for Angola since the end of the war in 2002, but had refrained from disbursing $150m. of emergency recovery credit, awaiting progress on improving economic governance. Attempts during 2003 by the Angolan Government to organize an international donor conference for the post-war reconstruction of Angola were rebuffed by donors, who stated that Angola should devote more of its own resource wealth to social and humanitarian action. Donors appeared unwilling to commit further funds until there was greater transparency in the management of Angola's vast petroleum revenues. As a result, the 2003 UN appeal for Angola received less than one-half of the funds requested. Undeterred, in November 2003 the UN launched its 2004 appeal, requesting a total of $262m., of which $202m. was to be allocated for relief and the remainder for reconstruction. However, donor take-up was again weak, and by the end of 2004 only $116m. had been raised. As a result the Angolan Government and UN agencies agreed not to launch a humanitarian appeal for 2005, and instead the Government pledged to organize a donor conference in the second half of the year to secure funding for reconstruction and post-conflict humanitarian projects. However, by early 2006 it appeared unlikely that donors would participate in a full-scale conference as Angola continued to benefit from record petroleum revenues and generous credits from the People's Republic of China.

The availability of foodstuffs remained critical in Angola, and in 2003 the UN World Food Programme (WFP) provided food assistance to 2.2m. Angolans, representing its largest operation in Angola for several years. In January 2006 WFP reported that food production had risen sharply in the 2004/05 season, greatly increasing the availability of food, and that as a result it would focus its future operations on targeted interventions. Nevertheless, WFP warned that food insecurity remained a problem in the central highlands and in Moxico and Cuando-Cubango. Angolan refugees and internally displaced persons (IDPs) have been returning to their homes in Angola in great numbers since the end of the war, the vast majority of their own accord and without any humanitarian assistance. In December 2003 the UN Office for the Coordination of Humanitarian Affairs estimated that 3.8m. Angolans had returned to their place of origin in Angola, leaving a total of 500,000 IDPs in Angolan camps and temporary areas and a further 400,000 living with relatives or host families. According to the office of the UN High Commissioner for Refugees (UNHCR), between mid-2002 and the end of 2005 a total of 360,000 refugees returned to Angola, of which 123,000 received assistance from UNHCR. A further 96,000 refugees remained in Zambia, the Republic of the Congo and the DRC. However, many returning refugees were unable to plant and harvest properly, partly owing to the presence of landmines in vast areas of Angola, and also as a result of unclear property rights in several areas. New land ownership legislation was drafted by the Government in November 2003, and was approved by the Assembléia Nacional in September 2004. The draft law was criticized for favouring powerful urban interests and weakening the land rights of rural populations and the urban poor, in particular by making it illegal to acquire land through long-term occupation. The legislation would also allow the authorities to expropriate land and conduct forced evictions, a policy that had already caused great controversy in the Boa Vista, Soba Kapassa and Benfica areas of Luanda where, between 2001 and 2003, numerous evictions were carried out, often at gunpoint.

In October 2004 President dos Santos began a series of government reshuffles in an effort to improve the MPLA's image in the run-up to legislative elections scheduled to take place in 2006. The dismissal of three ministers that month was followed in December by the removal of the Minister of Justice, Paulo Tjipilika—a former member of UNITA, who founded his own party, the Tendência de Reflexão Democrática, and who was replaced by his deputy, Manuel da Costa Aragão—the Minister of Health, Albertina Hamukuaya, and the Minister of

Hotels and Tourism, Jorge Valentim, and their replacement by Sebastião Sapuile Veloso and Eduardo Chingunji, respectively. All were members of UNITA, and the changes were reportedly made at the request of the UNITA President, Samakuva. In January 2005 President dos Santos dismissed the Minister of Social Communication, Pedro Hendrik Vaal Neto, replacing him with Manuel António Rabelais, the former director of Rádio Nacional de Angola. The series of reshuffles reflected a new MPLA policy of 'gradualism' in its attempts to reform the Government, and represented a move away from the 1990s when changes to the Government were carried out with full-scale reappointments, greatly increasing political instability. In a further move to improve the Government's image, in late 2004 a campaign was launched to combat corruption. In September the provincial director for social assistance in Zaire province was dismissed and subsequently arrested on charges of embezzlement of food aid funds, and in October the Governor of Bengo province, Ezelindo Mendes, was dismissed and fined over financial irregularities regarding a lucrative contract he signed as Governor in 1996. However, Angola was still ranked towards the bottom of Transparency International's 2004 Corruption Perceptions Index (joint 133rd out of 146 countries), and many donors and humanitarian organizations dismissed the Government's moves as purely cosmetic.

In a speech on 30 December 2004, President dos Santos announced that elections would finally take place in 2006, although he did not confirm whether legislative and presidential elections would occur at the same time, as demanded by the opposition. In January 2005 the Assembléia Nacional began debating new electoral legislation, with provisions made regarding regulations for the registration and financing of parties, and for the preparation of the electoral register. In April 2005 a package of seven electoral laws was passed by the Assembléia Nacional after much wrangling between the MPLA and UNITA. An 11-member Comissão Nacional Eleitoral (CNE—National Electoral Commission) was set up to oversee the electoral process and was composed of two members chosen by the President, six elected by the Assembléia Nacional, a Supreme Court judge, a representative of the Ministry of Territorial Administration and one from the National Council for Social Communication.

In June 2005 the Supreme Court ruled that President dos Santos was eligible to stand in the elections, and up to two more times subsequently, arguing that his current tenure in office was not covered by the new Constitution. In August the CNE was sworn into office. However, in October the CNE Chairman, António Caetano de Sousa, admitted that the registration of an estimated 8m. voters, which had been due to start in May, would not take place until early 2006, after the end of seasonal rains, and would run for six months. In early September 2005 dos Santos held a series of one-to-one audiences with Angola's leading opposition parties, arguing in favour of delaying the elections; however, they continued to insist that the elections be held in 2006. Also in that month Holden Roberto was removed from his post as President of the FNLA after more than 40 years as its leader. Roberto's ousting followed the signing of a pact with the FNLA leadership in October 2004 under which he promised to step down at the end of a 10-month transitional period, and triggered a prolonged leadership contest.

In November 2005 more than 600 families were forcibly evicted from the Luanda suburbs of Viana, Samba, Cambamba and Kilamba Kiaxi. Their homes were demolished to make way for a new urban development scheme, called *Nova Vida* ('New Life'), by the provincial governments, but the evictions drew heavy criticism in the local press and sparked protests by NGOs. During his end-of-year speech in December, President dos Santos hinted that elections would not take place in 2006 after all, and stated that there would need to be significant improvements to Angola's road and rail infrastructure before a credible vote could take place. In February 2006 he finally admitted that elections would not occur by September 2006 as indicated in the electoral timetable, and stated that they would take place either in late 2007 or early 2008. The opposition protested angrily at the delay, but were powerless to affect the timetable.

In January 2006 tensions within UNITA surfaced when 16 UNITA deputies in the Assembléia Nacional refused a request from Samakuva, to stand down in favour of his preferred candidates. Samakuva threatened to suspend the deputies from the Assembléia Nacional; however, the Constitutional Commission postponed its decision on expelling the deputies, enabling them to remain in their seats. In March Samakuva responded by expelling four UNITA members, including Valentim, the former Minister of Hotels and Tourism, who had been one of Samakuva's most outspoken critics, and suspended Eugénio Manuvakola, the party's former Secretary-General, for one year.

Meanwhile, in February 2006 the former Angolan ambassador to Russia, Gen. Roberto Leal Ramos Monteiro 'Ngongo' was appointed as the new Minister of the Interior, replacing Osvaldo de Jesus Serra Van-Dúnem who died earlier that month following surgery in São Paulo, Brazil. Also in that month, President dos Santos dismissed Gen. Fernando Garcia Miala, the director of the Serviço de Inteligência Externa (SIE—Angola's foreign intelligence service). A subsequent investigation chaired by the head of military affairs at the presidency, Gen. Helder Vieira Dias 'Kopelipa', accused Gen. Miala of carrying out unauthorized surveillance of certain ministers and of seeking to undermine the President's authority. However, rumours in the local press that Miala had been plotting a coup against President dos Santos were denied by the Government.

In February 2006 an outbreak of cholera in Luanda's slums spread quickly across the country, reaching 13 of Angola's 18 provinces by the end of May. In early June the World Health Organization reported a total of 41,475 cases and 1,576 deaths. By November there were nearly 60,000 reported cases and 2,400 deaths. A further 13,866 cases had been reported by May 2007 following heavy rains and flooding in January.

In April 2006 the CNE announced that voter registration would commence by July, with the process expected to take up to six months to complete, and with elections likely to take place by the end of 2007. However, after further delays, the Council of Ministers announced in August that the registration of an estimated 7.5m.–8m. Angolan voters would begin in November, and continue until June 2007. In October 2006 the Government launched a public campaign to encourage popular participation in the elections, and on 15 November the registration process officially began. According to the CNE, by the end of 2006 a total of 945,451 Angolans had been registered. In mid-January 2007 a second phase of registration began, following the Christmas break, and by the end of February over 2.2m. Angolans had been registered. In February President dos Santos declared that he expected the legislative elections to be held in 2008, to be followed by the presidential election in mid-2009.

In January 2007 Chivukuvuku announced that he would challenge Samakuva for the leadership of UNITA at the party congress which was scheduled to take place later that year. In February Samakuva took the issue of the 16 rebel deputies in the Assembléia Nacional to the country's Supreme Court; however, before a ruling could be made the MPLA used its majority in the Assembléia Nacional to confirm that the five expelled UNITA deputies could keep their seats, further complicating the dispute.

POST-WAR PROGRESS IN CABINDA

The conflict in Cabinda continued following the end of the civil war in April 2002, although on a smaller scale, with the army conducting several brutal attacks against FLEC in late 2002. Despite commanding the support of the majority of the Cabinda population, FLEC was weakened by the defection of a number of its members. The Angolan Government was keen to suppress FLEC activity so that foreign companies could begin onshore oil exploration in Cabinda, and in August 2003 one of FLEC's most senior leaders, Ranque Franque, was invited to Luanda to commence peace negotiations with the Government. In August 2004 FLEC's two main factions, FLEC—FAC and FLEC—R, joined forces to negotiate with the Government, but a power struggle between the movement's Secretary-General, António Bento Bembe, and its leader, N'zita Henriques Tiago, slowed progress. In February 2006 a group of civil-society organizations and pro-independence factions styling itself the Fórum Cabindês para o Diálogo (FCD) held talks with the Angolan Government aimed at ending the conflict. Broad agreement was reached on basic negotiating principles, and in late March it was announced that the enclave would be granted special status.

Following the introduction of a formal cease-fire in mid-June 2006 and the creation of a special statute for Cabinda in mid-July, on 1 August the Angolan Government signed a peace agreement with Bembe on the FCD's behalf. The agreement had five key elements: the full cessation of hostilities; the demobilization of all FLEC troops and their reintegration into the national army, police or civilian society; special status for Cabinda as an autonomous region of Angola; an amnesty for all fighters who surrendered to the authorities; and a significant reduction in the number of FAA troops in Cabinda. The agreement also provided for the appointment of three members of the FCD as deputy ministers in the Ministry of the Interior, the Ministry of Petroleum and the Ministry of Agriculture and Rural Development, of a deputy governor for Cabinda and to various positions in the Cabinda office of the national oil company, Sociedade Nacional de Combustíveis de Angola. However, the agreement was immediately rejected by Tiago, who questioned Bembe's authority to conclude the agreement and vowed that fighting would continue. In early January 2007 615 former FLEC fighters were incorporated into the FAA and another 113 into the national police force, but there remained as many as 1,000 FLEC fighters who had yet to demobilize. Meanwhile, sporadic attacks continued on army convoys and positions in Cabinda carried out by Tiago's faction of FLEC.

Economy

JOHN HUGHES

Revised by EDWARD GEORGE

INTRODUCTION

Prior to independence in 1975, Angola enjoyed a high-output economy, with a rapidly expanding manufacturing sector, near self-sufficiency in agriculture, with crop surpluses for export, and abundant natural resources, such as petroleum and iron ore. The petroleum sector has continued to prosper, but almost all other sectors of the economy are operating at a fraction of pre-independence levels. The civil war that began in 1975 disrupted output, made transport and distribution increasingly difficult and led to the displacement of a large part of the population. Resources were diverted towards defence; in the late 1980s annual defence spending absorbed as much as one-half of the Government's total budget expenditure. Following the resumption of hostilities in 1992, the purchase of arms was estimated to have surpassed the levels of the 1980s, with some analysts estimating government expenditure on arms (including unofficial spending) to amount to some 90% of total expenditure.

After the end of the civil war in 2002, Angola underwent an economic boom, fuelled by rising foreign direct investment (FDI), increased oil production and revenue, and rising volumes of Chinese finance, which is transforming the country's decrepit infrastructure. Angola's gross domestic product (GDP), according to the IMF, increased, in real terms, by an average of 7.5% per year in 1996–2005 (while population growth was 2.8%). In 2005 real GDP growth of 20.6% was recorded, the highest rate for a decade. Petroleum revenues were expected to increase greatly over the next four years, boosting annual real GDP growth to more than 10%. Petroleum has become the mainstay of the economy, accounting for 93.7% of export earnings in 2005. The oil sector provided an estimated 62.9% of GDP in 2005. However, a majority of the economically active population is dependent on the depressed agricultural sector, although millions of farmers have fled to the cities, particularly Luanda and Benguela and Lobito.

ECONOMIC POLICY

Following independence, the Government implemented a policy of state interventionism and wide-scale nationalization based on its Marxist-Leninist ideology, but also in response to the economic crisis caused by the war and the emigration of skilled Portuguese workers. The resulting damage to the economy, particularly the agricultural sector, which employed about 75% of the economically active population, was aggravated by the ongoing operations of the União Nacional para a Independência Total de Angola (UNITA) in rural areas. In 1987, however, President dos Santos announced that the Government intended to implement major reforms of the economy, aimed at reducing reliance on the state sector and at increasing productivity, purchasing power and consumption levels. He also declared Angola's intention to seek membership of the IMF in order to take advantage of Western financial assistance for economic reform.

Consequently, an economic and financial restructuring programme, the Saneamento Económico e Financeiro (SEF), was implemented in January 1988. The programme involved a reduction in government control over state enterprises; redeployment of civil servants to more productive enterprises; improvements in the supply and distribution systems; and more price incentives for smaller enterprises. External financial support was needed for the success of the programme, and the Government actively encouraged joint ventures between foreign and Angolan enterprises. Angola was admitted to the IMF in September 1989. In October 1990 the central committee of the ruling Movimento Popular de Libertação de Angola—Partido do Trabalho (MPLA—PT) proposed the introduction of a market economy.

Following an announcement by the Government in April 1991 that 100 companies nationalized after independence were to be returned to their original owners, and that some state-owned enterprises were to be partially privatized, a new programme of economic reforms was presented in November. The programme included reductions in personal income taxes and consumer taxes; the abolition of price 'ceilings' on all except a few basic commodities; salary increases for public-sector workers, to compensate for the withdrawal of ration cards; and a national minimum wage. In July 1996 the Government introduced a further reform programme known as *Nova Vida* ('New Life'). However, many components of the Government's economic reform objectives were never implemented, owing to the civil war.

Monetary Policy

As a result of the conflict and the Government's policy of monetizing large fiscal deficits, the rate of inflation regularly spiralled out of control from the early 1990s. Since 2000, however, the annual rate of inflation has fallen steadily from a peak of 325.0% in 2000 to an average of 43.6% in 2004, 23.0% in 2005 and an estimated 13.3% in 2006. It is likely that the Government suppressed inflation through artificial measures, including deferred state payments, delays in raising regulated prices on utilities and costly intervention in the currency markets to support the exchange rate (the 'hard kwanza' policy introduced in late 2003). As a result of chaotic monetary policy, the currency has also suffered ongoing, and at times severe, depreciation. After the kwanza was replaced, at par, by a new kwanza in September 1990, it was devalued by more than 50% in October to US \$1 = 60 new kwanza. The resumption of the war in 1992 prompted further devaluations, which brought the official exchange rate to $1 = 2,150,000 new kwanza in January 1995. In July 1995 a 'readjusted' kwanza, with a value equivalent to 1,000 new kwanza, entered into circulation. The currency continued to depreciate, but, following the introduction of the *Nova Vida* programme in 1996, the differential between the official and parallel exchange rates decreased to around 10%. By April 1999 the value of the currency had deteriorated considerably, with the official rate standing at $1 = 740,000 readjusted kwanza, compared with a free market rate of $1 = 1,620,000 readjusted kwanza.

The dual exchange rate was finally abolished in May 1999, despite strong opposition from powerful elements in the presidency, who had benefited from access to foreign exchange at artificially low rates. Banking transactions were liberalized, allowing commercial banks to trade among themselves in US dollars, thus creating an interbank money market. In December a new currency, the kwanza, replaced the readjusted kwanza at a rate of 1 kwanza = 1,000,000 readjusted kwanza. Following the establishment of free floating exchange rates, the rate for the new kwanza was set at US $1 = 5.5 kwanza. The continued high level of inflation brought the currency to an average of $1 = 74.6 kwanza in 2003. In that year the central bank adopted the 'hard kwanza' policy, using the country's large petroleum revenues to intervene in the foreign-exchange markets to prop up the value of the currency. As a result of this policy, and of the weakness of the dollar on international markets, the kwanza's depreciation against the dollar slowed, its value averaging $1 = 85.3 kwanza in 2004 and $1 = 87.2 kwanza in 2005, before appreciating moderately to an average of $1 = 80.4 kwanza in 2006. By May 2007 the currency had appreciated further, to $1 = 79.0 kwanza.

Budgetary Policy

The civil conflict has also meant that budgets have had little significance. In 1992 the budgetary deficit tripled, owing to unplanned (largely military) spending. Budgets since 1993 have focused on restoring economic and financial stability and promoting economic production, although defence has remained the sector with the largest allocation of funds. In 1998 a considerable decline in international petroleum prices resulted in a shortfall of some US $1,000m. in budget revenue. However, several sizeable petroleum deposits were discovered in 1998–99, and the Government was due to receive at least $800m. in signature bonuses from foreign petroleum companies in return for licences to operate in three ultra-deep-water petroleum blocks.

In late 1999 plans to reduce public expenditure were announced, and the tax revenue collection system was significantly improved. In January 2000 the Government abolished the much-criticized policy of recording foreign exchange transactions in the petroleum sector as 'off-budget' items and requiring all transactions to be registered with the Banco Nacional de Angola (BNA). The 2002 budget was revised following the death of the UNITA leader, Jonas Savimbi (see Recent History), with additional expenditure envisaged for demobilization and reconstruction. Moreover, the cessation of hostilities was likely to increase pressure on the Government to produce transparent and meaningful budget figures, something it had previously failed to do. (It was estimated that in 2001, for example, petroleum revenue of between US $1,000m. and $1,500m. bypassed the budget.) The budget for 2003, the first post-war budget, failed to meet these expectations, and a second revision in July 2003 failed to rectify these problems. The inflation forecast was raised to 65%, the fiscal surplus of 4.5% of GDP was changed to a fiscal deficit of 6.2% of GDP, and an oil price of $22 per barrel was assumed, 13% below analysts' estimates.

In December 2004 the Assembléia Nacional approved the 2005 budget and the Government's economic reform programme for 2005–06. Total expenditure in 2005 was set at US $11,100m., with real GDP growth forecast at 16.1% and annual inflation at 15%. The opposition parties again criticized the Government for failing to allocate enough expenditure to health, education and agriculture while overspending on defence and public order. The budget was also criticized for its assumption that oil prices would average only $26.50 per barrel when the average oil price in 2005 was in excess of $50 per barrel. However, budget implementation was poor, and by the end of 2005 only around 15% of expenditure had been executed.

In December 2005 the Assembléia Nacional approved the 2006 budget. Real GDP growth was forecast at 27.9% (driven by expanding oil production) and inflation at 10%. Total expenditure was set to increase massively, to US $23,100m., driven by a surge in public investment which was set to almost treble to $8,700m. The budget also proposed a four-fold increase in foreign lending to $7,200m., reflecting new Chinese, Brazilian, Russian, Portuguese and other credit lines. The budget was heavily criticized by the opposition for its implausibly low oil price projection (at $45 per barrel), its imprudent increase in borrowing and the massive rise in expenditure which the Government was expected to have difficulty executing. In August 2006 the Government revised the budget, increasing the oil price projection to $55 per barrel, and reducing the real GDP growth forecast to 15.5%, and the total expenditure forecast from $23,100m. to $20,054m.

In November 2006 the Assembléia Nacional approved the 2007 budget. Total expenditure was set to increase by a further 37%, mostly to finance large increases in public-sector salaries. However, given that only around 60% of budgeted expenditure was executed in 2006, a downwards revision was expected to occur later in 2007.

Relations with Foreign Donors

Talks between the Government and the IMF have continued since 1999 regarding an economic monitoring programme that would facilitate further donor assistance and a restructuring of the country's external debt. In April 2000 an agreement with the IMF provided for the implementation of a staff-monitored programme (SMP) for a nine-month period; however, no new disbursements of funds were agreed upon.

An IMF mission to Angola in February 2002 reported that the budgetary situation had considerably deteriorated by the end of 2001. In addition, the IMF noted that the Government remained unwilling to disclose the management of its petroleum revenue, as well as the accounts of the national petroleum company, the Sociedade Nacional de Combustíveis de Angola (SONANGOL). According to the IMF, expenditure unaccounted for by the Government between 1997 and 2001 amounted to about 12% of GDP. In late 2002 the Government admitted that it was facing serious problems over the repayment of its oil-backed commercial loans, with debt-service accounting for 30% of government revenue. It was estimated that foreign reserves were down to US $500m. at that time, compared with $1,000m. in July 2002. However, in January 2003 the Government was able to secure a $1,000m.–$1,500m. loan from several Western banks, part of which was to be used to refinance existing loans. More generally, in the wake of its victory over UNITA (see Recent History), the Government appeared to be placing its reform programme on hold.

In May 2003 the Angolan Government abandoned its previous course, and during an Article IV consultation with the IMF formally requested a new poverty reduction and growth facility (PRGF) programme. This seemed unlikely to occur, however, as in September the IMF published a highly critical report on Angola's economic mismanagement. Noting that little action had been taken to promote financial transparency, the report lamented Angola's continuing macroeconomic instability, poor fiscal management, stalled structural reforms and failure to tackle poverty. It also noted that 31% of total government spending, representing 14.7% of GDP, was still occurring outside the state budget. Relations with the IMF improved somewhat, however, following a visit by an IMF technical team to Luanda in December 2003, and during Article IV consultations in April 2004 Angola once again pressed the IMF for a new PRGF programme. While a formal lending agreement with the IMF still seemed unlikely, the IMF expressed interest in setting up a new SMP, provided the Government made significant progress with reforms. During a visit to Angola in July the IMF praised the Government for reducing inflation and boosting transparency, but again raised concerns over Angola's external debt, the low level of foreign reserves and the Government's lax fiscal discipline. Although a new SMP was expected to commence before the end of 2005, the

IMF remained concerned at the Government's slow progress in improving budgetary transparency and fiscal management, and in early 2005 the fund cancelled a mission to Angola after the Government failed to provide information on Angola's windfall revenue from high petroleum prices in 2004, estimated at over US $1,000m.

Following an IMF mission to Angola in April 2005 the country was close to agreeing a new 12-month SMP. However, in August the Minister of Finance, José Pedro de Morais, indicated that the Government wanted to implement its own 'home-grown' reform programme under a new IMF monitoring mechanism, the policy support instrument. Given the Government's poor record on economic reform, the IMF insisted that an SMP be successfully implemented first, and in November de Morais indicated that Angola would sign up to an SMP during the first half of 2006. However, following another IMF mission to Angola in March 2006, the Fund announced that it did not consider an economic programme necessary for Angola as it had access to sufficient resources to fund its reconstruction. The breakdown in negotiations was confirmed by the Angolan Government in late 2006 when it formally called off talks with the Fund on a new monitoring arrangement, insisting that it no longer required funding from the IMF and that its own 'home-grown' economic reform programme would be sufficient to ensure economic growth, macroeconomic stability and poverty reduction. However, the Angolan Government would continue with the IMF's biannual Article IV consultations, and it is expected to accept technical assistance offered by the Fund for the analysis of economic data.

AGRICULTURE

Owing to its large area and variety of climate, Angola is one of the most promising agricultural countries of southern Africa. However, only about 3% of Angola's total area has been cultivated as arable or permanent crop land, because of civil unrest, transport problems, and a lack of proper marketing facilities and incentives. As a result, shortages have been prevalent, and famine has been a frequent occurrence since independence. Less than one-half of the country's cereal requirements is produced locally, and high levels of cereal imports are required. The depopulation of the countryside, as a consequence of the civil war, resulted in crops being left unharvested and in a widespread failure to replant. Furthermore, severe food shortages following a period of drought in late 2000 worsened in 2001. Since the end of the civil war in April 2002 (see Recent History), the Government has made considerable efforts to effect a recovery in agricultural production.

Following the signing of the cease-fire agreement in April 2002, returning refugees suffered from lack of supplies, the effects of landmines and unclear property rights, which hampered planting and harvesting, and malnutrition continued to be a severe problem. The lack of food was particularly acute in UNITA demobilization areas.

One of the most serious impediments to increasing the level of agricultural production is the vast number of anti-personnel mines that remain concealed about the countryside as a result of the war. It is estimated that there are some 5m.–7m. unexploded mines in Angola, and around 80,000 civilians have suffered injuries necessitating the amputation of limbs as a result of accidentally detonating mines; this is the highest proportion of casualties among the civilian population of any country in the world. The UN has taken the lead in conducting demining operations and in supporting the Central Mine Action Training School, established by the UN Angola Verification Mission to instruct demobilized soldiers from both the government and UNITA forces. Efforts to demine the country stalled in 1998, as programmes were suspended owing to the resumption of hostilities, while both the Government and UNITA began to lay new mines. However, following the cessation of hostilities, the Government requested renewed assistance from the UN on the demining programme, and in July 2002 announced that Angola had ratified the Convention on the Prohibition of the Use, Stockpiling, Production and Transfer of Anti-personnel Mines and on their Destruction (which had originally been adopted at an international conference in Oslo, Norway, in September 1997). Between 2002 and 2005 demining operations in Angola cleared 33.2m. sq m of land and 13,000-km of roads, removing or destroying over 30,000 anti-personnel mines, 2,500 anti-tank mines and 160,000 unexploded devices. Landmines continue to kill and injure, however, and in 2005 there were 67 mine accidents, resulting in 26 deaths and 70 injuries.

Major Crops

In the mid-1970s Angola was the second largest African coffee producer and the world's main supplier of robusta coffee, cultivated mainly in the Uíge, Cuanza-Norte, Cuanza-Sul and Luanda provinces. Prior to independence, annual production of green coffee was more than 200,000 metric tons, with the USA being the main export customer. Coffee was cultivated on a variety of Portuguese plantations, ranging from substantial commercial holdings to family plantations. However, the subsequent departure of the Portuguese, neglect of the plantations, which were nationalized following independence, and civil conflict contributed to a decline, reducing production to about one-50th of pre-independence levels. In the 1990s output ranged between 2,160 tons in 1994 and 5,100 tons in 1998. Since 2002 output has risen from 1,250 tons to 3,000 tons in 2005, and was set to rise to 10,000 tons in 2006. The impact of the decline in agricultural production has been aggravated by falling world prices for robusta coffee, by increasing competition from Asian producers and by a shift in Western consumer demand to arabica varieties. Export earnings from coffee fell from US $80m. in 1984 to an estimated $300,000 in 2005.

Since the 1980s the Government has sought to reinvigorate the coffee sector, but plans have been hampered by the ongoing armed conflict. In 1983 the Government established the Empresa de Rebenefício e Exportação do Café de Angola (CAFANGOL), a state-controlled coffee-processing and trading organization. Plans to privatize CAFANGOL, together with the state-owned coffee plantations, commenced in 1997, although foreign ownership of the plantations was to be limited to 30%–40%. According to the Government, about US $20m. would be required for the rehabilitation of 60,000 ha of family plantations and 30,000 ha of private estates, compared with a potential revenue from coffee production as high as $15m. per year. The Angolan National Institute of Coffee (INCA) and the UN World Food Programme launched a project to provide employment for demobilized soldiers and their families on coffee plantations, and in late 2002 a plantation was set up outside Huambo for UNITA returnees. In May 2006 the Government announced an $8.5m. programme to boost coffee production in the municipality of Amboim, which was expected to raise annual production to 40,000 metric tons by the end of the decade.

Sisal exports reached 67,000 metric tons in 1974, when Angola was Africa's second most important producer. Production has since fallen sharply, principally as a result of a slump in world prices and the transition from private to state ownership, amounting to only an estimated 500 tons in 2005. Sorghum and millet are important staples for Angolans, and in 2006 157,000 tons were produced, the bulk of which was traded and consumed locally.

Maize formerly ranked fifth or sixth among Angola's agricultural exports, with a harvest of some 700,000 metric tons in 1973. As a consequence of a decline in cereal output since independence, Angola has been a recipient of food aid since 1975. Since independence, maize output has averaged between 180,000 tons in 1990 and 504,662 tons in 1998, fluctuating according to the intensity of the conflict. Maize production improved substantially as a result of the end of the war and better rains, reaching 720,275 tons in 2005. As a result of better rainfall and the increased area under cultivation, Angola's cereal import requirement dropped from 800,000 tons in 2004/05 to 701,000 tons in 2005/06, according to UN estimates. However, following a poor harvest in 2006 FAO forecast that Angola's cereal import requirement would rise to 847,000 tons in 2006/07.

Cotton was formerly one of the most promising products of Angola, and was both a concessionary and an African cultivation. In 1974 production of seed (unginned) cotton reached 104,000 metric tons. Organized planters in the Cuanza-Sul province were responsible for a large increase in mechanized production, and an increasing part of production was processed in Angola. The collapse of European-owned plantations reduced production of seed cotton, and in 2005 production was just 5,600 tons.

Prior to independence, sugar production was controlled by three Portuguese companies, and output of raw sugar was about 85,000 metric tons per year from annual sugar-cane production of just under 1m. tons. Following independence, the main sugar-cane plantations were reorganized as workers' co-operatives, with Cuban management and assistance. Production of raw sugar declined sharply. The withdrawal of Cuban personnel by 1991 led to further deterioration in the sector. Production of raw sugar stood at 32,000 tons in 2003, while sugar-cane production totalled an estimated 360,000 tons in 2005. Nearly all sugar for domestic consumption is now imported. In recent years the Angolan Government has sought private-sector investment for the rehabilitation of sugar production in Dombe Grande, near Benguela; the Government also planned to rehabilitate the sugar-cane plantations before their eventual privatization.

Cassava is the main Angolan crop in terms of volume produced, and is the staple food of the majority of the population. Most of the crop is consumed domestically, with no transaction above the local market level. Production rose from an estimated 6.6m. metric tons in 2004 to 8.6m. tons in 2005. The cultivation of bananas is being increased in the lower reaches of the rivers north of Luanda and of the Cuvo river. Estimated output was 300,000 tons in 2005.

Exports of palm oil totalled 4,400 metric tons in 1974, but ceased shortly after independence. According to FAO, total production of palm kernels was estimated at 280,000 tons in 2005, producing 53,000 tons of palm oil and 7,428 tons of palm kernel oil. Tobacco grows well on the formerly white-owned farms in the central and southern provinces of Benguela, Huíla and Namibe, with an estimated output of 3,300 tons in 2005. Other commodities (such as rice, sorghum, beans, tropical and temperate fruit, cocoa and groundnuts) are testimony to the agricultural potential of Angola.

Livestock, Forestry and Fisheries

Livestock-raising is concentrated in southern and central Angola, owing to the prevalence of the tsetse fly and the poor quality of the natural pastures in the north of the country. Some two-thirds of all cattle are found in Huíla province alone. The modern ranching sector, established by the Portuguese, was nationalized following independence, and has subsequently been adversely affected by civil war and drought. Meat shortages are prevalent in all cities, and imports of meat are indispensable. In 2005, according to FAO, Angola had only about 4.2m. head of cattle, 2.1m. goats, 780,000m. pigs and 340,000 sheep. (These figures appear to be inflated: the full extent of damage to the livestock industry in the civil war may not have been taken into account.)

Angola possesses important forestry resources, especially in the Cabinda, Moxico, Luanda and Cuanza-Norte provinces. Cabinda, in particular, has some valuable indigenous species, such as African sandalwood, rosewood and ebony. Softwood plantations of eucalyptus and cypress are used for fuel and grow along the Benguela railway and near Benguela, where they are used for wood pulp and paper manufacture. Exports of timber, however, ceased at independence. As in other sectors, output of logs fell sharply after independence, from over 550,000 cu m in 1973 to some 40,000 cu m in the early 1980s. Output recovered in the mid-1980s, but in 2005 it amounted to only an estimated 45,900 cu m.

The fishery industry is mainly centred around Namibe, Tombua and Benguela. However, the industry has suffered from the withdrawal of most Portuguese trawlers at independence. At present, few trawlers are operational, owing to lack of maintenance, while foreign trawlers operating off the coast have significantly depleted fish reserves in Angolan waters. Around two thirds of the annual catch is made by foreign and local trawlers, with the remainder being caught by around 20,000 local artisanal fishermen. The total catch declined from an average of 450,000 metric tons per year in the early 1970s to 240,000 tons in 2004.

MINERALS

Diamonds

Angola is believed to be one of the richest countries in mineral reserves of southern Africa, and is the second largest exporter of hydrocarbons in sub-Saharan Africa, after Nigeria. Angola's kimberlite pipes, first discovered in 1911, are believed to rank among the world's five richest deposits of embedded diamonds. In 2000 the country's diamond reserves were estimated at 40m. carats in alluvial deposits and 50m. carats in kimberlite rocks. The country's total output of diamonds was 2.4m. carats in 1974, but fell to about 300,000 carats following independence. Annual production remained below 1m. carats until 1989. During 1986–2000 full control of this sector was exercised by a state enterprise, the Empresa Nacional de Diamantes de Angola (ENDIAMA), which instigated a new national diamond policy, whereby mining was to be divided into blocks, to be exploited under production-sharing agreements with foreign concessionaires. Following the ratification of the Lusaka Accord in 1994, ENDIAMA announced plans to increase official diamond production to more than 2m. carats per year. Annual output reached 3.8m. carats in 1999, and increased to 5.1m. carats in 2001. Several new diamond fields have been explored in recent years. Annual diamond production was estimated by the Government at 7.0m. carats in 2005 and 9.7m. carats in 2006. ENDIAMA forecast that production would increase to 10m. carats in 2007 and to 19m. carats by 2010. In 2006 Angola was the world's fourth largest diamond producer, after Botswana, Russia and South Africa, and the world's fifth largest diamond producer by value.

Figures of diamond output have been deceptive, since a significant proportion of the real production has been mined and smuggled by UNITA, which partially controlled the diamond-producing area. Official sales of diamonds reached US $250m. in 1992, but reached only one-quarter of that level following the resumption of the civil war in late 1992, when diamond-mining areas again came under UNITA control. In 2000 official revenue from diamond exports increased significantly, to an estimated $739m., principally as a result of the restructuring of the diamond industry in Angola (see below), but declined slightly, to $688m., in 2001. However, the share of the formal sector in these exports is estimated to have increased from $367m. to $442m. Overall, losses incurred from the informal mining of diamonds (previously estimated at some $2m. daily) were believed to have been reduced to less than $1m. daily by 2001, as a consequence of gains by the Angolan armed forces in UNITA-controlled mining areas. A report issued by the diamond-producing Angolan Selling Corporation (ASCORP, see below) in mid-2002 indicated that annual profits in the diamond industry had fallen by some 87%, owing to a decline in demand. However, since UNITA surrendered control of its mines following the April 2002 peace agreement and the subsequent lifting of UN sanctions, official diamond exports have risen sharply, reaching an estimated $1,089m. in 2005, for which the Government earned $130m. in tax revenue.

In November 1996 ENDIAMA granted permission for UNITA representatives to commence negotiations with foreign corporations concerning the exploration and mining of diamond reserves in areas under de facto UNITA control. UNITA established its own legal mining company, the Sociedade Geral das Minas, which was awarded two prospecting concessions; UNITA was also party to two agreements signed in 1997 between ENDIAMA and foreign companies. However, following the fall, in May 1997, of UNITA's ally, the President of Zaire (now the Democratic Republic of the Congo—DRC), Mobutu Sese Seko, the Government launched several military offensives against UNITA-controlled mines, recovering about 10% of UNITA's productive areas. The fall, in October of that year, of another of UNITA's allies, the President of the Republic of the Congo, Pascal Lissouba, made unofficial mineral production increasingly difficult for UNITA, as lines of transport were severed. By the time of Savimbi's death in February 2002, UNITA-controlled mining areas were producing diamonds worth no more than an estimated US $120m. per year.

Under the terms of the agreement with ENDIAMA, De Beers began prospecting for alluvial and kimberlite diamonds in five areas of the country in May 1997. In May 2001 De Beers announced that it had suspended its activities and investments in Angola and in October 2002 the company announced that it would take the Government to international arbitration on three separate issues: an unpaid loan of US $50m., which had risen in value to $92m. by mid-2004; the Government's failure to honour a marketing contract for all diamonds produced in the Cuango valley; and the cancelling of three large prospecting licences on which De Beers had already spent $32m. in prospecting operations. After a temporary halt to the action, De Beers restarted arbitration in July 2003, and hearings held in Brazil during September and October were suspended after running out of time, with no final ruling having been reached. Arbitration proceedings were finally settled in the European courts in July 2004, after which De Beers began negotiations with the Government to restart operations in Angola. In May 2005 De Beers finally reached an agreement with the Government to resume operations in Angola, and in June it signed a new contract with ENDIAMA to prospect for kimberlite in a 3,000-sq-km area of north-eastern Angola. In January 2007 De Beers was awarded three new 3,000-sq-km concessions in Lunda-Norte province.

Other South African, Canadian, Brazilian, Portuguese and Russian interests were also involved in exploration activities. In conjunction with ENDIAMA, a Russian diamond corporation, Almazy Rossii-Sakha (Alrosa), opened a processing mill at the Catoca diamond field in north-eastern Angola in 1998. Covering an area of more than 660 ha, the Catoca kimberlite has been estimated to contain potential diamond reserves of up to 200m. carats, which would establish it as one of the world's largest deposits of diamonds. By 2003 the field produced 40% of all official Angolan diamond sales, and was the world's fourth largest diamond mine. Alrosa has stated its intention to upgrade Catoca, doubling the value of the field's output to US $350m. A Canadian mining company, DiamondWorks, also commenced commercial production in nearby alluvial diamond concessions, Camagico and Camatchia in the province of Lunda-Norte, in mid-1997. Operations were halted in 1998, after an attack by UNITA. Alrosa signed an agreement in December 2002 to resume operations at these two sites, in conjunction with a Portuguese consortium, Escom. The agreement was, however, contested by DiamondWorks. In all, Alrosa planned to invest $300m. in Angola in 2003–08. The end of hostilities was expected to open other areas to exploitation. A US company, American Mineral Fields, signed an agreement with ENDIAMA in April 2002 for two diamond licences in Lunda-Norte and Malanje provinces. In April 2003 a South African company, Trans Hex, also signed an agreement with ENDIAMA to operate the alluvial Luarica field in Lunda-Norte, which was previously exploited by UNITA. In May construction began on a new diamond ore mill at the Catoca kimberlite mine, increasing the annual value of output at the mine to $350m. The Catoca kimberlite mine, which started operations in 1996, was expected to produce 189m. carats, worth around $11,000m., during its 40-year lifespan.

The role played by the illicit diamond trade in perpetuating the civil war in Angola was highlighted in a high-profile campaign launched by the organization Global Witness, based in the United Kingdom. The resultant publicity forced De Beers to announce, in October 1999, that it would only purchase diamonds bearing government certificates of origin. The Government subsequently announced its decision to produce new certificates that were more difficult to tamper with. Pressure on the diamond industry was intensified following the publication, in March 2000, of a report by the UN Sanctions Committee, 'naming and shaming' the Presidents of Togo and Burkina Faso, as well as Belgian, Bulgarian and Ukrainian officials, accusing them of involvement in the illicit diamond trade and of providing military assistance to UNITA. As a result, the Diamond High Council in Antwerp, Netherlands, entered into an origin-verification agreement with the Angolan Government. Moreover, De Beers announced a complete restructuring of its own operations. In December 2002 the Angolan Government announced its participation in the Kimberley Process Certification Scheme, an international initiative that aims to identify the source mine of each diamond. Under the scheme, the Ministry of Geology and Mines was to issue unique certificates for Angolan diamonds.

Furthermore, in early 2000 a complete restructuring of the industry was initiated with the creation of a new state diamond monopoly, the Sociedade de Comercialização de Diamantes (SODIAM). The role of ENDIAMA was reduced to that of a prospecting company, retaining its joint ventures with foreign producers. All buying and marketing was transferred to the newly created ASCORP, a joint venture between SODIAM (which holds a 51% stake), the Israeli diamond trader, Lev Leviev, a Belgian company, Trans Africa Investment Services (TAIS), and members of President dos Santos's family. All existing marketing licences were terminated, and operators were given 30 days to sign new agreements with ASCORP. In April 2003 the Government finally abolished ASCORP's monopoly, and in August cancelled its marketing contract because of non-compliance with contractual obligations. Diamond companies had been extremely unhappy in their dealings with ASCORP, resulting in Brazil's Oderbrecht selling its entire stake in Angolan diamond concessions, and the rescinding of ASCORP's monopoly was hailed as a major step in the liberalization of Angola's diamond industry. The Government also approved plans in March 2003 to create a new company, ENDIAMA Prospecção e Produção, which was to develop a level of skills similar to that acquired by SONANGOL in the petroleum sector (see below). In March 2005 the new company announced its first project to develop a diamond mine at Camanjanja in north-eastern Lunda-Norte, with an eventual production of around 7,000 carats per year.

In October 2003 ENDIAMA signed a deal with three Angolan companies for the Cacolo alluvial diamond licence in Lunda-Norte province in which it would hold a 31% stake, and in November it agreed an alluvial licence in the diamond-rich Cuango area. In December the Angolan authorities stepped up their efforts to centralize and strengthen government control over Angola's historically chaotic diamond industry by establishing a new security agency, the Corpo de Segurança de Diamantes (CSD). The CSD was to be run by the domestic intelligence services, the Serviços de Informações (SINFO), and was to monitor, store, classify and transport diamonds, as well as set up new legal instruments. In late 2003 the Angolan security forces came under criticism from human rights groups for their violent eviction of hundreds of *garimpeiros* (miners) who had come into Angola illegally from the neighbouring DRC to mine alluvial diamonds. By early 2005 an estimated 256,000 foreign miners had been expelled from Angola's diamond zones.

In January 2005 ENDIAMA signed a three-year prospecting contract with two private Angolan companies, Hipergesta and Ngunga, and in February production started at the Muanga diamond mine in north-eastern Lunda-Norte under a partnership between ENDIAMA, Sociedade de Desenvolvimento Mineiro (SDM) and a private Angolan company, Di Oro. In November construction work began at the Camatchia and Camagico kimberlite mines on a US $199m. plant which was to process 1m. metric tons of raw material each year. In December Canada's Moydow Mines International signed an agreement with ENDIAMA to prospect for kimberlites in Lunda-Sul province. In mid-November the Catoca kimberlite mine expanded production following the opening of a new $90m. processing plant, which increased production at the mine to 5.5m. carats per year, worth around $400m. In April 2006 ENDIAMA entered into a five-year joint venture with Alrosa to explore for diamonds in the Cacolo area of Lunda-Sul province. By the end of 2006 there were 14 formal-sector mines in operation in Angola. More than 100 mining licences have been granted by the Government since 2002, most of which cover small areas, but many of these have not yet been developed.

In November 2006 the Government created the pan-African Association of Diamond Producing Nations (ADPA), to be headed by Angola with its headquarters in Luanda. The association's main objective will be to co-ordinate the policies of Africa's diamond producers to protect international prices, boost foreign investment in Africa's mining sector, and capture a greater share of profits.

Petroleum

The petroleum industry is the principal economic mainstay of the Government, with petroleum extraction, refining and distribution constituting Angola's most important economic activity. Output of petroleum expanded rapidly during the 1980s, from an average of 155,000 barrels per day (b/d) in late 1982 to 550,000 b/d in 1992. Following a small decline in 1993 due to the war, production again increased consistently, reaching an estimated 740,000 b/d in 2001. Output increased to an average of 981,000 b/d in 2004, following the start of production, in early 2002, at the Girassol field operated by Total (formerly TotalFinaElf, formed by the merger of Total, Petrofina and Elf Aquitaine). Production reached 1.2m. b/d in 2005 and an estimated 1.7m. b/d in 2006, and was forecast to reach 2m. b/d by the end of 2007 and over 2.5m. b/d by 2011. Total FDI was forecast to amount to US $26,000m. in 2003–07. Angola's export earnings from petroleum and petroleum products also increased steadily, to an estimated $22,583m. in 2005. According to the IMF, between 1998 and 2002 the Angolan Government received petroleum revenues of $15,000m. Prior to 2006 Angola was not a member of the Organization of the Petroleum Exporting Countries (OPEC), and as a result the country was not constrained by production quotas. In 2005 hydrocarbons accounted for 68% of total exports and around 90% of state revenues. In 2005 the petroleum and gas sectors accounted for 63% of GDP. Estimates of proven recoverable reserves of crude petroleum have more than doubled since 1997, to 13,000m.–16,000m. barrels in 2006.

In 1955 the Belgian-owned Petrofina discovered petroleum in the Cuanza valley. A petroleum company, Fina Petróleos de Angola (PETRANGOL), was subsequently established, under the joint ownership of the Angolan Government and Petrofina interests. PETRANGOL constructed a refinery in the suburbs of Luanda. The greatest impetus to expansion, however, came from the Cabinda Gulf Oil Company (CABGOC), which discovered petroleum off shore at Cabinda in 1966. After independence SONANGOL was established in 1976 to manage all fuel production and distribution and in 1978 was authorized to acquire a 51% interest in all petroleum companies operating in Angola, although the management of operations was to remain under the control of foreign companies. In the late 1970s SONANGOL divided the Angolan coast, excluding Cabinda, into 13 exploration blocks, which were leased to foreign companies under production-sharing agreements (PSAs). Although CABGOCs Cabinda offshore fields (which are operated by the US Chevron Corporation) remain the core of the Angolan petroleum industry (accounting for about two-thirds of total output), production was buoyant at other concessions close to the enclave, held by Agip, Total, Conoco and Chevron. In addition, SONANGOL itself operates a production block.

In 1992 Elf Aquitaine acquired a 10% interest in CABGOC, reducing SONANGOL's share to 41%, with Chevron holding 39% and Agip 10%. Onshore, Petrofina remained the operator. SONANGOL took a 51% interest in Petrofina's original Cuanza valley operations, including the Luanda refinery, whose capacity meets most domestic requirements. SONANGOL also had a 51% interest in an onshore venture by Petrofina in the River Congo estuary area, in which Texaco held a 16% share. A lingering maritime border dispute between Angola and the Republic of the Congo was settled in March 2002, which would allow ChevronTexaco (known as Chevron from May 2005) to begin prospecting in the area.

In recent years attention has focused on deep-water blocks (numbered 14–33), which have produced promising results. In August 1997 Elf Aquitaine announced the discovery of one of Africa's largest ever petroleum fields, Girassol, with estimated reserves of 3,500m. barrels, off the Angolan coast. In the same year the company discovered another giant deep-sea oilfield in Block 17, Dália. Girassol started production in early 2002 and contracts were finally awarded for Dália in late 2003. Production on the 1,000m.-barrel oilfield started in December 2006, and was expected to rise to 240,000 b/d by mid-2007. A total of 15 discoveries had been made in Block 17 by Total by mid-2003, including two in that year, Acácia and Horténsia. In November Block 17's Jasmin oilfield commenced production, reaching 15,000 b/d by the end of 2003. Production reached 50,000 b/d in 2004, raising production on the entire Girassol project to 230,000 b/d. Production also started in December 1999 at the company's Kuito field. However, Total's relations with the Government have been strained by France's ongoing judicial proceedings against Pierre Falcone for his alleged involvement in supplying the Angolan Government with arms in the early 1990s (see Recent History). In response, the Angolan Government refused to renew the company's production licence for Block 3 after it expired in late 2004, and rescinded the company's further exploration rights in Block 17. In 1998 Exxon announced a large petroleum discovery, Kizomba, in Block 15. Total reserves were estimated at 1,000m. barrels. Further discoveries were made in 1999 and 2000. Exxon began construction on the US $4,300m. project in June 2002, and production on the Kizomba-A project started in August 2004, one year ahead of schedule, with a plateau rate of 250,000 b/d. Production on Kizomba-B began in late 2005. Both fields were producing 550,000 b/d from recoverable reserves estimated at 2,000m. barrels. Combined with production of 80,000 b/d from the Xikomba field in the same block, this has meant that Exxon has overtaken Chevron as Angola's largest petroleum operator. Production from a third field, Kizomba-C, which includes the Batuque, Saxi and Mondo fields, was expected to begin in 2007.

In 2000 SONANGOL and BP announced the discovery of two petroleum wells in Block 18. BP's Greater Plutônio project in deep-water Block 18 was, however, only approved by SONANGOL in March 2002, after a dispute between SONANGOL and BP over the latter's announced policy of disclosing its revenue-sharing payments in Angola. The project was expected to begin in mid-2007 with an eventual capacity of 250,000 b/d. Three significant deposits were also discovered in Block 14, exploited by SONANGOL.

In June 2003 two new discoveries were announced in the ultra-deep maritime zone north-west of Luanda, the Gindungo-1 field in Block 32 (operated by Total) and the Saturno well on Block 31 (operated by BP). The discoveries were a boost for foreign companies after the disappointing results in other ultra-deep-water blocks, namely ExxonMobil's Block 33 and Norsk Hydro's Block 34 where non-commercial finds were discovered. Also in June ChevronTexaco awarded contracts for the development of its Benguela, Belize, Lobito and Tombôco (BBLT) project in deep-water Block 14. In January 2006 production started on the Benguela and Belize fields, followed by the Lobito and Tombôco fields in June 2006. Chevron forecasts that production will rise to 200,000 b/d by 2009. In February 2005 SONANGOL awarded the stake previously belonging to Total in shallow-water Block 3/80 to a joint venture between Sonangol and the China Petroleum Company (Sinopec)—SONANGOL Sinopec International (SSI)—and in March the Ministry of Petroleum also approved the transfer of SONANGOL's 50% stake in Block 18 to SSI. In May a group of petroleum companies paid a US $4.5m. signature bonus for shallow-water Block 10, which would be operated by Devon Energy. In October 2005 ExxonMobil announced two new discoveries in deep-water Block 15, Kakocha and Tchihumba, the 15th and 16th finds in the block. In November the Xikomba oilfield (with total recoverable reserves of 100m. barrels) in ExxonMobil's Block 15 began production, reaching 80,000 b/d by the end of 2005. It was estimated that these new fields would double Angolan production to 2m. b/d by 2008 or 2009, although the decline in older fields could reduce this rate of production. In an effort to maintain the increase in production, the Angolan Government was planning to relicense existing oil blocks on the expiry of their concessions. In November 2005 SONANGOL put up for tender exploration licences for shallow-water Blocks 1, 5 and 6, and deep-water Block 26, and relinquished acreages in deep-water Blocks 15, 17 and 18. In December SONANGOL announced that 29 companies had prequalified to bid for these licences, and in April and May 2006 SONANGOL awarded exploration licences for all seven blocks. Operatorship of Blocks 1, 5 and 15 was awarded to Tullow Oil of the United Kingdom, Vaalco Energy of the USA and Agip-ENI of Italy, respectively, while Brazil's PETROBRÁS secured large stakes in and operatorship of blocks 6, 18 and 26. The China Petroleum Corporation (Sinopec) became the largest equity partner, but not the operator, in Block 18, and acquired large stakes in Blocks 15 and 17 in partnership with SONANGOL. Total succeeded to win back the acreages on Block 17 which it had been forced to relinquish in 2005, although the award of the licence has been delayed by a dispute over the size of the signature bonus Total must pay. In October 2006 the Government created five new blocks in Angola's ultra-deep north-west, an area west of the existing ultra-deep-water Blocks 31–34 known as 'ultra-ultra-deep-water'. The five blocks, which have been designated Blocks 46–50, are due to be auctioned in a licensing round, which is expected to take place in late 2007.

The major portion of Angola's petroleum is exported to the USA and the People's Republic of China in its crude form, although the Luanda refinery processes 37,000 b/d of crude petroleum. The Government announced in April 1998 that it intended to invest US $10m. to upgrade and increase the capacity of the Luanda refinery to 60,000 b/d. There were also plans to construct a new refinery, capable of processing 240,000 b/d at Lobito, which would process oil from the Dália and Kuito fields. After lengthy delays, in March 2006 the Government signed a consortium agreement with SONANGOL and Sinopec to build and operate the refinery. Construction of the $3,500m. refinery was due to be carried out by the Republic of Korea's Samsung, and the refinery was due to be operational by 2010. However, in March 2007 the Government announced that it had suspended negotiations with Sinopec after both parties were unable to agree on the kind of petroleum products to produce at the refinery. SONANGOL then planned to complete the project on its own.

In 1998 the Government announced its intention to commence the production of liquefied natural gas (LNG), from a plant in Soyo. In March 2002 ChevronTexaco, SONANGOL, TotalFinaElf, BP, Norsk Hydro and ExxonMobil signed an agreement for this project, in which ChevronTexaco was to hold 32% of the equity, SONANGOL 20% and the other companies 12% each. By 2006 Chevron had increased its stake to 36.4%, with SONANGOL holding 22.8%, and BP and Total each holding 13.6%. In April 2007 Agip-ENI signed a memorandum of understanding to acquire the remaining 13.6% stake in the project from ExxonMobil. The $4,000m. project was expected to start production in 2010, at a rate of 5m. metric tons per year, eventually rising to 8m. tons per year. In December 2004 operations began in ChevronTexaco's $1,900m. Sanha-Bombôco gas and condensate field in Block 0, which was expected to produce 100,000 b/d of liquid hydrocarbons by 2007. Following the cessation of hostilities with UNITA and the decline in separatist activity in Cabinda, there were also plans to boost onshore petroleum exploration in Angola, particularly in the provinces of Cabinda and Zaire.

On 1 January 2007 Angola was formally admitted as OPEC's 12th member, becoming the organization's first new member since 1975. The terms of Angola's membership were still being negotiated in early 2007, but Angola has not yet been given a production quota in recognition of the fact that the country's output is rising rapidly.

Other Mining

Iron mining began in 1956 and production averaged 700,000–800,000 metric tons annually in the 1960s from mines in the Huambo and Bié provinces. The Cassinga mines in the Huíla province, which have proven reserves of more than 1,000m. tons of high-grade haematite, were the decisive factor in increasing production to around 40m. tons per year. However, they have been inoperative since 1975. In 1981 a state-owned iron company, Empresa Nacional de Ferro de Angola (FERRANGOL), was created. Angola holds considerable ore production stockpiles, which await the eventual rehabilitation of rail links to the coast. In October 2006 the Government launched a programme to encourage foreign investors to develop reserves of iron and manganese at both the Cassinga mine and at the Cassala-Kitungo deposits, which are believed to contain 200m. tons of iron ore.

Reserves of copper have been identified in the Uíge province, and other deposits are known to exist in the Namibe, Huíla and Moxico provinces. In 2006 a British mining company, Silverpritex, started mining for copper in Cachoeiras de Binga, Cuanza-Sul province, while important deposits of feldspar have been found in the southern province of Huíla. In May 2005 a US-based company, Mayfair Mining and Minerals, Inc., was awarded a 70% stake in the 1,300-sq-km Ucua licence in western Bengo province, where it would prospect for emeralds, aquamarines and minerals. Unexploited reserves of phosphate rock exist in the Zaire and Cabinda provinces, and deposits of uranium have been found along the border with Namibia.

POWER

Angola's power potential exceeds its needs, with an estimated hydroelectric potential of 15,000 MW. However, since independence there have been no significant additions to Angola's power-generating capacity. As a result, power supply is erratic and the situation is exacerbated by the fragmentation of the market into several independent producers, and the absence of a national grid. In 2002 Angola had 205 MW of installed hydroelectric capacity and 412 MW of thermal capacity, but several new projects boosted generation capacity to 1,200 MW by the end of 2006. In April 2007 the Minister of Energy and Water, José Maria Botelho de Vasconcelos, announced government plans to invest $2,000m. in the national power grid over the next five years.

Most of Angola's energy output is of hydroelectric origin, and there is an impressive dam on the Cuanza at Cambambe, constructed and operated by a Brazilian company; its generating capacity stood at 180 MW in 2006. Luanda's industries are the main beneficiaries of power from the dam. There is also an 18-MW dam at Mabubas on the Dande river. Construction of the Capanda dam in Malanje province began in 1985 but was repeatedly halted due to the war, only resuming in 2000. In January 2004 the first 130-MW turbine started operations, supplying power to Luanda and other large towns in north-central Angola. A second 130-MW turbine opened in June 2004, doubling capacity. In November 2005 construction began on a new 260-MW generating unit at Capanda. Scheduled for completion in July 2007, this second construction phase would double the dam's generating capacity to 520 MW. Separate projects were also underway to construct new power lines linking Cambambe with Luanda. In January 2007 the Government approved a US $218m. 15-month project, led by Brazil's Oderbrecht, to construct new power lines between the Capanda dam and Luanda. The same month the 30-MW Caminhos de Ferro de Angola power station started supplying power to Luanda. During the first half of 2007, France's Alstom was scheduled to start construction of a $10m., 35-MW power plant to supply Luanda.

Prior to independence Lobito and Benguela were provided with electricity by two privately owned dams, the Lomaum and the Biópio, both on the Catumbela river. The Gove dam, in the Huambo course of the Cunene river, was completed with South African capital, but was destroyed during the war. New power facilities for the dam were to be studied in the early 2000s, in conjunction with the Namibia Power Corporation (NamPower). In November 2003 the Russian company Alrosa commenced construction of the 16-MW Chicapa hydroelectric project, located on the Chicapa river in north-eastern Angola, which would provide power to Saurimo and the nearby Catoca diamond mine. Production at the first 4-MW turbine started in January 2007, and was expected to reach 16 MW by May. Further south, the 51-MW Matala dam serves Lubango, Namibe and Cassinga. This project was only a very small part of an ambitious Angolan-Namibian scheme for damming the Cunene river, thus providing Namibia, which is deficient in power and water, with cheap electricity and a permanent water supply. However, the construction of a major power station at the Ruacaná Falls, where the Cunene river reaches the Namibian border, has been impeded by the military and political instability in the region, although the first stage became operational in 1977. The potential annual output of the scheme was provisionally assessed at 1,000m. kWh. It was announced in December 2002 that feasibility studies were to be carried out, in conjunction with NamPower, for the construction of a hydroelectric dam on the Cunene, although the dam was heavily opposed by environmental campaigners. In June 2006 the Angolan press reported that Russia's Technopromexport planned to invest US $1,000m. in the construction of two new power stations at Nyanga (with a capacity of 450 MW) and Lauka.

INDUSTRY

Angola's industrial activity is centred on construction materials, petroleum refining, food processing, textiles, equipment for the petroleum industry, steel, chemicals, electrical goods and vehicle assembly. Angola's manufacturing sector has considerable potential, in view of the country's abundance of raw materials, such as petroleum and iron ore. During 1962–70 manufacturing output expanded at an average rate of 19% per year. The food-processing, brewing and tobacco industries were the most developed. The textile industry flourished after the ban on the creation of industries competing against metropolitan manufacturers was repealed in 1966. Cotton was the principal fibre used, and in 1973 textile industries occupied second place in Angola. However, output from Angola's industrial sector has dwindled to a fraction of pre-independence levels, owing to civil unrest, shortages of raw materials, unreliability of power supplies and disruption of the transport infrastructure. Most branches of the manufacturing sector continued to contract during the 1980s. Official figures showed manufacturing output in 1985 to be only one-half of its 1973 level. In 2005 manufacturing and construction contributed 3.6% and 3.3% of GDP, respectively.

Following the withdrawal of Portuguese owners, many enterprises were brought under state control and ownership, and by the mid-1980s about 80% of the industrial work-force was employed in state-owned companies. Under the SEF, introduced in January 1988, legislation was reformed, granting state enterprises autonomous control of management. A new foreign investment code was also introduced, which aimed to increase the rights of foreign companies regarding operation, transfer of profits, taxation, etc., while, in return, foreign investors were expected to expand the transfer of technical and managerial skills to Angolan industrial personnel. Under the new code, however, many sectors remained closed to foreign investment: these included the postal and telecommunications sectors, the news media, air transport and shipping, defence and security, and state banking. The Government's privatization programme was approved in 2001, but little progress has been made. In April 2003 the Government introduced several laws, which replaced the previous investment regime. The new laws aimed to promote foreign investment in Angola, by allowing companies to repatriate profit, and to bring the legal framework for private-sector operations in the country in line with international practice.

After independence, activity in the building trade effectively ceased, except for the reconstruction of a number of bridges destroyed in the conflict. However, following the end of the civil war in 2002 a major construction boom began in Luanda. In 2005 the US $43m. headquarters of the AAA insurance company and the $70m. US embassy were inaugurated, and several more skyscrapers opened in 2006, including SONANGOL's new headquarters. In December Luanda's first shopping centre, the $35m. Belas Shopping, opened for business. It was expected to attract up to 10,000 shoppers each day. Meanwhile, in May the Government announced plans to construct a new marketplace at Panguila, 18 km north of Luanda, to replace the Roque Santeiro Market. The work will be carried out by a Chinese construction firm, Jiangsu Construction Group, at a cost of $28m. However, the plan is being opposed by local traders who have threatened to boycott the new market because of its remote location from central Luanda and their main buyers. In November the Government launched a project, Programa de Reestruturação do Sistema de Logística e de Distribuição de Produtos Essenciais à População, to create a network of markets and shops across Angola selling basic goods at low prices. The project, which will cost an estimated $1,700m. over 2006–12, will involve the construction of 10,000 retail outlets, 16 municipal, suburban and rural markets, and 31 supermarkets (which will be known as 'Nosso Super'). Other projects under development include the 'Nova Vida' project in Luanda Sul district, which aims to build 2,500 luxury homes for civil servants; however, the forced eviction of more than 600 families from the proposed site has drawn criticism from humanitarian groups. The Luanda Waterfront Corporation is carrying out the redevelopment of Luanda's waterfront boulevard with office buildings, leisure centres, residential properties and hotels as part of a $2,000m., 13-year project. In March 2006 the Government announced that it would build 200,000 new homes by 2008 to meet the country's housing shortage.

The revival of the construction sector has spurred the revival of the main cement works, operated by the Empresa de Cimentos de Angola (Cimangola), in Luanda, and the sector should also benefit from the Capanda dam project. Nova Cimangola, a cement company formed as a public-private partnership with a Norwegian firm, Scancem, increased production from 182,000 metric tons in 1995 to 600,000 tons in 2002. The company planned to invest US $25m. in 2003–07, and by the end of 2005 it had increased production to 1.4m. tons per year. In January 2006 Portugal's second largest cement company, Secil, announced an investment of $100m. in the construction of a cement factory in Lobito. Operations were scheduled to start in 2009 with initial production of 600,000 tons per year, eventually rising to 1.7m. tons per year.

In March 2000 a Coca-Cola bottling plant, created as a US $36m. joint venture between the Angolan Government and Indol International (a subsidiary of South African Breweries), began production at Bom Jesus, some 60 km from Luanda. The plant, reportedly the first direct foreign investment in Angola for many years outside the petroleum and diamond sectors, employed some 400 people and produced 14m. cases in 2003. Another $6m. plant was subsequently built in Huíla province. Other plants were being considered in Benguela, Huambo and Cabinda, where Coca-Cola was to invest $50m. in 2003–08, in addition to the $130m. invested in Angola between 1998 and 2003. A Portuguese soft drinks company, Sumol, opened another $25m. plant in Luanda in December 2002. In April 2002 the Government and a German company, Ferrostaal, also signed an agreement to construct an aluminium smelter. In 2003 a Chinese company, Guangdong Overseas Construction Corporation, invested $7.2m. to construct a motorcycle assembly plant, the first of its kind in Angola. In January 2005 Volkswagen announced it was constructing a vehicle assembly plant and dealer network for Volkswagen and its subsidiary, Skoda, in Angola. The $48m. project was to employ up to 2,500 people and was expected to start operations by 2007. However, the project's future was in doubt when its director was dismissed after being implicated in a major corruption scandal at Volkswagen in Germany. In late 2005 Troller Jeeps announced it was constructing a vehicle assembly plant in Viana on the outskirts of Luanda. The plant was scheduled to begin operations in March 2006 and would produce 40 jeeps per month, rising to 80 in 2006 and 120 in 2007.

TRANSPORT AND COMMUNICATIONS

Angola's colonial administration made a considerable effort to improve the communications network, and in 1974 there were 8,317 km of tarred roads in a total road network of 72,323 km. These efforts were continued by the Government, in part to facilitate military transport. In 2001 Angola had 51,429 km of roads, of which about 10.4% were paved. Bus transportation was also fairly developed following independence, but from the early 1980s guerrilla warfare dramatically curtailed most road transportation. In 1988 an emergency programme was launched to rehabilitate the transport infrastructure. Under the programme, which was to cost a total of US $340m., $142m. was allocated to the rehabilitation of roads and $121m. to the rehabilitation of the Luanda and Namibe railways. The programme was also to include work on the ports of Luanda and Namibe, and on Saurino and Luena airports. However, in 1997 the Government estimated that 80% of the country's road network was in disrepair and estimated the total cost of rebuilding roads and bridges destroyed during the civil conflict at $4,000m. A substantial programme of road and bridge rehabilitation was announced in 2000, and further programmes followed in 2002 and 2005. In 2006–07 the Government planed to repair or rebuild approximately 1,300 bridges that were destroyed during the civil war. In February 2007 the national road institute, the Instituto Nacional de Estradas de Angola (INEA), announced that over 1,200 km of new roads would be built in Angola during 2007 as part of plans to connect all of Angola's 18 provincial capitals by asphalt roads by the end of 2008. In addition, in early 2007 work began on a $128m. project to rehabilitate 238 km of roads linking Cala, Ganda and Catengue in Huambo and Benguela provinces.

Prior to independence the Portuguese constructed a rail network totalling 2,722 km. However, by the end of the war in April 2002 the network had almost entirely ceased to function, with only small sections of line still operating along the coast. Railways served a dual purpose, to open the interior and to provide export channels for Zambia and the land-locked province of Katanga in the DRC, which export large volumes of minerals. Hence, all railway lines run towards the coast. The volume of freight handled on Angolan railways was 9,272,883 metric tons in 1973, but the annual total declined to 135,000 tons in 1994, only to recover slowly from the late 1990s (242,000 tons by 2001).

The 479-km Luanda railway, chiefly for local goods traffic and passengers, was the only line functioning with a degree of regularity during the late 1980s, albeit at a low level of activity. In April 1997 work was completed on the reconstruction of the 180-km rail link between Luanda and Dondo, in Cuanza-Norte province, which had been closed for seven years owing to the hostilities. Rehabilitation of the Luanda railway, which was damaged by the destruction of bridges by UNITA prior to 1991 and subsequently by further hostilities, commenced in November 2003. The project was being financed by the People's Republic of China, and was expected to be completed by the end of 2007. The 907-km Namibe railway, in the south, was assuming a new importance as a carrier of iron ore from Cassinga before the security situation resulted in the closure of the mines. In 2006 work began on a US $1,200m. project to rehabilitate and modernize the line. The project was to replace 856 km of track, build 73 new stations and purchase new locomotives, and was scheduled for completion by the end of 2007. Once complete, the line was expected to carry 2m. passengers and 15m. metric tons of goods per year. In February 2005 the President of Namibia, Sam Nujoma, announced that the construction of a new railway line to connect the Namibian port of Walvis Bay with Namibe had begun.

The 1,336-km Benguela railway was of international importance and was the strategic outlet for exports of copper and zinc from Zaire and Zambia, bypassing South Africa and providing the most direct link to the west coast. However, UNITA guerrilla attacks caused the suspension of all cross-border traffic after 1975. For the most part the domestic Lobito–Huambo section of the railway was maintained in operation, although at a reduced level. In April 2002 a 45-km section of the railway was finally opened in Huambo province. In April 2003 the Government announced that it planned to invest US $4,000m. in rebuilding the country's rail network, with the involvement of the private sector. By June tenders had already been invited from foreign companies for the existing transport corridors. Work began in February 2005 on the 11-year project, financed in part by a $2,000m. Chinese credit line, which involved the rehabilitation of Angola's three existing lines—from Lobito to the Zambian border, from Luanda to Malanje, and from Namibe to Menongue—as well as the construction of a new line along the coast linking Luanda, Lobito and Benguela. A feasibility study is also under way for a railway from Luanda to the northern enclave of Cabinda, via a new road bridge that is to be built over the Congo River. The Government anticipated that the Namibe and Benguela lines would be fully operational by the end of 2007. In the long term, the Government plans to connect Angola's rail network to those of Namibia and South Africa.

Internal air transport is well developed, with a network of good airports and rural landing strips, and has become the only moderately safe means of transportation, owing to the insecurity on road and rail routes. The Chinese Government helped finance the modernization of Angola's only international airport in Luanda, and is carrying out the US $60m. construction of a second airport in Bom Jesus, 40 km east of Luanda, which is due for completion in 2010. In February 2007 the Government announced plans to rehabilitate 32 airports and aerodromes by the end of 2010.

Angola's main harbours are Lobito, Luanda and Namibe. Cabinda has become the principal loading port, with 7.6m. metric tons (mostly petroleum) handled in recent years, and is due to undergo extensive rehabilitation in 2007. Luanda port has steadily increased its traffic in recent years, increasing the volume of goods handled from 2.6m. tons in 2002 to 4.1m. tons in 2005. The port of Lobito handled 1.15m. tons in 2005, an increase of 44% from the previous year, while Namibe handled 292,000 tons in 2002. As the country exports very little except petroleum, unloaded goods account for about 85% of traffic south of Cabinda. Passenger traffic is now almost negligible. The state-owned shipping company, Angonave, which had been insolvent, was finally liquidated in April 2002. In July 2003 Angola's main general cargo terminal, Luanda Commercial Port, announced a US $90m. modernization programme. Over five years Nile Dutch Line would invest $18m. in one terminal, while Unicargas would invest $23m. in another. The tender for a third terminal, originally won by a consortium of Gestão de Fundos and Maersk, was withdrawn after a court upheld a complaint by a rival firm regarding irregularities in the bidding process. In August 2005 a fourth terminal, operated by the state-owned Unicargas company, came into operation in Luanda port, handling 244,000 tons of cargo per year. In 2006 the Government announced that a fifth terminal supporting mining activity was to be added. In February Luanda port's three terminal operators announced they would invest $131m. in 2006–10 to modernize the port, with the aim of boosting traffic to 5.3m. tons by 2010.

Angola's telephone communications network, which was badly damaged during the years of war, benefited from considerable investment in the late 1990s. After inter-state communications were re-established with Menongue in March 1997, only three provincial capitals remained without inter-state communications: Ndalatando, Mbanza-Kongo and Malanje. The first step in Angola Telecom's plans for improving and extending services was the recovery of some US $18m. in service payments owed by government agencies. The next step was to begin an infrastructure investment plan, at a cost of $80m., focusing initially on the cities of Luanda and Benguela. Angola Telecom's infrastructure investment aims for compatibility with Africa One, the fibre-optic cable system, worth $1,600m., that will serve the African continent. In January 2001 the state monopoly on telecommunications was ended, and in March a new cellular communications network was inaugurated.

In December 2002 a second national operator, Mundo Star-Tel, was licensed, and in February 2004 Telecom Namibia purchased a 44% stake in the company, promising to invest N $19m. (US $14m.) over the next three years to install high-speed networks. In September 2003 Angola Telecom launched an ADSL broadband internet service in Luanda. A rival broadband internet service was introduced by a new cable television company in 2004. In late 2003 Movicel, the mobile cellular telephone subsidiary of Angola Telecom, awarded a contract to Nortel Networks of Canada to install a new network, the code division multiple access, that is compatible with the mobile telephone systems used in North America. Movicel's competitor, UNITEL, uses the Global System for Mobile Communications, which is common in Europe. Both companies planned to extend mobile phone coverage to all 18 of Angola's provincial capitals by the end of 2005. In 2006 UNITEL had 2.1m. subscribers, and planned to increase this to 3m. by the end of 2007 following a US $250m. network upgrade; in comparison, Movicel had around 500,000 subscribers at the end of 2006. In 2006 Angola had around 2.6m. mobile phone users, a large increase compared with just 20,000 when the first mobile phones were introduced in 1995. According to a survey in 2006, 75% of Luanda's inhabitants over the age of 15 owned a mobile phone.

TRADE AND FOREIGN PAYMENTS

The principal exported commodities in 2005 were crude petroleum (which, at US $22,583m., accounted for 93.7% of total export earnings) and diamonds ($1,092m., or 4.5%). The USA was Angola's principal customer in 2006 (38.6% of total exports), followed by the People's Republic of China (34.7%) and the European Union (EU—8.7%). The main sources of imports in 2005 were the EU (35.2%), South Korea (17.3%), the USA (14.3%) and South Africa (6.3%). In 2005 the total value of merchandise exports was $24,109m. and the value of merchandise imports was $8,353m., leaving a trade surplus of $15,756m., and a surplus of $5,138m. on the current account of the balance of payments. The country's large external debt was estimated by the World Bank at $11,755m. at the end of 2005, of which $9,428m. was medium- and long-term public debt. In 2005 the cost of debt-servicing was equivalent to 9.2% of the value of exports of goods and services.

In September 2003 an agreement was signed with Germany to cancel half of Angola's US $283m. debt, while in November Poland agreed to reduce Angola's $153m. debt (from Cold War arms sales) by 60%, to $61m., with the remaining 40% to be repaid from 2006. The same month the Brazilian Government agreed to reschedule Angola's $997m. debt, with payments stretching from 2005 to 2017. In March 2004 Angola agreed a $2,000m. oil-backed loan from China's Eximbank for infrastructure projects. The loan was repayable over 17 years with a five-year grace period. This was followed in April when SONANGOL agreed a $2,350m. loan from the United Kingdom's Standard Chartered Bank, the largest loan in Angola's history, for budgetary support, debt repayment and investment costs in Angola's ultra-deep-water blocks. In September 2005 the French bank, Calyon, arranged a $2,000m. syndicated loan for the Angolan Government to fund infrastructure development.

Economic relations with Portugal have developed since the conclusion of the Estoril peace agreement in 1991. In February 1992 Portugal agreed to lend US $325m. to enable Angola to import Portuguese goods. At the same time, it was agreed that Portugal would increase its purchases of petroleum from Angola. In November 2002 Portugal and Angola signed an agreement to restructure the latter's €2,200m. debt, at highly concessional interest rates, which was criticized by other donors. In August 2005 Angola signed an agreement with Portugal to reschedule its $958m. debt, under which it repaid $258m. immediately, with the remainder to be repaid in 25 equal annual instalments from 2009 onwards. Angola also agreed to pay $195m. to Portuguese banks, representing 35% of its debts to them, with the remainder of its debt to be written off. In April 2006 Angola started negotiations with the 'Paris Club' of official creditors to renegotiate its outstanding debts, and in December 2006 and January 2007 it repaid $2,300m. of debt, leaving an estimated $800m. in arrears, which the Government pledged to repay before the end of 2007. This has reduced Angola's total external debt stock to an estimated $10,700m. at the end of 2006.

Angola's inclusion in the African, Caribbean and Pacific (ACP) group of signatories of the third and fourth Lomé Conventions not only made more funds available from the EU, but also increased both the range and volume of its trading operations. In February 2003 Angola ratified the Cotonou Agreement (the successor to the fourth Lomé Convention), which had been concluded between the EU and the ACP states in June 2000. Angola participates fully in the Southern African Development Community, and has special responsibility for the co-ordination of energy development and conservation. In January 1999 Angola became a member of the Communauté économique des états de l'Afrique centrale.

Statistical Survey

Source (unless otherwise stated): Instituto Nacional de Estatística, Av. Ho Chi Minh, CP 1215, Luanda; tel. 222322776; e-mail ine@angonet.gn.apc.org.

Area and Population

AREA, POPULATION AND DENSITY

Area (sq km)	1,246,700*
Population (census results)	
30 December 1960	4,480,719
15 December 1970	
Males	2,943,974
Females	2,702,192
Total	5,646,166
Population (UN estimates at mid-year)	
2004	15,636,000
2005	16,095,000
2006	16,557,000
Density (per sq km) at mid-2006	13.3

* 481,354 sq miles.

Source: partly UN, *World Population Prospects: The 2006 Revision*.

DISTRIBUTION OF POPULATION BY PROVINCE
(provisional estimates, mid-1995)

	Area (sq km)	Population	Density (per sq km)
Luanda	2,418	2,002,000	828.0
Huambo	34,274	1,687,000	49.2
Bié	70,314	1,246,000	17.7
Malanje	87,246	975,000	11.2
Huíla	75,002	948,000	12.6
Uíge	58,698	948,000	16.2
Benguela	31,788	702,000	22.1
Cuanza-Sul	55,660	688,000	12.4
Cuanza-Norte	24,110	412,000	17.1
Moxico	223,023	349,000	1.6
Lunda-Norte	102,783	311,000	3.0
Zaire	40,130	247,000	6.2
Cunene	88,342	245,000	2.8
Cabinda	7,270	185,000	25.4
Bengo	31,371	184,000	5.9
Lunda-Sul	56,985	160,000	2.8
Cuando-Cubango	199,049	137,000	0.7
Namibe	58,137	135,000	2.3
Total	1,246,600	11,561,000	9.3

PRINCIPAL TOWNS
(population at 1970 census)

Luanda (capital)	480,613	Benguela	40,996
Huambo (Nova Lisboa)	61,885	Lubango (Sá da Bandeira)	31,674
Lobito	59,258	Malanje	31,559

Source: Direcção dos Serviços de Estatística.

Mid-2005 ('000, incl. suburbs, UN estimate): Luanda 2,766 (Source: UN, *World Urbanization Prospects: The 2005 Revision*).

BIRTHS AND DEATHS
(annual averages, UN estimates)

	1990–95	1995–2000	2000–05
Birth rate (per 1,000)	52.5	49.0	48.6
Death rate (per 1,000)	23.8	22.6	22.1

Source: UN, *World Population Prospects: The 2006 Revision*.

Expectation of life (years at birth, WHO estimates): 40 (males 38; females 42) in 2004 (Source: WHO, *World Health Report*).

ECONOMICALLY ACTIVE POPULATION
('000 persons, 1991, estimates)

	Males	Females	Total
Agriculture, etc.	1,518	1,374	2,892
Industry	405	33	438
Services	644	192	836
Total labour force	2,567	1,599	4,166

Source: UN Economic Commission for Africa, *African Statistical Yearbook*.

1996 (official estimates, '000 persons): Total employed 475,214; Unemployed 19,000; Total labour force 494,214 (males 379,166; females 115,049) (Source: ILO).

Mid-2004 (estimates in '000): Agriculture, etc. 4,521; Total (incl. others) 6,390 (Source: FAO).

Health and Welfare

KEY INDICATORS

Total fertility rate (children per woman, 2005)	6.6
Under-5 mortality rate (per 1,000 live births, 2005)	260
HIV/AIDS (% of persons aged 15–49, 2005)	3.7
Physicians (per 1,000 head, 2004)	0.08
Hospital beds (per 1,000 head, 1990)	1.29
Health expenditure (2004): US $ per head (PPP)	37.5
Health expenditure (2004): % of GDP	1.9
Health expenditure (2004): public (% of total)	79.4
Access to water (% of persons, 2004)	53
Access to sanitation (% of persons, 2004)	31
Human Development Index (2004): ranking	161
Human Development Index (2004): value	0.439

For sources and definitions, see explanatory note on p. vi.

Agriculture

PRINCIPAL CROPS
('000 metric tons)

	2003	2004	2005
Wheat*	4	4	4
Rice (paddy)	16	21†	7
Maize	619	577†	720
Millet	83	123†	138
Potatoes	302	332†	307
Sweet potatoes	543	525†	659
Cassava (Manioc)	6,892	6,650†	8,606
Sugar cane*	360	360	360
Dry beans	93	76†	108
Groundnuts (in shell)	60	57†	66
Sunflower seed*	11	11	11
Oil palm fruit*	280	280	280
Cottonseed*	6	6	6
Tomatoes*	13	13	13
Onions and shallots (green)*	13	13	13
Other vegetables*	245	245	245
Bananas*	300	300	300
Citrus fruit*	78	78	78
Pineapples*	40	40	40
Other fruits (excl. melons)*	32	32	32
Coffee (green)*	1	1	1

* FAO estimates.
† Unofficial figure.

Source: FAO.

LIVESTOCK
('000 head, year ending September, FAO estimates)

	2001	2002	2003
Cattle	4,100	4,150	4,150
Pigs	800	780	780
Sheep	350	340	340
Goats	2,150	2,050	2,050
Chickens	6,800	6,800	6,800

2004–05: Figures assumed to be unchanged from 2003 (FAO estimates).

Source: FAO.

LIVESTOCK PRODUCTS
('000 metric tons, FAO estimates)

	2000	2001	2002
Cattle meat	85.0	85.0	85.0
Goat meat	9.7	9.7	9.2
Pig meat	28.6	27.9	27.9
Chicken meat	8.6	8.6	8.6
Game meat	7.5	7.5	7.5
Sheep meat	1.3	1.3	1.3
Cows' milk	195.0	195.0	195.0
Hen eggs	4.3	4.3	4.3
Honey	23.0	23.0	23.0

2003–05: Figures assumed to be unchanged from 2002 (FAO estimates).

Source: FAO.

Forestry

ROUNDWOOD REMOVALS
('000 cubic metres, excluding bark, FAO estimates)

	2003	2004	2005
Sawlogs, veneer logs and logs for sleepers	46	46	46
Other industrial wood	1,050	1,050	1,050
Fuel wood	3,402	3,487	3,574
Total	4,498	4,583	4,670

Source: FAO.

SAWNWOOD PRODUCTION
('000 cubic metres, including railway sleepers, FAO estimates)

	1983	1984	1985
Total	6	2	5

1986–2005: Annual production as in 1985 (FAO estimates).

Source: FAO.

Fishing

('000 metric tons, live weight)

	2003	2004	2005*
Freshwater fishes	10.0	10.0*	10.0
West coast sole	n.a.	8.3	8.2
West African croakers	18.9	18.3	19.0
Dentex	18.2	17.9	17.8
Cunene horse mackerel	28.1	34.9	35.0
Sardinellas	45.0	58.6	55.0
Chub mackerel	9.7	6.6	7.0
Total catch (incl. others)	211.5	240.0*	240.0

* FAO estimate(s).

Source: FAO.

Mining

('000 metric tons, unless otherwise indicated)

	2003	2004	2005
Crude petroleum ('000 42-gallon barrels):			
crude	321,200	383,250	456,250
refinery products*	14,000	14,000	14,000
Salt (unrefined)	30	30	30
Diamonds ('000 carats):†			
industrial	570	610	700
gem	5,130	5,490	6,300

* Estimates; includes asphalt and bitumen.
† Reported figures, based on estimates of 90% of production at gem grade and 10% of production at industrial grade.

Source: US Geological Survey.

Industry

SELECTED PRODUCTS
('000 metric tons, unless otherwise indicated)

	2001	2002	2003
Frozen fish	57.8	43.9	36.2
Wheat flour	20.3	21.0	38.2
Bread	313.7	n.a.	261.0
Beer ('000 hectolitres)	82.0	80.0	192.0
Non-alcoholic beverages ('000 hectolitres)	82.0	56.0	88.8
Jet fuels	330.9	352.5	324.8
Motor spirit (petrol)	107.2	104.6	95.9
Kerosene	31.2	36.9	43.9
Distillate fuel oils	501.7	461.0	407.5
Residual fuel oils	552.8	590.7	639.3
Butane gas	31.5	34.3	30.0
Cement	465.5	312.7	500.6

Source: IMF, *Angola: Selected Issues and Statistical Appendix* (April 2005).

Finance

CURRENCY AND EXCHANGE RATES

Monetary Units
100 lwei = 1 kwanza.

Sterling, Dollar and Euro Equivalents (30 April 2007)
£1 sterling = 157.204 kwanza;
US $1 = 78.815 kwanza;
€1 = 107.228 kwanza;
1,000 kwanza = £6.36 = $12.69 = €9.33.

Average Exchange Rate (kwanza per US $)
2004 83.541
2005 87.159
2006 80.368

Note: In April 1994 the introduction of a new method of setting exchange rates resulted in an effective devaluation of the new kwanza, to US $1 = 68,297 new kwanza, and provided for an end to the system of multiple exchange rates. Further substantial devaluations followed, and in July 1995 a 'readjusted' kwanza, equivalent to 1,000 new kwanza, was introduced. The currency, however, continued to depreciate. Between July 1997 and June 1998 a fixed official rate of US $1 = 262,376 readjusted kwanza was in operation. In May 1999 the Central Bank announced its decision to abolish the existing dual currency exchange rate system. In December 1999 the readjusted kwanza was replaced by a new currency, the kwanza, equivalent to 1m. readjusted kwanza.

BUDGET
('000 million kwanza)

Revenue	2004*	2005*	2006†
Tax revenue	597.3	1,050.3	1,394.2
Petroleum	469.3	862.1	1,172.1
Income tax	42.4	62.2	84.6
Tax on goods and services	36.5	54.9	56.1
Taxes on foreign trade	33.2	47.0	54.8
Taxes on properties	0.7	1.0	1.2
Other taxes	15.2	23.1	25.4
Contributions to social welfare	—	21.0	19.1
Grants	7.5	6.4	9.4
Other revenue	4.9	8.2	18.5
Total	609.7	1,085.8	1,441.3

Expenditure	2004*	2005*	2006†
Current	518.6	725.0	798.2
Personnel‡	170.4	246.7	296.3
Goods and services	156.2	245.1	255.4
Interest payments	38.6	53.5	56.3
Transfers	153.4	179.7	190.3
Capital	73.3	134.7	540.2
Total	591.9	859.7	1,338.5

* Estimates.
† Projections.
‡ Including wages and salaries of defence and public order personnel.

Source: Ministry of Finance, Luanda.

INTERNATIONAL RESERVES
(US $ million at 31 December)

	2004	2005	2006
IMF special drawing rights	0.23	0.21	0.23
Foreign exchange	1,373.82	3,196.64	8,598.35
Total	1,374.05	3,196.85	8,598.58

Source: IMF, *International Financial Statistics*.

MONEY SUPPLY
(million kwanza at 31 December)

	2004	2005	2006
Currency outside banks	45,933.1	59,692.6	71,588.7
Demand deposits at banking institutions	49,970.9	92,991.6	123,634.8
Total (incl. others)	96,058.5	152,909.9	195,488.0

Source: IMF, *International Financial Statistics*.

COST OF LIVING
(Consumer Price Index for Luanda at December; base: 1994 average = 100)

	1999	2000	2001
Food	3,551.1	11,211.2	22,494.2
Clothing	5,189.4	21,449.2	45,733.9
Rent, fuel and light	28,392.7	157,756.4	434,224.6
All items (incl. others)	5,083.6	18,723.6	40,456.1

Source: IMF, *Angola: Selected Issues and Statistical Appendix* (September 2003).

All items (Consumer Price Index for Luanda at December; base: 2000 = 100): 1,501.2 in 2004; 1,872.8 in 2005; 2,091.5 in 2006 (Source: IMF, *International Financial Statistics*).

NATIONAL ACCOUNTS

Expenditure on the Gross Domestic Product
(US $ million at current prices)

	2003	2004	2005
Government final consumption expenditure	6,452.2	8,940.8	14,019.5
Private final consumption expenditure	4,698.4	5,732.5	6,356.3
Gross fixed capital formation / Increase in stocks	1,767.4	1,802.1	3,205.3
Total domestic expenditure	12,918.0	16,475.4	23,581.1
Exports of goods and services	9,709.1	13,756.0	22,435.0
Less Imports of goods and services	8,801.1	10,732.5	17,541.3
GDP in purchasers' values (market prices)	13,825.9	19,498.8	28,474.8
GDP at constant 2000 prices	11,135.7	12,374.5	14,304.9

Source: African Development Bank.

Gross Domestic Product by Economic Activity
(million kwanza at current prices, estimates)

	2001	2002	2003
Agriculture, forestry and fishing	16,077	37,661	79,579
Mining	113,055	235,820	549,284
Petroleum and gas	100,916	209,347	501,530
Manufacturing	7,634	17,566	37,063
Electricity and water	79	181	376
Construction	7,124	16,375	34,713
Trade	30,442	67,094	154,772
Other services	18,385	50,332	155,832
Sub-total	192,798	425,029	1,011,620
Import duties	4,313	8,524	25,421
GDP at market prices	197,111	433,553	1,037,040

Source: Banco Nacional de Angola.

GDP at market prices (million kwanza at current prices): 1,031,435 in 2003; 1,693,564 in 2004; 2,518,898 in 2005 (Source: IMF, *International Financial Statistics*).

BALANCE OF PAYMENTS
(US $ million)

	2003	2004	2005
Exports of goods f.o.b.	9,508.2	13,475.0	24,109.4
Imports of goods f.o.b.	–5,480.1	–5,831.8	–8,353.2
Trade balance	4,028.1	7,643.2	15,756.2
Exports of services	201.1	322.8	176.8
Imports of services	–3,321.1	–4,802.7	–6,791.0
Balance on goods and services	908.0	3,163.3	9,142.0
Other income received	12.3	33.0	25.8
Other income paid	–1,738.7	–2,516.6	–4,056.6
Balance on goods, services and income	–818.5	679.6	5,111.2
Current transfers received	186.2	124.4	172.5
Current transfers paid	–87.3	–117.9	–145.8
Current balance	–719.6	686.2	5,137.9
Direct investment abroad	–23.6	–35.2	–219.4
Direct investment from abroad	3,504.7	1,449.2	–1,303.9
Portfolio investment assets	1.0	–2.1	–1,267.0
Other investment assets	120.0	–1,951.5	–1,850.1
Investment liabilities	–2,231.5	–83.0	1,525.1
Net errors and omissions	–388.2	276.7	–377.9
Overall balance	262.8	340.3	1,644.9

Source: IMF, *International Financial Statistics*.

External Trade

SELECTED COMMODITIES

Imports (million kwanza)	1983	1984	1985
Animal products	1,315	1,226	1,084
Vegetable products	2,158	3,099	2,284
Fats and oils	946	1,006	1,196
Food and beverages	2,400	1,949	1,892
Industrial chemical products	1,859	1,419	1,702
Plastic materials	431	704	454
Textiles	1,612	1,816	1,451
Base metals	1,985	3,730	2,385
Electrical equipment	3,296	2,879	2,571
Transport equipment	2,762	2,240	3,123
Total (incl. others)	20,197	21,370	19,694

Exports (US $ million)	2003	2004	2005
Crude petroleum	8,530	12,442	22,583
Refined petroleum products	139	148	242
Gas (per barrel)	16	30	30
Diamonds	788	790	1,092
Coffee	0.8	0.3	0.3
Total (incl. others)	9,508	14,475	24,109

Total imports (US $ million): 2,597 in 1997; 2,079 in 1998; 3,109 in 1999; 3,040 in 2000; 3,179 in 2001; 3,760 in 2002; 5,480 in 2003; 5,832 in 2004; 8,353 in 2005.

Sources: Banco Nacional de Angola; African Development Bank.

PRINCIPAL TRADING PARTNERS
(US $ million)*

Imports c.i.f.	2004	2005	2006
Brazil	392	572	707
European Union	2,225	2,747	4,188
Portugal	920	1,093	1,677
Korea, Republic	1,996	1,669	2,063
South Africa	525	600	747
USA	654	1,021	1,705
Total (incl. others)	7,033	8,136	11,905

Exports f.o.b.	2004	2005	2006
China, People's Republic	4,121	5,982	9,937
European Union	1,107	2,966	2,484
Portugal	2	30	63
France	747	1,585	1,413
South Africa	261	296	366
USA	4,361	8,042	11,068
Total (incl. others)	11,541	20,194	28,664

* Data are compiled on the basis of reporting by Angola's trading partners.

Source: IMF, *Direction of Trade Statistics*.

Transport

GOODS TRANSPORT
(million metric tons)

	1999	2000	2001
Road	2,500.0	5,727.3	4,708.6
Railway	123.2	179.8	242.6
Water	2,009.0	5,981.0	3,045.6

Source: IRF, *World Road Statistics*.

PASSENGER TRANSPORT
(million passenger-km)

	1999	2000	2001
Road	73,644.9	111,455.7	166,044.7
Railway	3,467.3	3,194.9	3,722.3

Source: IRF, *World Road Statistics*.

ROAD TRAFFIC
(motor vehicles in use at 31 December, estimates)

	1997	1998	1999
Passenger cars	103,400	107,100	117,200
Lorries and vans	107,600	110,500	118,300
Total	211,000	217,600	235,500

2000–2002: data assumed to be unchanged from 1999 (estimates).

Source: UN, *Statistical Yearbook*.

SHIPPING

Merchant Fleet
(registered at 31 December)

	2003	2004	2005
Number of vessels	122	125	128
Total displacement (grt)	44,811	47,937	53,869

Source: Lloyd's Register-Fairplay, *World Fleet Statistics*.

International Sea-borne Freight Traffic
(estimates, '000 metric tons)

	1989	1990	1991
Goods loaded	19,980	21,102	23,288
Goods unloaded	1,235	1,242	1,261

Source: UN Economic Commission for Africa, *African Statistical Yearbook*.

CIVIL AVIATION
(traffic on scheduled services)

	2001	2002	2003
Kilometres flown (million)	3	3	4
Passengers carried ('000)	101	101	99
Passenger-km (million)	413	417	417
Total ton-km (million)	87	87	92

Source: UN, *Statistical Yearbook*.

Tourism

FOREIGN TOURIST ARRIVALS

Country of origin	2000	2001	2002
Belgium	597	1,303	2,162
Brazil	3,272	3,789	6,859
France	4,577	9,134	12,125
Germany	359	525	2,272
Italy	935	1,007	2,431
Philippines	1,175	1,963	1,034
Portugal	15,601	12,687	17,182
Russia	1,243	1,726	1,748
South Africa	3,774	6,880	9,674
Spain	1,361	1,569	2,005
United Kingdom	3,648	5,432	6,828
USA	3,013	3,924	5,409
Total (incl. others)	50,765	67,379	90,532

Total tourist arrivals 106,625 in 2003; 194,329 in 2004.

Tourism receipts (US $ million, incl. passenger transport): 51 in 2002; 63 in 2003; 82 in 2004.

Source: World Tourism Organization.

Communications Media

	2003	2004	2005
Telephones ('000 main lines in use)	96.3	96.3	94.3
Mobile cellular telephones ('000 subscribers)	332.8	940.0	1,094.1
Personal computers ('000 in use)	n.a.	27	n.a.
Internet users ('000)	84	172	n.a.

Source: International Telecommunication Union.

Radio receivers ('000 in use, 1999): 840 (Source: UN, *Statistical Yearbook*).

Daily newspapers (1998): 5 (average circulation 133,000 copies) (Source: UNESCO Institute for Statistics).

Book production (1995): 22 titles (all books) (Source: UNESCO, *Statistical Yearbook*).

Education

(1997/98)

	Teachers	Pupils
Pre-primary	n.a.	214,867*
Primary	31,062†	1,342,116
Secondary:		
general	5,138‡	267,399
teacher training	280§	10,772*
vocational	286‡	12,116*
Higher	776	8,337

* Figure for school year 1991/92.
† Figure for school year 1990/91.
‡ Figure for school year 1989/90.
§ Figure for school year 1987/88.

Source: mainly UNESCO, Institute for Statistics.

Adult literacy rate (UNESCO estimates): 67.4% (males 82.9%; females 54.2%) in 2004 (Source: UN Development Programme, *Human Development Report*).

Directory

The Constitution

The MPLA regime adopted an independence Constitution for Angola in November 1975. It was amended in October 1976, September 1980, March 1991, April and August 1992, and November 1996. The main provisions of the 1975 Constitution, as amended, are summarized below:

BASIC PRINCIPLES

The Republic of Angola shall be a sovereign and independent state whose prime objective shall be to build a free and democratic society of peace, justice and social progress. It shall be a democratic state based on the rule of law, founded on national unity, the dignity of human beings, pluralism of expression and political organization, respecting and guaranteeing the basic rights and freedoms of persons, whether as individuals or as members of organized social groups. Sovereignty shall be vested in the people, which shall exercise political power through periodic universal suffrage.

The Republic of Angola shall be a unitary and indivisible state. Economic, social and cultural solidarity shall be promoted between all the Republic's regions for the common development of the entire nation and the elimination of regionalism and tribalism.

Religion

The Republic shall be a secular state and there shall be complete separation of the State and religious institutions. All religions shall be respected.

The Economy

The economic system shall be based on the coexistence of diverse forms of property—public, private, mixed, co-operative and family—and all shall enjoy equal protection. The State shall protect foreign investment and foreign property, in accordance with the law. The fiscal system shall aim to satisfy the economic, social and administrative needs of the State and to ensure a fair distribution of income and wealth. Taxes may be created and abolished only by law, which shall determine applicability, rates, tax benefits and guarantees for taxpayers.

Education

The Republic shall vigorously combat illiteracy and obscurantism and shall promote the development of education and of a true national culture.

FUNDAMENTAL RIGHTS AND DUTIES

The State shall respect and protect the human person and human dignity. All citizens shall be equal before the law. They shall be subject to the same duties, without any distinction based on colour, race, ethnic group, sex, place of birth, religion, level of education, or economic or social status.

All citizens aged 18 years and over, other than those legally deprived of political and civil rights, shall have the right and duty to take an active part in public life, to vote and be elected to any state organ, and to discharge their mandates with full dedication to the cause of the Angolan nation. The law shall establish limitations in respect of non-political allegiance of soldiers on active service, judges and police forces, as well as the electoral incapacity of soldiers on active service and police forces.

Freedom of expression, of assembly, of demonstration, of association and of all other forms of expression shall be guaranteed. Groupings whose aims or activities are contrary to the constitutional order and penal laws, or that, even indirectly, pursue political objectives through organizations of a military, paramilitary or militarized nature shall be forbidden. Every citizen has the right to a defence if accused of a crime. Individual freedoms are guaranteed. Freedom of conscience and belief shall be inviolable. Work shall be the right and duty of all citizens. The State shall promote measures necessary to ensure the right of citizens to medical and health care, as well as assistance in childhood, motherhood, disability, old age, etc. It shall also promote access to education, culture and sports for all citizens.

STATE ORGANS

President of the Republic

The President of the Republic shall be the Head of State, Head of Government and Commander-in-Chief of the Angolan armed forces. The President of the Republic shall be elected directly by a secret universal ballot and shall have the following powers:

- to appoint and dismiss the Prime Minister, Ministers and other government officials determined by law
- to appoint the judges of the Supreme Court
- to preside over the Council of Ministers
- to declare war and make peace, following authorization by the Assembléia Nacional
- to sign, promulgate and publish the laws of the Assembléia Nacional, government decrees and statutory decrees
- to preside over the National Defence Council
- to decree a state of siege or state of emergency
- to announce the holding of general elections
- to issue pardons and commute sentences
- to perform all other duties provided for in the Constitution.

Assembléia Nacional

The Assembléia Nacional is the supreme state legislative body, to which the Government is responsible. The Assembléia shall be composed of 223 deputies, elected for a term of four years. The Assembléia shall convene in ordinary session twice yearly and in special session on the initiative of the President of the Assembléia, the Standing Commission of the Assembléia or of no less than one-third of its deputies. The Standing Commission shall be the organ of the Assembléia that represents and assumes its powers between sessions.

Government

The Government shall comprise the President of the Republic, the ministers and the secretaries of state, and other members whom the law shall indicate, and shall have the following functions:

- to organize and direct the implementation of state domestic and foreign policy, in accordance with the decision of the Assembléia Nacional and its Standing Commission
- to ensure national defence, the maintenance of internal order and security, and the protection of the rights of citizens
- to prepare the draft National Plan and General State Budget for approval by the Assembléia Nacional, and to organize, direct and control their execution.

The Council of Ministers shall be answerable to the Assembléia Nacional. In the exercise of its powers, the Council of Ministers shall issue decrees and resolutions.

Judiciary

The organization, composition and competence of the courts shall be established by law. Judges shall be independent in the discharge of their functions.

Local State Organs

The organs of state power at provincial level shall be the Provincial Assemblies and their executive bodies. The Provincial Assemblies shall work in close co-operation with social organizations and rely on the initiative and broad participation of citizens. The Provincial Assemblies shall elect commissions of deputies to perform permanent or specific tasks. The executive organs of Provincial Assemblies shall be the Provincial Governments, which shall be led by the Provincial Governors. The Provincial Governors shall be answerable to the President of the Republic, the Council of Ministers and the Provincial Assemblies.

National Defence

The State shall ensure national defence. The National Defence Council shall be presided over by the President of the Republic, and its composition shall be determined by law. The Angolan armed forces, as a state institution, shall be permanent, regular and non-partisan. Defence of the country shall be the right and the highest indeclinable duty of every citizen. Military service shall be compulsory. The forms in which it is fulfilled shall be defined by the law.

The Government

HEAD OF STATE

President: JOSÉ EDUARDO DOS SANTOS (assumed office 21 September 1979).

COUNCIL OF MINISTERS

(August 2007)

Prime Minister: FERNANDO (NANDO) DA PIEDADE DIAS DOS SANTOS.

Deputy Prime Minister: AGUINALDO JAIME.

Minister of National Defence: Gen. KUNDI PAIHAMA.

Minister of the Interior: Gen. ROBERTO LEAL RAMOS MONTEIRO (NGONGO).

Minister of Foreign Affairs: JOÃO BERNARDO DE MIRANDA.

Minister of Justice: MANUEL DA COSTA ARAGÃO.

Minister of Territorial Administration: VIRGÍLIO FERREIRA FONTES PEREIRA.

Minister of Planning: ANA AFONSO DIAS LOURENÇO.

Minister of Finance: JOSÉ PEDRO DE MORAIS.

Minister of Petroleum: DESIDÉRIO DA GRAÇA VERÍSSIMO DA COSTA.

Minister of Fisheries: SALOMÃO LUHETO XIRIMBIMBI.

Minister of Industry: JOAQUIM DUARTE DA COSTA DAVID.

Minister of Agriculture and Rural Development: AFONSO PEDRO CANGA.

Minister of Geology and Mines: MANUEL ANTÓNIO AFRICANO NETO.

Minister of Public Administration, Labour and Social Security: Dr ANTÓNIO DOMINGOS PITRA DA COSTA NETO.

Minister of Health: ANASTÁCIO ARTUR RUBEN SICATO.

Minister of Education: ANTÓNIO BURITY DA SILVA NETO.

Minister of Culture: BOAVENTURA CARDOSO.

Minister of Science and Technology: JOÃO BAPTISTA NGANDAJINA.

Minister of Transport: ANDRÉ LUÍS BRANDÃO.

Minister of Posts and Telecommunications: LICÍNIO TAVARES RIBEIRO.

Minister of Family and the Promotion of Women: CÂNDIDA CELESTE DA SILVA.

Minister of Former Combatants: PEDRO JOSÉ VAN-DÚNEM.

Minister of Youth and Sports: JOSÉ MARCOS BARRICA.

Minister of Public Works: FRANCISCO HIGINO CARNEIRO.

Minister of Commerce: JOAQUIM EKUMA MUAFUMUA.

Minister of Hotels and Tourism: EDUARDO JONATÃO CHINGUNJI.

Minister of Social Assistance and Reintegration: JOÃO BAPTISTA KUSSUMUA.

Minister of Social Communication: MANUEL ANTÓNIO RABELAIS.

Minister of Energy and Water: JOSÉ MARIA BOTELHO DE VASCONCELOS.

Minister of Urban Affairs and the Environment: SITA JOSÉ DIAKUMPUNA.

Ministers in the Office of the Presidency

Secretary of the Council of Ministers: JOAQUIM ANTÓNIO CARLOS DOS REIS.

Minister in the Presidency and Head of the Civil House: AMERICO MARIA DE MORAIS GARCIA.

Civil Affairs: JOSÉ DA COSTA DE SILVA LEITÃO.

Military Affairs: MANUEL HELDER DIAS.

General Secretariat: JOSÉ MATEUS DE ADELINO PEIXOTO.

MINISTRIES

Office of the President: Protocolo de Estado, Futungo de Belas, Luanda; tel. 222370150; fax 222370366.

Office of the Prime Minister: Luanda.

Office of the Deputy Prime Minister: Luanda; tel. 222371032; fax 222370842; e-mail ministro.adj1m@netangola.com.

Ministry of Agriculture and Rural Development: Av. Comandante Gika 2, CP 527, Luanda; tel. 222322694; fax 222320553; e-mail gabminander@netangola.com; internet www.angola-portal.ao/MINADER/.

Ministry of Commerce: Palácio de Vidro, Largo 4 de Fevereiro, CP 1242, Luanda; tel. 222310626; fax 222310335; e-mail gab.min.com@ebonet.net; internet www.angola-portal.ao/MINCO.

Ministry of Culture: Av. Comandante Gika, Luanda; tel. and fax 222323979; e-mail mincultura@mincultura.gv.ao; internet www.angola-portal.ao/MINCULT.

Ministry of Education: Av. Comandante Gika, CP 1281, Luanda; tel. 222320653; fax 222321592; internet www.angola-portal.ao/MED/.

Ministry of Energy and Water: Av. 4 de Fevereiro 105, CP 2229, Luanda; tel. 222393681; fax 222298687; internet www.angola-portal.ao/MINEA/.

Ministry of Family and the Promotion of Women: Palácio de Vidro, Largo 4 de Fevereiro, Luanda; tel. and fax 222311728; e-mail phildelgado@netangola.com; internet www.angola-portal.ao/MINFAMU.

Ministry of Finance: Av. 4 de Fevereiro 127, CP 592, Luanda; tel. and fax 222338548; e-mail cdi@minfin.gv.ao; internet www.angola-portal.ao/MINFIN/.

Ministry of Fisheries: Edif. Atlântico, Av. 4 de Fevereiro 30, CP 83, Luanda; tel. 222311420; fax 222310199; e-mail geral@angola-minpescas.com; internet www.angola-minpescas.com.

Ministry of Foreign Affairs: Rua Major Kanhangulo, Luanda; tel. 222397490; fax 222393246; e-mail webdesigner@mirex.ebonet.net; internet www.angola-portal.ao/MIREX/.

Ministry of Former Combatants: Av. Comandante Gika 2, CP 3828, Luanda; tel. 222323865; fax 222320876; internet www.angola-portal.ao/MACVG.

Ministry of Geology and Mines: Av. Comandante Gika, CP 1260, Luanda; tel. 222322766; fax 222321655; e-mail min.geominas@ebonet.net; internet www.angola-portal.ao/MGM.

Ministry of Health: Rua 17 de Setembro, CP 1201, Luanda; tel. and fax 222338052; internet www.angola-portal.ao/MINSA/.

Ministry of Hotels and Tourism: Palácio de Vidro, Largo 4 de Fevereiro, Luanda; tel. 222310899; fax 222310629; internet www.angola-portal.ao/MINHOTUR.

Ministry of Industry: Rua Cerqueira Lukoki 25, CP 594, Luanda; tel. 222390728; fax 222392400; e-mail gmi@ebonet.net; internet www.angola-portal.ao/MIND/.

Ministry of the Interior: Av. 4 de Fevereiro 204, CP 2723, Luanda; tel. 222391049; fax 222395133; internet www.angola-portal.ao/MININT.

Ministry of Justice: Rua 17 de Setembro, CP 2250, Luanda; tel. and fax 222339914; e-mail minijus20@hotmail.com; internet www.angola-portal.ao/MINJUS/.

Ministry of National Defence: Rua 17 de Setembro, Luanda; tel. 222337530; fax 222334276; e-mail minden1@ebonet.net; internet www.angola-portal.ao/MINDEN.

Ministry of Petroleum: Av. 4 de Fevereiro 105, CP 1279, Luanda; tel. and fax 222385847; internet www.angola-portal.ao/MINPET/.

Ministry of Planning: Largo do Palácio do Povo, Cidade Alta, Luanda; tel. 222390188; fax 222339586; e-mail lourenco@compuserve.com; internet www.angola-portal.ao/MINPLAN/.

Ministry of Posts and Telecommunications: Rua Major Kanhangulo, Luanda; tel. 222311004; fax 222330776; e-mail sg_mct@snet.co.ao; internet www.angola-portal.ao/MCT/.

Ministry of Public Administration, Labour and Social Security: Rua do 1° Congresso do MPLA 5, Luanda; tel. 222338940; fax 222399507; e-mail mapess@ebonet.net; internet www.mapess.gv.ao.

Ministry of Public Works: Rua Frederich Engels 92, Luanda; tel. 222336715; fax 222392539.

Ministry of Science and Technology: Ilha do Cabo, Luanda; tel. and fax 222309794; e-mail dgmk@ebonet.com; internet www.angola-portal.ao/MINCIT/.

Ministry of Social Assistance and Reintegration: Av. Hoji Ya Henda 117, CP 102, Luanda; tel. 222341460; fax 222342988; internet www.angola-portal.ao/MINARS.

Ministry of Social Communication: Av. Comandante Valódia, 1° e 2° andares, CP 2608, Luanda; tel. and fax 222443495; e-mail mcs@netangola.com; internet www.angola-portal.ao/MCS.

Ministry of Territorial Administration: Av. Comandante Gika 8, Luanda; tel. 222321729; fax 222323272; internet www.angola-portal.ao/MAT.

Ministry of Transport: Av. 4 de Fevereiro 42, CP 1250-C, Luanda; tel. 222311303; fax 222311582.

Ministry of Urban Affairs and the Environment: Luanda; tel. 222336717; internet www.angola-portal.ao/MINUA/.

Ministry of Youth and Sports: Av. Comandante Valódia 229, 4° andar, Luanda; tel. and fax 222321118; internet www.angola-portal.ao/MINJUD.

PROVINCIAL GOVERNORS

(August 2007)

All Provincial Governors are ex officio members of the Government.

Bengo: JORGE INOCENCIO DOMBOLO.

Benguela: DUMILDE DAS CHAGAS SIMÕES RANGEL.

Bié: JOSÉ AMARO TATI.

Cabinda: JOSÉ ANÍBAL LOPES ROCHA.

Cuando-Cubango: JORGE BIWANGO.

Cuanza-Norte: HENRIQUE ANDRÉ JÚNIOR.

Cuanza-Sul: SERAFIM MARIA DO PRADO.

Cunene: PEDRO MUTINDE.

Huambo: AGOSTINHO NJAKA.

Huíla: FRANCISCO JOSÉ RAMOS DA CRUZ.

Luanda: JOB CASTELO CAPAPINHA.

Lunda-Norte: MANUEL FRANCISCO GOMES MAIATO.

Lunda-Sul: FRANCISCO TSCHIWISSA.

Malanje: CRISTOVÃO DA CUNHA.

Moxico: JOÃO ERNESTO DOS SANTOS.

Namibe: ÁLVARO MANUEL DE BOAVIDA NETO.

Uíge: ANTÓNIO BENTO KANGULO.

Zaire: PEDRO SEBASTIÃO.

President and Legislature

PRESIDENT*

Presidential Election, 29 and 30 September 1992

	Votes	% of votes
José Eduardo dos Santos (MPLA)	1,953,335	49.57
Dr Jonas Malheiro Savimbi (UNITA)	1,579,298	40.07
António Alberto Neto (PDA)	85,249	2.16
Holden Roberto (FNLA)	83,135	2.11
Honorato Lando (PDLA)	75,789	1.92
Luís dos Passos (PRD)	59,121	1.47
Bengui Pedro João (PSD)	38,243	0.97
Simão Cacete (FPD)	26,385	0.67
Daniel Júlio Chipenda (Independent)	20,646	0.52
Anália de Victória Pereira (PLD)	11,475	0.29
Rui de Victória Pereira (PRA)	9,208	0.23
Total	3,940,884	100.00

*Under the terms of the electoral law, a second round of the presidential election was required to take place in order to determine which of the two leading candidates from the first round would be elected. A resumption of hostilities between UNITA and government forces prevented a second round from taking place. The electoral process was to resume only when the provisions of the Estoril peace agreement, concluded in May 1991, had been fulfilled. However, provision in the Lusaka peace accord of November 1994 for the second round of the presidential election was not pursued.

LEGISLATURE

Assembléia Nacional: CP 1204, Luanda; tel. 222334021; fax 222331118; e-mail assembleianacional@parlamento.ebonet.net; internet www.parlamento.ao.

President: ROBERTO DE ALMEIDA.

General Election, 29 and 30 September 1992

	Votes	% of votes	Seats*
MPLA	2,124,126	53.74	129
UNITA	1,347,636	34.10	70
FNLA	94,742	2.40	5
PLD	94,269	2.39	3
PRS	89,875	2.27	6
PRD	35,293	0.89	1
AD Coalition	34,166	0.86	1
PSD	33,088	0.84	1
PAJOCA	13,924	0.35	1
FDA	12,038	0.30	1
PDP—ANA	10,620	0.27	1
PNDA	10,281	0.26	1
CNDA	10,237	0.26	—
PSDA	19,217	0.26	—
PAI	9,007	0.23	—
PDLA	8,025	0.20	—
PDA	8,014	0.20	—
PRA	6,719	0.17	—
Total	3,952,277	100.00	220

*According to the Constitution, the total number of seats in the Assembléia Nacional is 223. On the decision of the National Electoral Council, however, elections to fill three seats reserved for Angolans resident abroad were abandoned.

Election Commission

Comissão Nacional Eleitoral (CNE): Av. Amílcar Cabral, 30–31, Luanda; tel. 222393825; e-mail info@cne.gv.ao; internet www.cne.gv.ao; f. 2005; government agency; Pres. ANTÓNIO CAETANO DE SOUSA.

Political Organizations

In 2007 there were over 130 political parties.

Aliança Democrática de Angola: Leader SIMBA DA COSTA.

Angolan Democratic Coalition (AD Coalition): Pres. EVIDOR QUIELA (acting).

Convenção Nacional Democrata de Angola (CNDA): mem. of POC; Leader PAULINO PINTO JOÃO.

Frente para a Democracia (FpD): Sec.-Gen. LUIS FERNANDES DO NASCIMENTO.

Frente de Libertação do Enclave de Cabinda (FLEC): f. 1963; comprises several factions, claiming total forces of c. 5,000 guerrillas, seeking the secession of Cabinda province; in Sept. 2004 the Frente de Libertação do Enclave de Cabinda—Forças Armadas Cabindesas (FLEC—FAC) and the Frente de Libertação do Enclave de Cabinda—Renovada (FLEC—R) merged under the above name; Leader N'ZITA HENRIQUES TIAGO; Sec.-Gen. ANTÓNIO BENTO BEMBE.

Frente de Libertação do Enclave de Cabinda—Conselho Superior Alargado (FLEC—CSA): f. 2004; political wing of FLEC; supports Cabindan independence through negotiation; Leader LIBERAL NUNO.

Frente Nacional de Libertação de Angola (FNLA): Av. Hoji Va Henda (ex Av. do Brasil) 91/306, CP 151, Luanda; tel. and fax 222344638; e-mail fnla@fnla-angola.org; internet www.fnla-angola.org; f. 1962; Pres. LUCAS NGONDA; Interim Sec.-Gen. NYMI A-SIMBI.

Movimento de Defesa dos Interesses de Angola—Partido de Consciência Nacional (MDIA—PCN) (Movement for the Defence of Angolan Interests—National Conscience Party): f. 1991; Pres. FILIPE PINTO SUAMINA; Sec.-Gen. AFONSO MAYTUKA.

Movimento Popular de Libertação de Angola (MPLA) (People's Movement for the Liberation of Angola): Luanda; e-mail mpla@ebonet.net; internet www2.ebonet.net/MPLA; f. 1956; in 1961–74 conducted guerrilla operations against Portuguese rule; governing party since 1975; known as Movimento Popular de Libertação de Angola—Partido do Trabalho (MPLA—PT) (People's Movement for the Liberation of Angola—Workers' Party) 1977–92; in Dec. 1990 replaced Marxist-Leninist ideology with commitment to 'democratic socialism'; absorbed the Fórum Democrático Angolano (FDA) in 2002; Chair. JOSÉ EDUARDO DOS SANTOS; Sec.-Gen. JULIÃO MATEUS PAULO.

Nova Democracia—União Eleitoral: f. 2006; a splinter group from the POC comprising the Frente Unida para Liberdade Democratica (FULD), the Movimento para Democracia de Angola (MPDA), the Partido Angolano Republicano (PAR), the Partido Social Independente de Angola (PSIA), the Partido Socialista Liberal (PSL) and the União Nacional para Democracia (UND); Sec.-Gen. QUINTINO DE MOREIRA.

Partido de Aliança de Juventude, Operários e Camponêses de Angola (PAJOCA) (Angolan Youth, Workers' and Peasants' Alliance Party): Pres. ALEXANDRE SEBASTIÃO ANDRÉ.

Partido Angolano Independente (PAI): Leader ADRIANO PARREIRA.

Partido de Apoio Democrático e Progresso de Angola (PADEPA): Luanda; f. 1995; Chair. JOSÉ CARLOS LEITÃO.

Partido Democrático Angolano (PDA): Leader ANTÓNIO ALBERTO NETO.

Partido Democrático Liberal de Angola (PDLA): Leader HONORATO LANDO.

Partido Democrático para o Progresso—Aliança Nacional de Angola (PDP—ANA): Interim Leader and Pres. SEDIANGANI MBIMBI.

Partido Democrático para o Progresso Social (PDPS): founded by members of the PRS; Pres. PAULO LUSENQUENY.

Partido Liberal Democrático (PLD): Rua Manuel Fernando Caldeira, 3c andar, Esquerda Município de Ingombotas, CP 10199, Luanda; tel. 222396968; fax 222395966; e-mail pld@ebonet.net; Leader ANÁLIA DE VICTÓRIA PEREIRA.

Partido Nacional Democrata de Angola (PNDA): Sec.-Gen. PEDRO JOÃO ANTÓNIO.

Partido Reformador de Angola (PRA): Leader RUI DE VICTÓRIA PEREIRA.

Partido Renovador Democrático (PRD): Leader LUÍS DOS PASSOS.

Partido Renovador Social (PRS): Pres. EDUARDO KWANGANA; Sec.-Gen. JOÃO BAPTISTA NGANDAJINA.

Partido Social Democrata (PSD): Leader BENGUI PEDRO JOÃO.

Partido Social Democrata de Angola (PSDA): Leader ANDRÉ MILTON KILANDONOCO.

Partidos de Oposição Civil (POC): Luanda; f. 2005; coalition comprising 13 small parties; formed to contest presidential and legislative elections; six parties left the coalition in December 2006 to form the Nova Democracia—União Eleitoral; Exec. Sec. MANUEL FERNANDES; Pres. PAULINO PINTO JOÃO.

Tendência de Reflexão Democrática (TRD): Luanda; Leader PAULO TJIPILIKA.

União Democrática Nacional de Angola (UDNA): Largo Teixeira de Pascoais 14/15, Vila Alice, Luanda; f. 1980s as underground movement; recognized by Supreme Court in 1994; Pres. FRANCISCO J. PEDRO KIZADILAMBA.

União Nacional para a Independência Total de Angola (UNITA): internet www.kwacha.net; f. 1966; to secure independence from Portugal; later received Portuguese support to oppose the MPLA; UNITA and the Frente Nacional de Libertação de Angola conducted guerrilla campaign against the MPLA Govt with aid from some Western countries, 1975–76; supported by South Africa until 1984 and in 1987–88, and by USA after 1986; obtained legal status in March 1998, but hostilities between govt and UNITA forces resumed later that year; signed cease-fire agreement with the MPLA Govt in April 2002; joined the Govt in Dec. 2002; support drawn mainly from Ovimbundu ethnic group; Pres. ISAÍAS SAMAKUVA.

Other parties include the **Partido Angolano para Unidade Democrática e Progresso (PAUPD)**.

The **Fórum Cabindês para o Diálogo (FCD)** was formed in 2004 to provide a united platform for Cabindan separatists and civil-society leaders with which to negotiate with the Government. Its leader was ANTÓNIO BENTO BEMBE.

Diplomatic Representation

EMBASSIES IN ANGOLA

Algeria: Rua Edif. Siccal, Rainha Ginga, CP 1389, Luanda; tel. 222332881; fax 222334785; e-mail ambalg@netangola.com; Ambassador TOUFIK DAHMANI.

Belgium: Av. 4 de Fevereiro 93, 3° andar, CP 1203, Luanda; tel. 222336437; fax 222336438; e-mail luanda@diplobel.org; internet www.diplomatie.be/luanda; Ambassador HUBERT COOREMAN.

Brazil: Rua Houari Boumedienne 132, Miramar, CP 5428, Luanda; tel. 222441307; fax 222444913; e-mail emb.bras@ebonet.net; Ambassador MARCELO DA SILVA VASCONCELOS.

Bulgaria: Rua Fernão Mendes Pinto 35/37, Alvalade, CP 2260, Luanda; tel. 222324213; fax 222321010; e-mail bulgemb@ebonet.net; Ambassador ELENKO ANDREEV.

Cape Verde: Rua Oliveira Martins 3, Luanda; tel. 222321765; fax 222320832; Ambassador SILVINO DA LUZ.

China, People's Republic: Rua Houari Boumedienne 196, Miramar, CP 52, Luanda; tel. 222341683; fax 222344185; e-mail shiguan@netangola.com; Ambassador ZHANG BEISAN.

Congo, Democratic Republic: Rua Cesário Verde 24, Luanda; tel. 222361953; Ambassador BOLANGAMBE YONGO.

Congo, Republic: Av. 4 de Fevereiro 3, Luanda; tel. 222310293; Ambassador CHRISTIAN GILBERT BEMBET.

Côte d'Ivoire: Rua Eng Armindo de Andrade 75, Miramar, CP 432, Luanda; tel. 222440878; fax 222440907; e-mail aciao@ambaci-angola.org; internet www.ambaci-angola.org; Ambassador ANNE GNAHOURET TATRET.

Cuba: Rua Che Guevara 42, Ingombotas, Luanda; tel. 222336749; fax 222339165; e-mail embcuba.ang@ebonet.net; Ambassador PEDRO ROSS LEAL.

Czech Republic: Rua Companhia de Jesus 43–45, Miramar, Luanda; tel. 222430646; fax 222447676; e-mail luanda@embassy.mzv.cz; Ambassador ROBERT KOPECKÝ.

Egypt: Rua Comandante Stona 247, Alvalade, CP 3704, Luanda; tel. 222321590; fax 222323285; e-mail embegipto@ebonet.net; Ambassador BELAL ABD EL-WAHED EL-MASRY.

Equatorial Guinea: Luanda; Ambassador Gen. EUSTAQUIO NZENG ESONO.

France: Rua Reverendo Pedro Agostinho Neto 31–33, CP 584, Luanda; tel. 222334841; fax 222391949; e-mail cad.luanda-amb@diplomatie.gouv.fr; internet www.ambafrance-ao.org; Ambassador GUY AZAÏS.

Gabon: Av. 4 de Fevereiro 95, Luanda; tel. 222372614; Ambassador RAPHAËL NKASSA-NZOGHO.

Germany: Av. 4 de Fevereiro 120, CP 1295, Luanda; tel. 222334516; fax 222399269; e-mail germanembassy.luanda@ebonet.net; internet www.luanda.diplo.de; Ambassador Dr INGO WINKELMANN.

Ghana: Rua Cirilo da Conceição E Silva 5, 1A, CP 1012, Luanda; tel. 222338239; fax 222338235; e-mail embassyghana@ebonet.net; Ambassador KWASI BAAH-BOAKYE.

Guinea: Luanda.

Holy See: Rua Luther King 123, CP 1030, Luanda; tel. 222330532; fax 222332378; e-mail nunc.nuncio@snet.co.ao; Apostolic Nuncio Most Rev. GIOVANNI ANGELO BECCIU (Titular Archbishop of Roselle).

India: Rua Marquês das Minas 18A, Macalusso, CP 6040, Luanda; tel. 222392281; fax 222371094; e-mail indembluanda@ebonet.net; Ambassador (vacant).

Israel: Edif. Siccal, 11° andar, Rua Rainha Ginga, Luanda; tel. 222395295; fax 222396366; e-mail info@luanda.mfa.gov.il; internet luanda.mfa.gov.il; Ambassador BAHIJ MANSOUR.

Italy: Rua Americo Boavida 49–51, Ingombotas, CP 6220, Luanda; tel. 222331245; fax 222333743; e-mail segreteria.luanda@esteri.it; internet www.ambluanda.esteri.it; Ambassador TORQUATO CARDILLI.

Japan: Rua Armindo de Andrade 183–185, Miramar, Luanda; tel. 222442007; fax 222449888; Chargé d'affaires a.i. HIROAKI SANO.

Kenya: Luanda; Ambassador MESHACK NYAMBATI.

Mali: Rua Padre Manuel Pombo 81, Maianga, Luanda; e-mail ambamali@netangola.com; Ambassador FAROUK CAMARA.

Morocco: Edif. Siccal, 10° andar, Rua Rainha Ginga, Luanda; tel. 222393708; fax 222338847; e-mail aluanda@supernet.ao; Ambassador ABDELLAH AIT EL HAJ.

Mozambique: Rua Amílcar Cabral 102, R/C CP 12117, Luanda; tel. and fax 222330811; fax 222332883; e-mail embamoc.Ida@netangola.com; Ambassador ANTÓNIO MATOSE.

Namibia: Rua dos Coqueiros 37, CP 953, Luanda; tel. 222395483; fax 222339234; e-mail embnam@netangola.com; Ambassador LINEEKELA MBOTI.

Netherlands: Edif. Secil, 6°, Av. 4 de Fevereiro 42, CP 3624, Luanda; tel. 222310686; fax 222310966; e-mail lua@minbuza.nl; internet mfa.nl/lua-en; Ambassador JAN GIJS SCHOUTEN.

Nigeria: Rua Houari Boumedienne 120, Miramar, CP 479, Luanda; tel. and fax 222340089; Ambassador Prince IHENEDEN EREDIAUWA.

Norway: Rua de Benguela 17, Bairro Patrice Lumumba, CP 3835, Luanda; tel. 222449936; fax 222449248; e-mail emb.luanda@mfa.no; internet www.noruega.ao; Ambassador ARILD R. ØYEN.

Poland: Rua Comandante N'zagi 21–23, Alvalade, CP 1340, Luanda; tel. 222323088; fax 222323086; e-mail embpol@netangola.com; internet www.luanda.polemb.net; Chargé d'affaires a.i. PIOTR MYŚLIWIEC.

Portugal: Av. de Portugal 50, CP 1346, Luanda; tel. 222333027; fax 222390392; e-mail secretariado.emb@netcabo.co.ao; Ambassador FRANCISCO RIBEIRO TELLES.

Romania: Rua Ramalho Ortigão 30, Alvalade, Luanda; tel. and fax 222321076; e-mail ambromania@ebonet.net; Chargé d'affaires a.i. IACOB PRADA.

Russia: Rua Houari Boumedienne 170, CP 3141, Luanda; tel. 222445028; fax 222445320; e-mail rusemb@netangola.com; Ambassador ANDREI KEMARSKY.

São Tomé and Príncipe: Rua Armindo de Andrade 173–175, Luanda; tel. 222345677; Ambassador ARMINDO BRITO FERNANDES.

Serbia: Rua Comandante N'zagi 25–27, Alvalade, CP 3278, Luanda; tel. 222321421; fax 222321724; e-mail yugoemb@snet.co.ao; Ambassador DOBRIVOJ KACANSKI.

South Africa: Edif. Maianga, 1° e 2° andar, Rua Kwamme Nkrumah 31, Largo da Maianga, CP 6212, Luanda; tel. 222330593; fax 222398730; e-mail saemb.ang@netangola.com; internet www.sambangola.info; Ambassador THEMBA M. N. KUBHEKA.

Spain: Av. 4 de Fevereiro 95, 1° andar, CP 3061, Luanda; tel. 222391166; fax 222332884; e-mail emb.luanda@mae.es; Ambassador FRANCISCO JAVIER VALLAURE DE ACHA.

Sweden: Rua Garcia Neto 9, CP 1130, Miramar, Luanda; tel. 222440706; fax 222443460; e-mail Erik.Åberg@foreign.ministry.se; internet www.swedenabroad.com/luanda; Ambassador ERIK ÅBERG.

United Kingdom: Rua Diogo Cão 4, CP 1244, Luanda; tel. 222334582; fax 222333331; e-mail ppa.luanda@fco.gov.uk; internet www.britishembassy.gov.uk/angola; Ambassador RALPH PUBLICOVER.

USA: Rua Houari Boumedienne 32, Miramar, CP 6468, Luanda; tel. 222641000; fax 222641232; e-mail econusembassyluanda@yahoo.com; internet luanda.usembassy.gov; Ambassador CYNTHIA G. EFIRD.

Viet Nam: Edif. Kalunga Atrium, 10° andar, Rua Engracia Fragoso, Ingombotas, CP 75, Luanda; tel. 222390684; fax 222390369; e-mail dsqvnangola@netangola.com; Ambassador NGUYEN DINH.

Zambia: Rua Rei Katyavala 106–108, CP 1496, Luanda; tel. 222331145; Ambassador FRANCISCO XAVIER MUSSONDA.

Zimbabwe: Edif. Secil, Av. 4 de Fevereiro 42, CP 428, Luanda; tel. and fax 222311528; e-mail embzimbabwe@ebonet.net; Ambassador JAMES MANZOU.

Judicial System

There is a Supreme Court and Court of Appeal in Luanda. There are also civil, criminal and military courts.

Supreme Court: Rua 17 de Setembro, Luanda; fax 222335411; Pres. Dr CRISTIANO ANDRÉ.

Office of the Attorney-General: Rua 17 de Setembro, Luanda; tel. 222333171; fax 222333172; Attorney-General AUGUSTO DA COSTA CARNEIRO.

Religion

In 1998 it was estimated that 47% of the population followed indigenous beliefs, with 53% professing to be Christians, mainly Roman Catholic. There is a small Muslim community, which comprises less than 1% of the population.

CHRISTIANITY

In early 2005 some 85 Christian denominations were registered in Angola.

Conselho de Igrejas Cristãs em Angola (CICA) (Council of Christian Churches in Angola): Rua 15 24, Bairro Cassenda, Luanda; tel. 222351663; fax 222356144; e-mail cica@angonet.org; f. 1977 as Conselho Angolano de Igrejas Evangélicas; 14 mem. churches; five assoc. mems; one observer; Pres. Rev. ALVARO RODRIGUES; Gen. Sec. Rev. LUÍS NGUIMBI.

Protestant Churches

Evangelical Congregational Church in Angola (Igreja Evangélica Congregacional em Angola—IECA): CP 1552, Luanda; tel. 222355108; fax 222350868; e-mail iecageral@snet.co.ao; f. 1880; 750,000 mems; Gen. Sec. Rev. AUGUSTO CHIPESSE.

Evangelical Pentecostal Church of Angola (Missão Evangélica Pentecostal de Angola): CP 219, Porto Amboim; 13,600 mems; Sec. Rev. JOSÉ DOMINGOS CAETANO.

United Evangelical Church of Angola (Igreja Evangélica Unida de Angola): CP 122, Uíge; 11,000 mems; Gen. Sec. Rev. A. L. DOMINGOS.

Other active denominations include the African Apostolic Church, the Church of Apostolic Faith in Angola, the Church of Our Lord Jesus Christ in the World, the Evangelical Baptist Church, the Evangelical Church in Angola, the Evangelical Church of the Apostles of Jerusalem, the Evangelical Reformed Church of Angola, the Kimbanguist Church in Angola, the Maná Church and the United Methodist Church.

The Roman Catholic Church

Angola comprises three archdioceses and 13 dioceses. At 31 December 2004 there were 10,947,439 adherents in the country, equivalent to 51.2% of the population.

Bishops' Conference

Conferência Episcopal de Angola e São Tomé (CEAST), CP 3579, Luanda; tel. 222443686; fax 222445504; e-mail ceast@snet.co.ao.

f. 1967; Pres. Most Rev. DAMIÃO ANTÓNIO FRANKLIN (Archbishop of Luanda).

Archbishop of Huambo: Most Rev. JOSÉ DE QUEIRÓS ALVES, Arcebispado, CP 10, Huambo; tel. 241220130; fax 241220133; e-mail bispado-huambo@huambo.angonet.org.

Archbishop of Luanda: Most Rev. DAMIÃO ANTÓNIO FRANKLIN, Arcebispado, Largo do Palácio 9, CP 87, 1230-C, Luanda; tel. 222331481; fax 222334433; e-mail spastoral@snet.co.ao.

Archbishop of Lubango: Most Rev. ZACARIAS KAMWENHO, Arcebispado, CP 231, Lubango; tel. and fax 261230140; e-mail arquidiocese.lubango@netangola.com.

The Press

A free press was reinstituted in 1991, after 15 years of government control. In 2004 there were seven privately owned newspapers in Angola.

DAILIES

Diário da República: CP 1306, Luanda; official govt bulletin.

O Jornal de Angola: Rua Rainha Ginga 18–24, CP 1312, Luanda; tel. 222335531; fax 222333342; e-mail jornaldeangola@nexus.ao; internet www.jornaldeangola.com; f. 1975; state-owned; Dir JOSÉ RIBEIRO; mornings and Sun.; circ. 41,000.

PERIODICALS

Actual: Rua Fernando Pessoa 103, Vila Alice, CP 6959, Luanda; tel. and fax 222332116; e-mail actuals@hotmail.com; f. 2003; weekly; Editor JOAQUIM ALVES.

Agora: Rua Commandante Valódia 59, 2° andar, CP 24, Luanda; tel. and fax 222344680; e-mail agora-as@ebonet.net; f. 1996; weekly; Dir AGUIAR DOS SANTOS.

Angolense: Rua Cónego Manuel das Neves 83B, Luanda; tel. 222341501; fax 222340549; e-mail angolense@netangola.com; f. 1998; weekly; Dir AMÉRICO GONÇALVES.

O Apostolado: Rua Comandante Bula 118, São Paulo, CP 3579, Luanda; tel. 222432641; fax 222440628; e-mail direccao@apostolado.info; internet www.apostolado.info; current and religious affairs; Dir MAURÍCIO AGOSTINHO CAMUTO.

A Capital: Luanda; f. 2003; weekly; Dir FRANCISCO TANDALA.

Comércio Actualidade: Rua da Missão 81, CP 6375, Luanda; tel. 222334060; fax 222392216; e-mail actualidade@ebonet.net; f. 1993; weekly; Editor VICTOR ALEIXO.

Eme: Luanda; tel. 222321130; f. 1996; fortnightly; MPLA publ; Dir FERNANDO FATI.

Folha 8: Rua Conselheiro Júlio de Vilhena 24, 5° andar, CP 6527, Luanda; tel. 222391943; fax 222392289; e-mail folha8@ebonet.net; f. 1994; two a week; Dir WILLIAM TONET.

Gráfica Popular: Luanda; state-owned.

Independente: Rua Gracia da Horta 9, Luanda; tel. and fax 222343968; weekly; Dir PEDRO NARCISO.

Jornal dos Desportos: Rua Rainha Ginga 18–24, CP 1312, Luanda; tel. 222335531; fax 222335481; e-mail jornaldosdesportos@hotmail.com; internet www.jornaldosdesportos.com; f. 1994; bi-weekly; Dir LUIS FERNANDO; Editorial Dir POLICARPO DA ROSA; circ. 5,000.

Lavra & Oficina: CP 2767-C, Luanda; tel. 222322421; fax 222323205; e-mail uea@uea-angola.org; internet www.uea-angola.org; f. 1975; journal of the União dos Escritores Angolanos (Union of Angolan Writers); monthly; circ. 5,000.

A Palavra: Luanda; f. 2003; weekly.

Semanário Angolense: Rua António Feliciano de Castilho 103, Luanda; tel. 222264915; fax 222263506; e-mail info@semanarioangolense.com; internet www.semanarioangolense.net; f. 2003; independent; current affairs; Dir FELIZBERTO GRAÇA CAMPOS; weekly.

Tempos Novos: Av. Combatentes 244, 2° andar, CP 16088, Luanda; tel. 222349534; fax 222349534; f. 1995.

NEWS AGENCIES

In early 2006 legislation was passed by the Assembléia Nacional ending the governmental monopoly over news agencies.

Agência Angola Press (ANGOP): Rua Rei Katyavala 120, CP 2181, Luanda; tel. 222447343; fax 222447342; e-mail angop@netangola.com; internet www.angolapress-angop.ao; f. 1975; Dir-Gen. MANUEL DA CONCEIÇÃO.

Centro de Imprensa Anibal de Melo (CIAM): Rua Cerqueira Lukoki 124, CP 2805, Luanda; tel. 222393341; fax 222393445; govt press centre; Dir Dr OLYMPIO DE SOUSA E SILVA.

Foreign Bureaux

Agence France-Presse (AFP): CIAM, Rua Cerqueira Lukoki 124, CP 2805, Luanda; tel. 2223979033; Bureau Chief MANUELA TEIXEIRA.

ITAR—TASS (Information Telegraphic Agency of Russia—Telegraphic Agency of the Sovereign Countries): Rua Marechal Tito 75, CP 3209, Luanda; tel. 222342524; Correspondent VLADIMIR BORISOVICH BUYANOV.

Inter Press Service (IPS) (Italy): CIAM, Rua Cerqueira Lukoki 124, CP 2805, Luanda; tel. 222334895; fax 222393445; Correspondent CHRIS SIMPSON.

Lusa (Agência de Notícias de Portugal, SA): Luanda; Bureau Chief MIGUEL SOUTO.

Prensa Latina (Cuba): Rua D. Miguel de Melo 92, Luanda; tel. 222336804; e-mail prela-ang@elebonet.net; Chief Correspondent ROBERTO SALOMÓN.

Reuters (United Kingdom): CIAM, Rua Cerqueira Lukoki 124, CP 2805, Luanda; tel. 222334895; fax 222393445; Correspondent CRISTINA MULLER.

RIA—Novosti (Russian Information Agency—News): Luanda; Chief Officer VLADISLAV Z. KOMAROV.

Xinhua (New China) News Agency (People's Republic of China): Rua Karl Marx 57, 3° andar E, Bairro das Ingombotas, Zona 4, Luanda; tel. 222332415; Correspondent ZHAO XIAOZHONG.

Publishers

Chá de Caxinde: Av. do 1° Congresso do MPLA 20–24, CP 5958, Luanda; tel. 222336020; fax 222332876; e-mail chacaxinde@ebonet.net; f. 1999; Dir JAQUES ARLINDO DOS SANTOS.

Editorial Kilombelombe: Luanda; Dir MATEUS VOLÓDIA.

Editorial Nzila: Rua Comandante Valódia 1, ao Largo do Kinaxixi, Luanda; tel. 222447137; e-mail edinzila@hotmail.com.

Plural Editores: Rua Lucrécia Paim 16A (ex-Marquês de Minas), Bairro do Maculusso, Luanda; e-mail plural@pluraleditores.co.ao; internet www.pluraleditores.co.ao; f. 2005; 49% owned by Porto Editora (Portugal); technical and educational.

Ponto Um Indústria Gráfica: Rua Sebastião Desta Vez 55, Luanda; tel. 222448315; fax 222449424.

União dos Escritores Angolanos (UEA): Luanda; tel. and fax 222323205; e-mail uea@uea-angola.org; internet www.uea-angola.org.

GOVERNMENT PUBLISHING HOUSE

Imprensa Nacional, UEE: CP 1306, Luanda; f. 1845; Gen. Man. ANA MARÍA SOUSA E SILVA.

Broadcasting and Communications

TELECOMMUNICATIONS

Angola Telecom (AT): Rua das Quipacas 186, CP 625, Luanda; tel. 222311889; fax 222311288; e-mail Sec_CA@angolatelecom.com; internet www.angolatelecom.com; state telecommunications co; Dir-Gen. JOÃO AVELINO AUGUSTO MANUEL.

Movicel Telecomunicaçõcs, Lda: Rua Mãe Isabel 1, Luanda; tel. 222692000; fax 222692090; internet www.movicel.co.ao; f. 2002; mobile cellular telephone operator; Chair. MANUEL AVELINO; Exec. Dir MICHAEL ROUBICEK.

Mundo StarTel: Rua Ndunduma 188, São Paulo, Município de Sambizanga, Luanda; tel. 222432417; e-mail mundostartel@netangola.com; 44% owned by Telecom Namibia.

Nexus Telecomunicações e Serviços SARL: Rua dos Enganos 1, 1° andar, Luanda; tel. 228740041; fax 228740741; e-mail nexus@nexus.ao; internet www.nexus.ao; began operations mid-2004; fixed-line operator.

Unitel SARL: Sede Miramar, Rua Marechal Bróz Tito 77–79, Ingombotas, Luanda; tel. 222199100; fax 222447783; e-mail unitel@unitel.co.ao; internet www.unitel.co.ao; f. 1998; 25% owned by Portugal Telecom; private mobile telephone operator; Dir-Gen. NICOLAU JORGE NETO.

Regulatory Authority

Instituto Angolano das Comunicações (INACOM): Av. de Portugal 92, 7° andar, CP 1459, Luanda; tel. 222338352; fax 222339356; e-mail inacom.dg@netangola.com; internet www.inacom.og.ao; f. 1999; monitoring and regulatory authority; Dir-Gen. JOÃO BEIRÃO.

BROADCASTING

Radio

A decree on the regulation of radio broadcasting was approved in 1997. Since that time private operators had reportedly experienced difficulty in gaining permission to broadcast; although four private stations were operating in Luanda in 2004.

Rádio Nacional de Angola: Rua Comandante Gika, CP 1329, Luanda; tel. 222320192; fax 222324647; e-mail rna.dg@netangola.com; internet www.rna.ao; state-controlled; operates Canal A, Radio 5, Radio FM Estério, Radio Luanda and Radio N'gola Yetu; broadcasts in Portuguese, English, French, Spanish and vernacular languages (Chokwe, Kikongo, Kimbundu, Kwanyama, Fiote, Ngangela, Luvale, Songu, Umbundu); Dir-Gen. ALBERTO DE SOUSA.

Luanda Antena Comercial (LAC): Rua Luther King 5, CP 3521, Luanda; tel. 222394989; fax 222396229; e-mail lac@ebonet.net; internet www.nexus.ao/lac; popular music.

Radio CEFOJOR: Rua Luther King 123/4, Luanda; tel. 222336140; e-mail cefojor@hotmail.com; f. 2003; commercial station, provides journalistic training; Dir-Gen. JOAQUIM PAULO DA CONCEIÇÃO.

Rádio Ecclésia—Emissora Católica de Angola: Rua Comandante Bula 118, São Paulo, CP 3579, Luanda; tel. 222443041; fax 222443093; e-mail recclesia@recclesia.org; internet www.recclesia.org; f. 1955; broadcasts mainly restricted to Luanda; coverage of politics and current affairs; Dir-Gen. JOSÉ PAULO.

Radio Escola: Luanda; educational.

Rádio Morena Comercial, Lda: Rua Comandante Kassanji, CP 537, Benguela; tel. 272232525; fax 272234242.

The Voice of America (internet www.ebonet.net/voa) also broadcasts from Luanda.

Television

In early 2006 legislation was passed by the Assembléia Nacional ending the Government's monopoly over television and simplifying the radio licensing process. A digital television system, TV Cabo Angola, began broadcasting in early 2006.

Televisão Pública de Angola (TPA): Rua Ho Chi Minh, CP 2604, Luanda; tel. 222320272; fax 222323027; e-mail carlos.cunha@netangola.com; internet www.tpa.ao; f. 1976; state-controlled; 2 channels; Man. Dir CARLOS CUNHA.

Finance

(cap. = capital; res = reserves; dep. = deposits; m. = million; brs = branches; amounts in kwanza (equivalent to 1m. readjusted kwanza), unless otherwise indicated)

BANKING

All banks were nationalized in 1975. In 1995 the Government authorized the formation of private banks. In 2006 there were 12 commercial banks in Angola.

Central Bank

Banco Nacional de Angola: Av. 4 de Fevereiro 151, CP 1243, Luanda; tel. 222399125; fax 222390579; e-mail bna.cri@ebonet.net; internet www.bna.ao; f. 1976; bank of issue; Gov. Dr AMADEU DE JESÚS CASTELHANO MAURÍCIO; 6 brs.

Commercial Banks

Banco Comercial Angolano (BCA): Av. Comandante Valódia 83A, CP 6900, Luanda; tel. 222349548; fax 222349516; e-mail bca@snet.co.ao; f. 1997; 50% owned by Absa; cap. 0.9m., res 347.4m., dep. 1,799.3m. (Dec. 2002); Pres. Dr BENVINDO RAFAEL PITRA; 4 brs (2005).

Banco de Fomento Angola—BFA: Rua Amílcar Cabral 58, Luanda; tel. 222638900; fax 222638925; internet www.bfa.ao; f. 1993 as Banco Fomento Exterior; name changed to above in 2001; 100% owned by Banco BPI, SA, Portugal; cap. 3,522.0m., res 2,613.0m., dep. 75,168.4m. (Dec. 2004); CEO EMIDIO PINHEIRO; 38 brs (2005).

Banco Internacional de Crédito (BIC): Rua Cerqueira Lukoki 78–80, Luanda; tel. 222391526; fax 222391407; e-mail bancobic@bancobic.ao; internet www.bancobic.ao; f. 2005; 25% owned by Américo Amorim, Portugal; Chair. FERNANDO MENDES TELES.

Banco de Poupança e Crédito (BPC): Largo Saydi Mingas, CP 1343, Luanda; tel. 222390841; fax 222372529; e-mail bpc@bpc.ao; internet www.bpc.ao; f. 1956 as Banco Comercial de Angola; 100% state-owned; undergoing privatization in 2006; cap. 1,304.0m., res 2,574.3m., dep. 64,072.4m. (Dec. 2004); Chair. PAIXÃO ANTÓNIO JÚNIOR; brs throughout Angola.

Banco Regional do Keve SARL: Edif. Robert Hudson, Rua Rainha Ginga 77, CP 1804, Luanda; tel. 222394100; fax 222395101; e-mail servicoscentrais@bankeve.com; internet www.bankeve.com; f. 2003; Pres. AMILCAR AZEVEDO DA SILVA.

Banco Sol: Rua Rei Katyavala 110–112, Maculusso, Zona 8, Ingombotas, CP 814, Luanda; tel. 222402215; fax 222440226; e-mail banco.sol@ebonet.net; internet www.bancosol.co.ao; f. 2000; cap. 96.9m., res 389.9m., dep. 5,474.0m. (Dec. 2004); Pres. SEBASTIÃO BASTOS LAVRADOR.

Development Bank

Banco de Comércio e Indústria SARL: Rua Rainha Ginga, Largo do Atlético 79–83, POB 1395, Luanda; tel. 222330209; fax 222334924; e-mail falfredo@bci.ebonet.net; f. 1991; 91% state-owned; privatization pending; provides loans to businesses in all sectors; cap. US $9.5m., res $34.4m., dep. $247.3m. (Dec. 2002); Chair. ADRIANO RAFAEL PASCOAL; 5 brs.

Banco de Desenvolvimento de Angola (BDA): Luanda; f. 2006; Pres. FRANCO PAIXÃO.

Investment Bank

Banco Africano de Investimentos SARL (BAI): Rua Major Kanhangulo 34, CP 6022, Luanda; tel. 222335749; fax 222335486; e-mail baisede@bancobai.co.ao; internet www.bancobai.co.ao; f. 1997; 17.5% interest owned by Sonangol; cap. 6.5m., dep. 91,253.3m. (Dec. 2005); Pres. Dr MÁRIO ABÍLIO PALHARES; 15 brs.

Foreign Banks

Banco Comercial Português—Atlântico SA: Rua Rainha Ginga 83, CP 5726, Luanda; tel. 222397922; fax 222397397; e-mail atlantico_luanda@netangola.com; Gen. Man. MARIA NAZARÉ FRANCISCO DANG.

Banco Espírito Santo Angola SARL (BESA): Rua do 1º Congresso do MPLA 29, Bairro Ingombotas, Luanda; tel. 222693600; fax 222693698; internet www.besa.ao; f. 2002; 99.96% owned by Banco Espírito Santo SA, Lisbon; cap. US $7.0m., res $6.1m., dep. $205.3m. (Dec. 2004); Gen. Mans Dr CARLOS SILVA, Dr HELDER BATAGLIA.

Banco Totta de Angola SARL: Av. 4 de Fevereiro 99, CP 1231, Luanda; tel. 222332729; fax 222333233; e-mail tottango@ebonet.net; 99.98% owned by Banco Santander Totta; cap. €15.5m. (Dec. 2003); Man. Dir Dr MÁRIO NELSON MAXIMINO; 7 brs.

NovoBanco: Rua N'Dunduma 253/257, Bairro Miramar, Município Sambizanga, Luanda; tel. 222430040; fax 222430074; e-mail secretariado@novobanco.ao; internet www.novobanco.net; f. 2004; Pres. GABRIELE HEBER; Dir STEFAN WOLFF.

BNP Paribas, Citigroup and Equator Bank Ltd maintain offices in Luanda.

STOCK EXCHANGE

Bolsa de Valores e Derivativos do Angola (BVDA): Mutamba, Luanda; f. 2006.

INSURANCE

AAA Seguros SA: Rua Lenine 58, Luanda; tel. 222691331; fax 222691342; e-mail saovicente@aaa.co.ao; f. 2000; life and non-life; Pres. Dr CARLOS MANUEL DE SÃO VICENTE.

ENSA Seguros de Angola (Empresa Nacional de Seguros e Resseguros de Angola, UEE): Av. 4 de Fevereiro 93, CP 5778, Luanda; tel. 222332990; fax 222332946; e-mail ensaio@ebonet.net; f. 1978; state-owned; to be privatized; Chair. MANUEL JOAQUIM GONÇALVES; Pres. and Dir-Gen. ALEIXO AUGUSTO.

GA Angola Seguros (Global Alliance Insurance Angola): Av. 4 de Fevereiro 79, 1° andar, Luanda; tel. 222330368; fax 222398815; e-mail blara@globalalliance.co.ao; internet www.globalalliance.co.ao; f. 2005; owned by Global Alliance Group (United Kingdom); Gen. Man BRIAN LARA.

Nova Sociedade de Seguros de Angola S.A. (Nossa Seguros): Av. 4 de Fevereiro 111, Luanda; tel. 222399909; fax 222399153; e-mail info@nossaseguros.com; internet www.nossaseguros.com.

Trade and Industry

GOVERNMENT AGENCIES

Corpo de Segurança de Diamantes (CSD): Luanda; f. 2004; security agency monitoring diamond mining sector.

Gabinete de Obras Especiais: Luanda; Dir MANUEL FERREIRA CLEMENTE JÚNIOR.

Gabinete de Reconstrução Nacional: Luanda; f. 2004; monitors economic and social reconstruction programmes; Dir MANUEL HELDER VIEIRA DIAS JÚNIOR.

Gabinete de Redimensionamento Empresarial: Rua Cerqueira Lukoki 25, 9° andar, CP 594, Luanda; tel. 222390496; fax 222392987; privatization agency.

Instituto de Desenvolvimento Agrário: Rua Comandante Gika, CP 2109, Luanda; tel. and fax 222323651; e-mail ida.canga@netangola.com; promotes agricultural development; Dir Eng. AFONSO PEDRO CANGA.

Instituto de Desenvolvimento Industrial de Angola (IDIA): Rua Cerqueira Lukoki 25, 8° andar, CP 594, Luanda; tel. and fax 222338492; e-mail idiadg@netangola.com; f. 1995; promotes industrial development; Dir KIALA NGONE GABRIELE.

Instituto de Investimento Estrangeiro (IIE): Rua Cerqueira Lukoki 25, 9º andar, CP 594, Luanda; tel. 222392620; fax 222393381; foreign investment agency.

Instituto Nacional de Cereais (INCER): Av. 4 de Fevereiro 101, CP 1105, Luanda; tel. and fax 222331611; promotes cereal crops; Dir-Gen. ESTEVÃO MIGUEL DE CARVALHO.

CHAMBER OF COMMERCE

Câmara de Comércio e Indústria de Angola (CCIA) (Angolan Chamber of Commerce and Industry): Largo do Kinaxixi 14, 1° andar, CP 92, Luanda; tel. 222444506; fax 222444629; e-mail ccira@ebonet.net; internet www.ccia.ebonet.net; Pres. ANTÓNIO JOÃO DOS SANTOS.

INDUSTRIAL AND TRADE ASSOCIATIONS

Associação Comercial de Benguela: Rua Sacadura Cabral 104, CP 347, Benguela; tel. 272232441; fax 272233022; e-mail acbenguela@netangola.com; internet www.netangola.com/acb; f. 1907; Pres. AIRES PIRES ROQUE.

Associação Comercial e Industrial da Ilha de Luanda (ACIL): Largo do Kinaxixi 9, Luanda; tel. 222341866; fax 222349677; Pres. PEDRO GODHINO DOMINGOS.

Associação Comercial e Industrial de Luanda (ACOMIL): Largo do Kinaxixi 14–30, Luanda; tel. 222335728; Pres. JOÃO ADÃO ANTÔNIO TIGRE.

Associação Comercial de Luanda (ASCANGOLA): Edif. Palácio de Comércio, 1° andar, CP 1275, Luanda; tel. 222332453.

Associação Industrial de Angola (AIA): Rua Manuel Fernando Caldeira 6, CP 6127, Luanda; tel. 222443504; fax 222392241; e-mail secretariado@aiaangola.com; internet www.aiaangola.com; Pres. JOSÉ SEVERINO.

Associação de Mulheres Empresárias: Largo do Kinaxixi 14, 3° andar, Luanda; tel. 222346742; fax 222343088; f. 1990; asscn of business women; Sec.-Gen. HENRIQUETA DE CARVALHO.

Rede Angolana do Sector Micro-Empresarial (RASME): Luanda; asscn of small businesses; Exec.-Co-ordinator BAY KANGUDI.

STATE TRADING ORGANIZATIONS

Angolan Selling Corporation (ASCORP): Edif. Soleil B, Rua Tipografia Mama Tita, Ingombotas, CP 3978, Luanda; tel. 222396465; fax 222397615; e-mail ascorpadmin@ebonet.net; f. 1999; 51% state-owned diamond-trading co; Pres. NOE BALTAZAR.

Direcção dos Serviços de Comércio (DNCI) (Dept of Trade): Palácio de Vidro, 3° andar, Largo 4 de Fevereiro 7, CP 1337, Luanda; tel. and fax 222310658; e-mail minco.dnci.gc@netangola.com; internet www.dnci.net; f. 1970; brs throughout Angola; Dir GOMES CARDOSO.

Exportang, UEE (Empresa de Exportações de Angola): Rua dos Enganos 1A, CP 1000, Luanda; tel. 222332363; co-ordinates exports.

Importang, UEE (Empresa de Importações de Angola): Calçada do Município 10, CP 1003, Luanda; tel. 222337994; f. 1977; co-ordinates majority of imports; Dir-Gen. SIMÃO DIOGO DA CRUZ.

Maquimport, UEE: Rua Rainha Ginga 152, CP 2975, Luanda; tel. 222339044; f. 1981; to import office equipment.

Mecanang, UEE: Rua dos Enganos, 1°–7° andar, CP 1347, Luanda; tel. 222390644; f. 1981; to import agricultural and construction machinery, tools and spare parts.

Nova Angomédica, UEE: Rua do Sanatório, Bairro Palanca, CP 2698, Luanda; tel. 222261366; fax 222260010; f. 1981; production and distribution of pharmaceutical goods; Gen. Dir JAILTON BATISTA DOS SANTOS.

Sociedade de Comercialização de Diamantes de Angola SARL (SODIAM): Edif. Endiama/De Beers, Rua Rainha Ginga 87, CP 1072, Luanda; tel. 222370217; fax 222370423; e-mail sodiamadmin@ebonet.net; f. 2000; part of the ENDIAMA group; diamond trading org.; Man. Dir MANUEL ARNALDO DE SOUSA CALADO.

STATE INDUSTRIAL ENTERPRISES

Bricomil: Rua Massano Amorim 79, Chicala, Luanda; tel. 222343895; fax 222342533; f. 1986; 55% state-owned; privatization planned; civil construction; 650 employees.

Companhia do Açúcar de Angola: Rua Direita 77, Luanda; production of sugar.

Empresa Abastecimento Técnico Material, UEE (EMATEC): Largo Rainha Ginga 3, CP 2952, Luanda; tel. 222338891; technical and material suppliers to the Ministry of National Defence.

Empresa de Construção de Edificações, UEE (CONSTROI): Rua Amílcar Cabral 167, 1° andar, Luanda; tel. 222333930; construction.

Empresa de Obras Especiais (EMPROE): Rua Ngola Kiluange 183–185, Luanda; tel. 222382142; fax 222382143; building and civil engineering.

Empresa de Pesca de Angola, UEE (PESCANGOLA): Luanda; f. 1981; state fishing enterprise, responsible to the Ministry of Fisheries.

Empresa de Rebenefício e Exportação do Café de Angola, UEE (CAFANGOL): Rua Robert Shields 4–6, CP 342, Luanda; tel. 222337916; fax 222332840; e-mail cafangol@nexus.ao; f. 1983; nat. coffee-processing and trade org.; Dir-Gen. ALVARO FARIA.

Empresa de Tecidos de Angola, UEE (TEXTANG): Rua N'gola Kiluanji-Kazenga, CP 5404, Luanda; tel. 222381134; production of textiles.

Empresa dos Tabacos de Angola: CP 1238, Luanda; tel. 222336995; fax 222336921; manufacture of tobacco products; Gen. Man. K. Bittencourt.

Empresa Nacional de Cimento, UEE (ENCIME): CP 157, Lobito; tel. 272212325; cement production.

Empresa Nacional de Comercialização e Distribuição de Produtos Agrícolas (ENCODIPA): Luanda; central marketing agency for agricultural produce; numerous brs throughout Angola.

Empresa Nacional de Diamantes de Angola (ENDIAMA), UEE: Rua Major Kanhangulo 100, CP 1247, Luanda; tel. and fax 222332718; f. 1981; commenced operations 1986; diamond mining; a number of subsidiary companies undergoing privatization; Pres. Dr Manuel Arnaldo de Sousa Calado.

Empresa Nacional de Ferro de Angola (FERRANGOL): Rua João de Barros 26, CP 2692, Luanda; tel. 222373800; iron production; Chair. Diamantino Pedro de Azevedo; Dir Armando de Sousa.

Empresa Nacional de Manutenção, UEE (MANUTECNICA): Rua 7, Av. do Cazenga 10, CP 3508, Luanda; tel. 222383646; assembly of machines and specialized equipment for industry.

Geotécnica Unidad Económica Estatal: Rua Angola Kilmanse 389–393, Luanda; tel. 222381795; fax 222382730; f. 1978; for surveying and excavation; Man. P. M. M. Elvino, Jr.

Siderurgia Nacional, UEE: Rua Farol Lagostas, Luanda; tel. 222383587; f. 1963; nationalized 1980; scheduled for privatization; steelworks and rolling mill plant.

Sonangalp, Lda: Rua Manuel Fernando Caldeira 25, Luanda; tel. 222334527; fax 222333529; internet www.sonangalp.co.ao; f. 1994; 51% owned by Sonangol, 49% owned by Petrogal Angola (Portugal); fuel distribution; Pres. António Silvestre.

Sociedade Nacional de Combustíveis de Angola (SONANGOL): Rua 1° Congreso do MPLA 8–16, CP 1316, Luanda; tel. 222632162; fax 2223919782; e-mail drh@sonangol.co.ao; internet www.sonangol.co.ao; f. 1976 for exploration, production and refining of crude petroleum, and marketing and distribution of petroleum products; sole concessionary in Angola, supervises on- and offshore operations of foreign petroleum cos; 11 subsidiaries, including shipping cos; holds majority interest in jt ventures with Cabinda Gulf Oil Co (Cabgoc), Fina Petróleos de Angola and Texaco Petróleos de Angola; CEO Manuel Vicente; c. 7,000 employees.

UTILITIES

Electricity

Empresa Nacional de Construções Eléctricas, UEE (ENCEL): Rua Comandante Che Guevara 185–187, CP 5230, Luanda; tel. 222446712; fax 222446759; e-mail encel@encel.co.ao; internet www.encel.co.ao; f. 1982; supplier of electromechanical equipment; Dir Gen. Daniel Simas.

Empresa Nacional de Electricidade, EP (ENE): Edif. Geominas 6°–7° andar, CP 772, Luanda; tel. 222321499; fax 222323433; e-mail enepdg@netangola.com; f. 1980; production and distribution of electricity; Pres. and Dir-Gen. Eng. Eduardo Gomes Nelumba.

Water

Empresa Provincial de Água de Luanda (EPAL): Rua Frederich Engels 3, CP 1387, Luanda; tel. 222335001; fax 222330380; e-mail epalsdg@sney.co.ao; state-owned; Dir Diógenes Oliveira.

MAJOR COMPANIES

Agip Angola, Lda: Rua Nicolau Gomes Spencer 140, CP 1289, Luanda; tel. 22391894; fax 22394133; subsidiary of ENI SpA, Italy; Chair. Pietro Cavanna; Man. Dir Piero Fraenzi; 85 employees.

Agroquímica de Angola SARL (AGRAN): CP 67, Luanda; tel. 222333594; fax 222339499; e-mail agran@netangola.com; f. 1960; 98.7% owned by Petrogal Angola; manufacture of agricultural chemicals.

Angola Polishing Diamond, SA: Luanda; f. 2005; 47% owned by LLD Diamonds Ltd (Israel), 48% owned by SODIAM; c. 600 employees.

BP Angola, Lda: Rua Rainha Ginga 87, Luanda; tel. 222637440; fax 222637333; subsidiary of BP PLC, UK; Man. Dir Richard Field; over 600 employees.

Chevron: Av. Lenine 77, CP 2950, Luanda; tel. 222392646; fax 222394348; owns Cabinda Gulf Oil Co (CABGOC); Man. Dir Jim Blackwell.

Coca-Cola Bottling SARL: Rua N'Gola Kiluange 370, Luanda; tel. 222381212; fax 222380047; e-mail angola@africa.coca-cola.com; internet www.angola.coca-cola.com; f. 1999; 55% owned by Coca-Cola, USA, 45% state-owned; bottling plant at Bom Jesus; Dir-Gen. Islay Rhind.

Companhia Fabril e Comercial de Angola SARL (COMFABRIL): Av. 4 de Fevereiro 79, CP 859, Luanda; tel. 222336393; fax 222336390; manufacture and sale of chemicals; Pres. José Manuel da Silva José Mello.

Fina Petróleos de Angola SARL (PETRANGOL): Rua Rainha Ginga 128, CP 1320, Luanda; tel. 222336855; fax 222391031; e-mail carlosalves@fpa.ebonet.net; f. 1958 for exploration, production and refining of petroleum and natural gas; operates Luanda petroleum refinery, Petrangol, with capacity of 40,000 b/d; also operates Quinfuquena terminal; 64.1% owned by Total (France); Gen. Man. Carlos Alves; 553 employees.

Indufer: Rua Maianga 40–44, Luanda; tel. 222398350; fax 222290054; e-mail indufame@ebonet.net; private co managing Fábrica de Tubos de Angola (FATA) and Metalúrgica de Angola (Metang) in preparation for privatization; Pres. José Pinto dos Santos Neto.

Nova Cimangola (Empresa de Cimentos de Angola): Av. 4 de Fevereiro 42, CP 2532, Luanda; tel. 222334941; fax 222334940; f. 1994; 49% owned by Cimpor, Portugal; 39% state-owned; production of cement and plaster; CEO Manuel Victor.

Petrogal Angola SA: Av. 4 de Fevereiro 3–4, Luanda; tel. 222397977; fax 222339499; 100% owned by Galpenergia (Portugal); exploration, production and distribution of petroleum; Chair. Prof. Manuel Ferreira de Oliveira.

Petromar UEM: Rua Georgi Dimitrov 5–7, Bairro Ingombotas, Luanda; tel. 222332424; fax 222330339; internet www.petromar.co.ao; f. 1984; exploration and production of petroleum and gas; Dir-Gen. Philippe Frederic.

Sociedade Angolana de Gases Comprimodos SARL (ANGASES): Estrada do Cacuaco, CP 524, Luanda; tel. 222310505; fax 222310099; e-mail angases@ebonet.net; f. 1951; production of medical and industrial gases and electrodes; Gen. Man. Julio De Melo Araujo.

Sociedade de Desenvolvimento Mineiro de Angola SARL: Parque Empresarial Odebrecht, Av. Pedro de Castro Van-Dúnem 'Loy' s/n, Bloco D, Luanda Sul, CP 6551, Luanda; tel. 222678300; fax 222678315; e-mail stinfo@sdm.net; internet www.sdm.net; owned by Odebrecht (Brazil) and ENDIAMA; Dir-Gen. Maurício Neves.

Sociedade Industrial dos Tabacos de Angola (SITAL): Av. Governador Sousa Coutinho 38, CP 343, Benguela; tel. 272232691; fax 272235077; 100% owned by British American Tobacco Company; wholesale trade in tobacco.

Sociedade Mineira de Catoca, Lda: Edif. Endiama, 4° andar, Rua Major Kanhangulo 100, Luanda; tel. 222676990; fax 222676991; e-mail contato@catoca.com; internet www.catoca.com; f. 1992; jt diamond mining and exploration operation owned by ENDIAMA, Alrosa (Russia), Odebrecht (Brazil) and Daumonty Financing BV; Admin. Dir Marcelo Gomes; 2,000 employees.

Sociedade Unificada de Tabacos de Angola, Lda (SUT): Rua Deolinda Rodrigues 530–537, CP 1263, Luanda; tel. 222360180; fax 222360170; f. 1919; tobacco products; 100% owned by British American Tobacco Company; Gen. Man. Dr Manuel Lamas.

TRADE UNIONS

Sindicato dos Jornalistas Angolanos (SJA): Rua Francisco Távora 8, 1° andar, CP 2140, Luanda; tel. 222331969; fax 222332420; e-mail sja@netangola.com; f. 1992; Pres. Avelino Miguel; Gen. Sec. Luisa Rogério; 1,253 mems in 2003.

Sindicato Nacional de Professores (Sinprof): Rua da Missão 71, 4° andar, Luanda; tel. 222371780; e-mail sinprof@angonet.org; teachers' union; Gen. Sec. Miguel João Filho.

União Nacional das Associações de Camponeses Angolanos (UNACA): Luanda; peasants' asscn; Gen. Sec. Paulo Uime.

União Nacional de Trabalhadores Angolanos (UNTA) (National Union of Angolan Workers): Av. 4 de Fevereiro 210, CP 28, Luanda; tel. 222334670; fax 222393590; e-mail untadis@netangola.com; f. 1960; Pres. Manuel Augusto Viage; c. 160,000 mems.

Transport

The transport infrastructure was severely dislocated by the civil war that ended in 2002. Subsequently, major rebuilding and upgrading projects were undertaken.

RAILWAYS

There are three main railway lines in Angola, the Benguela railway, which runs from the coast to the Zambian border, the Luanda–Malanje line, and the Moçamedes line, which connects Namibe and Cuando-Cubango. In 2004 only 850 km out of a total of almost 3,000 km of track were operational. A plan introduced in late 2004 to rehabilitate and extend the rail network was expected to take 11 years and to cost US $4,000m. In mid-2005 a project for rebuilding and upgrading the railway system was approved by the Southern African Development Community (SADC). The Benguela line—a significant export route—was scheduled to reopen in mid-2007, following demining and reconstruction work by Chinese workers.

Direcção Nacional dos Caminhos de Ferro: Rua Major Kanhangulo, CP 1250, Luanda; tel. 222370091; f. 1975; nat. network operating four fmrly independent systems covering 2,952 track-km; Dir JULIO BANGO.

Amboim Railway: Porto Amboim; f. 1922; 123 track-km; Dir A. GUIA.

Benguela Railway (Caminho de Ferro de Benguela—Empresa Pública): Praça 11 Novembro 3, CP 32, Lobito, Benguela; tel. 272222645; fax 272225133; e-mail cfbeng@ebonet.net; f. 1903; line completed 1928; owned by Govt of Angola; line carrying passenger and freight traffic from the port of Lobito across Angola, via Huambo and Luena, to the border of the Democratic Republic of the Congo (DRC, fmrly Zaire); 1,301 track-km; guerrilla operations by UNITA suspended all international traffic from 1975, with only irregular services from Lobito to Huambo being operated; the rehabilitation of the railway was a priority of a 10-year programme, planned by the Southern African Development Co-ordination Conference (SADCC, now SADC), to develop the 'Lobito corridor'; from 2001 rehabilitation of the line was under government control; in 2004 a consortium from China (People's Republic) agreed to rehabilitate the line to the DRC; Dir-Gen. DANIEL QUIPAXE; 1,700 employees.

Caminho de Ferro de Moçâmedes (CFM): CP 130, Lubango; tel. 261221752; fax 261224442; e-mail gab.dir.cfm@netangola.com; f. 1905; main line from Namibe to Menongue, via Lubango; br. lines to Chibia and iron ore mines at Cassinga; 838 track-km; Dir-Gen. Dr JÚLIO BANGO JOAQUIM.

Luanda Railway (Empresa de Caminho de Ferro de Luanda, UEE): CP 1250-C, Luanda; tel. 222370061; f. 1886; serves an iron-, cotton- and sisal-producing region between Luanda and Malanje; 536 track-km; Man. A. ALVARO AGANTE.

ROADS

In 2001 Angola had 51,429 km of roads, of which 7,944 km were main roads and 5,278 km were secondary roads. About 10.4% of roads were paved. It was estimated that 80% of the country's road network was in disrepair. In 2005–06 contracts were awarded to various foreign companies to upgrade the road network, including the main north–south coastal road. The Government planned a US $190m. programme to rebuild some 1,200 km of the network by 2008.

Direcção Nacional dos Transportes Rodoviárias: Rua Rainha Ginga 74, 1° andar, Luanda; tel. 222339390.

Instituto Nacional de Estradas de Angola (INEA): Rua Amílcar Cabral 35, 3° andar, CP 5667, Luanda; tel. 222332828; fax 222335754.

SHIPPING

The main harbours are at Lobito, Luanda and Namibe. The first phase of a 10-year SADCC (now SADC) programme to develop the 'Lobito corridor', for which funds were pledged in January 1989, was to include the rehabilitation of the ports of Lobito and Benguela. In January 2007 the Japanese authorities pledged US $9m. for the rehabilitation of the quays of Namibe and Lobito ports. The port of Luanda was due to be upgraded by 2010. In December 2005 Angola's registered merchant fleet comprised 128 vessels, totalling 53,869 grt.

Direcção Nacional da Marinha Mercante e Portos: Rua Rainha Ginga 74, 4° andar, Luanda; tel. 222332032.

Agenang, UEE: Rua Engracia Fragoso 47–49, Luanda; tel. 222336380; fax 222334392; state shipping co; scheduled for privatization.

Cabotang—Cabotagem Nacional Angolana, UEE: Av. 4 de Fevereiro 83A, Luanda; tel. 222373133; operates off the coasts of Angola and Mozambique; Dir-Gen. JOÃO OCTAVIO VAN-DÚNEM.

Empresa Portuária do Lobito, UEE: Av. da Independência 16, Lobito, Benguela; tel. 272222718; fax 272222719; e-mail eplobito@eplobito.com; internet www.eplobito.com; long-distance sea transport; Gen. Man. JOSÉ CARLOS GOMES.

Empresa Portuária de Luanda: CP 1229, Porto de Luanda; tel. 222393284; Pres. SÍLVIO BARROS VINHAS.

Empresa Portuária de Moçâmedes—Namibe, UEE: Rua Pedro Benje 10A e C, CP 49, Namibe; tel. 264260643; long-distance sea transport; Dir HUMBERTO DE ATAIDE DIAS.

Orey Angola, Lda: Largo 4 de Fevereiro 3, 3° andar, CP 583, Luanda; tel. 222310290; fax 222310882; e-mail orey@oreylad.ebonet.net; internet www.orey.com/angola; international shipping, especially to Portugal; Dir Commdt A. CARMONA E COSTA.

Sécil Marítima SARL, UEE: Edif. Secil, Av. 4 de Fevereiro 42, 1° andar, CP 5910, Luanda; tel. 222311334; fax 222311784; e-mail secilmaritima@msn.com; operates ports at Lobito, Luanda and Namibe; Gen. Man. MARIA AMÉLIA RITA.

CIVIL AVIATION

Angola's airport system is well-developed, but suffered some damage in the later years of the civil war. The 4 de Fevereiro airport in Luanda is the only international airport. During the mid-2000s airports at Luanda, Lobito, Soyo, Namibe, Saurimo, Uíge, Huambo and Bié were undergoing rehabilitation.

Direcção Nacional da Aviação Civil: Rua Frederich Engels 92, 6° andar, CP 569, Luanda; tel. 222339412.

Empresa Nacional de Aeroportos e Navegação Aerea (ENANA): Av. Amílcar Cabral 110, CP 841, Luanda; tel. and fax 222351267; e-mail cai_enana@snet.co.ao; administers airports; Chair. JORGE DOS SANTOS CORREIA MELO.

TAAG—Linhas Aéreas de Angola: Rua da Missão 123, CP 79, Luanda; tel. 222332338; fax 222390396; e-mail gci_taag@ebonet.net; internet www.nexus.ao/taag; f. 1938; internal scheduled passenger and cargo services, and services from Luanda to destinations within Africa and to Europe and South America; Chair. JESÚS NELSON PEREIRA MARTINS.

Angola Air Charter: Aeroporto Internacional 4 de Fevereiro, CP 3010, Luanda; tel. 222321290; fax 222320105; e-mail aacharter@independente.net; f. 1992; subsidiary of TAAG; CEO A. DE MATOS.

Air Nacoia: Rua Comandante Che Guevara 67, 1° andar, Luanda; tel. and fax 222395477; f. 1993; Pres. SALVADOR SILVA.

SONAIR SARL: Aeroporto Internacional 4 de Fevereiro, Luanda; tel. 222633502; fax 222321572; e-mail support.sonair@sonangol.co.ao; internet www.sonairsarl.com; f. 1998; subsidiary of SONANGOL; operates direct flights between Luanda and Houston, Texas, USA; Pres. Dr ANTÓNIO DOS SANTOS DOMINGOS.

Transafrik International Ltd: Aeroporto Internacional 4 de Fevereiro, Luanda; tel. 222353714; fax 222354183; e-mail info@transafrik.com; internet www.transafrik.com; f. 1986; operates international contract cargo services; CEO BJÖRN NÄF; Chief Financial Officer STEPHAN BRANDT.

Tourism

Angola's tourism industry is undeveloped as a result of the years of civil war, although its potential for development is great. Tourist arrivals totalled 194,329 in 2004.

National Tourist Agency: Palácio de Vidro, Largo 4 de Fevereiro, CP 1240, Luanda; tel. 222372750.

Defence

In accordance with the peace agreement concluded by the Government and the União Nacional para a Independência Total de Angola (UNITA) in May 1991 (see Recent History), a new 50,000-strong national army, the Forças Armadas de Angola (FAA), was established, comprising equal numbers of government forces, the Forças Armadas Populares de Libertação de Angola (FAPLA), and UNITA soldiers. After elections in 1992, UNITA withdrew its troops from the FAA and hostilities resumed. Following the signing of the Lusaka Accord in November 1994, the integration of the UNITA contingent into the FAA resumed. In 1995 agreement was reached between the Government and UNITA on the enlargement of the FAA to comprise a total of 90,000 troops, and discussions began concerning the potential formation of a fourth, non-combatant branch of the FAA, which would engage in public works projects. In mid-1997 the Government estimated that UNITA maintained a residual force numbering some 25,000–30,000 troops, while UNITA claimed to have a force of only 2,963 'police'. In March 1998 UNITA issued a declaration announcing the complete demobilization of its forces and by May some 11,000 UNITA soldiers had been integrated into the FAA. However, the integration process was abandoned following the resumption of hostilities between the Government and UNITA in December 1998. Following the ratification of a cease-fire in April 2002, only 5,000 UNITA fighters were integrated into the FAA; it was estimated that 80,000 had been reintegrated into civilian life by November 2003. As assessed at November 2006, the FAA had an estimated total strength of 107,000: army 100,000, navy 1,000 and air force 6,000. In addition, there was a paramilitary force numbering an estimated 10,000.

Defence Expenditure: Budgeted at 127,000m. kwanza for 2006.

Chief of General Staff of the Armed Forces: Gen. FRANCISCO PEREIRA FURTADO.

Chief of General Staff of the Army: Gen. JORGE BARROS NGUTÓ.

Chief of General Staff of the National Air Force: Gen. FRANCISCO GONÇALVES AFONSO.

Chief of General Staff of the Navy: Adm. AUGUSTO DA SILVA CUNHA.

Education

Education is officially compulsory for eight years, between seven and 15 years of age, and is provided free of charge by the Government. Primary education begins at the age of seven and lasts for four years. Secondary education, beginning at the age of 11, lasts for up to seven years, comprising a first cycle of four years and a second of three years. According to UNESCO estimates, enrolment at primary schools in 2000/01 included 37% of children in the relevant age-group (boys 39%; girls 35%), while secondary enrolment was equivalent to 18% of children in the relevant age-group (boys 19%; girls 16%). There are two universities, at Luanda, while in 2005 there were plans to open a further 32 higher-education establishments and a new university. In 1991 the Government approved legislation permitting the foundation of private educational establishments. Some 29,000 new teachers were recruited in 2003–04, according to the Ministry of Education. The 2006 budget allocated an estimated 83,500m. kwanza to education.

Bibliography

Andresen Guimarães, F. *The Origins of the Angolan Civil War: Foreign Intervention and Domestic Political Conflict.* Basingstoke, Palgrave, 2001.

Anstee, M. *Orphan of the Cold War: The Inside Story of the Collapse of the Angolan Peace Process.* London, Macmillan, and New York, St Martin's Press, 1996.

Bender, G. J. *Angola Under the Portuguese: The Myth and the Reality.* Lawrenceville, NJ, Africa World Press, 2004.

Bhagavan, M. R. *Angola's Political Economy: 1975–1985.* Uppsala, Nordic Africa Institute, 1996.

Birmingham, D. *Frontline Nationalism in Angola and Mozambique.* London, James Currey Publrs, and Trenton, NJ, Africa World Press, 1992.

Empire in Africa: Angola and its Neighbors. Columbus, OH, The Ohio State University Press, 2006.

Bridgland, F. *Jonas Savimbi: A Key to Africa.* Edinburgh, Mainstream, 1986.

Brittain, V. *Death of Dignity.* London, Pluto Press, 1998.

Broadhead, S. H. *Historical Dictionary of Angola.* 3rd Edn. Metuchen, NJ, Scarecrow Press, 1992.

Cann, J. P. *Counter-insurgency in Africa: The Portuguese Way of War 1961–1974.* Westport, CT, Greenwood Press, 1997.

Cilliers, J., and Dietrich, C. (Eds). *Angola's War Economy: The Role of Oil and Diamonds.* Pretoria, Institute for Security Studies, 2000.

Conçalves, J. *Economics and Politics of the Angolan Conflict: The Transition Re-Negotiated.* Bellville Centre for Southern Africa Studies, University of the Western Cape, 1995.

Crocker, C. A. *High Noon in Southern Africa: Making Peace in a Rough Neighbourhood.* New York, NY, W. W. Norton, 1992.

Fish, B., and Durost Fish, B. *Angola: 1980 to the Present: Slavery, Exploitation, and Revolt (Exploration of Africa).* London, Chelsea House Publications, 2001.

George, E. *The Cuban Intervention in Angola (1965–1991), from Che Guevara to Cuito Cuanavale.* London, Frank Cass, 2005.

Hare, P. *Angola's Last Best Chance for Peace (An Insider's Account of the Peace Process).* Washington, DC, United States Institute of Peace, 1998.

Hart, K., and Lewis, J. (Eds). *Why Angola Matters.* London, James Currey Publrs, 1995.

Henderson, L. W. *Angola: Five Centuries of Conflict.* Ithaca, NY, Cornell University Press, 1979.

Heywood, L. *Contested Power in Angola, 1840s to the Present.* Rochester, NY, University of Rochester Press, 2000.

Hodges, T. *Angola from Afro-Stalinism to Petro-Diamond Capitalism.* Oxford, James Currey Publrs, 2001.

Angola: Anatomy of an Oil State. Oxford, James Currey Publrs, 2004.

Jett, D. T. *Why Peacekeeping Fails.* Basingstoke, Palgrave, 2001.

Konczacki, Z. A., Parpart, J. L., and Shaw, T. M. (Eds). *Studies in the Economic History of Southern Africa.* Vol. I. London, Frank Cass, 1990.

MacQueen, N. *The Decolonization of Portuguese Africa: Metropolitan Revolution and the Dissolution of Empire.* Harlow, Longman, 1997.

McCormick, S. H. *The Angolan Economy: Prospects for Growth in a Postwar Environment.* Washington, DC, CSIS, 1994.

Maier, K. *Angola: Promises and Lies.* London, SERIF, 1996.

Marcum, J. *The Angolan Revolution.* 2 vols. Cambridge, MA, MIT Press, 1969 and 1978 (new Edn).

Martin, J. W. *A Political History of the Civil War in Angola, 1974–90.* New Brunswick, NJ, Transaction Publishers, 1992.

Martin, P. M. *Historical Dictionary of Angola.* London, 1980.

Minter, W. (Ed.). *Operation Timber: Pages from the Savimbi Dossier.* Trenton, NJ, Africa World Press, 1988.

Apartheid's Contras: An Inquiry into the Roots of War in Angola and Mozambique. London, Zed Press, 1994.

Mohanty, S. *Political Development and Ethnic Identity in Africa: A Study of Angola since 1960.* London, Sangham, 1992.

Núñez, B. *Dictionary of Portuguese-African Civilization.* Vol. I. London, Hans Zell, 1995.

Pélissier, R. *Explorar: Voyages en Angola.* Orgeval, Editions Pélissier, 1980.

Roque, F. *A Economia de Angola.* Lisbon, Bertrand, 1991.

Sogge, D. *Sustainable Peace: Angola's Recovery.* Harare, Southern African Resource and Documentation Centre, 1992.

Spikes, D. *Angola and the Politics of Intervention.* Jefferson, NC, McFarland Publishers, 1993.

Tvedten, I. *Angola: Struggle for Peace and Reconstruction.* Boulder, CO, Westview Press, 1997.

Venter, A. J. *War in Angola.* Hong Kong, Concord Publications, 1992.

Vincenti, S. *Angola e Africa do Sul.* Luanda, Eclicas do Autor, 1994.

Wheeler, D. L., and Pélissier, R. *Angola.* London, Greenwood Press, 1978.

Wright, G. *The Destruction of a Nation: United States Policy towards Angola since 1945.* London, Pluto Press, 1997.

BENIN

Physical and Social Geography

R. J. HARRISON CHURCH

The Republic of Benin, bordered on the east by Nigeria, on the west by Togo and to the north by Burkina Faso and Niger, covers an area of 112,622 sq km (43,484 sq miles). From a coastline of some 100 km on the Gulf of Guinea, the republic extends inland about 650 km to the Niger river. The population was 4,915,555 at the census of February 1992, rising to 6,769,014, according to the census of February 2002. At mid-2006, according to UN estimates, the population was 8,760,000, giving an average population density of 77.8 inhabitants per sq km. The population of Cotonou, the political capital and major port, was 665,100 at the 2002 census, and that of Porto-Novo, the official capital, was 223,552. Other large cities include Abomey-Calavi (with a population of 307,745), Djougou (181,895) and Banikoura (152,028).

The coast is a straight sandbar, pounded by heavy surf on the seaward side and backed by one or more lagoons and former shorelines on the landward side. Rivers flow into these lagoons, Lakes Ahémé and Nokoué being estuaries of two rivers whose seaward exits are obstructed by the sandbar. A lagoon waterway is navigable for barges to Lagos, in Nigeria.

North of Lake Nokoué the Ouémé river has a wide marshy delta, with considerable agricultural potential. Elsewhere the lagoons are backed northward by the Terre de Barre, a fertile and intensively farmed region of clay soils. North again is the seasonally flooded Lama swamp. Beyond are areas comparable with the Terre de Barre, and the realm of the pre-colonial kingdom of Dahomey.

Most of the rest of the country is underlain by Pre-Cambrian rocks, with occasional bare domes, laterite cappings on level surfaces, and poor soils. In the north-west are the Atacora mountains, whose soils, although less poor, are much eroded. On the northern borders are primary and other sandstones; soils are extremely infertile and short of water.

Deposits of low-grade iron ores, chromium, rutile, phosphates, kaolin and gold occur in the north of the country. Extraction of petroleum from a small oilfield, off shore from Cotonou, at Sémé, ceased in late 1998, although there were attempts at rehabilitation in the early 2000s. Reserves of natural gas, estimated to total 4,000m. cu m, were also being evaluated at that time. Limestone and marble are currently mined.

Southern Benin has an equatorial climate, most typical along the coast, although with a low rainfall of some 1,300 mm. Away from the coast the dry months increase until a tropical climate prevails over the northern half of the country. There a dry season alternates with a wet one, the latter being of seven months in the centre and four months in the north; nevertheless, the rainfall averages 1,300 mm per year.

In the colonial period the Fon and Yoruba of the south enjoyed educational advantages and were prominent in administration throughout French West Africa. After independence many were expelled to Benin, where there is great unemployment or underemployment of literates. The northern peoples, such as the Somba and Bariba, are less Westernized. The Fon were the most numerous ethnic group in the country, accounting for 39.2% of the population in 2002, followed by the Adja (15.2%) and Yoruba (12.3).

Recent History

PIERRE ENGLEBERT

Revised by KATHARINE MURISON

INDEPENDENCE AND ARMY RULE

Benin (then Dahomey) became a self-governing republic within the French Community in December 1958 and an independent state on 1 August 1960. Political life in the republic was extremely unstable following independence, as regionally based interests contended for power. Hubert Maga, the republic's first President, was deposed in October 1963 by an army *coup d'état*, and successive army-supported regimes governed the country for the ensuing decade.

In October 1972 Maj. (later Brig.-Gen.) Mathieu Kérékou, a northerner, seized power. Marxism-Leninism was introduced as the national ideology, and banking, insurance and the principal industrial sectors were nationalized; the Parti de la révolution populaire du Bénin (PRPB) became the sole authorized political party. In 1975 the country was renamed the People's Republic of Benin. In the early 1980s worsening economic conditions prompted Benin to move increasingly towards the Western bloc and the IMF. By the mid-1980s France had replaced the USSR as the principal supplier of military equipment, while also remaining predominant in trade, development assistance and other forms of co-operation. Amid rising social tensions and ethnic rivalries, Kérékou left the army in January 1987 to become a civilian Head of State. Ensuing tensions between the Government and the army culminated in attempted coups in March and June 1988.

'CIVILIAN COUP'

Although a period of repression in the aftermath of the coup attempts, in conjunction with popular dissatisfaction at IMF-stipulated austerity measures, engendered an atmosphere of increased social tension and instability, at legislative elections in June 1989 a single list of 206 candidates was approved by almost 90% of the votes cast. In August the legislature, the Assemblée nationale révolutionnaire (ANR), re-elected Kérékou to the presidency for a further five-year term. However, in December the abandonment of Marxism-Leninism as the state ideology was announced, and Benin's external creditors subsequently agreed to a partial funding of outstanding public-sector salaries.

In February 1990 a national conference of the 'active forces of the nation' voted to abolish the existing structure of government and its institutions. Pending elections to a new legislature, the functions of the ANR were assumed in March by an interim Haut conseil de la république (HCR), which included the principal opposition leaders. The President of the republic was for the first time to be elected by universal suffrage, with a five-year mandate, renewable only once. Nicéphore Soglo, a former official of the World Bank, was designated as interim Prime Minister, and named a transitional Government. Kérékou was obliged to relinquish the defence portfolio to Soglo, and also to accept the conference's resolution to change the country's name to the Republic of Benin. In May the military prefects of Benin's six provinces were replaced by civilians, and in June an extensive restructuring of the armed forces was implemented. In August legislation was promulgated to permit the registration of political parties.

Benin was thus the first sub-Saharan African country to experience a 'civilian coup'. A draft constitution was submitted to a national referendum in December 1990. Voters were asked to choose between two versions of the Constitution, one of which incorporated a clause stipulating upper and lower age-limits for presidential candidates (thereby automatically disqualifying several ex-presidents). In all, 95.8% of those who voted gave their assent to one or other of the versions, with 79.7% of voters endorsing the age restrictions.

Some 24 political parties participated in the legislative elections, which took place in February 1991. A pro-Soglo alliance secured the greatest number of seats (12) in the 64-member Assemblée nationale. The first round of the presidential election, on 10 March, was contested by 13 candidates. Reflecting regional ethnic divisions, Soglo, who secured 36.2% of the total, received his greatest support in the south of the country, while Kérékou, who received his greatest support in the north, took 27.3% of the overall vote. Soglo was elected President in a second round of voting, securing 67.7% of the total votes cast. Before its dissolution, in late March, the HCR granted Kérékou immunity from any legal proceedings arising from his years in power.

THE SOGLO PRESIDENCY, 1991–96

Soglo was inaugurated as President on 4 April 1991. He subsequently relinquished the defence portfolio. The Soglo administration intensified efforts at economic liberalization, and also began criminal proceedings against corrupt former state officials.

In May 1992 several soldiers were arrested and accused of plotting a coup. Among those detained was Capt. Pascal Tawes, a former deputy commander of Kérékou's presidential guard. Tawes and some of his associates subsequently escaped from custody, and in August gained control of an army base in the north. The rebellion was suppressed, but Tawes and several other mutineers evaded arrest. In September 1994 Tawes and 15 others were sentenced *in absentia* to life imprisonment with hard labour.

Although broad groupings of parties evolved, the absence of a majority party or coalition in the Assemblée nationale tended to delay the passage of legislation. However, the President's position was strengthened by the formation, in June 1992, of Le Renouveau, a pro-Soglo majority group, comprising some 34 deputies. Nevertheless, Soglo lost his majority support in the Assemblée nationale in October 1993, when 15 members of Le Renouveau withdrew from the coalition. In July, meanwhile, Soglo had aligned himself with the (Parti de la) Renaissance du Bénin (RB), formed by his wife, Rosine, in 1992; he was appointed leader of the RB in July 1994.

Electoral Tensions

Preparations for elections to the Assemblée nationale, scheduled for February 1995, engendered further friction between the executive and legislature. Soglo opposed the creation of an independent electoral commission, the Commission électorale nationale autonome (CENA), which the Assemblée nationale none the less approved in November 1994, and a planned increase in the number of deputies from 64 to 83. The elections were twice postponed as a result of organizational difficulties, and finally took place on 28 March 1995, contested by 31 political organizations. The Constitutional Court annulled the results of voting for 13 seats owing to irregularities. Following by-elections in May, the RB held 20 seats in the Assemblée nationale, and other supporters of Soglo a total of 13. Opposition parties held 49 seats, the most prominent being the Parti du renouveau démocratique (PRD), with 19 seats, and the Front d'action pour le renouveau et le développement—Alafia (FARD—Alafia), with 10. Bruno Amoussou, the leader of the opposition Parti social-démocrate (PSD), was elected President of the legislature. A new Government was announced in June.

Presidential Candidacies

Renewed institutional conflict followed the decision of the Assemblée nationale, in December 1995, to delay ratification of elements of the country's structural adjustment programme. The legislature rejected a revised programme twice during January 1996, and also rejected the draft budget for 1996, prompting the announcement that the budget and adjustment programme were to be implemented by presidential decree. Meanwhile, Soglo's policies of economic reform, while praised internationally, gave rise to domestic concern that social issues had been neglected, and criticism was increasingly levelled at the perceived authoritarianism of the Government.

The first round of the presidential election was held on 3 March 1996 and contested by seven candidates. Soglo secured 35.7% of the valid votes and Kérékou 33.9%, followed by Adrien Houngbédji, the leader of the PRD (19.7%). Most of the defeated candidates, among them Houngbédji, quickly expressed their support for Kérékou. A second round of voting took place on 18 March. On 24 March the Constitutional Court proclaimed that Kérékou had received the support of 52.5% of voters. Some 78.1% of those eligible had voted. Kérékou was inaugurated as President on 4 April.

THE RETURN OF KÉRÉKOU

Having sought authorization by the Constitutional Court for the appointment of a Prime Minister (provision for such a post is not stipulated in the Constitution), Kérékou named Houngbédji as premier in a Government that included representatives of eight parties that had supported his presidential campaign.

In September 1997 the Assemblée nationale approved an amnesty for perpetrators of acts seeking to undermine state security and what were termed election and media crimes committed between January 1990 and June 1996. The amnesty provoked protests by the RB, which warned that it would exacerbate ethnic and regional tensions (the majority of those amnestied were northerners). One of its principal beneficiaries, Tawes, returned to Benin in September 1997. In October, however, the Constitutional Court invalidated the amnesty legislation, on the grounds that the Government had not consulted the Supreme Court, whose involvement in the formulation of such legislation the Constitutional Court deemed obligatory.

From February 1998 a series of general strikes, involving some 37,000 civil servants, caused considerable disruption. In March agreement was reached on the payment of salary arrears to civil servants, one of the major causes of discontent. Nevertheless, a further general strike proceeded in May. Houngbédji resigned and withdrew the PRD from the Government. The most senior member of a new Government appointed by Kérékou in mid-May was Pierre Osho, as Minister-delegate to the Presidency, in charge of Defence and Relations with the Institutions. Only three ministers retained their previous positions. The new Government, which included representatives of seven parties, commanded the support of just 27 members of the Assemblée nationale. Further conflict between the executive and legislature thus appeared inevitable.

Legislative Elections of 1999

On 30 March 1999 some 35 parties and alliances contested the elections to the 83-member Assemblée nationale. The opposition parties won a narrow victory, securing 42 seats, while the pro-Kérékou parties won 41. Voting was divided on clear regional lines: the RB won 27 seats, principally in the centre and south of Benin, while parties supporting Kérékou performed strongly in the north. The CENA estimated the rate of participation at over 70%. The opposition was swift to reassure observers that it intended to co-operate with the President and to seek consensus where possible. In June Kérékou effected a minor cabinet reshuffle, as a result of which the number of parties represented in the Council of Ministers increased to 10.

In October 1999 an estimated 32,000 civil servants undertook a three-day general strike after public-sector unions and the Government failed to reach agreement on the payment of salary arrears and the abolition of a new system of promotion according to merit. Although further labour unrest was reported, agreement was subsequently reached on the creation of a bipartisan commission to investigate a new system of remuneration and promotion for the civil service, and on the payment of salary arrears.

In June 2000 one of Benin's principal trade union federations, the Centrale des syndicats autonomes du Bénin, undertook a 48-hour strike in protest at the rapid escalation of the cost of petroleum. Popular discontent at the rises intensified, and in early July an estimated 10,000 people attended a public demonstration in Cotonou, organized by Benin's six trade union federations. The Government later announced that funds would be made available for social measures to compensate those affected by the price increases, although protests continued.

Kérékou Re-elected

Of the 17 candidates permitted to contest the presidency on 4 March 2001, Soglo was, once again, widely regarded as the sole credible challenger to Kérékou. Corruption emerged as a leading issue during campaigning, as allegations were made of fraudulent behaviour by both Kérékou and Soglo with regard to large parastatal companies. Initially, the Court announced that Kérékou had gained the largest share of the votes, with Soglo in second place, but that, as no candidate had secured an absolute majority, a second round would be held on 18 March. As campaigning for the second round proceeded, the Constitutional Court conducted a review of the initially declared results of the first round. According to revised provisional results, issued on 13 March, Kérékou received 45.4% of the votes cast, Soglo 27.1%, Houngbédji 12.6% and Amoussou 8.6%. The revised results indicated an increase in the electoral roll of some 300,000, and measured turn-out at around 80%. Houngbédji endorsed the candidature of Soglo (although many of his supporters voiced support for Kérékou), while Amoussou encouraged his supporters to vote for Kérékou, who pledged to form a broad-based government of national unity, if re-elected.

As allegations of electoral irregularities persisted, Soglo appealed to the Constitutional Court to annul the disputed results, and to re-run the election, either in those constituencies, or on a nation-wide basis. On 16 March 2001, following the rejection of his appeal, Soglo withdrew from the election and urged his supporters to abstain from voting in the second round. Polling was postponed, initially until 19 March, and subsequently until 22 March, in order to permit Houngbédji to campaign. However, on 19 March Houngbédji also declared his dissatisfaction with the conduct of the election and withdrew. Despite having previously declared his support for Kérékou, Amoussou agreed to challenge him for the presidency. Following Houngbédji's withdrawal, nine opposition members of the CENA, including its Vice-President, resigned in protest at the alleged manipulation of the Commission by a small group close to its President, Charles Djrèkpo (who was a member of Amoussou's PSD).

The second round of the election duly took place on 22 March 2001. Voter participation was, at approximately 55%, notably lower than in the first round. Two days after the poll, the CENA announced that Kérékou had been re-elected, with 84.1% of the valid votes cast, despite supporters of Soglo protesting that the depleted CENA had no legitimacy to organize the elections.

Kérékou formed a 21-member Government in May 2001, including eight new ministers. Amoussou retained his post as Minister of State, responsible for the Co-ordination of Government Action, Future Planning and Development. In July it was announced that proposed municipal elections had been cancelled, as a result of overspending on the presidential election.

In August 2001 dissent within the RB became apparent, when 10 of the party's deputies, led by the party's Vice-Chairman, Nathaniel Bah, formed a separate grouping within the Assemblée nationale. Despite the expulsion of Bah from the RB, his supporters announced his assumption of the party leadership (displacing Rosine Soglo) at an extraordinary congress in September. In January 2002 a congress of the RB reinstated Rosine Soglo as the party chairperson.

In late 2001 and early 2002 up to 32,000 civil servants and workers, primarily in the health and education sectors, participated in a series of nation-wide strikes, in support of demands for higher salaries and the withdrawal of proposals to introduce promotion on grounds of merit within the public sector. In March 2002 the Government reached agreement with six of the seven trade unions that had organized the strikes; wage arrears were to be paid and an increase in civil servants' salaries granted, while the question of procedures for promotions was to be referred to the Assemblée nationale.

In November 2002 it was announced that legislative elections would be held on 30 March 2003. Meanwhile, the delayed municipal and local elections were held in two rounds in December 2002 and January 2003; some 5,700 candidates contested the 1,199 seats nation-wide. Although supporters of Kérékou, who formed an electoral alliance known as the Union pour le Bénin du futur (UBF), were the most successful grouping overall, the RB gained the majority of seats in Cotonou, where Nicéphore Soglo was elected mayor, while the PRD secured control of Porto-Novo, with Houngbédji elected mayor (although he resigned from this position in June 2003). Following the municipal elections the UBF formally constituted itself as a party, under the leadership of Amoussou; the PSD merged into the UBF.

Elections to the Assemblée Nationale, 2003

The legislative elections, which were held, as scheduled, on 30 March 2003, were contested by 1,162 candidates, representing 14 political groups, and were marked by an appreciably lower turn-out than previous legislative elections, estimated at around 50%. The elections resulted in the establishment of a clear pro-presidential majority in the Assemblée nationale for the first time since the introduction of multi-party elections, with supporters of Kérékou securing 52 of the 83 elective seats. The UBF emerged as the largest single party, with 31 seats, and the pro-presidential Mouvement africain pour la démocratie et le progrès (MADEP) won nine seats. The representation of the RB, the largest party in the outgoing assembly, was reduced from 27 to 15 seats. It was reported that as many as one-half of the deputies elected had not previously served in the legislature. On 10 April Houngbédji announced that the PRD, which secured 11 seats in the elections, would henceforth support the Government, as a result of which the pro-presidential bloc in the Assemblée nationale held 63 seats.

In April 2003 Antoine Idji Kolawolé of the MADEP, hitherto Minister of Foreign Affairs and African Integration, was elected as President of the Assemblée nationale, defeating Rosine Soglo. After lengthy consultations, the formation of a new Government was finally announced in June. Amoussou was appointed to the most senior ministerial position, as Minister of State, responsible for Planning and Development, while several principal members of the previous administration were reappointed.

A major political concern during the second half of 2003 was the alleged involvement of senior police and judicial officials with international criminal gangs based in Benin. The activities of these gangs, who were reported to be involved principally in the smuggling of stolen motor cars, had, in mid-August, resulted in the closure of the Beninois–Nigerian border for six days (see below). In September President Kérékou established a special commission to investigate alleged links between government officials and organized criminal groups. In October, following the publication of a report by the commission, the Beninois authorities announced that several senior police and judicial officials had been dismissed.

In a separate major case of corruption, in June 2004 37 civil servants from the judiciary and the finance ministry were sentenced to between 30 months' and five years' imprisonment for their involvement in the embezzlement of more than 8,000m. francs CFA in state funds between 1996 and 2000, while 25 defendants received suspended sentences and a further 25 were acquitted. Of the country's nine lower courts, only one was not implicated in the scandal, in which 27 magistrates were among the accused.

A sharp decline in economic conditions contributed to an outbreak of labour unrest in late 2004. Following a breakdown in negotiations between the Government and trade unions, a three-day general strike took place in mid-October in support of demands for higher pay and improved pensions for public-sector workers and a reduction in university fees. Further industrial action followed in November. Teachers seeking the payment of salary arrears and allowances, together with the permanent employment of teachers currently working under temporary contracts, commenced a nation-wide strike in October that did not end until January 2005, when, in order to avoid the entire academic year being invalidated, the Government reached an agreement with the teaching trade unions.

PRESIDENTIAL ELECTION OF 2006

By early 2005 there was already much discussion regarding possible contenders for the presidency at the election due in March 2006, which Kérékou was constitutionally barred from contesting, having served two consecutive terms of office and, at 72 years of age, having exceeded the 70-year age limit for candidates. Nicéphore Soglo was also ineligible to stand again owing to his age. In February 2005 Kérékou effected a major reshuffle of the Council of Ministers, notably dismissing Amoussou and the Minister of Finance and the Economy, Grégoire Laourou, who were replaced, respectively, by Zul Kifl Salami and Cosme Sèhlin. Pierre Osho, a close ally of the President, was retained as Minister of State, responsible for National Defence. It was suggested that Amoussou, who was regarded as a potential candidate for the presidency, had been removed from the Government to allow him to concentrate on preparing for the forthcoming election, although Kérékou remained silent over his preferred successor and his future intentions, prompting speculation that the President might attempt to extend his tenure by delaying the election or by amending the Constitution to allow himself to seek a further term in office. In July, however, Kérékou announced that he would not contest the forthcoming election.

Meanwhile, significant divisions had begun to emerge in the UBF. In October 2004 Joseph Gandaho, an adviser to Kérékou, announced the formation of the UBF 'Aller plus loin' by more than 30 pro-presidential political parties and associations. However, the new movement excluded many of the main pro-Kérékou parties, among them the PSD, FARD—Alafia, the MADEP and the PRD. In April 2005 there was a further split when Alain Adihou, the Minister of Technical Education and Professional Training, created the Alliance UBF. Most of the UBF's deputies and other elected representatives reportedly dissociated themselves from Adihou's organization, attending a special general assembly of the 'original' UBF called by Amoussou in May. The opposition RB was also divided, with eight deputies having resigned from the party by mid-May.

In November 2005 Sèhlin, suggested that the Government did not have sufficient resources to fund the presidential election, which was scheduled for 5 March 2006. In the following month the Assemblée nationale approved the cancellation of a planned electoral census, in an apparent attempt to reduce costs. Amid fears that the election would be postponed, a group of non-governmental organizations established an election support fund (which reportedly raised more than 7,000m. francs CFA), while 13 political parties formed a coalition to campaign for the election to be held on schedule. In January 2006 Osho resigned from the Council of Ministers in protest at the management of the election; he was controversially replaced by Col (retd) Martin Dohou Azonhiho, who had earlier declared himself in favour of a postponement. Later that month trade unions organized a two-day strike in support of their demands that the Government finance the poll. Kérékou dismissed the Minister of Foreign Affairs, Rogatien Biaou, in February, following allegations of his involvement in the illegal sale of land surrounding Benin's embassy in the USA.

Boni Yayi Elected

Despite the financial difficulties, the first round of the presidential election, contested by 26 candidates, was held on 5 March 2006, as scheduled. Dr Boni Yayi, until recently President of the Banque ouest-africaine de développement and standing as an independent, received the largest share of the votes cast, with 35.64%, followed by Houngbédji, with 24.13%, Amoussou, with 16.23%, and Léhadi Soglo, the eldest son of Nicéphore and Rosine Soglo, with 8.41%. Some 76% of the electorate participated in the first round. International observers were largely satisfied with the conduct of the poll, despite concerns regarding the high number of registered voters, which was widely regarded to be excessive considering the size of the population.

A second round of voting was contested by Yayi and Houngbédji on 19 March 2006, after the last-minute rejection by Kérékou of an appeal by the CENA, supported by the Constitutional Court, for a postponement until 22 March, owing to a delay in the announcement of the results of the first round (which had only been officially proclaimed by the Court on 15 March). Of the 24 candidates defeated in the first round, 11 urged their supporters to vote for Yayi, including Amoussou and Soglo. Yayi won a decisive victory in the second round, securing 74.52% of the votes cast. A lower turn-out, of around 67%, was recorded.

YAYI'S PRESIDENCY

Yayi was inaugurated to succeed Kérékou as Head of State on 6 April 2006. The new President pledged to reduce poverty, to combat corruption and to revive the economy, with the aim of achieving a double-digit rate of annual growth by 2010. Two days later the President announced the formation of a new Council of Ministers dominated by technocrats and comprising 22 members, none of whom had served in the outgoing Government. Pascal Koupaki, a former official at the Banque centrale des états de l'Afrique de l'ouest, was appointed as Minister of Development, the Economy and Finance, the most senior position in the Government.

In June 2006 the Assemblée nationale approved a constitutional amendment extending deputies' term of office from four years to five. Proponents of the reform claimed that it would allow the next general election, which had been due in March 2007, to be held concurrently with local elections in 2008, thus reducing costs. However, in July 2006 the Constitutional Court overturned the Assemblée nationale's decision, which had been criticized by civil society organizations, ruling it to be invalid. In December it was reported that several deputies had resigned from the PRD, the PSD, the MADEP and the Union pour la République to form a new parliamentary group, the Nouvelle Alliance, to be led by Corentin Kohoue, formerly of the PSD.

Organizational difficulties, mainly resulting from internal divisions within the CENA, forced the postponement of the legislative elections from 25 March 2007 to 31 March. The 83 seats in the Assemblée nationale were contested by 2,158 candidates representing 24 parties and alliances. The Force cauris pour un Bénin emergent (FCBE), a pro-presidential coalition of some 20 parties, became the largest grouping in the legislature, securing 35 seats, followed by the Alliance pour une dynamique démocratique (comprising the RB, the MADEP and the PSD, among others), which won 20 seats, and the PRD, which took 10. The remaining seats were shared by nine other parties or alliances. It was reported that only 20 deputies from the outgoing legislature had succeeded in retaining their seats. The CENA estimated voter turn-out at 58.7%. Meanwhile, earlier in March four members of the presidential guard were injured when gunmen opened fire on a convoy carrying Yayi near Parakou, some 450 km north of Cotonou; six people were later arrested in connection with the attack. In early May Mathurin Nago of the FCBE, hitherto Minister of Higher Education and Professional Training, was elected as President of the Assemblée nationale, defeating Amoussou.

In mid-June 2007 President Yayi announced a comprehensive reorganization of the Council of Ministers, in which the number of portfolios was increased to 26. The new Government included 17 new appointees; most notably, Gen. Félix Hessou became Minister of the Interior and Public Security, while Lawani Soule Mana was awarded the finance portfolio.

EXTERNAL AFFAIRS

Benin has contributed to several regional peace-keeping operations in recent years. In April 1998 Benin was one of eight countries to participate in the 'Cohésion Kompienga '98' military exercises (conducted as part of efforts to train regional armies in peace-keeping and humanitarian assistance operations). Benin subsequently contributed some 140 troops to the peace-keeping operations in Guinea-Bissau undertaken by the Cease-fire Monitoring Group of the Economic Community of West African States (ECOWAS), although it withdrew its force in June 1999, following the *coup d'état* in Guinea-Bissau. Troops from Benin participated in ECOWAS peace-keeping missions in Côte d'Ivoire from early 2003 and in Liberia from September of that year, and were subsequently incorporated into the UN operations that followed in both countries. Benin also contributed some 650 troops to UN peace-keeping operations in the Democratic Republic of the Congo from April 2005. Meanwhile, in late 2004 military training exercises involving some 1,500 West African troops who were to form an ECOWAS Task Force charged with intervening in conflicts in the region took place in Benin.

Benin maintains generally good relations with neighbouring countries, and joined the Community of Sahel-Saharan States in March 2002. None the less, in mid-2000 a long-term dispute between Benin and Niger over the ownership of various small islands in the Niger river erupted once more after Nigerien soldiers reportedly sabotaged the construction of a Beninois administrative building on Lété Island. Meetings between representatives of Benin and Niger, and subsequent arbitration by the Organization of African Unity (now the African Union), failed to resolve the dispute, and in April 2002 the two countries officially ratified an agreement (signed in June 2001) to refer the dispute to the International Court of Justice (ICJ) at The Hague, Netherlands, for arbitration. Benin and Niger filed confidential written arguments with the Court, and in November 2003 a five-member Chamber formed to consider the case held its first public sitting. Both countries subsequently submitted counter-arguments, and each filed a third pleading in December 2004. In June of that year the UN had awarded Benin and Niger US $350,000 each towards the cost of resolving their dispute. Final submissions were presented by the two Governments at public hearings before the Chamber in March 2005. In July the Chamber of the ICJ issued its judgment on the delineation of the border between Benin and Niger, ruling that 16 of the 25 islands, including Lété, belonged to Niger; both countries' Governments accepted the ruling. Meanwhile, in November 2004 Nigerien traders and haulage contractors commenced a boycott of the port of Cotonou in response to the fatal shooting in the city of two Nigeriens by Beninois gendarmes in September. President Kérékou visited Niger in December in an attempt to ease tensions resulting from the shooting. The boycott was ended in January 2005 following a meeting between the Nigerien President, Mamadou Tandja, and the Beninois Minister of Foreign Affairs and African Integration, Rogatien Biaou, in Niamey, the capital of Niger, during which Biaou announced that the Beninois Government would pay compensation to the families of the victims.

Benin and Nigeria launched joint police patrols along their common border in August 2001, following concerns about cross-border crime and the reported import of small arms from Benin to Nigeria. Renewed concerns about cross-border crime prompted the Nigerian authorities to close the border unilaterally in August 2003. Following a meeting between the Presidents of the two countries later in the month, the frontier was reopened and measures aimed at enhancing co-operation to combat cross-border crime were announced. Tensions between the two countries were further eased by the extradition, in September, from Benin to Nigeria, of Hamani Tidjani, a citizen of Niger resident in Cotonou, who was sought in Nigeria on suspicion of smuggling stolen motor cars, as well as for his alleged involvement in a suspected assassination attempt on a daughter of President Olusegun Obasanjo earlier in the year. Nevertheless, security around the common border was believed to have been the main focus of further discussions between Kérékou and Obasanjo in April 2004. In July it was reported that a joint commission had amicably resolved a dispute over the land and maritime boundary between Benin and Nigeria. None the less, tensions remained over the smuggling of goods, particularly fuel, from Nigeria to Benin, and in January 2005 enhanced joint patrols of the common border were launched. In April Presidents Obasanjo and Kérékou signed a bilateral trade agreement aimed at curbing smuggling and other cross-border crime, as well as enhancing trade relations. Shortly after his inauguration in April 2006, President Yayi's first official foreign visit was to Nigeria, where he held discussions with Obasanjo. In August Yayi and Obasanjo signed a treaty on the maritime boundary between Benin and Nigeria, while the two countries' Ministers of Foreign Affairs signed a memorandum of understanding on the establishment of a joint standing committee to delineate the land boundary. At a summit meeting held in the Nigerian capital, Abuja, in February 2007, Yayi, Obasanjo and the President of Togo, Faure Gnassingbé, announced the formation of a Co-Prosperity Alliance Zone, aimed at accelerating the integration of their national economies and promoting peace, stability and development in West Africa. Later that month the electricity networks of Benin and Nigeria were officially connected, enabling energy to be supplied from Nigeria to Benin (and also to Togo) at a lower cost. Furthermore, a pipeline to transport gas from Nigeria to Benin, Togo and Ghana was scheduled to commence deliveries by the end of the year.

From late April 2005 thousands of Togolese sought refuge in Benin, having fled the violence that followed a presidential election in their country. The Beninois Government appealed for some US $5m. in international aid to support its efforts to assist the refugees. By the end of the year the office of the UN High Commissioner for Refugees (UNHCR) had registered 26,632 Togolese refugees in Benin, many of whom were living with family and friends. Many refugees subsequently returned to Togo, following the restoration of stability in that country, and by the end of 2006 9,444 remained in Benin, according to UNHCR. In April 2007 Benin, UNHCR and Togo signed an agreement on the voluntary repatriation of the remaining refugees.

Economy

EDITH HODGKINSON

Revised by NADÈGE TCHOTCHOE

The dominant characteristics of the economy of Benin are its dualism and its dependence on Nigeria. There is an official, documented sector, covering government and relatively modern industry and agriculture, and an unofficial, largely unrecorded sector, consisting of basic food production and cross-border trade with Nigeria. Changes in the rate of economic growth are closely linked to trends in Nigeria and in other member countries of the Economic Community of West African States and of the Union économique et monétaire ouest-africaine. From 1985 Benin suffered a period of economic depression, caused by the closure of the border with Nigeria (which was in force between April 1984 and March 1986), the economic recession in Nigeria, and the decline in international prices for Benin's major export commodities, cotton and petroleum, while the strengthening of the CFA franc in relation to the US dollar reduced the proceeds from these commodities in local currency terms. Economic performance improved in the 1990s, with annual growth in gross domestic product (GDP) averaging 5.0%, in real terms, in 1990–2003.

The economic success of the 1990s owed much to a series of good harvests, but a significant contribution was also made by the reversal in economic policy from 1990–91 under the new civilian regime, which aimed to enhance and expand the role of the private sector. The structural reform programme undertaken by the administration of Nicéphore Soglo (1991–96) was supported by the significant rescheduling of debt that was agreed by bilateral official creditors in December 1991 (see below) and an Enhanced Structural Adjustment Facility (ESAF) at the IMF for the period 1993–95.

However, the context for the structural reform programme was fundamentally modified by the devaluation, by 50%, of the CFA franc in January 1994; notably, the imposition of price controls by the Government failed to counter fully the increase in the rate of inflation, which rose from near zero in 1993 to an average of 38.5% in 1994. Moreover, the domestic manufacturing sector, which is heavily dependent on foreign supplies, was adversely affected by the overnight doubling of import costs. None the less, devaluation had some positive effects—stimulating export growth and demand for local products, notably foodstuffs. Increased inflows of foreign aid, in conjunction with particularly good cotton crops, contributed to stronger GDP growth during the mid-1990s. However, the reduction in household income that devaluation entailed alienated popular support for the Soglo regime, and it was the urban areas (traditionally a stronghold for Soglo) that bore the brunt of the adjustment. Devaluation thus had a high political cost, which was paid by Soglo when he was defeated in the 1996 election.

Under the subsequent administrations of President Mathieu Kérékou (1996–2006), liberalization became well entrenched in many sectors, and the Government maintained a co-operative relationship with the IMF. In mid-1996 the terms were agreed for a new ESAF, to cover the period 1996–99. The programme the funding supported aimed to achieve a steady improvement in economic growth, with low inflation and both fiscal and current-account deficits falling as a ratio of GDP.

The Government's slow progress in implementing the privatization programme and a proposed retrenchment in the public-sector payroll caused the IMF to suspend disbursements in 1998, although the facility was resumed in January 1999. A decline in cotton prices and the suspension of petroleum output (see below) in 1998 also ensured that the implementation of proposed structural reforms was delayed. In July 2000 the IMF announced that disbursements equivalent to US $35.7m. would be granted to Benin in 2000–03 under the Poverty Reduction and Growth Facility (PRGF, the successor to ESAF). (In July 2002 the IMF announced that the PRGF arrangement was to be extended until March 2004.) In 2000 the Government began to instigate reforms in the cotton sector, ending the monopsony of the Société Nationale pour la Promotion Agricole (SONAPRA), although the anticipated reform of other sectors, including telecommunications and energy, was further delayed. Although allegations of malpractice and corruption in the privatization of the state enterprise responsible for the distribution of petroleum products, the Société Nationale de Commercialisation des Produits Pétroliers (SONACOP), heightened public concerns regarding the restructuring of the economy in 2000, the Government remained committed to extending its privatization programme and agreed to improve divestiture procedures.

Subsequent progress on privatization was slow, however, following the re-election of Kérékou in 2001. The state post and telecommunications company, the Office des Postes et des Télécommunications (OPT), was to be separated into two companies, with the proposed telecommunications company to undergo transfer to private ownership, while the divestiture of the electricity and water utility, the Société Béninoise d'Electricité et d'Eau (SBEE), was also anticipated. In 2002 the World Bank pledged a loan of US $30m. towards the restructuring of the SBEE, and in December of that year a plan for its financial rehabilitation was adopted. In June 2003 the Government approved the creation of a new company to assume the water activities of the SBEE, the Société Nationale des Eaux du Bénin (SONEB), which was to be transferred to local public-sector management. A decree establishing a regulatory body for the telecommunications sector was adopted by the Council of Ministers in October. Following lengthy delays, a company to assume the telecommunications activities of OPT, known as Bénin Télécoms, was established in 2004; it was intended that a 55% share in the company would be transferred to private ownership in 2005. The transfer of SONAPRA to private ownership began in mid-2003, but proceeded only sporadically during 2004 and despite hostility to the process from employees and trade unions. The process of privatization for these parastatals has advanced at a very gradual pace. It is now intended that SONAPRA will be fully privatized in 2007, whereas the transfer to private ownership of OPT and the SBEE's has been postponed until 2008/09. Additionally, reductions in state ownership were expected at the Port Autonome de Cotonou (PAC) and at various companies within the textiles, petroleum, cement, hotels and brewing sectors. In the longer term it was intended to encourage further private-sector participation in the economy by restructuring the banking sector and by improving the regulatory environment.

Projections suggested that the consistent economic growth recorded during the second half of the 1990s would continue, with real GDP growth of 6.0% and 5.6% recorded in 2002 and 2003, respectively. This growth was underpinned by good cotton harvests in 2001–03 (with a record crop being recorded in 2002), and expansion in the construction, manufacturing and services sectors in 2003. In 2005, according to estimates by the World Bank, Benin's gross national income (GNI), measured at average 2003–05 prices, was US $4,343.6m., equivalent to $510 per head (or $1,110 on an international purchasing-power parity basis). During 1995–2005, it was estimated, GDP per head increased, in real terms, by an average of 1.5% per year. In 2005 GDP increased by 3.9%. Aside from the low international prices for cotton, and the high cost of petroleum, Benin's economic growth was impeded by several other factors. Notably, there was a downturn in international trade through the PAC as neighbouring countries diverted their international transit trade to more efficient and competitive ports elsewhere in the region, while in August 2003 Nigeria (Benin's principal regional trading partner) prohibited the import of 44 goods. The consequent reduction of commercial activities reduced Benin's revenue by an estimated 25%–33% (equivalent to around 5% of Benin's GDP) in 2003. The imports ban from Nigeria was partially lifted in November 2004, resulting in some recovery in export activity; however, the volume of officially traded goods with Nigeria rose at a slower rate than the goods traffic to other neighbouring countries of Mali, Burkina Faso and Niger (by 133.4%, 52.6%, and 25.5%, respectively). In 2005 the volume of goods activity from the PAC increased by 29.8% and the total value of goods traded was 12,900m. francs CFA.

The practice of prudent monetary, fiscal and credit policies resulted in inflation decreasing to only 1.5% by 2003, and reducing further to 0.9% in 2004, according to IMF estimates. The increase in the rate of inflation to 2.4% in 2005 largely reflected high food prices that resulted from low rainfall, and continuing high international prices for fuel products. Consequently, GDP growth was restricted to 3.9% for that year. Improvements in cotton production in 2006 resulted in a change to the recent downward trend in real GDP growth (up to 4.1%), and although the economy remained vulnerable to exogenous shocks, the Organisation for Economic Co-operation and Development projected growth of 4.5% and 4.8%, respectively, in 2007 and 2008, subject to good levels of trade with Nigeria and ongoing efforts to restructure the cotton industry.

POPULATION AND EMPLOYMENT

Benin has for some time had a high standard of education. The existence of a large élite—for whom employment cannot easily be found in an underdeveloped, slowly growing economy—was at the root of Benin's unstable political situation following independence, as was the rift between three clearly defined regions: Parakou and the north, Abomey and the centre-south, and the narrow coastal zone around Cotonou (the main port) and Porto-Novo (the official capital). Almost three-quarters of the country's inhabitants—the population was estimated to total 8.76m. at mid-2006—reside in the southern regions, giving a population density there of more than 200 per sq km—one of the highest in West Africa. In the 1990s there was a pronounced movement to the towns. By the early 2000s about 40% of inhabitants were urban, around double the level in 1990. The population of the commune of Cotonou was measured at 665,100 in the 2002 census, although in the following year the UN estimated that the population of the surrounding agglomeration at 827,754. In 1995–2005 the population was estimated to have increased by an average of 3.1% per year. The rapid increase in population growth has, however, offset much of the country's economic growth in recent years.

While agriculture, livestock and fishing engage around one-half of the work-force, the public sector has also traditionally been a significant source of employment, accounting for about one-half of wage and salary earners in the early 1990s. This proportion has since declined, however, under the reform programmes implemented by the Soglo and subsequent Kérékou administrations, which aimed at reducing public expenditure. The number of civil servants declined from 40,053 in 1990 to 30,619 in 1999, as part of the public-sector restructuring process. The policy of limiting recruitment continues to be on the current Government's agenda. During the financial crisis in the late 1980s civil servants' wages were frozen and their grade-based benefits suspended. In 1991 the granting of annual wage increases resumed, but the gap between actual and grade-based salaries did not diminish until 2004, giving rise to an estimated wage arrears of 7.1% of GDP at the end of 2006. Civil servant authorities plan to keep 2007/08 wages and arrears payments at 6.2% of GDP.

AGRICULTURE, FORESTRY AND FISHERIES

The economy is largely dependent on the agricultural sector, which accounted for a projected 36.5% of GDP in 2006 and employed an estimated 50.0% of the labour force in 2004, according to FAO estimates. Output of the major food crops has risen strongly since the drought of 1981–83, reflecting both improved climatic conditions and a transfer of emphasis from cash crops to the cultivation of staple foods, and Benin is self-sufficient in basic foods. In 2005 output of cassava was 3,100,000 metric tons, yams 2,257,300 tons, maize 842,600 tons, and millet and sorghum 200,600 tons. Production of non-traditional food crops—notably rice (to substitute for imports), tomatoes, beans and onions—has also risen. The World Bank estimated that agricultural GDP increased at an average annual rate of 5.6% in 1995–2005; growth in 2005 was 4.4%.

In the past the major cash crop was oil palm, which remains the principal tree crop. Output of palm products, which was formerly based on natural plantations, covering 400,000 ha, benefited in the 1970s from intensive cultivation on some 30,000 ha of industrial plantations, partly financed by French aid. Production of palm kernels was estimated at 50,000 metric tons in 1976, palm kernel oil at more than 21,000 tons, and palm oil at almost 50,000 tons. However, output subsequently fell, owing to low producer prices and the overvalued CFA franc, and combined marketed production of palm oil and palm kernel oil was down to an average of only about 15,000–20,000 tons per year in the mid-1990s, although by the early 2000s output had recovered, reaching an estimated 46,800 tons in 2005. The figure for marketed production is distorted by the incidence of smuggling from Nigeria (in order to secure payment in the 'hard currency' CFA franc, rather than in the unstable naira).

By far the most valuable commercial crop is cotton, the production of which expanded rapidly in the 1980s, and which now accounts for over one-half of recorded export earnings. Benin's output of unginned (seed) cotton expanded dramatically in the mid-1980s, reaching 132,762 metric tons in 1986. With an expansion in the area under cultivation, output levels continued to increase in the early 1990s, and, boosted by the increase in producer prices following the currency's devaluation, production reached a record 430,398 tons in 1996. Output subsequently fell, however, owing to management problems at the cotton-marketing board and weaker international prices, although annual output consistently remained in excess of 300,000 tons. In 2002 the restructuring of SONAPRA contributed to a record output of 485,522 tons. According to unofficial figures, production of 404,800 tons was recorded in 2003, increasing to 411,300 tons in 2004. Production dropped in 2005, however, to just 366,100 tons. A draft framework on trade reached by members of the World Trade Organization at the beginning of August 2004 committed the USA and other wealthier developed countries to reducing subsidies to their cotton farmers—a key demand of West African cotton producers such as Benin—although further talks would be required prior to the conclusion of a final agreement, and substantive cuts in subsidies were not expected to take effect for several years.

An indication of the importance of the cotton sector can be seen in that it represents roughly 10% of GDP and approximately 350,000 cotton producers support almost 40% of the population of Benin. Some 240,000 metric tons were expected to be produced in 2006/07 after the disastrous 2005/06 harvest. The primary problem in recent years has been the lack of timely and effective distribution of inputs, disputes over cotton seed prices, diversion of fertilizers and late planting.

Whereas cotton is grown mainly in the north, other cash crops are produced in the south, where there are two rainy seasons. These include coffee, cocoa, groundnuts and karité nuts (sheanuts). Marketed production of cocoa and coffee tends to vary widely, since much of the recorded production originates in Nigeria. Recorded production of cash crops declined from the late 1980s because official purchase prices did not keep pace with the rise in the cost of living, prompting farmers to switch to subsistence food crops, or to sell their output outside official channels, either domestically, or in Nigeria. This situation was to some extent remedied by the 1994 devaluation, whose doubling of the local-currency value of foreign earnings benefited producers.

In 2005 cattle herds numbered 1.8m. head, sheep and goats an estimated 2.1m., and pigs (kept mainly in the south) 322,000. Livestock farming is practised in its traditional form in the north.

Exploitation of timber resources (mainly for fuel) is still limited, although rising, with annual roundwood removals reaching 494,000 cu m (according to FAO estimates) in 2004. In 2005, however, roundwood removals increased dramatically, to 6,393,000 cu m, the majority of which composed of fuel wood. A reafforestation programme, which was inaugurated in 1985 to counter desertification, was to concentrate on fast-growing species around populated areas.

Food supply is also supplemented by fishing, the majority of which takes place in inland waters, although in recent years the traditional sector has been in decline, owing to salination of the lagoons around Cotonou. The fishing sector accounted for some 2% of GDP in 2001. Fishing is mainly based on artisanal fishing, with the annual catch recorded at around 38,400 metric tons in 2005. Additionally, in the late 1990s many instances of unregulated fishing vessels, including Nigerian artisanal and semi-industrial vessels and other foreign vessels, operating illicitly within Benin's exclusive economic zone were reported.

MINING AND POWER

Although phosphates, kaolin, chromium, rutile, gold and iron ore have been located in the north, the only minerals so far exploited are limestone (for cement), marble, petroleum and natural gas, and mining contributed only a projected 0.3% of GDP in 2006. Production of petroleum in Benin began in the Sémé oilfield, 15 km off shore from Cotonou, in 1982, with initial output averaging 4,000 barrels per day (b/d). Production reached a peak of 9,000 b/d in 1985, with the entry into operation of a third well and of water-injection facilities; five new wells were also drilled. Despite an enhanced recovery programme backed by funds from the International Development Association, by 1996 output had declined to 1,500 b/d. Production ceased at the end of 1998, as a result of declining reserves, combined with low world prices for crude petroleum. In October 1999, however, Zetah Oil signed a contract to rehabilitate the oilfield, and subsequently signed a 25-year production contract for the field, which was estimated to retain petroleum reserves of some 22m. barrels. Exploration for oil and gas was accelerated in late 2002, with concessions being granted to Canadian and US companies. However, by 2003 output was negligible.

Electricity supply (512.8m. kWh in 2003) comes largely from the Akosombo hydroelectric dam in Ghana, as operations at the 62-MW installation on the frontier with Togo at Nangbeto, on the Mono river, which began in 1988, have tended to be sporadic. A second dam, with 104 MW capacity, was under construction at Adjarala, with the aim of achieving eventual self-sufficiency in power for both Benin and Togo. In 2000 the construction of a further electricity line, to run from Lagos, Nigeria, to Togo, through Benin, was proposed by the Governments of the three countries. A pipeline to supply natural gas from Nigeria to Benin, Togo and Ghana was under construction in the mid-2000s. The project was expected to be completed in November 2007, but it is feared that instability in Nigeria's oil delta may delay the project. Imports of mineral fuels and lubricants accounted for 23.0% of the value of total imports in 2004.

MANUFACTURING

Manufacturing activity is still small-scale and, apart from the construction materials, beer and soft drinks industries, is mainly confined to the processing of primary products for export (cotton ginning, oil palm processing), or import substitution of simple consumer goods. The manufacturing sector contributed a projected 8.5% of GDP in 2006. According to the World Bank, manufacturing GDP increased at an average annual rate of 4.8% in 1995–2005; the sector contracted by 2.1% in 2004, before growing once more, by 4.5%, in 2005. Cotton processing has been the most important activity since the late 1980s, after additional ginning plants came into operation, including three new ginneries in a joint venture between the cotton marketing agency, SONAPRA, and a French company in 1995/96. With capacity at 560,000 metric tons, there is excess capacity over national cotton production. In addition, other agricultural processing plants—for maize, cashew nuts and vegetables—have been rehabilitated to supply the stronger domestic and foreign markets. However, two of the principal cotton-oil processing plants in the country, operated by the Société des Huileries du Bénin and by Fludor, ceased operations in early 2005.

Two joint ventures that were established with Nigeria in the early 1980s have proved unprofitable. The cement plant at Onigbolo began production in 1982. Plans to sell one-half of the scheduled annual output of 600,000 metric tons to Nigeria failed to materialize, and the plant has, therefore, operated at only about one-half of its capacity. By the end of the Soglo regime the number of parastatals had been reduced from 120 to 15, although it had become increasingly difficult to attract financially viable bids. The debts accumulated at the Onigbolo cement plant and the Savé sugar complex delayed their privatization, which had been agreed in principle by the Nigerian and Beninois Governments. Following the re-election of Kérékou as President in 1996, the privatization programme was further delayed, although the new administration was obliged to continue the programme in order to secure a further ESAF. The conditions attached to the resumption of the ESAF in 1999, following its suspension in the previous year (see above), included the privatization of the petroleum company, SONACOP, and the textile enterprise, the Société Industrielle des Textiles, and the liberalization of the telecommunications and cotton sectors. A 55% stake in SONACOP was sold, and the management of the two loss-making joint ventures with Nigeria was leased out to overseas investors in 1999. A French group was given a five-year lease on the cement plant, to prepare it for privatization, while it was estimated in early 2001 that the rehabilitation of the Savé complex, under the management of a Mauritian company, would require investment of some 16,000m. francs CFA. Cement imports and prices were liberalized with effect from August 2002, although the long-term consequences of this measure for the Beninois cement industry remained uncertain. Annual output of hydraulic cement of 200,000–250,000 metric tons was recorded in 1999–2004.

THE SERVICES SECTOR

The services sector is the largest sector in economic terms, accounting for a projected 48.9% of GDP in 2006, and employing 36% of the economically active population in 1999. The sector consists mainly of trade and commerce (which contributed a projected 35.9% of the GDP of the tertiary sector in 2006), transport, telecommunications and other personal services, as well as the relatively large public administration. Five private banks were established in the 1990s, and a small regional stock exchange (the Bourse Régionale des Valeurs Mobilières, with its head office in Abidjan, Côte d'Ivoire) was founded in 1998. Tourism still remains underdeveloped in Benin, with most infrastructure being concentrated in Cotonou. According to the World Bank, the GDP of the services sector increased at an average annual rate of 4.1% in 1995–2005; output of the sector grew by 2.0% in 2004 and by 3.2% in 2005.

Transport Infrastructure

Benin's transport infrastructure is comparatively good. Most internal transportation uses the country's road network: in 2004 the classified road network totalled some 19,000 km, about 10% of which was paved. A number of major road construction schemes, including the upgrading of the 222-km Dassa–Parakou link of the Cotonou–Niger highway, have been implemented, with financial support from the European Community (now European Union—EU), the African Development Bank (ADB) and the Arab Bank for Economic Development in Africa. By the construction of new roads and the upgrading of existing routes, it is hoped to develop the country's status as an entrepôt for regional trade. Benin's foreign earnings benefit from the transit trade from Niger via the 579-km Benin–Niger railway. There have long been plans to extend the line from Parakou to Niamey, but, given Niger's economic circumstances and strained budget resources, the project's implementation is now only a remote possibility. In 1999 the network handled 269.0m. ton-km of goods, but this figure declined dramatically, to 153.2m. ton-km, in 2000.

The port of Cotonou handles 3.0m.–4.3m. tons of freight per year, of which up to 1m. tons has typically been transit trade with Niger and Burkina Faso, and some 300,000 second-hand motor vehicles, nearly all of which are destined for Burkina Faso, Chad, Mali, Niger and Nigeria. In the 1990s the port benefited from US $4m. in investment by the Danish company Maersk Line (now Maersk Sealand) in container facilities. The company began operations at the port in May 1998, thus ending the state company's monopoly on container trade (which had reached 739,000 tons in 1997). The port's petroleum-handling capacity was increased by around 60% in November 1999, with the opening of a new terminal. Following the onset of severe insecurity in Côte d'Ivoire in late 2002, the port at Cotonou also benefited from an increase in traffic diverted from Abidjan. Although a number of measures intended to improve the efficiency of the port have been implemented, partly in order to manage the increased traffic flow, opposition to these measures by trade unions has resulted in intermittent industrial action. With freight arriving at the port at Cotonou forecast to increase to 4.5m. tons by 2006, in May 2004 plans were announced to construct a dry port at Parakou, some 450 km north of Cotonou. The dry port will cover 100 ha, including a terminal with truck and rail facilities. Work on this was still underway in early 2007. In 2006 the EU under the eighth European Development Fund awarded Benin a grant of €23m. for the building of a new road network in Banikoara-Kandi (located in the Benin cotton belt), and it was anticipated that the building of the network would improve conditions for the transport of cotton to the processing facilities and to producers.

FINANCE

A wide-ranging austerity programme was implemented in 1987, with the aim of reducing current expenditure, in order to reduce Benin's chronic budget deficit, which had reached the equivalent of 7.3% of GDP in 1986. Public enterprises were transferred to private ownership, liquidated or rehabilitated, and public-sector salaries were initially 'frozen' and subsequently reduced. However, the political turmoil of late 1989 and early 1990 meant that revenue from taxation virtually ceased, and the accumulation of salary arrears precipitated the downfall of the Kérékou regime. The budget deficit (excluding grants) surged to 10.6% of GDP in 1989.

The Soglo administration succeeded in reducing the deficit to 4.8% by 1993. This was owing to several factors, including higher revenues (notably, as port trade was displaced to Benin from Togo), privatization, and a reduction in interest payments (following the rescheduling of foreign debt by the 'Paris Club' of official creditors in 1991). The devaluation of the CFA franc in 1994 put additional pressure on budget expenditure, and the deficit (excluding grants) rose to 7.3% of GDP in 1995. By 2001 the budget deficit (including grants) had declined to 26,200m. francs CFA, equivalent to 1.5% of GDP, before increasing to 44,900m. francs CFA (equivalent to 2.3% of GDP) in 2002. Following a series of strikes in 2001, the Government increased budgetary expenditure to meet demands for the payment of public-sector wage arrears, notably in the health and education sectors. In 2003 Benin recorded an overall budget deficit of 38,700m. francs CFA (equivalent to 1.9% of GDP). In 2004 the budgetary deficit was 22,400m. francs CFA, equivalent to 1.0% of GDP. The budget deficit worsened in 2005, when it was equivalent to 2.9% of GDP, before improving slightly to 2.7% of GDP in 2006,. These increases on previous years were a consequence of the decision to subsidize the cotton industry, and increased expenditure on poverty reduction programmes and the organization of the presidential elections.

As well as agreements with the IMF for debt relief and support for poverty reduction from the initiative for heavily indebted poor countries (HIPC), Benin has also benefited from a broad range of grants and loans from several donor organizations. Since 2000 development aid has been granted by the EU (to fund road construction and health care), the World Bank (for education, the national HIV/AIDS programme and the restructuring of the cotton sector), the ADB (for road improvements, rural electrification and debt relief), the Banque ouest-africaine de développement (for urban regeneration) and the World Food Programme (in the form of food aid). There have also been a number of bilateral finance initiatives, including finance from France (for poverty reduction, support of the cotton sector, decentralization, language training, development of the national parks, road rehabilitation and the development of the media), Denmark (for transport infrastructure, health care, the agricultural sector, the promotion of democracy and water supply and treatment) and Germany (for infrastructure and health-care projects). Non-EU countries that provided financial assistance to Benin in the early 2000s included Switzerland (to fund a population census), Canada (in support of the HIV/AIDS programme), the USA (for education, the promotion of democracy and good governance), the People's Republic of China (for rural development projects) and Japan (in the form of equipment finance, health care and food aid).

FOREIGN TRADE AND PAYMENTS

Benin has traditionally maintained a very substantial external trade deficit. During the 1980s export earnings were adversely affected by the recession in Nigeria, the closure of the border between the two countries during 1984–86, the impact of drought upon palm products, cocoa and coffee in 1981–83, and the decline in international cotton prices in 1986 and 1987. Despite a good recovery in exports in the early 1990s, the gap between exports and imports remained massive because the resumption of economic growth prompted an increase in the level of imports. The sharp depreciation of the currency in 1994 temporarily narrowed this gap, but by 1995 the trade deficit was at a record level of 101,000m. francs CFA. The trade deficit narrowed considerably in 1996, to 16,400m. francs CFA, but subsequently increased, reaching 239,700m. francs CFA in 2002, when the value of exports of cotton and textiles declined by 19.5% compared with the previous year. The trade deficit was reduced slightly, to 232,800m. francs CFA in 2003 before increasing to 243,300m. francs CFA in 2004. The fluctuations of the late 1990s reflected the impact on export earnings of trends in cotton prices, and the impact on the cost of imports of the international price of petroleum. In 2002 the principal source of imports (24.0%) was France; other major sources were the People's Republic of China, Côte d'Ivoire and Ghana. The principal market for exports in that year was Nigeria (22.2%); other important purchasers of Benin's textiles and cotton products were India, Ghana and Indonesia. In 2005 China became Benin's main destination for exports. According to figures from the General Administration of Customs, Sino-Beninois trade reached US $1,090m. in 2005, an increase of 58.7% compared with year on year. The principal imports were food products, mineral fuels and lubricants and capital goods.

Historically, the deficit on merchandise trade has been partly covered by remittances from Benin nationals overseas, which were estimated at an annual average of US $60m.–$70m. by the early 2000s. In 2004 the deficit on the current account of the balance of payments was 170,900m. francs CFA (some $323.5m.), while the overall deficit on the balance of payments was estimated at 53,600m. francs CFA (some $101.5m.). A significant offset is the inflow of overseas development aid, which amounted to an annual average (net) of $244m. in 2000–02, and was mainly sourced from France, the International Development Association, the European Commission, the USA, Denmark and Germany. The current account deficit grew slightly to an estimated 164,700m. francs CFA in 2006. Variations in the terms of the foreign debt have had a marked effect on the burden of debt service. After a structural reform programme was agreed with the IMF, and a three-year structural adjustment facility awarded in June 1989, the 'Paris Club' agreed to the rescheduling of $193m. in debt. Further relief was accorded in December 1991, when the 'Paris Club', recognizing the efforts of the new Government to resolve the country's public-financing difficulties, undertook to reduce the debt-service burden by one-half. There was a further rescheduling, on similar terms, in June 1993, after the IMF accorded Benin access to the ESAF.

The devaluation of the CFA franc in January 1994 greatly increased the burden on the Beninois economy of servicing foreign debt (the value of which had thereby doubled in local currency terms). Supplementary assistance was therefore arranged (for the entire Franc Zone in Africa) by the IMF, the World Bank and the EU, and France accorded debt waivers. In the case of Benin, 600m. French francs (equivalent to US $109m.) was cancelled with immediate effect. However, the increase in borrowing, particularly from multilateral institutions (borrowing from which is not eligible for rescheduling), had pushed Benin's debt to $1,614m. by the end of 1995. The ESAF extended to the new administration in August 1996 opened the way to a fourth round of debt rescheduling by the country's bilateral official creditors. About $208m. in non-concessionary debt was restructured on the highly concessionary 'Naples' terms. Under these terms, creditors either write off two-thirds of the liability (both principal and interest) and reschedule the balance over 23 years at market rates, or they reduce interest rates, with repayment over 33 years (effectively reducing the debt by two-thirds).

By the end of 1996 the debt had declined to US $1,592m., equivalent to 73.6% of GNI—compared with the 109% registered in 1994—while the debt-service ratio was 6.0% in 1996. At the end of 2004 external debt totalled some $1,916m., equivalent to 47.3% of GNI. In 2003 the cost of debt-servicing was equivalent to 7.6% of the value of exports of goods and services, having declined from 11.8% in 2000. In July 2000, as part of the HIPC initiative, the IMF and the World Bank announced the eventual cancellation of some $460m. of Benin's debt and announced a further three-year enhanced HIPC programme for 2000–03. In March 2003 Benin became the eighth country to reach 'completion point' under the enhanced HIPC initiative, as a result of which the country's creditors were committed to the debt relief provisionally agreed in 2000. In June 2005 Benin was among 18 countries to be granted 100% debt relief on multilateral debt agreed by the Group of Eight leading industrialized nations (G-8). The Government also prepared a Poverty Reduction Strategy Paper for the period 2003–05, which was intended to promote further strong economic growth and ensure financial stability. The formation of a stable pro-Government legislative majority for the first time since the introduction of a multi-party system in Benin, following elections in March 2003, also seemed likely to ease the implementation of further reforms. The peaceful transfer of power to the new president, Yayi Boni, the former head of the Banque ouest-africaine de développement, in elections held in March 2006, demonstrated Benin's continued adherence to the democratic process. Boni pledged further restructuring of both the public and private sectors and has since articulated a new economic vision for accelerating economic growth and poverty reduction.

Statistical Survey

Source (unless otherwise stated): Institut National de la Statistique et de l'Analyse Economique, BP 323, Cotonou; tel. 21-30-82-43; fax 21-30-82-46; e-mail insae@insae-bj.org; internet www.insae-bj.org.

Area and Population

AREA, POPULATION AND DENSITY

Area (sq km)	112,622*
Population (census results)	
15–29 February 1992	4,915,555
11 February 2002	
Males	3,284,119
Females	3,485,795
Total	6,769,914
Population (UN estimates at mid-year)†	
2004	8,224,000
2005	8,490,000
2006	8,760,000
Density (per sq km) at mid-2006	77.8

* 43,484 sq miles.

† Source: UN, *World Population Prospects: The 2006 Revision*.

ETHNIC GROUPS

2002 (percentages): Fon 39.2 (incl. Fon 17.6; Goun 6.3; Aïzo 4.3; Mahi 3.5; Ouémè 2.5; Torri 2.4; Kotafon 1.4; Tofin 1.3); Adja 15.2 (incl. Adja 8.7; Sahouè 2.6; Xwla 1.4; Mina 1.2); Yoruba 12.3 (incl. Nagot 6.8; Yoruba 1.8; Idaasha 1.5; Holli-Djè 1.4); Bariba 9.2 (incl. Bariba 8.3); Peulh 6.9 (incl. Peulh Fulfuldé 5.5); Otamari 6.1 (incl. Berba 1.4; Ditamari 1.3; Waama 1.0); Yoa Lokpa 4.5 (incl. Yoa 1.8; Lokpa 1.2); Dendi 2.5 (incl. Dendi 2.4); Others 2.7.

ADMINISTRATIVE DIVISIONS

(2002 census)

Département	Area (sq km)	Population	Population density (per sq km)
Alibori	25,683	521,093	20.3
Atacora	20,459	549,417	26.9
Atlantique	3,233	801,683	247.9
Borgou	25,310	724,171	28.6
Collines	13,561	535,923	39.5
Couffo	2,404	524,586	218.2
Donga	10,691	350,062	32.7
Littoral	79	665,100	8,419.0
Mono	1,396	360,037	257.9
Ouémé	2,835	730,772	257.8
Plateau	1,865	407,116	218.3
Zou	5,106	599,954	117.5
Total	112,622	6,769,914	60.1

PRINCIPAL TOWNS

(Communes, 2002 census)

Cotonou	665,100	Seme-Kpodji	115,238
Abomey-Calavi	307,745	Bohicon	113,091
Porto-Novo (capital)	223,552	Tchaourou	106,852
Djougou	181,895	Savalou	104,749
Banikoara	152,028	Malanville	101,628
Parakou	149,819	Ketou	100,499
Aplahoue	116,988	Kalale	100,026

Mid-2003 (incl. suburbs, UN estimate): Cotonou 827,754 (Source: UN, *World Urbanization Prospects: The 2003 Revision*).

Mid-2005 (incl. suburbs, UN estimate): Porto Novo 242,000 (Source: UN, *World Urbanization Prospects: The 2005 Revision*).

BIRTHS AND DEATHS

(annual averages, UN estimates)

	1990–95	1995–2000	2000–05
Birth rate (per 1,000)	46.3	44.0	42.2
Death rate (per 1,000)	13.9	12.8	12.6

Source: UN, *World Population Prospects: The 2006 Revision*.

2002: Birth rate 41.2 per 1,000; Death rate 12.3 per 1,000.

Expectation of life (years at birth, WHO estimates): 53 (males 52; females 53) in 2004 (Source: WHO, *World Health Report*).

ECONOMICALLY ACTIVE POPULATION

(persons aged 10 years and over, 1992 census)

	Males	Females	Total
Agriculture, hunting, forestry and fishing	780,469	367,277	1,147,746
Mining and quarrying	609	52	661
Manufacturing	93,157	67,249	160,406
Electricity, gas and water	1,152	24	1,176
Construction	50,959	696	51,655
Trade, restaurants and hotels	36,672	395,829	432,501
Transport, storage and communications	52,228	609	52,837
Finance, insurance, real estate and business services	2,705	401	3,106
Community, social and personal services	126,122	38,422	164,544
Activities not adequately defined	25,579	12,917	38,496
Total employed	1,169,652	883,476	2,053,128
Unemployed	26,475	5,843	32,318
Total labour force	1,196,127	889,319	2,085,446

Source: ILO, *Yearbook of Labour Statistics*.

2002 (census results): Total employed 2,811,753 (males 1,421,474, females 1,390,279); Unemployed 19,123 (males 12,934, females 6,189); Total labour force 2,830,876 (males 1,434,408, females 1,396,468).

Mid-2004 (estimates in '000): Agriculture, etc. 1,583; Total labour force 3,163 (Source: FAO).

Health and Welfare

KEY INDICATORS

Total fertility rate (children per woman, 2005)	5.6
Under-5 mortality rate (per 1,000 live births, 2005)	150
HIV/AIDS (% of persons aged 15–49, 2005)	1.8
Physicians (per 1,000 head, 2004)	0.04
Hospital beds (per 1,000 head, 2005)	.50
Health expenditure (2004): US $ per head (PPP)	40.4
Health expenditure (2004): % of GDP	4.9
Health expenditure (2004): public (% of total)	51.2
Access to water (% of persons, 2004)	67
Access to sanitation (% of persons, 2004)	33
Human Development Index (2004): ranking	163
Human Development Index (2004): value	0.428

For sources and definitions, see explanatory note on p. vi.

Agriculture

PRINCIPAL CROPS

('000 metric tons)

	2003	2004	2005*
Rice (paddy)	54.2	64.7	64.7
Maize	788.3	842.6	842.6
Millet	35.5	36.8	36.8
Sorghum	163.3	163.8	163.8
Sweet potatoes	51.1	50.0	50.0
Cassava (Manioc)	3,054.8	2,955.0	3,100.0
Yams	2,010.7	2,257.3	2,257.3
Sugar cane	75.4	70.0*	70.0
Dry beans	81.8	93.8	93.8
Pulses	18.4	25.6	25.6
Cashew nuts (in shell)*	40	40	40
Groundnuts (in shell)	125.0	130.0†	130.0
Coconuts*	20	20	20
Oil palm fruit*	244	244	244
Cottonseed	230†	235†	235
Tomatoes	141.8	144.2	144.2
Chillies and green peppers	25.2	33.6	33.6
Okra	85.3†	86.0*	86.0
Pineapples	105.9†	106.0*	106.0
Cotton (lint)	148†	150†	150

* FAO estimate(s).

† Unofficial figure.

Source: FAO.

LIVESTOCK

('000 head, year ending September)

	2003	2004	2005*
Cattle	1,689	1,745	1,800
Sheep	670*	700*	750
Goats	1,300*	1,350*	1,380
Pigs	297	309	322
Chickens	10,000*	13,000*	13,000

* FAO estimate(s).

Source: FAO.

LIVESTOCK PRODUCTS

('000 metric tons, FAO estimates)

	2003	2004	2005
Cattle meat	20.4	21.1	21.7
Goat meat	4.5	4.6	4.7
Pig meat	3.8	3.9	4.1
Chicken meat	11.6	15.2	15.2
Game meat	6.0	6.0	6.0
Cows' milk	26.3	27.2	28.1
Goats' milk	6.8	7.1	7.2
Hen eggs	7.2	9.4	9.4

Source: FAO.

Forestry

ROUNDWOOD REMOVALS

('000 cubic metres, excl. bark, FAO estimates)

	2003	2004	2005
Sawlogs, veneer logs and logs for sleepers	35	35	35
Other industrial wood	297	297	297
Fuel wood	162	162	6,061
Total	494	494	6,393

Source: FAO.

SAWNWOOD PRODUCTION

('000 cubic metres, incl. railway sleepers)

	2002	2003	2004*
Total (all broadleaved)	46	31	31

* FAO estimate.

2005: Production as in 2004 (FAO estimate).

Source: FAO.

Fishing

('000 metric tons, live weight)

	2003	2004	2005
Capture	41.6	40.0	38.0
Tilapias*	10.9	10.2	10.2
Black catfishes*	1.5	1.4	1.4
Torpedo-shaped catfishes*	1.5	1.4	1.4
Mullets	2.1	2.1	2.1
Sardinellas	1.8	1.6	1.2
Bonga shad	1.7	1.6	1.6
European anchovy	1.5	1.1	0.9
Bluefish	1.5	1.3	n.a.
Freshwater crustaceans*	4.6	4.3	4.3
Penaeus shrimps*	2.4	2.3	2.3
Aquaculture	0.0	0.0	0.4
Total catch (incl. others)*	41.7	40.0	38.4

* FAO estimates.

Note: Figures exclude catches by Beninois canoes operating from outside the country.

Source: FAO.

Mining

	2003	2004	2005
Clay ('000 metric tons)*	21	21	21
Gold (kg)	20	20	20

* Estimates.

Source: US Geological Survey.

Industry

SELECTED PRODUCTS

('000 metric tons, unless otherwise indicated)

	2000	2001	2002
Cement (hydraulic)*	250	250	250
Beer of barley†	35.0	35.0	35.0
Beer of sorghum†	32.8	35.0	41.8
Salted, dried or smoked fish†	2.0	2.0	2.0
Palm oil†	15	15	15
Palm kernel oil	9.7‡	9.7‡	9.7†
Electric energy (million kWh)	57	90	92

* Data from the US Geological Survey.

† Estimate(s).

‡ Unofficial figure.

Cement (hydraulic, '000 metric tons): 250 in 2003; 250 in 2004 (estimate); 250 in 2005 (estimate) (Source: US Geological Survey).

Salted, dried or smoked fish ('000 metric tons): 2.4 in 2003 (Source: FAO).

Sources: mainly UN, *Industrial Commodity Statistics Yearbook*; FAO.

Finance

CURRENCY AND EXCHANGE RATES

Monetary Units

100 centimes = 1 franc de la Communauté financière africaine (CFA).

Sterling, Dollar and Euro Equivalents (31 May 2007)

£1 sterling = 964.12 francs CFA;
US $1 = 487.59 francs CFA;
€1 = 655.96 francs CFA;
10,000 francs CFA = £10.37 = $20.51 = €15.24.

Average Exchange Rate (francs CFA per US $)

2004	528.29
2005	527.47
2006	522.89

Note: An exchange rate of 1 French franc = 50 francs CFA, established in 1948, remained in force until January 1994, when the CFA franc was devalued by 50%, with the exchange rate adjusted to 1 French franc = 100 francs CFA. This relationship to French currency remained in effect with the introduction of the euro on 1 January 1999. From that date, accordingly, a fixed exchange rate of €1 = 655.957 francs CFA has been in operation.

BUDGET

('000 million francs CFA)

Revenue*	2005	2006†	2007‡
Tax revenue	334.0	378.8	416.5
Taxes on international trade and transactions§	174.8	207.4	221.4
Direct and indirect taxes	159.2	171.4	195.1
Non-tax revenue	49.4	38.1	43.2
Total	383.4	416.9	459.7

Expenditure	2005	2006†	2007‡
Salaries	130.3	135.0	145.1
Pensions and scholarships	26.5	29.3	31.6
Other expenditure and current transfers	182.2	194.9	177.2
Investment	144.2	113.4	219.4
Budgetary contribution	76.3	48.6	106.2
Financed from abroad	67.9	64.8	113.2
Interest due	6.9	5.8	7.3
External debt	5.6	5.6	5.6
Net lending	-0.8	1.2	—
Total	489.3	479.6	580.6

* Excluding grants received ('000 million francs CFA): 47.9 in 2005; 55.7 in 2006 (estimate); 65.1 in 2007 (projection).

† Estimates.

‡ Projections.

§ Including value-added taxes on imports.

Source: IMF, *Benin: Second Review Under the Three-Year Arrangement Under the Poverty Reduction and Growth Facility and Request for Waiver of a Performance Criterion - Staff Report; Press Release on the Executive Board Discussion; and Statement by the Executive Director for Benin* (June 2007).

INTERNATIONAL RESERVES

(excluding gold, US $ million at 31 December)

	2004	2005	2006
IMF special drawing rights	—	0.2	0.1
Reserve position in IMF	3.4	3.1	3.3
Foreign exchange	636.5	653.5	908.9
Total	639.9	656.8	912.3

Source: IMF, *International Financial Statistics*.

MONEY SUPPLY

('000 million francs CFA at 31 December)

	2004	2005	2006
Currency outside banks	129.9	193.3	253.1
Demand deposits at deposit money banks	198.6	225.3	239.5
Checking deposits at post office	8.1	29.9	9.8
Total money (incl. others)	337.2	449.4	503.1

Source: IMF, *International Financial Statistics*.

COST OF LIVING

(Consumer Price Index; base: 2000 = 100)

	2003	2004	2005
Food, beverages and tobacco	105.5	104.7	114.4
Clothing	101.9	101.2	101.4
All items (incl. others)	108.1	109.0	114.9

Source: ILO.

NATIONAL ACCOUNTS

('000 million francs CFA at current prices)

Expenditure on the Gross Domestic Product

	2004	2005*	2006†
Final consumption expenditure	1,881.6	2,028.5	2,200.2
Households, incl. non-profit institutions serving households	1,622.9	1,753.5	1,906.1
General government	258.7	274.9	294.1
Gross capital formation	442.4	437.0	505.7
Gross fixed capital formation	415.5	444.9	481.1
Changes in inventories; Acquisitions, less disposals, of valuables	27.0	-8.0	24.6
Total domestic expenditure	2,324.0	2,465.5	2,705.9
Exports of goods and services	428.7	494.7	471.6
Less Imports of goods and services	612.7	656.2	708.7
GDP in market prices	2,140.0	2,304.0	2,468.8

Gross Domestic Product by Economic Activity

	2004	2005*	2006†
Agriculture, livestock, forestry, hunting and fishing	690.3	751.4	824.8
Mining	5.0	5.3	5.8
Manufacturing	167.6	184.6	192.5
Water, gas and electricity	25.9	28.4	30.1
Construction and public works	86.8	92.9	100.4
Trade	354.3	382.4	396.3
Transport and communications	163.7	173.9	184.6
Banks and insurance	39.6	41.6	44.1
Non-market services	224.4	238.9	255.9
Other services	199.5	210.9	222.3
Sub-total	1,957.1	2,110.3	2,256.8
Less Financial intermediation services indirectly measured	36.1	37.9	40.2
Import taxes and duties	219.0	231.6	252.2
GDP in purchasers' values	2,140.0	2,304.0	2,468.8

* Preliminary figures.

† Projected figures.

BALANCE OF PAYMENTS
('000 million francs CFA)

	2005	2006*	2007†
Exports of goods f.o.b.	171.6	147.2	192.3
Imports of goods f.o.b.	–393.3	–399.4	–454.1
Trade balance	–221.7	–252.3	–261.8
Exports of services	129.6	121.1	128.0
Imports of services	–154.4	–143.4	–155.0
Balance on goods and services	–246.5	–274.6	–288.8
Income (net)	–20.3	–18.1	–22.5
Balance on goods, services and income	–266.8	–292.7	–311.3
Private unrequited transfers	63.6	72.4	76.7
Public unrequited transfers	47.5	61.6	70.0
Current balance	–155.7	–158.7	–164.7
Capital account (net)	39.7	607.8	60.6
Medium- and long-term public capital	47.0	–517.4	61.6
Medium- and long-term private capital	58.7	56.4	27.7
Deposit money banks	–20.4	26.5	—
Short-term capital	55.0	53.5	—
Net errors and omissions	46.0	47.7	—
Overall balance	70.4	115.8	–14.8

* Estimates.
† Projections.

Source: IMF, *Benin: Second Review Under the Three-Year Arrangement Under the Poverty Reduction and Growth Facility and Request for Waiver of a Performance Criterion - Staff Report; Press Release on the Executive Board Discussion; and Statement by the Executive Director for Benin* (June 2007).

External Trade

PRINCIPAL COMMODITIES
('000 million francs CFA)

Imports c.i.f.	2002	2003	2004
Food products	119.0	124.0	115.7
Textiles, cotton products, etc.	44.6	34.2	30.3
Capital goods	74.0	93.0	82.5
Mineral fuels, lubricants, etc.	87.5	104.9	108.3
Chemicals, chemical products, etc.	35.3	23.9	21.1
Pharmaceutical products	27.2	21.6	20.7
Total (incl. others)	502.4	515.1	471.0

Exports f.o.b.	2002	2003	2004
Textiles, cotton products, etc.	93.5	111.1	110.3
Edible fruit, oil-bearing fruit	15.5	15.4	12.4
Tobacco products, cigarettes, etc.	2.5	5.7	10.3
Wood, wood products, etc.	5.5	2.9	2.0
Lime, cement, etc.	1.1	3.0	6.3
Total (incl. others)	167.5	157.8	158.7

PRINCIPAL TRADING PARTNERS
(US $ million)

Imports c.i.f.	2000	2001	2002
Belgium	10.5	17.4	13.8
China, People's Repub.	29.6	48.0	46.7
Côte d'Ivoire	50.9	32.7	40.8
France (incl. Monaco)	146.9	138.7	174.3
Germany	15.9	17.2	21.0
Ghana	26.7	29.4	40.4
India	8.9	8.5	14.1
Italy	20.1	22.1	23.5
Japan	16.9	18.5	20.5
Korea, Repub.	3.0	6.3	6.8
Mauritania	7.6	2.7	2.8
Netherlands	32.2	23.2	29.1
Nigeria	10.2	29.3	27.8
Pakistan	5.5	2.0	0.8
Saudi Arabia	9.5	6.5	4.7
Senegal	12.5	11.7	21.7
South Africa	3.2	11.0	18.1
Spain	16.1	13.5	13.3
Thailand	15.0	19.1	20.4
United Kingdom	18.2	20.9	36.0
USA	18.1	26.0	21.1
Total (incl. others)	547.1	601.9	727.0

Exports f.o.b.	2000	2001	2002
Bangladesh	7.2	2.0	3.0
Belgium	4.4	4.0	3.1
Brazil	16.8	10.4	0.9
China, People's Repub.	0.4	0.4	16.9
France (incl. Monaco)	3.2	4.7	11.9
Germany	4.0	3.2	3.2
Ghana	4.9	10.7	26.5
India	59.8	55.7	43.3
Indonesia	9.4	10.2	24.1
Italy	12.0	8.3	12.8
Morocco	7.1	4.4	9.0
Netherlands	0.8	1.1	6.5
Niger	7.4	4.5	5.6
Nigeria	2.8	9.7	67.6
Pakistan	1.5	1.3	12.8
Portugal	2.3	1.8	3.1
Saudi Arabia	2.0	2.3	0.7
Spain	5.6	4.8	4.7
Switzerland-Liechtenstein	2.6	1.5	3.6
Thailand	7.2	7.9	12.6
Turkey	8.9	3.7	3.7
United Kingdom	0.9	2.5	1.9
Viet Nam	0.8	3.3	1.2
Total (incl. others)	188.4	181.8	304.0

Source: UN, *International Trade Statistics Yearbook*.

Transport

RAILWAYS
(traffic)

	1998	1999	2000
Passengers carried ('000)	699.8	n.a.	n.a.
Passenger-km (million)	112.0	82.2	156.6
Freight ton-km (million)	218.7	269.0	153.2

Source: mainly IMF, *Benin: Statistical Appendix* (August 2002).

2001 (traffic, million): Passenger-km 101; Net ton-km 316 (Source: UN, *Statistical Yearbook*).

2002 (traffic, million): Net ton-km 482 (Source: UN, *Statistical Yearbook*).

ROAD TRAFFIC
(motor vehicles in use)

	1994	1995	1996
Passenger cars	26,507	30,346	37,772
Buses and coaches	353	405	504
Lorries and vans	5,301	6,069	7,554
Road tractors	2,192	2,404	2,620
Motorcycles and mopeds	220,800	235,400	250,000

Source: IRF, *World Road Statistics*.

Passenger cars ('000 in use): 135.7 in 2002; 135.7 in 2003 (Source: UN, *Statistical Yearbook*).

Commercial vehicles ('000 in use): 18.8 in 2002; 19.2 in 2003 (Source: UN, *Statistical Yearbook*).

SHIPPING

Merchant Fleet
(registered at 31 December)

	2003	2004	2005
Number of vessels	6	6	6
Total displacement ('000 grt)	1.0	1.0	1.0

Source: Lloyd's Register-Fairplay, *World Fleet Statistics*.

International Sea-borne Freight Traffic
(at Cotonou, including goods in transit, '000 metric tons)

	2001	2002	2003
Goods loaded	380.5	462.2	469.4
Goods in transit	6.5	5.6	8.6
Goods unloaded	2,929.3	3,007.7	3,808.9
Goods in transit	984.9	514.7	838.1

Source: IMF, *Benin: Statistical Appendix* (November 2004).

CIVIL AVIATION

(traffic on scheduled services, domestic and international)*

	1999	2000	2001
Kilometres flown (million)	3	3	1
Passengers carried ('000)	84	77	46
Passenger-km (million)	235	216	130
Total ton-km (million)	36	32	19

* Including an apportionment of the traffic of Air Afrique.

Source: UN, *Statistical Yearbook*.

Tourism

FOREIGN VISITORS BY COUNTRY OF ORIGIN*

	2002	2003	2004
Angola	110	8,592	9,613
Austria	5,000	4,000	3,000
Belgium	3,000	3,500	3,125
Burkina Faso	2,800	2,200	3,750
Burundi	250	2,100	2,157
Cameroon	2,200	9,814	10,599
Central African Republic	210	2,000	1,877
Chad	370	1,870	2,110
Congo, Republic	2,000	37,781	36,376
Côte d'Ivoire	7,600	12,000	10,705
France	10,000	11,000	14,210
Gabon	1,000	6,830	5,878
Germany	500	2,500	1,520
Ghana	1,340	7,311	7,511
Guinea	1,010	730	1,810
Madagascar	70	1,800	1,102
Malawi	5	2,100	2,330
Mali	2,310	1,300	1,210
Niger	4,310	6,810	5,900
Nigeria	15,250	19,800	20,200
Senegal	1,915	3,800	1,100
Togo	4,650	10,400	11,200
Tunisia	140	1,724	1,918
USA	1,000	350	211
Total (incl. others)	72,288	175,000	173,500

* Arrivals of non-resident tourists at national borders, by country of residence.

Receipts from tourism (US $ million, incl. passenger transport): 94.5 in 2002; 107.9 in 2003; n.a. in 2004.

Source: World Tourism Organization.

Communications Media

	2003	2004	2005
Telephones ('000 main lines in use)	66.5	72.8	76.3
Mobile cellular telephones ('000 subscribers)	236.2	386.7	n.a.
Personal computers ('000 in use)	26	30	32
Internet users ('000)	70	100	425

Facsimile machines (number in use): 1,064 in 1996.

Source: International Telecommunication Union.

Television receivers: ('000 in use): 272 in 2000 (Source: UNESCO, *Statistical Yearbook*).

1999: Radio receivers ('000 in use): 2,661; Daily newspapers 13 (average circulation 32,500 copies); Non-daily newspapers 2 (average circulation 44,000 copies); Periodicals 106 (average circulation 110,000 copies) (Sources: UNESCO, *Statistical Yearbook* and Institute for Statistics).

Book production: 84 titles (42,000 copies) in 1994 (first editions only); 9 titles in 1998. Sources: UNESCO, *Statistical Yearbook*, UNESCO Institute for Statistics.

Education

(2003/04, except where otherwise indicated)

			Students ('000)		
	Institutions	Teachers	Males	Females	Total
Pre-primary	283*	606	11.2	10.8	22.0
Primary	4,178†	25,583	755.0	564.7	1,319.6
Secondary	145‡	12,205	225.6	112.8	338.4
Tertiary§	n.a.	672	15.8	3.9	19.8

* 1995/96.
† 1999/2000.
‡ 1993/94.
§ 2000/01.

Source: UNESCO, *Statistical Yearbook* and Institute for Statistics.

Adult literacy rate (UNESCO estimates): 34.7% (males 46.9%; females 23.3%) in 2004 (Source: UN Development Programme, *Human Development Report*).

Directory

The Constitution

A new Constitution was approved in a national referendum on 2 December 1990. Its main provisions are summarized below:

PREAMBLE

The Beninois People reaffirm their opposition to any political regime founded on arbitrariness, dictatorship, injustice and corruption, reassert their attachment to the principles of democracy and human rights, as defined in the United Nations Charter, the Universal Declaration of Human Rights and the African Charter of the Rights of Man and Peoples, proclaim their attachment to the cause of African Unity and solemnly adopt this new Constitution as the supreme Law of the State.

I. THE STATE AND SOVEREIGNTY

Articles 1–6: The State of Benin is an independent, sovereign, secular, democratic Republic. The capital is Porto-Novo. The official language is French. The principle of the Republic is 'government of the People, by the People and for the People'. National sovereignty belongs to the People and is exercised through elected representatives and by referendums. Political parties operate freely, as determined by the Charter of Political Parties, and must respect the principles of national sovereignty, democracy, territorial integrity and the secular basis of the State. Suffrage is universal, equal and secret.

II. RIGHTS AND DUTIES OF THE INDIVIDUAL

Articles 7–40: The State is obliged to respect and protect the sacred and inviolable rights of the individual, and ensures equal access to health, education, culture, information, vocational training and employment. Primary education is compulsory. The State progressively assures the provision of free public education. Private schools are permitted. Torture and the use of cruel or degrading punishment are prohibited, and detention is subject to strict limitations. All persons have the right to property ownership, to freedom of conscience and expression. The State guarantees the freedoms of movement and association. All are equal before the law. The State recognizes the right to strike. Military service is compulsory.

III. THE EXECUTIVE

Articles 41–78: The President of the Republic is the Head of State. Candidates for the presidency must be of Beninois nationality by birth or have been naturalized for at least 10 years, and must be aged 40–70 years. The President is elected for a mandate of five years, renewable only once, by an absolute majority of votes cast. If no candidate receives an absolute majority, a second round is to be held between the two highest placed candidates. The Constitutional Court oversees the regularity of voting and announces the results. No President may serve more than two mandates.

The President of the Republic holds executive power. Following consultation with the Bureau of the Assemblée nationale, he names the members of the Government, who may not hold any parliamentary mandate. The President of the Republic chairs the Council of Ministers and has various defined powers of appointment.

The President of the Republic promulgates laws adopted by the Assemblée nationale, and may demand the resubmission of a law to the Assemblée nationale prior to its promulgation. In the event that the President of the Republic fails to promulgate a law, the Constitutional Court may, in certain circumstances, declare the law as binding.

After consultation with the President of the Assemblée nationale and the President of the Constitutional Court, the President of the Republic may call a referendum on matters pertaining to human rights, sub-regional or regional integration or the organization of public powers. The President of the Republic is the Supreme Chief of the Armed Forces.

The President of the Republic may delegate certain specified powers to ministers. The President of the Republic or any member of his Government may be called to account by the Assemblée nationale.

IV. THE LEGISLATURE

i. The Assemblée Nationale

Articles 79–93: Parliament exercises legislative power and controls the activities of the Government. Deputies of the Assemblée nationale, who must be civilians, are elected by direct universal suffrage for four years, and may be re-elected. The Assemblée nationale elects its President and a Bureau. Deputies enjoy various conditions of immunity from prosecution.

ii. Relations between the Assemblée Nationale and the Government

Articles 94–113: Members of the Government may attend sessions of the Assemblée nationale. Laws are approved by a simple majority, although organic laws require an absolute majority and approval by the Constitutional Court. The Assemblée nationale authorizes any declaration of war. States of siege and of emergency are declared in the Council of Ministers, although the Assemblée nationale must approve the extension of any such state beyond 15 days.

Deputies may, by a three-quarters' majority, decide to submit any question to referendum. If the Assemblée nationale has not approved a balanced budget by 31 December of any year, the measures foreseen by the finance law may be implemented by ordinance.

V. THE CONSTITUTIONAL COURT

Articles 114–124: The Constitutional Court is composed of seven members, of which four are named by the Bureau of the Assemblée nationale and three by the President of the Republic, each for a mandate of five years, renewable only once. The President of the Constitutional Court is elected by his peers for a period of five years and is a senior magistrate or lawyer. The decisions of the Constitutional Court are not subject to appeal.

VI. THE JUDICIARY

Articles 125–130: The judiciary is independent of the legislature and of the executive. It consists of the Supreme Court, and other courts and tribunals created in accordance with the Constitution. Judges may not be removed from office. The President of the Republic appoints magistrates and is the guarantor of the independence of the judiciary, assisted by the Higher Council of Magistrates, the composition, attributes, organization and function of which are fixed by an organic law.

i. The Supreme Court

Articles 131–134: The Supreme Court is the highest jurisdiction of the State in administrative and judicial matters, and with regard to the accounts of the State and to local elections. The decisions of the Court are not subject to appeal. The President of the Supreme Court is appointed for five years by the President of the Republic. The President of the Supreme Court may not be removed from office during his mandate, which is renewable only once.

ii. The High Court of Justice

Articles 135–138: The High Court of Justice comprises the members of the Constitutional Court (other than its President), six deputies of the Assemblée nationale and the President of the Supreme Court. The High Court of Justice elects a President from among its members and is competent to try the President of the Republic and members of the Government in cases of high treason, crimes committed during the exercise of their functions and plots against state security. In the event of an accusation of high treason or of contempt of the Assemblée nationale, and in certain other cases, the President of the Republic and members of the Government are to be suspended from their functions. In the case of being found guilty of such charges, they are dismissed from their responsibilities.

VII. THE ECONOMIC AND SOCIAL COUNCIL

Articles 139–141: The Economic and Social Council advises on proposed laws, ordinances or decrees that are submitted to it. Proposed laws of an economic or social nature must be submitted to the Council.

VIII. THE HIGH AUTHORITY FOR BROADCASTING AND COMMUNICATION

Articles 142–143: The High Authority for Broadcasting and Communication assures the freedom of the press and all other means of mass communication. It oversees the equitable access of political parties, associations and citizens to the official means of communication and information.

IX. INTERNATIONAL TREATIES AND ACCORDS

Articles 144–149: The President of the Republic negotiates and ratifies international treaties and accords. Peace treaties, those relating to international organization or territorial changes and to certain other matters must be ratified by law.

X. LOCAL AUTHORITIES

Articles 150–153: The local authorities of the Republic are created by law and are freely administered by elected councils. Their development is overseen by the State.

XI. ON REVISION

Articles 154–156: The initiative for the revision of the Constitution belongs jointly to the President of the Republic, after a decision has been taken in the Council of Ministers, and to the Assemblée nationale, given a majority vote of three-quarters of its members. A revision requires approval by referendum, unless it is supported by a majority of four-fifths of the members of the Assemblée nationale. The republican and secular basis of the State may not be the subject of any revision.

XII. TRANSITIONAL AND FINAL DISPOSITIONS

Articles 157–160: This new Constitution must be promulgated within eight days of its adoption by referendum. The President of the Republic must assume office and the Assemblée nationale convene by 1 April 1991. The Haut Conseil de la République and the transitional Government will continue to exercise their functions until the installation of the new institutions.

The Government

HEAD OF STATE

President: Boni Yayi (inaugurated 6 April 2006).

COUNCIL OF MINISTERS
(August 2007)

President: Dr Boni Yayi.

Minister of State, in charge of the Economy, Planning, Development and the Evaluation of Public Action: Irénée Koupaki.

Minister of State, in charge of National Defence: Issifou Kogui N'Douro.

Minister of the Interior and Public Security: Gen. Félix Hessou.

Minister of Decentralization, Local Communities and Territorial Development: Issa Démole Moko.

Minister of Foreign Affairs, African Integration, Francophone Affairs and Beninois Abroad: Moussa Okanla.

Minister of Finance: Lawani Soule Mana.

Minister of Agriculture, Stockbreeding and Fisheries: Roger Dovonou.

Minister of Trade, Industry and Small and Medium-sized Enterprises: Grégoire Akofodji.

Minister of Mining, Energy and Water: Sacca Lafia.

Minister of Health: Kessile Tchala.

Minister of Primary Education, Literacy and National Languages: Christine Ouinsavi.

Minister of Secondary Education and Professional Training: Bernadette Sohoudji Agbossou.

Minister of Higher Education and Scientific Research: Vicentia Bocco.

Minister of Youth, Sports and Leisure: Ganiou Soglo.

Minister of Labour and the Civil Service: Emmanuel Tiando.

Minister of Culture, Tourism and Crafts: Soumanou Seïbou Toléba.

Minister of Family and Children: Gnimbere Dansou.

Minister of Administrative and Institutional Reform: Bio Gounou Idrissou Sina.

Minister of the Environment and the Protection of Nature: Juliette Koudenoukpo Biaou.

Minister of Microfinance and Youth and Women's Employment: Sakinatou Abdou Alfa Orou.

Minister of Town Planning, Housing, Land Reform and the Fight against Coastal Erosion: François Gbenoupko Noudégbessi.

Keeper of the Seals, Minister of Justice, Legislation and Human Rights: Gustave Anani Cassa.

Minister in charge of Relations with the Institutions, Government Spokesperson: Alexandre Hountodji.

Minister-delegate at the Presidency, in charge of Communication and New Technologies: Désiré Adadja.

Minister-delegate at the Presidency, in charge of Transport and Public Works: Armand Zinzindohoué.

Minister-delegate at the Ministry of Finance, in charge of the Budget: Albert Segbégnon Houngbo.

MINISTRIES

Office of the President: BP 1288, Cotonou; tel. 21-30-00-90; fax 21-30-06-36; internet www.gouv.bj.

Ministry of Administrative and Institutional Reform: BP 302, Cotonou; tel. 21-30-12-47; fax 21-30-18-51.

Ministry of Agriculture, Stockbreeding and Fisheries: 03 BP 2900, Cotonou; tel. 21-30-04-10; fax 21-30-03-26; e-mail sgm@agriculture.gouv.bj; internet www.agriculture.gouv.bj.

Ministry of Culture, Tourism and Crafts: 01 BP 2037, Guincomey, Cotonou; tel. 21-30-70-10; fax 21-30-70-31; e-mail sg@tourisme.gouv.bj; internet www.tourisme.gouv.bj.

Ministry of Decentralization, Local Communities and Territorial Development: Cotonou.

Ministry of the Environment and the Protection of Nature: 01 BP 3621, Cotonou; tel. 21-31-55-96; fax 21-31-50-81; e-mail sg@environnement.gouv.bj; internet www.mehubenin.net.

Ministry of Family and Children: 01 BP 2802, Cotonou; tel. 21-31-67-08; fax 21-31-64-62; e-mail sgm@famille.gouv.bj; internet www.famille.gouv.bj.

Ministry of Finance: BP 302, Cotonou; tel. 21-30-02-81; fax 21-31-18-51; e-mail sgm@finance.gouv.bj; internet www.finance.gouv.bj.

Ministry of Foreign Affairs, African Integration, Francophone Affairs and Beninois Abroad: Zone Résidentielle, route de l'Aéroport, 06 BP 318, Cotonou; tel. 21-30-09-06; fax 21-30-19-70; e-mail sgm@etranger.gouv.bj; internet www.etranger.gouv.bj.

Ministry of Health: Immeuble ex-MCAT, 01 BP 882, Cotonou; tel. 21-33-21-63; fax 21-33-04-62; e-mail sgm@sante.gouv.bj; internet www.sante.gouv.bj.

Ministry of Higher Education and Scientific Research: 01 BP 348, Cotonou; tel. 21-30-06-81; fax 21-30-57-95; e-mail sgm@recherche.gouv.bj; internet www.recherche.gouv.bj.

Ministry of the Interior and Public Security: BP 925, Cotonou; tel. 21-30-11-06; fax 21-30-01-59; e-mail sgm@securite.gouv.bj; internet www.securite.gouv.bj.

Ministry of Justice, Legislation and Human Rights: BP 2493, Cotonou; tel. 21-30-08-90; fax 21-30-18-21; e-mail sgm@justice.gouv.bj; internet www.justice.gouv.bj.

Ministry of Labour and the Civil Service: BP 907, Cotonou; tel. 21-31-26-18; fax 21-31-06-29; e-mail sgm@travail.gouv.bj; internet www.travail.gouv.bj.

Ministry of Microfinance and Youth and Women's Employment: Cotonou.

Ministry of Mining, Energy and Water: 04 BP 1412, Cotonou; tel. 21-31-29-07; fax 21-31-35-46; e-mail sgm@energie.gouv.bj; internet www.energie.gouv.bj.

Ministry of National Defence: BP 2493, Cotonou; tel. 21-30-08-90; fax 21-30-18-21; e-mail sgm@defense.gouv.bj; internet www.defense.gouv.bj.

Ministry of Primary Education, Literacy and National Languages: 01 BP 10, Porto-Novo; tel. 20-21-33-27; fax 20-21-50-11; e-mail sgm@enseignement.gouv.bj; internet www.enseignement.gouv.bj.

Ministry of Secondary Education and Professional Training: 10 BP 250, Cotonou; tel. and fax 21-30-56-15; e-mail sgm@formation.gouv.bj; internet www.formation.gouv.bj.

Ministry of Trade, Industry and Small and Medium-sized Enterprises: BP 363, Cotonou; tel. 21-30-76-46; fax 21-30-30-24; e-mail sgm@commerce.gouv.bj; internet www.commerce.gouv.bj.

Ministry of Youth, Sports and Leisure: 03 BP 2103, Cotonou; tel. 21-30-36-14; fax 21-38-21-26; e-mail sgm@jeunesse.gouv.bj; internet www.jeunesse.gouv.bj.

President and Legislature

PRESIDENT

Presidential Election, First Ballot, 5 March 2006

Candidate	Votes	% of votes
Boni Yayi	1,074,308	35.64
Adrien Houngbédji	727,239	24.13
Bruno Ange-Marie Amoussou	489,122	16.23
Léhadi Vinagnon Vitoun Soglo	253,478	8.41
Antoine Kolawole Idji	97,595	3.24
Lazare Maurice Sehoueto	61,195	2.03
Séverin Adjovi	53,304	1.77
Antoine Dayori	37,436	1.24
Others	208,812	6.93
Total	3,014,167*	100.00

* Including 11,678 invalid votes, equivalent to 0.39% of the total.

Second Ballot, 19 March 2006

Candidate	Votes	% of votes
Boni Yayi	1,979,305	74.52
Adrien Houngbédji	673,937	25.37
Total	2,656,070*	100.00

* Including 2,828 invalid votes, equivalent to 0.11% of the total.

LEGISLATURE

Assemblée nationale

BP 371, Porto-Novo; tel. 20-21-22-19; fax 20-21-36-44; e-mail assemblee.benin@yahoo.fr; internet www.assembleebenin.org.

President: MATHURIN NAGO.

General Election, 31 March 2007, provisional results

Party	Seats
Force cauris pour un Bénin émergent (FCBE)	35
Alliance pour une dynamique démocratique (ADD)	20
Parti du renouveau démocratique (PRD)	10
Force clé (FC)	4
Union pour la relève (UPR)	3
Alliance du renouveau (AR)	2
Coalition pour un Bénin émergent (CBE)	2
Force espoir (FE)	2
Union nationale pour la démocratie et le progrès (UNDP)	2
Alliance des forces du progrès (AFP)	1
Restaurer l'espoir (RE)	1
Parti pour la démocratie et le progrès social (PDPS)	1
Total	83

Election Commission

Commission électorale nationale autonome (CENA): Porto-Novo; f. 1994; 25 mems, of whom 18 are appointed by the Assemblée nationale, two by the President of the Republic, one by civil society; there are additionally four members of the Commission's permanent administrative secretariat; Pres. EUGENE CAPO CHICHI.

Advisory Council

Economic and Social Council (CES): ave Jean-Paul II, 08 BP 679, Cotonou; tel. 21-30-03-91; fax 21-30-03-13; e-mail dasoul@cma.inbox.as; internet www.ces.gouv.bj; f. 1994; 30 mems, representing the executive, legislature and 'all sections of the nation'; reviews all legislation relating to economic and social affairs; competent to advise on proposed economic and social legislation, as well as to recommend economic and social reforms; Pres. RAPHIOU TOUKOUROU.

Political Organizations

The registration of political parties commenced in August 1990. In mid-2002 there were more than 160 registered parties. In mid-2007 the most important political parties included the following:

Alliance pour une dynamique démocratique (ADD): Leader NICÉPHORE SOGLO.

Mouvement africain pour la démocratie et le progrès (MADEP): BP 1509, Cotonou; tel. 21-31-31-22; f. 1997; Leader El Hadj SÉFOU L. FAGBOHOUN.

Parti social-démocrate (PSD): Leader BRUNO AMOUSSOU.

La renaissance du Bénin (RB): BP 2205, Cotonou; tel. 21-31-40-89; f. 1992; Hon. Pres. NICÉPHORE SOGLO; Chair. ROSINE VIEYRA SOGLO.

Rassemblement démocratique pour le développement—Nassara (RDD—Nassara): Leader RAMATOU BABA MOUSSA.

Union des forces démocratiques (UFD): Parakou; f. 1994; Leader GEORGE SACCA.

Alliance étoile: f. 2002; Leader SACCA LAFIA.

Union pour la démocratie et la solidarité nationale (UDS): BP 1761, Cotonou; tel. 21-31-38-69; Pres. SACCA LAFIA.

Les verts du Bénin—Parti écologiste du Bénin: 06 BP 1336, Cotonou; tel. and fax 21-35-19-47; e-mail greensbenin@yahoo.fr; internet www.greensbenin.org; f. 1995; Pres. TOUSSAINT HINVI; Sec. PIERRE AHOUANOZIN.

Alliance des forces du progrès (AFP): Assemblée nationale, BP 371, Porto-Novo; Leader VALENTIN ADITI HOUDE.

Alliance impulsion pour le progrès et la démocratie (Alliance IPD): 04 BP 0812, Cotonou; tel. 21-35-20-03; f. 1999; Leader THÉOPHILE NATA.

Alliance MDC-PS-CPP: Assemblée nationale, BP 371, Porto-Novo; Leader DAMIEN ZINSOU MODÉRAN ALAHASSA.

Congrès du peuple pour le progrès (CPP): Quartier Houéyiho, villa 061, cité BCEAO, BP 1565, Cotonou; tel. 21-38-52-55; Leader SÉDÉGNON ADANDE-KINTI.

Mouvement pour le développement par la culture (MDC): Quartier Zogbohoué, BP 10, Cotonou; Pres. CODJO ACHODÉ.

Parti du salut (PS): 06 BP 11, Cotonou; tel. 21-36-02-56; f. 1994; Leader DAMIEN MODÉRAN ZINSOU ALAHASSA.

Alliance du renouveau (AR): Leader MARTIN DOHOU AZONHIHO.

Coalition pour un Bénin émergent (CBE): Leader VENANCE GNIGLA.

Force cauris pour un Bénin émergent (FCBE): tel. 95-86-11-00; e-mail fcbe@gmail.com; internet www.fcbe2007.org; Pres. EXPÉDIT HOUESSOU; Sec.-Gen. DAVID NAHOUAN.

Force clé: Carré 315, ScoaGbéto, 01 BP 1435, Cotonou; tel. 21-35-09-36; f. 2003 on basis of Mouvement pour une alternative du peuple; Leader LAZARE SÈHOUÉTO.

Force espoir (FE): Leader ANTOINE DAYORI.

Mouvement pour le développement et la solidarité (MDS): BP 73, Porto-Novo; Leader SACCA MOUSSÉDIKOU FIKARA.

La nouvelle alliance (LNA): Assemblée nationale, BP 371, Porto-Novo; Leader SOULÉ DANKORO.

Union pour le progrès et la démocratie (UPD—Gamèsu): Assemblée nationale, BP 371, Porto-Novo; f. 2002 by mems of fmr Parti social démocrate; Pres. JEAN-CLAUDE HOUNKPONOU.

Nouvelle Alliance: Cotonou; f. 2006; Leader CORENTIN KOHOUE.

Parti pour la démocratie et le progrès social (PDPS): Leader EDMOND AGOUA.

Parti du renouveau démocratique (PRD): Immeuble Babo Oganla, 01 BP 1157, Porto-Novo; tel. 21-30-07-57; f. 1990; Leader ADRIEN HOUNGBÉDJI.

Rassemblement pour la démocratie et le panafricanisme (RDP): 03 BP 1050, Cotonou; tel. 21-32-02-83; fax 21-32-35-71; e-mail cotrans@leland.bj; f. 1995; Pres. DOMINIQUE O. HOUNGNINOU, GILLES AUGUSTE MINONTIN; Treas. JANVIER SETANGNI.

Restaurer l'espoir (RE): Leader CANDIDE AZANNAÏ.

Union pour le Bénin du futur (UBF): 03 BP 1972, Cotonou; tel. 21-33-12-23; e-mail amoussou@avu.org; f. 2002 by supporters of then Pres. Kérékou; separate faction, UBF 'Aller plus loin', formed Oct. 2004 under leadership of JOSEPH GANDAHO, comprising more than 30 pro-presidential parties and asscns; further, smaller, faction, the 'Alliance UBF' formed April 2005, led by ALAIN ADIHOU; Co-ordinator BRUNO AMOUSSOU.

Front d'action pour le renouveau, la démocratie et le développement—Alafia (FARD—Alafia): 01 BP 3238, Cotonou; tel. 21-33-34-10; f. 1994; Sec.-Gen. DANIEL TAWÉMA.

Union nationale pour la démocratie et le progrès (UNDP): Chair. EMILE DERLIN ZINSOU.

Union pour la relève (UPR): Gbégamey; Leader ISSA SALIFOU.

Diplomatic Representation

EMBASSIES IN BENIN

China, People's Republic: 2 route de l'Aéroport, 01 BP 196, Cotonou; tel. 21-30-07-65; fax 21-30-08-41; e-mail prcbenin@serv.eit.bj; internet bj.chineseembassy.org; Ambassador LI BEIFEN.

Congo, Democratic Republic: Carré 221, Ayélawadjè, Cotonou; tel. 21-30-00-01.

Cuba: ave de la Marina, face Hôtel du Port, 01 BP 948, Cotonou; tel. 21-31-52-97; fax 21-31-65-91; e-mail ecubaben@leland.bj; Ambassador MARTA FERNÁNDEZ PERAZA.

Denmark: Lot P7, Les Cocotiers, 04 BP 1223, Cotonou; tel. 21-30-38-62; fax 21-30-38-60; e-mail cooamb@um.dk; internet www.ambcotonou.um.dk; Ambassador ANDERS SERUP RASMUSSEN.

Egypt: Lot G26, route de l'Aéroport, BP 1215, Cotonou; tel. 21-30-08-42; fax 21-30-14-25; Ambassador OSAMA TAWFEEK BADR.

France: ave Jean-Paul II, BP 966, Cotonou; tel. 21-30-02-25; fax 21-30-07-57; e-mail ambafrance.cotonou@diplomatie.gouv.fr; internet www.ambafrance-bj.org; Ambassador JEAN-CLAUDE CHRISTIAN DAZIANO.

Germany: 7 ave Jean-Paul II, BP 504, Cotonou; tel. 21-31-29-67; fax 21-31-29-62; e-mail info@cotonou.diplo.de; internet www.cotonou.diplo.de; Ambassador Dr ALBRECHT CONZE.

Ghana: route de l'Aéroport, Lot F, Les Cocotiers, BP 488, Cotonou; tel. 21-30-07-46; fax 21-30-03-45; e-mail ghaemb02@leland.bj; Ambassador M. ADU.

Holy See: blvd de France, Quartier Awhouanléko/Djoméhountin, Zone des Ambassades, 08 BP 400, Cotonou; tel. 21-30-03-08; fax 21-30-03-10; e-mail noncia@intnet.bj; Apostolic Nuncio MICHAEL AUGUST BLUME (Titular Bishop of Alexanum).

Korea, Democratic People's Republic: Cotonou; Ambassador KIM PYONG GI.

Libya: Carré 36, Cotonou; tel. 21-30-04-52; fax 21-30-03-01; Ambassador TOUFIK ASHOUR ADAM.

Netherlands: ave Pape Jean Paul II, Route de l'aeroport, derrière le Tri Postal, 08 BP 0783, Cotonou; tel. 21-30-04-39; fax 21-30-41-50; e-mail cot@minbuza.nl; internet www.mfa.nl/cot; Ambassador C. G. WEIJERS.

Niger: derrière l'Hôtel de la Plage, BP 352, Cotonou; tel. 21-31-56-65; Ambassador LOMPO SOULEYMANE.

Nigeria: ave de France, Marina, BP 2019, Cotonou; tel. 21-30-11-42; fax 21-30-18-79; Ambassador EZEKEIL O. OLADEJI.

Russia: Zone résidentielle, ave de la Marina, face Hôtel du Port, BP 2013, Cotonou; tel. 21-31-28-34; fax 21-31-28-35; e-mail benamrus@leland.bj; internet www.benin.mid.ru; Ambassador VLADIMIR S. TIMOSHENKO.

USA: Carré 125, rue Caporal Anani Bernard, 01 BP 2012, Cotonou; tel. 21-30-06-50; fax 21-30-06-70; internet usembassy.state.gov/benin; Ambassador GAYLEATHA B. BROWN.

Judicial System

Constitutional Court: BP 2050, Cotonou; tel. 21-31-16-10; fax 21-31-37-12; e-mail cconstitutsg@yahoo.fr; internet www.gouv.bj/institutions/cour_constitutionnelle/presentation.php; f. 1990; inaug. 1993; seven mems; four appointed by the Assemblée nationale, three by the President of the Republic; exercises highest jurisdiction in constitutional affairs; determines the constitutionality of legislation, oversees and proclaims results of national elections and referendums, responsible for protection of individual and public rights and obligations, charged with regulating functions of organs of state and authorities; Pres. CONCEPTIA L.-DENIS-OUINSOU; Sec.-Gen. MARCELLINE-CLAIRE GBÈHA AFOUDA.

High Court of Justice: 01 BP 2958, Porto-Novo; tel. 20-21-26-81; fax 20-21-27-71; tel. hcjbenin@intnet.bj; internet www.gouv.bj/institutions/haute_cour/presentation.php; f. 1990; officially inaugurated in 2001; comprises the six members of the Constitutional Court (other than its President), six deputies of the Assemblée nationale and the First President of the Supreme Court; competent to try the President of the Republic and members of the Government in cases of high treason, crimes committed in, or at the time of, the exercise of their functions, and of plotting against state security; Pres. CLOTILDE MEDEGAN NOUGBODE.

Supreme Court: 01 BP 330, Cotonou; tel. and fax 21-31-31-05; e-mail contact@coursupreme.bj; internet www.coursupreme.gouv.bj; f. 1960; highest juridical authority in administrative and judicial affairs and in matters of public accounts; competent in disputes relating to local elections; advises the executive on jurisdiction and administrative affairs; comprises a President (appointed by the President of the Republic, after consultation with the President of the Assemblée nationale, senior magistrates and jurists), presidents of the component chambers, a public prosecutor, four assistant procurators-fiscal, counsellors and clerks; Pres. SALIOÙ ABDOUDOU; Attorney-Gen. NESTOR DAKO; Pres. of the Judicial Chamber EDWIGE BOUSSARI; Pres. of the Administrative Chamber GRÉGOIRE Y. ALAYÈ; Pres. of the Chamber of Accounts FIRMIN DJIMENOU; Chief Clerk FRANÇOISE QUENUM.

Religion

Religious and spiritual cults, which were discouraged under Kérékou's military regime, re-emerged as a prominent force in Beninois society during the 1990s. At the time of the 2002 census it was estimated that some 38% of the population were Christians (mainly Roman Catholics) around 24% were Muslims, and around 17% followed the traditional *vodoun* religion, with a further 6% being adherents of other traditional religions.

CHRISTIANITY

The Roman Catholic Church

Benin comprises two archdioceses and eight dioceses. At 31 December 2004 there were an estimated 1.8m. Roman Catholics (about 25.0% of the population), mainly in the south of the country.

Bishops' Conference

Conférence Episcopale du Bénin, Archevêché, 01 BP 491, Cotonou; tel. 21-30-66-48; fax 21-30-07-07; e-mail cepiscob@intnet.bj; Pres. Most Rev. NESTOR ASSOGBA (Archbishop Emeritus of Cotonou).

Archbishop of Cotonou: Most Rev. MARCEL HONORAT LÉON AGBOTON, Archevêché, 01 BP 491, Cotonou; fax 21-30-07-07; e-mail cotonou@cef.fr.

Archbishop of Parakou: Most Rev. FIDÈLE AGBATCHI, Archevêché, BP 75, Parakou; tel. 23-61-02-54; fax 23-61-01-99; e-mail archeveche@borgou.net.

Protestant Church

There are an estimated 257 Protestant mission centres in Benin.

Eglise Protestante Méthodiste en République du Bénin (EPMB): 54 ave Mgr Steinmetz, 01 BP 34, Cotonou; tel. and fax 21-31-11-42; e-mail epmbenin@intnet.bj; f. 1843; Pres. Rev. Dr SIMON K. DOSSOU; Sec. Rev. Dr CÉLESTIN GB. KIKI; 101,000 mems (1997).

VODOUN

The origins of the traditional *vodoun* religion can be traced to the 14th century. Its influence is particularly strong in Latin America and the Caribbean, owing to the shipment of slaves from the West African region to the Americas in the 18th and 19th centuries.

Communauté Nationale du Culte Vodoun (CNCV): Ouidah; Pres. ADAN YOSSI GUÊDÊHOUNGUÊ.

ISLAM

Union Islamique du Bénin (UIB): Cotonou; Pres. Imam El Hadj MOHAMED AMED SANNI.

BAHÁ'Í FAITH

National Spiritual Assembly: BP 1252, Cotonou.

The Press

In 2001 there were 18 daily newspapers and 37 periodicals published in Benin.

DAILIES

L'Araignée: siège du cyber DOPHIA, face Cité Houeyiho, 01 BP 1357, Cotonou; tel. 21-30-64-12; fax (44) 21-32-18-84; e-mail direction@laraignee.org; internet www.laraignee.org; f. 2001; online only; politics, public affairs, culture, society, sport; Dir of Publishing FÉLIX ANIWANOU HOUNSA; Editor-in-Chief WILLÉANDRE HOUNGBÉDJI.

L'Aurore: face Clinique Boni, 05 BP 464, Cotonou; tel. 21-33-70-43; Dir PATRICK ADJAMONSI; circ. 1,500.

Bénin-Presse Info: 01 BP 72, Cotonou; tel. 21-31-26-55; fax 21-31-13-26; e-mail abpben@bow.intnet.bj; internet www.gouv.bj/presse/abp/index.php; bulletin of Agence Bénin-Presse; Dir YAOVI R. HOUNKPONOU; Editor-in-Chief JOSEPH VODOUNON.

Les Echos du Jour: Carré 136, Sodjatimè, 08 BP 718, Cotonou; tel. 21-33-18-33; fax 21-33-17-06; e-mail echos@intnet.bj; independent; Dir MAURICE CHABI; Editor-in-Chief SÉBASTIEN DOSSA; circ. 3,000.

Fraternité: face Station Menontin, 05 BP 915, Cotonou; tel. 21-38-47-70; fax 21-38-47-71; e-mail fraternite@fraternite-info.com;

internet www.fraternite-info.com; Dir-Gen. MALICK SEIBOU GOMINA; Editor-in-Chief BRICE U. HOUSSOU.

L'Informateur: Etoile Rouge, Bâtiment Radio Star, Carré 1072C, 01 BP 5421, Cotonou; tel. and fax 21-32-66-39; f. 2001; Dir CLÉMENT ADÉCHIAN; Editor-in-Chief BRICE GUÈDÈ.

Le Matin: Carré 54, Tokpa Hoho, 06 BP 2217, Cotonou; tel. 21-31-10-80; fax 21-33-42-62; e-mail lematinonline@moncourrier.com; f. 1994; independent; Dir MOÏSE DATO; Editorial Dir LUC-AIMÉ DANSOU.

Le Matinal: Carré 153–154, Atinkanmey, 06 BP 1989, Cotonou; tel. 90-94-83-32; e-mail infodumatinal@yahoo.fr; internet www.actubenin.com; f. 1997; daily; Dir-Gen. CHARLES TOKO; Editor-in-Chief NAPOLÉON MAFORIKAN; circ. 5,000.

La Nation: Cadjèhoun, 01 BP 1210, Cotonou; tel. 21-30-02-99; fax 21-30-34-63; e-mail onip@communication.gouv.bj; internet www.gouv.bj/presse/lanation/index.php; f. 1990; official newspaper; Dir AKUÉTÉ ASSEVI; Editor-in-Chief HUBERT O. AKPONIKPE; circ. 4,000.

La Nouvelle Tribune: Lot 1409, Houéyiho II, 09 BP 336, Cotonou; tel. 21-30-65-16; Editor-in-Chief ALAIN ASSOGBA.

L'Oeil du Peuple: Carré 743, rue PTT, Gbégamey, 01 BP 5538, Cotonou; tel. 21-30-22-07; e-mail loeildupeuple@yahoo.fr; Dir CELESTIN ABISSI; Editor-in-Chief PAUL AGBOYIDOU.

Le Point au Quotidien: 332 rue du Renouveau, 05 BP 934, Cotonou; tel. 90-91-69-45; fax 21-32-25-31; e-mail info@lepointauquotidien.com; independent; Dir and Editor-in-Chief FERNANDO HESSOU; circ. 2,000.

Le Républicain: Les Presses d'Afrique, Carré 630, Tanto, 05 BP 1230, Cotonou; tel. and fax 21-33-83-04; e-mail lerepublicain@lerepublicain.org; independent; Editor-in-Chief ISIDORE ZINSOU.

Le Soleil: Carré 850, Sikècodji, 02 BP 8187, Cotonou; tel. 21-32-69-96; Dir MAURILLE GNANSOUNOU; Editor-in-Chief MATINI MARCOS.

La Tribune de la Capitale: Lot 03-46, Parcelle E, Houinmè, Maison Onifadé, Catchi, 01 BP 1463, Porto-Novo; tel. 20-22-55-69; e-mail latribunedelacapitale@yahoo.fr; internet www.latribunedelacapitale.com; Dir of Publication SETH EVARISTE HODONOU; Editor-in-Chief VINCENT LEZINME.

PERIODICALS

Afrique Identité: ave du Canada, Lot 1069 T, 02 BP 1215, Cotonou; Dir ANGELO AHOUANMAGMA; Editorial Dir SERGE AUGUSTE LOKO.

Agri-Culture: 03 BP 0380, Cotonou; tel. and fax 21-36-05-46; e-mail agriculture@uva.org; f. 1999; monthly; Editor-in-Chief JOACHIM SAÏZONOU; circ. 1,000.

L'Autre Gazette: 02 BP 1537, Cotonou; tel. 21-32-59-97; e-mail collegi@beninweb.org; Editor-in-Chief WILFRIED AYIBATIN.

L'Avenir: Carré 911, 02 BP 8134, Cotonou; tel. 21-32-21-23; fortnightly; political analysis; Dir CLAUDE FIRMIN GANGBE.

Bénin Hebdo: 03 BP 2332, Cotonou; tel. 90-92-24-09; Dir SANGARÉ NOUHOUN; Editor-in-Chief DENIS CHAUMEREUIL.

Bénin Info: 06 BP 590, Cotonou; tel. 21-32-52-64; fortnightly; Dir ROMAIN TOI.

Bénin Santé: 06 BP 1905, Cotonou; tel. 21-33-26-38; fax 21-33-18-23; fortnightly.

Le Canard du Golfe: Carré 240, Midombo, Akpakpa, 06 BP 59, Cotonou; tel. 21-32-72-33; e-mail lecanardugolfe@yahoo.fr; satirical; weekly; Dir F. L. TINGBO; Editor-in-Chief EMMANUEL SOTIKON.

Le Continental: BP 4419, Cotonou; Editor-in-Chief ARNAULD HOUNDETE.

La Croix du Bénin: Centre Paul VI, 01 BP 105, Cotonou; tel. and fax 21-32-11-19; e-mail andrequenum@yahoo.com; internet www.lacroixdubenin.com; f. 1946; twice a week; Roman Catholic; Editor Rev. Dr ANDRÉ S. QUENUM.

La Dernière Barque—Creuset de la Jeunesse Chrétienne Céleste: 06 BP 446, Cotonou; tel. 21-33-04-07; fax 21-33-42-14.

Emotion Magazine: 06 BP 1404, Cotonou; tel. 95-40-17-07; fax 21-32-21-33; e-mail emomagazine@yahoo.fr; f. 1998; every two months; cultural and social affairs; Dir of Publication ERIC SESSINOU HUANNOU; Editor-in-Chief BERNARD HERMANN ZANNOU; circ. 3,000 (2006).

L'Enjeu: 04 BP 0454, Cotonou; tel. 21-35-19-93; Editor-in-Chief MATHURIN ASSOGBA.

La Flamme: 01 BP 2582, Cotonou; tel. 21-30-69-03; Editor-in-Chief PHILIPPE NOUDJENOUME.

La Gazette du Golfe: Immeuble La Gazette du Golfe, Carré 902E, Sikècodji, 03 BP 1624, Cotonou; tel. 21-32-68-44; fax 21-32-52-26; e-mail gazettedugolfe@serv.eit.bj; f. 1987; weekly; Dir ISMAËL Y. SOUMANOU; Editor MARCUS BONI TEIGA; circ. 18,000 (nat. edn), 5,000 (international edn).

Le Gongonneur: 04 BP 1432, Cotonou; tel. 90-90-60-95; fax 21-35-04-22; e-mail dahoun@yahoo.com; Dir MATHIAS C. SOSSOU; Editor-in-Chief PASCALINE APHIA HOUNKANRIN.

Le Héraut: 03 BP 3417, Cotonou; tel. 21-36-00-64; e-mail heraut@syfed.bj.refer.org; monthly; current affairs; analysis; produced by students at Université nationale du Bénin; Dir GEOFFREY GOUNOU N'GOYE; Editor-in-Chief GABRIEL DIDEH.

Initiatives: 01 BP 2093, Cotonou; tel. 21-31-22-61; fax 21-31-59-50; e-mail cepepe@firstnet1.com; 6 a year; journal of the Centre de Promotion et d'Encadrement des Petites et Moyennes Entreprises.

Journal Officiel de la République du Bénin: BP 59, Porto-Novo; tel. 20-21-39-77; f. 1890; present name adopted 1990; official govt bulletin; fortnightly; Dir AFIZE DÉSIRÉ ADAMO.

Labari: BP 816, Parakou; tel. and fax 23-61-69-10; f. 1997; weekly; Dir DRAMANE AMI-TOURE; circ. 3,000.

La Lumière de l'Islam: Carré 163, 01 BP 4022, Cotonou; tel. and fax 21-31-34-59; monthly; Dir MOHAMED BACHIROU SOUMANOU.

Madame Afrique: Siège Mefort Inter Diffusion, Carré 1066, quartier Cadjehoun, 05 BP 1914, Cotonou; tel. 97-68-22-90; e-mail madafric@yahoo.fr; f. 2000; monthly; women's interest; Dir of Publication BERNARD G. ZANKLAN.

Le Magazine de l'Entreprise: BP 850, Cotonou; tel. 21-30-80-79; fax 21-30-47-77; e-mail oliviergat@hotmail.com; f. 1999; monthly; business; Dir A. VICTOR FAKÈYÈ.

Nouvel Essor: Cotonou; tel. 21-32-43-13; monthly; Editor-in-Chief JEAN-BAPTISTE HOUNKONNOU.

Opérateur Économique: ave du Général de Gaulle, 01 BP 31, Cotonou; tel. 21-31-20-81; fax 21-31-22-99; monthly; published by Chambre de Commerce et d'Industrie du Bénin; Dir WASSI MOUFTAOU.

Le Perroquet: Carré 478, Quartier Bar-Tito, 03 BP 880, Cotonou; tel. 21-32-18-54; e-mail leperroquet2003@yahoo.fr; f. 1995; two a month; independent; news and analysis; Dir DAMIEN HOUESSOU; Editor-in-Chief SEPTOME ATCHÉKPE; circ. 4,000 (2004).

Le Piment: Carré 1965, Zogbo, 07 BP 0665, Cotonou; tel. 21-30-26-01; fax 21-31-25-81; 2 a month; independent; Editor-in-Chief JOACHIM GBOYOU.

Le Radical: 03 BP 0408, Cotonou; Dir ALASSANE BAWA.

Le Recadaire: 02 BP 308, Cotonou; tel. 21-22-60-11; e-mail lerecadaire@yahoo.com; Dir GUTEMBERT HOUNKANRIN.

La Région: Carré 1030, 05 BP 708, Cotonou; Editor-in-Chief ROMAIN CODJO.

La Réplique: BP 1087, Porto-Novo; tel. and fax 20-21-45-77; Dir EMILE ADECHINA; Editor-in-Chief JERÔME AKLAMAVO.

La Sirène: Carré 357, Sènadé, 01 BP 122, Cotonou; tel. 21-33-40-17; Dir ETIENNE HOUSSOU.

Le Télégramme: 06 BP 1519, Cotonou; tel. 21-33-04-18; fortnightly; Editor-in-Chief RENÉ NANA.

Le Temps: Kouhounou, 04 BP 43, Cotonou; tel. 21-30-55-06; 2 a month; Dir YAYA YOLOU; Editor-in-Chief GUY CONDÉ.

Le Tribune de l'Economie: BP 31, Cotonou; tel. 21-31-20-81; fax 21-31-32-99; monthly; Editor-in-Chief MOUFTAOU WASSI.

Press Association

Union des Journalistes de la Presse Privée du Bénin (UJPB): blvd de la République, près Cadmes Plus, 03 BP 383, Cotonou; tel. 21-32-52-73; e-mail ujpb@h2com.com; internet www.h2com.com/ujpb; f. 1992; asscn of independent journalists; Pres. AGAPIT N. MAFORIKAN.

NEWS AGENCIES

Agence Bénin-Presse (ABP): BP 72, Cotonou; tel. and fax 21-31-26-55; e-mail abpben@intnet.bj; f. 1961; national news agency; section of the Ministry of Communication and the Promotion of New Technologies; Dir YAOVI R. HOUNKPONOU.

Associated Press (USA) is also represented in Benin.

Publishers

AFRIDIC: 01 BP 269, 01 Porto-Novo; tel. 20-22-32-28; e-mail afridic@caramail.com; f. 1996; poetry, essays, fiction; Dir ADJIBI JEAN-BAPTISTE.

Editions de l'ACACIA: 06 BP 1978, Cotonou; tel. 21-33-04-72; e-mail zoundin@yahoo.fr; f. 1989; fmrly Editions du Flamboyant; literary fiction, history, popular science; Dir OSCAR DE SOUZA.

Editions des Diasporas: 04 BP 792, Cotonou; e-mail camouro@yahoo.fr; poetry, essays; Editor CAMILLE AMOURO.

Editions Ruisseaux d'Afrique: 04 BP 1154, Cotonou; tel. and fax 90-94-79-25; fax 21-30-31-86; e-mail ruisseau@leland.bj; f. 1992; children's literature; Dir BÉATRICE GBADO.

Editions Souvenir: 01 BP 2589, Porto-Novo; tel. 97-88-49-04; e-mail editsouvenir@voila.fr; youth and adult literature; Dir JEAN-BAPTISTE KUNDA LI FUMU'NSAMU.

Graphitec: 04 BP 825, Cotonou; tel. and fax 21-30-46-04; e-mail lewado@yahoo.com.

Imprimerie Notre Dame: BP 109, Cotonou; tel. 21-32-12-07; fax 21-32-11-19; e-mail lacroixbenin@excite.fr; f. 1974; Roman Catholic publications; Dir BARTHÉLÉMY ASSOGBA CAKPO.

Société Tunde: 06 BP 1925, Cotonou; tel. 21-30-15-68; fax 21-30-42-86; e-mail tunde.sa@tunde-sa.com; internet www.tunde-sa.com; f. 1986; economics, management; Pres. BABATOUNDÉ RASAKI OLLOFINDJI; Dir-Gen. ALFRED LAMBERT SOMA.

Star Editions: 01 BP 367, Recette principale, Cotonou; tel. 90-94-66-28; fax 21-33-05-29; e-mail star_editions@yahoo.fr; business, economics, science, poetry; Editor JOACHIM ADJOVI.

GOVERNMENT PUBLISHING HOUSE

Office National d'Edition, de Presse et d'Imprimerie (ONEPI): 01 BP 1210, Cotonou; tel. 21-30-02-99; fax 21-30-34-63; f. 1975; Dir-Gen. INNOCENT ADJAHO.

Broadcasting and Communications

TELECOMMUNICATIONS

Bénin Télécoms: Ganhi, 01 BP 5959, Cotonou; tel. 21-31-20-45; fax 21-31-38-43; e-mail Mail@benintelecoms.bj; internet www.benintelecoms.bj; f. 2004 to assume responsibility for telecommunications activities of fmr Office des Postes et des Télécommunications (OPT), in advance of proposed transfer of 55% stake to private ownership, scheduled for 2007; Dir-Gen. PATRICK BENON.

Bell Bénin Communications (BBCOM): Cotonou; f. 2002; mobile cellular telephone operator; Chief Exec. ISSA SALIFOU.

Libercom: blvd Saint-Michel, face Hall des Arts et de la Culture, 01 BP 5959, Cotonou; tel. 21-31-68-01; fax 21-31-68-00; f. 2000; mobile cellular telephone operator in Cotonou and Porto-Novo; 23,000 subscribers (2001).

Spacetel Bénin-BéninCell: 01 BP 5293, Cotonou; tel. 21-31-66-41; internet www.areeba.com.bj; f. 2000; mobile cellular telephone operator in Cotonou, Porto-Novo and Parakou under network name Areeba; affiliate of Spacetel (United Kingdom); 6,000 subscribers (2001).

Telecel Bénin: Cotonou; tel. 21-31-66-60; internet www.telecel-benin.com; f. 2000; mobile cellular telephone operator in Cotonou, Porto-Novo, Abomey, Lokossa, other regions of southern Benin and in Parakou; subsidiary of Atlantique Telecoms (Côte d'Ivoire); Dir-Gen. ERIC TRONEL; 130,000 subscribers (Jan. 2004).

BROADCASTING

Since 1997 the Haute Autorité de l'Audiovisuel et de la Communication has issued licences to private radio and television stations.

Haute Autorité de l'Audiovisuel et de la Communication (HAAC): 01 BP 3567, Cotonou; tel. 21-31-17-45; fax 21-31-17-42; e-mail haac@planben.intnet.bj; internet www.gouv.bj/institutions/haac/presentation_top.php; f. 1992; Pres. ALI ZATO.

Radio

In early 2002 there were nine commercial radio stations, 17 non-commercial stations and five rural or local stations broadcasting in Benin.

Office de Radiodiffusion et de Télévision du Bénin (ORTB): 01 BP 366, Cotonou; tel. 21-30-46-19; fax 21-30-04-48; e-mail ortb@intnet.bj; state-owned; radio programmes broadcast from Cotonou and Parakou in French, English and 18 local languages; Dir-Gen. JULIEN PIERRE AKPAKI; Dir FIDÈLE EDOH AYIKOUE.

Atlantic FM: 01 BP 366, Cotonou; tel. 21-30-20-41; Dir JOSEPH OGOUNCHI.

Radiodiffusion nationale du Benin: BP 366, Cotonou; tel. 21-30-10-96; f. 1953; Dir MOUFALIOU LIADY.

Radio Régionale de Parakou: BP 128, Parakou; tel. 23-61-07-73; Dir SÉNI SOUROU.

Bénin-Culture: BP 21, Association pour l'Institutionnalisation de la Mémoire et de la Pensée Intellectuelle Africaine, 01 BP 21, Porto-Novo; tel. 20-22-69-34; Head of Station ARMAND COVI.

Golfe FM-Magic Radio: 03 BP 1624, Cotonou; tel. 21-32-42-08; fax 21-32-42-09; e-mail golfefm@serv.eit.bj; internet www.eit.bj/golfefm.htm; Dir ISMAËL SOUMANOU.

Radio Afrique Espoir: Carré 123, 03 BP 203, Porto-Novo; tel. 20-21-34-55; fax 20-21-32-63; e-mail afespoir@intnet.bj; Dir RAMANOU KOUFERIDJI.

Radio Carrefour: BP 2304, Goho, Bohicon; tel. 22-51-16-06; fax 22-51-16-55; e-mail chrisdavak@yahoo.fr; f. 1999; production and broadcast of radio and television programmes; Dir-Gen. CHRISTOPHE DAVAKAN.

Radio FM-Ahémé: BP 66, Bopa, Mono; tel. 95-05-58-18; f. 1997; informative, cultural and civic education broadcasts; Dir AMBROISE COKOU MOUSSOU.

Radio Immaculée Conception: BP 88, Allada; tel. 21-36-80-97; e-mail satric@immacolata.com; internet www.immacolata.com; operated by the Roman Catholic Church of Benin; broadcasts to Abomey, Allada, Bembéréke, Cotonou, Dassa-Zoume, Djougou and Parakou; Dir Fr ALFONSO BRUNO.

Radio Maranatha: 03 BP 4113, Cotonou; tel. and fax 21-32-58-82; e-mail maranatha.fm@serv.eit.bj; internet www.eit.to/RadioMaranatha.htm; operated by the Conseil des Eglises Protestantes Evangéliques du Bénin; Dir Rev. CLOVIS ALFRED KPADE.

Radio Planète: 02 BP 1528, Immeuble Master Soft, Cotonou; tel. 21-30-30-30; fax 21-30-24-51; e-mail janvier@planetefm.com; internet www.planetefm.com; Dir JANVIER YAHOUEDEHOU.

Radio Solidarité FM: BP 135, Djougou; tel. 23-80-11-29; fax 23-80-15-63; Dir DAOUDA TAKPARA.

La Voix de la Lama: 03 BP 3772, Cotonou; tel. 21-37-12-26; fax 21-37-13-67; e-mail voix_delalama@yahoo.fr; f. 1998; non-commercial FM station, broadcasting on 103.8 Mhz from Allada; Dir SÉRAPHINE DADY.

La Voix de l'Islam: 08 BP 134, Cotonou; tel. 21-31-11-34; fax 21-31-51-79; e-mail islamben@leland.bj; operated by the Communauté musulmane de Zongo; Dir El Hadj MAMAN YARO.

Radio Wêkê: 05 BP 436, Cotonou; tel. 20-21-38-40; fax 20-21-37-14; e-mail issabadarou@hotmail.com; Promoter ISSA BADAROU-SOULÉ.

Benin also receives broadcasts from Africa No. 1, the British Broadcasting Corporation World Service and Radio France International.

Television

ORTB: (see Radio); Dir of Television PIERETTE AMOUSSOU.

ATVS: BP 7101, Cotonou; tel. 21-31-43-19; owned by African Television System-Sobiex; Dir JACOB AKINOCHO.

LC2—La Chaîne 2 (LC2): 05 BP 427, Cotonou; tel. 21-33-47-49; fax 21-33-46-75; e-mail lc2@intnet.bj; internet www.lc2international.tv; commenced broadcasts 1997; Pres. and Dir-Gen. CHRISTIAN LAGNIDE; Dir-Gen. NADINE LAGNIDE.

Telco: 44 ave Delorme, 01 BP 1241, Cotonou; tel. 21-31-34-98; e-mail telco@serv.eit.bj; relays five international channels; Dir JOSEPH JÉBARA.

TV+ International/TV5: 01 BP 366, Cotonou; tel. 21-30-10-96; Dir CLAUDE KARAM.

Finance

(cap. = capital; res = reserves; dep. = deposits; m. = million; br(s). = branch(es); amounts in francs CFA)

BANKING

Central Bank

Banque centrale des états de l'Afrique de l'ouest (BCEAO): ave Jean-Paul II, BP 325, Cotonou; tel. 21-31-24-66; fax 21-31-24-65; e-mail akangni@bceao.int; internet www.bceao.int; HQ in Dakar, Senegal; f. 1962; bank of issue for the mem. states of the Union économique et monétaire ouest-africaine (UEMOA, comprising Benin, Burkina Faso, Côte d'Ivoire, Guinea-Bissau, Mali, Niger, Senegal and Togo); cap. and res 859,313m., total assets 5,671,675m. (Dec. 2002); Gov. DAMO JUSTIN BARO (acting); Dir in Benin IDRISS LYASSOU DAOUDA; br. at Parakou.

Commercial Banks

Bank of Africa—Bénin (BOAB): ave Jean-Paul II, 08 BP 0879, Cotonou; tel. 21-31-32-28; fax 21-31-31-17; e-mail boa.dg@sobiex.bj; internet www.bkofafrica.net/benin.htm; f. 1990; 35.2% owned by African Financial Holding; cap. 7,000m., res 12,884m., dep. 246,348m. (Dec. 2005); Chair. FRANÇOIS O. TANKPINOU; Dir-Gen. RENÉ FORMEY DE SAINT LOUVENT; 11 brs.

Banque Atlantique du Bénin: 109 rue des Cheminots, carré 107, 08 BP 682, Cotonou; tel. 21-31-81-63; fax 21-31-76-58; e-mail b.atlant@intnet.bj; Pres. SERGE GUETTA.

Banque Internationale du Bénin (BIBE): carrefour des Trois Banques, ave Giran, 03 BP 2098, Jéricho, Cotonou; tel. 21-31-55-49; fax 21-31-23-65; e-mail bibedi@leland.bj; f. 1989; owned by Nigerian commercial interests; cap. 9,000m., dep. 48,577m. (Dec. 2002); Chair. Dr G. A. T. OBOH; Man. Dir JEAN-PAUL K. AIDDO; 4 brs.

Continental Bank—Bénin (La Continentale): ave Jean-Paul II, carrefour des Trois Banques, 01 BP 2020, Cotonou; tel. 21-31-24-24; fax 21-31-51-77; e-mail contibk@intnet.bj; internet www.cbankbenin.com; f. 1993 to assume activities of Crédit Lyonnais Bénin; 43% state-owned; full transfer to private-sector ownership proposed; res 1,974m., dep. 23,230m., total assets 50,594m. (2005); Pres. NICOLAS ADAGBE; Gen. Man. JOSEPH AYEH; 4 brs.

Diamond Bank Bénin: 308 rue du Révérend Père Colineau, 01 BP 955, Cotonou; tel. 21-31-79-27; fax 21-31-79-33; e-mail bao@diamondbank.com; 80% owned by Diamond Bank (Nigeria); cap. and res 1,939m., total assets 20,645m. (Dec. 2003); Chair. PASCAL GABRIEL DOZIE; Dir-Gen. BENJAMIN OVIOSU; 2 brs.

Ecobank Bénin: rue Gouverneur Bayol, 01 BP 1280, Cotonou; tel. 21-31-40-23; fax 21-31-33-85; e-mail ecobnetbj@ecobank.com; internet www.ecobank.com; f. 1989; 78% owned by Ecobank Transnational Inc (operating under the auspices of the Economic Community of West African States); cap. 3,500m., res 5,869m. (Dec. 2003), dep. 107,814m. (Dec. 2004); Pres., Chair. and Dir GILBERT MEDJE; Man. Dir CHRISTOPHE JOCKTANE LAWSON; 8 brs.

Finadev: ave du Commandant Decoeur, 01 BP 6335, Cotonou; tel. 21-33-73-70; fax 21-31-31-02; e-mail info@finadev.org; internet www.finadev.org; f. 1998; 25% owned by Financial Bank Bénin, 25% owned by FMO (Netherlands), 25% owned by International Finance Corpn; cap. and res 1,471.2m., total assets 5,508.8m. (Dec. 2003); Pres. RÉMY BAYSSET; Dir-Gen. PATRICK LELONG; 4 brs.

Financial Bank Bénin (FBB): Immeuble Ganhi, rue du Commandant Decoeur, 01 BP 2700, Cotonou; tel. 21-31-31-00; fax 21-31-31-02; e-mail info@financial-bank-bj.com; f. 1996; 43.5% owned by Financial BC (Togo); cap. and res 2,672.5m., total assets 60,334.8m. (Dec. 2003); Pres. ABDOULAYE MALLAM IDI; Dir-Gen. JEAN-LUC LABONTE; 8 brs.

Société Générale de Banques au Bénin (SGBBE): ave Clozel, Quartier Ganhi, 01 BP 585, Cotonou; tel. 21-31-83-00; fax 21-31-82-95; f. 2002; 67% owned by Genefitec, a wholly owned subsidiary of Groupe Société Générale (France); cap. and res 2,044.0m., total assets 25,503.0m. (Dec. 2003); Pres. AXELLE DE SAINT-AFFRIQUE.

Savings Bank

Caisse Nationale d'Epargne: Cadjèhoun, route Inter-Etat Cotonou-Lomé, Cotonou; tel. 21-30-18-35; fax 21-31-38-43; internet www.cne.opt.bj; state-owned; cap. and res 948.0m., total assets 27,512.5m. (Dec. 2002); Pres. CHARLES PRODJINOTHO; Dir ZAKARI BOURAHIMA.

Credit Institutions

Crédit du Bénin: 08 BP 0936, Cotonou; tel. 21-31-30-02; fax 21-31-37-01; Man. Dir GILBERT HOUNKPAIN.

Crédit Promotion Bénin: 03 BP 1672, Cotonou; tel. 21-31-31-44; fax 21-31-31-66; wholly owned by private investors; cap. 150m., total assets 409m. (Dec. 1998); Pres. BERNARD ADIKPETO; Man. Dir DÉNIS OBA CHABI.

Equipbail Bénin: blvd Jean-Paul II, 08 BP 0690, Cotonou; tel. 21-31-11-45; fax 21-31-46-58; e-mail equip.be@bkofafrica.com; internet www.bkofafrica.net/equipbail.htm; f. 1995; 78.7% owned by Bank of Africa—Bénin; cap. and res 544.7m., total assets 3,447.6m. (Dec. 2003); Pres. PAUL DERREUMAUX.

Financial Institution

Caisse Autonome d'Amortissement du Bénin: BP 59, Cotonou; tel. 21-31-47-81; fax 21-31-53-56; manages state funds; Man. Dir IBRAHIM PEDRO-BONI.

STOCK EXCHANGE

Bourse Régionale des Valeurs Mobilières (BRVM): Antenne Nationale des Bourses du Bénin, Immeuble Chambre de Commerce et d'Industrie du Bénin, ave Charles de Gaulle, 01 BP 2985, Cotonou; tel. 21-31-21-26; fax 21-31-20-77; e-mail agnigla@brvm.org; internet www.brvm.org; f. 1998; national branch of BRVM (regional stock exchange based in Abidjan, Côte d'Ivoire, serving the member states of UEMOA); Man. in Benin YVETTE AISSI GNIGLA.

INSURANCE

A&C Bénin: Carré 21, 01 BP 3758, ave Delorme, Cotonou; e-mail info@acbenin.com; internet www.acbenin.com; all branches; Dir-Gen. JUSTIN HERBERT AGBOTON.

ASA Bénin: 01 BP 5508, Cotonou; tel. and fax 21-30-00-40; fmrly Société Nationale d'Assurance; Pres. EGOULETI MONTETCHO.

Assurances et Réassurance du Golfe de Guinée (ARGG): 04 BP 0851, Cadjehoun, Cotonou; tel. 21-30-56-43; fax 21-30-55-55; e-mail argg@intnet.bj; non-life insurance and re-insurance; Man. Dir COLETTE POSSET TAGNON.

Gras Savoye Bénin: Immeuble Aboki Hounkpehedji, 1er étage, ave Mgr Steinmetz, face de l'Immeuble Kougblenou, 01 BP 294 RP Cotonou; tel. 21-31-69-22; fax 21-31-69-79; e-mail gsbenin@leland.bj; affiliated to Gras Savoye (France); Man. GUY BIHANNIC.

SOBAC: Carré 5, ave Delorme, 01 BP 544, Cotonou; tel. 21-31-67-35; fax 21-31-67-34; e-mail sobac@intnet.bj; affiliate of AGF (France).

Union Béninoise d'Assurance-Vie: 08 BP 0322, Cotonou; tel. 21-30-06-90; fax 21-30-07-69; e-mail uba@firstnet.bj; f. 1994; cap. 400m.; 51% owned by Union Africaine Vie (Côte d'Ivoire); Man. Dir VENANCE AMOUSSOUGA.

Trade and Industry

GOVERNMENT AGENCIES

Cellule des Opérations de Dénationalisation (COD): 02 BP 8140, Cotonou; tel. 21-31-59-18; fax 21-31-23-15; Co-ordinator VICTORIN DOSSOU-SOGNON.

Centre Béninois de la Recherche Scientifique et Technique (CBRST): 03 BP 1665, Cotonou; tel. 21-32-12-63; fax 21-32-36-71; e-mail cbrst@bow.intnet.bj; f. 1986; promotes scientific and technical research and training; 10 specialized research units; Dir-Gen. Prof. THÉOPHILE ZOHOUN.

Centre Béninois du Commerce Extérieur (CBCE): pl. du Souvenir, BP 1254, Cotonou; tel. 21-30-13-20; fax 21-30-04-36; e-mail cbce@bow.intnet.bj; internet www.cbce.africa-web.org; f. 1988; provides information to export cos.

Centre de Promotion et de l'Artisanat: à côté du Hall des Arts et de la Culture, BP 2651, Cotonou; tel. and fax 21-30-34-91; e-mail cpa.info@netcourrier.com; f. 1987; Dir BOIGRA KOMBIÉNI.

Centre de Promotion et d'Encadrement des Petites et Moyennes Entreprises (CEPEPE): face à la Mairie de Xlacondji, 01 BP 2093, Cotonou; tel. 21-31-44-47; fax 21-31-59-50; e-mail cepepe@firstnet.bj; internet www.cepepe.firstnet.bj; f. 1989; promotes business and employment; offers credits and grants to small businesses; undertakes management training and recruitment; publishes bi-monthly journal, *Initiatives*; Dir-Gen. THÉOPHILE CAPO-CHICHI.

Institut National de Recherches Agricoles du Bénin (INRAB): 01 BP 884, Cotonou; tel. 21-30-02-64; fax 21-30-37-70; e-mail inrabdg4@intnet.bj; internet www.bj.refer.org/benin_ct/rec/inrab/inrab.htm; f. 1992; undertakes research into agricultural improvements; publicizes advances in agriculture; Dir DAVID Y. ARODOKOUN.

Office Béninois de Recherches Géologiques et Minières (OBRGM): Ministry of Mining, Energy and Water Resources, 04 BP 1412, Cotonou; tel. 21-31-03-09; fax 21-31-41-20; e-mail nestorved@yahoo.fr; internet www.energie.gouv.bj/obrgm/index.htm; f. 1996 as govt agency responsible for mining policy, exploitation and research; Dir-Gen. NESTOR VEDOGBETON.

Office National d'Appui à la Sécurité Alimentaire (ONASA): PK3, route de Porto-Novo, 06 BP 2544, Cotonou; tel. 21-33-15-02; fax 21-33-02-93; e-mail onasamdr@intnet.bj; internet www.isicad.org/infoprix; f. 1992; distribution of cereals; Pres. IMAROU SALÉ; Dir-Gen. MOUSSA ASSOUMA.

Office National du Bois (ONAB): BP 1238, Cotonou; tel. 21-33-10-30; fax 21-33-19-56; e-mail mifor@intnet.bj; f. 1983; reorganized and partially privatized in 2002; forest development and management, manufacture and marketing of wood products; transfer of industrial activities to private ownership pending; Dir-Gen. PIERRE HOUAYE.

DEVELOPMENT ORGANIZATIONS

Agence Française de Développement (AFD): blvd de France, 01 BP 38, Cotonou; tel. 21-31-35-80; fax 21-31-20-18; e-mail afdcotonou@groupe-afd.org; internet www.afd.fr; fmrly Caisse Française de Développement; Country Dir DIDIER ROBERT.

Association Française des Volontaires du Progrès (AFVP): BP 344, Recette Principale, Cotonou; tel. 21-30-06-21; fax 21-30-07-78; e-mail afvpbn@intnet.bj; internet www.afvp.org; f. 1964; Nat. Delegate RÉMI HALLEGOUËT.

Mission de Coopération et d'Action Culturelle (Mission Française d'Aide et de Coopération): BP 476, Cotonou; tel. 21-30-08-24; administers bilateral aid from France; Dir BERNARD HADJADJ.

SNV Bénin (Société Néerlandais de Développement): 01 BP 1048, Carré 107, Zone Résidentielle, Rue du PNUD, Cotonou; tel. 21-31-21-22; fax 21-31-35-59; e-mail snvben@intnet.bj.

CHAMBER OF COMMERCE

Chambre de Commerce et d'Industrie du Bénin (CCIB): ave du Général de Gaulle, 01 BP 31, Cotonou; tel. 21-31-20-81; fax 21-31-32-

99; e-mail ccib@bow.intnet.bj; internet www.ccib.bj; f. 1908; present name adopted 1962; Pres. ATAOU SOUFIANO; brs at Parakou, Mono-Zou, Natitingou and Porto-Novo.

EMPLOYERS' ORGANIZATIONS

Conseil National des Chargeurs du Bénin: 06 BP 2528, Cotonou; tel. 21-31-59-47; fax 21-31-59-07; e-mail cncb@intnet.bj; f. 1983; represents interests of shippers; Dir-Gen. PIERRE GANSARÉ.

Conseil National du Patronat du Bénin (CNP–Bénin): 01 BP 1260, Cotonou; tel. 21-30-74-06; fax 21-30-83-22; e-mail cnpbenin@yahoo.fr; internet www.cnpbenin.org; f. 1984 as Organisation Nationale des Employeurs du Bénin; Pres. SÉBASTIEN AJAVON; Sec.-Gen. VICTOR FAKEYE.

Fondation de l'Entrepreneurship du Bénin (FEB): pl. du Québec, 08 BP 1155, Cotonou; tel. 21-31-35-37; fax 21-31-37-26; e-mail fonda@intnet.bj; internet www.placequebec.org; non profit-making org.; encourages the devt of the private sector and of small and medium-sized businesses; Dir PIERRE DOVONOU LOKOSSOU.

Syndicat des Commerçants Importateurs et Exportateurs du Bénin: Cotonou; Pres. M. BENCHIMOL.

Syndicat Interprofessionnel des Entreprises Industrielles du Bénin: Cotonou; Pres. M. DOUCET.

Syndicat National des Commerçants et Industriels Africains du Bénin (SYNACIB): BP 367, Cotonou; Pres. URBAIN DA SILVA.

UTILITIES

Communauté Electrique du Bénin (CEB): Vedoko, BP 537, Cotonou; tel. 21-30-06-75; f. 1968; jt venture between Benin and Togo to exploit energy resources in the two countries; Dir N'PO CYR KOUAGOU.

Société Béninoise d'Electricité et d'Eau (SBEE): 01 BP 2047, Cotonou; tel. 21-31-21-45; fax 21-31-50-28; f. 1973; state-owned; production and distribution of electricity and water; separation of electricity and water sectors pending, prior to proposed privatization of electricity operations; Dir-Gen. SOULE MAMA LAWANI.

Société Nationale des Eaux du Bénin (SONEB): Cotonou; f. 2003 to assume water activities of Société Béninoise d'Electricité et d'Eau; Dir-Gen. ALASSANE BABA-MOUSSA.

MAJOR COMPANIES

The following are among the largest companies in terms of either capital investment or employment.

Bio-Benin: 04 BP 1227, Cotonou; tel. 21-30-14-20; fax 21-30-12-76; f. 1984; 99.9% state-owned; mfrs and wholesalers of pharmaceutical preparations; cap. 300m. francs CFA; Dir ALI ASSANI.

British American Tobacco Benin (BAT-Bénin): BP 07, Ouidah; tel. 21-34-13-04; fax 21-34-13-23; f. 1984; fmrly Société Béninoise des Tabacs et Allumettes (SOBETA); mfrs of tobacco products; Man. Dir JONATHAN D'SOUZA.

CAMIN SA—Centrale de l'Automobile et de Matériel Industriel: PK4, Akpakpa, route de Porto-Novo, Zone Industrielle, 01 BP 2636, Cotonou; tel. 21-33-01-95; fax 21-33-12-55; e-mail camin@leland.bj; f. 1986; import and export of motorcycles, vehicles, components and parts, and agricultural and industrial equipment; Chair. and Man. Dir RÉMY GAUDENS YESSOUFOU; 70 employees (2007).

CIMBENIN SA—Cimenterie du Bénin: Agbanlangandan, Sèkandji, BP 1224, Cotonou; tel. 21-33-07-32; fax 21-33-02-45; e-mail cimdg@bow.intnet.bj; internet www.heidelbergcement.com; f. 1991; cap. 1,950m. francs CFA; mfrs of cement and wholesalers of bldg materials; 54% owned by HeidelbergCement Group (Germany); Man. Dir JEAN-FRANÇOIS DEFALQUE; 156 employees (2004).

Colas-Bénin: PK4, route de Porto-Novo, 01 BP 228, Cotonou; tel. 21-33-40-10; fax 21-33-06-98; e-mail colascotonou@serv.eit.bj; internet www.eit.to/colas.htm; construction; mem. of Groupe Colas (France); Dir PIERRE MAJORAL.

Compagnie Béninoise de Négoce et de Distribution (CBND): ave Pierre Delorme, 01 BP 07, Cotonou; tel. 21-31-34-61; fax 21-31-34-63; e-mail cbnd@intnet.bj; internet www.groupecbnd.com; f. 1973; fmrly CFAO Bénin; import, export and distribution of consumer goods; sales 120,000 francs CFA (2000); Pres. EMMANUEL KOUTON; Dir-Gen. PATRICE CATHARIA; 75 employees (2002).

Complexe Textile du Bénin (COTEB): BP 231, Parakou; tel. 23-61-09-49; fax 23-61-11-99; production of textiles and garments; Man. Dir D. LENAERTS.

Grands Moulins du Bénin (GMB): Zone Industrielle d'Akpakpa, 01 BP 949, Cotonou; tel. 21-33-08-17; internet www.chagourygroup.com/grandmoulins.html; f. 1971; cap. 438m. francs CFA; owned by Chagoury Group (Nigeria); wheat-milling; Chair. GILBERT RAMEZ CHAGOURY; Chief Exec. RONALD CHAGOURY.

Groupe la Tour: Carré 161, carrefour de l'Eglise, Sacré-Coeur, Akpakpa, 01 BP 3900, Cotonou; tel. 21-33-47-56; fax 21-33-55-97; e-mail latour@latourafrique.com; distribution of construction materials, household and office equipment, electrical goods, clothing.

SCB—Société des Ciments du Bénin: Plakonji Ancien Wharf, 01 BP 448, Cotonou; tel. 21-31-37-03; fax 21-31-50-74; e-mail scb@serv.eit.bj; produces and distributes cement; owned by Amida Group (France).

SCB-Lafarge: BP 61, Pobé, Onigbolo; tel. 20-25-05-96; fax 20-25-05-59; e-mail scb.lafarge@scb-lafarge.bj; f. 1999 to replace Société des Ciments d'Onigbolo; 50% owned by Société des Ciments du Bénin (q.v.), 50% by Société Financière Lafarge (France); produces and markets cement; cap. 10,000m. francs CFA; Pres. TONY HADLEY; Man. Dir MARIUS ELEGBEDE.

Société Béninoise de Brasserie (SOBEBRA): route de Porto-Novo, BP 135, Cotonou; tel. 21-33-10-61; fax 21-33-01-48; f. 1957; cap. 3,200m. francs CFA; production and marketing of beer, soft drinks and ice; Pres. BARNABÉ BIDOUZO; Man. Dir ANDRÉ FONTANA.

Société Béninoise de Textiles (SOBETEX): 01 BP 90, Cotonou; tel. 21-33-09-16; f. 1968; cap. 500m. francs CFA; 49% state-owned; bleaching, printing and dyeing of imported fabrics; Pres. FRANÇOIS VRINAT; Dir EMILE PARAÏSO.

Société de Commerce d'Automobile et de Réprésentation (SOCAR Bénin): PK3, route de Porto-Novo, 01 BP 6, Cotonou; tel. 21-33-11-81; fax 21-33-11-84; e-mail socar.benin@intnet.bj; wholesale trade in motor vehicles and spare parts; Dir-Gen. JEAN-FRANÇOIS MEUNIER.

Société des Huileries du Bénin (SHB): BP 08, Bohicon; tel. 22-51-03-63; fax 22-51-15-83; e-mail davidkonan@hotmail.com; f. 1997; processes cottonseed for cooking oil, cottonseed cake and animal feed; suspended operations in early 2005.

Société Nationale de Commercialisation des Produits Pétroliers (SONACOP): ave Jean Paul II, 01 BP 245, Cotonou; tel. 21-31-22-90; fax 21-31-24-85; e-mail dirgene@sonacop.net; internet www.sonacop.net; f. 1974; 55% owned by La Continentale des Pétroles et d'Investissements (CPI), 35% state-owned; imports and distributes petroleum products; cap. 1,500m. francs CFA; Pres. and Dir-Gen. SÉFOU FAGBOHOUN; 310 employees (2005).

Société Nationale pour l'Industrie des Corps Gras (SONICOG): BP 312, Cotonou; tel. 21-33-07-01; fax 21-33-04-60; f. 1962; privatized in 1999; processes sheanuts (karité nuts), palm kernels and cottonseed; Man. Dir JOSEPH GABIN DOSSOU.

Société Nationale pour la Promotion Agricole (SONAPRA): 01 BP 933, Cotonou; tel. 21-33-08-20; fax 21-33-19-48; f. 1983; state-owned; privatization under way in 2005; manages 10 cotton-ginning plants; distributes and markets cotton fibre and cotton seed; sales of cotton US $75m. (2004/05); Dir-Gen. RAÏMATOU LALEYE ABDOU.

Total Bénin: ave Jean Paul II, 08 BP 701, Cotonou 08; tel. 21-30-65-47; distribution of petroleum.

TRADE UNIONS

Centrale des Organisations Syndicales Indépendantes (COSI): Cotonou; tel. 21-30-20-12; principally active in the health and education sectors; Sec.-Gen. JOSÉ DE SOUZA.

Centrale Syndicale des Travailleurs du Bénin (CSTB): 03 BP 0989, Cotonou; tel. 21-30-13-15; fax 21-33-26-01; actively opposes privatization and the influence of the international financial community; linked to the Parti Communiste du Bénin; Sec.-Gen. GASTON AZOUA.

Centrale des Syndicats Autonomes du Bénin (CSA—Bénin): 1 Blvd St Michel, Bourse du Travail, 04 BP 1115, Cotonou; tel. 21-30-31-82; fax 21-30-23-59; e-mail csabenin@intnet.bj; principally active in private-sector enterprises; Sec.-Gen. GUILLAUME ATTIGBÉ.

Centrale des Syndicats du Secteur Privé et Informel du Bénin (CSPIB): 03 BP 2961, Cotonou; tel. 21-33-53-53.

Centrale des Syndicats Unis du Bénin (CSUB): Cotonou; tel. 21-33-10-27.

Confédération Générale des Travailleurs du Bénin (CGTB): 06 BP 2449, Cotonou; tel. 21-31-73-11; fax 21-31-73-10; e-mail cgtbpdd@bow.intnet.bj; principally active in public administration; Sec.-Gen. PASCAL TODJINOU; 33,275 mems (2002).

Confédération des Organisations Syndicales Indépendantes du Bénin (COSI—Benin): Bourse du Travail, 03 BP 1218, Cotonou; tel. 21-30-39-65; fax 21-33-27-82; e-mail cosibenin@intnet.bj; Sec.-Gen. GOERGES KAKAÏ GLELE.

Union Nationale des Syndicats de Travailleurs du Bénin (UNSTB): 1 blvd Saint-Michel, BP 69, Recette Principale, Cotonou; tel. and fax 21-30-36-13; e-mail unstb@yahoo.fr; principally active in public administration; sole officially recognized trade union 1974–90; 40,000 members in 2005, of which 25,000 in the informal sector; Sec.-Gen. EMMANUEL ZOUNON.

Transport

In 1996 the World Bank approved a credit of US $40m., to be issued through the International Development Association, in support of a major programme of investment in Benin's transport network. The integrated programme aimed to enhance Benin's status as an entrepôt for regional trade, and also to boost domestic employment and, by improving the infrastructure and reducing transport costs, agricultural and manufacturing output.

RAILWAYS

Organisation Commune Bénin-Niger des Chemins de Fer et des Transports (OCBN): BP 16, Cotonou; tel. 21-31-28-57; fax 21-31-41-50; e-mail ocbn@intnet.bj; f. 1959; 50% owned by Govt of Benin, 50% by Govt of Niger; total of 579 track-km; main line runs for 438 km from Cotonou to Parakou in the interior; br. line runs westward via Ouidah to Segboroué (34 km); also line of 107 km from Cotonou via Porto-Novo to Pobé (near the Nigerian border); extension to the Republic of Niger proposed; Dir-Gen. FLAVIEN BALOGOUN.

ROADS

In 2004 there were some 19,000 km of roads, including 1,805 km of paved roads.

Agence Générale de Transit et de Consignation (AGETRAC): blvd Maritime, BP 1933, Cotonou; tel. 21-31-32-22; fax 21-31-29-69; e-mail agetrac@leland.bj; f. 1967; goods transportation and warehousing.

Compagnie de Transit et de Consignation du Bénin (CTCB Express): Cotonou; f. 1986; Pres. SOULÉMAN KOURA ZOUMAROU.

SHIPPING

The main port is at Cotonou. In 2003 the port handled some 4,278,300 metric tons of goods.

Port Autonome de Cotonou (PAC): BP 927, Cotonou; tel. 21-31-28-90; fax 21-31-28-91; e-mail pac@leland.bj; internet www.portdecotonou.com; f. 1965; state-owned port authority; Dir-Gen. JOSEPH TCHAFFA.

Association pour la Défense des Intérêts du Port de Cotonou (AIPC) (Communauté Portuaire du Bénin): Port Autonome de Cotonou; tel. 21-31-17-26; fax 21-31-28-91; f. 1993; promotes, develops and co-ordinates port activities at Cotonou; Pres. ISSA BADAROU-SOULÉ; Sec.-Gen. CAMILLE MÉDÉGAN.

Compagnie Béninoise de Navigation Maritime (COBENAM): Place Ganhi, 01 BP 2032, Cotonou; tel. 21-31-27-96; fax 21-31-09-78; e-mail cobenam@elodia.intnet.bj; f. 1974 by Govts of Algeria and Dahomey (now Benin); 100% state-owned; Pres. ABDEL KADER ALLAL; Man. Dir ARMAND PRIVAT KANDISSOUNON.

Maersk Bénin: Maersk House, Zone OCBN Lot 531, Parcelle B, 01 BP 2826, Cotonou; tel. 21-31-43-30; fax 21-31-56-60; e-mail BNNMKT@maersk.com; internet www.maerskline.com/bj; subsidiary of Maersk Line (Denmark); Dir DAVID SKOV.

SDV Bénin: route du Collège de l'Union, Akpakpa, 01 BP 433, Cotonou; tel. 21-31-21-19; fax 21-31-59-26; e-mail sdvbenin@bow.intnet.bj; f. 1986; affiliated to SDV Group (France); Pres. J. F. MIGNONNEAU; Dir-Gen. R. PH. RANJARD.

Société Béninoise d'Entreprises Maritimes (SBEM): BP 1733, Cotonou; tel. 21-31-23-57; fax 21-31-59-26; warehousing, storage and transportation; Dir RÉGIS TISSER.

Société Béninoise des Manutentions Portuaires (SOBEMAP): blvd de la Marina, BP 35, Cotonou; tel. 21-31-41-45; fax 21-31-53-71; e-mail infos@sobemap.com; internet www.sobemap.com; f. 1969; state-owned; Dir-Gen. WASSI BANKOLÉ.

Société Béninoise Maritime (SOBEMAR): Carré 8, Cruintomé, 08 BP 0956, Cotonou; tel. 21-31-49-65; fax 21-31-67-72; e-mail sobemar@intnet.bj.

CIVIL AVIATION

There is an international airport at Cotonou-Cadjehoun and there are secondary airports at Parakou, Natitingou, Kandi and Abomey.

Trans Air Bénin (TAB): Cotonou; f. 2000; regional flights; Dir BRICE KIKI.

Tourism

Benin's rich cultural diversity and its national parks and game reserves are the principal tourist attractions. About 173,500 tourists visited Benin in 2004. Receipts from tourism were estimated at US $107.9m. in 2003.

Direction de la Promotion et des Professions Touristiques: BP 2037, Cotonou; tel. 21-32-68-24; fax 21-32-68-23; e-mail dth@benintourism.com; internet www.benintourism.com.

Defence

As assessed at November 2006, the Beninois Armed Forces numbered an estimated 4,750 active personnel (land army 4,300, navy about 100, air force 350). Paramilitary forces comprised a 2,500-strong gendarmerie. Military service is by selective conscription, and lasts for 18 months.

Defence Expenditure: Estimated at 37,000m. francs CFA in 2005.

Chief of Defence Staff: Brig.-Gen. CHABI A. BONI.

Chief of Staff of the Army: Col DOMINIQUE M. AHOUANDJINOU.

Chief of Staff of the Navy: Capt. FERNAND MAXIME AHOYO.

Chief of Staff of the Air Force: Col CAMILLE MICHODJEHOUN.

Education

The Constitution of Benin obliges the state to make a quality compulsory primary education available to all children. All public primary and secondary schools in Benin finance themselves through school fees. Primary education begins at six years of age and lasts for six years. Secondary education, beginning at 12 years of age, lasts for up to seven years, comprising a first cycle of four years and a second of three years. According to UNESCO estimates, primary enrolment in 2003/04 included 83% of children in the appropriate age-group (males 93%; females 72%), while enrolment at secondary schools in 2000/01 included 17% of children in the appropriate age group (males 23%; females 11%). In the 1990s the Government sought to extend the provision of education. In 1993 girls in rural areas were exempted from school fees, and in 1999 the Government created a 500m. francs CFA fund to increase female enrolment. The Université Nationale du Bénin, at Cotonou, was founded in 1970 and had a student population of approximately 9,000 in 1999/2000. A second university, in Parakou, with a student capacity of approximately 3,000, opened in 2001. In 2001 public expenditure on education totalled 71,100m. francs CFA.

Bibliography

Adamon, A. D. *Renouveau démocratique au Bénin: la Conférence nationale des forces vives et la période de transition*. Paris, L'Harmattan, 1995.

Adekounte, F. L. *Entreprises publiques Béninoises: la descente aux enfers*. Cotonou, Les Editions du Flamboyant, 1996.

Adjovi, V. E. *Une élection libre en Afrique: la présidentielle du Bénin, 1996*. Paris, Editions Karthala, 1998.

Albert, I. *Des femmes. Une terre: une nouvelle dynamique sociale au Bénin*. Paris. L'Harmattan, 1993.

Alpern, S. B. *Amazons of Black Sparta: The Women Warriors of Dahomey*. New York, NY, New York University Press, 1998.

Banégas, R. *La démocratie à pas de caméléon. Transition et imaginaires politiques au Bénin*. Paris, Editions Karthala, 2003.

Bio Tchané, A., and Montigny, P. *Lutter contre la corruption: un impératif pour le développement du Bénin dans l'économie internationale*. Paris, L'Harmattan, 2000.

Campbell, W. D. *The Emergent Independent Press in Benin and Côte d'Ivoire*. Westport, CT, Praeger Publishers, 1998.

Cornevin, R. *La République populaire du Bénin, des Origines dahoméennes à nos jours*. Paris, Académie des Sciences d'Outremer, 1984.

Le Dahomey. Paris, Presses universitaires de France, 1965.

Histoire du Dahomey. Paris, Berger-Levrault, 1962; new edn as *Histoire du Bénin*. Paris, Maisonneuve et Larose.

Decalo, S. *Historical Dictionary of Benin*. Metuchen, NJ, Scarecrow Press, 1995.

Dissou, M. *Le Bénin et l'épreuve démocratique: leçons des élections de 1991 à 2001.* Paris, L'Harmattan, 2002.

Dunn, J. (Ed.). *West African States: Failure and Promise.* Cambridge, Cambridge University Press, 1978.

Eades, J. S., and Allen, C. *Benin.* Oxford, Clio, 1996.

Garcia, L. *Le royaume du Dahomé face à la pénétration coloniale.* Paris, Editions Karthala, 1988.

Gbago, B. G. *Le Bénin et les droits de l'homme.* Paris, L'Harmattan, 2001.

Harrison Church, R. J. *West Africa.* 8th Edn. London, Longman, 1979.

Heilbrunn, J. R. *Markets, Profits and Power: The Politics of Business in Benin and Togo.* Bordeaux, Centre d'étude d'Afrique noire, 1996.

Houngnikpo, M. C. *Determinants of Democratization in Africa: A Comparative Study of Benin and Togo.* Lanham, MD, University Press of America, 2001.

Manning, P. *Slavery, Colonialism and Economic Growth in Dahomey, 1640–1960.* Cambridge, Cambridge University Press, 1982.

Noudjenoume, P. *La démocratie au Bénin, 1988–1993: bilans et perspectives.* Paris, L'Harmattan, 1999.

Ogbemudia, S. O. *Years of Challenge.* Oxford, Heinemann Educational Books (Nigeria), 1991.

Onibon, Y. O. *Les Femmes Béninoises: de l'étalage a la conquête du marché international.* Paris, Université de Paris, 1995.

Passot, B. *Le Bénin Les hommes et leur milieu: guide pratique.* Paris, L'Harmattan, 2004.

Van Ufford, P. Q. *Trade and Traders: The Making of the Cattle Market in Benin.* Amsterdam, Thela Thesis, 1999.

BOTSWANA

Physical and Social Geography

A. MACGREGOR HUTCHESON

PHYSICAL FEATURES

The Republic of Botswana is a land-locked country, bordered by Namibia to the west and north, by the latter's Caprivi Strip to the north, by Zimbabwe to the north-east, and by South Africa to the south and south-east. Botswana occupies 581,730 sq km (224,607 sq miles) of the downwarped Kalahari Basin of the great southern African plateau, which has here an average altitude of 900 m above sea-level. Gentle undulations to flat surfaces, consisting of Kalahari sands overlying Archean rocks, are characteristic of most of the country but the east is more hilly and broken. Most of southern Botswana is without surface drainage and, apart from the bordering Limpopo and Chobe rivers, the rest of the country's drainage is interior and does not reach the sea. Flowing into the north-west from the Angolan highlands, the perennial Okavango river is Botswana's major system. The Okavango drains into a depression in the plateau, 145 km from the border, to form the Okavango swamps and the ephemeral Lake Ngami. From this vast marsh, covering 16,000 sq km, there is a seasonal flow of water eastwards along the Botletle river 260 km to Lake Xau and thence into the Makarakari salt pan. Most of the water brought into Botswana by the Okavango is lost through evaporation and transpiration in the swamps.

The Kalahari Desert dominates southern and western Botswana. From the near-desert conditions of the extreme south-west with an average annual rainfall around 130 mm, there is a gradual increase in precipitation towards the north (635 mm) and east (380–500 mm). There is an associated transition in the natural vegetation from the sparse thornveld of the Kalahari Desert to the dry woodland savannah of the north and east, and the infertile sands give way eastwards to better soils developed on granitic and sedimentary rocks.

POPULATION AND RESOURCES

The eastern strip, the best-endowed and most developed region of Botswana, possesses about 80% of the population, which totalled 1,680,863, according to the census of August 2001. (The total population was estimated at 1,858,000 at mid-2006.) Seven of the eight Batswana tribes, and most of the Europeans and Asians, are concentrated in the east. According to the census, in 2001 52.1% of all Batswana, compared with 45.7% in 1991, lived in settlements of 5,000 or more inhabitants. A substantial number of Batswana (the figure is unrecorded, but estimated to be at least 50,000) are employed in South Africa, many of them (an estimated 5,867 at the end of 2000) in mining. The absence of these workers helps to ease pressure on resources and contributes to the country's income through deferred pay and remittances sent home to their families. However, as a large proportion of the population is less than 15 years of age, there is a pressing need for improvements in agricultural productivity and in other sectors of the economy to provide work for the growing number of young people who are entering the labour market.

Shortage of water, resulting from the low annual rainfall and aggravated by considerable fluctuations in the monthly distribution and total seasonal rainfall, is the main hindrance to the development of Botswana's natural resources, although a number of projects have improved water supply to the main centres of economic activity. Limitations imposed by rainfall make much of the country more suitable for the rearing of livestock, especially cattle, but it has been estimated that in eastern Botswana 4.45m. ha are suitable for cultivation, of which only about 10% is actually cultivated. Although in the east the irrigation potential is limited, the Okavango-Chobe swamps offer substantial scope for irrigation (as much as an estimated 600,000 ha).

In recent years Botswana's economic base has been considerably widened. Exploitable deposits of diamonds (of which Botswana is the world's largest producer by value), gold, silver, uranium, copper, nickel, coal, manganese, asbestos, common salt, potash, soda ash and sodium sulphate have been identified, and some of these minerals are currently being mined. In particular, the major developments of diamond mining at Orapa, Letlhakane and Jwaneng, and copper-nickel mining focused on Selebi-Phikwe, with their attendant infrastructural improvements, are assisting in the diversification of the predominantly agricultural economy.

Recent History

CHRISTOPHER SAUNDERS

Based on an earlier article by RICHARD BROWN

What today is the Republic of Botswana was part of the territory that the British Government declared a protectorate in 1885, at the request of local Tswana rulers who wished to deter Boer encroachment from the Transvaal in the east. In 1895 the southern portion was incorporated into the Cape Colony, and the northern portion, which continued to be ruled directly by Britain through the High Commissioner, was then known as the Bechuanaland Protectorate. There was some expectation that Bechuanaland would join the new Union of South Africa after 1910, but the Tswana made clear their opposition to this, and the territory remained under direct British rule until it gained independence as Botswana in 1966.

It was not until 1960 that the first nationalist party, the Bechuanaland People's Party (BPP), was founded, with links to the African National Congress of South Africa (ANC). The BPP soon split, with one section later becoming the Botswana Independence Party (BIP) and the other the more important Botswana People's Party (BPP). In 1961 Seretse (later Sir Seretse) Khama gained a seat on the legislative council, and was appointed to the territory's Executive Council. In 1962 he formed the Bechuanaland (later Botswana) Democratic Party (BDP). Many white settlers gave their support to the BDP in preference to the more radical BPP. In the territory's first direct general election under universal adult suffrage, held in 1965, the BDP won 28 of the 31 seats, and Khama became Prime Minister. Independence followed on 30 September 1966, when Bechuanaland became the Republic of Botswana, with Khama as the first President. As a result of the discovery and exploitation of diamonds, independent Botswana was in the decades that followed to achieve a rate of economic growth unmatched anywhere else in Africa, and the country became known as the continent's most stable democracy.

When Khama died in July 1980, his Vice-President, Dr Quett (later Sir Quett) Ketumile Masire, succeeded to the presidency.

As Minister of Finance and Development Planning, Masire had played an important role in the country's economic development. He was to remain in office for 18 years, during which time the BDP retained its political dominance. In the election of 1989, the BDP won 31 of the 34 elective seats, and 65% of all votes cast. Weakened by internal dissent, the leading opposition party, the Botswana National Front (BNF), won only three seats, although it obtained 27% of the total votes.

In March 1992 the Vice-President, Peter Mmusi, and the Minister of Agriculture, Daniel Kwelagobe, resigned after being implicated by a commission of inquiry in a corruption scandal involving the illegal transfer of land. Festus Mogae, the Minister of Finance and Development Planning, who was known for his fiscal prudence and sound economic management, was appointed Vice-President and allocated the portfolio of local government and lands. Mmusi and Kwelagobe remained in the BDP but opposed the Government's economic liberalization policy, and sought to overturn the findings of the commission on illegal land dealings. Uncertainty about the future leadership of the BDP and the President's silence on this matter added to the divisions within the ruling party before the general election of October 1994. Although the Government rejected the BNF's demands for the appointment of an independent electoral commission and for the reduction of the voting age to 18 years, the party abandoned its threat to boycott the election and sought, instead, to mobilize popular support on the issues of government corruption and economic recession. The success of this strategy was demonstrated when the BNF fared unexpectedly well in the election, winning 37.7% of votes and increasing its representation to 13 of the 40 elective seats. The BDP, however, with 53.1% of the vote, won 26 seats. More than 70% of the electorate participated in the election. Only three ministers (among them Mogae) retained their portfolios in the new Cabinet, which included Kwelagobe, who had been acquitted by the High Court on charges relating to the corruption allegations made against him in 1992 and was reinstated as Minister of Agriculture.

A number of constitutional amendments were adopted in mid-1997. The President was now limited to two terms of office, and provision was made for the automatic succession to the presidency of the Vice-President, in the event of the death or resignation of the President. The electoral system was reformed, the age of eligibility to vote being reduced to 18 years and an independent electoral commission was established. In November 1997 Masire announced that he would retire in March the following year. A ceremony to mark his retirement was held on 31 March 1998 and the following day Mogae was inaugurated as President.

THE MOGAE PRESIDENCY

The only new minister in Mogae's Cabinet was Lt-Gen. Seretse Ian Khama, the son of Sir Seretse Khama and Commander of the Botswana Defence Force (BDF). Khama received the portfolio of presidential affairs and public administration, and was designated as Vice-President, subject to his election to the National Assembly. Once elected, he was duly sworn in as Vice-President and for a time feuding within the BDP decreased. Ponatshego Kedikilwe, who had been favoured for the vice-presidency by certain prominent members of the BDP leadership, was appointed Minister of Finance and Development Planning. In July 2003 Khama was elected chairman of the BDP and was emerging as Mogae's likely successor.

Meanwhile, hostility between Kenneth Koma, founder and long-time leader of the BNF, and his deputy, Michael Dingake, had led to a split in that party. At the BNF's annual congress in April 1998 relations deteriorated over the issue of dissident members who had been expelled from the party. Koma, supported by the dissidents, ordered the expulsion from the party of central committee members. In June some of these members formed the Botswana Congress Party (BCP), which was declared the official opposition in mid-July, after 11 of the BNF's 13 deputies decided to join the new party. There was discontent within the BDP over corruption and the conduct of the primary ballot to select candidates for the general election, but dissension among members of the opposition assisted the BDP in securing a decisive victory in the October 1999 election, winning 33 of the 40 seats. The BNF won six seats, and the BCP only one; Dingake, the BCP leader, was defeated in Gaborone. While the BDP regained five of the seats taken by the BNF in 1994, the BNF recovered seats it had lost to the BCP in mid-1998, and performed well in the urban centres, particularly Gaborone, Lobatse and Kgatleng.

In February 2000 eastern Botswana suffered the worst floods ever recorded in the country, and more than 11,000 houses were destroyed, leaving over 60,000 people homeless. However, this was a minor disaster compared with the HIV/AIDS pandemic, which had by then become the Government's primary health concern. Botswana was the first country in Africa to distribute antiretroviral drugs for those with HIV through its public health system under the Masa (New Dawn) programme funded by the African Comprehensive HIV/AIDS Partnership (ACHAP), a public-private partnership with the Bill and Melinda Gates Foundation and the Merck Foundation. By 2003 ACHAP believed that approximately 300,000 people in Botswana were HIV-positive, with an estimated 37.3% of 15–49 year olds infected, the highest proportion anywhere in the world. As a result, life expectancy fell to 40 years by early 2006 and Botswana dropped further down the UN Human Development index. The Masa programme initially provided free antiretrovirals and counselling at Gaborone, Francistown, Serowe and Maun, targeting priority groups of HIV-positive people, including pregnant women, children older than six months, and patients with tuberculosis. District and village AIDS committees and voluntary test centres were established and began to roll out the programme to deliver antiretrovirals to additional sites. Though HIV prevalence among pregnant women began to decline, people remained reluctant to discover their HIV status and it seemed unlikely that the aim of preventing new infections by 2016 would be achieved. A local development policy group estimated that within a decade the economy would be more than 30% smaller than it would have been without the AIDS pandemic. A major outbreak of diarrhoea among children in early 2006, which resulted in more than 500 deaths, was thought to have been caused in part by HIV-positive mothers not breast-feeding. Although Botswana still had the highest rate of HIV infection of any country in the world, the Minister of Health was able to announce in March 2007 that HIV prevalence had decreased to 32.4% and that over 80,000 people were receiving antiretroviral drugs. Botswana could claim to have one of Africa's most progressive and comprehensive programmes for dealing with the disease.

Meanwhile, based on the recommendations of a government commission established in July 2000 to investigate allegations of discrimination against minority ethnic groups, the Government presented a number of draft constitutional amendments to Parliament in 2002. Under the proposals, the House of Chiefs, Botswana's second legislative chamber, was to be renamed the Ntlo ya Dikgosi, and its membership increased from 15 to 35, comprising 30 members elected every five years by senior tribal authorities and five specially appointed members. In April 2002 the draft amendments were revised to allow the eight paramount chiefs from the Setswana-speaking 'principal tribes' to retain their ex officio status in the chamber, prompting criticism from opposition parties and from those who believed that discrimination was continuing against the minority ethnic groups, including the indigenous San. Long before the matter was resolved, the National Assembly approved legislation providing for the expansion of its membership from 40 to 57, with effect from the 2004 general election, at which time there were to be 17 additional constituencies.

The BDP remained politically dominant owing to the continued deep divisions in the opposition. Yet another split took place in the BNF in 2003, leading to the formation of the New Democratic Front (NDF). Koma, the former BNF leader, was suspended from the party for his support of Peter Woto, a rival to Otsweletse Moupo for the party leadership. Moupo consolidated his control of the BNF, and Woto and others joined the NDF. Inspired by the example of other African countries, in which coalitions of opposition parties had challenged parties long in power, three opposition parties signed an electoral pact, in an effort to unseat the BDP, but the BNF and the Botswana Alliance Movement (BAM) soon accused the BPP of not adhering to the terms of the pact, after the former BPP President, Motlatsi Molapisi, unveiled BPP candidates in constituencies where, under the terms of their agreement, representatives from the BNF or BAM were to stand.

Sensitive to the charge that it had been in power for such a lengthy period that it was no longer democratic in its practice, the BDP held parliamentary and council primary elections for the first time in 2003, using a process it named 'Bulela Ditswe'. This more democratic candidate-selection system, under which all party members could vote in primary elections in constituencies, led to bitter feuding within the party. In the wake of the primary elections, Mogae and Khama called for unity. Mogae asked those defeated in the party's primaries to rally behind the winners, but a number of key members of the party attempted to appeal against the defeats that they suffered in the primary elections, alleging that opposition party members had been recruited to vote, that civil servants and persons under the age of eligibility to vote had taken part in the primaries and that there had been widespread intimidation of voters. A BDP team investigated their claims and rejected them.

From the late 1990s the Botswana Government provoked much international criticism for its attempts to relocate some 3,000 San or Bushmen people, often referred to by the derogatory term Basarwa, meaning people without cattle, from their ancestral lands within the Central Kalahari Game Reserve (CKGR) to new settlements outside the reserve. A government study conducted in 1985 found that the San in the CKGR were abandoning their traditional means of hunting on foot in favour of guns, horses and even four-wheel drive vehicles. Permanent, settled agricultural communities, grazing livestock, were being established that were not consistent with the land-use patterns envisaged when the CKGR was formed. In an attempt to persuade the San to move out of the reserve, the Government began to disconnect water supplies, and offered them compensation if they relocated. The London-based minority-rights group Survival International (SI) alleged that the policy of resettlement had been devised to allow diamond mining to take place in the reserve.

The issue of the forced removal of the San from the CKGR came to the fore again in January 2002, when the Government cut off water supplies to those who had refused to leave the reserve. In April that year 243 San, assisted financially by SI and the First People of the Kalahari movement, began legal action, requesting a ruling that the termination of basic services was illegal and that they had been deprived of their land by force. The case was initially dismissed on a technicality but was subsequently taken to the High Court; in December 2006, at the end of what had become the longest and most expensive legal case in Botswana's history, the High Court ruled that the Government's refusal to issue San with hunting licences for the reserve was unlawful and that the San had the right to remain on their ancestral land. Following the judgment, the Government declared that it would not help the San to return, and some San were detained for hunting in the reserve. SI continued to claim that the Government wanted to drive them out.

In 2005, meanwhile, the Government had tabled legislation in the National Assembly to make the Constitution 'tribally neutral'. This removed a clause giving protection to San and other minorities, and critics argued that the amendment was designed to undermine the court challenge. When further evictions of San were threatened, an urgent application was made to the High Court to stop them. In February 2005 Professor Kenneth Good, an Australian-born lecturer in political science at the University of Botswana, was given 48 hours to leave the country because—it was widely believed—he supported SI's attempt to have Botswana's diamonds labelled 'blood diamonds' because of the removal of the San from the CKGR. Good rejected the idea that Botswana was a 'model democracy' and had criticized the President's nomination of Khama as his designated successor, alleging that Khama had awarded tenders to family members when head of the army and had commandeered military helicopters to aid the BDP's election campaign in 2004 (see below). Good challenged his deportation order in court, but failed to have the decision overturned, the Attorney-General stating that the matter was beyond judicial review. Appeals to Mogae by Good's supporters were unsuccessful and he was forced to settle abroad, where he continued to write articles criticizing Mogae and claiming that Botswana was a 'dysfunctional democracy' because of the immense power of the presidency and its control over the succession. This view was challenged by Mogae's supporters who indicated that although the Vice-President automatically succeeded to the presidency on the resignation or death of the President, both the Vice-President and President were confirmed in office by the democratically elected Parliament. The political dominance of the BDP was attributed to the failure of the opposition to unite.

In August 2004 members of the Botswana Mining Workers' Union (BMWU) commenced industrial action at the country's four diamond mines, demanding higher wages. The strike was called off after a salary increase was offered; however, the BMWU then demanded the reinstatement of those who had been identified as the chief organizers of the action and who had been dismissed without benefits. The Government also dismissed some civil servants who had engaged in industrial action and deducted money from the salaries of others. The unions argued that the existing Trade Disputes Act gave them inadequate protection and that taking industrial disputes to mediation or arbitration was too long, complicated and costly a process. Labour unrest continued and in May 2005 the Botswana Federation of Trade Unions and the Public Service Workers' Association threatened action to force the Government to protect workers from victimization, unfair dismissal and discrimination on the grounds of HIV/AIDS status.

After more than two years of negotiations, an agreement was signed in May 2006 by President Mogae and Nicky Oppenheimer, Chairman of the De Beers diamond-mining group, that renewed the licence for 25 years on the world's most valuable diamond mine, Jwaneng, and other mines at Orapa, Letlhakane and Damtshaa belonging to the Debswana Diamond Company (a joint venture between the Botswana Government and De Beers). As part of the agreement Botswana increased its shareholding in De Beers from 7.5% to 15%. Both parties also agreed to launch a new joint venture, the Botswana Diamond Trading Company (BDTC), to help the country diversify from its heavy reliance on the mining of diamonds. BDTC was to sort, polish and value rough diamonds mined in Botswana, as well as others from outside the country, and the process of aggregation, by which the best sales parcels of diamonds were arranged, was to be moved from London, United Kingdom, to Gaborone from 2009. President Mogae and his Government were strong supporters of the Kimberley Process Certification Scheme (see Economy), which regulated the trade in rough diamonds, and constantly stressed that the country could account for the origin of all its diamonds. In February 2005 Mogae opened a large new open-pit gold mine, funded mainly by Australian companies, close to the Zimbabwean border. When the Botswana currency was devalued, it was widely believed that this was to promote diversification away from mining, but relatively little manufacturing industry was attracted to Botswana.

The 2004 Election

At the legislative elections held on 30 October 2004 the rate of voter participation was recorded at 74.6%, compared with 77.3% five years before. The ruling BDP won 44 of the 57 seats, with 51.7% of the vote. The BNF increased its number of seats to 12, but the party's President, Otsweletse Moupo, lost his seat and the party's Secretary-General, Akanyang Magama, took over as leader of the opposition. The BCP, as in the 1999 election, won only one seat, but its share of the vote increased from 11.9% to 16.6% and its victory in Gaborone Central, where the former Minister of Lands and Housing, Margaret Nasha, was defeated, was the main surprise of the election. Mogae was re-elected President by the National Assembly for a second and final term and was sworn in on 2 November. He was expected to step down at the end of March 2008 to be succeeded by Khama. In an extensive reshuffle of his Cabinet, Mogae appointed 11 new ministers, nine of whom were new members of the National Assembly. Those appointed tended to support Khama, while supporters of Kedikilwe were excluded. Among those removed from the Cabinet was Kwelagobe, the Secretary-General of the BDP, who had held ministerial office since 1973. The President could also appoint four members of the National Assembly and his decision to select two defeated BDP candidates was criticized for breaking an unwritten rule that defeated candidates would not be appointed.

In the concurrently held local elections, most of the seats in the capital and in Lobatse, the hub of the beef industry, were secured by the opposition, while the majority of the seats in Francistown, the second largest city, went to the BDP. For some observers the election reinforced Botswana's reputation as a stable, liberal democracy, but the continued weakness of the opposition was the cause of much comment. The BCP claimed that the state media had given the ruling party unfair advantage and not allowed the opposition to present its case. Others argued for proportional representation as a way to give the opposition a larger presence in the National Assembly.

Domestic Developments

In February 2006 representatives of the four main opposition parties—the BNF, BCP, BPP and BAM—met in Francistown at talks convened by Lebang Mpotokwane (an external mediator and Chairman of the Committee for Strengthening Democracy in Botswana) in order to agree upon a consensus on co-operation in the run-up to the next general election, expected in 2009. For some time it appeared that progress was being made, but by early 2007 the talks had collapsed.

In late 2006 controversy surrounded the Government's Intelligence and Security Bill, which proposed that a new security directorate be established. Non-governmental organizations were concerned that there would be no parliamentary oversight of this, nor adequate means for recourse in cases of abuse. An emergency meeting was called by the Botswana Council of Non-Governmental Organisations to discuss how to oppose the legislation. Several members of the BDP also attended the meeting, prompting speculation of dissension within the party. Critics of the Government pointed to the legislation as further evidence that the country was no longer the model of democracy in Africa, but was moving in a more authoritarian direction. Further evidence brought forward included the proposed selection procedure for BDP candidates for the 2009 elections, and the announcement by the Government in March 2007 that 17 individuals from the United Kingdom, the USA, Australia and Canada—mainly human rights campaigners, journalists and academics—would henceforth require visas to visit Botswana. Tensions were expected to rise further as the 2009 elections approached. Meanwhile, in January 2007 President Mogae effected a reorganization of the Cabinet. Most notably, Kwelagobe was appointed to the newly created post of Minister for Public Service in the Office of the President, responsible for the Public Service, the Ombudsman, the Independent Electoral Commission and the National AIDS Co-ordinating Agency, while Kedikilwe assumed the minerals, energy and water affairs portfolio, replacing Charles Tibone, who became Minister of Labour and Home Affairs.

EXTERNAL RELATIONS

Following the unilateral declaration of independence by Rhodesia (now Zimbabwe) in 1965, Khama opposed the illegal regime, but was unable to implement effective economic sanctions against that country owing to Botswana's dependence on the Rhodesian-owned railways for its economic survival. Zimbabwe's achievement of internationally recognized independence in April 1980 brought considerable economic benefits to Botswana. Khama helped to forge the alliance of 'front-line' states against the apartheid regime in South Africa, and in 1979 Botswana was a founder member of the Southern African Development Co-ordination Conference (SADCC—reorganized in 1992 as the Southern African Development Community—SADC), to encourage regional development and reduce members' economic dependence on South Africa.

In the 1970s and 1980s it was Botswana's policy to accommodate South African refugees, while not allowing them to use the country as a base for attacks on South Africa. In June 1985 South African security forces raided alleged ANC bases in Gaborone, killing at least 15 people. Further raids followed in 1986 and 1988, but with the relaxation of the political climate within South Africa from 1990 onwards there was a gradual improvement in relations between the two countries; full diplomatic relations were established in June 1994, after which the two countries worked closely together in SADC.

While full diplomatic relations were established between Botswana and Zimbabwe in May 1983, tensions continued throughout the 1980s over the influx of Zimbabwean refugees. In 1982 supporters of Joshua Nkomo's Zimbabwe African People's Union, whom the Zimbabwean Government considered as insurgents, crossed into Botswana in considerable numbers. Nkomo himself fled to Botswana in March 1983, but soon left for the United Kingdom. After the general election in Zimbabwe in July 1985 a new influx of refugees again caused tensions. In May 1988 Masire expressed confidence that the remaining Zimbabwean exiles would return to their country voluntarily following an apparent improvement in the political climate in Zimbabwe. In the mid-1990s, however, the Government expressed concern at the growing number of illegal immigrants in the country, the majority of whom were from Zimbabwe. As instability in Zimbabwe increased following the seizure of white-owned farms in that country. Mogae expressed his commitment to respect for private property rights and described developments in Zimbabwe as 'regrettable'. He attempted, through behind-the-scenes diplomacy, to bring his influence to bear, but claimed that there was little that Botswana could do.

A joint permanent commission of the two countries continued to meet, and in early 2001 the Zimbabwean Minister of Foreign Affairs thanked Botswana for making representations to the US Congress against the imposition of sanctions on Zimbabwe. However, as Zimbabwe's economic crisis worsened, considerable numbers of Zimbabweans again moved into Botswana, and a number of violent incidents took place along the border. In July 2003 Botswana and Zimbabwe began operating joint patrols to prevent the passage of Zimbabwean refugees into Botswana, and by 2004 Botswana was repatriating some 2,500 illegal immigrants—mainly Zimbabweans—each month. It was not known how many remained within the country. Although President Mogae stated that Zimbabwe suffered from a 'drought of leadership', his Government hesitated openly to criticize its neighbour, either in SADC or in bilateral talks. In May 2006 Botswana's Minister of Finance and Development Planning, Baledzi Gaolathe, urged the IMF to help Zimbabwe deal with its foreign-exchange shortages, after the Fund had refused to provide new financial support. As the Zimbabwe crisis deepened, the Government of Botswana did not speak out strongly, despite the increasing number of refugees and the growth of xenophobia in Botswana. Although Botswana was now deporting tens of thousands of Zimbabweans each year, the influx continued and the increase in crime in Botswana, which had become a growing concern, was often blamed on Zimbabweans. The Botswana authorities appeared to accept that the country would not be able to escape the consequences if the already dire situation in Zimbabwe worsened.

Following the achievement of independence by Namibia in March 1990, presidential visits were exchanged by Botswana and Namibia and steps were taken to ensure bilateral co-operation. However, in 1992 a border dispute developed between the two countries regarding their rival territorial claims over a small island in the Chobe river, which Namibia called Kasikili and Botswana Sedudu. In early 1995 Botswana and Namibia agreed to present the case for arbitration at the International Court of Justice (ICJ), and in February 1996 the two countries signed an agreement committing themselves in advance to the court's eventual judgment. In the following month it was announced that Botswana and Namibia were to establish joint sub-committees at posts along the frontier in order to control illegal border crossings and smuggling. What were perceived as attempts by Botswana to extend the role and capabilities of its armed forces (most notably the completion of a large new airbase at Molepolole in 1995 and efforts during 1996–97 to procure military tanks) were, for a time, a source of friction between the two countries, although Botswana emphasized that it only sought to enable its military to fulfil a wider regional and international peace-keeping role. Namibia's decision to construct a pipeline to take water from the Okavango river, which feeds the Okavango delta, an important habitat for Botswana's varied wildlife and a major tourist attraction, created further tension in 1996.

In early 1997 it was reported that Namibia had been angered by Botswana's erection of a fence along Namibia's Caprivi Strip, which separates the two countries to the north; Botswana insisted, however, that the fence was simply a measure to control the spread of livestock diseases. In January 1998 an emergency meeting of the Botswana-Namibia Joint Commission on Defence and Security was held to discuss ownership of an island named Situngu in the Chobe river. The two countries agreed to set up a joint technical commission to demarcate the shared border and confirmed that they would accept the judgment of the ICJ on Sedudu-Kasikili. In December the ICJ awarded the island to Botswana. A joint commission to investigate other demarcation disputes along the Chobe and two other rivers was subsequently established, and in March 2003 its report was accepted by the Presidents of the two countries.

In late 1998 relations between the two countries were further strained by the arrival in Botswana of more than 300 refugees from the Caprivi Strip in Namibia. These included Mishake Muyongo, who had been suspended as President of the Democratic Turnhalle Alliance (the leading Namibian opposition party) in August, and other leading Caprivians who had been campaigning for the secession of their region from Namibia. Other refugees followed, claiming intimidation and harassment by the Namibian army, and by early 1999 more than 2,000 were living in a camp north of Gaborone. Demands by Namibia for their extradition were refused, although it was agreed by the two Governments in March 1999 that prominent dissidents among the refugees would be allowed to leave Botswana for another country, and that an amnesty was to be extended to other refugees returning to Namibia. A formal agreement to this effect was signed in May under the auspices of the office of the UN High Commissioner for Refugees (UNHCR), after which Muyongo and two others were granted asylum in Denmark. However, the programme to repatriate others to Namibia was suspended in August 1999, and some 2,400 refugees remained in Botswana. A new agreement for their repatriation to the Caprivi Strip was signed by UNHCR and the two countries involved in April 2002, and in August of that year those refugees who had registered for repatriation (mostly from the western Caprivi) began to return to Namibia. Between August and October around 800 refugees were repatriated to Namibia (although UNHCR reported that none of them originated from the Caprivi Strip), leaving some 1,200 in Botswana, who remained reluctant to return. A larger number, from the eastern Caprivi, refused to register, fearing possible mistreatment if they returned to Namibia. Meanwhile, in September 2001 the Gaborone Magistrate Court ruled in favour of the extradition of suspected Caprivi separatists who were wanted in Namibia for alleged high treason. However, this decision was reversed by Botswana's High Court in December 2002. In December 2003 UNHCR criticized the deportation from Botswana to Namibia of eight Caprivians, seven of whom were subsequently charged with high treason over alleged separatist activities; the authorities in Botswana claimed that the eight had lost their refugee status by visiting Namibia after being granted asylum in Botswana.

Botswana's principled stand on apartheid, its political stability and democratic record, and its reputation for moderation, gave the country a minor but effective voice in many international deliberations. The SADC Secretariat, located in Gaborone, was opened by Masire in 1990. In 2004 SADC agreed that an early-warning centre to collect information on developing crises in the region would also be located in Botswana, and it seemed likely that the planned SADC military force, part of the African Union's larger African Standby Force, would be stationed there because of its stability and proximity to the geographic centre of the region. In August 2005 the 25th meeting of SADC heads of state and government was held in Gaborone, and in August 2006 ministers from the 13 member states of SADC met again in Gaborone to prepare the agenda for the 26th summit.

From December 1999 former President Masire acted as facilitator in efforts to achieve peace in the Democratic Republic of the Congo (DRC). His efforts appeared for a long time to be unsuccessful, particularly when President Laurent-Désiré Kabila rejected his involvement. In March 2001, however, after Kabila had been succeeded by his son, Joseph, Masire helped to secure the withdrawal of some of the foreign forces stationed in the DRC, and in 2002 and 2003 he chaired various meetings in Sun City, South Africa, that brought together the rival Congolese factions in an effort to find a peaceful settlement to the conflict in the DRC.

Economy

LINDA VAN BUREN

Classed as an 'upper middle-income country' by the World Bank, Botswana's gross national income per head of US $5,590 in 2005, was the highest in continental Sub-Saharan Africa. Diamonds have transformed Botswana's economy, providing a level of stability that is rare in Africa. Over the years this precious commodity has significantly alleviated the effects of regional problems in other sectors, such as livestock and tourism. Botswana promotes its output as 'diamonds for development', as an alternative to so-called 'conflict diamonds' (see below), and much of the country's diamond revenue has funded, and continues to fund, its development. Overall, the target for real GDP growth of 5.5% per year over the period of National Development Plan 9 (NDP 9) was exceeded in 2002/03, when 6.7% was achieved, and in 2004/05, when 9.2% was recorded; however, GDP contracted in 2005/06, by 0.9%. Annual inflation reached double figures in 2006, at 11.6%, after having averaged 8.6% in 2005 and 6.8% in 2004. The rise in inflation is attributed to high prices for petroleum, which Botswana must import. The trend is downward, however, and inflation was reined in to 8.5% in the 12 months to December 2006. These figures—although comparing very favourably with many other African economies, especially in view of the hyperinflation prevailing in neighbouring Zimbabwe—are higher than Botswana's economic planners and consumers would wish. For this reason, parastatals were directed to exercise restraint in pricing and to achieve their revenue targets through improved productivity rather than through price increases.

The Bank of Botswana must execute a delicate balancing act in setting the value of the pula. On the one hand, its rate against the US dollar is crucial, as global diamond sales are denominated in dollars; on the other hand, the pula's rate against the South African rand is also important, because South Africa is Botswana's main trading partner. After several years during which the trends of the US dollar and the rand were at odds with each other, the Bank of Botswana introduced a new exchange-rate regime in May 2005, termed the 'crawling band'. This broadened the margins between the buy rate and the sell rate of the pula by the Bank of Botswana. The effect of this widening spurred a significant increase in inter-bank trading and fostered considerably more competition among banks in the foreign-exchange market. As a result, during the 12 months between June 2006 and June 2007, the pula depreciated against both currencies—by 9.7% against the US dollar and by 4% against the rand. At 30 November 2006 Botswana's foreign-exchange reserves stood at US $7,900m., compared with $6,300m. at 30 November 2005 and $5,700m. at 31 December 2004. Forward import cover lengthened from 22 months in November 2005 to 30 months in November 2006. (Botswana repeatedly scores the longest forward import cover in the world.)

Both the Botswana Ministry of Finance and Development Planning and the IMF forecast lower customs revenue and a levelling-off of diamond receipts in the next decade, while HIV/AIDS would continue to have a devastating effect on Botswana's bid to create a more highly skilled labour force (see below). Government estimates in February 2003 indicated that of a total of 41,000 pregnancies per year, 35.4% would produce HIV-positive babies. To address this situation, the Government introduced the Prevention of Mother-to-Child Transmission (PMTCT) programme. By February 2004 11,329 pregnant women had received counselling under the programme, of whom 71%, or about 8,000, were tested for HIV. Of those tested about 2,400 proved to be HIV-positive, and of those 1,697 had been placed on azidothymidine (AZT) treatment by September 2003. In 2006 92% of pregnant women who were known to be HIV-positive received treatment at the time of delivery, while 91% of HIV-exposed newborn babies received the programme's infant formula and drug therapy. Botswana's PMTCT programme has the highest uptake of any country in sub-Saharan Africa. The government-set target of enrolling 85,000 HIV patients in Anti-Retroviral Therapy (ART) by the end of 2006 was not met; however, the number enrolled did rise from 54,378 in 2005 to 75,785 in 2006. The 2004/05 budget allocated P415m. to the fight against HIV/AIDS, and the 2005/06 budget provided a further increase, to P650m. According to the Government, HIV prevalence is declining, especially among young people. The Sentinel Surveillance, which tests pregnant women aged between 15 and 49 years who were attending government clinics, found that HIV prevalence had declined from 37.4% in 2003 to 33.4% in 2005 and to 32.4% in 2006. It should also be noted that HIV/AIDS has reversed the achievements Botswana had made in infant mortality and life expectancy. The number of babies who died before reaching the age of one had gradually declined to a low of 37 per 1,000 live births in 1996 but had increased to an estimated 56 per 1,000 live births in 2005, and this trend was attributed almost entirely to the effects of HIV/AIDS.

AGRICULTURE

Botswana's agricultural sector employed about 45% of the economically active population in December 2006, a level that has changed little for more than a decade, yet contributed just 1.9% of total GDP in 2005/06. In the early 2000s the subsistence agricultural sector, both arable and livestock-based, employed a disproportionately large number of ageing workers and was failing to attract younger people in sufficient numbers. Pressure for job creation is particularly acute because of Botswana's youthful population: some 70% of all Batswana are under 29 years of age. The Government hopes that the agricultural sector as well as industry can provide jobs for young workers. Composed partly of semi-desert and partly of a savannah area, with erratic rainfall and relatively poor soils, the country is more suited to grazing than to arable production. During the 1990s attempts were made to compensate for this shortage of arable land by developing the country's irrigation potential, but agriculture remained dominated by the livestock sector generally and by the cattle industry in particular. Agricultural GDP declined at an average annual rate of 1.7% in 1995/06–2005/06; it decreased by 11.0% in 2004/05 and by 3.6% in 2005/06.

The improved management of the agricultural sector is a government priority, especially owing to its key role in providing employment, and the rains of early 2006 were described as 'widespread and significant'. The Government provided farmers with free seeds at the right time to take advantage of these rains, and the outlook for good agricultural performance was expected. Rains in early 2007 were more erratic, however. Of a national area of 325,000 ha of arable land, only 140,326 ha had been ploughed during the 2005/06 cropping season. Total cereal-crop production accounted for only 18% of Botswana's national annual cereal requirement, which was assessed at 200,133 metric tons in 2005/06. Lower agricultural output was attributed to a variety of causes, ranging from damage by quelea birds, infestation by rats, frost in two regions and leaching of nutrients out of the topsoil by excessive rainfall. Notably, however, although drought and HIV/AIDS have affected the entire southern African region, in 2003 the UN World Food Programme (WFP) deemed South Africa, Namibia and Botswana to be the only countries in the region capable of coping without WFP assistance.

In June 1998 the Botswana Government formulated a plan, now known as the National Master Plan for Arable Agriculture and Dairy Development (NAMPAADD), aimed at boosting productivity and at guiding investment to protect the country's fragile rangelands, which were at risk from overgrazing. The scheme focused on diversification into areas such as horticulture, forestry, game farming and beekeeping. The 2000/01 national budget allocated P5m. to fund pilot projects under NAMPAADD, including a demonstration dairy project at Sunnyside Farm near Lobatse, a 'horticultural cluster' at Dikabeya Production Training Farm, a one-stop service centre for agriculture at Barolong farms, and a scheme for reusing waste water for irrigation in the Glen Valley, near Gaborone. A 610-ha demonstration farm was established in 2003/04 at Ramatlabama to train 'pilot farmers' and agricultural extension workers in dryland farming of field crops. Nine 'pilot farmers' were selected from various regions to train in irrigation technology at Dikabeya and in the Glen Valley, in the expectation that they would return to their regions and train others. By 2007 seven of the eight hectares at Dikabeya had yielded crops of tomatoes, green mealies, butternut squash, green peppers, carrots and onions; the eighth hectare is earmarked for greenhouse use. Construction of the Sunnyside Dairy Training Farm was completed in 2006. NAMPAADD's risk-cover policy, aimed at insuring producers against production losses caused by unexpected extreme natural conditions, was tested in 2003/04 and 2004/05 during drought conditions.

A major study of the livestock sector was completed in 2005, and the Government was to consider its findings during 2007 with a view to formulating a long-term development strategy aimed at strengthening the sector. The study recommended major reforms of the sector, including a reduction in the 'excess regulatory burden' and a restructuring of the Botswana Meat Commission (BMC). The national cattle herd doubled in the first 16 years after independence, stimulated by improved beef export prices, the expansion of available grazing through the drilling of new boreholes, and the establishment of effective disease control, based on a system of cordon fences and vaccination, which kept most of the country free of foot-and-mouth disease (FMD) after 1981. The cordon system opened up the lucrative market within the European Union (EU), which offered preferential terms and price subsidies (in Botswana's case, a 92% levy rebate, with a quota of 18,910 metric tons of beef per year) to Lomé Convention signatories able to satisfy the stringent disease-control criteria, but it also involved the Government in international controversy over the impact of the cordon system on wildlife. The criticism was intensified by the fact that the economic benefit of beef exports largely accrued to the 5% of households that were estimated to own more than one-half of the national herd, with about one-fifth of the total held by 360 large-scale commercial farms. Approximately 50% of rural households neither owned nor had access to cattle.

In 1999 the Ministry of Agriculture initiated a computerized system of cattle identification and tracing in order to comply with an EU directive, issued in 1997 in response to the bovine spongiform encephalopathy (BSE) crisis in the European beef market, which required that all cattle slaughtered and exported to EU countries be traced to the farm on which they were born. Termed the Livestock Identification and Traceback System (LITS), the scheme involves the insertion of a reticular bolus containing a microchip into the animal's stomach. The microchip serves to identify each animal and to contribute to a national identification database. The LITS project, which began with a seven-month pilot scheme at a cost of P29.5m. in Kgatleng and Kweneng, was completed in August 2001, with 247,000 cattle in these districts—about 82% of the total—carrying the bolus insertions. In November replication of the system in other parts of Botswana began and by April 2004 1.3m. cattle were carrying boluses. The system encountered opposition from many farmers, who claimed that the previous system, which used electronic ear tags, was cheaper and more efficient. The LITS scheme was expected to cost P300m. in total. The Government's response to critics of the scheme was to agree to a review of the project.

In 2002 Botswana became one of only three countries in Africa (the other two being Namibia and Swaziland) to receive a 'geographical classification' from the EU, recognizing that its cattle were unlikely to be infected with BSE: this distinction enables Botswana's beef to be exported to any country in the world. The BMC is responsible for slaughtering cattle and is capable of handling the high levels of throughput that occur in times of drought, although in the absence of drought conditions, when owners are replenishing their herds, the BMC has excess capacity. The BMC slaughtered 168,763 head of cattle in 2001, the highest level since 1992/93; nevertheless, capacity utilization was 88% at the Francistown abattoir and just 54% at the huge abattoir in Lobatse. Botswana's national cattle herd stood at 3.1m. head in 2005. An outbreak of FMD in Zimbabwe in August 2001 placed Botswana farmers on alert along the length of the two countries' shared border, but despite this vigilance the disease was discovered in north-eastern Botswana in February 2002. The BMC immediately closed its abattoirs and implemented measures to contain the disease, restricting livestock movements and destroying more than 12,000 head of cattle. The Lobatse abattoir reopened shortly afterwards, and exports of beef to the EU resumed from those areas of Botswana that were unaffected by FMD. Exports to other countries gradually resumed following the EU's decision.

Singled out in the 2005 budget speech for its continued lack of profitability, the BMC has come under increasing pressure from its principal shareholder, the Government, to improve its performance. The Government offered the BMC a P16.7m. tax remission for the 2004/05 financial year and agreed a P63m. loan guarantee for the year to June 2005, to help the BMC obtain further credit, in addition to its reported P160m. overdraft as of May 2005. The Government also insisted that the BMC sell off some of its non-core business and assets, including houses and land. The BMC responded by removing utility subsidies for its employees; by placing non-core businesses, such as Mainline Couriers in Gaborone and Botswana Road Services in Francistown, on the market; and by closing the BMC Village in Lobatse, which had been home to more than 400 BMC employees. BMC Village residents were served eviction notices, and the area was rezoned for commercial use. In 2006 Tannery Industries Botswana Ltd had offered to buy the BMC tannery, and the BMC had already divested itself of Botswana Road Services and Botzam Services. Storage and chill-room facilities in Cape Town and London were also to be put up for sale.

The World Trade Organization (WTO) has proposed an end to the EU beef subsidies enjoyed by Botswana and other African, Caribbean and Pacific (ACP) nations. Beef quotas are to be gradually eliminated by the end of 2007; during the transitional period Botswana and the other ACP countries will prepare themselves for the establishment of reciprocity in trade with the EU in order to become WTO-compliant. The cattle sector is very strongly focused on beef production rather than dairy output, and milk has to be imported. A NAMPAADD study found that Botswana has the potential to increase local production of milk through increased dairy-herd size and more modern farm-management techniques. The BMC also processes cowhides to the wet-blue stage, thereby increasing the value of the hides by 125%. The hides are then marketed globally under tender. The BMC has the capability of tanning the hides all the way through to finished leathers, but stops at the wet-blue stage because further processing would not offer a sufficient return, owing to the small size of the local market for leather products. Tanning to finished leathers does take place in Botswana but on a smaller scale.

In contrast to the cattle sector, sheep and goat numbers have withstood the periodic droughts reasonably well. Principally a subsistence-sector resource, the national herd of sheep and goats increased from 776,000 head in 1982 to 2.25m. in 2005. The main commercial development other than beef has been in urban poultry farming; Botswana had about 4.0m. chickens in 2005, 1.2m. more than in 1999. Efforts have also been made to improve the availability of eggs and chickens in rural areas, and to improve local production of milk and fish. Diversification efforts have focused on ostrich and fish farming, and on improving the infrastructure for the marketing of fresh milk. Ostrich farming has become a promising new industry. In August 2004 the EU approved Botswana's ostrich abattoir, opening the way for the export of fresh and chilled ostrich meat to the EU market. Exports to Europe of the low-cholesterol red meat began in 2005. In 2005 Botswana had 46 registered ostrich farms, producing some 5,000 birds annually for slaughter. In 2006 it was announced that a P13m. model ostrich multiplication farm was to be established at Dibete. This farm experienced some teething problems in that year, which caused the temporary closure of the ostrich abbatoir, but it reopened in December 2006. The demand for ostrich meat far outweighs the supply.

In the arable sector commercial farmers provide a disproportionate share of crop production. Of the 85% of small-scale farms producing crops, almost one-third covered less than 3 ha, and only 6.8% covered more than the 10-ha minimum necessary for household self-sufficiency, even in years of adequate rains. As a result, two-thirds of rural households were reported to depend for as much as 40% of their income on members employed in the formal, predominantly commercial, agricultural sector.

In the mid-1980s land under irrigation totalled only 1,000 ha, the majority consisting of privately owned farms producing cash crops, primarily cotton, citrus fruits and tobacco. Botswana is considered to have substantial irrigation potential, particularly in the Okavango delta and Chobe areas. In view of the unique and fragile nature of the Okavango, especially, there are also significant possible environmental risks in realizing this potential, which became the subject of considerable study in the mid-1990s. Some experimentation, using flood-recession irrigation, was initiated at Molapo, on the eastern fringe of the Okavango. Pending the final outcome of environmental studies, it was planned to proceed with a scheme, costing P180m., to develop 5,000–10,000 ha of high-yielding crops by improving water- and crop-management systems. Other projects were also being studied under the Government's 'accelerated water-resource development programme'. According to government figures, even though Botswana is by and large an arid country, the proportion of the population who have sustainable access to safe drinking water is 98%, and the Government is continuing its efforts to bring this figure up to 100%.

MINERALS AND MINING

In 2005 Botswana was Africa's third largest mineral producer by value, but it was only after independence, in 1966, that the country was found to possess abundant reserves of diamonds, coal, copper-nickel, soda ash, potash and sodium sulphate. Substantial deposits of salts and plutonium, as well as smaller reserves of gold, silver and a variety of industrial minerals, were also identified. The mining sector contributed an estimated 40.8% of GDP in 2004/05, when the sector grew by 18.1% in a single year. In contrast, real mining-sector GDP declined by 4.4% in 2005/06, when it contributed 4.5% to GDP. The GDP of the sector increased, in real terms, at an average annual rate of 9.0% in 1995/96–2005/06. Botswana's diamond sector performed particularly well in 2000/01, despite the beginning of a global economic slowdown; growth was encouraged by the impact of the first full year of operations at the Orapa mine since its expansion. Global diamond prices were 14% higher in 2004 than in 2003. However, prices were sluggish in 2006, and despite a production increase from 31.9m. carats in 2005 to 33m. carats in 2006, revenue stagnated. Botswana produces about one-third of the world's total diamonds.

Large-scale mineral exploitation began in 1971, when the 117-ha Orapa diamond mine (the world's second largest, in terms of size) began production, and Botswana proceeded to develop a relatively diverse mining sector, with three major diamond mines, coal exploitation and copper-nickel production, as well as the mining of gold, industrial minerals and semi-precious stones. The Letlhakane pipe, near Orapa, began producing diamonds in 1977, and Jwaneng, 125 km west of Gaborone, came on stream in 1982. The Damtshaa mine, comprising four small diamond pipes 20 km east of Orapa, was formally commissioned in late October 2003. It was forecast to produce 5m. carats from 39m. metric tons of ore over the 31-year projected life of the mine. Output in 2003 was 292,270 carats, significantly exceeding the forecast of 250,050 carats. The diamond mines are owned and operated by the Debswana Diamond Co (Pty), a joint venture owned equally by the Botswana Government and De Beers Centenary AG of Switzerland, which employed more than 6,000 people in the mid-2000s. An expansion of plant capacity at Jwaneng was followed by a further expansion at Orapa, at a cost of P1,400m., which commenced in 1997. Orapa 2000 included an additional treatment plant and was expected to double Orapa's annual output from around 6m. carats to 11.9m. carats. Despite the depressed global demand at the time, the Government confirmed, in February 1999, that the Orapa expansion would proceed on schedule, and, indeed, President Mogae formally opened Orapa 2000 in May 2000. The result was that production at Orapa doubled in that year, coinciding with a marked upturn in global diamond sales. In 2001, the first full year after the opening of the Orapa expansion, Botswana produced 26.4m. carats, compared with 24.6m. in 2000. A further increase in capacity is planned, in the form of investment worth P223m. to develop the kimberlite pipes near Orapa. Although all current diamond-mining operations are carried out by Debswana, a number of other companies have become involved in diamond exploration, conducting extensive ground surveys. The Botswana Government and De Beers successfully negotiated Debswana's renewal of the Jwaneng mining lease, signing the Heads of Agreement document in December 2004. All financial terms had been agreed and were made retroactive to August 2004, when the previous lease expired.

Since the mid-1980s the diamond industry has continued to strengthen its role as the mainstay of Botswana's vigorous economic performance. In 2001 a UN initiative to boycott so-called 'conflict diamonds' gave a further boost to the industry, when overseas officials visited the country and proclaimed Botswana's diamonds to be 'blood-free'. The enforcement mechanism is a certification scheme aimed at excluding diamonds from the world market that have been traded for arms by rebel movements in conflict zones. Botswana rapidly became one of the major beneficiaries of this initiative, known as the Kimberley Process Certification Scheme. Botswana was elected to the position of Vice-Chair of the Kimberley Process for 2005, a post which led automatically to the Chair position in 2006. The number of diamond-cutting and -polishing factories in Botswana rose from four in 2005 to 16 in 2007. The number of workers employed by these factories rose from 650 in 2004 to 785 in 2005. The development of these diamond factories is an indication of a subtle but unmistakable shift in the power ratio of the two 50:50 partners in Debswana. Previously, De Beers would have simply vetoed any efforts towards vertical development or greater value added within Botswana in favour of the status quo—shipping all the diamonds off in rough form into Central Selling Organization coffers—however, Botswana is now exercising much more control over this commodity and is emerging as a global player in the diamond market. Furthermore, in 2006 the Government granted a licence to a company other than Debswana to mine diamonds in Botswana. DiamonEx (Pty) Ltd, also of Botswana, should begin production by the end of 2007 at a site near Lerala.

Production of copper-nickel matte at Selebi-Phikwe began in 1974, and output rose steadily, reaching some 50,000 metric tons per year by the late 1980s. However, the value of sales of matte per ton declined consistently during the 1980s, owing to depressed international prices for nickel and copper. These low prices created acute financial problems for the operating company, Bamangwato Concessions Ltd (BCL), and for its parent group, Botswana Roan Selection Trust. A resurgence of prices for base metals after mid-1987 improved BCL's financial position, allowing it to bring on stream two new copper-nickel mines, including the high-grade Selebi North mine, with a view to reaching full capacity of about 1,500 tons of ore per day by mid-1990. Nevertheless, another slump in international copper prices in 1993 rendered BCL unable to cover its operating costs. The Government subsequently warned that BCL would need a substantial level of new capital investment, together with stringent restraints on wages, if the mine were to survive as a viable operation; however, the reserves of ore at Selebi-Phikwe were expected to run out by 2010. The other copper-nickel mine (at Selkirk, east of Francistown) was opened at the end of 1988 by a consortium of Swiss and British investors, with an annual production capacity of 60,000 tons of high-grade ore. Plans to develop the adjacent, and larger, Phoenix deposit came to fruition, and the Phoenix expansion—making it the largest nickel mine in Africa—helped to raise BCL's output from 2m. tons in 2002 to 2.5m. tons in 2003. However, BCL was forced to close down for more than two months in 2004 in order to rebuild its smelter. The timing of the closure was particularly unfortunate as global copper prices experienced a 60% rise in 2004, while global nickel prices increased by 40% over the same period, and the company was unable to take full advantage of these favourable price trends. Fortunately, the global prices of these commodities continued at these higher levels during 2005, and BCL was eventually able to profit from them. As a result, the company did not apply for government borrowing during 2005 and even found itself in a position to pay back some of its previous loans. Output of copper nickel and cobalt declined slightly in 2006 in volume terms, but prices for these metals were buoyant. The nickel price doubled from US $6.80 per lb to more than $15.00 per lb during 2006, and the copper price also doubled, from $1.84 per lb to a high of $3.63 before falling back to $2.75 per lb in December 2006.

Plans to exploit Botswana's coal reserves have been restricted by the low level of international prices and by the great distance to major coal markets. Production amounted to 983,833 metric tons in 2006. Some 17,000m. tons of steam coal suitable for power-plant use have been identified in the east, and coal is extracted at Morupule Colliery (a subsidiary of Debswana), where output rose from 579,400 tons in 1987 to almost 1m. tons in 2001, before declining to 916,036 tons in 2004. Most of the coal was for electricity generation to service the mining industry and the soda ash plant at Sua Pan (see below). The Government has also encouraged domestic coal use, in order to conserve fuel wood. Prohibitive transport costs impeded the export of coal from Morupule, and capacity was limited to 1.2m. tons. In 2004 it was estimated that unmined deposits of coal at Morupule amounted to 5,000m. tons. A new P87m. coal-washing plant at Morupule received approval from the Government in 2006, with construction due to begin by the end of 2007. Studies have revealed that substantial exploitable coal-bed methane reserves exist at Kodibeleng, and pilot production wells were spudded in 2006. Construction is to begin in early 2008 on a 3,600-MW coal-fired power station at Mmamabula, the output of which would be exported mainly to the Electricity Supply Commission (ESKOM) of South Africa, with a target delivery date of early 2011. The US $6,000m. Phase I will create 6,000 temporary construction jobs over a four-year period as well as 1,350 permanent jobs after start-up. Power exports are forecast to earn $850m. per annum over 40 years; the scheme's capacity is more than five times the national power requirement of Botswana.

In 1986 South African interests began talks with the Botswana Government for a joint venture, Soda Ash Botswana (Pty) Ltd, to build a plant at Sua Pan, with forecast annual output of some 300,000 metric tons of soda ash and 650,000 tons of salt. The success of the project depended on the sale of the soda ash to South Africa. The scheme was troubled from the start, with output lower than expected, initially owing to technical problems, and subsequently to a lack of demand and increased competition in the South African market. Soda Ash Botswana was liquidated in May 1995, to be succeeded later that year by Botswana Ash (Pty) Ltd (Botash), 50% of which is owned by the Botswana Government, 14% by the Anglo American Corporation, 14% by De Beers and 14% by African Explosives and Chemical Industries, with the remaining 8% held by a consortium of banks. Despite being relieved of a heavy debt burden, Botash's problems continued at first, when floods in 1996 once again halted production. However, the company achieved a 69.1% rise in production in the first quarter of 1997, compared to the same period of 1996. In June 1999 the company achieved its highest-ever monthly production level for salt, at 32,300 tons, and by 2000 Botash had become a profitable concern. Production of soda ash increased from 276,218 metric tons in 2005 to an estimated 300,000 tons in 2006, while output of salt rose from 196,443 tons in 2005 to 217,014 tons in 2006.

For many years gold has been mined in Botswana, intermittently and on a small scale. In 1987 a joint venture, Shashe Mines, was formed by the Botswana Government and private US and Canadian interests to explore gold deposits at Map Nora near Francistown; exploitation of the mineral commenced in 1989. The Bonanza gold mine in Tati Schist, 40 km from Francistown, has proven reserves of 2,040 metric tons, with a gold content of 14.8 g per ton, in association with silver and other minerals. Kudu Mining also operates the Rainbow gold mine, some 60 km from Francistown. A new gold mine at Mupane, 30 km south-east of Francistown, commenced production in 2004. The mine was expected to produce about 3,100 kg of gold per year but has yet to reach this target; however, output rose from 2,705 kg in 2005 to 2,800 kg in 2006.

MANUFACTURING

The GDP of the manufacturing sector grew at an average annual rate of 2.4% in 1995/06–2005/06. It increased by 7.7% in 2004/05, but declined in 2005/06 by 3.3%. The largest factor inhibiting growth has been the small size of the Botswana market, at 1.86m. people, according to 2006 UN estimates. Trade barriers are another inhibiting factor, restricting Botswana-based manufacturers from operating in neighbouring, larger markets, particularly South Africa. Nevertheless, 2005 saw the establishment of a number of new ventures, albeit on a modest scale, including companies producing lead ingots, asphalt and bitumen, sewage pipes, leather, t-shirts, pasta, biscuits, float glass and bone china. A can-manufacturing company at Lobatse began production in February 2007. Manufacturers exporting to Zimbabwe were particularly hard hit by that country's inability to settle payments for goods from Botswana from 2000 onwards. However, in the late 1990s the percentage of Botswana's exports that went to Zimbabwe declined and by 2001 represented only about 2.6% of total exports. Botswana's weak infrastructure, which was once cited as a deterrent to export growth, is now being significantly improved, but import dependence and a shortage of skilled manpower remain. The Government is addressing the skills shortage, with some success, through concerted efforts to improve education and training. Import dependence remains a problem, however; the low percentage of value added to some products in Botswana is used by neighbouring states as an excuse to maintain trade barriers. Nevertheless, as the labour force becomes more skilled, there will be greater potential for higher proportions of value to be added.

The manufacturing sector is regarded as the primary stimulus for job creation, which is often cited as the Botswana economy's most serious challenge. Past performance indicates that the sector does hold considerable job-creation potential. Formal employment in manufacturing stood at 4,400 jobs in 1978, with more than one-third of those posts at the parastatal BMC (see above); by 1991 the sector had created more than six times as many jobs and was employing 27,548 people, while the BMC's proportion had dropped to 14%. Formal-sector employment increased 10-fold in the next decade; the 2001 census found that 270,300 people held formal-sector jobs in March 2001, the majority of them in the private sector. The manufacturing sector's generally strong performance can be attributed to a number of government policies, based on the Financial Assistance Policy, which provided a wide range of subsidies to potential entrepreneurs, particularly in the small-scale sector, and a highly attractive foreign investment code. An employment survey in late 2004 found that 11,005 new jobs were created between September 2003 and September 2004, twice as many as had been created between September 2002 and September 2003. Formal-sector employment grew by 2.8% between March 2004 and March 2005, down from 3.1% the previous year. The 2.8% figure is below the NDP 9 target but is higher than population growth. A 2006 labour force survey revealed that the manufacturing sector employed 6.6% of the working population.

The Government's current diversification programme also places priority on the country's need to develop manufacturing. The parastatal Botswana Development Corporation (BDC) has for three decades supported more than 100 enterprises, including companies involved in brewing, sugar packaging, furniture making, clothing manufacture, tourism, milling and concrete products. In the services sector the Corporation is considering supporting industrial and retail showrooms and a hotel and amusement park. The Botswana Export Development and Investment Authority (BEDIA) was established in the late 1990s to promote exports of the country's manufactured goods. In February 2002 the Government announced proposed changes aimed at reducing delays in licensing, liberalizing trade and promoting competition. BEDIA also seeks ways to add value locally to Botswana's own raw materials; schemes under consideration to this end range from jewellery to textiles, garment manufacture, glassmaking, tanneries, leather-goods manufacture and even information-technology products.

ENERGY AND WATER DEVELOPMENT

Rapid growth in the economy and in the population resulted in an equally rapid expansion in the demand for energy and water. The Botswana Power Corporation (BPC) has implemented a continuing programme of capacity expansion, of which a major project was the Morupule power station. Using coal mined at Morupule, the station became the focus of a new national grid system linking the existing northern and southern networks, based on the Selebi-Phikwe and Gaborone power stations, with six 30-MW units in operation. A project to link Botswana into the Zambian and Zimbabwean grids was completed in 1991; and in the late 1990s, as part of a major expansion into other areas of southern Africa by South Africa's ESKOM, a 400-kilovolt transmission line linking Bulawayo in Zimbabwe to Matimba in South Africa was to run across Botswana. In May 2002 the BPC announced the signing of two agreements with the Namibia Power Corporation, under which Namibia would supply power to Botswana. The arrangements included the construction of a 132-kilovolt transmission line, work on which had already begun, with joint funding from the two Governments. In 2006 the BPC embarked upon a US $600m. expansion of generating capacity at Morupule power station, with construction scheduled to start in November 2007 and with completion expected in 2009/10; this project will treble generating capacity from 132 MW in 2006 to 532 MW in 2010. Apart from the further work at Morupule, the main short-term focus of the electricity programme was the extension of the rural catchment area of the national grid, with the aim of conserving fuel wood and reducing petroleum demand. About 100 villages were brought into the national grid in 1997–2000. In 2002 about 30% of the households in Botswana had mains electricity; the government target was to increase that proportion to 70% by 2009. The challenge of meeting that objective is two-fold. First, many of the households without electricity lie beyond the current reach of the national-grid infrastructure; only further construction can electrify these households. Second, some households that lie within the reach of the national grid are not connected because the cost is prohibitive; a change in the tariff policy or subsidization of the connection charges will be required for the electrification of these households.

For an arid country such as Botswana, the provision of water is a formidable challenge. Water-development efforts are laid out in the National Water Master Plan (NWMP), which in 2004 underwent an extensive review. Beyond the remote Okavango and Chobe areas, the country has only minimal surface water supplies, and 80% of national demand is met from groundwater sources. Livestock is the largest single user, consuming about one-third, followed by mining, urban areas, and rural areas and villages. Although not fully assessed, groundwater supplies are not expected to exceed 4,000m. cu m per year, and intense competition for water resources has emerged in the main urban and mining areas in the east, leading to the postponement of plans for the development of industrial sites, particularly in Gaborone. The situation has been further exacerbated by recurrent drought. Aid from overseas is currently being used to develop water resources. In addition, an 'accelerated water resource development programme' sought to provide more dams, in an attempt to fulfil the projected requirements of the 1990s. Now part of the NWMP, the Ntimbale Dam was completed in 2006, with ancillary installations due to be completed in June 2007. Construction is to begin in the 2007/08 financial year on dams at Dikgathong, Thune, Lothane and Mosetse. Other water projects include the Maun Water Supply and Sanitation Design, the Kanye-Molepolole Emergency Water Supply Plan, the Tonota Emergency Water Supply Plan and the construction of a booster pump station for the Ramotswa water-supply system.

FOREIGN TRADE AND BALANCE OF PAYMENTS

Diamonds have been Botswana's principal export by value since the mid-1970s, accounting for as much as 88% of total earnings and for more than 50% of government revenue in some years. Other exports include copper-nickel matte, meat and meat products, soda ash, salt and textiles. Botswana's principal imports are machinery and electrical equipment, food, beverages and tobacco, vehicles and transport equipment, chemical and rubber products, wood and paper products, metals and metal products, and textiles and footwear. The United Kingdom is generally the principal client, purchasing some four-fifths of all exports. Other major clients include other countries of the Southern African Customs Union (SACU) and continental Europe. Botswana's main supplier is SACU, which provides more than three-quarters of all imports.

While diamond revenue stagnated in 2006 when lower global prices cancelled out higher export volume, between 2003 and 2006 export revenue from non-diamond exports grew by some 20% per annum in US dollar terms. The current account of the balance of payments for 2006 was estimated to have reached P11,926m., an increase from the record P8,360.2m. recorded in 2005. The overall account—which had registered a modest deficit of P272m. in 2004—rebounded in 2005, with a surplus of P7,036m., rising again in 2006 to P10,255.8m. The Government regards the high level of reserves as essential to sustain Botswana's future economic development as diamond earnings level out, with no single source of export revenue to replace them. The rapid escalation in reserves after 1985 was paralleled, however, by increasing criticism of the Government's concern with long-term financial security. According to critics, the Government's conservative fiscal policies were depressing productive investment, particularly by the private sector, and were subsequently hindering job creation.

Botswana operates an open economy, with combined import and export values exceeding GDP, making both the domestic economy and the external account vulnerable to fluctuations in the terms of trade and exchange rates. The Government has maintained a flexible, trade-orientated exchange-rate policy since the pula was established in 1976 as the national currency. In 2002 Botswana introduced a value-added tax (VAT), which replaced the old sales tax. For an economy as open as Botswana's, even in years of considerable global upheaval, such as 1998, the rate of inflation remained remarkably stable. Botswana's balance-of-payments situation was also helped by its low debt burden. The country's total debt-service costs in 2006 were P1,270m., of which P850m. was set aside for the redemption of a five-year domestic bond issued in 2003. The Government has already announced plans to re-issue this bond. Botswana's total external debt can be paid off completely out of the country's foreign reserves 50 times over.

GOVERNMENT FINANCE

At independence about one-half of Botswana's public expenditure was financed directly by the Government of the United Kingdom. This extreme level of reliance on external support was altered by Botswana's accession to SACU in 1969, and the country had become financially independent of the United Kingdom by 1972/73. From 1977/78 until 1982/83 customs revenue constituted the principal component of government income, but since then this source has been overtaken by mineral revenue, which in 2006/07 accounted for an estimated 40.6% of total revenue (excluding grants), compared with 27.5% for customs and excise revenue. A new SACU agreement was signed in October 2002, and in June 2003 negotiations began towards the creation of a SACU-USA Free Trade Area; these negotiations dragged on into 2006, protracted by the inability to reach agreement over intellectual property rights that would have hindered SACU member states' ability to import drugs needed to treat HIV/AIDS and talk stalled in April. In July an agreement was signed between SACU and the European Free Trade Area, granting SACU exporters free access to the Iceland, Liechtenstein, Norway and Switzerland markets. The balanced 2007/08 budget, presented in February 2007, called for total spending of P25,912m. and was in keeping with the Fiscal Rule enacted by Parliament in December 2005, which prevented budgets from totalling more than 40% of GDP. Projected total revenue was P27,179m. Recurrent expenditure amounted to P18,717m., while development expenditure was projected at P7,257m. The largest single allocation, at 23.2%, was for education.

POPULATION AND EMPLOYMENT

According to the census conducted in August 2001, between 1991 and 2001 the population grew by an average of 2.4% per year, a significantly smaller rate of increase compared with the 3.5% per year recorded between 1981 and 1991. In its 2000 revision of world population prospects, the UN estimated that in 1999 88% of the 33m. adults in the world infected by HIV resided in just 45 countries, of which 35 were in sub-Saharan Africa, with the most adversely affected country being Botswana, where about one in every three adults was infected by HIV. The average life expectancy at birth in Botswana, according to the UN, would have been 67 years in 1995–2000 in the absence of HIV/AIDS, but instead was estimated at 44.4 years for the same period. In 2000–05 the UN estimated the life expectancy to be 46.6 years. The UN's population-growth forecasts for Botswana have consequently been revised downward, to 2.0% per year in 1995–2000 and to 1.2% per year in 2000–05. The population was expected to increase by just 1.1% in 2010–15. According to the 2001 census, the population of Botswana was 1,680,863, compared to 1,326,796 at the previous census in August 1991.

The impact of the HIV/AIDS epidemic on the country's economy will certainly be significant. On the one hand, a slower growth rate will mean that the challenge to create jobs for school-leavers will not be quite so difficult; on the other, companies often point to a shortage of skills as a major constraint on investment, and government resources spent on training a skilled labour force will be diluted, if one in four people trained has a shorter working life. The IMF in October 2002 commended the Botswana Government for its 'head-on approach to the challenges of HIV/AIDS'. However, the Government itself recognized that its measures, such as government-funded universal availability of ART and its programme for the prevention of mother-to-child transmission of HIV/AIDS (see above) would need to achieve a higher take-up rate than had so far been recorded, if they were to attain their maximum effectiveness. The take-up rate has steadily improved since that assessment and is now above 90%, but the Government is aiming for 100% coverage.

During the 1980s Botswana experienced rapid urbanization; of the total population, only 18.2% lived in urban areas in 1981, whereas 52.1% lived in urban areas in 2001. This increase in the pressure for employment exceeded the downwardly revised rate of population growth, and the challenge of finding jobs for the continuing high number of school-leavers entering the labour market each year remained a priority. Whereas 57% of those in formal-sector employment worked in the private sector in March 1997, more than one-half of the 12,200 jobs created in the following 12 months were in the public sector. In 2002/03 the private sector accounted for the majority of newly created jobs. The Government estimated in 2004 that about 15,000 formal-sector jobs had been created in 2001–03. The informal sector, engaged mainly in wholesale and retail trade and in light manufacturing, comprised some 57,240 workers in 1998, of whom about 42% were self-employed. Manufacturing is seen as offering the greatest potential for job creation, but the

Government is also seeking to provide better living conditions in rural areas so that people will not have to move to towns and cities to have access to basic amenities, health care and jobs. A 2006 labour force survey showed that 548,594 were actively employed in Botswana (35,982 of which were employed in the manufacturing sector), while the unemployment rate stood at 17.6%.

The Government in 2000 studied the informal sector with some intensity, in view of its job-creation potential, and since then every aspect of the formal sector has also been studied to maximize that potential. Job creation had long been a stated priority in government planning, and the draft NDP 9 (see above), covering the period 2003/04–2008/09, continued to place emphasis on economic diversification as a means of generating employment and reducing poverty. The plan also embraced external-sector liberalization, the rationalization of public-sector activities through restructuring and so-called 'right-sizing', privatization, and measures to harness more of the country's limited agricultural potential. Clearly, challenges remain, and Botswana's leadership acknowledges this openly, but much has been achieved in the four decades since independence. At home, a Household Incomes and Expenditure Survey undertaken in 2002/03 found that the proportion of Botswana citizens living below the poverty datum line had fallen from 47% in 1993/94 to 30% in 2002/03. In the global context, Botswana's reputation for sound economic management is evidenced in a number of ways, not least the country's A-grade rating for four successive years by both Moody's and Standard and Poor's. In 2006, the 40th anniversary of Botswana's independence, Botswana's Governments—past and present—could point to a great deal of achievement in economic management. The motto 'diamonds for development' is no mere hollow phrase; it is an action plan that has seen much real implementation, with hard evidence to prove it. However, the greatest challenge facing Botswana is one that was unknown in 1966: HIV/AIDS. The Government acknowledges this and is proactively addressing the problem. Diamond revenue is of significant assistance in funding this challenge, as well as others, and statistics demonstrate that Botswana's measured approach to this disease is achieving some success.

Statistical Survey

Source (unless otherwise stated): Central Statistics Office, Private Bag 0024, Gaborone; tel. 352200; fax 352201; e-mail csobots@gov.bw; internet www.cso.gov.bw.

Area and Population

AREA, POPULATION AND DENSITY

Area (sq km)	581,730*
Population (census results)	
21 August 1991	1,326,796
17 August 2001	
Males	813,488
Females	867,375
Total	1,680,863
Population (UN estimates at mid-year)†	
2004	1,815,000
2005	1,836,000
2006	1,858,000
Density (per sq km) at mid-2006	3.2

* 224,607 sq miles.

† Source: UN, *World Population Prospects: The 2006 Revision*.

ADMINISTRATIVE DISTRICTS
(population at census of August 2001)

Barolong	47,477	Kweneng	230,535
Central	501,381	Lobatse	29,689
Central Kalahari Game Reserve	689	Ngamiland	122,024
Chobe	18,258	Ngwaketse West	10,471
Delta	2,688	North-East	49,399
Francistown	83,023	Orapa	9,151
Gaborone	186,007	Selebi-Phikwe	49,849
Ghanzi	32,481	South-East	60,623
Jwaneng	15,179	Southern	113,704
Kgalagadi	42,049	Sowa	2,879
Kgatleng	73,507		

PRINCIPAL TOWNS
(population at August 2001 census)

Gaborone (capital)	186,007	Serowe	42,444
Francistown	83,023	Kanye	40,628
Molepolole	54,561	Mahalapye	39,719
Selebi-Phikwe	49,849	Mochudi	36,692
Maun	43,776	Lobatse	29,689

Mid-2005 (incl. suburbs, UN estimate): Gaborone 210,000 (Source: UN, *World Urbanization Prospects: The 2005 Revision*).

BIRTHS AND DEATHS
(annual averages, UN estimates)

	1990–95	1995–2000	2000–05
Birth rate (per 1,000)	32.4	29.1	26.0
Death rate (per 1,000)	7.2	12.1	16.3

Source: UN, *World Population Prospects: The 2006 Revision*.

2001 (12 months prior to August 2001 census): Births 53,735 (birth rate 41.1 per 1,000); Deaths 20,823 (death rate 12.4 per 1,000) (Source: UN, *Demographic Yearbook*).

Expectation of life (years at birth, UN estimates): 34.9 (males 34.9; females 34.8) in 2004 (Source: UN Development Programme, *Human Development Report*).

ECONOMICALLY ACTIVE POPULATION
(number of persons aged 7 years and over, 2006 labour force survey)

	Males	Females	Total
Agriculture, hunting, forestry and fishing	103,924	65,407	169,331
Mining and quarrying	12,396	1,716	14,112
Manufacturing	16,020	19,963	35,982
Electricity, gas and water supply	2,697	1,537	4,234
Construction	22,169	4,265	26,434
Wholesale and retail trade; repair of motor vehicles, motorcycles and personal and household goods	28,791	50,804	79,596
Hotels and restaurants	3,848	10,968	14,816
Transport, storage and communications	10,292	5,381	15,674
Financial intermediation	3,018	5,406	8,424
Real estate, renting and business services	15,338	9,778	25,116
Public administration and defence; compulsory social security	34,372	25,417	59,789
Education	15,190	27,987	43,177
Health and social work	5,503	8,612	14,114
Other community, social and personal service activities	5,277	5,283	10,560
Private households with employed persons	8,013	18,247	26,261
Extra-territorial organizations and bodies	456	439	895
Activities not adequately defined	—	78	78
Total employed	287,303	261,290	548,594

Health and Welfare

KEY INDICATORS

Total fertility rate (children per woman, 2005)	3.0
Under-5 mortality rate (per 1,000 live births, 2005)	120
HIV/AIDS (% of persons aged 15–49, 2005)	24.1
Physicians (per 1,000 head, 2004)	0.40
Hospital beds (per 1,000 head, 2003)	2.20
Health expenditure (2004): US $ per head (PPP)	504.3
Health expenditure (2004): % of GDP	6.4
Health expenditure (2004): public (% of total)	62.9
Access to water (% of persons, 2004)	95
Access to sanitation (% of persons, 2004)	42
Human Development Index (2004): ranking	131
Human Development Index (2004): value	0.570

For sources and definitions, see explanatory note on p. vi.

Agriculture

PRINCIPAL CROPS
('000 metric tons)

	2003	2004*	2005*
Maize	1.6	7.1	7.4
Sorghum	32.3	19.6	15.9
Sunflower seed*	7	8	9
Roots and tubers*	93	96	99
Pulses*	18.5	17.1	16.6
Vegetables*	16.4	16.3	16.2
Fruit*	10.6	10.3	10.1

* FAO estimates.

Source: FAO.

LIVESTOCK
('000 head, year ending September, FAO estimates)

	2003	2004	2005
Cattle	3,100	3,100	3,100
Horses	33	33	33
Asses	332.5	332.5	332.5
Sheep	300	300	300
Goats	1,700	1,850	1,950
Pigs	8	8	8
Poultry	4,000	4,000	4,000

LIVESTOCK PRODUCTS
('000 metric tons)

	2003	2004	2005*
Cattle meat	26.9	26.6*	25.1
Goat meat*	4.7	5.1	5.4
Chicken meat*	5.4	5.4	5.4
Other meat*	14.0	14.1	14.1
Cows' milk*	101.5	101.5	101.5
Goats' milk*	3.9	3.9	3.9
Hen eggs*	64.3	64.3	64.3

* FAO estimate(s).

Source: FAO.

Forestry

ROUNDWOOD REMOVALS
('000 cubic metres, excl. bark, FAO estimates)

	2003	2004	2005
Industrial wood	105.0	105.0	105.0
Fuel wood	649.6	655.0	660.8
Total	754.6	760.0	765.8

Source: FAO.

Fishing

(metric tons, live weight)

	2003	2004	2005
Tilapias	72	102	83
Other freshwater fishes	50	59	49
Total catch	122	161	132

Note: Figures exclude aquatic mammals, recorded by number rather than weight. According to FAO estimates, the number of Nile crocodiles caught was: 9 in 2003; nil in 2004; nil in 2005.

Source: FAO.

Mining

(metric tons, unless otherwise indicated)

	2003	2004	2005*
Hard coal	822,780	913,087	984,876
Copper ore†‡	24,292	21,195	26,704
Nickel ore‡	27,400	22,292	28,212
Cobalt†‡	294	223	326
Salt	229,432	208,319	243,945
Diamonds ('000 carats)	30,412	31,125	31,890
Soda ash (natural)	309,350	263,358	279,085
Sand and gravel ('000 cu metres)	1,485	2,330	2,110

* Preliminary.

† Figures refer to the metal content of matte; product smelted was granulated nickel-copper-cobalt matte.

‡ Figures refer to the nickel content of matte and include some product not reported as milled.

Source: US Geological Survey.

Industry

SELECTED PRODUCTS

	2001	2002	2003
Beer ('000 hectolitres)	1,692	1,396	1,198
Soft drinks ('000 hectolitres)	431	389	405
Electric energy (million kWh)	1,044	1,009	n.a.

Source: UN, *Industrial Commodity Statistics Yearbook*.

Finance

CURRENCY AND EXCHANGE RATES

Monetary Units
100 thebe = 1 pula (P).

Sterling, Dollar and Euro Equivalents (31 May 2007)
£1 sterling = 12.304 pula;
US $1 = 6.223 pula;
€1 = 8.372 pula;
100 pula = £8.13 = $16.07 = €11.95.

Average Exchange Rate (pula per US $)
2004 4.693
2005 5.110
2006 5.8366

BUDGET

(million pula, year ending 31 March)

Revenue*	2005/06	2006/07†	2007/08‡
Taxation	20,130.0	24,417.3	24,555.7
Mineral revenue	11,045.1	11,374.2	10,890.0
Customs and excise	3,929.9	7,361.9	7,398.3
Non-mineral income taxes	3,003.2	3,315.6	3,553.4
Other taxes	2,151.8	2,365.6	2,714.0
General sales tax/VAT	1,978.9	2,190.8	2,519.4
Other current revenue	2,023.6	1,886.1	2,299.8
Interest	97.3	36.2	58.7
Other property income	912.0	696.6	999.9
Fees, charges, etc.	957.6	1,092.5	1,191.2
Sales of fixed assets and land	56.8	60.7	50.1
Total	22,153.6	26,303.4	26,855.5

Expenditure§	2005/06	2006/07†	2007/08‡
General services (incl. defence)	5,268.0	6,244.6	7,517.7
Social services	8,127.0	10,735.1	12,058.0
Education	4,197.4	5,481.4	6,009.9
Health	2,056.4	2,686.7	3,378.4
Housing, urban and regional development	1,082.8	1,601.1	1,541.4
Food and social welfare programme	189.5	151.0	119.2
Other community and social services	600.9	815.0	1,009.0
Economic services	2,347.1	3,473.6	4,368.9
Agriculture, forestry and fishing	791.8	689.6	757.0
Mining	–134.7	147.7	193.7
Electricity and water supply	931.7	1,013.7	1,064.1
Roads	324.5	814.5	840.3
Others	433.8	808.3	1,513.9
Transfers	1,889.8	1,956.2	1,967.6
Deficit grants to local authorities	1,571.9	1,678.6	1,823.1
Interest on public debt	317.9	277.6	144.5
Total	17,631.9	22,409.5	25,912.3

* Excluding grants received (million pula): 113.0 in 2005/06; 493.5 in 2006/07; 323.6 in 2007/08.
† Estimates.
‡ Budget estimates.
§ Including net lending (million pula): –306.1 in 2005/06; –47.2 in 2006/07; –60.8 in 2007/08.

Source: Bank of Botswana, Gaborone, *Annual Report 2006*.

INTERNATIONAL RESERVES

(US $ million at 31 December)

	2004	2005	2006
IMF special drawing rights	53.46	50.85	55.53
Reserve position in IMF	31.84	10.59	9.40
Foreign exchange	5,576.13	6,247.62	7,927.47
Total	5,661.43	6,309.06	7,992.40

Source: IMF, *International Financial Statistics*.

MONEY SUPPLY

(million pula at 31 December)

	2004	2005	2006
Currency outside banks	632	625	753
Demand deposits at commercial banks	2,989	3,206	4,387
Total money (incl. others)	4,225	3,998	5,157

Source: IMF, *International Financial Statistics*.

COST OF LIVING

(Consumer Price Index; base: 2000 = 100)

	2003	2004	2005
Food (incl. beverages)	125.0	130.9	137.9
Clothing (incl. footwear)	112.4	114.8	116.9
Housing	138.0	153.9	163.9
Fuel	118.0	125.2	147.1
All items (incl. others)	125.8	134.4	146.1

2006: All items 163.0.

Source: ILO.

NATIONAL ACCOUNTS

(million pula at current prices, year ending 30 June, provisional figures)

National Income and Product

	1998/99	1999/2000	2000/01
Domestic primary incomes	17,098.6	19,867.7	22,944.3
Consumption of fixed capital	2,647.4	3,068.5	3,623.2
Gross domestic product (GDP) at factor cost	19,746.0	22,936.2	26,567.5
Taxes on production and imports	1,887.8	2,106.9	2,188.9
Less Subsidies	110.0	100.0	120.0
GDP in market prices	21,523.8	24,943.1	28,636.5

Expenditure on the Gross Domestic Product

	2003/04	2004/05	2005/06
Government final consumption expenditure	9,286.2	10,811.2	11,785.6
Private final consumption expenditure	12,243.7	13,846.2	15,022.7
Increase in stocks	9,183.8	7,990.8	4,559.1
Gross fixed capital formation	8,867.8	9,797.9	10,402.9
Total domestic expenditure	39,581.5	42,446.1	41,770.3
Exports of goods and services	17,875.6	24,279.3	32,125.5
Less Imports of goods and services	14,624.1	17,104.5	16,758.3
Statistical discrepancy	–260.0	—	—
GDP in purchasers' values	42,573.0	49,620.9	57,137.4
GDP at constant 1993/94 prices	20,941.2	22,865.7	22,672.1

Source: Bank of Botswana, Gaborone, *Annual Report 2006*.

Gross Domestic Product by Economic Activity

	2003/04	2004/05	2005/06
Agriculture, hunting, forestry and fishing	951.8	899.9	1,027.9
Mining and quarrying	15,078.9	19,222.4	22,178.0
Manufacturing	1,647.5	1,772.5	1,895.6
Water and electricity	1,058.9	1,216.2	1,398.0
Construction	2,103.4	2,241.7	2,426.9
Trade, restaurants and hotels	4,894.4	5,082.5	6,116.0
Transport, post and telecommunications	1,398.6	1,519.1	2,040.5
Finance, insurance and business services	4,517.4	5,169.7	5,919.3
Government services	7,231.8	8,104.1	9,509.6
Social and personal services	1,594.7	1,884.7	2,259.2
Sub-total	40,477.5	47,112.7	54,771.0
Less Imputed bank service charge.	1,577.4	1,799.8	2,250.8
GDP at basic prices	38,900.1	45,312.9	52,520.2
Import duties	1,971.8	2,315.0	2,643.5
Taxes on products	1,918.9	2,240.4	2,254.8
Less Subsidies on products	217.8	247.4	281.1
GDP in purchasers' values	42,573.0	49,620.9	57,137.4

Source: Bank of Botswana, Gaborone, *Annual Report 2006*.

BALANCE OF PAYMENTS
(million pula)

	2004	2005*	2006†
Exports of goods f.o.b.	17,344.6	22,631.5	26,558.3
Imports of goods f.o.b.	–13,440.5	–14,440.1	–15,135.7
Trade balance	3,904.1	8,195.5	11,422.6
Exports of services	3,511.3	4,496.6	4,523.6
Imports of services	–3,715.3	–4,331.9	–3,911.5
Balance on goods and services	3,700.1	8,360.2	12,034.7
Other income received	1,065.5	2,330.1	2,604.5
Other income paid	–5,882.6	–6,478.3	–6,474.4
Balance on goods, services and income	–1,117.0	4,212.0	8,164.8
Current transfers received	3,486.7	4,578.9	4,949.2
Current transfers paid	–1,017.6	–1,112.8	–1,188.1
Current balance	1,352.0	7,678.5	11,926.0
Capital account (net)	149.2	160.8	125.7
Direct investment abroad	181.9	–285.5	–119.1
Direct investment from abroad	1,835.2	1,423.7	1,591.9
Portfolio investment assets	–2,055.3	–2,067.0	–3,448.1
Portfolio investment liabilities	–137.0	83.0	n.a.
Other investment assets	–985.1	–777.8	n.a.
Other investment liabilities	–396.0	1,328.1	484.4
Net errors and omissions	–216.8	–508.0	–102.7
Overall balance	–271.8	7,035.6	10,255.8

* Estimates.
† Provisional.

Source: Bank of Botswana, Gaborone, *Annual Report 2006*.

External Trade

PRINCIPAL COMMODITIES
(million pula, provisional figures)

Imports c.i.f.	2004	2005	2006
Food, beverages and tobacco	2,049.0	2,244.1	2,468.8
Fuels	1,705.1	2,205.4	3,074.2
Chemicals and rubber products	1,694.6	1,983.5	2,354.9
Wood and paper products	1,376.8	689.6	736.2
Textiles and footwear	705.7	792.1	898.7
Metals and metal products	1,180.9	1,239.5	1,451.7
Machinery and electrical equipment	2,475.8	2,713.6	2,986.2
Vehicles and transport equipment	1,883.7	2,079.0	1,701.2
Total (incl. others)	14,695.5	16,078.3	17,762.8

Exports f.o.b.	2004	2005	2006
Meat and meat products	240.5	376.4	477.0
Diamonds	12,434.5	16,863.9	19,431.8
Copper-nickel matte	1,578.3	2,316.1	3,618.9
Textiles	560.9	1,117.2	914.7
Vehicles and parts	556.1	573.1	178.7
Total (incl. others)	16,489.7	22,480.8	26,180.1

PRINCIPAL TRADING PARTNERS
(million pula, provisional figures)

Imports c.i.f.	2004	2005	2006
SACU*	13,172.9	13,596.9	15,364.2
Zimbabwe	240.8	247.5	265.2
United Kingdom	482.8	204.3	193.3
Other Europe	890.1	883.8	540.7
Korea, Repub.	21.5	29.5	32.2
USA	201.3	201.9	156.5
Total (incl. others)	15,788.0	16,078.3	17,762.8

Exports f.o.b.	2004	2005	2006
SACU*	1,587.0	2,027.5	1,617.8
Zimbabwe	614.4	935.8	1,419.0
Other Africa	39.7	109.7	190.4
United Kingdom	12,266.6	17,011.2	19,099.4
Other Europe	301.6	288.4	503.8
USA	264.4	498.0	470.7
Total (incl. others)	16,489.7	22,480.8	26,180.1

* Southern African Customs Union, of which Botswana is a member; also including Lesotho, Namibia, South Africa and Swaziland.

Transport

RAILWAYS
(traffic)

	2002	2003	2004
Number of passengers ('000)	528.1	572.0	406.2
Freight ('000 metric tons)	2,080.2	1,995.8	1,974.1

Source: Botswana Railways.

Passenger-km (million): 528.1 in 2002; 572.0 in 2003 (Source: International Road Federation, *World Road Statistics*).

Freight net ton-km (million): 920.2 in 2003; 636.7 in 2004 (Source: International Road Federation, *World Road Statistics*).

ROAD TRAFFIC
(registered vehicles)

	2003	2004	2005
Cars	65,479	74,465	83,039
Light duty vehicles	75,355	79,122	79,812
Trucks	9,394	9,942	10,349
Buses	7,407	8,749	9,490
Tractors	2,957	3,068	2,913
Others (incl. trailers, motorcycles and tankers)	13,236	13,919	14,461
Total	173,828	189,265	200,064

CIVIL AVIATION
(traffic on scheduled services, million)

	2001	2002	2003
Kilometres flown	3	3	3
Passenger-km	77	80	83
Total ton-km	7	8	8

Source: UN, *Statistical Yearbook*.

Passengers carried: 482,740 in 2003; 533,684 in 2004; 552,350 in 2005.

Freight carried (metric tons): 682.9 in 2003; 756.8 in 2004; 920.6 in 2005.

Tourism

FOREIGN TOURIST ARRIVALS

Country of origin	2002	2003	2004
Namibia	64,001	69,587	57,542
South Africa	527,505	514,708	626,207
United Kingdom	20,548	18,518	24,069
Zambia	25,637	83,588	72,492
Zimbabwe	454,847	550,994	576,328
Total (incl. others)	1,273,784	1,405,535	1,522,807

Receipts from tourism (US $ million, excl. passenger transport): 319 in 2002; 457 in 2003; 549 in 2004.

Source: World Tourism Organization.

Communications Media

	2003	2004	2005
Telephones ('000 main lines in use)	131.8	136.5	132.0
Mobile cellular telephones ('000 subscribers)	522.8	563.8	823.1
Personal computers ('000 in use)	75	80	n.a.
Internet users ('000)	60	60	n.a.

Source: International Telecommunication Union.

Television receivers ('000 in use): 40 in 2000 (Source: UNESCO, *Statistical Yearbook*).

Radio receivers ('000 in use): 237 in 1997 (Source: UNESCO, *Statistical Yearbook*).

Facsimile machines: 3,529 in use in 1997/98 (Source: UNESCO, *Statistical Yearbook*).

Book production (first editions only): 158 titles in 1991, including 61 pamphlets (Source: UNESCO, *Statistical Yearbook*).

Daily newspapers: 1 in 2000 (average circulation 50,000 copies) (Source: UNESCO, *Statistical Yearbook*).

Non-daily newspapers: 3 in 1996 (average circulation 51,000 copies) (Source: UNESCO, *Statistical Yearbook*).

Other periodicals: 14 titles in 1992 (average circulation 177,000 copies) (Source: UNESCO, *Statistical Yearbook*).

Education

(2003, unless otherwise indicated)

	Institutions	Teachers*	Students
Primary	770	11,375	330,376
Secondary	278	9,649	156,786
Vocational and technical education	50	1,221	11,133
Teacher training	4	195	1,526
Colleges of education	2†	170‡	1,802

* Number of teachers trained.

† 2001 figure.

‡ 1998 figure.

Source: Ministry of Education, Gaborone.

Agricultural college (2004): Teachers 120; Students 850 (Source: Botswana College of Agriculture).

University (2005): Teachers 791; Students 15,725 (Source: University of Botswana).

Adult literacy rate (UNESCO estimates): 81.2% (males 80.4%; females 81.8%) in 2004 (Source: UN Development Programme, *Human Development Report*).

Directory

The Constitution

The Constitution of the Republic of Botswana took effect at independence on 30 September 1966; it was amended in August and September 1997. Its main provisions, with subsequent amendments, are summarized below:

EXECUTIVE

President

Executive power lies with the President of Botswana, who is also Commander-in-Chief of the armed forces. Election for the office of President is linked with the election of members of the National Assembly. The President is restricted to two terms of office. Presidential candidates must be over 30 years of age and receive at least 1,000 nominations. If there is more than one candidate for the Presidency, each candidate for office in the Assembly must declare support for a presidential candidate. The candidate for President who commands the votes of more than one-half of the elected members of the Assembly will be declared President. In the event of the death or resignation of the President, the Vice-President will automatically assume the Presidency. The President, who is an ex officio member of the National Assembly, holds office for the duration of Parliament. The President chooses four members of the National Assembly.

Cabinet

There is also a Vice-President, whose office is ministerial. The Vice-President is appointed by the President and deputizes in the absence of the President. The Cabinet consists of the President, the Vice-President and other Ministers, including Assistant Ministers, appointed by the President. The Cabinet is responsible to the National Assembly.

LEGISLATURE

Legislative power is vested in Parliament, consisting of the President and the National Assembly, acting after consultation in certain cases with the Ntlo ya Dikgosi. The President may withhold assent to a Bill passed by the National Assembly. If the same Bill is again presented after six months, the President is required to assent to it or to dissolve Parliament within 21 days.

Ntlo ya Dikgosi

Formerly known as the House of Chiefs, the Ntlo ya Dikgosi comprises the Chiefs of the eight principal tribes of Botswana as ex officio members, four members elected by sub-chiefs from their own number, and three members elected by the other 12 members of the Ntlo ya Dikgosi. Bills and motions relating to chieftaincy matters and alterations of the Constitution must be referred to the Ntlo ya Dikgosi, which may also deliberate and make representations on any matter. Following a review, in December 2005 it was announced that the membership of the Ntlo ya Dikgosi would be increased from 15 to 35.

National Assembly

The National Assembly consists of 40 members directly elected by universal adult suffrage, together with four members who are elected by the National Assembly from a list of candidates submitted by the President; the President, the Speaker and the Attorney-General are also ex officio members of the Assembly. The life of the Assembly is five years. In June 2002 the National Assembly voted to increase its membership from 40 directly elected members to 57, with effect from the following general election.

The Constitution contains a code of human rights, enforceable by the High Court.

The Government

HEAD OF STATE

President: FESTUS G. MOGAE (took office 1 April 1998; sworn in 20 October 1999 and, for a second term, 2 November 2004).

Vice-President: Lt-Gen. SERETSE KHAMA IAN KHAMA.

CABINET
(August 2007)

President: FESTUS G. MOGAE.

Vice-President: Lt-Gen. SERETSE KHAMA IAN KHAMA.

Minister for the Administration of Justice, responsible for the Attorney-General's Chambers, the Botswana Defence Force, the Police and the Directorate of Corruption and Economic Crime and Security: PHANDU SKELEMANI.

Minister for Public Service in the Office of the President, responsible for the Public Service, the Ombudsman, the Independent Electoral Commission and the National AIDS Co-ordinating Agency: DANIEL KWELAGOBE.

Minister of Health: Prof. SHEILA TLOU.

Minister of Agriculture: JOHNNIE K. SWARTZ.

Minister of Foreign Affairs and International Co-operation: Lt-Gen. MOMPATI S. MERAFHE.

Minister of Minerals, Energy and Water Affairs: PONATSHEGO KEDIKILWE.

Minister of Trade and Industry: D. NEO MOROKA.

Minister of Local Government: Dr MARGARET N. NASHA.

Minister of Works and Transport: LESEGO MOTSUMI.

Minister of Communications, Science and Technology: PELONOMI VENSON-MOITOYI.

Minister of Environment, Wildlife and Tourism: Capt. KITSO MOKAILA.

Minister of Finance and Development Planning: BALEDZI GAOLATHE.

Minister of Education: JACOB NKATE.

Minister of Labour and Home Affairs: CHARLES TIBONE.

Minister of Lands and Housing: Brig. RAMADELUKA SERETSE.

Minister of Youth, Sports and Culture: Maj.-Gen. MOENG PHETO.

Attorney-General: ATHALIAH MOLOKOMME.

In addition, there were five Assistant Ministers.

MINISTRIES

Office of the President: Private Bag 001, Gaborone; tel. 3950825; fax 3950858; e-mail op.registry@gov.bw; internet www.gov.bw/government/ministry_of_state_president.html#office_of_the_president.

Ministry for the Administration of Justice: Gaborone.

Ministry of Agriculture: Private Bag 003, Gaborone; tel. 3950602; fax 3975805; internet www.gov.bw/government/ministry_of_agriculture.html.

Ministry of Communications, Science and Technology: Private Bag 00414, Gaborone; tel. 3910384; fax 3907236; internet www.gov.bw/government/ministry_of_communications_science_and_technology.html.

Ministry of Education: Chief Education Officer, Block 6 Bldg, 2nd Floor, Government Enclave, Gaborone; Private Bag 005, Gaborone; tel. 3655400; fax 3655458; e-mail moe.webmaster@gov.bw; internet www.moe.gov.bw/moe/index.html.

Ministry of Environment, Wildlife and Tourism: Private Bag 0047, Standard House, 2nd Floor, Main Mall, Gaborone; tel. 3953024; fax 3908675.

Ministry of Finance and Development Planning: Private Bag 008, Gaborone; tel. 3950201; fax 3956086; e-mail gsethebe@gov.bw; internet www.finance.gov.bw.

Ministry of Foreign Affairs and International Co-operation: Private Bag 00368, Gaborone; tel. 3600700; fax 3913366; e-mail csmaribe@gov.bw; internet www.gov.bw/government/ministry_of_foreign_affairs.html.

Ministry of Health: Private Bag 0038, Gaborone; tel. 3170585; e-mail moh-webmaster@gov.bw; internet www.moh.gov.bw.

Ministry of Labour and Home Affairs: Private Bag 002, Gaborone; tel. 3611100; fax 3913584; e-mail msetimela@gov.bw; internet www.gov.bw/government/ministry_of_labour_and_home_affairs.html.

Ministry of Lands and Housing: Private Bag 00434, Gaborone; tel. 3904223; fax 3911591.

Ministry of Local Government: Private Bag 006, Gaborone; tel. 354100; fax 352091; internet www.mlg.gov.bw.

Ministry of Minerals, Energy and Water Affairs: Khama Cres., Private Bag 0018, Gaborone; tel. 3656600; fax 3972738; internet www.gov.bw/government/ministry_of_minerals_energy_and_water_affairs.html.

Ministry of Trade and Industry: Private Bag 004, Gaborone; tel. 3601200; fax 3971539; internet www.mti.gov.bw.

Ministry of Works and Transport: Private Bag 007, Gaborone; tel. 3958500; fax 3913303; internet www.gov.bw/government/ministry_of_works_and_transport.html.

Ministry of Youth, Sports and Culture: Gaborone.

Legislature

NTLO YA DIKGOSI

The Ntlo ya Dikgosi has a total of 15 members. Following a review, in December 2005 it was announced that the membership would be increased from 15 to 35 members.

Chairperson: Chief MOSADI SEBOKO.

NATIONAL ASSEMBLY

Speaker: PATRICK BALOPI.

General Election, 30 October 2004

Party	Votes	% of votes	Seats
Botswana Democratic Party	213,308	51.7	44
Botswana National Front	107,451	26.1	12
Botswana Congress Party	68,556	16.6	1
Botswana Alliance Movement	11,716	2.8	—
Botswana People's Party	7,886	1.9	—
Others*	3,482	0.8	—
Total	412,399	100.0	57†

* Including independents and candidates representing the New Democratic Front and MELS Movement of Botswana.

† The President and the Attorney-General are also ex officio members of the National Assembly.

Election Commission

Independent Electoral Commission (IEC): Government Enclave, Block 8, 7th Floor, Private Bag 00284, Gaborone; tel. 3612400; fax 3900581; internet www.iec.gov.bw; f. 1997; Chair. J. Z. MOSOJANE.

Political Organizations

Botswana Alliance Movement (BAM): Private Bag BO 210, Gaborone; tel. 3913476; fax 3914634; f. 1998 as an alliance of opposition parties—the Botswana Labour Party, United Socialist Party (PUSO), Botswana People's Party (BPP), Botswana Progressive Union, United Action Party and Independence Freedom Party—to contest the 1999 general election; the BPP withdrew in July 2000; Pres. EPHRAIM LEPETU SETSHWAELO; Chair. MOTSAMAI K. MPHO; Sec.-Gen. MATLHOMOLA MODISE.

Botswana Congress Party (BCP): Plot 364, Extension 4, Independence Ave, Gabarone; POB 2918, Gaborone; tel. and fax 3181805; internet www.bcp.org.bw; f. 1998 following split from the BNF; Pres. GILSON SALESHANDO; Nat. Chair. BATISANI MASWIBILI; Sec.-Gen. TAOLO LUCAS.

Botswana Democratic Party (BDP) (Domkrag): POB 28, Tsholetsa House, Gaborone; tel. 3952564; fax 3913911; internet www.bdp.org.bw; f. 1962 as the Bechuanaland Democratic Party; Pres. FESTUS G. MOGAE; Chair. Lt-Gen. SERETSE KHAMA IAN KHAMA; Sec.-Gen. DANIEL K. KWELAGOBE; Exec. Sec. Dr BATLANY COMMA SEREMA.

Botswana National Front (BNF): POB 1720, Gaborone; tel. 3951789; fax 3184970; e-mail botswananationalfront@yahoo.com; f. 1966; incl. fmr mems of the United Socialist Party (PUSO), which split from the BNF in 1994 later to re-affiliate in 2005; Pres. OTSWELETSE MOUPO; Chair. NEHEMIAH MODUBULE; Sec.-Gen. AKANYANG MAGAMA.

Botswana People's Party (BPP): POB 484, Francistown; f. 1960; Leader BERNARD BALIKANI.

Botswana Workers' Front (BWF): POB 597, Jwaneng; tel. 5880420; f. 1993 following split from the BNF; mems may retain dual membership of the BNF; Leader SHAWN NTHAILE.

MELS Movement of Botswana: POB 501818, Gaborone; tel. 3906005; fax 3933241; e-mail joinaandass@botsnet.bw; f. 1984; Marxist-Leninist; Leader THEMBA JOINA; Vice-Pres. EPHRAIM MAKGETHO.

New Democratic Front (NDF): Gaborone; f. 2003 following split from the BNF; affiliated to the BCP since mid-2006; Leader DICK BAYFORD.

Social Democratic Party (SDP): POB 201818, Gaborone; tel. 3956516; f. 1994 following split from the BNF; Leader RODGERS SEABUENG.

Diplomatic Representation

EMBASSIES AND HIGH COMMISSIONS IN BOTSWANA

Angola: 2715 Phala Cres., Private Bag BR 111, Gaborone; tel. 3900204; fax 3975089; e-mail angolaemb@info.bw; Ambassador JOSÉ AGOSTINHO NETO.

China, People's Republic: 3096 North Ring Rd, POB 1031, Gaborone; tel. 3953270; fax 3900147; e-mail chinaemb_bw@mfa.gov.cn; internet bw.china-embassy.org; Ambassador DING XIAOWEN.

Cuba: Plot 5198, Village, POB 40261, Gaborone; tel. 3951750; fax 3911485; Ambassador JORGE LUIS LOPEZ TORMO.

France: 761 Robinson Rd, POB 1424, Gaborone; tel. 3973863; fax 3971733; e-mail frambbots@info.bw; Ambassador JEAN-PIERRE COURTOIS.

Germany: Professional House, 3rd Floor, Segoditshane Way, Broadhurst, POB 315, Gaborone; tel. 3953143; fax 3953038; e-mail info@gaborone.diplo.de; internet www.gaborone.diplo.de; Ambassador ULF HANEL.

India: Plot 5375, President's Dr., Private Bag 249, Gaborone; tel. 3972676; fax 3974636; e-mail administration@hci.org.bw; internet www.highcommissionofinida.org.bw; High Commissioner V. N. HADE.

Kenya: Plot 786, Independence Ave, Private Bag 297, Gaborone; tel. 3951408; fax 3951409; e-mail kenya@info.bw; internet www.kenyamission-botswana.com; High Commissioner CHARLES MBAKA.

Libya: Plot 8851 (Government Enclave), POB 180, Gaborone; tel. 3952481; fax 356928; Ambassador ASSED MOHAMED ALMUTAA.

Namibia: Plot 186, Morara Close, POB 987, Gaborone; tel. 3902181; fax 3902248; High Commissioner TSUKHOE GOWASES.

Nigeria: Plot 1086–92, Queens Rd, The Mall, POB 274, Gaborone; tel. 3913561; fax 3913738; High Commissioner MARIUS U. OFFOR.

Russia: Plot 4711, Tawana Close, POB 81, Gaborone; tel. 3953389; fax 3952930; e-mail embrus@info.bw; Ambassador IGOR S. LIAKIN.

South Africa: Plot 29, Queens Rd, Private Bag 00402, Gaborone; tel. 3904800; fax 3905501; e-mail sahcgabs@botsnet.bw; High Commissioner DIKGANG F. MOOPELOA.

Sweden: Development House, 4th Floor, The Mall, Private Bag 0017, Gaborone; tel. 3953912; fax 3953942; e-mail ambassaden.gaborone@foreign.ministry.se; internet www.swedenabroad.com/gaborone; Ambassador ANNIKA JAGANDER.

United Kingdom: Plot 1079–1084, Main Mall, off Queens Rd, Private Bag 0023, Gaborone; tel. 3952841; fax 3956105; e-mail bhc@botsnet.bw; internet www.britishhighcommission.gov.uk/botswana; High Commissioner FRANCIS (FRANK) JAMES MARTIN.

USA: Embassy Enclave, off Khama Cres., POB 90, Gaborone; tel. 3953982; fax 3956947; e-mail ircgaborone@state.gov; internet botswana.usembassy.gov; Ambassador KATHERINE H. CANAVAN.

Zambia: POB 362, Gaborone; tel. 3951951; fax 3953952; High Commissioner CECIL HOLMES.

Zimbabwe: Plot 8850, POB 1232, Gaborone; tel. 3914495; fax 3905863; Ambassador THOMAS MANDIGORA.

Judicial System

There is a High Court at Lobatse and a branch at Francistown, and Magistrates' Courts in each district. Appeals lie to the Court of Appeal of Botswana. The Chief Justice and the President of the Court of Appeal are appointed by the President.

Chief Justice: JULIAN NGANUNU.

High Court

Private Bag 1, Lobatse; tel. 5330396; fax 5332317.

Judges of the High Court: ISAAC K. B. LESETEDI, MARUPING DIBOTELO, UNITY DOW, MOATLHODI MARUMO, STANLEY SAPIRE.

President of the Court of Appeal: PATRICK TEBBUTT.

Justices of Appeal: STANLEY MOORE, JULIAN NGANUNU, HEIN GROSSKOPF, NEVILLE ZIETSMAN, NICHOLAS JOHN MCNALLY, RODGER KORSAH, CHRIS PLEWMAN.

Registrar and Master: GODFREY NTHOMIWA.

Office of the Attorney-General

Private Bag 009, Gaborone; tel. 3954700; fax 3957089.

Attorney-General: Dr ATHALIAH MOLOKOMME.

Religion

The majority of the population hold animist beliefs; an estimated 30% are thought to be Christians. There are Islamic mosques in Gaborone and Lobatse. The Bahá'í Faith is also represented.

CHRISTIANITY

Botswana Council of Churches (Lekgotla la Dikereke mo Botswana): POB 355, Gaborone; tel. and fax 3951981; e-mail bots.christ.c@info.bw; f. 1966; Pres. Rev. ODIRILE E. MERE; Gen. Sec. DAVID J. MODIEGA; 24 mem. churches and orgs.

The Anglican Communion

Anglicans are adherents of the Church of the Province of Central Africa, covering Botswana, Malawi, Zambia and Zimbabwe. The Church comprises 15 dioceses, including one in Botswana. The current Archbishop of the Province is the Bishop of Upper Shire in Malawi. The Province was established in 1955, and the diocese of Botswana was formed in 1972. There were some 10,500 adherents at mid-2000.

Bishop of Botswana: Rt Rev. MUSONDA TREVOR S. MWAMBA, POB 769, Gaborone; tel. 3953779; fax 3913015; e-mail acenter@info.bw.

Protestant Churches

There were an estimated 178,000 adherents in the country at mid-2000.

African Methodist Episcopal Church: POB 141, Lobatse; tel. 5407520; e-mail mobeat@bpc.bw; Presiding Elder Rev. MOSES P. LEKHORI.

Evangelical Lutheran Church in Botswana (Kereke ya Luthere ya Efangele mo Botswana): POB 1976, Gaborone; tel. 3952227; fax 3913966; e-mail elcb@info.bw; f. 1979; Bishop Rev. PHILIP J. ROBINSON; 43 congregations; c. 25,000 mems (2004).

Evangelical Lutheran Church in Southern Africa (Botswana Diocese): POB 400, Gaborone; tel. 3953976; Bishop Rev. M. NTUPING.

Methodist Church of Southern Africa (Gaborone Circuit): POB 260, Gaborone; tel. 3167627; Circuit Supt Rev. ODIRILE E. MERE.

United Congregational Church of Southern Africa (Synod of Botswana): POB 1263, Gaborone; tel. 3952491; synod status since 1980; Chair. Rev. D. T. MAPITSE; Sec. Rev. M. P. P. DIBEELA; c. 24,000 mems.

Other denominations active in Botswana include the Church of God in Christ, the Dutch Reformed Church, the Mennonite Church, the United Methodist Church and the Seventh-day Adventists.

The Roman Catholic Church

Botswana comprises one diocese and an apostolic vicariate. The metropolitan see is Bloemfontein, South Africa. The church was established in Botswana in 1928, and had an estimated 63,102 adherents (some 6.5% of the total population) in the country at 31 December 2004. The Bishop participates in the Southern African Catholic Bishops' Conference, currently based in Pretoria, South Africa.

Bishop of Gaborone: Rt Rev. BONIFACE TSHOSA SETLALEKGOSI, POB 218, Bishop's House, Gaborone; tel. 3912958; fax 3956970; e-mail gabs.diocese@botsnet.bw.

Vicar Apostolic of Francistown: Rt Rev. FRANKLYN NUBUASAH, POB 702, Francistown; tel. 2413601; fax 2417183.

The Press

DAILY NEWSPAPERS

Dikgang tsa Gompieno (Daily News): Mass Media Complex, Western Bypass, Private Bag 0060, Gaborone; tel. 3653065; fax 3901675; e-mail dailynews@gov.bw; internet www.mcst.gov.bw/dailynews; f. 1964; Mon.–Fri.; publ. by Dept of Information and Broadcasting; Setswana and English; Editor ME GOLEKANYE MOLAPISI; circ. 60,000.

Mmegi/The Reporter: Segogwane Way, Plot 8901, Broadhurst, Private Bag BR 50, Gaborone; tel. 3974784; fax 3905508; e-mail dikgang@mmegi.bw; internet www.mmegi.bw; f. 1984 as *Mmegi wa Dikgang*; daily; publ. by Dikgang Publishing Co; Setswana and English; Man. Editor TITUS MBUYA; circ. 20,000; also publishes the weekly *Mmegi Monitor* (f. 2000, Monday, circ. 16,000).

PERIODICALS

Botswana Advertiser/Northern Advertiser: 5634 Nakedi Rd, Broadhurst Industrial, POB 130, Gaborone; tel. 3914788; fax 3182957; publ. by Printing & Publishing Co Botswana (Pty) Ltd; weekly; English; circ. 90,000 (Botswana Advertiser), 35,000 (Northern Advertiser).

The Botswana Gazette: 125 Sedimosa House, Millennium Park, Kgale View, POB 1605, Gaborone; tel. 3912833; fax 3972283; e-mail production@gazette.bw; internet www.gazette.bw; f. 1985; publ. by News Co Botswana; weekly; Man. Dir CLARA OLSEN; Editor BATLHALEFHI LEAGAJANG; circ. 17,000.

Botswana Guardian: Plot 14442, Kamushungo Rd, G-West Industrial Site, POB 1641, Gaborone; tel. 3908432; fax 3908457; internet www.botswanaguardian.co.bw; f. 1983; weekly; publ. by Pula Printing & Publishing (Pty) Ltd; English; Editor OUTSA MOKONE; circ. 21,505.

Botswana Journal of Technology: University of Botswana, Private Bag 0061, Gaborone; tel. 3554210; fax 3952309; e-mail ngowiab@mopipi.ub.bw; 2 a year; science and technology; Reviews Editor Prof. ALFRED B. NGOWI.

Business and Financial Times: Unit 9, Plot 64, Gaborone International Commerce Park, POB 402396, Gaborone; tel. 3939911; fax 3939910; e-mail bftimes@info.bw; Publr JAFFAR KATERYA MBUI; Editor JIMMY SWIRA.

The Clarion: POB 397, Gaborone; tel. 3930709; fax 3930708; Editor SELLO MOTSETA.

Fame Magazine: F5, Fairground Mall, POB 2214, Gaborone; tel. and fax 3907711; e-mail kudadi@yahoo.com.

Flair Magazine: Plot 22055, Mocha House, Unit Z, POB 21606, Gaborone; tel. 3911349; fax 3911359; monthly; Editor BOITSHEPO BALOZWI.

Francistown News and Reviews: POB 632, Francistown; tel. and fax 2412040; weekly; English.

Kutlwano: Private Bag BR 139, Gaborone; tel. 3653500; fax 3653630; e-mail kutlwano@gov.bw; monthly; publ. by Dept of Information Services; Setswana and English; Editor BOME MATSHABA; circ. 15,000.

The Midweek Sun: Plot 14442, Kamushungo Rd, G-West Industrial Site, POB 00153, Gaborone; tel. 3908408; fax 3908457; internet www.midweeksun.co.bw; f. 1989; weekly; English; Editor MIKE MOTHIBI; circ. 17,971.

Mokgosi Newspaper: Plot 134, Madirelo, Tlokweng, POB 46530, Gaborone; tel. 3936868; fax 3936869; e-mail mokgosi@mmegi.bw.

Ngami Times: Mabudutsa Ward, Private Bag BO 30, Maun; tel. 6864807; fax 6860257; e-mail tnt@info.bw; internet www.ngamitimes.com; f. 1999; weekly; English; Editor NORMAN CHANDLER.

Sunday Standard: Postnet Kgale View, Private Bag 351, Suite 287, Gaborone; tel. 3188784; fax 3188795; internet www.sundaystandard.info; Editor OUTSA MOKONE.

Sunday Tribune: POB 41458, Gaborone; tel. and fax 3926431; weekly.

Tautona Times: Office of the President, Private Bag 001, Gaborone; tel. 3975154; fax 3902795; e-mail jramsay@gov.bw; f. 2003; weekly; electronic press circular publ. by the Office of the Pres.; Press Sec. Dr JEFF RAMSAY.

The Voice: Plot 170, Unit 7, Commerce Park, POB 40415, Gaborone; tel. 3161585; fax 3932822; e-mail voicebw@yahoo.com; internet www.thevoicebw.com; f. 1992 as *The Francistowner*; weekly; Publr BEATA KASALE; Man. Editor DONALD MOORE; Editor EMANG BOKHUTLO; circ. 29,000.

Wena Magazine: POB 201533, Gaborone; tel. and fax 3907678; e-mail environews@it.bw; f. 1998; 6 a year; English and Setswana; environmental issues; Editor and Publr FLORA SEBONI-MMEREKI; circ. c. 8,000.

The Zebra's Voice: National Museum, 331 Independence Ave, Private Bag 00114, Gaborone; tel. 3974616; fax 3902797; e-mail bemotswakhumo@gov.bw; internet www.botswana-museum.gov.bw; f. 1980; quarterly; cultural affairs; Editor BERLINAH MOTSWAKHUMO; circ. 5,000.

NEWS AGENCIES

Department of Information Services, Botswana Press Agency (BOPA): Private Bag BR 139, Gaborone; tel. 3653525; fax 3653626; e-mail bopa@gov.bw; f. 1981; News Editor MABEL KEBOTSAMANG.

Foreign Bureaux

Deutsche Presse-Agentur (Germany) and Reuters (UK) are represented in Botswana.

Press Organizations

Botswana Journalists' Association (BOJA): POB 60518, Gaborone; tel. 3974435; f. 1977; represents professional journalists; affiliated to the Int. Fed. of Journalists; Chair. SECHELE SECHELE; Sec.-Gen. RAMPHOLO MOLEFHE; 55 mems (1999).

Botswana Media Consultative Council (BMCC): POB 2679, Gaborone; tel. 71624382; e-mail botswanamedia@info.bw; internet www.botswanamedia.bw; f. 1998; promotes the devt of a democratic media; Chair. Dr JEFF RAMSAY; Exec. Sec. ANTOINETTE O. CHIGODORA; 40 mem. orgs (1999).

Publishers

A. C. Braby (Botswana) (Pty) Ltd: Unit 3/A/2, Western Industrial Estate, 22100 Phase 4 Industrial, POB 1549, Gaborone; tel. 3971444; fax 3973462; e-mail directory@bt.bw; internet www.brabys.com/bw/; business directories.

Botsalo Books: Gaborone International Commerce Park, Kgale, Plot 59/60, Unit 5, POB 1532, Gaborone; tel. 3912576; fax 3972608; e-mail botsalobooks@botsnet.bw; internet www.abcdafrica.com/botsalobooks.

The Botswana Society (BotSoc): Unispan Bldg, Lot 54, International Commerce Park, Kgale, POB 71, Gaborone; tel. 3919673; fax 3919745; e-mail baybooks@it.bw; internet www.botsoc.org.bw; f. 1968; archaeology, arts, history, law, sciences; Pres. FESTUS G. MOGAE.

Heinemann Educational Botswana (Pty) Ltd: Plot 20695, Unit 4, Magochanyana Rd, POB 10103, Village Post Office, Gaborone; tel. 3972305; fax 3971832; e-mail hein@info.bw; internet www.heinemann.co.za; Man. Dir LESEDI SEITEI.

Lentswe la Lesedi (Pty): POB 2365, Gaborone; tel. 314017; fax 314634; e-mail publisher@lightbooks.net; f. 1992

> **Lightbooks Publishers:** Digitec House, 685 Botswana Rd, The Mall, POB 2365, Gaborone; tel. 3903994; fax 3914017; e-mail publisher@lightbooks.net; internet www.lightbooks.net; f. 1992; commercial publishing division of Lentswe la Lesedi (Pty); scholarly, research, women's issues, journals, reports; Publr CHARLES BEWLAY.

Longman Botswana (Pty) Ltd: Plot 14386, West Industrial Site, New Lobatse Rd, POB 1083, Gaborone; tel. 3922969; fax 3922682; e-mail carlson@longman.info.bw; f. 1981; subsidiary of Pearson Education, UK; educational; Man. Dir J. K. CHALASHIKA.

Macmillan Botswana Publishing Co (Pty) Ltd: Plot 50635, Block 10, Airport Rd, Gaborone; tel. 3911770; fax 3911987; e-mail leburu.sianga@macmillan.bw; CEO FELICITY LEBURU-SIANGA.

Medi Publishing: Phakalane Phase 1, Medie Close, Plot No. 21633, POB 47680, Gaborone; tel. 3121110; e-mail medi@it.bw; f. 1995; scholarly; Publishing Dir PORTIA TSHOAGONG.

Mmegi Publishing House (MPH): Plot 8901, Segogwane Way, Broadhurst, Private Bag BR 298, Gaborone; tel. 3952464; fax 3184977; e-mail ntebela@mmegi.bw; academic and general.

Morula Press: Business School of Botswana, Ext. 2, 222 Independence Ave, Selemelo, POB 402492, Gaborone; tel. 3906134; fax 3904809; f. 1994; business, law.

Printing and Publishing Co (Botswana) (Pty) Ltd (PPCB): Plot 5634 Nakedi Rd, Broadhurst Industrial, POB 130, Gaborone; tel. 3914788; fax 3182957; e-mail ppcb@info.bw; internet www.ppcb.co.bw; educational; Man. Dir Y. MUSSA; Gen. Man. GAVIN BLAMIRE.

GOVERNMENT PUBLISHING HOUSE

Department of Government Printing and Publishing Service: Private Bag 0081, Gaborone; tel. 353202; fax 312001; Dir O. ANDREW SESINYI.

Broadcasting and Communications

TELECOMMUNICATIONS

Botswana Telecommunications Authority (BTA): 206–207 Independence Ave, Private Bag 00495, Gaborone; tel. 3957755; fax 3957976; internet www.bta.org.bw; f. 1996; independent regulator for the telecommunications industry; Chair. Dr JOHN MOTHIBI; CEO THARI G. PHEKO.

Botswana Telecommunications Corpn (BTC): POB 700, Gaborone; tel. 3958411; fax 3952777; internet www.btc.bw; f. 1980; state-owned; privatization pending; fixed-line telecommunications provider; Chair. WILFRED MANDLEBE; CEO VINCENT T. SERETSE.

Mascom: Tsholetsa House, Plot 4705/6, Botswana Rd, Main Mall, Private Bag BO298, Bontleng, Gaborone; tel. 3903396; fax 3903445; internet www.mascom.bw; f. 1998; 60% owned by DECI; 40% owned by Econet Wireless; mobile cellular telecommunications provider; CEO JOSE GERALDES.

Orange Botswana: Camphill Bldg, Plot 43002/1, Private Bag BO64, Bontleng, Gaborone; tel. 3163370; fax 3163372; internet www.orange.co.bw; f. 1998 as Vista Cellular; present name adopted in 2003; 49% owned by Orange SA, France; 46% owned by Mosokelatsebeng Cellular; mobile cellular telecommunications provider; CEO THAPELO LIPPE.

BROADCASTING

The Department of Information and Broadcasting operates 21 radio stations across the country from bureaux in Gaborone, Kanye, Serowe and Francistown. The National Broadcasting Board was preparing to issue three further licences for private commercial radio stations in addition to those already held by Ya Rona FM and GABZ FM.

Department of Information and Broadcasting: Private Bag 0060, Gaborone; tel. 3658000; fax 564416; internet www.dib.gov.bw; f. 1978 following merger between Information Services and Radio Botswana; Dir O. ANDREW SESINYI.

Radio

Radio Botswana (RB1): Private Bag 0060, Gaborone; tel. 3952541; fax 3957138; e-mail rbeng@info.bw; state-owned; f. 1965; fmrly Radio Bechuanaland; culture, entertainment, news and current affairs programmes; broadcasts 18 hours daily in Setswana and English; Dir ANDREW SESINYI; Head of Programmes M. GABAKGORE.

Radio Botswana (RB2) (FM 103): Private Bag 0060, Gaborone; tel. 3653000; fax 3653346; e-mail mmphusu@gov.bw; f. 1992; contemporary entertainment; Head of Programmes MONICA MPHUSU.

GABZ FM 96.2: Private Bag 319, Gaborone; tel. 3170905; fax 3181443; e-mail feedback@gabzfm.co.bw; f. 1999; owned by Thari Investment; entertainment, news and politics; broadcasts in Setswana and English; Man. Dir KENNEDY OTSHELENG.

Ya Rona FM 106.6: POB 1607, Gaborone; tel. 3912305; fax 3901063; e-mail info@yaronafm.co.bw; internet www.yaronafm.co.bw; f. 1999; owned by Copacabana Investment; Station Man. DUMI LOPANG.

Television

Botswana Television (BTV): Private Bag 0060, Gaborone; tel. 3658000; fax 3900051; internet www.btv.gov.bw; f. 2000; broadcasts local and international programmes eight hours daily (Mon.–Fri.) and 10 hours (Sat.–Sun.); 60% local content; Gen. Man. BANYANA SEGWE.

GBC TV: Plot 53996, Mogochama St, opposite Coca Cola, POB 921, Gaborone; tel. 3957654; fax 3901875; f. 1988; operated by Gaborone Broadcasting Co (Pty) Ltd; Setswana and English; rebroadcasts foreign TV programmes; Man. Dir MIKE KLINK.

TV Association of Botswana: Gaborone; relays SABC-TV and BOP-TV programmes from South Africa.

Finance

(cap. = capital; res = reserves; dep. = deposits; m. = million; brs = branches; amounts in pula)

BANKING

Central Bank

Bank of Botswana: POB 712, Private Bag 154,17938 Khama Cres., Gaborone; tel. 3606000; fax 3913890; e-mail webmaster@bob.bw; internet www.bankofbotswana.bw; f. 1975; bank of issue; cap. 25m., res 12,385.9m., dep. 10,339.1m. (Dec. 2003); Gov. LINAH MOHOHLO.

Commercial Banks

African Banking Corpn of Botswana Ltd (ABC): ABC House, Tholo Office Park, Plot 50669, Fairground Office Park, POB 00303, Gaborone; tel. 3905455; fax 3902131; e-mail bmoyo@africanbankingcorp.com; internet www.africanbankingcorp.bw; f. 1989 as ulc (Pty) Ltd; name changed to African Banking Corpn (Pty) Ltd in 2001; present name adopted in 2002; subsidiary of ABC Holdings Ltd; financial services and investment banking; operates in Botswana, Mozambique, Tanzania, Zambia and Zimbabwe; total assets 1,902.1m. (Dec. 2005); Chair. OLIVER M. CHIDAWU; Pres. JITTO KURIAN.

Bank of Baroda (Botswana) Ltd: Plot 1108, Queens Rd, Main Mall, Gaborone; POB 21559, Bontleng, Gaborone; tel. 3188878; fax 3188879; e-mail botswana@barodabank.co.bw; internet www.bankofbaroda.com; f. 2001; subsidiary of the Bank of Baroda, India; Man. Dir R. S. SETIA; Chief Man. G. V. SESHADRI.

Barclays Bank of Botswana Ltd: Barclays House, 6th Floor, Plot 8842, Khama Cres., POB 478, Gaborone; tel. 3953411; fax 3913672; internet www.barclays.com; f. 1975 as local successor to Barclays Bank Int. Ltd; 74.9% owned by Barclays Bank PLC, UK; total assets 5,239.5m. (Dec. 2004); Chair. MBIGANYI CHARLES TIBONE; Man. Dir THULISIZWE JOHNSON; 48 brs.

First National Bank of Botswana Ltd: Finance House, 5th Floor, Plot 8843, Khama Cres., POB 1552, Gaborone; tel. 3642600; fax 3906130; e-mail achalwe@fnbbotswana.co.bw; internet www.fnbbotswana.co.bw; f. 1991; 69.5% owned by First Nat. Bank Holdings Botswana Ltd; total assets 7,213.1m. (June 2006); Chair. HENRY C. L. HERMANS; Man. Dir DANNY H. ZANDAMELA; 14 brs.

Kingdom Bank Africa Limited: Plot 133, Ext. 3, Independence Ave, Gaborone; POB 45078, Riverwalk, Gaborone; tel. 3906863; fax 3906874; f. 2003; Chair. NIGEL CHANKIRA; Man. Dir IRENE CHAMNEY; Exec. Dir TAPIWA SHAMU.

Stanbic Bank Botswana Ltd: Stanbic House, 1st Floor, Plot 50672, Fairground (off Machel Dr.), Private Bag 00168, Gaborone; tel. 3901600; fax 3900171; internet www.stanbic.co.bw; f. 1992; subsidiary of Standard Bank Investment Corpn Africa Holdings Ltd; cap. and res 170.5m., total assets 2,443.1m. (Dec. 2004); Chair. G. H. ABDOOLA (acting); Man. Dir D. W. KENNEDY; Exec. Dir T. FERREIRA; 6 brs.

Standard Chartered Bank Botswana Ltd: Standard House, 5th Floor, Queens Rd, The Mall, POB 496, Gaborone; tel. 3601500; fax 3918299; internet www.standardchartered.com/bw; f. 1975; 75% owned by Standard Chartered Holdings (Africa) BV, Amsterdam; total assets 4,729.7m. (Dec. 2005); Chair. P. L. STEENKAMP; Man. Dir NIGEL R. JONES; 14 brs; 4 agencies.

Other Banks

Botswana Savings Bank: Tshomarelo House, POB 1150, Gaborone; tel. 3952326; fax 3952608; e-mail marketing@bsb.bw; internet www.bsb.bw; f. 1992; cap. and res 48.4m., dep. 101.5m. (March 2000); Chair. F. MODISE; Man. Dir MICHAEL LESOLLE.

Letshego: POB 318, Gaborone; tel. 3180635; fax 3957949; e-mail letshego@info.bw; f. 1998; micro-finance; 43.8% owned by Micro Provident Ltd; 34.9% owned by the Int. Finance Corpn, Netherlands Devt Finance Co, Pan-African Investment Partners and Pan-Commonwealth African Partners; total assets 328.0m. (Oct. 2005); Chair. C. M. LEKAUKAU; Man. Dir J. A. CLAASSEN.

National Development Bank: Development House, Queens Rd, Main Mall, POB 225, Gaborone; tel. 3952801; fax 3974446; e-mail bmojalemotho@ndb.bw; internet www.ndb.bw; f. 1963; total assets 566.9m. (March 2005); Chair. LESEDI SEITEI (acting); CEO OAITSE M. RAMASEDI; 5 brs.

STOCK EXCHANGE

Botswana Stock Exchange: Finance House, 4th Floor, Unit 11, Millennium Office Park, Kgale Mews, Private Bag 00417, Gaborone; tel. 3180201; fax 3180175; e-mail enquiries@bse.co.bw; internet www.bse.co.bw; f. 1989; commenced formal functions of a stock exchange in 1995; Chair. LOUIS G. NCHINDO; CEO Dr T. T. K. MATOME; 25 cos and 32 securities firms listed in 2004.

INSURANCE

Botswana Eagle Insurance Co Ltd: Eagle House, Plot 54479, Fairgrounds, POB 1221, Gaborone; tel. 588888; fax 588911; e-mail john.main@saeagle.co.za; f. 1976; subsidiary of SA Eagle, South Africa; Gen. Man. JOHN MAIN.

Botswana Insurance Holdings Ltd (BIHL): Block A, Fairgrounds Office Park, POB 336, Gaborone; tel. 3951791; fax 3906386; f. 1975; 54% owned by African Life Assurance Co Ltd (Aflife), South Africa; total income 1,182.9m. (March 2005); Chair. McLEAN C. LETSHWITI.

Botswana Life Insurance Ltd: Botswana Life Insurance House, Nyerere Dr., Private Bag 00296, Gaborone; tel. 3951791; fax 3905884; subsidiary of BIHL; life insurance; CEO REGINA VAKA.

Metropolitan Life of Botswana Ltd: Standard House, 3rd Floor, Queens Rd, Main Mall, Private Bag 231, Gaborone; tel. 3957761; fax 3906639; e-mail nkgabi@metropolitan.co.bw; internet www.metropolitan.co.bw; f. 1996; 75% owned by Metropolitan South Africa, 25% owned by the Botswana Devt Corpn; Chair. JUSTIN VAN DEN HOVEN; Man. Dir NATHAN KGABI.

Mutual and Federal Insurance Co of Botswana Ltd: Private Bag 00347, Gaborone; tel. 3903333; fax 3903400; e-mail bkelly1@mf.co.za; subsidiary of Mutual and Federal, South Africa; Man. Dir BRYAN KELLY.

Trade and Industry

GOVERNMENT AGENCIES

Botswana Housing Corpn (BHC): POB 412, Gaborone; tel. 3605100; fax 3952070; e-mail jbmolosankwe@bhc.bw; internet www.bhc.bw; f. 1971; provides housing for central govt and local authority needs and assists with private-sector housing schemes; Chair. MACLEAN C. LETSHWITI; CEO MOOTIEMANG R. MOTSWAISO.

Citizen Entrepreneurial Development Agency (CEDA): 205 Independence Ave, 1st Floor, Private Bag 00504, Gaborone; tel. 3170895; fax 3170896; internet www.ceda.co.bw; f. 2001; develops and promotes citizen-owned enterprises; provides business training and financial assistance; Chair. H. P. MAHLOANE; CEO Dr THAPELO C. MATSHEKA.

Department of Food Resources: POB 96, Gaborone; tel. 3954124; f. 1982; procurement, storage and distribution of food commodities under the Drought Relief Programme; Admin. Officer M. S. SEHLULANE.

Department of Town and Regional Planning: Private Bag 0042, Gaborone; tel. 3951935; f. 1972; responsible for physical planning policy and implementation.

Public Enterprises Evaluation and Privatisation Agency (PEEPA): Private Bag 00510, Gaborone; tel. 3188807; fax 3188662; f. 2001; responsible for commercializing and privatizing public parastatals; CEO JOSHUA GALEFOROLWE.

DEVELOPMENT ORGANIZATIONS

Botswana Council of Non-Governmental Organisations (BOCONGO): Tebelelo Kgethang, Private Bag 00418, Gaborone; tel. 3911319; fax 3912935; e-mail bocongo@bocongo.org.bw; internet www.bocongo.org.bw; Exec. Dir BABOLOKI TLALE; 84 mem. orgs.

Botswana Development Corpn Ltd: Private Bag 160, Moedi, Plot 50380, Gaborone International Showgrounds (off Machel Dr.), Gaborone; tel. 3651300; fax 3904193; e-mail enquiries@bdc.bw; internet www.bdc.bw; f. 1970; Chair. S. S. G. TUMELO; Man. Dir KENNETH O. MATAMBO.

Botswana Enterprise Development Unit (BEDU): POB 0014, Plot 1269, Lobatse Rd, Gaborone; f. 1974; promotes industrialization and rural devt; Dir J. LINDFORS.

Botswana Export Development and Investment Authority (BEDIA): Plot 28, Matsitama Rd, The Main Mall, POB 3122, Gaborone; tel. 3181931; fax 3181941; e-mail bedia@bedia.bw; internet www.bedia.bw; f. 1998; promotes and facilitates local and foreign investment; Chair. MORAGO NGIDI; CEO (vacant).

Botswana International Financial Services Centre (BIFSC): Plot 50676, Block B, Fairground Office Park, Private Bag 160, Gaborone; tel. 3605000; fax 3913075; e-mail ifsc@ifsc.co.bw; internet www.ifsc.co.bw; f. 2003; govt-owned; Chair. H. C. L. HERMANS; CEO ALAN P. BOSHWAEN.

Department of Trade and Investment Promotion (TIPA), Ministry of Trade and Industry: Private Bag 00367, Gaborone; tel. 3951790; fax 3905375; promotes industrial and commercial investment, diversification and expansion; offers consultancy, liaison and information services; participates in overseas trade fairs and trade and investment missions; Dir D. TSHEKO.

Financial Services Co of Botswana (Pty) Ltd: POB 1129, Finance House, Khama Cres., Gaborone; tel. 3951363; fax 3957815; f. 1974; hire purchase, mortgages, industrial leasing and debt factoring; Chair. M. E. HOPKINS; Man. Dir R. A. PAWSON.

Integrated Field Services: Ministry of Trade and Industry, Private Bag 004, Gaborone; tel. 3953024; fax 3971539; promotes industrialization and rural devt; Dir B. T. TIBONE.

RETENG: the Multicultural Coalition of Botswana: POB 402786, Gaborone; tel. 71654345; fax 3937779; f. 2003; umbrella org. composed of human rights advocacy and conservation groups, and public-service and private-sector unions; Sec.-Gen. Prof. LYDIA NYATHI-RAMAHOBO.

CHAMBER OF COMMERCE

Botswana National Chamber of Commerce and Industry: POB 20344, Gaborone; tel. 3952677.

INDUSTRIAL AND TRADE ASSOCIATIONS

Botswana Agricultural Marketing Board (BAMB): Plot 130, Unit 3–4, Gaborone International Finance Park, Private Bag 0053, Gaborone; tel. 3951341; fax 3952926; internet www.bamb.co.bw; Chair. E. M. MAPHANYANE; CEO M. MPHATHI.

Botswana Meat Commission (BMC): Plot 621, 1 Khama Ave, Private Bag 4, Lobatse; tel. 5330619; fax 5332228; e-mail marketing@bmc.bw; internet www.bmc.bw; f. 1966; slaughter of livestock, export of hides and skins, carcasses, frozen and chilled boneless beef; operates tannery and beef products cannery; Exec. Chair. Dr MOTSHUDI V. RABOROKGWE; Gen. Man. JOHNSON BOJOSI.

EMPLOYERS' ORGANIZATIONS

Botswana Confederation of Commerce, Industry and Manpower (BOCCIM): BOCCIM House, POB 432, Gaborone; e-mail boccim@info.bw; internet www.boccim.co.bw; f. 1971; Pres. IQBAL EBRAHIM; Exec. Dir ELIAS DEWAH; 1,700 mems.

Botswana Teachers' Union (BTU): Plot 0019, BTU Rd Mogoditshane; BTU Centre, Private Bag 0019, Mogoditshane; tel. 3906774; fax 3909838; e-mail btu@it.bw; internet www.btu.co.bw; f. 1937 as the Bechuanaland Protectorate African Teachers' Asscn; present name adopted 1966; affiliated to Education Int.; merger discussions under way in mid-2006 with Botswana Primary Teachers Asscn (BOPRITA—Pres. SAM MALETE), Asscn of Botswana Tertiary Lecturers (ABOTEL—Pres. ALLEN KEITSENG) and BOSETU; Pres. JAPHTA RADIBE; Sec.-Gen. KEORAPETSE A. KGASA; 13,000 mems.

UTILITIES

Electricity

Botswana Power Corpn (BPC): Motlakase House, Macheng Way, POB 48, Gaborone; tel. 3603203; fax 3973563; e-mail alidia@bpc.bw; internet www.bpc.bw; f. 1971; operates power stations at Selebi-Phikwe (capacity 65 MW) and Morupule (132 MW); Chair. E. RAKHUDU; CEO JOHN T. KALUZI.

Water

Department of Water Affairs: Khama Cres., Private Bag 0018, Gaborone; tel. 3656600; fax 3972738; provides public water supplies for rural areas.

Water Utilities Corpn: Private Bag 00276, Gaborone; tel. 3604400; fax 3973852; e-mail metsi@wuc.bw; internet www.wuc.bw; f. 1970; 100% state-owned; supplies water to main urban centres; Chair. NOZIPHO MABE; Chief Exec. FRED MAUNGE.

MAJOR COMPANIES

The following are among the leading companies in Botswana in terms of capital investment and employment. Amounts are in pula.

Bamangwato Concessions Ltd (BCL): BCL Mine, Box 3, Selebi Phikwe; tel. 2621200; fax 2610441; e-mail bcl@bcl.bw; internet www.bcl.bw; f. 1956; 85% owned by Botswana RST Ltd (Botrest); 7.5% owned by Lion Ore Mining Int. Ltd Group, Canada; 7.5% state-owned; sole copper mining co; copper mining, smelting and processing; Gen. Man. MONTWEDI MPHATHI; 4,000 employees (2006).

Bata Shoe Co Botswana (Pty) Ltd: Plot 17979, Ramogononwane Rd, POB 1882, Gaborone; tel. 3924575; fax 3161182; e-mail bata@info.bw; subsidiary of Bata a. s., Czech Republic; mfrs of footwear.

Botswana RST Ltd (Botrest): POB 3, Selebi-Phikwe; tel. 810211; fax 810441; e-mail bcl@bcl.bw; f. 1967 as Botswana Roan Selection Trust Ltd; holding co with 85% shareholding in copper-nickel producers, BCL Ltd; Chair. D. C. BAILEY; Gen. Man. MONTWEDI MPHATHI; 4,800 employees.

BP Botswana (Pty) Ltd: Plot 682/3, Botswana Rd, Main Mall, POB 183, Gaborone; tel. 3951077; fax 3912836; f. 1975; petroleum exploration and production.

Chobe Holdings Ltd: Plot 50371, Fairground Office Park, POB 32, Kasane; tel. 6250340; eco-tourism; interests in Botswana and Namibia; revenue 36,775m. (2005); Chair. M. C. TIBONE; Man. Dir J. M. GIBSON.

Debswana Diamond Co (Pty) Ltd: Debswana House, The Mall, POB 329, Gaborone; tel. 3614200; fax 3180778; e-mail jmatome@debswana.bw; internet www.debswana.com; owned equally by the Botswana Govt and De Beers Centenary AG, Switzerland; sole diamond-mining interest in Botswana; operates three mines in

Orapa and one at Jwaneng; Chair. Dr AKOLANG RUSSIA TOMBALE; Man. Dir BLACKIE MAROLE; 6,000 employees.

Engen Botswana Ltd: Plot 54026, Western Bypass, Gaborone West, POB 867, Gaborone; tel. 3922210; e-mail josiel.ndlovu@engenoil.com; fmrly Mobil; subsidiary of Engen Petroleum Ltd, South Africa; suppliers of petroleum-based fuels and lubricants; revenue 680.2m. (March 2006); Chair. M. S. SOLOMONS; Man. Dir JOHN THANGWANE.

Furniture Mart Ltd: Private Bag 115, Gaborone; tel. 3913051; e-mail ramani@cashb.bw; furniture and appliance retail; operates in Botswana, Namibia and Zimbabwe; revenue 133.7m. (July 2005); Chair. JOHN T. MYNHARDT; Man. Dir CHARLES WRIGLEY; 39 stores in Botswana; c. 1,000 employees.

Gold Fields Botswana (Pty) Ltd: Barclays House, 4th Floor, Khama Cres., POB 271, Gaborone; holds prospecting licences covering an area of 4,986 sq km.

MRI Botswana: Plot 20623, Block 3, cnr Samedupe Rd and Ramakukane Way, Broadhurst Industrial Estate, Private Bag BR 256, Gaborone; tel. 3903066; fax 3164728; internet www.mri.co.bw; f. 1992; suppliers of medical and rescue services; revenue 17.9m. (June 2005); Chair. D. J. ALEXANDER (acting); Man. Dir D. PHILIP MAKGALEMELE.

Northern Textile Mills (Pty) Ltd: Plot 9807, Phase 4 Industrial Area, POB 1508, Francistown; tel. 2414773; fax 2414947; e-mail info@nortex.info.bw; internet www.nortex.co.za; mfrs of household textiles; exports to Mauritius, South Africa, Tanzania, Zimbabwe and the USA; Man. Dir MUKESH JOSH; 432 employees.

RDC Properties Ltd: POB 1415, Gaborone; tel. 3912641; fax 3973441; f. 1996; property management, devt and retail; interests in Botswana, Madagascar and South Africa; revenue 18.7m. (Dec. 2005); Chair. M. A. GIACHETTI; Man. Dir GUIDO R. GIACHETTI.

RPC Data Ltd: Plot 39, Unit 5, International Commerce Park, Private Bag BR 5, Gaborone; tel. 3903644; fax 3903645; e-mail info@rpcdata.com; internet www.rpcdata.com; f. 1989 as Rob Pool Computing (Pty) Ltd; present name adopted in 1994; management consultancy and information technology services; operates in Botswana, South Africa, Uganda and Zambia; revenue 28.8m. (May 2003); Man. Dir ROB POOL; Exec. Dir MOMPATI NWAKO.

Sechaba Brewery Holdings Ltd (SBHL): Kgalagadi Breweries (Pty) Ltd, cnr Kubu Rd and Nelson Mandela Dr., Broadhurst Industrial Estate, POB 631, Gaborone; tel. 3971598; fax 3971594; e-mail birkholtzd@kbl.bw; 25.6% owned by Botswana Devt Corpn, 16.8% owned by SABMiller Africa BV, Netherlands; SABMiller controls 40% of KBL and BBL; mfrs of clear beer and soft drinks; distributors of wines and spirits (Kgalagadi Breweries Ltd) and traditional beers (Botswana Breweries Ltd); sales 920.4m. (March 2006); Chair. EDWARD W. KOMANYANE; Man. Dir LONWABO MTONGANA; 1,000 employees.

Securicor Botswana Ltd: POB 1488, Gaborone; tel. 3912211; fax 3972779; f. 2003 following acquisition of Inco Group; subsidiary of Group 4 Securicor PLC, UK; security and cash transportation services; revenue 59.2m. (Dec. 2005); Chair. L. M. MPOTOKWANE; Man. Dir ROCKIE G. M. MMUTLE; 800 employees.

Sefalana Holding Co Ltd: Plot 117, Kwena House, Unit 3, Kgale, Private Bag 0080, Gaborone; tel. 3913661; fax 3907613; miller, processor and distributor of cereals (Foods Botswana); motor vehicle dealership and travel agency (M. F. Holdings Ltd); soap production (Kgalagadi Soap Industries Ltd); revenue 70.6m. (April 2006); Chair. LAWRENCE D. LEKALAKE; Man. Dir C. D. CHAUHAN; 869 employees.

Metro Sefalana Cash and Carry Ltd (METSEF): Plot 49767, Samora Machel Dr., Private Bag 00422, Gaborone; tel. 3912700; f. 1994; wholesale retailer; 39% each owned by Sefalana Holding Co Ltd and Metcash South Africa; revenue 990.9m. (April 2005); Man. Dir B. DAVIS; 23 brs.

Turnstar Holdings Ltd: Acumen Park, Plot 50370, Fairground Office Park, POB 1172, Gaborone; tel. 3180156; fax 3180921; e-mail frabie@khumopam.co.bw; f. 2002; property investment; revenue 65.8m. (Oct. 2006); Chair. C. M. LEKAUKAU; Man. Dir G. H. ABDOOLA.

CO-OPERATIVES

Department of Co-operative Development: POB 86, Gaborone; tel. 3950721; fax 3951657; e-mail vmosele@gov.bw; f. 1964; promotes marketing and supply, consumer, dairy, horticultural and fisheries co-operatives, thrift and loan societies, credit societies, a co-operative union and a co-operative bank; Commissioner VIOLET MOSELE.

TRADE UNIONS

Botswana Federation of Trade Unions (BFTU): POB 440, Gaborone; tel. and fax 3952534; f. 1977; affiliated to the Int. Trade Union Confed., the Org. of African Trade Union Unity and the Southern African Trade Union Co-ordination Council (SATUCC); Pres. RONALD DUST BAIPIDI; 25,000 mems (2001).

Affiliated Unions

Botswana Bank Employees' Union (BOBEU): Ext. 4, South Ring Rd, Dilalelo, POB 111, Gaborone; tel. 3905893; Gen. Sec. ALFRED SELEKE.

Botswana Construction Workers' Union: POB 1508, Gaborone; tel. 352534; fax 357790; affiliated to the Building and Wood Workers Int.; Gen. Sec. JOSHUA KESIILWE.

Botswana Diamond Sorters and Valuators' Staff Union (BDSVU): POB 1186, Gaborone; affiliated to the Int. Fed. of Chemical, Energy, Mine and Gen. Workers' Unions; Gen. Sec. EDWARD KELONEILWE.

Botswana Hotel, Wholesalers, Furniture, Agricultural and Commercial General Workers' Union (BHWFACGWU): POB 62, Gaborone; tel. 3911874; fax 3959360; f. 2006 by merger of Botswana Agricultural Marketing Board Workers' Union, Botswana Commercial and Gen. Workers' Union (f. 1988), Botswana Hotel Travel and Tourism Union, and Botswana Wholesale Furniture and Retail Workers' Union.

Botswana Mining Workers' Union (BMWU): POB 86, Orapa; tel. 2970331; fax 2970067; affiliated to the Int. Fed. of Chemical, Energy, Mine and General Workers' Unions; Chair. CHIMBIDZANI CHIMIDZA; Sec.-Gen. JACK TLHAGALE.

Botswana Postal Services Workers' Union (BOPSWU): POB 87, Gaborone; Chair. AARON LEFU.

Botswana Power Corpn Workers' Union (BPCWU): Private Bag 0053, Gaborone; affiliated to the Int. Fed. of Chemical, Energy, Mine and General Workers' Unions; Gen. Sec. MAVIS KOOGOTSITSE.

Botswana Railways Amalgamated Workers' Union (BRAWU): POB 181, Gaborone; affiliated to the Int. Transport Workers' Fed.; Chair. LETLAMPONA MOKGALAJWE.

Botswana Telecommunications Employees' Union (BOTEU): Gaborone; Pres. LESETSWE KOFA.

National Amalgamated Local and Central Government, Parastatal, Statutory Body and Manual Workers' Union (NALCPMWU): Ext. 15, Plot No. 4946/7, Jawara Rd, POB 374, Gaborone; tel. 352790; fax 357790; e-mail nalcg.pwu@info.bw; affiliated to the Public Services Int.; Chair. DAVID OTHUSITSE BINA TSALAILE; Gen. Sec. SIMON KGAOGANANG.

Other affiliated unions include: the Air Botswana Employees' Union; the Botswana Beverages and Allied Workers' Union; the Botswana Central Bank Staff Union; the Botswana Housing Corpn Staff Union; the Botswana Institute of Development Management Workers' Union; the Botswana Manufacturing and Packaging Workers' Union; the Botswana Meat Industry Union; the Botswana National Development Bank Staff Union; the Botswana Private Medical and Health Services Workers' Union; the Botswana Savings Bank Employees' Union; the Botswana Vaccine Institute Staff Union; and the Rural Industry Promotions Co Workers' Union.

Principal Non-affiliated Unions

Botswana Secondary Teachers' Trade Union (BOSETU): Unit 5, Commerce Park, Broadhurst, POB 404341, Gaborone; tel. 3937472; fax 3170845; f. 1986 as Botswana Fed. for Secondary School Teachers; present name adopted on achieving union status in 2006; Pres. ERIC DITAU.

Botswana Unified Local Govt Service Asscn (BULGSA): Private Bag 40, Francistown; tel. and fax 2413312; internet www.bulgsa.org.bw; affiliated to the Public Services Int.; Pres. PELOTSHWEU A. D. S. BAENG; Sec.-Gen. MOTELEBANE SHEPPARD MOTELEBANE.

Transport

RAILWAYS

The 960-km railway line from Mafikeng, South Africa, to Bulawayo, Zimbabwe, passes through Botswana and has been operated by Botswana Railways (BR) since 1987. In 1997 there were 888 km of 1,067-mm-gauge track within Botswana, including three branches serving the Selebi-Phikwe mining complex (56 km), the Morupule colliery (16 km) and the Sua Pan soda-ash deposits (175 km). BR derives 85%–90% of its earnings from freight traffic, although passenger services do operate between Gaborone and Francistown, and Lobatse and Bulawayo. Through its links with Spoornet, which operates the South African railways system, and the National Railways of Zimbabwe, BR provides connections with Namibia and Swaziland to the south, and an uninterrupted rail link to Zambia, the Democratic Republic of the Congo, Angola, Mozambique, Tanzania and Malawi to the north. However, freight traffic on BR was severely reduced following Zimbabwe's construction, in 1999, of a rail link from Bulawayo to Beitbridge, on its border with South Africa.

Botswana Railways (BR): Private Bag 52, Mahalapye; tel. 4711375; fax 4711377; f. 1987; Chair. IQBAL EBRAHIM; CEO ANDREW LUNGA.

ROADS

In 1999 there were 10,217 km of roads, including 3,360 km of main roads, and 2,210 km of secondary roads. Some 55% of the road network was paved, including a main road from Gaborone, via Francistown, to Kazungula, where the borders of Botswana, Namibia, Zambia and Zimbabwe meet. (In 2004 some 6,116 km of road were bitumenized.) The construction of a 340-km road between Nata and Maun was completed in the late 1990s. Construction of the 600-km Trans-Kalahari Highway, from Jwaneng to the port of Walvis Bay on the Namibian coast, commenced in 1990 and was completed in 1998. A car-ferry service operates from Kazungula across the Zambezi river into Zambia.

Department of Road Transport and Safety: Private Bag 0026, Gaborone; tel. 3905442; responsible for national road network; responsible to the Ministry of Works and Transport; Dir MOSES K. SEBOLAI.

CIVIL AVIATION

The main international airport is at Gaborone. Four other major airports are located at Kasane, Maun, Francistown and Ghanzi. In 2000 there were also 108 airfields throughout the country. Scheduled services of Air Botswana are supplemented by an active charter and business sector. In September 2005 the Government announced that the Department of Civil Aviation would be converted into a parastatal company, the Civil Aviation Authority.

Air Botswana: POB 92, Sir Seretse Khama Airport, Gaborone; tel. 3952812; fax 3974802; e-mail commercial@airbotswana.co.bw; internet www.airbotswana.co.bw; f. 1972; 45% state-owned; transfer to private sector suspended in April 2004; domestic services and regional services to countries in eastern and southern Africa; Chair. G. N. THIPE; Gen. Man. LANCE BROGDEN; 150,000 passengers per year.

Tourism

There are five game reserves and three national parks, including Chobe, near Victoria Falls, on the Zambia–Zimbabwe border. Efforts to expand the tourism industry include plans for the construction of new hotels and the rehabilitation of existing hotel facilities. In 2004 foreign tourist arrivals were estimated at 1,522,807, compared with 1,405,535 in 2003. Receipts from tourism increased from an estimated US $319m. in 2002 to $457m. in 2003, and to $549m. in 2004.

Department of Tourism: Ministry of Environment, Wildlife and Tourism, Private Bag 0047, Standard House, 2nd Floor, Main Mall, Gaborone; tel. 3953024; fax 3908675; internet www.botswanatourism.org; f. 1994; Dir TLHABOLOGO NDZINGE.

Department of Wildlife and National Parks: POB 131, Gaborone; tel. 3971405; fax 3912354; e-mail dwnp@gov.bw; Dir J. MATLHARE.

Hospitality and Tourism Association of Botswana (HATAB): Private Bag 00423, Gaborone; tel. 3957144; fax 3903201; e-mail hatab@hatab.bw; internet www.hatab.bw; f. 1982; fmrly Hotel and Tourism Assen of Botswana; CEO MORONGOE NTLOEDIBE-DISELE.

Defence

Military service is voluntary. Botswana established a permanent defence force in 1977. As assessed at November 2006, the total strength of the Botswana Defence Force (BDF) was some 9,000, comprising an army of 8,500 and an air force of 500. In addition, there was a paramilitary police force of 1,500. There are plans to enlarge the strength of the army to 10,000 men. In August 2005 the Government announced plans to recruit women into the BDF, although no specific date was given.

Defence Expenditure: Estimated P1,600m. in 2006.

Defence Force Commander: Maj.-Gen. TEBOGO H. C. MASIRE.

Education

Although education is not compulsory, enrolment ratios are high. Primary education begins at seven years of age and lasts for up to seven years. Secondary education, beginning at the age of 13, lasts for a further five years, comprising a first cycle of three years and a second of two years. According to UNESCO estimates, enrolment at primary schools in 2003/04 included 82% of children in the relevant age-group (boys 81%; girls 83%), while the comparable ratio for secondary enrolment was 61% (boys 58%; girls 64%). The Government aims to provide universal access to 10 years of basic education. Botswana has the highest teacher-pupil ratio in Africa, but continues to rely heavily on expatriate secondary school teachers. School fees were abolished in 1987. However, in October 2005 legislation was approved to reintroduce fees for secondary education from January 2006. Tertiary education is provided by the University of Botswana (which was attended by 15,725 students in 2005) and the affiliated College of Technical and Vocational Education. There are also some 49 other technical and vocational training centres, including the Institutes of Health Sciences, the Botswana College of Agriculture, the Roads Training College, the Colleges of Education (Primary and Secondary), and the Botswana Institute of Administration and Commerce. Education was allocated some 15.5% of total projected expenditure under the National Development Plan for 1998–2003. Expenditure on education by the central Government in 2006/07 was budgeted at P5,512.9m. (representing 24.6% of total expenditure by the central Government).

Bibliography

Amanze, J. N. *African Traditional Religions and Culture in Botswana: A Comprehensive Textbook*. Gaborone, Pula Press, 2002.

Amanze, J. N. (Ed.). *African Christianity in Botswana*. Gweru, Mambo Press, 1998.

Bolaane, M., and Mgadla, P. T. *Batswana*. New York, NY, Rosen Publishing Group Inc., 1997.

Botswana Society. *Settlement in Botswana*. London, Heinemann Educational, 1982.

Chilisa, B., Mafela, L., and Preece, J. (Eds). *Educational Research for Sustainable Development*. Gaborone, Lightbooks Publishers, 2005.

Dale, R. *Botswana's Search for Autonomy in Southern Africa*. Westport, CT, Greenwood Press, 1995.

Dingake, M. *The Politics of Confusion: The BNF Saga 1984–1998*. Gaborone, Bay Publishing (Pty) Ltd, 2004.

Düsing, S. *Traditional Leadership and Democratisation in Southern Africa: A Comparative Study of Botswana, Namibia, and Southern Africa*. London, Lit, 2002.

Du Toit, P. *State Building and Democracy in Southern Africa: Botswana, Zimbabwe and South Africa*. Washington, DC, US Institute of Peace Press, 1995.

Good, K. *Realizing Democracy in Botswana, Namibia and South Africa*. Pretoria, Africa Institute, 1997.

Bushmen and Diamonds: (Un)Civil Society in Botswana. Uppsala, Nordic Africa Institute, 2003.

Harvey, C. (Ed.). *Banking Policy in Botswana: Orthodox but Untypical*. Brighton, Institute of Development Studies, 1996.

Hassan, Z. E. *Livelihood Diversification in Drought-prone Rural Botswana*. Kiel, Wissenschaftsverlag Vauk Kiel, 2002.

Hayward, M. F. *Elections in Independent Africa*. Boulder, CO, Westview Press, 1987.

Jackson, A. *Botswana, 1939–1945: An African Country at War*. Oxford, Clarendon Press, 1999.

Landau, P. S. *The Realm of the Word: Language, Gender and Christianity in a Southern African Kingdom*. London, James Currey Publishers, 1996.

Leith, J. C. *Why Botswana Prospered*. Montreal, McGill-Queen's University Press, 2005.

Levy, W. *A Chronicle of Print and Electronic Media for Aspiring Journalists*. Gaborone, Lightbooks Publishers, 2005.

Livingston, J. *Debility and the Moral Imagination in Botswana*. Bloomington, IN, Indiana University Press, 2005.

Maundeni, Z. *40 Years of Democracy in Botswana, 1965-2005*. Gaborone, Mmegi Publishing House, 2005.

Civil Society, Politics and the State in Botswana. Gaborone, Medi Publishers, 2004.

Women and Food Security in Rural Botswana. Arlington, VA, W1, 1998.

Mazonde, I. N. (Ed.). *Minorities in the Millennium: Perspectives from Botswana*. Gaborone, Lightbooks, 2002.

Mogalakwe, M. *The State and Organised Labour in Botswana*. Aldershot, Ashgate, 1997.

Molomo, M. G., and Mokopakgosi, B. T. *Multi-Party Democracy in Botswana*. Harare, SAPES Trust, 1991.

Morton, F., *et al. Historical Dictionary of Botswana*. 2nd Edn, Methuen, NJ, Scarecrow Press, 1989.

Motzafi-Haller, P. *Fragmented Worlds, Coherent Lives: The Politics of Difference in Botswana*. Westport, CT, Bergin and Garvey, 2002.

Ntanda Nsereko, D. *Constitutional Law in Botswana*. Gaborone, Pula Press, 2002.

Oommen, M. A., *et al. Botswana Economy since Independence*. New Delhi, Tate/McGraw-Hill, 1983.

Peters, P. E. *Dividing the Commons: Politics, Policy and Culture in Botswana*. London, University Press of Virginia, 1994.

Preece, J., and Mosweunyane, D. *Perceptions of Citizenship Responsibility Amongst Botswana Youth*. Gaborone, Lightbooks Publishers, 2004.

Rakner, L. *Botswana: 30 Years of Economic Growth, Democracy and Aid*. Bergen, CMI, 1996.

Sallein, J. S. (Ed.), *et al. Aspects of the Botswana Economy*. Oxford, James Curry Publishers, 1998.

Saugestad, S. *The Inconvenient Indigenous: Remote Area Development in Botswana*. Uppsala, Nordic Africa Institute, 2001.

Schmidt, D. A. *The Bechuanaland Pioneers and Gunners*. Westport, CT, Praeger, 2006.

Seidman, J. *In Our Own Image*. Gaborone, Foundation for Education with Production, 1990.

Seisa, S., and Youngman, F. (Eds). *Education For All in Botswana*. Gaborone, Macmillan Botswana, 1995.

Siphambe, H. K., *et al. Economic Development of Botswana: Facets, Policies, Problems and Prospects*. Gaborone, Bay Publishing (Pty) Ltd, 2005.

Stedman, S. J. *Botswana: The Political Economy of Democratic Development*. Boulder, CO, Lynne Rienner Publishers, 1993.

Tlou, T., *et al. Seretse Khama, 1921–1980*. Johannesburg, Macmillan, 1995.

Vanqa, T. P. *The Development of Education in Botswana*. Gaborone, Lightbooks Publishers, 2001.

Vaughn, O. *Chiefs, Power and Social Change: Chiefship and Modern Politics in Botswana, 1880s–1990s*. Trenton, NJ, Africa World Press, 2003.

Werbner, R. *Reasonable Radicals and Citizenship in Botswana: The Public Anthropology of Kalanga Elites*. Bloomington, IN, Indiana Univ. Press, 2004.

Williams, A. S. *Colour Bar: The Triumph of Seretse Khama and His Nation*. London; New York, NY, Allen Lane, 2006.

Colour Bar: Seretse Khama's Battle for Botswana and an Unconventional Marriage. London; New York, NY, Allen Lane, 2006.

Wiseman, J. *Botswana*. Oxford, ABC Clio, 1992.

THE BRITISH INDIAN OCEAN TERRITORY (BIOT)

The British Indian Ocean Territory (BIOT) was formed in November 1965, through the amalgamation of the former Seychelles islands of Aldabra, Desroches and Farquhar with the Chagos Archipelago, a group of islands 1,930 km north-east of Mauritius, previously administered by the Governor of Mauritius. Aldabra, Desroches and Farquhar were ceded to Seychelles when that country was granted independence in June 1976. Since then BIOT has comprised only the Chagos Archipelago, including the coral atoll Diego Garcia, with a total land area of 60 sq km (23 sq miles), together with a surrounding area of some 54,400 sq km (21,000 sq miles) of ocean.

BIOT was established to meet British and US defence requirements in the Indian Ocean. Previously, the principal economic function of the islands was the production of copra: the islands, together with the coconut plantations, were owned by a private company. The copra industry declined after the Second World War, and, following the purchase of the islands by the British Crown in 1967, the plantations ceased to operate and the inhabitants were offered the choice of resettlement in Mauritius or in Seychelles. The majority (which numbered about 1,200) went to Mauritius, the resettlement taking place during 1969–73, prior to the construction of the military facility. Mauritius subsequently campaigned for the immediate return of the Territory, and received support from the Organization of African Unity (now the African Union) and from India. A protracted dispute with the United Kingdom over compensation for those displaced ended in 1982 when the British Government agreed to an *ex-gratia* payment of £4m. In July 2000 a judicial review of the validity of the Immigration Ordinance of 1971, under which the islanders were removed from BIOT, and which continued to prevent them from resettling in the Territory, was instigated. Meanwhile, in March 1999 it was disclosed that the displaced islanders and their families, now estimated to number up to 4,000, were not to be included in the offer of full British citizenship, with the right of abode in the United Kingdom, that was to be extended to residents of other United Kingdom Overseas Territories by legislation pending in the British Parliament.

In November 2000 the British High Court ruled that the Chagos islanders (Ilois) had been illegally evicted from the Chagos Archipelago, and quashed Section 4 of the 1971 Ordinance, which prevented the return of the Ilois to BIOT. During the case it transpired that the British Government had received a subsidy of US $11m. on the purchase of Polaris submarines in the 1960s from the USA, in return for the lease of Diego Garcia for the US military. Furthermore, the Government had apparently termed the Ilois 'contract workers' in order to persuade the UN that the islanders were not an indigenous population with democratic rights. However, memorandums of the Foreign and Commonwealth Office revealed government knowledge of some of the Ilois living in the Chagos Archipelago for two generations. The British Secretary of State for Foreign and Commonwealth Affairs declined an appeal, thereby granting the islanders an immediate right to return to BIOT. Despite this, a new ordinance, issued in January 2001, allowed the residents to return to any of the islands in the Archipelago, except Diego Garcia, easing US fears of a population near its military base. The British Overseas Territories Act came into effect in May 2002, allowing the displaced islanders to apply for British citizenship. At that time the British Government was also examining the feasibility of a return to the Chagos Archipelago for the islanders, who continued to seek compensation. (However, a report had concluded that resettlement on the atolls of Salomon and Peros Banhos was logistically possible, if not necessarily economically viable.) In October 2003 the High Court ruled that although the islanders could claim to have been ill-treated, the British Government had not known at the time that its actions were unlawful and their claims for compensation were dismissed. Many of the islanders subsequently moved to the United Kingdom.

In December 2000 the Ilois announced their intention to sue the US Government for US $6,000m. in compensation. The hearing of the case, in which the Ilois alleged genocide, torture and forced relocation, opened in December 2001. In mid-2002 the Chagos islanders initiated legal action against the recruitment consultancy that supplies civilian employees for the US naval base on Diego Garcia, alleging that the company had discriminated against them when appointing staff to the base; the consultancy was the first of 12 entities that the islanders intended to sue in the USA. (In April 2006 the US Federal Court of Appeals of the District of Columbia ruled that it had no authority to order compensation to those evicted in order to make way for the establishment of a US military base on Diego Garcia.)

In June 2004 the British Government issued two decrees explicitly stating the country's control of immigration services within the archipelago and banning the Ilois from returning. Nevertheless, in a meeting with a British official in November the Chagossian group reached agreement for some 100 people to travel to Diego Garcia for the purpose of visiting the graves of relatives. In early April 2006 102 Chagossians commenced a visit to the archipelago. On 11 May the British High Court ruled that the exclusion of the islanders from their territory was irrational and unlawful. The British Government commenced proceedings to overturn the May ruling at the Court of Appeal in February 2007; however in May that court confirmed that the residents of the Chagos Archipelago had been unlawfully removed and upheld the displaced islanders' immediate right to return. It was estimated that only approximately 500 of the 2,000 deported during the 1960s and 1970s were still alive.

A 1966 agreement between the United Kingdom and the USA provided for BIOT to be used by both countries over an initial period of 50 years, with the option of extending this for a further 20 years. The United Kingdom undertook to cede the Chagos Archipelago to Mauritius when it was no longer required for defence purposes. Originally the US military presence was limited to a communications centre on Diego Garcia. In 1972, however, construction of a naval support facility was begun, apparently in response to the expansion of the Soviet maritime presence in the Indian Ocean. In August 1987 the US navy began to use Diego Garcia as a facility for minesweeping helicopters taking part in operations in the Persian (Arabian) Gulf. Following Iraq's invasion of Kuwait in August 1990, Diego Garcia was used as a base for US B-52 aircraft, which were deployed in the Gulf region. Runway facilities on Diego Garcia were again used in September 1996 and December 1998 as a base for US support aircraft during US missile attacks on Iraq. In October 2001 US forces used the Diego Garcia base to launch strikes on Afghanistan with B-52 aircraft. In March–April 2003 the base was used to launch bombing raids on Iraq in the US-led military campaign to oust the regime of Saddam Hussain.

In January 1988 Mauritius renewed its campaign to regain sovereignty over the Chagos Archipelago, and reiterated its support for a 'zone of peace' in the Indian Ocean. In November 1989, following an incident in which a military aircraft belonging to the US Air Force accidentally bombed a US naval vessel near Diego Garcia, a demonstration was held outside the US embassy in Mauritius, demanding the withdrawal of foreign military forces from the area. The Mauritius Government announced that it would draw the attention of the UN Security Council to the dangers that it perceived in the execution of US military air exercises. However, the US Assistant Secretary of State for African Affairs reiterated during an official visit to Mauritius, in the same month, that the USA would maintain its military presence in the Indian Ocean. In December 2000, following the British High Court's ruling, Mauritius once again staked its claim for sovereignty over the Chagos Archipelago. In April 2004 Paul Bérenger, the recently installed Prime Minister of Mauritius, renewed the campaign to reclaim sovereignty after specialists in international law advised him that the decree by which the United Kingdom separated the Chagos Archipelago from Mauritius was illegal. An attempt was made to block the Mauritian Government from pursuing the case at the International Court of Justice on the basis of a long-standing ruling, whereby members of the Commonwealth could not take the United Kingdom to court; in July the ruling was extended to former members of the Commonwealth, in order to prevent Mauritius from circumventing the obstacle by withdrawing from that organization. Mauritius announced that it would pursue the matter at the General Assembly of the UN.

The civil administration of BIOT is the responsibility of a non-resident commissioner in the Foreign and Commonwealth Office in London, United Kingdom, represented on Diego Garcia by a Royal Navy commander and a small British naval presence. A chief justice, a senior magistrate and a principal legal adviser (who performs the functions of an attorney-general) are resident in the United Kingdom.

Land Area: about 60 sq km.

Population: There are no permanent inhabitants. In November 2004 there were about 4,000 US and British military personnel and civilian support staff stationed in the Territory.

Currency: The official currency is the pound sterling, but the US dollar is also accepted.

Commissioner: LEIGH TURNER, Head of Overseas Territories Dept, Foreign and Commonwealth Office, King Charles St, London SW1A 2AH, United Kingdom; tel. (20) 7008-2890.

Administrator: TONY HUMPHRIES, Overseas Territories Dept, Foreign and Commonwealth Office, King Charles St, London SW1A 2AH, United Kingdom; tel. (20) 7008-2890.

Commissioner's Representative: Commdr NEIL HINCH, RN, Diego Garcia, c/o BFPO Ships.

BURKINA FASO

Physical and Social Geography

R. J. HARRISON CHURCH

Burkina Faso (formerly the Republic of Upper Volta) is a land-locked state of West Africa and is situated north of Côte d'Ivoire, Ghana and Togo. Burkina has an area of 274,200 sq km (105,870 sq miles). The December 1996 census recorded a total population of 10,312,609. According to UN estimates, the population had risen to 14,359,000 at mid-2006, giving an average density of 52.4 inhabitants per sq km. In recent years there has been large-scale emigration to neighbouring Côte d'Ivoire and Ghana by people seeking work on farms, in industries andin the service trades, although economic and political difficulties in these host countries (particularly the former) have prompted the return of large numbers of migrant workers to Burkina. The main ethnic groups are the Mossi in the north and the Bobo in the south-west. Along the northern border are the semi-nomadic Fulani, who are also present in the east of the country. The capital city, Ouagadougou, had a population of 709,736 in 1996; the second city, Bobo-Dioulasso, had 309,771 inhabitants at that time.

Towards the south-western border with Mali there are primary sandstones, terminating eastward in the Banfora escarpment. As in Guinea, Mali and Ghana, where there are also great expanses of these rocks, their residual soils are poor and water percolates deep within them. Although most of the rest of the country is underlain by granite, gneisses and schists, there is much loose sand or bare laterite; consequently, there are extensive infertile areas. Moreover, annual rainfall is only some 635–1,145 mm, and comes in a rainy season of at the most five months. Water is scarce except by the rivers or in the Gourma swampy area; by the former the simulium fly, whose bite leads to blindness, has been the target of extensive eradication projects, while in the latter the tsetse, a fly that can cause sleeping-sickness, is found. Given the grim physical environment, the density of population in the north-central Mossi area is remarkable. The area is, in fact, one of the oldest indigenous kingdoms of West Africa, dating back to the 11th century. Islam first penetrated the area during the 14th–16th centuries. At the end of the 18th century some local rulers, notably the leader of the Mossi, adopted Islam, but traditional religious practices among the population remained strong. Although Islam's expansion was facilitated by the circumstances of French rule, more than one-half of the population retain their traditional beliefs.

Burkina Faso has valuable deposits of gold, manganese and zinc, industrial exploitation of which is in progress or is planned. Reserves of silver, nickel, lead, phosphates and vanadium have also been identified.

Recent History

PIERRE ENGLEBERT

Revised by KATHARINE MURISON

Burkina Faso (then Upper Volta) became a self-governing republic within the French Community in December 1958. Full independence followed on 5 August 1960, with Maurice Yaméogo, the leader of the Union démocratique voltaïque (UDV), as President. Yaméogo's administration was autocratic in style. Opposition parties were banned, and popular support for the Government receded as the country's economic condition worsened. In January 1966 Yaméogo was deposed in an army coup, led by Lt-Col Sangoulé Lamizana. An elected civilian administration took office in December 1970, although effective power remained with the army. Further elections took place in May 1978, but all political parties except the UDV, the Union nationale pour la défense de la démocratie, led by Hermann Yaméogo, the son of the country's first President, and Prof. Joseph Ki-Zerbo's Union progressiste voltaïque were suppressed.

ARMY REGIMES, 1980–87

In November 1980, following a period of economic difficulty and popular unrest, Lamizana was overthrown in a bloodless coup led by Col Saye Zerbo, who formed a governing Comité militaire de redressement pour le progrès national (CMRPN) and banned political activity. By early 1982 serious rifts were evident within the CMRPN, and in November Zerbo and the CMRPN were supplanted by a military Conseil du salut du peuple (CSP), led by Maj. Jean-Baptiste Ouédraogo. Capt. Thomas Sankara, who had resigned from the CMRPN in 1981, was appointed Prime Minister.

It became increasingly apparent that Ouédraogo was presiding over a divided regime. In May 1983 Ouédraogo ordered the arrest of Sankara and his supporters in the CSP. Members of Sankara's commando unit, led by Capt. Blaise Compaoré, mutinied, and in August Sankara deposed Ouédraogo in a military coup. Sankara installed a Conseil national de la révolution (CNR) and formed a new Government, with himself as Head of State and Compaoré as Minister of State at the Presidency.

The CNR swiftly reorganized the country's public administration and installed 'revolutionary people's tribunals' to try former public officials charged with corruption. The army was purged, and civilian Comités pour la défense de la révolution (CDRs) were established throughout the country to implement government policy. In August 1984 Sankara renamed the country Burkina Faso ('Land of the Incorruptible Men'). A thorough reform of the judicial and education systems was conducted, and economic austerity measures implemented. Sankara's revolution became less identified with Marxism, and instead sought to accommodate a wider cross-section of society.

During 1987 divisions between Sankara and the three other leaders of the CNR became increasingly evident. On 15 October a commando unit loyal to Compaoré opened fire on Sankara, killing him and 13 allies. A Front populaire (FP) was proclaimed as successor to the CNR, and Compaoré, the Chairman of the FP, became Head of State.

THE FRONT POPULAIRE

While the FP pledged a continuation of the CNR's revolutionary politics, a phase of 'rectification', to incorporate economic liberalization, was announced. Negotiations for financial assistance with the IMF and the World Bank were instigated. The CDRs were abolished in 1988. In April 1989 the formation was announced of a new political grouping, the Organisation pour la démocratie populaire/Mouvement du travail (ODP/MT), under the leadership of a prominent supporter of Compaoré,

Clément Oumarou Ouédraogo. Leading members of groups that had refused to affiliate to the ODP/MT were removed from political office, while Ouédraogo was appointed as Minister-delegate to the Co-ordinating Committee of the FP. In September four leaders associated with the 1983 revolution were summarily executed, following the alleged discovery of a coup plot. Compaoré subsequently assumed the defence and security portfolio.

At the first congress of the FP in March 1990, delegates appointed a commission to draft a new constitution that would define a process of 'democratization'. In April Clément Oumarou Ouédraogo was dismissed from the leadership of the ODP/MT and subsequently removed from the Government. Roch Marc Christian Kaboré, whose political orientation was closer to that of Compaoré, assumed both the leadership of the ODP/MT and a senior position within the FP. Kaboré was promoted to the rank of Minister of State in September.

The first draft of the Constitution, published in October 1990, provided for a multi-party political system in what was to be designated the Fourth Republic. In March 1991 a congress of the ODP/MT adopted Compaoré as the party's official candidate for the forthcoming presidential election and abolished its adherence to Marxist-Leninist ideology. In May an appeal was made to political exiles to return to Burkina, and in August Compaoré declared an amnesty for all 'political crimes' committed since independence.

THE FOURTH REPUBLIC

The draft Constitution was endorsed by 93% of those who voted (reportedly one-half of the electorate) in a national referendum on 2 June 1991. The Constitution took effect on 11 June, whereupon the functions of the FP were separated from the organs of state. Compaoré remained Head of State, pending a presidential election, while the most senior member of the new transitional Council of Ministers was Kaboré. Many political parties criticized the dominant role of the ODP/MT, and several nominated government members declined to accept their appointments. A reorganized Government, appointed in July, included several opposition members, among them Hermann Yaméogo. (Yaméogo, himself now a presidential candidate, had been appointed to the FP in March 1990, only to be expelled three months later.) In August 1991, however, Yaméogo and two other members of his Alliance pour la démocratie et la fédération (ADF) resigned their government posts, in protest against proposed electoral procedures. In September opposition parties established a Coordination des forces démocratiques (CFD), and the remaining opposition members resigned from the transitional Government. In October five CFD representatives withdrew their presidential candidatures.

Compaoré (who had resigned his army commission in order to contest the presidency as a civilian) was the sole candidate in the presidential election, which took place, as scheduled, on 1 December 1991. He secured the support of 90.4% of those who voted, but an appeal by the CFD for a boycott of the poll was widely heeded, and an abstention rate of 74.7% was recorded. Shortly after the election Clément Oumarou Ouédraogo was assassinated. Compaoré was sworn in as President of the Fourth Republic on 24 December. In January 1992 the rehabilitation was announced of some 4,000 people who had been punished for political or trade union activity since 1983. In February 1992 the Government was reorganized to include Hermann Yaméogo and three other opposition members.

Some 27 parties contested postponed elections to the 107-seat Assemblée des députés populaires (ADP), which were held on 24 May 1992. The ODP/MT won 78 seats, while Pierre Tapsoba's Convention nationale des patriotes progressistes—Parti social-démocrate (CNPP—PSD) secured 12 seats, and the ADF four. An abstention rate of 64.8% was recorded. Compaoré appointed an economist, Youssouf Ouédraogo, as Prime Minister; the new Government included representatives of seven political organizations, although the ODP/MT retained control of most strategic ministries. In May 1993, following a split in the CNPP—PSD, six of the party's deputies joined Joseph Ki-Zerbo's newly formed Parti pour la démocratie et le progrès (PDP).

Following the 50% devaluation of the CFA franc, in January 1994, the Government introduced emergency measures, in an attempt to offset the immediate adverse effects of the currency's depreciation. Negotiations between trade unions, which denounced the measures as inadequate, and the Government failed to reach a compromise, and in March Youssouf Ouédraogo resigned. Kaboré was subsequently appointed Prime Minister; the ODP/MT and its associates dominated his administration, although Hermann Yaméogo received a ministerial post.

At municipal elections in February 1995 the ODP/MT won control of 26 of Burkina's 33 major towns, although less than 10% of those eligible were reported to have registered to vote. In December members were appointed to serve a three-year term in Burkina's second legislative chamber, the 178-member Chambre des représentants, which was to function in an advisory capacity.

In February 1996 Kadré Désiré Ouédraogo, hitherto Deputy Governor of the Banque centrale des états de l'Afrique de l'ouest, was appointed to succeed Kaboré as Prime Minister. Meanwhile, a new, social-democratic political organization, the Congrès pour la démocratie et le progrès (CDP), was formed, grouping the ODP/MT and 10 other parties. Ouédraogo assumed personal responsibility for the economy and finance in September.

Constitutional amendments and a new electoral code were approved by the ADP in January 1997: among the changes were the removal of restrictions on the renewal of the presidential mandate (which hitherto had been renewable only once), as well as an increase in the number of parliamentary seats to 111. The number of administrative provinces was also increased from 30 to 45. Elections to the enlarged legislature, now renamed the Assemblée nationale, took place on 11 May, contested by some 569 candidates from 13 political parties. The CDP won an overwhelming majority, with a total of 101 seats. The PDP secured six seats, and the Rassemblement démocratique africain and the ADF each took two seats. Kadré Désiré Ouédraogo retained the premiership in the new Government appointed in June.

In July 1998 an independent electoral body, the Commission électorale nationale indépendante (CENI), comprising six representatives of the legislative majority (the CDP and its allies), six opposition representatives and 14 representatives of civic society, was inaugurated. Shortly beforehand, however, several opposition parties announced their intention to boycott the forthcoming presidential election, stating that the measures in place were no guarantee of transparency at the poll.

Political Instability

As the presidential election approached, principal opposition leaders, including Ki-Zerbo and Hermann Yaméogo, the latter now leading the Alliance pour la démocratie et la fédération—Rassemblement démocratique africain (ADF—RDA), refused to participate. At the election, which was held on 15 November 1998, Compaoré was challenged by Ram Ouédraogo, leader of the ecologist Union des verts pour le développement du Burkina, and Frédéric Guirma, representing the Front de refus du rassemblement démocratique africain. The opposition denounced the election as fraudulent, but international monitors and national observers pronounced themselves largely satisfied with the conduct of the campaign. Turn-out by voters, at 56.1%, was appreciably higher than at the 1991 presidential election, despite opposition calls for a boycott. The results confirmed a decisive victory for Compaoré, with 87.5% of the valid votes cast. A new Government, again headed by Kadré Désiré Ouédraogo, was appointed in January 1999.

In December 1998 Norbert Zongo, an investigative journalist and managing editor of the newspaper *L'Indépendant*, was found dead, together with three colleagues, precipitating a major political crisis. Zongo, a frequent critic of Compaoré, had been investigating the death of David Ouédraogo, a chauffeur (employed by François Compaoré, the President's brother), who had allegedly been tortured to death by members of the presidential guard. Several opposition groups, demanding a full investigation into the matter, subsequently formed the Collectif d'organisations démocratiques de masse et de partis politiques. In January 1999 the formation of an independent commission of inquiry was announced. In early May the commission of inquiry (in which the Collectif refused to participate) submitted its final report, which suggested that members of the presidential guard implicated in the death of David Ouédraogo were also responsible for the murders of Zongo and his colleagues. In mid-May three prominent members of the opposition, including Halidou Ouédraogo, the Chairman of the Collectif, and Hermann Yaméogo, were briefly detained by the security forces, on charges that included plotting a *coup d'état*. In late May Compaoré announced that the presidential guard was to be reorganized, and that the state would pay compensation to the families of David Ouédraogo, Norbert Zongo and their associates.

In early June 1999 Compaoré established a Collège des sages, composed of state elders, religious and ethnic leaders, and other respected citizens, which was to work towards national reconciliation and to investigate unpunished political crimes committed since 1960. In mid-June 1999 the Collège ordered the arrest of three members of the presidential guard, accused of the murder of David Ouédraogo, and further implicated in the murder of Zongo. The Collège published its report in August, recommending that a government of national unity be formed, in addition to a 'commission of truth and justice', which would oversee the transition to a truly plural political system and investigate unresolved political murders, including that of former President Sankara. The Collège also suggested that amnesty be granted to those implicated during the commission's investigations, and that compensation be paid to the families of victims. The Collège further recommended that Compaoré not seek re-election and that fresh legislative elections be held. Although Compaoré praised the conclusions of the report, the opposition rejected the proposed amnesty and the requirement that Compaoré assent to the proposed reforms.

In September 1999 the Prime Minister began negotiations with the leaders of the major political parties in order to identify the key objectives of any government of national unity. Most political leaders indicated, however, that they would not participate in any such government until legal proceedings were expedited against those suspected of the murders of Ouédraogo and Zongo. Consequently, only two members of the opposition were included in the new Council of Ministers announced in October. In November, in accordance with the recommendations of the Collège des sages, two advisory commissions were inaugurated, one of which was to examine clauses of the Constitution and to formulate rules governing political parties, while the other was to promote national reconciliation. Many opposition parties refused to participate in the commissions.

In January 2000 the ruling CDP organized a public demonstration in favour of the proposals of the advisory commission on political reform, which had recommended the modification of the electoral code and the reform of the judiciary and the Constitution. In particular, the commission recommended the restriction of the presidential mandate to two successive terms. The legislature subsequently voted to revise the electoral code and to accord greater powers to the CENI. The opposition, however, expressed its continued determination to boycott elections until the Ouédraogo and Zongo cases were fully resolved. In February the advisory commission on national reconciliation published its report; among its demands were the prosecution of those suspected of involvement in so-called political killings, the granting of official apologies, compensation and a guarantee regarding the future security of victims of political violence or their relatives. The commission also called for greater freedom of speech and of assembly, the resolution of legal proceedings in the Ouédraogo and Zongo cases, the introduction of an amnesty law, and the construction of a monument to Sankara.

Constitutional and Electoral Reform

In April 2000 the Assemblée nationale adopted legislation revising the electoral code; under the new regulations, 90 deputies were to be elected from regional lists, while 21 would be elected from a national list. The Assemblée also approved a constitutional amendment reducing the presidential mandate from seven to five years, renewable only once. (However, as the new limits were to take effect from the next election, Compaoré would be able to stand again in 2005 and 2010.) In addition, the legislature adopted significant judicial reforms, providing for the eventual abolition of the Supreme Court and the replacement of its four permanent chambers with four new state institutions: a Constitutional Council, a Council of State, a Court of Cassation and a National Audit Court. The four new judicial institutions were finally inaugurated in late 2002. Meanwhile, the Government announced that it was to encourage the return to Burkina Faso of political exiles, and that a mausoleum for Sankara was to be constructed.

In April 2000 Hermann Yaméogo was expelled from the Groupe du 14 février (G-14f) opposition group for having criticized the group's policy of not co-operating with the Government on reform until the David Ouédraogo and Zongo cases had been resolved. In May the Government announced that municipal elections, which had been initially scheduled for February, would be held on 30 July. Although Compaoré held a meeting with Halidou Ouédraogo and other members of the Collectif in late May to discuss the process of reform, the death at the end of the month of a police officer who had been implicated in attempts to conceal the murder of David Ouédraogo provoked further suspicions. In July the elections were postponed until 24 September, owing to logistical difficulties. Meanwhile, three parties, including the ADF—RDA, were expelled from the Collectif and the G-14f after they nominated their own election candidates. The CDP won a clear victory in the municipal elections on 24 September, retaining outright control of 40 of the 49 municipalities. Although the G-14f and the PDP boycotted the poll, some 25 parties contested the elections, at which a turn-out of 68.4% was reported, and 14 parties gained representation.

The trial of the soldiers accused of murdering David Ouédraogo began in August 2000. Two of the defendants were acquitted by the military tribunal, but two members of Compaoré's presidential guard, including Marcel Kafando, head of the guard at the time of Ouédraogo's death, were sentenced to 20 years' imprisonment, with a third member sentenced to 10 years'. In February 2001 Marcel Kafando was charged additionally with arson and with the murder of Zongo and three others. However, the remaining charges against Kafando were dismissed in mid-2006 on the grounds of lack of evidence, prompting criticism from international press freedom groups and human rights organizations.

Meanwhile, in November 2000, amid heightened social unrest, Kadré Désiré Ouédraogo resigned as Prime Minister and was replaced by Paramanga Ernest Yonli, hitherto Minister of the Civil Service and Institutional Development. Compaoré subsequently formed a 36-member Council of Ministers, including 12 opposition members. The new appointments resulted from an accord reached by Yonli and representatives of seven political parties, specifying the parties' conditions for joining the Government, notably the prompt and thorough completion of pending legal cases. Those party to the agreement included the ruling CDP, and the ADF—RDA, although the PDP declined to participate. In December, following further unrest, the Government prohibited all demonstrations of a non-religious nature.

At the end of March 2001 relatives of Sankara and Zongo were among leading figures who boycotted a state-organized 'day of forgiveness', which had been proposed by the Collège des sages. None the less, some 30,000 people gathered in a stadium in the capital, Ouagadougou, where President Compaoré asked for forgiveness for some 176 unpunished crimes committed by representatives of the state since 1960. In June 2001 several thousand people participated in a demonstration in Ouagadougou, led by the Collectif, demanding that those whom they believed to have ordered the killing of Zongo, including François Compaoré, be brought to justice. Meanwhile, the PDP merged with the Parti socialiste burkinabè (PS), to form the PDP—PS.

In February 2002 the Assemblée nationale adopted a constitutional amendment providing for the abolition of the Chambre des représentants, following the failure to appoint replacement representatives for those whose terms had expired in December 2001. The Government announced proposals for the eventual replacement of the Chambre by a

Conférence générale de la nation, the membership and responsibilities of which were to be determined in due course; however, no such body had been established by mid-2007. Meanwhile, the Government denied reports, issued by a human rights organization, that the security forces had been implicated in the extrajudicial killings of more than 100 suspected criminals in late 2001, during a campaign against armed criminals.

Legislative Elections, 2002

Some 30 parties contested elections to the Assemblée nationale on 5 May 2002. The polls were the first to be conducted in Burkina with the use of a single ballot paper, in accordance with the demands of opposition parties. The CDP narrowly retained its majority in the new legislature, securing a total of 57 of the 111 seats, with 49.5% of the overall votes cast, although its representation was much reduced. The ADF—RDA won 17 seats, with 12.6% of the votes cast, and the PDP—PS 10 seats; 10 other parties were represented in the new legislature. Kaboré was elected as President of the Assemblée nationale in June, prior to the reappointment of Yonli as Prime Minister. Despite the slim majority held by the CDP in the Assemblée nationale and the precedent set by the inclusion of ministers from opposition parties in the outgoing administration, the new 31-member Government did not contain any representatives of the opposition.

In June 2003 Hermann Yaméogo resigned from the ADF—RDA and formed a new party, the Union nationale pour la démocratie et le développement (UNDD); Gilbert Ouédraogo was elected as President of the ADF—RDA in July.

In October 2003 the Government announced that the authorities had prevented a planned coup. By January 2004 15 members of the armed forces, including several members of the presidential guard, and two civilians, notably Norbert Tiendrébéogo, the Chairman of the Front des forces sociales, had been arrested on suspicion of involvement in the alleged plot. It was announced that the detainees were to be charged with threatening state security. The alleged leader of the group, Capt. Luther Ouali, was additionally to be charged with treason and complicity with a foreign power; reports, denied by the Governments of both countries, stated that Ouali had made contact with prominent officials in Côte d'Ivoire and Togo. In mid-January President Compaoré dismissed the Minister of Defence, Gen. Kouamé Lougué, appointing in his place Yéro Boly, hitherto head of the presidential administration. It subsequently emerged that Lougué had been questioned by the state prosecutor in connection with the alleged coup plot. Two other ministers were replaced in the reorganization. The trial of 11 of the soldiers and the two civilians was conducted by a military court in April. Ouali, who acknowledged during the trial that he had received some 50m. francs CFA from an aide to President Laurent Gbagbo of Côte d'Ivoire, but claimed that the money was intended for the establishment of a transport company, was sentenced to 10 years' imprisonment; six other defendants received lesser sentences, while a further six (including Tiendrébéogo) were acquitted.

In April 2004 the Assemblée nationale approved an amendment to the electoral code, changing the electoral unit from the region, which number 15, to the province, of which there are 45. The vote was boycotted by most opposition parties, which claimed that they would be disadvantaged by the revised electoral code as they would be unable to field candidates in all 45 electoral units. The amendment represented a return to the system in place prior to the reforms adopted in 2000: these were regarded as having contributed to the opposition's success in significantly increasing its legislative representation in the 2002 elections.

Opposition Arrests

In September 2004, on their return from a visit to Côte d'Ivoire, Hermann Yaméogo and his cousin, Noël Yaméogo, were detained and accused by the Burkinabè Government of passing false intelligence reports to the Ivorian and Mauritanian Governments regarding the alleged existence of mercenary training camps in Burkina Faso. In October Noël Yaméogo was indicted on charges of treason and violating state security, while police confiscated the passport of Hermann Yaméogo, who, as a deputy, benefited from immunity from prosecution. Both men denied the allegations made against them. Some 16 opposition parties held a rally in Ouagadougou in October to demand the release of Noël Yaméogo, and later called for an international inquiry to be conducted into the role of the Compaoré regime in regional crises. A further rally in support of the Yaméogos took place at the end of the month in Koudougou, an opposition stronghold. Noël Yaméogo was freed pending trial in February 2005.

Presidential Election, 2005

In March 2005 it was announced that the first round of the presidential election would take place on 13 November. Local elections, which had previously also been expected to be held in November, just before the presidential poll, were postponed until 12 February 2006. In June 2005 Compaoré announced his intention to seek a third term as the presidential candidate of the CDP. By this time several other candidates had already emerged, including three representing a 15-party opposition alliance, known as Alternance 2005, namely: Hermann Yaméogo of the UNDD; Philippe Ouédraogo of the Parti pour la démocratie et le socialisme; and Bénéwendé Stanislas Sankara of the Union pour la renaissance—Mouvement sankariste. Ram Ouédraogo, who had failed to secure a nomination under Alternance 2005, was to contest the election on behalf of his own party, the Rassemblement des écologistes du Burkina, while other declared candidates included Prof. Kilachia Laurent Bado, the President of the Parti de la renaissance nationale, and Prof. Ali Lankoandé, who had been elected to succeed Ki-Zerbo as the National President of the PDP—PS in February.

In September 2005 Compaoré effected a minor government reshuffle, notably removing two ministers belonging to the Parti africain de l'indépendance, which had decided not to support him in the forthcoming election, instead nominating the party's Secretary-General, Soumane Touré. In October the Constitutional Council approved the presidential candidacies of 13 of the 15 applicants, the highest number since the reintroduction of multi-party democracy in 1991 (the elections of that year and of 1998 having been largely boycotted by the opposition). The legitimacy of Compaoré's candidacy was disputed by several opposition parties, which claimed that the constitutional amendment approved in 2000 that limited a President to serving only two terms of office should be applied retroactively, and five opposition candidates subsequently lodged an appeal with the Constitutional Council to that effect. However, the Council rejected this appeal, prompting Yaméogo to announce his withdrawal from the election, although in the event his name remained on the ballot paper. In late October a two-day general strike was organized by some 17 trade unions in support of demands for an increase in salaries and pensions and a reduction in taxes on consumer goods.

DECISIVE VICTORY FOR COMPAORÉ

The presidential election was held on 13 November 2005, as scheduled. With the opposition divided, Compaoré was re-elected by an overwhelming majority of the votes cast, securing 80.35%, compared with the 4.88% won by his nearest rival, Bénéwendé Stanislas Sankara. Compaoré's candidacy had been supported by some 28 parties, including the second largest in the Assemblée nationale, the ADF—RDA. An electoral turn-out of 57.7% was reported. Compaoré was inaugurated to serve a third elected term of office on 20 December. A new Government was formed in early January 2006, again headed by Prime Minister Yonli; the allocation of the most strategic portfolios remained unchanged, although a number of new ministers were appointed from parties that had supported Compaoré in the presidential election, with the entry into government of Gilbert Ouédraogo, the President of the ADF—RDA, as Minister of Transport, particularly notable.

Compaoré and the CDP Consolidate Power

Following two further postponements, the municipal elections were finally held on 23 April 2006 in Burkina Faso's 351 municipalities (302 new communes having been created in rural areas since the last elections in 2000). Of the 73 political parties that contested the elections, around 30 secured municipal representation, although the CDP retained control of most principal towns and won 72% of the available council seats, according to final results released by the Constitutional Council. Only 49.1% of the electorate participated in the polls. In late May 2006 civil servants seeking increased pay observed a two-day strike, while several thousand people demonstrated in Ouagadougou against rising fuel prices.

Heavy fighting between the police and the army in December 2006, in which three soldiers and two police officers were killed, prompted the Government to postpone summits of the Economic Community of West African States (ECOWAS) and the Union économique et monétaire ouest-africaine, which had been due to take place in Ougadougou. The military and the police agreed to end hostilities after a week, and the summits were held in the Burkinabè capital in the following month.

Elections to the Assemblée nationale took place on 6 May 2007, contested by 47 parties fielding 3,748 candidates. The CDP strengthened its legislative majority, securing 73 of the 111 seats (compared with the 57 seats it won in the 2002 elections), according to provisional results, while the ADF—RDA, which had supported Compaoré in the 2005 presidential poll, took 14 seats. The remaining 24 seats were shared by 11 parties. The PDP—PS, whose founder, Ki-Zerbo, had died in December 2006, performed particularly poorly, its representation declining to two seats (from 10 following the 2002 elections).

FOREIGN RELATIONS

Compaoré has gained considerable respect as a regional mediator, although during the 1990s some regional and Western governments expressed concern at his perceived role in the conflicts in Liberia, Sierra Leone and Angola.

Following the escalation of the civil conflict in Liberia after early 1990, Burkina's relations with some members of ECOWAS deteriorated as a result of the Compaoré Government's open support for Charles Taylor's rebel National Patriotic Front of Liberia and refusal to contribute troops to the ECOWAS force (ECOMOG) that was sent to Liberia in mid-1990. In September 1995, however, the Compaoré administration announced that Burkina would contribute troops to ECOMOG. In February 1997 Burkinabè troops assisted in the preparations for elections in Liberia; members of the Burkinabè military subsequently remained in Liberia to assist in training new armed forces.

In early 1999 President Ahmed Tejan Kabbah of Sierra Leone and the Government of Nigeria alleged that Burkina and Liberia were co-operating to provide support and supply arms to the rebel fighters of the Revolutionary United Front (RUF) in Sierra Leone. In early 2000 a report to the UN Security Council accused Burkina Faso of having on several occasions supplied weapons to the RUF in exchange for diamonds. It was also alleged that Burkina Faso had supplied weapons to Liberia and to Angolan rebel groups, despite international embargoes on the supply of weapons to those countries. The report, which further accused Compaoré of having conducted personal negotiations with the Angolan rebel leader, Jonas Savimbi, was strenuously denied by the Burkinabè Government. In an attempt to forestall further international criticism of the Burkinabè Government's alleged involvement in arms-trafficking, it was announced in December 2000 that a mechanism to control the import of weapons to Burkina was to be established. Although Compaoré, in May 2001, criticized a UN decision to impose travel restrictions on Liberian officials, subsequent relations with the Taylor Government were more distant. Notably, Taylor's Government was not represented at a conference hosted by the Burkinabè Government in July 2002, intended to promote a peaceful resolution of the political crisis in Liberia, and Compaoré welcomed Taylor's resignation as President of Liberia in August 2003.

In November 1999 a dispute over land rights between Burkinabè settlers in the south-west of Côte d'Ivoire and the indigenous Krou population led to the violent and systematic expulsion from the region of several hundred Burkinabè plantation workers. Several deaths were reported, and it was estimated that up to 20,000 expatriates subsequently returned to Burkina. Following the *coup d'état* in Côte d'Ivoire in December, the military authorities assured the Government of Burkina that the expulsions would cease and that measures would be taken in order to allow workers to return. None the less, tensions between the two countries heightened as the former Prime Minister of Côte d'Ivoire, Alassane Ouattara, was excluded from participation in the Ivorian presidential election of October 2000 because of his Burkinabè origins. Following a coup attempt in Abidjan, Côte d'Ivoire, in January 2001, which the Ivorian Government attributed to the influence of unnamed, neighbouring states, attacks on Burkinabè expatriates in Côte d'Ivoire reportedly increased; by late January it was reported that up to 10,000 Burkinabè were returning to Burkina each week. In June the two countries announced that they would commence joint patrols of their common border. In July a meeting between Compaoré and the democratically elected Ivorian President, Laurent Gbagbo, in Sirte, Libya, was reported to have helped defuse tensions between the two countries, and Gbagbo made his first official visit to Burkina in December.

Following the outbreak of unrest in Côte d'Ivoire in September 2002, Gbagbo again alleged that an unnamed, neighbouring country (widely regarded as a reference to Burkina) was implicated in the rebellion. However, in November, following an attack on the residence of the Burkinabè President in Abidjan, the Ivorian Government expressed its regret for the attack. A statement by Compaoré in an interview with the French newspaper *Le Parisien*, in January 2003, to the effect that the restoration of peace in Côte d'Ivoire would necessitate the resignation of Gbagbo as President, led to a further deterioration in relations between the two countries. As a result of the upsurge in violence in Côte d'Ivoire, at least 350,000 Burkinabè citizens reportedly fled Côte d'Ivoire for Burkina. Compaoré welcomed the peace agreement signed in France in January, known as the Marcoussis Accords, which provided for a government of national reconciliation in Côte d'Ivoire, although at the end of the month the Burkinabè embassy in Abidjan was attacked and set on fire by opponents of the agreement. As greater stability appeared to return to Côte d'Ivoire later that year, the common border of the two countries, closed since the onset of the rebellion, was reopened in September. In October the Government of Côte d'Ivoire denied suggestions of Ivorian involvement in the alleged coup plot in Burkina (see above). In late 2003 Compaoré hosted meetings with several prominent Ivorian leaders, including Gbagbo, Prime Minister Seydou Diarra and former rebel leader Guillaume Soro, emphasizing the need to develop bilateral co-operation. In March 2004, however, the Burkinabè Government announced that four of its citizens were among hundreds of people allegedly killed by the Ivorian security forces as they quashed protests in Abidjan, and in July Burkina accused Côte d'Ivoire of violating its airspace. Later in July, at a meeting in Abidjan, representatives of the two countries pledged to combat 'destabilizing acts' against their respective countries and agreed to increase co-operation in security and defence matters. Nevertheless, relations between Burkina Faso and Côte d'Ivoire remained strained, and in September Gbagbo sent a letter to John Kufuor, the President of Ghana and then Chairman of ECOWAS, reportedly accusing Compaoré of supporting rebel forces in Côte d'Ivoire and alleging that foreign troops were undergoing training in Burkina Faso. The Burkinabè Government dismissed the allegations, which it claimed were based on false information provided to the Ivorian authorities by Hermann and Noël Yaméogo. Bilateral relations subsequently improved, and in early 2007 Compaoré facilitated direct talks between Gbagbo and Soro, which resulted in the signing of a new political agreement between the two sides in Ouagadougou in March. Meanwhile, Compaoré was presiding over a committee established to monitor the implementation of a political accord signed in August 2006 by Togo's Government and the main opposition parties of that country, following negotiations also chaired by the Burkinabè President.

Compaoré's first official visit to France, in June 1993, was widely interpreted as a recognition by the French authorities of his legitimacy following the installation of elected organs of state. Burkina swiftly forged close relations with Jacques

Chirac following his election to the French presidency in May 1995, and contacts remained frequent. Compaoré subsequently participated in a regional mediation effort, conceived at the meeting, to resolve the political crisis in the Central African Republic (CAR). The Assemblée nationale authorized the contribution of a Burkinabè military contingent to the surveillance mission for the CAR in February 1997, and a Burkinabè force remained in the CAR as part of the UN peacekeeping force that succeeded the regional mission between April 1998 and February 2000.

Links with Libya have generally been strong under the Compaoré regime; Burkina was, notably, a founder member of the Libyan-sponsored Community of Sahel-Saharan States, established in 1997.

Relations between Burkina Faso and Mauritania were severely strained from late August 2004 after the Mauritanian Government accused Burkina Faso of conspiring with Libya to destabilize the regime of President Col Maawiya Ould Sid'Ahmed Taya. It was alleged that Burkina Faso had provided refuge, weapons, funding and training to former army officers Saleh Ould Hnana, Mohamed Ould Sheikhna and Abderahmane Ould Mini, whom the Mauritanian authorities held responsible for leading an attempt to overthrow Taya that month and an earlier failed coup in June 2003. The Burkinabè Government strongly refuted the accusations. The Mauritanian Government reiterated its allegations against Burkina on several occasions during the following months and boycotted the 10th summit of La Francophonie, which was held in Ouagadougou in November 2004. In December, during the trial in Mauritania of the more than 190 people accused of participating in the coup attempts, Ould Hnana admitted conspiring to overthrow Taya, but denied receiving assistance from Burkina Faso or Libya. (In February 2005 Ould Hnana, Ould Sheikhna, Ould Mini and a fourth officer were sentenced to life imprisonment, while Sidi Mohamed Mustapha Ould Limam Chavi, a Mauritanian-born adviser to President Compaoré, was sentenced *in absentia* to 15 years' imprisonment.) Meanwhile, tensions arose between Burkina Faso and Guinea in October 2004 when the Burkinabè Minister of Security, Djibrill Yipéné Bassolet, claimed that Hermann Yaméogo, the President of the opposition UNDD, had organized a meeting in the Guinean capital, Conakry, of opponents of the Burkinabè Government, including Ivorian and Mauritanian participants, with the aim of destabilizing Compaoré's regime. The Guinean Government vehemently denied having hosted such a meeting. Relations between Burkina Faso and Mauritania improved following the overthrow of Taya's regime in August 2005. Col Ely Ould Mohamed Vall, who assumed the leadership of Mauritania, as President of a self-styled Military Council for Justice and Democracy, attended President Compaoré's inauguration to a new term of office in December, and in March 2006 Compaoré visited Nouakchott, the Mauritanian capital, at Vall's invitation.

In March 2007 it was reported that Burkina Faso's territorial disputes with both Niger and Benin were to be referred to the International Court of Justice in The Hague, Netherlands, for arbitration.

Economy

EDITH HODGKINSON

Revised by the editorial staff

A land-locked country in the savannah lands of the West African Sahel, Burkina Faso has been continually challenged in its efforts to ensure the survival of its agricultural and pastoral economy, and has only limited prospects for modernization, whether through industrialization or the expansion of external trade. The population (estimated at 14.36m. in mid-2006) is largely rural, depending on traditional farming methods for subsistence and receiving modest earnings from the sale of cash crops, fruit, vegetables, livestock or firewood. The climate is arid, and the rivers mostly seasonal, so supplies of water can run low during the long dry period, and the economy is very vulnerable to weather conditions.

Burkina is also highly dependent on the maintenance of good economic and political relations with its six neighbours. An estimated 2m. Burkinabè work abroad, some seasonally and some permanently, primarily in Côte d'Ivoire and Ghana; political and social upheaval in the former country, particularly following the *coup d'état* of December 1999, and the rebellion that commenced in September 2002, has been largely to the detriment of Burkinabè migrants there. This migration of workers reinforces Burkina's commercial contacts with its southern neighbours, where many consumer goods are purchased for resale in Burkina, and their remittances also contribute substantially to the national balance of payments, helping to offset the country's chronic trade deficit.

Manufacturing activity is restricted to small units, established principally in the second city, Bobo-Dioulasso and, to a lesser extent, in the capital, Ouagadougou. It takes the form of import substitution and the processing of local agricultural commodities, and, apart from cotton ginning, the manufacturing sector makes little contribution to exports. Small-scale artisanal production serves regional and tourist markets, with the active informal sector representing an important source of jobs and income. Burkina's mineral resources are only just beginning to be exploited on a significant basis, and there is considerable optimism regarding the country's deposits of gold (which has been mined in small quantities for centuries), zinc and manganese.

The economy's dependence on agriculture and on workers' remittances means that its performance can fluctuate widely from year to year. However, whereas in the late 1980s and early 1990s growth in gross domestic product (GDP) on average only just kept pace with the increase in population, since 1995 the rate of expansion has improved, with average annual growth of 6.5% in 1995–2006, according to the African Development Bank (ADB). The improvement in the second half of the 1990s can be attributed to the structural adjustment programme initiated in 1991, and to the enhancement of export earnings generated by the 50% devaluation of the CFA franc in January 1994. The strong growth of the cotton sector also contributed. Real GDP growth slowed in 2000, to 2.2%, largely owing to external factors, including a rise in petroleum prices and reduced income from workers' remittances, as a large number of Burkinabè returned from neighbouring countries. In addition, severe drought in that year resulted in lower output of cereal crops. GDP growth rates of 6.5% and 6.2% were achieved in 2001 and 2002, respectively. GDP growth of 8.7% in 2003 was substantially stronger than the 2.6% initially estimated, largely owing to higher than projected agricultural production. Growth slowed in 2004 to 3.9%, but recovered somewhat in 2005 and 2006, to 7.3% and 5.5%, respectively. The economy, however, remains small, so that, with gross national income (GNI) in 2005, measured at average 2003–05 prices, estimated by the World Bank at only US $5,240m., equivalent to $400 per head (less than one-half of the level in neighbouring Côte d'Ivoire), Burkina remains one of the world's poorest countries: on the UN Development Programme's human development index, Burkina ranked 174th of 177 countries in 2006, mainly because of its very poor health and education indicators. In October 2003 a $212m. government plan to reduce the number of people living below the poverty line from nearly 50% to 35% by 2006 was endorsed by non-governmental organizations and civil society. Improving access to education and health services was a priority of the initiative, which was projected to raise the country's GDP by some 4%.

Reversing the nationalization policy pursued by the Sankara regime in 1983–87, a major aspect of the structural adjustment implemented from the mid-1990s was a divestment programme designed to enhance the role of the private sector. Burkina's best prospects for modernization and economic growth appeared to lie in the development of the mining sector, small-scale, resource-based manufacturing, increased exports of horticultural products to Europe and in a modest expansion of the tourism industry.

AGRICULTURE

Agriculture (including livestock-rearing, forestry and fishing)—which accounted for 34.0% of Burkina's GDP in 2005 and, according to FAO, engaged about 92.2% of the labour force in 2004—is largely at subsistence level. In those years when conditions are favourable, the country rebuilds its food stocks to last through periods of unfavourable climatic conditions, when severe shortages have been experienced. In all years poor transport and storage facilities serve to reduce the supply that is effectively available. Cereal production is determined by climatic conditions, but has remained consistently in excess of 2m. metric tons since the early 1990s. Severe drought conditions in 2000 led to the lowest output recorded since 1990, with production measured at 2,286,227 tons. However, better climatic conditions resulted in record cereals crops being recorded in each of the three following years, reaching 3,649,533 tons in 2005. A major irrigation and water supply programme initiated in April 2004 was expected to allow the production of a further 122,000 tons of cereals per year through the treatment of 700 ha of land, as well providing 4,000 supply points for drinking water. The cereals crop in 2004, however, declined slightly compared with the previous year, to 2,901,973 tons. In late 2004 Burkina Faso was granted an International Development Association (IDA) credit of US $84m. to assist in countering the damage caused to cereal crops by locust swarms in the north of the country in that year and to fund programmes to reduce the region's future vulnerability to such infestations.

Burkina's cash crops were formerly the surplus of subsistence cultivation, mainly karité nuts (sheanuts), production of which was an estimated 70,000 metric tons in 2004, and sesame seeds, of which a record crop of 31,230 tons was recorded in 2001, reflecting a three-fold expansion in the area harvested that year, to some 60,921 ha, although production fluctuated in subsequent years, largely reflecting annual changes in the area harvested of the crop. Output reached 18,472 tons in 2003 before declining, to only 11,794 tons in 2004. It recovered slightly in 2005 to 17,717 tons. From the 1990s, however, there was considerable government investment in cotton, groundnuts, sugar, cashew nuts and market gardening, with financial aid from, among others, the European Development Fund.

The most important cash crop (and principal source of export earnings—an estimated 69.1% of the total in 2004) is cotton; the sector received a strong boost from the higher local-currency prices paid to producers after the devaluation of the CFA franc in January 1994. Moreover, a major investment programme for the cotton sector, announced in 1996, aimed to increase output by the then state-owned processing and marketing company, the Société burkinabè des fibres textiles (SOFITEX), to 345,000 metric tons of seed cotton within five years, through the modernization of facilities and an expansion in the area cultivated. Although output declined in subsequent years, reaching 212,545 tons in 2000, largely as a result of less favourable climatic conditions and parasite infestation, there was a marked increase in output in the early 2000s, and the area harvested increased more than two-fold in 2003, as compared with 2000, reflecting the reversal of a shift away from cotton to cereals production that had occurred in the late 1990s. Record seed cotton production of some 440,268 tons was registered in 2002, and further record crops, of 448,700 tons, 575,933 tons and 671,319, were recorded in 2003, 2004 and 2005, respectively, following three seasons of good rains. In late 2001 a number of market reforms were introduced into the sector: the monopoly held by SOFITEX on the collection and marketing of seed cotton was eliminated, and the involvement of the private sector, particularly in the eastern and central regions, was expanded. In early 2004 a consortium of European banks extended a loan of €62m. to Burkina Faso's cotton sector; SOFITEX intended to purchase fertilizers and pesticides with the funds, with the aim of increasing output to some 600,000 tons. A draft framework on trade reached by members of the World Trade Organization in August of that year committed the USA and other wealthier developed countries to reducing subsidies to their cotton farmers—a key demand of West African cotton producers such as Burkina Faso—although further talks would be required prior to the conclusion of a final agreement, and substantive cuts in subsidies were not expected to take effect for several years. West African cotton producers estimated that they had lost some US $150m. per year in export earnings since 1997 as a result of US subsidies.

The production of groundnuts has generally increased steadily since the mid-1980s. Although annual production fluctuates, according to climatic conditions, groundnut production increased from an average of 81,841 metric tons per year in 1980–85 to an average of 240,595 tons per year in 1997–2002. A record crop, of some 358,121 tons, was recorded in 2003, although production declined to 245,307 tons in 2004, before recovering to 331,234 tons in 2005. Output of raw sugar, which began in 1974/75, exceeded 30,000 tons annually in the late 1990s and amounted to around 40,000 tons per year in the first half of the 2000s.

The livestock sector (including livestock and livestock products, hides and skins) contributed 9.7% of GDP in 2002 and an estimated 12.1% of the country's export earnings in 2004, and would account for significantly more if unrecorded shipments were taken into account. Stock-rearing is practised by the semi-nomadic Fulani (Peul) in the sparsely populated areas of the north and east, although a large-scale programme is redeveloping livestock production in the west of the country. An FAO-supported West African regional development project for those areas affected by trypanosomiasis (sleeping-sickness) includes Burkina Faso. In 2005 there were an estimated 8.0m. cattle, 7.0m. sheep and 10.7m. goats. In 2002 some 802,400 head of livestock were exported, including 285,600 cattle.

The small fish catch (some 8,500–9,000 metric tons per year, according to FAO) is consumed locally. Timber production is insignificant, despite the large area under forest (almost one-quarter of the total); however, foreign agencies are now funding timber development projects in the Kompienga and Bagré dam regions. In 2003 the Government launched a 10-year plan to combat desertification and land erosion through reafforestation programmes covering 350 districts; it was anticipated that some 17,500 ha of forest would be developed as a result. During 1995–2006 agricultural GDP increased at an average annual rate of 5.8%. Agricultural GDP increased by 4.1% in 2006. The food harvest in that year was poor, however, leaving 12 of the country's 45 provinces under the threat of famine.

MINING AND POWER

A priority of the Compaoré administration has been the exploitation of Burkina's mineral resources, which include gold, manganese, zinc and silver. To bring in new capital to enhance production at the mine at Poura, in western-central Burkina, where reserves were estimated at 25,000–27,000 kg, the Government privatized the company involved in its development, the Société de recherche et d'exploitations minières du Burkina. Sahelian Goldfields of Canada, which took over the rehabilitation work at Poura in late 1995, bought a 90% stake, forming a new company, the Société aurifère du Sahel. The mine at Poura, which closed in March 1996, was reopened in October 1998. In October 2003 High River Gold Mines Ltd of Canada announced its intention to commence development of the Taparko gold mine, with the construction of a mill and infrastructure to process ore from both the Taparko deposits and the nearby Bouroum deposits; production was expected to average more than 90,000 troy oz (2,800 kg) of gold per year over an eight-year period. The short-term prospects for the sector suffered from a sharp decline in the price of gold in 1999; however, production increased from 209 kg in 2002 to 770 kg in the following year, increasing further to 1,395 kg in 2005. In early 2005 Etruscan Resources of Canada announced that it had received a positive feasibility study on the proposed development of an open-cast gold mine at Youga, some 180 km south-east of Ouagadougou. Construction of the mine, which had an expected annual output of 88,000 oz over a five-and-one-half year period, commenced later in the year. None the less, and although in the mid-1990s gold had been Burkina's third largest source of export revenue (after cotton, and livestock and livestock products) by 2004 gold amounted for only an estimated 3.0% of the country's export trade.

The potential for zinc-mining operations at Perkoa, in central Burkina, was investigated in the early 1990s by Boliden International of Sweden. Proven reserves of some 7m. metric tons of ore have been identified. Following the abandonment of the project by Boliden, a South African company, Metorex, acquired the joint venture established to develop the mine, Billiton Burkina Faso, in September 1999. In November 2004 AIM Resources of Australia acquired a majority stake in the project. Burkina's other mineral prospects include titanium, vanadium, nickel, bauxite, lead and phosphates, although none of these is considered to be commercially viable at present. A more immediate development prospect is for the quarrying of limestone deposits at Tin Hrassan, near Tambao, which can be developed for cement production. The Government has, meanwhile, signalled its intention to increase the contribution of mining (particularly gold mining) to the economy. As of January 2007 there were two mines under construction, at Tarparko-Bouroum and Youga, with a further five projects having either completed their feasibility studies or applied for permits, while another three were at the advanced source-definition stage. At mid-2006 230 mining permits had been granted, compared with just 145 a year earlier.

Electricity generating capacity was considerably expanded in the 1990s, while production in the energy sector more than doubled in 1990–2000, with growth continuing in the early 2000s. Total production of electricity increased from 216m. kWh in 1993 to an estimated 473m. kWh in 2004. The bulk of output (around 60%–80%) is thermal, with the remainder largely provided by two hydroelectric stations, on the Kompienga and Bagré rivers, with a combined capacity of 31 MW. Work on a 12-MW scheme at Diébougou began in 1998; agreement was reached in the same year for a 30-MW facility, Ouaga III, at the Kossodo industrial zone, to be built and run by an affiliate of the Aga Khan's Economic Development Fund. An electricity interconnection with Côte d'Ivoire, which was opened in April 2001, sought to overcome the difficulties of electricity production in Burkina associated with the country's climate. There were also plans for electricity interconnection with Ghana, which will be financed by France and the European Investment Bank (EIB). In the mid-2000s the Burkinabè authorities were seeking funding in order to construct a hydroelectric dam at Samendeni, in the west of the country. In order to stimulate increased private investment in the sector, the Government planned to end its monopoly on production and distribution. Electricity, gas and water contributed 2.4% of GDP in 2005.

MANUFACTURING

Manufacturing accounted for 12.7% of GDP in 2005, according to Banque centrale des états de l'Afrique de l'ouest. Growth has been hampered by the small size of the domestic market, the lack of indigenous raw materials and shortages of finance and management skills. The higher local cost of imports since devaluation contributed to some recovery in the sector in the second half of the 1990s, after several years of decline. However, the introduction at the beginning of 2000 of duty-free trade in industrial goods within the regional grouping, the Union économique et monétaire ouest-africaine, brought stiffer competition, which most local manufacturers were not well placed to counter. According to the ADB, manufacturing GDP increased at an average annual rate of 7.4% in 1995–2006; growth of 6.3% was recorded in 2006. Production takes the form of agricultural processing (in particular, cotton, leather and sugar) and the substitution of consumer goods imports. The first industrial plant of any significance was the textile plant at Koudougou, which entered production in 1970. Cotton-ginning capacity was increased in 1989 with the expansion of the SOFITEX complex in Bobo-Dioulasso, and further expansion occurred in the second half of the 1990s.

Under Sankara's administration, the Brasseries du Burkina brewery operation was one of the few major industries to retain a substantial private holding. The Compaoré administration has, by contrast, implemented an extensive divestment programme, aiming to reduce the Government's equity in industrial concerns to a maximum of 25%. Thus, part of the state's holding in the Société industrielle du Faso, which produces motorcycles and bicycles (important methods of transport in this predominantly rural country), was sold to private Burkinabè interests in 1993. In 1994–96 some 22 parastatals were identified for sale, and all but three were subsequently divested. Legislation was adopted in 1994 authorizing the privatization of a further 19 organizations, among them the Caisse de stabilisation des prix des produits agricoles du Burkina and the Société sucrière de la Comoé (SOSUCO). Progress on these privatizations was inhibited by their political sensitivity: SOSUCO ranks second only to the Government as a source of employment. When a 52% stake in the sugar complex was sold in 1998, the new owner, a consortium headed by an Aga Khan affiliate, pledged to retain all the permanent work-force. SOFITEX was transferred to majority private-sector ownership in 2001. By September 2002 a total of 26 enterprises had been transferred to the private sector, while a further 16 had been liquidated or were in the process of liquidation.

TRANSPORT INFRASTRUCTURE

Overall the transport network is relatively poor, although it has received considerable investment in recent years. An important transport artery is the railway line from the border with Côte d'Ivoire through Bobo-Dioulasso, Koudougou and Ouagadougou to Kaya. However, the track, vehicles and services have been in need of maintenance and further investment. Following the withdrawal, in 1987, of Côte d'Ivoire from the joint rail partnership, Burkina Faso and Côte d'Ivoire established separate rail companies, and in 1993 issued a joint tender for the transfer to private ownership of services on the line. SITARAIL, a consortium of French, Belgian, Ivorian and Burkinabè interests, assumed management of operations in 1995. Financing for the attendant investment programme was provided by IDA, the Caisse (now Agence) française de développement, the EIB, the West African Development Bank and the Belgian Government. There was a total road network of 15,272 km in 2004 (of which 31% was paved). World Bank funds supported the rehabilitation of the road network in the late 1990s, and seven African and Arab organizations pledged funds in 1997 for the paving of two major roads to the borders with Ghana and Côte d'Ivoire. In late 2000 the Government announced that some 6,000 km of roads would be constructed in rural areas over a period of three years. The country has two international airports (at Ouagadougou and Bobo-Dioulasso); infrastructure at Ouagadougou airport was updated, with financial assistance from France, in the 1990s and was to be further improved. It was reported in late 2006 that a new airport would be constructed 35 km north-east of Ouagadougou at an estimated cost of US $450m. The project was expected to be completed by 2011.

FINANCE

Since the early 1970s there has been a history of fiscal deficit, which has been chiefly attributable to the economy's low taxable capacity. Reducing the budget deficit, which was equivalent to 4.6% of GDP (including grants) in 1993, was a primary objective under the terms of the Enhanced Structural Adjustment Facility (ESAF) accorded by the IMF to Burkina in 1993 and again in 1996. In 1994, as a result of the currency devaluation and additions to the state payroll, the budget deficit (including grants) reached 5.1% of GDP. However, some progress was subsequently made, through controls on current spending and enhanced revenue from taxation, including higher rates of value-added tax from September 1996. The deficit (including grants) narrowed to 2.0% of GDP in 1996, but increased spending, encouraged by an impending election, resulted in the deficit rising to 3.8% of GDP in 1997. Although the divestiture of loss-making state enterprises and the restructuring of those that have remained under state ownership have reduced state expenditure, the Government's capital spending programme has remained dependent on external grants. Budgetary spending on capital projects was cut in 1999, in response to declining aid inflows. The loss of customs revenue under the new regional tariff structure necessitated a 1% reduction in total planned budget spending in 2000; the budget deficit was equivalent to 3.6% of GDP in that year, but declined to the equivalent of 3.0% in 2001, before increasing slightly, to 3.1% of GDP in 2002. In December 2003 it was reported that the civil war in Côte d'Ivoire had resulted in a shortfall of 77,000m. CFA francs in Burkinabè government revenues, partly owing to a decline in customs and excise revenue from trade with that country and a reduction in remittances from Burkinabè workers based there. In 2005 Burkina recorded an overall budget deficit of an estimated 158,500m. francs CFA, equivalent to an estimated 4.3% of GDP. The following year an estimated overall budget deficit of 178,300m. francs CFA was recorded

In September 1999 the IMF accorded a further ESAF (which later that year became the Poverty Reduction and Growth Facility—PRGF) to Burkina, equivalent to US $54m., to cover 1999–2002, and in April 2000 the authorities submitted a Poverty Reduction Strategy Paper, which was endorsed by the IMF and the World Bank in July of that year. Ongoing structural reforms included plans for the privatization of the telecommunications company, the Office national des télécommunications (by the end of 2004), the electricity company, the Société nationale burkinabè d'électricité (SONABEL), and the petroleum company, the Société nationale burkinabè d'hydrocarbures (SONABHY). In June 2003 the IMF accorded a further PRGF to Burkina, for 2003–06, approving the eventual release of funds equivalent to some $34m. In August 2006 the IMF completed its sixth review under the PRGF arrangement, and made a further $14m. in funds available. The Fund also praised the country's recent positive economic growth, highlighting the strong cereal and cotton production in 2005. Some success was also achieved in containing inflation, which had declined to 2.0% in 2003, while in 2004 deflation of 0.4% was estimated. Inflation, however, accelerated in 2005 and was estimated at 6.5%.

FOREIGN TRADE AND PAYMENTS

Burkina has suffered from a chronic and substantial trade deficit. Its export capacity is highly vulnerable to weather conditions and trends in international prices for cotton, while the import bill reflects a range of factors: the domestic food balance, international prices for petroleum and the level of investment spending, both public and private. Annual fluctuations in the size of the deficit have therefore been substantial. Over time it has tended to rise in nominal terms, registering a peak of US $367m. in 1993 (calculated in balance-of-payments terms, which exclude the cost of transportation—a significant item for this remote, land-locked country). Coverage by export earnings of the import bill rarely exceeded one-half. The immediate impact of the devaluation of the CFA franc in 1994 was a 27% fall in import spending in US dollar terms, while receipts from exports declined by only 5% (representing an 87% rise in CFA franc values). The trade deficit consequently fell to only $129m. (in payments terms) in 1994. In 2004 the trade deficit was 188,100m. francs CFA (equivalent to $224m.). In 2005 the principal sources of imports were France (which provided 18.7% of the total) and Côte d'Ivoire (18.0%). The principal market for exports in that year was Ghana (taking 16.6% of the total). The principal exports in 2004 were cotton, and livestock and livestock products (including hides and skins). In the same year the principal imports were capital equipment, intermediate goods, petroleum products and food products.

The merchandise deficit thus represents a large outflow on the current account, compounded by the substantial debit represented by transport costs. It is in part—and in some years wholly—offset by remittances from emigrants and aid inflows. Workers' remittances fluctuate in response to economic conditions in host countries, and have not yet regained the peak of US $187m. registered in 1988. In 1994–98 these inflows averaged $99m. per year, with the decline in part reflecting the depreciation in the currencies of host countries against the dollar. These remittances declined further thereafter, as a result of political and social insecurity in Côte d'Ivoire in the aftermath of the military coup in that country in December 1999, and the political crisis in that country after September 2002.

Meanwhile, net inflows of official development assistance from multilateral institutions and countries of the Organisation for Economic Co-operation and Development and the Organization of the Petroleum Exporting Countries increased from US $336m. in 2000 to $473m. in 2002. By far the major source of bilateral aid is France; the Netherlands and Denmark are also important donors. Given this significant inflow of concessionary funds, Burkina's external debt has remained comparatively low and its debt-service burden moderate, although difficulties in meeting debt-servicing payments prompted the country's bilateral creditors to agree, in 1991 and again in 1993, to rescheduling, and further concessions were made after the devaluation of the CFA franc in 1994. The application of 'Naples' terms to $70m. in non-concessionary debt (which effectively annulled two-thirds of the liability) was agreed in June 1996; in the same month France cancelled 60,300m. francs CFA in concessional debt. At the end of 1999 some 75.1% of debt owed was to multilateral institutions and therefore not open to rescheduling or cancellation. Thus, while the country's debt ratios are theoretically not excessive—with total debt at the end of 2004, at $1,967m., equivalent to 40.8% of GNI, with the debt-service ratio in 2003 at 10.3%—in practice, given the fragility of the economy, Burkina has very limited scope to increase its call on foreign funds other than on extremely concessionary terms. Burkina's total external public debt in 2005 was $1,920m., according to the ADB.

None the less, in recognition of its commitment to structural adjustment and a debt burden classified as 'unsustainable' because of the dependence on workers' remittances, Burkina was deemed eligible for debt reduction under the terms of the initiative for heavily indebted poor countries (HIPC), introduced by the World Bank and the IMF in 1997. In July 2000 the IMF and the World Bank agreed debt-reduction arrangements with Burkina Faso valued at $700m. It was estimated that the overall reduction in the country's debt-servicing obligations would thereby be reduced by around one-half in subsequent years, allowing, it was hoped, for increased government expenditure on social development. Burkina was also one of 19 poor countries to benefit from a cancellation of debt granted by France in January 2001. In April 2002 Burkina became the fifth country to reach completion point under the enhanced framework of the HIPC initiative, rendering it eligible for additional debt relief. In June 2005 Burkina Faso was among 18 countries to be granted 100% debt relief on multilateral debt agreed by the Group of Eight leading industrialized nations (G-8), subject to the approval of the lenders. In August 2006 the ADB granted $19.48m. to Burkina to aid rural development projects, while in October it awarded a further $3.6m. to improve the country's budget management, particularly in the areas of reliability and transparency. In early 2007 Burkina became eligible to receive funding from the US Millennium Challenge Account, with the possibility of receiving as much as 200,000m. francs CFA in aid.

Statistical Survey

Source (except where otherwise stated): Institut National de la Statistique et de la Démographie, 555 blvd de la Révolution, 01 BP 374, Ouagadougou 01; tel. 50-32-49-76; fax 50-32-61-59; e-mail insd@cenatrin.bf; internet www.insd.bf.

Area and Population

AREA, POPULATION AND DENSITY

Area (sq km)	274,200*
Population (census results)	
10–20 December 1985	7,964,705
10 December 1996	
Males	4,970,882
Females	5,341,727
Total	10,312,609
Population (UN estimates at mid-year)†	
2004	13,507,000
2005	13,933,000
2006	14,359,000
Density (per sq km) at mid-2006	52.4

* 105,870 sq miles.

† Source: UN, *World Population Prospects: The 2006 Revision*.

ETHNIC GROUPS

1995 (percentages): Mossi 47.9; Peul 10.3; Bobo 6.9; Lobi 6.9; Mandé 6.7; Sénoufo 5.3; Gourounsi 5.0; Gourmantché 4.8; Tuareg 3.1; others 3.1 (Source: La Francophonie).

PROVINCES

(population at 1996 census)

	Population	Capital	Population of capital
Balé	168,170	Boromo	11,232
Bam	211,551	Kongoussi	17,893
Banwa	215,297	Solenzo	n.a.
Bazèga	213,824	Kombissiri	16,821
Bougouriba	76,498	Diébougou	11,637
Boulgou	415,583	Tenkodogo	31,466
Boulkiemdé	421,302	Koudougou	72,490
Comoé	241,376	Banfora	49,724
Ganzourgou	256,921	Zorgo	17,466
Gnagna	307,372	Bogandé	8,960
Gourma	220,116	Fada N'Gourma	29,254
Houet	672,114	Bobo-Dioulasso	309,771
Ioba	161,484	Dano	n.a.
Kadiogo	941,894	Ouagadougou	709,736
Kénédougou	198,541	Orodara	16,581
Komandjari	50,484	Gayéri	n.a.
Kompienga	40,766	Pama	n.a.
Kossi	230,693	Nouna	19,105
Koulpélogo	187,399	Ouargaye	n.a.
Kouritenga	250,117	Koupéla	17,619
Kourwéogo	117,996	Boussé	n.a.
Léraba	92,927	Sindou	n.a.
Lorom	111,339	Titao	n.a.
Mouhoun	235,391	Dédougou	33,815
Nahouri	119,739	Pô	17,146
Namentenga	252,738	Boulsa	12,280
Nayala	136,393	Toma	n.a.
Noumbiel	51,431	Batié	n.a.
Oubritenga	197,237	Ziniaré	11,153
Oudalan	137,160	Gorom-Gorom	5,669
Passoré	271,864	Yako	18,472
Poni	195,900	Gaoua	6,424
Sanguié	249,583	Réo	22,534
Sanmatenga	464,032	Kaya	33,958
Séno	201,760	Dori	23,768
Sissili	153,434	Léo	18,988
Soum	252,993	Djibo	20,080
Sourou	188,512	Tougan	15,218
Tapoa	234,968	Diapaga	5,017
Tuy	160,722	Houndé	21,830
Yagha	116,419	Sebba	n.a.
Yatenga	444,563	Ouahigouya	52,193
Ziro	119,219	Sapouy	n.a.
Zondoma	127,654	Gourcy	16,317
Zoundwéogo	197,133	Manga	14,035
Total	10,312,609		

PRINCIPAL TOWNS

(population at 1996 census)

Ouagadougou (capital)	709,736	Ouahigouya	52,193
Bobo-Dioulasso	309,771	Banfora	49,724
Koudougou	72,490	Kaya	33,958

Mid-2005 (incl. suburbs, UN estimate): Ouagadougou 926,000 (Source: UN, *World Urbanization Prospects: The 2005 Revision*).

BIRTHS AND DEATHS

(annual averages, UN estimates)

	1990–95	1995–2000	2000–05
Birth rate (per 1,000)	49.0	47.7	45.9
Death rate (per 1,000)	17.1	16.4	15.7

Source: UN, *World Population Prospects: The 2006 Revision*.

Expectation of life (years at birth, WHO estimates): 48 (males 47; females 48) in 2004 (Source: WHO, *World Health Report*).

ECONOMICALLY ACTIVE POPULATION

(1996 census, persons aged 10 years and over)

	Males	Females	Total
Agriculture, hunting, forestry and fishing	2,284,744	2,229,124	4,513,868
Mining and quarrying	2,946	1,033	3,979
Manufacturing	46,404	25,161	71,565
Electricity, gas and water	2,279	534	2,813
Construction	20,678	398	21,076
Trade, restaurants and hotels	98,295	126,286	224,581
Transport, storage and communications	20,024	556	20,580
Finance, insurance, real estate and business services	10,466	2,665	13,131
Community, social and personal services	76,690	27,236	103,926
Activities not adequately defined	15,104	13,712	28,816
Total employed	2,577,630	2,426,705	5,004,335
Unemployed	51,523	19,757	71,280
Total labour force	2,629,153	2,446,462	5,075,615

Mid-2004 ('000, FAO estimates): Agriculture, etc. 5,747; Total labour force 6,235 (Source: FAO).

Health and Welfare

KEY INDICATORS

Total fertility rate (children per woman, 2005)	6.5
Under-5 mortality rate (per 1,000 live births, 2005)	191
HIV/AIDS (% of persons aged 15–49, 2005)	2.0
Physicians (per 1,000 head, 2004)	0.05
Hospital beds (per 1,000 head, 1996)	1.42
Health expenditure (2004): US $ per head (PPP)	76.5
Health expenditure (2004): % of GDP	6.1
Health expenditure (2004): public (% of total)	54.8
Access to water (% of persons, 2004)	61
Access to sanitation (% of persons, 2004)	13
Human Development Index (2004): ranking	174
Human Development Index (2004): value	0.342

For sources and definitions, see explanatory note on p. vi.

Agriculture

PRINCIPAL CROPS
('000 metric tons)

	2003	2004	2005
Rice (paddy)	95.5	74.5	93.5
Maize	665.5	481.5	799.1
Millet	1,184.3	937.6	1,196.3
Sorghum	1,610.3	1,399.3	1,552.9
Sweet Potatoes	28.5	40.9	51.5
Yams	35.5	89.7	85.4
Sugar cane*	450	442	440
Cow peas (dry)	456.6	276.3	127.7
Bambara beans	35.2	27.8	39.6
Other pulses*	25	25	25
Groundnuts (in shell)	358.1	245.3	331.2
Cottonseed	250*	315†	370†
Okra*	26	26	26
Other vegetables*	206	206	206
Fruit*	78.1	78.1	78.1
Cotton (lint)†	163	210	250

* FAO estimate(s).
† Unofficial figure(s).

LIVESTOCK
('000 head, year ending September)

	2003	2004*	2005*
Cattle	7,312	7,653	8,010
Sheep	6,703	6,854	7,009
Goats	10,306	10,367	10,709
Pigs	1,887	2,076	2,284
Chickens	24,384	25,052	25,739
Horses	36	37	39
Asses, mules or hinnies	915	970	1,028
Camels	15	15	15

* FAO estimates.

Source: FAO.

LIVESTOCK PRODUCTS
('000 metric tons, FAO estimates)

	2003	2004	2005
Cattle meat	100.6	103.0	108.6
Sheep meat	15.7	16.0	16.4
Goat meat	26.0	26.9	27.7
Pig meat	27.2	29.9	32.9
Chicken meat	29.3	30.1	31.0
Other meat	7.8	8.0	8.2
Cows' milk	160.9	168.4	190.8
Goats' milk	36.1	37.3	38.6
Hen eggs	42.7	43.8	45.0

Source: FAO.

Forestry

ROUNDWOOD REMOVALS
('000 cubic metres, excluding bark)

	2003	2004	2005*
Sawlogs, veneer logs and logs for sleepers	87	73	73
Other industrial wood	1,098	1,098*	1,098
Fuel wood	6,152	8,040	11,896
Total	7,337	9,211	13,067

* FAO estimate(s).

Source: FAO.

SAWNWOOD PRODUCTION
('000 cubic metres)

	2003	2004	2005
Total (all broadleaved)	1.5	1.2	1.2*

* FAO estimate.

Source: FAO.

Fishing

(metric tons, live weight)

	2003	2004*	2005
Capture	9,000	9,000	9,000
Freshwater fishes	9,000	9,000	9,000
Aquaculture	5	5	6*
Total catch	9,005	9,005	9,006*

* FAO estimate(s).

Source: FAO.

Mining

	2003	2004	2005*
Cement (metric tons)*	30,000	30,000	30,000
Gold (kg)	770	1,125	1,395

* Estimated production.

Source: US Geological Survey.

Industry

SELECTED PRODUCTS
(metric tons, unless otherwise indicated)

	2000	2001	2002
Edible oils	17,888	19,452	19,626
Shea (karité) butter	186	101	21
Flour	12,289	13,686	10,005
Pasta	211	n.a.	n.a.
Sugar	43,412	46,662	47,743
Beer ('000 hl)	494	500	546
Soft drinks ('000 hl)	221	222	250
Cigarettes (million packets)	85	78	78
Printed fabric ('000 sq metres)	275	n.a.	n.a.
Soap	12,079	9,240	9,923
Matches (cartons)	9,358	4,956	3,009
Bicycles (units)	22,215	17,718	20,849
Mopeds (units)	16,531	19,333	19,702
Tyres ('000)	397	599	670
Inner tubes ('000)	2,655	3,217	2,751
Electric energy ('000 kWh)	390,322	364,902	361,000

Electric energy ('000 kWh): 444,554 in 2003; 473,249 (estimate) in 2004.

Source: IMF, *Burkina Faso: Selected Issues and Statistical Appendix* (September 2005).

Finance

CURRENCY AND EXCHANGE RATES

Monetary Units

100 centimes = 1 franc de la Communauté financière africaine (CFA).

Sterling, Dollar and Euro Equivalents (31 May 2007)

£1 sterling = 964.116 francs CFA;
US $1 = 487.592 francs CFA;
€1 = 655.957 francs CFA;
10,000 francs CFA = £10.37 = $20.51 = €15.24.

Average Exchange Rate (francs CFA per US $)

2004	528.29
2005	527.47
2006	522.89

Note: An exchange rate of 1 French franc = 50 francs CFA, established in 1948, remained in force until January 1994, when the CFA franc was devalued by 50%, with the exchange rate adjusted to 1 French franc = 100 francs CFA. This relationship to French currency remained in effect with the introduction of the euro on 1 January 1999. From that date, accordingly, a fixed exchange rate of €1 = 655.957 francs CFA has been in operation.

BUDGET

('000 million francs CFA)

Revenue*	2005†	2006†	2007‡
Tax revenue	336.8	362.3	413.5
Income and profits	79.7	85.7	99.6
Domestic goods and services	185.8	194.3	224.4
International trade	60.7	71.3	73.3
Non-tax revenue	28.4	30.1	36.9
Total	365.2	392.4	450.4

Expenditure§	2005†	2006†	2007‡
Current expenditure	332.4	386.4	419.5
Wages and salaries	141.4	159.9	182.7
Goods and services	75.3	82.2	93.4
Interest payments	18.2	17.3	8.2
Current transfers	97.6	126.9	135.2
Capital expenditure	322.7	361.9	424.9
Total	655.1	748.3	844.4

* Excluding grants received ('000 million francs CFA): 131.5 in 2005; 177.6 in 2006; 178.0 in 2007.

† Estimates.

‡ Projected.

§ Excluding net lending ('000 million francs CFA): –13.2 in 2005; –14.6 in 2006; –2.9 in 2007.

Source: IMF, *Burkina Faso: Sixth Review Under the Arrangement Under the Poverty Reduction and Growth Facility and Request for Waiver of Performance Criteria and Augmentation of Access, and Ex Post Assessment of Longer-Term Program Engagement - Staff Reports; Press Release on the Executive Board Discussion; and Statement by the Executive Director for Burkina Faso* (October 2006).

INTERNATIONAL RESERVES

(excluding gold, US $ million at 31 December)

	2004	2005	2006
IMF special drawing rights	0.2	0.2	—
Reserve position in IMF	11.3	10.5	11.1
Foreign exchange	657.6	427.7	543.7
Total	669.1	438.4	554.8

Source: IMF, *International Financial Statistics*.

MONEY SUPPLY

('000 million francs CFA at 31 December)

	2004	2005	2006
Currency outside banks	175.0	153.3	141.2
Demand deposits at deposit money banks*	193.9	194.9	220.6
Checking deposits at post office	4.5	2.7	3.5
Total money (incl. others)	378.2	351.8	366.6

* Excluding the deposits of public establishments of an administrative or social nature.

Source: IMF, *International Financial Statistics*.

COST OF LIVING

(Consumer Price Index; base: 1996 = 100)

	2002	2003	2004
Food, beverages and tobacco	113.4	111.5	106.1
Clothing	107.8	118.7	117.9
Housing, water, electricity and gas	109.5	114.8	115.8
All items (incl. others)	114.3	116.6	116.1

2005: All items 123.6.

Source: Banque centrale des états de l'Afrique de l'ouest.

NATIONAL ACCOUNTS

('000 million francs CFA in current prices)

Expenditure on the Gross Domestic Product

	2003	2004	2005
Final consumption expenditure	2,308.9	2,601.2	2,808.0
Households, incl. non-profit institutions serving households	1,791.0	2,019.8	2,199.9
General government	517.9	581.4	608.1
Gross capital formation	515.6	479.9	565.1
Gross fixed capital formation	500.2	559.3	625.1
Changes in inventories	15.4	–79.4	–60.0
Total domestic expenditure	2,824.5	3,081.1	3,373.1
Exports of goods and services	212.9	286.5	294.1
Less Imports of goods and services	533.8	667.3	682.2
GDP in market prices	2,503.6	2,700.2	2,985.0

Gross Domestic Product by Economic Activity

	2003	2004	2005
Agriculture, livestock, forestry and fishing	799.4	803.2	940.5
Mining	1.5	1.6	1.8
Manufacturing	337.1	347.0	350.8
Electricity, gas and water	46.4	55.0	65.3
Construction and public works	92.5	111.5	125.9
Trade	309.8	364.8	388.2
Transport and communications	89.9	98.6	117.9
Other market services	260.0	297.2	324.8
Non-market services	398.4	426.0	452.8
Sub-total	2,335.0	2,504.9	2,768.0
Import taxes and duties	168.6	195.3	217.0
GDP in market prices	2,503.6	2,700.2	2,985.0

Source: Banque centrale des états de l'Afrique de l'ouest.

BALANCE OF PAYMENTS
('000 million francs CFA, estimates)

	2004	2005	2006
Exports of goods f.o.b.	249	252	319
Imports of goods f.o.b.	–498	–556	–621
Trade balance	–249	–304	–302
Services (net)	–121	–138	–142
Balance on goods and services	–370	–442	–444
Income (net)	–16	–22	–21
Balance on goods, services and income	—386	–464	–465
Private unrequited transfers (net).	20	21	29
Official unrequited transfers (net).	80	95	96
Current balance	–286	–348	–339
Capital transfers (net)	106	115	818
Official capital (net)	94	112	–506
Private capital (net)*	21	17	78
Net errors and omissions	8	—	—
Overall balance	–57	–103	50

* Including portfolio investment and direct foreign investment.

Source: IMF, *Burkina Faso: Request for a Three-Year Arrangement Under the Poverty Reduction and Growth Facility - Staff Report; Press Release on the Executive Board Discussion; and Statement by the Executive Director for Burkina Faso* (October 2006).

External Trade

PRINCIPAL COMMODITIES
('000 million francs CFA)

Imports f.o.b.	2003	2004	2005
Food products	66.1	65.2	85.5
Mineral fuels, lubricants and related products	76.6	93.9	123.5
Chemical products	67.0	83.7	94.1
Manufactured articles	102.4	129.0	139.5
Machinery and transport materials	113.6	131.9	145.0
Total (incl. others)	446.8	534.6	619.2

Exports f.o.b.	2003	2004	2005
Food	12.4	16.4	12.7
Beverages and tobacco	8.9	6.1	4.1
Oils and fats (animal and vegetable)	4.0	2.9	2.0
Machinery and transport materials	6.5	6.5	3.4
Manufactured articles	7.7	3.8	7.8
Total (incl. others)	182.5	206.6	175.0

PRINCIPAL TRADING PARTNERS
('000 million francs CFA)*

Imports c.i.f.	2003	2004	2005
Belgium-Luxembourg	25.5	28.8	26.7
Benin	45.5	36.6	42.1
Chile	3.3	3.2	7.6
China, People's Repub.	12.0	21.2	16.7
Côte d'Ivoire	39.9	85.2	111.4
France	97.8	112.9	115.9
Germany	13.8	12.2	9.9
Ghana	17.3	14.4	36.3
India	10.6	9.1	17.3
Italy	6.4	7.8	10.5
Japan	9.2	9.3	9.2
Netherlands	6.2	6.7	6.2
Pakistan	0.0	0.1	7.1
Russia	9.8	6.2	2.3
Senegal	10.3	22.4	7.9
Spain	6.0	5.8	10.4
Thailand	2.5	5.2	8.0
Togo	81.9	71.6	70.8
USA	9.1	11.4	16.2
Total (incl. others)	446.8	534.6	619.2

Exports f.o.b.	2003	2004	2005
Belgium-Luxembourg	0.9	0.2	2.4
Benin	5.5	3.8	1.4
Côte d'Ivoire	3.6	18.1	18.3
France	8.5	14.7	17.2
Ghana	49.3	34.9	29.1
Mali	6.7	1.7	3.2
Niger	6.8	7.8	4.0
Switzerland	7.4	20.5	16.5
Togo	89.5	97.1	71.9
United Kingdom	0.0	2.5	1.1
Total (incl. others)	182.5	206.6	175.0

* Figures refer to recorded trade only.

Transport

RAILWAYS

	2002	2003	2004*
Freight traffic ('000 metric tons)	869.7	179.7	293.9
Passengers ('000 journeys)	320.6	87.5	116.6

* Estimates.

Source: IMF, *Burkina Faso: Selected Issues and Statistical Appendix* (September 2005).

2005: Freight ton-km (million) 674,877.

2003: Passengers carried 87.5; Passenger-km (million) 9,980; Freight carried 179.7; Freight ton-km 128,795.

ROAD TRAFFIC
('000 motor vehicles in use)

	1998	1999	2000
Passenger cars	25.3	26.3	26.5
Commercial vehicles	14.9	19.6	22.6

2001–03: Figures as in 2000.

Source: UN, *Statistical Yearbook.*

2005 ('000): Private cars 84.2; Lorries 20.1; Vans 20.1; Public transport 5.7; Tractors 8.2; Motorbikes and mopeds 100.0.

CIVIL AVIATION
(traffic on scheduled services)*

	2001	2002	2003
Kilometres flown (million)	2	1	1
Passengers carried ('000)	100	53	54
Passenger-km (million)	158	29	29
Total ton-km (million)	22	3	3

* Including an apportionment of the traffic of Air Afrique.

Source: UN, *Statistical Yearbook.*

Tourism

FOREIGN VISITORS BY COUNTRY OF ORIGIN*

	2003	2004	2005
Belgium	4,984	6,482	6,438
Benin	6,443	8,765	9,186
Canada	3,000	4,548	6,048
Côte d'Ivoire	9,229	14,924	14,454
France	47,663	62,510	77,220
Germany	4,683	5,523	5,190
Ghana	3,831	5,456	4,914
Guinea	2,759	4,528	3,534
Italy	3,215	3,727	5,244
Mali	7,785	12,411	12,018
Mauritania	1,652	1,834	1,854
Netherlands	2,734	2,932	3,198
Niger	7,016	11,455	10,836
Nigeria	2,328	4,097	3,366
Senegal	5,950	9,882	9,792
Switzerland	4,025	5,192	3,828
Togo	5,394	6,961	7,974
United Kingdom	2,475	3,618	3,288
USA	6,030	6,872	7,290
Total (incl. others)	163,123	222,201	244,728

* Arrivals at hotels and similar establishments.

Receipts from tourism (US $ million, incl. passenger transport): 23 in 2000; 25 in 2001.

Source: World Tourism Organization.

Communications Media

	2003	2004	2005
Telephones ('000 main lines in use)	65.4	81.4	97.4
Mobile cellular telephones ('000 subscribers)	227.0	398.0	572.2
Personal computers ('000 in use)	26	29	31
Internet users ('000)	48	53	65

Source: International Telecommunication Union.

Television receivers ('000 in use): 140 in 2000 (Source: UNESCO, *Statistical Yearbook*).

Radio receivers ('000 in use): 370 in 1997 (Source: UNESCO, *Statistical Yearbook*).

Daily newspapers (national estimates): 4 (average circulation 14,200 copies) in 1997; 4 (average circulation 14,500 copies) in 1998 (Source: UNESCO Institute for Statistics).

Non-daily newspapers: 9 (average circulation 42,000 copies) in 1995 (Source: UNESCO, *Statistical Yearbook*).

Book production: 12 titles (14,000 copies) in 1996 (first editions only); 5 in 1997 (Sources: UNESCO, *Statistical Yearbook*, UNESCO Institute for Statistics).

Education

(2003/04, except where otherwise indicated, private and public institutions)

			Students ('000)		
	Institutions	Teachers	Males	Females	Total
Pre-primary	147*	473†	7.3†	6.6†	13.9†
Primary	n.a.	23,402	647.0	492.5	1,139.5
Secondary	496†	7,840	147.6	98.0	245.6
Tertiary	n.a.	561	14.6	4.2	18.9

* 1997/98.

† 2001/02.

Source: mostly UNESCO Institute for Statistics.

Adult literacy rate (UNESCO estimates): 21.8% (males 29.4%; females 15.2%) in 2004 (Source: UN Development Programme, *Human Development Report*).

Directory

The Constitution

The present Constitution was approved in a national referendum on 2 June 1991, and was formally adopted on 11 June. The following are the main provisions of the Constitution, as amended in January 1997, April 2000 and February 2002:

The Constitution of the 'revolutionary, democratic, unitary and secular' Fourth Republic of Burkina Faso guarantees the collective and individual political and social rights of Burkinabè citizens, and delineates the powers of the executive, legislature and judiciary.

Executive power is vested in the President, who is Head of State, and in the Government, which is appointed by the President upon the recommendation of the Prime Minister. With effect from the November 2005 election, the President is elected, by universal suffrage, for a five-year term, renewable only once (previously, a seven-year term had been served).

Legislative power is exercised by the multi-party Assemblée nationale. Deputies are elected, by universal suffrage, for a five-year term. The number of deputies and the mode of election is determined by law. The President appoints a Prime Minister and, at the suggestion of the Prime Minister, appoints the other ministers. The President may, having consulted the Prime Minister and the President of the Assemblée nationale, dissolve the Assemblée nationale. Both the Government and the Assemblée nationale may initiate legislation.

The judiciary is independent and, in accordance with constitutional amendments approved in April 2000 (see Judicial System), consists of a Court of Cassation, a Constitutional Council, a Council of State, a National Audit Court, a High Court of Justice, and other courts and tribunals instituted by law. Judges are accountable to a Higher Council, under the chairmanship of the Head of State, who is responsible for guaranteeing the independence of the judiciary.

The Constitution also makes provision for an Economic and Social Council, for a Higher Council of Information, and for a national ombudsman.

The Constitution denies legitimacy to any regime that might take power as the result of a *coup d'état*.

The Government

HEAD OF STATE

President: BLAISE COMPAORÉ (assumed power as Chairman of the Front populaire 15 October 1987; elected President 1 December 1991; re-elected 15 November 1998 and 13 November 2005).

COUNCIL OF MINISTERS
(August 2007)

President: BLAISE COMPAORÉ.

Prime Minister: TERTIUS ZONGO.

Minister of State, Minister of Agriculture, Water Resources and Fisheries: SALIF DIALLO.

Chad: Ouagadougou; Ambassador AGNÈS MAÏMOUNA ALLAH.

China (Taiwan): 994 rue Agostino Neto, 01 BP 5563, Ouagadougou 01; tel. 50-31-61-95; fax 50-31-61-97; e-mail ambachine@fasonet.bf; Ambassador TAO WEN-LUNG.

Côte d'Ivoire: pl. des Nations Unies, 01 BP 20, Ouagadougou 01; tel. 50-31-82-28; fax 50-31-82-30; e-mail ambci@cenatrin.bf; Ambassador RICHARD KODJO.

Cuba: rue 4/64, La Rotonde, Secteur 4, Ouagadougou; tel. 50-30-64-91; fax 50-31-73-24; e-mail embacuba.bf@fasonet.bf; Ambassador FERNANDO PRATS MARI.

Denmark: 316, ave Blaise Compaoré, 01 BP 1760, Ouagadougou 01; tel. 50-32-85-40; fax 50-32-85-77; e-mail ouaamb@um.dk; internet www.ambouagadougou.um.dk; Ambasssador MOGENS PEDERSEN.

Egypt: Zone du Conseil de L'Entente, blvd du Faso, 04 BP 7042, Ouagadougou 04; tel. 50-30-66-39; fax 50-31-38-36; e-mail egyptianembassy@liptinfor.bf; Ambassador MUHAMMAD MAMDOUH ALI EL-ASHMAWI.

France: ave du Trésor, 01 BP 504, Ouagadougou 01; tel. 50-49-66-66; fax 50-49-66-09; e-mail ambassade@ambafrance-bf.org; internet www.ambafrance-bf.org; Ambassador FRANÇOIS GOLDBLATT.

Germany: 399 ave Joseph Badoua, 01 BP 600, Ouagadougou 01; tel. 50-30-67-31; fax 50-31-39-91; e-mail amb.allemagne@fasonet.bf; Ambassador ULRICH HOCHSCHILD.

Ghana: 22 ave d'Oubritenga, 01 BP 212, Ouagadougou 01; tel. 50-30-76-35; e-mail embagna@fasonet.bf; Ambassador MOGTARI SAHANUN.

Korea, Democratic People's Republic: Ouagadougou; Ambassador KIL MUN YONG.

Libya: 01 BP 1601, Ouagadougou 01; tel. 50-30-67-53; fax 50-31-34-70; Ambassador ABD AN-NASSER SALEH MUHAMMAD YOUNES.

Mali: 2569 ave Bassawarga, 01 BP 1911, Ouagadougou 01; tel. 50-38-19-22; Ambassador Col TOUMANY SISSOKO.

Mauritania: Ouagadougou; Ambassador MOHAMED OULD SID AHMED LEKHAL.

Morocco: Ouaga 2000 Villa B04, place de la Cotière, 01 BP 3438, Ouagadougou 01; tel. 50-37-40-16; fax 50-37-41-72; e-mail maroc1@fasonet.bf; Ambassador ALI AHMAOUI.

Netherlands: 415 ave Dr Kwamé N'Krumah, 01 BP 1302, Ouagadougou 01; tel. 50-30-61-34; fax 50-30-76-95; e-mail oua@minbuza.nl; Ambassador Dr HAN GERARD DUIJFJES.

Nigeria: rue de l'Hôpital Yalgado, 01 BP 132, Ouagadougou 01; tel. 50-36-30-15; Ambassador AHMED KASHIM.

Saudi Arabia: Ouagadougou; Ambassador AID BIN MUHAMMAD ATH-THAKFI.

Senegal: Immeuble Espace Fadima, ave de la Résistance du 17 Mai, 01 BP 3226, Ouagadougou 01; tel. 50-31-14-18; fax 50-31-14-01; e-mail ambasenebf@cenatrin.bf; Ambassador CHEIKH SYLLA.

USA: 602 ave Raoul Follereau, Koulouba, 01 BP 35, Ouagadougou 01; tel. 50-30-67-23; fax 50-31-23-68; e-mail amembouaga@state.gov; internet ouagadougou.usembassy.gov; Ambassador JEANINE E. JACKSON.

Judicial System

In accordance with constitutional amendments approved by the Assemblée nationale in April 2000, the Supreme Court was abolished; its four permanent chambers were replaced by a Constitutional Council, a Council of State, a Court of Cassation and a National Audit Court, all of which commenced operations in December 2002. Judges are accountable to a Higher Council, under the chairmanship of the President of the Republic, in which capacity he is officially responsible for ensuring the independence of the judiciary. A High Court of Justice is competent to try the President and members of the Government in cases of treason, embezzlement of public funds, and other crimes and offences.

Constitutional Council: 11 BP 1114, Ouagadougou 11; tel. 50-31-06-24; internet www.conseil-constitutionnel.gov.bf; f. 2002 to replace Constitutional Chamber of fmr Supreme Court; Pres. IDRISSA TRAORÉ; Sec.-Gen. HONIBIPÈ MARIAM MARGUERITE OUÉDRAOGO.

Council of State: 01 BP 586, Ouagadougou 01; tel. 50-30-64-18; e-mail webmaster@conseil-etat.gov.bf; internet www.conseil-etat.gov.bf; f. 2002 to replace Administrative Chamber of fmr Supreme Court; comprises two chambers: a Consultative Chamber and a Chamber of Litigation; First Pres. HARIDIATA SERE DAKOURÉ; Pres. of Consultative Chamber THÉRÈSE SANOU TRAORÉ; Pres. of Chamber of Litigation SOULEYMANE COULIBALY.

Court of Cassation: 05 BP 6204, Ouagadougou 05; tel. 50-31-20-47; fax 50-31-02-71; e-mail cheick.ouedraogo@justice.gov.bf; internet www.cour-cassation.gov.bf; f. 2002 to replace Judicial Chamber of fmr Supreme Court; First Pres. CHEICK DIMKINSEDO OUÉDRAOGO.

High Court of Justice: Ouagadougou; f. 1998; comprises six deputies of the Assemblée nationale and three magistrates appointed by the President of the Court of Cassation; Pres. YARGA LARBA; Vice-Pres. DÉ ALBERT MILLOGO.

National Audit Court: 01 BP 2534, Ouagadougou 01; tel. 50-30-36-00; fax 50-30-35-01; e-mail infos@cour-comptes.gov.bf; internet www.cour-comptes.gov.bf; f. 2002 to replace Audit Chamber of fmr Supreme Court; comprises three chambers, concerned with: local government organs; public enterprises; and the operations of the State; First Pres. BOUREIMA PIERRE NEBIE; Procurator-Gen. THÉRÈSE TRAORÉ SANOU; Pres of Chambers PASCAL SANOU, SÉNÉBOU RAYMONDD MANUELLA OUILMA TRAORÉ, SABINE OUEDRAOGO YETA.

Religion

The Constitution provides for freedom of religion, and the Government respects this right in practice. The country is a secular state. Islam, Christianity and traditional religions operate freely without government interference. More than 50% of the population follow animist beliefs.

ISLAM

An estimated 30% of the population are Muslims.

Association Islamique Tidjania du Burkina Faso: Ouagadougou; Pres. CHEICK ABOUBACAR MAÏGA II.

CHRISTIANITY

The Roman Catholic Church

Burkina Faso comprises three archdioceses and 10 dioceses. At 31 December 2004 there were an estimated 1.6m. Roman Catholics in Burkina, comprising 12.5% of the total population.

Bishops' Conference

Conférence des Evêques de Burkina Faso et du Niger, 01 BP 1195, Ouagadougou 01; tel. 50-30-60-26; fax 50-31-64-81; e-mail ccbn@fasonet.bf.

f. 1966; legally recognized 1978; Pres. Rt Rev. PHILIPPE OUÉDRAOGO (Bishop of Ouahigouya).

Archbishop of Bobo-Dioulasso: Most Rev. ANSELME TITIANMA SANON, Archevêché, Lafiaso, 01 BP 312, Bobo-Dioulasso; tel. 20-97-04-35; fax 20-97-04-38; e-mail ddec.bobo@fasonet.bf.

Archbishop of Koupéla: Most Rev. SÉRAPHIN F. ROUAMBA, Archevêché, BP 51, Koupéla; tel. 40-70-00-30; fax 40-70-02-65; e-mail archevkou@fasonet.bf.

Archbishop of Ouagadougou: Most Rev. JEAN-MARIE UNTAANI COMPAORÉ, Archevêché, 01 BP 1472, Ouagadougou 01; tel. 50-30-67-04; fax 50-30-72-75; e-mail archidiocese.ouaga@liptinfor.bf.

Protestant Churches

Assemblées de Dieu du Burkina Faso: 01 BP 458, Ouagadougou 01; tel. 50-30-54-60; e-mail ad@adburkina.org; internet www.adburkina.org; f. 1921; Pres. Pastor JEAN PAWENTAORÉ OUÉDRAOGO.

Fédération des Eglises et Missions Evangéliques (FEME): BP 108, Ouagadougou; tel. 50-36-14-26; e-mail feme@fasonet.bf; f. 1961; 10 churches and missions, 82,309 adherents; Pres. Pastor FREEMAN KOMPAORÉ.

BAHÁ'Í FAITH

Assemblée spirituelle nationale: 01 BP 977, Ouagadougou 01; tel. 50-34-29-95; e-mail gnampa@fasonet.bf; Nat. Sec. JEAN-PIERRE SWEDY.

The Press

Direction de la presse écrite: Ouagadougou; govt body responsible for press direction.

DAILIES

24 Heures: 01 BP 3654, Ouagadougou 01; tel. 50-31-41-08; fax 50-30-57-39; f. 2000; privately owned; Dir BOUBAKAR DIALLO.

Bulletin de l'Agence d'Information du Burkina: 01 BP 2507, Ouagadougou 01; tel. 50-32-46-39; fax 50-32-46-40; e-mail aib.redaction@mcc.gov.bf; internet www.aib.bf; f. 1964 as L'Agence Voltaïque de Presse; current name adopted in 1984; Dir JAMES DABIRÉ.

L'Express du Faso: 01 BP 1, Bobo-Dioulasso 01; tel. 20-97-93-26; e-mail kami.express@caramail.com; f. 1998; privately owned; Dir of Publication KAMI MOUNTAMOU.

President and Legislature

PRESIDENT

Presidential Election, 13 November 2005

Candidate	Votes	% of votes
Blaise Compaoré	1,660,148	80.35
Bénéwendé Stanislas Sankara	100,816	4.88
Kilachia Laurent Bado	53,743	2.60
Philippe Ouédraogo	47,146	2.28
Ram Ouédraogo	42,061	2.04
Ali Lankoandé	35,949	1.74
Norbert Michel Tiendrébéogo	33,353	1.61
Soumane Touré	23,266	1.13
Gilbert Bouda	21,658	1.05
Pargui Emile Paré	17,998	0.87
Others	30,132	1.46
Total	2,066,270	100.00

LEGISLATURE

Assemblée nationale

01 BP 6482, Ouagadougou 01; tel. 50-31-46-84; fax 50-31-45-90.

President: ROCH MARC CHRISTIAN KABORÉ.

General Election, 6 May 2007

Parties	% of total votes*	National list seats	Total seats†
CDP	58.85	9	73
ADF—RDA	10.70	2	14
UPR	4.30	1	5
UNIR—MS	3.89	1	4
CFD/B‡	2.34	1	3
PDS	3.28	1	2
PDP—PS	2.51	—	2
RDB	2.09	—	2
UPS	1.74	—	2
PAREN	1.29	—	1
RPC	1.15	—	1
UDPS	1.03	—	1
PAI	0.83	—	1
Total (incl. others)	100.00	15	111

* Including votes from regional and national party lists.

† Including seats filled by voting from regional lists, totalling 96.

‡ The Coalition des forces démocratiques du Burkina, an electoral alliance of six parties.

Election Commission

Commission électorale nationale indépendante (CENI): 01 BP 5152, Ouagadougou 01; tel. 50-30-00-52; fax 50-30-80-44; e-mail ceni@fasonet.bf; internet www.ceni.bf; f. 2001; 15 mems; Pres. MOUSSA MICHEL TAPSOBA.

Advisory Council

Conseil économique et social: 01 BP 6162, Ouagadougou 01; tel. 50-32-40-91; fax 50-31-06-54; e-mail ces@ces.gov.bf; internet www.ces.gov.bf; f. 1985; present name adopted in 1992; 90 mems; Pres. THOMAS SANON.

Political Organizations

A total of 47 political parties contested the legislative elections held in May 2007. In that year the most important political parties included the following:

Alliance pour la démocratie et la fédération—Rassemblement démocratique africain (ADF—RDA): 01 BP 1991, Ouagadougou 01; tel. 50-30-52-00; f. 1990 as Alliance pour la démocratie et la fédération; absorbed faction of Rassemblement démocratique africain in 1998; several factions broke away in 2000 and in mid-2003; Pres. GILBERT NOËL OUÉDRAOGO.

Alliance pour le progrès et la liberté (APL): Ouagadougou; tel. 50-31-16-01; Sec.-Gen. JOSÉPHINE TAMBOURA-SAMA.

Congrès pour la démocratie et le progrès (CDP): 1146 ave Dr Kwamé N'Krumah, 01 BP 1605, Ouagadougou 01; tel. 50-31-50-18; fax 50-31-43-93; e-mail contact@cdp-burkina.org; internet www.cdp-burkina.org; f. 1996 by merger, to succeed the Organisation pour la démocratie populaire/Mouvement du travail as the principal political org. supporting Pres. Compaoré; social democratic; Pres. ROCH MARC CHRISTIAN KABORÉ.

Convention nationale des démocrates progressistes (CNDP): Ouagadougou; tel. 50-36-39-73; f. 2000; Leader ALFRED KABORÉ.

Convention panafricaine sankariste (CPS): BP 44, Bokin; tel. 40-45-72-93; f. 1999 by merger of four parties, expanded in 2000 to include two other parties; promotes the policies of fmr Pres. Sankara; Pres. NONGMA ERNEST OUÉDRAOGO.

Convention pour la démocratie et la fédération (CDF): Ouagadougou; tel. 50-36-23-63; f. 1998; Pres. AMADOU DIEMDIODA DICKO.

Convergence pour la démocratie sociale (CDS): Ouagadougou; f. 2002; socialist, opposed to Govt of Pres. Compaoré; Chair. VALERIE DIEUDONNÉ SOMÉ; Exec. Sec.-Gen. SESSOUMA SANOU.

Front des forces sociales (FFS): BP 255, Ouagadougou; tel. 50-32-32-32; f. 1996; Sankarist; member of the Groupe du 14 février and opposition Collectif d'organisations démocratiques de masse et de partis politiques; Chair. NORBERT MICHEL TIENDRÉBÉOGO.

Front patriotique pour le changement (FPC): BP 8539, Ouagadougou; tel. 70-25-32-45; Pres. TAHIROU IBRAHIM ZON.

Mouvement du peuple pour le socialisme—Parti fédéral (MPS—PF): BP 3448, Ouagadougou; tel. 50-36-50-72; f. 2002 by split from PDP—PS; Leader Dr PARGUI EMILE PARÉ.

Mouvement pour la tolérance et le progrès/Moog Teeb Panpaasgo (MTP): BP 2364, Ouagadougou; tel. 50-36-45-35; f. 2000; Sankarist; contested 2002 legislative elections as part of the Coalition des forces démocratiques (CFD); Pres. CONGO EMMANUEL NAYABTIGUNGU KABORÉ.

Parti africain de l'indépendance (PAI): Ouagadougou; tel. 50-33-46-66; f. 1999; Sec.-Gen. SOUMANE TOURÉ.

Parti pour la démocratie et le progrès—Parti socialiste (PDP—PS): 11 BP 26, Ouagadougou 11; tel. and fax 50-31-14-10; e-mail pdp-ps@fasonet.bf; f. 2001 by merger of the Parti pour la démocratie et le progrès and the Parti socialiste burkinabè; Nat. Pres. Prof. ALI LANKOANDÉ.

Parti pour la démocratie et le socialisme (PDS): Ouagadougou; tel. 50-34-34-04; Pres. FÉLIX SOUBÉIGA.

Parti de la renaissance nationale (PAREN): Ouagadougou; tel. 50-43-12-26; f. 2000; social-democratic; Pres. KILACHIA LAURENT BADO.

Parti socialiste unifié: Ouagadougou; f. 2001 by mems of fmr Parti socialiste burkinabè; Leader BENOÎT LOMPO.

Rassemblement pour le développement du Burkina.

Rassemblement populaire des citoyens (RPC): Ouagadougou; f. 2006; promotes an alternative style of politics; Pres. ANTOINE OUARÉ.

Union des démocrates et progressistes indépendants (UDPI): BP 536, Ouagadougou; tel. 50-38-27-99; expelled from Groupe du 14 février in mid-2000; Leader LONGO DONGO.

Union pour la démocratie et le progrès social (UDPS): Ouagadougou; Leader FIDÈLE HIEN.

Union nationale pour la démocratie et le développement (UNDD): 03 BP 7114, Ouagadougou 03; tel. 50-31-15-15; f. 2003 by fmr mems of the ADF—RDA (q.v.); liberal; Pres. Me HERMANN YAMÉOGO.

Union des partis sankarist.

Union pour la renaissance—Mouvement sankariste (UNIR—MS): Ouagadougou; tel. 50-36-30-45; f. 2000; Pres. BÉNÉWENDÉ STANISLAS SANKARA.

Union pour la république.

Diplomatic Representation

EMBASSIES IN BURKINA FASO

Algeria: Secteur 13, Zone du Bois, 295 ave Babanguida, 01 BP 3893, Ouagadougou 01; tel. 50-36-81-81; fax 50-36-81-79; e-mail ambalg@cenatrin.bf; Ambassador MOHAMED EL AMINE BEN CHERIF.

Belgium: Immeuble Me Benoit Sawadogo, 994 rue Agostino Neto, Koulouba, 01 POB 1624, Ouagadougou 01; tel. 50-31-21-64; fax 50-31-06-60; e-mail ouagadougou@diplobel.org; internet www.diplomatie.be/ouagadougou; Ambassador JANSEN PAUL.

Canada: rue Agostino Neto, 01 BP 548, Ouagadougou 01; tel. 50-31-18-94; fax 50-31-19-00; e-mail ouaga@dfait-maeci.gc.ca; internet www.dfait-maeci.gc.ca/burkina_faso; Ambassador LOUIS-ROBERT DAIGLE.

L'Observateur Paalga (New Observer): 01 BP 584, Ouagadougou 01; tel. 50-33-27-05; fax 50-31-45-79; e-mail lobservateur@zcp.bf; internet www.lobservateur.bf; f. 1973; privately-owned; also a Sunday edn, *L'Observateur Dimanche*; Dir EDOUARD OUÉDRAOGO; circ. 7,000.

Le Pays: Cité 1200 logements, 01 BP 4577, Ouagadougou 01; tel. 50-36-20-46; fax 50-36-03-78; e-mail ed.lepays@cenatrin.bf; internet www.lepays.bf; f. 1991; independent; Dir-Gen. BOUREIMA JÉRÉMIE SIGUE; Editor-in-Chief MAHOROU KANAZOE; circ. 5,000.

Sidwaya Quotidien (Daily Truth): 5 rue du Marché, 01 BP 507, Ouagadougou 01; tel. 50-31-22-89; fax 50-31-03-62; e-mail daouda.ouedraogo@sidwaya.bf; internet www.sidwaya.bf; f. 1984; state-owned; Editor-in-Chief DAOUDA EMILE OUEDRAOGO; circ. 3,000.

PERIODICALS

L'Aurore: 01 BP 5104, Ouagadougou 01; tel. 70-25-22-81; e-mail enitiema@yahoo.fr; Dir of Publication ELIE NITIÈMA.

Bendré (Drum): 16.38 ave du Yatenga, 01 BP 6020, Ouagadougou 01; tel. 50-33-27-11; fax 50-31-28-53; e-mail bendrekan@hotmail.com; internet www.journalbendre.net; f. 1990; weekly; current affairs; Dir SY MOUMINA CHERIFF; circ. 7,000 (2002).

Les Echos: Ouagadougou; f. 2002; weekly; Editor DAVID SANHOUIDI.

Evasion: Cité 1200 logements, 01 BP 4577, Ouagadougou 01; tel. 50-36-17-30; fax 50-36-03-78; e-mail ed.lepays@cenatrin.bf; internet www.lepays.bf/hebdo; f. 1996; publ. by Editions le Pays; weekly; current affairs; Dir-Gen. BOUREIMA JÉRÉMIE SIGUE; Editor-in-Chief ABDOULAYE TAO.

L'Evènement: 01 BP 1860, Ouagadougou 01; tel. and fax 50-31-69-34; e-mail bangreib@yahoo.fr; internet www.cnpress-zongo.net/evenementbf; f. 2001; bimonthly; Editor-in-Chief NEWTON AHMED BARRY.

L'Hebdomadaire: Ouagadougou; tel. 50-31-47-62; e-mail hebdcom@fasonet.bf; internet www.hebdo.bf; f. 1999; Fridays; Dir ZÉPHIRIN KPODA; Editor-in-Chief DJIBRIL TOURÉ.

L'Indépendant: 01 BP 5663, Ouagadougou 01; tel. 50-33-37-75; e-mail sebgo@fasonet.bf; internet www.independant.bf; f. 1993 by Norbert Zongo; weekly, Tuesdays; Dir LIERMÉ DIEUDONNÉ SOMÉ; Editor-in-Chief TALATO SIID SAYA.

Le Journal du Jeudi (JJ): 01 BP 3654, Ouagadougou 01; tel. 50-31-41-08; fax 50-30-01-62; e-mail info@journaldujeudi.com; internet www.journaldujeudi.com; f. 1991; weekly; satirical; Dir BOUBAKAR DIALLO; Editor-in-Chief DAMIEN GLEZ; circ. 10,000.

Laabaali: Association Tin Tua, BP 167, Fada N'Gourma; tel. 40-77-01-26; fax 40-77-02-08; e-mail info@tintua.org; internet www.tintua.org/Liens/Laabali.htm; f. 1988; monthly; promotes literacy, agricultural information, cultural affairs, in Gourmanché; Dir of Publishing BENOÎT B. OUOBA; Editor-in-Chief SUZANNE OUOBA; circ. 3,500.

Le Marabout: 01 BP 3564, Ouagadougou 01; tel. 50-31-41-08; e-mail info@marabout.net; f. 2001; monthly; publ. by the Réseau africain pour la liberté d'informer; pan-African politics; satirical; Dir BOUBAKAR DIALLO; Editor-in-Chief DAMIEN GLEZ.

L'Opinion: 01 BP 6459, Ouagadougou 01; tel. and fax 50-30-89-49; e-mail zedcom@fasonet.bf; internet www.zedcom.bf; weekly; Dir of Publishing ISSAKA LINGANI.

Regard: 01 BP 4707, Ouagadougou 01; tel. 50-31-16-70; fax 50-31-57-47; weekly; Dir CHRIS VALÉA; Editor PATRICK ILBOUDO; circ. 4,000.

San Finna: Immeuble Photo Luxe, 12 BP 105, Ouagadougou 12; tel. and fax 50-35-82-64; e-mail sanfinna@yahoo.fr; internet www.sanfinna.com; f. 1999; Mondays; independent; current affairs, international politics; Editor-in-Chief MATHIEU N'DO.

Sidwaya Hebdo (Weekly Truth): 5 rue du Marché, 01 BP 507, Ouagadougou 01; tel. 50-31-22-89; fax 50-31-03-62; e-mail daouda.ouedraogo@sidwaya.bf; internet www.sidwaya.bf; f. 1997; state-owned; weekly; Editor-in-Chief DAOUDA EMILE OUEDRAOGO.

Sidwaya Magazine (Truth): 5 rue du Marché, 01 BP 507, Ouagadougou 01; tel. 50-30-63-07; fax 50-31-03-62; e-mail sidwayas@mcc.gov.bf; internet www.sidwaya.bf; f. 1989; state-owned; monthly; Editor-in-Chief BONIFACE COULIBALY; circ. 2,500.

La Voix du Sahel: 01 BP 5505, Ouagadougou 01; tel. 50-33-20-75; e-mail voixdusahel@yahoo.fr; privately owned; Dir of Publication PROMOTHÉE KASSOUM BAKO.

Votre Santé: Cité 1200 logements, 01 BP 4577, Ouagadougou 01; tel. 50-36-20-46; fax 50-36-03-78; e-mail ed.lepays@cenatrin.bf; internet www.lepays.bf/mensuel; f. 1996; publ. by Editions le Pays; monthly; Dir-Gen. BOUREIMA JÉRÉMIE SIGUE; Editor-in-Chief SÉNI DABO.

NEWS AGENCY

Agence d'Information du Burkina (AIB): 01 BP 2507, Ouagadougou 01; tel. 50-32-46-39; fax 50-32-46-40; e-mail aib.redaction@delgi.gov.bf; internet www.aib.bf; f. 1964; fmrly Agence Voltaïque de Presse; state-controlled; Dir JAMES DABIRÉ.

PRESS ASSOCIATIONS

Association Rayimkudemdé—Association Nationale des Animateurs et Journalistes en Langues Nationales du Burkina Faso (ARK): Sigh-Noghin, Ouagadougou; f. 2001; Pres. RIGOBERT ILBOUDO; Sec.-Gen. PIERRE OUÉDRAOGO.

Centre National de Presse—Norbert Zongo (CNP—NZ): 04 BP 8524, Ouagadougou 04; tel. and fax 50-34-37-45; e-mail cnpress@fasonet.bf; internet www.cnpress-zongo.net; f. 1998 as Centre National de Presse; centre of information and documentation; provides journalistic training; incorporates Association des Journalistes du Burkina (f. 1988); Dir ABDOULAYE DIALLO.

Publishers

Editions Contact: 04 BP 8462, Ouagadougou 04; tel. 76-61-28-72; e-mail contact.evang@cenatrin.bf; f. 1992; evangelical Christian and other books in French.

Editions Découvertes du Burkina (ADDB): 06 BP 9237, Ouagadougou 06; tel. 50-36-22-38; e-mail jacques@liptinfor.bf; human and social sciences, poetry; Dir JACQUES GUÉGANÉ.

Editions Firmament: 01 BP 3392, Ouagadougou 01; tel. 50-38-44-25; e-mail brkabore@uemoa.int; f. 1994; literary fiction; Dir ROGER KABORÉ.

Editions Flamme: 04 BP 8921, Ouagadougou 04; tel. 50-34-15-31; fax 70-21-10-28; e-mail flamme@liptinfor.bf; f. 1999; owned by the Assemblées de Dieu du Burkina Faso; literature of Christian interest in French, in Mooré and in Dioula; Dir Pastor ZACHARIE DELMA.

Editions Gambidi: 01 BP 5743, Ouagadougou 01; tel. 50-36-59-42; e-mail jp.guigane@liptinfor.bf; politics, philosophy; Dir JEAN-PIERRE GUINGANÉ.

Graphic Technic International & Biomedical (GTI): 01 BP 3230, Ouagadougou 01; tel. and fax 50-31-67-69; e-mail hien.ignace@fasonet.bf; medicine, literary, popular and children's fiction, poetry; Dir ANSOMWIN IGNACE HIEN.

Editions Hamaria: 01 BP 6788, Ouagadougou 01; tel. 50-34-38-04; e-mail edition.hamaria@fasonet.bf; sciences, fiction.

Presses Africaines SA: 01 BP 1471, Ouagadougou 01; tel. 50-30-71-75; fax 50-30-72-75; general fiction, religion, primary and secondary textbooks; Man. Dir A. WININGA.

Editions Sankofa et Gurli: 01 BP 3811, Ouagadougou 01; tel. 70-24-30-81; e-mail sankogur@hotmail.com; f. 1995; literary fiction, social sciences, African languages, youth and childhood literature; in French and in national languages; Dir JEAN-CLAUDE NABA.

Editions Sidwaya: BP 810, Ouagadougou; f. 1998 to replace Société Nationale d'Editions et de Presse; state-owned; transfer to private ownership proposed; general, periodicals; Pres. PIERRE WAONGO.

Broadcasting and Communications

TELECOMMUNICATIONS

Regulatory Authority

Autorité nationale de Régulation des Télécommunications du Burkina Faso (ARTEL): ave Dimdolobsom, Porte 43, Rue 3 angle Rue 48, 01 BP 6437, Ouagadougou 01; tel. 50-33-41-98; fax 50-33-50-39; e-mail secretariat@artel.bf; internet www.artel.bf; f. 2000 prior to the proposed liberalization of the telecommunications sector; Pres. of the Council of Administration BAZONA BERNARD BATIONO; Dir-Gen. LOUHOUN J. CLÉMENT DAKUYO.

Service Providers

Office National des Télécommunications (ONATEL): ave de la Nation, 01 BP 10000, Ouagadougou 01; tel. 50-49-44-02; fax 50-31-03-31; e-mail dcrp@onatel.bf; internet www.onatel.bf; 51% owned by Maroc Telecom (Morocco, Vivendi); 23% state owned; Pres. PAUL BALMA; Dir-Gen. MOHAMMED MORCHID.

TELMOB: tel. 49-42-41; fax 50-49-42-78; e-mail wema.d@onatel.bf; internet www.onatel.bf/telmob/index.htm; f. 2002; mobile cellular telephone operator in 19 cities; Dir DIEUDONNÉ WEMA; 400,000 subscribers (Dec. 2006).

Celtel Burkina Faso: ave du Général Aboubacar Sangoulé Lamizana, 01 BP 6622, Ouagadougou 01; tel. 50-33-14-00; fax 50-33-14-06; e-mail service_clientele@bf.celtel.com; internet www.bf.celtel.com; f. 2001; mobile cellular telephone operator in Ouagadougou, Bobo-Dioulasso and 19 other towns; subsidiary of Celtel International

(United Kingdom); Dir-Gen. MOUHAMADOU NDIAYE; 55,000 subscribers (2003).

Telecel-Faso: ave de la Nation, 08 BP 11059, Ouagadougou 08; tel. 50-33-35-56; fax 50-33-35-58; e-mail infos@telecelfaso.bf; internet www.telecelfaso.bf; f. 2000; mobile cellular telephone operator in Ouagadougou, Bobo-Dioulasso and 19 other towns; 80% owned by Orascom Telecom (Egypt); Dir-Gen. AHMED CISSÉ; 80,000 subscribers (Dec. 2003).

BROADCASTING

Regulatory Authority

Higher Council of Communication (Conseil supérieur de la Communication): 290 ave Ho Chi Minh, 01 BP 6618, Ouagadougou 01; tel. 50-30-11-24; fax 50-30-11-33; e-mail info@csi.bf; internet www.csi.bf; f. 1995 as Higher Council of Information, present name adopted 2005; Pres. LUC ADOLPHE TIAO; Sec.-Gen. SONGRÉ ETIENNE SAWADOGO.

Radio

Radiodiffusion-Télévision du Burkina (RTB): 01 BP 2530, Ouagadougou 01; tel. 50-31-83-53; fax 50-32-48-09; f. 2001; Dir-Gen. MARCEL TOE.

Radio Nationale du Burkina (La RNB): 03 BP 7029, Ouagadougou 03; tel. 50-32-43-02; fax 50-31-04-41; e-mail mafarmas@hotmail.com; f. 1959; state radio service; comprises national broadcaster of informative and discussion programmes, music stations *Canal Arc-En-Ciel* and *Canal Arc-en-Ciel Plus*, and two regional stations, broadcasting in local languages, in Bobo-Dialasso and Gaoua; Dir MAFARMA SANOGO.

Radio Evangile Développement (RED): 04 BP 8050, Ouagadougou 04; tel. 50-43-51-56; e-mail redbf@laposte.net; internet www.red-burkina.org; f. 1993; broadcasts from Ouagadougou, Bobo-Dioulasso, Ouahigouya, Léo, Houndé, Koudougou and Yako; evangelical Christian; Dir-Gen. ETIENNE KIEMDE.

Horizon FM: 01 BP 2714, Ouagadougou 01; tel. 50-33-23-23; fax 50-30-21-41; e-mail hfm@grouphorizonfm.com; internet www.grouphorizonfm.com; f. 1990; private commercial station; broadcasts in French, English and eight vernacular languages; operates 10 stations nationally; Dir JUDITH IDA SAWADOGO.

Radio Locale-Radio Rurale: 03 BP 7029, Ouagadougou 03; tel. 50-31-27-81; fax 40-79-10-22; f. 1969; community broadcaster; local stations at Diapaga, Djibasso Gasson, Kongoussi, Orodara and Poura; Dir-Gen. BÉLIBIÉ SOUMAÏLA BASSOLE.

Radio Maria: BP 51, Koupela; tel. and fax 40-70-00-10; e-mail administration.bur@radiomaria.org; internet www.radiomaria.org; f. 1993; Roman Catholic; Dir BELEMSIGRI PIERRE CLAVER.

Radio Salankoloto-Association Galian: 01 BP 1095, Ouagadougou 01; tel. 50-31-64-93; fax 50-31-64-71; e-mail radiosalankoloto@cenatrin.bf; f. 1996; community broadcaster; Dir ROGER NIKIÉMA.

Radio Vive le Paysan: 05 BP 6274, Ouagadougou 05; tel. 50-31-16-36; fax 50-38-52-90; e-mail aeugene@fasonet.bf.

Radio la Voix du Paysan: BP 100, Ouahigouya; tel. 40-55-04-11; fax 40-55-01-62; community broadcaster; f. 1996; Pres. BERNARD LÉDÉA OUÉDRAOGO.

Television

La Télévision du Burkina: 955 blvd de la Révolution, 01 BP 2530, Ouagadougou 01; tel. 50-31-83-53; fax 50-32-48-09; e-mail television@rtb.bf; internet www.tnb.bf; branch of Radio-Télévision du Burkina (q.v.); Dir YACOUBA TRAORÉ.

Télévision Canal Viim Koéga—Fréquence Lumière: BP 108, Ouagadougou; tel. 50-30-76-40; e-mail cvktv@cvktv.org; internet www.cvktv.org; f. 1996; operated by the Fédération des Eglises et Missions Evangéliques.

Finance

(cap. = capital; res = reserves; dep. = deposits; m. = million; br(s). = branch(es); amounts in francs CFA)

BANKING

Central Bank

Banque centrale des états de l'Afrique de l'ouest (BCEAO): ave Gamal-Abdel-Nasser, BP 543, Ouagadougou; tel. 50-30-60-15; fax 50-30-63-76; e-mail akangni@bceao.int; internet www.bceao.int; HQ in Dakar, Senegal; f. 1962; bank of issue for the mem. states of the Union économique et monétaire ouest-africaine (UEMOA, comprising Benin, Burkina Faso, Côte d'Ivoire, Guinea-Bissau, Mali, Niger, Senegal and Togo); cap. and res 859,313m., total assets 5,671,675m. (Dec. 2002); Resident Representative JÉROME BRO GREBE; br. in Bobo-Dioulasso.

Other Banks

Bank of Africa—Burkina Faso (BOA—B): 770 ave de la Résistance du 17 mai, 01 BP 1319, Ouagadougou 01; tel. 50-30-88-70; fax 50-30-88-74; e-mail boadg@fasonet.bf; internet www.bkofafrica.net/burkina.htm; f. 1998; cap. 2,000m., res 609.9m., dep. 69,324.7m. (Dec. 2005); Chair. LASSINÉ DIAWARA; 2 brs.

Banque Agricole et Commerciale du Burkina (BAC-B): 2 ave Gamal Abdel Nasser, Secteur 3, 01 BP 1644, Ouagadougou 01; tel. 50-33-33-33; fax 50-31-43-52; e-mail bacb@bacb.bf; f. 1980; fmrly Caisse Nationale de Crédit Agricole du Burkina (CNCA-B); present name adopted 2002; 25% state-owned; cap. 3,500m., res 1,255m., dep. 56,417m. (Dec. 2003); Pres. TIBILA KABORE; Chair. and Gen. Man. LÉONCE KONÉ; 4 brs.

Banque Commerciale du Burkina (BCB): 653 ave Dr Kwam N'Krumah, 01 BP 1336, Ouagadougou 01; tel. 50-30-78-78; fax 50-31-06-28; e-mail bcb@bcb.bf; internet www.bcb.bf; f. 1988; 50% owned by Libyan Arab Foreign Bank, 25% state-owned, 25% owned by Caisse Nationale de Sécurité Sociale; res 1,360m., dep. 42,336m., total assets 57,994m. (Feb. 2005); Pres. JACQUES ZIDA; Gen. Man. MAHMUD HAMMUDA; 4 brs.

Banque Internationale du Burkina (BIB): 1340 ave Dimdolobsom, 01 BP 362, Ouagadougou 01; tel. 50-30-00-00; fax 50-31-00-94; e-mail bibouaga@fasonet.bf; f. 1974; 25% owned by Fonds Burkina de Développement Economique et Social, 24.2% owned by Compagnie de Financement et de Participation (Rep. of the Congo), 22.8% state owned; cap. 4,800.0m., res 5,648.8m., dep. 127,749.3m. (Dec. 2005); Pres. and Dir-Gen. GASPARD-JEAN OUÉDRAOGO; 21 brs.

Banque Internationale pour le Commerce, l'Industrie et l'Agriculture du Burkina (BICIA—B): 479 ave Dr Kwamé N'Krumah, 01 BP 08, Ouagadougou 01; tel. 50-31-31-31; fax 50 31-19-55; e-mail biciabdg@fasonet.bf; internet www.biciab.bf; f. 1973; affiliated to BNP Paribas (France); 25% state-owned; cap. 5,000m., res 5,455m., dep. 113,489m. (Dec. 2004); Pres. MICHEL KOMPAORÉ; Dir-Gen. JEAN-PIERRE BAJON-ARNAL; 11 brs.

Ecobank Burkina: Immeuble espace Fadima, 633 rue Maurice Bishop, 01 BP 145, Ouagadougou 01; tel. 50-31-89-80; fax 50-31-89-81; e-mail ecobank@ecobank.com; internet www.ecobank.com; f. 1996; 59% owned by Ecobank Transnational Inc., 14.4% by private Burkinabè enterprises, 12% by Ecobank Benin, 12% by Ecobank Togo; cap. 1,500.0m., res 3,315.5m., dep. 61,337.0m. (Dec. 2004); Chair. ANDREA BAYALA; Dir-Gen. ASSIONGBON EKUÉ.

Société Générale de Banques au Burkina (SGBB): 248 rue de l'Hôtel de Ville, 01 BP 585, Ouagadougou 01; tel. 50-32-32-32; fax 50-31-05-61; e-mail sgbb.burkina@socgen.com; internet www.sgbb.bf; f. 1998; 31% owned by Société Générale (France), 15% state-owned; cap. and res 5,510m., total assets 95,927m. (Dec. 2004); Dir-Gen. WILLIAM BERTHAULT.

Credit Institutions

Burkina Bail, SA: 1043 ave du Dr Kwame Nkrumah, Immeuble SODIFA, 01 BP 1913, Ouagadougou 01; tel. 50-30-69-85; fax 50-30-70-02; e-mail asory@burkinabail.bf; internet www.burkinabail.bf; 47% owned by BIB; cap. 1,000m., total assets 8,200m. (Dec. 2005); Dir-Gen. ABDOULAYE KOUAFILANN SORY.

Réseau des Caisses Populaires du Burkina (RCPB): Ouagadougou; tel. 50-30-48-41; Dir-Gen. DAOUDA SAWADOGA; 276,966 mems (June 2002), 104 co-operatives.

Société Burkinabè de Financement (SOBFI): Immeuble Nassa, 1242 ave Dr Kwamé N'Krumah, 10 BP 13876, Ouagadougou 10; tel. 50-31-80-04; fax 50-33-71-62; e-mail sobfi@fasonet.bf; f. 1997; cap. 500.0m., total assets 2,850.9m. (Dec. 2002); Pres. DIAWAR DIACK.

Bankers' Association

Association Professionnelle des Banques et Etablissements Financiers (APBEF-B): 1021 ave Houari, 01 BP 6215, Boumedienne 01, Ouagadougou 01; tel. 50-31-20-65; fax 50-31-20-66; e-mail apbef-b@cenatrin.bf; f. 1967; Pres. MICHEL KAHN.

STOCK EXCHANGE

Bourse Régionale des Valeurs Mobilières (BRVM): s/c Chambre de Commerce, d'Industrie et d'Artisanat du Burkina, 01 BP 502, Ouagadougou 01; tel. 50-30-87-73; fax 50-30-87-19; e-mail louedraogo@brvm.org; internet www.brvm.org; f. 1998; national branch of BRVM (regional stock exchange based in Abidjan, Côte d'Ivoire, serving the member states of UEMOA); Man. LÉOPOLD OUÉDRAOGO.

INSURANCE

FONCIAS—TIARD: 99 ave Léo Frobénius, 01 BP 398, Ouagadougou 01; tel. 50-30-62-04; fax 50-31-01-53; e-mail groupe-foncias@foncias.bf; f. 1978; 51% owned by AGF (France), 20% state-owned; non-life insurance and reinsurance; cap. 400m.; Dir-Gen. BERNARD GIRARDIN; also **Foncias-Vie**, life insurance; Dir-Gen. JOSEPH BARO.

Gras Savoye Burkina Faso: avenue de la Résistance du 17 mai, 01 BP 1304, Ouagadougou 01; tel. 50-30-51-69; fax 50-30-51-73; e-mail grassavoye@fasonet.bf; affiliated to Gras Savoye (France); Dir-Gen. LAURENT SAWADOGO.

Société Nationale d'Assurances et de Réassurances (SONAR): 284 ave de Loudun, 01 BP 406, Ouagadougou 01; tel. 50-33-46-66; fax 50-30-89-75; e-mail sonarinfo@sonar.bf; internet www.sonar.bf; f. 1974; 42% owned by Burkinabè interests, 33% by French, Ivorian and US cos, 22% state-owned; life and non-life; cap. 720m. (SONAR-IARD, non-life), 500m. (SONAR-Vie, life); Dir-Gen. ANDRÉ B. BAYALA; 8 brs and sub-brs.

Union des Assurances du Burkina (UAB): 08 BP 11041, Ouagadougou 08; tel. 50-31-26-15; fax 50-31-26-20; e-mail uab@fasonet.bf; f. 1991; 42% owned by AXA Assurances Côte d'Ivoire; cap. 500m.; Pres. APPOLINAIRE COMPAORÉ; Dir-Gen. (non-life insurance) SI SALIFOU TRAORÉ; Dir-Gen. (life insurance) SOUMAÏLA SORGHO.

Trade and Industry

GOVERNMENT AGENCIES

Bureau des Mines et de la Géologie du Burkina (BUMIGEB): 4186 route de Fada N'Gourma, 01 BP 601, Ouagadougou 01; tel. 50-36-48-02; fax 50-36-48-88; e-mail bumigeb@cenatrin.bf; internet www.bumigeb.bf; f. 1978; restructured 1997; research into geological and mineral resources; Pres. S. KY; Dir-Gen. PASCALE DIENDÉRÉ.

Commission de Privatisation: 01 BP 6451, Ouagadougou 01; tel. 50-33-58-93; fax 50-30-77-41; e-mail privatisation@fasonet.bf; Pres. PLACIDE SOME.

Comptoir Burkinabè des Métaux Précieux (CBMP): Ouagadougou; tel. 50-30-75-48; fax 50-31-56-34; promotes gold sector, liaises with artisanal producers; transfer to private management pending; Dir-Gen. YACOUBA BARRY.

Office National d'Aménagement des Terroirs (ONAT): 01 BP 3007, Ouagadougou 01; tel. 50-30-61-10; fax 50-30-61-12; f. 1974; fmrly Autorité des Aménagements des Vallées des Voltas; integrated rural development, including economic and social planning; Man. Dir ZACHARIE OUÉDRAOGO.

Office National des Barrages et des Aménagements Hydro-agricoles (ONBAH): 03 BP 7056, Ouagadougou 03; tel. 50-30-89-82; fax 50-31-04-26; e-mail onbah@cenatrin.bf; f. 1976; control and development of water for agricultural use, construction of dams, water and soil conservation; state-owned; Dir-Gen. AÏZO TINDANO.

Office National du Commerce Extérieur (ONAC): 30 ave de l'UEMOA, 01 BP 389, Ouagadougou 01; tel. 50-31-13-00; fax 50-31-14-69; e-mail info@onac.bf; internet www.tradepoint.bf; f. 1974; promotes and supervises external trade; Man. Dir BAYA JUSTIN BAYILI; br. at Bobo-Dioulasso.

DEVELOPMENT ORGANIZATIONS

Agence Française de Développement (AFD): 52 ave de la Nation, 01 BP 529, Ouagadougou 01; tel. 50-30-60-92; fax 50-31-19-66; e-mail afdouagadougou@bf.groupe-afd.org; internet www.afd.fr; Country Dir LOUIS L'AOT.

Association Française des Volontaires du Progrès (AFVP): 01 BP 947, Ouagadougou 01; tel. 50-30-70-43; fax 50-30-10-72; e-mail afvp.bf@liptinfor.bf; internet www.afvp.org; f. 1973; supports small business; Nat. Delegate EUGÈNE SOME.

Bureau d'Appui aux Micro-entreprises (BAME): BP 610, Bobo-Dioulasso; tel. 20-97-16-28; fax 20-97-21-76; e-mail bame@fasonet.bf; f. 1991; supports small business; Dir FÉLIX SANON.

Cellule d'Appui à la Petite et Moyenne Entreprise d'Ouagadougou (CAPEO): 01 BP 6443, Ouagadougou 01; tel. 50-31-37-62; fax 50-31-37-64; e-mail capeod@fasonet.bf; internet www.spid.com/capeo; f. 1991; supports small and medium-sized enterprises.

Promotion du Développement Industriel, Artisanal et Agricole (PRODIA): Secteur 8, Gounghin, 01 BP 2344, Ouagadougou 01; tel. 50-34-31-11; fax 50-34-71-47; e-mail prodia@cenatrin.bf; f. 1981; supports small business; Dir MAMADOU OUÉDRAOGO.

CHAMBER OF COMMERCE

Chambre de Commerce, d'Industrie et d'Artisanat du Burkina Faso: 118/220 ave de Lyon, 01 BP 502, Ouagadougou 01; tel. 50-30-61-14; fax 50-30-61-16; e-mail ccia-bf@ccia.bf; internet www.ccia.bf; f. 1948; Pres. El Hadj OUMAROU KANAZOÉ; Dir-Gen. HAMADÉ OUÉDRAOGO; brs in Bobo-Dioulasso, Koupéla and Ouahigouya.

EMPLOYERS' ORGANIZATIONS

Club des Hommes d'Affaires Franco-Burkinabé: Ambassade de France au Burkina Faso, 01 BP 4382, Ouagadougou 01; tel. 50-31-32-73; fax 50-31-32-81; e-mail chafb@liptinfor.bf; internet www.chafb.bf; f. 1990; represents 65 major enterprises and seeks to develop trading relations between Burkina Faso and France; Pres. OUMAR YUGO.

Conseil National du Patronat Burkinabè (CNPB): 01 BP 660, Ouagadougou 01; tel. 50-33-29-24; fax 50-30-25-21; e-mail belco@fasonet.bf; f. 1998; comprises 27 professional groupings; Pres. El Hadj OUMAROU KANAZOE; Exec. Sec. EMILE KABORÉ.

Groupement Professionnel des Industriels (GPI): Immeuble TELMOB, 447 ave de la Nation, 01 BP 5381, Ouagadougou 01; tel. and fax 50-30-11-59; e-mail gpi@fasonet.bf; internet www.gpi.bf; f. 1974; Pres. MARTIAL OUÉDRAOGO.

Fédération Nationale des Exportateurs du Burkina (FENEB): 01 BP 389, Ouagadougou 01; Permanent Sec. SEYDOU FOFANA.

Jeune Chambre du Burkina Faso: Ouagadougou; tel. 50-31-36-14; e-mail eras@fasonet.bf; internet www.jceburkina.bf; f. 1976; org. of entrepreneurs aged 18–40; affiliated to Junior Chambers International, Inc; Exec. Pres. J. P. L. AÏSHA TRAORÉ.

Maison de l'Entreprise du Burkina Faso (MEBF): rue 3-1119, porte 132, 11 BP 379, Ouagadougou 11; tel. 50-39-80-60; fax 50-39-80-62; e-mail info@me.bf; internet www.me.bf; f. 2002; promotes development of the private sector; Pres. ALAIN ROGER COEFE.

Syndicat des Commerçants Importateurs et Exportateurs du Burkina (SCIMPEX): 01 BP 552, Ouagadougou 01; tel. 50-31-18-70; fax 50-31-30-36; e-mail scimpex@fasonet.bf; internet www.scimpex-bf.com; Pres. LASSINÉ DIAWARA.

Union Nationale des Producteurs de Coton du Burkina Faso (UNPCB): 02 BP 1677, Bobo-Dioulasso 02; tel. 20-97-33-10; fax 20-97-20-59; e-mail unpcb@fasonet.bf; internet www.abcburkina.net/unpcb/unpcb_index.htm; f. 1998; Pres. FRANÇOIS TRAORÉ.

UTILITIES

Electricity

Société Générale de Travaux et de Constructions Electriques (SOGETEL): Zone Industrielle, Gounghin, 01 BP 429, Ouagadougou 01; tel. 50-34-29-80; fax 50-34-25-70; e-mail sogetel@cenatrin.bf; internet www.cenatrin.bf/sogetel; transport and distribution of electricity.

Société Nationale Burkinabè d'Electricité (SONABEL): 55 ave de la Nation, 01 BP 54, Ouagadougou 01; tel. 50-30-61-00; fax 50-31-03-40; e-mail info@sonabel.bf; internet www.sonabel.bf; f. 1984; state-owned; partial privatization proposed; production and distribution of electricity; Dir-Gen. SALIF LAMOUSSA KABORÉ.

Water

Office National de l'Eau et de l'Assainissement (ONEA): 01 BP 170, Ouagadougou 01; tel. 50-43-19-00; fax 50-43-19-11; e-mail onea@fasonet.bf; f. 1977; storage, purification and distribution of water; transferred to private management (by Veolia Water Burkina Faso) in 2001; Dir-Gen. MAMADOU LAMINE KOUATE.

Veolia Water Burkina Faso: 06 BP 9525, Ouagadougou 06; tel. and fax 50-34-03-00; manages operation of water distribution and sewerage services; subsidiary of Veolia Environnement (France).

CO-OPERATIVES

Union des Coopératives Agricoles et Maraîchères du Burkina (UCOBAM): 01 BP 277, Ouagadougou 01; tel. 50-30-65-27; fax 50-30-65-28; e-mail ucobam@zcp.bf; f. 1968; comprises 8 regional co-operative unions (6,500 mems, representing 35,000 producers); production and marketing of fruit, vegetables, jams and conserves; Dir-Gen. YASSIA OUEDRAOGO.

MAJOR COMPANIES

The following are some of the largest companies in terms of either capital investment or employment.

Brasseries du Burkina (BRAKINA—BGI): 01 BP 519, Ouagadougou 01; tel. 50-32-55-00; fax 50-35-60-22; e-mail g.lecluse@liptinfor.bf; f. 1960; cap. 2,530m. francs CFA; brewers, bottlers and mfrs of soft-drinks; 99% owned by BGI/CASTEL; Man. Dir GEORGES LECLUSE; 300 employees (2004).

Burkina et Shell: 01 BP 569, Ouagadougou 01; tel. 50-30-22-06; fax 50-31-22-47; e-mail roger.a.teko-folly@sburk.simis.com; f. 1976; marketing and distribution of petroleum products; cap.

US $362,829, sales US $54m. (2001); Dir-Gen. ROGER A. TEKO-FOLLY; 61 employees (2002).

Burkina Moto: 01 BP 1871, Ouagadougou 01; tel. 50-30-61-27; fax 50-30-84-96; e-mail bmoto@fasonet.bf; f. 1985; import and distribution of bicycles, motorcycles and tyres; private co; cap. 200m. francs CFA, sales US $7.9m. (2001); Pres. and Dir-Gen. APPOLINAIRE T. CAMPAORÉ; 109 employees (2002).

Comptoir Burkinabè de Papier (CBP): 907 ave Yennenga, 01 BP 1338, Ouagadougou 01; tel. 50-31-16-21; fax 50-31-37-06; e-mail cbp@fasonet.bf; f. 1989; paper producer; private co; Pres. and Dir-Gen. JOSEPH BAAKLINI.

Etablissement Tiko-Tamou: 08 BP 11244, Ouagadougou 08; tel. 50-31-37-73; fax 50-31-78-61; f. 1986; mfrs of traditional woven clothing, handicrafts and musical instruments; private co; sales US $0.3m. (1999); Pres. and Dir-Gen. SATA TAMINI.

FASOPLAST—Société des Plastiques du Faso: Zone Industrielle de Youghin, 01 BP 534, Ouagadougou 01; tel. 50-34-31-51; fax 50-34-20-67; e-mail fasoplast@fasoplast.bf; f. 1986; cap. 681m. francs CFA (2001); mfrs of plastics; Man. Dir MAMADY SANOH; 300 employees (2003).

Grands Moulins du Burkina (GMB—Faso Mugu): BP 64, Banfora; f. 1970; 25% state-owned; cap. 865m. francs CFA; flour-millers and mfrs of animal feed; Man. Dir ISSA BRUNO BICABA; 140 employees (2002).

Groupe Aliz Cuirs et Peaux: 01 BP 2069, Ouagadougou 01; tel. 50-35-74-97; fax 50-35-74-96; e-mail grpaliz@cenatrin.bf; f. 1986; processing and export of animal hides and skins; 2m. hides and skins processed, 600,000 raw hides exported annually; acquired Société Burkinabè de Manufacture de Cuir in 2001; Pres. and Dir-Gen. ALIZÈTA OUÉDRAOGO; 275 employees (2000).

Manufacture Burkinabè de Cigarettes (MABUCIG): 55 rue 19, 14 BP 94, Bobo-Dioulasso 14; e-mail mabucig.bobo@fasonet.bf; f. 1966; cap. 935m. francs CFA; cigarette production of 1,000 metric tons per year; Pres. LASSINE DIAWARA; Man. Dir JEAN-CLAUDE STARCZAN.

Perkoa Zinc Project: 01 BP 1463 Ouagadougou 01; tel. 50-31-66-35; f. 1999; zinc mining and exploration at Perkoa, Sanguié province; majority owned by AIM Resources Ltd (Australia) since Nov. 2004.

Société Africaine de Pneumatiques (SAP–Olympic): 01 BP 389, Bobo-Dioulasso 01; tel. 20-97-03-86; fax 20-97-11-18; e-mail sap@fasonet.bf; f. 1972; cap. 980m. francs CFA, sales 3,000m. francs CFA (1999); tyres and inner tubes; Pres. and Man. Dir K. LAZARE SORE; 350 employees (2002).

Société Burkinabè des Fibres Textiles (SOFITEX): 01 BP 147, Bobo-Dioulasso 01; tel. 20-97-00-24; fax 20-97-00-23; e-mail sg@sofitex.bf; f. 1979; 36% state-owned; development and processing of cotton and other fibrous plants; offers technical and financial support to growers; cap. 4,400m. francs CFA, sales US $173.1m. (2001); Man. Dir CÉLESTIN TIENDRÉBÉOGO; 1,500 employees (2002).

Société de Construction et de Gestion Immobilière du Burkina (SOCOGIB): 01 BP 1646, 01 Ouagadougou; tel. 50-30-01-97; fax 50-31-19-20; e-mail socogib@liptinfor.bf; internet www.socogib.bf; f. 1961; construction and housing management; cap. 1,843m. francs CFA; Man. Dir ANATOLE BELEMSAGA; 35 employees (2001).

Société Nationale Burkinabè d'Hydrocarbures (SONABHY): 01 BP 4394, Ouagadougou 01; tel. 50-43-00-01; fax 50-43-01-74; e-mail sonabhy@sonabhy.bf; internet www.sonabhy.bf; f. 1985; import, transport and distribution of refined hydrocarbons; state-owned; privatization proposed; sales US $133.7m. (2001); Pres. SÉRIBA OUATTARA; Man. Dir JEAN-HUBERT YAMÉOGO; 229 employees (Dec. 2005).

Société Nouvelle Huilerie et Savonnerie-Compagnie Industrielle du Textile et du Coton (SN-Citec): 01 BP 1300, Bobo-Dioulasso 01; tel. 20-97-77-89; fax 20-97-27-01; e-mail sncitec@fasonet.bf; internet www.dagris.fr/implantations/SN%20Citec.html; f. 1995; affiliated to Groupe Dagris (France); cap. 3,445m. francs CFA; production of groundnut oil; mfrs of karité (shea) butter, soap and animal feed; Pres. GUY SOMÉ; Man. Dir FULGENCE TOE; 360 employees (2005).

Société Nouvelle Sucrière de la Comoé (SN-SOSUCO): BP 13, Banfora; e-mail sosucodg@liptinfor.bf; f. 1972; cap. 6,031m. francs CFA (2002); 52% owned by Groupe IPS (Côte d'Ivoire); sugar refining; Pres. DIANGUINABA BARRO; Man. Dir MATHIEU BAYALA; 3,700 employees (2000).

Société de Promotion des Filières Agricoles (SOPROFA): Bobo-Dioulasso; f. 2001; 75% owned by Aiglon Holding Cheikna Kagnassi (Switzerland), 25% state-owned; promotion of agricultural products, including sesame, mangoes, strawberries, soybeans and oleaginous products for export; cap. 500m. francs CFA; Dir ABDOULAYE KAGNASSI.

Total Burkina: 1080 ave Dr Kwamé N'Krumah, 01 BP 21, Ouagadougou 01; tel. 50-30-50-00; fax 50-32-50-01; e-mail total@total.bf; internet www.total.bf; petroleum distribution; fmrly Elf Oil Burkina, subsequently renamed TotalFinaElf Burkina; present name adopted 2003; cap. 605m. francs CFA (2002), sales 56,873m. francs CFA (2000); Dir-Gen. PHILIPPE GORON.

Winner Industrie: BP 266, Bobo-Dioulasso; tel. 20-97-02-01; fax 20-97-03-64; f. 1971; mfrs of batteries; fmrly Société de Fabrication des Piles du Faso (SOFAPIL); Pres. SALIF OUÉDRAOGO; Man. Dir PATRICK LEYDET.

TRADE UNIONS

In 2001 there were more than 20 autonomous trade unions. The five trade-union syndicates were:

Confédération Générale du Travail Burkinabè (CGTB): 01 BP 547, Ouagadougou 01; tel. 50-31-36-71; f. 1988; confed. of several autonomous trade unions; Sec.-Gen. TOLÉ SAGNON.

Confédération Nationale des Travailleurs Burkinabè (CNTB): BP 445, Ouagadougou; tel. 50-31-23-95; e-mail cntb@fasonet.bf; f. 1972; Sec.-Gen. LAURENT OUÉDRAOGO; 10,000 mems.

Confédération Syndicale Burkinabè (CSB): 01 BP 1921, Ouagadougou 01; tel. and fax 50-31-83-98; e-mail cosybu2000@yahoo.fr; f. 1974; mainly public service unions; Sec.-Gen. JEAN MATHIAS LILIOU.

Organisation Nationale des Syndicats Libres (ONSL): 01 BP 99, Ouagadougou 01; tel. 50-34-34-69; fax 50-34-34-69; e-mail onslbf@yahoo.fr; f. 1960; 6,000 mems.

Union Syndicale des Travailleurs Burkinabè (USTB): BP 381, Ouagadougou; f. 1958; Sec.-Gen. BONIFACE SOMDAH; 35,000 mems in 45 affiliated orgs.

Transport

RAILWAY

SITARAIL—Transport Ferroviaire de Personnes et de Marchandises: rue Dioncolo, 01 BP 5699, Ouagadougou 01; tel. 50-31-07-35; fax 50-30-85-21; 67% owned by Groupe Bolloré, 15% state-owned, 15% owned by Govt of Côte d'Ivoire; national branch of SITARAIL (based in Abidjan, Côte d'Ivoire); responsible for operations on the railway line between Kaya, Ouagadougou and Abidjan (Côte d'Ivoire); Rep. in Burkina SOULEYMANE YAMÉOGO.

Société de Gestion du Patrimoine Ferroviaire du Burkina (SOPAFER—B): 01 BP 192, Ouagadougou 01; tel. 50-30-25-48; fax 50-31-35-94; railway network services; Dir-Gen. NÉBAMA KERE.

ROADS

In 2004 there were an estimated 15,272 km of roads, of which some 31% was paved. A major aim of current road projects is to improve transport links with other countries of the region. In 1999 a US $37m. project was begun to upgrade the road linking Ouagadougou with the Ghanaian border via the more isolated southern provinces.

Interafricaine de Transport et de Transit (IATT): 04 BP 8242, Ouagadougou 04; tel. 50-30-25-12; fax 50-30-37-04.

Société Africaine de Transit (SAT): 01 BP 4249, Ouagadougou 01; tel. 50-31-09-16.

Société Africaine de Transports Routiers (SATR): 01 BP 5298, Ouagadougou 01; tel. 50-34-08-62.

Société Nationale du Transit du Burkina (SNTB): 474 ave Bishop, 01 BP 1192, Ouagadougou 01; tel. 50-30-60-54; fax 50-30-85-21; f. 1977; 31% owned by Groupe SAGA (France), 12% state-owned; road haulage and warehousing; Dir-Gen. SEYDOU DIAKITÉ.

CIVIL AVIATION

There are international airports at Ouagadougou and Bobo-Dioulasso, 49 small airfields and 13 private airstrips. Plans were announced in 2006 for the construction of a new international airport at Donsin, 35 km north east of the capital; the first phase of the project from 2007–11 was to cost some 115,000m. francs CFA. Two subsequent phases were projected to extend until 2023. Ouagadougou airport handled an estimated 2756,367 passengers and 4,105 metric tons of freight in 2005.

Air Burkina: 29 ave de la Nation, 01 BP 1459, Ouagadougou 01; tel. 50-30-76-76; fax 50-31-48-80; e-mail airburkina@cenatrin.bf; internet www.air-burkina.com; f. 1967 as Air Volta; 56% owned by Aga Khan Group; 14% state-owned; operates domestic and regional services; Dir MOHAMED GHELALA.

Tourism

Burkina Faso, which possesses some 2.8m. ha of nature reserves, is considered to provide some of the best opportunities to observe wild animals in West Africa. Some big game hunting is permitted. Several important cultural events are also held in Burkina Faso: the biennial pan-African film festival, FESPACO, is held in Ouagadougou, as is the biennial international exhibition of handicrafts, while Bobo-Dioulasso hosts the biennial week of national culture. In 2005 there were 244,728 foreign visitors. Receipts from tourism were estimated at US $25m. in 2001.

Office National du Tourisme Burkinabè (ONTB): ave Frobénius, BP 1318, Ouagadougou; tel. 50-31-19-59; fax 50-31-44-34; e-mail ontb@ontb.bf; internet www.ontb.bf; Dir-Gen. ISIDORE NABALOUM.

Defence

National service is voluntary, and lasts for two years on a part-time basis. As assessed at November 2006, the armed forces numbered 10,800 (army 6,400, air force 200, paramilitary gendarmerie 4,200). There was also a 'security company' of 250 and a part-time people's militia of 45,000.

Defence Expenditure: Estimated at 44,000m. francs CFA in 2006.

Chief of the General Staff of the Armed Forces and Chief of Staff of the Army: Col ALI TRAORÉ.

Education

Education is provided free of charge, and is officially compulsory for six years between the ages of seven and 14. Primary education begins at seven years of age and lasts for six years. Secondary education, beginning at the age of 13, lasts for a further seven years, comprising a first cycle of four years and a second of three years. Enrolment levels are among the lowest in the region. According to UNESCO estimates, in 2003/04 primary enrolment included 40.5% of children in the relevant age-group, while secondary enrolment included only 9.5% of children in the appropriate age-group. In 2001/02 there were approximately 46 pupils to every teacher in secondary education. There is a university in Ouagadougou, a polytechnic university at Bobo-Dioulasso and an école normale supérieure at Koudougou. The number of students enrolled at tertiary-level institutions in 2001/02 was 15,535. A radio service has been established to further general and technical education in rural areas. In 2000 spending on education represented 11.0% of total budgetary expenditure.

Bibliography

Anderson, S. (Ed. and Trans.). *Thomas Sankara Speaks: The Burkina Faso Revolution 1983–87.* New York, NY, and London, Pathfinder Press, 1988.

Andrimirado, S. *Il s'appelait Sankara: Chronique d'une mort violente.* Paris, Jeune Afrique Livres, 1988.

Asche, H. *Le Burkina Faso contemporain: L'expérience d'un auto-développement.* Paris, L'Harmattan, 2000.

Balima, S. T., and Frère, M.-S. *Médias et Communications sociales au Burkina Faso: Approche socio-économique de la circulation de l'information.* Paris, L'Harmattan, 2003.

Bila Kaboré, R. *Histoire politique du Burkina Faso 1919–2000.* Paris, L'Harmattan, 2002.

Chaigne, R. *Burkina Faso, l'imaginaire du possible: témoignage.* Paris, L'Harmattan, 2002.

Cruise O'Brien, D. B., Dunn, J., and Rathbone, R. (Eds). *Contemporary West African States.* Cambridge, Cambridge University Press, 1989.

Duval, M. *Un totalitarisme sans état—essai d'anthropologie politique à partir d'un village burkinabè.* Paris, L'Harmattan, 1985.

Emerging Markets Investment Center. *Burkina Faso Investment and Business Guide.* 2nd Edn. USA, International Business Publications, 1999.

Englebert, P. *Burkina Faso: Unsteady Statehood in West Africa.* Boulder, CO, Westview Press, 1996.

Guion, J. R. *Blaise Compaoré: Réalisme et intégrité.* Paris, Mondes en devenir, 1991.

Guirma, F. *Comment perdre le pouvoir?: Le cas de Maurice Yaméogo.* Paris, Chaka, 1991.

Guissou, B. *Burkina Faso, un espoir en Afrique.* Paris, L'Harmattan, 1995.

Harrison Church, R. J. *West Africa.* 8th Edn. London, Longman, 1979.

Jaffré, B. *Burkina Faso: les années Sankara de la révolution à la rectification.* Paris, L'Harmattan, 1989.

Koulansouonthe Pale, F.O., *et al. Aspects du développement économique dans un pays enclave: Burkina Faso.* Talence, Centre de recherche sur le transport et la logistique, 1998.

Kuba, R., Lentz, C. and Nurukyor Somda, C. *Histoire du peuplement et relations interethniques au Burkina Faso.* Paris, Editions Karthala, 2004.

Lachaud, J.-P. *Pauvreté, vulnerabilité et marché du travail au Burkina Faso.* Pessac, Université de Bordeaux, 1997.

Madiega, G. and Nao, O. (Eds) *Burkina Faso: Cent ans d'histoire, 1895-1995.* 2 vols, Paris, Editions Karthala, 2003.

Martens, L., and Meesters, H. *Sankara, Compaoré et la révolution Burkinabè.* EPO, Antwerp, 1989.

Massa, G., and Madiéga, Y. G. (Eds). *La Haute-Volta coloniale: témoignages, recherches.* Paris, Editions Karthala, 1995.

McFarland, D. M., and Rupley, L. A. *Historical Dictionary of Burkina Faso.* 2nd Edn. Lanham, MD, Scarecrow Press, 1998.

Meijenfeldt, R. von, Santiso, C., and Otayek, R. *La démocratie au Burkina Faso.* Stockholm, International Institute for Democracy and Electoral Assistance, 1998.

Obinwa Nnaji, B. *Blaise Compaoré: The Architect of Burkina Faso Revolution.* Ibadan, Spectrum Books, 1989.

Savadogo, K., and Wetta, C. *The Impact of Self-Imposed Adjustment: The Case of Burkina Faso 1983–1989.* Florence, Spedale degli Innocenti, 1991.

Sawadogo, A. Y. *Le Président Thomas Sankara, chef de la revolution Burkinabè 1983-1987: portrait.* Paris, L'Harmattan, 2001.

Ye, B. A. *Profil politique de la Haute Volta coloniale et néo-coloniale ou les origines du Burkina Faso révolutionnaire.* Ouagadougou, Imprimerie Nouvelle du Centre, 1986.

BURUNDI

Physical and Social Geography

The Republic of Burundi, like its neighbour Rwanda, is exceptionally small in area, comprising 27,834 sq km (10,747 sq miles), but with a relatively large population of 8,173,000 at mid-2006, according to UN estimates. The result is a high population density, of 293.6 persons per sq km. The principal towns are the capital, Bujumbura (population estimated at 447,000 at mid-2005), and Gitega (population 15,943 in 1978).

Burundi is bordered by Rwanda to the north, by the Democratic Republic of the Congo (DRC) to the west and by Tanzania to the south and east. The natural divide between Burundi and the DRC is formed by Lake Tanganyika and the Ruzizi river on the floor of the western rift-valley system. To the east, the land rises sharply to elevations of around 1,800 m above sea-level in a range that stretches north into the much higher, and volcanic, mountains of Rwanda. Away from the edge of the rift valley, elevations are lower, and most of Burundi consists of plateaux of 1,400–1,800 m. Here the average temperature is 20°C and annual rainfall 1,200 mm. In the valley the temperature averages 23°C, while rainfall is much lower, at 750 mm.

Population has concentrated on the fertile, volcanic soils at 1,500–1,800 m above sea-level, away from the arid and hot floor and margins of the rift valley. The consequent pressure on the land, together with recurrent outbreaks of intense internal unrest, has resulted in extensive migration, mainly to Tanzania, the DRC and Uganda. The ethnic composition of the population is much the same as that of Rwanda: about 85% Hutu, 14% Tutsi and less than 1% Twa, pygmoid hunters. Historically, the kingdoms of Urundi and Ruanda had a strong adversarial tradition, and rivalry between the successor republics remains strong. The national language is Kirundi, while French is also officially used.

Recent History

GREGORY MTHEMBU-SALTER

Burundi and neighbouring Rwanda to the north, unlike most African states, were not entirely artificial creations of colonial rule. At the time of their absorption into German East Africa in 1899, most of Burundi and Rwanda had already been incorporated into two kingdoms for at least a century. When, in 1916, Belgium occupied Ruanda-Urundi (as the League of Nations mandated territory encompassing both Rwanda and Burundi was designated), it continued the system of 'indirect rule' operated by the German authorities. This choice of colonial policy had a particular impact, since an ethnic minority, the Tutsi (comprising about 14% of the population, according to an unreliable colonial census, which used cattle-ownership as the main criterion for ethnic membership), had by then established dominance over the majority Hutu (85%, according to the same census) and a hunter-gatherer group, the Twa (1%). However, the potential for conflict between Hutu and Tutsi in Burundi was contained to an extent by the existence of the Ganwa, a princely class whose clans were comprised of both ethnic groups. Relations between the ordinary Tutsi and the Hutu were more equal than they later became, and intermarriage was fairly common.

Rivalry within the Ganwa was intense, and especially so from the mid-19th century onwards between those of the Batare and Bezi clans. The Bezi Ganwa controlled the crown when German colonists arrived, and were permitted to retain it in return for submission to German rule. The Belgian colonial authorities continued the policy, with the result that Bezi predominated in 'native' administrative posts during the first part of Belgian rule. After the Second World War, however, relations between the Bezi Ganwa Mwami (king) and the Belgian administration worsened due to growing Bezi demands for Burundi's national independence, while relations between the administration and the Batare Ganwa improved. Reluctantly, but in order to fulfil criteria imposed by a UN Trusteeship Council after 1948, the Belgian administration moved towards a degree of democratization. Two main parties came to the fore. The Union pour le progrès national (UPRONA), led by Prince Louis Rwagasore (a Bezi Ganwa and eldest son of the Mwami), was a progressive nationalist movement, with wide support. The rival Parti démocrate chrétien (PDC), dominated by the Batare Ganwa, was more conservative, wanting internal reforms to improve Batare status relative to the Bezi before independence. The Belgian administration, which wanted to retain control, strongly favoured the PDC. At legislative elections, held in September 1961, prior to the granting of internal self-government in January 1962, UPRONA won 58 of the 64 seats in the new Assemblée nationale. Rwagasore, who became Prime Minister after the elections, was assassinated in October 1961 by a Greek agent of the PDC, with the probable assistance of the Belgian administration. Rwagasore's assassination proved a crucial event in the subsequent history of Burundi; the absence of his unifying influence resulted in the division of UPRONA and encouraged the emergence of open conflict between Hutu and Tutsi.

MICOMBERO AND BAGAZA

UPRONA was unable to contain the ethnic tensions that followed the attainment of independence on 1 July 1962. The Mwami, Mwambutsa IV, played an active role in the composition of the first post-independence Governments, none of which remained long in office. There were four short-lived Governments between 1963 and 1965, and tensions were exacerbated when Hutu Prime Minister Pierre Ngendandumwe was assassinated in January 1965, only a week after taking office. Hutu candidates won a decisive victory in parliamentary elections held in May, but Mwambutsa appointed a Tutsi Ganwa as the new Prime Minister. Incensed, in October a faction of the Hutu-dominated gendarmerie attempted to seize power. Tutsi armed forces retaliated by massacring almost the entire Hutu political establishment, and thousands of rural Hutu who had supported the revolt.

In July 1966 Mwambutsa was deposed by his son, who took the title of Ntare V, and appointed Capt. (later Lt-Gen.) Michel Micombero as Prime Minister. In November Ntare was himself deposed by Micombero, who declared Burundi a republic. Subsequent purges of Hutu officers and politicians further consolidated Tutsi supremacy. Following an abortive coup attempt in April 1972, which degenerated into indiscriminate killings of Tutsi near the capital, the Tutsi military retaliated with massacres of unprecedented size and brutality. An estimated 100,000–200,000 Hutus were killed, and a further 200,000 fled the country, mainly to Zaire (now the Democratic Republic of the Congo, DRC), Tanzania and Rwanda. Nearly all Hutu elements were eliminated from the armed forces.

In November 1976 Col Jean-Baptiste Bagaza seized power in a bloodless coup. Although the army remained the dominant

force in Burundi's politics, attempts were made by the Bagaza regime to increase democratic participation in government. The first legislative elections under universal adult suffrage were held in October 1982, and in August 1984 Bagaza, as sole candidate, was elected Head of State, for the first time by direct suffrage.

During the period 1984–87 there was a sharp deterioration in the Government's observance of human rights. This was particularly marked in relation to religious freedom, and led Bagaza's regime into conflict with several Christian denominations. The number of political prisoners rose considerably during this period, and many detainees were subjected to torture. The intensification of authoritarian rule led to strained relations with most donor countries, which put pressure on Bagaza by withholding development aid.

THE BUYOYA REGIME, 1987–93

In September 1987, during a visit abroad, Bagaza was deposed by an army-led coup instigated by his cousin, Maj. Pierre Buyoya, who accused him of corruption and formed a 31-member ruling Military Committee for National Salvation (CMSN). UPRONA was dissolved and the 1981 Constitution was suspended. On 2 October Buyoya was sworn in as President, at the head of a new Government, and Bagaza went into exile in Libya. Apart from its greater tolerance of religious freedom of expression, and the release of hundreds of political prisoners, the new regime did not differ much from Bagaza's, and was equally reliant on the support of a small Tutsi-Hima élite from Bururi province, with strong representation in the army, civil service, judiciary and educational institutions.

Hutu–Tutsi Tensions

In August 1988 groups of Hutu, claiming Tutsi provocation, slaughtered hundreds of Tutsi in the northern towns of Ntega and Marangara. In restoring order, the army massacred an estimated 20,000 Hutus, and more than 60,000 refugees, mainly Hutu, fled to neighbouring Rwanda. After initially resisting Hutu demands for an inquiry into the killings, and for political reform, in October Buyoya appointed a Hutu, Adrien Sibomana, as Prime Minister, and brought a number of other Hutus into the Government. In the same month a Commission for National Unity (comprising an equal number of Tutsi and Hutu) was established to investigate the massacres and to make recommendations for national reconciliation.

The reforms alarmed many Tutsis, and during the first half of 1989 there were several attempted coups by 'hardline' Tutsi activists and Bagaza supporters. Following the publication in April of the report of the Commission for National Unity, Buyoya announced plans to combat all forms of discrimination against Hutus, but inter-ethnic tensions continued to fester. In November 1991 violent confrontations occurred in Bujumbura, and in the north and north-west of the country, resulting in large numbers of casualties. In late April 1992 there were further violent disturbances along the border with Rwanda, blamed by the Government on the Parti de libération du peuple Hutu (PALIPEHUTU), which, the authorities claimed, had been trained and armed in Rwanda.

Constitutional Transition

In April 1990 the Commission for National Unity produced a draft charter, which was submitted to extensive national debate. Public discussion, however, was closely directed and monitored by the re-established UPRONA, and failed to satisfy the demands of opposition groups. Political tensions were renewed in August, when the exiled leader of PALIPEHUTU died in prison in Tanzania, and the leader of a smaller dissident group was killed in a motor accident in Rwanda. Opponents of UPRONA alleged that both men had been assassinated by Buyoya's agents.

In December 1990 UPRONA dissolved the CMSN and transferred its functions to an 80-member central committee of UPRONA, with a Hutu, Nicolas Mayugi, as its Secretary-General. The draft charter on national unity, overwhelmingly approved in a referendum in February 1991, was rejected by PALIPEHUTU and other opposition groups. A government reorganization later that month, in which Hutus were appointed to 12 of the 23 ministerial portfolios, was viewed with scepticism by political opponents. In March a commission was established to prepare a report on the 'democratization' of national institutions and political structures, in preparation for the drafting of a new constitution.

In September 1991 Buyoya presented the report of the constitutional commission on 'national democratization'. Among its recommendations were an increase in parliamentary powers, the introduction of a once-renewable five-year presidential mandate, proportional representation, press freedom, guarantees of human rights and a system of 'controlled multi-partyism' whereby political groupings seeking legal recognition would be required to comply with certain requirements, including ethnic, regional and religious 'impartiality' and acceptance of the charter on national unity.

In March 1992 a referendum resulted in a vote of 90% in support of the proposed new Constitution, which was promulgated on 13 March. Multi-partyism was legalized by Buyoya in April, and by October eight political parties had received legal recognition. Among them was the Front pour la démocratie au Burundi (FRODEBU), established by Hutu former political exiles, which rapidly gained prominence, with the apparent support of PALIPEHUTU activists in many areas. In February 1993 Buyoya announced that presidential and legislative elections would take place in June, with elections for local government officials to follow in November. Buyoya believed he would be legitimately elected, but he was defeated. The clear winner in the presidential poll, conducted on 1 June, with 64.8% of votes cast, was Melchior Ndadaye, the FRODEBU candidate, with the support of the Rassemblement du peuple burundien (RPB), the Parti du peuple (PP) and the Parti libéral (PL). Buyoya, the UPRONA candidate, received only 32.4% of the votes, with support from the Rassemblement pour la démocratie et le développement économique et social (RADDES) and the Parti social démocrate (PSD). Elections for 81 seats in the new legislature were held on 29 June. FRODEBU won the largest share of votes cast (71%), and 65 of the 81 seats in the new legislature. UPRONA, with 21.4% of the votes, secured the remaining 16 seats. The Parti de réconciliation du peuple (PRP), the PP, the RADDES and the RPB all failed to attract the minimum 5% of votes needed for representation in the legislature. The elections were followed in early July by an attempted coup by army officers, which was swiftly suppressed. Ndadaye assumed the presidency on 10 July, becoming Burundi's first ever Hutu Head of State. A new 23-member Council of Ministers was subsequently announced; the new Prime Minister, Sylvie Kinigi, was one of seven newly appointed Tutsis.

NDADAYE, NTARYAMIRA AND THE RESURGENCE OF ETHNIC UNREST

Ndadaye's Government immediately began bringing FRODEBU supporters into the civil service and began drafting plans for extensive reform of the armed forces. The plans alarmed many Tutsi soldiers, and on 21 October 1993 more than 100 army paratroopers occupied the presidential palace and the headquarters of the national broadcasting company. The insurgents detained and killed a number of prominent Hutu politicians and officials, including President Ndadaye and the parliamentary Speaker, Giles Bimazubute; François Ngeze, one of the only senior Hutu members of UPRONA, and a minister in the Government of former President Buyoya, was later proclaimed as head of a National Committee for Public Salvation (CPSN). While ministers sought refuge abroad and in the offices of foreign diplomatic missions in Bujumbura, the armed forces declared a state of emergency, closing national borders and the capital's airport. However, immediate and unanimous international condemnation of the coup, together with the scale and ferocity of renewed inter-ethnic massacres, undermined support for the insurgents from within the armed forces, and precipitated the collapse of the CPSN, which was disbanded on 25 October. Communications were restored on 27 October, and by the following day the FRODEBU Government had reassumed control of the country. Ngeze and 10 coup leaders were arrested, although at least 40 other insurgents had fled. In early December a commission of judicial inquiry was created to investigate the insurgency.

In early January 1994 FRODEBU deputies in the Assemblée nationale approved a draft amendment to the Constitution, enabling the republican President to be elected by the Assemblée nationale. After intense inter-party negotiations, the Assemblée nationale elected Ndadaye's Minister of Agriculture, Cyprien Ntaryamira, as President. Ntaryamira assumed office on 5 February. Anatole Kanyenkiko of UPRONA was appointed Prime Minister, while the composition of a new multi-party Council of Ministers was finally agreed in mid-February.

In November 1993, following repeated requests by the Government for an international force to protect its ministers, the Organization of African Unity (OAU), now the African Union (AU), agreed to the deployment of a protection force of 180 military personnel. Tutsi opposition parties protested at the arrival of the military contingent, claiming sovereignty and territorial integrity were being compromised.

On 11 February 1994 an international commission of inquiry, established by a number of human rights organizations, concluded that the majority of members of the armed forces were involved in or had supported the October coup attempt, in which an estimated 25,000–50,000 Burundians died. Well-armed Hutu and Tutsi militia fought each other during February to establish territorial strongholds within the country, but in mid-March, responding to Tutsi opposition to the deployment of a foreign military force, the Government convinced the OAU to reduce the strength of the mooted Mission d'observation au Burundi (MIOB) from 180 to only 47 officers. (MIOB was finally deployed in Burundi in February 1995.) Clashes between the armed forces and Hutu militia worsened divisions between FRODEBU's moderate faction, led by Ntaryamira (who supported the forced disarmament of both Hutu and Tutsi militia groups), and Léonard Nyangoma's 'hardline' faction, which opposed further military action against Hutu militias. However, Ntaryamira's insistence that several senior Tutsi army personnel and the chief of the national gendarmerie be replaced for having failed to address the security crisis, and that the armed forces should not overlook its own ranks in the enforcement of the pacification programme, provoked sections of the security forces to embark on a campaign of violent destruction in the capital, resulting in dozens of civilian deaths.

POLITICAL MANOEUVRES AND COALITION GOVERNMENT

On 6 April 1994, returning from a regional summit meeting in Dar es Salaam, Tanzania, Ntaryamira was killed (together with the Ministers of Development, Planning and Reconstruction, and of Communications), when the aircraft of Rwandan President Juvénal Habyarimana, in which the Burundi delegation was travelling, was brought down by a rocket attack above Kigali airport, and crashed on landing. (Habyarimana, who was also killed in the crash, was widely acknowledged to have been the intended victim of the attack.) In contrast to the genocide that ensued in Rwanda in the aftermath of the death of Habyarimana, Burundians responded positively to appeals for calm issued by FRODEBU President Sylvestre Ntibantunganya, who, on 8 April, was confirmed (in accordance with the Constitution) as interim President for a three-month period, after which a presidential election was to be held. Army dissidents attempted a coup shortly after Ntibantunganya's installation as President, but were swiftly apprehended by loyal elements within the armed forces.

In May Nyangoma was dismissed from the Government, having failed to return from government business abroad. It later emerged that Nyangoma had been establishing a new party, the Conseil national pour la défense de la démocratie (CNDD), with an armed wing known as the Forces pour la défense de la démocratie (FDD), with the aim of restoring the power FRODEBU won in the 1993 elections by force. During May UPRONA elected a Hutu, Charles Mukasi, as its new leader, who was radically opposed to Hutu political parties, particularly FRODEBU, which he accused of perpetrating genocide. In the same month former President Bagaza resumed political activity, at the head of a new party, the Parti pour le redressement national (PARENA).

Having discounted the possibility of organizing a general election, owing to security concerns, in June 1994 the major political parties engaged in lengthy negotiations, with mediation by the UN Secretary-General's special representative, Ahemdou Ould Abdallah, to establish a procedure for the restoration of an elected presidency. A new agreement on power-sharing, in addition to a tentative agreement concluded in mid-July, was announced on 10 September. This 'Convention of Government', which detailed the terms of government for a four-year transitional period (including the allocation of nearly one-half of cabinet posts to opposition parties), was incorporated into the Constitution on 22 September. The Convention also provided for the creation of a National Security Council (formally inaugurated on 10 October) to address the security crisis. On 30 September the Convention elected Ntibantunganya to the presidency from a list of six candidates. Ntibantunganya's appointment was endorsed immediately by the Assemblée nationale, and he was formally inaugurated on 1 October 1994. Anatole Kanyenkiko was reappointed as Prime Minister on 3 October, and two days later a coalition Government was formed, with a composition reflecting the terms of the September Convention.

In December 1994 UPRONA withdrew from the coalition Government and from the legislature, in protest at the election earlier that month of Jean Minani (a prominent FRODEBU member) to the post of Speaker of the Assemblée nationale. UPRONA members accused Minani of having incited genocide against Tutsi in the aftermath of the October 1993 attempted coup. Kanyenkiko, however, remained Prime Minister. In early January 1995 the political crisis was averted by agreement between FRODEBU and UPRONA on a compromise FRODEBU candidate for the post of Speaker, Léonce Ngendakumana. Minani subsequently assumed the FRODEBU party leadership, and in mid-January UPRONA announced that it was willing to rejoin the Government. A month later, however, Kanyenkiko was forced out of UPRONA for having failed to support its December withdrawal from Government; he was replaced as Prime Minister on 1 March by Antoine Nduwayo, a UPRONA candidate selected in consultation with other Tutsi opposition parties, amid allegations of extremist Tutsi militia intimidation.

Ethnic tension persisted in the second half of 1994, exacerbated first by the scale and proximity of the violence in Rwanda (see above), and then by the arrival in the country of an estimated 200,000 Rwandan Hutu refugees fleeing the advancing Front patriotique rwandais (FPR) in Rwanda. While large-scale civil war was averted, ethnically motivated atrocities became a daily occurrence in parts of the country, including Bujumbura, where several prominent politicians and government officials were murdered. Fears that the security crisis would develop into civil war were intensified by reports that the allegedly 30,000-member FDD had reached an advanced stage in its preparations for conflict with the armed forces. Worsening politically and ethnically motivated violence during 1995 prompted renewed international concern that the security crisis would precipitate genocide similar to that just witnessed in Rwanda.

ETHNIC CONFRONTATION

In late 1995, as reports multiplied of atrocities perpetrated against both Hutu and Tutsi civilians by the armed forces, Tutsi militias known as the 'Sans Echecs', and Hutu rebel groups, the UN Secretary-General, Boutros Boutros-Ghali, petitioned the Security Council to authorize international military intervention. In February 1996 Boutros-Ghali renewed these efforts in response to a UN report on human rights, which concluded that a state of near civil war existed in many areas of the country. However, the Government (and Tutsi political opinion) remained fiercely opposed to a foreign military presence and persuaded the UN Security Council, unwilling to deploy UN troops in a hostile environment, that a negotiated settlement to the conflict was still attainable. Reports delivered by representatives of the US Agency for International Development and the Humanitarian Office of the European Union (EU), following an official visit undertaken in early April, expressed doubts that effective power-sharing could be achieved within the terms of the 1994 Convention of Government, particularly under the leadership of a powerful Tutsi premier. The USA and the EU announced the immediate suspension of aid.

Violence continued to escalate during 1996, with aid agencies reporting atrocities perpetrated by units of the armed forces against Hutu civilians, prompting the suspension of French military co-operation at the end of May. In early June the International Committee of the Red Cross (ICRC) suspended all activities following the murder of three ICRC employees in the north-west of the country, while other aid agencies announced that future operations would be restricted to the capital. All ICRC staff were subsequently withdrawn from the country.

At a meeting of the member nations of the Economic Community of the Great Lakes Countries, convened in Cairo, Egypt, in November 1995, at the request of the UN Secretary-General, the Presidents of Burundi, Rwanda, Uganda and Zaire, and a Tanzanian presidential representative, announced a sub-regional initiative for a negotiated peace in Burundi, involving mediation by the former President of Tanzania, Julius Nyerere. Representatives of some 13 political parties (including FRODEBU and UPRONA) participated in discussions conducted in Mwanza, Tanzania, with Nyerere as mediator, in April. However, a second round of discussions, scheduled for May, was postponed, owing to UPRONA objections to the participation of the CNDD. Further talks were conducted in Mwanza in early June, again mediated by Nyerere, but only intensified political polarization, with Tutsi parties accusing FRODEBU deputies of seeking to abrogate the Convention of Government, an allegation denied by FRODEBU. In what was regarded at the time as a startling concession from Nduwayo, in view of the historic opposition to foreign intervention within the Tutsi political community, both he and Ntibantunganya (following strong pressure from Nyerere) requested international troop deployment to protect government installations in Burundi at a conference of regional heads of state in Arusha, Tanzania, in late June. By early July a regional technical commission to examine the request for foreign assistance had convened in Arusha and reached a preliminary agreement on an intervention force, to comprise units of the Ugandan and Tanzanian armed forces and police officers from Kenya. However, fundamental differences of interpretation regarding the purpose and mandate of such a force swiftly emerged between Ntibantunganya and Nduwayo, with the latter accusing the President of attempting to neutralize the country's military capability. At a mass rally of Tutsi-dominated opposition parties, organized in the capital on 5 July, Nduwayo joined other political leaders in rejecting foreign military intervention and denouncing Ntibantunganya for allegedly encouraging external interference in domestic affairs. Some days later, however, full endorsement of the Arusha proposal for intervention was recorded by member nations of the OAU at a summit meeting, convened in Yaoundé, Cameroon.

Tensions intensified still further when reports emerged of a massacre of more than 300 Tutsi civilians at Bugendana, allegedly committed by Hutu militia, including heavily armed Rwandan Hutu refugees. FRODEBU made an urgent appeal for foreign military intervention to contain the increasingly violent civil and military reaction to these events, while Bagaza urged (Tutsi) civil resistance to foreign intervention and advocated a general strike in the capital, which was partially observed. Meanwhile, Tutsi students (with the support of the Tutsi political opposition) protested against regional military intervention, and demonstrated in support of demands for Ntibantunganya's removal. On 23 July 1996 Ntibantunganya was forced to abandon an attempt to attend the funeral of the victims of the Bugendana massacre, following attacks on the presidential helicopter by rioting mourners, and was informed by the armed forces that they could no longer guarantee his safety. On the following day Ntibantunganya fled from the presidential office, and sought refuge in the US embassy. Several government ministers and the Speaker of the Assemblée nationale withdrew to the German embassy compound, and Minani fled the country.

THE RETURN OF BUYOYA

With the FRODEBU members of government in hiding, the armed forces staged a coup on 25 July 1996. The Minister of National Defence, Lt-Col Firmin Sinzoyiheba, announced the suspension of the Assemblée nationale and all political activity, the imposition of a nationwide curfew and the closure of national borders and the airport at Bujumbura. The military then declared former President Buyoya as the new interim President of a 'transitional' republic. Although still in hiding, Ntibantunganya refused to relinquish office, but Nduwayo immediately resigned.

There was widespread international condemnation of the coup. To soften opinion, Buyoya announced that a largely civilian, broadly based government of national unity would be promptly installed, and that future negotiations with all Hutu groups would be considered. Echoing his political strategy of the early 1990s, Buyoya appointed Pascal-Firmin Ndimira, a Hutu member of UPRONA, as Prime Minister, but this concession failed to secure support for the Government from the rest of the region. A summit of regional heads of state, convened in Arusha on 31 July, declared its intention to impose severe economic sanctions against the new regime, failing the immediate restoration of constitutional government. Western countries, which had until this point strongly supported regional initiatives in Burundi, were, however, unwilling to carry out the imposition of sanctions. In early August the composition of a new multi-ethnic Cabinet was announced, and later that month Buyoya announced that an expanded transitional Assemblée nationale, incorporating existing elected deputies, would be inaugurated during September for a three-year period. A consultative council of elders was also to be established to oversee a period of broad political debate, during which time formal political activity would remain proscribed. In mid-August, following the publication of a report by the UN on events preceding the 1993 coup, Buyoya dismissed the army Chief of Staff, Col Jean Bikomagu, and the Commander of the gendarmerie, Col Pascal Simbanduko, both of whom were implicated by the UN in planning the coup.

In the months following August 1996, military action in eastern Zaire temporarily disrupted FDD operations in the area, and prompted the repatriation of at least 30,000 Burundians. Most militia activists crossed into Tanzania, from where they staged frequent incursions into Burundi's southern provinces, attacking military targets and unarmed civilians. The shift in the balance of power in eastern Zaire weakened regional sanctions, enabling some Burundian exports to be transported via Uvira and Bukavu in Sud-Kivu, and a limited amount of imports from East Africa to reach Burundi. In addition, trade to and from Burundi continued to pass through Kenya, Tanzania, Uganda and Rwanda, despite each of their public commitment to enforcing sanctions.

In August 1996 Buyoya met Nyerere in Tanzania, in an unsuccessful attempt to obtain a relaxation of the sanctions. In the following month the Regional Sanctions Co-ordinating Committee (RSCC) held its first meeting, at which it agreed to ease restrictions on the importation of emergency relief supplies; however, it emphasized that economic sanctions would remain in force until the Assemblée nationale was restored, political parties legalized and unconditional negotiations opened with Hutu militias, including the FDD.

On 12 September 1996 most of the powers of the Assemblée nationale were restored, but not its vital authority to dismiss the Government, and exiled members of the Assemblée nationale were invited to return to the country. This earned Buyoya an invitation to a meeting of regional heads of state, though as a factional leader rather than the President. In the event, neither Buyoya nor Nyangoma, who was also approached by the RSCC, attended. The RSCC offered no further concessions, instead imposing a deadline of 31 October for the commencement of negotiations between the Government and Hutu militias. Buyoya stated that he was unwilling to enter into negotiations until economic sanctions were eased. The RSCC agreed to a limited degree, granting further exemptions for aid agencies in October 1996. In December there were further discussions in Arusha, at which Nyerere unsuccessfully sought to bring together the Government, FRODEBU, the CNDD and UPRONA. A further meeting of the regional heads of state also took place, at which it was agreed to retain economic sanctions, pending the opening of negotiations by the contending forces.

Successive reports by the UN, published in December 1996 and in January 1997, alleged widespread human rights abuses, carried out both by Hutu militias and the armed forces. The reports were rejected by the Government, with the threat to expel UN human rights observers if their 'unfounded' allegations continued.

A further meeting of regional heads of state was convened in mid-April at Arusha; on this occasion, Buyoya was invited to attend as President. In response to a subsequent easing of economic sanctions, the heads of state agreed to permit the import to Burundi of most goods except fuel, which remained at the discretion of the aid agencies. The export of goods through countries participating in the sanctions programme remained officially prohibited. The CNDD denounced the relaxation of sanctions and intensified its armed attacks. It was disclosed by Buyoya in May that dialogue had taken place in Rome, Italy, between the Government and the CNDD, but that no substantive peace negotiations were immediately contemplated. This announcement prompted violent protests by Tutsi university students and was denounced by the UPRONA leadership, although some sections of the party expressed cautious support for a peace initiative. In late July the Rome discussions were suspended.

Fighting between the army and Hutu militias spread across a number of provinces in July and August 1997, and reports also emerged of clashes between the FDD and PALIPEHUTU, particularly in Bubanza province. Armed incursions by Hutu militias from refugee camps in Tanzania increased tensions in border regions and in late September and October there was sporadic fighting between Tanzanian and Burundian troops. The Burundian Government repeatedly accused the Tanzanian authorities of complicity in Hutu militia attacks. Tanzania always denied this claim and accused Burundi of attempting to deflect international opinion from the internal nature of the conflict. At a meeting of regional foreign ministers, held in Kampala, Uganda, in mid-August, it was decided to maintain the export embargo on Burundi, despite vigorous appeals from the Burundian Government. The Burundian Government accused Tanzania of influencing other countries to continue the embargo, and subsequently withdrew from all-party talks, organized by Nyerere, which took place in Arusha later that month.

By the end of 1997 national courts had imposed 220 death sentences on Hutus found guilty of committing genocide in 1993. The trial of the Tutsis accused of involvement in the 1993 coup attempt, and of assassinating President Ndadaye and six others, however, was subject to repeated adjournments, and verdicts were not delivered until May 1999. Five members of the armed forces were sentenced to death and a number of others received prison terms; however, Hutu political parties expressed concern that all the senior officers implicated in the coup attempt, including Bikomagu, were acquitted.

On 1 January 1998 some 1,000 rebels, believed to include Rwandan militia, attacked a military camp and village close to Bujumbura airport. They advanced some way before having to retreat in the face of a sizeable army counter-attack; more than 250 people were reported to have been killed, including many Hutu civilians. At the end of the month the minister of defence, Firmin Sinzoyiheba, was killed in a helicopter crash; he was replaced by Alfred Nkurunziza, Buyoya's chief military adviser.

On 21 February 1998 a meeting of regional heads of state in Kampala again opted to maintain sanctions. Tensions on the border with Tanzania began to ease and on 12 March formal tripartite discussions were held between Burundi, Tanzania and the office of the UN High Commissioner for Refugees (UNHCR). UNHCR proposed the policing of Burundian refugee camps to ensure no military activity took place. The CNDD split on 8 May, leaving Nyangoma in charge of one faction (which retained the name CNDD), while the FDD Chief of Staff, Jean-Bosco Ndayikengurukiye, assumed leadership of the greater part of the party, including most of its armed forces, which became known as the CNDD—FDD.

POWER-SHARING AND A NEW TRANSITIONAL CONSTITUTION

With the imminent expiry of FRODEBU's electoral mandate, in March 1998 the Government initiated negotiations with the Assemblée nationale concerning the required course of action. FRODEBU demanded a return to the 1992 Constitution, while the Government proposed a continuation of the terms of office introduced by Buyoya after the July 1996 coup. A compromise was eventually reached, which Buyoya described as a new partnership between the Government and the Assemblée nationale. The partnership exacerbated division within FRODEBU, particularly between those in the leadership in exile and those still based in Burundi, with the former insisting that the Arusha discussions were the only legitimate negotiating forum. On 6 June 1998 the transitional Constitution, which combined elements of both the 1992 Constitution and the 1996 decree adopted by Buyoya after the July coup, was promulgated. Under this Constitution, the Assemblée nationale was expanded, the size of the Council of Ministers was reduced, and two vice-presidential posts were created. On 11 June 1998 Buyoya was sworn in as Head of State, and two days later a new Council of Ministers was announced. On 15–21 June the Government attended all-party talks in Arusha, under the chairmanship of Nyerere, at which all the participating delegations agreed to hold further talks on 20 July and to suspend hostilities at that date. However, both the Government and the CNDD—FDD immediately distanced themselves from the agreement, rendering it ineffective. Despite the decision to establish a small number of commissions to examine the key issues in the conflict, the negotiations made little progress. Frustrated donors demanded a review of the regional sanctions policy in order in a bid to force faster progress at the discussions.

In October 1998 Charles Mukasi, an opponent of the Arusha negotiations, was replaced, allegedly by improper means, as UPRONA President by the Minister of Information and Government Spokesman, Luc Rukingama (a Buyoya loyalist). Rukingama was more enthusiastic about the Arusha process than Mukasi, and at the next round of discussions later that month, three of the planned commissions were successfully constituted. The briefs of the three commissions were to examine the nature of the conflict, democracy and good governance, and peace and security, respectively. Other commissions, once constituted, examined the rehabilitation of refugees and economic development, transitional institutions, and the guarantees for the implementation of the eventual peace agreement.

The CNDD—FDD and PALIPEHUTU continued their attacks throughout 1998 and early 1999, particularly on camps for the internally displaced. The majority of reported incidents took place in Bujumbura Rural and Makamba provinces, and their intensity increased prior to each round of talks in Arusha. In late 1998 the armed forces increased their involvement in the civil war in the DRC (their presence there had been initially denied) and by May 1999 at least 3,000 troops were believed to have been deployed in the east, attempting to destroy CNDD—FDD camps. The effort largely failed. In August 1998 war broke out in the DRC, enabling the CNDD—FDD to increase its presence there, supporting Congolese government troops in Sud-Kivu and Katanga. The DRC Government objected to the presence of Burundian troops in the DRC and in May 1999 threatened to launch a retaliatory attack on Bujumbura. The Burundi Government responded that the presence of its troops in the DRC was necessary to confront the security threat posed by CNDD—FDD forces, and that it would respond to any attack on its territory.

A fourth round of discussions was held at Arusha in January 1999, with the CNDD—FDD again failing to participate. Regional heads of state decided at a meeting on 21–23 January 1999 to suspend the economic embargo, in the hope that this measure would strengthen the Arusha peace process. The decision was welcomed both internally and abroad, but dismissed by the CNDD—FDD as premature.

On 18 March 1999 changes were effected in the leadership of FRODEBU. Secretary-General Augustin Nzojibwami suspended former President Ntibantunganya from the party's executive committee, together with other senior members, for alleged ethnicism and ill discipline. However, Minani ordered Nzojibwami's expulsion from the party (although he refused to recognize the expulsion). By June distinct factions had emerged, centred around Minani and Nzojibwami.

In early May 1999 seven predominantly Hutu parties, including the CNDD and the external wing of FRODEBU, met in Moshi, Tanzania, to negotiate a common position prior to the commissions convening in mid-May. The parties assumed a joint stance on most issues and became known as G7. The Government and the internal wing of FRODEBU condemned G7 for allegedly encouraging ethnic polarization, while Nyerere supported it, arguing that it facilitated the talks by minimizing differences between parties. In response to the formation of G7, predominantly Tutsi parties formed a negotiating bloc (known initially as G8, and later as G10). Delegations representing UPRONA, the Government and the Assemblée nationale remained outside the two blocs. At the end of May Buyoya proposed a 10-year political transition, including plans for the establishment of an upper legislative chamber, the Sénat, and for the enlargement of the Assemblée nationale. Buyoya proposed that he rule for five years and a FRODEBU representative for the remaining five years. The proposals were rejected by all externally based political forces.

Commission meetings in Arusha resumed in early July 1999 for a fifth round, but made little progress. The fifth round of negotiations was eventually concluded, earlier than anticipated, on 17 July by Nyerere, who blamed the failure of the discussions on alleged government intransigence. The Government, meanwhile, stated that the talks could not succeed without the presence of the CNDD—FDD and a faction of PALIPEHUTU's armed wing, which had split from the party and was known as the Forces nationales de libération (FNL), and blamed their absence on Nyerere. A sixth round of discussions at Arusha was due to commence in September, but was postponed, owing to Nyerere's ill health. Nyerere subsequently died in London, United Kingdom, on 14 October. His death resulted in the suspension of the Arusha process.

In early August 1999 Hutu militia attacked Kanyosha, near the capital. A brutal counter-insurgency operation by the armed forces resulted in hundreds of civilian casualties, according to Amnesty International. Hutu militia attacked Bujumbura's Musega and Mutanga suburbs in late August, killing at least 50 people. The Government responded by intensifying regroupment in Bujumbura Rural province, and by mid-September a further 200,000 civilians had been gathered into camps.

MANDELA BECOMES MEDIATOR

Buyoya visited the South African President, Thabo Mbeki, in Pretoria in late August 1999, requesting that South Africa play an active role in the peace process. In early December regional heads of state, meeting in Arusha, unanimously selected the former South African President, Nelson Mandela, as the new Burundi mediator. The appointment received international support as well as the endorsement of the Burundi Government.

Immediately after his appointment, Mandela urged Hutu militia leaders to join the peace process. Mandela made his first official visit to Arusha in mid-January 2000, where he told participants that they were responsible for all the killings and should show greater urgency in reaching a solution. Mandela subsequently attended a meeting at the UN Security Council, which condemned the Burundi Government's regroupment policy, but resolved to encourage donors to resume substantial assistance.

Mandela attended his first round of Arusha discussions, the seventh of the process, in February 2000. Mandela prompted contention among delegates by criticizing Tutsi domination of public life and urging equal representation of Hutu and Tutsi in the armed forces, while also referring to Hutu rebel attacks on civilians as 'terrorism'. Mandela criticized Buyoya for his imprisonment of political opponents, and denounced regroupment, describing the camps as unfit for human habitation. After the Arusha discussions, the Government swiftly reassured the armed forces that it would not allow the imposition of ethnic quotas in the military. Mandela met senior army commanders and the Minister of Defence, Col Cyrille Ndayirukiye, in Johannesburg, South Africa, in mid-March, afterwards commending their 'realistic' stance, and later met the leadership of the CNDD—FDD and the FNL.

The next Arusha round of negotiations, which commenced on 27 March 2000, focused on the issue of army integration, despite the continued absence of the CNDD—FDD and FNL. The discussions concluded with the distribution of a draft accord to delegations for their consideration. Meanwhile, fierce fighting was reported during March and April in provinces bordering Tanzania, as well as skirmishes on the outskirts of Bujumbura. The fighting continued in May, particularly in Makamba, resulting in thousands of new displacements and refugees.

Mandela arrived in Burundi for the first time in late April 2000 for a brief visit that had been preceded by increased violence, particularly near Bujumbura. In late May Mandela met with senior army commanders and militia leaders in Johannesburg, although the CNDD—FDD declined to participate. Mandela met with Buyoya in Johannesburg in early June, and subsequently announced that Buyoya had agreed to ensure equal representation of Hutu and Tutsi in the army and had guaranteed the closure of regroupment camps by the end of that month.

In early July 2000 the CNDD—FDD said it would for the first time attend, but not negotiate at, peace discussions under Mandela's mediation, which were to commence on 19 July. The FNL maintained its boycott. Prior to the discussions, the mediators presented a draft peace accord, which brought together the positions previously agreed by the negotiating parties, but remained vague on main issues (including who should lead the transition, the nature of the electoral system and how to achieve a cease-fire), owing to the lack of consensus. The CNDD—FDD outlined its preconditions for a cease-fire and further talks with the Government, but Mandela's hopes that the parties might reach agreement on the key issues during the July discussions were disappointed.

THE ARUSHA AGREEMENT

Despite the failure of these talks, Mandela remained hopeful regarding the possibility of a rapid settlement, and announced that a further negotiating round would take place in late August. In the intervening period Mandela conducted bilateral discussions with the heads of party delegations at Arusha, to persuade them to commit to signing an accord. To increase the pressure, Mandela invited a number of heads of state, including the US President, Bill Clinton, and other senior international political figures to the August discussions. The round culminated on 28 August, with the signing of an agreement by all except for three parties, with the remainder signing in September. The agreement included arrangements for a pre-transitional, and then transitional, period, which would be followed by democratic elections, the creation of a Sénat and amendments to the Assemblée nationale, judicial reform, the establishment of an international force to assist during the transition, and an independent investigation into alleged crimes of genocide. The agreement did not, however, cover who should lead the transition, how to achieve a cease-fire, and the nature of the electoral system.

The CNDD—FDD and the FNL rejected the Arusha accord, and intensified their military campaigns, particularly in regions bordering Tanzania, and in rural areas surrounding Bujumbura and the second city, Gitega. Mandela arranged a meeting in Nairobi, Kenya, on 20 September 2000 between the militia leadership, the Government and regional heads of state, which Ndayikengurukiye declined to attend. The FNL leader, Kossan Kabura, was present, but was not prepared to talk to Buyoya, and would only converse with the regional heads of state, who instructed his forces and the CNDD—FDD observe a cease-fire within 30 days. After the signing of the accord, the South African Deputy President, Jacob Zuma, took over an increasing amount of the Burundi mediation work from Mandela, who had earlier announced that, with the peace agreement signed, he considered his involvement to be largely ended.

On 23 February 2001 a committee within the FNL announced that it had deposed Kabura from the post of party President and installed Agathon Rwasa in his place. Kabura insisted that he remained the militia's President. On 24 February, in its most daring military action, the FNL invaded Bujumbura and secured part of the city for several days, before the armed forces regained control. The fighting then shifted to rural areas outlying the capital, where more than 20,000 people were displaced in March. In early April there were fierce clashes between the armed forces and the FNL near Gitega, although by the end of the month most of the militia had taken refuge in the Kibira forestland, from where, it was feared, they were preparing a further offensive on the capital.

The FNL's attack immediately preceded a further round of discussions in Arusha on 27–28 February 2001, arranged by Mandela, and with the regional heads of state once again in attendance, to resolve the main remaining issues of disagreement. The talks again failed to resolve these issues, although Mandela's proposal that the leadership of the transition should be shared, with a Tutsi as Head of Government in the first period and a Hutu in the second, was eventually accepted by the delegations. A number of parties agreed to submit Col Epitace Bayaganakandi and FRODEBU's Domitien Ndayizeye as candidates for the transitional leadership, but this was rejected by the Government and regional heads of state.

After the talks, Buyoya stated that there would be no transition without a cease-fire, prompting accusations from some parties, including FRODEBU's external wing, that this amounted to a coup. On 19 March 2001 the peace implementation committee had its first substantive meeting, at which the parties did little more than restate their demands. Meanwhile, there were renewed clashes between the CNDD—FDD and Forces Armées Burundiais (FAB) in southern Burundi. Zuma met Ndayikengurukiye and the new Congolese President, Joseph Kabila, on 9 April in Kinshasa, DRC, and again, with Buyoya, in Libreville, Gabon, later that month. The meeting was abandoned on 18 April, in response to reports of a coup attempt in Bujumbura, which prompted Buyoya's return home; however, the attempt by Tutsi army officers, who briefly seized the state radio station, was suppressed after a few hours.

On 23 July 2001 Mandela convened a regional summit meeting in Arusha to resolve the impasse in the peace process and two days later an agreement was announced on the transitional leadership, namely that Buyoya was to remain in the office of President for a period of 18 months, after which time he would be replaced by a Hutu leader for the following 18 months. In October Mandela convened a summit meeting in Pretoria on Burundi, and announced that a South African force was to be deployed in the country to protect politicians returning from exile to participate in the forthcoming transitional Government and other transitional institutions. Ndayikengurukiye also attended a summit meeting, but hopes that this might mean a cease-fire could result were disappointed when the CNDD—FDD split after the Pretoria summit meeting, resulting in the emergence of a new faction, led by Pierre Nkurunziza, supported by nearly all CNDD—FDD combatants.

NEW TRANSITIONAL GOVERNMENT INSTALLED

The 700-member South African protection force was deployed in late October 2001, and, under the terms of the August 2000 agreement, a new 26-member transitional Government was installed on 1 November. Buyoya remained as head of state, the Secretary-General of FRODEBU, Domitien Ndayizeye, became Vice-President, and the Cabinet included members from all the signatory parties to the Arusha agreement but was dominated by UPRONA and FRODEBU.

Mandela, the UN Security Council, the EU and the OAU all expressed the view to the CNDD—FDD and the FNL that the installation of the new transitional Government rendered their armed struggle inappropriate, but the militia disagreed, insisting hostilities would continue as long as the Tutsi FAB remained the country's real power. At the beginning of November 2001 the CNDD—FDD intensified attacks in the eastern provinces, while the FNL carried out raids and ambushes in the region of Bujumbura. In late November the armed forces launched a major operation against the FNL near Tenga, north-east of Bujumbura, which resulted in the displacement of thousands of civilians.

The new transitional Assemblée nationale was inaugurated on 4 January 2002. In addition to 121 deputies from the previous Assemblée nationale, 57 new representatives had been nominated, most of them by parties that signed the Arusha agreement. FRODEBU was the largest party in the Assemblée, and Minani, its Chairman, was elected President (Speaker) of the Assemblée on 10 January, while Frédéric Ngenzebuhoro of UPRONA became Vice-President. In early February the transitional Sénat commenced operations, with Libère Bararunyeretse, a close associate of Buyoya and a senior UPRONA negotiator in Arusha, as its President.

Zuma travelled to Burundi and Tanzania for discussions concerning a possible cease-fire in early January 2002. There followed a series of meetings in Pretoria in February, attended by representatives of the Government and armed forces, and both factions of the CNDD—FDD, but not by the FNL. Nkurunziza's CNDD—FDD faction later announced that it had reached agreement with the Government on a general framework for negotiations that were intended to result in agreement on a cease-fire and an inclusive political settlement.

Zuma hosted new consultations between the militia groups and the Burundi Government in Pretoria in late April 2002, which the FNL again failed to attend. Nkurunziza was present, but his demand to negotiate directly with the armed forces was summarily rejected by the Government, for which, in part, Nkurunziza blamed Zuma. Ndayikengurukiye's CNDD—FDD faction was more ready to negotiate, although it did not declare a cease-fire, as Zuma had hoped it would. CNDD—FDD combatants launched repeated attacks in western Burundi during April and May, after crossing Lake Tanganyika from bases in the DRC, and in early June bombarded Bujumbura from a boat on the lake. The CNDD—FDD began a new offensive in the eastern province of Ruyigi, bordering Tanzania, in early July, prompting the Government again to accuse the Tanzanian Government of complicity, which the Tanzanian Government denied.

Peace negotiations, convened in Dar es Salaam on 12 August 2002, were boycotted once more by Rwasa, but attended for the first time by a newly emerged minority faction of the FNL, headed by Alain Mugabarabona, as well as both CNDD—FDD factions. Nkurunziza's CNDD—FDD faction finally agreed to negotiate with the Government at the Dar es Salaam talks, rather than, as it had previously demanded, the armed forces, but only on condition that the Government was prepared to accept responsibility for the armed forces' coup against Ndadaye in 1993. The government delegation refused, however, and the discussions were suspended. Fearing a permanent impasse, Zuma scheduled a regional summit meeting for 7 October 2002. The regional heads of state attended the discussions with the intention of imposing sanctions on the CNDD—FDD and FNL, but in the end granted a request by Zuma that they give the parties a further 30 days to negotiate. Also on 7 October Mugabarabona's faction of the FNL signed a cease-fire agreement with the Government (despite uncertainty as to whether Mugabarabona actually commanded any forces), and Ndayikengurukiye's faction of the CNDD—FDD signed a memorandum of understanding, which later resulted in a cease-fire agreement. Heavy fighting coincided with the peace talks. The FNL launched raids in the region of Bujumbura in August, while the CNDD—FDD concentrated its attacks near the second city of Gitega. A government counter-offensive around Gitega in September resulted in a massacre in Itaba district, in which 180 people were killed (the highest number of fatalities from a single attack in many years). Mukasi continued to denounce the peace process, and was arrested and detained for doing so on 6 October. In a further bid to suppress radical Tutsi opinion, Bagaza and other PARENA leaders were placed under house arrest one month later. Further discussions between the Government and Nkurunziza, beginning in Dar es Salaam on 26 October, were intended by Zuma to secure a cease-fire agreement before the deadline imposed by the regional heads of state. However, these talks also ended in failure. A demand by the CNDD—FDD that the entire Arusha agreement be renegotiated was refused by the government delegation, which argued that doing so would be rejected by some parties in the transitional Government, resulting in its collapse.

Nkurunziza and Buyoya were invited to attend a summit of regional heads of state on Burundi, which commenced in Arusha on 1 December 2002. This resulted in the signing of the long-awaited cease-fire agreement on 3 December, stipulating that a cease-fire be in effect by the end of that month. CNDD—FDD combatants would not be disarmed, but assembled, together with their armaments, in designated camps. The cease-fire and encampment of the CNDD—FDD were to be verified and monitored by an AU force. It was also agreed that a new national army, which would include fighters from the CNDD—FDD, would be established. Rukingama resigned as President of UPRONA on 7 December, and was replaced by Alphonse Kadege, also a Buyoya loyalist. Despite the official cease-fire between the armed forces and the CNDD—FDD, fighting continued, particularly in areas where the CNDD—FDD intended to assemble its fighters. With the need to deploy the AU force urgent, at a meeting in Addis Ababa, Ethiopia, on 12–13 January 2003, the Governments of South Africa, Ethiopia and Mozambique agreed to contribute troops. Buyoya and Nkurunziza met in Pretoria on 27 January to discuss the implementation of the cease-fire agreement, and agreed that CNDD—FDD fighters should assemble in camps in Bubanza and Ruyigi provinces. This agreement immediately exacerbated the conflict in both provinces, however, as the CNDD—FDD intensified its efforts to capture territory, while the armed forces moved aggressively to retain it. Clashes were also reported in Gitega, Cibitoke, Kayanza and Muramvya. Nkurunziza and Buyoya met once more in Pretoria on 21 February, but the discussions failed, with Nkurunziza accusing Buyoya of reneging on commitments made at their previous meeting. Regional heads of state, Buyoya and the CNDD—FDD's Secretary-General, Hassan Rajabu, met in Dar es Salaam on 1 March. Both Buyoya and Rajabu reiterated their commitment to the cease-fire agreement, but on the ground the conflict between their forces continued unabated.

NDAYIZEYE SECURES AGREEMENT WITH THE CNDD—FDD

In early March 2003 Buyoya attempted to persuade the South African Government that he should remain Head of State until an effective cease-fire was in place, but the South African Government refused; on 28 March Buyoya announced that he would transfer the presidency to Ndayizeye, when his 18-month period of office expired at the end of April. On 30 April Ndayizeye became President for the scheduled 18 months, and Kadege became Vice-President. Contingents of the AU force, known as the African Mission in Burundi (AMIB), commenced deployment in that month. (Meanwhile, in April the legislature adopted a bill providing for the establishment of an international judicial commission of inquiry into war crimes committed since mid-1962.) Ndayizeye's first Government, announced in early May, was little changed from Buyoya's previous administration.

Further discussions between the Government and Nkurunziza's faction of the CNDD—FDD in July and August 2003 made little progress, but Ndayizeye and Nkurunziza finally signed a power-sharing agreement in Pretoria on 8 October. The CNDD—FDD agreed to abandon hostilities and order its combatants to assemble in cantonments, in return for substantial representation in the Government and the armed forces. By that time AMIB had reached its maximum authorized strength of 3,128 troops (of which South Africa contributed 1,629, and the remainder were contributed by Mozambique and Ethiopia).

Ndayizeye and Nkurunziza returned to Pretoria in late October 2003, where the CNDD—FDD secured a key concession, namely a government promise of immunity from prosecution for its combatants, which was also extended to members of the armed forces. The immunity decision was denounced by Tutsi parties, and also received condemnation from international human rights groups, who denounced granting impunity for crimes against humanity. Nkurunziza's CNDD—FDD officially ended hostilities on 10 November, and fighting ceased soon after throughout most of the country, with the exception of Bujumbura Rural and Cibitoke provinces, where FNL forces remained active. On 16 November the peace agreement was formally signed at a summit of regional heads of state in Dar es Salaam, and on 23 November Ndayizeye announced the establishment of a new Government of national unity, incorporating CNDD—FDD representatives. Nkurunziza was appointed to the newly created post of Minister of State for Good Governance and State Inspection, which was officially designated as the third most important position in the administration.

Despite the terms of the peace agreement requiring CNDD—FDD combatants to assemble in cantonments in preparation for disarmament, the faction began conducting joint operations with members of the armed forces against the FNL in Bujumbura Rural and Cibitoke, with heavy fighting ensuing. On 29 December 2003 FNL forces ambushed and killed the papal envoy in Burundi attracting widespread international condemnation. Clashes were also reported in Bururi province between supporters of Nkurunziza and those loyal to Léonard Nyangoma, who had originally established the CNDD.

In January 2004 Ndayizeye appointed a new 33-member Joint Military High Command, comprising 21 members selected from the armed forces and 13 from Nkurunziza's faction of the CNDD—FDD. Ndayizeye announced that this measure would be followed by the establishment of a new reconstituted armed forces, the Forces de défense nationales (FDN). No representatives from either Ndayikengurukiye's faction of the CNDD—FDD or from Mugabarabona's minority FNL faction were included in the high command, apparently in violation of the Government's earlier agreements with them. Discussions between Ndayizeye and the FNL leadership, commencing in the Netherlands in mid-January, initially appeared positive, but in February ended with a unilateral suspension of dialogue by the FNL. During the following months continued heavy fighting between the FNL and CNDD—FDD, allied with members of the armed forces, caused the displacement of some 50,000 civilians.

HUTU AND TUTSI REPRESENTATION IN GOVERNMENT

Ndayizeye convened a series of meetings with members of parties represented in the Government during February and March 2004 in order to secure agreement on key unresolved issues, including the contents of a new draft constitution and electoral code. No agreement was reached, however, prompting Ndayizeye, who also cited concern at the ongoing civil war, to support a postponement in elections. In April Nkurunziza withdrew the CNDD—FDD from the Government until July, alleging its power-sharing accord was not being respected by Ndayizeye. Nevertheless, in May Ndayizeye presented a new draft electoral timetable, postponing for a year the presidential poll, which was originally due to be held by the end of October. FRODEBU and the CNDD—FDD rejected the proposed extension, which was supported by predominantly Tutsi parties. After a meeting of political parties, convened by Zuma in Pretoria, failed to reach agreement on the issue, a summit of regional heads of state in Dar es Salaam on 5–6 June ruled that elections must proceed according to the original schedule. Despite renewed contact between the FNL and Zuma just before the summit, the heads of state condemned the militia for remaining outside the peace process and imposed sanctions on its leadership, with further measures threatened.

Six months after Zuma made the initial request, on 21 May 2004 the UN Security Council approved the replacement of the AMIB mission with the Opération des Nations Unies au Burundi (ONUB), which officially commenced deployment on 1 June for an initial six-month period. Consequently, the UN, rather than South Africa, would be paying for the operation, which was to be expanded to include additional military personnel from a number of countries.

Mbeki and Zuma hosted prolonged discussions between the various political parties in Pretoria during late July 2004, in an attempt to resolve the deadlock on the key issue of political and ethnic representation in government after the election. A draft power-sharing accord specifying 60% Hutu and 40% Tutsi representation in the Government and Assemblée nationale was signed on 6 August by the main Hutu parties, but was rejected by predominantly Tutsi parties, which objected to a definition of representation in ethnic, rather than party political, terms that would allow predominantly Hutu parties to meet the required Tutsi quotas from within their own ranks, instead of by working with Tutsi parties. Hutu parties, however, refused to compromise on this point and were supported by the increasingly impatient South African Government and the regional heads of state. On 13 August the FNL, allegedly with the support of Rwandan Hutu militia and elements within the Congolese armed forces, massacred 152 Congolese Banyamulenge refugees at the Gatumba refugee camp near Bujumbura. (Large numbers of Banyamulenge had fled from Uvira, in the DRC's Sud-Kivu province, in June.) A subsequent UN report stated that there was insufficient evidence to establish with certainty who perpetrated the killings, although a report by Human Rights Watch unequivocably attributed responsibility to the FNL. The Gatumba massacre took place despite a significant nearby presence of members of the armed forces, who failed to take decisive action to prevent the attack. The impact of the massacre reverberated across the region, with one faction of the DRC Government suspending its participation in the political transition for a time, the Rwandan Government threatening to reinvade the DRC if the perpetrators were not penalized and Banyamulenge refugees in Bujumbura staging a demonstration, which was dispersed by the security forces. Many of the refugees subsequently fled to Banyamulenge refugee camps in Rwanda, which they considered more secure. A five-member independent electoral commission was established at the end of August. In continuing protests against the agreement signed in Pretoria, Tutsi parties boycotted government meetings throughout September. Undeterred, remaining Hutu party ministers approved a new draft Constitution incorporating the Pretoria accord, which was to be submitted to a referendum and adopted prior to national elections.

On 15–17 September 2004 Ndayizeye called an extraordinary joint session of the Assemblée nationale and the Sénat to ratify the draft Constitution. With delegates from Tutsi parties absent, Hutu delegates unanimously approved the constitutional text, which Ndayizeye then presented to the Constitutional Court for endorsement. However, the Constitutional Court declined to conduct a scheduled hearing, later declaring that its role was to interpret the Constitution, not rule on its legality. Insisting that this implied the Court's endorsement of the text, Ndayizeye announced a referendum would be conducted on 20 October, which was later rescheduled for 26 November. Since the interim Constitution was, however, due to expire on 1 November, the regional heads of state ruled that the disputed draft Constitution approved by the Sénat and Assemblée nationale replace it on this date. The regional heads of state further ruled that Ndayizeye's mandate, which was also due to expire at this time, be extended until 22 April 2005, which became the rescheduled date for national elections.

NKURUNZIZA AND THE CNDD—FDD'S ELECTORAL TRIUMPH

On 31 October 2004 the transitional Government's mandate was formally extended for a further six months, and the new Constitution came into effect. In mid-November Ndayizeye dismissed the Vice-President, Alphonse Kadege, owing to his alleged obstruction of government policy, and replaced him with another Tutsi member of UPRONA, Frédéric Ngenzebuhoro, who had previously been the Deputy Speaker of the Assemblée nationale. The referendum did not take place as scheduled on 26 November, and the next deadline in mid-December was also missed, with the electoral commission each time citing technical constraints. The long-awaited national military demobilization programme began on 2 December; about 55,000 combatants from Hutu militia and the mainly Tutsi existing armed forces were to be demobilized under the process within five years, leaving around 30,000 combatants to form the new FDN, which was formally established on 31 December. The referendum finally took place on 28 February 2005, with the results indicating an overwhelming endorsement of the Constitution. Turn-out was high, at more than 91% of registered voters, of whom 90.1% voted in favour of the Constitution. Despite allegations of fraud and electoral malpractice, the overall consensus of local and national observers was that the vote was generally free and fair. The new Constitution was subsequently signed into law by Ndayizeye on 19 March, thereby allowing legislative elections to proceed. The FNL observed a truce during the referendum period, and a meeting between its leadership and the Tanzanian President, Benjamin Mkapa, in early April resulted in a declaration from the militia that it was prepared to negotiate with the Government and would end fighting when talks began. The militia further undertook not to disrupt the electoral process. The FNL had previously been classified as a terrorist organization by the regional heads of state, but the Tanzanian Government pledged that it would urge a review of this position if dialogue began between the FNL and the Burundian Government. The next pre-election stage in the transitional process was for the legislature to agree on an electoral code. This measure was completed in late April, when, according to the timetable that regional heads of state had stipulated earlier, the transitional period was to end. Regional heads of state were consequently obliged, at a meeting in Kampala, to extend the transitional period once again, until 26 August. According to this schedule, there were to be local elections in June, legislative elections in July, and subsequently, on 19 August, the new Assemblée nationale and Sénat members were to elect a new President, who was to be inaugurated one week later.

On 3 June 2005 communal elections were conducted under the transitional schedule; turn-out was estimated at 81% of registered voters, and with voting largely taking place along ethnic lines, of the 3,225 contested seats, the CNDD—FDD secured 1,781, FRODEBU 822 and UPRONA 260 seats. The CNDD—FDD won control of 15 provinces, with FRODEBU winning in Bujumbura and Bururi. Voting was marred by violence in Bubanza and Bujumbura Rural provinces, despite an FNL promise of a truce during the elections, but proceeded peacefully elsewhere. In mid-June the Government approved a UN proposal for the establishment of a truth and reconciliation commission to investigate crimes perpetrated during the conflict from 1993. Elections to a reduced number of 100 seats in the Assemblée nationale took place, as scheduled, on 4 July 2005. Turn-out was lower than in the communal elections, but the polls were judged 'reasonably free and fair' by international observers. According to provisional official results, the CNDD—FDD won 59 seats, FRODEBU 25 and UPRONA 10. A further 18 deputies were subsequently nominated in accordance with the constitutional requirements of balance of ethnic representation (60% Hutu and 40% Tutsi) and a minimum 30% representation of women, with the result that representatives from the Twa ethnic group were allocated three seats, while the CNDD—FDD, FRODEBU and UPRONA each received five additional seats, leaving the CNDD—FDD with an absolute majority in the Assemblée of 13. Communal councillors participated in Sénat elections on 29 July. The CNDD—FDD won 30 of the 34 contested seats, and FRODEBU the remaining four. Four former Presidents were subsequently allocated seats, and Twa representatives were designated three seats. Eight further senators were later added in order to achieve the constitutionally stipulated minimum representation of women; the four political parties with the highest votes each nominated two women to the additional seats. Nkurunziza resigned as President of the CNDD—FDD on 28 July (he was replaced by Hussein Radjabu) and officially presented himself as the party's presidential candidate. On 19 August a joint session of the Assemblée nationale and the Sénat elected Nkurunziza as President. Nkurunziza was the only candidate, and won more than 81.5% of votes cast. On 26 August Nkurunziza was sworn in as President in Bujumbura.

THE CNDD—FDD BEGINS TO GOVERN

Nkurunziza appointed a 20-member Council of Ministers on 30 August 2005, seeking to reassure Tutsis by appointing Martin Nduwimana of UPRONA as First Vice-President, and the Tutsi former Chief of Staff, Maj. Germain Niyoyanka, as Minister of National Defence. FRODEBU objected to receiving only three ministerial portfolios, maintaining that it was entitled to five. The CNDD—FDD received 12 government posts. The establishment of the new Government was warmly welcomed by the international community, but denounced by the FNL as illegitimate. The FNL increased its military campaign after Nkurunziza's election, and in October the new President announced an intensification of the counter-insurgency against it. The result, according to international human rights groups, was a worsening of human rights abuses by both sides.

In early January 2006 Nkurunziza began a series of appointments to senior civil service and parastatal positions, almost all of which were awarded to CNDD—FDD supporters. Also in January, and to the consternation of local human rights groups, Nkurunziza ordered the provisional release of 'political prisoners', with the stated aim of promoting national reconciliation. By mid-March more than 3,000 prisoners had been released, most of whom were CNDD—FDD supporters. Frustrated by the party's weak representation in the new Government and angered at alleged human rights abuses, in mid-March FRODEBU President Léonce Ngendekumana ordered its representatives to withdraw from the Government. The ministers in question, however, refused to do so, and the strategy was denounced by Ngendekumana's rival in the party, Jean Minani. Raising international concerns about the stability of the administration, on 7 March Nkurunziza announced on national radio that senior members of the armed and security forces had planned a coup attempt against him. No arrests were made initially, however, and the allegations were dismissed as scaremongering by opposition parties. In his first ministerial reorganization on 17 March, Nkurunziza removed two CNDD—FDD ministers for alleged corruption and mismanagement. In mid-April there was a public confrontation between Radjabu and Mathias Basabose, a CNDD—FDD deputy, with each accusing the other of corruption. Radjabu instigated the expulsion of Basabose from the CNDD—FDD, following which a press conference called by Basabose to explain his version of events was forcibly broken up by the police.

Rwasa announced in Dar es Salaam in mid-March that the FNL would accept unconditional negotiations with the Government to end hostilities. The Government responded positively a few days later. In mid-May, following a request from Nkurunziza that South Africa assist in the negotiations, Mbeki appointed the South African Minister of Safety and Security, Charles Nqakula, as mediator. (Zuma, who had mediated in previous discussions, had been dismissed from the South African Government in 2005, after being charged with corruption.) Negotiations commenced in Dar es Salaam in late May. On 18 June government and FNL delegations signed an 'agreement of principles' but discussions continued throughout July without agreement being reached on a cease-fire.

In August 2006 the security forces arrested several prominent opposition politicians, including Ndayizeye and Kadege, on suspicion of involvement in the alleged coup plot announced by the Government in March. Despite protests from donors and human rights organizations that those detained be charged or released, they remained in detention without charge throughout September and October. On 5 September, Second Vice-President Alice Nzomukunda of the CNDD—FDD resigned her post, citing as her reason the allegedly destructive role played in the Government by Radjabu. A week later, Nzomukunda was replaced by Marina Barampana, a close ally of Radjabu.

Following further talks between the Government and the FNL, on 7 September the two parties signed a cease-fire agreement despite having failed to resolve several key issues, including the future composition of the Government and the armed forces. A month later, in Bujumbura, Nqakula formally inaugurated a cease-fire verification commission, but this was boycotted by the FNL, which demanded the release of its leaders from detention before it would agree to cease hostilities.

RADJABU SUFFERS REVERSES

The trial of Ndayizeye, Kadege and others charged with involvement in the coup plot began on 24 November 2006 but was immediately adjourned, resuming in late December. The prosecution alleged that the accused were part of a regional plot to overthrow the Government, also apparently involving the General Chief of Staff of the Rwandan armed forces Gen. James Kabareebe, Salim Saleh (the half-brother of Ugandan President Gen. (retd) Yoweri Kaguta Museveni), former Burundian President Buyoya and renegade Congolese General Laurent Nkunda. On 15 January 2007 the Constitutional Court acquitted Ndayizeye and Kadege citing a lack of evidence.

A week after the Constitutional Court decision, and in a clear sign of his fast-changing political fortunes, Radjabu took temporary refuge in the South African embassy in Bujumbura, stating that he feared for his life. On 7 February 2007 in Ngozi there followed an extraordinary congress of the CNDD—FDD, convened by Nkurunziza but boycotted by Radjabu and his supporters, at which Radjabu was replaced as party Chairman by Col Jérémie Ngendakumana. Ngendakumana was formerly Burundi's ambassador to Kenya, and was viewed as a loyal supporter of Nkurunziza. Radjabu denounced the congress as illegal and in late February appealed to the Supreme Court to have the decisions annulled, but in early April the court ruled against Radjabu. Shortly after the CNDD—FDD congress, meanwhile, Nkurunziza dismissed Barampana for alleged insubordination; she was replaced by Gabriel Ntisezerana. Barampana was subsequently arrested and charged with fraud. Several Radjabu supporters were removed from the Council of Ministers in a reshuffle on 12 February, and 10 days later another Radjabu supporter, First Vice-President Yolande Nzikoruriho, was removed from office and replaced by Anatole Manirakiza, a Nkurunziza-loyalist. In mid-March the President of the Assemblée nationale, Immaculée Nahayo, also a Radjabu supporter, was voted out of office, to be replaced by Pie Ntavyohanyuma. On 27 April the Assemblée nationale voted to strip Radjabu of his immunity from prosecution and he was arrested and detained the same day. Meanwhile, in mid-February the Government released several FNL leaders from detention, and a week later the militia began participation in the cease-fire verification commission.

FORCED POPULATION MOVEMENTS

The cross-border movement of vast numbers of refugees, provoked by regional ethnic and political violence, is a key factor in Burundi's relations with all neighbouring states. Nearly all Burundi's refugees are, and historically have been, Hutu. Most of these refugees have gone to Tanzania, and while numbers have fluctuated over the years, there have never been fewer than 200,000 since the killings of 1972 (see above). The substantial Burundian refugee presence has been an important motivation for the Tanzanian Government's involvement in Burundian politics. In 2003 more than 500,000 Burundian refugees were believed to be living in Tanzania (of whom at least 200,000 were not assisted by UNHCR), but the transitional process in Burundi, the restoration of peace to the country's border provinces with Tanzania, increasing hostility to their presence from the Tanzanian authorities and a UNHCR-sponsored programme have encouraged many to return. An estimated 145,000 refugees returned to Burundi during 2004–05, and a further 100,000 in 2006.

After the abortive coup in October 1993 (see above), while many of the Hutu refugees who subsequently fled the country went to Tanzania, at least 500,000 crossed into Rwanda and the DRC. The arrival of Burundian Hutu refugees fleeing persecution from the Tutsi military into Rwanda was undoubtedly a factor radicalizing Hutu sentiment prior to the Rwandan genocide. Following the Rwandan genocide and the subsequent victory of the FPR, thousands of Rwandan Hutus sought refuge in Burundi, while most of the Burundian refugees in Rwanda were repatriated at that time. During 1995 and 1996 most of the Rwandan refugees returned to Rwanda. Beginning in 2004, the two countries again exchanged refugees, with thousands of Rwandan Hutus fleeing to Burundi to escape the *gacaca* (traditional justice) process, which threatened to implicate them in the 1994 genocide, and Burundian Tutsis taking refuge from what they feared was a fast-approaching period of vengeful Hutu hegemony. Reassured by the accommodating stance taken by Nkurunziza's Government, most Burundian

Tutsi refugees returned. Rwandan Hutu refugees, by contrast, have been determined to stay in Burundi, despite exhortations by both Governments for them to return. Several thousand Rwandans were forcibly repatriated during mid-2005 but most, it appeared, had returned to Burundi by the end of that year. Most Burundian refugees from the 1993 conflict living in the DRC were forced to leave during 1997–98 by DRC government forces and the Burundian armed forces. Fighting between the main Goma faction of the Rassemblement congolais pour la démocratie (RCD—G), Mai-Mai and Banyamulenge militia in the DRC's Sud-Kivu province from 2002 caused substantial movements of Banyamulenge refugees from the DRC into Burundi. Clashes during mid-2004 between opposing factions of the Congolese government forces generated a further flow of Banyamulenge refugees into both Burundi and Rwanda. Following the massacre of Banyamulenge refugees in Burundi's Gatumba camp in August (see above), other Banyamulenge refugees felt unsafe in Burundi and many fled into Rwanda, although several thousand remained. In March 2007, the first refugees of a group of 500 Banyamulenge survivors of the Gatumba massacre were relocated to the USA under a resettlement programme.

Economy

FRANÇOIS MISSER

Revised by the editorial staff

In terms of average income, Burundi is one of the poorest countries in the world, and its economic performance is heavily dependent on the international price of coffee. Life expectancy at birth in 2004 was 45 years, one of the lowest in Africa. During 1995–2005, in the context of a high rate of population growth (2.1% per year), gross domestic product (GDP) per head decreased, in real terms, at an average annual rate of 1.6%. At the end of 2005 GDP per head was estimated at US $105. Overall GDP increased, in real terms, at an average rate of 7.1% per year during 1965–80, by an average of 4.4% per year in 1980–90, and, according to the African Development Bank (ADB), at an average annual rate of 1.4% in 1995–2006.

The new transitional Government that was established in November 2001 planned to increase the country's GDP by 6% annually during its three-year mandate and afterwards, in order to achieve a recovery to the level that had prevailed before the 1993 political crisis. However, these expectations, which were based on the projected increase of reconstruction-orientated investments and on the beginning of the exploitation of the country's substantial nickel resources, were not met. In 2003 Burundi's GDP actually decreased by an estimated 1.2%, owing to the impact of poor weather on the first crops of the season. Activity in non-farm sectors, however, remained strong. Despite difficult political and security conditions in 2004, Burundi's performance in that year was in accordance with the targets agreed by the IMF within the framework of a Poverty Reduction and Growth Facility (PRGF), which was approved in January (see below). The GDP growth rate for 2004 was 5.5%, slightly higher than projected, owing to increased coffee prices on the world market, larger transfers of funds by donors (foreign aid contributed the equivalent of 17% of GDP in 2004) and the benefits of structural reforms of the Ministry of Finance and the central bank administrations initiated by the Government. GDP growth of 5.0% was projected by the Bretton Woods institutions for 2005, in the context of a progressive return of peace. In that year, however, despite a significant improvement in the security situation and the Government's adherence to the PRGF-supported programme, real GDP growth was only about 1%, largely as a result of a severe decline in coffee production and worsening drought in the north of the country. According to the African Development Bank, growth of 6.1% was estimated in 2006, largely as a result of strong recovery in the coffee sector. The annual rate of inflation averaged 7.6% in 1980–90 and increased to an average rate of 14.3% in 1990–2001. Following the depreciation of the exchange rate throughout 2002 and higher food prices resulting from lower agricultural output, the annual rate of inflation, which had registered a decline of 1.5percentage points in 2002, rose to 7.9% in 2003. In 2004 the rate increased again to 10.8%. In 2005 the annual rate of inflation increased to 13.4%, but in 2006 it slowed to just 5.0%. An improvement in the stability of the Burundian franc was recorded throughout 2004, while the difference between the official and parallel rates of the national currency fell from 15% in 2003 to 2% in 2004. From mid-2005, however, the Burundian franc appreciated against the US dollar, which, together with the Government's tightening of monetary policy, resulted in a sharp decline in inflation, to about 1% at the end of that year. A World Bank-supported disarmament, demobilization and reintegration programme for former combatants was under way in 2005. New organs of government were successfully installed, following democratic elections in July. Progress in negotiations between the Government and the remaining rebel movement (see Recent History), was slow, but there were rising hopes for a cessation of hostilities in the first half of 2007.

At 2001 Burundi was one of the 34 sub-Saharan African countries designated by the UN as 'least developed countries'. According to the UN development index, between 1990 and 2004 almost 90% of the population were living on less than US $2 per day and Burundi ranked 169th on the list of 177 countries in 2004. Expenditure on health amounted to only about 3.2% of GDP in 2004. By early 2005 the implementation of the 'Politique Nationale de Santé 2005–15' was behind schedule. Malaria is the principal cause of mortality. According to the Joint UN Programme on HIV/AIDS (UNAIDS), in 2006 some 150,000 Burundians were infected with HIV/AIDS, with an infection rate of 3.3% of adults aged between 15 and 49. However, in 2006 70,000 people were tested at 135 voluntary centres around the country (a figure that had increased significantly from just 80 in 2003), while the rate of mother to child transmission has also decreased.

The situation of the education sector was precarious, owing to the lack of adequate infrastructure and qualified teachers. According to the Ministry of National Education, the primary-school enrolment rate was projected to increase from 69% in 2001 to 81% in 2004 and 85% in 2006, owing to the creation of more schools. However, the rate is 20% lower for girls. In October 2004 the Government of Burundi and the UN Children's Fund (UNICEF) launched a 'return to school' programme, involving 440,000 pupils in the nine provinces with the highest proportion of refugees.

Burundi's population density, estimated at 293.6 persons per sq km in 2006, is one of the highest in Africa and has been subject to significant fluctuation since mid-1993, as a result of the cross-border movement of vast numbers of refugees. The office of the UN High Commissioner for Refugees (UNHCR) estimated that 319,000 refugees have returned to Burundi since the end of the 12-year civil war, creating a number of land disputes throughout the country. Large numbers of Burundians have also been relocated under government plans aimed at removing them from areas of conflict. In April 1997 UN officials reported that this large-scale movement, combined with the shortage of food aid, had resulted in widespread childhood malnutrition in the 'regroupment' camps. This, in turn, provoked more cross-border movement, as did the attacks against Burundian refugee camps in Zaire (now the Democratic Republic of the Congo, DRC) by Zairean rebels and Rwandan troops in October 1996. In April 1997 the neighbouring states partially suspended regional economic sanctions (imposed following the coup of July 1996) to allow for the import of food aid. However, administrative obstacles resulted in insufficient supplies entering the country. Serious flooding also prevented about two-thirds of the food aid from reaching its destination, and by the end of 1998 some 350,000 people remained dependent on food aid for their survival. In 1999 increased insecurity further disrupted agricultural activities. By the end of 2000 the national food deficit amounted to 178,000 metric tons of cereals. National crop production decreased by 34% for food legumes and 15% for cereals during that year. By early 2001 the World Food Programme (WFP) estimated that 450,000 remained dependent on food aid. Throughout 2002 the deterioration of the security situation resulted in new displacements of people fleeing violence, particularly in central and eastern provinces; FAO anticipated that additional emergency food aid would be required to meet the needs of these newly displaced civilians. In 2003 a combination of floods and insect infestation resulted in a severe drop in coffee production.

In 2004 the northern provinces of Kirundo and Muyinga were severely affected by famine, owing to insufficient rainfall and a poor cassava crop caused by the mosaic virus. WFP, with the assistance of the European Community Humanitarian Aid Office, provided food to about 650,000 Burundian citizens throughout the country during that year. During 2004, according to UNHCR, some 90,000 Burundian refugees were repatriated from Tanzania, increasing pressure on local authorities. In late 2005 further severe food shortages were reported in the northern and eastern provinces, after continuing drought again had a negative impact on the cassava crop and also caused a fall of some 78% in coffee production, which had reduced farmers' incomes.

AGRICULTURE

At mid-2004, according to FAO, an estimated 89.7% of the labour force were engaged in agriculture (including forestry and fishing), mainly at subsistence level, and the sector provided an estimated 35.0% of GDP in 2005. During 1980–90 agricultural GDP increased, in real terms, by an average of 3.1% per year. During 1995–2006, according to the ADB, the sector grew by just 0.4%. In 2004 it increased by 3.4%, before contracting in 2005 by 6.3%. It recovered in 2006, posting growth of 7.7%.

Burundi's dominant cash crop is coffee. About 1m. farmers were involved in coffee production in 2001. However, the overwhelming dependence on coffee has had an adverse effect on the balance of payments in times of declining international coffee prices. The STABEX (Stabilization of Export Earnings) scheme, introduced in 1975 under the first Lomé Convention and retained in the three subsequent Conventions, helped to ease this difficulty. This mechanism was replaced with a further compensation scheme, known as FLEX, by the new Cotonou Agreement, signed in June 2000 between the European Union (EU) and the African, Caribbean and Pacific states. Additionally, in the early 1990s the Government acted to attract private-sector investment in the coffee industry. The state monopoly on coffee exports was relaxed, and a restructuring of the two factories that process Burundi's entire coffee crop was undertaken. The improvement in the international price of coffee resulted in revenue of some US $77m. in 1998, despite a declining crop caused by a shortage of fertilizers and the age of the plantations. However, the coffee price decline provoked a reduction in export revenue, from $42m. in 1999 to $31.4m. in 2000, $21.1m. in 2001 and $17.4m. in 2002.

In 2002 coffee production recovered dramatically, to 36,000 metric tons (the previous year output had amounted to just 15,834 tons), although nsufficient rainfall in November 2002 contributed to a decline in the 2003 crop, to 20,100 tons. However, the Office des Cultures Industrielles du Burundi (OCIBU), which supervises coffee exports, reported an improvement during the second half of 2004, owing to the abundant rainfall recorded in April, and output increased to about 37,000 tons in that year. The 2005 crop, however, was at its lowest level for more than 40 years, with an estimated output of only 6,000 tons, owing to insufficient rainfall and a combination of factors, including insecurity, diseases, lack of technical support, poor maintenance of the plantations and low world prices. The average price for the 2003 output was US $0.413 per kg, about one-half of the 1999 price.

Coffee accounted for 37.7% of total export revenues in 2006. In early 2007 the US-based coffee chain Starbucks pledged to work with local farmers and facilitate growth in the sector. In December of 2003 the Government announced plans to withdraw from the sector and sell its shares in the Société de Gestion, de Traitement et de Lavage (SOGESTAL) washing stations and in the Songa and Buterere coffee plants. The European Commission offered to support this operation with remaining funds from the STABEX. Owing to insufficient rainfall and continuing insecurity, together with substantial smuggling of the output to neighbouring countries, coffee exports dropped considerably, amounting to only 14,522 tons in the first 10 months of 2004, compared with 25,426 tons in the equivalent 2003 period. However, owing to a 50% rise in the international price, to US $0.66 per kg, in October 2004 in comparison with the previous year, the value of exports during that period was almost the same in nominal terms (21,130m. Burundian francs, compared with 21,980m. Burundian francs for the first 10 months of 2003). An improvement in the quality of exports was also recorded, with a proportion of 80.9% fully-washed quality in the output. In 2005 the authorities aimed to reform the OCIBU parastatal, which fixed the coffee price, provided agronomic expertise to the farmers and carried out market prospection activities. According to plans, these prerogatives would henceforth be transferred to the farmers' associations. In early 2005 the Ministry of Agriculture and Livestock created a new body, the Observatoire des Filières au Burundi (OFB), to assist Burundi's Confédération Nationale des Caféculteurs (CNC) in a number of tasks, including the commercialization of fertilizers, outside market prospection and establishment of the producer price. These measures were expected to contribute to curbing the smuggling of coffee to neighbouring countries. The Burundian Association of Coffee Exporters (ABEC) also began to prospect foreign markets in Europe and the USA. In mid-2006 the continuation of the reform strategy of the coffee sector, supported by the EU and the World Bank, was considered to be essential to poverty reduction, especially for some 800,000 small rural producers. At that time, however, a government invitation for applications to acquire two washing stations had been unsuccessful. According to a government schedule for reforms, a new regulatory, legal and institutional framework of the coffee sector, including restructuring of OCIBU, was to be implemented prior to the 2007/08 harvest.

The low international price for coffee is a permanent subject of concern for the Burundian authorities. OCIBU was unable to raise the producer price, owing to losses incurred during the embargo period. Indeed, in March 2002 OCIBU had not yet recovered a US $3.5m. debt, resulting from an exchange of coffee for imported goods (some of which were never delivered) during the embargo. However, the Government hoped that STABEX funds could assist the coffee sector in improving its performance by 2002. Nevertheless, in July of that year, owing to the continuing decline in the international price, the Government was again unable to raise the producer price, although Burundian coffee won several quality awards, in both Kenya and France, during that year. Meanwhile, Burundi's deparching and processing company, the Société de Déparchage et de Conditionnement du Café (SODECO), which had financed producers between 1996 and 2001, was experiencing difficulties. In response, the Government increasingly encouraged the development of alternative cash crops, such as essential oils for the perfume industry, and fruits (particularly mangoes and maracujas), vegetables (beans) and flowers for export.

Tea has become Burundi's second most important crop, generating export revenues of 10,238.4m. Burundian francs (representing 17.0% of total export earnings) in 2006. Despite the drought in 2000, tea production in that year increased to 7,134 tons, according to FAO, and in 2001 exceptionally high output of an estimated 9,045 tons was achieved. After the good harvest of 2001, production decreased to 6,605 tons in 2002 and increased to 7,380 tons in 2003. Production remained stable in 2004 and 2005, with 7,712 tons and 7,500 tons, respectively. In December 2003 the state announced its intention to privatize the management of the Office du Thé du Burundi (OTB), which was burdened by a debt of 13,000 Burundian francs. It also announced that the five tea estates and plants of Ijenda, Rwegura, Teza, Tora and Buhoro would be transferred to the private sector.

Output of cotton, which is mainly grown in the plain of Ruzizi, amounted to 2,585 metric tons in 2000 and the Compagnie de Gérance du Coton (COGERCO) parastatal aimed to increase output to 4,000 tons in 2001. In early 2001 heavy rain hindered efforts to develop cotton production in the northern province of Kirundo, and actual output was 2,880 tons. Nevertheless, COGERCO announced that the mid-2002 crop had increased by 20% compared with the previous year, and in August it announced higher prices for cotton producers in order to encourage them. Total output in that year amounted to 3,040 tons. However, these efforts were hampered by growing insecurity in the Imbo plain and in 2003 production was only some 2,163 tons, and remained at about that level in 2005. In the long term, COGERCO expected to increase the area of cotton fields by as much as 12,000 ha. Indeed, the high quality of Burundi's cotton is much appreciated both by the domestic textile industry and by foreign clients. COGERCO was undergoing difficulties in early 2005. It had accumulated a US $400,000 debt owed to the Banque Commerciale du Burundi (BANCOBU), and was unable to recover a $150,000 debt from its sole client, the Complexe Textile du Bujumbura (COTEBU) state-owned textile plant. An additional problem was that COTEBU was purchasing cotton from COGERCO at a price lower than the international one. By April 2005 the Burundian state was considering the divestment of COGERCO. Owing to COTEBU's insolvency, however, the Burundian Government allowed the parastatal to market Burundi's cotton abroad in that year.

Burundi has obtained foreign assistance for the development of other crops. On the Imbo plain, land is being reclaimed for the cultivation of cotton and rice in an integrated rural development scheme that is assisted by the UN Development Programme (UNDP) and FAO. However, rice development projects have also been disrupted by fighting in the region. Many fields have been abandoned, road maintenance has deteriorated and pumping stations have been sabotaged. In mid-2001 Belgium, FAO and the EU agreed to finance a programme to encourage rice production and to distribute seeds to peasants in the north of the country. In 2004 rice production reached 64,532 metric tons, according to FAO, and increased further in 2005, to 67,947 tons. An integrated sugar scheme was established in the south-east of the Mosso region, with finance provided mainly by the ADB, the Fund of the Organization for the Petroleum Exporting Countries and the Arab Bank for Economic Development in Africa (BADEA). Plantations of sugar cane have been established on the Mosso plain, near Bujumbura, in association with a refinery, which was projected to meet 90% of Burundi's demand for sugar by the early 1990s, with further potential for exports. However, both civil unrest and the inadequate size of the cultivated areas have prevented Burundi from becoming self-sufficient in cane. Attacks carried out by rebels from Tanzania have frequently disrupted production, and in October 2000 rebels attacked a pumping station and burnt tractors of the Société Sucrière du Mosso (SOSUMO). As a result of both civil unrest and drought, Burundi's sugar output decreased from 20,600 tons in 1999 to 18,308 tons in 2000, and remained at about that level in 2001. However, the country has become a net sugar exporter in recent times, albeit an irregular one, and exports fluctuate considerably. In 2004 sugar exports amounted to 8,378 tons and sugar export revenue to 3,272m. Burundian francs (6.2% of total export revenue). The following year sugar exports amounted to just 2,050 tons and sugar export revenue to 970m. Burundian francs (1.6% of total export revenue). In 2006 sugar exports decreased further, amounting to only 1,000 tons and sugar export revenue to 466m. Burundian francs (0.8% of total export revenue). These exports and the smuggling of sugar to neighbouring Rwanda and the DRC, where prices were higher than in Burundi, contributed to chronic shortages on the domestic market. In May 2005 the Minister of Commerce and Industry, Thomas Minani, acknowledged that the domestic production of 20,000 tons was insufficient to meet the requirements of the Burundian market, estimated at 23,000 tons.

Bananas, sweet potatoes, cassava, pulses and maize are other important, but mainly subsistence, crops. In March 2001 the Government requested assistance from foreign donors to combat the 'cassava mosaic' pest, which first appeared in Uganda in 1997 and subsequently spread to Rwanda, Tanzania, the DRC and Burundi. New varieties of potatoes were introduced by the agronomic department of the University of Burundi at Bujumbura, in the Imbo plain, in August 2003. In July 2003 the Institut des Sciences Agronomiques du Burundi (ISABU) announced plans to import varieties of eleusine from Ethiopia in order to revive the declining production of this traditional staple crop. In January 2004 agronomists recommended that returned refugees benefit from assistance to produce bananas and stressed the need to regenerate existing plantations. Palm oil was also produced in modest proportions (600 metric tons in 2000) by the Huilerie de Palme du Burundi installation. Production was expected to be increased significantly by the operations of a new oil installation, owned by the private Rumonge Palm Oil company, which commenced production in September 2001 at an annual level of 9,900 tons (far short of the plant's installed capacity of 50,000 tons of palm oil per year). In February 2003 a third private oil company, COGEMIMI, commenced production at Minago, near Rumonge, with the financial assistance of Luxembourg, which invested 195m. Burundian francs in the project. Most of the palm oil produced is sold on the domestic market. Palm oil exports amounted to only 52 tons in 2003. In June 2003 the state sold its 48% share in the Huilerie de Palme du Burundi (which was heavily indebted) to a private company, SAVONOR.

Although potentially self-sufficient in food production, civil disturbances and inclement weather have disrupted the country's infrastructure and have prevented supplies from reaching urban centres. In 2006 heavy rains destroyed a number of homes and farms, particularly in the Makamba province, where 1,500 people were left homeless. Continued flooding destroyed 50%–80% of November's harvest, according to WFP. The significant difference between the official and the parallel rates of the Burundian franc to the dollar encouraged large-scale illicit trade in staple products and sugar from Burundi to neighbouring countries. Another incentive for the smuggling of rice was the difference between the fixed price paid to peasants by the rice estate parastatal, which produced about one-third of the country's production in the Imbo plain, and the consumer price in Bujumbura, which was three times higher by the end of 1999. One of the main problems is the increasing fragmentation of rural land, with farms averaging 0.8 ha per household and soil problems reducing productivity. Rates of fertilizer use are among the lowest in Africa. The increased smuggling of fertilizers to neighbouring Rwanda in 2000 and 2001, together with the decline of the peasants' purchasing power, have aggravated conditions of access to these inputs. Nevertheless, by early 2001 WFP and FAO, which introduced a seeds distribution programme in February, were expecting a 17% increase in agricultural output in that year, principally owing to an improvement in climatic conditions. By June 16 seed production and distribution centres had been created, with the financial support of Belgium, the EU and the World Bank. Another important challenge was deforestation and soil erosion, which the Government and non-governmental organizations attempted to contain, with a programme of reafforestation, which envisaged the planting of 45m. trees during 2001–02. (By mid-2005, however, the Burundian authorities were expressing particular concern about deforestation in the Kibira region, in the north of the country.)

In early 2002 the new Government also initiated a policy of land redistribution, aimed specifically at meeting the needs of returned refugees and internally displaced persons. The authorities warned that unused land, particularly in the Gihanga and Mutinbuzi communes, would be redistributed. At the same time the Government announced plans to redistribute land that had been acquired or occupied illegally. In order to provide credit to farmers, in mid-2001 the Burundian authorities also created a Rural Fund of 2,000m. Burundian francs. These efforts were expected to be supplemented by donor contributions, directed both at supporting the rural sector and at creating revenue for returned refugees, internally displaced persons and demobilized combatants. At the end of March 2003 the Burundian Minister of Agriculture and Livestock announced a 6% decrease in agricultural output, owing to chronic insecurity, insufficient rains and inadequate supply of fertilizers. Meanwhile, WFP warned that more than 1m. civilians were in need of emergency food aid. In February WFP launched a US $164m. three-year programme of assistance to provide 24,000 metric tons of food to some 631,000 civilians. In December the Government announced a three-year plan of action to fight soil degradation, at a projected cost of 10,300m. Burundian francs. During 2004 the food situation deteriorated considerably; agricultural production decreased in most parts of the country, particularly in the provinces of Kirundo, Karusi, Bubanza and Bujumbura, and by the end of August WFP and FAO planned to provide the food requirements of more than 800,000 tons. Drought and ongoing insecurity were identified as the main causes. WFP estimated that 80% of the population of Kirundo province were threatened by famine at the end of 2004. In the southern province of Makamba, the food deficit was estimated at 30% in October. However, the Société Régionale pour le Développement de l'Imbo (SRDI) expected a 4,000-ton increase in rice output, to 20,000 tons, owing to improvements in the supply of fertilizers and irrigation. Meanwhile, the ISABU agronomists pursued their efforts to fight the mosaic cassava disease. In October the institute identified seven species that could resist the disease and were being disseminated among the peasants of the Kumoso region. In late 2005, following continued drought, WFP reported a food deficit of 334,000 tons.

The development of livestock is hindered by the social system, which encourages the maintenance of cattle herds that are both too large and too little exploited. As with other sub-sectors, livestock-rearing has been adversely affected by civil unrest, and in 1995 and early 1996 cattle rustlers removed entire herds (some cattle were used by rebel groups to explode mines around army barracks). In early 2003 the Agence française de développement announced a 70m. Burundian francs programme to assist 40 peasant communities in developing new ovine and bovine herds. In February 2004 the Ministry of Agriculture and Livestock announced co-operation with veterinary laboratories in Kenya, Malawi and South Africa to find a vaccine in order to eradicate the foot-and-mouth epidemic in the region. Exports of hides demonstrated a modest recovery in 2003, from 471 tons in 2002 to 646 tons, and reached 1,833 tons by 2006, accounting for 2.6% of total export revenue. The UN Industrial Development Organization (UNIDO) announced plans in 2004 to invest 200m. Burundian francs in order to enable the tannery of Burundi to resume its activities.

Fishing in the waters of Lake Tanganyika was banned by the Government in April 1996, following reports that the lake was being used as a transit point by extremist insurgents from Zaire and Tanzania. In 1998, however, as security on the lake improved, the resumption of fishing was authorized. However, fishing capacity decreased by 37% between 1993 and 2000, according to UN agencies. In 2002 the Government began to encourage better marketing and conservation of fish products from the smaller lakes of northern Burundi. By mid-2003 fishing was authorized only during the day on Lake Tanganyika, for security reasons. In September 2004, however, the relative improvement of the security situation in southern Burundi contributed to the resumption of fishing in the Rumonge region, on Lake Tanganyika.

MINERALS

Small quantities of bastnaesite and cassiterite have been exploited by the Karongo Mining Co (SOMIKA). Cassiterite exports amounted to only 39 metric tons in 2000, but increased to 44 tons in 2001 and to 67 tons in 2002, before decreasing to 24 tons in 2003 and to 16 tons in 2004. In conjunction with the rise in international prices of columbo-tantalite (of which niobium was a by-product), this increased production stimulated the country's mineral exports, which increased from 219.6m. Burundian francs in 2000 to 1,635.4m. Burundian francs in 2001. In 2002 niobium exports amounted to 72 tons, but, owing to the collapse of international prices, export earnings of this product totalled only 755m. Burundian francs. As columbo-tantalite is mined in small quantities in Burundi, this sharp increase in exports prompted UN officials to suspect that part of the total might be illicitly traded ore from the neighbouring DRC. In 2003 niobium ore exports amounted to 32 tons, valued at 161m. Burundian francs, about one-half of the quantity of 2001 exports, but hardly more than one-10th of their value. In 2004 exports remained at about that level, reaching 28 tons, valued at 91.8m. Burundian francs, by October. In April 2005 the Ministry of Energy and Mines admitted that these statistics failed to reflect the real situation, since some three-quarters of Burundian minerals were smuggled to Rwanda, where they could be sold at much higher prices (double in the case of cassiterite).

About 28 metric tons of wolframite (a tungsten-bearing ore) were produced at Nyarudende, in Kirundo province, in small-scale mining operations during 2004. In January 2002 the Burundian Government announced plans to facilitate a loan to relaunch the activities of the Compagnie Minière d'Exploitation du Burundi, which exploited tungsten. A small amount of alluvial gold is also produced, but output could increase significantly depending on the success of a project to exploit the Muyinga reserves, estimated at 60 tons of gold ore, associating a Canadian corporation, AMTEC, and the state-owned Burundi Mining Corpn (BUMINCO). In March 1999 the Preferential Trade Area Bank agreed to disburse a loan of US $297,500 to allow BUMINCO to purchase equipment for a gold-processing plant (which was to have a monthly capacity of 10 kg), pending completion of a feasibility study on an industrial project at Masaka. Initial prospecting on the Masaka site by BUMINCO was completed in May 1999, and further exploration commenced during the same month on sites at Rugomero and Butihinda. Production of gold increased from 483 kg in 2002 to 2,900 kg in 2004. Petroleum has been detected beneath Lake Tanganyika and in the Ruzizi valley, for which test drillings were carried out in the late 1980s by US petroleum interests, in association with the Burundian Government. However, petroleum experts stated that complete seismic surveys in Lake Tanganyika would also require prospecting in the DRC and Tanzanian parts of the lake. Stability in the DRC would consequently be an additional precondition to relaunching the project.

Surveys have estimated that Burundi's nickel deposits amount to about 300m. metric tons, containing 4m. tons of metal. In March 1999 an agreement was signed between the Burundian Government and an Australian company, Andover Resources, for the exploitation of deposits Musongati deposits. Andover Resources was to complete a feasibility study to assess the economic viability of the project, which envisaged the construction of a plant with an annual capacity of 45,000 tons of nickel by 2002, at a total estimated cost of US $700m.; the project was also to include the construction of employee housing, of a 35-MW power station and of rail or road access to the plant. In 1999 Andover Resources (which became a subsidiary of the Canadian enterprise Argosy Minerals Inc.) obtained concessions on further deposits at Nyabikere and Waga. In May 2000, however, Andover Resources declared that it was unable to proceed with the Musongati project, owing to instability in the region. In August the leader of the main rebel faction stated that he did not consider the mining contracts signed by the Burundian Government to be valid, criticizing more specifically the contract signed between Argosy Minerals and the Government, which accordingly took most of the profits. In April 2002, however, Argosy Minerals announced its intention to resume the Musongati project, owing to the improved political situation resulting from the installation of the new transitional coalition Government in November 2001. The Burundian Minister of Energy and Mines and Argosy Minerals agreed on a new programme, including feasibility studies on the cost of access infrastructure to the Musongati mine, which was also believed to contain some platinum group metal reserves. In December 2003 the Minister of Energy and Mines announced that work would resume soon on the site. One year later, however, he informed the legislature that not much progress had been made and expressed concern about Argosy Minerals' financial capacity to develop the Musongati project.

Burundi has estimated reserves of 15m. metric tons of phosphate rock, and sufficient reserves of carbonatite (7.3m. tons) to satisfy the domestic demand for cement have also been identified, near Gatara.

INDUSTRY

There is little industrial activity in Burundi, apart from the processing of agricultural products, such as cotton, coffee, tea and vegetable oil, and small-scale wood mills. Only 2.1% of the working population were employed in industrial activities at the census of 1990. During 1980–90 industrial GDP increased at an average annual rate of 4.5%. The sector's GDP increased by an average of 2.9% per year in 1995–2006. According to the ADB, industrial GDP grew by 7.2% in 2005, and by 7.5% in 2006. Industry contributed 20.1% to GDP in 2005.

Manufacturing GDP increased, in real terms, at an average annual rate of 5.7% in 1980–90, and of 1.1% in 1995–2006. The manufacturing sector accounted for some 13.5% of GDP in 2005. By the mid-1980s several small enterprises, including glass, cement, footwear, insecticide factories, a flour mill and a brewery, had been established. (The Brarudi brewery, 60% owned by Heineken and 40% owned by the Burundian Government, was reported to have provided almost 40% of total government tax receipts in 1996.) A textile industry was also developed, with aid from the People's Republic of China, which exported fabrics to the neighbouring states of Rwanda and Zaire until the end of 1995 when, as with most industry in Bujumbura, the plant was closed temporarily after the sabotage of electricity pylons, which left the capital without electric power for several weeks. However, the Government demonstrated its determination to keep the sector operational and the installations were repaired and placed in the custody of the army; textile production increased by 11% in 1997 and by a further 42% in 1998. A further increase of 15.7% was recorded in 1999, as a result of growing demand from neighbouring Rwanda, in conjunction with the much faster depreciation of the Burundian franc. However, the decrease of domestic cotton production forced the main company, COTEBU, to rely mainly on imports. In October 1999 it signed a contract for the import of 1,000 metric tons of cotton from Malawi. One sign of recovery was the company's rapidly increasing turnover, from 2,469m. Burundian francs in 1997 to 5,516m. Burundian francs in 1999. Otherwise, except for textiles, pharmaceutical products, matches and cigarettes, the output of most industries suffered a further decline in 1999. In early 2002, in an attempt to revive domestic consumption, the Government agreed to the Brarudi brewery's request for a reduction of 10% in the prices of their products. During the first half of 2002 industrial production rose by 2.1%. Except for that of chemicals, activity increased in most sectors. Brarudi's output increased by 5% in volume, and by the end of 2002 Brarudi's consolidated sales of beer and soft drinks had increased by 8.2%, compared with 2001.

Further progress was registered in 2002, with an 8.1% rise in COTEBU's output, a 6.4% increase in the production of cigarettes and a 0.8% rise in soap production. In February 2003 the Société Industrielle Pharmaceutique (SIPHAR) commenced production of generics and antiretroviral medicines at a new plant in Bujumbura. Meanwhile, like Brarudi, COTEBU announced plans to take advantage of Burundi's forthcoming integration into the Common Market for Eastern and Southern Africa (COMESA) free-trade area, by offering more competitive products, with the assistance of the Chinese Government. By contrast, managers from smaller industrial corporations expressed fears about their ability to compete with Kenyan, Ugandan or Egyptian products after the abolition of all tariffs on 1 January 2004.

At the end of 2004 COTEBU's deficit was 1,000m. Burundian francs, and the company's debt amounted to eight times this amount in January 2005. The smuggling of Asian products was partly responsible for this situation and contributed to the problems of the company, which experienced disruption in its imports of inputs (chemical products, fuel and lubricants) and delays in its maintenance programme. However, the commission of 50,000 uniforms by the national police and armed forces in early 2005 raised new expectations among the management. In addition, the People's Republic of China, which had supported the construction of the textile plant, extended a US $2m. loan to enable COTEBU to purchase modern printing equipment. COTEBU's difficulties were partially compensated by a 9.9% increase in the output of the Brarudi beer factory in 2004, which, nevertheless, had to import soft drinks and Amstel beer from its Rwandan holding company, Bralirwa, to meet the rising demand. In 2004 Brarudi achieved a record 10,000m. Burundian francs profit and doubled the value of its exports (1,106m. Burundian francs in 2003), which represented 4.6% of the country's export revenues.

Overall, industry performed reasonably in the mid-2000s. Beer production increased by 20.5%, to 1,220,297 hectolitres in 2006, while soft drinks sales rose by 79.5%. However, cigarette output declined by 2.2%, to 410m. units, and textile production continued to decrease, to 7.2m. units in 2005. Sales of pharmaceutical products decreased by 27.0% that year, while production of construction materials also declined, by 34.3% in 2006.

In January 1996, as a safeguard against electricity shortages or cuts in the future, the Government purchased a US $3.5m. thermal power station, comprising four generators with a total capacity of 5.2 MW. Burundi remained, however, a net importer of electricity, with domestic production of 99.2m. kWh in 2000, compared with a total consumption of 143.8m. kWh. At the end of March 2001 the main power line, which provided 70% of the country's electricity supplies, from both the Ruzizi II and Rwegura hydroelectric power installations, was accidentally damaged in an offensive by government forces against the rebels. In early April rebels also sabotaged the Rwegura power line. As a result, Bujumbura suffered substantial power cuts. Despite this incident, the 2001 production was 114.5m. kWh, 15.3% higher than the previous year. In 2002 Burundi's production of 127.3m. kWh was 10.9% higher than the 2001 levels, while total consumption amounted to 154m. kWh. In 2003, however, while consumption remained equivalent, production dropped by 20.5%, to 101.5m. kWh, owing to insufficient rainfall. In January 2004 the state water and electricity company, Régie de Distribution d'Eau et d'Electricité (REGIDESO), increased its prices by 20% and 25%, respectively. Throughout 2003 customers repeatedly complained about chronic power shortages. The situation deteriorated further in 2004, with a 10% decline in production, to 91.6m. kWh. However, Burundi's capacity to hold a referendum at the end of February 2005 and the prospect of peace negotiations with the Forces nationales de libération (FNL) rebels prompted the EU to proceed rapidly with plans to rehabilitate the country's electricity network. It decided to accelerate the disbursement of funds that it had pledged to finance the country's Rehabilitation Programme (Prebu) since 2000, comprising €9.3m. for the rehabilitation of the REGIDESO electricity infrastructure, the repair of hydroelectric power stations and the improvement of transport and distribution lines, which had suffered much damage during the conflict since its beginning in late 1993. The impact of the embargo imposed by neighbouring states from July 1996 to early 1999, the scarcity of foreign exchange and the reduction of foreign aid, had prevented REGIDESO from financing such rehabilitation work. In March 2005 the reconstruction of middle and low tension distribution lines in the northern outskirts of Bujumbura and of Kanyosha, in the south of the capital, began. Further measures included the rehabilitation of 30-kv lines in the provinces. The programme also included the connection of the Kayenzi, Marangara and Buhiga hydroelectric power stations to the national grid. The EU programme involved the rehabilitation of the installations of the Nyemanga hydroelectric power station, which was inaugurated in 1988 and supplies the Bururi, Makamba and Rutana provinces in southern Burundi.

Although Burundi is a net importer of power (essentially from the DRC), the Government signed an interconnection agreement in September 2002, which was to allow REGIDESO to export electricity to the Tanzanian province of Kigoma. However, the most promising opportunity to improve electricity supply was the commitment made in July 2004 by the EU, Belgium and the Netherlands to support the resumption of co-operation projects in the framework of the Economic Community of the Great Lakes Countries (CEPGL), which grouped Burundi, Rwanda and the DRC in the areas of energy, water, telecommunications, agriculture and customs. These projects included the rehabilitation of the Ruzizi I hydroelectric power station and its upgrading from 28.2 MW to 39.6 MW, and the interconnection of the Ruzizi I and Ruzizi II (40 MW) power dams. Ongoing border security issues, however, generated tensions between the DRC and its two neighbouring countries, which prevented further meetings from taking place during 2004. Nevertheless, at the end of March 2005 the DRC expressed new interest in reviving co-operation within the CEPGL framework. The International Development Association (IDA) was contributing towards financing a long-term programme to develop basic forestry services and promote tree-planting for the supply of wood for fuel, building-poles and timber. Industrial development is hampered by Burundi's distance from the sea (about 1,400 km to Dar es Salaam and 2,000 km to Mombasa), as a result of which only manufactures capable of absorbing the high costs of transport can be developed.

FOREIGN AID AND DEVELOPMENT PLANNING

Burundi is severely dependent on foreign assistance, both for capital projects and for budgetary support. Before early 1996 the main bilateral donors were Belgium, France, Japan and Germany. Multilateral agencies, such as IDA and the European Development Fund (EDF), have been involved in schemes to increase Burundi's production of coffee, and BADEA has also been a substantial source of development loans. Burundi was a considerable beneficiary of aid from the EU through the Lomé Conventions. The main focus of EU development aid has been the rural sector, while STABEX transfers have been of pivotal importance to the coffee, tea and cotton industries. Under the Lomé IV Convention, which operated until 2000, when it was succeeded by the Cotonou Agreement, the EDF allocated ECU 126m. for projects in Burundi during the period 1990–95, of which ECU 112m. was in grants and the balance in venture capital. However, the lack of regional security had prompted many donors (who had already withdrawn aid workers to the capital and even to their own countries) to 'freeze' disbursements and to suspend projects. Although Belgium released the first tranche of a 180m. Belgian franc aid package for primary health care and education projects in December 1998, EU development ministers stated at that time that the full resumption of aid was dependent on the successful conclusion of the peace talks in Arusha, Tanzania. A World Bank mission in November 1998 considered possible reconstruction measures, including increased support for community-based services, employment-generation schemes, protection of social expenditure and agricultural rehabilitation programmes. Burundi joined the Multilateral Investment Guarantee Agency in March 1998. In 1999 the World Bank was financing three projects in Burundi, totalling commitments of US $40m., in the sectors of health, population, social welfare and infrastructure (rural water supplies). The projects were restructured in that year to promote community-level activities. In April 2000 the World Bank approved a $35m. credit to help Burundi stabilize its economy. This emergency project aimed to assist the Government in preparing an environment for economic recovery and restoring essential social services to support peace and reconciliation negotiations. It was also to finance the recovery of the private sector, rehabilitation in health, education and agricultural infrastructure, and to improve economic productivity for conflict-affected private businesses. The World Bank prepared three additional projects in 2001, with a total commitment of $63m., concerning employment generation, transport rehabilitation and a leverage insurance facility for trade as guarantees for foreign investment. In June 2000 an EU rehabilitation programme of €48m. was to finance schools, housing and water-supply projects, to provide credit for small and medium-sized enterprises and communities, and also to support livestock-rearing, and the production and the distribution of seeds to farmers. Of this total, €3m. were allocated to finance the creation of jobs for demobilized combatants.

In December 2000, following the signature of the Arusha peace agreement on 28 August of that year, participants in an International Donors Conference, held in Paris, France, pledged US $440m. towards urgent humanitarian assistance, economic reconstruction and longer-term development needs. Donors pledged to increase their assistance in 2002 and thereafter, if the peace and reconciliation process continued to show progress, and if the country established a strong programme of economic reforms. Some donors also expressed their willingness to participate in a Trust Fund co-ordinated by the World Bank to provide debt-servicing relief until Burundi, which was eligible for assistance under the enhanced initiative for heavily indebted poor countries (HIPC), received such assistance. The HIPC initiative required the conception and implementation of a Poverty Reduction Strategy Paper, and the establishment of a record of good economic policy under IMF guidance. At the Paris meeting, Belgium pledged 1,000m. Belgian francs to finance humanitarian and rehabilitation projects in the health, agriculture and justice sectors and in February 2001 announced that it would provide FAO and Médecins sans frontières with 85m. Belgian francs to enable the distribution of seeds and medicine. An additional amount of 23m. Belgian francs would be channelled through UNICEF to finance an anti-malaria programme.

In December 2001 the World Bank and the main donors pledged US $764m. of loans and grants to alleviate Burundi's debt burden and finance programmes to combat the HIV/AIDS epidemic in the country. In April 2002 the Government welcomed support from Belgium and the United Kingdom, which each pledged several million dollars to the Trust Fund established by the World Bank to finance the reimbursement of the cost of debt-servicing. Total funding requirements for the 2001 UN Consolidated Inter-Agency Appeal for Burundi amounted to $101.9m., of which $40.6m. was allocated to food aid, $22.2m. to economic recovery and infrastructure, $10.3m. to multi-sectoral assistance, $8.3m. to health, $6.7m. to agriculture, $5.2m. to the protection of human rights and the promotion of the rule of law, $4.9m. to education, and $2m. to water and sanitation. In early March 2002 the World Bank approved a $187m. loan for the Transitional Support Strategy for Burundi for 2002–03. The proposed lending programme was to be divided between the two years, with $102m. for 2002. Of this amount, $54m. was to be allocated for economic rehabilitation, $12m. for the third phase of the national health and population project, and $36m. to support the AIDS and orphans project. Both loans were approved during the first half of 2003, following the August 2002 20% devaluation of the Burundian franc (a measure that was commended by the Bretton Woods institutions). Of the $85m. for 2003, $40m. was designated for an emergency road rehabilitation project, $10m. for the third phase of Burundi's social action project (Bursap), $15m. for a multi-sector capacity building project and the remaining $20m. for a demobilization and reintegration programme. Funding requirements for the 2003 UN Consolidated Inter-Agency Appeal for Burundi amounted to $70m.

The 2001 budget was revised in August of that year to increase revenue from 123,500m. Burundian francs to 130,200m. Burundian francs, while expenditure was reduced from 138,600m. Burundian francs to 130,500m. Burundian francs. In the event, however, according to the IMF, revenue and grants amounted to an estimated 119,300m. Burundian francs in 2001, while expenditure (including net lending) totalled 147,700m. Burundian francs. In October 2002 the Minister of Good Governance and Privatization emphasized the poor management of Burundi's embassies abroad, of the petroleum sector, and of the tax and customs departments of the administration. In 2002 the national budget was revised, with total expenditure amounting to 169,500m. Burundian francs, exceeding the preliminary budget figures by 5.2%.

Burundi's Structural Adjustment Programme, which had been agreed with the IMF in 1986, was interrupted by political and civil instability and was terminated in June 1995. Despite the introduction of adjustments, including a new labour code, a new banking law and central bank statutes, the promotion of exports, a duty drawback scheme and transport subsidies for exports, the Government failed to reduce the role of the state in the economy and to redirect public resources to support development or improve the efficiency, transparency and accountability of public-sector management. Military expenditure and subsidies for inefficient parastatals remained high and, in the view of the Bretton Woods institutions, adequate state divestment was not achieved. During 1985–95 military expenditure increased from 3.0% to 4.4% of GDP, and from 20.8% to 24.8% of the budget, while the size of the armed forces rose from some 9,000 to 22,000. In early 2000 a report submitted by the Ministry of Finance revealed that embezzlement and fraud at the expense of the Burundian parastatals amounted to 10,860m. Burundian francs. In January 2001 a legislative inquiry estimated the loss at more than 12,000m. Burundian francs. The OCIBU parastatal alone was owed some 2,188m. Burundian francs by three exporters, while the customs department was claiming a debt of 2,177m. Burundian francs from a private petroleum distribution company. In late December 2003 the independent Observatoire de Lutte contre la Corruption et les Malversations Economiques revealed that embezzlement committed between 1993 and 2003 represented a loss of 39,000m. Burundian francs for the state.

The successful implementation of plans to privatize one-half of all public enterprises and establish private management contracts for the remainder by the end of 1995 proved unattainable, given the unrest in the country, and by mid-1996 54 enterprises remained under state ownership and management. In 1998 the telecommunications sector was liberalized. (By February 2000 three operators were competing for the mobile cellular telephone market.) However, the process of privatizing the Office National des Télécommunications (ONATEL) proved protracted. The Government planned to retain a 35% share in the company, while the remaining 14% was to be distributed among ONATEL's employees. REGIDESO was also designated for transfer to the private sector. In July 2001 ONATEL commissioned a telecommunications centre with a total capacity of 50,000 lines, at a cost of US $40m. In November of that year ONATEL and the private mobile cellular telephone operator, Téléphonie Cellulaire du Burundi (TELECEL), agreed to interconnect their respective networks. In April 2003 the Multilateral Investment Guarantee Agency announced that it would provide $1m. for a cellular telecommunications project aimed at addressing the country's acute shortage of telephone services. The project was to involve the creation, operation and maintenance of a nation-wide mobile telephone network by Mauritius Telecom. In November ONATEL contracted two Chinese companies to build a 14,000m. Burundian francs centre of operations, enabling the parastatal to become an operator on the cellular telephone market. In 2004 ONATEL became an internet service provider. This new competition created problems for the mobile telephone market leader, TELECEL, and for the two other smaller operators, AFRICEL and SPACETEL. In addition, TELECEL entered into a dispute with the tax authorities, which claimed that the company had failed to declare 1,000m. Burundian francs of its 2002 revenue.

By April 2000 the financial crisis in the country was such that currency reserves were the equivalent of only two months of imports. Foreign-exchange reserves had already dwindled from US $200m. at the end of 1995 to $43.2m. at the end of February 1999. Burundi's external debt totalled $1,108m. at the end of 2000, and by the end of 2004 had increased to $1,385m., of which $1,325m. was long-term public debt. Debt-servicing in 2003 was equivalent to 66.0% of the value of exports of goods and services.

In October 2002 the IMF approved a credit of US $13m. in emergency post-conflict aid to support the Burundi Government's reconstruction and economic recovery programme. Under the programme, the central bank was to improve its capacity to monitor and control bank liquidity, and to develop more flexible monetary policy instruments. Rapid progress in the implementation of the programme would facilitate the delivery of external aid and provide for a medium-term programme that could be supported by the IMF, under a PRGF and HIPC initiative. An equivalent amount was disbursed by the IMF in May 2003. At the same time the World Bank also extended an SDR 15.1m. economic recovery loan and, through IDA, subsidized up to $14.2m. of the cost of constructing schools and primary health-care centres and of improving the water supply in the Makamba, Ruyigi and Rutana provinces. In March 2003 the EU contributed funds of €22.6m. to support Burundi's macroeconomic reforms and an additional €1.23m. to finance the African Union peace-keeping mission for six months. In November 2002 France committed €2m. for the supply of medicines, for the University of Burundi and for the reimbursement of the arrears owed by the Government to REGIDESO.

In mid-January 2004, at a conference organized by Belgium and UNDP, donors pledged US $1,032m. This amount was supposed to finance the budget of the following three years and also provide balance-of-payments support (about $440m.), assistance for displaced persons, returnees, and refugees and a demobilization and rehabilitation programme for the military ($500m.). The remaining funds were allocated for the organization of the forthcoming elections and good governance programmes. In late November 2003 Burundi had embarked on two major reforms. The Assemblé nationale adopted new legislation for the establishment of an independent Court of Auditors and the Ministry of Finance announced the reorganization of the public procurement procedures. The signature on 16 November 2003 of a cease-fire between the Government and the main rebel group contributed to create a favourable climate for such commitments. The principal donor was the EU, with a total of $279m., which included a $172m. package under the ninth EDF aimed at financing rural development and agricultural projects, institutional support, good governance projects, and macroeconomic support. The other donors were the World Bank ($140m.), the USA ($135m.), the IMF ($93m.), the United Kingdom ($50m.), Germany ($46.2m.), Belgium ($46.2) and France ($25.5m.). These funds were supposed to contribute to offset the budget deficit for 2004, which was estimated at 59,505m. Burundian francs (26.4% of total expenditure), despite a 14.4% increase in receipts, to 167,073m. Burundian francs. In January 2004 the IMF extended a $102m. loan to Burundi within the framework of the PRGF, which was intended to cover partially the estimated $200m. external financing deficit under the 2004 programme, and to help reschedule the external debt arrears. The IMF considered that the staff-monitored programme, initiated in the second half of 2001, with the aim of stabilizing the macroeconomic situation, facilitating the mobilization of external assistance, and providing the basis for growth and poverty reduction, had generally made satisfactory progress in 2003, with budget execution meeting projections. In its assessment, the IMF noted that Burundi's net international reserves were at comfortable levels, equivalent to the value of 3.5 months of imports at the end of September 2003. The IMF expressed the hope that implementation of the authorities' programme would provide conditions for a strong resumption of economic growth in 2004, allowing Burundi to qualify for much-needed debt relief under the enhanced HIPC initiative.

By mid-2005 external debt had reached the unsustainable level of US $1,351m., according to the Bretton Woods institutions. The donors' broad analysis was that sustainable economic development in Burundi depended on the permanent end of the conflict and on the scope and success of economic reforms designed to attract investments, develop the domestic market and modernize agriculture, privatize the coffee sector and the parastatals, establish a reliable legal framework, create new loan facilities for domestic and foreign investors and develop industry and services. In March 2005 an IMF delegation welcomed Burundi's efforts to qualify for the HIPC initiative, but considered that the year-on-year growth rate was below expectations and the rate of inflation too high, and urged the adoption of more reforms. Nevertheless, the IMF expressed confidence that Burundi would soon become eligible to benefit from debt relief under the HIPC initiative. During 2005 donors were to fund a 12% budget deficit, which was largely a result of the cost of national reconciliation. Indeed, defence expenditure, at a total of 72,000m. Burundian francs, absorbed 22% of the 2005 total budgeted expenditure of 326,000m. Burundian francs (a 33% increase compared with the 2004 budget). This amount was supposed to meet the cost of the integration of former rebel combatants into the national army and the national police. The cost of debt-servicing alone amounted to 32,000m. Burundian francs, while education, agriculture and health represented 91,000m. Burundian francs. However, the Ministry of Finance was confident that, with the decline in hostilities in the country, donors would contribute to 25% of the 2005 budget, with $82m. (compared to $35m. in 2004).

The improvement in security conditions and the prospect of a permanent peace settlement prompted the European Commission to pledge an additional €100m. in December 2004 to finance poverty eradication and peace process consolidation projects, ranging from road projects to the financing of the electoral process. This amount included a €7.6m. allocation to reduce Burundi's arrears on the debt owed to the multilateral institutions and a €19.5m. grant to reimburse the debt owed to the European Investment Bank. In addition, the European Commission decided to increase Burundi's National Indicative Programme for 2002–07 by €10m., to €182m., in order to contribute to the socio-economic reintegration of refugees and internally displaced persons, and to support the democratization process and the reform of the security sector. Other contributions for the 2004–07 period included a US $10m. loan and a $2.3m. grant from the African Development Fund in support of Burundi's Programme of Support to Economic Reform and Good Governance. The ADB resumed its co-operation with Burundi in September 2004, after five years of suspension owing to government default on arrears, and extended a $3m. loan in order to the strengthen the capacities of the administration. In order to maximize tax collection, the World Bank approved a $26m. loan to Burundi's Ministry of Finance in February 2005.

In August 2005 the IMF and IDA issued a joint statement agreeing that Burundi had taken the measures necessary to qualify for interim debt relief under the enhanced HIPC initiative. This decision enabled Burundi to reduce its average debt-servicing payments by 80%; the Government announced that savings, which were equivalent to 35% of the national budget, were to be used to improve the living standards of the population. In November the ADB also declared Burundi to be eligible for external debt assistance. The IMF urged the authorities to seek debt relief from non-'Paris Club' creditors that had not provided relief under the enhanced HIPC initiative on terms comparable to those obtained from 'Paris Club' creditors. A donor conference, organized by the Government in February 2006 to appeal for emergency assistance, resulted in pledges totalling US $85m., far below the target amount of $168m.; the funds were designated principally for famine relief and rehabilitation of the education sector. In August 2006 IDA granted $60m. to Burundian authorities to aid economic reform initiatives. In early 2007 the World Bank released a further $150m. to support social and economic projects over the next three years, while two agreements were signed with Germany to provide 23,000m. Burundian francs; over two-thirds of that amount has been set aside for water purification projects, with the remainder to be spent on reintegration of returning refugees. Belgium, meanwhile, had already granted €10m. in late 2006 for education, rural water projects and road works. Donor nations are, however, wary of how their money is spent. Thus, in June 2007 a conference was held in Bujumbura and attended by major donors, namely Belgium, France, the Netherlands and the World Bank. Burundian authorities pledged their commitment to transparency, promising to spend the aid responsibly.

Fiscal performance in 2005 was considered to be satisfactory: revenue of 172,100m. Burundian francs (equivalent to 20% of GDP) was much higher than the target of that year's programme, while current expenditure was consistent with projections and domestically financed project spending considerably lower than targeted. On a commitment basis, the overall deficit, after grants, but with a delay in programme grants, was 6.2% of GDP, compared with a target of 0.2% of GDP. The 2006 budget estimated revenue of 178,400m. Burundian francs (equivalent to 19.1% of GDP), with expenditure of 379,300m. Burundian francs. On a commitment basis, the overall deficit, after grants, was just 2.2% of GDP. The IMF envisaged a budget in 2007 with revenues of 185,200m. Burundian francs (equivalent to 19.7% of GDP) and expenditure of 436,800m. Burundian francs, leaving an overall deficit, after grants, on a commitment basis, of just 6,900m. Burundian francs (equivalent to 0.7% of GDP).

FOREIGN TRADE

Burundi's total export earnings amounted to US $80.7m. in 1994 and rose to $112.9m. in 1995 (owing to improved international coffee prices). In 1996, as a result of the trade embargo, total export earnings decreased to $40.4m., although in 1997, owing to improved international coffee prices and the partial suspension of the embargo, earnings increased to $87.5m. Total export earnings subsequently declined steadily, to $31.0m. in 2002, but increased to about $37.5m. in 2003. According to the Banque de la République du Burundi, export earnings reached 52,688.6m. Burundian francs in 2004, 61,488.3m. Burundian francs in 2005 and 60,359.4m. Burundian francs in 2006. The principal exports are traditionally coffee, tea, sugar, beer and minerals, which had become a significant export product by 2001, accounting for around 5% of all export earnings. In 1999 the Government established an exports promotion fund of 1,000m. Burundian francs to assist in the marketing efforts of exporting companies. Meanwhile, the cost of imports, totalling $172.6m. in 1994 and $175.6m. in 1995, fell to $100.0m. in 1996, as a result of the embargo, decreasing further to $96.1m. in 1997. The cost of imports declined from $123.5m. in 1998 to $104.8m. in 2002, before rising to $130.0m. in 2003 and to an estimated $142.8m. in 2004. According to the Banque de la République du Burundi, the cost of imports has increased in recent years, from 193,605.2m. Burundian francs in 2004, to 289,123.9m. Burundian francs in 2005 and to 442,511.1m. Burundian francs in 2006. The principal imports are chemical products, gas oil, motor cars, motor petroleum, trucks and mechanical devices and parts. In 2000 Tanzania recovered its status as a principal supplier of Burundi; however, in early 2001 the Burundian Government considered no longer using the Dar es Salaam port as its main transit point for import, owing to the Tanzanian Government's failure to conclude a bilateral tariff arrangement with Burundi. As an alternative, the Burundian Government envisaged the transportation of most of its foreign trade through the Kenyan port of Mombasa and the Zambian port of Mpulungu on Lake Tanganyika, despite attacks carried out by rebels on Burundian cargo ships on the lake. Nevertheless, in 2003 the volume of imports transported through Dar es Salaam increased by more than 50%, although Tanzania was overtaken as the main supplier of Burundi by Belgium. The EU countries (in particular Belgium, France and Germany), together with the USA, Tanzania, Kenya and Japan, are Burundi's main trading partners. South Africa, which trebled its exports to Burundi between 1997 and 2003, has also become an increasingly significant trade partner. In 2006 Burundi again recorded a substantial trade deficit, with total imports amounting to more than seven times the value of total exports ($60,359m. Burundian francs). In that year the principal supplier was Saudi Arabia (12.6% of total imports), followed by Belgium-Luxembourg (11.7%), Kenya (8.2%) and Japan (7.8%). Soaring oil prices and massive external funding, which allowed the country to purchase food and other humanitarian-related products, were the main causes of the considerable deficit.

The credibility of a free export zone, established in 1992, was seriously undermined in August 1993, when the new administration withdrew the financial advantages being offered to Affimet, a Belgian gold dealer and refiner, under the scheme, having calculated that the company's use of the zone was depriving the state of US $12m. per year in taxes. In 1994, however, these advantages were once again extended to the company. An estimated 9.6 metric tons of gold were exported from Burundi in that year. Almost 80% of this total was believed to have originated in Zaire, with the remainder proceeding from Tanzania and Uganda, and only an insignificant share mined locally. Import statistics from the Belgian office of foreign trade indicated that in 1992 Burundi exported precious stones and metals valued at 1,100m. Belgian francs to Belgium. In 1993 the value of these exports increased to 1,500m. Belgian francs, declining to 784m. Belgian francs (about $23m.) in 1994. However, despite official claims that such transactions involve 'goods in transit', the failure of official export statistics in Burundi to reflect the importance of the trade in gold has prompted concern as to the accuracy of official export figures in general. As a result of the embargo, the trade in gold fell considerably from the end of July 1996. This prompted Affimet to consider other locations for a gold-refining plant, in Rwanda or the DRC. In January 1999, however, the Government signed an agreement allowing Affimet to purchase, process and export all precious and semi-precious minerals from Burundi. In February the International Centre for Settlement of Investment Disputes eventually ruled that the Burundian Government reimburse $3m. to Affimet. This amount represented a deposit by Affimet corresponding to taxes and royalties, which the Belgian company should not have paid, according to the initial free export zone agreement. After the authorities failed to reimburse this amount by the deadline of 1 April, Affimet decided to seize Burundi's bank assets in Belgium by the end of that year. The measure initially included not only accounts of the Burundian state, but also those of the central bank of Burundi in Belgium. Lawyers for the central bank succeeded in ending the measure in March 2000. Meanwhile, the Burundian Ministry of Commerce ordered the closure of Affimet, together with an 'offshore' bank and an airline owned by the same Belgian gold trader in Burundi. The dispute obstructed attempts by the Burundian Government to attract other foreign companies to develop a free export zone in the country. It was finally resolved in February 2002, with an agreement between the Burundian central bank and the Belgian Belgolaise Bank to reimburse the $3.3m. of debt (including arrears) owed to Affimet. In August 2002 the Government amended the 1992 legislation establishing the free export zone, henceforth excluding minerals, together with coffee, tea, sugar and palm oil, and restricting the benefit of the tax exonerations attached to this status to companies that market or process non-traditional exports, such as fruits, vegetables and flowers.

In 1985 Burundi became a full member of the Preferential Trade Area for Eastern and Southern African States (superseded in 1993 by COMESA). Burundi was integrated into COMESA's free-trade area in January 2004. Meanwhile, a special compensation fund was to assist the economy in adapting to the consequences of the forthcoming ending of the tariff system. While Burundian businesses claimed that strong support was required to increase their competitiveness, the Government insisted that compensation was necessary to balance the projected losses in its customs revenue. A report from the Bujumbura-based Institut du Développement Économique emphasized that on average Burundian industries worked at 20% of their capacity, and that many would have to merge in order to be able to face regional competition on the domestic and export markets. In April 2003 the authorities announced measures to assist the textile sector in addressing the consequences of the dismantling of tariffs within COMESA. On 1 January 2004 Burundi began to implement a zero tariff on all imports from other COMESA member states, to the concern of the local private sector, which claimed that the Burundian companies were less advanced in many aspects, particularly in terms of equipment and of technology, but also in marketing expertise. In September 2003 Burundi submitted a formal request to become eligible for the US African Growth and Opportunity Act initiative, which was designed to promote bilateral trade and improved market access to sub-Saharan African countries. In February 2004 the Government announced its intention to introduce a new investment code, including incentives to attract foreign capital, despite obstacles such as the land-locked situation of the country, the small size of its market and the continuing political crisis. The new code was expected particularly to encourage initiatives in the transport sector. Burundi is also a full member of the Communauté économique des états d'Afrique centrale. In 2000 Burundi applied to join the East African Community and in December 2006 Burundi, together with Rwanda, was admitted to that organization.

TRANSPORT

The network of roads is dense, but few of the 12,322 km of routes are paved, and these are the roads that connect Bujumbura with Gitega, Kayanza and Nyanza-Lac. In 1992 the Government revealed that 600 km of roads had been rehabilitated during the previous three years, and announced a four-year programme of future road improvements, covering a further 1,000 km. A new crossing of the Ruzizi river, the Bridge of Concord (Burundi's longest bridge), was inaugurated in early 1992. However, recent improvements to Tanzania's road network, the reopening in 1994 of the Rwanda–Uganda border (facilitating road access to Mombasa) and competition between Burundian private road transport concerns and Tanzanian railways for the movement of goods from Burundi have all contributed to a reduction in transportation costs. In 2001 the World Bank allocated US $40m. to finance the rehabilitation of the road linking Bujumbura and the Tanzanian border town of Mugina, the maintenance of the Rugombo–Kayanza road in the north-west and the construction of the Nyakararo–Mwaro–Gitega road in the centre of the country. The reform of the National Road Fund was a condition attached by the World Bank for the disbursement of these funds. The EDF announced plans for the construction of roads linking Gitega and Muyinga, Muyinga and Cankuzo, and Cankuzo and Ruyigi. BADEA also announced in 2001 that it would fund feasibility studies for the construction of the Makamba–Bururi road in the southern part of the country and of the Rumonge–Bururi–Gitega road, between Lake Tanganyika and the centre of the country. In December 2004 the European Commission announced that it would finance the rehabilitation of the Gitega–Karusi–Muyinga road by up to €24m. and the roads in Bujumbura up to €15.5m.

Lake Tanganyika (of which Burundi has about 8% sovereignty) is a crucial component in Burundi's transport system, since most of the country's external trade is conducted along the lake between Bujumbura and Tanzania and the DRC. This trade became more difficult in 1996, owing to the embargo and also to guerrilla attacks on shipping. Traffic at the port of Bujumbura decreased from 211,900 metric tons in 1995 to 99,000 tons in 1997. However, traffic at the port increased to 151,200 tons in 1998, and to 170,700 tons in 1999, as a result of measures taken by the Government to curb guerrilla activity on the lake, combined with efforts to find an alternative trade route through Zambia to the port of Durban, South Africa. The Burundian authorities aimed to reduce traffic on the Tanzanian route to the port of Dar es Salaam, owing to the inability of both the Tanzanian and Burundian Governments to conclude a tariffs agreement for the goods in transit. By the end of November 2000 traffic had reached 179,000 tons, representing an increase of 7.1%, compared with 1999, and a further increase, to 198,500 tons, was recorded in 2000. In 2001, however, traffic decreased to 175,320 tons, owing to lower coffee exports through the port and lower imports. The traffic remained unchanged in 2002, but decreased by 10.9% on the previous year, to only 182,600 tons in 2006. However, owing mainly to the collapse of coffee exports, the volume of traffic dropped by 12.2% during the first 10 months of 2004. In 2005 the Burundian authorities expressed concern that the falling water levels of Lake Tanganyika (resulting from deforestation and climate change) had severely affected activities at the port of Bujumbura, making large amounts of dock space unusable.

Plans to construct a railway linking Burundi with Uganda, Rwanda and Tanzania were announced in 1987. The proposed line would connect with the Kigoma–Dar es Salaam line in Tanzania, substantially improving Burundi's isolated trade position. However, the civil unrest in Burundi has since caused these plans to be postponed. There is an international airport at Bujumbura. In 1999 passenger traffic reached 53,082 (the highest level since 1995). However, this record was exceeded in both 2000 and 2001, when passenger traffic totalled 58,402 and 72,112, respectively. Passenger traffic continued to increase, reaching 82,942 in 2002 and 86,353 in 2003. Freight traffic increased from 3,571 metric tons in 1996 to 25,891 tons in 1997. However, freight traffic fell to 10,830 tons in 1998, and to 3,626 tons in 1999, largely owing to the resumption of traffic at the port of Bujumbura and on Lake Tanganyika. Freight traffic continued to decline, to 2,240 tons, in 2003. During the first three-quarters of 2004, however, a spectacular increase in traffic was recorded: the number of passengers rose by 32.3%, from 63,634 to 84,223, while freight increased by 46%, from 1,657 tons to 2,420 tons. Following the suspension of sanctions in January 1999, several regional airlines resumed flights to Burundi. In September 2004 Rwandair Express inaugurated its first flight between Kigali and Bujumbura, under the conditions of a memorandum of understanding with Air Burundi, and commenced direct flights from Bujumbura to South Africa, Kenya, Uganda and Europe.

Statistical Survey

Area and Population

AREA, POPULATION AND DENSITY

Area (sq km)	27,834*
Population (census results)†	
15–16 August 1979	4,028,420
16–30 August 1990	
Males	2,473,599
Females	2,665,474
Total	5,139,073
Population (UN estimates at mid-year)‡	
2004	7,566,000
2005	7,859,000
2006	8,173,000
Density (per sq km) at mid-2006	293.6

* 10,747 sq miles.
† Excluding adjustment for underenumeration.
‡ Source: UN, *World Population Prospects: The 2006 Revision*.

Principal Towns: Bujumbura (capital), population 235,440 (census result, August 1990). *1978:* Gitega 15,943 (Source: Banque de la République du Burundi). *Mid-2005* (urban population, incl. suburbs, UN estimate): Bujumbura 447,000 (Source: UN, *World Urbanization Prospects: The 2005 Revision*).

BIRTHS AND DEATHS

(UN estimates, annual averages)

	1990–95	1995–2000	2000–05
Birth rate (per 1,000)	46.5	43.8	44.2
Death rate (per 1,000)	19.7	18.2	16.7

Source: UN, *World Population Prospects: The 2006 Revision*.

Expectation of life (years at birth, WHO estimates): 45 (males 42; females 47) in 2004 (Source: WHO, *World Health Report*).

ECONOMICALLY ACTIVE POPULATION*

(persons aged 10 years and over, 1990 census)

	Males	Females	Total
Agriculture, hunting, forestry and fishing	1,153,890	1,420,553	2,574,443
Mining and quarrying	1,146	39	1,185
Manufacturing	24,120	9,747	33,867
Electricity, gas and water	1,847	74	1,921
Construction	19,447	290	19,737
Trade, restaurants and hotels	19,667	6,155	25,822
Transport, storage and communications	8,193	311	8,504
Financing, insurance, real estate and business services	1,387	618	2,005
Community, social and personal services	68,905	16,286	85,191
Activities not adequately defined	8,653	4,617	13,270
Total labour force	1,307,255	1,458,690	2,765,945

* Figures exclude persons seeking work for the first time, totalling 13,832 (males 9,608, females 4,224), but include other unemployed persons.

Source: UN, *Demographic Yearbook*.

Mid-2004 (estimates in '000): Agriculture, etc. 3,355; Total labour force 3,739 (Source: FAO).

Health and Welfare

KEY INDICATORS

Total fertility rate (children per woman, 2005)	6.8
Under-5 mortality rate (per 1,000 live births, 2004)	190
HIV/AIDS (% of persons aged 15–49, 2005)	3.3
Physicians (per 1,000 head, 2004)	0.03
Hospital beds (per 1,000 head, 2006)	0.70
Health expenditure (2004): US $ per head (PPP)	16.2
Health expenditure (2004): % of GDP	3.2
Health expenditure (2004): public (% of total)	26.2
Access to water (% of persons, 2004)	79
Access to sanitation (% of persons, 2004)	36
Human Development Index (2004): ranking	169
Human Development Index (2004): value	0.384

For sources and definitions, see explanatory note on p. vi.

Agriculture

PRINCIPAL CROPS

('000 metric tons)

	2003	2004	2005
Wheat*	8.7	7.5	7.5
Rice (paddy)	61.3	64.5	67.9
Maize	127.0*	123.2	123.0*
Millet	10.6	10.6	7.8
Sorghum	71.5	74.2	67.8
Potatoes	28.0*	26.1	26.0*
Sweet potatoes	835.0*	834.4	835.0*
Cassava (Manioc)	750.0*	709.6	710.0*
Taro (Coco yam)	85.7*	61.7	62.0*
Yams	10.0*	9.9	10.0*
Sugar cane*	200.0	180.0	180.0
Dry beans	245.0*	220.2	220.0*
Dry peas*	33.5	33.5	33.5
Groundnuts (in shell)*	8.8	8.8	8.8
Oil palm fruit*	13.0	13.0	13.0
Vegetables (incl. melons)*	250.0	250.0	250.0
Bananas and plantains	1,600.0	1,600.0	1,600.0
Other fruits*	85.0	85.0	85.0
Coffee (green)	5.6	36.0	7.8†
Tea (made)	7.4	7.7	7.5†

* FAO estimate(s).
† Unofficial figure.

Source: FAO.

LIVESTOCK

('000 head, year ending September)

	2003	2004	2005
Cattle	355	374	396
Pigs*	70	70	70
Sheep	240	236	243
Goats*	750	750	750
Chickens*	4,300	4,300	4,300

* FAO estimates.

Source: FAO.

LIVESTOCK PRODUCTS
('000 metric tons)

	2003	2004	2005
Cattle meat	5.5	4.7	5.6
Sheep meat*	1.0	1.0	1.0
Goat meat*	2.9	2.9	2.9
Pig meat*	4.2	4.2	4.2
Chicken meat*	6.1	6.1	6.1
Cows' milk	14.8	14.3	16.2
Sheep's milk*	0.7	0.7	0.7
Goats' milk*	8.4	8.4	8.4
Hen eggs*	3.0	3.0	3.0

* FAO estimates.

Source: FAO.

Forestry

ROUNDWOOD REMOVALS
('000 cubic metres, excl. bark, FAO estimates)

	2003	2004	2005
Sawlogs, veneer logs and logs for sleepers	266	266	266
Other industrial wood	67	67	67
Fuel wood	8,241	8,390	8,542
Total	8,574	8,723	8,875

Source: FAO.

SAWNWOOD PRODUCTION
('000 cubic metres, incl. railway sleepers, FAO estimates)

	1998	1999	2000
Coniferous (softwood)	7	17	18
Broadleaved (hardwood)	26	63	65
Total	33	80	83

2001–05: Figures assumed to be unchanged from 2000 (FAO estimates).

Source: FAO.

Fishing

(metric tons, live weight)

	2003	2004	2005*
Capture	14,697	13,855	14,000
Freshwater perches	1,323	4,643	4,000
Dagaas	13,080	8,876	9,600
Aquaculture	200	200	200
Total catch (incl. others)	14,897	14,055	14,200

* FAO estimates.

Source: FAO.

Mining

(metric tons, unless otherwise indicated)

	2003	2004	2005
Tin ore*	5	9	4
Tantalum and niobium (columbium) concentrates†	24.4	23.4	42.6
Gold (kilograms)*	2,855	3,229	3,905
Peat	4,580	4,643	4,700‡

* Figures refer to the metal content of ores.

† The estimated tantalum content (in metric tons) was: 5.8 in 2003; 5.0 in 2004 and 9.2 in 2005.

‡ Estimate.

Source: US Geological Survey.

Industry

SELECTED PRODUCTS
('000 metric tons, unless otherwise indicated)

	2004	2005	2006
Beer ('000 hectolitres)	973.1	1,012.5	1,220.3
Soft drinks ('000 hectolitres)	119.6	143.6	257.7
Cottonseed oil ('000 litres)	157.9	135.9	101.2
Sugar	20.2	19.1	18.1
Cigarettes (million)	376.1	419.1	409.6
Paint	0.5	0.5	0.5
Polyethylene film (metric tons)	122.4	103.9	80.8
Soap (metric tons)	3,235.0	3,130.4	2,956.2
Plastic racks ('000)	233.0	112.0	234.9
Fabrics ('000 metres)	5,544.5	4,811.3	2,865.6
Blankets ('000)	106.8	43.3	n.a.
Fibro-cement products	0.4	0.4	—
Moulds (metric tons)	23.2	18.2	20.9
PVC tubing (metric tons)	91.9	114.9	137.1
Steel tubing (metric tons)	265.9	197.4	59.4
Electric energy (million kWh)	91.6	100.3	93.3

Source: Banque de la République du Burundi.

Finance

CURRENCY AND EXCHANGE RATES

Monetary Units

100 centimes = 1 Burundian franc.

Sterling, Dollar and Euro Equivalents (30 April 2007)

£1 sterling = 2,087.667 francs;
US $1 = 1,046.660 francs;
€1 = 1,423.981 francs;
10,000 Burundian francs = £4.79 = $9.55 = €7.02.

Average Exchange Rate (Burundian francs per US dollar)

2004 1,100.910
2005 1,081.580
2006 1,028.430

GOVERNMENT FINANCE

(central government operations, '000 million Burundian francs)

Summary of balances	2005	2006*	2007†
Revenue	172.1	178.4	203.0
Less Expenditure and net lending	316.7	379.3	436.8
Overall balance (commitment basis)	−144.6	−200.9	−233.8
Change in arrears	−10.8	−23.2	−4.3
External (interest)	−10.7	−1.8	—
Domestic	−0.1	−21.4	−4.3
Overall balance (cash basis)	−155.1	−224.1	−238.1
Grants	90.6	180.7	245.0
Overall balance after grants	−64.5	−43.4	6.9

Revenue	2005	2006*	2007†
Tax revenue	158.9	162.2	185.2
Income tax	41.8	43.8	48.1
Taxes on goods and services	78.3	82.9	97.2
Taxes on international trade	38.4	33.2	37.4
Non-tax revenue	13.2	16.1	17.8
Total	172.1	178.4	203.0

Expenditure and net lending	2005	2006*	2007†
Current expenditure	200.6	226.9	268.2
Compensation of employees	72.6	96.6	121.7
Civilian	41.9	58.5	74.9
Military	24.0	23.0	27.1
New police force	6.7	15.1	19.7
Goods and services	65.7	62.2	71.3
Civilian	26.7	27.1	35.5
Military	29.6	23.0	23.0
New police force	9.5	12.1	12.8
Transfers and subsidies	30.3	40.6	46.5
Interest payments	32.0	27.5	28.7
DDR project‡	8.7	35.0	33.0
Elections	24.5	—	—
Project expenditure	84.1	119.4	137.6
Net lending	−1.4	−2.0	−2.0
Total	316.4	379.3	436.8

* Estimates.

† Budget forecast.

‡ Demobilization, disarmament and reintegration.

Source: IMF, *Burundi: Fifth Review Under the Arrangement Under the Poverty Reduction and Growth Facility and Request for Waiver of a Performance Criterion - Staff Report; Press Release on the Executive Board Discussion; and Statement by the Executive Director for Burundi* (March 2007).

INTERNATIONAL RESERVES

(US $ million at 31 December)

	2004	2005	2006
Gold*	0.42	0.49	0.61
IMF special drawing rights	0.35	0.27	0.33
Reserve position in IMF	0.56	0.51	0.54
Foreign exchange	64.84	99.30	129.66
Total	66.17	100.57	131.14

* Valued at market-related prices.

Source: IMF, *International Financial Statistics*.

MONEY SUPPLY

(million Burundian francs at 31 December)

	2004	2005	2006
Currency outside banks	57,153	67,856	68,437
Deposits at central bank	1,218	1,348	1,225
Demand deposits at commercial banks	91,079	104,871	145,068
Demand deposits at other monetary institutions	1,910	3,192	3,416
Total money	151,360	177,267	218,145

Source: IMF, *International Financial Statistics*.

COST OF LIVING

(Consumer Price Index for Bujumbura; base: January 1991 = 100)

	2003	2004	2005
Food	415.1	446.8	546.7
Clothing	449.9	547.3	576.6
Housing, heating and light	462.4	472.3	563.4
Transport	473.2	471.5	565.9
All items (incl. others)	427.3	452.8	539.9

Source: IMF, *Burundi: Selected Issues and Statistical Annex* (August 2006).

NATIONAL ACCOUNTS

Expenditure on the Gross Domestic Product

(million Burundian francs at current prices)

	2004	2005	2006
Government final consumption expenditure	163,470	204,900	290,000
Private final consumption expenditure	638,547	759,900	803,200
Gross fixed capital formation	84,139	133,800	245,400
Changes in inventories	176	—	—
Total domestic expenditure	886,332	1,098,600	1,338,600
Exports of goods and services	60,201	76,100	121,500
Less Imports of goods and services	198,047	312,600	473,500
GDP in purchasers' values	748,486	862,100	986,600

Source: IMF, *International Financial Statistics*.

Gross Domestic Product by Economic Activity

('000 million Burundian francs at current prices, estimates)

	2003	2004	2005
Agriculture, hunting, forestry and fishing	232.5	264.0	271.1
Mining and quarrying / Electricity, gas and water	6.6	7.4	9.1
Manufacturing*	75.2	85.5	104.9
Construction	28.0	31.8	41.7
Trade, restaurants and hotels	30.7	34.8	44.7
Transport, storage and communications	32.2	36.6	46.9
Other services	174.9	198.7	256.0
GDP at factor cost	580.1	658.8	774.4
Indirect taxes, *less* subsidies	64.1	72.8	86.4
GDP in purchasers' values	644.2	731.5	860.8

* Including handicrafts ('000 million Burundian francs): 26.0 in 2003; 29.6 in 2004; 36.2 in 2005.

Source: IMF, *Burundi: Selected Issues and Statistical Appendix* (August 2006).

BALANCE OF PAYMENTS
(US $ million)

	2005	2006*	2007†
Exports of goods f.o.b.	57.2	60.8	70.0
Imports of goods f.o.b.	–239.0	–285.9	–335.2
Trade balance	–181.8	–225.1	–265.2
Services (net)	–89.5	–107.6	–110.9
Balance on goods and services	–271.3	–332.7	–376.1
Other income (net)	–19.3	–20.7	–20.1
Balance on goods, services and income	–290.7	–353.4	–396.2
Current transfers (net)	207.6	229.6	236.3
Current balance	–83.1	–123.8	–159.9
Capital account (net)	26.2	75.7	118.8
Direct investment	15.0	8.0	15.0
Official loans (net)	37.7	–1.0	–11.1
Other investment	13.9	25.8	35.0
Net errors and omissions	12.5	—	—
Overall balance	22.2	–15.3	–2.2

* Estimates.
† Projections.

Source: IMF, *Burundi: Fifth Review Under the Arrangement Under the Poverty Reduction and Growth Facility and Request for Waiver of a Performance Criterion - Staff Report; Press Release on the Executive Board Discussion; and Statement by the Executive Director for Burundi* (March 2007).

External Trade

PRINCIPAL COMMODITIES
(million Burundian francs)

Imports c.i.f.	2004	2005	2006
Portland cement	11,296.0	14,529.7	15,418.7
Motor spirit (gasoline)	10,017.4	13,075.3	23,631.1
Gas oils	11,664.6	15,083.6	26,002.0
Chemical products	17,851.5	18,193.0	28,769.3
Iron and steel and castings thereof	8,056.8	10,720.3	12,890.2
Products in castings of iron and steel	3,032.4	9,430.3	5,910.1
Mechanical devices and spare parts	11,787.7	32,210.7	18,712.7
Other electrical apparatus	5,302.8	18,836.1	17,505.9
Motor cars	8,564.2	8,667.4	25,565.8
Trucks	5,324.1	8,083.3	20,224.3
Total (incl. others)	193,605.2	289,123.9	442,511.1

Exports f.o.b.	2004	2005	2006
Coffee	32,341.6	43,586.6	40,838.3
Tea	11,245.8	9,564.8	10,238.4
Sugar	3,272.3	969.7	466.0
Beer	2,067.3	1,432.8	603.6
Minerals	543.2	1,026.5	2,959.7
Other articles (excl. personal items)	646.5	2,421.6	690.8
Total (incl. others)	52,688.6	61,488.3	60,359.4

Source: Banque de la République du Burundi.

PRINCIPAL TRADING PARTNERS

Imports c.i.f. (million Burundian francs)	2004	2005	2006
Belgium-Luxembourg	26,359.0	35,451.4	51,820.5
China, People's Repub.	6,987.6	12,794.8	19,312.2
Denmark	4,553.7	5,354.7	9,890.7
France	12,431.1	15,115.5	19,597.8
Germany	7,755.2	15,505.8	10,421.4
India	10,073.9	11,318.2	15,243.8
Italy	6,701.3	15,592.6	14,085.1
Japan	11,600.2	19,802.9	34,338.9
Kenya	30,275.9	36,824.3	36,463.7
Netherlands	3,726.8	4,886.7	5,728.9
Russia	54.2	525.7	20,791.3
Saudi Arabia	466.0	10,724.1	55,862.0
South Africa	4,980.8	16,198.9	9,773.6
Tanzania	16,402.1	13,934.8	7,803.3
Uganda	12,155.5	12,297.0	17,405.1
United Kingdom	1,778.3	6,794.9	20,366.7
USA	2,092.7	7,451.3	10,251.2
Zambia	7,356.0	10,742.7	13,294.9
Total (incl. others)	193,605.2	289,123.9	442,511.1

Source: Banque de la République du Burundi.

Exports f.o.b. (US $ million)	2002	2003	2004
Belgium	6.2	4.5	8.5
Germany	0.9	0.8	1.9
Kenya	0.5	0.6	1.7
Netherlands	1.7	1.5	2.1
Rwanda	3.2	2.2	5.1
Switzerland and Liechtenstein	6.2	43.1	46.3
Tanzania	0.1	0.3	0.2
United Kingdom	5.8	5.0	4.1
Total (incl. others)	26.5	65.9	82.7

Source: UN, *International Trade Statistics Yearbook*.

2005 (million Burundian francs): Total exports 61,488.3 (Source: Banque de la République du Burundi).

2006 (million Burundian francs): Total exports 60,359.4 (Source: Banque de la République du Burundi).

Transport

ROAD TRAFFIC
('000 motor vehicles in use, estimates)

	1998	1999	2000
Passenger cars	6.6	6.9	7.0
Commercial vehicles	9.3	9.3	9.3

2001–03 ('000 motor vehicles in use): Figures assumed to be unchanged from 2000.

Source: UN, *Statistical Yearbook*.

LAKE TRAFFIC
(Bujumbura, '000 metric tons)

	2004	2005	2006
Goods:			
arrivals	169.1	188.5	172.1
departures	14.6	16.5	10.5

Source: Banque de la République du Burundi.

CIVIL AVIATION
(traffic on scheduled services)

	1996	1997	1998
Passengers carried ('000)	9	12	12
Passenger-km (million)	2	8	8

Source: UN, *Statistical Yearbook*.

Tourism

TOURIST ARRIVALS BY REGION*

	2003	2004	2005
Africa	24,706	1,333	49,473
Americas	2,308	5,908	9,956
Asia	1,162	4,528	4,023
Europe	7,620	29,409	29,486
Unspecified	38,320	92,050	55,480
Total	74,116	133,228	148,418

* Including Burundian nationals residing abroad.

Tourism receipts (US $ million, incl. passenger transport): 1.2 in 2003; n.a. in 2004; n.a. in 2005.

Source: World Tourism Organization.

Communications Media

	2003	2004	2005
Telephones ('000 main lines in use)	23.9	27.7	27.7
Mobile cellular telephones ('000 subscribers)	64.0	100.6	153.0
Personal computers ('000 in use)	13	34	34
Internet users ('000)	14	25	25

Source: International Telecommunication Union.

Television receivers ('000 in use): 200 in 2001.

Radio receivers ('000 in use): 440 in 1997.

Facsimile machines (number in use): 4,000 in 1996.

Daily newspapers: 1 in 1998.

Non-daily newspapers: 5 in 1998 (circulation 8,000 copies).

Sources: International Telecommunication Union; UNESCO, *Statistical Yearbook*.

Education

(2003/04)

	Teachers	Students		
		Males	Females	Total
Pre-primary	318*	4,514	4,384	8,898
Primary	18,899	528,511	439,977	968,488
Secondary:				
general	8,047	80,818	59,917	140,735
technical and vocational		5,910	5,606	11,516
Higher	669	12,157	4,353	15,706

* Figure refers to 1988/89.

Institutions (1988/89): Primary 1,512; Secondary 400.

Source: UNESCO Institute for Statistics.

Adult literacy rate (UNESCO estimates): 59.3% in 2004 (Source: UN Development Programme, *Human Development Report*).

Directory

The Constitution

On 20 October 2004 an interim 'post-transitional' Constitution was officially adopted by the President, after its approval by both chambers of the legislature. The new Constitution, which extended the mandate of the transitional organs of government from 1 November until elections, scheduled for 22 April 2005, was endorsed at a national referendum on 28 February 2005 (replacing the Constitution of 28 October 2001). In April 2005 the Government announced that the presidential mandate was to be extended to allow elections to be rescheduled. Under the new timetable, elections were conducted to the Assemblée nationale on 4 July, and to the Sénat on 19 July; the new legislative chambers elected the President on 19 August, and the inauguration took place on 26 August. The main provisions of the Constitution are summarized below:

PREAMBLE

The transitional Constitution upholds the rights of the individual, and provides for a multi-party political system. The Government is based on the will of the people, and must be composed in order to represent all citizens. The function of the political system is to unite and reconcile all citizens and to ensure that the established Government serves the people. The Government must recognize the separation of powers, the primacy of the law and the principles of good governance and transparency in public affairs. All citizens have equal rights and are assured equal protection by the law. The civic obligations of the individual are emphasized.

POLITICAL PARTY SYSTEM

Political parties may be established freely, subject to conformity with the law. Their organization and activities must correspond to democratic principles and membership must be open to all civilians. They are not permitted to promote violence, discrimination or hate on any basis, including ethnical, regional or religious or tribal affiliation. Members of defence and security bodies, and acting magistrates are prohibited from joining political parties. A five-member Commission électorale nationale indépendante guarantees the freedom, impartiality and independence of the electoral process.

EXECUTIVE POWER

Executive power is vested in the President, who is the Head of State. The President is elected by universal direct suffrage for a term of five years, which is renewable once. (The first post-transitional President is to be elected by a majority of two-thirds of members in both legislative chambers.) The President is assisted in the exercise of his powers by two Vice-Presidents, whom he appoints, and presides over the Government.

GOVERNMENT

The President appoints the Government in consultation with the Vice-Presidents. The Government is required to comprise a 60% proportion of Hutu ministers and deputy ministers and 40% of Tutsi ministers and deputy ministers, and to include a minimum 30% of women. Political parties that secured more than 5% of votes cast in legislative elections are entitled to nominate a proportionate number of representatives to the Government. The President is obliged to replace a minister in consultation with the political party that the minister represents.

LEGISLATURE

Legislative power is vested in the bicameral legislature, comprising a lower chamber, the Assemblée nationale, and an upper chamber, the Sénat. The Assemblée nationale has a minimum of 100 deputies, with a proportion of 60% Hutu and 40% Tutsi representatives, and including a minimum 30% of women. Deputies are elected by direct universal suffrage for a term of five years, while the Twa ethnic group nominates three representatives. If the election results fail to conform to the stipulated ethnic composition, additional deputies may be appointed in accordance with the electoral code. The Sénat comprises a minimum of two senators elected by ethnically balanced colleges from each of the country's provinces, and three Twa representatives, and includes a minimum 30% of women. Both chambers have a President and Vice-Presidents.

JUDICIARY

The President guarantees the independence of the judiciary, with the assistance of the Conseil Supérieur de la Magistrature. The highest judicial power is vested in the Cour Suprême. All appointments to these organs are made by the President, on the proposal of the Minister of Justice and in consultation with the Conseil Supérieur de la Magistrature, and are endorsed by the Sénat. The Cour Constitutionnelle interprets the provisions of the Constitution and ensures the conformity of new legislation. The Cour Constitutionnelle comprises seven members, who are appointed by the President, subject to the approval of the Sénat, for a six-year renewable term.

DEFENCE AND SECURITY FORCES

The establishment and operations of defence and security forces must conform to the law. Members of defence and security forces are prohibited from belonging to, participating in the activities of, or demonstrating prejudice towards, any political parties. All citizens are eligible to join the defence and security forces. During a period to be determined by the Sénat, defence and security forces are not permitted to comprise more than 50% of one single ethnic group, in order to ensure an ethnic balance and guard against acts of genocide and military coups.

The Government

HEAD OF STATE

President: Maj. JEAN-PIERRE NKURUNZIZA (elected 19 August 2005; inaugurated 26 August 2005).

First Vice-President: MARTIN NDUWIMANA.

Second Vice-President: GABRIEL NTISZERANA.

COUNCIL OF MINISTERS
(August 2007)

A transitional Government, comprising representatives of the Conseil national pour la défense de la démocratie—Force pour la défense de la démocratie (CNDD—FDD), the Front pour la démocratie au Burundi (FRODEBU), the Mouvement pour la réhabilitation du citoyen—Rurenzangemero (MRC—Rurenzangemero), the Parti pour le redressement national (PARENA), the Union pour le progrès national (UPRONA) and Inkinzo y'Ijambo Ry'abarundi (Inkinzo).

Minister of the Interior and Public Security: Maj. Gen. EVARISTE NDAYISHIMYE.

Minister of External Relations and International Co-operation: ANTOINETTE BATUMUBWIRA.

Minister at the Presidency, in charge of Good Governance, and General Inspection of the State and Local Administration: VÉNANT KAMANA.

Minister of Justice, Keeper of the Seals: CLOTILDE NIRAGIRA.

Minister of Development Planning and National Reconstruction: TABU ABDALLAH MANIRAKIZA.

Minister of Finance: CLOTILDE NIZIGAMA.

Minister of National Defence and Former Combatants: Lt-Gen. GERMAIN NIYOYANKANA.

Minister of Information, Communications and Relations with Parliament, and Government Spokesman: HAFSA MOSSI.

Minister of Agriculture and Livestock: JEAN DE DIEU MUTABAZI.

Minister of Commerce and Industry: ESTELLA NICAYENZI.

Minister of Public Works and Equipment: JOSEPH HASABAMAGARA.

Minister of Transport, Posts and Telecommunications: PHILIPPE NJONI.

Minister of Land Management, Environment and Tourism: ODETTE KAYITESI.

Minister of Energy and Mines: HERMAN TUYAGA.

Minister of National Education and Culture: SAÏDI KIBEYA.

Minister of Public Health: Dr YVES SAHINGUVU.

Minister of Public Services, Labour and Social Security: DANIEL KINIGI.

Minister of Regional Integration: RAMADHAN KARENGA.

Minister of Youth and Sports: JEAN-JACQUES NYENIMIGABO.

Minister of National Solidarity, Human Rights and Gender: IMMACULÉE NAHAYO.

Minister at the Presidency, in charge of AIDS: MBONIMPA BARNABÉ.

MINISTRIES

Office of the President: Bujumbura; tel. 22226063.

Ministry of Agriculture and Livestock: Bujumbura; tel. 22222087.

Ministry of Commerce and Industry: BP 492, Bujumbura; tel. 22225330; fax 22225595.

Ministry of Development Planning and National Reconstruction: BP 224, Bujumbura; tel. 22225394; fax 22224193; e-mail ministre@miniplan.bi; internet www.cslpminiplan.bi.

Ministry of Energy and Mines: BP 745, Bujumbura; tel. 22225909; fax 22223337; e-mail dgee@cbinf.com.

Ministry of External Relations and International Co-operation: Bujumbura; tel. 22222150.

Ministry of Finance: BP 1830, Bujumbura; tel. 22225142; fax 22223128.

Ministry of Information, Communications and Relations with Parliament: BP 2870, Bujumbura.

Ministry of Justice: Bujumbura; tel. 22222148.

Ministry of National Solidarity, Human Rights and Gender: Bujumbura; tel. 22225039.

Ministry of Public Services and Social Security: BP 1480, Bujumbura; tel. 22225645; fax 22228715; e-mail mtpe@cbinf.com; internet www.burundi.gov.bi/appofre.htm.

Ministry of Public Works and Equipment: BP 1860, Bujumbura; tel. 22226841; fax 22226840; e-mail mtpe@cbinf.com; internet www.burundi.gov.bi/appoffre.htm.

Ministry of Transport, Posts and Telecommunications: BP 2000, Bujumbura; tel. 22222923; fax 22226900.

Ministry of Youth and Sports: Bujumbura; tel. 22226822.

President and Legislature

PRESIDENT

On 19 August 2005 the newly established Assemblée nationale and Sénat elected Jean-Pierre Nkurunziza, the leader of the Conseil national pour la défense de la démocratie—Force pour la défense de la démocratie (CNDD—FDD), as President; the sole candidate, he secured more than 81.5% of votes cast, according to provisional results.

SÉNAT

President: GERVAIS RUFYIKIRI (CNDD—FDD).

First Vice-President: ANATOLE MANIRAKIZA (CNDD—FDD).

Second Vice-President: GENEROSE BIMAZUBUTE (FRODEBU).

Elections, 29 July 2005

Party	Seats*
Conseil national pour la défense de la démocratie—Force pour la défense de la démocratie (CNDD—FDD)	30
Front pour la démocratie au Burundi (FRODEBU)	4
Total	34

* In accordance with constitutional requirements for balance of ethnic representation and a minimum 30% representation of women, a further four seats were allocated to former Presidents, three to the Twa ethnic group and eight to women, increasing the total number of senators to 49.

ASSEMBLÉE NATIONALE

President: PIE NTAVYOHANYUMA (CNDD—FDD).

First Vice-President: ALICE NZOMUKUNDA (CNDD—FDD).

Second Vice-President: MARTIN NDUWIMANA (UPRONA).

Elections, 4 July 2005

Party	Votes	% of votes	Seats*
Conseil national pour la défense de la démocratie—Force pour la défense de la démocratie (CNDD—FDD)	1,417,800	58.55	59
Front pour la démocratie au Burundi (FRODEBU)	525,336	21.69	25
Union pour le progrès national (UPRONA)	174,575	7.21	10
Conseil national pour la défense de la démocratie (CNDD)	100,366	4.14	4
Mouvement pour la réhabilitation du citoyen—Rurenzangemero (MRC—Rurenzangemero)	51,730	2.14	2
Independents and others	151,619	6.26	—
Total	2,421,426	100.00	100

* In accordance with constitutional requirements for balance of ethnic representation and a minimum 30% representation of women, a further 18 seats were allocated, including three to members of the Twa ethnic group, increasing the total number of deputies to 118. CNDD—FDD, FRODEBU and UPRONA each received an additional five seats.

Election Commission

Commission électorale nationale indépendante (CENI): Bujumbura; f. 2004; independent; Chair. PAUL NGARAMBE.

Political Organizations

Political parties are required to demonstrate firm commitment to national unity, and impartiality with regard to ethnic or regional origin, gender and religion, in order to receive legal recognition. By 2005 the number of registered political parties had increased to 34; these included former rebel organizations, with only the Forces nationales de libération remaining in conflict with government forces.

Alliance burundaise-africaine pour le salut (ABASA): Bujumbura; f. 1993; Tutsi; Leader TÉRENCE NSANZE.

Alliance des Vaillants (AV—Intware) (Alliance of the Brave): Bujumbura; f. 1993; Tutsi; Leader ANDRÉ NKUNDIKIJE.

Alliance libérale pour le développement (ALIDE): f. 2001; Leader JOSEPH NTIDENDEREZA.

Alliance nationale pour les droits et le développement économique (ANADDE): Bujumbura; f. 1992; Tutsi; Leader PATRICE NSABABAGANWA.

Alliance nouvelle pour la démocratie et le développement au Burundi: f. Aug. 2002; Leader JEAN-PAUL BURAFUTA.

Conseil national pour la défense de la démocratie (CNDD): Bujumbura; e-mail cndd_bur@usa.net; internet www.club.euronet.be/pascal.karolero.cndd.burundi; f. 1994; Hutu; Pres. LÉONARD NYANGOMA.

Conseil national pour la défense de la démocratie—Force pour la défense de la démocratie (CNDD—FDD): fmr armed wing of the Hutu CNDD; split into two factions in Oct. 2001, one led by JEAN-BOSCO NDAYIKENGURUKIYE and the other by JEAN-PIERRE NKURUNZIZA; Nkurunziza's faction incl. in Govt Nov. 2003, following peace agreement; registered as political org. Jan. 2005; Chair. JÉRÉMIE NGENDAKUMANA; Sec.-Gen. MANASSÉ NZOBONIMPA.

Forces nationales de libération (FNL): fmr armed wing of Hutu Parti de libération du peuple hutu (PALIPEHUTU, f. 1980); split in Aug. 2002 and in Dec. 2005; cease-fire with Govt announced Sept. 2006; Chair. JEAN-BOSCO SINDAYIGAYA; Leader SYLVESTRE NIYUNGEKO.

Front national de libération Icanzo (FNL Icanzo): reconstituted Dec. 2002 from fmr faction of Forces nationales de libération; Leader Dr ALAIN MUGABARABONA.

Front pour la démocratie au Burundi (FRODEBU): Bujumbura; f. 1992; split in June 1999; Hutu; Chair. LÉONCE NGENDAKUMANA.

KAZE—Force pour la défense de la démocratie (KAZE—FDD): f. May 2004; reconstituted as a political party from a faction of the armed CNDD—FDD (see above); Leader JEAN-BOSCO NDAYIKENGURUKIYE.

Mouvement pour la réhabilitation du citoyen—Rurenzangemero (MRC—Rurenzangemero): Bujumbura; f. June 2001; regd Nov. 2002; Leader Lt-Col EPITACE BAYAGANAKANDI.

Mouvement socialiste panafricaniste—Inkinzo y'Ijambo Ry'abarundi (MSP—Inkinzo) (Guarantor of Freedom of Speech in Burundi): Bujumbura; f. 1993; Tutsi; Pres. Dr ALPHONSE RUGAMBARARA.

Parti de la consensus nationale (PACONA): f. Feb. 2004; Leader JEAN-BOSCO NDAYIZAMBAYE.

Parti indépendant des travailleurs (PIT): Bujumbura; f. 1993; Tutsi; Chair. NICÉPHORE NDIMURUKUNDO.

Parti libéral (PL): BP 2167, Bujumbura; tel. 2214848; fax 2225981; e-mail liberalburundi@yahoo.fr; f. 1992; Hutu; Leader GAËTAN NIKOBAMYE.

Parti du peuple (PP): Bujumbura; f. 1992; Hutu; Leader MARORA SYLVESTRE.

Parti pour la démocratie et la réconciliation: f. May 2002; Leader AUGUSTIN NZOJLBWAMI.

Parti pour le développement et la solidarité des travailleurs (PML-Abanyamwete): Bujumbura; f. Oct. 2004; Leader PATRICIA NDAYIZEYE.

Parti pour la paix, la démocratie, la réconciliation et la reconstruction (PPDR): f. Dec. 2002 by fmr mems of FRODEBU (see above); regd March 2004; Leader JEAN-LÉOPOLD NZOBONIMPA.

Parti pour la réconciliation du peuple (PRP): Bujumbura; f. 1992; Tutsi; Leader MATHIAS HITIMANA.

Parti pour le redressement intégral du Burundi (PARIBU): Bujumbura; f. Sept. 2004; Leader BENOÎT NDORIMANA.

Parti pour le redressement national (PARENA): Bujumbura; f. 1994; Leader JEAN-BAPTISTE BAGAZA.

Parti pour la restitution de la monarchie et du dialogue (PRMD) (Abuhuza): Bujumbura; f. 2004; Leader GODEFROID KAMATARI.

Parti social démocrate (PSD): Bujumbura; f. 1993; Tutsi; Leader GODEFROID HAKIZIMANA.

Rassemblement pour la démocratie et le développement économique et social (RADDES): Bujumbura; f. 1992; Tutsi; Chair. JOSEPH NZEYZIMANA.

Rassemblement pour le peuple du Burundi (RPB): Bujumbura; f. 1992; Hutu; Leader BALTHAZAR BIGIRIMANA.

Sonovi-Ruremesha (Party for a Non-Violent Society): f. Aug. 2002; Tutsi; Chair. DEOGRATIAS NDAYISHIMIYE.

Union pour la paix et le développement (Zigamibanga): f. Aug. 2002; Leader FREDDY FERUVI.

Union pour le progrès national (UPRONA): BP 1810, Bujumbura; tel. 22225028; f. 1958 following the 1961 elections; the numerous small parties which had been defeated merged with UPRONA, which became the sole legal political party in 1966; party activities were suspended following the coup of Sept. 1987, but resumed in 1989; Chair. ALOYS RUBUKA.

Diplomatic Representation

EMBASSIES IN BURUNDI

Belgium: 9 blvd de la Liberté, BP 1920, Bujumbura; tel. 22226176; fax 22223171; e-mail bujumbura@diplobel.org; Ambassador FRANÇOIS CORNET D'ELZIUS.

China, People's Republic: 675 sur la Parcelle, BP 2550, Bujumbura; tel. 22224307; fax 22213735; Ambassador ZENG XIANQI.

Egypt: 31 ave de la Liberté, BP 1520, Bujumbura; tel. 22223161; Ambassador MUHAMMAD ABDUL EL-KHADER EL-KHASAB.

France: 60 ave de l'UPRONA, BP 1740, Bujumbura; tel. 22203000; fax 22203010; Ambassador JOËL LOUVET.

Germany: 22 rue 18 septembre, BP 480, Bujumbura; tel. 22226412; Ambassador THOMAS MANGARTZ.

Holy See: 46 ave des Travailleurs, BP 1068, Bujumbura; tel. 22225415; fax 22223176; e-mail nonciat@cbinf.com; Apostolic Nuncio Most Rev. PAUL RICHARD GALLAGHER (Titular Archbishop of Hodelm).

Korea, Democratic People's Republic: BP 1620, Bujumbura; tel. 22222881; Ambassador SOON CHUN LEE.

Russia: 78 blvd de l'UPRONA, BP 1034, Bujumbura; tel. 22226098; fax 22222984; Ambassador IGOR S. LIAKIN-FROLOV.

Rwanda: 24 ave du Zaïre, BP 400, Bujumbura; tel. 22223140; Ambassador JANVIER KANYAMASHULI.

Tanzania: 855 rue United Nations, BP 1653, Bujumbura; tel. 22248632; fax 22248637; e-mail tanzanrep@usan-bu.net; Ambassador FRANCIS MNDOLWA.

USA: ave des Etats-Unis, BP 1720, Bujumbura; tel. 22223454; fax 22222926; e-mail jyellin@bujumbura.us-state.gov; Ambassador PATRICIA N. MOLLER.

Judicial System

Constitutional Court: Bujumbura; comprises a minimum of seven judges, who are nominated by the President for a six-year term.

Supreme Court: BP 1460, Bujumbura; tel. and fax 22213544; court of final instance; three divisions: ordinary, cassation and administrative; Pres. MARIE ANCILLA NTAKABURIMVO.

Courts of Appeal: Bujumbura, Gitega and Ngozi.

Tribunals of First Instance: There are 17 provincial tribunals and 123 smaller resident tribunals in other areas.

Religion

Some 67% of the population are Christians, the majority of whom are Roman Catholics. Anglicans number about 60,000. There are about 200,000 other Protestant adherents, of whom about 160,000 are Pentecostalists. About 23% of the population adhere to traditional beliefs, which include the worship of the god Imana. About 10% of the population are Muslims. The Bahá'í Faith is also active in Burundi.

CHRISTIANITY

Conseil National des Eglises Protestantes du Burundi (CNEB): BP 17, Bujumbura; tel. 22224216; fax 22227941; e-mail cneb@cbninf.com; f. 1935; 10 mem. churches; Pres. Rt Rev. JEAN NDUWAYO (Anglican Bishop of Gitega); Gen. Sec. Rev. OSIAS HABINGABWA.

The Anglican Communion

The Church of the Province of Burundi, established in 1992, comprises five dioceses.

Archbishop of Burundi and Bishop of Buye: Most Rev. SAMUEL NDAYISENGA, BP 94, Ngozi; fax 22302317.

Provincial Secretary: Rev. PASCAL BIGIRIMANA, BP 2098, Bujumbura; tel. 22224389; fax 22229129; e-mail eebprov@cbinf.com.

The Roman Catholic Church

Burundi comprises one archdiocese and six dioceses. At 31 December 2004 there were an estimated 4,757,005 adherents, equivalent to 66.3% of the total population.

Bishops' Conference

Conférence des Evêques Catholiques du Burundi, 5 blvd de l'UPRONA, BP 1390, Bujumbura; tel. 22223263; fax 22223270; e-mail cecab@cbinf.com.

f. 1980; Pres. Rt Rev. JEAN NTAGWARARA (Bishop of Bubanza).

Archbishop of Gitega: Most Rev. SIMON NTAMWANA, Archevêché, BP 118, Gitega; tel. 22402160; fax 22402620; e-mail archigi@bujumbura.ocicnet.net.

Other Christian Churches

Union of Baptist Churches of Burundi: Rubura, DS 117, Bujumbura 1; Pres. PAUL BARUHENAMWO.

Other denominations active in the country include the Evangelical Christian Brotherhood of Burundi, the Free Methodist Church of Burundi and the United Methodist Church of Burundi.

BAHÁ'Í FAITH

National Spiritual Assembly: BP 1578, Bujumbura; tel. 79955840; e-mail bahaiburundi@yahoo.fr; Sec. YOLANDE KABERA.

The Press

National Communications Council (Conseil national de la communication—CNC): Bujumbura; f. 2001 under the terms of the transitional Constitution; responsible for ensuring press freedom; Pres. JEAN-PIERRE MANDA.

NEWSPAPER

Le Renouveau du Burundi: BP 2573, Bujumbura; tel. 22226232; f. 1978; daily; French; govt-owned; circ. 2,500 (2004); Dir THADDÉE SIRYUYUMUNSI.

PERIODICALS

Au Coeur de l'Afrique: Association des conférences des ordinaires du Rwanda et Burundi, BP 1390, Bujumbura; fax 22223027; e-mail cnid@cbinf.com; bimonthly; education; circ. 1,000.

Bulletin Économique et Financier: BP 482, Bujumbura; bimonthly.

Bulletin Mensuel: Banque de la République du Burundi, Service des études, BP 705, Bujumbura; tel. 22225142; monthly.

In-Burundi: c/o Cyber Média, BP 5270, ave du 18 septembre, Bujumbura; tel. 2244464; current affairs internet publication; Editor-in-Chief EDGAR C. MBANZA.

Ndongozi Y'uburundi: Catholic Mission, BP 690, Bujumbura; tel. 22222762; fax 22228907; fortnightly; Kirundi.

Revue Administration et Juridique: Association d'études administratives et juridiques du Burundi, BP 1613, Bujumbura; quarterly; French.

PRESS ASSOCIATION

Burundian Association of Journalists (BAJ): Bujumbura; Pres. FRANÇOIS SENDAZIRASA.

NEWS AGENCY

Agence Burundaise de Presse (ABP): ave Nicolas Mayugi, BP 2870, Bujumbura; tel. 22213083; fax 22222282; e-mail abp@cbinf.com; internet www.abp.info.bi; f. 1975; publ. daily bulletin.

Publishers

BURSTA: BP 1908, Bujumbura; tel. 22231796; fax 22232842; f. 1986; Dir RICHARD KASHIRAHAMWE.

Editions Intore: 19 ave Matana, BP 2524, Bujumbura; tel. 22223499; e-mail anbirabuza@yahoo.fr; f. 1992; philosophy, history, journalism, literature, social sciences; Dir Dr ANDRÉ BIRABUZA.

IMPARUDI: ave du 18 septembre 3, BP 3010, Bujumbura; tel. 22223125; fax 22222572; e-mail imparudi@yahou.fr; f. 1950; Dir-Gen. THÉONESTE MUTAMBUKA.

Imprimerie la Licorne: 29 ave de la Mission, BP 2942, Bujumbura; tel. 22223503; fax 22227225; f. 1991.

Les Presses Lavigerie: 5 ave de l'UPRONA, BP 1640, Bujumbura; tel. 22222368; fax 22220318.

Régie de Productions Pédagogiques: BP 3118, Bujumbura II; tel. 22226111; fax 22222631; e-mail rpp@cbinf.com; f. 1984; school textbooks; Dir ABRAHAM MBONERANE.

GOVERNMENT PUBLISHING HOUSE

Imprimerie Nationale du Burundi (INABU): BP 991, Bujumbura; tel. 22224046; fax 22225399; f. 1978; Dir NICOLAS NIJIMBERE.

Broadcasting and Communications

TELECOMMUNICATIONS

Agence de Régulation et de Contrôle des Télécommunications (ARCT): 360 Ave Patrice Lumumba, BP 6702, Bujumbura; tel. 22210276; fax 22242832; e-mail arct@cbinf.com; Dir.-Gen. JOSEPH NSEGANA.

Direction Générale des Transports, Postes et Télécommunications: BP 2390, Bujumbura; tel. 22225422; fax 22226900; govt telecommunications authority; Dir-Gen. APOLLINAIRE NDAYIZEYE.

Office National des Télécommunications (ONATEL): BP 60, Bujumbura; tel. 22223196; fax 22226917; e-mail onatel@cbinf.com; f. 1979; service provider; privatization pending; Dir-Gen. AUGUSTIN NDABIHORE.

Téléphonie Cellulaire du Burundi (TELECEL): Bujumbura; e-mail clareher@telecel.bi; f. 1993; 40% govt-owned; mobile telephone service provider; Dir-Gen. MARTIN BAKA.

BROADCASTING

Radio

Radio Isanganiro: Bujumbura; internet www.ijambo.net; f. Nov. 2002; controlled by Association Ijambo, f. by Studio Ijambo (see below); broadcasts on 89.7 FM frequency, in Kirundi, French and Swahili; services cover Bujumbura area, and were to be extended to all Great Lakes region.

Radio Publique Africain (RPA): Bujumbura; f. 2001 with the aim of promoting peace; independent; Dir Alexis Sinduhije.

Radio Umwizero/Radio Hope: BP 5314, Bujumbura; tel. 22217068; e-mail umwizero@cbinf.com; f. 1996; EU-funded, private station promoting national reconciliation, peace and development projects; broadcasts nine hours daily in Kirundi, Swahili and French; Dir Hubert Vieille.

Studio Ijambo (Wise Words): Bujumbura; e-mail burundi@sfcg.org; internet www.studioijambo.org; f. 1995 by Search for Common Ground; promotes peace and reconciliation.

Voix de la Révolution/La Radiodiffusion et Télévision Nationale du Burundi (RTNB): BP 1900, Bujumbura; tel. 22223742; fax 22226547; e-mail rtnb@cbinf.com; internet www.burundi-quotidien.com; f. 1960; govt-controlled; daily radio broadcasts in Kirundi, Swahili, French and English; Dir-Gen. Innocent Muhozi; Dir (Radio) Emmanuel Nzeyimana.

Television

Voix de la Révolution/La Radiodiffusion et Télévision Nationale du Burundi (RTNB): BP 1900, Bujumbura; tel. 22223742; fax 22226547; e-mail rtnb@cbinf.com; internet www.burundi-quotidien.com; f. 1960; govt-controlled; television service in Kirundi, Swahili, French and English; Dir (Television) David Hicuburumai.

Finance

(cap. = capital; res = reserves; dep. = deposits; m. = million; brs = branches; amounts in Burundian francs)

BANKING

Central Bank

Banque de la République du Burundi (BRB): BP 705, Bujumbura; tel. 22225142; fax 22223128; e-mail brb@brb.bi; internet www.brb.bi; f. 1964 as Banque du Royaume du Burundi; state-owned; bank of issue; total assets 229,503.9m. (Dec. 2004); Gov. Isaac Bizimana; Vice-Gov. Spésiose Baransata; 2 brs.

Commercial Banks

Banque Burundaise pour le Commerce et l'Investissement SARL (BBCI): blvd du Peuple Murundi, BP 2320, Bujumbura; tel. 22223328; fax 22223339; e-mail bbci@cbinf.com; f. 1988; cap. and res 2,645.8m., total assets 14,016.2m. (Dec. 2003); Pres. Celeslin Mizero; Dir-Gen. Charles Nihangaza.

Banque Commerciale du Burundi SARL (BANCOBU): Gaspard Sindayigaya, BP 990, Bujumbura; tel. 22222317; fax 22221018; e-mail bancobu@cbinf.com; f. 1988 by merger; cap. 1,100m., res 1,418.3m., dep. 39,506.6m. (Dec. 2004); Pres. Pierre-Claver Gahungu; Man. Dir Gaspard Sindayigaya; 8 brs.

Banque de Crédit de Bujumbura SM: ave Patrice Emery Lumumba, BP 300, Bujumbura; tel. 22201111; fax 22223007; e-mail direction@bcb.bi; internet www.bcb.bi; f. 1964; cap. 1,000.0m., res 6,236.7m., dep. 64,046.7m. (Dec. 2005); Pres. Rénilde Bazahica; 7 brs.

Banque de Financement et de Leasing S.A.: blvd de la Liberté, BP 2998, Bujumbura; tel. 22243206; fax 22225437; e-mail finalease@cbinf.com; cap. and res 1,400.5m., total assets 8,578.4m. (Dec. 2003); Pres. Audace Bireha; Dir-Gen. Eric Bonane Rubega.

Banque de Gestion et de Financement: 1 blvd de la Liberté, BP 1035, Bujumbura; tel. 22221352; fax 22221351; e-mail bgf@usan.bu.net; f. 1996; cap. 1,029.0m., res 860.6m., dep. 17,378.9m. (Dec. 2005); Pres. Béde Bedetse; Gen. Man. Mathias Ndikumana.

Interbank Burundi SARL: 15 rue de l'Industrie, BP 2970, Bujumbura; tel. 22220629; fax 22220461; e-mail info@interbankbdi.com; internet www.interbankbdi.com; cap. and res 5,370.9m., total assets 64,867.9m. (Dec. 2003); Pres. Georges Coucoulis.

Development Bank

Banque Nationale pour le Développement Economique SARL (BNDE): 3 ave du Marché, BP 1620, Bujumbura; tel. 22222888; fax 22223775; e-mail bnde@cbinf.com; f. 1966; cap. 3,241.9m., res 1,534.7m., dep. 6,045.6m. (Dec. 2005); Chair. and Man. Dir Jean Ciza.

Co-operative Bank

Banque Coopérative d'Epargne et de Crédit Mutuel (BCM): BP 1340, Bujumbura; operating licence granted in April 1995; Vice-Pres. Julien Musaragany.

Financial Institutions

Fonds de Promotion de L'Habitat Urbain (FPHU): BP 1996, Bujumbura; tel. 22227676; e-mail fphu@cbinf.com; cap. 818m. (2005); Dir-Gen. Audace Bukuru.

Société Burundaise de Financement: 6 rue de la Science, BP 270, Bujumbura; tel. 22222126; fax 22225437; e-mail sbf@cbinf.com; cap. and res 2,558.9m., total assets 11,680.4m. (Dec. 2003); Pres. Astère Girukwigomba; Dir-Gen. Darius Nahayo.

INSURANCE

Société d'Assurances du Burundi (SOCABU): 14–18 rue de l'Amitié, BP 2440, Bujumbura; tel. 22226520; fax 22226803; e-mail socabu@cbinf.com; f. 1977; cap. 180m.; Man. Dir Onesime Nduwimana.

Société Générale d'Assurances et de Réassurance (SOGEAR): BP 2432, Bujumbura; tel. 22222345; fax 22229338; f. 1991; Pres. Benoît Ndorimana; Dir-Gen. L. Saussez.

Union Commerciale d'Assurances et de Réassurance (UCAR): BP 3012, Bujumbura; tel. 22223638; fax 22223695; f. 1986; cap. 150m.; Chair. Lt-Col Edouard Nzambimana; Dir-Gen. Pascal Ntamashimikiro.

Trade and Industry

GOVERNMENT AGENCIES

Agence de Promotion des Echanges Extérieurs (APEE): BP 3535, Bujumbura; tel. 22225497; fax 22222767; promotes and supervises foreign exchanges.

Office du Café du Burundi (OCBU): BP 450, Bujumbura; tel. 22224017; fax 22225532; e-mail dgo@usan-bu.net; f. 1964; supervises coffee plantations and coffee exports; Dir-Gen. Barthélémy Niyikiza.

Office National du Commerce (ONC): Bujumbura; f. 1973; supervises international commercial operations between the Govt of Burundi and other states or private orgs; also organizes the import of essential materials; subsidiary offices in each province.

Office National du Logement (ONL): BP 2480, Bujumbura; tel. 22226074; f. 1974 to supervise housing construction.

Office du Thé du Burundi (OTB): 52 blvd de l'UPRONA, Bujumbura; tel. 22224228; fax 22224657; e-mail otb@cbinf.com; f. 1979; supervises production and marketing of tea; Man. Dir Salvatore Nimubona.

DEVELOPMENT ORGANIZATIONS

Compagnie Financière pour le Développement SA: Bldg INSS, 1 Route Nationale, BP 139, Ngozi; tel. 22302279; fax 22302296; Pres. Abbé Ephrem Girukwishaka.

Fonds de Développement Communal SP: BP 2799, Bujumbura; tel. 22221963; fax 22243268; e-mail fdc@cbinf.com; Pres. Béatrice Bukware.

Fonds de Promotion de l'Habitat Urbain: 6 ave de la Liberté, BP 1996, Bujumbura; tel. 22227676; fax 22223225; e-mail fphu@cbinf.com; cap. 818m. Burundian francs; Pres. Didace Birabisha.

Institut des Sciences Agronomiques du Burundi (ISABU): BP 795, Bujumbura; tel. 22227349; fax 22225798; e-mail isabu@usan-bu.net; f. 1962 for the scientific development of agriculture and livestock.

Office National de la Tourbe (ONATOUR): BP 2360, Bujumbura; tel. 22226480; fax 22226709; f. 1977 to promote the exploitation of peat deposits.

Société d'Economie pour l'Exploitation du Quinquina au Burundi (SOKINABU): 16 blvd Mwezi Gisabo, BP 1783, Bujumbura; tel. 22223469; fax 22218160; e-mail chiastos@yahoo.fr; f. 1975 to develop and exploit cinchona trees, the source of quinine; Dir Christian Remezo.

Société Régionale de Développement de l'IMBO (SRDI): Bujumbura; promotes development of IMBO region.

Société Régionale de Développement de Kayanza (SRD KAYANZA): Kayanza; promotes development of Kayanza region.

Société Régionale de Développement de Kirimiro (SRD KIRIMIRO): Bujumbura; promotes development of Kirimiro region.

Société Régionale de Développement de Kirundo (SRD KIRUNDO): Bujumbura; promotes development of Kirundo region.

Société Régionale de Développement de Mumirwa (SRD MUMIRWA): Bujumbura; promotes development of Mumirwa region.

Société Régionale de Développement de Rumonge (SRD RUMONGE): Bujumbura; promotes development of Rumonge region.

CHAMBER OF COMMERCE

Chambre de Commerce, d'Industrie, d'Agriculture et d'Artisanat du Burundi: BP 313, Bujumbura; tel. 22222280; fax 22227895; f. 1923; Pres. DIDACE NZOHABONAYO; Sec.-Gen. CYRILLE SINGEJEJE; 130 mems.

UTILITY

Régie de Distribution d'Eau et d'Electricité (REGIDESO): Ngozi, Bujumbura; tel. 22302222; state-owned distributor of water and electricity services; Dir JÉRÔME CIZA.

MAJOR COMPANIES

Brarudi: BP 540, Bujumbura; tel. 22215360; f. 1955; production of beer and soft drinks.

Burundi Mining Corpn (BUMINCO): BP 648, Bujumbura; tel. 22223299; f. 1986; part state-owned; mineral exploitation.

Compagnie de Gérance du Coton (COGERCO): BP 2571, Bujumbura; tel. 22222208; fax 22224370; e-mail cogerco@cbinf.com; f. 1984; development of cotton industry; Pres. SÉBASTIEN NDAVIZEYE; Dir FRANÇOIS KABURA.

Engen: BP 15, Bujumbura, 10 pl. de l'Indépendance; tel. 22222848; fax 22223163; e-mail engen@cbinf.com; fmrly Fina BP Burundi; petroleum and gas exploration; Dir-Gen. CHARLES NIKOBASA.

Société Sucrière du Moso (SOSUMO): BP 835, Bujumbura; tel. 22221662; fax 22223028; e-mail sosumo@cbinf.com; f. 1982 to develop and manage sugar cane plantations; Pres. BONAVENTURE KIDWINGIRA; Dir-Gen. NUMÉRIEN BARUTWANAYO.

TRADE UNIONS

Confédération des Syndicats du Burundi (COSYBU): Bujumbura; Chair. Dr PIERRE-CLAVIER HAJAYANDI.

Union des Travailleurs du Burundi (UTB): BP 1340, Bujumbura; tel. 22223884; f. 1967 by merger of all existing unions; closely allied with UPRONA; sole authorized trade union prior to 1994, with 18 affiliated nat. professional feds; Sec.-Gen. MARIUS RURAHENYE.

Transport

RAILWAYS

There are no railways in Burundi. Plans have been under consideration since 1987 for the construction of a line passing through Uganda, Rwanda and Burundi, to connect with the Kigoma–Dar es Salaam line in Tanzania. This rail link would relieve Burundi's isolated trade position.

ROADS

In 2004 Burundi had a total of 12,322 km of roads, of which 5,012 km were national highways and 282 km secondary roads. A new crossing of the Ruzizi river, the Bridge of Concord (Burundi's longest bridge), was opened in early 1992.

Office des Transports en Commun (OTRACO): BP 1486, Bujumbura; tel. 22231313; fax 22232051; 100% govt-owned; operates public transport.

INLAND WATERWAYS

Bujumbura is the principal port for both passenger and freight traffic on Lake Tanganyika, and the greater part of Burundi's external trade is dependent on the shipping services between Bujumbura and lake ports in Tanzania, Zambia and the Democratic Republic of the Congo.

Exploitation du Port de Bujumbura (EPB): Bujumbura; tel. 22226036; f. 1967; 43% state-owned; controls Bujumbura port; Dir-Gen. MÉTHODE SHIRAMBERE.

CIVIL AVIATION

The international airport at Bujumbura is equipped to take large jet-engined aircraft.

Air Burundi: 40 ave du Commerce, BP 2460, Bujumbura; tel. 22224609; fax 22223452; e-mail airbdi@cbinf.com; f. 1971 as Société de Transports Aériens du Burundi; state-owned; operates charter and scheduled passenger services to destinations throughout central Africa; CEO Col ANTOINE GATOTO; Dir C. KAGARI.

Tourism

Tourism is relatively undeveloped. The annual total of tourist arrivals declined from 125,000 in 1991 to only 10,553 in 1997. Total arrivals increased gradually thereafter, reaching 74,116 in 2003 and increasing to an estimated 148,418 in 2005. Tourism receipts amounted to an estimated US $1.2m. in 2003. However, continued failure fully to restore peace in the country effectively prevented any significant revival of tourism.

Office National du Tourisme (ONT): 2 ave des Euphorbes, BP 902, Bujumbura; tel. 22224208; fax 22229390; e-mail ontbur@cbinf.com; f. 1972; responsible for the promotion and supervision of tourism; Dir DÉO NGENDAHAYO.

Defence

Burundi's armed forces, as assessed at November 2006, comprised an army of 35,000 and a paramilitary force of 31,050 gendarmes (including a 50-strong marine police force). At the end of 2004 the Government had officially established a reconstituted armed forces (Forces de défense nationales—FDN—comprising equal proportions of Hutus and Tutsis), which incorporated some 23,000 former rebel combatants, and a new police force. In April 2003 the deployment of the first members of an AU Mission in Burundi (AMIB) commenced; the contingent (which comprised mainly South African troops, with reinforcements from Ethiopia and Mozambique) was mandated to assist in the enforcement of the cease-fire between the Government and rebel factions. In May 2004 the UN Security Council approved the deployment of a Opération des Nations Unies au Burundi (ONUB—with a maximum authorized strength of 5,650 military personnel), to replace AMIB. Under a resolution of 30 June 2006, the UN Security Council ended the mandate of ONUB at the end of December, when it was replaced by a UN office, the Bureau Intégré des Nations Unies au Burundi (BINUB). BINUB was established for an initial period of one year, with authorization to continue peace consolidation, including support for the demobilization and reintegration of former combatants and reform of the security sector. Some 850 South African peace-keeping troops previously belonging to ONUB were transferred to the authority of the AU, which announced plans to increase the size of the contingent deployed in the country to 1,700.

Defence Expenditure: Estimated at 50,000m. Burundian francs in 2005.

Chief of Staff of the Army: Gen. VINCENT NIYUNGEKO.

Chief of Staff of the Gendarmerie: Col SALVATOR NDAYIYUNVIYE.

Education

Education is provided free of charge. Kirundi is the language of instruction in primary schools, while French is used in secondary schools. Primary education, which is officially compulsory, begins at seven years of age and lasts for six years. Secondary education, which is not compulsory, begins at the age of 13 and lasts for up to seven years, comprising a first cycle of four years and a second of three years. In 2003/04, according to UNESCO estimates, 57% of children in the relevant age-group (males 60%; females 54%) were enrolled at primary schools. Enrolment at secondary schools in that year was equivalent to only an estimated 12% of the population in the appropriate age-group (males 14%; females 10%). There is one university, in Bujumbura; in 2002/03 11,915 students were enrolled there. Expenditure on education by the central Government was estimated at 23,000m. Burundian francs (15.2% of total government spending) in 2002.

Bibliography

Brennan, K. *Burundi.* Broomall, PA, Mason Crest Publishers, 2004.

Chrétien, J.-P. 'La société du Burundi: Des mythes aux réalités', in *Revue Française d'Etudes Politiques Africaines,* Nos. 163–164 (pp. 94–118). July–August 1979.

Histoire rurale de l'Afrique des Grands Lacs. Paris, Editions Karthala, 1983.

Chrétien, J.-P., Guichaoua, A., and Le Jeune, G. *La crise d'août 1988 au Burundi.* Paris, Editions Karthala, 1989.

Eggers, E. *Historical Dictionary of Burundi.* 2nd Edn. Metuchen, NJ, Scarecrow Press, 1997.

Emerging Markets Investment Center. *Burundi Investment and Business Guide.* Washington, DC, International Business Publications, 1999.

Gahama, J. *Le Burundi sous administration belge.* Paris, Editions Karthala, 1983.

Guichaoua, A. (Ed.). *Les crises politiques au Burundi et au Rwanda (1993–1994).* Paris, Editions Karthala, 1995.

Guillet, C., and Ndayishinguje, P. *Légendes historiques du Burundi.* Paris, Editions Karthala, 1987.

Hakizimana, A. *Naissances au Burundi: Entre Tradition et Planification.* Paris, L'Harmattan, 2002.

International Business Publications. *Burundi Foreign Policy and Government Guide.* Washington, DC, 2004.

Lambert, M. Y. *Enquête démographique Burundi (1970–1971).* Bujumbura, Ministère du Plan, 1972.

Lemarchand, R. *Rwanda and Burundi.* London, Pall Mall, 1970.

Selective Genocide in Burundi. London, Minority Rights Group, 1974.

African Kingships in Perspective. London, Frank Cass & Co, 1974.

Ethnocide as Discourse and Practice. Washington, DC, Woodrow Wilson Center Press and Cambridge, Cambridge University Press, 1994.

Burundi: Ethnic Conflict and Genocide. Cambridge, Cambridge University Press, 1996.

Longman, T. P. *Burundi—Proxy Target: Civilians in the War on Burundi.* New York, NY, Human Rights Watch, 1998.

Mpozagara, G. *La République du Burundi.* Paris, Berger-Levrault, 1971.

Mwakikagile, G. *Civil Wars in Rwanda and Burundi: Conflict Resolution in Africa.* New York, NY, Nova Science Publishers, 2004.

Mworoha, E. *Histoire du Burundi.* Paris, Hatier, 1987.

Nsanzé, T. *Le Burundi au carrefour de l'Afrique.* Brussels, Remarques africaines, 1970.

L'Edification de la République du Burundi. Brussels, 1970.

Ntahombaye, P. *Des noms et des hommes. Aspects du nom au Burundi.* Paris, Editions Karthala, 1983.

Ould Abdallah, A. *Burundi on the Brink 1993–95: A UN Special Envoy Reflects on Preventative Diplomacy (Perspectives Series).* Washington, DC, United States Institute of Peace, 2000.

Reyntjens, F. *Burundi 1972–1988. Continuité et changement.* Brussels, Centre d'étude et de documentation africaines (CEDAF—ASDOC), 1989.

Small States in an Unstable Region—Rwanda and Burundi 1999–2000 (Current African Issues, 23). Uppsala, Nordiska Afrikainstitutet, 2001.

Again at the Crossroads—Rwanda and Burundi, 2000–2001. Uppsala, Nordiska Afrikainstitutet, 2001.

Sommers, M. *Fear in Bongoland: Burundi Refugees in Urban Tanzania (Studies in Forced Migration, Vol. 8).* New York, NY, Berghahn Books, 2001.

Southall, R., and Bentley, K. *African Peace Process: Mandela, South Africa, and Burundi.* Pretoria, Human Sciences Research Council, 2005.

Tuhabonye, G., and Brozek, G. *This Voice in My Heart: A Genocide Survivor's Story of Escape, Faith, and Forgiveness.* New York, NY, Amistad, 2006.

United States Committee for Refugees. *From Coup to Coup: Thirty Years of Death, Fear and Displacement in Burundi.* Washington, DC, USCR, 1996.

CAMEROON

Physical and Social Geography

JOHN I. CLARKE

PHYSICAL FEATURES

The Republic of Cameroon covers an area of 475,442 sq km (183,569 sq miles), and contains exceptionally diverse physical environments. The country occupies a fairly central position within the African continent, with the additional advantage of a 200-km coastline. Its environmental diversity arises from various factors, including the country's position astride the volcanic belt along the hinge between west and central Africa, together with its intermediate location between the great basins of the Congo, the Niger and Lake Chad, its latitudinal extent between 2° and 13°N, its altitudinal range from sea-level to more than 4,000 m, and its spread from coastal mangrove swamp to remote continental interior.

In the south and centre of the country a large undulating and broken plateau surface of granites, schists and gneisses rises northwards away from the Congo basin to the Adamawa plateau (900–1,520 m above sea-level). North of the steep Adamawa escarpment, which effectively divides northern from southern Cameroon, lies the basin of the Benue river, a tributary of the Niger, which is floored by sedimentary rocks, interspersed with inselbergs and buttes. In the west of the country a long line of rounded volcanic mountains and hills extends from Mt Cameroun (4,095 m), the highest mountain in west and central Africa, north-eastwards along the former boundary between East and West Cameroon and then along the Nigerian border. Volcanic soils derived from these mountains are more fertile than most others in the country and have permitted much higher rural population densities than elsewhere.

Cameroon has a marked south-north gradation of climates, from a seasonal equatorial climate in the south (with two rainy seasons and two moderately dry seasons of unequal length), to southern savannah and savannah climates (with one dry and one wet season), to a hotter drier climate of the Sahel type in the far north. Rainfall thus varies from more than 5,000 mm in the south-west to around 610 mm near Lake Chad. Corresponding to this climatic zonation is a south-north gradation of vegetal landscapes: dense rain forest, Guinea savannah, Sudan savannah and thorn steppe, while Mt Cameroun incorporates a vertical series of sharply divided vegetation zones.

POPULATION

The population of Cameroon was enumerated at 10,493,655 at the census of April 1987, and was estimated to have risen to 18,175,000 in mid-2006, giving an average density of 38.2 inhabitants per sq km. Population growth has been rapid (an average rate of 2.1% per year in 1995–2005) and the composition and distribution of the population are extremely diverse. In the southern forest regions Bantu peoples predominate, although there are also pygmy groups in some of the more remote areas. North of the Bantu tribes live many semi-Bantu peoples including the ubiquitous Bamiléké. Further north the diversity increases, with Sudanese Negroes, Hamitic Fulani (or Foulbe) and Arab Choa.

The distribution of population is uneven, with concentrations in the west, the south-central region and the Sudan savannah zone of the north. An important religious and social divide lies across the country. While the peoples of the south and west have been profoundly influenced by Christianity and by the European introduction of an externally orientated colonial-type economy, the peoples of the north are either Muslim or animist and have largely retained their traditional modes of life. Consequently, the population of the south and west is much more developed, economically and socially, than that of the north, although the Government has made efforts to reduce this regional disparity.

One aspect of this disparity is the southern location of the capital, Yaoundé (estimated population 1,485,000 in 2005), and the main port of Douala (1,761,000), as well as most of the other towns. Much of their growth results from rural–urban migration; many of the migrants come from overcrowded mountain massifs in the west, and the Bamiléké constitute more than one-third of the inhabitants of Douala. Nevertheless, about two-thirds of all Cameroonians remain rural village-dwellers.

One other major contrast in the social geography of Cameroon is between anglophone north-west and south-west Cameroon, with less than one-10th of the area and just over one-fifth of the population, and the much larger, more populous francophone area of former East Cameroon. The contrasting influences of British and French rule remain evident in education, commerce, law and elsewhere, although unification of the civil services since 1972, official bilingualism and the integration of transport networks and economies have helped to reduce the disparities between the two zones.

Recent History

PIERRE ENGLEBERT

Revised by KATHARINE MURISON

The German protectorate of Kamerun, of which the Republic of Cameroon was formerly a part, was established in 1884. In 1916 the German administration was overthrown by combined French-British-Belgian military operations during the First World War, and in 1919 the territory was divided into British and French spheres of influence. In 1922 both zones became subject to mandates of the League of Nations, which allocated four-fifths of the territory to French administration as French Cameroun, and the other one-fifth, comprising two long, non-contiguous areas along the eastern Nigerian border, to British administration as the Northern and Southern Cameroons.

In 1946 the mandates were converted into UN trust territories, still under their respective French and British administrations. However, growing anti-colonial sentiment made it difficult for France and Britain to resist the UN Charter's promise of eventual self-determination for all inhabitants of trust territories. In 1957 French Cameroun became an autonomous state within the French Community, and on 1 January 1960 proceeded to full independence as the Republic of Cameroon. Ahmadou Ahidjo, the leader of the Union camerounaise, who had served as Prime Minister since 1958, was elected as the country's first President.

In the British Cameroons, which was attached for administrative purposes to neighbouring Nigeria, a UN-supervised plebiscite was held in February 1961 in both parts of the trust territory. Voters in the Southern Cameroons opted for union with the Republic of Cameroon (which took place on 1 October), while northern Cameroon voters chose to merge with Nigeria (becoming the province of Sardauna). The new Federal Republic of Cameroon thus comprised two states: the former French zone became East Cameroon, while the former British portion became West Cameroon. Ahidjo assumed the presidency of the federation. In June 1972 the country was officially renamed the United Republic of Cameroon. The sole legal party, the Union nationale camerounaise (UNC), assumed full supervision of Cameroon's organized political and social affairs. In its foreign policy, the UNC Government adopted a non-aligned stance and sought to reduce its dependence on France and the Western bloc.

Despite dissatisfaction in some quarters with the single-party system and discontent among English-speaking politicians about their relatively low representation in government, Ahidjo and the UNC retained popular support in subsequent single-list elections. In 1980 Ahidjo was again re-elected as sole candidate for a further five-year term.

THE BIYA PRESIDENCY

In November 1982 Ahidjo resigned on the grounds of ill health, and transferred the presidency to Paul Biya, the country's Prime Minister since 1975. Ahidjo, however, retained the chairmanship of the UNC. By mid-1983 divisions between Ahidjo and Biya had become evident, and in August Biya announced the discovery of a plot to overthrow the Government. Two close associates of Ahidjo were arrested and Ahidjo passed the chairmanship of the UNC to Biya and left the country, dying in exile in 1989. In January 1984 Biya was re-elected President, as sole candidate, and the country's original official name, the Republic of Cameroon, was subsequently restored.

Reassertion of Presidential Power

Following an unsuccessful attempt by an army faction to overthrow the Government in April 1984, Biya moved decisively to reassert his control. Members of the Government whose loyalty remained in doubt were gradually removed from office, and most of the major public enterprises experienced a change of leadership. In March 1985 the UNC was renamed the Rassemblement démocratique du peuple camerounais (RDPC).

From January to March 1986 elections took place for members of RDPC bodies on all levels; the choice of candidates presented for election indicated that a measure of democratization was beginning to emerge; new candidates were elected to more than 50% of the posts. The gradual appointment to the administration of a number of the formerly influential functionaries of the Ahidjo period also indicated Biya's increasing confidence in the stability of his regime.

Elections to the National Assembly were held in April 1988, together with a presidential election. Voters in the legislative elections were presented with a choice of RDPC-approved candidates. Biya, the sole candidate for the presidency, obtained 98.75% of the votes cast. In May 1988 Biya dismissed 24 ministers and several ministries were merged or abolished.

Opposition and the Pro-Democracy Movement

In February 1990 12 people were imprisoned, having been found guilty of subversion as a result of their alleged involvement in an unofficial opposition organization, the Social Democratic Front (SDF). In May six deaths were reported, after security forces violently suppressed a demonstration organized by the SDF, which took place in Bamenda (in the English-speaking north-west of the country) and was attended by at least 20,000 people. The SDF, led by John Fru Ndi, received the support of many prominent writers and lawyers (and was alleged by the Government to be receiving financial support from Nigeria).

In June 1990 a congress of the RDPC re-elected Biya as President of the party and carried out a major reorganization of the central committee. In response to continued civil unrest, Biya stated that the future adoption of a multi-party system was envisaged, and subsequently announced the abolition of laws governing subversion, the relaxation of restraints on the press, and the reform of legislation prohibiting political associations. In the same month a committee was established to formulate legislation on human rights. In August several political prisoners were released. In September the Vice-President of the RDPC resigned, in protest at alleged corruption and violations of human rights by the Government.

In December 1990 the National Assembly approved a constitutional amendment providing for the establishment of a multi-party system. Under the new arrangements, the Government was required to grant (or refuse) registration within three months to any political association seeking legal recognition. In addition, registered parties were to receive state support during election campaigns. A large number of political associations subsequently emerged.

During 1991 pressure for political reform intensified. In January anti-Government demonstrators protested at Biya's failure (despite previous undertakings) to grant an amnesty to prisoners implicated in the April 1984 coup attempt. In April 1991 the National Assembly formally granted a general amnesty to all political prisoners, and reintroduced the post of Prime Minister. Sadou Hayatou, hitherto Secretary-General to the presidency, was appointed to the position. Hayatou subsequently formed a 32-member transitional Government, which principally comprised members of the former Cabinet. In late April a newly established alliance of 11 leading opposition groups, the National Co-ordination Committee of Opposition Parties (NCCOP), demanded an unconditional amnesty for all political prisoners (the existing arrangements for an amnesty excluded an estimated 400 political prisoners jailed ostensibly for non-political offences), and the convening of a national conference before 10 May. The continuing reluctance of the Government to set a date for the national conference prompted the NCCOP to initiate a campaign of civil disobedience, initially comprising one-day strikes and demonstrations. Opposition leaders also demanded the resignation of Hayatou and his Cabinet as a precondition to multi-party elections. Later that month seven of Cameroon's 10 provinces were placed under military rule, and in June the Government prohibited meetings of opposition parties. In June the NCCOP intensified the campaign of civil disobedience, and orchestrated a general strike. In response, the Government prohibited opposition gatherings, and, following continued civil disturbances, banned the NCCOP, whose leaders declared that the campaign of civil disobedience was to continue. However, the effect of the general strike declined in subsequent months.

In October 1991 Biya announced that legislative elections were to take place in February 1992, and that a Prime Minister was to be appointed from the party that secured a majority in the National Assembly. In November the Government and about 40 of the 47 registered opposition parties signed an agreement providing for the establishment of a 10-member committee to draft constitutional reforms. The opposition pledged to suspend the campaign of civil disobedience, while the Government agreed to end the ban on opposition meetings and to release all prisoners who had been arrested during the demonstrations earlier that year. However, several parties within the NCCOP, including the SDF, subsequently rejected the agreement. In December the Government ended the military rule that had been imposed in seven provinces. In the same month the National Assembly approved a new electoral code.

In January 1992 the Government announced that legislative elections would be held on 1 March. However, a number of opposition groups, including the SDF and the Union démocratique du Cameroun (UDC), refused to participate in the elections, claiming that the scheduled date was too early and that the electoral code was biased in favour of the RDPC. In February the opposition parties that had not accepted the agreement in November 1991 formed a political coalition, the Alliance pour le redressement du Cameroun (ARC), which was to boycott the elections. Later in February 1992 the former Prime Minister, Bello Bouba Maigari, was elected as Chairman of one of the principal opposition movements, the Union nationale pour la démocratie et le progrès (UNDP).

At the legislative elections on 1 March 1992, which were contested by 32 political parties, the RDPC won 88 of the 180 seats in the National Assembly; the UNDP secured 68 seats, the Union des populations camerounaises (UPC) 18, and the Mouvement pour la défense de la République (MDR) six seats. An estimated 61% of registered voters took part in the elections, although the proportion was only 10% in regions affected by the general strike. The RDPC formed an alliance with the MDR after the elections, thereby securing an absolute majority in the National Assembly. In April Biya announced a new Cabinet, which retained the majority of ministers from the previous administration. Five members of the MDR, including its leader, Dakole Daissala, also received portfolios. Simon Achidi Achu, an anglophone member of the RDPC who had served in the Ahidjo administration, was appointed Prime Minister.

In August 1992 Biya announced that the forthcoming presidential election, due to take place in May 1993, was to be brought forward to October. This measure was widely believed to benefit the Government, following the failure of a large number of opposition supporters to register earlier that year, as a result of the SDF boycott of the legislative elections. Later that month the Government introduced legislation regulating the election of the President, which prohibited political parties from forming electoral alliances, and stipulated that, contrary to the system in operation in most other francophone African countries, the election was to comprise a single round of voting. Following protracted negotiations, two of the seven opposition candidates withdrew in favour of the leader of the SDF, John Fru Ndi, who received the endorsement of the ARC alliance.

At the presidential election, which took place on 11 October 1992, Biya was re-elected by 39.9% of votes cast, while Fru Ndi secured 35.9%, and Maigari, the candidate of the UNDP, 19.2% of the vote. Fru Ndi disputed the official results, and claimed that he had won the election. A number of protest demonstrations ensued, particularly in the North-West Province and in Douala. However, the Supreme Court ruled against a petition by Fru Ndi to invalidate the election results, despite confirmation from a US monitoring organization that it had detected widespread electoral irregularities. At the end of October, in response to continued unrest, the Government placed Fru Ndi and a number of his supporters under house arrest, and placed the North-West Province under a state of emergency for a period of three months.

Pressure for Constitutional Reform

Biya was inaugurated for a third term as President in November 1992. Although he undertook to carry out further constitutional reforms, international criticism of the Government increased, resulting in the suspension of economic aid by the USA and Germany in protest at the suppression of opposition activity and the continued enforcement of the state of emergency. At the end of November Biya appointed a new Cabinet, which included representatives of the UPC, the UNDP and the Parti national du progrès (PNP). In December the state of emergency in the North-West Province was lifted.

In March 1993 the Union pour le changement, an alliance of opposition parties, which included the SDF, co-ordinated a campaign of demonstrations and a boycott of French consumer goods (in protest at the French Government's continuing support for Biya) to reinforce demands that a new presidential election take place. In the same month, in response to international pressure, the Government announced that a national debate on constitutional reform was to take place by the end of May. In April, following SDF demands that a revised constitution be submitted for approval at a national referendum by a stipulated date, Fru Ndi stated that he was to convene a national conference to determine the political future of Cameroon. In the same month a meeting organized by the Cameroon Anglophone Movement (CAM), which took place in Buéa, the capital of the South-West Province, issued demands for the restoration of a federal system of government, as a counter to the dominance of the French-speaking section of the population in the country.

Following a meeting with the French President, François Mitterrand, in May 1993, Biya announced that the planned debate on the revision of the Constitution was to take place in early June. Instead of the envisaged national conference, however, a technical commission was established to prepare recommendations based on proposals from all sectors of the population. Later in May the Government published draft constitutional amendments, which provided for a democratic system of government, including the establishment of an upper legislative chamber, a council of supreme judiciary affairs, a council of state, and a high authority to govern the civil service. The constitutional provisions also limited the tenure of the President to two five-year terms of office. Elections were to comprise two rounds of voting (a system more favourable to the opposition). The draft legislation retained a unitary state, but, in recognition of demands by supporters of federalism, introduced a more decentralized system of government. The constitutional proposals were subject to amendment, following the recommendations of the technical commission. However, three representatives of the English-speaking community subsequently resigned from the technical commission, in protest at the Government's alleged control of the constitutional debate.

At a party congress, which took place in July 1993, the SDF adopted a draft constitution that provided for a decentralized federal state. At the end of August a two-day strike organized by the SDF failed to attract the support of other prominent opposition parties, and was only partially observed. In November security forces prevented Fru Ndi from conducting a press conference in Yaoundé, and about 30 SDF members were arrested. They were subsequently released, following representations by the French Government.

In February 1994 six principal opposition parties (excluding the SDF) formed an electoral coalition, the Front démocratique et patriotique, to contest municipal elections due to take place later that year. In July, in accordance with the Government's aim of promoting economic recovery, a new ministry with responsibility for the economy and finance was created as part of an extensive reorganization of the Cabinet. At the end of that month about eight people were killed in clashes in the northern town of Maroua, following agitation within the UNDP, which subsequently led to a split in the party, over the decision by its Vice-Chairman, Hamadou Moustapha, to accept a cabinet portfolio without obtaining the party's prior consent.

In September 1994 an informal alliance of 16 opposition movements, the Front des alliés pour le changement (FAC), was established under the leadership of Fru Ndi (effectively replacing the Union pour le changement); the FAC criticized alleged human rights violations on the part of the authorities, together with the indefinite postponement of the municipal elections and the proposed transfer of state-owned enterprises to the private sector. The UNDP and the UDC refused to join the alliance, however, on the grounds that it was dominated by the SDF. In November Biya announced that discussions on the revision of the Constitution were to resume, following the establishment of a 'consultative constitutional review committee' and that the municipal elections were to take place in 1995.

Constitutional discussions in December 1994 were boycotted by the opposition, which objected to limitations in the agenda of the debate. In early 1995 revised constitutional amendments were submitted to Biya for consideration. In February the leader of the Mouvement pour la démocratie et le progrès (MDP), Samuel Eboua, was elected President of the FAC, replacing Fru Ndi. In the same month the UNDP expelled Moustapha and another member of the Government from the party. In April Biya announced the creation of 64 new local government districts, in preparation for the forthcoming municipal elections.

In early July 1995 members of a newly emerged anglophone organization, the Southern Cameroons National Council (SCNC, which demanded that the former portion of the British Cameroons that had amalgamated with the Republic of Cameroon in 1961 be granted autonomy), staged a demonstration in Bamenda, subsequently clashing with security forces. Later that month English-speaking representatives of the Government criticized the demands for the establishment of an anglophone republic (which would be known as Southern Cameroons); the SCNC apparently intended to proclaim formally the independence of Southern Cameroons on 1 October 1996, following the adoption of a separate constitution for the new republic. In early August the SCNC was prohibited from staging a demonstration. In the same month representatives of anglophone movements, including the SCNC and the CAM, officially presented their demands for the establishment of an independent republic of Southern Cameroons at the UN, and urged the international community to assist in resolving the issue in order to avert civil conflict in Cameroon; the organizations claimed that the plebiscite of 1961, whereby the former southern portion of British Cameroons had voted to merge with the Republic of Cameroon on terms of equal status, had been rendered invalid by subsequent francophone domination.

In October 1995 a special congress of the RDPC re-elected Biya as leader of the party for a further term of five years. Meanwhile, Cameroon's pending application for membership of the Commonwealth (see below) prompted further controversy; opposition movements urged the Commonwealth to refuse admission to Cameroon on the grounds that no progress had been achieved with regard to Commonwealth stipulations on human rights and the democratic process, while the SCNC submitted a rival application for membership on behalf of the proposed independent republic of Southern Cameroons. (Nevertheless, Cameroon was admitted to the organization in November.) In December the National Assembly formally adopted the revised constitutional amendments, submitted by Biya earlier that month, which increased the presidential mandate from five to seven years (while restricting the maximum tenure of office to two terms) and provided for the establishment of an upper legislative chamber, to be known as the Senate.

Some 38 political parties participated in the municipal elections, which finally took place in January 1996. The RDPC retained about 56% of the 336 local government areas, while the SDF secured 27%, principally in the west of the country. In March the SDF and the UNDP (which had also achieved some success in the municipal elections, principally in the north) urged a campaign of civil disobedience in protest at the Government's appointment by decree of representatives to replace the elected mayors in principal towns.

In September 1996 Biya appointed Peter Mafany Musonge, hitherto the manager of the Cameroon Development Corporation, to the office of Prime Minister, replacing Achidi Achu. In January 1997 the Government announced that the legislative elections, which had been scheduled to take place in March, were to be postponed owing to organizational difficulties, following complaints from opposition parties that their supporters had been allowed insufficient time for registration. At the end of March about 10 people, including three police-officers, were killed when unidentified armed groups staged attacks against government and security buildings in Bamenda and other towns in the North-West Province; a curfew was imposed in the province and a number of people were subsequently detained in connection with the violence, which was generally attributed to members of the SCNC.

The legislative elections, which were contested on 17 May 1997 by 46 political parties, were monitored by a Commonwealth observer mission. The announcement later that month of provisional election results (which attributed a large majority of seats to the RDPC) prompted claims from the opposition parties of widespread electoral malpractice. (The Commonwealth observer group also expressed general dissatisfaction with the election process.) Three people were killed in clashes between RDPC and SDF members in the South-West Province, where the election result was disputed by the two parties. In June the Supreme Court announced the official election results: the RDPC had secured 109 of the 180 seats in the legislature, while the SDF had won 43, the UNDP 13 and the UDC five seats; the Mouvement pour la jeunesse du Cameroun (MLJC), the UPC and the MDR obtained one seat each. On 3 August further polls were conducted in seven constituencies where the results had been annulled owing to alleged irregularities; the RDPC won all of the seats, thus increasing its level of representation in the National Assembly to 116 seats.

A presidential election was held on 12 October 1997, contested by seven candidates. The SDF, UNDP, UDC and Union du peuple africain (UPA) boycotted the election in protest at the absence of an independent electoral commission. While official sources asserted that a record 81.4% of the electorate participated in the election, opposition leaders claimed that, in fact, the abstention rate was higher than 80%, and denounced the poll as an 'electoral masquerade'. As anticipated, Biya was re-elected, obtaining a reported 92.6% of the votes cast. Of the other candidates, Henri Hogbe Nlend of the UPC secured 2.5% of the vote, while Samuel Eboua of the MDP won 2.4%. On 3 November Biya was formally inaugurated, beginning, in accordance with the revised Constitution, a seven-year term in office. Biya reappointed Musonge as Prime Minister. Following negotiations between the RDPC and elements of the opposition, the new Government, announced in early December, included members from four of Cameroon's approximately 150 political parties; the RDPC retained 45 of the 50 ministerial posts. Among the non-RDPC appointees were Bello Bouba Maigari of the UNDP, one of several prominent figures to have boycotted the October election, and Henri Hogbe Nlend, who was appointed Minister of Scientific and Technical Research. It was reported that the SDF had declined an invitation to enter into a coalition Government. Following the failure of further negotiations between the RDPC and the SDF (reportedly over the issue of the establishment of an independent national electoral commission), in February 1998 the SDF and the UDC announced their intention to form a common front of opposition.

In July 1998 10 of the 43 SDF parliamentary deputies resigned from the party, in protest at the perceived tribalism and authoritarianism of its leadership. In October the SDF expelled its first national Vice-President, Soulaimane Mahamad, following the latter's criticism of Fru Ndi's authoritarian style of leadership. In January 1999 Fru Ndi announced that he was willing to engage in direct dialogue with President Biya. It was, however, alleged that Fru Ndi had announced this radical change of policy in the hope of securing a favourable verdict in his prosecution on charges of defaming a former SDF official. In April Fru Ndi was, nevertheless, found guilty, and was fined and given a three-year suspended sentence. At the SDF party conference in that month Fru Ndi was re-elected party leader. The conference also voted not to enter into dialogue with the Government until an independent electoral commission had been established.

In September 1998 it was reported that, following attacks on police premises, more than 40 anglophone Cameroonians, who were alleged to be secessionists campaigning for the independence of Southern Cameroon, were being detained without trial and tortured in Yaoundé. The opposition suggested, however, that the raids had been staged by government agents as a pretext for further suppression of demands for increased decentralization. In January 1999 the opposition condemned the Government for the alleged marginalization of the anglophone minority, noting that only three of the 2,000 soldiers recently recruited by the armed forces were English-speaking. The trial of the alleged anglophone secessionists (the majority of whom had been arrested in 1997) began in June 1999. The defendants claimed that confessions that they were members of the separatist SCNC had been extracted under torture and threats of summary execution. The human rights organization Amnesty International later claimed that, prior to the start of the trial, several of the detainees had died in prison either because of torture or lack of medical care. In August the accused formally denied all the charges against them, although several individuals admitted to being members of a cultural association linked to the SCNC. In October three of the defendants were sentenced to life imprisonment, others received lengthy prison sentences, while 29 were acquitted. (In December 2005 the prison sentences of six of the convicted secessionists were reduced on appeal, while a further two detainees were acquitted.) Amnesty International and the UN's Human Rights Committee both subsequently criticized Cameroon for its alleged failure to protect and to respect fundamental human rights. In April 2003 the US Department of State added to international criticism of Cameroon's human rights record, citing the continuing problem of overcrowding in the country's prisons and several cases of 'disappearances' of political opponents of the Government.

Meanwhile, in September 1999 Mounchipou Seydou was dismissed as Minister of Posts and Telecommunications and was subsequently arrested on charges of embezzlement of public funds. There was a cabinet reshuffle in March 2000, which was widely interpreted as a response to an escalation in urban crime (several foreign diplomats had been attacked). All ministers linked to security matters were involved in the reshuffle, most notably the Minister of Territorial Administration, Samson Ename, who was replaced by Ferdinand Kougou Edima, a former governor. Furthermore, some 70% of senior police officers were reportedly replaced.

In November 2000 deputies staged a sit-in outside the National Assembly building after the security forces prevented a protest march, from the legislative building to the presidential palace, from proceeding. The march had been organized by the SDF in support of demands for the creation of an independent electoral commission. In the following month the National Assembly adopted legislation on the establishment of a National Elections Observatory and on the regulation of state funding for political parties and electoral campaigns. However, five opposition parties boycotted the vote on the new body, claiming that it would be unconstitutional, as it would perform the same functions as the Constitutional Council. The President's role in appointing its 11 members was also criticized. President Biya subsequently postponed municipal elections, scheduled for mid-January 2001, until January 2002, ostensibly on the grounds that the new electoral legislation had yet to become fully operational, and that the 21st Franco-African summit was to convene in Yaoundé a few days prior to the original date.

The SCNC boycotted the municipal and legislative elections, which were eventually held concurrently on 30 June 2002. Their postponement by one week, owing to insufficient voting materials, led to the dismissal of the Minister of Territorial Administration, Ferdinand Koungou Edima. In the event 47 political parties contested the elections to the National Assembly, at which the RDPC increased its representation to 133 seats, while the SDF won 21 seats, the UDC five, the UPC three and the UNDP only one seat. However, the Supreme Court cancelled voting in nine constituencies, where 17 seats were at stake, because of voters' complaints. The rate of voter participation was estimated at less than 50%. The RDPC also won 286 of the 336 council seats contested in the municipal elections. Opposition parties claimed that widespread electoral irregularities had taken place and demanded that the results be annulled. The Government refused, and, in response, six opposition parties, including the SDF, refused to participate in the newly elected legislature. However, the SDF's resolve was weakened by internal divisions, which were exacerbated in July, when Fru Ndi's unilateral decision to end the SDF boycott of the legislative institutions prompted allegations that he was in covert negotiations to secure a role in government. Twelve senior officials subsequently resigned from the SDF and formed a new political party, the Alliance des forces progressistes. In August there was an extensive cabinet reshuffle, in which 18 new members of government were appointed. On 15 September voting took place for the 17 legislative seats that had remained vacant since June; the RDPC secured a further 16 seats, increasing its majority to 149 of the 180 seats in the National Assembly, while the SDF won the remaining seat.

In mid-2003 the activities of several independent media outlets were suspended. In December a further 12 independent radio stations, many of which were based in English-speaking regions of Cameroon, were ordered to cease transmission. International press freedom organizations claimed that the Government had taken this action in order to suppress speculation relating to the forthcoming presidential election, which was due in October 2004. Also in December 2003 the legislature approved a series of reforms to the National Elections Observatory, including the extension of appointees' terms from one year to three years and provisions for public consultations (undertaken in early 2004) on appointments to the organization.

Biya Re-elected

In November 2003 the SDF, the UDC and three other opposition parties announced the formation of an electoral coalition, with the intention of nominating a single candidate to contest the forthcoming presidential election. A further four parties later joined the grouping, named the Coalition nationale pour la réconciliation et la reconstruction (CNRR). In July 2004 several people were injured in Yaoundé when the police intervened to suppress a protest march organized by the CNRR in support of its demand for the computerization of the electoral register. Further opposition demonstrations were staged in the capital on a weekly basis during the following months, and were similarly dispersed by the security forces. Up to 8,000 people reportedly attended a series of marches and demonstrations held in Bamenda in August in response to the recent murder of a local SDF politician. The SDF claimed that a tribal leader, who was also an RDPC deputy, was involved in the killing, which had allegedly followed a disagreement between the two men over voter registration in the area. (In February 2005 the National Assembly lifted the deputy's immunity from prosecution, and in April 2006 he and nine other defendants were sentenced to 15 years' imprisonment for involvement in the murder.)

The opposition's attempt to unite behind a single presidential candidate failed in September 2004, when Fru Ndi refused to stand aside for Adamou Ndam Njoya, the leader of the UDC, who had been selected to represent the CNRR. A total of 16 candidates registered to contest the election, which was held on 11 October, although three withdrew their candidatures on the eve of the poll. Biya was re-elected for a further seven-year term in office, securing 70.92% of the votes cast, according to final results. His two main opponents, Fru Ndi and Njoya, received 17.40% and 4.48% of the vote, respectively. A turn-out of 82.2% was officially recorded. Opposition parties accused Biya and his supporters of widespread electoral fraud, but their petitions to the Constitutional Council for the annulment of the poll were rejected. International observers from the Commonwealth and the Organisation internationale de la Francophonie declared themselves broadly satisfied with the conduct of the election, although they acknowledged shortcomings in its organization, in particular the exclusion of large numbers of eligible voters from the electoral roll. It was reported that only around 4.6m. voters of an adult population of some 8m. had been registered.

In December 2004 Biya appointed a new Cabinet, headed by Prime Minister Ephraim Inoni (hitherto Assistant Secretary-General of the Presidency). Inoni was an anglophone, like his predecessor, Musonge. Five political parties were represented in the new administration, although a large majority of positions were allocated to RDPC members. Inoni announced that economic reform would be his priority. The previous Government had been criticized for failing to address high unemployment, corruption and a lack of transparency in public finances.

An anti-corruption campaign, organized by the newly appointed Minister of the Economy and Finance, Polycarpe Abah Abah, was launched in January 2005, with the publication in local newspapers of the names of 73 senior civil servants accused of embezzling public funds. Most were dismissed from their posts, and some were to be tried on criminal charges. In March the Government announced that an investigation had revealed that fraudulent practices by some 500 officials at the Ministry of the Economy and Finance had increased the payroll by some 1,000m. francs CFA per month over several years. In August 2006 Abah Abah revealed that some 45,000 fictitious employees had been discovered on the government payroll, resulting in the theft of some US $10m. of public money each month.

Meanwhile, from April 2005 students began protests in support of their demands for the restoration of student grants and improved academic and living conditions. Following the deaths of two students in clashes with the security forces, President Biya ordered the disbursement of some 2,400m. francs CFA to improve university conditions. Most students had returned to classes by mid-May after the Government offered a number of concessions to their demands, although violent disturbances continued at Buéa University until the end of the month, when strike action was finally suspended, following the intervention of the Minister of Higher Education, Jacques Fame Ndongo.

In July 2005 the National Assembly approved legislation harmonizing the penal code in Cameroon. Hitherto, the francophone and anglophone regions of Cameroon had been subject to distinct penal codes based, respectively, on the Code d'instruction criminelle of 1938 and the Criminal Procedure Ordinance of 1958. The new, unique penal code was to combine elements of the Napoleonic, British and pre-colonial legal traditions. Although the measure was broadly welcomed as beneficial to national unity, opposition groups warned that it alone would not be sufficient to improve the legal system and protect citizens' rights. In June 2006 it was reported that public distrust of the police and judiciary had led to the widespread lynching of suspected criminals by vigilante mobs.

Discontent persisted among anglophones in southern Cameroon. The SCNC remained active, and its members continued to be regularly arrested, particularly around 1 October, the anniversary of the union of Southern Cameroons with the Republic of Cameroon, and 20 May, Cameroon's National Day. In October 2005 a clandestine SCNC radio station, Radio Free Southern Cameroons, commenced broadcasting in southern Cameroon.

The initiation by the Government of another anti-corruption campaign in January 2006 coincided with the dismissal of around 20 heads of public enterprises, a number of whom were subsequently arrested and charged with misappropriating public funds. A new national commission charged with combating corruption was created by presidential decree in March, and further arrests followed. In April the National Assembly adopted legislation requiring government members and other senior state officials involved in the management of public funds to declare to a nine-member commission their assets and property at the beginning and end of their tenures of office. The SDF expressed doubts regarding the independence of the commission, but the party's proposal that the declarations be made public was rejected.

Internal divisions within the SDF intensified in February 2006, when Clément Ngwasiri, the President of the party's National Advisory Council (NAC), was expelled from the party for conducting 'anti-party activities'. The NAC had recently declared that it was assuming the leadership of the party, claiming that the mandate of the SDF's National Executive Committee (NEC) had expired in April 2003. The NAC had also announced that the next congress of the party, scheduled for 26 May 2006, at which a new NEC was to be elected, would be held in Yaoundé rather than Bamenda, as arranged by the current NEC. In May the NEC dismissed Bernard Muna, a candidate for the chairmanship of the SDF, and some 20 other activists apparently allied to Ngwasiri from the party. SDF congresses were held in both Bamenda and Yaoundé on 26 May, despite an earlier court order suspending their organization. In Bamenda Fru Ndi was re-elected as national Chairman of the SDF, while in Yaoundé dissident party members elected Muna to this position. Prior to the Yaoundé congress Grégoire Diboulé, a pro-Ngwasiri regional leader of the SDF, was killed in violent clashes between the two rival factions of the party. More than 20 members of the SDF were subsequently arrested and charged with involvement in Diboulé's murder; they remained in detention, awaiting trial, in early 2007. Fru Ndi was reportedly charged with complicity in the murder, but was not detained. Meanwhile, Fru Ndi announced the formation of a 36-member 'shadow' cabinet in July 2006. A court in Bamenda ruled that Fru Ndi was the sole legitimate leader of the SDF in November.

At an RDPC congress, held in July 2006, Biya was re-elected party leader and pledged to organize elections to a new Senate (provision for which had been made in constitutional amendments adopted in December 2005) before the end of his presidential mandate in 2011. In September 2006 Biya effected a minor cabinet reshuffle, retaining Inoni as Prime Minister.

In late November 2006 two students at Buéa University were killed in clashes with the security forces, following demonstrations by students claiming that francophone candidates had been unfairly favoured in an entrance examination to the University's newly established school of medicine.

Legislation providing for the creation of a new independent electoral commission, Elections Cameroon (ELECAM), was approved in December 2006, following a commitment made by the Government to the Commonwealth at a meeting in February. The SDF boycotted the vote, expressing dissatisfaction that members of ELECAM would be appointed by the President and that there would be a delay before the new body would become operational. Pending ELECAM's establishment (which was to be achieved within 18 months), the National Elections Observatory and the Ministry of Territorial Administration and Decentralization would remain responsible for organizing and supervising elections. In March 2007 it was reported that a group of RDPC deputies was seeking to amend the Constitution to allow Biya to stand for the presidency again in 2011 by abolishing the limitation on terms that had been adopted in December 2005. In April 2007 legislative and municipal elections were scheduled for 22 July.

REGIONAL CONCERNS

During 1989–93 President Biya actively sought Cameroon's admission to the Commonwealth, which, following the Government's agreement to comply with certain democratic conditions, was approved in 1993. Its membership took effect in November 1995. Apart from a border dispute with Nigeria, relations with neighbouring countries are generally harmonious. In March 2001 tensions arising from a series of incursions into Cameroonian territory by heavily armed troops from the Central African Republic (CAR) were defused following a negotiated withdrawal. In December 2005 the first meeting was held of a bilateral commission charged with addressing security concerns at the border between Cameroon and the CAR; insecurity at the border persisted in 2006–07, however. In November 2006 the office of the UN High Commissioner for Refugees (UNHCR) reported that some 30,000 people from the CAR were seeking refuge in Cameroon, having fled attacks by bandits and former rebels in their own country; the refugees were mainly nomadic cattle breeders, belonging to the Mbororo ethnic group.

The Bakassi Dispute

In June 1991 the Nigerian Government claimed that Cameroon had annexed nine Nigerian fishing settlements, following a long-standing border dispute, based on a 1913 agreement between Germany and the United Kingdom that ceded the Bakassi peninsula in the Gulf of Guinea (a region of strategic significance) to Cameroon. Subsequent attempts to negotiate the dispute achieved little progress. In January 1994 it was reported that members of the Cameroonian security forces had entered Nigeria and raided villages, killing several Nigerian nationals. Nigeria subsequently occupied the two nominally Cameroonian islands of Diamant and Jabane in the Gulf of Guinea. Cameroon also dispatched troops to the region. In February the Cameroon Government announced that it was to submit the matter to adjudication by the UN Security Council, the Organization of African Unity (OAU, now the African Union) and the International Court of Justice (ICJ), based in The Hague, Netherlands. However, subsequent clashes between Nigerian and Cameroonian forces in the disputed region prompted fears of a full-scale conflict. In May two members of the Nigerian armed forces were killed in further clashes in the region. Later that month negotiations between the two nations, which were mediated by the Togolese Government, resumed in Yaoundé. In September 10 members of the Cameroonian armed forces were killed in further confrontations.

In February 1996 renewed hostilities between Nigerian and Cameroonian forces in the Bakassi peninsula resulted in several casualties. Later that month Cameroon and Nigeria agreed to refrain from further military action, and delegations from the two countries resumed discussions, again with Togolese mediation. In March the ICJ ordered both nations to cease military operations in the region, to withdraw troops to former positions, and to co-operate with a UN investigative mission, which was to be dispatched to the area. In April, however, clashes continued, with each Government accusing the other of initiating the attacks. Claims by Nigeria that the Cameroonian forces were supported by troops from France were denied by the French Government. Tension between the two countries increased in July, after the Nigerian Government accused Cameroon of reinforcing its contingent in the Bakassi peninsula. In September both Governments assured the UN investigative mission of their commitment to a peaceful settlement of the dispute. In December and May 1997, however, the Nigerian authorities claimed that Cameroonian troops had resumed attacks in the region. Renewed fighting between Cameroonian and Nigerian forces was reported in December and February 1998. In September Nigeria moved more troops and equipment into the peninsula in response to reports, denied by the authorities in Yaoundé, that Cameroon had massed troops in the area. In October further contention arose when Nigeria alleged that Cameroon had awarded a Canadian company a concession to prospect for petroleum in the disputed area. Cameroon insisted that the concession had been granted for three areas, none of which was in the Bakassi peninsula.

From late 1998 relations between the two countries began to improve, and in November the International Committee of the Red Cross organized a prisoner exchange between the two sides. In April 1999 the President-elect of Nigeria, Gen. Olusegun Obasanjo, visited Cameroon, the first such visit since the beginning of the border conflict in 1994. The two countries were reported to have agreed to resolve the dispute 'in a fraternal way'. It was, however, announced that the ICJ proceedings would continue.

In October 2002 the ICJ issued its final verdict on the demarcation of the land and maritime boundary between Cameroon and Nigeria, notably ruling in favour of Cameroon's sovereignty over the Bakassi peninsula, citing the 1913 Anglo-German partition agreement. Despite having no option to appeal, Nigeria refused to accept the Court's decision, ostensibly in view of claims that some 90% of the peninsula's residents were Nigerian citizens. Troop deployments began to increase on both sides of the border, prompting fears of a full-scale armed conflict between the two countries. In November, however, at a meeting in Geneva, Switzerland, mediated by the Secretary-General of the UN, Kofi Annan, the Presidents of Cameroon and Nigeria signed a joint communiqué announcing the creation of a bilateral 12-member commission, to be headed by a UN Special Representative, with a mandate to achieve a peaceful solution to the Bakassi peninsula dispute. At its inaugural meeting in Yaoundé in December, the commission agreed on a 15-point peace agenda and decided to establish a sub-committee to undertake the demarcation of the boundary.

In August 2003 Nigeria and Cameroon adopted a framework agreement for the implementation of the ICJ's judgment, providing for the withdrawal of all military and administrative personnel from the Bakassi region; the process of demarcation of boundaries between the two countries was expected to take up to three years to complete. The bilateral commission requested that the international community support the cost of the exercise, which was estimated at some US $12m. In December the Nigerian Government ceded control of 33 villages on its north-eastern border to Cameroon, but sovereignty over the disputed territory with petroleum resources remained under discussion. In January 2004 Presidents Biya and Obasanjo, meeting in Geneva, with UN mediation, agreed to exchange consular envoys and to establish joint security patrols in the disputed region; the eventual signing of a treaty of friendship and non-aggression was envisaged. Following an amicable meeting in Yaoundé in July between Presidents Biya and Obasanjo, it was confirmed that Nigerian troops would withdraw from Bakassi by 15 September. However, just days before the expiry of the deadline the Nigerian Government announced that the transfer of authority in the peninsula had been delayed by technical difficulties in demarcating the maritime border. A meeting of the joint commission aimed at resolving the deadlock over the transfer ended without agreement in October. In April 2005 Cameroon and Nigeria signed an agreement with UNHCR providing for the voluntary repatriation of some 10,000 Nigerians who had entered Cameroon in 2002, fleeing inter-ethnic conflict in Taraba State, in eastern Nigeria.

In May 2005, at talks in Geneva, again mediated by Annan, Presidents Biya and Obasanjo agreed to accelerate the negotiation of a new programme for the withdrawal of Nigerian troops from Bakassi. In July the bilateral commission resumed its activities in Yaoundé, establishing a joint working group to draft a new timetable for the withdrawal of Nigerian troops from the peninsula. At a meeting in the Nigerian capital, Abuja, in October, the bilateral commission reached agreement on a new programme for Nigeria's withdrawal, based on the report of the joint working group. On 12 June 2006, at bilateral talks mediated by Annan in New York, USA, Obasanjo signed an agreement to withdraw Nigerian troops from Bakassi within 60–90 days. The deadline for the withdrawal was met, with Nigerian troops leaving the peninsula on 14 August. Pending a full transfer of authority in Bakassi, which was to be completed within two years, the southern part of the peninsula was to remain under Nigerian administrative control.

Economy

CHARLOTTE VAILLANT

Based on an earlier article by EDITH HODGKINSON

From independence until the mid-1980s Cameroon's record was one of strengthening, diversified economic growth. This was based on a flourishing agricultural sector, with a range of export and food crops (food self-sufficiency was attained relatively early), and the development of petroleum from the late 1970s. In the first half of the 1980s economic growth averaged 7%–8% annually (more than double the annual average in the previous two decades).

The situation deteriorated sharply, however, following the steep decline in the international price for petroleum in the second half of the 1980s, when reduced export and public revenues forced the Government to adopt austerity policies. As a result, Cameroon's economy contracted rapidly for almost a decade, with the rate of decline in real gross domestic product (GDP) reaching 10.4% in the year ending 30 June 1988. Economic decline was arrested with the devaluation of the CFA franc in January 1994. After falling by an average of about 4% per year between 1990/91 and 1993/94, GDP rose by 3.3% in 1994/95 and growth was maintained at 4%–5% per year throughout the following five years, representing a steady yet slow recovery in per capita income.

A continued decline in petroleum production adversely affected economic growth in the early 2000s. A weak business environment, combined with acute competition from abroad, hindered progress in manufacturing over the same period. As a result, the non-oil sector remained dominated by performance in agriculture. Rising performance in services, in particular telecommunications and transport, none the less, helped to maintain real GDP growth above 4% in 2001, 2002, and 2003. Two successive years of decelerating economic growth ensued, with growth of 3.7% and 2.0% recorded in 2004 and 2005, respectively. Because of a disappointing performance in forestry and agriculture, GDP growth remained sluggish in 2006, at an estimated 3.5%, despite a recovery in oil production. Cameroon's economic prospects depend on continued reforms to combat corruption, improve the business climate and resource allocation and to diversify the economy away from primary commodities, especially petroleum. Cameroon ranked

152nd out of 175 states in the World Bank's Doing Business 2007 index.

AGRICULTURE

Agriculture, forestry and fishing contributed an estimated 21% to Cameroon's GDP in 2005, and, according to FAO estimates, provided a livelihood for an estimated 54% of the labour force. This sector's share of GDP represented a significant decline from its 32% contribution in the year 1978/79, when the petroleum sector was not yet developed. Small-scale farmers dominate agricultural export production with the exception of rubber and palm oil. By contrast, timber production remains the sphere of large foreign firms, despite efforts to enhance Cameroonian participation. In the early 1980s the role of the national agricultural marketing board, the Office national de commercialisation des produits de base (ONCPB), was reduced, and responsibility for marketing was gradually transferred to the private sector.

The agricultural sector is well diversified, reflecting the country's varied ecology. The export-crop sector includes coffee, cocoa, palm oil, banana and sugar cane. The food-crop sector includes maize, millet, sorghum and rice. Cameroon is a significant world producer of cocoa, ranking sixth in recent years. Cocoa was grown on an estimated 400,000 ha in 2005, according to FAO. Coffee is also cultivated on some 250,000 ha, predominantly in the west and south. Nine-10ths of the coffee crop is robusta. Coffee and cocoa output can fluctuate widely from year to year, reflecting climatic and vegetative circumstances and fluctuations in international prices. Both coffee and cocoa yields have suffered as a result of the failure of replanting programmes to keep pace with the ageing of plantations. The coffee sector was also greatly affected by dwindling international prices from the mid-1990s until a slight recovery in recent years. Cocoa farmers in Cameroon benefited from the political crisis in Côte d'Ivoire (traditionally the world's leading producer) and rising international cocoa prices in the early 2000s. In 2005 cocoa and coffee production amounted to 178,500 metric tons and 43,620 tons, respectively.

Bananas also became a leading agricultural export, following the transfer to the private sector of the state-owned enterprise Organisation Camerounaise de la Banane in the late 1980s. The sector's prospects have deteriorated with the end of the banana-quota scheme operated by the European Union (EU), of which Cameroon is a beneficiary. The erosion in trade preferences from the EU in large part explains the fall in banana production from a peak 313,700 metric tons in 2003 to an estimated 270,800 tons in 2005.

Cotton production, which is concentrated in the north, totalled 306,000 metric tons in 2004/05. Output of palm oil averaged 100,000 tons per year in the mid-1990s, but production was an estimated 172,047 tons by 2004. Rubber has good prospects, with yields competing with those of the major Asian producers. Output was estimated at 61,000 tons in 2004. Commercial production of cane sugar began in 1966, and production stood at 1.5m. tons by 2004.

Cameroon's food production has been advancing at a higher rate than population growth, and the country is generally self-sufficient. In 2004 output of millet and sorghum reached an estimated 610,000 metric tons, while maize production amounted to an estimated 850,000 tons. The annual harvest of paddy rice, which is grown under both traditional and modern methods, increased from only 15,000 tons in 1979/80 to 107,400 tons in 1984/85, reflecting the Government's priority of achieving self-sufficiency in cereals. Output has since fluctuated fairly widely, mainly in response to drought. According to FAO, production reached 70,000 tons in 2005, against a previous five years average production of 65,000 tons. Nevertheless, the long-term target for annual rice production remains 280,000 tons. Livestock, mainly raised by traditional methods, makes a significant contribution to the food supply. In 2004 the national herd was estimated at 5.6m. cattle, 8.2m. sheep and goats and 1.4m. pigs, while commercial poultry farms had an estimated 31m. chickens. Poultry production increased markedly since the introduction of an import ban on frozen chickens in 2004. The development of the fisheries industry has been constrained by the relatively small area available for exploitation (because of boundary disputes and the presence of the offshore island of Bioko, part of Equatorial Guinea) and the poor level of fish stocks in these waters. In 2005 the total catch was estimated at some 142,700 metric tons by FAO, with industrial fishing accounting for less than one-10th of the total.

Almost one-half of the country is covered by forest, but an inadequate transport system has impeded the development of this sector, and only around one-third of the area has been exploited. Forestry is Cameroon's second most important source of export earnings after oil, with roundwood and sawnwood exports amounting to roughly 15% of total export receipts. The Government implemented forestry legislation in 1999, when unprocessed log exports of 23 endangered hardwood species, including mahogany and sapele, were banned. Some progress has been made as a result, with log production officially declining from 3,400,000 cu m in 2000/01 to 1,931,100 cu m in 2002/03 and to 1,738,200 cu m in 2003/04. At the same time, processed wood production has increased, with national sources estimating the 2003 increase at 12.5%. According to IMF and government estimates, production declined in 2005, as reforms to foster sustainable forestry production led to decreased utilization of forestry permits.

MINING AND POWER

While by far the largest source of foreign exchange earnings, mining (including petroleum production) amounted to just 4.3% of GDP in 2004. In 1976 the French petroleum company Elf (now part of Total) established a commercial oilfield in shallow water near the Nigerian border, and four fields came on stream in 1977–78. Production of crude petroleum reached a peak of 9.2m. metric tons in 1985, but declined to 5.4m. tons in 1995. A recovery was recorded in 1998, when output totalled 6.0m. tons, in response to improved incentives for the development of marginal fields. Output has since declined continuously, as a result of the maturation of the main fields. Crude oil production fell to 3.2m. tons in 2004 and 3.0m. tons in 2005. There was a slight recovery in production to an estimated 3.2m. tons in 2006, as new minor oil fields came on stream. Transparency in the management of oil revenues has meanwhile recently increased with Cameroon joining the Extractive Industry Transparency Initiative (EITI).

In October 2002 the International Court of Justice granted Cameroon sovereignty over the oil-rich Bakassi peninsula, settling a dispute with Nigeria. This, combined with new tax incentives introduced by the Cameroonian Government in 2002, could open new development prospects in the petroleum sector. Nigeria completed its withdrawal from the Bakassi peninsula on 14 August 2006 (see Recent History). Meanwhile, in July 2003 a consortium, involving Petronas of Malaysia, and the US companies ExxonMobil and ChevronTexaco, completed construction of a 1,070-km subterranean pipeline to transport oil from the Doba basin in southern Chad to a marine export terminal off the southern Cameroonian port of Kribi. Royalties from the new terminal were projected to total an estimated US $550m. over a 28-year period, which would partially offset the decline in direct revenue from petroleum mining. Exploration has, meanwhile, continued in the Río del Rey Basin and the Douala Basin, with the announcement of minor oil discoveries and the signing of two new production-sharing agreements in 2005 and 2006. In September 2006 the Socitété Nationale des Hydrocarbures launched a tender for exploration in six new blocks of the Río Del Rey basin. Total proven petroleum reserves in Cameroon were estimated at 400m. barrels at the end of 2004. Natural gas reserves, estimated by the US Energy Information Administration at 3,900m. cu ft at the end of 2004, are still unexploited. In June 2002 nine companies were invited to consider developing the Sanaga Sud gasfield. Six bids were received and in 2006 the Société Nationale des Hydrocarbures signed a production-sharing agreement with Perenco to develop and exploit the offshore gasfield.

Major bauxite deposits, at Minim Martap (900m. metric tons) and Ngoundal (200m. tons), have also yet to be exploited, although their development would enable the Edéa smelter, which produces some 95,000 tons of aluminium annually, but is dependent on imports of bauxite from Guinea, to be supplied locally. Deposits of iron ore near Kribi also remain unexploited (despite some recent Australian interest) and uranium reserves totalling up to 10,000 tons have been identified, but not developed, owing to low international prices. There is potential for gold mining, but so far all operations remain small-scale. Extensive limestone deposits near Garoua supply clinker and cement plants, and considerable nickel reserves also exist at Nkamouna in East Province. In mid-2003 new regulations were approved, replacing the somewhat restrictive mining law of 1964, and appeared to pave the way for wider commercial exploitation of the country's non-oil mineral resources.

In early 2006 total installed generating capacity in Cameroon amounted to 933 MW, consisting of 721 MW of hydroelectric capacity and 212 MW of thermal capacity. Heavy industry is the major consumer, with the aluminium plant, Alucam, taking nearly 50% of the total generation. The chief installations are at Edéa (total capacity 263 MW) and at Song-Loulou (total capacity 384 MW). These stations supply the network linking Yaoundé, Edéa, Douala and the west. The other major network supplies the north and draws principally on the 72-MW hydroelectric station at Lagdo. In 2001 the US company AES bought a majority share in the electricity provider, Société Nationale d'Electricité du Cameroun (SONEL). In August 2004 AES-SONEL completed the construction of a new 85-MW oil-fired plant at Limbé. The company has plans for a natural gas-fired, 150-MW plant at Kribi and an invitation for tenders for the construction of the plant was published in September 2006. The plant could become operational within a year after its construction begins. A dam at Lom Pangar on the Sanaga river was scheduled for completion in 2010. The Government also plans to increase electricity supply by building a new hydroelectric plant at Memve'ele in South province. In 2006 the Electricity Development Corporation (EDC) was established to manage all the infrastructure belonging to the state in the electricity sector, including the country's dams. Plans for these new investments are slow to materialize, however, and the energy shortage remains acute. Meanwhile, about 40 diesel-fuelled stations, with a total capacity of 82 MW, are used as back-up facilities.

MANUFACTURING

Manufacturing contributed an estimated 19% of GDP in 2005. In 2004 the housing and construction sectors comprised 3% of GDP, while utilities accounted for 1%. The GDP of the secondary sector (excluding mining) increased by 8.4% in 2002, as domestic demand increased with the construction of the Chad–Cameroon pipeline. Growth slowed to 1.3% in 2003 but increased to 2.3% in 2004. Growth slowed again in 2005 when an increase of just 0.7% was recorded, before rising once again in 2006 to 2.0%. The manufacturing sector is dominated by the processing of agricultural goods and raw materials, and the assembly of imported raw materials and components. The bulk of manufacturing industry is of post-independence origin, when the Government began to give priority to industrial development aimed at national and regional markets. To this end, extensive tax and financing incentives were made available, while the state took substantial share-holdings in major ventures, held through the Société Nationale d'Investissement du Cameroun. A number of projects initiated at the beginning of the 1980s were not generally successful. An integrated pulp and paper mill was developed at Edéa, but was in operation for only five years, closing down in 1986 after suffering heavy losses. A petroleum refinery began production at Cap Limboh in 1981. Its initial annual capacity was increased to 2m. metric tons, but output declined to less than 1m. tons, owing to competition from illicit imports from Nigeria. The refinery announced plans to increase production capacity in 2006. Local manufacturing, notably sugar, cement and textiles, has also been adversely affected by the widespread illicit trade in Nigerian goods, resulting from the strong CFA franc; the currency devaluation of 1994 provided only a temporary respite. Ageing plants and electricity rationing similarly explained why the industrial sector worked roughly 30% below capacity in 2000–01. Public works performed particularly well over this period, primarily as a result of the construction of the Chad–Cameroon pipeline.

The economic crisis in the 1980s prompted a reversal in government policies, with a programme for the privatization of state-owned companies and a tightening up or liquidation of those running at a loss. However, resistance from adversely affected interests meant that little progress was made until late 1990, when 15 companies were transferred to the private sector. Other parastatal enterprises were liquidated, and those remaining under the aegis of the state, such as SONEL, were obliged to sign performance contracts with the Government as part of the overall structural adjustment programme. Privatization continued in subsequent years, although the programme was constantly behind target, owing, in part, to the poor financial situation of the enterprises. Following renewed pressure from its multilateral creditors, the Government has expanded the programme since mid-1994, and by late 2003 some major disposals had been effected in manufacturing, including the sugar and palm oil companies, the tea component of the Cameroon Development Corporation (CDC), and SONEL. However, the sale of the largest single state enterprise, the CDC (with remaining interests in rubber, palm oil, and bananas), the water utility, Société Nationale des Eaux du Cameroun (SNEC), and SODECOTON, The Government has repeatedly renewed its commitment to privatization, in an effort to comply with IMF recommendations (see Foreign Trade and Aid). A new call for tenders for the lease management contract of SNEC was issued in November 2006.

TRANSPORT AND TELECOMMUNICATIONS

The transport infrastructure suffers from inadequate investment and maintenance, although major divestitures—including the shipping line, the state railway, and Douala harbour—have taken place in the past decade. The rail network, totalling some 1,104 km, forms the most important component. The main line is the 885-km Transcameroon, from Douala to Ngaoundéré. In July 2002 the World Bank disbursed a 15,600m.-francs CFA loan to Cameroon to help rehabilitate the main line. There are plans to connect the line with the proposed new port at Grand Batanga (see below) and, in the long term, to construct a 1,000-km line from Kribi to the Central African Republic (CAR).

According to the OECD, the road network totalled some 50,000 km in 2005, of which an estimated 5,000 km were paved. The privatization of road maintenance works, and strong foreign donor support, notably from the EU, has supported progress in this sub-sector since the late 1990s. Roads in the north have been improved to give access to the Ngaoundéré rail-head, and there are long-term plans to upgrade the east-west road linking Nigeria with the CAR. Work to rehabilitate the Wouri bridge in Douala began in 2004.

Cameroon has seaports at Douala-Bonabéri, Kribi and Limbé-Tiko (although the latter is now almost completely unusable), and a river port at Garoua. Total handling capacity is 7m. metric tons annually. Feasibility studies have been conducted for deep-water ports at Cap Limboh (near Limbé and the oil refinery) and Grand Batanga, south of the existing port handling wood and minerals at Kribi. The latter is dependent on the exploitation of the offshore gas reserve and iron ore reserves, neither of which seems likely in the near future.

The poor state of the road network has encouraged the development of internal air travel and of small domestic airports. There are international airports at Douala, Garoua and Yaoundé. In early 2006 one-half of Cameroon Airlines' (CAMAIR) 900 employees were made redundant, and the Government pre-selected four airlines to participate in a tender for the national carrier: SN Brussels, Royal Air Maroc, Kenya Airways, and Comair of South Africa. CAMAIR, which was highly indebted, was to be liquidated before the new operator takes over. CAMAIR held traffic rights on domestic flights and services to Africa and Europe. Negotiations with the provisional successful bidder began in mid-November 2006.

The telecommunication company Cameroon Telecommunications (CAMTEL) is also scheduled for privatization. After an abortive attempt to sell a majority share in the company in 1999, the Government issued a tender for pre-qualification in early 2006. Privatization was further delayed in 2006 to allow more time for preparation of the final documents.

CAMTEL was the sole fixed line company operating in the country. Created in 1998, it has currently 110,000 subscribers. In early 2006 there were three mobile phone providers in Cameroon: MTN Cameroon, which had 1.1m. subscribers in September 2005; Orange, which had 889,000 subscribers at that time; and Cameroon Mobile Telecommunications Corporation (launched by CAMTEL in March 2006).

FINANCE

Revenue from petroleum production profoundly changed the country's fiscal position, and allowed a rapid rise in both current and capital spending during the early 1980s. The situation was transformed by the collapse of international oil prices in 1986, which led to diminished petroleum royalties, and was followed by a general contraction in the economy. The Government initially tried to sustain the level of investment expenditure and imports by drawing on the accumulated oil revenue held in an extrabudgetary account. However, with the continued weakness in international prices for petroleum and for the country's major cash crops, these funds were largely depleted by the end of the decade. In this situation, the Biya Government was obliged to introduce austerity programmes, involving reductions in both current and capital expenditure. With the support of the World Bank, the ADB and France, the Government commenced an extensive, five-year programme of economic restructuring in 1989/90. This entailed the reform of the country's parastatal organizations (through the liquidation of unprofitable enterprises and the transfer to private ownership of others) and of the inefficient administrative structure. At the same time, the Government sought to impose strict controls on public spending, including a 'freeze' on civil service recruitment, and introduced measures to expand the tax base. The fiscal balance fluctuated thereafter, with a deficit reaching an equivalent 13.4% of GDP in 1990/91. The situation was compounded by social unrest in the early 1990s, and a politically motivated refusal to pay taxes. Performance subsequently improved after the CFA franc devaluation in 1994, to within the range 1%–2% (after grants) in 1995/96–1997/98. This was due to increased foreign assistance (at first, mostly from France) and a steady improvement in non-oil tax receipts (further helped by the restoration in 1994/95 of export taxes on agro-industrial products, made feasible by the currency's devaluation).

IMF support resumed in the wake of the devaluation, but relations proved difficult and disbursements were repeatedly suspended as the Government failed to comply with performance criteria. In August 1997, however, with a new Government showing convincing commitment to structural reform, the IMF extended a US $220m. enhanced structural adjustment facility (ESAF). The Government maintained fiscal restraint in 1998/99, despite a 34.8% fall in oil revenues that year, and in 1999/2000 the fiscal balance (on a commitment basis) turned into a surplus of 81,000m. francs CFA (equivalent to 1.4% of GDP). An increase in, and extension of, the sales tax also helped to improve the fiscal balance (a value-added tax was introduced in 1999), while the privatization or liquidation of parastatal companies further contributed to boosting non-oil revenues. After strengthening significantly in 1997–2000, Cameroon's fiscal position deteriorated in subsequent years. On the expenditure side, fiscal benchmarks continued to focus on efforts to mobilize non-oil revenue through more efficient and transparent tax and custom management. By 2002–03, however, non-oil revenue collection began falling, as a result of lower tax compliance and continuous delays in structural reforms. At the same time, petroleum revenue failed to increase (despite higher international prices for that commodity) owing to a decline in production volumes, an increase in the discount for lower quality petroleum and the appreciation of the CFA franc against the US dollar. The Government failed to shift spending allocation away from recurrent expenditure, despite a commitment to increase public investment and social spending under the Poverty Reduction Strategy Paper. The financial situation of state-owned enterprises also deteriorated over this period, primarily as a result of growing payment arrears by the Government and delays in financial restructuring. Budgetary slippage in 2004 led to the suspension of the IMF Poverty Reduction Growth Facility (PRGF) programme agreed in December 2000. Fiscal performance improved in 2005, prompting the IMF to approve a new three-year PRGF, worth $26.8m. in October of that year. According to IMF projections, in 2005 the fiscal balance (including grants) rose to a surplus equivalent to 2.0% of GDP. Fiscal performance in the first half of 2006 was also deemed satisfactory, with non-oil revenue benchmarks being met and oil revenues being higher than expected. There was some overall concern, however, that poverty-related expenditures were below target, while public-sector reforms (including CAMTEL, SNEC, and the post office) suffered continuous delays.

The financial sector is relatively sophisticated; however, the economic crisis of the late 1980s affected the sector rapidly and severely, as the Government withdrew its reserves with the commercial banks and private companies supplying the public sector suffered from accumulating arrears. By 1987 most commercial banks were technically insolvent. An important element of the structural adjustment programme in 1989–92 was a restructuring of the financial sector, with banks being liquidated or, in a few cases, merging. There was a new wave of reforms in 1995–98. The Banque Internationale pour le Commerce et l'Industrie du Cameroun was closed in 1996 and was renamed Banque Internationale du Cameroun pour l'Epargne et le Crédit, under French management, in 1997. The commercial banking sector had returned to profit by mid-1997, and later in that year two new commercial banks opened up, the Commercial Bank of Cameroon and Citicorp of Cameroon. Yet the banking sector remains dominated by three main banks (including the Société Générale de Banques au Cameroun and the Banque Internationale du Cameroun pour l'Epargne et le Crédit), while state-owned financial institutions, such as the Cameroon Postal Service (CAMPOST), require restructuring. In April 2003 Cameroon's first stock exchange opened in Douala; it was hoped that this might drive the expansion of the private sector by improving its access to finance. However, by mid-2005 no companies were listed on the exchange, reflecting concerns over relatively weak regulations, potential corruption and competition from the regional stock exchange in Libreville, Gabon. Trading started a year later, with the listing of shares from the company Société des eaux minérales du Cameroun (SEMC).

FOREIGN TRADE AND AID

The emergence of petroleum as a leading export in the late 1970s resulted in a considerable and growing surplus on foreign trade, despite significant increases in the level of import spending. Although petroleum earnings declined sharply in the late 1980s, trade remained in substantial surplus, sustained by earnings from agricultural exports. None the less, export coverage of imports narrowed from the 200% recorded in 1985 to an average of 140% by the late 1990s. A trade surplus of 73,000m. francs CFA was recorded in 2003, as a result of the hugely reduced import and services bill following the completion of the Chad–Cameroon oil pipeline. The continued rise in world petroleum prices since 2002 has boosted export revenues, despite a fall in petroleum production and the continued appreciation of the CFA franc against the US dollar. As a result, the trade balance turned into a small surplus in 2005. The current-account deficit (including grants) amounted to 3.4% of GDP in 2005 and, according to the IMF, was projected to fall to just 0.4% of GDP in 2006. In that year receipts from petroleum were estimated to amount to 54% of total exports.

The high level of earnings from the petroleum sector during the early 1980s enabled development expenditure to be financed without a substantial increase in the foreign debt. Servicing of the foreign debt was thus manageable, representing about 15% of export earnings in most years during the first half of the decade. However, the January 1994 devaluation of the CFA franc doubled overnight the local currency value of the foreign debt and special debt relief measures were agreed. A 'Paris Club' rescheduling agreement was suspended in 1995, as a result of policy shortcomings and withheld payments by the IMF and the World Bank. With the IMF's approval of a

US $220m. ESAF in August 1997, a major new debt-rescheduling agreement valued at some $2,000m. was signed with the 'Paris Club' in October. As a result, Cameroon cleared all its arrears on previously deferred debt to 'Paris Club' creditors and was up-to-date on non-rescheduled debt. The external debt continued to rise, to $9,917m. by the end of 1998, but declined in subsequent years, reaching $8,367m. at the end of 2001, equivalent to 103% of gross national income (GNI); the debt-service ratio in that year was 12.6%, compared with 20.4% at the end of 2000.

In October 2000 the IMF and World Bank agreed to grant Cameroon a debt-service relief package under the enhanced initiative for heavily indebted poor countries (HIPC), worth US $2,000m. This included $1,300m. of bilateral debt relief, as later formally agreed by the 'Paris Club' in December 2000. Interim HIPC debt relief began in 2001 and in August 2002 the British Government agreed to cancel 90% of Cameroon's external debt (worth 40,000m. francs CFA) and to reschedule the remaining 10% over a period of 23 years. External debt fell to $8,555m. (equivalent to 92.8% of GNI) by the end of 2002. In June 2003 the World Bank announced a 'soft' loan of $49.7m. to assist the country in buying back some $935m. of unpaid debt to commercial creditors. Cameroon's external debt stock was estimated at $7,000m. at the end of 2004, equivalent to 44% of GDP. After more than one year's delay resulting from policy slippages, Cameroon reached completion point under HIPC II in May 2006. This was expected to help reduce Cameroon's future debt-service payments by about $4,900m. in nominal terms. The 'Paris Club' subsequently negotiated a generous debt relief deal with the government, leading to a reduction in Cameroon's bilateral debt stock from $3,500m. to only $27m. Upon reaching the HIPC completion point, Cameroon also became eligible for further debt relief from the IMF, IDA, and the African Development Fund under the Multilateral Debt Relief Initiative. The stock of external debt as a percentage of GDP was projected to fall from 33.2% in 2005 to 3.1% in 2006 as the Government finalized the signing of bilateral agreements with its creditors.

Inflows of official development assistance (ODA), which had been falling in most years since 1994, when they had reached a peak of US $730.3m. (net of repayment), recovered in the late 1990s, after the currency devaluation made Cameroon—formerly a middle-income country—eligible for multilateral funds on concessionary terms. Net ODA receipts totalled $756m. in 2003, falling to $572m. in 2004 and $335m. in 2005. Despite great potential, Cameroon has failed to attract any significant flows in foreign direct investment (FDI) outside the petroleum sector. FDI inflows totalled $215m. in 2003. It was hoped that Cameroon's accession to the Fonds Africain de Garantie et de Co-opération Economique (African Guarantee and Economic Co-operation Fund) in April 2006 would promote foreign investment in the country.

Statistical Survey

Source (unless otherwise stated): Direction de la Prévision, Ministère de l'Economie et des Finances, BP 18, Yaoundé; tel. 223-4040; fax 223-2150.

Area and Population

AREA, POPULATION AND DENSITY

Area (sq km)	475,442*
Population (census results)	
9 April 1976†	7,663,246
9 April 1987	
Males	5,162,878
Females	5,330,777
Total	10,493,655
Population (UN estimates at mid-year)‡	
2004	17,409,000
2005	17,795,000
2006	18,175,000
Density (per sq km) at mid-2006	38.2

* 183,569 sq miles.

† Including an adjustment for underenumeration, estimated at 7.4%. The enumerated total was 7,090,115.

‡ Source: UN, *World Population Prospects: The 2006 Revision*.

PROVINCES
(population at 1987 census)

	Urban	Rural	Total
Centre	877,481	774,119	1,651,600
Littoral	1,093,323	259,510	1,352,833
West	431,337	908,454	1,339,791
South-West	258,940	579,102	838,042
North-West	271,114	966,234	1,237,348
North	234,572	597,593	832,165
East	152,787	364,411	517,198
South	104,023	269,775	373,798
Adamaoua	178,644	316,541	495,185
Far North	366,698	1,488,997	1,855,695
Total	3,968,919	6,524,736	10,493,655

PRINCIPAL TOWNS
(population at 1987 census)

Douala	810,000	Bamenda	110,000
Yaoundé (capital)	649,000	Nkongsamba	85,420
Garoua	142,000	Kumba	70,112
Maroua	123,000	Limbé	44,561
Bafoussam	113,000		

Mid-2005 ('000, incl. suburbs, UN estimates): Douala 1,761; Yaoundé 1,485 (Source: UN, *World Urbanization Prospects: The 2005 Revision*).

BIRTHS AND DEATHS
(annual averages, UN estimates)

	1990–95	1995–2000	2000–05
Birth rate (per 1,000)	40.9	37.9	37.9
Death rate (per 1,000)	13.1	13.8	15.0

Source: UN, *World Population Prospects: The 2006 Revision*.

Expectation of life (years at birth, WHO estimates): 50 (males 50; females 51) in 2004 (Source: WHO, *World Health Report*).

ECONOMICALLY ACTIVE POPULATION
(persons aged six years and over, mid-1985, official estimates)

	Males	Females	Total
Agriculture, hunting, forestry and fishing	1,574,946	1,325,925	2,900,871
Mining and quarrying	1,693	100	1,793
Manufacturing	137,671	36,827	174,498
Electricity, gas and water	3,373	149	3,522
Construction	65,666	1,018	66,684
Trade, restaurants and hotels	115,269	38,745	154,014
Transport, storage and communications	50,664	1,024	51,688
Financing, insurance, real estate and business services	7,447	562	8,009
Community, social and personal services	255,076	37,846	292,922
Activities not adequately defined	18,515	17,444	35,959
Total in employment	2,230,320	1,459,640	3,689,960
Unemployed	180,016	47,659	227,675
Total labour force	2,410,336	1,507,299	3,917,635

Source: ILO, *Yearbook of Labour Statistics*.

Mid-2005 (estimates in '000): Agriculture, etc. 3,695; Total labour force 6,900 (Source: FAO).

Health and Welfare

KEY INDICATORS

Total fertility rate (children per woman, 2005)	4.4
Under-5 mortality rate (per 1,000 live births, 2005)	149
HIV/AIDS (% of persons aged 15–49, 2005)	5.4
Physicians (per 1,000 head, 2004)	0.19
Hospital beds (per 1,000 head, 1990)	2.55
Health expenditure (2004): US $ per head (PPP)	82.7
Health expenditure (2004): % of GDP	5.2
Health expenditure (2004): public (% of total)	28.0
Access to water (% of persons, 2004)	66
Access to sanitation (% of persons, 2004)	51
Human Development Index (2004): ranking	144
Human Development Index (2004): value	0.506

For sources and definitions, see explanatory note on p. vi.

Agriculture

PRINCIPAL CROPS
('000 metric tons)

	2003	2004	2005
Rice (paddy)	47	50	53
Maize	912	966	1,023
Millet	50*	60†	52*
Sorghum	574	608	523
Potatoes	139	142	146
Sweet potatoes	186	190	190*
Cassava (Manioc)	2,048	2,093	2,139
Yams	280	286	293*
Taro (Coco yams)	1,103	1,128	1,152
Other roots and tubers*	15	15	15
Sugar cane*	1,400	1,380	1,373
Dry beans	193	200	207
Groundnuts (in shell)	218	226	234
Oil palm fruit*	1,250	1,214	1,222
Melonseed*	57	57	57
Tomatoes	399	408	418
Pumpkins, squash and gourds	122	125	128
Dry onions	72	74	75
Bananas	743	798	856
Plantains	1,275	1,315	1,356
Avocados*	52	54	56
Pineapples	47	48	50
Coffee (green)†	48	54	44
Cocoa beans†	155	167	179
Natural rubber	46	46*	46*

* FAO estimate(s).
† Unofficial figure(s).

Source: FAO.

LIVESTOCK
('000 head, year ending September, FAO estimates unless otherwise indicated)

	2003	2004	2005
Horses	17	17	17
Asses	39	40	40
Cattle	5,800	5,900	6,000*
Pigs	1,350	1,350	1,350
Sheep	3,800	3,800	3,800
Goats	4,400	4,400	4,400
Chickens	31,000	31,000	31,000

* Unofficial figure.

Source: FAO.

LIVESTOCK PRODUCTS
('000 metric tons, FAO estimates)

	2003	2004	2005
Cattle meat	90.5	93.3	94.8
Sheep meat	16.4	16.4	16.4
Goat meat	15.7	15.7	15.7
Pig meat	16.2	15.7	15.5
Chicken meat	30.0	31.8	33.1
Game meat	50.0	50.1	50.5
Cows' milk	130.0	130.0	130.0
Sheep's milk	17.2	17.2	17.2
Goats' milk	42.1	42.1	42.1
Hen eggs	335.0	335.0	335.0
Honey	3.0	3.0	3.1

Source: FAO.

Forestry

ROUNDWOOD REMOVALS
('000 cubic metres, excl. bark)

	2003	2004	2005
Sawlogs, veneer logs and logs for sleepers	1,400	1,450	1,450
Other industrial wood	250	350	350
Fuel wood	9,330	9,407	9,485
Total	10,980	11,207	11,285

Source: FAO.

SAWNWOOD PRODUCTION
('000 cubic metres, incl. railway sleepers)

	2003	2004	2005
Total (all broadleaved)	658	702	702*

* FAO estimate.

Source: FAO.

Fishing

('000 metric tons, live weight)

	2003	2004	2005
Capture	117.8	129.0	142.3
Freshwater fishes	55.0	65.0	75.0
Cassava croaker	1.3	0.9	0.4
Bobo croaker	1.5	2.0	2.4
Other croakers and drums	1.6	0.8	—
Sardinellas	21.8	11.8	1.8
Bonga shad	20.2	30.8	41.7
Aquaculture	0.3	0.3	0.3
Total catch	118.1	129.3	142.7

Source: FAO.

Mining

	2003	2004	2005*
Crude petroleum (million barrels)	24.8	34.7	21.9
Gold (kilograms)†	700	1,500	1,500
Pozzolan ('000 metric tons)	600	600	600
Limestone ('000 metric tons)	103	103	103

* Estimated production.
† From artisanal mining.

Source: US Geological Survey.

Industry

SELECTED PRODUCTS

('000 metric tons, unless otherwise indicated)

	2000	2001	2002
Palm oil	136	138	144
Raw sugar*	82	99	113
Veneer sheets ('000 cu metres)	70	55	53
Plywood ('000 cu metres)	37	35	42
Jet fuels†	57	61	69
Motor spirit (petrol)†	323	354	232
Kerosene†	250	260	140
Gas-diesel (distillate fuel) oil†	459	437	370
Residual fuel oils	397	344	317
Lubricating oils	16	16	17
Petroleum bitumen (asphalt)†	5	5	5
Liquefied petroleum gas	26	28	18
Cement	956	980	937
Aluminium (unwrought)	181	72	79
Electric energy (million kWh)	3,378	3,509	3,304

* FAO estimates.
† Estimates.

2003 Cement ('000 metric tons) 949; Veneer sheets ('000 cu metres) 47; Plywood ('000 cu metres) 39.

Sources: UN, *Industrial Commodity Statistics Yearbook*; FAO.

Finance

CURRENCY AND EXCHANGE RATES

Monetary Units

100 centimes = 1 franc de la Coopération financière en Afrique centrale (CFA).

Sterling, Dollar and Euro Equivalents (31 May 2007)

£1 sterling = 964.116 francs CFA;
US $1 = 487.592 francs CFA;
€1 = 655.957 francs CFA;
10,000 francs CFA = £10.37 = $20.51 = €15.24.

Average Exchange Rate (francs CFA per US $)

2004	528.29
2005	527.47
2006	522.89

Note: An exchange rate of 1 French franc = 50 francs CFA, established in 1948, remained in force until January 1994, when the CFA franc was devalued by 50%, with the exchange rate adjusted to 1 French franc = 100 francs CFA. This relationship to French currency remained in effect with the introduction of the euro on 1 January 1999. From that date, accordingly, a fixed exchange rate of €1 = 655.957 francs CFA has been in operation.

BUDGET

('000 million francs CFA)

Revenue*	2004	2005	2006
Oil revenue	325	439	643
Non-oil revenue	942	1,104	1,165
Direct taxes	228	262	264
Taxes on international trade	179	189	206
Other taxes on goods and services	370	462	522
Value-added tax	331	385	445
Non-tax revenue (excluding privatization proceeds)	96	126	100
Total	1,267	1,543	1,808

Expenditure	2004	2005	2006
Current expenditure	1,169	1,055	1,097
Wages and salaries	450	414	419
Other goods and services	414	337	381
Interest on public debt	164	129	87
Subsidies and transfers	141	175	211
Capital expenditure	167	206	271
Externally financed investment	67	44	64
Domestically financed investment	90	159	177
Restructuring	10	3	31
Other	–5	17	–5
Total	1,331	1,278	1,364

* Excluding grants received ('000 million francs CFA): 19 in 2004; 47 in 2005; 2,664 in 2006.

Source: IMF, *Cameroon: Statistical Appendix* (August 2007).

INTERNATIONAL RESERVES*

(US $ million at 31 December)

	2004	2005	2006
IMF special drawing rights	0.67	2.13	4.63
Reserve position in IMF	1.01	1.00	1.08
Foreign exchange	827.63	946.25	1,710.51
Total	829.31	949.38	1,716.22

* Excluding reserves of gold (30,000 troy ounces each year).

Source: IMF, *International Financial Statistics*.

MONEY SUPPLY

('000 million francs CFA at 31 December)

	2004	2005	2006
Currency outside banks	324.04	273.48	265.67
Demand deposits at deposit money banks	492.14	550.03	632.35
Total money (incl. others)	829.96	832.90	935.86

Source: IMF, *International Financial Statistics*.

COST OF LIVING

(Consumer Price Index; base: 2000 = 100)*

	2004	2005	2006
Food	109.2	110.3	117.9
All items	108.4	110.5	116.2

* Data prior to 2004 for Douala and Yaoundé only.

Source: ILO.

NATIONAL ACCOUNTS

Expenditure on the Gross Domestic Product
('000 million francs CFA at current prices)

	2004	2005	2006
Government final consumption expenditure	847.1	872.1	901.3
Private final consumption expenditure	5,946.8	6,298.1	6,709.1
Gross capital formation	1,521.1	1,546.9	1,564.5
Change in inventories	54.8	121.5	2.7
Total domestic expenditure	8,369.8	8,838.9	9,177.6
Exports of goods and services	1,616.8	1,789.7	2,159.5
Less Imports of goods and services	1,652.7	1,878.6	1,967.0
GDP in purchasers' values	8,333.9	8,749.6	9,370.1
GDP at factor cost at constant 2000 prices	7,754.5	7,932.6	8,173.2

Gross Domestic Product by Economic Activity
('000 million francs CFA at current prices)

	2002	2003
Agriculture, hunting, forestry and fishing	2,075.2	2,144.9
Petroleum	512.2	487.5
Manufacturing	1,060.7	1,137.1
Electricity, gas and water	124.7	144.9
Construction	538.4	546.5
Services	3,054.7	3,243.9
GDP at factor cost	7,365.9	7,704.8
Indirect taxes, *less* subsidies	229.5	246.2
GDP in purchasers' values	7,595.4	7,951.1

Source: Banque des états de l'Afrique centrale.

2005 (US $ million at constant 2000 prices): Agriculture, etc. 2,336.92; Industry 3,553.81 (Manufacturing 2,153.51); Services 5,425.79; GDP at factor cost 11,316.52 (Source: African Development Bank, *Statistical Yearbook*).

BALANCE OF PAYMENTS

('000 million francs CFA)

	2003	2004	2005
Exports of goods f.o.b.	1,332.9	1,348.5	1,637.4
Imports of goods f.o.b.	–1,251.6	–1,383.8	–1,524.7
Trade balance	81.3	–35.3	112.7
Services (net)	–456.4	–392.8	–293.9
Balance on goods and services	–375.1	–428.1	–181.2
Other income (net)	–308.2	–274.6	–200.1
Balance on goods, services and income	–683.3	–702.7	–381.3
Current transfers (net)	126.2	96.5	95.7
Current balance	–557.1	–606.2	–285.6
Capital account (net)	44.5	44.6	48.1
Direct investment (net)	222.6	168.7	118.5
Portfolio investment (net)	0.3	0.4	0.4
Other investments (net)	–231.1	131.6	–44.4
Errors and omissions	159	63.7	79.9
Overall balance	–361.8	–197.2	–83.1

Source: Banque des états de l'Afrique centrale.

External Trade

PRINCIPAL COMMODITIES

(US $ million)

Imports c.i.f.	2002	2003	2004
Food and live animals	314.2	342.9	407.4
Cereals and cereal preparations	171.4	173.7	212.0
Mineral fuels, lubricants, etc.	274.4	249.7	427.8
Petroleum, petroleum products and related materials	270.5	243.6	423.4
Crude petroleum and oils	213.7	170.8	366.6
Chemicals and related products	247.0	291.3	312.5
Manufactured goods	290.8	324.2	327.4
Iron and steel	56.7	65.6	60.7
Tubes, pipes and fittings	24.2	14.9	12.8
Machinery and transport equipment	540.6	558.5	642.6
Road vehicles	160.5	199.3	198.8
Total (incl. others)	1,866.3	2,020.7	2,407.0

Exports f.o.b.	2002	2003	2004
Food and live animals	358.2	419.4	456.5
Coffee, tea, cocoa, spices, etc.	290.3	314.1	344.9
Cocoa and cocoa products	235.2	242.5	266.9
Cocoa beans (raw, roasted)	191.6	179.5	230.3
Coffee (green, roasted)	53.4	69.8	76.7
Crude materials, inedible, except fuels	349.8	440.3	599.7
Textile fibres and wastes	93.9	108.1	144.6
Raw cotton (not carded or combed)	93.9	108.1	144.6
Mineral fuels, lubricants, etc.	886.2	1,109.7	1,157.0
Petroleum, petroleum products and related materials	886.2	1,109.7	1,157.0
Crude petroleum and oils	824.6	999.3	1,019.4
Petroleum products (refined)	61.6	110.3	137.6
Manufactured goods	160.9	191.2	205.4
Aluminium	76.9	92.9	114.2
Total (incl. others)	1,801.7	2,245.8	2,478.4

Source: UN, *International Trade Statistics Yearbook*.

PRINCIPAL TRADING PARTNERS

(US $ million, estimates)

Imports c.i.f.	2002	2003	2004
Belgium	75	85	118
Brazil	17	28	36
Canada	21	16	15
China, People's Repub.	67	87	111
Côte d'Ivoire	29	34	32
Finland	9	11	63
France (incl. Monaco)	435	391	540
Germany	87	77	111
Guinea	31	35	38
India	25	31	27
Italy	62	68	69
Japan	85	122	111
Mauritania	14	19	28
Netherlands	52	64	55
Nigeria	200	170	293
South Africa	38	44	36
Spain	28	27	35
Thailand	26	22	55
Turkey	14	21	22
United Kingdom	60	40	50
USA	156	102	127
Total (incl. others)	1,866	2,021	2,407

Exports f.o.b.	2002	2003	2004
Belgium	38	56	96
Chad	39	46	28
China, People's Repub.	78	98	63
Congo, Democratic Repub.	11	29	21
Congo, Repub.	21	20	23
France (incl. Monaco)	234	244	335
Gabon	19	43	38
Germany	26	26	22
Guinea	11	33	30
India	27	8	17
Ireland	7	13	27
Italy	342	302	285
Netherlands	231	238	212
Nigeria	15	17	25
South Africa	4	53	20
Spain	359	491	264
Turkey	12	11	28
United Kingdom	26	43	98
USA	122	169	142
Total (incl. others)	1,802	2,246	2,478

Source: UN, *International Trade Statistics Yearbook*.

Transport

RAILWAYS
(traffic, year ending 30 June)

	2001	2002	2003
Freight ton-km (million)	1,159	1,179	1,090
Passenger-km (million)	303	308	322

Source: UN, *Statistical Yearbook*.

ROAD TRAFFIC
('000 motor vehicles in use, estimates)

	2001	2002	2003
Passenger cars	134.5	151.9	173.1
Commercial vehicles	51.1	37.4	57.4

Source: UN, *Statistical Yearbook*.

SHIPPING

Merchant Fleet
(registered at 31 December)

	2003	2004	2005
Number of vessels	61	64	66
Total displacement ('000 grt)	186.8	185.1	55.3

Source: Lloyd's Register-Fairplay, *World Fleet Statistics*.

International Sea-borne Freight Traffic
(freight traffic at Douala, '000 metric tons)

	1995	1996	1997
Goods loaded	1,841	1,967	2,385
Goods unloaded	2,317	2,211	2,497

Source: Banque des états de l'Afrique centrale, *Etudes et Statistiques*.

CIVIL AVIATION
(traffic on scheduled services)

	2001	2002	2003
Kilometres flown (million)	4	9	8
Passengers carried ('000)	157	235	225
Passenger-km (million)	423	585	562
Total ton-km (million)	84	73	70

Source: UN, *Statistical Yearbook*.

Tourism

FOREIGN VISITORS BY COUNTRY OF ORIGIN*

	2002	2004†	2005
Belgium	4,383	3,885	3,046
Canada	2,600	2,399	5,918
France	53,167	40,611	80,057
Italy	4,628	4,426	8,915
Netherlands	3,214	4,217	6,959
Switzerland	8,674	5,668	7,188
United Kingdom	6,069	5,818	11,618
USA	10,906	9,194	21,779
Total (incl. others)	226,019	189,856	176,372

* Arrivals at hotels and similar establishments.
† Figures not available for 2003.

Receipts from tourism (US $ million, incl. passenger transport): 39 in 2000.

Source: World Tourism Organization.

Communications Media

	2003	2004	2005
Telephones ('000 main lines in use)	95.2	99.4	99.4
Mobile cellular telephones ('000 subscribers)	1,077	1,537	2,259
Personal computers ('000 in use)	100	160	160
Internet users ('000)	120	167	167

Radio receivers ('000 in use): 2,270 in 1997.

1996: Daily newspapers 2 in 1996 (average circ. 91,000); Non-daily newspapers 7 in 1996 (average circ. 152,000).

Sources: mainly UNESCO, *Statistical Yearbook*; International Telecommunication Union.

Education

(2003/04, unless otherwise indicated)

			Students ('000)		
	Institutions	Teachers	Males	Females	Total
Pre-primary	1,371*	8,882	88.8	87.2	176.0
Primary	9,459*	55,266	1,615	1,364	2,979
Secondary:					
general	700*	23,682	406.4†	355.7†	762.1
technical/ vocational	324*	11,861†	279.2	119.7	398.9
Universities	6‡	2,993†	51.4†	32.5†	83.9

* 1998 figures.
† Estimate.
‡ 1996/97 figure.

Source: UNESCO Institute for Statistics.

Adult literacy rate (UNESCO estimates): 67.9% (males 77.0%; females 59.8%) in 2004 (Source: UN Development Programme, *Human Development Report*).

Directory

The Constitution

In December 1995 the National Assembly formally adopted amendments to the 1972 Constiution that provided for a democratic system of government, with the establishment of an upper legislative chamber (to be known as the Senate), a Council of Supreme Judiciary Affairs, a Council of State, and a Civil Service High Authority, and restricted the power vested in the President, who was to serve a maximum of two seven-year terms. The restoration of decentralized local government areas was also envisaged. The main provisions of the 1972 Constitution, as amended, are summarized below:

The Constitution declares that the human being, without distinction as to race, religion, sex or belief, possesses inalienable and sacred rights. It affirms its attachment to the fundamental freedoms embodied in the Universal Declaration of Human Rights and the UN Charter. The State guarantees to all citizens of either sex the rights and freedoms set out in the preamble of the Constitution.

SOVEREIGNTY

1. The Republic of Cameroon shall be one and indivisible, democratic, secular and dedicated to social service. It shall ensure the equality before the law of all its citizens. Provisions that the official languages be French and English, for the motto, flag, national anthem and seal, that the capital be Yaoundé.

2–3. Sovereignty shall be vested in the people who shall exercise it either through the President of the Republic and the members returned by it to the National Assembly or by means of referendum. Elections are by universal suffrage, direct or indirect, by every citizen aged 21 or over in a secret ballot. Political parties or groups may take part in elections subject to the law and the principles of democracy and of national sovereignty and unity.

4. State authority shall be exercised by the President of the Republic and the National Assembly.

THE PRESIDENT OF THE REPUBLIC

5. The President of the Republic, as Head of State and Head of the Government, shall be responsible for the conduct of the affairs of the Republic. He shall define national policy and may charge the members of the Government with the implementation of this policy in certain spheres.

6–7. Candidates for the office of President must hold civic and political rights, be at least 35 years old and have resided in Cameroon for a minimum of 12 consecutive months, and may not hold any other elective office or professional activity. The President is elected for seven years, by a majority of votes cast by the people, and may serve a maximum of two terms. Provisions are made for the continuity of office in the case of the President's resignation.

8–9. The Ministers and Vice-Ministers are appointed by the President to whom they are responsible, and they may hold no other appointment. The President is also head of the armed forces, he negotiates and ratifies treaties, may exercise clemency after consultation with the Higher Judicial Council, promulgates and is responsible for the enforcement of laws, is responsible for internal and external security, makes civil and military appointments, provides for necessary administrative services.

10. The President, by reference to the Supreme Court, ensures that all laws passed are constitutional.

11. Provisions whereby the President may declare a state of emergency or state of siege.

THE NATIONAL ASSEMBLY

12. The National Assembly shall be renewed every five years, though it may at the instance of the President of the Republic legislate to extend or shorten its term of office. It shall be composed of 180 members elected by universal suffrage.

13–14. Laws shall normally be passed by a simple majority of those present, but if a bill is read a second time at the request of the President of the Republic a majority of the National Assembly as a whole is required.

15–16. The National Assembly shall meet twice a year, each session to last not more than 30 days; in one session it shall approve the budget. It may be recalled to an extraordinary session of not more than 15 days.

17–18. Elections and suitability of candidates and sitting members shall be governed by law.

RELATIONS BETWEEN THE EXECUTIVE AND THE LEGISLATURE

19. Bills may be introduced either by the President of the Republic or by any member of the National Assembly.

20. Reserved to the legislature are the fundamental rights and duties of the citizen; the law of persons and property; the political, administrative and judicial system in respect of elections to the National Assembly, general regulation of national defence, authorization of penalties and criminal and civil procedure etc., and the organization of the local authorities; currency, the budget, dues and taxes, legislation on public property; economic and social policy; the education system.

21. The National Assembly may empower the President of the Republic to legislate by way of ordinance for a limited period and for given purposes.

22–26. Other matters of procedure, including the right of the President of the Republic to address the Assembly and of the Ministers and Vice-Ministers to take part in debates.

27–29. The composition and conduct of the Assembly's programme of business. Provisions whereby the Assembly may inquire into governmental activity. The obligation of the President of the Republic to promulgate laws, which shall be published in both languages of the Republic.

30. Provisions whereby the President of the Republic, after consultation with the National Assembly, may submit to referendum certain reform bills liable to have profound repercussions on the future of the nation and national institutions.

THE JUDICIARY

31. Justice is administered in the name of the people. The President of the Republic shall ensure the independence of the judiciary and shall make appointments with the assistance of the Higher Judicial Council.

THE SUPREME COURT

32–33. The Supreme Court has powers to uphold the Constitution in such cases as the death or incapacity of the President and the admissibility of laws, to give final judgments on appeals on the Judgment of the Court of Appeal and to decide complaints against administrative acts. It may be assisted by experts appointed by the President of the Republic.

IMPEACHMENT

34. There shall be a Court of Impeachment with jurisdiction to try the President of the Republic for high treason and the Ministers and Vice-Ministers for conspiracy against the security of the State.

THE ECONOMIC AND SOCIAL COUNCIL

35. There shall be an Economic and Social Council, regulated by the law.

AMENDMENT OF THE CONSTITUTION

36–37. Bills to amend the Constitution may be introduced either by the President of the Republic or the National Assembly. The President may decide to submit any amendment to the people by way of a referendum. No procedure to amend the Constitution may be accepted if it tends to impair the republican character, unity or territorial integrity of the State, or the democratic principles by which the Republic is governed.

The Government

HEAD OF STATE

President: Paul Biya (took office 6 November 1982; elected 14 January 1984; re-elected 24 April 1988, 11 October 1992, 12 October 1997 and 11 October 2004).

CABINET
(August 2007)

A coalition of the Rassemblement démocratique du peuple camerounais (RDPC), the Union nationale pour la démocratie et le progrès (UNDP), the Union des populations camerounaises (UPC), the Mouvement pour la défense de la République (MDR) and the Alliance nationale pour la démocratie et le progrès (ANDP).

Prime Minister: Ephraim Inoni (RDPC).

Deputy Prime Minister, in charge of Justice: Amadou Ali (RDPC).

Ministers of State

Minister of State and Secretary-General of the Presidency: Laurent Esso (RDPC).

Minister of State in charge of Territorial Administration and Decentralization: Marafa Hamidou Yaya (RDPC).

Minister of State in charge of External Relations: Jean-Marie Antangana Mebara (RDPC).

Minister of State in charge of Posts and Telecommunications: Bello Bouba Maigari (UNDP).

Minister of State in charge of Planning, Programme Execution, Development and Territorial Administration: Augustin Frédéric Kodock (UPC).

Minister of State in charge of Culture: Ferdinand Léopold Oyono.

Minister of State, in charge of Agriculture and Rural Development: Jean Kuéte.

Ministers

Minister of the Economy and Finance: Polycarpe Abah Abah.

Minister of Scientific Research and Innovation: Madeleine Tchuenté (RDPC).

Minister of Small and Medium Businesses, Local Economy and Crafts: Laurent Etoundi Ngoa.

Minister of Employment and Professional Training: Zacharie Pérévet (RDPC).

Minister of Secondary Education: Louis Bapes Bapes.

Minister of Forests and Wildlife: Elvis Ngolle Ngolle (RDPC).

Minister of Urban Development and Housing: Colbert Tchatat (RDPC).

Minister of Higher Education: Jacques Fame Ndongo (RDPC).

Minister of Social Affairs: Catherine Bakang Mbock (RDPC).

Minister of Public Works: Bernard Messengue Avom (RDPC).

Minister of Energy and Water: Jean Bernard Sindeu.

Minister of Estates and Land Affairs: Loius Marie Abogo Nkono (RDPC).

Minister of Transport: Dakolé Daïssala (MDR).

Minister of Labour and Social Welfare: Robert Nkili (RDPC).

Minister of Industry, Mines and Technological Development: Charles Salé (RDPC).

Minister of the Environment and the Protection of Nature: Pierre Hélé (RDPC).

Minister of Trade: Luc Magloire Mbanga Atangana.

Minister of Communication: Ebenezer Mouelle Njoh.

Minister of Women's Affairs and the Family: Suzanne Bombak (RDPC).

Minister of Basic Education: Haman Adama (RDPC).

Minister of Livestock, Fisheries and Animal Industries: Dr Aboubakary Sarki (RDPC).

Minister of Public Service and Administrative Reform: Emmanuel Bonde (RDPC).

Minister of Youth: Adoum Garoua.

Minister of Sports and Physical Education: Edjoa Augustin.

Minister of Public Health: Urbain Olanguena Awono (RDPC).

Minister of Tourism: Baba Hamadou (RDPC).

Ministers-delegate

Minister-delegate at the Ministry of Finance and the Budget, in charge of the Budget: Essimi Menye (RDPC).

Minister-delegate at the Ministry of Economy and Finance, in charge of Programmes: Daniel Njankouo Lamere.

Minister-delegate at the Ministry of Planning, Programme Execution, Development and Territorial Administration: Abdoulaye Yaouba.

Minister-delegate at the Ministry of Defence: Rémy Ze Meka (RDPC).

Minister-delegate at the Ministry of External Relations, in charge of Relations with the Commonwealth: Joseph Dion Ngute (RDPC).

Minister-delegate at the Ministry of External Relations, in charge of Relations with the Islamic World: Adoum Gargoum (RDPC).

Minister-delegate at the Ministry of Territorial Administration and Decentralization: Emmanuel Edou (RDPC).

Minister-delegate at the Ministry of the Environment and the Protection of Nature: Nana Aboubakar Djalloh (UNDP).

Minister-delegate at the Ministry of Communication: Gervais Mendo Zé (RDPC).

Minister-delegate at the Ministry of Justice: Maurice Kamto (RDPC).

Minister-delegate at the Ministry of Relations with Parliament and the Economic and Social Council: Grégoire Owona (RDPC).

Minister-delegate, in charge of the Supreme State Audit: David Siegfried Etamé Massoma (RDPC).

Secretaries of State

Secretary of State for Estates and Land Affairs: Jean Claude Etogo (RDPC).

Secretary of State for the Economy and Finances: Denis Omarou (RDPC).

Secretary of State for Secondary Education: Cathérine Abena.

Secretary of State for Commerce: Ama tuta Muna.

Secretary of State for Public Health: Alim Hayatou (RDPC).

Secretary of State for Youth and Sports, in charge of Youth: Denis Oumarou (RDPC).

Secretary of State for Justice, in charge of Prisons: Emmanuel Ngafeeson.

Secretary of State for Agriculture and Rural Development: Aboubakar Abdoulaye (RDPC).

Secretary of State for Public Works: Abono Moampamb Paulin.

Secretary of State for Transport: Ndanga Ndinga Badel.

Secretary of State for Defence, in charge of the National Gendarmerie: Jean Baptiste Bokam.

Other Officials with the Rank of Minister

Ministers in charge of Special Duties at the Presidency: Hamadou Moustapha (ANDP), Mengot Victor Arrey Nkongho, Justin Ndioro (RDPC).

Director of the Cabinet of the President of the Republic: Ngo'o Mebe (RDPC).

MINISTRIES

Correspondence to ministries not holding post boxes should generally be addressed c/o the Central Post Office, Yaoundé.

Office of the President: Palais de l'Unité, Yaoundé; tel. 2223-4025; internet www.camnet.cm/celcom/homepr.htm.

Office of the Prime Minister: Yaoundé; tel. 2223-8005; fax 2223-5735; e-mail spm@spm.gov.cm; internet www.spm.gov.cm.

Ministry of Agriculture and Rural Development: Quartier Administratif, Yaoundé; tel. 2223-1190; fax 2222-5091.

Ministry of Communication: Quartier Hippodrome, Yaoundé; tel. 2223-3467; fax 2223-3022; e-mail mincom@mincom.gov.cm; internet www.mincom.gov.cm.

Ministry of Culture: Quartier Hippodrome, Yaoundé; tel. 2222-6579; fax 2223-6579.

Ministry of Defence: Quartier Général, Yaoundé; tel. 2223-4055.

Ministry of Economy and Finance: BP 13750, Quartier Administratif, Yaoundé; tel. and fax 7723-2099; internet www.camnet.cm/investir/minfi/.

Ministry of Employment and Professional Training: Yaoundé; tel. 2222-0186; fax 2223-1820.

Ministry of Energy and Water: Quartier Administratif, BP 955, Yaoundé; tel. 2223-3404; fax 2223-3400; e-mail minmee@camnet.cm; internet www.camnet.cm/investir/minmee.

Ministry of the Environment and the Protection of Nature: Yaoundé.

Ministry of Estates and Land Affairs: Yaoundé.

Ministry of External Relations: Yaoundé; tel. 2220-3850; fax 2220-1133; internet www.diplocam.gov.cm.

Ministry of Forests and Wildlife: BP 1341, Yaoundé; tel. 2220-4258; fax 2222-9487; e-mail onadef@camnet.cm; internet www.camnet.cm/investir/envforet/index.htm.

Ministry of Higher Education: 2 ave du 20 Mai, BP 1457, Yaoundé; tel. 2222-1770; fax 2222-9724; e-mail aowono@uycdc.uninet.cm; internet www.mineup.gov.cm.

Ministry of Industry, Mines and Technological Development: Quartier Administratif, BP 955, Yaoundé; tel. 2223-3404; fax 2223-3400; e-mail minmee@camnet.cm; internet www.camnet.cm/investir/minmee.

Ministry of Justice: Quartier Administratif, Yaoundé; tel. 2222-0189; fax 2223-0005.

Ministry of Livestock, Fisheries and Animal Industries: Yaoundé; tel. 2222-3311.

Ministry of National Education: Quartier Administratif, Yaoundé; tel. 2223-4050; fax 2223-1262.

Ministry of Posts and Telecommunications: Quartier Administratif, Yaoundé; tel. 2223-0615; fax 2223-3159; internet www.minpostel.gov.cm.

Ministry of Public Health: Quartier Administratif, Yaoundé; tel. 2222-2901; fax 2222-0233; internet www.camnet.cm/investir/hgy/index.htm.

Ministry of the Public Service and Administrative Reform: Yaoundé; tel. 2222-0356; fax 2223-0800.

Ministry of Public Works: Quartier Administratif, Yaoundé; tel. 2222-1916; fax 2222-0156.

Ministry of Relations with Parliament and the Economic and Social Council: Yaoundé.

Ministry of Scientific Research and Innovation: Yaoundé; tel. 2222-1331; fax 2222-1333; internet www.minrest.gov.cm.

Ministry of Secondary Education: Yaoundé.

Ministry of Small and Medium Businesses, Local Economy and Crafts: Yaoundé.

Ministry of Social Affairs: Quartier Administratif, Yaoundé; tel. 2222-5867; fax 2222-1121.

Ministry of Sports and Physical Education: Yaoundé; tel. 2223-1201.

Ministry of Technical and Professional Training: Yaoundé.

Ministry of Territorial Administration and Decentralization: Quartier Administratif, Yaoundé; tel. 2223-4090; fax 2222-3735.

Ministry of Trade: Yaoundé; tel. 2223-0216.

Ministry of Tourism: BP 266, Yaoundé; tel. 2222-4411; fax 2222-1295; e-mail mintour@camnet.cm; internet www.mintour.gov.cm.

Ministry of Transport: Quartier Administratif, Yaoundé; tel. 2222-8709; fax 2223-2238; e-mail mintrans@camnet.cm; internet www.camnet.cm/investir/transport.

Ministry of Urban Development and Housing: Yaoundé; tel. 2223-2282.

Ministry of Women's Affairs and the Family: Quartier Administratif, Yaoundé; fax 2223-3965.

Ministry of Youth: Quartier Administratif, Yaoundé; tel. 2223-3257; e-mail minjes@minjes.gov.cm; internet www.minjes.gov.cm.

President and Legislature

PRESIDENT

Election, 11 October 2004

Candidate	% of votes
Paul Biya (RDPC)	70.92
John Fru Ndi (SDF)	17.40
Adamou Ndam Njoya (UDC)	4.47
Garga Haman Adji (ADD)	3.37
Others*	3.84
Total	100.00

* There were 12 other candidates.

NATIONAL ASSEMBLY

President: CAVAYE YÉGUIÉ DJIBRIL.

General Election, 30 June 2002*

Party	Seats
Rassemblement démocratique du peuple camerounais (RDPC)	149
Social Democratic Front (SDF)	22
Union démocratique du Cameroun (UDC)	5
Union des populations camerounaises (UPC)	3
Union nationale pour la démocratie et le progrès (UNDP)	1
Total	180

* Includes the results of voting in nine constituencies (for 17 seats) where the elections were postponed until 15 September 2002, owing to irregularities.

Election Commission

Observatoire national des élections (ONEL) (National Elections Observatory): Yaoundé; tel. 2221-2543; internet www.onelcam.org; f. 2000; 11 dirs appointed by the Head of State; Pres. ENOCH KWAYEB.

Political Organizations

In mid-2006 the Observatoire national des élections listed 176 legal political parties, of which the most important are listed below:

Action for Meritocracy and Equal Opportunity Party (AMEC): BP 20354, Yaoundé; tel. 9991-9154; fax 2223-4642; e-mail Tabijoachim@yahoo.fr; Leader JOACHIM TABI OWONO.

Alliance des forces progressistes (AFP): BP 4724, Douala; f. 2002; Leader MAIDADI SAIDOU YAYA.

Alliance pour la démocratie et le développement (ADD): BP 231, Garoua; Sec.-Gen. GARGA HAMAN ADJI.

Alliance nationale pour la démocratie et le progrès: BP 5019, Yaoundé; tel. and fax 220-9898; Pres. HAMADOU MOUSTAPHA.

Alliance pour le progrès et l'émancipation des dépossédés (APED): Yaoundé; f. 1991; Leader BOHIN BOHIN.

Alliance pour le redressement du Cameroun (ARC): f. 1992 by a number of opposition movements.

Cameroon Anglophone Movement (CAM): advocates a federal system of govt.

Démocratie intégrale au Cameroun (DIC): BP 8282, Douala; f. 1991; Leader GUSTAVE ESSAKA.

Front des alliés pour le changement (FAC): Douala; f. 1994; alliance of 16 opposition movements; Leader SAMUEL EBOUA.

Front démocratique et patriotique (FDP): f. 1994; alliance of six opposition parties.

Mouvement africain pour la nouvelle indépendance et la démocratie (MANIDEM): fmrly a faction of the UPC; Leader ANICET EKANE.

Mouvement démocratique pour la défense de la République (MDR): BP 6438, Yaoundé; tel. 2220-8982; f. 1991; Leader DAKOLE DAÏSSALA.

Mouvement des démocrates camerounais pour la paix (MDCP): BP 3274, Yaoundé; f. 2002; Leader GAMEL ADAMOU ISSA.

Mouvement pour la démocratie et le progrès (MDP): BP 8379, Douala; f. 1992; Leader ARON MUKURI MAKA.

Mouvement pour la jeunesse du Cameroun (MLJC): Leader DIEUDONNÉ TINA.

Mouvement pour la libération et le développement du Cameroun (MLDC): BP 886, Edéa; tel. 3346-4431; fax 3346-4847; f. 1998 by a breakaway faction of the MLJC; Leader MARCEL YONDO BLACK.

Nouvelle force populaire (NFP): BP 1139, Douala; f. 2002; Leader LÉANDRE DJINO.

Parti des démocrates camerounais (PDC): BP 6909, Yaoundé; tel. 2222-2842; f. 1991; Leader LOUIS-TOBIE MBIDA.

Parti libéral-démocrate (PLD): f. 1991; Leader NJOH LITUMBE.

Parti populaire pour le développement (PPD): f. 1997.

Parti républicain du peuple camerounais (PRPC): BP 6654, Yaoundé; tel. 2222-2120; f. 1991; Leader ANDRÉ ATEBA NGOUA.

Parti socialiste camerounais (PSC): BP 12501, Douala; Sec.-Gen. EMMANUEL ELAME.

Parti socialiste démocratique du Cameroun (PSDC): Leader JEAN MICHEL TEKAM.

Rassemblement camerounais pour la république: BP 452, Bandjoun; tel. 3344-1349; f. 1992; Leader SAMUEL WAMBO.

Rassemblement démocratique du peuple camerounais (RDPC): Palais des Congrès, BP 867, Yaoundé; tel. and fax 2221-2417; e-mail rdpc@rdpc.cm; internet www.rdpc.cm; f. 1966 as Union nationale camerounaise by merger of the Union camerounaise, the Kamerun National Democratic Party and four opposition parties; adopted present name in 1985; sole legal party 1972–90; Pres. PAUL BIYA; Sec.-Gen. JOSEPH-CHARLES DOUMBA.

Social Democratic Front (SDF): BP 490, Mankon, Bamenda; tel. 3336-3949; fax 3336-2991; e-mail webmaster@sdfparty.org; internet www.sdfparty.org; f. 1990; Chair. NI JOHN FRU NDI; Sec.-Gen. Prof. TAZOACHA ASONGANYI.

Social Democratic Movement (SDM): BP 7655, Yaoundé; tel. 9985-9372; f. 1995; breakaway faction of the Social Democratic Front; Leader SIGA ASANGA.

Southern Cameroons National Council (SCNC): f. 1995; supports the establishment of an independent republic in anglophone Cameroon; Chair. Chief ETTE OTUN AYAMBA.

Union démocratique du Cameroun (UDC): BP 1638, Yaoundé; tel. 2222-9545; fax 2222-4620; f. 1991; Leader ADAMOU NDAM NJOYA.

Union des forces démocratiques du Cameroun (UFDC): BP 7190, Yaoundé; tel. 2223-1644; f. 1991; Leader VICTORIN HAMENI BIELEU.

Union nationale pour la démocratie et le progrès (UNDP): BP 656, Douala; tel. 2220-9898; f. 1991; split in 1995; Chair. BELLO BOUBA MAIGARI; Sec.-Gen. PIERRE FLAMBEAU NGAYAP.

Union nationale pour l'indépendance totale du Cameroun (UNITOC): BP 1301, Yaoundé; f. 2002; Leader DANIEL TATSINFANG.

Union des populations camerounaises (UPC): Douala; tel. 2222-8074; f. 1948; split into two main factions in 1996: UPC (N), led by WINSTON NDEH NTUMAZAH and UPC (K), led by AUGUSTIN FRÉDÉRIC KODOCK.

Diplomatic Representation

EMBASSIES AND HIGH COMMISSIONS IN CAMEROON

Algeria: 433 rue 1828, Quartier Bastos, BP 1619, Yaoundé; tel. 2221-5351; fax 2231-5354; Ambassador BAALLAL AZZOUZ.

Belgium: rue 1792, Quartier Bastos, BP 816, Yaoundé; tel. 2220-0519; fax 2220-0521; e-mail yaounde@diplobel.org; internet www.diplomatie.be/yaounde/; Ambassador FRANCK CARRUET.

Brazil: BP 348, Yaoundé; tel. 2223-3646; Chargé d'affaires a.i. ARNALDO CLARETE SALABERT.

Canada: Immeuble Stamatiades, pl. de l'Hôtel de Ville, BP 572, Yaoundé; tel. 2223-2311; fax 2222-1090; e-mail yunde@international.gc.ca; High Commissioner JULES SAVARIA.

Central African Republic: 41 rue 1863, Quartier Bastos, Montée du Carrefour de la Vallée Nlongkak, BP 396, Yaoundé; tel. and fax 2220-5155; Ambassador JEAN WENZOUÏ.

Chad: Quartier Bastos, BP 506, Yaoundé; tel. 2221-0624; fax 2220-3940; e-mail ambatchad_yaounde@yahoo.fr; Ambassador ANDRÉ SEKIMBAYE BESSANE.

China, People's Republic: Nouveau Bastos, BP 1307, Yaoundé; tel. 2221-0083; fax 2221-4395; e-mail chinaemb_cm@mfa.gov.cn; Ambassador WANG SIFA.

Congo, Democratic Republic: BP 632, Yaoundé; tel. 2220-5103; Chargé d'affaires a.i. KUSAMBILA ZOLA WAY.

Congo, Republic: Rheinallée 45, BP 1422, Yaoundé; tel. 2221-2458; Chargé d'affaires a.i JOSEPH NZIÉFÉ.

Côte d'Ivoire: BP 11354, Yaoundé; tel. 2221-3291; fax 2221-3295; Ambassador PAUL AYOMAN AMBOHALÉ.

Egypt: 718 rue 1828, Quartier Bastos, BP 809, Yaoundé; tel. 2220-3922; fax 2220-2647; Ambassador MOHAMED SA'AD M. AKL.

Equatorial Guinea: 82 rue 1851, Quartier Bastos, BP 277, Yaoundé; tel. and fax 2221-0804; Ambassador (vacant).

France: Plateau Atémengué, BP 1631, Yaoundé; tel. 2222-7900; fax 2222-7909; e-mail chancellerie.yaounde-amba@diplomatie.gouv.fr; internet www.ambafrance-cm.org; Ambassador GEORGES SERRE.

Gabon: Quartier Bastos, Ekoudou, BP 4130, Yaoundé; tel. 2220-2966; fax 2221-0224; Ambassador FERDINAND MASSALA MALONGA.

Germany: Nouvelle Bastos, Bastos-Usine, BP 1160, Yaoundé; tel. 2221-0566; fax 2220-7313; e-mail info@jaun.diplo.de; internet www.jaunde.diplo.de; Ambassador VOLKER SEITZ.

Greece: Quartier Mont Fébé, BP 82, Yaoundé; tel. 2221-0195; fax 2220-3936; e-mail ambgrece@camnet.cm; Ambassador CHARAKAMBOUS PAUL.

Holy See: rue du Vatican, BP 210, Yaoundé (Apostolic Nunciature); tel. 2220-0475; fax 2220-7513; e-mail nonce.cam@sat.signis.net; Apostolic Pro-Nuncio Most Rev. ELISEO ANTONIO ARIOTTI (Titular Archbishop of Vibiana).

Israel: rue du Club Olympique à Bastos 154, Longkak, BP 5934, Yaoundé; tel. 2221-1291; fax 2221-0823; e-mail info@yaounde.mfa.gov.il; internet yaounde.mfa.gov.il; Ambassador BENNY OMER.

Italy: Plateau Bastos, BP 827, Yaoundé; tel. 2220-3376; fax 2221-5250; e-mail ambasciata.yaounde@esteri.it; internet www.ambyaounde.esteri.it; Ambassador ANTONIO BELLAVIA.

Japan: 1513 rue 1828, Quartier Bastos, Ekoudou, BP 6868, Yaoundé; tel. 2220-6202; fax 2220-6203; Ambassador MASAKI KUNIEDA.

Korea, Democratic People's Republic: Yaoundé; Ambassador KIM RYONG YONG.

Liberia: Quartier Bastos, Ekoudou, BP 1185, Yaoundé; tel. 2221-1296; fax 2220-9781; Ambassador MASSA JAMES.

Libya: Quartier Nylon Nlongkak, Quartier Bastos, BP 1980, Yaoundé; tel. 2220-4138; fax 2221-4298; Chargé d'affaires a.i. IBRAHIM O. AMAMI.

Morocco: 32 rue 1793, Quartier Bastos, BP 1629, Yaoundé; tel. 2220-5092; fax 2220-3793; e-mail ambmaroccam@yahoo.fr; Ambassador ABDELFATTAH AMOUR.

Nigeria: Quartier Bastos, BP 448, Yaoundé; tel. 2223-5551; High Commissioner EDWIN ENOSAKHARE EDOBOR.

Romania: Immeuble Dyna Immobilier, rue de Joseph Mballa Elounden, BP 6212, Yaoundé; tel. and fax 2221-3986; Chargé d'affaires a.i. MIRCEA BONCU.

Russia: Quartier Bastos, BP 488, Yaoundé; tel. 2220-1714; fax 2220-7891; e-mail consrusse@camnet.cm; Ambassador POULATE ABDOULAYEV.

Saudi Arabia: rue 1951, Quartier Bastos, BP 1602, Yaoundé; tel. 2221-2675; fax 2220-6689; Ambassador AHMED HUSSEIN ALBEDEWI.

Spain: blvd de l'URSS, Quartier Bastos, BP 877, Yaoundé; tel. 2220-3543; fax 2220-6491; e-mail embespcm@mail.mae.es; Ambassador MARÍA JESÚS ALONSO JIMÉNEZ.

Tunisia: rue de Rotary, Quartier Bastos, BP 6074, Yaoundé; tel. 2220-3368; fax 2221-0507; Chargé d'affaires a.i. MOHAMED NACER KORT.

United Kingdom: ave Winston Churchill, BP 547, Yaoundé; tel. 2222-0545; fax 2222-0148; e-mail BHC.yaounde@fco.gov.uk; internet www.britcam.org; High Commissioner DAVID SYDNEY MADDICOTT.

USA: rue Nachtigal, BP 817, Yaoundé; tel. 2223-1500; internet usembassy.state.gov/yaounde; Ambassador JANET E. GARVEY.

Judicial System

Supreme Court

Yaoundé; tel. 2222-0164; fax 2222-0576.

Consists of a president, nine titular and substitute judges, a procureur général, an avocat général, deputies to the procureur général, a registrar and clerks.

President: ALEXIS DIPANDA MOUELLE.

High Court of Justice

Yaoundé.

Consists of nine titular judges and six substitute judges, all elected by the National Assembly.

Attorney-General: MARTIN RISSOUCK MOULONG.

Religion

It is estimated that 53% of the population are Christians (an estimated 25.1% of those are Roman Catholics), 25% adhere to traditional religious beliefs, and 22% are Muslims.

CHRISTIANITY

Protestant Churches

There are about 1m. Protestants in Cameroon, with about 3,000 church and mission workers, and four theological schools.

Fédération des Eglises et missions évangéliques du Cameroun (FEMEC): BP 491, Yaoundé; tel. and fax 2223-8117; e-mail femec_org@yahoo.fr; internet www.wagne.net/femec; f. 1968; 10 mem. churches; Pres. Rev. Dr JEAN KOTTO (Evangelical Church of Cameroon); Admin. Sec. Rev. Dr GRÉGOIRE AMBADIANG DE MENDENG (Presbyterian Church of Cameroon).

Eglise évangélique du Cameroun (Evangelical Church of Cameroon): BP 89, Douala; tel. 3342-3611; fax 3342-4011; f. 1957; 500,000 mems (1992); Pres. Rev. CHARLES E. NJIKE; Sec. Rev. HANS EDJENGUELE.

Eglise presbytérienne camerounaise (Presbyterian Church of Cameroon): BP 519, Yaoundé; tel. 3332-4236; independent since 1957; comprises four synods and 16 presbyteries; Gen. Sec. Rev. GRÉGOIRE AMBADIANG DE MENDENG.

Eglise protestante africaine (African Protestant Church): BP 26, Lolodorf; f. 1934; Dir-Gen. Rev. MARNIA WOUNGLY-MASSAGA.

Presbyterian Church in Cameroon: BP 19, Buéa; tel. 3332-2487; fax 332-2754; e-mail pcc_modoffice19@yahoo.com; 800,000 mems (2007); 302 ministers; Moderator Rev. NYANSAKO-NI-NKU.

Union des Eglises baptistes au Cameroun (Union of Baptist Churches of Cameroon): New Bell, BP 6007, Douala; tel. 3342-4106; autonomous since 1957; Gen. Sec. Rev. EMMANUEL MBENDA.

Other Protestant churches active in Cameroon include the Cameroon Baptist Church, the Cameroon Baptist Convention, the Church of the Lutheran Brethren of Cameroon, the Evangelical Lutheran Church of Cameroon, the Presbyterian Church in West Cameroon and the Union of Evangelical Churches of North Cameroon.

The Roman Catholic Church

Cameroon comprises five archdioceses and 18 dioceses. At 31 December 2004 adherents represented some 24.8% of the total population. There are several active missionary orders, and four major seminaries for African priests.

Bishops' Conference

Conférence Episcopale Nationale du Cameroun, BP 1963, Yaoundé; tel. 2231-1592; fax 7771-3542; e-mail ngoyambjulienne@yahoo.fr.

f. 1989; Pres. Most Rev. SIMON-VICTOR TONYÉ BAKOT (Archbishop of Yaoundé).

Archbishop of Bamenda: Most Rev. CORNELIUS FONTEM ESUA, Archbishop's House, BP 82, Bamenda; tel. 3336-1241; fax 3336-3487; e-mail archbishopshouse@yahoo.com.

Archbishop of Bertoua: Most Rev. ROGER PIRENNE, Archevêché, BP 40, Bertoua; tel. 2224-1748; fax 2224-2585; e-mail pirenner@yahoo.fr.

Archbishop of Douala: Cardinal CHRISTIAN WIYGHAN TUMI, Archevêché, BP 179, Douala; tel. 3342-3714; fax 3342-1837.

Archbishop of Garoua: Most Rev. ANTOINE NTALOU, Archevêché, BP 272, Garoua; tel. 2227-1353; fax 2227-2942.

Archbishop of Yaoundé: Most Rev. SIMON-VICTOR TONYÉ BAKOT, Archevêché, BP 207, Yaoundé; tel. 2220-2461; fax 2221-9735; e-mail mgrvictortonyeb@camnet.cm.

BAHÁ'Í FAITH

National Spiritual Assembly: BP 145, Limbé; tel. 3333-2146; mems in 1,744 localities.

The Press

DAILIES

Cameroon Tribune: route de l'Aéroport, BP 1218, Yaoundé; tel. 2230-4147; fax 2230-4362; e-mail cameroon-tribune@cameroon-tribune.cm; internet www.cameroon-tribune.net; f. 1974; govt-controlled; French and English; Publr MARIE CLAIRE NNANA; Man. Editor ABUI MAMA ELOUNDOU; circ. 25,000.

Mutations: South Media Corporation, BP 12348, Yaoundé; tel. 2222-5104; fax 2222-9635; e-mail journalmutations@yahoo.fr; internet quotidienmutations.info; daily; French; independent; Publr ALAIN BLAISE BATONGUE.

Politiks Matinal: Yaoundé; f. 1999; independent; French; circ. 10,000.

The Post: POB 91, Buéa; tel. 3332-3287; fax 7773-8904; e-mail thepostnp@yahoo.com; internet www.postnewsline.com; weekly; independent; English; Publr FRANCIS WACHE; Editor CHARLY NDI CHIA.

Le Quotidien: BP 13088, Douala; tel. 3339-1189; fax 3339-1819; French; circ 29,000.

PERIODICALS

Accord Magazine: BP 3696, Messa, Yaoundé; tel. 9969-0600; e-mail accordmag@hotmail.com; popular culture.

Affaires Légales: BP 3681, Douala; tel. 3342-5838; fax 3343-2259; monthly; legal periodical.

Afrique en Dossiers: Yaoundé; f. 1970; French and English; Dir EBONGUE SOELLE.

L'Anecdote: Face collège Vogt, BP 25070, Yaoundé; tel. 2231-3395; e-mail journalanecdote@yahoo.com; weekly; conservative; Editor-in-Chief FRANÇOIS BIKORO.

Aurore Plus: BP 7042, Douala; tel. 3342-9261; fax 3342-4917; e-mail jouraurplus@yahoo.fr; twice weekly.

Cameroon Outlook: BP 124, Limbé; f. 1969; 3 a week; independent; English; Editor JÉRÔME F. GWELLEM; circ. 20,000.

Cameroon Panorama: BP 46, Buéa; tel. 3332-2240; e-mail cainsbuea@yahoo.com; f. 1962; monthly; English; Roman Catholic; Editor Rev. Fr MOSES TAZOH; circ. 4,500.

Cameroon Review: BP 408, Limbé; monthly; Editor-in-Chief JÉRÔME F. GWELLEM; circ. 70,000.

Cameroon Times: BP 408, Limbé; f. 1960; weekly; English; Editor-in-Chief JÉRÔME F. GWELLEM; circ. 12,000.

Challenge Hebdo: BP 1388, Douala; weekly; Editor BENJAMIN ZEBAZE.

Le Combattant: Yaoundé; weekly; independent; Editor BENYIMBE JOSEPH; circ. 21,000.

Courrier Sportif du Bénin: BP 17, Douala; weekly; Dir HENRI JONG.

Dikalo: BP 4320, Douala; tel. 3337-2122; fax 3337-1906; f. 1991; independent; 2 a week; French; Publications Dir TETTEH M. ARMAH; Editor HENRI EPEE NDOUMBE.

Ecovox: BP 1256, Bafoussam; tel. 3344-6668; fax 3344-6669; e-mail ecovox@cipcre.org; internet www.cipcre.org/ecovox; 2 a year; French; ecological news.

L'Effort Camerounais: BP 15231, Douala; tel. 3343-2726; fax 3343-1837; e-mail leffortcamerounais@yahoo.com; internet www.leffortcamerounais.com; bi-monthly; Catholic; f. 1955; Editor-in-chief ANTOINE DE PADOU CHONANG.

La Gazette: BP 5485, Douala; 2 a week; Editor ABODEL KARIMOU; circ. 35,000.

The Herald: BP 1218, Yaoundé; tel. 2231-5522; fax 2231-8497; 3 a week; English; Dir Dr BONIFACE FORBIN; circ. 1,568.

Al Houda: BP 1638, Yaoundé; quarterly; Islamic cultural review.

L'Indépendant Hebdo: Yaoundé; Chief Editor EVARISTE MENOUNGA.

Le Jeune Observateur: Yaoundé; f. 1991; Editor JULES KOUM (imprisoned for libel in January 2005).

J'informe: Yaoundé; tel. 9993-6605; fax 2220-5336; f. 2002; weekly; French; Editor DELOR MAGELLAN KAMGAING.

Journal Officiel de la République du Cameroun: BP 1603, Yaoundé; tel. and fax 2221-5218; weekly; official govt notices; Man. Editor JOSEPH MARCEL; circ. 4,000.

Le Messager: rue des écoles, BP 5925, Douala; tel. 3342-0214; fax 3342-0439; internet www.lemessager.net; f. 1979; 3 a week; independent; Man. Editor PIUS N. NJAWE; circ. 20,000.

The Messenger: BP 15043, Douala; English-language edn of Le Messager; Editor HILARY FOKUM.

Nleb Ensemble: Imprimerie Saint-Paul, BP 763, Yaoundé; tel. 2223-9773; fax 2223-5058; f. 1935; fortnightly; Ewondo; Dir Most Rev. JEAN ZOA; Editor JOSEPH BEFE ATEBA; circ. 6,000.

La Nouvelle Expression: 12 rue Prince de Galles, BP 15333, Douala; tel. 3343-2227; fax 3343-2669; internet www.lanouvelleexpression.net; independent; 3 a week; French; Man. Editor SÉVERIN TCHOUNKEU.

La Nouvelle Presse: Face mairie de Yaoundé VIème/Biyem-Assi, BP 2625, Messa, Yaoundé; tel. 9996-6768; e-mail lanvellepresse@iccnet.cm; f. 2001; weekly; Publications Dir JACQUES BLAISE MVIE.

Ouest Echos: BP 767, Bafoussam; tel. and fax 3344-1091; e-mail ouechos@wagne.net; internet www.wagne.net/ouestechos/; weekly; regional; Dir MICHEL ECLADOR PÉKOUA.

Presbyterian Newsletter: BP 19, Buéa; quarterly.

Que Savoir: Douala; monthly; industry, commerce and tourism.

Recherches et Études Camerounaises: BP 193, Yaoundé; monthly; publ. by Office National de Recherches Scientifiques du Cameroun.

La Révélation: Yaoundé; Dir BOSCO TCHOUBET.

La Sentinelle: BP 24079, Douala; tel. and fax 3339-1627; weekly; lifestyle; circ. 3,200.

Le Serment: Yaoundé; newspaper; Editor-in-Chief ANSELME MBALLA.

Le Serviteur: BP 1405, Yaoundé; monthly; Protestant; Dir Pastor DANIEL AKO'O; circ. 3,000.

Le Travailleur/The Worker: BP 1610, Yaoundé; tel. 2222-3315; f. 1972; monthly; French and English; journal of Organisation Syndicale des Travailleurs du Cameroun/Cameroon Trade Union Congress; Sec.-Gen. LOUIS SOMBES; circ. 10,000.

Le Triomphe: BP 1862, Douala; tel. 3342-8774; f. 2002; weekly; Publications Dir SIPOWA CONSCIENCE PARFAIT.

L'Unité: BP 867, Yaoundé; weekly; French and English.

Weekly Post: Obili, Yaoundé; Publr Chief BISONG ETAHOBEN.

NEWS AGENCIES

CamNews: c/o SOPECAM, BP 1218, Yaoundé; tel. 2230-3830; fax 2230-4362; Dir JEAN NGANDJEU.

Foreign Bureaux

Xinhua (New China) News Agency (People's Republic of China): ave Joseph Omgba, BP 1583, Yaoundé; tel. 2220-2572; Chief Correspondent SUN XINGWEN.

Agence France-Presse (France), Reuters (United Kingdom) and ITAR—TASS (Russia) are also represented.

PRESS ASSOCIATIONS

Association des Journalistes Indépendants du Cameroun (AJIC): BP 2996, Yaoundé; tel. 2222-3572; independent journalists' asscn; Pres. CÉLESTIN LINGO.

Conseil Camerounais des Médias (CCM): Yaoundé; f. 2005; created by the UJC to strengthen the quality and independence of journalism in Cameroon; 9 mems.

Union des Journalistes du Cameroun (UJC): Yaoundé; Pres. CÉLESTIN LINGO.

Publishers

AES Presses Universitaires d'Afrique: BP 8106, Yaoundé; tel. 2222-0030; fax 2222-2325; e-mail aes@iccnet.cm; internet www .aes-pua.com; f. 1986; literature, social sciences and law; Dir-Gen. SERGE DONTCHUENG KOUAM.

Editions Akoma Mba: ave Germaine Ahidjo 20189, Yaoundé; tel. 9992-2955; fax 2222-4343; e-mail akomamba@hotmail.com; educational; Dir EDMOND VII MBALLA ELANGA.

Editions Clé (Centre de Littérature Evangélique): BP 1501, ave Maréchal Foch, Yaoundé; tel. 2222-3554; fax 2223-2709; e-mail editionscle@yahoo.fr; internet www.wagne.net/cle; f. 1963; African and Christian literature and studies; school textbooks; medicine and science; general non-fiction; Dir Dr MARCELIN VOUNDA ETOA.

Editions Le Flambeau: BP 113, Yaoundé; tel. 2222-3672; f. 1977; general; Man. Dir JOSEPH NDZIE.

Editions Ndzé: BP 647, Bertoua; tel. 9950-9295; fax 2224-2585; e-mail editions@ndze.com; internet www.ndze.com; fiction; Commercial Dir ALEXIS LIMBONA.

Editions Semences Africaines: BP 5329, Yaoundé-Nlongkak; tel. 9917-1439; e-mail renephilombe@yahoo.fr; f. 1974; fiction, history, religion, textbooks; Man. Dir RÉNÉ LÉA PHILOMBE.

New Times Publishing House: Presbook Compound, BP 408, Limbé; tel. 3333-3217; f. 1983; publishing and book-trade reference; Dir and Editor-in-Chief JÉRÔME F. GWELLEM.

Presses de l'Université catholique d'Afrique Centrale (PUCAC): BP 11628, Yaoundé; tel. 2230-5508; fax 2230-5501; e-mail p_ucac@yahoo.fr; internet www.pucac.com; Man. GABRIEL TSALA ONANA.

GOVERNMENT PUBLISHING HOUSES

Centre d'Edition et de Production pour l'Enseignement et la Recherche (CEPER): BP 808, Yaoundé; tel. 7723-1293; f. 1967; transfer pending to private ownership; general non-fiction, science and technology, tertiary, secondary and primary educational textbooks; Man. Dir JEAN CLAUDE FOUTH.

Imprimerie Nationale: BP 1603, Yaoundé; tel. 2223-1277; scheduled for transfer to private ownership; Dir AMADOU VAMOULKE.

Société de Presse et d'Editions du Cameroun (SOPECAM): route de l'Aéroport, BP 1218, Yaoundé; tel. 2230-4147; fax 2230-4362; e-mail mclairennana@yahoo.fr; f. 1977; under the supervision of the Ministry of Communication; Pres. PAUL TESSA; Dir-Gen. MARIE CLAIRE NNANA.

Broadcasting and Communications

TELECOMMUNICATIONS

A Telecommunications Regulation Agency was established in early 1999.

Cameroon Telecommunications (CAMTEL): BP 1571, Yaoundé; tel. 2223-4065; fax 2223-0303; e-mail camtel@camnet.cm; internet www.camnet.cm; f. 1999 by merger of INTELCAM and the Dept of Telecommunications; 51% privatization pending; Pres. NFON VICTOR MUKETE; Dir-Gen. DAVID NKOTO EMANE.

Cameroon Mobile Telecommunications Corporation: f. by CAMTEL in March 2006.

Mobile Telephone Networks (MTN) Cameroon Ltd: 360 rue Drouo, Bonamouti, Akwa, Douala; tel. 9900-9000; fax 9900-9040; f. 1999 as CAMTEL Mobile; acquired by MTN in 2000; mobile cellular telephone operator; 70% owned by MTN Ltd, 30% owned by Broadband Telecom Ltd.

Société Camerounaise de Mobiles: Yaoundé; internet www.fcr .fr/fr/identite/pays/cameroun.htm; f. 1999; mobile cellular telephone operator; operates in Yaoundé, Douala and Bafoussam; 100% owned by France Câbles et Radio; Dir-Gen. JEAN-PAUL GANDET.

BROADCASTING

Radio

Office de Radiodiffusion-Télévision Camerounaise (CRTV): BP 1634, Yaoundé; tel. 2221-4077; fax 2220-4340; internet www.crtv .cm; f. 1987; broadcasts in French and English; satellite broadcasts commenced in Jan. 2001, reaching some 80% of the national territory; Pres. of Council of Administration PIERRE MOUKOKO MBONJO (Minister of Communication); Dir-Gen. (vacant).

Radio Bertoua: BP 260, Bertoua; tel. 2224-1445; fax 2224-2275; Head of Station BAIVE NYONG PHILIP.

Radio Buéa: BP 86, Buéa; tel. 3332-2615; programmes in English, French and 15 vernacular languages; Man. PETERSON CHIA YUH; Head of Station GIDEON MULU TAKA.

Radio Douala: BP 986, Douala; tel. 3342-6060; programmes in French, English, Douala, Bassa, Ewondo, Bakoko and Bamiléké; Dir BRUNO DJEM; Head of Station LINUS ONANA MVONDO.

Radio Garoua: BP 103, Garoua; tel. 2227-1167; programmes in French, Hausa, English, Foulfouldé, Arabic and Choa; Dir BELLO MALGANA; Head of Station MOUSSA EPOPA.

Radio Ngaoundéré: BP 135, Ngaoundéré; tel. 2225-2148.

Radio Tam Tam: Yaoundé.

Radio Yaoundé FM 94: BP 1634, Yaoundé; tel. 2220-2502; Head of Station LOUISE POM.

There are also provincial radio stations at Abong Mbang, Bafoussam, Bamenda, Ebolowa and Maroua.

Television

Television programmes from France were broadcast by the Office de Radiodiffusion-Télévision Camerounaise from early 1990.

Office de Radiodiffusion-Télévision Camerounaise (CRTV): see Radio.

Finance

(cap. = capital; res = reserves; dep. = deposits; m. = million; brs = branches; amounts in francs CFA)

BANKING

Central Bank

Banque des Etats de l'Afrique Centrale (BEAC): rue du Docteur Jamot, BP 1917, Yaoundé; tel. 2223-4030; fax 2223-3329; e-mail beacyde@beac.int; internet www.beac.int; f. 1973; bank of issue for mem. states of the Communauté économique et monétaire de l'Afrique centrale (CEMAC, fmrly Union douanière et économique de l'Afrique centrale): Cameroon, the Central African Repub., Chad, the Repub. of the Congo, Equatorial Guinea and Gabon; cap. 45,000m., res 326,675m., total assets 2,150,301m. (Dec. 2003); Gov. JEAN-FÉLIX MAMALEPOT; Dir in Cameroon SADOU HAYATOU; 5 brs in Cameroon.

Commercial Banks

Afriland First Bank: pl. de l'Indépendance, BP 11834, Yaoundé; tel. 2223-2068; fax 2222-1785; e-mail firstbank@afrilandfirstbank .com; internet www.afrilandfirstbank.com; SBF & Co. (36.62%), FMO (19.80%), private shareholders (43.58%); cap. and res 10,017m., total assets 161,293m. (Dec. 2003); Pres. Dr PAUL KAMMOGNE FOKAM; Gen. Man. ALAMINE OUSAMANE MEY.

Amity Bank Cameroon SA: BP 2705, Douala; tel. 3343-2055; fax 3343-2046; e-mail amity@amitybank.cm; internet www.amitybank .cm; f. 1990; cap. and res −2,671m., total assets 24,717m. (June 2002); Pres. Prof. VICTOR ANOMAH NGU; Dir-Gen. MATHURIN NGASSA; 4 brs.

Banque Internationale du Cameroun pour l'Epargne et le Crédit (BICEC): ave du Général de Gaulle, BP 1925, Douala; tel. 3342-8843; fax 3342-6047; e-mail bicec@bicec.com; internet www .bicec.com; f. 1962 as Banque Internationale pour le Commerce et l'Industrie du Cameroun; name changed as above in 1997, following restructuring; 52.5% owned by Groupe Banques Populaires (France); cap. 3,000m., res 18,928m., dep. 258,615m. (Dec. 2003); Pres. JEAN-BAPTISTE BOKAM; Gen. Man. JEAN-PIERRE SCHIANO; 26 brs.

Citibank N.A. Cameroon: 96 rue Flatters, Bonanjo, BP 4571, Douala; tel. 3342-4272; fax 3342-4074; internet www.citigroup .com; f. 1997; Dir-Gen. ASIF ZAIDI; COO WILSON CHOLA.

Commercial Bank of Cameroon (CBC): Centre d'affaires Flatters, 96 rue Flatters, BP 4571, Douala; tel. 3342-4272; e-mail cbcbank@ccbc-bank.com; f. 1997; cap. and res. 12,596m., total assets 125,596m. (Dec. 2003); Pres. VICTOR FOTSO.

Crédit Lyonnais Cameroun SA: 220 Monsieur Vogt, BP 700, Yaoundé; tel. 3343-5400; fax 3342-5413; e-mail scb_cl_cameroun@ creditlyonnais.fr; f. 1989 as Société Commerciale de Banque—Crédit Lyonnais Cameroun; name changed as above in 2002; 35% state-owned; cap. and res 6,000m., total assets 258,316m. (Dec. 2004); Pres. MARTIN ARISTIDE OKOUDA; Gen. Man. FRANCIS DUBUS; Sec.-Gen. PIERRE SAM-NDOUMBE; 15 brs.

Ecobank Cameroun SA (Togo): blvd de la Liberté, BP 582, Douala; tel. 3343-8250; fax 3343-8487; e-mail ecobankcm@ecobank.com; internet www.ecobank.com; f. 2001; cap. 2,500m., res 2,953m., dep.

51,356m., total assets 72,038m. (Dec. 2005); Chair. André Fotso; Man. Dir Abou Kabassi Kassimou.

Highland Corporation Bank SA: Immeuble Hôtel Hilton, blvd du 20 mai, BP 10039, Yaoundé; tel. 2223-9287; fax 2232-9291; e-mail atnjp@camnet.cm; internet pcnet.ifrance.com/pcnet/hcb/; f. 1995; 100% privately owned; cap. 600m. (Dec. 1996); Exec. Pres. Paul Atanga Nji; Asst Dir-Gen. Johanes Mbati.

Société Générale de Banques au Cameroun (SGBC): 78 rue Joss, BP 4042, Douala; tel. 3342-7010; fax 3343-0353; e-mail sgbcdla@camnet.cm; f. 1963; 25.6% state-owned; cap. and res 17,213m., total assets 301,391m. (June 2001); Chair. Amadou Njifenjou Mouliom; Dir-Gen. Alain Bellissard; 15 brs.

Standard Chartered Bank Cameroon SA: blvd de la Liberté, BP 1784, Douala; tel. 3343-5200; fax 3342-8927; internet www.standardchartered.com/cm/index.html; f. 1980 as Boston Bank Cameroon; name changed 1986; 100% owned by Standard Chartered Bank (United Kingdom); cap. 7,000m., total assets 143,619m. (June 2002); CEO Paul Sagnia; 3 brs.

Union Bank of Cameroon, Ltd (UBC): BP 110, Bamenda, Douala; tel. 3336-2316; fax 3336-2310; e-mail ubc@unionbankcameroon.com; internet www.unionbankcameroon.com; total assets 7,278m. (June 2001); Pres. Gabriel Ikomé Njoh; CEO Julius Akene Ngawa.

Development Banks

Banque de Développement des Etats de l'Afrique Centrale: see Franc Zone.

Crédit Foncier du Cameroun (CFC): 484 blvd du 20 mai 1972, BP 1531, Yaoundé; tel. 2223-5216; fax 2223-5221; f. 1977; 75% state-owned; cap. and res 7,835m., total assets 87,000m. (Dec. 2003); provides assistance for low-cost housing; Pres. André Booto A. Ngon; 10 brs.

Société Nationale d'Investissement du Cameroun (SNI): pl. du 20 mai, BP 423, Yaoundé; tel. 2222-4422; fax 2223-1332; e-mail sni@sni.cm; internet www.sni.cm; f. 1964; state-owned investment and credit agency; cap. 19,000m., res 20,980m., total assets 33,426m. (June 2000); Dir-Gen. Esther Belibi Dang.

Financial Institutions

Caisse Autonome d'Amortissement du Cameroun: BP 7167, Yaoundé; tel. 2222-0187; fax 2222-0129; e-mail camtis@camnet.cm; f. 1985; cap. 5,000m. (1998); Dir-Gen. Daniel Lamere Njankouo.

Caisse Commune d'Epargne et d'Investissement (CCEI): pl. de l'Indépendance, BP 11834, Yaoundé; tel. 2223-3068; fax 2222-1785; e-mail kengnea@hotmail.com; total assets 88,551m. (June 2000); Pres. Dr Paul Kanmogne Fokam; Dir-Gen. Daniel Potouonjou Taponzié.

Fonds d'Aide et de Garantie des Crédits aux Petites et Moyennes Entreprises (FOGAPE): BP 1591, Yaoundé; tel. 2223-3859; fax 2222-3274; f. 1984; cap. 1,000m. (Oct. 1997); Pres. Joseph Henga; Vice-Pres. Armand Firmin Mvondo.

National Financial Credit Company Cameroon (NFCC): BP 6578, Yaoundé; tel. 2222-4806; fax 2222-8781; e-mail national_financial_credit@yahoo.com; cap. and res 2,350m., total assets 9,338m.; Pres. Abey Jerome Ongher; Gen. Man. Awanga Zacharia.

Société Camerounaise de Crédit Automobile (SOCCA): rue du Roi Albert, BP 554, Douala; tel. 3342-7478; fax 3342-1219; e-mail soccabail@socca-cm.cm; internet www.giefca.com/english/cameroun.htm; cap. and res 4,770m., total assets 23,748m. (Dec. 2003); Pres. Valentin Mouyombon; Dir-Gen. Johann Baudot.

Société Camerounaise de Crédit-Bail (SOCABAIL): rue du Roi Albert, BP 554, Douala; tel. 3342-7478; fax 3342-1219; e-mail soccabail@camnet.cm; cap. 500m., res 1,343m., total assets 5,880m. (June 1999); Pres. Alain Guyon.

STOCK EXCHANGE

Bourse des Valeurs de Douala (Douala Stock Exchange): 1450 blvd de la Liberté, BP 442, Douala; tel. 3343-8582; fax 3353-8584; e-mail dsx@dsx.cm; f. 2003; 23% state-owned; Chair. Bénédict Belibi; Dir-Gen. Pierre Ekoulé Mouangué.

INSURANCE

Activa Assurances: BP 12970, Douala; tel. 3343-4503; fax 3343-4572; e-mail activa.assur@camnet.cm; f. 1999; all branches except life insurance; cap. 400m.; 66% owned by Cameroonian investors, 33% by Ivorian investors; Chair. Jean Kacou Diagou; Gen. Man. Richard Lowe.

AGF Cameroun Assurances: rue Manga Bell, BP 105, Douala; tel. 3342-9203; fax 3343-0324; e-mail agf.cameroun@agf-cm.com; internet www.agf-afrique.com/filiales/cameroun.htm; f. 1974; 71% owned by AGF Afrique; all classes of insurance; cap. 700m.; Dir-Gen. Adrien Cozza.

Assurances Mutuelles Agricoles du Cameroun (AMACAM): BP 962, Yaoundé; tel. 2222-4966; f. 1965; cap. 100m.; state-owned; privatization pending; Pres. Samuel Ngbwa Nguele; Dir-Gen. Luc Claude Nanfa.

Compagnie Camerounaise d'Assurances et de Réassurances (CCAR): 11 rue Franqueville, BP 4068, Douala; tel. 3342-3159; fax 3342-6453; f. 1974; cap. 499.5m.; Pres. Yvette Chassagne; Dir-Gen. Christian Le Goff.

Compagnie Nationale d'Assurances (CNA): BP 12125, Douala; tel. 3342-4446; fax 3342-4727; f. 1986; all classes of insurance; cap. 600m.; Chair. Théodore Ebobo; Man. Dir Protais Ayangma Amang.

General and Equitable Assurance Cameroon Ltd (GEACAM): 56 blvd de la Liberté, BP 426, Douala; tel. 3342-5985; fax 3342-7103; cap. 300m.; Pres. V. A. Ngu; Man. Dir J. Chebaut.

Société Africaine d'Assurances et Réassurances (SAAR): BP 1011, Douala; tel. 3343-1765; fax 3343-1759; Dir Simon Ningahi.

Société Camerounaise d'Assurances et de Réassurances (SOCAR): 1450 blvd de la Liberté, BP 280, Douala; tel. 3342-5584; fax 3342-1335; f. 1973; cap. 800m.; Chair. J. Yonta; Man. Dir R. Biouele.

Trade and Industry

GOVERNMENT AGENCY

Economic and Social Council: BP 1058, Yaoundé; tel. 2223-2474; advises the Govt on economic and social problems; comprises 150 mems, which serve a five-year term, and a perm. secr.; Pres. Luc Ayang; Sec.-Gen. François Eyok.

DEVELOPMENT ORGANIZATIONS

Agence Française de Développement (AFD): Immeuble Flatters, rue de la Radio 2283, Douala; tel. 3342-5067; fax 3342-9959; e-mail afd.douala@camnet.cm; internet www.afd.fr; fmrly Caisse Française de Développement; Man. Pascal Collange.

Cameroon Development Corporation (CAMDEV): Bota Area, Limbé; tel. 3333-2251; fax 3343-2654; e-mail cdcbota@iccnet2000.com; f. 1947; reorg. 1982; cap. 15,626m. francs CFA; statutory corpn established to acquire and develop plantations of tropical crops for local and export markets; operates two oil mills, 11 banana-packing stations and seven rubber factories; Chair. Chief Okiah Namata Elangwe; Gen. Man. Henry Njalla Quan.

Direction Générale des Grands Travaux du Cameroon (DGTC): BP 6604, Yaoundé; tel. 2222-1803; fax 2222-1300; f. 1988; commissioning, implementation and supervision of public works contracts; Chair. Jean Fouman Akame; Man. Dir Michel Kowalzick.

Hévéa-Cameroun (HEVECAM): BP 1298, Douala and BP 174, Kribi; tel. 3346-1919; f. 1975; state-owned; development of 15,000 ha rubber plantation; 4,500 employees; transferred to private ownership in 1997; Pres. Elie C. Nyokwedi Malonga; Man. Dir Jean-Marc Seyman.

Institut de Recherche Agricole pour le Développement (IRAD): BP 2067, Yaoundé; tel. and fax 2222-3362; e-mail iradpnrua@yahoo.com; internet www.irad-cameroon.org; Dir Simon Zok.

Institut de Recherche pour le Développement (IRD): BP 1857, Yaoundé; tel. 2220-1508; fax 2220-1854; e-mail cameroun@ird.fr; internet www.ird.fr; f. 1984; Rep. in Cameroon Dr Xavier Garde.

Mission d'Aménagement et d'Equipement des Terrains Urbains et Ruraux (MAETUR): BP 1248, Yaoundé; tel. 2222-3113; fax 2223-3190; e-mail maetur@gcnet.cm; internet www.maetur.gcnet.cm; f. 1977; Pres. Pierre Hélé; Dir-Gen. André Mama Fouda.

Mission d'Aménagement et de Gestion des Zones Industrielles: Yaoundé; state-owned industrial land authority; Dir Georges Manon Christol.

Mission de Développement de la Province du Nord-Ouest (MIDENO): BP 442, Bamenda; Dir Andrew Waindim Ndonyi.

Mission Française de Coopération et d'Action Culturelle: BP 1616, Yaoundé; tel. 2223-0412; fax 2222-5065; e-mail mission.coop@camnet.cm; administers bilateral aid from France; Dir Luc Hallade.

Office Céréalier dans la Province du Nord: BP 298, Garoua; tel. 2227-1438; f. 1975 to combat effects of drought in northern Cameroon and stabilize cereal prices; Pres. Alhadji Mahamat; Dir-Gen. Gilbert Gourlemond.

Office National du Cacao et du Café (ONCC): BP 3018, Douala; tel. 3342-9482; fax 3342-0002; Dir-Gen. Michaël Monsieur Ndoping.

Société de Développement du Cacao (SODECAO): BP 1651, Yaoundé; tel. 2230-4544; fax 2230-3395; f. 1974; reorg. 1980; cap. 425m. francs CFA; development of cocoa, coffee and food crop production in the Littoral, Centre, East and South provinces; Pres. JOSEPH-CHARLES DOUMBA; Dir-Gen. JÉRÔME MVONDO.

Société de Développement du Coton (SODECOTON): BP 302, Garoua; tel. 2227-1556; fax 2227-2026; f. 1974; Chair. HAOUNAYE GOUNOKO; Man. MOHAMMED IYA.

Société de Développement de l'Elevage (SODEVA): BP 50, Kousseri; cap. 50m. francs CFA; Dir Alhadji OUMAROU BAKARY.

Société de Développement et d'Exploitation des Productions Animales (SODEPA): BP 1410, Yaoundé; tel. 2220-0810; fax 2220-0809; e-mail sodepa@iccnet.cm; f. 1974; cap. 375m. francs CFA; development of livestock and livestock products; Man. Dir BOUBA NDENGUE DIEUDONNÉ.

Société de Développement de la Haute-Vallée du Noun (UNVDA): BP 25, N'Dop, North-West Province; f. 1970; cap. 1,380m. francs CFA; rice, maize and soya bean cultivation; Dir-Gen. SAMUEL BAWE CHI WANKI.

Société d'Expansion et de Modernisation de la Riziculture de Yagoua (SEMRY): BP 46, Yagoua; tel. 2229-6213; f. 1971; cap. 4,580m. francs CFA; commercialization of rice products and expansion of rice-growing in areas where irrigation is possible; Pres. ALBERT EKONO; Dir-Gen. LIMANGANA TORI.

Société Immobilière du Cameroun (SIC): BP 387, Yaoundé; tel. 2223-3411; fax 2222-5119; f. 1952; cap. 1,000m. francs CFA; housing construction and development; Pres. ABDOULAYE HAMAN ADJI; Dir-Gen. BONIFACE NGOA NKOU.

CHAMBERS OF COMMERCE

Chambre d'Agriculture, d'Elevage et des Forêts du Cameroun: BP 6620, Yaoundé; tel. 2222-0441; fax 2222-2025; e-mail cfe_cameroun@yahoo.fr; f. 1955; 120 mems; Pres. PHILÉMON ADJIBOLO; Sec.-Gen. SOLOMON NFOR GWEI; other chambers at Yaoundé, Ebolowa, Bertoua, Douala, Ngaoundéré, Garoua, Maroua, Buéa, Bumenda and Bafoussam.

Chambre de Commerce, d'Industrie et des Mines du Cameroun (CCIM): rue de Chambre de Commerce, BP 4011, Douala; also at BP 36, Yaoundé; BP 211, Limbé; BP 59, Garoua; BP 944, Bafoussam; BP 551, Bamenda; tel. 7742-6855; fax 7742-5596; e-mail cride-g77@camnet.cm; internet www.g77tin.org/ccimhp.html; f. 1921; 138 mems; Pres. PIERRE TCHANQUE; Sec.-Gen. SAÏDOU ABDOULAYE BOBBOY.

EMPLOYERS' ORGANIZATIONS

Association Professionnelle des Établissements de Crédit (APECCAM): BP 133, Yaoundé; tel. 2223-5401; fax 2223-5402; Pres. JEAN LOUIS CHAPUIS.

Groupement des Femmes d'Affaires du Cameroun (GFAC): BP 1940, Douala; tel. 3342-464; Pres. FRANÇOISE FONING.

Groupement Interpatronal du Cameroun (GICAM): ave Nlongkak, BP 1134, Yaoundé; tel. 2220-0750; fax 2220-0752; e-mail gicam@legicam.org; internet www.legicam.org; f. 1957; Pres. ANDRÉ SIAKA; Sec.-Gen. FRANCIS SANZOUANGO.

Mouvement des Entrepreneurs du Cameroun (MECAM): BP 12443, Douala; tel. 3339-5000; fax 3339-5001; Pres. ALPHONSE BIBEHE.

Syndicat des Commerçants Importateurs-Exportateurs du Cameroun (SCIEC): 16 rue Quillien, BP 562, Douala; tel. 3342-0304; Sec.-Gen. G. TOSCANO.

Syndicat des Industriels du Cameroun (SYNDUSTRICAM): BP 1516, Quartier Akwa, Yaoundé; tel. 3342-3058; fax 3342-5616; e-mail syndustricam@camnet.cm; f. 1953; Pres. CHARLES METOUCK.

Syndicat des Producteurs et Exportateurs de Bois du Cameroun: BP 570, Yaoundé; tel. 2220-2722; fax 2220-9694; Pres. CARLO ORIANI.

Syndicat Professionnel des Entreprises du Bâtiment, des Travaux Publics et des Activités Annexes: BP 1134, Yaoundé; BP 660, Douala; tel. and fax 2220-2722; Sec.-Gen. FRANCIS SANZOUANGOU.

Syndicats Professionnels Forestiers et Activités connexes du Cameroun: BP 100, Douala.

Union des Syndicats Professionnels du Cameroun (USPC): BP 829, Douala; Pres. MOUKOKO KINGUE.

West Cameroon Employers' Association (WCEA): BP 97, Tiko.

Utilities

Electricity

Société Nationale d'Electricité du Cameroun (SONEL): BP 4077, 63 ave de Gaulle, Douala; tel. 3342-5444; fax 3342-2209; e-mail sonel@camnet.cm; f. 1974; 44% state-owned; 56% stake acquired by AES Sirocco in 2001; Gen. Man. JEAN-DAVID BILE.

Water

Société Nationale des Eaux du Cameroun (SNEC): BP 157, Douala; tel. 3342-5444; fax 3342-2247; e-mail contact@snec-cameroun.com; internet www.snec-cameroun.com; f. 1967; 73% state-owned; privatization suspended Dec. 2003; Pres. AMADOU ALI; Dir-Gen. BASILE ATANGANA KOUNA (acting).

MAJOR COMPANIES

The following are some of the largest companies in terms of either capital investment or employment:

ALUCAM, Compagnie Camerounaise de l'Aluminium: BP 1090, Douala; tel. 3342-2930; fax 3342-7669; f. 1984; 39% state-owned; manufacture of aluminium by electrolysis using imported alumina; Pres. and Man. Dir RAPHAËL DIDI MANYAKA.

British American Tobacco Cameroun (BAT Cameroun): BP 94, Yaoundé; tel. 2221-0875; fax 2220-9189; e-mail bat.cameroun@camnet.cm; internet www.bat.com; f. 1946; cap. 2,394.8m. francs CFA; 99.5% owned by British American Tobacco; manufacture of cigarettes; Chair. NICK HALES; Gen. Man. ALAN SCHACHER.

Cameroon Sugar Co, Inc (CAMSUCO): BP 1462, Yaoundé; tel. 2223-0956; fax 2223-6410; f. 1972; sugar plantations, refining and marketing; transferred to private ownership in 1999; Pres. SALOMON ELOGO METOMO; Man. Dir AMOUGOU MBEDJA.

Cimenteries du Cameroun (CIMENCAM): BP 1323, Douala; tel. 3339-1119; fax 3339-0984; e-mail sat.cim@camnet.cm; f. 1965; cement works at Figuil, clinker-crushing plant at Douala-Bonabéri, factory at Garoua; 44% owned by Lafarge of France; Pres. ADAMA MODI; Dir-Gen. JEAN JUNG.

Contreplaqués du Cameroun (COCAM): BP 154, Mbalmayo; tel. 2228-1120; fax 2228-1420; f. 1966; cap. 2,489m. francs CFA; 89% state-owned, of which 49% by Société nationale d'investissement du Cameroun; development of forest resources, production of plywood and slatted panels; Pres. PATRICE MANDENG; Dir-Gen. RAYMOND VINCENT ATAGANA ABENA.

Cotonnière Industrielle du Cameroun (CICAM): BP 7012, Douala-Bassa; tel. 3340-6215; fax 3340-7431; e-mail cicam@camnet.cm; f. 1967; factory for bleaching, printing and dyeing of cotton at Douala; Dir Gen. PIERRE REGENET; 1,340 employees.

Del Monte Cameroon Ltd: BP 13275, Douala; tel. 3342-4934; fax 3342-5482; f. 1938; technical food services; Gen. Man. J. A. PELÁEZ.

Les Grandes Huileries Camerounaises: Zone Industrielle de Bassa, Douala; f. 1982; cap. 1,400m. francs CFA; 50% state-owned; Pres. Alhadji BACHIROU; Man. Dir ERIC JACOBSEN.

Guinness Cameroun SA: BP 1213, Douala; tel. 3340-7000; fax 3340-7182; e-mail enquiries@guinness.com; f. 1967; cap. 6,410m. francs CFA; production and marketing of beers; Man. Dir BRIAN JOHNSON; 900 employees.

Nouvelles Brasseries Africaines (NOBRA): rue Tamaris 5, Douala; tel. 3342-8503; f. 1979; cap. 7,000m. francs CFA; manufacturers of soft drinks; Pres. PIERRE TCHANQUE; Dir-Gen. ANDERS ANDERSEN.

Plasticam: Zone Industrielle de Bassa, 2060 rue 3W854, BP 4071, Douala; tel. 3337-5057; fax 3337-1877; e-mail plasticamsg@iccnet2000.com; f. 1962; plastic packaging producers; Chair. DANIEL FORGET; Gen. Man. BERNARD GUILPIN.

Saga Cameroun: BP 280, Yaoundé; tel. 2220-5137; fax 2221-3722; e-mail sagadla.direction@cm.dti.bollore.com; internet www.saga.fr; f. 1959; transport services; Pres. CLAUDE BENITAH; 620 employees.

Société Africaine Forestière et Agricole du Cameroun (SAFA Cameroun): BP 100, Douala; tel. 3342-9758; fax 3342-7512; f. 1897; plantation of natural rubber and production of rubber and latex; rubber and palm plantations at Dizangué; Pres. LUC BOEDT; Man. Dir GILBERT SUJET; 1,571 employees.

Société Anonyme des Brasseries du Cameroun (SABC): BP 4036, Douala; tel. 3342-9133; fax 3342-7945; f. 1948; production of beer and soft drinks; Pres. ANDRÉ SIAKA; 1,651 employees.

Société Camerounaise des Dépôts Pétroliers (SCDP): rue de la Cité Chardy, BP 2272, Douala; tel. 3340-5445; fax 3340-4796; e-mail scdp@camnet.cm; f. 1978; storage and distribution of petroleum; Dir JAMES N. MOUKOKO.

Société Camerounaise de Fabrication de Piles Electriques (PILCAM): BP 1916, Douala; tel. 3342-2628; f. 1970; cap. 1,472m. francs CFA; Pres. VICTOR FOTSO; Dir ANDRÉ FONTANA; 745 employees.

Société Camerounaise de Métallurgie (SCDM): BP 706, Douala; tel. 3342-4256; fax 3342-0185; f. 1984; cap. 1,475m. francs CFA; steel processors and mfrs of metal products; Man. Dir ALAIN GILBERT-DESVALLONS.

Société Camerounaise de Palmeraies (SOCAPALM): rue du Général Leman, BP 691, Douala; tel. 3343-7783; fax 3343-8734; f. 1968; cap. 12,629,000m. francs CFA; 73% privatized in 2000; management of palm plantations and production of palm oil and manufactured products; Chair. JUIMO MONTHE; Gen. Man. MARC MUTSAARS; 1,380 employees.

Société Camerounaise de Sacherie (SCS): Zone Industrielle de Bassa, BP 398, Douala; tel. 3342-3104; f. 1971; cap. 2,075m. francs CFA; 39% owned by ONCPB; production of sacks; Pres. GUILLAUME NSEKE; Dir THOMAS DAKAYI KAMGA.

Société Camerounaise des Tabacs (SCT): rue Joseph-Clerc, BP 29, Yaoundé; tel. 2222-1488; f. 1964; cap. 1,750m. francs CFA; tobacco cultivation and curing; Pres. PHILÉMON ADJIBOLO; Man. Dir LUCIEN KINGUE EBONGUE.

Société Camerounaise de Transformation de l'Aluminium (SOCATRAL): BP 291, Edéa; tel. 3346-4024; fax 3346-4774; e-mail socalu1@yahoo.fr; f. 1960; 49% owned by ALUCAM (q.v.); production of corrugated sheets, aluminium strips and rolled discs; Pres. and Man. Dir RAFAËL TITIMANYAKA.

Société Camerounaise de Verrerie (SOCAVER): BP 1456, Douala; tel. 3340-0506; fax 3340-6403; e-mail socaver@camnet.cm; f. 1966; 52.9% owned by SABC (q.v.); mfrs of glassware; Pres. MICHEL PALU; Gen. Man. ANDRÉ SIAKA.

Société Cartonnière (SOCARTO): BP 5028, Douala; tel. 3342-8572; fax 3342-8552; e-mail socarto@camnet.cm; f. 1971; state-owned; producer of paper and pulp; Man. Dir SAMUEL KONDO.

Société Forestière et Industrielle de Belabo (SOFIBEL): Yaoundé; tel. 2223-2657; f. 1975; cap. 1,902m. francs CFA; 39% state-owned; sawmill; manufacturers of plywood; Pres. SADOU DAOUDOU; Man. Dir DENIS KEEDI ATOK.

Société Générale des Travaux Métalliques (GETRAM): Douala; tel. 3342-8068; fax 3342-7761; f. 1980; cap. 1,200m. francs CFA; Pres. BERNARD MOUNDIO; Dir-Gen. OLIVIER BOUYGUES.

Société Industrielle Camerounaise des Cacaos (SIC CACAOS): BP 570, Douala; tel. 3340-8810; fax 3340-3931; e-mail sic.cacaos@camnet.cm; f. 1949; cap. 1,147.5m. francs CFA; production of cocoa and cocoa butter; Pres. JEAN-MARC DIEUDONNÉ OYONO; Man. Dir DIDIER BUÉCHER.

Société Industrielle des Tabacs du Cameroun (SITABAC): BP 1105, Douala; tel. 3342-4919; fax 3342-5949; e-mail sitabac@camnet.cm; cap. 4,556.6m. francs CFA; manufacture and sale of cigarettes; Pres. and Dir-Gen. JAMES ONOBIONO.

La Société les Minotiers du Cameroun: BP 785, Douala; tel. 3337-7501; fax 3337-1761; f. 1986; cap. 1,010m. francs CFA; flour mill; Pres. BABA AHMADOU; Dir-Gen. ANDRÉ NGANDEU.

Société Nationale des Hydrocarbures (SNH): BP 955, Yaoundé; tel. 2220-1910; fax 2220-4651; e-mail info@snh.cm; internet www.snh.cm; f. 1980; national petroleum co; Pres. JEAN-MARIE ATANGANA; Dir-Gen. ADOLPHE MOUDIKI.

Société Nationale de Raffinage (SONARA): BP 365, Cap Limboh, Limbé; tel. 3342-3815; fax 3342-3444; e-mail sonara.coh@camnet.cm; f. 1976; cap. 17,800m. francs CFA; 66% state-owned; establishment and operation of petroleum refinery at Cap Limboh; Chair. JOHN EBONG NGOLE; 620 employees.

Société de Palmeraies de la Ferme Suisse (SPFS): BP 06, Edéa-Ongué; tel. 3347-2126; fax 3343-0324; f. 1976; cultivation of products for industrial processing, operates factory for processing palm oil and palm kernels; Pres. and Man. Dir ALAIN DOUAT; 375 employees.

Société de Recherches et d'Exploitation des Pétroles du Cameroun (SEREPCA): 83 blvd de la Liberté, BP 2214, Douala-Bassa; tel. 3342-1785; fax 3342-1366; f. 1951; cap. 1,000m. francs CFA; 20% state-owned; prospecting and exploitation of offshore petroleum; Pres. JEAN-LOUIS VERMEULEN; Dir-Gen. MICHEL CHARLES; 600 employees.

Société Shell du Cameroun: BP 4082, Douala; tel. 3342-2415; fax 3342-6031; f. 1954; cap. 1,600m. francs CFA; import and distribution of petroleum products; Dir-Gen. BANJI OGUNGBEMI.

Société Sucrière du Cameroun (SOSUCAM): BP 875, Yaoundé; tel. and fax 2223-0585; e-mail sosucam@camnet.cm; e-mail info@sosucam.jlv.com; f. 1965; cap. 13,925m. francs CFA (2003); 24% state-owned; sugar refinery at M'bandjock; owned by Vilgrain group of France; Pres. and Man. Dir L. YINDA.

Société Textile du Cameroun pour le Linge de Maison (SOLICAM): BP 2413, Douala; tel. 3342-9720; f. 1979; cap. 3,000m. francs CFA; textile complex; Pres. SIMON NGANNYON; Dir-Gen. MICHEL VIALLET.

Summit Motors Cameroon, SA (SUMOCA): BP 4181, Douala; tel. 3337-2286; fax 3337-0558; e-mail sumoca@sumoca.com; internet www.sumoca.com; state-owned; Man. Dir ICHIRO TOMINO.

Texaco Cameroun, SA: blvd de la Liberté, POB 214, Douala; tel. 3342-3028; fax 3342-8312; e-mail bennett@texaco.iccnet.cm; f. 1947; Man. Dir WILLIAM C. BENNETT.

TotalFinaElf Cameroun: BP 4048, Douala-Bassa; tel. 3342-6341; fax 3342-6871; e-mail total@camnet.cm; f. 1900; exploration for, exploitation and distribution of petroleum reserves; Man. BERTRAND DEVOS.

PRINCIPAL CO-OPERATIVE ORGANIZATIONS

Centre National de Développement des Entreprises Coopératives (CENADEC): Yaoundé; f. 1970; promotes and organizes the co-operative movement; bureaux at BP 43, Kumba and BP 26, Bamenda; Dir JACQUES SANGUE.

Union Centrale des Coopératives Agricoles de l'Ouest (UCCAO): ave Samuel Wonko, BP 1002, Bafoussam; tel. 3344-4296; fax 3344-1845; e-mail uccao@uccao-cameroun.com; internet www.uccao-cameroun.com; f. 1958; marketing of cocoa and coffee; 120,000 mems; Pres. JACQUES FOTSO KANKEU; Gen. Man. FRANÇOIS MEFINJA FOKA.

West Cameroon Co-operative Association Ltd: BP 135, Kumba; founded as cen. financing body of the co-operative movement; provides short-term credits and agricultural services to mem. socs; policy-making body for the co-operative movement in West Cameroon; 142 mem. unions and socs representing c. 45,000 mems; Pres. Chief T. E. NJEA.

TRADE UNION FEDERATION

Confederation of Cameroon Trade Unions (CCTU): BP 1610, Yaoundé; tel. 2222-3315; f. 1985; fmrly the Union Nationale des Travailleurs du Cameroun (UNTC); Pres. ANDRE JULE MOUSSENI; Sec.-Gen. LOUIS SOMBES.

Transport

RAILWAYS

There are some 1,008 km of track—the West Line running from Douala to Nkongsamba (166 km), with a branch line leading south-west from Mbanga to Kumba (29 km), and the Transcameroon railway, which runs from Douala to Ngaoundéré (885 km), with a branch line from Ngoumou to Mbalmayo (30 km). In July 2002 the World Bank disbursed a loan of 15,600m. francs CFA to Cameroon to help rehabilitate the main line. In November the French Government approved a loan of US $12.5m. to Cameroon, primarily to improve rolling stock.

CAMRAIL S.A.: Gare Centrale de Bessengué, blvd de la Réunification, BP 766, Douala; tel. 3340-8247; fax 3340-8252; e-mail camrail.dg@iccnet2000.cm; internet www.camrail.net; f. 1999; passenger and freight transport; Pres. MICHEL ROUSSIN; Dir-Gen. BENOÎT DU SOUICH.

Office du Chemin de Fer Transcamerounais: BP 625, Yaoundé; tel. 2222-4433; supervises the laying of new railway lines and improvements to existing lines, and undertakes relevant research; Dir-Gen. LUC TOWA FOTSO.

ROADS

In 2004 there were an estimated 50,000 km of roads, of which 10.0% were paved.

SHIPPING

There are seaports at Kribi and Limbé-Tiko, a river port at Garoua, and an estuary port at Douala-Bonabéri, the principal port and main outlet, which has 2,510 m of quays and a minimum depth of 5.8 m in the channels and 8.5 m at the quays. Total handling capacity is 7m. metric tons annually. Plans are under way to increase the annual capacity of the container terminal. There are also plans to modernize Limbé-Tiko and to promote it internationally.

Office National des Ports/National Ports Authority: 81 rue de la Chambre de Commerce, BP 4023, Douala; tel. 3342-0133; fax 3342-6797; e-mail onpc@camnet.cm; internet www.camnet.cm/investir/transport/onpc; f. 1971; Chair. DAKOLÉ DAÏSSALA (Minister of Transport); Dir-Gen. ALPHONSE SIYAM SIVE.

Cameroon Shipping Lines SA (CAMSHIP): BP 15788, Douala; tel. 3342-0064; fax 3342-0114; f. 1975; scheduled for transfer to private-sector ownership; 6 vessels trading with Western Europe, USA, Far East and Africa; Chair. FRANÇOIS SENGAT KUO; Man. Dir RENÉ MBAYEN.

Camafrica Liner Ltd: Centre des Affaires Maritimes, BP 4054, Douala; non-vessel owner container carrier co. trading between West Africa and Europe.

Camtainer: Para-maratime Area, Douala Port, BP 4993, Douala; tel. 3342-7704; fax 3342-7173; internet www.camnet.cm/investir/transpor/camtenair/sommaire.htm.

Compagnie Maritime Camerounaise SA (CMC): BP 3235, Douala; tel. 3342-8540; fax 3342-5842.

Conseil National des Chargeurs du Cameroun (CNCC): BP 1588, Douala; tel. 3342-3206; fax 3342-8901; f. 1986; promotion of the maritime sector; Gen. Man. AUGUSTE MBAPPE PENDA.

Delmas Cameroun: rue Kitchener, BP 263, Douala; tel. 3342-4750; fax 3342-8851; f. 1977; Pres. JEAN-GUY LE FLOCH; Dir-Gen. DANY CHUTAUX.

MAERSK CAMEROUN SA—Douala: BP 12414, Douala; tel. 3342-1185; fax 3342-1186; e-mail dlasal@maersk.com.

Société Africaine de Transit et d'Affrètement (SATA): Douala; tel. 3342-8209; f. 1950; Man. Dir RAYMOND PARIZOT.

Société Agence Maritime de l'Ouest Africain Cameroun (SAMOA): 5 blvd de la Liberté, BP 1127, Douala; tel. 3342-1680; f. 1953; shipping agents; Dir JEAN PERRIER.

Société Camerounaise de Manutention et d'Acconage (SOCAMAC): BP 284, Douala; tel. 3342-4051; e-mail socamac@camnet.cm; internet www.camnet.cm/investir/transpor/socamac.htm; f. 1976; freight handling; Pres. MOHAMADOU TALBA; Dir-Gen. HARRY J. GHOOS.

Société Camerounaise de Transport et d'Affrètement (SCTA): BP 974, Douala; tel. 3342-1724; f. 1951; Pres. JACQUES VIAULT; Dir-Gen. GONTRAN FRAUCIEL.

Société Camerounaise de Transport Maritime: BP 12351, Douala; tel. 3342-4550; fax 3342-4946.

Société Ouest-Africaine d'Entreprises Maritimes—Cameroun (SOAEM—Cameroon): 5 blvd de la Liberté, BP 4057, Douala; tel. 3342-5269; fax 3342-0518; f. 1959; Pres. JACQUES COLOMBANI; Man. Dir JEAN-LOUIS GRECIET.

SOCOPAO Cameroun: BP 215, Douala; tel. 3342-6464; f. 1951; shipping agents; Pres. VINCENT BOLLORE; Man. Dir E. DUPUY.

Transcap Cameroun: BP 4059, Douala; tel. 3342-7214; f. 1960; Pres. RENÉ DUPRAZ; Man. Dir MICHEL BARDOU.

CIVIL AVIATION

There are international airports at Douala, Garoua and Yaoundé; there are, in addition, 11 domestic airports, as well as a number of secondary airfields.

Aéroports du Cameroun (ADC): Aéroport de Douala; tel. 3342-3577; fax 3342-3758; f. 1999; manages major airports; 35% owned by Aéroports de Paris, 29% state-owned.

Air Affaires Afrique: BP 1225, Douala; tel. 3342-2977; fax 3342-9903; f. 1978; regional and domestic charter passenger services; CEO BYRON BYRON-EXARCOS.

Cameroon Airlines (CAMAIR): 3 ave du Général de Gaulle, BP 4092, Douala; tel. 3342-2525; fax 3342-3443; e-mail camair@camnet.cm; internet www.cameroon-airlines.com; f. 1971; domestic flights and services to Africa, North America and Europe; Dir-Gen. PAUL NGAMO HAMANI (interim); Inspector-Gen. of Administration and Finance ESTHER GOUETT.

Tourism

Tourists are attracted by Cameroon's cultural diversity and by its national parks, game reserves and sandy beaches. In 2005 176,372 tourists visited Cameroon. In 2000 receipts from tourism totalled US $39m.

Ministry of Tourism: see Ministries.

Defence

As assessed at November 2006, Cameroon's armed forces were estimated to total 23,100 men, including 9,000 in paramilitary forces. The army numbered 12,500, the navy about 1,300 and the air force 300. Cameroon has a bilateral defence agreement with France.

Defence Expenditure: Estimated at 134,000m. francs CFA in 2006.

Commander-in-Chief of the Armed Forces: PAUL BIYA.

Education

Since independence, Cameroon has achieved one of the highest rates of school attendance in Africa, but provision of educational facilities varies according to region. Education, which is bilingual, is provided by the Government, missionary societies and private concerns. Education in state schools is available free of charge, and the Government provides financial assistance for other schools. Primary education begins at six years of age. It lasts for six years in Eastern Cameroon (where it is officially compulsory), and for seven years in Western Cameroon. Secondary education, beginning at the age of 12 or 13, lasts for a further seven years, comprising two cycles of four years and three years in Eastern Cameroon, and two years in Western Cameroon. In 2003/04 there were some 3.0m. pupils enrolled at the primary level, while the number of pupils enrolled at secondary schools totalled some 1.2m. The State University at Yaoundé, which was established in 1962, has been decentralized, and consists of five regional campuses, each devoted to a different field of study. Expenditure on education by the central Government in 2004 was estimated at 213,143m. francs CFA (26.3% of total spending).

Bibliography

Ardener, E., and Ardener, S. *Kingdom on Mount Cameroon: Studies in the History of the Cameroon Coast 1500–1960*. Oxford, Berghahn Books, 2002.

Asuagbor, G. O. *Democratization and Modernization in a Multilingual Cameroon*. Edwin Mellin Press, 1998.

Bandolo, H. *La flamme et la fumée*. Yaoundé, Editions SOPECAM, 1988.

Bayart, J.-F. *L'état au Cameroun*. Paris, Presses de la Fondation Nationale des Sciences Politiques, 1985.

Belinga, E. *Cameroun: La Révolution pacifique du 20 mai*. Yaoundé, 1976.

Beti, M. *Lutte ouverte aux camerounais*. Rouen, Editions des Peuples Noirs, 1986.

Biya, P. *Communal Liberalism*. London, Macmillan, 1987.

Biyita bi Essam, J.-P. *Cameroun: Complots et Bruits de Bottes*. Paris, L'Harmattan, 1984.

Bjornson, R. *The African Quest for Freedom and Identity: Cameroonian Writing and the National Experience*. Bloomington, IN, Indiana University Press, 1994.

Burnham, P. *The Politics of Cultural Differences in Northern Cameroon*. Edinburgh, Edinburgh University Press, 1996.

Chem-Langhëë, B. *The Paradoxes of Self-Determination in the Cameroons under United Kingdom Administration: The Search for Identity, Well-Being and Continuity*. Lanham, MD, University Press of America, 2004.

Chiabi, E. M. *The Making of Modern Cameroon*. Lanham, MD, University Press of America, 1997.

Cruise O'Brien, D. B., Dunn, J., and Rathbone, R. *Contemporary West African States*. Cambridge University Press, 1989.

De Lancey, M. W. *Cameroon: Dependence and Independence*. Boulder, CO, Westview Press, 1989.

De Lancey, M. W., and Schrader, P. J. *Cameroon*. Oxford, Clio, 1986.

Donnat, G. *Afin que nul l'oublie*. Paris, L'Harmattan, 1986.

Epale, S. J. *Plantations and Development in Western Cameroon 1875–1975: A Study in Agrarian Capitalism*. New York, Vantage Press, 1985.

Eyinga, A. *Introduction à la politique camerounaise*. Paris, L'Harmattan, 1984.

Fonge, F. *Modernization Without Development: Patterns of Change and Continuity in Post-independence Cameroonian Public Service*. Trenton, NJ, Africa World Press, 1998.

Gabriel, R. *L'Administration publique camerounaise*. Paris, Librairie Générale de Droit et de Jurisprudence, 1986.

Gaillard, P. *Le Cameroun*. Paris, L'Harmattan, 1989.

Goheen, M. *Men Own the Fields, Women Own the Crops: Gender and Power in the Cameroon Grassfields*. Madison, WI, University of Wisconsin Press, 1996.

Gros, J.-G. *Cameroon: Politics and Society in Critical Perspective*. Lanham, MD, University Press of America, 2003.

Hugon, P. *Analyse du sous-développement en Afrique noire: L'exemple de l'économie du Cameroun*. Paris, Presses Universitaires de France, 1968.

Ignatowski, C. *Journey of Song: Public Life and Morality in Cameroon*. Bloomington, IN, Indiana University Press, 2006.

Joseph, R. A. *Radical Nationalism in Cameroon*. London, Oxford University Press, 1977.

Koenig, E. L., Chia, E., and Povey, J. (Eds). *A Socio-Linguistic Profile of Urban Centers in Cameroon*. Los Angeles, CA, UCLA (Crossroads Press), 1983.

Konings, P. *Labour Resistance in Cameroon*. London, James Currey Publishers, 1993.

Gender and Class in the Tea Estates of Cameroon. Brookfield, VT, Ashgate Publishing, 1996.

Le Vine, V. T., and Nye, R. P. *Historical Dictionary of the Republic of Cameroon*. 2nd Edn. Metuchen, NJ, Scarecrow Press, 1990.

Manga, E. J. *The African Economic Dilemma: The Case of Cameroon*. Lanham, MD, University Press of America, 1998.

Mbaku, J. M. and Takougang, J. (Eds). *The Leadership Challenge in Africa: Cameroon Under Paul Biya*. Trenton, NJ, Africa World Press, 2004.

Mehler, A. *Kamerun in der Ära Biya: Bedingungen, erste Schritte und Blockaden einer demokratischen Transition*. Hamburg, Institut für Afrika-Kunde, 1993. (Hamburger Beiträge zur Afrika-Kunde; 42).

Ndongko, W. A., and ViveKananda, F. *Economic Development of Cameroon*. Stockholm, Bethany Books, 1990.

Ngoh, V. J. *Cameroon 1884–1985: A Hundred Years of History*. Yaoundé, Imprimerie Nationale, 1988.

Southern Cameroons 1922–1961: A Constitutional History. Hampshire, Ashgate Publishing Ltd, 2001.

Previtali, S. *Le Cameroun par les ponts et par les routes*. Paris, Editions Karthala, 1988.

Regis, H. *Fulbe Voices: Marriage, Islam, and Medicine in Northern Cameroon*. Boulder, CO, Westview Press, 2002.

Sindjoun, L. *Comment Peut-On Etre Opposant au Cameroun?: Politique Parlementaire et Politique Autoritaire*. Dakar, Council for the Development of Social Science Research in Africa, 2005.

Stoecker, H. (Ed.). *German Imperialism in Africa*. London, Hurst Humanities, 1986.

Takougang, J., and Krieger, M. H. *African State and Society in the 1990s: Cameroon's Political Crossroads*. Boulder, CO, Westview Press, 1998.

Weiss, L. T. *Migrants nigérians, la diaspora dans le sud-ouest du Cameroun*. Paris, L'Harmattan, 1998.

Zeltner, J.-C., and Torneux, H. *L'arabe dans le bassin du Tchad*. Paris, Editions Karthala, 1986.

CAPE VERDE

Physical and Social Geography

RENÉ PÉLISSIER

The island Republic of Cape Verde, comprising 10 islands, of which nine are inhabited, and five islets, lies in the Atlantic Ocean, about 500 km west of Dakar, Senegal. The archipelago comprises the windward islands of Santo Antão (754 sq km), São Vicente (228 sq km), Santa Luzia (34 sq km), São Nicolau (342 sq km), Boa Vista (622 sq km) and Sal (215 sq km) to the north, while to the south lie the leeward islands of Maio (267 sq km), Santiago (992 sq km), Fogo (477 sq km) and Brava (65 sq km).

The total area is 4,036 sq km (1,558 sq miles) and the administrative capital is Praia (population of 94,757 at the 2000 census) on Santiago island. The other main centre of population is Mindelo (São Vicente), with an estimated 62,970 inhabitants in 2000, which is the principal port and, with Praia, the economic centre of the archipelago. The 2000 census recorded a total population of 434,625 (107.7 inhabitants per sq km). Santiago is the most populous of the inhabited islands, with an estimated population of 236,627 in 2000, followed by São Vicente (67,163), Santo Antão (47,170) and Fogo (37,421). Santa Luzia has no permanent inhabitants. The total population was estimated at 494,105 in 2007.

Except for the low-lying islands of Sal, Boa Vista and Maio, the archipelago is mountainous, craggy and deeply indented by erosion and volcanic activity. The highest point is Mt Fogo (2,829 m), an active volcano. Located in the semi-arid belt, the islands have an anaemic hydrography, and suffer from chronic shortages of rainfall, which, combined with high temperatures (yearly average 22°–26°C at Praia), cause intense periodic droughts. These droughts have an economically devastating effect on the islands and necessitate heavy dependence on international food aid, which provides most of Cape Verde's food requirements. A desalination plant on São Vicente serves the needs of Mindelo, which is otherwise without drinkable water.

Ethnically, about 71% of the inhabitants are of mixed descent, except on Santiago, where the majority is of pure African stock. Whites represent about 1% of the population. The two official languages are Portuguese and Crioulo, a creole Portuguese, which is influenced by African vocabulary, syntax and pronunciation. Illiteracy is still widespread. In 2004 the average life expectancy at birth was 67 years for men and 71 years for women.

Since independence, a significant number of islanders have emigrated, principally to the USA, the Netherlands, Italy and Portugal, where Cape Verdeans have replaced Portuguese migrants to other countries of the European Union. At least 700,000 Cape Verdeans live outside the country, and their remittances provide an important source of development capital.

Recent History

JONATHAN GREPNE

Revised by EDWARD GEORGE

The Cape Verde islands were colonized by Portugal in the 15th century. In the movement for independence from Portuguese rule during the 1950s, Cape Verde aligned itself with the mainland territory of Portuguese Guinea (now Guinea-Bissau) in a unified nationalist movement, the Partido Africano da Independência do Guiné e Cabo Verde (PAIGC). At Guinea-Bissau's independence in September 1974, however, the PAIGC leadership in Cape Verde decided to pursue its claims separately, rather than to seek an immediate federation with Guinea-Bissau, with which there were few unifying factors other than a common colonial heritage. In December 1974 the Portuguese Government and representatives of the islands' PAIGC formed a transitional administration. Elections to the Assembléia Nacional Popular (ANP—National People's Assembly) took place in June 1975, with independence, as the Republic of Cape Verde, following on 5 July.

Aristides Pereira, the Secretary-General of the PAIGC, became the country's first President. Pedro Pires was appointed Prime Minister, with effective control of the Government. In 1980 the PAIGC was constitutionally established as the sole legal party, and in November of the same year prospects of unification with Guinea-Bissau vanished when Luis Cabral, the President of Guinea-Bissau (and himself a Cape Verdean), was removed in a *coup d'état*. In 1981 the Cape Verdean branch of the PAIGC renamed itself the Partido Africano da Independência de Cabo Verde (PAICV). Although Cape Verde was until September 1990 a one-party state, government policies were generally pragmatic and sensitive. In the mid-1980s non-PAICV members began to take an increasingly prominent role in public and political life. Central control of the economy was eased, to allow a greater degree of private economic initiative, and in 1989 the Government introduced legislation to encourage Cape Verdeans abroad to become involved in the process of development.

DEMOCRATIC CHANGE

Moves towards a relaxation of the PAICV's political monopoly began to emerge in early 1990, as Cape Verde became affected by political changes in West Africa and the Eastern bloc. In February 1990 the PAICV announced the convening of an emergency congress to discuss the possible abolition of the constitutional provision that guaranteed its political monopoly. In April a newly formed opposition group, the Movimento para a Democracia (MpD), demanded the immediate introduction of a multi-party system. In the same month Pereira announced that the next presidential election, which was planned for December 1990, would be held, for the first time, on the basis of universal adult suffrage.

At the first public meeting of the MpD, held in Praia in June 1990, the movement's co-ordinator, Carlos Veiga, stated that the MpD was prepared to negotiate with the PAICV for a transition to political plurality. In July Pereira announced that legislative elections would be held on a multi-party basis before the end of the year, and in September Cape Verde officially became a multi-party state, with the approval by the ANP of the constitutional amendment abolishing the PAICV's monopoly of power. The MpD duly obtained registration and held its first congress in Praia in November, at which Veiga was elected party Chairman. The MpD subsequently declared its support for the candidacy of António Manuel Mascarenhas Gomes

Monteiro, a former Supreme Court judge, in the forthcoming presidential election.

The legislative elections held in January 1991 resulted in a clear victory for the MpD, which secured 56 of the 79 seats in the ANP. The PAICV held the remaining 23 seats. In the same month Veiga was sworn in as Prime Minister at the head of an interim Government, pending the result of the presidential election. This took place in February, and resulted in a decisive victory for Mascarenhas against Pereira, with the former securing 73.5% of the votes cast. Mascarenhas took office in March, and a new Government was formed in April.

THE SECOND REPUBLIC

A new Constitution, enshrining the democratic basis of the 'Second Republic', took effect in September 1992, when a new national flag and emblem were adopted. At its annual national congress in August 1993 the PAICV elected Aristides Lima to the post of Secretary-General of the party, replacing Pires, who was appointed to the newly created post of party Chairman. At an extraordinary convention of the MpD in February 1994 increasing internal dissent prompted about 15 senior members of the party, led by Dr Eurico Correia Monteiro (who had previously been dismissed as Minister of Justice and Labour), to leave the MpD and form a new opposition group, the Partido da Convergência Democrática (PCD).

At legislative elections held in December 1995 the MpD obtained an absolute majority, taking 50 seats in a smaller Assembléia Nacional (as the ANP had been renamed), reduced from 79 seats to 72 under legislation approved in 1994. The PAICV gained 21 seats and the PCD won the remaining seat. At the presidential election which followed in February 1996, Mascarenhas was re-elected unopposed. After the election, Veiga expressed his intention to continue the policies of liberal economic and social reform of his previous term in office, and to introduce further constitutional amendments. At the annual party congress of the PAICV, held in September 1997, Pires, who advocated traditional left-wing policies, was elected leader of the PAICV.

In March 1999 Veiga confirmed speculation that he would not seek re-election as the Chairman of the MpD at the next party convention. António Gualberto do Rosário, the Deputy Prime Minister, and the mayor of Praia, Jacinto Santos, subsequently announced their candidacies for the chairmanship of the MpD, and thus the premiership. The contest escalated into a bitter leadership battle, which seriously weakened the ruling party and was followed by substantial losses in municipal elections held in February 2000. Although the MpD retained eight of the 17 local councils, it came second after the PAICV, which won the capital, Praia. Following the resignation of Pedro Pires, who announced his candidacy for the presidential election, the PAICV elected José Maria Neves as the new President of the party in June. At the MpD convention, held in July, do Rosário was elected Chairman of the party. In the same month Veiga announced his resignation from the premiership and declared his intention to contest the forthcoming presidential election. Do Rosário succeeded him as Prime Minister.

THE RETURN OF THE PAICV

At legislative elections, held on 14 January 2001, the PAICV won an absolute majority of 40 seats (and 49.5% of the vote) against 30 seats (40.5%) for the MpD. A new political force, the Aliança Democrática para a Mudança (ADM), formed in October 2000 by the PCD, the Partido de Trabalho e Solidariedade (PTS) and the União Caboverdiana Independente e Democrática (UCID), obtained the remaining two seats. The performance of the ADM was, however, disappointing—its total share of the vote was 6.1%—and the alliance disbanded after the elections. The Partido para a Renovação Democrática (PRD), formed in July 2000 by Santos, following his defeat in the MpD leadership contest, failed to win any seats.

Shortly after the legislative elections José Maria Neves was appointed Prime Minister. His Government, inaugurated in February 2001, stated that its priority would be the reduction of unemployment and the rehabilitation of public finances. The appointment of a respected economist, Carlos Augusto Duarte de Burgo, as Minister of Finance and Planning, highlighted the Government's commitment to these objectives. The first round of the presidential election, held on 11 February, was inconclusive and a second round in which Pires narrowly defeated Veiga, securing 50.01% of votes cast, was held on 25 February. Official results eventually confirmed that Pires had defeated Veiga by a margin of only 17 votes. Appeals against the results by Veiga (citing voting irregularities) were rejected by the Supreme Court in March, which confirmed Pires as the new President.

The defeat of the MpD prompted do Rosário to resign from the party leadership in August 2001. At the party's congress in December, Agostinho Lopes, one of the party's founding members, was elected Chairman. Following Lopes' appointment, the MpD adopted a more confrontational stance towards the Government. A newspaper, *Expresso das Ilhas*, was established by the MpD in December to counter the perceived dominance by the PAICV of the media, and the party successfully opposed tax changes in the 2002 budget, which were subsequently declared unconstitutional by the Supreme Court. This prompted the Government, which did not have the parliamentary majority of two-thirds required for constitutional amendments, to propose a national consensus, a *pacto de regime*, on important political and economic themes. However, little progress was made, as the MpD remained obstructive, blocking, for example, the adoption of a new electoral code in April 2003 when the Government refused to accept an amendment making the National Electoral Commission (NEC) independent. As a result, local elections in March 2004 took place under the old electoral system, prompting accusations of electoral fraud in a number of municipalities.

In November 2003 two small opposition parties, the PCD and the PRD, signed an electoral pact for the forthcoming local elections. In mid-March 2004 Cape Verde held its fourth set of multi-party municipal elections. The governing PAICV presented candidates in 16 municipalities, the MpD in 15, the PCD-PRD in five, the UCID in two, and the PTS in one. The elections resulted in a resounding victory for the MpD which won in nine municipalities, while the PAICV managed to retain only six, with independents taking the remaining two. The smaller opposition parties failed to win a single municipality, prompting the resignation of the PCD President, Eurico Monteiro. The result put Cape Verde's second city, Mindelo, under MpD control, and pushed the PAICV back to control of only three of the archipelago's nine inhabited islands. Voter turn-out was poor, however, with 42.5% of the electorate failing to vote.

Responding to the Government's election defeat, in April 2004 Prime Minister Neves reorganized his cabinet, effecting the biggest shake-up of the executive since he took power in January 2001. Three ministries and four secretariats of state were abolished and replaced with a new structure of 13 ministries and four secretariats of state. (In September this was changed to 14 ministries and three secretariats of state, following the creation of the Ministry of Social Communication, headed by João Baptista Pereira.) Three new ministers, including João Pereira Silva as Minister of the Economy, Growth and Competitiveness, were brought into the cabinet. In July a new penal code, replacing the existing Portuguese-influenced post-colonial code, which had previously been in place, was adopted. The new code criminalized a range of new offences, including the negligent or deliberate transmission of illness (particularly HIV/AIDS), domestic abuse, sexual abuse against minors and crimes related to information technology.

In November 2005 President Pires confirmed that the legislative elections would take place on 22 January 2006, and that the presidential election would be held on 12 February. In December 2005 Pires announced that he would stand for re-election, while the MpD, as expected, nominated Veiga as its official candidate. Concerns about unemployment, the lack of opportunities for young Cape Verdeans and the recent crime wave on Santiago island dominated the election campaign, with little to distinguish between the two main parties' platforms.

On 6 February 2006 the Comissão Nacional de Eleições (National Elections Commission—CNE) announced that the PAICV had won a convincing victory in the legislative elections, securing 52.3% of the national vote and winning 41 out of 72 seats in the Assembléia Nacional, one more than in 2001. The MpD received 44.0% of the vote and won 29 seats, with the remaining two seats taken by the UCID. Later that month Pires was re-elected to the presidency after securing 50.98% of the votes cast, winning by a narrow majority of 3,342 votes; it was estimated that he secured an estimated two-thirds of the diasporan vote. The MpD complained of electoral fraud; however, their challenges were dismissed, prompting the resignation of Lopes as MpD leader. In early March Neves unveiled his new Council of Ministers, making only minor changes to the Government. Neves announced that his Government's priorities were to boost annual growth above 10%; to reduce unemployment to below 10%; to establish the country's first public university; to revise the electoral code; and to renew the fight against drug smuggling and drug-related crime. On 10 September Jorge Santos was elected as the new MpD leader, promising to reinvigorate and modernize the party. Santos was a founding member of the MpD and a former mayor of Ribeira Grande (Santiago) who narrowly lost the leadership election to Lopes in 2005.

In September 2006 the Minister of Finance and Public Administration, João Serra, resigned, reportedly on grounds of ill health, and was replaced by Cristina Duarte, an economist. In November the Minister for the Economy, Growth and Competitiveness, João Pereira Silva, was forced to resign following allegations of impropriety regarding a contract to manage the development of tourism on Boa Vista and Maio. The Government admitted that there were irregularities in the contract and annulled it, but insisted that there was no evidence of corruption. Two parliamentary commissions were subsequently set up to investigate the two companies involved in the scandal. In late December the former Cape Verdean ambassador to the USA, José Brito, replaced Pereira Silva.

In mid-February 2007 the PAICV and the MpD set up a 14-member commission (comprising seven deputies from each party) which was charged with reaching consensus on issues such as revisions to the Constitution and the creation of a parliamentary auditing commission that require a two-thirds majority in the National Assembly to become law. The cross-party commission's remit included agreeing changes to the electoral code, in particular regarding the membership and structure of the CNE. It was hoped that the new code would come into force prior to the municipal elections scheduled to be held in 2008.

EXTERNAL AFFAIRS

The MpD Government successfully sought to expand Cape Verde's range of international contacts, with special emphasis on potential new sources of development aid, including Israel, the Gulf states, Cuba and the People's Republic of China. However, Cape Verde has also maintained particularly good relations with the former colonial power, Portugal, and countries with large Cape Verdean expatriate communities, such as Luxembourg and the Netherlands. Ties have been developed with the neighbouring autonomous regions of the Canary Islands (Spain), the Azores (Portugal) and Madeira (Portugal), with official visits resulting in the signing of protocols aimed at promoting co-operation. In February 2003 Portugal announced its support for Cape Verde's plan to seek 'special status' within the European Union (EU), and was followed by Spain and Luxembourg. During a visit to Portugal in May 2005 the Prime Minister, José Maria Neves, announced that Cape Verde's long-term aim was to secure full membership of the EU, but this was likely to take many years. In February 2007 officials from the Cape Verdean and Portuguese Governments met with the European Commission and agreed to draw up an action plan for attaining 'special status'. EU officials have agreed to discuss Cape Verde's 'special partnership' with the EU as part of the EU's development programme for Cape Verde for 2008–13, which was scheduled to be completed by the end of 2007. In recent years the Government has strengthened co-operation with the EU on preventing illegal immigration via Cape Verde to Europe, and in August 2006 the EU agreed to extend its frontier-monitoring operations to the archipelago.

Cape Verde has maintained good relations with the USA, where 400,000 expatriate Cape Verdeans live, a community almost equal in size to the population of Cape Verde. Cape Verde has also maintained historically close relations with Brazil, and with other lusophone countries, in particular Angola. In 2003 the Cape Verdean and Angolan Governments announced that they had formed a 'strategic partnership'. Cape Verde also maintains close relations with Guinea-Bissau, Mozambique and São Tomé and Príncipe, known collectively, with Cape Verde and Angola, as the Países Africanos de Língua Oficial Portuguesa (PALOP). In July 1996 the Comunidade dos Países de Língua Portuguesa, comprising the five PALOP countries together with Portugal and Brazil, was formed with the intention of benefiting each member state through joint co-operation on technical, cultural and social matters. In December 1996 Cape Verde also became a full member of the Sommet francophone, a commonwealth comprising the world's French-speaking countries, having been an observer at its annual meetings since 1977. Cape Verde is a member of the African Union (formerly the Organization of African Unity), the Economic Community of West African States, the African Development Bank and the UN, and was a signatory to the Lomé Conventions, which promoted co-operation between the EU and African, Caribbean and Pacific countries. In October 2002 Cape Verde ratified the successor to the Lomé Conventions, the Cotonou Agreement. Cape Verde has traditionally maintained good relations with the IMF and the World Bank, which have regularly commended the country's economic reform programme.

In May 2006 Cape Verde hosted the first NATO exercise in Africa, known as Steadfast Jaguar 2006, which was designed as the first full test of the NATO Response Force. Much of the equipment used in the exercise was subsequently transferred to the Cape Verdean military.

Economy

JONATHAN GREPNE

Revised by EDWARD GEORGE

According to the World Bank, Cape Verde's estimated gross national income (GNI) was US $976m. in 2005, equivalent to about $1,930 per head (or $5,610 per head on an international purchasing-power parity basis). Cape Verde's GNI per head is therefore greater than any of the other four former Portuguese African colonies, and Cape Verde is the only lusophone African nation within the World Bank's lower middle-income bracket. However, according to a survey of household incomes carried out by the National Institute of Statistics (INE) between October 2001 and October 2002, 36% of the population are classified as poor. Rural areas suffer the most, with 51% of the population living in poverty compared with 25% in urban areas. Poverty therefore remains the dominant theme in this largely subsistence economy. In 2006 unemployment was estimated to affect 18.3% of the labour force, with a further 26% under-employed. In 2006 the Prime Minister, José Maria Neves, pledged to reduce unemployment to less than 10% by the end of his mandate in 2011.

Despite the country's physical disadvantages, the economy has grown fairly steadily since independence in 1975, benefiting from the considerable provision of official aid, on very favourable terms, the substantial remittances of Cape Verdean *émigrés*, whose number is almost double that of those actually living on the islands, and economic reforms since the 1990s. Remittances from *émigrés* totalled US $223m. in 2005, equivalent to 23.7% of gross domestic product (GDP). In 1997–2006 Cape Verde's GDP increased, in real terms, at an average annual rate of 5.9%, compared with only 1.3% in 1983–92. In comparison, the population increased by an average of 2.4% per year in 1997–2006. According to official projected figures, the total population was estimated at 484,904 in 2006. The Government introduced value-added tax (VAT) and reformed the tariff system in 2004, boosting domestic revenues from 18.8% of total revenue in 2003 to 21.1% in 2004. In 2005 the fiscal deficit dropped to 5.1% of GDP, and the current account deficit to 4.5% of GDP. In December 2006 gross international reserves stood at $255m., equivalent to the value of more than five months' imports, up from $174m. in December 2005. The annual rate of inflation averaged 2.5% in 1997–2006, compared with 10% in 1983–92. Annual inflation contracted by 1.9% in 2004 due to a tightening of monetary policy and a good harvest which caused a fall in food prices, and averaged just 0.4% in 2005. However, in 2006 it increased to an estimated 5.4% due to strong economic growth.

In November 2006 the Assembléia Nacional approved the 2007 budget. Total government expenditure was forecast to be lower than in the 2006 budget, at 40,200m. escudos (US $237m.), of which 41% was allocated to capital expenditure, reflecting the Government's priority of modernizing the archipelago's infrastructure. Spending on education was also set to rise substantially, in particular for vocational education. Total revenue was projected to rise by 5.3%, to 37,500m. escudos, leaving a fiscal deficit of 2,700m. escudos, equivalent to 2.5% of GDP. This would be lower than the fiscal deficit recorded in 2006 of 5.1% of GDP. The financing gap was expected to be met almost entirely by foreign funding, including grants, loans and counterpart funds from food aid. The Government forecast that real GDP growth would increase from an estimated 6.0% in 2006 to 6.5% in 2007, with inflation falling from an estimated 5.5% in 2006 to 0.2% in 2007.

AGRICULTURE AND FISHERIES

The Cape Verde archipelago is situated in the Sahelian climatic zone and thus suffers from severe periodic droughts. Less than 10% (39,000 ha) of Cape Verde's total surface area is cultivable (one-half of this is on Santiago). In the absence of the necessary infrastructure to combat the effects of droughts, Cape Verde has not been able to achieve self-sufficiency in food production. Cereal production covers on average only 15% of Cape Verde's annual food requirements, and the remainder, varying from 28,000 metric tons to 70,000 tons, needs to be imported. Most imports are provided through international food aid. Erratic rains, upon which most agriculture depends, have led to unpredictable harvests. In 2002 a disastrous drought reduced total production to less than 10,000 tons. A good harvest followed in 2003, in the wake of good rains during the planting season, but in September 2004 locust swarms from the West African mainland damaged maize crops in Santiago, Maio and Santo Antão. In addition, poor rainfall precipitated a drought on Fogo and Maio, and led to a two-thirds reduction in the maize harvest on Santiago. However, good rains led to a strong recovery in 2005 and 2006, although localized drought was reported in some agricultural areas. Agriculture (including forestry and fishing) contributed just 9.1% of GDP in 2005, although the sector is an important source of employment, involving 23% of the total labour force. About 54% of farms on cultivated land are smaller than 1 ha and fewer than 3% exceed 5 ha. According to the African Development Bank (ADB), in 1997–2006 agricultural GDP grew at an average annual rate of 4.5%. In 2006 it increased by 5.8%.

Since independence reafforestation plans have been put into effect with assistance from FAO. Some 23m., mostly drought-resistant, trees (American acacias) have been planted, in order to reduce soil erosion and increase groundwater levels. In 2000 some 20% of the total surface area of the archipelago was forested. In addition, about 7,200 rainwater dykes have been built, new wells have been sunk and a more efficient system of irrigation has been adopted. About 3,000 ha are currently irrigated but this could rise to 8,600 ha in the future. Estimates suggest that the total potentially exploitable groundwater and surface water resources of Cape Verde are around 150m. cu m per year. In January 2004 work began on constructing a reservoir at Poilão (Santiago island), with US $4m. of funding from the Chinese Government. The reservoir was opened in July 2006, and had a storage capacity of 1.7m. cu litres. The Government has also implemented several projects to construct smaller reservoirs in Santiago, Santo Antão, and São Nicolau.

Santiago is the main agricultural producer (contributing about one-half of total production), followed by Santo Antão and São Nicolau. Food crops are maize, beans, cassava and sweet potatoes, supplemented (wherever soils, terrain and rainfall permit) with bananas, vegetables, sugar cane and fruits. The main staples are beans and maize, which are intercropped. As a result of drought and damage by locusts, production of maize has varied. Production was 19,549 metric tons in 2001, dropping to just 5,067 tons in 2002 as a result of the devastating drought which hit the islands. Production recovered to 12,154 tons in 2003, before falling to 10,000 tons in 2004 and to just 3,650 tons in 2005 as a result of a localized locust infestation and drought on the islands of Fogo and Maio. Cape Verde's overall annual cereal requirement is estimated at around 110,000 tons. More than one-half of Cape Verde's total irrigated land is used for sugar cane (production totalled an estimated 14,000 tons in 2005), most of which is used in the production of a popular alcoholic beverage, grogue, for local consumption. The Government is seeking to reallocate this land to staple and cash crops by encouraging the manufacture (and future export) of an alternative liquor using imported molasses.

Cash crops, such as bananas, arabica coffee, groundnuts, castor beans and pineapples, are encouraged, but poor inter-island communications, low educational attainment, the shortage of government funds, lack of suitable available land and adverse climatic conditions hinder the development of a thriving agricultural sector. As a result, the islands' only significant export crop is bananas (with production of 6,000 metric tons in 2004). Cape Verde has a 4,800-ton quota with the European Union (EU), and bananas are mainly shipped to Portugal. A rather exotic commodity, locally known as purgueira (*jatropha curcas*), which grows wild, is also exported (for soap-making). In the past Cape Verde exported coffee, castor beans and tomatoes, but only in minimal quantities, owing to the prevailing climatic conditions. A small quantity of these commodities is produced on Fogo for national consumption. Wine production has been encouraged on Fogo, the volcanic terrain of which is suitable for viniculture. Most of the production is used for local consumption, notably in tourism resorts.

Livestock herds have been reduced to one-quarter, or even one-10th, of their pre-drought level, but are slowly recovering. In 2005 about 23,000 cattle, 112,750 goats, 10,000 sheep and 205,000 pigs were raised for food and milk. About 17,000 asses and horses provide the main form of transport in mountainous rural areas.

Fishing offers great development potential. Cape Verde's exclusive economic zone comprises 734,265 sq km and contains one of the last significantly underused fishing grounds in the world, with a total sustainable yield estimated at about 35,000 metric tons per year. Traditionally, fishing has been a small-scale industry, employing only about 7,000 local fishermen. However, in recent years output has increased strongly, increasing fishing's contribution to merchandise exports from 2.2% in 2004 to 8.3% in 2005. Fishing accounted for 40% of merchandise exports (including re-exports) in 2005. Of some 1,400 fishing boats, only around 40% are motorized, and of some 95 larger vessels used for industrial fishing, only 64 are fully operational. The Government, which privatized the state-owned fishing company, the Empresa Caboverdiana de Pescas, has sought to encourage private entrepreneurs by means of credit facilities, training and research. In February 2004 work was completed on a two-year US $16m. project, financed by the Japanese Government, to refurbish and enlarge Praia's fishing dock. In the same month the Arab Bank for Economic Development in Africa agreed to finance a project, costing $850,000, to modernize the Sucla fish-packing plant in Tarrafal (São Nicolau). The privatization of the loss-making Interbase fish-freezing plant was completed in April 2005 when the company was taken over by a Spanish-Cape Verdean consortium.

Fishing exports consist primarily of tuna. In 1997 the EU signed a three-year fishing agreement with Cape Verde, providing Spanish, French and Portuguese vessels with a licence to catch 5,000 metric tons of tuna fish annually in Cape Verdean waters. As a result of EU involvement, annual local fishing catches have increased to about 10,000 tons. In 2005 the total catch was 7,742 tons, according to FAO. The renewal of the fishing agreement with the EU, which had been delayed since 2000, because of disagreements between Cape Verde and the EU over the amount to be paid for the fishing licences, was finally achieved in September 2001. Under the agreement, the number of EU vessels allowed to fish in Cape Verdean waters was increased from 73 to 117 and the annual amount to be paid for licences was increased by 30%–50%. Cape Verde traditionally exports three-quarters of its fish to the EU. In November 2003 the EU extended its fisheries protocol with Cape Verde by a further year, to 30 June 2005. The protocol covered the fishing of tuna and demersal (sea floor) species in Cape Verde's territorial waters, and entitles Cape Verde to €680,000 per year for research, fishing surveillance programmes, infrastructure improvements, training and contributions to ship owners. In December 2005 Cape Verde signed a new fishing accord with the EU, covering the period September 2006–August 2011. Under the agreement, 84 EU ships would be allowed to catch 5,000 tons of fish each year in Cape Verde's territorial waters in return for an annual payment of €325,000 and a grant of €60,000 to promote sustainable fishing activities.

TRANSPORT AND TOURISM

Cape Verde is strategically located between Africa, Europe and America. International maritime and air transport, including transshipment, were identified as an important source of foreign exchange by both the Partido Africano da Independência de Cabo Verde (PAICV) and MpD administrations. The main port of the islands is Porto Grande at Mindelo on São Vicente. The container storage terminal at Porto Grande was expanded and modernized in 1997, while the port of Praia was also completely modernized and offers refrigerator and container storage. In June 2005 the US Millennium Challenge Account (MCA) agreed to fund a US $53m. project to further modernize and expand the port of Praia. New port facilities were opened on Maio and Boa Vista in 1997, on Fogo in 1999, and on Brava in 2000. In 1997 investors from the USA, Saudi Arabia and Pakistan founded an international ship registration agency in Mindelo, establishing the Cape Verdean flag as a 'flag of convenience'. The state ferry company, Arca Verde, was liquidated in 2003, and since December of that year a maritime transport company, Transnacional, has operated a passenger ferry service between the islands of Santiago, Maio, Boa Vista, Fogo and Brava. In 2006 the Government launched the bidding process for the privatization of the port operator, Empresa Nacional de Administração dos Portos (Enapor), which is due to be completed before the end of 2007.

There are 2,250 km of roads in Cape Verde, of which 1,750 km are paved (mostly with cobblestones). In June 2003 the Government established a US $1.1m. National Road Fund, to be administered by the Instituto das Estradas (Road Institute), to build, rehabilitate and maintain the archipelago's road network. The remote island of Santo Antão has received the Government's special attention because of its potential as an eco-tourism resort, and in July 2003 Prime Minister Neves laid the first stone of the Paul–Janela road, an internationally funded project to link the communities of Paul and Porto Novo on the island. In 2005 the Government launched a five-year programme, supported with $46m. in funding from the MCA, to upgrade and expand the road and bridge network in Santiago and Santo Antão. Major projects include the €20m. São Domingos–Assomada road and the €25m. ring-road project on Santiago island, both of which were financed by Portugal, and studies on the construction of a €20m. ring road on Fogo and new rural roads on the islands of Santiago, São Vicente, São Nicolau, Santo Antão and Maio.

The Government has pledged to improve air transport infrastructure on the islands, with the apparent objective of turning Cape Verde into a regional transport hub. The Amílcar Cabral international airport on Sal island has a throughput capacity of 1m. passengers per year (it currently handles more than 300,000 passengers per year) and can accommodate aircraft of up to 50 metric tons. The domestic and international flights terminals have been further improved since 1998, and in May 2004 a new air traffic control system was inaugurated. Financed by the European Investment Bank at a cost of €20m., the Sistema de Controlo de Tráfego Aéreo replaced Sal's existing air traffic control system, which had been in use since 1980, and gave Cape Verde the most sophisticated system currently in operation in Africa. The airport's facilities have been used as a strategic refuelling point, chiefly by South African Airways and Aeroflot (Russia), as well as a number of cargo transportation airlines, which account for around 30% of all landings. A new international airport in Praia, designed to accommodate large aircraft, became operational in November 2005. The airport's construction was financed by the EU and Portuguese banks. In December 2003 the regional development fund of the Economic Community of West African States (ECOWAS) pledged US $7m. to finance the construction of a priority passenger terminal and to complete the road serving the new airport. In 2000 the airport on São Vicente was also upgraded, and in June 2005 work began on an additional 1.7-km runway for the airport, as well as on a new international airport on Boa Vista, which was due for completion in July 2007. Concurrently, the Government plans to construct a further international airport on Maio, and further airport expansion was planned on Fogo, with the aim of meeting the current 11% annual increase in air traffic.

The national airline, Transportes Aéreos de Cabo Verde (TACV), operates a regular inter-island service and in 2000 embarked on an aggressive expansion of its international network, with flights to most West African airports, major European cities and, since 2002, to Brazil and the USA. However, by 2003 the company had begun to accumulate heavy losses, forcing it to implement a radical cost-cutting programme in preparation for privatization. By the end of that year it had reduced its losses by 93%, and in June 2004 it began restructuring with the help of a foreign management team and the World Bank. Privatization was expected to take place before the end of 2007.

Tourism has been identified as the area with the most potential for economic development. Cape Verde benefits from its proximity to the European market, enjoys a favourable climate for most of the year and offers white sandy beaches and some spectacular mountain scenery. Tourism has been the sector to benefit most from foreign investment, helped by the introduction of legislation, from 1991, aimed at providing increased incentives and guarantees to investors, and highlighted by the fact that the contribution of the sector to the country's GDP increased from 4.0% in 1998 to 10.4% in 2005. In 2004 there were 11 hotels of international standard on Sal, 10 on Santiago, four on São Vicente, three on Boa Vista and one on Fogo. By 2005 there were 9,500 hotel beds in Cape Verde, up from 5,239 in 2000. As a result, the number of tourists increased from around 60,000 in 1998 to 197,844 in 2005, mainly from Italy (35.2%), Portugal (25.4%) and Germany (10.7%). The Government aims to attract 400,000 tourists annually to Cape Verde by 2008, rising to 1m. by 2015. In 2004 earnings from tourism totalled US $125m.—more than double their 2000 level. However, the tourism industry is heavily concentrated in the three regions of Cape Verde—Sal, Santiago and São Vicente—with the rest of the archipelago receiving only 17% of trade. In September 2005 the Government began revising the foreign investment law in order to attract more foreign direct investment (FDI) to the sector. In December 2004 work restarted on the $715m. Santiago Golf Resort, which was due for completion in 2008. The 1,000-ha resort will have five hotels, 3,000 holiday apartments, a shopping centre, a hospital, tennis courts, a casino, nightclubs and restaurants, and is expected to create 4,000 jobs. In June

2005 work began on the $770m. Sambala Village project, set to be Cape Verde's largest tourism complex, which will develop a 930-ha site in the bay of São Francisco, 10 km from Praia. Four tourist villages are to be constructed, along with two luxury hotel resorts (one served by a marina) and an 18-hole golf course. In November 2006 an Irish company, Cape Verde Development, announced plans to invest €2,000m. in a tourist resort and golf courses on Sal island. In January 2007 a group of investors from the United Arab Emirates announced an investment of €160m. in a tourist resort on São Vicente. In 2007 work is due to start on the €250m. Ponta Bicuda tourist resort, located close to Praia's new international airport, which is scheduled for completion by 2009. The project includes six hotels, 1,300 houses and retail services.

MANUFACTURING

The industrial sector (including construction and power) remains largely undeveloped, accounting for 19.7% of GDP in 2005. According to the ADB, in 1997–2006 manufacturing GDP grew at an average annual rate of 4.1%, and by 5.8% in 2006. Manufacturing consists primarily of fish-canning, clothing, footwear, rum-distilling and bottling plants, contributing only 1.1% to GDP in 2005 and employing around 6% of the total labour force. In order to attract foreign investment and promote the expansion of industrial exports, the free-zone enterprise law was enacted in 1993, permitting enterprises producing goods and services exclusively for export to benefit from exemptions on tax and customs duties for a period of 10 years. The law also applied to new firms specializing in transhipment. Legislation enacted in 1999 provided for the transformation of industrial parks at Mindelo and Praia into free-trade zones and for the establishment of a further free-trade zone on Sal island. The free-trade zone in Mindelo is currently being extended with support from Portugal.

EXTRACTIVE INDUSTRIES

Until recently, mining was of little significance, representing less than 1% of GDP in 2001, with pozzolana, a volcanic ash used in cement manufacture (an estimated 1,000 metric tons in 2000), and unrefined salt (an estimated 1,600 tons in 2003) traditionally being the main products. However, in December 2003 the Chinese Government agreed to construct a US $55m. cement plant in Santa Cruz (Santiago island), its first investment in a Portuguese-speaking country. The new plant will have a production capacity of 350,000 tons per year, easily meeting Cape Verde's 200,000-ton domestic demand and enabling the country to export the surplus. Furthermore, in January 2004 construction began on a pozzolana cement factory in Porto Novo (Santo Antão), projected to produce 40,000 tons per year. The $5m. plant is being financed by a consortium of Italian and Cape Verdean investors and started production in late 2005.

AID AND INVESTMENT

Government policy in recent years has sought to attract private foreign investment, particularly towards tourism, fishing and light manufacturing, the latter benefiting from the country's geographical location, available work-force, low wage costs and beneficial trade agreements with the countries of ECOWAS, as well as the EU and the USA. In 1989 legislation was introduced to open the economy to private external investment, but this was limited to the Cape Verdean emigrant community. In 1993 an external investment law opened the economy to all foreign investment and a free-zone enterprise law was passed. Industrial parks at Praia and Mindelo were constructed with funding from the EU. Since 1996 an increasing proportion of foreign investment, principally from Italy, has been in the tourism sector. In 2005 total FDI inflows into Cape Verde amounted to US $19.3m., increasing the total FDI stock to $247.2m. Tourism continues to receive the largest share of FDI in Cape Verde, with 56.3% of the total in 2004, rising to 92.8% in 2005. In that year Cape Verde attracted an estimated $120m. in FDI to develop tourism in Sal, Maio and Boa Vista. In October 2004 a new investment agency, Cabo Verde Investimentos, replaced the tourism promotion board, Centro de Promoção Turística do Investimento e das Exportações, and the entrepreneurial support agency, Instituto de Apoio ao Desenvolvimento Empresarial. The new agency was to promote public-private partnerships for investment in the islands' infrastructure and the development of the tourism industry.

In 1995 40% of the state telecommunications company, Cabo Verde Telecom (CVT), was sold to Portugal Telecom International for US $20m., and a further 50% of CVT was divested in 1997–98. Some $90m. has been pledged for investment by the Portuguese company. As a result, the network has expanded from 21,500 main lines in use in 1995 to 71,400 in 2005, yielding the second highest density of fixed telephone lines in Africa, after Mauritius. The sector was further liberalized in January 2007 when the Government formally ended CVT's monopoly on fixed-line services. A fibre optic telecommunication line linking Santiago, Sal, São Nicolau and São Vicente, which began operating in 1997, offers online data communications and was linked in 2002 to a transatlantic network. CVT has also introduced a mobile cellular telephone network, Telemóvel, and in 2005 there were 81,700 active mobile telephone accounts. In 2005 the International Telecommunications Union estimated that there were 25,000 internet users in Cape Verde. In May 2004 CVT inaugurated the country's first broadband services in Praia. Improved telecommunications could, potentially, enable the Government to transform Cape Verde into an offshore banking centre.

The state-owned radio and television company, Rádio Televisão de Cabo Verde (RTC), is the only national television station, although a licence has been granted to a private channel. As of early 2007, however, the new channel (Tiver) was not yet operational. In June 2003 a group of senior French media experts arrived in Praia to modernize Cape Verde's national television network, which currently reaches only 65% of the population. Several large French media companies—including TV5 and Canal Plus France International—were to help Cape Verdean television switch from analogue to digital signals. In September 2006 the Government launched a tender for new licences for independent television stations. In May 2005 CVT and the Chinese Xiamen Xinouli secured an international tender to operate the first cable television network in Cape Verde. CVT launched its cable television service, ZAP TV, in 2006, and was followed by CVXTV, a subsidiary of Xiamen Xinouli, which launched a wireless television service in April 2007.

Foreign aid is indispensable to Cape Verde, which receives one of the highest levels of aid per head in the world (US $279.6 per head in 2004). According to the Organisation for Economic Co-operation and Development, total official development assistance was $160.6m. in 2004, with Portugal, the Netherlands, Spain and the USA being the largest bilateral donors. In May 2004 Cape Verde was selected, along with five other African countries, for generous development assistance from the MCA. Established to support countries deemed to have embraced reform, good governance and economic freedom, the MCA was expected to disburse up to $1,000m. of development aid to 16 selected countries during 2004, with disbursements rising to as much as $2,500m. in 2005. Cape Verde secured $73m. of MCA funding for 2005–06, $30m. of which was to be available in 2005, with the remaining $43m. to follow in 2006. MCA funds will finance a range of development projects. Cape Verde was excluded as a candidate country for the 2005 funding round on the grounds that its projected GDP per head in 2005 exceeded the permitted ceiling, but it was selected again for the 2006 funding round as part of a new, lower middle-income category.

Under the Lomé Conventions, Cape Verde was allocated EU aid of US $38m. for its 1991–95 development programme and of $42m. for 1996–2000. (In mid-2000 the Lomé Convention was succeeded by the Cotonou Agreement, which Cape Verde ratified in October 2002.) The EU aid programme was primarily directed at improving the provision of water, electricity and sanitation, particularly in Praia and Mindelo. In May 2002 the EU provided aid of some €32m. for the 2002–07 development programme, which was to focus on combating poverty and improving infrastructure on the islands.

In December 2003 the World Bank agreed to lend Cape Verde US $25m. for improvements to the road infrastructure in the archipelago. The first phase of the loan was to cover the rehabilitation of roads linking the Santa Catarina and Tarrafal districts, with further funding earmarked for the coastal ring-road on Santiago. In November 2004 Cape Verde signed a new, three-year Indicative Co-operation Plan with Portugal, valued at €55m. ($72.4m.), covering 2005–07. Projects in 2005 included the asphalting of the Praia–São Domingos road and the construction of Praia's ring road. Foreign aid to Cape Verde was expected to triple in 2005, reaching $139.8m. Most of this was to take the form of budgetary support, reflecting donors' confidence in the Government's economic management, with the bulk of the funding invested in infrastructure programmes. Further aid agreements reached in early 2005 included an additional €12.5m. from the EU, and €10m. for environmental projects provided by the Netherlands.

In 2005 the UN approved the upgrade of Cape Verde's status from a least-developed to a medium-developed country; the graduation was scheduled to take place in 2008. The change reflects the country's steady progress in social development and economic growth since the mid-1990s. The change in categorization will mean that Cape Verde loses access to the highly preferential loans from multilateral sources that are available to less-developed countries. However, given the Government's strong track record in macroeconomic management, donors have pledged to continue to provide funding and budget support for Cape Verde's development projects over the coming years.

PRIVATIZATION

The MpD Government planned to privatize 25 companies by 2002; only the post office and the air traffic control and airport handling firm were to remain under state control. The Banco Comercial do Atlântico, the Caixa Económica de Cabo Verde, Garantia (insurance) and Promotora (venture capital) were fully or partially privatized in 1999–2000. In April 1999 the Government also established a multi-sectoral regulatory agency for transport, aviation, communication, water, electricity and the environment, while a national agency for security of food provision was established to ensure that food imports were adequately distributed. By 2000 some US $93m. in revenue had been generated through privatization, and a total of 15 companies had been fully or partially privatized, rising to more than 30 by the end of 2005. The privatization of TACV has been delayed until late 2007, and that of the national electricity and water utility, Electra, was reversed in 2006, following a prolonged dispute over tariffs between the Government and Electra's consortium owners, which led to subsequent power cuts across the archipelago. The Government pledged to complete the privatization of five remaining state-owned enterprises by the end of 2006, but this was subsequently postponed until the end of 2007.

TRADE

Cape Verde's principal merchandise exports are clothing and footwear, canned tuna and mackerel, frozen fish and lobster. Small amounts of salt and pozzolana are exported. Among cash crops, only bananas are exported in significant quantities. Cape Verde also re-sells fuel (bunkering) to passing ships and aircraft, earning US $40.5m. in 2004. Exports of processed fish and light-manufactured goods are expected to increase substantially in the future, as new freezing and canning plants come into operation, as well as free-trade zones at Praia and Mindelo. The principal exports in 2004 were clothing and footwear.

Cape Verde traditionally operates a substantial trade deficit, which stems from the need to import some 85% of its food requirements (although most of this is provided free under aid schemes), as well as manufactured goods, fuel and other essential goods. Although merchandise exports, including fuel (bunkering), increased from US $9m. in 1993 to $86.7m. in 2005, merchandise imports rose even more, reaching $435.6m. in 2005, thus widening the trade deficit. The rise in imports resulted in part from the MpD Government's open market policies, notably the liberalization of previous restrictions on almost all imported goods, and the introduction of measures enabling local firms to borrow from domestic banks in order to purchase imported materials. In 1996 the Government began imposing import restrictions and tariffs on certain non-essential goods in order to reduce the trade deficit. The deficit narrowed to $172m. in 1997, but has since widened again, to $348.9m. in 2005.

In recent years Portugal has significantly increased its trading with Cape Verde. In 1989 Portugal exported goods worth US $34m. (32% of imports) to Cape Verde, but by 2006 the value of these transactions had reached 50.2% of imports. Other important sources of imports in 2006 were the Netherlands (11.2%), Brazil (6.4%) and Spain (5.6%). Portugal is also the principal market for exports, accounting for 53.2% of the total in 2006, followed by Spain (27.3%) and Guinea-Bissau (4.2%). Exports of services typically account for the larger share of total exports of goods and services. In 2005 exports of services provided revenue of $278.2m., although imports reached $438.1m. It was envisaged that export earnings from the services sector would increase significantly in the near future, particularly from tourism, transshipment and the servicing of aircraft belonging to foreign airlines.

In March 2004 Cape Verde completed the first round of negotiations to join the World Trade Organization (WTO). Cape Verde formally applied for WTO membership in November 1999, and presented a formal memorandum requesting membership in January 2004. Cape Verde received assistance from the US Agency for International Development, the EU, the United Kingdom and the UN Conference on Trade and Development in preparing its application, and it appeared likely that it would be accepted. A second round of talks took place in December 2004, but Cape Verde's accession has been delayed until it brings its legislation regarding import tariffs, the commercial code, VAT and intellectual property rights into line with WTO standards. The Government expects membership of the WTO to be approved by the end of 2007.

FINANCE

In 1993 the first commercial bank was established, the Banco Comercial do Atlântico (BCA), while new legislation provided for the creation of financial institutions to offer loans and credit to small and medium-sized entrepreneurs. Despite the fact that its capital was raised solely from state funds provided by the Banco de Cabo Verde (BCV), the BCA enjoyed relative independence from the central bank and had a high degree of autonomy in its administration and management. The state's shares in BCA were sold in 1999 to a consortium led by the Portuguese Caixa Geral de Depósitos. The BCV now functions solely as a central bank. The principal savings institutions are the Fundo de Solidariedade Nacional, which handles public investment, and the Instituto Caboverdiano de Solidariedade, which handles international aid. The establishment of Portuguese banks in Cape Verde was expected to raise the level of available credit lines through Portugal, and subsequently increase the level of investment and imports from that country. In July 2004 a group of Cape Verdean entrepreneurs established a private bank, Banco Caboverdiano de Negócios, following their purchase for US $3.3m. of Banco Totta Cabo Verde, a subsidiary of Banco Totta e Açores. In 2006 there were five banks operating in Cape Verde. A stock exchange which was founded in 1999 finally started operations in December 2005, trading treasury bonds and shares in local banks. In March 2007 the Government sold a 28.5% stake in the state-owned Empresa Nacional de Combustíveis on the exchange, and in May it sold a 51.2% stake in the tobacco company, the Sociedade Caboverdiana de Tabacos, to a consortium of four Cape Verdean businesses. The Government plans to float two other state-owned enterprises, the Empresa Nacional de Productos Farmacêuticos and Inpharma, as part of their privatization.

DEBT

Although Cape Verde's total external debt at the end of 2004 reached US $517m., equivalent to 55.2% of GNI, it is worth noting the low level of Cape Verde's debt-servicing costs, which the Government has kept to a minimum. As a proportion of the value of exports of goods and services, the debt-service ratio was 5.3% in 2003. In addition, about $25m. of debt owed to

Portugal was restructured in July 2001. Public domestic debt increased from about $40m. in 1992 to $180m. at the end of 1998, but was to be converted into lower-interest bonds to be managed by the central bank of Portugal in an offshore trust fund, from which 95% of the interest earned would be used to repay the national debt, with the remainder placed in a special development fund. The Government was to contribute $80m. in revenue from the accelerated privatization programme and international donors the remaining $100m. However, the debt-conversion operation only commenced in 1999, while a deterioration of public finances prompted the Government to resort to domestic financing. Only $37m. in privatization revenue had been used to support the trust fund by mid-2002. The larger portion, $52m., was used for budgetary support. As a result, public domestic debt increased again, to $140m., at the end of 2001, equivalent to 26% of GDP. During 2003 Cape Verde cleared its arrears with all of its multilateral creditors and successfully rescheduled those with all but two of its bilateral creditors (this was achieved in early 2005).

PLANNING

In April 2002 the IMF approved a Poverty Reduction and Growth Facility (PRGF), worth US $11m., to support the National Development Plan (the first time such a facility had been provided for Cape Verde). In May 2003 the IMF commended both the Government's economic policies and the performance of the economy, and in June the disbursement of a further tranche under the PRGF was approved. In July 2003 the IMF released a further Special Drawing Rights (SDR) 1.23m. ($1.7m.) from Cape Verde's SDR 8.64m. ($12m.) PRGF arrangement, bringing the total amount drawn so far to SDR 3.7m. ($5.2m.). A third IMF review in December 2003 noted some slippages in meeting targets for the fiscal deficit and international reserves, but nevertheless commended the Government for taking corrective action, and praised its track record of pursuing prudent fiscal and monetary policies, while redirecting public spending towards key social services. A further IMF review in May 2004 concluded that Cape Verde had met its macroeconomic targets, and approved a $2.5m. loan to strengthen the foreign exchange reserves of the BCV. In November 2004 an IMF mission reported that Cape Verde had failed to meet several objectives for economic and financial performance in the first six months of 2004. However, when the fund completed its fifth PRGF review in February 2005 it praised Cape Verde's improved economic and fiscal performance, which it attributed to the Government's adherence to prudent macroeconomic policies and commitment to structural reform. In July 2005 the IMF completed its sixth and final review of the PRGF, commending the Government's strong macroeconomic performance throughout the programme, but warning of the country's continuing vulnerability to external shocks. In July 2006 the IMF granted Cape Verde a policy support instrument (PSI), a new monitoring programme designed for low-income countries that no longer need IMF financial assistance, but still require its technical assistance and endorsement of their policies. Cape Verde's PSI is focused on completing the Government's reform agenda, and will support its medium-term expenditure framework for 2006–09. In November 2004 the Government presented its Growth and Poverty Reduction Strategy Paper (GPRSP) covering the period 2004–07, after lengthy consultations with the private sector and civil society. In February 2005 the World Bank approved an International Development Association credit of $15m. to support the programme's implementation. Two further credits of up to $15m. each were to be made available in 2006 and 2007, provided that Cape Verde maintains a good track record in implementing the GPRSP. In April 2007 Portugal agreed a new Indicative Cooperation Plan, worth €13.4m, including projects in education, health and poverty-reduction.

In March 1998 Cape Verde and Portugal signed an agreement providing for their respective currencies to become linked through a fixed exchange rate. The linking of the two currencies, in July 1998, not only transformed the Cape Verde escudo into a convertible currency, thus encouraging foreign investment and trade, but also established a firm monetary link to the single European currency following its introduction in January 1999. A further US $14m. in support of the currency peg was provided in July 2001. Under the terms of the agreement, Portugal agreed to underwrite the link with some $50m. to augment Cape Verde's foreign-currency reserves. Furthermore, the new development was expected to encourage trade with West African countries in the CFA franc zone, which is linked to the single European currency. The IMF has advised the Government that stronger reserves are necessary to maintain the country's currency peg with the euro (set at a rate of 110.27 escudos = €1), but there is concern among some economists that the cost of maintaining the peg may harm economic competitiveness by preventing devaluation. Nevertheless, the Government is strongly committed to the peg as part of its efforts to promote closer integration with the EU, a long-standing foreign policy objective.

Statistical Survey

Sources (unless otherwise stated): Instituto Nacional de Estatística, Av. Amílcar Cabral, CP 116, Praia, Santiago; tel. 613960; e-mail inecv@mail.cvtelecom.cv; internet www.ine.cv; Statistical Service, Banco de Cabo Verde, Av. Amílcar Cabral 117, CP 101, Praia, Santiago; tel. 2607060; fax 2614447; e-mail apericles@bcv.cv; internet www.bcv.cv.

AREA AND POPULATION

Area: 4,036 sq km (1,558 sq miles).

Population: 341,491 (males 161,494, females 179,997) at census of 23 June 1990; 436,863 (males 211,479, females 225,384) at census of 16 June 2000. *2006:* 494,105 (official estimate). *By Island* (2000 census): Boa Vista 4,209; Brava 6,804; Fogo 37,421; Maio 6,754; Sal 14,816; Santo Antão 47,170; São Nicolau 13,661; Santiago 236,627; São Vicente 67,163. *2002* (official estimates): Boa Vista 4,661; Brava 6,678; Fogo 37,607; Maio 7,042; Sal 15,889; Santo Antão 47,312; São Nicolau 13,535; Santiago 247,947; São Vicente 69,837.

Density (2007): 122.4 per sq km.

Principal Towns (population at 2000 census): Praia (capital) 94,757; Mindelo 62,970. *Mid-2005* (incl. suburbs, UN estimate): Praia 117,000 (Source: UN, *World Urbanization Prospects: The 2005 Revision*).

Births and Deaths: Birth rate 30.9 per 1,000 (2000–05); Death rate 5.3 per 1,000 (2000–05) (Source: UN, *World Population Prospects: The 2006 Revision*). *2003:* Live births 13,334 (birth rate 28.9 per 1,000); Deaths 2,786 (death rate 7.0 per 1,000) (Source: UN, *Demographic Yearbook*).

Expectation of Life (years at birth, WHO estimates): 70 (males 67; females 71) in 2004. (Source: WHO, *World Health Report*).

Economically Active Population (persons aged 10 years and over, 1990 census): Agriculture, hunting, forestry and fishing 29,876; Mining and quarrying 410; Manufacturing 5,520; Electricity, gas and water 883; Construction 22,722; Trade, restaurants and hotels 12,747; Transport, storage and communications 6,138; Financial, insurance, real estate and business services 821; Community, social and personal services 17,358; Activities not adequately defined 24,090; *Total labour force* 120,565 (males 75,786, females 44,779), including 31,049 unemployed persons (males 19,712, females 11,337) (Source: ILO). *2000 Census* (persons aged 10 years and over): Total employed 144,310; Unemployed 30,334; Total labour force 174,644. *Mid-2004* (FAO estimates): Agriculture, etc. 40,000; Total (incl. others) 196,000 (Source: FAO).

HEALTH AND WELFARE

Key Indicators

Total Fertility Rate (children per woman, 2005): 3.6.

Under-5 Mortality Rate (per 1,000 live births, 2005): 35.

Physicians (per 1,000 head, 2004): 0.49.

Hospital Beds (per 1,000 head, 2000): 1.60.

Health Expenditure (2004): US $ per head (PPP): 225.1.

Health Expenditure (2004): % of GDP: 5.2.

Health Expenditure (2004): public (% of total): 75.8.

Access to Water (% of persons, 2002): 80.

Access to Sanitation (% of persons, 2002): 42.

Human Development Index (2004): ranking: 106.

Human Development Index (2004): 0.722.

For sources and definitions, see explanatory note on p. vi.

AGRICULTURE, ETC.

Principal Crops ('000 metric tons, 2005, FAO estimates): Maize 3.6; Potatoes 3.5; Sweet potatoes 2.2; Cassava 2.7; Sugar cane 11.7; Pulses 3.4; Coconuts 6.0; Cabbages 4.9; Tomatoes 5.4; Dry onions 1.7; Green beans 2.9; Cucumbers and gherkins 1.2; Bananas 6.0; Guavas, mangoes and mangosteens 4.4; Other fruits 4.7.

Livestock ('000 head, 2005, FAO estimates): Cattle 23.0; Pigs 205.0; Sheep 10.0; Goats 112.8; Horses 0.5; Asses and mules 16.4; Chickens 460.

Livestock Products ('000 metric tons, 2005, FAO estimates): Pig meat 7.4; Other meat 1.4; Cows' milk 5.4; Goats' milk 5.6; Hen eggs 1.8.

Fishing (metric tons, live weight, 2005): Total catch 7,742 (Skipjack tuna 348; Yellowfin tuna 1,778).

Source: FAO.

MINING

Production (metric tons, 2005, estimates): Salt (unrefined) 1,600. Clay, gypsum, limestone and volcanic rock were also produced, at unreported levels. Source: US Geological Survey.

INDUSTRY

Production (metric tons, 2003, unless otherwise indicated): Canned fish 200; Frozen fish 900; Flour 15,901 (1999 figure); Beer 4,104,546 litres (1999 figure); Soft drinks 922,714 litres (1996 figure); Cigarettes and tobacco 77 kg (1999 figure); Paint 628,243 kg (1997 figure); Footwear 670,676 pairs (1996 figure); Soap 1,371,045 kg (1999 figure); Electric energy 164.3m. kWh (2001). Sources: mainly UN, *Industrial Commodity Statistics Yearbook*, and IMF, *Cape Verde: Statistical Appendix* (October 2001).

FINANCE

Currency and Exchange Rates: 100 centavos = 1 Cape Verde escudo; 1,000 escudos are known as a conto. *Sterling, Dollar and Euro Equivalents* (31 May 2007): £1 sterling = 162.07 escudos; US $1 = 81.97 escudos; €1 = 110.27 escudos; 1,000 Cape Verde escudos = £6.170 = $12.200 = €9.069. *Average Exchange Rate* (escudos per US dollar): 97.788 in 2003; 88.748 in 2004; 88.682 in 2005.

Budget (million escudos, 2006, preliminary): *Revenue*: Taxation 22,828 (Taxes on income and profits 6,952, Taxes on international trade 4,889, Consumption taxes 9,821, Other tax revenue 1,166); Non-tax revenue 2,017; Net lending 301; Grants 5,789; Total (incl. adjustment) 31,044. *Expenditure*: Recurrent 18,908 (Wages and salaries 11,547, Acquisition of goods and services 1,197, Transfers and other subsidies 3,464, Interest payments 1,920; Other recurrent expenditure 781); Capital 12,338; Other 3,678; Total 34,924. Source: IMF, *Cape Verde: Second Review Under the Policy Support Instrument—Staff Report; Press Release on the Executive Board Discussion; and Statement by the Executive Director for Cape Verde* (June 2007).

International Reserves (US $ million at 31 December 2006): Reserve position in the IMF 0.02; Foreign exchange 254.43; Total 254.45. Source: IMF, *International Financial Statistics*.

Money Supply (million escudos at 31 December 2006): Currency outside banks 7,731.2; Demand deposits at commercial banks 31,186.1; Total money (incl. others) 38,917.3. Source: IMF, *International Financial Statistics*.

Cost of Living (Consumer Price Index; base: 1989 = 100): 184.9 in 2004; 185.7 in 2005; 195.7 in 2006.

Expenditure on the Gross Domestic Product (million escudos at current prices, 2005): Government final consumption expenditure 16,148; Private final consumption expenditure 67,648; Gross fixed capital formation (incl. increase in stocks) 33,019; *Total domestic expenditure* 116,815; Exports of goods and services 14,719; *Less* Imports of goods and services 44,363; *GDP in purchasers' values* 87,171. Source: IMF, *Cape Verde: Statistical Appendix* (September 2006).

Gross Domestic Product by Economic Activity (million escudos at current prices, 2005): Agriculture, forestry and livestock 7,869; Fishing 1,035; Industry and energy 7,530; Construction 9,112; Commerce 18,200; Hotels 2,088; Transport and communications 18,621; Banks and insurance 3,727; Housing 5,048; Public service 11,813; Other services 2,078; *Sub-total* 87,121; *Less* Imputed bank service charges 2,756; *Total value added** 84,366; Import taxes 13,773; *GDP at market prices* 98,139. Source: IMF, *Cape Verde: Statistical Appendix* (September 2006).

* Including indirect taxes, net of subsidies, with the exception of taxes on imports.

Balance of Payments (US $ million, 2005): Exports of goods f.o.b. 88.85; Imports of goods f.o.b. –437.67; *Trade balance* –348.83; Exports of services 277.00; Imports of services –208.39; *Balance on goods and services* –280.21; Other income received 18.89; Other income paid –52.05; *Balance on goods, services and income* –313.38; Current transfers (net) 278.99; *Current balance* –34.39; Capital account (net) 20.37; Direct investment abroad –0.9; Direct investment from abroad 54.44; Other investment assets –55.14; Other investment liabilities 90.85; Net errors and omissions –23.70; *Overall balance* 52.35. Source: IMF, *International Finance Statistics*.

EXTERNAL TRADE

Principal Commodities (distribution by SITC, million escudos, 2005): *Imports c.i.f.*: Consumer goods 16,042 (Intermediate food products 8,819); Intermediary goods 9,553 (Construction materials 4,578); Capital goods 6,536 (Machines 3,296, Transportation 2,770); Petroleum imports 2,691 (Diesel oil 1,891); Other imports 3,422; Total 38,245. *Exports f.o.b.*: Fish and crustaceans 635.0; Footwear 245.0; Miscellaneous manufactured articles 691.4 (Articles of apparel and clothing accessories 614.3); Total (incl. others) 1,571.4; Re-exports 6,039.2. Source: IMF, *Cape Verde: Statistical Appendix* (September 2006).

Imports (distribution by SITC, US $ million, 2001): Food and live animals 63.4 (Milk and cream 12.0, Cereals and cereal preparations 16.5, Vegetables and fruit 9.1, Sugar, sugar preparations and honey 7.8); Beverages and tobacco 15.4 (Alcoholic beverages 8.9); Mineral fuels, lubricants, etc. 13.9 (Refined petroleum 13.4); Basic manufactures 40.5 (Cement 8.6, Manufactures of metals 9.4); Machinery and transport equipment 68.7 (Power generating machinery 9.7, General industrial machinery and parts 8.4, Electric machinery and apparatus 10.8, Passenger vehicles 12.8); Miscellaneous manufactured articles 21.3; Total (incl. others) 247.5. Source: UN, *International Trade Statistics Yearbook*.

Principal Trading Partners (million escudos, 2006): *Imports c.i.f.*: Brazil 3,024.7; Côte d'Ivoire 127.8; France 1,184.1; Germany 545.6; Italy 2,267.2; Netherlands 5,315.8; Portugal 23,878.1; Senegal 192.4; Spain 2,668.3; United Kingdom 649.5; USA 659.9; Total (incl. others) 47,578.9. *Exports f.o.b.*: Guinea-Bissau 75.9; Netherlands 10.5; Portugal 968.3; Spain 496.8; USA 25.0; Total (incl. others) 1,819.0.

TRANSPORT

Road Traffic (motor vehicles in use, 31 December 2003): Light vehicles 23,811; Heavy vehicles 5,032; Motorcycles 1,924.

Shipping: *Merchant Fleet* (registered at 31 December 2005): Number of vessels 42, total displacement ('000 grt) 25.8 (Source: Lloyd's Register-Fairplay, *World Fleet Statistics*). *International Sea-borne Freight Traffic* (estimates, '000 metric tons, 1993): Goods loaded 144, goods unloaded 299 (Source: UN Economic Commission for Africa, *African Statistical Yearbook*).

Civil Aviation (traffic on scheduled services, 2003): Kilometres flown 5,000,000; Passengers carried 253,000; Passenger-km 285,000,000; Total ton-km 27,000,000. (Source: UN, *Statistical Yearbook*).

TOURISM

Tourist Arrivals by Country of Residence (2005): Belgium 5,121; France 14,284; Germany 21,121; Italy 69,728; Portugal 50,240; South Africa 9,432; Spain 7,626; Switzerland 1,976; USA 2,102; Total (incl. others) 197,844.

Tourism Receipts (US $ million, incl. passenger transport unless otherwise indicated): 101 in 2002; 137 in 2003; 125 in 2004 (excl. passenger transport).

Source: World Tourism Organization.

COMMUNICATIONS MEDIA

Radio Receivers* (1997): 73,000 in use.

Television Receivers† (2000): 2,000 in use.

Telephones† (2005): 71,400 main lines in use.

Mobile Cellular Telephones† (2005): 81,700 subscribers.

Facsimile Machines‡ (1996): 1,000 in use.

Personal Computers† (2004): 48,000 in use.

Internet Users† (2004): 25,000.

Non-daily Newspapers* (1996): 4 titles (average circulation 20,000 copies).

Book Production* (1989): 10 titles.

* Source: UNESCO, *Statistical Yearbook*.

† Source: International Telecommunication Union.

‡ Source: UN, *Statistical Yearbook*.

EDUCATION

Pre-primary (2003/04): 446 schools; 969 teachers; 21,005 pupils.

Primary (2003/04, unless otherwise indicated): 425 schools (2002/03); 3,169 teachers; 85,138 pupils.

Total Secondary (2003/04): 33 schools; 2,193 teachers; 49,790 pupils.

Higher (2003/04): 425 teachers; 3,036 pupils. Note: In 2002/03 a further 1,743 pupils were studying abroad.

Teacher Training (2003/04): 3 colleges; 52 teachers; 948 pupils.

Adult Literacy Rate (UNESCO estimates): 75.7% (males 85.4%; females 68.0) in 2002 (Source: UN Development Programme, *Human Development Report*).

Source (unless otherwise indicated): Comunidade dos Países de Língua Portuguesa.

Directory

The Constitution

A new Constitution of the Republic of Cape Verde ('the Second Republic') came into force on 25 September 1992. The Constitution defines Cape Verde as a sovereign, unitary and democratic republic, guaranteeing respect for human dignity and recognizing the inviolable and inalienable rights of man as a fundament of humanity, peace and justice. It recognizes the equality of all citizens before the law, without distinction of social origin, social condition, economic status, race, sex, religion, political convictions or ideologies and promises transparency for all citizens in the practising of fundamental liberties. The Constitution gives assent to popular will, and has a fundamental objective in the realization of economic, political, social and cultural democracy and the construction of a society that is free, just and in solidarity.

The Head of State is the President of the Republic, who is elected by universal adult suffrage and must obtain two-thirds of the votes cast to win in the first round of the election. If no candidate secures the requisite majority, a new election is held within 21 days and contested by the two candidates who received the highest number of votes in the first round. Voting is conducted by secret ballot. Legislative power is vested in the Assembléia Nacional, which is also elected by universal adult suffrage. The Prime Minister is nominated by the Assembléia, to which he is responsible. On the recommendation of the Prime Minister, the President appoints the Council of Ministers, whose members must be elected deputies of the Assembléia. There are 17 local government councils, elected by universal suffrage for a period of five years.

A constitutional revision, adopted in July 1999, gave the President the right to dissolve the Assembléia Nacional, created a new advisory chamber (Conselho Económico e Social), and gave the State the right to adopt Crioulo as the country's second official language.

The Government

HEAD OF STATE

President: PEDRO DE VERONA RODRIGUES PIRES (elected 25 February 2001; re-elected 12 February 2006).

COUNCIL OF MINISTERS
(August 2007)

Prime Minister: JOSÉ MARIA PEREIRA NEVES.

Minister in Assistance to the Prime Minister and Minister of Qualifications, Employment and Parliamentary Affairs: SARA MARIA DUARTE LOPES.

Minister of State and of Infrastructure, Transport and the Sea: MANUEL INOCÊNCIO SOUSA.

Minister of State and of Health: BASÍLIO MOSSO RAMOS.

Minister of Foreign Affairs, Co-operation and Communities: VÍCTOR MANUEL BARBOSA BORGES.

Minister of Justice: JOSÉ MANUEL GOMES ANDRADE.

Minister of Internal Administration: JÚLIO LOPES CORREIA.

Minister of Culture: MANUEL MONTEIRO DA VEIGA.

Minister of the Environment and Agriculture: MARIA MADALENA BRITO NEVES.

Minister of Education and Higher Education: FILOMENA DE FÁTIMA RIBEIRO VIEIRA MARTINS.

Minister of Labour, Solidarity and the Family: SIDÓNIO FONTES LIMA MONTEIRO.

Minister of the Economy, Growth and Competitiveness: JOSÉ BRITO.

Minister of Finance and Public Administration: CRISTINA DUARTE.

Minister of Decentralization, Housing and Territorial Order: RAMIRO ANDRADE ALVES AZEVEDO.

Minister of the Presidency of the Council of Ministers, State Reform and National Defence: MARIA CRISTINA LOPES ALMEIDA FONTES LIMA.

Secretary of State in Assistance to the Minister of Finance and Public Administration: LEONESA MARIA LIMA FORTES.

Secretary of State for Public Administration: ROMEU FONSECA MODESTO.

Secretary of State for Education: OCTÁVIO RAMOS TAVARES.

Secretary of State for Youth and Sports: AMÉRICO SABINO SOARES NASCIMENTO.

Secretary of State for Foreign Affairs: DOMINGOS DIAS PEREIRA MASCARENHAS.

Secretary of State for Agriculture: ROSA LOPES ROCHA.

MINISTRIES

Office of the President: Presidência da República, Palácio do Plateau, CP 100, Plateau, Praia, Santiago; tel. 2616555; fax 2614356; internet www.presidenciarepublica.cv.

Office of the Prime Minister: Gabinete do Primeiro Ministro, Palácio do Governo, Várzea, CP 16, Praia, Santiago; tel. 2610411; fax 2613099; e-mail gab.imprensa@gpm.gov.cv; internet www.primeirominístro.cv.

Ministry of Culture: Praia, Santiago; tel. 2610567.

Ministry of Decentralization, Housing and Territorial Order: Praia, Santiago.

Ministry of the Economy, Growth and Competitiveness: Praia, Santiago; tel. 2605300; fax 2617299; e-mail jorge.borges@gov1.gov.cv.

Ministry of Education and Higher Education: Palácio do Governo, Várzea, CP 111, Praia, Santiago; tel. 2610509; fax 2612764; internet www.minedu.cv.

Ministry of the Environment and Agriculture: Ponta Belém, CP 115, Praia, Santiago; tel. 2615713; fax 2614054; internet www.maap.cv.

Ministry of Finance and Public Administration: 107 Av. Amílcar Cabral, CP 30, Praia, Santiago; tel. 2607400; e-mail aliciab@gov1.gov.cv; internet www.mf.cv.

Ministry of Foreign Affairs, Co-operation and Communities: Palácio das Comunidades, Achada de Santo António, Praia, Santiago; tel. 2615727; fax 2616262; e-mail mne@gov.cv.

Ministry of Health: Palácio do Governo, Várzea, CP 47, Praia, Santiago; tel. 2610501.

Ministry of Infrastructure, Transport and the Sea: Ponta Belém, Praia, Santiago; tel. 2615709; fax 2611595; e-mail GSoares@mih.gov.cv.

Ministry of Internal Administration: Praia, Santiago.

Ministry of Justice: Rua Serpa Pinto, CP 205, Praia, Santiago; tel. 2623257; fax 2623261.

Ministry of Labour, Solidarity and the Family: Praia, Santiago.

Ministry of the Presidency of the Council of Ministers, State Reform and National Defence: Praia, Santiago.

Ministry of Qualifications, Employment and Parliamentary Affairs: Praia, Santiago.

President and Legislature

PRESIDENT

Presidential Election, 12 February 2006

Candidate	Votes	% of votes
Pedro de Verona Rodrigues Pires (PAICV)	86,583	50.98
Carlos Alberto de Carvalho Veiga (MpD)	83,241	49.02
Total	169,824	100.00

LEGISLATURE

Assembléia Nacional: Achada de Santo António, CP 20 A, Praia, Santiago; tel. 2608000; fax 2622660; e-mail an-cv@cvtelecom.cv; internet www.parlamento.cv.

Speaker: ARISTIDES RAIMUNDO LIMA.

Legislative Elections, 22 January 2006

Party	Votes	% of votes	Seats
Partido Africano da Independência de Cabo Verde (PAICV)	88,965	52.28	41
Movimento para a Democracia (MpD)	74,909	44.02	29
União Cristã, Independente e Democrática (UCID)	4,495	2.64	2
Partido da Renovação Democrática (PRD)	1,097	0.64	—
Partido Socialista Democrático (PSD)	702	0.41	—
Total	170,168	100.00	72

Election Commission

Comissão Nacional de Eleições (CNE): Praia; e-mail cne@cne.cv; internet www.cne.cv; Pres. BARTOLOMEU LOPES VARELA.

Political Organizations

Movimento para a Democracia (MpD): Av. Cidade Lisboa, 4° andar, CP 90 A, Praia, Santiago; tel. 2614122; e-mail mpd@mpd.cv; internet www.mpd.cv; f. 1990; advocates administrative decentralization; governing party from 1991 to 2001; formed alliance with the PCD to contest 2006 legislative and presidential elections; Chair. JORGE SANTOS.

Partido Africano da Independência de Cabo Verde (PAICV): Av. Amílcar Cabral, CP 22, Praia, Santiago; tel. 2612720; fax 2611410; internet www.paicv.org; f. 1956 as the Partido Africano da Independência do Guiné e Cabo Verde (PAIGC); name changed in 1981, following the 1980 coup in Guinea-Bissau; sole authorized political party 1975–90; governing party since 2001; Pres. JOSÉ MARIA NEVES; Sec.-Gen. ARISTIDES LIMA.

Partido da Renovação Democrática (PRD): Praia, Santiago; f. 2000 by fmr mems of the MpD; Pres. JOSÉ LUÍS BARBOSA.

Partido Socialista Democrático (PSD): Praia, Santiago; f. 1992; Sec.-Gen. JOÃO ALÉM.

Partido de Trabalho e Solidariedade (PTS): Praia, Santiago; f. 1998; Interim Leader ISAÍAS RODRIGUES.

União Cristã, Independente e Democrática (UCID): Praia, Santiago.

Diplomatic Representation

EMBASSIES IN CAPE VERDE

Angola: Av. OUA, Achada de Santo António, CP 78 A Praia, Santiago; tel. 2623235; fax 2623234; e-mail emb.angola@cv.telecom.cv; Ambassador JOSÉ AUGUSTO CÉSAR 'KILUANGE'.

Brazil: Chã de Areia 2, CP 93, Praia, Santiago; tel. 2615607; fax 2615609; e-mail contato@embrasilpraia.org; Ambassador MARIA DULCE SILVA BARROS.

China, People's Republic: Achada de Santo António, CP 8, Praia, Santiago; tel. 2623029; fax 2623047; e-mail chinaemb_cv@mfa.gov.cn; Ambassador WU YUANSHAN.

Cuba: Achada de Santo António, Praia, Santiago; tel. 2619048; fax 2617527; e-mail ecubacpv@cvtelecom.cv; Ambassador PEDRO EVELIO DORTA GONZÁLEZ.

France: Achada de Santo António, CP 192, Praia, Santiago; tel. 2615591; fax 2615590; e-mail fransula@cvtelecom.cv; internet www.ambafrance-cv.org; Ambassador BERNARD DEMANGE.

Korea, Democratic People's Republic: Praia; Ambassador RI IN SOK.

Portugal: Av. OUA, Achada de Santo António, CP 160, Praia, Santiago; tel. 2626097; fax 2613222; e-mail embport@cvtelecom.cv; internet www.consuladopt.cv; Ambassador Dr GRAÇA ANDERSEN GUIMARÃES.

Russia: Achada de Santo António, CP 31, Praia, Santiago; tel. 2622739; fax 2622738; e-mail embrus@cvtelecom.cv; Ambassador VLADIMIR E. PETUKHOV.

Senegal: Rua Abílio Macedo, Plateau, CP 269, Praia, Santiago; tel. 2615621; fax 2612838; e-mail silcarneyni@hotmail.com; Ambassador MARIÈME NDIAYE.

USA: Rua Abílio Macedo 6, Praia, Santiago; tel. 2608900; fax 2611355; internet praia.usembassy.gov; Ambassador ROGER DWAYNE PIERCE.

Judicial System

Supremo Tribunal de Justiça (STJ)

Gabinete do Juiz Presidente, Edif. dos Correios, Rua Cesário de Lacerda, CP 117, Praia, Santiago; tel. 2615810; fax 2611751; e-mail stj@supremo.gov.cv; internet www.stj.cv.

f. 1975; Pres. BENFEITO MOSSO RAMOS.

Attorney-General: FRANQUILIM AFONSO FURTADO.

Religion

CHRISTIANITY

At 31 December 2004 there were an estimated 328,313 adherents of the Roman Catholic Church in the country, equivalent to 73.9% of the population. Protestant churches, among which the Church of the Nazarene is the most prominent, represent about 1% of the population.

The Roman Catholic Church

Cape Verde comprises two dioceses, directly responsible to the Holy See. The Bishops participate in the Episcopal Conference of Senegal, Mauritania, Cape Verde and Guinea-Bissau, currently based in Senegal.

Bishop of Mindelo: Rt Rev. ARLINDO GOMES FURTADO, CP 447, 2110 Mindelo, São Vicente; tel. 2318870; fax 2318872; e-mail diocesemindelo@cvtelecom.cv.

Bishop of Santiago de Cabo Verde: Rt Rev. PAULINO DO LIVRAMENTO ÉVORA, Av. Amílcar Cabral, Largo 5 de Outubro, CP 7600, Praia, Santiago; tel. 2611119; fax 2612126; e-mail pom.curia.pera@cvtelecom.cv.

The Anglican Communion

Cape Verde forms part of the diocese of The Gambia, within the Church of the Province of West Africa. The Bishop is resident in Banjul, The Gambia.

Other Christian Churches

Church of the Nazarene: District Office, Av. Amílcar Cabral, Plateau, Praia, Santiago; tel. 2613611.

Other churches represented in Cape Verde include the Church of the Assembly of God, the Church of Jesus Christ of Latter-day Saints, the Evangelical Baptist Church, the Maná Church, the New Apostolic Church, the Seventh-day Adventist Church and the Universal Church of the Kingdom of God.

BAHÁ'Í FAITH

National Spiritual Assembly: Rua Madragoa, Plateau, Praia, Santiago; tel. 2617739.

The Press

Agaviva: Mindelo, São Vicente; tel. 2312121; f. 1991; monthly; Editor GERMANO ALMEIDA; circ. 4,000.

Boletim Oficial da República de Cabo Verde: Imprensa Nacional, CP 113, Praia, Santiago; tel. 2614150; e-mail incv@cvtelecom.cv; weekly; official announcements.

O Cidadão: Praça Dr António Aurélio Gonçalves 2, Mindelo, São Vicente; tel. 2325024; fax 2325022; e-mail cidadao@caboverde.zzn.com; weekly; Editor JOSÉ MÁRIO CORREIA.

Expresso das Ilhas: Santiago; internet www.expressodasilhas.cv; f. 2001 by the MpD; daily; Dir VLADEMIRO MARÇAL.

Horizonte: Achada de Santo António, CP 40, Praia, Santiago; tel. 2622447; fax 2623330; f. 1999; daily; pro-Government; Editor FERNANDO MONTEIRO; circ. 5,000.

Raízes: CP 98, Praia, Santiago; f. 1977; quarterly; cultural review; Editor ARNALDO FRANÇA; circ. 1,500.

A Semana: Rotunda do Palmarejo, CP 36 C, Praia, Santiago; tel. 2629860; fax 2628661; e-mail asemana@cvtelecom.cv; internet www.asemana.cv; f. 1991; weekly; pro-PAICV; independent; Editor FILOMENA SILVA; circ. 5,000.

Terra Nova: Rua Guiné-Bissau 1, CP 166, Mindelo, São Vicente; tel. 2322442; fax 2321475; e-mail terranova@cabonet.cv; f. 1975; monthly; Roman Catholic; Editor P. ANTÓNIO FIDALGO BARROS; circ. 3,000.

There is also an online newspaper, Visão News (www.visaonews.com), based in the USA. Further news websites include Paralelo14 (www.paralelo14.com), AllCaboVerde.com (www.noscaboverde.com), Cabonet (www.cabonet.or) and Sport Kriolu (www.sportkriolu.com), dedicated to sport.

NEWS AGENCIES

Inforpress: Achada de Santo António, CP 40 A, Praia, Santiago; tel. 2623025; fax 2623023; internet www.inforpress.cv; f. 1988 as Cabopress; Pres. JOSÉ AUGUSTO SANCHES.

Foreign Bureaux

Agence France Presse: CP 26/118, Praia, Santiago; tel. 2613890.

Inter Press Service (IPS) (Italy): CP 14, Mindelo, São Vicente; tel. 2314550; Rep. JUAN A. COLOMA.

Lusa (Agência de Notícias de Portugal, SA): Prainha, Praia, Santiago; tel. 2613519; Bureau Chief FRANCISCO FONTES.

PRESS ASSOCIATION

Associação de Jornalistas de Cabo Verde (AJOC): CP 1 A, Praia, Santiago; tel. 2622655; fax 2623054; e-mail jornalistascaboverde@gmail.com; f. 1993; Pres. PAULO JORGE LIMA; 11 media cos and 159 individual mems.

Publishers

Instituto Caboverdeano do Livro e do Disco (ICL): Centro Cultural, CP 158, Praia, Santiago; tel. 2612346; books, journals, music.

GOVERNMENT PUBLISHING HOUSE

Imprensa Nacional: CP 113, Praia, Santiago; tel. 2614209; Admin. JOÃO DE PINA.

Broadcasting and Communications

TELECOMMUNICATIONS

Cabo Verde Telecom: Rua Cabo Verde Telecom, Várzea, CP 220, Praia, Santiago; tel. 2609200; fax 2613725; e-mail cvtelecom@cvtelecom.cv; internet www.nave.cv; f. 1995; 40% owned by Portugal Telecom; operates mobile network, Telemóvel; Chief Exec. ANTÓNIO PIRES CORREIA.

Cabo Verde Telecom was the sole telephone, cable and internet provider; however, in 2004 the Government announced plans to open the telecommunications market by 2010. There were plans to grant a licence for a second mobile provider.

Regulatory Authority

Agência Nacional das Comunicações (ANAC): Edifício do MIT, Ponta Belém, CP 892, Praia, Santiago; tel. 2604400; fax 2613069; e-mail info.anac@anac.cv; internet www.anac.cv; f. 2006; Pres. DAVID GOMES.

BROADCASTING

Rádio Televisão de Cabo Verde (RTC): Rua 13 de Janeiro, Achada de Santo António, CP 1 A, Praia, Santiago; tel. 2605200; fax 26052; e-mail rtc@mail.cvtelecom.cv; govt-controlled; 40 transmitters and relay transmitters; FM transmission only; radio broadcasts in Portuguese and Creole for 24 hours daily; one television transmitter and seven relay television transmitters; television broadcasts in Portuguese and Creole for eight hours daily with co-operation of RTP Africa (Portugal) and TV5 Honde; Pres. MARCOS OLIVEIRA.

Televisão de Cabo Verde: Praia, Santiago; sole television broadcaster; part of Radio Televisão de Cabo Verde; Dir DANIEL MEDINA.

Praia FM: Rua Visconde de S. Januario 19, 4° andar, CP 276 C, Praia, Santiago; tel. 2616356; fax 2613515; e-mail praiafm@cvtelecom.cv; internet www.praiafm.biz; Dir GIORDANO CUSTÓDIO.

Rádio Comercial: Achada de Santo António, Prédio Gomes Irmãos, 3° esq., CP 507, Praia, Santiago; tel. 2623156; fax 2622413; e-mail multimedia.rc@cvtelecom.cv; internet www.radiocomercial.net; f. 1997; Admin. HENRIQUE PIRES; Dir CARLOS FILIPE GONÇALVES.

Rádio Educativa de Cabo Verde: Achada de Santo António, Praia, Santiago; tel. 2611161.

Rádio Morabeza: Rua da Guiné Bissau 3A, CP 456, Mindelo, São Vicente; tel. 2324431; fax 2300069; e-mail radiomorabeza@cvtelecom.cv.

Rádio Nacional de Cabo Verde (RNCV): CP 26, Praia, Santiago; tel. 2613729.

Rádio Nova—Emissora Cristã de Cabo Verde: CP 166, Mindelo, São Vicente; tel. 2322082; fax 2321475; internet www.radionovaonline.com; f. 2002; Roman Catholic station; Dir ANTÓNIO FIDALGO BARROS.

Voz de São Vicente: CP 29, Mindelo, São Vicente; fax 2311006; f. 1974; govt-controlled; Dir JOSÉ FONSECA SOARES.

Radiotelevisão Portuguesa International and Canal Plus International began broadcasting in 1995. A further television channel, Pulu TV, began broadcasting in 2005, but was yet to be licensed. In 2005 there were estimated to be 12 radio stations.

Finance

(cap. = capital; res = reserves; dep. = deposits; m. = million; brs = branches; amounts in Cape Verde escudos, unless otherwise indicated)

BANKING

Central Bank

Banco de Cabo Verde (BCV): Av. Amílcar Cabral 117, CP 101, Praia, Santiago; tel. 2607000; fax 2607095; e-mail mcosta@bcv.cv; internet www.bcv.cv; f. 1976; bank of issue; cap. 200.0m., res 243.8m., dep. 16,630.4m. (Dec. 2005); Gov. CARLOS AUGUSTO DUARTE DE BURGO.

Other Banks

Banco Caboverdiano de Negócios (BCN): Rua Justino Lopes 1, CP 593, Praia, Santiago; tel. 2611662; fax 2614006; e-mail bcn@cvtelecom.cv; f. 1996 as Banco Totta e Açores (Cabo Verde); renamed as above in 2004; owned by a Cape Verdean consortium; cap. €2.7m. (Oct. 2004); 3 brs; Administrator RODRIGO BARCELOS NASCIMENTO.

Banco Comercial do Atlântico (BCA): Chã d'Areia, CP 474, Praia, Santiago; tel. 2615535; fax 2613235; e-mail bcd@bca.cv; internet www.bca.cv; f. 1993; privatized in 2000; main commercial bank; cap. 1,000m., res 615.1m., dep. 43,663.1m. (Dec. 2005); Pres. and Gen. Man. JOÃO HENRIQUE REAL PEREIRA; 24 brs.

Banco Interatlântico: Av. Cidade de Lisboa, CP 131 A, Praia, Santiago; tel. 2614008; fax 2614752; e-mail bi@bi.cv; internet www.bi.cv; f. 1999; Pres. JOÃO HENRIQUE REAL PEREIRA.

Caixa Económica de Cabo Verde, SA (CECV): Av. Cidade de Lisboa, CP 199, Praia, Santiago; tel. 2603601; fax 2615560; e-mail cecv@caixaeconomica.cv; internet www.caixaeconomica.cv; f. 1928; privatized in 1999; commercial bank; cap. 348.0m., res 926.4m., dep. 14,855.5m. (Dec. 2004); Pres. and Exec. Dir FRANCISCO JOSÉ GONÇALVES SIMÕES; 11 brs.

STOCK EXCHANGE

Bolsa de Valores de Cabo Verde, Sarl (BVC): Achada de Santo António, CP 115 A, Praia, Santiago; tel. 2603030; fax 2603038; e-mail bcv@bvc.cv; internet www.bvc.cv; f. 1998; reopened December 2005; Pres. VERÍSSIMO PINTO.

INSURANCE

Companhia Caboverdiana de Seguros (IMPAR): Av. Amílcar Cabral, CP 469, Praia, Santiago; tel. and fax 2613765; e-mail impar@cvtelecom.cv; f. 1991; Pres. Dr CORSINO ANTÓNIO FORTES.

Garantia Companhia de Seguros: Chã d'Areia, CP 138, Praia, Santiago; tel. 26086221; fax 2616117; e-mail garantia@cvtelecom.cv; f. 1991; privatized in 2000; Pres. JOÃO HENRIQUE REAL PEREIRA.

Trade and Industry

GOVERNMENT AGENCIES

Agência Nacional de Segurança Alimentar (ANSA): Achada de Santo António, Praia, Santiago; e-mail ansa@cvtelecom.cv; food security agency.

Cabo Verde Investimentos (CI): Praia, Santiago; e-mail CI@cvinvest.cv; f. 2004 to replace the Centro de Promoção Turística, de Investimento Externo e das Exportações (PROMEX); promotes public-private investment partnerships in infrastructure and tourism; Pres. VICTOR FIDALGO.

Comissão de Investimento Externo e Empresa Franca (CIEF): Praia, Santiago; foreign investment commission.

Gabinete de Apoio à Reestruturação do Sector Empresarial do Estado (GARSEE) (Cabo Verde Privatization): Largo do Tunis, Cruzeiro, CP 323, Praia, Santiago; tel. 2614748; fax 2612334; e-mail cvprivatization@mail.cvtelecom.cv; bureau in charge of planning and supervising restructuring and divestment of public enterprises; Project Dir Dr SÉRGIO CENTEIO.

DEVELOPMENT ORGANIZATION

Instituto Nacional de Investigação e Desenvolvimento Agrário (INIDA): CP 84, Praia, Santiago; tel. 2711147; fax 2711133; e-mail inida@mail.cvtelecom.cv; f. 1979; research and training on agricultural issues.

TRADE ASSOCIATION

Associação para a Promoção dos MicroEmpresários (APME): Fazenda, Praia, Santiago; tel. 2606056; f. 1988.

CHAMBERS OF COMMERCE

Câmara de Comércio, Indústria e Serviços de Barlavento (CCISB): Rua da Luz 31, CP 728, Mindelo, São Vicente; tel. 2328495; fax 2328496; e-mail camara.com@cvtelecom.cv; f. 1996; Pres. MANUEL J. MONTEIRO.

Câmara de Comércio, Indústria e Serviços de Sotavento (CCISS): Rua Serpa Pinto 160, CP 105, Praia, Santiago; tel. 2617234; fax 2617235; e-mail cciss@cvtelecom.cv.

STATE INDUSTRIAL ENTERPRISES

Empresa Nacional de Avicultura, SARL (ENAVI): Tira Chapéu Zona Industrial, CP 135, Praia, Santiago; tel. 2627268; fax 2628441; e-mail enavi@cvtelecom.cv; poultry-farming.

Empresa Nacional de Combustíveis, SARL (ENACOL): Largo John Miller's, CP 1, Mindelo, São Vicente; tel. 2306060; fax 2323425; e-mail enacolsv@mail.cvtelecom.cv; internet www.enacol.cv; f. 1979; supervises import and distribution of petroleum; Dir Dr MÁRIO A. RODRIGUES.

Empresa Nacional de Produtos Farmacêuticos, SARL (EMPROFAC): Tira Chapéu Zona Industrial, CP 59, Praia, Santiago; tel. 2627895; fax 2627899; e-mail emprofac@cvtelecom.cv; f. 1979; due to be privatized by early 2007; state monopoly of pharmaceuticals and medical imports.

UTILITIES

Electricity and Water

Empresa de Electricidade e Água, SARL (Electra): Av. Baltasar Lopes Silva 10, CP 137, Mindelo, São Vicente; tel. 2303030; fax 2324446; e-mail comercial@electra.cv; internet www.electra.cv; f. 1982; 51% government-owned; Pres. RUI EDUARDO FERREIRA RODRIGUES PENA.

MAJOR COMPANIES

Cimentos de Cabo Verde (CCV): Tira Chapéu, CP 14 A, Praia, Santiago; tel. 2603110; fax 2612086; e-mail cimentoscv@cimentoscv.com; internet www.cimentoscv.com; f. 1994; 86.6% owned by Cimpor (Portugal); imports and distributes construction materials.

Companhia dos Tabacos de Cabo Verde, SARL: CP 67, São Vicente; tel. 2314400; manufacture of tobacco and tobacco products.

Construções de Cabo Verde, SA (CVC): Achada Grande, CP 242, Praia, Santiago; tel. 2633879; fax 2633221; e-mail cvc@cvc.cv; 57.6% owned by Grupo SOMAGUE (Portugal); construction, mainly on govt infrastructure and building projects; Pres. Eng. JOÃO MANUEL NUNES SALVADOR.

Empresa Caboverdiana de Pescas (Pescave): Mindelo, São Vicente; tel. 6313118; formerly govt-owned; fishing company.

Maripesca, Lda: Rua de S. João, CP 696, Mindelo, São Vicente; tel. 2316542; fax 2316582; e-mail maripesca@cvtelecom.cv; fishing equipment.

Sociedade Caboverdiana de Cerveja e Refrigerantes, SARL: CP 320, Praia, Santiago; tel. 2615575; fax 2614488; production of beer and soft drinks.

Sociedade Caboverdiana de Tabacos, Lda (SCT): Av. 5 de Julho, CP 270, São Vicente; tel. 2323349; fax 2323351; e-mail sctabacos@cvtelecom.cv; internet www.sct.cv; f. 1996; Pres. EUCLIDES JESUS MARQUES OLIVEIRA; 41 employees.

Sociedade Industrial de Calçado, SARL (SOCAL): CP 92, Mindelo, São Vicente; tel. 2315059; fax 2312061; industrial shoe factory.

CO-OPERATIVE

Instituto Nacional das Cooperativas: Achada de Santo António, Praia, Santiago; tel. 2616376; central co-operative org.

TRADE UNIONS

Confederação Caboverdiana dos Sindicatos Livres (CCSL): Rua Dr Júlio Abreu, CP 155, Praia, Santiago; tel. and fax 2616319; e-mail ccsl@cvtelecom.cv; Sec.-Gen. JOSÉ MANUEL VAZ.

Federação Nacional dos Sindicatos dos Trabalhadores da Administração Pública (FNSTAP): CP 123, Praia; tel. 2614305; fax 2613629; Pres. MIGUEL HORTA DA SILVA.

Sindicato dos Transportes, Comunicações e Turismo (STCT): Praia, Santiago; tel. 2616338.

União Nacional dos Trabalhadores de Cabo Verde—Central Sindical (UNTC—CS): Av. Cidade de Lisboa, CP 123, Praia, Santiago; tel. 2614305; fax 2613629; e-mail untc@cvtelecom.cv; internet www.untc-cs.org; f. 1978; Chair. JÚLIO ASCENÇÃO SILVA.

Transport

ROADS

In 2004 there were an estimated 2,250 km of roads, of which 1,750 km were paved. In 2005 the Government planned to allocate €635m. to upgrade the road network, including building highways and a ring road around Praia.

Associação Apoio aos Reclusos e Crianças de Rua (AAPR): Achada de Santo António, CP 205 A, Praia, Santiago; tel. 2618441; fax 2619017; e-mail aapr@cvtelecom.cv; road development agency.

SHIPPING

Cargo-passenger ships call regularly at Porto Grande, Mindelo, on São Vicente, and Praia, on Santiago. There were plans to upgrade the ports at Praia, Sal, São Vicente and Porto Novo (Santo Antão). There are small ports on the other inhabited islands. Cape Verde's registered merchant fleet at 31 December 2005 consisted of 42 vessels, totalling 25,805 grt.

Comissão de Gestão dos Transportes Marítimos de Cabo Verde: CP 153, São Vicente; tel. 2314979; fax 2312055.

Empresa Nacional de Administração dos Portos, SA (ENAPOR, SA): Av. Marginal, CP 82, Mindelo, São Vicente; tel. 2324414; fax 2324337; e-mail enapor@mail.cvtelecom.cv; internet www.enapor.cv; f. 1982; due to be privatized by early 2007; Chair. and Man. Dir FRANKLIM DO ROSÁRIO SPENCER.

Arca Verde (Companhia Nacional de Navegação): Rua 5 de Julho, Plateau, Santiago; tel. 2615497; fax 2615496; e-mail cnnarcaverdepra@cvtelecom.cv; shipping co; undergoing privatization.

Cape Verde National Shipping Line, SARL (Cs Line): Rua Baltasar Lopez da Silva, CP 238, Mindelo, São Vicente.

Companhia Caboverdiana de Navegação: Rua Cristiano Sena Barcelos 3–5, Mindelo, São Vicente; tel. 2322852.

Companhia de Navegação Estrela Negra: Av. 5 de Julho 17, CP 91, Mindelo, São Vicente; tel. 2325423; fax 2315382.

Linhas Marítimas Caboverdianas (LINMAC): CP 357, Praia, Santiago; tel. 2614352; fax 2613715; Dir ESTHER SPENCER.

Seage Agência de Navegação de Cabo Verde: Av. Cidade de Lisboa, CP 232, Praia, Santiago; tel. 2615758; fax 2612524; e-mail seage@cvtelecom.cv; f. 1986; Chair. CÉSAR MANUEL SEMEDO LOPES.

Transnacional, a shipping company, operates a ferry service between some islands.

CIVIL AVIATION

The Amílcar Cabral international airport, at Espargos, on Sal island, can accommodate aircraft of up to 50 tons and 1m. passengers per year. The airport's facilities were expanded during the 1990s. A second international airport, Aeroporto da Praia, was opened in late 2005. There is also a small airport on each of the other inhabited islands. The airport on São Vicente was upgraded to international capacity in 2000. Plans were also under way for the construction of two further international airports, on Boa Vista and São Vicente. Transportes Aéreos de Cabo Verde (TACV) and the Portuguese carrier, TAP, operate flights to Cape Verde.

Agência de Aviação Civil (AAC): Praia, Santiago; f. 2005; regulatory agency; Pres. VALDEMAR CORREIA.

Empresa Nacional de Aeroportos e Segurança AEREA, EP (ASA): Aeroporto Amílcar Cabral, CP 58, Ilha do Sal; tel. 2412626; fax 2411570; e-mail pca@asa.cv; internet www.asa.cv; airports and aircraft security; Pres. MÁRIO LOPES.

Transportes Aéreos de Cabo Verde (TACV): Av. Amílcar Cabral, CP 1, Praia, Santiago; tel. 2608200; fax 2618323; e-mail pferreira@tacv.aero; internet www.tacv.cv; f. 1958; internal services connecting the nine inhabited islands; also operates regional services to Senegal, The Gambia and Guinea-Bissau, and long-distance services to Europe and the USA; due to be privatized by 2007; Pres. and CEO JOÃO HIGINO SILVA; Gen. Man. PAULO FERREIRA.

A private company, Inter Island Airlines, offers flights between the islands of Cape Verde, and a new inter-island carrier, Halcyon Air, was established in early 2005.

Tourism

The islands of Santiago, Santo Antão, Fogo and Brava offer attractive mountain scenery. There are extensive beaches on the islands of Santiago, Sal, Boa Vista and Maio. Some 197,844 tourists visited Cape Verde in 2005. In 2004 tourism receipts totalled some US $125m. The sector is undergoing rapid expansion, with development in a number of Zonas de Desenvolvimento Turístico Integral. In late 2003 the Government began steps to have Fogo, which contains the only live volcano on Cape Verde, designated a UNESCO world heritage site. Plans were unveiled in March 2004 to promote the island of Santa Luzia as an eco-tourism destination. Construction of a large tourist resort on Santiago, expected to cost €550m., commenced in early 2005. Tourist arrivals are projected to increase to about 400,000 annually by 2008.

Defence

The armed forces numbered about 1,200 (army 1,000, air force less than 100, coastguard 100), as assessed at November 2006. There is also a police force, the Police for Public Order, which is organized by the local municipal councils. National service is by selective conscription. In October 2002 the Government announced a programme of reform, involving the coastguard, the military police and special forces dealing with drugs-trafficking and terrorism offences.

Defence Expenditure: Budgeted at 640m. escudos in 2006.

Chief of Staff of the Armed Forces: Col ANTERO DE MATOS.

Education

Compulsory primary education begins at six or seven years of age and lasts for six years. Secondary education, beginning at 13 years of age, is divided into two cycles, the first comprising a three-year general course, the second a two-year pre-university course. There are three teacher-training units and two industrial and commercial schools of further education. According to UNESCO estimates, primary enrolment in 2003/04 included 91% of children in the relevant age-group (males 92%; females 91%), while secondary enrolment was equivalent to 55% of children in the relevant age-group (males 52%; females 58%). In 2002/03 there were 1,743 Cape Verdean students studying at overseas universities. In 2002 a private university, the Universidade Jean Piaget de Cabo Verde, opened in Praia. In 2003 expenditure on education was budgeted at 4,786,037 escudos, or 26% of the central Government's total public expenditure.

Bibliography

Almeida, R., and Nyhan, P. *Cape Verde and its People: A Short History*. Boston, MA, TCHUBA—American Committee for Cape Verde, 1978.

Amaral, I. *Santiago de Cabo Verde*. Lisbon, 1964.

Cabral, A. *Unity and Struggle*. New York, NY, Monthly Review Press, 1979.

Carreira, A. *Cabo Verde, Formação e Extinção de uma Sociedade Escravocrata*. Bissau, 1972.

Migrações nas Ilhas de Cabo Verde. Lisbon, Universidade Nova, 1977.

Cabo Verde: Classes sociais, estructura familiar, migrações. Lisbon, Ulmeiro, 1977.

The People of the Cape Verde Islands: Exploitation and Emigration (trans. and edited by C. Fyfe). London, Hurst, and Hamden, CT, Archon Books, 1983.

da Graça, A. *Cape Verdean Culture: An Interactive / Cooperative Approach*. New Bedford, MA, 1995.

Davidson, B. *The Fortunate Isles: A Study of Cape Verde*. London, Hutchinson, and Trenton, NJ, World Press, 1989.

de Pina, M.-P. *Les îles du Cap-Vert*. Paris, Editions Karthala, 1987.

Foy, C. *Cape Verde: Politics, Economics and Society*. London, Pinter Publishers, Marxist Regimes Series, 1988.

Langworthy, M., and Finan, T. J. *Waiting for Rain: Agriculture and Ecological Imbalance in Cape Verde*. Boulder, CO, Lynne Rienner, 1997.

Lesourd, M. *État et société aux îles du Cap-Vert: Alternatives pour un petit état insulaire*. Paris, Editions Karthala, 1995.

Lima, A. *Reforma Política em Cabo Verde: do Paternalismo à Modernização do Estado*. Praia, 1992.

Lobban, R. *Historical Dictionary of Cape Verde*. 3rd Edn. Metuchen, NJ, Scarecrow Press, 1995.

Cape Verde: Crioulo Colony to Independent Nation. Boulder, CO, Westview Press, 1995.

Cape Verde. Boulder, CO, Westview Press, 1998.

May, S. *Tourismus in der Dritten Welt: Das Beispiel Kapverde*. Frankfurt am Main, Campus Verlag, 1985.

Meintel, D. *Race, Culture and Portuguese Colonialism in Cabo Verde*. Syracuse, NY, Syracuse University Press, 1985.

Soares, J. B. *Cabo Verde: Um País em Transição*. Boston, MA, Praia Branca Production, 1993.

THE CENTRAL AFRICAN REPUBLIC

Physical and Social Geography

DAVID HILLING

Bordered to the north by Chad, to the east by Sudan, to the south by the Republic of the Congo and the Democratic Republic of the Congo, and to the west by Cameroon, the Central African Republic forms a geographic link between the Sudano-Sahelian zone and the Congo basin. The country consists mainly of plateau surfaces at 600 m–900 m above sea-level, which provide the watershed between drainage northwards to Lake Chad and southwards to the Oubangui-Congo river system. There are numerous rivers, and during the main rainy season (July–October) much of the south-east of the country becomes inaccessible as a result of extensive inundation. The Oubangui river to the south of Bangui provides near-year-round commercial navigation and is the main outlet for external trade. However, development of the country is inhibited by its land-locked location and the great distance (1,815 km) to the sea by way of the fluvial route from Bangui to Brazzaville, in the Republic of the Congo, and thence by rail to Pointe-Noire.

The Central African Republic covers an area of 622,984 sq km (240,535 sq miles). At the census of December 1988 the population was 2,463,616. According to UN estimates, the population numbered 4,265,000 in mid-2006, giving an average density of 6.8 inhabitants per sq km. The greatest concentration of population is in the western part of the country; large areas in the east are virtually uninhabited. Of the country's numerous ethnic groups, the Banda and Baya jointly comprise more than 50% of the population. Sango, a lingua franca, has been adopted as the national language.

Only in the south-west of the country is the rainfall sufficient (1,250 mm) to sustain a forest vegetation. The south-western Lobaye region is a source of coffee (the main cash crop), cocoa, rubber, palm produce and timber. Cotton, also an important cash crop, is cultivated in a belt beyond the forest. This area could benefit substantially from a proposed rail link with the Transcameroon railway.

Alluvial deposits of diamonds occur widely and are exploited, but uranium is potentially of much greater economic importance. The exploitation of ore-rich deposits at Bakouma, 480 km east of Bangui, which has been inhibited by inadequate access routes and by technical problems, awaits a sustained recovery in the present level of world uranium prices.

Recent History

PIERRE ENGLEBERT

Revised by RICHARD BRADSHAW and JUAN FANDOS-RIUS

In 1958 the French-administered territory of Oubangui-Chari was granted internal self-government and became the Central African Republic (CAR). However, the leader of the independence movement, Barthélémy Boganda, died in an unexplained plane crash in March 1959, and David Dacko became the republic's first President at independence on 13 August 1960. The ruling Mouvement d'évolution sociale de l'Afrique noire (MESAN) was declared the sole legal party in December 1962. In December 1965–January 1966 Col Jean-Bédel Bokassa, the Commander-in-Chief of the armed forces, seized power in a *coup d'état*. Bokassa's regime became increasingly despotic, inefficient and corrupt. Several external opposition groups were formed, including the Mouvement pour la libération du peuple centrafricain (MLPC), led by Ange-Félix Patassé (who had been dismissed as Prime Minister in 1978 and had fled to France). In September 1979 Bokassa, while in Libya, was deposed in a bloodless coup carried out by French troops who 'returned' Dacko to power. A multi-party system was restored in February 1981 and in March Dacko was elected with 50% of the votes cast while Patassé received 38%. Political opposition to Dacko increased during 1981 and in September Army Chief of Staff Gen. André Kolingba took power in a bloodless coup.

KOLINGBA'S RULE, 1981–93

Kolingba banned political activity and disenchantment with the military regime soon became evident. In March 1982 an unsuccessful coup attempt was staged by Patassé, who took refuge in the French embassy, which arranged for his transport to exile in Togo. In November 1986 some 91.2% of voters granted a further six-year mandate to Kolingba as President and approved a draft Constitution, which provided for wide-ranging powers for the Head of State. In February 1987 the constitutive assembly of Kolingba's Rassemblement démocratique centrafricain (RDC) stipulated a clear separation between party and State in the Constitution and membership of the party was made voluntary. In July the country's first legislative elections for 20 years were boycotted by the opposition and all 142 candidates contesting the 52 seats in the Assemblée nationale were RDC nominees.

Kolingba then sought reconciliation with opponents of his regime by inviting Gen. François Bozizé Yangovounda, a participant in the 1982 coup attempt, to return from exile, but Bozizé chose to remain in Benin. In July 1989 12 of Kolingba's opponents, including Bozizé, were arrested in Benin and subsequently extradited to the CAR and imprisoned.

In late 1990 opposition to Kolingba intensified. Civil servants had not received pay for several months and the Union syndicale des travailleurs de la Centrafrique (USTC) called a general strike. The RDC eventually agreed to pay workers one-quarter of the arrears owed them, to re-establish the post of Prime Minister and to initiate a fundamental review of the Constitution. In March 1991 former Minister of State Edouard Frank was nominated Prime Minister.

In December 1991 Kolingba pardoned Bozizé and in August 1992 he opened a Grand National Debate, which was dominated by pro-Kolingba nominees and thus boycotted by the Concertation des forces démocratiques (CFD) and the Roman Catholic Church. In May 1993 the new Prime Minister, Enoch Dérant Lakoué, announced that elections, which had been postponed for almost 12 months, would take place in October, but pressure from the French Government led Kolingba to bring the elections forward to August. In the first round of the presidential election on 22 August, Patassé received 37.3% of the votes cast, Prof. Abel Goumba won 21.7%, Dacko won 20.1%, and Kolingba received just 12.1%.

DEMOCRATIC TRANSITION

Patassé won the second round of the ballot on 19 September 1993, receiving 52.5% of votes cast, and was declared President by the Supreme Court on 27 September. In subsequent elections for seats in the Assemblée nationale, the MLPC won 34 seats (nine seats short of an absolute majority), the RDC 13 seats, the Front patriotique pour le progrès (FPP) and the Parti libéral-démocrate (PLD) seven seats each, and the Alliance pour la démocratie et le progrès (ADP) and supporters of Dacko, six seats each. Seven minor parties and independents shared the remaining 12 seats.

On 22 October 1993 Patassé was sworn in as President and soon appointed Jean-Luc Mandaba, Vice-President of the MLPC, as Prime Minister of a coalition Government which enjoyed a working majority of 53 seats in the Assemblée nationale. In December 1994 a draft Constitution was approved by 82% of voters in a national referendum and the new Constitution was adopted in January 1995.

ARMY DISCONTENT

In the mid-1990s the Government's repeated failure to pay the salaries of public-sector employees and members of the armed forces provoked frequent strikes and mounting political unrest. In mid-April 1996 the Conseil démocratique des partis politiques de l'opposition (CODEPO), a coalition of several opposition movements formed in December 1995, staged an anti-Government rally in Bangui and part of the national army mutinied in the capital demanding the immediate payment of all arrears. Patassé promised that part of the overdue salaries would be paid and that the mutineers would not be prosecuted. Faced with the presence of French troops (the Eléments français d'assistance opérationelle—EFAO) in Bangui that were ready to protect the presidential palace and other key installations, the rebellion swiftly collapsed. In late April Patassé appointed a new armed forces Chief of Staff, Col (later Gen.) Maurice Regonessa, and banned all public demonstrations. In mid-May, however, discontent again resurfaced and CODEPO demanded the resignation of the Government. Patassé ordered control of the national armoury to be transferred from the regular army to his own presidential guard, a move which provoked a second, more serious insurrection. Once again French troops were deployed to protect the Patassé Government but the mutineers managed to take five hostages, including Regonessa and Charles Massi, a government minister, before the French forces were able to suppress the rebellion. In all, 11 soldiers and 32 civilians were reported to have been killed in the second army mutiny. Following extended negotiations between the mutineers and government representatives, an accord was signed which provided for an amnesty for the rebels, the immediate release of hostages, and the installation of a new government of national unity.

In June 1996 a protocol was signed by the Government that provided for the establishment of a government of national unity under the leadership of a civilian Prime Minister with no official party ties. As a result, Gabriel Koyambounou's Government resigned and former ambassador to France Jean-Paul Ngoupandé was named Prime Minister. Ngoupandé nominated a new Council of Ministers but CODEPO was dissatisfied with the level of its representation in the Council and withdrew from the Government of National Unity. Patassé refused to transfer any effective power to Prime Minister Ngoupandé, who grew increasingly frustrated at the situation.

In October 1996, troops which had been involved in the insurrections of April and May refused to be transferred from the capital to a more remote location. In mid-November, another mutiny erupted. Parts of Bangui were occupied by the rebels and several hostages were taken. Many of the mutineers, who demanded the resignation of Patassé, belonged to the Yakoma ethnic group of Kolingba. EFAO troops were deployed once again to prevent the overthrow of Patassé.

In December 1996 a 15-day truce was agreed upon. French military involvement in the CAR was condemned by prominent opposition parties, which also sought unsuccessfully to initiate a parliamentary vote to bring impeachment proceedings against Patassé. After a resurgence of violence, former President of Mali, Brig.-Gen. Amadou Toumani Touré came to Bangui as mediator and helped negotiate the 'Bangui Accords' signed at the end of January 1997, which granted an amnesty to the mutineers and led to the formation of a new government of national unity and the replacement of the EFAO troops patrolling Bangui by peace-keeping forces from African nations. The opposition promptly opposed the appointment at the end of January of Michel Gbezera-Bria (a close associate of Patassé) as Prime Minister. Nevertheless, a 'Government of Action' was formed in mid-February and Gen. Bozizé replaced Col Regonessa as Chief of Staff of the armed forces.

MISAB AND MINURCA

During February 1997 peace-keeping operations were transferred to a newly formed Mission interafricaine de surveillance des accords de Bangui (MISAB), which included some 700 soldiers from Burkina Faso, Chad, Gabon, Mali, Senegal and Togo. When MISAB soldiers attempted to disarm former mutineers in late March, fighting broke out and some 20 MISAB soldiers were killed. A spokesman for the rebels, Capt. Anicet Saulet, insisted that the lack of representation of the former mutineers in the new Government constituted a breach of the Bangui Accords. Following a meeting between Saulet and Patassé in early April, the Council of Ministers was expanded to include two military officers as representatives of the rebels. Several hundred of the former mutineers then attended a ceremony officially recognizing their reintegration into the regular armed forces.

In June 1997 clashes between MISAB forces and former mutineers resulted in the arrest of more than 80 former mutineers, the deaths of about 100 soldiers and several civilians, and the destruction of numerous homes and business premises. Touré again visited Bangui in his capacity as Chairman of MISAB, and negotiated a four-day truce in late June and a 10-day cease-fire agreement in early July. All former mutineers were to be reintegrated into the regular armed forces and their safety and that of the people living in the districts under their control was guaranteed. The rebels, for their part, agreed to hand over their weapons. In early September the nine representatives of opposition parties in the Council of Ministers resumed their vacant posts.

In July 1997 France announced its intention to withdraw its troops from the CAR by April 1998. France's proposal for the formation of a UN force encountered initial resistance from the USA. A National Reconciliation Conference held in Bangui in February 1998 led to the signing on 5 March of a National Reconciliation Pact by Patassé and 40 representatives of all the country's political and social groups. The pact restated the main provisions of the Bangui Accords and of the political protocol of June 1996. The powers of the President were, however, guaranteed, and presidential elections were scheduled for late 1999.

The pact facilitated the authorization in March 1998 by the UN Security Council of the establishment of a peace-keeping mission, the UN Mission in the Central African Republic (MINURCA) to replace MISAB. MINURCA comprised 1,345 mostly African troops which were to remain in the country for at least three months, but its mission was subsequently extended until the end of February 1999 in order to support and verify the legislative elections.

The first round of elections finally took place on 22 November and 13 December 1998. Parties loyal to Patassé (the so-called Mouvance présidentielle) won 47 of the 109 seats, while the opposition won 55. In early January 1999 10 opposition ministers resigned from the Government in protest at what they termed the Mouvance présidentielle's disregard for the results of the elections. Patassé's choice of a close associate, Anicet Georges Dologuélé, to form a new Government, provoked public demonstrations and the opposition's formal withdrawal from the chamber. Dologuélé announced the composition of a Council of Ministers, which included members of the opposition Mouvement pour la démocratie et le développement (MDD), despite opposition agreement not to accept posts in the new Government. The MDD leadership ordered its members to resign their posts. Armand Sama, however, the nominated Minister of Town Planning, Housing and Public Buildings, defied the MDD leadership and retained his post.

In February 1999 the UN Security Council extended MINURCA's mandate until November of that year but the force was to be gradually reduced after the successful conclusion of the election. The Security Council expressed its concern at the political tension caused by the disputed legislative elections and reminded the Government that it had promised reform of the economy and of the armed forces. France opposed the extension of MINURCA's mandate and withdrew its troops from the CAR in February.

In April 1999 the UN Secretary-General, Kofi Annan, called on all factions in the CAR to co-operate in preparations for the presidential election. A 27-member Commission électorale mixte indépendante (CEMI) was inaugurated in May and in July the Constitutional Court authorized 10 candidates to stand in the presidential election. President Patassé presented himself as a candidate, as did two former Presidents (Kolingba and Dacko), two former Prime Ministers (Ngoupandé and Lakoué) and Goumba, who had been the most successful opposition candidate in the 1993 election. The election was held on 19 September, and on 2 October the Constitutional Court announced that Patassé had been re-elected, with 51.6% of the total votes cast. Patassé's nearest rivals were Kolingba, with 19.4%, Dacko, with 11.2%, and Goumba, with 6.1%. The defeated candidates demanded the annulment of the election results, which they claimed had been manipulated, but asked their supporters to remain calm. On 22 October Patassé was sworn in as President for a further six-year term. In early November reappointed Prime Minister Dologuélé announced the formation of a new Council of Ministers, which included members of parties loyal to Patassé as well as independents, three opposition representatives and two members of the armed forces. The Government stated that its main priorities were to improve human development in the CAR and to combat poverty. Particular emphasis was also laid on restructuring the public sector and the armed forces.

In October 1999 Kofi Annan requested the UN Security Council to authorize the gradual withdrawal of MINURCA from the CAR over a three-month period, but in December the UN announced proposals to establish a Bureau de soutien à la consolidation de la paix en Centrafrique (BONUCA), in Bangui. BONUCA began its operation on the same day as the final withdrawal of MINURCA, 15 February 2000, with a one-year mandate. In September 2000 BONUCA's mandate was extended until the end of 2001, and in September 2001, following continued unrest, it was extended for another one-year period.

Meanwhile, in April 2000 the Dologuélé Government survived a vote of 'no confidence' proposed by the opposition in the Assemblée nationale. In November, thousands of civil servants staged a strike in support of their demands for the payment of at least 12 of the 30 months' salary arrears owed to them. The paralysis of public services exacerbated social tensions, and youths joined the protest movement, erecting barricades. Then 15 opposition parties united to demand the resignation of President Patassé and to announce, in December, the formation of a co-ordination committee with the aim of organizing a peaceful transfer of power. In April 2001 Patassé dismissed Dologuélé and appointed Martin Ziguélé as Prime Minister.

On 28 May 2001 rebel soldiers attacked Patassé's official residence in an attempted coup. However, the insurgency was quickly suppressed and order restored by troops loyal to Patassé. Libyan troops and helicopters and a contingent of rebels from the Democratic Republic of the Congo (DRC) arrived to support the Patassé regime. About 20 people were killed during the unsuccessful coup. Heavy fighting in Bangui resulted in some 300 deaths and an estimated 60,000–70,000 civilians were reported to have fled the capital. According to aid agencies, only about 10,000 had returned by mid-July. In August 2002 Kolingba and 20 associates were sentenced to death *in absentia* for involvement in the attempted coup; a further 500 defendants were reported to have received prison terms of 10–20 years.

In August 2001 the Council of Ministers was reshuffled. The Minister of National Defence, Jean-Jacques Démafouth, suspected of involvement in the May coup attempt, was replaced, but he was acquitted of all charges at his trial in October 2002. Gen. Bozizé was dismissed from the post of Chief of Staff of the armed forces in October and in early November, after attempts were made to arrest Bozizé, violence erupted in Bangui between supporters of Bozizé and the presidential guard supported by forces from Libya. Bozizé soon fled to southern Chad, where he and some 300 of his armed supporters were granted asylum. In December the CAR judiciary abandoned legal proceedings against Bozizé and in January 2002, during a meeting held in Chad, a government delegation invited Bozizé and his supporters to return to the CAR.

At a meeting of the Communauté économique et monétaire de l'Afrique centrale (CEMAC) in Libreville, Gabon, in early December 2001 a commission, chaired by President Omar Bongo of Gabon, was created to find a lasting solution to the crisis in the CAR. In April 2002 the Government proposed reforms to improve public services, promote good governance and eradicate poverty. However, in July the Minister of State in charge of Finance and the Budget, Eric Sorongopé, was arrested on suspicion of embezzling government funds. More than 20 government officials were also detained on suspicion of involvement in the widespread corruption scandal. The withdrawal of IMF and World Bank representatives from Bangui aggravated the ongoing budget crisis, and protests continued owing to the Government's failure to pay public-sector wages. In September BONUCA's mandate was extended until December 2003.

On 25 October 2002 the northern suburbs of Bangui were invaded by forces loyal to Bozizé. After five days of heavy fighting, pro-Government forces, supported by Libyan troops and about 1,000 soldiers from a DRC rebel grouping, the Mouvement pour la libération du Congo (MLC), succeeded in repelling the insurgents. The Patassé Government failed to fully suppress the forces allied to Bozizé and by December the CAR was divided between loyalist areas in the south and east and rebel-held northern regions between the Chadian border and Bangui. The UN expressed concern for the welfare of the approximately 150,000 refugees and displaced civilians positioned between Bozizé's forces and pursuing pro-Government troops.

In December 2002 the first contingent of a CEMAC peacekeeping force (eventually to number 350) arrived in Bangui, and in January 2003 Libyan forces were withdrawn. The CEMAC forces were mandated to protect the President, enforce security along the CAR–Chad border and help restructure the military. In December 2002 CAR security forces dispersed residents of Bangui who had erected road-blocks in protest at the presence of rebel fighters from the DRC who were engaged in raping and looting. In February 2003 MLC fighters began to withdraw from the CAR, in response to international pressure on the Patassé Government.

Meanwhile, in November 2002 President Patassé pledged his support for a national dialogue in order to resolve the conflict in the CAR. However, co-ordination efforts undertaken by Bishop Paulin Pomodimo were undermined by the refusal of both internal and exiled opposition leaders to agree on a date or location for the discussions. Nevertheless, in February 2003 Patassé announced the establishment of a new commission to rehabilitate officials returning from exile, and in March the RDC and other opposition parties resumed their participation in the Assemblée nationale.

BOZIZÉ ASSUMES POWER

On 15 March 2003 armed supporters of Bozizé and mercenaries from Chad converged on Bangui, encountering little resistance from government troops. President Patassé, returning from a regional summit in Niger, was forced to fly on to the Cameroonian capital, Yaoundé, after shots were fired at his plane as it approached Bangui. Casualties during the coup were estimated at no more than 15 people, but following an outbreak of looting throughout Bangui, a curfew was imposed on 16 March. After the surrender of security forces in the capital and a lack of resistance from CEMAC troops, Bozizé declared himself Head of State, dissolved the Assemblée nationale and suspended the Constitution. Although the coup was condemned by France, the African Union (AU), the UN, CEMAC and the USA, it was alleged to have had the covert support of France, Gabon and Chad. Bozizé announced that a new consensus government would be formed in consultation with the former opposition, human rights groups and development agencies and soon secured the approval of the Governments of Gabon and the Republic of the Congo. Bozizé also gained the support of opposition parties, which pledged to oppose any attempt by Patassé to return to power. In March Abel Goumba, leader of the FPP and a hero of the independence movement, was appointed as Prime Minister. A new, broadly based transitional Government was then formed. Despite receiving only two positions in the new Council of Ministers, in mid-April the MLPC declared that it would adhere to the transitional arrangements decreed by Bozizé. Public support for the new regime increased following the payment of public-sector salaries for the first time in more than two years. In April 2003 an amnesty for those convicted of involvement in the coup attempt of May 2001 was proclaimed. On 30 May Bozizé inaugurated a 98-member advisory Conseil national de transition (CNT), which included representatives of political parties, trade unions, religious organizations and human rights groups, in order to assist him in exercising legislative power during the transitional period, which was to last 18–30 months. The CNT subsequently elected Nicolas Tiangaye, a prominent human rights activist, as its speaker. Bozizé confirmed his intention to return the country to civilian rule in January 2005, after presidential and legislative elections and the approval of a new constitution, to be drafted by the CNT.

In mid-2003 the Bozizé regime gained increasing international recognition for its efforts to reform the country's institutions and to promote reconciliation, and in July UN agencies announced the resumption of food aid to the CAR. The CNT resolved that the long-delayed national dialogue, towards which the previous administration had made tentative efforts, would take place in mid-September. Several prominent political figures agreed to participate, including former Presidents Kolingba and Dacko. Meanwhile, the Government began prosecuting corruption within the country's economic institutions and civil service. In June the executive boards of the state electricity and telecommunications companies were dismissed owing to alleged accounting irregularities, and in July 866 non-existent workers were removed from the public-sector payroll. Judicial authorities began investigating the whereabouts of some 4,800m. francs CFA donated by the Japanese Government for the Patassé administration's reconciliation plans, and ordered the suspension of mineral and timber interests controlled by the former President. The Government also considered possible changes to the country's mining code in July and, in an effort to improve transparency, issued guidelines obliging government officials and politicians to declare their personal assets. In August the state prosecutor issued an international arrest warrant for Patassé, now in exile in Togo, on charges including murder and embezzlement. In September BONUCA's mandate was extended until December 2004.

Some 350 delegates, representing the Government, political organizations, trade unions, civil society and ethnic groups, participated in the national dialogue, which ended in late October 2003, and a panel was created to oversee the implementation of the delegates' recommendations, which included the establishment of a Truth and Reconciliation Commission. The curfew imposed in March was lifted at the end of October. In December Prime Minister Goumba was appointed Vice-President and a former financier, Célestin-Leroy Gaombalet, was named Prime Minister. In a subsequent government reshuffle 14 ministers retained their portfolios and new appointees also included several political figures linked to previous administrations. In late December the chief of presidential security, Col Danzoumi Yalo, and his brother, Sani Yalo, a businessman, were arrested on suspicion of plotting a coup. In that month a new mining code was also promulgated and new legislation appeared to limit the President's discretion over awarding contracts for mineral exploitation and strengthened the role of the security forces in monitoring illegal mining.

In January 2004 an eight-member inter-ministerial committee, headed by Prime Minister Gaombalet, was established to oversee the forthcoming electoral process. It was decided that a referendum on a new constitution drafted by the CNT would be held in November, with municipal, presidential and legislative elections to follow between December and January 2005. Although Bozizé had previously announced that he would not be a candidate in the next elections, in mid-June 2004 he declared his candidature possible. In early December the newly appointed Transitional Constitutional Court (TCC) oversaw the planned referendum on a new constitution, which was approved by 87.2% of those who voted. The new Constitution provided for a presidential term of five years, renewable only once, and increased powers for the Prime Minister. Following the referendum, Bozizé announced that presidential and legislative elections were to be rescheduled for mid-February 2005 and that he would stand as an independent candidate for the presidency. In late December 2004 the TCC disqualified nine presidential candidates including former President Patassé and former Prime Minister Ngoupandé. This decision, however, provoked popular unrest and in early January 2005 Bozizé annulled the disqualification of Ngoupandé and two other candidates.

THE 2005 ELECTIONS

Presidential and legislative elections were held concurrently on 13 March 2005. The pro-Bozizé 'Kwa na kwa' coalition secured 42 of the 105 seats in the new Assemblée nationale, while the Mouvement de libération du peuple Centrafricain (supporting former Prime Minister Martin Ziguélé) won 11 seats; 34 independent candidates were also elected. In the presidential election Bozizé secured 43.0% of the votes cast, while Ziguélé obtained 23.5% and Kolingba 16.4%. Since no candidate had won an absolute majority, Bozizé and Ziguélé competed in a second round of voting on 8 May; Bozizé was elected with some 64.7% of the total votes. Despite allegations by opposition groups of electoral malpractice, Ziguélé conceded defeat and appealed for calm from his supporters. The new Assemblée nationale convened on 9 June and Bozizé was sworn in as President two days later. Elie Doté was appointed Prime Minister and he presented a new Council of Ministers composed primarily of Kwa na kwa members, although also including two members of both the MLPC and the RDC. Doté promised to rid the public-sector payroll of fictitious workers, in order to help pay salary arrears.

In August 2005 floods rendered 6,500 people homeless in Bangui, resulting in an international aid effort. In October civil servants launched a strike to procure salary arrears and raises, while Doté suspended three ministers temporarily, pending investigation for alleged financial impropriety. In November civil servants agreed to suspend their strike for six months, but as the Government failed subsequently to pay salaries as promised, they resumed the strike. Finally, on 6 January 2006 the strike ended, services resumed and schools reopened. In November 2005, meanwhile, the Food and Agriculture Organization announced that widespread banditry in farming areas had increased the risk of food shortages in the northern prefectures of Ouham, Ouham Pende, Ouaka, Nana-Gribizi and Kemo. In December the Fonds d'entretien routier was established in order to improve and maintain national, regional and rural roads; none the less, bandits still made road travel dangerous. In December the AU reported that criminal gangs were recruiting pro-Patassé soldiers from groups such as the Union des forces républicaines (UFR), led by Lt François-Florian N'Djadder-Bedaya, and the Armée populaire pour la restauration de la république et la démocratie (APRD).

In late December 2005 the Assemblée granted Bozizé's request to rule by decree for nine months, a move criticized by the CAR Human Rights League, and in late January 2006 a cabinet reshuffle was effected. In April 2006 the Government requested that the International Court of Justice to conduct an investigation into former President Patassé's activities.

On 2 September 2006 Bozizé formed a new Government with Doté retained as Prime Minister and also assuming the position of Minister of Finance and Budget. Later that month Ziguélé was elected President of the MLPC. Also in September the Criminal Court acquitted 14 people accused of attempting to depose President Bozizé. In October teachers at the University of Bangui called for the Dean's resignation because their salaries were insufficient.

REBEL INSURGENCIES

During mid-2006 rebel activity in the north of the country became President Bozizé's most serious problem. During fighting in late June 14 soldiers were killed by rebels and in early July four senior armed forces officers were dismissed by the President on suspicion of being sympathetic to rebel groups. The Chief of Staff Gen. Antoine Gambi was replaced by Gen. Jules Bernard Ouandé. Meanwhile, Patassé was said to be financing the training of mercenaries on the northern border. In August Jean-Jacques Larmassoum, a rebel leader of the APRD, was sentenced to life in prison, and former President Patassé was sentenced to 20 years of forced labour *in absentia*.

In late October 2006 the village of Birao in the north-east of the country was taken by rebels of the Union des forces démocratiques pour le rassemblement (UFDR), a coalition created in Kigali, Rwanda in September by the Groupe d'action patriotique de la libération de Centrafrique (GAPLC), led by Michel Am Nondroko Djotodia, the Mouvement des libérateurs centrafricains pour la justice (MLCJ), led by Capt. Abakar Sabone, and the Front démocratique centrafricain (FDC), led by Commdt Justin Hassan. Within one week the UFDR rebels had seized control of most of the prefecture of Vakaga; however, in late November government forces and French troops regained control of Vakaga. Several rebel leaders, including Djotodia and Sabone were arrested in Benin, although Bangui's attempts to extradite these leaders failed and they were released in February 2007.

In November 2006 UN aid began to reach the devastated region around Kaga-Bandoro, which had been raided by road bandits known as 'zaranguinas', and from where thousands of local residents had fled to the prefecture of Nana-Gribizi. The Fédération internationale des droits de l'homme estimated that at least 70,000 people also fled to neighbouring Cameroon and Chad to escape fighting in the region between APRD rebels and government troops. In early November former Prime Minister and Médiateur de la République (National Ombudsman), Prof. Abel Goumba, had called for talks between the Government and rebel leaders in order to end such violence. Also in November Sabone, as spokesman for the UFDR rebel coalition, insisted that a transitional Government with a Muslim Prime Minister be inaugurated, and that a quota for Muslim participation in the Government be established.

In mid-November 2006 President El Hadj Omar (Albert-Bernard) Bongo Ondimba of Gabon announced that troops from that country were to be deployed to the CAR to serve as part of the Force multinationale de la CEMAC (FOMUC). Days later humanitarian organizations decided to suspend their operations in the Paoua region due to ongoing conflict there. Also in that month France dispatched a further 100 troops to join the 200-strong force already based in Boali.

In late November 2006 the Forces armées centrafricaines (FACA), assisted by French troops, regained control of Birao, but UFDR rebels took control of Ndélé and Bamingui. In early December French troops forced the UFDR rebels to abandon Ndélé and went on to attack rebels in Ouanda-Djallé. Later that month Bozizé visited Birao to demonstrate government control of the region.

In early January 2007 the UFDR announced that the Front démocratique de libération du peuple centrafricain (FDPC), led by Abdoulaye Miskine, was not part of its coalition. APRD rebels attacked Paoua in mid-January but were unable to retain control of the town. On 25 January and 1 February in Sirte, Libya, President Bozizé met with Miskine and the APRD supporter André Ringui Le Gaillard, a former minister under Patassé. A peace agreement was signed on 2 February between the CAR Government, the FDPC and the APRD and the following day Bozizé returned to Bangui with Miskine, who was accused of war crimes by human rights organizations.

In late February 2007 Bozizé and Miskine returned to Libya, where Revolutionary Leader Col Muammar al-Qaddafi asked Miskine to persuade UFDR leaders to sign the Sirte agreement. However, in March 2007 rebels launched further attacks on Birao and FACA forces were obliged to assist the CAR to regain control of the region. Later that month Bozizé appealed to all rebel groups to sign the Sirte accord. In mid-April Gen. Raymond Ndougou of the CAR armed forces and the UFDR leader, Zakaria Damane, signed a new 10-point peace agreement at Birao. Both sides agreed to end their confrontation and the UFDR was granted permission to engage in politics. In mid-May Sabone announced that he did not accept the Birao agreement and that his MLCJ military front and the UFDR intended to continue their struggle. In late May 2007 approximately 1,000 UFDR rebels were reported to have entered the CAR from Darfur via the Sudanese Am Dafok border post. Damane explained that they had entered disguised as refugees.

In late June 2007 a local government source reported that gunmen, believed to have crossed the border from the CAR, had attacked civilians in a remote part of Cameroon, killing one person and kidnapping 22 others. Meanwhile, earlier in that month a Médecins sans frontières (MSF) employee was killed by gunfire during an assessment mission in north-west CAR. Following the incident, MSF-France and other non governmental organizations, including the International Committee of the Red Cross, temporarily suspended work around Paoua.

EXTERNAL RELATIONS

The CAR's relations with France, the former colonial power, have remained important. France is still the principal source of foreign aid, and French advisers oversee the CAR's security services. For many years France maintained a military presence in the CAR, which was regarded as a vital element of its strategy in the region, notably with regard to Chad. However, in accordance with a foreign policy decision by France during the late 1990s to disengage forces from its former African colonies, the French military presence in the CAR was substantially reduced during October 1997–April 1998. Following the overthrow of President Patassé in March 2003, the French Government deployed some 300 troops in Bangui, initially to protect foreign citizens, but later to provide training for CAR military units. In mid-2003 France was reported to have contributed some US $10.2m. in support of CEMAC's expanded peace-keeping operations throughout the CAR; these were reported in August 2003 to have been successful in restoring order in the north of the country, which had remained unstable since the coup in March. In December 2006 France granted the CAR €1m. to help that country pay its debt to the African Development Bank. Prime Minister Doté then travelled to Addis Ababa, Ethiopia to attend an AU Peace and Security Council meeting, where he thanked France for providing military support to the CAR armed forces.

In May 1997 the CAR recognized the administration of President Laurent Kabila in the DRC (formerly Zaire). In the same month the CAR and the DRC signed a mutual assistance pact, which provided for permanent consultation on internal security and defence. The pact also sought to guarantee border security; however, during mid-1997 armed soldiers of what had been the Zairean army were reported to be fleeing troops loyal to Kabila and crossing the Oubangui river into the CAR. In January 1999 some 5,000 Congolese civilians crossed the Oubangui to escape the fighting between government troops and the rebel soldiers occupying the northern part of the DRC. Although the CAR had not formally ratified the treaty of mutual assistance with the DRC, in early 1999 the authorities permitted DRC troops to enter CAR territory in order to try to halt the rebel advance in the north. In August 1999 the regional office of the UN High Commissioner for Refugees (UNHCR) reported that the CAR was sheltering about 54,000 refugees from conflicts in the DRC, Chad and Sudan. However, as the security situation within the CAR worsened, in December 2001 UNHCR announced plans to establish a new camp in the DRC for refugees fleeing political unrest in that country. Following the attempted coup in the CAR in May 2001, UNHCR estimated that 23,000 people had escaped to the DRC; further movements were reported in the aftermath of the attempted coup of October 2002.

In late 1994 the CAR and Chad agreed to establish a bilateral security structure to ensure mutual border security. Attacks on Chadian nationals resident in Bangui and on the Chadian contingent of the MISAB forces in late 1996 and early 1997 led the Chadian Government to issue a communiqué in March 1997 warning that further incidences of such aggression would not be tolerated. In June 1999 President Patassé issued an official apology to Chad following a disturbance at a market in Bangui in which five Chadian nationals were killed by members of the CAR security forces. In August the CAR Government agreed to pay compensation to the families of the victims. None the less, in December it was reported that some 1,500 Chadian refugees were preparing to leave the CAR, allegedly owing to fears for their security following the imminent departure of MINURCA forces. Relations between the CAR and Chad deteriorated when armed men, led by a Chadian rebel, raided southern Chad from the CAR on 29 and 31 December 2001; four people were killed during the raids. A further outbreak of violence in the border area was reported in April 2002, which resulted in at least one fatality. Despite pledges by both countries to increase co-operation, further clashes in August resulted in the deaths of 20 CAR soldiers. The CAR's decision to appoint Col Martin Koumtamadji as the head of a special unit in the CAR military, charged with securing the common border, further strained relations, as did Chad's reputed sponsorship of forces loyal to Bozizé. In early October a CEMAC summit in Libreville, Gabon, sought to defuse tensions between the two countries; in accordance with an agreement reached at the summit, Bozizé and Koumtamadji were subsequently granted asylum in France and Togo, respectively, and in December the first contingent of a CEMAC force was deployed in Bangui, initially to protect Patassé and later to monitor joint patrols of the border by Chadian and CAR troops. Meanwhile, at the end of October, following a coup attempt in the CAR (see above), Chad accused CAR security forces of the massacre of some 80–120 Chadian civilians in Bangui, a claim denied by the Patassé Government, which, in turn, accused Chad of planning the annexation of northern areas of the CAR. However, relations between the two countries subsequently began to improve somewhat, and in January 2003 the Governments of the CAR, Chad and Sudan announced their intention to establish a tripartite committee to oversee the security and stability of their joint borders. In February, following an official visit by Chadian President Idriss Deby Itno to the CAR, many Chadian nationals were released from imprisonment in the CAR. Following Bozizé's assumption of power in the CAR in March 2003, the Chadian Government dispatched some 400 troops to Bangui, apparently in order to reinforce CEMAC's peace-keeping force, although in May it was reported that only some 120 Chadian soldiers were to be formally integrated into CEMAC's operations in the CAR, which were initially scheduled to end in January 2005. However, CEMAC troops were still present in the CAR at the end of June 2005, when it was announced that operations would continue at least until the end of the year. By mid-2005 there were thought to be some 38,500 refugees living in Chad who had fled unrest in the CAR.

In April 1999 the CAR signed a treaty of friendship and co-operation with Togo. Patassé maintained a close association with the country and was granted asylum by the Togolese Government after being overthrown in March 2003. The Patassé Government was closely allied with Libya, and in April 1999 the CAR joined the Libyan-sponsored Community of Sahel-Saharan States (CEN-SAD). Relations were strained by the Bozizé Government's repossession of assets ceded to Libya by the previous administration, although the two countries resumed diplomatic relations in July 2003. In July 2004 Bozizé made his first state visit to Libya, praising that country's contribution to peace, stability and development in the CAR.

Following the successfully held legislative and presidential elections in 2005, the AU's Peace and Security Council voted in late June to reintegrate the CAR into the Union and to lift the sanctions imposed on the country following the coup of March 2003. In June 2005 Bozizé's new democratic mandate was welcomed by many countries, some of which donated funds to the CAR over the following months to support its democratic institutions. On 1 July heads of state of the CEMAC nations extended FOMUC's mandate for at least six months. In the following month France donated €4m. to post-conflict recovery projects. In early December the People's Republic of China and the CAR signed an accord on rural development and military co-operation, while later that month the Assemblée nationale ratified the non-aggression, solidarity and mutual assistance pact of CEMAC countries. Also in December, Bozizé forged ties with the Tripoli-based World Association for the Islamic Call while on an official visit to Libya, which he visited again in January 2006.

Meanwhile, in late December 2005 the mandate of FOMUC was again extended to help restore security and stability in the CAR, especially in the north. In January France and the CAR announced their support of a project intended to stimulate the use of the internet in the country. In February Sudan, the CAR and UNHCR agreed to allow the repatriation from the CAR to Sudan of several thousand refugees, thought to total some 16,000. In April the CAR asked France for military assistance following a border violation by an aircraft reportedly transporting unidentified armed men. Also in April, Bozizé made a brief visit to South Africa where an agreement was signed for greater co-operation between the two countries.

In August 2006 Bozizé travelled to Côte d'Ivoire and then to Gabon to attend Independence Day celebrations. In mid-September Bozizé attended the 14th Conference of the Non-aligned Movement held in Havana, Cuba, where he held talks with Esteban Lazo, a member of Cuba's Communist Party Political Bureau and later that month Bozizé attended the 11th La Francophonie Summit in Bucharest, Romania, where he met with French President Jacques Chirac.

In October 2006 the European Union (EU) granted €5m. for a health-irrigation project in Bangui. Also in that month Bozizé and a group of CAR businessmen travelled to the People's Republic of China for a 10-day visit aimed at strengthening economic and diplomatic ties between the two nations, although Bozizé was unable to attend a China-Africa Summit in Beijing the following month because of rebel activity in northern CAR. Nevertheless, in November China agreed to provide the CAR with approximately €5m. for development projects and in January 2007 the Chinese Minister of Foreign Affairs visited Bangui.

In November 2006 Bozizé accused Sudanese President Omar Hassan Ahmad al-Bashir of attempting to destabilize the CAR. A goodwill mission was then sent to Bangui by the Sudanese Government to reassure Bozizé that Sudan was not supporting the various rebel groups active in the border. However, a visit to Khartoum planned for early December by Bozizé was cancelled and relations between Bangui and Khartoum remain strained.

In November 2006 the World Bank granted US $82m. in subsidies to the CAR and in December the IMF granted $54.5m. in aid over a three-year period for a plan to reduce poverty. In early March 2007 the EU Commissioner for Development and Humanitarian Aid, Louis Michel, travelled to Bangui to discuss European financial support for the CAR and in mid-May 2007 KfW, the German Development Bank, granted aid to the CAR for the implementation of development projects in the Bossangoa area. In June Prime Minister Doté attended a Development Partner Consultation for the CAR, convened in Brussels, Belgium, and organized with the support of the UN Development Programme and the World Bank. That organization subsequently approved a regional operation, costing US $201m., to finance transport and trade improvements in Cameroon, Chad and the CAR.

Economy

CHARLOTTE VAILLANT

Based on an earlier article by EDITH HODGKINSON

While the economy of the Central African Republic (CAR) is constrained by the country's land-locked location and its small population, it has a good primary resource base, notably diamonds and rainforest timber, and relatively diversified agriculture. The record since independence has, however, been patchy. Under the first Government of President David Dacko (to 1965) the economy stagnated, as cotton output fell. In 1966 the new military Government, under Jean-Bédel Bokassa, introduced measures to revive agricultural production and to encourage rural development. During the early 1970s economic stagnation and recession recurred, and the country's economic plight was a prime factor in the military take-over in 1981. The new Government under Gen. André Kolingba immediately negotiated a standby credit from the IMF, paving the way for a rescheduling of the country's debt. The austerity programme that the Government was required to implement generated such severe political strains that the Kolingba Government temporarily reneged on its budgetary promises in 1983. However, it could not hold out for long, and the IMF-approved programme was soon reinstated. A significant step forward was the three-year structural adjustment facility agreed with the IMF in 1987. The programme this supported aimed to liberalize the economy, to foster private enterprise and to improve public finances, primarily through policies of retrenchment in the civil service and the liquidation or privatization of parastatal organizations. Considerable progress was made along these lines, and real growth in gross domestic product (GDP) was a steady 2% per year in 1988–90. A second structural adjustment programme was agreed in 1990.

By the early 1990s, however, the overvaluation of the CFA franc was having a markedly adverse effect on the economy, depressing the coffee and cotton sectors and stimulating a high level of diamond smuggling. In 1994 the 50% devaluation of the CFA franc gave a major immediate boost to local manufacturing and coffee and cotton exports, accelerating GDP growth to 4.9% in 1994 and 7.2% in 1995. However, the newly installed Ange-Félix Patassé Government procrastinated on the implementation of the reforms necessary to secure an Enhanced Structural Adjustment Facility (ESAF) from the IMF, thereby failing to take advantage of the willingness of the CAR's major aid donors to increase funding and to reduce the debt burden. Corruption and financial mismanagement, including the failure to pay arrears on public-sector and military salaries, caused the army mutinies of 1996, and contributed to the 4.0% fall in GDP in that year. The economy recovered substantially with the return of peace in 1997, with GDP growing by 7.5%. In June 1998, conscious of the political need to deliver regular growth and to guarantee the payment of salaries in the public sector, the Patassé Government accepted IMF conditions for an ESAF, valued at US $66m.; the CAR was thus the last Franc Zone country to secure this facility in the wake of the devaluation of the CFA franc.

The new programme, which covered the period to 2001, emphasized the implementation of privatizations and the enhancement of government revenue, rather than cuts in spending. Progress in 1999 was satisfactory, with movement on privatization of the two major commercial banks, as well as the petroleum distribution company, and strong growth in tax revenues. Economic growth was, meanwhile, maintained at 3.9% in 1998 and 3.6% in 1999.

In 2000 shortcomings in programme implementation delayed the approval of the second annual arrangement under the IMF facility (renamed Poverty Reduction and Growth Facility—PRGF). The accumulation of domestic payments arrears, including salaries, aggravated social tensions, leading to industrial action by public-sector workers across all sectors in late 2000 and early 2001. This, coupled with higher international petroleum prices and a doubling in petroleum transportation costs following a suspension of imports from the Democratic Republic of the Congo (DRC), caused growth in 2000 to decelerate significantly to 1.8%. Further unrest, following the attempted coup in May 2001, also destabilized the domestic economy in 2001, when GDP grew by only 0.3%. Negotiations with the IMF continued after the PRGF expired, leading to the approval of a six-month Staff Monitored Programme in October 2001 to monitor progress. However, the discovery of a widespread embezzlement scandal in the Ministry of Finance and the Budget in July 2002 further undermined creditor confidence in the CAR. The Government was unable to complete its IMF-approved programme of structural and fiscal reforms, and the IMF and the World Bank suspended operations in the country.

Between October 2002 and March 2003 economic activity was disrupted by fighting between government troops and those loyal to Gen. François Bozizé Yangovounda, the former Chief of Staff of the armed forces. As a result, GDP declined by 0.6% in 2002 and by 7.6% in 2003, with the formal economy shattered by the destruction and looting. Following his assumption of power in March 2003 Bozizé and his new transitional Government began diplomatic efforts to secure financial assistance from international donors. After two successive missions to the country, the IMF approved an Emergency Post-Conflict Assistance programme (EPCA) in July 2004 to support the Government's programme of reforms. However, the Government failed to meet the programme's targets and in February 2005 the IMF deferred discussions for the renewal of the EPCA until after the presidential election, which was eventually held on 13 March after administrative delays. Following two visits to the country, the IMF eventually approved a second EPCA (worth US $10.2m.) at the end of January 2006. A satisfactory implementation of the second EPCA triggered the approval of a new three-year PRGF (worth US $54.5m.) by the IMF in December 2006. Improved security conditions and the resumption of donor support contributed to a recovery in economic growth, with GDP rising by 1.3% in 2004, 2.2% in 2005 and an estimated 3.5% in 2006, according to the IMF.

AGRICULTURE

Agriculture, forestry and fishing dominate the economy, contributing an estimated 56.5% of GDP in 2005 and employing about 56% of the economically active population in that year. In 1995–2006 agricultural GDP grew at an average annual rate of 3.0%; growth in 2006 was 3.5%. Agriculture is concentrated in the tropical rain forest area of the south-west and the savannah lands in the central region and north-west. Output of the major food crops (cassava, maize, millet, sorghum, groundnuts and rice) increased in the late 1990s, as the Government put greater emphasis on this sector in its regional development programmes. As a result the CAR reached near self-sufficiency in staple foods, mostly cassava, sorghum and millet. Agricultural diversification was also promoted, mainly to substitute imports. This notably involved a palm oil complex at Bossongo, with an annual capacity of 7,500 metric tons, servicing 2,500 ha of plantations, and a sugar refinery at Ouaka, supplied from 1,300 ha of new plantations. The Government also encouraged the cultivation of vegetables for export to the European market, with peppers and green beans cultivated in an area within easy reach of the country's international airport at Bangui. Performance in agriculture has been particularly uneven in recent years. As a consequence of the fighting, agricultural production and supply declined sharply during 2003, especially in the north-west of the country, where the rebellion began. It recovered in 2004, supported by an improved security situation and increased planting, reaching 1.00m. tons in 2005. Agricultural production is estimated to have increased slightly in 2006, to 1,02m.

tons, according to the regional central bank, the Banque des Etats d'Afrique Centrale (BEAC). However, improved production did not prevent severe localized food shortages, a result of continued instability in the north of the country that has already caused the displacement of thousands of people. Given the importance of the agriculture sector, the Government has tried in recent years to revive it; in particular, a three-year recovery plan for cotton, coffee and tobacco was presented in early 2007.

Coffee was superseded by cotton as the CAR's major export crop from the mid-1990s, as falling international prices led to a reduction in coffee output; coffee export earnings slumped from 10.2% of recorded export earnings in 1999 to less than 2% in 2001. Formerly produced on large, European-owned plantations, it is now the domain of smallholders. The crop is cultivated mainly in the south-western and central-southern regions of the country, and more than 90% is of the robusta variety. The Agence de développement de la zone caféière is the parastatal organization responsible for the purchase, transportation and marketing of this commodity. After reaching a peak of 18,000 metric tons in 1996, production levels have rapidly declined, reflecting poor growing conditions, a decline in world prices and continued insecurity, which has hampered farming activities. Coffee production fell from 5,520 tons in 2002/03 to 2,700 tons in 2004/05, according to the International Coffee Organization (ICO). It recovered slightly, to 2,760 tons in 2005/06, and was projected to reach 6,000 tons in 2006/07, according to the ICO.

Cotton, the country's leading export crop, is also cultivated by smallholders, principally in the north-east of the country. Cotton export earnings have declined dramatically over the past decade. In 2002 cotton contributed 6.3% of total exports, compared with 17.5% in 1997. The sector increasingly suffered from the overvaluation of the CFA franc, which kept producer prices low, while the Government was unable to maintain its subsidy payments. By 1993 output of seed cotton was down to 15,966 metric tons, one-half of the average in the 1980s. Boosted by much higher prices since the 1994 currency devaluation, the area under cultivation has risen by one-third since the beginning of the decade, and the crop was at a record 46,037 tons in 1996/97, when cotton gins were operating at full capacity. Although the sector subsequently encountered difficulties the long-term outlook for the CAR's cotton crop is favourable, particularly as it is less vulnerable to drought than some other crops. With international cotton prices rising, seed cotton output increased by an estimated 34% from 24,500 tons in 2000/01 to 32,900 tons in 2001/02. In May 2002 the cotton utility, Société cotonnière centrafricaine (SOCOCA), was liquidated and replaced by partly state-owned Société centrafricaine de développement des textiles (SOCADETEX). The bulk of the cotton harvest in 2002/03 was left unpurchased, however, as a result of the political and civil disruption. In addition, the fighting and looting greatly damaged the industry's infrastructure, with five ginning complexes left in need of repair. Consequently, seed cotton production declined to 14,000 tons in 2002/03, 6,800 tons in 2003/04 and to an estimated 5,500 tons in 2004/05, according to the BEAC. Given continued instability in the north-west of the country—where most of the cotton is grown—and SOCADETEX's financial difficulties that have resulted in arrears in payments to cotton producers, cotton production is estimated to have remained at the same levels in 2005/06; a recovery to 6,600 tons was expected in 2006/07, once the reconstruction of a number ginneries is completed. Meanwhile, the Government stepped up efforts to revive the sector. In April 2006 specifically, it decided to liquidate SOCADETEX as a result of financial difficulties; meanwhile, it plans to acquire a controlling interest in the new company and negotiate a partnership with French company Dagris, which had owned a stake in SOCADETEX.

For decades efforts have been made to develop the livestock industry, and the number of cattle has increased substantially, despite the problems caused by droughts, the limitations of available fodder and the prevalence of the tsetse fly. Efforts are being made to improve marketing, and to encourage the sedentary raising of cattle to allow for treatment against disease. The herd has also grown as a result of migration from Chad and Sudan. Many herdsmen in the north fled the CAR during 2002–2003, as a result of the rebellion. In 2004 increased stability favoured the return of some herdsmen, and there were an estimated 3.4m. head of cattle and 3.1m. goats. The BEAC estimated a total of 13.8m. head of livestock in 2006, an increase of 4.4% compared with 2005. Nevertheless, domestic meat production fails to satisfy demand, and development of the sector is hindered by widespread land disputes between livestock producers and crop producers.

The CAR's large forest resources (an estimated 102,000 sq km of tropical rain forest) are at present under-exploited commercially, largely as a result of a lack of adequate roads and low-cost means of transportation to the coast. Only about 10% of the forest area is accessible to river transport. In addition, large areas are held as private hunting reserves. Nevertheless, timber exploitation expanded considerably from the late 1960s, following the formation of new companies geared to export and the establishment of new sawmills. The forestry sector continues to face major constraints, including low water levels on the traditional transport route along the Congo river and smuggling. In mid-2003 the new Government of Gen. Bozizé suspended all licences awarded under the previous administration, pending the results of a review of the sector. This led to a fall in annual wood production to 524,500 cu m. A total of 276,200 cu m was exported, mostly to Europe and neighbouring countries. According to the BEAC, wood production recovered slightly to 584,900 cu m in 2004, 530,022 cu m in 2005 and an estimated 709,970 cu m in 2006, while there are plans to improve the road network in the logging areas.

MINING

The contribution of mining to GDP is likely to be much greater than the IMF estimate of 6.9% in 2003, since an estimated one-half of the output of diamonds, the leading mineral, is thought to be smuggled out of the country and, so, escapes the official record. In the CAR diamonds are found in widely scattered alluvial deposits (mainly in the south-west and west of the country), rather than Kimberlite deposits, which are concentrated and, thus, more easily exploited and policed. The decline in recorded output, from a peak of 609,000 carats in 1968 to 416,400 carats in 2002, is partly attributable to increased smuggling, a concomitant of which has been a decline in the quality of officially traded stones. Independent observers have estimated illegal exports at some 500,000 carats per year. The Government aims to encourage the development of local cutting and polishing industries; by the early 2000s, however, there was still only one diamond-cutting centre and exports of diamonds remained almost entirely in uncut form. Exports of diamonds provided some 36% of total export revenue in 2002. In mid-2003 the new Bozizé Government initiated a thorough review of the CAR's mining code, suspended all mining permits and closed mining interests controlled by former President Patassé. It was estimated that 50% of potential revenue from taxes on diamond exports were lost to smuggling and corruption under the Patassé administration. As a result, diamond production fell to an estimated 332,700 carats in 2003. Furthermore, in July 2003 the CAR became a participant in the Kimberley Process, an international certification scheme aimed at excluding from the world market diamonds that have been traded for arms by rebel movements in conflict zones. A new mining code was finally adopted in December 2003, with new measures allowing for greater transparency in the issuing of licences and greater control on diamond-smuggling. The Government also initiated negotiations with the South African diamond company De Beers, which resulted in the attribution of exploration permits in 2004 and the signature of an agreement in April 2005. Meanwhile, the Central African Mining Company and the Central African Diamond Company, both subsidiaries of the Canadian company Energem, resumed mining operations in May 2004. Efforts to combat fraud in the sector continued in recent years, notably with the introduction of new export rules in November 2005. Overall diamond production rose to 585,600 carats in 2004 but fell back to 383,295 carats in 2005, according to the BEAC. Production was estimated to have increased by 8.4%, to 415,530 carats in 2006. Despite the temporary suspensions of permits in September the Government awarded more than 50 exploration licences in 2005.

Gold is also mined, although production levels have fluctuated sharply, from a peak of 538 kg in 1980 to just 7 kg in 2003. The signing of a first 25-year gold mining convention in January 2006 with Aurafrique, a subsidiary of the Canadian company Axim, was expected to increase gold production in the long-term. Uranium has been discovered near Bakouma, 480 km east of Bangui. Reserves are estimated at 20,000 metric tons, with a concentration ratio of some 50%. In recent years rising uranium prices and falling world stock have resulted in renewed interest from foreign companies in the Bakouma site; and a licence to mine uranium was eventually attributed to South Africa's Uramin in 2006. The Bakouma uranium mining project was officially inaugurated in October 2006. Reserves of iron ore, copper, tin, lignite and limestone have also been located, although the inadequacy of the country's transport infrastructure has deterred mining companies from attempting their commercial exploitation.

MANUFACTURING AND POWER

Manufacturing is based on the processing of primary products and is relatively undeveloped, contributing an estimated 2.4% of GDP in 2003. In the mid-1990s the major activities were the processing of foods, beverages and tobacco, furniture, fixtures and paper and textiles. Out of 250 enterprises that were in operation before the 1996 mutiny, only a dozen, often involving foreign participation, have survived: these include the Société centrafricaine de cigarettes (SOCACIG—tobacco, reopened in 2000), the Société de gestion des sucreries centrafricaines (SOGESCA—sugar, privatized in 2003), MOCAF (beverages), the Société centrafricaine de développement des textiles (SOCADETEX—as SOCOCA was renamed after being privatized), Centrafricaine des palmeraies (CENTRAPALM—palm oil, mooted for privatization), and a number of saw mills. A total of more than 3,000 jobs were lost, as a result of the continued unrest. The sector recovered a little during 1999 and 2001, despite energy rationing. Manufacturing activities suffered greatly from the political and civil disruption during October 2002 and March 2003, notably ginning activities, as SOCADETEX suspended operations and several ginneries were destroyed. In real terms, the GDP of the manufacturing sector declined by 9.5% in 2002 and by an estimated 22.4% in 2003. Many public and private enterprises and public administration buildings operating around Bangui were looted, contributing to a significant fall in production capacity not only in goods, but also in services. However, manufacturing activity was estimated by the BEAC to have increased by 6.5% in 2006.

The main source of power supply is hydroelectric, at the two stations at the Boali falls. Electricity coverage is low, at approximately 3% of the total population. Plans have been under way to construct a new hydroelectric plant at Kembe for several years, but no progress was made owing to the lack of funding. The Government has announced several projects in recent years to increase the country's hydroelectric capacity and reduce electricity shortages, but their implementation will depend on the Government's ability to secure sufficient funding. A significant strand of the Patassé Government's privatization programme was the divestment of its holdings in the state power utility, the Société énergie de Centrafrique (ENERCA), and the petroleum distribution company, the Société centrafricaine des pétroles (PETROCA). The latter was privatized in 1999, with the network taken over by Elf and Total of France (now Total) and Shell, while ENERCA's power distribution division was put out to tender in early 2000. In July 2003 Bozizé's Government announced that corruption and mismanagement at ENERCA, SODECA and at the state-owned telephone company over the previous two years had resulted in a total loss of 15,000m. francs CFA for the Government. There was little progress to redress the financial situation of the three state-owned companies, although the Government held discussions in order to establish a road-map aimed at the electricity sector's full liberalization. Given the company's parlous finances, the first step will be to restructure Enerca's debts.

TRANSPORT AND TELECOMMUNICATIONS

The transport infrastructure is underdeveloped and a major constraint on the country's economic development. There is an extensive network of roads (an estimated 23,810 km in 1999), but only about 2% of the system is paved. The road network has suffered serious deterioration, owing to lack of maintenance, due to the Government's budget crisis. However, international development organizations and bilateral donors have extended funds for road rehabilitation projects. There is no railway, but there are long-standing plans to extend the Transcameroon line to Bangui and also to link the CAR with the rail systems in Sudan and Gabon. A large volume of freight is carried by river; of a total of 7,000 km of inland waterways, some 2,800 km are navigable, most importantly the Oubangui river south of Bangui, which is the country's main outlet for external trade, and the Sangha and Lobaye rivers. Port facilities are being improved, with assistance from France and the European Union (EU).

The principal route for the import and export trade has traditionally been the trans-equatorial route, which involves 1,800 km by river from Bangui to Brazzaville, in the Republic of the Congo, and then rail from Brazzaville to Pointe-Noire. However, instability in the Republic of the Congo since 1997, and in the neighbouring DRC since 2000, have led to periodic suspension of this service. River traffic has therefore declined, as importers and exporters have turned to the new land route through Cameroon, although the outlet via Pointe Noire remains important for timber shipments. Improved security conditions in the CAR and the rest of the region, coupled with the Government's commitment to reduce the number of road blocks, could enhance transport in the foreseeable future. The rehabilitation of major road and river infrastructure will largely depend on forthcoming financial support from the EU and other donors.

There is an international airport at Bangui-M'Poko, and there are also 37 small airports. However, internal services are irregular, underserviced and dependent on the availability of fuel.

The telecommunications sector is limited but has grown rapidly in recent years, driven by mobile cellular telephone services. The privatization of the parastatal Société Centrafricaine de Télécommunications (SOCATEL) has been delayed indefinitely since 2003. Three mobile telephone companies, Telecel (since 1996, with an estimated 40,000 subscribers in 2006), Nationalink (since 2004, with an estimated 20,000 subscribers) and Atlantique Cellulaire (an estimated 20,000 subscribers) operate in the country. In addition, in April 2007 France Télécom acquired a mobile telephone and internet licence in the country and expected to launch operations by the end of the year. Most mobile phone services have been concentrated around the capital, Bangui.

PUBLIC FINANCE

The CAR's fiscal position remains extremely weak, a situation compounded by continued political instability. The narrow tax base is vulnerable to adverse trends in international prices for coffee and cotton and prone to erosion as a result of tax evasion and smuggling, while losses incurred by the parastatal organizations and personnel expenditure for the cumbersome civil service have put constant pressure on public spending. Salaries absorbed 76.9% of tax and non-tax revenue in 2005 according to IMF estimates, although salaries arrears continued to accumulate each year. Meanwhile, the combined debt of the three public utilities (electricity, water and telecommunication) was close to 8% of GDP in 2003.

The slow pace of economic reform meant that by 1994 the budget deficit had risen to 36,000m. francs CFA (7% of GDP; excluding grants the deficit was almost twice as high). The deficit before grants was brought down slightly in 1995 only through the non-payment of salaries. The resulting unrest and political insecurity damaged the domestic revenue base in 1996–97. In July 1999 the IMF noted that, while progress had been less than envisaged under the terms of the ongoing economic programme, the CAR had succeeded in improving budgetary receipts, from 6.1% of GDP in 1996 to an estimated 9.1% of GDP in 1999. Total revenues steadily increased, after value-added tax of 18% was introduced in January 2001, reaching the equivalent of 10.8% of GDP in 2002. Excluding grants excluded, the government budget fell from a deficit equivalent to 6.6% of GDP in 2000 to 4.3% of GDP in 2001, rising slightly to 5.0% of GDP in 2002. Improved revenue collection, coupled with continued donor support, permitted a much-needed rise in capital expenditures. This proved insufficient to avoid cash rationing, however, with the Government accumulating fresh external and domestic payment arrears, including wages, in 2000–02. Revenue fell by around 32% in nominal terms in 2003, to 7.7% of GDP, owing to the economic downturn and the collapse of public services (including tax administration). External grants, meanwhile, decreased by 57% to 10,100m. francs CFA, after most donors withheld their financial assistance to the country in the wake of the March 2003 coup. On the expenditure side, capital spending was curtailed from 46,000m. francs CFA in 2002 to 19,500m. francs CFA in 2003. Obligations on recurrent spending were only partly met, leading to a new accumulation of domestic and external payment arrears (including salaries and interest payments on multilateral debt) totalling 215,000m. francs CFA, or 31% of GDP, at the end of December 2003. The budget deficit, excluding grants and on a commitment basis, rose to 3.1% of GDP. In order to maintain a tight budget in 2004, the Government took measures to reduce the salaries of ministers and top-earning civil servants by 25%–30%, to reform taxes and regulations in the mining and forestry sectors, to overhaul tax and custom administration and to combat tax fraud. These measures helped to improve tax collection, and revenue was estimated at 11.4% of GDP in 2004.

Despite the Government's efforts to reduce the wage bill, expenditure rose to an estimated 13.5% of GDP, and the budget balance, excluding grants, deteriorated further, to an estimated 5.5% of GDP, according to the IMF. Meanwhile, payments of domestic arrears were suspended. Following the legislative and presidential elections of May 2005, which represented a return to democratic rule, it was hoped that external aid would resume rapidly. In July the EU resumed its €100m. aid allocation to the CAR for 2002–07, intended for infrastructural improvements, and it was announced that further EU aid would be dependent upon the approval of an IMF assistance plan. The IMF delegation to the CAR in that month praised efforts made by the Government to eradicate corruption and lower the public-sector wage bill. However, the Fund expressed concern at a number of shortcomings in the Government's macroeconomic management, especially the recorded year-on-year reduction in government revenues in the first half of 2005. The Government subsequently implemented austerity measures, including a 12-month 'freeze' on public-service recruitment and the conduct of a payroll audit and civil-servants census in order to reduce the number of civil servants. These measures, coupled with the holding of successful elections in 2005 and improved security conditions in the country, were positive signs, which contributed to the IMF's decision to approve a second EPCA at the end of January 2006. While agreeing a new aid programme, the IMF stressed the need for the Government to increase revenue and control the public-sector wage bill. Meanwhile, although revenue rose to an estimated 12.2% of GDP in 2005, expenditure increased more rapidly (as a result notably of election-related spending), to 16.7% of GDP, resulting in the widening of the fiscal deficit, to an estimated 8.5% of GDP. In 2006 the Government continued to pursue a prudent fiscal policy, containing spending—in particular the wage bill—while boosting revenue through reforms in the tax and customs administration. Overall, the IMF expected the fiscal deficit (excluding grants) to fall to 4% of GDP in 2006. The satisfactory implementation of the second EPCA programme, coupled with continued efforts by the Government to improve economic management and the fiscal position, contributed to the approval by the IMF of a three-year (2007–09) poverty reduction and growth facility (PRGF) in December 2006, providing for US $54.5m in funding.

FOREIGN TRADE AND THE BALANCE OF PAYMENTS

The CAR's foreign trade balance turned from historically persistent, but relatively modest, deficits in the 1980s and early 1990s to small surpluses from the mid-1990s. Structural weaknesses (especially in transport), political instability and fluctuations in the international prices for diamonds, coffee, timber and cotton have prevented the CAR's exports from reaching their full potential. In addition, a large proportion of diamond and wood exports are thought to be unrecorded. The impact of the 1994 devaluation of the CFA franc, notably on exports of cotton, was a significant factor in pushing the trade account into a marginal surplus in 1996 and 1997, although a deficit of 1,500m. francs CFA was recorded in 1998. The trade surplus rose from 9,400m. francs CFA in 1999 31,100m. francs CFA in 2000, mainly owing to a sharp increase in wood exports. However, a surge in the import of petroleum products (the country's fuel stocks were detained in the DRC through much of 2000) reduced the trade surplus to 25,800m. francs CFA in 2001. In 2002 the trade surplus totalled 18,500m. francs CFA, before falling sharply to 6,100m. francs CFA in 2003, owing to political instability. The decline in exports, by 27%, was particularly severe in cotton (a 91% decrease), but also in wood products (28%), diamonds (23%) and coffee (20%). The fall in diamond exports was also partly due to the Government's decision to suspend mining and forestry permits, thus forcing enterprises to re-apply. In 2004 exports decreased by 11.4%, while imports increased by 7.6%, mainly owing to higher oil-related imports. This resulted in a trade deficit of 7,500m. francs CFA. The trade deficit widened to an estimated 12,100m. francs CFA in 2005 and a projected 12,900m. francs CFA in 2006, according to the IMF.

The CAR has traditionally recorded large net outflow on services, reflecting transport costs stemming from the country's land-locked position. As a result, the country's current-account balance has remained in deficit, despite the trade surplus and a generally high net level of unrequited public transfers. The current-account deficit (including grants) represented 4.4% of GDP in 2004, before falling back to an estimated 2.8% of GDP in 2005. The IMF projected it to widen slightly, to 3.3% of GDP in 2006. The CAR has traditionally received substantial inflows of aid in grant form. In 1994–98 grants from members of the Development Assistance Committee of the Organisation for Economic Co-operation and Development averaged US $136m. per year. France has been the leading single source throughout, accounting for almost one-half of these inflows. However, net overseas development assistance (ODA) inflows steadily fell, from $118m. in 1999 to $59.8m. in 2002, primarily because of the slow implementation of reforms and political instability. In 2003 net ODA inflows fell again to $50m. In 2004 net ODA inflows recovered to $104.5m.

The deficit on the current account has largely been covered by borrowing from governments and multilateral institutions, since the CAR has not proved particularly attractive to foreign private investors (other than in the diamond sector). The total external debt has consequently been rising over a long period, reaching a peak of US $946m. in 1995. The Government benefited from two successive debt relief packages from bilateral creditors in 1994 and 1998, which helped to clear payment arrears and reduce the stock of external debt to $821.9m. by the end of 2001. Total debt stock stood at $1,082m. by the end of 2004 equivalent to 83% of gross national income (GNI), and at $1,016m. at the end of 2005, equivalent to 47.3% of GNI.

Statistical Survey

Source (unless otherwise stated): Division des Statistiques et des Etudes Economiques, Ministère de l'Economie, du Plan et de la Coopération Internationale, Bangui.

Area and Population

AREA, POPULATION AND DENSITY

Area (sq km)	622,984*
Population (census results)	
8 December 1975	2,054,610
8 December 1988	
Males	1,210,734
Females	1,252,882
Total	2,463,616
Population (UN estimates at mid-year)†	
2004	4,123,000
2005	4,191,000
2006	4,265,000
Density (per sq km) at mid-2006	6.8

* 240,535 sq miles.

† Source: UN, *World Population Prospects: The 2006 Revision*.

PRINCIPAL TOWNS

(estimated population at mid-1994)

Bangui (capital)	524,000	Carnot	41,000
Berbérati	47,000	Bambari	41,000
Bouar	43,000	Bossangoa	33,000

Mid-2005 (incl. suburbs, UN estimate): Bangui 541,000 (Source: UN, *World Urbanization Prospects: The 2005 Revision*).

BIRTHS AND DEATHS

(annual averages, UN estimates)

	1990–95	1995–2000	2000–05
Birth rate (per 1,000)	41.6	40.0	37.9
Death rate (per 1,000)	16.6	18.0	19.4

Source: UN, *World Population Prospects: The 2006 Revision*.

Expectation of life (years at birth, WHO estimates): 41 (males 40; females 41) in 2004 (Source: WHO, *World Health Report*).

ECONOMICALLY ACTIVE POPULATION

(persons aged 6 years and over, 1988 census)

	Males	Females	Total
Agriculture, hunting, forestry and fishing	417,630	463,007	880,637
Mining and quarrying	11,823	586	12,409
Manufacturing	16,096	1,250	17,346
Electricity, gas and water	751	58	809
Construction	5,583	49	5,632
Trade, restaurants and hotels	37,435	54,563	91,998
Transport, storage and communications	6,601	150	6,751
Financing, insurance, real estate and business services	505	147	652
Community, social and personal services	61,764	8,537	70,301
Activities not adequately defined	7,042	4,627	11,669
Total employed	565,230	532,974	1,098,204
Unemployed	66,624	22,144	88,768
Total labour force	631,854	555,118	1,186,972

Source: ILO.

Mid-2005 (estimates in '000): Agriculture, etc. 1,281; Total labour force 1,878 (Source: FAO).

Health and Welfare

KEY INDICATORS

Total fertility rate (children per woman, 2005)	4.8
Under-5 mortality rate (per 1,000 live births, 2005)	193
HIV/AIDS (% of persons aged 15–49, 2005)	10.7
Physicians (per 1,000 head, 2004)	0.08
Hospital beds (per 1,000 head, 1991)	0.87
Health expenditure (2004): US $ per head (PPP)	54.3
Health expenditure (2004): % of GDP	4.1
Health expenditure (2004): public (% of total)	36.8
Access to water (% of persons, 2004)	75
Access to sanitation (% of persons, 2004)	27
Human Development Index (2004): ranking	172
Human Development Index (2004): value	0.353

For sources and definitions, see explanatory note on p. vi.

Agriculture

PRINCIPAL CROPS

('000 metric tons)

	2003	2004	2005
Rice (paddy)	29.7	30.7*	32.3*
Maize	119.0	110.0†	90.0†
Millet*	10.0	10.5	10.7
Sorghum*	42.5	44.2	45.8
Cassava (Manioc)*	520.0	543.7	547.4
Taro (Coco yam)*	80.0	100.0	100.0
Yams*	330.0	381.8	404.4
Sugar cane*	90.0	90.0	90.0
Pulses*	27.0	27.0	27.0
Groundnuts (in shell)	133.6	140.0†	140.0†
Oil palm fruit*	28.0	17.7	11.1
Sesame seed	42.8	44.2*	45.8*
Melonseed	27.9	27.9*	27.9*
Pumpkins, squash and gourds*	5.9	5.9	6.0
Other vegetables*	63.9	63.9	64.0
Bananas*	110.0	119.1	123.0
Plantains*	80.0	84.5	86.5
Oranges*	20.0	23.4	24.7
Pineapples*	13.8	14.6	15.0
Coffee (green)†	5.5	4.3	3.3
Cottonseed*	0.6	6.4	7.5
Cotton (lint)*	0.4	0.4	0.4

* FAO estimate(s).

† Unofficial figure(s).

Source: FAO.

LIVESTOCK

('000 head, year ending September)

	2003	2004	2005
Cattle	3,347	3,423*	3,423†
Goats	3,087	3,087†	3,087†
Sheep	259	259†	259†
Pigs	771	805*	805†
Chickens	4,769	4,769*	259†

* Unofficial figure.

† FAO estimate.

Source: FAO.

LIVESTOCK PRODUCTS
('000 metric tons)

	2003	2004	2005
Cattle meat	71.0*	74.0†	74.0*
Sheep meat*	1.5	1.5	1.5
Goat meat*	11.5	11.5	11.5
Pig meat	12.9	13.5†	13.5*
Chicken meat*	4.0	4.0	4.0
Other meat*	8.8	8.8	8.8
Cows' milk*	65.0	65.0	65.0
Hen eggs*	1.5	1.5	1.5
Honey*	13.0	13.0	13.0

* FAO estimate(s).
† Unofficial figure.

Source: FAO.

Forestry

ROUNDWOOD REMOVALS
('000 cubic metres, excluding bark)

	2003	2004	2005
Sawlogs, veneer logs and logs for sleepers	475	524	524
Other industrial wood*	308	308	308
Fuel wood	2,000	2,000	2,000*
Total	2,783	2,832	2,832

* FAO estimate(s).

Source: FAO.

SAWNWOOD PRODUCTION
('000 cubic metres, including railway sleepers)

	2001	2002	2003
Total (all broadleaved)	150	97	69

2004–05: Figures assumed to be unchanged from 2003 (FAO estimate).

Source: FAO.

Fishing

('000 metric tons, live weight of capture, FAO estimates)

	2003	2004	2005
Total catch (freshwater fishes)	15.0	15.0	15.0

Source: FAO.

Mining

(estimates)

	2003	2004	2005
Gold (kg, metal content of ore)	7	7	7
Diamonds ('000 carats)	333	350	380

Source: US Geological Survey.

Industry

SELECTED PRODUCTS
('000 metric tons, unless otherwise indicated)

	2003	2004	2005
Beer ('000 hectolitres)	121.7	n.a.	n.a.
Sugar (raw, centrifugal)*	12	12	12
Soft drinks and syrups ('000 hectolitres)	38.4	n.a.	n.a.
Cigarettes (million packets)	16.1	n.a.	n.a.
Palm oil*	1.7	1.7	1.7
Groundnut oil*	31.6	33.2	33.2
Plywood ('000 cubic metres)	1.9	2.0*	2.0*

* FAO estimate(s).

Sources: IMF, *Central African Republic: Selected Issues and Statistical Appendix* (August 2004); FAO.

Electric energy (million kWh, estimates): 107 in 2000; 108 in 2001; 108 in 2002 (Source: UN, *Industrial Commodity Statistics Yearbook*).

Finance

CURRENCY AND EXCHANGE RATES

Monetary Units

100 centimes = 1 franc de la Coopération financière en Afrique centrale (CFA).

Sterling, Dollar and Euro Equivalents (31 May 2007)

£1 sterling = 964.116 francs CFA;
US $1 = 487.592 francs CFA;
€1 = 655.957 francs CFA;
10,000 francs CFA = £10.37 = $20.51 = €15.24.

Average Exchange Rate (francs CFA per US $)

2004 528.29
2005 527.47
2006 522.89

Note: An exchange rate of 1 French franc = 50 francs CFA, established in 1948, remained in force until January 1994, when the CFA franc was devalued by 50%, with the exchange rate adjusted to 1 French franc = 100 francs CFA. This relationship to French currency remained in effect with the introduction of the euro on 1 January 1999. From that date, accordingly, a fixed exchange rate of €1 = 655.957 francs CFA has been in operation.

BUDGET
('000 million francs CFA)

Revenue*	2004	2005†	2006‡
Tax revenue	48.3	50.6	59.5
Direct taxes	15.6	14.7	17.4
Indirect domestic taxes	22.1	26.4	28.9
Taxes on international trade	10.6	9.5	13.2
Taxes on imports	7.1	7.0	8.9
Non-tax revenue	7.5	8.0	9.6
Total	55.8	58.5	69.1

Expenditure§	2004	2005†	2006‡
Current primary expenditure	66.7	75.4	61.0
Wages and salaries	38.9	39.2	36.5
Other goods and services	17.8	22.2	13.3
Transfers and subsidies	10.0	14.0	11.2
Interest payments	8.5	6.6	15.5
Capital expenditure	18.2	38.4	23.8
Domestically financed	7.7	8.4	5.3
Externally financed	10.5	29.9	18.5
Total	93.4	120.4	100.3

* Excluding grants received ('000 million francs CFA): 22.7 in 2004; 29.5 in 2005 (estimate); 30.9 in 2006 (projected figure).
† Estimates.
‡ Projected figures.
§ Excluding adjustment for payment arrears ('000 million francs CFA): –21.15 in 2004; –26.9 in 2005 (estimate); –6.0 in 2006 (projected figure).

Source: IMF, *Central African Republic: Request for a Three-Year Arrangement Under the Poverty Reduction and Growth Facility - Staff Report; Staff Statement; Press Release on the Executive Board Discussion; and Statement by the Executive Director for the Central African Republic* (February 2007).

INTERNATIONAL RESERVES

(US $ million at 31 December)

	2004	2005	2006
Gold (national valuation)	4.88	5.71	7.06
IMF special drawing rights	2.46	0.12	0.71
Reserve position in IMF	0.25	0.23	0.24
Foreign exchange	145.62	138.87	124.40
Total	153.21	144.93	132.41

Source: IMF, *International Financial Statistics*.

MONEY SUPPLY

('000 million francs CFA at 31 December)

	2004	2005	2006
Currency outside banks	81.34	89.86	80.93
Demand deposits at commercial and development banks	16.38	23.85	24.53
Total money	97.72	113.70	105.46

Source: IMF, *International Financial Statistics*.

COST OF LIVING

(Consumer Price Index for Bangui; base: 2000 = 100)

	2003	2004	2005
Food	112.4	107.2	110.9
Fuel and light	n.a.	100.2	98.2
Clothing	n.a.	124.4	123.1
All items (incl. others)	110.9	108.6	111.7

Source: ILO.

NATIONAL ACCOUNTS

Expenditure on the Gross Domestic Product

(US $ million at current prices)

	2004	2005	2006
Government final consumption expenditure	133.91	179.43	131.18
Private final consumption expenditure	1,180.04	1,162.58	1,317.65
Gross fixed capital formation	79.90	121.30	122.65
Total domestic expenditure	1,393.85	1,463.31	1,571.48
Exports of goods and services	154.74	164.08	177.59
Less Imports of goods and services	241.29	256.45	279.44
GDP in purchasers' values	1,307.3	1,370.94	1,469.63
GDP at constant 2000 prices	838.10	856.54	886.52

Source: African Development Bank, *Statistical Yearbook*.

Gross Domestic Product by Economic Activity

('000 million francs CFA at current prices)

	2001	2002	2003*
Agriculture, hunting, forestry and fishing	365.2	370.4	378.8
Mining and quarrying	46.0	47.7	46.1
Manufacturing	24.6	21.5	16.1
Electricity, gas and water	5.4	5.2	5.4
Construction	29.0	29.7	30.9
Transport and communications	26.8	27.9	26.6
Commerce	75.2	75.7	72.3
Other merchant services	38.7	39.0	37.6
Government services	39.8	45.1	47.0
Technical assistance	21.8	19.9	4.5
GDP at factor cost	672.6	682.1	665.2
Indirect taxes	29.6	36.5	23.6
Customs duties	7.0	7.6	7.7
GDP in purchasers' values	709.2	726.2	696.4

* Estimates.

Source: IMF, *Central African Republic: Selected Issues and Statistical Appendix* (August 2004).

2006 (US $ million at constant 2000 prices): Agriculture, etc. 517.46; Industry 160.71 (Manufacturing 62.19); Services 208.35; GDP at factor cost 886.52 (Source: African Development Bank, *Statistical Yearbook*).

BALANCE OF PAYMENTS

('000 million francs CFA)

	2004	2005*	2006†
Exports of goods	66.0	67.6	75.3
Imports of goods	–73.6	–79.8	–88.3
Trade balance	–7.5	–12.1	–12.9
Services (net)	–38.2	–36.6	–36.8
Balance on goods and services	–45.7	–48.7	–49.8
Income (net)	–3.0	0.0	–0.6
Balance on goods, services, and income	–48.7	48.7	–50.4
Current transfers (net)	18.2	28.1	25.0
Current balance	–30.5	–20.5	–25.3
Capital account (net)	18.5	15.4	22.7
Project disbursements	2.6	3.2	3.0
Program disbursements	0.0	4.0	0.0
Scheduled amortization	–17.2	–11.8	–12.9
Private sector (net)	7.0	1.8	–28.5
Overall balance	–19.5	–7.9	–40.9

* Estimates.

† Projections.

Source: IMF, *Central African Republic: Request for a Three-Year Arrangement Under the Poverty Reduction and Growth Facility—Staff Report; Staff Statement; Press Release on the Executive Board Discussion; and Statement by the Executive Director for the Central African Republic* (February 2007).

External Trade

PRINCIPAL COMMODITIES
(distribution by SITC, US $ million)

Imports c.i.f.	2001	2002	2003
Food and live animals	14.0	13.0	18.3
Cereals and cereal preparations	9.5	8.2	9.4
Flour of wheat or meslin	6.2	5.3	6.1
Beverages and tobacco	3.6	3.1	4.0
Tobacco and tobacco manufactures	2.7	2.4	3.1
Crude materials (inedible) except fuels	3.8	3.7	8.1
Textile fibres (excl. wool tops) and waste	2.4	2.7	3.5
Mineral fuels, lubricants, etc.	3.4	8.2	11.0
Petroleum, petroleum products, etc.	3.4	8.1	10.9
Chemicals and related products	9.2	10.1	17.5
Medicinal and pharmaceutical products	5.8	6.1	13.5
Medicaments	4.6	5.3	13.1
Manufactured goods	9.4	10.5	16.0
Non-ferrous metals	1.1	1.2	1.5
Machinery and transport equipment	19.3	18.3	18.9
Machinery specialized for particular industries	1.5	1.4	0.5
Civil engineering and contractors' plant and equipment	0.7	0.3	0.3
Construction and mining machinery	0.7	0.3	0.2
General industrial machinery, equipment and parts	2.3	2.3	4.7
Telecommunications and sound equipment	0.7	1.5	1.3
Road vehicles and parts*	10.2	8.6	8.4
Passenger motor cars (excl. buses)	3.0	2.3	1.3
Motor vehicles for goods transport and special purposes	2.5	2.1	0.9
Goods vehicles (lorries and trucks)	2.5	2.1	0.9
Parts and accessories for cars, buses, lorries, etc.*	1.1	1.2	0.5
Miscellaneous manufactured articles	4.5	7.3	4.7
Total (incl. others)	67.6	74.7	99.6

* Excluding tyres, engines and electrical parts.

Exports f.o.b.	2001	2002	2003
Food and live animals	1.9	1.2	0.8
Crude materials (inedible) except fuels	35.7	33.7	40.3
Cork and wood	13.8	11.1	15.6
Textile fibres (excl. wool tops) and waste	6.9	7.6	1.0
Cotton	6.9	7.5	0.9
Crude fertilizers and crude minerals (excl. coal, petroleum and precious stones)	15.0	15.1	23.7
Industrial diamonds (sorted)	15.0	15.0	23.7
Basic manufactures	34.2	33.2	23.9
Diamonds (excl. sorted industrial diamonds), unmounted	33.3	32.6	23.6
Sorted non-industrial diamonds, rough or simply worked	26.3	32.4	17.3
Machinery and transport equipment	1.2	0.8	0.2
Road vehicles	0.9	0.5	0.1
Total (incl. others)	74.3	69.5	65.7

Source: UN, *International Trade Statistics Yearbook*.

PRINCIPAL TRADING PARTNERS
(US $ million)

Imports c.i.f.	2001	2002	2003
Belgium-Luxembourg	3.5	4.0	9.1
Brazil	—	0.5	1.1
Cameroon	8.5	8.5	10.0
Chad	1.0	0.5	0.6
China, People's Repub.	0.6	1.1	2.5
France (incl. Monaco)	27.1	25.9	29.8
Germany	1.1	2.6	1.5
Italy	1.3	1.0	0.8
Japan	6.8	7.3	2.9
Netherlands	0.9	0.7	8.8
USA	1.5	1.0	1.3
Total (incl. others)	67.6	74.7	99.6

Exports f.o.b.	2001	2002	2003
Belgium-Luxembourg	53.6	50.6	46.1
Cameroon	1.5	1.2	2.3
France (incl. Monaco)	2.1	1.8	4.3
Germany	4.1	4.1	4.7
Japan	0.5	0.7	0.2
Portugal	0.5	2.3	0.5
Spain	0.6	1.0	0.8
Sudan	1.3	0.5	0.4
Switzerland (incl. Liechtenstein)	0.9	1.1	0.9
Turkey	0.4	0.8	0.5
United Kingdom	—	0.8	2.0
Total (incl. others)	74.3	69.5	65.7

Source: UN, *International Trade Statistics Yearbook*.

Transport

ROAD TRAFFIC
(motor vehicles in use)

	1999	2000	2001
Passenger cars	4,900	5,300	5,300
Commercial vehicles	5,800	6,300	6,300

Source: UN, *Statistical Yearbook*.

SHIPPING
(international traffic on inland waterways, metric tons)

	1996	1997	1998
Freight unloaded at Bangui	60,311	56,206	57,513
Freight loaded at Bangui	5,348	5,907	12,524
Total	65,659	62,113	70,037

Source: Banque des états de l'Afrique centrale, *Etudes et Statistiques*.

CIVIL AVIATION
(traffic on scheduled services)*

	1999	2000	2001
Kilometres flown (million)	3	3	1
Passengers carried ('000)	84	77	46
Passenger-km (million)	235	216	130
Total ton-km (million)	36	32	19

* Including an apportionment of the traffic of Air Afrique.

Source: UN, *Statistical Yearbook*.

Tourism

FOREIGN VISITORS BY COUNTRY OF ORIGIN*

	2003	2004	2005
Cameroon	604	904	1,165
Chad	212	352	566
Congo, Democratic Rep.	103	142	248
Congo, Republic	411	418	468
Côte d'Ivoire	182	127	280
France	1,010	2,492	2,913
Gabon	32	166	251
Italy	130	383	475
Senegal	139	315	383
Total (incl. others)	5,687	8,156	11,969

* Arrivals at hotels and similar establishments.

Receipts from tourism (US $ million, incl. passenger transport): 4 in 2003; 4 in 2004; n.a. in 2005.

Source: World Tourism Organization.

Communications Media

	2002	2003	2004
Telephones ('000 main lines in use)	9.0	9.5	10.0
Mobile cellular telephones ('000 subscribers)	12.6	40.0	60.0
Personal computers ('000 in use)	8	10	11
Internet users ('000)	5.0	6.0	9.0

2005: Figures assumed to be unchanged from 2004 (estimates).

Source: International Telecommunication Union.

Radio receivers: 283,000 in use in 1997 (Source: UNESCO, *Statistical Yearbook*).

Daily newspapers: 3 in 1996 (average circulation 6,000) (Source: UNESCO, *Statistical Yearbook*).

Non-daily newspapers: 1 in 1995 (average circulation 2,000) (Source: UNESCO, *Statistical Yearbook*).

Education

(2003/04, unless otherwise indicated)

	Institutions*	Teachers	Students: Males	Students: Females	Students: Total
Pre-primary‡	162	572†	2,955	3,118	6,073
Primary‡	930	4,004	248,135	172,577	420,712
Secondary:					
general‡	46	1,005	43,706§	22,786§	66,492§
vocational	n.a.	(1,005)	n.a.	n.a.	6,778‖
Tertiary	n.a.	136	5,296¶	1,027¶	6,323¶

* 1990/91 figures.
† 1987/88 figure.
‡ Estimates.
§ 2002/03 figure.
‖ 2001/02 figure.
¶ 1999/2000 figure.

Source: UNESCO Institute for Statistics.

Adult literacy rate (UNESCO estimates): 48.6% (males 64.8%; females 33.5%) in 2004 (Source: UN Development Programme, *Human Development Report*).

Directory

The Constitution

Following the overthrow of President Ange-Félix Patassé in mid-March 2003, the Constitution of January 1995 was suspended. In December 2004 a new constitution was approved at a referendum by 87.2% of the electorate. The new Constitution provides for a presidential term of five years, renewable only once.

The Government

HEAD OF STATE

President of the Republic and Minister of National Defence, the Restructuring of the Armed Forces, Veterans and Disarmament: Gen. FRANÇOIS BOZIZÉ YANGOVOUNDA (assumed power 16 March 2003; elected by direct popular vote 8 May 2005).

COUNCIL OF MINISTERS
(August 2007)

Prime Minister and Head of Government: ELIE DOTÉ.

Minister of State for Communication, National Reconciliation, Democratic Culture and the Promotion of Human Rights: ABDOU KARIM MÉCKASSOUA.

Minister of Finance and the Budget, and of Mines, Energy and Hydraulics: Lt-Col SYLVAIN N'DOUTINGAÏ.

Minister of State for Rural Development: CHARLES MASSI.

Minister of National Education: CHARLES-ARMEL DOUBANE.

Minister of Planning, the Economy and International Co-operation: SYLVAIN MALICKO.

Minister of the Interior and Public Security: Gen. RAYMOND PAUL NDOUGOU.

Minister of Equipment and Promotion of the Regions: JEAN-PROSPER WODOBODÉ.

Minister of Justice: PAUL OTTO.

Minister in charge of the Secretariat-General of the Government and Relations with Parliament: LAURENT N'GON BABA.

Minister of Public Health: Dr LALHA KONAMNA.

Minister of the Reconstruction of Public Buildings, Urban Planning and Housing: TIMOLEON M'BAIKOUA.

Minister of Posts and Telecommunications, responsible for New Technologies: FIDÈLE NGOUANDJIKA.

Minister of the Civil Service: JACQUES BOTI.

Minister of Youth and Sports: DÉSIRÉ ZANGA-KOLINGBA.

Minister of Tourism Development and Artisanal Industries: YVONNE M'BOÏSSONA.

Minister of Social Affairs: MARIE SOLANGE PAGONENDJI.

Minister of Trade, Industry and the Promotion of the Public Sector: ROSALIE KOUDOUNGUÉRÉ.

Minister of Foreign and Francophone Affairs and Regional Integration: CÔME ZOUMARA.

Minister of Transport and Civil Aviation: Lt-Col PARFAIT-ANICET M'BAYE.

Minister of Water Resources, Forests, Hunting, Fishing and the Environment: EMMANUEL BIZZO.

Minister-delegate to the Minister of State for Rural Development, responsible for Agriculture: Dr David Banzokou.

Minister-delegate to the Prime Minister and Government Spokesperson: Aurélien-Simplice Zingas.

Minister-delegate to the Minister of Finance and the Budget: Nicolas Nganzé.

Minister-delegate to the State Minister of Foreign and Francophone Affairs and Regional Integration: Marie Reine Hassan.

MINISTRIES

Office of the President: Palais de la Renaissance, Bangui; tel. 61-46-63.

Ministry of the Civil Service: Bangui; tel. 61-21-88; fax 61-04-14.

Ministry of Communication, National Reconciliation, Democratic Culture and the Promotion of Human Rights: BP 940, Bangui; tel. 61-27-66; fax 61-59-85.

Ministry of Equipment and Promotion of the Regions: Bangui.

Ministry of Finance and the Budget: BP 696, Bangui; tel. 61-38-05.

Ministry of Foreign and Francophone Affairs and Regional Integration: Bangui; tel. 61-54-67; fax 61-26-06.

Ministry of the Interior and Public Security: Bangui; tel. 61-14-77.

Ministry of Justice: Bangui; tel. 61-52-11.

Ministry of Mines, Energy and Hydraulics: Bangui; tel. 61-20-54; fax 61-60-76.

Ministry of National Defence, the Restructuring of the Armed Forces, Veterans and Disarmament: Bangui; tel. 61-00-25.

Ministry of National Education: BP 791, Bangui; tel. 61-08-38.

Ministry of Planning, the Economy and International Cooperation: BP 912, Bangui; tel. 61-70-55; fax 61-63-98.

Ministry of Posts and Telecommunications and New Technologies: Bangui; tel. 61-29-66.

Ministry of Public Health: Bangui; tel. 61-16-35.

Ministry of the Reconstruction of Public Buildings, Urban Planning and Housing: Bangui; tel. 61-69-54.

Ministry of Rural Development: Bangui; tel. 61-28-00.

Ministry of Social Affairs: Bangui; tel. 61-55-65.

Ministry of Tourism Development and Artisanal Industries: Bangui; tel. 61-04-16.

Ministry of Trade, Industry and the Promotion of the Public Sector: Bangui; tel. 61-10-69.

Ministry of Transport and Civil Aviation: BP 941, Bangui; tel. 61-70-49; fax 61-46-28.

Ministry of Water Resources, Forests, Hunting, Fishing and the Environment: Bangui; tel. 61-79-21.

Ministry of Youth and Sports: Bangui; tel. 61-39-69.

President and Legislature

PRESIDENT

Presidential Election, First Round, 13 March 2005

Candidate	Votes	% of votes
Gen. François Bozizé Yangovounda	382,241	42.97
Martin Ziguélé	209,357	23.53
André Kolingba	145,495	16.36
Jean-Paul Ngoupandé	45,182	5.08
Charles Massi	28,618	3.22
Abel Goumba	22,297	2.51
Henri Pouzère	18,647	2.10
Josué Binoua	13,559	1.52
Jean-Jacques Demafouth	11,279	1.27
Auguste Bouanga	7,085	0.80
Olivier Gabirault	5,834	0.66
Total*	889,594	100.00

* Excluding 57,022 invalid votes.

Presidential Election, Second Round, 8 May 2005

Candidate	Votes	% of votes
Gen. François Bozizé Yangovounda	610,903	64.67
Martin Ziguélé	333,716	35.33
Total	944,619	100.00

ASSEMBLÉE NATIONALE

Speaker: Célestin-Leroy Gaombalet.

General Election, 13 March and 8 May 2005

Party	Seats
Convergence Kwa na kwa	42
MLPC	11
RDC	8
PSD	4
FPP	2
ADP	2
Löndö Association	1
Independents	34
Total	104*

* Following the second round of elections, one seat remained undeclared.

Election Commission

Commission électorale mixte indépendante (CEMI): Bangui; f. 2004; Pres. Jean Willybiro Sacko.

Political Organizations

Alliance pour la démocratie et le progrès (ADP): Bangui; f. 1991; progressive; Leader Jospeh Théophile Douaclé.

Armée populaire pour la restauration de la république et la démocratie (APRD): Bangui; armed insurrectionary group; Leader Martin Koumtamadji.

Collectif des Centrafricains en France (CCF): Paris (France); f. 1984; umbrella org. for political representatives resident in France; Gen. Sec. André Doungouma-Foky.

Concertation des partis politiques d'opposition (CPPO): Bangui; umbrella org. of 12 parties opposed to former President Patassé.

Conseil démocratique des partis politiques de l'opposition (CODEPO): Bangui; f. 1995; political alliance led by Auguste Boukanga; comprises the following parties.

Mouvement démocratique pour la renaissance et l'évolution de la République Centrafricaine (MDRERC): Bangui; Chair. Joseph Bendounga; Sec.-Gen. Léon Sebou.

Parti républicain centrafricain (PRC): Bangui.

Convention nationale (CN): Bangui; f. 1991; Leader David Galiambo.

Coordination des patriotes centrafricains (CPC): Paris (France) and Bangui; f. 2003; umbrella org. for groups opposed to former President Patassé and affiliated to the uprising of March 2003; Sec.-Gen. Abdou Karim Méckassoua.

Forum civique (FC): Bangui; Leader Gen. Timothée Malendoma.

Forum démocratique pour la modernité (FODEM): Bangui; tel. 61-29-54; e-mail eric.neris@wanadoo.fr; internet membres.lycos.fr/fodem/; f. 1998; Pres. Charles Massi.

Front démocratique de libération du peuple centrafricain (FDPC): Leader Abdoulaye Miskine.

Front patriotique pour le progrès (FPP): BP 259, Bangui; tel. 61-52-23; fax 61-10-93; f. 1972; aims to promote political education and debate; Leader Alexandre Goumba.

G11: Bangui; f. 1997; alliance of 11 opposition parties led by Prof. Abel Goumba; principal mems: ADP, FPP, MDD and RDC.

Mouvement d'évolution sociale de l'Afrique noire (MESAN): Bangui; f. 1949; comprises two factions, MESAN and MESAN-BOGANDA, led respectively by Fidèle Ogbami and Joseph Ngbangadibo.

Mouvement national pour le renouveau: Bangui; Leader Paul Bellet.

Mouvement pour la démocratie et le développement (MDD): Bangui; f. 1993; aims to safeguard national unity and the equitable distribution of national wealth; Leader LOUIS PAPENIAH.

Mouvement pour la démocratie, l'indépendance et le progrès social (MDI-PS): BP 1404, Bangui; tel. 61-18-21; e-mail mdicentrafrique@chez.com; internet www.chez.com/mdicentrafrique; Sec.-Gen. DANIEL NDITIFEI BOYSEMBE.

Mouvement pour la libération du peuple centrafricain (MLPC): Bangui; f. 1979; leading party in govt Oct. 1993–March 2003; Pres. MARTIN ZIGUÉLÉ; Sec.-Gen. JEAN-MICHEL MANDABA.

Nouvelle alliance pour le progrès (NAP): Bangui; internet www.centrafrique-nap.com; Leader JEAN-JACQUES DEMAFOUTH.

Parti libéral-démocrate (PLD): Bangui; Leader NESTOR KOMBO-NAGUEMON.

Parti social-démocrate (PSD): BP 543, Bangui; tel. 61-59-02; fax 61-58-44; Leader ENOCH DERANT LAKOUÉ.

Rassemblement démocratique centrafricain (RDC): BP 503, Bangui; tel. 61-53-75; f. 1987; sole legal political party 1987–91; Leader Gen. ANDRÉ KOLINGBA.

Rassemblement populaire pour la reconstruction de la Centrafrique (RPRC): Bangui; Leader Gen. FRANÇOIS BOZIZÉ YANGO-VOUNDA.

Union des démocrates pour le renouveau panafricain (UDRP): Bangui; Leader BENOÎT LIKITI.

Union des forces acquises à la paix (UFAP): Bangui; f. 1998; opposition alliance, including political parties, trade unions and human rights orgs; weakened by withdrawals in Nov. 1999; Pres. PAUL BELLÉT.

Union des forces démocratiques pour le rassemblement (UFDR): Bangui; f. 2006; Leader ZAKARIA DAMANE.

Front démocratique centrafricain (FDC): Bangui; Leader Commdt JUSTIN HASSAN.

Groupe d'action patriotique de la libération de Centrafrique (GAPLC): Bangui; Leader MICHEL AM NONDROKO DJOTODIA.

Mouvement des libérateurs centrafricains pour la justice (MLCJ): Bangui; Leader Capt. ABAKAR SABONE.

Union des forces républicaines de Centrafrique: Bangui; f. 2006; armed insurrectionary group; Leader Lt FRANÇOIS-FLORIAN N'DJADDER-BEDAYA.

Union pour un mouvement populaire de Centrafrique (UMPCA): Pres. YVONNE M'BOÏSSONA.

Union nationale démocratique du peuple centrafricain (UNDPC): Bangui; f. 1998; Islamic fundamentalist; based in south-east CAR; Leader MAHAMAT SALEH.

Union pour le progrès en Centrafrique (UPCA): Bangui; Leader FAUSTIN YERIMA.

Union pour la république (UPR): Bangui; leader PIERRE SAMMY MAKFOY.

Diplomatic Representation

EMBASSIES IN THE CENTRAL AFRICAN REPUBLIC

Cameroon: rue du Languedoc, BP 935, Bangui; tel. 61-18-57; fax 61-16-87; Chargé d'affaires a.i. GILBERT NOULA.

Chad: ave Valéry Giscard d'Estaing, BP 461, Bangui; tel. 61-46-77; fax 61-62-44; Ambassador MAHAMAT YAYA DAGACHE.

China, People's Republic: ave des Martyrs, BP 1430, Bangui; tel. 61-27-60; fax 61-31-83; e-mail chinaemb_cf@mfa.gov.cn; Ambassador HE SIJI.

Congo, Democratic Republic: Ambassador EMBE ISEA MBAMBE.

Congo, Republic: BP 1414, Bangui; tel. 61-20-79; Ambassador LIKIBI TSIBA NOBERT.

Egypt: angle ave Léopold Sédar Senghor et rue Emile Gentil, BP 1422, Bangui; tel. 61-46-88; fax 61-35-45; Ambassador HANI RIAD MO'AWAD.

France: blvd du Général de Gaulle, BP 884, Bangui; tel. 61-30-05; fax 61-74-04; e-mail chancellerie.bangui-amba@diplomatie.gouv.fr; internet www.ambafrance-cf.org; Ambassador ALAIN-JEAN GIRMA.

Holy See: ave Boganda, BP 1447, Bangui; tel. 61-26-54; fax 61-03-71; e-mail nonrca@intnet.cf; Apostolic Nuncio Most Rev. PIERRE NGUYÊN VAN TOT (Titular Archbishop of Rusticiana).

Japan: Temporarily closed; affairs handled through the Embassy of Japan, Yaoundé, Cameroon, since October 2003.

Libya: Bangui; tel. 61-46-62; fax 61-55-25; Ambassador (vacant).

Nigeria: ave des Martyrs, BP 1010, Bangui; tel. 61-40-97; fax 61-12-79; Ambassador A. A. ILEMIA.

Russia: ave du Président Gamal Abdel Nasser, BP 1405, Bangui; tel. 61-03-11; fax 61-56-45; e-mail ruscons@intent.cf; e-mail rusconsrca@yandex.ru; Ambassador IGOR P. LABUZOV.

Sudan: ave de France, BP 1351, Bangui; tel. 61-38-21; Ambassador Dr SULEIMA MOHAMED MUSTAPHA.

USA: ave David Dacko, BP 924, Bangui; tel. 61-02-00; fax 61-44-94; Chargé d'affaires a.i. JAMES PANOS.

Judicial System

Supreme Court: BP 926, Bangui; tel. 61-41-33; highest judicial organ; acts as a Court of Cassation in civil and penal cases and as Court of Appeal in administrative cases; comprises four chambers: constitutional, judicial, administrative and financial; Pres. TAGBIA SANZIA.

There is also a Court of Appeal, a Criminal Court, 16 tribunaux de grande instance, 37 tribunaux d'instance, six labour tribunals and a permanent military tribunal. A High Court of Justice was established under the 1986 Constitution, with jurisdiction in all cases of crimes against state security, including high treason by the President of the Republic. The 1995 Constitution (which was suspended by Gen. François Bozizé in mid-March 2003) established a Constitutional Court, the judges of which were to be appointed by the President. In December 2004 Bozizé appointed a Transitional Constitutional Court that oversaw the referendum on a new constitution held in the same month.

Religion

It is estimated that 24% of the population hold animist beliefs, 50% are Christians (25% Roman Catholic, 25% Protestant) and 15% are Muslims. There is no official state religion.

CHRISTIANITY

The Roman Catholic Church

The Central African Republic comprises one archdiocese and eight dioceses. There were an estimated 829,171 adherents at 31 December 2004.

Bishops' Conference

Conférence Episcopale Centrafricaine, BP 1518, Bangui; tel. 50-27-46; fax 61-46-92; e-mail ceca_rca@yahoo.fr.

f. 1982; Pres. Most Rev. FRANÇOIS-XAVIER YOMBANDJE (Bishop of Bossangoa).

Archbishop of Bangui: Most Rev. PAULIN POMODIMO, Archevêché, BP 1518, Bangui; tel. 03-77-31; fax 61-46-92; e-mail archbangui@yahoo.fr.

Protestant Church

Eglise Protestante du Christ Roi: BP 608, Bangui; tel. 61-14-35.

The Press

The independent press is highly regulated. Independent publications must hold a trading licence and prove their status as a commercial enterprise. They must also have proof that they fulfil taxation requirements. There is little press activity outside Bangui.

DAILIES

E le Songo: Bangui; f. 1986.

Le Citoyen: BP 974, Bangui; tel. 61-89-16; independent; Dir MAKA GBOSSOKOTTO; circ. 3,000.

Le Confident: BP 427, Bangui; tel. 04-64-14; e-mail leconfident2000@yahoo.fr; internet www.leconfident.net; f. 2001; Mon.–Sat.; Dir MATHURIN C. N. MOMET.

Le Novateur: BP 913, Bangui; tel. 61-48-84; fax 61-87-03; e-mail ccea_ln@intnet.cf; independent; Publr MARCEL MOKWAPI; circ. 750.

Top Contact: Bangui; independent.

PERIODICALS

Bangui Match: Bangui; monthly.

Centrafrique-Presse: BP 1058, Bangui; tel. and fax 61-39-57; e-mail redaction@centrafrique-presse.com; internet www.centrafrique-presse.com; weekly; Publr PROSPER N'DOUBA.

Le Courrier Rural: BP 850, Bangui; publ. by Chambre d'Agriculture.

Le Délit d'Opinion: Bangui; independent.

Demain le Monde: BP 650, Bangui; tel. 61-23-15; f. 1985; fortnightly; independent; Editor-in-Chief NGANAM NÖEL.

Journal Officiel de la République Centrafricaine: BP 739, Bangui; f. 1974; fortnightly; economic data; Dir-Gen. GABRIEL AGBA.

Nations Nouvelles: BP 965, Bangui; publ. by Organisation Commune Africaine et Mauricienne; politics and current affairs.

Le Peuple: BP 569, Bangui; tel. 61-76-34; f. 1995; weekly; Editor-in-Chief VERMOND TCHENDO.

Le Progrès: BP 154, Bangui; tel. 61-70-26; f. 1991; monthly; Editor-in-Chief BELIBANGA CLÉMENT; circ. 2,000.

Le Rassemblement: Bangui; organ of the RDC; Editor-in-Chief MATHIAS GONEVO REAPOGO.

La Tortue Déchainée: Bangui; independent; satirical; Publr MAKA GBOSSOKOTTO.

PRESS ASSOCIATION

Groupement des Editeurs de la Presse Privée Indépendante de Centrafrique (GEPAIC): Bangui; Pres. MAKA GBOSSOKOTO.

NEWS AGENCIES

Agence Centrafricaine de Presse (ACAP): BP 40, Bangui; tel. 61-22-79; f. 1974; Gen. Man. VICTOR DETO TETEYA.

Russia's ITAR—TASS (Information Telegraphic Agency of Russia—Telegraphic Agency of the Sovereign Countries) and Agence France-Presse are represented in the CAR.

Publisher

GOVERNMENT PUBLISHING HOUSE

Imprimerie Centrafricaine: ave David Dacko, BP 329, Bangui; tel. 61-72-24; f. 1974; Dir-Gen. PIERRE SALAMATE-KOILET.

Broadcasting and Communications

TELECOMMUNICATIONS

Société Centrafricaine de Télécommunications (SOCATEL): BP 939, Bangui; tel. 61-42-68; fax 61-44-72; e-mail dg-socatel@socatel.cf; internet www.socatel.cf; f. 1990; 60% state-owned; 40% owned by France Câbles et Radio (France Télécoms); further privatization suspended March 2003; Dir-Gen. VALENTIN NZAPAOKO.

CARATEL Entreprises: BP 2439, Bangui; tel. 61-44-10; fax 61-44-49; e-mail telecomp@intnet.cf; internet www.socatel.intnet.cf; mobile cellular telephone operator.

Centrafrique Telecom Plus: BP 2439, Bangui; tel. 61-44-10; fax 61-44-49; e-mail telecomp@intnet.cf; internet www.socatel.intnet.cf/index2.html; 40% owned by France Telecom; 22% owned by Socatel; f. 1996; supplies wireless and high-speed Internet services.

Telecel: BP 939, Bangui; tel. 61-19-30; fax 61-16-99; mobile cellular telephone operator.

BROADCASTING

Radiodiffusion-Télévision Centrafricaine: BP 940, Bangui; tel. 61-25-88; f. 1958 as Radiodiffusion Nationale Centrafricaine; govt-controlled; broadcasts in French and Sango; Sec.-Gen. DELPHINE ZOUTA.

Radio Rurale: community stations operating in Bouar, Nola, Berbérati and Bambari.

Radio Ndeke Luka: community station operated by UN.

Radio Nostalgie: commercial radio station in Bangui.

Radio Notre-Dame: radio station operated by Roman Catholic Church.

Finance

(cap. = capital; res = reserves; dep. = deposits; m. = million; br. = branch; amounts in francs CFA)

BANKING

Central Bank

Banque des Etats de l'Afrique Centrale (BEAC): BP 851, Bangui; tel. 61-40-00; fax 61-19-95; e-mail beacbgf@beac.int; HQ in Yaoundé, Cameroon; f. 1973; bank of issue for mem. states of the Communauté économique et monétaire de l'Afrique centrale (CEMAC, fmrly Union douanière et économique de l'Afrique centrale), comprising Cameroon, the CAR, Chad, the Repub. of the Congo, Equatorial Guinea and Gabon; cap. 45,000m., res 176,661m., total assets 2,144,626m. (Nov. 2003); Gov. JEAN-FÉLIX MAMALEPOT; Dir in CAR ENOCH DERANT LAKOUÉ.

Commercial Banks

Banque Internationale pour le Centrafrique (BICA): place de la République, BP 910, Bangui; tel. 61-00-42; fax 61-61-36; e-mail bica@intnet.cf; internet www.socatel.intnet.cf/bica.html; f. 1946; present name adopted 1996; 35% owned by Banque Belgolaise SA, Brussels, 15% by group of African investors (COFIPA), 40% by private citizens, 10% by Govt; cap. and res 1,117m., total assets 19,616m. (Dec. 2001); Pres. MARTIN BABA; Dir-Gen. JEAN-CLAUDE PORCHER; 1 br.

Banque Populaire Maroco-Centrafricaine (BPMC): rue Guérillot, BP 844, Bangui; tel. 61-31-90; fax 61-62-30; e-mail bpmc@intnet.cf; f. 1991; 57.5% owned by Groupe Banque Populaire (Morocco); cap. and res 4,183m., total assets 13,331m. (Dec. 2003); Gen. Man. MOHAMMED BENZIANI.

Commercial Bank Centrafrique (CBCA): rue de Brazza, BP 59, Bangui; tel. 61-29-90; fax 61-34-54; e-mail cbcabank@cbc-bank.com; internet www.cbc-bank.com/cb_centrafrique/page.php?langue=fr; f. 1962; 51% owned by Groupe Fotso; 39% owned by CAR private shareholders; 10% state-owned; cap. 1,500.m., res 1,856.3m., dep 22,941.2m. (Dec. 2005); Pres. SERGE PSIMHIS; Dir-Gen. RICHARD BORONG LIVE; 1 br.

Development Bank

Banque de Développement des Etats de l'Afrique Centrale: see Franc Zone.

Financial Institutions

Caisse Autonome d'Amortissement de la République Centrafricaine: Bangui; tel. 61-53-60; fax 61-21-82; management of state funds; Dir-Gen. JOSEPH PINGAMA.

Caisse Nationale d'Epargne (CNE): Office national des postes et de l'épargne, Bangui; tel. 61-22-96; fax 61-78-80; Pres. SIMONE BODEMO-MODOYANGBA; Dir-Gen. AMBROISE DAOUDA; Man. ANTOINE BEKOUANEBANDI.

Bankers' Association

Association Professionnelle des Banques: Bangui.

Development Agencies

Agence Française de Développement: rue de la Moyenne corniche, BP 817, Bangui; tel. 61-03-06; fax 61-22-40; e-mail afd@intnet.cf; e-mail afdbangui@yahoo.fr; internet www.afd.fr; administers economic aid and finances specific development projects; Man. DELPHINE DORBEAU.

Mission Française de Coopération et d'Action Culturelle: BP 934, Bangui; tel. 61-63-34; fax 61-28-24; administers bilateral aid from France; Dir HERVÉ CRONEL.

INSURANCE

Agence Centrafricaine d'Assurances (ACA): BP 512, Bangui; tel. 61-06-23; f. 1956; Dir R. CERBELLAUD.

Assureurs Conseils Centrafricains (ACCAF): ave Barthélemy Boganda, BP 743, Bangui; tel. 61-19-33; fax 61-44-70; e-mail centrafrique@ascoma.com; internet www.ascoma.com; f. 1968; owned by Ascoma (Monaco); Man. VENANT EBELA; Dir-Gen. SYLVAIN COUSIN.

Entreprise d'Etat d'Assurances et de Réassurances (SIRIRI): Bangui; tel. 61-36-55; f. 1972; Pres. EMMANUEL DOKOUNA; Dir-Gen. MARTIN ZIGUÉLÉ.

Legendre, A. & Cie: rue de la Victoire, BP 896, Bangui; Pres. and Dir-Gen. ANDRÉ LEGENDRE.

Union Centrafricaine d'Assurances et de Réassurances: rue du Général de Gaulle, BP 343, Bangui; tel. 61-36-66; fax 61-33-40; e-mail ucardg@intnet.cf; Dir-Gen. ALAIN BLANCHARD.

Trade and Industry

DEVELOPMENT ORGANIZATION

Société Centrafricaine de Développement Agricole (SOCADA): ave David Dacko, BP 997, Bangui; tel. 61-30-33; f. 1964; reorg. 1980; 75% state-owned, 25% Cie Française pour le Développement des Fibres Textiles (France); purchasing, transport and marketing of cotton, cotton-ginning, production of cottonseed oil and groundnut oil; Pres. MAURICE METHOT.

INDUSTRIAL AND TRADE ASSOCIATIONS

Agence de Développement de la Zone Caféière (ADECAF): BP 1935, Bangui; tel. 61-47-30; coffee producers' asscn; assists coffee marketing co-operatives; Dir-Gen. J. J. NIMIZIAMBI.

Agence Nationale pour le Développement de l'Elevage (ANDE): BP 1509, Bangui; tel. 61-69-60; fax 61-50-83; assists with development of livestock.

Bourse Internationale de Diamant de Bangui: BP 26, Bangui; tel. 61-58-63; fax 61-60-76; diamond exchange; supervised by the Ministry of Mines, Energy and Hydraulics.

Caisse de Stabilisation et de Péréquation des Produits Agricoles (CAISTAB): BP 76, Bangui; tel. 61-08-00; supervises marketing and pricing of agricultural produce; Dir-Gen. M. BOUNANDELE-KOUMBA.

Fédération Nationale des Eleveurs Centrafricains (FNEC): ave des Martyrs, BP 588, Bangui; tel. 61-23-97; fax 61-47-24.

Groupement des Industries Centrafricaines (GICA): Bangui; umbrella group representing 12 principal companies of various industries.

Office National des Forêts (ONF): BP 915, Bangui; tel. 61-38-27; f. 1969; reafforestation, development of forest resources; Dir-Gen. C. D. SONGUET.

CHAMBERS OF COMMERCE

Chambre d'Agriculture, d'Elevage, des Eaux, Forêts, Chasses, Pêches et du Tourisme: BP 850, Bangui; tel. 61-06-38; e-mail chagri_rca@hotmail.com; f. 1964; Sec.-Gen. HENRI OUIKON.

Chambre de Commerce, d'Industrie, des Mines et de l'Artisanat (CCIMA): blvd Charles de Gaulle, BP 823, Bangui; tel. 61-16-68; fax 61-35-61; e-mail ccima@intnet.cf; Pres. RIGOBERT YOMBO; Sec. GERTRUDE ZOUTA-YAMANDJA.

EMPLOYERS' ORGANIZATION

Union Nationale du Patronat Centrafricain (UNPC): Immeuble Tropicana, 1°, BP 2180, Bangui; tel. and fax 61-42-10; e-mail patronat@intnet.cf; Pres. FAUSTIN ZAGUI.

UTILITIES

Electricity

Société Energie de Centrafrique (ENERCA): ave de l'Indépendance, BP 880, Bangui; tel. 61-20-22; fax 61-54-43; e-mail enerca@intnet.cf; f. 1967; state-owned; production and distribution of electric energy; 119.1 GWh produced for the Bangui grid in 2003; Dir-Gen. SAMUEL TOZOUI.

Water

Société de Distribution d'Eau en Centrafrique (SODECA): BP 1838, Bangui; tel. 61-59-66; fax 61-25-49; f. 1975 as the Société Nationale des Eaux; state-owned co responsible for supply, treatment and distribution of water; Dir-Gen. SAMUEL RANGBA.

MAJOR COMPANIES

The following are among the largest companies in terms of either capital investment or employment.

Alpha Robusta Café: BP 320, Bangui; fax 61-44-49; purchase and distribution of coffee; Man. CHRISTELIN BANGANDOZOU.

Bata SA Centrafricaine: BP 364, Bangui; tel. 61-45-79; f. 1969; cap. 150m. francs CFA; footwear mfrs; Dir VICTOR DE RYCKE.

COLALU: rue Chavannes, BP 1326, Bangui; tel. 61-20-42; fax 61-55-29; e-mail colalu@intnet.dj; f. 1969; cap. 69m. francs CFA; 57% owned by ALUCAM (Cameroon); mfrs of household articles and sheet aluminium; Pres. CLAUDE MILLET; Dir-Gen. M. KAPPES.

Compagnie Industrielle d'Ouvrages en Textiles (CIOT): BP 190, Bangui; tel. 61-36-22; f. 1949; cap. 250m. francs CFA; mfrs of clothing and hosiery; Dir-Gen. MICHEL ROBERT.

Comptoir National du Diamant (CND): blvd B. Boganela, Bangui; tel. 61-07-02; f. 1964; 50% state-owned, 50% owned by Diamond Distributors (USA); mining and marketing of diamonds; Dir-Gen. M. VASSOS.

Entreprise Forestière des Bois Africains Centrafrique (EFBACA): BP 205, Bangui; tel. 61-25-33; f. 1969; 12% state-owned; exploitation of forests and wood processing; Pres. VICTOR BALET; Dir JEAN QUENNOZ.

Huilerie Savonnerie Centrafricaine (HUSACA): BP 1020, Bangui; tel. 61-58-54; fax 61-68-11; mfrs of soap, edible oil and animal feed; Dir BASSAM ABDALLAH.

Industrie Centrafricaine du Textile (ICAT): BP 981, Bangui; tel. 61-40-00; f. 1965; cap. 586m. francs CFA; state-owned; textile complex; Man. Dir M. NGOUNDOUKOUA.

Industries Forestières de Batalimo (IFB): BP 517, Bangui; tel. 61-28-77; f. 1970; cap. 100m. francs CFA; Dir JACQUES GADEN.

Motte-Cordonnier-Afrique (MOCAF): BP 806, Bangui; tel. 61-18-13; f. 1951; cap. 1,123m. francs CFA; production of beer, soft drinks and ice; Pres. BERTRAND MOTTE; Dir-Gen. PHILIPPE MAGNAVAL.

Société Centrafricaine des Cuirs (CENTRA-CUIRS): Bangui; f. 1975; cap. 75m. francs CFA; 20% state-owned; mfrs of leather goods.

Société Centrafricaine de Déroulage (SCAD): BP 1607, Bangui; tel. 61-09-44; fax 61-56-60; f. 1972; cap. 700m. francs CFA; exploitation of forests, mfrs of plywood; also operates a sawmill; Dir-Gen. J. KAMACH; 392 employees.

Société Centrafricaine de Développement des Textiles (SOCADETEX): BP 154, Bangui-Lakouanga; tel. 61-76-23; fax 61-06-17; plant at Bossangoa; cotton producer; frmly the Société Cotonnière Centrafricaine (SOCOCA) prior to privatization in 2002; liquidation announced in April 2006.

Société Centrafricaine du Diamant (SODIAM): BP 1016, Bangui; tel. 61-03-79; cap. 100m. francs CFA; export of diamonds; Dir DIMITRI ANAGNOSTELLIS.

Société Centrafricaine d'Exploitation Forestière et Industrielle (SOCEFI): BP 3, M'Bata-Bangui; f. 1947; nationalized 1974; cap. 880m. francs CFA; operates a sawmill; also timber exporters and mfrs of prefabricated dwellings; Man. Dir PIERRE OPANZOYEN.

Société Centrafricaine des Gaz Industriels (SOCAGI): blvd Bouganda, BP 905, Bangui; tel. 61-16-42; fax 61-12-74; e-mail socagi@yahoo.fr; f. 1965; cap. 53m. francs CFA; manufacture and sale of industrial and medical gases; Pres. and Dir-Gen. PAUL LALAGUE.

Société Centrafricaine des Palmiers (CENTRAPALM): BP 1355, Bangui; tel. 61-49-40; fax 61-38-75; f. 1975; state-owned; production and marketing of palm oil; operates the Bossongo agro-industrial complex; Pres. MATHIEU-FRANCIS NGANAWARA; Gen. Man. Dr JOËL BEASSEM.

Sylvicole (SLOVENIA-BOIS): BP 183 Lakouanga, Bangui; tel. 61-13-30; f. 1970; cap. 250m. francs CFA; partly Slovenian-owned; sawmill; frmly the Société d'Exploitation et d'Industrialisation Forestière en RCA; Dir FRANC BENKOVIĆ.

Société Industrielle Centrafricaine (SICA): BP 1325, Bangui; tel. 61-44-99; f. 1967; cap. 200m. francs CFA; sawmill at M'baiki in the Lobaye area, annual capacity 18,000 cu m; Dir CHARLES SYLVAIN.

Société Industrielle Forestière en Afrique Centrale (SIFAC): BP 156, Bangui; f. 1970; cap. 95m. francs CFA; sawmill and joinery; Dir JACQUES GADEN.

Société de Plantations d'Hévéas et de Caféiers (SPHC): BP 1384, Bangui; f. 1974; cap. 160m. francs CFA; rubber and coffee plantations.

Sucrière en Afrique (SUCAF-RCA): ave Boganda, km 4, BP 1370, Bangui; tel. 61-32-88; fax 61-34-09; acquired in 2003 by the Castel group (France); sugar producer; factory at Ouaka.

Taillerie Centrafricaine de Diamant: 117 ave Boganda, Bangui; tel. 61-66-19; fax 61-62-28; diamond production; Dir-Gen. ATNIAL LEVI.

Total Centrafricaine de Gestion (TOCAGES): BP 724, Bangui; tel. 61-05-88; f. 1950; cap. 200m. francs CFA; 51% state-owned; storage, retailing and transport of petroleum products; Dir CHRISTIAN-DIMANCHE SONGUET.

TRADE UNIONS

Confédération Chrétienne des Travailleurs de Centrafrique (CCTC): BP 939, Bangui; tel. 61-05-71; fax 61-55-81; Pres. LOUIS SALVADOR.

Confédération Nationale de Travailleurs de Centrafrique: BP 2141, Bangui; tel. 50-94-36; fax 61-35-61; e-mail cnt@intnet.cf; Sec.-Gen. JEAN-RICHARD SANDOS-OULANGA.

Confédération Syndicale des Travailleurs de Centrafrique (CSTC): BP 386, km 5, Bangui; tel. 61-38-69; Sec.-Gen. SABIN KPOKOLO.

Confédération Syndicale des Travailleurs de la Centrafrique: BP 386, Bangui; tel. and fax 61-38-69.

Organisation des Syndicats Libres du Secteur Public, Parapublic et Privé (OSLP): BP 1450, Bangui; tel. 61-20-00; Sec.-Gen. GABRIEL NGOUANDJI-TANGAS.

Union Générale des Travailleurs de Centrafrique (UGTC): BP 346, Bangui; tel. 61-05-86; fax 61-17-96; Pres. CÉCILE GUÉRÉ.

Union des Journalistes: Bangui; tel. 61-13-38.

Union Syndicale des Travailleurs de Centrafrique (USTC): BP 1390, Bangui; tel. 61-60-15; e-mail vvesfon@yahoo.fr; Sec. THÉOPHILE SONNY COLÉ.

Transport

RAILWAYS

There are no railways at present. There are long-term plans to connect Bangui to the Transcameroon railway. A line linking Sudan's Darfur region with the CAR's Vakaga province has also been proposed.

ROADS

In 1999 there were an estimated 23,810 km of roads. Only about 3% of the total network is paved. Eight main routes serve Bangui, and those that are surfaced are toll roads. Both the total road length and the condition of the roads are inadequate for current requirements. In 1997 the European Union provided 32,500m. francs CFA to improve infrastructure in the CAR. In September a vast road-improvement scheme was launched, concentrating initially on roads to the south and north-west of Bangui. The CAR is linked with Cameroon by the Transafrican Lagos–Mombasa highway. Roads are frequently impassable in the rainy season (July–October).

Bureau d'Affrètement Routier Centrafricain (BARC): Gare routière, BP 523, Bangui; tel. 61-20-55; fax 61-37-44; Dir-Gen. J. M. LAGUEREMA-YADINGUIN.

Compagnie Nationale des Transports Routiers (CNTR): Bangui; tel. 61-46-44; state-owned; Dir-Gen. GEORGES YABADA.

Fonds Routier: BP 962, Bangui; tel. 61-62-95; fax 61-68-63.

Projet Sectoriel de Transports (PST): BP 941, Bangui; tel. 61-62-94; fax 61-65-79.

TBC Cameroun SARL: BP 637, Bangui; tel. 61-20-16; fax 61-13-19; e-mail rca@tbclogistics.com; internet www.tbclogistics.com; f. 1963.

INLAND WATERWAYS

There are some 2,800 km of navigable waterways along two main water courses. The first, formed by the Congo river and its tributary the Oubangui, can accommodate convoys of barges (of up to 800 metric tons load) between Bangui and Brazzaville and Pointe-Noire in the Republic of the Congo, except during the dry season, when the route is impassable. The second is the river Sangha, also a tributary of the Congo, on which traffic is again seasonal. There are two ports, at Bangui and Salo, on the rivers Oubangui and Sangha, respectively. Bangui port has a handling capacity of 350,000 tons, with 350 m of wharfs and 24,000 sq m of warehousing. Efforts are being made to develop the Sangha upstream from Salo, to increase the transportation of timber from this area and to develop Nola as a timber port.

Agence Centrafricaine des Communications Fluviales (ACCF): BP 822, Bangui; tel. 61-09-67; fax 61-02-11; f. 1969; state-owned; supervises development of inland waterways transport system; Chair. GUY MAMADOU MARABENA.

Société Centrafricaine de Transports Fluviaux (SOCATRAF): rue Parent, BP 1445, Bangui; tel. and fax 61-43-15; e-mail socatraf@intnet.cf; f. 1980; 51% owned by ACCF; Man. Dir FRANÇOIS TOUSSAINT.

CIVIL AVIATION

The international airport is at Bangui-M'Poko. There are also 37 small airports for internal services.

Agence pour la sécurité de la navigation aérienne en Afrique et Madagascar (ASECNA): 32–38, ave Jean Jaurès, BP 828, Bangui; tel. 61-33-80; fax 61-49-18; e-mail contact@asecna.aero; internet www.asecna.com; Dir-Gen. OUSMANE ISSOUFOU OUBANDAWAKI.

Centrafrican Airlines (CAL): Aéroport Bangui-M'Poko; f. 1999; privately owned; internal flights.

Mondial Air Fret (MAF): BP 1883, Bangui; tel. 61-14-58; fax 61-62-62; f. 1998; Dir THÉOPHILE SONNY COLÉ.

Tourism

Although tourism remains relatively undeveloped, the CAR possesses considerable scenic attractions in its waterfalls, forests and wildlife. In 2005 11,969 tourists arrived. In 2004 receipts from tourism were estimated at US $4m.

Fonds du Développement et Touristique: BP 2327, Bangui; tel. 61-13-51; fax 61-09-75.

Office National Centrafricain du Tourisme (OCATOUR): rue Roger Guérillot, BP 645, Bangui; tel. 61-45-66.

Defence

As assessed at November 2006, the armed forces numbered about 3,150 men (army 2,000, air force 150 and gendarmerie 1,000). Military service is selective and lasts for two years. In April 1998 the UN Mission to the Central African Republic (MINURCA) commenced peace-keeping operations in the country; MINURCA completed its gradual withdrawal on 15 February 2000. In December 2002 the first contingent of a peace-keeping force from the Communauté économique et monétaire de l'Afrique centrale (CEMAC) arrived in Bangui; at November 2006 the force comprised 380 troops, from Gabon, Chad and the Republic of the Congo. Some 300 French troops, who had been dispatched following the overthrow of President Patassé in March 2003, also remained in the CAR in March 2007, as part of Operation Boali, charged with restructuring the local armed forces and supporting the Force multinationale de la CEMAC.

Defence Expenditure: Estimated at 8,200m. francs CFA in 2006.

Chief of Staff of the Armed Forces: Gen. JULES BERNARD OUANDÉ.

Education

Education is officially compulsory for eight years between six and 14 years of age. Primary education begins at the age of six and lasts for six years. Secondary education begins at the age of 12 and lasts for up to seven years, comprising a first cycle of four years and a second of three years. In 2003/04 enrolment at primary schools was equivalent to 56% of children in the relevant age-group (67% of boys; 44% of girls), according to UNESCO estimates, while in 2001/02 secondary enrolment was equivalent to only 12%. Current expenditure by the Ministry of Education in 1995 totalled 8,820m. francs CFA, equivalent to 1.6% of gross national income. The provision of state-funded education was severely disrupted during the 1990s and early 2000s, owing to the inadequacy of financial resources.

Bibliography

de Bayle des Hermens, R. *Recherches préhistoriques en République Centrafricaine*. Paris, Klincksieck, 2005.

Bigo, D. *Pouvoir et obéissance en Centrafrique*. Paris, Editions Karthala, 1989.

Binoua, J. *Centrafrique: l'instabilité permanente*. Paris, L'Harmattan, 2005.

Brégeon, J.-N. *Administrateurs en Oubangui-Chari*. Paris, Editions Denoël, 1998.

Carter, G. M. (Ed.). *National Unity and Regionalism in Eight African States*. Ithaca, NY, Cornell University Press, 1966.

de Dreux Brezé, J. *Le Problème du regroupement en Afrique équatoriale*. Paris, Librairie Gale de Droit et de Jurisprudence, 1968.

Emerging Markets Investment Center. *Central African Republic Investment and Business Guide*. 2nd Edn. USA, International Business Publications, 1998.

Central African Republic Business and Investment Yearbook. USA, International Business Publications, 2002.

Central African Republic Business Intelligence Report. USA, International Business Publications, 2003.

Germain, E. *Centrafrique et Bokassa 1965–1979: Force et déclin d'un pouvoir personnel*. Paris, L'Harmattan, 2001.

Kalck, P. *Central African Republic (World Bibliographical Series)*. Paris, ABC-Clio, 1992 and 2004.

Histoire de la République Centrafricaine. Paris, Berger Levrault, 1977.

N'Douba, P. *L'otage du général rebelle centrafricain François Bozizé: Journal d'un Captif des 'Libérateurs'*. Paris, L'Harmattan, 2006.

Ngoupandé, J.-P. *Chronique de la crise centrafricaine 1996–1997: le syndrome barracuda*. Paris, L'Harmattan, 1997.

O'Toole, T. *The Central African Republic. The Continent's Hidden Heart*. Boulder, CO, Westview Press, 1986.

Historical Dictionary of the Central African Republic. 3rd Edn. Metuchen, NJ, Scarecrow Press, 2004.

Pigeon, P. *Les activités informelles en République Centrafricaine.* Paris, L'Harmattan, 2000.

Saulnier, P. *Le Centrafrique: Entre mythe et réalité.* Paris, L'Harmattan, 1998.

Bangui raconte: Contes de Centrafrique. Paris, L'Harmattan, 2000.

Titley, B. *Dark Age: The Political Odyssey of Emperor Bokassa.* Liverpool, Liverpool University Press, 1997.

Wagon, J.-B. *L'économie centrafricaine: pour rompre avec la logique de rente.* Paris, L'Harmattan, 1998.

Woodfork, J. *Culture and Customs of the Central African Republic.* Westport, CT, Greenwood Press, 2006.

Zoctizoum, Y. *Histoire de la République Centrafricaine*, 2 vols. Paris, L'Harmattan, 1984.

CHAD

Physical and Social Geography

DAVID HILLING

The Republic of Chad is bordered to the north by Libya, to the south by the Central African Republic, to the west by Niger and Cameroon and to the east by Sudan. The northernmost of the four independent states that emerged from French Equatorial Africa, Chad is, with an area of 1,284,000 sq km (495,800 sq miles), the largest in terms of size and population (10,468,000 at mid-2006, according to UN estimates). Traditionally a focal point for equatorial and Saharan trade routes, the country's vast size, land-locked location and great distance from the coast create problems for economic development. The only large city is the capital, N'Djamena (known as Fort-Lamy during the colonial period), which had a population of 530,965 at the 1993 census.

The relief is relatively simple. From 240 m in the Lake Chad depression in the south-west, the land rises northwards through the Guéra massif at 1,800 m to the mountainous Saharan region of Tibesti at 3,350 m. Eastwards, heights of 1,500 m are attained in the Ouaddaï massif. In the south the watershed area between the Chari and Congo rivers is of subdued relief and only slight elevation. The only rivers of importance, both for irrigation and seasonal navigation, are the Chari and Logone, which traverse the south-west of the country and join at N'Djamena, before flowing into Lake Chad.

Extending across more than 16° of latitude, Chad has three well-defined zones of climate, natural vegetation and associated economic activity. The southern third of the country has annual rainfall in excess of 744 mm (increasing to 1,200 mm in the extreme south), and has a savannah woodland vegetation. This is the country's principal agricultural zone, providing the two main cash crops, cotton and groundnuts, and a variety of local food crops (especially rice). Northwards, with rainfall of 250–500 mm per year, there is a more open grassland, where there is emphasis on pastoral activity, limited cultivation of groundnuts and local grains, and some collection of gum arabic. This marginal Sahel zone was adversely affected by drought during most of the 1970s and 1980s, and the cattle herds were greatly reduced in number. The northern third of the country has negligible rainfall and a sparse scrub vegetation, which grades north into pure desert with little apparent economic potential, although the 'Aozou strip', a region of 114,000 sq km in the extreme north, is believed to contain significant reserves of uranium and other minerals. The development of substantial petroleum reserves in the Doba Basin, in the south of the country, and also at Sedigi commenced in the late 1990s and continued in the early 2000s, and production of petroleum at Doba commenced in 2003. There was also believed to be considerable potential for the commercial exploitation of gold, particularly at Mayo-Kebbi, in the south of the country.

Chad's total population is relatively small in relation to its large area, and is markedly concentrated in the southern half of the country. Religious and ethnic tensions between the people of the north and south have traditionally dominated the history of Chad. The population of the north is predominantly Islamic, of a nomadic or semi-nomadic character, and is largely engaged in farming and in breeding livestock. Rivalry between ethnic groups is strong. By contrast, the inhabitants of the south are settled farmers, who largely follow animist beliefs. The Sara tribes, some 10 ethnic groups with related languages and cultural links, comprise a large section of the population of the south. Since the end of the Second World War, the population of the south has inclined towards a more Westernized culture; the rate of literacy has increased rapidly, and Christianity has attracted a number of adherents. The population of the north, however, forms a traditional, Islamic society, and is largely unaffected by modern education. The state is secular and exercises neutrality in relation to religious affiliations. In 1995 the closely related Sara, Bongo and Baguirmi peoples represented the largest ethnic group, amounting to an estimated 20.1% of the population between them, followed by the Chadic (17.7%) and Arabs (14.3%). French and Arabic are the official languages. Karembou, Ouadi, Teda, Daza and Djonkor are the principal vernaculars.

Recent History

BERNARD LANNE

Revised by EDWARD GEORGE

Formerly part of French Equatorial Africa, Chad became an autonomous republic within the French Community in November 1958. François Tombalbaye, a southerner and leader of the Parti progressiste tchadien (PPT), was elected Prime Minister in March 1959. Chad became independent on 11 August 1960, under Tombalbaye's presidency. However, the sparsely populated northern territory of Borkou-Ennedi-Tibesti (BET), accounting for some 47% of the area of Chad, remained under French military administration until 1964. In 1963 the PPT was declared the sole legal party. Discontent with the party's political monopoly, and with mismanagement and corruption by government officials, precipitated a serious rebellion, focused mainly in the north, in 1965. The Front de libération nationale du Tchad (FROLINAT), formed in Sudan in 1966, later assumed leadership of the revolt. In August 1968 French troops intervened in support of the Government.

As a result of the French military intervention, the rebellion was contained, and in 1972 the French reinforcements left Chad. Libya, which maintained a claim to sovereignty over the 'Aozou strip' in northern Chad, continued to provide support to FROLINAT. Following a deterioration in relations between Chad and France, in 1972 Tombalbaye signed a pact of friendship with Libya, which none the less annexed the 'Aozou strip' in 1973.

In April 1975 Tombalbaye was killed in a military coup, and Gen. Félix Malloum, former army Chief of Staff, assumed power. FROLINAT remained in opposition to the new Government. Divisions subsequently emerged within FROLINAT, whose leader, Hissène Habré, an opponent of the Libyan annexation of the 'Aozou strip', was replaced by Goukouni Oueddei. (Habré continued, however, to lead a faction within FROLINAT.) FROLINAT launched renewed offensives during 1977 and 1978, and overran large areas of territory. The Government successfully sought French assistance to halt the advance of FROLINAT.

CIVIL CONFLICT AND LIBYAN INTERVENTION

In August 1978 Malloum appointed Habré as Prime Minister, to lead a civilian Government. Relations between Malloum and

Habré soon deteriorated, and in February 1979 fighting broke out in N'Djamena, the capital, between the Government's Forces armées tchadiennes (FAT) and Habré's troops, the Forces armées du nord (FAN). With the tacit support of France, the FAN seized control of N'Djamena, while the rebel faction led by Goukouni (the Forces armées populaires, FAP) gained territory in the north. In March Malloum resigned and fled the country, after appointing Lt-Col (later Gen.) Wadal Abdelkader Kamougué as his successor.

In April 1979 a provisional Government (Gouvernement d'union nationale de transition, GUNT) was formed by FROLINAT, the FAN, the Mouvement populaire pour la libération du Tchad (MPLT) and the FAT. The leader of the MPLT, Lol Mahamat Choua, was appointed President, while Goukouni and Habré took ministerial portfolios. However, a committee, headed by Kamougué, which rejected the authority of the new Government, was established at Moundou to govern the south. In August, following the failure of attempts to dislodge Kamougué's forces, a second GUNT was organized under the presidency of Goukouni, with Kamougué as Vice-President. In April 1980, following renewed conflict between the FAP and the FAN, Habré was dismissed from the GUNT. In accordance with France's stated policy of neutrality, its troops were withdrawn from Chad in May. In June, without the prior consent of the GUNT, a treaty of friendship and co-operation was signed in Tripoli between Libya and a representative of Goukouni. In October Libyan forces intervened in the hostilities, resulting in the defeat of Habré and the retreat of the FAN from N'Djamena. A 15,000-strong Libyan contingent subsequently entered Chad.

In January 1981 Goukouni signed a further agreement with Libya, providing for a gradual political union of Chad and Libya. In April Libyan troops intervened in clashes between the FAP and the Conseil démocratique révolutionnaire (CDR), one of the breakaway factions of FROLINAT, resulting in numerous casualties. In November Libyan forces were withdrawn, and, at the behest of France, the Organization of African Unity (OAU, now the African Union—AU) sent a peace-keeping force to Chad. In February 1982 the OAU proposed that a cease-fire be declared, with elections to take place, under its supervision, before 30 June. Goukouni rejected the OAU plan, which effectively comprised a political victory for the FAN, and hostilities intensified. The FAN continued to advance, capturing N'Djamena in early June. Goukouni fled the country, and the coalition of factions that constituted the GUNT began to fragment.

HABRÉ IN POWER, 1982–90

In mid-June 1982, following the capture of N'Djamena, the formation of a provisional Council of State, with Habré as Head of State, was announced. By the end of June the OAU force had withdrawn from Chad, and in October Habré was inaugurated as President. A new Government was formed, in which southerners held a large proportion of ministerial portfolios. However, Goukouni's troops regained control of the greater part of BET, with Libyan support. In January 1983 elements of the FAT joined the FAN to form the Forces armées nationales tchadiennes (FANT).

In March 1983, in negotiations with the Libyan Government, Habré rejected Libyan demands for the recognition of Chad's Islamic character and of the annexation of the 'Aozou strip', and for the signing of a treaty of alliance. By July Goukouni's rebel troops, with assistance from Libya, had occupied the entire BET region. Following further advances by the FANT and Goukouni's forces (with Libyan support), France dispatched some 3,000 troops to Chad, and by September all fighting between the factions had ceased.

Political and Military Initiatives

During early 1984 it became evident that Habré needed to regain support in the south to consolidate political power. In June Habré replaced the FROLINAT-FAN grouping with a new official party, the Union nationale pour l'indépendance et la révolution (UNIR). In a government reshuffle in July one-half of the ministerial posts (including the foreign affairs portfolio) were allocated to southerners.

Meanwhile, in September 1984 France and Libya agreed to the simultaneous withdrawal of their forces in Chad. The evacuation of French forces was completed in November, but Libyan troops remained, in contravention of the agreement. France subsequently stated that it would not enforce Libyan withdrawal from northern Chad, but would intervene if Libyan forces advanced towards N'Djamena. President François Mitterrand recognized Chad's claim to the 'Aozou strip', while criticizing Habré for jeopardizing national unity in favour of territorial gain. From October 1985 Libya began to reinforce its military presence in northern Chad. In February 1986 GUNT forces initiated Libyan-supported attacks on government positions to the south of the 16th parallel. The offensive was repelled by the FANT, and Habré appealed to France for increased military aid. Shortly afterwards French military aircraft, operating from the Central African Republic (CAR), bombed a Libyan-built airstrip north-east of Faya-Largeau. A retaliatory air attack on N'Djamena airport caused minor damage. France subsequently established an air-strike force at N'Djamena to counteract any further Libyan attack (an intervention designated 'Opération Epervier'), while the USA provided supplementary military aid to Habré's forces.

Reconciliation with Libya

In March 1986 Habré appointed several former opponents to the Council of Ministers. Meanwhile, divisions within the GUNT increased and by October Goukouni had indicated his willingness to negotiate with Habré, amid indications that the FAP had decided to join Habré's FANT. In November, with Libyan support, Acheikh Ibn Oumar of the CDR assumed the presidency of a reconstituted GUNT, comprising seven of the original 11 factions.

In December 1986 clashes broke out in Tibesti between Libyan forces and the now pro-Habré FAP. In January 1987 FANT troops recaptured a number of strategic targets in the north. Following a Libyan offensive on the southern town of Arada, France launched a retaliatory air attack. Libyan forces subsequently began to retreat, and by May Habré's troops had regained control of northern Chad, except for the Aozou region. In July reconciliation talks between Habré and Goukouni (the latter now resident in Algiers, Algeria) ended in failure. In August Kamougué (who had transferred his support to Habré in February) joined the Government. In that month the FANT seized control of the town of Aozou, but were subsequently forced by Libyan air attacks to withdraw to positions in Tibesti. In September an OAU-brokered cease-fire took effect. There was, however, a considerable reinforcement of the Libyan bases in the Aozou region and on the Niger–Libya border. In February 1988 a number of former opposition parties, including the FAP, merged with UNIR. In March, following a dispute with Oumar, the GUNT was reconstituted under Goukouni. In November, following the conclusion of a peace agreement in Iraq, forces led by Oumar declared support for Habré, and subsequently returned to Chad.

A meeting between the leaders of Chad and Libya, under the aegis of an OAU ad hoc committee (established in 1977 to debate the question of the sovereignty of the Aozou region), was, meanwhile, scheduled for May 1988. Shortly before the summit it was announced that the Libyan leader, Col Muammar al-Qaddafi (who had repeatedly boycotted meetings of the ad hoc committee), would not be attending. However, the Libyan Government, having subsequently announced its willingness to recognize the Habré regime, invited Habré and Goukouni to meet in Libya for reconciliation negotiations, and offered to provide financial aid for reconstruction in northern Chad. In October, following mediation by Togo, Chad and Libya issued a joint communiqué expressing their willingness to seek a peaceful solution to the territorial dispute, and diplomatic relations (which had been suspended in 1982) were resumed in November.

Despite the appointment of Oumar as Minister of Foreign Affairs in March 1989, political tensions persisted. In April the Minister of the Interior and Territorial Administration was arrested, following the discovery of an alleged coup plot. The Commander-in-Chief of the Armed Forces, Hassan Djamous, and his predecessor in that post, Idriss Deby, who were both implicated in the conspiracy, fled to Sudan with their supporters. FANT troops were dispatched to quell the mutiny, during which Djamous was killed. Deby escaped, with Sudanese assistance, to Libya, and in June formed a new opposition movement, the Action du 1 avril, based in Sudan.

Relations between Libya and Chad remained uneasy in mid-1989, when Habré accused Qaddafi of collusion with the Sudanese Government in preparing a military attack against Chad. In August Chad and Libya signed a draft agreement for the peaceful resolution of the dispute: if a political settlement was not achieved within one year, the issue would be submitted to arbitration by the International Court of Justice (ICJ). Provision was made for an OAU-supervised withdrawal of all armed forces from the Aozou region and for the release of all prisoners of war. In September, however, the first session of a Chad-Libya joint commission, which was to oversee the implementation of the agreement, broke down over arrangements for the release of Libyan prisoners of war. Later that year hostilities resumed between the FANT and pro-Libyan forces along Chad's border with Sudan.

A new Constitution was approved by referendum on 10 December 1989, reportedly receiving the support of 99.94% of votes cast. The new Constitution, promulgated on 20 December, confirmed Habré as President for a further seven-year term, upheld the principle of a single-party state and provided for the creation of an elected legislature, with a five-year mandate.

In March 1990 Deby and his supporters, the Forces patriotiques du salut (subsequently known as the Mouvement patriotique du salut, MPS), launched an invasion of eastern Chad from bases in Sudan. France dispatched military equipment and personnel to reinforce 'Opération Epervier' at Abéché; although the French contingent did not participate in the military engagements, its presence undoubtedly induced the rebel forces to retreat. In May the fifth session of the Chad-Libya joint commission was compromised by the seizure, by Chadian forces, of 10 Libyan vehicles on Sudanese territory. In July the Chadian Government alleged that Libya and Sudan were massing forces in Sudan, in preparation for an offensive against Chad. In August, none the less, shortly before the agreed deadline for a settlement, negotiations between Habré and Qaddafi took place in Morocco. Both Governments subsequently agreed to refer the territorial dispute to the ICJ. Meanwhile, 436 candidates contested 123 seats at legislative elections held in July 1990; the electoral turn-out was 56%.

DEBY TAKES POWER

On 10 November 1990 forces led by Deby invaded Chad from Sudan and launched an attack on positions held by Chadian government forces north-east of Abéché. The FANT initially forced the rebels to retreat to Sudan; however, attacks soon resumed, with territorial gains being reported for the MPS in the east, and many FANT units reportedly transferred their allegiance to Deby. Negotiations concerning the sovereignty of the Aozou region, scheduled for late November, were suspended by Qaddafi, who claimed that allegations of Libyan involvement in the rebel invasion had undermined conditions for the discussions.

On 30 November 1990 Habré, together with his entourage, fled Chad, after the MPS had seized control of Abéché. Deby arrived in N'Djamena two days later, and declared his commitment to the creation of a democratic multi-party political system. The Assemblée nationale was dissolved, the Constitution was suspended and a provisional 33-member Council of State was formed, with Deby as interim Head of State. The Council of State mainly comprised members of the MPS and allied parties, although Oumar was appointed Special Adviser to the Head of State. Following the publication of a report, compiled by the MPS, accusing Habré of violations of human rights and of corruption, Deby sought Habré's extradition from Senegal, where he had been granted political asylum. Later in December the Government announced that the FANT was to be restructured and designated the Armées nationales tchadiennes (ANT).

Following the accession to power of the MPS, it was announced that aid and co-operation agreements between France and the Habré Government would be honoured, and that new accords would be formulated. The USA, however, refused to extend formal recognition to the new regime, although it affirmed its commitment to existing aid agreements. The Libyan and Sudanese Governments declared support for the new regime, and undertook not to allow forces hostile to Deby to operate on their territory.

On 1 March 1991 a National Charter, drafted by the executive committee of the MPS, was adopted for a 30-month transitional period, at the end of which a constitutional referendum was to be held. The Charter confirmed Deby's appointment as President, Head of State and Chairman of the MPS, and required the Government to institute measures to prepare for the implementation of a multi-party system. Under the terms of the Charter, a new Council of Ministers and a 31-member legislative Conseil de la République were to replace the provisional Council of State. On 4 March Deby was formally inaugurated as President. The Council of State was dissolved, and the former President of the Assemblée nationale, Dr Jean Bawoyeu Alingué, was appointed Prime Minister in a new Government.

POLITICAL REFORM

In May 1991 Deby announced that a national conference, scheduled for May 1992, would prepare a new constitution to provide for the introduction of a multi-party system and would be followed by legislative elections. Constitutional amendments permitting the registration of opposition movements would enter into force in January 1992. In October the Council of Ministers adopted regulations regarding the authorization of political parties. Under the new legislation, each party was required to have a minimum of 30 founder members, three each from 10 of Chad's 14 prefectures; the formation of parties on an ethnic or regional basis was prohibited. However, the MPS was exempted from the conditions of registration and opposition groups denounced the legislation as biased in its favour.

OPPOSITION TO THE DEBY GOVERNMENT

In September 1991 rebels attacked military garrisons in Tibesti, killing 50 people. Deby alleged that the offensive was instigated from Niger by Habré loyalists. In October 1991 troops attacked an arsenal at N'Djamena airport in an attempt to seize power; some 40 people were killed in the ensuing fighting. France reaffirmed its support for the MPS, and announced that the 'Epervier' contingent would be reinforced by an additional 300 troops. Following the coup attempt, the Chadian Government abrogated a recent co-operation agreement with Libya, on the grounds that the sovereignty of the Aozou region remained in dispute.

In late December 1991 some 3,000 troops loyal to Habré attacked several towns in the region of Lake Chad. The rebels were reported to be members of the Mouvement pour la démocratie et le développement (MDD), an opposition group based in Libya, led by Goukouni Guët. By early January 1992 the rebels had captured the towns of Liwa and Bol, and were advancing towards N'Djamena, causing government forces to suffer heavy losses. France dispatched troops to reinforce the 'Epervier' force, ostensibly to protect French citizens. Shortly afterwards the Government claimed that the rebels had been defeated. A number of prominent members of the opposition and former members of the Habré Government were subsequently arrested and summary executions were reported. France condemned such violations of human rights, and warned that its continued support for Deby was dependent on the implementation of political reforms. Later in January the Government declared an amnesty for political prisoners.

In April 1992 France announced that the role of 'Opération Epervier' as a defensive strike force was to cease, although French troops were to remain in Chad to assist in the restructuring of the ANT. In May the national conference was postponed; later that month Joseph Yodoyman, a member of the Alliance nationale pour la démocratie et le développement (ANDD), replaced Alingué as Prime Minister. Deby formed a new Council of Ministers, which included, for the first time, five members of the opposition.

In late May 1992 MDD rebels launched a further attack in the Lake Chad region, provoking government forces to counter-attack from Nigerian territory In June the Government announced that it had pre-empted a coup attempt, led by Abbas Koti, who had recently been replaced as Minister of State for Public Works and Transport. Shortly afterwards members of the pro-Koti Conseil national de redressement du Tchad (CNRT) attacked ANT forces in the Lake Chad region; fighting was also reported near Faya-Largeau. In late June representatives of the Government and the MDD signed an agreement envisaging a cessation of hostilities and the immediate release of detained MDD activists, although renewed clashes between government forces and the MDD troops were reported in July. In August clashes between Comité de sursaut national pour la paix et la démocratie (CSNPD) forces and government troops were reported in Doba, in the south. In September, none the less, the Government signed further peace agreements with the MDD, the CSNPD and an opposition movement based in Sudan, the Front national du Tchad (FNT).

In July 1992 the trade union federation, the Union des syndicats du Tchad (UST), organized a series of strikes, to protest at government plans to reduce salaries and to increase taxes. In October the UST organized a one-month general strike, demanding higher public-sector salaries and the convening of the national conference. Two former opposition members resigned their ministerial portfolios, to protest at the subsequent ban imposed by the Government on the activities of the UST. In mid-October the Government announced that the national conference would take place in January 1993. At the end of October 1992 the MDD officially declared the peace agreement, signed in September, to be invalid, alleging that the Government had received armaments from Libya and was preparing to resume hostilities; renewed clashes were subsequently reported. In November a number of UST activists were arrested after the general strike was extended for a further month. Later in November the Government ended the ban on the UST, although the general strike continued to be largely observed until January 1993.

CIVIL TENSION AND TRANSITION

The national conference was finally convened in January 1993, attended by some 800 delegates (representing, among others, the institutions of state, trade unions, professional associations and 30 political organizations). In April the conference adopted a Transitional Charter, elected Dr Fidel Moungar, hitherto Minister of National and Higher Education, as Prime Minister, and established a 57-member interim legislature, the Conseil supérieur de la transition (CST). Former President Choua, now leader of the Rassemblement pour la démocratie et le progrès (RDP), was elected Chairman of the CST. It was agreed that Deby was to remain in office as Head of State and Commander-in-Chief of the Armed Forces for one year (with provision for one extension), while a transitional Government, under the supervision of the CST, was to implement economic, political and social programmes drafted by the conference; multi-party elections were to take place at the end of this period. Moungar's Government retained only four members of the former Council of Ministers, and included representatives of a number of opposition parties. However, the membership of the transitional Government was almost halved in June.

Meanwhile, in January 1993 it was reported that CSNPD forces had attacked government troops at Goré, in the south. Later in January troops loyal to Habré attempted a *coup d'état* while Deby was visiting France. In February government troops clashed with members of the Nigerien armed forces after attacking MDD bases in Niger, and renewed military engagements took place between government troops and the CSNPD in southern Chad. By March some 15,000 civilians had fled to the CAR.

In May 1993, following a report by a commission of inquiry, the transitional Government confirmed that members of the ANT engaged in hostilities with the CSNPD had perpetrated massacres of civilians in southern Chad earlier that year. Moungar stated that officials implicated in the violence had been arrested and that a judicial investigation was to take place. In June the CST refused to ratify a co-operation agreement that had been signed with Libya in November 1992, in view of the outstanding issue of the sovereignty of the Aozou region (which was to be reviewed by the ICJ later that month).

In response to widespread concern at the increasing incidence of violent crime involving the security forces, in July 1993 the Government announced a reorganization of the ANT and the security forces. In August some 82 civilians were killed in the Ouaddaï region, apparently during inter-ethnic clashes. Shortly afterwards it was reported that some 41 people had been killed when the Republican Guard violently suppressed a demonstration by residents of N'Djamena, protesting against the massacre. The CST accused the Government of exceeding its powers by thus deploying the Republican Guard, and by imposing a national curfew following the unrest. In mid-August Koti (who had been arrested in Cameroon in December 1992, before reportedly escaping from detention) returned to Chad, after a peace agreement was reached by the CNRT and the Government. In September, despite efforts by the Government to allay discontent in the south, the CSNPD threatened to impede plans to exploit petroleum reserves in the region of Doba—considered essential to future prospects of economic development—unless the Government conceded to demands for the establishment of a federal state. In October Koti signed a further agreement with the Government, whereby the CNRT was to be granted legal status as a political party, and its forces integrated into the ANT. Following the killing of Koti by security forces, the CNRT announced that operations against government forces would be resumed.

Increasing disagreement between supporters of Deby and Moungar culminated, in October 1993, in the approval by the CST of a motion expressing 'no confidence' in the Moungar administration. Moungar subsequently resigned and his Government was dissolved. In November the CST elected Nouradine Kassiré Delwa Coumakoye, hitherto Minister of Justice, as Prime Minister, and a new transitional Government, which retained 10 members of the former administration, was appointed. In December a committee was established to prepare a draft constitution, an electoral code and legislation governing the registration of political organizations.

Meanwhile, activity by what had come to be known as 'politico-military' groups continued. The MDD and the Union nationale pour la démocratie et le socialisme announced in January 1994 that they were to unite against government forces, while members of the FNT attacked a military garrison at Abéché.

LIBYA WITHDRAWS FROM THE 'AOZOU STRIP'

In February 1994 the ICJ ruled in favour of Chad in the dispute over the sovereignty of the 'Aozou strip'. Later that month, however, Chad claimed that Libya had deployed additional troops in the region. In April Libya agreed to commence the withdrawal of troops from the region, in an operation that was to be monitored by UN observers and officials from both countries. In May Libya and Chad issued a joint statement confirming that the withdrawal of Libyan troops had been completed as scheduled, and in June the two Governments signed a co-operation agreement.

CONSTITUTIONAL PROPOSALS

In March 1994 the constitutional committee presented its recommendations, including provisions for the election of a President for a term of five years, the installation of a bicameral legislature and a Constitutional Council, and the establishment of a decentralized administrative structure. (In the event, the proposed upper legislative chamber was never established, however.) In April the CST extended the transitional period for one year. A new electoral timetable was adopted, and preparatory measures, to be adopted by June, included the introduction of an electoral code, the establishment of a national reconciliation council, and the appointment of electoral and human rights commissions. The constitutional recommendations were to be submitted for approval at a national referendum in December, with legislative and presidential elections to be held by March 1995.

Government efforts to negotiate a settlement with the UST to end industrial unrest were impeded by further strike action by public-sector workers at the end of April 1994, in support of demands for an increase in salaries to compensate for the 50% devaluation of the CFA franc in January. Despite a presidential decree declaring the strike illegal, industrial action continued. In May the Government established a 12-member national reconciliation council, which was to initiate negotiations with insurgent opposition forces. Later in May Deby announced an extensive government reorganization. In July the Government reached agreement with the UST on a limited increase in salaries and the payment of wage arrears.

TRANSITIONAL POLITICS

In August 1994, following the resumption of negotiations between the Chadian authorities and the CSNPD, the two sides signed a cease-fire agreement, providing for the recognition of the CSNPD as a legal political organization, and the integration of its forces into the ANT; implementation of the agreement was to be supervised by a committee comprising representatives of the UN and of the CAR, France and Gabon. Later in August, however, it was reported that government troops had killed some 26 civilians in southern Chad, in reprisal for attacks by members of another rebel faction, the Forces armées pour la République fédérale/Victimes d'agression (FARF/VA).

In September 1994 it was reported that the Minister of Mines and Energy, Lt-Col Mahamat Garfa (who had recently been dismissed as Chief of Army Staff), had fled N'Djamena with substantial government funds, and, together with some 600 members of the ANT, had joined CNRT forces in eastern Chad. Garfa subsequently established a co-ordination of eight rebel groups operative in eastern Chad, the Alliance nationale de la résistance (ANR), while remaining in exile himself. In October Choua was replaced as Chairman of the CST by a member of the MPS, Mahamat Bachar Ghadaia.

Deby officially announced in November 1994 that the process of democratic transition would be completed in April 1995, following presidential and legislative elections. In December 1994 Deby proclaimed a general amnesty for political prisoners and, excluding Habré, opposition members in exile. In January 1995 the CST adopted a new electoral code, and a Commission électorale nationale indépendante (CENI) was established. Later in January the CST approved the draft of the Constitution, which had been amended in accordance with recommendations reached by a national conference in August 1994.

In late March 1995 the CST extended the transitional period for a further year, and amended the National Charter to the effect that the incumbent Prime Minister was henceforth prohibited from contesting the forthcoming presidential election or from belonging to a political party. These measures attracted strong criticism from opposition parties, which subsequently sought a legal challenge to the validity of the extension of the transitional period. In April the CST voted to remove Coumakoye as Prime Minister, after criticizing him for the lack of progress in the organization of democratic elections. Although Coumakoye rejected the attempt to dismiss him as unconstitutional, the CST elected Djimasta Koibla, a prominent member of Alingué's Union pour la démocratie et la République (UDR), as Prime Minister. A new transitional Government was subsequently formed. In May the CENI scheduled the constitutional referendum for November and the presidential election for February 1996, with legislative elections to follow, in two rounds, in April and May. A unilateral declaration by the Government, in July, of a national cease-fire was received with caution by the rebel movements.

In November 2005 the Government and the MDD signed a peace agreement providing for a cease-fire, an exchange of prisoners and the integration of a number of MDD troops into the ANT. Also in that month the CENI promulgated a further timetable whereby a constitutional referendum was to take place in March 1996, followed by a presidential election in June and legislative elections later that year. Reconciliation discussions were convened in Franceville, Gabon, in January 1996, with mediation by the Governments of Gabon, the CAR and Niger and in March, following protracted negotiations, the Government and 13 opposition parties signed an agreement providing for the imposition of a cease-fire and the establishment of a special security force to maintain order during the electoral period.

PRESIDENTIAL AND LEGISLATIVE ELECTIONS

The conclusion of the Franceville agreement allowed the electoral timetable to proceed as rescheduled. However, a number of opposition groups, particularly the southern-based federalist organizations, urged their members to reject the draft Constitution, which enshrined a unitary state, at the national referendum. None the less, the new Constitution was adopted by 63.5% of votes cast at the referendum on 31 March 1996, although support for the Constitution was notably higher in northern and central regions than in the south.

By April 1996 15 presidential candidates, including Deby, had emerged. In the first round of voting, on 2 June, Deby secured 43.8% of votes cast, with Kamougué (contesting the election on behalf of the Union pour le renouveau et la démocratie—URD) taking 12.4% and Saleh Kebzaboh (for the Union nationale pour le développement et le renouveau—UNDR) 8.5%. Although Kebzaboh announced his support for Deby, the majority of the eliminated candidates urged a boycott of the second round, alleging electoral fraud. In early July the Government suspended the activities of the UST, after it attempted to organize an electoral boycott.

The second round of the presidential election, contested by Deby and Kamougué, took place on 3 July 1996: according to official results, Deby was elected by 69.1% of votes cast. He was inaugurated as President on 8 August, and subsequently reappointed Koibla as premier. Koibla formed a new Government, which included several opposition members, notably Kebzaboh (as Minister of Foreign Affairs). The ban on the UST was revoked at the end of July.

Legislative voting eventually took place on 5 January and 23 February 1997. Although voting was reportedly conducted relatively peacefully, a number of opposition activists were arrested for disrupting the electoral process, and both the MPS and opposition parties challenged preliminary results in several constituencies. Later in March the Court of Appeal announced the final results, according to which the MPS secured an absolute majority, with 63 of the 125 seats, while the URD won 29 seats, the UNDR 15 and the UDR four. The Assemblée nationale was installed on 4 April, and in early May Kamougué was elected President of the legislature, following an accord between his party, the URD, the MPS and the UNDR. Later that month Nassour Guelengdouksia Ouaidou (hitherto Secretary-General at the President's Office) was appointed Prime Minister. His Government included representatives of several parties, although the MPS retained the most senior ministerial portfolios. Kebzaboh was redesignated Minister of State for Public Works, Transport, Housing and Town Planning.

INSURGENCY PROBLEMS

In April 1997 the transitional Government and the FARF/VA signed a further peace agreement, which provided for the integration of FARF/VA civilian and armed members into the state apparatus, and the legalization of the movement as a political party. In May the incoming administration was reported to have negotiated a peace agreement with the FAP. In October the Government extended a general amnesty to members of the FNT, the Front national du Tchad renové (FNTR) and the Mouvement pour la justice sociale et la démocratie, which were to be legalized as political parties. In late October clashes erupted in Moundou between members of the ANT and insurgent elements of the FARF/VA. According to official figures, 42 FARF/VA rebels, 52 civilians and four members of the ANT were killed. The FARF/VA accused the Government of reneging on elements of the April peace agreement, and renewed clashes were reported in late November, in which several civilians were killed.

The restoration of peace, particularly in the south, was regarded as imperative, as efforts continued to secure external funding for the development of petroleum resources. In May 1998 a new peace accord was signed by the Government and the FARF/VA providing for an immediate cease-fire in Logone

Oriental and Logone Occidental prefectures, a general amnesty for FARF/VA rebels and the withdrawal of élite elements of the security services from the south; the accord renewed the provision included in the agreement of April 1997 for the transformation of the FARF/VA into a political party and the integration of its forces into the Chadian army.

In May 1998 Kebzaboh was dismissed from the Government, together with two other members of the UNDR. In July Ngarledjy Yorongar, the sole representative of the federalist Fédération action pour la République (FAR) in the Assemblée nationale, was sentenced to three years' imprisonment. A southerner who had been an outspoken critic of provisions for the exploitation of petroleum in southern Chad, Yorongar had claimed that Kamougué had received payment of 1,500m. francs CFA from a French petroleum company, and had also alleged that Déby and his family were mismanaging the country's petroleum resources.

THE TIBESTI REBELLION

From late 1998 reports emerged of a rebellion in the Tibesti region of northern Chad by the Mouvement pour la démocratie et la justice au Tchad (MDJT), led by Youssouf Togoimi, who had been dismissed as Minister of Defence in June 1997. In March 1999 it was revealed that a 3,000-strong élite military force had been deployed to counter the MDJT. In April 1999 the MDJT, the MDD and the CDR announced that they were to join forces to end what they termed the 'bloody drift' of the past decade. In late June FROLINAT stated that it was giving political and logistical support to the MDJT. In November the MDJT claimed to have defeated ANT forces in Aozou, killing 80 and capturing 47 (a further 42 ANT troops were said to have defected to the rebellion). In February 2000 it was reported that the former armed wing of the MDD had renamed itself the Mouvement pour l'unité et la République (MUR), and that the MUR had subsequently allied itself with the MDJT and the CDR. Meanwhile, in December 1999 it was announced that 13 'politico-military' groups, including FROLINAT and the FNTR, had formed a new alliance in opposition to the Deby regime, the Coordination des mouvements armés et partis politiques de l'opposition (CMAP). In the same month another four 'politico-military' groups, led by Acheikh Ibn Oumar, formed the Comité politique d'action et de liaison (CPAL).

Ouaidou resigned as Prime Minister in mid-December 1999. He was replaced by Nagoum Yamassoum, whose new Government included five UNDR members, among them Kebzaboh. In July 2000 the MDJT attacked a garrison in Bardaï and proclaimed their control of four towns in Tibesti. Official military sources stated that 57 rebels and 13 government troops were killed during the fighting.

PRESIDENTIAL ELECTION

In July 2000 the Assemblée nationale approved proposals for the creation of a new structure for the CENI, which was to plan a reorganization of constituencies in advance of presidential and legislative elections due to be held in 2001. (The administrative structure of Chad had been changed in 1999, with the former 14 prefectures replaced by 28 departments.) The Government was to appoint 16 of the 31 CENI members, with a further 12 to be nominated by parties represented in the legislature, and the remaining three by non-parliamentary parties. Several opposition parties were concerned by their apparent exclusion from the CENI and threatened to boycott the forthcoming elections in protest against the new arrangements. An extensive reshuffle of the Government at the end of August 2000 followed the dismissal of ministers belonging to the URD, owing to their party's rejection of the new electoral code. Furthermore, a number of members of the MPS resigned from the ruling party, reportedly in protest against violent acts committed by government forces.

In September 2000 Togoimi met with Deby for the first time, in Sirte, Libya. Togoimi's proposal for multilateral peace discussions, incorporating all opposition groups and Deby's administration, was followed later that month by a conference at which Deby met representatives of some 30 opposition organizations (including trade unions and civil society groups, in addition to political parties), styling themselves the Forces vives, which were reportedly united, under the leadership of Abderaman Djasnabaille, in their disapproval of the new electoral code. Renewed fighting broke out in October between members of the MDJT and the ANT in the north of Chad, and later intensified, with the MDJT reportedly launching attacks from Libyan territory.

In February 2001 it was announced that the presidential election would take place on 20 May and that elections to the Assemblée nationale, which had initially been scheduled for April 2001, were to be postponed until March 2002. In April 2001 Deby dismissed all UNDR ministers from the Government, following Kebzaboh's announcement that he was to contest the presidential election. The Secretary-General of the Parti pour la liberté et le développement (PLD), Ibn Oumar Mahamat Saleh, who was also a presidential candidate, subsequently ordered his party's three ministers to withdraw from the Government; two of the three ministers reportedly offered their resignation, although Yamassoum expressed his willingness to retain them in their government posts.

In May 2001 the six opposition presidential candidates, including Kamougué, Alingué and Yorongar, signed an electoral pact, pledging to unite behind a single candidate in the event of a second round; observers noted that, with the exception of the federalist Yorongar, the opposition candidates had few distinct policies beyond the desire to remove Deby from office. Meanwhile, in addition to the MPS, 27 political organizations, including the RDP, rallied behind Deby.

The election took place, as scheduled, on 20 May 2001; international and national observers pronounced themselves largely satisfied with its conduct, despite organizational difficulties; however, the six opposition candidates subsequently complained of widespread fraud and malpractice. In late May, prior to the announcement of the results, eight members of the CENI resigned, alleging irregularities in the vote counting. Following the CENI's announcement of preliminary results crediting Deby with 67.4% of votes cast, all six opposition candidates were briefly arrested at Kebzaboh's home, apparently for breaching a ban on political meetings prior to the declaration of official election results. The unsuccessful candidates were subsequently rearrested on charges of inciting violence and civil disobedience, although the arrests were promptly rescinded. In early June the opposition presented a petition to the Constitutional Council, requesting that the election be annulled. On 13 June the Constitutional Council issued the final results of the election, according to which Deby had received 63.2% of the valid votes cast, followed by Yorongar, with 16.4%. A turn-out of 61.4% was declared by the Constitutional Council, compared with the 80.9% initially announced by the CENI. In July the insurgency in Tibesti escalated, as MDJT forces claimed to have captured the town of Fada, killing 86 government troops; however, although the Government acknowledged that an attack had taken place, it denied the losses and refuted the involvement of the MDJT in the incident.

Yamassoum was reappointed as Prime Minister in mid-August 2001 and named a 35-member Government, including 14 new appointees, which comprised 20 representatives from the MPS, five from the RDP and the remainder from other groups that had supported Deby in the presidential election. Despite a promise by Deby to review the voters' register, opposition parties urged a boycott of the legislative elections scheduled for early 2002.

NATIONAL RECONCILIATION SOUGHT

In August 2001 Deby announced that he was willing to engage in dialogue with both the CMAP and the CPAL. Although the CPAL rejected any negotiations, in late October the CMAP offered to send a delegation to N'Djamena to enter into discussions with Deby, if its security could be assured. Meanwhile, in September the CMAP accused FROLINAT-Conseil provisoire de la révolution, as the organization had been renamed, of having engaged in separate discussions with the Government and with unnamed foreign politicians; the grouping was consequently expelled from the CMAP. In October a further report by Amnesty International stated that 'disappearances', extra-judicial executions and torture continued to be committed in Chad; the claims were rejected by the Government. In December the CMAP presented the Government with proposals for a peace plan, and in January 2002 the Minister of Foreign Affairs, Mahamat Saleh Annadif, held discussions with CMAP members in France and with other opposition members in exile in Benin and Nigeria.

During December 2001 and January 2002 representatives of the Government and principal opposition leaders (with the notable exception of Yorongar) participated in negotiations intended to lead to opposition participation in the forthcoming legislative elections. Although opposition parties continued to demand a full reorganization of the voter registration procedures, in late January Deby announced that the elections would be held on 21 April; according to the revised electoral code, the new Assemblée nationale was to be enlarged to 155 members. In early February Djasnabaille was indicted on charges of fraud. In that month the FAR, the UNDR and the URD announced their intention to participate in the legislative elections.

Meanwhile, reports emerged in December 2001 that the Libyan Government, which was mediating between MDJT rebels and the Chadian Government, had assured the rebels of its support. The involvement of Libya in the peace process was regarded as a major factor in the beneficial terms offered to the MDJT in a peace agreement, signed by the group's deputy leader, Adoum Togoi Abbo (a former Chadian ambassador to Libya), and the Chadian Government in early January 2002. According to the agreement, both sides would institute an immediate cease-fire and a general amnesty for prisoners. Moreover, the MDJT was to participate in the Chadian Government and other state institutions, while the rebel forces were to be regularized. Notably, the Libyan Government was to be responsible for monitoring the implementation of the agreement. However, Togoimi did not give his approval to the arrangements, and, as a split in the MDJT became evident, in early April the group issued a statement accusing the Government of inhibiting the peace process by its refusal to postpone legislative elections in order to allow the appointment of MDJT representatives to the Government.

LEGISLATIVE ELECTIONS

Elections to the Assemblée nationale, which were held on 21 April 2002, were contested by 472 candidates, representing some 40 parties, although the UDR and PLD boycotted the polls. According to the final election results, which were issued on 19 May, the MPS won 110 seats in the Assemblée nationale, significantly increasing its representation. (It was reported that MPS candidates were unopposed in some 50 constituencies.) The RDP became the second largest party, with 12 seats, while the FAR became the largest opposition party, with nine seats. Coumakoye's VIVA—Rassemblement national pour la démocratie et le progrès (VIVA—RNDP) and the UNDR each won five seats, and the URD's representation was significantly reduced, to only three seats. The Constitutional Council annulled the results of voting in two constituencies. In June Deby appointed his special counsellor, Haroun Kabadi, a senior official in the MPS, as Prime Minister, to head a 28-member Council of Ministers.

Meanwhile, in May 2002 it was reported that Togoi was being held in detention by forces loyal to Togoimi, who had confirmed his rejection of the peace agreement signed in January. None the less, in July some 200 former MDJT fighters were reported to have joined government forces; Togoi was subsequently demoted to the position of Second Vice-Chairman of the MDJT, effectively leading his own faction within the organization. An attack, in September, on the eastern village of Tissi was attributed by the Chadian Government to troops supported by the CAR, although the ANR, which had been dormant for several years, claimed responsibility for the raid and, amid heightened tension with the CAR (see below), emphasized that the perpetrators of the attack were resident in Chad.

The death of Togoimi, in Libya, in September 2002, while being treated for injuries sustained in a landmine explosion in northern Chad, raised hopes that peace talks between the Government and the MDJT would be reconvened, and Deby visited the north in order to encourage a resumption of negotiations. However, in October renewed fighting broke out in the north; following an attack by the MDJT on an airport at Faya N'Gourma, in which some 20 ANT soldiers reportedly died, further clashes were reported near Fada, in which, according to official figures, 50 MDJT rebels were killed. Later in the month the Government announced that the ANT had mounted an offensive against the MDJT near Ennedi, killing 123 MDJT fighters and capturing a further 63, as well as releasing 20 Sudanese and four Libyan civilians held hostage by the rebels. In mid-November rebels of the Forces des organisations nationales pour l'alternance et les libertés au Tchad (FONALT), one of the constituent groups of the ANR, claimed to have killed 116 ANT soldiers in clashes near Adré, close to the borders with Sudan and the CAR, although the Chadian Government made no official confirmation or denial of these reports.

In January 2003, following negotiations in Libreville, Gabon, hosted by the Gabonese President, Omar Bongo, the Government and the ANR signed a peace memorandum, in which members of the ANR were granted a general amnesty prior to their reintegration into the civilian sector. Moreover, Garfa, the leader of the ANR, returned to Chad for the first time since 1994. However, the FONALT rejected the terms of the accord. A new Council of Ministers was appointed in late June, including 11 new ministers: the new Prime Minister was Moussa Mahamat Faki, a close ally of Deby and a fellow northerner, while Yamassoum was appointed to the position of Minister of State, Minister of Foreign Affairs and African Integration; the dismissal of Kabadi as Prime Minister followed his removal, earlier in June, from the executive committee of the MPS, reportedly in response to dissatisfaction with his performance in this role.

Meanwhile, during the first half of 2003 reports emerged of the formation of a new umbrella grouping of 'politico-military' organizations opposed to the Deby regime, the Front uni pour la démocratie et la paix (FUDP). The initiative to establish the grouping had apparently come from among Chadian exiles in Benin, although, following pressure from the Beninois authorities, several influential members of the group left Benin for Togo. By mid-July, when Togoi was elected as the President of the FUDP, at a congress reportedly held in Nigeria, several 'politico-military' organizations had announced their affiliation to the grouping, including the MDD and the faction of the MDJT loyal to Togoi. The FUDP stated as its objective the establishment of a new constitution and of a transitional government, prior to the holding of free and transparent elections.

CONSTITUTIONAL AMENDMENTS

In November 2003 some 20 opposition parties, including the URD, the UNDR and the RDP, issued a document calling for a programme of electoral reform; it was also reported that these parties were considering the establishment of a common platform in advance of the presidential election scheduled for 2006. Meanwhile, claims that supporters of Deby were seeking to amend the Constitution, in order to permit the President to contest a further term of office, prompted the two RDP ministers to resign from the Government in late November; they were replaced by two members of the MPS. Moreover, Choua, the leader of the RDP, subsequently announced that the party would no longer support the MPS in the Assemblée nationale.

In December 2003 the Government signed a peace agreement with Togoi in Ouagadougou, Burkina Faso (where Togoi had been resident since 2000), providing for an immediate cease-fire, an amnesty for MDJT fighters and supporters, and for the eventual inclusion of an undisclosed number of MDJT ministers in the Chadian Government. However, hard-line factions of the MDJT rejected the terms of the agreement, claiming to have killed as many as 30 government troops in renewed clashes in Tibesti shortly after the agreement had been signed. In February 2004 Radio Brakos, an independent radio station in Moissala, in southern Chad, was closed by the authorities after it broadcast an interview with an opposition politician.

In March 2004 six 'politico-military' organizations, including a faction of the MDJT, the MDD, the CDR and the MUR, formed the Union des forces pour le changement (UFC). Oumar was named as Provisional National Co-ordinator of the new grouping, which declared itself committed to the development of national unity and the holding of fair and free elections. In April Ahmat Hassaballah Soubiane, a founder member of the MPS and the former Chadian ambassador to the USA and Canada (a post from which he was reportedly dismissed earlier in the year after criticizing Deby's plans to change the Constitution and seek a third term in office), announced in Washington, DC, the formation of the Coalition pour la défense de la démocratie et des droits constitutionnels (CDDC). In May 25 opposition parties, including the URD, the UNDR and the RDP, announced that they had formed the Coordination des partis politiques pour la défense de la constitution (CPDC), which, like the CDDC, sought to resist Deby's proposed constitutional modifications.

In May 2004 the Assemblée nationale approved eight constitutional amendments, most notably the removal of the restriction limiting the President to serving two terms of office and the establishment of the proposed upper legislative chamber, the Sénat, provided for by the 1996 Constitution but never formed; an Economic and Social Council, the members of which were to be appointed by the President, was to be formed, while the Head of State was to be granted additional powers to instigate further constitutional reform. The changes, which required endorsement in a national referendum, were vigorously criticized by opposition parties, which boycotted the vote, called a national strike (not widely observed) and urged people to demonstrate outside the legislative building. In June the Constitutional Council rejected an opposition appeal to annul the constitutional revisions.

In late July 2004 Deby effected a major reorganization of the Council of Ministers, dismissing nine ministers and allocating representatives of a number of smaller parties that had supported Deby in the 2001 presidential election posts in the new Government. The MPS retained control of the most important portfolios and Faki remained Prime Minister. However, Faki resigned as Prime Minister on 3 February 2005; Deby nominated Pascal Yoadimnadji, hitherto the Minister of Agriculture, as the new premier.

On 6 June 2005, according to official results, announced later in the month, some 66.75% of the votes cast in a referendum approved the proposed constitutional amendments, which thereby took effect. Some 67.8% of the registered electorate were reported to have participated in the plebiscite, as a consequence of which Deby (despite earlier speculation about the President's health) would be permitted to seek re-election in 2006. The CPDC denounced the results of the referendum as fraudulent and refused to meet with the Government to discuss the organization of the presidential poll, vowing to oppose Deby's re-election. In August President Deby carried out a major cabinet reshuffle, his second of the year, increasing the number of posts from 29 to 35. Although Yoadimnadji remained as premier, many new appointments were of supporters and allies of Deby, as a reward for supporting his referendum campaign.

In October 2005 Deby announced that the Republican Guard was being dissolved following the defection of 600–800 Chadian troops to a new rebel movement, Socle pour le changement, l'unité et la démocratie (SCUD), operating in eastern Chad near the border with Sudan. The movement, led by Yahya Dillo, a former Chadian officer and a nephew of Deby, was formed following the referendum and vowed to overthrow the Deby regime. Responding to this new threat, in November President Deby reshuffled the senior military leadership, at national and at regional level. In late November SCUD forces carried out attacks on military camps near the capital, N'Djamena, seizing military supplies and extended their operations throughout eastern Chad. In early December another group of Chadian soldiers, including 82 senior officers, defected to SCUD.

On 15 March 2006 a coup plot within the army was discovered and suppressed without bloodshed, the coup's leaders fleeing to eastern Chad to join SCUD. In reprisal, one week later Chadian forces launched a series of attacks on rebel bases across the border in Sudan. On 9 April rebels from the Front uni pour le changement démocratique (FUCD), under the command of Capt. Mahamat Nour Adbelkerim, the leader of another rebel movement, the Rassemblement pour la démocratie et les libertés (RDL), launched an invasion of Chad from bases in Sudan, rapidly advancing towards N'Djamena. On 13 April the insurgents attacked the capital and, in fierce fighting, around 400 soldiers from both sides were killed before the rebels were driven out of the city. Some local reports put the death toll as high as 1,000. Government forces subsequently claimed to have killed a further 150 rebels in Adré as they drove them back towards the border with Sudan. Government forces were assisted by French troops stationed in N'Djamena, which provided intelligence and logistical support.

DEBY'S THIRD TERM

Despite the massive instability caused by the rebel incursion, the presidential election went ahead as scheduled on 3 May 2006, although a boycott was urged by the coalition of opposition parties. Three weeks later the Constitutional Council released the final results, which gave Deby (now renamed Deby Itno) a third successive five-year term as President, with 64.67% of the votes cast. Voter turn-out was poor, however, at only 53.1%, and the four competing presidential candidates were known allies of Deby-Itno. The opposition denounced the results, demanding a national dialogue, and was supported in its calls by the international community. On 8 August Deby Itno was inaugurated as President, and one week later he reappointed Yoadimnadji as Prime Minister. There were few changes to the 40-member Council of Ministers, the only notable new appointments being former premier Coumakoye as Minister of State, Minister of Land Management, Town Planning and Housing, and the former CENI chairman Ahmat Mahamat Bachir as Minister of Territorial Administration.

In late July 2006 DebyItno began a five-day session of dialogue with 54 political parties in N'Djamena. However, the meeting was boycotted by the most influential opposition parties, including the CPDC and FAR. They denounced the dialogue as a masquerade to mollify international opinion. Nevertheless, the meeting adopted measures to reinforce democracy, including changes to the composition of the CENI, amendments to the electoral code and the introduction of subsidies for political parties.

Meanwhile, clashes with rebel forces continued. In early July 2006 rebels attacked Adré and Kalonge on the Chad–Sudan border, triggering an outbreak of inter-ethnic violence in Ouaddaï and Salamat which, reportedly, caused hundreds of deaths and resulted in the burning of several villages. In response, in mid-November Prime Minister Yoadimnadji declared a state of emergency that covered all regions of Chad bordering Sudan and the CAR. Later in November the Assemblée nationale extended the state of emergency for six months after the army suffered heavy reverses at the hands of the rebels.

Following bitter divisions within the FUCD after its failed attack on N'Djamena, in October 2006 a new rebel movement, the Union des forces pour la démocratie et le développement (UFDD), was formed. This allied the CDR with the Union des forces pour le progrès et la démocratie (UFPD), under Gen. Mahamat Nouri, a former defence minister and ambassador to Saudi Arabia. Another Zaghawa rebel movement, the Rassemblement populaire pour la justice, led by Abakar Tolli, also joined the UFDD. In late October UFDD forces briefly occupied Goz Beïda and Am Timan, before retreating to the border with Sudan. In response, the army attacked UFDD forces at Saraf Bogou, near the Sudanese border. According to the UFDD, 70 government troops were killed in the fighting, including the army Chief of Staff Gen. Moussa Seugui, and 40 were taken prisoner. In late November UFDD forces occupied Abéché, seizing fuel, weapons, vehicles and food worth US $1.5m. from UN World Food Programme stores. The French Government dispatched a further 100 troops and two aircraft to bolster its forces in Chad. Three weeks of heavy fighting followed between rebel and government forces across Ouaddaï and Biltine provinces and the Sudanese border, with rebels belonging to the Rassemblement des forces démocratique (RAFD) seizing Guéréda and Koulbous.

In mid-December 2006 the Chadian army launched a counter-offensive in the east of the country with thousands of troops, recapturing a 150 km strip along the border between Tiné and Adré. During these manoeuvres Chadian troops crossed into Sudan in pursuit of RAFD rebels, advancing as far as Tendelti, 12 km north-west of El Geneina, before withdrawing into Chad. Later in December Deby Itno signed a peace accord with the de facto head of the FUCD, Nour, in Tripoli, Libya. Under the terms of the deal, Nour and those FUCD rebels loyal to him were granted an amnesty and were to be integrated into the national army, while Nour's aides were to receive government posts within three months. In accordance with the peace deal, on 15 February 2007 the army released 400 FUCD rebels who had been captured during the attack on N'Djamena the previous April.

Meanwhile, in mid-January 2007 fresh fighting broke out when UFDD rebels captured Gouro and Ounianga Kebir, 500 km north of Abéché, and several days later the border towns of Adé and Adré. In mid-February UFDD rebels claimed to have captured Faya, the capital of Borkou-Ennedi-Tibesti province, killing more than 60 government troops, although the army claimed the attack was repulsed. As a result of fighting in the east of Chad, international humanitarian agencies estimated that there were 100,000 internally displaced persons in Chad, in addition to 220,000 refugees from Darfur and 48,000 refugees from the CAR. In mid-January the UN Security Council had agreed to send a mission to Chad and the CAR to assess whether a UN force should be sent to protect the border with Sudan. Following the two-week mission, in late February the newly appointed UN Secretary-General, Ban Ki-Moon, proposed two options to the UN Security Council: a 6,000-strong force supported by helicopters; or a 10,900-strong ground-based force. However, in late February the Chadian Government rejected the proposed UN peace-keeping force, insisting that it would only allow an international civil police force to protect refugees.

On 23 February 2007 the Prime Minister Pascal Yoadimnadji died suddenly from a brain haemorrhage in Paris, France. Three days later Coumakoye was appointed as the new Prime Minister and on 4 March a new Council of Ministers was unveiled. Nine ministers were dismissed, and Nour was appointed Minister of National Defence, in accordance with the peace agreement signed in December 2006. In mid-March the legislature approved the Government's programme, which included commitments to peace and security, and promises to bolster social spending and engage in political dialogue.

Meanwhile, fighting continued in the east of the country. In early April 2007 there were clashes near Amdjirema between the army and rebels from the Concorde nationale tchadienne (CNT), which was allied to the UFDD. Several days later the Chadian army launched a cross-border raid on the Sudanese settlement of Forbaranga, killing 17 Sudanese citizens and provoking condemnation from the Sudanese and Egyptian Governments and the Arab League. In an attempt to defuse tensions between Chad and Sudan, on 3 May a peace deal was signed between President Deby Itno and Sudan's President, Lt-Gen. Omar Hassan Ahmed al-Bashir, under the mediation of Saudi Arabia's King Abdallah. Under the deal, both leaders pledged to cease training and funding rebel groups, and to stop all cross-border attacks.

On 10 June 2007, following a meeting with France's new foreign minister, Bernard Kouchner, Deby Itno announced that his Government had agreed in principle to the deployment of a UN or EU peacekeeping force along the Chadian border with Sudan.

EXTERNAL RELATIONS

Relations with France appeared uneasy in the first half of 1998, particularly following the expulsion of a French military attaché. In May Deby denounced what he termed the 'neo-imperialism' of the international media and of human rights groups, accusing the West of imposing multi-party politics on Africa. In June 30 French security agents, who had apparently been operating as Deby's protection agents, were dismissed. Deby, none the less, met President Jacques Chirac during a visit to France in July, while in September the French army Chief of Staff visited Chad in an effort to ease tensions. It was generally believed that France regarded the maintenance of its military presence in Chad as a priority, given the country's proximity to several potential conflict zones. However, in March 2000 the Chadian Government demanded the recall of the French ambassador in N'Djamena; it was alleged that France's refusal to provide military support to government forces in Tibesti was a factor in the dispute. The French Minister of Defence, Michèle Alliot-Marie, visited Chad and met Deby in April 2003, when she expressed support for the actions of Chadian troops in the force deployed by the Communauté économique et monétaire de l'Afrique centrale (CEMAC) in the CAR (see below). Deby established a close relationship with the French President, Jacques Chirac, which ensured him diplomatic and military support when his regime was under attack from rebels. French troops and military advisors helped secure N'Djamena for Deby Itno's regime during the attack by FUCD forces in April 2006.

From 1977 Chad maintained close diplomatic relations with Taiwan, which lavished aid on the country in return for diplomatic recognition. However, following intensive lobbying and financial inducements by the Chinese Government, on 6 August 2006 Chad formally established diplomatic ties with the People's Republic of China, prompting Taiwan to suspend diplomatic relations.

During the late 1990s Chad forged increasingly close relations with its neighbours, particularly Libya. Chad was a founder member of the Community of Sahel-Saharan States, established in Tripoli in 1997. Deby and members of his administration made several visits to Libya from 1997; some of these visits were made by air prior to the ending of the UN embargo on air links with Libya in April 1999. Following the conclusion of a peace agreement between the Chadian Government and the rebel MDJT in Tripoli in January 2002 (see above), Libya pledged aid for the development of Chad's Tibesti region. Since then Qaddafi has been involved in numerous attempts to broker peace agreements between the Chadian Government and rebel forces.

In December 1996 President Deby participated in efforts to mediate in the political crisis in the CAR, and in early 1997 Chadian troops joined the regional surveillance mission in that country. Chadian forces remained in the CAR as part of the UN peace-keeping mission (MINURCA) until its withdrawal in February 2000. In response to a coup attempt in the CAR in May 2001, Chad reportedly dispatched troops to defend the Government of President Ange-Félix Patassé. In November heightened unrest broke out in the CAR, following an attempt to arrest the recently dismissed Chief of Staff of the Armed Forces, Gen. François Bozizé, in connection with the May coup attempt. Bozizé crossed into southern Chad, with an estimated 300 armed supporters, and was granted refuge in Sarh. Meanwhile, as tension between the two countries remained high, repeated clashes were reported at the Chad–CAR border and, in mid-January 2002, CEMAC decided to send a mission of experts to the area. Relations between the two countries were further strained in March, when the killing of 11 Chadian cattle herdsmen in the border regions of the CAR precipitated a retaliatory attack against a village in the CAR. In mid-April a meeting of the Presidents of the two countries in N'Djamena resulted in the reopening of the border, which had been closed during the unrest.

In early August 2002 the CAR Prime Minister, Martin Ziguélé, accused Chadian troops of launching cross-border attacks on the CAR, precipitating an emergency CEMAC summit later that month, as well as the dispatch of a further observer mission to the affected region. An attack by the ANR in eastern Chad (see above), in early September, was attributed by the Chadian Government to troops supported by the CAR. In early October a CEMAC summit in Libreville sought to defuse tensions between the two countries; in accordance with an accord reached at the summit, Bozizé and Khoumtan-Madji were subsequently granted asylum in France and Togo, respectively. In late October it was reported that some 120 Chadians had been killed by troops in the CAR capital, Bangui, during disturbances that followed a further coup attempt, prompting the Chadian Government to call for an official inquiry into the events, and in November Patassé accused Chad of seeking to annex regions in the north of the CAR. In December a CEMAC force was deployed in Bangui, initially to protect Patassé and later to monitor joint patrols of the border by Chadian and CAR troops. Tensions subsequently abated somewhat, and in late January 2003 the Governments of Chad, the CAR and Sudan announced their intention to establish a tripartite committee to oversee the security and stability of their joint borders. In mid-February the Presidents of Chad and the CAR met in Bangui in an attempt to normalize relations between the two countries. Later that month some 20,000 refugees (many of whom were Chadian nationals who had been resident in the CAR for many years) entered southern Chad, fleeing renewed fighting in the CAR. Following Bozizé's forcible assumption of power in the CAR in mid-March, some 400 Chadian troops were reportedly dispatched to the CAR; around 120 Chadian troops were subsequently integrated into the CEMAC force that had been deployed in the CAR in late 2002. In July 2004 WFP warned that the 27,000 CAR refugees living in Chad were at risk of starvation; WFP had appealed for US $3.4m. in July 2003 to assist the refugees, but had only received $1.5m. In June 2005 a fresh wave of refugees fleeing an outbreak of fighting between rebel groups and government forces in the northern CAR started to flood into southern Chad. By early 2006 the new arrivals had swelled the number of CAR refugees in Chad to an estimated 50,000. In November Bozizé and Deby Itno issued a joint statement, accusing the Sudanese Government of trying to destabilize the region by supporting the rebels and allowing them to operate from bases in Sudan.

Following the outbreak of a violent rebellion in the Darfur region of western Sudan in February 2003, which the Sudanese authorities allegedly attempted to suppress through pro-Government ethnic Arab militias known as the *Janjaweed* (see the chapter on Sudan), Deby played a major role in promoting diplomatic measures intended to restore peace to the region, meeting Sudanese President al-Bashir in April, August and December. In early November Sudanese and Chadian officials agreed to establish a joint force to patrol the countries' common border, amid rising concerns about cross-border banditry associated with the rebellion. Peace talks between representatives of the Sudanese Government and the rebel Sudan Liberation Movement (SLM) were held in N'Djamena in December, but were inconclusive; the Chadian Government issued a statement blaming the SLM for the breakdown in negotiations.

At the end of March 2004 indirect peace talks between the Government, the SLM and the Sudan Justice and Equality Movement (SJEM), attended by international observers, commenced in Chad, and on 8 April a 45-day humanitarian cease-fire was signed by representatives of the three parties. Further talks were held in Chad between the Government, the SLM and the SJEM later that month, but little progress was made. Although it was agreed that the cease-fire could be renewed for additional 45-day periods, it failed to hold. In mid-June the Chadian Government announced that its troops had killed 69 *Janjaweed* fighters who had attacked the Chadian village of Birak, some 6 km from the Sudanese border. By August more than 170,000 Sudanese had fled to Chad, according to the office of the UN High Commissioner for Refugees (UNHCR), which had succeeded in relocating 118,000 of these refugees to camps away from the insecure border area, where raids by militias continued. None the less, by December the number of Sudanese refugees in Chad was estimated at 200,000, according to UNHCR, as a result of which considerable strain on food and water resources was reported in the border region. In that month the Sudanese Government concluded a cease-fire in N'Djamena with a previously unidentified rebel group, the National Movement for Reform and Development, which described itself as a breakaway faction of the SJEM.

During early 2005 serious disagreements between the Governments of Chad and Sudan led to Chad suspending its role as the AU's official mediator in the Darfur conflict, although in June the Government was persuaded to resume participation in the talks. In December tensions with Sudan resurfaced following alleged violations of Sudanese airspace by the Chadian air force and Sudan's continuing support for Chadian rebels from the RDL based in Darfur. Both sides agreed to resume talks in early January 2006, but, following the rebel attack on N'Djamena in April, President Deby accused Sudan of supporting the invasion, formally severed diplomatic relations, and threatened to expel the 200,500 Sudanese refugees sheltering in eastern Chad. However, he was persuaded to retract this threat after the personal intervention of Chad's UN High Commissioner for Refugees, Antonio Guterres. Chad formally withdrew from the AU-sponsored Darfur peace talks in protest, but despite that absence a tentative peace deal was signed on 5 May. The deal was backed by the Sudanese Government and the leader of the Sudan Liberation Army (SLA), Minni Minnawi, but was rejected by a smaller faction of the SLA and by the SJEM. On 8 August Chad formally re-established diplomatic relations with Sudan, following a meeting between the Chadian and Sudanese Presidents. This was followed mid-October by a meeting between Chadian and Sudanese military representatives in N'Djamena which led to the signing of another security accord. However, in November Deby Itno and Bozizé, issued a joint statement condemning Sudan for supporting rebellions in both the CAR and Chad, and for instigating genocide in Darfur. In January 2007, at the AU heads of state summit in Addis Ababa, Ethiopia, Deby Itno again condemned the Sudanese Government for supporting Chadian rebel groups, and threatened to suspend its membership of the AU if Sudan was elected to the AU presidency. In an attempt to defuse tensions, in February the outgoing French president, Jacques Chirac, mediated a meeting between the Chadian and Sudanese Presidents during the Franco-African summit in Cannes, France. This culminated with an agreement to promise to respect each other's sovereignty and stop supporting armed rebellions in neighbouring states. In late May the new French foreign minister, Bernard Kouchner, proposed establishing a humanitarian corridor through Chad for channelling aid to Darfuri refugees in Chad and Sudan.

Further concerns regarding regional security emerged in March 2004, when clashes at the Niger–Chad border between Islamist militants belonging to the Algerian-based Groupe salafiste pour la prédication et le combat (GSPC) and Chadian and Nigerien troops resulted in the deaths of some 43 GSPC fighters and three Chadian soldiers, according to the Chadian Government. It was announced that month that the Governments of Algeria, Chad, Mali and Niger were to reinforce security co-operation in the regions of their common borders. Meanwhile, the MDJT had reportedly captured a prominent GSPC leader, Amara Saïfi (also known as Abderrazak le Para). In July it was reported that the MDJT had released Saïfi, whose faction of the GSPC had apparently united with the Chadian rebel group to fight the Chadian army.

In 1998 it was reported that Chad was to seek the extradition from Senegal of former President Habré, with a view to his prosecution in relation to human rights abuses and in connection with the embezzlement of state funds. A committee of inquiry, established by the Deby regime, had held Habré's 'political police' responsible for the deaths of some 40,000 people and the torture of a further 200,000; the deposed President was also alleged to have taken some 7,000m. francs CFA in state funds when he fled Chad in 1990. In February 2000, following a ruling by a Senegalese court that he could be tried in that country for alleged crimes committed in Chad under his leadership, Habré was charged with complicity in acts of torture and barbarity, and placed under house arrest. The charges were rejected in July, however, on the basis that Senegal lacked the appropriate penal procedure to process such an international case; this ruling was upheld by Senegal's highest court of appeal in March 2001. None the less, in April 2001 President Abdoulaye Wade of Senegal stated that Habré's presence in the country was regarded as undesirable and gave him 30 days' notice to leave. Nevertheless, Habré remained in Senegal in 2006, while his alleged victims were seeking his extradition to stand trial in Belgium under a law that (as amended in 2003) gave that country's courts universal jurisdiction in cases of human rights abuses and war crimes if Belgian citizens or long-term residents were among the plaintiffs. (Several of the alleged victims of abuses committed under Habré's regime had been granted Belgian citizenship.) In early 2006 the AU appointed a panel of seven legal experts to decide Habré's fate; in July they urged an 'African solution', which appeared to preclude extradition to Belgium and returned the decision to Senegal. In February 2007 Senegal's legislature passed a law enabling domestic courts to try Habré on charges of human-rights violations.

Economy

CHARLOTTE VAILLANT

Based on an earlier article by EDITH HODGKINSON

Chad is one of the poorest and least developed countries of Africa, and its geographical isolation, climate and meagre natural resources have resulted in an economy of very narrow range. The construction of a pipeline linking the oilfields in southern Chad to the port of Kribi in Cameroon, which commenced operations in July 2003, offered the prospect of considerably higher incomes. Yet, despite the close involvement of the Bretton Woods Institutions and the finalization of the Poverty Reduction Strategy Paper (PRSP) by the Chadian Government in June 2003, by 2007 there was no marked acceleration in poverty reduction as a result of petroleum development. The country's economic construction task remained substantial and performance in the non-petroleum sector, where the bulk of the population makes a living, remained limited, because of great vulnerability to external shocks and continued instability, particularly in the east of the country. Overall, according to the World Bank, gross national income (GNI) per head amounted to around US $400 in 2005, compared with $180 in 2000.

The primary sector has traditionally dominated the economy. Hitherto, virtually all of the country's limited industrial and commercial production facilities have been located in or close to N'Djamena, the capital. Much economic activity is informal, and very few statistics are published. There are hardly any all-weather roads and no railways. The country is land-locked and its major economic centres are situated 1,400–2,800 km from the sea. Its structural problems of economic development, immense in any circumstances, have been rendered still more acute by civil conflict and by drought. Consequently, for most of the period since independence, the authorities have had to focus on 'crisis management' rather than on the pursuit of a longer-term economic strategy. In any event, policies formulated in N'Djamena have tended to have limited impact in the remote hinterland of the centre and north and also in large parts of the disaffected south.

The country's economic performance in the 1990s was poor. Gross domestic product (GDP) declined by nearly one-fifth in 1989–93. The 50% devaluation of the CFA franc in January 1994 benefited both cotton and livestock production, and GDP increased by 10.2% in that year. Lower rates of growth were recorded in subsequent years, although growth peaked at 6.6% in 1997, largely as a result of an increase in food and export crop output attributed to higher rainfall and a rise in manufacturing, before declining slightly to 6.0% in 1998. Real GDP declined by 0.6% in 1999. The energy crisis and intensified rebel fighting in northern regions were instrumental in reducing real GDP by 0.7% in 2000. In that year erratic rainfall resulted in the greatest food shortage in Chad for a decade. Petroleum development boosted economic growth in the following years. Real GDP increased by 9.5% in 2001 and by 9.6% in 2002, fuelled by pipeline-related construction in the petroleum sector and a boost in domestic consumption. Oil production started in 2003, with GDP growth reaching 14.7% in that year (exports began in October), according to the IMF; in 2004 GDP growth of 33.6% was recorded. Growth in the non-petroleum sector remained slow, however, because of the impact of harsh climatic conditions on agriculture performance. In 2005 overall growth slowed to 8.6%, despite satisfactory harvests, as the rise in petroleum production levelled off and public investment in priority sectors failed to pick up. Growth is estimated to have further slowed in 2006, to 1.3%, according to the IMF, reflecting lower oil production than initially projected, rising instability in the east of the country and disruption to government expenditure following the dispute with the World Bank over the management of oil revenue. The IMF anticipated this figure would declined further, with the economy projected to contract by 1.2% in 2007.

AGRICULTURE

Agriculture and livestock (but excluding fishing) accounted for 19.0% of GDP in 2005, and employed some 72% of the labour force in that year. The main area of crop production is situated in the south of the country, with cattle production prevailing in the more arid northern zones. In the extreme north camel- and sheep-rearing and date orchards are predominant. The principal food crops are sorghum and millet. Rice, maize, groundnuts and cassava are also grown for domestic consumption. A record cereal output of 1.7m. metric tons was recorded in 2003, as a result of exceptional weather conditions. Lower rainfall and the locust invasion resulted in a decline in cereal production to 1.3m. tons in 2004. This led to a significant depletion of food stocks and a threat of famine in the north. Cereal production is estimated to have recovered in 2005 and 2006, to around 1.9m. tons in both years, reflecting good weather conditions. Rural development schemes implemented in southern Chad, with assistance from France, the European Union (EU), Canada and the World Bank, aim to increase production of cereals and livestock. However, major problems remain in the area of distribution and marketing, which resulted in some localized scarcity. In addition, rising instability in the east of the country and in the Darfur region of neighbouring Sudan in recent years—causing the presence in eastern Chad of thousands of refugees that fled fighting in Darfur, as well as a rising number of internally displaced Chadians and people from the Central African Republic (CAR)—has caused severe localized food insecurity in some areas, as well as disruption to marketing activities and pricing mechanisms, raising the need for emergency food aid.

Some progress was made in the cultivation of rice by modern methods during the 1990s, with the area harvested appreciably increasing, from 36,854 ha in 1990 to 103,803 ha in 2002, although the area cultivated declined thereafter, to 95,000 ha in 2003 and to 91,000 ha in 2004, according to unofficial figures. Output has none the less varied markedly from year to year. In 2005 paddy rice production increased to an exceptional 141,000 metric tons, according to local sources, against a yearly average of 111,000 tons in 1999–2004, but fell back to an estimated 107,000 tons in 2006. Sugar cane is another food crop of significance (see Mining, Power and Manufacturing). According to local sources, production in 2004 totalled 280,000 tons and is estimated to have increased to 343,000 tons and 366,000 tons, in 2005 and 2006, respectively.

Cotton, which is Chad's main export crop, has encountered growing difficulties in recent years. In 2003 petroleum products replaced cotton and livestock as the main source of foreign exchange; consequently, cotton contributed an estimated 12.9% of total export revenue in 2003 and only 2.6% of total exports in 2005, compared with 41.1% in 2001. Cotton production has been widely encouraged since the 1920s, and seed cotton is now grown on some 280,000 ha, in the south of the country. On the verge of bankruptcy, the cotton marketing monopoly, the Société Cotonnière du Tchad (COTONTCHAD), streamlined its ginning operations and froze price support to farmers from 1986. The devaluation of the CFA franc in January 1994 was followed by a 50% increase in the producer price, which generated an immediate increase in output, to 156,746 metric tons in 1994. Production of seed cotton reached a record level of 263,476 tons in 1997. A new pricing mechanism was introduced in that year, to reflect movements in the world prices. The recovery was short-lived, however, as falling world cotton prices, coupled with poor road access and lack of fertilizers, compounded the sector's difficulties in the ensuing years. This from time to time prompted COTONTCHAD's decision to suspend the pricing mechanism to reduce the knock-on effect of falling world prices on farmers' income. Farm-gate prices were increased in April 2004, from 150 francs CFA per kg for the 2003/04 season to 190 francs CFA per kg for the 2004/05 season. As a result of these price incentives and satisfactory growing conditions in the south of the country, cotton production recovered from 102,200 tons in 2003 to 219,900 tons in 2004, according to official figures. However, a reduction in producer prices to 160 francs CFA per kg, reflecting falling world prices, coupled with continued financial difficulties at COTONTCHAD, contributed to a fall in cotton production, to an estimated 182,000 tons, in 2005. Cotton production is estimated to have further decreased in 2006 due to inadequate weather conditions. The IMF and World Bank regard the restructuring of COTONTCHAD, which remains 75% state-owned, as a priority. In late 2001 the oil- and soap-producing division of the business, the Direction huilerie savonnerie, was split from COTONTCHAD, and sold to private operators in 2003.

Following the agreement of a new Poverty Reduction and Growth Facility (PRGF) with the IMF in February 2005, the Government prepared a three-year 'road map' to accelerate structural reforms, which envisaged the withdrawal of the Government from the sector by 2008. The 'road map' also provided for the reintegration of the new Société Huilerie-savonnerie into COTONTCHAD, which was implemented in 2006.

Gum arabic, which is harvested from traditional plantations of acacia trees in the north, is Chad's fourth largest export, after petroleum products, livestock and cotton. As with cotton, currency devaluation stimulated exports, which were reported to have quadrupled in value in 1994. Despite a strong international demand, there has been little increase in levels of output in recent years, because of high transport costs and the lack of an organizational structure. According to local sources, in 2006 Chad produced an estimated 14,000 metric tons of gum arabic, up from 12,000 tons in 2003. Chad is the world's second largest producer of gum arabic, after Sudan.

Livestock production has a significant role in the Chadian economy and alone contributed 8.3% of total GDP in 2005, according to the IMF. Local sources estimated livestock contribution to GDP at 8.4% in 2006. It generally yields more in terms of cash income than the cotton industry, but much of this is not officially registered. Cattle-raising is concentrated in the central and southern regions of the country. Livestock is often exported illicitly, without payment of taxes, mainly to Nigeria, where it is sold or bartered for consumer goods. Livestock has replaced cotton as the primary source of foreign-exchange earnings (excepting petroleum products) since 2002; according to the IMF in 2003 livestock provided 38.4% of total export earnings, although this share fell to 13.9% and 10.2% of GDP, in 2004 and 2005, respectively, as the country started exporting petroleum. In 2004, according to the IMF, there were some 6.4m. head of cattle and 8.2m. sheep and goats. In the long term there is considerable potential for livestock exports, subject to the upgrading of the herds and improvements in marketing arrangements.

Fishing is an important economic activity in the Lake Chad region; in 2001–05, according to data published by FAO, the average annual catch amounted to around 75,000 metric tons.

MINING, POWER AND MANUFACTURING

The exploitation of proven deposits of petroleum in Chad has long been inhibited by the high cost of importing plant and machinery long distances with poor or non-existent transport facilities. In response to the increase in world petroleum prices during the 1970s, petroleum extraction began in the Sédigui region, to the north of Lake Chad, in 1977. However, output was very modest—about 1,500 barrels per day (b/d) in 1979/80—and the operation was subsequently suspended because of the precarious security situation. In 1993 exploration in the Doba Basin (in southern Chad) revealed reserves of petroleum, which were subsequently estimated at more than 900m. barrels. Proposals for the development of 300 wells and a processing facility were announced, and an agreement was signed in 1995 by the Governments of Chad and Cameroon for the construction and operation of a 1,070-km pipeline to transport petroleum from Doba to the port of Kribi in Cameroon. The project was subject to great controversy over the impact of the project on the environment, as well as concerns about the possible misuse of oil resources. In November 1999 the World Bank agreed to lend Chad and Cameroon US $93.0m. for the project, after overcoming environmental concerns and setting conditions for sound oil-revenue management; this triggered fresh lending from commercial banks. The cost of the project was estimated to be $1,500m. for Chad and $3,700m. overall. Construction began in late 2000 by a consortium, Esso Chad, consisting of ExxonMobil of the USA (40%), Petronas of Malaysia (35%) and the Chevron Corporation of the USA (25%). Objections by environmental and human rights organizations to the 25-year project were reinforced, after it was reported that the Government had spent $3m. of a bonus received from petroleum companies on armaments. The Chad–Cameroon pipeline was completed one year ahead of schedule and production commenced in July 2003. Initial output amounted to an average 50,000 b/d in 2003. Production reached at times more than 200,000 b/d by late 2004, close to the full production capacity of 225,000 b/d. In 2005, however, petroleum production from Miandoum and Komé, two of the three Doba oilfields, was lower than anticipated, because of a high water content and prospects for reaching such production levels became poor. Despite this, according to Esso Chad, petroleum production increased from an annual average of 24,000 b/d (an annual total of 8.6m. barrels) in 2003 to 168,000 b/d (61.4m. barrels) in 2004 and to 173,000 b/d (63.3m. barrels) in 2005, following the commencement of production at the Nya field. However, with production slowing at the three original Doba oil fields, despite the start of production at the Moundouli field, output fell to 153,000 b/d in 2006 (55.9m. barrels). Proven reserves in Lake Chad were estimated at 900m. barrels, but the country's total reserves are known to amount to at least 1,500m. barrels, if the rest of the country is included. Esso Chad is currently the only oil producer, but the Government continued to issue exploration permits after the pipeline came on stream, and other companies are involved in oil exploration in Chad, in particular the China National Petroleum Corporation, which is the majority shareholder in the H permit (437,000 sq km in three regions of Chad) following the acquisition of Canada's Encana 50% rights in February 2007 and previously Clivenden's rights in 2003 and 2005; and Taiwan's Overseas Petroleum and Investment Corporation, which was granted an exploration permit in early 2006. In order to increase its direct role in oil activities, in mid-2006 the Government created a national hydrocarbons company, the Société des hydrocarbures du Tchad. Additionally, a new oil law was passed in May 2007, providing for the establishment of production-sharing agreements for new oilfields.

Natron, found in pans on the northern edge of Lake Chad, is the only non-petroleum mineral of importance currently exploited in Chad. It is used as salt, for human and animal consumption, in the preservation of meats and hides and in soap production, and was exported to Nigeria via the Logone river from N'Djamena. Alluvial gold and materials for the construction industry are also extracted. There is believed to be considerable potential for the further exploitation of gold deposits, particularly in the former prefecture of Mayo-Kebbi, and for the development of bauxite, titanium and uranium reserves. In 2001 the first gold mine in Chad, at Ganboké, in the south of the country, was opened by Afko Corea (Republic of Korea).

The country's domestic energy crisis has remained largely unresolved, despite Chad becoming a significant producer of petroleum, with high energy prices and regular electricity shortages. Electricity in Chad is generated by two main oil-powered plants operated by a public corporation, the Société Tchadienne d'Eau et d'Électricité (STEE); installed capacity is 45.8 MW. The annual output of electricity has stagnated since the mid-1970s, as a result of ageing equipment and the prohibitive costs of importing petroleum, and was put at 84m. kWh in 2004. The utility has also been severely affected by persistent non-payment of bills, notably by other public-sector enterprises. It was anticipated that the development and liberalization of the energy sector in Chad would reduce the prohibitively high cost of electricity, which has been a major factor in rendering industrial enterprises uncompetitive. In September 2000 the Government and Vivendi (of France—subsequently renamed Veolia Water) signed a management and operating contract for the STEE, with plans to repair existing generators and increase capacity. Construction work meanwhile commenced on the rehabilitation of the Sédigui oilfield and the construction of a pipeline linking Sédigui to a proposed refinery at Farcha, near N'Djamena. The project, which was expected to produce up to 5,000 b/d and cover the bulk of Chad's energy requirements, stalled in 2001. Work on the project was still suspended at mid-2007. In April 2004 Veolia renounced its contract to manage and potentially acquire the STEE, causing another reverse in the country's electricity sector. Generating capacity increased in the short term, following the installation of new donor-funded, oil-powered generators in 2004. In late 2006 generating capacity for the capital, N'Djamena, improved following the installation of new generating station at Farcha.

Manufacturing (which contributed 4.6% of GDP in 2005) is centred in N'Djamena and Moundou, and is mainly devoted to the processing of agricultural products. The processing of cotton is the principal industry, and the recovery in cotton production during the mid-1990s prompted COTONTCHAD to increase capacity at its eight mills in 1996/97. As part of the restructuring of COTONTCHAD, in accordance with the demands of the Bretton Woods institutions, its oil and soap activities were legally separated from the company in late 2001 and sold to a private operator in 2003; however, they were reintegrated into COTONTCHAD in 2006. The transfer to majority private ownership of the Société nationale sucrière du Tchad (as the Compagnie Sucrière du Tchad) was completed in April 2000. Although the company was forced to temporarily suspend its operations in 2004 because of illicit imports from Cameroon and Nigeria, sugar production recovered in 2006, to a record level of 36,000 metric tons. Other manufacturing activities in Chad include cigarette production and brewing; there is also a wide range of small-scale enterprises operating outside the recorded sector, including crafts and the production of agricultural implements. This unofficial sector makes a significant contribution to employment and overall production.

TRANSPORT AND TELECOMMUNICATIONS

Transportation within Chad is inadequate and expensive. Communications with the outside world are difficult, slow and costly because of the great distance from the sea, the character of the trade, and poor facilities in neighbouring countries. In 1999 the Government adopted a new road classification system, in accordance with which Chad was deemed to possess a year-round national road network of 2,600 km, a dry-season-only road network of 3,600 km and a regional rural road network of some 3,000 km. The total length of the road network was an estimated 40,000 km, of which only 412 km was paved. Transport limitations are a major obstacle to the country's economic development and efforts are being made to improve the internal transport system (with help from the World Bank, the European Development Fund and the USA), including the rehabilitation and construction of an ancillary road network as part of rural development in the south. The EU and France are currently the largest financial providers in Chad's water and road rehabilitation sector. Transport infrastructural improvements in adjacent countries, especially in Cameroon, were also expected to benefit Chad. The EU contributed funds to the construction of a road linking Sarh with Léré, near the Cameroon border, and for a 400-km highway linking Moundou, in south-western Chad, and Ngaoundéré, in northern Cameroon. Inland waterways are significant, with 2,000 km of the Chari and Logone rivers navigable in all seasons. In January 2002 the Agence française de développement and the French defence ministry announced the release of funds to rehabilitate the international airport at N'Djamena, from where regular civilian and cargo services operate to Sudan, to northern Nigeria and to Paris, France. Concerning telecommunications, the parastatal, Société des télécommunications du Tchad (Soteltchad), is mooted for privatization. Soteltchad has a monopoly on fixed and international telecommunications services. Two mobile phone companies, Celtel (since 2004) and Tigo (since October 2005), operate in the country. Celtel reached 372,000 subscribers at the end of 2006, against around 190,000 for Tigo. Most mobile phone services have been concentrated around the capital, N'Djamena, although both operating companies had plans to expand them to other areas.

PUBLIC FINANCE

Chad has historically faced severe public-finance difficulties. Economic decline and civil strife have exacerbated the low level of tax revenue; saddled with deep and chronic budgetary deficits, the Government has largely relied on foreign aid to maintain basic public services. Since the mid-1980s, with the support of the IMF, the World Bank and the major bilateral donors, the Government has attempted to increase revenue receipts and to reduce spending. Limited progress was made after the devaluation in 1994, as spending came under pressure from the sharp inflationary impact of devaluation. The Government's economic programme, backed by an Enhanced Structural Adjustment Facility (ESAF) extended by the IMF in September 1995, again laid emphasis on improving revenue collection and also included the introduction of a single turnover tax, effective from the beginning of 1997. Spending was to be controlled through reform of the large state enterprises (in cotton, sugar and electricity) and of the civil service. Tax revenue consequently increased from 39,700m. francs CFA in 1995 (equivalent to 5.5% of GDP) to 68,000m. francs CFA in 1999 (equivalent to 7.2% of GDP), while recurrent expenditures were largely kept under control over the same period. In 1998 the adverse impact on the economy of the energy crisis meant that total revenue was below the budgeted target. Steps were taken to curtail non-essential expenditures, with the overall deficit (including grants) reduced to 2.4% of GDP, compared with 3.8% of GDP in 1997. Foreign assistance contributed 50,900m. francs CFA that year, equivalent to 5.0% of GDP.

Under pressure from the World Bank, the Government adopted legislation on petroleum revenue management in 1999. Budgetary efforts have since continued to focus on strengthening revenue transparency and the monitoring of priority expenditures. Under the new legislation, 80% of direct revenue (royalties and dividends) from the petroleum sector was to be allotted to the development of education, health and infrastructure, while 10% is to be held in trust for future generations. In January 2000 the IMF approved a three-year programme for Chad under the PRGF—the successor to the ESAF. The resources available under this arrangement were augmented in May 2001, in order to respond to food shortages, and again in January 2002, to address the decline in international prices of cotton. In 2000 Chad recorded an overall budgetary deficit (including grants) of 65,200m. francs CFA, equivalent to 6.6% of GDP. A value-added tax was introduced that year, but this failed to compensate for a 17.8% rise in nominal wages and salaries. An overall budgetary deficit of 69,100m. francs CFA, equivalent to 5.7% of GDP, was recorded in 2001. In 2002 the budgetary deficit was 83,000m. francs CFA, equivalent to 6% of GDP. In that year, donors raised concerns over high military spending and below-target priority outlays.

Public finances were expected to take a new turn in 2003, although revenue from the petroleum sector did not actually accrue until late in the year. In June 2003 the IMF announced that a disbursement equivalent to US $7.6m., issued under the terms of the PRGF in October 2002, had been deemed non-complying, as a result of the failure of the Chadian authorities to inform the Fund of new external payments arrears accumulated in mid-2002. The IMF ordered that this amount be repaid, with accrued interest, by October 2003. According to revised estimates, the overall budget deficit, on a commitment basis and including grants, increased to 100,700m. francs CFA in 2003, equivalent to 6.3% of GDP. Delays in establishing the stabilization and sterilization mechanisms, as well as several of the organizations provided for under the legislation on petroleum revenue management, including the Petroleum Revenue Control and Monitoring Board and the Fund for Future Generations (FFG), explained the late receipt of petroleum revenue. However, in 2004, oil receipts rose to 57,700m. francs CFA. This surge in revenue helped to compensate for a shortfall in aid flows following the expiration of the PRGF in

2004. The budget deficit (on a commitment basis, including grants) was reduced to 69,400m. francs CFA, or 3% of GDP. Despite rising petroleum revenues, domestic payment arrears (including wages) continued to accumulate in that year.

In February 2005 the IMF approved a new three-year PRGF, worth US $38.2m. According to IMF estimates, revenues from the petroleum sector (largely royalties and dividends) increased to 130,400m. francs CFA in 2005. There was also an increase in oil-financed spending in priority sectors. In December 2005, however, the law on petroleum revenue management was revised to free up more resources for the treasury—money was taken from the FFG and the definition of priority sectors was widened to include public administration and security. This decision was caused by problems in revenue management and rising urgent needs as a result of instability in the region. In reaction, the World Bank suspended all funding to the country and froze the escrow account into which Chad's oil revenue was deposited. Meanwhile, the completion of the first review under the PRGF was postponed because of fiscal difficulties and the IMF suspended its disbursements. An agreement was eventually signed with the World Bank in July 2006 committing the Chadian Government to allocate 70% of all petroleum revenues (direct and indirect) to priority spending, while the FFG was officially suppressed. Shortly after the signature of the July agreement, the Government accused two partners of the oil consortium, Esso Chad—Chevron and Petronas—of having paid insufficient taxes for the year and threatened to expel them from the country. This resulted in an additional tax payment of US $281.6m. by Chevron and Petronas at the end of 2006. This, coupled with increased oil production and the first payment of corporate income taxes from Esso Chad, contributed to increased revenue in 2006, estimated in the 2006 revised budget at 748,400m. francs CFA; expenditure also rose, to an estimated 726,900m. francs CFA, driven by increased military spending reflecting continued instability in the east of the country. Overall, the Government estimated that the fiscal balance posted a small surplus of 21,500m. francs CFA (or 0.6% of GDP, according to the IMF). Petroleum revenues are projected to peak in 2007, owing to increased income taxes payments from oil companies.

FOREIGN TRADE, AID AND PAYMENTS

While exports and imports have fluctuated widely as a result of the civil war and bad weather, Chad's foreign trade has, almost without exception, shown a very large deficit, owing to the low level of production in the economy and the high cost of transport. Before the development of the country's petroleum resources commenced in 2000, the principal imports had comprised food products (accounting for 19.1% of the cost of total imports in 1995). Total imports more than doubled in 2001, compared with the previous year, to reach 497,417m. francs CFA, before increasing more than two-fold again in 2002, to 1.1m. francs CFA, as a result of imports of machinery and other goods related to the Doba oil project. Cotton has traditionally been the principal export commodity, followed by livestock. A rise in output of cotton and an increase in international prices in the early 1990s generated an increase in export earnings and ensured a narrowing of the trade deficit; however, the devaluation of the CFA franc in 1994 failed to reduce the imbalance in that year—the deficit was 42,600m. francs CFA—as a result of the economy's high dependence on imports. In the following years sluggish export performance, coupled with a surge in pipeline-related imports, caused the trade deficit to widen dramatically, increasing to 359,117m. francs CFA in 2001. The trade deficit widened still further in 2002, to some 978,400m. francs CFA, as a result of import spending in the petroleum sector. There was a 35.9% decline in cotton export prices in 2002. This, combined with a 9.0% fall in the volume of cotton exports, and despite reasonably sound performances in other traditional sectors, caused total exports to decline in that year by 7.0%, to 128,900m. francs CFA.

Petroleum effectively became the primary source of foreign-exchange earnings for Chad when the first barrel left Kribi in October 2003. As a result, total exports more than doubled to 350,400m. francs CFA in 2003, before reaching an unprecedented 1.1m. francs CFA in 2004 and 1.6m. francs CFA in 2005. Meanwhile, imports slowed following the completion of the oil pipeline, to 453,200m. francs CFA in 2003 and remained broadly stable at 462,300m. francs CFA in 2005 and 428,100m. francs CFA in 2005. Chad's trade balance thereby resulted in a surplus of 679,800m. francs CFA being recorded in 2004, and of 1.2m. francs CFA in 2005, according to the IMF. The trade surplus is estimated to have further risen in 2006, helped by strong international petroleum prices.

The current account of the balance of payments has been persistently in deficit, owing to the very high outflows on services, mostly transport costs. The external current-account deficit (including external transfers) peaked at 1,390,500m. francs CFA in 2002, equivalent to 100.4% of GDP, the majority of which was financed through petroleum-related foreign direct investment (net inflows of foreign direct investment totalled US $924m. in 2002, according to the UN Conference on Trade and Development, UNCTAD). The current-account deficit declined to 750,300m. francs CFA (47.4% of GDP) in the following year and to 110,900m. francs CFA (4.8% of GDP) in 2004, according to the IMF. In 2005 the current-account deficit was estimated to have declined further, to 26,500m. francs CFA, an equivalent of 0.9 % of GDP, reflecting an improvement in the trade balance. Although this is a marked improvement compared with previous years, the balance of payment situation in the non-petroleum sector—where the majority of the population is employed—remains weak. In 2005 the trade deficit in the non-petroleum sector amounted to 75,900m. francs CFA. Foreign direct investment inflows, which declined significantly after the completion of the Chad–Cameroon pipeline from US $924m. in 2002 to US $478m. in 2004, before recovering to US $705m. in 2005, will continue largely to take place in the oil sector, despite plans to liberalize the cotton sector. The telecommunications sector is also likely to attract some foreign investment.

To offset the deficit, Chad relied heavily on foreign assistance, which was also needed to fund basic budgetary requirements and any development expenditure, as well as the episodes of military activity. France was the principal bilateral supplier of aid, including direct budgetary assistance (providing approximately 30% of all international financial assistance disbursed in 1990–98) until 2003. In 2004, however, France was overtaken by the USA. The People's Republic of China, the EU and other multilateral agencies, and, more recently, Arab countries (particularly Kuwait) have also granted substantial assistance, principally for agricultural and infrastructure projects. Throughout the 1990s multilateral aid exceeded bilateral inflows, accounting for US $438m. of aid received in 1995–2001, out of a total of $447m. Some 95.5% of this aid was issued on concessional terms. Overseas development assistance increased steadily from 2000, with net inflows totalling $319m. in 2004.

Most of Chad's borrowing was from government and other official sources, on highly concessionary terms (see above). Consequently, while external debt increased significantly, from US $284m. in 1980 to $1,590m. at the end of 2005 (equivalent to 61.1% of GNI), debt servicing remained relatively low. The relatively low debt-service ratio was also attributable to the frequent failure to pay liabilities as they fell due (arrears on repayment were 1,100m. francs CFA at the end of 2003), as well as debt relief. The CFA franc's devaluation in 1994—which represented an immediate increase in the cost of debt servicing—was followed by the cancellation of Chad's official debt to France. Moreover, in February 1995 Chad was granted enhanced relief on its debt to official bilateral creditors under the 'Naples terms'. In May 2001 Chad was declared eligible for debt-service relief under the Bretton Woods institutions' enhanced initiative for heavily indebted poor countries (HIPC). In June the 'Paris Club' of official creditors provided a rescheduling of Chad's debt on 'Cologne terms'. Following the IMF's approval of a new PRGF in February 2005, the Government hoped to reach completion point (where full debt relief begins) rapidly, although this failed to materialize following the postponement of the conclusion of the PRGF's first review due to the deterioration of the country's fiscal position. However, following a mission to Chad in March 2007, the IMF announced that it expected to conclude the first and second reviews under the PRGF by the end of June.

Statistical Survey

Source (unless otherwise stated): Institut national de la statistique, des études economiques et démographiques, BP 453, N'Djamena; tel. 52-31-64; fax 52-66-13; e-mail inseed@intnet.td; internet www.inseed-tchad.org.

Area and Population

AREA, POPULATION AND DENSITY

Area (sq km)	
Land	1,259,200
Inland waters	24,800
Total	1,284,000*
Population (sample survey)	
December 1963–August 1964	3,254,000†
Population (census result)	
8 April 1993‡	
Males	2,950,415
Females	3,208,577
Total	6,158,992
Population (UN estimates at mid-year)§	
2004	9,810,000
2005	10,146,000
2006	10,468,000
Density (per sq km) at mid-2006	8.3

* 495,800 sq miles.

† Including areas not covered by the survey.

‡ Figures are provisional. The revised total, including an adjustment for underenumeration (estimated at 1.4%), is 6,279,931.

§ Source: UN, *World Population Prospects: The 2006 Revision*.

ETHNIC GROUPS

1995 (percentages): Sara, Bongo and Baguirmi 20.1; Chadic 17.7; Arab 14.3; M'Bourn 6.3; Masalit, Maba and Mimi 6.1; Tama 6.1; Adamawa 6.0; Sudanese 6.0; Mubi 4.1; Hausa 2.1; Kanori 2.1; Massa 2.1; Kotoko 2.0; Peul 0.5; Others 4.5 (Source: La Francophonie).

PREFECTURES

(1993 census)

	Area (sq km)	Population*	Density (per sq km)	Principal city
Batha	88,800	288,458	3.2	Ati
Biltine	46,850	184,807	3.9	Biltine
Borkou-Ennedi-Tibesti (BET)	600,350	73,185	0.1	Faya-Largeau
Chari-Baguirmi†	82,910	1,251,906	15.1	N'Djamena
Guéra	58,950	306,253	5.2	Mongo
Kanem	114,520	279,927	2.4	Mao
Lac	22,320	252,932	11.3	Bol
Logone Occidental	8,695	455,489	52.4	Moundou
Logone Oriental	28,035	441,064	15.7	Doba
Mayo-Kebbi	30,105	825,158	27.4	Bongor
Moyen Chari	45,180	738,595	16.3	Sarh
Ouaddaï	76,240	543,900	7.1	Abéché
Salamat	63,000	184,403	2.9	Am-Timan
Tandjile	18,045	453,854	25.2	Lai
Total	1,284,000	6,279,931	4.9	

* Including adjustment for underenumeration.

† Including the capital district, N'Djamena (population 530,965).

Note: As a result of administrative reform, Chad's prefectures have been replaced by the following regions: Batha (principal city Ati), Borkou-Ennedi-Tibesti (Faya), Chari-Baguirmi (Massenya), Guéra (Mongo), Hadjer-Lamis (Massakory), Kanem (Mao), Lac (Bol), Logone Occidental (Moundou), Logone Oriental (Doba), Mandoul (Koumra), Mayo-Kebbi Est (Bongor), Mayo-Kebbi Ouest (Pala), Moyen-Chari (Sarh), Ouaddaï (Abéché) Salamat (Am-Timan), Tandjilé (Laï) and Wadi Fira (Biltine). The capital city, N'Djamena, also has the status of a region.

PRINCIPAL TOWNS

(population at 1993 census)

N'Djamena (capital)	530,965	Koumra	26,702
Moundou	99,530	Pala	26,115
Sarh	75,496	Am Timan	21,269
Abéché	54,628	Bongor	20,448
Kelo	31,319	Mongo	20,443

Mid-2005 (incl. suburbs, UN estimate): N'Djamena 888,000 (Source: UN, *World Urbanization Prospects: The 2005 Revision*).

BIRTHS AND DEATHS

(annual averages, UN estimates)

	1990–95	1995–2000	2000–05
Birth rate (per 1,000)	47.5	47.6	47.4
Death rate (per 1,000)	15.8	15.7	16.0

2001 (preliminary): Live births 397,896; Deaths 138,025.

Sources: UN, *World Population Prospects: The 2006 Revision* and *Population and Vital Statistics Report*.

Expectation of life (years at birth, WHO estimates): 46 (males 45; females 48) in 2004 (Source: WHO, *World Health Report*).

ECONOMICALLY ACTIVE POPULATION

('000 persons at mid-1990, ILO estimates)

	Males	Females	Total
Agriculture, hunting, forestry and fishing	1,179	1,102	2,281
Industry	105	9	115
Manufacturing	50	6	56
Services	245	100	344
Total labour force	1,529	1,211	2,740

Source: ILO.

1993 census (persons aged six years and over): Total employed 2,305,961; Unemployed 16,268; Total labour force 2,322,229.

Mid-2005 ('000, estimates): Agriculture, etc. 3,085; Total labour force 4,385 (Source: FAO).

Health and Welfare

KEY INDICATORS

Total fertility rate (children per woman, 2005)	6.7
Under-5 mortality rate (per 1,000 live births, 2005)	208
HIV/AIDS (% of persons aged 15–49, 2005)	3.5
Physicians (per 1,000 head, 2004)	0.04
Hospital beds (per 1,000 head, 2005)	0.40
Health expenditure (2004): US $ per head (PPP)	41.7
Health expenditure (2004): % of GDP	4.2
Health expenditure (2004): public (% of total)	36.9
Access to water (% of persons, 2004)	42
Access to sanitation (% of persons, 2004)	9
Human Development Index (2004): ranking	171
Human Development Index (2004): value	0.368

For sources and definitions, see explanatory note on p. vi.

Agriculture

PRINCIPAL CROPS

('000 metric tons)

	2002	2003	2004
Rice (paddy)	134.9	126.0	91.1
Maize	84.3	118.0	107.4
Millet	357.4	516.3	297.5
Sorghum	480.7	564.7	449.4
Other cereals	155.1	293.1	267.4
Potatoes*	27	27	27
Sweet potatoes*	64	64	64
Cassava (Manioc)	322†	325*	325*
Taro (Coco yam)*	38	38	38
Yams*	230	230	230

—continued	2002	2003	2004
Sugar cane*	355	366	366
Dry beans*	78	78	78
Other pulses*	43	43	43
Groundnuts (in shell)†	450	450	450
Sesame seed†	35	35	35
Melonseed*	20	20	20
Cottonseed†	113	80	128
Dry onions*	14	14	14
Other vegetables*	81	81	81
Dates*	18	18	18
Mangoes*	32	32	32
Other fruit*	63	63	63
Cotton (lint)†	71.0	49.0	81.5

* FAO estimate(s).
† Unofficial figure(s).

2005: Production assumed to be unchanged from 2004 (FAO estimates).

Source: FAO.

LIVESTOCK
('000 head, year ending September)

	2003	2004*	2005*
Cattle	6,268†	6,400	6,540
Goats	5,588†	5,717	5,843
Sheep	2,511†	2,569	2,628
Pigs	24*	25	25
Horses	267†	273	275
Asses	380*	388	388
Camels	730*	735	740
Poultry	5,000*	5,200	5,200

* FAO estimate(s).
† Unofficial figure.

Source: FAO.

LIVESTOCK PRODUCTS
('000 metric tons, FAO estimates)

	2003	2004	2005
Cattle meat	78.3	80.2	81.6
Sheep meat	13.0	13.3	13.6
Goat meat	20.9	21.4	21.9
Other meat	10.0	10.2	10.3
Cows' milk	169.3	172.8	176.6
Sheep's milk	9.4	9.6	9.9
Goats' milk	33.5	34.3	34.8
Poultry eggs	4.5	4.7	4.7

Source: FAO.

Forestry

ROUNDWOOD REMOVALS
('000 cubic metres, excl. bark, FAO estimates)

	2003	2004	2005
Sawlogs, veneer logs and logs for sleepers*	14	14	14
Other industrial wood†	747	747	747
Fuel wood	6,239	6,362	6,488
Total	7,000	7,123	7,249

* Output assumed to be unchanged since 1993.
† Output assumed to be unchanged since 1999.

Source: FAO.

SAWNWOOD PRODUCTION
('000 cubic metres, incl. railway sleepers)

	1994	1995	1996
Total (all broadleaved)	2.4*	2.4	2.4

* FAO estimate.

1997–2005: Annual production as in 1996 (FAO estimates).

Source: FAO.

Fishing

('000 metric tons, live weight, FAO estimates)

	2001	2002	2003
Total catch (freshwater fishes)	80.0	75.0	70.0

2004–05: Figure assumed to be unchanged from 2003 (FAO estimates).

Source: FAO.

Mining

	2003	2004	2005
Crude petroleum ('000 barrels)	8,600	61,400	63,300

Source: US Geological Survey.

Industry

SELECTED PRODUCTS

	2002	2003	2004
Sugar (centrifugal, raw, '000 metric tons)	23.1	38.0	40.0
Beer ('000 metric tons)	12.4	11.0	8.4
Cigarettes (million packs)	36.0	37.0	40.0
Electric energy (million kWh)	106.6	86.0	84.0

Source: IMF, *Chad: Selected Issues and Statistical Appendix* (January 2007).

Oil of groundnuts ('000 metric tons): 36.6 in 2002 (Source: FAO).

Finance

CURRENCY AND EXCHANGE RATES

Monetary Units
100 centimes = 1 franc de la Coopération financière en Afrique centrale (CFA).

Sterling, Dollar and Euro Equivalents (31 May 2007)
£1 sterling = 964.116 francs CFA;
US $1 = 487.592 francs CFA;
€1 = 655.957 francs CFA;
10,000 francs CFA = £10.37 = $20.51 = €15.24.

Average Exchange Rate (francs CFA per US $)
2004 528.29
2005 527.47
2006 522.89

Note: An exchange rate of 1 French franc = 50 francs CFA, established in 1948, remained in force until January 1994, when the CFA franc was devalued by 50%, with the exchange rate adjusted to 1 French franc = 100 francs CFA. This relationship to French currency remained in effect with the introduction of the euro on 1 January 1999. From that date, accordingly, a fixed exchange rate of €1 = 655.957 francs CFA has been in operation.

BUDGET

('000 million francs CFA)

Revenue*	2003	2004	2005
Non-petroleum revenue	124.6	140.3	159.2
Tax revenue	113.4	122.0	138.9
Taxes on income and profits	52.4	52.5	58.9
Companies	20.3	23.5	24.2
Individuals	30.2	26.9	32.4
Employers' payroll tax	1.9	2.1	2.3
Property tax	2.5	4.1	4.2
Taxes on goods and services	20.6	25.9	26.0
Turnover tax	14.4	15.4	17.9
Tax on petroleum products	4.7	5.1	5.4
Taxes on international trade	31.3	33.8	41.1
Import taxes	27.6	33.8	41.1
Export taxes	1.6	2.0	1.6
Other revenue	11.2	18.3	20.4
Property income	2.1	2.9	1.0
Administrative fees	1.9	1.2	2.3
Non-industrial sales	2.2	3.3	2.0
Petroleum-exploitation permits and share premium	—	8.3	13.6
Petroleum revenue	—	57.7	130.4
Total	124.6	198.0	289.7

Expenditure†	2003	2004	2005
Current expenditure	149.4	154.7	187.3
Wages and salaries	73.6	80.1	101.2
Civil service	56.2	60.9	73.3
Military	17.4	19.2	27.9
Goods and services	42.6	32.4	34.2
Transfers	19.2	30.1	37.1
Interest	9.5	10.2	10.4
External	8.6	8.2	7.2
Investment expenditure	198.6	182.1	217.7
Domestically financed	28.9	48.7	68.5
Foreign-financed	169.7	133.4	149.1
Total	348.0	336.8	404.9

* Excluding grants received ('000 million francs CFA): 122.7 in 2003; 69.4 in 2004; 104.2 in 2005.

† Excluding net lending ('000 million francs CFA): 76.6 in 2003; 68.0 in 2004; 53.3 in 2005.

Source: IMF, *Chad: Selected Issues and Statistical Appendix* (January 2007).

INTERNATIONAL RESERVES

(US $ million at 31 December)

	2004	2005	2006
Gold*	4.88	5.71	7.06
IMF special drawing rights	0.07	0.07	0.10
Reserve position in IMF	0.44	0.40	0.42
Foreign exchange	221.23	225.10	624.57
Total	226.62	231.28	632.15

* Valued at market-related prices.

Source: IMF, *International Financial Statistics*.

MONEY SUPPLY

('000 million francs CFA at 31 December)

	2004	2005	2006
Currency outside banks	110.11	154.10	217.21
Demand deposits at commercial and development banks	65.31	77.78	140.38
Total money (incl. others)	175.44	231.89	357.60

Source: IMF, *International Financial Statistics*.

COST OF LIVING

(Consumer Price Index for African households in N'Djamena; base: 2000 = 100)

	2004	2005	2006
All items	110.0	118.7	128.2

Source: IMF, *International Financial Statistics*.

NATIONAL ACCOUNTS

Expenditure on the Gross Domestic Product

('000 million francs CFA at current prices)

	2002	2003	2004*
Government final consumption expenditure	106.2	108.2	114.5
Private final consumption expenditure	1,745.1	1,111.0	1,035.5
Gross fixed capital formation	899.6	782.7	765.2
Variation in stocks	25.0	69.5	20.7
Total domestic expenditure	2,775.9	2,071.4	1,935.9
Exports of goods and services	175.6	391.7	1,199.9
Less Imports of goods and services	1,574.7	934.3	1,073.1
GDP in purchasers' values	1,376.8	1,528.8	2,062.7

* Estimates.

Source: Banque des états de l'Afrique centrale.

Gross Domestic Product by Economic Activity

('000 million francs CFA at constant 1995 prices)

	2003	2004	2005
Agriculture*	307.5	287.8	328.0
Mining and quarrying†	30.9	30.9	34.2
Electricity, gas and water	6.3	6.2	8.1
Manufacturing	97.9	91.9	107.2
Construction	20.4	23.5	26.9
Petroleum sector	123.5	485.0	486.9
Wholesale and retail trade, restaurants and hotels; Transport and communications	274.7	292.1	314.2
Public administration	128.6	143.8	160.6
Other services	104.7	85.6	157.8
GDP at factor cost	1,094.5	1,446.8	1,623.9
Indirect taxes, *less* subsidies	44.8	48.8	54.0
GDP in purchasers' values	1,139.3	1,495.6	1,677.9

* Excluding fishing.

† Including fishing.

Source: IMF, *Chad: Selected Issues and Statistical Appendix* (January 2007).

BALANCE OF PAYMENTS

('000 million francs CFA)

	2003	2004	2005
Exports of goods f.o.b.	350.4	1,142.1	1,639.2
Imports of goods f.o.b.	−453.2	−462.3	−428.1
Trade balance	−102.8	679.8	1,211.1
Exports of services	41.4	47.6	66.4
Imports of services	−481.2	−721.6	−802.6
Balance on goods and services	−542.6	5.8	474.9
Factor income (net)	−265.3	−231.5	−543.2
Balance on goods, services and income	−807.9	−225.7	−68.3
Private unrequited transfers (net)	14.6	41.9	32.5
Official unrequited transfers (net)	43.0	72.9	62.3
Current balance	−750.3	−110.9	26.5
Public long- and medium-term capital	149.0	165.3	137.7
Direct investment	414.0	252.6	323.8
Other investments	−22.2	−27.3	−40.9
Fund for future generations	—	5.0	13.0
Short-term capital	−120.7	−233.4	−372.2
Net errors and omissions	303.5	−33.8	−64.5
Overall balance	−26.7	17.5	23.5

Source: IMF, *Chad: Selected Issues and Statistical Appendix* (January 2007).

External Trade

PRINCIPAL COMMODITIES

Imports c.i.f. (US $'000)	1995
Food and live animals	41,182
Cereals and cereal preparations	16,028
Wheat and meslin (unmilled)	8,945
Sugar, sugar preparations and honey	17,078
Refined sugars, etc.	16,825
Beverages and tobacco	7,175
Mineral fuels, lubricants, etc.	38,592
Refined petroleum products	38,551
Motor spirit (gasoline) and other light oils	6,490
Kerosene and other medium oils	8,456
Gas oils	23,318
Chemicals and related products	15,507
Medicinal and pharmaceutical products	7,789
Basic manufactures	26,190
Non-metallic mineral manufactures	7,654
Metal manufactures	8,804
Machinery and transport equipment	51,246
General industrial machinery, equipment and parts	8,175
Road vehicles (incl. air-cushion vehicles) and parts*	17,873
Parts and accessories for cars, lorries, buses, etc.*	8,253
Miscellaneous manufactured articles	27,335
Printed matter	13,565
Postage stamps, banknotes, etc.	11,622
Total (incl. others)	215,171

* Excluding tyres, engines and electrical parts.

Source: UN, *International Trade Statistics Yearbook*.

Exports ('000 million francs CFA)	2000	2001	2002*
Cotton	50.6	56.9	33.2
Livestock	48.8	49.5	52.0
Total (incl. others)	130.2	138.3	118.0

* Estimates.

Source: La Zone Franc, *Rapport Annuel 2002*.

Total imports c.i.f. (million francs CFA): 169,733 in 1996; 194,732 in 1997; 210,207 in 1998; 194,523 in 1999; 224,386 in 2000; 497,417 in 2001; 1,146,934 in 2002; 459,100 in 2003; 365,200 in 2004 (Source: IMF, *International Financial Statistics*).

Total exports c.i.f. (million francs CFA): 349,100 in 2003; 1,191,300 in 2004 (Source: IMF, *International Financial Statistics*).

PRINCIPAL TRADING PARTNERS

Imports c.i.f. (US $'000)	1995
Belgium-Luxembourg	4,771
Cameroon	33,911
Central African Repub.	3,010
China, People's Repub.	6,251
France	88,887
Germany	2,988
Italy	6,452
Japan	5,121
Malaysia	2,234
Netherlands	2,843
Nigeria	25,269
Spain	3,402
USA	13,966
Total (incl. others)	215,171

Source: UN, *International Trade Statistics Yearbook*.

Transport

ROAD TRAFFIC
(motor vehicles in use at 31 December)

	1994	1995*	1996*
Passenger cars	8,720	9,700	10,560
Buses and coaches	708	760	820
Lorries and vans	12,650	13,720	14,550
Tractors	1,413	1,500	1,580
Motorcycles and mopeds	1,855	2,730	3,640

* Estimates.

Source: International Road Federation, *World Road Statistics*.

2006: Passenger cars 18,867; Vans 24,874; Buses 3,278; Tractors 3,132; Motorcycles 63,036 (Source: Ministère de Travaux Publics et de Transport).

CIVIL AVIATION
(traffic on scheduled services*)

	1999	2000	2001
Kilometres flown (million)	3	3	1
Passengers carried ('000)	84	77	46
Passengers-km (million)	235	216	130
Total ton-km (million)	36	32	19

* Including an apportionment of the traffic of Air Afrique.

Source: UN, *Statistical Yearbook*.

Tourism

FOREIGN VISITORS BY NATIONALITY*

	2003	2004	2005
Belgium	164	219	241
Canada	1,044	1,942	1,935
Egypt	370	440	426
France	7,897	9,986	11,757
Germany	405	508	547
Italy	166	202	246
Libya	473	563	549
Saudi Arabia	121	143	149
Switzerland	303	381	458
United Kingdom	270	336	363
USA	3,206	3,433	3,693
Total (incl. others)	20,974	25,899	29,356

* Arrivals at hotels and similar establishments.

Receipts from tourism (US $ million, incl. passenger transport): 14 in 2000; 23 in 2001; 25 in 2002; 2003–05 n.a.

Source: World Tourism Organization.

Communications Media

	2002	2003	2004
Telephones ('000 main lines in use)	11.8	12.4	13.0
Mobile cellular telephones ('000 subscribers)	34.2	65.0	123.0
Personal computers ('000 in use)	13	14	15
Internet users ('000)	15	30	35

2005: Mobile cellular telephones ('000 subscribers) 210.0.

Television receivers ('000 in use): 10.9 in 2000.

Radio receivers ('000 in use): 1,670 in 1997.

Facsimile machines (number in use): 182 in 1999.

Daily newspapers (national estimates): 2 in 1997 (average circulation 1,550 copies); 2 in 1998 (average circulation 1,560 copies).

Non-daily newspapers: 2 in 1995 (average circulation 10,000 copies); 14 in 1997; 10 in 1998.

Periodicals: 51 in 1997; 53 in 1998.

Sources: International Telecommunication Union; UNESCO, *Statistical Yearbook*; UNESCO Institute for Statistics; UN, *Statistical Yearbook*.

Education

(2003/04, unless otherwise indicated)

	Institutions	Teachers	Students		
			Males	Females	Total
Pre-primary*	24	67	938	735	1,673
Primary	2,660†	16,228	683,452	441,540	1,124,992
Secondary	n.a.	6,464	168,436	53,731	222,167
Tertiary‡	n.a.	423	5,190	916	6,106

* 1994/95 figures; public education only.

† 1995/96.

‡ 2000/01.

Source: mainly UNESCO Institute for Statistics.

Adult literacy rate (UNESCO estimates): 25.7% (males 40.8%; females 12.8%) in 2004 (Source: UN Development Programme, *Human Development Report*).

Directory

The Constitution

The Constitution of the Republic of Chad, which was adopted by national referendum on 31 March 1996, enshrines a unitary state. The President is elected for a term of five years by direct universal adult suffrage. The Prime Minister, who is appointed by the President, nominates the Council of Ministers. The legislature comprises a 155-member Assemblée nationale, which is elected by direct universal adult suffrage for a term of four years. The Constitution provides for an independent judicial system, with a High Court of Justice, and the establishment of a Constitutional Court and a High Council for Communication.

Constitutional amendments approved by the Assemblée nationale in May 2004 and confirmed by referendum in June 2005 provided for the abolition of the restriction on the number of terms that the President is permitted to serve (hitherto, the Head of State had been restricted to two terms in office), and for the abolition of an upper legislative chamber, the Sénat, provided for in the 1996 Constitution (which had not, however, been established). The amendments also provided for the establishment of a Conseil économique, social et culturel, the members of which would be appointed by the President of the Republic.

The Government

HEAD OF STATE

President: Gen. Idriss Deby Itno (assumed office 4 December 1990; elected President 3 July 1996; re-elected 20 May 2001 and 3 May 2006).

COUNCIL OF MINISTERS

(August 2007)

Prime Minister: Dr Nouradine Kassiré Delwa Coumakoye.

Minister of State, Minister of Infrastructure: Adoum Younousmi.

Minister of State, Minister of Mines and Energy: Mahamat Ali Abdallah Nassour.

Minister of State, Minister of Agriculture: Dr Haroun Kabadi.

Minister of External Relations: Ahmat Allam-Mi.

Minister of Justice, Keeper of the Seals: Pahimi Padacke Albert.

Minister of the Interior and Public Security: Ahmat Mahamat Bachir.

Minister of Finance and Information Technology: Abbas Mahamat Tolli.

Minister of the Economy and Planning: Ousmane Matar Breme.

Minister of the Civil Service and Labour: Fatimé Tchombi.

Minister of Public Health: Avocksouma Djona.

Minister of National Education: Abderamane Koko.

Minister of Higher Education, Scientific Research and Professional Training: Dr Oumar Idriss al-Farouk.

Minister of Petroleum: Emmanuel Nadingar.

Minister of National Defence: Capt. Mahamat Nour Abdelkarim.

Minister of Stockbreeding: Ahmat Abdoulaye Ogoum.

Minister of Trade, Industry and Crafts: Youssouf Abbassalah.

Minister of Land Management, Town Planning and Housing: Mahamat Abdoulaye Mahamat.

Minister of the Environment, National Parks and Quality of Life: Dr Haoua Outmane Djame.

Minister of Fisheries, Water Resources and Villages: Abakar Ramadane.

Minister of Social Welfare, National Solidarity and Families: Ngarmbatina Carmel Sou VI.

Minister of General State Control and the Promotion of Morality: Mahamat Bechir Okortomi.

Minister of Communication, Government Spokesperson: Hourmadji Moussa Doumgor.

Minister of Posts and New Communications Technologies: Mahamat Garfa.

Minister of Youth and Sports: Oumar Boukar.

Minister of Culture and the Arts: Dillah Lucienne.

Minister of the Development of Tourism: Brahim Koulamallah.

Minister in charge of Associative Development, Micro-credits and Poverty Prevention: Nadjalta Mirangaye.

Minister in charge of Human Rights: Fatime Issa Ramadane.

Secretary of State for Infrastructure, responsible for Transport: Goundoul Vikama.

Secretary of State for External Relations, responsible for International Co-operation: Djidda Moussa Outman.

Secretary of State for External Relations, responsible for African Integration: Ismael Idriss Ismael.

Secretary of State for Public Health, responsible for Sanitation: Oumar Boukar Gana.

Secretary of State for National Defence, responsible for War Veterans and Victims of War: Sauguelni Boniface.

Secretary of State for Agriculture, responsible for Professional Training and Food Security: Khadidja Hassaballah.

Secretary of State for Finance and Information Technology, responsible for the Budget: Abakar Mallah.

Secretary of State for the Interior, responsible for Public Security and Immigration: Oumar Boukar.

Secretary of State for the Interior, responsible for Communities of the Decentralized Territories: Abderahmane Djasnabaille.

Secretary of State for National Education, responsible for Literacy: HAPISTA ALBOUKHARI.

Secretary of State for the Secretary General of the Government, responsible for Relations with the National Assembly: LONA GONG RAOUL.

Minister, Secretary-General of the Government, in charge of Relations with the National Assembly: KALZEUBE PAYUIMI DEUBET.

MINISTRIES

Office of the President: Palais rose, BP 74, N'Djamena; tel. 51-44-37; fax 52-45-01; e-mail presidence@tchad.td; internet www.presidence-tchad.org.

Office of the Prime Minister: BP 463, N'Djamena; tel. 52-63-39; fax 52-69-77; e-mail cpcprimt@intnet.td; internet www.primature-tchad.com.

Ministry of Agriculture: BP 441, N'Djamena; tel. 52-65-66; fax 52-51-19; e-mail conacils@intnet.td.

Ministry of Associative Development, Micro-credits and Poverty Prevention: N'Djamena.

Ministry of the Civil Service and Labour: BP 637, N'Djamena; tel. and fax 52-21-98.

Ministry of Communication: BP 892, N'Djamena; tel. 52-40-97; fax 52-65-60.

Ministry of Culture and the Arts: BP 892, N'Djamena; tel. 52-40-97; fax 52-65-60.

Ministry of the Development of Tourism: BP 86, N'Djamena; tel. 52-44-21; fax 52-51-19.

Ministry of Economy and Planning: N'Djamena.

Ministry of the Environment, Quality of Life and National Parks: BP 905, N'Djamena; tel. 52-60-12; fax 52-38-39; e-mail facdrem@intnet.td.

Ministry of Finance and Information Technology: BP 816, N'Djamena; tel. 52-68-61; fax 52-49-08; e-mail d.dette@intnet.td.

Ministry of External Relations: BP 746, N'Djamena; tel. 51-80-50; fax 51-45-85.

Ministry of Fisheries, Water Resources and Villages: N'Djamena.

Ministry of General State Control and the Promotion of Morality: N'Djamena.

Ministry of Higher Education, Scientific Research and Professional Training: BP 743, N'Djamena; tel. 51-61-58; fax 51-92-31.

Ministry of Human Rights: N'Djamena.

Ministry of Infrastructure: N'Djamena.

Ministry of the Interior and Public Security: BP 916, N'Djamena; tel. 52-05-76.

Ministry of Justice: BP 426, N'Djamena; tel. 52-21-72; fax 52-21-39; e-mail justice@intnet.td.

Ministry of Land Management, Town Planning and Housing: BP 436, N'Djamena; tel. 52-31-89; fax 52-39-35.

Ministry of Mines and Energy: BP 816, N'Djamena; tel. 51-83-06; fax 52-75-60; e-mail cons.mines@intnet.td.

Ministry of National Defence: BP 916, N'Djamena; tel. 52-35-13; fax 52-65-44.

Ministry of National Education: BP 743, N'Djamena; tel. 51-92-65; fax 51-45-12.

Ministry of Petroleum: BP 816, N'Djamena; tel. 52-56-03; fax 52-36-66; e-mail mme@intnet.td; internet www.ministere-petrole.td.

Ministry of Posts and New Communications Technologies: BP 154, N'Djamena; tel. 52-15-79; fax 52-15-30; e-mail dabye@intnet.td.

Ministry of Public Health: BP 440, N'Djamena; tel. 51-51-14; fax 51-58-00.

Ministry of Social Welfare, National Solidarity and Families: BP 80, N'Djamena; tel. 52-25-32; fax 52-48-88.

Ministry of Stockbreeding: BP 750, N'Djamena; tel. 52-89-43.

Ministry of Territorial Administration: BP 742, N'Djamena; tel. 52-56-09; fax 52-59-06.

Ministry of Youth and Sports: BP 519, N'Djamena; tel. 52-26-58.

President and Legislature

PRESIDENT

Election, 3 May 2006

Candidate	Votes	% of vote
Idriss Deby Itno	1,863,042	64.67
Kassiré Delwa Coumakoye	436,002	15.13
Pahimi Padacke Albert	225,368	7.82
Mahamat Abdoulaye	203,637	7.07
Ibrahim Koullamallah	152,940	5.31
Total	2,880,989	100.00

LEGISLATURE

Assemblée nationale

Palais du 15 janvier, BP 01, N'Djamena; tel. 53-00-15; fax 31-45-90; internet www.primature-tchad.org/ass.php.

President: NASSOUR GUÉLENDOUKSIA OUAÏDOU.

General Election, 21 April 2002

Party	Seats
Mouvement patriotique du salut (MPS)	110
Rassemblement pour la démocratie et le progrès (RDP)	12
Fédération action pour la République (FAR)	9
VIVA—Rassemblement national pour la démocratie et le progrès (VIVA—RNDP)	5
Union nationale pour le développement et le renouveau (UNDR)	5
Union pour le renouveau et la démocratie (URD)	3
Others*	9
Vacant†	2
Total	155

* There were nine other parties.

† The Constitutional Council annulled the results of voting in two constituencies, in which by-elections were subsequently to be held.

Election Commission

Commission électorale nationale indépendante (CENI): N'djamena; f. 2000; 31 mems, incl. 12 mems appointed by the Government, 16 by political parties represented in the Assemblée nationale, three by extra-parliamentary political parties.

Political Organizations

Legislation permitting the operation of political associations, subject to official registration, took effect in October 1991. In mid-2006 there were 78 officially registered political organizations, of which the following were among the most important:

Action tchadienne pour l'unité et le socialisme (ACTUS): N'Djamena; e-mail actus@club-internet.fr; f. 1981; Marxist-Leninist; Sec.-Gen. Dr DJIMADOUM LEY-NGARDIGAL.

Alliance nationale pour la démocratie et le développement (ANDD): BP 4066, N'Djamena; tel. 51-46-72; f. 1992; Leader SALIBOU GARBA.

Alliance tchadienne pour la démocratie et le développement (ATD): N'Djamena; e-mail info@atd-tchad.com; Leader ABDERAMAN DJASNABAILLE.

Coalition pour la défense de la démocratie et des droits constitutionnels (CDDC): f. 2004 to unite opposition groups in resisting President Deby's proposed revision of the Constitution; Coordinator AHMAT HASSABALLAH SOUBIANE.

Convention pour la démocratie et le fédéralisme: N'Djamena; f. 2002; socialist; supports the establishment of a federal state; Leader ALI GOLHOR.

Convention nationale démocratique et sociale (CNDS): N'Djamena; Leader ADOUM DAYE ZERE.

Coordination des partis politiques pour la défense de la constitution (CPDC): f. 2004 to oppose President Deby's proposed constitutional modifications; mems include the RDP, the URD and the UNDR.

Fédération action pour la République (FAR): BP 4197, N'Djamena; tel. 51-79-67; fax 51-78-60; e-mail yorongarn@yahoo.fr;

internet www.yorongar.com; supports the establishment of a federal republic; Leader NGARLEDJY YORONGAR.

Mouvement patriotique du salut (MPS): Assemblée nationale, Palais du 15 janvier, BP 01, N'Djamena; e-mail administrateur@tchad-gpmps.org; internet www.tchad-gpmps.org; f. 1990 as a coalition of several opposition movements; other opposition groups joined during the Nov. 1990 offensive against the regime of Hissène Habré, and following the movement's accession to power in Dec. 1990; Pres. D'IDRISS NDELE MOUSSA.

Parti pour la liberté et le développement (PLD): N'Djamena; f. 1993; boycotted legislative elections in 2002; Sec.-Gen. IBN OUMAR MAHAMAT SALEH.

Rassemblement pour la démocratie et le progrès (RDP): N'Djamena; f. 1992; seeks to create a secure political environment by the establishment of a reformed national army; supported the re-election of Pres. Deby in 2001, but withdrew support from the Govt in Nov. 2003; Leader LOL MAHAMAT CHOUA.

Union pour la démocratie et la République (UDR): N'Djamena; f. 1992; supports liberal economic policies and a secular, decentralized republic; boycotted legislative elections in 2002; Leader Dr JEAN BAWOYEU ALINGUÉ.

Union nationale pour le développement et le renouveau (UNDR): N'Djamena; supports greater decentralization and increased limitations on the power of the state; Pres. SALEH KEBZABOH; Sec.-Gen. CÉLESTIN TOPONA.

Union pour le renouveau et la démocratie (URD): BP 92, N'Djamena; tel. 51-44-23; fax 51-41-87; f. 1992; Leader Gen. WADAL ABDELKADER KAMOUGUÉ.

VIVA—Rassemblement national pour la démocratie et le progrès (VIVA—RNDP): N'Djamena; f. 1992; supports a unitary, democratic republic; Pres. KASSIRÉ DELWA COUMAKOYE.

A number of unregistered dissident groups (some based abroad) are also active. In early 2006 these organizations, largely 'politico-military', included the following:

Alliance nationale de la résistance (ANR): f. 1996 as alliance of five movements; in early 2003 comprised eight rebel groups based in eastern Chad; signed peace agreement with Govt in Jan. 2003, although FONALT rejected this accord; Leader Col MAHAMAT GARFA.

Armée nationale tchadienne en dissidence (ANTD): f. 1994; Leader Col MAHAMAT GARFA.

Forces des organisations nationales pour l'alternance et les libertés au Tchad (FONALT): rejected cease-fire signed by ANR with Govt in Jan. 2003; Leader Col ABDOULAYE ISSAKA SARWA.

Coordination des mouvements armés et partis politiques de l'opposition (CMAP): internet www.maxpages.com/tchad/cmap2; f. 1999 by 13 'politico-military' organizations; a number of groups subsequently left, several of which later joined the FUDP (q.v.); Leader ANTOINE BANGUI.

Front extérieur pour la rénovation: Leader ANTOINE BANGUI.

Front de libération nationale du Tchad-Conseil provisoire de la révolution (FROLINAT-CPR): f. 1968 in Sudan; based in Algeria; Leader GOUKOUNI OUEDDEI.

Front uni pour le changement démocratique (FUCD): f. 2005; signed a peace agreement with the Government in Dec. 2006; Leader Capt. MAHAMAT NOUR ABDELKERIM.

Rassemblement pour la démocratie et les libertés (RDL): f. 2005 in Eastern Chad; Leader Capt MAHAMAT NOUR ABDELKERIM.

Socle pour le changement, l'unité nationale et la démocratie (SCUD): f. 2005 in Eastern Chad; Leaders TOM ERDIMI, YAYA DILLO DJÉROU.

Front uni pour la démocratie et la paix (FUDP): f. 2003 in Benin; seeks by all possible means to establish a new constitution and a transitional govt in advance of free and transparent elections; faction of MDJT (q.v.) led by Adoum Togoi Abbo claims membership, but this is rejected by principal faction of MDJT; Pres. Brig.-Gen. ADOUM TOGOI ABBO.

Conseil national de résistance (CNR): leadership of group forced to leave Benin for Togo in mid-2003; Pres. HISSÈNE KOTY YACOUB.

Convention populaire de résistance (CPR): e-mail cpr60@voila.fr; f. 2001 by fmr mems of CNR (q.v.); Leader ABDEL-AZIZ ABDALLAH KODOK.

Front national du Tchad renové (FNTR): Dabo; e-mail yasaid2001@yahoo.fr; internet www.maxpages.com/tchad/fntr; f. 1996 in Sudan by fmr mems of FNT (q.v.); based in Dabo (France); announced abandonment of armed struggle in 2002; new leadership elected in early 2003; seeks establishment of semi-presidential and social-democratic system of govt; publishes monthly bulletin, *Al-Widha*, in French and Arabic; Hon. Pres. MAHAMAT MOUSSA; Sec.-Gen. SALAHADINE MAHADI.

Mouvement nationale des rénovateurs tchadiens (MNRT): e-mail fpls@romandie.com; democratic opposition in exile; Sec.-Gen. ALI MUHAMMAD DIALLO.

Rassemblement des forces démocratique—Convention nationale Tchadienne ((RAFD—CNT)): f. 2006.

Union des forces pour le changement (UFC): f. 2004; advocates suspension of the 1996 Constitution and the composition of a new Charter of the Republic to develop national unity, free, transparent elections and the rule of law; National Co-ordinator ACHEIKH IBN OUMAR.

Conseil démocratique révolutionnaire (CDR): Leader ACHEIKH IBN OUMAR.

Front démocratique populaire (FDP): Leader Dr MAHAMOUT NAHOR.

Front populaire pour la renaissance nationale.

Mouvement pour la démocratie et le développement (MDD): tel. and fax 34-46-17; e-mail mdd@mdd-tchad.com; internet membres.lycos.fr/mddtchad; comprises two factions, led by ISSA FAKI MAHAMAT and BRAHIM MALLAH.

Mouvement pour la démocratie et la justice au Tchad (MDJT): based in Tibesti, northern Chad; e-mail admin@mdjt.net; internet www.mdjt.net; fmr deputy leader, Brig.-Gen. ADOUM TOGOI ABBO, signed a peace agreement with Govt in Jan. 2002, although this was subsequently rejected by elements close to fmr leader, YOUSSOUF TOGOIMI (who died in Sept. 2002); split into two factions in 2003; the faction led by Togoi claimed membership of the FUDP (q.v.) and signed a peace agreement with the Govt in Dec. 2003, which was rejected by the faction led by Chair. Col HASSAN ABDALLAH MARDIGUÉ; announced a proposed merger with FROLINAT—CPR in December 2006.

Mouvement pour l'unité et la République (MUR): f. 2000 by faction of the MDD (q.v.); Leader GAILETH GATOUL BOURKOUMANDAH.

Union des forces pour la démocratie et le développement (UFDD): f. 2006; Leader MAHAMAT NOURI.

Union des forces démocratiques (UFD): Leader Dr MAHAMAT NAHOUR.

Diplomatic Representation

EMBASSIES IN CHAD

Algeria: BP 178, rue de Paris, N'Djamena; tel. 52-38-15; fax 52-37-92; e-mail amb.algerie@intnet.td; Ambassador BOUBAKEUR OGAB.

Cameroon: rue des Poids Lourds, BP 58, N'Djamena; tel. 52-28-94; Chargé d'affaires a.i. ABBAS IBRAHIMA SALAHEDDINE.

Central African Republic: rue 1036, près du Rond-Point de la Garde, BP 115, N'Djamena; tel. 52-32-06; Ambassador DAVID NGUINDO.

China, People's Republic: BP 735, N'Djamena; tel. 52-29-49; fax 53-00-45; internet td.china-embassy.org; Ambassador WANG YINGWU.

Congo, Democratic Republic: ave du 20 août, BP 910, N'Djamena; tel. 52-21-83.

Egypt: Quartier Clemat, ave Georges Pompidou, auprès rond-point de la SONASUT, BP 1094, N'Djamena; tel. 51-09-73; fax 51-09-72; e-mail ambegyndj@africamail.com; Ambassador KHALED ABDALLAH SHEHATA.

France: rue du Lt Franjoux, BP 431, N'Djamena; tel. 52-25-75; fax 52-28-55; e-mail amba.france@intnet.td; internet www.ambafrance-td.org; Ambassador BRUNO FOUCHER.

Holy See: rue de Béguinage, BP 490, N'Djamena; tel. 52-31-15; fax 52-38-27; e-mail nonceapo@intnet.td; Apostolic Nuncio Most Rev. PIERRE NGUYÊN VAN TOT (Titular Archbishop of Rusticiana).

Korea, Democratic People's Republic: N'Djamena; Ambassador KIM PYONG GI.

Libya: BP 1096, N'Djamena; tel. 51-92-89; e-mail alibya1@intnet.td; Ambassador GHAYTH SALIM.

Nigeria: 35 ave Charles de Gaulle, BP 752, N'Djamena; tel. 52-24-98; fax 52-30-92; e-mail nigndjam@intnet.td; Ambassador M. ARGUNGU.

Russia: 2 rue Adjutant Collin, BP 891, N'Djamena; tel. 52-57-19; fax 51-31-72; e-mail rusam@intnet.td; Ambassador VLADIMIR N. MARTYNOV.

Saudi Arabia: Quartier Aéroport, rue Jander Miry, BP 974, N'Djamena; tel. 52-31-28; fax 52-33-28; e-mail najdiat.tchad@intnet.td.

Sudan: rue de la Gendarmerie, BP 45, N'Djamena; tel. 52-43-59; e-mail amb.soudan@intnet.td; Ambassador ABDALLAH CHEIKH.

USA: ave Félix Eboué, BP 413, N'Djamena; tel. 51-70-09; fax 51-56-54; e-mail YingraD@state.gov; internet usembassy.state.gov/ndjamena; Ambassador MARC M. WALL.

Judicial System

The highest judicial authority is the Supreme Court, which comprises a Judicial Chamber, an Administrative Chamber and an Audit Chamber. There is also a Constitutional Council, with final jurisdiction in matters of state. The legal structure also comprises the Court of Appeal, and magistrate and criminal courts. A High Court of Justice, which is competent to try the President or members of the Government in cases of treason, embezzlement of public funds, and certain other crimes and offences, was inaugurated in June 2003.

Supreme Court: rue 0221, Quartier Résidentiel, 1er arrondissement, BP 5495, N'Djamena; tel. 52-01-99; fax 52-51-81; e-mail ccsrp@intnet.td; internet www.coursupreme-tchad.org; Pres. ABDERAHIM BIREME HAMID; Pres. of the Judicial Chamber BELKOULAYE BEN COUMAREAUX; Pres. of the Administrative Chamber OUSMAME SALAH IDJEMI; Pres. of the Audit Chamber DOLOTAN NOUDJALBAYE; Prosecutor-Gen. EDOUARD NGARTA M'BAIOUROUM.

Constitutional Council: BP 5500, N'Djamena; tel. 52-03-41; e-mail conseil.sg@intnet.td; internet www.primature-tchad.org/cc.php; Pres. HOUDEÏNGAR DAVID NGARIMADEN.

Court of Appeal: N'Djamena; tel. 51-24-26; Pres. MAKI ADAM ISSAKA.

High Court of Justice: BP 1407, N'Djamena; tel. 52-33-54; fax 52-35-35; e-mail dchcj@intnet.td; internet www.primature-tchad.org/hdj.php; f. 2003; comprises 15 deputies of the Assemblée nationale, of whom 10 are titular judges and five supplementaries, who serve in the absence of a titular judge. All 15 are elected for the term of four years by their peers; competent to try the President and members of the Government in cases of treason, embezzlement of public funds, and certain other crimes and offences; Pres. ADOUM GOUDJA.

Religion

It is estimated that some 50% of the population are Muslims and about 30% Christians. Most of the remainder follow animist beliefs.

ISLAM

Conseil Suprême des Affaires Islamiques: POB 1101, N'Djamena; tel. 51-81-80; fax 52-58-84; Head of the Islamic Community Imam MOUSSA IBRAHIM.

CHRISTIANITY

The Roman Catholic Church

Chad comprises one archdiocese, six dioceses and one apostolic prefecture. At 31 December 2004 baptized Roman Catholics numbered approximately 754,904 (about 8.8% of the total population), most of whom resided in the south of the country and in N'Djamena.

Bishops' Conference

Conférence Episcopale du Tchad, BP 456, N'Djamena; tel. 52-37-79; fax 52-50-51; e-mail secreta.cet@intnet.td.

f. 1991; Pres. Most Rev. JEAN-CLAUDE BOUCHARD (Bishop of Pala).

Archbishop of N'Djamena: Most Rev. MATTHIAS N'GARTÉRI MAYADI, Archevêché, BP 456, N'Djamena; tel. 51-74-44; fax 52-50-51; e-mail diocndja@intnet.td.

Protestant Churches

Entente des Eglises et Missions Evangéliques au Tchad (EEMET): BP 2006, N'Djamena; tel. 51-53-93; fax 51-87-20; e-mail eemet@intnet.td; assen of churches and missions working in Chad; includes Assemblées Chrétiennes au Tchad (ACT), Assemblées de Dieu au Tchad (ADT), Eglise Evangélique des Frères au Tchad (EEFT), Eglise Evangélique au Tchad (EET), Eglise Fraternelle Luthérienne au Tchad (EFLT), Eglise Evangélique en Afrique Centrale au Tchad (EEACT), Eglise Evangélique Missionnaire au Tchad (EEMT); also five assoc. mems: Union des Jeunes Chrétiens (UJC), Groupe Biblique des Hôpitaux au Tchad (GBHT), Mission Evangélique contre la Lèpre (MECL), Croix Bleue du Tchad (CBT).

BAHÁ'Í FAITH

National Spiritual Assembly: BP 181, N'Djamena; tel. 51-47-05; e-mail ntirandaz@aol.com.

The Press

Al-Watan: N'Djamena; tel. 51-57-96; weekly; Editor-in-Chief MOUSSA NDORKOÏ.

Audy Magazine: BP 780, N'Djamena; tel. 51-49-59; f. 2000; 2 a month; women's interest; Dir TONGRONGOU AGOUNA GRÂCE.

Bulletin Mensuel de Statistiques du Tchad: BP 453, N'Djamena; monthly.

Carrefour: Centre al-Mouna, BP 456, N'Djamena; tel. 51-42-54; e-mail almouna@intnet.td; f. 2000; every 2 months; Dir Sister NADIA KARAKI; circ. 1,000 (2001).

Chronique: Association pour la Promotion des Libertés Fondamentales Tchad (APLFT), BP 4037, N'Djamena; tel. 51-91-14; monthly; promotes civic information and popular understanding of civic law; Dir MAOUNDONODJI GILBERT.

Comnat: BP 731, N'Djamena; tel. 51-46-75; fax 51-46-71; quarterly; publ. by Commission Nationale Tchadienne for UNESCO.

Grenier: BP 1128, N'Djamena; tel. 53-30-14; e-mail cedesep@intnet.td; monthly; economics; finance; Dir KOHOM NGAR-ONE DAVID.

Info-Tchad: BP 670, N'Djamena; tel. 51-58-67; news bulletin issued by Agence-Info Tchad; daily; French.

Informations Economiques: BP 458, N'Djamena; publ. by the Chambre de Commerce, d'Agriculture et d'Industrie; weekly.

La Lettre: BP 2037, N'Djamena; tel. and fax 51-91-09; e-mail ltdh@intnet.td; f. 1993; monthly; publ. by the Ligue Tchadienne des droits de l'Homme; Dir DOBIAN ASSINGAR.

N'Djamena Bi-Hebdo: BP 4498, N'Djamena; tel. 51-53-14; fax 52-14-98; e-mail ndjh@intnet.td; 2 a week; Arabic and French; f. 1989; Dir YALDET BÉGOTO OULATAR; Editor-in-Chief DIEUDONNÉ DJONABAYE; circ. 3,500 (2001).

Notre Temps: BP 4352, N'Djamena; tel. and fax 51-46-50; e-mail ntemps.presse@yahoo.fr; f. 2000; weekly; opposed to the Govt of Pres. Deby Itno; Editorial Dir NADJIKIMO BENOUDJITA; circ. 3,000 (2001).

L'Observateur: BP 2031, N'Djamena; tel. and fax 51-80-05; e-mail observer.presse@intnet.td; f. 1997; weekly; Dir NGARADOUMBE SAMBORY; circ. 4,000 (2001).

Le Progrès: 1976 ave Charles de Gaulle, BP 3055, N'Djamena; tel. 51-55-86; fax 51-02-56; e-mail progres@intnet.td; f. 1993; daily; Dir MAHAMAT HISSÈNE; circ. 3,000 (2001).

Revue Juridique Tchadienne: BP 907, N'Djamena; internet www.cefod.org/Droit_au_Tchad/Revuejuridique/Sommaire_rjt.htm; f. 1999; Dir MAHAMAT SALEH BEN BIANG.

Tchad et Culture: BP 907, N'Djamena; tel. 51-54-32; fax 51-91-50; e-mail cefod@intnet.td; internet www.cefod.org; f. 1961; monthly; Dir RONELNGUÉ TORIAÏRA; Editor-in-Chief NAYGOTIMTI BAMBÉ; circ. 4,500 (2002).

Le Temps: face Ecole Belle-vue, Moursal, BP 1333, N'Djamena; tel. 51-70-28; fax 51-99-24; e-mail temps.presse@intnet.td; f. 1995; weekly; Publishing Dir MICHAËL N. DIDAMA; circ. 6,000 (2001).

Victoire Al Nassr: N'Djamena; tel. 51-64-17; weekly; Dir ABOUBAKAR MAHAMAT BORGHO.

La Voix du Paysan: BP 1671, N'Djamena; tel. 51-82-66; monthly; Dir DJALDI TABDI GASSISSOU NASSER.

NEWS AGENCIES

Agence-Info Tchad: BP 670, N'Djamena; tel. 52-58-67; f. 1966; Dir ABAKAR HASSAN ACHEICK.

Foreign Bureau

Agence France-Presse (AFP): N'Djamena; tel. 51-54-71; Correspondent ALDOM NADJI TITO.

Publisher

Imprimerie du Tchad (IDT): BP 456, N'Djamena; tel. 52-44-40; fax 52-28-60; Gen. Dir D. E. MAURIN.

Broadcasting and Communications

TELECOMMUNICATIONS

Société des Télécommunications du Tchad (SOTEL TCHAD): BP 1132, N'Djamena; tel. 52-14-36; fax 52-14-42; e-mail sotel@intnet.td; internet www.sotel.td; f. 2000 by merger of telecommunications services of fmr Office National des Postes et des Télécommunications and the Société des Télécommunications Internationales du Tchad; privatization proposed; Dir-Gen. ALI MAHAMAT ZÈNE ALI FADEL.

Celtel-Tchad: ave Charles de Gaulle, BP 5665, N'Djamena; tel. 52-04-18; fax 52-04-19; e-mail info@td.celtel.com; internet www.td.celtel.com; f. 2000; affiliated to Celtel International (United Kingdom); provides mobile cellular telecommunications in N'Djamena, Moundou and Abéché, with expansion to further regions proposed; Dir-Gen. TSHINSELE VAN BELLIGEN BESTON.

Millicom Tchad: N'Djamena; internet www.millicom.com; f. 2005; 87.% owned by Millicom International Cellular (Luxembourg/Sweden); operates mobile cellular telecommunications network in N'Djamena (with expansion to other cities proposed) under the brand name 'Tigo'.

BROADCASTING

Regulatory Authority

High Council of Communication (HCC): BP 1316, N'Djamena; tel. 52-36-00; fax 52-31-51; e-mail hcc@intnet.td; f. 1994; responsible for registration and regulation of radio and television stations, in addition to the printed press; funds independent radio stations; Pres. MOUSSA MAHAMAT DAGO; Sec.-Gen. ADOUM GUEMESSOU.

Radio

Private radio stations have been permitted to operate in Chad since 1994, although private broadcasts did not begin until 1997. By mid-2002 15 private and community stations had received licences, of which nine had commenced broadcasts. There was, additionally, a state-owned broadcaster, with four regional stations.

Radio Nationale Tchadienne (RNT): BP 4589, N'Djamena; tel. 53-32-00; f. 1955; state-controlled; programmes in French, Arabic and 11 vernacular languages; four regional stations; Dir N'GUÉRÉBAYE ADOUM SALEH.

Radio Abéché: BP 36, Abéché, Ouaddaï; tel. 69-81-49.

Radio Faya-Largeau: Faya-Largeau, Borkou.

Radio Moundou: BP 122, Moundou, Logone Occidental; tel. 69-13-22; programmes in French, Sara and Arabic; Dir DIMANANGAR DJAÏNTA.

Radio Sarh: BP 270, Sarh, Bahr Kôh; tel. 68-13-61; programmes in French, Sara and Arabic; Dir BIANA FOUDA NACTOUANDI.

Union des radios privées du Tchad (URPT): N'Djamena; f. 2002; as a federation of nine private and community radio stations, including the following:

DJA FM: BP 1312, N'Djamena; tel. 51-64-90; fax 52-14-52; e-mail myzara@intnet.td; f. 1999; music, cultural and informative programmes in French, Arabic and Sara; Dir ZARA YACOUB.

Radio Brakoss (Radio de l'Agriculture): Moïssala, Mandoul; f. 1996; community radio station; operations suspended by the Govt in Feb. 2004, broadcasts resumed June 2004.

Radio Duji Lohar: BP 155, Moundou, Logone Occidental; tel. 69-17-14; fax 69-12-11; e-mail cdave@intnet.td; f. 2001.

Radio FM Liberté: BP 892, N'Djamena; tel. 51-42-53; f. 2000; financed by nine civil-society organizations; broadcasts in French, Arabic and Sara; Dir DOBIAN ASSINGAR.

Radio Lotiko: Diocese de Sarh, BP 87, Sahr; tel. 68-12-46; fax 68-14-79; e-mail lotiko@intnet.td; internet www.lotiko.org; f. 2001; community radio station; Dir FABRIZIO COLOMBO.

La Voix du Paysan: BP 22, Doba, Logone Oriental; f. 1996; Roman Catholic; Dir DJALDI TABDI GASSISSOU NASSER.

Television

TVT Télévision tchadienne: BP 274, N'Djamena; tel. 52-26-79; fax 52-29-23; state-controlled; broadcasts c. 12 hours per week in French and Arabic; Dir OUROUMADJI MOUSSA.

Broadcasts from Canal France International, TV5, CNN and seven Arabic television stations are also received in Chad.

Finance

(cap. = capital; res = reserves; dep. = deposits; m. = million; br(s). = branch(es); amounts in francs CFA)

BANKING

Central Bank

Banque des Etats de l'Afrique Centrale (BEAC): ave Charles de Gaulle, BP 50, N'Djamena; tel. 52-21-65; fax 52-44-87; e-mail beacndj@beac.int; internet www.beac.int; HQ in Yaoundé, Cameroon; f. 1973; bank of issue for mem. states of the Communauté économique et monétaire de l'Afrique centrale (CEMAC, fmrly Union douanière et économique de l'Afrique centrale), comprising Cameroon, the Central African Repub., Chad, the Repub. of the Congo, Equatorial Guinea and Gabon; cap. 45,000m., res 176,661m., total assets 2,144,626m. (Nov. 2003); Gov. JEAN-FÉLIX MAMALEPOT; Dir in Chad IDRISS AHMED IDRISS; brs at Moundou and Sarh.

Other Banks

Banque Agricole du Soudan au Tchad (BAST): ave el-Niméry, BP 1727, N'Djamena; tel. 51-90-41; fax 51-90-40; e-mail bast@intnet.td; cap. 1,200m. (2002), total assets 1,845m. (Dec. 1999); Pres. MOUHAMED OUSMAN AWAD; Dir-Gen. ABDELKADER OUSMAN HASSAN; 1 br.

Banque Commerciale du Chari (BCC): ave Charles de Gaulle, BP 757, N'Djamena; tel. 51-89-58; fax 51-62-49; e-mail bcc@intnet.td; 50% state-owned, 50% owned by Libya Arab Foreign Bank (Libya); cap. and res 3,567m., total assets 20,931m. (Dec. 2001); Pres. BIDJERE BINDJAKI; Dir-Gen. HAMED EL MISTIRI.

Banque Internationale pour l'Afrique au Tchad (BIAT): ave Charles de Gaulle, BP 87, N'Djamena; tel. 52-43-14; fax 52-23-45; e-mail biat@intnet.td; f. 1954; current name adopted 1981; 80.6% owned by Compagnie de Financement et de Participation (Bamako, Mali); cap. 3,000m. res 1,317m., dep. 24,876m. (Dec. 2003); Chair. BABER TOUNKARA; Dir-Gen. GUY MALLETT.

Banque Sahélo-Saharienne pour l'Investissement et le Commerce (BSIC): ave Charles de Gaulle, BP 81, N'Djamena; tel. 52-26-92; fax 62-26-93; e-mail bsic@bsic-tchad.com; internet www.bsic-tchad.com; f. 2004; Pres. and Dir-Gen. ALHADJI MOHAMED ALWARFALLI.

Commercial Bank Tchad (CBT): rue du Capitaine Ohrel, BP 19, N'Djamena; tel. 52-28-28; fax 52-33-18; e-mail expbdt@intnet.td; f. 1962; 50.7% owned by Groupe FOTSO (Cameroon), 17.5% state-owned; fmrly Banque de Développement du Tchad; cap. 4,020m., res 2,465m., dep. 38,624m. (Dec. 2005); Pres. YOUSSOUF ABBASALAH; Dir-Gen. GEORGES DJADJO; 1 br.

Financial Bank Tchad (FBT): BP 804, N'Djamena; tel. 52-33-89; fax 52-29-05; e-mail fbt@intnet.td; f. 1992; 67.8% owned by Financial BC (Togo); cap. and res 534m., total assets 22,216m. (Dec. 2003); Pres. RÉMY BAYSSET; Dir-Gen. MARC ATHIEL.

Société Générale Tchadienne de Banque (SGTB): 2–6 rue Robert Lévy, BP 461, N'Djamena; tel. 52-28-01; fax 52-37-13; e-mail sgtb@intnet.td; internet www.sgtb.td; f. 1963; 30% owned by Société Générale (France), 15% by Société Générale de Banque au Cameroun; cap. and res 3,603m., total assets 36,579m. (Dec. 2003); Pres. and Dir-Gen. CHEMI KOGRIMI; 3 brs.

Bankers' Organizations

Association Professionnelle des Banques au Tchad: 2–6 rue Robert Lévy, BP 461, N'Djamena; tel. 52-41-90; fax 52-17-13; Pres. CHEMI KOGRIMI.

Conseil National de Crédit: N'Djamena; f. 1965 to formulate a national credit policy and to organize the banking profession.

INSURANCE

Assureurs Conseils Tchadiens Cecar et Jutheau: rue du Havre, BP 139, N'Djamena; tel. 52-21-15; fax 52-35-39; e-mail biliou.alikeke@intnet.td; f. 1966; Dir BILIOU ALIKEKE.

Gras Savoye Tchad: rue du Général Thillo, BP 5620, N'Djamena; tel. 52-00-72; fax 52-00-71; e-mail gras.savoye@intnet.td; affiliated to Gras Savoye (France); Man. DOMKRÉO DJAMON.

Société Mutuelle d'Assurances des Cadres des Professions Libérales et des Indépendants (SMAC): BP 644, N'Djamena; tel. 51-70-19; fax 51-70-61.

Société de Représentation d'Assurances et de Réassurances Africaines (SORARAF): N'Djamena; Dir Mme FOURNIER.

Société Tchadienne d'Assurances et de Réassurances (La STAR Nationale): ave Charles de Gaulle, BP 914, N'Djamena; tel. 52-56-77; fax 52-51-89; e-mail star@intnet.td; internet www.lastarnationale.com; f. 1977; privatized in 1996; brs in N'Djamena, Moundou and Abéché; cap. 500m.; Dir-Gen. ALI ADOUM DJAYA.

Trade and Industry

DEVELOPMENT ORGANIZATIONS

Agence Française de Développement (AFD): route de Farcha, BP 478, N'Djamena; tel. 52-70-71; fax 52-78-31; e-mail afdndjamena@groupe-afd.org; internet www.afd.fr; Country Dir BENOÎT LEBEURRE.

Association Française des Volontaires du Progrès (AFVP): BP 448, N'Djamena; tel. 52-20-53; fax 52-26-56; e-mail afvptchd@intnet.td; internet www.afvp.org; f. 1965; Nat. Delegate ISMAÏLA DIAGNE.

Association Tchadienne pour le Développement: BP 470, Quartier Sabangali, N'Djamena; tel. 51-43-69; fax 51-89-23; e-mail darna.dnla@intnet.td; Dir DIGALI ZEUHINBA.

Mission Française de Coopération et d'Action Culturelle: BP 898, N'Djamena; tel. 52-42-87; fax 52-44-38; administers bilateral aid from France; Dir EDOUARD LAPORTE.

Office National de Développement Rural (ONDR): BP 896, N'Djamena; tel. 52-23-20; fax 52-29-60; e-mail psapdn@intnet.td; f. 1968; Dir HASSAN GUIHINI DADI.

Société de Développement du Lac (SODELAC): BP 782, N'Djamena; tel. 52-35-03; f. 1967; to develop the area of Lake Chad; cap. 179m. francs CFA; Pres. HASSANTY OUMAR CHAIB; Dir-Gen. ABBO YOUSSOUF.

CHAMBER OF COMMERCE

Chambre de Commerce, d'Industrie, d'Agriculture, des Mines et d'Artisanat: 13 rue du Col Moll, BP 458, N'Djamena; tel. 52-52-64; fax 52-52-63; e-mail cciama@intnet.td; f. 1935; brs at Sarh, Moundou, Bol and Abéché; Pres. Dr NICOLE FROUD; Dir-Gen. BEKOUTOU TAIGAM.

TRADE ASSOCIATIONS

Office National des Céréales (ONC): BP 21, N'Djamena; tel. 52-37-31; fax 52-20-18; e-mail oncl@intnet.td; f. 1978; production and marketing of cereals; Dir-Gen. MAHAMAT ALI HASSABALLAH; 11 regional offices.

Société Nationale de Commercialisation du Tchad (SONACOT): BP 630, N'Djamena; tel. 51-30-47; f. 1965; cap. 150m. francs CFA; 76% state-owned; nat. marketing, distribution and import-export co; Man. Dir MARBROUCK NATROUD.

EMPLOYERS' ORGANIZATIONS

Conseil National du Patronat Tchadien (CNPT): rue Bazelaire, angle ave Charles de Gaulle, BP 134, N'Djamena; tel. and fax 52-25-71; fax 51-60-65; Pres. RAKHIS MANNANY; Sec.-Gen. MARC MADENGAR BEREMADJI; 67 mem. enterprises with total work-force of 8,000 (2002).

Union des Transporteurs Tchadiens: N'Djamena; tel. 51-45-27.

UTILITIES

Veolia Water—STEE (Société Tchadienne d'Eau et d'Electricité): 11 rue du Col Largeau, BP 44, N'Djamena; tel. 51-28-81; fax 51-21-34; f. 1968; state-owned; managed privately by subsidiary of Veolia Environnement (France) since 2000; production and distribution of electricity and water; Pres. GOMON MAWATA WAKAG; Dir-Gen. ISMAEL MAHAMAT ADOUM.

MAJOR COMPANIES

The following are some of the largest private and state-owned companies in terms of capital investment or employment.

Boissons et Glacières du Tchad (BGT): Zone Industrielle de Farcha, BP 656, N'Djamena; tel. 51-31-71; fax 51-24-77; e-mail bgt@intnet.td; f. 1970; affiliate of Groupe Castel (France); cap. 110m. francs CFA; production of mineral water, soft drinks and ice; Pres. MARCEL ILLE; Dir GASTON BONLEUX.

Brasseries du Logone: ave du Gouverneur Général Félix Eboué, BP 170, Moundou, Logone Occidental; f. 1962; cap. 800m. francs CFA; brewery; Man. Dir BRUNO DELORME; 145 employees.

Compagnie Sucrière du Tchad (CST): BP 5763, N'Djamena; tel. 52-32-70; fax 52-28-12; e-mail cst@jlv.com; f. 1976; fmrly Société Nationale Sucrière du Tchad (SONASUT); affiliated to Groupe Somdiaa (France); cap. 6,460m. francs CFA (2001); refining of sugar; mfrs of lump sugar and confectionery; Dir-Gen. MA ISMAEL; 1,350 employees (2001).

Direction Huilerie Savonnerie (DHS): N'Djamena; f. 2001 by separation from Société Cotonnière du Tchad; production and marketing of cottonseed oil, soap and oilcake; transfer of state-held 75% stake to private ownership pending.

Esso Exploration & Production Chad: rue de Bordeaux, BP 694, N'Djamena; internet www.essochad.com; subsidiary of ExxonMobil Corpn (USA); prospecting for petroleum.

Grande Bijouterie du Tchad SA: BP 1233, N'Djamena; tel. 51-31-16; fax 51-58-84; sale of gold and diamond jewellery.

Les Grands Moulins du Tchad: BP 173, N'Djamena; f. 1963; cap. 158.25m. francs CFA; milling of flour; mfrs of pasta, biscuits and cattle feed; Pres. EMILE MIMRAN; Man. Dir in N'Djamena JEAN-PAUL BAILLEUX.

Manufacture de Cigarettes du Tchad (MCT): BP 572, N'Djamena; tel. 51-21-45; fax 51-20-40; f. 1968; cap. 340m. francs CFA; 15% state-owned; mfrs of cigarettes; Pres. PIERRE IMBERT; Man. Dir XAVIER LAMBERT.

Société Cotonnière du Tchad (COTONTCHAD): BP 151, Moundou, Logone Occidental; tel. 69-12-10; fax 69-13-32; f. 1971; 75% state-owned; restructured 2001; privatization proposed; buying, ginning and marketing of cotton; owns 11 cotton gins; Dir-Gen. DAVID HOUDEINGAR; 1,000 employees (2001).

Société d'Étude et d'Exploitation de la Raffinerie du Tchad (SEERAT): BP 467, N'Djamena; tel. 52-80-70; fax 52-71-08; f. 1991; construction of pipelines and petroleum refineries; Chair. YOUSSOUF MAINA.

Société Moderne des Abattoirs—Abattoir Frigorifique de Farcha (AFF): Farcha; e-mail abattoir.farcha@intnet.td; privatized 1998; industrial slaughterhouse for meat industry.

Société Shell Tchad: route de Farcha, BP 110, N'Djamena; tel. 51-24-90; fax 51-22-67; f. 1971; cap. 205m. francs CFA; Pres. DAVID LAWSON LOUGHMAN; Dir-Gen. JEAN-RENÉ MBIANDJEU.

Société Textile du Tchad (STT): BP 238, Sarh, Bahr Kôh; f. 1966; textiles complex.

Tchad Oil Transport Co (TOTCO): BP 694, N'Djamena; fax 52-47-90; f. 1998, commenced active operations 2003; 95% owned by consortium of Chevron Corpn (USA), ExxonMobil (USA) and Petronas (Malaysia), 5% state-owned; controls transportation of petroleum through pipeline between Doba and Cameroonian border, and owns and operates three pumping stations.

Total Tchad: Zone Industrielle de Farcha, route de Mara, BP 75, N'Djamena; tel. 52-77-27; distribution of petroleum.

TRADE UNIONS

Confédération Libre des Travailleurs du Tchad (CLTT): ave Charles de Gaulle, BP 553, N'Djamena; tel. 51-76-11; fax 52-44-56; Sec.-Gen. BRAHIM BAKAS; 22,500 mems (2001).

Union des Syndicats du Tchad (UST): BP 1114, N'Djamena; tel. 51-47-77; fax 51-44-40; f. 1988; federation of trade unions; Pres. DOMBAL DJIMBAGUE; Sec.-Gen. DJIBRINE ASSALI HAMDALLAH.

Transport

RAILWAYS

There are no railways in Chad. In 1962 the Governments of Chad and Cameroon signed an agreement to extend the Transcameroon railway from Ngaoundéré to Sarh, a distance of 500 km. Although the Transcameroon reached Ngaoundéré in 1974, its proposed extension into Chad remains indefinitely postponed.

ROADS

The total length of the road network in 1999 was an estimated 40,000 km, of which 3,100 km were principal roads and 1,400 km were secondary roads; only 412 km of the network was paved. There are also some 20,000 km of tracks suitable for motor traffic during the October–July dry season. The European Union is contributing to the construction of a highway connecting N'Djamena with Sarh and Léré, on the Cameroon border, and of a 400-km highway linking Moundou and Ngaoundéré.

Coopérative des Transportateurs Tchadiens (CTT): BP 336, N'Djamena; tel. 51-43-55; road haulage; Pres. SALEH KHALIFA; brs at Sarh, Moundou, Bangui (CAR), Douala and Ngaoundéré (Cameroon).

Société Générale d'Entreprise Routière (SGER): BP 175, N'Djamena; tel. and fax 51-55-12; e-mail itralu@intnet.td; devt and maintenance of roads; 95% owned by Arcory International (Sudan); Pres. PATRICK MORIN.

Société Tchadienne d'Affrètement et de Transit (STAT): 21 ave Félix Eboué, BP 100, N'Djamena; tel. 51-88-72; fax 51-74-24; e-mail stat.tchad@intnet.td; affiliated to Groupe Saga (France); road haulage.

INLAND WATERWAYS

The Chari and Logone rivers, which converge to the south of N'Djamena, are navigable. These waterways connect Sarh with N'Djamena on the Chari and Bongor and Moundou with N'Djamena on the Logone.

CIVIL AVIATION

The international airport is at N'Djamena. There are also more than 40 smaller airfields.

Air Affaires Tchad: BP 256, N'Djamena; tel. 51-06-20; e-mail airaffaires@yahoo.st; passenger and freight internal and charter flights.

Minair Tchad: ave Charles de Gaulle, BP 1239, N'Djamena; tel. 51-31-51; fax 51-07-80; passenger and freight air transport.

Toumaï Air Tchad (TAT): N'Djamena; tel. 52-28-29; fax 52-41-06; f. 2004; scheduled passenger and cargo flights on domestic routes, and between N'Djamena and destinations in central and West Africa; Pres. and Dir-Gen. MAHAMAT BABA ABATCHA.

Tourism

Chad's potential attractions for tourists include a variety of scenery from the dense forests of the south to the deserts of the north. Receipts from tourism in 2002 totalled an estimated US $25m. A total of 29,356 tourists visited Chad in 2005, compared with 20,974 in 2003.

Direction de la promotion touristique: BP 86, N'Djamena; tel. 52-44-16.

Defence

As assessed at November 2006, the Armée nationale tchadienne (ANT) was estimated to number 25,350 (army approximately 20,000, air force 350, Republican Guard 5,000). In addition, there was a 4,500-strong gendarmerie. The army has been undergoing restructuring since 1996. Military service is by conscription. Under defence agreements with France, the army receives technical and other aid: in April 2007 there were 1,300 French troops deployed in Chad.

Defence Expenditure: Estimated at 30,900m. francs CFA in 2006.

Chief of Staff of the Armed Forces: Brig.-Gen. BANYARA KOSSINGAR.

Chief of the Land Forces: Brig.-Gen. MASSOUD DRESSA.

Chief of Naval Staff: Lt MORNADJI MBAISSANEBE.

Chief of Air Force: Brig-Gen. NADJITA BÉASSOUMAL.

Education

Education is officially compulsory for six years between six and 12 years of age. Primary education begins at the age of six and lasts for six years. Secondary education, from the age of 12, lasts for seven years, comprising a first cycle of four years and a second of three years. In 2002/03 primary enrolment included 57% of children in the relevant age-group (males 68%; females 46%), while secondary enrolment in that year included only 11% of children in the appropriate age-group (males 16%; females 5%). The Université du Tchad was opened at N'Djamena in 1971. In addition, there are several technical colleges. Some 5,901 students were enrolled at higher education institutions in 1999/2000. Total expenditure on education by the central Government (including foreign-financed investment) in 1996 was 32,196m. francs CFA (21.2% of total government expenditure).

Bibliography

Azevedo, M. J. *Roots of Violence: A History of War in Chad.* Amsterdam, Gordon and Breach, 1998.

Azevedo, M. J., and Naadozie, E. U. *Chad: A Nation in Search of its Future.* Boulder, CO, Westview Press, 1998.

Bangoura, M. T. *Violence politique et conflits en Afrique: le cas du Tchad.* Paris, L'Harmattan, 2005.

Bangui-Rombaye, A. *Tchad: élections sous contrôle, 1996–1997.* Paris, L'Harmattan, 1999.

Britsch, J. *La mission Foureau-Lamy et l'arrivée des français au Tchad 1898–1990.* Paris, L'Harmattan, 1995.

Buijtenhuijs, R. *Le Frolinat et les révoltes populaires du Tchad (1965–1976).* The Hague, 1978.

Le Frolinat et les guerres civiles du Tchad (1977–1984). Paris, Editions Karthala, 1987.

Transition et élections au Tchad, 1993–1997: restauration autoritaire et recomposition politique. Paris, Editions Karthala, 1999.

Burr, M., and Collins, R. O. *Africa's Thirty Years' War: Libya, Chad and the Sudan 1963–1993.* Boulder, CO, Westview Press, 1999.

Chapelle, J. *Le peuple tchadien, ses racines et sa vie quotidienne.* Paris, L'Harmattan, 1986.

Cruise O'Brien, D. B., Dunn, J., and Rathbone, R. (Eds). *Contemporary West African States.* Cambridge, Cambridge University Press, 1989.

Decalo, S. *Historical Dictionary of Chad.* 3rd Edn. Metuchen, NJ, Scarecrow Press, 1997.

Djian, G. *Le Tchad et sa conquête (1900–1914).* Paris, L'Harmattan, 1996.

Kovana, V. *Précis des guerres et conflits au Tchad.* Paris, L'Harmattan, 2000.

Lanne, B. *Tchad-Libye. La querelle des frontières.* Paris, Editions Karthala, 1982.

Répertoire de l'administration territoriale du Tchad (1900–1994). Paris, L'Harmattan, 1995.

Histoire politique du Tchad de 1945 à 1958. Paris, Editions Karthala, 1999.

Le Cornec, J. *Histoire politique du Tchad de 1900 à 1962.* Paris, Librairie générale de Droit et Jurisprudence, 1963.

Lemoine, T. *Tchad, 1960–1990: trente années d'indépendance.* Paris, Lettres du monde, 1997.

Magnant, J.-P. (Ed.). *L'Islam au Tchad.* Talence, IEP, 1992.

Mays, T. M. *Africa's first peacekeeping operation: the OAU in Chad, 1981–1982.* Westport, CN, Praeger, 2002.

Nebardoum, D. *Le labyrinthe de l'instabilité politique au Tchad.* Paris, L'Harmattan, 1998.

Contribution à une pensée politique de développement pour le Tchad. Paris, L'Harmattan, 2001.

Nolutshungu, S. C. *Limits of Anarchy: Intervention and State Formation in Chad.* Virginia, University Press of Virginia, 1996.

Petry, M. and Bambe, N. *Le pétrole du Tchad: Rêve ou cauchemar pour les populations?* Paris, Editions Karthala, 2005.

Triaud, J.-I. *Tchad 1900–1902: Une guerre franco-libyenne oubliée?—Une confrérie musulmane: La Sanusiyya face à la France.* Paris, L'Harmattan, 2001.

Tubiana, J., Arditi, C., and Pairault, C. (Eds). *L'identité tchadienne: L'héritage des peuples et les apports extérieurs.* Paris, L'Harmattan, 1994.

Ye, M. N. *L'éducation de base au Tchad: Situation, enjeux et perspectives.* Paris, L'Harmattan, 1998.

Yorongar, N. *Tchad, le procès d'Idriss Déby: Témoignage à charge.* Paris, L'Harmattan, 2003.

THE COMOROS*

Physical and Social Geography

R. J. HARRISON CHURCH

The Comoro Islands, an archipelago of four small islands, together with numerous islets and coral reefs, lie between the east African coast and the north-western coast of Madagascar. The four islands cover a total land area of only 2,236 sq km (863 sq miles) and are scattered along a NW–SE axis, a distance of 300 km separating the towns of Moroni in the west and Dzaoudzi in the east. The French names for the islands, Grande-Comore (on which the capital, Moroni, is situated), Anjouan, Mohéli and Mayotte were changed in May 1977 to Ngazidja, Nzwani, Mwali and Mahoré, respectively, although the former names are still widely used. The islands are volcanic in structure, and Mt Karthala (rising to 2,440 m above sea-level) on Ngazidja is still active; it erupted in April 2005, causing an estimated 10,000 people to leave their homes, although no deaths were reported. Climate, rainfall and vegetation all vary greatly from island to island. There are similar divergences in soil characteristics, although in this instance natural causes have been reinforced by human actions, notably in deforestation and exhaustion of the soil.

The population was estimated at 818,000 in mid-2006. The population density in that year was 439.3 per sq km. (Average population density—excluding Mayotte—was 283.5 inhabitants per sq km in 1998.) Moroni had an estimated population of 53,420 in 2003. The ethnic composition of the population is complex. The first settlers were probably Melano-Polynesian peoples who came to the islands from the Far East by the sixth century AD. Immigrants from the coast of Africa, Indonesia, Madagascar and Persia, as well as Arabs, had all arrived by about 1600, when the Comoros were becoming established as a port of call on European trade routes to India and the Indonesian archipelago. The Portuguese, the Dutch and the French further enriched the ethnic pattern, the latter introducing into the islands Chinese (who have since left) and Indians. In Mayotte and Mwali Arabic features are less evident, mainly because the two islands were settled by immigrants from the African coast and Madagascar. In fact, while Arab characteristics are strong in the islands generally, in particular in the coastal towns, the African is predominant in the territory as a whole. Islam is the prevalent religion of the islands. The official languages are Comorian (a mixture of Swahili and Arabic), French and Arabic. In Mayotte, Shimaoré (a Mahorian dialect of Comorian) and Shibushi are spoken; French is little used outside of the administration and education systems.

Recent History

Revised by the editorial staff

The Comoros, acquired as a French possession during 1841–1909, became a French Overseas Territory in 1947. Internal autonomy was granted in 1961, although substantial powers were retained by France. At a referendum held in December 1974, there was a 96% vote in favour of independence. This was strongly opposed, however, by the island of Mayotte (Mahoré), which sought the status of a French overseas department. France sought to persuade the Comoran Government to draft a constitution for the islands that would allow a large measure of decentralization and thus satisfy the population of Mayotte, and proposed that any constitutional proposals should be ratified by referendum in each island separately before independence could be granted. These proposals were rejected by the Comoran Chambre des députés, and on 6 July 1975 the chamber approved a unilateral declaration of independence, and designated Ahmed Abdallah, the President of the Government Council, as President of the Republic. France retained control of Mayotte.

In August 1975 Abdallah was removed from office and replaced by Prince Saïd Mohammed Jaffar, who was in turn replaced as President in January 1976 by Ali Soilih. In February Mayotte voted overwhelmingly to retain its links with France. Preparations for the 1976 referendum in Mayotte were accompanied by a deterioration in relations between France and the Comoros. On 31 December 1975 France formally recognized the independence of Grande-Comore (Ngazidja), Anjouan (Nzwani) and Mohéli (Mwali), but all relations between the two Governments, together with aid and technical assistance programmes, were effectively suspended.

The Soilih regime initiated a revolutionary programme, blending Maoist and Islamic philosophies, aimed at creating an economically self-sufficient and ideologically progressive state. The excesses of Soilih's methods aroused widespread resentment among traditional elements of society, and his programme of reform seriously undermined the economy.

ABDALLAH IN POWER, 1978–89

In May 1978 Soilih was overthrown and subsequently killed in a *coup d'état*, carried out by a small mercenary force led by a French national, Col Robert Denard, on behalf of the ex-President, Ahmed Abdallah. Power was assumed by a 'politico-military directory', with Abdallah at its head. The new administration pledged to implement democratic reforms and to restore good relations with members of the Arab League and with France. French economic, cultural and military co-operation was duly resumed, and additional assistance was also forthcoming from Arab countries, the European Community (EC, now the European Union—EU) and the African Development Fund. A new Constitution approved by referendum in October 1978 was followed by presidential and legislative elections. Abdallah was elected President for a six-year term. Despite the constitutional guarantee of free activity for all political parties, the Assemblée fédérale established the Union comorienne pour le progrès (Udzima) as the sole legal party for a period of 12 years from 1982. A number of unofficial opposition groups, based mainly in France, were established. Abdallah's regime pursued an increasingly authoritarian course as the 1980s proceeded. Power was progressively centralized, reducing the role of the governors of the four islands, the federal Government became responsible for controlling the islands' economic resources and there were allegations of corruption and the ill-treatment of political detainees.

*Most of the information contained in this chapter relates to the whole Comoran archipelago, which the Comoros claims as its national territory and has styled 'The Union of the Comoros'. The island of Mayotte, however, is administered by France as an Overseas Collectivité Départementale, and is treated separately at the end of this chapter.

At a presidential election, which took place in September 1984, Abdallah, as sole candidate, was re-elected for a further six-year term by 99.4% of votes cast. Despite appeals by opposition groups for voters to boycott the election, some 98% of the electorate participated. In January 1985, following the adoption of constitutional amendments, the post of Prime Minister was abolished, and Abdallah assumed the powers of Head of Government.

In February 1987 the Government announced that elections to the Assemblée fédérale would take place in March. Although Abdallah had indicated that all political groups would be permitted to participate, opposition candidates were allowed to contest seats only on Ngazidja, where they obtained more than 35% of votes cast; Udzima retained full control of the legislature. In November, during Abdallah's absence in France, the Comoran authorities suppressed an attempted coup by a left-wing group.

In November 1989 a constitutional amendment permitting Abdallah to serve a third six-year term as President was approved by 92.5% of votes cast in a popular referendum. However, this result was challenged by the President's opponents, and violent demonstrations ensued.

Mercenary Intervention

On the night of 26–27 November 1989 Abdallah was assassinated by members of the presidential guard, under the command of Col Denard. As stipulated in the Constitution, the President of the Supreme Court, Saïd Mohamed Djohar, took office as interim Head of State, pending a presidential election. Denard and his supporters, however, staged a pre-emptive *coup d'état*, in which 27 members of the security forces were reportedly killed. In mid-December Denard agreed to withdraw peacefully from the islands and, following the arrival of French paratroops in Moroni, was flown to South Africa with 25 other mercenaries. (In May 1999 Denard stood trial in France and was acquitted of Abdallah's assassination.)

THE DJOHAR PRESIDENCY, 1990–95

At the end of December 1989 the main political groups agreed to form a provisional Government of National Unity. A general amnesty was extended to all political prisoners, and an inquiry was initiated into Abdallah's death. The presidential election duly took place on 18 February 1990, but voting was abandoned, amid opposition allegations of widespread fraud. Balloting was held again on 4 and 11 March; after an inconclusive first round, Djohar, who was supported by Udzima, obtained 55.3% of the total votes cast, while Mohamed Taki, the leader of the Union nationale pour la démocratie aux Comores (UNDC), secured 44.7% of the vote. In late March Djohar appointed a new Government, which included two of his minor opponents in the presidential election: Prince Saïd Ali Kemal, a grandson of the last sultan of the Comoros and the founder of the opposition Islands' Fraternity and Unity Party (CHUMA), and Ali Mroudjae, a former Prime Minister and the leader of the Parti comorien pour la démocratie et le progrès (PCDP). In April Djohar announced plans for the formal constitutional restoration of a multi-party political system, and indicated that extensive economic reforms were to be undertaken.

On 3 August 1991 the President of the Supreme Court, Ibrahim Ahmed Halidi, announced the dismissal of Djohar, on the grounds of negligence, and proclaimed himself interim President. Opposition leaders declared that the seizure of power was justified by the Constitution. Djohar responded by ordering the arrests of Halidi and several other members of the Supreme Court, and imposing a state of emergency. Later in August the Government banned all public demonstrations, following violent clashes between pro-Government demonstrators and members of the opposition. Djohar subsequently formed a new coalition Government, which included two members of the Front démocratique (FD). In an attempt to appease increasing discontent on the island of Mwali, which had repeatedly demanded greater autonomy, two members of Mwalian opposition groups were appointed to the Government. However, the two dominant parties in the coalition, Udzima and the PCDP, objected to the ministerial changes, and accused Djohar of attempting to reduce their influence. Shortly afterwards the PCDP and Udzima left the Government.

In November 1991 Udzima denounced the proposed constitutional amendments and joined the opposition. Opposition leaders demanded the dissolution of the Assemblée fédérale, which they declared to be unlawfully constituted on the grounds that it had been elected under the former one-party system, and the formation of a government of national unity. Later in November, however, Djohar reached an agreement with the principal opposition leaders, including Taki, to initiate a process of national reconciliation, which would include the formation of a government of national unity and the convening of a new constitutional conference. The agreement also recognized the legitimacy of Djohar's election as President.

In January 1992 a new transitional Government of National Unity was formed, under the leadership of Taki, who was designated as its 'Co-ordinator'. Later in January a national conference, comprising both representatives of political associations supporting Djohar and of opposition parties, was convened to draft a new constitution. However, the conference was boycotted by representatives of Mwali, which had announced plans to conduct its own referendum on self-determination. In April the conference submitted a number of constitutional reform proposals. In May 18 opposition parties demanded the resignation of Djohar's son-in-law, Mohamed M'Changama, as Minister of Finance, following allegations of irregularities in negotiating government contracts. Djohar subsequently redesignated Taki as Prime Minister and formed a new interim cabinet. In June, despite concerted opposition by eight parties, led by Udzima and the FD, the reform proposals were accepted by 74.3% of those voting in the constitutional referendum. The new constitutional provisions, which limited presidential tenure to a maximum of two five-year terms, also provided for a bicameral legislature, comprising an Assemblée fédérale, together with a 15-member Sénat, comprising five representatives from each island to be chosen by an electoral college. Elections at national and local level were to take place later in 1992. In early July Djohar dismissed Taki, on the grounds that he had allegedly appointed a former associate of Col Denard to a financial advisory post in the Government. Later that month a new Government was formed.

In mid-1992 social and economic conditions on the Comoros deteriorated, following renewed strikes in protest at economic austerity measures undertaken by the Government in conjunction with the IMF and World Bank. In early September Djohar announced that legislative elections were to begin in late October, but opposition parties claimed that the schedule provided insufficient time for preparation, and threatened to boycott the elections.

In late September 1992, during a visit by Djohar to Paris, France, a coup attempt was mounted by disaffected members of the armed forces. A number of the rebels were subsequently detained and charged with involvement in the insurgency. In mid-October rebel troops, led by a former member of Abdallah's presidential guard, attacked the military garrison of Kandani, in an attempt to release the detainees. Shortly afterwards, government forces attacked the rebels at Mbeni, to the north-east of Moroni; fighting was also reported on Nzwani. Later in October a demonstration was staged in protest at the French Government's support of Djohar. By the end of October some 25 people had been killed in clashes between rebels and government troops in Moroni.

In October 1992 Djohar agreed to postpone the legislative elections until late November, although opposition parties demanded a further delay, and Udzima and the UNDC maintained their electoral boycott. The first round of the elections, which took place on 22 November, was marred by widespread violence and electoral irregularities, and a boycott was implemented by Udzima and the UNDC. Results in six constituencies were subsequently annulled, while the second round of voting, on 29 November, took place in only 34 of the 42 constituencies. Following partial elections on 13 and 30 December, reports indicated that candidates supporting the President, including seven members of the Union des démocrates pour le développement (UDD), had secured a narrow majority in the Assemblée fédérale. The leader of the UDD, Ibrahim Abdérémane Halidi, was appointed Prime Minister on 1 January 1993, and formed a new Council of Ministers. Shortly after the new Government took office, political tensions began to emerge between Djohar and Halidi, while the parties supporting Djohar, which commanded a majority in the Assemblée, fragmented into three dissenting factions. A cabinet reshuffle in late February failed to resolve these divisions.

In April 1993 nine people, including two sons of former President Abdallah and two prominent members of Udzima, were convicted on charges of complicity in the coup attempt in September 1992, and sentenced to death. After domestic and international pressure the sentences were commuted. In May 1993 a number of deputies, proposed a motion of censure against the Government (apparently with the tacit support of Djohar), challenging Halidi's competence as Prime Minister. Following the approval of the motion by 23 of the 42 deputies in the Assemblée fédérale, Djohar replaced Halidi with Saïd Ali Mohamed. Mohamed subsequently formed a new Council of Ministers, which, however, received the support of only 13 of the 42 members of the Assemblée. In mid-June 19 deputies affiliated to Halidi proposed a motion of censure against the new Government, on the grounds that the Prime Minister had not been appointed from a party that commanded a majority in the Assemblée. However, Djohar declared the motion unconstitutional, dissolved the Assemblée, and announced legislative elections. Shortly afterwards, he appointed a former presidential adviser, Ahmed Ben Cheikh Attoumane, as Prime Minister. A new Council of Ministers was subsequently formed.

Following the dissolution of the Assemblée fédérale, opposition parties declared Djohar unfit to hold office, in view of the increasing political confusion, and demanded that legislative elections take place within the period of 40 days stipulated in the Constitution. In early July 1993, however, Djohar announced that the elections were to be postponed until October, and requested that the 24 registered political parties form themselves into three main groupings. Later in July opposition parties organized a widely observed one-day general strike as a prelude to a campaign of civil disobedience designed to force Djohar to bring forward the legislative elections or to resign. Opposition members who had allegedly participated in the campaign of civil disobedience were temporarily detained.

In early September 1993 a number of opposition movements, led by Udzima and the UNDC, established an informal electoral alliance, known as the Union pour la République et le progrès. The FD, the PCDP, CHUMA and the Mouvement pour la démocratie et le progrès (MDP) also announced that they would present joint candidates. Later in September Djohar postponed the legislative elections until November; in that month the legislative elections were rescheduled for 12 and 19 December.

Having failed to obtain party political support for an electoral alliance, Djohar announced in October 1993 the formation of a new party, the Rassemblement pour la démocratie et le renouveau (RDR), mainly comprising supporters of M'Changama and including several prominent members of the Government. Later that month 16 political parties, including several organizations that supported Djohar, threatened to boycott the elections unless the Government repealed legislation that redrew constituency boundaries and appointed a new electoral commission. Opposition supporters subsequently prevented government candidates from convening political gatherings. In November Djohar reshuffled the Council of Ministers, and established a new National Electoral Commission (NEC), in compliance with the demands of the opposition.

In the first round of the legislative elections, which took place on 12 December 1993, four opposition candidates secured seats in the Assemblée fédérale, apparently provoking official concern. Following the second round of polling, it was reported that three people had been killed in violent incidents on Nzwani. The electoral commission subsequently invalidated results in eight constituencies. Partial elections later took place in these constituencies and at Moroni, where the second round of voting had been postponed at the demand of two government candidates; however, opposition candidates refused to participate on the grounds that voting was to be conducted under government supervision rather than that of the electoral commission. The RDR consequently secured all 10 contested seats in the partial elections, and 22 seats in total, thereby gaining a narrow majority in the Assemblée. In early January 1994 Djohar appointed the Secretary-General of the RDR, Mohamed Abdou Madi, as Prime Minister. The new Council of Ministers included several supporters of M'Changama, who was elected Speaker of the Assemblée. Following the installation of the new Government, 12 prominent opposition parties adopted a joint resolution claiming that the RDR had obtained power illegally, and established a new alliance, known as the Forum pour le redressement national (FRN), led by Abbas Djoussouf.

In October 1994 Djohar dismissed Abdou Madi as Prime Minister, and appointed Halifa Houmadi to the post. The resultant new Council of Ministers included only two members of the former administration.

In February 1995 the Government announced that elections to the regional councils would take place in April, to be followed by the establishment of a Senate and a Constitutional Council (in accordance with the terms of the Constitution). The opposition, however, accused Djohar of resorting to unconstitutional tactics and electoral manipulation. In March Djohar announced that forthcoming elections to the regional councils were to be rescheduled for July 1996, ostensibly for financial reasons.

In April 1995 reports emerged of disagreements between Djohar and Houmadi, following accusations by Houmadi of financial corruption by Djohar and M'Changama. Djohar subsequently replaced Houmadi as Prime Minister with a former Minister of Finance, Mohamed Caabi El Yachroutu, who brought with him a reputation as a reformist, technocratic administrator, with good relations with the IMF and World Bank. A 13-member cabinet, including only five members of the previous administration, was formed. In May three former Prime Ministers, Mohamed, Abdou Madi and Houmadi, urged the removal of M'Changama (who, they claimed, exerted undue influence over Djohar) and the dissolution of the Assemblée fédérale. Meanwhile, it was feared that the further postponement of elections to the regional councils would delay the presidential election. At the end of July Djohar removed Issilame and a further three associates of M'Changama from the Council of Ministers.

INVASION, INTERVENTION AND INTERIM GOVERNMENT

In September 1995 about 30 European mercenaries, led by Denard, invaded Ngazidja, seized control of the garrison at Kandani and captured Djohar. The mercenaries, who were joined by about 300 members of the Comoran armed forces, released a number of prisoners (including those detained for involvement in the September 1992 coup attempt), and installed a former associate of Denard, Capt. Ayouba Combo, as a leader of a transitional military committee. The French Government denounced the coup and suspended economic aid to the Comoros, but initially refused to intervene, despite requests for assistance from El Yachroutu, who had taken refuge in the French embassy. In early October Combo announced that he had transferred authority to Mohamed Taki and the leader of CHUMA, Saïd Ali Kemal (both of whom had welcomed the coup), as joint civilian Presidents, apparently in an attempt to avert military action by the French Government. The FRN, however, rejected the new leadership and entered into negotiations with El Yachroutu. Following a further appeal for intervention from El Yachroutu, who invoked a defence co-operation agreement that had been negotiated in 1978, some 900 French military personnel landed on the Comoros. Shortly afterwards, Denard and his associates, together with the disaffected members of the Comoran armed forces, surrendered to the French troops. (The mercenaries were subsequently placed under arrest and deported to France. In mid-2006 Denard was awarded a suspended sentence of five years by a French court for his involvement in the coup.)

Following the French military intervention, El Yachroutu declared himself interim President in accordance with the Constitution and announced the formation of a Government of National Unity, which included members of the constituent parties of the FRN. Djohar rejected El Yachroutu's assumption of power and announced the reappointment of Saïd Ali Mohamed as Prime Minister. Later in October 1995 a National Reconciliation Conference agreed that El Yachroutu would remain interim President, pending the forthcoming election, which was provisionally scheduled for early 1996. The interim administration, which was supported by the armed forces, refused to recognize Djohar's appointments and announced that he would be prohibited from re-entering the country. At the end of October 1995 El Yachroutu granted an amnesty to all Comorans involved in the coup attempt and appointed representatives of the UNDC and Udzima (which had supported the coup) to the new Council of Ministers. In early November both Governments simultaneously convened cabinet meetings and held rival political rallies in the capital, and it was reported that separatist movements had become active on Nzwani and Mwali. It was widely believed that the French Government had tacitly encouraged Djohar's removal from power. Later in November, however, supporters of Djohar, including M'Changama, organized a political gathering to demand the resignation of El Yachroutu's administration. Meanwhile, political leaders on Mwali rejected the authority of both rival Governments, urged a campaign of civil disobedience and established a 'citizens' committee' to govern the island; discontent with the central administration also emerged on Nzwani.

THE TAKI PRESIDENCY, 1996–98

In the first round of the presidential election, which took place on 6 March 1996, Taki and the leader of the MDP, Abbas Djoussouf, secured the highest number of votes; it was subsequently reported that 12 of the 13 unsuccessful candidates had transferred their support to Taki in the second round of the election. Taki was duly elected to the presidency on 16 March, obtaining 64% of the vote, and was sworn in on 25 March. Taki appointed a new Council of Ministers, headed by Tadjidine Ben Saïd Massoundi, which included five of the presidential candidates who had given him their support in the second round of the election.

In early April 1996 Taki dissolved the Assemblée fédérale and announced that legislative elections would take place on 6 October. New governors, all belonging to the UNDC, were appointed to each of the three islands. In mid-June, during a visit to France, discussions took place between Taki and the French President, Jacques Chirac. Taki requested financial aid to enable him to liquidate the wage arrears owed to civil servants, and confirmed his wish for French troops to remain on the Comoros. It was subsequently announced that Chirac had agreed to these requests and, in addition, had offered French assistance in the reorganization of public finance, education, public health and the judicial system.

In a government reorganization in late August 1996, Saïd Ali Kemal and a representative of the Forces pour l'action républicaine were dismissed, following their parties' refusal to disband in order to join the single pro-presidential party that Taki intended to establish. A consultative committee on the Constitution, established in September, considered requests from Taki for the reinforcement of presidential powers, including the President's right to choose governors for each island, and an end to the two-term limit on presidential office. The constitutional committee was boycotted by the FRN and other opposition parties. At the referendum on the constitutional reforms, held on 20 October, 85% voted in favour of the new Constitution. Legislative elections were postponed until 1 December. Meanwhile, Taki had succeeded in building a single-party ruling group to support his presidency. On 5 October delegates from the UNDC, the RDR, Udzima and 20 other pro-Government parties merged, as the Rassemblement national pour le développement (RND). This prompted Abbas Djoussouf and other anti-Taki politicians to form the Collectif de l'opposition and announce, on 13 November, a boycott of the legislative elections. On 30 November a number of government opponents, including former Prime Ministers Ali Mroudjae and Mohamed Abdou Madi, were arrested on arson charges, as the boycott campaign continued. They were released on 2 December. Results from the polls held on 1 December gave the RND 32 seats out of a total of 43 in the Assemblée fédérale. There were widespread reports of irregularities. The second round awarded a further four seats to the RND, giving it 36 seats, with the Islamist Front national pour la justice (FNJ) obtaining three seats, and independent candidates four.

Following the elections, the Prime Minister, Tadjidine Ben Saïd Massoundi, resigned. A new Government was appointed on 27 December 1996, under Ahmed Abdou. The Government quickly came into conflict with opposition politicians and public servants. On 1 January 1997 workers went on strike in protest against salary arrears. Opposition politicians, including Djoussouf, were detained on several occasions in January, and 30 people were injured during a demonstration in Moroni late in the month when strikers clashed with the security forces. Meanwhile, tensions rose further on Nzwani and Mwali. On Nzwani there were serious clashes between workers and the security forces in mid-March, as up to 3,000 people erected barricades in the streets of the main town, Mutsamudu. Up to four people were reported to have been killed. In May it was reported that, in an attempt to resolve the crisis, Taki and Djoussouf had agreed to establish a joint commission to define terms for a proposed accord on the participation of the FRN in formulating national policy.

Separatist Problems

During July 1997 two people were killed on Nzwani in skirmishes between the security forces and separatist demonstrators. The unrest rapidly escalated into a full-scale movement for secession on Nzwani and Mwali, which was aggravated by the Government's unsuccessful attempts to subdue separatists on Nzwani, who had declared their intention to seek a return to French sovereignty. The relative economic wealth of neighbouring Mayotte as a French Overseas Collectivité Territoriale was thought to have influenced popular feeling on Nzwani. Several separatist movements had emerged, notably the Mouvement populaire anjouanais, whose leader, Abdallah Ibrahim, was chosen to chair a 'political directorate' on Nzwani. On 3 August the 'political directorate' unilaterally declared Nzwani's secession from the Comoros; Ibrahim was subsequently elected as president of a 13-member 'politico-administrative co-ordination'. Meanwhile, separatist activity on Mwali intensified, and on 11 August secessionists declared the island's independence and appointed their own government.

President Taki, influenced by extremists in the Moroni administration, dispatched a force of at least 200 men to invade Nzwani on 2–3 September 1997. Barricades were erected in Mutsamudu and an unknown number of people, reportedly far more than 100, were killed as the invasion failed to suppress the insurrection, after two days of heavy fighting. This failure prompted the dissolution of Ahmed Abdou's Government; Taki assumed absolute power for a three-week period, and then named a transitional commission, which excluded those who had advocated the invasion plan.

Underlying much of the unrest were attempts by Taki to centralize the administration of the archipelago; this was seen on Nzwani and Mwali as a bid for political and administrative supremacy on Ngazidja. At this stage the Organization of African Unity (OAU, now the African Union—AU) and the UN became increasingly involved with the unfolding crisis. A reconciliation conference was scheduled for the end of October 1997, at the OAU's headquarters in Addis Ababa, Ethiopia. Ibrahim held a referendum on Nzwani's secession on 26 October, despite the objections of the Moroni Government and the misgivings of some separatists, notably Abdou Madi; the reported result was 99.9% in favour of independence. France continued to reject absolutely demands for Nzwani to be reincorporated into the former colonial power.

As Taki steadily lost his remaining support on Ngazidja, amid administrative paralysis and economic decline, the crisis continued in deadlock for the remainder of 1997. A separatist government was appointed by the secessionists on Nzwani in October, further inflaming inter-island relations. Opposition parties in Moroni demanded that Taki be removed, declared that they would participate in the formation of a government of national unity only if separatists from Nzwani and Mwali were involved, and insisted that the dispute had to be resolved under the aegis of the OAU. In early December Taki named a new Council of Ministers, under Nourdine Bourhane, although the transitional commission appointed in September remained in existence. The inter-Comoran reconciliation conference that had been scheduled for October finally took place in December; a peace agreement between Nzwani and Moroni was signed under OAU auspices, but its provisions were never fully implemented.

Factional disputes were reported on Nzwani in early 1998; in February Abdou Madi, who had fled the island after the referendum of October 1997, returned in an unsuccessful attempt to mount resistance to the separatists, reportedly with the support of both Taki and the OAU. A referendum on a separatist constitution was carried by a reported 99.5% of votes cast on Nzwani in late February 1998. In March Ibrahim appointed a new government. In an effort to establish dialogue with the opposition, Taki named a three-member committee of political veterans in mid-May to examine the problem. At the end of the month the Council of Ministers was reshuffled in favour of moderates, and the President succeeded in bringing Abdou Madi back into government, although overtures to the Moroni opposition were unsuccessful, as they again demanded that Taki step down. As government employees' salaries remained unpaid, political unrest spread in Moroni itself, and more ominously within the army. Two days of anti-Government rioting in the capital resulted in at least three deaths in mid-May.

In July 1998, as social unrest on Nzwani escalated, a dispute over the future aims of the secessionist movement led to the dismissal of the island's government, provoking violent clashes between islanders loyal to Ibrahim, who favoured independence within the framework of an association of the Comoran islands, and supporters of the outgoing prime minister, Chamassi Saïd Omar, who continued to advocate reattachment to France. It was subsequently reported that Ahmed Mohamed Hazi, a former Comoran army Chief of Staff and ally of Omar, had failed in an attempt to depose Ibrahim.

Meanwhile, as social and economic conditions deteriorated further, with salaries still unpaid and strike action ongoing, Taki visited a number of countries, including Mozambique, South Africa and the United Kingdom, to seek assistance in resolving the crisis. In August 1998 the Government provisionally suspended transport links with both Nzwani and Mayotte. France later refused the Government's request for a suspension of links between Mayotte and Nzwani, thus worsening the already fragile relations between the two countries. At meetings later in the year with Djoussouf and the leadership of his own party, Taki proposed the establishment of a government of public salvation, an idea opposed by many members of the RND and several government ministers.

INTERIM GOVERNMENT AND ARMY COUP

On 6 November 1998 President Taki died unexpectedly. It was stated that he had suffered a heart attack, although several senior officials expressed serious doubts about the actual circumstances of the President's death. Tadjidine Ben Saïd Massoundi, the Nzwanian President of the High Council of the Republic and a former Prime Minister (March–December 1996), was designated acting President, in accordance with the Constitution, pending an election, which would be held after 30–90 days. Massoundi immediately revoked the ban on the movement of people and goods to Nzwani and, despite the continued opposition of several government ministers, proceeded with Taki's project for the formation of a government of public salvation. Djoussouf, the main opposition leader, was subsequently appointed Prime Minister, to head a Council of Ministers composed of members of the FRN and the RND. Divisions within the RND over its participation in the new Government led to a split in the party. In late January 1999 Massoundi extended his presidential mandate, which was soon to expire, pending a resolution of the crisis dividing the islands. In February an agreement was signed by the acting President and political parties opposed to the FRN-RND Government, which provided for the formation of a new government to be supported by up to three technical commissions. However, the FRN refused to participate in the agreement, declaring its intention to remain in power until a Comoran inter-island conference had been held.

Meanwhile, renewed tension within the separatist administration on Nzwani intensified in December 1998, provoking eight days of armed clashes between rival militias, which led to at least 60 deaths before a cease-fire agreement was signed. In January 1999 Ibrahim agreed to transfer some of his powers to a five-member 'politico-administrative directorate', as meetings commenced between the rival separatist factions. No consensus was achieved in the following months, however, and, when Ibrahim replaced the directorate with a 'committee of national security' in March, the new administration was immediately rejected by rival leaders. Resistance to the ruling administration in Moroni increased in March, when opposition leaders organized a protest meeting, during which they strongly denounced Massoundi; six people were later injured during clashes with the security forces after demonstrators, demanding the dismissal of Ngazidja's governor, attempted to occupy his official residence.

On 19–23 April 1999 an OAU-sponsored inter-island conference was held in Antananarivo, Madagascar. An accord was reached whereby the federal state would become a union within one year, with the presidency rotating among the three islands. However, the delegates from Nzwani failed to sign the agreement, insisting on the need for consultation prior to a full endorsement. Several days of rioting followed in Moroni, as demonstrators protested against Nzwani's refusal to ratify the accord, reportedly forcing more than 1,000 Nzwanians from their homes before order was restored.

On 30 April 1999 the Chief of Staff of the Comoran armed forces, Col Assoumani Azali, seized power in a bloodless coup, deposing Massoundi and dissolving the Government, the Assemblée fédérale and all other constitutional institutions. Having sought to justify his actions on the grounds that the authorities had failed to take the political measures necessary to control the security situation in the Comoros, Azali promulgated a new constitutional charter in which he proclaimed himself Head of State and of Government, and Commander-in-Chief of the armed forces. Full legislative functions were also vested in Azali, who undertook to relinquish power following the creation of the new institutions provided for in the Antananarivo accord. The appointment of a State Committee (composed of six members from Ngazidja, four from Mwali and two from Nzwani) was followed by that of a State Council, which was to supervise the activities of the State Committee and comprised eight civilians and 11 army officers. The OAU, which had not been represented at Azali's inauguration (although the UN had sent representatives), condemned the coup, withdrew its military observers from the Comoros and urged the international community not to recognize the new regime.

AZALI IN POWER

At the beginning of June 1999 Azali created five technical commissions, which were charged with directing the implementation of the Antananarivo accord. An electoral commission was established, while the other commissions were to oversee various projects, including the drafting of new constitutions for the union and the islands and the preparation of a donors' conference. However, despite an undertaking by Azali to transfer power to a civilian government within a year, domestic discontent with the new administration increased, as the main political parties boycotted a meeting at which they were to have nominated representatives to serve on the new commissions. Furthermore, France and the USA were reported to have suspended all military co-operation with the Republic.

In mid-June 1999 Lt-Col Abdérémane Saïd Abeid, who had previously occupied the role of national mediator on Nzwani, formed a government of national unity on the island, appointing himself as 'co-ordinator'. Relations between Ngazidja and Nzwani appeared to be improving to some extent in early July, when Azali and Abeid met on Mwali. The meeting represented the most senior-level contact between the islands since the secessions of August 1997. In mid-August 1999 elections to establish a 25-member national assembly on Nzwani were held. No official results were released, but reports indicated that the most staunch separatists won the majority of seats. In mid-September the Nzwani executive council announced its decision not to sign the Antananarivo peace agreement; Abeid stated that the signature of the accord would not be in accordance with the aspirations of the island's population. In December the OAU threatened the imposition of sanctions on the island should its leaders not have signed the peace accord by 1 February 2000. In retaliation, Abeid announced that a referendum would be held on Nzwani on 23 January 2000 regarding the signature of the Antananarivo accord. According to the separatist authorities of Nzwani, the results of the referendum revealed an overwhelming majority (94.5%) in favour of full independence for the island; the OAU, however, announced that it did not recognize the outcome of the ballot, following allegations of intimidation and repression of those in favour of reconciliation. In February the federal Government indefinitely suspended the movement of sea freight to and from Nzwani. Telephone communications as well as all air and sea links were subsequently suspended and banks were closed, in accordance with sanctions recommended by the OAU. Meanwhile, following a series of meetings between Azali and a number of political parties from all three islands regarding the establishment of a more representative and decentralized government in Moroni, the State Committee underwent an extensive reorganization in early December, including the appointment of a new Prime Minister, Bianrifi Tarmidi (from Mwali). Although Mwali was well represented in the new executive, only one Nzwanian minister was appointed.

In May 2000 the OAU announced that the possibility of lifting the sanctions against Nzwani separatists was also connected to the return to constitutional order on the Comoros; it advocated the restoration of the October 1996 constitution, the return of Tadjidine Ben Saïd Massoundi as head of state, as well as the appointment of an interim government and prime minister. The following month an OAU delegation arrived in Moroni in an attempt to revive peace talks. However, Abeid reiterated his rejection of the Antananarivo accord. In response, the OAU announced the possibility of armed intervention on Nzwani. This was rejected at the OAU summit, held in July 2000; however, it was agreed that a total maritime blockade of Nzwani would be established. In late July Azali announced that a new draft constitution was shortly to be presented to the State Committee for approval, in an attempt to satisfy the aspirations of those sections of the population demanding a return to constitutional order.

National Reconciliation

On 26 August 2000 an agreement, known as the Fomboni accord, was signed by Azali and Abeid. The accord provided for the drawing up of a new constitution, which would grant Nzwani, Ngazidja and Mwali considerable control over their own affairs. However, the central government would maintain jurisdiction over foreign affairs, external defence, currency, nationality and religion. There was to be a one-year transition period, following which the constitutional amendments were to be submitted to a referendum vote. However, the accord was severely criticized by the OAU on the grounds that it contravened the terms of the Antananarivo accord. Despite demonstrations organized by opposition members on Nzwani, a tripartite commission comprising delegates from each island was established in November to define the terms of the new constitution. In late November Tarmidi was replaced as Prime Minister by Hamada Madi 'Boléro', who formed a new Government. However, attempts to include opposition members in the new Government and the tripartite commission were unsuccessful.

Following OAU and Organisation internationale de la francophonie (OIF) mediation, on 17 February 2001 an agreement on national reconciliation was signed in Fomboni by representatives of the Comoran Government, the Nzwani administration, opposition parties and civil society. The OAU, the OIF and the EU were to be guarantors of the peace accord, which provided for the establishment of a new Comoran entity. Under the provisions of the agreement an independent tripartite commission, comprising equal numbers of delegates from each of the islands and representing all of the signatory groups, was to draft a new constitution, which would be submitted to a national referendum for approval by June 2001. The new constitution was to define the areas of jurisdiction of the new entity and the individual islands, although the central administration would retain control over religion, nationality, currency, foreign affairs and defence. An independent national electoral commission was also to be formed. Following the constitutional referendum, a transitional government of national unity would also be established, charged with creating the new institutions, holding elections and transferring power to civilians by 31 December. However, in mid-March, following disagreements over the composition of a follow-up committee intended to monitor progress on implementation of the Fomboni agreement, the opposition withdrew from the reconciliation process. In mid-April the Nzwani administration also withdrew from the process. In July it was announced that the constitutional referendum had been postponed until September, ostensibly owing to lack of available funds to administer it.

On 8–9 August 2001 a military coup on Nzwani ended in the removal from power of Saïd Abeid Abdérémane. Abeid, who was arrested and subsequently fled Nzwani, was replaced by a collective presidency, consisting of Maj. Mohamed Bacar, Maj. Hassane Ali Toihili and Maj. Charif Halidi; a government of eight civilian commissioners was appointed. The new leadership of Nzwani committed itself to the Fomboni agreement. However, on 24 September a further bloodless military coup was instigated by the deputy head of the Comoran army and close ally of Azali, Maj. Ayouba Combo. Although Combo was initially declared leader of the army, and Ahmed Aboubakar Foundi was installed as leader of Nzwani, they were captured the following day, before subsequently escaping the island. In November Abeid attempted unsuccessfully to regain control of Nzwani in a military coup; he was defeated by military forces loyal to Bacar and was obliged to flee the island. It was thought that Abeid had been motivated by his wish to prevent moves towards national reconciliation, and the attempted coup was strongly condemned by the Government, which reaffirmed its support for the island's authorities. Abeid, however, denied his involvement in the events, maintaining that the instigator had in fact been Allaoui Ahmed, who had reportedly allied himself with the Organisation pour l'indépendance d'Anjouan, a political alliance that favoured a 'no' vote in the upcoming referendum on constitutional changes.

NEW CONSTITUTION AND PRESIDENTIAL ELECTIONS

At the constitutional referendum, which was held on 23 December 2001, some 76.4% of the electorate voted in favour of the proposed new Constitution. The country, which was to change its name to the Union of the Comoros, was to be led by the President of the Union, who was to head the Council of the Union, and governed by a legislative assembly, the Assemblée de l'Union. The position of President was to rotate between the islands, while the Vice-Presidents, who were also members of the Council of the Union, were to be inhabitants of the two remaining islands; the first President was to come from Ngazidja. Each of the three islands was to become financially autonomous and was to be ruled by its own local government and institutions. The Union was to be responsible for matters of religion, nationality, currency, foreign affairs and external defence, while shared responsibilities between the Union and the islands were to be determined at a later date. A transitional government was to be installed to monitor the implementation of the new institutions.

In early January 2002 Prime Minister Hamadi Madi 'Boléro' tendered his resignation. A transitional Government of National Unity was installed on 20 January, with 'Boléro' reappointed as Prime Minister, and included members of the former Government, opposition representatives and two of Nzwani's separatist leaders. However, on the following day the Government collapsed, following the withdrawal of the opposition representatives, as a result of a disagreement over the allocation of ministerial portfolios. The opposition ministers had expressed their disappointment at not having been offered the position of Prime Minister, nor the portfolios of foreign affairs or finance, the budget and privatization, which they claimed had been part of the agreement on national reconciliation of February 2001. Meanwhile, Azali resigned as Head of State and announced his intention to stand as an independent candidate in the forthcoming presidential election; 'Boléro' was to serve as President *ad interim*. In mid-February 2002 the Government of National Unity was re-established.

On 10 March 2002 voters on Nzwani and Mwali approved new local Constitutions; this was followed on 7 April by the approval of a new Constitution on Ngazidja (an earlier draft had been rejected). In a first round of voting in the federal presidential election on 17 March, contested by nine candidates, Azali secured 39.8% of the vote. Mahamoud Mradabi of the Shawiri party won 15.7% and Saïd Ali Kemal of CHUMA 10.7%; however, both Mradabi and Kemal boycotted the second round. Consequently, on 14 April Azali was elected unopposed as Federal President of the Union of the Comoros, reportedly securing more than 75% of the votes cast. However, the result was declared invalid by the NEC, on the grounds that the election had not been free and fair. Nevertheless, following the dissolution of the NEC, and the appointment of an independent electoral body, Azali was declared Federal President. Meanwhile, in late March and early April Maj. Mohamed Bacar and Mohamed Saïd Fazul were elected as regional Presidents of Nzwani and Mwali, respectively; on 19 May Abdou Soule Elbak was elected regional President of Ngazidja, defeating Azali's preferred candidate, Bakari Abdallah Boina. The regional Presidents subsequently formed local Governments. In early June Azali announced the formation of a new Government of the Union of the Comoros, which replaced the transitional Government of National Unity.

However, the process of local devolution was complicated by uncertainty about areas of jurisdiction on Ngazidja, as Moroni was the seat of government for both Azali and Elbak. In mid-June 2001 disagreement over the new political structure prompted the occupation of a number of government buildings by troops. In response, the Government of Ngazidja boycotted the inauguration of the new head of the armed forces, Col Soilihi Ali Mohammed, and warned the OAU that it suspected a coup was being planned, to be led by Soilihi. President Elbak also dismissed a number of local government figures loyal to Azali. On 6 July Presidents Elbak and Bacar boycotted Independence Day celebrations. In mid-July Azali declared his intention to bring forward the process of national reconciliation, holding legislative elections in September instead of December. As a result of a meeting in mid-August, Ngazidja was also granted its own internal security forces by Azali. Nevertheless, at the end of August street barricades were erected in Moroni, in protest at incomplete devolution on Ngazidja, which left Elbak with less authority than the other islands' Presidents. Soldiers dispersed the protests, injuring five (a subsequent inquiry revealed that live ammunition had been used). In September Azali announced that the legislative elections would be delayed until October; they were soon postponed further, to March–April 2003, despite assertions from international representatives that the absence of institutions for dialogue was a threat to the national reconciliation process.

In late January 2003 the follow-up committee on the implementation of the reconciliation agreement proposed that elections to the islands' local assemblies be held on 13 and 20 April and elections to the Assemblée de l'Union on 11 and 19 May. In early March Elbak and Bacar denounced Azali's failure to implement measures to resolve the institutional crisis and accused the Federal President of repeated constitutional violations, requesting that the EU temporarily delay payment for fishing rights to the federal Government. Later in the month the federal Government announced the indefinite postponement of the legislative elections. In an attempt to resolve the continuing political crisis, which centred on control of taxation, customs, the police and other institutions on Ngazidja, in July an AU mission, led by the South African Minister of Foreign Affairs, Nkosazana Dlamini-Zuma, visited the Comoros. Talks brought together Azali and the regional Presidents with the aim of removing obstacles to legislative elections; the creation was proposed of a Constitutional Court, which would have jurisdiction over such power struggles in the future. Although the discussions were described as 'fruitful', and the AU delegation supported the position of Azali, no active progress was made. However, a deadline of three weeks was set for an agreement to be reached before a reconciliation meeting to be held in South Africa, chaired by President Thabo Mbeki. In August, at the subsequent meeting in Pretoria, South Africa, representatives of the federal and island Governments signed a memorandum, according to which the federal Government would retain control of the army, but the administration of the police force would be devolved to the island Governments. Agreement was also reached that, during a transitional period leading to legislative elections, the customs services would be managed by a joint board, with taxes shared between the federal and island administrations. In November 2003 opposition parties issued a statement calling for President Azali's immediate resignation, on the grounds that he was not committed to implementing the agreements reached in Pretoria and in previous conferences. On 20 December, following further mediation by the AU, the agreement reached in August was ratified by Azali and the three island Presidents in Moroni. A follow-up committee was appointed to monitor the implementation of the accord.

Elections to the three island assemblies were held on 14 and 21 March 2004 and were observed by an AU mission. Pro-Azali candidates won an overall total of only 12 seats in the assemblies, while candidates from 11 parties allied to Elbak secured 14 of the 20 seats in the Ngazidja assembly, supporters of Bacar won 18 of the 25 seats available on Nzwani (where the elections were to be rerun in two constituencies) and nine allies of Fazul were elected to the 10-member assembly on Mwali. The parliament of Ngazidja was installed in early April, and was followed by the swearing in of the Mwali and Nzwani parliaments on 15 and 16 May, respectively.

Elections to the Assemblée de l'Union took place on 18 and 25 April 2004. According to final results, declared on 28 April, the Convention pour le renouveau des Comores (CRC) won only six of the 18 directly elected seats, while a loose coalition supporting the three island Presidents secured 11 seats and CHUMA took one seat. The rate of voter participation in the second round was 68.5%. The 15 remaining seats in the 33-member federal assembly were taken by five nominees each from the island legislatures. Hamada Madi, the Minister of Defence and a close associate of President Azali, was defeated in Mwali—in early April he had, contrary to popular opinion, attempted to dismiss the directors of two state companies on the island—and subsequently resigned his post on 30 April. The inauguration of the assembly, scheduled for 27 May, was postponed by President Azali and finally took place on 4 June. In mid-July President Azali effected a cabinet reshuffle, granting responsibility for co-ordinating Union affairs on their home islands to the two Vice-Presidents. The new Government comprised the two Vice-Presidents, seven ministers of state and two secretaries of state and included a representative each from Nzwani and Mwali, and one member of CHUMA.

Municipal elections were scheduled to take place on Nzwani between 4 and 11 July 2004; however, the main opposition party on the island, the Front de l'action pour la démocratie et le développment, claiming that previous elections on the island had not been transparent and democratic, stated that it would boycott the elections. A demonstration was held by civil servants, including teachers, in mid-June to protest against five months of salary arrears. The Cour Constitutionelle (Constitutional Court) was inaugurated in September, and Abdallah Ahmed Sourette was elected as its President in October. On 19 November, in a follow-up to the 2001 agreement on national reconciliation signed in Fomboni, long-awaited legislation on the division of power between the national and island authorities was passed by the Assemblée de l'Union. The bill, which was supported by President Azali, had provoked much controversy as it sought to clarify authority over security forces and public assets. Authority over the gendarmerie was granted to the island Presidents, precipitating a demonstration by the armed forces. The island Presidents also expressed their dissatisfaction with the bill, which, they claimed, had been amended by the Assemblée without their consent. It was subsequently declared invalid by the Constitutional Court and returned to the Assemblée.

In early 2005 teachers commenced industrial action over salary arrears, and there were reports that two protesters had died in clashes with the police on Nzwani. It was reported, however, that classes resumed in late March. Meanwhile, on Nzwani, increasing vocal opposition to Bacar, led to the suspension of a local radio station and the arrest of five men on charges of attempting to overthrow the island President. In July President Azali effected a reorganization of the Union Government. Most notably, Oubeidi Mze Cheik, hitherto the Director of the Customs Office, became Minister of Finance and the Budget, while Aboudou Soefo was awarded the foreign affairs portfolio. Also in July Elbak reshuffled the island Government of Ngazidja. In early September government employees commenced industrial action in protest at salary arrears and proposed reforms to the public sector. Later that month further demonstrations took place over an increase in the price of fuel, and one person was reported to have died when police fired on protesters. The situation was resolved when President Azali announced a reduction in import duties to offset the rise in fuel costs.

THE 2006 PRESIDENTIAL ELECTION

In October 2005 the Assemblée de l'Union approved legislation granting Comorans living abroad the right to vote. (It was estimated that some 200,000 Comorans were resident in France.) In early 2006 the Commission nationale des élections aux Comores (CNEC) announced that the presidential election would be held on 16 April and 14 May.

At the first round of the presidential election, duly held on 16 April 2006 on the island of Nzwani, in accordance with the constitutional requirements of the rotating presidency, 13 candidates participated, with three qualifying for the second, nation-wide, round. In the second round, held as scheduled on 14 May, Ahmed Abdallah Sambi, a respected businessman and Islamic theologian, won 99,112 votes, equivalent to 58.02% of the valid votes cast. Ibrahim Halidi, a former Prime Minister who was supported by outgoing President Azali, won 48,378 votes (28.32%), while Mohamed Djaanfari received 23,322 votes (13.65%). Voter turn-out was reported to have been 58.1%, and the election was praised by international observers as having been 'free and fair'. All three candidates came from the island of Nzwani, in accordance with the constitutional requirement that the presidency rotate between the three islands comprising the Union of the Comoros. On 26 May Sambi was sworn in as President, and on 29 May the composition of a new administration, comprising six ministers and two Vice-Presidents, was announced. Notably, the defence portfolio was transferred to the President's office.

ISLAND ELECTIONS

On 10 June 2007 the first round of presidential elections were held on two of the three islands, Ngazidja and Mwali. The election on Nzwani was postponed until 17 June, at the request of the President Sambi and the AU, following outbreaks of violence and allegations of corruption and intimidation in the weeks leading to the elections. Nevertheless, Bacar proceeded to hold the election, claiming a to have secured victory with 73.22%% of the vote. He subsequently announced himself as President of Nzwani for a second term, despite both the AU and the Union Government declaring the results to be null and void. The political unrest continued on Nzwani while the second round of voting, largely agreed to have been free and fair, took place on Ngazidja and Mwali on 25 June. Mohamed Abdouloihabi was named as President of Ngazidja, while Mohamed Ali Said secured the presidency of Mwali. A delegation of officials from the AU met with President Sambi, and the Nzwani authorities on 24 June to discuss the situation. A statement was subsequently issued in which demands were made for the authorities of Nzwani to hold free and fair elections, in compliance with an AU security plan. The Union Government expressed disappointment over the AU's response, threatening to restore order on Nzwani through military force if necessary, but later conceded that a military response would require external assistance owing to an imbalance in the strength of the Union's military forces compared to the contingent of armed militia in Nzwani.

EXTERNAL RELATIONS

Diplomatic relations between the Comoros and France, suspended in 1975, were restored in 1978; in November of that year the two countries signed agreements on military and economic co-operation, apparently deferring any decision on the future of Mayotte. In subsequent years, however, member countries of the UN General Assembly repeatedly voted in favour of a resolution affirming the Comoros' sovereignty over Mayotte, with only France dissenting. Following Djohar's accession to power, diplomatic relations were established with the USA in June 1990. In September of that year the Comoros and South Africa signed a bilateral agreement providing for a series of South African loans towards the development of infrastructure in the Comoros. In September 1993 the League of Arab States (Arab League) accepted an application for membership from the Comoros. In November 1994 the Government signed an agreement with Israel that provided for the establishment of diplomatic relations between the two countries, prompting protests from the Arab League and from Islamic leaders in the Comoros. Djohar subsequently announced that the implementation of the agreement was to be postponed, pending a satisfactory resolution to the conflict in the Middle East. In mid-1999, following the military coup headed by Col Azali, France and the USA suspended all military co-operation with the Comoros; France re-established military co-operation in September 2002. In 2003 President Azali visited a number of countries, including the USA and the People's Republic of China, in an effort to encourage foreign investment in the Comoros. In mid-2004 a joint commission with Sudan was created. President Azali visited France in early 2005, and the Franco-Comoran commission resumed, after a hiatus of 10 years.

Economy

Revised by the editorial staff

The Comoros, with few natural resources, a chronic shortage of cultivable land, a narrow base of agricultural crops and a high density of population, is among the poorest countries of sub-Saharan Africa, and is highly dependent on external trade and assistance. In 2005, according to estimates by the World Bank, the gross national income (GNI) of the Comoros (excluding Mayotte), measured at average 2003–05 prices, was US $387m., equivalent to $640 per head (or $2,000 on an international purchasing-power parity basis). During 1995–2005, it was estimated, the population increased at an average annual rate of 2.1%, while gross domestic product (GDP) per head declined, in real terms, by an average of 0.2% per year. According to the African Development Bank (ADB), overall GDP increased, in real terms, at an average annual rate of 2.0% in 1995–2006; real GDP increased by 4.2% in 2005 and by 1.2% in 2006.

AGRICULTURE

Agriculture is the dominant economic activity in the Comoros (contributing 48.5% of GDP in 2005 and employing 71.8% of the labour force in 2004, according to FAO). In 2004 the sector accounted for some 98% of export earnings. At the census of September 1991, despite large-scale emigration to neighbouring countries, overall population density was 240 inhabitants per sq km (excluding Mayotte), with a density of 445.6 on the island of Nzwani (Anjouan). By 2006, according to UN estimates, population density had risen to 439.3 inhabitants per sq km. The problem of overpopulation on the three independent islands has worsened since the break with Mayotte, which has the largest area of unexploited cultivable land in the archipelago. Settlers from Nzwani and Ngazidja (Grande-Comore) have been compelled to leave Mayotte and return to their already overpopulated native islands, where the potential for agricultural development is extremely limited. Demographic pressure was considered to be one of the main causes of the attempted secession by Nzwani and Mwali (Mohéli) in 1997.

Local subsistence farming, using primitive implements and techniques, is inadequate to maintain the population. Despite a number of rural development projects financed by various international agencies, yields are very poor, storage facilities lacking, and much of the best land is reserved for export cash-crop production. Cassava, taro, rice, maize, pulses, coconuts and bananas are cultivated. Almost all meat and vegetables are imported.

The major export crops are vanilla (valued at 1,166m. Comoros francs in 2005, according to IMF figures), cloves (146m. Comoros francs) and ylang ylang ($747m. Comoros francs). The main production of these three crops comes from Nzwani. Political unrest has had a serious impact on both production and trade, and revenue from unofficial ('black market') sales has been used to pay for imports of staple foods and fuel for the island. The rise of this 'black market' trade was a major element in the imposition of economic sanctions by the Organization of African Unity (OAU, now the African Union).

Prices for vanilla, of which the islands traditionally have been one of the world's larger producers (with average outputs of 140–200 metric tons per year), have been affected in recent years by competition from low-cost producers, notably Indonesia and Madagascar, and from synthetic substitutes. According to the Banque Centrale des Comores, production has since declined to an estimated 60 tons per year. In 2004 world vanilla prices fell dramatically, to around US $50 per kg, as a result of a good harvest in Madagascar. It fell even further in early 2007, to around $17 per kg, from a high of $600 per kg three years earlier. It remained at a stable (albeit low) level of $20–$30 per kg in the first half of 2007. Sellers in the Comoros hope that the higher quality of vanilla that they produce will be able to sustain the industry until the market price increases. However, the timing of this is uncertain, as the cheaper vanilla produced in Madagascar continues to flood the market. France accounts for about one-third of the Comoros' vanilla exports.

The world clove market virtually collapsed in the mid-1980s. Export levels fluctuated considerably during the 1990s, but recovered to 3,200 tons in 2004, compared with 938 tons in 2000. During much of the 1990s prices remained depressed; however, as a result of the political instability in Indonesia (the world's main producer of cloves), prices increased substantially in late 1999, and continued to improve in the early 2000s.

The Comoros is the world's main supplier of ylang ylang, producing an estimated 80% of the world's supply, for which prices have been generally favourable, although unit values declined somewhat in the late 1990s. Ageing plantations and inadequate processing equipment, however, have prevented this export from achieving its full potential, and output declined from 72 tons in 1989 to an estimated 35 tons in 2004. However, it was announced in mid-2007 that the Comoros could increase their production of ylang ylang by as much as 20,000 tons per year as a result of the 70,000 plants that have been planted since 2005.

Shortfalls in foreign-exchange revenue from these three commodities have been met by funds, under the Stabex (Stabilization of Export Earnings) scheme of the European Union (EU). According to the ADB, agricultural GDP increased at an average annual rate of 4.1% in 1995–2006; it increased by 1.0% in 2006.

Fishing is practised on a small scale, with a total catch of 15,100 metric tons in 2005. According to recent studies, the Comoros has a potential annual catch of 25,000–30,000 tons of tuna. In October 1987 the Comoros and the European Community (EC, now the EU) signed a fishing agreement which permitted tuna-fishing vessels from EC countries to operate in Comoran waters and allowed the implementation of a scientific programme; this agreement was subsequently renewed. In late 2006, meanwhile, it was announced that a surveillance centre would be built in Moroni to monitor and prevent unlawful fishing in waters reserved for the Comoros.

MANUFACTURING AND SERVICES

The manufacturing sector contributed 4.1% of GDP in 2005. The sector consists primarily of the processing of vanilla and essential oils on Nzwani, and a few factories supplying the domestic market. According to the ADB, manufacturing GDP increased at an average annual rate of 1.3% in 1995–2006; it increased by 2.0% in 2006.

The Comoros has a fragile tourism industry, partly because of perceived political instability. Tourist arrivals increased from 7,627 in 1990 to 27,474 in 1998, but had decreased to 19,551 by 2005. In 2004 tourism receipts totalled US $10m. The majority of tourists are from France. According to the ADB, the GDP of the services sector increased at an average rate of 0.2% per year in 1995–2006; it increased by 1.6% in 2006.

TRANSPORT AND UTILITIES

Economic development in the Comoros is impeded by poor infrastructure, an increasingly erratic power and water supply, a very limited road system and a lack of reliable transportation between the islands and with the outside world. In late 2004 work, partially financed by France and the People's Republic of China, commenced on the upgrading of the international airport at Moroni-Hahaya on Ngazidja.

At the end of 1995 it was announced that the country's air carrier, Air Comores, was to be liquidated. Charter operations have taken its place, providing long-haul air links with Dubai, Paris (France) and Johannesburg (South Africa), although there have been constant problems in maintaining a regular service. In 1995–97 plans to privatize state-owned enterprises, such as Air Comores, and also the public utilities enterprise, Electricité et Eau des Comores (EEDC), and the Société Nationale des Postes et des Télécommunications, were impeded by inter-government dissension.

By mid-1997 it had been agreed that EEDC (to be renamed Comorienne de l'Eau et de l'Electricité) would pass into private management by the French company SOGEA, with finance provided by the Caisse française de développement (CFD, now the Agence française de développement). This project, involving 41m. French francs in CFD aid, was repeatedly delayed, and for much of 1997 there was no network electricity supply on the islands. In 2001 Comorienne de l'Eau et de l'Electricité was renationalized as the Service Public de l'Eau et de l'Electricité, only to be privatized for a second time in January 2002, as MA-MWE—Gestion de l'Eau et de l'Electricité aux Comores. In March 2001 the World Bank approved a US $11.4m. credit for the improvement of roads and water supply in urban areas. In May 2003 an agreement was signed with Egypt, whereby the latter would provide some $2.2m. in electrical equipment and training to help upgrade services in the islands. In October a contract to provide the Comoros with a Global Standard for Mobiles telephone network was awarded to Alcatel. In early 2005 it was announced that France had provided €1.5m. to upgrade rural water distribution networks on Nzwani and Mwali.

DEVELOPMENT, TRADE AND FINANCE

France represents the main source of economic support (see below), while the other member states of the EU, Japan, Saudi Arabia, Kuwait and the United Arab Emirates also provide financial assistance. Following the devaluation of the Comoros franc in January 1994, the French Government agreed to cancel outstanding debt arrears. At the end of 1994, however, France suspended budgetary assistance (which had totalled 24m. French francs in 1994), in response to the Comoran Government's failure to agree a structural adjustment programme with the IMF and the World Bank, but later agreed to continue to provide aid for projects in the social sector and education. Finance in the latter area was also to be forthcoming from the UN Development Programme, the World Bank and the UN Children's Fund. Following a bilateral agreement concluded between France and the Comoros in early 2005, it was expected that France would increase its dispersal of aid to the Comoros.

The Comoros' foreign-trade accounts have shown a persistent deficit; imports have tended to increase, while export receipts have fluctuated widely, in response to trends in international prices for vanilla, cloves and ylang ylang. In 2005, according to IMF estimates, the visible trade deficit was $90.6m., and there was a deficit of $12.3m. on the current account of the balance of payments. Principal export destinations in 2005 were the France (73.3%) and Germany (10.4%). The main source of imports was South Africa (15.4%), followed by France, Pakistan and Belgium-Luxembourg. Vanilla (providing 54.0% of the total), cloves (6.8%) and ylang ylang (34.6%) accounted for virtually all exports in 2005. The principal imports were petroleum products, meat, rice, cement, and iron and steel.

The annual rate of inflation averaged 3.9% during 2000–2005. In 2002 the budget deficit was 4% of GDP; however, in 2003 that figure had decreased to 3%. As a whole, the islands tended to achieve lower deficits than did the Union administration, which had relatively high spending on infrastructures and salaries, partly to avoid strike action. In January 2005 the budget for that year was passed by the Assemblée de l'Union (Assembly of the Union), along with legislation governing the division of revenue between the central and island administrations. The Union administration was to receive 33.8% of revenue, while Ngazidja, Nzwani and Mwali were to receive 30.7%, 26.8% and 8.8%, respectively. The budget deficit, including grants received, was 82m. Comoros francs in 2005.

At the end of 2004 the Comoros' external debt totalled US $305.8m. (of which $275.2m. was long-term public debt), while the cost of debt-servicing in 2001 was equivalent to 3.7% of the value of exports of goods and services, owing to the highly concessionary nature of the debt and accumulated interest arrears.

In January 1994 the devaluation of the Comoros franc led to a sharp increase in the price of imported goods, prompting strike action in the education and health sectors in support of higher salaries. In March, however, following the adoption of an economic reform programme for the period 1994–96, the IMF approved a one-year structural adjustment facility, equivalent to US $1.9m., while the World Bank also agreed to further credit. In mid-1995, in response to a further deterioration in the fiscal situation, the Government introduced a number of measures to limit budgetary expenditure under a public finance recovery programme, including tax increases and a reduction in civil servants' salaries. However, political instability continued to impede economic progress; following a coup attempt in September (see Recent History), a new interim Government initiated emergency financial measures, which included the payment of debts outstanding to the World Bank in order to qualify for agreements with international institutions. In early 1996 the Government failed to adopt a budget for that year, and interim financial procedures were instigated, with the resultant confusion contributing to a further decline in the economy. In April the World Bank outlined measures that needed to be taken by the Comoros to improve the economy: greater control of the wage bill; a reduction in public-sector staff; increased customs and fiscal revenues; and the privatization of state-owned companies. In February 1997 an IMF-supervised six-month surveillance programme was agreed. The Government hoped that this would lead to the approval of an enhanced structural adjustment facility, but the programme was soon beset by problems. By July the IMF was warning that insufficient progress had been made, especially where privatization and salary payments were concerned. Following a six-month extension of the monitoring programme, in February 1998 the IMF again concluded that the Comoros had failed to meet its economic objectives. In August increasing arrears on loan repayments led the World Bank to suspend the disbursement of funds to the Comoros. In early 1999 the EU suspended all aid to the islands. The intensification of political instability, following the seizure of power by the military in April (see Recent History), had a particularly adverse effect on maritime trade and on tourism. In January 2000, following the required repayment of arrears by the Comoran authorities, the World Bank resumed the disbursement of funds to the Comoros. Furthermore, in March a joint delegation of the World Bank and the IMF suggested measures to reduce the Comoros' state deficit. These included cuts in government spending and the possibility of a reduction of, or moratorium on, the Comoran foreign debt. In early 2000 the Comoran authorities reduced customs duties by 80% on products from member countries of the Indian Ocean Commission (IOC), as part of moves to comply with the integrated regional programme for trade development. However, even though trade with IOC countries represents less than 5% of imports, there were some fears that this would lead to a shortfall in customs revenue, which usually represents up to three-quarters of the state budget. In July 2001 a group of 'Friends of the Comoros', co-ordinated by the World Bank, pledged aid of $11.5m. for the alleviation of poverty and to assist with constitutional developments towards the establishment of a new Comoran entity. The funds were granted by the World Bank itself, the EU, the Organisation internationale de la francophonie, France, Mauritius and Morocco. Moreover, it was hoped that a number of agreements reached later that year, worth an estimated €5.9m., would encourage the further development of the production of vanilla, ylang ylang and cloves, and increase international demand for those crops.

In February 2000 the Ministers of the Interior, Finance and Transport indefinitely suspended the movement of sea freight to and from Nzwani. Moreover, in March the OAU suspended telephone communications and restricted petroleum deliveries by sea and air. It was subsequently reported that there were serious fuel shortages on the island and that petroleum prices had dramatically increased. General political instability, and in particular the difficulties in resolving the secessionist movement on Nzwani, has restricted the Comoros' access to international aid in recent years. Concern has also existed over allegations of mismanagement and corruption.

Following a mission to the Comoros in July 2002, the IMF announced that, owing to the current unstable economic situation, notably the tensions surrounding the sharing of political power on Ngazidja (see Recent History), it would not be possible to approve a Poverty Reduction and Growth Facility (PRGF) for the country. This statement was reiterated by the World Bank, which had also sent a delegation to the islands. Nevertheless, the IMF also stated that the Comoran economy had benefited from an increase in export prices and from the lifting, in 2001, of the OAU embargo on Nzwani (see above). Furthermore, earlier in July 2002 the IMF had proposed that a budget for the entire Union of the Comoros be drawn up, and also that the Government of the Union of the Comoros be responsible for the running of all state-owned companies. In November the federal Government and the EU signed a National Indicator Programme on co-operation during 2002–07; the Comoros was to receive €27.3m. under the Programme, mostly for education. Throughout late 2002 and early 2003 considerable economic disruption was caused on Ngazidja by the crisis over the distribution of political power on the island, following partial devolution, and many businesses were threatened by dual taxation by the local and federal Governments.

In February 2004 the IMF released the results of an Article IV consultation that had taken place in late 2002. The delay was the result of divisions between the Union and island Governments. However, the IMF stated that economic development had been positive in the 18 months preceding the consultation. In May the IMF issued the results of a further Article IV consultation with the Comoros, which had ended the previous month. The report maintained that, as a result of recent elections and ongoing tensions between President Azali and the three island Presidents, economic and structural reforms had almost stopped. In 2005 the Government agreed a 12-month staff-monitored programme with the IMF, with a view to reaching agreement on a (PRGF) programme. Among the proposals made by the IMF were the reform of the tax system and the privatization of the state-owned telecommunications and petroleum companies. In late 2005 an IMF mission visited the Comoros and, while maintaining that progress had been made in addressing the budget deficit, it stated that more time would be required fully to assess the progress of reforms. The Fund did, however, advocate the diversification of agricultural production and envisaged a moderate economic revival in the last quarter of the year. In March 2006 it was announced that although the Comoros had not met the requirements for a PRGF the monitoring programme would continue, and that it was hoped that negotiations on a PRGF would commence in late 2006. Meanwhile, in December 2005 a donors' conference was held in Mauritius, at which some $200m. was pledged to assist with the Comoros' four-year development and poverty reduction plan. In December of 2006 an IMF team visited the Comoros in order to assess their Interim Poverty Reduction Strategy Paper. It was hoped that a positive evaluation would lead to a Fund-supported PRGF programme.

In January 2006 the Comoros joined the Common Market for Eastern and Southern Africa.

Statistical Survey

Sources (unless otherwise stated): *Rapport Annuel*, Banque Centrale des Comores, place de France, BP 405, Moroni; tel. (73) 1814; fax (73) 0349; e-mail bancecom@comorestelecom.km; internet www.bancecom.com.

Note: Unless otherwise indicated, figures in this Statistical Survey exclude data for Mayotte.

AREA AND POPULATION

Area: 1,862 sq km (719 sq miles). *By Island*: Ngazidja (Grande-Comore) 1,146 sq km, Nzwani (Anjouan) 424 sq km, Mwali (Mohéli) 290 sq km.

Population: 335,150 (males 167,089, females 168,061), excluding Mayotte (estimated population 50,740), at census of 15 September 1980; 446,817 (males 221,152, females 225,665), excluding Mayotte, at census of 15 September 1991; 527,900 in 1998; 575,660, excluding Mayotte, at census of 1 September 2003. *Mid-2006* (UN estimate): 818,000 (Source: UN, *World Population Prospects: The 2006 Revision*). *By Island* (1991 census): Ngazidja (Grande-Comore) 233,533; Nzwani (Anjouan) 188,953; Mwali (Mohéli) 24,331.

Density (per sq km, mid-2006): 439.3.

Principal Towns ('000, incl. suburbs, mid-2005, UN estimate): Moroni (capital) 44,000. Source: UN, *World Urbanization Prospects: The 2005 Revision*.

Births and Deaths (including figures for Mayotte, UN estimates, 2000–05): Average annual birth rate 36.5 per 1,000; average annual death rate 7.4 per 1,000. Source: UN, *World Population Prospects: The 2006 Revision*.

Expectation of Life (years at birth, including Mayotte, WHO estimates): 64 (males 62; females 67) in 2004. Source: WHO, *World Health Report*.

Economically Active Population (ILO estimates, '000 persons at mid-1980, including figures for Mayotte): Agriculture, forestry and fishing 150; Industry 10; Services 20; Total 181 (males 104, females 77) (Source: ILO, *Economically Active Population Estimates and Projections, 1950–2025*). *1991 Census* (persons aged 12 years and over, excluding Mayotte): Total labour force 126,510 (males 88,034, females 38,476) (Source: UN, *Demographic Yearbook*). *Mid-2004* (official estimates in '000): Agriculture, etc. 270; Total labour force 376 (Source: FAO).

HEALTH AND WELFARE

Key Indicators

Total Fertility Rate (children per woman, 2005): 4.6.

Under-5 Mortality Rate (per 1,000 live births, 2005): 71.

HIV/AIDS (% of persons aged 15–49, 2005): 0.1.

Physicians (per 1,000 head, 2004): 0.15.

Hospital Beds (per 1,000 head, 2006): 2.20.

Health Expenditure (2004): US $ per head (PPP): 24.9.

Health Expenditure (2004): % of GDP: 2.8.

Health Expenditure (2004): public (% of total): 56.9.

Access to Water (% of persons, 2004): 86.

Access to Sanitation (% of persons, 2004): 33.

Human Development Index (2004): ranking: 132.

Human Development Index (2004): value: 0.556.

For sources and definitions, see explanatory note on p. vi.

AGRICULTURE, ETC.

Principal Crops ('000 metric tons, unless otherwise indicated, 2005, FAO estimates): Rice (paddy) 17.5; Maize 4.0; Potatoes 0.9; Sweet potatoes 5.7; Cassava (Manioc) 58.1; Taro 9.2; Yams 4.1; Pulses 14.3; Groundnuts (in shell) 0.9; Coconuts 80.5; Tomatoes 0.7; Other vegetables 3.0; Bananas 64.8; Other fruits 3.6; Vanilla (dried, metric tons) 65; Cloves 1.5.

Livestock ('000 head, year ending September 2005, FAO estimates): Asses 5.0; Cattle 45.0; Sheep 21.0; Goats 115.0; Chickens 510.

Livestock Products (metric tons, 2005, FAO estimates): Beef and veal 1,100; Sheep and goat meat 435; Chicken meat 560; Cow milk 4,550; Hen eggs 776.

Fishing ('000 metric tons, live weight, 2005): Total catch 15.1 (Sardinellas 1.0; Anchovies, etc. 1.0; Seerfishes 0.6; Skipjack tuna 3.2; Yellowfin tuna 5.9; Carangids 0.6; Indian mackerels 0.2).

Source: FAO.

INDUSTRY

Electric Energy (million kWh): 35.2 in 2003; 35.8 in 2004; 36.0 in 2005. Source: IMF, *Union of the Comoros: Selected Issues and Statistical Appendix* (October 2006).

FINANCE

Currency and Exchange Rates: 100 centimes = 1 Comoros franc. *Sterling, Dollar and Euro Equivalents* (31 May 2007): £1 sterling = 723.087 Comoros francs; US $1 = 365.694 Comoros francs; €1 = 491.968 Comoros francs; 1,000 Comoros francs = £1.383 = $2.735 =

€2.033. *Average Exchange Rate* (Comoros francs per US $): 396.214 in 2004; 395.601 in 2005; 392.168 in 2006. Note: The Comoros franc was introduced in 1981, replacing (at par) the CFA franc. The fixed link to French currency was retained, with the exchange rate set at 1 French franc = 50 Comoros francs. This remained in effect until January 1994, when the Comoros franc was devalued by 33.3%, with the exchange rate adjusted to 1 French franc = 75 Comoros francs. This relationship to French currency remained in effect with the introduction of the euro on 1 January 1999. From that date, accordingly, a fixed exchange rate of €1 = 491.968 Comoros francs has been in operation.

Budget (million Comoros francs, 2007, projected): *Revenue*: Tax revenue 22,163; Other revenue 4,089; Total 26,252 (excluding grants received 13,419). *Expenditure*: Budgetary current expenditure 29,298 (Wages and salaries 12,784, Goods and services 6,591, Transfers 3,463, Interest payments 859, Foreign-financed project assistance 2,340, Technical assistance programmes 3,296); Capital expenditure 11,121 (Externally financed 9,421, Domestically financed 1,700); Total 40,419.

International Reserves (US $ million at 31 December 20056): Gold 0.33; Reserve position in IMF 0.82; Foreign exchange 92.70; Total 93.85. Source: IMF, *International Financial Statistics*.

Money Supply (million Comoros francs at 31 December 2006): Currency outside deposit money banks 12,765; Demand deposits at deposit money banks 10,199; Total money (incl. others) 24,652. Source: IMF, *International Financial Statistics*.

Cost of Living (Consumer Price Index; base: 1999 = 100): All items 120.1 in 2003; 125.5 in 2004; 128.0 in 2005. Source: IMF, *Union of the Comoros: Selected Issues and Statistical Appendix* (October 2006).

Expenditure on the Gross Domestic Product (million Comoros francs at current prices, 2005): Government final consumption expenditure 18,678; Private final consumption expenditure 154,245; Gross fixed capital formation 14,253; *Total domestic expenditure* 187,176; Exports of goods and services 19,102; *Less* Imports of goods and services 53,166; *GDP in purchasers' values* 153,112. Source: IMF, *Union of the Comoros: Selected Issues and Statistical Appendix* (October 2006).

Gross Domestic Product by Economic Activity (million Comoros francs at current prices, 2005, estimates): Agriculture, hunting, forestry and fishing 78,110; Manufacturing 6,666; Electricity, gas and water 2,292; Construction and public works 7,876; Trade, restaurants and hotels 27,261; Transport and communications 14,111; Finance, insurance, real estate and business services 8,698; Government services 15,854; Other services 130; *Sub-total* 160,998; *Less* Imputed bank service charge 7,886; *GDP in purchasers' values* 153,112. Source: IMF, *Union of the Comoros: Selected Issues and Statistical Appendix* (October 2006).

Balance of Payments (US $ million, 2005, estimates): Exports of goods f.o.b. 13.8; Imports of goods f.o.b. –90.6; *Trade balance* –76.8; Services (net) –5.3; *Balance on goods and services* –82.1; Income (net) –2.3; *Balance on goods, services and income* –84.4; Private transfers (net) 65.0; Government transfers (net) 7.1; *Current balance* –12.3; Net capital account (incl. errors and omissions) 4.7; *Overall balance* –7.6. Source: IMF, *Union of the Comoros: Selected Issues and Statistical Appendix* (October 2006).

EXTERNAL TRADE

Principal Commodities (million Comoros francs, 2005): *Imports c.i.f.*: Meat and fish 3,771; Rice 3,417; Petroleum products 4,196; Cement 2,686; Iron and steel 1,373; Total (incl. others) 35,344. *Exports f.o.b.*: Vanilla 1,166; Cloves 146; Ylang ylang 747; Total (incl. others) 2,160. Source: IMF *Union of the Comoros: Selected Issues and Statistical Appendix* (October 2006).

Principal Trading Partners (US $ million, 2000): *Imports*: Belgium 1.3; France-Monaco 13.9; Indonesia 1.5; Kenya 3.9; Pakistan 4.9; South Africa 39.0; United Arab Emirates 1.8; Total (incl. others) 71.9. *Exports*: Canada 0.3; France-Monaco 3.0; Germany 0.5; Israel 0.2; Singapore 1.1; United Kingdom 0.6; USA 1.1; Total (incl. others) 6.9. Source: UN, *International Trade Statistics Yearbook*.

TRANSPORT

Road Traffic (motor vehicles in use, 1999, estimates): Passenger cars 692; Total 790. Source: International Road Federation, *World Road Statistics*.

Shipping: *Merchant Fleet* (registered at 31 December 2005): Number of vessels 205; Total displacement (grt) 608,544 (Source: Lloyd's Register-Fairplay, *World Fleet Statistics*). *International Sea-borne Freight Traffic* (estimates, '000 metric tons, 1991): Goods loaded 12; Goods unloaded 107 (Source: UN Economic Commission for Africa, *African Statistical Yearbook*).

Civil Aviation (traffic at Prince Said Ibrahim international airport, 1999): Passengers carried ('000) 130.4; Freight handled 1,183 metric tons.

TOURISM

Tourist Arrivals (2004): France 9,460; Madagascar 656; Réunion 1,429; Zimbabwe 786; Total (incl. others) 17,603. *2005:* Total arrivals 19,551.

Receipts from Tourism (US $ million, incl. passenger transport): 11 in 2002; 8 in 2003; 10 in 2004.

Source: partly World Tourism Organization.

COMMUNICATIONS MEDIA

Radio Receivers (1997): 90,000 in use. Source: UNESCO, *Statistical Yearbook*.

Television Receivers (1997): 1,000 in use. Source: UNESCO, *Statistical Yearbook*.

Telephones (2005): 16,900 main lines in use. Source: International Telecommunication Union.

Mobile Cellular Telephones (2005): 16,100 in use. Source: International Telecommunication Union.

Facsimile Machines (1998): 173 in use. Source: UN, *Statistical Yearbook*.

Personal Computers (2004): 5,000 in use. Source: International Telecommunication Union.

Internet Users (2005): 20,000. Source: International Telecommunication Union.

EDUCATION

Pre-primary (2003/04): 483 teachers; 2,279 pupils. Source: UNESCO Institute for Statistics.

Primary: 348 schools (1998); 2,967 teachers (2003/04); 103,809 pupils (2003/04). Sources: UNESCO Institute for Statistics and IMF, *Comoros: Statistical Appendix* (August 2005).

Secondary: Teachers: general education 3,091 (2003/04); teacher training 11 (1991/92); vocational 20 (2003/04). Pupils: 42,919 (2003/04). Sources: UNESCO Institute for Statistics and IMF, *Comoros: Statistical Appendix* (August 2005).

Post-secondary Vocational (2003/04): 51 teachers; 734 pupils. Source: UNESCO Institute for Statistics.

Tertiary (2003/04): 130 teachers; 1,779 pupils. Source: UNESCO Institute for Statistics.

Adult Literacy Rate: 56.2% (males 63.5%; females 49.1%) in 2002. Source: UN Development Programme, *Human Development Report*.

Directory

The Constitution

In accordance with an agreement on national reconciliation, signed on 17 February 2001 by representatives of the Government, the separatist administration on Nzwani, opposition parties and civil society, a new Constitution was presented in August and approved by referendum on 23 December. Under the terms of the new Constitution, the country was renamed the Union of the Comoros, and each of the three islands, Ngazidja, Nzwani and Mwali, were to be granted partial autonomy and were to be headed by a local government. The Union, governed by a central government, was to be headed by the President. The main provisions of the Constitution are summarized below.

PREAMBLE

The preamble affirms the will of the Comoran people to derive from the state religion, Islam, inspiration for the principles and laws that the State and its institutions govern; to guarantee the pursuit of a common future; to establish new institutions based on the rule of law, democracy and good governance, which guarantee an equal division of power between the Union and those islands that compose it; to adhere to the principles laid down by the Charters of the UN, the Organization of African Unity (now the African Union) and the Organization of the Islamic Conference and by the Treaty of the League of Arab States; and to guarantee the rights of all citizens, without discrimination, in accordance with the UN Declaration of Human Rights and the African Charter of Human Rights.

The preamble guarantees solidarity between the Union and the islands, as well as between the islands themselves; equality amongst the islands and their inhabitants, regardless of race, origin, or religion; the right to freedom of expression, education, health and justice; the freedom and security of individuals; the inviolability of an individual's home or property; and the right of children to be protected against abandonment, exploitation and violence.

THE UNION OF THE COMOROS

The Comoros archipelago constitutes a republic. Sovereignty belongs to the people, and is exercised through their elected representatives or by the process of referendum. There is universal secret suffrage, which can be direct or indirect, for all citizens who are over the age of 18 and in full possession of their civil and political rights. Political parties and groups operate freely, respecting national sovereignty, democracy and territorial integrity.

COMPETENCIES OF THE UNION AND THE ISLANDS

Each island freely administers its own affairs, while respecting the unity of the Union and its territorial integrity. Each island establishes its own fundamental laws, which must respect the Constitution. All Comorans within the Union have equal rights, freedoms and duties. All the islands are headed by an elected executive and assembly. The Union has ultimate authority over the individual islands and legislates on matters of religion, nationality, currency, foreign affairs, external defence and national identity. As regards those competencies shared by both the Union and the islands, the Union has ultimate jurisdiction only if the issue concerned affects more than one island, if the matter cannot be resolved by one island alone, or if the judicial, economic or social integrity of the Union may be compromised. The islands are responsible for those matters not covered by the Union, or by shared responsibility. The islands are financially autonomous.

THE UNION'S INSTITUTIONS

Executive Power

The President of the Union is the symbol of national unity. He is the guarantor of national independence, the unity of the Republic, the autonomy of the islands, territorial integrity and adherence to international agreements. He is the Head of State and is responsible for external defence and security, foreign affairs and negotiating and ratifying treaties.

The Council of the Union is composed of the President and two Vice-Presidents, selected from each island. The members of the Council are elected for a four-year term, and the position of President rotates between the islands, while the Vice-Presidents are inhabitants of the two remaining islands. The President appoints the members of the Government (ministers of the Union) and determines their respective portfolios. The composition of the Government must represent all of the islands equally.

Legislative Power

Legislative power is vested in the Assembly of the Union (Assemblée de l'Union), which is composed of 33 deputies, elected for a period of five years. Fifteen of the deputies are selected by the islands' local assemblies (five deputies per island) and 18 are directly elected by universal suffrage. The Assemblée de l'Union sits for two sessions each year and, if necessary, for extraordinary sessions.

Judicial Power

Judicial power is independent of executive and legislative power. The President of the Union is the guarantor of the independence of the judicial system and is assisted by the Higher Council of the Magistracy (Conseil Supérieur de la Magistrature). The Supreme Court (Cour Suprême) is the highest ruling authority in judicial, administrative and fiscal matters, and its rulings are final and binding. A Constitutional Court (Cour Constitutionelle) was created in 2004.

THE HIGH COUNCIL

The High Council considers constitutional matters, oversees the results of elections and referendums and guarantees basic human rights and civil liberties. Moreover, the High Council is responsible for ruling on any conflicts regarding the separate competencies of the Union and the islands. The President of the Union, the Vice-Presidents, the President of the Assemblée de l'Union, and each President of the local island executives appoint one member to the High Council. Members are elected for a six-year mandate, renewable once; the President of the High Council is appointed by the members for a six-year term.

REVISION OF THE CONSTITUTION

The power to initiate constitutional revision is jointly vested in the President of the Union and the members of the Assemblée de l'Union. Constitutional revision must be approved by a majority of two-thirds of the deputies in the Assemblée de l'Union and by two-thirds of the members of the islands' local assemblies. However, the organizational structure of the Union cannot be revised, and any revision that may affect the unity and territorial boundaries of the Union is not permitted.

PROVISIONAL ARRANGEMENTS

The Union's institutions, as defined in the Constitution, are to be established in accordance with the terms laid out in the agreement on national reconciliation of 17 February 2001. Institutions on the island of Mayotte will be established within a maximum period of six months following the island's decision to rejoin the Union of the Comoros.

The Government

HEAD OF STATE

Federal President: AHMED ABDALLAH SAMBI (elected 14 May 2006).

REGIONAL PRESIDENTS

Mwali: MOHAMED ALI SAID.

Ngazidja: MOHAMED ABDOULOIHABI.

Nzwani: (vacant).

GOVERNMENT OF THE UNION OF THE COMOROS

(August 2007)

Vice-President, with responsibility for Transport, Post, Telecommunications and Tourism: IDI NADHOIM.

Vice-President, with responsibility for Health, Solidarity and Gender Empowerment: IKILILOU DHOININE.

Minister of Finance, Budget and Planning: MOHAMED ALI SOLIHI.

Minister of Justice, the Civil Service, Penitentiary Administration and Administrative Reforms and Keeper of the Seals: MOURAD SAID IBRAHIM.

Minister of External Relations and Co-operation, with responsibility for the Diaspora and Francophone and Arab Relations: AHMED BEN SAÏD DJAFFAR.

Minister of Agriculture, Fisheries and the Environment: SITI KASSIM.

Minister of Territorial Management, Infrastructure, Urban Planning and Housing: NAÏLANE MHADJI.

Minister of National Education, Research, the Arts, Culture, Youth and Sports: ABDOURAHIM SAÏD BACAR.

Minister of Islamic Affairs, Human Rights and Information, responsible for Relations with Parliament and the Island Institutions: M'MADI ALI.

Minister of Energy: HOUMADI ABDALLAH.

Minister of the Economy, Labour, Employment and the Promotion of Female Entrepreneurs: HASSANI HAMADI.

Minister of Investment Promotion, Micro-Finance and Decentralized Co-operation: FOUAD BEN MOHADJI.

MINISTRIES

Office of the Head of State: Palais de Beit Salam, BP 521, Moroni; tel. (74) 4808; fax (74) 4829; e-mail presidence@comorestelecom.km; internet www.beit-salam.km.

Ministry of Agriculture, Fisheries and the Environment: Moroni.

Ministry of the Economy, Foreign Trade, Industrial Promotion and Employment: Moroni; tel. (73) 0951; fax (73) 1981.

Ministry of Energy: Moroni.

Ministry of External Relations and Co-operation, with responsibility for the Diaspora and Francophone and Arab Relations: BP 428, Moroni; tel. (73) 2306; fax (73) 2108; e-mail mirex@snpt.km.

Ministry of Finance, Budget and Planning: BP 324, Moroni; tel. (74) 4140; fax (74) 4141.

Ministry of Health, Solidarity and Gender Empowerment: Moroni.

Ministry of Investment Promotion, Micro-Finance and Decentralized Co-operation: Moroni.

Ministry of Islamic Affairs, Human Rights and Information: Moroni.

Ministry of Justice, the Civil Service, Penitentiary Administration and Administrative Reforms: BP 2028, Moroni; tel. (74) 4040; fax (73) 4045.

Ministry of National Education, Research, the Arts, Culture, Youth and Sports: BP 73, Moroni; tel. (74) 4180; fax (74) 4181.

Ministry of Territorial Management, Infrastructure, Urban Planning and Housing: BP 12, Moroni; tel. (74) 4500; fax (73) 2222.

Ministry of Transport, Post, Telecommunications and Tourism: BP 1315, Moroni; tel. (73) 4266; fax (73) 2222.

President and Legislature

PRESIDENT

Presidential Election, 14 May 2006

Candidate	Votes cast	% of votes
Ahmed Abdallah Sambi	99,112	58.02
Ibrahim Halidi	48,378	28.32
Mohamed Djaanfari	23,322	13.65
Total	170,812	100.00

LEGISLATURE

Assemblée de l'Union: BP 447, Moroni; tel. (74) 4000; fax (74) 4011.

President: SAÏD DHIUFFUR BOUNOU.

Elections, 18 and 25 April 2004

Party	Seats
Convention pour le renouveau des Comores (CRC)	6
CHUMA	1
Coalition supporting the three regional Presidents*	11
Total	33†

* A loose coalition supporting the three regional Presidents.

† The remaining 15 seats were filled by nominees from the islands' local assemblies, members of which had been elected on 14 and 21 March 2004.

Election Commission

Commission électorale nationale indépendante aux Comores (CENI): Moroni; f. 2007 to succeed the Commission nationale des élections aux Comores; 10–13 mems; each island has a Commission électorale insulaire, consisting of 7 mems.

Political Organizations

CHUMA (Islands' Fraternity and Unity Party): Moroni; e-mail chuma@pourlescomores.com; f. 1985; Leader SAÏD ALI KEMAL.

Convention pour le renouveau des Comores (CRC): f. 2002; Leader Col ASSOUMANI AZALI; Sec.-Gen. ABOUDOU SOEFOU.

Djawabu: Leader YOUSSOUF SAÏD SOILIHI.

Forces pour l'action républicaine (FAR): Leader Col ABDOURAZAK ABDULHAMID.

Front de l'action pour la démocratie et le développment (FADD): Nzwani; main opposition party on Nzwani.

Front démocratique (FD): BP 758, Moroni; tel. (73) 3603; e-mail idriss@snpt.km; f. 1982; Chair. MOUSTOIFA SAÏD CHEIKH; Sec.-Gen. ABDALLAH HALIFA.

Front national pour la justice (FNJ): Islamic fundamentalist orientation; Leader AHMED RACHID.

Mouvement des citoyens pour la République (MCR): f. 1998; Leader MAHAMOUD MRADABI.

Mouvement populaire anjouanais (MPA): f. 1997 by merger of Organisation pour l'indépendance d'Anjouan and Mouvement séparatiste anjouanais; principal separatist movement on Nzwani (Anjouan).

Mouvement pour la démocratie et le progrès (MDP—NGDC): Moroni; Leader ABBAS DJOUSSOUF.

Mouvement pour la République, l'ouverture et l'unité de l'archipel des Comores (Mouroua) (Movement for the Republic, Openness and the Unity of the Comoran Archipelago): Moroni; f. 2005; advocates institutional reform; Pres. SAÏD ABBAS DAHALANI.

Mouvement pour le socialisme et la démocratie (MSD): Moroni; f. 2000 by splinter group of the FD; Leader ABDOU SOEFOU.

Parti comorien pour la démocratie et le progrès (PCDP): Route Djivani, BP 179, Moroni; tel. (73) 1733; fax (73) 0650; Leader ABDOU SOULE ELBAK.

Parti républicain des Comores (PRC): BP 665, Moroni; tel. (73) 3489; fax (73) 3329; e-mail prc@online.fr; internet www.chez.com/prc; f. 1998; Leader MOHAMED SAÏD ABDALLAH M'CHANGAMA.

Parti socialiste des Comores (Pasoco): tel. (73) 1328; Leader AHMED AFFANDI ALI.

Rassemblement pour une initiative de développement avec une jeunesse avertie (RIDJA): BP 1905, Moroni; tel. and fax (73) 3356; f. 1999; Leader SAÏD LARIFOU; Sec.-Gen. AHAMED ACHIRAFI.

Rassemblement national pour le développement (RND): f. 1996; Chair. OMAR TAMOU; Sec. Gen. ABDOULHAMID AFFRAITANE.

Shawiri: Moroni; Leader Col MAHAMOUD MRADABI.

Shawiri—Unafasiya (SU): Moroni; f. 2003 following a split in Shawiri; Sec.-Gen. HADJI BEN SAÏD.

Union nationale pour la démocratie aux Comores (UNDC): Moroni; f. 1986; Pres. KAMAR EZZAMANE MOHAMED.

There are also a number of Islamist groups.

Diplomatic Representation

EMBASSIES IN THE COMOROS

China, People's Republic: Coulée de Lave, C109, BP 442, Moroni; tel. (73) 2521; fax (73) 2866; e-mail ambassadechine@snpt.km; Ambassador TAO WEIGUANG.

France: blvd de Strasbourg, BP 465, Moroni; tel. (73) 0615; fax (73) 3347; e-mail pierre.lanners@snpt.km; internet www.ambafrance-km.org; Ambassador CHRISTIAN JOB.

South Africa: Itsandra Royal Hotel, Rm 112, Moroni; Ambassador MASILO MABETA.

Judicial System

Under the terms of the Constitution, the President is the guarantor of the independence of the judicial system, and is assisted by the Higher Council of the Magistracy (Conseil Supérieur de la Magistrature). The highest ruling authority in judicial, administrative and fiscal matters is the Supreme Court (Cour Suprême). The High Council considers constitutional matters. A Constitutional Court (Cour Constitutionelle), comprising seven members, appointed by the President of the Union of the Comoros, the two Vice-Presidents and the three regional Presidents, was established in 2004.

Constitutional Court: Moroni; Pres. ABDALLAH AHMED SOURETTE.

Religion

The majority of the population are Muslims, mostly Sunni. At 31 December 2004 there were an estimated 4,300 adherents of the Roman Catholic Church, equivalent to 0.5% of the total population.

ISLAM

Organisation Islamique des Comores: BP 596, Coulée, Moroni; tel. (73) 2071.

CHRISTIANITY

The Roman Catholic Church

Office of Apostolic Administrator of the Comoros: Mission Catholique, BP 46, Moroni; tel. and fax (76) 1996; e-mail mcatholique@comorestelecom.km; Apostolic Pro-Admin. Fr JAN GEERITS.

The Press

Al Watwan: Nagoudjou, BP 984, Moroni-Coulée; tel. and fax (73) 4448; fax (73) 3340; e-mail alwatwan@snpt.km; internet www.comores-online.com/al-watwan; f. 1985; weekly; state-owned; Dir-Gen. MOHAMED ABDOU SOIMADOU; Editor-in-Chief AHMED ALIAMIR; circ. 1,500.

L'Archipel: Moroni; f. 1988; privately owned; monthly; French; Editor-in-Chief ABOUBACAR MCHANGAMA.

Comores Aujourd'hui: Moroni; Dir HAMADA MADI.

La Gazette des Comores: BP 2216, Moroni; tel. (73) 5234; e-mail la_gazette@snpt.km; weekly; Publication Dir ALLAOUI SAÏD OMAR.

Kashkazi: BP 5311, Moroni; internet www.kashkazi.com; f. 2005; weekly; French.

Le Matin des Comores: BP 1040, Moroni; tel. (73) 2995; fax (73) 2939; daily; Dir ALILOIAFA MOHAMED SAÏD.

NEWS AGENCY

Agence comorienne de presse (HZK-Presse): BP 2216, Moroni; tel. (73) 9121; e-mail hzk_presse2@yahoo.fr; internet www.hzk-presse.com; f. 2004; Dir EL-HAD SAID OMAR.

PRESS ASSOCIATION

Organisation comorienne de la presse écrite (OCPE): Moroni; f. 2004; Pres. ABOUBACAR MCHANGAMA.

Publisher

KomÉdit: BP 535, Moroni; e-mail edition@komedit.com; f. 2000; general.

Broadcasting and Communications

TELECOMMUNICATIONS

Comores Télécom (Comtel): BP 7000, Moroni; tel. (74) 4300; fax (73) 1079; e-mail webmaster@comorestelecom.km; internet www.comorestelecom.km; formerly Société Nationale des Postes et des Télécommunications; post and telecommunications operations separated in 2004; scheduled for privatization; there were further plans to divide the mobile telecommunications and fixed-line branches of Comtel; Dir-Gen. CHARIKANAE BOUCHRANE.

BROADCASTING

Transmissions to the Comoros from Radio France Internationale commenced in early 1994. A number of privately owned radio and television stations also broadcast in the Comoros. In 2004 a Comoran television station was being established with funds from the People's Republic of China.

Office de la Radio Télévision des Comores (ORTC): Moroni; Comoran state broadcasting company; broadcasts Radio Comoros (f. 1960) and Télévision Nationale Comorienne (TNC; f. 2006); Dir-Gen. RADHUIA WAHAB.

Radio-Télévision Anjouanaise (RTA): Mbouyoujou-Ouani, Nzwani; tel. (71) 0124; e-mail contact@rtanjouan.org; internet www.rtanjouan.org; f. 1997; television station f. 2003; owned by the Nzwani regional government; Dir (Radio) FAHARDINE ABDOULBAY; Dir (Television) AMIR ABDALLAH.

Radio

Radio-Comoro: BP 250, Moroni; tel. (73) 2531; fax (73) 0303; govt-controlled; domestic programmes in Comoran and French; international broadcasts in Swahili, Arabic and French; Dir-Gen. ISMAIL IBOUROI; Tech. Dir ABDULLAH RADJAB.

Radio Dzialandzé Mutsamudu (RDM): Mutsamudu, Nzwani; f. 1992; broadcasts on Nzwani; Co-ordinator SAÏD ALI DACAR MGAZI.

Radio KAZ: Mkazi, BP 1933; tel. (73) 5201.

Radio Ngazidja: Moroni; broadcasts on Ngazidja; also known as Radio Mdjidjengo; represents Ngazidja regional government; Man. ABDOU DJIBABA.

Television

Djabal TV: Iconi, BP 675, Moroni; tel. (73) 6767.

Mtsangani Television (MTV): Mtsangani, BP 845, Moroni; tel. (73) 3316; f. 1996; owned by Centre d'Animation Socio-culturelle de Matsangani; cultural and educational programmes.

TV—SHA: Shashagnogo; tel. (73) 3636.

Finance

BANKING

(cap. = capital; res = reserves; dep. = deposits; m. = million; brs = branches; amounts in Comoros francs)

Central Bank

Banque Centrale des Comores: pl. de France, BP 405, Moroni; tel. (73) 1814; fax (73) 0349; e-mail bancecom@snpt.km; internet www.bancecom.com; f. 1981; bank of issue; cap. 1,100m., res 7,260m., dep. 5,640m. (Dec. 1999); Gov. IBRAHIM BEN ALI.

Commercial Bank

Banque pour l'Industrie et le Commerce—Comores (BIC): pl. de France, BP 175, Moroni; tel. (73) 0243; fax (73) 1229; e-mail bic@snpt.km; f. 1990; 51% owned by Le Groupe Banque Populaire (France); 34% state-owned; cap. 300.0m., res 1,673.0m., dep. 20,247.9m. (Dec. 2004); Dir-Gen. CHRISTIAN GOULT; 6 brs.

There are a number of offshore financial institutions based in the Comoros. In 2005 the Madagascar-based bank BNI–Crédit Lyonnais announced plans to open a branch in the Comoros. In 2006 it was announced that EXIM Bank (Tanzania) would open a subsidiary in Moroni and that a merchant bank would open during that year.

Savings Bank

Société Nationale de la Poste et des Services Financiers (SNPSF): Moroni; internet www.snpsf.km; f. 2004.

Development Bank

Banque de Développement des Comores: pl. de France, BP 298, Moroni; tel. (73) 0818; fax (73) 0397; e-mail bdc.moroni@snpt.km; f. 1982; provides loans, guarantees and equity participation for small- and medium-scale projects; 50% state-owned; cap. and res 1,242.0m., total assets 3,470.5m. (Dec. 2002); Pres. MZE CHEI OUBEIDI; Gen. Man. SAÏD ABDILLAHI.

Trade and Industry

GOVERNMENT AGENCIES

Office National du Commerce: Moroni; state-operated agency for the promotion and development of domestic and external trade.

Office National d'Importation et de Commercialisation du Riz (ONICOR): BP 748, Itsambouni, Moroni; tel. (73) 5566; fax (73) 0144; e-mail onicor_moroni@snpt.km; Gen. Man. MUSLIME MOUSSA.

Société de Développement de la Pêche Artisanale des Comores (SODEPAC): Moroni; state-operated agency overseeing fisheries development programme.

DEVELOPMENT ORGANIZATION

Centre Fédéral d'Appui au Développement Rural (CEFADER): Moroni; rural development org. with branches on each island.

CHAMBERS OF COMMERCE

Union des Chambres de Commerce des Comores: BP 763, Moroni; tel. (73) 0958; fax (73) 1983; privatized in 1995; Pres. MOINSALIMA MAHAMOUD SOIDIKI.

TRADE ASSOCIATION

Organisation Comorienne de la Vanille (OCOVA): BP 472, Moroni; tel. (73) 2709; fax (73) 2719.

There is a further association, the **Fédération du secteur privé comorien** (FSPC).

EMPLOYERS' ORGANIZATIONS

Club d'Actions des Promoteurs Economiques: Moroni; f. 1999; Head SAÏD HASSANE DINI.

Organisation Patronale des Comores (OPACO): Oasis, BP 981, Moroni; tel. (73) 0848; f. 1991; Pres. CHAMSOUDINE AHMED.

UTILITIES

MA-MWE—Gestion de l'Eau et de l'Electricité aux Comores: BP 1762, Moroni; tel. (73) 3130; fax (73) 2359; e-mail cee@snpt.km; f. as Electricité et Eau des Comores; transferred to private management and renamed Comorienne de l'Eau et de l'Electricité in 1997; renationalized and renamed Service Public de l'Eau et de l'Electricité in 2001; reprivatized in Jan. 2002 and renamed as above; responsible for the production and distribution of electricity and water; Dir-Gen. ALLOUI SAÏD ABASSE.

Société d'Electricité d'Anjouan (EDA): Nzwani; Technical Dir YOUSSOUF ALI OICHEH.

STATE-OWNED ENTERPRISE

Comores Hydrocarbures: BP 3840, Moroni; tel. (73) 0490; fax (73) 1818; imports petroleum products; scheduled for privatization; Man. Dir MOHAMED EL-AMINE SOEFOU.

MAJOR COMPANIES

Agecom: BP 2242, Oasis, Moroni; tel. (73) 3677; importation of food products and construction material.

Exportations Salimamoud: BP 287, Magoudjou, Moroni; tel. (73) 2394; fax (73) 2395; import and export of meat products, vanilla.

TRADE UNION

Confédération des Travailleurs/euses des Comores (CTC): BP 1199, Moroni; tel. and fax (73) 5143; f. 1996; Sec.-Gen. IBOUROI ALI TABIBOU.

Transport

ROADS

In 1999 there were an estimated 880 km of classified roads. About 76.5% of the network was paved in that year.

SHIPPING

The port of Mutsamudu, on Nzwani, can accommodate vessels of up to 11 m draught. Goods from Europe are routed via Madagascar, and coastal vessels connect the Comoros with the east coast of Africa. The country's registered merchant fleet at 31 December 2005 numbered 205 vessels, totalling 608,544 grt. Mayotte suspended ferry services to the other islands in the archipelago in late 2004 due to safety issues.

Société Comorienne de Navigation: Moroni; services to Madagascar.

CIVIL AVIATION

The international airport is at Moroni-Hahaya on Ngazidja. Work began on the upgrading of the airport in late 2004. Each of the other islands has a small airfield. International services were operated by Air Austral (Réunion), Air Mayotte, Air Tanzania, Sudan Airways, Precision Air (Tanzania) and Yemenia. Blue Line (France) also offered charter flights between June and September. Kenya Airways commenced flying to the Comoros and Mayotte in November 2006.

Comores Air Services: Moroni; tel. (73) 3366; internal services and international flights to Madagascar.

Comores Aviation International: Moroni; tel. (73) 3400; fax (73) 3401; internet www.comores-aviation.com; f. 1999; twice-weekly charter flights between Moroni and Mayotte; Dir JEAN-MARC HEINTZ.

Tourism

The principal tourist attractions are the beaches, underwater fishing and mountain scenery. Increasing numbers of Comorans resident abroad were choosing to visit the archipelago; in 2004 it was estimated that 58.3% of visitors to the Comoros were former Comoran residents. In 2005 hotel capacity amounted to an estimated 836 beds. Receipts from tourism totalled US $26m. in 1997, but had decreased to $10m. by 2004. Tourist arrivals increased to 27,474 in 1998, but had decreased to 19,551 by 2005. In late 2004 the ferry service to Mayotte was suspended, disrupting the tourism sector as many tourists travel via Mayotte.

Société Comorienne de Tourisme et d'Hôtellerie (COMOTEL): Itsandra Hotel, BP 1027, Moroni; tel. (73) 2365; national tourist agency; Dir-Gen. SITTI ATTOMANE.

Defence

The national army, the Force comorienne de défense (FCD), comprised about 1,500 men in mid-1997. In December 1996 an agreement was ratified with France, which provided for the permanent presence of a French military contingent in the Comoros. Following the military coup in April 1999, French military co-operation with the Comoros was suspended, but resumed in September 2002.

Defence Expenditure: Estimated at US $3m. in 1994.

Chief of Staff of the Comoran Armed Forces: Lt-Col SAÏD HAMZA.

Education

Education is officially compulsory for 10 years between six and 16 years of age. Primary education begins at the age of six and lasts for six years. Secondary education, beginning at 12 years of age, lasts for seven years, comprising a first cycle of four years and a second of three years. According to UNESCO estimates, enrolment at primary schools in 2003/04 included 86% of children in the relevant age-group (males 91%; females 80%), while enrolment at secondary schools in that year was equivalent to 35% of children in the relevant age-group (males 40%; females 30%), according to UNESCO estimates. Children may also receive a basic education through traditional Koranic schools, which are staffed by Comoran teachers. The Comoros' first university opened in December 2003, and in 2004/05 there were 2,187 students enrolled at that institution. Current expenditure by the Ministry of Education in 1995 was 3,381m. Comoros francs, representing 21.1% of total current government expenditure.

Mayotte

Introduction

Since the Comoros unilaterally declared independence in July 1975, Mayotte (Mahoré) has been administered separately by France. The independent Comoran state claims Mayotte as part of its territory and officially represents it in international organizations, including the UN. In December 1976, following a referendum in April (in which the population voted to renounce the status of an overseas territory), France introduced the special status of 'Collectivité territoriale' for the island. Following public consultation in 2000, in July 2001 Mayotte was declared a Collectivité départementale. The French Government is represented on Mayotte by an appointed Prefect. There is a Conseil général (General Council) with 19 members, who are elected by universal adult suffrage. Mayotte has one representative in the Assemblée nationale (National Assembly) in Paris, France, and two in the Sénat (Senate).

Following the coup in the Comoros in May 1978, Mayotte rejected the new Government's proposal that it should rejoin the other islands under a federal system, and reaffirmed its intention of remaining linked to France. Until 1999 the main political party on Mayotte, the Mouvement Populaire Mahorais (MPM), sought full departmental status for the island, but France was reluctant to grant this in view of Mayotte's underdeveloped condition. In December 1979 the French Assemblée nationale approved legislation to prolong Mayotte's special status for another five years, during which period a referendum was to be conducted on the island. In October 1984, however, the Assemblée nationale further extended Mayotte's status, and the referendum on the island's future was postponed indefinitely. The UN General Assembly has adopted several resolutions reaffirming the sovereignty of the Comoros over the island, and urging France to reach an agreement with the Comoran Government as soon as possible. The Organization of African Unity (OAU, now the African Union) has endorsed this view.

Following elections to the Assemblée nationale in March 1986, Henry Jean-Baptiste, representing an alliance of the Centre des Démocrates Sociaux (CDS) and the Union pour la Démocratie Française (UDF), was elected as deputy for Mayotte. Relations between the MPM and the French Government rapidly deteriorated following the Franco-African summit in November 1987, when the French Prime Minister, Jacques Chirac, expressed his reservations to the Comoran President concerning the elevation of Mayotte to the status of a full overseas department (despite his announcement, in early 1986, that he endorsed the MPM's aim to upgrade the status of Mayotte).

In November 1989 the Conseil général demanded that the French Government introduce measures to curb immigration to Mayotte from neighbouring islands, particularly from the Comoros. In January 1990 pressure by a group from the town of Mamoudzou resulted in increasing tension over the presence of Comoran refugees on the island. A paramilitary organization, 'Caiman' (which demanded the expulsion of illegal immigrants), was subsequently formed. In May the Comoran President, Saïd Mohamed Djohar, undertook to pursue peaceful dialogue to resolve the question of Mayotte's sovereignty, and issued a formal appeal to France to review the island's status. Mayotte was used as a strategic military base in late 1990, in preparation for French participation in multinational operations during the 1991 Gulf War.

In June 1992 increasing tension resulted in further attacks against Comoran immigrants resident in Mayotte. In early September representatives of the MPM met the French Prime Minister, Pierre Bérégovoy, to request the reintroduction of entry visas in order to restrict immigration from the Comoros. Later that month the MPM organized a boycott (which was widely observed) of Mayotte's participation in the French referendum on the Treaty on European Union, in protest at the French Government's refusal to introduce entry visas. In February 1993 a general strike, staged in support of wage increases, culminated in violent rioting; security forces were subsequently dispatched from Réunion and mainland France to restore order. At the end of February, following legal proceedings against him, Jean-Paul Costes was replaced as Prefect by Jean-Jacques Debacq.

At elections to the Assemblée nationale, which took place in March 1993, Jean-Baptiste was returned by 53.4% of votes cast, while Mansour Kamardine, the Secretary-General of the local branch of the right-wing French mainland party, the Rassemblement pour la République (RPR), obtained 44.3% of the vote. Kamardine subsequently accused Jean-Baptiste of illegally claiming the support of an electoral alliance of the RPR and the UDF, known as the Union pour la France, by forging the signatures of the Secretary-General of the RPR and his UDF counterpart on a document. However, Jean-Baptiste denied the allegations, and, in turn, began legal proceedings against Kamardine for alleged forgery and defamation. Elections to the Conseil général (which was enlarged from 17 to 19 members) took place in March 1994; the MPM secured 12 seats, the local branch of the RPR four seats, and independent candidates three seats.

At elections to the French Sénat, held in September 1995, the incumbent MPM representative, Marcel Henry, was returned by a large majority. During a visit to Mayotte in October, the French Secretary of State for Overseas Departments and Territories pledged that a referendum on the future status of the island would be conducted by 1999. In October 1996 he confirmed that two commissions, operating from Paris and Dzaoudzi, were preparing a consultation document, which would be presented in late 1997, and announced that the proposed referendum would take place before the end of the decade.

In July 1997 the relative prosperity of Mayotte was thought to have prompted separatist movements on the Comoran islands of Nzwani and Mwali to demand the restoration of French rule, and subsequently to declare their independence in August. Illegal immigration from the Comoros has continued to be a major concern for the authorities on Mayotte; during January–February 1997 some 6,000 Comorans were expelled from the island, with many more agreeing to leave voluntarily.

Meanwhile, uncertainty remained over the future status of Mayotte. In April 1998 one of the commissions charged with examining the issue submitted its report, which concluded that the present status of Collectivité territoriale was no longer appropriate, but did not advocate an alternative. In May the MPM declared its support for an adapted form of departmental administration, and urged the French authorities to decide on a date for a referendum. Two rounds of preparatory talks on the island's constitutional future took place in December between local political organizations and senior French government officials; a project was drafted which addressed various options, although no consensus was reached. Further talks, expected to take place in February 1999, were suspended, apparently owing to France's concerns over the continuing political instability in the Comoros, particularly as French sovereignty over Mayotte remained unrecognized by the UN and the OAU. In the following months Jean-Baptiste and Younoussa Bamana, the President of the Conseil général, increased pressure on the French Government to organize a referendum by the end of 1999. In August, following negotiations between the French Secretary of State for Overseas Departments and Territories, Jean-Jack Queyranne, and island representatives, Mayotte members of the RPR and the PS, as well as the leader of the MPM, Bamana, signed a draft document providing for the transformation of Mayotte into a 'Collectivité départementale', if approved at a referendum. However, both Henry and Jean-Baptiste rejected the document. The two politicians subsequently announced their departure from the MPM and formed a new political party entitled the Mouvement Départementaliste Mahorais (MDM), whilst reiterating their demands that Mayotte be granted full overseas department status. Following the approval of Mayotte's proposed new status by the Conseil général (by 14 votes to five) and the municipal councils, an accord to this effect was signed by Queyranne and political representatives of Mayotte on 27 January 2000. On 2 July a referendum was held, in which the population of Mayotte voted overwhelmingly in favour of the January accord, granting Mayotte the status of 'Collectivité départementale' for a period of 10 years. In November the commission established to define the terms of Mayotte's new status published a report which envisaged the transfer of executive power from the Prefect to the Conseil général by 2004, the dissolution of the position of Prefect by 2007 and the concession of greater powers to the island Government, notably in the area of regional co-operation.

At elections to the Conseil général held in March 2001 no party established a majority. The MPM experienced significant losses, with only four of its candidates being elected, while the RPR won five seats, the Mouvement des Citoyens (MDC) two, the MDM one, the PS one and various right-wing independent candidates six. Bamana was re-elected as President of the Conseil général. The French Parliament approved Mayotte's status as a 'Collectivité départementale' in July. Philippe de Mester replaced Pierre Bayle as Prefect in September.

At the first round of the French presidential election, which was held on 21 April 2002, Chirac received the highest number of votes on Mayotte (and overall), winning 43% of votes cast on the island; the second round, held on 5 May, was also won by Chirac, who secured 88.3% of votes on the island, defeating the candidate of the Front National, Jean-Marie Le Pen. At elections to the Assemblée nationale, held in June, Kamardine, the candidate for the Union pour la Majorité Présidentielle (UMP, which incorporated the RPR, the Démocratie Libérale and significant elements of the UDF), defeated the MDM-UDF candidate, Siadi Vita. Jean-Jacques Brot replaced de Mester as Prefect in July.

At elections to the Conseil général held in March 2004, in an alliance with the MPM, the UMP (renamed Union pour un Mouvement Populaire in November 2003) won nine seats, the same number won by a centre-left list (Force de Rassemblement et d'Alliance pour le Progrès—FRAP) comprising the MDM, the MDC and two independent candidates. Saïd Omar Oili, also an independent candidate, tipped the balance in favour of FRAP and was elected President of a coalition government. In June 2004 Mansour Kamardine successfully introduced a proposal to abrogate the statute authorizing polygamy, bringing Mayotte into line with metropolitan French law. While all those already married to more than one person would not be affected, anyone reaching the age of consent after 1 January 2005 would no longer be permitted to marry again until any previous marriage had been legally dissolved. Some 98% of the population of Mayotte were adherents of Islam, a religion that accepts polygamy. In January 2005 Jean-Paul Kihl replaced Jean-Jacques Brot as Prefect. In late January 2007 Vincent Bouvier was appointed to replace Kihl as Prefect, although that position was scheduled to be abolished in 2007.

Nicolas Sarkozy of the UMP secured 30.5% of the votes cast on Mayotte in the first round of the French presidential election, held on 22 April 2007. However, in the second round, which took place on 6 May, Ségolène Royal of the PS won 60.0% of the votes cast, although Sarkozy was elected to the presidency. At elections to the Assemblée nationale, held on 10 and 17 June, Kamardine, was defeated by Abdoulatifou Aly, who was affiliated to the Mouvement Démocrate (MoDem), which had been formed following the presidential election by François Bayrou, the leader of the UDF, to oppose Sarkozy's UMP.

Mayotte's gross domestic product (GDP) per head was estimated at 4,050 French francs in 1991. Between the censuses of 1991 and 2002 the population of Mayotte increased at an average annual rate of 10.1%. The economy of Mayotte is based mainly on agriculture. In 2002 10.2% of the employed labour force were actively engaged in this sector. Vanilla, ylang ylang (an ingredient of perfume), coffee and copra are the main export products, but exports are limited by production costs and the local market is small. In 2005 no vanilla was exported, owing to global oversupply. Rice, cassava and maize are cultivated for domestic consumption; in 2003 it was estimated that some 44% of the population was dependent on *gratte* (subsistence) farming. Mayotte's total fishing catch declined from an estimated 10,055 metric tons in 2001 to 2,378 tons in 2005. Industry (which is dominated by the construction sector) engaged 23.0% of the employed population in 2002. There are no mineral resources on the island; in 2003 imports of mineral products comprised 3.5%, and base metals and metal products 7.8% of the cost of total imports. Total electricity production in 2004 was 139m. kWh. In 2005 electricity charges were reduced by more than one-fifth in line with new legislation that pegged local charges to those of metropolitan France until January 2007. Services engaged 66.8% of the employed population in 2002. The annual total of tourist arrivals (excluding cruise-ship passengers) increased from 6,700 in 1995 to 38,763 in 2005. Receipts from tourism in 2005 totalled €14.5m. In that year some 29% of tourists came from metropolitan France and 59% from Réunion.

In 2005 Mayotte's total budget revenue was €269.4m., while total expenditure was €252.0m. Official debt totalled 435.7m. francs at 31 December 1995. Mayotte recorded deflation of 2.0% in the year to December 2003. As Mayotte's labour force has continued to increase, mostly owing to a high birth rate and continued illegal immigration, youth unemployment has caused particular concern. In 1997 41% of the population were unemployed, of whom some 37.8% were under 25 years of age; by late 2003, however, unemployment had declined to 29%. The principal source of imports in 2003 was France (55.1%). France was also the principal market for exports (taking 61.4% of exports in that year); the other significant purchaser was the Comoros (24.7%). The principal exports in 2003 were fish products, ylang ylang and vanilla. The principal imports in that year were foodstuffs, machinery and appliances, chemicals and related products, base metals and metal products and transport equipment. At the end of 2003 the annual trade deficit was calculated at €180.4m. attributed largely to a 35% fall in exports; in terms of volume, exports declined by some 34% (2,117 metric tons, at a value of €4,088m.) during 2003. Exports of oil of ylang ylang had decreased in value by 40%; however, a revaluation of the price of vanilla meant that exports increased in value by 22% even though their volume had fallen by some 17%. Exports of farmed fish increased by 20% in terms of both volume and value following changes in European Union regulation, introduced in July, governing aquaculture in Mayotte. Of the total catch in 2004 some 170 tons was supplied by fish farms; although it was thought that there was potential for development of aquaculture in the export market, the sector's expansion was limited by the cost of air freight. In 2003 Mayotte imported goods worth €184.8m.

In April 1995 an economic and social programme was agreed with the French Government for the period 1995–99. Later in that year Mayotte received credit from France to finance further investment in infrastructure, particularly in the road network. In 1996 construction began on a plant to produce Coca-Cola products in the industrial zone around Longoni; construction costs were estimated at 16m.–18m. francs. In September 2000 an economic and social development agreement was signed with the French Government for the period 2000–04, under which Mayotte was to receive 4,386m. French francs for development assistance. The construction of a new quay at Longoni, at a cost of €120m., was expected to provide an additional 1,500 jobs, bringing the total to 2,000 by the time of its scheduled completion in 2007.

The official population of Mayotte was 160,265 at the census of 30 July 2002. The principal communes are Mamoudzou (population 45,485 at the 2002 census), Dzaoudzi (the capital, 12,308) and Koungou (15,383). The census showed that there were some 55,000 foreign nationals living in Mayotte, of whom 53,000 were Comorans. In 2002 there were less than 10,000 valid residence permits and it was estimated that around 12% of the population were illegal immigrants. However, in November 2003 Jean-Jacques Brot claimed that as many as one in four people in Mayotte were illegal immigrants; President Bamana went as far as to claim that some 70% of the prison population were foreigners. Studies that year suggested that, while the average number of immigrants between 1997 and 2002 had risen to 4,300, some 3,600 people were leaving Mayotte every year. According to official figures, more than two-thirds of the women who gave birth in Mayotte in 2004 were from the Comoros. The 2004 budget allocated €2m. towards the creation of an office for study of the immigration issue and purchase of a radar system. Some €6.7m. was allocated towards the expansion of Majicavo prison. France is responsible for the defence of the island: in August 2005 there were 1,100 French troops and gendarmes stationed on Mayotte and Réunion.

Statistical Survey

Source (unless otherwise indicated): Institut National de la Statistique et des Etudes Economiques de Mayotte; Z.I. Kawéni, BP 1362, 97600 Mamoudzou; tel. 269-61-36-35; fax 269-61-39-56; e-mail antenne-mayotte@insee.fr; internet www.insee.fr/mayotte.

AREA AND POPULATION

Area: 374 sq km (144 sq miles).

Population (before adjustment for double counting): 131,368 (males 66,600, females 64,768) at census of 5 August 1997; 160,301 (males 80,281, females 80,020) at census of 30 July 2002. After adjustments for double counting, the net population was recorded as: 131,320 in 1997; 160,265 in 2002.

Density (30 July 2002, based on population after adjustment for double counting): 428.5 per sq km.

Population by Country of Origin (2002, before adjustment for double counting): Mayotte 103,705; France 6,323; Comoros 45,057; Madagascar-Mauritius-Seychelles 4,601; Total (incl. others) 160,301.

Principal Towns (population of communes at 2002 census, after adjustment for double counting): Mamoudzou 45,485; Koungou 15,383; Dzaoudzi (capital) 12,308.

Births and Deaths (2004): Registered live births 7,452 (birth rate 39.0 per 1,000); Registered deaths 513 (death rate 3.0 per 1,000).

Expectation of Life (years at birth): 74.5 (males 72.0; females 76.0) in 2004.

Economically Active Population (persons aged 15 years and over, census of 30 July 2002): Agriculture and fishing 3,229; Electricity, gas and water 519; Industry 1,105; Construction 5,614; Wholesale and retail trade 5,435; Transport and telecommunications 2,007; Other marketable services 852; Finance and insurance 145; Other non-marketable services 12,608; *Total employed* 31,514 (males 22,182, females 9,332); Unemployed 13,044 (males 5,179, females 7,865); *Total labour force* 44,558 (males 27,361, females 17,197). *December 2005:* Unemployed 12,920.

HEALTH AND WELFARE

Key Indicators

Total Fertility Rate (children per woman, 2004): 4.5.

Physicians (per 1,000 head, 1997): 0.4.

Hospital Beds (per 1,000 head, 1997): 1.4.

For definitions see explanatory note on p. vi.

AGRICULTURE, ETC.

Livestock (2003): Cattle 17,235; Goats 22,811; Chickens 80,565.

Fishing (metric tons, live weight, 2005): Capture 2,214 (Skipjack tuna 472; Yellowfin tuna 302; Tuna-like fishes 274); Aquaculture 164; *Total catch* 2,378. Source: FAO.

INDUSTRY

Electric Energy (million kWh, net production): 139 in 2004.

FINANCE

Currency and Exchange Rates: 100 cent = 1 euro. *Sterling and Dollar Equivalents* (31 May 2007): £1 sterling = €1.4698; US $1 = €0.7433; €100 = £68.04 = US $134.53. *Average Exchange Rate* (euros per US dollar): 0.805 in 2004; 0.804 in 2005; 0.797 in 2006. The French franc was used until the end of February 2002. Euro notes and coins were introduced on 1 January 2002, and the euro became the sole legal tender from 18 February. Some of the figures in this Survey are still in terms of French francs.

Budget of the Collectivity (€ million, 2005): Total revenue 269.4; Total expenditure 252.0.

French State Expenditure (€ million, 2005): Direct expenditure 249.7; Indirect expenditure 73.6; Total expenditure 324.3.

Money Supply (million French francs at 31 December 1997): Currency outside banks 789; Demand deposits 266; Total money 1,055.

Cost of Living (Consumer Price Index for December; base: December 1996 = 100): 105.0 in 2003; 108.5 in 2004; 107.6 in 2005.

Expenditure on the Gross Domestic Product (€ million, 2001, provisional estimates): Government final consumption expenditure 288; Private final consumption expenditure 357; Gross fixed capital formation 151; *Total domestic expenditure* 796; Exports of goods and services 11; *Less* Imports of goods and services 183; *GDP in purchasers' values* 624. Note: Recorded accounts are not available; figures represent the findings of the working group (Comptes Economiques Rapides sur l'Outre-Mer—CEROM) set up to find a methodology to produce reliable GDP estimates.

EXTERNAL TRADE

Principal Commodities (€ million, 2005): *Imports c.i.f.:* Foodstuffs 55.9; Mineral products 40.5; Chemical products 19.5; Plastic materials and rubber 8.2; Base metals and metal products 19.2; Machinery and appliances 36.4; Transport equipment 30.7; Total (incl. others) 274.3. *Exports f.o.b.* (incl. re-exported goods): Foodstuffs 1.0; Chemical products 0.8 (Ylang-ylang 0.5); Plastic materials and rubber 0.8; Base metals and metal products 0.2; Machinery and appliances 1.2; Transport equipment 1.4; Total (incl. others) 5.2.

Principal Trading Partners (€ million, 2003): *Imports*: France 101.8; South Africa 8.9; Thailand 6.5; People's Republic of China 5.9; Germany 5.2; Spain 5.0; Mauritius 4.6; Italy 4.3; Total (incl. others) 184.8. *Exports*: France 2.7; Comoros 1.1; Réunion 0.3; Total (incl. others) 4.4. Source: Service des Douanes.

TRANSPORT

Road Traffic (1998): Motor vehicles in use 8,213.

Shipping (2005): *Maritime Traffic* Vessel movements 530; Goods unloaded 297,783 metric tons; Goods loaded 54,809 metric tons; Passengers 7,631 (arrivals 3,625, departures 4,006). *Barges* (2002): Passengers 11,845; Light vehicles 532. *Cruise Ships:* Vessel movements 36; Passengers 6,857.

Civil Aviation (2005): *Passengers Carried*: 200, 389 (arrivals 91,627, departures 108,762); *Freight Carried*: 1,395 metric tons; *Post Carried* 308 metric tons.

TOURISM

Foreign Tourist Arrivals (excluding cruise-ship passengers): 23,000 in 2003; 32,191 in 2004; 38,763 in 2005.

Foreign Tourist Arrivals by Country of Residence (2005): France (metropolitan) 11,074; Réunion 22,803; Total (incl. others) 38,763.

Tourism Receipts (€ million): 12.3 in 2003; 13.7 in 2004; 14.5 in 2005.

COMMUNICATIONS MEDIA

Telephones ('000 main lines in use, 2005, estimate): 10.0.

Mobile Cellular Telephones ('000 subscribers, 2005, estimate): 48.1.

Internet Users ('000, 2000): 1.8.

Source: International Telecommunication Union.

EDUCATION

Pre-primary (2005): 67 schools; 10,651 pupils.

Primary (2005): 113 schools; 31,164 pupils.

General Secondary (2005): 16 schools; 14,569 pupils.

Vocational and Technical (2005): 8 institutions; 6,298 students.

Students Studying in France or Réunion (2005): Secondary 2,293; Higher 2,345; Total 4,638.

Teaching Staff (2005): Primary 2,169; Secondary 1,419.

Directory

The Constitution

Mayotte has an elected General Council (Conseil général), comprising 19 members, which assists the Prefect in the administration of the island. Under the status of Collectivité départementale, which was adopted by the French Parliament in July 2001, executive power was transferred from the Prefect to the President of the Conseil général in April 2004, and the position of Prefect was to be dissolved by 2007.

The Government

(August 2007)

Prefect: VINCENT BOUVIER.

Secretary-General: GUY MASCRES.

Deputy to the French National Assembly: ABDOULATIFOU ALY (MoDem).

Representatives to the French Senate: ADRIEN GIRAUD (MDM, Union Centriste), SOIBAHADDINE IBRAHIM (UMP).

Economic and Social Adviser: ANZIZA MOUSTOIFA.

GOVERNMENT DEPARTMENTS

Department of Agriculture and Forestry: 15 rue Mariazé, BP 103, 97600 Mamoudzou; tel. 269-61-12-13; fax 269-61-10-31.

Department of Education: BP 76, 97600 Mamoudzou; tel. 269-61-10-24; fax 269-61-09-87; e-mail vice-rectorat@ac-mayotte.fr; internet www.ac-mayotte.fr.

Department of Health and Social Security: rue de l'Hôpital, BP 104, 97600 Mamoudzou; tel. 269-61-12-25; fax 269-60-19-56.

Department of Public Works: rue Mariazé, BP 109, 97600 Mamoudzou; tel. 269-61-12-54; fax 269-60-92-85; e-mail de-mayotte@equipement.gouv.fr.

Department of Work, Employment and Training: pl. Mariazé, BP 174, 97600 Mamoudzou; tel. 269-61-16-57; fax 269-61-03-37.

Department of Youth and Sports: rue Mariazé, BP 94, 97600 Mamoudzou; tel. 269-61-10-87; fax 269-61-01-26.

Conseil général

108 rue de l'Hôpital, BP 101, 97600 Mamoudzou; tel. 269-61-12-33; fax 269-61-10-18.

The Conseil général comprises 19 members. At elections held on 21 and 28 March 2004, the Union pour un Mouvement Populaire (UMP) won eight seats in alliance with the Mouvement Populaire Mahorais (MPM), which secured one seat, while the Mouvement Départementaliste Mahorais (MDM) and the Mouvement des Citoyens (MDC), also in alliance, obtained five and two seats, respectively; independent candidates were elected to the remaining three seats.

President: SAÏD OMAR ALI (Independent).

Political Organizations

Fédération de Mayotte de l'Union pour un Mouvement Populaire (UMP): route nationale, Immeuble 'Jardin Créole', 97600 Mamoudzou; tel. 269-61-64-64; fax 269-60-87-89; e-mail ahamed.attoumani@wanadoo.fr; centre-right; local branch of the metropolitan party; Sec.-Gen. MANSOUR KAMARDINE; Departmental Sec. AHAMED ATTOUMANI.

Fédération du Front National: route nationale 1, M'tsahara, 97630 M'tzamboro; BP 1331, 97600 Mamoudzou Cédex; tel. and fax 269-60-50-24; e-mail fatna@frontnational.com; Regional Sec. HUGUETTE FATNA.

Fédération du Mouvement National Républicain (MNR) de Mayotte: 15 rue des Réfugiers, 97615 Pamandzi; tel. and fax 269-60-33-21; Departmental Sec. ABDOU MIHIDJAY.

Mouvement de la Gauche Ecologiste de Mayotte: 33 ave des Jardins, Localité de Pamandzi, 97600 Pamandzi; tel. and fax 269-61-09-70; internet www.lesverts.fr; fmrly Les Verts Mayotte; affiliated to Mouvement de la Gauche Réunionnaise; Gen. Sec. AHAMADA SALIME.

Mouvement Départementaliste Mahorais (MDM): 97610 Dzaoudzi; f. 1999 by fmr mems of the MPM; seeks full overseas departmental status for Mayotte; Pres. ZOUBERT ADINANI.

Mouvement des Citoyens (MDC): Chirongui; Leader ALI HALIFA.

Mouvement Populaire Mahorais (MPM): 97610 Dzaoudzi; seeks departmental status for Mayotte; Leader YOUNOUSSA BAMANA.

Parti Socialiste (PS): Dzaoudzi; local branch of the metropolitan party; Fed. Sec. AHMADA FAHARDINE.

Judicial System

Palais de Justice: 12 rue de l'Hôpital, BP 106 (Kawéni), 97600 Mamoudzou; tel. 269-61-11-15; fax 269-61-19-63.

Tribunal Supérieur d'Appel

16 rue de l'Hôpital, BP 106, 97600 Mamoudzou; tel. 269-61-11-15; fax 269-61-19-63; Pres. JEAN-BAPTISTE FLORI; Prosecutor JEAN-LOUIS BEC.

Procureur de la République: JEAN-LOUIS BEC.

Tribunal de Première Instance: Pres. ALAIN CHATEAUNEUF.

Religion

Muslims comprise about 98% of the population. Most of the remainder are Christians, mainly Roman Catholics.

CHRISTIANITY

The Roman Catholic Church

Mayotte is within the jurisdiction of the Apostolic Administrator of the Comoros.

Office of the Apostolic Administrator: BP 1012, 97600 Mamoudzou; tel. and fax 269-61-11-53.

The Press

Flash Infos Mayotte: BP 60, 97600 Mamoudzou; tel. 269-61-54-45; fax 269-61-54-47; e-mail flash-infos@wanadoo.fr; internet www.mayottehebdo.com; f. 1999; daily e-mail bulletin; Dir LAURENT CANAVATE.

Le Mahorais: 15 Lot. Bamcolo, Majicavo, 97600 Mamoudzou; tel. 269-61-66-75; fax 269-61-66-72; weekly; French; Publ. Dir SAMUEL BOSHER; Editor-in-Chief CHLOÉ REMONDIÈRE.

Le Mawana: BP 252, Z.I. Kawéni, 97600 Mamoudzou; tel. 269-61-73-84; internet www.lemawana.fr; f. 2005; weekly; French; Publ. Dir MADI ABDOU N'TRO.

Mayotte Hebdo: BP 60, 97600 Mamoudzou; tel. 269-61-20-04; fax 269-60-35-90; e-mail mayotte.hebdo@wanadoo.fr; internet www.mayottehebdo.com; f. 2000; weekly; French; incl. the economic supplement *Mayotte Eco* and cultural supplement *Tounda* (weekly); Dir LAURENT CANAVATE; circ. 2,000.

Zan'Goma: Impasse du Jardin Fleuri, Cavani, 97600 Mamoudzou; f. 2005; monthly; French; Publ. Dir MONCEF MOUHOUDHOIRE.

Broadcasting and Communications

TELECOMMUNICATIONS

France Télécom Mayotte: Résidence Allamanda, rue de la Grande Traversée, 97600 Mamoudzou; tel. 269-61-00-14; fax 269-61-19-02; e-mail richard.roques@francetelecom.com.

Mayotte Télécom Mobile: mobile cellular telephone operator; local operation of Société Réunionnaise du Radiotéléphone based in Réunion.

RADIO AND TELEVISION

Réseau France Outre-mer (RFO): 1 rue du Jardin, BP 103, 97615 Pamandzi; tel. 269-60-10-17; fax 269-60-16-06; e-mail annick.henry@rfo.fr; internet www.rfo.fr; f. 1977; acquired by Groupe France Télévisions in 2004; fmrly Société Nationale de Radio-Télévision Française d'Outre-mer; radio broadcasts in French and more than 70% in Mahorian; television transmissions began in 1986; a satellite service was launched in 2000; Gen. Man. FRANÇOIS GUILBEAU; Regional Dir JEAN-FRANÇOIS MOENNAN.

Finance

(br(s). = branch(es);)

BANKS

Issuing Authority

Institut d'Emission d'Outre-mer: ave de la Préfecture, BP 500, 97600 Mamoudzou; tel. 269-61-05-05; fax 269-61-05-02; Dir MAX REMBLIN.

Commercial Banks

Banque Française Commerciale Océan Indien: pl. du Marché, BP 222, 97600 Mamoudzou; tel. 269-61-10-91; fax 269-61-17-40; e-mail mayotte@bfcoi.com; internet www.bfcoi.com; f. 1976; jtly owned by Société Générale and Mauritius Commercial Bank Ltd; Pres. GÉRALD LACAZE; Dir.-Gen. JEAN-MARIE D'ESPAGNAC; br. at Dzaoudzi.

Banque de la Réunion: 30 pl. Mariage, 97600 Mamoudzou; tel. 269-61-20-30; fax 269-61-20-28; 3 brs.

BRED Banque Populaire: Centre d'Affaires Mayotte, pl. Mariage, Z.I. 3, 97600 Mamoudzou; tel. 269-90-71-60; fax 269-90-29-57.

INSURANCE

AGF: pl. Mariage, BP 184, 97600 Mamoudzou; tel. 269-61-44-33; fax 269-61-14-89; e-mail jl.henry@wanadoo.fr; Gen. Man. JEAN-LUC HENRY.

Groupama: BP 665, Z.I. Nel, Lot 7, 97600 Mamoudzou; tel. 269-62-59-92; fax 269-60-76-08.

Prudence Créole: Immeuble Sana, rue du Commerce, BP 480, 97600 Mamoudzou; tel. 269-61-11-10; fax 269-61-11-21; e-mail prudencecreolemayotte@wanadoo.fr; 87% owned by Groupe Générali; 2 brs.

Vectra Paic Océan Indien: BP 65, 55 champs des Ylangs, 97680 Combani; tel. 269-62-44-54; fax 269-62-46-97; e-mail cfonteneau@wanadoo.fr.

Trade and Industry

DEVELOPMENT ORGANIZATION

Agence Française de Développement (AFD): ave de la Préfecture, BP 500, 97600 Mamoudzou; tel. 269-61-05-05; fax 269-61-05-02; internet www.afd.fr; Dir JEAN-FRANÇOIS HOARAU.

EMPLOYERS' ORGANIZATIONS

Mouvement des Entreprises de France Mayotte (MEDEF): Z.I. Kawéni, Immeuble GMOI, BP 570, 97600 Mamoudzou; tel. 269-61-44-22; fax 269-61-46-10; e-mail contact@medef-mayotte.com; internet www.medef-mayotte.com; Pres. SERGE CASTEL.

Ordre National des Médecins: BP 675 Kawéni, 97600 Mamoudzou; tel. 269-61-02-47; fax 269-61-36-61.

UTILITIES

Electricity

Electricité de Mayotte (EDM): BP 333, Z.I. Kawéni, 97600 Kawéni; tel. 269-61-44-44; fax 269-60-10-92; e-mail edm.mayotte@wanadoo.fr; f. 1997; subsidiary of SAUR.

Water

Syndicat des Eaux: BP 289, 97600 Mamoudzou; tel. 269-62-11-11; fax 269-62-10-31.

Major Companies

TRADE UNIONS

Confédération Inter-Syndicale de Mayotte (CISMA-CFDT): 18 rue Mahabou, BP 1038, 97600 Mamoudzou; tel. 269-61-12-38; fax 269-61-36-16; f. 1993; affiliated to the Confédération Française Démocratique du Travail; Gen. Sec. SAÏD BOINALI.

Affiliated unions incl.:

ScDEN-CGT: BP 793 Kawéni, 97600 Mamoudzou; tel. and fax 269-61-10-97; e-mail scdencgt.mayotte@free.fr; internet cgtprofsmayotte.free.fr; affiliated to the Confédération Générale du Travail; represents teaching staff; Sec.-Gen. NOEL JEGOU.

SGEN-CFDT: c/o CISMA, 18 rue Mahabou, BP 1038, 97600 Mamoudzou; tel. 269-61-12-38; fax 269-61-18-09; e-mail mayotte@sgen.cfdt.fr; internet etranger.sgen-cfdt.org/mayotte/sgenmayo.htm; affiliated to the Fédération des Syndicats Généraux de l'Education Nationale et de la Recherche; represents teaching staff; Sec.-Gen. FRANÇOISE HOLZAPFEL.

Fédération Départementale des Syndicats d'Exploitants Agricoles de Mayotte (FDSEAM): 150 rue Mbalamanga-Mtsapéré, 97600 Mamoudzou; tel. and fax 269-61-34-83; e-mail fdsea.mayotte@wanadoo.fr; affiliated to the Fédération Nationale des Syndicats d'Exploitants; Pres. AMBODY ALI; Dir MOUHTAR RACHIDE.

SNES Mayotte (SNES-FSU): 12 Résidence Bellecombe, 110 Lotissement Les Trois Vallées, Majicavo, 97600 Mamoudzou; tel. 269-62-50-58; fax 269-62-53-39; e-mail mayotte@snes.edu; internet www.mayotte.snes.edu; affiliated to the Syndicat National des Enseignements de Second Degré; represents teaching staff in secondary education; Sec. FRÉDÉRIC LOUVIER.

Union Départementale Force Ouvrière de Mayotte (FO): 20, rue Mahabou, BP 1109, 97600 Mamoudzou; tel. 269-61-18-39; fax 269-61-22-45; e-mail el.hadi@wanadoo.fr; Sec. Gen. EL HADI SOUMAILA.

Transport

ROADS

In 1998 the road network totalled approximately 230 km, of which 90 km were main roads.

SHIPPING

Coastal shipping is provided by locally owned small craft. There is a deep-water port at Longoni. Construction of a second quay at Longoni was proposed under the 2006 budget.

Service des Affaires Maritimes Mayotte: BP 37, 97615 Pamandzi; tel. 269-60-31-38; fax 269-60-31-39; e-mail sam-mayotte@equipement.gouv.fr; Head of Service MATTHIEU LE GUERN.

Service des Transports Maritimes (STM): BP 186, 97610 Dzaoudzi; tel. 269-60-10-69; fax 269-60-80-25; internet www.mayotte-stm.com; Dir MICHEL KERAMBRUN; 8 vessels.

CIVIL AVIATION

There is an airport at Dzaoudzi, serving daily commercial flights to the Comoros; four-times weekly flights to Réunion; twice-weekly services to Madagascar; and weekly services to Kenya and Mozambique. In January 2004 plans were approved for the construction a new runway to allow the commencement of direct flights to Paris, France. The proposed establishment of Air Mayotte International was abandoned in September 2004. Expansion and modernization of the airport at Pamandzi was envisaged under the 2006 budget.

Air Austral: pl. Mariage, BP 1429, 97600 Mamoudzou; tel. 269-60-90-90; fax 269-61-61-94; e-mail mayotte@air-austral.com; internet www.air-austral.com; Pres. GÉRARD ETHÈVE.

Tourism

Tropical scenery provides the main tourist attraction. Excluding cruise-ship passengers, Mayotte received 38,763 visitors in 2005; tourism receipts totalled €14.5m. in 2005. In 2002 there were nine hotels with some 350 rooms.

Comité du Tourisme de Mayotte: rue de la Pompe, BP 1169, 97600 Mamoudzou; tel. 269-61-09-09; fax 269-61-03-46; e-mail contact@mayotte-tourisme.com; internet www.mayotte-tourisme.com; Dir GEORGE MECS.

Bibliography

Abdelaziz, M. R. *Comores: Les institutions d'un état mort-né*. Paris, L'Harmattan, 2001.

Caminade, P. *Comores-Mayotte, une histoire néocoloniale*. Marseille, Agone, 2004.

Chamoussidine, M. *Comores: L'enclos ou une existence en derivé*. Moroni, KomÉdit, 2002.

Cornu, H. *Paris et Bourbon, La politique française dans l'Océan indien*. Paris, Académie des Sciences d'Outre-mer, 1984.

Mattoir, N. *Les Comores de 1975 à 1990: Une histoire politique mouvementée*. Paris, L'Harmattan, 2004.

Mmadi, A. *Pourquoi les Comores s'enfoncent-elles?* Grenoble, Thot, 2003.

Newitt, M. *The Comoros Islands: Struggle against Dependency in the Indian Ocean*. Aldershot, Gower, 1985.

Perri, P. *Les nouveaux mercenaires*. Paris, L'Harmattan, 1994.

Salesse, Y. *Mayotte: L'illusion de la France, propositions pour une décolonisation*. Paris, L'Harmattan, 1995.

Weinberg, S. *Last of the Pirates: The Search for Bob Denard*. London, Jonathan Cape, 1994.

Vérin, E., and P. *Histoire de la révolution comorienne: Décolonisation, idéologie et séisme social*. Paris, L'Harmattan, 1999.

THE DEMOCRATIC REPUBLIC OF THE CONGO

Physical and Social Geography

PIERRE GOUROU

PHYSICAL FEATURES

Covering an area of 2,344,885 sq km (905,365 sq miles), the Democratic Republic of the Congo (DRC, formerly Zaire) is bordered by the Republic of the Congo to the north-west, by the Central African Republic and Sudan to the north, by Uganda, Rwanda, Burundi and Tanzania to the east, and by Zambia and Angola to the south. There is a short coastline at the outlet of the River Congo. The DRC is, after Sudan, the largest country of sub-Saharan Africa. Despite its vast size, it lacks any particularly noteworthy points of relief, affording it a considerable natural advantage. Lying across the Equator, the DRC has an equatorial climate in the whole of the central region. Average temperatures range from 26°C in the coastal and basin areas to 18°C in the mountainous regions. Rainfall is plentiful in all seasons. In the north (Uele) the winter of the northern hemisphere is a dry season; in Katanga (formerly Shaba) in the south, the winter of the southern hemisphere is dry. The only arid region (less than 800 mm of rain per annum) is an extremely small area on the bank of the lower Congo.

The basin of the River Congo forms the country's dominant geographical feature. This basin had a deep tectonic origin; the continental shelf of Africa had given way to form an immense hollow, which drew towards it the waters from the north (Ubangi), from the east (Uele, Arruwimi), and from the south (Lualaba—that is the upper branch of the River Congo, Kasaï, Kwango). The crystalline continental shelf levels out at the periphery into plateaux in Katanga and the Congo-Nile ridge. The most broken-up parts of this periphery can be found in the west, in Bas-Congo, where the river cuts the folds of a Pre-Cambrian chain by a 'powerful breach', and above all in the east. Here, as a result of the volcanic overflow from the Virunga, they are varied by an upheaval of the rift valleys (where Lakes Tanganyika, Kivu, Edward and Albert are located).

The climate is generally conducive to agriculture and wood-forestry. Evergreen equatorial forest covers approximately 1m. sq km in the equatorial and sub-equatorial regions. In the north as in the south of this evergreen forest, tropical vegetation appears, with many trees that lose their leaves in the dry season. Vast stretches from the north to the south are, probably as a result of frequent fires, covered by sparse forest land, where trees grow alongside grasses (*biombo* from east Africa), and savannah dotted with shrubs.

The natural resources of the DRC are immense: its climate is favourable to profitable agriculture; the forests, if rationally exploited, could yield excellent results; the abundance of water should eventually be useful to industry and agriculture; and finally, there is considerable mineral wealth. The network of waterways is naturally navigable. The Congo carries the second largest volume of water of any river in the world. With the average flow to the mouth being 40,000 cu m per second, there are enormous possibilities for power generation, some of which are being realized at Inga. Indeed, the potential hydroelectric resources are considerable in the whole of the Congo basin.

The major exports of the DRC derive from the exploitation of its mineral resources. Copper is mined in upper Katanga, as are other metals—tin, silver, uranium, cobalt, manganese and tungsten. Diamonds are found in Kasaï, and tin, columbite, etc. in the east, around Maniema. In addition, many other mineral resources (such as iron ore and bauxite) await exploitation.

POPULATION

The DRC's population comprises numerous ethnic groups, which the external boundaries separate. The Kongo people are divided between the DRC, the Republic of the Congo and Angola; the Zande between the DRC and Sudan; the Chokwe between the DRC and Angola; the Bemba between the DRC and Zambia; and the Alur between the DRC and Uganda. Even within its frontiers, the ethnic and linguistic geography of the DRC is highly diverse. The most numerous people are: the Kongo; the people of Kwangu-Kwilu, who are related to them; the Mongo, with their many subdivisions, who inhabit the Great Forest; the Luba, with their related groups the Lulua and Songe; the Bwaka; and the Zande. The majority speak Bantu languages, of which there is a great diversity. However, the north of the DRC belongs linguistically to Sudan. The extreme linguistic variety of the DRC is maintained to some extent by the ability of the people to speak several languages, by the existence of 'intermediary' languages (a Kongo dialect, a Luba dialect, Swahili and Lingala) and by the use of French.

According to UN estimates, the country's population was 60,644,000 at mid-2006. About 80% of the DRC's inhabitants reside in rural areas. The average density of population is low (estimated by the UN to be 25.9 per sq km at mid-2006), and the population is unevenly distributed. The population density in the Great Forest is only about one-half of the national average, with stretches of several tens of thousands of sq km virtually deserted, although this is not because the area cannot accommodate more people. However, it is clear that the population (with the exception of some pygmies) cannot increase in density as long as the forest is preserved. Indeed, certain areas belonging to the forest belt but partly cleared for cultivation, although they have no particular natural advantages, have higher than average densities. At the northern edge of the Great Forest the population density increases up to 20 people per sq km, and is then reduced to one or two in the extreme north of the country. Certain parts of Mayombé (Bas-Congo) have 100 people per sq km, but the south of the republic is sparsely populated (at 1–3 people per sq km). The capital, Kinshasa, had 6,049,000 inhabitants in mid-2005, according to UN estimates, and is the principal urban centre. The second most important town, Lubumbashi, had an estimated 1,179,000 inhabitants in mid-2005, while other major centres of population were Kolwezi (1,270,000) and Mbuji-Mayi (1,024,000).

Recent History

GREGORY MTHEMBU-SALTER

The European colonization of the area now comprising the Democratic Republic of the Congo (DRC, formerly Zaire) dates from 1879, when the Association internationale du Congo (AIC), under the control of King Léopold II of Belgium, established a chain of trading stations along the River Congo. Economic exploitation of the surrounding territory expanded rapidly in response to the increasing international demand for wild rubber following the invention of rubber tyres for motor vehicles. The AIC's collection of rubber involved the systematic infliction of atrocities on the indigenous population, and, as a result, by 1908 as much as one-third of the population was estimated to have died prematurely or been killed, in what was arguably the first genocide of the modern era. Largely as a result of British and US diplomatic pressure following sustained pressure from civil society groupings and churches, responsibility for the administration of the territory was transferred from the King to the Belgian Government, and the Congo became a Belgian colony, known as the Belgian Congo.

Under Belgian rule, African political activity in the Congo was forbidden, and instead radical Congolese organized in 'cultural associations'. The most prominent of the associations was the Alliance des Ba-Kongo (ABAKO), led by Joseph Kasavubu. Following a violent demonstration organized by ABAKO in January 1959, the Belgian Government, which had previously been highly complacent about the need to move towards independence, was alarmed at the prospect of a prolonged colonial war, and greatly accelerated the independence process. Belgium favoured the creation of a unitary state, based on the centralized colonial system, while the ABAKO and most other Congolese political groups, except Patrice Lumumba's Mouvement national congolais (MNC), demanded a federal structure. The constitutional arrangements that eventually emerged were a compromise, affirming the unitary character of the state, but allowing each province its own government and legislature, and equal representation in a national senate.

THE FIRST REPUBLIC

The independence of the Republic of the Congo was proclaimed on 30 June 1960, with Kasavubu installed as President and Lumumba as Prime Minister. Five days later the armed forces mutinied. Their demands were partly satisfied by the replacement of the Belgian Chief of Staff by Col (later Marshal) Joseph-Désiré Mobutu, who was aligned with Lumumba's MNC. Belgian troops intervened to protect their nationals, and at the same time, with the apparent connivance of Belgium, the USA and South Africa, the provinces of Katanga (subsequently Shaba) and South Kasaï resolved to secede. Lumumba requested help from the UN to prevent this, which Kasavubu opposed, and the disagreement culminated in Lumumba's dismissal by Kasavubu in September. Lumumba challenged his dismissal, and appealed to the legislature to remove Kasavubu. The deadlock was resolved later that month by the intervention of the armed forces, and in September Col Mobutu assumed control of the country, ruling with the assistance of a hastily assembled collège des commissaires généraux (CCG). The CCG governed the Congo for a year, but failed to establish control of the north-eastern region, where some of Lumumba's former ministers had established a rival Government in Stanleyville (later Kisangani).

Mobutu restored power to President Kasavubu in February 1961. A few days later Lumumba was murdered on Mobutu's orders, but other involvement was also suspected, and in 2002 the Belgian Government finally conceded a measure of responsibility. The furious reaction to Lumumba's death from African Governments and the UN forced negotiations between Kasavubu and the MNC, and in August 1961 a new Government was formed, with Cyrille Adoula as Prime Minister. Most political groups supported the new administration, except Katanga separatists, led by Moïse Tshombe. A new Constitution entered into force on 1 August 1964, establishing a presidential system of government and a federalist structure.

Meanwhile, the Katanga secession bid collapsed in January 1963, when its leader, Tshombe, went into exile. During early 1964 rebellions broke out in the Kwilu region and in Sud-Kivu and northern Katanga provinces, and within a few months rebels had established their capital at Stanleyville. In July Kasavubu invited Tshombe to become interim Prime Minister, pending legislative elections, and in the following month the country was renamed the Democratic Republic of the Congo. In early 1965 the rebellion in the east was defeated by the army, assisted by Belgian troops and mercenaries.

In March and April 1965 the Tshombe Government organized legislative elections. The coalition led by Tshombe, the Convention nationale congolaise (CONACO), won a majority in the Chamber of Deputies, but was strongly challenged by an opposition bloc known as the Front démocratique congolais and political deadlock ensued. Led by Mobutu, the armed forces again intervened, and on 24 November Mobutu assumed full executive powers, declaring himself President of the 'Second Republic'.

'PRESIDENTIALISM' AND THE PARTY STATE

Moving swiftly to consolidate his power, Mobutu banned party politics and in 1966 established the Mouvement populaire de la révolution (MPR), while granting himself the sole right to legislate. Mobutu reduced the number of provinces from 21 to eight, and replaced provincial assemblies with governors appointed by and answerable to himself only. In June of that year a new Constitution was approved by referendum, establishing a presidential regime, with a new legislature to be elected at a date to be determined by the President. The Constitution provided for two legally authorized political parties, but the claims of existing political groups to official recognition were rejected. Later, the Constitution was amended so that the Government, the legislature and the judiciary all became institutions of the MPR, and all citizens automatically became party members. By 1970 Mobutu had eliminated almost all potential opposition. In October 1971 the country was renamed the Republic of Zaire. In 1972 the President took the name Mobutu Sese Seko Kuku Ngbendu Wa Za Banga, as part of a national policy of 'authenticity', which also resulted in the renaming of many towns and cities and the promotion of Congolese culture.

From the 1960s onwards Mobutu gave shelter to one of the factions fighting for independence in neighbouring Angola, the Frente Nacional de Libertação de Angola (FNLA), which established guerrilla bases and refugee camps along the border in Bas-Zaïre province. However, in 1976, after a rival faction, the Movimento Popular de Libertação de Angola (MPLA), won power, Mobutu agreed with the new Angolan President, Augustino Neto, that Angolan refugees in Zaire would be repatriated and that Angola would return to Zaire several thousand former members of Tshombe's forces, who would then receive amnesty. In March 1977, however, some of the latter, distrusting the pledge of an amnesty, instead invaded Katanga (now renamed Shaba) from Angola, receiving support from many of the disaffected inhabitants. Mobutu secured military assistance from France and Morocco, whose troops defeated the Katangese forces, ending the 'First Shaba War'. The Zairean armed forces subsequently exacted retribution on Katangese who had supported the rebellion, helping to provoke the 'Second Shaba War'. In early May 1978 several thousand Katangese based in Angola crossed the Zambian border and entered Shaba, occupying the important mining town of Kolwezi. French paratroops again intervened and recaptured the town, and in June a pan-African peace-keeping force arrived in Shaba, remaining there for more than a year.

ORGANIZATION OF OPPOSITION

During 1982 Zaire-based opponents of the country's one-party system formed a new party, the Union pour la démocratie et le progrès social (UDPS), which was quickly banned by the Government, while Nguza Karl-I-Bond, formerly a close political associate of Mobutu, emerged as spokesman for a new coalition of opposition exile groups, the Front congolais pour le rétablissement de la démocratie (FCD).

In May 1983, following the publication of a highly critical report on Zaire by the human rights organization Amnesty International, Mobutu offered an amnesty to all political exiles who returned to Zaire by 30 June. Some returned, but a substantial opposition movement remained in Belgium. Internal opposition to Mobutu's regime continued during 1984, when a rebel force briefly occupied the town of Moba, in Shaba province. Karl-I-Bond returned to Zaire in mid-1985 and was rewarded with the posting of US ambassador a year later, while Mobutu also ended restrictions on senior members of the banned UDPS.

In June 1987 several members of the UDPS, including Etienne Tshisekedi Wa Mulumba (its Secretary-General and a former Minister of the Interior), accepted Mobutu's offer of amnesty, and in October four other former UDPS leaders joined the MPR central committee. At the same time, Mobutu appointed other reconciled opponents of the Government to senior posts in state-owned enterprises. The improvement in relations was short-lived and in January 1988 Tshisekedi was placed under temporary house arrest. In April Tshisekedi was again arrested, after urging a boycott of legislative elections scheduled to take place that month in Kinshasa.

In February 1990 the UDPS organized demonstrations in Kinshasa and three other towns to commemorate the 29th anniversary of the assassination of Lumumba. Further unrest followed in April, when students staged protests in Kinshasa to demand larger study grants and the removal of Mobutu from power. In what was seen by many observers as an attempt to defuse the growing tension, Mobutu ordered Tshisekedi's release, and announced the imminent establishment of a multi-party political system, initially comprising three parties (including the MPR). At the same time Mobutu declared the inauguration of the 'Third Republic' and announced his resignation as Chairman of the MPR. The National Executive Council was dissolved, and Prof. Lunda Bululu, the Secretary-General of the Communauté économique des états de l'Afrique centrale (CEEAC) and formerly a legal adviser to Mobutu, replaced Kengo Wa Dondo as First State Commissioner.

In early May 1990 a new transitional Government was formed. Mobutu announced that a special commission would draft a new Constitution by the end of April 1991, and that presidential elections would be held before December of that year, with legislative elections to follow in 1992. He also promised the imminent 'depoliticization' of the armed forces, the gendarmerie, the civil guard, the security services and civil service.

Mobutu's reforms were widely viewed as inadequate, and there was more unrest in May 1990, when students at Lubumbashi University staged anti-Government demonstrations. Up to 150 students were massacred by the presidential guard on Mobutu's orders, prompting international outrage and suspensions of bilateral aid from several donors. Mobutu initially denied the massacre but later ordered an official parliamentary inquiry, as a result of which the Governor of Shaba and other senior local officials were arrested and charged with having organized the killing.

The USA announced in October 1990 that it was terminating all military and economic aid to Zaire. In November an anti-Government rally in Kinshasa, organized by the UDPS, was violently suppressed, but there were nonetheless anti-Government demonstrations during the following months in Kinshasa and Matadi. In February 1991 hundreds of thousands of workers, civil servants and public service employees in Kinshasa staged a three-day general strike to protest against working and living conditions and to demand the resignation of the Government. Later that month 20,000 people attended a UDPS rally in Kinshasa.

NATIONAL CONFERENCE

The Government's announcement of a timetable for the restoration of multi-party politics prompted a proliferation of political parties. Prominent among them was the Union des fédéralistes et républicains indépendants (UFERI), led by Karl-I-Bond. A new and enlarged transitional Government, appointed in March 1991, included several representatives of minor political parties, while more substantial and influential opposition parties refused to participate. In April Mobutu announced that a National Conference would convene at the end of the month, with the task of drafting a new constitution, but major opposition parties responded that they would not participate unless Mobutu relinquished power. Widespread anti-Government demonstrations followed, and in mid-April the security forces killed and injured scores of people when they opened fire on demonstrators in the diamond-mining town of Mbuji-Mayi.

The Parti démocrate et social chrétien (PDSC), the UDPS and the UFERI persisted with their opposition to the National Conference, and formed the Union sacrée de l'opposition radicale (USOR), which urged a boycott. By the end of July 1991 the USOR had expanded to include 130 parties, whereupon it decided that its growing influence and Mobutu's increased weakness justified its participation in the National Conference.

The National Conference opened on 7 August 1991, with 2,850 delegates attending, including representatives of 900 opposition political parties. USOR delegates immediately threatened to withdraw unless all their political demands were met, and there followed widespread opposition to the election of Isaac Kalonji Mutambay, a Protestant pastor, as President of the Conference.

On 2 September 1991 there were violent clashes between the security forces and opposition supporters protesting at massive inflation and the lack of progress in the National Conference, resulting in heavy civilian casualties. By late September the political unrest had escalated into widespread rioting and looting, firstly by the military and then spreading to the civilian population. Massive destruction of property took place and a large number of deaths were reported, until the riots were suppressed by French and Belgian troops.

After the riots, France, Belgium and the USA urged Mobutu to install a new government, and he obliged, appointing Tshisekedi as First State Commissioner on 2 October 1991. Only 12 days later, however, Tshisekedi was dismissed by Mobutu, after he refused to swear an oath of allegiance but instead publicly denounced the President. Mobutu then installed a 'Government of Crisis'.

It rapidly became evident that the 'Government of Crisis' lacked credibility both domestically and internationally, and President Abdou Diouf of Senegal undertook a new initiative to break the impasse. Diouf's proposals committed both Mobutu and opposition supporters to the convening of a sovereign National Conference with legislative power, and to the appointment of a First State Commissioner from the opposition. A new Government was sworn in on 28 November 1991, with Nguza Karl-I-Bond as First State Commissioner. The USOR, however, was largely excluded from the Government while key portfolios were retained by Mobutu's allies, including defence and security, external relations and international co-operation. The National Conference resumed in December, under the presidency of the Roman Catholic Archbishop of Kisangani, Laurent Monsengwo Pasinya. Serious divisions soon arose within the Conference, and Karl-I-Bond, following consultations with Mobutu, suspended it in January 1992, citing cost and its alleged responsibility for exacerbating ethnic tension. Karl-I-Bond proposed that each party have only one representative at the National Conference from any ethnic group, and Mobutu endorsed this, accusing the Conference of being unrepresentative, and alleging that far too many of the delegates originated from the two Kasaï provinces.

Violence intensified during early 1992 as the USOR and Christian churches mobilized demonstrations against the suspension of the Conference. On 16 February more than 30 people were killed by security forces in mass protests in Kinshasa. Such incidents further worsened Mobutu's international standing, leading to pressure from donor countries for the National Conference to be reinstated, and their continued suspension of aid. On 22–23 January troops briefly seized the national radio station, urging the removal of the Government and resumption of the National Conference. There were also strikes to demand both better wages and resumption of the Conference.

Increasingly isolated and under pressure, Mobutu, against the wishes of Karl-I-Bond, reconvened the Conference on 6 April 1992. On 17 April the Conference declared itself 'sovereign', with power to take binding legislative and executive decisions, and announced that it would draft a constitution and a timetable for legislative and presidential elections. After initially threatening to 'call the Conference to order', as he had done in the past, by late July Mobutu appeared to have conceded to its demands, while insisting, however, on retaining control of the armed forces. On 15 August the Conference overwhelmingly elected Tshisekedi as the transitional Prime Minister with a two-year mandate, replacing Nguza Karl-I-Bond, who had not sought re-election. Tshisekedi then appointed a transitional 'Government of National Union', which included known opponents of Mobutu.

Tshisekedi and Mobutu clashed almost immediately, following an announcement by the President of his intention to promote the adoption of a 'semi-presidential constitution', in opposition to the parliamentary system favoured by the Conference. In October 1992 attacks on opposition leaders and the offices of newspapers critical of Mobutu became increasingly frequent in Kinshasa, while ethnic violence worsened in Shaba. On 14 November the National Conference (without the participation of Mobutu's supporters) adopted a Constitution providing for the establishment of a 'Federal Republic of the Congo', the introduction of a bicameral legislature and the election, by universal suffrage, of a non-executive President to fulfil largely ceremonial functions. Executive and military power was to be exercised by the Prime Minister. The draft document was rejected by Mobutu (who had unsuccessfully attempted in early December to declare the Tshisekedi Government dissolved).

HIGH COUNCIL OF THE REPUBLIC

On 6 December 1992 the National Conference dissolved itself and was succeeded by a 453-member High Council of the Republic (HCR), retaining Archbishop Monsengwo as its President. Alarmed at the imminent seizure of his powers, Mobutu ordered the suspension of the HCR and the Government, and decreed that civil servants should usurp ministers in the supervision of government ministries (a demand that they refused). Attempts by the presidential guard to obstruct the convening of the HCR were defeated by a public demonstration in Kinshasa, organized by the HCR in protest at the actions of the armed forces. The HCR received the support of the USA, Belgium and France, in its declaration of Tshisekedi as Head of Zaire's Government.

In mid-January 1993 the HCR declared Mobutu guilty of treason and threatened impeachment proceedings unless he recognized the legitimacy of the transitional Government. At the end of the month several units of the army rioted in protest at an attempt by the President to pay them with discredited banknotes. Order was eventually restored, but only after the deaths of some 65 people (including the French ambassador to Zaire), and the intervention of French troops.

Rival Governments

In early March 1993, in an attempt to reassert his political authority, Mobutu convened a 'conclave' of political forces to debate the country's future, but the HCR and the USOR declined to participate. In mid-March the 'conclave' appointed Faustin Birindwa, a former UDPS member and adviser to Tshisekedi, as Prime Minister, charged with the formation of a 'government of national salvation'. Mobutu also reconvened the dormant National Assembly as a rival to the HCR. In early April Birindwa appointed a Cabinet, which included Karl-I-Bond (as First Deputy Prime Minister in charge of Defence), and three members of the USOR, who were immediately expelled from that organization. While the Birindwa administration was denied official recognition by most Western countries, Tshisekedi sought the intervention of the UN and in July 1993 the Secretary-General of the UN appointed Lakhdar Brahimi, a former Minister of Foreign Affairs in Algeria, as his special envoy to Zaire and mediator there. Meanwhile, in late June six of Birindwa's ministers, all former activists in the USOR, had announced the formation of the Union sacrée rénovée (USR), claiming that the USOR had abandoned its original political objectives. Mobutu was widely recognized to be fostering such divisions in the opposition through the extensive use of his personal patronage, since, despite the reduction of his formal political powers, he retained access to much of the country's capital and assets.

In late September 1993 Mobutu and the principal opposition groups agreed on the adoption of a single constitutional text for the transitional period, which was to be subject to approval by a national referendum. This would be followed by presidential and legislative elections, prior to the establishment of a new republic in January 1995.

In December 1993, at a rally in Kolwezi attended by Karl-I-Bond, the Governor of Shaba declared the autonomy of the province (reverting to the name of Katanga). Mobutu's subdued response to the Shaba declaration was attributed to his reluctance to engender further political opposition during negotiations that might dictate his political future.

EMERGENCE OF THE HCR—PT

A new agreement to form a transitional government was signed by most significant political parties in early January 1994. Encouraged by the level of political support for the initiative, Mobutu announced the dissolution of the HCR, the National Legislative Council and the Government, and a contest for the premiership between two candidates, Tshisekedi and Molumba Lukoji, to be decided by a transitional legislature (the Haut Conseil de la République—Parlement de Transition, HCR—PT) within 15 days of its inauguration. The PT was duly convened six days later, despite widespread protests, under the presidency of Archbishop Monsengwo. The HCR—PT immediately rejected Mobutu's procedure for the selection of a new Prime Minister, but its subsequent attempts to formulate a new procedure were frustrated by the increasingly divergent interests of the member parties of the USOR, and by Tshisekedi's insistence of his legitimate claim to the office.

On 8 April 1994 the HCR—PT endorsed a new transitional Constitution Act, according to which the Government would be accountable to the HCR—PT, and would assume some relinquished powers of the President, including the control of the central bank and the security forces and the nomination of candidates for senior posts in the civil service. In addition, a new Prime Minister was to be appointed from opposition candidates.

On 14 June 1994 the HCR—PT elected Léon Kengo Wa Dondo Prime Minister by a clear majority, but opposition leaders and the HCR—PT President rejected the election as invalid. A new transitional Government, announced on 6 July, was similarly rejected by the radical opposition, despite the offer of two ministerial posts to the UDPS. On 11 July, however, during a motion of confidence, the Government received overwhelming support from the HCR—PT, and the Prime Minister swiftly sought to restore the faltering confidence of the international donor community by committing the new administration to the implementation of political reform and economic structural adjustment. In mid-1994 Mobutu and the Government's international standing was enhanced by its readiness to accommodate more than 2m. Rwandan refugees, who had fled into Zaire from the former Rwandan Government following its defeat by the Rwandan Patriotic Front after the 1994 genocide there.

In early July 1994, citing problems in the Kivu provinces caused by the mass influx of Rwandan refugees, the transitional Government extended its original 15-month tenure by two years. Meanwhile, opposition frustration at the absence of an electoral timetable escalated, and there were further violent demonstrations in the capital. In early December opposition groups rejected a government offer to join a national coalition administration, and reiterated their demands for a timetable for multi-party elections. At the end of December the HCR—PT formalized the establishment of the National Electoral Commission (NEC), which was formally installed in April 1996.

At the same time it was announced that a referendum on a new constitution in December 1996 would be followed by presidential, legislative, regional and municipal elections in 1997. A draft of the new Constitution, which provided for a federal state with a semi-presidential parliamentary system of government, was adopted in late May 1996, and by the HCR—PT in October.

THE FALL OF MOBUTU

In August 1996 Mobutu left for Switzerland for four months to receive treatment for cancer, which was then at an advanced stage, and this, combined with the political and military legacy of the 1994 Rwandan refugee crisis, proved the turning-point in his rule. Kengo Wa Dondo's Government confronted a rapid escalation of violence in the eastern provinces of Nord- and Sud-Kivu. Rwandan Hutu militias and former soldiers of the Forces Armées Rwandais (ex-FAR) had by then, with the active assistance of the Zairean armed forces (Forces Armées de Zaïre—FAZ), converted Rwandan refugee camps into bases for rearmament and preparation for the future reconquest of Rwanda. By mid-1996 Rwandan Hutu militias, known as Interahamwe, with the support of Congolese Hutu Banyarwanda and the FAZ, were killing and displacing Congolese Tutsis and other ethnic groups. The situation was complicated by long-term rivalries in the area, including widespread resentment of Tutsis resident in Sud-Kivu (known as the Banyamulenge), and a dispute dating from the early days of the National Conference over their entitlement to Zairean nationality. In early October the Deputy Governor of Sud-Kivu ordered Banyamulenge to leave the country within a week. The order was subsequently suspended, but none the less provoked a powerful reprisal from Banyamulenge militias, who, with the full support of the Rwandan and Ugandan Governments, made rapid advances against the combined forces of the ex-FAR, Interahamwe and the poorly trained FAZ. What had initially been a localized movement seeking to defend the Banyamulenge and combat extremist Hutus rapidly gathered momentum and became a national coalition fighting to overthrow the Mobutu regime. Banyamulenge rebels were joined by other dissidents to form the Alliance des forces démocratiques pour la libération du Congo-Zaïre (AFDL). Soon to join the AFDL were the Katangese gendarmes, who had fought for the Angolan Government in its long-term civil conflict against the União Nacional para a Independência Total de Angola (UNITA), and who retained close contact with the Angolan Government. Laurent-Désiré Kabila was initially the AFDL's spokesman, but, on the agreement of the Rwandan, Ugandan and Angolan Governments, and also the probable influence of the Tanzanian Government, he was rapidly installed as the AFDL's leader. Kabila had been a ministerial aide under Lumumba and an occasionally active opponent of the Mobutu regime since the 1960s, and had spent most of his time prior to the mid-1990s in Tanzania. By early November AFDL forces controlled a substantial area adjoining the border with Rwanda, Burundi and parts of Uganda, including the key towns of Goma, Bukavu and Uvira, and by the end of the month they had captured most of Nord- and Sud-Kivu. Mobutu's absence, and uncertainties as to the state of his health, weakened the Zairean Government's response to the AFDL, although the main reasons for the loss of territory were the strength of the foreign (and particularly) Rwandan armed forces, who were supporting the AFDL, and the complete lack of commitment within the FAZ to defending the Government.

The AFDL's success in the east exacerbated anti-Tutsi sentiment in Kinshasa. In November 1996 the HCR—PT demanded the expulsion of all Tutsis from Zairean territory; following attacks on Tutsis and their property, many Tutsi residents of Kinshasa fled across the river to Brazzaville, in the Republic of the Congo. In the same month repeated public demonstrations demanded the resignation of Kengo Wa Dondo (himself part-Tutsi in origin) for having failed to respond effectively to the insurrection. Mobutu returned to Kinshasa on 17 December and while retaining Kengo Wa Dondo as Prime Minister ordered the formation of a crisis government, which included some opposition members, although it excluded the UDPS and was not approved by the HCR—PT. Before long, Tshisekedi's faction of the UDPS announced its support for the AFDL. In February 1997, following an effective general strike in Kinshasa, Mobutu banned all demonstrations and industrial action.

In late January 1997, assisted by foreign mercenaries, the FAZ launched a counter-offensive, but made no significant territorial gains. In February the AFDL advanced south and east, capturing Shabunda, Kalemie and Kindu, meeting almost no resistance on each occasion, except from the Zairean air force. In March, after brief hostilities, the AFDL took the strategically important northern town of Kisangani (which had until then been the centre of military operations for the Government), and in early April Mbuji-Mayi was captured by the rebels. AFDL troops entered Lubumbashi on 9 April, and government troops fled the city. Attempts at mediation between the two sides, undertaken by foreign Governments (most notably that of South Africa) and international organizations, during February–April had no impact, since Kabila was determined to capture Kinshasa and the presidency.

After the capture of Kisangani in March 1997, the HCR—PT, although technically inquorate, voted to dismiss Kengo Wa Dondo, who resigned at the end of that month, and was replaced by Tshisekedi. Tshisekedi, after offering government posts to members of the AFDL (which they refused), dissolved the HCR—PT, which voted, in turn, to dismiss Tshisekedi. On 8 April Mobutu declared a national state of emergency, dismissing the Government and ordering the deployment of security forces throughout Kinshasa. Gen. Likulia Bolongo was appointed Prime Minister at the head of a new 28-member National Salvation Government, in which major opposition parties refused to participate. Following inconclusive peace talks between Mobutu and Kabila, mediated by the South African President, Nelson Mandela, in early May, Mobutu refused to resign and Kabila reiterated his intention to seize the capital by force.

KABILA ASSUMES POWER

On 16 May 1997 Mobutu left Kinshasa and travelled to Togo, and then to Morocco, where he died on 7 September. On 17 May AFDL troops entered Kinshasa, encountering no resistance, and Kabila, from Lubumbashi, declared himself President of the Democratic Republic of the Congo (DRC, the name used in 1964–71). Kabila promised the rapid formation of a provisional government and of a constituent assembly within 60 days; presidential and legislative elections were, he stated, to take place within two years. On 20 May 1997 Kabila arrived in Kinshasa, and on 23 May formed a new Government, which, while dominated by members of the AFDL, also included members of the UDPS and of the Front patriotique, and avoided a potentially unpopular dominance of Tutsis. No Prime Minister was appointed, and Tshisekedi was not offered a cabinet post; he refused to recognize the new Government, and advocated public protest against the administration, but failed to raise the mass support that he had previously enjoyed. On 26 May Kabila issued a decree banning all political parties and public demonstrations. A public gathering on 28 May in support of Tshisekedi was dispersed by the army.

On 28 May 1997 Kabila issued another decree, granting himself legislative and executive power and control over the armed forces and the treasury. Of the previously existing institutions, only the judiciary was not dissolved. On the following day Kabila was sworn in as President of the DRC.

In September 1997 Kabila ordered most Rwandan army units to leave the DRC, and began replacing Banyamulenge units of the DRC armed forces with those from elsewhere in the country. In November the presidential security advisor, Masasu Nindaga, a founder member of the AFDL, was dismissed by Kabila and imprisoned. Clashes between troops supporting Nindaga and those loyal to Kabila in early December resulted in at least 20 casualties. Nindaga was later sentenced by a military court to 20 years' imprisonment for treason.

On 4 January 1998 a cousin of Kabila, Gaëtan Kakudji, was appointed Minister of the Interior as part of a cabinet reorganization that effected a general shift in power from Kivu politicians to those from Katanga. On 23 January two UDPS leaders were sentenced by a military tribunal to two years' imprisonment for 'agitating the public', and on 12 February Tshisekedi was once again arrested and this time banished to his home village in Kasaï Oriental until 1 July.

On 3 February 1998, after considerable international pressure, the Government announced the closure of the Kapalata military camp near Kisangani, where about 3,000 local Mai-Mai child soldiers were based. However, the Government rejected international calls for an early general election, with Kabila announcing in mid-February that there would be no elections until 'peace prevailed'.

Clashes between Banyamulenge and other army units, and Banyamulenge desertions were reported in Kivu in February 1998. Most returned to barracks in March, after being offered an amnesty, but later in the month reports emerged that a number of them had been interrogated and tortured in Bukavu. Banyamulenge activists complained of a return to conditions experienced during the Mobutu era. Also in March, the Zairean Association for the Defence of Human Rights (AZADHO) released a report chronicling a series of abuses allegedly committed by the new Government since coming to power, including massacres, pillage and corruption. The organization was subsequently banned.

In late March 1998 a constitutional commission appointed earlier by Kabila submitted its draft Constitution, which envisaged a five-year presidency, with the President enjoying extensive executive powers. On 26 May a transitional Constituent Assembly was established by presidential decree, specifically excluding anyone who held public office during Mobutu's presidency. The Assembly, holding legislative powers, was to review the draft Constitution and prepare it for approval by a national referendum. Kabila repeated his promise to hold a general election during 1999.

REBELLION AND REGIONAL INTERVENTION

On 28 July 1998 Kabila expelled all remaining Rwandan army units from the country. Shortly afterwards, a rebellion assisted by the Rwandan armed forces was launched in Nord- and Sud-Kivu. Rebel forces, operating as the Rassemblement congolais pour la démocratie (RCD), swiftly captured Goma, Bukavu and Uvira, which was denounced by Kabila as a Rwandan invasion of the DRC. Rwanda denied any involvement. On 4 August the RCD and Rwandan troops hijacked a plane from Goma airport and flew to the Kitona military base, near the Atlantic coast. They swiftly captured Kitona and the nearby Banana naval installation, and within one week had captured Matadi and the Inga hydroelectric dam, which enabled them to cut off Kinshasa's electricity supply. At this point, several government ministers, including the Minister of Foreign Affairs, Bizima Karaha, a Congolese Tutsi, defected to the rebels. On 19 August, at a meeting of Ministers of Defence of the Southern African Development Community (SADC, which the DRC had joined in September 1997), Zimbabwe and Namibia pledged to assist Kabila. Zimbabwean troops arrived in Kinshasa the following day and secured the international airport. Although the Rwandan Government believed that it had secured the agreement of the Angolan administration in its plan to overthrow Kabila, Angola also sent troops in late August, which succeeded in recapturing Banana and Kitona, and by the end of August had defeated the RCD in the west of the country. The RCD, however, assisted by Rwandan and Ugandan troops, consolidated its control of the eastern DRC, seizing Kisangani, the country's third largest town, apparently without resistance, in late August and subsequently captured a series of smaller towns in the east throughout September.

Diplomatic initiatives to end the war began on 7–8 September 1998, when regional Heads of State met in Victoria Falls, Zimbabwe, under the chairmanship of the Zambian President, Frederick Chiluba. A cease-fire was agreed at the meeting, but was rejected both by the RCD, which had been denied the opportunity to meet directly with the Heads of State, and by Kabila, who first demanded the withdrawal of Ugandan and Rwandan troops. On 15 September the annual SADC meeting in Mauritius endorsed the legitimacy of the intervention by Zimbabwe, Namibia and Angola and formally authorized Chiluba to continue his mediation efforts. Two weeks later, at a summit organized by Gabonese President Omar Bongo in Libreville, Gabon, the Governments of Gabon, Chad, the Republic of the Congo, the Central African Republic, Equatorial Guinea, Cameroon, Namibia and Angola recognized Kabila as the legitimate Head of State of the DRC and condemned the 'external aggression' against him.

In the first major government counter-attack in the eastern DRC, hundreds of Mai-Mai fighters (by then allied to Kabila) and Rwandan Interahamwe attacked Goma on 14 September 1998, but were defeated by the RCD and Rwandan forces. Rwanda subsequently accused Kabila of rearming the Interahamwe (a claim later endorsed by the UN commission of inquiry into illicit trade in armaments in the Great Lakes region). Meanwhile, Kabila continued his efforts to enlist further support for his Government, which resulted in Chad dispatching 2,000 troops to the DRC on 28 September. The RCD continued its military offensive and on 14 October captured the strategic town of Kindu, which allowed RCD forces to advance into Kasaï and Katanga. Concerned at developments, the Presidents of Angola, Namibia and Zimbabwe increased their military deployment in DRC. In November a new rebel group emerged called the Mouvement de libération du Congo (MLC), led by Jean-Pierre Bemba Gombo(the son of a prominent Mobutuist, Bemba Saolona, who joined Kabila's Cabinet in 1999). The MLC was based in Équateur and had large numbers of former FAZ soldiers among its ranks. It soon developed increasingly close ties with the Ugandan Government, while Rwanda remained committed to the RCD.

In November 1998, following talks with Mandela, the Rwandan Vice-President, Paul Kagame, finally admitted that Rwandan troops were fighting in support of the RCD against Kabila. Diplomatic efforts continued, but in the meantime the RCD extended its control over the eastern DRC, until by the end of 1998 it held about one-third of the country, from Isiro in the north-east to the Zambian border in the south-east, extending west as far as Bumba on the River Congo and Kindu and Kabalo further south. In June the RCD captured the railway junction town of Kamina, on the route to Lubumbashi, and advanced on Mbuji-Mayi, which it was prevented from seizing by Zimbabwean troops. In July the MLC captured the strategically significant town of Gbadolite, in Equateur.

Divisions emerged in the RCD in 1999, with the Vice-Chairman, Arthur Z'ahidi Ngoma, resigning in mid-February, after describing the movement as being under the control of the Rwandan and Ugandan Governments. In mid-May the RCD, in an action supported by Rwanda, but condemned by Uganda, deposed Ernest Wamba dia Wamba as Chairman, and replaced him with Emile Ilunga. Wamba dia Wamba denounced this move as illegitimate and established a faction in Kisangani, while Goma became the headquarters of Ilunga's Rwanda-backed faction, subsequently known as RCD—Goma. Violence in Kisangani subsequently forced Wamba dia Wamba in October to relocate once more, to Bunia, where he remained under Ugandan army protection. Wamba dia Wamba's faction became known as the RCD—Mouvement de libération (RCD—ML). Despite efforts by Wamba dia Wamba to contain them, ethnic tensions between Hema and Lendu communities in Bunia erupted into violence in late 1999, and have caused fierce fighting ever since, resulting in the death of many thousands, and the displacement of more than 200,000.

The Lusaka Accord

A peace summit was convened in Lusaka in late June 1999, and culminated in the signing of an accord on 10 July by the Presidents of the DRC, Zimbabwe, Angola, Rwanda and Uganda, but by none of the rebel leaderships. The accord provided for an immediate cease-fire, and for combatant forces inside the DRC to establish a Joint Military Commission (JMC), and to disarm identified militia groups, which included the Rwandan Interahamwe, Burundi's Force pour la défense de la démocratie, the Congolese Mai-Mai and Angola's UNITA. The accord also provided a timetable for the withdrawal of foreign forces, the deployment of UN peace-keepers and the organization of inter-Congolese political negotiations. Bemba signed the Lusaka Accord on 1 August, and on 6 August the UN

Security Council authorized the dispatch of 80 UN military observers to Kinshasa and regional capitals as the first stage of the UN's deployment in the DRC, which commenced on 13 September. At the end of November the UN Security Council established the Mission de l'organisation des nations unies en République démocratique du Congo (MONUC). Signalling the final collapse of Rwanda and Uganda's increasingly precarious relationship in the DRC, and the increased significance of control of the DRC's mineral and other resources in the schemes of the combatant factions, serious fighting erupted between Rwandan and Ugandan forces in Kisangani in mid-August and continued for four days. At the end of August all 51 founder members of the RCD signed the Lusaka Accord, following a compromise agreement (which was intended to resolve an acrimonious dispute between the two RCD factions over which grouping had the right to sign).

Kabila named a Mai-Mai commander, Sylvestre Louetcha, as the DRC Chief of Defence Staff in early September 1999. Some Mai-Mai commanders subsequently asserted that the Mai-Mai were therefore part of the Congolese armed forces and should, accordingly, be removed from the Lusaka list of negative forces. (However, the amendment was never made.)

Internal Political Developments

In early 1999 Kabila announced the formation of village-level Comités du pouvoir populaire (CPP—known popularly in Kinshasa as 'ce n'est pas possible'), and in April dissolved the AFDL, accusing many of its members of corruption. In March Kabila had announced that a national debate involving a wide range of DRC political opinion was to be organized. This was welcomed by Tshisekedi and other opposition politicians, until it transpired that the Government alone would decide who would be allowed to participate. The leadership of RCD—Goma was invited to attend, but declined. In December the Organization of African Unity (OAU) Secretary-General nominated the former Botswanan President, Sir Ketumile Masire, as mediator in the DRC's political dialogue. Masire recommended in January 2000 that 150 representatives from the Government, rebels, political opposition and civil society be invited to participate in the negotiations, but rejected the Government's suggestion that the discussions be conducted in Kinshasa.

In February 2000 Masire made his first visit to Kinshasa, where he was received with hostility by the Government. Masire visited the DRC again in March, but was denied permission by the Government to travel to rebel-held areas of the DRC. In April Masire proposed that the dialogue begin in July, and suggested Botswana, Ethiopia or Zambia as suitable locations for the discussions. These proposals were, however, rejected by the DRC Government on 22 April, which again demanded that the talks take place in Kinshasa. This was immediately rejected by the RCD—Goma. In early May Kabila announced that he could no longer wait for the proposed national dialogue, and that a new National Assembly would be installed on 1 July. Masire, meanwhile, visited rebel-held areas of eastern DRC for the first time, and announced that consultations would take place in Benin from early June, involving the DRC Government, opposition figures, prominent members of civil society and the three rebel groups, prior to the commencement of the dialogue on 3 July. However, the DRC Government declined to send a delegation to Benin, and prevented political opposition and civil society delegates from attending. On 11 June the DRC Government announced that it no longer had any confidence in Masire and requested that the OAU nominate a replacement.

Reaffirmation of the Lusaka Accord

Following a UN Security Council debate on the DRC conflict in late January 2000, the UN Secretary-General, Kofi Annan, recommended that MONUC be increased in size to 500 military observers, supported by some 5,000 combat troops with powers of enforcement, and the possibility of more troops being added if the Lusaka Accord was respected by its signatories. Annan's proposal was approved by the Security Council on 24 February, and the mandate of the force was extended to the end of August. Recognizing that the 1999 cease-fire agreement had been widely ignored, participants at a meeting of the JMC in early April 2000 agreed to a new cease-fire, which came into effect on 14 April. Fighting subsequently subsided in most areas, although serious clashes continued for a time in Equateur between the MLC and DRC government forces.

In early May 2000 fierce fighting erupted once more between Ugandan and Rwandan forces in Kisangani. Kagame and Museveni met in Tanzania in mid-May, and promised to withdraw their troops from Kisangani, leaving the town under the control of an expanded MONUC force. However, both armies remained in the city, and further hostilities between them in early June resulted in a costly military victory for Rwanda, causing more than 160 deaths, widespread destruction within the city, and thousands of residents being displaced. Uganda subsequently pledged a unilateral withdrawal from the city, while Rwanda indicated that its troops would remain in position until MONUC forces assumed control. The fighting attracted international condemnation, although a suggestion from Annan that Uganda and Rwanda be subject to sanctions until they withdrew from the DRC was never implemented.

In May 2000 Kabila announced the formation of a 300-member transitional Parliament, whose delegates were selected by a committee supervised by the Ministry of the Interior and subsequently approved by presidential decree. In July Kabila decreed the transfer of the transitional Parliament to Lubumbashi, and rebel-held Kisangani as the new location of the Supreme Court. On 22 August Kabila inaugurated the new Parliament in Lubumbashi, and on the following day unilaterally declared the Lusaka Accord invalid. The Government authorized the deployment of MONUC troops in government-held territory on 24 August, but then refused permission for them to arrive.

Kabila reorganized his Cabinet on 4 September 2000, appointing Gen. Likulia Bilongo, who was Mobutu's last Prime Minister, as the head of the newly created Ministry of Public Finance, and Dominique Sakombi Inongo, who had been, by his own admission, Mobutu's chief propagandist, as Minister of Information.

DRC government forces captured the town of Pepa, which was held by RCD—Goma, in mid-October 2000, after launching an unexpected attack, at the same time as a regional summit on the DRC conflict, convened in Maputo, Mozambique, where it was agreed that all combative forces should withdraw 15 km from their current positions. The 15-km withdrawal plan was taken up by another summit in Maputo later in the month, chaired by the South African President, Thabo Mbeki, who eventually secured agreement from all rebel forces. RCD—Goma reorganized its leadership in late October, with Ilunga being replaced as President by Adolphe Onusumba. Shortly afterwards, there was an attempted coup against Wamba dia Wamba's leadership of the struggling RCD—ML by his deputy, Mbusa Nyamwisi, which was suppressed by Ugandan troops.

RCD—Goma, strongly assisted by Rwandan troops, recaptured Pepa on 11 November 2000, and then continued its counter-offensive, capturing Pweto on the Zambian border in early December. Thousands of DRC and Zimbabwean government forces were forced to abandon the town, with most fleeing to Zambia, together with at least 60,000 civilian refugees.

Although Kabila's main allies, the Zimbabwean and Angolan Governments, announced support for Masire, the DRC President continued to reject him, and launched a parallel initiative to the national dialogue that Masire had been mandated to organize. On 22 December 2000 the DRC Government duly transported 200 specially selected participants to a meeting in Libreville, Gabon, described as a 'preparatory national dialogue'. The dialogue was then abruptly postponed until January 2001, after which participants issued a statement urging the revision of the Lusaka Accord, in accordance with earlier DRC Government demands.

JOSEPH KABILA ASSUMES POWER

Kabila was assassinated, apparently by a member of his presidential guard, on 16 January 2001. Three days later the Presidents of Angola, Zimbabwe and Namibia met in Luanda, Angola, and agreed to leave their troops in the DRC. Increased Zimbabwean and Angolan troop levels were subsequently reported in Kinshasa, and provided security when, on 23 January, Kabila's son, Joseph Kabila, was formally installed as the new President. During his first address, Kabila promised internal political liberalization and increased dialogue with the DRC's neighbours in order to end the war.

Kabila's inauguration as President immediately boosted the peace process. On 15 February 2001 the warring parties in the DRC revived their earlier agreement to withdraw 15 km from positions of military engagement, and in early March Masire visited Kinshasa at Kabila's invitation. Masire subsequently toured the region, and returned to Kinshasa in early April. The withdrawal from positions of military engagement commenced on 15 March, with the retreat from Pweto of RCD—Goma and Rwandan forces. The first contingent of MONUC troops arrived in RCD-held Kalemie in mid-March, followed shortly afterwards by the deployment of MONUC troops in government-held Kananga. After some delay, MONUC forces were dispatched to RCD-held Kisangani in late April, closely followed by the dispatch of more UN troops to government-held Mbandaka, which completed the initial MONUC deployment.

Kabila appointed a new Government on 14 April 2001. Mwenze Kongolo, the former Minister of Justice, with associations to the Zimbabwean Government, was appointed Minister of National Security and Public Order, in a measure widely interpreted as indicating the consolidation of Zimbabwean influence on the new DRC Government. Opposition parties urged Kabila to allow political activity, and Tshisekedi returned to Kinshasa after a 16-month absence on 23 April. Kabila ended some restrictions on political activity in mid-May, thus partially removing one of the obstacles to the national dialogue being organized by Masire, and ordered the release of a number of detained human rights activists.

In mid-October the UN Security Council voted to extend MONUC's mandate into a 'third phase', which was to involve the disarmament, demobilization, reintegration, repatriation and resettlement (DDRRR) of combatants identified as 'negative forces' by the Lusaka Accord, including the Interahamwe and the Mai-Mai.

Wamba dia Wamba was ousted as the RCD—ML leader in August 2001 by Mbusa Nyamwisi, who was based in the eastern town of Beni. The Ugandan Government was forced to recognize Nyamwisi as the new RCD—ML leader, despite Wamba dia Wamba's protests, and his open hostility to Bemba, Uganda's principal DRC ally. Bemba's anger at Museveni's recognition of Nyamwisi prompted the MLC to participate in a series of discussions with the Rwandan Government and RCD—Goma in Kigali, Rwanda, during late 2001 and early 2002, although these failed to result in a durable agreement.

Following preparatory discussions between the DRC Government and rebel and civil society representatives in Gaborone, Botswana, in late August 2001, it was agreed that the official inter-Congolese dialogue was to commence in mid-October in the Ethiopian capital, Addis Ababa. Annan travelled to the DRC in early September for an official visit, which was intended to maintain the momentum of the peace process.

In early November 2001 a UN committee investigating the illegal exploitation of the DRC's resources by the armed factions presented an updated version of a report originally produced in May. The report accused Rwanda and Uganda of illegal exploitation of the DRC's mineral resources, and was angrily rejected by both Governments, which defended the right of their nationals to conduct business in the country. Also in November the next round of the inter-Congolese dialogue was postponed until January 2002, and later rescheduled for 25 February, at Sun City, South Africa. In mid-December 2001 representatives of RCD—Goma, the MLC and the DRC Government met in Abuja, Nigeria, for UN-mediated talks. The main outcome was a tentative agreement between the three parties over the nature of Mai-Mai representation in Sun City. MONUC's DDRRR campaign started in December 2001, with the monitoring of nearly 2,000 Rwandan Hutu combatants, who had assembled in camps in Kamina, in DRC government territory, to present themselves for disarmament and demobilization.

The inter-Congolese dialogue commenced in Sun City in late February 2002, with all the major parties and numerous minor ones in attendance. The discussions generated intense debate and some significant agreements, but failed to find a formula to bring Kabila's Government, the MLC and RCD—Goma into a power-sharing partnership. Instead, Kabila, who in late March formed a new association, the Parti pour la réconciliation et le développement (PPRD), concluded a power-sharing agreement with the MLC and the RCD—ML on 17 April (the final day of the discussions). Despite this, mistrust persisted between the DRC Government and the MLC and the agreement was never implemented.

Two military challenges to RCD—Goma's control of eastern DRC erupted during mid-2002. On 14 May members of the FAC seized the official radio station in Kisangani and appealed to the population to assist them in overthrowing RCD—Goma and removing Rwandan troops. RCD—Goma quickly launched a counter-offensive, assisted by the RPA, which resulted in the massacre of up to 200 people (although RCD—Goma claimed that only 49 people had been killed). Meanwhile, in Sud-Kivu, RCD—Goma and Rwandan forces clashed with a breakaway RCD—Goma unit, led by Patrick Masunzu, in the Haut Plateau region in June, and widely supported within the Banyamulenge community, which had become increasingly disillusioned with RCD—Goma rule.

On 30 July 2002 a peace agreement, mediated by Mbeki, was signed by Kabila and Kagame in Pretoria, South Africa. Under the accord, Kabila pledged to arrest and disarm the Interahamwe militia in the DRC, while the Rwandan Government was to withdraw its troops from the country. President Robert Mugabe of Zimbabwe subsequently pledged to withdraw the remaining Zimbabwean troops supporting the DRC Government, and by the end of October most, if not all, had left. In mid-August the DRC and Uganda reached an accord in the Angolan capital, Luanda, providing for the normalization of relations between the two countries, and the full withdrawal of Ugandan troops in the DRC. Donors linked continued assistance to Rwanda to its troops leaving the DRC, and Rwandan troops were officially withdrawn in the first week of October. The withdrawal was verified by MONUC, but it lacked the resources to perform this task thoroughly, and it was widely alleged that it was incomplete.

Rwandan troop withdrawals were swiftly followed by Mai-Mai attacks on areas controlled by RCD—Goma, apparently with assistance from the DRC Government. Uvira was seized by the Mai-Mai in mid-October 2002, but was reoccupied by RCD—Goma one week later. The DRC Government began to implement its part of the Pretoria Agreement by expelling 25 leaders of the Forces démocratiques pour la libération du Rwanda (FDLR). The FDLR claimed to represent Rwandans in the DRC, and denied any link to the genocide, but appeared, nevertheless, to be linked to the Interahamwe. Controversially, eight of the leaders were repatriated to Rwanda, provoking a rebellion among Rwandan Hutu combatants encamped in Kamina, following which an unknown number fled the town. There were no further DDRRR campaigns by the DRC Government, which claimed instead that most Rwandan Hutu combatants had left government-held territory and crossed into territory occupied by RCD—Goma. The RCD—ML lost control of its stronghold, Bunia, in the Ituri region of Nord-Kivu, in mid-August to a breakaway faction, headed by Thomas Lubanga, which subsequently became known as the Union des patriotes congolais (UPC). The RCD—ML relocated to the nearby town of Beni, from where it was reported to be receiving supplies from the DRC Government. During late 2002 the RCD—ML was engaged in fierce hostilities, in the region of Isiro, in the north-east, with another breakaway faction of the RCD, known as the RCD—National (RCD—N), which was led by Roger Lumbala and supported by the MLC. In December the UN Secretary-General's special representative to the DRC, Amos Namanga Ngongi, mediated a cease-fire agreement between the RCD—ML, RCD—N and MLC, which led to a reduction in fighting for a short time, although skirmishes were again reported around Beni in early 2003. Meanwhile, in Bunia the UPC initially allied itself with Ugandan forces, but in December 2002 concluded an agreement with RCD—Goma, and subsequently received military supplies from the Rwandan Government. In late October the UN commission investigating the illegal exploitation of the DRC's resources by nations involved in the conflict published a new report, detailing the systematic exploitation of the DRC by 'élite networks' from Zimbabwe, Angola, Uganda, Rwanda, and the DRC itself. The report failed to support demands for a ban on the export of raw materials from the DRC, but recommended that certain sanctions be imposed on all the individuals and companies named in the report, and reduced aid to countries accused of involvement in exploiting the DRC. The findings of the commission were rejected by every accused nation, and, although welcomed by the UN Security Council, no action was taken against those accused of exploitation in the report.

A New Transitional Government

Talks resumed in Pretoria in November 2002 between groups participating in the inter-Congolese national dialogue, which on 17 December signed a new agreement, providing for a transitional Government, to be headed by Kabila, with four Vice-Presidents. The Vice-Presidents were to be representatives of the incumbent DRC Government, the MLC, RCD—Goma and the political opposition. It was agreed that the new Government would comprise at least 35 ministers from all parties involved in the inter-Congolese national dialogue. To include all groups, most ministries were divided into several components (creating, for example, three education ministries and four finance and economy ministries). The new transitional Parliament was to comprise a 500-member National Assembly and a 120-member Senate. In addition, new Congolese armed forces, composed of elements of the existing military, were to be established, although details remained undecided. In late March Masire convened a plenary meeting of all the participants in the inter-Congolese national dialogue, and on 2 April all parties officially signed a final accord providing for the adoption of the transitional organs of government (endorsing the Sun City and Pretoria Agreements). However, Kabila failed to attend the signing ceremony, attracting much criticism from the other delegates.

Following the predominantly Hema UPC's alliance with RCD—Goma in Ituri, the Ugandan armed forces transferred support to a militia mainly comprising members of the rival Lendu ethnic group, the Front de l'intégration pour la pacification de l'Ituri (FIPI). On 6 March 2003 FIPI and Ugandan armed forces seized Bunia from the UPC. In early April the UPC was implicated in the massacre of up to 800 Lendu civilians in the Ituri region. In the same month a new multi-faction Commission pour la pacification de l'Ituri (CPI) was established to assume control of the troubled region, but was weakened immensely by the refusal of the UPC to join. The Rwandan Government, alleging that the Ugandan armed forces were assisting the Interahamwe, threatened to invade again if Uganda's troops failed to leave the country. Following pressure from the South African Government, Ugandan troops left at the end of April. The UPC immediately attacked Bunia, and recaptured it after fierce fighting, during which many civilians were massacred by all sides. At that time MONUC had a 700-member force (mainly Uruguayan) in Bunia, but the limitations of its mandate hindered its ability to respond decisively, apart from sheltering several thousand people in its compound. The continuing violence in Ituri prompted increasing international calls for action. In mid-May Mkapa convened a peace summit in Dar es Salaam, Tanzania, which was attended by Kabila and most of the factions and resulted in a cease-fire agreement, which reduced the scale of the fighting in Ituri, but failed to end it. On 30 May the UN Security Council authorized the deployment of a French-led Interim Emergency Multinational Force of 1,500 troops to stabilize the situation, which commenced deployment in early June.

After extensive disputes over security, an RCD—Goma delegation finally arrived in Kinshasa on 27 April 2003. The nomination of the four Vice-Presidents, due to have been completed by 5 May, was impeded by dissension within opposition ranks, but on 29 June all former combatant groups finally signed an agreement on power-sharing in the future integrated transitional armed forces. This final stage in the peace process allowed Kabila on the following day to nominate a transitional Government, in which ministries were divided between rebel groups, the incumbent administration, political opposition and civil society organizations. The four Vice-Presidents were sworn in on 17 July and the first session of the new power-sharing Government took place on 25 July. On 20 August Kabila announced the nominations to the military leadership of the new unified armed forces, which was to incorporate elements of all the former rebel groups and the Mai-Mai militia; former RCD—Goma and MLC commanders were appointed to senior posts, including services chiefs of staff. On 22 August the inaugural session of the new bicameral transitional Parliament was conducted at the People's Palace, in Kinshasa; seats in the 500-member National Assembly and 120-member Senate were likewise divided between the former rebel groups, the Mai-Mai, the incumbent Government, political opposition and civil society.

In August 2003 William Swing, who had previously served as the US ambassador to DRC during 1998–2001, was appointed the new Special Representative of the UN Secretary-General in the DRC. Shortly afterwards, at the beginning of September, the French-led contingent officially transferred control of the Ituri region to MONUC reinforcements (after the UN Security Council at the end of July considerably increased MONUC's authorized maximum strength).

Tshisekedi returned to Kinshasa in late September 2003 for the first time since his alliance with the RCD—Goma in May 2002. Although Tshisekedi retained some support in the capital, he was widely criticized for boycotting talks with the unarmed opposition over the appointment of a Vice-President for the transitional Government, which resulted in the exclusion of the UDPS from the administration and its marginalization from mainstream politics.

In mid-January 2004 three senior officers were appointed to the posts left vacant by Gen. Laurent Nkunda and several other RCD—Goma officers who had earlier refused to assume them, but there was little progress towards forming the new reintegrated armed forces, nor in developing the eagerly awaited national DDRRR programme.

Kabila presented new nominations for the provincial governors in mid-May 2004. The PPRD secured three provinces (Kinshasa, Bas-Congo and Kasaï Occidental). The appointed Governor of Katanga, Kisula Ngoy, was, according to the Government, a Mai-Mai representative, but was widely held to be a Kabila supporter, resulting in protests in Lubumbashi. The RCD—Goma was allocated the governorship of Province Orientale and Nord-Kivu and the vice-governorship in Sud-Kivu, while the MLC was allocated Bandundu and Kasaï Oriental provinces.

The Government finally presented its DDRRR plan to donors in May 2004, and later that month the World Bank approved a US $100m. grant to fund it. The difficulties in implementing the programme were almost immediately emphasized, when, in late May, troops loyal to Kabila and the RCD—Goma clashed in Bukavu, resulting in several thousand Banyamulenge fleeing across the border into Rwanda. MONUC demanded that pro-RCD—Goma troops enter a cantonment camp established for integrating rebel forces, which most duly did by the end of the month. Two days later, however, several thousand troops loyal to Nkunda attacked the pro-Kabila forces, led by Col. Mbuza Mabe, and seized control of Bukavu on 2 June. Failure of MONUC troops to prevent this caused protest riots in Kinshasa, Lubumbashi and several other towns. Kabila accused Rwanda of redeploying troops on DRC territory, a charge that the Rwandan Government denied. As MONUC pressure on him increased, Nkunda later withdrew from Bukavu, allowing Mabe to reoccupy the city.

Soon after the anti-UN riots in Kinshasa, there was a short-lived coup attempt in the city during the night of 10–11 June 2004. The national radio and television station was briefly seized by about 20 dissident members of the armed forces, led by Maj. Eric Lenge, a member of the presidential guard, but loyal troops soon regained control of Kinshasa, arresting 12 of the dissidents, and Lenge fled into hiding.

In August 2004 some 160 Banyamulenge, numbering among 20,000 who had fled from Bukavu in June when Mabe retook the city to take refuge in Burundi, were massacred at a refugee camp at Gatumba, near the border between the two countries. Although a Burundian Hutu rebel faction, Forces nationales de libération (FNL), admitted responsibility for the atrocity, the Governments of Burundi and Rwanda maintained that DRC-based Hutu militia, Mai-Mai and even the DRC armed forces had been involved and threatened to resume military engagement in the DRC. The US-based Human Rights Watch (HRW) later reported that the evidence for significant participation in the massacre by militia other than the FNL was slight, but this was dismissed by Banyamulenge community leaders. A UN report into the massacre failed to reach a conclusion on who executed it. Soon after the massacre, Ruberwa briefly suspended his participation in the transitional Government in protest, but rejoined it, following talks with Mbeki in Kinshasa.

In early December 2004 the Rwandan President Paul Kagame twice threatened to redeploy the Rwandan armed forces in the DRC, if neither MONUC nor DRC government forces acted decisively against the FDLR, but rescinded this threat later in the month, following intense pressure from donors. There were subsequent reports of Rwandan troop movements on the border, and, covertly, inside the DRC, leading to increasing concern that conflict might resume between the two countries. At the same time clashes erupted in Kanyabayonga, Nord-Kivu, between competing factions of the armed forces, loyal to the RCD—Goma and to Kabila, forcing at least 60,000 people from their homes. In mid-November the transitional National Assembly adopted new legislation on the definition of Congolese nationality, specifying that anyone belonging to an ethnic group whose members or territory constituted the DRC at independence was Congolese. According to this definition, Banyamulenge and other Kinywarwanda-speaking residents of the Kivu provinces (except for those who crossed over in 1994) were Congolese, thereby fulfilling a main demand of the RCD—Goma and the Rwandan Government.

Following a parliamentary inquiry that accused a number of government members of corruption, in late November 2004 Kabila suspended six cabinet ministers and 12 heads of parastatals. Affected political parties protested, and the MLC suspended participation in the Government for a time (prompting a visit to Kinshasa by Mbeki to resolve the dispute), but in mid-January 2005 all except one of the ministers were replaced. Efforts by MONUC during 2004 to demobilize combatants in Ituri made little progress, and by the end of the year only about 500 combatants had registered for the disarmament programme, nearly one-half of whom were children. In December 2004 Kabila appointed the chief commanders of the six main Ituri militia as generals in the armed forces, attracting strong criticism from human rights organizations that they were being rewarded for the atrocities they had committed. There was further fighting in Ituri in January 2005, displacing thousands of people into Uganda; nevertheless, progress was made in demobilization, and by the end of February an estimated 3,000 Ituri-based combatants had been demobilized.

Delays in Election Timetable

In January 2005 Abbé Apollinaire Malu-Malu, the head of the Commission électorale indépendante (CEI), annouced that elections would be delayed, leading to large public protests in Kinshasa and other towns, which were suppressed by the security forces. In late January the UN panel of experts monitoring an international armaments embargo on the eastern DRC produced a second report, alleging numerous instances of the embargo's violation in Ituri, Nord- and Sud-Kivu. It documented a close link between mining interests and the conflict, with Ituri militia battling for control of gold exports, and rival factions of the armed forces and the Mai-Mai fighting over cassiterite and coltan deposits in Nord-Kivu. The report alleged ongoing links between the Mai-Mai, which had been incorporated into the armed forces, and the FDLR, contrary to the DRC Government's official position that it had ended all contacts with the Rwandan militia. The UN panel also concluded that the Rwandan, Burundian and Ugandan Governments were still supporting militia in eastern DRC, again contrary to their official undertakings. All three countries subsequently denied any involvement. In mid-February the Front des nationalistes et intégrationnistes (FNI), one of the main Ituri militias, killed nine MONUC personnel. Several militia leaders were subsequently arrested, including the FNI's leader, Floribert Ndjabu Ngabu, and Thomas Lubanga of the UPC.

The FDLR announced in February 2005 that it would end its armed struggle, providing the Rwandan Government allowed it to return home and transform itself into a political party. The Rwandan Government replied that the FDLR could return but that its members would be investigated for possible involvement in the 1994 genocide. The offer was rejected by the FDLR. In January 2005 African Union (AU) Heads of State, meeting in Abuja, Nigeria, had agreed to deploy an African force in eastern DRC to assist in the forcible disarmament of the FDLR, but despite a promise of European Union (EU) funds, the plan was not implemented. The UN Security Council voted in mid-April to adopt the recommendation of the UN panel of experts investigating implementation of the armaments embargo in eastern DRC, that the embargo be extended to the entire country. The Council issued a special appeal to regional governments to ensure that aircraft flying out of their countries were not used to transport weapons, but refrained from threatening sanctions against them should they fail to do so. Later in the month a number of military personnel and civilian politicians were arrested in the Katangan capital Lubumbashi, on suspicion of organizing a bid for the province's secession. André Tshombe, the son of Moïse Tshombe, who led Katanga to secession in the early 1960s, was among those arrested. Kabila then travelled to Lubumbashi in May, in an effort to calm the situation, and rally support for himself.

New Constitution Approved

On 13 May 2005 the transitional National Assembly adopted a new Constitution, which was scheduled to be submitted to a popular referendum within six months. The Constitution provided for a President, who was to appoint the Prime Minister and his administration, which were then to formulate policy. The President, however, was to remain head of the Council of Ministers. Ministers, but not the President, were to be answerable to the National Assembly. The National Assembly was empowered to dismiss the Government, but not the President, while the President was to retain the right to dissolve the National Assembly. The new Constitution also increased the 11 provinces in existence to 26, which were to receive greater autonomy than previously. The transitional process was scheduled to end following elections on 29 March 2006.

In mid-June 2005 the CEI began registering voters, and by the end of the process in November had impressed many international observers by having registered about 25m. Tshisekedi, however, urged his supporters not to register, on the grounds that the electoral process was flawed. Tshisekedi's claims were dismissed by Malu-Malu, but the veteran politician proved that he had a substantial following when more than 15,000 attended a UDPS rally in Kinshasa on 9 July.

The demobilization and disarmament campaign in Ituri, meanwhile, made further progress during early 2005, and by late June MONUC estimated that 15,000 combatants had been demobilized. A coalition of three militia groups, however, known as the Mouvement Révolutionnaire Congolais (MRC), formed in Uganda in June, determined to continue fighting, denouncing the demobilization campaign and demanding Iturian autonomy. Following the formation of the MRC, a Congolese government delegation travelled to Uganda to discuss the matter with Ugandan President Yoweri Museveni, who promised not to allow MRC leaders to assemble in Kampala in future. After a period of relative quiet, there was further violence in Ituri in October, particularly in Mongbwalu, the site of a gold-mining concession operated by the South African company Anglogold Ashanti, prompting government troops to increase deployment in the area.

With no prospect of political negotiations between the FDLR and the Rwandan Government, MONUC began in mid-2005 to become more involved in the Government's ongoing military campaign in Sud- and Nord-Kivu against the militia. In late July the Government announced a deadline of 30 September for all foreign troops to leave the country and soon afterwards MONUC announced that it was ready to assist the armed forces in also expelling the anti-Ugandan Government movement, the Lord's Resistance Army (LRA). Uganda had increasingly complained that anti-Ugandan Government militias were based in eastern DRC and warned that, if the DRC authorities failed to take action, the Ugandan armed forces might intervene instead. Meanwhile, in August Nkunda threatened from a secret location in Nord-Kivu to overthrow the Government. The Government then formally stripped Nkunda of his rank, and during September carried out a number of arrests of those suspected of links with him. There were clashes between Nkunda's supporters and a joint force of government and MONUC troops near Rutshuru, in Nord-Kivu, in mid-January 2006, forcing over 50,000 civilians to flee from the region.

A UN Security Council delegation visited the country in early November, and urged the Government to accelerate electoral preparations. The delegation also met with Tshisekedi, in an unsuccessful attempt to persuade him to participate in the elections. Also in November Bemba expelled the President of the National Assembly, Olivier Kamitatu Etsou, from the MLC. Kamitatu Etsou subsequently established his own party, the Alliance pour le renouveau du Congo.

The long-awaited constitutional referendum was conducted on 18 December 2005. According to the official results, announced in mid-January 2006, the new Constitution was approved by 84.3% of votes cast, although only 62% of the registered electorate had participated in the ballot. Fewer than 10,000 copies of the Constitution had been circulated before the vote, the pre-referendum campaign lasted only two weeks and was focused on major urban areas, indicating that few people had an idea of what they were voting for. Later in January the CEI once again postponed elections, citing logistical difficulties.

Military reforms, meanwhile, which were to integrate previously warring factions into the armed forces, were proceeding slower than originally envisaged. By the end of 2005 only six of 18 planned integrated brigades had been established, trained and deployed. Government and MONUC troops carried out further joint operations against the MRC in Ituri during late 2005 and early 2006, and in late December 2005 the Ugandan Government arrested and transferred 51 MRC combatants to the DRC. Government and MONUC troops also attacked Ugandan militia bases in Nord-Kivu and Haut-Zaire provinces, near the Sudanese border. On 24 January 2006 eight MONUC soldiers from Guatemala were killed by militia suspected to be LRA in the Garamba National Park in Haut-Zaire. At the same time as pursuing rebel militia in the east, in late 2005 the Government also launched military operations against Mai-Mai militia, under the command of Kyungu Mutanga (also known as Gédeon), in Katanga. The government initiative prompted mass population displacement, but managed to achieve the disarmament of some 2,000 Mai-Mai by the end of the year.

Kabila Wins Democratic Elections

The new Constitution was formally promulgated by Kabila on 18 February 2006. On 21 February the National Assembly approved the keenly awaited electoral legislation allowing presidential and parliamentary candidates to register, although this was only enacted by Kabila on 9 March. The CEI announced at this time that elections would be rescheduled again, to 18 June, only 12 days before the official end of the political transition period. Within the two-week deadline 33 presidential candidates, including Kabila, Bemba and Ruberwa (but not Tshisekedi), had emerged, while some 9,700 had registered to contest the 500 seats in the National Assembly. In March Lubanga was transferred from MONUC custody to the International Criminal Court (ICC) in The Hague, Netherlands, becoming the first person ever to be arrested by the Court, and in May government and MONUC troops intensified operations in Ituri, in an effort to ensure that elections were conducted peacefully. Seven Nepalese members of MONUC were captured by the FNI in late May, but were released following negotiations between the FNI, the Government and MONUC, after which the FNI also pledged to stop fighting. In return, the Government announced in mid-July that it would integrate FNI units into its forces. A few days later the MRC agreed also to end hostilities in return for integration into the armed forces. Meanwhile, in Haut-Katanga in May Gédeon and several hundred of his supporters surrendered to MONUC forces. In an attempt to ensure peaceful elections in the capital (and the evacuation of foreign nationals if necessary), on 26 April the UN Security Council authorized the temporary deployment of an EU military force (EUFOR RD Congo), led by Germany, in Kinshasa and neighbouring Gabon. The European Council of Ministers gave its approval in mid-June and the troops began arriving shortly afterwards. In a highly controversial announcement, the CEI announced on 1 May that the elections would be rescheduled one further time, to 30 July. Consequently, the elections were to take place after the official end of the transition agreed at Sun City, and the UDPS and many representatives of civil society and the churches argued that Malu-Malu lacked the authority to do this. However, Malu-Malu insisted that the new Constitution superseded the Sun City agreement, and allowed the transitional period to continue until elections were held.

The country's first democratic presidential and legislative elections in over 40 years took place on 30 July 2006. Despite reports of some procedural irregularities and violent incidents in the Kasaï region, where Tshisekedi received most support, most international observer missions announced that the elections had been conducted fairly. However, several presidential candidates subsequently accused the authorities of perpetrating mass falsification of the results, and in early August six poll officials were arrested on suspicion of malpractice. Prior to the announcement of partial results of the presidential election on 20 August, some five people were killed in fighting between members of the security forces and Bemba's supporters in Kinshasa. According to the CEI, Kabila had secured 44.81% and Bemba 20.03% of votes cast; about 70.5% of the electorate had voted. Most of Kabila's support came from Katanga, and eastern provinces that had been controlled by the RCD during the war, while Bemba received the most votes in western provinces and Kinshasa. Kabila's failure to secure an absolute majority of votes cast necessitated a second round of the presidential election, scheduled for 29 October (when deputies were also to be elected to the provincial Assemblies), to be followed by elections to the Senate at the end of December. Hostilities between forces loyal to Kabila and Bemba's supporters continued in Kinshasa following the CEI's announcement of the first round results, and MONUC troops intervened to rescue from Bemba's residence 14 foreign diplomats who had attempted to mediate between the factions. EUFOR reinforcements were dispatched to Kinshasa from Gabon, in an effort to restore peace in the capital. After three days of fighting, Kabila and Bemba reached an agreement to withdraw their forces from central Kinshasa.

In September 2006 in The Hague, Netherlands, the ICC charged Lubanga with recruiting children to fight in the UPC, much to the disappointment of human rights campaigners, who had hoped he would also be charged with committing gross human rights violations. Earlier that month the CEI released provisional results of the legislative elections, according to which the Parti du peuple pour la reconstruction et la démocratie, as the PPRD had been restyled, secured 111 seats, while the MLC won 64. The other main winners in the legislative poll were the Parti lumumbiste unifié (PALU), which gained 34 seats, the Mouvement social pour le renouveau, which secured 27, the Forces du renouveau (FR), which won 26, and the RCD 15. Some 63 other parties also secured parliamentary representation.

In mid-September 2006 PALU president Antoine Gizenga agreed to join Kabila's Alliance pour la majorité présidentielle (AMP), giving the multi-party coalition 285 seats, and thus an absolute majority in the National Assembly. In return, PALU was to be allowed to select the next prime minister. The second round of the presidential poll took place as scheduled, and on 15 November the CEI proclaimed Kabila the winner with 58.05% of the vote, compared to Bemba's 41.95%. Bemba officially contested the result before the Supreme Court, which rejected his petition on 27 November, upholding Kabila's victory. Bemba conceded defeat, while still alleging electoral fraud. Kabila was officially sworn in as President at a ceremony on 6 December.

Kabila appointed Gizenga as Prime Minister on 30 December 2006 and after prolonged and intense negotiations, Gizenga announced a new Government in February 2007: a total of 13 cabinet ministers were from the PPRD, five from PALU, and the remainder were members of the AMP. Despite international pressure, no ministerial seats were allocated to the MLC or its alliance partners. François Mobutu, son of the former president, was appointed Minister of State, in charge of Agriculture, while the interior, decentralization and security portfolio was retained by Denis Kalume Numbi, who was named in a 2002 UN report on the illegal exploitation of the country's resources. Antipas Mbusa Nyamwisi, leader of the FR, was appointed Minister of State, in charge of Foreign Affairs and International Co-operation.

Meanwhile, provincial election results were announced in early December 2006, according to which the AMP won majorities in seven provincial Assemblies, while the Union pour la Nation won majorities in four. The provincial Assemblies voted in senatorial elections on 19 January 2007, in which the AMP won 48 seats and the MLC 14; 26 senators were elected as independent. On 27 January the provincial Assemblies elected governors in nine provinces. Despite having majorities in four provincial Assemblies, Bemba's alliance secured only one governorship (that of his home province of Equateur), allegedly due to widespread bribery by the AMP. The election of an AMP governor in Bas-Congo province led to violent protests by Bundu dia Kongo, a secessionist religious organization that advocates independence for the province. At least 135 people were killed in a subsequent crackdown by the authorities in the provincial capital Matadi. The court of appeal in Matadi subsequently annulled the poll result, but it was later upheld by the Supreme Court in Kinshasa.

Violent clashes broke out in Nord-Kivu in November 2006, after Nkunda relaunched military operations in its Rutshuru and Masisi districts. Nkunda and Congolese government representatives met for talks hosted by the Rwandan Government in Kigali in January 2007, at which it was agreed that Nkunda's forces would eventually be integrated into the Congolese armed forces. In the meantime, a process known as 'mixage' was agreed on, according to which Nkunda's troops would fight alongside the Congolese armed forces in their ongoing campaign against the FDLR. A formal ceremony took place in Nord-Kivu, marking the integration of Nkunda's fighters into the armed forces in late March, but by May the agreement had disintegrated, and Nkunda relaunched an aggressive campaign to capture territory in the province, resulting in the displacement of tens of thousands of people. Meanwhile, in Ituri an agreement was signed in late November 2006 between the Government, the MRC, the FNI and the Forces de résistance patriotique en Ituri (FRPI), according to which their fighters would be granted amnesty in return for disarmament by the end of the year. The MRC and FRPI largely adhered to the agreement, but the FNI did not, and fighting resumed in Ituri between the FNI and the Congolese armed forces in February 2007. After several weeks of clashes, the FNI reversed its position, and its forces were formally integrated into the Congolese armed forces at a ceremony in Ituri on 7 April.

In late February 2007 the Government established 15 March as the deadline for the disbanding of private militia. In place of his substantial private army, Bemba was offered 12 policemen as bodyguards, which he rejected as inadequate. The deadline passed and on 22 March fighting erupted in central Kinshasa between the Congolese armed forces and Bemba's troops. The clashes lasted two days, and resulted in at least 150 casualties, as well as extensive damage to property. The Congolese armed forces eventually prevailed and Bemba fled to the South African embassy. Chief Prosecutor Tsaimanga Mukenda issued a warrant for his arrest, seeking to charge Bemba with high treason. Meanwhile, government troops broke into and looted the MLC headquarters in Kinshasa. International diplomatic efforts subsequently secured an agreement that Bemba could leave the country, ostensibly for medical treatment, and he flew to Portugal on 11 April. In a surprise result, veteran politician Kengo Wa Dondo was elected President of the Senate on 11 May, defeating Leonard She Okitundu, who had been the AMP candidate for the post.

FOREIGN RELATIONS

Patrice Lumumba was removed in 1961, and Mobutu Sese Seko installed with the forceful assistance of Western powers, on the understanding that he would protect against Communist expansion in Africa. Mobutu used this leverage skilfully, and extracted substantial aid from the West, particularly the USA, France and Belgium, until the late 1980s, when the collapse of first Eastern European and then Soviet Communism reduced the concern of Western powers about the advance of Communism in Africa, while at the same time increasing prominence was given in development assistance practices to issues of democracy and human rights, making it harder for donors to justify continued funds being made available for the likes of Mobutu. French and Belgian troops took control of Kinshasa following riots in September 1991, and two months later the French Government formally withdrew support from Mobutu. In the following months Western powers became more interventionist, pressurizing Mobutu to cede power, while urging the opposition to accept Mobutu as titular Head of State, lest Mobutu's sudden removal lead to anarchy.

Zaire's relations with the West improved in 1994 after Kengo Wa Dondo became Prime Minister, and his Government agreed to co-operate with international humanitarian agencies over the crisis arising from the arrival in eastern Zaire of more than 2m. Rwandan refugees in 1994. Most international and regional powers (with the exception of France) welcomed Mobutu's deposition in 1997, although most would have preferred a negotiated settlement, rather than the outright victory through force of arms that was eventually achieved by the AFDL.

Donors declined to finance an ambitious three-year economic programme announced by Kabila's Government in August 1997, and the war that began in the following year resulted in the cancellation of virtually all of the previously pledged development assistance; all balance-of-payments support and debt-rescheduling was also suspended. Some emergency humanitarian assistance reached the country, although most was directed through international aid agencies.

During the war, international bodies, including the UN Security Council and the OAU, repeatedly stressed their support for the DRC's territorial integrity and their wish for foreign forces to withdraw. However, no influential donor nations took practical measures to support Kabila or the countries allied with him, and the USA and the United Kingdom continued to provide substantial financial assistance to Rwanda and Uganda, the two countries with troops in the DRC in conflict with government forces. The assassination of President Laurent Kabila in January 2001 and the election of George W. Bush's Republican Administration in the USA the year before altered the situation. Donors had never had good relations with Kabila, but were immediately more favourable towards his urbane son, Joseph Kabila, whose accommodating stance, particularly regarding economic policy, was in marked contrast to that of his father. In addition, Bush demonstrated less interest in Rwanda's grievances than did President Bill Clinton, his Democratic predecessor, and more concern for the DRC's development into a country safe to invest in. Eighteen months into Kabila's presidency, in June 2002, the IMF granted the DRC access to credit, under a three-year Poverty Reduction and Growth Facility (PRGF), which was the first formal lending programme from a multilateral agency for a decade. In August the World Bank approved an assistance package, and preparations began for the DRC to gain access to debt relief under the initiative for heavily indebted poor countries initiative. The first few reviews of the Government's performance under the PRGF proceeded well, resulting in the release of successive tranches of credit, but completion of the fifth review was delayed, amid growing IMF concern over the rapid deterioration in the quality and transparency of public expenditure. The sixth and final PRGF review was abandoned by the IMF in mid-2006, although the Fund agreed to consider a new arrangement once a new government was installed. Despite the suspension of formal lending by the IMF, international donors remained strongly engaged in the country, not least to fund the elections, which cost more than US $460m. In addition, donors were strongly urged by international pressure groups to take stronger action against apparently systemic corruption and graft, particularly in customs and the mining and forestry sectors.

The transitional Government maintained strong relations with Laurent Kabila's war allies, Zimbabwe, Angola and Namibia, but Zimbabwe's hard-won political and economic influence was overtaken by that of South Africa, owing to Mbeki's strong involvement in the peace process and preparation for elections, and the much stronger South African economy. Following the example of Mbeki, South African companies demonstrated strong interest in the DRC, particularly in the mining and construction sectors. The South African energy parastatal ESKOM has ambitious (and expensive) plans to utilize the DRC's Inga dam to provide energy for the whole of southern Africa.

MONUC was able to achieve little during Laurent Kabila's presidency, and only began substantial deployment in 2001. Despite serious failures, including the inability of MONUC troops to prevent the capture of Bukavu by rebel armed forces officers, MONUC is generally recognized as having contributed to increased peace and security in the country, particularly during the critical immediate pre-election period, when it succeeded in securing conditions reasonably conducive to free and fair elections in most of the country's most unstable regions, such as Ituri and Haut-Katanga. In Nord- and Sud-Kivu, MONUC's increased anti-FDLR operations during 2006 succeeded in mollifying the Rwandan Government, which had previously accused MONUC of culpable ineffectiveness, with the result that Rwanda appeared to do little to foment trouble in the region prior to the elections. The DRC's new Constitution recognized the Congolese Banyarwanda (those of Rwandan origin) as Congolese citizens, which was a main demand of the Rwandan Government, contributing to a further easing of tension. In Ituri, the Rwandan and Ugandan Governments have apparently retained links with ethnic militia involved in illicit gold mining, although their networks have come under increasing scrutiny from UN and non-governmental investigators.

Relations between Joseph Kabila's newly elected Government and the Rwandan and Ugandan Governments have thus far been cordial, but formal diplomatic relations between them have yet to be established. During a visit to Angola by President Kabila in July 2007 an accord was signed with Angola's President Eduardo Dos Santos regarding the clarification of the two countries' borders. It was agreed to return their boundaries to their colonial borders and that a team from the former colonial powers, Portugal and Belgium, would demarcate the border, which would then be ratified by the AU.

Economy

FRANÇOIS MISSER

Revised by the editorial staff

MINING AND PETROLEUM

Although the Democratic Republic of the Congo (DRC, formerly Zaire) commands enormous economic potential and is richly endowed with a wide range of resources, the mining sector dominates the economy. The mining sector contributed an estimated 10.4% of gross domestic product (GDP) and some 83.2% of export earnings in 2004, when it registered growth of 16.3%. The country possesses an abundance of mineral resources, the most important being copper, diamonds, cobalt and zinc; there are also deposits of gold, cassiterite, manganese, cadmium, germanium, silver, wolframite and columbo-tantalite, most of which are exploited only on a small-scale industrial or artisanal basis. Copper, cobalt, zinc and germanium are found mainly in the south-eastern Katanga province, adjoining the Zambian Copperbelt; diamonds are located mainly in the Kasaï provinces, particularly around the towns of Mbuji-Mayi and Tshikapa, although some mining activity is conducted in Bandundu and Province Orientale (formerly Haut-Zaïre) regions. Cassiterite, wolframite, gold and columbo-tantalite are exploited mainly in the Kivu region in the east.

The state-owned mining corporation, the Générale des Carrières et des Mines (GÉCAMINES), was the dominant producer in the 1980s, accounting for more than 90% of copper output, and all production of cobalt, zinc and coal. Production of copper ore declined from 1988 onwards as other world producers, such as Chile, established new opencast, lower-cost mines. Consequently, GÉCAMINES has pursued a policy of vertical integration and increased value added, rather than the accelerated production of ore. Production had declined to 30,800 metric tons by 2000 and in 2002 national output (including GÉCAMINES and other producers) was estimated at 34,000 tons. Cobalt is mined mainly in association with copper, and world prices for this metal are among the most volatile of all minerals. By 2000 GÉCAMINES' cobalt production had declined to 3,739 tons. Intense international pressure to privatize GÉCAMINES prompted the Government to attempt to reduce operating costs by merging the three branches of the company in 1995. Subsequent negotiations regarding the privatization of GÉCAMINES were abandoned, after doubts were raised concerning the integrity of the tender process.

With the capture of Lubumbashi early in April 1997, Katanga's mining concerns were seized by the Alliance des forces démocratiques pour la libération du Congo-Zaïre (AFDL), led by Laurent-Désiré Kabila, who agreed to honour existing contracts. It was estimated that full rehabilitation of GÉCAMINES would require investment amounting to US $1,000m. A controversial framework agreement was signed in April between the AFDL and American Mineral Fields International (AMFI), awarding AMFI exclusive rights to conduct feasibility studies for the rehabilitation of a zinc mine and facilities at Kipushi. Prior to its closure in 1993, the mine also produced copper, gold, silver, cadmium, germanium and cobalt. AMFI was also awarded the Kolwezi copper-cobalt tailings project. A further contract was signed in June 1997 between the Belgian group Forrest International, the US-Finnish OM Group and GÉCAMINES for the processing of tailings in Lubumbashi, with a projected annual output of 5,000 metric tons of cobalt, 3,500 tons of copper and 15,000 tons of zinc by mid-1999. However, some confusion arose when the Government cancelled AMFI's contract for the Kolwezi tailings project in late 1997; AMFI subsequently alleged that the South African-based Anglo-American Corporation had wrongfully sought to invalidate the AMFI agreement. AMFI initiated court proceedings to this effect, although the action was later withdrawn. At that time several international corporations, including Anglo-American, agreed in principle to join a consortium with GÉCAMINES to develop a vast mining project (over 20,000 sq km) in the Kolwezi area. Geologists have estimated that the area has the potential for an annual output of 400,000 tons of copper and 8,000 tons of cobalt; the project has been forecast to cost $1,200m. In early 1998, however, the Congolese Government decided to cancel some 15 mining contracts, owing to the failure of foreign enterprises to invest in these projects. In addition, civil conflict, which commenced in early August of that year, acted as a deterrent to foreign investors.

In September 1998 a joint-venture agreement was signed between GÉCAMINES and Ridgepoint, a Zimbabwean company. Under this agreement, 80% of the Central Mining Group of GÉCAMINES was transferred to Ridgepoint, which retained the right to market the whole of the joint venture's production. In return, Ridgepoint endeavoured to assist GÉCAMINES to increase substantially the annual production of both copper and cobalt by the end of 1999, to 240,000 metric tons and 6,000 tons, respectively. In early 1999 a London-based trader, MRG Cobalt Sales, became the exclusive cobalt marketing agent for GÉCAMINES. A sharp rise in world cobalt prices followed the announcement of the deal. However, the trader withheld these stocks in an attempt to maintain high world prices. As a result, deprived of its cash resources, GÉCAMINES was unable to meet its obligation to its staff and creditors. This provoked strong reactions. In March about 1,000 tons of cobalt, one-quarter of the company's annual output, were seized in South Africa and Belgium, by a group of creditors from those countries. All these problems deterred foreign mining companies from implementing projects in Katanga. The Canadian Tenké Mining company closed its offices in the DRC, while ISCOR abandoned plans to rehabilitate the Kamoto mine. In March 2000 the GÉCAMINES' CEO and the DRC Government revoked the joint venture between GÉCAMINES and Ridgepoint, the Central Mining Group Corporation, which, according to its management, produced 3,000 tons of cobalt in 1999. In December 2000 the Canadian corporation Melkior Resources signed a contract to undertake the mineral development of about 2,800 sq km near Likasi for a period until mid-2002.

Meanwhile, Forrest International was discussing with Union Minière plans to develop Rwashi-Etoile deposits, of which reserves were estimated at 1.7m. metric tons of copper and 224,000 tons of cobalt. In October 1999 Union Minière showed a renewed interest in the Congolese copper belt by acquiring a 20% share in AMFI's interests in Congo Mineral Development (CMD), the joint venture between AMFI and the Anglo-American Corporation for the exploitation of the Kolwezi tailings. Potential production levels of 75,000 tons per year of copper and up to 12,000 tons per year of cobalt were estimated. By late 1999 CMD decided to proceed with an experimental plant programme and an environment impact study as part of a larger feasibility study, valued at US $5.5m. In April 2000 the DRC Government announced the creation of a Metals Exchange of Lubumbashi to market non-ferrous metals.

During 2001 GÉCAMINES' poor performance contributed largely to the Government's decision to dismiss the management boards of the main parastatals. In January 2002 the World Bank announced financial support of $25m., in order to allow GÉCAMINES to relaunch its production and, in particular, the exploitation of the Etoile tailings at Rwashi. However, the World Bank also urged both the Government and the mining companies to abstain from signing 'unethical contracts' at a donors' conference, held in December 2001 in Brussels, Belgium. A memorandum from GÉCAMINES employees, sent to President Joseph Kabila in October 2001, coincided with a statement by the DRC Court of Auditors' Chairman in attributing part of the decline to the failure of the contracts signed with foreign corporations to generate positive results for the Congolese parastatal. Of the total 33 contracts signed by the Congolese parastatal, only two were actually being implemented at that time, according to GÉCAMINES' unions. Between mid-2001 and mid-2002 GÉCAMINES' employees staged strike action several times to protest against agreements which they considered detrimental to the parastatal's interest, and also to demand the payment of salary arrears. GÉCAMINES' unions claimed that such contracts deprived the company of its most productive units.

The combined effect of the fall in international copper prices and the decline in output, which contributed to a year-on-year drop in export earnings generated by GÉCAMINES, from US $139m. in 2001 to $110m. in 2002, further increased tension among employees of the company. This situation and the World Bank's demands for the revision of all partnership contracts prompted the Government in early 2002 to amend some contracts. In March the Congolese authorities decided that the Kambove concentrating plant should no longer be operated by Tremalt Ltd. This measure followed the decision of the new manager of the KMC (a joint venture between GÉCAMINES and Tremalt Ltd) to take legal proceedings against the Congolese parastatal at the International Centre for the Settlement of Investment Disputes over the cancellation of the Ridgepoint-GÉCAMINES contract. By May the projects of only three foreign companies had been approved: Anvil Mining of Australia (which planned to develop the Dikulushi copper and silver mines); Tenké Mining; and Costamin International (a joint venture between the Canadian company Gold City Industries, the Peter Ewert International Group and Congo Stars Mining), owned by a Congolese expatriate, who aimed to develop the exploitation of the Etoile and Kansuki deposits. Despite this advantage, Tenké Mining estimated in early 2002 that the development of the huge Tenké and Fungurumé deposits would not commence before 2004, since this project would be heavily dependent on the improvement of road, electricity and railway infrastructures in Katanga. By contrast, First Quantum Minerals was considering the start of production at the Lonshi copper mine and the refinement of the copper ore at its Bwana Mkubwa installations in Zambia. Meanwhile, Anvil Mining proceeded with the development of the Dikulushi project, and in early 2002 signed a contract with the Australian Metallurgical Design and Management company for the construction of a treatment plant, due to commence production by August. Zincor, a subsidiary of the South African corporation Kumba, also signed a joint venture agreement with AMFI to rehabilitate the Kipushi copper and zinc mines. At that time many mining enterprises reaffirmed their interest in the abundant mineral reserves of Katanga, as prospects for a peace settlement increased shortly before the inter-Congolese peace discussions in Sun City, South Africa. This assisted in creating awareness among GÉCAMINES and government officials that they could benefit more from their joint venture agreements. In early 2002 a dispute arose between GÉCAMINES and the OM Group, which was accused of not providing sufficient returns for the benefits derived from the sale of germanium, a by-product of copper and cobalt obtained from the processing in Finland of products mined in the DRC. According to US mining experts, GÉCAMINES provided as much as one-third of the international production of this strategic mineral (of which the price was estimated at $840–$880 per kg by April 2002), used as an optic fibre component in the armament industry and for space technology purposes. A new mining code, aimed at providing incentives to investors, with the assistance of the World Bank and of the Congolese Federation of Diamond Traders, was approved by the legislature in June. According to the Ministry of Mines, the new code was expected to provide a liberalized foreign-exchange regime, a more transparent and predictable licensing system and to accelerate the process of approving projects. In July the Anglo-American Corporation withdrew from the venture with AMFI, which managed in February 2003 to find two other enterprises for joint development of the Kolwezi tailings project: the World Bank's International Financial Corporation and the Industrial Development Corporation of South Africa.

At the end of November 2002 the DRC's total cobalt production was 9,376 metric tons (compared with 10,767 tons in 2001), of which 5,470 tons were produced by the joint venture between Forrest International and GÉCAMINES at Lwiswishi, while output of the STL joint venture was 1,731 tons for the first eleven months of 2002. Meanwhile, GÉCAMINES' own production, excluding output from joint ventures with other partners, had declined to 1,579 tons, compared with 3,564 tons in November 2001. Apart from legal production, however, the mass illicit exploitation of heterogenite (a cobalt ore with a high content of 20%) by thousands of artisan diggers in the GÉCAMINES concessions, was causing much concern for the producers of the formal sector. This phenomenon, which started in 2001, not only deprived GÉCAMINES of high value minerals, but also threatened to affect the future profitability of mining in the area and contributed to the decline of international cobalt prices. The crisis of the global commercial airline industry, a major consumer of superalloys, following the 11 September 2001 terrorist attacks in the USA, adversely affected international prices. Unfortunately, this trend coincided with an excess of supplies from established producers, combined with higher sales from the US National Defense Stockpile and larger recycled scrap sales. All these circumstances prompted the Forrest Group and GÉCAMINES, which jointly operated the Lwiswishi opencast mine, to suspend operations until early May 2003, in order to carry out planned maintenance works that had been long postponed. The interruption of this operation for four months and the erosion of the stocks contributed to a substantial rise in the international price of cobalt, which was US $4.2 per kg by mid-May. As a result, the DRC's 2003 cobalt output was expected to be substantially lower than the previous year. In May the Forrest Group announced plans to invest $55m. for the construction of a new metallurgic plant at Lwiswishi to process the concentrates. In order to increase the profitability of such investment, the Forrest Group also acquired a majority share in the Kisenda copper mine at Kasumbalesa, with a potential annual output of 40,000 tons of copper, thereby taking advantage of the opportunities offered by the new mining code, which authorized the sale of some mining assets to private partners. The exploitation of manganese ore by the Société Minière Kisenge-Manganèse had ceased altogether in October 2001, when the mines were completely flooded. (In September 2005 Copper Resources Corporation announced that it had agreed to buy 75% of the Forrest Group's 80% ownership of the Kinsenda mine, in exchange for issuing shares to the Forrest Group representing a 40% stake in the company.)

In 2003 mine production of cobalt rose to 7,300 metric tons, compared with 11,900 tons in 2002, while refined cobalt output fell to 1,200 tons, compared with 2,149 tons in 2002. Mine production of copper increased to 59,800 tons in 2003, compared with an estimated 34,000 tons in 2002. Nevertheless, GÉCAMINES and its joint venture partners produced only 16,400 tons of copper in 2003, compared with 29,600 tons in 1999. Zinc output had declined to negligible levels. By mid-2004 the retrenchment of 10,000 employees of a total workforce of 24,000 at GÉCAMINES, which was financed by the World Bank, had failed to bring palpable results. Theft was identified as one of the main causes for the ongoing crisis of the parastatal; other factors were lack of investment, fuel and spare parts, and poor infrastructure.

AMFI announced in February 2004 that the Kingamyambo Musonoi Tailings (KMT), in which it held a 82.5% share (while GÉCAMINES and the state retained respectively 12.5% and 5% of the remaining stock), had successfully completed the first stage of an environmental and social impact assessment for its Kolwezi copper and cobalt project. However, progress was expected to be slow to materialize. Indeed, production was scheduled to begin only in 2007, at an annual level of 42,000 metric tons of copper and 7,000 tons of cobalt. During the visit of the South African President, Thabo Mbeki, to the DRC in January 2004, a memorandum of agreement was signed for a number of mining, tourism and railways projects, totalling $10,000m. The list included the development of GÉCAMINES Ruashi copper and cobalt mine.

By the end of April 2004, in an attempt to clarify the situation in the mining sector, the Government suspended the lease contract of GÉCAMINES' Etoile copper and cobalt concession to a company called CHEMAF, on the grounds that the price offered by this corporation was 10 times lower than the estimated potential of US $50m. for this mine. In May the Government also decided to dismiss the management of the Cadastre Minier (Cami), the entity in charge of the distribution of mining permits, owing to its failure to organize open tenders.

In 2004 an improvement was recorded, with copper production increasing substantially to 73,300 metric tons, while the cobalt output rose to 8,900 tons. STL alone expected to produce 4,000 tons of cobalt, 2,500 tons of copper and 15,000 tons of zinc in 2005. New investors emerged in the Katangese mining sector, such as the South African company Metorex, which planned to develop the Ruashi and Etoile copper mines near Lubumbashi, and Tiger Resources Ltd, an Australian company, which announced in May 2005 plans to complete a feasibility study on its newly acquired 3.7m.-ton copper and cobalt resource at Kabolela, to the north-west of Lubumbashi. The acquisition follows from a joint venture with the Belgian-owned Groupe Orgaman trading house. Meanwhile, Chinese businessmen began to express strong interest in the Congolese market. Since President Joseph Kabila's visit to Beijing, People's Republic of China, in March 2005, the Chinese Cobec corporation offered to rehabilitate the Kamatanda copper and cobalt mines and three copper-processing plants in Katanga for US $27.5m. In April Feza Mining, a joint venture between the Chinese company Wambao Resources and the Congolaises des Mines et de Development (COMIDE), inaugurated in Likasi a plant with a production capacity of 4,000 tons of cobalt-copper alloys. Chinese expertise is also provided to equip the Congolese Société de Développement Industriel et Minière du Congo (SODIMICO) with a 14,600-ton capacity furnace to process cobalt and copper ore. These measures were part of a broader strategy from the People's Republic of China to access essential inputs for its expanding economy. By 2004 China was purchasing about $100m. of Congolese cobalt. The continuing smuggling of Katanga's mineral products remained a important problem.

Good governance in the mining sector increasingly became a major concern of both the donors and the Congolese legislature. In November 2004 the IMF announced that its financial assistance to the DRC would be conditional to an audit of the mining sector. Concern for good governance also arose from the many crises undergone by the official bodies in charge of the mining sector since July 2003, when the transitional Government was installed. In August 2004 the head of the Cami was charged with mismanagement and prosecuted by the Minister of Mines. In March 2005 the Cami resumed its operations, after 10 months of interruptions. One of its first challenges was to recover the mining rights owed by the main companies, including the Congolese parastatals, which amounted to over US $30m. In early 2006 a report by a parliamentary commission into the mining industry recommended that no further partnership agreements be signed between GÉCAMINES and foreign mining concerns, on the grounds that the joint ventures resulted in a reduction in profits for the loss-making parastatal. In late 2005 Phelps Dodge Corporation acquired a 57.75% interest in the Tenké-Fungurumé copper-cobalt deposits in Katanga province; Tenké Mining owned 24.75% of the concession, while GÉCAMINES retained 17.5%. A feasibility study was undertaken in mid-2006 and copper production was expected to commence in early 2008. In November 2005 Mining Company Katanga signed a 25-year agreement with GÉCAMINES for the mining and exploitation of Kinsevere and Nambulwa copper-cobalt deposits in Katanga province. In July 2006 Anvil Mining increased its interest in the joint venture from 70% to 80%. The first stage of development of the Kinsevere deposits was scheduled for completion by mid-2007 and the project was expected to produce about 23,000–25,000 tons of black copper per year.

Until 1986 Zaire was the world's leading producer of industrial diamonds. Although about 98% of the country's production, from Kasaï Oriental, is of industrial diamonds, gemstones are also found. Official production figures fluctuate and are inaccurate, as a result of extensive and elaborate smuggling networks. The only large-scale producer is the Société Minière de Bakwanga (MIBA), which produced 8.2m. carats in 1987 and 7.3m. carats in 2004. The remainder of the diamond output is accounted for by artisan diggers (whose share of total output reached 72% in 2004), who are responsible for the majority of smuggling. Combined with MIBA's output, the total official production was 26m. carats in 1998, but declined to 20.1m. carats in 1999, and further, to 16m. carats, in 2000.

Diamonds, which became Zaire's principal source of foreign exchange in 1993, accounted for US $716m. in 1997. In March the AFDL decided to end De Beers' monopoly on the marketing of MIBA's production, allowing American Diamond Buyers, a company associated with AMFI, to open a buying office in Kisangani. Production became auctioned on a monthly basis, although De Beers remained the principal purchaser. De Beers' local subsidiary, SEDICO (formerly SEDIZA), continued to purchase diamonds from artisan diggers. In January 1999 a presidential decree banned all foreign currency transactions and a further decree stipulated that all diamond dealers were to sell their gems in exchange for new Congolese francs (the currency introduced in June 1998—see below). Instead of curbing the fraud, this decision prompted dealers to smuggle a greater proportion of their diamonds out of the DRC, with the result that the value of official production fell from $35m. in December 1998 to $16m. in February 1999, when the Bourse congolaise des matières précieuses (BCMP, Congolese

Precious Materials Exchange), through which all trade in diamonds was to be conducted, commenced operations. The value of artisanal production for the first 10 months of 1999 was $169m., 42.9% lower than that of the corresponding period in 1998.

In March 2000 the trade unions representing MIBA employees criticized the Ministry of Mines' decision to allocate the company's kimberlite deposits of Tshibwe and its alluvial deposits of Senga-Senga, to Nouvelle Minière de Senga Senga (SENGAMINES), a Congolese-Zimbabwean joint venture. According to the MIBA trade union representative, the Government had allocated the company's future reserves to SENGAMINES without any significant compensation. Moreover, such a measure was decided in particularly difficult circumstances for MIBA during the first quarter of 2000, as a result of periodic power shortages, MIBA had to interrupt frequently the production of its processing units. In addition, spare parts and fuel supplies imported from Zambia and South Africa by MIBA were often intercepted on their way to Kasaï Oriental by the Katanga authorities.

Government policies in the diamond sector have been erratic and subject to several reversals. In early June 2000 the state security seized the largest gem ever discovered in the Congo, a 265-carat stone and arrested its owner, the chairman of the Congolese Federation of Diamond Traders. After unsuccessful attempts to sell it without the owner's approval, the gem was eventually returned to him and sold in Tel-Aviv, Israel, in November by International Diamond Industries (IDI), which had obtained a controversial monopoly on all Congolese diamond exports in July. However, IDI proved unable to mobilize the stipulated amount of money to purchase DRC output. According to UN experts, this situation encouraged the smuggling of diamonds out of the country, which were valued by government sources at an estimated US $400m. per year. After the assassination of President Laurent-Désiré Kabila in January 2001, government policies in the sector changed radically. By mid-April the diamond market was fully liberalized, while IDI's monopoly was abolished in early May. In an attempt to prevent illicit trade in diamonds by identifying the origin of the gems, the DRC Government signed an agreement with the Antwerp Diamond High Council on 27 April, which provided for the establishment of a system of certification for all Congolese exports to Belgium. The signature took place at the end of an international conference, organized in the context of the Kimberley Process, which was also designed to prevent trafficking in 'conflict diamonds'.

In 2001 figures for total diamond exports combined both official production and estimates of illicit exports, smuggled from the government-held territory or traded with the consent of the administration of the rebel movement in the eastern part of the country. In 2001 estimates of exports from rebel zones by non-governmental organizations, UN sources and the rebel administrations varied considerably, between US $16m. and $42m. There was also a very wide discrepancy between government export figures for 2001 and those of Belgian imports from the DRC in that year, which were much higher. Since the DRC also exported to several other countries, particularly South Africa, it was likely that the malpractice was even higher and might amount to several hundred million dollars. In addition to smuggled gems, the Congolese press revealed in November that deliberate under-valuations by official agents were common practice. In any case, according to official figures, diamond exports amounted to 29m. carats, $462m. in value, in 2001, following the abolition of IDI Diamond's marketing monopoly in May of that year. An ascending trend was confirmed in 2002, when diamond exports (including parallel-market exports) amounted to $653m. and 36m. carats, showing increases of some 41% in value and 24% in volume, compared with the previous year. This performance was largely due to a rise in the quality and the volume of artisanal production, which accounted for about 81% of the value of total exports. Owing to the deterioration of equipment, which it could not afford to replace, MIBA was forced to exploit its own tailings, instead of mining more diamond-bearing resources (which were near depletion anyway). The main problem of the company was that, due to government injunctions, it was forced in February 2000 to transfer its best kimberlite concessions of Tshibwe to the SENGAMINES consortium. A small proportion of the output was contributed by GÉCAMINES (368,039 carats, valued at $3.1m.) and from the National Service production brigades established by the former President Laurent-Désiré Kabila (16,000 carats, valued at $190,000). Much of the improved performance was due to the valuation of gems by the newly created Centre d'Expertise et d'Evaluation du Congo (CEEC). However, CEEC figures for 2002 failed to mention SENGAMINES exports. The difficulties of MIBA were partly attributable to the discovery, by a committee established by the Belgian Senate to investigate the illegal exploitation of the DRC's natural resources and connections with the conflict, that the company had been instructed by the DRC Government in 1999 and in 2001 to purchase armaments from Eastern European countries. At that time MIBA concessions continued to be invaded by large numbers of illicit artisan diggers. In early 2003 the company adopted extensive measures for improved security, which included the introduction of a South African corporation, Overseas Security Services. The company's recovery plan for 2002–06 also envisaged important investments to increase the exploitation of kimberlite in order to compensate for the exhaustion of the detritic (surface) reserves. MIBA was considering the investment of some $120m. for the construction of a new tailings processing plant, the rehabilitation of the sorting station, the completion of a kimberlite processing unit, and the purchase of three turbines at the Lubilanji II hydro-electric power station. At that time MIBA's concessions also included nickel reserves, estimated at 324,000 metric tons, at Lutshasha, chrome deposits, estimated at 1.8m. tons, at Nkonko and four gold and silver concessions in the Kasaï Oriental province.

In 2003 the DRC achieved record production of 27.0m. carats of diamonds, valued at US $642m. Artisanal production accounted for about 71% of the total in volume and 81.5% in value. The rest was provided by MIBA, which improved its performance substantially, to 6.9m. carats, valued at $102.4m., and by SENGAMINES, which produced 1.1m. carats, worth $16.1m. The 23% increase in volume and 62.3% increase in value of total production were credited to stricter valuation controls performed by the CEEC and to the implementation of the Kimberley Process at all stages. However, controversy emerged in September concerning the marketing of MIBA's production. Indeed, the Minister of Mines considered that the terms of the sale of 22.2m. carats of MIBA's diamonds between August 2003 and July 2007 to Emaxon, an Israeli-owned company based in London, United Kingdom, would result in a $160m. loss for the Congolese mining company. According to the agreement, MIBA would receive only a $15m. loan, which would be used to purchase mining equipment in order to enable MIBA to exploit alluvial diamond deposits and to finance the construction of washing and sorting installations. Eventually, all parties agreed that the contract should be implemented, but that more favourable price conditions should be renegotiated. MIBA's decision to obtain such a loan was due to the company's financial crisis. A Belgian state investigation discovered that the main cause of all MIBA's problems was embezzlement of company funds amounting to $80m., by its former chief executive, Jean-Charles Okoto, who transferred the money to a Belgian bank account. In June 2004 an international warrant of arrest was issued against Okoto.

Despite the diamond production increase registered in 2003, illegal trade remained considerable. In May 2004 a Kimberley Process Certification Scheme (KPCS) investigated allegations that about 2m. carats of diamonds, valued at US $400m., mainly comprising smuggled gems from the DRC, were re-exported from the Republic of the Congo. Evidence of massive fraud in the trade of DRC diamonds, discovered through the KPCS, resulted in the expulsion of the Republic of the Congo from the system in July. Indeed, according to the DRC authorities, the Republic of the Congo authorities had been unable to prove that the diamonds exported from their country were produced locally. Also in May the DRC Minister of Mines requested that the Belgian authorities and Interpol seize a diamond of 822 carats, which was sold in Antwerp for $17m. without a certificate issued by the CEEC and which was exported illicitly through the Republic of the Congo capital, Brazzaville. However, illegal Angolan diamonds (mainly mined by Congolese and West African illegal migrants in the Angolan provinces of Bié and Lunda-Norte) were also smuggled through the DRC during 2003 and 2004. This prompted the Government of Angola to expel 70,000 Congolese from the country between December 2003 and April 2004. In September 2004 Angola resumed the expulsion of Congolese illegals from the diamond-producing areas, in collaboration with the DRC authorities.

The establishment of a transitional Government in July 2003 prompted major mining houses, such as De Beers and BHP Billiton, to request exploration permits in Kasaï Oriental. In August 2004 the Canadian company Southern Era obtained 41 permits, covering a total area of 1,300 sq km in the two Kasaï provinces. Meanwhile, new discoveries were made at Mpendjwa in Bandundu and near Boma (Bas-Congo) in 2003. In principle, the restoration of peace in much of the country should have resulted in an increase of tax and customs revenue generated by the trade of the diamonds from the Kisangani region. In April, however, the Government dispatched police, customs and CEEC agents to recover unpaid taxes from the Kisangani diamond dealers.

In 2004 diamond exports (including parallel-market exports) were estimated at 33m. carats, valued at US $828m. According to CEEC sources, one of the main reason for the good performance was the exclusion of the Republic of the Congo from the KPCS. The largest part of the exports was provided by artisanal production (22.1m. carats, valued at $617m.) Meanwhile, the production of SENGAMINES dropped sharply to 618,058 carats, valued at $11.8m., compared with 1.1m. carats, valued at $16.1m., in 2003. By early June 2005 the company's activities had been completely suspended. A new industrial company, the Kasaï Diamond Company (KDC), commenced operating in April 2004 and exported 4,456 carats, valued at $379,591. In December MIBA announced that it expected its output to rise from 7.3m. carats in 2004 to 8.5m. carats by 2006 and to 10m. carats by 2008, as a result of upgrading its installations. Indeed, during the first half of 2005 MIBA acquired $9m. of equipment, which was supposed to increase from 12 MW to 18 MW the capacity of its Tshiala hydroelectric power station and increase the supply of electricity to its new kimberlite washing plant and to its recently acquired dragline, which was to collect more quality diamonds from the swamps around Mbuji-Mayi. MIBA also planned to raise the percentage of gem-quality diamond mined to 6% in 2008, compared with less than 4% in 2003. During the first 10 months of 2005, diamond exports continued to increase by 23% in value, to $745m., compared with the previous year.

Artisanal and small-scale miners produce gold in Ituri province, in the east of the country. Rehabilitation work commenced in 1989 at the main gold mine, in the north-eastern part of the country, owned by the Office des Mines d'Or de Kilo-Moto (OKIMO). In 1990 two foreign companies in the Belgo-Canadian MINDEV consortium were given management contracts for OKIMO. A new company, the US Barrick Gold Corporation, obtained other exploitation permits from OKIMO in 1996 for 80,000 sq km, of a total of 82,000 sq km. However, by late 1997 the Government reviewed the contract and the area under Barrick Gold's control was reduced to 20,000 sq km. In early 1998, however, a legal dispute arose between Ashanti Goldfields of Ghana and an Australian company, Russel Resources, which both claimed the rights to a 2,000-sq km concession, formerly operated by MINDEV. At the end of 2002 Ashanti Goldfields' rights over the property were recognized, but the company was unable to carry out operations at its Mongbwalu property, owing to chronic insecurity. The private Société Minière du Kivu (SOMINKI) was expected to increase its potential under the new ownership of the Canadian Banro International Capital Inc (known from May 1996 as Banro Resources Corporation—later Banro Corporation). The reserves of both the former SOMINKI concessions and of the OKIMO concessions have been estimated to exceed 250 metric tons of gold. In February 1997 Affimet, a Belgian gold dealer and refiner, initiated negotiations with the AFDL to transfer its gold-refining activities from Burundi to the Kivu region, while the Ugandan company Caleb International expressed an interest in obtaining gold concessions in the region. However, the Fédération des Entreprises du Congo (FEC) protested in March against the continuing smuggling of gold to Rwanda and Uganda. On 31 July 1998 the Government dissolved by decree the Société Aurifère du Kivu et Maniema (SAKIMA, formed in 1997 as the successor to SOMINKI, 93% owned by Banro, 7% by the DRC Government), which held 47 concessions, totalling 10,271 sq km, in eastern DRC. In August Banro made a request for arbitration to the US-based International Centre for Settlement of Investment Disputes. The company, which protested that the measure was taken without prior warning, claimed $1,000m. from the Government. However, the rebels of the Rassemblement congolais pour la démocratie (RCD), who controlled the area, announced in October 1998 that they had suspended the decree. The capture by the RCD of substantial areas of the country has blocked the Government's access to the DRC's main gold mines, including both the SAKIMA and OKIMO concessions. In January 2002, one year after the International Centre for Settlement of Investment Disputes declined to rule on the case of Banro against the DRC Government, and five months after the Canadian company submitted a claim against the DRC at a US District Court, both sides finally reached an amicable agreement over the SAKIMA dispute. Accordingly, the DRC Government committed itself to recognizing Banro's right over the concessions through a presidential decree.

Gold output in 1998 declined sharply to an estimated 4,800 kg (compared with 9,600 kg in 1997), principally as a result of the occupation of the main gold mines in the east of the country by Ugandan and Rwandan forces from August of that year. According to US Geological Survey estimates, gold production had recovered to 7,200 kg by 2000. Owing to insecurity, estimated gold output again fell to only 4,100 kg in 2003. During that year, however, new developments suggested that the DRC could become a significant producer. In November Banro launched a two-year exploration programme on its Twangiza, Kamituga, Lugushwa and Namoya permit regions in Sud-Kivu, of which the confirmed and presumed resources were estimated at about 3.2m. troy oz. By mid-2005 OKIMO had concluded a number of joint-venture agreements with foreign companies, including AngloGold Ashanti, Borgakim, Kibali-Gold, Amani Gold, Moto GoldMines (formerly Equs), Tangold, Goldfields, Blue Rose, Mwana Africa and Rambi Gold. OKIMO's purpose was to use the revenues from the leasing rights paid by these companies to finance its own mining operations and also to establish a new geological database on its concessions in order to negotiate new contracts. However, gold exploitation in Ituri province (where unrest continued) proved to be a difficult exercise. Indeed, the joint venture between OKIMO and AngloGold Ashanti, Ashanti Gold Kilo, which in April 2005 received the authorization to exploit the Mongbwalu mine in a 8,000-sq km concession containing an estimated resource of 100 metric tons of gold ore, was accused by a UN report of having provided support and paid taxes to a local militia (charges that the company denied). At a meeting in Bukavu, the Sud-Kivu small-scale mining companies', traders' and gold-panners' associations requested the Ministry of Mines in May for a substantial reduction of taxes and of licensing costs, arguing that it would also reduce the temptation to engage in illegal activities.

Since August 1998, when civil conflict commenced, the DRC Government has condemned the illicit trade in diamonds, gold, columbo-tantalite (coltan) and timber from the rebel territories to Rwanda and Uganda. In April 2000 the UN Secretary-General proposed that a team of experts investigate the illegal exploitation of the natural resources of the DRC since the beginning of the civil conflict. One year later the experts produced a report, which condemned the Congolese rebels and their allies, the Governments of Rwanda, Uganda and Burundi. The report urged a UN embargo on exports of minerals (cassiterite, coltan, diamonds and gold) and timber from those countries and from rebel-controlled areas of the Congo, for the prosecution of rebel leaders and for the payment of compensation to the DRC Government. However, the UN Security Council extended the duration of the mandate of the team of experts to allow them to investigate more into the illegal exploitation of other Congolese resources, including copper and cobalt and diamonds, mined in government-held territory by Zimbabwean and Namibian interests. A further, similar report was issued in November 2001. A third interim report, published in May 2002, emphasized the role of transit countries, including the Republic of the Congo, the Central African Republic (CAR) and South Africa, and identified some final destination Western European countries, such as Belgium, France, Germany and the United Kingdom. However, the UN Security Council failed to follow the experts' recommendations in favour of an embargo on Rwandan, Ugandan and Burundian mineral exports, which increased dramatically in volume and value during 2001, when the international price for coltan rose sharply. During 2001 a decline in trafficking was reported, partly as a result of the collapse of coltan prices, which fell from US $100 per kg at the end of December 2000 to $22 per kg in July 2001. One of the effects, however, of the UN reports on the illegal exploitation of resources in the DRC was to convince Belgium's Société Générale des Minerais (SOGEM), a subsidiary of UMICORE (formerly Union Minière), to end its coltan purchases from the rebel zones of the DRC in June. In October 2002 the UN published its final report recommending sanctions, including a travel ban and 'freezing' of the assets of individuals allegedly involved in illegal exploitation of the country's resources. The report named more than 80 companies that had violated the Organisation for Economic Co-operation and Development (OECD) guidelines for multinational enterprises. However, these conclusions prompted strong protests from the companies named in the report, which demanded that the UN withdraw its accusations.

In January 2003 the DRC made progress towards stricter control of the illicit trade in its resources by introducing a diamond certification programme, in accordance with the Kimberley Process, which aimed to curb the trade in 'conflict diamonds'. The UN final report had important political consequences. In November 2002 President Joseph Kabila suspended seven senior officials named in the report, including three ministers and the managing directors of both GÉCAMINES and MIBA. In September 2003 the Dian Fossey Gorilla Fund convened a meeting in Durban, South Africa, of all the interests involved in coltan mining in the DRC, in order to address the threat posed by the incursions of poachers and illegal miners to the wildlife in the Kahuzi-Biega national park of Sud-Kivu. In mid-April 2004 DRC officials, mining companies, traders, diggers and civil society representatives held another meeting in Tanzania, to discuss how to accommodate conservation and coltan mining. It recommended seeking donors' support to finance mining activities outside the national park. Despite the withdrawal of the Rwandan and Ugandan armies from the DRC, illicit trade in coltan continued in the mid-2000s, particularly in the Sud-Kivu region.

Zaire became a producer of offshore petroleum in 1975, operating from fields on the Atlantic coast and at the mouth of the River Congo. In 1988 output totalled 10.7m. barrels, declining to 8.5m. by 2000. The reserves in the Atlantic fields, operated by Zaire Gulf Oil, have declined, but a Belgian-Zairean consortium, ZAIREP, operating in the mouth of the River Congo, slightly increased output in 1990. Campaigns of prospecting, undertaken by both companies, were hampered by political instability, and only began to benefit the sector in 1996.

In the face of the prolonged economic recession, the country's petroleum output has been broadly equivalent to domestic demand, although the DRC is reliant on imports, since the local refinery is not equipped to treat this exceptionally heavy petroleum. In the longer term, unless onshore exploration plans near the border with Uganda prove successful, petroleum reserves will be exhausted and, in all probability, the DRC will have to continue to import its domestic requirements. In January 2000 the US corporation Chevron announced that it would invest US $75m. to develop offshore exploration and production. In late 2000 the French corporation Perenco bought out TotalFinaElf's upstream interests in the DRC and became the operator for the onshore Tshiende, Liawenda, Kinkasi, Makelekese and Muanda fields, which produced around 7,000 barrels per day (b/d). Henceforth, the new equity interests in these fields were Perenco and Shell. By early 2001 Chevron's annual output was estimated at 19,000 b/d. The company announced plans to raise production to 21,000 b/d in 2002. Meanwhile, Perenco, which bought Royal Dutch/Shell's interest in the four onshore fields, announced in April 2002 its intention to increase output from 7,000 b/d to 12,000 b/d by the end of that year, as a result of a programme to rehabilitate abandoned wells on those fields. In 2001, as a result of an increase in international prices, earnings from petroleum rose by 23%, to $210.6m., and became the second most important export (after diamonds), accounting for 25% of the country's export revenue in that year. Nevertheless, prospects for the sector in 2002 did not appear to be very favourable, after the Government announced plans to double the taxation on petroleum companies to $5m. per month. Moreover, according to central bank statistics, the DRC's total petroleum production decreased from 25,700 b/d in 2001 to 23,080 b/d in 2002. In June the Government signed an agreement with the Canadian company Heritage Oil, granting it exclusive rights on a 30m.-sq km onshore block in the east of the country, on the shores of Lake Albert, at the Ugandan border. However, in May 2003 the two parties failed to agree on a production-sharing deal. Meanwhile, the DRC initiated a round of talks with Angola in May to find an amicable arrangement on the delimitation of the offshore border. The DRC Government argued that the maritime zone was arbitrarily demarcated in 1984 and that, as a result, the DRC was being denied access to deepwater blocks off shore, of which the potential annual output was estimated at 200,000 b/d. Angola proposed the establishment of a 'common interest area' to exploit the resources and avoid further conflicts. In mid-September 2004 the Angolan Government approved the memorandum of understanding establishing a joint offshore exploration and exploitation zone, which had been signed in June 2003 by officials from both countries. It was expected to resume activities in the zone. However, the agreement failed to include the fields that had already been discovered by operators with Angolan permits. In April 2004 Congo-Bitume announced that it was to commence the extraction of bitumen at the Mavuma deposits in Bas-Congo province, with the aim of meeting domestic demand for road asphalting and exporting the remainder.

In 2003 total petroleum production was estimated at 9.2m. barrels, of which 70% was offshore production. In July 2004 the main operator, ChevronTexaco, which has a 50% share in the DRC offshore operation, with the participation of Union Oil of California (32%) and Teikoku of Japan (18%), announced plans to sells its Congolese interests to Perenco. In that year total petroleum output increased to 10.1m. barrels, while exports of crude petroleum amounted to US $360m. (20% of total exports). By the end of 2004 Perenco announced plans to develop the Liawendo field and increase onshore production to 16,000 b/d, which, added to the offshore 21,000 b/d, could increase total output to 37,000 b/d. Meanwhile, the DRC Ministry of Energy has made efforts to encourage petroleum companies to bid for onshore permits on two blocks of 10,250 sq km and 10,125 sq km (1 and 2, respectively) in the Lake Albert area. The Congolese authorities also aimed to encourage exploration of blocks 3 and 4 of the Lake Tanganyika region, which covered 4,717 sq km and 41,527 sq km, respectively, of onshore and offshore surface, at the Burundian border. At the end of November the Governor of Bandundu announced in Kinshasa the discovery of petroleum reserves in the Kutu, Oshwe and Bagata districts, located in the north-east and the south-east of the province.

Before the second round of voting in the presidential elections in late 2006 foreign investors were already looking to take advantage of strong world mineral prices. BHP Billiton confirmed that they would be building an exploration office in the country. The new Prime Minister Antione Gizenga suggested in February 2007 that in the future sub-Saharan Africa would provide more than one-half of the world's diamond production. Meanwhile, GÉCAMINES continued to perform poorly, with debts of US $1,000m. at November 2006, and it laid off thousands of workers. Analysts claim, however, that if the company could eradicate smuggling and curb corruption the plant could reach annual capacities of around 470,000 metric tons of copper, 17,000 tons of cobalt and 70,000 tons of zinc. Meanwhile, in a significant development in early 2007, the country's power-sharing Government handed over interests in uranium mining to British-based Brinkley Mining. The company's African subsidiary will handle the production of nuclear materials when work on the project begins in October 2007. In March, however, the agreement came under scrutiny when the Minister of Scientific Research denounced it as 'criminal'. Uranium prices, meanwhile rose to a new high of $85 per pound. Following the inauguration of the new Government, it announced that reviews of all mining contracts would begin on 15 May to improve transparency in the sector. However, that date was pushed back to early June.

AGRICULTURE AND FORESTRY

The DRC's wide range of geography and climate produces an equally wide range of both food and cash crops. The main food crops are cassava, plantains, maize, groundnuts and rice, grown mainly by small-scale subsistence farmers. Cash crops include coffee, palm oil and palm kernels, rubber, cotton, sugar, tea and cocoa, many of which are grown on large plantations. The DRC has the potential to be not only self-sufficient in food but also to be a net exporter. In addition, with the exception of some parts of Kivu and Katanga, it has escaped the droughts that have caused such great damage in other parts of Africa in the last 20 years. The share of agriculture's contribution to GDP remained almost constant throughout the 1980s, accounting for 32% in 1989. However, the decline of the mining sector (excluding diamonds) contributed to an increase, to 48.4%, in the agricultural sector's share of GDP in 2004. According to the African Development Bank (ADB), in 1995–2006 the agricultural sector contracted by 1.3%; in 2006, however, it grew by 2.0%. At mid-2005 the agricultural sector employed approximately 60.8% of the working population, according to FAO.

The economic condition of agriculture in the DRC has been adversely affected both by the widespread expropriations of privately owned plantations in the early 1970s and the subsequent decline in output and from poor government funding (only 1% of GDP). The trend improved since the end of the 1980s, with a strong growth in production of food crops. However, the efficient supply of food to urban population centres continued to be impeded by the lack of infrastructure for the transportation of agricultural produce. There have been indications of an improvement in production of local food crops, but this is difficult to assess accurately, since a large proportion are subsistence crops and do not enter the money economy. More recent developments present a mixed outlook. Since the beginning of the 1990s, in most urban centres, an increasing number of inhabitants are growing their own food, either in their own gardens or in public open spaces.

The outbreak of civil war in August 1998 considerably aggravated the food security situation in the country. By May 1999 over one-half of the population of Kinshasa was suffering from acute shortages of food, owing to a sharp increase in petrol prices and the inability to transport food from the fertile regions of Nord-Kivu, which came under rebel control in August 1998. The general climate of unrest deterred peasants from growing and marketing food and the shortage of foreign currency needed for imports. The situation deteriorated further during 1999 and 2000, resulting in the reversal of the trade flow of agricultural products. The DRC, which was a net exporter of food staples to the neighbouring Republic of the Congo, commenced the import of Thai rice via Brazzaville. Government attempts to introduce 'magasins du peuple' ('people's stores') to act as price regulators of essential commodities were not successful, since traders were not willing to sell their goods at government prices. All this contributed to disrupt further the supply to Kinshasa, and to the other main cities, of food products.

Prospects for 2000 were obscured by a drought in the north and in the north-east of the country during the first quarter of the year. In November FAO estimated that the food deficit of Kinshasa alone would total 1m. metric tons by the end of 2000. Despite the growing deficit, the DRC's food imports decreased by one-half in 2000, according to FAO. Unsurprisingly, malnutrition was spreading throughout the country by the end of 2000, particularly in Mbandaka and in Katanga (where 60% of the peasants were lacking seeds, owing to the foreign currency shortages, which prevented their import). In January 2001 France and FAO pledged US $390,000 to finance the cultivation of resistant varieties of cassava, which was the basic staple for 70% of the Congolese population. Several districts of the Bandundu region were adversely affected by famine in that year. In March 2002 cassava, bean and sweet potato plantations, including those of the FAO experimental farm of Kinzau Mwuete, were destroyed by a locust plague. Early that year the Government admitted a complete shortage of fertilizers, which was attributed to the suspension of international co-operation and to the DRC's failure to establish an adequate supply policy, relying exclusively on foreign donations. During 2001 and 2002, however, donors attempted through various measures to assist the DRC in solving its domestic food problems. At the end of 2001 the European Union (EU) offered a €45m. grant for the rehabilitation of branch roads in Bandundu province to allow peasants to supply the cities. Part of the eighth European Development Fund €120m. package, signed in early 2002 in Kinshasa, was allocated to the rehabilitation of a principal section of the essential Matadi–Kinshasa road. In April a Chinese corporation commenced work on the rehabilitation of a further section of the same road, financed by a $50m. World Bank aid package. In late April, as a result of an agreement between the rebel Mouvement pour la libération du Congo (MLC) and the Kabila Government for the establishment of a joint transitional administration, signed in Sun City, South Africa, traffic resumed on the River Congo, between Kinshasa and the town of Bumba (Équateur), thereby increasing prospects of an improvement in food supplies to the capital. The 2002 UN Consolidated Inter-Agency Appeal for the Democratic Republic of the Congo included an agricultural component prepared by FAO, which comprised several projects, totalling $24.8m. The main priority was to provide assistance to 400,000 rural households with malnourished children through distribution of agricultural inputs and establish for them a permanent source of local food crops and vegetable seeds. The package also included a project of emergency assistance to rehabilitate feeder roads in order to give agricultural producers from 60,000 households access to markets and hence stimulate production. In March 2004 the Government requested the assistance of the international community to support the rehabilitation of the ecosystem, which had been destroyed during the conflict in Nord- and Sud-Kivu, and at the Angolan border in Bas-Congo.

In 2005 of an estimated population of 57m. inhabitants, nearly 42m. were undernourished accordingly. About 48% of the deaths of children less than five years old were attributed to malnutrition by the Programme National de Nutrition (PRONANUT) in March. In May of that year FAO announced that US $200m. would be spent in relaunching agriculture programmes. The shortage of essential inputs (seeds, veterinary products) and the poor state of the road network were identified as obstacles to food production and distribution. New varieties of cassava yielding between 20 to 30 metric tons per ha were introduced in 2005, in order to increase food security (about three to five times the current yields). During 2004 and 2005 USAID and Belgium assisted with various programmes, including the distribution of seeds to the farmers. The EU financed the rehabilitation of 4,000 km of rural feeder roads in Kinshasa, Équateur, Bandundu, Nord-Kivu and Sud-Kivu, and contributed €12m. to agricultural development projects and food security. Belgium also contributed to the rehabilitation of feeder roads in Bas-Congo. In 2005 the International Agriculture Development Fund announced a $14.7m. loan to relaunch agricultural projects in the Bumba and Mbandaka regions of Équateur. In some parts of the country, however, food production was hampered by insecurity and the lack of fertilizers and pesticides. Continuing instability in the Masisi area of Nord-Kivu prompted the German non-governmental organization (NGO) Agro Action Allemande to suspend activities in January 2005. In Kasaï, an unidentified disease was affecting the maize, cassava, peanuts and beans crops in Kamiyi territory by April. Chronic food shortages during the dry season have also caused deaths. However, the potential of the DRC's large and fertile territory might attract farmers interested in developing farming or ranching projects. In April a mission of 60 South African farmers prospected the market to identify projects.

Export earnings from agriculture, which accounted for approximately 40% of total revenue in 1960, had fallen to only 12.5% by 1994. This decline has been caused in part by the smuggling of coffee (the major agricultural export); it has been estimated that quantities of smuggled coffee are approximately equal to official production figures. From 1996 onwards, production fell substantially, with the destruction of numerous plantations in Nord-Kivu during the civil war. In 1997, as the result of these factors, disease and poor seed quality, output fell to 17,299 tons. High taxes on coffee exports also contributed to continued smuggling throughout the year towards Rwanda and Uganda. However, in that year the Office national du Café (ONC) launched a US $3.5m. recovery programme, financed by the International Coffee Organization (ICO), the UN Development Programme (UNDP) and a South African commercial bank. In 1998 output in the government-held areas was 21,172 tons, according to the DRC Central Bank, but declined to 18,578 tons in 1999, to 11,000 tons in 2000 and to 7,000 tons in 2001, while export earnings from coffee fell to a record low of $2.7m. in the latter year, owing to the decline in output and international prices. Meanwhile, according to the leadership of the rebel MLC, plantations in the province of Équateur produced about 15,000 tons in 2000, but encountered serious problems in transporting supplies, owing to both the interruption in traffic on the River Congo and difficulties in shipment to the Cameroonian port of Douala, following chronic unrest in the neighbouring CAR. By that time the MLC was making efforts to attract investors in order to stimulate recovery at the ageing plantations, and to increase annual output to 25,000 tons. During 2000, 2001 and 2002 the principal arabica production areas in the east of the country remained under the control of various other rebel groups, which exported the coffee from these zones through Uganda and Rwanda. As a result of the interruption of the supply from these main producing areas, the Kinshasa-based Nocafex coffee treatment and exporting company, which was formerly processing up to 1,000 tons of robusta coffee per year, closed in the second half of 2001. In May 2002 the International Coffee Council announced it would launch a biological survey in the southern part of the country to assess the needs of the sector. During the first nine months of 2002 coffee exports increased by more than 900%, to $24.8m., compared with the previous year, as a result of the resumption of the commercial traffic on the River Congo between the government-held zone and the area under the control of the MLC rebels. Estimates for coffee production vary considerably from one source to another. The official figure for the 2002 output was 7,200 tons, whereas data from the ICO estimated the quantity at 41,280 tons. In any case, owing to low prices and diseases, no major progress was expected for 2003 and 2004. In the long term, however, if the Government managed to secure the amount of $105m. recommended by the ONC to relaunch the activity, prospects might improve. In late 2003 plans to invest in quality improvement, disease control, expansion of the cultivated surfaces and rejuvenation of the plantations were announced; however, results were expected to prove slow. According to official figures, coffee output was 4,664 tons at mid-2004. In that year coffee accounted for 0.9% of total export earnings (compared with 8.8% in 1999). In January 2005 coffee producers of the Bas-Fleuve district in Bas-Congo were urging the ONC to buy their stocks, which they had accumulated for two years since traders had lost interest as a result of the low prices. The DRC is also a marginal producer of cocoa, with output estimated at 2,617 tons in 2002 by the Central Bank.

Production of sugar declined in the 1990s, reflecting continued civil and industrial unrest. In 1995 output at the Sucrerie de Kiliba totalled only 7,000 metric tons, declining further thereafter, as a result of the occupation of the Kiliba installation by rebels in August 1998. In addition, some 1,000 ha of the Kwilu-Ngongo sugar estate in Bas-Congo were destroyed by flooding in December 1999. In 2002 the output totalled 63,187 tons, compared with 57,739 tons in the previous year. A further production increase of 16.5%, to 73,630 tons, was recorded in 2003, despite some financial problems which delayed the supplies of spare parts to the sugar estate, owing to technical improvements. The differential between the production costs of about US $400 per ton by mid-2004 and the price of imported Brazilian sugar sold only at $220, posed a major difficulty for the Compagnie Sucrière de Kwilu-Ngongo. Meanwhile, in Sud-Kivu, the management of the Sucrerie de Kiliba initiated in 2004 a plan to relaunch the activities of the company. Yet insecurity in the region was inhibiting shareholders, who postponed investment decisions concerning the recovery of the company. In 2004 cotton output was estimated at 1,000 tons, less than 1% of the independence level of 180,000 tons. However, the Caisse de Stabilisation Cotonnière parastatal was making efforts to revive production by encouraging the development of the domestic textile industry, which was operating at only 20% of its installed annual capacity, and by promoting loans to farmers.

Palm oil production was estimated at 95,000 metric tons in 1988, but only a small percentage was exported. In 1999 production declined sharply, owing to the conflict prevailing in producing regions, such as Équateur and Province Orientale, and the DRC became a net importer. In October 2001, however, the Société des Plantations et Industries Huilières (SIPH) announced plans to resume palm oil production in the plantations of the Kwilu area, in Bandundu province, formerly operated by Unilever, which had been abandoned for the previous three years. In 2001 a record low output of 4,472 tons was registered, but recovered to 5,439 tons by mid-2004, as a result of the restoration of peace in the country. In the colonial period Zaire had been a sizeable rubber producer. In 1991 it still produced 10,644 tons of rubber, but by 1999 production had collapsed to 2,946 tons. The lack of investment and maintenance of ageing plantations, and the decline in international demand, owing to competition from synthetic products, were the main causes for the crisis in the sector. In 2000 output fell to 23 tons, due to the occupation of the main producing areas by the MLC rebels in Équateur. By 2003, however, a recovery to 2,307 tons was recorded.

In April 1999, in order to increase agricultural production, which was severely disrupted by the civil war and in particular by the suspension of traffic on the River Congo, the Government decided to requisition and rehabilitate abandoned farms and plantations in the areas still under its control. Villagers, prisoners and reconstruction brigades were to work on these properties, many of which had belonged to government opponents or to officials of the Mobutu regime. However, widespread looting of these properties followed the announcement of the project. The River Congo basin and Lake Tanganyika offered considerable potential for the development of the fisheries sector. A government report, published in April 2000, estimated the potential catch at 220,000 metric tons of fish (almost twice as much as the country's requirements, estimated at 120,000 tons). The rehabilitation of a berth in the port of Matadi and the construction of cold storage facilities were planned before the beginning of operations, scheduled for July 2002. In the first quarter of 2003 a new corporation, the Congolaise d'Industrie Agro-Alimentaire (CIAL), commenced production of dry fish at its new plant at Boma, on the Atlantic, with an initial modest target of 342 tons a year. In May a new company, the Société Congolaise de Pêche (SOCOPE), landed 1,300 tons of fish for the domestic market at Ango-Ango port, and was actively pressurizing the DRC Government in order to obtain fishing rights in Angolan, Namibian and Mozambican waters.

More than 1m. sq km of the DRC's land area is covered by forest (an estimated 6% of the world's forestland), representing a potential annual production of 6m. cu m. However, only a small proportion of this resource is currently exploited. Canada provided considerable technical assistance for the sector during the 1980s, including the preparation of an exhaustive inventory of forest resources. About 416,500 cu m of logs were felled in 1988, and 107,700 cu m were exported. Output declined to 149,160 cu m in 1998. The rebel uprising in early 1999 in Équateur deprived the companies based in government areas of access to the most significant concessions. As a result, production continued to decline to only 16,478 cu m in 2000.

Government measures in the late 1990s were aimed at increasing local value added in the sector, since activity was hitherto mainly limited to sawing the wood, with only minimal production of veneer and plywood. A substantial proportion of logging and sawing activity was carried out by SIFORZAL, a subsidiary of the German Danzer Group, with concessions of 2.6m. ha, although in 1996 a Malaysian enterprise considered the possibility of seeking logging concessions covering 1.5m. ha in Province Orientale and Équateur regions. However, the scarcity of foreign exchange and the lack of alternative means of revenue for the local inhabitants prompted fears that excessive logging might be undertaken, devastating the forest environment. In 1996 SIFORZAL expressed concern over the Government's failure to allocate taxes imposed on logging towards reafforestation programmes. Further disruption in the forestry sector was caused by the extension of the civil war to the forests of Province Orientale and Équateur and by President Kabila's decision, in January 1999, to impose a state monopoly on the logging sector, officially in order to impose an environmentally friendly policy. In February the seizure of 40,000 cu m of timber owned by 11 European companies operating in the DRC was ordered, prompting further legal action against the DRC. As a result of this action, in March 6,500 cu m of timber, shipped by the DRC Government, was seized in the port of Lisbon, Portugal, at the request of the European companies. As a result of an expansion of the rebel control over the forests of Orientale and Équateur provinces, in March 2000 SIFORCO (formerly SIFORZAL) decided to transfer its headquarters from the DRC to the Republic of the Congo. The inability to exploit the Équateur resources had prompted the Government to launch tenders in September 1999 for the allocation of 60,000 ha of concessions in Bas-Congo. In May 2000 the Government indicated that the Bas-Congo forests were over-exploited. In June the Bimpe-Kempili logging corporation resumed its activities in the Mai-Ndombe district of Bandundu province. However, prospects appeared less favourable at Nioki, where Canadian investors were disappointed by the local SODEFOR branch's inability to supply their planned paper factory with wood, despite an advance of US $28m. to SODEFOR by the investors.

During 2001 the disruption to traffic on the Rivers Congo and Ubangi prevented any resumption of logging activity in the main producing regions of Équateur, and output fell by 30%, to below 12,000 cu m. The Government attempted, nevertheless, to attract investors in other parts of the country. However, UN experts investigating the illegal exploitation of the country's resources criticized in their November 2001 report the terms of a huge logging agreement between the Congolese Government and the Société Congolaise pour l'Exploitation du Bois (SOCEBO), a subsidiary of COSLEG (the joint venture between the Zimbabwean military-controlled OSLEG corporation and COMIEX). Accordingly, SOCEBO obtained concession rights for the exploitation of 330,000 sq km of forests in Katanga, Bandundu, Kasaï and Bas-Congo provinces. However, the poor state of the roads and underestimation of the initial investment delayed implementation of the project. In 2002 SIFORCO's annual turnover was only US $2m., compared with $12m. before the war, as a result of the company's inability to supply timber from its concessions in the rebel territories. One concession, at Boliba, in Kasaï Occidental province, was completely looted, but another, at Buruba, resumed its activities in early 2003. During that year, however, SIFORCO produced 40,000 cu m at its Bumba concession in Équateur, envisaging an increase in output, to 70,000 cu m in 2004 and to 120,000 cu m in 2005.

In 2003, owing to the restoration of peace in the country and to the resumption of the traffic on the River Congo, according to central bank figures, timber production increased nearly fourfold, from 16,854 cu m in 2002 to 60,296 cu m; output continued to rise in 2004. By the end of November output already exceeded 86,000 cu m. With the World Bank's support, a new forestry code, introduced in September 2002, raised substantially concession leasing rights and logging rights to bring them in line with those practised in the region. The aim was to increase government revenue and discourage dubious foreign companies. As a result, some 25m. ha of 'speculative concessions' were cancelled. However, the World Bank was criticized by the British-based Rainforest Foundation, which alleged in February 2004 that the Bank's support for the forestry code would result in a 60-fold increase in logging. At the end of 2002 the USA, the EU and other donors reiterated their support for a regional programme of environmental protection in central Africa. In November the Government announced a three-year plan of reafforestation in Katanga, covering a total area of 22,000 ha. A further reafforestation programme was launched in the Nkamba area of Bas-Congo in 2004. At the beginning of 2005, as the improvement of security conditions allowed more experts to travel to the most remote forest zones, alarming revelations were made on the damaging impact of the conflict and of the statelessness on the country's environment. In early 2007, according to British-based Greenpeace, the rainforest stretching across five central African countries (including the DRC) was the second largest in the world at 21m. ha, but 40% of the DRC's share is under threat, which could have serious consequences for global warming. In early 2007 the British Government pledged £50m. for rainforest protection. Meanwhile, in addition to transparency in mining, analysts are also calling for closer scrutiny of the forestry sector.

In February 2005 the US Wildlife Conservation Society (WCS) reported that poachers and militias had sold 17 metric tons of ivory from between 450 and 950 elephants in the Epulu Okapi fauna reserve during the last half of 2004. According to this source, the elephant population of the reserve was reduced by one-half in the previous 10 years. In March 2005 the DRC Government banned the trade of ivory in order to abide by the Convention on International Trade of Endangered Species (CITES), which was ratified in 1982 by the Congolese state. According to the Institut Congolais pour la Conservation de la Nature (ICCN), the population of white rhinos in the Garamba national park, at the Sudanese border, was nearly extinct in early 2005: between 1980 and 2004 the number fell from 1,200 to only 15, owing to intensive poaching. Meanwhile, the number of hippos in the Virunga national park decreased from 23,000 to only 1,500 in just 10 years, between 1992 and 2002, according to the WCS. These concerns were partly taken into consideration by the participants of a donor conference, convened by the UN Organisation for Education, Science and Culture (UNESCO), in May 2005 in Paris, France, which pledged US $40m. for the protection of the Virunga, Maïko, Salonga and Kahuzi-Biega national parks and of the Epulu Okapi reserve (which are on the list of endangered world heritage sites). In 2005 the US National Aerospace Agency and the Woods Hole Institute of Massachussets established a surveillance system of the last 380 mountain gorillas of the Virunga park in order to help prevent further destruction of their habitat by neighbouring Congolese and Rwandan farmers. The DRC's crucial importance for global biodiversity has won increasing recognition internationally. The WCS emphasized in early 2005 that the Congo basin hosts 415 species of mammals, 1,094 species of birds, 268 species of reptiles, 80 of amphibians, more than 1,000 of fishes, over 1,300 of butterflies and 11,000 different sorts of plants. Beside this, the Congo forests provide vast carbon wells, which have a crucial role for the regulation of carbon dioxide and influence the regional climate in such a way that the Congo basin provides water to a large part of the African continent. Meanwhile, the FAO reminded that the sustainable management of the DRC forest resources is essential, since the country hosts 45% of the continent's forest. At the same time FAO deplored that the annual rate of deforestation in the DRC ranged between 0.4% and 0.6% and represented an ecological catastrophe.

INDUSTRY AND MANUFACTURING

Heavy industrial activity is concentrated in the mining sector and in GÉCAMINES' refineries in Katanga province. Prior to the decline in copper production of the late 1980s and early 1990s, the Shituru refinery processed about 225,000 metric tons of copper ore per year and a similar volume was refined 'on toll' in Belgium. In 1990 GÉCAMINES completed a large-scale five-year investment plan to improve copper-mining equipment and related infrastructure. However, GÉCAMINES' copper operation in Katanga suffered severe damage during regional unrest in 1992–93, and rehabilitation costs were estimated at US $1,000m. The GÉCAMINES recovery programme (1996–2000) included projects to modernize the Shituru plant, to process tailings at Lubumbashi and Kipushi, and to build a new cobalt-processing unit at Kakanda. A steel mill was set up at Maluku in 1972, during the era of high commodity prices, but it proved to be unprofitable and was closed down in 1986. In July 2001 the state's Fund for the Promotion of Industry decided to finance by up to $100,000 the resumption of activities at Maluku by the Société d'Exploitation Sidérurgique (Sosider), which was part of the targeted actions included in the IMF-monitored Strengthened Interim Programme. In early 2003 the Kazakhstan Mineral Resources Corporation (KMR) started negotiations with the Kinshasa authorities in order to purchase the Maluku plant. In February a memorandum of agreement was signed between the DRC Government and KMR's partners for a five-year lease of the plant, proposing to increase production to 70,000 tons per year and rehabilitate the installations for a total investment of $25m. In March Sosider signed an agreement with the British company Steelmarkers International (which is associated with KMR) to resume production at the Maluku plant. The UN Industrial Development Organisation offered its technical support. In February 2005 Sosider announced the resumption of operations at the Maluku steel plant by the joint venture it had established with steelmakers known as Sosteel. This company again urged the Government to prohibit all exports of scrap metal, since the plan was to use this material to produce 14,000 tons of steel products in 2005. Following an invitation launched in March by the Congolese Vice-President in charge of Economic Affairs, Jean-Pierre Bemba, a delegation from the Indian Izpat steel company expressed interest in the exploitation of the Banalia iron ore deposits in Kasaï Oriental, but announced that abundant electricity supply was a precondition to proceeding with the project.

The manufacturing sector is dominated by textiles, cement, engineering and agro-industries producing consumer goods. In 2004 manufacturing contributed an estimated 5.3% of GDP (compared with 14.4% in 1980). Production of most commodities in 1995 was much lower than the 1990 capacity. The sector has been consistently held back on three fronts: first, by the lack of foreign exchange to import badly needed spare parts; secondly, by the continuing decline in domestic purchasing power; and, finally, by chronic electricity cuts. It is estimated that throughout most of the 1980s manufacturers were operating at just 30% of installed capacity levels. During 1980–90 manufacturing production increased by an annual average of 2.3%. Manufacturing GDP, according to the IMF, declined at an average annual rate of 12.4% in 1990–95. According to the ADB, in 1995–2006 the sector contracted at an average annual rate of 0.8%; in 2006, however, it grew by 9.5%. As a whole the industrial sector performed better in 1995–2006, growing at an annual average rate of 3.4%; it grew by 10.0% 2006. In 1999 output of cement reached 158,100 metric tons. Small quantities of cement are exported to the CAR and to the Republic of the Congo. In 1995 170m. litres of beer were produced in Zaire. A new brewery near Mbuji-Mayi, with an annual production capacity of 96m. litres, entered into production late in that year. Owing to the decline in the population's purchasing power, however, output decreased to 140m. litres in 1996. In September 2002 the Dutch group Heineken, which owned the Bralima Breweries, announced a five-year investment plan of $60m. to modernize its Lubumbashi, Mbandaka and Kisangani plants.

Difficulties for the textile industry have been caused by the inadequate road infrastructure, preventing access to domestic cotton production, and by the smuggling of Chinese-made products; in 1997 the discovery of Chinese-made products resulted in the closure of three textile factories in Katanga. The production of cotton fabrics fell dramatically, from 23.3m. sq m in 1996 to 8.6m. sq m in 1997, as a result of the general disruption of the economy during the so-called 'liberation war'. In 1998 output rose slightly, to 10.2m. sq m, but the resumption of military activity and the currency shortages contributed to a further decline, to 8.7m. sq m, in 1999. By mid-2000 only two textile plants were still operating. In October the management of the main textile and fabrics corporation, UTEXAFRICA, decided to close temporarily its huge Kinshasa plant, one of the largest in sub-Saharan Africa, which employed 2,000 workers. The aim was again to attract the authorities' attention to the illicit trade in Asian-made printed fabrics across the River Congo, from Brazzaville. The authorities were, however, unable to curb the smuggling, and in April 2002 the management of UTEXAFRICA announced the indefinite closure of the plant. In July the Government announced a ban of printed fabrics imports in order to stimulate the activities of UTEXAFRICA and of another company, SINTEXKIN; however, the ban proved largely ineffective. Output of cotton fabrics declined to 1.3m. sq m and printed fabrics to 4.3m. sq m in 2003, while production fell further, to 0.3m. sq m and 4.2m. sq m respectively, in 2004. In July 2004 the Belgian management of UTEXAFRICA sold a majority of the shares to the Chinese Cha corporation, which renamed the company CONGOTEX. This measure, however, caused much concern among the Congolese trade unions, which expressed fears that the Chinese would stop the production and transform the Congolese subsidiary into a sales office for Chinese-made products. In February 2005 the Kisangani-based Société Textile de Kisangani (SOTEXKI) complained against the failure by the authorities to suppress imports of illegal and counterfeit products from Asia.

One of the most important areas of expansion in the manufacturing sector in the 1990s was informal light industry, especially in the shipyards at Kinshasa and in furniture manufacture. During 1999, however, the restrictions on trading in foreign currency deprived the sector of the funds to import the necessary resources to maintain production. During the first half of 1999 many companies, including the French car manufacturer Peugeot, the cardboard plant Cartoncongo and the Plastica company, ceased operations.

Throughout 2000 and 2001 the industrial sector, together with the rest of the economy, was seriously disrupted in the government-held areas, accounting for about one-half of the territory, by chronic shortages of fuel caused by the Government's imposition of lower-than-cost retail prices for petroleum products, calculated according to the official exchange rate of the Congolese franc to the US dollar (which until late May 2001 was six times lower than the parallel rate). Consequently, traders preferred to buy or sell on the parallel market, rather than at a severe loss. In the second half of 2001 fuel supplies improved considerably. Overall, however, the sector's activities were a complete failure, to which erratic government policies contributed to a certain extent. In early 2001 managers of several companies were arrested, and in September that year enterprises were forced to pay weekly taxes in cash. In early 2002 the Government ordered the suspension of the construction of the Africa Food plant, as a result of an unresolved dispute over land occupation. In Kasaï Occidental alone, about 500 similar conflicts were reported at that time. Consequently, the decision of the Cimenterie de Lukala (CILU) cement plant to increase output from 180,000 metric tons in 2001 to 200,000 tons in 2002, was viewed as very optimistic. Evidently, the company was relying on an increase in demand, generated by the hope of a resumption of donor funding for the reconstruction of the country. The decision of the management of Congo Metal, a company specializing in the production of metallic roofs, to resume operations in September 2001, was motivated by similar reasons. The US World Transport Authority's announcement in 2002 that it was to invest US $2m. in the construction of a car assembly plant was also unprecedented. In March the Fédération des Entreprises du Congo and Belgian interests made a joint declaration on the necessary conditions for economic recovery. This included the restoration of the rule of law, the creation of a legal framework for the promotion of investments, the simplification of tax legislation, the reform of the administration, anti-corruption measures, the rehabilitation of infrastructure, and the commitment of the state not to take reprisals against legitimate companies that continued to operate in regions under rebel control.

In 2002 a negative trend was observed in the manufacturing sector, affecting light metallurgy, the production of beer and soft drinks and output of chemicals. Nevertheless, other sectors in the industry performed well. The cement industry output increased by 28.2%, from 192,122 metric tons in 2001 to 246,248 tons in 2002, owing to a rise in demand generated by rehabilitation projects. In 2003 production increased again by 27.6%, to 314,326 tons, and in 2004 the mid-year production reached 211,905 tons, well above the figures of the previous year. One year later, in June 2005, however, despite indications that cement production would continue to increase, with plans by the CILU plant to raise its output from 312,000 tons in 2004 to 360,000 tons at the end of the year, there was a shortage of cement on the Congolese market, owing to an even faster growth in the demand generated by reconstruction projects. In 2003 a general increase was observed in the DRC's agrofood industry. The output of wheat flour rose by 75.2%, to 154,373 tons, whereas the production of beer and soft drinks increased by 12.6% and 15.5%, respectively, to 1.3m. hl and to 883,000 hl. In 2004 production of wheat flour was about 185,000 tons, demonstrating an increase of about 20%, compared with the previous year. Likewise, beer production reached 1.6m. hl, showing a 23.1% increase in comparison with 2003, while the soft drinks output was 1.2m. hl, about 32% higher than the 2003 figure. By 2003 the Indo-Pakistani Beltexco company was emerging as a leading enterprise in the DRC's industrial sector, with the acquisition of a soap-producing company, Marsavco, from Unilever, of a bicycle-assembling plant and of a coffee-roasting plant.

ENERGY

The DRC's potential for producing hydroelectric power is matched on the African continent only by that of Cameroon. Total potential is considered to be 100,000 MW, while the state electricity board, Société Nationale d'Electricité (SNEL), estimated installed capacity in 1987 at 2,486 MW. The country's most ambitious infrastructure project (which is estimated to account for a substantial proportion of the DRC's foreign indebtedness) is the Inga hydroelectric power project, based near the port of Matadi, at the mouth of the River Congo. This comprises two hydroelectric stations, which in 1986 produced 3,100m. kWh, and a 1,725-km high-voltage power line, extending almost the entire length of the country, from Inga to Kolwezi in the heart of the mining region. Inga produces some of the cheapest power in the world, but the ZOFI industrial free zone established beside the power stations, with the hope of attracting major heavy-industry projects (and, in particular, an aluminium smelter) has proved unsuccessful, attracting only a small number of small-scale industrial operations. In early 1990 a project costing 390m. French francs, funded by France and the African Development Bank (ADB), aimed to double the capacity of the high-voltage power line over the section from Inga to Kinshasa. The project also included a new transformer post and the reinforcement of the Inga-2 and Lingwala stations. The Inga plant supplies some power to the Republic of the Congo. SNEL is also linked to the grid of the Zambia Electricity Supply Corporation (ZESCO), and the South African Electricity Supply Commission (ESKOM) has carried out joint studies to optimize the connection with those companies and the Zimbabwe Electricity Supply Authority (ZESA). One of ESKOM's strategic objectives is the creation of a southern African grid, which could benefit from the energy of the Inga dam. In 1996 ESKOM, SNEL, the Angolan power company, Empresa Nacional de Electricidade (ENE), and the Namibia Power Corporation initiated a study to interconnect their national electricity grids, in order to utilize the potential of the Inga dam. In early 1998 ESKOM offered to collaborate with SNEL to improve electricity distribution networks in the DRC.

In 1999 the DRC Government requested Italy's financial and technical support to complete the construction of Inga-3, while the Nigerian Government expressed interest in a project to install a high-power line between Inga to supply the electricity to Nigeria, through the Republic of the Congo, Gabon and Cameroon. In April 2000 SNEL disclosed new plans, which included a project to construct a 330-KV high-power line between Kolwezi in Katanga, and Solwezi in Zambia, to export 1,000 MW to the southern African countries, the rehabilitation of Inga-1 and Inga-2, and the construction of Inga-3 in two phases (1,700 MW and 3,500 MW) by 2010. The total cost, including the high-power lines to Egypt and to western Africa, was by then estimated at US $11,000m. In January 2000 SNEL and ZESA concluded an agreement for the export of 150 MW to Zimbabwe annually at a cost of $7.2m. However, by March the total capacity of the DRC had slightly decreased compared with that of the late 1980s, totalling only 2,475 MW, including the Inga-1 power plant (351 MW), Inga-2 (1,426 MW), 493 MW for all the power stations of Katanga and 207 MW for the rest of the country. By this time Kinshasa was suffering from frequent power cuts, as a result of SNEL's inability to meet the growing demand. In September the German company Siemens and the DRC Government signed a $700m. agreement for the rehabilitation of the Inga-1 and Inga-2 power plants, for the strengthening of the Inga-Katanga high-power line, for the construction of a second high-power line between Inga and Kinshasa, for the rehabilitation of the power distribution network in the capital and for the supply of electricity to Kasaï Oriental and Occidental. According to DRC government sources, in compensation for these investments Siemens would receive a share in several joint ventures in the precious minerals sector. The Japanese consortium Kashin also offered to construct a second high-power line between Inga and Katanga. The enhancement of SNEL's production capacity was envisaged, in order to enable it to increase its sales of energy to ZESA, which signed a $82m. contract in April 2001 for the import of energy from the DRC to Zimbabwe. However, by that time, owing to Zimbabwe's own hard currency shortages, ZESA was having problems in paying its monthly $600,000 debt to SNEL. Moreover, the price of only $0.015 per kWh charged by SNEL to ZESA raised much critical comment from electricity engineers world-wide, who estimated that it did not cover the cost of transport from the Inga dam to Zimbabwe, while consumers in Katanga were complaining that the prices they had to pay were five times higher. SNEL was also experiencing difficulties in obtaining the reimbursement of a $20m. debt owed by the Republic of the Congo's Société Nationale d'Electricité (SNE). In order to resolve the difficulty, it was agreed that SNE would supply timber as a payment for part of its debt to SNEL, for power supplies from the Inga dam. According to SNEL's management, Burundi and Rwanda's failure to pay for the power from the Ruzizi I and II power station represented a $15m. loss for the company. Meanwhile, feasibility studies were under way to export energy from Inga to the Angolan enclave of Cabinda. Other plans were discussed in 2001 by the DRC and the CAR Governments for the construction of a 300-MW hydropower plant at Palambo, on the River Ubangi. In January 2002 the Belgian Government approved an $8m. loan to finance the rehabilitation of the Tshopo hydroelectric dam near Kisangani and the improvement of the electricity networks in Kinshasa and Kananga (Kasaï Occidental). From late 2000 SNEL demonstrated an increasing determination to collect its debts, in view of increasing anger from the population of Kinshasa, where several districts had been deprived of electricity for months. In June 2002 ESKOM was about to start the rehabilitation of the 75-MW hydropower station of Zongo and the 15-MW station of Nsanga in Bas-Congo, in order to improve the electricity supply in Kinshasa, under a $20m. 'rehabilitate, operate and transfer' contract. Such a contract was viewed as a first step towards the privatization of the DRC's electricity sector, which was first envisaged at the end of May 2001. One year later discussions were taking place between SNEL and several foreign corporations, including ESKOM, about the creation of an international consortium to rehabilitate and operate the existing Inga-1 and Inga-2 power stations, but also to construct and operate Inga-3. At that time the Government was also relying on the World Bank's financial support, and on other donors to pledge up to $400m. towards the development of energy projects in the country. However, the adoption of new legislation on energy was a precondition to donor assistance. Other projects included the restoration of electricity to the capital of the Bandundu province, Kikwit, in July 2001.

In the first half of 2003 Siemens was contracted by the World Bank to rehabilitate and expand the electricity and water distribution networks in Kinshasa and in the Bas-Congo region, as part of a US $450m. package under the country's Emergency Multi-Sector Rehabilitation and Reconstruction Programme (EMRRP). The works include the construction of an $83m. second high-power line between the Inga hydropower electric stations and Kinshasa. The German company was planning to start the first phase of the rehabilitation of the Inga-1 and Inga-2 power stations. The financing of power projects remained problematic. The South African engineering corporation Bateman and the diamond-trading company Steinmetz were invited by the Congolese authorities in early 2003 to become involved in energy rehabilitation projects in exchange for mining concessions. In March the DRC Government was also discussing plans with the World Bank and Hydro-Québec for the restructuring of SNEL and its transformation into a holding company formed by four distinct corporations, specializing, respectively, in generation, transport, distribution and development. This restructuring would be a preliminary stage before the much-awaited privatization of the company. The Canadian International Development Agency (CIDA) offered in January to finance a master plan for the electrification of the country.

A positive factor for the development of Inga was the political support of the New Partnership for Africa's Development (NEPAD) promoters, Presidents Thabo Mbeki of South Africa and Olusegun Obasanjo of Nigeria. Both considered Inga to be the potential centre of a future pan-African electricity grid. The ADB was requested to conduct an environmental-impact assessment of the Great Inga power station and of the Northern Energy Highway (to Sudan and Egypt) in 2003. In the second half of 2002 the Chairman of the Nigeria Electricity and Power Authority (NEPA), on a visit to Kinshasa, confirmed his interest in the construction of a 1,500-km high-power line (projected to cost US $700m.) between Inga and Lagos, which would deliver 1,000 MW. During 2003 SNEL devoted more efforts to improving its extremely poor financial situation, which was partly a result of the failure of customers such as GÉCAMINES and the state-owned railway corporation to pay their bills. The basis of SNEL's strategy to increase its revenue and contribute to development projects was the stimulation of exports. SNEL was planning to increase supplies from Inga to the Republic of the Congo's SNE to up to 50 MW in 2003. In October 2002 it signed a contract to supply 50 MW to Zambia with the Copperbelt Electricity Corporation (CEC) and the South African PB Power corporation. Under the contract, SNEL and CEC agreed to invest $20m. each in the construction of a 147-km, 330-KV high-power line between Karavia (in the DRC) and Zambia. The target was to supply a total of 500 MW to southern Africa by 2004, of which 50 MW would be generated for Zambia and the remainder for Botswana, Zimbabwe and South Africa. In October 2003 the German consultant Fichtner was awarded a €6m. contract to determine the rehabilitation requirements of both Inga-1 and Inga-2 power stations. The rehabilitation was badly needed; by the end of November only four of the five 58.5-MW turbines of Inga-1 and two of the eight 178-MW turbines of Inga-2 were operating. Tenders were to be launched in 2004. Fichtner was considering guaranteeing a capacity of 800 MW by mid-2005 and restoring the 1,775 MW total combined capacity of both stations by 2009. According to SNEL's management, the full rehabilitation of Inga-1 and Inga-2 would allow the export of 800 MW to Nigeria, which had already expressed the wish to build a high power line from Inga, with links to the Gabonese and Cameroonian grids. According to SNEL's management, the Western Corridor (Westcor) project, linking Inga to Angola, Namibia and South Africa, with a further connection to Botswana, could be the first expansion project to be implemented. It was to depend on the construction of the Inga-3 power station (1,700 MW–3,500 MW) by a consortium grouping the companies of the five countries involved. At a World Bank consultative group meeting in Paris, France, in late December 2003, the restoration of electricity supply in the main towns of the former rebel-occupied territories and the improvement of the supply to Kinshasa, were established as priorities. Emphasis was also laid on the privatization of the sector. Its guidelines were to be established by a new energy code due to be approved during 2004. In April a SDR-129.2m. loan was approved by the World Bank group, as a contribution to the first phase of the Southern African Power Market Project (SAPMP). The objective was to increase SNEL's export capacity to guarantee 500 MW of supply to its Southern African customers, through the strengthening and the expansion of the existing Inga–Katanga–Kasumbalesa corridor and the support to the rehabilitation of the Inga dam power stations. In March 2004 SNEL signed a new supply contract with ZESA, under more favourable terms. The sale price was increased by 60%, to $0.148 per kWh. The supplies were scheduled to rise from 100 MW to 150 MW, from 1 October of that year. SNEL also obtained in March the reimbursement by the Republic of the Congo's SNE of a 15-year-old $32m. debt. Meanwhile, SNEL claimed that it had significantly improved the recovery of the bills owed by the domestic clients from 35% to 60%, as a result of the identification of several thousand consumers in Kinshasa, who were benefiting from energy distribution but did not appear in the clients registers.

Prospects for increasing the generation capacity at regional and provincial levels began to improve in early 2004. In mid-March the Minister of Energy appointed new representatives to the board of the Société Internationale d'Electricité des Pays des Grands Lacs (SINELAC), the joint venture established by SNEL, Rwanda's ELECTROGAZ and Burundi's Régie de Distribution d'Eau et d'Electricité (REGIDESO) to exploit the Ruzizi dams in Sud-Kivu, thereby possibly allowing the rehabilitation of Ruzizi II to proceed. Independent projects were also in the process of being developed. In the first half of 2004 the South African company Clackson Power announced a US $9m. investment for the construction of a dam and a hydroelectric power station at Kakobola, in Bandundu. At the end of 2003 the company had also announced the construction of the KatendeI (10 MW) hydropower station in partnership with SNEL and the Conférence pour le Développement Socio-Economique du Kasaï Occidental.

On 11 July 2004 Burundi, the DRC and Rwanda announced their intention to relaunch the activities of the Communité Economique des Pays des Grands Lacs (CEPGL). The initiative was supported by Belgium, the Netherlands, the EU, the African Union, the UN and the World Bank. The main energy projects which were identified were the rehabilitation of the Ruzizi I hydroelectric power station, of which capacity was to be upgraded from 28.2 MW to 39.6 MW. This would enable Ruzizi I, which at that time only supplied power to SNEL, to sell electricity to Rwanda's power company ELECTROGAZ and to Burundi's REGIDESO. The second project was the interconnection between Ruzizi I and Ruzizi II (40 MW), which aimed at improving the flexibility of exploitation of ELECTROGAZ's grid, offering it a choice between the supply by Ruzizi I or by Ruzizi II. At a later stage, the revision of the Ruzizi II power station, which was currently operated by SINELAC, the joint venture formed by ELECTROGAZ (73%), Régie de Distribution d'Eau (REGIDESO) (21%) and SNEL (6%), was also envisaged. Donors also discussed the financing of the activities of the Banque de Développement des Etats des Grands Lacs (BDEGL), which aimed to become the vehicle for the implementation of the NEPAD projects in the region, including the construction of three 110-KV lines between Goma and Beni (304 km) in the DRC, between Bukavu and Kindu (300 km) in the DRC, and between Goma (DRC) and Mukungwa (Rwanda) around Lake Kivu. The Société Commerciale et Industrielle du Gaz (SOCIGAZ), which was created in 1990 by the DRC and Rwanda to develop methane gas projects, also badly needs financial and technical support to increase its activities. However, renewed political and military tensions between the DRC and its neighbouring countries in the second half of 2004 delayed the implementation of the projects.

During July and August 2004 the potential of the Inga dam was seriously reduced by a drought and, as a result, the supply to Kinshasa was considerably affected. However, prospects of increasing Inga's potential were expected to improve in the future. Indeed, in September the Canadian mining company Magnesium Alloy offered the DRC authorities to rehabilitate two turbines at Inga. This would enable Magnesium Alloy to obtain the 120 MW required to start operations at its magnesium plant in Kouilou (Republic of the Congo) at an annual level of 60,000 metric tons per year, which represented a total investment of US $750m. and would create 1,500 jobs. The Reynolds-Rusal consortium, which planned the construction of a 250,000-ton aluminium plant in the same area of the Republic of the Congo has also entered into talks with the DRC authorities and SNEL. However, this ambitious project would require the supply of 500 MW, which Inga is not able to offer before its entire rehabilitation (not envisaged before five years). The SNEL management expected that the recent reimbursement of a $32m. debt by the Republic of the Congo in early 2004 would enable it to improve the distribution network in the capital. In August the then Minister of Energy, Jean-Pierre Kalema Losona, ruled out the option of a privatization of the company. Accordingly, the World Bank pledged $50m. to improve the reliability of the Inga power stations' equipment. Kalema Losona announced that this, together with an additional funding of $30m. from the Government, would guarantee the supply of 750 MW, which estimated the cost of the full rehabilitation of Inga at $350m.

The regional interest for Inga's potential was confirmed in October 2004, with the signature of a memorandum of understanding in Johannesburg, South Africa, by the Ministers of Energy of South Africa, Namibia, Botswana, Angola and the DRC to establish the Western Corridor (Westcor) joint venture, with headquarters in the capital of Botswana, Gaborone. Each of the utilities owns 20% of the shares of the company, which has become a NEPAD flagship project. The US $5,000m. project was expected to be finalized by 2011, deriving its main electricity source from the DRC's proposed new 3,500-MW Inga-3 hydropower plant, on the River Congo. Analysts claim that the river has the potential to light the whole of Africa, and that it could be transmitted as far as Cape Town, South Africa. Meanwhile, only 6% of the DRC's population have access to electricity. The estimated cost of the project also included the construction of about 1,864 miles of 500-KV high-voltage direct-current and of 400-KV high-voltage alternating-current power transmission lines from the DRC through Angola and Namibia to South Africa, and the building of associated infrastructures, such as two sub-stations in Namibia and in Angola. It also encompasses the construction of hydropower stations in Angola on the Kwanza river and in Namibia. In November 2004 the World Bank announced the injection of loans amounting to $178.6m. to develop the Southern African Power Pool and help increase the power supply from the Inga dam through the upgrading and rehabilitation of transmission corridors from the DRC. In February 2007 the ADB granted $21.48m. to the new Government to fund its reconstruction programmes, specifically the Inga hydroelectric project

Meanwhile, companies are actively preparing for the future. During the DRC-Zambia joint commission meeting in November 2004, the Zambian Electricity Supply Corporation (Zesco) and SNEL agreed on the terms of a 210-MW contract for the supply of electricity from the future Inga-3 hydropower station. In February 2005 ESKOM of South Africa presented plans to harness the River Congo at the 'Africa Business and Sustainable Development' conference, organized in Nairobi, Kenya, by the UN Environment Programme. Accordingly, the plans envisaged engineering works that would siphon off the river, divert it through electricity-generating turbines, before channelling the water back into the Congo. The management of ESKOM announced that the project would qualify for carbon offset projects, which were controlled by the Kyoto Protocol's Clean Development Mechanism. In April the Japanese company Hundai also expressed its interest in this so-called 'energy highways project', which aimed to supply southern, central, eastern and northern Africa and southern Europe and the Middle East. In mid-2006 the Minister of Energy reiterated the Government's plans to attract investors to fund the hydroelectric project (the world's largest). Smaller projects were also underway. By mid-November 2004 the South African company Clackson Power brought equipment to Tshimbulu, prior to commencing the construction of the Katende-I (10 MW) hydropower station. Following a visit to the Iranian capital, Teheran, by the Congolese Vice-Minister of Energy, Electricité du Congo (EDC), announced plans in September to build a 1.6-MW hydroelectric plan at Lungudi, in Kasaï Occidental. EDC was to operate the plant. Meanwhile, SNEL's Southern African partners were dealing with a company which was undergoing a severe financial and political crisis. An audit carried out during the third quarter of 2004 by the Court of Auditors and the General Inspection of Finances revealed serious mismanagement practices and a dire financial situation at SNEL. The audit questioned Kalema Losona's approval of the transfer of a US $48m. debt owed to SNEL by the Republic of the Congo's SNE to a Bahamas-based company known as Consulco, which eventually meant a net loss of $14m. for SNEL. Kalema Losona was replaced in January 2005. In that month SNEL's total debt was estimated at $503m.; the company's 'rescue and recovery' three-year plan aiming at improving substantially the domestic and regional needs would cost up to $262m., but would not be implemented without external funding. In mid-2006 the DRC Government signed an agreement with the Canadian enterprise MagEnergy to develop the Busanga hydroelectric dam on the Lualaba River, thereby allowing the company to operate as an independent power producer.

WATER

The DRC's huge water reserves have since the late 1980s prompted a number of proposed projects, which, although not implemented due to their huge costs, have, nevertheless, retained the interest of potential investors. In 1988 an Italian company attempted unsuccessfully to establish a project, known as 'Transaqua', to transport water from the River Congo to the Sahel region. Twelve years later, in early 2000, the Kinshasa-based Water Trade Corpn and the US-based Sapphire Aqua Corpn announced plans to construct a 2,000-km pipeline from the River Congo, via Port Sudan, to the Middle East and another pipeline of 1,000 km to southern Africa, via the Okavango delta. However, by mid-2000 both companies, which had received the required permission from the DRC Government to construct and operate the pipelines, were still seeking financing to initiate their project, to be known as the 'Solomon pipelines'. In January 2002 the member states of the Lake Chad Basin International Commission (Chad, the CAR, Nigeria, Cameroon and Niger) discussed plans to divert water from the River Ubangi to help replenish Lake Chad, which had fallen in surface area from 25,000 sq km in 1972 to 2,000 sq km in 2002. However, the three member states of another regional organization, the Congo-Ubangi-Sangha Basin International Commission, the DRC, the Republic of the Congo and the CAR, immediately objected to this project, in which both the ADB and the Islamic Development Bank had expressed interest. DRC officials voiced concern that, since the River Ubangi is an important tributary of the River Congo, lower water levels would deplete the energy potential of the Inga hydroelectric dam. Officials from the three countries also protested that lower levels would make navigation more difficult on both the Rivers Ubangi and Congo, and that the diversion of Ubangi water would undermine the security of their food stocks, owing to the ensuing loss in fish catch. In May 2004, however, participants in a Southern African Development Community meeting in Dar es Salaam, Tanzania, proposed the diversion of River Congo basin waters to those member states affected by drought.

By May 2003 the water distribution parastatal Régie de Distribution d'Eau (REGIDESO) was planning to resume the production of drinking water in the rebel-occupied territories. REGIDESO's management estimated that a minimum of US $180m. would be necessary to guarantee the distribution of drinking water to the largest part of the Congolese population. By April 2004 REGIDESO envisaged the construction of a water treatment plant, with a daily 100,000 cu m capacity, near Kinshasa, which could increase domestic access to safe water by 16%. By that time Dutch and US investors were discussing plans with the Government for the construction of a water treatment plant, at an estimated cost of $90m., in the diamond-rich area of Tshikapa (Kasaï Occidental).

In February 2005 the Government estimated that it would be necessary to invest US $2,000m. in order to meet the UN's Millennium Development Goals on safe water distribution in the DRC. At that time the Government had only been able to commit $200m. for this objective. Three-quarters of the population consequently did not have access to safe drinking water. The improvement of the water distribution network was hampered by the magnitude of the fraud by customers who managed to access the water without paying for it. The REGIDESO parastatal registered 36,884 cases of fraud during 2004 in the city of Kinshasa alone, which caused serious financial losses to the company. In 2004 total unpaid bills owed to REGIDESO amounted to 49,263m. new Congolese francs, of which 31,816m. new Congolese francs were owed by public administrations, and the remainder by private customers. In January 2005 the EU pledged €24m. to improve water distribution and sanitation projects in Kinshasa and in the provinces.

TRANSPORT AND COMMUNICATIONS

Poor transport and communications infrastructure has proved a major handicap to the DRC's economic development. With a small strip of coastline of just 40 km, the DRC has no deep-water port and depends on the port of Matadi, close to the mouth of the River Congo, for its maritime traffic. In March 2000 the Government was attempting to relaunch the activities of the former state-owned Compagnie Maritime Zaïroise (renamed Compagnie Maritime du Congo), and requested that donors provide US $40m. to finance the purchase of two vessels for the resumption of the country's international traffic, which had been suspended in the mid-1990s. In 1989 Matadi handled 273,300 metric tons of mineral exports, compared with 53,000 tons sent via the Tanzanian port of Dar es Salaam and 160,000 tons by the 'southern route' through South Africa. However, in recent years inadequate maintenance and dredging of the port, together with extremely high charges, have contributed to a transfer of activity to the port of Pointe-Noire (Republic of the Congo). Traffic decreased from 980,556 tons in 1998 to 823,280 tons in 1999, as a result of the ban on foreign currency transactions, which had a negative impact on the country's external trade. The traffic of the port of Boma, on the Atlantic Ocean, decreased from 39,675 tons in 1998 to 36,110 tons in 1999, whereas the river port of Kinshasa handled only 46,360 tons in 1999, compared with 69,404 tons in 1998. In 2000 the infrastructure of the DRC's ports deteriorated sharply: in September of that year a Ministry of Transport study revealed that one-half of the berths of the port of Matadi could no longer be used, and that the rest required urgent rehabilitation works. In addition, access to the ports of Matadi, Boma and Banana (also on the Atlantic) had become increasingly difficult for high-sea vessels since the Régie des Voies Maritimes (RVM) parastatal was unable to implement plans for the dredging of the ports themselves and of the River Congo between the ocean and Matadi. Some improvements were expected after the completion of the rehabilitation of two dredging vessels in August 2000.

During the first seven months of 2002 traffic at Matadi rose by 9.5%, to 681,565 metric tons, compared with the same period in 2001. This improvement was due to the purchase of new equipment worth some US $1.9m. by the Office National des Transports (ONATRA) parastatal. Indeed, by July of that year only one-half of the 43 electric cranes were operating. In May 2003 ONATRA planned to increase traffic at Matadi to some 1.4m. tons per year, with financial support amounting to $1.7m. from the World Bank to rehabilitate the Matadi harbour equipment. The target for 2004 traffic at Matadi was again 1.4m. tons. In total, ONATRA expected traffic of 1.9m. tons in 2004, compared with 1.6m. tons in 2003, at Matadi, Boma and the river ports. The rehabilitation of the port of Matadi was one of the 10 main projects presented by the Association Nationale pour la Promotion des Investissements at the World Bank meeting in December 2003. In April 2004 the Government announced that it was to invest $13m. to bring the ports of Matadi and Boma to the security standards introduced by the International Maritime Organization on 1 July of that year. In March 2005 Belgium announced it would disburse €1m. to finance an emergency rehabilitation of the ports of Matadi and Kinshasa, with the assistance of the Antwerp and Brussels port authorities. The programme included the dredging of the River Congo between the port of Matadi and the Atlantic Ocean by a Dutch company and training courses for the staff of both Congolese port authorities. However, the complete rehabilitation of these infrastructures was estimated to be much more costly. At that time ONATRA considered that $16m. would be needed just to rehabilitate a portion of four berths in the port of Matadi. Belgium promised to request the World Bank to provide additional funds to finalize the rehabilitation of both harbours. By the end of March a sharp increase of the traffic was recorded in the port of Kinshasa. The passenger traffic between Kinshasa and Brazzaville increased by 44%, to 12,520 persons, during that month, whereas the volume of freight increased by 51%, to 2,297 tons. However, passengers between the two capitals complained about the corruption and fraud perpetrated at their expense by the DRC police, according to official media reports in April.

Communications between Kasaï, Katanga and southern Africa, and also in the eastern DRC, improved somewhat as a result of a management contract, signed in 1995 between the national railways company, Société Nationale des Chemins de Fer Zaïrois (SNCZ), and a joint Belgian-South African company, Sizarail, for the management of two SNCZ subsidiaries with a total rail network of 4,121 km. In 1996 traffic on the Sizarail network increased to 409,000 metric tons from 259,000 tons in 1995. However, in May 1997 the incoming administration nationalized Sizarail, and transferred its assets, without compensation, to the renamed Société Nationale des Chemins de Fer du Congo (SNCC). These assets included 14 locomotives and 100 wagons of the South African railway operator, Spoornet (a member of the Sizarail consortium); moreover, the SNCC defaulted on debts of some US $22m. owed to Spoornet and of $3.3m. owed to Zambia Railways. In protest, rail traffic via the Zambian border was suspended for several weeks.

In October 2001 ONATRA announced plans to rehabilitate 130 km of the 350-km railway line between Kinshasa and the port of Matadi. It also expressed the wish to purchase 20 locomotives, in order to increase traffic and compete more efficiently with road transport between the two cities. In April 2003 the Namibian authorities made efforts to attract the DRC Government's interest to the Walvis Bay–Ndola–Lubumbashi Corridor Development project. The aim was to gather regional support in order to obtain external funding for the construction of a railway line between Sesheke at the Zambian–Namibian border and Tsumeb (Namibia). Such a railway link, according to the Namibian authorities, would complement the existing road link and allow the Katanga and Zambian Copperbelt mining industry to benefit from a second corridor for its exports, pending the long-awaited rehabilitation of the Benguela railway. In mid-2003 the ONATRA management estimated the total cost of its railway and river transport rehabilitation projects at US $240m. ONATRA anticipated a 46.3% rise of passenger traffic, to 2.6m., in 2004. In April the SNCC announced the resumption of traffic between Kisangani and Ubundu (125 km), which had been interrupted for many years. In 2005 the SNCC railways company was, however, undergoing considerable problems. In March 280 railway wagons carrying more than 10,000 tons of maize and cassava were blocked at the Kime station, 200 km north of Kamina, as a result of the poor state of the line and of the lack of locomotives and diesel to transport these commodities to Kasaï Oriental. Furthermore, Congolese businessmen were complaining that the delivery of food products to the Kasaï Oriental region was being delayed at the Mwene-Ditu station by the constant racketeering and harassment perpetrated by the customs, intelligence and migration officers, who endeavoured to extort bribes from them.

Transport to the north and north-east is possible along the River Congo, and river traffic has been historically probably the single most important means of transport in the country. ONATRA is responsible for almost 14,000 km of waterways. Since mid-1999 traffic on the main waterways, the Rivers Congo and Ubangi, has declined sharply, as a result of the advance of rebel forces along those rivers towards the capital of Équateur, Mbandaka, which, nevertheless, remained under government control in mid-2000. However, in May 2000 UNDP financed the purchase of 1,000 river boats in order to facilitate the transportation of staple commodities from Bandundu towards Kinshasa. From June the situation worsened considerably with a succession of offensives and counter-offensives opposing the government troops and the rebels on the Rivers Ubangi and Congo, upstream of Mbandaka. International traffic was also disrupted. On several occasions vessels from the Republic of the Congo and the CAR were searched both by the DRC government troops and by the rebels. Following the April 2002 Sun City agreement between the Kabila Government and the rebel MLC, traffic was resumed in May of that year between Kinshasa and Bumba (Équateur). Later that month a convoy, escorted by UN peace-keepers, reached

Kisangani, which was under the control of the Rwandan-supported RCD. In 2003 traffic continued to increase and the Belgian Chanimetal shipyards recorded an increase of 25% in their operations during that year. Despite the resumption of traffic on the River Congo, the lack of regular and systematic dredging of the river was still causing many problems for the vessels operating between Kinshasa and Kisangani.

The road network is wholly inadequate for a country of the DRC's size: of the estimated 157,000 km of roads in 1999, only some 33,000 km were main roads, and most of the road network is in a very poor state of repair. In recent years the situation has become so critical that in Bas-Congo and Province Orientale, local businessmen and churches have contributed to the maintenance of the roads, as the Office des Routes has been unable to cope with this task. A plan to build a road bridge across the River Congo to link Kinshasa with Brazzaville, the capital of the Republic of the Congo, has frequently been proposed, and the EU has sponsored feasibility studies. The deterioration of the roads was so serious by May 1999, with traffic threatening to be interrupted on four different points on the Kinshasa–Kikwit road, that USAID, Shell RDC, Fina-Congo, Bracongo and Sulfo Industries decided jointly to finance rehabilitation works. At that time there were also plans to impose a road tax to pay for maintenance work on the Kinshasa–Matadi road, which was also in a poor state of repair. In January 2000 the Office des Routes announced that it had repaired 2,500 km of roads and 14 bridges throughout the country. At the end of that year FAO expressed concern regarding the poor state of the road network and, more particularly, of the Matadi–Kinshasa and Kikwit–Kinshasa roads, which were vital for the supply of essential commodities and staples to the capital. FAO also urged donors to finance their rehabilitation. A positive response came from the EU, which expressed, in March 2001, its readiness to resume development co-operation, pending progress in the implementation of the Lusaka peace process and in the dialogue between all the DRC parties. The rehabilitation of main and subsidiary roads was considered both in the framework of emergency rehabilitation programmes and of a larger reconstruction programme, which was due to be presented to the European Council of Ministers at the end of June. The €120m. programme was eventually signed in February 2002 and included rehabilitation work on the Kinshasa–Matadi road. In April a US $14.7m. programme, financed by the World Bank, to rehabilitate another main part of this road, was initiated. Furthermore, the EU also pledged in December 2001 €45m. for the rehabilitation of roads in Bandundu province, of which €20m. was to be allocated to the improvement of subsidiary roads. In total, the government projects identified by June 2001 in the public works, housing and urban architecture sectors amounted to $1,600m. Nevertheless, the Kinshasa authorities announced that they could only provide up to $200m. of this amount.

In February 2003 the South African company Reef Industrial Painters was contracted by the DRC Government to undertake, for the first time since its construction in 1983, maintenance works on a 722-m road-rail bridge at Matadi. In early 2003 the World Bank and the EU also announced plans to rehabilitate the Kananga–Tshikapa (265 km) and Kananga–Mbuji-Mayi (190 km) roads. In May of that year the World Bank was also planning a feasibility study for the rehabilitation of the Lubumbashi–Likasi road, which was of vital importance for the Copperbelt, and of other roads in Katanga province. Meanwhile, the Zambian and Congolese authorities were discussing plans for the construction of a paved road between Mokambo and Chembe and of a bridge on the Luapula river. Roads, with an allocation of US $605m., accounted for one third of the Government's Multi-Sector Emergency Rehabilitation and Reconstruction programme for the 2004–06 period. Following World Bank recommendations, the Government envisaged at the end of 2003 the privatization of road maintenance on some main roads. Part of the financing came from the EU, which allocated €60m. to the rehabilitation of the road network in Kinshasa, and from Kuwait, which announced a $15m. contribution to the programme. In Kasaï Occidental, the rehabilitation of 150 km of rural feeder roads was being implemented by local non-profit organizations. Meanwhile, the SODEFOR logging company rehabilitated 120 km in Bandundu province between October 2003 and June 2004. In July 2005 the Belgian company George Forrest International started the rehabilitation of Lubumbashi–Likasi–Nguba road in the Katanguese Copperbelt, commissioned by the Office des Routes, of which the cost was estimated at $28m. Similar works were also carried out by a Chinese company in the same area. At the beginning of 2005 the Office des Routes also started the rehabilitation of the Tshela–Singhini road in Bas-Congo province. Elsewhere, European NGOs were active during 2005 in carrying out road rehabilitation projects, such as the British-based Action Aid, which improved a 147-km dust road between Muja and Nyiragongo, in Nord-Kivu, and Dan Church, which initiated at Kalemie a programme to clear the roads around the city, the airport and the shores of Lake Tanganyika of land-mines (after 150 people had already been killed in the region). However, a deterioration of the network was reported during the first half of 2005 in several parts of the country. The failure of maintenance was mainly because the local administrations fail to pay the workers who are supposed to carry out these works, as recorded in the area of Mushenge, in Kasaï Occidental and in the Tshilenge area of Kasaï Oriental.

A sharp increase in petrol prices in February 2000 contributed to a general suspension of the transport system in the DRC, particularly in the capital, where severe petrol shortages were reported. The crisis was such that in June the DRC Government decided to seize the petrol and natural gas stocks belonging to the CAR Petroca distribution company, which were in storage in Kinshasa. The incident led to acute petrol shortages in Bangui, the capital of the CAR, and also to political tension between the two countries. In September, however, Lubumbashi was also adversely affected by a fuel crisis. On 28 May 2001 the Government decided to end the fixed exchange rate of the Congolese franc and allowed a fourfold increase in petrol prices, with immediate and dramatic repercussions on public transport and all commodity prices. This decision, together with an agreement, signed in late March 2001, between the Congolaise des Hydrocarbures parastatal (COHYDRO) and the South African Thebe Investment Company, for the supply of US $30m. of petroleum products, financed by the Rand Merchant Bank of South Africa, contributed to the reduction of Kinshasa's chronic fuel shortages. The situation improved further in September when, in accordance with IMF recommendations, the Government decided to liberalize all imports of petroleum products. From the second half of 2003 a substantial improvement in the supply of petroleum products was reported in the interior of the country, owing to the resumption of traffic on the River Congo and its tributaries. In December 2004 a new interim head of COHYDRO, Bomesi wa Bomesi, was appointed, following an audit carried out jointly by the court of auditors and by the general inspection of finances, which found serious irregularities in the management of 20 state-owned companies, including COHYDRO. The managers of the companies, a presidential adviser and six ministers (including the former Minister of Energy, Jean-Pierre Kalema Losona) were suspended by presidential decree at the end of November. In December Bomesi wa Bomesi warned that drastic and unpopular measures were necessary to restore the balance between COHYDRO's revenue and expenditure. Indeed, the company made sizeable investments during 2004, and began the construction of two new stations in the Kinshasa area, increasing to six the total number in the capital. A new station, representing a $700,000 investment, was inaugurated in the diamond capital, Mbuji-Mayi, in August 2004, and a further six were to be constructed in the provinces during 2005. COHYDRO, together with the other distribution companies, also suffered from the disruption in the supply of petroleum products on several occasions during 2004. That was particularly the case in Katanga, where public transport prices doubled in September, owing to a shortage provoked by the Zambian Government's decision to suspend exports of petroleum products to Zimbabwe and to the DRC, as a result of technical problems at the Indeni refinery. In 2005, following a severe lack of public transport in Kinshasa, the Indian Government announced an investment of $16m. to fund a new transport company, which would operate 250 buses supplied by Tata Motors Ltd from September.

Domestic air services deteriorated rapidly during the 1980s, as a result of Zaire's economic crisis. Some relief has been provided by a private carrier, Scibe Airlift Cargo, which began operations in 1982. Scibe operates services between the DRC's regional capitals and major towns and by 1985 was carrying more domestic passengers than Air Zaïre. Since the early 1990s Scibe, together with a smaller operator, Shabair, has undertaken services to Europe and South Africa. In late 1996 Zaire Express and Shabair merged to form Zaire Airlines (renamed Congo Airlines in April 1997). In 1997 the new Government of the DRC tried to relaunch the activities of the national carrier, renamed Lignes Aériennes du Congo (LAC). However, according to the management, an investment of US $234m. would have been necessary to make the LAC fully operational. Safety conditions are poor at the DRC's airports, and accidents have become commonplace.

Meanwhile, Air Tanzania and the LAC signed an agreement to commence flights from Dar es Salaam to Kinshasa and Lubumbashi. The explosion of an arsenal, close to Ndjili airport at Kinshasa in April 2000, killed more than 100 persons and destroyed a large part of the airport's installations. As a result, the private carrier Congo Airlines (CAL) lost two Boeing 707 aircraft and a Boeing 727 aircraft. The loss of these aircraft was a disaster for CAL, which had obtained authorization from the DRC Government to commence flights to Italy and Angola by the end of 1999. There are several other private airlines, including Katangair and Blue Air Lines. Part of the disaster at Ndjili airport was to be offset, however, by the Canadian Government's decision in late April 2000 to finance a US $28m. project to rehabilitate the airport's telecommunications and navigation equipment, in order to bring its installations in line with the regulations of the International Civil Aviation Organization (ICAO). In February 2000 the airstrip of the Mbuji-Mayi airport was extended from 1,900 m to 2,300 m, enabling it to become the fifth international airport of the DRC, after Kinshasa and Lubumbashi, then under government control, and the rebel-held cities of Goma and Gbadolite. In September 2001 the Bandundu and Mbandaka airports received distance-measuring equipment, bringing them in line with ICAO regulations.

In September 2000 a new private airline, Hewa Bora Airways (HBA), was allowed to operate on both domestic and international routes. The company, which had adopted the name of Kabila's guerrilla base in the east of the country during 1967–85, benefited from this advantage over all its competitors to import duty-free aircraft and spare parts. In February 2001 HBA, in which the late President had a share, purchased a 430-seat Lockheed Tristar aircraft in order to enable the company to operate on the international market. In November HBA inaugurated its flights to Johannesburg, while South African Airways (SAA) resumed its flights to Kinshasa after two years of interruption. Following the bankruptcy of the Belgian national carrier, Sabena, which was the main link between Kinshasa and Western Europe by late 2001, Air France also resumed its flights between Paris and Kinshasa in January 2002, and added connections to Brussels. At the end of April a new Belgian company, SN Brussels Airlines, and HBA restored direct flights between the Belgian and the Congolese capitals. Meanwhile, Kenya Airways increased the number of weekly flights between Nairobi and Kinshasa from four to five. The main development within the DRC was the resumption of flights in May between Kinshasa and several cities under rebel control, such as Lisala, Basankusu and Bumba, in Équateur, and Beni, in Nord-Kivu. In April 2003 HBA announced plans to purchase two Boeing 737 aircraft, following its decision to open new connections between Kinshasa and other African capitals. At the same time, however, Trans Kasaï Air, which had been created in May 2000, requested the Government's financial support to resume its activities, after their interruption in February 2002. In May 2003 the Régie des Voies Aériennes (RVA) parastatal airport authority estimated the total cost of the rehabilitation and improvement of the country's main airstrips at US $144.5m. By mid-2004 Air France, Air Gabon, Camair, Ethiopian Air Lines, HBA, Kenya Airways, SAA, SN Brussels and TAAG were operating international flights to and from Kinshasa. Significant improvements in infrastructures were expected in 2006, since the 2004–06 Multi-Sector Emergency Rehabilitation and Reconstruction programme allocated $256m. for rehabilitation, extension and increased security in more than 10 airports, including Ndjili international airport. The Ndolo airport at Kinshasa, which in the past had been used for domestic traffic, was reopened in May 2004.

Telecommunications facilities within the DRC, operated by the state telecommunications concern, the Office Congolais des Postes et des Télécommunications (OCPT, formerly known as the ONPTZ), are among the worst in Africa and international lines, apart from those to Brussels and Paris, are erratic. In 1980, when Zaire had an estimated 30,000 telephone lines, the ratio to the population was less than one line per 1,000 inhabitants. In September 1996 it was estimated that the ONPTZ network had shrunk to some 13,000 lines, with the private companies operating an additional 10,000 lines. Government estimates in the mid-1990s indicated that investment of US $200m. would be necessary to rehabilitate the telecommunications infrastructure; SAIT Holland and Inforindus, a Congolese company, subsequently undertook to repair, and temporarily to manage, the network of the OCPT. In early 1998 the US corporation Qualcomm Inc announced plans to invest up to $70m. to establish a wireless local loop system in the DRC. In September 1998 the Government seized a 45% stake, owned by a Tutsi businessman, in Telecel-Congo (a subsidiary of the US corporation Telecel International). The Government justified its decision (which was denounced as nationalization by the other shareholders) by accusing a number of individuals within Telecel of providing technical assistance to the RCD rebels.

A Global System for Mobile (GSM) Communications network was established in mid-1999, operated by Congolese Wireless Network (CWN). In late 1999 CWN also promised to establish mobile cellular telephone systems in 14 Congolese cities within the next three years. None of the three satellite communications networks (those of Telecel-Congo, Comcell or CWN) were interconnected by the end of 1999. Like Telecel, Comcell has experienced politics-related difficulties with the Kinshasa authorities. In July 2000 SAIT Telecom announced a plan to invest US $30m. in the establishment of a new GSM network with an estimated capacity of 50,000 lines. During that year new wireless operators, such as Celtel, Sogetel, Afritel, Microcom and Libertés, emerged. By early 2001 the OCPT network had decreased to 5,000 lines, although the company was attempting to develop joint-venture operations. In February the OCPT signed an agreement with a new operator, Millicom International, in order to offer fixed phone services, wireless connections and internet access to their clients. In July 2000 the Chinese company ZTE signed an agreement with the Congolese Government, providing for the creation of a joint Congo-Chine Telecom corporation, which would benefit from a $10m. loan from China's Export and Import Bank to develop several projects in the DRC's telecommunications sector. ZTE's plans were to establish 300,000 mobile telephone lines in Kinshasa. However, in April 2001 the DRC was excluded from the International Telecommunications Satellite (Intelsat) network, since it had been unable to pay up to $2.4m. of debt arrears to that organization. Moreover, the African Post and Telecommunications Union warned the DRC authorities that it might take similar action, if they failed to reimburse $300,000 in arrears. In mid-2001 the OCPT and the Korean company Komyung signed an agreement for the installation of a cable network, with a capacity of 1m. lines, for Kinshasa by the end of 2002, representing a total investment of $100m. According to both companies, this system would enable the OCPT to interconnect all existing cellular networks. In February 2002 the South African corporation Vodacom also expressed its intention of investing several hundred million US dollars in the DRC telecommunications sector. By May 2003 Vodacom had pledged to invest $475m. in several projects, which were to generate 3,000 jobs, and had emerged as the most important private investor in the DRC. Meanwhile, Congo-Korea Telecoms announced plans to establish 50,000 lines in Kinshasa during May and June 2003, with a further 30,000 in Mbuji-Mayi, Matadi and Lubumbashi. In April 2004 Congo-Korea Telecoms announced a six-year plan to invest up to $8,000m. in the establishment of an optic-fibre cable telephone network and the installation of 2m. lines. In January 2005 Vodacom announced it had 1m. subscribers in the DRC and the management reiterated its commitment to invest $500m. during 2002–07 in order to cover 80% of the country's territory. Another important development in that year was the decision in March by the Tanzania-based company Lucent to invest $60m.–$100m. in the construction of two new telecommunications stations in Kinshasa and in Lubumbashi, on behalf of the OCPT parastatal. By the end of June the DRC had six cellular telephone operators and three fixed-line telephone operators, in addition to the networks developed by several companies such as GÉCAMINES.

EXTERNAL TRADE

In common with most commodity-producing developing countries, throughout the 1980s Zaire experienced a steady deterioration in its terms of trade, as world market prices for most of its exports failed to keep pace with import price rises. Many of the problems now faced by the DRC have their origins in the early 1970s, when commodity prices were relatively high. At that time, following OPEC's first initiative in raising petroleum prices, the international banks found themselves with substantial deposits of 'petro-dollars' and were eager to utilize the funds as loans to developing countries from which they could obtain high rates of interest. With money flowing into the country to support grandiose development projects, such as the Inga hydroelectric station and the steelworks in Maluku, Zaire's import bill rose sharply and a recurrent trade deficit began to accrue, although for several years this was offset to some extent by external borrowing and inflows of foreign aid.

With the benefit of these inflows of funds, the Government made little serious effort to regulate the economic situation until the early 1980s. As the flow of aid and, in particular, commercial loans began to decrease, the import bill had to be reduced. However, in 1995 imports increased sharply, to US $924m., and reached an estimated $1,002m. in 1996. Owing to circumstances created by the civil war, the cost of imports fell to $807m. in 1997, to $546.3m. in 1998 and to $458m. in 1999. Imports subsequently registered an increase, to $807m., in 2001, while exports declined from $974m. in 1999 to $880m. in 2001. Consequently, the trade surplus declined from $516m. in 1999 to $73m. in 2001. Estimates for 2002 indicated a general increase in trade, owing to stricter control of the diamond trade and to higher levels of foreign assistance. During the first nine months of 2002, according to central bank statistics, exports reached $904m., compared with $722m. for the same period in 2001, whereas imports increased from $575m. to $669m.

Until the 1990s the composition of exports remained fairly constant, with minerals accounting for about 80%, of which GÉCAMINES produced more than one-half (diamonds between 10% and 15%, according to world prices, crude oil about 10% and gold about 1%). By 1993, however, diamonds accounted for more than one-half of total exports (53.8%), while all GÉCAMINES' products represented only 22.7% of the total. Cotton, which was an important source of revenue before independence, is no longer exported, and such output as still exists is used locally. Coffee is the only significant agricultural export, but its share in export revenue has fluctuated widely in recent years, together with international coffee prices, contributing 25% of export revenue in 1986, but only 4.2% in 1990. An increase in world coffee prices in 1994, however, helped to increase the share of coffee in export earnings to almost 40%. An analysis of Zaire's export revenue in 1990 by the World Bank showed earnings from copper at US $1,001m., diamonds at $240m., petroleum at $227m. and coffee at $120m. In 1994 the structure of exports had changed dramatically, with diamonds and coffee exports both overtaking GÉCAMINES products and petroleum. The DRC's principal imports comprise equipment and spare parts, food and beverages, as well as a substantial amount of luxury goods for resident expatriates and the affluent Congolese business community, and crude oil (when the local refinery is operating) or, more often, petroleum products. In 1999 diamonds were again the leading export product ($579m.—including estimates of smuggled gold and diamond exports), accounting for 59.4% of the total, followed by petroleum ($116m. and 11.9%), coffee ($86m. and 8.8%) and cobalt (8.2%). In 2000 revenue from diamonds was estimated at $444m., followed by crude petroleum ($207m.), cobalt ($97m.) and copper ($47m.), with earnings from coffee declining sharply to $7m. In 2001 diamond exports increased to $462m., while exports of crude petroleum amounted to $201m. However, coffee exports dropped to $2m., while copper and cobalt exports were together only $112m. Diamond exports reached $653m. (about 41% more than in 2001) in 2002, $816m. in 2003 and an estimated $828m. in 2004, while petroleum exports slightly declined in value to $199m. in 2001, but increased to $251m. in 2003 and to an estimated $360m in 2004. Coffee exports rose steadily, to $9m. in 2002, $13m. in 2003 and to an estimated $16m. in 2004.

As the former colonial power, Belgium has traditionally been the DRC's main trading partner. Approximately 60% of Zaire's exports went directly to Belgium, but this figure included the substantial amount of blister copper refined in Belgium, most of which was subsequently re-exported. Faltering relations between the two countries since 1988 have intermittently halted the flow of trade and assistance. A 'freeze' on foreign aid and export insurance guarantees, imposed by Belgium and many other Western countries, made Zaire increasingly reliant on trade with South Africa. In 1993 South Africa became Zaire's second largest supplier (South African imports amounted to some US $100m.), while Zaire became South Africa's fifth largest African market. By 1997 South Africa's exports to the DRC had nearly doubled, to $192m., while Belgium and Luxembourg accounted for $165m., Nigeria $71m., Hong Kong $48m., and the USA $42m. The USA is an important trading partner. Its percentage share of exports fluctuates, but can reach 30% or more in years when the US Administration replenishes strategic stocks such as cobalt. However, the recent reduction in GÉCAMINES' production capacity may oblige the USA to consider other suppliers, such as Zambia. In 2003 Belgium was the principal market for DRC exports (55.5%), followed by the USA (15.5%), Zimbabwe (11.2%) and Finland (4.8%). During that year South Africa retained its leadership among the DRC's suppliers, accounting for 18.0% of the value of total imports, followed by Belgium (15.8%), France (13.4%) and Germany (7.2%). During that year the value of exports increased by 24.5% to $1,340m., owing to an increase in diamond exports and higher international petroleum prices, despite lower copper exports; however, imports grew faster, to $1,496m., largely owing to the resumption of important donors' projects, which was made possible by the end of the conflict.

In 2003 the US Administration announced that the DRC would benefit from improved access to US markets under the African Growth and Opportunity Act, as a result of economic and political progress. In 2004 exports continued to increase to an estimated US $1,813m., mainly as a result of stricter controls on diamonds exports and of a reduction in the smuggling of gems to neighbouring Republic of the Congo, but again were lower than imports, which were estimated at $2,056m. In the future, both China and India could become significant destinations for Congolese products. Whereas Indian industrialists showed interest in April 2005 in the exploitation of the Banalia iron deposits, China's involvement in several mining projects and its purchases of cobalt of an estimated value totalling $100m. per year also boded favourably for an increase in trade with the DRC.

BALANCE OF PAYMENTS AND EXTERNAL DEBT

During the 1980s the Government's extensive deficit spending of the 1970s generated recurrent deficits on the balance-of-payments current account as new sources of external funding evaporated and service payments on debts incurred in earlier years fell due. Faced with this economic deterioration and with no local remedies available, Mobutu became, in 1982, one of the first African leaders to submit his country to an IMF-prescribed austerity programme. Subsequent visits by the state commissioner for finance to the 'Paris Club' of official creditors to request reschedulings of the official portion of external debt (accruing to Western Governments) became virtually an annual event, and 'Paris Club' rescheduling agreements were negotiated in each of the years from 1983–86.

Initially, the Zairean Government's apparent enthusiasm to fulfil IMF performance targets was favourably received by creditors. By 1986, however, following five years of economic austerity, there were few tangible results. Despite a further IMF programme agreed in May 1987, the economy continued to deteriorate. The zaire continued to depreciate. Disbursement of the IMF funds was also suspended because Fund officials would not accept the projected deficit in the national budget.

The political and social deterioration from late 1991 brought all negotiations with the IMF to a halt and rescheduling talks also ceased. No funds were to flow into Zaire for the purpose of structural adjustment or balance-of-payments support until a satisfactory settlement of Zaire's internal crisis had been achieved. In 1992 Zaire suspended virtually all payments on its foreign debt. In February 1994 the World Bank closed its office in Kinshasa, and in June Zaire was suspended from the IMF. Various donors, including Belgium, made it clear that suspension from the IMF could only be ended by the installation of a credible government with a feasible economic adjustment programme and plans to exert greater control over the armed forces and increase the efficiency of the central bank. Hopes for a prompt end to the suspension were encouraged by the announcement in July 1994 of the intention of the new Prime Minister, Kengo Wa Dondo, to regulate treasury disbursements to available resources, and to consider granting autonomous status to the central bank. However, following the visit of an IMF mission to Kinshasa at the end of 1994, the Board concluded that Zaire's draft budget for 1995 did not correspond to its own projections, with expenditure exceeding revenue by some US $30m. The control of inflation and the stabilization of the exchange rate were awaited as the concrete signs of recovery upon which donors were prepared to build a support programme. By September 1995, however, there were few signs that Kengo Wa Dondo's Government had managed to reduce inflation: within one year the exchange rate against the US dollar had decreased from NZ 1,400 = $1 to NZ 7,000 = $1. Despite Zaire's inability to fulfil the minimum requirements of the Bretton Woods institutions, its strategic position in central Africa and Kengo Wa Dondo's apparent efforts to sponsor a transition process and avert a humanitarian crisis prompted the EU to consider the resumption of aid in the autumn of 1995. An ECU 90m. rehabilitation project, aimed at restoring basic infrastructures and at stimulating food production, was subsequently adopted by the EU. However, the outbreak of civil war in September 1996 caused the inflation rate to rise once again, reaching 741% at the end of the year. The need to finance the war effort also prompted the Government to cease the repayment of debt arrears to the IMF altogether.

By the end of 1997 total external debt was US $12,330m., of which $8,617m. was long-term debt. This situation, combined with the accumulation of arrears to the World Bank and to the IMF, prevented these institutions from resuming lending to the DRC and from negotiating debt rescheduling. In December, at the 'Friends of Congo' meeting in Brussels, the World Bank sought to mobilize funding through a trust fund for the reconstruction of the DRC's economy, but the response was well below expectations. Failure to co-operate with the UN investigative mission in eastern DRC (see Recent History) contributed to a lack of donor enthusiasm; this was further compounded by the Government's refusal to endorse the commitments made by the Minister of Finance to begin monthly payments of $5m. to the IMF from the end of March 1998. Faced with expulsion from the IMF, in June the Government agreed to resume monthly repayments of $1.5m.

On 30 June 1998 a new currency, the Congolese franc (CF), was introduced, equivalent to 100,000 new zaires and to US $1.405. As a result of the civil war, however, its value had fallen to CF 3.3 = $1 by September. A presidential decree on 8 January 1999 banned the use of foreign currency for commercial transactions within the DRC, with the aim of strengthening the value of the national currency and increasing central bank and budget revenues through a tight control of foreign exchange. However, this measure had an adverse effect on the economy. Diamond and gold exporters tended to smuggle a higher proportion of their output rather than trade it for Congolese francs, and, following the ban, foreign suppliers decreased their sales or ceased to supply goods to the DRC (US dollars had accounted for 80% of the value of money in circulation in the DRC). At the same time a substantial decrease in the supply of imported spare parts and petrol, caused by the shortage of currency, reduced both production capacity and the ability to transport food from neighbouring regions to the capital. These factors contributed to a further sharp decline of the Congolese franc, which was valued at CF 5.2 = $1 in government-held areas in May 1999 and at CF 3.6 = $1 in rebel-held areas at that time. The new zaire was finally removed from circulation in June. A devaluation of the Congolese franc, to CF 9 = $1, took place in January 2000. However, the difference continued to increase between the official rate and the parallel rate, which was CF 50 = $1 by the end of May. The scarcity of Congolese franc banknotes in the rebel-controlled territories prompted the rebel groups to maintain the legal currency of the old zaire and the new zaire in these areas. A lucrative practice in which some diplomats were involved, according to the DRC authorities, was reported during the first half of 2000; the profiteers bought currency at the lower price of CF 40 = $1 at May in the rebel-controlled territories, which they would subsequently sell at CF 50 = $1 in Kinshasa. The depreciation of the Congolese franc coincided with a sharp resumption of inflation, which reached 285% in 1999, compared with an estimated 29% in 1998. The main cause for the depreciation was the acute shortage of foreign currency, together with high monetary growth as the Government continued to finance its growing budget deficits by printing banknotes.

Total external debt had increased to US $15,172m. by the end of 1998, owing to the accumulation of arrears. In January 2000 a meeting between President Kabila and an IMF delegation in Libreville prompted expectations regarding an improvement in relations between the DRC Government and the Bretton Woods institutions. In February, however, an exploratory mission from the IMF visited Kinshasa without being able to meet President Kabila and concluded that, in addition to the civil conflict, government policies were also responsible for the economic crisis in the DRC. Some amendments to the ban on transactions in foreign currency were nevertheless introduced in March by a presidential decree, which authorized, within some limits, the circulation of foreign currency in 'monetary free zones'.

The granting of a monopoly on diamond exports to the Israeli corporation IDI Diamonds in July 2000 resulted in a lack of foreign exchange, owing to its inability to mobilize sufficient resources to buy domestic production, which, in turn, encouraged the smuggling of diamonds. This contributed to a one-third devaluation of the Congolese franc in October, of which the official exchange rate was fixed at CF 50 = US $1, compared with CF 23.5 = $1 previously. On the parallel rate, the Congolese franc continued to depreciate and was at CF 142 = $1 at the time of President Kabila's assassination in January 2001. Shortly before, in mid-November 2000, the Governor of the central bank attempted to introduce some elements of liberalization into the economy, such as the use of foreign exchange in a greater number of transactions (notably the buying and selling of goods destined for export, the sale of services to non-residents and the money transfers to holders of foreign currency accounts).

The new President's speech at his inauguration on 26 January 2001, announcing the liberalization of the economy, new mining and investment codes, incentives for investors, more transparent tender procedures, the independence of the judiciary, and a wish to embark on a national reconciliation policy and to implement the Lusaka peace agreement, led to a resumption of dialogue with the Bretton Woods institutions. A joint IMF and World Bank mission, which visited Kinshasa early that year, urged the Government to engage in good governance and budgetary discipline, starting with the control of public expenditure and the freezing of banknotes printed in order to curb hyperinflation (estimated at over 520% by the end of 2000). A six-month interim programme of reforms was also discussed by the Government and the joint IMF-World Bank mission. The Bretton Woods institutions welcomed the cancellation of the IDI monopoly on diamond exports by early May, since it might contribute to the recycling of revenue from diamond exports within the formal economy and increase tax revenue. After a second IMF mission, which took place in early May, the Governor of the central bank announced the adoption of a 'floating' exchange rate for the Congolese franc, of which the official value was decreased sixfold, from CF 50 = US $1, to CF 315 = $1. On the following day the rate was already CF 342 = $1.

The authorities and Bretton Woods institutions hoped that these reforms might contribute to a change in government policy, in order to enable the country to benefit from the initiative for heavily indebted poor countries (HIPC), for which the DRC was declared eligible, and from the Poverty Reduction Strategy Programme. Extensive discussions were held in that context to streamline the economy and establish an adequate framework to initiate the privatization of the parastatals. An agreement on such policies was essential, prior to an arrangement regarding the debt situation, which had become totally unsustainable: by the end of 2000 total foreign debt was estimated by the World Bank at US $11,692m., equivalent to 298.6% of gross national income (GNI). At the end of 2001 total external debt amounted to $11,519m. (of which $7,587m. was long-term debt). In order to resolve the issue, at a meeting held in Paris, in May 2002, the World Bank proposed the establishment of a trust fund to facilitate the reimbursement of arrears to the multilateral institutions. On that occasion, several delegations pledged to contribute to the financing of the settlement programme prepared by the ADB, following progress made by the DRC Government in the implementation of the IMF Staff Monitored Programme (SMP) during the second half of 2001. By the end of 2001 the inflation rate had been reduced to 135%, compared with 514% in 2000, while the exchange rate had stabilized at CF 315 = $1 by September. The Government adopted a cash-basis budget, adhering strictly to a monthly cash-flow plan, under which expenditure was limited by actual revenue collection, although it admitted that total cumulative expenditure in September was 16% higher than envisaged in the SMP, owing to security-related expenses and salary increases to members of parliament and ministry staff. Extensive structural measures were implemented, notably price liberalization and the removal of 21,652 'ghost workers' from civil service payrolls. Donors also noted the Government's intention to prepare an anti-corruption action programme and initiate other reforms, ranging from the publication of a new investment code and the approval of new mining legislation in 2002, to the preparation of a realistic budget for that year. The Government's decision to declare the autonomy of the central bank was also welcomed. In September the Paris Club announced the cancellation of $4,600m of debt.

In February 2003 the World Bank expressed hopes that the DRC would qualify under the HIPC initiative for a cancellation of 80% of total external debt by March of that year. However, the resignation in February of the Minister of Finance caused concern among the Bretton Woods institutions, after he explained publicly that his decision was motivated by his objection to a US $8m. increase in extra-budgetary military expenditure. Nevertheless, on 24 March the IMF board approved the disbursement of $35m. from the Poverty Reduction and Growth Facility (PRGF), following the positive review of the government reforms until September 2002. At the end of April 2003, however, the new Minister of Economy, also in charge of the finance portfolio, expressed his disappointment, after the announcement by the World Bank and the IMF that they would only assess in July whether or not the DRC had made sufficient progress. The criteria imposed by the Bretton Woods institutions included: the formation of the transitional Government, the effective restoration of peace in the country and amendments to the 2003 draft budget, in order to include expenditure and revenue from the rebel-held zones. In May the second review of the interim programme supported by the PRGF, covering the September 2002–March 2003 period, took place in Kinshasa. It was supposed to assess the progress made in several areas, including the liquidation of three commercial banks, the restructuring of GÉCAMINES and of the OCPT telecommunications parastatal and the establishment of an ethical code of conduct for the public administration. At the end of May the Governor of the central bank, Jean-Claude Masangu Mulongo, declared that, in the event of a failure by the DRC to meet the IMF criteria in 2003, the country would face serious debt sustainability problems. However, some bilateral debt rescheduling and cancellation took place during the first half of 2003. In April the Italian Government announced the rescheduling of $900m. In May the European Commission announced its decision to allocate €100m. to reimburse the DRC's arrears to the European Investment Bank, thereby allowing this financial institution to resume its loans to the DRC. In July the IMF and the World Bank announced that the DRC had qualified for debt reduction, amounting to about $10,000m. in total, under the enhanced HIPC initiative. The World Bank's International Development Association (IDA) was to provide a total of $1,031m. in nominal debt-servicing relief, which was to be delivered in part through a 90% reduction in debt-servicing on IDA credit during 2003–26. The IMF pledged to provide assistance of $472m., which was to be delivered in part through an average annual reduction in debt-servicing of about 50% until 2012. In March 2004 the IMF announced that it had successfully conducted its third review of the programme supported by the PRGF, providing for further rescheduling from other donors. In April Belgium and Japan rescheduled €62m. and $700m. of bilateral debt, respectively. HIPC initiative assistance amounted to 6,505m. new Congolese francs in 2003 and an estimated 22,698m. new Congolese francs in 2004. At the end of 2004, according to the World Bank, total external debt was $11,841m. (of which $10,532m. was long-term debt), equivalent to 186.4% of GNI.

The IMF's PRGF arrangement with the DRC expired at the end of March 2006, before the completion of the final review, owing to fiscal slippages and delays in implementing structural measures. Overruns in expenditure, amounting to 2.5% of GDP, in the second half of 2005 were the result of spending by political institutions and the military, and to increases in wages granted to ease social tensions. Higher than expected revenue from petroleum production had limited the underlying fiscal deficit to 0.2% of GDP, which was, nevertheless, significantly lower than the target surplus of 1.6% of GDP. The authorities requested a staff-monitored programme for the period until the end of 2006, with the aim of maintaining macroeconomic stability during the elections, and policy implementation prior to the adoption of a successor PRGF arrangement. A final poverty reduction strategy was expected to be adopted subsequently, and it was possible that the DRC would reach completion point under the HIPC initiative and qualify for debt relief under a Multilateral Debt Reduction Initiative in the second half of 2007. Main conditions for eligibility were satisfactory implementation of the staff-monitored programme and completion of the first review of a new PRGF arrangement covering at least a six-month period. Total debt relief was to amount to more than US $7,000m., in net present value terms.

THE DOMESTIC ECONOMY

The last budget to balance was that for 1989. However, since inflation, and the economy in general, had become seemingly uncontrollable after 1990, the draft budget exercise had become somewhat academic. In November 1993 the Government introduced a new currency, the new zaire (each new unit being equivalent to 3m. old zaires), in an attempt at monetary reform. Nevertheless, in the absence of comprehensive adjustment and stabilization programmes, the measure was unable to stem the erosion of the national currency. The unequal allocation of primary expenditure between the executive and the public sector, and between ministries, was singled out as one major reason for the deterioration of the situation. As a result of a lack of budgetary discipline and of a widespread lack of confidence in the new currency, the value of the new zaire collapsed in a matter of months. Between November 1993 and the end of August 1995, the exchange rate against the US dollar decreased from NZ 3 = $1 to NZ 15,000 = $1. Annual inflation averaged 79.9% in 1985–90 and 2,477.7% in 1990–96, although by 1996 the inflation rate had fallen to 657%. In 1997 the rate of inflation decreased to just 13.7%, a result of the limitation of civil service salary increases, the partial freezing of public enterprises, the decision to cease issuing new banknotes and the effects of the civil war. The decline in demand, which led to a 4.1% contraction in GDP in 1997, has also been cited as a factor. The first post-Mobutu budget, which balanced at $744m., was adopted for 1998. In that year, however, there was a resurgence of inflation, which had surpassed 70% by November. The 1999 budget, which was adopted only in May, envisaged a deficit of 859m. new Congolese francs from expenditure of 2,958m. new Congolese francs and receipts of 2,099m. new Congolese francs. Capital expenditure amounted to 30% of the total, a higher proportion than in previous years. This was intended to provide financing for infrastructure works and for the funding of the activities of the Comités de pouvoir populaire (CPP), which were established in April 1999. In 1999 GDP contracted by 4.4%, while inflation increased to 333%. Statistics from the central bank indicated that production declined in almost all sectors in 1999, particularly in the mining and agricultural sectors. The occupation by the rebels of large parts of the DRC deprived the economy of the proceeds of the gold, arabica coffee and tea production. In addition, the main diamond-producing company, MIBA, underwent serious difficulties. The situation deteriorated further in May 1999 when the entire production for that month, some 400,000 carats, worth $10m., was seized under the President's orders at Kinshasa airport. In view of the dwindling capacity to collect taxes within this adverse environment, on 1 June 2000 the Government launched a campaign to recover forcibly arrears from taxpayers. Real GDP declined further, by 7.0%, in 2000, while inflation soared to 514% and consumer purchasing power fell by 83%, compared with the previous year. Macroeconomic targets for 2002 were generally achieved, with an inflation rate of 15%, and a GDP growth rate of 3.5% (compared with a decline of 2.0% in the previous year). During 2002 the new Congolese franc depreciated by 18.4%, from CF 311.5 = US $1 to CF 382.14 = $1, according to the central bank.

The 2003 budget, approved in March of that year, was prepared on the basis of a 5% GDP growth rate, of a 6% inflation rate and of an average exchange rate of CF 399 = US $1. The draft anticipated a 78.9% increase in the budget, with current revenue accounting for 50.3% of the total. The actual overall budget deficit in 2003 was 89,016m. new Congolese francs, according to the IMF. GDP growth of 5.6% (slightly higher than anticipated) was recorded, while the inflation rate stabilized at about 13% per annum. In December the year-on-year inflation rate was only 4.4% and the new Congolese franc was also stable at CF 385 = $1, having only depreciated by less than 1% since the end of 2002. Prior to the approval in March 2004 of the budget for that year, parliamentary deputies deplored that it was not sufficient to meet the additional costs of the preparations for the forthcoming elections. The Minister of the Budget, François Muamba Tsishimbi, conceded during a December 2003 donor conference in Paris that, despite the political reunification of the country, his administration continued to face difficulties in collecting taxes from the former rebel territories.

The overall budget deficit in 2004 increased to an estimated 98,475m. new Congolese francs. Real GDP growth in that year was 6.6%, slightly above projections, while end-of-year inflation increased to 9.2%. The new Congolese franc, which had remained stable against the US dollar until the end of July, began depreciating, and at the end of December had lost 16.9% of its value since the beginning of 2004. The exchange rate was only CF 444.09 = US $1, compared with CF 372.52 = $1 at the end of December 2003. Despite two interventions from the central bank, which sold $25m. in October 2004 and $12m. in January 2005, the central bank did not manage to reverse the trend and at the beginning of June 2005, the new Congolese franc had lost 9.1% of its value since the beginning of the year with an exchange rate of CF 482.31 = $1. According to the central bank Governor, Jean-Claude Masangu Mulongo, the main causes for the inflation was the increase of the price of petroleum products on the world markets. However, macroeconomic indicators improved in 2005 and generally met targeted levels. Real GDP growth was estimated at 6.5%, while end-of-year inflation was 21.3% (slightly below the target of 22.6%). The overall budget deficit for 2005 was projected at 81,032m. new Congolese francs, with exceptional expenditure (including spending for the demobilization, disarmament and reintegration—DDR—programme and the cost of the elections) of 157,015m. new Congolese francs. The 2007 budget, amounting to $2,170m., was announced in May. Although it was expected to be approved, there was criticism even within the ruling party that both revenue and expenditure targets were unrealistic. It was based on a growth prediction of 6.5% and 12.0% year-on-year inflation. The budget represented a 15% increase on the previous year's. Expenditure increased by 67% on the previous budget, one-third of which was allocated to debt-servicing. In the first month of 2007, however, inflation already stood at 25% on a annual basis, while the currency had depreciated by 10%. It was estimated that 84% of commercial transactions were made outside the banking system, while people continue to prefer the smaller denomination of US dollar notes to local currency.

With the assistance of both the South African and Belgian Governments, the Congolese Government initiated in February 2004 a census of its civil servants in order to remove 'ghost workers'. According to the Ministry of the Civil Service, of an estimated total of 600,000 civil servants, 100,000 should retire and 300,000 were either 'ghost workers', deceased or no longer working for the public administration. In late 2004 the court of auditors and the Ministry of Finance General Inspection Department revealed serious mismanagement in the parastatals. Of 20, only 12 had a board of administration. Public procurement procedures were not transparent and serious embezzlement practices were taking place. Beside this, many failed to pay taxes and, conversely, several of them were meeting serious financial problems and were close to bankruptcy, owing to the considerable debts owed to them by the Congolese state: by the end of October US $288m. was owed to the OCPT post and telephone company, $274m. was owed to the electricity company SNEL and the water parastatal REGIDESO was trying desperately to recover a $186m. debt. As a result, at the end of 2004 the managers of eight parastatals (SNEL, COHYDRO, Régie des Voies Maritimes, RVA, Compagnie Maritime du Congo, ONATRA, Institut national de la sécurité sociale and Institut national de préparation professionnel) were removed by the Government. In addition, the ministers responsible for public works, energy, mines, transport and communications, higher and university education and foreign trade were also dismissed. Nevertheless, much remained to be done to restore transparency in the contracts signed by the Congolese state and parastatals with the local and foreign sector. In mid-2006 the IMF stated that corruption remained a major problem, particularly in natural resource management.

ECONOMIC DEVELOPMENT

Unlike the majority of francophone African countries, Zaire never pursued conventional five-year economic development plans. Although substantial effort and money were expended on the preparation of a five-year plan (1986–90), prevailing economic conditions hampered its realization. The plan was not officially abandoned, but economic policy in the second half of the 1980s was almost entirely devoted to reducing budget deficits and the level of inflation. In November 1989 a paper presented to the legislature stated that expenditure under the plan to date had only been at an implementation rate of 49%, and referred to the 'ambitious and costly five-year plan and the restrictive programme of structural adjustment'. Following serious problems being experienced by GÉCAMINES, the progressive substitution of copper by other materials in world industry (and with Chile having opened one of the world's largest and lowest-cost copper mines in 1990), it became clear that national economic activity in the DRC must become more diversified. Economic growth has been hampered by the recent civil war. According to the ABD, GDP growth in 1995–2006 was just 0.5%, though since the civil war ended in 2003 conditions have improved. Growth was strong in 2006, estimated at 6.5%. The tourism sector in particular has seen improvement. In 2002, the year before the civil war ended, tourism arrivals totalled just 35,141. In 2005, however, that figure had almost doubled, to 61,007 arrivals. The majority of visitors came from Belgium (7.8% of the total), followed by France (5.3%).

There is vast potential both to rehabilitate and expand the agricultural sector, and to tap the country's huge forestry resources. The DRC's population represents a potentially large consumer base and offers great incentives for developing industry and manufacturing. One of the most immediate obstacles to development remains the lack of infrastructure of all categories. It is to be hoped, moreover, that the implementation of constitutional and political reform will clear the way for the eradication of endemic financial corruption that has long been an inhibiting factor in the country's economic betterment. However, the context for such fundamental reform is difficult, since the new administration has not been able to pay wages regularly to its civil servants. In December 1997 the Government asked the international donor community to contribute to a three-year stabilization and economic recovery programme of US $1,682m. Of this total, $946m. was allocated to the rehabilitation of the transport, agriculture and energy sectors, $440m. for political and economic stabilization and $296m. in human capital expenditures, such as health and education. As the result of several factors, including the refusal to resume the payment of arrears owed to the Bretton Woods institutions, a poor human rights record, the cancellation of mining contracts, which undermined investors' confidence, and accusations of sponsorship of terrorism against some donors, including Belgium, by mid-June 1998 the new authorities had been unable to secure the levels of external funding with which they planned to finance this programme. Relations with donors deteriorated further owing to the nationalization of gold concessions in Sud-Kivu and the seizure of private shares in Telecel, both of which undermined investor confidence in the DRC. This, combined with a difficult relationship with the IMF, the Government's poor human rights record and its refusal to open talks with the RCD rebels, contributed to the failure to secure commitments from Belgium, France and the EU during Kabila's visit to Europe at the end of November 1998. In early 1999, as a result of the reluctance of Western donors, the Government decided to pursue an African co-operation strategy with Zimbabwe and Namibia, which had offered revolving credit facilities of $15m. and $25m., respectively, for the purchase of imports.

By 2000 foreign aid had almost come to a halt, with the exception of a US $4.5m. loan from the ADB, allocated in February to finance a capacity-building programme in order to improve the management of the DRC's public administration. In March UNDP announced that it had allocated $47m. to finance several projects in the DRC, but also made apparent that its operational capacity was dependent on an improvement in the economic environment in the country.

The shift of policy towards a more market-orientated economy, which was advocated from the outset by the new President, contributed significantly to improve the climate between the DRC Government and the donor community. On 26 February 2001 the European Council stated that if the planned reforms announced by President Joseph Kabila were implemented, the EU would be willing to engage in substantive discussions with the DRC on a gradual resumption of development co-operation. At the end of Kabila's visit to Brussels on 16 March, the Chairman of the European Commission, Romano Prodi, announced a €28m. contribution to finance a rehabilitation programme of the Congolese judiciary, in order to restore the rule of law in the DRC. At the end of May, after significant improvements concerning the implementation of the Lusaka peace accord, including an agreement on the date for a preparatory meeting to the inter-Congolese dialogue, the European Commission announced a €169m. loan for the DRC, including €74m. for food security and transport management. Action was to focus on developing agricultural production capacity and rehabilitating roads in order to improve the supply of urban markets with staples from the rural areas, and the distribution of seeds and medicines among the peasants. The agreement also included a €17m. capacity-building programme to strengthen key institutions, such as the central bank, the Customs and Excise Office and the Roads Office, as well as health, sanitation, and education measures. By the end of June Belgium, which was to hold the EU presidency for the following six months, was planning to propose an integrated development plan for the Great Lakes region to its EU partners. All these contributions were expected mostly to finance the consolidated appeal from the UN agencies launched in November 2000, which required US $140m. to fund projects in the food, agriculture, health, education, human rights, economic recovery and infrastructure sectors. In March 2001 Canada and the DRC signed a co-operation agreement on a C $3.5m. capacity-building programme for the central bank. The People's Republic of China also proved active in the co-operation field: in October 2000 the Chinese Government announced a US $4.7m. grant to finance the rehabilitation of the People's Palace and of the Martyrs' Stadium. In February 2001 the Chinese embassy in Kinshasa also announced that the Beijing authorities were prepared to cancel all the DRC's debts to China. In May 2002 the World Bank announced it would contribute $454m. to the programme in a number of sectors (roads, railways, river transport, schools, hospitals and agriculture). Throughout 2002 the World Bank devoted much effort to mobilizing funds to support a $1,700m. Emergency Multi-Sector Rehabilitation and Reconstruction Programme (EMRRP). On 5 December the participants in a Consultative Group, meeting in Paris, announced or confirmed financial contributions amounting to more than $2,500m. There was a consensus that the recent period had been marked by progress on both the economic and political fronts. The donors welcomed the return to economic growth in 2002 and pledged additional resources to support the EMRRP. The donors discussed a working plan under the lead of UNDP, aimed at restoring the basic capacity needed to launch policy and administrative reforms, and to manage key programmes in areas such as governance, social sectors, infrastructure and economic recovery. This effort was complementary to bilateral donations, such as a €8.6m. grant from France pledged in early 2003 to reform the Customs and Excises Office, and the computerization of the tax collection department. In February the World Bank representative in Kinshasa announced the first disbursements under the EMRRP and pledged $40m. for projects in the health sector. He also announced a $50m. loan to finance GÉCAMINES' restructuring efforts, aimed partly at financing the voluntary retrenchment of some 12,000 workers. In March the International Finance Corporation was considering investment in the textile industry and in the tourism sector. In June the ADF announced a $38.3m. loan for the rehabilitation of water supply installations, hospitals and primary health care centres. At the same time the ADF pledged a $4.6m. grant to finance a national study on the preparation of a poverty reduction strategy for the DRC. In January Belgium planned to spend €14.5m. on health, rural roads and micro-credit projects. The USA also announced plans in March to spend up to $53m. by 2025 on conservation projects to protect Central African forests, preserve their biodiversity and support sustainable timber exploitation, through USAID and the Wildlife Conservation Society. While international donors were making efforts to assist the DRC's reconstruction efforts, in early 2003 Zimbabwe requested that the DRC Government pay $1,800m. in compensation for its contribution to the war effort.

In December 2003, at a further World Bank Consultative Group meeting, US $3,980m. was pledged to finance the country's reunification and recovery during the 2004–06 period. According to the World Bank, new and confirmed financial contributions were to reach $1,080m. in 2004. This amount was to increase to $1,200m. in 2005 and continue in subsequent years, according to both political and economic progress. About 70% of the total was to be allocated to infrastructure projects and the remaining 30% was to be allocated to social sectors. The United Kingdom emerged as one of the most important bilateral donors, with a total of $120m. over three years, followed by the USA, which pledged $330m. Japan promised to finance the rehabilitation of the port of Matadi, at an estimated cost of $16m., after China abandoned an earlier commitment to support these projects. Belgium committed to increase its bilateral aid from €18m. in 2003 to €25m. in 2004. The new funds were expected to finance the second phase of the EMRRP, which also concerned the eastern and north-eastern parts of the country. The list of projects included the rehabilitation of the river ports of Kisangani, Bumba and Lisala ($12m.), the acquisition of new wagons and locomotives and railway rehabilitation works ($70.6m.), the rehabilitation of 10 airports ($35m.), the acquisition of dredging and signalization materials for the RVF river transport authority ($4.5m.) and the rehabilitation of meteorological services ($6m.). During the Consultative Group meeting, the National Agency for the Promotion of Investments submitted a list of priorities, including the rehabilitation and the modernization of the Kinshasa Ndjili international airport, the construction of a railway between Kinshasa and Ilebo, housing projects in Kinshasa and the provincial capitals, the construction of two medium-sized hydroelectric power stations at Katende (Kasaï Occidental) and Tshiala (Kasaï Oriental), the rehabilitation of the Maluku steel plant, the revival of production of GÉCAMINES and of the export crops (cotton, coffee, tea, cocoa and rubber), the creation of logging companies, and of new urban transport companies in Kinshasa and the capitals of the provinces. After the meeting, the Vice-President in charge of the economy and finance, Jean-Pierre Bemba, urged businesses to invest in the DRC, declaring that the country would offer increased legal security for investors by joining Organisation pour l'Harmonisation en Afrique du Droit des Affaires, an organization furthering the standardization of business legislation between the francophone countries, and that the services, water and electricity sectors would soon be liberalized. Bemba also announced restructuring of the banking sector and reforms of tax legislation through the introduction of value-added tax before 2005. Participants of the meeting also indicated that funds would be conditional on the restoration of security in the country. For that reason, in May 2004 the World Bank board approved an IDA grant of $100m. to finance an Emergency Demobilization and Reintegration Project in the DRC, in order to support the DRC Government's efforts to demobilize an estimated 150,000 former combatants and to assist their reintegration into civilian life. Private companies operating in the DRC also emphasized that the Government's failure to reimburse the $690m. owed to the domestic private sector was a major obstacle to investment. They also urged the authorities to simplify customs clearing formalities, particularly at the port of Matadi. In May Bemba presented a plan to turn public procurement procedures into a more transparent exercise. However, some reforms appeared difficult to implement: indeed, by the end of June 2004, owing to internal conflicts, the Parliament was unable to respect its commitment to review the controversial public contracts signed during the war. In March the EU's Court of Auditors offered to assist the DRC's equivalent institution in its efforts to monitor the management of public expenditure. However, during a review carried out in May, the IMF expressed satisfaction with the DRC's economic performances, although it stressed that much remained to be achieved in the areas of good governance, the fight against corruption and transparency. Meanwhile, the Association nationale pour la promotion des investissements announced that in the first quarter of 2004 it had approved 22 investment projects, totalling $1,780m. During the first half of 2004 various public investments were also announced. The ADF pledged funds of $45m. for the health sector to assist in the eradication of malaria, HIV/AIDS and tuberculosis in Province Orientale, and also announced a $7.6m. grant towards an 'education for all' project, a $24.1m. loan for rural rehabilitation, and a $10.2m. grant to improve food security in Bas-Congo and Bandundu. The World Bank also approved a $102m. loan to finance a programme to combat the HIV/AIDS pandemic.

The adoption of a constitution, followed by local, legislative and presidential elections, was viewed as a main priority by the donor community in order to provide a stable political framework to undertake the reconstruction and the development of the country. The cost of this operation, which was initially estimated at US $285m., was constantly revised upwards, partly owing to the extension of the transition period at least for another six months beyond the initial 30 June 2005 deadline. By mid-June, however, the EU Special Envoy in the Great Lakes expressed concern about the availability of funds to finance these operations. Accordingly, the total cost was $467m., of which $103m. was for logistics and $43m. to guarantee the security of the electoral process. In principle, the DRC Government was to finance 10% of the total cost, but by mid-June only $197m. were pledged by the donors, including $90m. by the EU. At that time only $99m., or slightly over 20% of the required amount, were available, according to the Independent Electoral Commission. The other main priorities of the donors community was the reduction of poverty in a country which in 2003 ranked 168th of 174 countries, according the UNDP's Human Development Index, and where revenue per capita and per day decreased from $1.31 in 1973 to $0.23 in 2000. In March 2005 the Bureau Central de Coordination (BCECO), which channels the funds of various donors, announced that in 2004 it had approved projects valued at $974.26m., of which $847.8m. were pledged by the World Bank and $130.2m. by the ADB. Institutional reforms absorbed 32% of the total, followed by water and electricity (22%), road and sanitation infrastructures (19%), agriculture (12%), rural development (6%), community development (5%) education (3%) and social protection (1%).

In April 2005 the World Bank considered that the implementation of the US $1,700m. EMRRP focused on infrastructure, agriculture and social sectors and financed by the donors community was satisfactory and announced that it had already disbursed $440m. under this programme which should end by 30 June 2007. However, the Congolese Minister of Public Works and Infrastructure deplored in June 2005 that the implementation of the programme during the first three months of that year had suffered several delays. Disbursements accordingly amounted only to $95m., or 28.8% of the total commitments for the period ($329.2m.). The delays were particularly alarming as far as infrastructure was concerned. Only 10% of the pledged $224.6m. were actually disbursed during the first quarter of 2005. As a result, the rehabilitation of the Kinshasa–Matadi and Kinshasa–Kikwit–Kananga roads failed to begin on schedule. However, works for the rehabilitation of the Kinshasa–Matadi road by the Chinese Sinohydro company eventually commenced in April. However, the Minister of the Budget deplored that in 2004 only 25.5% of the 15,700m. new Congolese francs committed to finance anti-poverty programmes were spent. The implementation of new projects was, nevertheless, recorded during the first half of 2005. In March the EU launched the second phase of its €80m. Public Administration Reform (PAR) II Programme for rehabilitation support, of which 70% were to finance urban rehabilitation projects. During the previous month the EU Commission approved a €38m. programme for health, food security and support to internally displaced persons and rape victims. In June the UNDP announced that $67m. would be available to finance anti-HIV/AIDS, tuberculosis and malaria programmes during the following two years. One of the main bilateral interventions was a $57m. loan from the Indian Government to finance energy, metallurgy and mining, railway, pharmaceutical and information technology projects throughout the country. In May Sweden announced that it would contribute €15m. to various projects, of which €10m. was for humanitarian aid, for the peace process and the organization of elections and the remaining €5m. for the education sector. During the 2003/04 fiscal year, one the DRC's main partners was the United Kingdom, which contributed $24m. bilaterally, $13.5m. through the EU, $39m. through the World Bank and $54m. through the UN agencies. In addition, the United Kingdom pledged that it would finance the DRC's DDR programme by as much as $25m. and would contribute $16m. in humanitarian assistance.

In January 2006 a report published in the medical journal *The Lancet* concluded that the humanitarian situation in the DRC was the most severe in the world, with some 38,000 people continuing to die every month, owing to insecurity, lack of a public health system and inadequate international aid. It was estimated that a total of 3.9m. people had died since 1998, mainly as a result of disease. At a donor conference, which was organized in Brussels in February, the UN secured pledges of US $681m. to alleviate the crisis and support long-term development in the DRC. The UN and European Commission subsequently initiated a humanitarian action plan, which allocated the funds to a number of sectors. Belgium, which contributed $11.3m. to the plan, was the largest single donor. The European Commission was to provide $45m. in humanitarian aid in 2006, following a total of $78m. in 2004 and 2005. Political tensions were high prior to the presidential and legislative elections on 30 July 2006, and the EU dispatched troops to reinforce the extended mandate of the UN mission. In August the authorities announced that a second round of the presidential election would take place on 29 October, and in view of the time required in confirming nationwide results, a new government was not expected to be installed until at least November.

In late 2006 IMF members in Kinshasa expressed concerns that the power-sharing Government was ignoring previously agreed upon resolutions and failing to implement IMF-sponsored projects. Under the SMP the fiscal deficit was to be tightened to 1.5% of GDP, down from 9.5% recorded in 2005. This, however, did not happen, and instead spending had increased by 50% by mid-2006. At that time the World Bank was considering instigating a US $10,000m. programme of debt relief to the DRC. Meanwhile, Belgium resumed its co-operation with DRC, donating €195m. to improve infrastructure in the health and education sectors. The World Bank also recognized the need to provide aid for reconstruction, granting an initial $180m. (part of funding measures worth $380m. for 2007). Nevertheless, IMF reports continue to reflect a deteriorating economy and in early 2007 it warned the Government to curb spending. In May the United Kingdom granted $14m. to fund projects dedicated to improving education, health, the quality of drinking water and general governance. A more pressing concern, however, may be food shortages. An estimated 40m. people (72% of the DRC population) face food insecurity.

Statistical Survey

Sources (unless otherwise stated): Département de l'Economie Nationale, Kinshasa; Institut National de la Statistique, Office Nationale de la Recherche et du Développement, BP 20, Kinshasa; tel. (12) 31401.

Area and Population

AREA, POPULATION AND DENSITY

Area (sq km)	2,344,885*
Population (census result)	
1 July 1984	
Males	14,543,800
Females	15,373,000
Total	29,916,800
Population (UN estimates at mid-year)†	
2004	56,918,000
2005	58,741,000
2006	60,644,000
Density (per sq km) at mid-2006	25.9

* 905,365 sq miles.

† Source: UN, *World Population Prospects: The 2006 Revision*.

REGIONS*

	Area (sq km)	Population (31 Dec. 1985)†
Bandundu	295,658	4,644,758
Bas-Zaïre	53,920	2,158,595
Équateur	403,293	3,960,187
Haut-Zaïre	503,239	5,119,750
Kasaï Occidental	156,967	3,465,756
Kasaï Oriental	168,216	2,859,220
Kivu	256,662	5,232,442
Shaba (formerly Katanga)	496,965	4,452,618
Kinshasa (city)‡	9,965	2,778,281
Total	2,344,885	34,671,607

* In October 1997 a statutory order redesignated the regions as provinces. Kivu was divided into three separate provinces, and several of the other provinces were renamed. The Constitution of February 2006 increased the existing 11 provinces to 26: Bas-Uele, Équateur, Haut-Lomami, Haut-Katanga, Haut-Uele, Ituri, Kasaï, Kasaï Oriental, Kongo Central, Kwango, Kwilu, Lomami, Lualaba, Lulua, Mai-Ndombe, Maniema, Mongala, Nord-Kivu, Nord-Ubangi, Sankuru, Sud-Kivu, Sud-Ubangi, Tanganyika, Tshopo, Tshuapa and Kinshasa (city).

† Provisional.

‡ Including the commune of Maluku.

Source: Département de l'Administration du Territoire.

PRINCIPAL TOWNS

(population at census of July 1984)

Kinshasa (capital)	2,664,309	Likasi	213,862
Lubumbashi	564,830	Boma	197,617
Mbuji-Mayi	486,235	Bukavu	167,950
Kolwezi	416,122	Kikwit	149,296
Kisangani	317,581	Matadi	138,798
Kananga	298,693	Mbandaka	137,291

Source: UN, *Demographic Yearbook*.

Mid-2005: ('000, incl. suburbs, UN estimates) Kinshasa 6,049; Kolwezi 1,270; Lubumbashi 1,179; Mbuji-Mayi 1,024 (Source: UN, *World Urbanization Prospects: The 2005 Revision*).

BIRTHS AND DEATHS

(annual averages, UN estimates)

	1990–95	1995–2000	2000–05
Birth rate (per 1,000)	48.7	49.2	49.6
Death rate (per 1,000)	19.0	21.1	19.3

Source: UN, *World Population Prospects: The 2006 Revision*.

Expectation of life (years at birth, WHO estimates): 44 (males 42; females 47) in 2004 (Source: WHO, *World Health Report*).

Economically Active Population (mid-2005, estimates in '000): Agriculture, etc. 14,433; Total labour force 23,736 (Source: FAO).

Health and Welfare

KEY INDICATORS

Total fertility rate (children per woman, 2005)	6.7
Under-5 mortality rate (per 1,000 live births, 2005)	205
HIV/AIDS (% of persons aged 15–49, 2005)	3.2
Physicians (per 1,000 head, 2004)	0.11
Hospital beds (per 1,000 head, 1990)	1.43
Health expenditure (2004): US $ per head (PPP)	15.3
Health expenditure (2004): % of GDP	4.0
Health expenditure (2004): public (% of total)	28.1
Access to water (% of persons, 2004)	58
Access to sanitation (% of persons, 2004)	27
Human Development Index (2004): ranking	167
Human Development Index (2004): value	0.391

For sources and definitions, see explanatory note on p. vi.

Agriculture

PRINCIPAL CROPS
('000 metric tons)

	2003	2004	2005
Rice (paddy)	315	315	315
Maize	1,155	1,155	1,155
Millet	36	37	37
Sorghum	6	6	6
Potatoes	92	92	93
Sweet potatoes	223	224	230
Cassava (Manioc)	14,945	14,951	14,974
Taro (Coco yam)	66	66	66
Yams	85	85	85
Other roots and tubers*	70	70	70
Sugar cane	1,579	1,551	1,552
Dry beans	108	109	110
Dry peas	1	1	1
Groundnuts (in shell)	360	364	268
Oil palm fruit	1,065	1,079	1,092
Melonseed	40	40	40
Cottonseed*	20	20	20
Cabbages*	23	23	23
Tomatoes*	40	40	40
Onions (dry)*	58	53	53
Pumpkins, squash and gourds	29	30	30
Other vegetables*	354	294	298
Bananas	314	313	314
Plantains	1,207	1,199	1,193
Oranges	180	180	180
Avocados	61	62	63
Mangoes	200	202	203
Pineapples	194	195	195
Papayas	212	214	216
Other fruit*	77	77	77
Coffee (green)	32	32	32
Pimento and allspice*	33	33	33

* FAO estimates.

Source: FAO.

LIVESTOCK
('000 head, year ending September)

	2003	2004	2005
Cattle	760	758	757
Sheep	898	899	900
Goats	4,010	4,016	4,022
Pigs	955	957	959
Chickens	19,651	19,710	19,769

Source: FAO.

LIVESTOCK PRODUCTS
('000 metric tons)

	2003	2004	2005
Cattle meat	12.5	12.4	12.4
Goat meat	18.4	18.5	18.5
Pig meat	23.8	23.8	23.9
Chicken meat	10.6	10.6	10.6
Game meat	88.5	88.0	88.7
Other meat*	57.8	57.8	57.8
Cows' milk*	5.0	5.0	5.0
Hen eggs*	6.0	6.0	6.0

* FAO estimates.

Source: FAO.

Forestry

ROUNDWOOD REMOVALS
('000 cubic metres, excl. bark, FAO estimates)

	2003	2004	2005
Sawlogs, veneer logs and logs for sleepers	170	170	170
Other industrial wood	3,483	3,483	3,483
Fuel wood	68,517	69,777	71,066
Total	72,170	73,430	74,719

Source: FAO.

SAWNWOOD PRODUCTION
('000 cubic metres, incl. railway sleepers)

	2003	2004	2005
Total (all broadleaved)	15	15	15

Source: FAO.

Fishing

('000 metric tons, live weight)

	2000	2001	2002
Capture*	209.3	214.6	220.0
Aquaculture	2.1	2.7	3.0
Total catch*	211.4	217.3	223.0

* FAO estimates.

2003–05 : Figures assumed to be unchanged from 2002 (FAO estimates).

Source: FAO.

Mining

(metric tons, unless otherwise indicated)

	2003	2004	2005*
Hard coal*	1,000	1,000	1,000
Crude petroleum ('000 barrels)	9,200	10,100	10,000
Copper ore†	59,800	73,300	92,000
Tantalum and niobium (columbium) concentrates	71‡	42‡	45
Cobalt concentrates†*	14,500‡	20,500‡	22,000
Gold (kilograms)*	4,100	5,700	4,200
Silver (kilograms)	35,501	32,953	53,553
Germanium (kilograms)	2,500	2,500	2,500
Diamonds ('000 carats)§	26,981	30,880	30,300

* Estimated production.

† Figures refer to the metal content of mine output.

‡ Revised figure.

§ An estimated 20% of the diamond is gem quality; the majority of production is from artisanal mining.

Source: US Geological Survey.

Industry

SELECTED PRODUCTS

('000 metric tons, unless otherwise indicated)

	2002	2003	2004*
Maize flour	13	13	14
Wheat flour	88	154	185
Sugar	63	74	81
Cigarettes ('000 cartons)	3,707	2,462	2,922
Beer (million litres)	135	131	169
Soft drinks (million litres)	76	88	116
Soaps	15	8	6
Acetylene	21	14	9
Tyres ('000 units)	42	45	49
Cement	265	331	402
Steel	150	140	130
Explosives	34	32	30
Bottles ('000 units)	17	21	9
Cotton fabrics ('000 sq metres)	3,454	1,291	263
Printed fabrics ('000 sq metres)	5,526	4,277	4,200
Footwear ('000 pairs)	5,676	2,930	3,223
Blankets ('000 units)	20	14	14
Electric energy (million kWh)	5,937	5,980	6,904

* Estimates.

Source: IMF, *Democratic Republic of the Congo: Selected Issues and Statistical Appendix* (October 2005).

Finance

CURRENCY AND EXCHANGE RATES

Monetary Units

100 centimes = 1 new Congolese franc.

Sterling, Dollar and Euro Equivalents (28 February 2007)

£1 sterling = 1,100.88 new Congolese francs;
US $1 = 562.62 new Congolese francs;
€1 = 743.28 new Congolese francs;
1,000 new Congolese francs = £0.91 = $1.78 = €1.35.

Average Exchange Rate (new Congolese francs per US $)

2004 395.93
2005 473.91
2006 468.28

Note: In June 1967 the zaire was introduced, replacing the Congolese franc (CF) at an exchange rate of 1 zaire = CF 1,000. In October 1993 the zaire was replaced by the new zaire (NZ), equivalent to 3m. old zaires. On 30 June 1998 a new Congolese franc, equivalent to NZ 100,000, was introduced. The NZ was withdrawn from circulation on 30 June 1999. Some of the figures in this survey are still given in terms of a previous currency.

BUDGET

('000 million new Congolese francs)*

Revenue†	2003	2004‡	2005§
Customs and excises	72,500	104,105	149,414
Direct and indirect taxes (excl. petroleum)	49,038	71,355	97,721
Petroleum royalties and taxes	36,386	52,096	74,663
Other	16,793	20,447	38,427
Non-budget revenue	2,100	—	—
Total	176,817	248,003	360,226

Expenditure‖	2003	2004‡	2005§
Current expenditure	248,394	324,358	345,522
Wages and salaries	57,104	93,223	123,967
Interest on public debt	79,146	85,708	106,662
Transfers and subsidies	19,867	14,842	15,899
Other current expenditure	92,277	130,585	98,994
Non-budget expenditure	2,100	—	—
Capital expenditure	61,756	72,059	233,607
Externally financed investment	47,154	56,999	217,267
Domestically financed investment	14,603	15,060	16,340
Other operations	89	398	157,015
Total	312,339	396,815	736,144

* Figures refer to the consolidated accounts of the central Government.

† Excluding grants received ('000 million new Congolese francs): 46,506 in 2003; 51,354 in 2004 (estimate); 313,919 in 2005 (projection).

‡ Estimates.

§ Projections.

‖ Excluding expenditure related to the Highly Indebted Poor Countries (HIPC) initiative, introduced by the IMF and World Bank in 2003 ('000 million new Congolese francs): 0 in 2003; 1,018 in 2004 (estimate); 19,032 in 2005 (projection).

Source: IMF, *Democratic Republic of the Congo: 2005 Article IV Consultation, Fifth Review Under the Three-Year Arrangement Under the Poverty Reduction and Growth Facility, Requests for Waiver of Performance Criteria, Additional Interim Assistance Under the Enhanced Initiative for Heavily Indebted Poor Countries, and Request for an Extension of Arrangement—Staff Report; Staff Statement; Public Information Notice and Press Release on the Executive Board Discussion; and Statement by the Executive Director for the Democratic Republic of the Congo* (October 2005).

INTERNATIONAL RESERVES

(US $ million at 31 December)

	1993	1994	1995
Gold	8.59	10.71	10.83
Foreign exchange	46.20	120.69	146.60
Total	54.79	131.40	157.43

1996 (US $ million at 31 December): Foreign exchange 82.50.

1997 (US $ million at 31 December): Gold 15.80.

2002 (US $ million at 31 December): IMF special drawing rights 8.32.

2003 (US $ million at 31 December): IMF special drawing rights 7.96.

2004 (US $ million at 31 December): IMF special drawing rights 5.50.

2005 (US $ million at 31 December): IMF special drawing rights 1.38.

2006 (US $ million at 31 December): IMF special drawing rights 0.26.

Source: IMF, *International Financial Statistics*.

MONEY SUPPLY

(million new Congolese francs at 31 December)

	2003	2004	2005
Currency outside banks	63,148	101,467	119,937
Demand deposits at deposit money banks	8,606	15,364	18,952
Total money (incl. others)	72,110	117,078	139,097

Source: IMF, *International Financial Statistics*.

COST OF LIVING

(Consumer Price Index for Kinshasa; base: August 1995 = 100)

	2000	2001	2002
Food	171,392	363,385	416,203
Rent	146,696	413,753	486,604
Clothing	255,363	718,795	787,276
All items (incl. others)	179,368	421,685	485,086

Source: IMF, *Democratic Republic of the Congo: Selected Issues and Statistical Appendix* (October 2005).

All items (Consumer Price Index; base 2000 = 100): 571.3 in 2002; 644.9 in 2003; 670.6 in 2004; 813.6 in 2005 (Source: IMF, *International Financial Statistics*).

NATIONAL ACCOUNTS

Expenditure on the Gross Domestic Product
(US $ million at current prices)

	2004	2005	2006
Government final consumption expenditure	537.89	588.96	661.16
Private final consumption expenditure	5,770.90	6,054.38	7,659.96
Gross capital formation	840.22	1,008.34	1,465.90
Total domestic expenditure	7,149.01	7,651.68	9,787.02
Exports of goods and services	1,993.72	2,242.47	2,760.96
Less Imports of goods and services	2,573.39	2,792.36	3,750.29
GDP in purchasers' values	6,569.34	7,101.80	8,797.69

Source: African Development Bank.

Gross Domestic Product by Economic Activity
('000 million new Congolese francs at current prices)

	2002	2003	2004*
Agriculture, forestry, livestock, hunting, and fishing	962.1	1,150.6	1,226.9
Mining†	166.1	198.7	262.4
Manufacturing	102.3	122.3	135.4
Construction and public works	78.3	93.6	110.0
Electricity and water	58.9	70.4	85.1
Transport and telecommunications	70.7	84.6	97.8
Trade and commerce	421.3	450.9	514.3
Public administration	21.7	26.0	44.6
Other services	4.9	58.8	58.8
GDP at factor cost	1,886.3	2,255.8	2,535.1
Import duties	35.9	42.9	52.4
GDP at market prices	1,922.2	2,298.7	2,587.5

* Estimates.
† Including processing.

Source: IMF, *Democratic Republic of the Congo: Selected Issues and Statistical Appendix* (October 2005).

BALANCE OF PAYMENTS

(US $ million)

	2002	2003	2004*
Exports of goods f.o.b.	1,076	1,340	1,813
Imports of goods f.o.b.	–1,093	–1,496	–2,056
Trade balance	–17	–156	–244
Exports of services	99	144	172
Imports of services	–354	–398	–505
Balance on goods and services	–272	–410	–576
Other income received	20	73	91
Other income paid	–318	–243	–385
Balance on goods, services and income	–569	–580	–870
Current transfers (net)	417	497	496
Current balance	–152	–83	–375
Capital and financial account (net)	150	–113	–124
Net errors and omissions	–159	–257	242
Overall balance	–161	–452	–257

* Estimates.

Source: IMF, *Democratic Republic of the Congo: Staff-Monitored Program* (July 2006).

External Trade

PRINCIPAL COMMODITIES

(US $ million)

Imports c.i.f.	2002	2003	2004*
Petroleum	53	75	130
Total (incl. others)	1,093	1,495	2,056

Exports f.o.b.	2002	2003	2004*
Copper	51	19	60
Cobalt	70	102	250
Gold	18	10	10
Diamonds	653	816	828
Crude petroleum	199	251	360
Coffee	9	13	16
Total (incl. others)	1,076	1,340	1,813

* Estimates.

Source: IMF, *Democratic Republic of the Congo: Selected Issues and Statistical Appendix* (October 2005).

SELECTED TRADING PARTNERS

(US $ million)

Imports c.i.f.	1995
Belgium-Luxembourg	147.2
Canada	9.8
China, People's Repub.	26.8
Côte d'Ivoire	35.5
Ecuador	65.1
Germany	48.2
India	9.9
Iran	10.3
Italy	26.5
Japan	11.8
Kenya	22.5
Morocco	9.2
Netherlands	36.5
Nigeria	72.5
South Africa	89.3
Togo	22.5
United Kingdom	50.2
Zambia	9.4
Total (incl. others)	889.2

Exports f.o.b.	1995
Angola	51.0
Belgium-Luxembourg	90.9
Canada	11.6
Germany	8.7
Israel	17.2
Italy	29.6
Philippines	30.2
Senegal	9.5
South Africa	219.7
Switzerland	29.7
United Kingdom	29.7
USA	107.6
Total (incl. others)	742.8

Source: UN, *International Trade Statistics Yearbook*.

Transport

RAILWAYS

(traffic)*

	1999	2000	2001†
Passenger-km (million)	145.2	187.9	222.1
Freight (million ton-km)	386.5	429.3	459.1

* Figures refer to Société Nationale des Chemins de Fer Congolaise (SNCC) services only.
† Estimates.

Source: IMF, *Democratic Republic of the Congo: Selected Issues and Statistical Appendix* (June 2003).

ROAD TRAFFIC
(motor vehicles in use at 31 December)

	1994	1995*	1996*
Passenger cars	698,672	762,000	787,000
Buses and coaches	51,578	55,000	60,000
Lorries and vans	464,205	495,000	538,000
Total vehicles	1,214,455	1,312,000	1,384,000

* Estimates.

Source: IRF, *World Road Statistics*.

1999: Passenger cars 172,600; Commercial vehicles 34,600 (Source: UN, *Statistical Yearbook*).

SHIPPING

Merchant Fleet
(registered at 31 December)

	2004	2005	2006
Number of vessels	20	21	21
Total displacement ('000 grt)	12.9	13.9	13.9

Source: Lloyd's Register-Fairplay, *World Fleet Statistics*.

International Sea-borne Freight Traffic
(estimates, '000 metric tons)

	1988	1989	1990
Goods loaded	2,500	2,440	2,395
Goods unloaded	1,400	1,483	1,453

Source: UN, *Monthly Bulletin of Statistics*.

CIVIL AVIATION
(traffic on scheduled services)

	1992	1993	1994
Kilometres flown (million)	4	4	6
Passengers carried ('000)	116	84	178
Passenger-km (million)	295	218	480
Total ton-km (million)	56	42	87

Source: UN, *Statistical Yearbook*.

Tourism

FOREIGN TOURIST ARRIVALS BY ORIGIN

	2003	2004	2005
Africa	20,380	14,531	36,489
Congo, Republic	121	109	437
America	2,568	4,592	3,824
East Asia	3,156	3,998	5,943
Europe	9,037	13,117	14,751
Belgium	2,337	4,446	4,788
France	2,012	3,348	3,245
Germany	384	637	951
Italy	475	785	1,038
Total	35,141	36,238	61,007

Tourism receipts (US $ million): 2 in 1998.

Source: World Tourism Organization.

Communications Media

	2003	2004	2005
Telephones ('000 main lines in use)	9.7	10.5	10.6
Mobile cellular telephones ('000 subscribers)	1,000.0	1,990.7	2,746.0
Internet users ('000)	75.0	112.5	140.6

Radio receivers ('000 in use): 18,030 in 1997.

Television receivers ('000 in use): 100 in 1998.

Facsimile machines (estimated number in use): 5,000 in 1995.

Personal computers ('000 in use): 200 in 1998; 500 in 1999.

Book production (titles published): 112 in 1996.

Daily newspapers: 9 in 1998 (estimated average circulation 129,000).

Sources: International Telecommunication Union; UNESCO Institute for Statistics.

Education

(1998/99, unless otherwise indicated)

	Teachers	Students		
		Males	Females	Total
Pre-primary*†	1,670	n.a.	n.a.	41,435
Primary	154,618	2,116,752	1,905,659	4,022,411
General secondary	89,461	554,895	307,830	862,725
Technical and vocational		256,313	115,490	371,803
Tertiary	3,788	n.a.	n.a.	60,341*

* Estimate(s).

† 2001/02.

Institutions (1998/99): Primary 17,585; Secondary 6,007.

Source: UNESCO Institute for Statistics.

Adult literacy rate (UNESCO estimates): 67.2% (males 80.9%; females 54.1%) in 2004 (Source: UN Development Programme, *Human Development Report*).

Directory

The Constitution

A new Constitution was approved by the transitional legislature in May 2005, and endorsed by a national referendum in December. The Constitution officially entered into effect on 18 February 2006; its main provisions are summarized below:

GENERAL PROVISIONS

The state of the Democratic Republic of the Congo is divided for the purposes of administration into 25 provinces and the capital of Kinshasa (which has the status of a province). The provinces are granted autonomous powers for managing local resources, and also powers that are exercised in conjunction with the central Government, including control of between 40% and 60% of public funds. Each province has a Government and Assembly. The Constitution reaffirms the principle of democracy, guarantees political pluralism, and protects fundamental human rights and freedoms. The establishment of a one party system is prohibited and punishable by law as an act of treason.

PRESIDENT

The President is the Head of State and Commander-in-Chief of the armed forces. He is elected by direct universal suffrage for a term of five years, which is renewable once. Presidential candidates must be of Congolese nationality and a minimum of 30 years of age. The President nominates a Prime Minister from the political party that commands a majority in the legislature and other members of the Government on the proposal of the Prime Minister. He exercises executive powers in conjunction with the Government and subject to the approval of the legislature. The areas of defence, security and foreign affairs are conducted jointly by the President and the Government.

GOVERNMENT

The Government comprises the Prime Minister and a number of ministers and deputy ministers. The Government is responsible for conducting national politics, which it determines in conjunction with the President. The Government is accountable to the Assemblée nationale, which is empowered to adopt a motion of censure against it.

LEGISLATURE

Legislative power is vested in a bicameral Parlement, comprising a lower chamber, the Assemblée nationale, and an upper chamber, the Sénat. Members of the Assemblée nationale are elected by direct universal suffrage for a renewable term of five years. The number of deputies is determined by electoral law. Members of the Sénat are indirectly elected by the Assemblies of each of the country's provinces for a renewable term of five years. Both chambers have a President and two Vice-Presidents.

JUDICIARY

The Constitution guarantees the independence of the judicial system. Members of the judiciary are under the authority of the Conseil Supérieur de la Magistrature. The Cour de Çassation has jurisdiction over legal decisions and the Conseil d'État over administrative decisions. The Cour Constitutionnelle interprets the provisions of the Constitution and ensures the conformity of new legislation. The system also comprises a Haute Cour Militaire, and lower civil and military courts and tribunals. The Conseil Supérieur de la Magistrature has 18 members, including the Presidents and Chief Prosecutors of the main courts. The Cour Constitutionnelle comprises nine members, who are appointed by the President (three nominated by Parlement and three by the Conseil Supérieur de la Magistrature) for a term of nine years. The Head of State appoints and dismisses magistrates, on the proposal of the Conseil Supérieur de la Magistrature.

The Government

HEAD OF STATE

President: Maj.-Gen. JOSEPH KABILA KABANGE (inaugurated 26 January 2001, 7 April 2003 and 6 December 2006).

CABINET

(August 2007)

Prime Minister: ANTOINE GIZENGA.

Minister of State, in charge of Agriculture: FRANÇOIS JOSEPH MOBUTU NZANGA NGBANGAWE.

Minister of State, in charge of the Interior, Decentralization and Security: DENIS KALUME NUMBI.

Minister of State, in charge of Foreign Affairs and International Co-operation: ANTIPAS MBUSA NYAMWISI.

Minister of State, in charge of Higher and University Education: SYLVAIN NGABU CHUMBU.

Minister of State, in charge of Infrastructure, Public Works and Reconstruction: PIERRE LUMBI OKONGO.

Minister of State at the Presidency: NKULU MITUMBA KILOMBO.

Minister in Assistance to the Prime Minister: GODEFROID MAYOBO MPWENE NGANTIEN.

Minister of National Defence and War Veterans: CHIKEZ DIEMU.

Minister of Justice: GEORGES MINSAY BOOKA.

Minister of Planning: OLIVIER KAMITATU ETSU.

Minister of Regional Integration: IGNACE GATA MAVINGA.

Minister of Finance: ATHANASE MATENDA KYELU.

Minister of the Budget: ADOLPHE MUZITO.

Minister without Portfolio: JEANNINE MABUNDA LIOKO.

Minister of the National Economy: SYLVAIN JOËL BIFWILA TCHAMWALA.

Minister of Information, Press and Communications: TOUSSAINT TSHILOMBO SEND.

Minister of Industry: SIMON MBOSO KIAMPUTU.

Minister of Foreign Trade: KASONGO ILUNGA.

Minister of Small and Medium-sized Enterprises: JEAN-FRANÇOIS EKOFO PANZOKO.

Minister of Transport and Communication Routes: REMY HENRI KUSEYO GATANGA.

Minister of Rural Development: CHARLES MWANDO NSIMBA.

Minister of Primary and Secondary Education: MAKER MWANGU FAMBA.

Minister of Scientific Research: (vacant).

Minister of Public Health: VICTOR MAKWENGE KAPUT.

Minister of Mines: MARTIN KABWELULU LABILO.

Minister of Energy: SALOMON BANAMUHERE BALIENE.

Minister of Hydrocarbons: LAMBERT MENDE OMALANGA.

Minister of Employment and Social Planning: MARIE-ANGE LUKIANA MUFWANKOL.

Minister of the Civil Service: ZÉPHYRIN MUTU DIAMBU-DI-LUSALA NIEVA.

Minister of Social Affairs and National Solidarity: MARTIN BITIJULA MAHIMBA.

Minister of Women's Affairs: PHILOMÈNE OMATUKU ATSHAKAWO AKATSHI.

Minister of Youth and Sports: PARDONNE KALIBA MULANGA.

Minister of Land Affairs: LILIANE PANDE MUABA.

Minister of Town Planning and Housing: LAURENT-SIMON IKENGE LISAMBOLA.

Minister of Post, Telephones and Telecommunications: KYAMUSOKE BAMUSULANGA NTA-BOTE.

Minister of the Environment: DIDACE PEMBE BOKIAGA.

Minister of Tourism: ELIAS KAKULE MBAHINGANA.

Minister of Culture and the Arts: MARCEL MALENSO NDODILA.

Minister of Human Rights: EUGÈNE LOKWA ILWALOMA.

Minister of Humanitarian Affairs: JEAN-CLAUDE MUYAMBO KYASSA.

MINISTRIES

Office of the President: Hôtel du Conseil Exécutif, ave de Lemera, Kinshasa-Gombe; tel. (12) 30892; internet www.presidentrdc.cd.

Office of the Prime Minister: Kinshasa.

Ministry of the Budget: Kinshasa.

Ministry of the Civil Service: Kinshasa.

Ministry of Culture and the Arts: BP 8541, Kinshasa 1; tel. (12) 31005.

Ministry of Employment and Social Planning: blvd du 30 juin, BP 3840, Kinshasa-Gombe.

Ministry of Energy: Immeuble Snel, 239 ave de la Justice, BP 5137 KIN I, Kinshasa-Gombe; tel. (12) 22570.

Ministry of the Environment: 76 ave des Cliniques, Kinshasa-Gombe; internet www.minenv.itgo.com.

Ministry of Finance: blvd du 30 juin, BP 12998 KIN I, Kinshasa-Gombe; tel. (12) 33232; internet www.minfinrdc.cd.

Ministry of Foreign Trade: Kinshasa.

Ministry of Human Rights: Kinshasa.

Ministry of Humanitarian Affairs: Kinshasa.

Ministry of Hydrocarbons: Kinshasa.

Ministry of Industry: Kinshasa.

Ministry of Information, Press and Communications: ave du 24 novembre, BP 3171, KIN I, Kinshasa-Kabinda; tel. (12) 23171.

Ministry of the Interior, Decentralization and Security: ave de Lemera, Kinshasa-Gombe; tel. (12) 23171.

Ministry of Justice: 228 ave de Lemera, BP 3137, Kinshasa-Gombe; tel. (12) 32432.

Ministry of Land Affairs: Kinshasa.

Ministry of Mines: Kinshasa; internet www.miningcongo.cd.

Ministry of National Defence and War Veterans: BP 4111, Kinshasa-Gombe; tel. (12) 59375.

Ministry of the National Economy: Kinshasa.

Ministry of Planning: 4155 ave des Côteaux, BP 9378, Kinshasa-Gombe 1; tel. (12) 31346.

Ministry of Post, Telephones and Telecommunications: Immeuble Kilou, 4484 ave des Huiles, BP 800 KIN I, Kinshasa-Gombe; tel. (12) 24854.

Ministry of Primary and Secondary Education: Enceinte de l'Institut de la Gombe, BP 3163, Kinshasa-Gombe; tel. (12) 30098.

Ministry of Public Health: blvd du 30 juin, BP 3088 KIN I, Kinshasa-Gombe; tel. (12) 31750.

Ministry of Regional Integration: Kinshasa.

Ministry of Rural Development: Immeuble Sozacom, 3rd floor, blvd du 30 juin, BP 8722 KIN I, Kinshasa-Gombe; tel. (12) 31821.

Ministry of Scientific Research: Kinshasa.

Ministry of Small and Medium-sized Enterprises: Kinshasa.

Ministry of Social Affairs and National Solidarity: Kinshasa.

Ministry of Tourism: Kinshasa.

Ministry of Town Planning and Housing: 15 ave des Cliniques, BP 12348 KIN I, Kinshasa-Gombe; tel. (12) 31252.

Ministry of Transport and Communication Routes: Immeuble Onatra, blvd du 30 juin, BP 3304, Kinshasa-Gombe; tel. (12) 23660.

Ministry of Women's Affairs: Kinshasa.

Ministry of Youth and Sports: 77 ave de la Justice, BP 8541 KIN I, Kinshasa-Gombe.

President and Legislature

PRESIDENT

Presidential Election, First Round, 30 July 2006

Candidate	Votes	% of votes
Joseph Kabila Kabange (Independent)	7,590,485	44.81
Jean-Pierre Bemba Gombo (Mouvement de libération du Congo)	3,392,592	20.03
Antoine Gizenga (Parti lumumbiste unifié)	2,211,280	13.06
François Joseph Mobutu Nzanga Ngbangawe (Union des démocrates mobutistes)	808,397	4.77
Oscar Kashala Lukumuenda (Union pour la reconstruction du Congo)	585,410	3.46
Azarias Ruberwa (Rassemblement congolais pour la démocratie)	285,641	1.69
Pierre wa Syakassighe Pay-Pay (Coalition des démocrates congolais)	267,749	1.58
Vincent de Paul Lunda Bululu (Rassemblement des forces sociales et fédéralistes)	237,257	1.40
Others	1,558,723	9.20
Total	16,937,534	100.00

Presidential Election, Second Round, 29 October 2006

Candidate	Votes	% of votes
Joseph Kabila Kabange (Independent)	9,436,779	58.05
Jean-Pierre Bemba Gombo (Mouvement de libération du Congo)	6,819,822	41.95
Total	16,256,601	100.00

LEGISLATURE

The bicameral Parlement of the Democratic Republic of the Congo comprises a lower chamber, or Assemblée nationale, and an upper chamber, or Sénat, members of which are elected by the deputies of the provincial Assemblées.

Assemblée nationale

President: VITAL KAMERHE.

General Election, 30 July 2006

Party	Seats
Parti du peuple pour la reconstruction et la démocratie	111
Mouvement de libération du Congo	64
Parti lumumbiste unifié	34
Mouvement social pour le renouveau	27
Forces du renouveau	26
Rassemblement congolais pour la démocratie	15
Coalition des démocrates congolais	10
Convention des démocrates chrétiens	10
Union des démocrates mobutistes	9
Camp de la patrie	8
Démocratie chrétienne fédéraliste—Convention des fédéralistes pour la démocratie	8
Parti démocrate chrétien	8
Union des nationalistes fédéralistes du Congo	7
Others*	100
Independents	63
Total	500

* Comprising 56 political parties that won less than five seats.

Sénat

President: PIERRE MARINI BODHO.

Election, 19 January 2007

Party	Seats
Parti du peuple pour la reconstruction et la démocratie	22
Mouvement de libération du Congo	14
Forces du renouveau	7
Rassemblement congolais pour la démocratie	7
Parti démocrate chrétien	6
Convention des démocrates chrétiens	3
Mouvement social pour le renouveau	3
Parti lumumbiste unifié	2
Others*	18
Independents	26
Total	108

* Comprising 18 political parties that each won one seat.

Election Commission

Commission électorale indépendante (CEI): 4471 blvd du 30 juin, Commune de la gombe, Kinshasa; tel. (81) 10613; e-mail ceirdc@yahoo.fr; internet www.cei-rdc.cd; f. 2004; Chair. ABBÉ APOLLINAIRE MALU-MALU.

Political Organizations

In January 1999 a ban on the formation of political associations was officially ended, and in May 2001 remaining restrictions on the registration and operation of political parties were removed. Despite a peace agreement between the Government and rebel factions, reached in December 2002 and the subsequent installation of power-sharing institutions in 2003, heavy fighting continued in the east of the country. Some 260 political parties registered to contest presidential and legislative elections on 30 July 2006.

Camp de la patrie: Kinshasa; Leader ARTHUR NGOMA Z'AHIDI.

Coalition des démocrates congolais (CODECO): f. 2006; Leader PIERRE WA SYAKASSIGHE PAY-PAY.

Convention des démocrates chrétiens: Kinshasa; FLORENTIN MOKONDA BONZA.

Démocratie chrétienne féderaliste—Convention des fédéralistes pour la démocratie chrétienne (DCF—COFEDEC): 2209 ave des Etoiles, Kinshasa-Gombe; Leader VENANT TSHIPASA VANGI.

Forces du renouveau: Kinshasa; Leader ANTIPAS MBUSA NYAMWISI.

Forces novatrices pour l'union et la solidarité (FONUS): 13 ave de l'Enseignement, Kasa-Vubu, Kinshasa; f. 2004; advocates political pluralism; Pres. JOSEPH OLENGHANKOY; Sec.-Gen. JOHN KWET.

Front des nationalistes intégrationnistes (FNI): Bunia; f. 2003 in Uganda; ethnic Lendu rebel group, in conflict with Union des patriotes congolais in north-east; Leader FLORIBERT NDJABU NGABU.

Mouvement de libération du Congo (MLC): 6 ave du Port, Kinshasa-Gombe; f. 1998; fmr Ugandan-supported rebel movement; incl. in Govt in July 2003; Leader JEAN-PIERRE BEMBA GOMBO; Sec.-Gen. THOMAS LUHAKA.

Mouvement populaire de la révolution (MPR): 5448 ave de la Justice, Immeuble Yoko, Kinshasa-Gombe; f. 1966 by Pres. Mobutu; sole legal political party until Nov. 1990; advocates national unity and opposes tribalism; Leader Prof. VUNDWAWE TE PEMAKO; Sec.-Gen. KITHIMA BIN RAMAZANI.

Mouvement social pour le renouveau (MSR): Kinshasa; f. 2006; Leader PIERRE LUMBI.

Parti démocrate chrétien: Leader JOSÉ ENDUNDO BONONGE.

Parti démocrate et social chrétien (PDSC): 3040 route de Matadi, C/Ngaliema, Kinshasa; tel. (12) 21211; f. 1990; centrist; Pres. ANDRÉ BOBOLIKO; Sec.-Gen. TUYABA LEWULA.

Parti lumumbiste unifié (PALU): 9 rue Cannas, C/Limete, Kinshasa; Leader ANTOINE GIZENGA.

Parti du peuple pour la reconstruction et la démocratie (PPRD): Croisement des aves Pumbu et Batetela, Kinshasa-Gombe; f. March 2002 by Pres. Joseph Kabila; Sec.-Gen. VITAL KAMERHE.

Parti pour l'unité et la sauvegarde de l'intégrité du Congo (PUSIC): Bunia; coalition of four tribal militia groups, led by Hema; Leader ROBERT PIMBU.

Rassemblement congolais pour la démocratie (RCD—Goma): 26 ave Lukusa, Kinshasa-Gombe; e-mail congorcd@congorcd.org; internet www.congorcd.org; f. 1998; rebel movement until Dec. 2002 peace agreement; incl. in Govt July 2003; main Ilunga faction; supported by Rwanda; Leader AZARIAS RUBERWA; Sec.-Gen. FRANCIS BEDY MAKHUBU MABELE.

Rassemblement congolais pour la démocratie—Mouvement de libération (RCD—ML): 290 ave Libenge, Lingwala; broke away from main RCD in 1999; supported by Uganda; a number of groups were merged into the FLC (see above) in Jan. 2001; Pres. MBUSA NYAMWISI.

Rassemblement congolais pour la démocratie—National (RCD—N): blvd du 30 juin, S.V./64 Haut-Uélé (Isiro); broke away from RCD—ML in Oct. 2000; Leader ROGER LUMBALA.

Rassemblement des forces sociales et fédéralistes (RSF): 98 rue Poto-poto, Kimbanseke; Leader VINCENT DE PAUL LUNDA BULULU.

Rassemblement pour une nouvelle société (RNS): 1 bis rue Lufu, C/Bandalungwa; e-mail info@congozaire.org; Leader Dr ALAFUELE M. KALALA.

Union des démocrates mobutistes (UDEMO): f. by son of fmr Pres. Mobutu; Leader FRANÇOIS JOSEPH MOBUTU NZANGA NGBANGAWE.

Union des nationalistes fédéralistes du Congo (UNAFEC): 5 ave Citronniers, Kinshasa-Gombe; Leader GABRIEL KYUNGA WA KUMWANZA.

Union des patriotes congolais (UPC): 25 blvd de la Libération, Bunia; rebel group of Hema ethnic group, fmrly in conflict with Lendu in north-east; registered as political org. 2004, after peace agreement with Govt; Leader THOMAS LUBANGA.

Union pour la démocratie et le progrès social (UDPS): 10 rue, ave Cannas, Limete, Kinshasa; e-mail udps@globalserve.net; internet www.udps.org/udps.html; f. 1982; Leader ETIENNE TSHISEKEDI WA MULUMBA; Sec.-Gen. RÉMY MASSAMBA.

Union pour la reconstruction du Congo (UREC): Leader OSCAR LUKUMWENA KASHALA.

Union pour la République (UPR): 622 ave Monts des Arts, Kinshasa-Gombe; f. 1997; by fmr mems of the MPR; Leader BOBOY NYABAKA.

Diplomatic Representation

EMBASSIES IN THE DEMOCRATIC REPUBLIC OF THE CONGO

Angola: 4413–4429 blvd du 30 juin, BP 8625, Kinshasa; tel. (12) 33003; fax (13) 98971; e-mail consangolakatanga@voila.fr; Ambassador MAWETE JOÃO BAPTISTA.

Belgium: Immeuble Le Cinquantenaire, place du 27 octobre, BP 899, Kinshasa; tel. (12) 20110; fax (12) 22120; e-mail kinshasa@diplobel.org; Ambassador JOHAN SWINNEN.

Benin: 3990 ave des Cliniques, BP 3265, Kinshasa-Gombe; tel. (98) 128659; e-mail abkin@raga.net; Ambassador GEORGES S. WHANNOU DE DRAVO.

Cameroon: 171 blvd du 30 juin, BP 10998, Kinshasa; tel. (12) 34787; Chargé d'affaires a.i. DOMINIQUE AWONO ESSAMA.

Canada: 17, ave Pumbu, Commune de la gombe, BP 8341, Kinshasa 1; tel. (89) 50310; fax (99) 75403; e-mail kinshasa@international.gc.ca; Ambassador JEAN-PIERRE BOLDUC.

Central African Republic: 11 ave Pumbu, BP 7769, Kinshasa; tel. (12) 30417; Ambassador BERNARD LE SISSA.

Chad: 67–69 ave du Cercle, BP 9097, Kinshasa; tel. (12) 22358; Ambassador MAITINE DJOUMBE.

Congo, Republic: 179 blvd du 30 juin, BP 9516, Kinshasa; tel. (12) 34028; Ambassador EDOUARD ROGER OKOULA.

Côte d'Ivoire: 68 ave de la Justice, BP 9197, Kinshasa; tel. (12) 21208; Ambassador GUILLAUME AHIPEAU.

Cuba: 4660 ave Cateam, BP 10699, Kinshasa; tel. (12) 8803823; Ambassador JOSÉ SIVILA DE LA TORRE.

Egypt: 519 ave de l'Ouganda, BP 8838, Kinshasa; tel. (51) 10137; fax (88) 03728; Ambassador MORTDA ALY MOHAMED LASHIN.

Ethiopia: BP 8435, Kinshasa; tel. (12) 23327; Ambassador DIEUDEONNE A. GANGA.

France: 97 ave de la République du Tchad, BP 3093, Kinshasa; tel. (81) 5559999; fax (81) 5559937; e-mail ambafrance@ic.cd; internet www.ambafrance-cd.org; Ambassador BERNARD PREVOST.

Gabon: ave du 24 novembre, BP 9592, Kinshasa; tel. (12) 68325; Ambassador MICHEL MADOUNGOU.

Germany: 82 ave Roi Baudouin, BP 8400, Kinshasa-Gombe; tel. (81) 5561380; e-mail amballemagne@ic.cd; internet www.kinshasa.diplo.de; Ambassador KARL-ALBRECHT RICHARD WOKALEK.

Greece: Immeuble de la Communauté Hellénique, 3ème étage, blvd du 30 juin, BP 478, Kinshasa; tel. (99) 70521; e-mail gremb.kin@mfa.gr; Ambassador IOANNIS CHRISTOPHILIS.

Holy See: 81 ave Goma, BP 3091, Kinshasa; tel. (88) 08814; fax (88) 48483; e-mail nuntius@raga.net; Apostolic Nuncio Most Rev. GIOVANNI D'ANIELLO (Titular Archbishop of Paestum).

Israel: 141 blvd du 30 juin, BP 8343, Kinshasa; tel. (99) 87218; fax (88) 07494; e-mail daniel.saada@mfa.gov.il; Ambassador DANIEL SAADA.

Japan: Immeuble Citibank, 2ème étage, ave Colonel Lukusa, BP 1810, Kinshasa; tel. (88) 45305; fax (satellite) 871-761-21-41-42; e-mail ambj@ic.cd; Ambassador YASUO TAKANO.

Kenya: 4002 ave de l'Ouganda, BP 9667, Kinshasa; tel. (81) 5554797; fax (81) 5554805; e-mail kinshasa@mfa.go.ke; Ambassador KARUCHU SYLVESTER GAKUMU.

Korea, Democratic People's Republic: 168 ave de l'Ouganda, BP 16597, Kinshasa; tel. (81) 8801443; fax (81) 5300194; e-mail ckc.kin168@yahoo.com; Ambassador RI WON SON.

Korea, Republic: 65 blvd Tshatshi, BP 628, Kinshasa; tel. (81) 9820302; e-mail amb-rdc@mofat.go.kr; Chargé d'affaires KIM JONG SOEK.

Lebanon: 3 ave de l'Ouganda, Kinshasa; tel. (12) 82469; Chargé d'affaires a.i. CHEHADE MOUALLEM.

Liberia: 3 ave de l'Okapi, BP 8940, Kinshasa; tel. (12) 82289; Ambassador JALLA D. LANSANAH.

Mauritania: BP 16397, Kinshasa; tel. (12) 59575; Ambassador Lt-Col M'BARECK OULD BOUNA MOKHTAR.

Netherlands: 11 ave Zongontolo, 55 Immeuble Residence, BP 10299, Kinshasa; tel. (99) 8001140; fax (99) 9975326; e-mail kss@minbuza.nl; Ambassador E. C. W. VAN DER LAAN.

Nigeria: 141 blvd du 30 juin, BP 1700, Kinshasa; tel. (81) 7005142; fax (81) 2616115; e-mail nigemb@jobantech.cd; Ambassador Dr ONUORAH JONIKUL OBODOZIE.

Portugal: 270 ave des Aviateurs, BP 7775, Kinshasa; tel. (81) 5161277; e-mail ambassadeportugal@micronet.net; Ambassador ALFREDO MANUEL SILVA DUARTE COSTA.

Russia: 80 ave de la Justice, BP 1143, Kinshasa 1; tel. (12) 33157; fax (12) 45575; Ambassador VALERII GAMAIVNE.

South Africa: 77 ave Ngongo Lutete, BP 7829, Kinshasa-Gombe; tel. (88) 48287; fax (88) 04152; e-mail ambasud@ckt.cd; Ambassador Rev. Dr MOLEFE S. TSELE.

Spain: blvd du 30 juin, Bldg Communauté Hellénique, Commune de la gombe, BP 8036, Kinshasa; tel. (81) 8843195; e-mail emb.kinshasa@mae.es; Dr MIGUEL FERNÁNDEZ-PALACIOS MARTÍNEZ.

Sudan: 24 ave de l'Ouganda, Kinshasa; tel. (99) 37396; Chargé d'affaires a.i. ABDEL RA'OUF AMIR.

Sweden: 93 ave Roi Baudouin, Commune de la gombe, BP 11096, Kinshasa; tel. (99) 8174289; fax (satellite) 870-600-147849; e-mail ambassaden.kinshasa@foreign.ministry.se; internet www.swedenabroad.com/kinshasa; Ambassador MAGNUS WERNSTEDT.

Tanzania: 142 blvd du 30 juin, BP 1612, Kinshasa; tel. (12) 81700; fax (12) 88081; e-mail amb.tanzanie@ic.cd; Ambassador GORDON LUHWANO NGILANGWA.

Togo: 3 ave de la Vallée, BP 10117, Kinshasa; tel. (12) 30666; Ambassador MAMA GNOFAM.

Tunisia: 67–69 ave du Cercle, BP 1498, Kinshasa; tel. (88) 03901; e-mail atkinshasa@yahoo.fr; Ambassador AZOUZ ENNIFAR.

Turkey: 18 ave Pumbu, BP 7817, Kinshasa; tel. (88) 01207; fax (88) 04740; e-mail tckinsbe@raga.net; Ambassador DENIZ UZMEN.

United Kingdom: 83 ave Roi Baudouin, BP 8049, Kinshasa; tel. (81) 7150761; fax (81) 3464291; e-mail ambrit@ic.cd; Ambassador NICHOLAS KAY.

USA: 310 ave des Aviateurs, BP 397, Kinshasa; tel. (81) 5560151; fax (81) 5560173; e-mail AEKinshasaConsular@state.gov; internet kinshasa.usembassy.gov; Ambassador ROGER A. MEECE.

Zambia: 54–58 ave de l'Ecole, BP 1144, Kinshasa; tel. (81) 9999437; fax (88) 45106; e-mail ambazambia@ic.cd; Ambassador TENS C. KAPOMA.

Judicial System

Under the Constitution that entered into effect in February 2006, the judicial system is independent. Members of the judiciary are under the authority of the Conseil Supérieur de la Magistrature. The Cour de Cassation has jurisdiction over legal decisions and the Conseil d'État over administrative decisions. The Cour Constitutionnelle interprets the provisions of the Constitution and ensures the conformity of new legislation. The judicial system also comprises a Haute Cour Militaire, and lower civil and military courts and tribunals. The Conseil Supérieur de la Magistrature has 18 members, including the Presidents and Chief Prosecutors of the main courts. The Cour Constitutionnelle comprises nine members, who are appointed by the President (three nominated by the legislature and three by the Conseil Supérieur de la Magistrature) for a term of nine years. The Head of State appoints and dismisses magistrates, on the proposal of the Conseil Supérieur de la Magistrature.

Cour de Cassation

cnr ave de la Justice and ave de Lemera, BP 3382, Kinshasa-Gombe; tel. (12) 25104.

President of the Cour de Cassation: LWAMBA BINDU.

Procurator-General of the Republic: MONGULU T'APANGANE.

Religion

Many of the country's inhabitants follow traditional beliefs, which are mostly animistic. A large proportion of the population is Christian, predominantly Roman Catholic, and there are small Muslim, Jewish and Greek Orthodox communities.

CHRISTIANITY

The Roman Catholic Church

The Democratic Republic of the Congo comprises six archdioceses and 41 dioceses. An estimated 56% of the population are Roman Catholics.

Bishops' Conference

Conférence Episcopale de la République Démocratique du Congo, BP 3258, Kinshasa-Gombe; tel. (12) 34528; fax (88) 44948; e-mail conf.episc.rdc@ic.cd.

f. 1981; Pres. Most Rev. LAURENT MONSENGWO PASINYA (Archbishop of Kisangani).

Archbishop of Bukavu: (vacant), Archevêché, BP 3324, Bukavu; tel. (761) 470721; fax (761) 470723; e-mail archevechebk@yahoo.fr.

Archbishop of Kananga: Most Rev. GODEFROY MUKENG'A KALOND, Archevêché, BP 70, Kananga; tel. (81) 5013942; e-mail archidiocesekananga@yahoo.fr.

Archbishop of Kinshasa: Cardinal FRÉDÉRIC ETSOU-NZABI-BAMUNGWABI, Archevêché, ave de l'Université, BP 8431, Kinshasa 1; tel. (12) 3723546; e-mail archikin@ic.cd.

Archbishop of Kisangani: Most Rev. LAURENT MONSENGWO PASINYA, Archevêché, ave Mpolo 10B, BP 505, Kisangani; tel. (81) 2006715; fax (761) 608336.

Archbishop of Lubumbashi: Most Rev. FLORIBERT SONGASONGA MWITWA, Archevêché, BP 72, Lubumbashi; tel. (2) 48601; e-mail archidiolub@mwangaza.cd.

Archbishop of Mbandaka-Bikoro: Most Rev. JOSEPH KUMUONDALA MBIMBA, Archevêché, BP 1064, Mbandaka; tel. (98) 849988; e-mail mbandakabikoro@yahoo.fr.

The Anglican Communion

The Church of the Province of the Congo comprises six dioceses.

Archbishop of the Province of the Congo and Bishop of Boga: Most Rev. PATRICE BYANKYA NJOJO, CAC-Boga, POB 25586, Nairobi, Kenya.

Bishop of Bukavu: Rt Rev. FIDÈLE BALUFUGA DIROKPA, CAC-Bukavu, POB 53435, Nairobi, Kenya.

Bishop of Katanga: Rt Rev. ISINGOMA KAHWA, BP 16482, Kinshasa; tel. (88) 06533; e-mail peac_isingoma@yahoo.fr.

Bishop of Kindu: Rt Rev. ZACHARIA MASIMANGE KATANDA, CAC-Kindu, POB 53435, Nairobi, Kenya; e-mail angkindu@antenna.nl.

Bishop of Kisangani: Rt Rev. SYLVESTRE MUGERA TIBAFA, CAC-Kisangani, BP 861, Kisangani.

Bishop of Nord Kivu: Rt Rev. METHUSELA MUNZENDA MUSUBAHO, CAC-Butembo, POB 21285, Nairobi, Kenya; fax (satellite) 871-166-1121.

Kimbanguist

Eglise de Jésus Christ sur la Terre par le Prophète Simon Kimbangu: BP 7069, Kinshasa; tel. (12) 68944; f. 1921; officially est. 1959; c. 5m. mems (1985); Spiritual Head HE SALOMON DIALUNGANA KIANGANI; Sec.-Gen. Rev. LUNTADILLA.

Protestant Churches

Eglise du Christ au Congo (ECC): ave de la Justice 75, BP 4938, Kinshasa-Gombe; f. 1902; a co-ordinating agency for all the Protestant churches, with the exception of the Kimbanguist Church; 62 mem. communities and a provincial org. in each province; *c.* 10m. mems (1982); Pres. Bishop MARINI BODHO; includes:

Communauté Baptiste du Congo-Ouest: BP 4728, Kinshasa 2; f. 1970; 450 parishes; 170,000 mems (1985); Gen. Sec. Rev. LUSAKWENO-VANGU.

Communauté des Disciples du Christ: BP 178, Mbandaka; tel. 31062; f. 1964; 250 parishes; 650,000 mems (1985); Gen. Sec. Rev. Dr ELONDA EFEFE.

Communauté Episcopale Baptiste en Afrique: 2 ave Jason Sendwe, BP 2809, Lubumbashi 1; tel. and fax (2) 348602; e-mail kitobokabwe@yahoo.fr; f. 1956; 1,300 episcopal communions and parishes; 150,000 mems (2001); Pres. Bishop KITOBO KABWEKA-LEZA.

Communauté Evangélique: BP 36, Luozi; f. 1961; 50 parishes; 33,750 mems (1985); Pres. Rev. K. LUKOMBO NTONTOLO.

Communauté Lumière: BP 10498, Kinshasa 1; f. 1931; 150 parishes; 220,000 mems (1985); Patriarch KAYUWA TSHIBUMBU WA KAHINGA.

Communauté Mennonite: BP 18, Tshikapa; f. 1960; 40,000 mems (1985); Gen. Sec. Rev. KABANGY DJEKE SHAPASA.

Communauté Presbytérienne: BP 117, Kananga; f. 1959; 150,000 mems (1985); Gen. Sec. Dr M. L. TSHIHAMBA.

Eglise Missionaire Apostolique: 375 ave Commerciale, BP 15859, Commune de N'Djili, Kinshasa 1; tel. (98) 165927; e-mail buzi4@hotmail.com; f. 1986; 5 parishes; 2,600 mems; Apostle for Africa Rev. LUFANGA-AYIMOU NANANDANA.

The Press

DAILIES

L'Analyste: 129 ave du Bas-Congo, BP 91, Kinshasa-Gombe; tel. (12) 80987; Dir and Editor-in-Chief BONGOMA KONI BOTAHE.

L'Avenir: Kinshasa; internet www.groupelavenir.net; owned by Groupe de l'avenir; Chair. PIUS MUABILU.

Boyoma: 31 blvd Mobutu, BP 982, Kisangani; Dir and Editor BADRIYO ROVA ROVATU.

Elima: 1 ave de la Révolution, BP 11498, Kinshasa; tel. (12) 77332; f. 1928; evening; Dir and Editor-in-Chief ESSOLOMWA NKOY EA LINGANGA.

Mjumbe: BP 2474, Lubumbashi; tel. (2) 25348; f. 1963; Dir and Editor TSHIMANGA KOYA KAKONA.

Le Palmarès: 220 ave Mpolo, BP 63, Kinshasa-Gombe; supports Union pour la démocratie et le progrès social; Editor MICHEL LADELUYA.

Le Phare: bldg du 29 juin, ave Col Lukusa 3392, BP 15662, Kinshasa-Gombe; tel. (12) 45896; e-mail info@le-phare.com; f. 1983; Editor POLYDOR MUBOYAYI MUBANGA; circ. 4,000.

Le Potentiel: Immeuble Ruzizi, 873 ave du Bas-Congo, BP 11338, Kinshasa; tel. (12) 891053; e-mail potentiel@ic.cd; f. 1982; Editor MODESTE MUTINGA MUTUISHAYI; circ. 8,000.

La Référence Plus: BP 22520, Kinshasa; tel. (12) 45783; f. 1989; Dir ANDRÉ IPAKALA.

PERIODICALS

Afrique Editions: Kinshasa; tel. (88) 43202; e-mail bpongo@raga.net.

Allo Kinshasa: 3 rue Kayange, BP 20271, Kinshasa-Lemba; monthly; Editor MBUYU WA KABILA.

L'Aurore Protestante: Eglise du Christ au Congo, BP 4938, Kinshasa-Gombe; French; religion; monthly; circ. 10,000.

BEA Magazine de la Femme: 2 ave Masimanimba, BP 113380, Kinshasa 1; every 2 weeks; Editor MUTINGA MUTWISHAYI.

Bingwa: ave du 30 juin, zone Lubumbashi no 4334; weekly; sport; Dir and Editor MATEKE WA MULAMBA.

Cahiers Economiques et Sociaux: BP 257, Kinshasa XI, (National University of the Congo); sociological, political and economic review; quarterly; Dir Prof. NDONGALA TADI LEWA; circ. 2,000.

Cahiers des Religions Africaines: Faculté de Théologie Catholique de Kinshasa, BP 712, Kinshasa/Limete; tel. (12) 78476; f. 1967; English and French; religion; 2 a year; circ. 1,000.

Le Canard Libre: Kinshasa; f. 1991; Editor JOSEPH CASTRO MULEBE.

Circulaire d'Information: Association Nationale des Entreprises du Congo, 10 ave des Aviateurs, BP 7247, Kinshasa 1; tel. (12) 22565; f. 1959; French; legal and statutory texts for the business community; monthly.

La Colombe: 32B ave Tombalbaye, Kinshasa-Gombe; tel. (12) 21211; organ of Parti démocrate et social chrétien; circ. 5,000.

Congo-Afrique: Centre d'Etudes pour l'Action Sociale, 9 ave Père Boka, BP 3375, Kinshasa-Gombe; tel. (12) 34245; e-mail cepas@raga.net; f. 1961; economic, social and cultural; monthly; Editors FRANCIS KIKASSA MWANALESSA, RENÉ BEECKMANS; circ. 2,500.

Le Conseiller Comptable: 51 rue du Grand Séminaire, Quartier Nganda, BP 308, Kinshasa; tel. (88) 01216; fax (88) 00075; f. 1974; French; public finance and taxation; quarterly; Editor TOMENA FOKO; circ. 2,000.

Documentation et Information Protestante (DIP): Eglise du Christ au Congo, BP 4938, Kinshasa-Gombe; tel. and fax (88) 46387; e-mail eccm@ic.cd; French and English; religion.

Documentation et Informations Africaines (DIA): BP 2598, Kinshasa 1; tel. (12) 33197; fax (12) 33196; e-mail dia@ic.cd; internet www.peacelink.it/dia/index.html; Roman Catholic news agency reports; 3 a week; Dir Rev. Père VATA DIAMBANZA.

L'Entrepreneur Flash: Association Nationale des Entreprises du Congo, 10 ave des Aviateurs, BP 7247, Kinshasa 1; tel. (12) 22565; f. 1978; business news; monthly; circ. 1,000.

Etudes d'Histoire Africaine: National University of the Congo, BP 1825, Lubumbashi; f. 1970; French and English; history; annually; circ. 1,000.

Horizons 80: Société Congolaise d'Edition et d'Information, BP 9839, Kinshasa; economic affairs; weekly.

JuriCongo: coin des aves Commerce et Plateau, Galerie du 24 Novembre, Kinshasa; fax (12) 20320; e-mail cavas@ic.cd; guide to judicial affairs; Pres. EMERY MUKENDI WAFWANA.

Les Kasaï: 161 9e rue, BP 575, Kinshasa/Limete; weekly; Editor NSENGA NDOMBA.

Kin-Média: BP 15808, Kinshasa 1; monthly; Editor ILUNGA KASAMBAY.

KYA: 24 ave de l'Equateur, BP 7853, Kinshasa-Gombe; tel. (12) 27502; f. 1984; weekly for Bas-Congo; Editor SASSA KASSA YI KIBOBA.

Libération: Kinshasa; f. 1997; politics; supports the AFDL; weekly; Man. NGOYI KABUYA DIKATETA M'MIANA.

Mambenga 2000: BP 477, Mbandaka; Editor BOSANGE YEMA BOF.

Le Moniteur de l'Economie (Economic Monitor): Kinshasa; Man. Editor FÉLIX NZUZI.

Mwana Shaba: Générale des Carrières et des Mines, BP 450, Lubumbashi; monthly; circ. 25,000.

Ngabu: Société Nationale d'Assurances, Immeuble Sonas Sankuru, blvd du 30 juin, BP 3443, Kinshasa-Gombe; tel. (12) 23051; f. 1973; insurance news; quarterly.

Njanja: Société Nationale des Chemins de Fer Congolais, 115 pl. de la Gare, BP 297, Lubumbashi; tel. (2) 23430; fax (2) 61321; railways and transportation; annually; circ. 10,000.

NUKTA: 14 chaussée de Kasenga, BP 3805, Lubumbashi; weekly; agriculture; Editor NGOY BUNDUKI.

Post: Immeuble Linzadi, 1538 ave de la Douane, Kinshasa-Gombe; e-mail thepostrdc@yahoo.com; internet www.congoonline.com/thepost; 2 a week; Editor-in-Chief MUKEBAYI NKOSO.

Problèmes Sociaux Zaïrois: Centre d'Exécution de Programmes Sociaux et Economiques, Université de Lubumbashi, 208 ave Kasavubu, BP 1873, Lubumbashi; f. 1946; quarterly; Editor N'KASHAMA KADIMA.

Promoteur Congolais: Centre du Commerce International du Congo, 119 ave Colonel Tshatshi, BP 13, Kinshasa; f. 1979; international trade news; six a year.

Sciences, Techniques, Informations: Centre de Recherches Industrielles en Afrique Centrale (CRIAC), BP 54, Lubumbashi.

Le Sport Africain: 13è niveau Tour adm., Cité de la Voix du Congo, BP 3356, Kinshasa-Gombe; monthly; Pres. TSHIMPUMPU WA TSHIMPUMPU.

Taifa: 536 ave Lubumba, BP 884, Lubumbashi; weekly; Editor LWAMBWA MILAMBU.

Telema: Faculté Canisius, Kimwenza, BP 3724, Kinshasa-Gombe; f. 1974; religious; quarterly; edited by the Central Africa Jesuits; circ. 1,200.

Umoja: 23 Bunkeye Matonge, Kinshasa; weekly; Publr LÉON MOUKANDA LUNYAMA.

Vision: Kinshasa; 2 a week; independent; Man. Editor XAVIER BONANE YANGANZI.

La Voix des Sans-Voix: ave des Ecuries 3858, commune de Ngaliema, BP 11445, Kinshasa-Gombe; tel. (88) 40394; fax (88) 01826; e-mail vsv@ic.cd; internet www.congonline.com/vsv.

NEWS AGENCIES

Agence Congolaise de Presse (ACP): 44–48 ave Tombalbaye, BP 1595, Kinshasa 1; tel. (12) 22035; e-mail acpresse@rd-congo.com; internet www.rd-congo.com/acp.html; f. 1957; state-controlled; Dir-Gen. ALI KALONGA.

Digital Congo: 3335 ave Kabasele Tshiamala, Kinshasa-Gombe; tel. (88) 06269; e-mail info@multimediacongo.net; internet www.digitalcongo.net; news service owned by Multimedia Congo.

Documentation et Informations Africaines (DIA): BP 2598, Kinshasa 1; tel. (12) 34528; f. 1957; Roman Catholic news agency; Dir Rev. Père VATA DIAMBANZA.

Foreign Bureaux

Agence France-Presse (AFP): Immeuble Wenge 3227, ave Wenge, Zone de la Gombe, BP 726, Kinshasa 1; tel. (12) 27009; Bureau Chief JEAN-PIERRE REJETTE.

Agenzia Nazionale Stampa Associata (ANSA) (Italy): BP 2790, Kinshasa 15; tel. (12) 30315; Bureau Chief (vacant).

Pan-African News Agency (PANA) (Senegal): BP 1400, Kinshasa; tel. (12) 23290; f. 1983; Bureau Chief ADRIEN HONORÉ MBEYET.

Xinhua (New China) News Agency (People's Republic of China): 293 ave Mfumu Lutunu, BP 8939, Kinshasa; tel. (12) 25647; Correspondent CHEN WEIBIN.

Press Association

Union de la Presse du Congo: BP 4941, Kinshasa 1; tel. (12) 24437.

Publishers

Aequatoria Centre: BP 276, Mbandaka; f. 1980; anthropology, biography, ethnicity, history, language and linguistics, social sciences; Dir HONORÉ VINCK.

CEEBA Publications: BP 246, Bandundu; f. 1965; humanities, languages, fiction; Man. Dir (Editorial) Dr HERMANN HOCHEGGER.

Centre de Linguistique Théorique et Appliquée (CELTA): BP 4956, Kinshasa-Gombe; tel. (81) 8129998; e-mail anyembwe@yahoo.fr; f. 1971; language arts and linguistics; Dir-Gen. ANDRÉ NYEMBWE NTITA.

Centre de Documentation Agricole: BP 7537, Kinshasa 1; tel. (12) 32498; agriculture, science; Dir PIERTE MBAYAKABUYI; Chief Editor J. MARCELLIN KAPUKUNGESA.

Centre de Recherches Pédagogiques: BP 8815, Kinshasa 1; f. 1959; accounting, education, geography, language, science; Dir P. DETIENNE.

Centre de Vulgarisation Agricole: BP 4008, Kinshasa 2; tel. (12) 71165; fax (12) 21351; agriculture, environment, health; Dir-Gen. KIMPIANGA MAHANIAH.

Centre International de Sémiologie: 109 ave Pruniers, BP 1825, Lubumbashi.

Centre Protestant d'Editions et de Diffusion (CEDI): 209 ave Kalémie, BP 11398, Kinshasa 1; tel. (12) 22202; fax (12) 26730; f. 1935; fiction, poetry, biography, religious, juvenile; Christian tracts, works in French, Lingala, Kikongo, etc.; Dir-Gen. HENRY DIRKS.

Commission de l'Education Chrétienne: BP 3258, Kinshasa-Gombe; tel. (12) 30086; education, religion; Man. Dir Abbé MUGADJA LEHANI.

Connaissance et Pratique du Droit Congolais Editions (CDPC): BP 5502, Kinshasa-Gombe; f. 1987; law; Editor DIBUNDA KABUINJI.

Editions Lokole: BP 5085, Kinshasa 10; state org. for the promotion of literature; Dir BOKEME SHANE MOLOBAY.

Editions Saint Paul: BP 8505, Kinshasa; tel. (12) 77726; e-mail fspkin10@ic.cd; f. 1988; fiction, general non-fiction, poetry, religion; Dir Sister MASTAKI GODELIEVE; Sec. Sister M. ROSARIO ZAMBELLO.

Facultés Catholiques de Kinshasa: 2 ave de l'Université, Kinshasa-Limete; tel. and fax (12) 46965; e-mail facakin@ic.cd; f. 1957; anthropology, art, economics, history, politics, computer science; Rector Prof. Mgr HIPPOLYTE NGIMBI NSEKA.

Les Editions du Trottoir: BP 1800, Kinshasa; tel. (12) 9936043; e-mail smuyengo@yahoo.fr; f. 1989; communications, fiction, literature, drama; Pres. CHARLES DJUNJU-SIMBA.

Librairie les Volcans: 22 ave Pres. Mobutu, BP 400, Goma, Nord-Kivu; f. 1995; social sciences; Man. Dir RUHAMA MUKANDOLI.

Presses Universitaires du Congo (PUC): 290 rue d'Aketi, BP 1800, Kinshasa 1; tel. (12) 9936043; e-mail smuyengo@yahoo.fr; f. 1972; science, arts and communications; Dir Abbé SÉBASTIEN MUYENGO.

GOVERNMENT PUBLISHING HOUSE

Imprimerie du Gouvernement Central: BP 3021, Kinshasa-Kalina.

Broadcasting and Communications

TELECOMMUNICATIONS

Comcell: Commune de la Gombe, 6 ave du Port, BP 614, Kinshasa; tel. (12) 20241; fax (satellite) 377-97-990026; e-mail comcell@raga.net; provides satellite communications network; 4,000 subscribers.

Office Congolais des Postes et des Télécommunications (OCPT): Hôtel des postes, blvd du 30 juin, BP 13798, Kinshasa; tel. (12) 21871; fax (88) 45010; e-mail ocpt@ic.cd; state-owned; 13,000 lines; 40,000 subscribers; Dir-Gen. KAPITAO MAMBWENI.

Telecel-Congo: ave de la Justice 25, Kinshasa; provides satellite communications network; largest private operator; 45% nationalized in 1998; 12,000 subscribers.

BROADCASTING

Radio-Télévision Nationale Congolaise (RTNC): BP 3171, Kinshasa-Gombe; tel. (12) 23171; state radio terrestrial and satellite television broadcasts; Dir-Gen. JOSE KAJANGUA.

Radio

Several private radio broadcasters operate in Kinshasa.

Radio Candip: Centre d'Animation et de Diffusion Pédagogique, BP 373, Bunia.

La Voix du Congo: Station Nationale, BP 3164, Kinshasa-Gombe; tel. (12) 23175; state-controlled; operated by RTNC; broadcasts in French, Swahili, Lingala, Tshiluba, Kikongo; regional stations at Kisangani, Lubumbashi, Bukavu, Bandundu, Kananga, Mbuji-Mayi, Matadi, Mbandaka and Bunia.

Television

Several private television broadcasters operate in Kinshasa.

Antenne A: Immeuble Forescom, 2e étage, ave du Port 4, POB 2581, Kinshasa 1; tel. (12) 21736; private and commercial station; Dir-Gen. IGAL AVIVI NEIRSON.

Canal Z: ave du Port 6, POB 614, Kinshasa 1; tel. (12) 20239; commercial station; Dir-Gen. FRÉDÉRIC FLASSE.

Tele Kin Malebo (TKM): Kinshasa; private television station; nationalization announced 1997; Dir-Gen. NGONGO LUWOWO.

Télévision Congolaise: BP 3171, Kinshasa-Gombe; tel. (12) 23171; govt commercial station; operated by RTNC; broadcasts for 5 hours daily on weekdays and 10 hours daily at weekends.

Finance

(cap. = capital; res = reserves; dep. = deposits; m. = million; br(s). = branch(es); amounts in new Congolese francs unless otherwise indicated)

BANKING

The introduction as legal tender of a new currency unit, the new Congolese franc (CF), was completed on 30 June 1998. However, as a result of the civil conflict, its value immediately declined dramatically. In late 2003, following the restoration of relative peace and installation of new transitional authorities, the Central Bank introduced new notes in an effort to revive the national currency and nation-wide operations were gradually restored.

Central Bank

Banque Centrale du Congo: 513 blvd Colonel Tshatshi au nord, BP 2697, Kinshasa; tel. (12) 20704; fax (12) 8805152; e-mail cabgouv@bcc.cd; internet www.bcc.cd; f. 1964; res 1,030m. (2002); Gov. JEAN-CLAUDE MASANGU MULONGO; 8 brs.

Commercial Banks

Banque Commerciale du Congo SARL (BCDC): blvd du 30 juin, BP 2798, Kinshasa; tel. (81) 8845704; fax (99) 631048; e-mail dir@bcdc.cd; internet www.bcdc.cd; f. 1952; as Banque du Congo Belge, name changed as above 1997; cap. 3,544.9m., res 1,733.0m., dep. 61,141.6m. (Dec. 2004); Pres. NKEMA LILOO; Man. Dir YVES CUYPERS; 29 brs.

Banque Congolaise SARL: Immeuble Flavica 14/16, ave du Port, BP 9497, Kinshasa 1; tel. (12) 819982003; fax (12) 1398801; e-mail bank@rayventures.com; f. 1988; cap. and res NZ 3,000.2m., total assets NZ 9,579.1m. (Dec. 2003); Pres. BEYA KALAMBA; Admistrator-Delegate ROGER A. YAGHI.

Banque Internationale de Crédit SARL (BIC): 191 ave de l'Equateur, BP 1299, Kinshasa 1; tel. (81) 3330730; fax (81) 2616000; e-mail bic@ic.cd; f. 1994; cap. and res 946.2m., dep. 12,352.7m. (Dec. 2003); Pres. PASCAL KINDUELO LUMBU.

Banque Internationale pour l'Afrique au Congo (BIAC): Immeuble Nioki, ave de la Douane, BP 8725, Kinshasa 1; tel. (81) 7004001; e-mail com@biac.cd; internet www.biac.cd; cap. and res 945.6m., total assets 5,248.5m. (Dec. 2002); Pres. CHARLES SANLAVILLE.

Citibank (Congo) SARL Congo: Immeuble Citibank Congo, angle aves Col Lukusa et Ngongo Lutete, BP 9999, Kinshasa 1; tel. (81) 8840015; fax (12) 40015; e-mail singa.boyenge@citicorp.com; f. 1971; cap. and res NZ 199,425.2m., total assets NZ 1,928,804.9m. (Dec. 1996); Pres. ROBERT THORNTON; 1 br.

Rawbank Sarl: 3487 blvd du 30 juin, Immeuble Concorde Commune de la Gombe, Kinshasa; tel. (99) 8320000; fax (99) 631042; e-mail contact@rawbank.cd; internet www.rawbank.cd; f. 2002; cap. 1,233.6m., res 507.0m., dep. 12,056.3m. (Dec. 2004); MAZHAR RAWJI.

Société Financière de Développement SARL (SOFIDE): Immeuble SOFIDE, 9–11 angle aves Ngabu et Kisangani, BP 1148, Kinshasa 1; tel. (12) 816601531; e-mail sofide2001@yahoo.fr; f. 1970; partly state-owned; provides tech. and financial aid, primarily for agricultural devt; cap. and res 285.3m., total assets 1,202.0m. (Dec. 2003); Pres. and Dir-Gen. RAPHAËL SENGA KITENGE; 4 brs.

Stanbic Bank Congo SARL: 12 ave de Mongala, BP 16297, Kinshasa 1; tel. (12) 817006000; fax (12) 813013848; e-mail sbiccongo@raga.net; internet www.stanbic.co.cd; f. 1973; subsidiary of Standard Bank Investment Corpn (South Africa); cap. and res 59.3m., total assets 11,415.8m. (Dec. 2003); Chair. M. MUMBA; Administrator Delegate LOUIS NALLET; 1 br.

INSURANCE

INTERAFF: Bldg Forescom, ave du Port 4, Kinshasa-Gombe; tel. (88) 01618; fax (320) 2091332; e-mail interaff@raga.net; internet www.ic.cd/interaff.

Société Nationale d'Assurances (SONAS): 3443 blvd du 30 juin, Kinshasa-Gombe; tel. (12) 5110503; e-mail sonask@hotmail.com; f. 1966; state-owned; cap. US $5m.; 9 brs.

Trade and Industry

GOVERNMENT AGENCY

Bureau Central de Coordination (BCECO): ave Colonel Mondjiba 372, Complexe Utex Africa, Kinshasa; tel. (81) 9999180; e-mail bceco@bceco.cd; internet www.bceco.cd; f. 2001; manages projects funded by the African Development Bank and the World Bank; Dir-Gen. MAPON MATATA PONYO.

DEVELOPMENT ORGANIZATIONS

Bureau pour le Développement Rural et Urbain: Mont Ngafula, Kinshasa; e-mail bdru_kin@yahoo.fr.

Caisse de Stabilisation Cotonnière (CSCo): BP 3058, Kinshasa-Gombe; tel. (12) 31206; f. 1978 to replace Office National des Fibres Textiles; acts as an intermediary between the Govt, cotton ginners and textile factories, and co-ordinates international financing of cotton sector.

La Générale des Carrières et des Mines (GÉCAMINES): 450 blvd Kamanyola, BP 450, Lubumbashi; tel. (2) 222118; fax (2) 223655; f. 1967 to acquire assets of Union Minière du Haut-Katanga; state-owned corpn engaged in mining and marketing of copper, cobalt, zinc and coal; also has interests in agriculture; Exec. Chair. YUMA MONGA (acting).

Institut National pour l'Etude et la Recherche Agronomiques: BP 1513, Kisangani; f. 1933; agricultural research.

Office National du Café: ave Général Bobozo, BP 8931, Kinshasa 1; tel. (12) 77144; f. 1979; state agency for coffee and also cocoa, tea, quinquina and pyrethrum; Pres. FERUZA WA GHENDA.

Pêcherie Maritime Congolaise: Kinshasa; DRC's only sea-fishing enterprise.

CHAMBER OF COMMERCE

Chambre de Commerce, d'Industrie et d'Agriculture du Congo: 10 ave des Aviateurs, BP 7247, Kinshasa 1; tel. (12) 22286.

INDUSTRIAL AND TRADE ASSOCIATION

Association Nationale des Entreprises du Congo: 10 ave des Aviateurs, BP 7247, Kinshasa; tel. (12) 24623; f. 1972; represents business interests for both domestic and foreign institutions; Man. Dir EDOUARD LUBOYA DIYOKA; Gen. Sec. ATHANASE MATENDA KYELU.

EMPLOYERS' ASSOCIATION

Fédération des Entreprises du Congo (FEC): Kinshasa; e-mail feccongo@hotmail.com; Pres. PASCAL KINDUEL LUMBU; Sec.-Gen. JOSEPH MUKADULA KABUE.

UTILITIES

Electricity

Société Nationale d'Electricité (SNEL): 2831 ave de la Justice, BP 500, Kinshasa; tel. (12) 26893; fax (12) 33735; f. 1970; state-owned; Dir-Gen. MUYUMBA KALEMBE.

Water

Régie de Distribution d'Eau (REGIDESO): 65 blvd du 30 juin, BP 12599, Kinshasa; tel. (12) 22792; water supply admin; Pres. LUBUNGU PENE SHAKO.

MAJOR COMPANIES

The following are some of the largest companies in terms either of capital investment or employment.

Manufacturing and Trading

BAT Congo SARL: 973 ave Gen. Bobozo, Kingabwa, BP 621, Kinshasa I; tel. (12) 20289; fax (satellite) 871-682-340868; f. 1950; wholly owned subsidiary of British American Tobacco Co Ltd, London; mfrs of tobacco products; Chair. and Man. Dir B. MAVAMBU ZOYA.

Brasseries, Limonaderies et Malteries du Congo (BRALIMA): 912 ave du Flambeau, BP 7246, Kinshasa; tel. (12) 22141; f. 1923; production of beer, soft drinks and ice; Gen. Man. J. L. HOME.

Compagnie des Margarines, Savons et Cosmétiques au Congo SARL (MARSAVCO CONGO): 1 ave Kalemie, BP 8914, Kinshasa; tel. (12) 24821; f. 1922; subsidiary of Unilever NV; mfrs of detergents, foods and cosmetics; Pres. C. GODDE; 1,100 employees.

Compagnie Sucrière: blvd du 30 juin, bldg BCDC, BP 8816, Kinshasa, and BP 10, Kwilu Ngongo, Bas-Congo; tel. (12) 20476; internet www.finasucre.com; f. 1925; mfrs of sugar, alcohol, acetylene, oxygen and carbon dioxide; Dir ERIC VAN EECKHOUT.

IBM World Trade Corporation (Congo): 6 ave du Port, BP 7563, Kinshasa 1; tel. (12) 23358; fax (12) 24029; f. 1954; sale and maintenance of computers and business machines and associated materials; Gen. Man. MUKADI KABUMBU.

Industries Congolaises des Bois (ICB): 23 ave de l'Ouganda, BP 10399, Kinshasa; state forestry and sawmilling enterprise.

Plantations Lever au Congo: 16 ave Colonel Lukusa, BP 8611, Kinshasa I; f. 1911; subsidiary of Unilever NV; plantations of oil palm, rubber, cocoa and tea; Man. Dir A. J. RITCHIE.

Société BATA Congolaise: 33 ave Général Bobozo, BP 598, Kinshasa I; tel. (12) 27414; f. 1946; principal shoe mfr in the DRC; Man. Dir JEAN-LOUIS ANTZ; 100 employees.

Société Commerciale et Minière du Congo SA: BP 499, Kinshasa; subsidiary of Lonrho Ltd; engineering, motor trade, insurance, assembly and sale of earth-moving equipment.

Société Congo-Suisse de Produits Chimiques SARL: BP 14096, Kinshasa 1; tel. (12) 24707; sales agent for Ciba-Geigy pharmaceutical products.

Société Générale d'Alimentation (SGA): BP 15898, Kinshasa; state enterprise; import, processing and distribution of foodstuffs; largest chain of distributors in the DRC.

Tabacongo SARL: BP 621, Kinshasa; tel. (12) 20289; fax (12) 40105; internet www.bat.com; owned by British American Tobacco plc; Pres. and Dir-Gen. MAVAMBU ZOYA.

Minerals

Fina Recherche Exploitation Pétrolière (FINA REP SARL): BP 700, Kinshasa; tel. (12) 20103; fax (12) 20101; e-mail sofimmo@ic.cd; exploitation of petroleum; Pres. A. NOMMER.

Mobil Oil Congo: BP 2400, Kinshasa; tel. (88) 46265; fax (88) 04672; e-mail cobil@cobil.cd; marketing and sale of petroleum; Pres. GUILLAUME BOLENGA.

Office des Mines d'Or de Kilo-Moto (OKIMO): BP 219–220, Bunia; state-owned; operates gold mines; Pres. and Sec.-Gen. ISSIKATA TABU.

SHELL RDC: ave du Port 14/16, BP 2799, Kinshasa-Gombe; tel. (99) 23700; fax (88) 01447; f. 1978; marketing of petroleum products; Man. Dir P. MERCKX; 74 employees.

Société Aurifère du Kivu et Maniema (SAKIMA): f. 1997 as successor to Société Minière du Kivu; 93% owned by Banro Resources Corpn, 7% by DRC Government; exploitation of gold; Man. Dir MARIO FLOCCHI.

Société Congo Gulf Oil: blvd du 30 juin, BP 7189, Kinshasa I; tel. (12) 23111; international mining consortium exploiting offshore petroleum at Muanda.

Société Congo—Italienne de Raffinage: BP 1478, Kinshasa I; tel. (12) 22683; fax (12) 25998; f. 1963; petroleum refinery; Pres. LESSEDJINA IKWAME IPU'OZIA; 600 employees.

Société de Développement Industriel et Minière du Congo (SODIMICO): 4219 ave de l'Ouganda, BP 7064, Kinshasa; tel. (12) 32511; subsidiary of GÉCAMINES; see Development Organizations; copper-mining consortium exploiting mines of Musoshi and Kinsenda in Katanga.

Société Minière de Bakwanga (MIBA): BP 377, Mbuji-Mayi, Kasaï Oriental; f. 1961; cap. 27m. zaires; 80% state-owned; industrial diamond mining; CEO (vacant).

Société Minière du Tenké-Fungurume: Immeuble UCB Centre, 5ème étage, BP 1279, Kinshasa; f. 1970 by international consortium comprising Charter Consolidated of London, Govt of Zaire, Mitsui (Japan), Bureau de Recherches Géologiques et Minières de France, Léon Tempelsman and Son (USA) and COGEMA (France); copper and cobalt mining; Dir B. L. MORGAN.

Sonangol-Congo: 1513 blvd du 30 juin, BP 7617, Kinshasa 1; tel. (12) 25356; f. 1974; bought by the Sociedade Nacional de Combustíveis de Angola (SONANGOL) in 1998; petroleum refining, processing, stocking and transporting; Dir-Gen. NKOSI PEDRO.

TRADE UNIONS

The Union Nationale des Travailleurs was founded in 1967 as the sole trade-union organization. In 1990 the establishment of independent trade unions was legalized, and by early 1991 there were 12 officially recognized trade-union organizations.

Union Nationale des Travailleurs du Congo: BP 8814, Kinshasa; f. 1967; comprises 16 unions; Pres. KATALAY MOLELI SANGOL.

Transport

Compagnie des Transports du Congo: ave Muzu 52/75, Kinshasa; tel. (88) 46249; fax (322) 7065718; e-mail ros@ic.cd; road transport; Dir ROGER SENGER.

Office National des Transports (ONATRA): BP 98, Kinshasa 1; tel. (12) 21457; fax (12) 1398632; e-mail onatradf@ic.cd; f. 1935; operates some 14,000 km of waterways, 366 km of railways and road and air transport; administers ports of Kinshasa, Matadi, Boma and Banana; Pres. JULES IBULA MWANA KATAKANGA.

RAILWAYS

The main line runs from Lubumbashi to Ilebo. International services run to Dar es Salaam (Tanzania) and Lobito (Angola), and also connect with the Zambian, Zimbabwean, Mozambican and South African systems. In May 1997 the railway system was nationalized. In late 2003, under a major government programme, the rehabilitation of 500 km of railway linking northern and southern regions of the country commenced.

Kinshasa–Matadi Railway: BP 98, Kinshasa 1; 366 km operated by ONATRA; Pres. JACQUES MBELOLO BITWEMI.

Société Nationale des Chemins de Fer du Congo (SNCC): 115 pl. de la Gare, BP 297, Lubumbashi; tel. (2) 46306; fax (2) 342254; e-mail sncc01aie-lubum-cd; f. 1974; 3,606 km (including 858 km electrified); administers all internal railway sections as well as river transport and transport on Lakes Tanganyika and Kivu; man. contract concluded with a Belgian-South African corpn, Sizarail, in 1995 for the man. of the Office des Chemins de Fer du Sud (OCS) and the Société des Chemins de Fer de l'Est (SFE) subsidiaries, with rail networks of 2,835 km and 1,286 km, respectively; assets of Sizarail nationalized and returned to SNCC control in May 1997; Pres. and Gen. Man. KIBWE MIBUYA KAKUDJI.

ROADS

In 1999 there were an estimated 157,000 km of roads, of which some 33,000 km were main roads. Following the installation of transitional authorities in July 2003, an extensive infrastructure rehabilitation programme, financed by external donors, including the World Bank, was initiated. Work on a principal road, connecting the south-western town of Moanda with Kinshasa and Lubumbashi, commenced late that year.

Office des Routes: Direction Générale, ave Ex-Descamp, BP 10899, Kinshasa-Gombe; tel. (12) 32036; construction and maintenance of roads.

INLAND WATERWAYS

The River Congo is navigable for more than 1,600 km. Above the Stanley Falls the Congo becomes the Lualaba, and is navigable along a 965-km stretch from Ubundu to Kindu and Kongolo to Bukama. The River Kasai, a tributary of the River Congo, is navigable by shipping as far as Ilebo, at which the line from Lubumbashi terminates. The total length of inland waterways is 14,935 km.

Régie des voies fluviales: 109 ave Lumpungu, Kinshasa-Gombe, BP 11697, Kinshasa 1; tel. (12) 26526; fax (12) 42580; administers river navigation; Gen. Man. NGIAM KIPOY.

Société Congolaise des Chemins de Fer des Grands Lacs: River Lualaba services: Bubundu–Kindu and Kongolo–Malemba N'kula; Lake Tanganyika services: Kamina–Kigoma–Kalundu–Moba–Mpulungu; Pres. and Gen. Man. KIBWE MBUYU KAKUDJI.

SHIPPING

The principal seaports are Matadi, Boma and Banana on the lower Congo. The port of Matadi has more than 1.6 km of quays and can accommodate up to 10 deep-water vessels. Matadi is linked by rail with Kinshasa. The country's merchant fleet numbered 21 vessels and amounted to 13,922 gross registered tons at 31 December 2005.

Compagnie Maritime du Congo SARL: USB Centre, pl. de la Poste, BP 9496, Kinshasa; tel. (88) 20396; fax (88) 26234; e-mail cmdckin@ic.cd; f. 1946; services: North Africa, Europe, North America and Asia to West Africa, East Africa to North Africa; Gen. Man. ALEX MUKENDI KAMAMA.

CIVIL AVIATION

International airports are located at Ndjili (for Kinshasa), Luano (for Lubumbashi), Bukavu, Goma and Kisangani. There are smaller airports and airstrips dispersed throughout the country.

Blue Airlines: BP 1115, Barumbu, Kinshasa 1; tel. (12) 20455; f. 1991; regional and domestic charter services for passengers and cargo; Man. T. MAYANI.

Business Aviation: 1345 ave de la Plaine, Kingabwa-Kinshasa; tel. (88) 45588; fax (99) 42260; e-mail businessaviation@ic.cd; internet www.businessaviation.cd; regional services.

Compagnie Africaine d'Aviation: 6ème rue, Limete, Kinshasa; tel. (88) 43072; fax (88) 41048; e-mail ltadek@hotmail.com; f. 1992; Pres. DAVID BLATTNER.

Congo Airlines: 1928 ave Kabambare, N'dolo-Kinshasa, BP 12847, Kinshasa; tel. (12) 43947; fax (12) 00235; e-mail cal-fih-dg@ic.cd; f. 1994 as Express Cargo; assumed present name in 1997; international, regional and domestic scheduled services for passengers and cargo; Pres. JOSÉ ENDUNO; CEO STAVROS PAPAIOANNOU.

Hewa Bora Airways (HWA): ave Kabambare 1928, BP 1284, Kinshasa; tel. (12) 20643; internet www.hba.cd; national and international services.

Lignes Aériennes du Congo (LAC): 4, ave du Port, Kinshasa-Gombe, BP 8552, Kinshasa 1; tel. 819090001; Pres. LOUISE L. LONGANGE; Man. Dir PROSPER MAZIMPAKA FAATY.

Malila Airlift: ave Basoko 188, Kinshasa-Gombe; tel. (88) 46428; fax (satellite) 1-5304817707; e-mail malila.airlift@ic.cd; internet www.malila.cd; f. 1996; regional services; Man. VÉRONIQUE MALILA.

Waltair Aviation: 9ème rue 206, Limete, Kinshasa; tel. (88) 48439; fax (satellite) 1-3094162616; e-mail waltair.rdc@ic.cd; regional services; Dir VINCENT GILLET.

Zairean Airlines (Congo): 3555–3560 blvd du 30 juin, BP 2111, Kinshasa; tel. (88) 48103; f. 1981; international, regional and domestic services for passengers and cargo; Dir-Gen. Capt. ALFRED SOMMERAUER.

Tourism

The country offers extensive lake and mountain scenery, although tourism remains largely undeveloped. In 2005 tourist arrivals totalled 61,007. Receipts from tourism amounted to an estimated US $2m. in 1998.

Office National du Tourisme: 2A/2B ave des Orangers, BP 9502, Kinshasa-Gombe; tel. (12) 30070; f. 1959; Man. Dir BOTOLO MAGOZA.

Société Congolaise de l'Hôtellerie: Immeuble Memling, BP 1076, Kinshasa; tel. (12) 23260; Man. N'JOLI BALANGA.

Defence

The total strength of the armed forces of the Democratic Republic of the Congo, as assessed at November 2006, was 64,800 (army 60,000; navy 1,800; air force 3,000). A civil war began in August 1998 in the east of the country. A number of other regional West African countries became involved in the conflict, with Burundian, Rwandan and Ugandan troops supporting the opposition. A Mission de l'organisation des nations unies en République démocratique du Congo (MONUC), with an authorized military strength of 16,700 military personnel, was deployed in the country from November 1999. Following a peace agreement signed between the Governments of the DRC and Rwanda in July 2002, it was announced in October that the withdrawal of an estimated 30,000 Rwandan forces from the country had been completed. Although peace was partially restored, following a power-sharing agreement reached by the Government and rebel groups in December, hostilities continued in the east of the country, and in late 2004 Rwandan troops were reported to have been redeployed in the region. As part of the power-sharing agreement, a new unified armed forces, in which former rebel combatants and militia were integrated, was established in December 2003. Under a military co-operation agreement, signed in June 2004, South Africa was to assist in the integration and training of the new armed forces; the Belgian Government was also to support the programme. At the end of October 2005 the UN Security Council authorized a temporary increase of personnel in the military strength of MONUC for the period of legislative and presidential elections (which were rescheduled for 30 July 2006). In April 2006 the UN Security Council authorized the temporary deployment of a European Union force (EUFOR RD Congo) to provide military support to MONUC during the electoral period. At the end of November 2006 MONUC comprised 18,473 total uniformed personnel, including 16,622 troops, 776 military observers and 1,075 police, supported by 953 international civilian personnel, 2,079 local civilian staff and 660 UN volunteers. (EUFOR RD Congo) was temporarily deployed in the country during the electoral period.

Defence Expenditure: Estimated at US $174m. in 2006.

Commander-in-Chief: Maj.-Gen. JOSEPH KABILA KABANGE.

Chief of Staff of the Armed Forces: Lt-Gen. DIEUDONNE KAYEMBE MBANDAKULU.

Chief of Staff of the Army: Maj.-Gen. SYLVAIN BUKI.

Chief of Staff of the Navy: Vice-Adm. DIDIER ETUMBA LONGILA.

Chief of Staff of the Air Force: Maj.-Gen. RIGOBERT MASAMBA MUSUNGUI.

Education

Primary education, beginning at six years of age and lasting for six years, is officially compulsory. Secondary education, which is not compulsory, begins at 12 years of age and lasts for up to six years, comprising a first cycle of two years and a second of four years. In 2002/03, according to UNESCO estimates, primary enrolment was equivalent to 62% of pupils in the relevant age-group (69% of boys; 54% of girls), while the comparable ratio for secondary enrolment was 22% (28% of boys; 16% of girls). There are four universities, located at Kinshasa, Kinshasa/Limete, Kisangani and Lubumbashi. In the budget for 1997, education received an estimated 144,000m. new zaires (less than 1% of central government expenditure).

As a result of the prolonged civil conflict, government funding for education was effectively suspended, contributing to a decline in enrolment. In addition, large numbers of children had been internally displaced or recruited by combatant factions. In 2002 an emergency programme for education, with an estimated cost of US $101m., was introduced to restore rapidly access to basic education.

Bibliography

Abdulai, N. *Zaire: Background to the Civil War*. London, ARIB, 1997.

Abi-Saab, G. *The United Nations Operations in the Congo 1960–64*. London, Oxford University Press, 1978.

Adelman, H. (Ed.). *War and Peace in Zaire/Congo: Analysing and Evaluating Intervention, 1996–1997*. North Woodmere, NY, World Press, 2003.

Afoaku, O. G. *Explaining the Failure of Democracy in the Democratic Republic of the Congo: Autocracy and Dissent in an Ambivalent World*. New York, NY, Edwin Mellen Press, 2005.

African Rights. *The Cycle of Conflict: Which Way Out in the Kivus?* London, 2000.

Asch, S. *L'Eglise du Prophète Kimbangu*. Paris, Editions Karthala, 1983.

Bontinck, F. *L'évangélisation du Zaïre*. Kinshasa, Saint Paul Afrique, 1980.

Brooke Simons, P. *Cullinan Diamonds: Dreams and Discoveries*. Constantia, Fernwood Press, 2004.

Camiller, P. *The African Dream: the Diaries of the Revolutionary War in the Congo*. New York, NY, Grove Press, 2001.

Clark, J. *The African Stakes of the Congo War*. London, Palgrave, 2002.

Clement, J. A. P. (Ed.). *Postconflict Economics in Sub-Saharan Africa: Lessons from the Democratic Republic of the Congo*. Washington, DC, International Monetary Fund, 2004.

De Witte, L. *The Assassination of Lumumba*. New York, NY, Verso Books, 2001.

Dunn, K. *Imagining the Congo: The International Relations of Identity*. New York, NY, Palgrave Macmillan, 2003.

Edgerton, R. *The Troubled Heart of Africa: A History of the Congo*. New York, NY, St Martin's Press, 2002.

Ekpebu, L. B. *Zaire and the African Revolution*. Ibadan, Ibadan University Press, 1989.

Ekwe-Ekwe, H. *Conflict and Intervention in Africa: Nigeria, Angola and Zaire*. London, Macmillan, 1990.

Ewans, M. *European Atrocity, African Catastrophe: Leopold II, the Congo Free State and its Aftermath*. London, Curzon Press, 2001.

Gondola, D. *The History of Congo*. Westport, CT, Greenwood Press, 2002.

Hayward, M. F. *Elections in Independent Africa*. Boulder, CO, Westview Press, 1987.

Hochschild, A. *King Leopold's Ghost*. London, Macmillan, 1999.

Hoyt, M. P. E., and Stearns, M. *Captive in the Congo: A Consul's Return to the Heart of Darkness*. Washington, DC, United States Naval Institute, 2000.

Human Rights Watch. *The Curse of Gold: Democratic Republic of Congo*. New York, NY, 2005.

Huybrechts, A. *Transports et structures de développement au Congo. Etude de progrès économique de 1900 à 1970*. Paris and The Hague, Editions Mouton, 1970.

Institute for Global Dialogue. *The Transition in the Democratic Republic of the Congo: Problems and Prospects*. Midrand, 2006.

Jewsiewicki, B. (Ed.). *Etat indépendant du Congo, Congo belge, République démocratique du Congo, République du Zaïre?* Sainte-Foy, Québec, SAFI Press, 1984.

Kabamba, N. *Songye of the Democratic Republic of Congo*. Hallandale, FL, Aglob Publications, 2004.

Kadima, D., Kabemba, C. and Sharpe, K. *Whither Regional Peace and Security: The Democratic Republic of Congo After the War*. Pretoria, Africa Institute of South Africa, 2003.

Kamitatu-Massamba, C. *Zaïre, le pouvoir à la portée du peuple*. Paris, L'Harmattan, 1977.

Kanza, T. *Conflict in the Congo. The Rise and Fall of Lumumba*. Harmondsworth, Penguin, 1972.

Kelly, S. *America's Tyrant: The CIA (Central Intelligence Agency) and Mobutu of Zaire*. Lanham, MD, University of America Press, 1993.

Kitenge bin Kitoko, E. T., and Makosso, A.-C. *RDCongo, les élections et après: intellectuels et politiques posent les enjeux de l'après-transition*. Paris, L'Harmattan, 2006.

Leslie, W. J. *Zaire: Continuity and Political Change in an Oppressive State*. Boulder, CO, Westview Press, 1993.

MacGaffey, J. *The Real Economy of Zaire: An Anthropological Study*. London, James Currey, 1991.

MacGaffey, J., and Mukohya, V. *The Real Economy of Zaire: The Contribution of Smuggling and Other Unofficial Activities to National Wealth*. London, James Currey, 1991.

MacGaffey, J., and Bazenguissa-Ganga, R. *Congo-Paris: Transnational Traders on the Margins of the Law* (African Issues Published in Association with International African Institute). Bloomington, IN, Indiana University Press, 2000.

Marysse, S. *La libération du Congo dans le contexte de la mondialisation*. Antwerp, UFSIA, 1997.

Mbaya, K. (Ed.). *Zaire: What Destiny?* Dakar, CODESRIA, 1993.

Mokoli, M. M. *State Against Development: The Experience of Post-1965 Zaire*. Westport, CT, Greenwood Press, 1992.

Mukenge, T. *Culture and Customs of the Congo (Culture and Customs of Africa)*. Westport, CT, Greenwood Publishing Group, 2001.

Nest, M., Grignon, F. and Kisangani, E. F. (Eds.). *Democratic Republic of Congo: Economic Dimensions of War and Peace*. Boulder, CO, Lynne Rienner, 2006.

Nzongola-Ntalaja, G. *From Zaire to the Democratic Republic of the Congo*. Uppsala, Nordiske Afrikainstitutet, 1999.

The Congo from Leopold to Kabila: A People's History. London, Zed Books, 2002.

Pongo, M. K. *Transitions et Conflits au Congo-Kinshasa*. Paris, Éditions Karthala, 2001.

Sanqmpam, S. N. *Pseudo-capitalism and the Overpolitical State: Reconciling Politics and Anthropology in Zaire*. Brookfield, VT, Ashgate Press, 1994.

Schatzberg, M. G. *The Dialectics of Oppression in Zaire*. Bloomington, IN, Indiana University Press, 1988.

Shapiro, D., and Tambashe, B. O. *Kinshasa in Transition: Women's Education, Employment and Fertility (Population and Development)*. Chicago, IL, University of Chicago Press, 2003.

Trefon, T. (Ed.). *Reinventing Order in the Congo: How People Respond to State Failure in Kinshasa*. London, Zed Books, 2004.

Twain, M. *King Leopold's Soliloquy*. Long Island City, NY, U.S. International Publishers, 1961.

Vellut, J.-L., Loriaux, F., and Morimont, F. *Bibliographies historiques du Zaïre à l'époque coloniale (1880–1960)*. Louvain-la-Neuve, Tervuren, 1996.

Weiss, H. *War and Peace in the Democratic Republic of the Congo* (Current African Issues, No. 22). Uppsala, Nordiske Afrikainstitutet, 2000.

Willame, J. C. *Eléments pour une lecture du contentieux Belgo-Zaïrois*. Les Cahiers du CEDAF, Vol. VI. Brussels, Centre d'etude et de documentation africaines, 1988.

Patrice Lumumba—La crise congolaise revisitée. Paris, Editions Karthala, 1990.

Wrong, M. *In the Footsteps of Mr. Kurtz: Living on the Brink of Disaster in Mobutu's Congo*. London, Harper Collins, 2001.

Wynaden, J., and Kushner, N. *Welcome to the Democratic Republic of the Congo (Welcome to my Country)*. Milwaukee, WI, Gareth Stevens, 2002.

Young, M. C. *Politics in the Congo: Decolonization and Independence*. Princeton, NJ, Princeton University Press, 1965.

Young, M. C., and Turner, T. *The Rise and Decline of the Zairean State*. Madison, WI, University of Wisconsin Press, 1985.

THE REPUBLIC OF THE CONGO

Physical and Social Geography

DAVID HILLING

POPULATION

The Congo river forms approximately 1,000 km of the eastern boundary of the Republic of the Congo, the remainder of which is provided by the Oubangui river from just south of the point at which the Equator bisects the country. Across these rivers lies the Democratic Republic of the Congo. To the north, the republic is bounded by the Central African Republic and Cameroon. Gabon lies to the west, and the Cabinda exclave of Angola to the south, adjoining the short Atlantic coastline. Covering an area of 342,000 sq km (132,047 sq miles) the country supported a population of 2,591,271 at the census of 1996. The population was estimated by the UN to have increased to 3,689,000 by mid-2006, giving an average density of 10.8 inhabitants per sq km. About one-third of the population are dependent on agriculture, mainly of the bush-fallowing type, but this is supplemented where possible by fishing, hunting and gathering. The main ethnic groups are the Vili on the coast, the Kongo (centred on Brazzaville), and the Téké, Mbochi and Sanga of the plateaux in the centre and north of the country. The principal centres of urban population are the capital, Brazzaville (with a population of 856,410 at the 1996 census), and the main port of Pointe-Noire (455,131).

PHYSICAL FEATURES AND RESOURCES

The exploitation of substantial offshore petroleum deposits represents a major sector of the economy. The immediate coastal zone is sandy in the north, more swampy south of Kouilou, and in the vicinity of Pointe-Indienne yields small amounts of petroleum. A narrow coastal plain does not rise above 100 m, and the cool coastal waters modify the climate, giving low rainfall and a grassland vegetation. Rising abruptly from the coastal plain are the high-rainfall forested ridges of the Mayombé range, parallel to the coast and achieving a height of 800 m, in which gorges, incised by rivers such as the Kouilou, provide potential hydroelectric power sites. At Hollé, near the Congo-Océan railway and at the western foot of the range, there are considerable phosphate deposits. Mayombé also provides an important export commodity, timber, of which the main commercial species are okoumé, limba and sapele.

Inland, the south-western Niari valley has lower elevation, soils that are good by tropical African standards and a grassland vegetation, which facilitates agricultural development. A variety of agricultural products such as groundnuts, maize, vegetables, palm oil, coffee, cocoa, sugar and tobacco, is obtained from large plantations, smaller commercial farms and also peasant holdings. These products provide the support for a more concentrated rural population and the basis for some industrial development.

A further forested mountainous region, the Chaillu massif, is the Congo basin's western watershed, and this gives way north-eastwards to a series of drier plateaux, the Batéké region and, east of the Likoula river, a zone of Congo riverine land. Here are numerous watercourses, with seasonal inundation, and dense forest vegetation, which supports some production of forest products, although the full potential has yet to be realized. The rivers Congo and Oubangui, with tributaries, provide more than 6,500 km of navigable waterway, which are particularly important, owing to the lack of a developed network of roads.

Recent History

PIERRE ENGLEBERT

Revised by KATHARINE MURISON

The Republic of the Congo became autonomous within the French Community in November 1958, with Abbé Fulbert Youlou as Prime Minister. Full independence followed on 15 August 1960; in March 1961 Youlou was elected President. In 1963 Youlou transferred power to a provisional Government led by Alphonse Massamba-Débat, who was elected President in December. In 1964 the Marxist-Leninist Mouvement national de la révolution (MNR) was formed as the sole political party. In August 1968 Capt. (later Maj.) Marien Ngouabi deposed Massamba-Débat in a coup. A new Marxist-Leninist party, the Parti congolais du travail (PCT), replaced the MNR, and in January 1970 the country was renamed the People's Republic of the Congo.

In March 1977 Ngouabi was assassinated during an attempted coup by supporters of Massamba-Débat, who was subsequently executed. In April Col (later Brig.-Gen.) Jacques-Joachim Yhombi-Opango, a former Chief of Staff of the armed forces, was appointed Head of State. In February 1979 Yhombi-Opango surrendered his powers to a Provisional Committee appointed by the PCT. In March the President of the Committee, Col (later Gen.) Denis Sassou-Nguesso, was appointed President of the Republic and Chairman of the Central Committee of the PCT.

The Sassou-Nguesso regime adopted an increasingly pro-Western foreign policy and a liberal economic policy. Ethnic rivalries and economic problems resulted in an increase in opposition to Sassou-Nguesso during the late 1980s, and in September 1987 an armed uprising was suppressed.

At the PCT congress in July 1989 Sassou-Nguesso was re-elected Chairman of the party and President of the Republic for a further five-year term. At legislative elections, held in September, the single list of 133 candidates, including, for the first time, candidates who were not members of the PCT, was reportedly approved by 99.19% of those who voted.

POLITICAL TRANSITION

In August 1990 Sassou-Nguesso announced the release of several political prisoners, including Yhombi-Opango, who had been imprisoned for alleged complicity in a coup plot in 1987. In December 1990 an extraordinary congress of the PCT abandoned Marxism-Leninism as its official ideology, and formulated constitutional amendments legalizing a multi-party system. The amendments were subsequently approved by the Assemblée nationale populaire, and took effect in January 1991. An interim Government, led by Gen. Louis Sylvain Goma as Prime Minister (a position he had previously held in 1975–84), was subsequently installed.

A national conference was convened in February 1991. Opposition movements were allocated seven of 11 seats on the conference's governing body and were represented by 700 of the 1,100 delegates. The conference voted itself a sovereign body whose decisions were to be binding. In April the conference announced that the Constitution was to be abrogated and that the Assemblée nationale populaire and other national and regional institutions were to be dissolved. In June a 153-member legislative Haut conseil de la République (HCR) was established, in order to supervise the implementation of these measures, pending the adoption of a new constitution and the holding of elections. In the same month the Prime Minister replaced Sassou-Nguesso as Head of Government, and the country reverted to the name Republic of the Congo. André Milongo, a former World Bank official without formal political affiliation, succeeded Goma as Prime Minister. Independent trade unions were also legalized. In December the HCR adopted a draft Constitution, which provided for legislative power to be vested in an elected Assemblée nationale and Sénat and for executive power to be held by an elected President.

Army Discontent

In January 1992, following a reallocation of senior army posts by Milongo, members of the army, who were reputed to be supporters of Sassou-Nguesso, occupied strategic positions in Brazzaville and demanded the reinstatement of military personnel, who had allegedly been dismissed because of their ethnic affiliations, the removal of the newly appointed Secretary of State for Defence and payment of overdue salaries. Following at least five civilian deaths in armed clashes between government supporters and mutinous troops, the Secretary of State for Defence resigned, and Milongo agreed to appoint a candidate preferred by the army as Minister of Defence, although the Prime Minister assumed personal control of the armed forces.

Electoral Discord

The draft Constitution was approved by 96.3% of those who voted at a referendum in March 1992. At elections to the new Assemblée nationale in June and July, the Union panafricaine pour la démocratie sociale (UPADS) became the largest party, winning 39 of the 125 contested seats, followed by the Mouvement congolais pour la démocratie et le développement intégral (MCDDI), with 29 seats, and the PCT (18). At elections to the Sénat, held in late July, the UPADS also became the largest party, with 23 of the 60 contested seats. At the presidential election, held in two rounds in August, Pascal Lissouba, the leader of the UPADS and a former Prime Minister, was victorious, winning 61.32% of the votes cast in the second round to defeat Bernard Kolélas, the leader of the MCDDI; Sassou-Nguesso and Milongo were among the other 14 candidates who unsuccessfully contested the first round. In September Lissouba appointed Maurice-Stéphane Bongho-Nouarra as Prime Minister. Shortly after a new Council of Ministers had been named, however, the PCT terminated a pact it had formed with the UPADS and instead formed an alliance with the Union pour le renouveau démocratique (URD), a new grouping of seven parties, including the MCDDI. The URD-PCT alliance, which now had a majority of seats in parliament, won a vote of 'no confidence' in the Government in October, precipitating its resignation in November. Lissouba subsequently dissolved the Assemblée nationale, announcing that new legislative elections would be held. Claude Antoine Dacosta, a former FAO and World Bank official, was appointed Prime Minister of a transitional administration in December.

INTERNAL CONFRONTATION

At the first round of legislative elections, held in May 1993, the Mouvance présidentielle (MP), comprising the UPADS and its allies, won 62 of the 125 seats in the Assemblée nationale, while the URD-PCT coalition, led by Kolélas, secured 49. Protesting that serious electoral irregularities had occurred, the URD-PCT refused to contest the second round of elections in early June (for seats where no candidate had received more than 50% of votes cast in the first round). After the second round the MP held an absolute majority (69) of seats in the Assemblée nationale. In late June Lissouba appointed a new Council of Ministers, under Yhombi-Opango's premiership. Kolélas nominated a rival government and urged his supporters to instigate a campaign of civil disobedience. The political crisis soon precipitated violent conflict between armed militias, representing party political and ethnic interests, and the security forces. In late June the Supreme Court ruled that electoral irregularities had occurred at the first round of elections. In July the Government and the opposition negotiated a truce, and in August it was agreed that the disputed first-round results should be examined by a committee of impartial international arbitrators and that the second round of elections should be restaged. Following the repeated second round of elections, held in October, the MP retained its control of the Assemblée nationale, with 65 seats. The URD-PCT, with 57 seats, agreed to participate in the new Assemblée. In November, however, confrontations between armed militias and the security forces erupted again, with some 2,000 deaths reported during the second half of 1993. A cease-fire was agreed by the MP and the opposition in January 1994, although sporadic fighting continued.

In September 1994 six opposition parties formed an alliance, the Forces démocratiques unies (FDU), chaired by Sassou-Nguesso. The alliance, which was affiliated with the URD, included about 15 members of the Assemblée nationale. In December, following reconciliation talks between the Government and the opposition, a co-ordinating body was established to oversee the disarmament of the militias and the restoration of judicial authority. Meanwhile, Lissouba, Sassou-Nguesso and Kolélas signed an agreement that sought an end to hostilities between their respective supporters. In January 1995 a new coalition Council of Ministers, led by Yhombi-Opango, was appointed, including members of the MCDDI. The FDU refused to participate in the new administration. In December the major political parties signed a pact, requiring the disarmament of all party militias and the integration into the national security forces of 1,200 former militia members.

In August 1996 Yhombi-Opango resigned as Prime Minister. In September the new Prime Minister, David Charles Ganao, the leader of the Union des forces démocratiques, appointed an expanded Council of Ministers, including representatives of the URD. Following partial elections to the Sénat, held in October, the MP remained the largest grouping in the upper chamber.

Factional Violence

In February 1997 19 opposition parties (including the PCT and the MCDDI) demanded a number of reforms, including the expedited establishment of republican institutions, the disarmament of civilians and the deployment of a multinational peace-keeping force. During May renewed unrest was reported, and in June an attempt by the Government to disarm the militia group associated with Sassou-Nguesso's Forces démocratiques et patriotiques (FDP—as the FDU had been renamed) swiftly developed into a fierce conflict involving militia groups and opposing factions within the regular armed forces. Brazzaville was split effectively into three zones, controlled by supporters of Sassou-Nguesso, Lissouba and Kolélas, respectively. The conflict soon became polarized between troops loyal to the Lissouba administration and the 'Cobra' forces of Sassou-Nguesso. Despite efforts to mediate—led by Kolélas, President Omar Bongo of Gabon and the joint special representative of the UN and the Organization of African Unity (now the African Union—AU) to the Great Lakes region—none of the numerous cease-fires signed during mid-1997 endured. Sassou-Nguesso opposed an attempt by Lissouba to postpone presidential and legislative elections scheduled for July and August, and both sides were unable to agree on the composition of a proposed government of national unity. In June French troops assisted in the evacuation of foreign residents from Brazzaville; in mid-June they themselves departed, despite mediators' requests that they remain.

Fighting intensified in August 1997, spreading to the north. In September Lissouba appointed a Government of National Unity, under the premiership of Kolélas, thereby compromising the latter's role as a mediator. Sassou-Nguesso refused to accept the offer of five ministerial posts for his allies.

SASSOU-NGUESSO RESUMES POWER

In October 1997 Sassou-Nguesso's 'Cobra' forces, assisted by Angolan government troops, won control of Brazzaville and the strategically important port of Pointe-Noire. Lissouba and

Kolélas fled the Congo. Sassou-Nguesso was inaugurated as President, and appointed a transitional Government in early November. It was reported that some 10,000 people had been killed during the civil war and about 800,000 displaced. Upon his accession to power, Sassou-Nguesso decreed that party militias would be disarmed and outlawed as a matter of priority.

In January 1998 a Forum sur l'unité et la reconstruction was convened, comprising some 1,420 delegates; political organizations loyal to Lissouba refused to participate. The Forum approved the immediate commencement of a three-year transitional period (which could, however, be shortened or prolonged depending on economic and security conditions), pending the organization of presidential and legislative elections in 2001 and the approval by referendum of a new constitution. Meanwhile, a 75-member Conseil national de transition (CNT) was to act as legislative body. The Forum also recommended that the leaders of the previous administration be charged with 'genocide and war crimes'; warrants for the arrest of Lissouba, Kolélas and Yhombi-Opango were issued in November.

Continued Instability

Despite attempts to obtain an enduring peace settlement, clashes continued throughout 1998 in the Pool region, south of Brazzaville, a stronghold of the 'Ninja' militia loyal to Kolélas, causing thousands of refugees to flee the area. In December a full-scale battle for control of Brazzaville broke out between forces loyal to Kolélas (who remained in exile), allegedly supported by Angolan dissident groups, and Congolese government forces, augmented by Sassou-Nguesso's militia and Angolan government troops. More than 8,000 refugees were reported to have fled to the Democratic Republic of the Congo (DRC). In late December government forces launched offensives against Kolélas' forces in the south and west of the Congo.

In January 1999 sporadic fighting continued in Brazzaville and in the south-west, where the 'Cocoye' militia loyal to Lissouba was involved in skirmishes with government forces around the city of Loubomo (Dolisie), in the south-western Niari region. In late February the conflict in the area immediately south of Brazzaville intensified, and a further 10,000 people were estimated to have taken refuge in the DRC. By early March, however, the rebel militias had been obliged to withdraw to the Pool region. In May the army secured the city of Kinkala, capital of the Pool region, and captured the main rebel base in the south-west of the Congo.

Peace Initiatives

In September 1999 it was reported that some 600 militiamen loyal to Kolélas had surrendered, and several prominent opposition members voluntarily returned from exile. In October the authorities announced that the armed forces had regained control of all towns in the Pool region.

In November 1999 the Government announced that it had reached an agreement with the militias loyal to Lissouba and Kolélas, which included provision for a cease-fire and a general amnesty. The agreement was, however, rejected by Lissouba and Kolélas themselves, and the Government announced its intention to continue to seek their prosecution for alleged war crimes. In December the CNT adopted legislation providing for an amnesty for those militiamen who surrendered their weapons before mid-January 2000.

In December 1999 President Bongo was designated the official mediator between the Government and the militias. Following further discussions in Gabon, representatives of the armed forces and of the rebel militias signed a second peace agreement, which provided for the integration of militiamen into the armed forces and for measures to facilitate the return of displaced persons. Militia leaders continued, however, to demand the withdrawal of Angolan troops from the Congo. None the less, in late December a ceremony of reconciliation was held in Brazzaville between senior government figures and members of the previous Lissouba administration.

In February 2000 the committee in charge of observing the implementation of the peace process announced that the civil war was definitively over. It was estimated that around one-half of the estimated 810,000 people displaced by the conflict had returned to their homes. In May Kolélas and his nephew, Col Philippe Bikinkita, the Minister of the Interior in the previous Lissouba administration, were convicted, *in absentia*, of operating personal prisons in Brazzaville and of mistreating prisoners and causing their deaths during the 1997 civil war. Kolélas and Bikinkita, both in exile in the USA, were sentenced to death and ordered to pay compensation to their victims.

In November 2000 the Government adopted a draft Constitution, which included provisions for a presidential system of government, with a bicameral legislature and an independent judiciary. It was proposed that the Head of State be elected for a term of seven years, renewable once only. In December it was announced that some 12,000 militiamen had been disarmed during 2000, although both national and international observers reported that at least an equivalent number of militiamen remained at large in the Congo. (Earlier in the year the Government had acknowledged that it would not be feasible to integrate all former rebels into the armed forces or the police force.) In late December it was announced that the PCT had signed an agreement with the Rassemblement pour la démocratie et le progrès social, led by Jean-Pierre Thystère Tchicaya, to bring the latter party into the Government.

National Dialogue and Constitutional Reform

In February 2001 the Government established a commission to prepare for a period of national dialogue. However, internal and exiled opposition groups, displeased by their exclusion from this commission, and also citing security concerns, boycotted both the opening ceremony of the national dialogue in mid-March and regional debates that took place later in that month. None the less, some 2,200 delegates, representing public institutions, civil society associations, political parties loyal to the Government and independent parties, attended the debates, reportedly reaching a consensus on the draft Constitution. The national convention met in April, with the participation of several of those who had boycotted the first phase of national dialogue. Kolélas and Lissouba were notably absent from the convention, although it was reported that Kolélas had twice attempted to enter the Congo to participate, despite having been condemned to death in the previous year. The convention concluded with the adoption of an 'Agreement for Peace and Reconstruction'.

Meanwhile, in March 2001 a Congolese human rights organization reported the discovery of a number of mass graves, containing the bodies of people believed to have been executed by members of the security forces in 1998–99 in the Pool region. The Government denied the existence of any such graves, and Sassou-Nguesso denounced the human rights organization as attempting to disrupt the peace process. In May Martin Mberi, the Secretary-General of the UPADS and the Minister of Construction, Urban Development, Housing and Land Reform, resigned from the Government, reportedly to express dissent at the exclusion of Lissouba from the national dialogue and at the increased presidential powers envisaged in the proposed Constitution.

In July 2001 a new coalition of opposition parties sympathetic to Milongo, the Alliance pour la démocratie et le progrès (ADP), was formed, with the intention of fielding a single candidate in the presidential election due to be held in 2002. Meanwhile, the FDP reverted to its original name, the Forces démocratiques unies (FDU), and was expanded to consist of some 29 parties, with the purpose of uniting behind Sassou-Nguesso in the election (although the PCT was to contest the subsequent legislative elections independently of the FDU).

In September 2001 the CNT approved the text of the proposed Constitution, which was to be submitted to referendum following the compilation of an electoral census. Although the national convention had recommended that opposition parties participate in the electoral commission, only one opposition grouping, the ADP, was represented in the Commission nationale d'organisation des élections (CONEL), which was, moreover, to be responsible to the Ministry of the Interior, Security and Territorial Administration. In mid-December Lissouba, Kolélas and Yhombi-Opango issued a joint statement from abroad condemning the electoral process as lacking impartiality, and urging the international community to assist in the establishment of an independent electoral commission. Several opposition parties subsequently threatened to boycott the elections in protest at the composition of the CONEL. In late December the Supreme Court sentenced Lissouba, *in absentia*, to 20 years' imprisonment with hard labour for the mismanagement of public funds in association with the state petroleum company.

SASSOU-NGUESSO AND THE PCT CONSOLIDATE POWER

In December 2001 the electoral schedule was announced: the constitutional referendum was to be held on 20 January 2002, followed by the presidential election on 10 March, elections to the Assemblée nationale on 12 May and 9 June, and indirect elections to the Sénat on 30 June. The new Constitution was approved on 20 January by some 84.5% of votes cast, with a participation rate of some 77.5% of the electorate.

Presidential Election

In mid-February 2002 10 presidential candidates were approved by the Supreme Court, among them Sassou-Nguesso, Milongo, Mberi and Joseph Kignoumbi Kia Mbougou, of the UPADS. It was reported that Sassou-Nguesso's candidacy had the support of more than 50 political organizations, including a faction of the MCDDI. Meanwhile, six political parties supportive of Milongo formed an opposition alliance, the Convention pour la démocratie et le salut (CODESA), which effectively supplanted the ADP. However, in mid-February six candidates threatened to withdraw from the polls unless the Supreme Court ruled that the electoral law conformed with the transitional fundamental law of 1997, which made no explicit provision for the holding of general elections. In early March 2002, having received no reply to their submission to the Supreme Court, Mberi, Milongo and an unaffiliated opposition candidate announced the withdrawal of their candidacies. Milongo, who had been widely regarded as the sole credible challenger to Sassou-Nguesso, urged his supporters to boycott the poll, stating that his concerns about the transparency of electoral procedures and the impartiality of the CONEL remained unresolved.

With the principal opposition candidates thereby excluded, Sassou-Nguesso won an overwhelming victory in the presidential election contested by seven candidates on 10 March 2002, securing 89.41% of the votes cast. According to official figures, 69.36% of the electorate participated in the election. Although EU observers recorded a significant number of irregularities, it was noted that these were primarily of an administrative nature. After the presidential election CODESA called for the postponement of the elections to the Assemblée nationale, so that amended electoral registers could be compiled. The Government subsequently delayed the elections until 26 May and 23 June; local elections, initially scheduled to be held concurrently with the second round of voting for deputies, were further postponed until 30 June.

Renewed Violence in the South

Meanwhile, in late March 2002 renewed violence erupted in the Pool region, apparently instigated by members of a 'Ninja' militia group, led by Rev. Frédéric Bitsangou (also known as Ntumi). The conflict widened in early April, when two people were killed in an attack on a train on the Congo-Océan railway by members of the militia, although Ntumi denied his forces had initiated the attack. Following further insurgency in Mayama, some 80 km west of Brazzaville, government forces, reportedly assisted by Angolan troops, were dispatched to the region, and air attacks were launched against the rebels. By mid-April the unrest had spread to southern Brazzaville, and by late May some 50,000 people were reported to have been displaced. In late April government forces announced that they had regained control of the Congo-Océan railway, facilitating a normalization in the supply of fuel and food to the capital, although fighting continued in Pool. At the end of May government troops regained control of the rebel stronghold of Vindza.

Legislative Elections

The first round of elections to the 137-member Assemblée nationale, which was held on 26 May 2002, was contested by some 1,200 candidates from more than 100 parties. As a result of the unrest in the Pool region, voting was indefinitely postponed in eight constituencies, while disruption caused by protesters and administrative irregularities necessitated a rerun of polling in a further 12 constituencies on 28–29 May. Moreover, the CONEL subsequently disqualified 15 candidates. Turn-out in the first round, at which the PCT and its allies in the FDU won 38 of the 51 seats decided, was around 65%.

Prior to the second round of elections to the Assemblée, the security situation in Brazzaville deteriorated markedly. In mid-June 2002, while President Sassou-Nguesso was in Italy, a group of 'Ninja' militiamen attacked the capital's main military base, near to the international airport. In the subsequent fighting 72 rebels, three army officers and five civilians were killed, according to official reports, while some 100 rebel fighters were captured. In spite of requests by Milongo's party, the Union pour la démocratie et la République—Mwinda (UDR—Mwinda), for a postponement of the elections in those areas of western Brazzaville where fighting had occurred, and which were largely deserted, the elections went ahead on 23 June, as scheduled, although the rate of participation, at an estimated 30% nation-wide, was appreciably lower than in the first round, and was as low as 10% in some constituencies in Brazzaville and in Pointe-Noire. Following the polls, supporters of Sassou-Nguesso held an absolute majority in the new Assemblée; the PCT emerged as the largest party, with 53 seats, while the FDU alliance held a total of 30 seats. Moreover, many of the 19 nominally independent deputies elected were believed to be loyal to Sassou-Nguesso. The UDR—Mwinda became the largest opposition party, with only six seats, while the UPADS held four seats. Although 17 deputies from smaller parties were elected, the MCDDI notably failed to secure representation in the Assemblée.

The local and municipal elections, held on 30 June 2002, were also marked by a low turn-out and further entrenched Sassou-Nguesso's power; the PCT itself gained 333 of the 828 elective seats, while the success of constituent parties of the FDU ensured that supporters of the President held more than two-thirds of the elective seats. (CODESA had urged a boycott, citing allegations of widespread fraud in recent voting, although the UDR—Mwinda, the principal party in the alliance, encouraged its supporters to vote.) As the councillors elected on 30 June were those who would, in turn, elect the members of the Sénat on 7 July, the victory of those loyal to Sassou-Nguesso in the upper parliamentary chamber was also to be expected. Following these elections, the 66-member Sénat comprised 56 supporters of the President (44 from the PCT and 12 from the FDU), two representatives of civil society organizations, one independent and only one member of a small opposition party. Thus, supporters of President Sassou-Nguesso had gained clear control of both executive and legislative power. In August Tchicaya was elected as President of the Assemblée nationale, and the Secretary-General of the PCT, Ambroise-Edouard Noumazalay, was elected as President of the Sénat. Sassou-Nguesso was inaugurated as elected President on 14 August; a few days later he announced the formation of a new Government, which included no representatives of the opposition (although several representatives from civil society were appointed to ministerial positions).

Sporadic attacks by 'Ninja' militias in the Pool region, in particular against freight trains on the Congo-Océan railway, continued during the second half of 2002. In October unrest intensified, and several deaths of civilians were reported; up to 10,000 civilians were reported to have fled Pool between early October and mid-November. In early November an *ad hoc* presidential committee, comprising prominent citizens from the Pool region and politicians allied to Sassou-Nguesso or to Lissouba, proposed a cease-fire between government forces and the 'Ninja' forces allied to Ntumi, and the replacement of government army units in the region with gendarmerie patrols. In mid-November Sassou-Nguesso, rejecting the proposals of the committee, announced that a 'safe passage' would be provided from Pool to Brazzaville until mid-December for fighters who surrendered their arms, and reiterated that the terms of the peace agreement concluded in 1999 remained valid. However, fighting subsequently intensified and only 371 rebels were reported to have surrendered (estimates of the number of rebels at large varied from 3,000–10,000). Although Sassou-Nguesso announced an extension of the amnesty, as a result of which a further 90 rebels surrendered in early January 2003, some 15 civilians were killed in an attack in Pool at the beginning of that month, and in February the first outbreak of political violence in the neighbouring Bouenza region since 1999, in which a local police chief was killed, was reported.

PEACE AGREEMENT SIGNED

In mid-March 2003 the Government and Ntumi's 'Ninja' militia group signed an agreement aimed at restoring peace to the Pool region. The rebels agreed to end hostilities and disarm, while the Government was to guarantee an amnesty for the rebels and integrate former combatants into the national armed forces. In April the European Commission announced that it was to extend a grant of €731,000 to assist with the demobilization and reintegration of former 'Ninja' rebels in the Pool region. At the end of August the Assemblée nationale formally approved an amnesty for former 'Ninja' fighters, to cover the period from January 2000. By September 2003 the situation in Pool had stabilized sufficiently to allow an electoral commission to be formed in the region. None the less, in October renewed clashes between 'Ninja' fighters and government forces near Mindouli resulted in at least 13 deaths. In December, following reports that Kolélas had unsuccessfully attempted to re-enter the Congo under an assumed identity from the DRC, clashes were reported in Brazzaville between 'Ninja' groupings allied to Ntumi and Kolélas, although peace was soon restored.

In January 2004 Ntumi announced a series of conditions for his return to Brazzaville from his base in Loukouo, in the Pool region, including the installation of a government of national unity, the return of exiled former leaders, the definition of his status and an agreement on the number of his fighters to be integrated into the army, police and gendarmerie. The Government largely rejected Ntumi's demands in March, insisting that the peace agreement signed a year earlier made no provision for the formation of a government of national unity or the return of exiles, and announced that working groups had recently been formed to monitor the demobilization, disarmamemt and reintegration of former rebels and to consider Ntumi's status. At least seven militiamen and two members of the armed forces were killed in clashes near Kinkala later that month, according to the Government.

Divisions within the FDU emerged in April 2004 when five constituent parties issued a statement denouncing the alliance's inaction and demanding that a convention be held in an effort to address issues such as state reform, the consolidation of peace, and combating corruption and fraud. In early May the rail service linking Brazzaville to the Pool region resumed operations, and the Government announced that it had closed seven sites that had been established south of Brazzaville in October 2002 to shelter some 12,000 people who had fled fighting in Pool, following the completion of a programme to return them to their home villages. Later in May 2004 the European Commission withdrew the €731,000 that it had granted in April 2003 to assist with the disarmament and reintegration of former 'Ninja' rebels in the Pool region, owing to the failure of the former combatants to surrender their weapons. However, in the following month the Commission extended a new grant of €2m. to finance a wider programme of disarmament and reintegration, to be conducted over a period of between two and three years by the UN Development Programme, covering all areas of the Congo affected by civil war. In August some 20 opposition parties and associations, including the MCDDI, formed a coalition, the Coordination de l'opposition pour une alternance démocratique (CODE-A), with the stated aim of fostering non-violent political change in the Congo.

In July 2004 the Congo was suspended from the Kimberley Process, an international initiative to eliminate the illegal trade in diamonds to fund conflicts, after a report identified irregularities in the country's diamond exports. Sassou-Nguesso subsequently suspended diamond trading pending the implementation of reforms in the sector aimed at securing recertification by the Process. In November the Congo hosted a meeting of Central African government ministers responsible for mining, at which agreement was reached on the establishment of a regulatory body to monitor the trade in diamonds in the region.

ONGOING INSECURITY IN POOL

Instability persisted in the Pool region in late 2004. In mid-October the rail service between Brazzaville and Pointe-Noire was suspended following numerous attacks on trains in Pool. Ntumi denied claims that the attacks had been perpetrated by his 'Ninja' rebel group, also known as the Conseil national de la résistance (CNR), and demanded an independent inquiry into the incidents. A combined force of former 'Ninja' militiamen and gendarmes had been responsible for escorting trains between the two cities until earlier that month, when the Government had decided to replace them with army troops owing to alleged looting by the 'Ninjas'. Meanwhile, displaced persons who had fled hostilities in Pool continued to return gradually during 2004 with government assistance, although the humanitarian situation in the region remained poor and it was reported that armed fighters were still intimidating civilians, despite the peace agreement signed in March 2003. (It was estimated that between 100,000 and 147,000 people had fled Pool between 1998 and 2002.)

President Sassou-Nguesso reorganized the Council of Ministers in January 2005, notably creating a new post of Prime Minister, which was allocated to Isidore Mvouba, hitherto Minister of State, Minister of Transport and Privatization, responsible for the Co-ordination of Government Action. New appointees included Pacifique Issoibeka, formerly Deputy Governor of the Banque des états de l'Afrique centrale, who replaced Roger Rigobert Andely as Minister of Finance, the Economy and the Budget, and Bruno Itoua, hitherto Managing Director of the Société Nationale des Pétroles du Congo, who became Minister of Energy and Hydraulics. CODE-A criticized the creation of the post of Prime Minister, accusing Sassou-Nguesso of violating the Constitution, which made no provision for the position.

In January 2005 Ntumi established a commission to supervise the recovery of weapons held by militiamen in the region. Ntumi, who had yet to return to Brazzaville and whose status remained undefined, also called for talks with the Government prior to the organization of local and legislative elections in the eight constituencies of Pool where voting had been indefinitely postponed in 2002. In early March 2005 clashes between the security forces and the 'Ninja' militia, which followed the arrest of a member of the rebel group, resulted in the temporary closure of businesses and schools in two southern districts of Brazzaville. Meanwhile, the UN Office for the Co-ordination of Humanitarian Affairs released a report describing a social and economic crisis in the Pool region, where lack of access to health services, exacerbated by insecurity and logistical problems that had prevented assistance reaching the area, had led to an increased mortality rate and malnutrition. It was estimated that most towns and villages had regained only between one-half and two-thirds of their original populations.

DEMOBILIZATION EFFORTS

In March 2005 the Government initiated a new programme for the disarmament, demobilization and reintegration of 450 former combatants in the Pool region, for which it had allocated 201m. francs CFA. (More than 500 weapons were subsequently collected and destroyed under this programme.) Earlier demobilization efforts, funded by donors, had reportedly reintegrated some 8,000 former militias into society. The Congolese Government condemned an attack on a convoy of UN officials who were on a mission to evaluate the humanitarian situation in Pool in late April, blaming the 'Ninja' militia group for the incident. It was later reported that the CNR had disarmed those responsible for the attack and recovered property that had been seized from the UN officials. In May it was announced that the Government had commenced power-sharing talks with the CNR with the aim of bringing members of the movement into 'all national institutions'.

Meanwhile, in mid-April 2005 the Government announced that it had uncovered a coup plot planned by a group of around 20 army and police officers who were arrested earlier that year in connection with an arms theft at a paramilitary police barracks in Brazzaville. In March human rights organizations had expressed concern about the welfare of the detainees and urged the Government either to charge or release them. The Minister of Security and Public Order, Gen. Paul Mbot, claimed that the alleged coup leader, Capt. Pandi Ngouari, had received support from an exiled former Minister of the Economy and Finance, Guila Mougounga Kombo, who had served in the Lissouba administration in 1995–97, and two unnamed foreign businessmen, who were being sought by the authorities. Mbot also suggested that several senior officials were implicated in the foiled coup, including two parliamentary deputies. Opposition leaders, who were sceptical about the Government's claims, called for a judicial inquiry to be conducted into the affair.

The PCT's representation in the 66-member Sénat was reduced to 39 seats as a result of partial elections held on 2 October 2005. The ruling party secured 23 of the 30 seats contested at the elections, which were boycotted by opposition parties from CODE-A and CODESA, partly in protest at the composition of a new CONEL recently appointed by presidential decree. Of the remaining seven seats, six were won by pro-presidential parties, while one independent was elected to the upper chamber.

Having obtained authorization from the Congolese authorities, Kolélas returned to the Congo in October 2005 to attend the burial of his wife, who had died in Paris, France. At least six people were subsequently killed in heavy fighting between 'Ninja' rebels and government troops in southern Brazzaville. Earlier that month Ntumi had again demanded the formation of a government of national unity, in return for which the CNR would surrender the weapons it had collected from former combatants. In December, at the request of Sassou-Nguesso, the legislature granted amnesty to Kolélas, overturning his death sentence in the interests of national reconciliation. A few days later Kolélas apologized to the Congolese people for the harm he had caused during the 1997 civil war. Similarly, in March 2006 the acting President of the UPADS, Pascal Gamassa, requested forgiveness for his party's involvement in the civil war, on behalf of former President Lissouba.

In December 2005 the agreement of the European Union to disburse funds for the construction of a highway linking Kinkala with Brazzaville was attributed to improving security in Pool. It was hoped that the road would facilitate the provision of development aid to the region. The population of Pool had reportedly increased from 186,481 in 2000 to 362,358 in 2005 as people returned following the signing of the 2003 peace agreement. Nevertheless, the fragility of the security situation in Pool was evident in January 2006, when two international aid organizations, the International Committee of the Red Cross and Médecins sans frontières, temporarily suspended their operations in the region after a number of their staff were threatened or attacked by armed bandits. Meanwhile, the World Bank granted the Congo US $17m. to disarm, demobilize and reintegrate 30,000 former fighters in eight regions. According to government figures, there were some 43,000 former combatants throughout the country. In March some 500 weapons, 800 grenades and 80,000 pieces of ammunition that had been collected from former militias since the beginning of the year were destroyed in a ceremony in Brazzaville attended by Sassou-Nguesso and the Secretary-General of the UN, Kofi Annan. Those who agreed to surrender their arms were provided with agricultural tools and development aid in return. However, an estimated 34,000 illegally held firearms remained in circulation, posing a serious threat to security, and Ntumi declared that his troops would not fully disarm until an agreement on 'political partnership' had been signed by the CNR and the Government. In August it was reported that the commission responsible for reintegrating former combatants into society had recovered and destroyed a total of 11,776 weapons and reintegrated 17,459 people.

In March 2006 21 opposition parties and associations, including the UDR—Mwinda and the UPADS, formed the Front démocratique pour la commission électorale indépendante to campaign for the appointment of a new, independent electoral commission to organize the legislative elections due in 2007 and the presidential election due in 2009. In April Michel Mampouya, who had led the MCDDI during Kolélas's exile, left the party as a result of divisions that had emerged since Kolélas's return, and formed a new political party, the Parti de la sauvegarde des valeurs républicaines; the party held its inaugural congress in July.

Sassou-Nguesso resigned from the leadership of the PCT in early January 2007, on the grounds that the Constitution states that the role of President of the Republic is incompatible with holding office within a political party. At the end of that month one of the constituent parties of the FDU, the Rassemblement pour la démocratie et la République, announced that it was withdrawing from the pro-presidential majority, accusing the PCT of having reneged on an accord on collaboration signed in February 2002 by refusing to share power. The party, which had one representative in the Assemblée nationale, had never been allocated any government or other official posts. Meanwhile, Ntuni announced that the CNR was to be transformed into a legitimate political party, the Conseil national des républicains, and would participate in the forthcoming elections to the Assemblée nationale. In February the Government announced that the legislative elections would be held on 24 June and 22 July, under the supervision of a new, independent electoral commission, as demanded by the opposition. However, following the rejection of their demands for a review of electoral constituencies, in late April opposition parties boycotted the vote at which the Assemblée nationale approved the creation of the new commission and the nomination of its members by presidential decree.

In early March 2007 the President effected a minor government reshuffle, notably creating a new Ministry of Tourism and the Environment and appointing his former cabinet chief, Aimé Emmanuel Yoka, as Minister of State, Keeper of the Seals, Minister of Justice and Human Rights; most of the principal portfolios remained unchanged. In April the PCT and the MCDDI agreed to form an electoral alliance to contest the next legislative, local and presidential elections. A day later, as a result of the negotiations that commenced in 2005, the Government and the CNR signed an agreement providing for the destruction of weapons held by members of the movement, the integration of 250 former combatants into the national armed forces and the appointment of Ntumi to the Government. In late May, in accordance with the agreement, Sassou-Nguesso designated Ntumi as delegate-general to the President, in charge of promoting peace and reconciliation. On his return to Brazzaville, Ntumi was to be permitted to retain a 60-strong personal guard.

THE 'BEACH AFFAIR'

In July 2001 the families of some 353 missing Congolese citizens demanded a parliamentary inquiry into their disappearance from the Beach area of Brazzaville; it was reported that the missing people, former refugees from the civil war in the southern regions who had sought asylum in the DRC, had been arrested following their voluntary repatriation to the Congo in May 1999. In April 2004 the Congolese Government announced that six of the people believed to have disappeared in 1999 had been identified among a group of refugees being repatriated from the DRC, and claimed that more were still based in a camp in south-west DRC. Sassou-Nguesso subsequently ordered that a Congolese judicial inquiry be conducted into what had become known as the 'Beach affair', and in July 2004 four senior officers from the Congolese armed forces, including Dabira (also sought in France, see below), were indicted, having apparently volunteered to be tried in an attempt to clear their names. The trial of 15 senior army and police officers suspected of involvement in the 'Beach affair', on charges of murder, genocide, crimes against humanity and war crimes, commenced in Brazzaville in mid-July 2005. Many of the families of those missing and CODE-A had opposed the case being heard in the Congo, claiming that the judiciary was not truly independent of the executive. A month later all 15 defendants were acquitted of the charges against them. However, the court ordered the Government to pay compensation of 10m. francs CFA (one-10th of the amount sought) for each missing person to the families of 86 acknowledged victims, in recognition of the state's civil responsibility for the safety of its citizens.

FOREIGN RELATIONS

Since the 1997 civil war the principal aim of Congolese foreign policy has been to gain international recognition of the legitimacy of the Sassou-Nguesso Government, and to ensure the continued support of the Congo's bilateral and multilateral donors. These efforts have been largely successful, particularly since Sassou-Nguesso's election to the presidency in March 2002. In June of that year Sassou-Nguesso was also elected President of the Communauté économique des états de l'Afrique centrale, a position he still held in mid-2007. In October 2005 the Republic of the Congo was elected to serve as a non-permanent member of the UN Security Council during 2006–07. In January 2006 Sassou-Nguesso was elected to chair the AU for a one-year term of office, after the withdrawal of the candidacy of the Sudanese President, which several member states had opposed owing to the ongoing conflict in the Darfur region of western Sudan (q.v.).

France, the former colonial power, is the source of more than one-half of total assistance to the Republic of the Congo, the major supplier of imports and the primary business partner in the extraction of petroleum. During the 1997 civil war President Lissouba accused France of favouring the rebel forces of Sassou-Nguesso (who was reported to have allied himself with French petroleum interests) over the elected administration. In 1998 Lissouba and Kolélas attempted, unsuccessfully, to sue the French petroleum company Elf Aquitaine (now Total), claiming that it had provided support for Sassou-Nguesso. In May of that year France normalized relations with the Congo, resuming the supply of aid and instituting military co-operation, and Sassou-Nguesso made an official visit to France in September 2002, when he met President Jacques Chirac.

Relations between the Congo and France were, however, strained from mid-2002, as a result of an investigation by a French court into several Congolese officials, including President Sassou-Nguesso, in connection with the reported disappearance of 353 Congolese citizens, following their return from asylum in the DRC to the Congo in 1999 (see above). In December 2002 the Congo filed a case against France at the International Court of Justice (ICJ) at The Hague, Netherlands, claiming that the investigations represented a violation of Congolese sovereignty and disregarded Sassou-Nguesso's immunity as a Head of State. Hearings into the case at the ICJ commenced in April 2003, and in June the ICJ ruled that investigations into the Inspector-General of the Congolese armed forces, Gen. Norbert Dabira, could continue, while noting that no action that warranted the intervention of the ICJ had yet been undertaken against Sassou-Nguesso or other government ministers. However, the ICJ was not expected to issue an imminent ruling on the legitimacy of the jurisdiction of French courts over actions that were alleged to have occurred on Congolese territory; the ICJ also stated that the ruling would not prevent the Court conducting further investigations into the case. On four occasions between December 2004 and January 2006 the ICJ extended the time limits for certain written pleadings to be submitted to the Court by both parties, at the Congo's request. Meanwhile, the head of Congo's national police force, Col Jean-François Ndenguet, was detained briefly during a visit to France at the beginning of April 2004 in connection with the investigation into the disappearances, but was released after claiming diplomatic immunity.

In November 2004 the Court of Appeal in Paris ruled that all French legal proceedings relating to the so-called 'Beach affair' should be halted, as the French judiciary did not have legitimate jurisdiction in the case. Human rights organizations condemned the decision, accusing the Court of Appeal of succumbing to political pressure. During a visit to the Congo in February 2005, President Chirac dismissed this suggestion, insisting that the French judiciary was entirely independent of the executive. In January 2007, however, the French Court of Cassation overturned the ruling of the Paris Court of Appeal, prompting Sassou-Nguesso to accuse France of interfering in Congolese affairs. A resumption of French legal proceedings was under consideration in June. Meanwhile, the French Government continued to provide considerable assistance to the Congo. France granted the Congolese Government €24m. in April 2005 to enable it to settle its arrears with the African Development Bank, and a framework agreement was signed providing for French assistance with the restructuring of the Congolese armed forces and national police force. A further €116m. was promised in March 2007, to be disbursed during 2007–11, principally for projects related to health, the environment and education.

In the 1997 conflict Angolan government troops provided support to Sassou-Nguesso, including the occupation of Pointe-Noire, the Congo's main seaport and focus of the petroleum industry. Angola had accused the Lissouba Government of providing assistance both to rebels of the União Nacional para a Independência Total de Angola and to Cabindan separatist guerrillas. In response to international criticism of his role, President dos Santos of Angola announced in early 1998 that the majority of his forces had departed the Congo. However, Angolan troops played an important role in the defeat of the rebel attack on Brazzaville in December 1998. In January 1999 the Heads of State of Angola, the Congo, and the DRC met to agree a common policy on the conflicts in their countries. In December the interior ministers of the three countries met in Luanda, Angola, and signed a co-operation accord. The accord created a tripartite commission to ensure border security, the free movement of people and goods, the training of personnel, and the provision of assistance to displaced persons. Angolan troops assisted the Congolese Government in the renewed insurgency in the Pool region from early 2002, but the last contingent of Angolan soldiers was withdrawn from the Congo in December of that year. In late 2006 the office of the UN High Commissioner for Refugees (UNHCR) increased efforts to repatriate around 2,900 Angolan refugees who had fled to the Congo during the civil war in their own country.

Relations between the Republic of the Congo and the DRC steadily improved from the late 1990s. In December 1999 Sassou-Nguesso paid a brief visit to President Kabila in order to discuss bilateral co-operation and the implementation of the tripartite Luanda accord, and further discussion on issues of common interest, including, notably, border security and the rehabilitation of refugees and displaced persons, took place in 2000–04. In May 2001 some 19 DRC nationals suspected of involvement in the assassination of President Laurent-Désiré Kabila in January of that year were extradited from the Republic of the Congo to Kinshasa, DRC. In September 2002 Congolese authorities announced that, in accordance with a programme established in association with the International Organization for Migration, up to 4,000 soldiers from the DRC who had sought refuge or deserted in the Congo were to be repatriated. Delegations from the Congo and the DRC, meeting in Brazzaville in May 2004, reached agreement on the urgent need to repatriate voluntarily and reintegrate former combatants who had taken refuge in their respective countries, and formed a joint technical committee charged with monitoring the implementation of national programmes of demobilization, disarmament and reintegration; the presence of these former soldiers and militiamen had often created tensions between the two countries. At least 400 Congolese refugees returned home from the DRC during 2004, and in April 2005 the repatriation of some 57,000 refugees from the Congo to the DRC's Equateur province commenced under an agreement signed in September 2004 by officials from the two countries and UNHCR. In November 2006 it was reported that an estimated 51,000 DRC refugees remained in the Congo. The voluntary repatriation programme was expected to be intensified in 2007. Meanwhile, in June 2003 the Congo, Rwanda and UNHCR signed an agreement providing for the voluntary repatriation of up to 5,000 Rwandan refugees believed to be resident in the Congo; the first group of refugees returned to Rwanda in June 2004. However, many of the refugees were reluctant to return to Rwanda, and by August 2005 only around 130 had done so. At the end of 2005 there were some 12,500 Congolese refugees in the DRC and Gabon.

Economy

CHARLOTTE VAILLANT

Based on an earlier article by EDITH HODGKINSON

Since independence in 1960 economic policy in the Republic of the Congo has moved from one end of the ideological spectrum to close to the other. For the first decade and a half a systematic policy of state participation in productive enterprise was pursued, although the private sector was initially permitted to continue its activities, especially in mining, forestry and transport. Upon becoming Head of State in 1977, Joachim Yhombi-Opango emphasized that the Congo would benefit from the expertise that private investment and a 'mixed' economy could provide. Under Gen. Denis Sassou-Nguesso, who ousted Yhombi-Opango two years later, foreign management consortia were introduced to restructure highly inefficient nationalized companies, while the petroleum sector was further opened to private foreign investment. However, full-scale economic restructuring was only undertaken following the devaluation of the CFA franc in January 1994, albeit with limited success.

The Government of President Pascal Lissouba (1992–97) and the IMF agreed in May 1994 on a programme for the privatization of the major public-sector industries (including rail, air and water transport, electricity, the petroleum industry and postal services) and a substantial reduction in the number of civil servants. On the basis of progress achieved on economic liberalization and budgetary stabilization, the Congo was accorded an Enhanced Structural Adjustment Facility (ESAF) by the IMF in 1996. Progress was impeded, however, by the civil war that broke out in 1997, which severely disrupted economic activity in Brazzaville, and by the sharp decline in the international price of petroleum, the mainstay of the economy.

The new administration of Sassou-Nguesso, which took power in October 1997, inheriting a devastated infrastructure, immediately confirmed its commitment to privatization. In July 1998 the IMF agreed to a special post-conflict recovery credit, which was intended to be followed by another ESAF in 1999. The condition for the support—crucial to obtaining further relief on Congo's very heavy foreign debt burden (see below)—was a comprehensive programme of structural reform. However, the attainment of the programme's objectives was undermined in 1999 by the resumption of fighting in the south. In June 2000 the Government announced a provisional three-year programme for the rehabilitation and development of the country's social and economic infrastructure. In November the IMF agreed to further emergency post-conflict assistance, in support of the Government's reconstruction and economic recovery programme. The programme's priorities included the normalization of relations with external creditors, the reform of the civil service and the transfer of various state-owned enterprises to the private sector. The Government was also to implement measures to improve the management of petroleum revenue. An IMF Staff Monitored Programme (SMP) was signed in July 2001. Further post-conflict credits were approved by the World Bank in July 2001 and July 2002. It was hoped that the successful completion of the agreed programme of reforms would lead to further disbursement of funds, under the IMF's Poverty Reduction and Growth Facility (PRGF—the successor to the ESAF). However, talks with the IMF broke down in 2002–03 over delays in implementing structural reforms and deteriorating fiscal performance. In 2004 the Government stepped up its commitment to macroeconomic stabilization, financial soundness and transparency in the petroleum sector, and in December of that year the IMF approved a new three-year PRGF. This paved the way for additional loans from bilateral and multilateral creditors, notably the World Bank, and a new debt relief deal with bilateral lenders. In its first and second review of the PRGF, the IMF concluded that programme implementation had been satisfactory. The programme, however, went off-track in the first half of 2006 owing to expenditure over-run and lack of progress in the implementation of structural reforms. The PRGF was consequently suspended, prompting negotiations to establish an SMP. A six-month SMP was finally agreed in mid-July.

Partly as a result of Brazzaville's former status as the capital of French Equatorial Africa, and partly because the Congo and Oubangui rivers have long provided the main access to the Central African Republic (CAR) and Chad, services, transport and public administration in particular, traditionally played an unusually large role in the economy, and accounted for close to one-half of gross domestic product (GDP) in the early 1990s. The relative importance of services has since declined with the development of the petroleum sector, and the impact of the civil war on transport activities. In 2005 public administration accounted for an estimated 11.3% of GDP, while other services, including transport, accounted for 27.9% of GDP. Government employees totalled 69,868 in 2005, with one-third employed in the education sector. Some 38.1% of the country's inhabitants earned their livelihood from agriculture, fishing and forestry in 2003, which is low by sub-Saharan African standards. This sector accounted for an estimated 11.5% of GDP in 2005. An estimated 54.4% of the population reside in urban areas.

Economic growth has fluctuated widely, reflecting a combination of periods of political instability and the development of the petroleum sector. Improved output of petroleum, from 1979 onwards, coincided with increases in international prices for that commodity, which stimulated very high rates of investment by both the public sector and the petroleum companies, and hence strong GDP growth. The collapse of world petroleum prices in 1986 had severe repercussions throughout the economy, initially most acutely felt in major cuts in government spending. GDP initially declined (by 6.8% in 1986) and only slowly recovered over the next few years, with the rise in most years below the rate of population growth. Political turmoil led to a 2.8% decrease in GDP in 1993, and the decline deepened in 1994, to 4.8%, in part because of the impact on domestic demand of the 50% devaluation of the CFA franc in January of that year. Economic performance subsequently improved, with GDP growth reaching 4.3% in 1996, as the Nkossa oilfield came on stream and production for the domestic market derived some stimulus from the 1994 devaluation. The economic recovery was short-lived, however, with the outbreak of civil war bringing a 0.6% decline in GDP in the following year. The downturn was relatively limited because the petroleum industry, based at Pointe-Noire, was largely unaffected by the disorder. The onset of peace in 2000–02 boosted economic activity in the non-petroleum sector, with non-petroleum GDP growth averaging 16.6% in 2000, 12.1% in 2001 and 9.7% in 2002. At the same time, petroleum production started to decline and overall GDP growth rates decelerated from a peak of 8.2% in 2000 to 3.6% in 2001, before rising slightly to 5.4% in 2002. Despite a relatively strong growth in the non-petroleum sector, at 5.3%, a further decline in petroleum output reduced overall GDP growth to 0.8% in 2003. Performance in the non-petroleum sector continued to explain growth in 2004, at 3.5%. Economic growth has accelerated since 2005 on the back of a recovery in petroleum production. In 2005 real GDP increased by 7.8% and in 2006 real GDP grew by 6.1%. This reflected higher output in the petroleum sector and a robust contribution of the non-petroleum sector to growth, notably in construction and manufacturing (see below).

AGRICULTURE

Since the 1970s the agricultural sector has suffered from the lack of appropriate government policy, the poor management of state farms and the abandonment of farm-work in favour of salaried employment in the towns. With the exception of palm products, sugar and tobacco, which are grown on modern plantations (particularly in the south-western Niari valley), most agricultural crops are grown by families on small farms. In 2003 the Government announced a 10-year plan to revitalize the agricultural sector, in order to reduce the country's reliance on food imports. The Congo's food crop production has increased since the end of the civil war, although the volatile security situation has continued to disrupt farming and marketing activities in some parts of the country. Donors have also come forward with new financial packages. The country is far from self-sufficient, however, and as a result, the Congo was still listed as one of the African countries that faced an exceptional food emergency in 2007. The country produced an estimated 8,700 metric tons of cereals in 2004, bringing Congo's cereal import requirement for 2005 to an estimated 288,000 tons. Statistics recently compiled by the IMF show a strong recovery in the country's main crops. Output of cassava—the main subsistence crop—had recovered to 932,200 tons in 2003/04, against a production of 739,000 tons in 2000/01. Output of plantains amounted to 135,600 metric tons in 2003/04, compared with 73,000 tons in 2000/01. Secondary food crops include sweet potatoes, rice, yams, groundnuts and maize.

Sugar cane and tobacco have traditionally been the most important cash crops. The state corporation that ran the sugar industry, the Sucrerie du Congo, was replaced in 1991 by a joint venture between the Government and a French company. The Société agricole et de raffinage de sucre (SARIS-Congo), which is based in Nkayi, south-west of Brazzaville, reorganized and re-equipped the plantations, allowing them to satisfy domestic demand. As a result, annual production of raw sugar had almost doubled by the early 2000s, with production reaching a new record of 67,400 tons in 2005, just below its annual capacity of 70,000 tonnes. Poor infrastructure and insecurity in the region are a major hindrance to this activity. In addition, the country is soon to lose preferential market access to the EU as a result of ongoing reforms of the EU's Common Agricultural Policy.

Other traditional export crops—cocoa, coffee and oil palm—have become marginal since the late 1980s, with cocoa and coffee production averaging no more than 2,000 metric tons each year. Oil palm has fared somewhat better, with annual production of palm oil estimated at 16,700 tons in 1999–2003.

Animal husbandry has developed slowly, owing to the prevalence of the tsetse fly and the importance of the forestry sector, which has restricted the availability of pasture. Although numbers of livestock are increasing, the country is not self-sufficient in meat and dairy products. While river fishing remains artisanal, sea fishing is carried out commercially on a small scale, especially for tuna. The total fish catch was estimated at 58,400 metric tons in 2005.

Forestry

Forestry is a major economic activity. Forests cover about 55% of the Congo's total area and are a significant natural resource. Timber was the main export until it was superseded by petroleum in the mid-1970s, and presently accounts for roughly two-third of Congo's non-petroleum exports. The principal woods exploited are okoumé, limba and sapele, and there are substantial plantations of eucalyptus in the south-west of the country. Until 1987 the purchase and sale of logs was a monopoly of the state-owned Office Congolais des Bois. By 2001 some 95% of timber production was carried out by the private sector, with foreign companies accounting for a majority share in production. The exploitation by foreign investors of forest resources, particularly in the north of the country, has been encouraged, and in 2003 the Government announced measures intended to promote greater private-sector involvement in the forestry sector. The Government also attempted to relieve the pressure on virgin forest by requiring forestry companies to engage in reafforestation and also by increasing production within managed plantations, partly to fulfil local demand for fuel wood. A 2002 revision to the forestry code, compelling companies to process at least 85% of their production locally, has had some limited success.

Production of timber received an initial boost from the devaluation of the CFA franc in 1994, although the outbreak of fighting in the late 1990s greatly hindered the production and export of timber. Companies established in the south-west of the Congo were frequently obliged to suspend their activities owing to military activity, while the frequent suspension of traffic on the Congo-Océan railway caused congestion and protracted delays in the movement of timber from Brazzaville to the port at Pointe-Noire. As a result, the majority of timber companies in the north of the country exported produce by road to the port of Douala in Cameroon. Use of this route increased both transport costs and delays, however, as the roads were frequently impassable in the rainy season. Activity in forestry recovered significantly with the onset of peace in 2000–2002, when the railway line was re-opened to freight traffic. The route has remained subject to occasional disruptions since then, however. Meanwhile, the construction of the new river port at Lékéti, 600 km north of Brazzaville, has suffered serious delays.

The exploration of fast-growing trees began in 1978, when the first eucalyptus plantations were introduced to produce paper pulp and electricity and telephone poles for exports. Production of eucalyptus encountered major difficulties, after the majority shareholder, Shell Holding Bermuda, withdrew from Eucalyptus du Congo (ECO) in 2001, which thereby reverted to state ownership. Production subsequently declined dramatically, from 531,100 metric tons in 2000 to 61,200 tons in 2003. Production was nil in 2004 and 2005. The Canadian company, MagIndustries, finally acquired the newly-formed Eucalyptus Fibre Congo (EFC) through its forestry division, MagForestry in July 2005, but there has been continuous delay in resuming production. According to statistics recently compiled by the IMF, timber production amounted to 1,479,000 cu m in 2005, of which 710,000 cu m were exported as logs. In that year an estimated 248,000 cu m of wood was processed, compared with 202,000 cu m in 2002.

Mining and Energy

In the early 2000s the Congo was the fifth largest producer of crude petroleum in Africa, after Nigeria, Angola, Gabon and Equatorial Guinea. The country also holds significant reserves of natural gas. The petroleum sector's contribution to GDP declined in the first half of 2000s, as a result of economic recovery in the non-petroleum sector and the maturing of major oil fields. The sector contribution was down to 50% of GDP in 2003, compared with 58.9% in 2001. This trend was none the less reversed in 2005, as a result of a recovery in petroleum production and in 2006 the petroleum sector accounted for 60.4% of GDP. Oil has maintained an overwhelming dominance in export earnings and government revenue. According to preliminary estimates, petroleum revenue accounted for 89% of export earnings and 81.8% of total budget revenue in 2005. Earnings from crude petroleum exports more than doubled to 2,282,000m. francs CFA in that year, despite the continued depreciation of the US dollar, the currency in which international petroleum sales are denominated. This increase in earnings reflected both buoyant world petroleum prices (the average price increased by 40% in CFA franc terms) and a 12.8% recovery in domestic production.

At the end of 2006 the BP Statistical Review of World Energy estimated the proven petroleum reserves of the Congo at some 1,800m. barrels, an increase of some 500m. barrels compared with estimates made in the 1990s. This increase in reserves is mostly explained by recent discoveries associated with the intensification of oil exploration activities in deep and ultra-deep water fields. Onshore deposits were first discovered, at Pointe-Indienne, in 1957. In 1971, when these deposits were almost exhausted, new offshore petroleum fields were discovered, and their subsequent development has roughly maintained production levels. Nkossa, Congo's largest field with estimated reserves of 400m. barrels, came into production in 1996. By the mid-1990s average annual output was some 9.5m. metric tons per year. The development of the Nkossa field increased annual output to 12.6m. tons by 1998, and, with AGIP's Kitina field coming on line, output again increased in 1999, to 13.2m. tons. Petroleum production peaked at 13.3m. tons in 2000, before declining every year to 11.2m. tons in 2004, as a result of lower production in maturing fields (including Nkossa). Production has since recovered to 12.5m. tons in 2005 and 13.9m. tons in 2006, as a result of new fields, including

Mboundi and Nsoko, coming on stream. Production was expected to increase further in the following year.

Natural gas production in Nkossa, the only place where natural gas is produced in the Congo, totalled 233,925 metric tons in 2005. The exploration of other areas, both onshore and offshore, has continued, and in 2003 the Government launched a new round of licensing for the exploration of several offshore petroleum fields. In 2006 the deep-water Moho-Bilondo field was the largest petroleum field under development in Congo. Output was expected to begin in 2008, with production expected to peak at 91,000 barrels per day. Total Congo is the operator, holding a 53.5% stake, followed by Chevron of the USA, with a 31.5% stake, and the state oil company, Société Nationale des Pétroles du Congo (SNPC), with a 15% stake. Total Congo (formerly Elf Congo) and AGIP Congo, respectively wholly-owned subsidiaries of French/Belgian and Italian companies, together account for 98% of the Congo's petroleum production.

In line with the continuing programme of privatization, the Government's stake in the petroleum industry has been declining. In 1995 the Government announced that, henceforth, instead of demanding royalty payments from producers, it would enter into production-sharing agreements. Thus, it sold its 25% share in Elf Congo to the French company Elf Aquitaine (which previously held 75% of the share capital), and its 20% share in AGIP Recherches Congo to the majority shareholder, Italy's AGIP-Eni. The Société nationale des pétroles du Congo (SNPC) was formally created in April 1998 to take over the downstream activities of the state-owned Société nationale de recherches et d'exploitation pétrolière (HYDRO-CONGO). In 2002 Total, ChevronTexaco and Puma Energy/X-oil assumed the sale and distribution activities formerly conducted by HYDRO-CONGO. However, by mid-2005, the petroleum refinery formerly controlled by HYDRO-CONGO, La Congolaise de Raffinage (CORAF), had yet to be privatized. Based in Point-Noire, the 1m.-metric ton capacity refinery resumed production in 2000 after a four-year hiatus. CORAF's output has remained well below capacity, however. In 2005 production of refined petroleum products amounted to 514,775 metric tons, less than had been anticipated, as a result of leakages and the destruction by fire of some production units. The Government has taken steps to increase transparency in managing the country's petroleum-sector revenue, for example by completing the audit of the 1999–2001 SNPC accounts in 2003 and by formally joining the Extractive Industry Transparency Initiative (EITI) in June 2004, although some irregularities continued to be recorded in 2005.

Lead, zinc, gold and copper are produced in small quantities, and deposits of phosphate and bauxite are known. Foreign interest in the non-petroleum mining sector has been increasing in recent years. Magnesium Alloy Corpn of Canada planned to develop magnesium deposits at a rate of 60,000 metric tons per year at Kouilou by 2007, once financing and equity investment for the project had been secured, and a subsidiary of Anglo-American, of South Africa, planned the construction of a ferro-silicon smelter. In June 2006 the Kamoto Copper Company (jointly owned by Canadian and Democratic Republic of the Congo—DRC—interests) started the exploitation of its mining site in Kolwezi. Copper and cobalt productions were expected to reach an eventual annual output of 150,000 metric tons and 5,000 tons respectively. In 2004 the Congolese Government granted diamond exploration rights to an Israeli-owned company, Brazzaville Mining Resource; and in 2007 three diamond exploration concessions were awarded to the Canadian-based company Mexiva Mining. Congo was disqualified from the Kimberley Certification Scheme in 2004, as a result of discrepancies between the country's diamond production and exports. The country applied for readmission in 2006.

Production and distribution of electricity have been in the hands of a state-owned corporation, the Société Nationale d'Electricité, since 1967; proposals for its privatization have been repeatedly delayed since the late 1990s, particularly because of infrastructural damage caused during the civil conflict. Net generating capacity was 118 MW in 2003, of which about three-quarters was accounted for by the hydroelectric stations on the Bouenza and Djoué. National electricity production totalled an estimated 434m. kWh in 2005, some 355m. kWh of which was hydroelectric. An estimated 417m kWh was imported from the neighbouring DRC.

The country's enormous hydroelectric potential remains underexploited, owing to the low level of domestic consumption and also because the infrastructure is lacking to export output to regional markets. The construction of a 120-MW hydroelectric power station on the Lefini River by the Congolese Government and two Chinese companies started in late 2003; completion was scheduled for 2009. This new power station would double the power-generating capacity of the country. The Government also intended eventually to use the country's natural gas resources for electricity production. In December 2002 AGIP and ChevronTexaco (of the USA—now Chevron) completed the country's first natural gas-fired power station near Pointe-Noire, with a capacity of 25 MW.

MANUFACTURING

Administrative bottlenecks and engrained corruption have continued to hinder private sector activities. Manufacturing mainly takes the form of the processing of agricultural and forest products, and most of the industry is in Brazzaville, Pointe-Noire and N'Kayi. The sector has been disadvantaged by the high value of the CFA franc, which has undermined its competitiveness. The sector is also hindered by energy rationing. Nevertheless, brewing is a significant industry, followed by sugar-cane processing and eucalyptus plantations, which are used to supply a telegraph-pole and charcoal factory. All these products also sell to export markets. Cement production started in 2004, leading to an estimated production of 62,000 tons in 2005. The manufacturing sector received a further boost in 2005 and 2006, as a result of increased capacity at the country's brewery and soft drink plants, production from which is principally destined for the domestic and sub-regional markets.

TRANSPORT AND TELECOMMUNICATIONS

The Republic of the Congo plays an important role in the trans-equatorial transport system that links Chad, the CAR and parts of Cameroon and Gabon with the Atlantic coast; all of the rail and much of the river portion of the system is located in the Congo. The deep-water port at Pointe-Noire is the terminus of this network, and is central Africa's second most important gateway, after Douala in Cameroon. Traffic at the port at Pointe-Noire resumed at the end of the civil war in 2000, when the port was dredged. In the first ten months of 2005, the port handled 1.1m. metric tons of import freight and 772,234 tons of export freight. The river system (in all more than 4,000 km is navigable) is also of great significance as a transport artery throughout the country, reaching areas that would otherwise be isolated (particularly in the north). The Port of Brazzaville handled 126,000 tons of freight in 2001, compared with 90,000 tons in the previous year.

Some 60%–70% of the traffic on the 518-km Congo-Océan railway (which links Pointe-Noire and Brazzaville) is of an international nature. Operations were suspended by fighting in the area from late 1998 to mid-2000, and again in mid-2002. Improved security conditions in the aftermath of the 2002 general elections and the 2003 peace agreement with rebels in the Pool region have since permitted rail traffic to resume. Rehabilitation work has been slow, however, and the railway has continued to encounter frequent disruption. A 10-year investment programme, worth US $623m., was announced in 2007. Rail transport amounted to an estimated 253,900 metric tons of freight and 167,300 passengers per year.

Other transport facilities, and especially the road network, are little developed, owing to the great distances and dense equatorial forest. Large areas in the north of the country have no road access, but proposals to build roads there have encountered opposition from environmental groups, as well as funding constraints. In 2004 there were an estimated 17,289 km of roads; only about 5.0% of the total network was paved, while a substantial proportion of the road network (as much as one-half of the total) became impassable as a result of the civil war, and some towns, particularly in the Pool region, become isolated, and without reliable access to major roads.

Poor communications and a poorly maintained transport infrastructure continued to constitute a major obstacle to economic development.

Spending on infrastructure remains a priority in the Government's public investment programme. The major highways from Brazzaville to Kinkala, the capital of the Pool region, were being ameliorated, with the support of the European Union. Plans for a year-round river port was being constructed at Lékéti, from where an upgraded road would extend to Lékoni, in Gabon, thereby facilitating trade, have been slow to materialize. There are international airports at Brazzaville and Pointe-Noire, as well as five regional airports and 12 smaller airfields. Construction of a new international airport at Ollombo, approximately 500 km north of Brazzaville began in early 2001; the airport, which was expected to open in 2008, was subject to much controversy. The refurbishment of the international airport at Brazzaville was completed in the early 2000s and new airlines, including Royal Air Maroc, have resumed flights to the capital in recent years.

The telecommunications sector has expanded, with two private-sector mobile phone companies, Celtel and Libertis, now operating in the country. The state-owned telecommunications company, Société des Télécommunications du Congo (Sotelco) has been mooted for privatization since 2002, following its separation from the postal functions of the Office national des postes et télécommunications.

PUBLIC FINANCE

The rise in petroleum taxes and royalties from 1978 onwards (constituting 70% of budget revenue in 1981) stimulated a sharp increase in budget development spending at the beginning of the 1980s. This increased 17-fold between 1979 and 1983, and formed the basis of the rapid growth in the economy at the beginning of the 1980s. Following a significant fall in petroleum revenues (as a result of a decline in market prices for petroleum products) from 1986, the Government turned to the IMF for support and adopted a structural adjustment programme, which aimed to restore balance to public finances through cuts in both current and capital spending. The reduction in the former was achieved by means of a wide range of measures, including a 'freeze' on government salaries and the rationalization of several loss-making state-owned companies. The improvement registered in 1990 with the surge in international petroleum prices after the Iraqi invasion of Kuwait proved short-lived, as tax receipts were affected by domestic political unrest in 1991–92. There was a substantial decrease in the deficit in subsequent years, as increased petroleum revenues in 1996 reflected the commencement of production at Nkossa and an increase in the share of revenues, from 17.5% to 31.0%, due to be paid to the Government in accordance with production-sharing agreements. Extra expenditure and a slump in revenues owing to the civil war resulted in a severe imbalance in 1997. In 1998 a deficit of 229,800m. francs CFA was recorded on a commitments basis (equivalent to 20.0% of GDP), as a result of the sharp decline in international petroleum prices and the resumption of fighting in late 1998. This led to a sharp accumulation in external payment arrears of 338,300m. francs CFA. In 1999 the budget deficit (on a commitments basis) narrowed to 84,800m. francs CFA, equivalent to 5.9% of GDP, with the decline attributable to cuts in spending and a recovery in international prices for petroleum. The Government continued to fall behind its debt-service obligations and payment arrears increased by 262,500m. francs CFA in that year. Reflecting the general recovery in economic activity and a nominal increase in petroleum revenue of 69.8%, the overall budget balance (on a commitment basis) turned into a surplus of 27,800m. francs CFA (equivalent to 1.2% of GDP) in 2000. A small deficit of 14,100m. francs CFA (0.7% of GDP) was recorded in 2001. Despite buoyant petroleum revenues, public finances deteriorated sharply in 2002 (an election year), as a result of expenditures over-runs. This led to an overall budget deficit of 171,000m. francs CFA, equivalent to 8.1% of GDP. The Government restored some fiscal discipline in 2003, when capital and recurrent spending were reduced by an average 18.9% and wages were frozen in accordance with the social truce that the Government signed with trade unions in August 2002. Tighter control of spending and higher-than-expected petroleum revenues (despite a decrease in production) led to a budgetary surplus of 7.4m. francs CFA, equivalent to 0.4% of GDP, being recorded in 2003. In 2004 the Government took additional steps to increase transparency in the petroleum sector and centralize government revenues. Expenditures remained within budget, which, combined with rising petroleum-sector revenue as a result of stronger international petroleum prices, induced an estimated budget surplus (including grants and on commitment basis) of 89,000m. francs CFA, equivalent to 3.9% GDP. In that year alone the Government settled 1,613,000m. francs CFA in external payment arrears. Revenues from petroleum increased almost two-fold in 2005, reaching the equivalent of 32% of GDP. As a result, 170,000m. francs CFA, equivalent to 5.4% of GDP, were transferred to the central bank's newly created petroleum stabilization account. Non-oil revenues were lower than expected, owing to poor customs collections, but the Government continued to maintain a tight control over both current and capital expenditures. As a result, the budget surplus increased to an estimated 500,300m. francs CFA in 2005, equivalent to 15.9% of GDP. Large expenditure slippage was recorded in 2006, however, prompting the IMF to suspend its PRGF.

FOREIGN TRADE AND PAYMENTS

The expansion of the Congo's petroleum sector, which began in the late 1970s, supported significant annual trade surpluses until 1986, when the fall in petroleum prices almost halved export earnings in that year. This, in conjunction with higher interest payments on the rapidly escalating foreign debt, prompted a sharp and sudden deterioration in the country's current account balance, which remained in deficit throughout the 1990s. Signs of a recovery started in 2000. The current account balance turned positive again in that year, at an equivalent 7.9% of GDP, as a result of rising international oil prices. Strong petroleum prices continued to offset declining oil output and the weakness of the US dollar against the franc CFA in subsequent years. According to revised figures, the current account balance recorded a deficit, equivalent to 5.6% of GDP, in 2001, before turning into a surplus equivalent to 0.6% of GDP in 2002 and 1% of GDP in 2003, on the back of rising petroleum export earnings. However, imbalances in the external capital account are such that the Government has traditionally struggled to meet its external debt obligations through much of the past two decades. This also reflected poor public finance management in selected years. Tighter fiscal discipline in 2004, combined with rising petroleum production and prices in the following year, has allowed the government to clear much of its external debt payment arrears. In the meantime, the current account surplus rose from 42,000m. francs CFA (an equivalent 2.2% of GDP) in 2004 to 344,000m. francs CFA (11.7% of GDP) in 2005.

In most years the Congo has received relatively low levels of foreign aid because of its petroleum wealth and poor record of economic management. Net inflows of official development assistance from countries of the Organisation for Economic Co-operation and Development and multilateral agencies were running at around US $120m. annually in the early and mid-1990s, but they surged to $362m. in 1994 (because of additional French aid in the aftermath of the devaluation of the CFA franc), and were again at unusually high levels in 1996 ($430m.) and 1997 ($268m.). With spending disrupted by the civil war, net inflows declined to an annual average of only $79m. in 1998–2001. Official assistance has since been slow to resume, reflecting slow peace reconciliation and delays in securing a new financial deal with the IMF. Net official transfers increased from $70m. in 2003 to $116m. in 2004.

While borrowing from official creditors expanded only slowly, borrowing from private creditors rose sharply in the early 1980s, mainly reflecting the expansion in imports and the excessive use of petroleum-collateralized loans. By the end of 1990 the external debt had risen to US $4,947m., or 212.9% of gross national income (GNI), making the Congo the most heavily indebted African nation, on a per-head basis. The debt-service ratio was 35.3%, a dangerously high level in view of the Government's practice of borrowing against future petroleum earnings. Backed by the new agreement with the IMF, a new programme of support by external donors, led by France, commenced in 1990, enabling the Congo to pay off some of its debt arrears, notably to the World Bank. Foreign indebtedness fluctuated slightly in the following three years, before reaching a new high of $6,004m. in 1995, equivalent to 488.8% of GNI (at the new US $: CFA franc parity). The situation eased in the following years, as a result of the rescheduling of $989m. in liabilities after the currency was devalued and, more significantly, the new round of debt relief extended in 1996, subsequent to IMF approval of an ESAF. Bilateral official creditors granted 'Naples terms' on all liabilities incurred before 1986. The debt-service ratio consequently decreased markedly, from 35.3% in 1990 to 13.1% in 1995, before decreasing further in the second half of the 1990s. The debt-service ratio fluctuated in the early 2000s, declining to only 1.0% in 2002, before increasing to 4.0% in the following year.

Interest and principal payment arrears again increased during the civil war and in 2003 amounted to US $1,042m. and $2,649m., respectively. By the end of that year the country's outstanding debt had increased to $5,527m., equivalent to 206.2% of GNI. While the country's total debt stocks increased, to $5,829m., in 2004, interest and principal payments arrears both declined, to $443m. and $1,778m., respectively. The Government made steady progress to regularize its situation with external creditors in 2004 and 2005. In December 2004, following the IMF approval of a three year financial facility, the 'Paris Club' of official creditors agreed to cancel $1,680m. and reschedule $1,336m. of Congo's debt. The country also owed substantial arrears to the 'London Club' of commercial creditors. The country subsequently reached 'decision point' under the enhanced initiative for heavily indebted poor countries (HIPC) of the Bretton Woods institutions in 2006. Debt relief under HIPC should lower Congo's debt-service payments by about $2,900m. in nominal terms. 'Completion point', however, which is when a country receives its full amount of debt relief, will depend on significant progress being made on aspects of governance and transparency, including public finance management and regular auditing of the oil and forestry sectors.

Statistical Survey

Source (unless otherwise stated): Direction Générale, Centre National de la Statistique et des Etudes Economiques, Immeuble du Plan, Rond point du Centre Culturel Français, BP 2031, Brazzaville; tel. and fax 81-59-09; e-mail cnsee@hotmail.com; internet www.cnsee.org.

Area and Population

AREA, POPULATION AND DENSITY

Area (sq km)	342,000*
Population (census results)	
22 December 1984	1,909,248
30 July 1996	2,591,271
Population (UN estimates at mid-year)†	
2004	3,530,000
2005	3,610,000
2006	3,689,000
Density (per sq km) at mid-2006	10.8

* 132,047 sq miles.

† Source: UN, *World Population Prospects: The 2006 Revision*.

ETHNIC GROUPS

1995 (percentages): Kongo 51.4; Téké 17.2; Mbochi 11.4; Mbédé 4.7; Punu 2.9; Sanga 2.5; Maka 1.8; Pygmy 1.4; Others 6.7 (Source: La Francophonie).

REGIONS

(population at 1996 census)

	Area (sq km)	Population	Capital
Bouenza	12,260	189,839	Madingou
Cuvette	74,850	112,946	Owando
Cuvette ouest		49,422	Ewo
Kouilou	13,650	77,048	Pointe-Noire
Lékoumou	20,950	75,734	Sibiti
Likouala	66,044	66,252	Impfondo
Niari	25,925	103,678	Loubomo (Dolisie)
Plateaux	38,400	139,371	Djambala
Pool	33,955	265,180	Kinkala
Sangha	55,795	39,439	Ouesso
Total*	341,829	1,118,909	

* Excluding the municipalities of Brazzaville (100 sq km, population 856,410), Pointe-Noire (45 sq km, population 455,131), Loubomo (Dolisie—18 sq km, population 79,852), Nkaya (8 sq km, population 46,727), Ouesso (population 17,784) and Mossendjo (population 16,458).

PRINCIPAL TOWNS

(population at 1996 census)

Brazzaville (capital)	856,410	Loubomo (Dolisie)	79,852
Pointe-Noire	455,131	Nkaya	46,727

BIRTHS AND DEATHS

(annual averages, UN estimates)

	1990–95	1995–2000	2000–05
Birth rate (per 1,000)	38.5	37.2	35.1
Death rate (per 1,000)	11.1	12.6	12.7

Source: UN, *World Population Prospects: The 2006 Revision*.

Expectation of life (years at birth, WHO estimates): 54 (males 53; females 55) in 2004 (Source: WHO, *World Health Report*).

EMPLOYMENT

('000 persons at 1984 census)

	Males	Females	Total
Agriculture, etc.	105	186	291
Industry	61	8	69
Services	123	60	183
Total	289	254	543

Mid-2005 (estimates in '000): Agriculture, etc. 584; Total labour force 1,603 (Source: FAO).

Health and Welfare

KEY INDICATORS

Total fertility rate (children per woman, 2005)	6.3
Under-5 mortality rate (per 1,000 live births, 2005)	108
HIV/AIDS (% of persons aged 15–49, 2005)	5.3
Physicians (per 1,000 head, 2004)	0.20
Hospital beds (per 1,000 head, 1990)	3.35
Health expenditure (2004): US $ per head (PPP)	30.1
Health expenditure (2004): % of GDP	2.5
Health expenditure (2004): public (% of total)	49.2
Access to water (% of persons, 2004)	58
Access to sanitation (% of persons, 2004)	27
Human Development Index (2004): ranking	140
Human Development Index (2004): value	0.520

For sources and definitions, see explanatory note on p. vi.

Agriculture

PRINCIPAL CROPS
('000 metric tons)

	2003	2004	2005
Maize	9.0	9.2	8.0*
Sweet potatoes†	6.0	5.8	5.6
Cassava (Manioc)	877.8	932.2	900.0†
Cassava leaves	48.6	50.3	52.0†
Yams	11.0	11.4	11.0†
Sugar cane	601.7	616.8	550.0
Groundnuts (in shell)†	23.7	22.2	21.3
Oil palm fruit†	90.0	90.9	91.5
Vegetables (incl. melons)†	95.9	98.1	99.9
Bananas†	88.0	92.5	96.9
Plantains	58.8	61.4	65.0†
Guavas, mangoes and mangosteens	25.0	26.0	26.8
Avocados	6.3	6.6	6.5†

* Unofficial figure.
† FAO estimate(s).

Source: FAO.

LIVESTOCK
('000 head, year ending September, FAO estimates)

	2003	2004	2005
Cattle	100	110	115
Pigs	46.3	46.3	46.5
Sheep	98	98	99
Goats	294.2	294.2	295.0
Chickens	2,230	2,300	2,400

Source: FAO.

LIVESTOCK PRODUCTS
('000 metric tons, FAO estimates)

	2003	2004	2005
Cattle meat	1.9	2.0	2.2
Pig meat	2.1	2.1	2.1
Chicken meat	5.2	5.4	5.6
Game meat	18.0	20.0	20.0
Sheep and goat meat	1.1	1.1	1.1
Cows' milk	1.1	1.1	1.1
Hen eggs	1.2	1.2	1.2

Source: FAO.

Forestry

ROUNDWOOD REMOVALS
('000 cubic metres, excluding bark)

	2003	2004	2005
Sawlogs, veneer logs and logs for sleepers	194	165	165*
Pulpwood*	361	361	361
Other industrial wood*	370	370	370
Fuel wood*	1,202	1,219	1,237
Total	2,127	2,115	2,133

* FAO estimate(s).

Source: FAO.

SAWNWOOD PRODUCTION
('000 cubic metres, including railway sleepers)

	2002	2003	2004
Total (all broadleaved)	169.7	168.0	157.0

2005: Production as in 2004 (FAO estimate).

Source: FAO.

Fishing

('000 metric tons, live weight)

	2003	2004	2005
Capture	54.7	54.2	58.4
Freshwater fishes	31.2	30.3	32.5
West African croakers	3.0	2.3	2.8
Sardinellas	7.3	7.9	9.7
Aquaculture	0.0	0.0	0.0
Total catch	54.7	54.3	58.4

Source: FAO.

Mining

	2003	2004	2005
Crude petroleum ('000 barrels)	81,646	82,069	92,550
Gold (kg)*	75	60	20

* Estimated metal content of ore.

Source: US Geological Survey.

Industry

SELECTED PRODUCTS
('000 metric tons, unless otherwise indicated)

	2002	2003	2004
Raw sugar	56	45	65
Veneer sheets ('000 cu metres)	23	3	8
Jet fuels	43	38	47
Motor gasoline (petrol)	41	53	49
Kerosene	19	21	19
Distillate fuel oils	75	119	120
Residual fuel oils	228	287	295
Electric energy (million kWh)	397	343	399

Source: UN, *Industrial Commodity Statistics Yearbook*.

Finance

CURRENCY AND EXCHANGE RATES

Monetary Units

100 centimes = 1 franc de la Coopération financière en Afrique centrale (CFA).

Sterling, Dollar and Euro Equivalents (31 May 2007)

£1 sterling = 964.12 francs CFA;
US $1 = 487.59 francs CFA;
€1 = 655.957 francs CFA;
10,000 francs CFA = £10.37 = $20.51 = €15.24.

Average Exchange Rate (francs CFA per US $)

2004	528.29
2005	527.47
2006	522.89

Note: The exchange rate of 1 French franc = 50 francs CFA, established in 1948, remained in force until January 1994, when the CFA franc was devalued by 50%, with the exchange rate adjusted to 1 French franc = 100 francs CFA. The relationship to French currency remained in effect with the introduction of the euro on 1 January 1999. From that date, accordingly, a fixed exchange rate of €1 = 655.957 francs CFA has been in operation.

BUDGET

('000 million francs CFA)

Revenue*	2003	2004	2005†
Petroleum revenue	422	530	1,020
Royalties	149	n.a.	n.a.
Government profit share sold by SNPC	251	n.a.	n.a.
Other revenue	182	208	220
Domestic taxes	134	149	168
Direct	64	72	43
Indirect	70	78	125
Customs receipts	43	50	43
Non-tax revenue	5	9	10
Total	604	738	1,240

Expenditure‡	2003	2004	2005†
Current expenditure	471	496	575
Wages and salaries	120	123	130
Materials and supplies	50	55	62
Transfers	131	123	142
Common charges	43	52	66
Interest payments	118	128	158
External	94	111	128
Domestic	23	17	30
Local authorities	9	15	17
Capital expenditure	135	161	170
Externally financed	24	32	16
Domestically financed	111	128	154
Total	605	656	745

* Excluding grants received ('000 million francs CFA): 10 in 2003; 8 in 2004; 6 in 2005 (estimate).

† Estimates.

‡ Excluding net lending ('000 million francs CFA): 1 in 2003; 0 in 2004; 0 in 2005 (estimate).

Source: IMF, *Republic of Congo: Statistical Appendix* (June 2007).

INTERNATIONAL RESERVES

(US $ million at 31 December)

	2004	2005	2006
Gold (national valuation)	4.88	5.71	7.06
IMF special drawing rights	7.23	2.43	0.19
Reserve position in IMF	0.83	0.77	0.81
Foreign exchange	111.54	728.63	429.08
Total	124.48	737.54	437.14

Source: IMF, *International Financial Statistics*.

MONEY SUPPLY

('000 million francs CFA at 31 December)

	2004	2005	2006
Currency outside banks	155.89	207.24	271.24
Demand deposits at active commercial banks	110.72	159.98	273.02
Total money (incl. others)	278.79	396.19	584.61

Source: IMF, *International Financial Statistics*.

COST OF LIVING

(Consumer Price Index for Brazzaville; base: 2000 = 100)

	2004	2005	2006
Food	90.8	95.6	105.3
Clothing	106.7	n.a.	n.a.
Fuel and electricity	110.3	n.a.	n.a.
All items (incl. others)	106.4	109.6	116.8

Source: ILO.

NATIONAL ACCOUNTS

('000 million francs CFA at current prices)

Expenditure on the Gross Domestic Product

	2003	2004	2005*
Final consumption expenditure	1,008	1,118	1,300
Households; Non-profit institutions serving households	656	751	883
General government	353	368	417
Gross capital formation	532	556	707
Gross fixed capital formation	520	541	692
Changes in inventories; Acquisitions, less disposals, of valuables	12	15	15
Total domestic expenditure	1,540	1,774	2,007
Exports of goods and services	1,642	1,935	2,722
Less Imports of goods and services	1,112	1,315	1,579
GDP in market prices	2,072	2,294	3,150
GDP at constant 1990 prices	961	995	1,072

* Estimates.

Gross Domestic Product by Economic Activity

	2003	2004	2005*
Agriculture, hunting, forestry and fishing	133	136	148
Mining and manufacturing†	1,170	1,349	2,073
Electricity, gas and water	19	20	23
Construction	86	91	105
Trade, restaurants and hotels	184	197	225
Transport, storage and communications	130	140	163
Government services	148	152	173
Other services	138	147	170
GDP at factor cost	2,009	2,230	3,080
Import duties	63	65	69
GDP in purchasers' values	2,072	2,294	3,150

* Estimates.

† Including petroleum sector ('000 million francs CFA): 1,036 in 2003; 1,205 in 2004; 1,902 in 2005 (estimate).

Source: IMF, *Republic of Congo: Statistical Appendix* (June 2007).

BALANCE OF PAYMENTS
(US $ million)

	2003	2004	2005
Exports of goods f.o.b.	2,636.5	3,433.2	4,729.8
Imports of goods f.o.b.	−831.1	−969.0	−1,356.1
Trade balance	1,805.4	2,464.2	3,373.7
Exports of services	194.1	196.7	234.7
Imports of services	−875.4	−1,016.3	−1,560.5
Balance on goods and services	1,124.1	1,644.6	2,047.9
Other income received	10.3	13.3	15.4
Other income paid	−596.4	−961.8	−1,137.7
Balance on goods, services and income	538.0	696.0	925.6
Current transfers received	26.5	34.5	31.5
Current transfers paid	−44.0	−56.0	−53.8
Current balance	520.5	674.4	903.2
Capital account (net)	16.9	12.7	5.7
Direct investment abroad	−1.7	−4.5	n.a.
Direct investment from abroad	323.1	−8.5	724.0
Portfolio investment liabilities	−0.2	2.1	−13.1
Other investment assets	−180.3	−440.7	n.a.
Other investment liabilities	−842.4	−323.3	−1,534.1
Net errors and omissions	−116.0	−92.8	325.8
Overall balance	−280.1	−180.7	411.5

Source: IMF, *International Financial Statistics*.

External Trade

PRINCIPAL COMMODITIES
(distribution by SITC, US $ million)

Imports c.i.f.	2003
Food and live animals	144.3
Meat and meat preparations	39.0
Fish, crustaceans, molluscs and preparations thereof	29.3
Cereals and cereal preparations	36.2
Chemicals and related products	97.2
Medicinal and pharmaceutical products	39.0
Basic manufactures	134.2
Non-metallic mineral manufactures	22.7
Iron and steel	47.6
Machinery and transport equipment	196.7
Road vehicles and parts*	41.5
Miscellaneous manufactured articles	62.7
Total (incl. others)	681.5

Exports f.o.b.	2001	2002	2003
Crude materials (inedible) except fuels	111.9	140.7	216.3
Cork and wood	111.9	140.7	216.3
Wood in the rough or roughly squared	71.7	108.8	167.6
Wood, simply worked and railway sleepers of wood	40.2	31.9	48.7
Mineral fuels, lubricants, etc.	1,177.4	2,252.6	1,465.2
Petroleum, petroleum products, etc.	1,177.4	2,148.8	1,418.3
Crude petroleum oils, etc.	1,129.9	2,102.6	1,418.3
Refined petroleum oils, etc	47.5	46.2	n.a.
Total (incl. others)	1,313.1	2,423.2	1,722.0

* Data on parts exclude tyres, engines and electrical parts.

Source: UN, *International Trade Statistics Yearbook*.

PRINCIPAL TRADING PARTNERS
(US $ million)

Imports c.i.f.	2000	2001	2002
Belgium	23.5	24.3	31.8
Cameroon	19.7	22.2	23.0
China, People's Rep.	4.1	6.8	26.0
Côte d'Ivoire	7.1	6.9	7.0
France (incl. Monaco)	139.4	127.2	166.4
Gabon	8.1	9.0	2.9
Germany	11.4	16.3	23.3
India	6.1	6.0	11.9
Indonesia	4.2	6.2	5.6
Italy	41.2	79.7	53.2
Japan	21.0	27.6	21.4
Lebanon	0.2	0.6	38.1
Netherlands	29.3	29.2	29.0
Saudi Arabia	3.0	3.6	9.1
Senegal	5.7	5.1	5.7
South Africa	10.8	14.7	11.8
Thailand	7.2	7.2	7.5
United Kingdom	19.7	21.5	24.1
USA	66.6	59.2	66.4
Total (incl. others)	517.6	564.2	643.5

Exports f.o.b.	2001	2002	2003
Brazil	21.7	16.5	56.5
Cameroon	1.1	26.7	10.2
Chile	10.9	33.6	—
China, People's Rep.	78.0	168.8	375.8
France (incl. Monaco)	25.1	175.5	68.4
Germany	4.4	142.7	8.8
Iceland	1.5	63.0	47.5
India	20.6	18.8	—
Indonesia	—	21.3	24.9
Israel	0.8	36.7	2.9
Italy	38.0	39.3	21.9
Japan	1.7	97.1	0.4
Korea, Democratic People's Rep.	207.0	271.5	131.0
Korea, Rep.	20.6	174.7	239.1
Netherlands	21.2	35.3	8.6
Portugal	17.7	24.9	38.9
Singapore	0.3	44.3	0.1
Spain	15.8	18.2	26.7
USA	273.3	252.4	165.3
Total (incl others)	1,313.1	2,423.2	1,722.0

Source: UN, *International Trade Statistics Yearbook*.

Transport

RAILWAYS
(traffic)

	1999	2000	2001
Passengers carried ('000)	56.5	546.0	742.0
Freight carried ('000 metric tons)	65.7	236.0	548.0

Passenger-km (million): 9 in 1999.

Freight ton-km (million): 21 in 1999.

Sources: UN, *Statistical Yearbook;* IMF, *Republic of Congo: Selected Issues and Statistical Appendix* (July 2004).

ROAD TRAFFIC
(estimates, '000 motor vehicles in use)

	1999	2000	2001
Passenger cars	26.2	29.7	29.7
Commercial vehicles	20.4	23.1	23.1

Source: UN, *Statistical Yearbook*.

SHIPPING

Merchant Fleet
(registered at 31 December)

	2004	2005	2006
Number of vessels	18	19	19
Total displacement ('000 grt)	3.4	3.6	3.6

Source: Lloyd's Register-Fairplay, *World Fleet Statistics*.

Freight Traffic at Pointe-Noire
(metric tons)

	1996	1997	1998
Goods loaded	670,150	708,203	n.a.
Goods unloaded	584,376	533,170	724,000*

* Rounded figure.

Source: mainly Banque des états de l'Afrique centrale, *Etudes et Statistiques*.

CIVIL AVIATION
(traffic on scheduled services)*

	2001	2002	2003
Kilometres flown (million)	3	1	1
Passengers carried ('000)	95	47	52
Passenger-km (million)	157	27	31
Total ton-km (million)	22	3	3

* Including an apportionment of the traffic of Air Afrique.

Source: UN, *Statistical Yearbook*.

Tourism

FOREIGN VISITORS BY COUNTRY OF RESIDENCE*

	2000	2001	2002
Angola	1,747	1,767	2,169
Belgium	230	443	477
Cameroon	591	832	950
Central African Republic	238	208	172
Congo, Democratic Rep.	2,172	2,481	2,402
Côte d'Ivoire	401	1,380	633
France	4,831	8,576	6,196
Gabon	906	1,192	907
Germany	230	119	103
Italy	869	841	382
Senegal	354	379	253
Togo	270	86	58
United Kingdom	640	584	505
USA	518	408	414
Total (incl. others)	18,797	27,363	21,611

* Arrivals at hotels and similar establishments.

Receipts from tourism (US $ million, incl. passenger transport): 12.4 in 2000; 22.6 in 2001; 25.6 in 2002.

Source: World Tourism Organization.

Communications Media

	2002	2003	2004
Telephones ('000 main lines in use)	22.0	7.0	13.8
Mobile cellular telephones ('000 subscribers)	221.8	330.0	383.7
Personal computers ('000 in use)	13	15	17
Internet users ('000)	5	15	36

2005: Mobile cellular telephones ('000 subscribers) 490.0.

Source: International Telecommunication Union.

1997: Radio receivers ('000 in use): 341; Television receivers ('000 in use): 33 (Source: UNESCO, *Statistical Yearbook*).

Daily newspapers (national estimates): 6 in 1997 (average circulation 20,500 copies); 6 in 1998 (average circulation 20,600 copies) (Source: UNESCO Institute for Statistics).

Non-daily newspapers: 15 in 1995 (average circulation 38,000 copies) (Source: UNESCO, *Statistical Yearbook*).

Education

(2003/04, except where otherwise indicated)

	Institutions*	Teachers	Students: Males	Students: Females	Students: Total
Pre-primary	95	1,120	10,512	11,135	21,647
Primary	1,168	7,058	303,104	281,266	584,370
Secondary	n.a.	76,866	128,149	107,145	235,294
Tertiary†	n.a.	894	10,487	1,969	12,456

* 1998/99.
† 2002/03.

Sources: mostly UNESCO Institute for Statistics.

Adult literacy rate (UNESCO estimates): 82.8% (males 88.9%; females 77.1%) in 2002 (Source: UN Development Programme, *Human Development Report*).

Directory

The Constitution

The 1992 Constitution was suspended following the assumption of power by Gen. Denis Sassou-Nguesso on 15 October 1997. A new Constitution, which was approved by the Conseil national de transition (interim legislative body) on 2 September 2001 and endorsed by a public referendum on 20 January 2002, took effect following presidential and legislative elections in March–July 2002. Its main provisions are summarized below:

PREAMBLE

The Congolese people, having chosen a pluralist democracy as the basis for the development of the country, condemn the tyrannical use of power and political violence and declare that the fundamental principles proclaimed and guaranteed by the UN Charter, the Universal Declaration of Human Rights and other international treaties form an integral part of the present Constitution.

I. THE STATE AND SOVEREIGNTY

Articles 1–6: The Republic of the Congo is a sovereign, secular, social and democratic State. The principle of the Republic is government of the people, by the people and for the people. National sovereignty belongs to the people, who exercise it through universal suffrage by their elected representatives or by referendum. The official language of the Republic is French. The national languages of communication are Lingala and Kituba.

II. FUNDAMENTAL RIGHTS AND LIBERTIES

Articles 7–42: All citizens are equal before the law. Arbitrary arrest and all degrading forms of punishment are prohibited, and all accused are presumed innocent until proven guilty. Incitement to ethnic hatred, violence or civil war and the use of religion to political ends are forbidden. Equal access to education, which is compulsory until the age of 16, is guaranteed to all. The State is obliged to create conditions that enable all citizens to enjoy the right to work. All citizens, excluding members of the police and military forces, may participate in trade union activity. Slavery is forbidden, and forced labour permitted only as a judicial punishment.

III. DUTIES

Articles 43–50: All citizens have duties towards their family, society, the State and other legally recognized authorities. All citizens are obliged to conform to the Constitution, the laws of the Republic and to fulfil their obligations towards the State and society.

IV. POLITICAL PARTIES

Articles 51–55: Political parties may not be identified with an ethnic group, a region, a religion or a sect. They must protect and promote fundamental human rights, the rule of law, democracy, individual and collective freedoms, national territorial integrity and sovereignty, proscribe intolerance, ethnically based extremism, and any recourse to violence, and respect the secular form of the State.

V. EXECUTIVE POWER

Articles 56–88: The President of the Republic is the Head of State, Head of the Executive and Head of Government. The President is directly elected by an absolute majority of votes cast, for a term of seven years, renewable once. Presidential candidates must be of Congolese nationality and origin, aged between 40 and 70 years and have resided on national territory for at least 24 successive months prior to registering as a candidate. If required, a second round of voting takes place between the two highest-placed candidates in the first ballot. In the event of the death, resignation, or long-term incapacity of the President of the Republic, the President of the Sénat assumes limited executive functions for up to 90 days, pending an election, which he may not contest.

The President appoints ministers, senior civil servants, military staff and ambassadors. Ministers may not hold a parliamentary mandate or civic, public or military post, and their professional activity is restricted. The President of the Republic is the Supreme Head of the armed forces and the President of the Higher Council of Magistrates, and possesses the right of pardon. The President of the Republic chairs the Council of Ministers.

VI. LEGISLATIVE POWER

Articles 89–113: The Parliament is bicameral. Deputies are directly elected to the Assemblée nationale for a renewable term of five years. Senators are elected indirectly to the Sénat by local councils for a term of six years. One-half of the Sénat is elected every three years. Deputies and senators must be Congolese nationals, aged over 25 years in the case of deputies, or over 45 years in the case of senators, residing in national territory. A deputy or senator elected as a member of a political grouping may not resign from the grouping without simultaneously resigning his parliamentary position.

VII. RELATIONS BETWEEN THE LEGISLATIVE AND EXECUTIVE INSTITUTIONS

Articles 114–132: The President of the Republic may not dissolve the Assemblée nationale. The Assemblée nationale may not remove the President of the Republic. The legislative chambers consider proposed legislation in succession, with a view to adopting an identical text. If necessary, the President of the Republic may convene a joint commission to present a revised text to the two chambers. The President of the Republic may then call the Assemblée nationale to make a final decision. Special conditions apply to the passage of certain laws, including the national budget, and to a declaration of war or state of emergency.

VIII. JUDICIAL POWER

Articles 133–143: Judicial power is exercised by the Supreme Court, the Revenue and Budgetary Discipline Court, appeal courts and other national courts of law, which are independent of the legislature. The President of the Republic chairs a Higher Council of Magistrates, which guarantees the independence of the judiciary. The President of the Republic nominates judges to the Supreme Court and to the other courts of law, at the suggestion of the Higher Council of Magistrates. Judges of the Supreme Court may not be removed from office.

IX. CONSTITUTIONAL COURT

Articles 144–151: The Constitutional Court consists of nine members, each with a renewable mandate of nine years. One-third of the Court is renewed every three years. The President of the Republic nominates three members of the Constitutional Court independently, and the others at the suggestion of the President of each legislative chamber and of the Bureau of the Supreme Court. The President of the Republic nominates the President of the Constitutional Court. The Court ensures that laws, treaties and international agreements conform to the Constitution and oversees presidential elections.

X. HIGH COURT OF JUSTICE

Articles 152–156: The High Court of Justice is composed of an equal number of deputies and senators elected by their peers, and of members of the Supreme Court elected by their peers. It is chaired by the First President of the Supreme Court and is competent to try the President of the Republic in case of high treason. Members of the legislature, the Supreme Court and the Constitutional Court and government ministers are accountable to the High Court of Justice for crimes or offences committed in the execution of their duties, subject to a two-thirds' majority in a secret vote at a joint session of Parliament.

XI. ECONOMIC AND SOCIAL COUNCIL

Articles 157–160: The Economic and Social Council is a consultative assembly, which may become involved in any economic or social problem concerning the Republic, either of its own will or at the request of the President of the Republic or the President of either legislative chamber.

XII. HIGHER COUNCIL FOR THE FREEDOM OF COMMUNICATION

Articles 161–162: The Higher Council for the Freedom of Communication ensures freedom of information and communication, formulating recommendations on applicable issues.

XIII. MEDIATOR OF THE REPUBLIC

Articles 163–166: The Mediator of the Republic is an independent authority responsible for simplifying and humanizing relations between government and citizens, and may be addressed by any person dissatisfied with the workings of any public organization.

XIV. NATIONAL COMMISSION FOR HUMAN RIGHTS

Articles 167–169: The National Commission for Human Rights seeks to promote and protect human rights.

XV. POLICE AND MILITARY FORCES

Articles 170–173: The police and military bodies consist of the national police force, the national gendarmerie and the Congolese armed forces. These bodies are apolitical and subordinate to the civil authority. The creation of militia groups is prohibited.

XVI. LOCAL AUTHORITIES

Articles 174–177: The local administrative bodies of the Republic of the Congo are the department and the commune, and any others created by law.

XVII. INTERNATIONAL TREATIES AND AGREEMENTS

Articles 178–184: The President of the Republic negotiates, signs and, with the approval of Parliament, ratifies international treaties and agreements. Any proposed change to the territorial boundaries of the Republic must be submitted to popular referendum.

XVIII. ON REVISION

Articles 185–187: The Constitution may be revised at the initiative of the President of the Republic or members of Parliament. The territorial integrity of the Republic, the republican form of government, the secular nature of the State, the number of presidential terms of office permitted and the rights outlined in sections I and II (above) may not be the subject of any revision. Any constitutional amendments proposed by the President of the Republic are submitted directly to a referendum. Any constitutional changes proposed by Parliament must be approved by two-thirds of the members of both legislative chambers convened in congress, before being submitted to referendum. In both cases the Constitutional Court must have declared the acceptability of the proposals.

The Government

HEAD OF STATE

President: Gen. DENIS SASSOU-NGUESSO (assumed power 15 October 1997; inaugurated 25 October 1997; elected 10 March 2002).

COUNCIL OF MINISTERS

(August 2007)

Prime Minister, responsible for the Co-ordination of Government Action and Privatization: ISIDORE MVOUBA.

Minister at the Presidency, responsible for National Defence, Veterans and the War Disabled: Gen. JACQUES YVON NDOLOU.

Minister at the Presidency, responsible for Co-operation, Humanitarian Action and Solidarity: CHARLES ZACHARIE BOWAO.

Minister at the Presidency, responsible for Regional Integration and NEPAD: JUSTIN BALLAY MEGOT.

Minister of State, Keeper of the Seals, Minister of Justice and Human Rights: AIMÉ EMMANUEL YOKA.

Minister of State, Minister of Planning and Land Management: PIERRE MOUSSA.

Minister of State, Minister of Foreign Affairs and the Francophonie: BASILE IKOUÉBÉ.

Minister of State, Minister of the Civil Service and the Reform of the State: JEAN-MARTIN MBEMBA.

Minister of State, Minister of Hydrocarbons: JEAN-BAPTISTE TATI LOUTARD.

Minister of the Economy, Finance and the Budget: PACIFIQUE ISSOÏBEKA.

Minister of Mining, Extractive Industry and Geology: Gen. PIERRE OBA.

Minister of Capital and Public Works: Gen. FLORENT NTSIBA.

Minister of Agriculture, Stockbreeding and Fisheries: JEANNE DAMBANDZET.

Minister of the Forest Economy: HENRI DJOMBO.

Minister of Construction, Town Planning and Living Conditions: CLAUDE ALPHONSE NSILOU.

Minister of Territorial Administration and Decentralization: FRANÇOIS IBOVI.

Minister of Transport and Civil Aviation: EMILE OUSSO.

Minister of Land Reform and the Preservation of the Public Domain: LAMYR NGUELÉ.

Minister of Technical Education and Vocational Training: PIERRE MICHEL NGUIMBI.

Minister of Higher Education: HENRI OSSEBI.

Minister of Industrial Development and the Promotion of the Private Sector: EMILE MABONZOT.

Minister of Trade, Consumption and Supplies: ADÉLAÏDE MOUNDÉLÉ-NGOLLO.

Minister of Posts and Telecommunications, responsible for New Technologies: GABRIEL ENTCHA EBIA.

Minister of Primary and Secondary Education and Literacy: ROSALIE KAMA.

Minister of Culture and the Arts: JEAN-CLAUDE GAKOSSO.

Minister of Labour, Employment and Social Security: GILBERT ONDONGO.

Minister of Energy and Water Resources: BRUNO JEAN-RICHARDS ITOUA.

Minister of Communication, responsible for Relations with Parliament, Government Spokesperson: ALAIN AKOUALA-ATIPAULT.

Minister of Security and Public Order: Gen. PAUL MBOT.

Minister of Scientific Research and Technical Innovation: PIERRE ERNEST ABANDZOUNOU.

Minister of Sports and Youth Redeployment: MARCEL MBANI.

Minister of Health, Social Affairs and Families: EMILIENNE RAOUL.

Minister of the Maritime Economy and the Merchant Navy: LOUIS-MARIE NOMBO MAVOUNGOU.

Minister of the Promotion of Women and the Integration of Women into Development: JEANNE FRANÇOISE LÉKOMBA LOUMÉTO-POMBO.

Minister of Small and Medium-sized Enterprises and Crafts: MARTIN PARFAIT AIMÉ COUSSOUD-MAVOUNGOU.

Minister of Tourism and the Environment: ANDRÉ OKOMBI SALISSA.

MINISTRIES

Office of the President: Palais du Peuple, Brazzaville; tel. 81-17-11; e-mail contact@presicongo.cg; internet www.presidence.cg.

Office of the Prime Minister: Brazzaville; tel. 81-10-67; internet www.congo-site.net.

Office of the Minister at the Presidency, responsible for Co-operation, Humanitarian Action and Solidarity: Brazzaville; tel. 81-10-89.

Office of the Minister at the Presidency, responsible for National Defence, Veterans and the War Disabled: Brazzaville; tel. 81-22-31.

Office of the Minister at the Presidency, responsible for Regional Integration and NEPAD: Brazzaville.

Ministry of Agriculture, Stockbreeding and Fisheries: BP 2453, Brazzaville; tel. 81-41-31; fax 81-19-29.

Ministry of Capital and Public Works: BP 2099, Brazzaville; tel. 81-59-41; fax 81-59-07.

Ministry of the Civil Service and the Reform of the State: BP 12151, Brazzaville; tel. 81-41-68; fax 81-41-49.

Ministry of Communication, responsible for Relations with Parliament: BP 114, Brazzaville; tel. 81-41-29; fax 81-41-28; e-mail depcompt@congonet.cg.

Ministry of Construction, Town Planning and Living Conditions: BP 1580, Brazzaville; tel. 81-34-48; fax 81-12-97.

Ministry of Culture and the Arts: BP 20480, Brazzaville; tel. 81-02-35; fax 81-40-25.

Ministry of the Economy, Finance and the Budget: ave de l'Indépendance, croisement ave Foch, BP 2083, Brazzaville; tel. 81-45-24; fax 81-43-69; internet www.mefb-cg.org.

Ministry of Energy and Water Resources: Brazzaville.

Ministry of Foreign Affairs and the Francophonie: BP 2070, Brazzaville; tel. 81-10-89; fax 81-41-61.

Ministry of the Forest Economy: Immeuble de l'Agriculture, Face à Blanche Gomez, BP 98, Brazzaville; tel. 81-41-37; fax 81-41-34; e-mail secretariat@minifor.com; internet www.minifor.com.

Ministry of Health, Social Affairs and Families: BP 20101, Brazzaville; tel. 81-30-75; fax 81-14-33.

Ministry of Higher Education: Ancien Immeuble de la Radio, BP 169, Brazzaville; tel. 81-08-15; fax 81-52-65.

Ministry of Hydrocarbons: BP 2120, Brazzaville; tel. 81-10-86; fax 81-10-85.

Ministry of Industrial Development and the Promotion of the Private Sector: Centre Administratif, Quartier Plateau, BP 2117, Brazzaville; tel. 81-30-09; fax 81-06-43.

Ministry of Justice and Human Rights: BP 2497, Brazzaville; tel. and fax 81-41-49.

Ministry of Labour, Employment and Social Security: Immeuble de la BCC, ave Foch, BP 2075, Brazzaville; tel. 81-41-43; fax 81-05-50.

Ministry of Land Reform and the Preservation of the Public Domain: Brazzaville; tel. 81-34-48.

Ministry of the Maritime Economy and the Merchant Navy: Brazzaville; tel. 81-10-67; fax 82-55-14.

Ministry of Mining, Extractive Industry and Geology: BP 2124, Brazzaville; tel. 81-02-64; fax 81-50-77.

Ministry of Planning, Land Management: BP 64, Brazzaville; tel. 81-06-56; fax 81-58-08.

Ministry of Posts and Telecommunications, responsible for New Technologies: BP 44, Brazzaville; tel. 81-41-18; fax 81-19-34.

Ministry of Primary and Secondary Education and Literacy: BP 5253, Brazzaville; tel. 81-24-52; fax 81-25-39.

Ministry of the Promotion of Women and the Integration of Women into Development: Brazzaville; tel. 81-19-29.

Ministry of Scientific Research and Technical Innovation: Ancien Immeuble de la Radio, Brazzaville; tel. 81-03-59.

Ministry of Security and Public Order: BP 2474, Brazzaville; tel. 81-41-73; fax 81-34-04.

Ministry of Small and Medium-sized Enterprises and Crafts: Brazzaville.

Ministry of Social Affairs, Solidarity, Humanitarian Action and the Family: BP 2066, Brazzaville; tel. 81-53-39; fax 81-57-56.

Ministry of Sports and Youth Redeployment: BP 2061, Brazzaville; tel. 60-89-24.

Ministry of Technical Education and Vocational Training: BP 2076, Brazzaville; tel. 81-17-27; fax 81-56-82; e-mail metp_cab@yahoo.fr.

Ministry of Territorial Administration and Decentralization: BP 880, Brazzaville; tel. 81-40-60; fax 81-33-17.

Ministry of Tourism and Environment: Brazzaville.

Ministry of Trade, Consumption and Supplies: BP 2965, Brazzaville; tel. 81-41-16; fax 81-41-57; e-mail mougany@yahoo.fr.

Ministry of Transport and Civil Aviation: Immeuble Mafoua Virgile, BP 2066, Brazzaville; tel. 81-53-39; fax 81-57-56.

President and Legislature

PRESIDENT

Presidential Election, 10 March 2002

Candidate	Votes	% of votes
Denis Sassou-Nguesso	1,075,247	89.41
Joseph Kignoumbi Kia Mbougou	33,154	2.76
Angèle Bandou	27,849	2.32
Jean-Félix Demba Ntello	20,252	1.68
Luc Adamo Matéta	19,074	1.59
Côme Mankassa	15,054	1.25
Bonaventure Mizidi Bavouenza	11,981	1.00
Total	1,202,611	100.00

LEGISLATURE

The legislature, Parlement, comprises two chambers: a directly elected lower house, the Assemblée nationale; and an indirectly elected upper house, the Sénat.

Assemblée nationale

Palais du Parlement, BP 2106, Brazzaville; tel. 81-11-12; fax 81-41-28; e-mail dsancongo@yahoo.fr.

President: JEAN-PIERRE THYSTÈRE TCHIKAYA.

General Election, 26 May and 23 June 2002*

Party	Seats
Parti congolais du travail (PCT)	53
Forces démocratiques unies (FDU) †	30
Union pour la démocratie et la République—Mwinda (UDR—Mwinda)	6
Union panafricaine pour la démocratie sociale (UPADS)	4
Independents	19
Others	17
Vacant‡	8
Total	137

* Including the results of voting in 12 constituencies where the elections were rerun on 28–29 May 2002, owing to procedural irregularities on 26 May.

† An alliance of 29 parties.

‡ Voting was postponed indefinitely in eight constituencies in the Pool region as a result of unrest.

Sénat

Palais du Parlement, Brazzaville; tel. and fax 81-18-34.

President: AMBROISE-EDOUARD NOUMAZALAYE.

The upper chamber comprises 66 members, elected by representatives of local, regional and municipal authorities for a six-year term. After the most recent elections to the Sénat, held on 2 October 2005, the strength of the parties was as follows:

Party	Seats
Parti congolais du travail (PCT)	39
Forces démocratiques unies (FDU) *	12
Parti pour la reconstruction du Congo	1
Civil society organizations	1
Independent	6
Vacant†	7
Total	66

* An alliance of 29 parties.

† Six seats remained vacant, as unrest had led to the postponement, in June 2002, of local elections in the Pool region and continued insecurity there. Additionally, one seat remained vacant, following irregularities in voting in the elections held in October 2005, pending a new election to that seat.

Election Commission

Commission nationale d'organisation des élections (CONEL): Brazzaville; f. 2001; mems appointed by President of the Republic, Commission is responsible to the Ministry of the Interior, Security and Territorial Administration.

Advisory Council

Economic and Social Council: Brazzaville; f. 2003; 75 mems, appointed by the President of the Republic; Pres. AUGUSTE-CÉLESTIN GONGARAD NKOUA.

Political Organizations

In early 2004 there were more than 100 political parties and organizations in the Republic of the Congo. The following were among the most important of those believed to be active in mid-2007.

Alliance pour la Démocratie et le Développement National (ADDN): Brazzaville; f. 2005; supports Govt of Pres. Sassou-Nguesso; Pres. BRUNO MAZONGA.

Conseil national de la résistance: formed as political wing of 'Ninja' rebel group; Leader Rev. FRÉDÉRIC BITSANGOU (NTUMI).

Convention pour la démocratie et le salut (CODESA): Brazzaville; f. 2002; opposition alliance; Pres. ANDRÉ MILONGO.

> **Convention nationale pour la République et la solidarité (CNRS):** Brazzaville; f. 2001; Leader MARTIN MBERI.
>
> **Parti pour la reconstruction du Congo:** Brazzaville.
>
> **Rassemblement pour la démocratie et le développement (RDD):** Brazzaville; f. 1990; advocates a mixed economy; Pres. JOACHIM YHOMBI-OPANGO; Chair. SATURNIN OKABÉ.
>
> **Union pour la démocratie et le progrès social (UDPS):** Brazzaville; f. 1994 by merger; Leader JEAN-MICHEL BOUKAMBA-YANGOUMA.
>
> **Union pour la démocratie et la République—Mwinda (UDR—Mwinda):** Brazzaville; e-mail journalmwinda@presse-ecrite.com; internet www.mwinda.org; f. 1992; Leader ANDRÉ MILONGO.

Coordination de l'opposition pour une alternance démocratique (CODE-A): Brazzaville; f. 2005; opposition alliance; Leader HERVE AMBROISE MALONGA.

Forces démocratiques unies (FDU): Brazzaville; f. 1994; fmrly Forces démocratiques et patriotiques; 29 constituent parties in 2002; supports Govt of Pres. Sassou-Nguesso; Pres. LÉKOUNDZOU ITIHI OSSÉTOUMBA (acting).

> **Alliance pour le Congo (APC):** Brazzaville; Leader JUSTIN COUMBA.
>
> **Alliance congolaise pour l'ouverture, le salut et la solidarité (ACOSS):** Brazzaville; f. 1998; social-liberal; Pres. Dr LÉON-ALFRED OPIMBAT.
>
> **Club 2002:** Brazzaville; f. 2002; Pres. WILFRID NGUESSO.
>
> **Rassemblement pour la démocratie et le progrès social (RDPS):** Pointe-Noire; f. 1990; Pres. JEAN-PIERRE THYSTÈRE TCHIKAYA.
>
> **Rassemblement pour la démocratie et la République (RDR):** Brazzaville; Leader Gen. (retd) RAYMOND DAMASE NGOLLO.
>
> **Union patriotique pour la démocratie et le progrès (UPDP):** Brazzaville; Pres. AUGUSTE-CÉLESTIN GONGARAD-NKOUA.
>
> **Union pour le progrès (UP):** Brazzaville; Pres. JEAN-MARTIN MBEMBA; Sec.-Gen. OMER DEFOUNDOUX.
>
> **Union pour le redressement national (URN):** Mpila, Brazzaville; f. 1999; Pres. GABRIEL BOKILO.

Mouvement congolais pour la démocratie et le développement intégral (MCDDI): Brazzaville; e-mail info@mcddi.net; internet www.mcddi.org; f. 1990; Leader BERNARD KOLÉLAS.

Parti congolais du travail (PCT): Mpila, Brazzaville; f. 1969; sole legal political party 1969–90; fmrly member of FDU; Pres. (vacant); Sec.-Gen. AMBROISE-EDOUARD NOUMAZALAY.

Parti de la sauvegarde des valeurs républicaines (PSVR): Brazzaville; f. 2006 by fmr mems of MCDDI (q.v.); Pres. MICHEL MAMPOUYA.

Union congolaise des républicains (UCR): Brazzaville; Leader CÔME MANKASSA.

Union des forces démocratiques (UFD): Brazzaville; supports Govt; Pres. DAVID CHARLES GANOU.

Union panafricaine pour la démocratie sociale (UPADS): Brazzaville; e-mail courrier@upads.org; internet www.upads.org; Pres. PASCAL LISSOUBA; Sec.-Gen. PAULIN MKITA (acting).

Diplomatic Representation

EMBASSIES IN THE REPUBLIC OF THE CONGO

Algeria: rue Col Brisset, BP 2100, Brazzaville; tel. 81-17-37; fax 81-54-77; Ambassador ABDELAH LAOUARI.

Angola: BP 388, Brazzaville; tel. 81-47-21; fax 81-52-87; e-mail miranotom@yahoo.fr; Ambassador Dr MIRANO EDUARDO TOMAS.

Belgium: ave Patrice Lumumba, BP 225, Brazzaville; tel. 81-37-12; fax 81-37-04; e-mail brazzaville@diplobel.org; internet www.diplomatie.be/brazzaville.

Cameroon: BP 2136, Brazzaville; tel. 81-10-08; fax 81-56-75; Chargé d'affaires a.i. GUILLAUME NSEKE.

Central African Republic: BP 10, Brazzaville; tel. 83-40-14.

China, People's Republic: blvd Lyauté, BP 213, Brazzaville; tel. 83-11-32; fax 81-11-35; e-mail chinaemb_cg@mfa.gov.cn; Ambassador WO RUIDI.

Congo, Democratic Republic: Brazzaville; tel. 83-29-38; Ambassador FÉLIX MUMENGUI OTTHUW.

Cuba: 28 rue Lacien Fourneaux, BP 80, Brazzaville; tel. 81-03-79; e-mail embacuba@congonet.cg; Ambassador SIDENIO ACOSTA ADAY.

Egypt: 7 bis ave Bayardelle, BP 917, Brazzaville; tel. 81-07-94; fax 81-15-33; Ambassador MEDHAT KAMAL ABD EL-RAOF EL-KADI.

France: rue Alfassa, BP 2089, Brazzaville; tel. 81-55-41; e-mail webmestre@mail.com; internet www.ambafrance-cg.org; Ambassador NICHOLAS NORMAND.

Guinea: Brazzaville; tel. 81-24-66.

Holy See: rue Col Brisset, BP 1168, Brazzaville; tel. 81-55-80; fax 81-55-81; e-mail nonapcg@yahoo.com; Apostolic Nuncio Most Rev. ANDRES CARRASCOSA COSO (Titular Archbishop of Elo).

Italy: 2 blvd Lytautey, BP 2484, Brazzaville; tel. 81-58-41; fax 81-11-52; e-mail ambasciata.brazzaville@esteri.it; internet www.ambbrazzaville.esteri.it/Ambasciata_Brazzaville; Ambassador ANGELO TRAVAGLINI.

Korea, Democratic People's Republic: Brazzaville; tel. 83-41-98; Ambassador RI WON SON.

Libya: BP 920, Brazzaville.

Nigeria: 11 blvd Lyauté, BP 790, Brazzaville; tel. 83-13-16; Ambassador GREG MBADIWE.

Russia: ave Félix Eboué, BP 2132, Brazzaville; tel. 81-19-23; fax 81-50-85; e-mail amrussie@ic.cd; internet www.congo.mid.ru; Ambassador MIKHAIL S. TSVIGUN.

Judicial System

The 2002 Constitution provides for the independence of the judiciary from the legislature. Judges are to be accountable to the Higher Council of Magistrates, under the chairmanship of the President of the Republic. The constituent bodies of the judiciary are the Supreme Court, the Revenue and Budgetary Discipline Court and the appeal courts. The High Court of Justice is chaired by the First President of the Supreme Court and is competent to try the President of the Republic in case of high treason, and to try members of the legislature, the Supreme Court, the Constitutional Court and government ministers for crimes or offences committed in the execution of their duties.

Supreme Court: BP 597, Brazzaville; tel. 83-01-32; First Pres. PLACIDE LENGA.

High Court of Justice: Brazzaville; f. 2003; Pres. PLACIDE LENGA (First Pres. of the Supreme Court); Chief Prosecutor GEORGES AKIERA.

Constitutional Court: Brazzaville; Pres. GÉRARD BITSINDOU; Vice-Pres. AUGUSTE ILOKI; Mems SIMON-PIERRE NGOUONIMBA NCZARY, THOMAS DHELLO, MARC MASSAMBA-NDILOU, JACQUES BOMBÈTE, JEAN-PIERRE BERRI, DELPHINE-EMMANUELLE ADOUKI, JEAN-BERNARD ANAËL SAMORY.

Religion

At least one-half of the population follow traditional animist beliefs. Most of the remainder are Christians (of whom a majority are Roman Catholics).

CHRISTIANITY

The Roman Catholic Church

The Congo comprises one archdiocese, five dioceses and an apostolic prefecture. At 31 December 2004 there were an estimated 2.2m. Roman Catholics in the Republic of the Congo, accounting for some 52.9% of the population.

Bishops' Conference

Conférence Episcopale du Congo, BP 200, Brazzaville; tel. 63-83-91; fax 81-18-28; e-mail confepiscongo@yahoo.fr.

f. 1992; Pres. Most Rev. KOMBO ERNEST (Bishop of Owando).

Archbishop of Brazzaville: Most Rev. ANATOLE MILANDOU, Archevêché, BP 2301, Brazzaville; tel. 81-53-63; fax 81-38-17; e-mail archebrazza@yahoo.fr.

Protestant Church

Eglise Evangélique du Congo: BP 3205, Bacongo-Brazzaville; tel. and fax 81-04-54; f. 1909; Presbyterian; autonomous since 1961; 145,000 mems (2005); 105 parishes (1998); Pres. (vacant).

ISLAM

In 1997 an estimated 2% of the population were Muslims.

Comité Islamique du Congo: 77 Makotipoko Moungali, BP 55, Brazzaville; tel. 82-87-45; f. 1988; Leaders HABIBOU SOUMARE, BACHIR GATSONGO, BOUILLA GUIBIDANESI.

BAHÁ'Í FAITH

Assemblée spirituelle nationale: BP 2094, Brazzaville; tel. 81-36-93; e-mail congolink1@aol.com.

The Press

In July 2000 legislation was adopted on the freedom of information and communication. The legislation, which confirmed the abolition of censorship and reduced the penalty for defamation from imprisonment to a fine, specified three types of punishable offence: the encouragement of social tension (including incitement to ethnic conflict), attacks on the authorities (including libels on the Head of State or on the judiciary), and libels against private individuals. The terms of the legislation were to be guaranteed by a regulatory body, the Higher Council for the Freedom of Communication.

DAILIES

ACI Actualité: BP 2144, Brazzaville; tel. and fax 81-01-98; publ. by Agence Congolaise d'Information; Dir-Gen. THÉODORE KIAMOSSI.

Aujourd'hui: Brazzaville; tel. and fax 83-77-44; f. 1991; Man. Dir and Editor-in-Chief FYLLA DI FUA DI SASSA.

Mweti: BP 991, Brazzaville; tel. 81-10-87; national news; Dir MATONGO AVELEY; Editor-in-Chief HUBERT MADOUABA; circ. 7,000.

PERIODICALS

L'Arroseur: Immeuble Boulangerie ex-Léon, BP 15021, Brazzaville; tel. 58-65-51; fax 58-37-60; e-mail larroseur@yahoo.fr; f. 2000; weekly; satirical; Dir GERRY-GÉRARD MANGONDO; Editor-in-Chief JEAN-MARIE KANGA.

L'Autre Vision: 48 rue Assiéné-Mikalou, BP 5255, Brazzaville; tel. 51-57-06; e-mail lautrevision@yahoo.fr; 2 a month; Dir JEAN PAULIN ITOUA.

Capital: 3 ave Charles de Gaulle, Plateau Centre Ville, BP 541, Brazzaville; tel. 58-95-10; fax 51-37-48; e-mail capital@hotmail.com; 2 a month; economics and business; Dir SERGE-DENIS MATONDO; Editor-in-Chief HERVÉ SAMPA.

Le Choc: BP 1314, Brazzaville; tel. 41-25-39; fax 82-04-25; e-mail groupejustinfo@yahoo.fr; internet www.lechoc.info; weekly, news concerning several African states; Dir-Gen. and Publr ASIE DOMINIQUE DE MARSEILLE; Dir of Publication HERMAN BANGUI BAYO.

Co Co Ri Co: 201 rue Dolisie-Ouenzé, Brazzaville; tel. 66-39-80; fax 58-59-22; weekly; satirical; Dir AIMÉ-SERGE BAZOUNGOULA BISSEMO TURBO; Editor-in-Chief MOKABI DAWA.

Le Coq: Brazzaville; e-mail sosolecoq@yahoo.fr; f. 2000; weekly; Editor-in-Chief MALONGA BOUKA.

Le Défi Africain: Brazzaville; f. 2002; Dir of Publication JEAN ROMUALD MBEPA.

Les Dépêches de Brazzaville: Résidence Méridien, BP 15457, Brazzaville; tel. and fax 81-28-13; e-mail redaction@brazzaville-adiac.com; internet www.brazzaville-adiac.com; 6 a year; publ. by Agence d'Information de l'Afrique Centrale; Dir-Gen. JEAN-PAUL PIGASSE; Dir and Editor-in-Chief BELINDA AYESSA.

Les Echos du Congo: Immeubles Fédéraux 036, Centre-ville, Brazzaville; tel. 51-57-09; e-mail wayiadrien@yahoo.fr; weekly; pro-government; Dir-Gen. ADRIEN WAYI-LEWY; Editor-in-Chief INNOCENT OLIVIER TATY.

Epanza Makita: Brazzaville; f. 2004.

Le Flambeau: BP 1198, Brazzaville; tel. 66-35-23; e-mail congolink1@aol.com; weekly; independent; supports Govt of Pres. Sassou-Nguesso; Dir and Man. Editor PRINCE-RICHARD NSANA.

La Lettre de Brazzaville: Résidence Méridien, BP 15457, Brazzaville; tel. and fax 81-28-13; e-mail redaction@adiac.com; f. 2000; weekly; publ. by Agence d'Information de l'Afrique Centrale; Man. Dir JEAN-PAUL PIGASSE; Editor-in-Chief BELINDA AYESSA.

Le Nouveau Stade: BP 2159, Brazzaville; tel. 68-45-52; 2 a month; sports; Dir-Gen. LOUIS NGAMI; Editor-in-Chief S. F. KIMINA MAKUMBU.

La Nouvelle République: 3 ave des Ambassadeurs, BP 991, Brazzaville; tel. 81-00-20; state-owned; two a week; Dir-Gen. GASPARD NWAN; Editorial Dir HENRI BOUKOULOU.

L'Observateur: 165 ave de l'Amitié, BP 13370, Brazzaville; tel. 66-33-37; fax 81-11-81; e-mail lobservateur_2001@yahoo.fr; f. 1999; weekly; independent; opposes Govt of Pres. Sassou-Nguesso; Dir GISLIN SIMPLICE ONGOUYA; circ. 2,000 (2004).

Le Pays: BP 782, Brazzaville; tel. 61-06-11; fax 82-44-50; e-mail heblepays@yahoo.fr; f. 1991; weekly; Editorial Dir SYLVÈRE-ARSÈNE SAMBA.

La Référence: BP 13778, Brazzaville; tel. 56-11-37; fax 62-80-13; 2 a month; supports Govt of Pres. Sassou-Nguesso; Dir PHILIPPE RICHET; Editor-in-Chief R. ASSEBAKO AMAIDJORE.

La Rue Meurt (Bala-Bala): BP 1258, Brazzaville; tel. 66-39-80; fax 81-02-30; e-mail laruemeurt@yahoo.fr; f. 1991; weekly; satirical; opposes Govt of Pres. Sassou-Nguesso; Publr MATTHIEU GAYELE; Editorial Dir JEAN-CLAUDE BONGOLO; circ. 2,000 (2004).

La Semaine Africaine: blvd Lyautey, face Chu, BP 2080, Brazzaville; tel. and fax 81-23-35; e-mail lasemaineafricaine@yahoo.fr; internet www.lasemaineafricaine.com; f. 1952; weekly; Roman Catholic; general news and social comment; circulates widely in francophone equatorial Africa; Dir JEAN-PIERRE GALLET; Editorial Dir JOACHIM MBANZA; circ. 7,500.

Le Soleil: f. 1991; weekly; organ of the Rassemblement pour la démocratie et le développement.

Le Stade: BP 114, Brazzaville; tel. 81-47-18; f. 1985; weekly; sports; Dir HUBERT-TRÉSOR MADOUABA-NTOUALANI; Editor-in-Chief LELAS PAUL NZOLANI; circ. 6,500.

Tam-Tam d'Afrique: 97 rue Moussana, Ouenzé, BP 1675, Brazzaville; tel. 51-03-95; e-mail gouala@yahoo.fr; weekly; economics, finance; circ. 1,500 (2004).

Le Temps: BP 2104, Brazzaville; e-mail kiala_matouba@yahoo.fr; weekly; owned by supporters of former Pres. Lissouba; Editor-in-Chief HENRI BOUKOULOU.

Vision pour Demain: 109 rue Bakongo Poto-Poto, BP 650, Brazzaville; tel. 41-14-22; 6 a year; Dir SAINT EUDES MFUMU FYLLA.

NEWS AGENCIES

Agence Congolaise d'Information (ACI): ave E. P. Lumumba, BP 2144, Brazzaville; tel. and fax 81-01-98; e-mail agencecongoinfo@yahoo.fr; Gen. Man. BERNARD MANTELE.

Agence d'Information d'Afrique Centrale (ADIAC): Hôtel Méridien, BP 15457, Brazzaville; tel. and fax 81-28-13; e-mail belie@congonet.cg; internet www.brazzaville-adiac.com; f. 1997; Dirs JEAN-PAUL PIGASSE, BELINDA AYESSA; br. in Paris (France).

Foreign Bureaux

Agence France-Presse (AFP): c/o Agence Congolaise d'Information, BP 2144, Brazzaville; tel. 83-46-76.

Associated Press (AP) (USA): BP 2144, Brazzaville.

Inter Press Service (IPS) (Italy): POB 964, Brazzaville; tel. 81-05-65.

Pan-African News Agency (PANA) (Senegal): BP 2144, Brazzaville; tel. 83-11-40; fax 83-70-15.

Xinhua (New China) News Agency (People's Republic of China): Brazzaville; tel. 83-44-01.

Publishers

Editions ADIAC—Agence d'Information d'Afrique Centrale: Hôtel Méridien, BP 15457, Brazzaville; tel. and fax 81-28-13; e-mail redaction@brazzaville-adiac.com; internet www.brazzaville-adiac.com; f. 1997; publishes chronicles of current affairs; Dirs JEAN-PAUL PIGASSE, BELINDA AYESSA.

Editions 'Héros dans l'Ombre': BP 1678, Brazzaville; tel. 768-11-49; e-mail leopold_mamo@yahoo.fr; f. 1980; literature, criticism, poetry, essays, politics, drama, research; Chair. LÉOPOLD PINDY MAMONSONO.

Editions Lemba: BP 2351, Brazzaville; tel. 67-65-58; fax 81-00-17; e-mail editions_lemba@yahoo.fr; literature; Dir APOLLINAIRE SINGOU-BASSEHA.

Editions PAARI—Pan African Review of Innovation: BP 1622 Brazzaville; tel. 51-86-49; e-mail edpaari@yahoo.fr; f. 1991; social and human sciences, philosophy.

Editions Renaissance Congolaise: Brazzaville.

Imprimerie Centrale d'Afrique (ICA): BP 162, Pointe-Noire; f. 1949; Man. Dir M. SCHNEIDER.

Mokandart: BP 939, Brazzaville; tel. 68-46-69; e-mail mokandart@yahoo.fr; adult and children's literature; Pres. ANNICK VEYRINAUD MAKONDA.

GOVERNMENT PUBLISHING HOUSE

Imprimerie Nationale du Congo (INC): BP 58, Brazzaville; Dir JULES ONDZEKI.

Broadcasting and Communications

Higher Council for the Freedom of Communication: Brazzaville; f. 2003; 11 mems, nominated by the President of the Republic; Pres. JACQUES BANANGANZALA.

TELECOMMUNICATIONS

Celtel Congo: blvd Charles de Gaulle, angle allée Maikmba, BP 1267, Pointe-Noire; tel. 520-00-00; fax 94-88-75; e-mail celtelcongo@yahoo.fr; internet www.cg.celtel.com; f. 1999; mobile cellular telephone operator; network covers Brazzaville, Pointe-Noire, Loubomo (Dolisie), Ouesso, Owando and other urban areas; subsidiary of Celtel International (United Kingdom); Dir-Gen. ANTOINE PAMBORO; 30,000 subscribers (Dec. 2000).

Cyrus International (CYRTEL): Brazzaville; mobile cellular telephone operator; operates as jt venture between Nexus International (70%), a subsidiary of France Telecom and SOTELCO.

Libertis: 22 rue Behagle, BP 1150, Brazzaville; tel. 81-47-70; fax 81-44-16; f. 2000; mobile cellular telephone operator; network covers Brazzaville and Pointe-Noire; subsidiary of Orascom Telecom (Egypt).

Société des Télécommunications du Congo (SOTELCO): BP 39, Brazzaville; tel. 81-16-66; f. 2001 by division of postal and telecommunications services of the fmr Office National des Postes et Télécommunications; mobile cellular telephone system introduced in 1996; majority Govt-owned, part-owned by Atlantic TeleNetwork; further transfer to private ownership pending; Dir-Gen. RENÉ-SERGE BLANCHARD OBA (acting).

RADIO AND TELEVISION

Radio Brazzaville: face Direction Générale, SOTELCO, Brazzaville; tel. 51-60-73; f. 1999; official station; Man. JEAN-PASCAL MONGO SLYM.

Canal FM: BP 60, Brazzaville; tel. 83-03-09; f. 1977 as Radio Rurales du Congo; present name adopted 2002; community stations established by the Agence de coopération culturelle et technique; transmitters in Brazzaville, Sembé, Nkayi, Etoumbi and Mossendjo; Dir ETIENNE EPAGNA-TOUA.

Radio Liberté: BP 1660, Brazzaville; tel. 81-57-42; f. 1997; operated by supporters of Pres. Sassou-Nguesso.

Radiodiffusion-Télévision Congolaise (RTC): BP 2241, Brazzaville; tel. 81-24-73; state-owned; Pres. JEAN-GILBERT FOUTOU; Dir-Gen. GILBERT-DAVID MUTAKALA.

Radio Congo: BP 2241, Brazzaville; tel. 81-50-60; radio programmes in French, Lingala, Kikongo, Subia, English and Portuguese; transmitters at Brazzaville and Pointe-Noire; Gen. Man. ALPHONSE BOUYA DIMI; Dir of Broadcasting THÉOPHILE MIETE LIKIBI.

Télévision congolaise (TVC): BP 975, Brazzaville; tel. 81-01-16; f. 1963; operates for 46 hours per week, with most programmes in French but some in Lingala and Kikongo; Gen. Man. WAMÉNÉ EKIAYE-ACKOLI.

Télédiffusion du Congo: BP 2912, Brazzaville; tel. 81-06-08; Gen. Man. MÉDARD BOKATOLA.

Finance

(cap. = capital; res = reserves; dep. = deposits; m. = million; br(s). = branch(es); amounts in francs CFA)

BANKING

Central Bank

Banque des Etats de l'Afrique Centrale (BEAC): BP 126, Brazzaville; tel. 81-10-73; fax 81-10-94; e-mail beacbzv@beac.int; internet www.beac.int; HQ in Yaoundé, Cameroon; f. 1973; bank of issue for mem. states of the Communauté économique et monétaire en Afrique centrale (CEMAC, fmrly Union douanière et économique de l'Afrique centrale) comprising Cameroon, the Central African Repub., Chad, the Repub. of the Congo, Equatorial Guinea and Gabon; cap. 45,000m., res 176,661m., total assets 2,144,626m. (Nov. 2003); Gov. JEAN-FÉLIX MAMALEPOT; Dir in Repub. of the Congo MATHIAS DZON; br. at Pointe-Noire.

Commercial Banks

BGFI Bank Congo: BP 14579, Angle rue Reims, face à Pairie de France, Brazzaville; tel. 81-40-50; fax 81-50-89; state-owned; cap. 1,000m. (2002); Pres. MATHIAS DZON; Dir-Gen. ALAIN MOUSSIROU MABIALA; 2 brs.

COFIPA—Compagnie de Financement et de Participation: ave Amílcar Cabral, BP 147, Brazzaville; tel. 81-58-34; fax 81-03-73; e-mail cofipabzv@caramail.com; f. 2001 on privatization of Union Congolaise de Banques; cap. and res 2,868.2m., total assets 57,523.9m. (Dec. 2003); Dir-Gen. XAVIER ALIBERT; 14 brs.

La Congolaise de Banque (LCB): ave Amílcar Cabral, BP 2889, Brazzaville; tel. 81-09-78; fax 81-09-77; e-mail caic20@calva.com; f. 2004 on privatization of Crédit pour l'Agriculture, l'Industrie et le Commerce (CAIC); Dir-Gen. GILBERT BOPOUNZA; 4 brs.

Crédit Lyonnais-Congo (CL Co): ave Emmanuel Daddet, BP 1312, Pointe-Noire; tel. 94-24-00; fax 94-16-65; e-mail clpn10@valva.com; f. 2002 to replace Banque Internationale du Congo; 81% owned by Crédit Lyonnais (France), 9% state-owned; cap. and res 2,868.2m., total assets 57,523.9m. (Dec. 2003); Dir-Gen. PASCAL PETRIS; 2 brs.

Société Congolaise de Financement (SOCOFIN): BP 899, Pointe-Noire; tel. 67-10-44; fax 94-37-93; e-mail socofin.pnr@cg.celtelplus.com; f. 2001; cap. and res 370.0m., total assets 7,993.6m. (Dec. 2002); Dir-Gen. ERIC LECLERE.

Co-operative Banking Institution

Mutuelle Congolaise d'Epargne et de Crédit (MUCODEC): ave Paul Doumer, BP 13237, Brazzaville; tel. 81-07-57; fax 81-01-68; e-mail mucodec@wanadoo.fr; f. 1994; cap. and res 2,080m., total assets 29,000m. (Dec. 2003); Pres. JULIEN BOBOUNNGA; 45 brs.

Development Bank

Banque de Développement des Etats de l'Afrique Centrale: BP 1177, Brazzaville; tel. 81-17-61; fax 81-18-80; internet www.bdeac.org; cap. 22,240.0m., res 6,775.2m., dep. 6,579.9m. (Dec. 2005); Pres. and Chair. ANICET G. DOLOGUÉLÉ.

Financial Institution

Caisse Congolaise d'Amortissement (CCA): ave Foch, BP 2090, Brazzaville; tel. 81-57-35; fax 81-52-36; f. 1971; management of state funds; Dir-Gen. GEORGES NGUEKOUMOU.

INSURANCE

Assurances et Réassurances du Congo (ARC): BP 1033, Pointe-Noire; tel. 94-08-00; f. 1973; 50% state-owned; privatization pending; Dir-Gen. RAYMOND IBATA; brs at Brazzaville, Loubomo and Ouesso.

Gras Savoye Congo: 13 rue Germain Bikouma, angle Route de la Radio, Immeuble Guenin, BP 1901, Pointe-Noire; tel. 94-79-72; fax 94-79-74; e-mail grassavoye.congo@cg.celtelplus.com; affiliated to Gras Savoye (France); insurance brokers and risk managers; Man. PHILIPPE BAILLÉ.

Société de Courtage d'Assurances et de Réassurances (SCDE): BP 13177, Immeuble Foch, ave Foch, Brazzaville; tel. 81-17-63.

Trade and Industry

GOVERNMENT AGENCY

Comité des Privatisations et de Renforcement des Capacités Locales: Immeuble ex-SCBO, 7ème étage, BP 1176, Brazzaville; tel. 81-46-21; fax 81-46-09; e-mail privat@aol.com; oversees and co-ordinates transfer of state-owned enterprises to the private sector.

DEVELOPMENT ORGANIZATIONS

Agence Française de Développement (AFD): rue Béhagle, BP 96, Brazzaville; tel. 81-53-30; fax 81-29-42; e-mail afdbrazzaville@groupe-afd.org; internet www.afd.fr; French fund for economic co-operation; Country Dir ALAIN DALHEM.

Mission Française de Coopération et d'Action Culturelle: BP 2175, Brazzaville; tel. 83-15-03; f. 1959; administers bilateral aid from France; Dir JEAN-BERNARD THIANT.

Société Nationale d'Elevage (SONEL): BP 81, Loutété, Massangui; f. 1964; development of semi-intensive stock-rearing; exploitation of cattle by-products; Man. Dir THÉOPHILE BIKAWA.

CHAMBERS OF COMMERCE

Chambre de Commerce, d'Agriculture, d'Industrie et des Métiers de Brazzaville: BP 92, Brazzaville; tel. and fax 81-16-08; f. 1935; Pres. PAUL OBAMBI; Sec.-Gen. GÉRARD DONGO.

Chambre de Commerce, d'Agriculture et d'Industrie de Kouilou: BP 665, Pointe-Noire; tel. 94-12-80; fax 94-07-13; f. 1948; fmrly Chambre de Commerce, d'Industrie et des Métiers de Pointe-Noire; Chair. NARCISSE POATY PACKA; Sec.-Gen. JEAN-BAPTISTE SOUMBOU.

Chambre de Commerce, d'Agriculture et d'Industrie de Loubomo: BP 78, Loubomo; tel. 91-00-17.

Chambre Nationale d'Industrie et d'Agriculture du Congo: BP 1119, Brazzaville; tel. 83-29-56; fmrly Conférence Permanente des Chambres de Commerce du Congo; Pres. PAUL OBAMBI.

EMPLOYERS' ORGANIZATIONS

Forum des Jeunes Entreprises du Congo (FJEC): BP 2080, Brazzaville; tel. 81-56-34; e-mail fjec@inmarsat.francetelecom.fr; f. 1996; Sec.-Gen. PAUL KAMPAKOL.

Union Nationale des Opérateurs du Congo (UNOC): BP 5187, Brazzaville; tel. 81-54-32; operates a professional training centre; Pres. El Hadj DJIBRIL ABDOULAYE BOPAKA.

Union Patronale et Interprofessionnelle du Congo (UNICONGO): BP 42, Brazzaville; tel. 81-47-68; fax 81-47-66; f. 1958; Nat. Pres. JEAN-CHRISTOPHE TRANCEPAIN; Sec.-Gen. JEAN-JACQUES SAMBA; membership of 10 feds, representing 400 enterprises, with a total work-force of 25,000 (2001).

UTILITIES

Electricity

Société Nationale d'Electricité (SNE): 95 ave Paul Doumer, BP 95, Brazzaville; tel. 81-05-66; fax 81-05-69; e-mail snecongo@caramail.com; f. 1967; transfer to private management proposed; operates hydroelectric plants at Bouenza and Djoué; Pres. ALBERT CAMILLE PELLA; Dir-Gen. ALPHONSE BOUDONESA.

Water

Société Nationale de Distribution d'Eau (SNDE): rue du Sergent Malamine, BP 229, Brazzaville; tel. 83-73-26; fax 83-38-91; f. 1967; transferred to private-sector management by Bi-Water (United Kingdom) in 2002; water supply and sewerage; holds monopoly over wells and import of mineral water; Dir-Gen. AMBROISE BONGOUANDÉ.

MAJOR COMPANIES

The following are some of the largest companies in terms of either capital investment or employment.

AGIP Congo: ave Beagle, BP 2047, Brazzaville; tel. 81-11-52; fax 94-07-00; f. 1968; cap. US $7m.; wholly-owned by Eni (Italy); exploration and exploitation of petroleum resources; Chair. PIETRO CAVANNA; Man. Dir ANTONIO ROSSANI.

Boissons Africaines de Brazzaville (BAB): BP 2193, Brazzaville; tel. 83-20-06; f. 1964; mfrs of carbonated drinks and syrups.

Brasseries du Congo (BRASCO): POB 1147, Pointe-Noire; tel. 94-02-44; fax 94-15-30; mfrs of beer and soft drinks, fruit juices, soda, ice and carbon dioxide; 50% owned by CFAO (France), 50% by Heineken (Netherlands); Pres. J. L. HOME; Man. Dir G. J. BOUR; 570 employees.

La Congolaise des Bois Imprégnés (CBI): Pointe-Noire; f. 1986; production of electricity poles from eucalyptus trees; restructuring or privatization pending; 33 employees (2001).

La Congolaise de Raffinage: BP 755, Pointe-Noire; tel. 94-22-85; fax 94-04-18; e-mail coraf@coraf.com; f. 1982; state-owned; production of petroleum and petroleum products; Pres. LOUTARD TATY.

Eucalyptus Fibre Congo (EFC): BP 1227, Pointe-Noire; tel. 94-04-17; fax 94-40-54; f. 2005 to replace Eucalyptus du Congo (ECO); subsidiary of MagIndustries Corpn (Canada); production of wood-pulp and other products for export from eucalyptus plantations.

Groupe COFICO: BP 13359, Brazzaville; e-mail groupecofico@smartnet.ca; four cos: Congo Finance Corpn, International Import-

Export Corpn, Constructions et Gestion Immobilières, Société Agropastorale et d'Aménagement de Boko.

Impressions de Textiles de la République du Congo (IMPRECO): BP 188, Brazzaville; tel. 81-02-74; fax 83-01-96; f. 1973; 30% state-owned; textile printing.

Industrie Forestière d'Ouesso (IFO): BP 300, Loubomo; tel. 91-02-04; fax 91-06-66; e-mail ifo1@inmarsat.francetelecom.fr; f. 1964; cap. 400m. francs CFA; timber mills; fmrly Société Congolaise des Bois; owned by Danzer Group (Germany); Dir OTTO SCHLUMBOHM.

Minoterie du Congo (MINOCO): BP 871, Pointe-Noire; tel. 94-37-07; fax 94-44-56; e-mail direction@minoco.cg; f. 2000; affiliated with Seaboard Corpn, (USA); fmrly Minoterie et Aliments du Bétail; production of flour and animal feed; cap. 3,200m. francs CFA; Pres. and Dir-Gen. STEVE BRESKY.

Nouvelle Société des Ciments du Congo (SONOC): BP 72, Loutété; tel. 92-61-26; f. 2002 to replace Les Ciments du Congo; 56% owned by Chinese National Highway and Bridge Engineering Co (People's Republic of China), 44% state-owned; cap. 6,700m. francs CFA.

Régie Nationale des Palmeraies du Congo (RNPC): BP 8, Brazzaville; tel. 83-08-25; f. 1966; state-owned; transfer to private ownership proposed in 2006; production of palm oil; Man. Dir RENÉ MACOSSO.

Société Commune de Logistique Petrolière (SCLOG): Pointe-Noire; f. 2002; 25% state-owned, privately managed; distribution of petroleum products.

Société Congolaise Française (SOCOFRAN): BP 1148, Pointe-Noire; tel. 94-00-18; fax 94-23-36; e-mail transit@cg.celtelplus.com; f. 1961; building, construction, public works; cap. 60m. francs CFA (2001); Chief Exec. HUBERT PANDINO.

Société Congolaise Industrielle des Bois (CIB): BP 145, Brazzaville; tel. 24-90-21; fax 81-19-21; e-mail cibpokola@cibpokola.com; f. 1969; logs and timber production; sales 285m. francs CFA (2001); Pres. Dr HEINRICH LÜDER STOLL; Dir-Gen. JEAN-MARIE MEVELLEC; 1,500 employees (2002).

Société des Huiles du Congo (HUILCA): N'Kayi; tel. 92-11-60; f. 1988; 40% state-owned; production of oils and fats, vegetable oil refinery at Brazzaville; Pres. ANTOINE TABET; Dir-Gen. EMMANUEL PAMBOU.

Société Industrielle Agricole du Tabac Tropical (SIAT): BP 50, Brazzaville; tel. 83-16-15; fax 83-16-72; f. 1948; mfrs of cigarettes; Dir-Gen. BERNARD PUILLET; 70 employees (2001).

Société Industrielle de Déroulage et de Tranchage (SIDETRA): BP 1202, Pointe-Noire; tel. 94-20-07; f. 1966; 35% state-owned; forestry, production of sawn wood and veneers; 650 employees.

Société Libanaise de Bois de Placage: Likouala; f. 2000; factory producing logs and plywood from a region of forestry covering 199,000 hectares; 15-year licence granted in 2000.

Société Nationale de Construction (SONACO): Brazzaville; tel. 83-06-54; f. 1979; state-owned; building works; Man. Dir DENIS M'BOMO.

Société Nationale d'Elevage (SONEL): BP 81, Loutété, Massangui; f. 1964; state-owned; development of semi-intensive stock-rearing; exploitation of by-products; Man. Dir THÉOPHILE BIKAWA.

Société Nationale d'Exploitation des Bois (SNEB): Pointe-Noire; tel. 94-02-09; f. 1970; state-owned; production of timber; Chair. BRUNO ITOU.

Société Nationale des Pétroles du Congo (SNPC): BP 2008, Brazzaville; tel. 83-40-22; fax 83-12-38; internet www.snpc-group.com; f. 1998; petroleum research and exploration; owns refinery at Pointe-Noire; cap. 900m. francs CFA; Pres. and Dir-Gen. DENIS AUGUSTE MARIE GOKANA.

Total Congo: rue de la Corniche, BP 1037, Brazzaville; tel. 81-11-12; fax 83-24-22; f. 1969; cap. US $17.2m.; fmrly Elf Congo, subsequently renamed TotalFinaElf Congo; present name adopted 2003; wholly-owned by Total (France); exploration and exploitation of petroleum resources; Dir-Gen. S. LOUIS HEUZÉ.

TRADE UNION FEDERATIONS

Independent trade unions were legalized in 1991.

Confédération Générale des Travailleurs du Congo (CGTC): Brazzaville; f. 1995; Chair. PAUL DOUNA.

Confédération Nationale des Syndicats Libres (CNASYL): Brazzaville; f. 1994; Sec.-Gen. MICHEL KABOUL MAOUTA.

Confédération Syndicale Congolaise (CSC): BP 2311, Brazzaville; tel. 83-19-23; f. 1964; 80,000 mems.

Confédération Syndicale des Travailleurs du Congo (CSTC): BP 14743, Brazzaville; tel. 61-47-35; f. 1993; fed. of 13 trade unions; Chair. MICHEL SOUZA; 40,000 mems.

Confédération des Syndicats Libres Autonomes du Congo (COSYLAC): BP 14861, Brazzaville; tel. 82-42-65; fax 83-42-70; e-mail b.oba@congonet.cg; Pres. RENÉ BLANCHARD SERGE OBA.

Fédération nationale des travailleurs du Congo (FENATRAC): Brazzaville; f. 2001 by split from CSTC (q.v.); Sec. JULIEN NGOULOU.

Transport

RAILWAYS

In 1999 there were 1,152 km of railway track in the Congo. A 286-km section of privately owned line was used until 1991 to link the manganese mines at Moanda (in Gabon) with the main line to Pointe-Noire. Rail traffic has been severely disrupted since the 1997 civil war. The main line (of some 518 km) between Brazzaville and Pointe-Noire reopened briefly in November 1998 for freight traffic, but was subsequently closed following further unrest and sabotage. In early 2000 the Government signed two agreements with the Société Nationale des Chemins de Fer Français (France) relating to the repair of the line and associated infrastructure, and to the management of the network. Freight services resumed in August 2000, followed by passenger services in January 2001, although there was further disruption to the railways during unrest in mid-2002. In May 2004 the rail service linking Brazzaville to the Pool region resumed operations.

Chemin de Fer Congo-Océan (CFCO): BP 651, Pointe-Noire; tel. 94-11-84; fax 94-12-30; f. 1969; entered partnership with Rail Afrique International in June 1998; transfer to private management proposed; Dir-Gen. JACKY TRIMARDEAU.

ROADS

In 2004 there were an estimated 17,289 km of roads. Only about 5.0% of the total network was paved. The principal routes link Brazzaville with Pointe-Noire, in the south, and with Ouesso, in the north. A number of major construction projects initiated by President Sassou-Nguesso in 2000 and 2001 have involved the highways from Brazzaville to Kinkala, and from Brazzaville to the Pool region.

Régie Nationale des Transports et des Travaux Publics: BP 2073, Brazzaville; tel. 83-35-58; f. 1965; civil engineering, maintenance of roads and public works; Man. Dir HECTOR BIENVENU OUAMBA.

INLAND WATERWAYS

The Congo and Oubangui rivers form two axes of a highly developed inland waterway system. The Congo river and seven tributaries in the Congo basin provide 2,300 km of navigable river, and the Oubangui river, developed in co-operation with the Central African Republic, an additional 2,085 km.

Coordination Nationale des Transports Fluviaux: BP 2048, Brazzaville; tel. 83-06-27; Dir MÉDARD OKOUMOU.

Transcap—Congo: BP 1154, Pointe-Noire; tel. 94-01-46; f. 1962; Chair. J. DROUAULT.

SHIPPING

The deep-water Atlantic seaport at Pointe-Noire is the most important port in Central Africa and Brazzaville is one of the principal ports on the Congo river. A major rehabilitation programme began in October 1999, with the aim of establishing Pointe-Noire as a regional centre for container traffic and as a logistics centre for offshore oil exploration. In 1997 708,203 metric tons of goods were loaded at the port of Pointe-Noire, and 533,170 tons were unloaded.

La Congolaise de Transport Maritime (COTRAM): Pointe-Noire; f. 1984; national shipping co; state-owned.

Maersk Congo: 10 rue Massabi, Zone Portuaire, Pointe-Noire; tel. 94-21-41; fax 94-23-25; e-mail pnrmkt@maersk.com; f. 1997; represents Maersk Sealand (Denmark).

Port Autonome de Brazzaville: BP 2048, Brazzaville; tel. 83-00-42; f. 2000; port authority; Dir JEAN-PAUL BOCKONDAS.

Port Autonome de Pointe-Noire (PAPN): BP 711, Pointe-Noire; tel. 94-00-52; fax 94-20-42; e-mail info@papn-cg.com; internet www.papn-cg.com; f. 2000; port authority; Dir-Gen. JEAN-MARIE ANIÉLÉ.

SAGA Congo: 18 rue du Prophète Lasse Zephirin, BP 674, Pointe-Noire; tel. 94-10-16; fax 94-34-04; e-mail saga.congo@cg.dti.bollone.com.

Société Congolaise de Transports Maritimes (SOCOTRAM): BP 4922, Pointe-Noire; tel. 94-49-21; fax 94-49-22; e-mail info@socotram.com; internet www.socotram.fr; f. 1990.

CIVIL AVIATION

There are international airports at Brazzaville (Maya-Maya) and Pointe-Noire (Agostinho Neto). There are also five regional airports, at Loubomo (Dolisie, Ngot-Nzounzoungou), Nkaye, Owando, Ouesso and Impfondo, as well as 12 smaller airfields. In early 2001 the construction of a new international airport at Ollombo, some 500 km north of Brazzaville, began; the airport was expected to open by 2008. The refurbishment of Brazzaville airport commenced in 2001.

Aéro-Service: ave Charles de Gaulle, BP 1138, Pointe-Noire; tel. 94-23-80; fax 94-14-41; e-mail info@aero-service.net; internet www.aero-service.net; f. 1967; scheduled and charter passenger and freight services; operates nationally and to regional destinations; Pres. and Dir-Gen. R. GRIESBAUM.

Trans Air Congo: Immeuble City Center, ave Amílcar Cabral, BP 2422, Brazzaville; tel. 81-10-46; fax 81-10-57; e-mail info@flytransaircongo.com; internet www.transaircongo.org; f. 1994; private airline operating internal scheduled and international charter flights; Pres. and Dir-Gen. BASSAM ELHAGE.

Tourism

The tourism sector was severely disrupted in the late 1990s by political instability and internal unrest. Tourist visitors numbered 4,753 in 1999 (compared with tourist arrivals of 25,082 in 1998). In 2001, however, the number of tourist arrivals increased to 27,363, but declined slightly, to 21,611 in 2002. In 2002 earnings from tourism were estimated at US $26m.

Direction Générale du Tourisme et des Loisirs: BP 456, Brazzaville; tel. 83-09-53; f. 1980; Dir-Gen. ANTOINE KOUNKOU-KIBOUILOU.

Defence

As assessed at November 2006, the army numbered 8,000, the navy about 800 and the air force 1,200. In addition, there was a 2,000-strong Gendarmerie. National service is voluntary for men and women, and lasts for two years.

Defence Expenditure: Estimated at 34,000m. francs CFA for 2005.

Supreme Commander of the Armed Forces: Gen. DENIS SASSOU-NGUESSO.

Chief of General Staff of the Congolese Armed Forces: Gen. NORBERT ROBERT MONDJO.

Chief of Staff of the Air Force: Col JEAN-BAPTISTE FÉLIX TCHIKAYA.

Chief of Staff of the Navy: Col FULGOR ONGOBE.

Commander of the Ground Forces: Gen. NOËL LEONARD ESSONGO.

Sec.-Gen. of the National Security Council: Col JEAN-DOMINIQUE OKEMBA.

Education

Education is officially compulsory for 10 years between six and 16 years of age. Primary education begins at the age of six and lasts for six years. Secondary education, from 12 years of age, lasts for seven years, comprising a first cycle of four years and a second of three years. According to UNESCO estimates, enrolment at primary schools in 2003/04 was equivalent to 89% of children in the relevant age-group (boys 92%; girls 85%). In that year, enrolment at secondary schools was equivalent to 39% of children in the relevant age-group (boys 35%; girls 42%). In 1999/2000 13,403 students were attending tertiary institutions. In 2000 there were some 20,000 students enrolled in the Marien Ngouabi University in Brazzaville. Some Congolese students also attend further education establishments abroad. Expenditure on education by all levels of government was 52,274m. francs CFA in 1995. In September 2004 the World Bank approved a grant of US $20m. to assist with the reconstruction of the country's educational sector, which had been severely damaged by years of civil conflict.

Bibliography

Amin, S., and Coquery-Vidrovitch, C. *Histoire économique du Congo 1880–1968*. Paris, Anthropos, 1969.

Ayessa, B., and Pigasse, J. P. *Brazzaville: Chroniques 2001*. Brazzaville, Editions ADIAC, 2001.

Babu-Zale, R., *et al. Le Congo de Pascal Lissouba*. Paris, L'Harmattan, 1996.

Baniafouma, C. *Congo démocratie*. 5 vols. Paris, L'Harmattan, 1995–2003.

Dabira, N. *Brazzaville à feu et à sang: 5 juin–15 octobre 1997*. Paris, L'Harmattan, 1998.

Decalo, S., Thompson, V., and Adloff, R. *Historical Dictionary of Congo*. 3rd Edn. Lanham, MD, Scarecrow Press, 1996.

Eliou, M. *La formation de la conscience nationale en République populaire du Congo*. Paris, Anthropos, 1977.

Gouemo, R. *Le Congo-Brazzaville: de l'état postcolonial à l'état multinational*. Paris, L'Harmattan, 2004.

Idourah, S. N. *Justice et pouvoir au Congo-Brazzaville 1958–92: La confusion des rôles*. Paris, L'Harmattan, 2002.

Kinata, C. *Les ethnochefferies dans le Bas-Congo français : collaboration et résistance : 1896-1960*. Paris, L'Harmattan, 2001.

Kouvibidila, G.-J. *Histoire du multipartisme au Congo-Brazzaville. Volume 1: La marche à rebours 1940–1991*. Paris, L'Harmattan, 2001.

Histoire du multipartisme au Congo-Brazzaville. Volume 2: Les débuts d'une crise attendue 1992–1993. Paris, L'Harmattan, 2001.

Histoire du multipartisme au Congo-Brazzaville. Volume 3: La République en otage mai–octobre 1993. Paris, L'Harmattan, 2003

Lissouba, P. *Congo: Les fruits de la passion partagée*. Paris, Odilon, 1997.

Mabeko-T.,J.-M. *Barbares et citoyens, l'identité nationale à l'épreuve des transitions africaines: Congo-Brazzaville, Angola*. Paris, L'Harmattan, 2005

MacGaffrey, J., and Bazenguissa-Ganga, R. *Congo-Paris: Transnational Traders on the Margins of the Law*. Oxford, James Currey Publishers, 2000.

Makouta-Mboukou, J. P. *La destruction de Brazzaville ou la démocratie guillotinée*. Paris, L'Harmattan, 1999.

M'Kaloulou, B. *Dynamique paysanne et développement rural au Congo*. Paris, L'Harmattan, 1984.

Ndaki, G. *Crises, mutations et conflits politiques au Congo-Brazzaville*. Paris, L'Harmattan, 1998.

Nkaya, M. (Ed.) *Le Congo-Brazzaville à l'aube du XXIe siècle: Plaidoyer pour l'avenir*. Paris, L'Harmattan, 2004.

Nsafou, G. *Congo: de la démocratie à la démocrature*. Paris, L'Harmattan, 1996.

Obenga, T. *L'Histoire sanglante du Congo-Brazzaville (1959–1997)*. Paris, Présence Africaine, 1998.

Pigasse, J.-P. *Congo: Chronique d'une guerre annoncée (5 juin–15 octobre 1997)*. Brazzaville, Editions ADIAC, 1998.

Rabut, E. *Brazza, commissaire général. Le Congo français (1886–1897)*. Paris, Editions de l'école des hautes études en sciences sociales, 1989.

Sassou-Nguesso, D. *Le Manguier, le fleuve et la souris*. France, Jean-Claude Lattes, 1997.

Soni-Benga, P. *La guerre inachevée du Congo-Brazzaville (15 octobre 1997–18 décembre 1998)*. Paris, L'Harmattan, 2001.

West, R. *Brazza of the Congo: European exploration and exploitation in French Equatorial Africa*. Newton Abbot, 1973.

Zika, J.-R. *Démocratisme et misère politique en afrique: Le cas du Congo-Brazzaville*. Paris, L'Harmattan, 2002.

CÔTE D'IVOIRE

Physical and Social Geography

R. J. HARRISON CHURCH

The Republic of Côte d'Ivoire is situated on the west coast of Africa, between Ghana to the east and Liberia to the west, with Guinea, Mali and Burkina Faso to the north. Côte d'Ivoire is economically the most important of the states of sub-Saharan francophone Africa. The country has an area of 322,462 sq km (124,503 sq miles), and at the 1998 census the population was 15,366,671, rising to 19,657,738 by mid-2006 (giving an average population density of 61.0 inhabitants per sq km), according to official estimates. There is a diversity of peoples, with the Agni and Baoulé having cultural and other affinities with the Ashanti of Ghana. At the time of the 1998 census more than one-quarter of the population of the country were nationals of other states, with some 14.6% of the population nationals of Burkina Faso. The largest city is the former capital, Abidjan, which remains the principal commercial centre in Côte d'Ivoire, and which had a population of 3,576,000 in 2005. The second-largest city is Bouaké, in the north, with a population of 573,700 at that time. The official capital, the central city of Yamoussoukro, had a population of 299,243 in 1998.

From the border with Liberia eastwards to Fresco, the coast has cliffs, rocky promontories and sandy bays. East of Fresco the rest of the coast is a straight sandbar, backed, as in Benin, by lagoons. None of the seaward river exits is navigable, and a canal was opened from the sea into the Ebrié lagoon at Abidjan only in 1950, after half a century's battle with nature.

Although Tertiary sands and clays fringe the northern edge of the lagoons, they give way almost immediately to Archaean and Pre-Cambrian rocks, which underlie the rest of the country. Diamonds are obtained from gravels south of Korhogo, and near Séguéla, while gold is mined at Ity, in the west. The Man mountains and the Guinea highlands on the border with Liberia and Guinea are the only areas of vigorous relief in the country. Substantial deposits of haematite iron ore may be developed near Man for export through the country's second deep-water port of San-Pédro. There is considerable commercial potential for large offshore deposits of petroleum and also of natural gas, exploitation of which began in 1995: Côte d'Ivoire aims to become self-sufficient in (and, in the medium term, a net exporter of) hydrocarbons. Plans for the development of nickel reserves are proceeding.

Except for the north-western fifth of Côte d'Ivoire, the country has an equatorial climate. This occurs most typically in the south, which receives annual rainfall of 1,250 mm–2,400 mm, with two maxima, and where the relative humidity is high. Much valuable rainforest survives in the south-west, but elsewhere it has been extensively planted with coffee, cocoa, bananas, pineapple, rubber and oil palm. Tropical climatic conditions prevail in the north-west, with a single rainy season of five to seven months, and 1,250 mm–1,500 mm of rain annually. Guinea savannah occurs here, as well as in the centre of the country, and projects southwards around Bouaké.

Recent History

PIERRE ENGLEBERT

Revised by EDWARD GEORGE

THE HOUPHOUËT-BOIGNY ERA, 1960–93

From independence from French rule in August 1960 until his death in 1993, political life in Côte d'Ivoire was dominated by Dr Félix Houphouët-Boigny. He was the sole candidate for the presidency at every election until 1990, and his Parti démocratique de la Côte d'Ivoire—Rassemblement démocratique africain (PDCI—RDA) was the only legal political party until the same year. During his years in power, President Houphouët-Boigny guided the economic and political evolution of the country without any effective challenge to his rule. Sporadic political unrest was usually without cohesion, and political patronage was successfully used to defuse potential unrest. From the late 1960s efforts were made to 'Ivorianize' public administration and the economy. None the less, France has remained influential in Côte d'Ivoire's political and economic life, and French financial backing, together with membership of the Franc Zone, has been of major influence in Côte d'Ivoire's economic development.

Houphouët-Boigny supervised wide-ranging economic and political changes in 1980, following a period of economic and social malaise. The question then began to arise of an eventual successor to the ageing President. Although Houphouët-Boigny remained reluctant to nominate a Vice-President who would automatically succeed him, two likely contenders came to the fore: Philippe Yacé, a former President of the Assemblée nationale and Secretary-General of the PDCI—RDA, and Henri Konan Bédié, a former ambassador to the USA and Minister of Finance. The succession issue re-emerged prior to the October 1985 presidential election, with the abolition of the unfilled post of Vice-President in a constitutional amendment that allowed only for the President of the legislature to succeed to the presidency on an interim basis. The declared result of the presidential election was a 100% vote for Houphouët-Boigny, although at legislative elections in the following month only 64 of the 147 incumbent deputies were returned. In January 1986 Bédié was re-elected President of the Assemblée nationale, and in February Yacé was elected President of the Economic and Social Council, the country's third most senior political office. (Yacé held this post until his death in November 1998.)

In 1990 Côte d'Ivoire experienced unprecedented political upheaval. Demonstrations centred on the Government's austerity policies, which had been introduced to comply with a precondition for assistance by international creditors. Persistent unrest led to the deployment of troops in Abidjan. In response, Houphouët-Boigny appointed Alassane Ouattara, the Governor of the Banque centrale des états de l'Afrique de l'ouest (BCEAO, the regional central bank), to head a commission to formulate adjustment measures both more economically effective and more politically acceptable than previously proposed levies on income. In May, furthermore, Houphouët-Boigny agreed to the establishment of a plural political system. At the end of May a less stringent programme of austerity measures was announced, based on the recommendations of the Ouattara commission.

Opposition groups that had previously operated unofficially now acquired legal status and numerous new parties were swiftly formed. Côte d'Ivoire's first contested presidential election took place on 28 October 1990, with Houphouët-

Boigny challenged by Laurent Gbagbo, the candidate of the Front populaire ivoirien (FPI). The incumbent was elected for a seventh term of office by 81.7% of those who voted (69.2% of the electorate). In November the Assemblée nationale approved two constitutional amendments. The first effectively strengthened Bédié's position by providing for the President of the Assemblée nationale to assume the functions of the President of the Republic, should this office become vacant, until the expiry of the mandate of the previous incumbent. The second allowed for the appointment of a Prime Minister, a post subsequently awarded to Ouattara.

According to the official results of the parliamentary elections held in November 1990, the PDCI—RDA secured 163 seats in the new legislature, while the FPI won nine (Gbagbo was among the successful FPI candidates). Francis Wodié, the leader of the Parti ivoirien des travailleurs (PIT), was also elected, as were two independent candidates. The incoming Assemblée nationale reconfirmed Bédié as its President.

Dissension, Repression and Succession

In May 1991 security forces used violent methods to disperse a students' meeting at the University of Abidjan. Students and academic staff joined demonstrations in protest against the brutality, prompting further intervention by the security forces. The situation deteriorated in June, when members of the Fédération estudiantine et scolaire de Côte d'Ivoire (FESCI) attacked and killed a student who had defied an order to boycott classes. The Government ordered that the students' association be disbanded and deployed security forces on the campus. Tensions eased in August, when the Government withdrew troops from the campus. However, the political and social climate again deteriorated following the publication, in January 1992, of the findings of a commission of inquiry into the security forces' actions at the university. Although the commission found the Chief of the General Staff of the armed forces, Brig.-Gen. Robert Gueï, directly responsible for the acts of violence committed by his troops, Houphouët-Boigny emphasized that none of those incriminated by the report would be subject to disciplinary proceedings. In February, following further violent demonstrations, 16 FESCI activists, including the union's Secretary-General, were arrested. A demonstration, organized by the FPI, degenerated into violence, and more than 100 protesters were arrested following clashes with security forces. Among those detained was Gbagbo; it was announced that opposition leaders would be prosecuted under the terms of a new presidential ordinance that rendered political leaders responsible for acts of violence committed by their supporters. In late February the FESCI leader was fined and sentenced to three years' imprisonment, convicted of reconstituting a banned organization. In March Gbagbo and eight others were fined and sentenced to two-year prison terms. As the trials continued, opposition deputies began a boycott of the Assemblée nationale. In July Houphouët-Boigny declared an amnesty for all those convicted of political offences since the time of the 1990 disturbances.

President Houphouët-Boigny died on 7 December 1993. Later the same day Bédié announced his assumption of the duties of President of the Republic, with immediate effect, in accordance with the Constitution. Ouattara initially refused to recognize Bédié's right of succession, but resigned the premiership two days later, after France had acknowledged Bédié's legitimacy as President. Daniel Kablan Duncan, hitherto Minister-delegate, responsible for the Economy, Finance and Planning, was appointed Prime Minister.

THE BÉDIÉ PRESIDENCY

Several months of sporadic labour unrest were brought to an end by Houphouët-Boigny's death, and reactions to the 50% devaluation, in January 1994, of the CFA franc were generally more muted in Côte d'Ivoire than in other countries of the region. Despite Bédié's earlier criticism of Ouattara's economic policies, the new President and Prime Minister confirmed their commitment to adjustment measures initiated under Ouattara, including an accelerated programme of privatization. Meanwhile, Bédié conducted an effective purge of Ouattara sympathizers, appointing his own supporters to positions of influence in government agencies, the judiciary and in the state-owned media.

Bédié was elected Chairman of the PDCI—RDA in April 1994. His position as Head of State was further strengthened by Ouattara's departure for Washington, DC, USA, to take up the post of Deputy Managing Director of the IMF. In June a group of Ouattara loyalists left the PDCI—RDA to form what they termed a moderate, centrist organization, the Rassemblement des républicains (RDR). By the end of the year the new party had supplanted the FPI as the principal parliamentary opposition. Ouattara officially announced his membership of the RDR in early 1995.

Considerable controversy was caused by the adoption, in December 1994, of a new electoral code, in preparation for the following year's presidential and legislative elections. Opposition parties denounced clauses imposing restrictions on eligibility for public office, in particular requirements that candidates be of direct Ivorian descent and have been continuously resident in Côte d'Ivoire for five years prior to seeking election, both of which were interpreted as being directly aimed at preventing Ouattara from contesting the presidency. An FPI congress formally adopted Gbagbo as its candidate for the presidency, while the RDR invited Ouattara to stand as its presidential candidate; Ouattara, none the less, announced that he would not attempt to contest the presidency in violation of the law. The PDCI—RDA officially adopted Bédié as the party's presidential candidate.

As the presidential election approached both the FPI and the RDR (whose Secretary-General, Djény Kobina, had been expected to replace Ouattara as the party's candidate) stated that they would not be contesting the election as long as the conditions were not 'clear and open'; however, Wodié intended to contest the presidency as the candidate of the PIT.

The 1995 Elections

The presidential election took place, as scheduled, on 22 October 1995, following a week of violent incidents in several towns. The opposition, grouped in a Front républicain (FR), claimed that its call for an 'active boycott' of the poll had been largely successful, while the Government claimed that voters had participated both peacefully and in large numbers. Troops were deployed, ostensibly to prevent the disruption of voting by the opposition, although it was reported that polling had proceeded in only one of 60 designated centres in the FPI stronghold of Gagnoa. The official results of the presidential election were announced by the Constitutional Council five days after the poll. As had been expected, Bédié, with 95.2% of the valid votes cast, secured an overwhelming victory.

Efforts were intensified to reach an accommodation between the Government and opposition prior to the legislative elections, which were scheduled for 26 November 1995. In early November it was announced that the FR had agreed to abandon its boycott of the elections, in return for government concessions regarding the revision of voters' lists. The opposition suffered a reverse when the authorities announced that voting in three of Gagnoa's four constituencies, including the constituency that was to have been contested by Gbagbo, was to be postponed, owing to the disruption arising from the recent disturbances; moreover, Kobina's candidacy was disallowed, on the grounds that he had been unable to prove direct Ivorian descent. Voting for the legislature was reported to have proceeded generally without incident and the earliest indications were that the PDCI—RDA had retained a decisive majority. In late December the Constitutional Council annulled the results of the elections in three constituencies. The PDCI—RDA thus held 146 seats, the RDR 14 and the FPI nine.

In October 1995, shortly before the presidential election, Brig.-Gen. Gueï was replaced in his armed forces command and appointed to the Government; it was subsequently reported that he had refused to involve his troops in maintaining order during the election campaign. Duncan reshuffled his Government in January 1996, giving a position of less responsibility to Gueï.

Undercurrents of Unrest

Reports emerged in the independent press in May 1996 of a coup attempt by disaffected members of the armed forces at the time of the civil unrest that preceded the 1995 presidential election. Gueï's January 1996 demotion to a relatively minor government post was thus now interpreted as a reaction to unrest in the forces under his command.

A government reshuffle in August 1996 appeared to reflect Bédié's desire to remove from positions of influence figures connected with the insecurity prior to the 1995 elections. Among those to leave the Government were Gueï and Léon Konan Koffi. In January 1997 Gueï was dismissed from the army; a government communiqué stated that the investigative commission had found that the then armed forces chief had committed 'serious disciplinary offences' in the discharge of his duties.

A commission of inquiry into the 1995 pre-election unrest was inaugurated in December 1996. The RDR and the FPI refused to take up their allotted seats, however, protesting that the opposition had been judged responsible in advance of the inquiry. By-elections for eight parliamentary seats (including those for which voting did not take place or was cancelled in 1995) took place in that month: the FPI won five seats and the PDCI—RDA three.

Institutional Reforms

In August 1997 Bédié inaugurated a new National Security Council, directly responsible to the Head of State. He also announced that a general audit of the military was to be undertaken and that the armed forces were to be given additional responsibilities in areas such as countering illegal immigration, smuggling and organized crime, and in distributing humanitarian assistance.

Wide-ranging constitutional amendments were approved by the Assemblée nationale in June 1998. The session was boycotted by the RDR, and FPI deputies left the chamber during the debate: the opposition parties objected, in particular, to provisions conferring wider powers on the Head of State—specifically a clause allowing the President to delay elections or the proclamation of election results, on the grounds of 'events, serious troubles or *force majeure*'. The presidential mandate was, furthermore, to be extended to seven years, with no limit on the number of times an incumbent might seek re-election. Conditions of eligibility to seek public office were to be enshrined in the Constitution for the first time: most notably, candidates would be required to be Ivorian by birth, of direct Ivorian descent and to have been continuously resident in Côte d'Ivoire for 10 years. The opposition also denounced arrangements for the composition of a new upper house of the legislature, the Sénat, as two-thirds of its members were to be indirectly elected, with the remainder appointed by the Head of State. In September Gbagbo and Kobina led a demonstration in Abidjan to denounce the amendments.

In August 1999 Ouattara, who had returned to Côte d'Ivoire in July, and who had acquired a certificate confirming his Ivorian identity, was selected as the RDR's presidential candidate. Thereafter the long-simmering confrontation between Bédié and Ouattara quickly escalated, as Bédié continued to insist that he regarded his rival as a Burkinabè citizen and warned that he would suppress any protests on his behalf. When Ouattara's claim to citizenship was subjected to a new inquiry by judicial police, clashes occurred in September between police and supporters of Ouattara in Abidjan. In late October a court in Dimbokro, Ouattara's birthplace, cancelled his nationality certificate. The news prompted further violent demonstrations in Abidjan, during which a number of senior RDR leaders were arrested. The Secretary-General of the party since late 1998, Henriette Dagri-Diabaté, having been found guilty of inciting violence, was subsequently sentenced to two years' imprisonment. In early December, while Ouattara was in Paris, France, publicly denouncing the Government's actions, a warrant was issued for his arrest.

BRIG.-GEN. GUEÏ ASSUMES POWER

With Bédié's authority and his personal popularity rapidly declining, a mutiny among soldiers who converged on Abidjan on 23 December 1999 quickly escalated into a national crisis. The President initially sought to appease the soldiers, who seized most public buildings in the city, with the promise of improved pay and conditions; however, the troops subsequently altered their demands to include the reinstatement of Brig.-Gen. Gueï as Chief of Staff, some four years after his dismissal. On 24 December Gueï established a Comité national de salut publique (CNSP) to govern the country. Bédié fled to the French embassy, from where he moved to a French military base. The unexpected coup was apparently widely welcomed within Côte d'Ivoire, where the Bédié regime had been increasingly regarded as authoritarian and corrupt. In separate statements of support for the coup, both the RDR and FPI leaders speedily returned to Côte d'Ivoire from abroad. France also promptly accepted the coup and announced that it was to establish a dialogue with the new administration.

The new authorities rapidly succeeded in restoring order and calm. The CNSP did not at first announce a timetable for a return to civilian rule, but, having swiftly released the RDR's imprisoned leaders, it was initially interpreted as being solidly behind Ouattara, especially as Intendant-Gen. Lassana Palenfo, a prominent member of the CNSP, had previously held a ministerial portfolio in Ouattara's Government. The subsequent formation of an all-party Government in January 2000 provoked prolonged disagreements, particularly with the FPI, which, as a result, was eventually better represented than either the RDR or the PDCI—RDA (the latter did not officially approve the participation of two of its members in the new Government).

In late January 2000 Gueï promised that presidential and legislative elections would be held before 31 October, following a proposed constitutional referendum, scheduled for July. As the parties, with the exception of the PDCI—RDA, hurriedly confirmed their presidential candidates, the CNSP imposed a temporary ban on political gatherings until after the referendum. Despite the ban, a group of influential PDCI—RDA members began to canvass openly for Gueï himself to stand as the presidential candidate of the party, although Gueï seemed reluctant to declare his intentions publicly.

The publication of the draft constitution in May 2000 provoked a renewed political crisis, as the articles referring to the eligibility of candidates for the presidency restated the position that only candidates of solely Ivorian nationality and parentage could stand. In reaction to the protests of the RDR about the clause, Gueï announced a government reshuffle, in which all of the RDR ministers, with the exception of Dagri-Diabaté, were dismissed. In the reshuffle Gueï also appointed a Prime Minister, Seydou Elimane Diarra, an experienced civil servant and diplomat, widely regarded as an impartial figure. In the same month the authorities in Côte d'Ivoire issued an international warrant for the arrest of Bédié, who was living in exile in France, on charges of embezzlement.

The constitutional referendum proceeded in relative calm on 23 July 2000, although serious organizational difficulties caused voting to carry on into a second day. It was subsequently announced that 86.5% of voters had expressed their approval of the new Constitution, which had been supported by all the major parties, and which, *inter alia*, granted immunity from prosecution to members of the CNSP and to all those involved in the *coup d'état*. Turn-out in the referendum was estimated at 56%.

PRESIDENTIAL AND LEGISLATIVE ELECTIONS

In July 2000 Ouattara, who asserted that he complied with all the restrictions on eligibility, announced his intention to contest the presidential election, scheduled for 17 September, as the RDR candidate. Former President Bédié also announced that he intended to seek the nomination of the PDCI—RDA, although Gueï was reported to have refused to grant permission for Bédié's return from France. In mid-August Gueï announced that the country's four main political parties had agreed in advance to form a coalition government of national unity following the legislative elections. In the same month Gueï announced that he was to contest the election as an independent, contrary to previous reports that he had applied to become the candidate of the PDCI—RDA.

On 17 September 2000 members of the armed forces, angered by the late payment of bonuses and by Gueï's decision to contest the presidency, attacked Gueï's residence, killing two of his bodyguards. Troops loyal to Gueï successfully repelled the mutineers, several of whom were later arrested. The Supreme Court upheld a ban on the participation of both Ouattara and Bédié in the presidential election, which had been postponed until 22 October, leaving the field clear for the two main contenders, Gueï and Gbagbo. Following a further minor government reshuffle at the end of September, the FPI became the sole political party to be represented in the transitional Government.

After the election, as preliminary results indicated that Gbagbo was taking the lead, Gueï suspended the electoral commission and proclaimed himself as the winner. This, in turn, prompted Gbagbo's supporters to stage mass protests on the streets of Abidjan, until, on the morning of 25 October 2000, key units of the army and gendarmerie proclaimed their support for Gbagbo. Gueï promptly fled the country, while Gbagbo reinstated the electoral commission, which published official results showing that he had received 59.4% of the votes to Gueï's 32.7%. However, a low rate of participation (an estimated 33.2% overall, but markedly lower in the largely Muslim and RDR-supporting regions in the north, as well as in Yamoussoukro and other strongholds of the PDCI—RDA) cast doubt on the legitimacy of Gbagbo's victory. Concern was raised that Gbagbo had voiced support, during his campaign, for the notion of strengthening national identity, or 'ivoirité', in potentially inflammatory terms, similar to those used previously by Bédié. Gbagbo was sworn in on 26 October. On 27 October Pascal Affi N'Guessan, Minister of Industry and Tourism in the outgoing Government, was appointed as Prime Minister. In the three days following Gbagbo's accession to the presidency violent clashes between the security forces and RDR demonstrators demanding the annulment of the election resulted in 203 deaths, according to official figures. The discovery of a mass grave, containing the bodies of 57 people, in Yopougon, Abidjan, prompted the Government to announce an investigation into the violence. The UN subsequently established a commission of inquiry into the killings.

In continuing protest at Ouattara's exclusion, the RDR boycotted both the legislative elections held on 10 December 2000 and those held in January 2001 in a number of constituencies in the north, where unrest had led to the postponement of voting, with the result that the Assemblée nationale was now dominated by the FPI, with 96 seats, and the PDCI—RDA, with 94 seats. (A 'moderate' wing of the RDR, which subsequently called on Ouattara to resign his leadership of the party, did participate in the elections, winning five seats, while elections did not take place at all in two constituencies in Ouattara's home town of Kong, owing to continuing unrest.) N'Guessan remained at the head of a new Government appointed in late January, which included, in addition to members of the FPI, ministers from the PDCI—RDA and the PIT, and two independents.

ATTEMPTS AT RECONCILIATION

An atmosphere of political uncertainty prevailed throughout 2001, amid repeated rumours of attempted coups by disaffected army officers and reports that military contingents were being deployed to regions bordering Burkina Faso, Guinea and Liberia. Human rights campaigners expressed alarm at a rise in harassment of northerners and immigrants. In an attempt to secure his fragile authority, Gbagbo made new efforts at reconciliation between the principal political players; however, the issue of Ouattara's continued exclusion from the political process still proved divisive. In July N'Guessan was elected to replace Gbagbo as leader of the FPI. An official national reconciliation forum, chaired by Diarra and attended by some 700 representatives of political, religious and civil society organizations, opened in October; although Bédié and Ouattara returned from exile to attend the latter part of the forum, which continued until mid-December, a meeting between Gbagbo, Bédié, Gueï and Ouattara proved impossible to realize. Nevertheless, more substantial negotiations between the four leaders took place in Yamoussoukro during January 2002, and further such meetings were promised. Thereafter, it appeared that Gueï had decided to support Ouattara's case for Ivorian nationality.

A struggle for control of the PDCI—RDA, which had become increasingly split along ethnic lines, was apparent ahead of its national conference in April 2002, when Bédié was challenged for the party presidency by two northerners, Laurent Dona Fologo and Lamine Fadika. In the event, Bédié secured 82.5% of the votes cast in the leadership election and Dona Fologo was replaced as Secretary-General by Alphonse Djédjé Mady.

Ouattara was finally granted Ivorian citizenship in late June 2002, although he remained barred from contesting the presidency, as a result of having held Burkinabè citizenship. None the less, renewed inter-ethnic unrest erupted prior to local elections in mid-July, particularly in Daloa, where clashes broke out between supporters of the RDR and the FPI. At the elections, which were marred by logistical difficulties, the FPI and the PDCI—RDA won the largest number of seats, ahead of the RDR and a party formed in early 2001 by supporters of Gueï, the Union pour la démocratie et la paix de la Côte d'Ivoire (UDPCI). A further attempt at reconciliation was evident in the appointment of four RDR ministers to a reshuffled 'Government of National Unity', which remained under N'Guessan's premiership, in early August 2002. However, discontent at the membership of the Government became evident almost immediately; in particular, opposition parties expressed their dissatisfaction at the overruling of their preferred candidates for ministerial appointments by Gbagbo. Consequently, the UDPCI withdrew its support from the Government, although its sole minister remained in his post, in an independent capacity; similar disputes also arose within the PIT and the PDCI—RDA, while Gueï became an increasingly vocal critic of the Government.

MUTINY LEADS TO CIVIL CONFLICT

In mid-September 2002, while Gbagbo was on a state visit to Italy, Côte d'Ivoire entered its most serious political crisis since independence. On 19 September groups of soldiers (who were mainly supporters of Gueï) defied orders to surrender their arms, precipitating a mutiny that quickly split the armed forces throughout the country. In Abidjan dissidents killed the Minister of State, Minister of the Interior and Decentralization, Emile Boga Doudou, a close ally of Gbagbo, and attacked the home of the Minister of State, Minister of Defence and Civil Protection, Moïse Lida Kouassi. Gueï was killed in Abidjan, apparently by soldiers loyal to Gbagbo, either out of revenge or panic; it was subsequently suggested that Gueï had been about to announce a *coup d'état* at the national radio station, although reports as to the exact identity of the mutineers remained confused. Gbagbo, following his return to Côte d'Ivoire on 20 September, implied that an unnamed foreign country (widely understood to refer to Burkina Faso) was implicated in the insurgency. Amid renewed inter-ethnic tension and an upsurge in violence directed against northern Muslims and citizens of neighbouring states, and following an attack on his residence in Abidjan, Ouattara took up residence in the French embassy. (At the end of November he sought refuge in Gabon.) As the mutiny spread rapidly across the country, gendarmes were sent into immigrant shanty towns near Abidjan, where they burned and destroyed homes, killing hundreds of immigrants and northerners. With the situation deteriorating rapidly, on 22 September France dispatched 200 troops, who established a base at Yamoussoukro airport, in order to co-ordinate the evacuation of expatriates from Bouaké. On 24 September the USA deployed some 200 special forces to Korhogo, to airlift foreigners from the rebel-held town. Moreover, an emergency summit of the Economic Community of West African States (ECOWAS), which was convened in Accra, Ghana, in late September, resolved to dispatch a peace-keeping force to act as a 'buffer' between government and rebel troops, and mandated the Presidents of Ghana, Guinea-Bissau, Niger, Nigeria and Togo, in addition to the South African President, Thabo Mbeki, in his capacity as the Chairman of the African Union (AU), to form a 'contact group' to undertake negotiations between Gbagbo and the insurgents.

In early October 2002 Master-Sgt Tuo Fozié, who had been sentenced to 20 years' imprisonment *in absentia* earlier in the year for his purported role in an attempted *coup d'état* in January 2001, emerged as a spokesman for the rebels, who identified themselves as the Mouvement patriotique de la Côte d'Ivoire (MPCI) and stated as their principal demand the removal of Gbagbo from the presidency and the holding of fresh presidential and legislative elections; the MPCI emphasized that, although elements within the group had returned to Côte d'Ivoire from exile in various countries, it had no connection with any government. Negotiations between the MPCI and ECOWAS mediators took place in early October. Meanwhile, Gbagbo announced that the Government was prepared to enter into a cease-fire with the rebels, subject to their disarmament and the nation-wide restoration of government authority. However, the signature of the proposed cease-fire accord by the Government, initially scheduled for 5 October, was delayed on two occasions, and subsequently cancelled, precipitating the departure of the ECOWAS contact group from Côte d'Ivoire. Thereafter, the Government's forces consistently failed to make any advances in rebel-held areas, especially around Bouaké, which had become the main rebel stronghold, but across the south, which remained under government control, the apparently systematic destruction of the homes of suspected rebel supporters (often ethnic Dioula in addition to people of Burkinabè, Malian or Guinean origin) occurred, resulting in both large-scale migration of foreign citizens away from the south and further loss of life. Although the Government was quick to invoke its 1961 defence treaty with France, the French role soon came to consist primarily of holding the line that now effectively divided the country between north and south. The Government began to seek military support elsewhere, reportedly hiring the services of military advisers from South Africa and Angola, private defence companies from the United Kingdom and the USA, as well as more conventional mercenary troops from Eastern Europe.

In mid-October 2002 Gbagbo effectively assumed personal responsibility for defence. On the following day the MPCI gained control of Daloa, although, following several days of clashes, in which at least 17 people were killed, government forces recaptured the town. On 17 October Fozié unilaterally signed a cease-fire agreement on behalf of the MPCI, to take effect from the following day; Gbagbo, speaking in a 'live' television broadcast, announced his acceptance of the accord.

Regional diplomatic efforts began to get under way during October 2002. At the end of the month the Government and the MPCI entered into their first substantive negotiations in Lomé, Togo, under the aegis of ECOWAS; the government delegation was led by Laurent Dona Fologo, the President of the Economic and Social Council, while the rebel delegation was headed by the Secretary-General of the recently formed political wing of the MPCI, Guillaume Soro Kigbafori, a former leader of the FESCI. In early November the Government announced an amnesty for the rebels and the acceptance of their eventual reintegration into the national armed forces. For their part, regional leaders indicated that they would be willing to provide troops, under Senegalese command, to monitor a cease-fire. However, the negotiations between the Government and the MPCI broke down later in November, following the apparently politically motivated assassination of the brother of a co-founder of the FPI, Louis Dakoury-Tabley, who had defected to join the MPCI negotiators. In protest, Soro walked out of the talks, calling on Gbagbo to stop the killings of foreigners and northerners. By mid-November the office of the UN High Commissioner for Refugees (UNHCR) estimated that more than 200,000 people had been forced out of their homes, of whom at least 40,000 had formerly resided in Abidjan, where the destruction of shanty towns was ongoing. Later in November Gbagbo announced that he was prepared to call a referendum, to be held in 2003 or early 2004, on the need for constitutional amendments. At the end of the month, however, the four RDR representatives of the Government resigned, in protest at alleged human rights abuses in which the Government was implicated.

Meanwhile, the rebellion had spread to western regions of Côte d'Ivoire, bordering Guinea and Liberia. In late October 2002 two new rebel groups, apparently comprising supporters of Gueï and also including mercenaries from Liberia, emerged. The Mouvement populaire ivoirien du grand ouest (MPIGO) and the Mouvement pour la justice et la paix (MJP) rapidly gained control of the western cities of Danane and Man. As clashes continued in the west, France steadily increased its overall presence to some 3,000 troops by January 2003, and the first contingent of ECOWAS forces, comprising 179 Senegalese troops, arrived in Côte d'Ivoire in mid-January.

The Marcoussis Accords

In mid-January 2003 France succeeded in calling all sides together for detailed talks at Marcoussis, near Paris. After 10 days of negotiations, it was eventually agreed that a government of national reconciliation would be formed under the premiership of Diarra. The proposed interim government was to comprise a total of 41 representatives, including members of each of the main parties and several smaller parties, as well as of the rebel groups. The Marcoussis Accords were signed on 24 January, but immediately provoked a violent reaction among government supporters in Abidjan, where stones and petrol bombs were thrown at the French embassy and other French-linked institutions, amid further assaults on immigrants. Moreover, on his return to Côte d'Ivoire, Gbagbo appeared to repudiate the terms of the Marcoussis Accords, which he referred to as no more than 'proposals'. Over several days there was looting of French homes and businesses, prompting France to advise the departure of all its 'non-essential' nationals at the end of the month (other Western countries subsequently followed suit). Many businesses suspended operations, and the African Development Bank announced that it was relocating its headquarters, on a temporary basis, from Abidjan to Tunis, Tunisia. When Gbagbo made a long-awaited public announcement on 7 February, he continued to resist the terms agreed at Marcoussis, although he was coming under mounting international pressure, particularly from the UN Security Council, to honour the agreement.

Further rounds of negotiations and diplomacy took place throughout February 2003, with France continuing to urge the formation of the proposed government of national reconciliation, which remained in abeyance as a result of the insistence of the MPCI that it had been promised the defence and security portfolios. Nevertheless, Diarra was officially inaugurated as Prime Minister on 10 February. On the regional front, Ghana began to play an increasingly important role as an effective mediator among the parties and the rebel groups. A breakthrough came at the beginning of March, when the MPCI was persuaded to back down on its demands for control of these important ministries. A new agreement was signed by the main parties and rebel movements in Accra on 8 March. The agreement provided for a six-month peace process, involving the deployment of more than 4,000 peace-keeping personnel, mainly provided by France, but also including ECOWAS troops. It was agreed that an international monitoring group would be provided by the UN, ECOWAS and the AU.

Formation of the Government of National Reconciliation

In the first step towards implementing the Accra agreement, several principal positions in the new Government were announced in mid-February 2003, but those appointed were mostly members of the FPI and the PDCI—RDA. The rebel movements, which now referred to themselves as the 'new forces', and the RDR refused to attend the initial meetings of the Council of Ministers, although the MPCI, MPIGO and MJP sent a delegation to Yamoussoukro to express their reservations. Moreover, the allocation of the defence and security portfolios remained a source of disagreement within the Government, as the FPI refused to accept the appointment of Gaston Ouassénan Koné, of the PDCI—RDA, as Minister of Defence. In mid-March two existing ministers assumed these responsibilities, in an acting capacity.

Six months after the rebellion began the prevailing political and military difficulties in the country were beginning to create a humanitarian crisis. The continuing removal of people from their homes in the south was estimated to have forced 250,000 to head for neighbouring countries, while a further 600,000 people were reckoned to be internally displaced. By early April 2003 a 1,260-strong ECOWAS military mission in Côte d'Ivoire (ECOMICI) had been deployed to take over a section of the 'front line' near Yamoussoukro from French troops. It was intended that this force would eventually number around 3,400, with the additional troops to be deployed in two phases. Meanwhile, the number of killings mounted in the west of the country; the MPIGO leader, Félix Doh, was killed in late April after attempting to distance himself from his Liberian supporters. Nevertheless, on 1 May the Chief of Staff of the Ivorian armed forces, Gen. Mathias Doué, and the military leader of the MPCI, Col Michel Gueu, signed a cease-fire agreement, which was intended to apply to all rebel groups operating in Côte d'Ivoire. Later in May Soro confirmed that the MPCI's military activities had ceased, while a meeting of the Council of Ministers in Bouaké in late May was regarded as a significant symbolic measure. In mid-June the national army and rebel forces agreed to the eventual confinement of troops, and by the end of the month it was reported that order had been restored in western regions. At the end of June the Government announced that all former rebels would be disarmed by mid-September. Also in late June, the UN mission in Côte d'Ivoire (MINUCI), authorized by the UN Security Council in May and charged with overseeing the implementation of the Marcoussis Accords, commenced operations in Abidjan. On 4 July, in a ceremony held at the presidential palace, MPCI leaders formally announced the end of the conflict. Although tensions continued, in early August the Assemblée nationale approved legislation providing for an amnesty for those involved in political unrest between 17 September 2000 and 19 September 2002; those involved in abuses of human rights or violations of international humanitarian law were, however, to be excluded from this amnesty. By the end of August 2003 more than 50 political prisoners had been released. Meanwhile, the MPCI effectively absorbed the MPIGO and MJP, and announced that the organization was henceforth to be known as the Forces nouvelles (FN).

In late August 2003 the French authorities announced that 16 people, including a former close ally of Gueï, Ibrahim Coulibaly, had been arrested in Paris, on suspicion of seeking to destabilize the Ivorian Government. (Coulibaly was released on bail by the French authorities in mid-September, pending further investigations.) At the end of August some 50 people were arrested in Côte d'Ivoire, on suspicion of planning a *coup d'état*. Also in late August two French solders were killed in clashes with rebels in central Côte d'Ivoire, becoming the first peace-keeping troops to lose their lives in the conflict; the FN subsequently apologized for the incident and the alleged perpetrators of the killings were captured and brought before a military tribunal in early September.

On 13 September 2003 appointments to the defence and security portfolios were finally announced: René Amani, a close associate of Diarra, was appointed as Minister of Defence; and Martin Bleou, a human rights activist and professor of law, was named as Minister of Security. However, the FN and the RDR stated that they would not accept these nominations. On 22 September the FN suspended its participation in the Government, accusing Gbagbo of delaying the process of reconciliation, although one of its nine ministers announced his intention to remain in post. Moreover, the former rebels declared that they would not co-operate with the proposals for the disarmament and reintegration of former combatants. In late September, after an attack on a branch of the BCEAO and an outbreak of fighting in which at least 23 people were killed, French troops entered Bouaké and restored order, with the approval of the FN. In mid-October the Government prohibited demonstrations for a period of three months and also resolved to dissolve the Coordination des jeunes patriotes (CJP), a nationalist militia led by Charles Blé Goudé, a former leader of the FESCI and an ally of Gbagbo; these measures followed several violent demonstrations in Abidjan, led by the CJP, which had demanded the expedited disarmament of the FN and had criticized the peace-keeping role of French troops in the conflict.

Ongoing diplomatic efforts, under the aegis of ECOWAS, to advance the peace process appeared to have little short-term success. Negotiations between Diarra and Soro, convened in Accra in mid-November 2003 by the Ghanaian President, John Kufuor, and attended by six heads of state from the region, failed to satisfy FN demands for greater security and increased devolution of powers from the President to the Prime Minister.

Reconciliation Delayed

In early December 2003 Gbagbo announced that the former rebel forces in the north of the country would commence disarmament later that month, although the FN initially denied that such an agreement had been reached. In the event the disarmament process was further delayed, although some 40 government soldiers who had been held as prisoners-of-war in FN-controlled areas were released. Also that month the Council of Ministers approved proposed legislation that permitted presidential candidates to have only one parent of Ivorian origin, rather than two; as a constitutional amendment, this measure would require the approval of a two-thirds' majority of the Assemblée nationale and endorsement by public referendum before it could enter into force. Gbagbo announced that two other items of legislation, intended to grant greater security to migrant workers in Côte d'Ivoire—with regard to the right to apply for Ivorian citizenship and to own agricultural land—would also be subject to approval by referendum, although without having been presented to the Assemblée nationale. Soro criticized the proposal to hold three referendums, stating that the two measures concerning migrant workers could be adopted by the legislature.

On 22 December 2003 the FN announced that its ministers were to resume participation in the Government. In early January 2004 French peace-keeping troops began to enter regions of northern Côte d'Ivoire, with the agreement of the FN, reportedly in order to assist in the provision of humanitarian aid, although tensions persisted, particularly in Korhogo. In late February the UN Security Council established the UN Operation in Côte d'Ivoire (UNOCI); with an authorized military strength of 6,240, the peace-keeping operation was to be deployed for an initial period of 12 months from 4 April, on which date authority was to be transferred from MINUCI and ECOMICI to UNOCI. Some 4,000 French troops were to remain in the country, with a mandate to act as a rapid deployment force if required by the UN mission. Nevertheless, the process of national reconciliation appeared to be stalling somewhat, with Soro's announcement, at the end of February, that former rebel fighters would not disarm prior to legislative and presidential elections scheduled for 2005. In early March 2004 the PDCI—RDA announced that its ministers were to suspend their participation in the Government, with immediate effect, in response to what it termed acts of humiliation and aggression against the party by supporters of Gbagbo; all parties represented in the Government, with the exception of Gbagbo's FPI and the PIT, expressed support for the action of the PDCI—RDA. A few days later the disarmament process was indefinitely postponed.

On 25 March 2004 a protest march in Abidjan, organized by seven of the 10 signatory parties of the Marcoussis Accords (known collectively as the G7), in defiance of a six-week ban on demonstrations announced by Gbagbo earlier that month, prompted clashes between protesters and members of the security forces. According to official figures, 37 were killed, including two police-officers, although the G7, comprising the PDCI—RDA, the RDR, the UDPCI, the Mouvement des forces d'avenir (MFA) and the three former rebel movements now united in the FN, estimated the number of deaths at more than 300. An inquiry, conducted by the office of the UN High Commissioner for Human Rights (UNHCHR), later reportedly concluded that at least 120 civilians had been killed by the security forces in a 'carefully planned operation' organized by 'the highest authorities of the state'. Following the outbreak of violence, the RDR, the FN and the MFA announced that they were to suspend their participation in the Government and refused to negotiate with Gbagbo. The first contingent of UNOCI forces arrived in Côte d'Ivoire in early April.

The Accra Agreement

In mid-April 2004, following a two-day visit by President Mamadou Tandja of Niger, President Gbagbo acceded to the G7's principal demands in an attempt to restore some stability, agreeing to respect the right to demonstrate, to ensure the security of the people and to allow equal access to the state media to all political organizations. The peace process remained stalled, however, and in mid-May Gbagbo dismissed three opposition ministers from the Government, including

Soro. On the previous day Soro had urged ministers belonging to the FN to return to Bouaké from Abidjan, after Gbagbo had threatened to suspend their salaries and restrict their freedom to travel in response to their boycott of government meetings. Moreover, the dismissals provoked tension between Gbagbo and Prime Minister Diarra, who claimed they were in violation of the Marcoussis Accords. In early June the CJP and other Gbagbo loyalists, who accused France of favouring the rebel movements, attacked the French embassy and erected a barricade near the French military headquarters; UN vehicles were also vandalized during the attacks, which Gbagbo condemned. Later that month clashes between rival FN factions associated with Soro and Ibrahim Coulibaly led to the deaths of 22 people in Bouaké and Korhogo. In mid-July a UN commission of inquiry, established by the UNHCHR, commenced a three-month investigation into human rights violations committed in Côte d'Ivoire between 19 September 2002 and 24 January 2003. In early August 2004 the UN announced the discovery of three mass graves containing the bodies of 99 people believed to have been killed in the rebel fighting in June.

At the end of July 2004 all parties to the conflict, attending a meeting of West African heads of state that had been convened in Accra by the UN Secretary-General and the President of Ghana, signed an agreement on means of implementing the Marcoussis Accords. Under the agreement, which was to be monitored by UNOCI, ECOWAS and the AU, disarmament of the FN troops was to commence by 15 October and progress on amending the Constitution with regard to presidential eligibility and other political reforms was to be made by the end of September. In mid-August, in accordance with the agreement, Gbagbo reinstated the three government ministers dismissed in May, and all ministers from opposition parties and the former rebel groups resumed participation in the Government. Shortly afterwards the President signed a decree delegating some of his powers to the Prime Minister pending a presidential election due to be held in October 2005. However, the 15 October 2004 disarmament deadline was not observed by the rebels, who declared that insufficient progress had been made towards the realization of the proposed political reforms.

Renewed Violence

In early November 2004 the 18-month cease-fire was broken when the Ivorian air force launched bombing raids on Bouaké and other targets in the north of the country, reportedly resulting in the deaths of more than 80 civilians. On the third day of the offensive, nine French peace-keeping troops were killed when a French military base in Bouaké was bombed. In retaliation, French forces, acting on the direct orders of President Jacques Chirac, destroyed the entire fleet of the Ivorian air force on the ground. This precipitated several days of violence in Abidjan and elsewhere, with thousands of Ivorians, in particular members of the CJP, rioting, looting and attacking French and other foreign targets. French troops intervened to take control of Abidjan's airport and major thoroughfares and to protect French and other foreign nationals, clashing with rioters and protesters in the process; some 50 deaths were reported in the clashes. In response to the unrest, the Ivorian authorities appointed a new Chief of Staff of the armed forces, Maj.-Col (later Brig.-Gen.) Philippe Mangou. On 15 November the UN Security Council voted unanimously in favour of imposing an arms embargo, drafted by France, on Côte d'Ivoire. Meanwhile, Soro and eight other opposition ministers announced that they would not attend meetings of the Government, claiming that their security in Abidjan could not be guaranteed.

MEDIATION OF MBEKI AND THE PRETORIA AGREEMENT

In November and December 2004 the South African President, Thabo Mbeki, designated as mediator by the AU, held talks with both the Ivorian Government and the FN, aiming to re-establish the Marcoussis Accords as the basis for a solution of the crisis. Following concessions made by Gbagbo during these talks, a series of political reforms proposed by the Accords were submitted to the legislature for approval. On 17 December the Assemblée nationale voted in favour of amending the Constitution to permit persons with only one, rather than two, Ivorian parents to contest the presidency (thus allowing Ouattara to contest the elections scheduled for October 2005). Gbagbo, however, insisted that any constitutional change would require ratification at a referendum, while the G7 objected that such a plebiscite, which could only effectively be organized if the country were united, was unnecessary. Soro and his fellow opposition ministers continued their boycott of government meetings in early 2005, while the FN failed to observe a further proposed deadline for disarmament set for 15 January. Unrest intensified in February–March, with clashes between police forces and a pro-Government militia in early February resulting in at least two deaths. Attacks on FN forces in western regions by another pro-Government militia reportedly led to some 30 deaths, according to an FN commander, while supporters of the Government, led by the CJP, issued demands for French troops to leave Côte d'Ivoire. On 4 April the mandate of UNOCI and French peace-keeping troops was extended for a period of one month. (The mandate was extended for a further month on 4 May, and for an interim period of 21 days on 3 June, pending a reassessment of the mandate of UNOCI.)

In early April 2005 President Mbeki hosted a summit in Pretoria, South Africa, attended by Bédié, Diarra, Gbagbo, Ouattara and Soro, as a result of which an agreement was signed, on 6 April, committing all parties to the disbandment of militia groups and to the disarmament of the former rebel troops. Conditions for eligibility of presidential candidates at the election due to be held in October were to be decided subsequently, following consultation between Mbeki, the UN Secretary-General, Kofi Annan, and the Chairman of the AU, the President of Nigeria, Olusegun Obasanjo. On 14 April Mbeki issued a statement ruling that the Ivorian Constitutional Council should confirm the candidates of those parties that signed the Marcoussis Accords of 2003; this statement was thereby interpreted as permitting Ouattara's eventual candidacy. Following this statement, two of the FN ministers resumed participation in the Government. The first moves towards resolving the military aspects of the conflict commenced on 21 April, when both parties moved heavy weaponry away from the 'buffer zone' dividing the country. Later in the month Gbagbo declared that he would accept Ouattara as a legitimate candidate at the presidential election, but implied that in so doing, normal constitutional provisions would be temporarily lifted. At the end of May an attack on two villages in Duékoué resulted in 70 civilian fatalities.

In early May 2005 negotiations between the FN and the Ivorian armed forces concluded without agreement being reached on the programme for disarmament of the former rebel troops. Following a further round of discussions, however, it was agreed that disarmament would commence at the end of June, and that a new republican army would be established to incorporate both members of the existing armed forces and former rebel fighters. In accordance with this programme, disarmament was to be completed by 20 August. Meanwhile, in mid-May Ouattara, on behalf of the RDR, Bédié, on behalf of the PDCI—RDA, and the leaders of the MFA and the UDPCI signed an agreement to the effect that, in the event of the presidential election progressing to a second round (which would occur if no candidate received an absolute majority of votes cast in the first round), all four parties would support a common candidate in opposition to Gbagbo. In late June the UN Security Council agreed to extend the mandate of UNOCI and the French peace-keeping forces for a further seven months, until January 2006, broadening the mandate granted to UNOCI to include an active role in disarmament, support for the organization of elections and the establishment of the rule of law. The UN Security Council also authorized an increase of 1,225 troops, enlarging UNOCI to 7,200 men, in addition to 4,000 French troops.

At the end of June 2005 representatives of the Government and the FN, meeting in South Africa, agreed a deadline for the disarmament of pro-Government militias of 20 August, while legislation providing for the establishment of an independent electoral commission was to be agreed by 15 July. The South African authorities also stated that they would press for the imposition of sanctions against any parties perceived to be inhibiting the peace process. In mid-July another revised timetable for the disarmament of former rebels and militias was announced, following further negotiations between the FN and the Government: some 40,000 former rebels and 15,000 pro-Government militia were to disarm by early October. The FN troops were now due to commence disarming on 1 August, although several prominent members of the FN stated that they would not disarm before the pro-Government militias had done so. Later in the month Gbagbo signed legislation on the establishment of an independent electoral commission and on nationality, using his exceptional constitutional powers to override the requirement for parliamentary approval.

On 1 August 2005 the FN declared that they were not ready to begin disarming, despite further negotiations between the former rebels and the Ivorian armed forces, stating that the terms of the legislation recently decreed by Gbagbo differed from those that had been agreed in Pretoria in April. Although the presidential election remained scheduled for October, the failure to implement the peace accords made it increasingly improbable that the poll would be held as proposed. On 8 September Annan announced that the presidential election would not take place in October but would be delayed indefinitely, owing to the failure of the country's political parties to co-operate. His announcement was followed, on 27 September, by a televised address by Gbagbo during which he confirmed the postponement of the election, blaming the delay on the FN's refusal to disarm and the continuing division of the country between government-held and rebel-held zones. Three days later ECOWAS met in an emergency summit in Abuja, Nigeria, to discuss the crisis, referring the matter to the AU's Peace and Security Council, which met in Addis Ababa, Ethiopia, the following week. On 6 October the AU announced its decision, authorizing the extension of Gbagbo's mandate as President for up to 12 months and establishing 31 October 2006 as the new deadline for holding elections. The AU also urged the appointment of a new Prime Minister acceptable to all parties and the setting up of a working group to monitor the situation in the country, as well as a mediation group to push the peace process forward. In mid-October 2005 the UN Security Council adopted Resolution 1633, endorsing the AU's recommendations and previous peace agreements. The AU mediation team immediately proceeded to Côte d'Ivoire to hold consultations on the selection of a new premier. On 16 November Presidents Obasanjo and Mbeki announced a shortlist of four candidates, including a senior civil servant, Gervais Coulibaly, the president of the PDCI parliamentary group, Gaston Ouassénan Koné, a former justice minister, Jacqueline Oble-Lohouess, and an RDR militant, Tiémoko Yadé Coulibaly. However, in a surprise move on 4 December the AU mediation team nominated Charles Konan Banny, the governor of the regional central bank, BCEAO, to be the new Prime Minister.

Meanwhile, sporadic outbreaks of violence continued. In December 2005 the main police camp in Abidjan was attacked and in January 2006 an attack on a military camp at Akouédou, east of Abidjan, killed 10 soldiers. Following these attacks, 34 soldiers were arrested, prompting rumours that they had mutinied over pay.

GOVERNMENT OF NATIONAL UNITY

On 28 December 2005 Prime Minister Banny announced his new Government of national unity, comprising 32 ministries (fewer than in the previous Government). Each of the main parties was represented, with seven ministries for the FPI, six for the FN and five each for the PDCI—RDA and the RDR. Banny also assumed the finance and communications portfolios, while the former finance minister, Bohoun Bouabré, became Minister of State for Planning and Development, and the Secretary-General of the MPCI, Guillaume Kigbafori Soro, was appointed to the new role of Minister of State for the Programme of Reconstruction and Reintegration. In mid-January 2006 the Government met formally for the first time. However, only three days later it faced its first crisis, when the UN-mandated International Working Group (IWG) issued a statement rejecting the extension of the mandate of the Assemblée nationale, which had expired in December 2005. Interpreting the statement as a formal dissolution of the legislature, CJP militias loyal to President Gbagbo seized control of main roads and government buildings in Abidjan and the south-west of the country, attacking businesses and clashing with UN troops who were forced to withdraw from their bases in Guiglo and Douékoué. Once calm had been restored, the FPI threatened to withdraw from the transitional Government, but was persuaded to stay by President Obasanjo, who issued a statement confirming that the Assemblée nationale had not been dissolved. On 27 January 2006 Banny defused tensions by issuing a decree that prolonged the mandate of the Assemblée nationale.

In late January 2006 the UN Security Council extended the mandate of UNOCI to 15 December, approving the transfer of an additional 200 peace-keepers from Liberia to Côte d'Ivoire. It also extended the arms embargo for a further year. In late February Banny called a meeting in Yamoussoukro of the leaders of the main political parties—Gbagbo, Ouattara, Bédié and Soro—to resolve outstanding political issues. However, the only significant agreement reached was the recognition by all parties of the legitimacy and composition of the electoral commission, the Commission électorale indépendante (CEI).

On 29 March 2006 a fresh crisis arose after Prime Minister Banny announced his intention to restart the identification campaign for the registration of voters. This was strongly opposed by Gbagbo, who argued that the existing voter registers from 2000 were adequate and only needed updating. However, the opposition supported Banny's initiative, arguing that up to 3m. Ivorians had no identification papers, preventing them from voting. Following mediation in early April 2006 by the new AU president, Denis Sassou-Nguesso of the Republic of the Congo, a compromise was reached that was termed *concomitance*. This stipulated that the disarmament and identification processes would occur at the same time and in a co-ordinated manner, along with the redeployment of the public administration in the north. The agreement was rejected, however, by the FPI chairman, Pascal Affi N'Guessan, and the CJP leaders. Banny announced that a one-week pilot phase of *concomitance* would start on 18 May, to be followed by a national programme of identification and disarmament at the end of July. The pilot programme would involve local hearings, (*audiences foraines*), where government officials would issue new identification papers to those without them. It was subsequently judged a success and was concluded that only small adjustments were necessary to extend the project nationwide. At the same time, the military authorities on both sides took the first steps towards redeploying their forces in preparation for disarmament. This was followed in late May by the resumption of talks between government and FN forces on the sequencing of the disarmament process. The two sides agreed to start disarming on 8 June, after which talks would start on the creation of a new national army comprising elements from both forces. On 8 June the Government announced that the start of disarmament had been delayed for a further week to allow for the necessary security conditions to be met. However, as a result of poor organization and a shortage of funds to pay rebel soldiers, little progress was made with the disarmament and cantonment of rebel forces in preparation for their demobilization.

On 12 July 2006 the two-month identification process was officially launched by a team of magistrates in the Abidjan area, with the first hearings occurring on 15 July. However, it was severely delayed by procedural challenges and claims of electoral fraud by both the FPI and the FN. On 15 July CJP militias erected barricades in Abidjan's suburb of Abobo in order to disrupt the hearings, and on 19 July they extended the blockade across the whole city. The following day the CJP leader, Blé Goudé, called on his supporters to end their protest, and two days later he met with leaders of the opposition parties' youth movements to defuse tensions. However, on 25 July CJP militias again disrupted the identification process in Grand-Bassam, near Abidjan.

In early August 2006 Gbagbo delivered his annual televised address, reiterating his wish that elections be held before the end of the year. He pledged to remain as President until then, and to issue a decree naming new magistrates to carry out the identification process. In protest, the FN withdrew from disarmament talks, claiming Gbagbo had tampered with the identification process. Given the political deadlock, at a meeting in early September the UN-mandated IWG agreed that the elections scheduled for October should be postponed, and it called on the UN to draw up a new timetable to extend beyond the 31 October 2006 deadline.

However, before this deadline was reached in mid-August 2006 a fresh political crisis emerged, after a Panamanian-registered ship, *Probo Koala*, illegally unloaded 525 metric tons of toxic waste at several locations around Abidjan. Over the following week this caused an estimated 15 deaths and required more than 100,000 people to seek medical treatment. On 5 September it was revealed that the ship had been in the custody of Trafigura, a Dutch company linked with Nigerian and Ivorian business interests. Taking responsibility for the disaster, the following day Banny presented his Government's resignation to Gbagbo, and promised to punish those civil servants who had been involved in the dumping. Gbabgo accepted the resignation but requested that Banny remain in office and form a new Council of Ministers. However, this was rejected by the FN which claimed that Gbagbo did not have the authority to accept the resignation, and it refused to serve in a new administration. On 11 September a crisis meeting was held in Abidjan between Gbabgo, Banny, Ouattara, Bédié and Soro, under the mediation of the AU President Sassou-Nguesso. However, no agreement was reached, and two days later Gbagbo reinstated the Government. The ministers responsible for transport and the environment, water and forestry were replaced as a result of the scandal. In late November the official inquiry into the toxic waste scandal released its findings, blaming a wide range of authorities, including the port authority, the customs service, the municipal authorities and the transport and environment ministries, for negligence and fraud. In mid-February 2007 Gbagbo signed an agreement with Trafigura, under which the company agreed to pay 100,000m. francs CFA towards a clean-up operation, the construction of a local waste-processing factory and in compensation to the victims of the dumping.

On 1 November 2006 the UN Security Council adopted Resolution 1721, which renewed the transitional period established by Resolution 1633 for a maximum of 12 months, and called for presidential and legislative elections to be held by 31 October 2007. The resolution extended the mandates of Gbagbo and Banny for the duration of the transitional period, and increased Banny's powers to enable him to issue decrees without the consent of the Assemblée nationale. The resolution also designated Sassou-Nguesso as official mediator (formally ending the role played by the Mbeki) and confirmed the UN High Representative for elections in Côte d'Ivoire, Gerard Stoudmann, as the sole arbitrator for disputes arising during the election process. On 2 November Gbagbo made a televised address, accepting Resolution 1721 in principle, but implicitly rejecting Banny's authority over the armed forces. The following day Gbagbo received a public pledge of allegiance from the Chief of Staff of the Armed Forces, Gen. Philippe Mangou. The opposition parties, led by the FN, were also cautious in their acceptance of Resolution 1721, expressing doubts that it could be successfully implemented. Ostensibly to build a consensus for the implementation of the resolution, on 8 November 2006 Gbagbo started a two-week period of public consultations across the country.

In mid-December 2006 the UN Security Council extended the arms and diamond embargo against Côte d'Ivoire to October 2007, as well as UNOCI's mandate until 30 June 2007.

GBAGBO PURSUES DIALOGUE WITH THE FN

In December 2006 Gbagbo moved to break the political deadlock by proposing 'direct dialogue' with the FN within the context of Resolution 1721. In mid-January 2007 Soro and Banny met in Yamoussoukro at the monthly meeting of the IWG, which endorsed the principle of direct dialogue within the context of Resolution 1721. This view was subsequently endorsed by ECOWAS and the AU, which proposed the President of Burkina Faso, Blaise Compaoré, as a mediator. In early February talks started in the Burkinabè capital Ouagadougou between representatives of the Government and the FN and early the following month Gbagbo and Soro met for direct talks in Ouagadougou, under the mediation of Compaoré, with the close involvement of the Burkinabè Minister of Security, Djibrill Bassolé.

On 4 March 2007 Gbagbo and Soro signed an agreement, committing them to reach a solution to Côte d'Ivoire's political and military crisis. The accord called for the resumption of the *audiences foraines*, which would be limited to issuing temporary birth certificates; the drawing up of a new electoral register under the supervision of the CEI, with a view to holding fresh national elections; the resumption of the demobilization process and the integration of the FN into the national army; and the dissolution of the 'buffer zone', to be followed by the deployment of joint army and FN patrols in the area and the extension of the Government's control across the whole country. The agreement also provided for two new bodies to be set up: the Cadre permanent de concertation, comprising Gbagbo, Soro, Bédié, Ouattara and Compaoré; and the Comité d'évaluation et d'accompagnement, comprising representatives appointed by Gbagbo, Soro and Compaoré. The agreement envisaged the formation of a new government by no later than 8 April, with national elections scheduled to be held by 4 January 2008.

In mid-March 2007 Gbagbo signed a decree setting up an integrated central command for the armed forces (the Centre de commandement integré—CCI), which would be jointly headed by the army Chief of Staff Gen. Mangou and the FN Chief of Staff Gen. Soumaïla Bakayoko. The CCI was tasked with completing the disarmament and demobilization process, and ensuring security during the identification campaign and elections.

In mid-March 2007 the Government and the FN met for a second phase of talks in Ouagadougou, which focused on designating a new premier. On 29 March Gbagbo named Soro as Prime Minister, and on 5 April Soro officially took office. Two days later a new, 33-member transitional Government was announced, which was dominated by FPI and FN figures but retained several members of the previous administration. The FPI was awarded the second most powerful post in the Government, namely Minister of State for Planning and Development, which was taken by Paul Bouhoun Bouabré, as well as the justice and communication portfolios. The PCDI and RDR received the foreign affairs and agriculture portfolios, respectively. In mid-April Gbagbo issued an amnesty for crimes committed during the extended conflict, and the following day Soro gave his first televised address as Prime Minister, calling for reconciliation and forgiveness. On 16 April the 'buffer zone' was officially abolished, following five days of talks between the army, the FN and the UN.

However, progress with disarmament and electoral registration was again slow, and the deadline of 21 April 2007 to restart both processes was not met. Government meetings on these issues were marred by bitter infighting between FN and FPI ministers. On 19 May a ceremony was held in Guiglo, 500 km west of Abidjan, to mark the handover by pro-Gbagbo troops of over 1,000 weapons for destruction. However, the disarmament did not take place under the supervision of the CCI, and was dismissed by the opposition as a public relations exercise designed to put pressure on the FN to begin disarmament. In May the Government designated 60 teams for deployment around the country to restart the identification process, the cost of which was estimated at US $37m., and in mid-June Gbagbo issued a decree redeploying territorial administrators to the rebel-held north of the country. However, progress with the identification process was expected to be slow as a result of ongoing disagreements between the FN and the FPI.

Meanwhile, in mid-May 2007 violence broke out in Abidjan when militants from the student union destroyed the offices of two local human rights organizations, claiming that they had given shelter to professors who were in conflict with FESCI.

FOREIGN RELATIONS AND REGIONAL CONCERNS

Throughout his presidency Houphouët-Boigny was active in regional and international affairs, assisting in the peace process in Angola and, despite strong criticism by the Organization of African Unity (OAU, now the AU), favouring black African dialogue with the apartheid regime in South Africa. In regional affairs, Côte d'Ivoire under Houphouët-Boigny tended to favour the maintenance of close links with the West. Relations with France were generally close, and remained cordial following Bédié's accession to the presidency. Ivorian troops joined the UN peace-keeping mission in the Central African Republic in April 1998: this was Côte d'Ivoire's first involvement in such an operation. Following the destruction of the Ivorian air force by the French military on 6 November 2004, in retaliation for an Ivorian bombing raid that had resulted in the deaths of nine French peace-keeping troops (see above), numerous French targets in Abidjan, including schools, businesses and homes, were attacked. French troops entered Abidjan to secure the international airport and to protect French citizens, airlifting many of them out of the city. (In total it was estimated that 9,000 foreign citizens, the majority of them French, were evacuated from Abidjan during the crisis.) Some 600 troops were dispatched to reinforce France's military presence in Côte d'Ivoire, while diplomatic relations between the two countries remained tense. The French Government subsequently admitted that its forces had killed some 20 Ivorian civilians during clashes with rioters in Abidjan; the Ivorian authorities claimed the number was significantly higher.

In 1999 the deterioration in the political situation in Côte d'Ivoire attracted considerable concern among the country's regional and international allies. In mid-November it was suggested that the Bédié administration's emphasis on the promotion of a sense of national identity or 'ivoirité' had helped to provoke outbreaks of violence against Burkinabè migrant workers, who were systematically expelled in November from areas bordering Burkina Faso by indigenous Krou militants. Despite international disapproval of many of the aspects of the Bédié regime, the *coup d'état* in December, which brought Brig.-Gen. Robert Gueï to power, was, initially, widely condemned by France, the USA and the OAU, although intervention to restore Bédié was ruled out. In January 2000 the OAU ordered the military regime to announce a schedule for democratic elections or face exclusion from the OAU summit, to be held in July. Gueï's subsequent announcement that he intended to stand as a presidential candidate was criticized by the international community, and the resumption of international support for Côte d'Ivoire was stated to be dependent upon the conduct of the forthcoming presidential and legislative elections. Despite expressing disapproval at the exclusion of Alassane Ouattara from elections in 2000, France recommenced limited co-operation with Côte d'Ivoire in January 2001, with bilateral aid resumed from May. In the following month the European Union agreed to resume its financial assistance, on the condition that substantive progress be made towards national reconciliation. From late 2002 France dispatched additional troops to Côte d'Ivoire, to supplement the 550 already stationed in the country, and the French Government played an active role in the diplomatic efforts that led to the signature of the Marcoussis Accords in late January 2003 (see above). However, France stated that it regarded the civil conflict as an internal Ivorian matter, disregarding Gbagbo's statements relating to the alleged involvement of external forces in the rebellion; such involvement would have resulted in the invocation of a clause in a defence treaty between the two countries, necessitating the active military support of France for the Ivorian authorities. None the less, there was widespread anti-French feeling, particularly in Abidjan, following the conclusion of the Marcoussis Accords, and several thousand French citizens resident in Côte d'Ivoire reportedly left the country. French businesses nevertheless remain dominant in Côte d'Ivoire; in December 2005 the Government renewed the concession for the power distribution utility, Compagnie ivoirienne d'électricité (in which the French telecommunications company Bouygues holds a 54% stake), for a further 15 years.

Despite considerable evidence to the contrary, Houphouët-Boigny consistently denied that his Government was supporting Charles Taylor's National Patriotic Front of Liberia (NPFL), which was instrumental in the overthrow of President Samuel Doe in mid-1990 (see Recent History of Liberia). In mid-1995 Côte d'Ivoire, which had hitherto tended to promote the full integration of refugees into Ivorian society (a process facilitated by the common ethnic origin of communities on both sides of the Côte d'Ivoire–Liberia border), announced that, henceforth, reception camps for Liberian refugees would be established. In early 1996 the Ivorian authorities announced that security measures were to be increased in the west (in an effort to prevent rebel incursions and the infiltration of refugee groups by Liberian fighters) and in July the Government proclaimed western Côte d'Ivoire to be a military 'operational zone', extending the powers of the armed forces to act in response to rebel activity. The installation of elected organs of state in Liberia in 1997 facilitated the return of refugees; UNHCR estimated the number of Liberian refugees in Côte d'Ivoire at 119,900 at the end of 1998, compared with 327,700 at the end of 1996. Although it had initially been intended that the full repatriation of Liberian refugees should be completed by the end of December 1999, the programme of repatriation proceeded more slowly than anticipated, and some 76,000 of a total of more than 100,000 Liberian refugees remaining in Côte d'Ivoire were still receiving limited support from UNHCR at the end of that year. Many of the 122,846 Liberian refugees in Côte d'Ivoire at the beginning of 2002 had left the country by the end of that year; however, an estimated 43,000 remained. Conversely, some 25,000 Ivorian nationals were thought by UNHCR to have fled to Liberia in 2002 to escape fighting in western Côte d'Ivoire, while in 2004 some 10,000 Ivorians were reported to have sought refuge in Liberia following the renewed outbreak of violence in Côte d'Ivoire in November.

After the mutiny of 19 September 2002 and the effective division of Côte d'Ivoire into two parts, at least 1m. immigrants living and working in the south were forced out of their homes, losing their jobs and property. A massive migration of Burkinabè, Malian and Guinean workers followed the rampages of government gendarmes, militias and FPI youth organizations in immigrant areas of Abidjan and other southern towns. Many Burkinabè businesses were destroyed. Gbagbo and his ministers further heightened tension by accusing certain foreign countries, and by implication Burkina Faso, of providing military support to the rebel movements, although no evidence was produced to support such claims. As stability appeared to return to Côte d'Ivoire, the border with Burkina Faso, closed since the onset of the rebellion, was reopened in September 2003. In July 2004, at a meeting in Abidjan, representatives of the two countries pledged to combat 'destabilizing acts' against their respective countries and agreed to increase co-operation in security and defence matters; Burkina Faso had accused Côte d'Ivoire of violating its airspace earlier that month. Following the renewed outbreak of violence in Côte d'Ivoire in November, the Burkinabè President, Blaise Compaoré, commented in the French daily *Le Figaro* that it would be impossible to resolve the Ivorian conflict under the present regime in that country, reiterating previous statements. In 2005 Ivorian exports to Burkina Faso recovered to record levels, while in May 2006 a trial convoy of Burkinabè cotton successfully passed through rebel-held territory to reach Abidjan, raising the prospect of the reopening of traditional trade routes through the country. In late 2006 relations with the Burkinabè Government began to improve after Compaoré offered to mediate in the crisis. In January 2007 Compaoré was officially proposed as a mediator by the AU, and in February and March he hosted talks between representatives of the Ivorian Government and the FN in Ouagadougou, resulting in the peace accord signed in that city on 4 March. A second phase of peace talks were also held under Compaoré's mediation in March, leading to the appointment of Soro as Ivorian Prime Minister on 5 April.

Economy

RICHARD SYNGE

Based on an earlier article by EDITH HODGKINSON

For some 20 years following independence, Côte d'Ivoire was remarkable for its very high rate of economic growth. Gross domestic product (GDP) increased, in real terms, at an average annual rate of 11% in 1960–70 and 6%–7% in 1970–80, bringing it into the ranks of middle-income developing countries. During the 1980s the economy entered a period of overall decline. By late 1994, however, a marked recovery was in progress, with annual GDP growth reaching 1.8%, then accelerating to an average of 6.3% per year in 1995–98. A stimulus for this recovery was the 50% devaluation of the CFA franc in January 1994, which improved the competitiveness, in price terms, of Côte d'Ivoire's timber and non-traditional exports such as fish and rubber at a time when a boom in international prices for coffee was coming to an end. The economy's promising performance was subsequently knocked off course by Henri Konan Bédié's Government's loss of policy control in 1998 and 1999, and the suspension of disbursements by the European Union (EU) and the IMF (see below). The economy's performance was also negatively affected by a downturn in international cocoa prices and by the military overthrow of the Bédié Government in December 1999. The subsequent political instability that persisted after 2000 severely limited new foreign investment. Fiscal deficits and payments arrears increased, as the treasury struggled to keep financial control. In 2006 Prime Minister Charles Konan Banny attempted to assure creditors that the Government was committed to a resumption of normal relations. This was made credible by the possibility of a general improvement in Côte d'Ivoire's financial health resulting from surging exports of both crude and refined petroleum, as well as by modestly renewed inflows of foreign investment. Nevertheless, fiscal management remained vulnerable to the wider political developments ongoing in 2007.

The Government's relations with international financial institutions and with creditors were formerly close, but, amid reports of massive embezzlement of public funds by individuals in the Government, the EU suspended all financial disbursements in 1998, while the IMF, the support of which was required for Côte d'Ivoire's bid for substantial debt relief, suspended disbursements of its Enhanced Structural Adjustment Facility (ESAF) during 1999. The funds that were unaccounted for included US $26m. of EU aid and $18m. from the accounts of the agricultural marketing board, the Caisse de stabilisation et de soutien des prix des productions agricoles (Caistab). Following the withdrawal of financial support from the EU and IMF, uncertainty about Côte d'Ivoire's economic future intensified; the burden of its massive international debt could no longer attract negotiated relief, and there was inconsistency in the economic policies pursued by the successive leaderships of Brig.-Gen. Robert Gueï (1999–2000) and Laurent Gbagbo (2000–). Corruption also became a major problem, and morale in the public services deteriorated rapidly. The Government failed to adjust the prices of electricity and fuel in line with the costs of production and a number of state-owned institutions, including banks, were close to collapse. Eventually, the Gbagbo Government appeared to acknowledge the severity of the crisis and recommenced the process of reform that had been aborted under Bédié's presidency (1993–99).

After prolonged negotiations, the IMF approved a new staff-monitored programme for the period July–December 2001, with a view to strengthening the management of public finances, relaunching the process of structural reform, improving financial relations with creditors and creating the conditions for sustained economic recovery. The main focus of reform was in the cocoa marketing sector (see below) and measures were proposed to restore the financial health of the financial and energy sectors. The Government also announced a resumption of the stalled privatization programme. In March 2002 formal agreement was reached with the IMF for the release of US $365m. under the Poverty Reduction and Growth Facility (PRGF—which had replaced the ESAF), but the major political crisis that commenced in September severely disrupted the Government's economic policy-making and the programme was suspended. As people fled for safety to either rebel-controlled or state-controlled regions, plantations and other businesses dependent on immigrant labour were thrown into disarray. Normal transport services were suspended, as a result of widespread road-blocks and the closure of the commercially significant railway line from Abidjan to Ouagadougou, Burkina Faso. Activity at the ports of Abidjan and San-Pédro declined markedly, as trade was diverted to neighbouring countries. Nevertheless, the 2002 cocoa harvest was mostly harvested and shipped, with the crop fetching higher than usual prices, in part because of the fear of market shortages. During 2003, with the country divided in two, there was a general decrease in economic activity, with a sharp decline in agro-processing and manufacturing. The country's crisis after 2002 posed the most serious economic problems in the north, which was forced to trade almost exclusively with neighbouring Mali and Burkina Faso, countries that were themselves feeling the economic impact of the suspension of their transport links through Abidjan. In the main northern towns of Bouaké and Korhogo, banks remained closed and most transactions were conducted in cash or through informal arrangements. The decline in northern production and trade was estimated to have caused GDP to contract by 3.8% in 2003.

In the south, the Government of President Gbagbo was affected by the economic slowdown and the loss of customs revenues. Public sector indebtedness rose sharply. New taxes on cocoa and coffee exports were heavily used to finance the budget, and there was evidence of a rising level of off-budget expenditure, particularly on military supplies. International financial support remained suspended, as were the funds committed at the peace talks of January 2003 held in Paris, France. Only emergency funds were available from the international community and the situation worsened in 2004 when the Government suspended debt repayments to the World Bank and the African Development Bank (ADB). The economic crisis deepened after cocoa farmers withheld their crop in protest against the low prices being offered by the marketing companies. Revenue collection slumped and public-sector salaries went unpaid. Further reverses followed the attacks on French citizens and businesses in November 2004, causing investor confidence to collapse even more than hitherto. However, the coming on stream of new crude oil production facilities in 2005 and 2006 helped to limit the economic damage and to improve the prospects of an eventual recovery. During 2006 renewed prospects of international support for post-conflict assistance emerged, although these were dependent both on progress in the political field and in the settlement of arrears to the international financial institutions. Inflation has remained low, averaging 2.9% in 2003–06. According to the ADB, in 1995–2006 GDP increased at an annual average rate of 1.7%; growth was 1.8% in 2005 and 1.5% in 2006.

Population growth averaged about 3.6% per year in the late 1980s and early 1990s, one of the highest rates in the world, and, according to official sources, it grew at an average annual rate of 3.2% in 1995–2006. Expanding employment opportunities attracted immigrants from less prosperous neighbouring countries, particularly Burkina Faso, Mali and Guinea, and at the time of the 1998 census foreign citizens constituted 26% of the population, providing vital manpower for plantations and urban services. Mounting political instability and inter-ethnic tensions in the early 2000s prompted a significant proportion of the immigrant population to leave Côte d'Ivoire. The rate of urban growth had been rapid (at around 150% the overall rate of population growth), with some 44% of the population residing in urban areas in 1995—more than double the proportion recorded in 1960. Abidjan's population was measured at 2.9m. in the 1998 census, representing almost one-fifth of the country's population. This pressure on Abidjan was a significant factor in the designation of Yamoussoukro as the country's new political capital, from 1983, although Abidjan remains the principal centre for economic activity. The country's demographic patterns were, however, drastically altered by the upheavals that commenced in 2002, with up to 1m. people believed to have been displaced.

AGRICULTURE, FORESTRY AND FISHING

Although the Ivorian economy is relatively diversified, it remains strongly dependent on agriculture, which contributed 25.1% of GDP in 2005 and employed 43.7% of the economically active population in that year, according to FAO. Agriculture has long provided about three-quarters of export earnings, and the sector's rapid growth was the basis for the economic expansion of the 1960s and 1970s, although it has been complemented since 2005 by an increase in exports of crude and refined petroleum. In 1995–2006, according to the ADB, agricultural GDP increased at an average annual rate of 3.1%; it grew by 1.3% in 2005 and by 1.5% in 2006.

Coffee was formerly the leading cash crop, providing the main source of income for about one-half of Ivorians. However, it was superseded from the beginning of the 1980s by cocoa, production of which doubled between 1970 and 1979. The country became the world's largest cocoa producer after 1977, when its level of production overtook that of Ghana. Overall output continued to rise, with some fluctuations, and in the main crop season of 1999/2000 it reached 1.4m. metric tons. This increase in the cocoa harvest owed much to a major replanting programme implemented by the Government in the 1980s, aimed at eliminating ageing cultivation in the traditional cocoa belt, in the south-east, and developing it in the west, where rainfall is abundant. The expansion in cocoa production was also attributable to the transfer to the cultivation of cocoa by many former coffee producers. Cocoa production was maintained at more than 1.3m. tons in the 2004/05 season. In 2004 farmers refused to accept very low price levels (300 francs CFA per kg, compared with 704 francs CFA per kg in 2002) and the buying season did not begin until late November. Exports fell below 1m. tons in 2005. There were reports that increasing quantities of cocoa were being smuggled out of the country, especially to Ghana, where prices paid were considerably higher. Cocoa production in 2005/06 was 1.3m. tons. According to the crop marketing organization Bourse du café et du cacao (BCC), the average farm-gate price paid was 343 francs CFA per kg, up from the previous year, while the export tax revenue received by the authorities was 323,000m. francs CFA (US $617m.), 15% more than in the previous year.

Output of coffee reached a record level of some 366,800 metric tons in 1981. It was in overall decline thereafter and the surge in international coffee prices in 1993–94 and the leeway provided by the currency devaluation, which allowed increases in the price paid to producers, elicited a relatively modest response in terms of Ivorian output—the crop in 1995 was 194,968 tons. By 1998 the strength of prices had stimulated a sharp improvement in output, to 341,000 tons, the most substantial crop recorded since 1981. In subsequent years, further switching into cultivation of cocoa because of the narrowing in price differentials took place; although a large crop, of 336,273 tons, was recorded in 2000, there was a decline in coffee production in the 2000s, with output recorded at 154,000 tons in 2003/04 and only 95,600 tons in 2004/05, before recovering to 166,200 tons in 2005/06.

The former state marketing agency, Caistab, traditionally purchased all cocoa and coffee production. After the failure of its attempt to sustain world prices through stockpiling cocoa, the Ivorian Government was forced to halve producer prices in the 1989/90 season, to 200 francs CFA per kg for cocoa—their lowest level since 1978—and to 100 francs CFA per kg for coffee. Producer prices for both cocoa and coffee were increased immediately after the January 1994 devaluation. In January 1999 Caistab, which in recent years had operated principally as a consultative body, was privatized, and in August the market for cocoa and coffee was opened to competition. However, in November of that year cocoa and coffee farmers undertook a series of protests at the low prices they received for their crops and at what they termed the failure of the Nouvelle Caistab (as the organization had been renamed) to prepare adequately for the liberalization of the market. Following the discovery of large-scale embezzlement in the new body, its directors were dismissed in late 1999. Nouvelle Caistab was dissolved and replaced, in March 2001, by the BCC, which was to be operated by farmers' representatives. In the wake of the political crises of 2000 and 2001 it emerged that several exporters owed substantial sums of money to the former Caistab, with the result that the authorities were still trying to recover these funds by the time that it was finally liquidated at the end of 2001. After that date, several rival organizations competed for dominance in cocoa and coffee marketing including: the Autorité pour la régulation du café et du cacao (ARCC); the Fonds de regulation et de contrôle café-cacao (FRCC); the Association nationale des producteurs de café-cacao de Côte d'Ivoire (ANAPROCI), a group of wealthier farmers with strong political connections, dominated by Henri Amouzou; the Syndicat autonome des producteurs de café-cacao de Côte d'Ivoire (SYNAPROCI), established in 2003 by Tapé Koulou, a former associate of President Gbagbo (Koulou was removed as its head in 2004); and the Fédération ivoirienne des producteurs de café-cacao (FIPCC). A consultancy report commissioned by the EU into the functioning of the cocoa and coffee sector found that the new bodies had been mismanaged, had operated with no clear legal status and had received public funding without accountability. In 2006 EU auditors recommended the liquidation of ANAPROCI.

The high levels of taxation on cocoa exports—not only through the Droit unique de sortie, which was set at 220 francs CFA per kg in October 2006—have been blamed for the low prices paid to farmers and the emergence of new formal and informal trading networks with neighbouring countries (the areas controlled by the Forces nouvelles—New Forces—still accounted for 10%–15% of production in 2005/06; the beans were collected in the city of Man for forwarding to either Guinea or Burkina Faso). Some other levies are assumed to have been diverted to off-budget expenditure. The farmers' organizations have from time to time supervised disruptive protests against the levies they do not themselves control.

From the 1960s Côte d'Ivoire became a major producer of palm oil, and local processing of palm products developed. A series of replanting programmes was supported by the World Bank, the European Community (now EU), France and the United Kingdom. However, the target of becoming the world's leading palm oil producer was abandoned after the sharp fall in world prices in 1987, and only one of the two planned processing mills was constructed. Nevertheless, output of palm oil showed an overall increase in the 1990s, from an average of 208,885 metric tons per year in 1985–91 to 261,350 tons per year in 1995–2001. Output in 2005 was reported as 251,200 tons.

Cotton cultivation has become established in the north of the country. In the 1990s output of seed cotton averaged more than 200,000 metric tons per year, with a record crop of 399,933 tons achieved in the 1999 season. Most of the cotton was processed locally in eight ginning complexes, both for export (some 80% of total production) and for the local textile industry. A new ginning plant, reportedly the largest in West Africa, was opened in M'bengue in May 2001, with planned output of more than 200,000 tons per year. The political upheavals since 2002 have directly affected national cotton production, most of which takes place in the rebel-held area, but the Banque centrale des états de l'Afrique de l'ouest estimated output at 327,100 tons in 2004/05 and 336,200 tons in 2005/06.

The rubber industry underwent strong growth from the mid-1980s, registering an average 70,825 metric tons per year in 1989–91, and an annual average of 115,874 tons in 1998–2000, as the Government pursued plans for Côte d'Ivoire to become Africa's leading rubber producer. Output was 138,600 tons in 2004 and 116,200 tons in 2005. Exports were estimated to be somewhat higher than local production, on account of the smuggling of rubber produced in Liberia. The country is also a significant producer of bananas and pineapples, with exports directed principally at the European market. Pineapple output fell from 226,700 tons in 2004 to 188,700 tons in 2005. Banana output was 280,500 tons in 2004 and 260,500 tons in 2005.

The country is normally self-sufficient in maize, cassava, yams and plantains, and the Government has encouraged the production of rice, large quantities of which are imported. Two of the country's sugar mills have been converted to rice processing. By the mid-1980s the rice development programme was proving successful, and output of paddy rice averaged 1.21m. metric tons per year in 1996–2000 and 1.08m. tons per year in 2001–03. None the less, output still failed to meet domestic demand, which increased rapidly as the population moving from rural areas to town tended to switch its grain preference to rice.

A deficiency in sugar supply and the need to save foreign exchange on sugar imports led the Government to initiate a sugar development programme in the 1970s. Two complexes were in operation by 1980, but were producing sugar at twice the cost on the world market. This situation, in conjunction with the need to reduce foreign borrowing, led to the cancellation of six more planned complexes and the reduction of sugar-cane plantations, resulting in a decline in sugar production from the 1.82m. metric tons recorded in 1983 to an average of 1.17m. tons per year in 1997–2000. The industry has witnessed no recovery since 2000, with provisional estimates of production in 2004 at 930,000 tons.

Forestry has always been a significant source of export earnings, from both logs and sawn timber, and was the fourth largest source of export earnings (after cocoa beans, petroleum and coffee) in 2000. Most production is carried out by large integrated firms, many of which are foreign-owned. The area of exploitable timber had fallen to only about 1m. ha by 1987, compared with some 15.6m. ha at independence, because of inadequate reafforestation and the encroachment of agriculture on forest areas. In an attempt to conserve resources, the Government restricted commercial production to 3m. cu m per year. With domestic demand rising, the volume available for export declined, with exports falling from 3.1m. cu m (logs) in 1980 to only 29,000 cu m (and 521,000 cu m of sawn timber) in 1992. Export volumes subsequently recovered, to a total of 997,099 cu m in 1994, under the stimulus of much higher earnings in local currency terms. Meanwhile, the World Bank and other external agencies supported a reafforestation programme. Nevertheless, exports declined precipitously from the 1990s, and measured only 523,000 cu m in 2001.

Livestock herds are small—in 2005 there were an estimated 1.5m. head of cattle, 1.5m. sheep, 1.2m. goats and 33.0m. chickens—and meat production satisfies only one-third of national demand. Fishing is a significant activity, with industrial fishing accounting for about two-thirds of the annual catch of 55,000–70,000 metric tons. Ivorian participation in this sector is still low, and most traditional fishing is undertaken by non-Ivorians. Domestic production currently meets only about one-third of local demand.

MANUFACTURING AND MINING

The manufacturing sector, which accounted for 17.1% of GDP in 2005, has been dominated by agro-industrial activities—such as the processing of cocoa, coffee, cotton, oil palm, pineapples and fish. It was stimulated, immediately after independence, by the need to replace goods traditionally imported from Senegal, the manufacturing centre for colonial French West Africa, and it formed one of the most dynamic areas of the economy during this period. The sector was given a sharp boost by the 1994 devaluation of the CFA franc, which greatly enhanced the competitiveness of the local product. Growth in the GDP of the industrial sector (including mining, construction and utilities, in addition to manufacturing) reached 8.4% in 1996, and then surged to 13.1% in 1997 as output of petroleum and gas expanded (see below). However, industrial GDP declined by 9.5% in 2000 and by 2.4% in 2001 and has declined further in the wake of the political crisis of 2002, contracting by 4.6% in that year, by 3.5% in 2003 and by 8.6% in 2004. The industrial sector had been developing new export capacities but many firms were now forced to curtail or suspend production, and further new investment was placed on hold. According to the ADB, in 1995–2006, the industrial sector grew at an average annual rate of 2.3%; it increased by 9.9% in 2005 and by 5.0% in 2006.

The privatization of parastatal organizations in the mid-1990s included the state-owned telecommunications company, Côte d'Ivoire Télécom, as well as sugar, palm oil and cotton companies. Subsequent political uncertainties brought the privatization of other state enterprises to a halt.

The only significant activity in the mining sector (apart from hydrocarbons) is the extraction of diamonds and gold. Output from the two diamond mines, at Tortiya and Séguéla, is some 15,000 carats annually, but very much larger quantities are produced in illicit operations. Total output of some 306,500 carats was recorded in 2002, declining to an estimated 230,000 carats in 2003. In December 2005 the UN Security Council imposed a 12-month import ban on imports of rough diamonds from Côte d'Ivoire. Most production of diamonds is by artisanal methods from the north of the country, the area controlled by the Forces nouvelles, which is thought to have benefited from any resulting income. The exploitation of deposits of gold-bearing rock at Ity began in 1991, in a joint venture with the Compagnie française des mines. A second gold mine, at Aniuri, began operations in 1993, in a joint venture between Eden Roc of Canada and the state mining company. Production reached 3,672 kg in 2001 before declining to 3,570 kg in 2002. The heightened political tension from late 2002 had a detrimental impact on gold production, which declined sharply, to 1,313 kg in 2003. There is considerable potential for nickel mining. In 1996 Falconbridge of Canada signed an agreement with the Government to invest in the development of reserves at Sipilou and Gounguessou in the north-west, where tests indicated 54m. metric tons of nickel ore, but no further progress has been reported. In addition, there are substantial iron ore, bauxite and manganese reserves, all largely unworked.

ENERGY

Electricity generating capacity rose very rapidly, from 41 MW in 1962 to 675 MW in the early 1980s, as a result of the development of hydroelectric plants, which came to account for 90% of all power generated. However, the focus of development switched after the 1982–84 drought severely reduced the contribution of hydroelectric power, and policy is now to develop thermal capacity. Long-discussed plans for a thermal plant at Vridi, utilizing offshore reserves of natural gas, were finally realized in 1994. A consortium led by United Meridian of the USA has developed the Panthère gas field to supply a 100-MW plant at Vridi, which began to supply the national grid in 1997. With gas output from Panthère more than doubling in 1997, to 139m. cu m, plans were developed to use these resources to expand Côte d'Ivoire's exports of electricity. The first 144-MW phase of a gas-fired complex at Azito, close to Abidjan, opened in January 1999. Meanwhile, natural gas output has increased, with the commencement of production in mid-1999 at the Foxtrot offshore gas field, which is being developed by a US, French and Ivorian consortium. A new gas well was discovered in 2005. Applications for the development of other fields have been submitted to the Government. In addition to gas generation, the Compagnie ivoirienne d'électricité (CIE) has been developing plans to build a new hydro-electric power dam at Soubré on the Sassandra river. As of January 2003 Côte d'Ivoire had installed electric generation capacity of 919 MW; the majority is generated through thermal stations (68%) with the rest by hydroelectric stations (32%) at Ayame, Kossou, Taabo, Buyo and Grah. The country's power grid is connected to neighbouring countries. The CIE manages the state-owned generation facilities as well as electricity transmission and distribution, and it has a monopoly on electricity supply.

Côte d'Ivoire has experienced mixed success in the development of its petroleum reserves. Offshore petroleum was discovered in 1975, with reserves at the Bélier field estimated at 75m. metric tons. A larger discovery was made in the Espoir field (also off shore) in 1980. Output from the two fields reached a peak of 1.1m. tons in 1984. Production then declined and operations at the Espoir field were suspended in 1989, while those at the Bélier field ceased in 1990. Although offshore exploration for petroleum had virtually ceased by 1984, a new round of exploration undertaken in the early 1990s proved successful, with a major discovery of offshore petroleum, near Jacqueville and Grand-Lahou, in 1994. A joint venture by United Meridian of the USA and the state-owned Société nationale d'opérations pétrolières de la Côte d'Ivoire (PETROCI) began production at the Lion field in April 1995. Redevelopment and extension of the Espoir field commenced in 1999. After production-sharing arrangements were renegotiated, Canadian Natural Resources (CNR) of Calgary, with Tullow Oil as partner, developed the East Espoir field, and production resumed in 2002 with an estimated potential output of 35,000 barrels per day (b/d) CNR also operates the West Espoir field, which started production in mid-2006, and the Baobab field, which started producing from 11 wells in mid-2005 and is currently the largest single source of crude oil, with an estimated output potential of 65,000 b/d. The Lion field, producing 20,000 b/d, is operated by Devon Energy Corporation of the USA. Total national petroleum production has risen, increasing from 2.1m. barrels in 2001 to 21.9m. barrels in 2006. According to government figures, the value of crude oil exports totalled 267,000m. francs CFA in 2005, and that of petroleum products amounted to 793,600m. francs CFA. The figures have to be treated with caution and have been awaiting verification by the Extractive Industries Transparency Initiative, but the first official estimate of the value of crude oil exports in 2006 was 684,000m. francs CFA.

Exploration for both oil and gas increased in the mid-2000s with the involvement of a range of companies, including Vanco, CNR and Tullow, following the award of new exploration licences covering much of the country's offshore waters. Other incoming shareholders in exploration efforts have included Al Thani of the United Arab Emirates, ONGC of India, Sinopec of the People's Republic of China, Dana Petroleum of the United Kingdom and a local company, Yam's Petroleum.

The principal oil refinery, owned by Société ivoirienne de raffinage, has a capacity of 65,000 b/d, which is expected to be increased in the future. It receives oil directly by pipeline from the Lion field and it also processes crude shipped from Nigeria. The state owns 47% of the company.

Natural gas has primarily been used to generate electricity. The largest source of natural gas is the Foxtrot field, producing around 80m. cu ft per day, followed by the Manta field, producing 32m. cu ft per day. Both of these are operated by Foxtrot International. Devon Energy has been operating the Panthère field, with production of around 70m. cu ft per day, and CNR has announced the start of natural gas production from its West Espoir field.

TRANSPORT AND TELECOMMUNICATIONS

The most important transport facility is the deep-water port of Abidjan, rivalled in francophone West Africa only by the iron-ore-handling port of Nouadhibou in Mauritania. The freight handled at the port declined in 2002 and 2003, reaching 14.5m. metric tons in the latter year, rising again to 16.6m. tons in 2004 and 17.5m. tons in 2005. In 2006 there was significant growth in the volume of petroleum shipments through Abidjan, accounting for more than one-half of the port's traffic, which grew overall by 9.3% in the first six months over the same period of 2005.

Côte d'Ivoire has about 68,000 km of classified roads. In all, some 6,000 km of roads are now paved, almost six times the extent in 1970. Repair and extension of the road network has received funding from both multilateral agencies and donor governments (notably France, Germany and Japan) A railway line links Abidjan to Ouagadougou, Burkina Faso, with 660 km of line in Côte d'Ivoire. Management responsibility for the railway lies with SITARAIL, a consortium of French, Belgian, Ivorian and Burkinabè investors. All movement on the railway ceased in 2002, but resumed again in 2004, although at a much reduced level. SITARAIL's total freight traffic amounted to 455,703 tons in the first half of 2006, an increase of 13% compared with the same period in 2005. Côte d'Ivoire has international airports at Abidjan, Bouaké and Yamoussoukro, and there are several regional airports. The management of Abidjan airport was ceded to a French consortium, Aeria, and its capacity now stands at 2m. passengers per year. Passenger movements declined from a level of 1.4m. in 2000 to only 700,000 in 2003, showing no significant growth in the following two years as many long-haul carriers suspended their services.

Two mobile telephone companies, Orange Côte d'Ivoire and Télécel, dominated the market in 2005, with about 1m. subscribers each. In July South Africa's MTN purchased Télécel. At the end of the year a new firm, Acell, was licensed; the latter is a joint venture between a local company, Atlantique Télécoms, and a company from the United Arab Emirates, Unis Elisalat. After investment of US $100m., it started services under the name Moov Telecom in July 2006, capturing 500,000 new subscribers in the following three months.

TOURISM

Tourism developed strongly in the 1970s, with a newly created ministry stimulating diversification in location (away from the Abidjan area) and in type of visitor (away from business travellers, who previously accounted for almost two-thirds of arrivals). Special tax incentives and government guarantees on loans were offered for hotel construction. The number of tourists increased from some 93,000 in 1974 to 198,900 in 1979, with business visitors accounting for 40% of arrivals. Thereafter, visitor arrivals fluctuated in the range of 200,000–300,000 per year, broadly reflecting trends in world tourism. All tourism came to an abrupt halt after September 2002. Receipts from tourism in 2002 amounted to US $490m.

PUBLIC FINANCE

Following a strong economic recovery in 1995–98, revenue increased sufficiently to allow the Government to raise the level of its capital spending while maintaining a surplus on the primary budget (of 210,200m. francs CFA in 1998). The Government was thus able to pay off some arrears on its domestic debt. Under the programme agreed with the IMF for 1998–2000, the budget deficit was to be steadily reduced, to only 0.3% of GDP by the end of the period, with the support provided by the debt relief that was accorded after the granting of the ESAF. The failure to adhere to programme targets and the lack of transparency in government finances prompted the IMF to suspend the ESAF in mid-1999. Thereafter, there was a continuation of budget deficits and the Government fell behind in many of its repayments to international lenders.

The political crises of 2000 and 2001 severely worsened the Government's overall financial position. By the end of 2001 there was an accumulated stock of domestic payments arrears of 361,000m. francs CFA, estimated at 4.7% of GDP. In an attempt to increase government revenues, new measures were announced in 2002, including a 5% tax on new-project-related imports, an increase in the tax on cocoa exports, the reform of customs clearing procedures and the computerization of import-management systems. In 2003 the Government began collecting a number of additional taxes on the cocoa trade. In 2004 it announced a new tax on incomes to provide for its war effort and put pressure on businesses to contribute to a special reconstruction fund. The budget deficit was estimated at 1.0% of GDP in 2003, and it was assumed to have widened in subsequent years, although there was no formal reporting as the Government resorted to more ad hoc taxation measures to maintain an inflow of revenues. The authorities had difficulty in maintaining payments of public-sector salaries and ceased service all debts to development banks falling due after 2004. The Government's domestic arrears were estimated at 3% of GDP and there was an ongoing crisis in the banking sector, with the Caisse autonome d'amortissement unable to collect on 90% of its loans, and an estimated 24% of non-performing loans in the domestic banking system as a whole. The accumulation of arrears, both foreign and domestic, amounted to 26% of GDP at the end of 2005. The fiscal deficit was estimated at 1.9% of GDP in 2006, financed largely by further domestic borrowing, and was expected to widen in 2007.

Prime Minister Charles Konan Banny, appointed in 2005, resumed dialogue with the IMF and in May 2006 an IMF mission concluded that the fiscal position had improved on previous years and that control of expenditure had improved slightly. There was an agreement in principle on the main features of an economic programme that might receive IMF assistance. In April 2007 agreement was reached with the World Bank whereby Côte d'Ivoire would resume paying current debt service while working to clear arrears to the Bank of US $422m. by early 2008. If achieved, this would allow the resumption of full country programmes by the World Bank and other donors.

FOREIGN TRADE AND PAYMENTS

Côte d'Ivoire's balance of trade has regularly been in surplus because of the strength of its exports, which have largely been determined by the level of earnings from sales of coffee and cocoa. Trade surpluses of US $2,627.9m. and $2,394.2m. were recorded in 2004 and 2005, respectively. Nevertheless there was a small current-account deficit on the balance of payments of $12.4m. in 2005. Transfers have remained stable but imports have shown a propensity to rise sharply in all branches of goods (including military equipment and armaments). However, the surge in crude oil exports after 2005 could be expected to boost both the trade payments surplus and foreign exchange reserves (estimated as US $1,400m. in 2006). The Direction générale des douanes reported that crude oil exports were worth 391,500m. francs CFA in the first half of 2006, up from 64,900m. francs CFA in the same period of 2005 (crude oil and petroleum products provided a combined value of 839,900m. francs CFA, compared to cocoa's value of 330,100m. francs CFA). On the capital account inflows of foreign direct investment have been comparable with those benefiting other countries in the region, at $283m. in 2004 and $192m. in 2005; this reflected ongoing investments in oil, gas and telecommunications and the continued potential interest of foreign investors from all countries.

At the end of 1993 the external debt of US $19,071m. was more than twice the level of 1980. The devaluation of the CFA franc in January 1994 threatened to precipitate a crisis, since it doubled the external debt in local currency terms overnight. In common with other Franc Zone countries in Africa, Côte d'Ivoire was the beneficiary of special measures of compensation and relief. The 'Paris Club' of official creditors agreed a new round of debt reschedulings and cancellation, which reduced total debt to $17,395m. by the end of 1994. Côte d'Ivoire also received critically important aid from members of the Organisation for Economic Co-operation and Development and the Organization of the Petroleum Exporting Countries, net assistance from which doubled in 1994, to $1,594m., with most of the increase coming from the International Development Association (the concessionary lending agency of the World Bank), the IMF and France. As the short-term pressure eased, these net inflows declined over the following two years, to $446m. in 1996. However, Côte d'Ivoire's external position remained very problematic, with arrears on debt obligations reaching $3,504m. by the end of 1996, while its external debt had risen to $19,524m.

The debt relief that was agreed following the IMF's approval of a new ESAF in February 1998 had a considerable positive impact. The 'London Club' of commercial creditors agreed to implement a restructuring of US $8,600m. in liabilities that had originally been agreed in November 1996. As a result of the backdating of this arrangement to the end of 1997, the country's foreign debt was reduced by more than $4,000m. from the level at the end of 1996, to $15,609m. However, with the ESAF suspended and the new uncertainties generated by the military coup of December 1999, the implementation of a heavily indebted poor countries (HIPC) debt relief programme was inevitably postponed. At the end of 2003 total debt stocks amounted to $12,187m. (equivalent to 93.8% of gross national income), including short-term arrears of $917m. In that year the debt-servicing ratio was 8.5%, significantly less than in previous years. Debt repayments to most international financial institutions ceased during the course of 2004. Arrears to the World Bank amounted to $64m. and, as a result, all new lending ceased. The arrears had increased to $422m. by the time agreement was reached in Washington, DC, in April 2007 on a plan to repay them, the results of which would be tested in 2008.

Statistical Survey

Source (unless otherwise stated): Institut National de la Statistique, BP V55, Abidjan; tel. 20-21-05-38; fax 20-21-44-01; e-mail site-ins@globeaccess.net; internet www.ins.ci.

Area and Population

AREA, POPULATION AND DENSITY

Area (sq km)	322,462*
Population (census results)	
1 March 1988	10,815,694
20 December 1998	
Males	7,844,621
Females	7,522,050
Total	15,366,671
Population (official estimates at December)	
2004	18,545,968
2005	19,096,988
2006	19,657,738
Density (per sq km) at December 2006	61.0

* 124,503 sq miles.

ETHNIC GROUPS

1998 census (percentages, residents born in Côte d'Ivoire): Akan 42*; Voltaïque 18†; Mandé du nord 17‡; Krou 11; Mandé du sud 10§; Naturalized Ivorians 1; Others 1.

* Comprising the Baoulé, Agni, Abrou, Ebrié, Abouré, Adioukrou and Appollonien groupings.

† Comprising the Sénoufo, Lobi and Koulango groupings.

‡ Comprising the Malinké and Dioula groupings.

§ Comprising the Yacouba and Gouro groupings.

NATIONALITY OF POPULATION

(numbers resident in Côte d'Ivoire at 1998 census)

Country of citizenship	Population	%
Côte d'Ivoire	11,366,625	73.97
Burkina Faso	2,238,548	14.57
Mali	792,258	5.16
Guinea	230,387	1.50
Ghana	133,221	0.87
Liberia	78,258	0.51
Other	527,375	3.43
Total	15,366,672	100.00

POPULATION BY REGION
(1998 census)

Region	Population
Centre	1,001,264
Centre-Est	394,758
Centre-Nord	1,189,424
Centre-Ouest	2,169,826
Nord	929,686
Nord-Est	696,292
Nord-Ouest	740,175
Ouest	1,445,279
Sud	5,399,220
Sud-Ouest	1,400,748
Total	15,366,672

Note: In January 1997 the Government adopted legislation whereby Côte d'Ivoire's regions were to be reorganized. Further minor reorganizations were effected in April and July 2000. The new regions (with their regional capitals) are: Agnéby (Agboville), Bas-Sassandra (San-Pédro), Bafing (Touba), Denguélé (Odienné), 18 Montagnes (Man), Fromager (Gagnoa), Haut-Sassandra (Daloa), Lacs (Yamoussoukro), Lagunes (Abidjan), Marahoué (Bouaflé), Moyen-Cavally (Guiglo), Moyen-Comoé (Abengourou), N'zi-Comoé (Dimbokro), Savanes (Korhogo), Sud-Bandama (Divo), Sud-Comoé (Aboisso), Vallée du Bandama (Bouaké), Worodougou (Mankono) and Zanzan (Bondoukou).

PRINCIPAL TOWNS
(population at 1998 census)

Abidjan*	2,877,948	Korhogo	142,093
Bouaké	461,618	San-Pédro	131,800
Yamoussoukro*	299,243	Man	116,657
Daloa	173,107	Gagnoa	107,124

* The process of transferring the official capital from Abidjan to Yamoussoukro began in 1983.

2005 ('000, official estimates): Abidjan 3,576.0; Bouaké 573.7; Daloa 215.1.

BIRTHS AND DEATHS
(annual averages, official estimates)

	2004	2005	2006
Birth rate (per 1,000)	38.6	38.3	37.9
Death rate (per 1,000)	14.3	14.3	14.0

Expectation of life (years at birth, WHO estimates): 44 (males 41; females 47) in 2004 (Source: WHO, *World Health Report*).

ECONOMICALLY ACTIVE POPULATION*
(persons aged 6 years and over, 1988 census)

	Males	Females	Total
Agriculture, hunting, forestry and fishing	1,791,101	836,574	2,627,675
Mining and quarrying Manufacturing }	78,768	6,283	85,051
Electricity, gas and water	13,573	1,092	14,665
Construction	82,203	2,313	84,516
Trade, restaurants and hotels	227,873	302,486	530,359
Transport, storage and communications	114,396	3,120	117,516
Other services	434,782	156,444	591,226
Activities not adequately defined	998	297	1,295
Total labour force	2,743,694	1,308,609	4,052,303

* Figures exclude persons seeking work for the first time, totalling 210,450 (males 142,688; females 67,762).

Source: UN, *Demographic Yearbook*.

1988 census (revised figures): Total employed 4,025,478; Unemployed 237,275; Total labour force 4,262,753.

1998 census: Total employed 6,084,487; Unemployed 163,647; Total labour force 6,248,134.

Mid-2005 ('000,estimates): Agriculture, etc. 3,224; Total labour force 7,379 (Source: FAO).

2005 (official estimates): Total employed 7,561,116; Unemployed 207,743; Total labour force 7,768,859.

Health and Welfare

KEY INDICATORS

Total fertility rate (children per woman, 2005)	4.8
Under-5 mortality rate (per 1,000 live births, 2005)	196
HIV/AIDS (% of persons aged 15–49, 2005)	7.1
Physicians (per 1,000 head, 2004)	0.12
Hospital beds (per 1,000 head, 1990)	0.81
Health expenditure (2004): US $ per head (PPP)	63.6
Health expenditure (2004): % of GDP	3.8
Health expenditure (2004): public (% of total)	23.8
Access to water (% of persons, 2004)	84
Access to sanitation (% of persons, 2004)	37
Human Development Index (2004): ranking	164
Human Development Index (2004): value	0.421

For sources and definitions, see explanatory note on p. vi.

Agriculture

PRINCIPAL CROPS
('000 metric tons)

	2003	2004	2005
Rice (paddy)	659.8*	673.0	703.9
Maize	600.1*	608.0	640.2
Millet	45	60	50
Sorghum	48	75	80
Sweet potatoes	43*	45	50
Cassava (Manioc)	2,060.3	2,128.0	2,198.0
Taro (Coco yam)	370*	360	355
Yams	4,837.0	4,970.9	5,160.3
Sugar cane*	1,045	1,000	1,100
Cashew nuts	84.8	88.2†	94.0*
Kolanuts	57.6	65.2	73.8
Groundnuts (in shell)†	150	150	150
Coconuts*	240	223	213
Oil palm fruit	1,300.4	1,564.3	1,881.9
Cottonseed†	175.0	161.0	140.0
Tomatoes	24.6	25.4	26.2
Aubergines (Eggplants)	67.8	70.0	72.4
Chillies and green peppers*	22.5	23.4	23.9
Green corn (Maize)*	240	240	240
Other vegetables*	115.8	115.8	115.8
Bananas	234.7	241.2	222.0
Plantains	1,497.6	1,519.7	1,900
Oranges*	30	30	30
Other citrus fruit*	31.0	32.6	33.5
Pineapples	242.2	249.0	194.5
Guavas, mangoes and mangosteens	117	121	125
Other fruit*	26.2	26.2	26.2
Cotton (lint)	172	79	139
Coffee (green)	140.0	251	230
Cocoa beans	1,351.5	1,407.2	1,360.0†
Natural rubber (dry weight)	115.6	136.8	134.8

* FAO estimate(s).
† Unofficial figure(s).

Source: FAO.

LIVESTOCK
('000 head, year ending September)

	2003	2004	2005*
Cattle	1,460*	1,500*	1,500
Pigs	336	343	345
Sheep	1,523*	1,523*	1,523
Goats	1,192*	1,192*	1,192
Poultry	33,000*	33,000*	33,000

* FAO estimate(s).

Source: FAO.

LIVESTOCK PRODUCTS
('000 metric tons)

	2003	2004	2005*
Cattle meat	51.1	52.2	51.8
Sheep meat	5.1	5.1	5.0
Goat meat	3.9*	4.3*	4.3
Pig meat	12.3*	11.8*	11.8
Chicken meat	69.3*	69.3*	69.3
Game meat	13*	13*	13
Other meat	15*	15*	15
Cows' milk	25.9*	25.9*	25.9
Hen eggs	34.6	29.4	32.0

* FAO estimate(s).

Source: FAO.

Forestry

ROUNDWOOD REMOVALS
('000 cubic metres, excluding bark)

	2003	2004	2005*
Sawlogs, veneer logs and logs for sleepers	1,556	1,678	1,678
Fuel wood	8,615*	8,655*	8,700
Total	10,171	10,333	10,378

* FAO estimate(s).

Source: FAO.

SAWNWOOD PRODUCTION
('000 cubic metres, including railway sleepers)

	2002	2003	2004
Total (all broadleaved)	620	503	512

2005: Production assumed to be unchanged from 2004 (FAO estimate).

Source: FAO.

Fishing

('000 metric tons, live weight)

	2003	2004	2005*
Capture*	68.9	54.4	55.0
Freshwater fishes	21.0*	4.9	5.0
Bigeye grunt	2.1	2.4	2.4
Round sardinella	8.3	10.6	9.7
Madeiran sardinella	0.4	6.0	5.0
Bonga shad	8.5*	7.5*	8.0
Aquaculture	0.9	0.9	0.9
Total catch*	69.8	55.3	55.9

* FAO estimate(s).

Source: FAO.

Mining

	2003	2004	2005
Diamonds ('000 carats)	230.0*	300.0	300.0*
Gold (kg)	1,313	1,219	1,638
Natural gas (million cubic metres)	1,457	2,000	2,200
Crude petroleum ('000 barrels)	7,506	8,125	14,574

* Estimate.

Source: US Geological Survey.

Industry

SELECTED PRODUCTS
('000 metric tons, unless otherwise indicated)

	2000	2001	2002
Beer of barley*†	160	160	205
Salted, dried or smoked fish*	15	15	n.a.
Canned fish*	57.1	58.8	121.8
Palm oil—unrefined*	278.0	204.9	276.0‡
Raw sugar*‡	179	177	177
Cocoa powder and cake*†	54.4	59.1	61.0
Cocoa butter*†	48.2	52.4	54.1
Plywood ('000 cubic metres)	80	81	76
Jet fuel	96	92	92
Motor gasoline (petrol)	554	480	487
Kerosene	536	561	547
Gas-diesel (Distillate fuel) oils	1,103	1,128	1,084
Residual fuel oils	443	643	337
Cement§	650	650	650
Electric energy (million kWh)	4,813	4,903	5,309

Cotton yarn (pure and mixed, '000 metric tons): 24.7† in 1989.

Electric energy (million kWh): 5,531 in 2005.

Cement ('000 metric tons, estimates): 650 in 2003–05 (Source: mainly US Geological Survey).

* Data from FAO.

† Provisional or estimated figures.

‡ Unofficial figure(s).

§ Data from the US Geological Survey.

Source: mainly UN, *Industrial Commodity Statistics Yearbook*.

Finance

CURRENCY AND EXCHANGE RATES

Monetary Units

100 centimes = 1 franc de la Communauté financière africaine (CFA).

Sterling, Dollar and Euro Equivalents (31 May 2007)

£1 sterling = 964.116 francs CFA;
US $1 = 487.592 francs CFA;
€1 = 655.957 francs CFA;
10,000 francs CFA = £10.37 = $20.51 = €15.24.

Average Exchange Rate (francs CFA per US $)

2004	528.29
2005	527.47
2006	522.89

Note: An exchange rate of 1 French franc = 50 francs CFA, established in 1948, remained in force until January 1994, when the CFA franc was devalued by 50%, with the exchange rate adjusted to 1 French franc = 100 francs CFA. This relationship to French currency remained in effect with the introduction of the euro on 1 January 1999. From that date, accordingly, a fixed exchange rate of €1 = 655.957 francs CFA has been in operation.

BUDGET
('000 million francs CFA)

Revenue*	2000	2001	2002
Tax revenue	1,077.5	1,168.4	1,259.3
Direct taxes	334.4	327.2	333.1
Taxes on profits	143.3	115.8	111.5
Individual income taxes	128.2	133.5	145.8
Employers' contributions	23.6	24.8	24.7
Indirect taxes†	258.3	289.1	293.9
Value-added tax and withholding tax	142.5	167.3	174.7
Taxes on petroleum products	95.5	93.6	94.4
Taxes on imports†	225.9	262.0	281.5
Value-added tax	109.1	127.3	129.0
Taxes on exports	163.4	196.5	256.4
Coffee and cocoa	156.1	188.0	246.9
Non-tax revenue	159.5	167.9	169.1
Social security contributions	102.7	114.2	113.1
Total	1,237.0	1,336.3	1,428.4

Expenditure‡	2000	2001	2002
Current expenditure	1,148.6	1,154.0	1,264.2
Wages and salaries	448.1	484.1	523.5
Other operating expenses	392.4	406.4	531.5
Interest due on public debt	308.1	259.7	265.6
Internal	28.9	24.0	23.2
External	279.2	235.7	242.4
Capital expenditure	209.6	143.3	257.1
Domestically funded	104.3	84.0	145.9
Funded from abroad	105.3	59.3	111.2
Crisis-related expenditure	—	—	57.5
Total	1,358.2	1,297.3	1,591.6

* Excluding grants received ('000 million francs CFA): 33.6 in 2000; 40.3 in 2001; 41.1 in 2002.

† Excluding taxes on petroleum products.

‡ Excluding net lending ('000 million francs CFA): 9.0 in 2000; 9.6 in 2001; 12.9 in 2002.

Source: IMF, *Côte d'Ivoire: Statistical Appendix* (June 2004).

2003 ('000 million francs CFA): Revenue 1,351.9 (Tax revenue 1,190.1, Non-tax revenue 161.8), Expenditure 1,611.0 (Wages and salaries 539.4; Interest due on public debt 217.4; Capital expenditure 213.7). Figures exclude grants received ('000 million francs CFA): 39.1, and net lending ('000 million francs CFA): 9.1.

2004 ('000 million francs CFA): Revenue 1,440.3 (Tax revenue 1,241.4, Non-tax revenue 198.9); Expenditure 1,665.0 (Wages and salaries 545.8; Interest due on public debt 186.1; Capital expenditure 258.6). Figures exclude grants received ('000 million francs CFA): 75.9, and net lending ('000 million francs CFA): 10.6.

2005 ('000 million francs CFA): Revenue 1,472.5 (Tax revenue 1,251.1; Non-tax revenue 221.3); Expenditure 1,713.8 (Wages and salaries 563.4; Interest due on public debt 177.1; Capital expenditure 235.3). Figures exclude grants received ('000 million francs CFA): 94.6, and net lending ('000 million francs CFA): 20.3.

2006 ('000 million francs CFA): Revenue 1,602.4 (Tax revenue 1,372.1; Non-tax revenue 230.3); Expenditure 1,747.3 (Wages and salaries 589.0; Interest due on public debt 131.9; Capital expenditure 239.1). Figures exclude grants received ('000 million francs CFA): 15.1, and net lending ('000 million francs CFA): 22.1.

INTERNATIONAL RESERVES

(excluding gold, US $ million at 31 December)

	2004	2005	2006
IMF special drawing rights	0.2	0.6	1.0
Reserve position in IMF	0.9	0.9	1.0
Foreign exchange	1,692.5	1,320.0	1,795.7
Total	1,693.6	1,321.5	1,797.7

Source: IMF, *International Financial Statistics*.

MONEY SUPPLY

('000 million francs CFA at 31 December)

	2004	2005	2006
Currency outside banks	671.5	754.1	815.2
Demand deposits at deposit money banks*	619.0	628.3	710.7
Total money (incl. others)	1,300.4	1,397.3	1,551.0

* Excluding the deposits of public establishments of an administrative or social nature.

Source: IMF, *International Financial Statistics*.

COST OF LIVING

(Consumer Price Index for African households in Abidjan; base: 1996 = 100)

	2003	2004	2005
Food, beverages and tobacco	116.1	111.6	114.3
Clothing and footwear	99.9	100.2	101.9
Rent	114.4	116.3	126.1
All items (incl. others)	111.1	112.7	117.1

Source: ILO.

NATIONAL ACCOUNTS

('000 million francs CFA at current prices)

Expenditure on the Gross Domestic Product

	2003	2004	2005
Final consumption expenditure	6,335.3	6,528.8	6,839.0
Households; Non-profit institutions serving households	5,241.8	5,400.3	5,770.4
General government	1,093.5	1,128.5	1,068.6
Gross capital formation	779.8	818.8	773.9
Change in stocks	32.0	78.2	102.0
Total domestic expenditure	7,147.1	7,425.8	7,714.9
Exports of goods and services	3,749.6	3,741.6	4,184.8
Less Imports of goods and services	2,912.4	2,955.7	3,449.0
Statistical discrepancy	—	–33.2	—
GDP in purchasers' values	7,984.3	8,178.5	8,450.7

Gross Domestic Product by Economic Activity

	2003	2004	2005
Agriculture, livestock-rearing, forestry and fishing	2,039.9	1,896.0	1,965.4
Mining and quarrying	89.4	116.4	145.9
Manufacturing	1,246.0	1,331.3	1,341.0
Electricity, gas and water	179.5	190.4	196.3
Construction and public works	214.0	248.9	254.4
Trade	1,054.0	1,141.1	1,175.6
Transport, storage and communications	356.4	381.2	395.6
Non-market services	1,147.0	1,113.3	1,261.7
Other services	1,079.7	1,065.7	1,088.0
Sub-total	7,405.9	7,484.3	7,823.9
Import duties and taxes	578.4	694.3	626.8
GDP in purchasers' values	7,984.3	8,178.5	8,450.7

Source: Banque centrale des états de l'Afrique de l'ouest.

BALANCE OF PAYMENTS

(US $ million)

	2004	2005	2006
Exports of goods f.o.b.	6,919.3	7,697.4	8,190.8
Imports of goods f.o.b.	–4,291.4	–5,251.1	–5,038.9
Trade balance	2,627.9	2,446.3	3,151.9
Exports of services	762.7	832.4	818.7
Imports of services	–2,032.6	–2,123.5	–2,217.5
Balance on goods and services	1,358.0	1,155.2	1,753.1
Other income received	189.7	193.9	197.9
Other income paid	–841.3	–847.1	–926.0
Balance on goods, services and income	706.3	502.0	1,025.1
Current transfers received	187.4	194.8	204.4
Current transfers paid	–652.8	–657.2	–700.3
Current balance	240.9	39.6	529.2
Capital account (net)	145.9	185.2	27.5
Direct investment from abroad	283.0	311.9	315.0
Portfolio investment assets	–37.5	–50.0	–40.7
Portfolio investment liabilities	8.9	48.1	48.2
Financial derivatives assets	–6.0	–5.2	—
Financial derivatives liabilities	10.2	0.9	—
Other investment assets	–402.5	–374.4	–568.0
Other investment liabilities	–119.6	–400.3	–195.5
Net errors and omissions	26.6	–57.5	52.1
Overall balance	149.9	–301.6	167.8

Source: IMF, *International Financial Statistics*.

External Trade

PRINCIPAL COMMODITIES

(distribution by SITC, US $ million)

Imports c.i.f.	2000	2002*	2003
Food and live animals	377.9	523.0	655.1
Fish, crustaceans and molluscs, and preparations thereof	131.4	180.4	202.1
Fish, frozen, excl. fillets	127.9	175.3	196.5
Cereals and cereal preparations	153.4	218.4	250.2
Rice	97.5	134.3	157.7
Rice, semi-milled or wholly milled	91.2	130.6	156.7
Rice, semi-milled or wholly milled (unbroken)	76.5	102.0	122.3
Mineral fuels, lubricants, etc.	838.0	534.8	606.3
Petroleum, petroleum products, etc.	837.7	534.5	605.8
Crude petroleum and oils obtained from bituminous materials	679.5	419.2	537.8
Petroleum products, refined	154.9	109.9	61.5
Fuel oils, etc.	132.9	88.6	22.1
Chemicals and related products	352.1	447.6	499.7
Medical and pharmaceutical products	94.8	100.6	123.5
Medicaments (incl. veterinary medicaments)	89.3	91.6	114.7
Artificial resins and plastic materials, cellulose esters, etc.	90.7	101.0	118.4
Polymerization and copolymerization products	79.4	87.0	102.8
Basic manufactures	319.1	359.0	360.8
Iron and steel	64.7	84.1	74.9
Machinery and transport equipment	406.6	524.9	756.2
Road vehicles	104.7	115.9	249.2
Other transport equipment	7.0	138.6	191.3
Special purpose vessels, floating docks, etc.	—	134.5	174.1
Miscellaneous manufactured articles	84.6	88.9	119.0
Total (incl. others)†	2,482.2	2,599.0	3,536.3

Exports f.o.b.	2000	2002*	2003
Food and live animals	1,744.3	2,843.9	2,982.9
Fish, crustaceans and molluscs, and preparations thereof	128.9	139.7	141.0
Fish, prepared or preserved	120.1	135.7	136.2
Vegetables and fruit	179.5	183.9	189.0
Fruit and nuts, fresh, dried	171.6	179.6	183.4
Coffee, tea, cocoa, spices and manufactures thereof	1,327.2	2,353.7	2,418.8
Coffee and coffee substitutes	303.0	119.4	142.3
Coffee, green, roasted; coffee substitutes containing coffee	257.8	73.2	79.0
Coffee, not roasted; coffee husks and skins	244.1	72.1	77.8
Cocoa	1,017.9	2,203.0	2,230.4
Cocoa beans, raw, roasted	845.6	1,757.1	1,735.4
Cocoa butter and paste	160.7	390.1	409.1
Cocoa paste	98.2	244.7	233.9
Cocoa butter	62.5	145.4	175.2
Crude materials (inedible) except fuels	511.6	427.9	522.2
Cork and wood	271.7	190.0	198.1
Wood, simply worked and railway sleepers of wood	239.8	160.9	164.4
Wood, non-coniferous species, sawn, planed, tongued, grooved, etc.	237.2	158.1	162.8
Wood, non-coniferous species, sawn lengthwise, slices or peeled	218.0	135.5	131.1
Textile fibres (not wool tops) and their wastes (not in yarn)	148.9	134.6	178.4
Raw cotton, excl. linters, not carded or combed	148.0	133.8	177.6
Mineral fuels, lubricants, etc.	737.5	564.8	703.4
Petroleum, petroleum products, etc.	735.0	563.5	703.3
Crude petroleum and oils obtained from bituminous materials	69.7	90.9	195.9
Petroleum products, refined	644.7	457.5	489.9
Gasoline and other light oils	294.2	204.2	395.1
Motor spirit, incl. aviation spirit	61.3	47.8	313.6
Sprit type jet fuel	232.9	156.3	81.5
Gas oils	211.0	139.1	52.6
Chemicals and related products	142.9	234.3	215.2
Basic manufactures	244.3	258.6	240.4
Machinery and transport equipment	37.4	441.3	532.1
Road vehicles	13.6	13.2	364.1
Passenger motor vehicles (excl. buses)	3.4	3.1	189.4
Other transport equipment	4.7	409.3	113.2
Ships, boats and floating structures	2.4	407.6	109.0
Special purpose vessels, floating docks, etc.	1.9	407.5	108.8
Total (incl. others)	3,627.9	4,971.9	5,493.4

* No data were available for 2001.

† Including commodities and transactions not classified elsewhere in the SITC (US $ million): 0.2 in 2000, 0.0 in 2002, 382.4 in 2003 (Armoured fighting vehicles, war firearms, ammunition, parts, etc. 0.2 in 2000, 0.0 in 2002, 377.2 in 2003; Tanks and other armoured fighting vehicles, motorized, parts, etc. 0.2 in 2000, 0.0 in 2002, 368.6 in 2003).

Source: UN, *International Trade Statistics Yearbook*.

PRINCIPAL TRADING PARTNERS

(US $ million)

Imports c.i.f.	2000	2002*	2003
Bahrain	45.5	9.2	—
Belgium	100.3	62.6	80.2
Brazil	23.2	28.8	31.7
China, People's Republic	66.6	62.4	123.4
France (incl. Monaco)	504.7	555.6	1,152.6
Germany	89.5	93.6	100.4
India	17.6	72.3	70.3
Indonesia	8.0	17.5	36.3
Italy	90.5	121.7	111.3
Japan	72.2	71.1	58.3
Korea, Republic	24.6	38.2	39.1
Netherlands	76.0	93.1	117.2
Nigeria	659.8	366.8	509.8
Russia	62.5	77.1	57.6
Senegal	16.1	26.7	43.0
Singapore	1.2	141.2	7.3
South Africa	38.1	48.4	53.1
Spain	81.4	83.7	82.8
Thailand	54.6	64.1	74.1
United Kingdom	56.3	64.7	247.6
USA	89.0	89.8	114.1
Venezuela	25.8	11.1	8.3
Total (incl. others)	2,482.2	2,599.0	3,536.3

Exports f.o.b.	2000	2002*	2003
Belgium	138.7	128.9	147.1
Benin	43.2	41.7	74.3
Burkina Faso	129.5	146.6	112.8
Cameroon	34.1	41.0	59.7
Equatorial Guinea	19.0	17.3	130.9
France (incl. Monaco)	540.5	653.5	1,047.0
Germany	110.0	137.8	119.9
Ghana	134.9	106.0	124.4
India	93.3	85.8	75.3
Indonesia	33.5	57.0	57.2
Italy	172.5	189.0	188.4
Liberia	41.2	24.9	18.7
Mali	207.8	179.3	97.9
Netherlands	353.4	940.2	974.3
Niger	40.2	51.9	49.8
Nigeria	68.8	465.8	164.4
Poland	43.9	78.0	91.8
Russia	62.2	137.1	116.5
Senegal	145.8	57.3	95.7
Spain	136.5	246.8	309.5
Togo	88.6	80.9	121.2
United Kingdom	89.4	131.1	169.1
USA	301.3	374.7	389.3
Total (incl. others)	3,627.9	4,971.9	5,493.4

* No data were available for 2001.

Source: UN, *International Trade Statistics Yearbook*.

Transport

RAILWAYS
(traffic)

	2001	2002	2003
Passengers ('000)	399.5	320.0	87.5
Freight carried ('000 metric tons)	1,016.3	900.7	149.7

Passenger-km (million): 93.1 in 1999 (Source: SITARAIL—Transport Ferroviaire de Personnel et de Marchandises, Abidjan).

Freight ton-km (million): 537.6 in 1999 (Source: SITARAIL—Transport Ferroviaire de Personnel et de Marchandises, Abidjan).

ROAD TRAFFIC
('000 motor vehicles in use)

	1998	1999	2000
Passenger cars	98.4	109.6	113.9
Commercial vehicles	45.4	54.1	54.9

2001–02 ('000 motor vehicles in use): Figures assumed to be unchanged from 2000.

Source: UN, *Statistical Yearbook*.

SHIPPING

Merchant Fleet
(registered at 31 December)

	2003	2004	2005
Number of vessels	33	34	35
Total displacement ('000 grt)	8.9	9.1	9.2

Source: Lloyd's Register-Fairplay, *World Fleet Statistics*.

International Sea-borne Freight Traffic
(freight traffic at Abidjan, '000 metric tons)

	2001	2002	2003
Goods loaded	5,787	5,710	6,108
Goods unloaded	9,858	9,018	8,353

Source: Port Autonome d'Abidjan.

Freight traffic at San-Pédro ('000 metric tons, 2000): Goods loaded 1,102; Goods unloaded 251.

CIVIL AVIATION
(traffic on scheduled services)*

	1999	2000	2001
Kilometres flown (million)	6	3	1
Passengers carried ('000)	260	108	46
Passenger-km (million)	381	242	130
Total ton-km (million)	50	34	19

* Including an apportionment of the traffic of Air Afrique.

Source: UN, *Statistical Yearbook*.

Tourism

ARRIVALS BY COUNTRY OF RESIDENCE
('000)

	1996*	1997†	1998†
Belgium	4.3	4.2	4.5
Benin	12.5	11.1	14.3
Burkina Faso	11.0	11.9	17.1
Congo, Repub.	6.0	n.a.	7.6
France	66.7	69.0	73.2
Gabon	3.0	n.a.	5.4
Germany	3.2	3.8	3.9
Ghana	5.4	n.a.	6.7
Guinea	8.1	n.a.	12.5
Italy	5.0	14.0	7.6
Mali	10.7	n.a.	15.2
Niger	5.0	n.a.	5.4
Nigeria	7.9	n.a.	14.1
Senegal	13.0	12.1	16.6
Togo	8.7	8.2	10.8
United Kingdom	5.1	4.5	5.6
USA	15.3	17.0	18.8
Total (incl. others)	236.9	274.1	301.0

* Figures refer only to air arrivals at Abidjan—Félix Houphouët-Boigny airport.

† Figures refer to air arrivals at Abidjan—Félix Houphouët-Boigny airport and to arrivals at land frontiers.

Receipts from tourism (US $ million, excl. passenger transport): 317 in 1997; 331 in 1998; 337 in 1999; 291 in 2000; 289 in 2001; 490 in 2002.

Source: World Tourism Organization.

Communications Media

	2002	2003	2004
Telephones ('000 main lines in use)	324.8	238.0	257.9
Mobile cellular telephones ('000 subscribers)	1,027.1	1,280.7	1,674.3
Personal computers ('000 in use)	154	201	262
Internet users ('000)	90	140	160

2005: Mobile cellular telephones ('000 subscribers) 2,190.0.

Source: International Telecommunication Union.

Television receivers ('000 in use): 887 in 2000 (Source: UNESCO, *Statistical Yearbook*).

Radio receivers ('000 in use): 2,260 in 1997 (Source: UNESCO, *Statistical Yearbook*).

Daily newspapers (national estimates): 12 (average circulation 235,000 copies) in 1997; 12 (average circulation 238,000 copies) in 1998 (Source: UNESCO Institute for Statistics).

Non-daily newspapers: 15 in 1996 (average circulation 251,000 copies) (Source: UNESCO, *Statistical Yearbook*).

Education

(2002/03, unless otherwise indicated)

	Teachers	Students		
		Males	Females	Total
Pre-primary	2,179	24,786	23,861	48,647
Primary	48,308	1,141,762	904,403	2,046,165
Secondary	20,124*	474,203†	262,446†	736,649†
Tertiary*	n.a.	71,283	25,398	96,681

* 1998/99.

† 2001/02.

Institutions: 207 pre-primary in 1995/96; 7,599 primary in 1996/97.

Source: mostly UNESCO Institute for Statistics.

Adult literacy rate (UNESCO estimates): 45.9% (males 18.1%; females 42.6%) in 2004 (Source: UN Development Programme, *Human Development Report*).

Directory

The Constitution

Following the *coup d'état* of 24 December 1999, the Constitution that had been in force, with amendments, since 1960 was suspended. A new Constitution was subsequently prepared by a consultative committee, and was approved by referendum in July 2000. The main provisions of the Constitution are summarized below:

PREAMBLE

The people of Côte d'Ivoire recognize their diverse ethnic, cultural and religious backgrounds, and desire to build a single, unified and prosperous nation based on constitutional legality and democratic institutions, the rights of the individual, cultural and spiritual values, transparency in public affairs, and the promotion of sub-regional, regional and African unity.

FREEDOMS, RIGHTS AND DUTIES

Articles 1–28: The State guarantees the implementation of the Constitution and guarantees to protect the rights of each citizen. The State guarantees its citizens equal access to health, education, culture, information, professional training, employment and justice. Freedom of thought and expression are guaranteed to all, although the encouragement of social, ethnic and religious discord is not permitted. Freedom of association and demonstration are guaranteed. Political parties may act freely within the law; however, parties must not be created solely on a regional, ethnic or religious basis. The rights of free enterprise, the right to join a trade union and the right to strike are guaranteed.

NATIONAL SOVEREIGNTY

Articles 29–33: Côte d'Ivoire is an independent and sovereign republic. The official language is French. Legislation regulates the promotion and development of national languages. The Republic of Côte d'Ivoire is indivisible, secular, democratic and social. All its citizens are equal. Sovereignty belongs to the people, and is exercised through referendums and the election of representatives. The right to vote freely and in secret is guaranteed to all citizens over 18 years of age.

HEAD OF STATE

Articles 34–57: The President of the Republic is the Head of State. The President is elected for a five-year mandate (renewable once only) by direct universal suffrage. Candidates must be aged between 40 and 65, and be Ivorian citizens holding no other nationality, and resident in the country, with Ivorian parents. If one candidate does not receive a simple majority of votes cast, a second round of voting takes place between the two most successful candidates. The President holds executive power, and appoints a Prime Minister to co-ordinate government action. The President appoints the Government on the recommendation of the Prime Minister. The President presides over the Council of Ministers, is the head of the civil service and the supreme head of the armed forces. The President may initiate legislation and call referendums. The President may not hold any other office or be a leader of a political party.

ASSEMBLÉE NATIONALE

Articles 58–83: The Assemblée nationale holds legislative power. The Assemblée nationale votes on the budget and scrutinizes the accounts of the nation. Deputies are elected for periods of five years by direct universal suffrage. Except in exceptional cases, deputies have legal immunity during the period of their mandate.

INTERNATIONAL AGREEMENTS

Articles 84–87: The President negotiates and ratifies treaties and international agreements. International agreements, which modify internal legislation, must be ratified by further legislation. The Constitution must be amended prior to the ratification of certain agreements if the Constitutional Council deems this necessary.

CONSTITUTIONAL COUNCIL

Articles 88–100: The Constitutional Council rules on the constitutionality of legislation. It also regulates the functioning of government. It is composed of a President, of the former Presidents of Côte d'Ivoire and of six councillors named by the President and by the President of the Assemblée nationale for mandates of six years. The Council supervises referendums and announces referendum and election results. It also examines the eligibility of candidates to the presidency and the legislature. There is no appeal against the Council's decisions.

JUDICIAL POWER

Articles 101–112: The judiciary is independent, and is composed of the High Court of Justice, the Court of Cassation*, the Council of State, the National Audit Court, and regional tribunals and appeals courts. The Higher Council of Magistrates examines questions relating to judicial independence and nominates and disciplines senior magistrates. The High Court of Justice judges members of the Government in cases relating to the execution of their duties. The High Court, which is composed of deputies elected by the Assemblée nationale, may only judge the President in cases of high treason.

* Although the Constitution of 2000 refers to the highest court of appeal as the Court of Cassation, in early 2004 this court retained its previous designation, as the Supreme Court.

THE ECONOMIC AND SOCIAL COUNCIL

Articles 113–114: The Economic and Social Council gives its opinion on proposed legislation or decrees relating to its sphere of competence. The President may consult the Council on any economic or social matter.

THE MEDIATOR OF THE REPUBLIC

Articles 115–118: The Mediator is an independent mediating figure, appointed for a non-renewable six-year mandate by the President, in consultation with the President of the Assemblée nationale. The

Mediator, who may not hold any other office or position, receives immunity from prosecution during the term of office.

OTHER ISSUES

Articles 119–133: Only the President or the Assemblée nationale, of whom a two-thirds' majority must be in favour, may propose amending the Constitution. Amendments relating to the nature of the presidency or the mechanism whereby the Constitution is amended must be approved by referendum; all other amendments may be enacted with the agreement of the President and of a four-fifths' majority of the Assemblée nationale. The form and the secular nature of the republic may not be amended. Immunity from prosecution is granted to members of the Comité national de salut public and to all those involved in the change of government of December 1999.

The Government

HEAD OF STATE

President of the Republic: LAURENT GBAGBO (took office 26 October 2000).

COUNCIL OF MINISTERS

(August 2007)

Prime Minister: GUILLAUME SORO KIGBAFORI.

Minister of State for Planning and Development: ANTOINE BOHOUN BOUABRÉ.

Minister of Defence: N'GUESSAN MICHEL AMANI.

Minister of the Interior: ASSÉGNINI DÉSIRÉ TAGRO.

Keeper of the Seals, Minister of Justice and Human Rights: MAMADOU KONÉ.

Minister of Foreign Affairs: YOUSSOUF BAKAYOKO.

Minister of the Economy and Finance: KOFFI CHARLES DIBY.

Minister of Agriculture: AMADOU GON COULIBALY.

Minister of Mines and Energy: LÉON-EMMANUEL MONNET.

Minister of Construction, Town Planning and Housing: MARCEL BENOÎT AMON TANOH.

Minister of National Reconciliation and Relations with the Institutions: SÉBASTIEN DANO DJÉ DJÉ.

Minister of Economic Infrastructure: PATRICK ACHI.

Minister of Health and Public Hygiene: RÉMI ALLAH KOUADIO.

Minister of National Education: GILBERT BLEU-LAINE.

Minister of Higher Education and Scientific Research: IBRAHIMA CISSÉ.

Minister of Technical Education and Professional Training: MOUSSA DOSSO.

Minister of the Civil Service and Employment: HUBERT OULAYE.

Minister of Transport: TOIKEUSSE MABRI.

Minister of African Integration: AMADOU KONÉ.

Minister of Culture and Francophone Affairs: KOMOÉ AUGUSTIN KOUADIO.

Minister of Solidarity and the Victims of War: LOUIS ANDRÉ DAKOURY-TABLEY.

Minister of Animal Production and Fisheries: ALPHONSE DOUATI.

Minister of the Environment, Water and Forestry: DANIEL AHIZI AKA.

Minister of the Family, Women and Social Affairs: JEANNE BROU PEUHMOND ADJOUA.

Minister of the Struggle against AIDS: CHRISTINE NEBOUT ADJOBI.

Minister of Industry and the Promotion of the Private Sector: MARIE TÉHOUA AMAH.

Minister of Trade: YOUSSOUF SOUMAHORO.

Minister of Tourism and Crafts: SIDIKE KONATÉ.

Minister of Information and Communication Technology: HAMED BAKAYOKO.

Minister of Youth, Sport and Leisure: BANZIO DAGOBERT.

Minister of Reconstruction and Reintegration: FATOUMATA BAMBA.

Minister of Communication: IBRAHIM SY SAVANE.

Minister of Cities and Urban Health: THÉODORE MEL EG.

MINISTRIES

Office of the President: 01 BP 1354, Abidjan 01; tel. 20-22-02-22; fax 20-21-14-25; internet www.presidence.ci.

Office of the Prime Minister: blvd Angoulvant, 01 BP 1533, Abidjan 01; tel. 20-31-50-00; fax 20-22-18-33; e-mail pm@primature.gov.ci.

Ministry of African Integration: 5e–6e étages, Immeuble AMCI, 15 ave Joseph Anoma, Plateau, Abidjan; tel. 20-33-90-09.

Ministry of Agriculture: 25e étage, Immeuble Caisse de Stabilisation, BP V82, Abidjan; tel. 20-21-38-58; fax 20-21-46-18; e-mail minagra@cimail.net.

Ministry of Animal Production and Fisheries: 11e étage, Immeuble Caisse de Stabilisation, Plateau, Abidjan; tel. 20-21-33-94.

Ministry of Cities and Urban Health: Abidjan.

Ministry of the Civil Service and Employment: Immeuble Fonction Public, blvd Angoulvand, BP V93, Abidjan; tel. 20-21-42-90; fax 20-21-12-86.

Ministry of Communication: 22e étage, Tour C, Tours Administratives, Plateau, Abidjan; tel. 20-21-11-16.

Ministry of Construction, Town Planning and Housing: 26e étage, Tour D, Tours Administratives, 20 BP 650, Abidjan; tel. 20-21-82-35; fax 20-21-35-68.

Ministry of Culture and Francophone Affairs: 22e étage, Tour E, Tours Administratives, BP V39, Abidjan; tel. 20-21-40-34; fax 20-21-33-59; e-mail culture.ci@ci.refer.org.

Ministry of Defence: Camp Galliéni, côté Bibliothèque nationale, BP V241, Abidjan; tel. 20-21-02-88; fax 20-22-41-75.

Ministry of Economic Infrastructure: 23e étage, Immeuble Postel 2001, BP V6, Plateau, Abidjan; tel. 20-34-73-01; fax 20-21-37-30; e-mail minie@aviso.ci.

Ministry of the Economy and Finance: 16e étage, Immeuble SCIAM, ave Marchand, BP V163, Abidjan; tel. 20-20-08-42; fax 20-21-32-08.

Ministry of the Environment, Water and Forestry: 10e étage, Tour D, Tours Administratives, BP V06, Abidjan; tel. 20-22-61-35; fax 20-22-20-50.

Ministry of the Family, Women and Social Affairs: Tour E, Tours Administratives, BP V200, Abidjan; tel. 20-21-76-26; fax 20-21-44-61.

Ministry of Foreign Affairs: Bloc Ministériel, blvd Angoulvand, BP V109, Abidjan; tel. 20-22-71-50; fax 20-33-23-08; e-mail infos@mae.ci; internet www.mae.ci.

Ministry of Health and Public Hygiene: 16e étage, Tour C, Tours Administratives, Plateau, Abidjan; tel. 20-21-52-40.

Ministry of Higher Education and Scientific Research: 20e étage, Tour C, Tours Administratives, BP V151, Abidjan; tel. 20-21-57-73; fax 20-21-22-25.

Ministry of Industry and the Promotion of the Private Sector: 15e étage, Immeuble CCIA, rue Jean-Paul II, BP V65, Abidjan; tel. 20-21-64-73.

Ministry of Information and Communication Technology: 21e étage, Immeuble Postel 2001, BP V138, Abidjan; tel. 22-34-73-65; fax 22-44-78-47.

Ministry of the Interior: Immeuble SETU, en face de la préfecture, BP V241, Abidjan; tel. 20-22-38-16; fax 20-22-36-48.

Ministry of Justice and Human Rights: Bloc Ministériel, blvd Angoulvand A-17, BP V107, Plateau, Abidjan; tel. 20-21-17-27; fax 20-33-12-59.

Ministry of Mines and Energy: 15e étage, Immeuble SCIAM, ave Marchand, BP V40, Abidjan; tel. 20-21-66-17; fax 20-21-37-30.

Ministry of National Education: 28e étage, Tour D, Tours Administratives, BP V120, Abidjan; tel. 20-21-85-27; fax 20-22-93-22; e-mail menfb@ci.refer.org.

Ministry of National Reconciliation and Relations with the Institutions: Cocody, 08 BP 590, Abidjan 08; tel. 22-48-89-82; fax 22-48-92-82.

Ministry of Planning and Development: 23e étage, Immeuble CCIA, rue Jean-Paul II, Abidjan; tel. 20-22-20-04.

Ministry of Reconstruction and Reintegration: Abidjan.

Ministry of Solidarity and the Victims of War: derrière ENA, Cocody-les-Deux-Plateau, BP V241, Abidjan; tel. 22-41-45-38.

Ministry of the Struggle against AIDS: 7e étage, Immeuble Caisse de Stabilisation, Plateau, Abidjan; tel. 20-21-08-46.

Ministry of Technical Education and Professional Training: 10e étage, Tour C, Tours Administratives, Plateau, Abidjan; tel. 20-21-17-02.

Ministry of Tourism and Crafts: 15e étage, Tour D, Tours Administratives, BP V184, Abidjan 01; tel. 20-34-79-13; fax 20-44-55-80.

Ministry of Trade: 26e étage, Immeuble CCIA, rue Jean-Paul II, BP V65, Abidjan; tel. 20-21-76-35; fax 20-21-64-74.

Ministry of Transport: 14e étage, Immeuble Postel 2001, BP V06, Abidjan; tel. 20-34-48-58; fax 20-21-37-30.

Ministry of Youth, Sport and Leisure: 8e étage, Tour B, Tours Administratives, BP V136, Abidjan; tel. 20-21-92-64; fax 20-22-48-21.

President and Legislature

PRESIDENT

Presidential Election, 22 October 2000

Candidate	Votes	% of votes
Laurent Gbagbo (FPI)	1,065,597	59.36
Robert Gueï (Ind.)	587,267	32.72
Francis Wodié (PIT)	102,253	5.70
Théodore Mel-Eg (UDCY)	26,331	1.47
Nicolas Dioulo (Ind.)	13,558	0.76
Total*	1,795,006	100.00

* Excluding invalid votes (25,413).

LEGISLATURE

Assemblée nationale

01 BP 1381, Abidjan 01; tel. 20-21-60-69; fax 20-22-20-87.

President: MAMADOU KOULIBALY.

General Election, 10 December 2000*

Party	Seats
Front populaire ivoirien (FPI)	96
Parti démocratique de la Côte d'Ivoire—Rassemblement démocratique africain (PDCI—RDA)	94
Rassemblement des républicains (RDR) †	5
Parti ivoirien des travailleurs (PIT)	4
Union démocratique citoyenne (UDCY)	1
Mouvement des forces d'avenir (MFA)	1
Independents	22
Total‡	223

* These figures include the results of voting in 26 constituencies where elections were postponed until 14 January 2001, owing to unrest.

† The RDR officially boycotted the elections, and these seats were won by a faction within the party that did not participate in the boycott.

‡ Voting for the remaining two seats was postponed indefinitely.

Advisory Councils

Constitutional Council: blvd Carde, BP 4642, Abidjan 01; tel. 20-25-38-50; fax 20-21-21-68; internet www.gouv.ci/conseilconstitutionnel.php; f. 2000 to replace certain functions of the fmr Constitutional Chamber of the Supreme Court; Pres. YANON YAPO GERMAIN.

Economic and Social Council: 04 BP 301, Abidjan 04; tel. 20-21-14-54; internet www.gouv.ci/conseileco.php; Pres. LAURENT DONA FOLOGO; Vice-Pres. DIGBEU HILAIRE ANY, ETIENNE KOUDOU BOTI, NICOLE DEIGNA, MARTIN KOUAKOU N'GUESSA, VAKABA DEMOVALY TOURÉ; 120 mems.

Political Organizations

In mid- 2007 there were more than 100 registered political organizations.

Alliance pour la paix, le progrès et la souverainété (APS): Abidjan; f. 2003 by fmr members of the UDPCI (q.v.); Pres. HILAIRE DIGBEU ANI.

Forces nouvelles (FN): Bouaké; tel. 20-20-04-04; e-mail senacom@fnci.info; internet www.fnci.info; f. 2003 by the Mouvement patriotique de Côte d'Ivoire (MPCI), following its absorption of the Mouvement populaire ivoirien du grand ouest (MPIGO) and the Mouvement pour la justice et la paix (MJP), both of which were based in Man, in the west of Côte d'Ivoire; representatives of these three 'politico-military' groups, which had emerged following the outbreak of civil conflict in September 2002, were included in the Government of National Reconciliation formed in March 2003; Sec.-Gen. GUILLAUME SORO KIGBAFORI.

Front populaire ivoirien (FPI): Marcory Zone 4C, 22 BP 302, Abidjan 22; tel. 21-24-36-76; fax 21-35-35-50; e-mail infoservice@fpi-ci.org; internet www.fpi-ci.org; f. 1990; socialist; Pres. PASCAL AFFI N'GUESSAN; Sec.-Gen. SYLVAIN MIAKA OURETO.

Mouvement des forces d'avenir (MFA): Adjamé, face Fraternité Matin, 01 BP 4137, Abidjan 01; tel. 07-57-47-13; f. 1995; mem. of alliance, Rassemblement des Houphouëtistes pour la démocratie et la paix, formed in advance of proposed (but subsequently postponed) presidential elections in 2005; Pres. INNOCENT KOBENA ANAKY.

Parti africain pour la renaissance ivoirienne (PARI): Abidjan; f. 1991; Sec.-Gen. DANIEL ANIKPO.

Parti démocratique de la Côte d'Ivoire—Rassemblement démocratique africain (PDCI—RDA): Maison du parti, Cocody, 01 BP 79, Abidjan 01; e-mail sg@pdcirda.org; internet www.pdcirda.org; f. 1946; mem. of alliance, Rassemblement des Houphouëtistes pour la démocratie et la paix, formed in advance of proposed (but subsequently postponed) presidential elections in 2005; Pres. HENRI KONAN BÉDIÉ; Sec.-Gen. ALPHONSE DJÉDJÉ MADY.

Parti ivoirien des travailleurs (PIT): 20 BP 43, Abidjan 20; e-mail pit@abc.ci; social-democratic; f. 1990; First Nat. Sec. FRANCIS WODIÉ.

Parti pour le progrès et le socialisme (PPS): Abidjan; f. 1993; Sec.-Gen. Prof. BAMBA MORIFÉRÉ.

Rassemblement des républicains (RDR): 8 rue Lepic, Cocody, 06 BP 1440, Abidjan 06; tel. 22-44-33-51; e-mail rdrci@rdrci.org; internet www.rdrci.org; f. 1994 following split from PDCI—RDA (q.v.); officially boycotted the general election of Dec. 2000, except for a faction of some 60 candidates, led by ALPHONSE OULAÏ TOUSSÉA; mem. of alliance, Rassemblement des Houphouëtistes pour la démocratie et la paix, formed in advance of proposed (but subsequently postponed) presidential elections in 2005; Pres. Dr ALASSANE DRAMANE OUATTARA; Sec.-Gen. HENRIETTE DAGRI-DIABATÉ.

Union démocratique citoyenne (UDCY): 37 bis rue de la Canebière—PISAM, 01 BP 1410, Abidjan 01; tel. 05-07-77-77; f. 2000 following split from PDCI—RDA (q.v.); Sec.-Gen. THÉODORE MEL-EG.

Union des sociaux-démocrates (USD): Abidjan; Sec.-Gen. Me JÉRÔME CLIMANLO COULIBALY.

Union pour la démocratie et pour la paix de la Côte d'Ivoire (UDPCI): Deux Plateaux, derrière SOCOCE, 06 BP 6647, Abidjan 06; tel. 22-41-31-21; fax 20-22-22-20; e-mail dougbo@voila.fr; f. 2001 following split from PDCI—RDA by supporters of fmr head of state Gen. Robert Gueï; mem. of alliance, Rassemblement des Houphouëtistes pour la démocratie et la paix, formed in advance of proposed (but subsequently postponed) presidential elections in 2005; Pres. PAUL AKOTO YAO; Sec.-Gen. ALASSANE SALIF N'DIAYE.

Diplomatic Representation

EMBASSIES IN CÔTE D'IVOIRE

Following the onset of civil conflict in 2002 and subsequent unrest in Abidjan, many diplomatic missions have suspended or terminated their operations, or have transferred to other countries of the region.

Algeria: 53 blvd Clozel, 01 BP 1015, Abidjan 01; tel. 20-21-23-40; fax 20-22-37-12; Ambassador SALEH LEBDIOUI.

Angola: Lot 2461, rue des Jardins, Cocody-les-Deux-Plateaux, 01 BP 1734, Abidjan 01; tel. 22-41-38-79; fax 22-41-28-89; Ambassador (vacant).

Belgium: Immeuble Alliance, ave Terrasson des Fougères, 01 BP 1800, Abidjan 01; tel. 20-21-00-88; fax 20-22-41-77; e-mail abidjan@diplobel.org; internet www.diplomatie.be/abidjan; Ambassador DIRK VERHEYEN.

Benin: rue des Jasmins, Lot 1610, Cocody-les-Deux-Plateaux, 09 BP 283, Abidjan 09; tel. 22-41-44-13; fax 22-42-76-07; Ambassador OMER JEAN-GILLES DE SOUZA.

Brazil: Immeuble Alpha 2000, rue Gourgas, 01 BP 3820, Abidjan 01; tel. 20-22-23-41; fax 22-22-64-01; e-mail brascote@aviso.ci; Ambassador FAUSTO CARMELLO.

Burkina Faso: Immeuble SIDAM, 5e étage, 34 ave Houdaille, 01 BP 908, Plateau, Abidjan 01; tel. 20-21-15-01; fax 20-21-66-41; e-mail amba.bf@africaonline.ci; Ambassador EMILE ILBOUDO.

Cameroon: Immeuble le Général, blvd Botreau Roussel, 06 BP 326, Abidjan 06; tel. 20-21-33-31; fax 20-21-66-11; Ambassador (vacant).

Canada: Immeuble Trade Center, 23 ave Noguès, 01 BP 4104, Abidjan 01; tel. 20-30-07-00; fax 20-30-07-20; e-mail abdjn@dfait-maeci.gc.ca; internet www.dfait-maeci.gc.ca/abidjan; Ambassador MARIE-ISABELLE MASSIP.

Central African Republic: 9 rue des Jasmins, Cocody Danga Nord, 01 BP 3387, Abidjan 01; tel. 20-21-36-46; fax 22-44-85-16; Ambassador YAGAO-N'GAMA LAZARE.

China, People's Republic: Lot 45, ave Jacques Aka, Cocody, 01 BP 3691, Abidjan 01; tel. 22-44-59-00; fax 22-44-67-81; e-mail ambchine@aviso.ci; Ambassador MA ZHIXUE.

Congo, Democratic Republic: Carrefour France-Amérique, RAN Treichville, ave 21, 01 BP 541, Abidjan 01; tel. 21-24-69-06; Ambassador ISABELLE I. NGANGELLI.

Egypt: Immeuble El Nasr, rue du Commerce, 01 BP 2104, Abidjan 01; tel. 20-32-79-25; fax 20-22-30-53; e-mail amegypteci@afnet.net; Ambassador SHERIF YOUSSEF ABBAS SOLIMAN.

Ethiopia: Immeuble Nour Al-Hayat, 01 BP 3712, Abidjan 01; tel. 20-21-33-65; fax 20-21-37-09; e-mail ambethio@gmail.com; Ambassador YOHANNES GENDA GINBI.

France: rue Lecoeur, 17 BP 175, Abidjan 17; tel. 20-20-04-04; fax 20-20-04-47; e-mail scac.abidjan-amba@diplomatie.gouv.fr; internet www.ambafrance-ci.org.

Gabon: Immeuble Les Heveas, blvd Carde, 01 BP 3765, Abidjan 01; tel. 22-44-51-54; fax 22-44-75-05; Ambassador HENRI BEKALÉ-AKWÉ.

Germany: 39 blvd Hassan II, Cocody, 01 BP 1900, Abidjan 01; tel. and fax 22-44-20-41; e-mail d.bo.abj@africaonline.co.ci; internet www.abidjan.diplo.de; Ambassador ROLF ULRICH.

Ghana: Lot 2393, rue J 95, Cocody-les-Deux-Plateaux, 01 BP 1871, Abidjan 01; tel. 20-33-11-24; fax 20-22-33-57; e-mail ghembci@africaonline.co.ci; Ambassador KABRAL BLAY-AMIHERE.

Guinea: Immeuble Duplessis, 08 BP 2280, Abidjan 08; tel. 20-22-25-20; fax 20-32-82-45; Ambassador (vacant).

Holy See: Apostolic Nunciature, rue Jacques Aka, 08 BP 1347, Abidjan 08; tel. 22-40-17-70; fax 22-40-17-74; e-mail nuntius@aviso.ci; Apostolic Nuncio Mgr MARIO ROBERTO CASSARI.

India: Cocody Danga Nord, 06 BP 318, Abidjan 06; tel. 22-42-37-69; fax 22-42-66-49; e-mail indeamadj@africaonline.co.ci; Ambassador AMARENDRA KHATUA.

Israel: Immeuble Nour Al-Hayat, 01 BP 1877, Abidjan 01; tel. 20-21-49-53; fax 20-21-87-04; e-mail info@abidjan.mfa.gov.il; Ambassador MICHAËL ARBEL.

Italy: 16 rue de la Canebière, Cocody, 01 BP 1905, Abidjan 01; tel. 22-44-61-70; fax 22-44-35-87; e-mail ambitali@aviso.ci; internet www.ambabidjan.esteri.it; Ambassador GIOVANNI POLIZZI.

Japan: Immeuble Alpha 2000, ave Chardy, 01 BP 1329, Abidjan 01; tel. 20-21-28-63; fax 20-21-30-51; Ambassador TETSUO SHIOGUCHI.

Korea, Democratic People's Republic: Abidjan; Ambassador RI JAE RIM.

Korea, Republic: Immeuble le Mans, 8e étage, 01 BP 3950, Abidjan 01; tel. 20-32-22-90; fax 20-22-22-74; e-mail ambcoabj@mofat.go.kr; Ambassador KIM JONG-IL.

Lebanon: Immeuble Trade Center, ave Noguès, 01 BP 2227, Abidjan 01; tel. 20-33-28-24; fax 20-32-11-37; Ambassador ALI AJAMI.

Liberia: Immeuble La Symphonie, ave Général de Gaulle, 01 BP 2514, Abidjan 01; tel. 20-22-23-59; fax 22-44-14-75; Ambassador KRONYANH M. WEEFUR.

Libya: Immeuble Shell, 01 BP 5725, Abidjan 01; tel. 20-22-01-27; fax 20-22-01-30; Ambassador FATHI NASHAD.

Mali: 46 blvd Lagunaire, 01 BP 2746, Abidjan 01; tel. 20-32-31-47; fax 20-21-55-14; Ambassador SADA SAMAKÉ.

Mauritania: rue Pierre et Marie Curie, 01 BP 2275, Abidjan 01; tel. 22-41-16-43; fax 22-41-05-77; Ambassador ABDERRAHIM OULD HADRAMI.

Morocco: 24 rue de la Canebière, 01 BP 146, Cocody, Abidjan 01; tel. 22-44-58-73; fax 22-44-60-58; e-mail sifmaabj@aviso.ci; Ambassador HASSAN BENNANI.

Niger: 23 ave Angoulvant, 01 BP 2743, Abidjan 01; tel. 21-26-28-14; fax 21-26-41-88; Ambassador ADAM ABDOULAYE DAN MARADI.

Nigeria: Immeuble Maison du Nigéria, 35 blvd de la République, 01 BP 1906, Abidjan 01; tel. 20-22-30-82; fax 20-21-30-83; e-mail info@nigeriaembassy-ci.org; internet www.nigeriaembassy-ci.org; Ambassador ALBERT O. SOYOMBO.

Norway: Immeuble N'Zarama, blvd Lagunaire, 01 BP 607, Abidjan 01; tel. 20-22-25-34; fax 20-21-91-99; e-mail emb.abidjan@mfa.no; internet www.norvege.ci; Ambassador ODD-EGIL ANDHØY.

Russia: BP 583, Riviera, Abidjan 01; tel. 22-43-09-59; fax 22-43-11-66; e-mail ambrus@globeaccess.net; Ambassador OLEG V. KOVALCHUK.

Saudi Arabia: Plateau, Abidjan; Ambassador (vacant).

Senegal: Immeuble Nabil Choucair, 6 rue du Commerce, 08 BP 2165, Abidjan 08; tel. 20-33-28-76; fax 20-32-50-39; Ambassador MOUSTAPHA SÈNE.

South Africa: Villa Marc André, rue Mgr René Kouassi, Cocody, 08 BP 1806, Abidjan 08; tel. 22-44-59-63; fax 22-44-74-50; e-mail ambafsudpol@aviso.ci; Ambassador G. DUMISANI GWADISO.

Spain: impasse Abla Pokou, Cocody Danga Nord, 08 BP 876, Abidjan 08; tel. 22-44-48-50; fax 22-44-71-22; e-mail embespci@correo.mae.es; Ambassador FRANCISCO ELIAS DE TEJADA LOZANO.

Switzerland: Immeuble Botreau Roussel, 28 ave Delafosse, Plateau, 01 BP 1914, Abidjan 01; tel. 20-21-17-21; fax 20-21-27-70; e-mail vertretung@abi.rep.admin.ch; Ambassador JOHANNES KUNZ.

Tunisia: Immeuble Shell, ave Lamblin, 01 BP 3906, Abidjan 01; tel. 20-22-61-23; fax 20-22-61-24; Ambassador ZINE EL ABIDINE TERRAS.

USA: Cocody Riviera Golf, 01 BP 1712, Abidjan 01; tel. 22-49-40-00; fax 22-49-43-23; e-mail abjpress@state.gov; internet abidjan.usembassy.gov; Ambassador AUBREY HOOKS.

Judicial System

Since 1964 all civil, criminal, commercial and administrative cases have come under the jurisdiction of the courts of first instance, the assize courts and the Courts of Appeal, with the Supreme Court (referred to in the Constitution of 2000 as the Court of Cassation) as the highest court of appeal.

Supreme Court: rue Gourgas, Cocody, BP V30, Abidjan; tel. 20-22-73-72; fax 20-21-63-04; e-mail consetat@africaonline.co.ci; internet www.gouv.ci/courssupreme.php; comprises three chambers: judicial, administrative and auditing; Pres. TIA KONÉ; Pres. of the Judicial Chamber KAMA YAO; Pres. of the Administrative Chamber GEORGES AMANGOUA.

Courts of Appeal: Abidjan: First Pres. MARIE-FÉLICITÉ ARKHUST HOMA YAO; Bouaké: First Pres. CHRISTIAN ANIBIÉ KAKRÉ ZÉPHIRIN; Daloa: First Pres. GONHI SAHI.

Courts of First Instance: Abidjan: Pres. ANTOINETTE MARSOUIN; Bouaké: Pres. KABLAN AKA EDOUKOU; Daloa: Pres. WOUNE BLEKA; there are a further 25 courts in the principal centres.

High Court of Justice: composed of deputies elected from and by the Assemblée nationale; has jurisdiction to impeach the President or other member of the Government.

Constitutional Council: blvd Carde, BP 4642, Abidjan 01; tel. 20-25-38-50; fax 20-21-21-68; internet www.gouv.ci/conseilconstitutionnel.php; f. 2000 to replace certain functions of the fmr Constitutional Chamber of the Supreme Court; Pres. YANON YAPO GERMAIN; Mems Prof. RENÉ DEGNI SÉGUI, ANDRÉ KOUASSI KOUAKOU, ABRAHAM AKENOU SOUGBRO, MARIE-AGATHE BAROUAN DIOUMINCY LIKAGNÉNÉ, DOMINIQUE RÉGINE SUZANNE THALMAS TAYORO, LOUIS METAN AMANI.

Religion

The Constitution guarantees religious freedom, and this right is generally respected. Religious groups are required to register with the authorities, although no penalties are imposed on a group that fails to register. At the 1998 census it was estimated that about 34% of the population were Christians (mainly Roman Catholics), 27% of the population were Muslims, 15% followed traditional indigenous beliefs, 3% practised other religions, while 21% had no religious affiliation. It is, however, estimated that the proportion of Muslims is in fact significantly higher, as the majority of unregistered foreign workers are Muslims. Muslims are found in greatest numbers in the north of the country, while Christians are found mostly in the southern, central, western and eastern regions. Traditional indigenous beliefs are generally prevalent in rural areas.

ISLAM

Conseil National Islamique (CNI): Mosquée d'Aghien les deux Plateaux, BP 174 Cédex 03, Abidjan 08; tel. and fax 22-42-67-79; e-mail cni@africaonline.co.ci; internet www.cni-cosim.ci; f. 1993; groups more than 5,000 local communities organized in 13 regional and 78 local organizations; Chair. Imam El Hadj IDRISS KOUDOUSS KONÉ.

Conseil Supérieur Islamique (CSI): 11 BP 71, Abidjan 11; tel. 21-25-24-70; fax 21-24-28-04; f. 1978; Chair. El Hadj MOUSTAPHA KOWEÏT DIABY.

CHRISTIANITY

The Roman Catholic Church

Côte d'Ivoire comprises four archdioceses and 10 dioceses. At 31 December 2004 there were approximately 3.2m. Roman Catholics in the country, comprising about 15.8% of the total population.

Bishops' Conference

Conférence Episcopale de la Côte d'Ivoire, BP 713 Cédex 03, Abidjan-Riviera; tel. 22-47-20-00.

f. 1973; Pres. Most Rev. LAURENT AKRAN MANDJO (Bishop of Yopougon).

Archbishop of Abidjan: Most Rev. JEAN-PIERRE KUTWA, Archevêché, ave Jean Paul II, 01 BP 1287, Abidjan 01; tel. 20-21-23-08; fax 20-21-40-22.

Archbishop of Bouaké: Most Rev. VITAL KOMENAN YAO, Archevêché, 01 BP 649, Bouaké 01; tel. and fax 31-63-24-59; e-mail archebke@aviso.ci.

Archbishop of Gagnoa: Most Rev. JEAN-PIERRE KUTWÂ, Archevêché, BP 527, Gagnoa; tel. 32-77-25-68; fax 32-77-20-96; e-mail evechegagnoa@africaonline.co.ci.

Archbishop of Korhogo: Most Rev. MARIE-DANIEL DADIET, Archevêché, BP 12, Korhogo; tel. 36-86-01-18; fax 36-86-05-26.

Protestant Churches

Eglise CMA—Christian and Missionary Alliance: BP 585, Bouaké 01; tel. 31-63-23-12; fax 31-63-54-12; f. 1929; 13 mission stations; Nat. Pres. Rev. CÉLESTIN COFFI.

Eglise du Nazaréen (Church of the Nazarene): 22 BP 623, Abidjan 22; tel. 22-41-07-80; fax 22-41-07-81; e-mail awfcon@compuserve.com; f. 1987; active in evangelism, ministerial training and medical work; Dir JOHN SEAMAN.

Eglise Evangélique des Assemblées de Dieu de Côte d'Ivoire: 04 BP 266, Abidjan 04; tel. 20-37-05-79; fax 20-24-94-65; f. 1960; Pres. JEAN-BAPTISTE NIELBIEN.

Eglise Harriste: Bingerville; f. 1913 by William Wade Harris; affiliated to World Council of Churches 1998; allows polygamous new converts; 100,000 mems, 1,400 preachers, 7,000 apostles; Sec.-Gen. DOGBO JULES.

Eglise Protestante Baptiste Oeuvres et Mission Internationale: 03 BP 1032, Abidjan 03; tel. 23-45-20-18; fax 23-45-56-41; e-mail epbomi@yahoo.com; internet www.epbomi.net; f. 1975; active in evangelism, teaching and social work; medical centre, 6,000 places of worship, 400 missionaries and 193,000 mems; Pres. Rev. Dr YAYE ROBERT DION.

Eglise Méthodiste Unie de Côte d'Ivoire: 41 blvd de la République, 01 BP 1282, Abidjan 01; tel. 20-21-17-97; fax 20-22-52-03; e-mail emuciconf@yahoo.fr; f. 1923; publ. Le Méthodiste (monthly); autonomous since 1985; c. 800,000 mems; Pres. BENJAMIN BONI.

Mission Evangélique de l'Afrique Occidentale (MEAO): BP 822, Bouaflé; tel. and fax 30-68-93-70; e-mail wirci@aviso.ci; f. 1934; 16 missionaries, 5 staff at mission school; Field Dirs HARRY EUVING, PAULINE EUVING; affiliated church: Alliance des Eglises Evangéliques de Côte d'Ivoire (AEECI); 260 churches, 68 full-time pastors; Pres. KOUASSI ALAINGBRÉ PASCAL.

Mission Evangélique Luthérienne en Côte d'Ivoire (MELCI): BP 196, Touba; tel. 33-70-77-11; e-mail melci@aviso.ci; f. 1984; active in evangelism and social work; Dir GJERMUND VISTE.

Union des Eglises Evangéliques du Sud-Ouest de la Côte d'Ivoire and Mission Biblique: 08 BP 20, Abidjan 08; f. 1927; c. 250 places of worship.

WorldVenture: BP 109, Korhogo; tel. 36-86-01-07; fax 36-86-11-50; f. 1947; fmrly Conservative Baptist Foreign Mission Society, subsequently CB International; active in evangelism, medical work, translation, literacy and theological education in the northern area and in Abidjan.

The Press

DAILIES

24 Heures: rue St Jean, duplex 65, Cocody–Val Doyen I, 10 BP 3302, Abidjan 10; tel. 22-41-29-53; fax 22-41-37-82; e-mail infos@24heures.net; internet www.24heuresci.com; f. 2002; Dir-Gen. ABDOULAYE SANGARÉ; Dir of Publication and Editor-in-Chief JOACHIM BEUGRÉ; circ. 21,000 (2005).

Actuel: Cocody-les-Deux-Plateaux, 06 BP 2868, Abidjan 06; tel. 22-42-63-27; fax 22-42-63-32; f. 1996; organ of the FPI; Dir EUGÈNE ALLOU WANYOU; Editor-in-Chief DIABATÉ A. SIDICK.

L'Aurore: 18 BP 418, Abidjan 18; tel. 05-61-65-75; Editor-in-Chief EHOUMAN KASSY.

Le Courrier d'Abidjan: Riviera Bonoumin, 25 BP 1682, Abidjan 25; tel. 22-43-38-22; fax 22-43-30-46; internet www.lecourrierdabidjan.info; f. 2003.

Douze: rue Louis Lumière, Zone 4C, 10 BP 2462, Abidjan 10; tel. 21-25-54-00; fax 21-24-47-27; e-mail douze@afnet.net; publ. by Editions Olympe; f. 1994; sport; Dir MAZÉ SOUMAHORO; Editor-in-Chief FRANÇOIS BINI.

Fraternité Matin: blvd du Général de Gaulle, 01 BP 1807, Abidjan 01; tel. 20-37-06-66; fax 20-37-25-45; e-mail contact@fratmat.net; internet www.fratmat.net; f. 1964; official newspaper; Dir-Gen. HONORAT DÉ YÉDAGNE; Editorial Dir ALFRED DAN MOUSSA; circ. 26,000 (2005).

L'Intelligent d'Abidjan: Villa 12S, Bâtiment Star 4, 19 BP 1534, Abidjan 19; tel. 22-42-55-56; e-mail intelliabidjan@yahoo.fr; internet www.lintelligentdabidjan.org; f. 2003; Dir-Gen. W. ALAFÉ ASSÉ.

L'Inter: 10 BP 2462, Abidjan 10; tel. 21-21-28-00; fax 21-21-28-05; e-mail inter@linter-ci.com; internet www.linter-ci.com; f. 1998; publ. by Editions Olympe; national and international politics and economics; Dir RAYMOND N'CHO NIMBA; Editor-in-Chief CHARLES A. D'ALMÉIDA; circ. 18,000 (2002).

Le JD (Jeune Démocrate): 23 BP 3842, Abidjan 23; tel. 23-51-62-45; fax 23-51-63-75; e-mail lejd@africaonline.co.ci; f. 1999; Dir IGNACE DASSOHIRI; Editor-in-Chief OCTAVE BOYOU.

Le Jour: 26 Cocody-les-Deux-Plateau, 25 BP 1082, Abidjan 25; tel. 20-21-95-78; fax 20-21-95-80; internet www.lejourplus.com; f. 1994; publ. by Editions Le Nere; independent; Dir of Publication KOUAMÉ KOUAKOU; Editor-in-Chief VICKY DELORE; circ. 15,000 (2002).

Le Journal: Abidjan; internet www.lejournalci.com; f. 2003; supports PDCI—RDA; Dir of Publication NAZAIRE BREKA.

Le Libéral: 01 BP 6938, Abidjan 01; tel. and fax 22-52-21-41; e-mail leliberal@aviso.ci; f. 1997; Dir YORO KONÉ; Editor-in-Chief BAKARY NIMAGA; circ. 15,000.

Le National: Angré, Cocody, 16 BP 165, Abidjan 16; tel. 22-52-27-43; fax 22-52-27-42; f. 1999; nationalist; Publr LAURENT TAPÉ KOULOU; Editor-in-Chief (vacant); circ. 20,000 (2002).

Nord-Sud: Abidjan; f. 2005; Dir MEÏTÉ SINDOU; circ. 18,000 (2005).

Notr'Aurore: Immeuble SICOGI, Bâtiment K, Appartement 124, Deux-Plateaux Aghien, blvd Latrille, Abidjan; tel. 22-42-08-21; fax 22-42-08-24; f. 2002; nationalist; Editor-in-Chief EMMANUEL GRIÉ.

Notre Voie: Cocody-les-Deux-Plateaux, 06 BP 2868, Abidjan 06; tel. 22-42-63-31; fax 22-42-63-32; e-mail gnh@africaonline.co.ci; internet www.notrevoie.com; f. 1978; organ of the FPI; Dir WANYOU EUGÈNE ALLOU; Editor-in-Chief CÉSAR ETOU; circ. 20,000 (2002).

Le Nouveau Réveil: Adjamé Sud 80 Logements, Tours SICOGI, face Frat-Mat, Bâtiment A, 2e étage, porte 6, 01 BP 10684, Abidjan 01; tel. 20-38-42-00; fax 20-38-67-91; e-mail lenouveaureveil@yahoo.fr; internet www.lenouveaureveil.com; f. 2001 to replace weekly *Le Réveil-Hebdo*; supports PDCI—RDA; Dir of Publication DENIS KAH ZION; Editor-in-Chief EDDY PEHE; circ. 18,000 (2005).

Le Patriote: 23 rue Paul Langevin, Zone 4C, 22 BP 509, Abidjan 22; tel. 21-21-19-45; fax 21-35-11-83; e-mail info@lepatriote.net; internet www.lepatriote.net; organ of the RDR; Editor-in-Chief MOUSSA TOURÉ; circ. 40,000 (2002).

Le Populaire: 19 blvd Angoulvant, résidence Neuilly, Plateau, 01 BP 5496, Abidjan 01; tel. 21-36-34-15; fax 21-36-43-28; Dir RAPHAËL ORE LAKPÉ.

Soir Info: 10 BP 2462, Abidjan 10; tel. 21-21-28-00; fax 21-21-28-06; e-mail soirinfo@soirinfo.com; internet www.soirinfo.com; f. 1994; publ. by Editions Olympe; independent; Dir MAURICE FERRO BI BALI; Editor-in-Chief ZOROMÉ LOSS; circ. 22,000 (2002).

La Voie: face Institut Marie-Thérèse Houphouët-Boigny, 17 BP 656, Abidjan 17; tel. 20-37-68-23; fax 20-37-74-76; organ of the FPI; Dir ABOU DRAHAMANE SANGARÉ; Man. MAURICE LURIGNAN.

SELECTED BI-WEEKLIES AND WEEKLIES

L'Agora: Immeuble Nana Yamoussou, ave 13, rue 38, Treichville, 01 BP 5326, Abidjan 01; tel. 21-34-11-72; f. 1997; weekly; Dir FERNAND DÉDÉ; Editor-in-Chief BAMBA ALEX SOULEYMANE.

Argument: 09 BP 3328, Abidjan 09; tel. 20-37-63-96; f. 1998; weekly; Dir GUY BADIETO LIALY; Editor-in-Chief JEAN-LOUIS PÉHÉ.

Le Démocrate: Maison du Congrès, ave 2, Treichville, 01 BP 1212, Abidjan 01; tel. 21-24-45-88; fax 21-24-25-61; f. 1991; weekly; organ of the PDCI—RDA; Dir NOËL YAO.

Le Front: Immeuble Mistral, 3e étage, 220 Logements, 11 BP 11 2678, Abidjan 11; tel. 20-38-13-24; fax 20-38-70-83; e-mail quotidienlefront@yahoo.fr; internet www.lefront.com; two a week; Editorial Dir FATOUMATA COULIBALY; Editor KPOKPA BLÉ.

Gbich!: 10 BP 399, Abidjan 10; tel. and fax 21-26-31-94; e-mail gbich@assistweb.net; internet www.gbichonline.com; weekly; satirical; Editor-in-Chief MATHIEU BLEDOU.

Le Nouvel Horizon: 220 Logements, blvd du Général de Gaulle, Adjamé, 17 BP 656, Abidjan 17; tel. 20-37-68-23; f. 1990; weekly; organ of the FPI; Dir ABOU DRAHAMANE SANGARÉ; circ. 15,000.

La Nouvelle Presse: rue des Jardins, Cocody-les-Deux-Plateaux, 01 BP 8534, Abidjan 01; tel. 22-41-04-76; fax 22-41-04-15; e-mail jvieyra@africaonline.co.ci; f. 1992; weekly; publ. by Centre Africain de Presse et d'Edition; current affairs; Editors JUSTIN VIEYRA, JÉRÔME CARLOS; circ. 10,000.

Le Repère: 220 Logements, Adjamé Sud-Tours SICOGI, face Frat-Mat, Bâtiment A, 2e étage P6, 04 BP 1947, Abidjan 04; tel. and fax 20-38-67-91; supports PDCI—RDA; two a week; Dir of Publication DENIS KAH ZION; circ. 10,000 (2004).

Sports Magazine: Yopougon-SOGEFIHA, 01 BP 4030, Abidjan 01; tel. 23-45-14-02; f. 1997; weekly; Dir JOSEPH ABLE.

Téré: 220 Logements, blvd du Général de Gaulle, Adjamé-Liberté, 20 BP 43, Abidjan 20; tel. and fax 20-37-79-42; weekly; organ of the PIT; Dir ANGÈLE GNONSOA.

Top-Visages: rue du Commerce, 23 BP 892, Abidjan 23; tel. 20-33-72-10; fax 20-32-81-05; e-mail contact@topvisages.net; internet www.topvisages.net; weekly; Editor-in-Chief E. TONGA BÉHI; circ. 40,000 (2004).

La Voie du Compatriote: Adjamé St-Michel, 09 BP 2008, Abidjan 09; tel. 20-37-50-13; f. 1998; weekly; Dir SINARI KAL.

SELECTED PERIODICALS

Côte d'Ivoire Magazine: Présidence de la République, 01 BP 1354, Abidjan 01; tel. 20-22-02-22; f. 1998; quarterly; Dir JEAN-NOËL LOUKO.

Juris-Social: Centre National de Documentation Juridique (CNDJ), Villa 381 ilôt 43, face Polyclinique Saint Jacques, blvd Latrille, Cocody-les-Deux-Plateaux, 01 BP 2757, Abidjan 01; tel. 20-22-74-85; fax 20-22-74-86; e-mail cndj@aviso-ci; internet www.cndj.ci; monthly; jurisprudence; CNDJ also publishes quarterly periodical *Juris OHADA*.

La Lettre de l'Afrique de l'Ouest: rue des Jardins, Cocody-les-Deux-Plateaux, 01 BP 8534, Abidjan 01; tel. 22-41-04-76; fax 22-41-04-15; e-mail jvieyra@africaonline.co.ci; f. 1995; publ. by Centre Africain de Presse et d'Edition; six a year; politics, economics, regional integration; Editors JUSTIN VIEYRA, JÉRÔME CARLOS.

Maisons et Matériaux: 08 BP 2150, Abidjan 08; tel. 22-42-92-17; monthly; Dir THIAM T. DJENEBOU.

Roots-Rock Magazine: Abidjan; tel. 22-42-84-74; f. 1998; monthly; music; Dir DIOMANDÉ DAVID.

RTI-Mag: 08 BP 663, Abidjan 08; tel. 20-33-14-46; fax 20-32-12-06; publ. by Radiodiffusion-Télévision Ivoirienne; listings magazine.

Sentiers: 26 ave Chardy, 01 BP 2432, Abidjan 01; tel. 20-21-95-68; fax 20-21-95-80; e-mail redaction@aviso.ci; Editor-in-Chief DIÉGOU BAILLY.

Stades d'Afrique: blvd du Général de Gaulle, 01 BP 1807, Abidjan 01; tel. 20-37-06-66; fax 20-37-25-45; e-mail fratmat@africaonline.co.ci; f. 2000; sports; monthly; Dir-Gen. EMMANUEL KOUASSI KOKORÉ; Editor-in-Chief HÉGAUD OUATTARA.

Le Succès: 21 BP 3748, Abidjan 21; tel. 20-37-71-64; monthly; Dir AKPLA PLAKATOU.

Univers jeunes: 01 BP 3713, Abidjan 01; tel. 20-21-20-00; fax 21-35-35-45; e-mail univers@africaonline.co.ci; monthly; Editor-in-Chief MOUSSA SY SAVANÉ.

La Voix d'Afrique: rue des Jardins, Cocody-les-Deux-Plateaux, 01 BP 8534, Abidjan 01; tel. 22-41-04-76; fax 22-41-04-15; e-mail jvieyra@africaonline.co.ci; publ. by Centre Africain de Presse et d'Edition; monthly; Editor-in-Chief GAOUSSOU KAMISSOKO.

NEWS AGENCIES

Agence Ivoirienne de Presse (AIP): ave Chardy, 04 BP 312, Abidjan 04; tel. 20-22-64-13; fax 20-21-35-39; e-mail aip@ci.refer.org; f. 1961; Dir DALLI DEBY.

Foreign Bureaux

Agence France-Presse (AFP): 18 ave du Docteur Crozet, 01 BP 726, Abidjan 01; tel. 20-21-90-17; fax 20-21-10-36; e-mail afp@aviso.ci; internet www.afp.com; Dir SERGE ARNOLD.

Associated Press (AP) (USA): 01 BP 5843, Abidjan 01; tel. 22-41-38-95; fax 22-41-28-94; e-mail iromauld@yahoo.fr; Bureau Chief ELLEN KNICKMAYER.

PANA-Presse (Senegal): 09 BP 2744, Abidjan 09; tel. and fax 20-33-40-79; e-mail odji@bobley.africaonline.co.ci.

Reuters West Africa (United Kingdom): Résidence Les Acacias, 2e étage, appt 203–205, 20 blvd Clozel, 01 BP 2338, Abidjan 01; tel. 20-21-12-22; fax 20-21-30-77; e-mail abidjan.newsroom@reuters.com; West Africa Man. MICHEL CLÉMENT; Bureau Chief NICHOLAS PHYTHIAN.

Xinhua (New China) News Agency (People's Republic of China): Immeuble SGBCI, 4e étage, ave Lamblin, Plateau, 01 BP V321, Abidjan 01; tel. 20-32-52-20; fax 20-32-22-49; internet www.xinhua.org; Chief Correspondent LINGHU DAOCHENG.

PRESS ASSOCIATIONS

Association de la Presse Démocratique Ivoirienne (APDI): Abidjan; tel. 20-37-06-66; f. 1994; Chair. JEAN-BAPTISTE AKROU.

Union nationale des journalistes de Côte d'Ivoire (UNJCI): 06 BP 1675, Plateau, Abidjan 06; tel. 20-21-61-07; e-mail prunjci@unjci.org; internet unjci.org; f. 1991; Pres. HONORAT NDJOMOU DE YÉDAGNE.

Publishers

Centre Africain de Presse et d'Edition (CAPE): rue des Jardins, Cocody-les-Deux-Plateaux, 01 BP 8534, Abidjan 01; tel. 22-41-04-76; fax 22-41-04-15; e-mail jvieyra@africaonline.co.ci; Man. JUSTIN VIEYRA.

Centre d'Edition et de Diffusion Africaines (CEDA): 17 rue des Carrossiers, 04 BP 541, Abidjan 04; tel. 20-24-65-10; fax 21-25-05-67; e-mail infos@ceda-ci.com; internet www.ceda-ci.com; f. 1961; 20% state-owned; general non-fiction, school and children's books, literary fiction; Pres. and Dir-Gen. VENANCE KACOU.

Centre de Publications Evangéliques: 08 BP 900, Abidjan 08; tel. 22-44-48-05; fax 22-44-58-17; e-mail cpe@aviso.ci; internet www.editionscpe.com; f. 1967; evangelical Christian; Dir JULES OUOBA.

Editions Bognini: 06 BP 1254, Abidjan 06; tel. 20-41-16-86; social sciences, literary fiction.

Editions Eburnie: 01 BP 1984, 01 Abidjan; tel. 20-21-64-65; fax 20-21-45-46; e-mail eburnie@aviso.ci; f. 2001; illustrated books for children, social sciences, poetry.

Editions Neter: 01 BP 7370, Abidjan 01; tel. 22-52-52-68; f. 1992; politics, culture, history, literary fiction; Dir RICHARD TA BI SENIN.

Nouvelles Editions Ivoiriennes: 1 blvd de Marseille, 01 BP 1818, Abidjan 01; tel. 21-24-07-66; fax 21-24-24-56; e-mail edition@nei-ci.com; internet www.nei-ci.com; f. 1972; literature, criticism, essays, drama, social sciences, history, in French and English; Dir GUY LAMBIN.

Presses Universitaires et Scolaires d'Afrique (PUSAF—Editions Cissé): 08 BP 177, Abidjan 08; tel. 22-41-12-71; mathematics, economics, medicine.

Université Nationale de Côte d'Ivoire: 01 BP V34, Abidjan 01; tel. 22-44-08-59; f. 1964; academic and general non-fiction and periodicals; Publications Dir GILLES VILASCO.

GOVERNMENT PUBLISHING HOUSE

Imprimerie Nationale: BP V87, Abidjan; tel. 20-21-76-11; fax 20-21-68-68.

Broadcasting and Communications

TELECOMMUNICATIONS

Regulatory Authorities

Agence des Télécommunications de Côte d'Ivoire (ATCI): Immeuble Postel 2001, 4e étage, rue Lecoeur, 18 BP 2203, Abidjan 18; tel. 20-34-43-74; fax 20-34-43-75; e-mail courrier@atci.ci; internet www.atci.ci; f. 1995; Dir-Gen. SYLVANUS KLA.

Conseil des Télécommunications de Côte d'Ivoire: 17 BP 110, Abidjan 17; tel. 20-34-43-04; f. 1995; deals with issues of arbitration.

Service Providers

Atlantique Telecom—Moov (Moov): Immeuble N'Zarama, blvd Lagunaire, 01 BP 10204, Abidjan 01; tel. 20-30-21-19; fax 20-30-21-10; e-mail hfo@atlantiquetelecom.net; internet www.moov.com; f. 2005 as jt venture by Atlantique Télécoms (Côte d'Ivoire) and Elisalat (United Arab Emirates); owned by Etisalat (United Arab Emirates); mobile cellular telecommunications; Dir ABOUBACAR TOURÉ.

Côte d'Ivoire-Télécom (CI-Télécom): Immeuble Postel 2001, rue Lecoeur, 17 BP 275, Abidjan 17; tel. 20-34-40-00; fax 20-21-28-28; e-mail info@citelecom.ci; internet www.citelecom.ci; f. 1991; 51% owned by France Télécom, 49% state-owned; Pres. YAYA OUATTARA; Man. Dir ALAIN PETIT; 327,000 subscribers (June 2002).

MTN Côte d'Ivoire: Immeuble Loteny, 12 rue Crossons Duplessis, 01 BP 3685, Abidjan 01; tel. 20-31-63-16; fax 20-31-84-50; internet www.mtn.ci; f. 1996 as Loteny Télécom-Télécel; present name adopted 2005; mobile cellular telephone operator in more than 110 urban centres and on principal highway routes; 51% owned by Mobile Telephone Network International (South Africa); Chief Exec. RON ALLARD; 965,524 subscribers (Aug. 2005).

Orange Côte d'Ivoire: Immeuble Saha, blvd Valéry Giscard d'Estaing, Zone 4C, 11 BP 202, Abidjan 11; tel. 21-23-90-07; fax 21-23-90-11; internet www.orange.ci; f. 1996 as Ivoiris, present name adopted 2002; mobile cellular telephone operator in more than 60 urban centres; 85% owned by France Télécom; Man. Dir BERNARD CLIVET; 1.1m. subscribers (Oct. 2005).

BROADCASTING

Radio

In 1993 the Government permitted the first commercial radio stations to broadcast in Côte d'Ivoire; of the five licences initially granted, four were to foreign stations. Between 1998 and early 2001, a further 52 licences were granted.

Radiodiffusion-Télévision Ivoirienne (RTI): blvd des Martyrs, Cocody, 08 BP883, Abidjan 08; tel. 22-48-61-62; fax 22-44-78-23; e-mail info.rti@rti.ci; internet www.rti.ci; f. 1962; state-owned; two national TV channels, La Première and TV2, and two national radio channels, La Nationale and Fréquence II; Pres. MAURICE BANDAMA; Dir-Gen. AMESSAN BROU; Dir, La Première VICTOR DEBASS KPAN; Dir, TV2 ADÈLE DJEDJE; Dir, Radiodiffusion ELOI OULAÏ.

City FM: Immeuble Alpha Cissé, avant la piscine d'Etat, Treichville, 01 BP 7207, Abidjan 01; tel. 21-25-10-28; f. 1999; Pres. and Man. Dir Me ALIOU SIBI.

Radio Espoir: 12 BP 27, Abidjan 12; tel. 21-75-68-02; fax 21-75-68-04; e-mail respoir@aviso.ci; internet www.radioespoir.ci; f. 1990; Roman Catholic; broadcasts in French, local and sub-regional languages; Dir Fr BASILE DIANÉ KOGNAN.

Radio Nostalgie: 01 BP 157, Abidjan 01; tel. 20-21-10-52; fax 20-21-85-53; internet www.nostalgie.ci; f. 1993; Dir-Gen. HERVÉ CORNUEL.

Radio Peleforo Gbon: Route Ferké km 2, BP 841, Korhogo; tel. 21-86-22-62; fax 21-86-20-33.

Radio Soleil: 16 BP 1179, Abidjan 16; tel. 21-99-17-64; fax 21-79-12-48; e-mail ebadouel@irisa.fr.

Côte d'Ivoire also receives broadcasts from the Gabon-based Africa No 1 radio station, from the French-language Africa service of the BBC (United Kingdom), and from Radio France Internationale.

Television

Radiodiffusion-Télévision Ivoirienne (RTI): see Radio section.

Canal Plus Horizons: Abidjan; tel. 20-31-67-67; fax 20-22-72-22; e-mail abonne@canalhorizons.ci; internet www.canalhorizons.com; broadcasts commenced 1994; subsidiary of Canal Plus (France).

Finance

(cap. = capital; res = reserves; dep. = deposits; m. = million; br(s). = branch(es); amounts in francs CFA)

BANKING

Central Bank

Banque Centrale des Etats de l'Afrique de l'Ouest (BCEAO): 01 BP 1769, Abidjan 01; tel. 20-20-84-00; fax 20-22-28-52; internet www.bceao.int; f. 1962; HQ in Dakar, Senegal; bank of issue for the mem. states of the Union économique et monétaire ouest-africaine (UEMOA, comprising Benin, Burkina Faso, Côte d'Ivoire, Guinea-Bissau, Mali, Niger, Senegal and Togo); cap. and res 859,313m., total assets 5,671,675m. (Dec. 2002); Gov. DAMO JUSTIN BARO (acting); Dir in Côte d'Ivoire LANSINA BAKARY; 5 brs in Côte d'Ivoire.

Commercial Banks

Bank of Africa—Côte d'Ivoire (BOA—CI): ave Terrasson de Fougères, angle Rue Gourgas, 01 BP 4132, Abidjan 01; tel. 20-30-34-00; fax 20-30-34-01; e-mail boaci@bkofafrica.com; internet www.bkofafrica.net/cote_d_ivoire.htm; f. 1980; 66.7% owned by Groupe African Financial Holding; cap. and res 4,135m., total assets 81,072m. (Dec. 2003); Dir-Gen. RENÉ FORMEY DE SAINT LOUVENT; 1 br.

Banque Atlantique de Côte d'Ivoire: Immeuble Atlantique, ave Nogues, Plateau, 04 BP 1036, Abidjan 04; tel. 20-31-59-50; fax 20-21-68-52; e-mail baci1@baci.ci; f. 1979; cap. 7,000.0m., total assets 58,830m. (Dec. 2003); Pres. KONE DOSSONGUI; Dir-Gen. JEAN-PIERRE COTI; 3 brs.

Banque de l'Habitat de Côte d'Ivoire (BHCI): 22 ave Joseph Anoma, 01 BP 2325, Abidjan 01; tel. 20-25-39-39; fax 20-22-58-18; e-mail info@bhci.ci; internet www.bhci.ci; f. 1993; cap. and res 1,755m., total assets 16,834m. (Dec. 1999); Chair. DAVID AMUAH; Man. Dir LANCINA COULIBALY; 3 brs.

Banque Internationale pour le Commerce et l'Industrie de la Côte d'Ivoire SA (BICI-CI): ave Franchet d'Espérey, 01 BP 1298, Abidjan 01; tel. 20-20-16-00; fax 20-20-17-00; e-mail michel.lafont@africa.bnpparibas.com; internet www.bicici.org; f. 1962; 67.5% owned by BNP Paribas (France); absorbed BICI Bail de Côte d'Ivoire in 2003 and Compagnie Financière de la Côte d'Ivoire in 2004; cap. and res 38,436.7m., total assets 276,432.1m. (Dec. 2004); Chair. ANGE KOFFY; 35 brs.

Banque Nationale d'Investissement: Immeuble SCIAM, ave Marchand, Plateau, 01 BP 670, Abidjan 01; tel. 20-20-98-00; fax 20-21-35-78; e-mail info@caa.ci.com; cap. and res 28,408m., total assets 253,668m. (Dec. 2003); Pres. and Dir-Gen. VICTOR JÉRÔME NEMBELESSINI-SILUÉ.

Banque Paribas Côte d'Ivoire (Paribas—CI): 17 ave Terrasson de Fougères, 17 BP 09, Abidjan 17; tel. 20-21-86-86; fax 20-21-88-23; f. 1984; 85% owned by BNP Paribas (France); cap. and res 2,938m., total assets 30,697m. (Dec. 1999); Pres. and Dir-Gen. FRANÇOIS DAUGE.

BIAO—Côte d'Ivoire (BIAO—CI): 8–10 ave Joseph Anoma, 01 BP 1274, Abidjan 01; tel. 20-20-07-20; fax 20-20-07-00; e-mail info@biao.co.ci; internet www.biao.co.ci; f. 1980; fmrly Banque Internationale pour l'Afrique de l'Ouest—Côte d'Ivoire; 80% owned by Banque Belgolaise (Belgium), 20% state-owned; cap. 10,000.0m., res 169.9m., dep. 162,074.7m. (Dec. 2003); Pres. SEYDOU ELIMANE DIARRA; 31 brs.

Citibank Côte d'Ivoire: Immeuble Botreau-Roussel, 28 ave Delafosse, 01 BP 3698, Abidjan 01; tel. 20-20-90-00; fax 20-21-76-85; e-mail citibank@odaci.net; total assets US $198.7m. (2003); Dir-Gen. CHARLES KIE.

COFIPA Investment Bank CI: Immeuble Botreau Roussel, ave Delafosse, 04 BP 411, Abidjan 04; tel. 20-30-23-02; fax 20-30-23-01; e-mail dg@cofipa.ci; cap. and res 2,382.5m., total assets 19,171.2m. (Dec. 2002); Pres. BABER TOUNKARA; Dir-Gen. JACKIE VASSEUR.

Compagnie Bancaire de l'Atlantique Côte d'Ivoire (COBACI): Immeuble Atlantique, ave Noguès, 01 BP 522, Abidjan 01; tel. 20-21-28-04; fax 20-21-07-98; e-mail cobaci@africaonline.co.ci; 65% owned by Banque Atlantique–Côte d'Ivoire; cap. 3,002m., res 710m., total assets 38,502m. (Dec. 2003); Pres. DOSSONGUI KONÉ; Dir-Gen. RENÉ MAX DELAFOSSE.

Ecobank Côte d'Ivoire: Immeuble Alliance, 1 ave Terrasson de Fougères, 01 BP 4107, Abidjan 01; tel. 20-21-10-41; fax 20-21-88-16; e-mail ecobankci@ecobank.com; internet www.ecobank.com; f. 1989; 94% owned by Ecobank Transnational Inc (Togo); cap. and res 6,199m., dep. 118,761m. (Dec. 2003); Chair. AKA AOUÉLÉ; 1 br.

Omnifinance: 6e étage, Immeuble Alliance, 17 ave Terrasson de Fougères, 01 BP 6028, Abidjan 01; tel. 20-21-42-08; fax 20-21-42-58; 30% owned by Afriland First Bank (Cameroon); cap. and res 2,400m., total assets 38,322m. (Dec. 2003); Pres. and Dir-Gen. JACOB AMEMATEKPO.

Société Générale de Banques en Côte d'Ivoire (SGBCI): 5–7 ave Joseph Anoma, 01 BP 1355, Abidjan 01; tel. 20-20-12-34; fax 20-20-14-92; e-mail ddl.dir@sgbci.net; internet sgbci.groupe.socgen.com; f. 1962; 56.8% owned by Société Générale (France); cap. 15,333m., res 31,822m., total assets 417,424.5m. (Dec. 2003); Pres. TIÉMOKO YADÉ COULIBALY; Dir-Gen. BERNARD LABADENS; 55 brs.

Société Générale de Financement et de Participations en Côte d'Ivoire (SOGEFINANCE): 5–7 ave Joseph Anoma, 01 BP 3904, Abidjan 01; tel. 20-22-55-30; fax 20-32-67-60; f. 1978; 58% owned by SGBCI; cap. and res 2,409m., total assets 5,215m. (Dec. 2003); Pres. JEAN-LOUIS MATTEI; Dir-Gen. MICHEL MIAILLE.

Société Ivoirienne de Banque (SIB): Immeuble Alpha 2000, 34 blvd de la République, 01 BP 1300, Abidjan 01; tel. 20-20-00-00; fax 221-97-41; e-mail info@sib.ci; internet www.sib.ci; f. 1962; 51% owned by Calyon Corporate & Investment Bank (France), 49% state-owned; reduction of state holding to 19% proposed; cap. and res 15,733m., total assets 173,809m. (Dec. 2002); Administrator and Dir-Gen. PASCAL FALL; 14 brs.

Standard Chartered Bank Côte d'Ivoire (SCBCI): 23 blvd de la République, face Commissariat du 1er arrondissement, 17 BP 1141, Abidjan 17; tel. 20-30-32-00; fax 20-30-32-01; e-mail mylene.oule@standardchartered.com; internet www.standardchartered.com/ci/index.html; f. 2001; subsidiary of Standard Chartered Bank (United Kingdom); cap. and res 9,218m., total assets 76,289m. (Dec. 2003); Pres. EBENEZER ESSOKA; Dir-Gen. SERGE PHILIPPE BAILLY; 4 brs.

Versus Bank: Immeuble CRAAE-UMOA, blvd Botreau Roussel, angle ave Joseph Anoma, 01 BP 1874, Abidjan 01; tel. 20-25-60-60; fax 20-25-60-99; e-mail infos@versusbank.com; internet www.versusbank.com; f. 2004; Pres. ANDRÉ SIMONE TCHINAH.

Credit Institutions

Afribail—Côte d'Ivoire (Afribail—CI): 8–10 ave Joseph Anoma, 01 BP 1274, Abidjan 01; tel. 20-20-07-20; fax 20-20-07-00; 95% owned by BIAO—CI; cap. and res 334m., total assets 2,651m. (Dec. 2002); Chair. RENÉ AMANY; Pres. and Dir-Gen. ERNEST ALLOU TOGNAN.

Coopérative Ivoirienne d'Epargne et de Crédit Automobile (CIECA): 04 BP 2084, Abidjan 04; tel. 20-22-77-13; fax 20-22-77-35; cap. and res 805m. (Dec. 1998), total assets 1,169m. (Dec. 1999); Dir-Gen. DALLY ZABO.

Société Africaine de Crédit Automobilier (SAFCA): 1 rue des Carrossiers, Zone 3, 04 BP 27, Abidjan 04; tel. 21-21-07-07; fax 21-21-07-00; e-mail safca@aviso.ci; f. 1956; cap. and res 5,681.8m., total assets 22,511.1m. (Dec. 2001); Pres. and Dir-Gen. DIACK DIAWAR.

Société Africaine de Crédit-Bail (SAFBAIL): Immeuble SAFCA, 1 rue des Carrossiers, Zone 3, 04 BP 27, Abidjan 04; tel. 21-24-91-77; fax 21-35-77-90; e-mail safca@aviso.ci; f. 1971; cap. and res 2,922m., total assets 13,414m. (Dec. 1999); Chair. and Man. Dir DIACK DIAWAR.

SOGEFIBAIL—CI: 26 ave Delafosse, 01 BP 1355, Abidjan 01; tel. 20-32-85-15; fax 20-33-14-93; 35% owned by GENEFITEC, 35% by SOGEFINANCE, 25% by SGBCI; cap. and res 2,560.2m., total assets 4,452.3m. (Dec. 2003); Pres. JEAN-LOUIS MATTEI.

Bankers' Association

Association Professionnelle des Banques et Etablissements Financiers de Côte d'Ivoire (APBEFCI): 01 BP 3810, Abidjan 01; tel. 20-21-20-08; affiliated to Conseil National du Patronat Ivoirien (q.v.); Pres. JEAN-PIERRE MEYER.

Financial Institution

Caisse Autonome d'Amortissement de Côte d'Ivoire (CAA): Immeuble SCIAM, ave Marchand, 01 BP 670, Abidjan 01; tel. 20-20-98-00; fax 20-21-35-78; e-mail pdgbni@aviso.ci; f. 1959; management of state funds; cap. 10,000m., total assets 308,080m. (Dec. 2000); Chair. ABDOULAYE KONÉ; Man. Dir SÉKOU BAMBA.

STOCK EXCHANGE

Bourse Régionale des Valeurs Mobilières (BRVM): 18 ave Joseph Anoma, 01 BP 3802, Abidjan 01; tel. 20-32-66-85; fax 20-32-66-84; e-mail brvm@brvm.org; internet www.brvm.org; f. 1998 to succeed Bourse des Valeurs d'Abidjan; regional stock exchange serving mem. states of UEMOA; Dir-Gen. JEAN-PAUL GILLET.

BRVM (Antenne Nationale de Côte d'Ivoire): 18 ave Joseph Anoma, 01 BP 1541, Abidjan 01; tel. 20-31-55-50; fax 20-32-47-77; e-mail tbah@brvm.org; internet www.brvm.org; f. 1996; Pres. TIÉMOKO YADE COULIBALY; Man. AMADOU TIDIANE BAH.

INSURANCE

Abidjanaise d'Assurances: Immeuble Woodin Center, ave Noguès, 01 BP 2909, Abidjan 01; tel. 20-22-46-96; fax 20-22-64-81; e-mail abjassur@africaonline.co.ci; Dir-Gen. MARC RICHMOND.

African American Insurance Co (AFRAM): Immeuble ex-Monopris, 2 ave Noguès, 01 BP 7124, Abidjan 01; tel. 20-31-30-44; fax 20-32-69-72; Dir-Gen. CHRISTIAN CASEL.

Alliance Africaine d'Assurances (3A): 17 BP 477, Abidjan 17; tel. 20-32-42-52; fax 20-32-54-90; Pres. DAM SARR; Dir-Gen. CORINNE SARR.

AXA Assurances Côte d'Ivoire: ave Delafosse Prolongée, 01 BP 378, Abidjan 01; tel. 20-31-58-98; fax 20-31-88-00; e-mail johnson.boa@AXA-Assurances.ci; f. 1981; fmrly l'Union Africaine—IARD; insurance and reinsurance; Dir-Gen. JACQUES BOUDOU.

AXA Vie Côte d'Ivoire: 9 ave Houdaille, 01 BP 2016, Abidjan 01; tel. 20-22-25-15; fax 20-22-37-60; f. 1985; fmrly Union Africaine Vie; life assurance and capitalization; Chair. JOACHIM RICHMOND; Dir PATRICE DESGRANGES.

Colina: Immeuble Colina, blvd Roume, 01 BP 3832, Abidjan 01; tel. 20-21-65-05; fax 20-22-59-05; e-mail c-dg@colina-sa.com; internet www.colina-sa.com; f. 1980; Chair. MICHEL PHARAON; Dir-Gen. RAYMOND FARHAT.

Compagnie Nationale d'Assurances (CNA): Immeuble Symphonie, 30 ave du Général de Gaulle, 01 BP 1333, Abidjan 01; tel. 20-21-49-19; fax 20-22-49-06; f. 1972; cap. 400m.; insurance and reinsurance; transfer to private ownership pending; Chair. SOUNKALO DJIBO; Man. Dir RICHARD COULIBALY.

Gras Savoye Côte d'Ivoire: Immeuble Trade Center, ave Noguès, 01 BP 5675, Abidjan 01; tel. 20-25-25-00; fax 20-25-25-25; e-mail olivier.dubois@grassavoye.ci; affiliated to Gras Savoye (France); Man. OLIVIER DUBOIS.

Mutuelle Centrale d'Assurances: 15 Immeuble Ebrien, 01 BP 1217, Abidjan 01; tel. 20-21-11-24; fax 20-33-18-37.

Nouvelle Société Africaine d'Assurances (NSIA AGCI): Immeuble Manci, rue A43, 01 BP 1571 Abidjan 01; tel. 20-31-75-00; fax 20-31-98-00; e-mail nsia@africaonline.co.ci; f. 1995; Pres. and Dir-Gen. JEAN KACOU DIAGOU.

NSIA-Vie: Immeuble Zandaman, ave Noguès, 01 BP 4092, Abidjan 01; tel. 20-31-98-00; fax 20-33-25-79; e-mail agci@africaonline.co.ci; f. 1988; fmrly Assurances Générales de Côte d'Ivoire—Vie (AGCI-Vie); life; Pres. and Dir-Gen. JEAN KACOU DIAGOU.

Société Africaine d'Assurances et de Réassurances en République de Côte d'Ivoire (SAFARRIV): 01 BP 1741, Abidjan 01; tel. 20-21-91-57; fax 20-21-82-72; e-mail groupe-safarriv@safarriv.ci; f. 1975; affilated to AGF Afrique; Pres. TIÉMOKO YADÉ COULIBALY; Man. Dir CHRISTIAN ARRAULT.

Trade and Industry

GOVERNMENT AGENCIES

Autorité pour la Régulation du Café et du Cacao (ARCC): blvd Botreau Roussel, Immeuble CAISTAB, Plateau, 25 BP 1501, Abidjan 25; tel. 22-44-46-15; fax 20-21-29-03; e-mail p.zoungrana@arcc-ci.org; f. 2000; implements regulatory framework for coffee and cocoa trade; Pres. PLACIDE ZOUNGRANA.

Bureau National d'Etudes Techniques et de Développement (BNETD): ancien hôtel 'Le Relais', blvd Hassan II, Cocody, 04 BP 945, Abidjan 04; tel. 22-48-34-00; fax 22-44-56-66; e-mail info@bnetd.ci; f. 1978; as Direction et Contrôle des Grands Travaux; management and supervision of major public works projects; Dir-Gen. AHOUA DON-MELLO.

Comité de Privatisation: 6 blvd de l'Indénié, 01 BP 1141, Abidjan 01; tel. 20-22-22-31; fax 20-22-22-35; e-mail cpct@africaonline.co.ci; state privatization authority; Pres. PAUL AGODIO; Dir-Gen. AHOUA DON MELLO.

Compagnie Ivoirienne pour le Développement des Cultures Vivrières (CIDV): Abidjan; tel. 20-21-00-79; f. 1988; production of food crops; Man. Dir BENOÎT N'DRI BROU.

Fonds de Régulation et de Contrôle du Café et du Cacao (FRCC): Abidjan; f. 2002; assists small-scale producers and exporters of coffee and cocoa; administrative bd comprises five representatives of producers, two of exporters, three of banks and insurance cos, two of the state; Pres. ANGELINE KILI; Dir-Gen. KOUAKOU FIRMIN.

Nouvelle PETROCI: Immeuble les Hévéas, 14 blvd Carde, BP V194, Abidjan 01; tel. 20-20-25-00; fax 20-21-68-24; e-mail petrociholding@globeaccess.net; f. 1975 as Société Nationale d'Opérations Pétrolières de la Côte d'Ivoire (PETROCI); restructured 2000 to comprise three companies—Petroci Exploration Production, SA, Petroci Gaz and Petroci Industries Services; all aspects of hydrocarbons development; Pres. PAUL GUI DIBO; Man. Dir KOFFI ERNEST.

Société pour le Développement Minier de la Côte d'Ivoire (SODEMI): 31 blvd des Martyrs, 01 BP 2816, Abidjan 01; tel. 22-44-29-94; fax 22-44-08-21; e-mail sodemidg@aviso.cg; f. 1962; geological and mineral research; Pres. NICOLAS KOUANDI ANGBA; Man. Dir JEAN-YVES LIKANE.

Société de Développement des Forêts (SODEFOR): blvd François Mitterrand, 01 BP 3770, Abidjan 01; tel. 22-48-30-00; fax 22-44-02-40; e-mail info@sodefor.ci; f. 1966; establishment and management of tree plantations, sustainable management of state forests, marketing of timber products; Man. Dir N'GORAN YAO.

Société pour le Développement des Productions Animales (SODEPRA): 01 BP 1249, Abidjan 01; tel. 20-21-13-10; f. 1970; rearing of livestock; Man. Dir PAUL LAMIZANA.

DEVELOPMENT AGENCIES

Agence Française de Développement (AFD): blvd François Mitterrand, 01 BP 1814, Abidjan 01; tel. 22-40-70-40; fax 22-44-21-78; e-mail afdabidjan@groupe-afd.org; internet www.afd.fr; Country Dir MICHEL GAUTHEY.

Association Française des Volontaires du Progrès (AFVP): 01 BP 2532, Abidjan; tel. 20-22-85-09; fax 20-22-05-96; e-mail afvp-ci@africaonline.co.ci; internet www.afvp.org; f. 1965; Nat. Delegate JEAN-PIERRE JUIF.

Centre de Promotion des Investissements en Côte d'Ivoire (CEPICI): Tour CCIA, 5e étage, BP V152, Abidjan 01; tel. 20-21-40-70; fax 20-21-40-71; e-mail infocepici@bnetd.ci; internet www.cepici.net; f. 1993; investment promotion authority; Dir-Gen. TCHÉTCHÉ N'GUESSAN.

CHAMBERS OF COMMERCE

Chambre d'Agriculture de la Côte d'Ivoire: 11 ave Lamblin, 01 BP 1291, Abidjan 01; tel. 20-32-92-13; fax 20-32-92-20; Sec.-Gen. GAUTHIER N'ZI.

Chambre de Commerce et d'Industrie de Côte d'Ivoire: 6 ave Joseph Anoma, 01 BP 1399, Abidjan 01; tel. 20-33-16-00; fax 20-32-39-42; e-mail cci@africaonline.co.ci; f. 1992; Pres. JEAN-LOUIS BILLON; Dir-Gen. YAO KOUAME.

TRADE ASSOCIATIONS

Bourse du Café et du Cacao (BCC): 04 BP 2576, Abidjan 04; tel. 20-20-27-20; fax 20-20-28-14; e-mail info@bcc.ci; internet www.bcc.ci; f. 2001 to replace marketing, purchasing and certain other functions of La Nouvelle Caistab (Caisse de Stabilisation et de

Soutien des Prix des Productions Agricoles); Pres. LUCIEN TAPÉ DOH; Dir-Gen. TANO KASSI KADIO.

Fédération Ivoirienne des Producteurs de Café et de Cacao (FIPCC): Yamoussoukro; f. 1998; coffee and cocoa growers' asscn; Chair. CISSÉ LOCINÉ; c. 3,000 mems.

Organisation de Commercialisation de l'Ananas et de la Banane (OCAB): Abidjan; pineapple and banana growers' asscn; Exec. Sec. EMMANUEL DOLI.

EMPLOYERS' ORGANIZATIONS

Association Nationale des Producteurs de Café-Cacao de Côte d'Ivoire (ANAPROCI): BP 840, San-Pédro; tel. 34-71-20-98; fax 34-71-14-65; Pres. HENRI KASSI AMOUZOU; Sec.-Gen. THOMAS EYIMIN.

Conseil National du Patronat Ivoirien: 01 BP 8666, Abidjan 01; tel. 20-32-17-97; fax 20-32-39-73; e-mail cnpi@aviso.ci; f. 1993; Pres. DIACK DIAWAR; Sec.-Gen. ABOUBAKAR COULIBALY; nine affiliated federations, including the following:

Fédération Maritime de Côte d'Ivoire (FEDERMAR): Treichville, ave Christiani, 01 BP 4082, Abidjan 01; tel. 21-22-08-09; fax 21-22-07-90; e-mail issouf.fadika@ci.dti.bollore.com; f. 1958; Pres. ISSOUF FADIKA; Sec.-Gen. VACABA TOURÉ DE MOVALY.

Fédération Nationale des Industries et Services de Côte d'Ivoire (FNISCI): 01 BP 1340, Abidjan 01; tel. 20-21-71-42; fax 20-21-72-56; f. 1993; Pres. JOSEPH-DESIRÉ BILEY; Dir-Gen. DANIEL TEURQUETIL; 230 mems.

Groupement Ivoirien du Bâtiment et des Travaux Publics (GIBTP): 25 rue des Carrossiers, Concession SIDELAF, zone 3, 01 BP 464, Abidjan 01; tel. 21-25-29-46; fax 21-25-29-57; f. 1934 as Syndicat des Entrepreneurs et des Industriels de la Côte d'Ivoire; present name adopted 1997; Pres. KONGO KOUADIO KOUASSI.

Syndicat des Commerçants Importateurs et Exportateurs (SCIMPEX): 01 BP 3792, Abidjan 01; tel. 20-21-54-27; fax 20-32-56-52; Pres. JACQUES ROSSIGNOL; Sec.-Gen. M. KOFFI.

Syndicat Autonome des Producteurs de Café-Cacao de Côte d'Ivoire (SYNAPROCI): Abidjan; f. 2003; Pres. BANNY KOFFI GERMAIN (acting).

Syndicat des Exportateurs et Négociants en Bois de Côte d'Ivoire: Immeuble CCIA, 3e étage, 01 BP 1979, Abidjan 01; tel. 20-21-12-39; fax 20-21-26-42; e-mail unemaf@africaonline.co.ci; f. 1960; Pres. SOULEYMANE COULIBALY.

Syndicat des Producteurs Industriels du Bois (SPIB): Immeuble CCIA, 3e étage, 01 BP 318, Abidjan 01; tel. 20-21-12-39; fax 20-21-26-42; e-mail unemaf@africaonline.co.ci; f. 1943; Pres. WILFRIED BIRKENMAIER.

Union des Entreprises Agricoles et Forestières: Immeuble CCIA, 3e étage, 01 BP 2300, Abidjan 01; tel. 20-21-12-39; fax 20-21-26-42; e-mail unemaf@africaonline.co.ci; f. 1952; Pres. M. YORO BITIZIE.

UTILITIES

Electricity

Compagnie Ivoirienne d'Electricité (CIE): ave Christiani, 01 BP 6932, Abidjan 01; tel. 21-23-33-00; fax 21-24-63-22; e-mail info@cie.ci; internet www.cie.ci; f. 1990; 71% controlled by Société Bouygues group (France); Pres. MARCEL ZADI KESSY; Dir-Gen. MARCEL PELISSOU.

Compagnie Ivoirienne de Production d'Electricité (CIPREL): Tour Sidom, 12e étage, ave Houdaille, 01 BP 4039, Abidjan 01; tel. 20-22-60-97; independent power production; Pres. OLIVIER BOUYGUES.

Gas

Gaz de Côte d'Ivoire (GDCI): 01 BP 1351, Abidjan; tel. 22-44-49-55; f. 1961; transfer to majority private ownership pending; gas distributor; Man. Dir LAMBERT KONAN.

Water

Société de Distribution d'Eau de la Côte d'Ivoire (SODECI): 1 ave Christiani, Treichville, 01 BP 1843, Abidjan 01; tel. 21-23-30-00; fax 21-24-20-33; f. 1959; production, treatment and distribution of drinking water; 46% owned by Groupe Bouygues (France), 51% owned by employees; Chair. MARCEL ZADI KESSY; Man. Dir PIERRE LE TAREAU.

MAJOR COMPANIES

The following are among the largest companies in terms of either capital investment or employment.

Air Liquide-Société Ivoirienne d'Oxygène et d'Acetylène (SIVOA): 131 blvd de Marseille, 01 BP 1753, Abidjan 01; tel. 21-35-44-71; fax 21-35-66-72; f. 1962; cap. 873m. francs CFA; 20% state-owned, 72% owned by Air Liquide (France); mfrs of industrial and medical gases; CEO CLAUDE BOURAYNE; Man. Dir VINCENT SERAIN; 120 employees.

Bois Transformés d'Afrique (BTA): 01 BP 958, Abidjan 01; tel. 20-22-74-31; fax 20-22-74-69; e-mail BTA@afnet.net; f. 1972; cap. 233.5m. francs CFA; sawmills, plywood factory at Zagné; Dir-Gen. PHILIPPE DEKEULENEER.

Carnaud Metalbox SIEM: blvd Giscard d'Estaing, 01 BP 1242, Abidjan 01; tel. 21-35-89-74; fax 21-35-03-94; f. 1954; subsidiary of Carnaud Metalbox (France); cap. 1,889m. francs CFA; mfrs of cans; Man. Dir M. MOREAU.

Compagnie des Caoutchoucs du Pakidie (CCP): 01 BP 1191, Abidjan 01; tel. 20-37-15-38; fax 20-37-15-40; f. 1960; cap. 856m. francs CFA; rubber plantations and factory; Chair. FULGENCE KOFFI.

La Compagnie Cotonnière Ivoirienne (LCCI): M'Bengue, Korhogo; cotton ginning; f. 2001; 80% owned by Groupe Aiglon (Switzerland), 20% by Groupe Bolloré (France); Gen. Man. SIDI KAGNASSY; Dir ROBERT GANSAH.

Compagnie Ivoirienne pour le Développement des Textiles Nouvelle (CIDT Nouvelle): route de Béoumi, 01 BP 622, Bouaké 01; tel. 31-63-30-13; fax 31-63-41-67; f. 1974; cap. 7,200m. francs CFA; transferred to majority private ownership in 1998; present name adopted 1999; development of cotton production, cotton ginning; Man. Dir SAMBA COULIBALY.

Cosmivoire: Zone Industrielle de Vridi, 01 BP 3576, Abidjan 01; tel. 21-75-77-70; fax 21-27-28-13; e-mail cosmidm@sifca.ci; internet www.cosmivoire.ci; f. 1974; owned by SIFCA; cap. 702m. francs CFA; mfrs of soaps, cosmetics, oils, margarine, butter and alcohol; Pres. JEAN-BAPTISTE FOFANA; Man. Dir ANGORA TANO.

Ets R. Gonfreville (ERG): route de l'Aéroport, BP 584, Bouaké; tel. 31-63-32-13; fax 31-63-46-65; f. 1921; cap. 2,999m. francs CFA; spinning, weaving, dyeing and printing of cotton textiles; clothing mfrs; Man. Dir JACQUES RIVIÈRE; 2,500 employees (2001).

Filatures, Tissage, Sacs–Côte d'Ivoire (FILTISAC): Km 8, Autoroute Abobo–Adjamé, 01 BP 3962, Abidjan 01; tel. 20-30-46-00; fax 20-30-46-11; e-mail mail@filtisac.com; internet www.filtisac.com; f. 1965; cap. 4,407m. francs CFA (June 2002); sales US $44.9m. (2001); mfrs of jute bags and other packaging; CEO FRANÇOIS DE CHASSEY; Man. Dir NIZAR HASSAM; 2,000 employees (June 2002).

Grands Moulins d'Abidjan (GMA): Quai 1, Zone Portuaire, 01 BP 1743, Abidjan 01; tel. 20-21-28-33; fax 20-29-09-42; f. 1963; cap. 2,000m. francs CFA; flour milling and production of animal feed; Dir KOUASSI KOUADIO; 331 employees (2001).

Groupe FIBAKO–IVOIREMBAL: Km 8, route d'Abobo Gare, 01 BP 3962, Abidjan 01; tel. 31-63-32-12; fax 31-63-18-92; f. 1946; fmrly Ficelleries de Bouaké–Société Industrielle Ivoirienne d'Emballage; cap. 950m. francs CFA; spinning, mfrs of sacking and plastic packaging; Man. Dir PHILIPPE GODIN.

Industrie de Transformation des Produits Agricoles (API): Zone Industrielle de Vridi, 15 BP 431, Abidjan 15; tel. 21-35-20-09; f. 1968; cap. 900m. francs CFA; wholly owned by Cacao Barry Group (France); marketing of cocoa products, processing of cocoa beans; Man. Dir HONORÉ AKPANGNI.

Mobil Oil Côte d'Ivoire: Route de Petit Bassam, 15 BP 900, Abidjan 15; tel. 21-75-37-00; fax 21-75-38-00; f. 1974; cap. 2,000m. francs CFA; distribution of petroleum products; Chair. MICHEL BONNET; Dir J. LABAUNE.

National Electric-Côte d'Ivoire (NELCI): 16 BP 131, Abidjan 16; f. 1983; cap. 1,000m. francs CFA; assembly of radio and television receivers; Chair. TAMADA TAKASHI.

Nestlé Côte d'Ivoire: rue du Lycée Technique, 01 BP 1840, Abidjan 01; tel. 22-40-45-45; fax 22-44-43-43; e-mail annick.coulibaly@ci.nestle.com; f. 1959; cap. 5,518m. francs CFA (Dec. 1998); subsidiary of Nestlé (Switzerland); production of coffee and cocoa products, manufacture and sale of food products; sales US $117.6m. (2001); Chair. GEORGES N'DIA KOFFI; Man. Dir M. DESPONT; 710 employees (2001).

Palmindustrie: Pointe des Fumeurs, 01 BP V239, Abidjan 01; tel. 21-27-00-70; fax 21-25-47-00; f. 1969; cap. 34,000m. francs CFA; development of palm, coconut and copra products; Man. Dir BONIFACE NAMA BRITO; 10,700 employees (2001).

Plantations et Huileries de la Côte d'Ivoire (PHCI): 01 BP 715, Dabou; tel. and fax 23-57-27-15; f. 1954; production of palm oil; 82.64% owned by Blohorn HSL; Chair. PIERRE BONNEIL; Pres. and Dir-Gen. GEORGES BROU; 530 employees (2001).

Produits Ruraux de Négoce Côte d'Ivoire (PRN CI): rue de Textile, Zone Industrielle de Vridi; 01 BP 3836, Abidjan 01; tel. 21-27-00-60; fax 21-27-00-64; processing, storage and marketing of cocoa and coffee; Man. Dir THOMAS SEGUI.

Shell Côte d'Ivoire: Zone Industrielle de Vridi, 15 BP 378, Abidjan 15; tel. 21-27-00-18; fax 21-27-24-99; internet www.shell.com/home/Framework?siteId=ci-en; f. 1974; cap. 3,150m. francs CFA, sales

62,618m. francs CFA (1999); 67% owned by Royal Dutch Shell (Netherlands); distribution of petroleum products; Pres. GEORGE BRUNTON.

SIFCA: Zone Portuaire, 01 BP 1289, Abidjan 01; tel. 21-75-75-75; fax 21-25-45-65; e-mail communication@sifca.ci; internet www.sifca.ci; f. 1958; export of cocoa and coffee; sales US $677.9m. (2000); Pres. JEAN-LOUIS BILLON; Dir-Gen. YVES LAMBELIN; 290 employees (2002).

Société Africaine de Cacao (SACO): Zone 4, site 6, rue Pierre et Marie Curie, 01 BP 1045, Abidjan 01; tel. 21-75-02-00; fax 21-35-94-96; f. 1956; cap. 1,733m. francs CFA; 65% owned by Groupe Barry Callebaut (France/Belgium), 35% state-owned; sale of state holding pending; mfrs of cocoa powder, chocolate products, cocoa butter and oil-cake; Dir-Gen. DIDIER BUECHER; 700 employees (2001).

Société Africaine de Plantations d'Hévéas (SAPH): 01 BP 1322, Abidjan 01; tel. 20-21-18-91; fax 20-22-18-67; e-mail saphci@globeaccess.net; f. 1956; cap. 16,149m. francs CFA (Dec. 1998); 38.7% owned by SIFCA, 30.9% by Société Internationale des Plantations d'Hévéas (France); production of rubber on 17,000 ha of plantations; sales US $28.9m. (2000); Pres. and Man. Dir BÉATRICE AMOAKON; 4,206 employees (2002).

Société des Caoutchoucs de Grand-Béréby (SOGB): 17 BP 18, Abidjan 17; tel. 20-21-99-47; fax 20-33-25-80; f. 1979; 15% state-owned; rubber plantations and processing; cap. 21,602m. francs CFA; sales US $31.4m. (2001); Pres. FULGENCE KOFFI; Gen. Man. MARC MUTSAARS; 4,000 employees (2002).

Société de Conserves de Côte d'Ivoire (SCODI): Quai de Pêche, Zone Industrielle de Vridi, 01 BP 677, Abidjan 01; tel. 21-25-66-74; fax 21-25-07-52; f. 1960; cap. 908m. francs CFA; tuna canning; restructured 2006; Chair. PAUL ANTONIETTI; Gen. Man. FRANCIS AMBROISE.

Société de Construction et d'Exploitation d'Installations Frigorifiques (SOCEF): Port de Pêche, 04 BP 154, Abidjan 04; tel. 21-35-54-42; f. 1962; cap. 900m. francs CFA; mfrs of refrigeration units; Dir GÉRARD CLEMENT.

Société Cotonnière Ivoirienne (COTIVO): 01 BP 4037, Abidjan; tel. 23-51-70-01; fax 23-51-73-34; f. 1972; cap. 3,600m. francs CFA; textile complex; 27% state-owned; Pres. MICHEL HEMONNOT; Man. Dir MICHEL DUTRONC.

Société de Galvanisation de Tôles en Côte d'Ivoire (Tôles Ivoire): 15 BP 144, Abidjan 15; tel. 21-27-33-33; fax 21-27-43-24; e-mail ivoiral@globeaccess.net; f. 1970; cap. 975m. francs CFA; mfrs of galvanized corrugated sheets and other roofing materials; Pres. and Dir-Gen. PHILIPPE MIGNARD.

Société de Gestion des Stocks Pétroliers de Côte d'Ivoire (GESTOCI): blvd de Vridi, 15 BP 89, Abidjan 15; tel. 21-75-98-00; fax 21-27-17-82; e-mail gestoci@gestoci.ci; f. 1983; management of petroleum stocks; cap. 240m. francs CFA (June 2002); Man. Dir ATSÉ BENJAMIN YAPO; 187 employees (June 2002).

Société Ivoirienne de Béton Manufacturé (SIBM): 12 rue Thomas Edison, 01 BP 902, Abidjan 01; tel. 21-35-52-71; fax 21-35-82-27; e-mail sibm@ivoireb.com; f. 1978; cap. 800m. francs CFA; mem. of Société Africaine de Béton Manufacturé group; mfrs of concrete; Man. Dir DANIEL PAUL.

Société Ivoirienne de Câbles (SICABLE): Zone Industrielle de Vridi, 15 BP 35, Abidjan 15; tel. 21-27-57-35; fax 21-27-12-34; e-mail sicable@globeaccess.net; f. 1975; 51% owned by Pirelli SpA (Italy); mfrs of electricity cables; cap. 740m. francs CFA; sales €8.1m. (2002); Chair. ANDRÉ BOURG; Man. Dir CLAUDE REAU; 89 employees (2002).

Société Ivoirienne de Ciments et Matériaux (SOCIMAT): blvd du Port, 01 BP 887, Abidjan 01; tel. 21-75-51-00; fax 21-75-51-18; e-mail marfil@cimbelier.co.ci; f. 1952; cap. 707m. francs CFA; clinker-crushing plant; Man. Dir JOHANN PACHLER.

Société Ivoirienne de Raffinage (SIR): blvd de Petit-Bassam, Vridi, 01 BP 1269, Abidjan 01; tel. 21-27-01-60; fax 21-27-28-05; e-mail info@sir.ci; internet www.sir.ci; f. 1962; 53.73% owned by Nouvelle PETROCI, 20.35% by Total CI, 10.29% owned by Shell CI; operates petroleum refinery at Abidjan; cap. 39m. francs CFA, sales 107,895m. francs CFA (2006); Pres. LAURENT OTTRO ZIRIGNON; Dir-Gen. JOËL DERVAIN; 674 employees (2006).

Société Ivoirienne des Tabacs (SITAB): Zone Industrielle, 01 BP 607, Bouaké 01; tel. 20-20-23-12; fax 31-63-46-80; f. 1956; cap. 4,489m. francs CFA (Dec. 1998); mfrs of cigarettes; Chair. FRANÇOISE AIDARA; Man. Dir PIERRE MAGNE; 830 employees (2000).

Société de Limonaderies et Brasseries d'Afrique (SOLIBRA): 27 rue du Canal, 01 BP 1304, Abidjan; tel. 21-24-91-33; fax 21-35-97-91; f. 1955; mfrs of beer, lemonade and ice at Abidjan and Bouaflé; cap. 4,110m. francs CFA; sales US $96.5m. (2001); Pres. PIERRE CASTEL; Dir-Gen. JEAN-CLAUDE PALU; 600 employees (2001).

Société des Mines d'Ity (SMI): ave Joseph Blohorn, Impasse des Chevaliers de Malte, Cocody, 08 BP 872, Abidjan 08; tel. 22-44-63-63; fax 22-44-41-00; e-mail smiphp@aviso.ci; f. 1989; cap. 600m. francs CFA; 51% owned by COGEMA, 49% by SODEMI; mining of gold reserves (2.0 metric tons per year) at Ity; Pres. ABDOULAYE KONÉ; Man. Dir PHILIPPE. PALANQUE.

Société Multinationale de Bitumes (SMB): blvd de Petit-Bassam, Zone Industrielle de Vridi, 12 BP 622, Abidjan 12; tel. 21-23-70-70; fax 21-27-05-18; e-mail info.smb@siz.ci; f. 1978; cap. 1,218m. francs CFA (Dec. 1998); 53% owned by SIR; Pres. VINCENT TIOKO-DJEDJE; Dir-Gen. ADAMA DAO; 50 employees (2000).

Société Nationale Ivoirienne de Travaux (SONITRA): route d'Anyama, 01 BP 2609, Abidjan 01; tel. 20-37-13-68; f. 1963; cap. 2,273m. francs CFA; 55% state-owned; building and construction; Chair. FERNAND KONAN KOUADIO; Man. Dir AMOS SALOMON; 1,393 employees.

Société Nouvelle Abidjanaise de Carton Ondulé (SONACO): Zone Industrielle de Yopougon, 01 BP 1119, Abidjan; tel. 23-51-52-00; fax 23-46-65-06; e-mail sonaco@rossman.com; internet www.rossmann.com/fr/implantations/international/sonaco.html; f. 1963; cap. 1,200m. francs CFA; mfrs of paper goods and corrugated cardboard; owned by Groupe Rossman (France); Dir-Gen. JEAN-MICHEL RUEDA; 258 employees (2005).

Société de Stockage de Côte d'Ivoire (STOCACI): rue des Thoniers, Zone Portuaire, 01 BP 1798, Abidjan 01; f. 1980; cap. 1,000m. francs CFA; treatment and storage of cocoa and other products; Chair. JEAN ABILE GAL; Vice-Chair. and Man. Dir MADELEINE TCHICAYA.

Société Sucrière de la Côte d'Ivoire (SUCRIVOIRE): 16 ave du Docteur Crozet, 01 BP 2164, Abidjan 01; tel. 20-21-04-79; fax 20-21-07-75; f. 1997 following majority privatization of Société pour le Développement des Cannes à Sucre, l'Industrialisation et la Commercialisation du Sucre (SODESUCRE); 45% state-owned; sugar production; Chair. and Man. Dir JOSEPH KOUAMÉ KRA.

Société de Tubes d'Acier et Aluminium en Côte d'Ivoire (SOTACI): Zone Industrielle de Yopougon, 01 BP 2747, Abidjan 01; tel. 23-51-54-54; fax 23-46-69-25; e-mail sotaci@sotaci.co.ci; internet www.sotaci.ci; f. 1977; cap. 3,461m. francs CFA; sales US $66.8m. (2006); mfrs of steel and aluminium tubing and pipes; Pres. and Dir-Gen. ADHAM EL-KHALIL; Man. Dir DOMINIQUE MARCHAL; 619 employees (2006).

Total Côte d'Ivoire: 01 BP 555, Abidjan 01; tel. 20-22-27-29; fax 20-21-82-52; f. 1967; petroleum marketing and distribution; fmrly Elf Oil-CI, subsequently renamed TotalFinaElf Côte d'Ivoire, present name adopted 2003; subsidiary of Total (France); cap. 3,148.1m. francs CFA; sales US $200.5m. (2001); Pres. FRANCIS JAN; Dir-Gen. CHRISTOPHE GIRARDOT; 93 employees (2002).

TRITURAF: 01 BP 1485, Bouaké 01; tel. 31-63-26-42; fax 31-63-17-91; f. 1973; fmrly Société Ivoirienne de Trituration de Graines Oléagineuses et de Raffinage d'Huiles Végétales; 60% owned by Unilever, Netherlands/UK; operations in Bouaké suspended following outbreak of civil conflict in 2002; processing of cotton; cap. 2,600m. francs CFA (Dec. 1999); Pres. RIK BOSMAN; 342 employees (2001).

Unilever Côte d'Ivoire (Blohorn HSL): 01 BP 1751, Abidjan 01; tel. 21-24-90-60; fax 21-24-68-14; f. 1932; cap. 6,040m. francs CFA; 90% owned by Unilever Group (Netherlands/United Kingdom); fmrly Blohorn Huilerie-Savonnerie-Lipochimie (Blohorn HSL); production and marketing of edible oils, incl. margarine, and of palm oil products, incl. soap; sales US $208m. (2006); Chair. MARC DESENFANS; 740 employees (2006).

Union Industrielle Textile de Côte d'Ivoire (UTEXI): Zone Industrielle de Vridi, 15 BP 414, Abidjan 15; tel. 21-27-44-81; fax 21-27-16-16; f. 1972; cap. 3,700m. francs CFA; 12.75% state-owned; spinning and weaving mill at Dimbokro; operations suspended from 2002; Chair. JACQUES ROSSIGNOL; Man. Dir NOBOYUKI YOSHIDA.

Union Ivoirienne de Traitement de Cacao (UNICAO): Zone Industrielle de Vridi, 15 BP 406, Abidjan 15; tel. 21-27-14-49; fax 21-27-56-82; e-mail unicao@globeaccess.net; f. 1989; cap. 6,000m. francs CFA; subsidiary of SIFCOM group; processing of cocoa beans; Man. Dir H. KORNER; 263 employees (2001).

Uniwax: Zone Industrielle de Yopougon, 01 BP 3994, Abidjan 01; tel. 23-46-64-15; fax 23-46-69-42; e-mail uniwax@odaci.net; f. 1967; mfrs of batik fabrics; owned by Vlisco Group (Netherlands); cap. 1,750m. francs CFA; sales US $34.8m. (2001); Pres. PIERRE BONNEIL; Man. Dir JEAN-LOUIS MENUDIER; 540 employees (2002).

TRADE UNIONS

Dignité: 03 BP 2031, Abidjan 03; tel. 21-39-26-02; fax 21-37-74-89; Sec.-Gen. BASILE MAHAN-GAHE; 10,000 mems (2001).

Fédération des Syndicats Autonomes de la Côte d'Ivoire (FESACI): Abidjan; breakaway group from the Union Générale des Travailleurs de Côte d'Ivoire; Sec.-Gen. MARCEL ETTÉ.

Union Générale des Travailleurs de Côte d'Ivoire (UGTCI): 05 BP 1203, Abidjan 05; tel. 20-21-26-65; f. 1962; Sec.-Gen. HYACINTHE ADIKO NIAMKEY; 100,000 individual mems; 190 affiliated unions.

Transport

RAILWAYS

The rail network in Côte d'Ivoire totalled 1,316 km in 1999, including 660 km of track from Abidjan to Niangoloko, on the border with Burkina Faso; from there, the railway extends to Kaya, via the Burkinabè capital, Ouagadougou.

SITARAIL—Transport Ferroviaire de Personnel et de Marchandises: Résidence Memanou, blvd Clozel, Plateau, 16 BP 1216, Abidjan 16; tel. 20-20-80-00; fax 20-22-48-47; f. 1995 to operate services on Abidjan–Ouagadougou–Kaya (Burkina Faso) line; Man. Dir PIERRE MARTINEAU.

ROADS

In 2004 there were about 80,000 km of roads, of which some 6,500 km were paved. Some 68,000m. francs CFA was invested in the road network in 1994–98; projects included the upgrading of 3,000 km of roads and 30,000 km of tracks. Tolls were introduced on some roads in the mid-1990s, to assist in funding the maintenance of the network.

Société des Transports Abidjanais (SOTRA): 01 BP 2009, Abidjan 01; tel. 21-24-90-80; fax 21-25-97-21; e-mail sotra@access.net; f. 1960; 60% state-owned; urban transport; Dir-Gen. PHILIPPE ATTEY.

SHIPPING

Côte d'Ivoire has two major ports, Abidjan and San-Pédro, both of which are industrial and commercial establishments with financial autonomy. Abidjan, which handled some 15.0m. metric tons of goods in 2001, is the largest container and trading port in West Africa. Access to the port is via the 2.7-km Vridi Canal. The port at San-Pédro, which handled 1.2m. tons of goods in 1999, remains the main gateway to the south-western region of Côte d'Ivoire. As a result of widespread civil unrest from September 2002, much international freight transport that formerly left or entered the West African region through ports in Côte d'Ivoire was transferred to neighbouring countries.

Port Autonome d'Abidjan (PAA): BP V85, Abidjan; tel. 21-23-80-00; fax 21-23-80-80; e-mail info@paa-ci.org; internet www.paa-ci.org; f. 1992; transferred to private ownership in 1999; Pres. ANGE-FRANÇOIS BARRY-BATTESTI; Man. Dir MARCEL GOSSIO.

Port Autonome de San-Pédro (PASP): BP 339/340, San-Pédro; tel. 34-71-20-00; fax 34-71-27-15; e-mail pasp@pasp.ci; internet sanpedro-portci.com; f. 1971; Man. Dir OGOU ATTEMENE.

AMICI: Km 1, blvd de Marseille, 16 BP 643, Abidjan 16; tel. 21-35-28-50; fax 21-35-28-53; e-mail amici.abj@aviso.ci; f. 1998; 45% owned by Ivorian interests, 25% by Danish interests, 20% by German interests and 10% by French interests.

Compagnie Maritime Africaine—Côte d'Ivoire (COMAF—CI): rond-point du Nouveau Port, 08 BP 867, Abidjan 08; tel. 20-32-40-77; f. 1973; navigation and management of ships; Dir FRANCO BERNARDINI.

SDV—Côte d'Ivoire (SDV—CI): 01 BP 4082, Abidjan 01; tel. 20-20-20-20; fax 20-20-21-20; f. 1943; sea and air transport; storage and warehousing; affiliated to Groupe Bolloré (France); Pres. GILLES CUCHE.

SAGA Côte d'Ivoire: rond-point du Nouveau Port, 01 BP 1727, Abidjan 01; tel. 21-23-23-23; fax 21-24-25-06; f. 1959; merchandise handling, transit and storage; privately owned; Pres. M. GEORGES; Dir-Gen. DAVID CHARRIER.

Société Agence Maritime de l'Ouest Africain—Côte d'Ivoire (SAMOA—CI): rue des Gallions, 01 BP 1611, Abidjan 01; tel. 20-21-29-65; f. 1955; shipping agents; Man. Dir CLAUDE PERDRIAUD.

Société Ivoirienne de Navigation Maritime (SIVOMAR): 5 rue Charpentier, Zone 2B, Treichville, 01 BP 1395, Abidjan 01; tel. 20-21-73-23; fax 20-32-38-53; f. 1977; shipments to ports in Africa, the Mediterranean and the Far East; Dir SIMPLISSE DE MESSE ZINSOU.

Société Ouest-Africaine d'Entreprises Maritimes en Côte d'Ivoire (SOAEM–CI): 01 BP 1727, Abidjan 01; tel. 20-21-59-69; fax 20-32-24-67; f. 1978; merchandise handling, transit and storage; Chair. JACQUES PELTIER; Dir JACQUES COLOMBANI.

SOCOPAO–Côte d'Ivoire: Km 1, blvd de la République, 01 BP 1297, Abidjan 01; tel. 21-24-13-14; fax 21-24-21-30; e-mail socopao@africaonline.co.ci; shipping agents; Shipping Dir OLIVIER RANJARD.

CIVIL AVIATION

There are three international airports: Abidjan–Félix Houphouët-Boigny, Bouaké and Yamoussoukro. In addition, there are 25 domestic and regional airports, including those at Bouna, Korhogo, Man, Odienné and San-Pédro.

Agence Nationale de l'Aviation Civile: 07 BP 148, Abidjan 07; tel. 21-27-74-24; fax 21-27-63-46; civil aviation authority; Dir JEAN KOUASSI ABONOUAN.

Air Inter Ivoire: Aéroport de Port Bouët, 07 BP 62, Abidjan 07; tel. 21-27-84-65; internal flights.

Société Nouvelle Air Ivoire: Immeuble République, pl. de la République, 01 BP 7782, Abidjan 01; tel. 20-25-15-61; fax 20-32-04-90; e-mail info@airivoire.com; internet www.airivoire.com; f. 2000 to replace Air Ivoire (f. 1960); privatized in 2001; 76.42% owned by All Africa Airways, 23.58% state-owned; internal and regional flights.

Tourism

The game reserves, forests, lagoons, coastal resorts, rich ethnic folklore and the lively city of Abidjan are tourist attractions; Côte d'Ivoire also has well-developed facilities for business visitors, including golfing centres. Some 301,000 tourists visited Côte d'Ivoire in 1998; receipts from tourism in that year totalled US $331m. In 2002 receipts from tourism totalled $490m. Tourism has been negatively affected by instability resulting from the *coup d'état* in December 1999, the disputed elections of October 2000, and the widespread civil unrest that commenced in September 2002.

Office Ivoirien du Tourisme et de l'Hôtellerie: Immeuble ex-EECI, pl. de la République, 01 BP 8538, Abidjan 01; tel. 20-20-65-00; fax 20-20-65-31; e-mail oith@africaonline.co.ci; f. 1992; Dir CAMILLE KOUASSI.

Defence

As assessed at November 2006, Côte d'Ivoire's active armed forces comprised an army of 6,500 men, a navy of about 900, an air force of 700, a paramilitary presidential guard of 1,350 and a gendarmerie of 7,600. There was also a 1,500-strong militia, and reserve forces numbered 10,000 men. Military service is by selective conscription and lasts for 18 months. France supplies equipment and training, and had increased its military presence in Côte d'Ivoire from 550 to some 3,800 by August 2004, in order to monitor and enforce the cease-fire agreed in October 2002 between the Ivorian Government and rebels of the Mouvement patriotique de Côte d'Ivoire. The deployment by the Economic Community of West African States of a military mission (ECOMICI) commenced in Côte d'Ivoire in January 2003; by August an estimated 1,300 ECOMICI troops, of an authorized maximum of 3,411, were in Côte d'Ivoire. In June 2003 the UN Mission in Côte d'Ivoire (MINUCI) commenced operations in Abidjan, comprising 26 military liaison officers and 30 international civilian personnel. In late February 2004 the UN Security Council established the UN Operation in Côte d'Ivoire (UNOCI); with an authorized military strength of 6,240, the peace-keeping operation was deployed for an initial period of 12 months from early April, when authority was transferred from MINUCI and ECOMICI to UNOCI; the mandate of UNOCI was subsequently extended, on several occasions. In November 2004, following the death of nine French troops in an airstrike conducted by Ivorian military aircraft, the entire Ivorian air force, reportedly consisting of two Sukhoi-25 warplanes and five helicopters, was destroyed on the ground by French retaliatory action. Later that month the UN imposed a 13-month arms embargo on Côte d'Ivoire.

Defence Expenditure: Estimated at 100,000m. francs CFA in 2005.

Chief of Staff of the Armed Forces: Gen. PHILIPPE MANGOU.

Commander of Land-based Forces: Col DENIS BOMBET.

Commander of the Navy: Frigate Capt. GAGBÉI FAUSSIGNAUX VAGBA.

Commander of the Air Force: Maj.-Col ADAMA DOSSO.

Education

Education at all levels is available free of charge. Primary education, which is officially compulsory for six years between the ages of seven and 13 years, begins at six years of age and lasts for six years. According to UNESCO estimates, enrolment at primary schools in 2002/03 included 56% of children in the relevant age-group (males 62%; females 50%). The Ivorian Government's long-term objective is to provide primary education for all children by 2010. Secondary education, from the age of 12, lasts for up to seven years, comprising a first cycle of four years and a second cycle of three years. In 2001/02 total enrolment at secondary level included 20% of children in the relevant age-group (males 26%; females 15%), according to UNESCO estimates. The Université de Cocody (formerly the Université Nationale de Côte d'Ivoire), in Abidjan, has six faculties, and there are two other universities, at Abodo-Adjamé (also in Abidjan) and at Bouaké. Some 47,187 students were enrolled at university-level institutions in 1997/98. Expenditure on education in 1999 was estimated at 303,700m. francs CFA, equivalent to 25.3% of total government expenditure (excluding spending on the public debt). Education in the north of the country was badly disrupted following the failed coup in 2002.

Bibliography

Abo, F. K. *Pour un véritable réflexe patriotique en afrique: Le cas ivoirien.* Paris, L'Harmattan, 2002.

Bailly, D. *La restauration du multipartisme en Côte d'Ivoire: ou la double mort d'Houphouët-Boigny.* Paris, L'Harmattan, 1995.

Bassett, T. J. *The peasant cotton revolution in West Africa: Côte d'Ivoire, 1880-1995.* Cambridge, Cambridge University Press, 2001.

Baulin, J. *La succession d'Houphouët-Boigny.* Paris, Editions Karthala, 2000.

Bédié, H. Konan. *Les chemins de ma vie: Entretiens avec Eric Laurent.* Paris, Plon, 1999.

Boa-Thiémélé, R. L. *L'Ivoirité entre culture et politique.* Paris, L'Harmattan, 2003.

Boni, T. (Ed.) *Africulture 56: Côte d'Ivoire: le pari de la diversité.* Paris, L'Harmattan, 2003.

Contamin, B., and Fauré, Y.-A. *La bataille des entreprises publiques en Côte d'Ivoire: L'histoire d'un ajustement interne.* Paris, Editions Karthala, 1990.

Coulibaly, A. A. *Le système politique ivoirien de la colonie à la IIe République.* Paris, L'Harmattan, 2002.

Coulibaly, L. G. *Côte-d'Ivoire: Au coeur du bois sacré.* Paris, L'Harmattan, 2004.

Cruise O'Brien, D. B., Dunn, J., and Rathbone, R. (Eds). *Contemporary West African States.* Cambridge, Cambridge University Press, 1989.

Daniels, M. *Côte d'Ivoire.* Santa Barbara, CA, ABC Clio, 1996.

Diabaté, I., Dembele, O., and Akindes, F. (Eds). *Intellectuels ivoiriens face à la crise.* Paris, Editions Karthala, 2005.

Diarra, S. *Les faux complots d'Houphouët-Boigny.* Paris, Editions Karthala, 1997.

Doh-Djanhoundy, T. *Autopsie de la crise ivoirienne: la nation au coeur du conflit.* Paris, L'Harmattan, 2006.

Du Parge, A. *Parmi les rebelles: carnets de route en Côte d'Ivoire, 19 septembre 2002–19 septembre 2003.* Paris, L'Harmattan, 2003.

Dubresson, A. *Villes et industries en Côte d'Ivoire. Pour une géographie de l'accumulation urbaine.* Paris, Editions Karthala, 1989.

Ellenbogen, A. *Succession d'Houphouët-Boigny: Entre tribalisme et démocratie.* Paris, L'Harmattan, 2003.

Fauré, Y. A., and Médard, J.-F. *Etat et bourgeoisie en Côte d'Ivoire.* Paris, Editions Karthala, 1983.

Gbagbo, L. *Côte d'Ivoire: Fonder une nation africaine démocratique et socialiste en Côte d'Ivoire.* Paris, L'Harmattan, 1999.

Gombeaud, J.-L., Moutout, C., and Smith, S. *La Guerre du cacao, histoire secrète d'un embargo.* Paris, Calmann-Lévy, 1990.

Harrison Church, R. J. *West Africa.* 8th Edn. London, Longman, 1979.

Hilaire, G. G. *Le rempart: attaque terroriste contre la Côte d'Ivoire.* Paris, L'Harmattan, 2004.

Jarret, M. F., and Mahieu, F.-R. *La Côte d'Ivoire de la destabilisation à la refondation.* Paris, L'Harmattan, 2002.

Kokora, P. D. *Le Front populaire ivoirien: de la clandestinité à la légalité: le vécu d'un fondateur.* Paris, L'Harmattan, 1999.

Koné, A. *Houphouët Boigny et la Crise ivoirienne.* Paris, Editions Karthala, 2003.

Le Pape, M. and Vital, C. (Eds). *Côte d'Ivoire: l'année terrible, 1999–2000.* Paris, Editions Karthala, 2002.

Lisette, G. *Le Combat du Rassemblement Démocratique Africain.* Paris, Présence Africaine, 1983.

Lubeck, P. M. (Ed.). *The African Bourgeoisie: Capitalist Development in Nigeria, Kenya, and the Ivory Coast.* Boulder, CO, Lynne Rienner Publishers, 1987.

Miran, M. *Islam, histoire et modernité en Côte d'Ivoire.* Paris, Editions Karthala, 2006.

Nandjui, P. *Houphouët-Boigny: l'homme de la France en Afrique.* Paris, L'Harmattan, 1995.

La prééminence constitutionnelle du Président de la République en Côte d'Ivoire. Paris, L'Harmattan, 2004.

Navarro, R. *Côte d'Ivoire: Le culte du blanc: Les territoires culturels et leurs frontières.* Paris, L'Harmattan, 2003.

Rapley, J. *Ivorien Capitalism: African Entrepreneurs in Côte d'Ivoire.* London, Lynne Rienner Publishers, 1993.

World Bank. *Côte d'Ivoire Living Standards Survey: Design and Implementation.* Washington, DC, International Bank for Reconstruction and Development, 1986.

Zike, M. A. *Café/cacao: la rébellion ivoirienne contre les multinationales.* Abidjan, Edition Ami, 1990.

DJIBOUTI

Physical and Social Geography

I. M. LEWIS

The Republic of Djibouti is situated at the southern entrance to the Red Sea. It is bounded on the far north by Eritrea, on the west and south by Ethiopia, and on the south-east by Somalia. Djibouti covers an area of 23,200 sq km (8,958 sq miles), consisting mostly of volcanic rock-strewn desert wastes, with little arable land and spectacular salt lakes and pans. The climate is torrid, with high tropical temperatures and humidity during the monsoon season. The average annual rainfall is less than 125 mm. Only in the upper part of the basaltic range north of the Gulf of Tadjoura, where the altitude exceeds 1,200 m above sea-level, is there continuous annual vegetation.

At 31 December 1990 the population was officially estimated at 519,900, including refugees and other resident non-nationals. According to UN estimates, the population was 819,000 at mid-2006. In 1989 the capital town, Djibouti (whose port and railhead dominate the country's economy), had a population of about 329,337; by 2005 this was estimated to have risen to 550,000. The indigenous population is almost evenly divided between the Issa (who are of Somali origin) and the Afar, the former having a slight predominance. Both are Muslim Cushitic-speaking peoples with a traditionally nomadic economy and close cultural affinities, despite frequent local rivalry. The Afar inhabit the northern part of the country, the Issa the southern, and both groups span the artificial frontiers separating the Republic of Djibouti from Ethiopia, Eritrea and Somalia.

Since the development of the port of Djibouti in the early 1900s, the indigenous Issas have been joined by immigrants from the adjoining regions of Somalia. The Afar generally follow more restricted patterns of nomadic movement than the Issa, and a more hierarchical traditional political organization. While they formed a number of small polities, these were linked by the pervasive division running throughout the Afar population between the 'noble' Asaimara (or 'red') clans and the less prestigious Asdoimara (or 'white') clans. There is also a long-established Arab trading community. European expatriates are mainly French, mostly in government employment, commerce and the armed forces.

Recent History

THOMAS OFCANSKY

Revised by WALTER S. CLARKE

French interest in the territory that now comprises the Republic of Djibouti began modestly in the mid-19th century when the United Kingdom signalled its disapproval of French actions in Indo-China by denying coaling facilities in Aden to the French Navy. After executing treaties with local chiefs in 1862, France subsequently established a colonial government in Obock, on the north side of the Gulf of Tadjoura, in 1884. The unprotected roadstead and lack of water in the area of Obock caused the relocation of the colonial administration to the more favourable Bay of Djibouti six years later. At that time the area that quickly became the town of Djibouti was nothing more than a collection of reef outcroppings, mangrove swamps, and mud-flats. Djibouti town was well placed to serve as a focal point for trade with Addis Ababa, Ethiopia; in 1894 construction of a narrow-gauge railroad began and in 1917 the Djibouti–Addis Ababa railway was completed.

The territory's indigenous inhabitants, the Afar and the Somali Issa, are closely linked to larger Afar and Issa groups in Ethiopia and Somalia. During the colonial period these were major concerns to France, which wished to maintain its strategic position in the Horn of Africa. When independence was granted to British Somaliland and the Italian-administered UN Trust Territory of Somalia in 1960, the French Government decided that the ideal counter to Somali nationalism would be to install an Afar-led autonomous government in the colony. From 1960–76, the local government was led by an Afar, Ali Aref Bourhan. Following Somali-led nationalist rioting during a visit in 1967 by French President Gen. Charles de Gaulle, the colony was renamed the French Territory of the Afars and the Issas.

Demands for independence led by the Somali Issa community continued until 1976, when a unified political movement, the Ligue populaire africaine pour l'indépendance (LPAI), was formed under Abdallah Mohamed Kamil, an Afar notary. Following a popular referendum held in May 1977, the territory became independent on 27 June, the last French African possession to attain independence. Hassan Gouled Aptidon, a senior Issa politician and leader of the LPAI, became the first President of the Republic. Ethnic balance was ensured by the appointment of an Afar as Prime Minister, a practice that still continues.

However, initial efforts to maintain a careful ethnic balance in government were not successful, as the first Afar appointees (Kamil followed later by Ahmed Dini Ahmed) believed that no real power was delegated to them. In March 1979 Gouled replaced the LPAI with a new political party, the Rassemblement populaire pour le progrès (RPP), to reinforce his control. The two principal Afar-dominated pre-independence parties responded by merging into a clandestine opposition movement, the Front démocratique pour la libération de Djibouti (FDLD).

In June 1981 the first presidential election was held; Gouled, as the sole candidate, received 84% of the popular vote and was thus elected for a further six-year term. The FDLD rejected the election results and demanded a return to democracy and the release of political prisoners. Soon afterwards a new opposition party, the Parti populaire djiboutien (PPD), was formed under the leadership of Afar leader, and former premier, Ahmed. The leadership was arrested in September and the party banned, but in October, following the adoption of legislation to establish a one-party state, the PPD leaders were released.

THE PERIOD OF TROUBLES

In January 1986 a bomb was exploded at the RPP headquarters, killing two people. The bombing and the subsequent assassination of a prominent local businessman were followed by intensive security operations, resulting in the arrest of more than 1,000 people. Evidence of open opposition to Gouled attracted wider international attention in May, when Aden Robleh Awalleh, a former government minister, was charged with conducting 'massive propaganda campaigns' against the RPP, and was expelled from the party. Awalleh fled to Ethiopia, where he announced the formation of a new opposition group, the Mouvement national djiboutien pour l'instauration de la démocratie (MNDID), with the stated aim of restoring a multi-party parliamentary democracy.

At the presidential election held in April 1987 Gouled, the sole candidate, received more than 90% of the votes cast. Concurrently, a single list of candidates for the legislature was endorsed by 87% of those voting. In November Gouled dissolved the Government and appointed a 16-member Council of Ministers.

In January 1990 the FDLD, the MNDID and independent members of the opposition merged to form the Union des mouvements démocratiques (UMD), whose declared aim was to 'unite all the ethnic groups and different political persuasions' and to resolve the 'chaotic situation' existing in the country. In May intra-ethnic strife erupted between the Issa and the Somali Gadabursi communities in the capital. Prior to the country's independence, the Gadabursi controlled a significant portion of Djibouti's local trade; this commercial advantage was quickly overcome after independence by prominent Issas, giving rise to resentment between the two groups. In June units of the Djibouti armed forces raided Tadjoura and arrested Afar who were suspected of involvement in the UMD.

At the fifth RPP congress, held in March 1991, the party declared that it would remain Djibouti's sole legal political organization. This rejection of political pluralism was widely interpreted as a sign of its increasing insecurity in response to mounting discontent among Djibouti's various clans and clan branches—especially the Afar—at their exclusion from political power.

CIVIL INSURRECTION

New challenges to Gouled's authority appeared in April 1991 with the formation of a new and powerful armed opposition group, the Front pour la restauration de l'unité et de la démocratie (FRUD), which comprised three militant Afar groups, under the leadership of Ahmed. In November the FRUD launched an insurrection, and by the end of the month controlled many towns and villages in the north of the country, while besieging Tadjoura and Obock, then held by the national army. The Government conscripted all men between 18 and 25 years of age, and requested military assistance from France (see below) to repel what it described as external aggression by soldiers loyal to deposed President Mengistu Haile Mariam of Ethiopia. The FRUD denied that it constituted a foreign aggressor (although many of its officers had received training in Ethiopian military camps), claiming that its aim was to achieve political parity for all ethnic groups.

In December 1991 Gouled stated that a national referendum regarding proposed changes in the system of government would be held, but only when the 'external aggressors' had been expelled from the country. Under pressure from France and African leaders to halt a conflict that affected the economies of the region, Gouled appointed a committee to draft a new constitution, intended to provide for a plural political system. Following a meeting in January 1992 with senior French officials, the FRUD agreed to open a dialogue with the Government, based on an immediate bilateral cease-fire and progress on the promised democratic reforms. The Government, however, continued to insist that the FRUD was controlled by foreign interests, describing its military activities as an 'invasion' and responded to French mediation attempts with complaints that France had failed to honour its defence agreement. By late January the Government had lost control of most of northern Djibouti, with its garrisons in Tadjourah and Obock receiving supplies by sea across the Gulf of Tadjourah.

Attempts by France at achieving a rapprochement appeared to be more successful in February 1992, when, following meetings with the FRUD and the Djibouti Government, it was announced that the FRUD would declare a cease-fire and that France would deploy troops from its Djibouti garrison as a peace-keeping force in the north.

Constitutional Manoeuvres

A presidential commission on constitutional reform submitted its report in March 1992, and in April Gouled announced his plans for reform, which, while conceding the principle of political pluralism, proposed few other changes and retained a strong executive presidency. The proposals were rejected by the opposition, which demanded the holding of a national constitutional conference, and by the FRUD; however, the proposed reforms were cautiously welcomed by France. The President announced that the reforms would be determined in a national referendum and that legislative elections would follow. In late June Gouled declared that the referendum would be held in early September, followed by the introduction of a multi-party system in mid-September. Legislative elections were scheduled for November.

In July 1992 Gouled granted pardons to a number of opposition figures, including Awalleh, the exiled leader of the Parti national démocratique (PND), and the leader of the Front des forces démocratiques, Omar Elmi Khaireh. However, in the same month Ali Aref Bourhan, who had been France's choice as premier during most of the period 1960–76, and five others (who had been arrested for treason in January 1991) were sentenced to 10 years' imprisonment. Others among the 47 accused received prison sentences of up to six years. The Government sustained another defection in August with the announcement that Elaf Orbiss Ali, an Afar, had resigned as Minister of Labour, in protest against the continuing civil war and deteriorating economic situation, and was joining the Front uni de l'opposition djiboutienne (FUOD), a coalition of opposition parties, including the FRUD.

The draft Constitution prepared by Gouled was approved by referendum on 4 September 1992, with 96.8% voting in favour, according to the Ministry of the Interior, which claimed a voter turn-out of 75.2%. A proposition to restrict the number of political parties to four was also approved. However, with two-thirds of the country controlled by the FRUD, which had urged its supporters to boycott the referendum, and no independent observers present, the voting figures were received with some scepticism, notably by France, which refused to endorse the results. The referendum nevertheless facilitated the registration of political parties and the holding of multi-party elections, which were scheduled for December.

Attempts by France to foster negotiations between the Government and the FRUD appeared to have achieved success following the announcement in November 1992 that representatives of the two sides were to meet for the first time, under French auspices. However, the meeting was cancelled at short notice by the Government, which claimed that the FRUD had failed to honour preconditions, including the release of prisoners of war. In late November France withdrew its troops from northern Djibouti, where they had acted as a buffer between government and rebel forces.

With the opposition largely excluded from the process, elections were held on 18 December 1992, monitored by observers from France, the Organization of African Unity (OAU, now the African Union) and the League of Arab States (Arab League). The RPP won all 65 seats in the Assemblée nationale and 76.7% of the popular vote. Only the Parti pour le renouveau démocratique (PRD) contested the elections, taking one-third of the votes cast in the capital; The army claimed a series of successes during February and March 1993, recapturing FRUD strongholds in the south of the country and severing the rebels' supply routes to the sea. Nevertheless, the FRUD achieved a propaganda victory with its first guerrilla attack on the capital in mid-March.

Gouled reorganized the Council of Ministers in February 1993, preserving a careful ethnic balance, with Issa ministers receiving eight portfolios, and Afar representatives seven, with one portfolio each held by representatives of three other minorities. Five candidates stood in Djibouti's first contested presidential election, which was held on 7 May: Gouled himself, Mohamed Farah Elabe (for the PRD), Awalleh (PND) and two independents, Mohamed Moussa Ali 'Tourtour' (of the still proscribed Mouvement pour l'unité et la démocratie, but not representing his party) and Ahmed Ibrahim Abdi. The level of electoral participation was low (at 49.9% of those registered to vote), suggesting an Afar boycott. Official results indicated that Gouled received 60.8% of the votes cast, followed by Elabe (22.0%), Awalleh (12.3%), 'Tourtour' (3.0%) and Abdi (2.0%). The opposition alleged that there had been widespread electoral fraud.

During the electoral period, continuing pressure from the national army and internal disputes seriously weakened the Afar forces, and in 1994 the two sides signed a peace agreement. Some minor Afar groups, having rejected the agreement, made their peace with the Government in 2000. Ahmed returned from exile in France and led the opposition until his death in 2004.

Meanwhile, the health of the ageing Gouled began to decline seriously in 1995. In February 1999 he announced that he would not stand in the April 1999 presidential election, by which time his security chief (and nephew), Ismail Omar Gelleh, had organized his own power base in the RPP. Opposition leaders abstained from the election, and Gelleh secured an easy victory, taking 74.4% of the votes cast. Gouled died in November 2006.

DOMESTIC POLITICS UNDER PRESIDENT GELLEH

Shortly after his election, Gelleh pledged to continue the process of political decentralization and to accelerate the reintegration of demobilized soldiers. In mid-May 1999 Gelleh reappointed Barkat Gourad Hamadou as Prime Minister; a new Council of Ministers was announced shortly afterwards. In March 2000 the RPP convened its eighth congress, at which its 170-member central committee agreed to the formation of three party commissions (covering discipline, internal co-operation and press communications) in an attempt to enhance the ruling party's performance. Gelleh was also elected to the presidency of the RPP ensuring he retained his position of power. After a long period of ill-health, Djibouti's Prime Minister Gourad announced his retirement on 4 March 2001, having held the position for 22 years. His successor Dileita Mohamed Dileita immediately took his place. This appointment was seen as a further gesture to Afar hard-liners because Dileita had been one of Ahmed's most trusted advisers.

President Gelleh failed to improve Djibouti's unfavourable human rights reputation, especially with regard to the media and opposition leaders. According to the annual US Report on Human Rights Practices published in March 2007, Djibouti's human rights record 'remained poor'. The report noted electoral abuses, harsh prison conditions, official impunity, arbitrary arrest and detention, prolonged pre-trial detention, interference with privacy rights and restrictions on freedom of press, assembly and association. Other actions include police actions against demonstrators and strikers, continued discrimination against women, ethnic and clan groups and policies directed at trade unions and harassment of union leaders. In March 2007 the Government arrested Jean-Paul Noël Abdi, the Director of the Djibouti League of Human Rights, for falsely accusing a presidential bodyguard of rape. He was sentenced to six months' imprisonment and fined US $350.

Meanwhile, in early September 2002, to coincide with the 10th anniversary of the approval of the Constitution, the Government removed the constitutional limit (previously fixed at four) on the number of permitted political parties. On 10 January 2003 nine parties, organized into two blocs, contested the legislative elections. According to official results, the Union pour la majorité présidentielle (UMP), a coalition comprising the RPP, the FRUD, the PND and the Parti populaire social démocrate, secured 62.7% of the total votes cast, winning the majority of the votes in each of the country's five constituencies, and, thus, in accordance with the electoral laws, took all 65 seats in the Assemblée nationale. Therefore, despite obtaining 37.3% of the votes cast, the opposition Union pour l'alternance démocratique (UAD) coalition, headed by Ahmed, failed to secure any legislative representation. The day after the election the UAD protested against the results, claiming that it should have won 22 seats, and demanded that the elections be annulled. However, in mid-February the Constitutional Council rejected the coalition's request.

In mid-February 2005 trade union leaders criticized a proposed new labour code, approved by the Council of Ministers, which would require trade unions to be authorized by the Attorney-General, the Labour Inspectorate and the Ministries of the Interior and Decentralization, Justice, Muslim and Penal Affairs, and Human Rights and Labour and Vocational Training. The proposals would also grant the Attorney-General the authority to dissolve a trade union should one of the above ministries issue such a request. It has been reported that since the code entered into force in January 2006 a number of prominent trade union activists have been detained by the security services. Attention has also been drawn to the lack of press freedom and the Government's refusal to relinquish its monopoly on radio and television broadcasting, especially with regard to statements by opposition political parties.

In mid-February 2005 the UAD announced that it would not participate in the presidential election, scheduled to be held in early April, primarily because President Gelleh had rejected UAD demands to establish an independent national electoral commission composed of equal numbers of government and opposition members and to sanction free and fair access to the media by opposition political parties. As a result, Mohamed Daoud Chehem, the President of the Parti djiboutien pour le démocratie (PDD), which had been a member of the UAD coalition, announced that he would contest the presidency. Chehem criticized the UAD's boycott of the election, claiming that it would help Gelleh remain in power; however, he eventually withdrew from the election, citing 'government harassment and lack of transparency'. On 10 March the FRUD released a statement indicating that free and fair voting was 'almost impossible' and called on France and the USA to support a 'democratic transition in Djibouti'. On 8 April Gelleh, who was the sole candidate, won 100% of the vote in the country's presidential election, thus enabling him to serve a second and final six-year presidential term. According to official figures, some 78.9% of the country's estimated 197,000 registered voters cast their ballot; however, officials declared about 5.7% of the votes cast void. All opposition parties had boycotted the election and characterized the results as 'ridiculous, rigged and rubbish'. Nevertheless, observers from the Arab League reported that the polling stations had been improved and that the election had been peaceful.

REFUGEES AND RELIEF OPERATIONS

According to estimates by the office of the UN High Commissioner for Refugees (UNHCR), in 2005 Djibouti sheltered some 25,000 Somali refugees and a limited number of Ethiopian refugees in camps at Ali Addeh and Hol-Hol, south of Djibouti town. UNHCR continues to co-ordinate the voluntary departure of refugees from Somalia and Ethiopia. Djibouti government officials insist that there remain tens of thousands of economic migrants in Djibouti.

In late July 2004 the Djibouti Government, ostensibly for security and economic reasons, ordered all illegal immigrants to leave the country by the end of August or face forcible expulsion. Given the magnitude of the operation, the Government was forced to postpone the deadline until 15 September, by which time some 80,000 foreign nationals, primarily from Eritrea, Ethiopia, Somalia and Yemen, had left Djibouti. While most illegal immigrants departed voluntarily, a number sought protection among the thousands of refugees in UNHCR's Hol-Hol and Ali Addeh camps. The International Federation of Human Rights denounced the mass expulsion and accused the US Administration of engineering the deportations as part of its 'war on terrorism'. Other observers suggested that Gelleh ordered the expulsions in order to reduce unemployment in preparation for the presidential election of April 2005.

EXTERNAL RELATIONS

Owing to its geographical position, the maintenance of peaceful relations with Eritrea, Ethiopia and Somalia remains a vital consideration in Djibouti's foreign policy. Gouled artfully avoided the enticements of Somali President Maj.-Gen. Mohamed Siad Barre to join with the Somali Republic in the months following Djibouti's independence. After the collapse of the Siad Barre regime in 1991, the Somali state disintegrated. The 'Republic of Somaliland' (the former British Somaliland) soon declared itself independent in an effort to negate the decision to affiliate with the former UN Trust territory (Italian Somaliland) in 1960; the north-eastern region of 'Puntland' declared itself autonomous, while chronic anarchy characterized much of the south. Djibouti's major concern was with

'Somaliland', with which it shares a border. During the early 1990s relations between the two deteriorated, following numerous border clashes and the establishment of contacts between the 'Somaliland' authorities and the FRUD. In June 1996, however, Djibouti and 'Somaliland' concluded a 10-point agreement, which included provisions for co-operation on border security and the establishment of trade relations. In November 1997 Djibouti granted the republic official recognition, and shortly afterwards 'Somaliland' established a liaison bureau in Djibouti.

At the seventh Intergovernmental Authority on Development (IGAD) conference, which was held in Djibouti in November 1999, Gelleh announced his proposal to hold a Somali national reconciliation conference in Djibouti. This alarmed the leaders of 'Somaliland', which opposed attempts to recreate a unified Somali state, and they expressed their vehement opposition to the plan. The day after the IGAD conference 'Somaliland' closed its border with Djibouti and deployed troops to the Loyada border crossing. The border was reopened the following month. In April 2000, however, relations deteriorated again after 'Somaliland' refused to allow a Djiboutian delegation to leave its aircraft after landing in Hargeisa, and on the following day 'Somaliland' closed its border with Djibouti. In response, the Djiboutian authorities closed the 'Somaliland' liaison office in Djibouti town and ordered the 'Somaliland' representative to leave the country. 'Somaliland' officials justified their actions by claiming that Djibouti was encouraging ethnic violence and was responsible for a series of bombings in Hargeisa. In late May 2001 91.7% of the voters in 'Somaliland' approved a new constitution for the territory. At the time, some political associates of President Egal voiced anti-Djibouti sentiments causing tensions between pro- and anti-Egal factions in Djibouti's Issa community. Nevertheless, in mid-October Djibouti and 'Somaliland' concluded several bilateral agreements, notably pledging to cease hostile propaganda, to facilitate the movement of goods and people across the common border, and to enhance mutual security. Following the death of President Egal in May 2002, Gelleh quickly established cordial relations with the new President of 'Somaliland', Dahir Riyale Kahin. Djibouti and 'Somaliland' subsequently agreed to relocate the border crossing between the two countries back to Loyada; to work together to repatriate 'Somaliland' refugees from Djibouti; to improve trade relations; to strengthen bilateral co-operation; and to establish a committee to resolve existing and future disputes. However, it remains to be seen whether Djibouti and 'Somaliland' can successfully stabilize their contentious border.

Meanwhile, the Somali national reconciliation conference, the 13th such reconciliation effort to have been attempted since the fall of Siad Barre, opened in early May 2000 at Arta, about 40 km west of Djibouti town. Some 2,000 Somali delegates attended the proceedings and in late August established a Government-in-exile. In September President Gelleh sought to convince the UN General Assembly to provide support to the embryonic Somali Transitional National Government (TNG). In November Gelleh made a similar appeal at the summit meeting of the Organization of the Islamic Conference in Qatar.

In October 2002 the 'Arta group' and a number of other Somali politicians restarted the national reconciliation process in Eldoret, Kenya, under the auspices of IGAD, which includes Djibouti, Ethiopia, Kenya, Uganda, Somalia, Sudan and Eritrea. By mid-2003 there was no indication of any genuine progress in the Eldoret process. In May Djibouti pledged to send an envoy to reconcile differences between various TNG officials. In October 2003 Djibouti threatened to withdraw from the Somali peace talks because of Kenyan and Ethiopian 'high-handedness'; however, the USA reportedly persuaded Djibouti to remain engaged in the Eldoret process. Also that month Kahin visited Djibouti and agreed to reopen the 'Somaliland' diplomatic office in Djibouti and the two states signed several security agreements. In January 2004 'Puntland', which disputes 'Somaliland's' claim to the Sool and Sanaag provinces, accused Djibouti of providing weapons to Kahin's administration. Djibouti rejected the accusation.

Following the removal of Ethiopia's President Mengistu Haile Mariam, in May 1991, Djibouti re-established good relations with the successor transitional Government. During 1991–96 relations between Ethiopia and Djibouti focused primarily on economic development projects. In March 1997 the two countries pledged to fight against smuggling, drugs-trafficking and other cross-border crimes along their common frontier. During a visit to Addis Ababa in May, Gouled held discussions with the Prime Minister of Ethiopia, Meles Zenawi, on increasing co-operation between IGAD members and on the effect of Djibouti's demobilization programme on Ethiopia's Ogaden region. It was feared that a massive influx of Issa warriors from Djibouti could destabilize the region further. In August the two countries pledged to enhance co-operation in matters concerning foreign affairs, trade and industry, education, culture and immigration. In November Djiboutian and Ethiopian officials affirmed their intention to increase bilateral trade. President Gouled, in his capacity as the current Chairman of IGAD, visited Ethiopia and Eritrea in May 1998 to mediate in the border dispute between the two countries; Gouled's efforts proved unsuccessful.

The Eritrean–Ethiopian border dispute, which erupted into open warfare in June 1998, had a beneficial impact on Djibouti, largely because it resulted in the rerouting of Ethiopian military and non-military imports via Djibouti port. There were allegations, which the Djiboutian Government denied, that Ethiopian military forces had operated in Djibouti as part of its campaign against Eritrea. Other reports suggested that Ethiopian troops had been deployed to Yoboki, an area some 50 km inside Djibouti, to prevent attacks against Ethiopian truck convoys returning from Djibouti port. In November 1999 President Gelleh began a four-day visit to Ethiopia, during which he held meetings with President Negasso Gidada, Meles and several other Ethiopian ministers. Apart from pledging the full integration of the economies of the two countries, Gelleh and Meles released a joint statement, which expressed 'grave concern' about terrorist activities along their common border and laid the groundwork for greater security co-operation. In December Djibouti and Ethiopia concluded a military co-operation protocol, whereby Ethiopia agreed to provide maintenance, spare parts and equipment for the Djiboutian air force. In October 2001 Djibouti and Ethiopia created a joint council, which was to meet twice annually to promote commercial relations and resolve trade disputes. In December bilateral relations temporarily deteriorated after Djibouti increased handling charges at Djibouti port by more than 150%; the Ethiopian authorities rejected the tariff changes, claiming that they violated a 1999 trade agreement between the two countries. A subsequent visit by Ethiopian officials convinced Djibouti to reduce the increase from a proposed $2.50 per metric ton to US $2 per ton.

By late 2001 it was evident that Djibouti and Ethiopia were sharply divided over Somalia. Djibouti supported Somalia's TNG, while Ethiopia opposed the re-establishment of any strong central administration in Somalia.

Relations with Eritrea improved after the resolution of the border dispute between the two countries in 1998 and the restoration of diplomatic relations in 2000. In January 2002 an Eritrean delegation, led by the Minister of Foreign Affairs, arrived in Djibouti to attend a meeting of the countries' Joint Ministerial Commission. In December Afewerki visited Djibouti and, during talks with Gelleh, reportedly reached an agreement regarding anti-terrorism. In February 2004 the second Eritrea-Djibouti Joint Ministerial Commission meeting opened in the Eritrean capital, Asmara. Commission members held discussions on a number of themes, including foreign relations, security, transport, telecommunications, trade, maritime resources, agriculture and tourism.

Franco-Djiboutian relations historically have been vital to the latter's security and economic well-being. In late June 2002 President Gelleh informed France that Djibouti wished to modify the defence agreement between the two countries (concluded in 1999) by annulling provisions that allowed French forces to use Djibouti's port and international airport at no cost. In October Gelleh met with President Jacques Chirac, who acknowledged Djibouti's growing strategic importance as a result of the 'war on terror' (see below), but refused to acquiesce to Gelleh's demand to alter the defence agreement. Nevertheless, Gelleh asked Chirac for €20m. to erase the arrears of the civil service. Chirac agreed to review the amount of aid France granted Djibouti. French officials also implored Djibouti to join the Organisation de l'harmonisation en Afrique du droit des affaires (OHADA) in order to make the business environment safer for French companies and to maintain Djibouti's financial standing. Djibouti, demurred, stating that as OHADA primarily represented West Africa's French-speaking nations, Djibouti preferred to remain within the Common Market for Eastern and Southern Africa (COMESA). France eventually agreed to implement a 'new mechanism' for increasing its contribution to the Djiboutian treasury, but stressed that this did not represent payment for the use of Djiboutian military facilities. In May 2003 Djibouti announced that it had reached a 10-year agreement with France whereby the latter would provide it with €30m. annually. Under the agreement, the Djiboutian armed forces would receive €5m., while the remainder would be used to finance development projects. In August Djibouti and France signed a military agreement that defined the status of the French military garrison in Djibouti.

The so-called Borrel affair continues to disrupt relations between the two countries. Bernard Borrel, a French judge attached to the Djibouti Ministry of Justice, disappeared and was later found dead in suspicious circumstances in 1995. The Djibouti authorities declared that he had committed suicide, but in 2002 a French magistrate concluded that this ruling was 'implausible'. Some French intelligence sources allegedly accused President Gelleh, who was head of the security services at the time of Borrel's disappearance, of involvement in his murder. In April 2004 Gelleh charged the French Government with organizing an anti-Djiboutian media campaign to embarrass and weaken his Government. The French Government eventually released a statement denouncing reports in the French press and withdrew accusations that Gelleh had been involved in the murder. In late 2004 Borrel's wife succeeded in persuading the French authorities to reopen the case. Sophia Clement, a Paris magistrate, rejected an earlier finding that Borrel had committed suicide and accepted the theory that the judge had been murdered. In early January 2005 the French Cour d'appel summoned Hassan Said, the chief of Djibouti's security services, to determine whether he had suppressed evidence from Mohammed Alkhoumekani, a key witness who belonged to the Presidential Guard. Alkhoumekani testified that Gelleh, then the presidential chief of staff, and a number of other senior officials had stated that Borrel had been assassinated. The Djiboutian Government rejected this testimony on the grounds that France lacked jurisdiction in Djibouti. It did, however, respond by closing the local transmitter of Radio France Internationale. Nevertheless, the French Cour d'appel refused to exclude the possibility of issuing international arrest warrants against the suspects or summoning President Gelleh. In mid-January 2006 Djibouti requested that the International Court of Justice, based in The Hague, Netherlands, intervene in the affair following suggestions by French investigators that Borrel could have been assassinated.

In July 2004 Michèle Alliot-Marie, then French Minister of Defence, visited Djibouti to confirm the agreement made in August 2003 under which France would pay €30m. per year to secure usage of Djiboutian military facilities for the 2,850 French troops stationed in the country for the next nine years. The payment replaced all taxes on goods imported by the French forces and the income tax (totalling some €18m.) paid by French military personnel. It was reported that Djibouti's economy would benefit by up to €40m. annually for serving the French base and from the spending of French military personnel. Furthermore, it was rumoured that France was to double its annual military assistance contribution to Djibouti to €10m., in addition to providing some €25m. in bilateral aid per year.

In January 2005 the President of 'Somaliland', Dahir Riyale Kahin, met with President Gelleh and other Djiboutian officials and businessmen to discuss bilateral relations, illegal trade and the general security situation in the region. Although Kahin's reception included all the ceremonial symbols of an official visit by a foreign Head of State, Djibouti declined to extend diplomatic recognition to 'Somaliland'.

DJIBOUTI AND THE 'WAR ON TERROR'

Djibouti has long permitted relatively free access by friendly states to its airfield and port facilities. Although always cautious about any indication of supporting military actions against neighbouring states, it permitted the US Air Force to base C-130H gunships when they were deployed in Mogadishu, Somalia, in July–August 1993. The attacks on the World Trade Center in New York and the Pentagon in Washington, DC, on 11 September 2001 resulted in a significant enhancement of Djibouti's strategic importance to the USA and its allies. In early October Djibouti established a seven-member Comité national de lutte contre le terrorisme to monitor security conditions in Djibouti. Djibouti again agreed to grant access to its port and airfields as a base from which to monitor developments in Somalia, Sudan and other countries in the region. In mid-December 2002 the Combined Joint Task Force-Horn of Africa (CJTF-HOA) began operations in Djibouti to detect, disrupt and defeat transnational terrorism in conjunction with coalition partners across the region. In early May 2003 CJTF-HOA moved its headquarters to Camp Lemonier in Djibouti. There are now some 1,800 military personnel from Djibouti, Ethiopia, France, Germany, Italy, Kenya, the Republic of Korea, Romania, Spain, the United Kingdom and Yemen at Camp Lemonier. Germany, which remains one of the major coalition partners, initiated its participation in CJTF-HOA in January 2002, when it signed a memorandum of understanding with Djibouti regarding the status of its military and civilian personnel in Djibouti. The accord granted German military personnel access to Djibouti's port and airfields to conduct surveillance missions in the region, monitor sea traffic between Somalia and Yemen, and detect suspected al-Qa'ida and Taliban members fleeing Afghanistan. In March a senior US military commander visited Djibouti to discuss the 'war on terror' and the terrorist threat from Somalia. In May the USA announced that it would hand over the command of naval 'anti-terror' operations in the Horn of Africa to Germany. By mid-2004 Germany had three frigates, four supply ships, around 750 German sailors, and 150–200 other military personnel who operate a logistics support base. Despite the presence of this force, the German President, Johannes Rau, cancelled a scheduled visit to Djibouti in March because of a reported plot to assassinate him. The United Kingdom's presence in the region included HMS *Campbeltown*, which was assisting German navy observation aircraft with their daily aerial surveillance of the Indian Ocean waters off the Horn of Africa. Spain planned to deploy a P-3B surveillance aircraft to Djibouti, while France disclosed that it had dispatched two further ATL-2 surveillance aircraft to Djibouti to conduct patrol and intelligence missions in the sea off Oman and off the Somali coast. In December the US Secretary of Defense, Donald Rumsfeld, visited US forces in Djibouti.

In mid-January 2003 Gelleh and a number of Djiboutian ministers met US President George W. Bush and other senior US officials during a visit to Washington, DC. According to Gelleh, the USA agreed to provide US $8m. over the next two years for education and health projects in Djibouti and promised to reopen the US Agency for International Development office in the country. The following month Djibouti and the USA concluded an agreement that allowed US forces to use Djiboutian military installations. In recognition of its support of the 'war on terror', in late 2003 the USA announced that Djibouti would receive some $90m. worth of aid in 2003 and 2004, making Djibouti the largest recipient of development aid of any sub-Saharan African country. In earlier years aid had totalled only about $7m. annually.

In late December 2004 the Commander of CJTF-HOA claimed that terrorist organizations, including al-Qa'ida, were active in the Horn of Africa region. As a result, the USA believed there to be a terrorist threat in Djibouti because of its strategic location and the presence of a large number of US and coalition forces in the country. CJTF-HOA also maintains a very active civic action programme in the Horn of Africa. In Djibouti it has constructed school dormitories in Dikhil, improved the port facility in Obock, constructed several wells in the northern and southern areas of the country and surveyed the sea bottom in Djibouti's old port. In February 2006 it held a conference on 'religion as a force for peace' for religious leaders from Ethiopia, Kenya, Seychelles, the Comoros, Mauritius and Djibouti at Camp Lemonier. In May it was alleged that the command financed certain 'anti-terrorist' faction leaders in Mogadishu in order to pre-empt alleged al-Qa'ida activities in Somalia.

The Djiboutian Government does not wish to be associated with any US military actions directed against Somalia. In the wake of the Ethiopian successful campaign against the Union of Islamic Courts (UIC) in late 2006, President Gelleh asserted that no military operations were launched from Djibouti (it appeared that the C-130H gunships flew out of Ethiopia). In March 2007, after Ethiopian forces supported by US troops drove the UIC forces out of Somalia, President Gelleh was reported to have claimed that the Horn of Africa was no safer since the departure of the Islamists.

In an effort to maintain cordial relations with fellow members of the Arab League, Djiboutian diplomacy was particularly active throughout 2006 and early 2007. President Gelleh also attended the Beijing Summit of the Forum on China-Africa Cooperation in November 2006. In February 2007 two sports officials visited Cuba to discuss common interests.

Economy

THOMAS OFCANSKY

Revised by WALTER S. CLARKE

INTRODUCTION

Although a small resource-poor state populated by about 800,000 people, the Republic of Djibouti's strategic position at the southern mouth of the Red Sea during a period of heightened tension in the Middle East is bringing it new prosperity. It has developed significant financial support from Arab banks while permitting the deployment of US and European military forces on its soil. President Ismael Omar Gelleh proclaimed that 2007 would be the 'year of Djibouti' and announced that Djibouti intended to develop its port to be the most significant in eastern Africa. The World Bank, which published a comprehensive economic memorandum on Djibouti in August 2006, agreed that the economic and financial situations in the country were generally improving, but noted that a number of problems must be resolved if the country was to be able to achieve sustained growth. Despite recent positive developments, Djibouti remains one the 50 poorest countries in the world, with 74% of the population living on less than US $1 per day according to the UN World Food Programme.

There are a number of unique aspects to Djibouti's economic and financial system which have complicated its historical economic development. Alone among French colonies, it was decided in 1949 to tie Djibouti to the dollar zone: the Government of Ethiopia insisted that the US dollar be the currency used for the Djibouti–Addis Ababa railway and port; and the French Government hoped eventually to establish a tax-free trade zone in Djibouti. At the time, it was also difficult to persuade French *fonctionnaires* and military personnel to accept postings to the isolated colony, but currency instability in France following the Second World War made payment in dollars an attractive prospect.

Some of the results of this history were outlined in the 2006 World Bank economic memorandum: the country has very high civil service costs, about 10 times higher than in Ethiopia or Yemen; while the education and health standards are lower than Middle East or sub-Saharan averages. Only 55% of lower school age students (aged 6–11) complete their primary school education. Life expectancy is just 49 years, and infant mortality rates, at 85 per 1,000 live births, fall well below regional standards. According to the World Bank, the country's gross national income per head was about US $1,040, which would normally place it in the middle income countries bracket. However, it has some of the highest rates of illiteracy, morbidity and mother and infant mortality in the developing world. To break out of the low growth-high unemployment-high poverty trap, it is likely that Djibouti will need to increase private investment, improve efficiency in its public sector and lower its service delivery costs. About 84% of the country's inhabitants live in Djibouti town, making the country something of a 'city-state'. Unemployment in the town of Djibouti is estimated at 56%; there is little in the way of social services to alleviate poverty.

Other than a Coca-Cola bottling plant (which also bottles water), Djibouti has no real manufacturing capacity. The country is forced to rely upon its position astride the main Middle East-European maritime lines of communication to build a service economy which now contributes 70% of gross domestic product (GDP). Currently the focus of countries looking for a stable foothold in the Middle East region, Djibouti is dependent upon foreign assistance for over 80% of its public investment.

Djibouti's annual economic indicators are generally positive. GDP at market prices has increased annually from US $573.2m. in 2001 to an estimated $709m. in 2005. Real GDP growth increased from 1.9% in 2001 to an estimated 3.2% in 2005, while inflation in that year was low, at 3.2%, and was projected to decline to 2.5% in 2007. Djibouti's total external debt was an estimated $415m. at the end of 2005.

During 1995–2005 the population increased by an average of 2.7% per year (according to World Bank estimates), owing partly to the influx of refugees from Ethiopia and Somalia (although the population was expected to have decreased in 2004/05 due to the mass expulsion of foreign migrants). The last census in Djibouti was in 1983, and population estimates vary according to different sources.

A substantial share of the country's receipts are generated by the provision of services to the French military garrison (with about 2,850 men in November 2006) and the US base at Camp Lemonier (about 1,800 men and women). Revenues from the military presence contributed 2% of GDP in 2001, but rose to 6.3% in 2004, a figure that the World Bank estimated would remain fairly constant over the next 10 years.

TRANSPORT AND TRADE

Before the Ogaden war began in 1977, when the Victorian era narrow-gauge railway was among the first targets of Somali insurgents, nearly all of the colony's fresh food was imported from Ethiopia. The railway has not been well maintained, but Ethiopia and Djibouti agreed to grant a concession to the private sector to attempt to restore it to a competitive standard in the international freight market. In July 2004 the Chemin de Fer Djibouti-Ethiopien board of directors asked six companies to submit bids to manage and operate the railway. The firms included Transnet (South Africa), Comazar (South Africa), Rail India Technical and Economic Services, Africa Initiative 2020 (USA), Canac (USA), and Dubai International (which already manages Djibouti's port, airport, and the industrial and commercial free-trade zone). The Djibouti Government stated that the railway's privatization and upgraded infrastructure would increase cargo capacity from the current estimated 240,000 metric tons per year to 1.5m. tons per year. A European Union (EU) loan of €40m. to upgrade the sections of the track most in need of repair was awarded in 2006. At a meeting in Addis Ababa in March 2006 the Djibouti Minister of Equipment and Transport and his Ethiopian counterpart reaffirmed their commitment to modernizing the railway, and announced that Comazar had been awarded a contract to manage the railway for 25 years.

Because of the inefficiency and high costs of both the railway and Djibouti's port, the Government of Ethiopia gradually shifted its trade to Massawa and Assab (both now in Eritrea) during the 1970s and 1980s, with only around 10% of its trade being processed through Djibouti. The violent border dispute between Ethiopia and Eritrea in mid-1998 resulted in a substantial and immediate increase in activity at Djibouti port after Ethiopia stopped using the Eritrean ports. In the first three months of the conflict Djibouti port handled almost as much cargo as it did during 1997. During the first 11 months of 1998 Ethiopian imports via Djibouti port increased by 370%, while exports grew by 113%. In 1998 Ethiopia leased additional storage capacity in the port area to facilitate the delivery of some 1.6m. metric tons of cargo a year. To cope with the increased traffic, the Government invested considerable sums to upgrade port facilities; more than 1,000 additional workers were hired and the port was opened 24 hours a day. There were problems, however, as local importers experienced delays in the clearing of their shipments because Ethiopian imports received priority, and the lack of space for lorries, containers and storage delayed the processing and onward shipment of imports. In February 2000 Djibouti announced that the shipment of Ethiopian goods through Djibouti port had doubled to an annual total of 4m. tons since mid-1998, and during January–November 2000 the port handled 3.7m. tons of cargo, 2.8m. tons of which was transit trade with Ethiopia. Ethiopia's increased use of the port, however, caused some friction between the two countries. In October 1999 the Ethiopian authorities refused to allow Ethiopian petroleum importers to pay an increase of US $1 per ton on petroleum tariffs. During a visit to Ethiopia in November President Gelleh reduced the tariff to $0.50 per ton; however, tensions remained regarding the activities of Djiboutian and Ethiopian import-export and forwarding agents. Despite these problems, increased Ethiopian use of the port convinced Djibouti officials to launch a $15m. expansion programme, which was expected to triple the handling of the port's yard capacity.

In April 2000 the UN started work on a US $2.7m. expansion programme, which was to increase the port's handling capacity from 100,000 metric tons to 147,000 tons per month. In May the Dubai Ports Authority (DPA) signed a 20-year contract to manage Djibouti port. The agreement also empowered the DPA to develop Djibouti's free-trade zone. The DPA claimed that the agreement would boost the port's handling capacity from 125,000 tons to 300,000 tons per year by improving container facilities. The DPA also announced that it planned to implement a $2m. computerization and training scheme. In an attempt to attract foreign investors, Djibouti issued tax exemptions to several companies, including the Société d'Exploration du Lac, which received permission to import $8.5m. worth of equipment tax-free. Other companies that took advantage of the concessions included Trans African Transit Service and Djibouti Dry Port, both connected to Djibouti port. In mid-October President Gelleh announced the completion of a $1.64m. upgrade of the port at Tadjoura. According to Gelleh, the project reflected his determination to facilitate trade with the northern part of the country and his commitment to the decentralization of the economy. From July 2003 there was an increase in the number of companies forwarding freight to Ethiopia with a number of new companies, including Taran Transit Services, Continental Transit Services and Al Amana Transit Services, establishing businesses in Djibouti. The Djibouti Global Transit and Shipping Company concentrated on other port and airport activities, while the Djibouti Maritime Management Investment Company focused on port operations, supplying ships and operating fish farms.

In mid-December 2000 tensions between Djibouti and Ethiopia resurfaced after Djibouti, acting on a DPA recommendation, announced a significant increase in the tariffs applied to goods entering the port. Ethiopia strenuously objected to the increase in fees, from US $1 to $2.50 per metric ton for cargo in transit, and in February 2001, following discussions between the Ethiopian and Djibouti authorities, the two countries reached an agreement that the new charge would be $2 per ton, while the previous flat rate of $1 per ton on fertilizer, medicines and fuel would remain unchanged. According to the Djibouti port authority, there was a 14% increase in transit traffic at Djibouti port during the first six months of 2001. In July President Gelleh approved new legislation barring foreign companies from undertaking handling and transit operations in Djibouti port. As a result, foreign companies would have to carry out such operations in conjunction with Djiboutian business partners. Critics believed this legislation reflected the determination of Djibouti and Ethiopia to enforce a monopoly on the port's handling and transit operations and claimed that the main beneficiaries of the legislation would be the Compagnie Maritime et de Manutention de Djibouti, which was owned by members of Djibouti's political élite, and Ethiopia's state-owned Maritime and Transit Services Enterprise. There are also social consequences to the modernization of the ports; with increased containerization in the old port, and improved handling of liquid products at Dorale, many longshoremen are being made redundant. This predominantly affects the mainly Afar port labourers and several union leaders were imprisoned in 2006 as a consequence of their protest actions.

The Djibouti Government is very proud of its strategic financial relationship with the Persian Gulf Emirates. In 2005 the DPA received a 21-year contract to run Djibouti's customs service. In 2004 Jebel Ali Free Zone International was provided with a 30-year franchise to manage Djibouti's free-trade zone. Through a subsidiary, the Emirates National Oil Company, it is constructing the Dorale petroleum terminal and has also signalled its intention to invest US $300m. (equal to one-half of the country's annual GDP) in a new deep-water port and free zone. The $533m. refinery is expected to produce 100,000 barrels per day of petroleum, kerosene and liquified petroleum gas (LPG). In March 2006, using a $21.3m. facility from the Emirates Bank, Horizon Djibouti Terminals Ltd announced that it would expand its petroleum, chemicals and LPG storage area in the Djibouti port by 50%.

In 2001 the Government issued a decree providing for the principle of 'open skies' for access to its international airport, eliminating any restrictions on frequencies and destinations. In June 2002 the airport was privatized, with a 20-year management contract accorded to Dubai Ports International. The airport has only one bonded warehouse, which appears inadequate for current and anticipated needs. The airport is shared with military flights; according to the World Bank, in the first quarter of 2003 there were 3,332 commercial flights and 913 military movements.

Djibouti's place in the Horn of Africa and the world will certainly be broadened if a dramatic project announced to build a bridge to cross the Red Sea is brought to fruition. In April 2007 Middle East Development LLC (MED), a Dubai-based developer, announced that it had agreed with Noor City Development Corporation in Napa, USA, to plan, develop, construct and manage a bridge between Yemen and Djibouti. The first phase in the construction will be to build a 3.5-km bridge from the Yemeni mainland to Perim island in the Bab el Mandeb. The second phase comprised the construction of a 13-km suspension bridge and an 8-km girder bridge from Perim to the Djibouti mainland. The total cost of the connection between continents is estimated by MED to be US $10,000m.–$20,000m. and is expected to take up to nine years to complete. The ultimate goal of the project is to facilitate the movement of goods and services between the two continents.

At the end of 2004 Djibouti's trade deficit was US $197.8m. and this figure had increased to $216.8m. by March 2006. In 2003 the principal sources of imports were Saudi Arabia (20.2%), Ethiopia (11.2%), the People's Republic of China (9.5%), France (6.7%), and the United Kingdom (5.2%). The principal markets for exports in 2003 were Somalia (61.4%), Yemen (21.7%), Pakistan (6.0%), Ethiopia (4.8%), and the Republic of Ireland (1.0%). The principal imports in 2002 were food and beverages (31.2%), petroleum products (14.5%), qat—a mild narcotic leaf—(10.4%), and machinery and electrical appliances (8.7%). The principal exports in 2002 included re-exports (81.5%) and locally produced goods (18.5%) which included basic manufactures, food and live animals, and coffee and derivatives.

Approximately 11–12 metric tons of qat arrive from Ethiopia each day and are subsequently transported throughout Djibouti. The Société Générale d'Importation de Khat, has exclusive control of the trade. In March 2005 a report by the International Development Association (IDA) estimated that the purchase of qat consumes about 30% of family income. The well-regulated trade, which amounts to about 4,000 tons per year, produces substantial revenues for the Government.

RELATIONS WITH DONORS

Djibouti has been working with the IMF since the mid-1990s, with stand-by arrangements between 1996–1999, and with a Poverty Reduction and Growth Facility (PRGF), from 1999 to 2002. According to the IMF, these programmes made it possible to stabilize fiscal revenue, improve fiscal spending and cut back on the country's significant fiscal arrears. In May 2003 a Djiboutian delegation visited Washington, DC, to negotiate an agreement with the IMF that would not involve drawing on IMF funds that had attached conditions. The Djibouti authorities hoped to avoid taking on difficult commitments because of dramatic increases in French and US aid (see below). However, President Gelleh subsequently reversed his decision not to negotiate with the IMF after he learned that the absence of an IMF agreement could jeopardize budgetary support from other donors (France's 2003 pledge of €3m. in budgetary support had been conditional on an IMF agreement). In July Gelleh therefore received an IMF delegation to discuss several issues, including the country's next poverty reduction strategy paper. In June the World Bank approved a US $12m. grant from IDA to help Djibouti implement medical campaigns against HIV/AIDS, malaria and tuberculosis. Public-sector agencies, private and non-governmental organizations, and community-based organizations will support projects for the prevention and treatment of the diseases and for the care of sufferers. An IMF structural reform programme, designed to facilitate growth, did not reach its goals and did not stimulate employment or reduce poverty. As a consequence, in 2004 Djibouti began a staff-monitored programme with the Fund. The results of the first year did not achieve the goals established in the programme, and Djibouti negotiated a new agreement with the IMF in which it pledged to achieve two consecutive quarters of satisfactory performance in order to qualify for a new PRGF. Among the commitments made to the IMF, the Government pledged to revise the country's investment code, draft new commercial and labour codes and restructure the electricity and water industries.

Djibouti is a member of the African Development Bank (ADB), the IMF, the Islamic Development Bank (IDB), the World Bank and its affiliate, the International Finance Corpn, and receives considerable financial support from these organizations. In March 2002 the ADB concluded a number of agreements with Djibouti worth a total of US $7.22m. Two loans were aimed at reducing poverty, by promoting good governance, improving the legal framework for business and facilitating civil society's participation in development, and at the improvement of women's rights, while a further two grants focused on an institutional capacity-building project for the good governance of public finances and strengthening the ability of government departments, civil society organizations and the media to promote women's rights and advocacy programmes. These four projects brought the ADB's total commitment to Djibouti to some $109m. In early 2004 the ADB announced that it had approved a $10m. loan to help finance a $30m. project to build new bulk terminal facilities at Djibouti port.

Despite the steady reduction in French aid levels from the late 1990s onwards, France remains Djibouti's largest bilateral donor. Aside from the aid issue, the presence of the French military garrison in Djibouti continued to be of importance to both countries. In October 1999 the French army announced the cessation of further troop withdrawals. In May 2003 Djibouti announced that it had reached a 10-year agreement with France whereby the latter would provide it with €30m. annually. According to the terms of the agreement, the Djiboutian armed forces would receive €5m., while the remainder would be used to finance development projects. In 2004 France provided public development aid of some €20m. (compared with €22m. in 2002); €9m. of this amount represented intervention credits, 75% of which was to be used in the education, health and institutional sectors. The remaining 25% was for university study grants. Military co-operation accounted for €3.8m. worth of direct aid (deployment and payment of overseas workers, mission operations and internships). The French contribution to Djibouti through the EU was an estimated €1.6m. Police co-operation has been reduced to two technical assistants (one in airport security and the other as an adviser to the Djiboutian director of police). Franco-Djiboutian co-operation in the 'war on terror' involved port security, aerial and border surveillance, airport patrols, and the training of intelligence and anti-terrorist personnel.

In late July 2003 the US Agency for International Development (USAID) reopened its office in Djibouti town and announced plans to spend US $5m. on educational projects and $10m. on health projects during 2003. USAID also financed the construction of a livestock export centre near the village of Damerjog, south of Djibouti town. A private company was to manage the centre, which envisaged the export of 35,000–40,000 head of livestock annually. Eventually, some 200,000 head of livestock will be exported annually.

Djibouti is an eligible member of the Africa Growth and Opportunity Act that grants preferential access to the US market. Since the USAID office in Djibouti was reopened, the country has become the largest beneficiary of USAID assistance in Africa. Djibouti concluded bilateral investment agreements with Egypt, Ethiopia, India, Iran, Malaysia, and Yemen. Djibouti also concluded a partnership agreement with the members of the African, Caribbean and Pacific Group of States; an agreement for Promotion, Protection and Guarantee of Investment among member states of the Organization of the Islamic Conference; Articles of Agreement of the Islamic Corporation for the Insurance of Investment and Export Credit; and the Unified Agreement for the Investment of Arab Capital in Arab States. As a result of these initiatives, foreign direct investment, which was negligible prior to 2002, reached US $51.7m. in 2004. The Economic Funds for Development is another government initiative that offers low-interest financing to facilitate the creation of small industries to service domestic and international markets. Other donors have funded a variety of projects, including the approval in September 2004 of a $13.5m. loan by the Arab Fund for Economic and Social Development, with additional funding from the Organization of the Petroleum Exporting Countries, to expand electricity generation. In the same month, Italy approved an $11.7m. loan to improve health and sanitary conditions and the US Trade and Development Agency financed a feasibility study for a water desalination project. In October the Kuwait Fund for Arabic Economic Development agreed to a $20m. loan for the construction of a road between Tadjourah and Obock. Djibouti also belongs to the Common Market for Eastern and Southern Africa.

AGRICULTURE, WATER AND ENERGY

There is little arable farming in Djibouti, as the land is mainly volcanic desert, one of the least hospitable and most unproductive terrains in Africa, and the country was able to produce only about 3% of its food requirements. About one-third of the population are pastoral nomads, herding goats, sheep and camels, with nearly all of the remaining population living in Djibouti town. In 1990 the IDB agreed to finance the construction of a fish-canning factory with an annual capacity of 1,500 metric tons. In March 2004 the Government established the Djibouti Maritime Management Investment Company to increase fish production from 500 tons to 2,000–3,000 tons annually.

Water remains a very scarce resource in Djibouti and there were significant livestock losses during the three-year drought that ended in 2006. The development of underground water supplies for irrigation continues to be studied, and deep-water wells have been sunk in an attempt to alleviate the effects of chronic drought. Over-exploitation of ground water has led to shortages in Djibouti town and Ali-Sabieh. According to a report published by the Ministry of the Environment, the country's sole source of ground water has an annual renewal rate of 15m. cu m but national demand is 16m. cu m. A 1997

World Bank study predicted that by 2012 consumption would be twice the capacity of ground water renewal.

Geologically, Djibouti lies at the junction of three tectonic plates and these spreading cleavages in the earth's mantle are forcing Africa away from Arabia and consequently generating often violent seismic activities in Djibouti. With all of this energy so close to the surface, it has long been the aim of power experts to discover a means of harnessing Djibouti's volcanic heritage. Work began in 1986 on a major geothermal exploration project, funded by the World Bank. Although the objective of the scheme was to make Djibouti self-sufficient in energy, and possibly to export gas to neighbouring countries, by the mid-2000s Djibouti still relied on imported fuels for a large proportion of its energy requirements.

In 1986 Saudi Arabia granted Djibouti US $21.4m. for the purchase and installation of three electricity generators, with a combined capacity of 15 MW. Total electricity-generating capacity rose from 40 MW to 80 MW in 1988, when the second part of the Boulaos power station became operative. In 2000 a US company, Geothermal Development Associates (GDA), conducted a feasibility study for electricity production from the geothermal reserves at Lake Assal. GDA and Electricité de Djibouti also agreed to examine the possibility of building a geothermal power station with a 30-MW generating capacity. In December 2004 the African Development Fund, which is part of the ADB, approved a $27m. loan to Djibouti and a $32m. loan to Ethiopia to finance the Multinational Power Interconnection Project to connect the two countries' electricity grids. The Powergrid Corpn of India will conduct a feasibility study of the proposed project. It was predicted that 60% of the population of Djibouti would have access to electricity by 2015. In 2004 Djibouti produced some 266.6 MW of electricity.

TELECOMMUNICATIONS

Djibouti is now believed to have one of the most modern and efficient telecommunications systems in Africa. If the country is successful in developing the most modern and efficient port in East Africa, the telecommunications system will provide a powerful parallel support to it. Since the 1980s Djibouti has made considerable advances in developing telecommunications networks. In 1985 a second earth station was inaugurated, linking Djibouti to the telecommunications network of the Arab Satellite Communication Organization, while an undersea telecommunications cable to Saudi Arabia was also installed. In early 1997 the Société des Télécommunications Internationales de Djibouti (STID, a subsidiary of France Câble et Radio) launched a cellular telephone network, enabling the country to have internet services. In May 2000 Djibouti Télécom (DT—formed earlier that year to replace the STID) invited tenders to provide the country with a mobile cellular telephone system. DT officials hoped to attract investment of US $8m.–$10m. In February 2001 DT and Hanaro Telecom, of the Republic of Korea, signed a contract to upgrade Djibouti's internet services.

In April 2002 Djibouti granted a licence to Telesat Djibouti, which had been established by the French company Etablissements Seito, to operate a 24-channel television transmission system. It hoped that by offering cheaper subscription fees it would attract customers away from Djibnet, Djibouti's other television company, which commenced operations in 2000. In early 2003 Radiodiffusion-Télévision de Djibouti acquired the Telesat company that had been authorized to retransmit television programmes to Djibouti, thus competing directly with the French-owned Djibnet for the growing Djiboutian television market. In 2003 Zhongxing Telecommunications Equipment, of the People's Republic of China, was awarded a contract to improve DT following a US $12m. loan from China's Eximbank.

A project to tie together the communications systems of more than 20 African countries was agreed at a conference in Washington, DC, in July 2006. The Eastern Africa Submarine Cable System will consist of a high bandwidth, undersea optical cable system with links to Africa and the rest of the world. Among the organization financing the project were the World Bank, the European Investment Bank, the Development Bank of South Africa, the ADB, the Agence Française de Développement and the German Development Bank. The northern end of the cable system will be in Djibouti.

EDUCATION

In January 2006 President Gelleh signed a decree authorizing the creation of the University of Djibouti. The university welcomed its first students in September, with the courses available ranging from literature to management to earth sciences. Yemen and Djibouti reached an agreement to collaborate on Arabic education in November, while Djibouti and Morocco agreed to strengthen their co-operation in education, teaching and training in May 2007. Djibouti will host the first Horn of Africa intellectuals conference in November to develop a common long-term vision favouring 'stability, sustainable development and regional integration', according to Dr. Ismail Wais, the conference co-ordinator.

Statistical Survey

Source (unless otherwise stated): Ministère de l'Economie, des Finances et de la Planification, chargé de la Privatisation, Cité Ministérielle, BP 13, Djibouti; tel. 353331; fax 356501; e-mail cabmefpp@intnet.dj; internet www.ministere-finances.dj.

AREA AND POPULATION

Area: 23,200 sq km (8,958 sq miles).

Population: 220,000 (1976 estimate), including Afars 70,000, Issas and other Somalis 80,000, Arabs 12,000, Europeans 15,000, other foreigners 40,000; 519,900 (including refugees and resident foreigners) at 31 December 1990 (official estimate); 819,000 (UN estimate) at mid-2006 (Source: UN, *World Population Prospects: The 2006 Revision*).

Density (mid-2006): 35.3 per sq km.

Principal Towns (estimated population in 1991): Djibouti (capital) 329,337; Ali-Sabieh 16,423; Tadjourah 7,309; Obock 6,476; Dikhil 20,480 (Source: Thomas Brinkhoff, *City Population*, internet www.citypopulation.de. *Mid-2005* (incl. suburbs, UN estimate): Djibouti 555,000 (Source: UN, *World Urbanization Prospects: The 2005 Revision*).

Births, Marriages and Deaths (2000–05, UN estimates): Average annual birth rate 31.4 per 1,000; Average annual death rate 12.0 per 1,000 (Source: UN, *World Population Prospects: The 2006 Revision*). *1999* (capital district only): Births 7,898; Marriages 3,808.

Expectation of Life (years at birth, WHO estimates): 56 (males 54; females 57) in 2004. Source: WHO, *World Health Report*.

Economically Active Population (estimates, '000 persons, 1991): Agriculture, etc. 212; Industries 31; Services 39; *Total* 282 (males 167, females 115) (Source: UN Economic Commission for Africa, *African Statistical Yearbook*). *Mid-2004* ('000 persons, estimates): Agriculture, etc. 272; Total labour force 354 (Source: FAO).

HEALTH AND WELFARE

Key Indicators

Total Fertility Rate (children per woman, 2005): 4.8.

Under-5 Mortality Rate (per 1,000 live births, 2005): 133.

HIV/AIDS (% of persons aged 15–49, 2005): 3.10.

Physicians (per 1,000 head, 2004): 0.18.

Hospital Beds (per 1,000 head, 2000): 1.61.

Health Expenditure (2004): US $ per head (PPP): 87.2.

Health Expenditure (2004): % of GDP: 6.3.

Health Expenditure (2004): public (% of total): 69.2.

Access to Water (% of persons, 2004): 73.

Access to Sanitation (% of persons, 2004): 82.

Human Development Index (2004): ranking: 148.

Human Development Index (2004): index: 0.494.

For sources and definitions, see explanatory note on p. vi.

AGRICULTURE, ETC.

Principal Crops ('000 metric tons, 2005, FAO estimates): Tomatoes 1.3; Other vegetables 24.0 (incl. melons); Lemons and limes 1.8; Other fruit 1.6.

Livestock ('000 head, 2005, FAO estimates): Cattle 297; Sheep 466; Goats 512; Asses 9; Camels 69.

Livestock Products ('000 metric tons, 2005, FAO estimates): Cattle meat 6.1; Sheep meat 2.2; Goat meat 2.4; Camel meat 0.7; Cows' milk 8.1; Camels' milk 5.9.

Fishing (metric tons, live weight, 2005, FAO estimates): Groupers 60; Snappers and jobfishes 60; Porgies and seabreams 30; Barracudas 15; Carangids 15; Seerfishes 50; Other tuna-like fishes 15; Total catch (incl. others) 260.

Source: FAO.

INDUSTRY

Electric Energy (million kWh): 263.6 in 2003; 266.6 in 2004; 303.0 in 2005. Source: Banque Centrale de Djibouti, *Rapport Annuel 2005*.

FINANCE

Currency and Exchange Rates: 100 centimes = 1 Djibouti franc. *Sterling, Dollar and Euro Equivalents* (31 May 2007): £1 sterling = 351.41 Djibouti francs; US $1 = 177.72 Djibouti francs; €1 = 239.09 Djibouti francs; 1,000 Djibouti francs = £2.85 = $5.63 = €4.18. *Exchange Rate:* Fixed at US $1 = 177.721 Djibouti francs since February 1973.

Budget (million Djibouti francs, 2005): *Revenue*: Tax revenue 30,725 (Direct taxes 11,572, Indirect taxes 12,287, Registration fees, etc. 6,866); Other revenue (incl. property sales) 8,202; Total 38,927 (excl. official grants 7,783). *Expenditure*: Current expenditure 34,667; Capital expenditure 11,711 (Foreign-financed 8,207); Total 46,378. Source: Banque Centrale de Djibouti, *Rapport Annuel 2005*.

International Reserves (US $ million at 31 December 2006, excl. gold): IMF special drawing rights 0.82; Reserve position in IMF 1.65; Foreign exchange 117.85; Total 120.32. Source: IMF, *International Financial Statistics*.

Money Supply (million Djibouti francs at 31 December 2005): Currency outside banks 13,272; Demand deposits at commercial banks 34,456; Total money 47,728. Source: IMF, *International Financial Statistics*.

Cost of Living (Consumer Price Index; base: 2000 = 100): All items 107.5 in 2004; 111.3 in 2005; 114.6 in 2006. Source: African Development Bank.

Expenditure on the Gross Domestic Product (US $ million at current prices, 2006): Government final consumption expenditure 193.29; Private final consumption expenditure 472.38; Gross capital formation 247.59; *Total domestic expenditure* 913.26; Exports of goods and services 276.48; *Less* Imports of goods and services 428.96; *GDP in purchasers' values* 760.77. Source: African Development Bank.

Gross Domestic Product by Economic Activity (million Djibouti francs at current factor cost, 2005): Agriculture, hunting, forestry and fishing 4,051; Manufacturing (incl. mining) 3,145; Electricity and water 6,688; Construction and public works 9,314; Trade and tourism 18,518; Transport and communications 30,061; Finance and insurance 14,961; Public administration 20,096; Other services 2,156; *GDP at factor cost* 108,990; Indirect taxes, *less* subsidies 16,384; *GDP in purchasers' values* 125,376. Source: Banque Centrale de Djibouti, *Rapport Annuel 2005*.

Balance of Payments (US $ million, 2006): Exports of goods f.o.b. 55.2; Imports of goods f.o.b. –335.7; *Trade balance* –280.5; Exports of services 257.1; Imports of services –95.6; *Balance on goods and services* –119.0; Other income received 34.9; Other income paid –11.8; *Balance on goods, services and income* –96.0; Current transfers received 3.7; Current transfers paid –6.8; Current balance –99.1; Capital account (net) 16.8; Direct investment from abroad 108.3; Other investment assets –62.0; Other investment liabilities 18.8; Net errors and omissions –57.8 *Overall balance* –75.0. Source: IMF, *International Financial Statistics*.

EXTERNAL TRADE

Principal Commodities: *Imports c.i.f.* (million Djibouti francs, 1999): Food and beverages 6,796; Qat 3,300; Petroleum products 2,944; Chemical products 1,620; Clothing and footwear 1,251; Metals and metal products 1,355; Machinery and electrical appliances 3,399; Vehicles and transport equipment 2,781; Total (incl. others) 27,131. *Exports f.o.b.* (distribution by SITC, US $ '000, 1992): Food and live animals 3,292 (Rice 726, Coffee and coffee substitutes 1,773); Crude materials (inedible) except fuels 867; Basic manufactures 771; Machinery and transport equipment 1,260 (Road vehicles and parts 585, Other transport equipment 501); Commodities not classified according to kind 9,481; Total (incl. others) 15,919. Source: UN, *International Trade Statistics Yearbook*.

Principal Trading Partners: *Imports c.i.f.* (percentage of total trade, 2002): Ethiopia 11.1; France 7.6; Italy 3.1; Japan 2.5; Netherlands 4.4; Saudi Arabia 15.8; Singapore 2.2; United Kingdom 3.3; Yemen 1.3. *Exports f.o.b.* (percentage of total trade, 2002): Ethiopia 4.4; Somalia 57.2; Yemen 24.5. Source: IMF, *Djibouti: Statistical Appendix* (March 2004).

TRANSPORT

Railways (traffic, 2002): Passengers ('000) 570; Freight ton-km (million) 201. Source: IMF, *Djibouti: Statistical Appendix* (March 2004).

Road Traffic (estimates, motor vehicles in use, 1996): Passenger cars 9,200; Lorries and vans 2,040. Source: International Road Federation, *World Road Statistics*.

Shipping: *Merchant Fleet* (registered at 31 December 2005): 14 vessels (displacement 4,847 grt) (Source: Lloyd's Register-Fairplay, *World Fleet Statistics*). *Freight Traffic* ('000 metric tons, 2005): Goods 3,838; Fuels 1,544 (Source: Banque Centrale de Djibouti, *Rapport Annuel 2005*).

Civil Aviation (international traffic, 2005): *Passengers:* 19,985; *Freight:* 10,973 metric tons. Source: Banque Centrale de Djibouti, *Rapport Annuel 2005*.

TOURISM

Tourist Arrivals ('000): 20 in 1996; 20 in 1997; 20 in 1998.

Receipts from Tourism (US $ million): 4 in 1996; 4 in 1997; 4 in 1998.

Source: World Tourism Organization.

COMMUNICATIONS MEDIA

Newspapers (1995): 1 non-daily (estimated circulation 1,000).

Periodicals (1989): 7 (estimated combined circulation 6,000).

Radio Receivers (1997): 52,000 in use.

Television Receivers (2000): 45,000 in use.

Telephones (2004): 11,100 main lines in use.

Facsimile Machines (1999): 69 in use.

Mobile Cellular Telephones (2004): 34,500 subscribers.

Personal Computers (2004): 21,000 in use.

Internet Users (2004): 9,000.

Sources: mainly UNESCO, *Statistical Yearbook;* UN, *Statistical Yearbook;* International Telecommunication Union.

EDUCATION

Pre-primary (2003/04): 2 schools; 612 pupils.

Primary (2005/06): 82 schools; 46,523 pupils.

Secondary (2005/06): First cycle 17,180 pupils; Second cycle 6,767 pupils.

Higher (2004/05): 1,746 students; 96 teaching staff.

Sources: UNESCO, *Statistical Yearbook*; Ministère de l'éducation nationale et de l'enseignement supérieur; Pôle Universitaire de Djibouti.

Adult Literacy Rate (UNESCO estimate): 65.5% in 2003. Source: UN Development Programme, *Human Development Report*.

Directory

The Constitution

A new Constitution was approved by national referendum on 4 September 1992 and entered into force on 15 September.

The Constitution of Djibouti guarantees the basic rights and freedoms of citizens; the functions of the principal organs of state are delineated therein.

The President of the Republic, who is Head of State and Head of Government, is directly elected, by universal adult suffrage, for a period of six years, renewable only once. The President nominates the Prime Minister and, following consultation with the latter, appoints the Council of Ministers. The legislature is the 65-member Assemblée nationale, which is elected, also by direct universal suffrage, for a period of five years.

The 1992 Constitution provided for the establishment of a maximum of four political parties. On 4 September 2002, however, this limit on the number of political parties was revoked.

The Government

HEAD OF STATE

President and Commander-in-Chief of the Armed Forces: ISMAEL OMAR GELLEH (inaugurated 7 May 1999, re-elected 8 April 2005).

COUNCIL OF MINISTERS
(August 2007)

Prime Minister: DILEITA MOHAMED DILEITA.

Minister of Justice, Muslim and Penal Affairs, in charge of Human Rights: MOHAMED BARKAT ABDILLAHI.

Minister of the Interior and Decentralization: YACIN ELMI BOUH.

Minister of Defence: OUGOUREH KIFLEH AHMED.

Minister of Foreign Affairs and International Co-operation: MAHAMOUD ALI YOUSSOUF.

Minister of the Economy, Finance and Planning, in charge of Privatization: ALI FARAH ASSOWEH.

Minister of Trade and Industry: RIFKI ABDULKADER BAMAKHRAMA.

Minister of Agriculture, Livestock and Fishing: ABDULKADER KAMIL MOHAMED.

Minister of Communication and Culture, in charge of Post and Telecommunications, and Government Spokesman: ALI ABDI FARAH.

Minister of National and Higher Education: ABDI IBRAHIM ABSIEH.

Minister of Employment and National Solidarity: HOUMED MOHAMED DINI.

Minister of Energy and Natural Resources: MOHAMED ALI MOHAMED.

Minister of Equipment and Transport: ISMAÏL IBRAHIM HOUMED.

Minister of Health: ABDALLAH ABDILLAHI MIGUIL.

Minister of Presidential Affairs, in charge of Investment Promotion: OSMAN AHMED MOUSSA.

Minister of Housing, Urban Planning, the Environment, and National and Regional Development, in charge of relations with Parliament: ELMI OBSIEH WAISS.

Minister of Youth, Sports, Leisure and Tourism: HASSAN FARAH MIGUIL.

Minister-delegate to the Prime Minister, in charge of the Promotion of Women's, Family and Social Affairs: AÏCHA MOHAMED ROBLEH.

Minister-delegate to the Minister of Foreign Affairs and International Co-operation, in charge of International Co-operation: HAWA AHMED YOUSSOUF.

Minister-delegate to the Minister of Justice, Muslim and Penal Affairs, and Human Rights, in charge of Mosque Properties and Muslim Affairs: CHEIK MOGUEH DIRIR SAMATAR.

MINISTRIES

Office of the Prime Minister: BP 2086, Djibouti; tel. 351494; fax 355049.

Ministry of Agriculture, Livestock and Fishing: BP 453, Djibouti; tel. 351297.

Ministry of the Civil Service and Administrative Reform: BP 155, Djibouti; tel. 351464.

Ministry of Communication and Culture: BP 32, 1 rue de Moscou, Djibouti; tel. 355672; fax 353957; e-mail mccpt@intnet.dj; internet www.mccpt.dj.

Ministry of Defence: BP 42, Djibouti; tel. 352034.

Ministry of the Economy, Finance and Planning: BP 13, Djibouti; tel. 353331; fax 356501; e-mail cabmefpp@intnet.dj; internet www.ministere-finances.dj.

Ministry of Employment and National Solidarity: Djibouti; tel. 351838; fax 357268; e-mail adetip@intnet.dj.

Ministry of Energy and Natural Resources: BP 175, Djibouti; tel. 350340.

Ministry of Equipment and Transport: Palais du Peuple, BP 2501, Djibouti; tel. 350990; fax 355975.

Ministry of Foreign Affairs, International Co-operation and Parliamentary Relations: blvd Cheik Osman, BP 1863, Djibouti; tel. 352471; fax 353049.

Ministry of Health: BP 296, Djibouti; tel. 353331; fax 356300.

Ministry of Housing, Urban Planning, the Environment, and National and Regional Development: BP 11, Djibouti; tel. 350006; fax 351618.

Ministry of the Interior and Decentralization: BP 33, Djibouti; tel. 352542; fax 354862; internet www.elec.dj.

Ministry of Justice, Muslim and Penal Affairs, and Human Rights: BP 12, Djibouti; tel. 351506; fax 354012.

Ministry of Labour and Vocational Training: BP 170, Djibouti; tel. 350497.

Ministry of National and Higher Education: BP 16, Cité Ministérielle, Djibouti; tel. 350997; fax 354234; e-mail education .gov@intnet.dj; internet www.education.gov.dj.

Ministry of Presidential Affairs: Djibouti.

Ministry for the Promotion of Women's, Family and Social Affairs: BP 458, Djibouti; tel. and fax 350439; e-mail minfemme@ intnet.dj; internet www.ministere-femme.dj.

Ministry of Trade and Industry: BP 1846, Djibouti; tel. 351682.

Ministry of Youth, Sports, Leisure and Tourism: BP 2506, Djibouti; tel. 355886; fax 356830.

President and Legislature

PRESIDENT

At the presidential election held on 8 April 2005 the incumbent Ismael Omar Gelleh of the Rassemblement populaire pour le progrès secured 100% of the valid votes cast. Gelleh was the sole candidate at the election following the withdrawal, in March, from the contest of Mohamed Daoud Chehem, the representative of the Parti djiboutien pour la démocratie.

ASSEMBLÉE NATIONALE

Assemblée Nationale: BP 138, pl. Lagarde, Djibouti; tel. 350172; internet www.assemblee-nationale.dj.

Speaker: IDRISS ARNAOUD ALI.

General Election, 10 January 2003

Party	Valid votes	% of votes	Seats
Union pour la majorité présidentielle* . . .	53,293	62.73	65
Union pour l'alternance démocratique† . . .	31,660	37.27	—
Total	84,953	100.00	65

* A coalition comprising the FRUD, the PND, the PPSD and the RPP.

† A coalition comprising the ARD, the PDD, the PRD (renamed the MRD in November 2002) and the UDJ.

Election Commission

Commission électorale nationale indépendante: Djibouti; f. 2002; President ALI ISMAÏL YABEH.

Political Organizations

On 4 September 2002, to coincide with the 10th anniversary of the approval of the Constitution, restrictions on the number of legally permitted political parties (hitherto four) were formally removed. The following organizations contested the legislative elections of January 2003:

Alliance républicaine pour le développement (ARD): BP 1488, Marabout, Djibouti; tel. 250919; internet www.ard-djibouti.org; f. 2002; Leader AHMAD YOUSSOUF HOUMED; Sec.-Gen. KASSIM ALI DINI.

Front pour la restauration de l'unité et de la démocratie (FRUD): Djibouti; tel. 250279; f. 1991 by merger of three militant Afar groups; advocates fair representation in govt for all ethnic groups; commenced armed insurgency in Nov. 1991; split into two factions in March 1994; the dissident group, which negotiated a settlement with the Govt, obtained legal recognition in March 1996 and recognizes the following leaders; Pres. ALI MOHAMED DAOUD; Sec.-Gen. OUGOUREH KIFLEH AHMED; a dissident group, FRUD-Renaissance (led by IBRAHIM CHEHEM DAOUD), was formed in 1996.

Mouvement pour le renouveau démocratique et le développement (MRD): BP 3570, ave Nasser, Djibouti; internet www.mrd-djibouti.org; f. 1992 as the Parti du renouveau démocratique; renamed as above in 2002; Pres. DAHER AHMED FARAH; Sec.-Gen. SOULEIMAN HASSAN FAIDAL.

Parti djiboutien pour le développement (PDD): BP 892, Djibouti; tel. 353243; f. 2002; Pres. MOHAMED DAOUD CHEHEM; Sec.-Gen. ABDILLAHI MOHAMED SALAH.

Parti national démocratique (PND): BP 10204, Djibouti; tel. 342194; f. 1992; seeks formation of a 'govt of national unity' to supervise implementation of democratic reforms; Pres. ADEN ROBLEH AWALLEH.

Parti populaire social démocrate (PPSD): BP 434, Route Nelson Mandela, Djibouti; f. 2002; Pres. MOUMIN BAHDON FARAH; Sec.-Gen. HASSAN IDRISS AHMED.

Rassemblement populaire pour le progrès (RPP): Djibouti; e-mail rpp@intnet.dj; internet www.rpp.dj; f. 1979; sole legal party 1981–92; Pres. ISMAEL OMAR GELLEH; Sec.-Gen. IDRISS ARNAOUD ALI.

Union djiboutienne pour la démocratie et la justice (UDJ): Djibouti.

The following organizations are proscribed:

Coordination de l'opposition djiboutienne: f. 1996; alliance of the PND, the FUOD and the RPP–GDR; Leader ISMAEL GEDI HARED.

Front des forces démocratiques (FFD): Leader OMAR ELMI KHAIREH.

Front de libération de la côte des Somalis (FLCS): f. 1963; Issa-supported; has operated from Somalia; Chair. ABDALLAH WABERI KHALIF; Vice-Chair. OMAR OSMAN RABEH.

Front uni de l'opposition djiboutienne (FUOD): f. 1992; based in Ethiopia; united front of internal opposition groups, incl. some fmr mems of the RPP; Leader MAHDI IBRAHIM A. GOD.

Mouvement de la jeunesse djiboutienne (MJD): Leader ABDOULKARIM ALI AMARKAK.

Mouvement pour l'unité et la démocratie (MUD): advocates political pluralism; Leader MOHAMED MOUSSA ALI 'TOURTOUR'.

Organisation des masses Afar (OMA): f. 1993 by mems of the fmr Mouvement populaire de libération; Chair. AHMED MALCO.

Parti centriste et des reformes démocratiques (PCRD): f. 1993 in Addis Ababa, Ethiopia, by a breakaway faction of the FRUD; seeks official registration as an opposition party; Chair. HASSAN ABDALLAH WATTA.

Parti populaire djiboutien (PPD): f. 1981; mainly Afar-supported; Leader MOUSSA AHMED IDRIS.

Union des démocrates djiboutiens (UDD): affiliated to the FUOD; Chair. MAHDI IBRAHIM AHMED.

Union démocratique pour le progrès (UDP): f. 1992; advocates democratic reforms; Leader FARAH WABERI.

Union des mouvements démocratiques (UMD): f. 1990 by merger of two militant external opposition groups; Pres. MOHAMED ADOYTA.

Diplomatic Representation

EMBASSIES IN DJIBOUTI

China, People's Republic: BP 2021, rue Addis Ababa, Lotissement Heron, Djibouti; tel. 352246; fax 354833; e-mail chinaemb_dj@mfa.gov.cn; Ambassador SHEN JIANG KUAN.

Egypt: BP 1989, Djibouti; tel. 351231; fax 356657; e-mail ambegypte2004@gawab.com; Ambassador AHMED ABDEL WAHED ZEIN.

Eritrea: BP 1944, Djibouti; tel. 354961; fax 351831; Ambassador MOHAMED SAÏD MANTAY.

Ethiopia: rue Clochette, BP 230, Djibouti; tel. 350718; fax 354803; e-mail ethemb@intnet.dj; Ambassador SHEMSUDIN AHMED.

France: 45 blvd du Maréchal Foch, BP 2039, Djibouti; tel. 350963; fax 350272; e-mail ambfrdj@intnet.dj; internet www.ambafrance-dj.org; Ambassador DOMINIQUE DECHERF.

Libya: BP 2073, Djibouti; tel. 350202; Ambassador KAMEL AL-HADI ALMARASH.

Oman: Djibouti; tel. 350852; Ambassador SAOUD SALEM HASSAN AL-ANSI.

Qatar: Ambassador HADI NASSER MANSOUR AL-HAJIRI.

Russia: BP 1913, Plateau du Marabout, Djibouti; tel. 350740; fax 355990; e-mail russiaemb@intnet.dj; Ambassador MIKHAIL TSVIGOUN.

Saudi Arabia: BP 1921, Djibouti; tel. 351645; fax 352284; Ambassador ABDULAZIZ MUHAMMAD AL-EIFAN.

Somalia: BP 549, Djibouti; tel. 353521; Ambassador MUSE HIRSI FAHIYE.

Sudan: BP 4259, Djibouti; tel. 356404; fax 356662; Ambassador OSAMA SALAHUDDIN.

United Arab Emirates: Djibouti; Ambassador SAÏD BEN HAMDAM BEN MUHAMMAD AN-NAGHI.

USA: Villa Plateau du Serpent, blvd du Maréchal Joffre, BP 185, Djibouti; tel. 353995; fax 353940; e-mail amembadm@bow.intnet.dj; internet djibouti.usembassy.gov; Ambassador MARGUERITA DIANNE RAGSDALE.

Yemen: BP 194, Djibouti; tel. 352975; Ambassador ABDOURAB ALI AS-SALAFI.

Judicial System

The Supreme Court was established in 1979. There is a high court of appeal and a court of first instance in Djibouti; each of the five administrative districts has a 'tribunal coutumier'.

President of the Court of Appeal: KADIDJA ABEBA.

Religion

ISLAM

Almost the entire population are Muslims.

Qadi of Djibouti: MOGUE HASSAN DIRIR, BP 168, Djibouti; tel. 352669.

CHRISTIANITY

The Roman Catholic Church

Djibouti comprises a single diocese, directly responsible to the Holy See. There were an estimated 7,000 adherents in the country at 31 December 2004.

Bishop of Djibouti: GIORGIO BERTIN, Evêché, blvd de la République, BP 94, Djibouti; tel. 350140; fax 354831; e-mail evechcat@intnet.dj.

The Anglican Communion

Within the Episcopal Church in Jerusalem and the Middle East, Djibouti lies within the jurisdiction of the Bishop in Egypt.

Other Christian Churches

Eglise Protestante: blvd de la République, BP 416, Djibouti; tel. 351820; fax 350706; e-mail eped@intnet.dj; internet membres.lycos.fr/missiondjibouti; f. 1957; Pastor NATHALIE PAQUEREAU.

Greek Orthodox Church: blvd de la République, Djibouti; tel. 351325; c. 350 adherents; Archimandrite STAVROS GEORGANAS.

The Ethiopian Orthodox Church is also active in Djibouti.

The Press

L'Atout: Palais du peuple, Djibouti; twice a year; publ. by the Centre National de la Promotion Culturelle et Artistique.

Carrefour Africain: BP 393, Djibouti; fax 354916; fortnightly; publ. by the Roman Catholic mission; circ. 500.

La Nation de Djibouti: pl. du 27 juin, BP 32, Djibouti; tel. 352201; fax 353937; internet www.lanation.dj; e-mail lanation@intnet.dj; three times a week; Dir Abdoulrashid Idriss; circ. 4,300.

Le Progrès: Djibouti; weekly; publ. by the RPP; Publr Ali Mohamed Humad.

Le Renouveau: BP 3570, ave Nasser, Djibouti; tel. 351474; weekly; independent; publ. by the MRD; Editor-in-Chief Daher Ahmed Farah.

La République: Djibouti; weekly; independent; Editor-in-Chief Amir Adaweh.

Revue de l'ISERT: BP 486, Djibouti; tel. 352795; twice a year; publ. by the Institut Supérieur d'Etudes et de Recherches Scientifiques et Techniques (ISERT).

Le Temps: Djibouti; opposition newspaper; Owners Moussa Ahmed Idris, Ali Meidal Wais.

NEWS AGENCIES

Agence Djiboutienne d'Information (ADI): 1 rue de Moscou, BP 32, Djibouti; tel. 354013; fax 354037; e-mail adi@intent.dj; internet www.adi.dj; f. 1978.

Foreign Bureau

Agence France-Presse (AFP): BP 97, Djibouti; tel. 350484; Correspondent Khalid Haidar.

Broadcasting and Communications

TELECOMMUNICATIONS

Djibouti Télécom: 3 blvd G. Pompidou, BP 2105, Djibouti; tel. 352777; fax 359200; e-mail adjib@intnet.dj; internet www.adjib.dj; f. 1999 to replace Société des Télécommunications Internationales; 100% state-owned; Dir-Gen. Abdirahman M. Hassan.

BROADCASTING

Radio and Television

Djibnet: BP 1409, Djibouti; tel. 354288; e-mail webmaster@djibnet.com; internet www.djibnet.com.

Radiodiffusion-Télévision de Djibouti (RTD): BP 97, 1 ave St Laurent du Var, Djibouti; tel. 352294; fax 356502; e-mail rtd@intnet.dj; internet www.rtd.dj; f. 1967; state-controlled; programmes in French, Afar, Somali and Arabic; 17 hours radio and 5 hours television daily; Dir-Gen. (Radio) Abdi Atteyeh Abdi; Dir-Gen. (Television) Mohamed Djama Aden.

Telesat Djibouti: Route de l'Aéroport, BP 3760, Djibouti; tel. 353457.

Finance

(cap. = capital; res = reserves; dep. = deposits; m. = million; brs = branches; amounts in Djibouti francs)

BANKING

Central Bank

Banque Centrale de Djibouti: BP 2118, ave St Laurent du Var, Djibouti; tel. 352751; fax 356288; e-mail bndj@intnet.dj; internet www.banque-centrale.dj; f. 1977 as Banque Nationale de Djibouti; present name adopted 2002; bank of issue; cap. and res 6,056m. (Feb. 2005); Gov. Djama Mahamoud Haid; Gen. Man. Ahmed Osman.

Commercial Banks

Banque pour le Commerce et l'Industrie—Mer Rouge (BCI—MR): pl. Lagarde, BP 2122, Djibouti; tel. 350857; fax 354260; e-mail bcimr@africa.bnpparibas.com; f. 1977; 51% owned by Banque Nationale de Paris Intercontinentale; cap. 2,092.5m., res 209.3m., dep. 46,389.2m. (Dec. 2004); Pres. Jean-Jacques Santini; CEO François du Peuty; 6 brs.

Banque Indosuez—Mer Rouge (BIS—MR): 10 pl. Lagarde, BP 88, Djibouti; tel. 353016; fax 351638; e-mail secretariat@bimr-banque.com; f. 1908 as Banque de l'Indochine; present name adopted 1977; owned by Crédit Agricole, France; cap. 1,500.0m., res 526.7m., dep 43,322.0m. (Dec. 2006); Chair. and CEO Luc Beiso.

Investment Bank of Africa: Djibouti; f. 2000; subsidiary of AFH Holding (Luxembourg); cap. 300m.; CEO Ilia Karas.

Development Bank

Banque de Développement de Djibouti: angle ave Georges Clemenceau et rue Pierre Curie, BP 520, Djibouti; tel. 353391; fax 355022; f. 1983; 39.2% govt-owned; cap. and res 1,233m., total assets 3,081m. (Dec. 1997); Dir-Gen. Abdourahman Ismael Gelleh.

Banking Association

Association Professionnelle des Banques: c/o Banque pour le Commerce et l'Industrie—Mer Rouge, pl. Lagarde, BP 2122, Djibouti; tel. 350857; fax 354260; Pres. Mohamed Aden.

INSURANCE

Les Assureurs de la Mer Rouge et du Golfe Arabe (AMERGA): 8 rue Marchand, BP 2653, Djibouti; tel. 352510; fax 355623; e-mail direction.m@amerga.com; internet www.amerga.com; f. 2000; Dirs Thierry Marill, Luc Marill, Abdourahman Barkat Abdillahi, Mohamed Aden Aboubaker.

Ethiopian Insurance Corpn: rue de Marseille, BP 2047, Djibouti; tel. 352306.

GXA Assurances: rue Marchand, BP 200, Djibouti; tel. 353636; fax 353056; e-mail gxa@intnet.dj; Country Man. Christian Boucher.

Trade and Industry

CHAMBER OF COMMERCE

Chambre de Commerce de Djibouti: BP 84, pl. Lagarde, Djibouti; tel. 351070; fax 350096; e-mail ccd@intnet.dj; f. 1906; 24 mems, 12 assoc. mems; Pres. Saïd Omar Moussa; First Vice-Pres. Abdourahman Mahamoud Boreh.

TRADE ASSOCIATION

Office National d'Approvisionnement et de Commercialisation (ONAC): BP 79, Djibouti; tel. 350327; fax 356701; Chair. Mohamed Abdoulkader.

UTILITIES

Electricity

Electricité de Djibouti (EdD): blvd de la République, BP 175, Djibouti; tel. 352851; fax 354396; e-mail clientele@edd.dj; internet www.edd.dj; Dir-Gen. Djama Ali Gelleh.

Water

Office National des Eaux de Djibouti (ONED): blvd de la République, BP 1914, Djibouti; tel. 351159; fax 354423.

Société des Eaux de Tadjourah: c/o Ministry of Trade and Industry, BP 1846, Djibouti; tel. 351682.

TRADE UNIONS

Union Djiboutienne du Travail: rue Pierre Pascal, BP 2767, Djibouti; tel. 823979; fax 355084; e-mail udt_djibouti@yahoo.fr; f. 1992; confed. of 21 trade unions; Chair. Hassan Cher Hared; Sec.-Gen. Aden Mohamed Abdou.

Union Générale des Travailleurs Djiboutiens (UGTD): Sec.-Gen. Abdo Sikieh.

Transport

RAILWAYS

Chemin de Fer Djibouti–Ethiopien (CDE): BP 2116, Djibouti; tel. 350280; fax 351256; f. 1909; adopted present name in 1981; jtly owned by govts of Djibouti and Ethiopia; 781 km of track (121 km in Djibouti) linking Djibouti with Addis Ababa; Pres. Ismail Ibrahim Houmed.

ROADS

In 1996 there were an estimated 2,890 km of roads, comprising 1,090 km of main roads and 1,800 km of regional roads; some 12.6% of the roads were paved. Of the remainder, 1,000 km are serviceable throughout the year, the rest only during the dry season. About one-half of the roads are usable only by heavy vehicles. In 1981 the 40-km Grand Bara road was opened, linking the capital with the south. In 1986 the Djibouti–Tadjoura road, the construction of which was financed by Saudi Arabia, was opened, linking the capital with the north. In 1996 the Islamic Development Bank granted Djibouti a loan of US $3.6m. to finance road construction projects. In May 2004 the European Development Fund approved a $38.4m. road construction project between Djibouti and Addis Ababa, and in October the Kuwait Fund for Arabic Economic Development approved a $20m. loan to build a road between Tadjourah and Obock.

SHIPPING

Djibouti, which was established as a free port in 1981, handled 4,847,200 metric tons of freight in 2004.

Djibouti Maritime Management Investment Company (DMMI): Djibouti; f. 2004 to manage Djibouti's fishing port.

Port Autonome International de Djibouti: BP 2107, Djibouti; tel. 351031; fax 356187; e-mail david.hawker@port.dj; managed by Dubai Ports World, UAE since 2000; Gen. Man. DAVID HAWKER.

Maritime and Transit Services Enterprise: rue de Marseille, BP 680, Djibouti; tel. 353204; fax 354149; e-mail mtsdjib@bowintnet.dj.

Principal Shipping Agents

Almis Shipping Line & Transport Co: BP 85, Djibouti; tel. 356998; fax 356996; Man. Dir MOHAMED NOOR.

Cie Maritime et de Manutention de Djibouti (COMAD): ave des Messageries Maritimes, BP 89, Djibouti; tel. 351028; fax 350466; e-mail hettam@intnet.dj; stevedoring; Man. Dir ALI A. HETTAM.

Global Logistics Services Djibouti: rue Clemenceau, POB 3239, Djibouti; tel. 839000; fax 352283; e-mail gls.djibouti@gls-logistics.tk; shipping, clearing and freight-forwarding agent; Gen. Man. MOHAMED A. ELMI.

Global Shipping Services (GSS): POB 2666, Djibouti; tel. 251302; fax 353395; e-mail gss@intnet.dj; shipping agents; Man. Dir ALI A. HETTAM.

Inchcape Shipping Services & Co (Djibouti) SA: 9–11 rue de Genève, BP 81, Djibouti; tel. 353844; fax 353294; internet www.iss-shipping.com; e-mail iss.dj@iss-shipping.com; f. 1942; Dir-Gen. AHMED OSMAN GELLEH.

International Transit Services: POB 1177, Djibouti; tel. 251155; fax 353258; e-mail its02@intnet.dj; Man. Dir ROBLEH MOHAMED.

J. J. Kothari & Co Ltd: rue d'Athens, BP 171, Djibouti; tel. 350219; fax 351778; e-mail kothari@intnet.dj; shipping agents; also ship managers, stevedores, freight forwarders; Dirs S. J. KOTHARI, NALIN KOTHARI.

Société Djiboutienne de Trafic Maritime (SDTM): blvd Cheik Osman, BP 640, Djibouti; tel. 352351; fax 351103.

Société Maritime L. Savon et Ries: blvd Cheik Osman, BP 2125, Djibouti; tel. 352351; fax 351103; e-mail smsr@intnet.dj; Dir FRANÇOIS CAPIOMONT; Gen. Man. JEAN-PHILIPPE DELARUE.

CIVIL AVIATION

The international airport is at Ambouli, 6 km from Djibouti. There are six other airports providing domestic services.

Air Djibouti (Red Sea Airlines): BP 499, rue Marchand, Djibouti; tel. 356723; fax 356734; f. 1971; fmrly govt-owned, transferred to private ownership in 1997; internal flights and international services to destinations in Africa, the Middle East and Europe; Chair. SAÂD BEN MOUSSA AL-JANAIBI.

Daallo Airlines: BP 2565, Djibouti; tel. 340672; e-mail daallo@intnet.dj; f. 1992; operates services to Somalia, Saudi Arabia, the United Arab Emirates, France and the Netherlands; Man. Dir MOHAMED IBRAHIM YASSIN.

Djibouti Airlines (Puntavia Airline de Djibouti): BP 2240, pl. Lagarde, Djibouti; tel. 351006; fax 352429; e-mail djibouti-airlines@intnet.dj; internet www.djiboutiairlines.com; f. 1996; scheduled and charter regional and domestic flights; Man. Dir Capt. MOUSSA RAYALEH WABERI.

Tourism

Djibouti offers desert scenery in its interior and watersport facilities on its coast. A casino operates in the capital. There were about 20,000 tourist arrivals in 1998, when receipts from tourism totalled US $4m.

Office National du Tourisme de Djibouti (ONTD): pl. du 27 juin, BP 1938, Djibouti; tel. 353790; fax 356322; e-mail onta@intnet.dj; internet www.office-tourisme.dj; Dir MOHAMED ABDILLAHI WAIS.

Defence

Arrangements for military co-operation exist between Djibouti and France, and in November there were about 2,850 French military personnel stationed in Djibouti, while the US-led Combined Joint Task Force-Horn of Africa also had its headquarters in the country. As assessed at November 2006, the total armed forces of Djibouti itself, in which all services form part of the army, numbered some 10,950 (including 200 naval and 250 air force personnel). There were also paramilitary forces numbering 1,400 gendarmes, as well as a 2,500-strong national security force. Conscription of all men between 18 and 25 years of age was introduced in 1992.

Defence Expenditure: Budgeted at 4,500m. Djibouti francs in 2006.

Commander-in-Chief of the Armed Forces: Pres. ISMAEL OMAR GELLEH.

Chief of Staff of the Army: Gen. ZAKARIA CHEIK IBRAHIM.

Education

The Government has overall responsibility for education. Primary education generally begins at six years of age and lasts for six years. Secondary education, usually starting at the age of 12, lasts for seven years, comprising a first cycle of four years and a second of three years. In 2004/05 primary enrolment included 33% of pupils in the relevant age-group (36% of boys; 29% of girls), and secondary enrolment was equivalent to 19% of pupils in the relevant age-group (22% of boys; 15% of girls). Budgetary current expenditure on education in 2002 was 3,937m. Djibouti francs, equivalent to 12.8% of total government expenditure. In 2005/06, according to UNESCO estimates, there were 46,523 primary school pupils and 23,947 pupils receiving general secondary and vocational education. Djibouti's sole university, the Université de Djibouti, was formed in January 2006 as a replacement for the Pôle Universitaire de Djibouti, which opened in 2000 and had over 1,700 students in 2004/05.

Bibliography

Alwan, D. A., and Mibrathu, Y. *Historical Dictionary of Djibouti*. Lanham, MD, Scarecrow Press, 2001.

Coubba, A. *Djibouti: Une nation en otage*. Paris, L'Harmattan, 1993.

Dubois, C., and Soumille, P. *Des chrétiens à Djibouti en terre d'Islam: XIXe-XXe siècles*. Paris, Karthala, 2004.

Koburger, C. W. *Naval Strategy East of Suez: The Role of Djibouti*. New York, Praeger, 1992.

Laudouze, A. *Djibouti, Nation carrefour*. Paris, Editions Karthala, 1982.

Oberle, P., and Hugot, P. *Histoire de Djibouti: des origines à la république*. Paris, Editions Présence Africaine, 1985.

Schrader, P. J. *Djibouti*. Oxford, Clio Press, 1991.

'Ethnic Politics in Djibouti: From the "Eye of the Hurricane" to "Boiling Cauldron"', in *African Affairs*, Vol. 92, No. 367 (April 1993), pp 203–221.

Tholomier, R. *Djibouti: Pawn of the Horn of Africa*. Metuchen, NJ, Scarecrow Press, 1981.

Thompson, V., and Adloff, R. *Djibouti and the Horn of Africa*. London, Oxford University Press, 1968.

Tramport, J. *Djibouti Hier: de 1887 à 1939*. Paris, Hatier, 1990.

Weiss, E. *Djibouti: Évasion*. Paris, Editions du Fer à Marquer, 1990.

Woodward, P. *The Horn of Africa: State Politics and International Relations*. London, Tauris, 1996.

EQUATORIAL GUINEA

Physical and Social Geography

RENÉ PÉLISSIER

The Republic of Equatorial Guinea occupies an area of 28,051 sq km (10,831 sq miles). Geographically, the main components of the republic are the islands of Bioko (formerly known as Fernando Póo), covering 2,017 sq km, and Annobón (also known as Pagalu), 17 sq km; and, on the African mainland, bordered to the north by Cameroon, to the south and east by Gabon and westwards by the Gulf of Guinea, lies the province of Río Muni (also formerly known as Mbini), 26,017 sq km, including three coastal islets, Corisco (15 sq km) and the Great and Little Elobeys (2.5 sq km).

Bioko is a parallelogram-shaped island, 72 km by 35 km, formed from three extinct volcanoes. To the north lies the Pico de Basilé (rising to 3,007 m above sea-level), with an easy access. In the centre of the island are the Moka heights, while, further south, the Gran Caldera forms the remotest and least developed part of the island. The coast is steep to the south. Malabo is the only natural harbour. Crop fertility is high, owing to the combination of volcanic soils and plentiful rainfall. At the southern extremity of the Guinean archipelago lies the remote island of Annobón, south of the island of São Tomé.

Mainland Río Muni is a jungle enclave, from which a coastal plain rises steeply toward the Gabonese frontier. Its main orographic complexes are the spurs of the Monts de Cristal of Gabon. The highest peaks are Piedra de Nzas, Monte Mitra and Monte Chime, all rising to 1,200 m. The main river is the Mbini (formerly known as the Río Benito), non-navigable except for a 20-km stretch, which bisects the mainland province. On the Cameroon border is the Río Campo; its tributary, the Kye, is the de facto eastern border with Gabon. The coast is a long beach, with low cliffs towards Cogo. There is no natural harbour.

The country has an equatorial climate with heavy rainfall, especially in Bioko. The average temperature of Malabo is 25°C and the average rainfall is in excess of 2,000 mm. Humidity is high throughout the island, except on the Moka heights. Río Muni has less debilitating climatic conditions.

According to the July 1983 census, which recorded a total population of 300,000, there were 240,804 inhabitants in Río Muni, 57,190 on Bioko and 2,006 on Annobón. The population was estimated by the UN to be 496,000 at mid-2006. The main city is Malabo (with 96,000 inhabitants, including suburbs, according to UN estimates in 2005), the capital of Bioko and of the republic, as well as the main economic, educational and religious centre. The other town of note is Luba. Bubi villages are scattered in the eastern and western parts of the island. On the mainland the only urban centre is the port of Bata, which had a population of 24,100 in 1983. Other ports are Mbini and Cogo. Inland, Mikomeseng, Nkumekie, Ebebiyín and Evinayong are small market and administrative centres. The country is divided into seven administrative provinces: Bioko Norte, Bioko Sur and Annobón for the two main islands; Centro-Sur, Kié-Ntem, Litoral and Wele-Nzas for the mainland and its adjacent islets.

The ethnic composition of Equatorial Guinea is unusually complex for so small a political unit. The Fang are the dominant group in Río Muni, where they are believed to comprise 80%–90% of the population. North of the Mbini river are the Ntumu Fang, and to the south of it the Okak Fang. Coastal tribes—notably the Kombe, Balengue and Bujeba—have been pushed towards the sea by Fang pressure. Both Fang and coastal peoples are of Bantu origin. Since independence in 1968, many inhabitants of Río Muni have emigrated to Bioko, where they have come to dominate the civil and military services. The Bubi, who are the original inhabitants of Bioko, may now number about 5,000. The Fernandino, of whom there are a few thousand, are the descendants of former slaves liberated by the British, mingled with long-settled immigrants from coastal west Africa. The working population of Annobón are mainly seafarers and fishermen.

The official languages are Spanish and, since February 1998, French. In Río Muni the Fang language is spoken, as well as those of coastal tribes. Bubi is the indigenous language on Bioko, although Fang is also widely used in Malabo, and Ibo is spoken by the resident Nigerian population.

Recent History

MARISÉ CASTRO

The Republic of Equatorial Guinea, comprising the region of Río Muni, on the African mainland, and the islands of Bioko, Annobón, Corisco and the Elobeys, was granted independence on 12 October 1968, after 190 years of Spanish colonial rule. Francisco Macías Nguema, a mainland Fang from the Esangui clan, took office as President of the new republic, following multi-party elections in which he had received the support of a moderate coalition grouping.

In office, Macías Nguema moved swiftly to suppress opposition, and to assert his absolute power through a 'reign of terror'. The brutal nature of the regime led to the flight of as many as one-third of the total population, including nearly all of the skilled and educated elements of Equato-Guinean society. Macías Nguema obtained much of his economic and military aid from Eastern bloc countries; relations with Spain deteriorated, and serious disputes arose regionally with Gabon and Nigeria. The country's economy, centred on cocoa plantations on Bioko and relying on imported African labour, was devastated by the excesses of Macías Nguema's regime.

OBIANG NGUEMA'S PRESIDENCY

In August 1979 Lt-Col (now Gen.) Teodoro Obiang Nguema Mbasogo, the Commander of the National Guard and a nephew of the President, deposed Macías, who fled from the capital but was captured, tried and executed in September. Obiang Nguema announced the restoration of the rule of law, but banned all political parties and ruled through a Supreme Military Council (SMC), which continued to be dominated by the Esangui clan. In December 1981 the first civilians were appointed to the SMC, and in August 1982 a new Constitution was approved by 95% of voters in a referendum. Provisions for the protection of human rights and for a limited form of popular representation were incorporated in the Constitution, and Obiang Nguema was appointed to a seven-year term as President. At elections held in August 1983 all candidates were nominated by the President, to serve for a term of five years in a unicameral legislature with virtually no independent legislative powers.

Under Obiang Nguema there have been numerous allegations of coup plots and attempted coups, particularly in the

1980s and the early 2000s. These allegations have seldom been substantiated. Obiang Nguema created a 'governmental party', the Partido Democrático de Guinea Ecuatorial (PDGE), while still resisting demands for multi-party democracy. The higher ranks of the civil service and armed forces remained firmly in the hands of the President's Esangui clan, and elections continued to be overtly manipulated by the Government. At legislative elections held in July 1988, all of the PDGE candidates were returned, receiving 99.2% of the votes cast.

The first presidential election since 1968 took place in June 1989, with Obiang Nguema, the sole candidate, receiving 99% of the votes cast. The election was not conducted by secret ballot. An amnesty for political detainees was proclaimed in August. However, the international human rights organization Amnesty International has since reiterated long-standing accusations against the Government of detaining and mistreating its political opponents.

Opposition Pressures

Under growing internal and international pressure, Obiang Nguema eventually conceded the principle of political plurality in July 1991. A new Constitution containing such provisions was approved by referendum in mid-November; however, the few human rights safeguards contained in the 1982 Constitution were removed. In January 1992 a number of new laws were promulgated, which included legislation on political parties and on freedom of assembly and demonstration. This was followed by the formation of a new transitional Government (including only PDGE members) and the implementation of a general amnesty that included all political exiles. Provisions of the new Constitution exempted Obiang Nguema from any judicial procedures arising from his presidential tenure, while Equato-Guinean citizens who also held foreign passports and persons not continuously resident in Equatorial Guinea for 10 years were barred from standing as election candidates. This measure thus effectively excluded virtually all exiled political opponents from participation in national political life. The President indicated that legislative and presidential elections would not be held until the current mandates of the legislature and of the President had expired, in 1993 and 1996, respectively. The first two opposition parties, the Unión Popular (UP) and the Partido Liberal, were legalized in June 1992, and in September an alliance of opposition parties, the Plataforma de Oposición Conjunta (POC), was created.

Multi-party legislative elections took place in November 1993. They were, however, boycotted by most of the parties in the POC alliance, in protest at Obiang Nguema's refusal to review contentious clauses of the electoral law or to permit international observers to inspect the electoral register. Although representatives of the Organization of African Unity (now the African Union—AU) attended as observers, the UN declined a request by the Equato-Guinean authorities to monitor the elections, on the grounds that correct procedures were evidently not being implemented. Following a turn-out variously estimated at 30%–50% of the electorate, the PDGE won 68 of the 80 seats in the legislative House of Representatives (Cámara de Representantes del Pueblo); of the six opposition parties that presented candidates, the Convención Socialdemocrática Popular won six seats, the Unión Democrática y Social de Guinea Ecuatorial secured five seats and the Convención Liberal Democrática obtained one seat. Prior to the elections, opposition politicians were reported to have been harassed by the security forces and during the polling widespread irregularities in procedures were alleged. In December the Government announced that henceforth all party political gatherings would be subject to prior official authorization. Later that month Silvestre Siale Bileka, Prime Minister in the interim Government, became Prime Minister of the new administration. His Council of Ministers included no opposition representatives.

In June 1994, in response to pressure from international aid donors, the Government agreed to modify the controversial electoral law and to conduct a preliminary electoral census prior to the holding of local elections. In September, however, the authorities began to compile a full population census, instead of preparing for the local elections, which had been scheduled for November. The census was boycotted by opposition parties, and there were numerous arrests of political opponents. The local elections were postponed. During late November and early December the Convergencia para la Democracia Social (CPDS) held the first congress of an opposition political party to take place within Equatorial Guinea.

In early 1995 the Constitution and electoral law were amended to reduce from 10 to five years the minimum time required for presidential candidates to have been resident in Equatorial Guinea. In April several leaders of the opposition Partido del Progreso de Guinea Ecuatorial (PPGE), including its President, Severo Moto Nsa, were sentenced to terms of imprisonment, having been convicted of treason by a military court. These proceedings were widely condemned by the international community, and in August Obiang Nguema unexpectedly pardoned all the convicted PPGE members.

Local elections eventually took place in September 1995. Contested by 14 parties, they were the first truly representative multi-party elections to take place since independence. The electoral roll had been drafted with assistance from the UN, and the elections were monitored by a team of 27 international observers; observers representing the Government and opposition parties were also present at polling stations. The six member parties of the POC presented a united front, offering a single candidate in each constituency. Although no major problems were reported during the election campaigns, the ruling PDGE was accused of electoral fraud and harassment once polling was under way. The initial results indicated that opposition parties had won an overwhelming victory; however, the official results credited the ruling party with a majority of the votes cast in two-thirds of local administrations. Judicial appeals by the opposition against the outcome, supported by the team of international observers, were rejected.

At the presidential election held in February 1996 Obiang Nguema was returned to office for a third term, securing more than 90% of the votes cast. The election was boycotted by influential opposition parties, in protest at alleged electoral irregularities and official intimidation, and because their preferred candidate, Armancio Gabriel Nze, was not permitted to run for the POC. The electoral roll drawn up by the UN in 1995 was discarded in favour of an allegedly fraudulent list produced by the Government, and the conduct of the elections was severely criticized by foreign observers. One month later Obiang Nguema appointed a new Prime Minister, Angel Serafin Seriche Dougan; a new, enlarged Council of Ministers was announced the following month.

In February 1997 Obiang Nguema conceded that human rights violations (particularly in Río Muni) were damaging his Government's international reputation. The announcement by the Government of measures to prevent official torture and to punish those responsible were dismissed by human rights organizations and opposition politicians as an empty gesture aimed solely at appeasing potential foreign donors; acts of violence and intimidation allegedly carried out by members of the security forces continued to be reported.

In April 1997 a new national pact was signed by representatives of the Government and of 13 opposition parties, following two months of negotiations; the CPDS, a leading opposition party instrumental in the establishment of the POC, was excluded from the talks. One month later Moto Nsa was arrested by the Angolan authorities, having been discovered on board a boat carrying a consignment of arms, which were reportedly intended for use in a planned *coup d'état* in Equatorial Guinea. Moto Nsa was released in June and subsequently sought refuge in Spain. The PPGE was banned and the party subsequently split, with one faction demanding Moto Nsa's expulsion from the party; other party members defected to the ruling PDGE. In August Moto Nsa and 11 others were convicted *in absentia* of treason; Moto Nsa was sentenced to 101 years' imprisonment. During July and August 1997 a large number of people belonging to the PPGE and the (not yet legalized) Fuerza Demócrata Republicana (FDR) were arrested.

In January 1998 the Government resigned. Shortly afterwards Seriche Dougan was reappointed as Prime Minister and a new, enlarged Council of Ministers was formed. A notable appointment was that of Teodoro Nguema Obiang, the President's eldest son, as Minister of Forestry and Environment. In the following month a new electoral law was passed, which banned political coalitions; this was expected to disadvantage the opposition at the next legislative elections.

In late January 1998 armed protesters launched three successive attacks against mainly military targets on Bioko, killing four soldiers and three civilians. The attacks were alleged to have been perpetrated by members of the secessionist Movimiento para la Autodeterminación de la Isla de Bioko (MAIB), which was founded in 1993 to represent the island's indigenous Bubi population, who, following independence, had become outnumbered and marginalized by the dominant Fang. A wave of repressive measures against the Bubi and the local resident Nigerian community ensued; hundreds of people were arrested and many severely tortured. A maximum security alert was declared throughout the country. In May 1998 15 people were sentenced to death for their involvement in the attacks; in response to international pressure, however, the death sentences were commuted to terms of life imprisonment in September.

The country's second multi-party legislative elections (which had been postponed in November 1998) were finally held in March 1999, amid numerous allegations concerning electoral fraud and the harassment of opposition candidates and election workers, many of whom were expelled from the voting stations that they were monitoring. During the electoral campaign several members of opposition parties were arrested, including election candidates. In many districts of the mainland voters were required to cast their votes publicly. The elections were contested by 13 parties, and an estimated 99% of the electorate participated. The ruling PDGE claimed to have obtained more than 90% of the votes cast, increasing its representation from 68 to 75 of the 80 parliamentary seats. Two opposition parties, the UP and the CPDS, gained four seats and one seat, respectively, but refused to participate in the new administration. Together with five other opposition parties they rejected the results and demanded the annulment of the elections on the grounds that the electoral law had been violated. The Malabo Court of Appeal dismissed their petition, accusing the opposition of dishonesty; the case was subsequently taken to the Supreme Court. Following the election Seriche Dougan was reappointed to the premiership; a new Council of Ministers was announced in late July. The new Government instituted measures to purge corruption. During the first three months in office, the new administration dismissed hundreds of civil servants, including a number of high-ranking officials. This was followed in January 2000 by the dismissal of judicial officials, including the President of the Supreme Court and the President of the Constitutional Court. Silvestre Siale Bileka, a former Prime Minister, was appointed President of the Supreme Court

In March 2000 the new Special Representative for Equatorial Guinea at the office of the UN High Commissioner for Human Rights (UNHCHR) severely criticized the Equato-Guinean authorities for systematic and serious human rights violations. The Special Representative further stated that, despite some minor advances, real democracy did not exist in the country and accused the Government of refusing to authorize the formation of human rights non-governmental organizations. Despite serious ongoing human rights violations in the country, UNHCHR terminated the mandate of the Special Representative in April 2002, following intense lobbying by an unofficial alliance of African states in the UN.

In February 2001 Seriche Dougan's Government was dismissed. Two days later a new Council of Ministers was appointed, which included two sons and two nephews of President Obiang Nguema, and Cándido Muatetema Rivas as the new Prime Minister. Following the change of government, several opposition parties in exile in Spain urged President Obiang to call legislative elections, pointing to the dismissal of the previous Government as an indication of the failure of his political programme. In March 2002 more than 100 people were arrested on allegations that they had plotted a coup in October 2001. In June 2002 68 people were imprisoned for between six and 20 years for plotting to oust President Obiang. Opposition parties, the European Union (EU) and Amnesty International condemned the judicial process as seriously flawed, citing procedural irregularities, allegations of torture and lack of evidence.

Meanwhile, in May 2002 Obiang Nguema was declared a candidate for the presidential election, which was scheduled for February 2003. In October 2002, however, the President announced that elections would take place on 15 December. Four opposition candidates withdrew on the day of the election in protest at alleged irregularities, including intimidation of voters and expulsion of, and threats to, opposition parties' electoral monitors, as well as the presence of military personnel in some voting booths. President Obiang Nguema was returned to office for a fourth term, having obtained 97.1% of the votes cast. The EU did not consider the election free and fair and supported the opposition's call for new elections. This, however, was rejected by the Supreme Court. A month later President Obiang Nguema was sworn in as President. During the ceremony the President called for the formation of a government of national unity, including representatives from all political groups. The Government was dismissed, and in February 2003 a new, enlarged Government, again led by Prime Minister Muatetema Rivas, was appointed. The new Government included some of the presidential candidates in the December 2002 election. The CPDS, however, declared it would decline the invitation to join the Government, unless all the political prisoners imprisoned in June 2002 (including its Secretary-General, Plácido Micó Abogo) were released. Micó Abogo was eventually granted a conditional presidential pardon in August 2003, along with some 17 other political opponents of the regime sentenced in the previous year.

Attempted Coup

In late October 2003 reports circulated of a failed coup attempt. Dozens of military officers, including a close relative of President Obiang Nguema, as well as a number of civilians were arrested between November and December. They were tried secretly in February 2004. Details of the trial and sentences were not provided. The authorities claimed to have foiled at least three further coups in March, May and October 2004, one involving foreign nationals. In March 15 foreigners, mainly South African and Armenian nationals resident in the country, were arrested following intelligence allegedly received from South Africa. Their trial began in open court in Malabo on 23 August. Together with Severo Moto Nsa and the members of his so-called government-in-exile, who were tried *in absentia*, the accused were convicted, in November, of attempting to overthrow the Government and kill President Obiang Nguema. They received prison terms ranging from 14 to 63 years; Moto Nsa was sentenced to 63 years' imprisonment. The authorities accused some Western governments, businessmen and multinational companies of involvement in the alleged coup plot, which, they claimed, had been organized by Moto Nsa. He denied any involvement in the affair. The arrest of the 15 foreign nationals in March followed that of 70 South African nationals at Harare airport (Zimbabwe) for complicity in the alleged conspiracy to overthrow the Equato-Guinean Government. In late August they were convicted in a Zimbabwean court of contravening immigration laws; two were also convicted of contravening aviation laws, while Simon Mann, the suspected operational leader of the alleged coup attempt, was convicted of attempting to purchase weapons. The Equato-Guinean authorities relentlessly sought his extradition from Zimbabwe for him to face charges of plotting to overthrow the Government in Equatorial Guinea. In May 2007 the Harare Magistrates' Court granted the application requesting his extradition; however, an appeal against the Court's decision was lodged. Mann was the founder of Executive Outcomes, an international security consultancy that was subsequently liquidated. Also in August 2004, Sir Mark Thatcher (a businessman and son of former British Prime Minister Baroness Thatcher) was arrested in South Africa on suspicion of having financed the alleged coup attempt. Although Thatcher initially denied involvement in the affair, in January 2005 he admitted contravening South African anti-mercenary legislation by agreeing to finance the use of a helicopter. He was fined R3m. (more than US $500,000) and was given a four-year suspended sentence. In June six of the Armenian nationals convicted of involvement in the coup attempt were pardoned by

President Obiang Nguema and released from prison, although according to Equato-Guinean law, sentences, and convictions, can only be overturned by an appeal court. In mid-2006 one of the South African prisoners was pardoned on humanitarian grounds. Dozens of other political prisoners and detainees were released at the same time, including some convicted of involvement in attempted coups in June 2002 and in September 2005.

Legislative and municipal elections were held concurrently on 25 April 2004. Political opponents complained of intimidation by the authorities preceding the elections. As expected, the ruling PDGE obtained 68 of the 100 parliamentary seats (a coalition of eight parties allied to Obiang Nguema secured a further 30 seats) and won, with its allies, 237 of the 244 council seats in the 30 local councils, while the CPDS won the remaining two parliamentary seats and had just eight councillors elected in five local councils. The CPDS contested the results of the two polls, alleging serious irregularities, but the Malabo Appeals Court upheld the result and rejected the CPDS's charges. In June the new House of Representatives was sworn in. The CPDS took up its two seats, but refused to sit on any committees. Later in June a new Government was formed, led by Prime Minister Miguel Abia Biteo Borico, who demanded, as an anti-corruption measure, that the new ministers declare their assets before being sworn in.

On 10 August 2006 President Obiang Nguema accepted the resignation of all 51 members of the Council of Ministers, accusing them of corruption and incompetence. Nevertheless, the majority of the new Government, comprising 28 ministers and 31 vice-ministers and secretaries, had held portfolios in the previous administration. All but two ministers in the new Government were affiliated to the ruling PDGE. Controversially, the tradition of appointing a Prime Minister of the minority Bubi ethnicity was broken with the appointment of Ricardo Mangué Obama Nfubea, a member of the Fang majority. The new Prime Minister pledged to combat corruption, and in October he requested that members of his Government declare their personal wealth. The declaration of private wealth was made compulsory for all civil servants, who in December were urged to denounce acts of corruption committed by their colleagues. In January 2007, during the swearing in ceremony of senior civil servants, President Obiang vowed to root out corruption and incompetence in his Government. One month later a Presidential decree established the Agencia Nacional de Investigación Financiera, set up to fight money-laundering and the financing of terrorism.

Opposition from Exiles

Equato-Guinean exiles have reacted cautiously to Obiang Nguema's efforts to encourage their return. His regime's authoritarian ethos, together with reports of persistent human rights abuses, corruption and economic stagnation, have discouraged the great majority of émigrés from returning. During the Macías period the most influential exiled opposition party had been the Alianza Nacional para la Restauración Democrática de Guinea Ecuatorial (ANRD). Based in Geneva, Switzerland, it achieved a semi-representative, if unofficial, standing with UN bodies. Following Obiang Nguema's accession to power, however, ANRD's influence declined, and the exiled opposition split into numerous small and shifting groups, many of which were based in Spain. The PPGE, founded in 1983, emerged as a particularly influential opposition party during the late 1980s. Moto Nsa, the PPGE's leader during 1983–97, was appointed Secretary-General of the short-lived Junta Coordinadora de las Fuerzas de Oposición Democrática, which was formed in Zaragoza, Spain, in 1983, as a co-ordinating body for exiled opposition groups. Political liberalization in Gabon led during 1990 to the emergence of Libreville as a new centre of activity for the Equato-Guinean opposition in exile. The most significant of these groups was the Unión para la Democracia y el Desarollo Social (UDDS), founded in September 1990 and led by Antonio Sibacha Bueicheku. A coalition of parties dominated by the UDDS was formed in Libreville, in April 1991, under the title of Coordinación Democrática de los Partidos de Oposición de Guinea Ecuatorial, which has since been disbanded. Following the Government's amnesty for political exiles in January 1992 and the enactment of legislation in that month legalizing a multi-party political system, the opposition began to prepare for the legislative elections due to take place in 1993 (see above). The POC was dissolved in March 1996. In early 1999 opposition parties exiled in Spain formed the Coordinadora de la Oposición Conjunta (CODE), which grouped Moto Nsa's faction of the PPGE, the MAIB, the FDR, the Foro-Democracia Guinea Ecuatorial, the Unión Democrática Independiente (UDI) and the Unión para la Reconciliación y el Progreso. Following the March legislative elections, CODE announced the creation of a civil-military front and a government-in-exile, which aimed to overthrow President Obiang Nguema and promote democratic change. However, within a year the CODE had effectively ceased to exist.

In November 2000 six political parties (including the CPDS, the PPGE, the UP and the FDR) formed the Frente de Oposición Democrática (FOD), whose declared objective was to promote a speedy transition to democracy. One month later another coalition, the Resistencia Nacional de Guinea Ecuatorial, was created by five opposition parties in exile in Spain (including the PPGE, the FDR, the UDI and the MAIB) and was joined in March 2001 by the CPDS and the UP in Equatorial Guinea. By 2004, however, they had all collapsed. Numerous groups and associations have continued to emerge in Spain, all short-lived and of little impact in Equatorial Guinea.

In September 2003 three political parties in Spain formed a 10-minister government-in-exile, with Moto Nsa, leader of the banned PPGE, as its President. In March 2005 Moto Nsa fled to Croatia, fearing assassination by agents of the Equato-Guinean Government. Moto Nsa returned to Spain in April, having received assurances over his safety from the Spanish authorities, whom he had accused of complicity in the alleged assassination plot. In June the Equato-Guinean embassy in Madrid, Spain, was forcibly occupied and damaged by opposition activists who blamed the Obiang Nguema regime for the attempted murder that month of Manuel Tomo, the brother of FDR leader Germán Tomo, in a suburb of Madrid. In April several people were found guilty of the attempted murder of Manuel Tomo, but the court failed to find evidence of Equato-Guinean government involvement. Following the attack, the embassy was temporarily closed by the Equato-Guinean Government, which demanded as a condition for its re-opening that the Spanish Government should guarantee its safety and deal firmly with Equato-Guinean opposition militants exiled in Spain. In December Spain revoked Moto Nsa's status of political asylum.

FOREIGN RELATIONS

Equatorial Guinea's relations with Spain, the former colonial power (which has traditionally provided substantial economic aid), have been consistently strained by reports of internal corruption, the misuse of aid funds and abuses of human rights. In December 1993 the Spanish consul in Bata was expelled 'for interference in the country's internal affairs', following an alleged meeting between the consul and members of opposition parties. The Spanish Government recalled its ambassador and reduced aid to the country by 50%, excluding humanitarian assistance, from the beginning of January 1994. The ban was extended to all forms of aid at the end of the month. The EU has also withdrawn financial assistance and the UN Development Programme suspended a number of projects. In April 1994 negotiations commenced between the Equato-Guinean and Spanish Governments, with a view to resuming full Spanish financial assistance. In June aid donors met representatives of the Obiang Nguema administration and opposition parties; it was agreed that assistance would be resumed gradually, on condition that improvements were made in both the human rights situation and the democratization process. Relations with Spain improved considerably in 1996, with the election of a new Spanish Government; in 1997 negotiations recommenced between the two countries concerning the resumption of economic co-operation and aid. Opposition politicians expressed dismay at the *rapprochement*, which they believed would reduce international pressure on the Obiang Nguema Government to install a truly democratic political system in Equatorial Guinea. However, bilateral relations became strained once again during the second half of 1997, when Spain granted refugee status to the Equato-Guinean dissident Moto Nsa (see above), and deteriorated further in 1998. The Obiang Nguema regime has continued to accuse Spain of interfering in Equatorial Guinea's domestic affairs, of attempting to destabilize the country by providing funds to opposition organizations, and of trying to recolonize the country. Spanish citizens were frequently subjected to detention and expulsion. Spanish assistance to Equatorial Guinea resumed after the two Governments signed, in October 1999, a new three-year co-operation pact, which was not conditional on improvements in the Government's observance of human rights and democratization. During brief visits to Madrid, Spain, in March and October 2001 Obiang Nguema held talks with Spanish Prime Minister José María Aznar, who agreed to normalize relations with Equatorial Guinea in the economic field and discussed the possible restructuring of the outstanding debts owed to Spain. Spain was willing to help strengthen the Equato-Guinean institutions, in order to promote economic development, in exchange for the promotion and protection of human rights within Equatorial Guinea and legal guarantees for foreign investment.

In mid-2003 the two countries signed a commercial agreement aimed at promoting and protecting reciprocal investments. Other agreements signed between the two countries during 2003 included the pardoning of part of the Equato-Guinean debt to Spain, estimated at more than €70m. In exchange, Spanish companies were given exclusive rights to invest in private and public projects. One of the first companies to benefit from the agreement was Repsol, the Spanish petroleum company, which was granted 25% of the Corisco Deep oilfield, which had previously been granted in its totality to Vancon, a US oil company. Relations deteriorated in 2004, however, as the Spanish authorities repeatedly refused to extradite Moto Nsa, whom the Equatorial Guinean authorities accused of involvement in the alleged March coup attempt. They also accused Spain of withholding information about the planning of the alleged coup. The Equato-Guinean ambassador to Spain was recalled for one month. He was recalled again in July 2005 when the embassy was temporarily closed after an attack by opposition exiles (see above). Meanwhile, relations between the two countries began to improve in December 2004, after Spain announced that it was to pardon more than US $17m. of Equatorial Guinea's debt and provide an aid package for Equatorial Guinea up to 2006 worth €24m. In December 2005 relations between the two countries improved after Spain revoked Moto Nsa's political asylum, although the Spanish authorities refused to return him to Equatorial Guinea. In January 2006 the Equato-Guinean embassy in Madrid was finally reopened and a new ambassador was appointed. Meetings between high-level officials from the two countries were held throughout 2006, followed by a two-day visit to Spain by President Obiang in November, amid much criticism from Equato-Guinean exiles as well as from Spanish opposition parties.

In the early 1980s Obiang Nguema attempted to move the country away from Spanish influence and into France's economic sphere. In December 1983 Equatorial Guinea became a member of the Union douanière et économique de l'Afrique centrale (which was replaced by the Communauté économique et monétaire en Afrique centrale—CEMAC—in 1999), and in August 1984 it joined the Banque des états de l'Afrique centrale (BEAC). Full entry to the Franc Zone followed in January 1985, when the CFA franc replaced the epkwele as the national currency. The increasing level of French economic influence was reflected in the President's regular attendance at Franco-African summit meetings, and in an extended curriculum of French-language classes in Equato-Guinean schools. In February 1998 French became Equatorial Guinea's second official language. In March 2001 Obiang Nguema travelled to Paris, France, where he discussed with France's President Chirac the desirability of expanding economic relations, particularly in the petroleum industry. However, France's importance in that sector was beginning to wane. Equatorial Guinea has also sought in recent years to establish or improve relations with other European countries, particularly the United Kingdom, where it opened an embassy in May 2005. The Equato-Guinean Government also solicited British support in its attempt to prosecute several British businessmen accused of financing the alleged coup attempt of March 2004, adding that a lack of co-operation on the part of the British authorities could adversely affect British business interests in Equatorial Guinea. However, in September the British High Court turned down President Obiang Nguema's suit against several of the British businessmen. Also in September 2004 President Obiang Nguema travelled to Ukraine with the aim of strengthening relations between the two countries. During the visit he signed several agreements in spheres including military and technical co-operation. The agreements were ratified in December 2005 during the visit to Ukraine of the Equato-Guinean foreign minister.

During the late 1990s Obiang Nguema sought to improve Equatorial Guinea's relations with the EU. In July 2001 an EU delegation visited Equatorial Guinea to discuss co-operation under the European Development Fund, whereby the EU was to release more than US $11m. for development projects over a five-year period. Throughout 2002 and 2003 the EU remained critical of government policy, repeatedly calling for the release of the 68 prisoners sentenced in June 2002 and urging the Government to begin the process of democratization without delay. In February 2004 further talks were held between the EU and the Government of Equatorial Guinea, aimed at strengthening co-operation, particularly in the areas of good governance, human rights, democracy and civil society. A protocol on these matters was finally signed in November of that year. In June 2006 the EU banned Equato-Guinean aircraft, including the presidential plane, from using EU airspace. Despite the Equato-Guinea authorities denouncing the ban, further co-operation projects on human rights and law and order were agreed with the EU in July.

Obiang Nguema has also sought to establish amicable relations with countries outside Europe, particularly the People's Republic of China and the Democratic People's Republic of Korea. In September 1996 an agreement on economic co-operation was signed with China, which was renewed in November 2001, when President Obiang visited China. Co-operation agreements were signed on computing and infrastructure development, as well as on health care. In addition, China agreed to pardon some of Equatorial Guinea's debt and to provide interest-free loans. In November 2002 China also agreed to finance the construction of the headquarters of Equatorial Guinea's national radio and television company in Malabo and Bata at a cost of US $6.2m. Co-operation expanded in 2005, following several reciprocal visits by senior government officials of both countries. At the end of a visit to China in October 2005, President Obiang Nguema stated that thenceforth China would be Equatorial Guinea's main development partner. Agreements were signed in areas of infrastructure and housing, natural resource exploitation, agriculture, silviculture and fishing, as well as health and service provision. In exchange for a share in Equatorial Guinea's petroleum exploitation, China cancelled a reportedly large but undisclosed part of the debt owed by Equatorial Guinea. There were further reciprocal visits throughout 2006 and the first quarter of 2007, during which additional economic agreements were reached. These include an accord signed in Malabo in August 2006 whereby some 15 Chinese companies were contracted to build thousands of social housing units and some 2,000 km of roads, and to undertake other infrastructure projects throughout the country, including a hydro-electricity terminal which would supply electricity to 23 towns in the mainland region. In November China granted Equatorial Guinea more than US $2,000m. in loans for infrastructure projects and, in January 2007, cancelled $75m. of Equatorial Guinea's debt. During President Obiang Nguema's visit to the Philippines in May 2006, the two countries signed several co-operation agreements in economic, cultural and technological spheres. Equatorial Guinea also signed an agreement with the Banco de Comercio of the Philippines to create a national bank in Equatorial Guinea, to be called the Banco Nacional de Guinea Ecuatorial, which was expected to become operational later that year.

Meanwhile, in July 1998, during a visit to Iran by the Equato-Guinean Minister of Foreign Affairs and Co-operation, it was agreed that the two countries would establish full diplomatic relations, and several co-operation arrangements were signed in the areas of agriculture, health and technology. Links with Israel were strengthened during 2005. In July a major programme for improving health-care provision was started in conjunction with the Shiba Hospital in Tel-Aviv, Israel, which was to train over 100 Equato-Guinean nurses, including nursing trainers. Co-operation has also been promoted with Latin American countries, notably Mexico and Cuba. During Obiang Nguema's visit to Cuba in November 1999, a co-operation agreement between the two countries was signed in the areas of health, education and agriculture. The co-operation agreement was renewed in May 2007 and expanded to include training in telecommunications and the media. Military aid from Morocco, which replaced that from Cuba after 1979, remained crucial to the maintenance of Obiang Nguema's regime until 1994, when most Moroccan troops were withdrawn from Equatorial Guinea, apart from a small number of guards overseeing the President's security.

Some military aid has also been received from the USA. After a period of tense relations in the 1990s, the US embassy in Malabo was eventually closed in 1996, apparently as part of a programme of cost-saving measures. With relations between the two countries improving in the early years of the 21st century, the US Department of State reopened its embassy in Malabo in October 2003, headed by a chargé d'affaires. US investment in Equatorial Guinea was estimated at US $5,000m. in 2002. According to numerous reports, in the wake of the terrorist attacks on the USA on 11 September 2001, the US Administration approved further military aid to train a coastguard service to protect petroleum installations in Equatorial Guinea. It has been estimated that by 2015 Equatorial Guinea, together with Angola and Nigeria, will provide 25% of the USA's petroleum imports. In a sign of increasing co-operation between the USA and Equatorial Guinea, in June 2006 Donald Johnson was nominated to succeed US Ambassador Niels Marquardt, who was resident in Cameroon, as resident US Ambassador in Malabo. In January 2007 Equatorial Guinea signed a five-year deal with a private US firm to train its armed forces and presidential guard.

Regionally, Equatorial Guinea's relations with Nigeria deteriorated when, in 1988, Nigeria threatened to invade Bioko to eject South African personnel, who were alleged to be installing a satellite-tracking station and extending Malabo airport, in preparation for a military assault on the Niger delta oilfields. The affair was eventually resolved in 1990 by reciprocal state visits by the two Heads of State. In mid-1994 the two countries agreed to co-operate in the establishment of an international commission to demarcate maritime borders in the Gulf of Guinea. These negotiations between Equatorial Guinea and Nigeria were complicated by the presence of substantial reserves of petroleum in the disputed offshore areas. In August 2000 the two countries signed seven agreements covering a number of areas, including bilateral air services, fishing rights, technical aid corps and defence co-operation. Relations between the two countries continued to improve, and in March 2002 Equatorial Guinea supported Nigeria in its dispute with Cameroon over the Bakassi peninsula. However, opposition groups in and outside Equatorial Guinea viewed the rapprochement between the two Governments with suspicion, and have accused Nigerian security personnel of connivance with Equato-Guinean security forces in the abduction and subsequent repatriation of Equato-Guinean exiles in Nigeria in January and July 2005. Over the years relations with Cameroon have been intermittently tense. There was renewed tension between the two countries after Equatorial Guinea supported Nigeria's claim to the Bakassi peninsula. Relations deteriorated sharply in March 2004, as the Government of Equatorial Guinea effected a major clamp-down on alleged illegal immigrants. Hundreds were forcibly expelled from the country, the vast majority of whom were from Cameroon. Many were detained and ill-treated, and had their property stolen or destroyed by the Equato-Guinean security forces. The Cameroon Government recalled its ambassador, while in Cameroon the Equatorial Guinean diplomatic missions were attacked. In December 2006 the Equato-Guinean authorities unilaterally closed its border with Cameroon at Kye-Ossi following an assault on an Equato-Guinean nun by Cameroonian traders. The border remained closed for several weeks.

Relations with Gabon have come under strain, as a result of unresolved frontier disputes, revived by petroleum exploration activity in southern Río Muni. In March 2003 Gabonese forces occupied the small island of Mbañé, over which both countries have long claimed ownership; in June Equatorial Guinea rejected a Gabonese proposal to share any petroleum revenues from the island. In January 2004 both countries agreed to seek UN mediation to settle the dispute, and a mediator was sent to the area in June. In an attempt to settle the territorial dispute amicably, in May President Obiang Nguema proposed joint exploitation of the petroleum in the area. At a meeting in the Gabonese capital in January 2005 the Presidents of both countries expressed optimism that an amicable agreement would soon be finalized. In February 2006 the Presidents of the two countries met under the auspices of the UN at its headquarters in Geneva, Switzerland, to establish definitively the sea and land borders between the two countries and sovereignty over the islands of Mbañé, Cocoteros and Conga. The two Presidents agreed to rescind the 2004 agreement jointly to exploit the natural resources in the disputed area. They agreed to meet again as soon as negotiations were concluded to ratify an agreement. However, no further meetings took place, and in April 2007 the Equatorial Guinean Government accused the Gabonese of unwillingness to discuss sovereignty over the islands and of blocking the negotiations initiated a year earlier.

In May 1993 Equatorial Guinea and South Africa established diplomatic relations, and in 1999 several South African companies became involved in various economic and social projects in Equatorial Guinea. In March 2001 South Africa's largest petroleum company reached agreement with two Equato-Guinean companies to drill for petroleum and gas off shore. Relations have continued to improve, and in 2004 South Africa opened an embassy in Malabo.

Since 2000 Equatorial Guinea has actively sought to establish diplomatic and economic relations with other African countries. Close ties were formed with Angola during 2000 and were strengthened with the opening, in January 2006, of an Equato-Guinean embassy in the Angolan capital, Luanda. In February President Obiang Nguema and several of his ministers visited Angola to sign several co-operation agreements in the areas of defence, internal and external security and public order, oil and transport. Angolan president José Eduardo dos Santos reciprocated the visit in February 2007. In February 2001 diplomatic relations were established with Libya. In 2004, following a visit by President Obiang Nguema to Ghana in June, the two countries signed economic agreements providing, *inter alia*, for a study into refining Equato-Guinean oil in Ghana. Closer links were also forged with Zimbabwe following the arrest at Harare International Airport, Zimbabwe, in March of 70 alleged mercenaries accused of planning to overthrow the Government of Equatorial Guinea. In June the two countries signed an agreement to open diplomatic delegations in Malabo and Harare, and in November President Robert Mugabe visited Equatorial Guinea where he was acclaimed as the 'saviour of the nation' and Equatorial Guinea's 'favourite son' by the host country's authorities. President Obiang Nguema reciprocated the visit in April 2006. During his visit to Zimbabwe economic and trade agreements were signed between the two countries, although both countries denied reports that they had signed an agreement whereby Equatorial Guinea would supply petroleum to Zimbabwe. None the less, in late May, press reports maintained that such an agreement in fact had been reached. Immediately after a visit in March 2007 by President Mugabe, Equatorial Guinea began to supply petroleum to Zimbabwe on favourable terms. Stronger links with other lusophone African countries were being developed in the mid-2000s.

Economy

MARISÉ CASTRO

The economy of Equatorial Guinea was traditionally based on agriculture and forestry, the principal products being timber, cocoa, coffee, palm oil, bananas and cassava. During the 1990s, however, the petroleum sector became increasingly important, leading to unprecedented levels of economic growth. By 2002 it had become the country's most valuable asset, responsible for turning Equatorial Guinea into the fastest growing economy in the world and, by 2005, Africa's sixth largest oil producer (after Nigeria, Algeria, Libya, Angola and Egypt), when, according to the IMF, production reached 355,000 barrels per day (b/d), representing a rise of 7.9% on the previous year. According to the World Bank, in 2001 Equatorial Guinea's gross national income (GNI), measured at average 1999–2001 prices, was US $327m., equivalent to $710 per head. During 1995–2004 gross domestic product (GDP) per head increased, in real terms, at an average annual rate of 18.8%. Over the same period the population increased by an estimated average of 2.6% per year. Overall GDP increased, in real terms, at an average annual rate of 21.6% in 1995–2004. According to the World Bank, real GDP advanced by 16.9% in 2000, but by only 1.3% in 2001, before increasing by 17.6% in 2002. However, according to figures from the regional central bank, the Banque des États de l'Afrique Centrale (BEAC), real GDP increased by 65.6% in 2001, by an estimated 20.9% in 2002 and by 15.0% in 2003. In 2004 GDP growth reached 26.6%, (48.6%, according to the IMF), attributable mainly to the expansion of hydrocarbon production. In the same year non-oil GDP increased by 13% (9.9%, according to the IMF), owing primarily to the expansion in construction, infrastructure and services. According to the IMF, this increased to 10.8% in 2005 and remained at that level in 2006. Overall GDP growth was estimated by the IMF at 45.8% in 2005. However, according to the Equato-Guinean authorities GDP growth in 2005 was only 9.2% (while according to the IMF real GDP growth in 2005 was 6.5%) and the forecast for growth in 2006 was 8.3% and for 2007–10 was 5.0%. This decrease was attributed to the decline in production by the Zafiro oilfield, exploited by ExxonMobil. GDP per head in 2002 was $4,364, increasing to $4,741 in 2003 and to $5,753 in 2004. Inflation fell to 4% in 2005, below the regional average of 4.8%.

In 2003 petroleum revenue totalled 409,709m. francs CFA, constituting 87% of total revenue (excluding grants), compared with approximately 133,199m. francs CFA in 2000; the figure for 2004 had risen considerably, to 766,278m. francs CFA (91% of total revenue, excluding grants). In 2005 petroleum revenue almost doubled in nominal terms, reaching 1,440,885m. francs CFA (94% of total revenue, excluding grants). In 2005 the country exported US $7,049.5m. worth of petroleum, according to preliminary IMF figures. Hydrocarbons production and timber accounted for nearly all of the country's total exports in 2005 with oil and gas accounting for an estimated 93.2% of GDP and a preliminary 98.9% of exports. Despite the large revenues brought by oil, some 65% of the population continued to live in abject poverty. A report published in October 2005 by the UN Development Programme (UNDP) showed that, in one year, Equatorial Guinea had dropped 12 places on the Index of Human Development, from 109th to 121st, and that life expectancy had fallen from 49.1 years in 2001 to 43.3 in 2005. In January 2006 UNDP estimated that 60% of the population had no access to running water or electricity and that 70% had lived on less than $2 per day. In the same year the IMF stated that Equatorial Guinea had sufficient resources to be able to end poverty. However, an estimated 80% of the national revenue is concentrated in the hands of the ruling oligarchy.

AGRICULTURE, FORESTRY AND FISHING

Agriculture, including hunting, forestry and fishing, contributed an estimated 2.1% of GDP in 2005 (compared with 51.6% of GDP in 1995). However, by 2006 its contribution had recovered to over 10%. In 2004 agriculture employed an estimated 68.4% of the active population. In May 2007 the Government announced plans to increase investment in the agricultural sector via a project worth US $3.5m. which will also include the revamping of the Institute for Agricultural Promotion. Timber, primarily, from the mainland province of Río Muni is the second largest revenue earner after petroleum and accounted for 25.8% of export revenue in 1996; however, by 2004 it accounted for only an estimated 1.2% of export revenue. There are some 1.3m. ha of timber suitable for lumbering operations. The devaluation of the national currency, the CFA franc, in 1994, stimulated timber exploration and output, and by the end of 1997 all timber land had been granted in concessions. This massive growth in the forestry exploitation sector has called into question its sustainability. The environmental impact on easily accessible areas close to the coast or to navigable waterways has already been devastating. It is estimated that during 1990–2000 Equatorial Guinea lost 0.6% of its forest annually. According to the IMF, at the current rate of extraction, available resources would be exhausted by the year 2012. The principal exploited species of wood are okoumé (most of which is exported, with only 3% processed locally) and akoga. Output rose throughout the 1990s, reaching an estimated 811,000 cu m in both 1995 and 1996. By 1997 exports totalled 510,000 cu m, and reached 514,800 cu m in 2001. In 2004 FAO estimated the value of Equatorial Guinea's forestry exports for that year at around US $96.6m. Exploitation rights to sizeable areas of forest were granted by President Obiang Nguema to foreign (mainly French and Spanish) concessionaires. By the end of 1995 there were 38 timber concessions, compared with 15 at the end of 1993. In 1997 the private timber industry was dominated by 20 companies, primarily European in origin. However, by 1999 the sector came to be dominated by Asian firms, and the People's Republic of China became the main importer of Equato-Guinean timber.

Cocoa, which provided 2.9% of export earnings in 1996, is the main crop of Bioko, where its cultivation accounts for about 90% of the country's total output. In 2003 cocoa production totalled some 2,000 metric tons and by 2005 it had declined further to 1,993 tons. Prior to independence an area in excess of 41,000 ha was under cocoa cultivation, underpinned by high guaranteed prices on the Spanish domestic market. More than 800 plantations belonged to Africans, but most of the land and production was controlled by Europeans. Nationalized under Macías Nguema, the cocoa plantations were initially offered back to their former owners after the coup of 1979. However, many plantations remained unclaimed and others were subsequently reconfiscated; most are now owned by members of the presidential entourage, and are managed by two Spanish companies. They are worked on a share-cropping basis by local small farmers. Only about one-third of the land that was cultivated before independence is now exploited, and most of the trees are old and poorly tended. In 1991 the World Bank initiated a 10-year rehabilitation scheme, under which strictly commercial criteria were to be applied, to preclude any accusations of anti-competitive subsidies. Under the programme, it was hoped that yields would be increased through replanting and the control of plant pests and diseases. The programme also provided for a gradual expansion in the areas under cultivation, with the promotion of diversification into other crops in areas of marginal cocoa production. The cocoa rehabilitation scheme was part of a wider agricultural project, which attracted a pledge of US $18m. from the World Bank and lesser sums from other donors. Cocoa still employs the highest proportion of Equatorial Guinea's work-force. However, despite considerable pay increases in recent years, many workers are leaving cocoa plantations to work in the more lucrative petroleum industry.

In the 1980s the economy of Equatorial Guinea was entirely dependent on coffee and cocoa. Coffee is still an important agricultural export commodity, although it is believed that about two-thirds of the coffee harvest is smuggled into Gabon to benefit from that country's higher producer prices. In 1988 it was estimated that there were nearly 20,000 ha planted with coffee, divided among some 25,000 households. The quality is poor and the yields are extremely low.

Cassava, coco yam, sweet potatoes, plantain, bananas, rice, maize, palm oil and eggs are all produced for the domestic market. In July 2002 the Instituto de Promoción Agraria began to grant credit to small farmers in Malabo as an incentive for them to grow food for the internal market, in an attempt to limit the country's dependence on imports. There are eventual prospects of substantial food exports to Gabon, which is persistently short of foodstuffs and already imports plantain from Río Muni. The Government is promoting the production of spices (vanilla, pepper and coriander) for export.

Livestock raising almost disappeared from the country during the Macías Nguema period. In 1986 the African Development Bank (ADB) provided a loan of US $12.6m. to revive cattle-rearing on the high pastures of Moka, in Bioko, to a level comparable to that prevailing prior to independence, when the island was self-sufficient in beef and dairy products. The cattle herd was estimated at 5,000 head in 2004, and a slaughterhouse was in operation.

Fisheries constitute one of the most abundant resources of Equatorial Guinea, but have been seriously neglected. At independence, some 5,000 people worked in the fishing industry, and those of Annobón (Pagalu) were renowned as skilled fishermen. Tuna from the waters around Annobón and shellfish from Bioko were processed locally and exported. Under Macías Nguema, the fishing industry collapsed, and the USSR was granted a fishing monopoly. This was terminated in 1980, and replaced by agreements with Spain in 1980, with Nigeria in 1982 (renewed in 1991), and with the European Community (EC, now the European Union—EU) in 1983 (renewed in 1986 and 1989). In 1989 the EC paid ECU 6m. for an agreed monthly tonnage catch by European fishing vessels, mainly Spanish and French. The agreement was renewed for a period of three years from July 2001. Under the renewed agreement, annual financial compensation for Equatorial Guinea was increased from €320,000 to €412,500, while the annual level of captures available to the 62 permitted European vessels was increased from 4,000 metric tons to 5,500 tons. The agreement was renewed in 2004 and again in 2007. The EU has also financed research and training schemes to improve Equatorial Guinea's own artisanal fishing operations. The total catch rose to 7,001 tons in 1999, but declined to an estimated 3,500 tons in 2004. Given the importance of the primary sector, particularly with regard to employment, in 2003 the Government pledged commitment to the diversification and development of agro-fisheries production, including food conservation, food processing, transportation and marketing. It was expected that by implementing the rural development programme Equatorial Guinea would eventually produce a surplus for the export market, particularly in the fishing industry, which remained underdeveloped.

INDUSTRY, MINING, POWER AND COMMUNICATIONS

In 1984 the offshore Alba gas and condensate field was discovered by Spain's Repsol on behalf of Empresa Guineano-Española de Petróleos (Gepsa), a joint venture between the Government and Repsol. However, Gepsa was dissolved in 1990, and the concession was taken over, on a production-sharing basis, by a consortium of US independent operators, led by Walter International. Production began in late 1991, at a rate of 1,200 b/d. The first consignment of condensates left Bioko in early 1992. Output rose to 6,700 b/d in 1995, and increased further during the late 1990s. Walter International carried out further successful exploration work in neighbouring blocks near Bioko, and between April 1992 and March 1993 it was reported that the company had exported some 1.2m. barrels of high-grade petroleum valued at US $23m. In 1999 Equatorial Guinea exported 36m. barrels valued at $400m. In 1995 the Northern Michigan Electric Co (NOMECO) took over the operation of the Alba wells. By 2000 Alba's production of condensate reached 14,500 b/d, with an additional 1,800 b/d of natural gas liquids. By 2006 Alba's production of condensate had risen to 40,000 b/d. In January 2002 CMS Energy, the majority partner and operator of the Alba field and NOMECO's parent company, sold all its interests in Equatorial Guinea to the US company Marathon Oil for $993m. Marathon Oil also acquired a majority interest in the Bioko Block and Atlantic Methanol Plant in Malabo, which began production in 2001.

Petroleum production has greatly increased since October 1995, when Exxon Mobil's (then Mobil Oil Corpn's) Zafiro field came on stream; Exxon Mobil, which has invested $130m. in the country, began to produce 40,000 b/d from Zafiro in August 1996; by 2002 Zafiro was producing 150,000 b/d and in 2004 production stood at an estimated 280,000 b/d. The Zafiro field is Equatorial Guinea's largest producer, producing about 70% of all Equatorial Guinea's oil, or about 300,000 b/d, with an estimated 600m. barrels in crude oil reserves. Exxon Mobil's total production in the country reached 100,000 b/d by 1999 and with the entry into production of the new field, Jade, in March 2000 output rose to 145,000 b/d, and to 200,000 b/d by the end of 2002. Jade's production reached 60,000 b/d by mid-2002. In May 2002 the company announced further investment in the Zafiro oilfield of $900m., and the installation of a second production rig, which was expected to increase the field's output by about 70%, bringing ExxonMobil's (as the company had been renamed in late 1999) total oil production in Equatorial Guinea to about 250,000 b/d by the end of 2003. ExxonMobil was due to return to Equatorial Guinea in 2006 part of block B, in which the Zafiro field is located, making it available for the Government to negotiate exploration rights on new terms. Other parcels, including some in block F, operated by Marathon Oil, were also expected to become available in 2006. In September that year a new licensing round for new offshore acreage was opened. It consisted of 28 blocks, eight of which were located in the Bioko Basin and 16 in the Río Muni Basin. The remaining four were located around Annóbon Island. The results were expected to be announced in January 2007. Test drilling is now under way in the Topacio prospect, also controlled by ExxonMobil, in which United Meridien International Corporation (UMIC) has a 25% stake. The Topacio prospect could potentially yield a further 40,000 b/d. Ocean Energy Inc. has acquired the exploration rights of blocks A, C and D to the north of Bioko, where drilling commenced in late 1996, from UMIC, the previous majority shareholder and operator for those blocks.

In 1996 the French company Elf Aquitaine (now part of Total) was planning to set up several Equato-Guinean-Gabonese joint ventures in order to circumvent a territorial dispute between the two countries regarding offshore fields in the vicinity of the islands of Corisco and the Great and Little Elobeys. However, the disputed ownership of several islands was reported still to be obstructing development of the area in 2003. In an attempt to settle the territorial dispute amicably, in May President Obiang Nguema proposed the joint Equato-Guinean-Gabonese exploitation of the oil in the area. In addition, in early 2001 the US company Triton Energy (now owned by Amerada Hess), in partnership with the South African oil and gas exploration group Energy Africa, began production at the Ceiba oilfield in the Río Muni basin on the coast opposite Mbini, the second most important field after Zafiro and ahead of Alba. In the same year new discoveries increased the field's estimated proven reserves to 300,000m. barrels; in mid-2003 output from the field totalled about 45,000 b/d, and reached a reported 100,000 b/d by the first quarter of 2004. Production was expected to rise as other wells came onstream. In 2003 efforts were continuing to develop blocks in the Ceiba field's immediate vicinity; in March Energy Africa announced that it had acquired a 20% stake in ChevronTexaco's production in block L, immediately north of Ceiba. Original estimates of reserves in the Alba field stood at 69m. barrels of oil equivalent. However, new discoveries have increased the estimates to nearly 1,000m. barrels of oil equivalent. Production in the Okume field, next to Ceiba and owned by Amerada Hess (85%) and GEPetrol (15%), started in December 2006 and was expected to produce 60,000 b/d by 2008. Total petroleum production in 2001 was estimated at 250,000 b/d. By 2004 it had reached 371,700 b/d, according to estimates of the US Energy Information Administration (EIA). Various sources estimated total oil production in 2005 at 450,000–500,000 b/d. However, a study by the BEAC in early 2006 indicated that, as with other oil-producing countries in the region, production in Equatorial Guinea would begin to decrease in 2007 after peaking in 2006 at 18.6m. metric tons and would only reach 16.2m. tons in 2009. Nevertheless, by the end of 2006 total oil production was estimated at 3390,000 b/d, increasing to 420,000 b/d by the second half of 2007 and reaching some 580,000 b/d in 2008.

In February 2001 the Government created Petróleos de Guinea Ecuatorial (renamed Guinea Ecuatorial de Petróleo—GEPetrol—in October), a mixed venture with predominantly Equato-Guinean capital, to safeguard the country's interests against the foreign petroleum companies operating in the country. In July President Obiang Nguema announced plans to renegotiate hydrocarbons contracts to increase the country's participation in petroleum licences, which stood at around 5%. This increased to 15% with the granting of the first licence in 2001. In September 2002 a law was passed that officially designated oilfields as under state control. A new hydrocarbons law was passed in September 2006 aimed at increasing royalties due to the state, hitherto set at a minimum of 10% of production, and at extending state involvement in oil projects overall.

The USA is the main source of investment in the petroleum industry of Equatorial Guinea, which is the fourth largest beneficiary of US foreign investment in sub-Saharan Africa. Some 65% of the petroleum produced is exported to the USA. Nevertheless, contracts have also been signed with companies from other countries. In July 2005 the Norwegian company Equity Resources signed a contract for the exploration with the Equato-Guinean state-owned GEPetrol of part of block E (south-east of Bioko), which was abandoned by Total Oil in 2002. In January 2006 the Brazilian oil company PETROBRÁS obtained 50% of exploration rights of block L, where the Ceiba oilfield is located, near the River Muni. PETROBRÁS's partners in block L were Chevron Equatorial Guinea, Ltd (with a 22.5% stake); Amerada Hess (12.5%); Energy Africa (10%) and Sasol Petrolium International (5%). In February the Chinese hydrocarbons company China National Offshore Oil Company, Ltd signed a five-year production-sharing contract with GEPetrol for an offshore block south of Bioko. Following the visit of President Obiang to Spain in November, it was announced that Spanish oil company Repsol-YPF would form part of the consortium contracted to undertake exploration of the Corisco Deep Block. Exclusive exploration rights were granted to American company Vanco Energy in 2003. With the formation of the consortium Vanco Energy and Repsol-YPF each hold 25% of the concession, while Mexxen Petroleum, the main operator, holds 50%.

The Equato-Guinean petroleum fields also contain considerable reserves of natural gas. Since 2001 natural gas resources had been extracted by the US-based Atlantic Methanol Production Company (AMPCO). In February 1988 the US companies CMS Energy and Samedan Oil signed a deal with the Equato-Guinean Government to construct a petrochemical plant near Malabo, at a cost of US $300m. A $400m. methanol plant, completed during the second half of 2001, was designated to process most of the natural gas that was previously being flared. In 2006 it was estimated that 70,000m. cu ft of gas was flared every year. The Government pledged to eliminate all gas flaring by 2008. The plant initially produced 19,000 b/d. The condensate output of the Alba fields, in particular, rose substantially, and has been forecast to generate as much as $300,000 per day in the coming years. In mid-2001 the Alba field was producing 225m. cu ft, an increase of about 150% since late 2000, and output was expected to increase by 40% in 2003. A new condensate plant, with an annual capacity of 3.4m. tons, constructed by Marathon Oil at a cost of $1,500m., was completed six months ahead of schedule and loaded its first cargo in May 2007. BP agreed to buy the total plant production for 17 years at a cost of approximately $15,000m., with a view to exporting to the USA and other markets. In 2006 the country was exporting 45,000m. cu ft of natural gas annually. GEPetrol, meanwhile, was reported to be seeking a 25% stake in further concessions for the Alba field's natural gas, which were valued at $1,000m. in mid-2003. Altogether, in 2005 Equatorial Guinea was estimated by the EIA to have gas reserves of between 1,300,000m. and 4,400,000 cu ft. In January 2005 the Sociedad Nacional de Gas de Guinea Ecuatorial (SONAGAS) was created to oversee gas exploration and development. In May 2006 Nigeria and Equatorial Guinea signed an agreement whereby Nigeria would provide 600m.–800m. cu ft per to be processed in the liquified natural gas (LNG) plant in Bioko. In September SONAGAS and the Russian company Gazprom agreed to establish a joint venture for gas infrastructure projects and the production of LNG. Total proven oil reserves stood between 1,770m. and 2,500 m barrels at the end of 2004; however, estimates of total reserves continue to rise as a result of new discoveries. This included the discovery in October 2005 by American company Noble Energy Inc, of oil block O, some 34 km east of Bioko and with capacity to produce over 8m. cu m of natural gas per day and 1,225 b/d of condensed gas. Equatorial Guinea also has reserves of gold, iron ore, manganese, tantalum and uranium, but these have yet to be exploited.

Electricity is provided only to the main towns both on Bioko and the mainland. In 1989 a 3.6-MW hydroelectric power station, built on the Riaba river (Bioko), was officially opened. The plant was constructed at a cost of US $32.1m., and provides most of the power on Bioko. There have been commissioning problems with the power station, and disputes over electricity tariffs with a French company, Saur-Afrique, which manages the distribution of electricity on the island. During the dry season the Malabo diesel plant supplements output from Riaba. A further 3.6-MW power station, constructed with aid from the People's Republic of China, at Bikomo, near Bata, supplies 90% of Río Muni's energy requirements. In February 2000 a new thermal power station to supply Malabo, which had been under construction for two years, at a cost of $13.5m., came on stream. Nevertheless, electricity supply remains erratic, and blackouts are common. Furthermore, 60% of the population do not have access to electricity. This is partly due to ageing power installations and poor management. At the end of 2002 Equatorial Guinea was estimated to have 15.4 MW of installed generation capacity, of which 80% was thermal and the remainder hydroelectric.

Before independence, there was a diversified and flourishing light industrial sector, centred in Malabo; this infrastructure was effectively ruined by Macías Nguema and has yet to be fully restored. The manufacturing sector contributed only 0.1% of GDP in 2002. Two sawmills in Bata currently account for most of the country's industrial activity; the town also has a small cement works and a bleach factory. Food-processing and soap production are carried out on a small scale. Cocoa fermenting and drying is the only significant manufacturing industry on Bioko.

Since independence the entire Equato-Guinean road network has fallen into disrepair. There are about 700 km of paved roads in the country. During the early 1990s Spain allocated much of its economic aid towards the repair of roads on Bioko, in order to allow the cocoa plantations in the Luba and Riaba areas to re-enter production. In the late 1990s Equatorial Guinea embarked on a programme of nation-wide road repair and the rehabilitation of buildings and infrastructure in the main cities. The ADB was supporting the programme to improve the paved roads from Malabo to Luba and Riaba in 2002. A group of international donors are providing assistance for the upgrading of road access from the town of Mbini in Río Muni to Cogo on the Gabonese frontier, much of which is impassable in the rainy season; it is hoped that this will stimulate exports of foodstuffs to Gabon. The People's Republic of China was financing a project to link Mongomo to Bata, and the EU was supporting an inter-state road project to link Equatorial Guinea to Gabon and Cameroon. 'Food for work' programmes are also being introduced, in order to maintain the network of feeder roads. In mid-2000 Incat Petroleum Services won a contract to construct the main roads leading to and from Malabo, including a four-lane 7.5-km road linking the city to the airport, as well as to repair the Malabo–Luba highway. In January 2001 a French company won a contract worth US $21m. to resurface the road linking Mbini to Bata. In August 2006 an agreement was signed with China to build 2,000 km of road throughout the country. There are no railways.

Equatorial Guinea has two of the deepest seaports in the region at Bata and Malabo. The harbour that handles by far the largest volume of exports is Bata, in Río Muni; the port is used by the timber companies, and handled nearly 125,990 metric tons of exports in 1990. The Italian Government provided some US $5m. for the rehabilitation of the port in 1987, on condition that the facility be operated by a joint Italian-Equato-Guinean company. The initial aim was to increase the handling capacity of Bata to 500,000 tons per year, and eventually to 1m. tons. There have, however, been long delays in implementing this project. Malabo has an excellent natural harbour (formed by a sunken volcanic crater), which has been rehabilitated by a French company. There are regular shipping services to Europe, but maritime communications between Malabo, Bata and Annobón are erratic, and there is little maritime traffic with neighbouring mainland states. Construction, by the Dutch firm Pils, of a new port in Malabo to service the oil industry began in early 2003, and in March a major new free-trade port, constructed by Incat Petroleum Services at Luba, on the south-west coast of Bioko island, was inaugurated. The new port was to handle much of Equatorial Guinea's petroleum production in the future, and many of the petroleum companies operating in the country were expected to relocate to Luba.

There is an international airport at Malabo; a larger international airport at Bata, constructed with Italian aid, was completed in 1995. France has provided funds to upgrade facilities at the Malabo airport. Attempts to form a national airline have been beset by mismanagement and alleged corruption. Aerolíneas Guinea Ecuatorial, founded in 1982, had collapsed by 1985. Its successor, Ecuato Guineana de Aviación, was established in 1986 as a partnership between the Government and Air Inter-Gabon. After incurring heavy losses, the company went into liquidation in 1990, but has continued to operate limited regional and domestic services. In early 2006 there were 20 small airlines in the country, most operating domestically. Eighteen of them were temporarily grounded in May because they failed to meet the standards laid down by the Interntional Civil Aviation Organization. In March, meanwhile, the EU banned Equatorial Guinean aircraft from flying over EU territory. Scheduled international services are provided four times a week by Iberia and Spanair, between Malabo and Madrid, Spain, and Cameroon Airlines (CAMAIR), between Malabo and Douala, Cameroon. Swiss International Airlines (formerly Crossair) operates flights between Zürich, Switzerland, and Malabo twice a week, while KLM and Air France operate flights three times a week between Malabo, and Amsterdam and Paris, respectively. There is also a weekly flight to and from Houston, TX, USA.

AID, FINANCE AND DEVELOPMENT

Traditionally, the economy relied to a great extent on good relations with Spain and during the early 1990s Spanish assistance to Equatorial Guinea totalled about 350m. pesetas annually. However, in January 1994 Spain suspended one-half of its aid following a diplomatic contretemps. A tentative agreement for the gradual resumption of full assistance was made in mid-1994, and further negotiations took place in the late 1990s. In 1998 Spanish aid totalled just over 1.5m. pesetas, of which some two-thirds were allocated to health and education. In April 2004 Spain pardoned one-half of Equatorial Guinea's debt, estimated at €70m. In December 2004 Spain pardoned a further US $17m., and in February 2005 a Spanish aid package for Equatorial Guinea worth €24m. up to 2006 was announced.

France is the second main provider of aid; French assistance rose sharply after Equatorial Guinea joined the various French-sponsored regional economic associations for Central Africa in 1983–85. The EU, China and Cuba also provide project-specific aid. Economic relations with China have increased markedly since 2000. China has became a major player as an economic partner and provider of development aid. In October the Equato-Guinean authorities declared China to be their main development partner; at the same time China cancelled a large part of the debt owed to it by Equatorial Guinea, in exchange for a share of Equatorial Guinea's oil and construction industries. In May 2006 Equatorial Guinea and the Philippines signed an agreement for bilateral investment projects. Also in 2006 the US Agency for International Development and the Equatorial Guinean Government agreed to establish a Social Development Fund, with Equatorial Guinea's contribution set at US $15m. over a five-year period, to provide technical assistance in the implementation of health and education projects.

In January 1985 Equatorial Guinea entered the Franc Zone. The Banco de Guinea Ecuatorial (the former central bank and bank of issue) ceased operation, and the epkwele, which had been linked to the Spanish peseta, was replaced by the franc CFA at a rate of 4 bipkwele = 1 franc CFA. It was hoped that Equatorial Guinea's entry into the Franc Zone would bring the country out of isolation by encouraging foreign trade and investment. In July 1985 the 'Paris Club' of Western creditor Governments granted a rescheduling, over 10 years, of 246m. French francs of debt, with a five-year period of grace. According to the IMF, during 1991–95 total scheduled external debt-servicing amounted to an annual average of 89% of GDP; however, total cash payments on the external debt (including payments on arrears) averaged some 14% of domestic revenue over the same period. According to the World Bank, Equatorial Guinea's total external debt was US $238.9m. at the end of 2001, equivalent to 52.6% of GNI. In that year the cost of debt-servicing was equivalent to only 0.1% of the value of exports of goods and services. In 2004 the external debt was estimated at $115m., less than 3% of the GDP, with external debt-servicing considered insignificant.

The commencement in 1992 of petroleum exports was expected to generate a significant improvement in both the balance-of-payments and budgetary deficits,. On the basis of the then promising economic outlook, the IMF agreed to unblock the disbursement of structural adjustment facility funds in December 1991. The Government introduced an economic programme for 1994–96, supported by an SDR 12.9m. three-year enhanced structural adjustment facility (ESAF) from the IMF, which aimed to accelerate the diversification of the economy and the reform of the public sector, and to restructure the financial sector. Under the programme it was expected that the real rate of economic growth could be increased, while containing inflation at 35% and reducing the current-account deficit. However, while petroleum exports initially had a significant effect on the deficit on the current account of the balance of payments, which decreased, according to the IMF, from US $45.5m. in 1991 to only $0.6m. in 1994, the sector had little direct impact on the budgetary deficit (which totalled 8,318m. francs CFA in 1996 and an estimated 3,754m. francs CFA in 1998). By 1996 the current-account deficit had soared to $344m. Potential revenue from the profitable petroleum and timber sectors has been undermined by the inefficient taxation system. In addition, it has been alleged that members of the Equato-Guinean regime have profited personally from national oil revenues. While non-tax revenue from the petroleum sector did increase during 1992–95, it amounted on average only to some 10% of export earnings, which is low by regional standards.

Since 1996 there has been no formal agreement between the IMF and the Government of Equatorial Guinea, although there have been periodic consultations. The IMF has repeatedly stressed the need for Equatorial Guinea to establish greater fiscal discipline, accountability and transparency in the management of public-sector resources, particularly as regards revenue from the energy sector. In August 2001 the Government sought assistance from the IMF to restructure the economy. However, negotiations broke down when the Government refused to comply with IMF demands for greater fiscal transparency, full disclosure of government bank accounts and external audits of the petroleum sector, claiming that the information was a state secret. There were further contacts between the Government of Equatorial Guinea and the World Bank and the IMF in 2003, and in November the Government agreed to disclose the contents of Article IV, which relates to consultations on the need for transparency of statistical information, particularly with regard to the revenue from the oil sector, and improvements in macroeconomic management and governance. In April 2006 the IMF reported that Equatorial Guinea still held offshore accounts for oil revenue worth US $718m.

The devaluation of the CFA franc had a limited positive impact on Equatorial Guinea's economic prospects, although it was found necessary to impose price restraints on bread, medicines and petroleum to protect vulnerable sections of the population from economic hardship brought about by the reduction in their consumer purchasing power. Products for export were rendered more competitive on the international market and inflationary pressures were initially successfully contained. However, recent improvements in the trade balance are in part the result of a decreased purchasing power brought about by reductions in foreign aid; the re-establishment of good relations with the international donor community remains a priority, particularly in view of the reliance of the export base on timber and petroleum, and the finite nature of the reserves of these commodities. In May 2006 the IMF praised the Government's macroeconomic management and attempts at economic diversification. Nevertheless, given the frequent allegations of corruption in Equato-Guinean public life, greater public accountability in the use of government funds is also much to be desired.

Statistical Survey

Source (unless otherwise stated): Dirección Técnica de Estadística, Secretaría de Estado para el Plan de Desarrollo Económico, Malabo.

AREA AND POPULATION

Area: 28,051 sq km (10,831 sq miles): Río Muni 26,017 sq km, Bioko 2,017 sq km, Annobón 17 sq km.

Population: 300,000 (Río Muni 240,804, Bioko 57,190, Annobón 2,006), comprising 144,268 males and 155,732 females, at census of 4–17 July 1983 (Source: Ministerio de Asuntos Exteriores, Madrid); 406,151 at census of 4 July 1994 (provisional). *Mid-2006* (UN estimate): 496,000 (Source: UN, *World Population Prospects: The 2006 Revision*).

Density (mid-2006): 17.7 per sq km.

Provinces (population, census of July 1983): Kié-Ntem 70,202; Litoral 66,370; Centro-Sur 52,393; Wele-Nzas 51,839; Bioko Norte 46,221; Bioko Sur 10,969; Annobón 2,006.

Principal Towns (population at 1983 census): Bata 24,100; Malabo (capital) 15,253. *Mid-2005* (incl. suburbs, UN estimate): Malabo 96,000 (Source: UN, *World Urbanization Prospects: The 2005 Revision*).

Births and Deaths (UN estimates, annual averages): Birth rate 39.8 per 1,000 in 2000–05; Death rate 16.4 per 1,000 in 2000–05. Source: UN, *World Population Prospects: The 2006 Revision*.

Expectation of Life (years at birth, WHO estimates): 43 (males 42; females 44) in 2004. Source: WHO, *World Health Report*.

Economically Active Population (persons aged 6 years and over, 1983 census): Agriculture, hunting, forestry and fishing 59,390; Mining and quarrying 126; Manufacturing 1,490; Electricity, gas and water 224; Construction 1,929; Trade, restaurants and hotels 3,059; Transport, storage and communications 1,752; Financing, insurance, real estate and business services 409; Community, social and personal services 8,377; Activities not adequately defined 984; *Total employed* 77,740 (males 47,893, females 29,847); Unemployed 24,825 (males 18,040, females 6,785); *Total labour force* 102,565 (males 65,933, females 36,632). Note: Figures are based on unadjusted census data, indicating a total population of 261,779. The adjusted total is 300,000 (Source: ILO, *Yearbook of Labour Statistics*). *Mid-2005* ('000 persons, official estimates): Agriculture, etc. 139; Total labour force 204 (Source: FAO).

HEALTH AND WELFARE

Key Indicators

Total Fertility Rate (children per woman, 2005): 5.9.

Under-5 Mortality Rate (per 1,000 live births, 2005): 205.

HIV/AIDS (% of persons aged 15–49, 2005): 3.2.

Physicians (per 1,000 head, 2004): 0.3.

Hospital Beds (per 1,000 head, 2005): 2.2.

Health Expenditure (2004): US $ per head (PPP): 223.2.

Health Expenditure (2004): % of GDP: 1.6.

Health Expenditure (2004): public (% of total): 77.1.

Access to Water (% of persons, 2004): 43.

Access to Sanitation (% of persons, 2004): 53.

Human Development Index (2004): ranking: 120.

Human Development Index (2004): value: 0.653.

For sources and definitions, see explanatory note on p. vi.

AGRICULTURE, ETC.

Principal Crops ('000 metric tons, 2005, FAO estimates unless otherwise indicated): Sweet potatoes 36; Cassava 45; Coconuts 6; Oil palm fruit 35; Bananas 20; Plantains 31; Cocoa beans 3 (unofficial figure); Green coffee 4 (unofficial figure).

Livestock ('000 head, year ending September 2005, FAO estimates): Cattle 5; Pigs 6; Sheep 38; Goats 9.

Forestry (2005, FAO estimates): Roundwood removals ('000 cubic metres): Fuel wood 447 (assumed to be unchanged since 1983); Saw-logs, veneer logs and logs for sleepers 419; Total 866.

Fishing (metric tons, live weight, 2005, FAO estimates): Freshwater fishes 1,000; Clupeoids 1,900; Sharks, rays, skates, etc. 100; Total catch (incl. others) 3,500.

Source: FAO.

MINING

Production (2005, estimates): Crude petroleum 144 million barrels; Natural gas 2,300 million cubic metres. Source: US Geological Survey.

INDUSTRY

Palm Oil ('000 metric tons): 4.5 in 1999; 4.5 in 2000–05 (FAO estimates). Source: FAO.

Veneer Sheets ('000 cubic metres, FAO estimates): 9.3 in 1997; 15.0 in 1998–2005. Source: FAO.

Electric Energy (million kWh, estimates): 23 in 2000; 23 in 2001; 26 in 2002. Source: UN, *Industrial Commodity Statistics Yearbook*.

FINANCE

Currency and Exchange Rates: 100 centimes = 1 franc de la Coopération financière en Afrique centrale (CFA). *Sterling, Dollar and Euro Equivalents* (31 May 2007): £1 sterling = 964.116 francs CFA; US $1 = 487.592 francs CFA; €1 = 655.957 francs CFA; 10,000 francs CFA = £10.37 = $20.51 = €15.24. *Average Exchange Rate* (francs CFA per US dollar): 528.285 in 2004; 527.468 in 2005; 522.890 in 2006. *Note:* An exchange rate of 1 French franc = 50 francs CFA, established in 1948, remained in force until January 1994, when the CFA franc was devalued by 50%, with the exchange rate adjusted to 1 French franc = 100 francs CFA. This relationship to French currency remained in effect with the introduction of the euro on 1 January 1999. From that date, accordingly, a fixed exchange rate of €1 = 655.957 francs CFA has been in operation.

Budget (million francs CFA, 2005): *Revenue:* Petroleum sector 1,440,885; Non-oil revenue 87,940; Total revenue 1,528,825 (excl. grants 1,417). *Expenditure:* Current expenditure 158,958 (Interest payments 2,134); Capital expenditure 446,003 (Foreign-financed 1,417); Total expenditure 604,961 (excl. net lending and other 92,987). Source: IMF, *Republic of Equatorial Guinea: Selected Issues and Statistical Appendix* (June 2006).

International Reserves (US $ million at 31 December 2006, excl. gold): IMF special drawing rights 0.66; Foreign exchange 3,066.08; Total 3,066.74. Source: IMF, *International Financial Statistics*.

Money Supply ('000 million francs CFA at 31 December 2006): Currency outside deposit money banks 68.21; Demand deposits at deposit money banks 192.10; *Total money* (incl. others) 261.01. Source: IMF, *International Financial Statistics*.

Cost of Living (Consumer Price Index; base: 2000 = 100): 126.2 in 2003; 132.7 in 2004; 139.1 in 2005 (estimate). Source: IMF, *Republic of Equatorial Guinea: Selected Issues and Statistical Appendix* (June 2006).

Expenditure on the Gross Domestic Product ('000 million francs CFA at factor cost, 2005, estimates): Government final consumption expenditure 111.0; Private final consumption expenditure

270.6; Gross fixed capital formation 1,188.4; *Total domestic expenditure* 1,570.0; Exports of goods and non-factor services 3,791.5 *Less* Imports of goods and services 1,803.9; *GDP at factor cost* 3,557.8. Source: IMF, *Republic of Equatorial Guinea: Selected Issues and Statistical Appendix* (June 2006).

Gross Domestic Product by Economic Activity ('000 million francs CFA, 2005, estimates): Agriculture, hunting, forestry and fishing 74.3; Petroleum sector 3,299.5; Industry (incl. manufacturing, electricity and construction) 61.1; Services (incl. trade, transport and communications; finance and housing, government services and other services) 90.3; *Sub-total* 3,525.2; Import duties and subsidies 32.6; *GDP at market prices* 3,557.8. Source: IMF, *Republic of Equatorial Guinea: Selected Issues and Statistical Appendix* (June 2006).

Balance of Payments ('000 million francs CFA, 2005, preliminary figures): Exports of goods f.o.b. 7,124.6; Imports of goods c.i.f. –1,905.6; *Trade balance* 5,219.1; Exports of services 71.2; Imports of non-factor services –1,517.9; Net other income –4,603.4; *Balance on goods, services and income* –831.0; Private transfers (net) –86.7; Official transfers (net) 20.1; *Current balance* –897.6; Direct foreign investment 1,564.8; Medium- and long-term capital (net) –23.8; Short-term capital (net) 684.3; Errors and omissions 72.4; *Overall balance* 1,400.0. Source: IMF, *Republic of Equatorial Guinea: Selected Issues and Statistical Appendix* (June 2006).

EXTERNAL TRADE

Principal Commodities (distribution by SITC, US $ '000, 1990): *Imports c.i.f.:* Food and live animals 4,340; Beverages and tobacco 3,198 (Alcoholic beverages 2,393); Crude materials (inedible) except fuels 2,589 (Crude fertilizers and crude minerals 2,102); Petroleum and petroleum products 4,738; Chemicals and related products 2,378; Basic manufactures 3,931; Machinery and transport equipment 35,880 (Road vehicles and parts 3,764, Ships, boats and floating structures 24,715); Miscellaneous manufactured articles 2,725; Total (incl. others) 61,601. *Exports f.o.b.:* Food and live animals 6,742 (Cocoa 6,372); Beverages and tobacco 3,217 (Tobacco and tobacco manufactures 2,321); Crude materials (inedible) except fuels 20,017 (Sawlogs and veneer logs 12,839, Textile fibres and waste 7,078); Machinery and transport equipment 24,574 (Ships, boats and floating structures 23,852); Total (incl. others) 61,705. Source: UN, *International Trade Statistics Yearbook*. *2002* ('000 million francs CFA): Imports c.i.f. 768.9; Exports 1,547.0 (Petroleum 1,468.0; Timber 67.2). Source: IMF, *Equatorial Guinea: Selected Issues and Statistical Appendix* (December 2003).

Principal Trading Partners ('000 million francs CFA, 2002; figures are approximate): *Imports c.i.f.:* France 80; Italy 36; Netherlands 37; United Kingdom 122; USA 114; Yugoslavia, Fed. Repub. 224; Total (incl. others) 769. *Exports f.o.b.:* Cameroon 76; China, People's Repub. 269; Germany 22; Italy 40; Spain 391; USA 438; Total (incl. others) 1,547. Source: IMF, *Equatorial Guinea: Selected Issues and Statistical Appendix* (December 2003).

TRANSPORT

Road Traffic (estimates, motor vehicles in use at 31 December 1996): Passenger cars 1,520; Lorries and vans 540. Source: IRF, *World Road Statistics* **1997:** Passenger cars 1,173.

Shipping: *Merchant Fleet* (at 31 December 2005): Vessels 43; Total displacement 31,042 grt (Source: Lloyd's Register-Fairplay, *World Fleet Statistics*). *International Sea-borne Freight Traffic* ('000 metric tons, 1990): Goods loaded 110; Goods unloaded 64 (Source: UN, *Monthly Bulletin of Statistics*).

Civil Aviation (traffic on scheduled services, 1998): Passengers carried ('000) 21; Passenger-km (million) 4. Source: UN, *Statistical Yearbook*.

COMMUNICATIONS MEDIA

Radio Receivers (1997): 180,000 in use.

Television Receivers (1997): 4,000 in use.

Newspaper (1996): 1 daily (estimated circulation 2,000).

Book Production (1998): 17 titles.

Telephones (2005): 10,000 main lines in use.

Facsimile Machines (1998): 65 in use.

Mobile Cellular Telephones (2005): 96,900 subscribers.

Personal Computers (2005): 7,000 in use.

Internet Users (2005): 5,000.

Sources: UNESCO, *Statistical Yearbook;* UN, *Statistical Yearbook;* International Telecommunication Union.

EDUCATION

Pre-primary (2002/03): Schools 180*; Teachers 600; Students 23,644.

Primary (2001/02): Schools 483*; Teachers 1,810†; Students 78,390.

Secondary (2001/02, estimates): Teachers 894‡; Students 21,173.

Higher (1999/2000): Teachers 206†; Students 1,003.

* 1998 figure.

† Estimate.

‡ 1999/2000 figure.

Source: UNESCO Institute for Statistics.

Adult Literacy Rate: 87.0% (males 93.4%; females 80.5%) in 2004. Source: UN Development Programme, *Human Development Report*.

Directory

The Constitution

The present Constitution was approved by a national referendum on 16 November 1991 and amended in January 1995. It provided for the introduction of a plural political system and for the establishment of a legislative House of Representatives (Cámara de Representantes del Pueblo). The term of office of the President is seven years, renewable on an indefinite number of occasions. The President is immune from prosecution for offences committed before, during or after his tenure of the post. The Cámara de Representantes serves for a term of five years. Both the President and the Cámara de Representantes are directly elected by universal adult suffrage. The President appoints a Council of Ministers, headed by a Prime Minister.

The Government

HEAD OF STATE

President and Supreme Commander of the Armed Forces: Brig.-Gen. (retd) (TEODORO) OBIANG NGUEMA MBASOGO (assumed office 25 August 1979; elected President 25 June 1989; re-elected 25 February 1996 and 15 December 2002).

COUNCIL OF MINISTERS

(August 2007)

All ministers are affiliated to the Partido Democrático de Guinea Ecuatorial (PDGE), except where otherwise indicated.

Prime Minister and Head of Government: RICARDO MANGUÉ OBAMA NFUBEA.

First Deputy Prime Minister: ANICETO EBIACA MUETE.

Second Deputy Prime Minister: DEMETRIO ELO NDONG NSEFUMU.

Minister at the Presidency of the Republic in Charge of Political and Administrative Affairs: CARMELO MODÚ AKUSE BINDANG (UDS).

Minister at the Presidency of the Republic in Charge of Information, Culture and Tourism: ALFONSO NSUE MOKUY (CLD).

Minister at the Presidency of the Republic in Charge of Missions: ALEJANDRO EVUNA OWONO ASANGONO.

Minister in Charge of Relations with Parliament and Legal Affairs of the Government: ANGEL MISI MIBUY.

Minister at the Prime Minister's Office in charge of Sub-regional Integration: BALTASAR ENGONGA EJO.

Minister of External Relations, International Co-operation and Francophone Affairs: PASTOR MICHA ONDO BILE.

Minister of Justice, Religion and Penitentiary Institutions: MAURICIO BOKUNG ASUMU.

Minister of the Interior and Local Corporations: CLEMENTE ENGONGA NGUEMA ONGUENE.

Minister of National Defence: ANTONIO NDONG NGUEMA MIKWE.

Minister of National Security: MANUEL NGUEMA MBA.

Minister of Transport, Technology, Post and Telecommunications: ENRIQUE MERCADER COSTA.

Minister of Infrastructure and Urban Development: MIGUEL NSUE MICHA.

Minister of the Economy, Trade and Business Development: JAIME ELA NDONG.

Minister of Planning, Economic Development and Public Investment: JOSÉ ELA OYANA.

Minister of Finance and the Budget: MARCELINO OWONO EDU.

Minister of Mines, Industry and Energy: ATANASIO ELA NTOUGOU NSA.

Minister of Education, Science and Sports: CRISTOBAL MEÑANA ELA.

Minister of Health and Social Welfare: ANTONIO MARTIN NDONG NCHUCHUMA.

Minister of Labour and Social Security: EVANGELINA OYO EBULE.

Minister of Social Affairs and Women's Advancement: EULALIA ENVO BELA.

Minister of Agriculture and Forestry: TEODORO (TEODORÍN) NGUEMA OBIANG MANGUE.

Minister of Fisheries and the Environment: VICENTE RODRÍGUEZ SIOSA.

Minister of Information, Culture and Tourism, Government Spokesperson: SANTIAGO NSOBEYA EFUMAN NCHAMA.

Minister of Public Service and Administrative Planning: VICENTE EYATE TOMI.

In addition, there are 18 Deputy Ministers and 13 Secretaries of State.

MINISTRIES

Ministry of Agriculture and Forestry: Apdo 504, Malabo.

Ministry of the Economy, Trade and Business Development: BP 404, Malabo; tel. (09) 31-05; fax (09) 20-43.

Ministry of External Relations, International Co-operation and Francophone Affairs: Malabo; tel. (09) 32-20; fax (09) 31-32.

Ministry of Finance and the Budget: Malabo; internet www.ceiba-guinea-ecuatorial.org/guineees/indexbienv1.htm.

Ministry of the Interior and Local Corporations: Malabo; fax (09) 26-83.

Ministry of Justice, Religion and Penitentiary Institutions: Malabo; fax (09) 21-15.

Ministry of Mines, Industry and Energy: Calle 12 de Octubre s/n, Malabo; tel. (09) 35-67; fax (09) 33-53; e-mail d.shaw@ecqc.com; internet www.equatorialoil.com.

Ministry of National Defence: Malabo; tel. (09) 27-94.

Ministry of National Security: Malabo; tel. (09) 34-69.

Ministry of Social Affairs and Women's Advancement: Malabo; tel. (09) 34-69.

Ministry of Transport, Technology, Post and Telecommunications: Malabo; internet www.ceiba-guinea-ecuatorial.org/guineees/transport.htm.

President and Legislature

PRESIDENT

Gen. (Teodoro) Obiang Nguema Mbasogo was re-elected to the presidency unopposed on 15 December 2002, securing 97.1% of votes cast, following the withdrawal of all other candidates.

CÁMARA DE REPRESENTANTES DEL PUEBLO
(House of Representatives)

Speaker: Dr SALOMÓN NGUEMA OWONO.

General Election, 25 April 2004

Party	Seats
Partido Democrático de Guinea Ecuatorial (PDGE)	68
Democratic opposition*	30
Convergencia para la Democracia Social (CPDS)	2
Total	100

* A coalition of eight parties allied to President Obiang Nguema, including the Convención Socialdemocrática Popular (CSDP), the Partido de la Convergencia Social Democráta (PCSD) and the Unión Popular (UP).

Election Commission

Constitutional Court: Malabo; Pres. FRANCISCO NGOMO MBENGONO.

Political Organizations

Alianza Democrática Progresista (ADP): Pres. FRANCISCO MBÁ OLÚ BAHAMONDE.

Alianza Nacional para la Restauración Democrática de Guinea Ecuatorial (ANRD): 95 Ruperto Chapi, 28100 Madrid, Spain; tel. (91) 623-88-64; f. 1974; Sec.-Gen. LUIS ONDO AYANG.

Alianza Popular de Guinea Ecuatorial (APGE): pro-Government party; Pres. CARMELO MBA; Vice-Pres. TOMÁS BUEICHEKÚ.

Convención Liberal Democrática (CLD): Pres. ALFONSO NSUE MOKUY.

Convención Socialdemocrática Popular (CSDP): Leader SECUNDINO OYONO.

Convergencia para la Democracia Social (CPDS): Calle Tres de Agosto, Apdo 72, 2º andar, 1 Malabo; tel. (09) 20-13; e-mail cpds@intnet.gq; internet www.cpds-gq.org; Pres. SANTIAGO OBAMA NDONG; Sec.-Gen. PLÁCIDO MICÓ ABOGO.

Demócratas por el Cambio (DECAM): coalition based in Madrid, Spain; e-mail press@guinea-ecuatorial.org; internet www.guinea-ecuatorial.org; f. 2005; 16 mem. orgs; Gen. Co-ordinator JUSTO BOLEKIA BOLEKÁ.

Foro-Democracia Guinea Ecuatorial (FDGE).

Fuerza Demócrata Republicana (FDR): f. 1995; opposition grouping based in Spain; Leader GERMÁN TOMO.

Movimiento para la Autodeterminación de la Isla de Bioko (MAIB): e-mail info@maib.org; internet www.maib.org; f. 1993; by Bubi interests seeking independence of Bioko; clandestine; Gen. Co-ordinator WEJA CHICAMPO (arrested on 4 March 2004); Spokesman Dr ENRIQUE BONEKE.

Movimiento Nacional de Liberación de Guinea Ecuatoriana: POB 1484, Brooklyn, New York 11202-1484, USA; e-mail monalige@equatorialguinea-monalige.com; internet www.equatorialguinea-monalige.com; clandestine opposition party based in USA.

Partido de la Convergencia Social Demócrata (PCSD): Pres. BUENAVENTURA MESUY.

Partido Democrático de Guinea Ecuatorial (PDGE): Malabo; f. 1987; sole legal party 1987–92; Chair. Gen. (TEODORO) OBIANG NGUEMA MBASOGO; Sec.-Gen. FILIBERTO NTUTUMU NGUEMA NCHAMA.

Partido para el Desarrollo (PPD): based in Spain; f. 2001; Pres. ELOY ELO MVE MBENGOMO.

Partido del Progreso de Guinea Ecuatorial (PPGE): Madrid, Spain; e-mail ppge@telepolis.com; internet www.guinea-ecuatorial.org; f. 1983; Christian Democrat faction led by SEVERO MOTO NSA.

Partido de Reconstrucción y Bienestar Social (PRBS): Pres. FLORENTINO ECOMO NSOGO.

Partido Social Demócrata (PSD): Pres. BENJAMÍN BALINGA.

Partido Socialista de Guinea Ecuatorial (PSGE): Sec.-Gen. TOMÁS MECHEBA FERNÁNDEZ-GALILEA.

Resistencia Nacional de Guinea Ecuatorial (RENAGE): Apdo de Correos 40, 28930 Móstoles, Madrid, Spain; f. 2000; alliance of seven opposition groups; Leader DANIEL M. OYONO.

Unión para la Democracia y el Desarrollo Social (UDDS): f. 1990; Sec.-Gen. ANTONIO SIBACHA BUEICHEKU.

Unión Democrática Independiente (UDI): Leader DANIEL M. OYONO.

Unión Democrática Nacional (UDEMA): Pres. JOSÉ MECHEBA.

Unión Democrática y Social de Guinea Ecuatorial (UDS): Pres. CARMELO MODÚ ACUSÉ BINDANG.

Unión Popular (UP): f. 1992; conservative; Pres. JEREMÍAS ONDO NGOMO.

Unión Popular—Progresista (UP—Progresista): Leader PEDRO EKONG.

Unión para la Reconciliación y el Progreso (URP).

Diplomatic Representation

EMBASSIES IN EQUATORIAL GUINEA

Angola: Malabo; Ambassador EMILIO JOSÉ DO CARVALHO.

Cameroon: 37 Calle Rey Boncoro, Apdo 292, Malabo; tel. and fax (09) 22-63; Ambassador JOHN NCHOTU AKUM.

China, People's Republic: Carretera del Aeropuerto, Apdo 44, Malabo; tel. (09) 35-05; fax (09) 23-81; e-mail chinaemb_gq@mfa.gov.cn; Ambassador LI ZHONGLIANG.

France: Carretera del Aeropuerto, Apdo 326, Malabo; tel. (09) 20-05; fax (09) 23-05; e-mail chancellerie.malabo-amba@diplomatie.gouv.fr; internet www.ambafrance-gq.org; Ambassador HENRI DENIAUD.

Gabon: Calle de Argelia, Apdo 18, Malabo; Ambassador JEAN-BAPTISTE MBATCHI.

Guinea: Malabo.

Korea, Democratic People's Republic: Malabo; tel. (09) 20-47; Ambassador (vacant).

Morocco: Avda Enrique, Apdo 329, Malabo; tel. (09) 26-50; fax (09) 26-55; e-mail armge1@wanadoo.gq; Chargé d'affaires a.i. ELHASSAN DAHMAN.

Nigeria: 4 Paseo de los Cocoteros, Apdo 78, Malabo; tel. and fax (09) 33-85; Chargé d'affaires a.i. A. ONAH.

Russia: Malabo; Ambassador LEV A. VAKHRAMEYEV.

South Africa: Parque de las Avenidas de Africa s/n, POB 5, Malabo; tel. (09) 77-37; fax (09) 27-46; e-mail malabo@foreign.gov.za; Ambassador MOKGETHI MONAISA (resident in Gabon).

Spain: Parque de las Avenidas de Africa s/n, Malabo; tel. (09) 20-20; fax (09) 26-11; e-mail embespgq@correo.mae.es; Ambassador CARLOS ROBLES FRAGA.

USA: K-3, Carretera de Aeropuerto, Malabo; tel. (09) 88-95; fax (09) 88-94; e-mail usembassymalabo@yahoo.com; internet malabo.usembassy.gov; Ambassador DONALD C. JOHNSON.

Judicial System

The Supreme Court of Justice and the Constitutional Court sit in Malabo. The Supreme Court has four chambers (Civil and Social, Penal, Administrative and Common) and consists of a President and 12 magistrates, from whom the President of each chamber is selected. There are Territorial High Courts in Malabo and Bata, which also sit as courts of appeal. Courts of first instance sit in Malabo and Bata, and may be convened in the other provincial capitals. Local courts may be convened when necessary.

President of the Supreme Court of Justice: SERGIO ESONO ABESO TOMO.

Attorney-General: JOSÉ OLO OBONO.

Religion

More than 90% of the population are adherents of the Roman Catholic Church. Traditional forms of worship are also followed.

CHRISTIANITY

The Roman Catholic Church

Equatorial Guinea comprises one archdiocese and two dioceses. An estimated 91.5% of the population were adherents at 31 December 2004.

Bishops' Conference

Arzobispado, Apdo 106, Malabo; tel. (09) 29-09; fax (09) 21-76; e-mail arzobispadomalabo@hotmail.com.

f. 1984; Pres. Most Rev. ILDEFONSO OBAMA OBONO (Archbishop of Malabo).

Archbishop of Malabo: Most Rev. ILDEFONSO OBAMA OBONO, Arzobispado, Apdo 106, Malabo; tel. (09) 29-09; fax (09) 21-76; e-mail arzobispadomalabo@hotmail.com.

Protestant Church

Iglesia Reformada Evangélica de Guinea Ecuatorial (Evangelical Reformed Church of Equatorial Guinea): Apdo 195, Malabo; f. 1960; c. 8,000 mems.

The Press

Ebano: Malabo; f. 1940; weekly; government-controlled.

El árbol del centro: Apdo 180, Malabo; tel. (09) 21-86; fax (09) 32-75; Spanish; cultural review; 6 a year; publ. by Centro Cultural Español de Malabo; Dir GLORIA NISTAL.

Hoja Parroquial: Malabo; weekly.

La Gaceta: Malabo; f. 1996; bi-weekly.

La Verdad: Talleres Gráficos de Convergencia para la Democracia Social, Calle Tres de Agosto 72, Apdo 441, Malabo; publ. by the Convergencia para la Democracia Social; 5 annually; Editor PLÁCIDO MICÓ ABOGO.

Poto-poto: Bata; f. 1940; weekly; government-controlled.

Voz del Pueblo: Malabo; publ. by the Partido Democrático de Guinea Ecuatorial.

FOREIGN NEWS BUREAU

Agencia EFE (Spain): 50 Calle del Presidente Nasser, Malabo; tel. (09) 31-65; Bureau Chief DONATO NDONGO-BIDYOGO.

PRESS ASSOCIATION

Asociación para la Libertad de Prensa y de Expresión en Guinea Ecuatorial (ASOLPEGE Libre): Calle Isla Cabrera 3, 5°, 46026 Valencia, Spain; tel. (660) 930629; e-mail asopge_ngo@hotmail.com; f. 1997; name changed as above following relocation to Spain in 2003; Pres. PEDRO NOLASCO NDONG OBAMA.

Publisher

Centro Cultural Hispano-Guineano: Apdo 180, Malabo; tel. (09) 27-20; fax (09) 27-22; Spanish support withdrawn 2002.

Broadcasting and Communications

TELECOMMUNICATIONS

Dirección General de Correos y de Telecomunicaciones: Malabo; tel. (09) 28-57; fax (09) 25-15; Man. Dir M. DAUCHAT.

Guinea Ecuatorial de Telecomunicaciones, SA (GETESA): Calle Rey Boncoro 27, Apdo 494, Malabo; tel. (09) 28-15; fax (09) 33-13; e-mail contact@getesa.gq; internet www.getesa.gq; f. 1987; 60% state-owned, 40% owned by France Telecom; Man. FRANCISCO NVE NSOGO.

RADIO

Radio Africa and Radio East Africa: Apdo 851, Malabo; e-mail pabcomain@aol.com; commercial station; owned by Pan American Broadcasting; music and religious programmes in English.

Radio Nacional de Guinea Ecuatorial: Apdo 749, Barrio Comandachina, Bata; Apdo 195, 90 Avda 30 de Agosto, Malabo; tel. (08) 25-92; fax (08) 20-93; tel. (09) 22-60; fax (09) 20-97; govt-controlled; commercial station; programmes in Spanish, French and vernacular languages; Dir (Bata) SEBASTIÁN ELÓ ASEKO; Dir (Malabo) JUAN EYENE OPKUA NGUEMA.

Radio Santa Isabel: Malabo; Spanish and French programmes.

Radio Televisión Asonga: Bata; private.

TELEVISION

Televisión Nacional: Malabo; broadcasts in Spanish and French; Dir ANTONIO NKULU OYE.

Finance

(cap. = capital; res = reserves; dep. = deposits; m. = million; brs = branches; amounts in francs CFA)

BANKING

Central Bank

Banque des Etats de l'Afrique Centrale (BEAC): Apdo 501, Malabo; tel. (09) 20-10; fax (09) 20-06; e-mail beacmal@beac.int; HQ in Yaoundé, Cameroon; agency also in Bata; f. 1973; bank of issue for mem. states of the Communauté économique et monétaire de l'Afrique centrale (CEMAC, fmrly Union douanière et économique de l'Afrique centrale), comprising Cameroon, the Central African Repub., Chad, the Repub. of the Congo, Equatorial Guinea and Gabon; cap. 45,000m., res 176,661m., total assets 2,144,626m. (Nov. 2003); Gov. JEAN-FÉLIX MAMALEPOT; Dir in Equatorial Guinea FRANCISCO GARCÍA BERNICO; 2 brs in Equatorial Guinea.

Commercial Banks

Banco Nacional de Guinea Ecuatorial (BANGE): Bata; f. 2005.

BGFIBANK Guinea Ecuatorial: Calle de Bata s/n, Apdo 749, Malabo; tel. (09) 63-52; fax (09) 63-73; e-mail bgfi.ge@internet.gq; internet www.bgfi.com/htm/en/bgfibank/branch-malabo.html; 55% owned by BGFIBANK, 35% owned by private shareholders, 10% state-owned; incorporated June 2001; cap. 25,065m., total assets 270,877m. (Dec. 2004); Chair. PATRICE OTHA; Gen. Man. HENRI-CLAUDE OYIMA.

Caisse Commune d'Epargne et d'Investissement Guinea Ecuatorial (CCEI-GE): Calle del Presidente Nasser, Apdo 428, Malabo; tel. (09) 22-03; fax (09) 33-11; e-mail geccei@hotmail.com; 51% owned by Afriland First Bank (Cameroon); f. 1995; cap. and res 5,172m., total assets 81,191m. (Dec. 2003); Pres. BÁLTASAR ENGONGA EDJO'O; Dir-Gen. JOSEPH CÉLESTIN TINDJOU DJAMENI.

Commercial Bank Guinea Ecuatorial (CBGE): Carretera de Luba, Apdo 189, Malabo; e-mail cbgebank@cbc-bank.com; internet www.cbc-bank.com; f. 2003; cap. 1,500m. (Jan. 2003).

Société Générale des Banques GE (SGBGE): Calle Argelia 6, Apdo 686, Malabo; tel. (09) 93-37; fax (09) 33-66; e-mail jmjgarcia@yahoo.fr; internet groupe.socgen.com/bhfm/sgbge/home_f.htm; f. 1986; present name adopted 1998; 32.44% owned by Société Générale SA (France), 31.78% state-owned, 11.45% owned by Société Générale de Banques au Cameroun, 10.97% owned by local investors; cap. and res 2,780m., total assets 48,624m. (Dec. 2001); Chair. MARCELINO OWONO EDU; Man. Dir CHRISTIAN DELMAS; brs in Bata and Malabo.

Development Banks

Banco de Fomento y Desarrollo (BFD): Malabo; f. 1998; 30% state-owned; cap. 50m.

Banque de Développement des Etats de l'Afrique Centrale: see Franc Zone.

Financial Institution

Caja Autónoma de Amortización de la Deuda Pública: Ministry of the Economy, Trade and Business Devt, Apdo 404, Malabo; tel. (09) 31-05; fax (09) 20-43; management of state funds; Dir-Gen. RAFAEL TUN.

INSURANCE

Equatorial Guinean Insurance Company, SA (EGICO): Avda de la Libertad, Malabo; state-owned.

Trade and Industry

GOVERNMENT AGENCIES

Cámaras Oficiales Agrícolas de Guinea: Bioko and Bata; purchase of cocoa and coffee from indigenous planters, who are partially grouped in co-operatives.

Empresa General de Industria y Comercio (EGISCA): Malabo; f. 1986; parastatal body jtly operated with the French Société pour l'Organisation, l'Aménagement et le Développement des Industries Alimentaires et Agricoles (SOMDIA); import-export agency.

Oficina para la Cooperación con Guinea Ecuatorial (OCGE): Malabo; f. 1981; administers bilateral aid from Spain.

DEVELOPMENT ORGANIZATIONS

Agencia Española de Cooperación Internacional (AECI): Parque de las Avenidas de Africa, Malabo; tel. (09) 16-21; fax (09) 29-32; e-mail ucemalabo@wanadoo.gq; internet www.aeci.es.

Asociación Bienestar Familiar de Guinea Ecuatorial: BP 984, Malabo; tel. and fax (09) 33-13; e-mail abifage1@hotmail.com; family welfare org.

Asociación Hijos de Lommbe (A Vonna va Lommbe): Malabo; e-mail avvl@bisa.com; internet www.bisala.com/avvl.html; f. 2000; agricultural development org.

Camasa: Finca Sampaka, Km 7 Camino a Luba, Malabo; tel. (09) 86-92; e-mail casamallo@hotmail.com; internet www.camasa.net; f. 1906; agricultural devt on Bioko island; operates projects for the cultivation and export of cocoa, pineapple, coffee, vanilla, nutmeg, peppers and tropical flowers.

Centro de Estudios e Iniciativas para el Desarrollo de Guinea Ecuatorial (CEIDIGE): Malabo; e-mail ceidbata@intnet.gq; internet www.eurosur.org/CEIDGE/portada.html; umbrella group of development NGOs; Pres. JOSÉ ANTONIO NSANG ANDEME.

Family Care Guinea Ecuatorial (FGCE): Malabo; f. 2000; health and education development; Dir LAUREN TAYLOR STEVENSON.

Instituto Nacional de Promoción Agropecuaria (INPAGE): Malabo; govt agricultural development agency; reorganized 2000.

Sociedad Anónima de Desarrollo del Comercio (SOADECO-Guinée): Malabo; f. 1986; parastatal body jtly operated with the French Société pour l'Organisation, l'Aménagement et le Développement des Industries Alimentaires et Agricoles (SOMDIA); development of commerce.

CHAMBERS OF COMMERCE

Cámara de Comercio, Agrícola y Forestal de Malabo: Avda de la Independencia, Apdo 51, Malabo; tel. (09) 23-43; fax (09) 44-62; Dir ENRIQUE MERCADER COASTA.

Cámara Oficial de Comercio de Bioko: Avda de la Independencia 43, Apdo 51, Malabo; tel. and fax (09) 45-76; e-mail camara@orange.gq; Pres. VIDAL CHONI BECOBA.

INDUSTRIAL AND TRADE ASSOCIATIONS

Guinea Ecuatorial de Petróleo (GEPetrol): Calle Acacio Mane 39, BP 965, Malabo; tel. (09) 67-69; fax (09) 66-92; e-mail bonifacio.monsuy@ge-petrol.com; internet www.equatorialoil.com/pages/GEPetrol%20page.htm; f. 2001; state-owned petroleum company; National Dir CÁNDIDO NSUE OKOMO.

INPROCAO: Malabo; production, marketing and distribution of cocoa.

Sociedad Nacional de Gas de Guinea Ecuatorial (SONAGAS, G.E.): Malabo; f. 2005; oversees gas exploration and devt; Dir-Gen. JUAN ANTONIO NDONG.

Total Ecuatoguineana de Gestión (GE—Total): Malabo; f. 1984; 50% state-owned, 50% by Total (France); petroleum marketing and distribution.

Unión General de Empresas Privadas de la República de Guinea Ecuatorial (UGEPRIGE): Apdo 138, Malabo; tel. (09) 35-63; fax (09) 24-24.

Utilities

Electricity

ENERGE: Malabo; state-owned electricity board.

Sociedad de Electricidad de Guinea Ecuatorial (SEGESA): Carretera de Luba, Apdo 139, Malabo; tel. (09) 34-66; fax (09) 33-29; e-mail segesa@internet.gq; state-owned electricity distributor; Man. Dir BENITO ONDO.

TRADE UNIONS

A law permitting the establishment of trade unions was introduced in 1992.

Transport

RAILWAYS

There are no railways in Equatorial Guinea.

ROADS

In 1999 there were an estimated 2,880 km of roads and tracks.

Bioko: a semi-circular tarred road serves the northern part of the island from Malabo down to Batete in the west and from Malabo to Bacake Grande in the east, with a feeder road from Luba to Moka and Bahía de la Concepción.

Río Muni: a tarred road links Bata with the town of Mbini (Río Benito) in the west; another road, partly tarred, links Bata with the frontier post of Ebebiyín in the east and then continues into Gabon; other earth roads join Acurenam, Mongomo and Anisok.

SHIPPING

The main ports are Bata (general cargo and most of the country's export timber), Malabo (general), Luba (bananas, timber and petroleum), Mbini and Cogo (timber).

CIVIL AVIATION

There are two international airports, at Malabo (Santa Isabel Airport) and Bata. The national carrier, EGA—Ecuato Guineana de Aviación (which has been in liquidation since 1990), continues to provide limited regional and domestic services, as well as a weekly service to Madrid, Spain. Scheduled services between Malabo and Madrid are operated by Iberia and Líneas Aéreas de España. Direct flights to Paris, France, London, United Kingdom, and Zürich, Switzerland, are also available. SONAGESA, jointly operated by GEPetrol and SONAIR of Angola, offers direct connections between Malabo and Houston, TX, USA.

Air Consul: Apdo 77, Malabo; tel. and fax (09) 32-91; e-mail airconsul@intnet.gq; Man. FERNANDEZ ARMESTO.

EGA—Ecuato Guineana de Aviación: Apdo 665, Malabo; tel. (09) 23-25; fax (09) 33-13; internet www.ecuatoguineana.com/ega/ega.htm; regional and domestic passenger and cargo services; Pres. MELCHOR ESONO EDJO.

Swissair Guinée Equatoriale: Malabo; tel. (09) 18-81; fax (09) 18-80; two flights weekly between Malabo and Zürich, Switzerland; Man. M. HOFFSTETTER.

Tourism

Tourism remains undeveloped. Future interest in this sector would be likely to focus on the unspoilt beaches of Río Muni and Bioko's scenic mountain terrain.

Defence

As assessed at November 2006, there were 1,100 men in the army, 120 in the navy and 100 in the air force. There was also a paramilitary force, referred to both as 'Antorchas' and 'Ninjas', which was trained by French military personnel. Military service is voluntary. Spain and Morocco have provided military advisers and training since 1979. Military aid has also been received from the USA.

Defence Expenditure: Estimated at 3,800m. francs CFA in 2005.

Supreme Commander of the Armed Forces: Gen. (TEODORO) OBIANG NGUEMA MBASOGO.

Inspector-Gen. of the Armed Forces and the Security Forces: Rear Adm. JOAQUÍN NDONG NVÉ.

Education

Education is officially compulsory and free for five years between the ages of six and 11 years. Primary education starts at six years of age and normally lasts for five years. Secondary education, beginning at the age of 12, spans a seven-year period, comprising a first cycle of four years and a second cycle of three years. In 1982 the total enrolment at primary and secondary schools was equivalent to 81% of the school-age population. According to UNESCO estimates, in 2001/02 total enrolment at primary schools included 85% of children in the relevant age-group (males 92%; females 78%), while secondary enrolment in 2000/01 included 24% of children in the relevant age-group (males 30%; females 18%). In 1999/2000 there were 1,003 pupils in higher education. Since 1979, assistance in the development of the educational system has been provided by Spain. Two higher education centres, at Bata and Malabo, are administered by the Spanish Universidad Nacional de Educación a Distancia. The French Government also provides considerable financial assistance. In September 2002 a new National Plan for Education was ratified. Its aims were to improve basic literacy and to introduce education on health-related topics. In 1993 budgetary expenditure on education by the central Government amounted to an estimated 9.3% of total expenditure.

Bibliography

Agencia Española de Cooperación Internacional. *Segundo plano marco de cooperación entre el Reino de España y la República de Guinea Ecuatorial*. Madrid, AECI, 1990.

Boneke, J. B. *La transición de Guinea Ecuatorial: Historia de un fracaso.* Madrid, Labrys 54 Ediciones, 1998.

Castro A., Mariano, and de la Calle Muñoz, M. L. *Geografía de Guinea Ecuatorial.* Madrid, Programa de Colaboración Educativa con Guinea Ecuatorial, 1985.

Castroviejo Bolívar, J., Juste Balleste, J., and Castelo Alvarez, R. *Investigación y conservación de la naturaleza en Guinea Ecuatorial.* Madrid, Oficina de Cooperación con Guinea Ecuatorial, 1986.

Cohen, R. (Ed.). *African Islands and Enclaves.* London, Sage Publications, 1983.

Cronj, S. *Equatorial Guinea: The Forgotten Dictatorship.* London, 1976.

Cusack, I. *Equatorial Guinea: The Inculcation and Maintenance of Hispanic Culture.* Bristol, University of Bristol, 1999.

Eman, A. *Equatorial Guinea during the Macías Nguema Régime.* Washington, DC, 1983.

Equatorial Guinea Research Group. *Executive Report On Strategies in Equatorial Guinea.* San Diego, CA, Icon Group International, annual.

Fegley, R. *Equatorial Guinea: An African Tragedy.* New York, Peter Lang, 1989.

González-Echegaray, C. *Estudios Guineos: Filología.* Madrid, IDEA, 1964.

Estudios Guineos: Etnología. Madrid, IDEA, 1964.

International Business Publications. *Equatorial Guinea Foreign Policy and Government Guide.* 3rd Edn. USA, 2001.

Equatorial Guinea. 4th Edn. USA, 2002.

Equatorial Guinea Business Intelligence Report. 3rd Edn. USA, 2003.

Jakobeit, C. 'Äquatorialguinea' in Hanisch, R., and Jakobeit, C. (Eds). *Der Kakaoweltmarkt.* Vol. 2. Hamburg, Deutsches Übersee-institut, 1991.

Klitgaard, R. *Tropical Gangsters.* London, I. B. Tauris, 1990.

Liniger-Goumaz, M. *Guinea Ecuatorial: Bibliografía General.* 5 vols. Bern and Geneva, 1976–85.

Equatorial Guinea: An African Historical Dictionary. Metuchen, NJ, Scarecrow Press, 2000.

De la Guinée équatoriale nguemiste. Eléments pour le dossier de l'afro-fascisme. Geneva, Editions du Temps, 1983.

Statistics of Nguemist Equatorial Guinea. Geneva, Editions du Temps, 1986.

Small is not always Beautiful: The Story of Equatorial Guinea. London, Hurst, 1988.

Martín de Molino, A. *Los Bubis, ritos y creencias.* Malabo, Centro Cultural Hispano-Guineano, 1989.

La ciudad de Clarence: Primeros años de la actual ciudad de Malabo, capital de Guinea Ecuatorial, 1827-1859. Malabo, Centro Cultural Hispano-Guineano, 1993.

Ndongo Bidyogo, D. *Historia y Tragedia de Guinea Ecuatorial.* Madrid, Cambio, 1977.

Nerín, G. *Guinea Ecuatorial: Historia en Blanco y Negro.* Barcelona, Atalaya Península, 1997.

Nfumu, A. N. *Macías: ¿Verdugo o Víctima?* Madrid, Herrero y asociados, Pool de Servicios Editoriales, S.L., 2004.

Nguema-Obam, P. *Aspects de la religion fang.* Paris, Editions Karthala, 1984.

Obiang Nguema, T. *Guinea Ecuatorial, País Joven: Testimonios Políticos.* Malabo, Ediciones Guinea, 1985.

Pélissier, R. *Los Territorios Españoles de Africa.* Madrid, 1964.

Africana. Bibliographies sur l'Afrique luso-hispanophone (1800–1980). Orgeval, Editions Pélissier, 1981.

Reeves, P. *Equatorial Guinea: 1996 Presidential Elections Observation Report.* Washington, DC, International Foundation for Election Systems, 1996.

Roberts, A. *The Wonga Coup.* London, Profile Books, 2006.

Sundiata, I. K. *Equatorial Guinea.* Boulder, CO, Westview Press, 1990.

From Slaving to Neoslavery. Madison, WI, University of Wisconsin, 1996.

ERITREA

Physical and Social Geography

MILES SMITH-MORRIS

The State of Eritrea, which formally acceded to independence on 24 May 1993, covers an area of 121,144 sq km (46,774 sq miles). Its territory includes the Dahlak islands, a low-lying coralline archipelago offshore from Massawa. Eritrea, which has a coastline on the Red Sea extending for almost 1,000 km, is bounded to the north-west by Sudan, to the south and west by Ethiopia, and to the south-east by Djibouti. The terrain comprises the northern end of the Ethiopian plateau (rising to more than 2,000 m above sea-level), where most cultivation takes place, and a low-lying semi-desert coastal strip, much of which supports only pastoralism. Lowland areas have less than 500 mm of rainfall per year, compared with 1,000 mm in the highlands. Average annual temperatures range from 17°C in the highlands to 30°C in Massawa. The Danakil depression in the south-east descends to more than 130 m below sea-level and experiences some of the highest temperatures recorded on earth, frequently exceeding 50°C. Much of the coniferous forest that formerly covered the slopes of the highlands has been destroyed by settlement and cultivation; soil erosion is a severe problem.

The extent of Eritrea's natural resources awaits fuller exploration and evaluation. Copper ores and gold were mined from the Eritrean plateau in prehistoric times and there has been some extraction of iron ore. The Dallol depression, south of Massawa, is known to have valuable potash deposits. Some exploration for petroleum has taken place in Red Sea coastal areas; oil seepages and offshore natural gas discoveries have been reported.

The population of Eritrea was enumerated at just over 2.7m. in the Ethiopian census of 1984, but the war for independence resulted in large-scale population movements. Some 500,000 refugees fled to neighbouring Sudan and a significant, but unquantified, number of Eritreans has remained in Ethiopia. At mid-1991, according to official Ethiopian sources, the population of the Eritrean territory was estimated at 3,435,500. A total of 1.2m. people registered to vote in the April 1993 referendum, 860,000 of them within Eritrea, leading to estimates of a domestic population of about 2m. At mid-2006, according to UN estimates, Eritrea's population totalled 4,692,000. The population is fairly evenly divided between Tigrinya-speaking Christians, the traditional inhabitants of the highlands, and the Muslim communities of the western lowlands, northern highlands and east coast.

Recent History

ALAN RAKE

With subsequent revisions by SARA RICH DORMAN

Revised by GREG CAMERON

Modern Eritrea dates from the establishment of an Italian colony in the late 19th century. From a small concession gained near Assab in 1869, the Italians extended their control to Massawa in 1885 and to most of Eritrea by 1889. In the same year the Ethiopian emperor, Menelik, and the Italian Government signed the Treaty of Ucciali, which effectively recognized Italian control over Eritrea (and from which Italy derived its subsequent claim to a protectorate over Ethiopia). The period of Italian rule (1889–1941) and the subsequent years under British military administration (1941–52) created a society, economy and polity more advanced than in the semi-feudal Ethiopian empire. Following the Second World War, Ethiopia, which historically regarded Eritrea as an integral part of its territory, intensified its claims to sovereignty. The strategic interests of the USA and its influence in the newly founded UN resulted in a compromise, in the form of a federation between Eritrea and Ethiopia. No federal institutions were established, and Eritrean autonomy was systematically stifled. In 1962 Eritrea was reconstituted as a province of Ethiopia.

THE LIBERATION STRUGGLE

The dissolution of the federation brought forth a more militant Eritrean nationalism, whose political roots had been established during the process of consultation for the disposal of the Italian colony in the latter part of the period of British rule. The Eritrean Liberation Movement, founded in 1958, was succeeded by the Eritrean Liberation Front (ELF), which began an armed struggle in 1961. Organizational and ideological differences erupted into violence within the ELF in the mid-1960s, as a result of demands for reform from the increasing numbers of educated guerrilla fighters, particularly those from the Christian highlands and the Muslim eastern lowland towns. A reformist group separated from the ELF and formed the Popular Liberation Forces (renamed the Eritrean People's Liberation Front, EPLF, in 1977). A major consequence of the split was the civil war of 1972–74. The most influential groups remaining outside the EPLF have been those associated with Ahmed Nasser, leader of the ELF—Revolutionary Council (ELF—RC), and an Islamic movement that emerged during the 1980s among refugees in Sudan. The EPLF leadership consolidated a highly centralized and disciplined political and military organization, in contrast to the more loosely organized and factionalized ELF.

The 1974 revolution in Ethiopia and its violent aftermath brought thousands of new recruits into the resistance groups. Even greater numbers of recruits joined the EPLF after the Mengistu regime launched its 'red terror' campaign in Asmara, and following its capture of smaller cities such as Keren and Decamhare in 1977. From 1978 the EPLF consolidated the defence of its base area in the north and throughout the 1980s it pushed back the Ethiopian forces on all fronts, capturing large quantities of heavy artillery and tanks, and transforming itself from a guerrilla force into a regular army. The EPLF gained control of the north, the west (formerly the ELF's heartland) and, finally, the east coast with the capture of Massawa port in 1990. In May 1991 the EPLF broke through the Decamhare front and entered Asmara, the capital. The retreating Ethiopian forces left the city largely undamaged. The discipline of the Eritrean People's Liberation Army (EPLA) and the extensive network of secret cells in the capital helped to ensure a smooth transition from liberation movement to government.

Representatives of the EPLF attended the London Conference in a delegation separate from the Ethiopian People's Revolutionary Democratic Front, which was in control of Ethiopia and sympathetic to Eritrean nationalist aspirations. Both the USA and the Ethiopian delegation accepted the EPLF as the provisional Government, and the latter agreed to hold a referendum on independence in 1993. Ethiopian assent to this process played an important role in the international legitimation of Eritrea's path to independence. In advance of the referendum, the EPLF formed a Government and established ministries, most of whose key personnel were drawn from the EPLF. Although the international and regional political context was favourable for the transition to independence, the international economic context, prolonged warfare, drought and the legacy of neglect and destruction left by the Ethiopian forces placed the new Government in straitened circumstances; 80% of the population were still dependent on food aid and urban economic activity had virtually ceased. Over and above these domestic problems was the task of attracting back and reintegrating around 750,000 refugees. Of these, some 500,000 were in Sudan, 90% of whom would require extensive financial assistance to return.

In the absence of any significant sources of domestic revenue for reconstruction, the task of rebuilding fell largely to the EPLA, the members of which received a small stipend for their work. Finance for reconstruction came largely from contributions by Eritreans abroad and from assistance by foreign governments and non-governmental organizations (NGOs). Without full legal sovereignty, access to loans and assistance from international financial institutions was limited, but in 1993 this formal constraint was removed. In April a UN-supervised referendum took place in an atmosphere of national celebration. Of the 1,102,410 Eritreans who voted, 99.8% endorsed national independence. The anniversary of the liberation of Asmara, 24 May, was proclaimed Independence Day, and on 28 May the State of Eritrea formally attained international recognition.

INDEPENDENCE AND TRANSITIONAL GOVERNMENT

Following Eritrea's accession to independence, a four-year transitional period was declared, during which preparations were to proceed for establishing a constitutional and pluralist political system. At the apex of the transitional Government were three state institutions: the Consultative Council (the executive authority formed from the ministers, provincial governors and heads of government commissions); the National Assembly (the legislative authority formed from the Central Committee of the EPLF, together with 30 members from the Provincial Assemblies and 30 members appointed by the Central Committee); and the judiciary. In one of the National Assembly's first acts, Issaias Afewerki, the Secretary-General of the EPLF, was elected as Head of State, by a margin of 99 votes to five.

Transitional Politics

President Afewerki appointed a new Consultative Council in June 1993, comprising 14 ministers (all members of the EPLF politburo) and 10 regional governors. The third congress of the EPLF was convened at Nakfa, in Sahel province, in February 1994. There the EPLF formally transformed itself from a military front into a national movement (the People's Front for Democracy and Justice—PFDJ), hoping to embrace all Eritreans (except those accused of collaboration during the liberation struggle). The party congress also confirmed its support for a plural political system which was to be included in the final draft of a new constitution, which (together with legislation to regulate the formation of political parties) was to be submitted for approval by a national referendum. Afewerki was elected Chairman of an 18-member Executive Committee (while remaining Head of State, and leader of the PFDJ). A 75-member PFDJ Central Committee was elected (an additional 75 members were to be elected by PFDJ regional committees).

In March 1994 the National Assembly adopted a series of resolutions whereby the former executive body, the Consultative Council, was formally superseded by a State Council. Other measures adopted by resolutions of the Assembly included the creation of a 50-member Constitutional Commission and the establishment of a committee charged with the reorganization of the country's administrative divisions. It was decided that the National Assembly would henceforth comprise 75 members of the PFDJ Central Committee, and 75 directly elected members. However, no mechanism was announced for their election. All but eight of the 50-member Constitutional Commission were government appointees, and there was no provision for any opposition participation in the interim system. Later in the month Afewerki carried out a ministerial reshuffle, which was widely interpreted as an attempt to formalize a separation of the functions of the Government and the PFDJ executive.

International conferences on the draft constitution were held in the capital in July 1994 and in January 1995, presided over by Dr Bereket Habteselassie, the Chairman of the Constitutional Commission. Many foreign constitutional experts were invited to attend and discuss the draft document and there was extensive popular consultation; however, no opposition parties or opponents of the regime were invited to contribute. A third stage of consultation began in October 1995, when former soldiers of the EPLF armed forces were invited to discuss the draft law.

In May 1995 the National Assembly approved a law reducing the previous 10 administrative regions to six, each with regional, sub-regional and village administrations. In November the Assembly approved new names for the regions, unrelated to the ethnic groups that inhabit them, and finalized details of their exact boundaries and sub-divisions.

In early 1997 a Constituent Assembly was established to discuss and ratify the draft constitution. The Constituent Assembly comprised 527 members, of whom 150 were from the National Assembly, and the remainder selected from representatives of Eritreans residing abroad or elected by regional assemblies (adhering to a 30% quota for women). On 23 May the Constituent Assembly unanimously adopted the Constitution, instituting a presidential regime, with a President elected for a maximum of two five-year terms. According to the Constitution, the President, as Head of State, was empowered to appoint, with the approval of the National Assembly, the ministers, the commissioners, the Auditor-General, the President of the central bank and judges of the Supreme Court. The President's mandate could be revoked should two-thirds of the members of the National Assembly so demand. 'Conditional' political pluralism was authorized. Following the adoption of the Constitution, the Constituent Assembly was disbanded, having empowered a Transitional National Assembly (comprising the 75 members of the PFDJ, 60 members of the Constituent Assembly and 15 representatives of the Eritrean diaspora) to act as the legislative body until the holding of national elections. The outbreak of war in 1998 delayed the implementation of the Constitution, although government officials continued to insist that it would be implemented gradually, once peace returned.

CONFLICT WITH ETHIOPIA

Relations with Ethiopia deteriorated in late 1997 as disagreements arose following Eritrea's introduction of a new currency, the nakfa (see Economy). In late December there was a military confrontation around an Eritrean army post on the frontier in northern Dankalia, an area where Ethiopian rebels were reported to be operating. In May 1998 fighting erupted between Eritrean and Ethiopian troops in the border region after both countries accused the other of having invaded their territory. The subsequent fighting was particularly damaging for both Eritrea and Ethiopia. Despite a series of peace initiatives by various regional and international parties, including the Organization of African Unity (OAU, now the African Union—AU), Rwanda and the USA, conflicts between the two countries continued intermittently over a period of two years.

The scale of the conflict was without parallel in Africa. Hundreds of thousands of troops were involved in the fighting; both sides were exceptionally well armed with modern weapons. Ethiopian troops advanced several miles into Eritrean territory, occupying the Badme area. In mid-May 2000 Ethiopia launched an offensive near the disputed towns of Badme and Zalambessa and succeeded in repulsing the Eritrean forces. Hostilities continued despite growing fears of a mounting humanitarian crisis. It was estimated that between 500,000 and 1m. Eritreans had fled as the conflict spread into Eritrea, with many seeking refuge in Sudan. The crisis was exacerbated by drought and food shortages, with about 850,000 Eritreans and an estimated 8m. Ethiopians in need of emergency assistance. The UN Security Council voted unanimously to impose a 12-month arms embargo on the two countries in an attempt to prevent any further intensification of hostilities; however, hours after this announcement Ethiopia declared that it had captured the key strategic town of Barentu, in south-west Eritrea, and had taken full control of the western front. As Ethiopian forces continued to drive deeper into Eritrean territory, foreign diplomats and other expatriates were urged to leave the country. Ethiopia launched a massive new offensive, which led to the capture of Zalambessa, and on 25 May the Eritrean Government announced that it would withdraw troops from the disputed areas.

Ethiopian forces continued to capture Eritrean towns over the following days, although both sides had by this stage agreed to attend peace talks under the auspices of the OAU, which began on 29 May 2000 in Algiers, Algeria. On 18 June a peace agreement was signed, which provided for an immediate cease-fire and the deployment of a UN peace-keeping force in a 25-km buffer zone until the disputed 966-km border had been demarcated.

In mid-September 2000 the UN Security Council approved the deployment of a 4,200-strong UN Mission in Ethiopia and Eritrea (UNMEE) peace-keeping force. UNMEE, which was placed under the command of the Special Representative of the UN Secretary-General, Legwaila Joseph Legwaila, was charged with monitoring and ensuring that both Eritrea and Ethiopia comply with the agreement. A definitive peace agreement, formally bringing the war to an end, was signed in Algiers on 12 December. Both sides agreed to a permanent cessation of all hostilities and the release and repatriation of all prisoners of war. The UN pledged to establish two separate independent commissions to delineate the border and assess compensation claims. The border commission was to demarcate the border in accordance with colonial maps. By late January 2001 the UNMEE force, drawn from more than 30 member countries, had been fully deployed and began making provisions for the establishment of a Temporary Security Zone (TSZ) in the 25-km area between the two countries' troops.

In mid-April 2002 the five-member Boundary Commission at the International Court of Justice at The Hague, Netherlands, delivered its findings, which both countries had pledged to accept and respect. However, the Commission failed to locate Badme, the village where the war had begun, in either Eritrea or Ethiopia, and the village itself did not appear on any of the published maps. After the initial confusion, the Boundary Commission announced in March 2003 that Badme was indeed in Eritrean territory. Border demarcation, budgeted to cost US $7.6m., was scheduled to begin that year, but Ethiopia's rejection of the border ruling put demarcation on indefinite hold.

The peace process suffered a further reverse in mid-November 2003, when Eritrea withdrew its ambassador to the AU and accused the organization of neglecting its responsibilities over the dispute with Ethiopia. However, in the following month both countries agreed to establish three Sector Military Coordination Committees, under the chairmanship of UNMEE's Sector Commanders, in order to improve the mechanism for dealing with incidents in the border areas; it was hoped that the committees would prevent any minor border incidents from escalating into wider conflict. Later in December Lloyd Axworthy, a former Canadian Minister of Foreign Affairs, was appointed as the UN's special envoy to the region, tasked with resolving the stalled peace process between Eritrea and Ethiopia. While Ethiopia welcomed the appointment and pledged to work closely with Axworthy, the Eritrean Government expressed its opposition to the appointment, as it feared that it would result in amendments to the Boundary Commission's ruling. In November 2004 Ethiopia stated that it approved the ruling 'in principle' but called for dialogue over the implementation of the decision in sensitive areas. This was rejected by Eritrea, which insisted on 'full implementation' of the ruling. Eritrea continued to refuse to meet with Axworthy and the initiative collapsed shortly thereafter.

The Eritrean Government, increasingly infuriated over the inaction of the international community, initiated a more assertive strategy on 31 August 2005 when it declared that its decision to expel the US Agency for International Development from Eritrea was irreversible. Two weeks later a UN Security Council resolution merely called for Ethiopia to honour the border ruling, prompting the Eritrean Minister of Finance, Berhane Abrehe, addressing the UN General Assembly, to warn that Eritrea was 'determined, and has the right, to defend and preserve its territorial integrity by any means possible'. The Eritrean Government termed the resolution as 'toothless and pathetic'. In October Eritrea banned UN helicopters from its airspace and as a result, the UN was forced to close several of its bases along the border. In November UNMEE stated that troop movements had occurred on both sides of the border. Later that month UN Security Council Resolution 1640 threatened both nations with economic sanctions, demanding that Ethiopia pull back its troops from the border, demarcate the border without preconditions, and that Eritrea lift restrictions on UNMEE. Terming the threat of sanctions 'deplorable', Eritrea accused the Security Council of bias and in December ordered all UN personnel from the USA, Russia, Canada and European Union (EU) member states to leave the country. In the wake of the relocation of its Western staff, UNMEE claimed that it had lost its ability to monitor much of the border, while India and Jordan, the major troop contributors, warned that their forces were in danger.

Eritrea suffered a reversal when in December the Claims Commission, based in The Hague, set up to investigate war violations, ruled that Eritrea had triggered the border war with Ethiopia: since there was no armed attack against Eritrea, its attack on Ethiopia could not be justified as lawful self-defence under the UN charter. Eritrea was thus liable to compensate Ethiopia for damages caused. The Claims Commission also announced a series of awards regarding abuses against civilians and the seizure of property. The Eritrean Government subsequently announced that it respected the ruling.

In January 2006 the US ambassador to the UN, John Bolton, sought to revive the stalled process, stating that Ethiopian refusal to demarcate the border was the source of Eritrean restrictions against UNMEE operations. In that month Ethiopia duly complied with the UN demand to withdraw troops from the border area. Eritrea, however, refused to lift restrictions on UN peace-keepers. In mid-January, US and Eritrean officials held talks in Washington, DC, over the border crisis but Eritrea refused to allow the US Assistant Secretary of State for African Affairs, Jendayi Frazer, to travel to the Eritrean side of the border. In March the President of the Boundary Commission, Elihu Lauterpacht, called a meeting seeking to move the process forward. (In February 2005 the Boundary Commission had invited the two countries to a similar meeting in London, United Kingdom, which Ethiopia declined to attend. The Boundary Commission closed its field offices the following month, citing Ethiopia's obstructive stance.) There was no substantial progress and further talks, scheduled for April 2005, were later postponed to May. During this time Ethiopian Prime Minister Meles Zenawi accused Eritrea of complicity in a series of explosions in Addis Ababa. On 31 March, at the end of his term as Special Representative to the UN Secretary-General, Legwaila expressed his shock and profound disappointment that border demarcation was still pending. The Security Council extended UNMEE's mandate to 31 May and threatened sanctions against both countries should they continue to ignore Resolution 1640. The Eritrean Government, however, remained defiant, refusing to lift restrictions imposed on UNMEE's activities, and stated that the restrictions were by-products of the international community's failure to enforce Ethiopian compliance with the Boundary Commission's ruling. In May officials from the two countries met in London, but no progress was made. Eritrea continued to demand demarcation, while Ethiopia insisted on a process of dialogue. In late May the USA pressed the Security

Council to scale back UNMEE's operations. On 31 May Resolution 1681 extended UNMEE's mandate until 30 September 2006, while reducing the number of troops from 3,300 to 2,300. The Security Council demanded that both countries fully comply with Resolution 1640. The resolution fell short, however, of reconstituting UNMEE into an observer mission. Eritrean officials declared Resolution 1681 to be 'unjust' and demanded the full implementation of the Boundary Commission's ruling.

Relations with UNMEE continued to deteriorate and in August 2006 UNMEE members were apprehended while allegedly moving young people and goods out of the country by hiding them in their vehicles. The government-controlled press indicated that the UNMEE staff members, from the Democratic Republic of the Congo, had received large cash payments from each youth. Shortly thereafter five UN staff members were deported, accused of espionage. Relations were further strained by the shooting of a civilian by UNMEE soldiers who alleged that the Eritrean had broken into one of its bases. The government-controlled press also launched a vitriolic attack against the conduct of UNMEE personnel, along with a critique against aid dependency. In July the Government strongly criticized UNMEE and peace-keeping missions in general, claiming that peace-keeping missions did not bring peace. Also that month Ethiopian Brig. Gen. Kemal Gelchu, along with numerous soldiers, defected to the Eritreans, citing the oppression of the Oromo peoples and the undemocratic nature of the regime dominated by the Tigrai People's Liberation Front (TPLF). His group subsequently joined the Oromo Liberation Front (OLF). In October 2006 Eritrea moved some 1,500 troops and 14 tanks into the TSZ. The UN Secretary General, Kofi Annan, demanded that Eritrea withdraw its troops from the zone immediately. The eruption of war in Somalia compounded the border standoff. Ethiopia supported the transitional Government while Eritrea backed the Somali Supreme Islamic Courts Council (SSICC). The conflict in Somalia quickly morphed into a proxy war between Eritrea and Ethiopia; it also exacerbated the tensions between UNMEE and the Eritrean Government which accused it of being pro-Ethiopian. Eritrea's move into the TSZ was interpreted by the USA and the Ethiopian Government as part of a regional strategy to place military pressure on Ethiopia's northern front while it was simultaneously engaged in offensive action against the SSICC. An earlier UN report had alleged that Eritrea had supplied weapons to the SSICC.

In November 2006 the Boundary Commission announced that it would demarcate the Ethiopian–Eritrean border on maps using high resolution aerial photography to identify points where pillars should be placed to mark the boundary in the remaining disputed areas. The Commission also announced that it would allow the two countries to establish the physical boundary themselves, a move immediately rejected by both governments. Eritrea demanded that the border be physically laid out on the ground, while Ethiopia, which rejected the boundary, stated that the Commission was acting outside its mandate. Due to obstruction of its work on the ground by both parties, and despite UN Security Council Resolution 1710 of September 2006 urging full co-operation with the Boundary Commission, the Commission subsequently declared that both parties had to demarcate the border by the end of November 2007. Failing this, the boundary would stand as demarcated by the points the Commission had identified, following which the work would be completed and the Commission closed down. In reaching this decision, the Boundary Commission referred to a similar case from 1966, where aerial photography had been employed to identify points on the boundary between Argentina and Chile.

In January 2007 the new UN Secretary General, Ban Ki-Moon, warned that Ethiopia and Eritrea needed to do much more than settle their border issue if they were to establish sustainable peace, reconciliation and normalized relations. Subsequently UN Security Council Resolution 1741 extended UNMEE's mandate to 31 July 2007 while reducing the UN peace-keeping force from 2,300 to 1,700. The Security Council again demanded that Ethiopia accept fully and move to implement the border ruling. At the same time the Security Council requested that Eritrea immediately withdraw its forces from the TSZ and reverse its restrictions on UNMEE. In May Eritrea dismissed UN demands to resolve its border deadlock with Ethiopia through alternative mechanisms, and once again blamed the UN and USA for the impasse. In June 2007 press reports suggested that the Ethiopian Government had given its unconditional acceptance of the Boundary Commission's decision. However, Eritrea immediately dismissed Ethiopia's announcement, claiming that Ethiopia had attached conditions that undermined the spirit of the border ruling. Ethiopian Prime Minister Zenawi shortly thereafter stated that the Government was strengthening the Ethiopian army against potential attacks from Eritrea.

In late 2006 the ongoing conflict in Somalia continued to exacerbate the deadlock between Eritrea and Ethiopia and external powers. In December 2006 Eritrea accused Ethiopia of fabricating identity cards to support claims that Eritrea had sent troops to back the SSICC. The Eritrean Government vehemently opposed the UN authorizing of a regional force from the Intergovernmental Authority on Development (IGAD—comprising Djibouti, Eritrea, Ethiopia, Kenya, Somalia, Sudan and Uganda) and the AU to protect the Transitional Federal Government (TFG) in Somalia. In January 2007 President Afewerki stated that any AU peace-keeping mission sent into Somalia was doomed to failure, claiming that the SSICC had not been defeated, and adding that the AU lacked the organizational capability to deploy troops effectively in Somalia. In April Eritrea suspended its membership of IGAD due to deteriorating relations with Somalia. Eritrea subsequently fell into arrears with AU membership fees and lost its right to vote in the organization in June. In April two state media journalists were held by the Ethiopian authorities after the invasion by Ethiopian forces. In June Frazer claimed that Eritrea was undermining the Somali National Reconciliation Conference by harbouring 'extremist elements' linked to violent Islamist groups. It was reported that a Somali opposition coalition, established in late May 2007, had consolidated itself in Asmara and was believed to be made up of at least four major groups: the SSICC, Ethiopia's Ogaden National Liberation Front, the OLF and anti-Ethiopian former parliamentarians of the TFG.

POST-WAR POLITICS

Eritrea, with its smaller population came off worse in the conflict with Ethiopia, resulting in growing challenges to President Afewerki. While internal party conflicts had been experienced in the period before the war with Ethiopia, the war intensified these divisions. Afewerki adopted a policy of *mdskal* (freezing), in an attempt to exclude high-ranking officials and military commanders from participating in the decision-making process.

A number of senior military officials were subjected to *mdskal*, as was the Minister of Transport and Communications, and head of the presidential office, Saleh Idris Kekia, Moreover, Abraha Kassa, the head of national security, was held responsible for several intelligence failures during the war. Divisions between the President and senior PFDJ officials had initially surfaced at a meeting of the party's Executive Committee in August 2000, when Afewerki was criticized for failing to consult senior party figures, ignoring the party hierarchy and refusing to implement the Constitution. Furthermore, Afewerki was attacked for relying on a coterie of personal advisers. As a result of this pressure, the President reluctantly accepted the National Assembly's decision to hold multi-party elections in December 2001. The Minister of Local Government, Mahmoud Ahmed Sherifo, was appointed to head the commission that was to draft the electoral law. However, upon completion of the draft in January 2001, Sherifo distributed the document directly to members of the National Assembly and announced his intention to hold a press conference to publicize his findings. Afewerki cancelled the scheduled press conference and, in mid-February, dissolved the electoral law commission and summarily dismissed Sherifo from the Government.

In September 2000 a group of Eritreans, comprising mainly expatriate academics and professionals, including Bereket Habteselassie, met in Germany and drafted a letter addressed to the President that became known as 'the Berlin Manifesto'. In the letter, which was leaked to the media, they criticized several aspects of Afewerki's leadership and called for the implementation of the Constitution and for reform of the PFDJ. The group subsequently travelled to Eritrea and met with President Afewerki, but no reform followed.

During 2001 Afewerki was again the subject of criticism from within the PFDJ. In May 15 senior party officials signed an open letter to party members, accusing the President of working in an 'unconstitutional manner'. This group was composed of Central Council members, including Woldetensai, Sherifo, Petros Solomon and Mesfin Hagos. In mid-June Woldetensai and Solomon were dismissed from their posts. Later that month Solomon called for a new generation to lead the country. In August the Minister for Justice was dismissed after delivering a paper critical of the Eritrean justice system during an international conference held in Asmara.

In mid-September 2001 six of the G-15, as the signatories of the letter had become known, were detained, and the Government announced a temporary suspension of the independent press. Days later a further five members of the G-15 were arrested. Nine journalists and two Eritreans employed at the US embassy were also detained. Three other G-15 members, who were outside Eritrea at the time of the dispute, had their passports revoked. Afewerki insisted that his former allies had become threats to national security. The wives of two imprisoned G-15 politicians were also arrested, although one was later released. The others detained at the time remain imprisoned.

In October 2001 the Eritrean authorities expelled the Italian ambassador after he expressed concern at recent events in Eritrea on behalf of the EU. The Italian Government responded by expelling the Eritrean ambassador in Rome. Later that month Denmark, France, Germany and the Netherlands recalled their ambassadors from Eritrea for consultations. The four returned to Asmara in mid-November followed later by the Italian ambassador.

In late January 2002 the National Assembly ratified the electoral law, which stipulated that 30% of the seats in the new legislative chamber would be reserved for women. The PFDJ announced in February that, following extensive consultations with local and regional representatives, the National Assembly had decided not to permit the formation of political parties, although it conceded that the principle of establishing political parties was 'acceptable'.

In 2003 elections of local administrators and magistrates were held in villages throughout Eritrea and in May 2004 elections took place for regional assemblies. These elections were hailed as fair and successful by the National Election Committee, with turn-out at the regional elections officially recorded at 92%. The administration remained reluctant to implement a framework centred around a constitutional process of democratization and international human rights treaties and, in an interview with the Al-Arabiya television station in May 2007, President Afewerki stated that Eritrea would not import foreign models of democracy at the expense of Eritrea's national interests. The prospect of a general election in the near future appeared remote. In April 2007 Eritrea moved its Minister of Education, Osman Salih Muhammad, to the foreign affairs portfolio, while Semere Rusom assumed the education post.

POST-WAR STATE AND SOCIETY

The state's relations with churches, NGOs and other potential interest groups, also came under scrutiny in the post-war period, although the roots of conflict can be found in the period before 1998. The EPLF's experiences in the liberation war had made it intensely committed to secularism, with strong control over societal groups, which were subsumed into the movement. The major faiths in Eritrea include the Orthodox Church, Islam, the Evangelical Lutheran Church and the Roman Catholic Church. The Eritrean Orthodox Church, which dominates highland culture, had been a notable casualty of the Ethiopian occupation of the country at the time of the liberation war. Several monasteries were occupied by Ethiopian soldiers and many of the monks and their students were killed. After independence, a movement promoting secession from the Ethiopian church gained widespread support. In June 1994 Eritrea sent five abbots from Eritrean monasteries to the headquarters of the Coptic church in Cairo, Egypt, where they were inducted as bishops by Shenouda III, the Coptic Orthodox pontiff. In September the first bishops of the Eritrean Orthodox Church were consecrated at a ceremony conducted in Cairo. These consecrations signified the formal separation of the Eritrean Orthodox Church from the Ethiopian Orthodox Church as an independent body. In May 1998 Abuna Philippos was consecrated as the first Eritrean Patriarch by Shenouda III in Alexandria. Following Philippos' death in 2002, Abuna Yakob was anointed as the second Patriarch. Yakob died in December 2003; Abuna Antonios was elected as his successor in March 2004.

In January 2006, authorities reportedly placed Antonios under formal house arrest for protesting against the arrest of three Orthodox priests of the Medhane Alem Church, and for refusing to co-operate with the Government in closing down that Church. Antonios argued that his dismissal was in direct violation of long-established Church canons, under which a Patriarch's election is a lifetime appointment that cannot be revoked. He was, however, stripped of his Patriarchal vestments and holy artifacts in January 2007.

It is believed that one-half of Eritrea's population follows Islam; these populations are mainly found in lowland areas and pastoralist communities. The secular state respects Islamic holidays and traditions, and is vigilant against sectarianism. However, there is some concern among Muslim communities that language policies, which promote mother-tongue education, discriminate against Arabic (the mother tongue of less than 3% of the population), and in favour of Tigrinya. In practice, Tigrinya functions as an official language of government and the military. At the same time as evangelical churches were closed in 2002, opposition websites reported that mosques in some areas were also targeted by security forces, but these reports have proved impossible to verify. Eritrean Islamic Jihad (EIJ), which operates out of Sudan, has been held responsible for several bombs and landmines in the western lowlands.

Although Jehovah's Witnesses form only a small group, their post-independence history has been marked by conflicts with the state, as have been, to a lesser extent, the experiences of Evangelical and Pentecostal churches. Jehovah's Witnesses had first clashed with the new Government in 1993, when they refused to participate in the independence referendum. Their subsequent refusal to participate in national service led the Government to deny them citizenship rights in 1995. Other 'new' churches grew rapidly in the 1990s, as Eritreans returned from the diaspora, bringing new ways of worshipping with them or joining Evangelical churches that had been suppressed under the Ethiopian Dergue regime. A revival movement within the Orthodox Church also emerged at this time, demanding liturgical and institutional change, which was suppressed. In April 2002 all churches with less than 40 years' presence in Eritrea were ordered to close their branches outside Asmara, and churches in Asmara were similarly ordered to close in May. Church leaders were told that they could 'reapply' for licences to operate. Throughout 2003 and 2004 hundreds of church leaders and followers were detained for holding meetings and weddings. The controversy continues and is an increasing source of tension between the US and Eritrean Governments.

In 2002 it was announced that 11th-grade students were obliged to attend Sawa Military Camp for their final year of high school instead of graduating. Final-year university students were assigned to Sawa as their teachers. Those students who graduated from Sawa high school with good marks were sent to technical institutes, which comprise Mai Nefhi Institute of Science and Technology, Halhale College of Business and Economics, Adi Keyeh College of Social Sciences, Hamelmalo Agricultural College, the Marine Training College of Dongolo, and the Massawa Institute of Technology, and each reporting to a relevant ministry. These technical schools are financed by the World Bank's Education Sector Development Program. In September 2006 the University of Asmara was closed down. The reform was officially intended to decentralize education to the regions, but the quality of service delivery has undoubtedly deteriorated as Indian expatriate staff, Eritrean staff of the now-defunct university, and recently-graduated Eritrean undergraduates cope with large classroom sizes, poorly motivated students, transport bottlenecks, and a less than satisfactory infrastructure.

In early 2007 the emasculation of Eritrean civil society continued unabated. The private media remained banned and party and government leaders and journalists arrested in 2001 remained in detention. Opposition parties alleged that they were being held incommunicado at Era Ero, with one confirmed death, that of Gen. Oqbe Abraha. Human Rights Watch noted unconfirmed reports that another 31 had died in captivity. Amnesty International cited harsh conditions for those arrested, including being packed into cargo containers, starvation rations, lack of sanitation, solitary confinement, hard labour and limited medical treatment.

From the first years of independence both international and local NGOs have been tightly controlled. Religious organizations were required to keep their proselytization and welfare activities completely separate. Financial controls were also tightly mandated, with organizations only allowed to maintain an office in-country if administration comprised less than 10% of the overall budget. The 14 local organizations are required by law to rely mainly on local, rather than international financial support, although in practice this requirement is not met. In 1996 these restrictions were tightened with the result that international organizations could only work in the areas of health and education. Many NGOs left in 1997, when foreign staff were required to pay high rates of local tax. Some NGO representatives insisted that they were 'asked to leave'. Although a few NGOs returned in the aftermath of the Ethiopia–Eritrea border war, donor reluctance to fund non-humanitarian aid has diminished the sector. In June 2005 the Minister of Labour and Human Welfare, Askalu Menkerios, addressed the 93rd International Labour Organization conference where she outlined the salient features of the newly promulgated legislation regarding NGOs. Henceforth, NGOs were to be restricted to relief and rehabilitation activities, and were required to have a minimum operational capital of US $2m. In light of efforts at food self-reliance, and a state media increasingly hostile to Western NGOs as the 'other face of colonialism', in March 2006 the Eritrean Government revoked the operating permits of three NGOs: US charity Mercy Corps, the Irish agency Concern, and Acord of the United Kingdom. The Eritrean authorities claimed that the agencies had failed to meet the requirements for operational permits. In November 2006 the Eritrean Government ordered a further two international charities to leave the country, International Rescue Committee and Samaritans' Purse; the official reason cited was that their operations in eastern Sudan would be no longer needed in the wake of the peace agreement between Khartoum and eastern Sudanese rebels. The most significant domestic NGOs are the former mass movements of women, workers and youth, which function as interest-aggregating groups, recipients of donor funds, and quasi-ministerial bodies. During the political crisis of 2001 the National Union of Eritrean Youths and Students (NUEYS) was an important element in the Government's propaganda machine, using its newspapers to condemn both the G-15 and dissident university students. The NUEYS has also organized significant support for the Government among youth in the diaspora. However, in May 2004 Muheidin Shengeb, the NUEYS Chairman and a member of the PFDJ Executive Council, sought political asylum in the USA, claiming that he had been targeted for arrest by the Eritrean authorities. In May 2006 the eighth Congress of the NUEYS elected a new 51-member Central Council and Sultan Said to the role of Chairman.

Private newspapers had been allowed to publish in 1997, and had contributed to the vibrant public debates on the G-15 in 2000–01 (see above). In September 2001 all eight of Eritrea's independent newspapers (including those that were pro-Government) were forcibly closed and nine journalists were arrested, accused of accepting foreign funding. Government sources insist that newspapers may re-apply for permission to operate, if they agree to abide by the law, but no permits have since been issued. An estimated 16 journalists remained in gaol in 2005, while a number of other journalists have sought sanctuary abroad. The Committee to Protect Journalists (CPJ) denounced the Eritrean Government's continued detention of journalists seized since 2001. According to the CPJ, Eritrea was the only country in sub-Saharan Africa without a private media outlet. Foreign correspondents were occasionally subject to restrictions and television and radio broadcasters were controlled by the Government, although some opposition groups broadcast on short-wave and via the internet; Ethiopian television is widely watched by those with satellite receivers. In response to such criticisms, in November 2006 Eritrea accused the western media of focusing on the interests of the wealthy minority and routinely ignoring development issues of critical importance to much of the world's population.

Eritrea was the last African state to gain access to the internet (in 2000) and mobile cellular telephones (in 2004). Internet cafés spread rapidly throughout urban areas, despite frequent rumours of government control or enforced closures. Internet use increased from 2.3% of the population in 2003 to 12% in 2004. Work to distribute mobile telephone lines to Nakfa, Afabet and Assab has already commenced and was due to be completed in Nakfa and Afabet by late 2006. A satellite link has connected Assab to the regions and abroad.

The Military and National Service

Relations between war veterans and the state, and those Eritreans in national service and the state have fluctuated. Eritrea values its military veterans highly, and compulsory military service has existed since 1994. In 1997 it was written into the Constitution. All Eritreans between 18 and 40 years of age (with certain exceptions) were obliged to undertake six months' military training and 12 months' service. However, in July 1994 disillusioned war veterans took the director of the rehabilitation centre at Mai Habar hostage and demanded to meet the President to discuss their meagre rehabilitation benefits. Following that confrontation many veterans were integrated into the civil service and given selective access to higher education and tax exemptions on imported vehicles.

In 1998 a National Development Campaign was briefly implemented, which called upon all of those who had participated in national service since 1994 to remobilize for one month and carry out development projects. The programme, designed to mobilize 50,000–60,000 Eritreans, was scheduled to start at the end of April 1998 and to continue throughout May. When the border conflict with Ethiopia started in mid-May, the development projects were abandoned, but the mobilized youth were transferred to the front, along with remobilized veterans. Youth and students mobilized willingly, indeed enthusiastically, throughout the war, but since its conclusion reports of youths evading national service have multiplied. '*Gffas*' or 'round-ups' of those avoiding conscription have intensified, with soldiers stationed on street corners throughout urban areas, and on roads leading out of cities, checking passes and detaining those without service records. In some cases soldiers have reportedly entered houses and encountered violent resistance. In early 2004 the office of the UN High Commissioner for Refugees (UNHCR) in Ethiopia reported that some 250 Eritreans per month were seeking sanctuary in a refugee camp near the border. In March 2005 restrictions on exit visas were increased, raising the minimum age for an Eritrean man to gain an exit visa to 50 years.

According to UN figures, an estimated 202,000 out of the country's 4.7m. people serve in the armed forces. The army is the largest in sub-Saharan Africa and has the highest proportion of a nation's population in military service in the world. With national service likely to continue, dispirited youth seek to avoid conscription by hiding from gangs of military police. Flight across the borders remains the exit option of choice and refugee agencies estimated that during 2006 approximately 700 Eritreans each month fled to Sudan and another 400 to Ethiopia. Reports indicated that some 80–100 Eritreans every day were fleeing into UNHCR camps in Sudan. The refugees included youth of conscription age and, increasingly, young professional men and women who flee across the border to Ethiopia or Sudan, despite a reported 'shoot-to-kill' policy. During peace negotiations for the agreement signed with

Sudan in October 2006 (see below), allegations emerged that Eritrean government agents were in Sudan and forcibly returning those attempting to escape. Other counter-measures employed by the Government included the decentralization of military training bases away from the Sudanese border and, since mid-2005, the detention of family members of illegal refugees, and training young civil servants in an effort to encourage them not to defect. For many of these 'new breed' Eritrean refugees, entering Sudan was only the beginning of a hazardous journey north to Libya and then on to southern Europe. Others languish in refugee camps in Malta and Italy. Several asylum-seekers forcibly returned from Malta in 2002 and Libya in 2003 were still detained in early 2007.

REGIONAL AND INTERNATIONAL RELATIONS

Following its formal accession to independence in 1993, Eritrea gradually increased its international contacts, establishing diplomatic ties with Sudan, Ethiopia, Israel, Australia and Pakistan, and several international organizations. In July Eritrea and Ethiopia signed an agreement for the joint use of the ports of Assab and Massawa, while in August it was reported that 90,000 Ethiopian prisoners of war had been released by the Eritrean Government. In September the first meeting of the Ethiopian-Eritrean joint ministerial commission was held in Asmara, during which agreement was reached on measures to allow the free movement of nationals between each country, and on co-operation regarding foreign affairs and economic policy. However, cordial relations with several Arab states deteriorated following the publication and dissemination of articles critical of the Afewerki regime by the EIJ, a militant group based in Sudan.

The influence of regional organizations in the border conflict with Ethiopia remains limited. In March 2006 the newly appointed Chairman of IGAD, Kenyan President Mwai Kibaki, urged both countries to exercise restraint and to negotiate an end to their border dispute.

Relations between the transitional Government and Sudan, which had supported the EPLF during the war, deteriorated in December 1993, following an incursion by members of the EIJ from Sudan. In a clash with Eritrean forces, all the members of the group, and an Eritrean commander, were killed. In response to the incident, President Afewerki stressed the links between the EIJ and the Sudanese National Islamic Front, led by Dr Hassan at-Turabi, implying that the latter had prior knowledge of the incursion. However, following a swift denial by the Sudanese Government that it would ever interfere in the affairs of neighbouring states, Afewerki reaffirmed his commitment to improving bilateral relations.

In August 1994 Eritrea and Sudan signed an agreement concerning borders, security and the repatriation of refugees, and in November UNHCR initiated a repatriation programme for Eritrean refugees currently in Sudan. Some 500,000 Eritreans had taken refuge in Sudan in the early 1990s as a result of conflict, although by 1995 an estimated 125,000 had returned spontaneously, particularly following independence. Owing to delays in the implementation of the UNHCR programme, an estimated 342,300 Eritrean refugees remained in Sudan in late 1998. It was estimated that, as a result of the conflict between Ethiopia and Eritrea in 2000 (see above), a further 90,000 Eritreans had sought refuge in Sudan during May–June. In July, however, following the cessation of hostilities, UNHCR began operations to repatriate tens of thousands of Eritrean refugees. During 2001–02 Eritrea and Sudan co-operated closely with UNHCR on the repatriation of Eritrean refugees from Sudan. In mid-2002 Eritrean officials stated that 52,000 of the estimated 174,000 Eritrean refugees had returned, mainly to the Gash-Barka region, and that another 16,000 were registered to leave. In May 2002 UNHCR announced that with effect from January 2003 it would cease to regard Eritreans in Sudan as refugees, as it maintained that Eritreans there should no longer fear persecution. Many of the refugees contested this ruling, however, and 27,000 heads of families, representing an estimated total of 100,000 individuals, re-applied for refugee status, the majority citing their religious beliefs and political affiliations as sources of conflict with the Afewerki regime. According to provisional UNHCR figures, 116,746 Eritrean refugees were in Sudan at the end of 2005.

Relations between Eritrea and Sudan deteriorated in late 1994, when the Eritrean authorities accused Sudan of training 400 terrorists. Sudan, for its part, accused Eritrea of training some 3,000 Sudanese rebels in camps within Eritrea. In December Eritrea severed diplomatic relations with Sudan. Further destabilization followed in early 1995 after attacks in the Barka region by EIJ forces. The Eritrean authorities subsequently identified six alleged terrorist training camps on the Sudanese side of the border, and also claimed that the Sudanese security forces had arrested a large number of Eritrean refugees. Sudan responded by proposing Eritrea's suspension from IGAD, which had been attempting to mediate in Sudan's civil war. Sudan strongly criticized Eritrea for hosting a series of conferences in Asmara for the Sudanese opposition grouping, the National Democratic Alliance (NDA), in December 1994–January 1996. In February 1996 the Eritrean Government granted permission for Sudanese opposition leaders to use the Sudanese embassy in Asmara as their headquarters.

In January 1997 the NDA launched an attack from Eritrea on Sudanese forces in the border area, resulting in numerous casualties. Meanwhile, Eritrea claimed that the EIJ was training more than 4,000 Eritrean Muslims in Sudan to launch an attack against the Government. In June the Minister of Foreign Affairs announced that the security forces had foiled a plot by the Sudanese Government to assassinate President Afewerki. This prompted further clashes between Eritrean and Sudanese troops in the border area during July; Eritrean forces had been sent to reinforce the NDA units already operating near the border. In August there were reports that Sudanese military aircraft had entered Eritrean airspace, bombing the area around the town of Karora. In February 1998 Sudan closed the border with Eritrea to prevent further incursions by rebel groups.

By mid-1999, however, Sudan had indicated its willingness to improve its relations with Eritrea. In May Afewerki and President Lt-Gen. Omar Hassan Ahmad al-Bashir of Sudan signed a reconciliation agreement following a meeting in Qatar, which, *inter alia*, restored full diplomatic relations. In June Sudan accused Eritrea of violating the agreement by allowing a Sudanese opposition group to hold a rally in Asmara. Afewerki subsequently ordered all Sudanese anti-government activists to vacate the former embassy building in the capital, and in January 2000 Eritrea returned the building to the possession of the Sudanese authorities and the embassies in Asmara and Khartoum were later reopened. Moreover, the Minister of Foreign Affairs pledged that no further military or hostile acts would be launched from Eritrea into Sudan, and concurrently oversaw the reopening of the border. In August al-Bashir made an unplanned visit to Asmara where he and Afewerki agreed to further improve bilateral relations between the two countries. In December, however, al-Bashir accused Eritrea of continuing to support Sudanese rebel groups. Relations deteriorated further in March 2001 following claims, denied by Eritrea, that Sudanese rebel forces were gathered on the Eritrean side of the border. In July the two countries signed an agreement on border security.

Tensions between Eritrea and Sudan were exacerbated in October 2002 by intensified fighting in eastern Sudan. The Sudanese Government alleged that Eritrean forces were responsible for the attacks, and neither the visit of an AU delegation, nor the intervention of Libyan leader Col Muammar al-Qaddafi proved successful in resolving the dispute. Sudan subsequently closed the common border. In November the PFDJ accused Ethiopia, Yemen and Sudan of forming an 'axis of belligerence' with the aim of overthrowing the Eritrean Government. The Sudanese regime was also accused of continuing to support the EIJ, which was held responsible for a number of landmine attacks along the border in 2002, as well as the murder of a British national in 2003. The PFDJ and the NDA enhanced their political co-operation throughout 2005, including discussions with opposition movements based in the troubled Darfur region of Sudan. On 21 June 2005 President Afewerki held talks with Dr John Garang of the southern Sudan People's Liberation Movement. In July Afewerki sent congratulations to Garang and to the leadership in Khartoum, on the formation of a Government of national unity, on the basis of Naivasha Peace Accords (see Recent History of Sudan). However, Garang's death in a helicopter crash on 30 July caused palpable consternation within the Eritrean Government due to the uncertainty, albeit temporary, it brought to Eritrean-Sudanese relations. In April 2006, following the first meeting of the Sudanese-Eritrean Joint Committee, the two countries agreed to raise diplomatic ties to the ambassadorial level.

Relations between Eritrea and Sudan appeared to improve during 2007 despite accusations made by the Sudanese Government in July 2006 that Eritrea was supporting rebel factions from Dafur headquartered in Asmara. In September 2006 al-Bashir urged Eritrea to expel the members of Darfur rebel groups from its territories. On 14 October the Sudanese Government and rebels from the Eastern Front signed a peace accord, negotiated with Eritrean assistance, which was aimed at ending the 10-year armed conflict. The signing of the agreement in Eritrea was welcomed by Khartoum, which had been struggling to suppress rebellions across the country, and to maintain the unstable peace that had followed the civil war. All of the recognized Darfur rebel groups have offices in Eritrea and in June the Sudan Justice and Equality Movement, a breakaway faction of the Sudan Liberation Movement and the Sudan Federal Democratic Alliance, formed the National Redemption Front. In November Eritrea and Sudan restored full cross-border links. It was expected that Sudan would establish trade links to supply petroleum and goods to ease food shortages.

In November 1995 Eritrea's Minister of Foreign Affairs held talks with President Gouled in Djibouti. As a result, both countries pledged to enhance bilateral co-operation. Allegations made in a Yemeni newspaper in December that Eritrean troops had made an incursion into north-east Djibouti were vehemently denied by Eritrea. In April 1996 Gouled reportedly rejected a map (produced in Italy in 1935) which apparently indicated that a 20-km strip of land currently claimed by Djibouti was, in fact, Eritrean territory. Concurrently, reports emerged of the attempted occupation of a border post in Djibouti (within the disputed territory) by Eritrean troops. Relations between the two countries subsequently improved; however, in November 1998 Djibouti suspended diplomatic relations with Eritrea, following allegations by the Eritrean authorities that it was supporting Ethiopia in the Eritrea–Ethiopia border conflict. In March 2000 Djibouti announced that it had resumed diplomatic relations with Eritrea, and in January 2002 they agreed to resume bilateral co-operation and signed a number of accords relating to trade, transport and immigration. In September 2006 a Djiboutian delegation headed by the Minister of Defence, Ougoureh Kifleh Ahmed, met with the Eritrean Minister of Defence, Sebhat Ephrem.

In November 1995 there were reports that Eritrean troops had attempted to land on the Red Sea island of Greater Hanish, one of three islands (the others being Lesser Hanish and Zuqar) claimed by both Eritrea and Yemen. The invasion attempt had reportedly been prompted by Yemen's announced intention to develop Greater Hanish as a tourist resort, and its subsequent refusal to comply with an Eritrean demand that the island be evacuated. The disputed islands had been used by Eritrea (with apparent Yemeni approval) during its struggle for independence from Ethiopia. Yemen subsequently resumed its claims to the islands, because of both their strategic importance (located close to a principal shipping lane) and the possibility of discovering lucrative petroleum reserves in their surrounding waters. Negotiations in Eritrea and Yemen failed to defuse the crisis, and in mid-December fighting erupted between the two sides, resulting in the deaths of six Eritrean and three Yemeni soldiers. Two days later Eritrea and Yemen agreed to a cease-fire, but fighting resumed on the following day, and Eritrean forces succeeded in occupying Greater Hanish. The cease-fire was adhered to thenceforth, and some 180 captured Yemeni soldiers were released at the end of the month. The Ethiopian and Egyptian Governments attempted, unsuccessfully, to broker an agreement, and in January 1996 France assumed the mediatory role. In May representatives of Eritrea and Yemen signed an arbitration accord in Paris, France, whereby the two sides agreed to submit the dispute to an international tribunal. France subsequently undertook to observe and supervise military movements in the area around the disputed islands. In August, despite the accord, Eritrean troops occupied Lesser Hanish; however, later in the month Eritrea withdrew its soldiers after mediation by France and a UN Security Council edict to evacuate the island forthwith. In October Eritrea and Yemen confirmed that they would submit the dispute to an international tribunal. A five-judge arbitration court was established in the United Kingdom and started work in April 1997. In October 1998 the tribunal ruled that the Hanish islands belonged to Yemen and had been illegally occupied by Eritrea. Both countries accepted the ruling, and shortly afterwards they agreed to establish a joint committee to strengthen bilateral co-operation. In March Eritrea and Yemen had exchanged ambassadors. In December 1999 the Hanish arbitration tribunal announced that Eritrean fishermen would still be permitted to engage in artisanal fishing around the Hanish islands. Since 2005 technical experts from both countries have met in order to formulate a programme for joint development of the fisheries sector. In July 2006 President Ali Abdullah Saleh of Yemen paid a state visit to Asmara, where he met President Afewerki. The two men discussed trade and investment and the recent events in Somalia. This was followed in November by the signing of an agreement to establish a joint fisheries company to undertake fishing activities as well as the processing and canning of various fish products.

The USA has long had a military and security interest in Eritrea. In December 1997 the US Department of Defense financed two projects associated with Massawa port, justifying the expenditure by arguing that future military manoeuvres in the area around the Red Sea would involve US forces. There were also reports that the USA was considering transferring its military base from Saudi Arabia to Eritrea. An important US airbase and listening station had existed at Kagnew some 30 years earlier. Relations with the USA became complicated in 2001, with the arrest of Eritrean nationals working in the US embassy in Asmara (see above). None the less, at the same time, Eritrea made great efforts to ingratiate itself with the USA, pledging its support for the 'war on terrorism', and participating in the US-led coalition's campaign to oust the regime of Saddam Hussain in Iraq. Persistent rumours of the establishment of a US military base in the Dahlak islands were followed by Eritrean efforts to entice the USA to use Assab as an anti-terrorism base, instead of Djibouti, including a lobbying campaign in Washington, DC, which was estimated to be costing US $50,000 per month. The US Secretary of Defense, Donald Rumsfeld, visited Eritrea briefly in late 2002, leading commentators to suggest that US military advisers were less wary of entanglement in Eritrea than their counterparts at the Department of State.

In July 2005 President Afewerki held talks with the Commander of US Central Command, Gen. John Abizaid, making clear his view that border demarcation was paramount over the 'war on terror', especially given that the USA was a guarantor of the Algiers peace agreement. In November Afewerki reiterated the Government's support for the peace process and its rejection of US hegemony. In March 2006 Eritrea accused the USA of hypocrisy over the annual State Department Country Report on Human Rights Practices, which criticized alleged Eritrean government crackdowns on those evading national service, the continued detention of political prisoners, and measures forcing parents to pay substantial fines if their children fled the country illegally. The Government retaliated by claiming that, in the wake of prison abuse scandals in Iraq and at the US naval base in Guantánamo Bay in Cuba, the US Administration had no moral grounds to criticize other countries. Increasingly vitriolic in tone, the Eritrean Government, in April 2006, stated that military, diplomatic and economic support from Washington to Addis Ababa outweighed John Bolton's January diplomatic initiative. In his annual Independence Day speech Afewerki claimed that the USA was responsible for allowing Ethiopia to ignore the Boundary Commission's ruling, prompting the US Ambassador to walk out in protest of the National Stadium where the rally was being held. On Martyr's Day in June 2006 the Eritrean Government accused the USA once again of favouring the Ethiopian Government in the border dispute, and of interfering in the Somalia conflict on the pretext of fighting terrorism. In March 2007 Eritrea joined Belarus, the People's Republic of China, Cuba, Iran, Myanmar, the Democratic People's Republic of Korea and Zimbabwe on the State Department's list of 'the world's most systematic human rights violators'. The USA accused Eritrea of aiding rebel groups trying to destabilize Ethiopia, the main US counter-terrorism ally in the region, as well as the SSICC in Somalia. Eritrean presidential advisor Yemane Ghebremeskel stated that many problems in the Horn of Africa were a result of US policy, a trend dating back to the times of the independence struggle. In early 2007 visa services for Eritreans were suspended until diplomatic delegations were allowed unimpeded entry into Eritrea.

Relations with European donor countries, and the provision of non-humanitarian aid, seem unlikely to improve until the resolution of the political situation in Eritrea. In particular, relations with Italy came under strain in 2005. In July Italy withdrew its military police officers from the UN mission in Asmara, after Eritrea imposed restrictions on their activities. Relations between the two countries deteriorated further in 2006. In March Eritrea arrested and expelled Ludovico Serra, the First Secretary of the Italian embassy in the capital; Italy responded by ordering an Eritrean diplomat in Rome to leave the country. Serra had sought a resolution to a dispute regarding the status and value of a colonial-era villa in Massawa, owned by wealthy Italians. Shortly after Serra's departure, the villa was demolished to make way for a reconstruction project, according to Eritrean officials. In late September 2006 President Afewerki met with the French Minister-Delegate for Co-operation, Development and La Francophonie, Brigitte Girardin. The talks were believed to have focused on the prevailing situation in the region as well as the role of the USA in the Horn of Africa. In December Afewerki paid an official visit to Italy to meet with Prime Minister Romano Prodi, and to hold a press conference with Italian journalists, during which he denied that Eritrea had sent troops to Somalia and reiterated the Boundary Commission's ruling on demarcation. In August 2006 The European Commission (EC) considered halting aid to Eritrea in protest at food aid being sold and the proceeds used for government work programmes, which violated the conditions under which the EC donated the food. However, relations with the EU appeared to show signs of improvement in 2007. The EU adopted a new partnership for peace, security and development in the Horn of Africa. According to reports the new European strategy would be defined in close co-operation with the governments concerned. It planned to draw on the EU's recently announced €3,000m. fund for improving governance in developing nations.

Since 2001 Eritrea has increasingly looked beyond the West for support. China and Eritrea have developed their diplomatic and economic ties, including the signing of a US $1.8m. development agreement in June 2004. Eritrean-Chinese ties were strengthened in mid-2005 with further trade and aid agreements in place by July in the areas of infrastructure, trade and investment, and agriculture. China has recently sought to improve its relations with a number of African countries, especially with regard to raw materials. Political ties were further strengthened when the Secretary of the PFDJ received the Head of the Political Studies Bureau of the Chinese Communist Party. The PFDJ official noted that Eritrean-Chinese relations had deep roots going back to the 1960s (on a state visit the year before Afewerki had visited the Nanjing military college, where he had studied as a young guerrilla leader). This was followed by the visit of a Chinese military delegation to Asmara in August 2005. In July 2006 the Governments of Eritrea and China signed a loan agreement worth US $22m. to modernize the telecommunications infrastructure. In August President Afewerki held talks with a delegation from the Export and Import Bank of China interested in investment opportunities in Eritrea, including in the mining and fisheries sectors. The possibility of conducting a feasibility study on a proposed cement factory in the northern Red Sea region was also discussed and agreements on the provision of expatriate medical professionals were renewed. In November Afewerki attended the Africa-China Summit in Beijing, China.

In June 2006 Ephrem, the Minister of Defence, signed an agreement on military co-operation with his Pakistani counterpart during an official visit to Islamabad. The agreement envisaged the exchange of troops between the two countries for training purposes and the possible expansion of co-operation into other areas. In March 2007, at the conclusion of the fourth session on economic and scientific-technical co-operation, Cuba and Eritrea signed an agreement in the areas of agriculture, education and fishing, and a long term agreement on the permanence of the Cuban Medical Brigade, where 59 doctors were already employed. In December 2006 Iran welcomed an Eritrean proposal to establish diplomatic relations between the two countries, an initiative consolidated in June 2007 when the new Iranian ambassador, Reza Ameri, presented his credentials to President Afewerki.

CONCLUSION

Eritrea in 2007 remains one of the most militarized countries in the world. The stand-off with Ethiopia continues and Western powers in the UN Security Council have failed to move beyond resolutions and the periodic renewal of UNMEE's mandate. Although renewed war is not yet imminent, the scene is set for an ongoing stalemate that undermines international law and corrodes Eritrea's relationship with Western powers. The chronic 'no war, no peace' stalemate in turn infects all aspects of Eritrean polity, society and economy, ranging from a growing securitization of public life to deepening poverty and disaffection.

Economy

ALAN RAKE

With subsequent revisions by SARA RICH DORMAN

Revised by GREG CAMERON

The economic realities of Eritrea are dominated by the legacies of war, drought and continued mobilization. The economy is highly dependent on external sources of funding and has few dynamic export sectors. Until relations with Ethiopia are resolved, domestic politics are normalized (see Recent History), and a peacetime economy is developed, economic recovery will continue to be slow and incremental. Although statistical reporting on the country's economy improved markedly from the late 1990s, the previously weak statistical base and economic dislocation mean that all figures should be regarded with caution. The Government's failure to publish regular budgets further complicates assessment of Eritrea's economic health.

Eritrea remained one of Africa's poorest countries in 2006 with a United Nations Development Programme (UNDP) Human Development Index (HDI) ranking of 157 out of 177, a slight improvement on its ranking of 161 in 2005. Two-thirds of the population were unable to obtain sufficient calories, and food security remained an acute problem. Good rains in the 2005 season led to a relatively strong recovery in agriculture, which, combined with a temporary construction boom, helped the gross domestic product (GDP) growth rate to reach an estimated 4.8% in 2005, despite a downturn in most other sectors. Per caput gross national income (GNI) in 2005 was US $220. However the World Bank estimates that GDP will decline by 1.2% in 2005–09. The inflation rate has been persistently high in recent years: the general retail price index was 147% higher in July 2003 than in 1997, and the food price index rose by 178% over the same period. The average annual inflation rate, recorded at 25% in 2004, declined to an estimated 12% in 2005 due to the appreciation of the exchange rate and stricter price controls (see Foreign Trade and Payments, below). According to the African Development Bank (ADB), the rate of inflation was recorded at 14.2% in 2006, while World Bank figures estimated that consumer prices increased by some 20% in that year. Nevertheless, some advances have been made in social development, and hopes of further economic development centred on investment initiatives in the mining and free port sectors.

ECONOMIC ASPECTS OF WAR

One of the contributing factors to the start of the war with Ethiopia (1998–2000) was the creation of a new national currency, the nakfa, in July 1997. (Eritrea had retained the Ethiopian birr as its monetary unit since independence.) The war itself generated deep and long-lasting impacts on agricultural production, labour, exports, and governmental expenditure. The Government also had to cope with hundreds of thousands of displaced persons and some 65,000 Eritreans expelled from Ethiopia. In addition, trade with Ethiopia, which previously accounted for two-thirds of Eritrean exports, virtually ceased. Activity at the port of Assab declined sharply as most of Eritrea's war *matériel* was routed through Massawa.

Despite the signing of a peace accord in December 2000, levels of defence expenditure remained high. Total government expenditure on defence increased by 48% in 1998, and remained at 23% of GDP in 2002. Following considerable pressure, and the first open internal criticism of the President, in June 2001 President Issaias Afewerki announced that the total number of Eritreans killed during the two-year war amounted to 19,000. Since the end of the war, 1m. displaced people have returned home; however, according to the World Food Programme (WFP), nearly one-half of them are still dependent on food aid. There are still an estimated 45,000 internally displaced people (IDPs) in Eritrea; the majority live in refugee camps and are entirely dependent on humanitarian aid. According to the International Committee of the Red Cross, 85% of them are women and children. Most of the IDP camps are situated in or close to the UN-patrolled Temporary Security Zone, a 25-km buffer zone along the disputed border between Eritrea and Ethiopia. Ongoing tensions near the border and the presence of landmines have prevented the displaced from accessing their communal lands. The Eritrean armed forces laid 240,000 mines and Ethiopian forces 150,000–200,000 during the border war, according to International Campaign to Ban Landmines' 2005 Landmine Monitor Report. In Eritrea landmines were laid in some of the most populated and fertile regions of the country. An estimated 12,000 ha in Debub Province, and most of the sub-region of Lalai Gasin in Gash-Barka Province, are completely unusable owing to the presence of unexploded landmines.

With 45 of every 1,000 Eritreans enrolled in the armed forces, Eritrea maintains the highest proportion of its population in the army of any country in the world. The need to demobilize an estimated 200,000 troops will undoubtedly place further strain on the country's already fragile economy, although donors have pledged around US $124m. of a total $197m. required for this crucial programme. Under a pilot scheme, which concluded in June 2002, more than 5,000 soldiers, including 3,600 women, were demobilized. In 2004 the first phase of demobilization began, which was expected to process 65,000 soldiers. The National Commission for Demobilization and Reintegration Programme is currently seeking World Bank funding to compensate those demobilized in 2004, although Government ministries and the six regional administrations have instigated a number of training programmes. However, the current 'no war, no peace' impasse could continue indefinitely, thereby delaying the demobilization programme. Until full demobilization occurs, labour shortages will continue to have a negative effect on the financial viability of private enterprise and the ability of families to plough and harvest crops. There has been no large-scale resettlement in rural areas during this post-border-war phase. Moreover, many soldiers have become urbanized in the army and face limited economic prospects in poorly developed rural villages.

A study by the University of Asmara noted that approximately 33% of Eritrea's poorest citizens live in urban areas, of which 11% are in Asmara. In 2002 the Government launched the 'Warsai-Yikealo' initiative, which employs members of the armed forces in economic development projects in various sectors. In addition, the armed forces have been involved in farming, the digging of wells and the construction of dams for irrigation.

ECONOMIC POLICY AND AID

Eritrea's efforts to rebuild the economy, which had been shattered by the war of independence, proved further constrained by drought and the war with Ethiopia. Economic reforms announced in August 1994 targeted investment, land tenure, monetary and fiscal policy and trade. The programme represented a major change from a wartime command economy to a liberal market economy, designed for peace. Private investment was to be liberalized, and government involvement reduced to a regulatory capacity (with the exception of the provision of assistance for depressed regions). While some progress was made towards these goals in the 1990s, many of these policies have since been reversed. In October 1994 a new tariff regime, aimed at curbing inflation but encouraging trade and investment, was adopted. Capital goods and raw materials were subject to minimal tariffs of less than 3%, whereas tariffs on some luxury goods were fixed as high as 50%. Private and foreign investors were to be treated equally, and remission of capital and profits was to be unrestricted, but employment for Eritrean nationals would be prioritized. The 43 state enterprises were scheduled for privatization, and 11 state-owned hotels were also expected to be sold. It was announced that small export-orientated businesses would qualify for competitive exchange rates and loans under the Recovery and Rehabilitation Programme (see Construction, Transport and Tourism, below). The privatization programme began to make serious progress in the second half of 1997, and by 2003 37 government enterprises had been privatized. International investors purchased the Eritrea Shoe factory, the Gash Cigarette factory, the Asmara Textiles factory and the Red Sea Soap factory, but expressed little interest in the Asmara Brewery, which produces far below current levels of demand using outdated machinery.

Import restrictions on private-sector companies were imposed in 2003, and further restrictions were announced in 2005. Domestic entrepreneurs have complained that only firms closely affiliated to the ruling People's Front for Democracy and Justice (PFDJ) have been able to expand their operations or purchase privatized businesses. The PFDJ and, to a lesser extent, the National Union of Eritrean Youths and Students (NUEYS), are also increasingly active in the manufacturing and service sectors. Relatively little is known about the wide range of ventures owned wholly or partially by the PFDJ, but they include businesses in the construction, information technology and tourism sectors. The NUEYS's most financially successful ventures have been in the distribution of liquid petroleum gas for home cooking and the distribution of filtered, bottled water for domestic consumption. Allegations are increasingly being made that businesses are owned by Eritrea's senior military officers, or that officers use military conscript labour to build their villas. Many private businessmen have migrated to neighbouring Sudan, Kenya and Uganda, and those who remain in Eritrea face stringent foreign currency regulations, harsh penalties for 'black' market exchanges, and a strong market disadvantage *vis-à-vis* the

PFDJ enterprises. Private sector fixed capital formation was estimated at 5.3% of GDP in 2004.

Eritrea's first donor conference was convened by the World Bank in France in December 1994. Donors pledged US $250m. in international aid for 1995. In the 1990s loans were forthcoming for projects in irrigation, improving the drinking water network, port rehabilitation, support to the health sector, and recruitment and training programmes. However, in September 1999 the World Bank announced that it was to halt all new funding for Eritrea until the conflict with Ethiopia had been brought to a peaceful conclusion. World Bank aid duly resumed following the signing of a peace accord in December 2000. The current World Bank portfolio comprises eight projects worth a total of US $294m. Additionally, the World Bank administers Trust Funds worth $102.1m., supporting parallel development programmes by donors including the USA, the European Union (EU) and Italy. Specific programmes in education and health include early childhood development, and the HAMSET (HIV/AIDS, malaria, sexually transmitted diseases and tuberculosis) disease control project. The social protection portfolio encompasses demobilization and reintegration programmes and the rehabilitation of cultural assets. The infrastructure portfolio includes port rehabilitation and power distribution, parts of which are funded by grants.

World Bank disbursements in 2005 amounted to US $57m. Overall net aid from all donors in 2004 was $242m., which comprised 28% of GDP. A Post-crisis Rural Recovery and Development Programme, has been proposed, funded by the International Fund for Agricultural Development (IFAD), which comprises a component part of the Integrated Rural Development Programme, co-financed by the ADB, the EU and the World Bank.

FOREIGN TRADE AND PAYMENTS

In July 1994 Eritrea became the 179th member of the IMF, with an initial quota of SDR 11.5m. Eritrea sought to show the international donor community its commitment to implementing a liberal trade and exchange regime and developing an export-orientated domestic economy. As early as January 1992 Eritrea and Ethiopia signed an agreement whereby the port of Assab became a free port for Ethiopia, and which provided for tax-free trade between the two countries, using the Ethiopian birr as currency. In October 1994 Eritrea and Ethiopia signed a further agreement to allow the free movement of goods between the two countries without payment of customs dues. A tariff agreement providing for a free-trade zone and the basis for future economic union between the two countries was announced by the Ethiopian Government in May 1995. However, the outbreak of war between the two countries in May 1998 brought a sharp halt to trade, and discussions regarding future trading relations did not receive high priority during peace talks in December 2000.

With a significant number of Eritreans living outside the country, taxes paid directly to the Government by expatriates (accounting for 2% of their annual income) and remittances to families play a key role in the economy. Over a 10-year period private transfers from the diaspora accounted for an average of 37% of GDP. Expatriates have also invested in Eritrea through the purchase of bonds, which in 1999 represented 3.1% of GDP. Some analysts have suggested that remittances may decline as a result of recent political turmoil (see Recent History). It bears repeating that economic data should be treated with caution due to the closed nature of the policy-making process.

Preliminary World Bank data for 2005 by country unit staff show exports of both goods (total exports being US $13m. in 2004) and services at $64m., and imports of goods and services at $572m. with a trade deficit of $508m. Net current transfers, after net income, totalled $371m., with an overall current account deficit of $145m.

Preliminary IMF data for 2004 indicated that the principal markets for Eritrean exports were Italy (21.7%), Sudan (5.8%) and Japan (5.3%); while the main sources of imports were the United Arab Emirates (19.1%), the USA (11.8%) and Saudi Arabia (9.9%). Imports from the People's Republic of China are significant; however, precise figures for trade between Eritrea and China are not available. Principal exports included salt, semi-processed leather goods, flowers, livestock and textiles; while the main imports were machinery and transport equipment, spare parts, food, manufactured goods, intermediate goods, and petroleum and chemical products. The collapse of Eritrea's regional export trade is a major economic constraint, in recent years attributed to the closed or restricted border between Eritrea and Sudan (See Recent History). The border was, however, reopened in late 2006. Ethiopia was formerly the main destination for Eritrean exports.

Foreign officials maintain that fiscal and debt sustainability remain the key challenges facing the Eritrean Government. By 2005, due to unsustainable budget deficits, the Government increasingly reverted to a closely controlled economic model. The IMF estimated the 2005 fiscal deficit to be around 20% of GDP, the bulk of it financed domestically (16%). Eritrea's external debt in 2004 was US $681m. GDP that year was $930m. According to preliminary data, Eritrea's GDP in 2005 totalled $990m.

Despite the heavy debt burden, external-debt servicing has been manageable due to the foreign-exchange controls in the context of an appreciating real exchange rate. Domestic debt service payments have been kept under control through high negative real interest rates on treasury bills. The foreign exchange shortage has been addressed with foreign currency controls. In 2005 the Government unified the dual exchange rate system into a single official rate at 15 nakfa to every US $1, which represented a nominal appreciation of approximately 20%. Official exchange rates have remained much lower than those available on the 'black' market. The use of foreign currency was declared illegal in April 2005, in an attempt to curb the growing 'black' market in foreign exchange; persons involved in such transactions faced gaol sentences of up to two years and fines of more than 2m. nakfa. Inflation was tackled through price controls imposed on 16 'declared goods', including basic foodstuffs, textiles, and building materials. In May 2005 the Government issued coupons, which can be obtained at state-owned 'fair-price' shops, for a limited number of 'priority goods' such as sugar, sorghum, wheat, teff (the staple indigenous grain), coffee, tea powder, lentils and cooking oil. Some of these commodities can be purchased at prices as much as 50% below market prices. There are also controls on housing rent, a measure that has brought relief for many lower-income families in Asmara, although the long-term impact on investment in affordable housing remains unclear. Import permits for most private imports have been effectively denied to all but priority goods since February 2005. Though the controls appear to have been relaxed recently, the impact on the private trader and retail sectors has been severe.

In 2005 reserves of foreign exchange were equal to just one month's worth of import revenues. Defence expenditure was equivalent to 25% of GDP, whilst budgetary expenditure on education and health was around 4%. None the less, the pattern of government expenditure has altered since 2003. Savings have been made on the defence wage bill due to the demobilization programme; civil service salaries have been frozen and cuts made in capital expenditure. However, there has been an increase in social spending, primarily in the pension and war victims' funds. Payments to the families of war victims rose from 158m. nakfa in 2003 to 390m. nakfa in 2005. Increases in pension payments have been even steeper, increasing from 20m. nakfa in 2003 to some 280m. nakfa in 2005. The Government's current budgetary planning framework contains two key elements: the containment of domestic capital expenditure at 5.5% of GDP; and a projected decrease in expenditure on grants to follow an improvement in the food security situation (although multilateral agencies predict a long term decline in agricultural production). General government fixed capital formation was estimated to be 17.5% of GDP in 2004. The Government has also expressed an interest in pursuing Eritrea's eligibility for debt relief under the enhanced heavily indebted poor countries (HIPC) initiative.

AGRICULTURE

For most Eritreans, by far the most important sector of the economy is agriculture, which despite a reduction in food production of some 40% over the period 1980–90, still sustains 80% of the population.

Preliminary figures from the World Bank show that agriculture contributed 22.6% of GDP in 2005, due to the relative decline in the shares of industry (22.6%) and services (54.8%) in that same year. The rate of growth in agriculture in 2005 was 8.4%, a significant increase over the average annual rate of growth of 7.0% in 2004. According to 2004 data, 3.7% of cropland was irrigated. Most sedentary agriculture is practised in the highlands, where rainfall is sufficient to cultivate the main crops: teff, sorghum, millet, barley and wheat. According to WFP, up to 40% of households are headed by females and are especially vulnerable to food insecurity. In addition to smallholder agriculture, the Government also allocates land concessions to investors to enable crop production over relatively large areas. Concessions vary in size depending on location and water availability (rain-fed or irrigation) as well as on crops. Those near seasonal river beds normally measure between 10 ha–30 ha and produce vegetables (onions, okra, carrots, etc.) and fruits such as bananas and oranges, while those in arid or semi-arid areas can be as large as 400 ha and are used primarily for cereals and oilseed crops. The contribution of concessions to the country's food economy remains mediocre. Pastoralists and livestock production predominate in the lowlands, with herding patterns, both within the lowlands and between the lowlands and highlands, in search of grazing areas. The main animals are sheep and goats, followed by cattle, camels, donkeys and horses. On average rural households possess between three and five sheep or goats; and apart from oxen, which are often put to graze in areas reserved for them, most livestock are reared on an extensive system that relies on natural pasture and crop residues. As a result, there is a marked annual fluctuation in stock condition, which reflects the availability of fodder and water. For pastoralists, the border war with Ethiopia largely halted the movement of livestock both to traditional grazing lands across the border and to grazing areas within Eritrean territory that are still heavily mined; it has also closed important livestock trade routes.

Rural development programmes are operated by a variety of international organizations, including UNDP, the World Bank (in credit and community development), IFAD (irrigation in lowland areas), FAO (extension and research), the Danish International Development Agency (various agricultural sectors), the ADB (national livestock project), the EU (eradication of rinderpest), and the United States Agency for International Development (rural business).

In 1992, which was described as a satisfactory year in agricultural terms, some 315,000 ha of land were cultivated, and 250,000 metric tons of grain harvested, a more than threefold increase from the previous year. However, land under cultivation had increased only to some 393,300 ha in 2002. Grain production dropped back to 85,000 tons in 2000, rose briefly and fell again to 85,000 tons in 2004. As this suggests, the years since independence have been marked by erratic production patterns, negatively affected by droughts, crop pests and war, despite government programmes to rehabilitate communications, transportation and irrigation. The failure of rains throughout much of Eritrea in June–October 2002 marked the onset of another catastrophic drought, during which crop production was estimated to have fallen by 77%. The early rains failed and the late rains were unusually short, preventing crops from completing their growth cycle. In some areas fields were left fallow owing to lack of rain. In others, crops withered in the dry soil. Drought elsewhere on the continent and Eritrea's own political crisis seemed to slow the response to appeals for support from the international donor community, and while the 2003 appeal for support was 57% funded, a similar appeal in 2004 received only 38% of the funds required.

Given the concerns about food security, restrictions on the travel of diplomats and international aid workers inside Eritrea, announced in early 2004, were greeted with dismay. Restrictions were further tightened for foreign nationals in May 2006: travel permits must be obtained 10 days in advance in order to travel outside of Asmara. In July 2005 the Minister of Agriculture announced that he expected the 2005 harvest to produce 440,000 metric tons of output, on an area of 556,600 ha. During the summer of 2005 President Afewerki toured the regions, inspecting agricultural and infrastructural projects, and assessing the impact of the plentiful rains on the production base, particularly Eritrea's so-called 'bread basket' province of Gash-Barka. His tour signified a dramatic shift in agricultural policy previously declared at a Cabinet meeting in January 2006, and the evolving food security document which called for the identification of areas rich in fertile soil and water and the introduction of modern farming practises, both private and collective.

Insisting it is self-reliant and that the 2005 harvest had proved a success, Eritrea has maintained restrictions on aid distribution since September 2005 when the number of people receiving free food was reduced by 94%, from 1.3m. people to 72,000. Aid agencies expected food from the 2005 harvest to last for around two or three months, and have predicted a humanitarian crisis should the 2006 harvest fail. Reports have suggested that some people are already moving around or out of the country in search of food, and some hospitals are struggling to cope with malnutrition. The HDI report indicated that the situation had deteriorated, with the percentage of undernourished having increased from 61% of the population in 2004 to 73% in 2005. Malnutrition of children under the age of five stood at 40% in 2005. The UN Secretary General's Special Humanitarian Envoy for the Horn of Africa, Kjell Magne Bondevik, sought to raise the international community's concerns when he held talks with Afewerki in April 2006. Stressing his view that the free distribution of food aid paralyses productivity and leads to dependency, and that a 'food-for-work' programme would be equally ineffective, Afewerki insisted that the most viable solution to dependency would be to create employment opportunities, enabling Eritreans to buy food for themselves. The Government announced that existing stocks of food aid had been integrated into Asmara's long-term food security scheme. Greater stocks of flour subsequently appeared in the markets in Asmara; however, it was unclear clear how the new scheme would benefit the rural poor.

The 2005 harvest improved markedly from previous years, however, the UN warned it was not sufficient for the country to recover from damage caused by years of rain failures, exacerbated by conflict. In good years the harvest can meet up to two-thirds of domestic demand (roughly 600,000 metric tons of cereal), while in bad years less than one-third is supplied. The deficit must be met by either aid donations, or commercial imports necessitating foreign exchange. Contradicting the Government's figure of 440,000 tons, international agencies unofficially estimated that the 2005 harvest yielded no more than 150,000–250,000 tons.

Land reform legislation was promulgated in 1994, whereby the Government was to maintain ownership of all land, but farmers would be allowed a life-long lease on currently held land. In addition, every Eritrean citizen would automatically qualify for the right to use a specific plot throughout their life in their home village. The implications of this policy for pastoralist communities were unclear. Little research has been conducted on the impact of the land reform for agriculture in rural areas, although preliminary evidence suggests that urban land pressure is such that peripheral residential developments are encroaching on arable land. There is also little evidence of land tenure change. Land tenure reform remains controversial *vis-à-vis* the traditional peasant communal form (*diessa*) and the merits of pro-market reforms in Eritrean agriculture will remain a moot point until substantial investment is made in human capital.

Few farmers' associations exist in Eritrea and even government agencies, such as the Ministry of Agriculture, lack sufficient capacity in areas such as research, extension, regulation, and information provision. Co-operative legislation, backed by technical support from the International Labour Organization in the late 1990s, remains in hiatus. Without an independent co-operative movement there are few channels for village-level input in areas such as government technical assistance, management training, and pricing policy, a situation which could potentially undermine attempts to resettle demobilized soldiers in their home villages. A series of recommendations by agricultural professionals in March 2006 recognized the need for a more farmer-centred approach, but it remains to be seen if these recommendations will be incorporated into the forthcoming food security document.

In June 2006 1.3m. cattle were vaccinated against rinderpest and other diseases in the Gash-Barka region, where 44% of domestic animals are located, according to the Livestock Resources Office of the Ministry of Agriculture. In mid-July President Afewerki conducted an inspection tour of that region, including water diversion activities in the Golij subzone and at Hashenkit, a number of animal feed and reproduction centres, and a sugar and tomato paste factory in Afhimobl. In September, at a joint Cabinet meeting that included regional administrators and operation commanders, Afewerki urged the attainment of food security as the national priority. In October Afewerki again visited the Gash-Barka region and inspected the vast agricultural estate of Kach'ero, located 15 km from Omahajer, and private farms. Also in that month the Head of Planning and Statistics of the Ministry of Agriculture, Solomon Haile, assessed the 2006 rainfall, which started as usual in Debub, Anseba, and Maekel, but commenced late in Gash-Barka. Compared with the long-term average, the records of the rainfall activities were closer to normal for most of the meteorological stations. However, the amount of the rainfall recorded, the number of rainy days, and the intervals between the rainy days all varied greatly from location to location, although notably the north of Gash-Barka and Anseba received low rainfall.

A government spokesman reported that 494,235 ha of land were cultivated in 2006. The major crops cultivated that year were sorghum, which covers almost 53% of the cultivated area, followed by barley at 9.1%. Other crops included pearl millet (8.5%), finger millet (5.8%), teff (5.2%), sesame (5.0%), and maize (4.3%). In June 2007 Bondevik accepted that Eritrea would only receive food assistance as part of a government-run programme whereby donated food would be monitored and sold in markets, not as free distribution, as part of its 'cash-for-work' programme. He also expressed concern over the future political and humanitarian direction of the country.

Fisheries are a potential growth area for the Eritrean economy. Sardines, anchovies, tuna, shark and mackerel are fished in the Red Sea. UN fishery experts have estimated that Eritrea has the potential to achieve annual yields of around 70,000 metric tons. Although fishing activity has traditionally been on a very small scale, FAO figures indicated a greatly increased total catch from an estimated 225 tons in 1997 to a peak of 12,612 tons in 2000, before declining to 6,689 tons in 2003. There was a slight increase in the total catch in 2004 to 7,404 tons. In 2005 FAO data indicated a catch totalling 4,027 tons, significantly below the Government's optimistic forecasts of 24,000 tons.

INDUSTRY

Although in the 1930s Eritrea was substantially more industrialized than most of its neighbours, by the time of independence infrastructure was aged and desperately needed rehabilitation. Eritrea's industrial base traditionally centred on the production of glass, cement, footwear and canned goods. Although some of the 42 public-sector factories—producing textiles, footwear, beverages and other light industrial goods—were operating in 1991, they were doing so at only one-third of capacity. By 1995 production had increased considerably, mostly as a result of substantial government aid. The Government calculated that the cost of industrial recovery would be US $20m. for the private sector and $66m. for the state sector. The sector's growth decelerated in 2004 by 0.4%, although in 1995–2004 the average annual growth rate was 6.2%, according to World Bank data. In 2005 industry contributed an estimated 22.6% of GDP. There are plans to increase the production of footwear and leather goods, as well as the amount of those goods exported to other countries in the region. The Government and UNDP launched a three-year integrated programme in 2000 to rehabilitate the industrial sector, which has focused on the leather industry and agricultural machinery. A second phase of this programme was initiated in 2004. Since its inception in 1996, the Saving and Micro Credit Program (SMCP) has loaned 100m. nakfa, and in the first six months of 2006, the SMCP lent over 11.5m. nakfa to about 1,600 beneficiaries, mainly for business activities, although the scheme was recently extended to government employees.

The manufacturing sector provided an estimated 10.7% of GDP in 2004, rising to an estimated 22.6% in 2006, according to the IMF. All public enterprises in the sector were scheduled for divestment or liquidation, following the initiation of a programme of privatization in 1995. Since independence several small manufacturing companies have been established, including an innovative high-quality surgical intraocular lens factory that exports to countries in Europe, Africa and Asia. Until mid-1997 imported petroleum was processed at the Assab refinery, whose entire output of petroleum products was delivered to Ethiopia. However, the ageing and inefficient refinery at Assab was closed in late 1997, and the Government announced that it would import refined petroleum for the immediate future.

During a meeting of ministers in April 2005 the Minister of Trade and Industry outlined steps being taken to assess the status of industrial plants, new investment ventures, the promotion of export activities and import substitution industrialization, and the enhancing of the viability of public trading agencies. The ministerial meeting followed Eritrea's participation in a meeting of six African countries—Kenya, Uganda, Tanzania, Burundi, Ethiopia and Eritrea—in Zanzibar, Tanzania, in March on ways to improve the quality of their export-orientated products in line with the sixth World Trade Organization (WTO) ministerial conference held in December 2005 in Hong Kong. Eritrea is an observer but not a full member of the WTO. Eritrea's non-membership of the WTO allows it to pursue an export-orientated strategy without the reciprocal opening of its domestic economy, particularly in the service sector. Eritrean officials are hopeful that the Massawa Free Port Zone will attract significant investment. Eritrea's 29 Economic Processing Zones (EPZs), including Massawa EPZ, have been given preferential access to the markets of countries with less than US $1,000 per caput GNI. This may give the Massawa EPZ a competitive advantage *vis-à-vis* countries with EPZs, with per caput income of greater than $1,000. Production in the EPZs requires 40% local input.

The opening of Free Zones was officially announced at a meeting held with the Eritrean business community at the National Chamber of Commerce in November 2006. Investors in Free Zones are exempt from import or export taxes. The Government would only have an administrative role through the Free Zone Authority. Eritrea is expected to benefit from the exchange of hard currency, indirect revenue and tax from the thousands of Eritreans who are expected to be employed there.

In terms of overall business environment, the World Bank listed the number of procedures required successfully to start up a business at 13 in 2006, while in that year the World Bank estimated foreign direct investment (including net inflows) at US $11.4m.

MINING AND POWER

Eritrea's mineral resources are believed to be of significant potential value, although in 2002 mining and quarrying accounted for less than 0.1% of GDP. Gold-bearing seams exist in many of the igneous rocks forming the highlands of Eritrea. There are at least 15 gold mines and a large number of prospects close to Asmara, and the potential for new discoveries in the area is considered good. There are two regions of widespread gold mineralization in the western lowlands, at Tokombia and Barentu. Other mineral resources include potash, zinc, magnesium, copper, iron ore and marble. In April 1995 a new mining law was promulgated, which declared all mineral resources to be state assets, but recognized an extensive role for private investors in their exploitation. Investor companies would enjoy a concessionary tax regime, pay royalties of 2%–5% and encounter no restriction on repatriating profits. The Government retained the right to acquire a 10% share in any mining undertaking. In December applications to explore for gold and base metals were received from numerous foreign companies. Particular interest was expressed in the old Eritrean mines that had been exploited until the early 1940s.

In March 1996 Canada's Reese Mining Co signed two agreements for the exploration of gold and copper reserves. In the following month the Government signed exploration agreements with Western Mining of Australia and Ghana's Ashanti Goldfields. Gold production is reported to have fallen by 57% between 1997 and 2000. The value of gold produced in Eritrea in 2000 amounted to US $1.7m., according to officials from the Ministry of Energy and Mines, cited by the US Geological Survey. Prospecting, which also declined during the 1998–2000 war, seemed to be reviving with the cessation of hostilities, although incidents along the Sudanese border threatened development. In early 2003 Canada's Nevsun Resources announced the discovery of new, high-grade ore in Bisha. In 2004 and 2005 two further Canadian companies, Sunridge and Northern Mining, substantially expanded their gold prospecting in areas mined prior to independence. Nevsun's Bisha mine is expected to be the first to begin production, in 2008, commencing with gold, followed by zinc and copper. The Government estimates that the Bisha project alone will directly employ up to 400 people and provide 10 times that number with indirect jobs, such as truck drivers and port workers. Diplomatic sources say the Bisha mine could generate hundreds of millions of dollars a year. In June 2007 the Nevsun Bisha Mining Share Company released a summary document of its Social and Environmental Impact Assessment (SEIA) in order to provide residents in Eritrea with a brief plain language version of the proposed Bisha Mine SEIA. The Eritrean authorities are also currently seeking to enhance exploitation of marble in the Chain Mountains, in the Gash-Barka region.

In view of Eritrea's acute energy shortage, the possibility of large reserves of petroleum and natural gas beneath the Red Sea is of particular importance. In early 1993 the Government made petroleum exploration regulations more stringent, and BP, which had signed a contract for petroleum exploration with the former Ethiopian regime, had its exploration rights invalidated. A US petroleum company, Amoco (now BP), and the International Petroleum Corpn of Canada were the only two remaining companies with concessions. The latter had operating rights in the 31,000-sq-km Danakil block along the Eritrean coast, where there are believed to be good prospects for petroleum and gas discoveries. In November 1993 a new code of practice regulating the petroleum sector was promulgated, allowing companies a 25-year licence, renewal periods of 10 years and fiscal advantages. Several prominent international petroleum companies expressed an interest in exploration and distribution. A local company, Prima, backed by expatriate Eritrean shareholders and Shell-Eritrea, was expected to handle internal distribution. In October 1995 the Government signed an agreement with Anadarko Petroleum Corpn of the USA for a seven-year prospecting contract, worth US $28.5m. Anadarko began its seismic studies for petroleum in the Zula block (containing the Dahlak islands) in November 1996. In September 1997 Anadarko signed a second production-sharing agreement to explore the Edd block, extending more than 6.7m. acres south of its Zula permit and stretching almost as far as the Hanish islands. Anadarko undertook to spend a further $23m. on prospecting and announced that it would begin drilling in both blocks in 1998. However, the war with Ethiopia effectively brought a halt to exploration activities. Following the cessation of hostilities, the Eritrean Government signed a petroleum exploration agreement with CMS Oil and Gas of the USA in May 2001.

Eritrea's economic performance is also hampered by its lack of capacity to produce energy. Total production of electricity in 1998 was 186m. kWh, 74% of which was in Asmara. An estimated 249m. kWh were produced in 2002. Electricity is provided to only some 10% of the population, the remainder relying on fuel wood and animal products. However, in 2003 the Government reported that their programme of rural electrification had reached 90 villages. Imports of fuel and energy comprised an estimated 8.9% of the total cost of imports in 2000. Attempts are being made to harness the plentiful and clear sunlight for solar energy. With an increase in the use of solar power, it was hoped that the demand for wood for fuel (from the rapidly diminishing forests, already severely denuded by the war of independence) would decline. In mid-1997 work commenced on the construction of the Hirgigo power station at Massawa. Financed by Arab and Italian donors, and World Bank loans, the completed station cost US $172m., of which $22m. was dedicated to repairing damage caused by Ethiopian bombardment in 2000. The Hirgigo power station officially came on stream in March 2003.

CONSTRUCTION, TRANSPORT AND TOURISM

In 1993 the Government adopted a two-year Recovery and Rehabilitation Programme, which was to be funded by a series of loans on concessionary terms (involving total investment of US $147m.). The World Bank's International Development Association (IDA) approved a credit of SDR 18.1m. (some $25m.), and Italy pledged $24.3m. Contributions were also promised by a number of other European countries, the EU and UNDP. The programme focused on infrastructure and construction projects. Public enterprises, particularly cement, metalworks and limestone factories, underwent rehabilitation, while emphasis was also placed on rebuilding government offices, commercial and residential buildings and the reconstruction of roads and infrastructure.

In 1993 the Government announced plans for the rehabilitation of the Asmara–Massawa railway line, which had been severely damaged during the war of independence. Construction work began in 1997 and was completed in February 2003. There are also plans to construct a rail link from Massawa to the Sudanese border near Tessenei. Extending the line would establish a freight route for goods from the newly opened Massawa free port zone, in addition to providing for the transport of zinc and gold from the Nevsun mines, which are due to start production in 2008, to the port. The opening of the Sudanese–Eritrean border has added impetus to the project. Comparatively speaking, Eritrea has a long road network for its land base, totalling 18,540 km. In 2006 six large bridges were constructed along the Barentu–Tessenei road.

In late 1997 the World Bank approved an IDA loan of US $30m. for the improvement of Massawa and Assab ports. Significant progress has also been made in rehabilitating the port of Massawa, which was heavily bombed by Ethiopia during the 1998–2000 war. In Massawa priority was given to the dredging of the harbour and the extension of the docks; in Assab the main objective was to accelerate the transfer of cargo through the purchase of cargo-handling equipment. Both ports were virtually closed to Ethiopian trade with the outbreak of hostilities between the two countries in May 1998. As a result of the conflict, activity at Assab port declined markedly: some 322 vessels docked at the port in 1998, compared with 628 in the previous year.

TOURISM

Tourism in Eritrea remains undeveloped and has been further damaged by the war, meaning that visitors from Eritrea's vast diaspora, primarily in Organisation for Economic Co-operation and Development (OECD) countries and the Middle East, form the bulk of arrivals, numbering 87,298 in 2004. There are plans to promote architectural (Eritrea possesses a number of fine Italian modernist colonial-era buildings) and archaeological (pre-Axumite discoveries) tourism, to be financed in part by a World Bank loan for the Government's Cultural Assets Rehabilitation Project. Construction of Gash Setit Wildlife Reserve is ongoing. According to the IMF, tourism revenue in 2004 was US $73m.

A regional conference on conserving biodiversity and expanding natural reserves in the Horn of Africa was conducted in August 2006 in Asmara by ecology experts from Somalia, Djibouti and Eritrea. The authorities are confident that the construction of the Serejeca–Shebah road will enhance wildlife tourism in the Semenawi Keyhi Bahri region. In addition, since the road passes through the agricultural centre of the eastern lowlands, it may play a leading role in transportation and marketing for the farmers and could also serve as a subsidiary to the Asmara–Massawa road. According to World Bank figures, 4.3% of the total Eritrean land area is nationally protected.

THE SOCIAL SECTOR

The Government has sought to protect and build upon achievements in the social sphere, particularly health and education, while maintaining a modicum of state involvement in the economy. In terms of government spending, the education budget has risen from 164m. nakfa in 2000 to 431m. nakfa in 2005. According to the HDI, male literacy increased from 38.2% in 2004 to 68.2% in 2005; female literacy was constant at 45.6% over the same period. Taking Gash Barka as an example, the Ministry of Education reported a rise in the literacy rate of 24%, progress attributable to adult literacy learning centre programmes in the regions. Gross primary enrolment in 2005 stood at 64%, with males comprising 71% of school-age enrolment and females 57%. In March 2007 legislation came into force making female genital mutilation punishable by fine and imprisonment. The National Union of Eritrean Women has reported that more than 90% of Eritrean women are circumcized.

According to the World Bank, in 2005 the average life expectancy in Eritrea was 55 years. Infant mortality per 1,000 births was 50 and child deaths before the age of five declined to 78 per 1,000 in 2005. Similarly, the percentage of underweight children under the age of five decreased to 40%. In 2005 the Eritrean authorities reported that the number of malaria cases had fallen by 85% over the past five years due to the increased use of treated bed nets provided by the Government. More than 1m. free nets were distributed over four years. New regional hospitals were opened in 2005 in Ghinda, Mendefera, Assab and Barentu. By November 2006 the Eritrean Government had paid over 709m. nafka in a benefit scheme for families of fallen soldiers over the last two years. World Bank figures for 2000–04 indicated that 57% of the population (72% urban and 54% rural) had sustainable access to improved water sources, while only 9% of the population had sustainable access to improved sanitation (34% urban and 3% rural). The rate of HIV/AIDS infection among those aged between 15 and 49 was relatively low, at 2.4% in 2005. Nevertheless, according to the UN in 2004, the prevalence of HIV/AIDS among men and women aged 15–24 in 2001 was 4.3% and 2.8%, respectively, and it is thought to have increased in recent years. HIV/AIDS is now judged to be the second leading cause of death in patients over five years of age. Particular concern was being raised over the rates of infection in the military and the implications of the return of these men and women to their home communities after demobilization. Tuberculosis cases are also on the rise, from 268 per 100,000 people in 2005 to 271 per 100,000 in 2006. In that year the Ministry of Health, with technical and financial assistance from the Fred Hollows Foundation of Australia, the Christian Blind Mission in Germany, the Norwegian Association for the Blind and Partially Sighted and WHO conducted a cross sectional survey on trachoma in order to determine the prevalence of active trachoma in children and blinding trachoma in adults. According to the survey the prevalence of trachoma in children between the ages of one and five years old was 9%.

Statistics can, however, hide the human dimension to the realities faced by Eritreans, who enjoy domestic social peace. Crime rates are low, making Asmara one of the safest cities in the world and state social service provision is generally efficient and honest. Underpinning this relative cohesiveness, and striking to all foreigners, is the sense of social and public purpose that makes Eritrea stand out in contemporary sub-Saharan Africa. Yet life is becoming a crushing burden of declining real wages, poorly paid jobs, queues for basic commodities, incredible hardship in the rural areas and indefinite national conscription. The possibility of further regional conflict also weighs on the minds of many citizens. Moreover many observers are doubtful that the leadership would accede to political pluralism even were the border stalemate with Ethiopia resolved. Likewise, the exiled Eritrean opposition remains fragmented and no domestic dissent is tolerated. There is also a growing xenophobia against foreigners, with indications that those Eritreans who associate with them may come under scrutiny. The alienation between state and society is widening, perhaps irrevocably, and the current geopolitical matrix suggests little in the way of optimism.

Statistical Survey

Source (unless otherwise stated): Ministry of Trade and Industry, POB 1844, Asmara; tel. (1) 118386; fax (1) 110586.

Area and Population

AREA, POPULATION AND DENSITY*

Area (sq km)	121,144†
Population (census results)	
9 May 1984	
Males	1,374,452
Females	1,373,852
Total	2,748,304
Population (UN estimates at mid-year)‡	
2004	4,354,000
2005	4,527,000
2006	4,692,000
Density (per sq km) at mid-2006	38.7

* Including the Assab district.

† 46,774 sq miles.

‡ Source: UN, *World Population Prospects: The 2006 Revision*.

PRINCIPAL TOWNS

(estimated population at January 2006)

Asmara (capital)	1,062,676	Keren	59,534
Assab	74,405	Mitsiwa (Massawa)	38,395

Source: Stefan Helders, *World Gazetteer* (internet www.world-gazetteer.com).

BIRTHS AND DEATHS

(averages per year, UN estimates)

	1990–95	1995–2000	2000–05
Birth rate (per 1,000)	40.2	39.6	40.5
Death rate (per 1,000)	14.3	11.8	10.6

Source: UN, *World Population Prospects: The 2006 Revision*.

Expectation of life (years at birth, WHO estimates): 60 (males 59; females 62) in 2004 (Source: WHO, *World Health Report*).

Health and Welfare

KEY INDICATORS

Total fertility rate (children per woman, 2005)	5.3
Under-5 mortality rate (per 1,000 live births, 2004)	78
HIV/AIDS (% of persons aged 15–49, 2005)	2.40
Physicians (per 1,000 head, 2004)	0.05
Health expenditure (2004): US $ per head (PPP)	27.4
Health expenditure (2004): % of GDP	4.5
Health expenditure (2004): public (% of total)	39.2
Access to water (% of persons, 2004)	60
Access to sanitation (% of persons, 2004)	9
Human Development Index (2004): ranking	157
Human Development Index (2004): value	0.454

For sources and definitions, see explanatory note on p. vi.

Agriculture

PRINCIPAL CROPS
('000 metric tons)

	2003	2004	2005
Wheat	3.4	5.1	0.7
Barley	8.6	11.1	9.3
Maize	4.5	3.2	2.5
Millet	11.7	8.0	17.4
Sorghum	64.1	44.6	114.3
Potatoes	10.9	16.0	17.5
Other roots and tubers*	85.0	85.0	85.0
Dry beans	0.3	0.6	0.2
Dry broad beans*	1.8	1.8	1.8
Dry peas	1.4	0.1	0.1
Chick-peas	0.1	3.5	3.5*
Lentils	0.1	0.1	0.2
Vetches*	4.5	4.5	4.5
Other pulses*	27.0	25.0	25.0
Groundnuts (in shell)	1.2*	0.8	2.5
Sesame seed	7.0	5.0	18.5
Linseed	0.1*	0.1	0.0
Vegetables*	23.0	23.0	23.0
Fruits*	2.0	2.0	2.0

* FAO estimate(s).

Source: FAO.

LIVESTOCK
('000 head, year ending September, FAO estimates)

	2003	2004	2005
Cattle	1,927	1,930	1,950
Sheep	2,100	2,100	2,100
Goats	1,700	1,700	1,700
Camels	75	75	75
Chickens	1,370	1,370	1,370

Source: FAO.

LIVESTOCK PRODUCTS
('000 metric tons, FAO estimates)

	2003	2004	2005
Cattle meat	16.7	16.7	16.7
Sheep meat	6.7	6.7	5.6
Goat meat	5.8	5.8	5.8
Chicken meat	2.3	2.3	2.1
Camels' milk	5.1	5.1	5.1
Cows' milk	39.2	39.2	39.2
Goats' milk	8.5	8.5	8.5
Sheep's milk	3.9	3.9	3.9
Hen eggs	2.0	2.0	2.0
Wool: greasy	0.8	0.8	0.8

Source: FAO.

Fishing

(metric tons, live weight of capture)

	2003	2004	2005
Lizardfishes	1,688	3,886	2,364
Sea catfishes	207	217	57
Threadfin breams	525	819	615
Snappers and jobfishes	227	102	27
Barracudas	1,845	411	208
Carangids	343	301	120
Queenfishes	387	212	38
Penaeus shrimps	451	413	235
Total catch (incl. others)	6,689	7,404	4,027

Source: FAO.

Mining

('000 metric tons, unless otherwise indicated, estimates)

	2003	2004	2005
Gold (kilograms)	9	33	25
Marble ('000 sq m)	1,777.8	780.3	36.0
Limestone	3	3	3
Salt	5	3	6

Source: US Geological Survey.

Finance

CURRENCY AND EXCHANGE RATES

Monetary Units
100 cents = 1 nakfa.

Sterling, Dollar and Euro Equivalents (30 April 2007)
£1 sterling = 30.667 nakfa;
US $1 = 15.375 nakfa;
€1 = 20.918 nakfa;
1,000 nakfa = £32.61 = $65.04 = €47.81.

Note: Following its secession from Ethiopia in May 1993, Eritrea retained the Ethiopian currency, the birr. An exchange rate of US $1 = 5.000 birr was introduced in October 1992 and remained in force until April 1994, when it was adjusted to $1 = 5.130 birr. Further adjustments were made subsequently. In addition to the official exchange rate, the Bank of Eritrea applied a marginal auction rate (determined at fortnightly auctions of foreign exchange, conducted by the National Bank of Ethiopia) to aid-funded imports and to most transactions in services. A more depreciated preferential rate applied to remittances of foreign exchange by Eritreans abroad, to proceeds from exports and to most payments for imports. On 1 April 1997 Eritrea unified the official and preferential exchange rates at $1 = 7.20 birr (which had been the preferential rate since January 1996). In November 1997 the Government introduced a separate national currency, the nakfa, replacing (and initially at par with) the Ethiopian birr. The exchange rate in relation to the US dollar was initially set at the prevailing unified rate, but from 1 May 1998 a mechanism to provide a market-related exchange rate was established.

Average Exchange Rate (nakfa per US $)
2004 13.7875
2005 15.3679
2006 15.3750

BUDGET
(million nakfa)

Revenue*	2000	2001†	2002‡
Tax revenue	982.7	1,278.8	1,538.2
Direct taxes	473.5	572.9	552.8
Taxes on personal income	122.7	136.9	159.6
Taxes on business profits	299.9	387.5	337.2
Rehabilitation tax	10.4	2.9	1.8
Domestic sales tax (incl. stamp duties)	238.1	297.0	368.3
Import duties and taxes	271.0	409.0	617.1
Port fees and charges	59.4	103.3	148.5
Other current revenue	743.4	429.4	575.6
Extraordinary revenue	322.9	174.9	29.2
Total	2,108.3	1,986.4	2,291.4

Expenditure	2000	2001†	2002‡
Current expenditure	4,333.8	4,160.4	4,147.2
General services	2,722.2	2,444.7	2,619.5
Internal affairs	25.9	36.4	46.9
Regional administration	328.8	326.7	164.8
Foreign affairs	102.7	103.6	179.1
Defence§	2,220.3	1,883.6	2,104.4
Economic services	55.7	64.6	71.1
Agriculture and natural resources	32.9	34.3	37.5
Mining and energy	2.9	3.1	3.4
Construction and urban development	7.8	9.2	13.7

Expenditure—*continued*	2000	2001†	2002‡
Transport and communications	5.6	5.7	6.7
Social services	361.8	345.6	394.8
Education and training	163.8	182.0	182.9
Health	99.3	97.6	110.8
Demobilization of ex-combatants	—	6.9	7.8
Capital expenditure	1,064.9	2,005.0	1,991.1
General services	117.4	241.2	227.8
Economic development	581.4	1,359.0	955.6
Agriculture and natural resources	116.2	164.7	131.3
Trade, industry and tourism	1.2	4.7	5.8
Construction, transport and communications	262.7	551.2	378.4
Social development	366.1	404.8	807.7
Education	262.2	231.2	284.3
Health	85.9	143.2	478.2
Total	5,398.7	6,165.4	6,138.3

* Excluding grants received (million nakfa): 1,204.8 in 2000 (current 1,165.5, capital 39.3); 1,375.6 (preliminary) in 2001 (current 913.6, capital 462.0); 1,118.4 (estimate) in 2002 (current 510.0, capital 608.4).

† Preliminary figures.

‡ Estimates.

§ Including some demobilization costs.

Source: IMF, *Eritrea: Selected Issues and Statistical Appendix* (June 2003).

INTERNATIONAL RESERVES
(US $ million at 31 December)

	1999	2000	2001
Gold (national valuation)	19.7	10.4	10.5
Reserve position in IMF	0.0	0.0	0.0
Foreign exchange	34.2	25.5	39.7
Total	53.9	35.9	50.3

Foreign exchange:30.3 in 2002; 24.7 in 2003; 34.7 in 2004; 27.9 in 2005; 25.3 in 2006.

Source: IMF, *International Financial Statistics*.

MONEY SUPPLY
(million nakfa at 31 December)

	2004	2005	2006
Currency outside banks	3,253	3,654	3,515
Demand deposits at banks	4,491	5,414	6,056
Total money (incl. others)	7,799	9,102	9,636

Source: IMF, *International Financial Statistics*.

COST OF LIVING
(Consumer Price Index at December; base: 2000 = 100)

	2004	2005	2006
All items	196.2	225.6	257.7

Source: African Development Bank.

NATIONAL ACCOUNTS

Expenditure on the Gross Domestic Product
(US $ million)

	2004	2005	2006
Final consumption expenditure	1,462.92	1,298.41	1,467.93
Gross capital formation	201.36	185.74	218.29
Total domestic expenditure	1,664.28	1,484.15	1,686.22
Exports of goods and services	95.24	63.69	74.13
Less Imports of goods and services	831.50	585.64	675.86
GDP in market prices	928.01	962.20	1,084.49
GDP at factor cost at constant 2000 prices	671.39	703.62	714.17

Source: African Development Bank.

Gross Domestic Product by Economic Activity
(million nakfa at current prices)

	2000	2001*	2002*
Agriculture, forestry and fishing	871.1	1,279.2	941.3
Mining and quarrying	5.8	2.8	3.3
Manufacturing†	644.2	772.6	939.1
Electricity and water	68.4	80.8	100.8
Construction	607.8	746.3	954.0
Wholesale and retail trade	1,136.2	1,369.5	1,672.6
Transport and communications	727.8	877.0	1,071.3
Financial services	189.2	228.0	278.5
Dwellings and domestic services	121.9	143.5	169.5
Public administration and services	1,037.7	1,197.7	1,387.6
Other services	362.7	436.6	528.0
GDP at factor cost	5,772.8	7,134.0	8,045.8
Indirect taxes, *less* subsidies	427.7	637.0	985.4
GDP in purchasers' values	6,200.5	7,771.0	9,031.2

* Preliminary figures.

† Including handicrafts and small-scale industry.

Source: IMF, *Eritrea: Selected Issues and Statistical Appendix* (June 2003).

2005 (million nafka at current prices): Agriculture, hunting, forestry, fishing 1,959; Mining, manufacturing and utilities 1,649 (Manufacturing 1,477); Construction 1,511; Wholesale, retail trade, restaurants and hotels 2,669; Transport, storage and communication 1,678; Other activities 3,804; Sub-total 13,270. Source: UN Statistics Division, National Accounts Main Aggregates Database.

BALANCE OF PAYMENTS
(US $ million)

	2000	2001*	2002†
Exports of goods f.o.b.	36.7	19.9	51.8
Imports of goods c.i.f.	−470.3	−536.7	−533.4
Trade balance	−433.5	−516.7	−481.7
Exports of services	60.7	127.5	132.6
Imports of services	−28.3	−33.4	−30.3
Balance on goods and services	−401.1	−422.6	−379.4
Other income (net)	−1.4	−4.6	−6.1
Balance on goods, services and income	−402.5	−427.2	−385.5
Private unrequited transfers (net)	195.7	175.0	205.6
Official unrequited transfers (net)	102.4	120.8	80.3
Current balance	−104.5	−131.4	−99.6
Capital account (net)	—	7.3	3.6
Financial account	98.7	94.8	64.6
Short-term capital (net)	−14.7	18.7	15.9
Net errors and omissions	−9.5	36.5	−7.6
Overall balance	−15.2	7.2	−39.0

* Preliminary figures.

† Estimates.

Source: IMF, *Eritrea: Selected Issues and Statistical Appendix* (June 2003).

External Trade

PRINCIPAL COMMODITIES
(distribution by SITC, US $ '000)

Imports c.i.f. (excl. petroleum)	2001	2002	2003
Food and live animals	110.9	153.0	175.2
Animal and vegetable oils, fats and waxes	13.6	7.4	19.3
Chemicals and related products	45.5	36.4	26.2
Basic manufactures	101.5	115.6	63.3
Machinery and transport equipment	107.4	155.9	97.2
Miscellaneous manufactured articles	34.0	46.9	40.7
Total (incl. others)	422.9	537.9	432.8

Exports f.o.b.	2001	2002	2003
Food and live animals	8.8	37.7	2.4
Crude materials (inedible) except fuels	3.0	6.0	2.1
Chemicals and related products	0.7	0.6	0.1
Basic manufactures	5.6	4.8	1.1
Miscellaneous manufactured articles	0.5	1.5	0.7
Total (incl. others)	19.0	51.8	6.6

Source: UN, *International Trade Statistics Yearbook*.

PRINCIPAL TRADING PARTNERS
(US $ million)

Imports c.i.f.	2001	2002	2003
Belgium	11.9	13.7	8.6
Germany	11.8	16.4	6.7
Italy	79.0	70.4	50.1
Netherlands	13.9	17.4	10.4
Saudi Arabia	70.0	70.0	45.4
United Arab Emirates	64.6	90.7	52.9
United Kingdom	9.6	10.0	11.7
USA	20.4	38.5	68.9
Total (incl. others)	422.9	537.9	432.8

Exports f.o.b.	2001	2002	2003
Djibouti	—	0.8	—
Germany	0.7	0.5	0.1
India	3.2	0.5	0.5
Italy	2.1	1.8	0.8
Netherlands	0.4	0.3	0.7
Saudi Arabia	0.3	0.1	—
Sudan	9.7	43.4	1.3
Total (incl. others)	19.0	51.8	6.6

Source: UN, *International Trade Statistics Yearbook*.

Transport

ROAD TRAFFIC
(motor vehicles in use)

	1996	1997	1998
Number of registered vehicles	27,013	31,276	35,942

SHIPPING

Merchant Fleet
(registered at 31 December)

	2003	2004	2005
Number of vessels	12	12	11
Displacement (grt)	21,092	21,092	20,755

Source: Lloyd's Register-Fairplay, *World Fleet Statistics*.

CIVIL AVIATION

	1996	1997	1998
Passengers ('000)	168.1	173.8	105.2

Tourism

ARRIVALS BY COUNTRY OF ORIGIN

	2003	2004	2005
Germany	1,252	1,005	1,045
India	2,580	2,420	2,985
Italy	2,334	3,476	3,246
Japan	103	1,063	1,018
Kenya	695	1,481	796
Sudan	717	992	664
United Kingdom	1,106	1,079	888
USA	1,745	1,611	1,611
Total (incl. others)	80,029	87,298	83,307

Tourism receipts (US $ million, incl. passenger transport): 73 in 2002; 73 in 2004 (data for 2003 not available); n.a. in 2005.

Source: World Tourism Organization.

Communications Media

	2003	2004	2005
Telephones ('000 main lines in use)	38.1	39.3	37.7
Mobile cellular telephones ('000 subscribers)	n.a.	20	40.4
Personal computers ('000 in use)	12	15	35
Internet users ('000)	9.5	50.0	70.0

2000: Television receivers ('000 in use) 100; Facsimile machines 1,771 in use.

Radio receivers ('000 in use): 345 in 1997.

Book production (1993): 106 titles (including 23 pamphlets) and 420,000 copies (including 60,000 pamphlets). Figures for books, excluding pamphlets, refer only to school textbooks (64 titles; 323,000 copies) and government publications (19 titles; 37,000 copies).

Sources: mainly UNESCO, *Statistical Yearbook*; International Telecommunication Union.

Education

(2004/05, unless otherwise indicated)

	Institutions*	Teachers	Pupils
Pre-primary	95	829	31,244
Primary	695	7,642	377,512
Secondary: General	44	4,058	215,080
Secondary: Teacher-training	2	47*	922*
Secondary: Vocational	n.a.	168	1,864
University and equivalent level	n.a.	429†	4,612†

* 2001/02 figure(s).
† 2003/04 figure.

Sources: UNESCO; Ministry of Education, Asmara.

Adult literacy rate (UNESCO estimates): 56.7% (males 68.2%; females 45.6%) in 2003 (Source: UN Development Programme, *Human Development Report*).

Directory

The Constitution

On 23 May 1997 the Constituent Assembly unanimously adopted the Eritrean Constitution. A presidential regime was instituted, with the President to be elected for a maximum of two five-year terms. The President, as Head of State, has extensive powers and appoints, with the approval of the National Assembly (the legislature), the ministers, the commissioners, the Auditor-General, the President of the central bank and the judges of the Supreme Court. The President's mandate can be revoked if two-thirds of the members of the National Assembly so demand. 'Conditional' political pluralism is authorized. Pending the election of a new National Assembly, legislative power was to be held by a Transitional National Assembly, comprising the 75 members of the People's Front for Democracy and Justice (PFDJ) Central Committee, 60 members of the former Constituent Assembly and 15 representatives of Eritreans residing abroad.

The Government

HEAD OF STATE

President: ISSAIAS AFEWERKI (assumed power May 1991; elected President by the National Assembly 8 June 1993).

CABINET
(August 2007)

President: ISSAIAS AFEWERKI.

Minister of Defence: Gen. SEBHAT EPHREM.

Minister of Justice: FAWZIA HASHIM.

Minister of Foreign Affairs: OSMAN SALIH MUHAMMAD.

Minister of Information: ALI ABDU.

Minister of Finance: BERHANE ABREHE.

Minister of Trade and Industry: Dr GIORGIS TEKLEMIKAEL.

Minister of Agriculture: AREFAINE BERHE.

Minister of Labour and Human Welfare: ASKALU MENKERIOS.

Minister of Marine Resources: AHMED HAJI ALI.

Minister of Construction: ABRAHA ASFAHA.

Minister of Energy and Mines: TESFAI GEBRESELASSIE.

Minister of Education: SEMERE RUSOM.

Minister of Health: Dr SALIH MEKKI.

Minister of Transport and Communications: WOLDEMIKAEL ABRAHA.

Minister of Tourism: AMNA NUR HUSSEIN.

Minister of Land, Water and the Environment: WOLDEMICHAEL GEBREMARIAM.

Minister of Local Government: NAIZGHI KIFLU.

MINISTRIES AND COMMISSIONS

Office of the President: POB 257, Asmara; tel. (1) 122132; fax (1) 125123.

Ministry of Agriculture: POB 1048, Asmara; tel. (1) 181499; fax (1) 181415.

Ministry of Construction: POB 841, Asmara; tel. (1) 114588; fax (1) 120661.

Ministry of Defence: POB 629, Asmara; tel. (1) 165952; fax (1) 124990.

Ministry of Education: POB 5610, Asmara; tel. (1) 113044; fax (1) 113866; internet www.erimoe.gov.er.

Ministry of Energy and Mines: POB 5285, Asmara; tel. (1) 116872; fax (1) 127652.

Ministry of Finance: POB 896, Asmara; tel. (1) 118131; fax (1) 127947.

Ministry of Fisheries: POB 923, Asmara; tel. (1) 120400; fax (1) 122185; e-mail mofisha@eol.com.er.

Ministry of Foreign Affairs: POB 190, Asmara; tel. (1) 127838; fax (1) 123788; e-mail tesfai@wg.eol.

Ministry of Health: POB 212, Asmara; tel. (1) 117549; fax (1) 112899.

Ministry of Information: POB 872, Asmara; tel. (1) 120478; fax (1) 126747; internet www.shabait.com.

Ministry of Justice: POB 241, Asmara; tel. (1) 127739; fax (1) 126422.

Ministry of Labour and Human Welfare: POB 5252, Asmara; tel. (1) 181846; fax (1) 181760; e-mail mlhw@eol.com.er.

Ministry of Land, Water and the Environment: POB 976, Asmara; tel. (1) 118021; fax (1) 123285.

Ministry of Local Government: POB 225, Asmara; tel. (1) 114254; fax (1) 120014.

Ministry of Tourism: POB 1010, Asmara; tel. (1) 126997; fax (1) 126949; e-mail eritrea_tourism@cts.com.er; internet www.shaebia.org/mot.html.

Ministry of Trade and Industry: POB 1844, Asmara; tel. (1) 118386; fax (1) 120586.

Ministry of Transport and Communications: POB 1840, Asmara; tel. (1) 114222; fax (1) 127048; e-mail motc.rez@eol.com.er.

Eritrean Relief and Refugee Commission: POB 1098, Asmara; tel. (1) 182222; fax (1) 182970; e-mail john@errec.er.punchdown.org.

Land and Housing Commission: POB 348, Asmara; tel. (1) 117400.

Provincial Administrators

There are six administrative regions in Eritrea, each with regional, sub-regional and village administrations.

Anseba Province: SALMA HASSAN.

Debub Province: MUSTAFA NUR HUSSEIN.

Debubawi Keyih Bahri Province: TSEGEREDA WOLDEGERGIS.

Gash-Barka Province: KAHSAI GEBREHIWOT.

Maakel Province: SEMERE RUSOM.

Semenawi Keyih Bahri Province: ABDALLA MUSA.

Legislature

NATIONAL ASSEMBLY

In accordance with transitional arrangements formulated in Decree No. 37 of May 1993, the National Assembly consists of the Central Committee of the People's Front for Democracy and Justice (PFDJ) and 60 other members: 30 from the Provincial Assemblies and an additional 30 members, including a minimum of 10 women, to be nominated by the PFDJ Central Committee. The legislative body 'outlines the internal and external policies of the government, regulates their implementation, approves the budget and elects a president for the country'. The National Assembly is to hold regular sessions every six months under the chairmanship of the President. In his role as Head of the Government and Commander-in-Chief of the Army, the President nominates individuals to head the various government departments. These nominations are ratified by the legislative body. In March 1994 the National Assembly voted to alter its composition: it would henceforth comprise the 75 members of the Central Committee of the PFDJ and 75 directly elected members. In May 1997, following the adoption of the Constitution, the Constituent Assembly empowered a Transitional National Assembly (comprising the 75 members of the PFDJ, 60 members of the former Constituent Assembly and 15 representatives of Eritreans residing abroad) to act as the legislature until elections were held for a new National Assembly.

Chairman of the Transitional National Assembly: ISSAIAS AFEWERKI.

Election Commission

Electoral Commission: Asmara; f. 2002; 5 mems appointed by the President; Commissioner RAMADAN MOHAMMED NUR.

Political Organizations

Afar Federal Alliance: e-mail afa_f@hotmail.com; f. 2003.

Democratic Movement for the Liberation of Eritrean Kunama: e-mail kcs@baden-kunama.com; internet www.baden-kunama.com.

Eritrean Democratic Party (EDP): e-mail info@selfi-democracy.com; internet www.selfi-democracy.com; f. 2001 as the Eritrean People's Liberation Front—Democratic Party (EPLF—DP); breakaway group from the PFDJ; name changed to above in 2004; Leader MESFIN HAGOS.

Eritrean Islamic Jihad (EIJ): radical opposition group; in Aug. 1993 split into a mil. wing and a political wing.

Eritrean Islamic Party for Justice and Development (EIPJD) (Al-Hizb Al-Islami Al-Eritree Liladalah Wetenmiya): internet www.alkhalas.org; f. 1988 as Eritrean Islamic Jihad Movement; changed name to al-Khalas in 1998; political wing of EIJ; Leader KHALIL MUHAMMAD AMER.

Eritrean Liberation Front (ELF): f. 1958; commenced armed struggle against Ethiopia in 1961; subsequently split into numerous factions (see below); mainly Muslim support; opposes the PFDJ; principal factions:

Eritrean Liberation Front—Central Command (ELF—CC): f. 1982; Chair. ABDALLAH IDRISS.

Eritrean Liberation Front—National Council (ELF—NC): Leader Dr BEYENE KIDANE.

Eritrean Liberation Front—Revolutionary Council (ELF—RC): Chair. AHMED WOLDEYESUS AMMAR.

Eritrean Democratic Alliance (EDA): internet www.erit-alliance.com; f. 1999 as the Alliance of Eritrean National Forces, became Eritrean National Alliance in 2002, adopted present name in 2004; broad alliance of 16 parties opposed to PFDJ regime; Chair. BERHANE YEMANE 'HANJEMA'; Sec.-Gen. HUSAYN KHALIFA.

Eritrean People's Democratic Front (EPDF): e-mail main-office@sagem-eritra.org; internet www.democrasia.org; f. 2004 by merger of People's Democratic Front for the Liberation of Eritrea and a faction of ERDF; Leader TEWOLDE GEBRESELASSIE.

Eritrean Popular Movement (EPM): f. 2004; Leader ABDALLAH ADEM.

Eritrean Revolutionary Democratic Front (ERDF): e-mail webmaster@eritreana.com; internet www.eritreana.com; f. 1997 following merger of Democratic Movement for the Liberation of Eritrea and a faction of People's Democratic Front for the Liberation of Eritrea; Leader BERHANE YEMANE 'HANJEMA'.

Gash Setit Organization: Leader ISMAIL NADA.

Movement for Democratic Change: Leader Dr TESFAI BRINJI.

People's Front for Democracy and Justice (PFDJ): POB 1081, Asmara; tel. (1) 121399; fax (1) 120848; e-mail webmaster@shaebia.org; internet www.shaebia.org; f. 1970 as the Eritrean Popular Liberation Forces, following a split in the Eritrean Liberation Front; renamed the Eritrean People's Liberation Front in 1977; adopted present name in Feb. 1994; Christian and Muslim support; in May 1991 took control of Eritrea and formed provisional Govt; formed transitional Govt in May 1993; Chair. ISSAIAS AFEWERKI; Sec.-Gen. ALAMIN MOHAMED SAID.

Red Sea Afar Democratic Organization: Afar opposition group; Sec.-Gen. IBRAHIM HAROUN.

Diplomatic Representation

EMBASSIES IN ERITREA

China, People's Republic: 16 Ogaden St, POB 204, Asmara; tel. (1) 185271; fax (1) 185275; e-mail chemb@eol.com.er; Ambassador SHU ZHAN.

Djibouti: POB 5589, Asmara; tel. (1) 354961; fax (1) 351831; Ambassador AHMAD ISSA.

Egypt: 5 Dej Afworki St, POB 5570, Asmara; tel. and fax (1) 123294; Ambassador IBRAHIM KHALIL ABDALLAH.

France: POB 209, Asmara; tel. (1) 126599; fax (1) 123298; e-mail af@gemel.com.er; Ambassador PIERRE COULONT.

Germany: SABA Building, 8th Floor, Warsay St, POB 4974, Asmara; tel. (1) 186670; fax (1) 186900; e-mail info@asmara.diplo.de; internet www.asmara.diplo.de; Ambassador ALEXANDER BECKMANN.

Iran: Asmara; Ambassador REZA AMERI.

Israel: 32 Abo St, POB 5600, Asmara; tel. (1) 188521; fax (1) 188550; e-mail info@asmara.mfa.gov.il; Ambassador MENAHEM KANAFI.

Italy: POB 220, 11 171–1 St, Asmara; tel. (1) 120160; fax (1) 121115; e-mail ambasciata.asmara@esteri.it; internet www.ambasmara.esteri.it; Ambassador GAETANO MARTINEZ TAGLIAVIA.

Libya: Asmara.

Netherlands: 16 Bihat Street, POB 5860, Asmara; tel. (1) 127628; fax (1) 127591; e-mail asm@minibuza.nl; internet www.mfa.nl/asm; Ambassador NELLEKE LINSSEN.

Norway: 11 173–1 St, POB 5801, Asmara; tel. (1) 122138; fax (1) 122180; internet www.norway.gov.er; Chargé d'affaires a.i. ARMAN AARDAL.

Russia: POB 5667, Asmara; tel. (1) 127172; fax (1) 127164; e-mail rusemb@eol.com.er; Ambassador ALEXANDER OBLOV.

Saudi Arabia: POB 5599, Asmara; tel. (1) 120171; fax (1) 121027; Ambassador NASSER AR-RASHEIDAN.

Sudan: Asmara; tel. (1) 202072; fax (1) 200760; e-mail sudanemb@eol.com.er; Ambassador MOHAMED AL-HASSAN.

United Kingdom: 66–68 Mariam Ghimbi St, POB 5584, Asmara; tel. (1) 120145; fax (1) 120104; e-mail asmara.enquiries@fco.gov.uk; Ambassador NICHOLAS ASTBURY.

USA: POB 211, 179 Ala St, Asmara; tel. (1) 120004; fax (1) 127584; e-mail usembassyasmara@state.gov; internet asmara.usembassy.gov; Ambassador RONALD K. MCMULLEN.

Yemen: POB 5566, Asmara; tel. (1) 114434; fax (1) 117921; Ambassador Dr AKRAM ABD AL-MARIK AL-QABRI.

Judicial System

The judicial system operates on the basis of transitional laws which incorporate pre-independence laws of the Eritrean People's Liberation Front, revised Ethiopian laws, customary laws and post-independence enacted laws. The independence of the judiciary in the discharge of its functions is unequivocally stated in Decree No. 37, which defines the powers and duties of the Government. It is subject only to the law and to no other authority. The court structure is composed of first instance sub-zonal courts, appellate and first instance zonal courts, appellate and first instance high courts, a panel of high court judges, presided over by the President of the High Court, and a Supreme Court presided over by the Chief Justice, as a court of last resort. The judges of the Supreme Court are appointed by the President of the State, subject to confirmation by the National Assembly.

Supreme Court: Asmara.

High Court: POB 241, Asmara; tel. (1) 127739; fax (1) 201828; e-mail prshict@eol.com.er.

Religion

Eritrea is almost equally divided between Muslims and Christians. Most Christians are adherents of the Orthodox Church, although there are Protestant and Roman Catholic communities. A small number of the population follow traditional beliefs.

CHRISTIANITY

The Eritrean Orthodox Church

In September 1993 the separation of the Eritrean Orthodox Church from the Ethiopian Orthodox Church was agreed by the respective church leaderships. The Eritrean Orthodox Church announced that it was to create a diocese of each of the country's then 10 provinces. The first five bishops of the Eritrean Orthodox Church were consecrated in Cairo in September 1994. In May 1998 Eritrea's first Patriarch (Abune) was consecrated in Alexandria. In January 2006 Eritrea's third Patriarch, Abune Antonios I (who had been under house arrest since August 2005), was deposed by the Holy Synod.

Patriarch (Abune): DIOSKOROS.

The Roman Catholic Church

At 31 December 2004 there were an estimated 149,788 adherents in the country.

Bishop of Asmara: Rt Rev. ABBA MENGHISTEAB TESFAMARIAM, 19 Gonder St, POB 244, Asmara; tel. (1) 120206; fax (1) 126519; e-mail kimehret@gemel.com.er.

Bishop of Barentu: Rt Rev. THOMAS OSMAN, POB 9, Barentu; tel. and fax (1) 127283.

Bishop of Keren: Rt Rev. KIDANE YEBIO, POB 460, Keren; tel. (1) 401907; fax (1) 401604; e-mail cek@gemel.com.er.

The Anglican Communion

Within the Episcopal Church in Jerusalem and the Middle East, Eritrea lies within the jurisdiction of the Bishop in Egypt.

Leader: ASFAHA MAHARY.

ISLAM

Eritrea's main Muslim communities are concentrated in the western lowlands, the northern highlands and the eastern coastal region.

Leader: Sheikh AL-AMIN OSMAN AL-AMIN.

The Press

There is no independent press in Eritrea.

Business Perspective: POB 856, Asmara; tel. (1) 121589; fax (1) 120138; monthly; Tigrinya, Arabic and English; publ. by Eritrean National Chamber of Commerce; Editor MOHAMMED-SFAF HAMMED.

Chamber News: POB 856, Asmara; tel. (1) 120045; fax (1) 120138; monthly; Tigrinya, Arabic and English; publ. by Asmara Chamber of Commerce.

Eritrea Profile: POB 247, Asmara; tel. (1) 114114; fax (1) 127749; e-mail eritreaprofile@yahoo.com; internet www.shabait.com; f. 1994; twice-weekly; English; publ. by the Ministry of Information; Editor-in-Chief IDRIS AWAD AL-KARIM (acting).

Hadas Eritra (New Eritrea): Asmara; f. 1991; six times a week; in English, Tigrinya and Arabic; govt publ; Editor PAULOS NETABAY ABRAHAM; circ. 49,200.

Newsletter: POB 856, Asmara; tel. (1) 121589; fax (1) 120138; e-mail encc@aol.com.er; monthly; Tigrinya, Arabic and English; publ. by Eritrean National Chamber of Commerce; Editor MOHAMMED-SFAF HAMMED.

Broadcasting and Communications

Ministry of Transport and Communications (Communications Department): POB 4918, Asmara; tel. (1) 115847; fax (1) 126966; e-mail motc.rez@eol.com.er; Dir-Gen. ESTIFANOS AFEWERKI.

TELECOMMUNICATIONS

Eritrea Telecommunication Services Corpn (EriTel): 11 Semaetat St, POB 234, Asmara; tel. (1) 124655; fax (1) 120938; e-mail eritel@tse.com.er; internet www.tse.com.er; f. 1991; operates fixed-line and mobile cellular networks; Gen. Man. TESFASELASSIE BERHANE.

TFanus: 46 Daniel Comboni Street, POB 724, Asmara; tel. (1) 202590; fax (1)126457; e-mail webmaster@tfanus.com.er; internet www.tfanus.com.er; f. 1996; internet service provider.

BROADCASTING

Radio

Voice of the Broad Masses of Eritrea (Dimtsi Hafash): POB 242, Asmara; tel. (1) 120426; fax (1) 126747; govt-controlled; programmes in Arabic, Tigrinya, Tigre, Saho, Oromo, Amharic, Afar, Bilien, Nara, Hedareb and Kunama; Dir-Gen. TESFAI KELETA; Technical Dir BERHANE GEREZGIHER.

Voice of Liberty: Asmara; e-mail VoL@selfi-democracy.com; internet selfi-democracy.com; radio programme of the EDP; broadcasts for one hour twice a week.

Television

ERI-TV: Asmara; f. 1992; govt station providing educational, tech. and information service; broadcasting began in 1993; programming in Arabic, English, Tigre and Tigrinya; transmissions limited to Asmara and surrounding areas; Dir-Gen. ALI ABDU.

Finance

(cap. = capital; res = reserves; dep. = deposits; m. = million; brs = branches; amounts in nakfa)

In November 1997 Eritrea adopted the nakfa as its unit of currency, replacing the Ethiopian birr, which had been Eritrea's monetary unit since independence.

BANKING

Central Bank

Bank of Eritrea: POB 849, 21 Victory Ave, Asmara; tel. (1) 123036; fax (1) 123162; e-mail kibreabw@boe.gov.er; f. 1993; bank of issue; Gov. TEKIE BEYENE.

Other Banks

Commercial Bank of Eritrea: POB 219, 208 Liberty Ave, Asmara; tel. (1) 121844; fax (1) 124887; e-mail gm.cber@gemel.com.er; f. 1991; cap. 400.0m., res 344.5m., dep. 13,791.6m. (Dec. 2004); Chair. BERHANE ABREHE; Gen. Man. YAMANE TESFAI; 15 brs.

Eritrean Development and Investment Bank: POB 1266, 29 Bedho St, Asmara; tel. (1) 126777; fax (1) 201976; e-mail edib@gemel.com.er; f. 1996; cap. 45m., total assets 194.2m. (Dec. 2003); provides medium- to long-term credit; Chair. HABTEAB TESFATSION; Gen. Man. Dr GOITOM W. MARIAM; 4 brs.

Housing and Commerce Bank of Eritrea: POB 235, Bahti Meskerem Sq., Asmara; tel. (1) 120350; fax (1) 202209; internet www.shaebia.org/new-hcb.html; e-mail hcb@gemel.com.er; f. 1994; cap. 33m., total assets 1,824.7m. (Dec. 1999); finances residential and commercial construction projects and commercial loans; Chair. HAGOS GHEBREHIWET; Gen. Man. BERHANE GHEBREHIWET; 10 brs.

INSURANCE

National Insurance Corporation of Eritrea (NICE): NICE Bldg, 171 Bidho Ave, POB 881, Asmara; tel. (1) 123000; fax (1) 123240; e-mail nice@nic-eritrea.com.er; internet www.nice-eritrea.com; f. 1992; partially privatized in 2004; general and life; Gen. Man. ZERU WOLDEMICHAEL.

Trade and Industry

CHAMBER OF COMMERCE

Eritrean National Chamber of Commerce: POB 856, Asmara; tel. (1) 121589; fax (1) 120138; e-mail encc@gemel.com.er.

TRADE ASSOCIATION

Red Sea Trading Corporation: 29/31 Ras Alula St, POB 332, Asmara; tel. (1) 127846; fax (1) 124353; f. 1983; import and export services; operated by the PFDJ; Gen. Man. KUBROM DAFLA.

UTILITIES

Electricity

Eritrean Electricity Authority (EEA): POB 911, Asmara; fax (1) 121468; e-mail eeahrg@eol.com.er.

Water

Dept of Water Resources: POB 1488, Asmara; tel. (1) 119636; fax (1) 124625; e-mail wrdmlwe@eol.com.er; f. 1992.

Transport

Eritrea's transport infrastructure was severely damaged during the three decades of war prior to independence. International creditors have since provided loans for the repair and reconstruction of the road network and for the improvement of port facilities.

RAILWAYS

The 306-km railway connection between Agordat, Asmara and the port of Massawa was severely damaged during the war of independence and ceased operation in 1975. However, in 1999 an 81-km section of the Asmara–Massawa line (between Massawa and Embatkala) became operational, and in 2001 a further 18-km section, connecting Embatkala and Ghinda, was added. In February 2003 the reconstruction of the entire Asmara–Massawa line was completed.

Eritrean Railway: POB 6081, Asmara; tel. (1) 123365; fax (1) 201785; Co-ordinator, Railways Rehabilitation Project AMANUEL GEBRESELLASIE.

ROADS

In 1999 there were an estimated 4,010 km of roads in Eritrea, of which some 874 km were paved. Roads that are paved require considerable repair, as do many of the bridges across seasonal water courses destroyed in the war. The programme to rehabilitate the road between Asmara and the port of Massawa was completed in 2000.

SHIPPING

Eritrea has two major seaports: Massawa, which sustained heavy war damage in 1990, and Assab, which has principally served Addis Ababa, in Ethiopia. Under an accord signed between the Ethiopian and Eritrean Governments in 1993, the two countries agreed to share the facilities of both ports. Since independence, activity in Massawa has increased substantially; however, activity at Assab declined following the outbreak of hostilities with Ethiopia in May 1998. In 1998 a total of 463 vessels docked at Massawa, handling 1.2m. metric tons of goods; 322 vessels docked at Assab, which handled 1.0m. tons of goods. At 31 December 2005 Eritrea's registered merchant fleet numbered 11 vessels, with a total displacement of 20,755 grt.

Dept of Maritime Transport: POB 679, Asmara; tel. (1) 121317; fax (1) 121316; e-mail motc.rez@eol.com.er; Dir-Gen. ALEM TZEHAIE.

Port and Maritime Transport Authority: POB 851, Asmara; tel. (1) 111399; fax (1) 113647; Dir WELDE MIKAEL ABRAHAM.

BC Marine Services: 189 Warsay St, POB 5638, Asmara; tel. (1) 202672; fax (1) 12747; e-mail info@bc-marine.com; internet www.bc-marine.com; f. 2000; services include marine consultancy, marine survey and ship management; branches in Assab and Massawa; Dir Capt. NAOD GEBREAMLAK HAILE.

Cargo Inspection Survey Services: St No. 171-5-171, POB 906, Asmara; tel. (1) 120369; fax (1) 121767; e-mail gellatly@eol.com.er.

Eritrean Shipping Lines: 80 Semaetat Ave, POB 1110, Asmara; tel. (1) 120359; fax (1) 120331; f. 1992; provides shipping services in Red Sea and Persian (Arabian) Gulf areas and owns and operates four cargo ships; Gen. Man. TEWELDE KELATI.

Maritime Ship Services Enterprise: POB 99, Massawa; tel. (1) 552729; fax (1) 552483; e-mail ersasmsw@tse.co.er; shipping agents.

CIVIL AVIATION

The international airport is at Asmara.

Civil Aviation Department: POB 252, Asmara; tel. (1) 124335; fax (1) 124334; e-mail motc.rez@eol.com.er; handles freight and passenger traffic for eight scheduled carriers which use Asmara airport; Dir-Gen. PAULOS KAHSAY.

Eri-Air: Asmara; f. 2001; weekly charter flights to Italy; Man. Dirs TEWOLDE TESFAMARIAM, HAILEMARIAM GEBRECHRISTOS.

Eritrean Airlines: POB 222, Asmara; tel. (1) 125500; fax (1) 125465; internet www.flyeritrea.com; Man. Dir ABRAHA GHIRMAZION.

Tourism

The Ministry of Tourism is overseeing the development of this sector, although its advance since independence has been inhibited by the country's war-damaged transport infrastructure, and by subsequent conflicts with Ethiopia and other regional tensions. Eritrea possesses many areas of scenic and scientific interest, including the Dahlak Islands (a coralline archipelago rich in marine life), offshore from Massawa, and the massive escarpment rising up from the coastal plain and supporting a unique ecosystem. In 2005 83,307 tourists visited Eritrea. Tourist receipts in 2004 amounted to US $73m. Since May 2006 it has been necessary for foreign nationals to obtain a permit 10 days in advance in order to travel outside of the capital.

Eritrean Tourism Service Corporation: Asmara; operates govt-owned hotels.

Defence

As assessed at November 2006, Eritrea's active armed forces included an army of about 200,000, a navy of 1,400 and an air force of about 350. National service is compulsory for all Eritreans between 18 and 40 years of age (with certain exceptions), for a 16-month period, including four months of military training. Defence expenditure in 2005 was budgeted at US $74m. In September 2000 the UN Security Council approved the establishment of the UN Mission in Ethiopia and Eritrea (UNMEE, comprising 4,200 peace-keeping troops), which was subsequently deployed on the Eritrean side of the two countries' common border. At the end of December 2006 UNMEE numbered 2,063 troops, 222 military observers, as well as 149 international civilians and 194 local civilians.

Education

Education is provided free of charge in government schools and at the University of Asmara. There are also some fee-paying private schools. Education is officially compulsory for children between seven and 13 years of age. Primary education begins at the age of seven and lasts for five years. Secondary education, beginning at 12 years of age, lasts for as much as six years, comprising a first cycle of two years and a second of four years. In 2003/04, according to UNESCO estimates, the total enrolment at primary schools included 48% of children in the relevant age-group (males 52%; females 44%), while the comparable ratio for secondary enrolment was only 24% (males 28%; females 19%). Government expenditure on education in 2002 was 467.2m. nakfa (7.6% of total spending). By mid-1994 Eritrea had about 600 schools, almost three times as many as in 1991. In 2004/05 there were some 5,500 students enrolled on bachelor degree courses at the University of Asmara. The University of Asmara was officially closed in September 2006. Higher education would henceforth be provided by six newly-established technical institutes, each associated with a relevant Government ministry. The institutes provide education in the fields of science, technology, business and economics, social sciences, agriculture and marine training.

Bibliography

Abbay, A. *Identity Jilted or Re-imagining Identity? The Divergent Paths of the Eritrean and Tigrayan Nationalist Struggles.* Lawrenceville, NJ, Red Sea Press, 1998.

Bariagaber, A. *Conflict and the Refugee Experience: Flight, Exile, and Repatriation in the Horn of Africa*. Aldershot, Ashgate, 2006.

Bekoe, D. A.(Ed.). *East Africa and the Horn: Confronting Challenges to Good Governance*. Boulder, CO, Lynne Rienner Publishers, 2006.

Bereketeab, R. *Eritrea: The Making of a Nation* Trenton, NJ, Red Sea Press, 2007.

Cliffe, L., and Davidson, B. (Eds). *The Long Struggle of Eritrea for Independence and Constructive Peace*. Nottingham, Spokesman, 1988.

Connell, D. *Against All Odds: A Chronicle of the Eritrean Revolution.* Trenton, NJ, Red Sea Press, 1993.

Building a New Nation: Collected Articles on the Eritrean Revolution (1983–2002), Vol. 2. Trenton, NJ, Red Sea Press, 2004.

Conversations with Eritrean Political Prisoners. Trenton, NJ, Red Sea Press, 2004.

Constitutional Commission of Eritrea. *Constitutional Proposals for Public Debate*. Asmara, Adulis Printing Press, 1995.

Denison, E., Ren Yu, G., and Begremedhin, N. *Asmara*. London, Merrell Publishers, 2003.

Doornbos, M., Cliffe, L., and Markakis, J. (Eds). *Beyond Conflict in the Horn: The Prospects of Peace and Development in Ethiopia, Somalia, Eritrea and Sudan*. Lawrenceville, NJ, Red Sea Press, 1992.

Doornbos, M., and Tesfai, A. (Eds). *Post-conflict Eritrea: Prospects for Reconstruction and Development.* Lawrenceville, NJ, Red Sea Press, 1999.

Duffield, M., and Prendergast, J. *Without Troops and Tanks: Humanitarian Intervention in Ethiopia and Eritrea.* Lawrenceville, NJ, Red Sea Press, 1995.

Ellingson, L. *The Emergence of Eritrea, 1958–1992.* London, James Currey Publishers, 1993.

Erlich, H. *The Struggle over Eritrea 1962–78*. Stanford, CA, Hoover Institution, 1983.

Fegley, R. *Eritrea.* Oxford, Clio Press, 1995.

Fekadu, T. *Journey from Nakfa to Nakfa: Back to Square One, 1976-1979*. Asmara, Sabur Printing Press, 2002.

Firebrace, J., and Holland, S. *Never Kneel Down.* Trenton, NJ, Red Sea Press, 1985.

Fukui, K., and Markakis, J. (Eds). *Ethnicity and Conflict in the Horn of Africa*. London, James Currey, 1994.

Henze, P. B., *Eritrea's War: Confrontation, International Response, Outcome, Prospects.* Addis Ababa, Shama Books, 2001.

Gebregergis, T. *Eritrea: An Account of an Eritrean Political Exile on his Visit to Liberated Eritrea: December 1991–March 1992.* Amsterdam, Liberation Books, 1993.

Gebre-Medhin, J. *Peasants and Nationalism in Eritrea*. Trenton, NJ, Red Sea Press, 1989.

Ghebre-Ab, H. (Ed.). *Ethiopia and Eritrea: A Documentary Study.* Trenton, NJ, Red Sea Press, 1993.

Gorke, I., Klingebiel, S., *et al. Promoting the Reintegration of Former Female and Male Combatants in Eritrea.* Berlin, German Development Institute, 1995.

Iyob, R. *The Eritrean Struggle for Independence: Domination, Resistance, Nationalism 1941–93.* Cambridge, Cambridge University Press, 1995.

Jacquin-Berdal, D., and Plaut, M. (Eds). *Unfinished Business: Ethiopia and Eritrea at War*. Trenton, NJ, Red Sea Press, 2005.

Kibreab, G. *Ready and Willing...But Still Waiting: Eritrean Refugees in Sudan and the Dilemmas of Return.* Uppsala, Life and Peace Institute, 1996.

Killion, T. *Historical Dictionary of Eritrea.* Lanham, MD, Scarecrow Press, 1998.

Legum, C., and Lee, B. *Conflict in the Horn of Africa*. London, Rex Collings, 1977.

Lewis, I. M. (Ed.). *Nationalism in the Horn of Africa*. London, Ithaca Press, 1983.

Machida, R. *Eritrea: The Struggle for Independence.* Trenton, NJ, Red Sea Press, 1987.

Markakis, J. *National and Class Conflict in the Horn of Africa*. Cambridge, Cambridge University Press (African Studies Series No. 55), 1988.

Maundi, M. O., Zartman, I. W., Khadiagala, G. M. and Nuamah, K. *Getting In: Mediators' Entry into the Settlement of African Conflicts* Washington, DC, United States Institute of Peace Press, 2006.

Medhanie, T. *Eritrea: The Dynamics of a National Question*. Amsterdam, B. R. Grunner, 1986.

Eritrea and Neighbours in the 'New World Order': Geopolitics, Democracy and 'Islamic Fundamentalism'. Munster, LIT, 1994.

Mehreteab, A. *Wake Up, Hanna!* Reintegration and Reconstruction Challenges for Post-War Eritrea. Lawrenceville, NJ, Red Sea Press, 2004.

Mengisteab, K., and Yohannes, O. *Anatomy of an African Tragedy: Political, Economic and Foreign Policy Crisis in Post-Independence Eritrea*. Trenton, NJ, Red Sea Press, 2005.

Mesghenna, Y. *Italian Colonialism: A Case Study of Eritrea 1869–1934*. Lund, University of Lund, 1989.

Müller, Tanya. *Making of Elite Women: Revolution and Nation Building in Eritrea*. Leiden, Brill Academic Publishers, 2005.

Murtaza, N. *The Pillage of Sustainability in Eritrea, 1600s-1900s Rural Communities and the Creeping Shadows of Hegemony*. Westport, CT, Greenwood Press, 1998.

Negash, T. *Italian Colonialism in Eritrea, 1882–1941: Policies, Praxis and Impact*. Uppsala, Almqvist and Wiksell International, 1987.

No Medicine for the Bite of a White Snake: Notes on Nationalism and Resistance in Eritrea 1890–1940. Uppsala, University Press, 1987.

Eritrea and Ethiopia: The Federal Experience. New Brunswick, NJ, Transaction Publishers, 1997.

Negash, T., and Tronvoll, K. *Brothers at War*. Oxford, James Currey Publishers, 2000.

Papstein, R. *Eritrea: A Tourist Guide*. Lawrenceville, NJ, Red Sea Press, 1995.

Eritrea: Revolution at Dusk. Lawrenceville, NJ, Red Sea Press, 2001.

Pateman, R. *Eritrea: Even the Stones are Burning*. Trenton, NJ, Red Sea Press, 1990.

Pool, D. *From Guerrillas to Government*. Oxford, James Currey Publishers, 2000.

Prouty, C., and Rosenfeld, E. *Historical Dictionary of Ethiopia and Eritrea*. 2nd Edn. Lanham, MD, and London, Scarecrow Press, 1994.

Rena, R. *A Handbook on the Eritrean Economy: Problems and Prospects for Development* Dar es Salaam, New Africa Press, 2006.

Sherman, R. *Eritrea: The Unfinished Revolution*. New York, Praeger, 1980.

Tekle, A. (Ed.). *Eritrea and Ethiopia: From Conflict to Co-operation*. Lawrenceville, NJ, Red Sea Press, 1994.

Tesfagiorgis, G. H. (Ed.). *Emergent Eritrea: Challenges of Economic Development*. Lawrenceville, NJ, Red Sea Press, 1993.

Tesfamichael, A., Sebahtu, S. H. *Commercial Fish of the Eritrean Red Sea*. Clacton on Sea, Apex Publishing, 2006.

Trevaskis, G. K. *Eritrea: A Colony in Transition*. London, Oxford University Press, 1960.

Tronvoll, K. *A Small Village in the Highlands of Eritrea: a Study of the People, their Livelihood and Land Tenure during the Times of Turbulence*. Lawrenceville, NJ, Red Sea Press, 1998.

United Nations. *The United Nations and the Independence of Eritrea*. New York, United Nations Department of Public Information, 1996.

With, P. *Politics and Liberation: the Eritrean Struggle, 1961–1986*. Aarhus, Denmark, University of Aarhus, 1987.

Wolde-Yesus, A. *Eritrea: Root Causes of War and Refugees*. Baghdad, Sinbad, 1992.

Wrong, M. *I Didn't Do It for You: How the World Betrayed a Small African Nation*. London, HarperCollins, 2005.

Yohannes, O. *Eritrea, a Pawn in World Politics*. Gainesville, FL, University Press of Florida, 1991.

ETHIOPIA

Physical and Social Geography

G. C. LAST

The Federal Democratic Republic of Ethiopia is a land-locked country in the Horn of Africa, covering an area of 1,133,380 sq km (437,600 sq miles). Ethiopia's western neighbour is Sudan; to the south it has a common border with Kenya; and to the east and south-east lie the Republic of Djibouti and the Somali Democratic Republic. To the north and north-east lies the State of Eritrea.

PHYSICAL FEATURES

Elevations range from around 100 m below sea-level in the Dallol Depression (Kobar Sink), on the north-eastern border with Eritrea, to a number of mountain peaks in excess of 4,000 m above sea-level, which dominate the plateaux and of which the highest is Ras Dashen, rising to 4,620 m.

The southern half of Ethiopia is bisected by the rift valley, ranging between 40–60 km in width and containing a number of lakes. In the latitude of Addis Ababa, the western wall of the rift turns north and runs parallel to the west coast of Arabia, leaving a wide plain between the escarpment and the Red Sea coast of Eritrea. The eastern wall of the rift turns to the east in the latitude of Addis Ababa, forming an escarpment looking north over the Afar plains. The escarpments are nearly always abrupt, and are broken at only one point near Addis Ababa where the Awash river descends from the rim of the plateau.

The plateaux to the west of the rift system dip gently towards the west and are drained by right-bank tributaries of the Nile system, which have carved deep and spectacular gorges. The plateaux to the north of Lake Tana are drained by the Tekeze and Angareb rivers, headwaters of the Atbara. The central plateaux are drained by the Abbai (Blue Nile) river and its tributaries. The Abbai rises in Lake Tana and is known as the Blue Nile in Sudan. Much of the flood water in the Blue Nile system comes from the left-bank tributaries, which rise in the high rainfall region of south-west Ethiopia. This southern region is also drained by the Akobo, Gilo and Baro rivers, which form the headwaters of the Sobat river. The only river of significance to the west of the rift valley that is not part of the Nile system is the Omo, which drains southwards into Lake Turkana and is known in its upper course as the Gibie. The lower trough of the Omo has, in recent years, been the site of interesting archaeological discoveries of early human occupation, pre-dating the early remains at Olduvai in Tanzania. The rift valley itself contains a number of closed river basins, including the largest, the Awash, which flows north from the rift valley proper into the Afar plain and terminates in Lake Abe. It is in the middle and lower Awash regions of the rift valley that even earlier remains of man have been discovered, in the locality of Hadow, below the escarpment to the east of Dessie. The highlands to the east of the rift are drained south-eastwards by the headstreams of the Webi-Shebelli and Juba river systems.

The location of Ethiopia across a series of major fault lines and its association with earth movements, particularly in the Afar plains, which are related to the continuing drift of the African continent away from the Asian blocks, makes it highly susceptible to minor earth tremors.

CLIMATE, VEGETATION AND NATURAL RESOURCES

Ethiopia lies within the tropics but the wide range of altitude produces considerable variations in temperature conditions, which are reflected in the traditional zones of the *dega* (the temperate plateaux), the *kolla* (hot lowlands) and the intermediate frost-free zone of the *woina dega*. The boundaries between these three zones lie at approximately 2,400 m and 1,700 m above sea-level. Average annual temperature in the *dega* is about 16°C, in the *woina dega* about 22°C and in the *kolla* at least 26°C. A main rainy season covers most of the country during June–August, when moist equatorial air is drawn in from the south and west.

Ethiopia is extremely vulnerable to drought conditions, particularly in the low-lying pastoral areas, and along the eastern escarpment where there is a widespread dependence upon the spring rains (*belg*). The development of cultivation in areas of marginal rainfall has accentuated this problem.

Despite the significant variations in local climates and in the distribution of rainfall, Ethiopia's climatic conditions can be described generally in terms of well-watered highlands and uplands, mostly receiving at least 1,000 mm of rain a year with the exception of the Tigraian plateau, and dry lowlands, generally having less than 500 mm of rain, with the significant exception of the Baro and Akobo river plains in the south-west, which lie in the path of summer rain-bearing winds.

The natural vegetation of the plateaux and highlands above 1,800 m is coniferous forest (notably *zigba* and *tid*), but these forests have now largely disappeared, existing only in the more inaccessible regions of the country. In the south-west higher rainfall, with lower elevations and higher temperatures, has produced extensive broad-leafed rain forests with a variety of species, including abundant *karraro*. Previously densely forested areas in the former Illubabor and Kaffa Administrative Regions of the south-west have now, with the extension of all-weather road systems, been subject to extensive commercial exploitation and the activities of a growing population of traditional cultivators, with devastating impact on the natural vegetation.

Above the tree line on the plateaux are wide expanses of mountain grassland. The highlands are the site of settled agriculture in which some 4m. farmers produce a variety of grain crops. The growth of population and the depletion of resources in forest cover and soil have led to the practice of farming in areas that are very marginal and unreliable in rainfall, notably along the eastern escarpment. This has exacerbated drought and famine conditions. In particular, the most important traditional grain crop, teff, used in the highlands for the production of the staple food, injera, has been most seriously affected. This has had a notable impact, as the populations there do not adapt easily to replacement crops (and relief supplies) of maize and rice.

In the lowlands, dependent on rainfall conditions, there is a range of dry-zone vegetation. Extensive natural range-lands, particularly in the Borena and Ogaden plains in the south, are an important resource in Ethiopia and currently support some 30m. head of cattle.

Drought conditions, which began in 1972–73, in association with abnormal conditions affecting the whole Sahel region of Africa, have completely disrupted the pastoral economy in many areas, resulting in a high mortality rate both of humans and livestock and severely depleting vegetation cover.

To add to Ethiopia's problems is the frequent invasion by the so-called 'desert' locust. There are breeding grounds of this insect in the drier regions of the country, but much of the damage is done by large swarms of adults, which can contain more than 25m. locusts, each eating its own weight in vegetation daily, and which originate in the semi-desert areas of Sudan, Saudi Arabia, Somalia and Kenya.

Although the exploitation of gold and copper ores on the Eritrean plateau dates from prehistoric times, relatively little is known of the potential mineral resources of Ethiopia; by the mid-1990s only about one-quarter of the country had been geologically mapped. Probably the area with the highest mineral potential lies in the west and south-west (in the

Wollega, Illubabor and Kaffa regions). There are alluvial gold workings in the Adola area of the Sidamo region, and platinum deposits near Yubdo in the Wollega region. Potentially valuable deposits of potash have been located in the Dallol Depression; their exploitation awaits the development of other infrastructure and effective joint operations between Ethiopia and Eritrea.

Exploration for petroleum was carried out for some years in the Ogaden region without success. More recently, attention has been diverted to the southern borders of Ethiopia. In the Bale region between the rivers Web and Webi-Shebelli, it has been reported that petroleum reserves have been identified. The geothermal power potential of extensive sources in the Afar plain region is being evaluated.

Ethiopia commands excellent potential for the generation of hydroelectric power. A number of plants are in operation along the course of the Awash river, while numerous sites have been identified along the Blue Nile river basin, at which power production could be coupled with irrigation schemes.

POPULATION

According to a census conducted in October 1994, the total population was 53,477,265 (males 26,910,698; females 26,566,567). The population of the capital had increased to 2,084,588, while a further eight towns each had more than 105,000 inhabitants. The growth rates in these larger urban settlements are high. At mid-2007 the Central Statistical Authority estimated the population to be 77,127,000, with overall density of population of 68.1 inhabitants per sq km. However, this average conceals a very wide variation among the regions, as might be expected from the multiplicity of natural environments.

The distribution of population generally reflects the pattern of relief. The highlands, having a plentiful rainfall, are the home of settled agriculture and contain nearly all of the major settlements. Land more than 2,000 m above sea-level was, in the past, free of the malarial mosquito, a factor contributing to the non-occupation of lowlands that are suitable for farming. However, recent evidence shows that this traditional limit is being breached as average temperatures rise and the mosquito adapts to higher elevations. It would not be unreasonable to assume that 10% of the population live below 1,000 m, 20% at 1,000 m–1,800 m and 70% above the 1,800 m contour line. The distribution of population has been affected by recurrent droughts, which have forced many people to leave their traditional areas in search of emergency aid, and by the erstwhile government policy of resettling famine victims from the former Tigrai and Wollo Administrative Regions in newly established villages in the lowlands of the south-west; additionally, the civil war, which intensified in 1989–91, caused the displacement of large numbers of the population.

The implementation of new administrative regions ('States'), which are based on ethnic distributions, has resulted in movement of minority groups, and the massive recruitment of young men for the war with Eritrea (1998–2000) is likely to have had long-term implications for population growth and distribution.

Recent History

PATRICK GILKES

With subsequent revisions by SARAH VAUGHAN

Revised for this edition by GREG CAMERON and MANICKAM VENKATARAMAN

THE ETHIOPIAN EMPIRE

Ethiopia's history as an organized and independent polity dates back to the beginning of the second century during the Auximite rule in the northern regional state (*killil*) of Tigrai, which covered the present-day northern part of Ethiopia and included parts of Eritrea down to the coast around Massawa and Zula. Conversion to Christianity took place in the fourth century AD. In the fifth and sixth centuries it extended across the Red Sea, but its core lay in the northern Ethiopian highlands (present-day Tigrai and Eritrea). When Axum collapsed in the eighth century, power shifted south to Lasta, and later to Shoa. In the 16th century, 50 years of conflict with the Muslim sultanate of Adal exhausted both; they fell an easy prey to the Oromos, a pastoral people who expanded from the south.

Ethiopian political history has been marked by constant power struggle for supremacy between ambitious individuals such as Menelik of Shoa, Kassa Hailu of Gondar (named as Emperor Tewodros in 1855–68) and later Kassa Mircha of Tigrai (crowned as Emperor Yohannes IV in 1872–89) and Gobeze of Amhara regions. Internal and external invasions led to instability. While Yohannes IV was fighting the Egyptians, Italians and Sudanese Mahdists on the northern border, Menelik directed his energies to acquire modern armaments and continued Shoan expansion to the east, south and west of Shoa, conquering areas rich in coffee, gold, ivory and slaves. In 1896 he defeated the Italians at the battle of Adwa, but Italy retained control of the northern part of the country to create its colony Eritrea.

The first stage of Ethiopia's modernization was undertaken by Menelik II (1889–1913) and later by Haile Selassie (1930–1974). The creation of modern schools, for which teachers from abroad—especially from India—were recruited, a professional army, a written Constitution and an elected Parliament were the results of Haile Selassie's efforts towards modernization of the state. This process was interrupted by the Italian invasion and conquest of 1935–41, but after Ethiopia's liberation, Haile Selassie continued a largely successful policy of centralization. However, Ethiopia remained essentially feudal, with small Amhara-dominated modern sectors in the bureaucracy and in industry. In 1952, after protracted discussions, Eritrea, a UN-mandated territory after the Second World War, was federated with Ethiopia. Severe hardships, which were a result of frequent wars and periodic famine, particularly in Tigrai, were not addressed adequately by Menelik nor by Haile Selassie and thus caused much resentment among non-Amhara nationalities. Haile Selassie himself preferred to concentrate on international affairs. Addis Ababa became the headquarters of the Organization of African Unity (OAU, now the African Union—AU), and the UN Economic Commission for Africa. His main ally was the USA: Ethiopia, the main recipient of US aid in Africa in the 1950s and 1960s, provided the USA with a major communications base at Kagnew, in Asmara, the capital of Eritrea.

The incorporation of Eritrea under Selassie's centralized control led to the dismantling of its institutions, including the press, trade unions, political parties and the elected Parliament. In 1962 Eritrea became a province of Ethiopia, igniting the Eritrean struggle for independence. Originally led by the Eritrean Liberation Front (ELF), supported mainly by Muslim pastoralists from lowland areas, by the early 1970s disaffected ELF members had founded the Popular Liberation Forces (renamed the Eritrean People's Liberation Front—EPLF—in 1977), which was more representative of the Tigraian Christian highland agriculturalists.

Long-term weaknesses of the regime included a growing agrarian crisis, inequitable distribution of land, and lack of development. More immediately, the costs of the revolt in Eritrea after 1961, drought and famine in Wollo in 1972–74, and, by 1973, Haile Selassie's own near-senility and his failure to designate an heir, fuelled the grievances of the military, students and workers. A series of army mutinies, started in January 1974, were paralleled by civilian strikes. Attempts at reform by a new Prime Minister made little progress, and from June a co-ordinating committee of the armed forces began to arrest leading officials. Haile Selassie was deposed in September, with little dissent, and was murdered the following year. His remains were finally reburied in Trinity Cathedral, Addis Ababa, in November 2000, with many of the exiled royal family in attendance. The monarchy was formally abolished in March 1975.

MILITARY RULE

The imperial regime was replaced by the Provisional Military Administrative Council (PMAC), or *Dergue* (Committee), which adopted Marxism as its ideology and declared Ethiopia a socialist state in December 1974. Lt-Gen. Aman Andom, from Eritrea, was drafted in as Head of State, but disagreements over the Eritrean revolt led to his death only two months later. At the same time, 57 former high-ranking military and civilian officials were summarily executed, including two former Prime Ministers and 17 generals.

As part of the Government's revolutionary reforms, known as *Ethiopia Tikdem* (Ethiopia First), more than 100 companies were nationalized or partly taken over by the state; trade unions were restructured; rural and urban land was nationalized in March and July 1975, respectively; thousands of students were dispatched to the countryside on a national campaign for development; more than 30,000 local peasant associations were created with responsibility for tax collection, judicial affairs and administration; and similar associations, *kebeles*, were established in towns, with pyramids of higher-level organizations, district, regional and national. In April 1976 the theory of the revolution was outlined in the 'national democratic revolution programme', essentially the work of a Marxist-Leninist group, the All-Ethiopia Socialist Movement (MEISON), which wanted a Soviet-style communist party, but was prepared to accept the need for temporary military rule. Its rival, the Ethiopian People's Revolutionary Party (EPRP), another and more popular Marxist-Leninist grouping, argued for the immediate creation of a civilian government, and also supported the Eritrean struggle. Their disputes, over ideology and control of the new institutions, intensified into urban terrorism, and spilt over into the PMAC. In December 1976 pro-EPRP *Dergue* members appeared to have won the arguments; in February 1977 the first Vice-Chairman of the *Dergue*, Lt-Col Mengistu Haile Mariam, seized power with MEISON support. Mengistu became Head of State and Chairman of the PMAC and launched, originally on behalf of MEISON, the 'red terror' campaign, aimed at eliminating the EPRP. Tens of thousands were killed or tortured, particularly in urban areas. In mid-1977 Mengistu turned against MEISON too and by late 1978 both organizations had been virtually eliminated. The *Dergue's* initial and principal support came from Oromo peasantry who had benefited from the land reforms of 1975, aimed at restoring their lands from the Northerners.

The ideological and power struggles were intensified by a deteriorating military situation in Eritrea, where the guerrillas had captured all but five towns, and in the south and south-east where Somalia attempted to take advantage of the weakness of the central administration and the army. In July 1977 Somalia, claiming the Somali-inhabited area of the Ogaden, invaded to support the Western Somali Liberation Front (WSLF) guerrillas which it had been arming and training. Within five months Somali forces had overrun most of the south and south-east, and the town of Harar was under attack. However, the overstretched Somali army ran out of supplies, just as Ethiopia, with Cuban help in training a 300,000-strong militia force, received a massive influx of Soviet military equipment. Somalia, previously a close ally of the USSR, expelled its Soviet military advisers and severed relations with Cuba; Ethiopia, in turn, suspended relations with the USA. In early 1978, with its new weaponry and the help of 16,000 Cuban troops, the Ethiopian army drove out the Somali army.

The Ethiopian army then moved to Eritrea. Within a few months it had retaken most of the towns, forcing the ELF to revert to guerrilla operations, and pushing the EPLF into the far north around the remote town of Nakfa. There the Ethiopian forces lost their momentum, and over several years accumulated serious losses in a series of unsuccessful attacks including the 'Red Star' offensive, personally commanded by Mengistu. Meanwhile, continuing religious, ethnic and ideological differences among the Eritrean movements erupted into civil war in 1981; the EPLF, in alliance with the Tigrai People's Liberation Front (TPLF), forced the ELF into Sudan in 1982, where they were disarmed and later fragmented.

After the military successes of 1978, Mengistu turned his attention to organizing a political party. The Commission for Organizing the Party of the Working People of Ethiopia was established in 1979. Various revolutionary women's, youth, peasant and trade-union associations were founded, and the Workers' Party of Ethiopia was formally inaugurated in September 1984. It failed to attract either support or loyalty from the general population, which regarded it as a vehicle for the regime's control.

NATIONALITIES ISSUES AND THE OVERTHROW OF MENGISTU

The rhetoric of the revolution raised expectations among various nationalities, particularly Oromos, Somalis, Afars and Tigraians all of whom were vying for autonomy and/or independence. The Government had one partial success with the Afars when a 'progressive' Afar National Liberation Movement (ANLM) appeared, prepared to accept the PMAC's version of regional autonomy. ANLM members were appointed local administrators, but the speed of progress towards autonomy was unsatisfactory.

By the early 1980s the Oromo Liberation Front (OLF), advocating self-determination for the Oromo people and the use of Oromo culture and language, was gaining support from peasants critical of government efforts to establish co-operatives; originally, the *Dergue's* greatest support had been among Oromo peasantry who had benefited from the land reforms of 1975. Most serious for the Government was the success of the TPLF. Established in 1975, it received arms and training from the EPLF. In 1977–78 it drove out other opponents, notably the Ethiopian Democratic Union, an exile-based group which included former aristocracy, and the left-wing EPRP, which had taken up armed struggle. Relations between the TPLF and the EPLF were strained for several years in the 1980s, but after 1988, when they were once more co-operating, the TPLF was rapidly able to take over the whole of Tigrai region.

The regime's response to the growth of the nationality movements was, originally, only military. A political response was attempted following the disastrous famine of 1984–85, which had eradicated any gains made by state farms, and a heavily criticized and ill-organized resettlement programme, abandoned after two years, which had moved some 600,000 people into the south and west. The new Constitution of 1987 provided for an 835-seat elected legislature, the National Shengo, and for the creation of several autonomous regions based on ethnicity: Tigrai for the Tigraian people; Dire Dawa for Issa Somalis; the Ogaden region for other Somalis; and Assab for Afars in both Eritrea and Ethiopia. These allowed for elected assemblies with control over health, education, development, finance and taxation. In 1990, following an attempted coup the previous year, Mengistu made further concessions. Ethiopian socialism was abandoned; opposition groups were invited to participate in a unity party; free-market principles replaced economic planning; and peasants were allowed to bequeath land to their children. The peasantry were quick to abandon the highly unpopular enforced 'villagization' policy, and the area of land under cultivation increased significantly.

However, Mengistu's overtures failed to satisfy either the TPLF or the EPLF; both were determined to oust him, regarding this as a prerequisite for achievement of their respective aims. Mengistu's military situation deteriorated steadily after 1988 following a major defeat at Afabet in Eritrea, and at Shire in Tigrai the following year; Massawa was captured by the EPLF in February 1990, severing supply lines for the army in

Eritrea. Disillusionment grew steadily within the army, which previously supported Mengistu owing to his determination to keep Eritrea and his commitment to a united Ethiopia; his apparent refusal to accept any political solution was finally seen as a liability. The economy was collapsing as fast as the military and political situation. The price of coffee, Ethiopia's sole foreign-exchange earner, was falling, and supplies of cheap Soviet petroleum ceased in mid-1989. The revolution in Eastern Europe precipitated a complete collapse of Ethiopia's overseas alliances, and the loss of critical arms supplies. Mengistu attempted to replace his Soviet allies with Israel, promising to allow the Ethiopian Jews (Falashas) to leave (13,000 had been flown from Sudan to Israel in a secret airlift in 1984); Israel initially provided cluster bombs and anti-guerrilla training, but, under strong US pressure, this support was stopped. However, in May 1991 as the regime collapsed, with government consent the Israelis took control of Addis Ababa airport for 36 hours to evacuate a further 14,000 of the remaining Falasha population.

Once in control of Tigrai region in 1989, the TPLF orchestrated a united front, the Ethiopian People's Revolutionary Democratic Front (EPRDF) with the Ethiopian People's Democratic Movement, a largely Amhara organization whose development had allowed the TPLF to spread the struggle outside Tigrai region, and which was subsequently renamed the Amhara National Democratic Movement (ANDM). As the EPRDF advanced further south it supported or created other organizations: the Oromo People's Democratic Organization (OPDO), after the OLF refused to join the EPRDF, and a short-lived officers' movement. The TPLF remained the major element in the front, but its own original demands for self-determination were replaced by its commitment to the removal of Mengistu and the establishment of a democratic government in Addis Ababa.

On 21 May 1991 Mengistu fled to Zimbabwe where he was granted political asylum. The USA presided over peace talks in London, in an attempt to provide an orderly transfer of power from the Government. The government delegation did not even have time to surrender before the USA, fearing a collapse of law and order in Addis Ababa, agreed that the EPRDF should enter the city. On 28 May the EPRDF entered the capital and subsequently established an interim Government. The EPLF attended the founding conference but as an observer only, to mark Eritrea's de facto independence; it subsequently established a provisional Government in Eritrea pending the holding of a referendum in April 1993, when 99.8% of voters approved independence. *De jure* independence came in May 1993. Relations with Ethiopia were formalized by a series of agreements covering defence, security, trade and the economy, and on the use of Assab, given free port status because of its particular importance to Ethiopia, land-locked by the independence of Eritrea.

THE EPRDF AND FEDERAL POLITICS

In July 1991 the EPRDF convened a national conference attended by representatives of some 20 political organizations to discuss Ethiopia's political future and establish a transitional Government. The EPRDF drafted a national charter providing for an 87-seat Council of Representatives to govern during a two-year transition period. The EPRDF Chairman, Meles Zenawi, was elected Head of State; the Vice-Chairman of the EPRDF, Tamirat Layne, became Prime Minister. Some 32 political organizations were subsequently represented on the Council, with the EPRDF's component parts occupying 32 of the 87 seats. The next largest group on the council was the OLF with 12 seats. Oromos were allocated a total of 27 seats, but they were divided between five different organizations. The portfolios of the Council of Ministers were similarly distributed, with 17 ministers from seven different organizations being appointed.

From the outset, the EPRDF made it clear it would support Eritrean independence, and emphasized self-determination for Ethiopia's nationalities within a federal system as the answer to the political problem of a multi-ethnic state. The EPRDF originally established 12 self-governing regions with two chartered cities. After changes, including the merger of four regions in the south west, the new Constitution of 1994 created the regional states (*killil*) of Tigrai, Afar, Amhara, Oromia, Benishangul-Gumuz, Southern Peoples, Somali, Gambela, and Harari, together with Addis Ababa and the administrative area of Dire Dawa. The basis of the new states was ethnicity and language, although equally they reflected political power. Regions were expected, in theory at least, to raise their own funding, but this proved difficult; by the mid-2000s the bulk of revenue was still coming from central government sources.

In 1994 there was a significant decline in agricultural production, and the threat of large-scale famine was only averted with substantial imports. Agricultural production subsequently improved, but government claims of food self-sufficiency in 1996–97 were premature. There were significant food shortages in 1999 and 2000, when the effect of poor rainfall was intensified by the impact of the war with Eritrea (see below) on transport and production. Several years of high production saw the collapse of grain prices, precipitating a debt crisis amongst farmers, whose consumption of fertilizer dropped sharply in 2002. Inadequate and erratic rainfall followed in 2002, as a result of which an estimated 13.2m. people required 1.5m. metric tons of food aid during 2003, including increased numbers in pockets of the south of the country. Better rains and production during 2003 reduced those expected to require aid in 2004 to an estimated 7.2m. people, of whom 5m. were considered to be chronically food insecure. While good rainfall in 2004 raised crop production by an estimated 24% compared with the previous year, 387,500 tons of emergency food aid were still required, and the number of people considered to be chronically food insecure did not decrease. Particular concern continued to focus on the southern and eastern pastoralist areas of the country. None the less, successive good harvests did not reduce the need for food aid. In 2005 an estimated 9m. people required food aid; by early 2006 this figure had risen to 10m. A new Food Security Co-ordination Bureau was established in April 2004 to address chronic problems. This was supported by a Food Security Coalition of Donors and government plans to purchase surpluses at fixed prices if necessary, in order to stabilize a fragmented market, and implement a new Productive Safety Net Programme. The planned voluntary resettlement of 400,000 households (2.2m. people), which began in 2002, had relocated approximately 300,000 people to more fertile areas within Tigrai, Oromia, Amhara, and the Southern Region by June 2004. Resettlement was accompanied by an aggressive policy of water harvesting. Together with the implementation of resettlement, the distribution of resources remained a matter of controversy, and resettlement was consequently brought to a halt in 2004.

Numerous political parties emerged in the period after 1991, mostly ethnically based. However, their participation in elections was poor until the May 2005 legislative elections, which saw a significant increase in participation both by the people as well as by political parties. Notably, since 1992 the EPRDF has been victorious in all elections (regional, constituent assembly and national) and has retained power ever since the overthrow of the *Dergue* regime. As Tigraians constitute about 5% of the population, the EPRDF fostered parallel political parties such as the Southern Ethiopian People's Democratic Front (SEPDF) with which it could form alliances to manoeuvre for political control. The existence of the EPRDF's OPDO was a major reason for the breakdown in relations with the OLF, despite the OLF's position in government. In the months preceding the 1992 elections, there were numerous clashes as the two organizations manoeuvred for position in the Oromo regions. Both also sought to remove other nationalities from their areas. Just before the elections the OLF and several other groups pulled out, and the OLF also withdrew from the Government.

In 1992–2001 the EPRDF and its supporting parties did extremely well in almost every region, and even in Addis Ababa it repeatedly won the vast majority of the regional seats. In 1992 elections were briefly postponed in Afar and Somali regions, where EPRDF support was less well organized. After its withdrawal from government, the OLF attempted to revive guerrilla activity. Most of its fighters were quickly apprehended but small groups continued to operate, and the OLF claimed responsibility for several bomb explosions along the Addis Ababa–Djibouti railway in 1996. Western diplomatic efforts to reconcile the OLF and the EPRDF made little progress, and an OLF congress in April 1998 took a stronger line towards the idea of an independent Oromo state. With relations between the Popular Front for Democracy and Justice (PFDJ—formerly EPLF), the ruling regime in Asmara and the EPRDF plummeting as a consequence of the war of 1998–2000, Eritrea began supporting the Ethiopian opposition forces, notably offering the OLF an operating base in Asmara.

In 1999, with Eritrean support, the OLF infiltrated hundreds of Eritrean-trained fighters through Somalia into southern Ethiopia; most were rounded up by the end of the year. In October 2000 a conference in Eritrea, brought together six Oromo opposition parties, including the OLF and the Islamic Front for the Liberation of Oromia, as the United Liberation Forces of Oromia. In late 2004 international observers participated in a meeting of the OLF in Norway, and attempts were made to hold the 2005 OLF congress in Europe. In the event these failed, and the OLF National Congress held in Asmara, in December 2004, consolidated relations between the OLF and the Eritrean Government, removing the chance that the OLF might participate in the May 2005 Ethiopian legislative elections.

In early March 2006 four people were injured in a bomb explosion in Addis Ababa. On 27 March one person was killed and at least 15 wounded in a series of bomb attacks in the capital. Further blasts occurred in the capital, in the town of Jijiga in the east of the country and Gedo in the west, during April–May, killing 11 people. In a parliamentary address in late March Meles had accused Eritrea and the OLF of carrying out the attacks in that month and the police continued to suspect the OLF of involvement, despite a denial issued by the group in mid-May. In November 2006 the OLF indicated that it had approached Kenya, Nigeria and South Africa for help in mediating between itself and the Ethiopian Government to end decades of sporadic conflict in the remote but resource-rich Oromia region. At the same time fighting appeared to be continuing between the OLF and the Government. The Tigrai People's Democratic Movement and the Southern Ethiopian Peoples' Front for Justice and Equality also claimed to have made attacks against government forces in March 2007.

Meanwhile, in June 2005 the Government claimed to have captured the OLF military commander in ongoing operations against the organization. Continuing tension between the Somali State and Oromia regarding the allocation of up to 700 *kebeles* along the disputed border resulted in a referendum on 24 October 2004 in 440 *kebeles* where agreement could not be reached. Referendums were postponed in 22 *kebeles*, particularly around Moyale, where the registration of voters proved controversial.

Armed opposition to the Government surfaced in several other regional states, including Afar and Gambela, as well as from the externally based Ogaden National Liberation Front (ONLF), formed as a result of defection from within the WSLF in the 1980s. The OLF and the ONLF signed a military co-operation agreement in July 1996, but have made few inroads in their demands for greater autonomy and firm commitments for possible independence despite Eritrean support and training since 1998. They claim that the EPRDF had no intention of allowing secession, deliberately making the process lengthy and difficult—secession would require a two-thirds' majority in the regional legislature, a majority vote in a federally organized referendum, and an agreed transfer of power over a three-year period. The ONLF also received support from another Somali organization, the Islamic Union Party (al-Ittihad al-Islam), which has been fighting for an Islamic state in Somalia. Al-Ittihad claimed responsibility for bomb explosions in hotels in Addis Ababa and Dire Dawa in early 1996. The EPRDF responded from 1996 with a series of cross-border attacks into Somalia, aiming to disrupt al-Ittihad and its allies, occupying several towns and villages, and supplying arms to movements opposed to al-Ittihad in Somalia. These operations intensified in 1999 when Eritrea attempted to distract Ethiopia's attention from the war along the Ethio-Eritrean border by supplying weapons to the OLF and various Somali factions opposed to Ethiopia. Ethiopian troops again crossed the Somalia border in early 2001, following increased ONLF activity, and have subsequently been active in Somalia on numerous occasions, claiming legitimate security interests.

The situation in Gambela State deteriorated from late 2002, primarily as a result of the increasingly militant activities of Anywaa nationalist groups, concerned at what they saw as the growing influxes and regional influence of the Nuer. A series of inter-communal clashes between Nuer and Anuak communities broke out in Itang in July 2002 and continued into 2003, with dozens of people killed. From mid-2003 attacks on regional civil servants, particularly highlanders, escalated. Tensions between Anywaa and the highlander community culminated in the massacre of hundreds of Anywaa men in Gambella town with the alleged participation of the Ethiopian army. In December eight officials from the office of the UN High Commissioner for Refugees and the Federal Agency for Refugee and Returnee Affairs were killed whilst surveying a new site for Nuer refugees 25 km from Gambela town, apparently by Anuak militants opposed to the relocation. Angered at the killings, Gambela townspeople targeted Anuak residents, and, according to government sources, 56 were killed, 74 wounded, and 410 houses were razed to the ground, before government forces intervened. (Opposition sources stated that the actual casualty figures were much higher.) The intervention of federal security forces in pursuit of suspected militants led to 37 arrests relating to the killings in Gambela town, and an estimated 10,000 Anuak fled to Pochalla in neighbouring Sudan in early January 2004. Later that month Anuak militants killed 180 highlanders panning alluvial gold on the Baro River, and in February a highlander settlement was attacked. Intensive military and political efforts by the Federal Government appeared to have calmed, if not resolved, the situation by mid-2004, and by June 7,900 of those who had fled Ethiopia in January were reported to have returned to the region. In late 2004 a Commission of Inquiry led by the President of the Federal Supreme Court placed a proportion of blame for some of the killings in late 2003 on the collusion and inappropriate action of the military and police.

ELECTIONS AND GOVERNMENT CONTROL

Elections for a Constituent Assembly in June 1994 demonstrated that the EPRDF had become a disciplined, tightly organized and highly centralized front using government resources to great effect. The main opposition groups boycotted the elections. In December the Constituent Assembly ratified the draft Constitution (including controversial articles on the right to self-determination and secession, and state ownership of land) with little change from the approved draft, although recognition of *Shari'a* law for Muslims was included, following a major demonstration in Addis Ababa.

The final stage in the creation of the Federal Democratic Republic of Ethiopia came in May 1995 with elections to the Federal Parliamentary Assembly (the House of People's Representatives) and to the regional State Councils, which elect representatives to the upper house (the House of the Federation). Executive power lies with a Prime Minister, chosen by the majority party in the Federal Assembly. The EPRDF and its allies won an overwhelming victory, and Meles Zenawi, as Chairman of the EPRDF and of the TPLF, which remained the dominant element in the EPRDF, became Prime Minister in August 1995; Dr Negasso Gidada of the OPDO was elected President. In Tigrai region the TPLF took all seats for both the federal and state assemblies; EPRDF parties were equally successful in the Amhara, Oromia and Southern regions. Despite Addis Ababa's reputation as a centre for opposition, the EPRDF won all 92 local assembly seats; independents took only two of the city's 23 Federal Assembly seats. In Afar and Somali regions, after postponements, pro-EPRDF parties won narrow victories; in neither case did this stop guerrilla activity by opposition parties seeking greater autonomy or secession. Pro-EPRDF parties had equal problems in the remaining regions. Overall the election results were seriously undermined by the decision of most opposition parties to boycott, claiming insufficient access to media, extensive arrest and harassment of their officials and closure of party offices. International observers generally agreed with the criticisms;

there was a consensus that, whilst the elections represented an advance on past experience, they were not entirely free or fair.

A similar pattern appeared in the next national legislative elections on 14 May 2000. The EPRDF, as expected, won an overwhelming victory. Voting was postponed for several months in Somali State (owing to severe drought in the region) and was repeated in several constituencies of the Southern Nations, Nationalities and Peoples State after opposition accusations of irregularities were upheld by the National Election Board (NEB). The Ethiopian-based opposition parties claimed numerous irregularities had occurred, including physical abuse, intimidation of monitors and vote-rigging. International observers largely accepted opposition complaints and, as in 1995, classified the elections as neither free nor fair. The OPDO won the largest number of seats in the House of People's Representatives, taking 178 of 546 seats available; the ANDM won 134 seats and the TPLF 38. In elections to the House of the Federation opposition parties had some successes, although the EPRDF coalition parties won by huge margins in their respective regions. In other regional states, pro-EPRDF parties all managed to win majorities, although there were again claims of extensive voting irregularities. In February 2004 the Ethiopian Somali Democratic League won a majority of seats in local elections, which were finally held for the first time in 48 out of 51 districts of the Somali State, with the opposition Western Somali Democratic Party winning seats in several districts.

Until mid-2005 EPRDF control of the political process and of the political debate kept the opposition in disarray. The Council of Alternative Forces for Peace and Democracy in Ethiopia (CAFPDE), bringing together some 30 groups, was established in 1993, following a conference in Paris, France. The CAFPDE finally achieved official registration in July 1996, and has been a major critic of EPRDF policies on land, rents and leases, the economy and human rights. However, EPRDF pressure and its control of the media, coupled with CAFPDE's own divisions and weakness, limited its impact. An attempt to provide an alternative umbrella opposition grouping came when eight organizations met in Paris in September 1998 and formed the Coalition of Ethiopian Opposition Political Organizations (CEOPO). It included groups based both in Ethiopia and abroad, but the choice of prominent anti-EPRDF exiles for its leadership meant it did not participate in the May 2000 elections. A new coalition, the United Ethiopian Democratic Forces (UEDF), emerged in March 2003. In February 2004 senior members of the UEDF held discussions with Prime Minister Meles on a range of issues relating to the May 2005 legislative elections. They requested changes to the NEB and to the electoral law, the investigation and compensation of past abuses and access for international observers. In May 2004 they presented Meles with a detailed critique of existing 'first-past-the-post' electoral legislation, and by mid-year arrangements for observers from the AU had been agreed. By September a new party—Rainbow Ethiopia: Movement for Democracy and Social Justice—emerged, led by two prominent Ethiopian academics, Prof. Mesfin Woldemariam, a former head of the Ethiopian Human Rights Council, and Dr Berhanu Nega, a respected economist. By October Rainbow Ethiopia, together with the All Ethiopia Unity Party (AEUP, previously the All Amhara People's Organization—AAPO), the Ethiopian Democratic Unity Party (EDUP—a merger of the Ethiopian Democratic Party and the Ethiopian Democratic Union), and the Ethiopian Democratic League, had jointly formed the Coalition for Unity and Democracy (CUD).

Alliance formation was thus a notable feature of the May 2005 legislative elections at which the CUD and the UEDF competed against the EPRDF. Although it brought about a dynamic change in Ethiopia, the two opposition alliances could not reach agreement on the fundamental political issues, namely the Ethiopian state and its institutions. The UEDF, a coalition of largely ethnic-based opposition groups, supported the democratization of existing ethnic federal arrangements, whereas the CUD, a coalition of multi-ethnic composition, endorsed a reformed economic federalism, which stressed Ethiopian rather than ethno-national identity, removing the right to secession. Determined to open up the political process, the Government sanctioned the conduct of live televised debates between the EPRDF and opposition parties on all aspects of economic and social policy, and on federalism, good governance, and human rights. The CUD and the UEDF won a high degree of recognition, particularly among urban populations. International election observers appreciated the move towards a more competitive electoral process. Voter turnout (except in Somali State, where voting was scheduled for August 2005) was in excess of 90%. Although the pre-election scenario was peaceful, the aftermath of elections was highly controversial in view of the competing claims by the opposition and the ruling party on the vote counting process where 299 constituencies were disputed. The NEB issued preliminary results for 517 of the seats in which the ruling EPRDF won 302, the CUD 122, the UDEF 57 and others 13. Many of the CUD's victories were won in urban areas, with all but one of the seats in Addis Ababa's municipal assembly taken by the opposition, along with national legislative and regional council seats in almost every town across the country. Provisional results also suggested that the CUD had made significant inroads in rural areas of Amhara, winning strong support in much of Gojjam, Gondar, and Simien Shoa, as well as some parts of the south. The UEDF, meanwhile, gained strongholds in Oromia and the Southern region. EPRDF-allied organizations dominated the vote in the smaller and border regions of Gambela, Benishangul-Gumuz, Harari and Afar.

The declaration of final results, due on 8 June 2005, was consequently postponed to 8 July and both sides continued to claim victory. Political passions ran high and in early June violent clashes were reported in Addis Ababa. A city-wide taxi strike hardened on 8 June as demonstrators attempted to barricade roads in the city's commercial centre (Merkato and Piassa). Police and the military responded with force, reportedly using live ammunition to disperse crowds and some 36 people were killed with more than 100 injured. The Government accused the opposition, particularly the CUD, of inciting unrest, and thousands of CUD members were detained in centres at Zwai and Sendafa. Several opposition leaders, including the CUD leader, Hailu Shawel, were placed under house arrest and prevented from travelling overseas. On 10 June the EPRDF, CUD and UEDF signed an agreement, committing themselves to accepting the outcome of an NEB complaints review procedure. The international donor community exerted pressure on all sides to resolve the electoral process peacefully.

Final results, including those from 31 constituencies where voting had been reheld and the 15 August 2005 elections in the Somali region, were declared on 5 September by the NEB, according to which the EPRDF won 327 seats (67.8% of the votes), while the combined opposition took 172 seats (the CUD 109, the UEDF 52 and the Oromo Federalist Democratic Movement 11); this represented an increase of 160 seats compared with the 2000 elections. The CUD, however, refused to accept the final results and in early October 100 CUD deputies boycotted the opening of Parliament and have since refused to take up their seats.

In mid-October 2005 Meles effected a reorganization of the Council of Ministers, replacing 11 ministers. He retained his Deputy Prime Minister and Minister of Agriculture and Rural Development, Addiso Leggese, and the key posts of Minister of Foreign Affairs and Minister of Finance and Economic Development remained unchanged. The revised Council included seven ministers from Amhara, five from Oromia and three from Tigrai (including Prime Minister Meles). Later that month 34 CUD members were arrested in Oromia, allegedly having been discovered by police in possession of firearms and ammunition. During 1–4 November protests against the results of the May elections erupted into violent clashes between protesters and the security forces. At least 46 people were reported to have been killed and hundreds injured. The 15 members of the CUD's central committee, including Shawel, were among around 3,000 people arrested following the disturbances. In mid-December they, along with 114 others, were charged with treason and attempted genocide, a move condemned by the USA, the European Union (EU) and international human rights organizations. Criminal proceedings against the accused, 35 of whom were to be tried *in absentia*, commenced on 23 February 2006. In March charges against 18 of those accused were withdrawn. In June 2007 the Federal High Court convicted 38 people, among them senior leaders of the CUD, of violating the Constitution. However, in mid-July all 38 were pardoned and freed from prison just days after being given life sentences over the election protests. Meanwhile, an independent commission of inquiry was established by the legislature in April 2006 to investigate the incidents. It reported that the security forces did not use excessive force when they killed 193 demonstrators in 2005 (more than the 78 reported by the police), but defecting commissioners alleged that their more critical findings had been altered by the Government.

HUMAN RIGHTS

Human rights continue to be a contentious issue, with international and local human rights organizations making serious criticisms, many of which were loudly renewed in the wake of the Addis Ababa killings of 8 June 2005 (see above). Since 1992 reports by the Ethiopian Human Rights Council have detailed alleged extrajudicial killings, disappearances and numerous cases of arbitrary arrest and imprisonment. Amnesty International and Human Rights Watch have condemned detentions without trial, disappearances and the increasing use of torture. In its 2007 annual report Amnesty International referred to many human rights violations, including torture, rape and extrajudicial killing, to several thousand people held in long-term detention without charge or trial and to harsh prison conditions. Journalists were among those arrested in November 2005 and all private newspapers which had criticized the Government in connection with the elections were suspended from operating, according to Amnesty International.

The majority of the 20,000 Oromos detained in 1992 on suspicion of guerrilla activity were released by late 1994, and detention camps closed. About 100 remained in detention and were brought to trial in 1995; in February 2002 two were sentenced to death and others given prison sentences. Most of those detained after the demonstrations in March and April 2002 in Oromia State were released in mid-year, but some continued to be held without charge or trial, apparently accused of links with the OLF. More than 20 people were arrested after the OLF bombing of a railway office in Dire Dawa in June 2002. In March 2005 Human Rights Watch issued a report detailing alleged harassment and detentions in Oromia, in the run-up to the national elections. According to Amnesty International, hundreds of people detained in November 2005 were still incarcerated during 2006 without trial or charge, together with others accused of OLF membership. In addition, in Gambela region, members of the Anuak ethnic group were arrested in the aftermath of the mass killings in Gambela town in 2003 and detained without charge or trial. There were also reports of torture of political prisoners suspected of supporting armed groups such as the OLF and the ONLF.

In the wake of the Ethiopian offensive in Somalia in 2006 international human-rights groups pressed the Ethiopian Government to release details of detainees from 19 countries held at secret prisons, where US agents allegedly carried out interrogations in the search for al-Qa'ida operatives. In April 2007 the ONLF killed 65 Ethiopians and nine Chinese citizens in an attack on a petroleum exploration field run by a Chinese company. It accused the Ethiopian army of moving nomads away from their grazing lands in order to prospect for oil. The Ethiopian Government suspected Eritrea of supporting the ONLF attack. Shortly afterwards another attack attributed to the ONLF occurred in Jijiga, which killed several people and injured the President of the Ogaden region and leader of Somali People's Democratic Party Abdullahi Hassan. Sources say the region is now subject to a crackdown by government soldiers who are targeting ONLF fighters. In late July the International Committee of the Red Cross was ordered to leave the Ogaden region by the Ethiopian Government, who accused the humanitarian organization of 'collaborating with the enemy'. The ONLF alleged that the Government was imposing a food blockade on the region.

In mid-March 2002 violence erupted in the Southern Nations, Nationalities and Peoples State between rival ethnic groups and the security forces. According to official figures, 128 people were killed in the disturbances at Tepi; according to Amnesty International up to 200 demonstrators, protesting against administrative changes, were shot dead by police. Opposition sources initially claimed that as many as 1,000 were killed. The EU subsequently demanded a 'transparent, public and open' inquiry into the incidents and expressed its concern that a large number of those believed to have been killed were the victims of 'revenge attacks' by local police-officers. In August some 90 state employees, including 41 police-officers, were arrested for their roles in the violence and charged with human rights violations, instigation of violence and abuse of office. Meanwhile, in May, in Awassa, the capital of Sidama zone, hundreds of protesters were arrested after another demonstration over planned administrative changes was forcibly dispersed, with as many as 35 people killed by the police. Following international disquiet, the Southern regional Government established an inquiry, which resulted in extensive changes and a planned restructuring of the regional police. Dozens of officials and members of the police force were dismissed or detained, although none faced trial. During 2004 human rights concerns focused on events in Gambela (see above).

The continued delays over the trials of senior officials of the former regime have raised comment, although few disagreed with the decision to charge them with crimes against humanity. In February 1994 Ethiopia requested the extradition of Mengistu, but the Zimbabwean Government consistently refused to grant this, and in March 2001 granted him permanent residence; in November 1999 South Africa refused an extradition request while Mengistu was receiving medical treatment on its territory. The trial of 69 former senior officials (23 *in absentia*, including Mengistu) on charges of crimes against humanity and war crimes began in December 1994, although proceedings have been adjourned on numerous occasions. The prosecution finally concluded its case in November 2001, having called a total of 725 witnesses, and the defence commenced its case a year later. The trial concluded in December 2006 with the conviction of more than 50 individuals, including Mengistu who continued to be protected from extradition by the Zimbabwean Government.

In February 1997 the special prosecutor's office announced that it was to try a further 5,198 people on charges of genocide and war crimes, nearly 3,000 of them *in absentia*. These trials proceeded more quickly, with some 60% of the accused having been sentenced to up to 20 years' 'rigorous imprisonment' by mid-2003. A number of sentences, including five death penalties, were handed down in late 2003. The 1995 Constitution provided for the establishment of a human rights commission and the post of ombudsman. Legislation approving both bodies was finally passed in 2000, and a Human Rights Commissioner and Ombudsman were appointed in late 2004.

EPRDF DIVISIONS AND DOMESTIC POLITICAL ISSUES

In March 2001 major divisions emerged within the TPLF central committee and among senior members and politburo members of the EPDRF, of which the TPLF was the leading party. In part a power struggle, the arguments also reflected major ideological shifts. After the signing of a peace agreement with Eritrea in December 2000 (see below), the EPRDF commenced a comprehensive audit of its 10 years in power, preceded by a similar evaluation in its component parties. The extensive self-awareness (*gimgema*) sessions within the TPLF's central committee, prior to a planned congress later in 2001, led to detailed criticisms of government policies. Critics, who included several of the leading ideologues in the TPLF, argued that the Government had subverted the Tigraian revolution, abandoning its Marxist principles, shifting from democratic centralism to bourgeois democracy, and accused Meles of 'selling out to capitalism and western powers'. Furthermore, Meles was criticized over political liberalization, devolution and federalism. The disagreements were fierce, and Meles survived a motion of 'no confidence' in March by a slender majority of five votes, although two of his critics subsequently recanted and pledged their support for him. His opponents, who included Siye Abraha, a former Minister of Defence, and Gebru Asrat, President of Tigrai Regional State, were ousted from the TPLF central committee, as well as from their official government positions. The Government subsequently used claims of corruption to take action against Siye, as well as members of his family, and other dissident government officials and business executives, many of whom remained in detention in mid-2005. Dozens of officials from the Commercial Bank of Ethiopia and the sugar industry were also detained, although a few were released without charge in May 2005, and several changes were made to the board of the Endowment Fund for the Rehabilitation of Tigrai, a consortium of TPLF-controlled private-sector enterprises, previously chaired by Siye. The issue of corruption had initially been raised in September 2000 in President Gidada's New Year message, and a central anti-corruption office was established in November of that year as part of the civil service reform programme.

The extent of corruption began to cause concern in 1996 when the then Deputy Prime Minister and Minister of Defence, Tamirat Layne, was dismissed and detained; he was finally sentenced to 18 years' imprisonment in 2000. Hundreds of officials in different *killil* have been removed since 1996, following *gimgema* sessions. During 2001 Meles called on the other parties in the EPRDF—the ANDM, the OPDO and the SEPDF—for support. The OPDO and the SEPDF leaderships proved lukewarm, and later in the year both Kumsa Demksa, President of Oromia State and Secretary-General of the OPDO, and Abate Kisho, President of the Southern Nations, Nationalities and Peoples State, were removed from their posts after *gimgema* sessions, although the former was later rehabilitated. In October 2002 the administration of Addis Ababa was dissolved, and Prime Minister Meles appointed a new temporary administration pending new elections, due in 2005. Chairman Arkebe Oqubay Mitiku's energetic administration rapidly gained a degree of popularity in the capital, following swift moves to clean up and speed up service provision, reform the structures of local municipal government and improve the appearance of the city. Voters were less enthusiastic about the demolition of large areas of the city and the imposition of a raft of new taxes and municipal charges. The detention of the CUD leadership (see above) prevented the party from gaining control of the Addis Ababa municipal assembly, despite having won 22 of the 23 seats available in the May 2005 elections. In early May 2006 assembly members approved the nomination by Meles of an interim Chairman, Berhanu Deressa, and a nine-member Cabinet to administer the city for one year. In late May 2006, following a conference in Utrecht, Netherlands, several opposition parties and armed rebel groups announced the formation of a new coalition opposed to the ruling EPRDF. The Alliance for Freedom and Democracy (AFD) brought together the CUD, the OLF, the ONLF and the Ethiopian People's Patriotic Front (EPPF—a rebel group active in north-west Ethiopia) and has considerably reduced the nationalist and unitary constituency of these parties. This has led to divisions within the CUD, which split into a number of factions.

One of those dismissed from the OPDO was President Gidada, who was also expelled from the EPRDF, although he was allowed to complete his term of office. He was succeeded as President in October 2001 by Lt Girma Wolde Giorgis, a former President of the Parliament during the reign of Haile Selassie and a member of the House of Representatives since 1995. Prior to the expiry of his presidential term, Gidada accused the Government of embarking on a campaign of propaganda against him and complained of pressure from Meles. The OPDO lost 22 of the 27 members of its central committee, and several defected to the OLF. Among them was Yonatan Dibissa, the Oromia State Minister for Justice, and Almaz Meko, the Speaker of the House of the Federation, who was replaced in early 2004 by Mulatu Teshome, also an Oromo. The Minister of Defence, Gen. Abadula Gameda, was appointed Chairman of the OPDO, but difficulties persisted. After the student disturbances in Oromia State in March and April 2002 (see above), a considerable number of OPDO officials were detained and accused of links with the OLF.

The creation of a number of super-ministries in 2001 to co-ordinate policy in rural development, capacity building, infrastructural development, trade and industry, and federal affairs was expected to assist with the implementation of 'free markets', 'revolutionary democracy' and 'renewal' policies and form a central part of the Government's principal policy objectives of poverty reduction and securing the support of international donors. Great emphasis was placed on capacity building, with World Bank and donor funding for a US $200m. programme for public-sector capacity building over five years due to commence in July 2004 in the areas of civil service, local government, tax, information technology, justice and municipal reform. The newly created Ministries of Federal Affairs and Capacity Building were to implement these reforms, with the former providing support particularly to the weaker peripheral 'emergent' regional states. Another planned aspect of the reforms was a reorganization of the EPRDF, in order to establish it as a national party, rather than a regional front, with the aim of converting the ethnically based TPLF, ANDM, OPDO and SEPDF parties into regional branches of a central EPRDF, although no substantive progress has been made with this issue. The informal influence of the political party *vis-à-vis* a bureaucratized and professionalized state sector, however, seemed to have declined markedly, with the bureau of capacity building taking over responsibilities for popular mobilization, both political and developmental. Commentators have suggested that the decline of the influence of the party correlated with the fall of EPRDF electoral support in 2005.

EXTERNAL AFFAIRS

Internationally, the EPRDF continued to maintain good relations with the USA and with European powers, despite difficulties associated in recent years with the Ethiopia-Eritrea Boundary Commission and the 2005 elections. The 'Paris Club' of official creditors and international agencies have provided generous amounts of loans and grants, although the IMF, concerned about delays in liberalizing trade, interest and exchange rates, suspended a structural adjustment facility in October 1997 for one year. There was concern over expenditure on the war with Eritrea and over the possible diversion of resources; at least US $1,000m. of aid was suspended during the conflict. Shortly after the signing of a peace treaty in December 2000 to bring a formal end to the war the World Bank resumed aid, and in November 2001 Ethiopia qualified for debt relief under the initiative for heavily indebted poor countries (HIPC). In mid-June 2005 the British Government suspended £20m. in direct budget support to the Ethiopian Government, in the wake of the killings earlier that month. In January 2006, during a visit to Ethiopia, the British Secretary of State for International Development, Hilary Benn, announced the suspension of a further £30m. in direct budget support, citing concerns over the detention and trial of opposition leaders, journalists and civil society activists on charges related to the Addis Ababa protests in late 2005 (see above). It was announced in July 2006 that the USA was to double its diplomatic representation in Ethiopia by opening an additional embassy that will be responsible for relations with the AU. The US Agency for International Development also signed deals with the Government worth several million US dollars. During a visit to Ethiopia in July 2006 the World Bank President, Paul Wolfowitz, described the Bank's resumption of aid to Ethiopia as a sign of improved confidence in the country. The World Bank recently resumed work in Ethiopia with the approval of the Protection of Basic Services (PBS) project, which provides water, health and education. In the wake of EU disquiet over the controversy surrounding the findings of the independent commission on the 2005 post-election violence (see above), in October 2006 EU officials condemned a decision by Ethiopia to expel two EU diplomats, accused of trying to smuggle criminals into Kenya, and demanded an explanation from the Ethiopian ambassador. In March 2007 Russia announced that it would cancel the remaining $160m. debt owed to it by Ethiopia.

Relations with Sudan deteriorated sharply in 1995, following apparent Sudanese complicity in the attempted assassination of President Mubarak of Egypt in Addis Ababa in June. Ethiopia, together with Uganda and Eritrea, and with US support, backed Sudanese opposition forces, providing arms, training and, in 1996, artillery support. Relations have steadily improved since 1998, following Ethiopia's conflict with Eritrea; Eritrea has been supporting Sudanese opposition movements since 1994. A series of development and security agreements between Sudan and Ethiopia were signed prior to the signing of the 2005 Comprehensive Peace Agreement that ended Sudan's civil war after more than 21 years, although implementation of these has been slow; road links have been upgraded to allow Ethiopian use of Port Sudan and Ethiopia has become a substantial purchaser of Sudanese petroleum, easing pressure on the port of Djibouti.

Regionally, Ethiopia has adopted an assertive role, heading OAU efforts to foster a peace settlement in Somalia; it hosted reconciliation conferences in Addis Ababa in 1993 and at Sodere in January 1997, where 26 Somali factions agreed on a process to establish a transitional government. No further progress was made, however, and Ethiopia ascribed the failure in part to Egypt's subsequent Cairo conference of Somali factions. In turn, Egypt considers Ethiopian plans to construct dams on the Blue Nile as a serious threat to its water supplies. In November 1999 Ethiopia, Egypt and Sudan signed an agreement for strategic co-operation on the Nile, and a World Bank donor group, the International Consortium for Co-operation on the Nile, has been established; recent Nile conferences have been amiable but tensions remain between Ethiopia and Egypt over the future use of the river, and Ethiopian rhetoric became more aggressive in early 2005.

Ethiopia has supported efforts to give the Djibouti-based Intergovernmental Authority on Development (IGAD), which includes Djibouti, Eritrea, Ethiopia, Kenya, Sudan and Uganda, a more active political and security role regionally, including mediation in the conflicts in Somalia and Sudan. IGAD's effectiveness has been severely limited, however, by its internal relationships, particularly the poor relations of Eritrea with Ethiopia and Sudan. In 1994 Ethiopia provided a battalion of troops for UN peace-keeping operations in Rwanda and sent a battalion to Burundi in mid-2003. Meles has supported US proposals for an AU peace-keeping force, and backed both the US-led 'war on terrorism' and the war against Iraq. Meles also made a successful visit to the United Kingdom in February 2003, and was appointed a senior member of the British Prime Minister's Commission for Africa. Meles was OAU Chairman in 1995–96 and Ethiopia's House of People's Representatives was supportive of the idea for the creation of the AU to replace the OAU. Addis Ababa, previously the headquarters of the OAU, has continued in the same role for the AU, with an opening summit in 2003 followed by a meeting in July 2004 attended by the UN Secretary-General, Kofi Annan. African embassies and the AU have been allocated extensive additional plots for construction in the city. Ethiopia has established close relations with Israel, formed closer links with Saudi Arabia, and signed a security agreement with Yemen in October 1999. In April 2007 IGAD was accused of supporting Ethiopia's intervention in Somalia which led to Eritrea's withdrawal from its membership. Earlier, Eritrea along with Djibouti refused to send their delegates to the IGAD's emergency summit held in September 2006.

Relations with Djibouti appeared to be consolidated when Djibouti replaced Assab as Ethiopia's main outlet to the sea, and with the election of Ethiopian-born Ismail Omar Gelleh as Djibouti's new President in May 1999. However, relations deteriorated after the Dubai Port Authority (now Dubai Ports World—DP World) took over the management of Djibouti port in 2000. This increased capacity, but attempts to raise tariffs resulted in disagreements between the two countries. Furthermore, Ethiopia became concerned by Djibouti's improved relations with Eritrea in 2000.

Further differences arose over Djibouti's organization of a Somali national reconciliation conference at Arta, Djibouti, in 2000, which led to the establishment of a Somali Transitional National Assembly (TNA) and a Transitional National Government (TNG). Ethiopia was unimpressed by the election of a President unwilling to engage with the self-proclaimed 'Republic of Somaliland', with which Ethiopia has close relations. The TNA made little effort to reach accommodation with the political elements excluded from the Djibouti conference, including 'Puntland'. With Ethiopian support, these elements subsequently established the Somali Reconciliation and Restoration Council (SRRC), which aimed to overthrow the TNG. While Ethiopia accepted the idea of a single Somali state excluding 'Somaliland', it wished for an alternative to the TNG and remained concerned by Islamic support for the Somali President, Abdulkassim Salad Hasan, the upsurge of guerrilla activity by the ONLF in Ethiopia's Somali Regional State in 2002, and by Eritrea's decision to recognize the TNG and provide it with arms in early 2002. Ethiopia backed IGAD proposals for another reconciliation conference, which finally opened at Eldoret, Kenya, in October 2002.

Relations with Kenya have remained cordial, with Ethiopia exploring the possibility of using Mombasa as a port; however, OLF activity along the border led to a number of cross-border operations and to several clashes between Ethiopian militia and Kenyan security forces in 2000 and 2001. Significant numbers of OLF fighters were reported to have been detained by Kenya in June 2004, with Ethiopian incursions into Northern Kenya drawing protests in early 2005. In mid-2006 at least 50 people were reported to have been killed on both sides of the border in renewed clashes between the Ethiopian Borena and Kenyan Gabra pastoralist tribes, exacerbated by prolonged drought in the region and the resulting decimation of livestock.

CONFLICT WITH SOMALIA

Ethiopia strongly supported the election of Col Abdullahi Yussuf Ahmed as Somali President in January 2005. As President of the autonomous region of 'Puntland', Yussuf had previously enjoyed Ethiopian support in his attempts to defeat armed Islamist militias operating in the region. The new Transitional Federal Government (TFG—the successor to the TNG) was relocated to Somalia from Kenya in mid-2005 but failed to gain a strong foothold outside of the towns of Baidoa and Jowhar. In March Meles joined with other IGAD leaders in an offer to send peace-keeping troops to Somalia; Meles' intervention was vehemently opposed by a large section of the Somali population, particularly in the capital, Mogadishu, where demonstrators burned Ethiopian flags in protest at the proposed deployment of Ethiopian troops in the country. The Ethiopian authorities grew increasingly concerned for the TFG's future in 2006. In January fighting erupted in Mogadishu between the Union of Islamic Courts (UIC) militia, accused by Ethiopia of having links with the al-Qa'ida (Base) organization of Saudi-born Islamist Osama bin Laden, and an alliance of former militia leaders and TFG ministers. The UIC subsequently gained control of the capital and much of southern Somalia and was thought to be planning an assault on Baidoa. Meles warned in late June that the Islamists threatened to destabilize the whole region, and stated that Ethiopia was prepared to use force to defend itself against any perceived threat. It has been reported that Ethiopian forces were operating, albeit discreetly, in the area. The claim of the UIC over the Ogaden, its support for the ONLF, the possible spread of radical Islam throughout Ethiopia's large Muslim population and access to the sea are the reasons for Ethiopia's strong opposition to the UIC coming to power in Somalia. Meles issued strong support for Yussuf, who had earlier called upon Ethiopia to provide troops to defend the TFG from the Islamists' advance. In early July reports suggested that around 500 Ethiopian troops and armoured vehicles had been deployed in Baidoa and a neighbouring town. Ethiopia, however, denied that any of its troops had entered Somalia, whilst reiterating its support for the TFG. Tensions increased later that month when the Somali Supreme Islamic Courts Council (SSICC, as the UIC had been restyled in June) leader, Sheikh Hassan Dahir Aweys, threatened to declare a *jihad* (holy war) to remove Ethiopian troops from Somali territory. In late July the UN Secretary-General's Special Representative for Somalia, François Lonseny Fall, urged Ethiopia and Eritrea, which had been suspected of arming the SSICC, not to intervene, amid fears that the two countries could begin a 'war-by-proxy' in Somalia.

The SSICC's success in capturing the port city of Kismayo and other areas surrounding Mogadishu in September 2006 further raised fears that Ethiopia would intervene directly to support the TFG. This external conflict helped to bolster government relations with Ethiopian opposition forces and the Government's actions enticed support from the Ethiopian diaspora. When the Government sought parliamentary approval for military intervention in Somalia on 30 November, the opposition vote was split with parties such as the UEDF and the Temesghen Zewdie faction of the CUD objecting to intervention, while Ayele Chamiso's faction of the CUD and the UEDP–Medhin group endorsed it. Further inflaming the situation were reports that in March Eritrea had supplied the UIC with arms. The defection of some prominent members of the TFG to Eritrea has reinforced the perception that Eritrea is waging a 'war-by-proxy' against Ethiopia. The defeat of SSICC militias with the help of Ethiopian forces in December has brought a semblance of peace that has yet to be consolidated and periodic clashes have occurred since January 2007. The US training of Ethiopian troops is seen as a tacit US support for Ethiopian intervention in Somalia. Facing economic constraints, there are now increasing internal pressures for Ethiopia to withdraw from Somalia. At the same time the USA and the AU have warned Ethiopia not to withdraw its troops before peace-keepers are deployed to replace them. However, the replacement of Ethiopian troops by an AU mission continued to be delayed by disagreements between AU and IGAD members over the issues of funding, logistics, and the duration of the force's mandate.

Conflict with Eritrea

Political and economic policies since May 1998 have been influenced, and occasionally dominated, by the war with Eritrea and its consequences. Relations were cordial until 1997, with Eritrean independence generally, if sometimes reluctantly, accepted in Ethiopia, and the abrupt expulsion of 150,000 Ethiopian soldiers and civilians from Eritrea in 1991–92 had largely been ignored by the Ethiopian Government. Eritrea was offended by Ethiopia's reaction to its new currency, the nakfa, introduced in 1997, by Ethiopia's subsequent insistence on using 'hard' currencies in all transactions, and by its unilateral improvement in relations with Sudan. Despite close links between Prime Minister Meles and President Issaias Afewerki of Eritrea, a minor border dispute in May 1998 escalated. Following the death of several Eritrean troops at Badme, Eritrea dispatched substantial reinforcements, taking over three areas previously under Ethiopian administration, and advancing into Ethiopia. When Eritrea refused to withdraw its forces, Ethiopia promptly declared war. The resulting conflict was calamitous for both countries with estimates of 70,000–100,000 killed and countless more wounded and displaced. The war lasted for nearly two years before Ethiopian forces gained the upper hand with significant inroads into Eritrean territory. After OAU-sponsored talks in Algiers, Algeria, collapsed in April 2000, Ethiopia launched a short, but highly successful, offensive in May–June. Despite the UN Security Council's imposition of a 12-month arms embargo on both countries, Ethiopian forces won a series of victories, breaking the Eritrean defences, rapidly capturing a number of towns, and threatening an advance on Asmara. On 25 May the Eritrean Government announced that it would withdraw its troops from all disputed areas. A cessation of hostilities was agreed in Algiers on 18 June. The terms were largely favourable to Ethiopia and included a return to the pre-May 1998 border positions, the establishment of a 25-km wide demilitarized security zone inside the Eritrean frontier, the deployment of a UN peace-keeping force and the future demarcation of the border. A formal peace agreement, signed in Algiers on 12 December 2000, provided for a permanent cessation of all hostilities, the return of all prisoners of war, the demarcation of the common border by an independent commission, and the establishment of a commission to assess compensation claims. Both countries also pledged to co-operate with an independent investigation into the origins of the conflict.

In September 2000 the UN Security Council approved the deployment of a 4,200-strong UN Mission in Ethiopia and Eritrea (UNMEE), to police the Temporary Security Zone (TSZ); in April 2001 UNMEE announced that both Eritrea and Ethiopia had withdrawn all forces from the TSZ. The Claims Commission held its first meeting in May 2001, and a total of 40 claims have been filed covering the conduct of military operations, the treatment of POWs and of civilians and their property, and the economic impact of government actions. The Claims Commission completed the majority of its work by the end of 2004, and a series of rulings were handed down at the end of April 2005. In December 2005 the Claims Commission ruled that Eritrea was 'liable to compensate Ethiopia' for an attack in May 1998. The Boundary Commission held its first meeting in May 2001, and issued its decisions on delineation in April 2002. Both Ethiopia and Eritrea committed themselves to accepting these in advance, agreeing that they should be 'final and binding' and that there should be no appeal procedure. The Boundary Commission accepted the 1908 boundary line in the region of Badme, but did not identify on which side of the line the village lay, stating that it awaited delineation on the ground. This allowed both sides to claim victory, although it soon emerged that the Boundary Commission had placed Badme on the Eritrean side of the border. While Eritrea quickly accepted the Boundary Commission's decisions, Ethiopia's concerns grew.

In September 2003 Meles wrote to Annan formally rejecting significant parts of the decision of the Boundary Commission, which he described as 'illegal', while insisting on Ethiopia's commitment to the framework of the peace agreement. Physical delineation of the border, which had been due to start in November 2003 in the relatively uncontroversial eastern sector, was postponed indefinitely, and UNMEE's mandate was extended for a further six months, to September 2004. The UN Secretary-General's envoy, Lloyd Axworthy, held talks in Addis Ababa in February 2004, although the Eritrean authorities refused to meet him. While there had been few violent incidents on the border, the situation was considered increasingly fragile. Tension along the border escalated significantly towards the end of 2004, and by November Ethiopia was taking steps to protect its northern airspace against Eritrean aggression. On 25 November Prime Minister Meles unexpectedly announced to Parliament a five-point plan, pledging that his Government would accept the Boundary Commission's ruling 'in principle'; conduct dialogue on its implementation; would normalize relations between the two countries; would pay Ethiopian dues to the Commission; and would resolve the dispute only by peaceful means. These overtures were abruptly rejected by Eritrea, and also drew widespread domestic criticism of what some interpreted as capitulation in agreeing to the demarcation.

Tensions along the disputed border escalated in early 2005. In February significant new troop deployments by Ethiopia and Eritrea in the border area were criticized by the international community and raised fears of renewed conflict. The UN Security Council extended UNMEE's mandate by six months in March, and again in September. In October Meles affirmed that Ethiopia was willing to accept the Boundary Commission's ruling 'in principle' and urged Eritrea to participate in talks regarding the delineation process. However, the Eritrean Government immediately rejected any further talks. The following month the Security Council approved Resolution 1640, which demanded that Ethiopia accept the Boundary Commission's ruling, and that troops be withdrawn from both sides of the border, threatening the imposition of economic sanctions should both countries refuse to comply. Ethiopian troops entered the TSZ, thus breaching the terms of the Algiers peace agreement, for a period of five days later in November. In December Minister of Foreign Affairs Seyoum Mesfin announced that an unspecified number of troops would be redeployed away from the border area in a gesture of goodwill aimed at restarting negotiations with Eritrea. Later that month UNMEE staff were relocated to Ethiopia following the expulsion by the Eritrean Government of all UNMEE personnel from the USA, Canada, Russia and EU member states. Although the move was initially described as temporary, Eritrea continued to impose restrictions upon UNMEE activities, and by mid-2006 UNMEE staff remained in Ethiopia.

On May 31 2006 the UN Security Council adopted Resolution 1681, which reduced the size of UNMEE's peace-keeping force by 1,000 to 2,300, citing the impasse in the delineation process and intransigence on the part of both countries. In mid-June an Ethiopian spokesman accused Eritrea of obstructing the path to peace and of seeking to destabilize the region after its refusal to attend a meeting of the Boundary Commission led to its cancellation. Later that month the Ethiopian authorities announced that the army had killed some 111 insurgents, whom it alleged had entered the country from Eritrea 'in a bid to realize the Eritrean Government's objectives'. A further 86 rebels were reportedly captured and 18 injured in the operation. Meles later reiterated the view that Eritrea was a destabilizing force in the region, and accused it of providing arms and logistical support to an Islamist militia which had taken control of much of southern Somalia (see Recent History of Somalia), in an attempt to foment unrest on Ethiopia's southern border and to widen the border conflict.

In September 2006, expressing deep concern about the 'untenable' stalemate in the peace process between Ethiopia and Eritrea, UN Secretary-General Kofi Annan called on the Security Council to extend the mandate of the UN monitoring mission until January 2007, warning of the potential for disaster in the Horn of Africa if the situation was not resolved. Subsequently, the Security Council extended the peace-keepers' mandate by four months, but threatened to overhaul the mission if Ethiopia and Eritrea did not make progress toward demarcating their border. Both countries continued to express claims and counter-accusations throughout the remainder of 2006 and into 2007, which the Somali conflict only exacerbated. Accusing the UN and USA of being pro-Ethiopian, Eritrea demanded that Ethiopia abide by the Boundary Commission ruling and demarcate the border, while Ethiopia for its part continued to insist on some degree of negotiation to complement the implementation of the border ruling. Ethiopia also demanded that Eritrean troops withdraw from the TSZ. Eritrea's move was interpreted by the US and the Ethiopian Governments as part of a regional strategy to place military pressure on Ethiopia. The UN reported that Eritrea had sent weapons to the SSICC in order to keep Ethiopian troops engaged in the north so that they could not move into Somalia. In November 2006 the Boundary Commission announced that it would demarcate the Ethiopian–Eritrean border on maps and leave the rival nations to establish the physical boundary themselves; both Ethiopia and Eritrea rejected this plan. The two nations subsequently boycotted a meeting of the Boundary Commission in The Hague, Netherlands. Eritrea accepted the panel's ruling, which awarded it Badme, but wanted it to be physically enforced on the ground, while Ethiopia, which rejected the boundary, said the Commission was acting outside its mandate. In the wake of the boycott by both countries, the Boundary Commission announced that it would give both parties one year to demarcate their border. As a result of obstruction of its work on the ground, the Commission stated it had used modern techniques, including high resolution aerial photography, to identify points where pillars should be placed to mark the boundary in the disputed areas and that it was now the responsibility of both countries to finish marking the boundary themselves. If they failed to do so by the end of November 2007, the boundary would stand as demarcated by the points the Boundary Commission had identified.

In January 2007, under the new Secretary-General, Ban Ki-Moon, the UN Security Council extended the UNMEE Mission until 31 July 2007 and reduced the UN peace-keeping force in Ethiopia and Eritrea from 2,300 to 1,700. The Council reiterated its demand that Ethiopia accept fully and without delay the final and binding decision of the Boundary Commission, and take immediate steps to enable, without preconditions, the complete demarcation of the border between the two countries. It demanded that Eritrea withdraw its troops and equipment from the TSZ, and reiterated its demand that it reverse all restrictions on UNMEE's movement and operations, including those of the Secretary-General's acting Special Representative, and provide the Mission with the access, assistance, support and protection required for the performance of its duties. In June there were press reports that the Ethiopian Government had given its unconditional acceptance of the Boundary Commission decision. Eritrea dismissed Ethiopia's announcement that it had accepted the border ruling, stating that Ethiopia attached conditions that undermined the spirit of the decision. Shortly thereafter Meles stated that the Government was strengthening the Ethiopian army to defend against an attack by Eritrea.

Economy

DAVID STYAN

With subsequent revisions by SARAH VAUGHAN

Revised for this edition by GREG CAMERON and MANICKAM VENKATARAMAN

With a population of 77.1m. in mid-2007 (although estimates do vary) Ethiopia is Africa's second most populous country, after Nigeria. It has the ninth largest land area on the continent, and has abundant agricultural, mineral and hydrological resources. Despite this, most Ethiopians face acute rural impoverishment, their livelihoods critically dependent upon unstable, rain-fed agriculture. Ethiopians live some of the hardest, shortest lives in the world, with some of the lowest consumption levels per head and among the highest incidences of malnutrition and infant mortality. Although more than 32m. Ethiopians are under 16 years of age, poverty and minimal infrastructure mean access to health and education services is chronically low. The lowest road-density in Africa exacerbates the isolation and vulnerability of many rural communities, particularly in years of drought. The share of the rural population within 2 km of an all-season road is just under 20% and people live predominantly in rural areas. According to the National Office of Population estimates, in 2005 61.4m. people lived in rural areas while 11.7m. lived in urban areas. Estimated gross national income (GNI) per head in 2005 of US $160 per head is less than one-quarter of the average for sub-Saharan Africa and it appeared unlikely that the UN's Millennium Development Goals (MDGs) would be met in the area of extreme poverty reduction.

Economic reforms since 1991 have brought significant improvements in both economic policy and performance, but they have so far failed to produce sustained economic growth and poverty reduction. While the number of people living under the poverty line outside the cities has remained stable—at around 45% of the rural population—government statistics indicate that poverty rates in the expanding urban population rose from 33% in 1996 to 37% in 2000. Reforms remain overshadowed by the legacy of decades of stagnation and daunting structural weaknesses. In 1998–2000 economic prospects were undermined by an internecine war with Eritrea. In the early 2000s deep divisions within the ruling party and the army further compromised both the coherence of policy-making and economic prospects. By 2002, however, the new constellation had settled into place, and new strategies for public-sector capacity building and urban, rural, and pastoral development, begun in 2004, started to come to fruition in 2005. Changes to policy-making and administration in Addis Ababa, however, were unable to deliver economic benefits or to secure electoral support for the Government: urban populations across the country voted heavily against the ruling Ethiopian People's Revolutionary Democratic Front (EPRDF) in the May 2005 legislative elections.

ECONOMIC STRUCTURES

Ethiopians' individual livelihoods and aggregate economic well-being depend almost entirely upon agriculture. National accounts, the accuracy of which, as with most official Ethiopian data, should be treated with considerable caution, suggest that in the financial year ending July 2005 over 48% of gross domestic product (GDP) stemmed from agriculture. With the lowest level of urbanization in Africa, it was estimated that 80.2% of the economically active population was employed in the agricultural sector in 2005. Until recent years, coffee alone accounted for more than one-half of export earnings; its share fell to only 34% during 2002/03, reflecting the collapse of world prices, although it rose to 37% in 2003/04, owing to an increase of 30% in the volume of sales and a small price increase. Hides, skins and the stimulant qat constitute the other significant earners, with new sectors, including fruit and fresh flowers, beginning to emerge following the construction of chilled export facilities at Bole International Airport. Industry represented only 11% of national income during the 1990s, rising to 13% in recent years, and grew at an annual average rate of 5.5% during 2000–04, while services, including the state bureaucracy and the defence forces, accounted for more than one-third of formal economic activity.

Ethiopia has a diverse agricultural profile, with cropping patterns and livelihoods differing widely both between and within highland communities. Coffee and root crops are grown in the fertile central and southern areas, while the semi-arid eastern and southern lowlands are characterized largely by pastoral economies, notably of Somalis and Afars. Ethiopia contains the largest total livestock herds in Africa.

Despite such significant internal economic and geographical disparities, poverty is endemic throughout the country. The level of poverty, according to 2004/05 data, was 36%. This is despite the fact that the economically active population as a proportion of the total population, stood at an aggregate of 78.4%, according to the 2005 National Labour Survey by the Central Statistical Agency of Ethiopia, with the rate among males found to be higher (86.1%) compared with females (71.2%). The employment to population ratio is also high, with 76.7% of the country's total population in employment. In 2005 about 77.0% of the total population of the country aged 10 years and over were working (84.7% of males and 69% of females). The rate of unemployment at the national level was 8.1%.

The fragmented aggregate national and international data available suggests that Ethiopia has some of the weakest development indicators in the world. In 2005, according to preliminary World Bank data, life expectancy at birth was 42 years and the rate of infant mortality was 110 per 1,000 live births, while child malnutrition as a percentage of children under five years of age was 47%. These figures contradict those published by the National Office of Population, which shows life expectancy at birth for males as 45 and for females as 47, with the infant mortality rate in 2005 at 77 per 1,000 births. By 2004 total enrolment at primary-school age had risen to 51%, and enrolment in secondary education was equivalent to 28% of children in the relevant age group. Recent data shows improvement with gross primary enrolment standing at 93%. In 2004 the adult literacy rate was 37.9% of the total population. Male literacy was far higher than females (49.9% compared with 26.6%, respectively). Young children suffer the brunt of poverty; some 12.3% of children do not survive beyond their fifth birthday. Nevertheless, according to a report compiled by the Ministry of Finance and Economic Development, access to sanitation, safe water and health care facilities had improved markedly, with about 35.9% of total population having access to safe water (rural 25.2% and urban 92.4%) and 16.9% to sanitation. The utilized budget in the health sector for 2004/05 was 1,229.7m. birr, which was a marked increase compared with previous years. While Ethiopia's HIV/AIDS infection rates, estimated at 4.4% in 2003 (12.6% urban, 2.6% rural), are significantly lower than other east African countries, there are some 1.5m. people living with the disease. Recent trends indicate an increasing prevalence in rural areas and stabilization in urban areas. The Government's approach to address this includes the integration of HIV/AIDS education in schools and mainstreaming HIV/AIDS programmes in all government branches.

In the light of these statistics, it is little surprise that Ethiopia lies 170th out of the 177 countries listed in the UN Development Programme's 2006 Human Development Index. A Ministry of Finance and Economic Development report published in July 2006 indicated that, on average, 2.5m. children are born each year in Ethiopia and at current rates of growth the population is expected to reach 100m. by 2015.

The largest single unexploited resource is rivers. The chronic instability of agricultural production could be partially alleviated by increased irrigation. At present only an estimated 4% of cultivable land is even partially irrigated. Much of this is along the southern Awash valley. Similarly, Ethiopia's hydroelectric potential was largely untapped until recently, when generating capacity rose by one-third with the opening of the 184-MW Gilgel Gibe facility in February 2004 at a cost of 2,200m. birr. In late July 2006 construction work began on a 1,870-MW hydroelectric power plant and dam in the Omo Gibe basin in the south-west of the country, which is expected to be completed in 2011. The Government has sought concessions from Nile Basin countries in order to begin projects before gaining their consent.

In May 2006 the Ethiopian Electric Power Corpn signed an agreement with the Kenya Electricity Generating Co and the Kenya Power and Lighting Co to connect the two countries' electricity grids and for the joint development of power-generation facilities in Ethiopia. The project is due to be completed in 2009. Ethiopia's installed capacity in 2000–04 was 533.8 MW.

With the partial exception of gold, Ethiopia's mineral resources also remain mostly unexploited, representing 1.1% of GDP by 2004/05. The country has considerable proven reserves of gold, coal, potassium, tantalum and iron ore. In the mid-1990s a series of foreign mining companies bought concessions to explore for gold in the country's three main goldfields. In 1997 the Government sold the largest operating mine, Lega Dembi, to the Ethio-Saudi Al-Amoudi group. Minerals used in construction, such as limestone and marble, are produced, the latter also being exported. In addition, since 1995 there has been limited exploration for semi-precious gemstones. In early 2004 the one-year contract signed in April 2003 between the Ethiopian Government and the Malaysian company Petronas for oil exploration in the Ogaden, was renewed and extended geographically. The company has also been active in the Gambela region and has signed a total of four contracts with the Government for petroleum exploration. In early August 2006 Petronas was awarded a contract to develop reserves of natural gas in the Calub and Hilala areas in the Ogaden basin, first discovered in the early 1970s. There are plans to construct a gas refinery at Calub and eventually a pipeline to Djibouti for export. Meanwhile, in March 2006 licences were granted to the Malaysian-based company Pexco for exploration and development of petroleum reserves in the Ogaden and to Afar Exploration of the USA for exploratory work in the Afar region. Lundin Petroleum AB of Sweden, through its subsidiary, Lundin East Africa, was expected to commence oil exploration in Ethiopia before the end of 2007.

ECONOMIC STAGNATION AND REFORM

Given the country's structural constraints, sustained economic improvement is difficult, even with policies conducive to growth. However, between the revolution in 1974 and the late 1980s, economic policy was largely unfavourable to growth. The Government's emphasis on state farms, large-scale rural resettlement and collectivization schemes undermined agricultural production, while civil war in the provinces of Eritrea and Tigrai, recurrent drought and environmental decay reinforced economic stagnation.

Initial land reforms resulted in limited increases in productivity, but these were often undermined by insecure tenures and disincentives to production. Social indicators did improve, notably in health and literacy, although rarely to the levels claimed. Despite nationalization and state control of banks, inbred fiscal and monetary conservatism helped check inflation. However, the nationalization of industry, centralized control of distribution and considerable investment in state farms and prestige industrial projects failed to produce sustained industrial growth. Peasants' quotas, lack of agricultural incentives, poor access to credit and fertilizers, and tight political control via hierarchical peasants' associations were all inimical to rural investment and entrepreneurship. Poor agrarian production was further stunted by the famine of 1984–85. Modest economic recovery came with subsequent harvests, and from 1988 there was a loosening of economic controls. Such liberalization was too little too late. Successive military defeats in the north from 1989 weakened central government and further disrupted the highland economy.

REFORMS SINCE 1991

Economic dislocation owing to war, culminating in the overthrow of the Government in 1991, saw the collapse of tax collection and export earnings, while poor harvests further stunted growth in 1991–93. In addition to managing the economic consequences of the rapid demobilization of some 300,000 troops, the new Government had to disentangle the assets, liabilities, infrastructure and personnel of the Ethiopian and nascent Eritrean states. The Eritrean economy was, de facto, managed entirely independently from May 1991. Until late 1997 it continued to use the Ethiopian birr in what was in effect a currency union, buttressed by a series of bilateral agreements guaranteeing free movement of people and goods between the two countries. However, this arrangement ruptured in 1998 with the outbreak of hostilities (see below).

Upon taking power, the EPRDF rapidly jettisoned its *dirigiste* Marxist dogma, and immediately embarked on market reform and structural adjustment. Despite limited experience and personnel, the Government has retained tight control of the content and timing of the reform programme. Relations with donors and allies have occasionally been frosty; in 1997–98 a dispute with the IMF over the pace of financial-sector reform sparked a nine-month break in relations. However, the authorities won praise from donors for resolute 'ownership' of reform, and by 1998 had become one of the World Bank's favoured clients in sub-Saharan Africa.

The Government has implemented extensive economic reforms in four broad areas: the dismantling of direct controls and deregulation of both domestic and foreign trade; the overhaul of government taxation and expenditure, implemented in tandem with the restructuring of the civil service along federal lines; financial liberalization, including the devaluation of the birr and the fostering of private banking and insurance markets; and privatization.

In rural areas market reforms have produced largely positive results, with increased output, prices and revenues for peasants, although marketing weaknesses have repeatedly tended to undermine prices during good harvests. In towns the benefits of liberalization have been less clear: wholesale and retail trade is now almost exclusively in private hands, but significant barriers to investment, including poor infrastructure, state bureaucracy and convoluted systems of urban land-leases, remain. The urban poor and middle classes have been adversely affected since 2003, as the cost of living has risen with the introduction of a range of new rental tariffs and municipal charges. The Government has formulated extensive sectoral investment programmes, notably for transport, health and education, to be implemented at federal and state level. However, these are critically dependent upon external donor funding, and also require improvements in capital budget and project implementation, particularly by smaller regional administrations.

The EPRDF has eschewed comprehensive planning, but it does have a loose, medium-term economic framework for federal and regional economic development. This 'agricultural development-led industrialization' strategy aims to promote medium-scale industries based on agricultural processing in the larger regional capitals. It envisages the integration of such agro-processing plants with programmes to improve productivity in smallholder agriculture as well as larger-scale commercial farms. Despite deregulation and the ability of regional governments to grant licences for commercial farming, large-scale commercial agriculture remains beset with problems of infrastructure, land tenure and licensing.

Although several hundred small state-owned retail outlets were quickly sold, the privatization of larger companies has been piecemeal, slow and far from transparent. In April 1999 the Government announced plans to dispose of interests in 120 of the remaining 163 state-owned companies over the next three years. Despite financial liberalization, banking and insurance remain dominated by the state. A similar situation prevails in terms of attempts to encourage foreign direct investment. Ethiopia's investment code has been liberalized four times since 1992, most recently in April 2003. Privatization and the encouragement of foreign investment were hampered during 2001–02 by the arrest on corruption charges of senior officials overseeing the sale of state-owned assets and the promotion of foreign direct investment—six former executives of the state-owned Commercial Bank of Ethiopia (CBE) were released without charge in mid-August 2006. Five others had previously been released on bail; however, the former CBE Chairman, Moges Chemere, was returned to gaol, accused of two charges of corruption. Chemere reportedly faced up to 10 years' imprisonment if found guilty. Meanwhile, in mid-2002 it was announced that a further 114 public enterprises had been scheduled for privatization by the end of 2003; the Government also invited expressions of interest for a 30% stake in the Ethiopian Telecommunications Corpn (ETC) and signed a contract with the Royal Bank of Scotland to provide management consultancy services to the CBE for two years. The privatization of the ETC has since been put on hold and the process is not expected to recommence in the near future. Overall private-sector fixed capital formation amounted to 9.6% of GDP in 2000–04. Foreign direct investment was US $454m. in 2004.

RECENT DEVELOPMENTS

Since 1991 government economic policy has been characterized by continuity, caution and slow but steady reform. Despite the shift from 'transitional' to federal government in 1995, a progressive restructuring and devolution of regional and local government since 1992, and the conflict with Eritrea during 1998–2000, there have been few changes to the broad orientation of economic policy as laid out in 1991–93. This coherence and consistency is largely due to the continuity of personnel. Changes to the ruling party leadership following the divisions in March 2001 (see Recent History) resulted in new emphasis on policy areas such as the urban and pastoral economies along with a renewed vigour associated with capacity building and continuities in economic reform. Notwithstanding what is often perceived as an obsession with secrecy and national autonomy, disagreements with key donors have surfaced only over the sequencing and timing of reforms, notably in the financial sector. The gradual pace of reform, and the secondary role accorded to foreign donors' advice, have contributed to economic stability.

According to World Bank figures, GDP increased by an average of 5.3% per year during 1998–2005, despite two successive years of crop failure in the late 1990s. Buoyant agricultural output resulted in an increase in GDP of 7.7% in 2000/01, but only 1.1% in 2001/02. Although growth of 6.0% was predicted for 2002/03, following crop failures GDP in fact contracted by 3.8%. The IMF estimated that GDP had expanded by 11.1% in 2003/04 and by 8.8% in 2004/05. With annual population growth averaging 2.3% during 1995–2005, and, according to some estimates, as much as 3% in subsequent years, these increases, with intermittent contractions, represented only marginal per capita improvements. Aggregate data mask erratic fluctuations, due primarily to variations in rain-fed agriculture. Preliminary data suggest that real income per head fell significantly in the two fiscal years from July 1998–July 2000, and even more severely during 2002/03.

Annual inflation averaged 2.3% during 2000–05. Official measurements of inflation are driven primarily by fluctuations in grain prices, in turn determined by harvest and supply conditions. Thus in years of good harvests prices fall. Prices increased by 1.9% in 2000, but declined by 6.7% in 2001 and by a similar percentage in early 2002, owing to improved harvests simultaneously increasing food supplies and depressing grain prices. By mid-2002 this trend had prompted concern among policy-makers and peasants at what appeared to be a cyclical structural weakness; good harvests driving down grain prices, and consequently rural incomes, below subsistence levels. This, in turn, undermined agricultural productivity, with farmers unable and unwilling to invest in improved seeds, fertilizer and pesticides, on which hopes of improved aggregate output rested. This undermining of rural livelihoods was exacerbated by falling world coffee prices—farm-gate prices paid to Ethiopia's smallholder producers declined by 18% in 2001 and still further in 2002, depressing demand for livestock. The situation reversed rapidly following poor harvests in 2002, and annual average inflation had risen to 18.6% by October 2003, as a result of high grain prices. The Government raised fuel prices by 15%–30% in April 2004, reflecting international prices, and increasing non-food inflation rates for the year to 7.8% (from 1.3% the previous year). Inflation fell to 3.3% in 2003/04 as a result of good harvests, but rose again to 11.6% in 2005 as a result of continued high grain prices and increases in the price of fuel. In early 2006 the Government imposed a ban on the export of teff, maize, sorghum and wheat in an effort to curb sharp rises in the prices of those commodities.

Even following good harvests, many millions of Ethiopians remain dependent on food aid, as they are simply too poor to purchase food. Indeed, in mid-2003 the Disaster Prevention and Preparedness Commission (DPPC) stated that the country's lack of purchasing power was Ethiopia's greatest problem. This prompted a review of food security policy and the establishment of a Co-ordinating Bureau in 2004 to seek means of stabilizing the livelihoods of an estimated 5m. people, who remained chronically dependent on food aid. Heavy flooding during the summer rains compounded these problems, with hundreds reported killed and thousands displaced in Dire Dawa, Oromia and Tigrai provinces.

Recurrent government expenditure in 2003/04 contracted by 11.6% compared with the previous year, to a total of 11,961m. birr, but rose again to 13,036m. birr in 2004/05. The IMF estimated that the Government's overall budget deficit rose in real terms during 2004/05 to 4,519m. birr (US $519m.), falling to 4.7% of GDP from 4.8% in 2003/04. World Bank figures showed an overall budget deficit of 5.0% of GDP in 2004/05 and 5.3% of GDP in 2005/06. The GDP deflator decreased from 9.6% in 2004, to an estimated 6.0% in 2005.

The structures of the Ethiopian state's expenditure and revenues have been reformed in conjunction with the elaboration of a federal state with nine regional states. The country's two significant urban commercial centres, Addis Ababa and Dire Dawa, are administered separately. The formulas delineating tax-raising and expenditure prerogatives of central and regional governments remain somewhat convoluted, prompting accusations of poor transparency and accountability of regional authorities. The two small western regions bordering Sudan, and the mainly pastoral Afar and Somali regional administrations have all experienced corruption and frequent changes in personnel. However, despite evidence of increasing dishonesty in recent years, large-scale graft and corruption remains much lower in Ethiopia than in other sub-Saharan states. Transparency International ranked Ethiopia 130th out of 163 countries in its 2006 report. Moreover, Ethiopia rates comparatively well in regards to the number of procedures required, totalling seven, successfully to start up a new business, according to the World Bank in 2006.

EXTERNAL TRADE

External tariffs have been simplified and reduced extensively since 1992. Falling coffee prices, coupled with significant planned increases of imports under successive adjustment and investment programmes, mean that both Ethiopia's overall trade position and terms of trade weakened from the mid-1990s. In 1998 Ethiopia earned US $382m. from coffee exports; by 2000 this had declined to $255m., despite a higher export volume of 118,911 metric tons (115,027 tons having been exported in 1998). According to IMF data, a current-account deficit of $149.5m. was registered in 2002, compared with a surplus of $14.6m. in 2000. Primarily as a result of a 35% increase in the value of coffee exports, between 2002/03 and 2003/04 the value of exports totalled $608.9m.—an increase of over 26% on the previous year. In 2004/05 the total value of exports was estimated at $818m. and the following financial year revenues from coffee exports totalled $427m. from an export volume of 183,000 tons. The value of qat exports, meanwhile, continued to increase exponentially, overtaking hides and skins (for which European prices had dropped) as Ethiopia's second largest export in 2002/03, and earning the country more than $100m. in 2003/04, largely as a result of price rises. Ethiopia runs a surplus of invisible earnings, largely owing to the performance of Ethiopian Airlines and Ethiopian Shipping Lines Corpn, the latter having prospered, in spite of the lack of a home port. In 2000–04 imports exceeded exports by 17.3%. In 2005 exports of goods and services represented 16.4% of GDP. There were reports of fuel shortages in parts of the country in July 2007 and fuel imports have contributed to the country's trade deficit. Meanwhile, meetings between officials from Ethiopia and Sudan in early February 2007 failed to create any new agreement on border trade zones. The current border trade agreements help Ethiopia to export products such as natural honey, leeks, horse beans, butter and sorghum, which have a combined estimated annual value of 1.9m. birr.

The Ethiopian birr has been devalued progressively since 1992, moving from US $1 = 2.07 birr to $1 = 8.59 birr in March 2003 and to $1 = 8.84 in March 2007. Since mid-1993 the rate of the birr has been determined by auctions supervised by the national bank. In 1998 these became essentially wholesale auctions, supplying foreign exchange to an increasingly liberalized retail banking sector. The cautious pace of reform was successful, achieving a phased devaluation with minimal inflation and a steady narrowing of the parallel market premium.

PROBLEMS AND PROSPECTS

Acute, perennial food shortages remain the most immediate and protracted economic problem confronting the majority of Ethiopians. Since 1991 the Government, via the DPPC, and donors have made significant improvements to the country's famine early-warning systems. An emergency food security reserve has been established and food relief storage and distribution networks have been improved. Nevertheless, most rural communities remain highly vulnerable, owing to acute poverty and the vagaries of weather and pests. In times of shortage, aid efforts are hampered by the rural isolation of many highlanders. Most settlements are inaccessible by road, particularly during the long rainy season (June–September) when need is often greatest. In both 1994/95 and 1999 harvest failures left an estimated 4.5m. people in need of food assistance. Erratic regional harvests in 1999 created additional severe shortages in both highland and pastoral areas. In July 2002, following two consecutive poor rainy seasons, the DPPC revised its estimates of the number of Ethiopians in need of food aid from 5.2m. to 8m. By mid-2003 some 13.2m. people had been affected by the ongoing drought, and appeals were again made to donors to provide large amounts of aid. The number of people requiring food assistance during 2004 was estimated at 7.2m. Despite an improved harvest in 2004, UN estimates for 2005 indicated that up to 9m. people were in need of food aid and in 2006 that number had risen to 10m.

Since 1998 Afar and Somali pastoralists have also endured severe hardship as a result of prolonged drought and the collapse of livestock prices. The latter was triggered by Saudi Arabia's ban on livestock imports from the Horn of Africa. While the ban was lifted in May 1999, prices, herds and pastoral livelihoods have been slow to recover. In an attempt to counteract the effects of protracted severe drought, between November 2004 and May 2005 Afar areas were given 9,000 metric tons of relief grain per month, more than any other region.

In the longer term, without significant improvements in agricultural productivity and the pastoral way of life, the Ethiopian economy will be unable to generate the agricultural surplus necessary both to fund economic diversification and support the inevitable acceleration of urbanization. Growth in agricultural output in recent years has been primarily due to an expansion in cultivated land, rather than sustained increases in productivity. According to the IMF, yield growth between 1991/92–2004/05 remained at an average of around 0.2% per year. Only via sustained improvements in rural productivity, primarily via irrigation and increased fertilizer application, can living standards be improved. Some 2.5% of the country's cropland was being irrigated in 2003, while fertilizer consumption was 0.15 kg per ha of arable land in 2002. Although the Government is heavily promoting the use of fertilizer, many peasants resist, not least because of high cost, unreliable returns and fears of exacerbating the acute soil erosion experienced in the highlands. There is also minimal use of pesticides, further contributing to low and inconsistent yields.

The Ethiopian Government's national poverty reduction strategy for 2006–10, the Plan for Accelerated and Sustained Development to End Poverty, acknowledged agriculture's significant and decisive role in the social and economic development of the country. Government policy seeks the transformation of subsistence agriculture to a market-orientated development, both in terms of food security and the commercialization of agriculture. Priority areas, known as 'growth corridors', have been identified by the Government as areas with comparative advantages that can play a critical role in accelerating growth and ensuring food security. The Government is advocating increased productivity (including reducing post-harvest losses), improving marketing systems and promoting high value crops for export, while ensuring natural resource conservation for these areas. The Jimma region is a good example due to its fertile soils and year-round rainfall (1,500 mm). There is also provision in the strategy explicitly to link small enterprises with agriculture. To promote commercialization the Ethiopia Commodity Exchange (ECEX) project aims to establish a commodity exchange. This formal market institution will facilitate premium prices for quality produce, decrease transaction costs for market participation and increase information and transparency for all market actors. Meanwhile, the planned Canadian International Development Agency programme will aid agricultural colleges through university linkages in order to support its private-sector development initiatives. The US Agency for International Development's Ethiopia Agribusiness and Trade Expansion Activity aims to improve the competitiveness and productivity of farmers, traders, and processors through the identification of export market opportunities. Meanwhile, the World Bank Rural Capacity Building project was approved in June 2006. One component of this project is the training of extension agents.

Another weakness is Ethiopia's dependence upon a single export crop, coffee. For almost four decades coffee has routinely accounted for up to two-thirds of Ethiopia's foreign exchange earnings and an estimated 260,000 metric tons of coffee is produced annually. Fluctuations in international coffee prices greatly accentuate the inherent instability of the Ethiopian economy (see above), although Ethiopia is unique among African coffee producers in consuming much of the crop at home. Since 1996 limited steps have been taken to improve the quality of Ethiopian coffee exports. Washing and processing facilities have been advanced, and the production of premium brands has been promoted. Most coffee is produced by smallholders. Since 1991 the marketing and export of coffee has increasingly been in private hands. Attempts to diversify exports away from coffee have so far shown few results. Flowers, fruit and vegetables for export are produced, but the quality of finishing, packaging and marketing lags behind that of neighbouring competitors such as Kenya.

Ethiopia's economy is, and will remain for the foreseeable future, highly dependent on external donor funding, which amounted to 7.8% of GDP in 2003/04. The total trade deficit was around 15% of GDP in 1998–2001, once services and private transfers were taken into account, and an overall current-account deficit of around 8.5% of GDP was estimated, leaving an external financing requirement of some US $8,600m. over the three-year period. Some $5,000m. of this represented concessional debt relief, much of this sum being the cancellation of rouble debts to the former USSR accumulated prior to 1991. The current-account deficit at the end of 2002/03 was estimated to total 2.2% of GDP, a decrease from 4.7% in the previous year. In 2003/04 the current-account deficit was equivalent to an estimated 5.1% of GDP, rising to 9.1% in 2004/05. In 2005 the current-account deficit reached $1,567.8m.

Discussions regarding Ethiopia's eligibility for the IMF/World Bank debt-relief initiative for heavily indebted poor countries (HIPC) were delayed in 1999, owing to the hostilities between Ethiopia and Eritrea. Other important donors effectively suspended new project-lending in mid-1999. However, by 1998 actual disbursement was already lagging significantly behind pledges, largely owing to constraints in implementation capacity, which was further restricted by the war effort. In September 2000 the World Bank announced that it was to resume financial assistance to Ethiopia, which had been suspended for more than two years. Discussions of HIPC terms resumed in early 2001, with donors linking additional debt relief to the elaboration of the country's poverty reduction strategy paper, a draft of which was published early in 2001. Full HIPC debt reduction was agreed in principle in November 2001.

In March 2001 the IMF approved a three-year arrangement for a total of US $112m. under its Poverty Reduction and Growth Facility (PRGF) to support the Government's 2000/01–2002/03 economic programme. In early August 2001 the IMF completed the first review of Ethiopia's economic programme and disbursed credit of $22m., with immediate effect. The second review and disbursement was completed in March 2002, and subsequent reviews proceeded as anticipated, with a fifth review in November 2003 making downward revisions owing to the lingering impact of the drought, but releasing a penultimate disbursement of $15m. in February 2004. Ethiopia's progress was endorsed at the final review in September 2004, and a second smaller-phase PRGF was considered in March 2005, after the relatively favourable second-round review of Ethiopia's sustainable development and poverty reduction programme in February. The Ethiopian Government used the review to request a doubling of aid inflows, to some $4,000m. per annum, to boost the chances of reaching its MDGs.

In late April 2004 it was announced that Ethiopia had reached its completion point under the HIPC initiative, the 13th out of 37 possible countries to have done so. In March 2006 the World Bank approved debt cancellation for 17 countries, including Ethiopia, under the HIPC initiative and the process was due to begin in mid-year. Top-up funds were agreed to keep debt/export ratios down to 150%–175%, although they reached 216% in mid-2004, as a result of falling coffee export revenues, before dropping back to acceptable levels over the subsequent year. As a result, Ethiopia benefits from the following debt relief: US $1,300m. in net present value from multilateral donors; $700m. from bilateral donors; and $300m. from 'Paris Club' creditors. This is against a total external debt nominally valued at $7,151m. in 2003. Recent figures show an estimated total nominal debt service relief of $3,275m. Figures from 2005 show that total outstanding and disbursed debt from the World Bank International Development Association programme stood at $3,359m. World Bank disbursements for 2005 amounted to $162m. Total aid received from all donors in 2004 was $1,682m., which represented 22.6% of GDP.

Transparency and accountability in economic policy-making remain problematic. Despite extensive liberalization, many markets remain far from competitive. The piecemeal privatization process and the allocation of urban land-leases in particular have attracted accusations of favouritism and regional bias in policy-making. An Ethio-Saudi entrepreneur, Muhammad Hussein al-Amoudi, has established extensive interests in real estate, hotels, beverages, banking, insurance, agriculture and mining. A second group of conglomerates are owned and managed by members or affiliates of the ruling party, particularly in the media and distribution sectors, prompting allegations that public contracts are awarded on the basis of party ties or ethnic favouritism. Critics of the Government claim that the economic influence and political connections of such consortia have squeezed smaller, genuinely independent entrepreneurs out of crucial markets, undermining private investor confidence. Such issues are not helped by the constrained nature of public debate of economic issues. Although the situation has improved since 1991, particularly in the run-up to elections in May 2005, there is little press debate or general public understanding of economic policy-making. In January 2002 economic confidence was further eroded when 40 senior figures linked to the CBE, which controls over 80% of retail banking, were arrested. The overall restructuring of Ethiopia's financial sector has long been a demand of external donors, with the Government insisting the IMF should recognize the validity of its opposition to banking liberalization in the absence of a functioning money market. Value-added tax was introduced at 15% to replace sales tax on 1 January 2003.

THE ECONOMIC IMPACT OF WAR WITH ERITREA

The initial, short-term, aggregate economic impact of the 1998–2000 conflict with Eritrea was surprisingly limited. Disruption to agricultural production was restricted largely to Tigrai, where 385,000 people were reportedly displaced. Disturbance to land-locked Ethiopia's foreign trade was also less than initially forecast. The decision to suspend use of the Eritrean ports of Assab and Massawa and to channel all foreign trade via Djibouti was taken unilaterally by Ethiopia. The flexibility of Djibouti's port facilities and the efficiency of road haulage from Djibouti to Addis Ababa and the highlands ensured a continuous flow of goods to and from Ethiopia. Currency and trade questions played a key role in the genesis of the conflict. The signing of a peace accord in December 2000, and the announcement of the Boundary Commission's decision regarding the demarcation of the Ethio-Eritrean border in April 2002 (see Recent History), resulted in a considerable reduction in levels of defence spending. In March 2003 a study by the Ethiopian Economic Policy Research Institute estimated that the total cost of the war to the Ethiopian Government amounted to US $29,000m. The war inevitably diminished the reporting and transparency of economic and fiscal data. During the war senior government officials stated that the cost of conflict had been met largely by deferring capital expenditure, implying severe cuts in sectoral investment programmes, and sharp reductions in health and education expenditure. These have been reversed since 2000, with rises in social-sector spending central to Ethiopia's externally monitored poverty reduction strategy approved by donors in February 2005. An elaborate timetable and targets for further reform—notably in the financial sector—outlined in September 1998 were rendered obsolete by the financial pressures of war and increased military expenditure. The war also led to markedly reduced investment in the economy, rapid deflation, rising public-sector borrowing and a widening budget deficit; Ethiopia urgently requires a prolonged period of political stability, if it is to attract much-needed foreign investors back into the country.

Finally, war further eroded domestic and international confidence in the economy. The expulsion of more than 50,000 largely urban Ethiopians with family ties to Eritrea undermined both the Government's legal commitment to property rights and general investor confidence. The apparently arbitrary criteria and rationale behind the expulsions exacerbated economic uncertainty, which was somewhat reduced when, in early 2004, the Government introduced legislation granting citizenship rights to long-term residents of Eritrean origin.

The crisis of the war with Eritrea added to the deeper pressures of rapid population growth and slow agrarian change. Political uncertainty, low economic growth and investment undermine already limited opportunities for employment and education, and inevitably fuelled an increase in migration, which amounted to 662,444 people in 2000–04. Over the past 15 years or so middle-class and urban youths have fled to the USA and the northern countries of the European Union. Given the high level of poverty at home, such external migration is likely to intensify in the immediate future, thus heightening the role that remittances from abroad, which totalled US $133m. in 2004, will play in Ethiopia's economy.

Statistical Survey

Source (unless otherwise stated): Central Statistical Authority, POB 1143, Addis Ababa; tel. (1) 553010; fax (1) 550334; internet www.csa.gov.et.

Note: Unless otherwise indicated, figures in this Survey refer to the territory of Ethiopia after the secession of Eritrea in May 1993.

Area and Population

AREA, POPULATION AND DENSITY

Area (sq km)	1,133,380*
Population (census results)	
9 May 1984†	39,868,501
11 October 1994	
Males	26,910,698
Females	26,566,567
Total	53,477,265
Population (official estimates at mid-year)	
2005	73,908,000
2006	75,067,000
2007	77,127,000
Density (per sq km) at mid-2007	68.1

* 437,600 sq miles.

† Including an estimate for areas not covered by the census.

ADMINISTRATIVE DIVISIONS

(estimated population at mid-2007)

	Population ('000)		
	Males	Females	Total
Regional States			
1 Tigrai	2,193	2,256	4,449
2 Afar	787	631	1,418
3 Amhara	9,805	9,819	19,624
4 Oromia	13,626	13,678	27,304
5 Somali	2,384	2,060	4,444
6 Benishangul/Gumuz	322	318	640
7 Southern Nations, Nationalities and Peoples	7,619	7,702	15,321
8 Gambela	129	124	253
9 Harari	104	99	203
Chartered Cities			
1 Dire Dawa	206	206	412
2 Addis Ababa	1,469	1,590	3,059
Total	38,644	38,483	77,127

PRINCIPAL TOWNS
(official estimates at mid-2007)

Addis Ababa (capital)	3,059,000	Mekele	177,090
Dire Dawa	293,173	Bahir Dar	175,185
Nazret	239,525	Jimma	166,592
Gondar	204,001	Debre Zeit	137,413
Dessie	177,116	Awasa	131,300

BIRTHS AND DEATHS
(annual averages, UN estimates)

	1990–95	1995–2000	2000–05
Birth rate (per 1,000)	46.9	44.1	40.7
Death rate (per 1,000)	17.2	15.8	14.4

Source: UN, *World Population Prospects: The 2006 Revision*.

Expectation of life (years at birth, WHO estimates): 50 (males 49; females 51) in 2004 (Source: WHO, *World Health Report*).

ECONOMICALLY ACTIVE POPULATION
('000 persons aged 10 years and over, March 2005)*

	Males	Females	Total
Agriculture, hunting, forestry and fishing	14,209.4	10,998.8	25,208.2
Mining and quarrying	51.4	30.6	82.1
Manufacturing	444.0	1,085.3	1,529.4
Electricity, gas and water	25.2	7.7	32.9
Construction	349.9	95.7	445.6
Wholesale and retail trade; repair of motor vehicles, motorcycles and personal and household goods	652.2	984.9	1,637.1
Hotels and restaurants	96.8	672.3	769.1
Transport, storage and communications	132.0	14.5	146.4
Financial intermediation	21.6	16.3	37.9
Real estate, renting and business services	36.1	16.2	52.3
Public administration and defence; compulsory social security	242.0	125.9	367.9
Education	178.2	104.5	282.7
Social work	45.6	32.5	78.1
Community, social and personal services	303.5	135.2	438.7
Households with employed persons	23.1	225.5	248.6
Extra-territorial organizations and bodies	42.7	25.1	67.9
Not classifiable by economic activity	6.5	3.8	10.3
Total employed	16,860.3	14,574.8	31,435.1
Unemployed	427.9	1,225.8	1,653.7
Total labour force	17,288.2	15,800.6	33,088.8

* Excluding armed forces.

Source: ILO.

Health and Welfare

KEY INDICATORS

Total fertility rate (children per woman, 2005)	5.7
Under-5 mortality rate (per 1,000 live births, 2005)	164
HIV/AIDS (% of persons aged 15–49, 2003)	4.40
Physicians (per 1,000 head, 2003)	0.03
Hospital beds (per 1,000 head, 1990)	0.24
Health expenditure (2004): US $ per head (PPP)	21.1
Health expenditure (2004): % of GDP	5.3
Health expenditure (2004): public (% of total)	51.5
Access to water (% of persons, 2004)	22
Access to sanitation (% of persons, 2004)	13
Human Development Index (2004): ranking	170
Human Development Index (2004): value	0.371

For sources and definitions, see explanatory note on p. vi.

Agriculture

PRINCIPAL CROPS
('000 metric tons)

	2003	2004	2005
Wheat	1,618	2,177	2,307
Barley	1,087	1,376	1,398
Maize	2,744	2,906	3,343
Oats	39	58	57
Millet (Dagusa)	305	313	397
Sorghum	1,784	1,718	2,200
Potatoes	510	510	450
Sweet potatoes	497	452	409
Yams	222	193	172
Sugar cane	2,456*	2,454	n.a.
Dry beans	117.5	175.5	176.0*
Dry broad beans	430.2	426.9	601.7
Dry peas	170.4	170.4	197.0
Chick-peas	135.9	135.9	216.9
Lentils	35.3	35.3	63.4
Vetches	79	125	146
Soybeans (Soya beans)	457	835	3,812
Groundnuts (in shell)	29.3	29.1	34.2
Castor beans*	15	15	15
Rapeseed	19.9	29.3	30.0*
Safflower seed	5	7	6
Sesame seed	61.5	115.4	148.9
Cottonseed†	37.0	37.0	43.0
Cotton (lint)†	20	20	23
Linseed	77.4	151.9	125.9
Cabbages*	152	164	174
Tomatoes	55	36	35
Green onions and shallots*	20	20	20
Dry onions	217	230	176
Garlic*	71	79	86
Bananas	175	182	211
Oranges	13	17	16*
Mangoes	163.3	135.0*	135.0*
Avocados	81.3	82.3*	83.4*
Papayas	230.5	246.9*	259.2*
Coffee (green)†	221.6	260.0	300.0

* FAO estimate(s).

† Unofficial figures.

Source: FAO.

LIVESTOCK
('000 head, year ending September)

	2003*	2004	2005*
Cattle	39,000	38,103	38,500
Sheep	15,000	16,576	17,000
Goats*	9,623	9,626	1,626
Asses and mules	4,130	4,091	4,125
Horses	1,450	1,447	1,500
Camels	470	468	470
Pigs*	28	28	29
Poultry	38,000	35,656	39,000

* FAO estimates.

Source: FAO.

LIVESTOCK PRODUCTS
('000 metric tons, FAO estimates)

	2003	2004	2005
Cattle meat	338.3	331.5	336.0
Sheep meat	49.9	55.1	56.6
Goat meat	28.7	28.7	28.7
Pig meat	1.6	1.6	1.7
Chicken meat	50.2	47.1	52.0
Game meat	74	75	77
Other meat	50	50	50
Cows' milk	1,500	1,500	1,500
Goats' milk	17.2	17.3	17.3
Sheep's milk	37.5	41.5	42.5
Hen eggs	37.1	36.6	36.6
Honey	37.8	38.1	39.0
Wool: greasy	12	12	12

Source: FAO.

Forestry

ROUNDWOOD REMOVALS
('000 cubic metres, excl. bark)

	2003	2004	2005
Sawlogs, veneer logs and logs for sleepers	6	4	4*
Pulpwood*	7	7	7
Other industrial wood	2,917	2,917	2,917*
Fuel wood*	91,603	93,029	94,481
Total	94,533	95,957	97,409

* FAO estimate(s).

Source: FAO.

SAWNWOOD PRODUCTION
('000 cubic metres, incl. railway sleepers)

	2001	2002	2003
Coniferous (softwood)	25*	1	0
Broadleaved (hardwood)	35*	13	17
Total	60	14	17

* FAO estimate.

2004–05: Figures assumed to be unchanged from 2003 (FAO estimates).

Source: FAO.

Fishing

(metric tons, live weight of capture)

	2003	2004	2005
Rhinofishes	668	100	267
Other cyprinids	394	415	427
Tilapias	4,653	5,590	3,604
North African catfish	2,662	2,532	2,366
Nile perch	168	919	2,260
Total catch (incl. others)	10,113	10,451	9,797

Source: FAO.

Mining

('000 metric tons, unless otherwise indicated, year ending 7 July, estimates)

	2002/03	2003/04	2004/05
Gold (kilograms)	3,875	3,443	3,900
Limestone	2,290	2,380	2,800
Gypsum and anhydrite	48	51	52
Pumice	219	271	320

Source: US Geological Survey.

Industry

SELECTED PRODUCTS
('000 metric tons, year ending 7 July, unless otherwise indicated)

	2000/01	2001/02	2002/03
Wheat flour	165	143	137*
Macaroni and pasta	26	23	30*
Raw sugar	251	248*	268*
Wine ('000 hectolitres)	25	27*	32*
Beer ('000 hectolitres)	1,605	1,812*	2,123*
Mineral waters ('000 hectolitres)	395	395*	433*
Soft drinks ('000 hectolitres)	677	995	845*
Cigarettes (million)	1,904	1,511*	1,511*
Cotton yarn	5.7	7.7*	5.5*
Woven cotton fabrics ('000 sq m)	45,000	45,000*	41,000*
Nylon fabrics ('000 sq m)	1,300	1,000*	1,400*
Footwear (including rubber, '000 pairs)	n.a.	6,677	7,138
Soap	14.8	19.2*	11.6*
Tyres ('000)*	209	198	191
Clay building bricks ('000)*	20	22	21
Quicklime*	11	8	11
Cement*	819	919	890

* Year ending 31 December of later year.

Source: UN, *Industrial Commodity Statistics Yearbook*.

Cement (hydraulic, '000 metric tons, year ending 7 July): 1,130.1 in 2003; 1,315.9 in 2004; 1,568.0 in 2005 (estimate) (Source: US Geological Survey).

Beer of millet ('000 metric tons): 220.7 in 2001; 208.0 in 2002; 244.1 in 2003 (Source: FAO).

Beer of barley ('000 metric tons): 388.2 in 2001; 411.7 in 2002; 322.0 in 2003 (Source: FAO).

Finance

CURRENCY AND EXCHANGE RATES

Monetary Units
100 cents = 1 birr.

Sterling, Dollar and Euro Equivalents (28 February 2007)
£1 sterling = 17.300 birr;
US $1 = 8.842 birr;
€1 = 11.681 birr;
100 birr = £5.78 = $11.31 = €8.56.

Average Exchange Rate (birr per US $)

2004	8.636
2005	8.666
2006	8.699

GENERAL BUDGET

(rounded figures, million birr, year ending 7 July)

Revenue	2002/03	2003/04	2004/05
Taxation	8,244	10,907	12,265
Taxes on income and profits	2,878	2,832	3,569
Personal income	833	948	1,132
Business profits	1,639	1,303	1,714
Domestic indirect taxes	1,668	2,200	2,589
Import duties	3,564	5,276	5,746
Export duties	1	0	0
Other revenue	2,906	3,011	3,202
Reimbursements and property sales	204	185	193
Sales of goods and services	190	376	873
Total*	11,149	13,917	15,467

Expenditure	2002/03	2003/04	2004/05
Current expenditure	13,527	11,961	13,036
General services	4,679	5,048	5,767
Economic services	1,223	1,356	1,468
Social services	3,183	3,253	3,775
Interest and charges	1,219	1,080	1,011
External assistance (grants)†	2,890	699	721
Capital expenditure	6,313	8,271	11,515
Economic development	3,342	4,773	7,766
Social development	1,331	2,233	3,310
General services and compensation	444	1,265	455
External assistance (grants)†	1,196	1,047	1,513
Total	19,840	20,232	24,551

* Excluding grants received from abroad (million birr): 4,533 in 2002/03; 4,001 in 2003/04; 4,565 in 2004/05.

† Imputed value of goods and services provided, mainly aid in kind.

Source: IMF, *Federal Democratic Republic of Ethiopia: Selected Issues and Statistical Appendix* (May 2006).

INTERNATIONAL RESERVES

(US $ million at 31 December, excluding gold)

	2004	2005	2006
IMF special drawing rights	0.5	0.2	0.1
Reserve position in IMF	11.2	10.3	11.0
Foreign exchange	1,485.1	1,111.0	821.6
Total	1,496.8	1,121.5	832.7

Source: IMF, *International Financial Statistics*.

MONEY SUPPLY

(million birr, at 31 December)

	2004	2005	2006
Currency outside banks	8,274.5	9,623.3	11,606.4
Demand deposits at commercial banks	13,933.1	16,132.1	20,207.0
Total money (incl. others)	22,312.0	25,980.7	32,056.2

Source: IMF, *International Financial Statistics*.

COST OF LIVING

(Consumer Price Index; base: 2000 = 100)

	2003	2004	2005
All items	109.8	113.4	126.6

Source: IMF, *International Financial Statistics*.

NATIONAL ACCOUNTS

Expenditure on the Gross Domestic Product

(million birr at current prices; year ending 7 July)

	2002/03	2003/04	2004/05
Government final consumption expenditure	10,904	11,739	13,766
Private final consumption expenditure	52,096	68,745	79,466
Statistical discrepancy	–1	0	0
Gross capital formation	15,502	17,827	25,402
Total domestic expenditure	78,501	98,311	118,634
Exports of goods and services	9,779	12,913	15,826
Less Imports of goods and services	20,136	27,333	37,784
GDP in purchasers' values	68,144	83,892	96,676

Source: IMF, *Federal Democratic Republic of Ethiopia: Selected Issues and Statistical Appendix* (May 2006).

Gross Domestic Product by Economic Activity

(at constant 1999/2000 factor cost; year ending 7 July)

	2001/02	2002/03	2004/05
Agriculture, hunting, forestry and fishing	27,361	32,100	35,948
Mining and quarrying	350	378	408
Manufacturing	3,561	3,752	3,939
Electricity and water	1,577	1,688	1,789
Construction	3,176	3,437	3,729
Trade and related services	7,694	8,194	8,686
Hotels and restaurants	1,348	1,436	1,522
Transport and communications	3,470	3,713	3,973
Finance and insurance	1,301	1,377	1,466
Real estate and renting	4,815	5,012	5,213
Public administration and defence	3,268	3,333	3,433
Education	1,966	2,182	2,422
Health	734	793	857
Domestic and other services	1,310	1,375	1,444
Private households with employed persons	191	198	206
Statistical discrepancy	–468	–496	–528
Total	61,654	68,472	74,506

Source: IMF, *Federal Democratic Republic of Ethiopia: Selected Issues and Statistical Appendix* (May 2006).

BALANCE OF PAYMENTS

(US $ million)

	2003	2004	2005
Exports of goods f.o.b.	496.4	678.3	917.3
Imports of goods f.o.b.	–1,895.0	–2,768.5	–3,700.9
Trade balance	–1,398.6	–2,090.2	–2,783.5
Exports of services	761.7	1,005.5	1,012.1
Imports of services	–708.7	–958.3	–1,193.8
Balance on goods and services	–1,345.6	–2,043.0	–2,965.2
Other income received	18.9	31.7	43.4
Other income paid	–43.1	–60.3	–48.0
Balance on goods, services and income	–1,369.8	–2,071.6	–2,969.8
Current transfers received	1,266.5	1,420.6	1,426.0
Current transfers paid	–33.1	–16.8	–23.9
Current balance	–136.4	–667.8	–1,567.8
Direct investment from abroad	—	—	265.1
Other investment assets	68.8	–261.8	302.2
Investment liabilities	178.1	335.0	191.2
Net errors and omissions	–390.1	–354.1	486.3
Overall balance	–279.6	–948.8	–322.9

Source: IMF, *International Financial Statistics*.

External Trade

PRINCIPAL COMMODITIES

(distribution by SITC, US $ '000)

Imports c.i.f.	2001	2002	2003
Food and live animals	218.9	151.8	499.6
Cereals and cereal preparations	197.9	133.6	458.1
Unmilled wheat and meslin	136.4	107.1	362.8
Unmilled durum wheat	47.6	52.8	188.7
Mineral fuels, lubricants, etc.	316.3	197.0	320.7
Refined petroleum products	315.8	196.2	320.2
Chemicals and related products	210.6	207.0	239.7
Manufactured fertilizers	44.6	66.1	26.1
Basic manufactures	346.6	298.9	463.2
Textile yarn, fabrics, etc.	71.2	65.7	90.6
Iron and steel	104.2	100.6	172.9
Universals, plates and sheets	47.6	40.5	61.3
Machinery and transport equipment	503.9	514.3	822.1
Machinery specialized for particular industries	75.0	77.6	115.3
General industrial machinery equipment and parts	60.3	48.7	76.1
Telecommunications, sound recording and reproducing equipment	45.2	47.4	102.0
Electrical machinery, apparatus, etc.*	67.2	65.9	133.1
Road vehicles and parts†	169.3	191.7	255.3
Passenger motor cars (excl. buses)	53.5	69.4	79.2
Lorries and special purposes motor vehicles	73.2	75.4	87.9
Motor vehicles for goods transport, etc.	66.3	72.3	83.7
Miscellaneous manufactured articles	138.0	170.0	213.6
Total (incl. others)	1,810.9	1,593.5	2,685.9

* Excluding telecommunications and sound equipment.
† Excluding tyres, engines and electrical parts.

Exports f.o.b.	2001	2002	2003
Food and live animals	203.1	244.2	255.3
Unmilled cereals	18.1	12.0	11.3
Vegetables and fruit	29.6	41.5	27.1
Beans, peas and other leguminous vegetables, dried and shelled	20.8	30.5	18.5
Raw sugar beet and cane, solid	0.9	20.4	15.6
Coffee, not roasted, coffee husks and skins	145.1	159.8	181.4
Crude materials (inedible) except fuels	140.7	107.3	197.3
Raw hides and skins (excl. furs)	27.9	8.7	2.3
Oil seeds and oleaginous fruit	37.7	40.0	61.1
Sesame seeds	24.5	31.3	47.9
Miscellaneous manufactured articles	50.4	57.1	50.6
Leather	46.7	53.4	43.1
Sheep and lamb skin leather	26.5	29.0	28.5
Commodities and transactions not elsewhere specified	4.5	3.5	0.0
Non-monetary gold, unwrought or semi-manufactured	4.5	3.5	0.0
Total (incl. others)	402.6	414.9	512.7

Source: UN, *International Trade Statistics Yearbook*.

Exports (million birr, 2004): Coffee, tea, mate and spices 1,649.1; Oil seeds and oleaginous fruits, miscellaneous grains, seeds and fruit; industrial or medicinal plants; straw and fodder 530.6; Vegetable plaiting materials; vegetable products not elsewhere specified or included 948.1; Sugars and sugar confectionery 134.0; Raw hides and skins (excluding fur) and leather 389.6; Cotton 160.1; Total 4,470.9.

PRINCIPAL TRADING PARTNERS

(US $ million)

Imports c.i.f.	2001	2002	2003
Belgium	37.9	40.9	28.4
China, People's Republic	134.8	144.8	313.7
Denmark	21.0	10.3	19.6
Djibouti	48.9	60.3	26.8
Egypt	17.8	19.4	29.9
France (incl. Monaco)	58.2	25.9	74.3
Germany	87.0	83.6	89.0
India	91.1	93.5	175.5
Indonesia	28.2	26.0	41.3
Italy	135.2	140.5	245.9
Japan	78.5	113.0	195.8
Kenya	15.1	17.4	23.1
Korea, Republic	42.8	21.5	43.5
Kuwait	1.0	0.3	128.3
Malaysia	12.1	7.3	29.2
Netherlands	41.8	38.9	60.4
Russia	8.8	15.7	30.0
Saudi Arabia	201.1	111.0	131.3
Sweden	38.4	30.1	32.7
Turkey	22.8	35.1	62.2
United Arab Emirates	112.1	114.3	40.5
United Kingdom	61.7	73.0	150.5
USA	167.5	126.5	384.4
Yemen	132.4	7.9	5.8
Total (incl. others)	1,811.0	1,593.5	2,685.9

Exports f.o.b.	2001	2002	2003
Belgium	7.3	12.4	14.5
China, People's Republic	4.5	7.4	5.0
Djibouti	71.4	54.3	99.4
Egypt	2.6	4.9	2.2
France (incl. Monaco)	11.6	11.1	8.5
Germany	23.1	49.5	57.6
Greece	2.9	4.8	3.7
Iceland	11.8	2.3	0.3
India	17.4	11.0	7.4
Indonesia	3.4	2.4	1.4
Israel	14.0	15.1	14.4
Italy	42.6	41.0	31.7
Japan	37.2	37.3	43.7
Netherlands	4.6	4.2	5.7
Pakistan	2.1	13.8	1.3
Saudi Arabia	37.8	28.1	35.4
Somalia	13.4	9.6	28.9
Switzerland-Liechtenstein	8.3	10.2	16.1
Turkey	0.2	5.6	10.9
United Arab Emirates	6.4	8.1	10.8
United Kingdom	15.8	17.3	15.6
USA	19.6	16.7	22.7
Yemen	8.0	7.6	16.1
Total (incl. others)	402.6	414.9	512.7

Source: UN, *International Trade Statistics Yearbook*.

Transport

RAILWAYS

(traffic, year ending 7 July)*

	2002/03	2003/04	2004/05
Addis Ababa–Djibouti:			
Passenger-km (million)	253	40	34
Freight (million net ton-km)	—	81	56

* Including traffic on the section of the Djibouti–Addis Ababa line which runs through the Republic of Djibouti. Data pertaining to freight include service traffic.

ROAD TRAFFIC

(motor vehicles in use, year ending 7 July)

	2000	2001	2002
Passenger cars	59,048	59,737	67,614
Buses and coaches	9,334	11,387	18,067
Lorries and vans	34,355	43,375	34,102
Motorcycles and mopeds	n.a.	2,198	2,575
Road tractors	6,809	1,275	1,396
Total	109,546	117,972	123,754

Source: IRF, *World Road Statistics*.

SHIPPING

Merchant Fleet

(registered at 31 December)

	2003	2004	2005
Number of vessels	9	8	8
Displacement (grt)	81,933	79,441	79,441

Source: Lloyd's Register-Fairplay, *World Fleet Statistics*.

International Sea-borne Shipping

(freight traffic, '000 metric tons, year ending 7 July)

	1996/97	1997/98	1998/99
Goods loaded	242	201	313
Goods unloaded	777	1,155	947

Source: former Ministry of Transport and Communications, Addis Ababa.

CIVIL AVIATION

(traffic on scheduled services)

	2002	2003	2004
Passenger-km (million)	3,300	3,600	4,400
Total ton-km ('000)	83,500	93,500	117,100

Source: UN, *Monthly Bulletin of Statistics*.

Tourism

TOURIST ARRIVALS BY COUNTRY OF ORIGIN

	2003	2004	2005
Canada	4,434	5,169	8,396
Djibouti	21,708	14,627	4,179
France	5,482	4,501	5,899
Germany	5,719	6,256	6,731
India	3,602	4,641	7,125
Italy	6,348	7,696	7,983
Japan	1,622	1,658	1,708
Kenya	7,072	7,217	9,277
Netherlands	3,044	3,227	4,387
Saudi Arabia	6,283	9,778	5,382
Sudan	3,769	3,787	5,343
United Kingdom	8,978	10,627	11,254
USA	22,496	28,112	32,282
Yemen	2,651	2,975	3,102
Total (incl. others)*	179,910	184,079	227,398

* Including Ethiopian nationals residing abroad.

Receipts from tourism (US $ million, incl. passenger transport): 336 in 2003; 457 in 2004; n.a. in 2005.

Source: World Tourism Organization.

Communications Media

	2003	2004	2005
Telephones ('000 main lines in use)	435.0	484.4	610.3
Mobile cellular telephones ('000 subscribers)	97.8	178.0	410.6
Personal computers ('000 in use)	150	225	n.a.
Internet users ('000)	75	113	n.a.

Book production: 444 titles in 1999.

Non-daily newspapers: 78 in 1998 (average combined circulation 402,000).

Daily newspapers: 2 in 1998 (average circulation 23,000 copies).

Radio receivers ('000 in use): 11,340 in 2000.

Television receivers ('000 in use): 1,260 in 2000.

Facsimile machines (number in use): 3,594 in 2000.

Sources: UNESCO, *Statistical Yearbook*; UN, *Statistical Yearbook*; International Telecommunication Union.

Education

(1999/2000 unless otherwise indicated)

	Institutions	Teachers	Students
Pre-primary	834	4,584*	153,280*
Primary	11,490	110,945*	8,019,287*
Secondary: general	410	77,775*	4,382,571*
Secondary: teacher training	12	294	4,813
Secondary: skill development centres	25	367	2,474
Secondary: technical and vocational	25	4,957*	106,336*
University level	6	4,803†	172,111†
Other higher:			
Government	11	578	18,412
Non-government	4	140	8,376

* 2004/05 figure.

† 2003/04 figure.

Sources: Ministry of Education, Addis Ababa; UNESCO Institute of Statistics.

Adult literacy rate (UNESCO estimates): 41.5% (males 49.2%; females 33.8%) in 2002 (Source: UN Development Programme, *Human Development Report*).

Directory

The Constitution

The Constitution of the Federal Democratic Republic of Ethiopia was adopted by the transitional Government on 8 December 1994. The following is a summary of the main provisions of the Constitution, which came into force on 22 August 1995.

GENERAL PROVISIONS

The Constitution establishes a federal and democratic state structure and all sovereign power resides in the nations, nationalities and peoples of Ethiopia. The Constitution is the supreme law of the land. Human rights and freedoms, emanating from the nature of mankind, are inviolable and inalienable. State and religion are separate and there shall be no state religion. The State shall not interfere in religious matters and vice versa. All Ethiopian languages shall enjoy equal state recognition; Amharic shall be the working language of the Federal Government.

FUNDAMENTAL RIGHTS AND FREEDOMS

All persons are equal before the law and are guaranteed equal and effective protection, without discrimination on grounds of race, nation, nationality, or other social origin, colour, sex, language, religion, political or other opinion, property, birth or other status. Everyone has the right to freedom of thought, conscience and religion and the freedom, either individually or in community with others, and in public or private, to manifest his religion or belief in worship, observance, practice and teaching. Every person has the inviolable and inalienable right to life, privacy, and the security of person and liberty.

DEMOCRATIC RIGHTS

Every Ethiopian national, without discrimination based on colour, race, nation, nationality, sex, language, religion, political or other opinion, or other status, has the following rights: on the attainment of 18 years of age, to vote in accordance with the law; to be elected to any office at any level of government; to freely express oneself without interference; to hold opinions without interference; to engage in economic activity and to pursue a livelihood anywhere within the national territory; to choose his or her means of livelihood, occupation and profession; and to own private property.

Every nation, nationality and people in Ethiopia has the following rights: an unconditional right to self-determination, including the right to secession; the right to speak, to write and to develop its own language; the right to express, to develop and to promote its culture, and to preserve its history; the right to a full measure of self-government which includes the right to establish institutions of government in the territory that it inhabits. Women shall, in the enjoyment of rights and protections provided for by this Constitution, have equal rights with men.

STATE STRUCTURE

The Federal Democratic Republic of Ethiopia shall have a parliamentarian form of government. The Federal Democratic Republic shall comprise nine States. Addis Ababa shall be the capital city of the Federal State.

STRUCTURE AND DIVISION OF POWERS

The Federal Democratic Republic of Ethiopia comprises the Federal Government and the member States. The Federal Government and the States shall have legislative, executive and judicial powers. The House of People's Representatives is the highest authority of the Federal Government. The House is responsible to the people. The State Council is the highest organ of state authority. It is responsible to the people of the State. State government shall be established at state and other administrative levels deemed necessary. Adequate power shall be granted to the lowest units of government to enable the people to participate directly in the administration of such units. The State Council has legislative power on matters falling under state jurisdiction. Consistent with the provisions of this Constitution, the Council has the power to draft, adopt and amend the state constitution. The state administration constitutes the highest organ of executive power. State judicial power is vested in its courts. The States shall respect the powers of the Federal Government. The Federal Government shall likewise respect the powers of the States. The Federal Government may, when necessary, delegate to the States powers and functions granted to it by the Constitution.

THE FEDERAL HOUSES

There shall be two Federal Houses: the House of People's Representatives and the House of the Federation.

Members of the House of People's Representatives shall be elected by the people for a term of five years on the basis of universal suffrage and by direct, free and fair elections held by secret ballot. Members of the House, on the basis of population and special representation of minority nationalities and peoples, shall not exceed 550; of these, minority nationalities and peoples shall have at least 20 seats. The House of People's Representatives shall have legislative power in all matters assigned by this Constitution to federal jurisdiction. The political party or coalition of political parties that has the greatest number of seats in the House of People's Representatives shall form and lead the Executive. Elections for a new House shall be concluded one month prior to the expiry of the House's term.

The House of the Federation is composed of representatives of nations, nationalities and peoples. Each nation, nationality and people shall be represented in the House of the Federation by at least one member. Each nation or nationality shall be represented by one additional representative for each one million of its population. Members of the House of the Federation shall be elected by the State Councils. The State Councils may themselves elect representatives to the House of the Federation, or they may hold elections to have the representatives elected by the people directly. The House of the Federation shall hold at least two sessions annually. The term of mandate of the House of the Federation shall be five years. No one may be a member of the House of People's Representatives and of the House of the Federation simultaneously.

PRESIDENT OF THE REPUBLIC

The President of the Federal Democratic Republic of Ethiopia is the Head of State. The House of People's Representatives shall nominate the candidate for President. The nominee shall be elected President if a joint session of the House of People's Representatives and the House of the Federation approves his candidacy by a two-thirds' majority vote. The term of office of the President shall be six years. No person shall be elected President for more than two terms. The President's duties include the opening of the Federal Houses; appointing ambassadors and other envoys to represent the country abroad; granting, upon recommendation by the Prime Minister and in accordance with law, high military titles; and granting pardons.

THE EXECUTIVE

The highest executive powers of the Federal Government are vested in the Prime Minister and in the Council of Ministers. The Prime Minister and the Council of Ministers are responsible to the House of People's Representatives. In the exercise of state functions, members of the Council of Ministers are collectively responsible for all decisions they make as a body. Unless otherwise provided in this Constitution, the term of office of the Prime Minister is the duration of the mandate of the House of People's Representatives. The Prime Minister is the Chief Executive, the Chairman of the Council of Ministers, and the Commander-in-Chief of the national armed forces. The Prime Minister shall submit for approval to the House of People's Representatives nominees for ministerial posts from among members of the two Houses or from among persons who are not members of either House and possess the required qualifications. The Council of Ministers is responsible to the Prime Minister and, in all its decisions, is responsible to the House of People's Representatives. The Council of Ministers ensures the implementation of laws and decisions adopted by the House of People's Representatives.

STRUCTURE AND POWERS OF THE COURTS

Supreme Federal judicial authority is vested in the Federal Supreme Court. The House of People's Representatives may, by a two-thirds' majority vote, establish nation-wide, or in some parts of the country only, the Federal High Court and First-Instance Courts it deems necessary. Unless decided in this manner, the jurisdictions of the Federal High Court and of the First-Instance Courts are hereby delegated to the state courts. States shall establish State Supreme, High and First-Instance Courts. Judicial powers, both at federal and state levels, are vested in the courts. Courts of any level shall be free from any interference or influence of any governmental body, government official or from any other source. Judges shall exercise their functions in full independence and shall be directed solely by the law. The Federal Supreme Court shall have the highest and final judicial power over federal matters. State Supreme Courts shall have the highest and final judicial power over state matters. They shall also exercise the jurisdiction of the Federal High Court.

MISCELLANEOUS PROVISIONS

The Council of Ministers of the Federal Government shall have the power to decree a state of emergency in the event of an external invasion, a breakdown of law and order that endangers the constitutional order and cannot be controlled by the regular law enforcement agencies and personnel, a natural disaster or an epidemic. State executives can decree a state-wide state of emergency should a natural disaster or an epidemic occur.

A National Election Board independent of any influence shall be established, to conduct free and fair elections in federal and state constituencies in an impartial manner.

The Government

HEAD OF STATE

President: Lt GIRMA WOLDE GIORGIS (took office 8 October 2001).

COUNCIL OF MINISTERS
(August 2007)

Prime Minister: MELES ZENAWI.

Deputy Prime Minister and Minister of Agriculture and Rural Development: ADDISO LEGGESE.

Minister and Economic Adviser to the Prime Minister: NEWAYEKRISTOS GEBRAB.

Minister and Public Organization and Participation Adviser to the Prime Minister: ABAY TSEHAYE.

Minister and Public Relations Adviser to the Prime Minister: BEREKET SIMON.

Minister and Special Adviser to the Prime Minister: Dr FASIL NAHOM.

Minister and National Security Affairs Adviser: MULUGETA ALEMSEGED.

Minister and Adviser to the Deputy Prime Minister: Prof. MESFIN ABEBE.

Minister of Foreign Affairs: SEYOUM MESFIN.

Minister of Health: Dr TEWEDROS ADHANOM.

Minister of Capacity Building: TEFERA WALWA.

Minister of Defence: KUMA DEMEKESA.

Minister of Energy and Mines: ALEMAYEHU TEGENU.

Minister of Finance and Economic Development: SUFYAN AHMED.

Minister of Information: BERHAN HAILU.

Minister of Education: Dr SINTAYEHU WOLDEMIKAEL.

Minister of Federal Affairs: SIRAJ FEGETA.

Minister of Trade and Industry: GIRMA BIRU.

Minister of Justice: ASSEFA KESSITO.

Minister of Transport and Communications: JUNEDI SADO.

Minister of Cabinet Affairs: BIRHANU ADELO.

Minister of Labour and Social Affairs: HASAN ABDELLA.

Minister of Water Resources: ASEFAW DINGAM.

Minister of Revenues: MELUKA FENTA.

Minister of Youth and Sports: ASTER MAMO.

Minister of Women's Affairs: HIRUT DILEBO.

Minister of Culture and Tourism: MAHMUD DIRIR.

MINISTRIES

Office of the President: POB 1031, Addis Ababa; tel. (11) 1551000; fax (11) 1552030.

Office of the Prime Minister: POB 1013, Addis Ababa; tel. (11) 1552044; fax (11) 1552020.

Ministry of Agriculture and Rural Development: POB 62347, Addis Ababa; tel. (11) 5538134; fax (11) 5530776; e-mail moav@telecom.net.et.

Ministry of Capacity Building: Addis Ababa; tel. (11) 1552800; fax (11) 1553338.

Ministry of Culture and Tourism: POB 2183, Addis Ababa; tel. (11) 5512310; fax (11) 5512889; e-mail tourismethiopia@ethionet.et; internet www.tourismethiopia.org.

Ministry of Defence: POB 1373, Addis Ababa; tel. (11) 5511777; fax (11) 5516053.

Ministry of Education: POB 1367, Addis Ababa; tel. (11) 1553133; fax (11) 1550877; e-mail heardmoe@telecom.net.et.

Ministry of Energy and Mines: POB 486, Addis Ababa; tel. (11) 5153689; fax (11) 5517874; e-mail mme@telecom.net.et.

Ministry of Federal Affairs: POB 1031, Addis Ababa; tel. (11) 5512766; fax (11) 1552030.

Ministry of Finance and Economic Development: POB 1037, Addis Ababa; tel. (11) 1552800; fax (11) 1550118; e-mail meda2@telecom.net.et.

Ministry of Foreign Affairs: POB 393, Addis Ababa; tel. (11) 5517345; fax (11) 5514300; e-mail mfa.addis@telecom.net.et; internet www.mfa.gov.et.

Ministry of Health: POB 1234, Addis Ababa; tel. (11) 5517011; fax (11) 5519366; e-mail moh@telecom.net.et.

Ministry of Information: Addis Ababa; tel. (11) 1551100; fax (11) 1569678; internet www.moinfo.gov.et.

Ministry of Infrastructure: POB 1238, Addis Ababa; tel. (11) 5516166; fax (11) 5515665; e-mail publicrelation@moi.gov.et; internet www.moi.gov.et.

Ministry of Justice: POB 1370, Addis Ababa; tel. (11) 512288; fax (11) 517775; e-mail ministry-justice@telecom.net.et; internet www.mojet.gov.et.

Ministry of Labour and Social Affairs: POB 2056, Addis Ababa; tel. (11) 5517080; fax (11) 5518396; e-mail moisa-comt@telecom.net.et.

Ministry of Revenue: POB 2559, Addis Ababa; tel. (11) 4667466; fax (11) 4662628; e-mail mor@telecom.net.et; internet www.mor.gov.et.

Ministry of Trade and Industry: POB 704, Addis Ababa; tel. (11) 5518025; fax (11) 5514288.

Ministry of Water Resources: POB 5744, Addis Ababa; tel. (11) 6611111; fax (11) 6611700; e-mail mowrl@telecom.net.et.

Ministry of Women's Affairs: Addis Ababa.

Ministry of Works and Urban Development: POB 1238, Addis Ababa; tel. (11) 5518292; fax (11) 527969.

Ministry of Youth and Sports: POB 1364, Addis Ababa; tel. (11) 5517020.

Regional Governments

Ethiopia comprises nine regional governments, one chartered city (Addis Ababa) and one Administrative Council (Dire Dawa), which are vested with authority for self-administration. The executive bodies are respectively headed by Presidents (regional states) and Chairmen (Addis Ababa and Dire Dawa).

PRESIDENTS
(August 2007)

Tigrai: TSEGAYE BERHE.

Afar: ESMAEL ALISERO.

Amhara: AYALEW GOBEZE.

Oromia: Gen. ABEDULA GEMEDA.

Somali: ABDULAHI HASAN MOHAMMED.

Benishangul/Gumuz: YAREGAL AYSHESHIM.

Southern Nations, Nationalities and Peoples: SHIFERAW SHIGUTTE.

Gambela: UMED UBONG.

Harari: MURAD ABDULHADIN.

CHAIRMEN
(August 2007)

Dire Dawa: ABDULAZIZ MOHAMMED.

Addis Ababa: BERHANU DERESSA.

Legislature

FEDERAL PARLIAMENTARY ASSEMBLY

The legislature comprises an upper house, the House of the Federation (Yefedereshn Mekir Bet), with 108 seats (members are selected by state assemblies and are drawn one each from 22 minority nationalities and one from each professional sector of the remaining nationalities, and serve for a period of five years), and a lower house of no more than 550 directly elected members, the House of People's Representatives (Yehizbtewekayoch Mekir Bet), who are also elected for a five-year term.

Speaker of the House of the Federation: DEGIFE BULA.

Deputy Speaker of the House of the Federation: MOHAMMED SIREE.

Yehizbtewekayoch Mekir Bet
(House of People's Representatives)

Speaker: TESHOME TOGA.

Deputy Speaker: SHITAYE MINALE.

General Election, 15 May 2005*

Party	Seats
Ethiopian People's Revolutionary Democratic Front (EPRDF)	327
Coalition for Unity and Democracy (CUD)	109
United Ethiopian Democratic Forces (UEDF)	52
Oromo Federalist Democratic Movement (OFDM)	11
Somali People's Democratic Party (SPDP)	24
Benishangul Gumuz People's Democratic Unity Front (BGPDUF)	8
Afar National Democratic Party (ANDP)	8
Gambela People's Democratic Movement (GPDM)	3
Sheko-Majenger People's Democratic Unity Organization (SMPDUO)	1
Harari National League (HNL)	1
Argoba National Democratic Organization (ANDO)	1
Independent	1
Total	546

* Owing to alleged electoral irregularities at some polling stations, voting was repeated in 31 constituencies on 21 August, when a by-election for a further seat was also conducted. Voting for 24 seats in the Somali Regional State additionally took place on that date.

Election Commission

National Electoral Board of Ethiopia (NEBE): POB 40812, Addis Ababa; tel. (1) 514911; fax (1) 514929; internet www.electionsethiopia.org; f. 1993; independent board of seven politically non-affiliated mems appointed, on the Prime Minister's recommendation, by the House of People's Representatives; Chair. Kemal Bedri Kelo.

Political Organizations

Afar People's Democratic Organization (APDO): fmrly Afar Liberation Front (ALF); based in fmr Hararge and Wollo Admin. Regions; Leader Ismail Ali Sirro.

Alliance for Freedom and Democracy (AFD): Addis Ababa; f. 2006; broad coalition of political parties and rebel groups opposed to the Government.

Coalition for Unity and Democracy (CUD): POB 882, Addis Ababa; tel. (11) 553506; fax (11) 553155; e-mail kinijitheadquarter@kinijit.org; internet www.kinijit.org; f. 2004 as a coalition of four parties opposed to the EPRDF; the All Ethiopia Unity Party, the Ethiopian Democratic League, the Ethiopian Democratic Unity Party and the Rainbow Ethiopia: Movement for Democracy and Justice merged in late 2005 to form a single party; Pres. Hailu Shawel; Vice-Pres. Birtukan Mideksa.

Ethiopian People's Patriotic Front (EPPF): e-mail info@eppf.net; internet www.eppf.net; armed anti-Govt group.

Ogaden National Liberation Front (ONLF): e-mail foreign@onlf.org; internet www.onlf.org; f. 1984; seeks self-determination for the Ogaden region; Chair. Mohamed Omar Osman.

Oromo Liberation Front (OLF): e-mail olfinfodesk@earthlink.net; internet www.oromoliberationfront.org; seeks self-determination for the Oromo people; participated in the Ethiopian transitional Govt until June 1992; Chair. Dawud Ibsa Ayana; Vice-Chair. Abdulfattah A. Moussa Biyyo.

Sidama Liberation Front (SLF).

Coalition of Ethiopian Democratic Forces (COEDF): f. 1991 in the USA by the Ethiopian People's Revolutionary Party—EPRP (the dominant member), together with a faction of the Ethiopian Democratic Union (EDU) and the Ethiopian Socialist Movement (MEISON); opposes the EPRDF; Chair. Mersha Yoseph.

Ethiopian National Congress (ENC): e-mail tsehaibs@eircom.net; internet www.ethiopiannationalcongress.org; f. 1997; USA-based org.; aims to form a unified opposition among anti-Govt parties; Chair. Tsehai Berhane-Selassie.

Ethiopian National Democratic Party (ENDP): f. 1994 by merger of five pro-Govt orgs with mems in the Council of Representatives; comprises: the Ethiopian Democratic Organization, the Ethiopian Democratic Organization Coalition (EDC), the Gurage People's Democratic Front (GPDF), the Kembata People's Congress (KPC), and the Wolaita People's Democratic Front (WPDF); Chair. Fekadu Gedamu.

Ethiopian People's Revolutionary Democratic Front (EPRDF): Addis Ababa; f. 1989 by the TPLF as an alliance of insurgent groups seeking regional autonomy and engaged in armed struggle against the EDUP Govt; Chair. Meles Zenawi; Vice-Chair. Addiso Leggese; in May 1991, with other orgs, formed transitional Govt.

Amhara National Democratic Movement (ANDM): based in Tigrai; represents interests of the Amhara people; fmrly the Ethiopian People's Democratic Movement (EPDM); adopted present name in 1994; Chair. Addiso Leggese.

Oromo People's Democratic Organization (OPDO): f. 1990 by the TPLF to promote its cause in Oromo areas; based among the Oromo people in the Shoa region; Leader Gen. Abedula Gemeda.

Tigrai People's Liberation Front (TPLF): f. 1975; the dominant org. within the EPRDF; Chair. Meles Zenawi; Vice-Chair. Seyoum Mesfin.

Gambela People's Democratic Front (GPDF): pro-Govt group based in the Gambela region; Chair. Akilo Nigilio.

Oromo Federalist Democratic Movement (OFDM): Chair. Bulcha Demeksa.

Sheko-Majenger People's Democratic Unity Organization (SMPDUO).

Sidama Liberation Movement (SLM): Awassa.

Somali Abo Liberation Front (SALF): operates in fmr Bale Admin. Region; has received Somali military assistance; Sec.-Gen. Masurad Shu'abi Ibrahim.

Somali People's Democratic Party: f. 1998 by merger of Ogaden National Liberation Front (ONLF) and the Ethiopian Somali Democratic League (ESDL—an alliance comprising the Somali Democratic Union Party, the Issa and Gurgura Liberation Front, the Gurgura Independence Front, the Eastern Gabooye Democratic Organization, the Eastern Ethiopian Somali League, the Horyal Democratic Front, the Social Alliance Democratic Organization, the Somali Abo Democratic Union, the Shekhash People's Democratic Movement, the Ethiopian Somalis' Democratic Movement and the Per Barreh Party); Chair. Mohamoud Dirir Gheddi; Sec.-Gen. Sultan Ibrahim.

Southern Ethiopian People's Democratic Front (SEPDF): f. 1992; as an alliance of 10 ethnically based political groups from the south of the country; was represented in the transitional Council of Representatives, although five of the participating groups were expelled from the Council in April 1993.

United Ethiopian Democratic Forces (UEDF): Addis Ababa; internet www.hebret.com; f. 2003; Chair. Fasika Belete.

Afar Revolutionary Democratic Unity Front (ARDUF): f. 1993.

All Amhara Unity Party (AAUP).

All Ethiopian Socialist Movement (MEISON): f. 1968.

Ethiopian Social Democratic Federal Party (ESDFP): f. 1993 as the Council of Alternative Forces for Peace and Democracy in Ethiopia; adopted present form in November 2004; opposes the EPRDF; Chair. Dr Beyene Petros.

Ethiopian Medhin Democratic Party (MEDHIN): internet www.medhin.org; US-based org.; Chair. Prof. Seyoum Gelaye.

Ethiopian National United Front (ENUF): tel. 7851618; e-mail info@enufforethiopia.net; internet www.enufforethiopia.net; f. 2001; USA-based org.; Chair. Bekele Molla.

Ethiopian People's Federal Democratic Unity Party (HibreHizb): Vice-Sec. Lt Ayalsew Dessie.

Ethiopian People's Revolutionary Party (EPRP): e-mail espic@aol.com; internet www.eprp.com; f. 1972; Leader Mersha Yoseph.

Oromo National Congress (ONC): Addis Ababa; tel. (1) 512104; Chair. Dr Merere Gudina.

Southern Ethiopian People's Democratic Coalition (SEPDC): opposition alliance; Chair. Dr Beyene Petros.

Tigraian Alliance for National Democracy (TAND): Leader Mekonnen Zellelew.

United Ethiopian Democratic Party (UEDP): POB 101458, Addis Ababa; tel. (11) 5508727; fax (11) 5508730; e-mail uedpmedhinpr@gmail.com; internet www.uedpmedhin.org; f. 2003 by the merger of Ethiopian Democratic Unity Party and the Ethiopian Democratic Party; Sec.-Gen. Dr Admassu Gebreyehu.

United Oromo Liberation Forces (UOLF): f. 2000 in Asmara, Eritrea, as a common Oromo Front seeking to overthrow the Ethiopian Govt; Sec.-Gen. Galasa Dilbo; alliance comprises:

Islamic Front for the Liberation of Oromia: Leader Abdelkarim Ibrahim Hamid.

Oromo Liberation Council (OLC).

Oromo Liberation Front (OLF): see above.

Oromo People's Liberation Front (OPLF).

Oromo People's Liberation Organization (OPLO).

United Oromo People's Liberation Front (UOPLF).

Western Somali Liberation Front (WSLF): POB 978, Mogadishu, Somalia; f. 1975; aims to unite the Ogaden region with Somalia; maintains guerrilla forces of c. 3,000 men; has received support from regular Somali forces; Sec.-Gen. ISSA SHAYKH ABDI NASIR ADAN.

The following parties have parliamentary representation: **Afar National Democratic Party (ANDP); Argoba National Democratic Organization (ANDO); Benishangul Gumuz People's Democratic Unity Front (BGPDUF); Gambela People's Democratic Movement (GPDM); Harari National League (HNL); Somali People's Democratic Party (SPDP).**

Diplomatic Representation

EMBASSIES IN ETHIOPIA

Algeria: Woreda 23, Kebele 13, House No. 1819, POB 5740, Addis Ababa; tel. (11) 3719666; fax (11) 3719669; e-mail algemb@telecom.net.et; Ambassador NOUREDDINE AOUAM.

Angola: Woreda 18, Kebele 26, House No. 6, POB 2962, Addis Ababa; tel. (11) 5510085; fax (11) 5514922; e-mail angola.embassy@telecom.net.et; Ambassador MANUEL DOMINGOS AUGUSTO.

Austria: POB 1219, Addis Ababa; tel. (11) 3712144; fax (11) 3712140; e-mail addis-abeba-ob@bmeia.gv.at; internet www.aussenministerium.at/addisabeba; Ambassador RUDOLF AGSTNER.

Belgium: Comoros St, Kebele 8, POB 1239, Addis Ababa; tel. (11) 6611813; fax (11) 6613646; e-mail addisababa@diplobel.org; internet www.diplomatie.be/addisababa; Ambassador GUNTHER SLEEUWAGEN.

Benin: Addis Ababa; Ambassador EDOUARD AHO-GELLE.

Botswana: POB 22282, Addis Ababa; tel. (11) 715422; fax (11) 714099; Ambassador ZIBANE JOHN NTAKHWANA.

Brazil: Bole Sub-City, Kebele 2, House No. 2830, POB 2458, Addis Ababa; tel. (11) 6620401; fax (11) 6620412; e-mail embradisadm@ethionet.et; Ambassador RENATO XAVIER.

Bulgaria: Haile Gabreselassie Rd, Woreda 17, Kebele 13, POB 987, Addis Ababa; tel. (11) 6610032; fax (11) 6613373; e-mail bulemba@ethionet.et; Chargé d'affaires a.i. EMIL TRIFONOV.

Burkina Faso: Kebele 19, House No. 281, POB 19685, Addis Ababa; tel. (11) 6615863; fax (11) 6625857; e-mail ambfet@telecom.net.et; Ambassador BRUNO ZIDOUEMBA.

Burundi: POB 3641, Addis Ababa; tel. (11) 4651300; e-mail burundi.emb@telecom.net.et; Ambassador PHILIPPE NTAHONKURIYE.

Cameroon: Bole Rd, Woreda 18, Kebele 26, House No. 168, POB 1026, Addis Ababa; tel. (11) 5504488; fax (11) 5518434; Ambassador JEAN-HILAIRE MBÉA MBÉA.

Canada: Nefas Silk Lafto Kifle Ketema 3, Kebele 4, House No. 122, POB 1130, Addis Ababa; tel. (11) 3713022; fax (11) 3713033; e-mail addis@international.gc.ca; internet www.dfait-maeci.gc.ca/africa/ethiopia-contact-en.asp; Ambassador YVES BOULANGER.

Cape Verde: Kebele 3, House No. 107, POB 200093, Addis Ababa; tel. (11) 6635466; e-mail embcv@ethionet.et; Chargé d'affaires a.i. CUSTODIA LIMA.

Chad: Bole Rd, Woreda 17, Kebele 20, House No. 2583, POB 5119, Addis Ababa; tel. (11) 6613819; fax (11) 6612050; Ambassador MAITINE DJOUMBE.

China, People's Republic: Jimma Rd, Woreda 24, Kebele 13, House No. 792, POB 5643, Addis Ababa; tel. (11) 3711960; fax (11) 3712457; e-mail chineseembassy@telecom.net.et; internet et.china-embassy.org; Ambassador LIN LIN.

Congo, Democratic Republic: Makanisa Rd, Woreda 23, Kebele 13, House No. 1779, POB 2723, Addis Ababa; tel. (11) 3710111; fax (11) 3713485; e-mail rdca@telecom.net.et; Ambassador GÉRARD MAPANGO KEMISHANGA.

Congo, Republic: Woreda 3, Kebele 51, House No. 378, POB 5639, Addis Ababa; tel. (11) 5514188; fax (11) 5514331; Ambassador RAYMOND SERGE BALE.

Côte d'Ivoire: Woreda 23, Kebele 13, House No. 1308, POB 3668, Addis Ababa; tel. (11) 3711213; fax (11) 3712178; e-mail coted.aa@telecom.net.et; Ambassador MDALO GBOUAGBRE.

Cuba: Woreda 17, Kebele 19, House No. 197, POB 5623, Addis Ababa; tel. (11) 620459; fax (11) 620460; e-mail embacuba@ethiopia.cubaminrex.cu; Ambassador RICARDO GARCÍA DÍAZ.

Czech Republic: Kebele 15, House No. 29, POB 3108, Addis Ababa; tel. (11) 5516132; fax (11) 5513471; e-mail addisababa@embassy.mzv.cz; internet www.mzv.cz/addisababa; Ambassador ZDENĚK DOBIÁŠ.

Denmark: c/o Embassy of Norway, Nefas Silk Lafto Kifle Ketema, Kebele 3, House No. 1019, POB 12955, Addis Ababa; tel. (11) 3711377; fax (11) 3711399; e-mail addambdk@ethionet.et; internet www.ambaddisababa.um.dk; Ambassador PERNILLE DAHLER KARDEL.

Djibouti: POB 1022, Addis Ababa; tel. (11) 6613200; fax (11) 6612786; Ambassador IBRAHIM MOHAMMED KAMIL.

Egypt: POB 1611, Addis Ababa; tel. (11) 1226422; fax (11) 1226432; e-mail egyptian.emb@ethionet.et; Ambassador SHAMEL NASSER.

Equatorial Guinea: Bole Rd, Woreda 17, Kebele 23, House No. 162, POB 246, Addis Ababa; tel. (11) 6626278; Ambassador (vacant).

Eritrea: POB 2571, Addis Ababa; tel. (11) 5512844; fax (11) 5514911; Chargé d'affaires a.i. SAHIH OMER.

Finland: Mauritania St, Kebele 12, House No. 1431, POB 1017, Addis Ababa; tel. (11) 3205920; fax (11) 3205923; e-mail sanomat.add@formin.fi; Ambassador KIRSTI AARNIO.

France: Kabana, POB 1464, Addis Ababa; tel. (11) 1236022; fax (11) 1236029; e-mail scacamb@ethionet.et; internet www.ambafrance-ethiopie.org; Ambassador STÉPHANE GOMPERTZ.

Gabon: Woreda 17, Kebele 18, House No. 1026, POB 1256, Addis Ababa; tel. (11) 6611075; fax (11) 6613700; Ambassador EMMANUEL ISSOZE-NGONDET.

The Gambia: Kebele 3, House No. 79, POB 60083, Addis Ababa; tel. (11) 6624647; fax (11) 6627895; e-mail gambia@ethionet.et; Ambassador Dr OMAR A. TOURAY.

Germany: Yeka Kifle Ketema, Kebele 6, POB 660, Addis Ababa; tel. (11) 1235139; fax (11) 1235152; e-mail germemb@ethionet.et; internet www.addis-abeba.diplo.de; Ambassador Dr CLAAS DIETER KNOOP.

Ghana: Jimma Rd, Woreda 24, Kebele 13, House No. 108, POB 3173, Addis Ababa; tel. (11) 3711402; fax (11) 3712511; e-mail ghmfa24@telecom.net.et; Ambassador JOHN EVONLAH AGGREY.

Greece: off Debre Zeit Rd, POB 1168, Addis Ababa; tel. (11) 4654911; fax (11) 4654883; e-mail greekembassy@telecom.net.et; internet www.telecom.net.et/~greekemb; Ambassador DIONISIOS KOUNTOUREAS.

Guinea: Debre Zeit Rd, Woreda 18, Kebele 14, House No. 58, POB 1190, Addis Ababa; tel. (11) 4651308; fax (11) 4651250; Ambassador SEKOU CAMARA.

Holy See: POB 588, Addis Ababa (Apostolic Nunciature); tel. (11) 3712100; fax (11) 3711499; e-mail vatican.embassy@telecom.net.et; Apostolic Nuncio Most Rev. MOLINER INGLÉS RAMIRO (Titular Archbishop of Sarda).

India: Kabena, POB 528, Addis Ababa; tel. (11) 1552100; fax (11) 1552521; e-mail indembassy@telecom.net.et; Ambassador GURJIT SINGH.

Indonesia: Mekanisa Rd, POB 1004, Addis Ababa; tel. (11) 3712104; fax (11) 3710873; e-mail indoeth@hotmail.com; Ambassador DEDDY SUDARMAN.

Iran: 317–318 Jimma Rd, POB 1144, Addis Ababa; tel. (11) 3710037; fax (11) 3712299; e-mail ir.em.et@telecom.net.et; internet www.iranembassy-addis.net; Ambassador ABABA KIUMARS FOTOUHI QIYAM.

Ireland: Sierra Leone St, Kebele 6, House No. 21, POB 9585, Addis Ababa; tel. (11) 4665050; fax (11) 4665020; e-mail ireland.emb@ethionet.et; Chargé d'affaires a.i. DON SEXTON.

Israel: Woreda 16, Kebele 22, House No. 283, POB 1266, Addis Ababa; tel. (11) 6460999; fax (11) 64619619; e-mail embassy@addisababa.mfa.gov.il; internet addisababa.mfa.gov.il; Ambassador YAACOV AMITAI.

Italy: Villa Italia, POB 1105, Addis Ababa; tel. (11) 1235717; fax (11) 1235689; e-mail ambasciata.addisabeba@esteri.it; Ambassador RAFFAELE DE LUTIO.

Japan: Woreda 18, Kebele 7, House No. 653, POB 5650, Addis Ababa; tel. (11) 5511088; fax (11) 5511350; e-mail japan-embassy@telecom.net.et; Ambassador KINICHI KOMANO.

Kenya: Woreda 16, Kebele 1, POB 3301, Addis Ababa; tel. (11) 610033; fax (11) 611433; e-mail kenya.embassy@telecom.net.et; Ambassador FRANKLIN ESIPILA.

Korea, Democratic People's Republic: Woreda 20, Kebele 40, House No. 892, POB 2378, Addis Ababa; tel. (11) 6182828; Ambassador O UL ROK.

Korea, Republic: Jimma Rd, Old Airport Area, POB 2047, Addis Ababa; tel. (11) 4655230; e-mail skorea.emb@telecom.net.et; Ambassador JHUNG BYUNG KUCK.

Kuwait: Woreda 17, Kebele 20, House No. 128, POB 19898, Addis Ababa; tel. (11) 6615411; fax (11) 6612621; Ambassador FAISAL MUTLAQ AL-ADWAHI.

Lesotho: Asmara Rd, Woreda 17, Kebele 16, House No. 157, POB 7483, Addis Ababa; tel. (11) 6614368; fax (11) 6612837; Ambassador MOTLATSI RAMAFOLE.

Liberia: Roosevelt St, Woreda 21, Kebele 4, House No. 237, POB 3116, Addis Ababa; tel. (11) 5513655; Ambassador Dr Edward Gboloco Howard Clinton.

Libya: Ras Tessema Sefer, Woreda 3, Kebele 53, House No. 585, POB 5728, Addis Ababa; tel. (11) 5511077; fax (11) 5511383; Ambassador Ali Abdalla Awidan.

Madagascar: Woreda 17, Kebele 19, House No. 629, POB 60004, Addis Ababa; tel. (11) 612555; fax (11) 610127; e-mail emb.mad@telecom.net.et; Ambassador Jean Pierre Rakotoarivony.

Malawi: Bole Rd, Woreda 23, Kebele 13, House No. 1021, POB 2316, Addis Ababa; tel. (11) 3711280; fax (11) 3719742; e-mail malemb@telecom.net.et; Ambassador James Donald Kalilagnwe.

Mali: Kebele 03, House No. 418, Addis Ababa; tel. (11) 168990; fax (11) 162838; e-mail keitamoone@maliembassy-addis.org; internet www.maliembassy-addis.org; Ambassador Al-Maamoun Baba Lamine Keïta.

Mauritania: Lidete Kifle Ketema, Kebele 2, House No. 431 a, POB 200015, Addis Ababa; tel. (11) 3729165; fax (11) 3729166; e-mail mauritania@ethionet.et; Ambassador Mohamed Abdellahi Ould Babana.

Mauritius: Kebele 03, House No. 750, POB 200222, Kifle Ketema, Addis Ababa; tel. (1) 6615997; fax (1) 6614704; e-mail mmaddis@ethionet.et; Ambassador Taye Wan Chat Kwong.

Morocco: 210 Bole Rd, POB 60033, Addis Ababa; tel. (11) 5508440; fax (11) 5511828; e-mail morocco.emb@ethionet.et; Ambassador Abdeljebbar Brahime.

Mozambique: Woreda 17, Kebele 23, House No. 2116, POB 5671, Addis Ababa; tel. (11) 3712905; fax (11) 3710021; e-mail embamoc-add@telecom.net.et; Ambassador Manuel Tomás Lubisse.

Namibia: Woreda 17, Kebele 19, House No. 2, POB 1443, Addis Ababa; tel. (11) 6611966; fax (11) 6612677; e-mail namemb@ethionet.et; Ambassador George Liswaniso.

Netherlands: Woreda 24, Kebele 13, House No. 1, POB 1241, Addis Ababa; tel. (11) 3711100; fax (11) 3711577; e-mail add@minbuza.nl; internet www.netherlandsembassyethiopia.org; Ambassador Alphons Hennekens.

Niger: Woreda 9, Kebele 23, POB 5791, Addis Ababa; tel. (11) 4651305; fax (11) 4651296; Ambassador Diamballa Maimouna.

Nigeria: POB 1019, Addis Ababa; tel. (11) 1550644; Chargé d'affaires a.i. Chigozie Obi-Nnadozie.

Norway: POB 8383, Addis Ababa; tel. (11) 3710799; fax (11) 3711255; e-mail emb.addisabeba@mfa.no; internet www.norway.org.et; Ambassador Jens-Petter Kjemprud.

Poland: Bole Sub-City, Kebele 3, House No. 2111, POB 27207, Addis Ababa; tel. (11) 6185401; fax (11) 6610000; e-mail polemb@ethionet.et; internet www.addisabeba.polemb.net; Ambassador Mariusz Woźniak.

Portugal: Sheraton Addis, Taitu Street, POB 6002, Addis Ababa; tel. (11) 171717; fax (11) 173403; e-mail embportadis@hotmail.com; Ambassador Dr Vera Maria Fernandes.

Romania: Houses 9–10, Bole Kifle Ketema, Kebele 03, POB 2478, Addis Ababa; tel. (11) 6610156; fax (11) 6611191; e-mail roembaddis@ethionet.et; Chargé d'affaires a.i. Gabriel Branzaru.

Russia: POB 1500, Addis Ababa; tel. (11) 6612060; fax (11) 6613795; e-mail russemb@ethionet.et; Ambassador Mikhail Y. Afanasiev.

Rwanda: Africa House, Woreda 17, Kebele 20, POB 5618, Addis Ababa; tel. (11) 6610300; fax (11) 6610411; e-mail rwanda.emb@telecom.net.et; Ambassador Nyilinkindi Gaspard.

Senegal: Africa Ave, POB 2581, Addis Ababa; tel. (11) 6611376; fax (11) 6610020; e-mail ambassene-addis@ethionet.et; Ambassador Amadou Kébé.

Serbia: POB 1341, Addis Ababa; tel. (11) 5517804; fax (11) 5514192; e-mail serbembaddis@ethionet.et; Ambassador Ivan Zivković.

Sierra Leone: POB 5619, Addis Ababa; tel. (11) 3710033; fax (11) 3711911; e-mail sleon.et@telecom.net.et; Ambassador Ibrahim M. Kamara.

Somalia: Bole Kifle Ketema, Kebele 20, House No. 588, POB 1643, Addis Ababa; tel. (11) 6180673; fax (11) 6180680; Ambassador Abdikarim Farah.

South Africa: POB 1091, Addis Ababa; tel. (11) 3713034; fax (11) 3711330; e-mail sa.embassy.addis@telecom.net.et; Ambassador L. C. Pepani.

Spain: Entoto Ave, POB 2312, Addis Ababa; tel. (11) 1222544; fax (11) 1222541; e-mail emb.addisabeba@mae.es; Ambassador María del Carmen de la Peña Corcuera.

Sudan: Kirkos, Kebele, POB 1110, Addis Ababa; tel. (11) 5516477; fax (11) 5519989; e-mail sudan.embassy@telecom.net.et; Ambassador Abu Zaid al-Hassan.

Sweden: Ras Tessema Sefer, Woreda 3, Kebele 53, House No. 891, POB 1142, Addis Ababa; tel. (11) 5511255; fax (11) 5514558; e-mail ambassaden.addis-abeba@foreign.ministry.se; internet www.swedenabroad.com/addisabeba; Ambassador Staffan Tillander.

Switzerland: Jimma Rd, Old Airport Area, POB 1106, Addis Ababa; tel. (11) 3711107; fax (11) 3712177; e-mail add.vertretung@eda.admin.ch; Ambassador Peter Reinhardt.

Tanzania: POB 1077, Addis Ababa; tel. (11) 5511063; fax (11) 5517358; e-mail tz@telecom.net.et; Ambassador Msuya W. Mangachi.

Togo: Addis Ababa; Ambassador Tilioufei Koffi Esaw.

Tunisia: Wereda 17, Kebele 19, Bole Rd, POB 100069, Addis Ababa; tel. (11) 6612063; fax (11) 6614568; e-mail embassy.tunisia@telecom.net.et; Ambassador Muhammad Adel Smaoui.

Turkey: POB 1506, Addis Ababa; tel. (11) 6613161; fax (11) 6611688; e-mail turk.emb@ethionet.et; Ambassador Can Altan.

Uganda: Kirkos Kifle Ketema, Kebele 35, House No. 31, POB 5644, Addis Ababa; tel. (11) 5513088; fax (11) 5514355; e-mail uganda.emb@telecom.net.et; Ambassador Edith Grace Ssempala.

Ukraine: Woreda 17, Kebele 23, House No. 2111, POB 2358, Addis Ababa; tel. (11) 661698; fax (11) 6621288; e-mail ukremb@ethionet.et; Ambassador Vladyslav Demyanenko.

United Kingdom: POB 858, Addis Ababa; tel. (11) 6612354; fax (11) 6610588; e-mail britishembassy.addisababa@fco.gov.uk; internet www.britishembassy.gov.uk/ethiopia; Ambassador Norman Ling.

USA: Entoto St, POB 1014, Addis Ababa; tel. (11) 5174000; fax (11) 5174001; e-mail pasaddis@state.gov; internet addisababa.usembassy.gov; Ambassador Donald Y. Yamamoto.

Venezuela: Bole Kifle Ketama, Kebele 21, House No. 314–16, POB 1909, Addis Ababa; tel. (11) 6460601; fax (11) 5154162; Ambassador Luis Mariano Joubertt Mata.

Yemen: POB 664, Addis Ababa; Ambassador Dr Amin Muhammad al-Yousfi.

Zambia: POB 1909, Addis Ababa; tel. (11) 3711302; fax (11) 3711566; Ambassador Lazarous Kapambwe.

Zimbabwe: POB 5624, Addis Ababa; tel. (11) 6613877; fax (11) 6613476; e-mail zimbabwe.embassy@telecom.net.et; Ambassador Dr Andrew Hama Mtetwa.

Judicial System

The 1994 Constitution stipulates the establishment of an independent judiciary in Ethiopia. Judicial powers are vested in the courts, both at federal and state level. The supreme federal judicial authority is the Federal Supreme Court. This court has the highest and final power of jurisdiction over federal matters. The federal states of the Federal Democratic Republic of Ethiopia can establish Supreme, High and First-Instance Courts. The Supreme Courts of the federal States have the highest and the final power of jurisdiction over state matters. They also exercise the jurisdiction of the Federal High Court. According to the Constitution, courts of any level are free from any interference or influence from government bodies, government officials or any other source. In addition, judges exercise their duties independently and are directed solely by the law.

Federal Supreme Court: Addis Ababa; tel. (11) 5448425; comprises civil, criminal and military sections; its jurisdiction extends to the supervision of all judicial proceedings throughout the country; the Supreme Court is also empowered to review cases upon which final rulings have been made by the courts (including the Supreme Court) where judicial errors have occurred; Pres. Kemal Bedri.

Federal High Court: POB 3483, Addis Ababa; tel. (11) 2751911; fax (11) 2755399; e-mail fedhc@telecom.net.et; hears appeals from the state courts; has original jurisdiction; Pres. Adil Ahmed.

Awraja Courts: regional courts composed of three judges, criminal and civil.

Warada Courts: sub-regional; one judge sits alone with very limited jurisdiction, criminal only.

Religion

About 45% of the population are Muslims and about 40% belong to the Ethiopian Orthodox (Tewahido) Church. There are also significant Evangelical Protestant and Roman Catholic communities. The Pentecostal Church and the Society of International Missionaries carry out mission work in Ethiopia. There are also Hindu and Sikh religious institutions. It has been estimated that 5%–15% of the population follow animist rites and beliefs.

CHRISTIANITY

Ethiopian Orthodox (Tewahido) Church

The Ethiopian Orthodox (Tewahido) Church is one of the five oriental orthodox churches. It was founded in AD 328, and in 1989 had more than 22m. members, 20,000 parishes and 290,000 clergy. The Supreme Body is the Holy Synod and the National Council, under the chairmanship of the Patriarch (Abune). The Church comprises 25 archdioceses and dioceses (including those in Jerusalem, Sudan, Djibouti and the Western Hemisphere). There are 32 Archbishops and Bishops. The Church administers 1,139 schools and 12 relief and rehabilitation centres throughout Ethiopia.

Patriarchate Head Office: POB 1283, Addis Ababa; tel. (11) 1116507; Patriarch (Abune) Archbishop PAULOS; Gen. Sec. L. M. DEMTSE GEBRE MEDHIN.

The Roman Catholic Church

At 31 December 2004 Ethiopia contained an estimated 75,536 adherents of the Alexandrian-Ethiopian Rite and 460,156 adherents of the Latin Rite.

Bishops' Conference: Ethiopian and Eritrean Episcopal Conference, POB 2454, Addis Ababa; tel. (11) 1550300; fax (11) 1553113; e-mail ecs@ethionet.et; internet www.ecs.org.et; f. 1966; Pres. Most Rev. BERHANEYESUS DEMEREW SOURAPHIEL (Metropolitan Archbishop of Addis Ababa).

Alexandrian-Ethiopian Rite

Adherents are served by one archdiocese (Addis Ababa) and two dioceses (Adigrat and Emdeber).

Archbishop of Addis Ababa: Most Rev. BERHANEYESUS DEMEREW SOURAPHIEL, Catholic Archbishop's House, POB 21903, Addis Ababa; tel. (11) 1111667; fax (11) 1551348.

Latin Rite

Adherents are served by the five Apostolic Vicariates of Awasa, Harar, Meki, Nekemte and Soddo-Hosanna, and by the Apostolic Prefectures of Gambela and Jimma-Bonga.

Other Christian Churches

The Anglican Communion: Within the Episcopal Church in Jerusalem and the Middle East, the Bishop in Egypt has jurisdiction over seven African countries, including Ethiopia.

Armenian Orthodox Church: St George's Armenian Church, POB 116, Addis Ababa; f. 1923; Deacon VARTKES NALBANDIAN.

Ethiopian Evangelical Church (Mekane Yesus): POB 2087, Addis Ababa; tel. (11) 5533293; fax (11) 5534148; e-mail eecmy.co@telecom.net.et; internet www.eecmy.org; Pres. Rev. ITEFFA GOBENA; f. 1959; affiliated to Lutheran World Fed., All Africa Confed. of Churches and World Council of Churches; c. 4.67m. mems (2006).

Greek Orthodox Church: POB 571, Addis Ababa; tel. and fax (11) 1226459; Metropolitan of Axum Most Rev. PETROS YIAKOUMELOS.

Seventh-day Adventist Church: POB 145, Addis Ababa; tel. (11) 5511319; e-mail info@ecd.adventist.org; internet www.ecd.adventist.org; f. 1907; Pres. TINSAE TOLESSA; 130,000 mems.

ISLAM

Leader: Haji MOHAMMED AHMAD.

JUDAISM

A phased emigration to Israel of about 27,000 Falashas (Ethiopian Jews) took place during 1984–91. In February 2003 the Israeli Government ruled that the Falashmura (Ethiopian Christians whose forefathers had converted from Judaism) had been forced to convert to Christianity to avoid religious persecution and that they had the right to settle in Israel. In January 2004 Ethiopia and Israel agreed to allow the Falashmura to be flown to Israel; some 17,000 Falashmura and a further 3,000 Falashas were expected to arrive in Israel by 2007.

The Press

DAILIES

Addis Zemen: POB 30145, Addis Ababa; f. 1941; Amharic; publ. by the Ministry of Information; circ. 40,000.

The Daily Monitor: POB 22588, Addis Ababa; tel. (11) 1560788; e-mail themonitor@telecom.net.et; f. 1993; English; Editor-in-Chief NAMRUD BERHANE TSAHAY; circ. 6,000.

Ethiopian Herald: POB 30701, Addis Ababa; tel. (11) 5156690; f. 1943; English; publ. by the Ministry of Information; Editor-in-Chief TSEGIE GEBRE-AMLAK; circ. 37,000.

PERIODICALS

Abyotawit Ethiopia: POB 2549, Addis Ababa; fortnightly; Amharic.

Addis Tribune: Tambek International, POB 2395, Addis Ababa; tel. (11) 6615228; fax (11) 6615227; e-mail tambek@telecom.net.et; internet www.addistribune.com; f. 1992; weekly; English; Editor-in-Chief YOHANNES RUPHAEL; circ. 6,000.

Addis Zimit: POB 2395, Addis Ababa; tel. (11) 1118613; fax (11) 1552110; f. 1993; weekly; Amharic; Editor-in-Chief (vacant); circ. 8,000.

Al-Alem: POB 30232, Addis Ababa; tel. (11) 5158046; fax (11) 5516819; f. 1941; weekly; Arabic; publ. by the Ministry of Information; Editor-in-Chief TELSOM AHMED; circ. 2,500.

Asqual: Editor-in-Chief DAWIT FASSIL.

Berisa: POB 30232, Addis Ababa; f. 1976; weekly; Oromogna; publ. by the Ministry of Information; Editor BULO SIBA; circ. 3,500.

Beza: Addis Ababa; weekly; Editor-in-Chief YARED KEMFE.

Birhan Family Magazine: Addis Ababa; monthly; women's magazine.

Birritu: National Bank of Ethiopia, POB 5550, Addis Ababa; tel. (11) 5530040; fax (11) 5514588; e-mail birritu@ethionet.et; internet www.nbe.gov.et; f. 1982; quarterly; Amharic and English; banking, insurance and macroeconomic news; circ. 2,500; Editor-in-Chief SEMENEH ADGE; Editor MULUGETA AYALEW.

Capital: POB 95, Addis Ababa; tel. (11) 5531759; fax (11) 5533323; e-mail syscom@telecom.net.et; internet www.capitalethiopia.com; f. 1998; weekly; Sunday; publ. by the Ministry of Trade and Industry; business and economics; Editor-in-Chief BEHAILU DESALEGN.

Ethiopian Reporter: Woreda 19, Kebele 56, House No. 221, POB 7023, Addis Ababa; tel. and fax (11) 4421517; e-mail mcc@telecom.net.et; internet www.ethiopianreporter.com; weekly; English and Amharic.

Ethiopis Review: Editor-in-Chief TESFERA ASMARE.

Mabruk: Addis Ababa; weekly; Editor-in-Chief TESAHALENNE MENGESHA.

Maebel: Addis Ababa; weekly; Amharic; Editor-in-Chief ABERA WOGI.

Menilik: Editor-in-Chief ZELALEM GEBRE.

Meskerem: Addis Ababa; quarterly; theoretical politics; circ. 100,000.

Negarit Gazeta: POB 1031, Addis Ababa; irregularly; Amharic and English; official gazette.

Nigdina Limat: POB 2458, Addis Ababa; tel. (11) 5513882; fax (11) 5511479; e-mail aachamber1@telecom.net.et; monthly; Amharic; publ. by the Addis Ababa (Ethiopia) Chamber of Commerce; circ. 6,000.

Press Digest: POB 12719, Addis Ababa; tel. (11) 5504200; fax (11) 5513523; e-mail phoenix.universal@telecom.net.et; f. 1993; weekly.

Satenaw: Editor-in-Chief TAMRAT SERBESA.

Tequami: Addis Ababa; weekly; Editor-in-Chief SAMSON SEYUM.

Tinsae (Resurrection): Addis Ababa; tel. (1) 116507; Amharic and English; publ. by the Ethiopian Orthodox Church.

Tobia Magazine: POB 22373, Addis Ababa; tel. (11) 1556177; fax (11) 1552654; e-mail akpac@telecom.net.et; monthly; Amharic; Man. GOSHU MOGES; circ. 30,000.

Tobia Newspaper: POB 22373, Addis Ababa; tel. (11) 1556177; fax (11) 1552654; e-mail akpac@telecom.net.et; weekly; Amharic; Man. GOSHU MOGES; circ. 25,000.

Tomar: Benishangul; weekly; Amharic; Editor-in-Chief BEFEKADU MOREDA.

Wetaderna Alamaw: POB 1901, Addis Ababa; fortnightly; Amharic.

Yezareitu Ethiopia (Ethiopia Today): POB 30232, Addis Ababa; weekly; Amharic and English; publ. by the Ministry of Information; Editor-in-Chief IMIRU WORKU; circ. 30,000.

NEWS AGENCIES

Ethiopian News Agency (ENA): Patriot St, POB 530, Addis Ababa; tel. (11) 1550011; fax (11) 1551609; e-mail feedback@ena.gov.et; internet www.ena.gov.et; f. 1942; Chair NETSANET ASFAW.

Foreign Bureaux

Agence France-Presse (AFP): POB 3537, Addis Ababa; tel. (11) 5531430; fax (11) 5511006; e-mail emmanuel.goujon@afp.com; Chief SABA SEYOUM.

Agenzia Nazionale Stampa Associata (ANSA) (Italy): POB 1001, Addis Ababa; tel. (11) 1111007; Chief BRAHAME GHEBREZGHI-ABIHER.

Associated Press (AP): Addis Ababa; tel. (11) 4161726; Correspondent ABEBE ANDUALAM.

Deutsche Presse-Agentur (dpa) (Germany): Addis Ababa; tel. (11) 5510687; Correspondent GHION HAGOS.

ITAR—TASS (Information Telegraphic Agency of Russia—Telegraphic Agency of the Sovereign Countries): Addis Ababa; tel. (11) 6181255; Bureau Chief GENNADII G. GABRIELYAN.

Prensa Latina (Cuba): Gen. Makonnen Bldg, 5th Floor, nr Ghion Hotel, opp. National Stadium, Addis Ababa; tel. (11) 5519899; Chief HUGO RIUS BLEIN.

Reuters (UK): Addis Ababa; tel. (11) 5156505; Correspondent TSEGAYE TADESSE.

RIA—Novosti (Russian Information Agency—News): POB 239, Addis Ababa; Chief VITALII POLIKARPOV.

Xinhua (New China) News Agency (People's Republic of China): POB 2497, Addis Ababa; tel. (11) 5515676; fax (11) 5514742; Correspondent CHEN CAILIN.

PRESS ASSOCIATIONS

Ethiopian Free Press Journalists' Association (EFJA): POB 31317, Addis Ababa; tel. and fax (11) 1555021; e-mail efja@telecom.net.et; f. 1993; granted legal recognition in 2000; activities suspended in late 2003; Pres. KIFLE MULAT.

Ethiopian Journalists' Association: POB 30288, Addis Ababa; tel. (11) 1117852; fax (11) 5513365; Pres. KEFALE MAMMO.

Publishers

Addis Ababa University Press: POB 1176, Addis Ababa; tel. (11) 1119148; fax (11) 1550655; e-mail aau.pres@telecom.net.et; f. 1968; educational and reference works in English, general books in English and Amharic; Editor MESSELECH HABTE.

Berhanena Selam Printing Enterprise: POB 980, Addis Ababa; tel. (11) 1553233; fax (11) 1553939; e-mail bspe@telecom.net.et; f. 1921; fmrly Government Printing Press; publishes and prints newspapers, periodicals, books, security prints and other miscellaneous commercial prints; Gen. Man. MULUWORK G. HIWOT.

Educational Materials Production and Distribution Enterprise (EMPDE): POB 27444, Addis Ababa; fax (11) 6461295; e-mail empde@telecom.net.et; f. 1999; textbook publishers.

Ethiopia Book Centre: POB 1024, Addis Ababa; tel. (11) 1123336; f. 1977; privately owned; publr, importer, wholesaler and retailer of educational books.

Kuraz Publishing Agency: POB 30933, Addis Ababa; tel. (11) 1551688; state-owned.

Mega Publishing: POB 423, Addis Ababa; tel. (11) 1571714; fax (11) 1571715; e-mail MegaPub@telecom.net.et; general publishers.

Broadcasting and Communications

TELECOMMUNICATIONS

Ethiopian Telecommunication Agency (ETA): Bekelobet, Tegene Bldg, Kirkos District, Kebele 02/03, House No. 542, POB 9991, Addis Ababa; tel. (11) 4668282; fax (11) 4655763; e-mail gm@eta.gov.et; internet www.eta.gov.et; aims to promote the development of high quality, efficient, reliable and affordable telecommunication services in Ethiopia; Gen. Man. ALEMU ALEMU.

Ethiopian Telecommunications Corpn (ETC): POB 1047, Addis Ababa; tel. (11) 5510500; fax (11) 5515777; e-mail etc.commun@ethionet.et; internet www.ethionet.et; f. 1894; CEO AMARE AMSALU; Chair. DEBRE TSION GEBRE MICHAEL.

BROADCASTING

Radio

Radio Ethiopia: POB 654, Addis Ababa; tel. (11) 1551011; internet www.angelfire.com/biz/radioethiopia; f. 1941; Amharic, English, French, Arabic, Afar, Oromifa, Tigre, Tigrinya and Somali; Gen. Man. KASA MILOKO.

Radio Torch: POB 30702, Addis Ababa; f. 1994; Amharic; operated by the EPRDF; Gen. Man. MULUGETA GESEE.

Radio Voice of One Free Ethiopia: broadcasts twice a week; Amharic; opposes current Govts of Ethiopia and Eritrea.

Voice of the Revolution of Tigrai: POB 450, Mekele; tel. (34) 4410545; fax (34) 4405485; e-mail vort@telecom.net.et; f. 1985; Tigrinya and Afargna; broadcasts 57 hours per week; supports Tigrai People's Liberation Front.

Television

Ethiopian Television: POB 5544, Addis Ababa; tel. (11) 5155326; fax (11) 5512685; f. 1964; semi-autonomous station; accepts commercial advertising; programmes transmitted from Addis Ababa to 26 regional stations; Chair. BEREKET SIMON; Gen. Man. SELOME TADDESSE.

Finance

(cap. = capital; res = reserves; dep. = deposits; m. = million; br(s). = branch(es); amounts in birr)

BANKING

Central Bank

National Bank of Ethiopia: POB 5550, Addis Ababa; tel. (11) 5517430; fax (11) 5514588; e-mail nbe.vgov@telecom.net.et; internet www.nbe.gov.et; f. 1964; bank of issue; cap. 50.0m., res 2,356.4m., dep. 12,138.4m. (June 2002); Gov. TEKLEWOLD ATNAFU; Vice-Gov. ALEMSEGED ASSEFA; 1 br.

Other Banks

Awash International Bank SC: Africa Ave, POB 12638, Addis Ababa; tel. (11) 6614482; fax (11) 6614477; e-mail awash.bank@telecom.net.et; internet www.awash-bank.com; f. 1994; cap. 110.1m., res 20.4m., dep. 1,042.9m. (Dec. 2002); Chair. and Pres. HAMBISSA WAKWAYA; 32 brs.

Bank of Abyssinia: POB 12947, Addis Ababa; tel. (11) 5530663; fax (11) 5510409; e-mail info@bankofabyssinia.com; internet www.bankofabyssinia.com; f. 1905; closed 1935 and reopened 1996; commercial banking services; cap. and res 188m., total assets 1,651.8m. (June 2005); Chair. ASELEFECH MULUGETA; 24 brs.

Commercial Bank of Ethiopia: Unity Sq., POB 255, Addis Ababa; tel. (11) 5511271; fax (11) 5514522; e-mail cbe.plng@telecom.net.et; internet www.combanketh.com; f. 1943; reorg. 1996; state-owned; cap. 619.7m., res 606.5m., dep. 19,514.9m. (June 2003); Chair. MEKONNEM MANYAZEWAL; Pres. GEZAHEGN YILMA DANTEW; 175 brs.

Construction and Business Bank: Higher 21, Kebele 04, POB 3480, Addis Ababa; tel. (11) 5512300; fax (11) 5515103; e-mail cbb@telecom.net.et; f. 1975 as Housing and Savings Bank; provides credit for construction projects and a range of commercial banking services; state-owned; cap. and res 80.8m., total assets 1,019.1m. (June 2003); Chair. ATO TADESSE HAILE; Gen. Man. ATO ADDISU HABBA; 20 brs.

Dashen Bank: Garad Bldg, Debre Zeit Rd, POB 12752, Addis Ababa; tel. (11) 4661380; fax (11) 4653037; e-mail dashen.bank@ethionet.et; internet www.dashenbanksc.com; cap.and res 385.9m., dep. 3,691.6m. (June 2006); Pres. LULSEGED TEFERI; Chair. TEKLU HAILE; 40 brs.

Development Bank of Ethiopia: Zosip Broz Tito St, POB 1900, Addis Ababa; tel. (11) 5511188; fax (11) 5511606; e-mail dbe@telecom.net.et; provides devt finance for industry and agriculture, technical advice and assistance in project evaluation; state-owned; cap. and res 418.8m., total assets 3,163.2m. (June 2002); Chair. ABI W. MESKEL; Gen. Man. WONDWOSSEN TESHOME; 32 brs.

NIB International Bank SC: Africa Avenue, Dembel City Centre, POB 2439, Addis Ababa; tel. (11) 5503288; fax (11) 5504349; e-mail nibbank@ethionet.et; internet www.addischamber.com/nibbank.htm; f. 1999; cap. 285.0m., res 44.7m., dep. 1451.8m. (June 2006); Chair. LEMMA H. GIORGISS; Pres. AMERGA KASSA; 27 brs.

United Bank: Mekwor Plaza Bldg, Debe Zeit Rd, POB 19963, Addis Ababa; tel. (11) 4655222; fax (11) 4655243; e-mail hibretbank@telecom.net.et; f. 1998; commercial banking services; cap. and res 96m., dep. 532.7m. (June 2004); Chair. EYESSUS W. ZAFU; Pres. ADMASSU TECHANE; 14 brs.

Wegagen Bank: POB 1018, Addis Ababa; tel. (11) 5532800; fax (11) 5523521; e-mail wegagen@telecom.net.et; f. 1997; commercial banking services; cap. 95.4m., total assets 1,660m. (Feb. 2004); Chair. WONDWOSSON KEBEDE; CEO KIDANE NIKODIMOS; 23 brs.

Bankers' Association

Ethiopian Bankers' Association: Addis Ababa; f. 2001; Pres. LEIKUN BERHANU.

INSURANCE

Africa Insurance Co: POB 12941, Addis Ababa; tel. (11) 6637716; fax (11) 6638253; e-mail africains@ethionet.et; internet www.africainsurance.com.et; f. 1994; Gen. Man. KITOS JIRANIE.

Awash Insurance Co: POB 12637, Addis Ababa; tel. (11) 6614420; fax (11) 6614419; Gen. Man. TSEGAYE KEMAS.

Ethiopian Insurance Corpn: POB 2545, Addis Ababa; tel. (11) 5512400; fax (11) 5517499; e-mail eic.mdxvs@ethionet.et; internet www.eic.com.et; f. 1976; life, property and legal liabilities insurance cover; Man. Dir TEWODROS TILAHUN.

Global Insurance SC: POB 180112, Addis Abba; tel. (11) 1567400; fax (11) 1566200; e-mail globalinsu@ethionet.et; f. 1997; cap. 16.8m.; Man. Dir AHMED IBRAHIM; 8 brs; 86 employees.

National Insurance Co of Ethiopia: POB 12645, Addis Ababa; tel. (11) 4661129; fax (11) 4650660; e-mail nice@telecom.net.et; Man. Dir and CEO HABTEMATIAM SHUMGIZAW.

Nile Insurance Co: POB 12836, Addis Ababa; tel. (11) 5537709; fax (11) 5514592; e-mail nileinsu@mail.telecom.net.et; f. 1995; Gen. Man. MAHTSENTU FELEKE.

Nyala Insurance SC: Mickey Leland St, POB 12753, Addis Ababa; tel. (11) 6626667; fax (11) 6626706; e-mail nisco@telecom.net.et; internet www.nyalainsurance.com; Man. Dir NAHU-SENAYE ARAYA.

United Insurance Co SC: POB 1156, Addis Ababa; tel. (11) 5515656; fax (11) 5513258; e-mail united.insurance@telecom.net .et; Chair. GETAMESSAY DEGEFU; Man. Dir IYESUSWORK ZAFU.

Trade and Industry

CHAMBERS OF COMMERCE

Ethiopian Chamber of Commerce: Mexico Sq., POB 517, Addis Ababa; tel. (11) 5514005; fax (11) 5517699; e-mail ethchamb@ ethionet.et; internet www.ethiopianchamber.com; f. 1947; city chambers in 26 localities; Pres. SOLOMON AFEWORK; Sec.-Gen. MESFIN SHIMELES.

Addis Ababa Chamber of Commerce: POB 2458, Addis Ababa; tel. (11) 5513882; fax (11) 5511479; e-mail AAchamber1@telecom.net .et; internet www.addischamber.com; Chair. BERHANE MEWA; Sec.-Gen. SEMUNESH DEMETROS.

INDUSTRIAL AND TRADE ASSOCIATIONS

Ethiopian Beverages Corpn: POB 1285, Addis Ababa; tel. (11) 6186185; Gen. Man. MENNA TEWAHEDE.

Ethiopian Cement Corpn: POB 5782, Addis Ababa; tel. (11) 1552222; fax (11) 1551572; Gen. Man. REDI GEMAL.

Ethiopian Chemical Corpn: POB 5747, Addis Ababa; tel. (11) 6184305; Gen. Man. ASNAKE SAHLU.

Ethiopian Coffee Export Enterprise: POB 2591, Addis Ababa; tel. (11) 5515330; fax (11) 5510762; f. 1977; Chair. SUFIAN AHMED; Gen. Man. DERGA GURMESSA.

Ethiopian Food Corpn: Addis Ababa; tel. (11) 5518522; fax (11) 5513173; f. 1975; produces and distributes food items, including edible oil, ghee substitute, pasta, bread, maize, wheat flour, etc.; Gen. Man. BEKELE HAILE.

Ethiopian Fruit and Vegetable Marketing Enterprise: POB 2374, Addis Ababa; tel. (11) 5519192; fax (11) 5516483; f. 1980; sole wholesale domestic distributor and exporter of fresh and processed fruit and vegetables, and floricultural products; Gen. Man. KAKNU PEWONDE.

Ethiopian Grain Trade Enterprise: POB 3321, Addis Ababa; tel. (11) 4652436; fax (11) 4652792; e-mail egte@ethionet.et; Gen. Man. BERHANE HAILU.

Ethiopian Handicrafts and Small-Scale Industries Development Agency: Addis Ababa; tel. (11) 5157366; f. 1977.

Ethiopian Import and Export Corpn (ETIMEX): Addis Ababa; tel. (11) 5511112; fax (11) 5515411; f. 1975; state trading corpn under the supervision of the Ministry of Trade and Industry; import of building materials, foodstuffs, stationery and office equipment, textiles, clothing, chemicals, general merchandise, capital goods; Gen. Man. ASCHENAKI G. HIWOT.

Ethiopian Oil Seeds and Pulses Export Corpn: POB 5719, Addis Ababa; tel. (11) 1550597; fax (11) 1553299; f. 1975; Gen. Man. ABDOURUHMAN MOHAMMED.

Ethiopia Peasants' Association (EPA): f. 1978 to promote improved agricultural techniques, home industries, education, public health and self-reliance; comprises 30,000 peasant asscns with c. 7m. mems; Chair. (vacant).

Ethiopian Petroleum Enterprise: POB 3375, Addis Ababa; fax (11) 5512938; e-mail ethpetroleum@telecom.net.et; f. 1976; Gen. Man. YIGZAW MEKONNEN.

Ethiopian Pharmaceuticals and Medical Supplies Corpn (EPHARMECOR): POB 21904, Addis Ababa; tel. (11) 2134577; fax (11) 2752555; f. 1976; manufacture, import, export and distribution of pharmaceuticals, chemicals, dressings, surgical and dental instruments, hospital and laboratory supplies; Gen. Man. GIRMA BEPASSO.

Ethiopian Sugar Corpn: POB 133, Addis Ababa; tel. (11) 5519700; fax (11) 5513488; Gen. Man. ABATE LEMENGH.

Green Star Food Co LLC: POB 5579, Addis Ababa; tel. (11) 5526588; fax (11) 5526599; e-mail greenstar@telecom.net.et; f. 1984; fmrly the Ethiopian Livestock and Meat Corpn; production and marketing of canned and frozen foods; Gen. Man. DAWIT BEKELE.

National Leather and Shoe Corpn: POB 2516, Addis Ababa; tel. (11) 5514075; fax (11) 5513525; f. 1975; produces and sells semi-processed hides and skins, finished leather, leather goods and footwear; Gen. Man. GIRMA W. AREGAI.

National Textiles Corpn: POB 2446, Addis Ababa; tel. (11) 5157316; fax (11) 5511955; f. 1975; production of yarn, fabrics, knitwear, blankets, bags, etc.; Gen. Man. FIKRE HUGIANE.

Natural Gum Processing and Marketing Enterprise: POB 62322, Addis Ababa; tel. (11) 5527082; fax (11) 5518110; e-mail natgum@ethionet.et; internet www.naturalgum.ebigchina.com; f. 1976; state-owned; Gen. Man. TEKLEHAIMANOT NIGATU BEYENE.

UTILITIES

Electricity

Ethiopian Electric Power Corpn (EEPCO): De Gaulle Sq., POB 1233, Addis Ababa; tel. (11) 1560042; fax (11) 1550822; e-mail eelpa@ telecom.net.et; internet www.eepco.gov.et; Chair. HAILEMELEKOT TEKLE GIORGIS; Gen. Man. MIHRET DEBEBE.

Water

Addis Ababa Water and Sewerage Authority: POB 1505; Addis Ababa; tel. (11) 6623902; fax (11) 6623924; e-mail aawsa.ha@ethionet .et; f. 1971; Gen. Man. H. GIORGIS GETACHEW ESHETE.

Water Resources Development Authority: POB 1045, Addis Ababa; tel. (11) 6612999; fax (11) 6611245; Gen. Man. GETACHEW GIZAW.

TRADE UNION

Confederation of Ethiopian Trade Unions (ETU): POB 3653, Addis Ababa; tel. (11) 5155473; fax (11) 5514532; e-mail eef@telecom .net.et; f. 1975; comprises nine industrial unions and 22 regional unions with a total membership of 320,000 (1987); President KASAHUN FULLO.

Transport

RAILWAYS

Chemin de Fer Djibouti-Ethiopien (CDE): POB 1051, Addis Ababa; tel. (11) 5517250; fax (11) 5513533; f. 1909; adopted present name in 1981; jtly owned by Govts of Ethiopia and Djibouti; 781 km of track (660 km in Ethiopia), linking Addis Ababa with Djibouti; Pres. ISMAIL IBRAHIM HOUMED.

ROADS

In 2004 the total road network comprised an estimated 36,469 km of primary, secondary and feeder roads, of which 6,980 km were paved, the remainder being gravel roads. In addition, there are some 30,000 km of unclassified tracks and trails. A highway links Addis Ababa with Nairobi in Kenya, forming part of the Trans-East Africa Highway. In mid-2003 work commenced on the second phase of the Road Sector Development Programme, which aimed to upgrade 80% and 63% of paved and gravel roads, respectively, to an acceptable condition by 2007.

Comet Transport SC: POB 2402, Addis Ababa; tel. (11) 4403963; fax (11) 4426024; e-mail cometrans@telecom.net.et; f. 1994; Gen. Man. FELEKE YIMER.

Ethiopian Freight Transport Corpn: POB 2538, Addis Ababa; tel. (11) 5515211; fax (11) 5519740; restructured into five autonomous enterprises in 1994.

Ethiopian Road Transport Authority: POB 2504, Addis Ababa; tel. (11) 5510244; fax (11) 5510715; e-mail kasahun_khmariam@ yahoo.com; enforces road transport regulations, promotes road safety, registers vehicles and issues driving licences; Gen. Man. KASAHUN H. MARIAM.

Ethiopian Roads Authority: POB 1770, Addis Ababa; tel. (11) 5517170; fax (11) 5514866; e-mail era2@ethionet.et; internet www .era.gov.et; f. 1951; construction and maintenance of roads, bridges and airports; Dir-Gen. ZAID WOLDE GEBREAL.

Public Transport Corpn: POB 5780, Addis Ababa; tel. (11) 5153117; fax (11) 5510720; f. 1977; urban bus services in Addis Ababa and Jimma, and services between towns; restructured into three autonomous enterprises in 1994 and scheduled for privatization; Man. Dir AHMED NURU.

SHIPPING

The formerly Ethiopian-controlled ports of Massawa and Assab now lie within the boundaries of the State of Eritrea (q.v.). Although an agreement exists between the two Governments allowing Ethiopian access to the two ports, which can handle more than 1m. metric tons of merchandise annually, in mid-1998 Ethiopia ceased using the ports, owing to the outbreak of hostilities. Ethiopia's maritime trade currently passes through Djibouti (in the Republic of Djibouti), and also through the Kenyan port of Mombasa. An agreement was also signed in July 2003 to allow Ethiopia to use Port Sudan (in Sudan). At 31 December 2005 Ethiopia's registered merchant fleet numbered eight vessels, with a total displacement of 79,441 grt.

Ethiopian Shipping Lines Corpn: POB 2572, Addis Ababa; tel. (11) 5518280; fax (11) 5519525; e-mail esl@telecom.net.et; internet www.ethiopianshippinglines.com.et; f. 1964; serves Red Sea, Europe, Mediterranean, Gulf and Far East with its own fleet and chartered vessels; Chair. GETACHEW BELAY; Gen. Man. AMBACHEW ABRAHA.

Marine Transport Authority: Ministry of Infrastructure, POB 1238, Addis Ababa; tel. (11) 5158227; fax (11) 5515665; e-mail ketecom@telecom.net.et; f. 1993; regulates maritime transport services; Dept Head ASKAL W. GEORGIS.

Maritime and Transit Services Enterprise: POB 1186, Addis Ababa; tel. (11) 5517564; fax (11) 5518197; e-mail mtse@telecom.net.et; internet www.telecom.net/~mtse; f. 1979; services include stevedoring, storehandling, bagging, forwarding and trucking; Chair. GETACHEW GEBRE; Gen. Man. AHMED YASSIN.

CIVIL AVIATION

Ethiopia has two international airports (at Addis Ababa and Dire Dawa) and around 40 airfields. Bole International Airport in the capital handles 95% of international air traffic and 85% of domestic flights. A programme to modernize the airport, at an estimated cost of 819m. birr (US $130m.), was undertaken during 1997–2001. Construction of airports at Axum, Lalibela and Gondar was completed in April 2000.

Ethiopian Airlines: Bole International Airport, POB 1755, Addis Ababa; tel. (11) 6612222; fax (11) 6611474; e-mail publicrelations@ethiopianairlines.com; internet www.flyethiopian.com; f. 1945; operates regular domestic services and flights to 47 international destinations in Africa, Europe, Middle East, Asia and the USA; Chair. SEYOUM MESFIN; CEO GIRMA WAKE.

Ethiopian Civil Aviation Authority: POB 978, Addis Ababa; tel. (11) 6650252; fax (11) 6650269; e-mail civil.aviation@ethionet.et; regulatory authority; provides air navigational facilities; Dir-Gen. MESFIN FIKRU WOLDE-YOHANNES.

Tourism

Ethiopia's tourist attractions include the early Christian monuments and churches, the ancient capitals of Gondar and Axum, the Blue Nile (or Tississat) Falls and the National Parks of the Simien and Bale Mountains. Tourist arrivals in 2005 totalled 227,398. In 2004 receipts from tourism (including passenger transport) amounted to US $457m.

Ministry of Culture and Tourism: POB 2183, Addis Ababa; tel. (11) 5512310; fax (11) 5512889; e-mail tourismethiopia@ethionet.et; internet www.tourismethiopia.org.

Defence

Following the fall of Mengistu's Government and the defeat of his army in May 1991, troops of the Eritrean People's Liberation Front (EPLF) and the Ethiopian People's Revolutionary Democratic Front (EPRDF) were deployed in Eritrea and in Ethiopia, respectively. In June 1993 EPRDF forces were estimated at about 100,000. In October 1993 it was announced that preparations were under way to create a 'multi-ethnic defence force'. Extensive demobilization of former members of the Tigrai People's Liberation Front has since taken place. In September 1996 the Government sold its naval assets. Owing to hostilities with Eritrea in 1998–2000, there was a large increase in the size of the armed forces and in defence expenditure during this period. As assessed at November 2006, Ethiopia's active armed forces numbered an estimated 152,500, including an air force of some 2,500. In July 2000 the UN Security Council adopted a resolution (No. 1312) establishing the UN Mission in Ethiopia and Eritrea (UNMEE), which was to supervise the ceasefire and the implementation of a peace agreement between the two countries. At the end of December 2006 UNMEE numbered 2,063 troops, 222 military observers, as well as 149 international civilians and 194 local civilians.

Defence Expenditure: Budgeted at 3,000m. birr in 2006.

Chief of Staff of the Armed Forces: Lt-Gen. SAMORA YUNIS.

Education

Education in Ethiopia is available free of charge, and, after a rapid growth in numbers of schools, it became compulsory between the ages of seven and 13 years. Since 1976 most primary and secondary schools have been controlled by local peasant associations and urban dwellers' associations. Primary education begins at seven years of age and lasts for eight years. Secondary education, beginning at 15 years of age, lasts for a further four years, comprising two cycles of two years, the second of which provides preparatory education for entry to the tertiary level. According to UNESCO estimates, in 2004/05 total enrolment at primary schools included 56% of children in the appropriate age-group (58% of boys; 55% of girls); in that year enrolment at secondary schools included 28% of children in the relevant age-group (34% of boys; 22% of girls). There are 21 institutions of higher education in Ethiopia, including six universities (in Addis Ababa, Bahir Dar, Alemanya, Jimma, Awassa and Makele). A total of 91,655 students were enrolled in higher education in 2004/05, according to government statistics. The 2004/05 budget allocated an estimated 10.9% (2,956m. birr) of total expenditure to education.

Bibliography

Abbink, J. *Ethiopian Society and History: A Bibliography of Ethiopian Studies 1957–1990*. Leiden, African Studies Centre, 1990.

Abegaz, B. (Ed.). *Essays on Ethiopian Economic Development*. Aldershot, Avebury, 1994.

Abir, M. *Ethiopia and the Red Sea: The Rise and Decline of the Solomonic Dynasty and Muslim–European Rivalry in the Region*. London, Frank Cass, 1980.

Abraham, K. *Ethiopia: from Bullets to the Ballot Box: The Bumpy Road to Democracy and the Political Economy of Transition*. Lawrenceville, NJ, Red Sea Press, 1994.

Ad-din Arabfaqih, S., Ad-din Ahmad Bin Abdul Qader, S. and Stenhouse, P. L. (trans.). *The Conquest of Abyssinia: Futuh Al Habasa*. Hollywood, CA, Tsehai Publishers, 2005.

Africa Watch. *Evil Days: 30 Years of War and Famine in Ethiopia*. New York, Human Rights Watch, 1991.

Agyeman-Duah, B. *The United States and Ethiopia: Military Assistance and the Quest for Security 1953–1993*. Lanham, MD, University Press of America, 1994.

Attilo, A., Berhanu, K., and Ketsella, Y. *Ethiopia: Politics, Policy Making and Rural Development*. Addis Ababa, Addis Ababa University Press, 2006.

Bariagaber, A. *Conflict and the Refugee Experience: Flight, Exile, and Repatriation in the Horn of Africa*. Aldershot, Ashgate, 2006.

Bekele, S. (Ed.). *An Economic History of Ethiopia. Vol. I: The Imperial Era, 1941–1974*. Dakar, CODESRIA, 1995.

Bekoe, D. A.(Ed.). *East Africa and the Horn: Confronting Challenges to Good Governance*. Boulder, CO, Lynne Rienner Publishers, 2006.

Benti, G. *Addis Ababa: Migration and the Making of a Multiethnic Metropolis, 1941–1974*. Lawrenceville, NJ, Red Sea Press, 2007.

Berhanu, K., Olika, T., Kefale, A., and Erega, J. *Electoral Politics, Decentralized Governance and Constitutionalism in Ethiopia*. Addis Ababa, Addis Ababa University Press, 2007.

Clapham, C. *Transformation and Continuity in Revolutionary Ethiopia*. Cambridge, Cambridge University Press, 1988.

Crummey, D. *Land and Society in the Christian Kingdom of Ethiopia*. Chicago, University of Illinois Press, 2001.

Del Boca, A. *The Ethiopian War 1935–1941*. Chicago, University of Chicago Press, 1969.

Doornbos, M., Cliffe, L., Ahmed, A.G.M., and Markakis, J. (Eds). *Beyond Conflict in the Horn: The Prospects of Peace and Development in Ethiopia, Somalia, Eritrea and Sudan*. Lawrenceville, NJ, Red Sea Press, 1992.

Dugan, J., and Lafore, L. *Days of Emperor and Clown, The Italo-Ethiopian War 1935–1936*. New York, Doubleday, 1973.

Erlich, H. *Ethiopia and the Middle East*. Boulder, CO, and London, Lynne Rienner Publishers, 1994.

Saudi Arabia and Ethiopia: Islam, Christianity, and Politics Entwined. Boulder, CO, Lynne Rienner Publishers, 2007.

Fukui, K., and Markakis, J. (Eds). *Ethnicity and Conflict in the Horn of Africa*. London, James Currey, 1994.

Ghebre-Ab, H. (Ed.). *Ethiopia and Eritrea: A Documentary Study*. Trenton, NJ, Red Sea Press, 1993.

Gilkes, P. *The Dying Lion: Feudalism and Modernization in Ethiopia*. London, Julian Friedmann, 1974.

Griffin, K. (Ed.). *The Economy of Ethiopia*. New York, St Martin's Press, 1992.

Gurdon, C. (Ed.). *The Horn of Africa*. London, University College London Press, 1994.

Haile Selassie I. *The Autobiography of Emperor Haile Selassie I. 'My Life and Ethiopia's Progress'*. Oxford, Oxford University Press, 1976.

Haile-Selassie, T. *The Ethiopian Revolution, 1974–1991: From a Monarchical Autocracy to a Military Oligarchy*. London, Kegan Paul International, 1997.

Hameso, S.Y., and Hassen, M. (Eds). *Arrested Development in Ethiopia: Essays on Underdevelopment, Democracy, and Self-Determination*. Lawrenceville, NJ, Red Sea Press, 2006.

Hammond, J. *Fire from the Ashes: A Chronicle of the Revolution in Tigray, Ethiopia, 1975–1991*. Lawrenceville, NJ, Red Sea Press, 1999.

Hammond, Laura C. *This Place Will Become Home: Refugee Repatriation to Ethiopia*. Ithaca, NY, Cornell University Press, 2004.

Hansson, G. *The Ethiopian Economy 1974–94: Ethiopia, Tikdem and After*. London, Routledge, 1995.

Harbeson, J. W. *The Ethiopian Transformation*. Boulder, CO, Westview Press, 1988.

Henze, P. *Layers of Time: A History of Ethiopia*. London, Hurst, 2000.

Jacquin-Berdal, D. and Plaut, M. (Eds). *Unfinished Business: Ethiopia and Eritrea at War*. Lawrenceville, NJ, Red Sea Press, 2006.

Jalata, A. *Oromia and Ethiopia: State Formation and Ethnonational Conflict, 1868–2000*. Piscataway, NJ, Transaction Publishers, 2005.

Katsuyoski, F., and Markakis, J. (Eds). *Ethnicity and Conflict in the Horn of Africa*. London, James Currey, 1994.

Kebbede, G. *The State and Development in Ethiopia*. Atlantic Highlands, NJ, Humanities Press, 1992.

Keller, E. J. *Revolutionary Ethiopia: From Empire to People's Republic*. Bloomington, Indiana University Press, 1989.

Levine, D. Greater *Ethiopia: The Evolution of a Multicultural Society*. Chicago, University of Chicago Press, 1974.

Lockot, H. W. *The Mission: The Life, Reign and Character of Haile Selassie I*. London, Hurst, 1992.

A History of Ethiopia. Berkeley, University of California Press, 2001.

Haile Selassie I: The Formative Years 1892–1936. Berkeley, University of California Press, 1987.

Maundi, M. O., Zartman, I. W., Khadiagala, G. M. and Nuamah, K. *Getting In: Mediators' Entry into the Settlement of African Conflicts* Washington, DC, United States Institute of Peace Press, 2006.

Markakis, J. *National and Class Conflict in the Horn of Africa*. Cambridge, Cambridge University Press (African Studies Series, No. 55), 1988.

Ethiopia: Anatomy of a Traditional Polity. Addis Ababa, Shama Books, 2006.

Markakis, J. and Ayele, N. *Class and Revolution in Ethiopia*. Addis Ababa, Shama Publishers, 2006.

Negash, T. *Rethinking Education in Ethiopia*. New Brunswick NJ, Transaction Publishers, 1996.

Eritrea and Ethiopia: The Federal Experience. Uppsala, Nordiska Africainstitutet, 1997.

Negash, T., and Tronvoll, K. *Brothers at War*. London, James Currey, 2000.

Ofcansky, T. P., and Berry, L. (Eds). *Ethiopia: A Country Study*. Washington, DC, USGPO, 1991.

Ofcansky, T. P., and Shinn, D. H. (Eds). *Historical Dictionary of Ethiopia*. Lanham, MD, Scarecrow Press, 2004.

Olmstead, J. *Woman between Two Worlds: Portrait of an Ethiopian Rural Leader*. Champaign, IL, University of Illinois Press, 1997.

Ottaway, M. *Soviet and American Influence in the Horn of Africa*. New York, Praeger, 1982.

(Ed.). *The Political Economy of Ethiopia*. New York, Praeger, 1990.

Pankhurst, A. *Resettlement and Famine in Ethiopia: The Villagers' Experience*. Manchester, Manchester University Press, 1992.

Pankhurst, R. *Economic History of Ethiopia, 1880–1935*. Addis Ababa, 1968.

History of Ethiopian Towns: From Middle Ages to Early Nineteenth Century. Stuttgart, Steiner Verlag, 1982.

History of Ethiopian Towns: From Mid Nineteenth Century to 1935. Stuttgart, Steiner Verlag, 1985.

The Ethiopians. Oxford, Blackwell, 1999.

Patman, R. G. *The Soviet Union in The Horn of Africa*. Cambridge, Cambridge University Press, 1990.

Pausewang, S., *et al.* (Eds). *Ethiopia: Rural Development Options*. London, Zed Books, 1990.

Ethiopia Since the Derg: A Decade of Democratic Pretension and Performance. London, Zed Books, 2003.

Phillipson, D. W. *Ancient Ethiopia*. London, British Museum Press, 1998.

Praeg, B. *Ethiopia and Political Renaissance in Africa*. New York, NY, Nova Science Publishers, 2006.

Prouty, C. *Empress Taytu and Menilek II: Ethiopia 1883–1910*. London, Ravens Educational and Development Services, 1986.

Prouty, C., and Rosenfeld, E. *Historical Dictionary of Ethiopia and Eritrea*. 2nd Edn. Lanham, MD, and London, Scarecrow Press, 1994.

Sbacchi, A. *Ethiopia under Mussolini: Fascism and the Colonial Experience*. London, Zed Press, 1985.

Schwarz, Tanya. *Ethiopian Jewish Immigrants in Israel*. Curzon Press, 2000.

Teferra, Daniel. *Economic Development and Nation Building in Ethiopia*. Lanham, MD, University Press of America, 2005.

Turton, D. *Ethnic Federalism: The Ethiopian Experience in Comparative Perspective*. Oxford, James Currey Ltd, 2006.

Woube, Mengistu. *Effects of Resettlement Schemes on the Biophysical and Human Environments: The Case of the Gambela Region, Ethiopia*. Boca Raton, FL, Universal Publishers, 2005.

Young, J. *Peasant Revolution in Ethiopia: The Tigray People's Liberation Front, 1975–91*. Cambridge: Cambridge University Press, 1997.

GABON

Physical and Social Geography

DAVID HILLING

Lying along the Equator, on the west coast of Africa, the Gabonese Republic covers an area of 267,667 sq km (103,347 sq miles) and comprises the entire drainage basin of the westward-flowing Ogooué river, together with the basins of several smaller coastal rivers such as the Nyanga and Como.

The low-lying coastal zone is narrow in the north and south but broader in the estuary regions of the Ogooué and of Gabon. South of the Ogooué numerous lagoons, such as the N'Dogo, M'Goze and M'Komi, back the coast, and the whole area is floored with cretaceous sedimentary rocks, which at shallow depth yield oil. The main producing oilfields are in a narrow zone stretching southwards from Port-Gentil, both on and off shore. The interior consists of Pre-Cambrian rocks, eroded into a series of plateau surfaces at heights of 450–600 m and dissected by the river system into a number of distinct blocks, such as the Crystal mountains, the Moabi uplands and the Chaillu massif. This area is one of Africa's most mineralized zones, with the large-scale exploitation of manganese and uranium contributing significantly to Gabon's economy. There are also deposits of high-grade iron ore, gold and diamonds.

Gabon has an equatorial climate, with uniformly high temperatures, high relative humidities and mean annual rainfalls of 1,500–3,000 mm. More than 80% of the country's area is covered with rainforest, one of the highest national proportions in the world, and wood from the okoumé tree provided the basis for the country's economy until superseded by minerals in the 1960s. Grassland vegetation is restricted to the coastal sand zone south of Port-Gentil and parts of the valleys of the Nyanga, upper N'Gounié and upper Ogooué.

Agricultural development in the potentially rich forest zone has been limited by the small size of the country's population. At the July 1993 census the population was enumerated at 1,014,976, and in mid-2006, according to UN estimates, totalled 1,311,000, giving an average density of only 4.9 inhabitants per sq km. As the population is small in relation to national income, Gabon has one of the highest levels of income per head in mainland sub-Saharan Africa, although many of the country's enterprises depend on labour imported from neighbouring countries. The three main urban concentrations may now account for more than one-half of the population; in 1993 Libreville, the capital, had 419,596 inhabitants; Port-Gentil, the centre of the petroleum industry, 79,225; and Franceville and Moanda, the mining centres, had 31,183 and 21,882, respectively. By 2003 the population of Libreville was estimated to have increased to some 611,000. The major rural concentrations are found in Woleu N'Tem, where coffee and cocoa are the main cash crops, and around Lambaréné, where palm oil and coffee are important. The country's principal ethnic groups are the Fang (30%) and the Eshira (25%).

Recent History

PIERRE ENGLEBERT

Revised by RALPH YOUNG

ONE-PARTY GOVERNMENT

Formerly part of French Equatorial Africa, Gabon was granted internal autonomy in 1958 and became fully independent on 17 August 1960. Léon M'Ba, the new republic's first President, died in November 1967, and was succeeded by his Vice-President, Albert-Bernard (later El Hadj Omar) Bongo, who reconstituted the ruling party as the Parti démocratique gabonais (PDG), while imposing a one-party state in March 1968. Gabon enjoyed relative political stability during the 1970s and experienced an economic 'boom' driven by its petroleum sector. Economic problems in the early 1980s triggered the emergence of political opposition, led by the Mouvement de redressement national (MORENA), formed by exiles in France in 1976. Accusing Bongo of corruption and personal extravagance, MORENA demanded the restoration of democratic institutions. Bongo, however, resisted reform. In the presidential election of November 1986, Bongo was re-elected for a further seven-year term, with a reported 99.97% of the vote.

Following a deterioration in the economy, compulsory salary reductions for public-sector employees in October 1988 provoked a wave of strikes, forcing Bongo to declare that economic reforms would be pursued only to the extent compatible with social and political stability. MORENA, though experiencing internal divisions, resumed its campaign against the Government in early 1989. In May, however, Fr Paul M'Ba Abessole, the movement's Chairman (and a Catholic priest), visited Gabon and met Bongo. M'Ba Abessole subsequently declared his support for Bongo's regime and in early 1990, following his removal from the leadership of MORENA, formed a new organization, MORENA des bûcherons.

CONSTITUTIONAL TRANSITION

Strikes and demonstrations by workers and students in early 1990 reflected increasing public discontent. In late February a 'special commission for democracy', established by the PDG, submitted a report critical of the one-party system. The following day Bongo promised fundamental political reforms, subsequently announcing that legislative elections, scheduled for April, would be postponed for six months to allow time for constitutional changes. He also proposed that a multi-party system be introduced after a five-year transitional period. However, a national conference of some 2,000 delegates, convened in late March to formulate a reform programme, demanded an immediate political liberalization and the formation of an interim government, to hold office until competitive legislative elections. Bongo accepted these demands, and in April Casimir Oye Mba, the Governor of the Banque des états de l'Afrique centrale, was appointed Prime Minister in a transitional administration including several opposition members.

In May 1990 the legislature approved constitutional amendments facilitating the transition to a multi-party system. The existing presidential mandate (effective until January 1994) would continue; thereafter, elections to the presidency would be contested, and the tenure of office would be reduced to five years, renewable only once. Bongo then resigned as Secretary-General of the PDG, claiming that a party political role was now incompatible with his position as Head of State. Following the death, in suspicious circumstances, of Joseph Rendjambe, the Secretary-General of the Parti gabonais du progrès (PGP), demonstrators attacked property belonging to Bongo and his associates. A country-wide curfew was imposed as unrest increased. French troops arrived to protect the estimated 20,000 French residents, and several hundred Europeans were evacuated. As the violence spread to Port-Gentil (threatening the oil sector), a state of emergency was imposed in the region, and at least two deaths were reported. The national curfew was lifted in early July, although the state of emergency remained in force in the area surrounding Port-Gentil.

Legislative Elections

Legislative elections were held in September 1990; however, only parties registered during the national conference in March could contest these. The first round of voting, on 16 September, was disrupted by violent protests over suspected fraud. Following opposition allegations of widespread irregularities, the results in 32 constituencies were invalidated. The transitional Government subsequently conceded that malpractice had occurred and the second electoral round was postponed until late October. A commission with both PDG and opposition members was established to supervise polling. At the elections, the PDG won an overall majority, with 62 seats, while opposition candidates secured 55.

A Government of National Unity was announced on 27 November 1990; Oye Mba was reappointed as Prime Minister. The PDG received 16 portfolios, with the remaining eight distributed among five opposition parties. Three other opposition movements refused cabinet posts. The new Constitution, promulgated on 22 December, endorsed reforms included in May's transitional Constitution. A proposed senate, or upper chamber, was blocked by the opposition. A constitutional council was to replace the Supreme Court's administrative chamber, and a national communications council was to be introduced to ensure the impartial treatment of information by the state media.

The Assemblée nationale's final composition was determined in March 1991, with elections in the five constituencies where results had been annulled. The PDG held 66 seats, the PGP 19, the Rassemblement national des bûcherons (RNB, formerly MORENA des bûcherons) 17, MORENA—originels seven, the Association pour le socialisme au Gabon (APSG) six, the Union socialiste gabonais (USG) three, and two smaller parties one seat each.

Opposition Realignments and Social Unrest

In May 1991 six opposition parties formed the Coordination de l'opposition démocratique (COD). Announcing its withdrawal from the Assemblée nationale, it demanded the full implementation of the new Constitution, the appointment of a new Prime Minister, and access to the state-controlled media. Following a general strike organized by the COD, Bongo dissolved the Council of Ministers, affirmed his intention to implement the new Constitution and announced that a Constitutional Court and a National Communications Council had been created. In a further attempt to diffuse discontent, Bongo pardoned over 200 political prisoners. When opposition deputies ended their boycott of the legislature, a new coalition Government was formed, on June 22, which retained 14 members of the previous Council of Ministers and included representatives of MORENA—originels, the USG and the APSG.

In February 1992 the Government announced that a multiparty presidential election would take place in December 1993, two months before the expiry of Bongo's term of office. The same month, following student protests over their scholarship grants, the university was closed and a ban on public demonstrations was imposed. The COD subsequently organized a one-day general strike in Port-Gentil (which was only partially observed), followed by a one-day 'dead city' campaign in Port-Gentil and Libreville. In late February the Government reopened the university and lifted the ban on demonstrations. In July the Assemblée nationale adopted a new electoral code, despite protests that the Government had not complied with the COD's demands.

By late October 1992 16 candidates had emerged for the forthcoming presidential election, including Bongo, M'Ba Abessole, Pierre-Louis Agondjo Okawé (the leader of the PGP) and a former Prime Minister, Léon Mébiame. In early November five political groups (the PDG, the USG, the APSG, the Cercle des libéraux réformateurs—CLR and the Parti de l'unité du peuple gabonais) agreed to support Bongo's candidacy, while eight opposition candidates established an informal alliance, known as the Convention des forces du changement (CFC).

Presidential Election and Political Retrenchment

At the presidential election on 5 December 1993, Bongo was re-elected with 51.2% of votes cast; M'Ba Abessole secured 26.5%. The official announcement of the results provoked rioting, with several foreign nationals being attacked. A national curfew and state of alert were imposed. Rejecting the results, M'Ba Abessole established an Haut conseil de la République (HCR), which included a majority of the presidential candidates, as part of a parallel government. Bongo strongly denounced this move and invited the unsuccessful candidates to take part in a government of national consensus. Amidst the political confusion, local government elections, due to take place in late December, were postponed until March 1994.

On 22 January 1994, after the Constitutional Court endorsed the election results, Bongo was inaugurated as President. M'Ba Abessole subsequently redesignated the HCR as the Haut conseil de la résistance and urged his supporters to refuse to pay taxes and to boycott the local government elections (which were again postponed, to August). In mid-February the national curfew and the state of alert were lifted, only to be reimposed later that month after a general strike in support of demands for salary increases to compensate for the substantial devaluation of the CFA franc in January degenerated into violence. Security forces destroyed the transmitters of Radio Liberté (owned by the RNB) and attacked M'Ba Abessole's private residence, provoking further clashes with protesters. Strike action was suspended after four days, following negotiations between the Government and trade unions; according to official figures, nine people had been killed (compared with opposition claims that 38 had died).

In March 1994 Oye Mba resigned and dissolved the Council of Ministers; later that month he was reappointed as Prime Minister and, following the opposition's rejection of his offer to create a government of national unity, a 38-member administration was formed. The size of the new Government attracted widespread criticism. In the same month the Assemblée nationale approved a constitutional amendment establishing a Sénat and repealing legislation that prohibited unsuccessful presidential candidates from participating in the Government within a period of 18 months. In September negotiations between the Government and the opposition took place in Paris, under the auspices of the Organization of African Unity (OAU, now the African Union—AU), which produced an agreement over a transitional coalition government; local government elections were to take place after a period of one year, followed by legislative elections six months later. The electoral code was to be revised and an independent electoral commission established, to ensure that the elections were seen to be conducted fairly. In early October Oye Mba resigned from office and dissolved the Council of Ministers. Bongo replaced him with Dr Paulin Obame-Nguema, an experienced PDG figure and former Prime Minister; Obame-Nguema formed a 27-member Council of Ministers which included six opposition members.

In January 1995 the HCR refused to participate in drafting the new electoral code until the Paris Accord was ratified; subsequently the Constitutional Court ruled that the Assemblée nationale was not empowered to ratify the agreement. In early February, however, opposition deputies ended a boycott of the legislature following a further ruling by the Constitutional Court that the Assemblée nationale was entitled to act as a parliamentary body, pending the installation of an upper chamber after the legislative elections in 1996, but that the constitutional provisions adopted under the terms of the Paris agreement would require endorsement by referendum. In April, in accordance with the Paris Accord, the Council of Ministers approved legislation providing for the release of prisoners detained on charges involving state security. At the national referendum in July, the constitutional amendments were approved by 96.48% of the votes cast, with 63.45% of registered voters participating.

LOCAL AND LEGISLATIVE ELECTIONS

After opposition complaints over the delay in implementing the electoral timetable stipulated in the Paris Accord, Bongo met all the officially recognized parties in May 1996. He agreed to establish a national electoral commission to formulate a timetable for local, legislative and senatorial elections, in consultation with the opposition. It was also decided that access to state-controlled media and election funding should be equitably divided. However, when the national electoral commission adopted a timetable for legislative elections in early October, HCR representatives withdrew from the commission and demanded the postponement of the local and legislative elections. In mid-October Pierre-Claver Maganga Moussavou, the leader of the Parti social-démocrate (PSD), was compelled to resign from the Government, following his condemnation of the electoral timetable.

Organizational problems disrupted the local elections, which were held on 20 October 1996; according to reports, only 15% of the electorate participated. The PDG gained control of the majority of the municipalities, although the PGP secured victory in Port-Gentil, while the RNB was successful in the north of the country. Elections in Fougamou (where voting had not taken place) and Libreville (where the results had been invalidated) were eventually rescheduled for 24 November, when the RNB secured 62 of the 98 seats in Libreville; M'Ba Abessole was subsequently elected mayor.

Legislative elections were delayed owing to the release of the local election results and the failure to revise electoral registers in time. From the two rounds of voting on 15 and 29 December 1996, the PDG emerged with 84 seats, while the RNB obtained seven, the PGP six and independent candidates four, with the remaining 14 seats shared by the CLR, the Union du peuple gabonais (UPG), the USG and others. Polling was unable to proceed for the five remaining seats and results in a number of other constituencies were later annulled, owing to irregularities. Following by-elections held in August 1997, during which five people reportedly died in violent incidents in north-east Gabon, the PDG held 88 seats, the PGP nine and the RNB five. Obame-Nguema was reappointed Prime Minister on 27 January 1997; the new Council of Ministers was dominated by PDG members.

Elections to the new Sénat took place on 26 January and 9 February 1997, with senators being elected by members of municipal councils and departmental assemblies. The PDG won 53 of the Sénat's 91 seats, while the RNB secured 20, the PGP four, the Alliance démocratique et républicaine (ADERE) three; smaller parties and independents shared the remaining seats. The results for a number of seats were annulled, however, and in subsequent by-elections, held later that year, the PDG increased its representation to 58 seats, while the RNB retained 20 seats and the PGP four.

INSTITUTIONAL CHANGES AND ELECTORAL DISCORD

On 18 April 1997, at a congress of deputies and senators, constitutional amendments, which extended the presidential term to seven years, provided for the creation of the post of Vice-President and formally designated the Sénat as an upper chamber of a bicameral legislature, were adopted, despite the protests of opposition leaders who objected to the creation of a vice-presidency and demanded that a referendum be held. The Vice-President was to deputize for the President when required, but was not to have any power of succession. In late May Bongo appointed Didjob Divungui-di-N'Dingue, a senior member of the ADERE (formally part of the HCR) and a candidate in the 1993 presidential election as Vice-President.

With a presidential election due in December 1998, the opposition leaders withdrew their representatives from the national electoral commission in September in protest at alleged irregularities in the voter registration. By late October President Bongo's candidature was confirmed, along with those of M'Ba Abessole and Alain Egouang Nze for the RNB, Pierre Mamboundou for the HCR, Maganga Moussavou for the PSD and two independents. A final candidate was Pierre-André Kombila, the RNB's former Secretary-General.

At the presidential election, which was held on 6 December 1998, Bongo was re-elected by 66.6% of votes cast, while Mamboundou received 16.5% of the votes and M'Ba Abessole secured 13.4%. The reported turnout was 53.8%. Opposition parties rejected the results, alleging malpractice amid confusion over the size of the newly registered electorate (after official statements gave contradictory figures). A proposal by Bongo for discussions was rejected by the main parties, which demanded the annulment of the election results prior to commencing talks. None the less, Bongo was inaugurated as President on 21 January 1999, and a new 42-member Council of Ministers, headed by Jean-François Ntoutoume Emane, was appointed.

In August 2000 four opposition parties, including the RNB (which subsequently changed its name to the Rassemblement pour le Gabon—RPG), formed a coalition, the Front des parties du changement, in preparation for legislative and local elections scheduled to be held in December 2001. In August 2001, however, the Government requested a postponement of the local elections owing to financial difficulties; the Constitutional Court concurred and they were scheduled for April 2002 (though they were later further postponed until September), with the legislative elections to proceed as planned.

THE 2001 LEGISLATIVE ELECTIONS

Elections to the Assemblée nationale took place on 9 and 23 December 2001. Three opposition parties accused the Government of inflating voter registration lists and boycotted the elections, while others called for the first round to be annulled as a result of reputed irregularities and high abstention rates, reported to have reached 56% nationally and 80% in Libreville and Port-Gentil. In the event, the elections were postponed until January 2002 in three constituencies and repeated in two others, owing to violent incidents. The PDG won 86 seats in the Assemblée, which were supplemented by 19 seats secured by independents with links to the PDG and other parties affiliated to the ruling party. Opposition parties obtained a total of 14 seats, of which the RPG won eight, the PSD two and the UPG one.

An enlarged Council of Ministers was announced in late January 2002, with Ntoutoume Emane reappointed as Prime Minister and President Bongo's son, Ali, continuing as Minister of National Defence. President Bongo was careful to include four opposition representatives—Moussavou (PSD) and three figures from the RPG, including its leader, M'Ba Abessole, hitherto a prominent critic of the Bongo regime. During March and April the Constitutional Court annulled the results of the December 2001 legislative elections in 12 constituencies, including eight in which the PDG had been successful, owing to irregularities. On 26 May and 9 June 2002 by-elections took place in these 12 constituencies and in Zadie (where voting had been postponed); the PDG won 10 of the 13 seats, increasing its representation to 88 seats. The PDG further consolidated its grip on power with a landslide victory in local elections held in late December.

In January 2003 Vice-President Divungui-di-N'Dingue was reportedly the target of an assassination attempt, in the south-west regional capital of Mouila, for which PSD activists were blamed. Despite denying involvement, Moussavou was removed from the Council of Ministers. M'Ba Abessole was awarded Moussavou's rural development portfolio to add to his existing responsibility for human rights; at the same time he became one of three Vice-Prime Ministers. Elections to the Sénat took place on 9 February; the PDG won more than 60 of the upper chamber's 91 seats, followed by the RPG, which secured eight seats. The continuity of the Bongo regime was further assured in July when the Assemblée nationale approved a constitutional amendment that abolished the two-term limit on the period of office the President could serve and reduced presidential elections from two rounds to one.

BONGO'S SEVENTH TERM

In September 2004 President Bongo Ondimba (who had added his father's name to his own in November 2003) reshuffled the Council of Ministers, increasing its size from 39 to 44 members. Ntoutoume Emane continued as Prime Minister, while most other key ministers also retained their positions, including M'Ba Abessole, whose RPG had voted in April 2004 to join the 'presidential majority', the coalition of parties committed to supporting Bongo Ondimba's presidential candidacy. Moussavou returned to the Council of Ministers after the PDS also agreed, in June 2004, to join the 'presidential majority'. By January 2005 this coalition embraced 29 of 35 registered parties and, of the remaining opposition politicians, only Mamboundou (UPG) and Agondjo Okawé (PGP) had well-established support bases (in the south-west and Port-Gentil, respectively). Agondjo Okawé died of a heart attack in August, leaving his party paralysed by divisions over who would become his successor.

In power for almost 40 years, Bongo Ondimba became Africa's longest-serving Head of State following the death in February 2005 of Togo's President, Gnassingbé Eyadéma, and observers anticipated that with a weakened opposition he would face no serious challenge at the presidential election scheduled for November. In April 2005, however, Zacherie Myboto, a senior minister who left the Government in early 2001 following press allegations that he had spread rumours concerning Bongo's health, announced the formation of the Union gabonaise pour la démocratie et le développement (UGDD). Myboto, formerly a member of the regime's leadership, also enjoyed access to members of the French Government, and his frequent visits to Paris, the media attention he received and two meetings with Dominique de Villepin, the French Prime Minister, aroused concern. In September Bongo Ondimba asked the French authorities to inform him of press conferences given by Gabonese politicians in Paris; when this was refused, he warned that his Government would revoke the passport of any politician who used a foreign platform to insult the President.

At the presidential election on 27 November 2005 Bongo Ondimba won easily against four opponents, after a two-week campaign that drew heavily on state resources. The incumbent took 79.2% of the vote, with turnout reported to be 63.3%. Pierre Mamboundou of the UPG took 13.6%, while Myboto, forced to stand as an independent because his party was not yet officially recognized, was accorded only 6.6%. Two other candidates attracted little support. Although international observers judged the election free and transparent, the opposition charged the regime with massive fraud, and sporadic outbreaks of unrest occurred in both Port-Gentil and Libreville, reportedly causing several deaths. In early December the authorities banned all public meetings nation-wide, although a new cabinet announced in late January 2006appeared to indicate a return to normality. While Ntoutoume Emane was replaced as Prime Minister by another economic reformer, Jean Eyéghé Ndong, key senior ministers retained their posts. However, underlying tensions were evident when police raided the UPG headquarters in mid-March, seizing files and computers. Mamboundou fled to the South African embassy, where he remained until mid-April, when he emerged for a meeting with President Bongo Ondimba. Their talks produced an agreement by the UPG to accept the election results in return for negotiations over electoral reform and the creation of an official post of Leader of the Opposition. These discussions led to agreement regarding changes to the electoral registration process, the elimination of a separate polling day for the security forces, and the reinstatement of two-round presidential elections. However, the ruling party resisted the official recognition of an opposition leader, as it did M'Ba Abessole's separate demand that the PDG be replaced by a unified structure allowing the smaller members of the 'presidential majority' greater influence than they had within a loose alliance. In June the Government was the subject of an embezzlement scandal involving the Caise nationale de sécurité sociale; one of the individuals accused of wrongdoing was the son of former Prime Minister Emane.

In legislative elections, held on 17 December 2006, the PDG's retained its grip on power. However, with no opposition boycott on this occasion, the PDG's number of seats was reduced by six to 82. The other parties in the 'presidential majority' secured 17 seats, including eight for the RPG; in an acrimonious campaign, M'Ba Abessole was defeated by Eyéghé Ndong, having beaten him in a Libreville constituency election in 2001. When the new Government was announced in January 2007 the number of ministers was increased from 39 to 44, including M'ba Abessole, although he was denied a portfolio. Of the opposition parties Mamboundou's UPG won eight seats and Myboto's UGDD just four. (Four seats also went to independents.) At by-elections in June, following the annulment of 20 results by the Constitutional Court, the UPG lost two constituencies while the UGDD gained one; overall the opposition's net gain was one seat.

Although faced with a considerable opposition challenge in the first years after the restoration of multi-party politics, Bongo Ondimba, who turned 71 in 2006, had demonstrated a mastery of domestic politics in his own country unmatched by any of the current francophone African leaders, except perhaps for Cameroon's Paul Biya. He had managed to balance regional and ethnic interests within the senior organs of the ruling party and the state, as well as to divide and, when useful, to co-opt opponents from other parties. The ruling PDG remained the only party with an effective national reach. Since the December 2001 elections there was evidence of a growing centralization of power, and many key positions in the military and security services were in the hands of allies from Bongo Ondimba's Haut-Ogooué province. The independent press had its autonomy eroded between 2001 and 2005 as Gabon's strict libel laws were used to suspend or ban 11 privately owned papers. With a fragmented political opposition and an underdeveloped civil society, Bongo Ondimba seemed secure for the foreseeable future. Although speculation over his succession had increased, manoeuvres among aspirant factions within the leadership remained discreet.

EXTERNAL CONCERNS

President Bongo Ondimba has pursued a policy of close co-operation with France. Gabon remains one of France's principal African trading partners and is one of four African states still providing France with permanent military base facilities (in Gabon's case, to accommodate a 600-strong battalion). However, relations were strained after March 1997, when allegations that Bongo had been a beneficiary in an international fraud emerged during a French judicial investigation of the state-owned petroleum company Elf-Aquitaine (now part of Total). In response, Bongo cancelled a visit to France and reportedly threatened to impose economic sanctions against French petroleum interests in Gabon. Bongo insisted that Elf's 'bonus' payments had been made only to the Gabonese Government. Nevertheless, further documentation of Elf's illicit links with the Bongo regime surfacing in late 1999 as a result of an investigation by Swiss authorities, the publication of a US congressional committee report on 'money-laundering' by US banks and the publication of the findings of the foreign affairs committee of the French Assemblée nationale. Between March and November 2003 the trial in Paris of Elf's former Director-General, its Director of General Affairs, the head of Elf-Gabon and 34 other company officials and business associates produced allegations of embezzlement by Elf executives, the secret funding of French political parties and of substantial illicit payments to foreign leaders (among them President Bongo).

None the less, Franco-Gabonese relations entered a phase of renewed intimacy following the re-election of Jacques Chirac as French President in May 2002 and the victory of his Union pour la majorité présidentielle in legislative elections the following month. President Bongo Ondimba has long enjoyed cordial relations with Chirac. The new French Government quickly made clear its intention to restore the special relationship between France and its African allies, which the previous Socialist Government had downgraded. Yet change returned to the agenda during the French presidential campaign of April–May 2007, with both the leading candidates promising to reform the existing 'Francafrique' relationship. Though Bongo was among the first foreign heads of state to personally congratulate the victor, Nicolas Sarkozy, he had earlier criticized both Sarkozy and his socialist opponent, Ségolène Royale, for their lack of understanding of African priorities.

France now faced growing competition for influence from the USA, which in the wake of the September 2001 terrorist attacks on New York's World Trade Center sought to diversify its sources of petroleum. In September 2002 US Secretary of State Colin Powell paid an official visit to Gabon, the most senior US official ever to do so; he was followed in March 2004 by a high-ranking US general and a senior senator. Relations with the People's Republic of China have also gained significance, with substantial Chinese investment in the hydrocarbons, mineral and timber sectors. Chinese President Hu Jintao visited Gabon in February 2004, and an agreement on energy and mining was signed in May. Trade between the two countries in 2004 was valued at some US $300m.

Bongo Ondimbahas been a significant intermediary actor in both regional and extra-regional disputes. The President had encouraged dialogue between Angola and the USA. In 1997 Bongo intervened in civil conflicts in Zaire (now the Democratic Republic of the Congo—DRC), the Central African Republic (CAR) and the Republic of Congo. At a Gulf of Guinea summit held in Libreville in November 1999, the seven countries represented agreed to form the Commission du golfe de Guinée (CGG), a consultative framework designed to promote co-operation and prevent conflicts among the member states. In December Bongo was designated as the official mediator in negotiations between the Government and militia groups in the Republic of Congo, which subsequently led to the conclusion of a peace agreement. During 2000 Bongo sought to mediate in the renewed civil war in the DRC, and in January 2001 the DRC President, Laurent-Désiré Kabila, shortly before his assassination, chose Libreville as the venue for an unsuccessful peace conference aimed at bringing an end to the fighting.

In January 2000 and July 2003 Gabon hosted military exercises with other central African states under the French-sponsored Renforcement des capacités africaines de maintien de la paix. At a Libreville meeting of the Communauté économique et monétaire de l'Afrique centrale (CEMAC) in early December 2001 Bongo had been appointed to chair a commission, also comprising Presidents Idriss Deby and Denis Sassou-Nguesso of Chad and the Republic of the Congo, respectively, to find a lasting solution to instability in the CAR (q.v.). In August 2002 a commission was established, chaired by Bongo, to examine conflicts along the border between the CAR and Chad. In October a CEMAC summit in Libreville further sought to defuse tensions between the CAR and Chad, and in November Gabonese soldiers arrived in the CAR as part of a CEMAC peace-keeping force, to replace a small Libyan contingent. The border region became increasingly insecure amid the external repercussions of the Darfur crisis in neighbouring Sudan, and the force remained in place in mid-2007. At the invitation of the European Union (EU), Gabon also deployed 200 troops in August 2006 to join the EU's rapid reaction force stationed in Kinshasa, the capital of the DRC, after the announcement of the results of the July presidential election sparked serious violence.

During 2004 President Bongo Ondimba became actively involved, alongside France, the AU and the UN, in efforts to find a political solution to the Côte d'Ivoire civil war, although after the Gabonese leader publicly rebuked the Ivorian President, Laurent Gbagbo, at the annual AU summit in July 2004 over his unwillingness to seek a political settlement to the conflict, relations between the two Governments became strained. Bongo and other African leaders were also involved in helping to resolve the political *impasse* between the Togolese Government and that country's opposition during August and September 2006. Reflecting Gabon's prominent role in African affairs, Minister of State for Foreign Affairs Jean Ping was elected President of the 29th Session of the UN General Assembly, which opened in September 2004, playing an important role in the negotiations over a key security and development document drafted to mark the UN's 60th anniversary meeting in September 2005. During 2005 Gabon ratified the UN Convention against Corruption. It also agreed to participate in the African Peer Review Mechanism, concerning both governance and economic management, which was inaugurated in July 2002 under the New Partnership for Africa's Development (NEPAD). Gabon was expected to be evaluated in 2007 (with a public report to be published by late 2008).

In February 2003 tension arose between Gabon and neighbouring Equatorial Guinea, following Gabon's occupation of the island of Mbañé, strategically located in the oil-rich waters off their shores. Mbañé and two other islets in Corisco Bay had been the focus of a simmering dispute between the two countries since 1972. Despite the rancour surrounding this issue, Gabon and Equatorial Guinea agreed to the appointment of a Canadian UN mediator in January 2004, and the following month accepted the terms of mediation for settling the dispute. However, the serious divisions within the Equato-Guinean leadership over the eventual succession to President Obiang Nguema Mbasogo and the ramifications of the failed coup attempt in March—not least that country's suspicions of Gabonese awareness of the plot—promised to prolong the process of resolving the boundary dispute in so sensitive a zone. Progress was made in early July 2004, when both countries' Presidents pledged to explore jointly for petroleum in the disputed offshore region, pending the results of UN mediation. The two Presidents again committed themselves in February 2006 to finding a negotiated settlement to the dispute. In early October, however, a month's ban was imposed on the independent weekly *L'Echo du Nord* for questioning Gabon's claim to the islands after the pro-government *L'Union* had revealed two weeks earlier that two ministers had plotted to sell the islands for cash. With Obiang Nguema having avoided the apparent trap, the issue remained unresolved in mid-2007.

Economy

EDITH HODGKINSON

Revised by RALPH YOUNG

The combination of a small population, of 1.3m., according to the 2003 census, and plentiful petroleum resources has given Gabon one of the highest incomes per head in sub-Saharan Africa. Gabon's gross national income (GNI) per head in 2005 was estimated by the World Bank at US $5,280. It therefore ranks as an upper-middle-income country, although only placed 124th of 177 countries in the UN Development Programme's 2006 Human Development Index; Gabon's position was more than 40 positions below countries with a similar gross national product per head. However, reflecting the dominance of the petroleum sector, and hence the vulnerability to trends in world prices, the rate of economic growth has fluctuated widely in recent decades. While growth in gross domestic product (GDP) averaged 9.5% per year in 1965–80, after the collapse in petroleum prices in 1986 the annual average declined to 0.8% in 1985–90. The 1990s saw an improvement, because of the development of the Rabi-Kounga oilfield, to an average of 2.5% per year in 1990–2003. In 2004 Gabon recorded only a modest increase in real GDP of 1.4%; however, growth reached 2.2% in 2005 and was expected to strengthen further in 2006.

The earlier period of rapid growth contained the petroleum 'boom' of the mid-1970s, when the surge in domestic production, prompted by higher world prices, generated government investment spending and borrowing, which left the country with a heavy debt burden and increased its vulnerability to adverse international trends in petroleum prices, interest rates and the value of the US dollar. Consequently, from the mid-1980s, the Government undertook a series of economic adjustment programmes, designed to reduce the external current-account deficit, while promoting the development of non-petroleum activities. Progress over economic reform was limited, however, and the non-petroleum economy failed to provide an alternative growth dynamic.

Following the devaluation of the CFA franc by 50% in relation to the French franc in January 1994, the Government adopted a more extensive programme for economic recovery, supported by IMF funding. However, shortcomings in implementation and the Fund's dissatisfaction with financial transparency delayed the award of an extended fund facility (EFF) until November 1995. The targets of the 1995–98 programme included: an improvement in the rate of return on petroleum resources; a reform of the tax system; a reduction in current budget spending (including payroll retrenchments); higher implementation of the budget's capital expenditure programme; and privatization of public-sector enterprises. Significant tax reforms were initiated, and an investment code consistent with IMF recommendations was introduced; several major privatizations were also completed (including the power utility).

Tight monetary and fiscal policies offset the strong inflationary impact of the currency's devaluation to reduce the rate from an average 36% in 1994 to 2.3% in 1998—well below the 5.0% target agreed with the IMF. However, slippage in other sectors in the run-up to the December 1998 presidential election caused the IMF to abandon the programme. An economic downturn in 1999, however, brought a sharp rise in Gabon's debt arrears, necessitating a new agreement with the IMF. The IMF wanted more far-reaching economic reform than the Government envisaged, including larger reductions in government spending and a greater contraction of the civil service. In October 2000 the IMF approved an 18-month stand-by credit, worth some US $119m., but this arrangement collapsed in April 2002, requiring the Government to negotiate a 14-month stand-by arrangement in May 2004 (worth around $105m.), accompanied by stricter conditions. This paved the way for a 'Paris Club' agreement in June 2004 to reschedule $849m. of debt owed to its members. By early 2005 Gabon was on course to meeting many of the terms set. The IMF praised the Government's decision to devote most of the extra revenue resulting from the current oil-price 'boom' to reducing Gabon's external debt, clearing other payment arrears and boosting the special Fund for Future Generations (established in 1998). With assistance from the World Bank, a poverty-reduction strategy was adopted by the Government in August 2005.

The tight fiscal and monetary policies as well as the social truce negotiated with the trade unions and employers in September 2003 (after a wave of strikes) had seen annual inflation fall from 2.1% in late 2003 to 0.5% in 2004. However, the increased government spending linked to the 2005 and 2006 elections sharply boosted domestic debt and raised inflation to over 6% by December 2006. In contrast to 1999, the IMF avoided sanctions. The privatization programme was well advanced, despite its political sensitivity for regime patronage networks and also the risks of labour unrest. The Government had responded promptly to criticism of its budgetary procedures and financial accountability arrangements published in October 2006. The proportion of public contracts awarded without competitive tendering (90% in 2004) had fallen to 65% by late 2006, and further falls were promised. Petrol and diesel prices were raised in March 2007 by around 25%, with accompanying measures to protect low-income families. The National Commission Against Unlawful Enrichment, while lacking strong enforcement powers, had instructed 3,000 senior civil servants to file statements of personal assets; in April 2007 it warned the 1,300 not complying that it would publish their names in late June. In May the IMF approved Gabon's request for a $117.3m. three-year stand-by agreement.

AGRICULTURE

Owing to the density of the tropical rainforest, only a small proportion of land area is suitable for agricultural activity and only 2% is estimated to be under cultivation. With over 80% of the population living in towns and a poor road infrastructure, the contribution to GDP of the agriculture, forestry and fishing sector is very modest, at an estimated 7.7% in 2005. Agricultural GDP rose by an average of only about 1.0% per year in the 1980s. It increased at an average annual rate of 3.1% in 1995–2005; growth in 2004 was 3.5%.

Among cash crops, palm oil is the most important. Export potential is limited, however, owing to intense competition from Far Eastern producers. A parastatal organization, the Société de développement de l'agriculture au Gabon (AGROGABON), formerly managed plantations covering 4,000 ha, which in 2005 produced an estimated 32,000 metric tons of oil-palm fruit. Production of refined sugar increased from negligible levels to 21,000 tons in 1989, with the development of a large-scale complex at Franceville. It has since decreased, although it stood at 17,500 tons in 2003, covering domestic requirements. In the 1980s the Government decided to promote rubber as an export crop, and four plantations covering 11,000 ha were developed by the state-owned Société de développement de l'hévéaculture (HEVEGAB), though by 2003 HEVEGAB was struggling to maintain its operations. Cocoa and coffee were once relatively significant cash crops, with a small amount available for export, but output has fallen since the 1980s, with annual cocoa crops down from 1,500–2,000 tons to some 300 tons in recent years. Coffee declined to only 120 tons in 2005, from around 1,000 tons per year in the early 1990s.

Tetse fly hindered animal husbandry before 1980, when the first tsetse-resistant cattle were imported. Livestock numbers have risen, with 35,000 head of cattle estimated in 2005 (compared with an average of 31,000 in 1989–91), 212,000 pigs (169,000) and 285,000 sheep and goats (241,000). Poultry farming is mainly on a smallholder basis. The 32,200 metric tons of meat products from local sources accounted for only 40% of Gabon's 2005 meat consumption. The Société gabonaise de développement d'élevage (an offshoot of AGROGABON) managed three cattle ranches; in 2004, along with AGROGABON and HEVEGAB, it was sold to SIAT of Belgium.

The total fishing catch was 30,500 metric tons in 2005. Resources are still not fully exploited, but under an agreement signed with the European Union (EU) in 1998 and renewed in 2003, EU trawlers are allowed to fish up to 9,000 tons per year, in return for aid funds and a levy on the catch. A new fish-processing centre at Port-Gentil, financed by Japanese aid worth 4,480m. francs CFA, was inaugurated in 2002, while Japan granted a further 3,800m. francs CFA in late 2003 to improve freshwater fishing facilities at Lambaréné. In July 2004 FAO granted Gabon US $270,000 to plan a long-term development strategy for the fishing industry.

FORESTRY

Tropical forests cover over 80% of Gabon's total land area. Until the commencement of mineral exploitation in the early 1960s, the timber industry dominated the economy. Okoumé and ozigo are the most important timbers, accounting for 75% of Gabon's timber exports. Gabon's forests contain an estimated 100 other species of commercially exploitable hard and soft woods. Gabon currently ranks as Africa's fourth largest producer of tropical wood, and the world's largest exporter of okoumé wood. Though forestry activities accounted for only some 1.7% of GDP in 2004, the industry was Gabon's second largest source of foreign-exchange earnings (9.1%) and the second largest employer of labour, after government. Some 50 companies are active in the forestry sector, which is dominated by a small number of European and, more recently, Chinese enterprises. Gabonese enterprises are involved in small-scale timber production.

The output of timber has fluctuated, mainly in response to international demand and the changing value of the US dollar in relation to the CFA franc, which affect the sector's competitiveness as regards suppliers in South-East Asia. Exports averaged some 1.4m. cu m of industrial roundwood per year in 1990–92, but then increased steadily because of production controls in some Asian countries and the unsettled political climate in several of Gabon's African competitors. Devaluation in 1994 gave an additional boost by doubling local currency earnings. The short-term fall in demand from Asian countries following the region's financial crisis in 1997 resulted in a one-third fall in both export volumes and earnings in 1998, to 1.8m. cu m, worth 130,900m. francs CFA. Exports increased in 1999 and 2000 (to 2.8m. cu m worth 281m. francs CFA in the latter year), but then declined, standing at around 1.7m. cu m in 2004 and 1.6m. cu m in 2005. The total amount of timber cut is thought to be much higher than official production figures, and there is concern that continuing expansion in the sector may prove unsustainable with the present low level of reafforestation.

A new Forestry Code was promulgated in 2001 that required logging companies to produce plans for the sustainable management of their concessions, although, as the deadline for these approached in late 2005, only six of the larger firms had done so. The Government also agreed to publish the lists of logging-permit holders and to award new permits by public auction. The cumbersome tax system was considerably rationalized. Tax evasion under the previous arrangements was costing Gabon an estimated US $10m. per year; in April 2007, as a signal of its commitment to reform this sector, the Government revoked 116 logging permits, covering an area of 1.8m. ha, over non-payment of taxes. The much criticized Société nationale des bois du Gabon (SNBG) lost its monopoly over the export of okoumé and ozigo logs in January 2006. The operations of SNGB were to be reduced to oversight of the sector. The Government's aim to raise the share of locally processed wood from its present level of 10%–15% would be possible, because the infrastructure for exporting logs is already well established and the trade very lucrative.

Gabon's forest reserves contain a significant proportion of the world's gorilla and chimpanzee populations, offering possibilities for eco-tourism, which the Government has begun actively to exploit. In 2002, following a US proposal at the Summit on Sustainable Development in Johannesburg, South Africa, to establish a Congo Basin partnership, the Government created 13 new national parks, covering 3m. ha or 10.6% of the country's land area. Besides US support, the World Bank, the EU, the London Zoological Society of the United Kingdom and several environmental groups have contributed funding or become engaged in conservation projects. Gabon's gorilla and chimpanzee populations have already been seriously reduced by logging and hunting, and by periodic outbreaks of Ebola haemorrhagic fever.

MINING

The source of Gabon's economic growth since the 1970s has been the exploitation of its mineral wealth, principally petroleum but also manganese and uranium. In 2005 petroleum and petroleum products accounted for over 80% of total export earnings, while the contribution of manganese was around 9%. Originally joining the Organization of the Petroleum Exporting Countries (OPEC) in 1975, Gabon withdrew in 1996, after production from the Rabi-Kounga field had raised national output well above OPEC'S quota.

While the petroleum industry remains the economy's dominant sector, its contribution fluctuates annually with trends in world prices and the value of the US dollar. Thus its share of GDP, totalling 40.4% in 1980, fell to a low of 16.5% in 1986; the development of Rabi-Kounga, however, increased this to 46.2% by 2001. After falling to 43.3% in 2003, surging oil prices caused its share to rise to some 46.6% in 2004 and to 50% in 2005.

Exploitation of petroleum began in 1956, but significant growth only commenced after 1967, with the coming into production of the Gamba-Ivinga deposits and the exploitation of the offshore Anguille deposit. Production remains largely off shore. Output increased every year until 1996, when they reached a peak of 365,000 barrels per day (b/d). Although once sub-Saharan Africa's third largest petroleum producer, by 2005 Gabon had slipped to sixth place. Rabi-Kounga has been Gabon's major producing field, but its output has fallen sharply in recent years. Although small new fields continue to be developed, national output slipped to 232,000 b/d in 2006. While Gabonese authorities were expecting that production would fall by 10% annually during 2005–2010, supportive world petroleum prices in 2005 and 2006 allowed economically more marginal fields to sustain Gabon's production levels. Gabon had 2,500m. barrels of proven petroleum reserves at the beginning of 2005, sufficient to support the industry for another three decades at current levels of extraction. However, exploration activity has been diminishing for some years; Gabon has also suffered from the greater attractiveness of exploration in Angola, Equatorial Guinea and the Republic of the Congo.

The main producer was previously Elf-Gabon (a 25:75 joint venture between the Government and Elf-Aquitaine, now part of Total), but it was overtaken in 1993 by Shell-Gabon, which operates the Rabi-Kounga field in association with Elf-Gabon and Amerada-Hess. By 2001 36 oilfields had been discovered, with several other foreign companies participating, including AGIP (which had replaced Elf as the largest holder of exploration acreage), Conoco, Marathon, Amoco, Pioneer and Vaalco. In recent years, smaller independent oil firms have arrived to exploit more marginal deposits, bringing a short-term boost to production.

The bulk of production is exported as crude—with the USA, France, Argentina and Brazil as the major markets—although there is a refinery at Port-Gentil with a capacity of 17,000 b/d. In the wake of the terrorist attacks in the USA in September 2001, and recognizing the priority of diversifying its energy sources, the USA began showing considerable interest in West and Central Africa, with Africa's share of US petroleum imports expected to rise from an estimated 15% in 2002 to 25% by 2015. The US Assistant Secretary of State for African Affairs, Walter Kansteiner, visited the region twice in mid-2002, while in September the US Secretary of State, Colin Powell, visited both Gabon and Angola. The increasing importance of Asian demand was underlined by a state visit in February 2004 by the President of the People's Republic of China, Hu Jintao, which resulted in a US $7m. aid agreement and a contract to supply China with significant amounts of petroleum.

Export earnings have mirrored both output and price trends, with an increase in most years since 1986, to 1.4m. francs CFA in 1997. Reflecting the fall in world prices in 1998, earnings in that year declined to 833,400m. francs CFA. Earnings increased in 1999 and 2000, reaching 1.8m. francs CFA in the latter year, but declined slightly in 2001, to an estimated 1.5m. francs CFA. Underpinned by buoyant oil prices, it climbed to 2.5m. francs CFA in 2005 and an estimated 2.6m. francs CFA in 2006. Yielding income to the Government in the form of royalties, taxes on company profits, exploration permits, and dividends and returns from the 15 fields in which it has equity, petroleum provided an estimated 54% of budget revenue in 2004 and 60% in 2005. The rising petroleum prices on international markets after August 2003 masked the domestic impact of Gabon's own production decline, if only temporarily. As a participant in the Extractive Industries Transparency Initiative sponsored by the British Government at the 2002 Summit on Sustainable Development, the Gabonese Government in 2005 established a technical working party to establish a framework for ensuring transparency in the financial relations between the oil companies and the state. A first report, in 2005, proved able to account for only 60% of oil revenues; a second report in April 2007 showed improved accounting procedures, and covered mining as well.

Since 1962 manganese ore has been mined at Moanda, near Franceville, by the Compagnie minière de l'Ogooué (COMILOG). Gabon had estimated reserves of 250m. metric tons. Until 1988 most ore was exported through the neighbouring Congo to the port of Pointe-Noire. The opening of a new port at Owendo near Libreville stimulated export volumes. In 1993 the South African group Gencor acquired a 15% holding in COMILOG from US Steel; other shareholders are Eramet of France, which in early 2006 held a 58% stake, the Société nationale d'investissement and private Gabonese interests. Production stood at 1.3m. tons of the metal in 2005 and 1.6m. tons in 2006. In 2006 Gabon was Africa's second largest manganese producer, after South Africa.

In April 2005 the Government signed an agreement with a consortium led by Chinese companies to exploit one of the largest iron-ore depositions in the world (estimated at 850m. metric tons), at Belinga in north-east Gabon. The project includes the construction of a 237-km spur to the Transgabonais railway, a new deep-water port at Cape Santa Clara and a hydroelectric dam. Work on the US $3,000m. project is expected to begin in 2007. Uranium had been mined at Mouana between 1958 and 1999, when declining world demand and the approaching exhaustion of reserves halted activities; during the 1990s production had averaged 500–600 tons per year. Alluvial deposits of gold are exploited on a small scale, with output estimated at some 70 kg per year. Stimulated by the decline in costs after the 1994 devaluation and changes in the mining code introduced in 2000, foreign companies are showing strong interest, both in gold mining and in the exploitation of niobium deposits. Lead, zinc and baryte deposits are known to exist. Marble is quarried at Doussé-Oussou.

MANUFACTURING AND POWER

Gabon's manufacturing sector accounted for an estimated 4.5% of GDP in 2005, and was centred on oil refining and timber processing. Other manufacturing industries include the processing of agricultural products, cement, soap, paint, industrial gas, cigarettes and textiles. Gabon has sought to develop large-scale natural-resource-based industries, but since its own domestic market is very small, these can for the most part be viable only in the context of the Communauté économique et monétaire en Afrique centrale (CEMAC), the successor to the Union douanière et économique de l'Afrique centrale, of which Gabon is one of six member countries. Gabon imports substantial quantities of manufactured products from other CEMAC countries, but apart from refined petroleum has exported little to its CEMAC partners. A bourse, eventually expected to serve the entire CEMAC region, opened in Libreville in January 2007. With 7.9% of 15–49-year-old Gabonese people believed to be infected with HIV in 2005, the Government opened a factory in Libreville in February 2005 that was to use Brazilian technology to manufacture drugs for the CEMAC area to treat HIV/AIDS, malaria and tuberculosis.

Electricity is produced and distributed by the Société d'énergie et d'eau du Gabon (SEEG), a parastatal, the management of which was taken over by a consortium of French and Canadian interests in 1993 and which was then privatized in 1997, with 51% going to a consortium led by France's Compagnie générale des eaux (since renamed Vivendi) and the balance sold to the Gabonese public. This was the first major privatization under the programme agreed with the IMF in 1996. In 1999 71.3% of electrical energy was provided by hydroelectric power, 17.8% by petroleum and 10.9% by natural gas. The contribution of hydroelectric power to total production was estimated at 41% in early 2003.

TRANSPORT AND COMMUNICATIONS

Gabon's surface transportation system remains inadequate. Until 1979 there were no railways except for the cableway link between the Congo border and the Moanda manganese mine, and the main rivers are navigable only for the last 80 km–160 km of their course to the Atlantic Ocean. The road network is poorly developed and much of it is unusable during the rainy seasons. In 2004 there were an estimated 9,170 km of roads, of which 10.2% were asphalted.

The Transgabonais railway scheme is among the most prestigious achievements of President Bongo Ondimba, opening up hitherto inaccessible areas and those more accessible from the Republic of the Congo, such as the mineral-rich Franceville area. The 679-km railway required a total investment of 800,000m.–900,000m. francs CFA between 1974 and 1986, which was not likely to be paid off, and external donors have been highly critical of the expenditure involved. The line finally became operational in 1989, although lack of finance prevented the completion at that time of the 237-km Booué–Belinga link, intended to enable exploitation of the large iron-ore deposits in the north-east (see above). In 1996 the Office du chemin de fer transgabonais (OCTRA) earned revenue of 21,757m. francs CFA, of which 57% came from the transport of logs, 8% from manganese and 13% from passengers. OCTRA was one of the major state assets due to be sold under the programme agreed with the IMF for 1995–98. In July 1999 Le Transgabonais, a consortium of timber interests headed by the state-owned timber concern, SNBG, took over the rail line on a 20-year operating concession, although this was cancelled in 2003 over the failure of Le Transgabonais to meet its financial obligations. In August 2005 a new 30-year concession was awarded to an affiliate of the manganese mining firm COMILOG. In 2007 it was decided to restructure and commercialize (rather than liquidate) the virtually bankrupt urban transport company SOGATRA.

The main port for petroleum exports is Port-Gentil, which also handles logs (floated down the Ogooué river) as does Owendo, the principal mineral port (though its facilities are currently overstretched). A third deep-water port operates at Mayumba. In September 2003 an Italian group won a 25-year concession for the management of port facilities at Libreville and Port-Gentil.

In the communications sector, Maroc Télécom, a subsidiary of the French telecommunications group Vivendi, acquired a 51% share of Gabon Télécom in February 2007. Also in early 2007 Gabon Post, having been liquidated, was being replaced by La Poste, a public agency of smaller size and with limited budgetary support.

Air transport plays an extremely important role in the economy, particularly because the dense forest, which covers much of the country, makes other modes of transport impracticable. Libreville's Léon M'Ba International Airport was modernized and expanded in the late 1980s, bringing capacity to 1.5m. passengers by 1990. As well as five domestic airports (Libreville, Port-Gentil, Franceville, Lambaréné and Moanda), there are various small airfields owned mainly by large companies working in the region. In 1977, following its withdrawal from Air Afrique, Gabon established its own international air carrier, Air Gabon, in which the state had an 80% interest. After drastic restructuring measures, the company was initially scheduled to be sold in 2002. However, owing to a lack of satisfactory international bids for the company, the Gabonese Government repurchased Air France's stake and, following consultations, recapitalized the company. In February 2006 the Government finally decided to liquidate Air Gabon, a process expected to be completed by September 2007. In January 2007 Gabon Airlines, a private venture intended to replace Air Gabon, commenced its services.

FINANCE

In the first period of petroleum exploitation the government budget was sustained by rapidly increasing income, but the investment requirements of the Transgabonais railway were largely met by borrowing at non-concessionary rates in the late 1970s, resulting in a serious deterioration in the fiscal position; the budget was in deficit by 1983. The situation was gravely exacerbated by the collapse in petroleum prices in 1986, which reduced government revenue from petroleum by one-quarter. In that year the deficit peaked at 186,700m. francs CFA (equivalent to 11.7% of GDP). Despite the completion of the Transgabonais and the surge in petroleum revenue in 1990 and 1991, the budget deficit remained because of debt servicing needs and the mounting civil-service costs. The gap was narrowed in 1993–94, and in 1995 a small surplus, of 16,100m. francs CFA, was registered due to rising petroleum production, the January 1994 devaluation (which doubled petroleum operators' incomes in local currency terms), and a major rescheduling of Gabon's bilateral debt (see below). As a result of a sharp fall in petroleum prices and increased capital expenditure, there was a return to deficit in 1997 and 1998. Modest budget surpluses were recorded in 1999 and 2000, with a more substantial surplus of 213,900m. francs CFA in 2001, equivalent to 6.3% of GDP. By 2006 the budgetary surplus stood at 460.5m. francs CFA, owing principally to rising petroleum prices.

FOREIGN TRADE AND PAYMENTS

Gabon has maintained a considerable surplus on its foreign trade, even through periods of instability in petroleum prices.

With Gabon's small population, exports have been, on average, about three times the value of imports. Even in the crisis year of 1986, when spending on the Transgabonais railway was still high and export earnings were halved, the value of imports was still 10% lower than that of exports. The trade surplus remained healthy through most of the 1990s, and reached 2.27m. francs CFA in 2005, and an estimated 2.34m. francs CFA in 2006.

On the other hand, the surplus on foreign trade has been exceeded by the deficit on services and transfers in nearly every year since 1985. This deficit was the result of high outflows of interest payments on the foreign debt and of remittances of profits and dividends by the petroleum industry. The current-account balance remains very sensitive to petroleum price fluctuations. Thus, the current-account deficit increased dramatically from US $163m. in 1985 to $1,058m. in 1986, when petroleum prices collapsed, while the surge in petroleum prices after the Iraqi invasion of Kuwait in 1990 produced a surplus of $168m. in 1990. Devaluation generated a surplus on the current account of $320m. in 1994, as spending on imported goods and services was depressed, and the increase in petroleum earnings in 1996, as Rabi-Kounga's output reached its peak, boosted the current-account surplus to $599m. The surplus was eliminated in 1998, when the fall in petroleum and timber earnings produced a current-account deficit of $596m. In both 1999 and 2000 there was a comfortable current-account surplus; in 2001, 2002 and 2003 Gabon registered successive deficits of $51m., $188m. and $30m., respectively, before a recovery to a surplus of $757m. in 2004 and an estimated $550m. in 2005 (or 10.5% and 6.8% of GDP, respectively).

The overall deficit on the balance of payments has been augmented by outflows on the capital account, as the heavy foreign borrowing that characterized the late 1970s and early 1980s came to an end, while the debt-repayment burden has been high. 'Exceptional financing' (the postponement of due debt-service payments) has made the most significant contribution in recent years to covering the payments gap, as Gabon has built up foreign debt arrears. That debt reached US $4,223m. in 1991, equivalent to 87% of GNI; of this, $539m. represented arrears. The situation deteriorated in 1992–93, with arrears increasing to $1,100m., or 28% of the country's total foreign debt of $3,861m. Yet its high GDP per head, and its poor record of compliance with commitments to the IMF, meant that Gabon was not a priority candidate for debt relief. The currency devaluation of January 1994 changed the environment. After a stand-by agreement with the IMF, both the 'Paris Club' of official bilateral creditors and the 'London Club' of commercial creditors agreed to debt rescheduling. Maturities on the official debt falling due in the period April 1994–March 1995, and all arrears, were rescheduled over 15 years, with a two-year period of grace. The 'London Club' restructured all commercial debt contracted before 1986. The debt situation was alleviated further by France's cancellation in 1994 of 50% of the loans contracted through the Caisse (now Agence) française de développement and by the cancellation of some $78m. in obligations in July 1996. The sharp deterioration in the current payments balance in 1999 led to an accumulation of arrears on the foreign debt, totalling $164m. and causing the total external debt to rise to $4,425m. At the end of 2004 total debt amounted to an estimated $3,795m., with debt repayments that year amounting to $493m. With a financing gap anticipated until 2014, the Government negotiated a new debt rescheduling agreement with the 'Paris Club' in June 2004 and another with the 'London Club' in mid-2005. However, higher than expected petroleum earnings meant that the external debt as a proportion of GDP decreased from 56% in 2003 to 50% in 2004, to 39% in 2005, and to 32.5% in 2006.

Despite Gabon's high income levels and the foreign investment its petroleum sector attracts, inflows of foreign aid, while relatively modest, were significant in underpinning both the budget and the balance of payments. In the period 1991–93 net aid disbursements averaged US $105m. per year, with 85% coming from France, much of it representing support for the overvalued CFA franc. The devaluation of 1994, and the associated external support, brought a sudden surge in inflows, to a net $182m. in that year (of which $150m. came from France) and an average of $135m. per year in 1995–96. Net inflows of aid fell back sharply in 1997 and 1998, to an average of $41.7m. a year, as Gabon's short-term needs eased; this figure stood at $53.9m. in 2005. However, the economy's downturn in 1998 highlighted the fragility of the country's balance-of-payments situation, and for most of 1999 foreign-exchange reserves were between $1m. and $2m., or less than one day's import cover; they have since strengthened, but remain vulnerable to sharp swings, year-on-year. The economy's fragility will continue while the country remains dependent on the export of a limited range of raw materials and restricted by the infrastructural and funding constraints on the economy's diversification. The solution of these problems is becoming ever more urgent; in the absence of major new petroleum discoveries, Gabon's petroleum production—which currently generates around one-half of GDP—is forecast to fall significantly in coming years, having already decreased by 36% between 1996 and 2006. The authorities' priorities since 2003 have been to restructure the economy in order to reduce dependency on the petroleum sector, to lessen this sector's distorting effects on agriculture and industry and to lower the level of public debt. At the same time, the predicted decline of petroleum revenues threatens seriously to weaken the financial underpinnings of the state and, so, reduce its capacity to act in furtherance of economic diversification and the welfare of the Gabonese people.

Statistical Survey

Source (unless otherwise stated): Direction Générale de la Statistique et des Etudes Economiques, Ministère de la Planification et de la Programmation du Développement, BP 2119, Libreville; tel. 72-13-69; fax 72-04-57; e-mail plan.dgsee.yahoo.fr; internet www.stat-gabon.ga.

Area and Population

AREA, POPULATION AND DENSITY

Area (sq km)	267,667*
Population (census results)	
31 July 1993	
Males	501,784
Females	513,192
Total	1,014,976
1 December 2003	1,269,000†
Population (UN estimates at mid-year)‡	
2004	1,270,000
2005	1,291,000
2006	1,311,000
Density (per sq km) at mid-2006	4.9

* 103,347 sq miles.

† Provisional (Source: UN, *Population and Vital Statistics Report*).

‡ Source: UN, *World Population Prospects: The 2006 Revision*.

REGIONS

(1993 census)

Region	Area (sq km)	Population	Density (per sq km)	Chief town
Estuaire	20,740	463,187	22.3	Libreville
Haut-Ogooué	36,547	104,301	2.9	Franceville
Moyen-Ogooué	18,535	42,316	2.3	Lambaréné
N'Gounié	37,750	77,781	2.1	Mouila
Nyanga	21,285	39,430	1.9	Tchibanga
Ogooué-Ivindo	46,075	48,862	1.1	Makokou
Ogooué-Lolo	25,380	43,915	1.7	Koula-Moutou
Ogooué-Maritime	22,890	97,913	4.3	Port-Gentil
Woleu-N'Tem	38,465	97,271	2.5	Oyem
Total	267,667	1,014,976	3.8	

PRINCIPAL TOWNS

(population at 1993 census)

Libreville (capital)	419,596	Mouila	16,307
Port-Gentil	79,225	Lambaréné	15,033
Franceville	31,183	Tchibanga	14,054
Oyem	22,404	Koulamoutou	11,773
Moanda	21,882	Makokou	9,849

Mid-2005 (incl. suburbs, UN estimate): Libreville (capital) 556,000 (Source: UN, *World Urbanization Prospects: The 2005 Revision*).

BIRTHS AND DEATHS

(annual averages, UN estimates)

	1990–95	1995–2000	2000–05
Birth rate (per 1,000)	30.2	27.7	25.7
Death rate (per 1,000)	10.2	11.7	11.7

Source: UN, *World Population Prospects: The 2006 Revision*.

Expectation of life (years at birth, WHO estimates): 57 (males 55; females 59) in 2004 (Source: WHO, *World Health Report*).

ECONOMICALLY ACTIVE POPULATION

('000 persons, 1991, estimates)

	Males	Females	Total
Agriculture, etc.	187	151	338
Industry	62	9	71
Services	69	26	95
Total labour force	318	186	504

Source: UN Economic Commission for Africa, *African Statistical Yearbook*.

1993 (census figures, persons aged 10 years and over): Total employed 308,322; Unemployed 67,622; Total labour force 375,944.

Mid-2005 (estimates in '000): Agriculture, etc. 197; Total 624 (Source: FAO).

Health and Welfare

KEY INDICATORS

Total fertility rate (children per woman, 2005)	3.8
Under-5 mortality rate (per 1,000 live births, 2005)	91
HIV/AIDS (% of persons aged 15–49, 2005)	7.9
Physicians (per 1,000 head, 2004)	0.29
Hospital beds (per 1,000 head, 1990)	3.19
Health expenditure (2004): US $ per head (PPP)	264.2
Health expenditure (2004): % of GDP	4.5
Health expenditure (2004): public (% of total)	68.8
Access to water (% of persons, 2004)	88
Access to sanitation (% of persons, 2004)	36
Human Development Index (2004): ranking	124
Human Development Index (2004): value	0.633

For sources and definitions, see explanatory note on p. vi.

Agriculture

PRINCIPAL CROPS

('000 metric tons)

	2003	2004	2005
Maize	31*	31†	30†
Cassava (Manioc)†	230	230	232
Taro (Coco yam)	59†	59†	n.a.
Yams†	155	155	165
Sugar cane †	190	190	180
Groundnuts (in shell)†	20	20	20
Oil palm fruit†	32	32	32
Vegetables	35	35	n.a.
Bananas†	12	12	13
Plantains†	270	270	274
Natural rubber†	11	11	11

* Unofficial figure.

† FAO estimate(s).

Source: FAO.

LIVESTOCK
('000 head, year ending September, FAO estimates)

	2001	2002	2003
Cattle	36	36	35
Pigs	213	212	212
Sheep	198	195	195
Goats	90	90	90
Chickens	3,200	3,100	3,100
Rabbits	300	300	300

2004–05: Figures assumed to be unchanged from 2003 (FAO estimates).

Source: FAO.

LIVESTOCK PRODUCTS
('000 metric tons, FAO estimates)

	2003	2004	2005
Cattle meat	0.7	1.1	1.1
Pig meat	3.1	3.2	3.3
Chicken meat	3.6	3.9	4.0
Rabbit meat	2.0	1.9	2.0
Game meat	21.0	21.0	n.a.
Cows' milk	1.6	1.6	1.6
Hen eggs	2.0	2.0	n.a.

Source: FAO.

Forestry

ROUNDWOOD REMOVALS
('000 cubic metres)

	2003	2004	2005
Sawlogs, veneer logs and logs for sleepers	3,563	3,500	3,200
Fuel wood	1,069	1,070	528
Total	4,632	4,570	3,728

Source: FAO.

SAWNWOOD PRODUCTION
('000 cubic metres, incl. railway sleepers)

	2003	2004	2005
Total	231	133	232

Source: FAO.

Fishing

('000 metric tons, live weight)

	2003	2004	2005
Capture	45.3	46.0	43.9
Tilapias	3.8	3.8	3.8
Other freshwater fishes	6.0	4.8	6.3
Barracudas	1.5	1.6	1.0
Bobo croakers	1.3	2.1	1.7
West African croakers	3.4	5.1	4.5
Lesser African threadfin	0.8	0.7	1.7
Bonga shad	12.0	10.6	8.6
Sardinellas	1.8	1.8	2.4
Penaeus shrimp	2.8	1.8	1.4
Aquaculture	0.1	0.1	0.1
Total catch	45.4	46.0	43.9

Source: FAO.

Mining

	2003	2004*	2005*
Crude petroleum ('000 barrels)	87,965	87,235†	85,469†
Natural gas (million cu metres)*	79	80	80
Diamonds (carats)*	500	500	500
Hydraulic cement ('000 metric tons)*	260	260	260
Manganese ore ('000 metric tons): gross weight‡	1,950*	2,400	2,800
Manganese ore ('000 metric tons): metal content§	50*	60	59
Gold (kilograms)*‡‖	70	300	300

* Estimated production.
† Reported figure.
‡ Figures refer to the metal content of ore.
§ Figures refer to the weight of chemical-grade pellets.
‖ Excluding production smuggled out of the country (estimated at more than 400 kg annually).

Source: US Geological Survey.

Industry

PETROLEUM PRODUCTS
('000 metric tons)

	2002	2003	2004
Butane	9.8	8.8	9.2
Motor spirit (petrol)	64.5	64.3	65.9
Kerosene	79.4	69.7	61.8
Distillate fuel oils	218.8	198.1	223.0
Residual fuel oils and asphalt	288.5	285.1	347.5

Source: IMF, *Gabon: Statistical Appendix* (May 2005).

2005 ('000 metric tons): Butane 9.5.

SELECTED OTHER PRODUCTS

	2003	2004	2005
Plywood ('000 cu metres)	37.8	52.8	68.1
Veneer sheets ('000 cu metres)	198.2	120.7	175.2
Cement ('000 metric tons)*	260	260	260
Alcoholic beverages ('000 hectolitres)	755.9	750.1	852.1
Soft drinks ('000 hectolitres)	568.4	537.9	587.0
Electric energy (million kWh)	1,314.6	1,337.1	1,363.7

* Estimated data from the US Geological Survey.

Finance

CURRENCY AND EXCHANGE RATES

Monetary Units

100 centimes = 1 franc de la Coopération financière en Afrique centrale (CFA).

Sterling, Dollar and Euro Equivalents (31 May 2007)

£1 sterling = 964.116 francs CFA;
US $1 = 487.592 francs CFA;
€1 = 655.957 francs CFA;
10,000 francs CFA = £10.37 = $20.51 = €15.24.

Average Exchange Rate (francs CFA per US $)

2004 528.29
2005 527.47
2006 522.89

Note: An exchange rate of 1 French franc = 50 francs CFA, established in 1948, remained in force until January 1994, when the CFA franc was devalued by 50%, with the exchange rate adjusted to 1 French franc = 100 francs CFA. This relationship to French currency remained in effect with the introduction of the euro on 1 January 1999. From that date, accordingly, a fixed exchange rate of €1 = 655.957 francs CFA has been in operation.

BUDGET

('000 million francs CFA)

Revenue*	2004	2005	2006†
Petroleum revenue	600.0	907.2	1,012.9
Non-petroleum revenue	511.5	525.0	569.7
Direct taxes	137.3	138.6	159.4
Indirect taxes	115.1	113.7	113.7
Value-added tax	82.6	80.5	78.4
Taxes on international trade and transactions	200.5	215.3	240.4
Import duties	172.9	179.6	210.1
Export duties	27.6	35.7	30.2
Other revenue	58.7	57.4	56.2
Total	1,111.5	1,432.2	1,582.6

Expenditure‡	2004	2005	2006†
Current expenditure	627.8	789.3	827.5
Wages and salaries	226.3	227.8	252.4
Other goods and services	125.1	153.2	167.2
Transfers and subsidies	125.6	279.1	291.3
Interest payments	150.8	129.2	116.6
Domestic	31.4	29.3	24.5
External	119.4	99.9	92.2
Capital expenditure	160.0	193.4	238.8
Domestically financed investment	142.2	146.1	190.0
Externally financed investment	17.8	47.3	48.8
Total	787.8	982.7	1,066.3

* Excluding grants received ('000 million francs CFA): 2.1 in 2004; 2.0 in 2005; nil in 2006 (preliminary).

† Preliminary figures.

‡ Excluding net lending, restructuring cost of public enterprises, and road maintenance and other special funds ('000 million francs CFA): 39.3 in 2004 (funds only); 58.4 in 2005; 55.8 in 2006 (funds only, preliminary).

Source: IMF, *Gabon: Request for Stand-By Arrangement - Staff Report; Staff Statement; Press Release on the Executive Board Discussion; and Statement by the Executive Director for Gabon* (May 2007).

INTERNATIONAL RESERVES

(US $ million at 31 December)

	2004	2005	2006
Gold*	5.63	6.59	8.14
IMF special drawing rights	6.26	0.12	0.88
Reserve position in IMF	0.28	0.31	0.37
Foreign exchange	436.88	668.13	1,112.19
Total	449.05	675.15	1,121.58

* Valued at market-related prices.

Source: IMF, *International Financial Statistics*.

MONEY SUPPLY

('000 million francs CFA at 31 December)

	2004	2005	2006
Currency outside banks	138.69	198.03	219.06
Demand deposits at commercial and development banks	248.06	326.41	396.99
Total money (incl. others)	387.45	528.29	617.99

Source: IMF, *International Financial Statistics*.

COST OF LIVING

(Consumer Price Index; base: 1975 = 100)

	2003	2004	2005
Food	481.0	472.1	473.7
Clothing	367.0	397.6	389.9
Housing	411.8	400.5	395.9
All items (incl. others)	489.2	490.4	490.0

NATIONAL ACCOUNTS

Expenditure on the Gross Domestic Product

(US $ million)

	2004	2005	2006
Government final consumption expenditure	940.21	999.30	1,046.65
Private final consumption expenditure	2,578.46	2,717.46	2,917.43
Gross fixed capital formation	1,997.07	2,010.82	2,151.00
Total domestic expenditure	5,515.74	5,727.58	6,115.08
Exports of goods and services	4,329.97	5,736.53	6,617.15
Less Imports of goods and services	2,667.58	2,798.37	3,241.41
GDP at market prices	7,178.13	8,665.74	9,490.81

Source: African Development Bank, *Selected Statistics on African Countries*.

Gross Domestic Product by Economic Activity

('000 million francs CFA at current prices)

	2002	2003	2004*
Agriculture, livestock, hunting and fishing	148.2	151.7	155.8
Forestry	60.0	59.6	58.8
Petroleum exploitation	1,380.4	1,416.6	1,654.7
Other mining	51.7	53.7	66.3
Manufacturing†	228.5	236.9	231.3
Electricity and water	45.2	47.0	51.3
Construction and public works	83.1	78.0	81.2
Trade	241.1	244.5	238.3
Transport	191.7	197.6	206.6
Financial services	20.4	20.9	20.0
Government services	293.4	301.0	308.6
Other services	459.9	461.3	475.2
GDP at factor cost	3,203.6	3,268.7	3,548.0
Indirect taxes	245.3	250.2	270.0
GDP in purchasers' values	3,448.9	3,518.9	3,818.0

* Estimates.

† Includes processing of primary products and research and oil services.

Source: IMF, *Gabon: Selected Issues and Statistical Appendix* (May 2005).

BALANCE OF PAYMENTS

('000 million francs CFA)

	2005*	2006†	2007‡
Exports of goods f.o.b.	2,989	3,166	3,101
Petroleum	2,489	2,602	2,480
Imports of goods f.o.b.	–716	–828	–953
Trade balance	2,273	2,338	2,148
Services and other income (net)	–1,275	–1,314	–1,238
Balance on goods, services and income	998	1,024	910
Current transfers (net)	–107	–103	–49
Current balance	891	920	861
Capital transfers (net)	3	3	0
Medium- and long-term capital	–361	–457	–322
Direct and portfolio investment	–146	–159	–86
Short-term capital	–435	–273	–340
Overall balance	98	194	200

* Preliminary.

† Estimates.

‡ Forecasts.

Source: IMF, *Gabon: Request for Stand-By Arrangement - Staff Report; Staff Statement; Press Release on the Executive Board Discussion; and Statement by the Executive Director for Gabon*(May 2007).

External Trade

PRINCIPAL COMMODITIES
('000 million francs CFA)

Imports	2002	2003	2004
Prepared foodstuffs (excl. beverages)	119.9	121.5	124.8
Beverages	12.6	11.0	9.5
Base metals and their manufactures	51.0	51.8	37.8
Machinery and mechanical appliances	145.6	106.4	130.8
Machines and electrical appliances	60.3	49.8	54.3
Vehicles	64.6	74.4	54.1
Consumption goods (excl. foodstuffs and beverages)	129.9	98.7	104.1
Intermediary products imported for construction and public works	20.6	17.1	18.2
Other	47.1	75.3	115.7
Total	651.7	605.9	649.3

Exports	2002	2003	2004*
Petroleum and petroleum products	1,430	1,499	1,801
Manganese	101	104	159
Timber	203	221	198
Total (incl. others)	1,781	1,850	2,245

* Estimates.

Source: IMF, *Gabon: Selected Issues and Statistical Appendix* (May 2005).

PRINCIPAL TRADING PARTNERS
(US $ million)

Imports c.i.f.	2002	2003	2004
Austria	12.4	10.6	1.8
Belgium	37.1	31.4	106.1
Brazil	0.0	7.9	16.4
Cameroon	0.0	31.7	30.1
China, People's Republic	0.0	8.6	14.5
Côte d'Ivoire	0.0	5.4	19.1
France (incl. Monaco)	443.8	308.4	393.8
Germany	31.3	21.2	14.1
India	0.0	4.1	10.3
Italy	34.1	25.3	26.5
Japan	0.0	40.4	29.1
Netherlands	44.8	34.2	40.0
Norway	33.9	6.8	1.1
Singapore	0.0	7.7	4.6
South Africa	0.0	7.6	20.3
Spain	34.2	10.8	21.9
Switzerland-Liechtenstein	12.1	3.4	2.4
Thailand	0.0	5.6	27.2
United Arab Emirates	0.0	3.4	9.8
United Kingdom	29.9	27.6	40.0
USA	0.0	105.8	44.2
Total (incl. others)	745.2	770.0	964.9

Exports f.o.b.	2001	2002	2004
Brazil	62.0	58.1	0.0
China, People's Republic	129.1	108.1	175.2
France (incl. Monaco)	350.2	183.7	246.2
Iceland	50.1	47.4	117.0
India	13.7	89.1	45.4
Italy	24.2	27.2	54.8
Japan	3.9	26.5	2.0
Korea, Republic	89.2	24.6	2.5
Nigeria	1.6	27.1	2.8
Norway	4.9	8.0	31.1
Portugal	33.2	8.0	13.0
Singapore	1.5	57.8	3.4
South Africa	61.2	52.9	38.4
Spain	35.6	14.0	33.6
Switzerland-Liechtenstein	96.0	39.8	53.4
Trinidad and Tobago	9.3	35.1	1.9
USA	1,418.9	1,430.0	1,363.6
Total (incl. others)	2,521.5	2,411.1	2,780.0

Note: data for exports for 2003 not available.

Source: UN, *International Trade Statistics Yearbook*.

Transport

RAILWAYS
(traffic)

	2003	2004	2005
Passengers carried ('000)	206.8	214.4	218.5
Freight carried ('000 metric tons)	2,967.7	3,455.8	3,923.8

ROAD TRAFFIC
(estimates, motor vehicles in use)

	1994	1995	1996
Passenger cars	22,310	24,000	24,750
Lorries and vans	14,850	15,840	16,490

Source: IRF, *World Road Statistics*.

SHIPPING

Merchant Fleet
(registered at 31 December)

	2003	2004	2005
Number of vessels	45	46	48
Total displacement ('000 grt)	12.7	12.8	13.5

Source: Lloyd's Register-Fairplay, *World Fleet Statistics*.

International Sea-borne Freight Traffic
('000 metric tons, Port-Gentil and Owendo)

	2002	2003	2004
Goods loaded	15,429	16,005	17,144
Goods unloaded	763	739	776

Source: IMF, *Gabon: Statistical Appendix* (May 2005).

CIVIL AVIATION
(traffic on scheduled services)

	2000	2001	2002
Kilometres flown (million)	8	7	7
Passengers carried ('000)	447	374	366
Passenger-kilometres (million)	847	637	643
Total ton-kilometres (million)	135	107	106

Source: UN, *Statistical Yearbook*.

Passengers carried ('000): 838.1 in 2002; 854.8 in 2003; 698.6 in 2004; 635.4 in 2005.

Tourism

	2001	2002	2003
Tourist arrivals	169,191	208,348	222,257
Tourism receipts (US $ million, incl. passenger transport)	46	77	84

Source: World Tourism Organization.

Communications Media

	2003	2004	2005
Telephones ('000 main lines in use)	38.4	38.7	39.1
Mobile cellular telephones ('000 subscribers)	300.0	489.4	649.8
Personal computers ('000 in use)	30	40	45
Internet users ('000)	35	40	67

1997: 501 facsimile machines in use.

1998: 2 daily newspapers (estimated average circulation 34,800 copies).

1999: 600,000 radio receivers in use.

2001: 400,000 television receivers in use.

Sources: UNESCO Institute for Statistics; UN, *Statistical Yearbook*; International Telecommunication Union.

Education

(2003/04 unless otherwise indicated, estimates)

	Institutions	Teachers	Pupils		
			Males	Females	Total
Pre-primary	9*	517†	7,784†	7,784†	15,568†
Primary	1,175*	7,764	142,268	139,103	281,371
Secondary:					
General	88§	3,102†	43,892‡	39,303‡	97,604†
Technical and vocational	11§	394†	5,025‖	2,562‖	7,587‖
Tertiary	2*	585¶	4,806¶	2,667¶	7,473¶

* 1991/92 figure.
† 2000/01 figure.
‡ 1999/2000 figure.
§ 1996 figure.
‖ 2002/03 figure.
¶ 1998/99 figure.

Source: UNESCO Institute for Statistics.

Adult literacy rate (UNICEF estimate): 71% in 2004 (Source: UN Development Programme, *Human Development Report*).

Directory

The Constitution

The Constitution of the Gabonese Republic was adopted on 14 March 1991. The main provisions are summarized below.

PREAMBLE

Upholds the rights of the individual, liberty of conscience and of the person, religious freedom and freedom of education. Sovereignty is vested in the people, who exercise it through their representatives or by means of referendums. There is direct, universal and secret suffrage.

HEAD OF STATE*

The President is elected by direct universal suffrage for a five-year term, renewable only once. The President is Head of State and of the Armed Forces. The President may, after consultation with his ministers and leaders of the Assemblée nationale, order a referendum to be held. The President appoints the Prime Minister, who is Head of Government and who is accountable to the President. The President is the guarantor of national independence and territorial sovereignty.

EXECUTIVE POWER

Executive power is vested in the President and the Council of Ministers, who are appointed by the Prime Minister, in consultation with the President.

LEGISLATIVE POWER

The Assemblée nationale is elected by direct universal suffrage for a five-year term. It may be dissolved or prorogued for up to 18 months by the President, after consultation with the Council of Ministers and President of the Assemblée. The President may return a bill to the Assemblée for a second reading, when it must be passed by a majority of two-thirds of the members. If the President dissolves the Assemblée, elections must take place within 40 days.

The Constitution also provides for the establishment of an upper chamber (the Sénat), to control the balance and regulation of power.

POLITICAL ORGANIZATIONS

Article 2 of the Constitution states that 'Political parties and associations contribute to the expression of universal suffrage. They are formed and exercise their activities freely, within the limits delineated by the laws and regulations. They must respect the principles of democracy, national sovereignty, public order and national unity'.

JUDICIAL POWER

The President guarantees the independence of the judiciary and presides over the Conseil Supérieur de la Magistrature. Supreme judicial power is vested in the Supreme Court.

* A constitutional amendment, adopted by the legislature on 18 April 1997, extended the presidential term to seven years and provided for the creation of the post of Vice-President. On 29 July 2003 the Constitution was further amended to remove the restriction on the number of terms of office the President may serve.

The Government

HEAD OF STATE

President: El Hadj OMAR (ALBERT-BERNARD) BONGO ONDIMBA (took office 2 December 1967, elected 25 February 1973, re-elected December 1979, November 1986, December 1993, December 1998 and November 2005).

Vice-President: DIDJOB DIVUNGUI-DI-N'DINGUE.

COUNCIL OF MINISTERS
(August 2007)

Prime Minister and Head of Government: JEAN EYÉGHÉ NDONG (PDG).

Vice-Prime Minister, Minister of the Environment, the Protection of Nature, Research and Technology: GEORGETTE KOKO.

Vice-Prime Minister, Minister of Reform, Human Rights, Co-ordination of Major Projects and the Fêtes Tournantes Independence Festival: PAUL MBA ABESSOLE (RPG).

Vice-Prime Minister, Minister of Relations with Parliament, in charge of Missions and Interministerial Commissions: EMMANUEL ONDO METHOGO (PDG).

Vice-Prime Minister, Minister of Foreign Affairs, Co-operation, Francophonie and Regional Integration: JEAN PING (PDG).

Minister of State for Social Affairs, National Solidarity, Well-being and the Fight against Poverty: JEAN-FRANÇOIS NDONGOU.

Minister of State for Planning and Programming Development: Casimir Oyé Mba (PDG).

Minister of State the Economy, Finance, the Budget and Privatization: Paul Toungui (PDG).

Minister of State for Public Health: Paulette Missambo (PDG).

Minister of State for Housing, Accommodation and Town Planning: Jacques Adiahénot (PDG).

Minister of State for Transport, Civil Aviation and Tourism: Pierre Claver Maganga Moussavou (PSD).

Minister of State for Public Works, Infrastructure and Construction: Gen. (retd) Idriss Ngari (PDG).

Minister of State for National Defence: Ali Bongo Ondimba (PDG).

Minister of State for the Interior, Public Security and Immigration: André Mba Obame (PDG).

Minister of State for Technical Instruction, Professional Training and Reintegration and the Professional Integration of Youths: Prof. Pierre André Kombila.

Minister of State for Agriculture, Livestock and Rural Development: Faustin Boukoubi (PDG).

Minister of Public Affairs, Administrative Reform and Modernization of the State: Gen. Jean Boniface Assélé.

Minister of Mining, Energy, Petroleum and Water Resources: Richard August Onouviet (PDG).

Minister of the Merchant Navy and Port Equipment: Honorine Doussou Naki (PDG).

Minister of Forestry, Water, Fishing and National Parks: Emile Doumba (PDG).

Minister of Communication, Post and Telecommunications and New Information Technologies, Spokesperson for the Government: René Ndemezo Obiang.

Minister of Justice, Guardian of the Seals: Martin Mbala (PDG).

Minister of Commerce and Industrial Development, in charge of NEPAD: Paul Biyoghé-Mba (PDG).

Minister of Family Affairs, the Protection of Children and the Promotion of Women: Angélique Ngoma (PDG).

Minister of National Education and Civic Instruction, in charge of Educating the Population: Michel Menga (PDG).

Minister of Youth and Sports: Egide Boundono Simangoye (PDG).

Minister for the Prevention and Management of Natural Disasters: Jean Massima (PDG).

Minister of State Control, Inspections, the Fight against Corruption and the Illegal Accumulation of Wealth: Pierre Amoughé Mba (RPG).

Minister for Small and Medium-Sized Businesses: Senturel Ngoma Madoungou (PDG).

Minister for the Fight against AIDS and for the Protection of Orphans and Widows: Denise Mekamne.

Minister of National and Regional Development and Decentralization: Dieudonné Pambou.

Minister of Higher Education and Research: Fr Albert Ondo Ossa.

Minister of Labour and Employment: Christiane Bitoughat.

Minister for the Social Economy and Crafts: Marie Missouloukagne.

Minister of Culture and the Arts: Blandine Marundu.

There were also 15 Ministers-delegate.

MINISTRIES

Office of the Prime Minister: BP 546, Libreville; tel. 77-89-81.

Ministry of Agriculture, Livestock and Rural Development: BP 551, Libreville; tel. 77-59-22; fax 76-38-34.

Ministry of Commerce and Industrial Development: Libreville.

Ministry of Decentralization and Territorial Administration: Libreville; tel. 72-29-83; fax 77-29-62.

Ministry of Economic Affairs, Finance, the Budget and Privatization: BP 165, Libreville; tel. 76-12-10; fax 76-59-74.

Ministry of the Environment, the Protection of Nature, Research and Technology: BP 2217, Libreville; tel. and fax 76-39-09.

Ministry of Family Affairs, the Protection of Children and the Promotion of Women: BP 5684, Libreville; tel. 77-50-32; fax 76-69-29.

Ministry for the Fight against AIDS and for the Protection of AIDS Orphans: Libreville.

Ministry of Foreign Affairs, Co-operation and Francophone Affairs: BP 2245, Libreville; tel. 72-95-21; fax 72-91-73.

Ministry of Government Auditing: Libreville.

Ministry of Housing, Urbanization and Cadastral Services: BP 512, Libreville; tel. 77-31-04; fax 74-04-62.

Ministry of the Interior, Public Security and Immigration: BP 2110, Libreville; tel. 74-35-06; fax 72-13-89.

Ministry of Justice: BP 547, Libreville; tel. 74-66-28; fax 72-33-84.

Ministry of Labour and Employment: BP 4577, Libreville; tel. 74-32-18.

Ministry of the Merchant Navy and Port Equipment: Libreville.

Ministry of Mining, Energy, Petroleum and Water Resources: BP 576, Libreville; tel. 77-22-39.

Ministry of National Defence: BP 13493, Libreville; tel. and fax 77-86-96.

Ministry of National and Higher Education: BP 6, Libreville; tel. 72-44-61; fax 72-19-74.

Ministry of National Solidarity, Social Affairs, Welfare and the Fight against Poverty: Libreville.

Ministry of Planning and Development: Libreville.

Ministry of Post and Telecommunications and New Technologies: Libreville.

Ministry for the Prevention and Management of Natural Disasters: Libreville.

Ministry for the Promotion of the Private Sector, the Social Economy and Crafts: BP 178, Libreville; tel. 76-34-62.

Ministry of Public Affairs, Administrative Reform and Modernization of the State: BP 496, Libreville; tel. 76-38-86.

Ministry of Public Health: BP 50, Libreville; tel. 76-36-11.

Ministry of Public Works, Equipment and Construction: BP 49, Libreville; tel. 76-38-56; fax 74-80-92.

Ministry of Reform, Human Rights, the Fight against Poverty and Illicit Enrichment: Libreville.

Ministry of Small and Medium-sized Businesses: BP 3096, Libreville; tel. 74-59-21.

Ministry of Technical Instruction, Professional Training and Reintegration and the Professional Integration of Youths: Libreville; tel. 73-37-35; fax 73-37-39.

Ministry of Territorial Waters, Forestry, Fishing and National Parks: BP 3974, Libreville; tel. 76-01-09; fax 76-61-83.

Ministry of Towns, the Promotion of Collective Life and Protection of Widows and Orphans: Libreville; tel. 31-68-98.

Ministry of Transport and Civil Aviation: BP 803, Libreville; tel. 74-71-96; fax 77-33-31.

Ministry of Youth and Sports: BP 2150, Libreville; tel. 74-00-19; fax 74-65-89.

President and Legislature

PRESIDENT

Presidential Election, 27 November 2005

Candidate	Votes	% of votes
El Hadj Omar (Albert-Bernard) Bongo Ondimba (PDG)	275,819	79.18
Pierre Mamboundou (UPG)	47,410	13.61
Zacharie Myboto (Ind.)	22,921	6.58
Augustin Moussavou King (PSG)	1,149	0.33
Christian Serge Maroga (RDD)	1,045	0.30
Total	348,344	100.00

ASSEMBLÉE NATIONALE

President: Guy Ndzouba Ndama.

Secretary-General: Jean-Baptiste Yama-Legnongo.

General Election, 17 December 2006*

Party	Seats
Parti démocratique gabonais (PDG)	82
Rassemblement pour le Gabon (RPG)	8
Union du peuple gabonais (UPG)	8
Union gabonaise pour la démocratie et le développement (UGDD)	4
Alliance démocratique et républicaine (ADERE)	3
Cercle des libéraux réformateurs (CLR)	2
Parti gabonais du progrès (PGP)	2
Parti social-démocrate (PSD)	2
Forum africain pour la reconstruction (FAR)	1
Rassemblement des démocrates républicains (RDR)	1
Congrès pour la démocratie et la justice (CDJ)	1
Mouvement africain de développment (MAD)	1
Rassemblement national des bûcherons—Democratique (RNB)	1
Independents	4
Total	120

* Elections in seven constituencies were postponed until 24 December 2006, owing to organizational difficulties. Results in 20 constituencies were annulled, following allegations of irregularities and fraud. By-elections were held on 10 June 2007 at which the PDG won 11 of the 20 seats available. Parties allied to the PDG won six seats, the opposition took two, and the remaining seat was secured by an independent candidate.

SÉNAT

President: RENÉ RADEMBINO-CONIQUET.

Secretary-General: FÉLIX OWANSANGO DEACKEU.

Indirect elections to the 91-member Sénat were held on 9 February 2003. The PDG won more than 60 seats and the RPG secured eight seats.

Election Commission

Commission électorale nationale autonome et permanente (CENAP): Libreville; f. 2006 to replace the Commission nationale électorale; Pres. appointed by the Constitutional Court; Pres. RENÉ ABOGHÉ ELLA.

Political Organizations

Alliance démocratique et républicaine (ADERE): Pres. MBOUMBOU NGOMA; Sec.-Gen. DIDJOB DIVUNGUI-DI-N'DINGUE.

Association pour le socialisme au Gabon (APSG): Pres. V. MAPANGOU MOUCANI MOUETSA.

Cercle des libéraux réformateurs (CLR): f. 1993 by breakaway faction of the PDG; Leader JEAN-BONIFACE ASSELE.

Congrès pour la démocratie et la justice (CDJ): Pres. JULES BOURDES OGOULIGUENDE.

Convention des forces du changement: f. 1993 as an informal alliance of eight opposition presidential candidates.

Forum africain pour la reconstruction (FAR): f. 1992; Leader Prof. LÉON MBOU-YEMBI.

Parti socialiste gabonais (PSG): f. 1991; Leader AUGUSTIN MOUSSAVOU KING.

Union socialiste gabonais (USG): Leader Dr SERGE MBA BEKALE.

Front national (FN): f. 1991; Leader MARTIN EFAYONG.

Front des parties du changement (FPC): f. 2000 as an alliance of four opposition parties to contest the 2001 legislative elections.

Gabon Avenir: f. 1999; Leader SYLVESTRE OYOUOMI.

Mouvement africain de développement (MAD): Leader PIERRE CLAVER NZENG EBOME.

Mouvement pour la démocratie, le développement et la réconciliation nationale (Modern): Libreville; f. 1996; Leader GASTON MOZOGO OVONO.

Mouvement d'emancipation socialiste du peuple: Leader MOUANGA MBADINGA.

Parti démocratique gabonais (PDG): BP 268, Libreville; tel. 70-31-21; fax 70-31-46; f. 1968; sole legal party 1968–90; Leader OMAR BONGO ONDIMBA; Sec.-Gen. SIMPLICE GUEDET MANZELA.

Parti gabonais du centre indépendant (PGCI): allied to the PDG; Leader JÉRÔME OKINDA.

Parti gabonais du progrès (PGP): f. 1990; Pres. (vacant); Vice-Pres. JOSEPH-BENOÎT MOUITY; Sec.-Gen. PIERRE LOUIS AGONDJO OKAWE.

Parti radical des républicains indépendants (PARI): Leader ANACLÉ BISSIELO.

Parti social-démocrate (PSD): f. 1991; Leader PIERRE-CLAVER MAGANGA MOUSSAVOU.

Rassemblement des démocrates (RDD): f. 1993; Leader CHRISTIAN SERGE MAROGA.

Rassemblement des démocrates républicains (RDR): Leader MAX MEBALE M'OBAME.

Rassemblement pour la démocratie et le progrès (RDP): Pres. PIERRE EMBONI.

Rassemblement pour le Gabon (RPG): f. 1990 as MORENA des bûcherons; renamed Rassemblement national des bûcherons in 1991, name changed as above in 2000; allied to the PDG; Leader Fr PAUL M'BA ABESSOLE; Vice-Pres. Prof. VINCENT MOULENGUI BOUKOSSO.

Rassemblement des Gaullois: Libreville; f. 1994; registered 1998; 5,000 mems; Pres. MAX ANICET KOUMBA-MBADINGA.

Rassemblement national des bûcherons—Démocratique (RNB): Libreville; f. 1991; Leader PIERRE ANDRÉ KOMBILA.

Rassemblement national des républicains (RNR): Libreville; f. 2002; Pres. GÉRARD ELLA NGUEMA; Sec-Gen. CHRISTIAN ABIAGHE NGOMO.

Union démocratique et sociale (UDS): f. 1996; Leader HERVÉ ASSAMANET.

Union gabonaise pour la démocratie et le développement (UGDD): Libreville; e-mail ugdd@ugdd.org; internet www.ugdd.org; f. 2005; Pres. ZACHARIE MYBOTO.

Union nationale pour la démocratie et le développement (UNDD): f. 1993; supports President Bongo.

Union pour la nouvelle République: f. 2007 following the merger of the Front pour l'unité nationale (FUNDU) and the Rassemblement des républicains indépendants (RRI); Leader LOUIS-GASTON MAYILA.

Union du peuple gabonais (UPG): f. 1989 in Paris, France; Leader PIERRE MAMBOUNDOU; Sec.-Gen. DAVID BADINGA.

Union pour le progrès national (UPN): Leader DANIEL TENGUE NZOUNDO.

Diplomatic Representation

EMBASSIES IN GABON

Algeria: Batterie 4, BP 4008, Libreville; tel. 73-23-18; fax 73-14-03; e-mail ambalgabon@komo.tiggabon.com; Ambassador (vacant).

Angola: BP 4884, Libreville; tel. 73-04-26; fax 73-78-24; Ambassador EMILIO JOSÉ DE CARVALHO GUERRA.

Belgium: Quartier Bas de Gué-Gué, Bord de Mer à côté de la Délégation de la Commission Européenne, BP 4079, Libreville; tel. 73-29-92; fax 73-96-94; e-mail libreville@diplobel.org; internet www.diplomatie.be/libreville; Ambassador IVO GOEMANS.

Benin: BP 3851, Akebe, Libreville; tel. 73-76-82; fax 73-77-75; Ambassador El Hadj LASSISSI ADÉBO.

Brazil: blvd de l'Indépendance, BP 3899, Libreville; tel. 76-05-35; fax 74-03-43; e-mail emblibreville@inet.ga; internet www.ambassadedubresil-gabon.org; Ambassador CARLOS A. FERREIRA GUIMARÃES.

Cameroon: BP 14001, Libreville; tel. 73-28-00; Ambassador JEAN KOÉ NTONGA.

Central African Republic: Libreville; tel. 72-12-28; Ambassador (vacant).

China, People's Republic: blvd Triomphale Omar Bongo, BP 3914, Libreville; tel. 74-32-07; fax 74-75-96; e-mail gzy@internetgabon.com; Ambassador XUE JINWEI.

Congo, Democratic Republic: BP 2257, Libreville; tel. 74-32-53; Ambassador KABANGI KAUMBU BULA.

Congo, Republic: BP 269, Libreville; tel. 73-29-06; Ambassador LIKIBI NTSIBA.

Côte d'Ivoire: Charbonnages, BP 3861, Libreville; tel. 73-82-70; fax 73-82-87; Ambassador CLAUDINE YAPOBI RICCI.

Egypt: Immeuble Floria, 1 blvd de la Mer, Quartier Batterie IV, BP 4240, Libreville; tel. 73-25-38; fax 73-25-19; Ambassador AHMED MUHAMMAD TAHA AWAD.

Equatorial Guinea: BP 1462, Libreville; tel. 75-10-56; Ambassador JOSÉ ESONO BACALE.

France: 1 rue du pont Pirah, BP 2125, Libreville; tel. 79-70-00; fax 79-70-09; e-mail ambafran@inet.ga; internet www.ambafrance-ga.org; Ambassador JEAN MARC SIMON.

Germany: blvd de l'Indépendance, Immeuble les Frangipaniers, BP 299, Libreville; tel. 76-01-88; fax 72-40-12; e-mail amb-allegmagne@inet.ga; Ambassador HANS-DIETRICH BERNHARD.

Guinea: BP 4046, Libreville; tel. 73-85-09; Ambassador MOHAMED SAMPIL.

Holy See: blvd Monseigneur Bessieux, BP 1322, Libreville (Apostolic Nunciature); tel. 74-45-41; e-mail nonapcg@yahoo.com; Apostolic Nuncio Mgr ANDRÉS CARRASCOSA COSO (Titular Archbishop of Elo).

Italy: Immeuble Personnaz et Gardin, rue de la Mairie, BP 2251, Libreville; tel. 74-28-92; fax 74-80-35; e-mail ambasciata.libreville@esteri.it; internet www.amblibreville.esteri.it; Ambassador MARIO SAMMARTINO.

Japan: blvd du Bord de Mer, BP 2259, Libreville; tel. 73-22-97; fax 73-60-60; Ambassador SADAMU FUJIWARA.

Korea, Democratic People's Republic: Ambassador KIM RYONG YONG.

Korea, Republic: BP 2620, Libreville; tel. 73-40-00; fax 73-99-05; e-mail gabon-ambcoree@mofat.go.kr; internet www.mofat.go.kr/mission/emb/embassy_en.mof?si_dcode=GA-GA; Ambassador CHO WON-HO.

Lebanon: BP 3341, Libreville; tel. 73-14-77; e-mail amb.lib.gab@inet.ga; Ambassador MICHELIN BAZ.

Mali: BP 4007, Quartier Batterie IV, Libreville; tel. 82-73-82; fax 73-82-80; e-mail ambamaga@yahoo.fr; Ambassador TRAORÉ ROKIATOU GUIKINE.

Mauritania: BP 3917, Libreville; tel. 74-31-65; Ambassador El Hadj THIAM.

Morocco: blvd de l'indépendance, Immeuble CK 2, BP 3983, Libreville; tel. 77-41-51; fax 77-41-50; e-mail sifamalbv@inet.ga; Ambassador ALI BOJI.

Nigeria: ave du Président Léon-Mba, Quartier blvd Léon-M'Ba, BP 1191, Libreville; tel. 73-22-03; fax 73-29-14; e-mail nigeriamission@internetgabon.com; Ambassador Chief IGNATIUS H. AJURU.

Russia: BP 3963, Libreville; tel. 72-48-69; fax 72-48-70; e-mail ambrusga@inet.ga; Ambassador VSEVOLOD SOUKHOV.

São Tomé and Príncipe: BP 489, Libreville; tel. 72-09-94; Ambassador URBINO JOSÉ GONHALVES BOTELÇO.

Senegal: Quartier Sobraga, BP 3856, Libreville; tel. 77-42-67; fax 77-42-68; e-mail ambasengab@yahoo.fr; Ambassador IBRAHIMA CABA.

South Africa: Immeuble les Arcades, 142 rue des Chavannes, BP 4063, Libreville; tel. 77-45-30; fax 77-45-36; e-mail saegabon@internetgabon.com; Ambassador MAHLOMOLA JOMO KHASU.

Spain: Immeuble Diamant, 2ème étage, blvd de l'Indépendance, BP 1157, Libreville; tel. 72-12-64; fax 74-88-73; e-mail ambespga@mail.mae.es; Ambassador Dr RAMIRO FERNÁNDEZ BACHILLER.

Togo: BP 14160, Libreville; tel. 73-29-04; fax 73-32-61; Ambassador AHLONKO KOFFI AQUEREBURU.

Tunisia: BP 3844, Libreville; tel. 73-28-41; Ambassador EZZEDINE KERKENI.

USA: blvd du Bord de Mer, BP 4000, Libreville; tel. 76-20-03; fax 74-55-07; e-mail clolibreville@state.gov; internet libreville.usembassy.gov; Ambassador R. BARRIE WALKLEY.

Judicial System

Supreme Court: BP 1043, Libreville; tel. 72-17-00; three chambers: judicial, administrative and accounts; Pres. BENJAMIN PAMBOU-KOMBILA.

Constitutional Court: Libreville; tel. 72-57-17; fax 72-55-96; Pres. MARIE MADELEINE MBORANTSUO.

Courts of Appeal: Libreville and Franceville.

Court of State Security: Libreville; 13 mems; Pres. FLORENTIN ANGO.

Conseil Supérieur de la Magistrature: Libreville; Pres. El Hadj OMAR BONGO ONDIMBA; Vice-Pres. BENJAMIN PAMBOU-KOMBILA (ex officio).

There are also Tribunaux de Première Instance (County Courts) at Libreville, Franceville, Port-Gentil, Lambaréné, Mouila, Oyem, Koula-Moutou, Makokou and Tchibanga.

Religion

About 60% of Gabon's population are Christians, mainly adherents of the Roman Catholic Church. About 40% are animists and fewer than 1% are Muslims.

CHRISTIANITY

The Roman Catholic Church

Gabon comprises one archdiocese, four dioceses and one apostolic prefecture. At 31 December 2004 the estimated number of adherents in the country was equivalent to 50.1% of the total population.

Bishops' Conference

Conférence Episcopale du Gabon, BP 2146, Libreville; tel. 72-20-73. f. 1989; Pres. Most Rev. TIMOTHÉE MODIBO-NZOCKENA (Bishop of Franceville).

Archbishop of Libreville: Most Rev. BASILE MVÉ ENGONE, Archevêché, Sainte-Marie, BP 2146, Libreville; tel. and fax 72-20-73.

Protestant Churches

Christian and Missionary Alliance: Gabon Field, BP 13021, Libreville; e-mail gabonfd@inet.ga; active in the south of the country; Field-Dir REV. ALBERT STOMBAUGH; 16,000 mems.

Eglise Evangélique du Gabon: BP 10080, Libreville; tel. 72-41-92; f. 1842; independent since 1961; 120,000 mems; Pres. Pastor SAMUEL NANG ESSONO; Sec. Rev. EMILE NTETOME.

The Evangelical Church of South Gabon and the Evangelical Pentecostal Church are also active in Gabon.

The Press

Afric'Sports: BP 3950, Libreville; tel. 76-24-74; monthly; sport; CEO SERGE ALFRED MPOUHO; Man. YVON PATRICE AUBIAN; circ. 5,000.

Le Bûcheron: BP 6424, Libreville; tel. 72-50-20; f. 1990; weekly; official publ. of the Rassemblement pour le Gabon; Editor DÉSIRÉ ENAME.

Bulletin Evangélique d'Information et de Presse: BP 80, Libreville; monthly; religious.

Bulletin Mensuel de Statistique de la République Gabonaise: BP 179, Libreville; monthly; publ. by Direction Générale de l'Economie.

La Concorde: Libreville; f. 2005; owned by TV+ group; daily; Dir FRANÇOIS ONDO EDOU; circ. 10,000.

L'Economiste Gabonais: BP 3906, Libreville; quarterly; publ. by the Centre gabonais du commerce extérieur.

Gabon d'Aujourd'hui: BP 750, Libreville; weekly; publ. of the Ministry of Culture, the Arts and Popular Education.

Gabon Libre: BP 6439, Libreville; tel. 72-42-22; weekly; Dir DZIME EKANG; Editor RENÉ NZOVI.

Gabon-Matin: BP 168, Libreville; daily; publ. by Agence Gabonaise de Presse; Man. HILARION VENDANY; circ. 18,000.

Gabon Show: Libreville; f. 2004; independent; satirical; printed in Cameroon; Man. Editor FULBERT WORA; weekly; circ. 3,000.

Gris-Gris International: Paris; f. 1990; weekly; independent; satirical; distribution forbidden in 2001; Editor-in-Chief RAPHAEL NTOUTOUME NKOGHE; Editor MICHEL ONGOUNDOU.

Journal Officiel de la République Gabonaise: BP 563, Libreville; f. 1959; fortnightly; Man. EMMANUEL OBAMÉ.

Le Misamu: BP 887, Libreville; tel. 74-74-59; fortnightly; Founder NOËL NGWA NGUEMA.

Ngondo: BP 168, Libreville; monthly; publ. by Agence Gabonaise de Presse.

Le Progressiste: blvd Léon-M'Ba, BP 7000, Libreville; tel. 74-54-01; f. 1990; Dir BENOÎT MOUITY NZAMBA; Editor JACQUES MOURENDE-TSIOBA.

La Relance: BP 268, Libreville; tel. 72-93-08; weekly; publ. of the Parti démocratique gabonais; Pres. JACQUES ADIAHÉNOT; Dir RENÉ NDEMEZO'O OBIANG.

Le Réveil: BP 20386, Libreville; tel. and fax 73-17-21; weekly; Man. ALBERT YANGARI; Editor RENÉ NZOVI; circ. 8,000.

La Sagaie: tel. Libreville; fortnightly; satirical; distribution suspended September 2003.

Sept Jours: BP 213, Libreville; weekly.

Sub-Version: Libreville; fortnightly; f. 2003; independent; satirical; printed in Douala, Cameroon; publ. suspended in 2003.

La Tribune des Affaires: BP 2234, Libreville; tel. 72-20-64; fax 74-12-20; monthly; publ. of the Chambre de Commerce, d'Agriculture, d'Industrie et des Mines du Gabon.

L'Union: Sonapresse, BP 3849, Libreville; tel. 73-58-61; fax 73-58-62; e-mail mpg@inet.ga; f. 1974; 75% state-owned; daily; official govt publ.; Dir-Gen. ALBERT YANAGRI; circ. 20,000.

La Voix du Peuple: BP 4049, Libreville; tel. 76-20-45; f. 1991; weekly; Editor-in-Chief JEAN KOUMBA; Editor MAURICE-BLAISE NDZADIENGA MAYILA; circ. 4,000.

Zoom Hebdo: Carrefour London, BP 352, Libreville; tel. 76-44-54; fax 74-67-50; e-mail actismedia@inet.ga; internet www.zoomhebdo.com; Friday; f. 1991; Dir-Gen. HANS RAYMOND KWAAITAAL; circ. 12,000–20,000.

NEWS AGENCIES

Agence Gabonaise de Presse (AGP): BP 168, Libreville.

Association Professionnelle de la Presse Ecrite Gabonaise (APPEG): BP 3849, Libreville; internet www.gabon-presse.org.

BERP International: BP 8483, Libreville; tel. 33-80-16; fax 77-58-81; e-mail berp8483@hotmail.com; f. 1995; Dir ANTOINE LAWSON.

Foreign Bureau

Agence France-Presse (AFP): ave du Colonel Parent, Immeuble Sogapal, Les Filaos, BP 788, Libreville; tel. 76-14-36; fax 72-45-31; e-mail afp-libreville@tiggabon.com; Dir JEAN-PIERRE REJETE.

Publishers

Gabonaise d'Imprimerie (GABIMP): BP 154, Libreville; tel. 70-22-55; fax 70-31-85; e-mail gabimp@inet.ga; f. 1973; Dir BÉATRICE CAILLOT.

Multipress Gabon: blvd Léon-M'Ba, BP 3875, Libreville; tel. 73-22-33; fax 73-63-72; e-mail mpg@inet.ga; monopoly distributors of magazines and newspapers; f. 1973; Chair. PAUL BORY.

Société Imprimerie de Gabon: BP 9626, Libreville; f. 1977; Man. Dir AKWANG REX.

Société nationale de Presse et d'Edition (SONAPRESSE): BP 3849, Libreville; tel. and fax 73-58-60; e-mail unionplus@intergabon.com; f. 1975; Pres. and Man. Dir NARCISSE MASSALA-TSAMBA.

Broadcasting and Communications

TELECOMMUNICATIONS

Gabon Télécom: Immeuble du Delta Postal, BP 20000, Libreville; tel. 78-76-05; fax 78-67-70; f. 2001; provider of telecommunications, including satellite, internet and cellular systems; 51% owned by Maroc Telecom; Dir-Gen. HERVÉ FULGENCE OSSAMY.

Société des Télécommunications Internationales Gabonaises (TIG): BP 2261, Libreville; tel. 78-77-56; fax 74-19-09; f. 1971; cap. 3,000m. francs CFA; 61% state-owned; privatization pending; planning and devt of international telecommunications systems; Man. Dir A. N'GOUMA MWYUMALA.

Celtel Gabon, Libertis and Telecel Gabon operate mobile telecommunication services covering 85% of Gabon's territory.

BROADCASTING

Radio

The national network, 'La Voix de la Rénovation', and a provincial network broadcast for 24 hours each day in French and local languages.

Africa No. 1: BP 1, Libreville; tel. 76-00-01; fax 74-21-33; e-mail africa@africa1.com; internet www.africa1.com; f. 1980; 35% state-controlled; international commercial radio station; daily programmes in French and English; Pres. LOUIS BARTHÉLEMY MAPANGOU; Sec.-Gen. MICHEL KOUMBANGOYE.

Radiodiffusion-Télévision Gabonaise (RTG): BP 150, Libreville; tel. 73-20-25; f. 1959; state-controlled; Dir-Gen. JOHN JOSEPH MBOUROU; Dir of Radio GILLES TERENCE NZOGHE.

Radio Fréquence 3: f. 1996.

Radio Génération Nouvelle: f. 1996; Dir JEAN-BONIFACE ASSELE.

Radio Mandarine: f. 1995.

Radio Soleil: f. 1995; affiliated to Rassemblement pour le Gabon.

Radio Unité: f. 1996.

Television

Radiodiffusion-Télévision Gabonaise (RTG): BP 10150, Libreville; tel. 73-21-52; fax 73-21-53; f. 1959; state-controlled; Dir-Gen. JOHN JOSEPH MBOUROU; Dir of Television JULES CÉSAR LEKOGHO.

Télé-Africa: Libreville; tel. 76-10-42; f. 1985; private channel; daily broadcasts in French.

Télédiffusion du Gabon: f. 1995.

TV Sat (Société de Télécommunications Audio-Visuelles): Immeuble TV SAT BP 184, Libreville; tel. 72-49-22; fax 76-16-83; f. 1994.

Finance

(cap. = capital; res = reserves; dep. = deposits; m. = million; brs = branches; amounts in francs CFA)

BANKING

Central Bank

Banque des Etats de l'Afrique Centrale (BEAC): BP 112, Libreville; tel. 76-13-52; fax 74-45-63; e-mail beaclbv@beac.int; HQ in Yaoundé, Cameroon; f. 1973; bank of issue for mem. states of the Communauté économique et monétaire de l'Afrique centrale (CEMAC, fmrly Union douanière et économique de l'Afrique centrale), comprising Cameroon, the Central African Repub., Chad, the Repub. of the Congo, Equatorial Guinea and Gabon; cap. 45,000m., res 176,661m., total assets 2,144,626m. (Nov. 2003); Gov. JEAN-FÉLIX MAMALEPOT; Dir in Gabon PHILIBERT ANDZEMBÉ; 4 brs in Gabon.

Commercial Banks

Banque Internationale pour le Commerce et l'Industrie du Gabon, SA (BICIG): ave du Colonel Parant, BP 2241, Libreville; tel. 77-76-80; fax 74-64-10; e-mail bicigdoi@inet.ga; internet www.bicig.com; f. 1973; 26.30% state-owned, 46.67% BNP Paribas SA; cap. and res 23,673.0m., total assets 268,199.0m. (Dec. 2003); Pres. ETIENNE GUY MOUVAGHA TCHIOBA; Dir-Gen. CLAUDE AYO-IGUENDHA; 9 brs.

Banque Internationale pour le Gabon: Immeuble Concorde, blvd de l'Indépendance, BP 106, Libreville; tel. 76-26-26; fax 76-20-53.

BGFIBANK: blvd du Bord de Mer, BP 2253, Libreville; tel. 76-40-35; fax 76-08-94; e-mail bgfi@internet.com; internet www.bgfi.com; f. 1972 as Banque Gabonaise et Française Internationale (BGFI); name changed as above in March 2000; 8% state-owned; cap. 25,065.4m., res 27,683.0m., dep. 309,751.4m. (Dec. 2005); Chair. PATRICE OTHA; Gen. Man. HENRI-CLAUDE OYIMA; 3 brs.

Citibank: 810 blvd Quaben, rue Kringer, BP 3940, Libreville; tel. 73-19-16; fax 73-37-86; total assets 1,000m. (Dec. 2004); Dir-Gen. FUNMI ADE AJAYI; Dep. Dir-Gen. JULIETTE WEISTFLOG.

Financial Bank Gabon: Immeuble des Frangipaniers, blvd de l'Indépendance, BP 20333, Libreville; tel. 77-50-78; fax 72-41-97; e-mail financial.gabon@financial-bank.com; cap. and res 719.0m., total assets 5,342.0m. (Dec. 2004); 69.78% owned by Financial BC, SA (Togo), 1.58% state-owned; Pres. RENÉ-HILAIRE ADIAHENO; Dir-Gen. PIERRE LECLAIRE.

Union Gabonaise de Banque, SA (UGB): ave du Colonel Parant, BP 315, Libreville; tel. 77-70-00; fax 76-46-16; e-mail ugbdio@internetgabon.com; internet ugb-interactif.com; f. 1962; 26.09% state-owned, 58.71% owned by Crédit Lyonnais (France); cap. 7,400.0m., res 6,076.1m., dep. 204,541.4m. (Dec. 2006); Chair. MARCEL DOUPAMBY-MATOKA; Man. Dir FRANÇOIS HOFFMANN; 6 brs.

Development Banks

Banque Gabonaise de Développement (BGD): rue Alfred Marche, BP 5, Libreville; tel. 76-24-29; fax 74-26-99; e-mail bdg@internetgabon.com; internet www.bgd-gabon.com; f. 1960; 69.01% state-owned; cap. and res 33,238.5m., total assets 52,339.0m. (Dec. 2003); Pres. MICHEL ANCHOVEY.

Banque Nationale de Crédit Rural (BNCR): ave Bouet, BP 1120, Libreville; tel. 72-47-42; fax 74-05-07; f. 1986; 74% state-owned; under enforced administration since March 2002; total assets 5,601m. (Dec. 2000); Pres. GÉRARD MEYO M'EMANE; Man. JOSEPH KOYAGBELE.

Banque Populaire du Gabon: 413 blvd de l'Indépendance, BP 6663, Libreville; tel. 72-86-89; fax 72-86-91.

BICI-Bail Gabon: Immeuble BICIG, 5ème étage, ave du Colonel Parant, BP 2241, Libreville; tel. 77-75-52; fax 77-48-15; internet www.bicig.ga/bicibail.htm; BNP Paribas-owned.

Société Financière Transafricaine (FINATRA): blvd de l'Indépendance, BP 8645, Libreville; tel. and fax 77-40-87; e-mail bgfi@internetgabon.com; internet www.bgfi.com; 50% owned by BGFIBANK; cap. 2,000m., total assets 14,613m. (Dec. 2003); Dir-Gen. MARIE CÉLINE NTSAME-MEZUI.

Société Gabonaise de Crédit Automobile (SOGACA): Immeuble SOGACA, BP 63, Libreville; tel. 76-08-46; fax 76-01-03; car finance; 43% CFAO Gabon, 10% state-owned; cap. and res

2,828.0m., total assets 18,583.0m. (Dec. 2003); Pres. THIERRY DE LAPLAGNOLLE; Dir-Gen. M. DE PAPILLION.

Société Gabonaise de Crédit-Bail (SOGABAIL): Immeuble Sogaca, BP 63, Libreville; tel. 77-25-73; fax 76-01-03; e-mail sogaca@assala.net; 25% CFAO Gabon, 14% state-owned; cap. and res 2,980.4m., total assets 4,123.2m.; Pres. M. LAPLAGNOLLE; Dir-Gen. THIERRY PAPILLON.

Société Nationale d'Investissement du Gabon (SONADIG): BP 479, Libreville; tel. 72-09-22; fax 74-81-70; f. 1968; state-owned; cap. 500m.; Pres. ANTOINE OYIEYE; Dir-Gen. NARCISSE MASSALA TSAMBA.

Financial Institution

Caisse Autonome d'Amortissement du Gabon: BP 912, Libreville; tel. 74-41-43; management of state funds; Dir-Gen. MAURICE EYAMBA TSIMAT.

INSURANCE

Agence Gabonaise d'Assurance et de Réassurance (AGAR): BP 1699, Libreville; tel. 74-02-22; fax 76-59-25; f. 1987; Dir-Gen. ANGE GOULOUMES.

Assinco: BP 7812, Libreville; tel. 72-19-25; fax 72-19-29; e-mail assinco@internetgabon.com; Dir EUGÉNIE DENDÉ.

Assurances Mutuelles du Gabon (AMG): Libreville; tel. 72-13-90; fax 74-17-02; Dir-Gen. M. VERON.

Assurances Nouvelles du Gabon: ave du Colonel Parant, BP 2225, Libreville; tel. 72-13-90; fax 74-17-02; fmrly Mutuelle Gabonaise d'Assurances; Dir-Gen. EKOMIE CÉSARE AFENE.

Assureurs Conseils Franco-Africains du Gabon (ACFRA-GABON): BP 1116, Libreville; tel. 72-32-83; Chair. FRÉDÉRIC MARRON; Dir M. GARNIER.

Assureurs Conseils Gabonais (ACG): Immeuble Shell-Gabon, rue de la Mairie, BP 2138, Libreville; tel. 74-32-90; fax 76-04-39; e-mail acg@ascoma.com; represents foreign insurance cos; Dir MICHELLE VALETTE.

Axa Assurances Gabon: BP 4047, Libreville; tel. 76-28-97; fax 76-03-34; e-mail axa.gabon@inet.ga; internet www.axa.com; Dir BERNARD BARTOSZEK.

Commercial Union: Libreville; tel. 76-43-00; Exec. Dir M. MILAN.

Fédération gabonaise des assureurs (FEGASA): BP 4005, Libreville; tel. 74-45-29; fax 77-58-23; Pres. JACQUES AMVAMÉ.

Gras Savoye Gabon: ave du Colonel Parant, BP 2148, Libreville; tel. 76-09-73; fax 76-57-41; e-mail contact@ga.grassavoye.com; internet www.ga.grassavoye.com; Dir CHRISTOPHE ROUDAUT.

Groupement Gabonais d'Assurances et de Réassurances (GGAR): Libreville; tel. 74-28-72; f. 1985; Chair. RASSAGUIZA AKEREY; Dir-Gen. DENISE OMBAGHO.

OGAR Gabon: BP 201, Libreville; tel. 76-15-96; fax 76-58-16; e-mail ogar@inet.ga; Dir EDOUARD VALENTIN.

Omnium Gabonais d'Assurances et de Réassurances (OGAR): 1811 blvd de l'Indépendence, BP 201, Libreville; tel. 76-15-96; fax 76-58-16; e-mail ogar@inet.ga; internet www.assurances-gabon.com; f. 1976; owned by Assurances Générales de France; general; Pres. MARCEL DOUPAMBY-MATOKA; Exec. Dir BLAISE NOYON.

Sécurité Gabonaise Assureurs Conseils (SGAC): Libreville; tel. 74-24-85; fax 74-60-07.

Société Librevilloise de Courtage d'Assurance et de Réassurance (SOLICAR): Libreville; tel. 74-01-23; fax 76-08-03.

Société Nationale Gabonaise d'Assurances et de Réassurances (SONAGAR): ave du Colonel Parant, BP 3082, Libreville; tel. 72-28-97; f. 1974; owned by l'Union des Assurances de Paris (France); Dir-Gen. JEAN-LOUIS MESSAN.

SOGERCO-Gabon: BP 2102, Libreville; tel. 76-09-34; f. 1975; general; Dir M. RABEAU.

UAG-Vie: ave du Colonel Parant, Libreville; tel. 72-48-58; fax 72-48-57; life insurance; Chair. FRANÇOIS SIMON; Dir LAURENT ARGOUET.

L'Union des Assurances pour le Gabon (UAPG): ave du Colonel Parant, BP 2141, Libreville; tel. 76-28-97; fax 74-18-46; f. 1976; Chair. GASTON OLOUNA; Dir-Gen. JACQUES BARDOUX.

Trade and Industry

GOVERNMENT AGENCIES

Conseil Economique et Social de la République Gabonaise: BP 1075, Libreville; tel. 73-19-46; fax 73-19-44; comprises representatives from salaried workers, employers and Govt; commissions on economic, financial and social affairs and forestry and agriculture; Pres. LOUIS GASTON MAYILA.

Agence de Promotion des Investissements Privés (APIP): BP 13740, Front de Mer, Libreville; tel. 76-87-65; fax 76-87-64; e-mail apip@netcourrier.com; internet www.invest-gabon.com; f. 2002; promotes private investment; Dir-Gen. LUDOVIC OGNAGNA OCKOGHO.

DEVELOPMENT ORGANIZATIONS

Agence Française de Développement (AFD): BP 64, Libreville; tel. 74-33-74; fax 74-51-25; e-mail afdlibreville@ga.groupe-afd.org; internet www.afd.fr; fmrly Caisse Française de Développement; Dir YVES BOUDOT.

Agence Nationale de Promotion de la Petite et Moyenne Entreprise (PROMOGABON): BP 2111, Libreville; tel. 26-79-19; fax 74-89-59; e-mail promogabon@inet.ga; f. 1964; state-controlled; promotes and assists small and medium-sized industries; Pres. SIMON BOULAMATARI; Man. Dir JEAN-FIDÈLE OTANDO.

Centre Gabonais de Commerce Extérieur (CGCE): Immeuble Rénovation, 3ème étage, BP 3906, Libreville; tel. 72-11-67; fax 74-71-53; promotes foreign trade and investment in Gabon; Gen. Dir PIERRE SOCKAT.

Commerce et Développement (CODEV): BP 2142, Libreville; tel. 76-06-73; f. 1976; 95% state-owned; import and distribution of capital goods and food products; Chair. and Man. Dir JÉRÔME NGOUA-BEKALE.

Conservation et Utilisation Rationelle des Ecosystèmes Forestiers en Afrique Centrale (ECOFAC): BP 15115, Libreville; tel. 73-23-43; fax 73-23-45; e-mail coordination@ecofac.org; internet www.ecofac.org.

Groupes d'Etudes et de Recherches sur la Démocratie et le Développement Economique et Social (GERDDES): BP 13114, Libreville; tel. 76-62-47; fax 74-08-94; e-mail gerddes@firstnet1.com; internet www.gerddes.org; Pres. MARYVONNE NTSAME NDONG.

Institut Gabonais d'Appui au Développement (IGAD): BP 20423, Libreville; tel. and fax 74-52-47; e-mail igad@inet.ga.

Mission Française de Coopération: BP 2105, Libreville; tel. 76-10-56; fax 74-55-33; administers bilateral aid from France; Dir JEAN-CLAUDE QUIRIN.

Office Gabonais d'Amélioration et de Production de Viande (OGAPROV): BP 245, Moanda; tel. 66-12-67; f. 1971; development of private cattle farming; manages ranch at Lekedi-Sud; Pres. PAUL KOUNDA KIKI; Dir-Gen. VEYRANT OMBÉ EPIGAT.

Palmiers et Hévéas du Gabon (PALMEVEAS): BP 75, Libreville; f. 1956; state-owned; palm-oil development.

Programme Régionale de Gestion de l'Information Environnementale en Afrique Centrale (PRGIE): BP 4080, Libreville; tel. 76-30-19; fax 77-42-61; e-mail urge@adie-prgie.org; internet www.adie-prgie.org.

Société de Développement de l'Agriculture au Gabon (AGRO-GABON): BP 2248, Libreville; tel. 76-40-82; fax 76-44-72; f. 1976; 93% state-owned; acquired by the Société Industrielle Agricole du Tabac Tropical in April 2004; Man. Dir ANDRÉ PAUL-APANDINA.

Société de Développement de l'Hévéaculture (HEVEGAB): BP 316, Libreville; tel. 72-08-29; fax 72-08-30; f. 1981; acquired by the Société Industrielle Agricole du Tabac Tropical in April 2004; development of rubber plantations in the Mitzic, Bitam and Kango regions; Chair. FRANÇOIS OWONO-NGUEMA; Man. Dir JANVIER ESSONO-ASSOUMOU.

Société Gabonaise de Recherches et d'Exploitations Minières (SOGAREM): Libreville; state-owned; research and development of gold mining; Chair. ARSÈNE BOUNGUENZA; Man. Dir SERGE GASSITA.

Société Gabonaise de Recherches Pétrolières (GABOREP): BP 564, Libreville; tel. 75-06-40; fax 75-06-47; exploration and exploitation of hydrocarbons; Chair. HUBERT PERRODO; Man. Dir P. F. LECA.

Société Nationale de Développement des Cultures Industrielles (SONADECI): Libreville; tel. 76-33-97; f. 1978; state-owned; agricultural development; Chair. PAUL KOUNDA KIKI; Man. Dir GEORGES BEKALÉ.

CHAMBER OF COMMERCE

Chambre de Commerce, d'Agriculture, d'Industrie et des Mines du Gabon: BP 2234, Libreville; tel. 72-20-64; fax 74-12-20; f. 1935; regional offices at Port-Gentil and Franceville; Pres. JOACHIM BOUSSAMBA-MAPAGA; Sec.-Gen. DOMINIQUE MANDZA.

EMPLOYERS' ORGANIZATIONS

Confédération Patronale Gabonaise: Immeuble les Frangipaniers, BP 410, Libreville; tel. 76-02-43; fax 74-86-52; e-mail infocpg@confederation-patronale-gabonaise.org; internet www.confederation-patronale-gabonaise.org; f. 1959; represents industrial, mining, petroleum, public works, forestry, banking, insurance, commercial and shipping interests; Pres. HENRI-CLAUDE OYIMA; Sec.-Gen. CHRISTIANE QUINIO.

Conseil National du Patronat Gabonais (CNPG): Libreville; Pres. RAHANDI CHAMBRIER; Sec.-Gen. THOMAS FRANCK EYA'A.

Syndicat des Entreprises Minières du Gabon (SYNDIMINES): BP 260, Libreville; Pres. ANDRÉ BERRE; Sec.-Gen. SERGE GREGOIRE.

Syndicat des Importateurs Exportateurs du Gabon (SIMPEX): Libreville; Pres. ALBERT JEAN; Sec.-Gen. R. TYBERGHEIN.

Syndicat des Industries du Gabon: BP 2175, Libreville; tel. 72-02-29; fax 74-52-13; e-mail sociga@ga.imptob.com; Pres. JACQUES-YVES LAUGE.

Syndicat des Producteurs et Industriels du Bois du Gabon: BP 84, Libreville; tel. 72-26-11; fax 77-44-43; e-mail synfoga@inet.ga.

Syndicat Professionnel des Usines de Sciages et Placages du Gabon: Port-Gentil; f. 1956; Pres. PIERRE BERRY.

Union des Représentations Automobiles et Industrielles (URAI): BP 1743, Libreville; Pres. M. MARTINENT; Sec. R. TYBERGHEIN.

Union Nationale du Patronat Syndical des Transports Urbains, Routiers et Fluviaux du Gabon (UNAPASYTRUFGA): BP 1025, Libreville; f. 1977; represents manufacturers of vehicle and construction parts; Pres. LAURENT BELLAL BIBANG-BI-EDZO; Sec.-Gen. AUGUSTIN KASSA-NZIGOU.

UTILITIES

Société d'Energie et d'Eau du Gabon (SEEG): BP 2187, Libreville; tel. 76-78-07; fax 76-11-34; e-mail laroche.lbv@inet.ga; internet www.seeg-gabon.com; f. 1950; 51% owned by Vivendi (France); controls 35 electricity generation and distribution centres and 32 water production and distribution centres; Pres. FRANÇOIS LAROCHE.

MAJOR COMPANIES

The following are some of the largest private and state-owned companies in terms of either capital investment or employment.

L'Auxiliaire du Bâtiment J.-F. Aveyra (ABA): BP 14382, Libreville; tel. 70-44-80; f. 1977; cap. 1,000m. francs CFA; production of construction materials, plastics; Chair. JEAN-FRANÇOIS AVEYRA; Man. Dir G. DUTILH.

CIMGABON: BP 477, Libreville; tel. 70-20-23; fax 70-27-05; e-mail dg.cimgabon@inet.ga; f. 1976; cap. 19,000m. francs CFA; privatized in Jan. 2001, 75% owned by Scancem International (Norway); clinker crushing works at N'Toum, Owendo (Libreville) and Franceville; Man. Dir ENDRE RYGH.

Compagnie Forestière du Gabon (CFG): BP 521, Port-Gentil; tel. 55-20-45; fax 55-36-43; f. 1945; cap. 6,785m. francs CFA; 52% state-owned; scheduled to be privatized; production of okoumé plywood and veneered quality plywoods; Chair. MICHEL ESSONGHÉ; 1,975 employees.

Compagnie Minière de l'Ogooué (COMILOG): BP 27-28, Moanda; tel. 66-40-02; fax 66-11-57; e-mail dg@comilogsa.com; internet www.erachem-comilog.com; f. 1953; cap. 32,812.5m. francs CFA; owned by Eramet (France); manganese mining at Moanda; Pres. CLAUDE VILLAIN; Man. Dir MARCEL ABEKE; 1,137 employees.

Foraid Gabon: BP 579, Port-Gentil; tel. 56-14-19; fax 56-54-72; e-mail foraidgabon@internetgabon.com; petrol logistics and construction; Dir MAX MERCIER.

Gabon Service Matériel Pétrolier (GSMP): BP 1067, Port-Gentil; tel. 55-53-21; e-mail gsm@inet.ga.

Gabonaise de Chimie (GCIAE): BP 20375, Z.I. d'Ouloumi, Libreville; tel. 72-17-61; fax 74-70-67; e-mail gciae@internetgabon.com; f. 1990; wholesalers of pharmaceuticals and agricultural chemicals; Pres. L. PHILIBERT.

Gabo-Ren: Port-Gentil; f. 1975; cap. 1,600m. francs CFA; 33% state-owned, 32% owned by Elf-Gabon, 35% owned by N'Ren Corpn; mfrs of artificial ammonia and urea.

Leroy-Gabon: BP 69, Libreville; tel. 74-23-11; f. 1976; cap. 2,080m. francs CFA; forestry; Chair. and Man. Dir JEAN LEPRINCE.

Marathon Petroleum: BP 1976, Port-Gentil; tel. 56-23-07; fax 56-23-06; oil exploration and works; Dir Gen. RICHARD POLLOCK.

Mobil Oil Gabon: Zone Industrielle Sud Owendo, BP 145, Libreville; tel. 70-05-48; fax 70-05-87; e-mail mobil@komo.tiggabon.com; f. 1972; cap. 547m. francs CFA; storage and distribution of petroleum products; Gen. Man. J. L. VINET.

PanOcean Energy Corporation, Ltd: Base DPS (face à la SBOM), BP 452, Port-Gentil; tel. 55-57-59; e-mail gabonoffice@paegabon.com; internet www.panafricanenergy.com; f. 1996; name changed as above in 2001; oil exploration and distribution; CEO PAUL L. KEYES.

PIZO Shell SA: Libreville; tel. 74-01-01; fax 76-02-44; f. 1987; cap. 1,875m. francs CFA; subsidiary of Shell Group; Man. Dir JEAN-BAPTISTE BIKULOU.

Rougier Océan Gabon SA (ROG): BP 130, Libreville; tel. 74-31-50; fax 74-31-48; e-mail gabon@groupe-rougier.com; cap. 1,200m. francs CFA; forestry and mfr of plywood; Chair. MAURICE ROUGIER; Dir HERVÉ BOZEC.

Shell-Gabon: BP 146, Port-Gentil; tel. 55-26-62; fax 55-45-29; f. 1960; cap. 15,000m. francs CFA; produced 69,000 barrels of oil in 2004; owned 75% by Royal Dutch-Shell group, 25% state-owned; exploration and production of hydrocarbons; Pres. and Man. Dir FRANCK DENELLE.

Société Bernabé Gabon: BP 2084, Libreville; tel. 74-34-32; fax 76-05-21; cap. 1,000m. francs CFA; metallurgical products, construction materials, hardware; Man. Dir MARC BABUIN; Finance Dir SYLVIAN HAMOUD.

Société des Brasseries du Gabon (SOBRAGA): 20 blvd Léon M'Ba, BP 487, Libreville; tel. 70-19-69; fax 70-09-21; e-mail info@sobraga.com; internet www.sobraga.com; f. 1966; cap. 1,558m. francs CFA; mfrs of beer and soft drinks; Chair. and Dir Gen. PIERRE CASTEL.

Société d'Exploitation des Produits Oléagineux du Gabon (SEPOGA): BP 1491, Libreville; tel. 76-01-92; fax 74-15-67; f. 1977; cap. 732m. francs CFA; 25% state-owned, 14% owned by Shell-Gabon; production and marketing of vegetable oils; Chair. PAUL KOUNDA-KIKI; Man. Dir EDMUND SCHEFFLER.

Société Gabonaise des Ferro-Alliages (SOGAFERRO): BP 2728, Moanda; f. 1974; cap. 1,000m. francs CFA; 10% state-owned; manganese processing; Chair. Dr HERVÉ MOUTSINGA; Man. Dir GILLES DE SEAUVE.

Société Gabonaise Industrielle (SOGI): BP 837, Libreville; tel. 76-15-37; fax 74-10-53; e-mail sogi@sogafric.ga; internet www.sogigabon.com; f. 1975; cap. 950m. francs CFA (2004); industrial construction, metal smelting; Dir-Gen. CHRISTIAN NISIO.

Société Gabonaise d'Oxygène et Acétylène (GABOA): BP 545, Zone Industrielle d'Owendo, Libreville; tel. 70-07-46; fax 70-27-15; e-mail gaboa@internetgabon.com; Dir-Gen. KHADIM THIAM.

Société Gabonaise de Peintures et Laques (GPL): BP 4017, Libreville; tel. 72-02-34; fax 70-02-44; e-mail gpldir@internetgabon.com; f. 1975; 30% state-owned; mfrs of paints and varnishes; Dir CHARLES MARTIN.

Société Gabonaise de Raffinage (SOGARA): BP 530, Port-Gentil; tel. 56-30-00; fax 55-15-28; f. 1965; cap. 1,200m. francs CFA; 25% state-owned; refines locally produced crude petroleum; Chair. RENÉ RADEMBINO CONIQUET; Man. Dir JEAN FIDÈLE OTANDO; 450 employees.

Société Gabonaise des Textiles (SOGATEX): f. 1987; 36.5% state-owned; mfrs of garments.

Société de la Haute Mondah (SHM): BP 69, Libreville; tel. 72-22-29; f. 1939; cap. 888m. francs CFA; forestry, plywood and sawmilling; Man. Dir M. DEJOIE.

Société Industrielle d'Agriculture et d'Elevage de Boumango (SIAEB): BP 68, Franceville; tel. 67-72-88; f. 1977; cap. 1,740m. francs CFA; 38% state-owned; in the process of liquidation since July 2001; maize, soya, rice and poultry production; Pres. SIMON BOULAMATARI; Man. Dir MARCEL LEKIBI.

Société Industrielle Textile du Gabon (SOTEGA): Libreville; tel. 72-19-29; f. 1968; cap. 260m. francs CFA; 15% state-owned; textile printing; Chair. RAPHAËL EBOBOCA; Man. Dir M. MARESCAUX.

Société Italo-Gabonaise des Marbres (SIGAMA): BP 3893, Libreville; tel. 72-25-83; f. 1974; cap. 542m. francs CFA; operates a marble quarry and factory at Doussé-Oussou; Man. Dir FRANCO MARCHIO.

Société Meunière et Avicole du Gabon (SMAG): BP 462 Z.I. d'Oloumi, Libreville; tel. 70-18-76; fax 70-28-12; e-mail smagb@internetgabon.com; f. 1968; cap. 1,341m. francs CFA; 30% state-owned; production of eggs, cattle feed, flour, bread; Chair. J. LOUIS VILGRAIN; Dir-Gen. XAVIER THOMAS.

Société des Mines de Fer de Mekambo (SOMIFER): Libreville; tel. 73-28-58; f. 1960; cap. 900m. francs CFA; 49% state-owned; mineral prospecting and mining; Chair. ADAMA DIALLO; Dir JEAN AUDIBERT.

Société de Mise en Valeur du Bois (SOMIVAB): BP 3893, Libreville; tel. 78-18-27; cap. 1,550m. francs CFA; forestry, sawmill, mfrs of sleepers for Transgabon railway; Chair. HERVÉ MOUTSINGA; Man. Dir FRANCO MARCHIO.

Société Nationale des Bois du Gabon (SNBG): BP 67, Libreville; tel. 79-98-71; fax 77-24-01; e-mail direction.commerciale@snbg-gabon.com; internet www.snbg-gabon.com; f. 1944; cap. 4,000m. francs CFA; 51% state-owned; has a monopoly of marketing all okoumé production; Pres. JEAN-PROSPER MOUSSOUAMY; 285 employees.

Société National Immobilière (SNI): BP 515, Libreville; tel. 76-05-81; fax 74-76-00; e-mail snigabon@internetgabon.com; f. 1976; cap. 1,250m. francs CFA; 77% state-owned; scheduled to be privatized; housing management and development; CEO ANTOINE N'GOUA.

Société Pizo de Formulation de Lubrifiants (PIZOLUB): BP 699, Port-Gentil; tel. 55-28-40; fax 55-03-82; e-mail pizolub@internetgabon.com; f. 1978; cap. 860m. francs CFA; scheduled to be privatized; mfrs of lubricating materials; Chair. MARCEL SANDOUNGOUT; Dir-Gen. LUCIEN OZOUAKI; 45 employees.

SOCIGA (Société de cigarettes Gabonaise): BP 2175, Libreville; tel. 72-02-29; fax 74-52-13; e-mail sociga@ga.imptop.com; Dir-Gen. JEAN-CLAUDE STARCZAN.

Sucreries d'Afrique Gabon (SUCAF Gabon): BP 610, Franceville; tel. 67-03-61; fax 67-03-63; e-mail sdg_sucaf@sucafgabon.com; f. 1974; cap. 4,000m. francs CFA; 53% state-owned; sugar production and agro-industrial complex at Ouélé; Chair. SAMUEL MBAYE; Dir-Gen. GUILLAUME SORDET; 533 employees.

Total Gabon: bvld Hourcq, BP 525, Port-Gentil; tel. 77-62-10; fax 76-41-85; e-mail martin.amegasse-efoe@total.com; internet www.total-gabon.com; f. 1934; cap. 76,500m. francs CFA; 36.6m. barrels of petroleum produced in 2004; 25% state-owned, 57% owned by Total group (France); petroleum exploration and extraction; Pres. JEAN PRIVEY; Dir-Gen. JEAN BIE.

TRADE UNIONS

Confédération Gabonaise des Syndicats Libres (CGSL): BP 8067, Libreville; tel. 77-37-82; fax 74-45-25; f. 1991; Sec.-Gen. FRANCIS MAYOMBO; 16,000 mems.

Confédération Syndicale Gabonaise (COSYGA): BP 14017, Libreville; tel. 72-17-98; fax 70-07-04; f. 1969 by the Govt, as a specialized organ of the PDG, to organize and educate workers, to contribute to social peace and economic development, and to protect the rights of trade unions; Gen. Sec. MARTIN ALLINI.

Transport

RAILWAYS

The construction of the Transgabonais railway, which comprises a section running from Owendo (the port of Libreville) to Booué (340 km) and a second section from Booué to Franceville (357 km), was completed in 1986. By 1989 regular services were operating between Libreville and Franceville. Some 2.9m. metric tons of freight and 215,000 passengers were carried on the network in 1999. In 1998 the railways were transferred to private management.

Société d'Exploration du Chemin de Fer Transgabonais (SETRAG): BP 578, Libreville; tel. 70-24-78; fax 70-20-38; operates Transgabonais railway; 84% owned by COMILOG; Chair. MARCEL ABEKE.

ROADS

In 2004 there were an estimated 9,170 km of roads, including 2,793 km of main roads and 6,377 km of secondary roads; about 10.2% of the road network was paved.

AGS Frasers: BP 9161, Libreville; tel. 70-23-16; fax 70-41-56; e-mail ags-gabon@ags-demenagement.com; internet www.agsfrasers.com; Dir CHRISTIAN POITTIER.

APRETRAC: BP 4542, Libreville; tel. 72-84-93; fax 74-40-45; e-mail apretrac@assala.net; Dir CHRISTOPHE DISSOU.

A.R.T.: BP 9391, Libreville; tel. 70-57-26; fax 70-57-28; e-mail bergon@inet.ga; freight; Dir-Gen. PHILIPPE BERGON.

Compagnie Internationale de Déménagement Transit (CIDT): BP 986, Libreville; tel. 76-44-44; fax 76-44-55; e-mail cidg@internetgabon.com; Dir THIERRY CARBONIE.

GETMA Gabon: BP 7510, Libreville; tel. 70-28-14; fax 70-40-20; e-mail claude.barone@assala.net; Dir CLAUDE BARONE.

Transform: BP 7538, Libreville; tel. 70-43-95; fax 70-21-91; e-mail transform@voila.fr; Dir J. P. POULAIN.

Transitex: BP 20323, Libreville; tel. 77-84-26; fax 77-84-35; e-mail helenepedemonte@transitex.ga; freight; Man. FRÉDÉRIC GONZALEZ.

INLAND WATERWAYS

The principal river is the Ogooué, navigable from Port-Gentil to Ndjolé (310 km) and serving the towns of Lambaréné, Ndjolé and Sindara.

Compagnie de Navigation Intérieure (CNI): BP 3982, Libreville; tel. 72-39-28; fax 74-04-11; f. 1978; scheduled for privatization; responsible for inland waterway transport; agencies at Port-Gentil, Mayumba and Lambaréné; Chair. JEAN-PIERRE MENGWANG ME NGYEMA; Dir-Gen. JEAN LOUIS POUNAH-NDJIMBI.

SHIPPING

The principal deep-water ports are Port-Gentil, which handles mainly petroleum exports, and Owendo, 15 km from Libreville, which services mainly barge traffic. The main ports for timber are at Owendo, Mayumba and Nyanga, and there is a fishing port at Libreville. The construction of a deep-water port at Mayumba is planned. A new terminal for the export of minerals, at Owendo, was opened in 1988. In 2004 the merchant shipping fleet numbered 46 and had a total displacement of 12,829 grt. In 1997 the Islamic Development Bank granted a loan of 11,000m. francs CFA for the rehabilitation of Gabon's ports.

Compagnie de Manutention et de Chalandage d'Owendo (COMACO): BP 2131, Libreville; tel. 70-26-35; f. 1974; Pres. GEORGES RAWIRI; Dir in Libreville M. RAYMOND.

Office des Ports et Rades du Gabon (OPRAG): BP 1051, Libreville; tel. 70-00-48; fax 70-37-37; f. 1974; 25-year management concession acquired in April 2004 by the Spanish PIP group; national port authority; Pres. ALI BONGO; Dir-Gen. JEAN PIERRE OYIBA.

SAGA Gabon: BP 518, Port-Gentil; tel. 55-54-00; fax 55-21-71; e-mail sagalbv@internetgabon.com; Chair. G. COGNON; Man. Dir DANIEL FERNÁNDEZ.

SDV Gabon: Zone Portuaire d'Owendo, BP 77, Libreville; tel. 70-26-36; fax 70-23-34; e-mail sdvg10@calva.com; internet www.sdv.com; freight by land, sea and air.

Société Nationale d'Acconage et de Transit (SNAT): BP 3897, Libreville; tel. 70-04-04; fax 70-13-11; e-mail marc.gérard@ga.dti.bollore.com; freight transport and stevedoring; Dir-Gen. MARC GÉRARD.

Société Nationale de Transports Maritimes (SONATRAM): BP 3841, Libreville; tel. 74-44-04; fax 74-59-87; f. 1976; relaunched 1995; 51% state-owned; river and ocean cargo transport; Man. Dir RAPHAEL MOARA WALLA.

Société du Port Minéralier d'Owendo: f. 1987; majority holding by Cie Minière de l'Ogooué; management of a terminal for minerals at Owendo.

SOCOPAO–Gabon: Immeuble Socapao, Zone Portuaire d'Owendo, BP 4, Libreville; tel. 56-09-13; fax 55-45-43; e-mail socopaolibreville@vpila.fr; f. 1983; freight transport and storage; Dir DANIEL BECQUERELLE.

CIVIL AVIATION

There are international airports at Libreville, Port-Gentil and Franceville, and 65 other public and 50 private airfields, linked mostly with the forestry and petroleum industries.

Air Affaires Gabon: BP 3962, Libreville; tel. 73-25-13; fax 73-49-98; f. 1975; domestic passenger chartered and scheduled flights; Chair. RAYMOND BELLANGER.

Air Service Gabon (ASG): BP 2232, Libreville; tel. 73-24-08; fax 73-60-69; f. 1965; charter flights; Chair. JEAN-LUC CHEVRIER; Gen. Man. FRANÇOIS LASCOMBES.

Gabon Airlines SA: Aéroport International Léon M'ba, Libreville; tel. 72-02-02; internet www.gabonairlines.com; f. July 2006 following liquidation of Compagnie Nationale Air Gabon in February; 51% owned by Royal Air Maroc (Morocco); internal and international cargo and passenger services.

Gabon Fret: BP 20384, Libreville; tel. 73-20-69; fax 73-44-44; e-mail info@gabonfret.com; internet www.gabonfret.com; f. 1995; air freight handlers; Dir DOMINIQUE OYINAMONO.

Société de Gestion de l'Aéroport de Libreville (ADL): BP 363, Libreville; tel. 73-62-44; fax 73-61-28; e-mail adl@inet.ga; f. 1988; 26.5% state-owned; management of airport at Libreville; Pres. CHANTAL LIDJI BADINGA; Dir-Gen. PIERRE ANDRÉ COLLET.

Tourism

Tourist arrivals were estimated at 222,257 in 2003, and receipts from tourism totalled US $84m. in that year. The tourism sector is being extensively developed, with new hotels and associated projects and the promotion of national parks.

Centre Gabonais de Promotion Touristique (GABONTOUR): ave du Colonel Parant, BP 2085, Libreville; tel. 72-85-04; fax 72-85-03; e-mail gabontour2006@yahoo.fr; f. 1988; Dir-Gen. LOUIS BARRY OGOULA OLINGO.

Office National Gabonais du Tourisme: BP 161, Libreville; tel. 72-21-82.

Defence

As assessed at November 2006, the army consisted of 3,200 men, the air force of 1,000 men and the navy of an estimated 500 men. Paramilitary forces (gendarmerie) numbered 2,000. Military service is voluntary. France maintains a detachment of 800 troops in Gabon.

Defence Expenditure: Budgeted at an estimated 10,000m. francs CFA for 2005.

Commander-in-Chief of the Armed Forces: Gen. AUGUSTIN ANGUILEY.

Education

Education is officially compulsory for 10 years between six and 16 years of age. According to UNESCO estimates, in 2000/01 77% of children in the relevant age-group (77% of boys; 77% of girls) attended primary schools, while in 2001/02 enrolment at secondary schools was equivalent to 50% of children in the relevant age-group. Primary and secondary education is provided by the State and mission schools. Primary education begins at the age of six and lasts for six years. Secondary education, beginning at 12 years of age, lasts for up to seven years, comprising a first cycle of four years and a second of three years. The Université Omar Bongo is based at Libreville and the Université des Sciences et des Techniques de Masuku at Franceville. In 1998 7,473 students were enrolled at institutions providing tertiary education. Many students go to France for university and technical training. The 1994 budget allocated 78,850m. francs CFA (19% of total administrative spending) to expenditure on education.

Bibliography

Aicardi de Saint-Paul, M. *Le Gabon du roi Denis à Omar Bongo.* Paris, Editions Albatros, 1987. Trans. by Palmer, A. F., and Palmer, T., as *Gabon: The Development of a Nation*. New York and London, Routledge, 1989.

Ambouroué-Avaro, J. *Un peuple gabonais à l'aube de la colonisation.* Paris, Editions Karthala, 1983.

Barnes, J. F. *Gabon: Beyond the Colonial Legacy.* Boulder, CO, Westview Press, 1992.

Culture, Ecology and Politics in Gabon's Rainforest (African Studies). New York, Edwin Mellen Press, 2003.

Bongo, O. *El Hadj Omar Bongo par lui-même.* Libreville, Multipress Gabon, 1988.

Bory, P. *The New Gabon.* Monaco, 1978.

Bouquerel, J. *Le Gabon.* Paris, Presses universitaires de France, 1970.

Deschamps, H. *Traditions orales et archives du Gabon.* Paris, Berger-Levrault, 1962.

Fernandez, J. W. *Bwiti.* Princeton, NJ, Princeton University Press, 1982.

Gardinier, D. E. *Historical Dictionary of Gabon.* Lanham, MD, Scarecrow Press, 1994.

Gaulme, F. *Le Pays de Cama Gabon.* Paris, Editions Karthala, 1983.

Le Gabon et son ombre. Paris, Editions Karthala, 1988.

Gray, C. *Colonial Rule and Crisis in Equatorial Africa: Southern Gabon, 1880–1940.* Rochester, NY, University of Rochester Press, 2002.

Mianzenza, A. D. *Gabon: l'agriculture dans une economie de rente.* Paris, L'Harmattan, 2001.

McKay, J. 'West Central Africa' in Mansell Prothero, R. (Ed.). *A Geography of Africa*. London, 1969.

Obiang, J.-F. *France-Gabon: pratiques clientélaires et logiques d'état dans les relations franco-africaines.* Paris, Editions Karthala, 2007.

Péan, P. *Affaires africaines.* Paris, Fayard, 1983.

Raponda-Walker, A. *Notes d'histoire du Gabon.* Montpellier, Imprimerie Charité, 1960.

Vennetier, P. 'Problems of Port Development in Gabon and Congo' in Hoyle, B. S., and Hilling, D. (Eds). *Seaports and Development in Tropical Africa.* London, 1970.

Les Plans de Développement des Pays d'Afrique Noire. 4th Edn. Paris, Ediafric, 1977.

Weinstein, B. *Gabon: Nation Building on the Ogooue.* Boston, MA, MIT Press, 1967.

L'Economie Gabonaise. Paris, Ediafric, 1977.

Yates, D. *The Rentier State in Africa: Oil Dependency and Neocolonialism in the Republic of Gabon.* Trenton, NJ, Africa World Press, 1996.

THE GAMBIA

Physical and Social Geography

R. J. HARRISON CHURCH

The Republic of The Gambia occupies an area of 11,295 sq km (4,361 sq miles). Apart from a very short coastline, The Gambia is a semi-enclave in Senegal, with which it shares some physical and social phenomena, but differs in history, colonial experience and certain economic affiliations. Its population (enumerated at 1,364,507 in April 2003, according to provisional census results, giving a density of 120.8 inhabitants per sq km) was one of the fastest growing of mainland Africa during the 1990s: the Government reported a rate of population growth of 4.2% in 1993. However, the rate had been reduced to 2.7% by 2005. The capital is Banjul, with a population of 34,828 in 2003, but it is exceeded in size by both Brikama (42,480 inhabitants in 1993) and Serrekunda (151,450 inhabitants in 1993). In mid-2006, according to UN estimates, the country's total population was 1,663,000, with a density of 147.2 inhabitants per sq km.

The Gambia essentially comprises the valley of the navigable Gambia river. Around the estuary (3 km wide at its narrowest point) and the lower river, the state is 50 km wide, and extends eastward either side of the navigable river for 470 km. In most places the country is only 24 km wide with but one or two villages within it on either bank, away from mangrove or marsh. The former extends about 150 km upstream, the limit of the tide in the rainy season, although in the dry season and in drought years the tide penetrates further upstream. Annual rainfall averages 1,150 mm. Coastal erosion has been increasing since 1980, and it is estimated that between 4 m and 5 m of coastal land was lost during the period 1990–94.

Small ocean-going vessels can reach Kaur, 190 km upstream, throughout the year; Georgetown, 283 km upstream, is accessible to some small craft. River vessels regularly call at Fatoto, 464 km upstream, the last of 33 wharf towns served by schooners or river boats. Unfortunately, this fine waterway is underutilized because it is separated from most of its natural hinterland by the nearby frontier with Senegal.

Some mangrove on the landward sides has been removed for swamp rice cultivation. Behind are seasonally flooded marshes with freshwater grasses, and then on the upper slopes of Tertiary sandstone there is woodland with fallow bush and areas cultivated mainly with groundnuts and millet.

The Gambia has no commercially exploitable mineral resources, although deposits of petroleum have been identified.

The principal ethnic groups are the Mandinka, Fula, Wolof, Jola, Serahule, Serere, Manjago and Bambara. There is also a small but influential Creole (Aku) community. Each ethnic group has its own vernacular language, although the official language is English.

Recent History

JOHN A. WISEMAN

Revised by KATHARINE MURISON

Following the establishment of a coastal trading settlement at Bathurst (now Banjul) in 1816, the extension of British control over the territory now comprising the Republic of The Gambia was completed by the close of the 19th century. Political life during the colonial period developed slowly, but following the extension of the franchise to all adults after 1960 two political parties came to the fore: the United Party (UP), which attracted support from urban coastal interests, and the rurally based Protectorate People's Party (PPP, subsequently the People's Progressive Party), led by Dr (later Sir) Dawda Jawara. The PPP emerged as the dominant party in elections in 1962. On 18 February 1965 The Gambia became an independent state, within the Commonwealth, with Jawara as Prime Minister.

JAWARA AND THE PPP, 1965–94

From independence in 1965 until the military *coup d'état* of July 1994, political life and government control were firmly concentrated in the hands of Jawara and the PPP. Jawara remained the central figure in Gambian politics, becoming President when the country opted for republican status in 1970. The UP went into decline after independence, and in 1975 was eclipsed by a new opposition party, the National Convention Party (NCP), whose leader, Sheriff Dibba, had formerly been a leading figure in the PPP.

In July 1981 dissident members of the paramilitary field force (the country had no army at this time) allied with a number of small radical groupings to attempt a coup. Following a week of fierce fighting in and around Banjul, in which at least 1,000 people were killed, the rebellion was crushed with support from Senegalese troops. There were two important ramifications of the coup attempt. The first was the establishment of a confederation with Senegal in February 1982. The Senegambian confederation was, however, always more favoured by the Senegalese authorities than it was by the Gambians, and in September 1989 it was formally dissolved. The second was the establishment of a Gambian army.

At elections held in May 1982 Jawara was re-elected President, with 72% of the votes, overwhelmingly defeating Dibba (who conducted his campaign from detention, having been charged in connection with the abortive coup; he was subsequently acquitted and released). The PPP again emerged with a clear majority in parliament, winning 27 seats, compared with three obtained by the NCP and five by independent candidates. Two new political parties appeared during 1986: the Gambia People's Party (GPP), under the leadership of Assan Musa Camara, who had previously been a leading figure in the PPP; and the People's Democratic Organization for Independence and Socialism (PDOIS), led by Halifa Sallah and Sam Sarr. However, at the May 1987 elections neither of the new parties took a single parliamentary seat. The NCP increased its representation to five elective seats, but the remainder were won by the PPP. In the presidential election Jawara won 59% of the votes, defeating Dibba (27%) and Camara (14%). In the presidential election held in April 1992 Jawara secured 58% of the vote, defeating Dibba (with 22%), Camara and two others. In concurrent parliamentary elections the PPP retained a comfortable majority, although its representation was reduced to 25 members. The NCP won six seats, while the GPP took two, and independent candidates three.

Following the 1992 elections, the appointment to the vice-presidency of Saihou Sabally, regarded by many as tainted by allegations of corruption, fuelled increasingly outspoken allegations of corruption and mismanagement in public life. In January 1994 Jawara announced the establishment of an independent public complaints commission, with the aim of combating corruption in public life. However, while public dissatisfaction with the PPP regime appeared to be increasing in late 1993 and early 1994, there was little indication of the dramatic political change that was shortly to occur.

MILITARY GOVERNMENT

On 22 July 1994 Jawara and his Government were overthrown by a military *coup d'état*. Although the coup appeared to have had little or no advance planning, it took place without bloodshed and met with very little resistance. Soldiers seized key installations and marched on government buildings in Banjul. It was announced that government was now in the hands of an Armed Forces Provisional Ruling Council (AFPRC), led by Lt (later Col) Yahya Jammeh. The other members of the Council were Lts Sana Sabally, Sadibou Hydara, Edward Singhateh and Yankuba Touray (all of whom were subsequently promoted to the rank of captain). The AFPRC announced the suspension of the Constitution, a ban on all political parties and activity, the temporary closure of the country's borders and a dusk-to-dawn curfew, and gave warning that they would 'mercilessly crush' any opposition to the take-over. Jammeh formed a provisional Cabinet, comprising both soldiers and civilians. Almost immediately, however, two military members of the Cabinet were dismissed and arrested. The frequency of cabinet changes has been a continuous feature of the Jammeh regime. Jammeh's early speeches, justifying the coup by portraying the Jawara regime as corrupt, inefficient and not truly democratic, while promising 'a new era of freedom, progress, democracy and accountability', resembled many post-coup speeches in other African states.

International reaction to the military take-over, especially from major aid donors such as the USA, the European Union (EU), the United Kingdom and Japan, was generally unfavourable, and, when attempts to persuade the AFPRC to restore the elected regime failed, efforts were concentrated on a return to democratic rule. Arab donor states such as Saudi Arabia and Kuwait agreed to continue funding aid projects; relations with Libya improved significantly, and full diplomatic relations were restored in 1994. Diplomatic links were established with Taiwan in July 1995, whereupon the People's Republic of China suspended relations.

In September 1994 the AFPRC established several commissions of inquiry to examine allegations of corruption and maladministration under Jawara. Even allowing for the fact that the commissions were designed, in part, to discredit the previous regime, they were seen to act according to due legal process and without direct interference from the AFPRC, and they undoubtedly uncovered significant and genuine evidence of widespread, systematic corruption, as well as high levels of bureaucratic confusion and chaos.

The AFPRC survived an attempted military counter-coup in November 1994 in which the coup leader and several other officers were killed. Several senior PPP figures were arrested but later released. A more serious attempt at a coup took place in January 1995, when two senior AFPRC members, Vice-Chairman Sabally and the Minister of the Interior, Hydara, reportedly attempted to assassinate Jammeh and seize power. The attempt was defeated, and Sabally and Hydara were removed from office and imprisoned. Hydara died in prison in June; Sabally subsequently received a nine-year prison sentence. Singhateh was promoted to the post of AFPRC Vice-Chairman. Persistent rumours in The Gambia suggested that Jammeh had fabricated allegations of a coup in order to eliminate those whom he regarded as potential rivals.

The frequency of arrests of politicians and journalists, as well as allegations of the harassment of civilians by the military, fuelled accusations of authoritarianism on the part of the Jammeh regime. There was considerable outrage in June 1995, when the body was discovered of the hitherto Minister of Finance, Ousman Koro Ceesay; although the authorities attributed his death to a motor accident, rumours circulated of more suspicious circumstances. In that month the AFPRC established a new police organization, the National Intelligence Agency (NIA), which was given wide powers of surveillance and arrest, and in August the restoration of the death penalty (abolished in 1993) was attributed to an increase in the incidence of murder. A government decree issued in November 1995 accorded the Minister of the Interior unlimited powers of arrest and detention without charge; the decree appeared to have been frequently used against suspected opponents of the regime, and there were increasingly frequent allegations of the torture of political detainees.

Constitutional Debate

Much public debate at this time focused on the timetable for, and manner of, a restoration of democratic civilian rule. In October 1994 the AFPRC announced what it termed a programme of rectification and transition to democratic constitutional rule, which provided for the restitution of elected civilian organs of state in 1998—four years after the seizure of power. The intended duration of military rule was denounced domestically and internationally. In November 1994 Jammeh announced the establishment of a 23-member National Consultative Committee (NCC) to examine the question of the transition. The NCC included representatives of trade unions, religious groups, women's organizations, professional associations and traditional chiefs. In January 1995 the NCC recommended that the transition period be reduced to two years from the time of the coup. Jammeh subsequently agreed to accept the revised programme, but rejected a further NCC suggestion that an interim civilian government be established while he remained as Head of State. Although the reduction in the proposed duration of military rule was generally welcomed, prominent creditors, including the EU and the USA, continued to withhold assistance.

The AFPRC established a Constitutional Review Commission (CRC) in April 1995. The CRC began a series of public hearings, at which one of the most contentious issues was the question of a proposed minimum age for presidential candidates. Underlying this debate was the widespread belief that Jammeh was himself planning to contest the presidency in 1996, although Jammeh consistently refused to confirm or deny this. There was increasing criticism that Jammeh's tours of the country resembled an election campaign, while civilian politicians were still forbidden by military decree to organize political meetings of any sort. Jammeh's cause was, moreover, now supported by the July 22 Movement: although ostensibly a non-governmental organization, the movement appeared to be functioning politically.

The CRC submitted its draft document to the AFPRC in November 1995, although its findings were not made public until March 1996, prompting suspicions that in the intervening period the AFPRC might have accepted, amended, or rejected the Commission's recommendations without public consultation. In April the elections were postponed, on the grounds that there was insufficient time to complete preparations, and in May voting was set for September (presidential) and December (legislative); the ban on political parties was to remain in place until after the constitutional referendum, which was to be held in August. Many aspects of the proposed constitution and the new electoral arrangements provoked concern among opponents of the AFPRC. The stipulation that presidential candidates must be aged between 30 and 65 years ensured Jammeh's eligibility for office, while preventing many veteran politicians from participating; there was to be no restriction on the number of times a President might seek re-election. The revised demarcation of constituency boundaries, it was alleged, would unduly favour the incumbent regime, and significant financial obstacles to political organizations seeking elected public office had been presented by raising both the deposit required from candidates and the proportion of the vote necessary to secure the deposit's return.

In January 1996 Jawara was charged *in absentia* with embezzlement, following investigations into the alleged diversion of proceeds (estimated at more than US $11m.) from the sale of petroleum donated by Nigeria. During March–April the confiscation was ordered of the assets in The Gambia of Jawara and 11 former government members.

The constitutional referendum took place on 8 August 1996. The rate of participation was more than 85%, and more than 70.4% of voters were reported to have endorsed the new document. A presidential decree was issued on 14 August, reauthorizing party political activity. Shortly afterwards, however, it was announced that the PPP, the NCP and the GPP were to be prohibited from contesting the forthcoming elections, as were all holders of executive office in the 30 years prior to the 1994 military take-over; thus, the only pre-coup parties authorized to contest the elections were the PDOIS and the People's Democratic Party. The effective ban on participation in the restoration of elected institutions of all those associated with political life prior to July 1994 provoked strong criticism from the Commonwealth, whose Ministerial Action Group on the Harare Declaration (CMAG) had hitherto made a significant contribution to the transition process.

THE JAMMEH PRESIDENCY

As the ban on all political organizations remained in force until only weeks before the presidential election, the formation of parties was a fairly rushed affair. As had been widely anticipated, the July 22 Movement transformed itself into an official political grouping to support Jammeh's campaign for the presidency, styling itself the Alliance for Patriotic Reorientation and Construction (APRC). Some of the elements associated with the pre-1994 parliamentary parties formed the United Democratic Party (UDP) under the leadership of a prominent human rights lawyer, Ousainou Darboe, who became the party's presidential candidate, while the PDOIS and the National Reconciliation Party (NRP) also selected candidates to contest the election. In September 1996 Jammeh and his AFPRC colleagues formally retired from the army: Jammeh was to contest the presidency as a civilian, as required by the Constitution.

The short presidential campaign was widely condemned as having been neither free nor fair, while international observers, including CMAG, expressed doubts as to the credibility of the election. The state-owned media promoted Jammeh while offering minimal coverage of the other candidates' campaigns. Moreover, the APRC enjoyed privileged access to government finance and resources. There were reports of violence and intimidation, often involving military personnel, directed especially at the UDP. As polling proceeded, on 26 September 1996, Darboe sought refuge in the Senegalese embassy in Banjul, having received threats to his life. The official results of voting gave Jammeh 55.8% of the votes and Darboe, his nearest rival, 35.8%. A further set of 'leaked' results later indicated a victory for Darboe, but these had limited credibility. The dissolution of the AFPRC was announced on 27 September; pending the legislative elections, the Cabinet was to be the sole provisional governing body. Jammeh was inaugurated as President on 18 October.

The legislative elections took place on 2 January 1997. Only the APRC had the resources to field candidates in all 45 constituencies (in five of these they were unopposed); the UDP contested 34 seats, the PDOIS 17 and the NRP five. The Gambian authorities, opposition groups and most international observers expressed broad satisfaction at the conduct of the poll. The official results of the elections gave the APRC a clear majority in the new National Assembly, with 33 seats. The UDP won seven seats, the NRP two seats and the PDOIS one seat; two independent candidates were also elected. As Head of State, Jammeh was empowered by the Constitution to nominate four additional members of parliament, from whom the Speaker (and Deputy Speaker) would be chosen. The opening session of the National Assembly accordingly elected Mustapha Wadda, previously Secretary-General of the APRC and Secretary at the Presidency, as Speaker. This session denoted the full entry into force of the Constitution and thus the inauguration of the Second Republic.

In February 1997 most remaining long-term political detainees, including army and police personnel, were released. Later in the month, none the less, there were new arrests: among those detained was the Commander of the State Guard, Lt Landing Sanneh. The title of Secretary of State was now given to all members of the Cabinet; ministries were similarly renamed Departments of State. Most of the powers and duties hitherto associated with the vice-presidency were transferred to the Secretary of State for the Office of the President, a post now held by Singhateh (who, at 27, was too young to hold the office of Vice-President).

In July 1997 CMAG reiterated its previous concerns regarding the lack of a 'fully inclusive' political system in The Gambia, urging the immediate removal of the ban on political activities by certain parties and individuals and the investigation of allegations of the harassment of opposition members. The tax on the registration of independent radio stations was more than doubled in January 1998, prompting opposition protests of censorship. In the following month the main independent station, Citizen FM, was ordered to cease broadcasts shortly after its director and a station journalist were arrested. (The station had recently broadcast information regarding the NIA, although the authorities attributed the closure to the station's failure to pay taxes.) In July 2000 the High Court reversed the original judgment, following an appeal by the director of Citizen FM, Baboucar Gaye. The state of the independent media again gave cause for concern in May 1999, when *The Daily Observer*, the only remaining newspaper that openly criticized the Government, was bought by a Gambian businessman closely associated with Jammeh; several journalists associated with criticisms of government policy were subsequently removed from their posts. In July *The Independent* newspaper was ordered to suspend publication because of alleged irregularities in its registration, although it was suggested that the suspension had been provoked by an article written by a member of the UDP, which accused the Jammeh regime of widespread corruption.

Meanwhile, opposition activists continued to allege harassment by the Government. In May 1998 nine people were arrested in a raid on the mosque at Brikama; among those detained was a prominent critic of Jammeh, Lamine Wa Juwara. A member of the UDP, Juwara had initiated a lawsuit seeking compensation for alleged wrongful imprisonment during the transition period. Darboe was also briefly imprisoned. In July Juwara's claim for damages was rejected by the Supreme Court on the grounds that the Constitution contained a clause granting immunity to the former AFPRC in connection with the transition period.

In December 1999 Jammeh called an extraordinary congress of the APRC in order to discuss the culture of embezzlement described in a report into official corruption by the Auditor-General. Jammeh announced that corrupt officials would be pursued through the courts irrespective of their political affiliation and subsequently dismissed the Gambian ambassadors to France and Belgium, whose embassies had been criticized by the report. Further allegations of government corruption emerged in January 2000 after the disclosure, during legal proceedings in the United Kingdom, that significant sums generated by the sale of petroleum had been paid into an anonymous Swiss bank account. The crude petroleum had been granted to The Gambia for trading purposes by the Nigerian Government between August 1996 and June 1998, reportedly in recognition of Jammeh's opposition in 1995 to the imposition of sanctions by the Commonwealth against Nigeria. Darboe subsequently alleged that Jammeh had illegally diverted more than US $1.9m. of the proceeds of the sale of the petroleum, although Jammeh vigorously denied any involvement in the matter.

In January 2000 the security forces announced that they had forestalled an attempted military coup. It was reported that, during efforts to arrest the conspirators, a member of the State Guard had been killed, and the Commander of the State Guard, Lt Sanneh, who was the officer in charge of security at the presidential palace, had been wounded. Another member of the State Guard was killed on the following day while attempting to evade arrest. The Secretary of State for the Interior, Ousman Badjie, strenuously denied rumours that the authorities had invented the plot as a pretext to purge the State Guard and as a means of diverting press attention from the petroleum scandal. In June several army officers and civilians were arrested on suspicion of plotting to overthrow Jammeh's Government. Seven were subsequently charged with treason, but all had been acquitted by July 2004.

Meanwhile, in March 2000 it was announced that municipal and rural elections were to be held in November, while a presidential election was to be held in October 2001. Five political parties announced their intention of contesting the local elections, the first since 1992. In August 2000, however, the APRC suggested that it would not be possible to hold municipal elections in November as scheduled, since the National Assembly had yet to approve the local government bill.

The continued failure of the Government to enact the local government bill prompted the Chairman of the Independent Electoral Commission (IEC), Anglican Bishop Solomon Tilewa Johnson, to instigate a court case against the Government. In December 2000, in a move that opponents of the Government described as unconstitutional, Jammeh dismissed Johnson from his position on the IEC; his predecessor, Gabriel Roberts, was reappointed, despite allegations that he had engaged in fraudulent behaviour in support of the APRC at the time of the 1996 elections.

In January 2001 a commission of inquiry published a report into student unrest in April 2000 that had followed the death of a student in firemen's barracks and the alleged rape of a schoolgirl by a member of the security forces. It was claimed that the security forces had used live ammunition to suppress the protests, during which 14 people had been killed and 30 people injured. The Government rejected the commission's recommendation that Badjie and senior police officials should accept responsibility for the disturbances.

In February 2001 Jammeh assured the Secretary-General of the Commonwealth that Decree 89 (which prohibited all holders of executive office in the 30 years prior to July 1994 from seeking public office) would be repealed in the near future; Jammeh was warned that if the ban were not lifted by October 2001, the Commonwealth would consider imposing sanctions against The Gambia. In April widespread public dissent was reported, after the National Assembly passed legislation, proposed by Badjie, which effectively granted indemnity from prosecution to those (including Badjie himself) found responsible for the disturbances and killings that had occurred during the student protests of April 2000.

During mid-2001 opposition figures claimed that a number of constitutional amendments envisaged by the Government, including proposals to extend the presidential term from five to seven years and to confer upon the President the power to appoint local chiefs, would precipitate acts of electoral fraud at the forthcoming parliamentary and presidential elections. In July Jammeh announced the abrogation of Decree 89, although it emerged that prominent individuals who had participated in pre-1994 administrations, including Jawara and Sabally, were still prohibited from seeking public office under separate legislation. None the less, the PPP, the NCP and the GPP were subsequently re-established. In August the UDP, the PPP and the GPP formed a coalition to contest the forthcoming presidential election.

Jammeh and the APRC Retain Power

The presidential election was held on 18 October 2001, in relatively calm conditions. A turn-out of some 90% was recorded. In addition to Darboe, the candidate of the opposition UDP-PPP-GPP coalition, Jammeh was challenged by Dibba for the NCP, Hamat Bah for the NRP and Sidia Jatta for the PDOIS. (Bah and Jatta had also contested the presidential election in September 1996, when their combined share of votes cast was somewhat less than 10%.) Jammeh was re-elected to the presidency, with 52.8% of the votes cast, according to official results, ahead of Darboe, who won 32.6% of the votes. Although Darboe conceded defeat, members of the opposition subsequently disputed the legitimacy of the results, reiterating claims of incorrect practice in the distribution of voting credentials and in the counting of ballots. Opposition supporters and other observers had earlier alleged that the compilation of voters' lists had been accompanied by widespread fraud. None the less, international observers, including representatives of the Commonwealth, described the poll as being largely free and fair.

Up to 60 opposition supporters were reportedly arrested in the week after the election, and the homes of prominent members of the UDP were attacked, allegedly by members of the youth wing of the APRC. A leading Gambian human rights activist, Lamin Sillah, was detained by the security forces, after he alleged that members of the opposition had been subject to harassment and sustained detention. Following pressure from international human rights campaigners, Sillah was released. Baboucar Gaye was also arrested, and his Citizen FM radio station again closed, officially on the grounds that it had defaulted on tax payments. In November 2001 Darboe announced his party's intention to take legal action to secure the release of UDP activists who remained in prison. Additionally, in October it was reported that several senior civil servants who were believed to be sympathetic to opposition parties, including the director of the national radio and television stations and a number of military officers, had been dismissed. Such dismissals appeared to reflect the implementation of a pledge made by Jammeh, in his election campaign, that he would ensure the loyalty to the President of civil and military organizations. Meanwhile, the IEC announced the postponement of the referendum on proposed constitutional changes, which had been scheduled for mid-November. In December, at his inauguration, Jammeh granted an unconditional amnesty to Jawara, guaranteeing the former President's security should he decide to return to The Gambia.

In December 2001 the UDP-PPP-GPP coalition announced that it would boycott legislative elections scheduled to be held in January 2002, as a result of the alleged addition of some 50,000 foreign citizens to electoral lists and the reputed transfer of voters between the electoral lists of different constituencies. Having denied these accusations, the IEC announced that the APRC had secured 33 of the 48 elective seats in the enlarged National Assembly, in constituencies where the party was unopposed owing to the boycott. At the elections, which took place on 17 January 2002, the APRC won 12 of the 15 contested seats, giving the party an overall total of 45 elective seats, the PDOIS obtained two seats and the NRP one. Electoral turn-out was reportedly low. An additional five members of parliament were appointed by President Jammeh, in accordance with the Constitution. Dibba, whose NCP had formed an alliance with the APRC prior to the elections, was appointed Speaker of the new National Assembly.

The long-delayed municipal elections, which were finally held on 25 April 2002, were boycotted by the UDP and the PDOIS; consequently, the APRC was unopposed in some 85 of the 113 local seats and won a total of 99 seats, securing control of all seven regional authorities. The NRP was the only other political organization to gain representation in local government, winning five seats; the remaining nine seats were won by independent candidates.

In June 2002 former President Jawara returned to The Gambia from exile in the United Kingdom; at the end of the month he was officially received by Jammeh at the presidential residence, and later tendered his resignation as leader of the PPP. In August Juwara alleged that the UDP's campaign funds had been diverted prior to the April elections to pay for Darboe's outstanding income-tax debts. The UDP expelled Juwara, who formed a new party, the National Democratic Action Movement (NDAM), in October. In November the leader of the youth wing of the UDP, Shyngle Nyassi, was arrested in connection with information from the NIA that allegedly implicated him in the sale of forged documents to Gambians seeking asylum abroad. Nyassi claimed that his arrest was a response to his criticism of the Government's economic policies. Nyassi was soon arrested again, however, along with Darboe and two other members of the UDP, in connection with the murder of an APRC supporter, Alieu Njie, in June 2000; their trial commenced in early 2003, but was adjourned in July. All four were finally acquitted in June 2005, owing to insufficient evidence. In November 2002 the opposition UDP-PPP-GPP coalition split, following the resignation of its Chairman, Assan Musa Camara, while President Jammeh dismissed a number of members of his Cabinet, accusing them of lacking seriousness. Notably, Jammeh took over the agriculture portfolio himself, amid opposition doubts about his qualification for the position.

Press Freedom

In May 2002 the National Assembly approved legislation to impose stricter regulations on the print media, in accordance with which all journalists would be required to register with a National Media Commission. The law was condemned as draconian by The Gambia Press Union, which announced that it would not co-operate with the new Commission. In June 2003 the state-run National Media Commission was created, despite continuing opposition from journalists, and was given far-reaching powers, including the authority to imprison journalists for terms of up to six months. All media organizations and independent journalists had to register with the Commission by 14 May 2004; however, after four leading newspapers, a magazine and a radio station held a week-long self-imposed suspension of publishing and broadcasting in protest at the Commission's powers, the deadline was extended by three months. In September 2003 the editor-in-chief of *The Independent*, Abdoulaye Sey, was reportedly detained for four days, soon after the newspaper published an article criticizing Jammeh. In October the offices of *The Independent* in Banjul were set on fire, and in April 2004 the printing press was set alight and destroyed. In August Demba Jawo, the President of The Gambia Press Union, reported that he had received an anonymous letter threatening him with death. Later that month, in an open letter to Jammeh, journalists called for increased security to prevent further attacks on the private media.

In mid-December 2004 the National Assembly repealed the controversial law that had created the National Media Commission, but approved legislation requiring newspapers and radio stations to reregister with the authorities within two weeks of the enactment of the law and abolishing the option of a fine for those convicted of libel or sedition, which would instead be punishable by prison terms of between six months and three years. Moreover, the bond for media registration was to be increased from D100,000 to D500,000. The murder in Banjul a few days later of Deyda Hydara, the editor of the private newspaper *The Point*, who had criticized the new legislation, prompted a protest march in the capital, reportedly attended by some 300 journalists, and a one-week strike by workers in the independent media. The Gambia Press Union called for an independent inquiry into the killing, amid suggestions that it had been politically motivated. The Government condemned Hydara's murder and pledged to find those responsible. Meanwhile, Reporters sans frontières, an international organization concerned with press freedom, urged Jammeh not to enact the new legislation. In March 2005 it emerged that the legislation had been signed into law in late December 2004, although its promulgation had not been made public until two months later, in apparent contravention of the Constitution. In May 2005 Reporters sans frontières called on President Jammeh to accept external assistance in the investigation into Hydara's murder, owing to lack of progress in the case. In May 2006 the Secretary of State for Justice, Sheikh Tijan Hydara, stated that the Government's investigation into Deyda Hydara's murder was ongoing. Meanwhile, in late March *The Independent* was closed down by the authorities and its general manager and editor-in-chief arrested, apparently in connection with an article naming people who had been arrested on suspicion of participating in an alleged coup attempt (see below). They were released without charge some three weeks later, although Lamin Fatty, a journalist for the newspaper, was arrested in April. In June 2007, nearly one year after his trial had commenced, Fatty was convicted of publishing false information and was ordered to pay a fine of some US $1,850 or serve one year's imprisonment. Meanwhile, *The Independent* remained closed.

Anti-Corruption Campaign

In September 2003 President Jammeh dismissed Badjie and Famara Jatta, the Secretary of State for Finance and Economic Affairs. Bakary Njie, the Secretary of State for Communication, Information and Technology, was removed from his post in the following month. Also in October Juwara was arrested on a charge of sedition, after urging Gambians to demonstrate in protest at price rises. Although his arrest was later ruled to be illegal, in December his bail was revoked. In February 2004 Juwara was sentenced to six months' imprisonment; an appeal against the ruling was filed later that month and he was released in June.

In October 2003 the President launched an anti-corruption drive, named 'Operation No Compromise', which led to a number of high-profile arrests. In November the leader of the APRC in the National Assembly, Baba Jobe, was charged with fraud and the Director-General of Customs and Excise was arrested. (In March 2004 Baba Jobe was convicted of various economic crimes and sentenced to nine years' imprisonment.) Moreover, in December 2003 Yankuba Touray, only recently appointed to replace Njie as Secretary of State for Communication, Information and Technology (having previously been responsible for the tourism and culture portfolio), was dismissed. In May 2004 Sulayman Masanneh Ceesay was replaced as Secretary of State for the Interior and Religious Affairs by Samba Bah. In April Amadou Scattred Janneh was appointed Secretary of State for Communication, Information and Technology, while Sulayman Mboob became Secretary of State for Agriculture, thus bringing to 84 the number of secretarial changes since President Jammeh was proclaimed Head of State in 1994. A coalition of opposition parties defeated the APRC at a by-election in Jarra West in July.

A Presidential Anti-Corruption Commission of Inquiry, chaired by a Nigerian judge, Madubochi Azubuike Paul, commenced hearings in Banjul in July 2004, in a continuation of 'Operation No Compromise'. During the following months government secretaries of state and other current and former senior public officials were questioned regarding their financial affairs, but there was some criticism that the President and parliamentary deputies were exempt from appearing before the commission, which was to examine the period from 22 July 1994 to 22 July 2004. In September Jammeh announced a minor cabinet reshuffle. In October Blaise Baboucar Jagne was replaced as Secretary of State for Foreign Affairs by Sidi Moro Sanneh. Several other public servants were dismissed in the same week, including Adama Deen, the Managing Director of The Gambia Ports Authority, Andrew Sylva, the Managing Director of the Social Security and Housing Finance Corporation, and Tamsir Jasseh, the Director of Immigration. Jasseh and Deen were both detained for nearly a week before being released without charge, while Sylva was arrested and later charged with perjury, reportedly in connection with his testimony before the anti-corruption commission, during which he had claimed that President Jammeh had taken an electricity generator from a state-owned hotel for use at his private residence. In November the Chief of Staff of the Armed Forces, Col Baboucar Jatta, was unexpectedly dismissed and retired from the military, having led the armed forces since Jammeh seized power in 1994. His successor was also dismissed in the following month and replaced by Lt-Col Assan Sarr.

There were further arrests of prominent figures in February 2005, including the head of the police force, Landing Badjie, and the head of the criminal investigation unit, Ousman Jatta. The Government dismissed Badjie from his post, accusing him of 'serious dereliction of duty' and citing his failure to solve a series of crimes. Badjie and Jatta were reportedly released several days later without being charged.

Jammeh effected a cabinet reshuffle in March 2005, dismissing Mousa Bala Gaye, the Secretary of State for Finance and Economic Affairs, Yankuba Kassama, the Secretary of State for Health and Social Welfare, and Mboob, the Secretary of State for Agriculture. The President assumed personal responsibility for agriculture. Jammeh defended the high rate of turnover in his Cabinet as being necessary to ensure transparency and accountability in government. Further cabinet changes followed later that month. Gaye, notably, made a swift return, as Secretary of State for Foreign Affairs, replacing Sanneh, who became Secretary of State for Trade, Industry and Employment. However, less than a week later Sanneh was removed from office and replaced by Neneh Macdouall-Gaye. At the same time Col (retd) Baboucar Jatta joined the Government as Secretary of State for the Interior, succeeding Samba Bah. Meanwhile, Jammeh appointed Raymond Sock as Secretary of State for Justice and Attorney General and Ismaila Sambou as Secretary of State for Local Government and Lands to replace Sheikh Tijan Hydara and Malafi Jarju, who were both dismissed in connection with the findings of the anti-corruption commission. Hydara was reappointed as Secretary of State for Justice and Attorney General in early October, while Lamin Kaba Bajo replaced Gaye as Secretary of State for Foreign Affairs later that month, as part of a minor government reshuffle. Gaye was initially appointed as Secretary of State for Trade, Industry and Employment, but in November returned to the position of Secretary of State for Finance and Economic Affairs.

Meanwhile, in March 2005 the Presidential Anti-Corruption Commission of Inquiry submitted its report to Jammeh. A number of civil servants and government officials allegedly implicated in the report were dismissed, and more than 30 senior current and former officials accused of corruption were reportedly given a two-week deadline to reimburse the Government for assets that they had allegedly acquired illicitly. The commission recommended the implementation of measures to ensure effective monitoring of tax payments, the adoption of new anti-corruption legislation and the creation of a permanent and independent commission to combat corruption. The Public Accountability and Anti-Corruption Unit was accordingly established in April. In June opposition leaders condemned the reappointment to the Cabinet, as Secretary of State for Agriculture, of Yankuba Touray, who had been ordered to repay some D2m. to the state following his appearance before the anti-corruption commission.

Opposition Realignments

In January 2005 the NDAM, the NRP, the PDOIS, the PPP and the UDP agreed to form a coalition, the National Alliance for Democracy and Development (NADD), with the aim of fielding a single opposition candidate to challenge Jammeh in the presidential election due in late 2006. In June 2005 four opposition deputies who had joined the recently registered NADD were expelled from the National Assembly, in accordance with the Constitution, which states that deputies choosing to change party must vacate their seats. The four deputies—Hamat Bah, the leader of the NRP, Sidia Jatta and Halifa Sallah, both leaders of the PDOIS, and Kemeseng Jammeh, of the UDP—subsequently lost an appeal against the decision at the Supreme Court, which declared their seats vacant as the NADD had been registered as a separate political party rather than an alliance of parties. Jatta, Sallah and Jammeh retained three of the four seats for the NADD at by-elections held in September, but Bah was defeated by the APRC candidate in the constituency of Upper Saloum. The NADD disputed the result in Upper Saloum, citing electoral irregularities.

In November 2005 Bah, Sallah and another senior member of the NADD, Omar Jallow, the Chairman of the PPP, were arrested. Sallah and Jallow were charged with sedition, while Bah was charged with the unauthorized possession of official documents. All three were released on bail in December, and in February 2006 they were acquitted when the state withdrew the charges against them. Their acquittal followed a meeting aimed at reconciliation between President Jammeh, other representatives of the APRC and opposition leaders, mediated by the Nigerian President, Olusegun Obasanjo, under the auspices of the Commonwealth, at which participants signed an electoral code of conduct ahead of the forthcoming presidential election and legislative polls due in early 2007. Meanwhile, divisions within the NADD leadership prompted the NRP and the UDP to withdraw from the movement and form a separate coalition. In March 2006 the NADD, now comprising the NDAM, the PDOIS and the PPP, announced that it had selected Sallah to be its presidential candidate. Darboe was to contest the election for the UDP-NRP coalition. The failure of the NADD and UDP-NRP candidates to defeat the APRC at a by-election in May led observers to suggest that only a united opposition could defeat Jammeh in the presidential election.

In late March 2006 the Gambian Government announced that the security forces had thwarted a plan by a group of army officers to overthrow the Government while President Jammeh was visiting Mauritania. More than 40 people were reportedly arrested in connection with the alleged coup plot, although its purported leader, the Chief of Staff of the Armed Forces, Lt-Col Ndure Cham, was believed to have fled to Senegal. The Gambian Government requested Senegalese assistance in detaining Cham, who had only been appointed as head of the armed forces in November 2005, after his predecessor, Lt-Col Sarr, was dismissed for allegedly mistreating soldiers. In early April 2006 it was announced that five detainees, including the former Director-General of the NIA, had escaped from custody while being transferred to another prison, although there was speculation that they may have been executed. Later that month Sheriff Dibba was dismissed as Speaker of the National Assembly and detained for several days on suspicion of complicity in the foiled coup; he was replaced as Speaker by Belinda Bidwell. In April 2007 a court martial convicted 10 military officers of involvement in the plot, sentencing them to prison terms ranging from 10 years to life.

Meanwhile, in July 2006 the Chairman of the IEC was unexpectedly dismissed, to be replaced by his deputy; no reason was given for his departure. The Gambia Party for Democracy and Progress joined the UDP-NRP coalition in August, after the presidential candidacy of its leader, Henry Gomez, was rejected by the IEC on the grounds that he did not meet a constitutional requirement to have resided in the country for at least five years. Meanwhile, opposition parties alleged that non-Gambian nationals were being registered to vote in the election; these voters, principally from the Senegalese province of Casamance, were expected to support Jammeh owing to ethnic allegiances.

Presidential and Legislative Elections

Jammeh was re-elected to a third term of office at the presidential election, which was held on 22 September 2006, winning 67.33% of the vote. Darboe secured 26.69% and Sallah 5.98%. The turn-out, at 58.6%, was considerably lower than that recorded in the 2001 election. None the less, Darboe alleged that unregistered voters had been allowed to cast ballots. A new Cabinet was appointed in late October, although many secretaries of state were retained from the previous administration.

Elections to the National Assembly took place on 25 January 2007. The ruling APRC secured 42 seats (including five unopposed), while the UDP won four seats, the NADD one seat and an independent candidate the remaining seat. Notably, Bah, Sallah and Kemeseng Jammeh were defeated by APRC candidates. The polls were again marked by a low rate of participation, reported to be 41.7%. Fatoumata Jahumpa-Ceesay replaced Bidwell as Speaker of the National Assembly in the following month. In April the opposition became further divided when the NDAM withdrew from the NADD.

FOREIGN RELATIONS

The Gambia maintains generally good relations with most countries in the region. Despite the presence in Senegal of prominent opponents of his regime, Jammeh has sought to improve relations with that country, and signed two agreements, in 1996 and 1997, aimed at increasing bilateral trade and at minimizing cross-border smuggling. In June 1997 the two countries agreed to take joint measures to combat insecurity, illegal immigration, arms-trafficking and drugs-smuggling. In January 1998 the Senegalese Government welcomed an offer by Jammeh to mediate in the conflict in the southern province of Casamance (see Recent History of Senegal): the separatist Mouvement des forces démocratiques de la Casamance (MFDC) is chiefly composed of the Diola ethnic group, of which Jammeh is a member. The Gambian Government subsequently took part in further initiatives to promote reconciliation in the province. At the end of 2002 there were some 4,230 refugees from Casamance registered with the office of the UN High Commissioner for Refugees (UNHCR) in The Gambia, although this number had declined to 548 by the end of 2003, and remained at this level at the end of 2005. However, an estimated 4,000 undocumented Senegalese refugees also remained in The Gambia. It was hoped that a peace agreement signed by the MFDC and the Senegalese Government in December 2004 would lead to an improvement in conditions in Casamance and the eventual repatriation of the refugees. However, in August 2006 UNHCR reported that more than 4,500 people had fled to The Gambia from Senegal that month following renewed fighting in Casamance between a faction of the MFDC and Senegalese government forces; some 1,600 Senegalese had crossed into The Gambia earlier that year.

Meanwhile, tensions arose between The Gambia and Senegal in August 2005 when The Gambia Ports Authority doubled the cost of using the ferry across the Gambia river. With the support of their Government, many Senegalese lorry drivers refused to pay the increased fare and blockaded the main border crossings between the two countries, adversely affecting regional trade. Despite a 15% reduction in the ferry tariff in October, Senegalese trade union leaders insisted that the blockade would continue. Later that month, however, at talks mediated by President Obasanjo of Nigeria, under the aegis of the Economic Community of West African States (ECOWAS), Jammeh agreed to reverse the price increase that took effect in August pending further consultations, while the Senegalese President, Abdoulaye Wade, pledged to end the blockade of the border. Agreement was also reached on the construction of a bridge over the Gambia river. In December the Gambian and Senegalese Governments decided that the bridge project should be a regional initiative, to be undertaken by the Gambia River Basin Development Organization. Plans for the establishment of a permanent secretariat for bilateral co-operation were also announced. Relations were again strained in March 2006, however, following allegations of Senegalese complicity in an abortive coup in The Gambia (see above). One of those arrested in connection with the plot reportedly claimed to have been instructed by Lt-Col Cham, the alleged leader of the coup, to liaise with the Senegalese embassy in Banjul. The Senegalese Government denied any involvement in the plot, which it condemned, and recalled its ambassador to The Gambia for consultations; a new ambassador was appointed in June.

In June 1998 Jammeh offered to mediate in the conflict between the Government and rebel forces, led by Brig. Ansumane Mané, in Guinea-Bissau. In January 1999 The Gambia agreed to provide troops for the ECOWAS Cease-fire Monitoring Group (ECOMOG) in Guinea-Bissau. After the defeat of government forces in Guinea-Bissau in May 1999, the Gambian authorities secured in June the safe passage of former President João Vieira to The Gambia on medical grounds, from where he departed for Portugal. The killing of Mané in December 2000 was widely regarded as a serious set-back for Gambian regional policy. In June 2002 the Gambian Government issued a statement refuting allegations made by the Guinea-Bissau President, Kumba Yalá, that Guinea-Bissau dissidents based in The Gambia had been involved in an attempted *coup d'état* in his country.

In January 2001 the Gambian Government denied that it was implicated, as stated in a UN report, in the illicit trafficking of diamonds to benefit dissident groups in Angola and Sierra Leone. The Gambia maintains particularly cordial relations with Nigeria, Libya and Taiwan, and in May 2004 a memorandum of understanding to promote economic and cultural co-operation was signed with Libya.

Relations with the United Kingdom were strained in 2001, following the expulsion of the British Deputy High Commissioner, Bharat Joshi, from The Gambia in late August. The Gambian authorities alleged that the diplomat had interfered in the country's internal affairs, following his attendance at an opposition meeting, but emphasized that the action had been taken against Joshi, and not the United Kingdom. However, in late September the Gambian Deputy High Commissioner in London was expelled from the United Kingdom, and further retaliatory measures were implemented against The Gambia. In January 2002 the EU representative, George Marc-André, was declared *persona non grata* by the Gambian authorities and requested to leave the country. The UN Development Programme's representative in Banjul was expelled from The Gambia in February 2007 after criticizing controversial claims made by President Jammeh that he had developed a cure for HIV/AIDS.

In September 2003 The Gambia contributed 150 troops to the ECOWAS Mission in Liberia (ECOMIL). In October the Gambian troops were transferred to a longer-term UN stabilization force, the UN Mission in Liberia (UNMIL), which replaced ECOMIL, with a mandate to support the implementation of a comprehensive peace agreement in that country. In December 2004 The Gambia contributed 196 troops to the African Union Mission in Sudan. At mid-2007 military personnel from The Gambia were also participating in UN peace-keeping operations in Côte d'Ivoire, and Ethiopia and Eritrea, as well as Liberia. At the end of 2005 there were 5,955 Sierra Leonean refugees and 780 Liberian refugees in The Gambia, according to UNHCR.

Economy

JOHN A. WISEMAN

Revised by the editorial staff

Apart from the development of a significant tourism industry, the principal features of the Gambian economy have altered relatively little in the post-independence period. The country has remained poor, underdeveloped and dependent. With a small population (of 1,663000 in mid-2006, according to UN estimates), high levels of illiteracy, no significant mineral resources, a poorly developed infrastructure and an erratic, arid climate, the prospects for dramatic economic development are slight. Official statistics on the economy have not been noted for their reliability, partly owing to administrative weakness and partly owing to a significant (and inherently unmeasurable) informal sector. More positively, in recent years there has been a moderate improvement in health and education provision, access to safe drinking water has widened, and life expectancy has increased, while infant mortality has declined. Most importantly, the country has, despite widespread poverty, avoided the famine and food insecurity experienced in many other African states.

AGRICULTURE AND FISHING

More than 70% of the Gambian population are directly dependent on agriculture for their livelihood, making this sector overwhelmingly the largest employer of labour, accounting for an estimated 77.7% of the labour force in 2004, according to FAO figures. Agriculture contributed 32.6% of gross domestic product (GDP) in 2005. For the most part, agricultural production is still organized through small-scale peasant units in which kinship predominates: over 90% of agricultural production is derived from this type of farming. Traditional patterns of shifting cultivation are widely used, and the bulk of production is for subsistence purposes. Large-scale plantation agriculture, whether privately operated or state-run, is minimal. The most crucial factor affecting agricultural production is the level of rainfall. Since the mid-1960s the country has experienced recurrent drought, of varying severity, which has adversely affected production levels and led to significant environmental degradation, especially the damage caused by the penetration of saline river water.

The predominant cash crop in The Gambia is groundnuts, first introduced from America in the 18th century. Groundnuts accounted for 28.7% of the value added by agriculture in 2005. Although the proportion of cultivated land devoted to groundnuts declined slowly for most of the 1990s, it began to increase again from 1997, and the area used to grow groundnuts in 2003, at 138,900 ha according to the IMF, was the largest recorded since independence. While the country produces less than 1% of the world's exported groundnuts, the national significance of the crop is immense. Some 20% of groundnut production is for domestic consumption by growers, the rest being cultivated for export, particularly in a processed form (groundnut-processing constitutes the major industrial activity). The cultivation of groundnuts is almost entirely undertaken by men, who therefore have major control over cash income in rural areas. In common with other crops, fluctuations in rainfall levels have a major effect on production levels from year to year. Additionally, the relative levels of official prices paid to producers in The Gambia and in neighbouring Senegal are a major determinant in groundnut sales. In years when producer prices are high in Senegal much of the Gambian crop is smuggled across the border into Senegal. Official statistics on groundnut production tend to be somewhat misleading. Even allowing for problems of measurements, the 1996 groundnut crop was reported to be the worst in living memory. Recorded production of 45,822 metric tons was little more than one-half that of 1995 and only about one-third of annual crops during the boom years of the 1970s. The dramatic decline was officially attributed to a number of factors, including poor seed varieties, low rainfall, shortage of fertilizers, bureaucratic inefficiency and labour shortages caused by migration to urban areas. Production recovered, however, from the late 1990s, as the area cultivated with groundnuts increased; the 2001 crop, of 151,100 tons, was the highest recorded since 1982, although, according to FAO, this figure declined by more than 50% in 2002, to just 71,500 tons, before recovering to 135,700 tons in 2004. FAO estimates that groundnut production subsequently contracted to some 100,000 tons in both 2005 and 2006. Groundnuts and groundnut products accounted for some 21.6% of total export earnings in 2002, but this figure declined to an estimated 13.3% in 2004. This decline became more dramatic in 2005 with groundnuts and groundnut products accounting for just 1.3% of total merchandise exports. While transport problems disrupted the processing of the groundnuts, the collapse in 2005 was partly due to changes in licensing requirement for the new crop season, which left a new company, the Gambian Agricultural Marketing Corporation, as the sole operator.

For subsistence purposes, rice is a more important crop than groundnuts. Most of the crop is consumed by producers and their families, although some is sold locally; the country remains a net importer of rice. Traditionally, rice has been grown (almost entirely by women) in the swamplands along the edge of the Gambia river, but since independence there have been several projects intended to expand pump-irrigated rice production, the majority of which were supported by foreign technical assistance. While increased rice production would provide the best route to the goal of self-sufficiency in basic foodstuffs, the rate of population growth has generally exceeded increases in output. Nevertheless, output in 2000, at 34,100 metric tons, was almost twice the level recorded in 1998, and was the largest crop recorded since 1982; low rainfall in 2002 led to an output of only 20,452 tons in that year, although FAO estimated an increase in output in 2004, to 32,600 tons. This figure was projected to have fallen to 17,934 tons in 2005, with a similar forecast for the following year.

Other important subsistence crops include millet (output of 84,618 metric tons in 2002 had risen to 127,563 tons in 2006), sorghum (production of 15,209 tons in 2002 rose to an estimated 30,499 tons in 2006) and cassava. In recent years there has been some expansion of fruit cultivation (bananas, mangoes, papayas and oranges) and horticulture. Produced mainly for subsistence purposes and local sales, fruit and vegetables accounted for an estimated 4.8% of export earnings in 2003. This figure collapsed in 2004, with fruit and vegetables accounting for a negligible amount of exports, increasing only marginally in 2005 when it represented under 0.1% of the total.

Livestock-rearing makes a contribution to subsistence in many parts of the country. Cattle, especially the more disease-resistant N'Dama strain, are an important source of meat, milk and hides. Most peasant farmers raise small numbers of goats, sheep and chickens. Fishing, largely using traditional methods, is an important source of local food, although the export of fish and fish products, which accounted for an estimated 2.6% of the value of total exports in 2002, made no recorded contribution to exports in 2004 and 2005. The total catch in 2005 was an estimated 32,000 metric tons.

The Gambia's overriding dependence on the groundnut sector remains an obstacle to sustained growth. The sector lags behind others in terms of modernization and productivity, although the gradual introduction of reforms, which sought to improve relations between public- and private-sector interests in the sector, commenced in 2000. In early 2006 African Development Bank projects, worth US $20.7m., to improve rice farming and irrigation were inaugurated.

TOURISM

The post-independence development of the tourism industry represents the most important and successful attempt at economic diversification and expansion in The Gambia. Prior to the 1994 *coup d'état* tourism had risen to become the country's largest source of foreign exchange. The industry began in 1965, but it was not until 1972 that its development was seriously undertaken by the Government, with the creation of 'tourism development areas'. Tourists initially came mainly from Sweden, but these were rapidly overtaken in numbers by British visitors, who came to constitute between one-third and one-half of tourist arrivals. Despite some diversification, the vast majority of tourists are still from north-western Europe. Tourism in The Gambia is mostly in the form of 'packages' organized by major western European (especially British) tour operators, whose decisions on whether or not to expand the promotion of tourism to The Gambia have a major impact on the development of the industry. The independent tourism sector has remained very small. Largely for climatic reasons, the main tourism season runs from October to April, during which time The Gambia has the considerable advantage of warm, dry conditions. Apart from rainfall in May–September, climatic disadvantages in this period include extreme heat and humidity, rendering The Gambia much less attractive to tourists. Attempts to promote off-season tourism have been generally ineffective, and most employees in the sector are thus laid off during these months. The rainy season marks the most active period in farming, but evidence suggests that very few workers in tourism return to farming during the tourism low-season. Despite its significant attractions for ornithologists and for those with an interest in African life and culture, The Gambia is mainly perceived by visitors as a 'beach' destination. Hotel development, to international standards, has therefore taken place mainly in the coastal areas and especially in the strip running from Bakau to Kotu Point. Attempts to attract tourists up-river for at least part of their stay have largely met with little success, apart from short day-trips organized by the hotels and tour companies. However, by 2003 some 10 camps for eco-tourism had been established, and in July of that year the former slaving fortress James Island was declared a UNESCO World Heritage Site. In a good year The Gambia might expect to receive up to 100,000 tourists, but actual numbers are sensitive to a number of factors, including economic conditions in western Europe and political uncertainty in The Gambia itself. A considerable amount of tourism-related employment lies in the informal sector, which is not amenable to statistical measurement. Although there are official, government-recognized tourist guides, there are very many more unofficial guides who make their living by providing a variety of services for tourists. Wood-carvers, silversmiths, potters, tailors, weavers and—especially—taxi drivers receive considerable income from tourism.

Inevitably, tourism is extremely vulnerable to political developments. The aftermath of the 1994 *coup d'état* posed serious problems for the sector. European tour operators had emphasized the image of the democratic stability of the country for many years, but this image was negated by the military's seizure of power. Following the November 1994 attempted coup, the British Government advised travellers that The Gambia was an 'unsafe' destination, and as a consequence most of the major British tour operators withdrew from the country; the Swedish and Danish Governments offered similar warnings. Although the official advice was changed by March 1995, tourist numbers for 1994/95, at some 43,000, were less than one-half of the level in 1993/94, causing the closure of many hotels and mass unemployment in the tourism sector. To compensate for the decline in arrivals from western Europe, the Government inaugurated an annual 'Roots Festival' in May 1996, designed to attract African-American visitors. During 1996/97 there was for the first time some success in attracting significant numbers of German tourists. In 1997 the volume of tourists began to return to pre-coup levels, reaching some 96,126 tourist arrivals (counting only those on air charter tours) in 1999. Arrivals had fallen to 57,231 by 2001, but increased to 90,095 by 2004, and again to 110,815 in 2005. The United Kingdom provided the greatest proportion of foreign visitors in 2004, with 53.6% of the total. The Gambia Tourist Authority was established in 2001, a Tourism Development Master Plan was implemented during 2003, partly funded by the African Development Bank. In 2003 tourism accounted for 6.6% of GDP.

FINANCE, AID AND TRADE

At independence the Gambian pound replaced the colonial West African Currency Board pound, at parity with sterling. This parity was maintained up to the inauguration of the Central Bank of The Gambia in March 1971. In July of that year the dalasi (divided into 100 butut) was adopted as the new national currency, with an exchange rate of D5 = £1. With minor adjustments this rate was retained until, as part of the Economic Recovery Programme (ERP—see below), the fixed exchange was abandoned and replaced by a floating rate. In recent years the dalasi has weakened considerably reaching a rate of D46.0 = £1 at 30 June 2003, and subsequently D54.9 = £1 at 30 April 2007, and there has been very little difference between official and informal rates (unlike in many sub-Saharan African countries, the latter is only slightly higher than the former).

Since independence The Gambia has been heavily dependent on external funding. Development assistance has frequently exceeded more than one-half of gross national income (GNI). Until the 1994 coup the major foreign donors were the European Union (EU), the USA, the United Kingdom, Canada, the Nordic countries, Japan, Saudi Arabia and the People's Republic of China. Opposition by most of the donor community to the imposition of military rule resulted in significant reductions in disbursements of development aid. The EU, for example, halved financial assistance (from US $20m. to $10m.), and announced that it had no plans to renew its aid programme until elected civilian government had been restored. Most bilateral aid programmes were either scaled down or abandoned. In an attempt to compensate for these losses, the Jammeh regime has tried to foster new sources of foreign assistance. Taiwan, notably, agreed to lend some $35m. following the restoration of diplomatic relations (severed in 1974) in July 1995. By 1998 Taiwan had become the country's biggest unilateral aid donor. (It was widely believed that The Gambia's accession to a non-permanent seat on the UN Security Council influenced this increase in Taiwanese assistance.) The Gambia was also reported to have received significant financial assistance from Libya upon the restoration of diplomatic relations in November 1994, and co-operation accords have, additionally, been signed with Cuba and with Iran. In March 2002 the USA finally lifted economic sanctions imposed on The Gambia following the 1994 *coup d'état*, and at the end of the year The Gambia's eligibility to benefit from favourable trading terms with the USA, under its African Growth and Opportunity Act (AGOA), in 2003 was confirmed. The country has continued to receive considerable amounts of aid from a wide variety of, mostly Western, non-governmental organizations; such aid is mainly targeted at projects designed to help the rural poor, although in June 2005 $4m. for urban poverty alleviation was made available by the International Development Association. In 2001 official development assistance and aid totalled some $51m., which represented 13.3% of GNI. A further source of external finance is the remittances of Gambians working abroad, mainly in western Europe and the USA, to their families in The Gambia. In mid-2005 The Gambia was one of nine 'second wave' countries deemed eligible for debt cancellation under the terms of the agreement reached by the Group of Eight industrialized nations (G-8) at a summit in Gleneagles, United Kingdom. This remained dependent on The Gambia fulfilling a number of criteria.

About one-third of The Gambia's GDP is derived from re-exports: goods imported into The Gambia under low import tariffs are then re-exported (not always in a legal manner) to other countries of the region, principally to Senegal, but also to Guinea, Guinea-Bissau and Mali. Some aspects of this trade are politically sensitive, and have periodically led to border problems with Senegal (see below). By the late 1990s political instability in Guinea-Bissau and in the Casamance region of Senegal was causing disruption in the re-export trade and was blamed, in the 1999 budget speech, for a 12% shortfall in tax revenue arising from decreases in import revenues associated with this trade. Export revenue increased from US $101.6m. in 2001 to $127.0m. in 2004, when re-exports accounted for some $101.2m. of revenue. Re-exports accounted for 91.9% of total merchandise exports in 2005, equivalent to $132.7m., according to preliminary IMF figures The principal market for exports in 2003 was the United Kingdom, while the principal source of imports was Germany.

ECONOMIC RESTRUCTURING

Having performed relatively strongly in the 10 years after independence, the Gambian economy then entered a decline, which reached crisis proportions in the mid-1980s. The balance of payments was in increasing deficit, leading to an accumulation of external payments' arrears and increased external borrowing. Government expenditure continued to expand, unsupported by a parallel expansion of state revenue. Increased government intervention in the economy through loan-guarantee schemes, extended parastatal activity, subsidized interest rates and exchange and price controls had the effect of distorting the economy. By 1984 The Gambia was unable to meet its obligations to the IMF, causing the latter to consider a ban on further drawings by the country. In response to this crisis, the Jawara administration adopted its ERP in August 1985: drawn up in consultation with, and with support from, the Bretton Woods institutions, this represented a significant attempt to restructure the Gambian economy, primarily by reducing unprofitable state involvement and liberalizing economic mechanisms. One of the first measures of the ERP was the flotation, in January 1986, of the dalasi; the creation of an inter-bank market for foreign exchange resulted in the devaluation of the national currency. There was a 120% depreciation in the first six months, with further falls recorded thereafter, until a de facto stabilization was achieved by the early 1990s. This policy resulted in the rechannelling of significant amounts of foreign exchange from the informal sector into the official sector. The ERP also entailed considerable retrenchment in the civil service, with the loss of about 20% of jobs in the government sector. Meanwhile, producer prices for groundnuts were increased, and these two measures went some way towards correcting the urban bias in the Gambian economy. The central bank first raised, then decontrolled, interest rates. Parastatal organizations were either privatized or subjected to strict financial discipline through performance contracts. For a time at least efforts were made to combat customs fraud, which led to an increase of one-third in revenue from such duties. The positive medium-term effects of the ERP included fiscal stabilization, significant reductions in inflation and higher rates of GDP growth. The programme for sustained development (PSD), inaugurated in 1990, was essentially a continuation of the economic policies of the ERP. The Gambia Produce Marketing Board, which had a monopoly over the purchase and export marketing of groundnuts from 1973 until 1990, and The Gambia Utilities Corpn were privatized under the PSD in 1993. However, the privatization programme stalled in 1994, and was further reversed in 1999 with the expropriation of The Gambia Groundnut Corpn (GGC) from Swiss-owned Alimenta. A settlement reached with Alimenta in 2001 and the formation of The Gambia Divestiture Agency enabled the continuation of privatization in 2003. The resale of the GGC is a criterion for the 'floating' completion point of debt relief under the initiative for heavily indebted poor countries (HIPC, see below).

Although, as noted above, the Gambian economy was damaged by reductions in foreign aid and the temporary collapse of the tourism industry following the military takeover, the Jammeh regime has not pursued any significant reversals of macroeconomic policy, and has consistently pledged its commitment to free-market capitalism. Following a decline of 4.0% in 1994/95, GDP was estimated to have increased by 3.1% in 1995/96—largely reflecting the partial recovery in tourist numbers—and by 2.1% in 1996/97. Currency exchange rates remained relatively stable following the *coup d'état*, with only minor depreciations against the US dollar and the pound sterling. Despite the apparent stabilization of the economy in the post-coup period, there has been criticism in some quarters of the new regime's enthusiasm for ambitious infrastructural and other 'prestige' projects, which have been mostly financed by international loans. At the end of 2002 The Gambia's long-term debt stood at US $503.6m., equivalent to 163.8% of GNI, while the debt-service ratio was 6.4%. The Government's long-term aim, outlined in its *Vision 2020* document published in September 1996, setting targets for all sectors of the economy, for education, health care, welfare, the environment and public administration, is to achieve the status of a middle-income economy by 2020.

Crucial support for the Gambian economy came from the IMF, which in mid-1998 approved funding under its Enhanced Structural Adjustment Facility (ESAF) for 1998–2000. The programme, which subsequently operated under the terms of the Poverty Reduction and Growth Facility (PRGF), aimed to achieve real GDP growth averaging some 4.5% annually, and to restrict average inflation to 3% per year. The fiscal deficit (excluding grants) was to be reduced to the equivalent of 1.9% of GDP by the end of the period covered by the PRGF (although this figure was subsequently revised to 5.9%), from the equivalent of 7.8% of GDP in 1997, while the deficit on the current account of the balance of payments (before official transfers) was to be maintained at about 10% of GDP. A fundamental aim of the programme was to encourage further private-sector development: to this end, the Government had undertaken in the 1998 budget to sign binding agreements with several parastatals, notably the port authority, public transport corporation, social security and housing fund and the telecommunications and utilities operators, to reduce the role of the state on condition of the attainment of certain performance criteria. The Government's decision to take over the struggling GGC was therefore criticized by the IMF as injurious to the programme's stated aim of increasing the role of the private sector and of enhancing investor confidence in The Gambia. Indeed, the increased budgetary expenditure associated with repayments resulting from the seizure of the company's property was regarded as being a major contributory factor in the failure to reach the PRGF targets on the fiscal deficit in 2001. In the event, although the fiscal deficit declined to the equivalent of 3.6% of GDP in 2000, in 2001 it increased to 8.7%; notably, the state-owned telecommunications company and one of the two water and electricity distribution companies owed tax arrears amounting to a total of D59m. As a result of legislation approved by the National Assembly in 2001, The Gambia Divestiture Agency was established to oversee the privatization programme. In the same year The Gambia Investment Promotion and Free Zones Agency was established to encourage private investment in the country, especially in the underdeveloped manufacturing sector. A US $16m. loan from the World Bank was granted in 2002 to develop a Free Zone at Banjul International Airport as part of The Gambia Trade Gateway Project. In December 2000 it was announced that The Gambia was to receive $91m. in debt-service relief under the terms of the HIPC initiative of the World Bank and the IMF. In June 2002 the Government presented a Poverty Reduction Strategy Paper, and a further PRGF, for the period 2002–05, equivalent to $27m., was agreed with the IMF in the following month. In December 2003 the IMF suspended PRGF assistance to The Gambia, however, owing to concerns regarding concealed government spending. The principal objectives of the PRGF were to maintain real GDP growth of some 6% annually, to limit inflation to below 4% annually and to reduce the overall deficit (excluding grants) to some 2% of GDP by 2005. In January 2003 The Gambia became eligible for funding under the AGOA. In December 2004 the Government repaid two non-complying disbursements worth $10.1m. that had been requested by the IMF. A staff-monitored programme, designed to improve growth and reduce poverty, was successfully completed in March 2006, and a new three-year PRGF was approved in February 2007.

Overall GDP increased, in real terms, at an average annual rate of 5.2% in 1995–2006; GDP increased by 6.5% in 2006, and the IMF estimated growth of 7.0% would be achieved in 2007. In 2006 the deficit in the current account of the balance of payments was US $73m., equivalent to 14.3% of GDP. This figure was estimated by the IMF to fall marginally to $72m. the following year.

The budget for 2007, presented to the National Assembly in December 2006, anticipated revenue of D3,342.7m., over 90% of which would be derived from tax revenue. It was anticipated that expenditure and net lending would amount to D4,408.3m., leaving a projected deficit of D1,065.6m. Inflation had reached 17.0% in 2003 when the IMF suspended the PRGF. This figure was reduced substantially in the following years, to 3.2% in 2005 and to 1.5% in 2006. The IMF anticipated that inflation would increase to 3.2% in 2007.

ECONOMIC RELATIONS WITH SENEGAL

The formal dissolution, in September 1989, of the Senegambia confederation (see Recent History), and subsequent allegations regarding Senegal's economic 'harassment' of The Gambia, raised serious questions regarding future economic relations between the two countries. During 1990 the Senegalese authorities eased restrictions on cross-border traffic, and the conclusion, in January 1991, of a new co-operation treaty confirmed several existing bilateral agreements governing such areas as defence and security, transport and telecommunications, health, trade, fishing, agriculture and energy.

Economic relations with Senegal did not improve following the imposition of military rule in The Gambia. Although Jammeh announced that the Senegalese restrictions on cross-border trade, in force since September 1993, were to be revoked following a visit to Senegal in September 1994, this failed to materialize. In retaliation, in April 1995 the Gambian authorities raised the tolls on the Yellitenda–Bambatenda ferry (Senegal's main link with its southern province of Casamance) by 1,000% for Senegalese vehicles, effectively forcing these to use the much longer Tambacounda route; the increase was, however, abandoned in June. In January 1996 the Senegalese and Gambian Governments agreed to end restrictions on cross-border trade between the two countries, subject to the implementation of measures designed to prevent smuggling. A further agreement, concluded in April 1997, was to facilitate trans-border movement of goods destined for re-export. A dispute between the two countries arose in August 2005 when the Gambian authorities increased the cost of crossing the Gambia river at Banjul by ferry; in retaliation Senegalese lorry drivers commenced a blockade of the common border. The conflict was resolved in October, under the mediation of the Nigerian President, Olusegun Obasanjo, and an agreement was reached to construct a bridge over the Gambia river. Both countries have maintained their membership of the sub-regional Gambia River Basin Development Organization, to which Guinea and Guinea-Bissau also belong. This organization is principally concerned with promoting development by means of regional co-operation and the joint exploitation of shared natural resources.

Statistical Survey

Sources (unless otherwise stated): Department of Information Services, 14 Daniel Goddard St, Banjul; tel. 4225060; fax 4227230; Central Statistics Department, Central Bank Building, 1/2 Ecowas Ave, Banjul; tel. 4228364; fax 4228903; e-mail director@csd.gm; internet www.gambia.gm/Statistics/statistics.html.

Area and Population

AREA, POPULATION AND DENSITY

Area (sq km)	11,295*
Population (census results)	
15 April 1993	1,038,145
15 April 2003†	
Males	687,781
Females	676,726
Total	1,364,507
Population (UN estimate at mid-year)‡	
2004	1,571,000
2005	1,617,000
2006	1,663,000
Density (per sq km) at mid-2006	147.2

* 4,361 sq miles.
† Provisional.
‡ Source: UN, *World Population Prospects: The 2006 Revision*.

ETHNIC GROUPS

1993 census (percentages): Mandinka 39.60; Fula 18.83; Wolof 14.61; Jola 10.66; Serahule 8.92; Serere 2.77; Manjago 1.85; Bambara 0.84; Creole/Aku 0.69; Others 1.23.

ADMINISTRATIVE DIVISIONS
(population at 2003 census, provisional results)

Banjul	34,828	Kanifing	322,410
Basse	183,033	Kerewan	172,806
Brikama	392,987	Kuntaur	79,098
Georgetown	106,799	Mansakonko	72,546

PRINCIPAL TOWNS
(population at 1993 census)

Serrekunda	151,450	Lamin	10,668
Brikama	42,480	Gunjur	9,983
Banjul (capital)	42,407	Basse	9,265
Bakau	38,062	Soma	7,925
Farafenni	21,142	Bansang	5,405
Sukuta	16,667		

Mid-2005 (incl. suburbs, UN estimate): Banjul 381,000 (Source: UN, *World Urbanization Prospects: The 2005 Revision*).

BIRTHS AND DEATHS
(annual averages, UN estimates)

	1990–95	1995–2000	2000–05
Birth rate (per 1,000)	42.7	40.6	38.1
Death rate (per 1,000)	14.1	12.3	11.2

Source: UN, *World Population Prospects: The 2006 Revision*.

Expectation of life (years at birth, WHO estimates): 57 (males 55; females 59) in 2004 (Source: WHO, *World Health Report*).

ECONOMICALLY ACTIVE POPULATION*
(persons aged 10 years and over, 1993 census)

	Males	Females	Total
Agriculture, hunting and forestry	82,886	92,806	175,692
Fishing	5,610	450	6,060
Mining and quarrying	354	44	398
Manufacturing	18,729	2,953	21,682
Electricity, gas and water supply	1,774	84	1,858
Construction	9,530	149	9,679
Wholesale and retail trade; repair of motor vehicles, motorcycles and personal and household goods	33,281	15,460	48,741
Hotels and restaurants	3,814	2,173	5,987
Transport, storage and communications	13,421	782	14,203
Financial intermediation	1,843	572	2,415
Other community, social and personal service activities	25,647	15,607	41,254
Activities not adequately defined	10,421	6,991	17,412
Total labour force	207,310	138,071	345,381

* Figures exclude persons seeking work for the first time, but include other unemployed persons.

Mid-2004 (estimates in '000): Agriculture, etc. 577; Total labour force 743 (Source: FAO).

Health and Welfare

KEY INDICATORS

Total fertility rate (children per woman, 2005)	4.5
Under-5 mortality rate (per 1,000 live births, 2005)	137
HIV/AIDS (% of persons aged 15–49, 2005)	2.4
Physicians (per 1,000 head, 2003)	0.11
Hospital beds (per 1,000 head, 2005)	0.8
Health expenditure (2004): US $ per head (PPP)	87.5
Health expenditure (2004): % of GDP	6.8
Health expenditure (2004): public (% of total)	27.1
Access to water (% of persons, 2004)	82
Access to sanitation (% of persons, 2004)	53
Human Development Index (2004): ranking	155
Human Development Index (2004): value	0.479

For sources and definitions, see explanatory note on p. vi.

Agriculture

PRINCIPAL CROPS
('000 metric tons)

	2003	2004	2005
Rice (paddy)	20.5*	32.6*	17.9
Maize	33.4	29.2	29.0
Millet	120.3	132.5	127.6
Sorghum	30.1	29.0	30.5
Cassava (Manioc)†	7.5	7.5	7.5
Pulses†	3.2	3.2	3.2
Groundnuts (in shell)	92.9	135.7	100.0
Oil palm fruit†	35.0	35.0	35.0
Other vegetables†	9.0	9.0	9.0
Mangoes†	0.6	0.6	0.6
Other fruits†	3.6	3.6	3.6

* Unofficial estimate.
† FAO estimates.

Source: FAO.

LIVESTOCK
('000 head, year ending September, FAO estimates)

	2003	2004	2005
Cattle	327.0	328.0	330.0
Goats	262.0	265.0	270.0
Sheep	146.0	147.0	148.0
Pigs	17.5	17.8	19.0
Asses, mules or hinnies	35.0	35.0	35.0
Horses	17.0	17.0	17.0
Chickens	600	620	650

Source: FAO.

LIVESTOCK PRODUCTS
('000 metric tons, FAO estimates)

	2003	2004	2005
Cattle meat	3.2	3.2	3.2
Goat meat	0.7	0.7	0.7
Sheep meat	0.4	0.4	0.4
Chicken meat	0.9	0.9	1.0
Game meat	1.0	1.0	1.0
Cows' milk	7.6	7.6	7.7
Hen eggs	0.7	0.7	0.7

Source: FAO.

Forestry

ROUNDWOOD REMOVALS
('000 cubic metres, excluding bark, FAO estimates)

	2003	2004	2005
Sawlogs, veneer logs and logs for sleepers*	106	106	106
Other industrial wood†	7	7	7
Fuel wood	629	638	647
Total	742	751	760

* Assumed to be unchanged since 1994.
† Assumed to be unchanged since 1993.

Source: FAO.

Fishing

('000 metric tons, live weight of capture)

	2003	2004	2005
Tilapias	1.1	1.1	1.1
Hairtails, scabbardfishes, etc.	0.0	4.0	3.0
Sea catfishes	0.7	0.8	0.8
Bonga shad	22.1	16.8	18.0
Sharks, rays, skates	1.1	0.5	0.5
Total catch*	36.9	31.4	32.0

* FAO estimates.

Source: FAO.

Mining

	2003	2004*	2005*
Clay (metric tons)	12,375	13,655	13,700
Laterites (metric tons)	227	245	250
Silica sand ('000 metric tons)	1,534	1,389	1,390
Zircon (metric tons)	13†	—	—

* Estimate.
† Data derived from sales figures.

Source: US Geological Survey.

Industry

SELECTED PRODUCTS
('000 metric tons, unless otherwise stated)

	2003	2004	2005
Palm oil—unrefined*	2.5	2.5	2.5
Groundnut oil*	24.0	38.5	34.8
Beer of millet*	50.4	55.4	55.4
Electric energy (million kWh)†	150.3	128.1	156.3

* FAO estimates.
† State Department for Trade, Industry and Employment.

Source: mainly FAO.

Finance

CURRENCY AND EXCHANGE RATES

Monetary Units
100 butut = 1 dalasi (D).

Sterling, Dollar and Euro Equivalents (30 April 2007)
£1 sterling = 54.8515 dalasi;
US $1 = 27.5000 dalasi;
€1 = 37.4137 dalasi;
1,000 dalasi = £18.23 = $36.36 = €26.73.

Average Exchange Rate (dalasi per US $)
2004 30.030
2005 28.575
2006 28.066

BUDGET
(million dalasi)

Revenue*	2003	2004	2005
Tax revenue	1,380.7	2,244.7	2,263.2
Direct taxes	441.0	606.3	682.5
Taxes on personal incomes	154.2	207.2	231.1
Taxes on corporate profits	265.8	367.1	406.6
Indirect taxes	939.7	1,638.4	1,580.8
Domestic taxes on goods and services	205.7	291.4	374.5
Taxes on international trade	734.0	1,347.0	1,206.2
Non-tax revenue	193.5	273.1	340.1
Total	1,574.2	2,517.8	2,603.4

Expenditure†	2003	2004	2005
Current expenditure	1,707.0	2,035.8	2,420.4
Wages and salaries	452.6	517.5	554.0
Other goods and services	594.5	583.8	735.6
Interest payments	607.6	867.9	1,130.9
Internal	444.2	633.3	890.1
External	163.4	234.6	240.8
Capital expenditure	608.3	1,733.5	1,449.6
Gambia Local Fund	57.2	88.8	106.3
External loans	340.7	1,121.3	1,138.3
External grants	132.0	395.7	203.0
Total	2,315.3	3,769.3	3,870.0

* Excluding grants received (million dalasi): 246.2 in 2003; 547.2 in 2004; 220.1 in 2005.

† Excluding lending minus repayments (million dalasi): −22.6 in 2003; −23.4 in 2004; −30.4 in 2005.

Source: IMF, *The Gambia: Selected Issues and Statistical Appendix* (March 2007).

INTERNATIONAL RESERVES

(US $ million at 31 December)

	2004	2005	2006
IMF special drawing rights	0.75	0.16	1.46
Reserve position in IMF	2.31	2.12	2.23
Foreign exchange	80.72	96.03	116.92
Total	83.77	98.31	120.61

Source: IMF, *International Financial Statistics*.

MONEY SUPPLY

(million dalasi at 31 December)

	2004	2005	2006
Currency outside banks	1,416.27	1,424.20	1,937.30
Demand deposits at commercial banks	1,691.34	1,896.41	2,248.10
Total money	3,107.61	3,320.61	4,185.40

Source: IMF, *International Financial Statistics*.

COST OF LIVING

(Consumer Price Index for Banjul and Kombo St Mary's; base: 1974 = 100)

	1997	1998	1999
Food	1,511.8	1,565.8	1,628.8
Fuel and light	2,145.8	1,854.9	2,076.0
Clothing*	937.5	981.8	999.9
Rent	1,409.6	1,431.3	1,428.6
All items (incl. others)	1,441.5	1,457.3	1,512.8

* Including household linen.

All items (Consumer Price Index for Banjul and Kombo St Mary's; base: 2000 = 100): 132.8 in 2003; 151.7 in 2004; 156.4 in 2005. (Source: ILO).

NATIONAL ACCOUNTS

(million dalasi at current prices)

Expenditure on the Gross Domestic Product

	2003	2004	2005
Government final consumption expenditure	877.7	986.2	1,310.9
Private final consumption expenditure	8,121.6	9,913.7	10,999.7
Increase in stocks Gross fixed capital formation	1,953.6	3,259.7	3,464.7
Total domestic expenditure	10,952.9	14,159.5	15,775.3
Exports of goods and services	4,739.3	6,067.5	6,815.8
Less Imports of goods and services	5,666.3	8,190.5	9,215.3
Statistical discrepancy	—	—	195.9
GDP in purchasers' values	10,025.9	12,036.6	13,179.9
GDP at constant 1976/77 prices	809.1	850.1	892.4

Gross Domestic Product by Economic Activity

	2003	2004	2005
Agriculture, hunting, forestry and fishing	2,822.4	3,610.0	3,899.6
Manufacturing	485.4	582.8	617.9
Electricity and water	123.7	117.4	128.9
Construction and mining	665.1	751.0	818.5
Trade	1,012.7	1,151.3	1,230.4
Restaurants and hotels	611.4	753.1	836.3
Transport and communications	1,740.8	2,073.9	2,404.7
Real estate and business services	567.1	658.6	714.2
Government services	712.9	810.0	872.5
Other services	344.8	400.5	421.6
GDP at factor cost	9,086.3	10,908.5	11,944.7
Indirect taxes, *less* subsidies	939.7	1,128.1	1,235.3
GDP in purchasers' values	10,025.9	12,036.6	13,179.9

Source: IMF, *The Gambia: Selected Issues and Statistical Appendix* (March 2007).

BALANCE OF PAYMENTS

(US $ million, year ending 30 June)

	2003	2004	2005
Exports of goods f.o.b.	77.63	109.16	100.98
Imports of goods f.o.b.	−156.37	−207.24	−215.47
Trade balance	−78.74	−98.08	−114.49
Exports of services	83.84	73.14	79.58
Imports of services	−36.26	−45.72	−45.38
Balance on goods and services	−31.17	−70.66	−80.30
Other income received	4.70	1.78	3.13
Other income paid	−31.94	−29.57	−35.37
Balance on goods, services and income	−58.40	−98.45	−112.54
Current transfers received	88.92	78.23	88.01
Current transfers paid	−32.91	−24.24	−25.90
Current balance	−2.39	−44.46	−50.44
Capital account (net)	4.80	5.15	0.58
Direct investment from abroad	21.90	56.75	51.93
Other investment assets	−19.64	−15.37	13.60
Investment liabilities	−12.10	5.56	2.93
Net errors and omissions	2.52	−8.88	−54.32
Overall balance	−4.90	−1.24	−35.73

Source: IMF, *International Financial Statistics*.

External Trade

PRINCIPAL COMMODITIES
(US $ '000)

Imports c.i.f.	2002	2003	2004
Food and live animals	37,581	40,456	64,687
Beverages and tobacco	8,231	8,592	12,374
Mineral fuels, lubricants, etc.	17,008	21,777	23,921
Animal and vegetable oils	6,078	6,104	11,404
Chemicals	16,201	9,965	17,414
Machinery and transport equipment	27,262	26,325	42,778
Miscellaneous manufactured articles	15,563	14,559	24,536
Total (incl. others)	160,105	152,607	236,604

2005: Total imports (US $ '000) 279,657.

Exports f.o.b.	2003	2004	2005*
Groundnut products	9,143	16,896	1,860
Fruit and vegetables	5,100	6	77
Fish and fish products	421	—	—
Cotton products	235	6,045	6,683
Total (incl. others†)	106,986	127,044	144,465

* Preliminary figures.
† Of which, re-exports: 83,454 in 2003; 101,190 in 2004; 132,733 in 2005.

Source: IMF, *The Gambia: Selected Issues and Statistical Appendix* (March 2007).

PRINCIPAL TRADING PARTNERS
(US $ million)

Imports c.i.f.	2001	2002	2003
Belgium	6.1	4.1	4.3
Brazil	5.4	7.9	5.9
China, People's Repub.	8.6	6.6	8.3
Côte d'Ivoire	10.7	5.7	5.1
Cyprus	2.1	0.5	1.8
Denmark	1.2	1.3	3.3
France (incl. Monaco)	8.2	8.0	10.2
Germany	34.3	61.2	58.8
Hong Kong	3.7	2.2	3.9
India	2.7	3.8	5.7
Italy	2.1	2.1	2.9
Japan	2.8	4.0	2.4
Netherlands	7.9	3.3	4.5
Senegal	2.4	6.9	7.5
Singapore	0.3	0.9	2.2
Spain	3.1	3.8	3.2
Thailand	0.3	3.2	0.5
Turkey	0.8	0.5	1.8
United Arab Emirates	1.1	0.9	2.3
United Kingdom	13.7	15.9	16.8
USA	3.9	7.2	3.4
Viet Nam	1.6	0.0	0.0
Total (incl. others)	132.3	156.3	162.6

Exports f.o.b.	2001	2002	2003
Belgium	0.8	0.1	0.0
China, People's Repub.	0.0	0.0	0.5
France (incl. Monaco)	2.2	0.0	0.1
Germany	0.1	0.1	0.5
Guinea	0.4	0.1	0.0
Guinea-Bissau	0.0	0.1	0.0
Hong Kong	0.0	0.0	0.1
Italy	0.0	0.4	0.9
India	0.0	0.0	0.1
Netherlands	0.0	0.1	0.4
Portugal	0.1	0.0	0.0
Senegal	0.2	0.3	0.2
Sierra Leone	0.1	0.4	0.1
Spain	0.5	0.2	0.2
Switzerland-Liechtenstein	0.0	1.2	0.0
United Kingdom	1.7	0.5	1.2
Total (incl. others)	6.3	3.8	5.1

Source: UN, *International Trade Statistics Yearbook*.

2005 (percentage of total): *Imports:* China, People's Republic 21.3; Côte d'Ivoire 8.4; Hong Kong 1.5; India 2.9; Japan 0.6; Senegal 11.3; Thailand 2.5; USA 5.3. *Exports* China, People's Republic 0.6; Ghana 1.3; Guinea 1.0; Guinea-Bissau 2.1; Hong Kong 0.6; India 40.4; Japan 2.2; Senegal 4.6; Thailand 3.7; USA 1.0 (Source: IMF, *The Gambia: Selected Issues and Statistical Appendix*—March 2007).

Transport

ROAD TRAFFIC
(motor vehicles in use, estimates)

	2002	2003	2004
Passenger cars	7,919	8,168	8,109
Buses	2,261	1,300	1,200
Lorries and vans	1,531	1,862	1,761

Source: IRF, *World Road Statistics*.

SHIPPING

Merchant Fleet
(registered at 31 December)

	2003	2004	2005
Number of vessels	9	13	13
Total displacement (grt)	2,183	33,159	33,159

Source: Lloyd's Register-Fairplay, *World Fleet Statistics*.

International Sea-borne Freight Traffic
('000 metric tons)

	1996	1997	1998
Goods loaded	55.9	38.1	47.0
Goods unloaded	482.7	503.7	493.2

CIVIL AVIATION
(traffic on scheduled services)

	1992	1993	1994
Kilometres flown (million)	1	1	1
Passengers carried ('000)	19	19	19
Passenger-km (million)	50	50	50
Total ton-km (million)	5	5	5

Source: UN, *Statistical Yearbook*.

Tourism

FOREIGN VISITORS BY COUNTRY OF ORIGIN*

	2002	2003	2004
Belgium	4,268	1,707	4,961
Denmark	2,260	2,616	1,997
Germany	3,707	4,253	2,891
Netherlands	10,419	7,262	13,112
Norway	711	999	5,513
Sweden	5,594	4,205	3,954
United Kingdom	48,894	40,872	48,297
USA	866	445	3,059
Total (incl. others)	81,005	73,485	90,095

* Air charter tourist arrivals.

Receipts from tourism (US $ million, incl. passenger transport): 48 in 2002; 51 in 2003; 59 in 2004.

Source: World Tourism Organization.

2005: Total foreign visitors 110,815 (Source: Source: IMF, *The Gambia: Selected Issues and Statistical Appendix*—March 2007).

Communications Media

	2003	2004	2005
Telephones ('000 main lines in use)	38.4	38.4	44.0
Mobile cellular telephones ('000 subscribers)	149.3	175.0	247.5
Personal computers ('000 in use)	21	23	23
Internet users ('000)	35	49	49

Television receivers (number in use): 4,000 in 2000.

Radio receivers ('000 in use): 196 in 1997.

Facsimile machines (number in use, year ending 31 March): 1,149 in 1997/98.

Daily newspapers: 1 in 1998 (average circulation 2,100 copies).

Non-daily newspapers: 4 in 1996 (estimated average circulation 6,000 copies).

Book production: 10 titles in 1998 (10,000 copies).

Sources: UNESCO Institute for Statistics; UNESCO, *Statistical Yearbook*; UN, *Statistical Yearbook*; International Telecommunication Union.

Education

(2004/05)

	Institutions	Teachers	Students		
			Males	Females	Total
Primary	402	4,819	91,741	89,241	180,982
Junior Secondary	160	1,004	30,173	26,892	57,065
Senior Secondary	49	409	16,740	11,795	28,535

Source: Department of State for Education, Banjul.

Adult literacy rate (UNESCO estimates): 37.8% (males 45.0%; females 30.9%) in 2002 (Source: UN Development Programme, *Human Development Report*).

Directory

The Constitution

Following the *coup d'état* of July 1994, the 1970 Constitution was suspended and the presidency and legislature, as defined therein, dissolved. A Constitutional Review Commission was inaugurated in April 1995; the amended document was approved in a national referendum on 8 August. The Constitution of the Second Republic of The Gambia entered into full effect on 16 January 1997.

Decrees issued during the transition period (1994–96) are deemed to have been approved by the National Assembly and remain in force so long as they do not contravene the provisions of the Constitution of the Second Republic.

The Constitution provides for the separation of the powers of the executive, legislative and judicial organs of state. The Head of State is the President of the Republic, who is directly elected by universal adult suffrage. No restriction is placed on the number of times a President may seek re-election. Legislative authority is vested in the National Assembly, comprising 48 members elected by direct universal suffrage and five members nominated by the President of the Republic. The Speaker and Deputy Speaker of the Assembly are elected, by the members of the legislature, from among the President's nominees. The Constitution upholds the principle of executive accountability to parliament. Thus, the Head of State appoints government members, but these are responsible both to the President and to the National Assembly. Ministers of cabinet rank take the title of Secretary of State. Committees of the Assembly have powers to inquire into the activities of ministers and of government departments, and into all matters of public importance.

In judicial affairs, the final court of appeal is the Supreme Court. Provision is made for a special criminal court to hear and determine all cases relating to the theft and misappropriation of public funds.

The Constitution provides for an Independent Electoral Commission, an Independent National Audit Office, an Office of the Ombudsman, a Lands Commission and a Public Service Commission, all of which are intended to ensure transparency, accountability and probity in public affairs.

The Constitution guarantees the rights of women, of children and of the disabled. Tribalism and other forms of sectarianism in politics are forbidden. Political activity may be suspended in the event of a state of national insecurity.

The Government

HEAD OF STATE

President: Col (retd) Alhaji Yahya A. J. J. Jammeh (proclaimed Head of State 26 July 1994; elected President 26 September 1996, re-elected 18 October 2001 and 22 September 2006).

Vice-President: Isatou Njie-Saidy.

THE CABINET
(August 2007)

President: Col (retd) Alhaji Yahya A. J. J. Jammeh.

Vice-President and Secretary of State for Women's Affairs: Isatou Njie-Saidy.

Secretary of State for Finance and Economic Affairs: Musa Gibril Bala Gaye.

Secretary of State for Foreign Affairs: Balla Garba-Jahumpa.

Secretary of State for the Interior: Maj. (retd) Ousman Sonko.

Secretary of State for Justice and Attorney-General: Kebba Sanyang.

Secretary of State for Agriculture: Kanja Sanneh.

Secretary of State for Fisheries and Water Resources: YANKOUBA TOURAY.

Secretary of State for Forestry and the Environment: Capt. (retd) EDWARD DAVID SINGHATEY.

Secretary of State for Health and Social Welfare: Dr TAMSIR MBOWE.

Secretary of State for Local Government and Lands: ISMAILA K. SAMBOU.

Secretary of State for Education: FATOU L. FAYE.

Secretary of State for Higher Education and Research: CRISPIN GREY-JOHNSON.

Secretary of State for Tourism and Culture: ANGELA COLLEY.

Secretary of State for Communication, Information and Technology: NENEH MACDOUALL-GAYE.

Secretary of State for Trade, Industry and Employment: ABDOU KOLLEY.

Secretary of State for Youth, Sports and Religious Affairs: Sheikh OMAR FAYE.

DEPARTMENTS OF STATE

Office of the President: PMB, State House, Banjul; tel. 4223811; fax 4227034; e-mail info@statehouse.gm; internet www.statehouse.gm.

Office of the Vice-President: State House, Banjul; tel. 4227605; fax 4224012; e-mail vicepresident@statehouse.gm.

Department of State for Agriculture: The Quadrangle, Banjul; tel. 228291; fax 223578.

Department of State for Communication, Information and Technology: Half-Die, Banjul; tel. 4227668; e-mail amjanneh@aol.com.

Department of State for Education: Willy Thorpe Bldg, Banjul; tel. 4227236; fax 4224180; internet www.edugambia.gm.

Department of State for Finance and Economic Affairs: The Quadrangle, POB 9686, Banjul; tel. 4228291; fax 4227954.

Department of State for Fisheries and Water Resources: 5 Marina Parade, Banjul; tel. 4228702; fax 4228628.

Department of State for Foreign Affairs: 4 Col. Muammar Ghadaffi Ave, Banjul; tel. 4223577; fax 4223578.

Department of State for Health and Social Welfare: The Quadrangle, Banjul; tel. 4225712; fax 4223178; e-mail dpi@dosh.gm.

Department of State for Higher Education and Research: Banjul.

Department of State for the Interior: ECOWAS Ave, Banjul; tel. 4228511; fax 4223063.

Department of State for Justice and Attorney-General's Chambers: Marina Parade, Banjul; tel. 4228181; fax 4225352; e-mail sthydara@hotmail.com.

Department of State for Local Government and Lands: The Quadrangle, Banjul; tel. 4228291.

Department of State for Tourism and Culture: New Administrative Bldg, The Quadrangle, Banjul; tel. 4227593; fax 4227753; e-mail masterplan@gamtel.gm.

Department of State for Trade, Industry and Employment: Central Bank Bldg, Independence Dr., Banjul; tel. 4228868; fax 4227756; e-mail tiewebmaster@qanet.gm; internet www.gambia.gm.

Department of State for Youth, Sports and Religious Affairs: The Quadrangle, Banjul; tel. 4225264; fax 4225267; e-mail dosy-s@qanet.gm.

President and Legislature

PRESIDENT

Presidential Election, 22 September 2006

Candidate	Votes	% of votes
Yahya A. J. J. Jammeh (APRC)	264,404	67.33
Ousainou N. Darboe (UDP)	104,808	26.69
Halifa Sallah (NADD)	23,473	5.98
Total	392,685	100.00

NATIONAL ASSEMBLY

Speaker: FATOUMATA JAHUMPA-CEESAY.

National Assembly: Parliament Buildings, Independence Dr., Banjul; tel. 4227241; fax 4225123; e-mail assemblyclerk@yahoo.com; internet www.nationalassembly.gm.

General Election, 25 January 2007

Party	Seats
Alliance for Patriotic Reorientation and Construction (APRC)	42
United Democratic Party (UDP)	4
National Alliance for Democracy and Development (NADD)	1
Independent	1
Total	48*

* The President of the Republic is empowered by the Constitution to nominate five additional members of parliament. The total number of members of parliament is thus 53.

Election Commission

Independent Electoral Commission (IEC): 7 Kairaba Ave, Latrikunda, Kanifing, POB 793, Banjul; tel. 4373804; fax 4373803; e-mail info@iec.gm; internet www.iec.gm; f. 1997; Chair. Alhaji MUSTAPHA CARAYOL.

Political Organizations

In 2006 eight parties were registered with the Independent Electoral Commission (IEC). In that year the most active parties included:

Alliance for Patriotic Reorientation and Construction (APRC): Gambisara White House, Kairaba Ave, Banjul; tel. 4377550; fax 4377552; f. 1996; governing party; Chair. President YAHYA A. J. J. JAMMEH.

Gambia People's Party (GPP): Banjul; f. 1986; socialist; not registered with the IEC; Leader ASSAN MUSA CAMARA.

The Gambia Party for Democracy and Progress (GPDP): POB 4014, Kombo St Mary, Serrekunda; tel. 9955226; f. 2004; Sec.-Gen. HENRY GOMEZ.

National Alliance for Democracy and Development (NADD): Banjul; f. Jan. 2005 to contest 2006 elections; Co-ordinator HALIFA SALLAH; comprises parties listed below:

National Democratic Action Movement (NDAM): 1 Box Bar Rd, Nema, Brikama Town, Western Division, Banjul; tel. 4484990; e-mail ndam_gambia@hotmail.com; f. 2002; reformist; Leader and Sec.-Gen. LAMIN WAA JUWARA.

People's Democratic Organization for Independence and Socialism (PDOIS): POB 2306, 1 Sambou St, Churchill, Serrekunda; tel. and fax 4393177; e-mail foroyaa@qanet.gm; f. 1986; socialist; Leaders HALIFA SALLAH, SAM SARR, SIDIA JATTA.

People's Progressive Party (PPP): c/o Omar Jallow, Ninth St East, Fajara M Section, Banjul; tel. and fax 4392674; f. 1959; fmr ruling party in 1962–94; centrist; Chair. OMAR JALLOW.

National Convention Party (NCP): 47 Antouman Faal St, Banjul; tel. 4229440; f. 1977; left-wing; Leader SHERIFF MUSTAPHA DIBBA.

National Reconciliation Party (NRP): 69 Daniel Goddard St, Banjul; tel. 4201371; fax 4201732; f. 1996; formed an alliance with the UDP in 2006; Leader HAMAT N. K. BAH.

United Democratic Party (UDP): 1 ECOWAS Ave, Banjul; tel. 4221730; fax 4224601; e-mail info@udpgambia.org; f. 1996; formed an alliance with the NRP in 2006; reformist; Sec.-Gen. and Leader OUSAINOU N. DARBOE; Nat. Pres. Col (retd) SAM SILLAH.

Diplomatic Representation

EMBASSIES AND HIGH COMMISSIONS IN THE GAMBIA

China (Taiwan): 26 Radio Gambia Rd, Kanifing South, POB 916, Banjul; tel. 4374046; fax 4374055; e-mail rocemb@gamtel.gm; Ambassador PATRICK CHANG PEI-CHI.

Cuba: C/801, POB 1487, Banjul; tel. and fax 4460789; e-mail embacuba@ganet.gm; Ambassador JORGE MARTÍNEZ SALSAMENDI.

Libya: Independence Dr., Banjul; tel. 4223213; fax 4223214; Chargé d'affaires a.i. TAHER S. DALOUB.

Nigeria: 52 Garba Jalumpa Ave, Bakau, POB 630, Banjul; tel. 4495803; fax 4496456; e-mail nigeriahc@qanet.gm; High Commissioner MARIAM MUHAMMED.

Senegal: 159 Kairaba Ave, POB 385, Banjul; tel. 4373752; fax 4373750; Ambassador MAMADOU FALL.

Sierra Leone: 67 Daniel Goddard St, Banjul; tel. 4228206; fax 4229819; e-mail mfodayyumkella@yahoo.co.uk; High Commissioner MOHAMMED FODAY YUMKELLA.

United Kingdom: 48 Atlantic Rd, Fajara, POB 507, Banjul; tel. 4495133; fax 4496134; e-mail bhcbanjul@fco.gov.uk; internet www.britishhighcommission.gov.uk/thegambia; High Commissioner PHILIP SINKINSON.

USA: The White House, Kairaba Ave, Fajara, PMB 19, Banjul; tel. 4392856; fax 4392475; e-mail consularbanjul@state.gov; internet www.usembassybanjul.gm; Ambassador JOSEPH D. STAFFORD.

Judicial System

The judicial system of The Gambia is based on English Common Law and legislative enactments of the Republic's Parliament which include an Islamic Law Recognition Ordinance whereby an Islamic Court exercises jurisdiction in certain cases between, or exclusively affecting, Muslims.

The Constitution of the Second Republic guarantees the independence of the judiciary. The Supreme Court is defined as the final court of appeal. Provision is made for a special criminal court to hear and determine all cases relating to theft and misappropriation of public funds.

Supreme Court of The Gambia

Law Courts, Independence Dr., Banjul; tel. 4227383; fax 4228380.

Consists of the Chief Justice and up to six other judges.

Chief Justice: ABDOU KARIM SAVAGE.

The **Banjul Magistrates Court**, the **Kanifing Magistrates Court** and the **Divisional Courts** are courts of summary jurisdiction presided over by a magistrate or in his absence by two or more lay justices of the peace. There are resident magistrates in all divisions. The magistrates have limited civil and criminal jurisdiction, and appeal from these courts lies with the Supreme Court. **Islamic Courts** have jurisdiction in matters between, or exclusively affecting, Muslim Gambians and relating to civil status, marriage, succession, donations, testaments and guardianship. The Courts administer Islamic *Shari'a* law. A cadi, or a cadi and two assessors, preside over and constitute an Islamic Court. Assessors of the Islamic Courts are Justices of the Peace of Islamic faith. **District Tribunals** have appellate jurisdiction in cases involving customs and traditions. Each court consists of three district tribunal members, one of whom is selected as president, and other court members from the area over which it has jurisdiction.

Attorney-General: Sheikh TIJAN HYDARA.

Solicitor-General: HENRY D. R. CARROLL.

Religion

About 85% of the population are Muslims. The remainder are mainly Christians, and there are a few animists, mostly of the Diola and Karoninka ethnic groups.

ISLAM

Banjul Central Mosque: King Fahd Bun Abdul Aziz Mosque, Box Bar Rd, POB 562, Banjul; tel. 4228094; Imam Ratib Alhaji ABDOULIE M. JOBE; Dep. Imam Ratib Alhaji TAFSIR GAYE.

Supreme Islamic Council: Banjul; Chair. Alhaji BANDING DRAMMEH; Vice-Chair. Alhaji OUSMAN JAH.

CHRISTIANITY

Christian Council of The Gambia: MDI Rd, Kanifing, POB 27, Banjul; tel. 4392092; e-mail gchristianc@hotmail.com; f. 1966; seven mems (churches and other Christian bodies); Chair. Rt Rev. ROBERT P. ELLISON (Roman Catholic Bishop of Banjul); Sec.-Gen. Rev. WILLIE E. E. CARR.

The Anglican Communion

The diocese of The Gambia, which includes Senegal and Cape Verde, forms part of the Church of the Province of West Africa. The Archbishop of the Province is the Bishop of Koforidua, Ghana. There are about 1,500 adherents in The Gambia.

Bishop of The Gambia: Rt Rev. SOLOMON TILEWA JOHNSON, Bishopscourt, POB 51, Banjul; tel. 4227405; fax 4229495; e-mail anglican@qanet.gm.

The Roman Catholic Church

The Gambia comprises a single diocese (Banjul), directly responsible to the Holy See. At 31 December 2004 there were an estimated 41,500 adherents of the Roman Catholic Church in the country, equivalent to 2.4% of the population. The diocese administers a development organization (Caritas, The Gambia), and runs 63 schools and training centres. The Gambia participates in the Inter-territorial Catholic Bishops' Conference of The Gambia and Sierra Leone (based in Freetown, Sierra Leone).

Bishop of Banjul: Rt Rev. ROBERT PATRICK ELLISON, Bishop's House, POB 165, Banjul; tel. 4391957; fax 4390998.

Protestant Churches

Abiding Word Ministries: New Covenant Worship Centre, 156 Mosque Rd, POB 207, Serrekunda; tel. 4392569; fax 4394035; e-mail awm@qanet.gm; internet www.awmgambia.com; f. 1988; Senior Pastor Rev. FRANCIS FORBES.

Methodist Church: 1 Macoumba Jallow St, POB 288, Banjul; tel. 4227506; fax 4228510; e-mail methodist@qanet.gm; f. 1821; Chair. and Gen. Supt Rev. NORMAN A. GRIGG.

BAHÁ'Í FAITH

National Spiritual Assembly: POB 583, Banjul; tel. 4229015; e-mail alsalihi@commit.gm.

The Press

All independent publications are required to register annually with the Government and to pay a registration fee.

The Daily Express: Banjul; f. 2006; independent; Man. Dir SAM OBI.

The Daily Observer: POB 131, Banjul; tel. 4496608; fax 4496878; e-mail webmaster@observer.gm; internet www.observer.gm; f. 1992; daily; pro-Government; Gen. Man. Dr SAJA TAAL.

Foroyaa (Freedom): 1 Sambou St, Churchill's Town, POB 2306, Serrekunda; tel. and fax 4393177; e-mail foroyaa@qanet.gm; internet www.foroyaa.com; 2 a week; publ. by the PDOIS; Editors HALIFA SALLAH, SAM SARR, SIDIA JATTA.

The Gambia Daily: Dept of Information, 14 Daniel Goddard St, Banjul; tel. 4225060; fax 4227230; e-mail gamna@gamtel.gm; f. 1994; govt organ; Dir of Information EBRUMA COLE; circ. 500.

The Gambia News and Report: Banjul; weekly; magazine.

The Independent: next to A–Z Supermarket, Kairaba Ave, Banjul; e-mail independent@qanet.gm; f. 1999; 2 a week; independent; Gen. Man. MADI CEESAY; Editor-in-Chief MUSA SAIDYKHAN.

The Point: 2 Garba Jahumpa Rd, Fajara, Banjul; tel. 4497441; fax 4497442; e-mail thepoint13@yahoo.com; internet www.thepoint.gm; f. 1991; 3 a week; Editor-in-Chief PAP SAINE; circ. 3,000.

The Toiler: 31 OAU Blvd, POB 698, Banjul; Editor PA MODOU FALL.

The Worker: 6 Albion Place, POB 508, Banjul; publ. by the Gambia Labour Union; Editor MOHAMED M. CEESAY.

NEWS AGENCY

The Gambia News Agency (GAMNA): Dept of Information, 14 Daniel Goddard St, Banjul; tel. 4225060; fax 4227230; e-mail gamna@gamtel.gm; Dir EBRIMA COLE.

PRESS ASSOCIATION

The Gambia Press Union (GPU): 78 Mosque Rd, Serrekunda, POB 1440, Banjul; tel. and fax 4377020; e-mail gpu@qanet.gm; affiliated to West African Journalists' Association; Pres. MADI CEESAY.

Publishers

National Printing and Stationery Corpn: Sankung Sillah St, Kanifing; tel. 4374403; fax 4395759; f. 1998; state-owned.

Baroueli: 73 Mosque Rd, Serrekunda, POB 976, Banjul; tel. 4392480; e-mail baroueli@qanet.gm; f. 1986; educational.

Observer Company: Bakau New Town Rd, Kanifing, PMB 131, Banjul; tel. 4496087; fax 4496878; e-mail webmaster@observer.gm; internet www.observer.gm; f. 1995; indigenous languages and non-fiction.

Sunrise Publishers: POB 955, Banjul; tel. 4393538; e-mail sunrisepublishers@yahoo.com; internet www.sunrisepublishers.net; f. 1985; regional history, politics and culture; Man. PATIENCE SONKO-GODWIN.

Broadcasting and Communications

TELECOMMUNICATIONS

Africell (Gambia): 43 Kairaba Ave, POB 2140, Banjul; tel. 4376022; fax 4376066; e-mail mmakkaoui@africell.gm; internet www.africell.gm; f. 2001; provider of mobile cellular telecommunications; CEO MEKIEDDIUE MAKKAOUI.

The Gambia Telecommunications Co Ltd (GAMTEL): Gamtel House, 3 Nelson Mandela St, POB 387, Banjul; tel. 4225262; fax 4224511; e-mail gen-info@gamtel.gm; internet www.gamtel.gm; f. 1984; state-owned; also operates mobile cellular telecommunications network, Gamcel, www.gamcel.gm; Man. Dir KATIM TOURAY.

BROADCASTING

Radio

The Gambia Radio and Television Services (GRTS): Serrekunga Exchange Complex, Karaiba Ave, POB 307 Serrekunda; tel. 4495101; fax 4495102; e-mail bora@gamtel.gm; f. 1962; state-funded, non-commercial broadcaster; radio broadcasts in English, Mandinka, Wolof, Fula, Diola, Serer and Serahuli; Dir-Gen. Alhaji MODOU SANYANG.

Citizen FM: Banjul; independent commercial broadcaster; broadcasts news and information in English, Wolof and Mandinka; rebroadcasts selected programmes from the British Broadcasting Corpn; operations suspended in Oct. 2001; Propr BABOUCAR GAYE; News Editor EBRIMA SILLAH.

Farafenni Community Radio: Farafenni; tel. 5735527.

FM B Community Radio Station: Brikama; tel. 4483000; FM broadcaster.

Radio 1 FM: 44 Kairaba Ave, POB 2700, Serrekunda; tel. 4396076; fax 4394911; e-mail george.radio1@qanet.gm; f. 1990; private station broadcasting FM music programmes to the Greater Banjul area; Dir GEORGE CHRISTENSEN.

Radio Gambia: Mile 7, Banjul; tel. 4495101; fax 4495923; e-mail semafye@hotmail.com.

Radio Syd: POB 279, Banjul; tel. 4228170; fax 4226490; e-mail radiosyd@gamtel.gm; f. 1970; commercial station broadcasting mainly music; programmes in English, French, Wolof, Mandinka and Fula; also tourist information in Swedish; not broadcasting at present, due to antenna problems; Dir CONSTANCE WADNER ENHÖRNING; Man. BENNY HOLGERSON.

Sud FM: Buckle St, POB 64, Banjul; tel. 4222359; fax 4222394; e-mail sudfm@gamtel.gm; licence revoked in 2005; Man. MAMADOU HOUSSABA BA.

West Coast Radio: Manjai Kunda, POB 2687, Serrekunda; tel. 4460911; fax 4461193; e-mail info@westcoast.gm; internet www.westcoast.gm; FM broadcaster.

The Gambia also receives broadcasts from Radio Democracy for Africa (f. 1998), a division of the Voice of America, and the British Broadcasting Corpn.

Television

The Gambia Radio and Television Services (GRTS): see Radio; television broadcasts commenced 1995.

There is also a private satellite channel, Premium TV.

Finance

(cap. = capital; res = reserves; dep. = deposits; m. = million; br(s). = branch(es); amounts in dalasi)

BANKING

Central Bank

Central Bank of The Gambia: 1–2 ECOWAS Ave, Banjul; tel. 4228103; fax 4226969; e-mail info@cbg.gm; internet www.cbg.gm; f. 1971; bank of issue; monetary authority; cap. 1.0m., res 3.0m., dep. 993.6m. (Dec. 1998); Gov. FAMARA JATTA; Gen. Man. HADDY A. SALLA.

Other Banks

Arab-Gambian Islamic Bank: 7 ECOWAS Ave, POB 1415, Banjul; tel. 4222222; fax 4223770; e-mail agib@qanet.gm; internet www.agib.gm; f. 1996; 21.1% owned by The Gambia National Insurance Co Ltd, 20.0% owned by Islamic Development Bank (Saudi Arabia); cap. and res 9.0m., total assets 116.9m. (Dec. 2001); Man. Dir MAMOUR MALICK JAGNE; 1 br.

First International Bank Ltd: 6 OAU Blvd, POB 1997, Banjul; tel. and fax 4202000; e-mail fib@gamtel.gm; internet www.fibgm.com; f. 1999; 61.9% owned by Slok Ltd (Nigeria); cap. 29.4m., dep. 88.3m. (Dec. 2004); Chair. Prof. J. O. IRUKWU; Man. Dir and CEO MOMODOU S. MUSA.

Guaranty Trust Bank (Gambia): 55 Kairaba Ave, Fajara, POB 1958, Banjul; tel. 4376371; fax 4376398; e-mail webmaster@gambia.gtbplc.com; internet www.gambia.gtbplc.com; f. 2002; subsidiary of Guaranty Trust Bank PLC (Nigeria); Man. Dir AYO RICHARDS.

International Bank for Commerce (Gambia) Ltd: 11A Liberation Ave, POB 211, Banjul; tel. 4228144; fax 4229312; e-mail ibc@qanet.gm; f. 1968; owned by Banque Mauritanienne pour le Commerce International; cap. and res 58,170m., dep. 307.0m. (Dec. 2003); Man. Dir MORY GUEBA CISSÉ; 2 brs.

International Commercial Bank (Gambia) Ltd: 48 Kairaba Ave, Serrekunda, KMC, POB 1600, Banjul; tel. 4377878; fax 4377880; e-mail yiphean01@yahoo.com; CEO TAN YIP HEAN.

Standard Chartered Bank (Gambia) Ltd: 8 ECOWAS Ave, POB 259, Banjul; tel. 4227744; fax 4227714; e-mail stsik@scbgamb.mhs.compuserve.com; internet www.standardchartered.com; f. 1978; 75% owned by Standard Chartered Holdings BV, Amsterdam; cap. 8.9m., res 62.8m., dep. 1,843.2m. (Dec. 2004); Chair. MOMODOU B. A. SENGHORE; 5 brs.

Trust Bank Ltd (TBL): 3–4 ECOWAS Ave, POB 1018, Banjul; tel. 4225777; fax 4225781; e-mail info@trustbank.gm; internet www.trustbank.gm; f. 1992; fmrly Meridien BIAO Bank Gambia Ltd; 30% owned by Data Bank, 25% by Social Security and Housing Finance Corpn, 10% by Boule & Co Ltd; cap. 40.0m., res 55.0m., dep. 1,358.2m. (Dec. 2004); Chair. KEN OFORI ATTA; Man. Dir PA MACOUMBA NJIE; 4 brs.

INSURANCE

Capital Insurance Co Ltd: 22 Anglesea St, POB 268, Banjul; tel. 4227480; fax 4229219; e-mail capinsur@gamtel.gm; f. 1985; CEO DODOU TAAL.

The Gambia National Insurance Co Ltd (GNIC): 19 Kairaba Ave, Fajara, KSMD, POB 750, Banjul; tel. 4395725; fax 4395716; e-mail info@gnic.gm; internet www.gnic.gm; f. 1974; privately owned; Chair. M. O. DRAMMEH; Man. Dir WILLIAM B. COKER; 3 brs.

Gamstar Insurance Co Ltd: 79 Daniel Goddard St, POB 1276, Banjul; tel. 4226021; fax 4229755; internet www.gamstarinsurance.net; f. 1991; Man. Dir BAI NDONGO FAAL.

Global Security Insurance Co Ltd: 73A Independence Dr., POB 1400, Banjul; tel. 4223716; fax 4223715; e-mail global@gamtel.gm; f. 1996; Man. Dir KWASU DARBOE.

Great Alliance Insurance Co: 10 Nelson Mandela St, POB 1160, Banjul; tel. 4227839; fax 4229444; e-mail gaichq@qanet.gm; f. 1989; Pres. BAI MATARR DRAMMEH; Man. Dir DEBORAH H. FORSTER.

Londongate (Gambia) Insurance Co: 1–3 Liberation Ave, POB 602, Banjul; tel. 4201740; fax 4201742; e-mail izadi@londongate.gm; internet www.londongate.co.uk/gambia_profile.htm; f. 1999; owned by Boule & Co Ltd; Marketing Man. T. OGOH.

New Vision Insurance Co. Ltd: 3–4 ECOWAS Ave, POB 239, Banjul; tel. 4223045; fax 4223040; Dir ANTHONY G. CARVALHO.

Prime Insurance Co Ltd: 10C Nelson Mandela St, POB 277, Banjul; tel. 4222476; e-mail prime@qanet.gm; f. 1997; Exec. Dir JARREH F. M. TOURAY; Man. Dir PA ALASSAN JAGNE.

Insurance Association

Insurance Association of The Gambia (IAG): Banjul.

Trade and Industry

GOVERNMENT AGENCIES

The Gambia Divestiture Agency (GDA): 80 OAU Blvd, POB 391, Banjul; tel. 4202530; fax 4202533; e-mail gda@gda.gm; internet www.gda.gm; f. 2001; advisory body; Man. Dir (vacant).

The Gambia Investment Promotion and Free Zones Agency (GIPFZA): 48 Kairaba Ave, Serrekunda, KMC, POB 757, Banjul; tel. 4377377; fax 4377379; e-mail info.gipfza@qanet.gm; internet www.gipfza.gm; CEO KEBBA A. TOURAY.

Indigenous Business Advisory Services (IBAS): POB 2502, Bakau; tel. 4496098; e-mail payibas@gamtel.gm.

National Investment Promotion Authority (NIPA): Independence Dr., Banjul; tel. 4228332; fax 4229220; f. 1994 to replace the National Investment Bd; CEO S. M. MBOGE.

DEVELOPMENT AGENCY

The Gambia Rural Development Agency (GARDA): Soma Village, Jarra West, PMB 452, Serrekunda; tel. 4496676; fax 4390095.

CHAMBER OF COMMERCE

The Gambia Chamber of Commerce and Industry (GCCI): 55 Kairaba Ave, KSMD, POB 3382, Serrekunda; tel. 4378929; fax 4378936; e-mail gcci@gambiachamber.com; internet www .gambiachamber.com; f. 1967; Pres. Bai Matarr Drammeh; CEO Mam Cherno Jallow.

INDUSTRIAL AND TRADE ASSOCIATIONS

Association of Gambian Entrepreneurs (AGE): POB 200, Banjul; tel. 4393494.

Gambia Produce Marketing Board (GPMB): Marina Foreshore, POB 284 Banjul; tel. 4227278; fax 4228037.

UTILITIES

Public Utilities Regulatory Authority (PURA): 1 Paradise Beach Pl., Bertil Harding Highway, Kololi; tel. 4465180; e-mail pura@pura.gm; internet www.pura.gm; f. 2001; monitors and enforces standards of performance by public utilities; Chair. Abdoulie Touray; Dir-Gen. Alagi B. Gaye.

National Water and Electricity Co Ltd (NAWEC): POB 609, Banjul; tel. 4496430; fax 4496751; f. 1996; in 1999 control was transferred to the Bassau Development Corpn, Côte d'Ivoire, under a 15-year contract; electricity and water supply, sewerage services; Chair. Momodou A. Jeng; Man. Dir Baboucar M. Jobe.

CO-OPERATIVES

Federation of Agricultural Co-operatives: Banjul.

The Gambia Co-operative Union (GCU): Dept of Co-operatives, 14 Marina Parade, Banjul; tel. 4227507; fax 4392582; Chief Officer Bakary Sonko.

MAJOR COMPANIES

Banjul Breweries Ltd: Kanifing Industrial Estate, Kombo St Mary Division, POB 830, Banjul; tel. 4391863; fax 4392266; e-mail banbrew@gamtel.gm; internet www.julbrew.gm; f. 1975; owned by Brauhaase (Germany); Gen. Man. A. F. Huberts; 112 employees (2005).

BIMEX Co Ltd: Kanifing Industrial Estate, POB 2588, Serrekunda; tel. 4372395; fax 4390601; e-mail bimex.banjul@commit.gm; building materials; Man. Dir Hubert Consol.

Boule & Co Ltd: NTC Complex, 1–3 Liberation Ave, POB 602, Banjul; tel. 4228818; fax 4226694; e-mail info@bouleco.com; internet www.bouleco.com; f. 1976; general merchants; Chair. and Man. Dir Charbel N. Elhajj.

CFAO Gambia: 14 Wellington St, POB 297, Banjul; tel. 4227473; fax 4227472; f. 1887; fmrly Compagnie Française de l'Afrique Occidental; general merchants; Man. Dir G. Durand; 100 employees (2001).

K. Chellaram & Sons (Gambia) Ltd: Kanifing Industrial Estate, POB 275, Banjul; tel. 4392912; fax 4392910; e-mail nchellaram@aol .com; internet www.chellaramsgambia.com; f. 1958; importers and general merchants; Man. Dir Nitin R. Chellaram.

Elof Trading Co Ltd: 40 Kanifing Industrial Estate, POB 95, Banjul; tel. 4394522; fax 4390599; f. 1991; general merchants; Dirs Kamal Melki, Nawal Melki.

Fass Upper Saloum Enterprises: 80 Garba Juhumpa Rd, POB 1328, Banjul; tel. 4497878; electrical supplies and building materials.

The Gambia Cotton Company (GAMCOT): Banjul; state-owned; scheduled for privatization.

The Gambia Groundnut Corpn (GGC): Banjul; distribution and marketing of groundnuts; subject to a take-over by the Government in Jan. 1999; scheduled for privatization in 2006; 528 employees.

The Gambia Oilseeds Processing and Marketing Corpn (GOPMAC): Marina Foreshore, Banjul; tel. 4227572; fax 4228037; assumed 'core' assets of The Gambia Produce Marketing Board in 1993.

Gamsen Construction: 50 Garba Jahumpa Rd, Bakau, POB 2844, Serrekunda; tel. 4497448; fax 4394766; construction and civil engineering; jtly owned by ALFRON and ATEPA Technologies, Senegal; Man. Dir Amadou Samba.

General Suppliers and Construction Services: Kairaba Ave, POB 316, Banjul; tel. 4461795; fax 4461795; construction services and suppliers.

International Pelican Seafood Ltd: Bund Rd, Banjul; e-mail hmcfood@erols.com; f. 1997; seafood processing and export; Man. Dir Ron Riggs.

S. Madi (Gambia) Ltd: 10c Nelson Mandela St, POB 255/256, Banjul; tel. 4227281; fax 4226192; e-mail s-madi@qanet.gm; general merchants, agents for Lloyd's of London; Man. Dir Jane H. Clement.

Maurel and Prom: 22 Buckle St, Banjul; fax 4228942; general merchants; Man. J. Eschenlohr.

Moukhtara Holding Co Ltd (MHC): 10 Moukhtara St, Kanifing Industrial Estate, POB 447, Banjul, Banjul; tel. 4392574; fax 4393085; e-mail moukhtara.gambia@gamtel.gm; internet www .moukhtara.com; f. 1975; holding co with interests in confectionery, educational books and stationery, timber, bricks, plastics, cosmetics and tissue paper; Man. Dir Sayed Moukhtara.

New Gambia Industrialists: 3 Essa Joof Rd, Kombo St, Kanifing, POB 954, Banjul; tel. 4373185; fax 4373185; e-mail ngi@qanet.gm; f. 1991; civil, mechanical and electrical design and construction; 20 employees.

Shell Marketing (Gambia) Ltd: POB 263, Banjul; tel. 4228028; fax 4227992; marketing and sale of petroleum products; Gen. Man. Adama Faal.

Sosseh & Sons Engineering Co Ltd: 34 Liberation Ave, POB 701, Banjul; marine and production engineering.

TAF Holding Co Ltd: Cemetery Rd, Kanifing Industrial Estate, POB 121, Banjul; tel. 4392333; fax 4390033; e-mail information .services@tafgambia.com; internet www.tafgambia.com; f. 1990; has subsidiaries in construction, real estate and tourism; Dir Mustapha Njie; 500 employees.

Zingli Manufacturing Co Ltd: Kanifing Industrial Estate, POB 2402, Serrekunda; tel. 4392282; mfrs of corrugated iron and wire.

TRADE UNIONS

Agricultural Workers' Association (AWA): Banjul; Pres. Sheikh Tijan Sosseh; 247 mems.

Association of Gambian Sailors: c/o 31 OAU Blvd, POB 698, Banjul; tel. 4223080; fax 4227214.

Dock Workers' Union: Albert Market, POB 852, Banjul; tel. 4229448; fax 4225049.

The Gambia Labour Union: 6 Albion Pl., POB 508, Banjul; f. 1935; Pres. B. B. Kebbeh; Gen. Sec. Mohamed M. Ceesay; 25,000 mems.

The Gambia National Trades Union Congress (GNTUC): Trade Union House, 31 OAU Blvd, POB 698, Banjul; Sec.-Gen. Ebrima Garba Cham.

Gambia Teachers' Union (GTU): POB 133, Banjul; tel. and fax 4392075; e-mail gtu@gamtel.gm; f. 1937; Pres. Omar J. Ndure.

The Gambia Workers' Confederation: Trade Union House, 72 OAU Blvd, POB 698, Banjul; tel. and fax 4222754; e-mail gambiawc@ hotmail.com; f. 1958 as The Gambia Workers' Union; present name adopted in 1985; Sec.-Gen. Pa Momodou Faal; 30,000 mems (2001).

Transport

The Gambia Public Transport Corpn: Factory St, Kanifing Housing Estate, POB 801, Kanifing; tel. 4392230; fax 4392454; f. 1975; operates road transport and ferry services; Man. Dir Bakary Huma.

RAILWAYS

There are no railways in The Gambia.

ROADS

In 2004 there were an estimated 3,742 km of roads in The Gambia, of which 1,652 km were main roads, and 1,300 km were secondary roads. In that year only 19.3% of the road network was paved. Some roads are impassable in the rainy season. The expansion and upgrading of the road network is planned, as part of the Jammeh administration's programme to improve The Gambia's transport infrastructure. Among intended schemes is the construction of a motorway along the coast, with the aid of a loan of US $8.5m. from Kuwait. In early 1999 Taiwan agreed to provide $6m. for road construction programmes, and in early 2000 work began on the construction of a dual carriageway between Serrekunda, Mandina and Ba, supported by funds from the Islamic Development Fund and the Organization of the Petroleum Exporting Counties. In 2006 the European Union provided a grant of €44m. to rehabilitate five roads.

SHIPPING

The River Gambia is well suited to navigation. A weekly river service is maintained between Banjul and Basse, 390 km above Banjul, and a ferry connects Banjul with Barra. Small ocean-going vessels can reach Kaur, 190 km above Banjul, throughout the year. Facilities at the port of Banjul were modernized and expanded during the mid-1990s, with the aim of enhancing The Gambia's potential as a transit point for regional trade. In 1999 three advanced storage warehouses were commissioned with total storage space of 8,550 sq m. The Gambia's merchant fleet consisted of 13 vessels, totalling 33,159 grt, at 31 December 2005.

The Gambia Ports Authority: 34 Liberation Ave, POB 617, Banjul; tel. 4229940; fax 4227268; e-mail info@gamport.gm; internet www.gamport.gm; f. 1972; Man. Dir ADAMA M. DEEN.

Gambia River Transport Co Ltd: 61 Wellington St, POB 215, POB 215, Banjul; tel. 4227664; river transport of groundnuts and general cargo; Man. Dir LAMIN JUWARA; 200 employees.

The Gambia Shipping Agency Ltd: 1A Cotton St, POB 257, Banjul; tel. and fax 4227518; e-mail gamship@qanet.gm; f. 1984; shipping agents and forwarders; Man. Dir N. LANGGAARD-SORENSEN; 30 employees.

Interstate Shipping Co (Gambia) Ltd: 43 Buckle St, POB 220, Banjul; tel. 4229388; fax 4229347; e-mail interstate@gamtel.gm; transport and storage; Man. Dir B. F. SAGNIA.

Maersk Gambia Ltd: 80 OAU Blvd, POB 1399, Banjul; tel. 4224450; fax 4224025; e-mail gamsalimp@maersk.com; f. 1993; owned by Maersk Line.

CIVIL AVIATION

Banjul International Airport, is situated at Yundum, 27 km from the capital. Construction of a new terminal, at a cost of some US $10m., was completed in late 1996. Facilities at Yundum have been upgraded by the US National Aeronautics and Space Administration (NASA), to enable the airport to serve as an emergency landing site for space shuttle vehicles.

The Gambia Civil Aviation Authority (GCAA): Banjul International Airport, Yundum; tel. 4472831; fax 4472190; e-mail dggcaa@qanet.gm; internet www.gambia.gm/gcaa; f. 1991; Dir-Gen. FANSU BOJANG.

The Gambia International Airlines: PMB 353, Banjul; tel. 4472770; fax 4223700; internet www.gia.gm; f. 1996; state-owned; sole handling agent at Banjul, sales agent; Chair. (vacant); Man. Dir (vacant).

Slok Air International (Gambia) Ltd: Banjul International Airport, Yundum; internet www.slokairinternational.com; commenced operations in The Gambia in 2004; Chair. AMADOU SAMBA; Man. Dir Capt. ERNEST I. BELL.

Tourism

Tourists are attracted by The Gambia's beaches and also by its abundant birdlife. A major expansion of tourism facilities was carried out in the early 1990s. Although there was a dramatic decline in tourist arrivals in the mid-1990s (owing to the political instability), the tourism sector recovered well. In 2004 some 90,095 air charter tourists visited The Gambia. In 2004 estimated earnings from tourism were US $59m. An annual 'Roots Festival' was inaugurated in 1996, with the aim of attracting African-American visitors to The Gambia.

The Gambia Hotels' Association: c/o The Bungalow Beach Hotel, POB 2637, Serrekunda; tel. 4465288; fax 4466180; e-mail info@bbhotel.gm; Chair. ARDY SARGE.

The Gambia Tourist Authority: Kololi, POB 4085, Bakau; tel. 4462491; fax 4462487; e-mail info@gta.gm; internet www.visitthegambia.gm; f. 2001; Dir KALIBA SENGHORE.

Defence

As assessed at November 2006, the Gambian National Army comprised 800 men, including a marine unit of about 70 men and the National Guards. The Armed Forces comprise the Army, the Navy and the National Guards. Military service has been mainly voluntary; however, the Constitution of the Second Republic, which entered into full effect in January 1997, makes provision for conscription.

Defence Expenditure: Estimated at D45m. in 2006.

Chief of Staff of the Armed Forces: Lt-Col LANG TOMBONG TAMBA.

Commander of the Gambian National Army: (vacant).

Commander of the National Guards: (vacant).

Commander of the Navy: SARJO FOFANA.

Education

Primary education, beginning at seven years of age, is free but not compulsory and lasts for nine years. It is divided into two cycles of six and three years. Secondary education, from 16 years of age, comprises two cycles, lasting three and two years. According to UNESCO estimates, in 2003/04 total enrolment at primary schools included 75% of children in the relevant age-group (boys 73%; girls 77%), while secondary enrolment included 45% of the appropriate age-group (boys 49%; girls 41%). The Jammeh administration has, since 1994, embarked on an ambitious project to improve educational facilities and levels of attendance and attainment. A particular aim has been to improve access to schools for pupils in rural areas. Post-secondary education is available in teacher training, agriculture, health and technical subjects. Some 1,591 students were enrolled at tertiary establishments in 1994/95. The University of The Gambia, at Banjul, was officially opened in 2000. In 2004 current expenditure by the central Government on education was an estimated D224.3m., equivalent to 17.5% of non-interest current expenditure.

Bibliography

Amnesty International. *The Gambia: Democratic Reforms Without Human Rights.* London, 1997.

Cooke, D., and Hughes, A. 'The Politics of Economic Recovery: The Gambia's Experience of Structural Adjustment, 1985–94', in *The Journal of Commonwealth and Comparative Politics,* Vol. 35, No. 1. London, Frank Cass, 1997.

The Gambia (World Bibliographical Series, Vol. 91). Oxford, Clio Press, 1988.

Gray, J. M. *A History of the Gambia.* New York, Barnes & Noble, and London, Frank Cass, 1966.

Harrison Church, R. J. *West Africa.* 8th Edn. London, Longman, 1979.

Hughes, A. 'From Colonialism to Confederation: The Gambian Experience of Independence 1965–1982', in Cohen, R. (Ed.), *African Islands and Enclaves.* London, Sage Publications, 1983.

'The Senegambian Confederation', in *Contemporary Review*, February 1984.

'The Collapse of the Senegambian Confederation', in *The Journal of Commonwealth and Comparative Politics,* Vol. 30, No. 2. London, Frank Cass, 1992.

Hughes, A. (Ed.). *The Gambia: Studies in Society and Politics.* Birmingham, University of Birmingham, Centre of West African Studies, 1991.

Hughes, A., and Gailey, A. *Historical Dictionary of The Gambia.* Metuchen, NJ, Scarecrow Press, 2000.

Hughes, A., and Perfect, D. *Political History of The Gambia, 1816–1922.* London, C. Hurst & Co, 1996.

Kanyongolo, E., and Norris, C. *The Gambia: Freedom of Expression Still Under Threat: The Case of Citizen FM.* London, Article 19, 1999.

Luom, M. *An Analysis of the Gambian Coup of 1994.* Ottawa, ON, Carleton University Press, 2001.

People's Progressive Party Special Editorial Commission. *The Voice of the People, the Story of the PPP, 1959–1989.* Banjul, The Gambia Communications Agency and Barou-Ueli Enterprises, 1992.

Radelet, S. 'Reform without Revolt: The Political Economy of Economic Reform in The Gambia', in *World Development*, Vol. 28, No. 8. Oxford, Pergamon Press, 1992.

Rice, B. *Enter Gambia: The Birth of an Improbable Nation.* London, Angus & Robertson, 1968.

Schroeder, R. A. *Shady Practices: Agroforestry and Gender Politics in The Gambia.* Berkeley, CA, University of California Press, 1999.

Sweeney, P. (Ed.). *The Gambia and Senegal.* London, APA, 1996.

Tomkinson, M. *Gambia.* 2nd Edn. London, Michael Tomkinson Publishing, 2001.

Touray, O. *The Gambia and the World: A History of the Foreign Policy of Africa's Smallest State, 1965–1995.* Hamburg, Hamburg Institute of African Affairs, 2000.

Wiseman, J. A. *Democracy in Black Africa: Survival and Revival.* New York, Paragon House, 1990.

'Military Rule in The Gambia: An Interim Assessment', in *Third World Quarterly,* Vol. 17, No. 5. London, 1996.

'The Gambia: From Coup to Elections', in *Journal of Democracy,* Vol. 9, No. 2. Washington, DC, 1998.

Wiseman, J. A., and Chongan, E. I. *Military Rule and the Abuse of Human Rights in The Gambia: The View from Mile 2 Prison.* Trenton, NJ, Africa World Press, 2000.

Wiseman, J. A., and Vidler, E. 'The July 1994 Coup d'Etat in The Gambia: The End of an Era', in *The Round Table,* No. 333. Abingdon, Carfax, 1995.

Wright, D. R. *The World and A Very Small Place in Africa.* Armonk, NY, M. E. Sharpe, 1997.

GHANA

Physical and Social Geography

E. A. BOATENG

PHYSICAL FEATURES

Structurally and geologically, the Republic of Ghana exhibits many of the characteristics of sub-Saharan Africa, with its ancient rocks and extensive plateau surfaces marked by prolonged sub-aerial erosion. About one-half of the surface area is composed of Pre-Cambrian metamorphic and igneous rocks, most of the remainder consisting of a platform of Palaeozoic sediments believed to be resting on the older rocks. These sediments occupy a substantial area in the north-central part of the country and form the Voltaic basin. Surrounding this basin on all sides, except along the east, is a highly dissected peneplain of Pre-Cambrian rocks at an average of 150–300 m above sea-level but containing several distinct ranges of up to 600 m. Along the eastern edge of the Voltaic basin and extending right down to the sea near Accra is a narrow zone of highly folded Pre-Cambrian rocks forming the Akwapim-Togo ranges. These ranges rise to 300–900 m above sea-level, and contain the highest points in Ghana. Continuing northwards across Togo and Benin, they form one of west Africa's major relief features, the Togo-Atakora range.

The south-east corner of the country, below the Akwapim-Togo ranges, is occupied by the Accra-Ho-Keta plains, which are underlain by the oldest of the Pre-Cambrian series (known as the Dahomeyan) and contain extensive areas of gneiss, of which the basic varieties weather to form heavy but agriculturally useful soils. Extensive areas of young rocks, formed between the Tertiary and Recent ages, are found only in the broad delta of the Volta in the eastern part of the Accra plains, and in the extreme south-west corner of the country along the Axim coast; while in the intervening littoral zone patches of Devonian sediments combine with the rocks of the Pre-Cambrian peneplain to produce a coastline of sandy bays and rocky promontories.

Most of the country's considerable mineral wealth, consisting mainly of gold, diamonds, manganese and bauxite, is associated with the older Pre-Cambrian rocks, although there are indications that petroleum may be available in commercial quantities in some of the younger sedimentaries.

The drainage is dominated by the Volta system, which occupies the Voltaic basin and includes the vast artificial lake of 8,502 sq km formed behind the hydroelectric dam at Akosombo. A second dam is sited at Kpong, 8 km downstream from Akosombo. Most of the other rivers in Ghana, such as the Pra, Birim, Densu, Ayensu and Ankobra, flow between the southern Voltaic or Kwahu plateau and the sea. Most are of considerable local importance as sources of drinking water, but are hardly employed for irrigation purposes.

CLIMATE AND VEGETATION

Climatic conditions are determined by the interaction of two principal airstreams: the hot, dry, tropical, continental air mass or harmattan from the north-east, and the moist, relatively cool, maritime air mass or monsoon from the south-west across the Atlantic. In the southern part of the country, where the highest average annual rainfall (of 1,270–2,100 mm) occurs, there are two rainy seasons (April–July and September–November), while in the north, with annual averages of 1,100–1,270 mm, rainfall occurs in only a single season between April and September, followed by a long dry season dominated by the harmattan. There is much greater uniformity as regards mean temperatures, which average 26°–29°C. These temperatures, coupled with the equally high relative humidities, which fall significantly only during the harmattan, tend to produce oppressive conditions, relieved only by the relative drop in temperature at night, especially in the north, and the local incidence of land and sea breezes near the coast.

Vegetation in Ghana is determined mainly by climate and soil conditions. The area of heavy annual rainfall broken by one or two relatively short dry seasons, to be found in the south-west portion of the country and along the Akwapim-Togo ranges, is covered with evergreen forest in the wetter portions and semi-deciduous forest in the drier portions, while the area of rather lower rainfall, occurring in a single peak in the northern two-thirds of the country and the anomalously dry area around Accra, is covered with savannah and scrub. Prolonged farming activities and timber exploitation have reduced the original closed forest vegetation, while in the savannah areas prolonged cultivation and bush burning have also caused serious degradation of the vegetation.

POPULATION

Ghana covers an area of 238,537 sq km (92,100 sq miles). The March 2000 census recorded a population of 18,845,265, giving an approximate density of 79.0 inhabitants per sq km. In 2006, according to UN estimates, the population was 23,008,000, with a density of 96.5 inhabitants per sq km. The high rate of population growth during the 1980s and 1990s, together with the influx of large numbers—mostly youth from the rural areas into the urban centres—coupled with a virtually stagnant economy and the lack of adequate employment openings, has created serious social and political problems. In view of these demographic trends, the Government has initiated a campaign of family planning and population control, and aims to improve living standards through increased economic development. The highest densities occur in the urban and cocoa-farming areas in the southern part of the country, and also in the extreme north-eastern corner, where intensive compound farming is practised.

There are no less than 75 spoken languages and dialects, each more or less associated with a distinct ethnic group. The largest of these groups are the Akan (comprising about one-half of Ghana's population), Mossi, Ewe and the Ga-Adangme. Any divisive tendencies which might have arisen from this situation have been absent, largely as a result of government policies; however, a distinction can be made between the southern peoples, who have come most directly and longest under the recent influence of European life and the Christian religion, and the northern peoples, whose traditional modes of life and religion have undergone relatively little change, owing mainly to their remoteness from the coast. One of the most potent unifying forces has been the adoption of English as the official language, although it is augmented by eight major national languages.

Recent History

RICHARD SYNGE

Based on an earlier article by T. C. McCASKIE

Following the Second World War, a sustained political campaign to secure independence for the Gold Coast from British colonial rule led to the emergence in 1949 of the Convention People's Party. Its leader, Dr Kwame Nkrumah, became Prime Minister of an indigenous ministerial Government popularly elected in 1951. Subsequent progress towards full independence followed a UN-supervised plebiscite in May 1956, when the British-administered section of Togoland, a UN Trust Territory, voted to join the Gold Coast in an independent state. On 6 March 1957 the new state of Ghana was granted independence within the Commonwealth, becoming the first British dependency in sub-Saharan Africa to attain independence under majority rule. Ghana became a republic on 1 July 1960, with Nkrumah as executive President.

Under Nkrumah's leadership, Ghana established close relations with the USSR and its allies, while remaining economically dependent on Western countries. Following widespread discontent at the country's worsening economic problems, and at widespread political corruption, Nkrumah was deposed by a military coup in February 1966, led by Gen. Joseph Ankrah. In October 1969 power was returned to an elected civilian Government led by Dr Kofi Busia, a prominent opposition activist from the Nkrumah period. In January 1972 the armed forces again took power, under the leadership of Lt-Col (later Gen.) Ignatius Kutu Acheampong. In 1977 his military junta announced its intention to relinquish power to a new government following a general election, to take place in June 1979. These arrangements, however, were forestalled in July 1978 by Lt-Gen. (later Gen.) Frederick Akuffo, the Chief of the Defence Staff, who assumed power in a bloodless *coup d'état*.

THE RAWLINGS COUPS

Tensions within the armed forces became evident in May 1979 when a group of junior military officers led by Flt-Lt Jerry Rawlings staged an unsuccessful coup attempt. Following a brief period in detention, Rawlings and his associates successfully seized power, amid great popular acclaim. In June Rawlings formed an Armed Forces Revolutionary Council (AFRC), and Acheampong, Akuffo and other senior officers were swiftly tried, convicted of corruption and executed.

The AFRC indicated that its assumption of power was temporary, and the general election took place in June 1979, as scheduled. The People's National Party (PNP), led by Dr Hilla Limann, emerged with the largest number of parliamentary seats and formed a coalition government with support from the smaller United National Convention. Dr Limann took office as President in September. However, dissatisfaction with measures taken by the Government to improve the economy provoked renewed discontent within the armed forces. On 31 December 1981 Rawlings seized power for the second time, assuming the chairmanship of a Provisional National Defence Council (PNDC). On this occasion, Rawlings expressed no intention of restoring power to civilian politicians; instead, the PNDC adopted measures to 'democratize' political decision-making and to decentralize power. City and district councils were replaced by People's Defence Committees, in an attempt to create mass participation at local level, and to encourage public vigilance.

The 'democratization' of the army led to the creation of factions, and to increasing divisions between military personnel along ethnic lines. Unsuccessful attempts to overthrow Rawlings were reported in November 1982 and in early 1983. Although Rawlings and the PNDC remained under challenge from exiled opponents there was some improvement in economic conditions during 1984. During 1985, however, the PNDC detected a further attempt from within the army to overthrow the regime.

INTERNAL CONCERNS

The PNDC became increasingly preoccupied with domestic security in 1986 and 1987. In March 1986 a number of people were tried for involvement in a conspiracy to overthrow the Government; several executions were subsequently carried out. In June 1987 the PNDC announced arrests in connection with another alleged conspiracy. Seven further arrests took place in November; on this occasion the detainees included former officials of the PNDC.

Elections to district assemblies were held in three stages, between December 1988 and February 1989. The PNDC reserved one-third of seats for its own nominees, and retained the power to scrutinize and disqualify individual candidates, although it was envisaged that the elected district assemblies would move towards regional representation, and ultimately form a national body that would supersede the PNDC.

However, the envisaged adoption of democratic reforms continued to be overshadowed by grave economic problems, while economic reforms were impeded by widespread mismanagement and corruption in the commercial sector. In September 1989 an attempted coup took place, led by Maj. Courage Quashigah, a former commander of the military police and a close associate of Rawlings. Rawlings assumed control of the armed forces until June 1990. Quashigah and four other members of the security forces were charged with conspiring to assassinate Rawlings.

CONSTITUTIONAL TRANSITION

In 1990 there were increasing demands for an end to the ban on political activities and associations, and for the abolition of a number of laws, particularly those concerning the detention of suspects. In July of that year, in response to pressure from Western donors to increase democracy in return for a continuation in aid, the PNDC announced that a National Commission for Democracy (NCD), under the chairmanship of Justice Daniel Annan, a member of the PNDC, would organize a series of regional debates, which would review the decentralization process, and consider Ghana's political and economic future. In August, however, a newly formed political association, the Movement for Freedom and Justice (MFJ), criticized the NCD, claiming that it was too closely associated with the PNDC. In addition, the MFJ demanded the abolition of a number of laws, the release of political prisoners, the end of press censorship and the immediate restoration of democratic government. The PNDC, however, advocated a 'national consensus', rather than a return to the discredited multi-party political system.

In late March 1991 the NCD presented its report, which recommended the election of an executive President for a fixed term, the establishment of a legislature and the creation of the post of Prime Minister. In May the PNDC endorsed the restoration of a plural political system, and accepted the NCD's recommendations. A 260-member Consultative Assembly was established, which was to review recommendations by a government-appointed committee of constitutional experts. A new constitution was subsequently to be submitted for endorsement by a national referendum.

In March 1992 Rawlings announced a programme for constitutional transition and the Consultative Assembly endorsed the majority of the constitutional recommendations, which were subsequently presented for approval by the PNDC. However, the proposed creation of the post of Prime Minister was rejected by the Assembly; executive power was to be vested solely in the President, who would appoint a Vice-President. In addition, the draft constitution included a provision that members of the Government be exempt from prosecution for acts committed during the PNDC's rule. At a national referendum held on 28 April, however, the adoption of the draft constitution was approved by 92% of votes cast, with 43.7% of the electorate voting. In May the Government introduced legislation that ended the ban on the formation of political associations; political parties were required to apply to the Interim National Electoral Commission (INEC) for legal recognition. Under the terms of the legislation, however, 21 former political organizations remained proscribed, while emergent parties were not permitted to use the names or slogans of these organizations.

In June 1992 a number of political organizations emerged, many of which were established by supporters of former politicians; six opposition groups subsequently obtained legal status. In the same month a coalition of pro-Government organizations, the National Democratic Congress (NDC), was formed to contest the elections on behalf of the PNDC. However, an existing alliance of supporters of Rawlings, known as the Eagle Club, refused to join the NDC, and formed the Eagle Party of Ghana, subsequently known as the EGLE (Every Ghanaian Living Everywhere) Party.

In September 1992, in accordance with the new Constitution, Rawlings retired from the armed forces (although he retained the title of Commander-in-Chief of the Armed Forces in his capacity as Head of State), and was subsequently chosen as the presidential candidate of the NDC. (The NDC later formed an electoral coalition with the EGLE Party and the National Convention Party—NCP.) A member of the NCP, Kow Nkensen Arkaah, became Rawlings' vice-presidential candidate. Four other political groups nominated presidential candidates: the People's Heritage Party (PHP); the National Independence Party (NIP); the People's National Convention (PNC, which nominated ex-President Limann); and the New Patriotic Party (NPP). Although the establishment of a united opposition to Rawlings was discussed, the parties failed to achieve agreement, owing, in part, to the apparent conviction of the NPP (which was recognized as the strongest of the movements) that its presidential candidate could defeat Rawlings.

Less than 48.3% of the registered electorate voted in the presidential election, which took place on 3 November 1992. Rawlings secured 58.3% of the vote, defeating the NPP candidate, Prof. A. A. Boahen, who won 30.4%. The Commonwealth observers declared that the election had been free and fair. However, the opposition parties, led by the NPP, claimed that widespread electoral irregularities had taken place. A curfew was imposed in Kumasi (in Ashanti Region), following incidents of violence, and rioting by opposition supporters, in which an NDC ward chairman was killed; in addition, a series of explosive devices were detonated in Accra and Tema. A prominent member of the PHP was later detained, together with other opposition supporters, accused of complicity in the bombings. The Government rescheduled the legislative elections for 22 December.

In early December 1992 Boahen announced that the opposition had direct evidence of electoral fraud perpetrated by the Government. The opposition parties declared, however, that they would not legally challenge the result of the presidential election, but that they would boycott the forthcoming general election. Accordingly, these elections (which had been again postponed until 29 December) were contested only by the NDC and its allies, the EGLE Party and the NCP. On this basis, the NDC obtained 189 of the 200 seats in the Parliament, while the NCP secured eight seats, the EGLE Party one seat and independent candidates two seats. On 7 January 1993 Rawlings was sworn in as President of the Fourth Republic, the PNDC was dissolved and the new Parliament was inaugurated.

THE FOURTH REPUBLIC

In early January 1993 a number of severe economic austerity measures were introduced under the 1993 budget. The NPP, the PNC, the NIP and the PHP subsequently formed an alliance, known as the Inter-Party Co-ordinating Committee (ICC), which strongly criticized the budget (widely believed to have been formulated under terms approved by the World Bank and the IMF), and announced that it was to act as an official opposition to the Government, despite its lack of representation in Parliament. In mid-April elections were held for the 10 regional seats in the consultative Council of State, and in May a new Council of Ministers (which included several members of the former PNDC administration) was sworn in. International approval of the series of election results was apparently indicated by subsequent pledges of economic assistance for Ghana. However, the member parties of the ICC continued to dispute the results of the presidential election. In August the NPP announced that it was prepared to recognize the legitimacy of the election results, thereby undermining the solidarity of the ICC. In December the PHP, the NIP and a faction of the PNC (all of which represented supporters of ex-President Nkrumah) merged to form the People's Convention Party (PCP).

Ethnic Tensions

In February 1994 long-standing hostility between the Konkomba ethnic group, which originated in former Togoland, and the land-owning Nanumba escalated, following demands by the Konkomba for traditional status that would entitle them to own land; some 500 people were killed in ethnic clashes in the Northern Region. The Government subsequently dispatched troops to the Northern Region to restore order and imposed a state of emergency in seven districts for a period of three months; however, skirmishes between a number of ethnic factions continued, and it was reported that some 6,000 Konkomba had fled to Togo.

In June 1994 the seven ethnic factions involved in the fighting signed a peace agreement that provided for the imposition of an immediate cease-fire and renounced violence as a means of settling disputes over land-ownership. The Government subsequently announced that troops were to be permanently stationed in the Northern Region in order to pre-empt further conflict, and appointed a negotiating team, which was to attempt to resolve the inter-ethnic differences. In August the state of emergency was finally ended. In March 1995 the Government again imposed a curfew in the Northern Region, in response to renewed ethnic violence, in which about 100 people were killed. In April a joint committee, comprising prominent members of the Konkomba and Nanumba ethnic groups, was established in an effort to resolve the conflict.

Meanwhile, the imposition, in February 1995, of value-added tax (VAT) under that year's budget prompted widespread protests. A series of demonstrations, which was organized by a grouping of opposition leaders, Alliance for Change, culminated in May, when five people were killed in clashes between government supporters and protesters. Later that month the national executive committee of the NCP decided to withdraw the party from the ruling coalition, claiming that the NDC had dominated the alliance. However, Vice-President Arkaah subsequently announced that he was to retain his office on the grounds that his mandate had not expired. In June the authorities agreed to suspend VAT, and reinstated the sales tax that had previously been in force. (However, VAT was subsequently reintroduced, with effect from December 1998.)

Elected Government

In the approach to the 1996 presidential and parliamentary elections, the NPP and PCP formed an electoral coalition, known as the Great Alliance, with John Kufuor of the NPP as presidential candidate and Arkaah of the PCP as the candidate for the vice-presidency. The NCP stated that it would support the NDC in the forthcoming elections, while the PNC announced its intention to contest the elections alone. In September Rawlings was nominated as the NDC's presidential candidate. The selection of common candidates provoked a lengthy dispute between the NPP and the PCP, with the parties contradicting each other regarding previous agreements on the distribution of seats.

The presidential and legislative elections took place, as scheduled, on 7 December 1996. Rawlings was re-elected President by 57.2% of the votes cast, while Kufuor secured 39.8% of the votes. In the parliamentary poll the NDC's representation was reduced to 133 seats, while the NPP won 60 seats (and a further one in June 1997, owing to a postponed contest), the PCP five and the PNC one seat. Despite opposition claims of malpractice, international observers declared that the elections had been conducted fairly, and an electoral turn-out of 76.8% was reported. At the end of December the PCP announced that its electoral alliance with the NPP had broken down. On 7 January 1997 Rawlings was again sworn in as President.

The lengthy process of appointing a new Council of Ministers resulted in a protracted dispute between the NDC and the opposition, prompting a series of parliamentary boycotts by the NPP, which insisted that all ministerial appointees be approved by the legislature's appointments committee prior to assuming their duties. In late February 1997 opposition parties filed a writ in the Supreme Court preventing Kwame Peprah, the reappointed Minister of Finance, from presenting the budget. Owing to the NDC's parliamentary majority, however, procedures were approved to allow those ministers who had been retained from the previous Government to avoid the vetting process. Nevertheless, in June the Supreme Court ruled that all presidential nominees for ministerial positions had to be approved by Parliament, even if they had served in the previous Government. Following the ruling, the NPP left the chamber on several occasions when ministers attempted to address Parliament. The Government subsequently announced that ministers who had participated in the previous administration were prepared to undergo vetting procedures.

In August 1998 the NCP and the PCP merged to form a new movement, the Convention Party (CP, later renamed the Convention People's Party—CPP, in honour of Nkrumah's party of the same name). In October the NPP again nominated Kufuor as its presidential candidate, to contest the election scheduled to take place in 2000. Under the terms of the Constitution, Rawlings was prohibited from seeking re-election to a third term in office, and had announced that the incumbent Vice-President, Prof. John Evans Atta Mills, was to contest the election on behalf of the NDC. At an NDC congress, which took place in December, the party constitution was amended to create the position for Rawlings of 'Life Chairman' of the party. In March 1999 a Ghanaian officer, Capt. James Owoo, who had allegedly been involved in attempts to remove the PNDC Government in the 1980s, was arrested by forces of the Economic Community of West African States (ECOWAS) Cease-fire Monitoring Group (ECOMOG) in Sierra Leone (see below), and was transported to Accra. It was subsequently announced that Owoo had been charged with conspiring to overthrow the Rawlings Government in 1998. Following dissatisfaction within the NDC at the changes carried out at the party congress, in June 1999 a disaffected group of party members formed a new political group, the National Reform Party (NRP).

In April 2000 the electoral register was reviewed in preparation for the election and the President ordered an amnesty for about 1,000 prisoners, including two former army officers convicted of subversion more than 10 years previously. Atta Mills was officially nominated as the NDC presidential candidate at the end of that month.

RAWLINGS REPLACED BY KUFUOR

Despite instances of pre-election violence, voting took place relatively peacefully on 7 December 2000. One of the principal concerns of voters in the preceding months was the deteriorating state of the economy (during 2000 alone there was a surge in inflation and a collapse in the value of the cedi), but there was also a strong movement in favour of political change, particularly in the more prosperous southern and western parts of the country. In the first round of the presidential election, which was contested by seven candidates, Kufuor secured 48.2% of the votes, compared to 44.5% for Atta Mills, a result that necessitated a second round of voting later in the month. In the legislative elections, the NPP won 100 of the 200 seats, performing particularly strongly in Accra and Kumasi and in Ashanti, Brong Ahafo and Eastern Regions. The NDC lost its majority in Parliament and returned 92 seats. Its main sources of support were the more impoverished regions of the north and east of the country. In the second round of the presidential election, Kufuor, benefiting from declarations of support from all the minor parties, defeated Atta Mills, with 56.9% of the votes.

The transfer of power took place in an atmosphere of remarkable good will. Nevertheless, the incoming Government indicated that it would undertake investigations into cases of suspected corruption by members of the former NDC administration. The Kufuor Government's primary concern was, however, to restore stability and growth to the economy, and, controversially, it opted to seek full debt relief under the initiative for heavily indebted poor countries of the World Bank and the IMF. The Government also moved to establish a 'truth and reconciliation' process to examine human rights abuses committed in Ghana since independence. An important example of this new political emphasis was the exhumation of the remains of the military officers executed in 1979 and the return of these remains to their families in December 2001. This gesture went some way towards providing a long-overdue reconciliation between Ghanaians on either side of the political divide that had emerged throughout the country following the first Rawlings coup in June 1979. The establishment of the National Reconciliation Commission (NRC) in May 2002 opened up a channel for complaints about human rights abuses and torture committed by previous Governments. By the end of that year the NRC had received nearly 3,000 complaints, mostly relating to events that took place under previous military regimes, and it commenced a series of public hearings in January 2003. One of the first to testify was a member of Nkrumah's presidential guard, who was held after the 1966 coup for 22 months. Other witnesses recounted torture suffered under the Rawlings regime. The NDC accused the Government of conducting a political witch-hunt against members of the former regime, but Rawlings himself appeared before the NRC in February 2004, when he denied direct knowledge of extra-judicial killings.

'Fast-track' court procedures were established to accelerate the delivery of justice in general, as well as specifically to deal with the cases that involved former office-holders. In December 2001 a former Deputy Minister of Finance in the Rawlings administration, Victor Selormey, was found guilty of diverting US $1.3m. of public money and was sentenced to eight years' imprisonment. A similar case involved the former Chief Executive of the Ghana National Petroleum Corpn, Tsatsu Tsikata, who was accused of causing wilful loss to the state; however in March 2002, Tsikata's lawyers succeeded in obtaining a ruling from the Supreme Court that the 'fast-track' courts were unconstitutional. In response, the Attorney-General, Nana Akuffo Addo, applied for a judicial review of the ruling, and the case resumed later in the year. In April 2003 a 'fast-track' court jailed three former officials of the NDC for their involvement in securing a $20m. loan for a rice-growing project that never materialized.

Among the first signs of economic improvement was a fall in the rate of depreciation of the cedi during 2001. There was also an increase in remittances by private individuals and companies abroad, but, despite an overall increase in business confidence, the new Government encountered significant political difficulties in pushing forward its liberalization policies and in persuading public opinion of the need for more comprehensive privatization of state-owned enterprises, in part because of a widespread sentimental attachment to long-established national institutions and in part because of the fear of further inflation. Although occasionally challenged by Rawlings and by reports of potentially inappropriate financial dealings, the Kufuor administration's authority appeared to be enhanced by its commitment to reconciliation and accountability. At an NPP delegates' conference in January 2003, Kufuor was selected unopposed as the party's presidential candidate for the election due in 2004. The NDC was much less united and underwent a more contentious selection process, although Atta Mills successfully defeated his challengers and was again nominated as the party's candidate.

There was further ethnic tension in the north of the country in 2002, in the wake of the violent abduction and murder of the King of the Dagomba, Ya-na Yakubu Andani, in Yendi in late March. The event was the culmination of unresolved and long-standing rivalries between the two ruling Dagomba clans, the Andani and the Abudu, and provoked violent clashes between clan members, in which more than 30 people were killed. In the light of subsequent reports that the King's abduction and murder were carried out by a heavily armed paramilitary unit, the Government was criticized for failing to ensure the King's security, and at the end of March the Minister of the Interior and the Minister for the Northern Region resigned. At least two suspects were arrested, and a curfew was imposed across the Northern Region. By early 2006 a process of consultation in the Dagomba area of the Northern Region had produced an apparent solution to the crisis in Yendi, involving the formal burial of the assassinated King and the appointment of a regent, Kampakuya Naa Abdulai Andani, a 34-year-old teacher. Meanwhile, there was an upsurge in tension in a long-running chieftaincy dispute in Bimbilla, 60 km south of Yendi.

Presidential and legislative elections were held concurrently on 7 December 2004, and were notable for their high rate of voter participation, officially recorded at 85.1%. The elections were conducted without violence and were widely judged to be free and fair. Kufuor was re-elected President, with 52.45% of the vote, while Atta Mills secured 44.64%. Of the 230 parliamentary seats, the NPP won 128, the NDC 94, the PNC four, the CPP three and an independent candidate one. The new Parliament was inaugurated on 7 January 2005; Ebenezer Begyina Seki Hughes was elected to the post of Speaker. Kufuor and Aliu Mahama were sworn in as President and Vice-President, respectively.

At the national congresses of the NPP and the NDC in December 2005 there were significant changes among party office holders. The NPP Chairman, Haruna Esseku, was replaced by Pete Mac Manu following allegations of financial abuse, prompting an inquiry by the Serious Fraud Office, while several senior NDC office holders, known to be opposed to the continued dominance of Rawlings, were voted out of office, prompting others in the party to resign. Dr Kwabena Adjei was elected Chairman of the NDC. Observers noted considerable jockeying for senior positions in both parties; none the less, in 2006 the NDC once again chose Atta Mills as its presidential candidate for 2008. Possible contenders for future presidential candidature in the NPP included Nana Akufo-Addo, Yaw Osafu-Maafo, Alan Kyeremanteng, Kwame Addo Kufuor and Hackman Owusu Agyeman, while Vice-President Aliu Mahama was widely regarded as a potential compromise candidate.

In July 2007 Kufuor effected substantial changes to the Government, following the resignations of a number of ministers who intended to contest the 2008 presidential election. The number of ministers and deputy ministers was reportedly increased to 82; most notably Albert Kan Dapaah, hitherto Minister of the Interior, was appointed Minister of Defence, while the former Minister for Information and National Orientation, Kwamena Bartels, assumed the interior portfolio.

FOREIGN RELATIONS

In 1984 the PNDC established close links with the Government of Capt. Thomas Sankara in the neighbouring state of Burkina Faso. Sankara, who seized power in August 1983, based the working structure of his 'revolution' on that of the PNDC. In August 1986 the Governments of Ghana and Burkina Faso agreed to establish a high-level political commission, which would be responsible for preparing a 10-year timetable for the political union of the two countries. Agreements were also made to harmonize their currencies and their energy, transport, trade and educational systems, and in September and October a joint military exercise was held. Following a military coup in Burkina Faso in October 1987, relations between the two countries were temporarily strained, but subsequently improved, after meetings between Rawlings and Sankara's successor, Capt. Blaise Compaoré, although the ambitious proposals for union announced in 1986 were abandoned.

Relations with Togo have frequently been strained, in particular as a result of the presence in Ghana of opponents of the Togolese President, Gnassingbé Eyadéma (see the chapter on Togo). By late 1992 more than 100,000 Togolese had taken refuge in Ghana, following the deterioration in the political situation in Togo. In January 1993 Ghana announced that its armed forces were to be mobilized, in reaction to concern at the increasing civil unrest in Togo. In March the Government of Togo accused Ghana of supporting an armed attack on the military camp at Lomé, the Togolese capital, where Eyadéma resided. In January 1994 a further attack on Eyadéma's residence was attributed by the Togolese authorities to armed dissidents based in Ghana, again contributing to a deterioration in relations between the neighbouring states. The Ghanaian chargé d'affaires in Togo was subsequently arrested, while Togolese forces killed 12 Ghanaians and bombarded a customs post at Aflao and several villages near the two countries' common border. Ghana, however, denied the accusations of involvement in the coup attempt and threatened to retaliate against further acts of aggression. In May allegations by the Togolese Government that Ghana had been responsible (owing to lack of border security) for bomb attacks in Togo further heightened tensions. Later that year, however, relations between the two countries improved, and in November full diplomatic links were formally restored, with the appointment of a Ghanaian ambassador in Togo. In February 1996 both parliaments established friendship groups to examine ways of easing tensions. By the end of 1996 some 48,000 Togolese refugees were estimated to have received payment for voluntary repatriation. Against this background of strained relations with Togo, the election of Kufuor in December 2000 quickly resulted in an improvement. There was a resumption of normal movements across the common border and a restoration of regular business dealings. Subsequently, Kufuor's Government played a conciliatory role after the death of Eyadéma in February 2005, at a time when other countries were expressing outrage at the unconstitutional seizure of power on behalf of the late Togolese President's son, Faure Gnassingbé. Following the presidential election held in Togo in April 2005, at which Gnassingbé secured a decisive victory, bilateral relations were expected further to improve. However, following Gnassingbé's election, by July some 15,000 Togolese refugees had registered in Ghana.

Ghana participated in the ECOMOG peace-keeping force, which was dispatched to Liberia in August 1990 following the outbreak of conflict between government and rebel forces in that country (see the chapter on Liberia). The Ghanaian contingent remained in ECOMOG while Rawlings (in his role as Chairman of the Conference of Heads of State and Government of ECOWAS) mediated continuing negotiations between the warring Liberian factions. Financial assistance was received from the Government of Canada for the care of the Liberian refugees, whose numbers had risen to 42,000 by late 2004, by which time many were beginning to be repatriated. In June 1997 the Ghanaian Government announced the establishment of a task force to monitor the situation in Sierra Leone, following a military coup in the previous month (see the chapter on Sierra Leone). By late 1998 most of the ECOMOG forces in Liberia had been redeployed in Sierra Leone, in response to the mounting conflict in that country. After the expansion of peace-keeping efforts in 2000, military and civilian police personnel from Ghana participated fully in the expanded UN Mission in Sierra Leone. Ghana has remained a leading contributor to UN peace-keeping missions around the world. In 2005 Ghana's armed forces participated in land and sea military exercises in West Africa in co-operation with forces from the USA, Spain and Italy.

As ECOWAS Chairman for 2002/03, President Kufuor played an active role in searching for solutions to the severe ethnic and political divisions that emerged in Côte d'Ivoire from September 2002. In a series of meetings staged in Accra, he was able to keep lines of communication open between the Ivorian President, Laurent Gbagbo, and the opposition parties and rebel movements within Côte d'Ivoire. As negotiations progressed towards the implementation of a peace process from March 2003, Ghanaian troops were despatched to participate in an ECOWAS peace-keeping mission in Côte d'Ivoire, the only troops from an English-speaking country to do so. During 2005 there were several reports of infiltration by armed groups across the border from northern Côte d'Ivoire into northern Ghana, although Ghana's armed forces succeeded in preventing any continued occupation by such groups.

President Kufuor was elected as Chairman of the African Union (AU) in January 2007 at the beginning of Ghana's 50th independence anniversary year, and he was acknowledged as an important figure in the context of Africa's international relations, attending the Franco-African summit in Cannes, France, in February and the African Partnership Forum held in Berlin, Germany, in May. At the AU summit of heads of state, held in Accra in July, it was agreed to set up a committee to establish a timetable for a pan-African government. The idea of a single pan-African government was first promoted by Kwame Nkrumah, Ghana's first post-independence President, in 1957. However, there was no agreement among AU leaders on how this goal was to be achieved.

Economy

LINDA VAN BUREN

Strong positive economic growth, spurred by agriculture and especially by the cocoa sector, continued in 2006 for the third consecutive year, despite inflationary pressures brought on primarily by high global petroleum prices. In May 2007 the IMF commended the Government for its implementation of macroeconomic policies and stated that Ghana was beginning to win the fight against poverty. The poverty headcount declined from around 52% in 1991/92 to 28.5% in 2005/06. At the current pace Ghana was likely achieve the Millennium Development Goal of halving poverty well before the target date of 2015.

At independence in 1957 Ghana possessed one of the strongest economies in Africa. However, the economy declined sharply in the following 25 years. During that period real per-head income fell by more than one-third, and the government tax base was diminished. The resulting large deficits led to rising inflation and a burgeoning external debt burden. It also resulted in lower expenditure on, and a general neglect of, the country's infrastructure, as well as its education and health services. By 1981 average annual price inflation was running at 142%. The Rawlings Government introduced two Economic Recovery Programmes (ERPs), developed in close collaboration with the World Bank and the IMF. The first ERP (ERP I), launched in 1983, was the stabilization phase of the economy's recovery, while ERP II, covering the period 1987–90, was the structural adjustment and development stage of that recovery.

The international community continued to support Ghana's reform efforts throughout the 1990s and into the 21st century. Ghana was often cited as the IMF's 'most senior star pupil' during the 1980s and the 1990s, and although the relationship has not always been a flawless one, Ghana's 'star-pupil' status still endures. This was reconfirmed in May 2003, when the IMF approved a three-year, US $258m. Poverty-Reduction and Growth Facility (PRGF) arrangement. In July 2004 the Fund, in its review of Ghana's PRGF arrangement, waived the non-observance of the quantitative performance criterion on the banking-sector credit to the Tema oil refinery and two structural performance criteria on the adjustment of petrol prices and for electricity and water tariffs. A third review of the PRGF, in July 2005, resulted in the disbursement of a further $38.7m. and also in the extension of the overall life of the arrangement to October 2006, awarding Ghana a greater opportunity to receive the full allocated amount. In mid-2006 following the fifth review of the PRGF arrangement, the Fund intimated it would waive Ghana's non-observance of two quantitative and one structural performance criteria. The October 2006 final review also granted a waiver for non-performance criteria concerning the assets of the Bank of Ghana and resulted in the release of the final $39m. tranche.

Ghana's return to high inflation shortly after President John Agyekum Kufuor took office, in January 2001, proved to be short-lived. The rate of inflation peaked at 41.9% in the 12 months to March 2001, but it had been reduced to 15.2% by the end of 2002. Higher global petroleum prices, coupled with a removal of fuel subsidies in early 2003, placed upward pressure on inflation, which at the end of December 2003 was running at 23.6% on a year-on-year basis. The 2004 budget set a target of reducing inflation to below 10% during the 2004/05 financial year; this target was not met, but year-on-year inflation was lowered to 11.8% at the end of December 2004. However, rising global petroleum prices in 2005 increased inflation to 14.9% as of September 2005. In December the IMF commended Ghana's economic planners for deregulating the petroleum sector and for adopting a new petroleum-product pricing mechanism in 2005, especially in the face of high world prices for that commodity. By 31 October 2006 the Government had succeeded in reducing the rate of inflation to 10.5%, but single-digit status remained elusive. The Kufuor administration also re-established stability for the cedi. During 2005 the cedi's value against the US dollar remained almost unchanged, while its value against the pound sterling and against the euro appreciated, in line with the dollar's fluctuation against these currencies. In May 2007 the Government announced that cedi notes in circulation were to be demonetized. For a six-month period, commencing on 7 July 2007, both old and new notes would circulate as legal tender, with the new notes being equal in face value to the old notes. After six months the old notes would cease to be legal tender.

Severe political instability in neighbouring Côte d'Ivoire from September 2002 coincided with bad weather in other cocoa-growing areas of the world to create a mini-boom for Ghana's cocoa growers. The international cocoa price briefly rose above US $2,400 per metric ton in October 2002; although it declined to $1,900 per ton in the following month, this was still twice the price on offer in November 2001. The price declined to $1,470 per ton in May 2005, but recovered to $1,980 per ton in May 2007.

The Ghanaian economy is based primarily on the country's lucrative gold and cocoa sectors, although some success has been achieved towards diversification; in 2003 these two commodities together contributed 58% of export revenue, although the proportion rose to 71% in 2004, owing mainly to the success of the cocoa sector against the relatively flat performance of other sectors. The production of cocoa was established in Ghana, mainly as an African smallholder crop, in the latter part of the 19th century. In the late 1950s, at the time of its political independence, Ghana was the world's leading exporter of cocoa, and this crop continued to account for 45%–70% of commodity exports in most years from the early 1970s until the 1990s, when increased mineral revenues led to a decline in cocoa's share of exports, to some 18% in 2000. In 2006, according to provisional figures, the sale of cocoa beans and cocoa products earned 34% of total merchandise export revenue. The country has been known as a source of gold for many centuries; large-scale extraction commenced in the 1880s, and the sector underwent a major revival in the 1990s, which subsequently proved to be sustainable, despite a weakness in the international price of gold. Export revenue from gold rose steeply in 2006, as a result of both a 13.2% rise in export volume and a 26% increase in the global price. Exports of timber from Ghana's forests also began in the 1880s. Exports of timber and timber products fell below $200m. in 2006, a decline of some 13%.

POLICY OBJECTIVES OF THE ERP

Exchange-rate and trade-policy reforms were given priority in the recovery programmes. A weekly foreign-exchange auction was introduced in September 1986. Two further main reforms in exchange and trade arrangements followed. The first of these was the release of foreign exchange for importers of consumer goods by allowing their participation in the auction. The second was the licensing of a number of foreign-exchange bureaux, which were empowered to buy and sell foreign exchange independently. Policies adopted in 1992 included the abolition of the weekly foreign auction, with the aim of making exchange-rate determination a function of a freely operating interbank market. The cedi steadily depreciated in value, however, losing 86% of its value between 1993 and 2000. Meanwhile, the Ghanaian Government stressed the need to protect the poorest people from the weakness of the cedi and from the resultant high prices of many items on the domestic market. On 31 May 2006 the exchange rate stood at 9,145 cedis to the US dollar, compared with 9,066 a year earlier; by May 2007, the rate had changed little and amounted to 9,075 cedis to the dollar. In December 1998 the Government introduced a value-added tax (VAT) at an initial rate of 10%. It was subsequently raised to 12.5%. The ERP also sought to rationalize the import tariff as the central instrument of trade protection. Finally, and as a by-product of exchange-rate policies, the major devaluations of the currency significantly boosted, in cedi terms, tax revenues on cocoa earnings.

The 1983 ERP also provided for changes to the policy of state ownership. At an early stage a consultant study recommended that 80 of 235 state enterprises be converted into joint ventures with the private sector, be completely divested or, in a few cases, be liquidated. Progress was initially slow; in the first decade only 52 enterprises were divested, of which 33 were sold to foreign investors. The pace then quickened, and more than 180 had been disposed of by 1996. In addition, some parastatal companies previously considered to be 'strategic', such as Ghana Airways and the Posts and Telecommunications Corpn, were designated for transfer to the private sector. (Ghana Telecom was created from the division of the Posts and Telecommunications Corpn in 1995, and was partially privatized in 1997.) In December 2004 the Government announced the creation of Ghana International Airlines Limited (GIA), which was to replace Ghana Airways and was to become the new national carrier. GIA was a joint venture between the Ghanaian Government and a US consortium GIA-USA. By April 2006, however, the carrier had experienced a number of difficulties, resulting in the dismissal of the company's Chief Executive. As of May 2007, the carrier was operating a daily service between Accra's Kotoka International Airport and London Gatwick in the United Kingdom.

In December 2001 the Government confirmed that 264 enterprises had been divested; of these, 155 had been sold outright (of which 38 were the subject of share offers on the Ghana Stock Exchange), while 21 had become joint ventures. A further 43 entities had been liquidated. The International Finance Corpn (IFC), the private-sector organ of the World Bank, became very active in Ghana during the late 1980s and the 1990s, adding no fewer than 25 Ghanaian companies to its portfolio during that period. Assistance was sometimes in the form of an equity participation, but was more often a loan, varying in size from $120,000 for a corrugated-carton manufacturer in 1991 to $6.58m. for an open-pit gold-mining operation in 1988.

ECONOMIC PERFORMANCE SINCE THE 1980S

By the end of 1982 Ghana's economy was severely flawed. Against this general background, economic performance since 1983 can be considered very successful, although further progress is necessary to achieve broad-based growth at all levels of the economy.

Real GDP increased at an average rate of 3% per year in 1980–90 and 4.4% in 1990–2003. Real GDP growth rates achieved were 5.2% in 2003, 5.8% in 2004, 5.9% in 2005 and 6.2% in 2006, with 6.5% growth forecast for 2007. The deficit on the current account of the balance of payments (excluding official transfers) was US $1,278.7m. (10.5% of GDP) in 2006, a slight improvement over 2005's shortfall of $1,378.5m. (14.3% of GDP). The overall balance of payments recorded a surplus of $178.8m. in 2006, double the surplus of $84.3m. in 2005. Private investment was deterred in the early 1990s by perceptions both of financial instability and of political obstacles placed in the way of businesses owned by known opponents of the Rawlings Government, while anticipated flows of foreign and Ghanaian private capital were not realized. New investment was concentrated in relatively few areas, principally in gold-mining and, to a lesser extent, in tourism. Much of the economy is based on short-term trading activity, and it was the services sector that exhibited the strongest growth during the recovery period. In 2005 the highest level of growth, 6.5%, was recorded by the agricultural sector, according to provisional figures, boosted by cocoa in particular. Industry grew by 5.6% in 2005, while the services sector grew by 5.4% in that year. The agricultural sector made the largest contribution to GDP in 2005, at 40.6%, according to provisional figures, compared with 41.5% in 2004. The services sector share of total GDP was 32.3% in 2005, up from 31.4% in 2004, while industry contributed 27.1% in 2004, a figure that remained the same in 2005. In 2006 GDP growth of 6.2% was attributed to strong performance in the industrial and service sectors.

Exports provisionally totalled $3,857.7m. in 2006, led by cocoa exports of $1,258,8m., while imports provisionally amounted to $6,852.4m. Gross international reserves stood at $1,782.69m. at 30 September 2007, enough to cover 3.3 months' worth of imports of goods and services. This compares unfavourably with the forward import cover of 3.9 months at the end of 2005 and 3.8 months at the end of 2004.

POPULATION

By November 2005 just over 60% of the labour force worked in the agricultural sector, while only 8% were employed in the services sector, largely as a result of the Government's efforts to reduce public-sector employment. In order to help those affected by its economic retrenchment policies, the Rawlings Government launched the Programme of Action to Mitigate the Social Costs of Adjustment (PAMSCAD) in 1988 and obtained pledges of US $140m. from donors to finance it. The first part of the PAMSCAD comprised a series of schemes to generate employment for those (about 45,000) affected by the job losses in the public sector during 1988–90. The second part aimed to strengthen community social programmes, including self-help groups. The final part was intended to provide the most vulnerable groups in society with basic needs, such as water and sanitation, health care, nutrition and housing. In 1995 redundant staff of the Ghana Cocoa Board (COCOBOD, see below) were to be retrained under an 890m. cedi national programme, funded by the European Union (EU) and the Government.

AGRICULTURE

In 2005, according to provisional figures, the agricultural sector (including forestry and fishing) accounted for 35.8% of GDP and employed more than one-half of the working population. Cocoa is traditionally Ghana's most important cash crop, occupying more than one-half of all the country's cultivated land; in 2004 cocoa alone contributed 17.9% of total GDP, but by 2006 this proportion had declined to 4.7%. In October 1983 the Government initiated a US $130m. campaign under ERP I to revitalize the cocoa sector. The Cocoa Marketing Board (CMB) was reorganized to implement the campaign more efficiently. Cash incentives were offered to farmers to replant crops, and producer prices were increased by 67% in cedi terms, though in terms of real purchasing power the price rise had little effect. Essential inputs, such as insecticides, building materials and sprayers, were made available, and improvements were made to transport and distribution services. Attention was also focused on estate rehabilitation and disease control in the major growing areas in the Ashanti and Western Regions (although the areas worst affected by disease were the Eastern and Central Regions). Progress was slow, owing to shortages of labour, resistance by farmers to the uprooting of old trees in order to prevent the spread of disease to new pods, and continued doubts about the adequacy of price incentives. Although more than 3m. hybrid cocoa pods were distributed to private farmers for planting in 1985, many farmers chose to plant food crops rather than cocoa, because they preferred to be provided with essential commodities rather than receive payment in cedis. Also in 1985 the CMB was reorganized as COCOBOD, and in July 1986 a new agreement, proposed by the World Bank, fixed the level of producer prices. In Ghana 320,000 ha of cocoa farming land was designated as special zones for rehabilitation and spraying to prevent black pod disease.

Under ERP II, the Government aimed to increase cocoa production to more than 350,000 metric tons per year. However, this target initially proved to be over-optimistic, and output remained below 300,000 tons per year. Subsidies on fertilizers were abolished, and high rates of interest discouraged farmers from seeking credit from the commercial banks. In late 1997, however, global cocoa prices reached a nine-year high, enabling the Government to act swiftly to make good on its promise of sharing out this good fortune with the farmers. In June 1997 the Government raised the producer price of cocoa from 1.2m. cedis per ton to 1.8m. cedis. Following this measure, the farmer received 54% of the estimated f.o.b. price received from the sale of cocoa by the Government to overseas purchasers, and it was announced that this proportion was to rise to 60% by 2000; in October 1998 the proportion increased to 56%. Kufuor's Government increased the producer price by 35% in 2001 and by 40% in February 2002, bringing it to 4.38m. cedis per ton. A further rise in October 2003 brought the producer price to 9m. cedis per ton. Consequently, the grower's share of the f.o.b. cocoa price increase achieved the target of 70% by the 2004/05 growing season. In October 2004, and again in November 2005, the Government took the decision not to raise the producer price, leaving it at 9m. cedis per ton; however, as international cocoa prices had declined, the growers' share of total cocoa revenue rose to 73% in 2004 before declining to 70%—the target—in 2005. The 2004 cocoa harvest of 736,911 tons was the largest ever recorded in Ghana and was almost 50% larger than the 2003 crop. In 2006 715,660 tons of cocoa beans were exported.

In July 1993 COCOBOD was formally deprived of its monopoly over the internal marketing of cocoa. Nevertheless, in 1998 the Rawlings Government restated its intention to resist pressure from the IMF and the World Bank to liberalize the external marketing of cocoa, which was still carried out exclusively by the Government. The Kufuor Government began the licensing of private cocoa-exporting companies in 2001. By 1999 18 companies in Ghana had been licensed to buy cocoa from the producers.

Ghana has also achieved some diversity in cash-crop production since the 1990s. On a small scale, both for local consumption and for export, Ghanaian farmers have begun to grow such crops as cashew nuts, brazil nuts, oranges, lemons, limes, apples, melons, papayas (pawpaws), mangoes, avocados, tomatoes, cucumbers, onions, green beans, aubergines (eggplants), chillies, okra, peppercorns, ginger and raspberries. In 1996 export-promotion villages were established to produce a number of high-value export crops. Cotton growers, however, complained in 2001 that the government policy of 'zoning' deterred competition. Thus, although two companies were allowed to buy cotton from farmers, each of the two was allocated sole rights over one-half of the cotton-growing regions, leaving individual farmers still with no choice as to buyer.

Food production is based principally on the farming of cassava, yams, cocoyams (taro), plantains and maize. In 1997 the Government announced that the outgrower scheme in the cultivation of oil palms and other cash crops had been so successful that it was to be used as the basis for similar schemes in other food and cash crops, particularly cereals and tubers. The yield of yams was to be improved by the use of better cultivation techniques.

Cattle farming is restricted to the Northern Region and the Accra plains; the national herd stood at 1.5m. head in 2005. Production of meat is insufficient to meet local annual demand of about 200,000 metric tons. Imports of livestock from adjacent countries have been considerable, though declining in recent years, owing to shortages of foreign exchange. The country had about 300,000 pigs in 2005. In February 2003 a 20% duty was imposed on imported poultry products to protect the local sector; Ghana had about 30m. chickens in 2005. Consumers ate more chicken than any other meat, mainly because the price of imported chicken had been relatively low. The worldwide fear of bird flu in 2005–06 was also a concern for Ghana's poultry farmers. Domestic fisheries (marine and Lake Volta) supply only between one-half and two-thirds of the country's total annual demand of 600,000 metric tons. The total catch in 2005 was 420,000 tons. In that year the Government introduced a steel vessel on Lake Volta to patrol the lake and curtail the use of illegal fishing gear. An estimated 80,000 Ghanaians fish in Lake Volta, using 17,500 canoes and netting some 82,000 tons of fish per year.

Ghana has extensive forests, mostly in the south-west, and developed a substantial timber export industry during the 1960s. The establishment of a Timber Marketing Board (TMB), with powers to fix minimum contract prices, marked the beginning of a decline in this sector, and in 1985 the TMB was replaced by the Forest Products Inspection Bureau and the Timber Export Development Board. Efforts are proceeding to promote timber exports, which are projected eventually to reach 700,000 cu m per year. However, exports declined from 902,860 cu m in 1994 to an annual average of 257,925 cu m in 1996–99. The Government has undertaken to phase out exports of raw logs and to encourage local processing of timber products, following the introduction in late 1993 of duty incentives for imports of sawmilling and other equipment. Ghana, however, possesses enough timber to meet its foreseeable domestic and export requirements until 2030. The forestry sector accounted for 3.6% of GDP in 2006, and was forecast to contribute 3.4% in 2007. Timber and timber products contributed $196.7m. in export revenue in 2006 and accounted for 7.2% of all exports by value. In that year more than 95% of all roundwood removals in Ghana were for locally consumed fuelwood.

MANUFACTURING

Apart from traditional industries such as food-processing, Ghana has a number of long-established large and medium-sized enterprises, including a petroleum refinery and plants producing textiles, vehicles, cement, paper, chemicals and footwear, and some export-based industries, such as cocoa-processing and wood-processing plants.

The manufacturing industries have traditionally been under-used, high-cost and strongly dependent on imported equipment and materials. Expansion was deterred by low levels of investment, by transport congestion and by persistent shortages of imported materials and spares. Moreover, the consistent overvaluation of the cedi and the irregularity of supply increased the attractiveness of imports relative to home-produced goods.

Manufacturing output declined sharply in the early 1980s, and the sector's contribution to Ghana's total GDP fell from 22% in 1973 to under 5% before the commencement of ERP I in 1983. Almost all industries continue to be affected by shortages of raw materials, spare parts and other imported machinery, irregular electricity supplies, and inflation. Nevertheless, according to the World Bank, manufacturing GDP increased at an average annual rate of 4.3% in 1995–2005; the contribution of the subsector to total GDP declined from 9.6% in 2002 to a provisional 8.6% in 2005. Most of the decline was attributable to the growing contribution of the cocoa sector to GDP, rather than to a decline in manufacturing output, as the sector grew by 4.6% in 2004, by 5.0% in 2005 and by a provisional 4.2% in 2006. The Kufuor Government placed heavy upward pressure on companies' costs by raising the minimum wage by 31% to 5,500 cedis per day (about US $0.76), fuel prices by an average of 64%, water tariffs by 96% and electricity tariffs by 103%. Higher global prices for oil also took their toll. Nevertheless, the Government has stated its intention to add more value to its exports locally, thereby opening up investment opportunities for companies interested in processing cocoa, timber and other commodities.

Among the largest capital-intensive industries in Ghana is an aluminium smelter at Tema, operated by the Volta Aluminium Co (Valco), which was owned by the multinational Kaiser Aluminum and Chemical Corpn (90%) and Alcoa (10%). Although the Tema plant has a potential output capacity of 200,000 metric tons of primary aluminium per year, annual production was less than 50,000 tons in the mid-1980s, owing to lower world demand and reduced energy supplies from the drought-stricken Akosombo hydroelectricity plant. Although production at Tema recovered to 152,000 tons in 1997, output of only 56,000 tons was recorded in 1998, owing to electricity shortages; high production during 2000 and 2001, with five potlines in operation, was reduced in 2002 and 2003 by cuts in power allocation. The contract governing the supply of electric power to Valco by the state-owned Volta River Authority (VRA) expired in April 1997, and agreement between Valco and the VRA on a renewal was never achieved, although the VRA continued to supply power to Valco without a renewal until January 2003. In that month 3 the VRA and Valco submitted the matter to mediation in Washington, DC, USA. Valco and Kaiser subsequently broke off mediation talks and instead applied for arbitration by the International Chamber of Commerce. The dispute centred on the price that Valco was to pay the VRA for electric power; the VRA wanted the price to reflect its own cost of electricity production, while Valco wanted to pay a price based on a global average cost of producing electricity. The Ghanaian Government relented to the extent of offering a price of US $0.03 per kWh, which would reduce, but not eliminate, a subsidization of power to Valco by the Ghanaian taxpayer. By mid-2003 this offer had not been accepted by Valco. In May 2004 the Consultative Group on International Agricultural Research allocated $18m. to fund 11 projects in the Volta Basin designed to improve the availability of water and food. In the end, in November 2004 Kaiser Aluminum completed the sale of its remaining interest in Valco to the Ghanaian Government. In January 2005 Alcoa and the Government signed a memorandum of understanding for the revitalization of Valco, with Alcoa, paving the way for further agreements about mining, refining, smelting, rail upgrades and ownership structure. The initial agreement called for the restart of three of the five existing potlines, with a total capacity of 120,000 tons per year.

Meanwhile, privatization of the manufacturing sector accelerated in 1993, and the Divestiture Implementation Committee (DIC) undertook to sell the Government's shares in a number of enterprises, including the Tema food complex, the Ghana Industrial Holding Co (GIHOC) pharmaceutical subsidiary, the Bonsa Tyre Co (including its rubber estate) and cocoa-processing factories in Tema and Takoradi. Buyers for Bonsa Tyre were still being sought in May 2007. In 2001, through the Ghanaian Investment Fund and venture capital funds, the Kufuor Government established a Small Business Assistance Programme to provide finance to small-scale enterprises. Sectors where these small-scale enterprises could make a large contribution with improved technologies were food-processing (especially fish), textiles, wood-processing and packaging. Companies that export from Ghana are allowed to retain 100% of their export proceeds in foreign-exchange accounts at Ghanaian banks under the Export Proceeds Retention Scheme. However, in May 2001 the Government expressed concern that some firms were keeping their export proceeds in banks outside Ghana, even though the scheme allows companies unqualified access to these sums. Among the companies scheduled for privatization in 2007 were Komenda Sugar, the GIHOC cannery at Pwulugu, the Paga Motel, Ejura Farms, the State Hotel Training School at Tema, Subri Industrial Plantation and Western Veneer & Lumber.

Evidence of increasing foreign investor confidence is apparent in the repurchase by multinationals, such as Unilever and Guinness, of shares in their Ghanaian operations that had been government-held. In an attempt to encourage new investments by foreign corporations, the Government repealed some restrictive legislation, and in early 1993 reduced the minimum capital requirements for new foreign investment and reserved very few activities exclusively for Ghanaians. Dividends, profits and the original investment capital could be repatriated freely in convertible currency, and tax incentives and benefits were improved. In 1995 the Government established the Ghana Free Zones Board and invited companies to invest in export-processing activities in Ghana, to be concentrated in export-processing zones (EPZs). The Board's role was strictly regulatory, and companies were allowed 100% ownership of free-zone enterprises. Investors were granted total exemption from duties on imported raw materials, exemption from withholding tax on dividends and exemption from income tax in the first 10 years (with an income tax rate of not more than 8% in the second 10 years). In addition, companies were allowed to sell up to 30% of their output into the Ghanaian market. By 1997 over 60 companies had applied for free-zone licences. In February 2000 the Government acknowledged that measures were required to prevent 'leakages' from the zone into the domestic market. In February 2002 the Government again expressed concern at abuses of the free-zone concept by some companies and vowed to take measures to correct the situation. The largest EPZ is the 480-ha Tema EPZ, in Ghana's principal port city. The 439-ha Ashanti EPZ is near the inland port of Ghana Boankra. The 880-ha Sekondi EPZ, formerly known as the Shama EPZ is currently under development; located in Ghana's second port city with a nearby rail link, this is aimed at heavy industries.

MINING

Gold is overwhelmingly the largest component of Ghana's mineral production. Non-gold mining output was sluggish in 2006, but gold output grew by 9%. The principal mine is situated at Obuasi and is the ninth largest in the world. In 2004 the merger of Ashanti Goldfields of Ghana with AngloGold Ltd of South Africa became effective, and the company, renamed AngloGold Ashanti, became the world's largest gold-mining company. AngloGold Ashanti continues to operate the Obuasi, Siguiri, Iduapriem and Geita mines in Ghana while also maintaining mining activities in Argentina, Australia, Brazil, Namibia and South Africa. The Obuasi mine alone produced 92,000 oz of gold in the first quarter of 2005. Total gold output in 2006 amounted to 2.1m. oz.

Following the political changes in South Africa in the 1990s, investors from that country bought Tarkwa Goldfields from the State Gold Mining Corpn in the mid-1990s, and almost immediately the inflow of new investment became evident as new facilities were constructed, virtually transforming the Tarkwa site (where gold reserves are measured at 13m. oz). The South African company Gold Fields announced a new investment in Tarkwa of R1,100m. in May 2003. The expansion would boost Tarkwa's output by 175,000 oz per year, to 700,000 oz per year from 2005. Goldfields Ghana Ltd invested US $162m. in the Tarkwa and Daman mines in 2003/04. In December 2003 the US company Newmont Mining Corpn of Denver, Colorado, announced a $350m. investment in the Ahafo gold-mining project, in Brong-Ahafo Region of western Ghana. The 269.5 sq m Ahafo project has 12 ore bodies, and a 'recently updated' feasibility study found that the project had the capacity to produce 500,000 equity oz per year (even more in initial years) and that 'proven and probable' reserves amounted to 108.6m. metric tons. Newmont, which owns 100% of the Ahafo project, is also proceeding with the 1,468 sq m open-pit Akyem gold-mining project, in Birim North district in Eastern Region. Newmont owns 85%, and the Ghanaian company Kenbert Mines Ltd owns the remaining 15%. Akyem has 80m. tons of 'proven and probable' reserves, and production is forecast at between 350,000–400,000 equity oz per year. The first gold output was expected in 2007. The Newmont Mining and Goldfields Ghana investments amount to more than $500,000 of new foreign investment in a single year. Gold Fields of South Africa holds a 71.1% interest in the Tarkwa and Damang mines; Tarkwa has multiple open pits and two heap-leaching plants, and Damang has two open pits and a carbon-in-leach (CIL) plant.

Diamonds, which are mainly industrial stones, are mined both by Ghana Consolidated Diamonds (formerly Consolidated Africa Selection Trust) at Akwatia and by local diggers. Total recorded production dwindled from 3.2m. metric carats (640 kg) in 1960 to 300,000 carats in 1988. Diamond output recovered as a result of efforts to regularize small-scale mining after 1990, and the Precious Minerals Marketing Co (PMMC) reported output of 686,551 carats in 2000, excluding Ghana Consolidated Diamonds production. Total output of diamonds in 2004 was reportedly 905,000 carats. In May 2003 the PMMC's efforts to achieve a clean bill of health with regard to the sale of 'conflict diamonds' received a reverse, when it was alleged that it had sold some stones to an Israeli company for less than US $3 per carat. The PMMC denied that the stones were 'conflict diamonds'.

Ghana entered petroleum production in 1978, when a US company began extracting petroleum from the continental shelf near Saltpond. Reserves at Saltpond were estimated at

7m. barrels, but average output during the early 1980s was only 1,250 barrels per day (b/d). In 1983 the Government established the Ghana National Petroleum Corpn (GNPC) to develop offshore areas under production-sharing contracts. Exploration and production rights were set out under the 1984 Petroleum Law, which allowed the Government to take an initial 10% share in any venture, with the option of buying 50% of production and holding a 50% royalty on output. In 1995 the decision was taken to reappraise a natural-gas deposit at Cape Three Points, discovered initially in 1974, and in 1997 the GNPC signed agreements with two foreign consortia for offshore exploration and production in the area. The 2006/07 budget promised a review of the Petroleum Exploration Law in order to make Ghana more attractive to oil prospectors. In 2006 the Government ratified four oil exploration contracts. These were with GASOP Oil for a concession at West Cape Three Point; with Amerada Hess for concessions at Deep Water Tano and West Cape Three Point; with Tullow Oil Ghana Limited (TOGL) and Sabre Oil and Gas Limited (SOGL) for a concession at Shallow Water West Tano; and with TOGL, SOGL and Kosmos Energy Ghana Limited for a concession at Deep Water West Tano.

In September 1995 Ghana joined Nigeria, Togo and Benin in signing an agreement to proceed with the construction of a West African Gas Pipeline from Nigeria. In May 2003 Ghana and other partners signed a further agreement for the creation of the West African Pipeline Company (WAPC) to operate the pipeline. The Ghanaian Government reported that it had paid for its 16.3% share of WAPC in full during 2004. The pipeline had been expected to deliver its first methane gas by the end of 2006, but this was later delayed until 2007. Ghana's sole refinery, the 45,000 b/d Tema oil refinery (TOR), was operated by the Ghanaian-Italian Petroleum Co and was owned by GNPC. A new unit was to be built at the refinery to convert excess residual fuel into petrol and liquefied petroleum gas (LPG). Plans for a partial privatization of the TOR were announced, with 30% to be sold to a 'strategic investor' with management control and 25% to be floated on the stock exchange, but in November 1998 Parliament objected to the sale of the TOR, as well as of the Ghana Oil Co (GOC), on the grounds that these were 'strategic assets'. This prompted the IMF in January 1999 to urge the Government to continue its privatization plans as scheduled. In 2004 TOR's activities were restricted to the refining of crude oil only; the procurement and importation of finished petroleum products was opened to private-sector oil-marketing companies (OMCs), but only by tender, and limited to the incremental amount between the TOR supply and the national demand. The first such tender was held in March 2004. Ghana's Petroleum Deregulation Policy came into effect in mid-February 2005 with the announcement that new prices for petroleum products would be set by the OMCs under the supervision of an independent National Petroleum Authority (NPA). Legislation to support the regulatory functions of the NPA was enacted in 2005.

In October 2002 Dana Petroleum PLC of the United Kingdom announced the discovery of large fan structures in the Deep Water West Tano Contract Area that could potentially contain several hundred million barrels of crude oil; a further find in shallow water nearby was announced a few days later. The quality of the sandstone target proved disappointing, but the exploratory well discovered 75 ft of high-quality oil-bearing sandstone reservoir in a shallower formation, at a depth of about 6,100 ft. Subsequent remapping indicated the potential for significant oil-in-place volumes of some 200m. barrels. As the oil is relatively viscous, future commercial viability will depend on how technology can be applied to maximise recovery efficiency, and this was the focus of development studies commenced in 2003. In light of this and other developments, the Ghanaian authorities offered Dana a three-year extension of its exploration licence. Nigeria is the principal supplier of crude petroleum to Ghana; other suppliers include Iran, Libya and Algeria.

Ghana possesses substantial reserves of bauxite, although only a small proportion, at Awaso in the Western Region, is currently mined. Exploitation of these deposits is carried out by the Ghana Bauxite Co (GBC), in which the Government holds a 20% interest. Bauxite output, which is all exported, fell from more than 300,000 metric tons per year during the 1950s to less than 30,000 tons by the mid-1980s, owing to the rapid deterioration of the railway line linking Awaso with port facilities at Takoradi. Repairs on the railway line ensured production recovered from 1985 and into the 1990s. Ghana now exports some 500,000 metric tons of bauxite ore per year.

Manganese ore is mined at Nsuta, in the Western Region, by the Ghana Manganese Co. Obsolete equipment and limited transport facilities at Takoradi Port and the main railway held ore production down in the 1980s. Output increased in the latter part of the decade, to reach 319,000 metric tons by 1991, but then declining to 100,000 tons by 1995, the year in which the Ghana Manganese Co was privatized. Thereafter, manganese production increased dramatically, reaching 448,000 tons in 1996 and 1.6m. tons in 2004. Ghana ranks as one of the world's largest producers of manganese, and Nsuta is the world's third-largest manganese mine.

ELECTRICITY

Until the opening of the Akosombo hydroelectricity plant on Lake Volta in 1966, electricity production came solely from diesel generators operated by the Electricity Co of Ghana (ECG) or by the mines. In 1986 the Akosombo plant, with an installed generating capacity of 912 MW, and later the 160-MW Kpong plant, together provided virtually all of Ghana's electricity needs, and allowed electricity to be exported to Togo and Benin when rain was sufficient. Drought in the early 1980s and again in 1998 caused the plants to operate far below capacity, leading to power interruptions. In the early 1980s the VRA, which operates electricity supply from Lake Volta, was forced to restrict output, and major commercial consumers, such as Valco (which takes, on average, more than 60% of the power supply from Akosombo), were forced to reduce production levels. To reduce Valco's dependence on the Akosombo facility, Valco is to invest US $1,000m. in a new 1,000-MW thermal plant at Tema, to make use of Nigerian gas to be delivered by the West African Gas Pipeline. A project to extend the electricity supply to the Northern, Upper West and Upper East Regions from Brong-Ahafo, in order to curtail reliance on diesel generators in the north, was financed by bilateral and multilateral credits. Drought again led to power rationing in February–June 1998, with the Government seeking emergency sources of electricity from abroad and many domestic enterprises, including Valco, operating at markedly reduced capacity. Aware that power shortages severely restrict industrial output and result in substantial levels of lost revenue, the Government in 1999 announced that it was to establish a transitional power system development plan to prevent the recurrence of power shortages following drought. To help alleviate the situation, the Government proposed the building of a 400-MW, $600m. hydroelectric facility at Bui, on the Black Volta River in western Ghana. An environmental group, Ghana Energy Foundation, opposed the scheme, suggesting in April 2001 that a series of micro-hydro projects, along small rivers in the country, would be both better for the ecosystem and more cost-effective, as the large scheme would flood a wide area, including the Bole Game Reserve, and would necessitate a huge outlay in compensation and resettlement costs. In 2007 the Government was pressing ahead with the Bui scheme and was negotiating with the People's Republic of China for financing. During 1999 480 communities were brought within the national grid.

The construction of the country's first gas-fired power generation plant (at a projected cost of US $400m.) at Aboadze, near Takoradi, was completed in December 1997, adding 200 MW to the national grid. CMS Energy Corpn of the USA announced in February 1999 that it was to build, own and operate a $60m., 110-MW electricity-generating unit at the site of the VRA's Takoradi thermal power plant near Aboadze. Initially, CMS was to hold 90% of the equity, with the VRA owning the other 10%, although as part of the agreement the VRA was to have an option to increase its share later to up to 50%. The VRA was to be the main customer for the scheme's electricity output, under a long-term contract. The facility constituted the first stage of a 330-MW expansion of the existing Takoradi plant. Takoradi, due to commence commercial operations in late 1999, initially using light crude petroleum as fuel, was to be converted to natural gas, sourced from Nigeria and Côte d'Ivoire. The 220-MW Takoradi T2 scheme came into operation in 2000, comprising two 110-MW turbine generators fuelled by light crude petroleum; the first commenced production in March and the second in November. A third 110-MW generator was to run on steam power. Under pressure from the World Bank, a new Public Utilities Regulatory Commission introduced a 90% increase in water and electricity tariffs in February 1998 and a further 100% rise in September, with the aim of eliminating all arrears of the power utilities by the end of 1999. In the event, further price increases were in store, and in 2001 Kufuor's Government raised the electricity tariff by more than 100%.

PUBLIC FINANCE

Since 1983 fiscal policies have been designed to reduce the imbalances in government finances and to foster economic growth. Capital spending, and the proportion of both revenue and expenditure to GDP, have increased significantly. The generally declining contribution of receipts from the cocoa tax to total revenue reflected substantial real increases in producer prices paid to farmers and greater efficiency in the collection of other taxes, notably income taxes and VAT. In 2001 Ghana collected 5% more tax revenue than forecast, reversing a long-standing trend of collection shortfalls. Tax revenue for 2005 was 21,302.1m. cedis. Ghana's heavy use of IMF facilities contributed significantly to the country's foreign debt. Total external debt stood at US $6,347.9m. at 31 December 2005, of which 64% was multilateral debt denominated in Special Drawing Rights. During 2006 the provisions of the IMF's heavily indebted poor countries initiative and the Multilateral Debt Relief Initiative reduced Ghana's total external debt by 66.2%, to $2,143.79m. at 30 September 2006. Not affected, however, was Ghana's domestic debt, which stood at 17,061,200m. cedis (equivalent to $1.91m.) at that date.

Private banks have proved increasingly willing to extend short-term credit to Ghana for a variety of financial operations, including $40m. to COCOBOD for the purchase of the cocoa crop for the 1993/94 season, followed by $150m. for 1994/95, $225m. in 1995/96, $225m. in 1996/97 and $275m. in 1997/98. The 1998 budget pledged to keep money-supply growth to a maximum of 20%, and the 2000 budget aimed to restrain it to below 16%. The Kufuor Government, however, allowed broad money-supply (M2) growth of 50% in the year to December 2002, before reducing it to 38% in the year to December 2003. This was further reduced, to 18.6% in the year to December 2005, but it increased sharply in the year to September 2006, to 33.6%.

DOMESTIC COMMERCE AND FINANCE

A small number of large and long-established foreign companies continue to be important in the import trade, though they have now largely withdrawn from retail transactions, except for department stores in the major towns and for certain 'technical' goods. Since 1962 the publicly owned Ghana National Trading Corpn (GNTC), created by purchase of A. G. Leventis and Co, has existed alongside the expatriate companies. At the retail level, independent Ghanaian and other African traders compete with the GNTC and with Lebanese and a few Indian businesses. The complex and highly fragmented trade in locally produced foodstuffs is almost wholly in African ownership. The 2004 Newmont Mining investment in the gold sector further illustrates that 100% foreign ownership in mining ventures is achievable in Ghana.

Prior to 1983 many aspects of trade in Ghana were reserved for Ghanaian ownership, but by the mid-1980s foreign investment was again encouraged. In 1986 the Government introduced a new investment code, offering a range of fiscal and trade incentives and inducements. The priority sectors, designated for special treatment under the new code, were agriculture, import-substitution industries, construction and tourism. The Government continues to stress the importance of private investment and has reduced public-sector investment in the development of basic key industries. Public-sector investment accounted for only 28% of total proposed investment under ERP I. Shares were floated on the Ghana Stock Exchange in such groups as Paterson Zochonis Ghana Ltd, UTC Estates, CFAO (Ghana) Ltd and Unilever Ghana Ltd.

The banking sector has expanded and undergone substantial reform since the mid-1980s. In 2003 there were nine commercial banks, as well as three development banks, five merchant banks and some 115 rural banks. The Bank of Ghana has strengthened its supervisory role and in June 1992 assumed control of the assets of the Ghana Co-operative Bank. CAL Bank Limited, Ecobank (Ghana) Ltd, Ghana Commercial Bank Ltd, HFC Bank Ltd, Standard Chartered Bank Ghana Ltd, and Trust Bank Limited of The Gambia were listed on the Ghana Stock Exchange in 2007.

TRANSPORT

The country's two major ports are both artificial: Takoradi, built in the 1920s, and Tema, which was opened in 1961 to replace the Accra roadstead and which became an industrial centre. The Ghana merchant shipping fleet's total displacement declined from 225,000 grt in 1982 to 115,200 grt in 2005, owing in large measure to the national Black Star Line's disposal of some of its ships.

There are 1,300 km of railway, forming a triangle between Takoradi, Kumasi and Accra-Tema. Exports traditionally accounted for the greater part of railway freight tonnage, but cocoa and timber were diverted to the roads as rail facilities deteriorated, and the railways have required a regular government subsidy since 1976. In 1996 the Government committed US $150m. towards upgrading the Western Line to link the mining areas with Takoradi port. In 1995 Ghana Railway Corpn took delivery of three new locomotives and 60 goods wagons, funded by Germany's Kreditanstalt für Wiederaufbau and Japan's Overseas Economic Co-operation Fund.

In 2005 Ghana had a total road network of approximately 57,6134 km, of which just 15% was paved. The road system is good by tropical African standards, but its maintenance has been a constant problem. The overwhelming focus of construction in the transport sector in the late 1990s was on roads, with work being completed on four new roads in 1996. In addition, 87 km of roads were gravelled in that year and a further 213 km were resurfaced. Government spending on road construction in 2006 totalled 783,200m. cedis, down from 863,900m. cedis in 2001. In 2003 the Government established Metro Mass Transit (MMT) Limited with the aim of creating a mass transit public bus company in the country. By the end of 2005 MMT had branches in Accra, Cape Coast, Koforidua, Kumasi, Sunyanit, Swedru, Takoradi and Tamale. MMT's fleet comprises 250 Yaxing buses, 150 Tata buses and 21 of the 100 DAF/Neoplan buses being assembled at the Neoplan Manufacturing Plant in Kumasi. The creation of Lake Volta, stretching some 400 km inland from the Akosombo dam, opened up new possibilities for internal transportation, but lake transport is still relatively modest. There is an international airport at Kotoka, near Accra, and other airports at Kumasi, Sunyani, Takoradi, Tamale and Wa serve inland traffic.

FOREIGN TRADE AND AID

Ghana has traditionally been an exporter of primary products, mainly gold, cocoa and timber, and an importer of capital goods, foodstuffs and mineral fuels. By 2001 revenue from non-traditional exports had increased to US $300.6m., an increase from $226.3m. in 2000. Ghana's visible trade balance was in deficit throughout the 1990s, increasing steadily to a shortfall of $1,227m. in 1999. Substantial deficits on invisible trade (services and transfers), accentuated by high payments to service the external debt, resulted in increasing deficits on the current account during the 1980s and the 1990s. In the 1990s the Western industrialized nations comprised Ghana's major trading partners, although useful links were maintained with countries of the former Soviet bloc, with which Ghana had developed trade relations in the early 1980s (in 1984 the USSR accounted for one-quarter of Ghanaian exports). In 2005 the principal export destination was Switzerland-Liechtenstein (representing 22% of the total), followed by the United Kingdom, the USA and the Netherlands. In 2005 the major sources of imports were the United Kingdom (8.5%), the USA, Nigeria and Germany.

Although the level of donor pledges has risen dramatically since 1980, disbursement of funds has often been slow. In 1999 efforts by the Ghanaian Government to meet IMF and World Bank requirements continued to be impeded by popular resistance to reform measures, including the introduction of VAT, increased electricity tariffs and road tolls. During 1997–2007, the IMF continually backed Ghana's development and poverty-reduction strategy with financial support and debt relief. In almost every instance, the Fund also waived Ghana's non-compliance on various issues. Since 2003 the IMF has expressed some concern at the level of debt that the Ghanaian Government owed on the domestic market and at monetary policy. However, it has concluded that with the monetary targets that the Government had set, single-digit inflation would be achievable, even though it has not yet been achieved. Most importantly, however, 2005 and especially 2006 were years in which Ghana's debt burden was significantly alleviated. In May 2007 the IMF commended Ghana for its 'sound economic policies and structural reforms'; it added that fiscal prudence had slipped in 2006 but noted that the Ghanaian authorities were addressing this 'slippage' with a package of corrective measures.

Statistical Survey

Source (except where otherwise stated): Ghana Statistical Service, POB GP1098, Accra; tel. (21) 671732; fax (21) 671731; internet www.bog.gov.gh.

Area and Population

AREA, POPULATION AND DENSITY

Area (sq km)	238,537*
Population (census results)	
11 March 1984	12,296,081
26 March 2000	
Males	9,320,794
Females	9,524,471
Total	18,845,265
Population (UN estimates at mid-year)†	
2004	22,057,000
2005	22,535,000
2006	23,008,000
Density (per sq km) at mid-2006	96.5

* 92,100 sq miles.

† Source: UN, *World Population Prospects: The 2006 Revision*.

POPULATION BY REGION
(2000 census)

Region	Population	Capital
Ashanti	3,600,358	Kumasi
Brong-Ahafo	1,798,058	Sunyani
Central	1,593,888	Cape Coast
Eastern	2,101,650	Koforidua
Greater Accra	2,903,753	Accra
Northern	1,805,428	Tamale
Upper East	919,549	Bolgatanga
Upper West	575,579	Wa
Volta	1,630,254	Ho
Western	1,916,748	Takoradi
Total	18,845,265	

PRINCIPAL TOWNS
(population at 1984 census)

Accra (capital)	867,459	Takoradi	61,484
Kumasi	376,249	Cape Coast	57,224
Tamale	135,952	Sekondi	31,916
Tema	131,528		

Mid-2005 ('000, incl. suburbs, UN estimate): Accra 1,981 (Source: UN, *World Urbanization Prospects: The 2005 Revision*).

BIRTHS AND DEATHS
(annual averages, UN estimates)

	1990–95	1995–2000	2000–05
Birth rate (per 1,000)	37.8	34.3	32.2
Death rate (per 1,000)	10.7	10.0	10.0

Source: UN, *World Population Prospects: The 2006 Revision*.

Expectation of life (years at birth, WHO estimates): 57 (males 56; females 58) in 2004 (Source: WHO, *World Health Report*).

ECONOMICALLY ACTIVE POPULATION
(1984 census)

	Males	Females	Total
Agriculture, hunting, forestry and fishing	1,750,024	1,560,943	3,310,967
Mining and quarrying	24,906	1,922	26,828
Manufacturing	198,430	389,988	588,418
Electricity, gas and water	14,033	1,404	15,437
Construction	60,692	3,994	64,686
Trade, restaurants and hotels	111,540	680,607	792,147
Transport, storage and communications	117,806	5,000	122,806
Financing, insurance, real estate and business services	19,933	7,542	27,475
Community, social and personal services	339,665	134,051	473,716
Total employed	2,637,029	2,785,451	5,422,480
Unemployed	87,452	70,172	157,624
Total labour force	2,724,481	2,855,623	5,580,104

2000 census ('000 persons aged 7 years and over): Total economically active population 9,039.3.

Source: ILO.

Mid-2005 (estimates in '000): Agriculture, etc. 6,245; Total 11,203 (Source: FAO).

Health and Welfare

KEY INDICATORS

Total fertility rate (children per woman, 2005)	4.1
Under-5 mortality rate (per 1,000 live births, 2005)	112
HIV/AIDS (% of persons aged 15–49, 2005)	2.3
Physicians (per 1,000 head, 2004)	0.15
Hospital beds (per 1,000 head, 2005)	0.90
Health expenditure (2004): US $ per head (PPP)	94.7
Health expenditure (2004): % of GDP	6.7
Health expenditure (2004): public (% of total)	42.2
Access to water (% of persons, 2004)	75
Access to sanitation (% of persons, 2004)	18
Human Development Index (2004): ranking	136
Human Development Index (2004): value	0.532

For sources and definitions, see explanatory note on p. vi.

Agriculture

PRINCIPAL CROPS
('000 metric tons)

	2003	2004	2005
Rice (paddy)	238.8	241.8	287.0
Maize	1,288.6	1,157.6	1,171.0
Millet	175.7	143.8	185.0
Sorghum	337.7	287.0	305.0
Sweet potatoes*	90.0	92.8	94.6
Cassava (Manioc)	10,239.3	9,738.8	9,567.0
Taro (Coco yam)	1,804.7	1,716.0	1,686.0
Yams	3,812.8	3,892.3	4,101.6*
Sugar cane	140.0	140.0	140.0*
Groundnuts (in shell)	439.0	389.6	420.0
Coconuts†	315.0	315.0	315.0
Copra†	11.0	11.0	11.7
Oil palm fruit	1,518.0*	1,955.3	2,024.6
Tomatoes*	200.0	200.0	200.3
Chillies and green peppers*	270.0	306.4	328.6
Dry onions*	38.5	38.5	38.5
Green beans*	20.0	20.0	20.0
Okra*	100.0	100.0	100.0
Bananas	10.0*	10.0*	52.6
Plantains	2,328.6	2,380.9	2,792.0
Oranges	300.0*	396.2*	500.0
Lemons and limes*	30.0	30.0	30.0
Pineapples*	60.0	66.7	71.2
Cottonseed†	7.8	9.5	12.5
Cocoa beans	497.0†	7367.0†	740.0
Natural rubber†	9.2	9.3	8.6

* FAO estimate(s).
† Unofficial figure(s).

Source: FAO.

LIVESTOCK
('000 head, year ending September)

	2003	2004	2005
Horses*	3.0	3.0	3.0
Asses, mules or hinnies*	13.5	13.7	13.7
Cattle	1,344.0	1,365.0*	1,385.0*
Pigs	303.0	300.0	305.0*
Sheep	3,015.0	3,111.5*	3,211.1*
Goats	3,560.0	3,595.6*	3,631.6*
Chickens	26,395	29,500*	30,000*

* FAO estimate(s).

Source: FAO.

LIVESTOCK PRODUCTS
('000 metric tons)

	2003	2004	2005
Cattle meat	24.4*	23.1	25.4
Sheep meat	10.4*	10.3	9.9
Goat meat	11.7*	12.1	11.8
Pig meat	10.2*	4.8	4.8
Chicken meat*	25.5	28.3	28.8
Game meat*	57.0	57.0	57.0
Cows' milk*	35.1	35.5	36.0
Hen eggs*	24.4	25.2	25.2

* FAO estimate(s).

Source: FAO.

Forestry

ROUNDWOOD REMOVALS
('000 cubic metres, excl. bark)

	2003	2004	2005
Sawlogs, veneer logs and logs for sleepers	1,400	1,350	1,350
Fuel wood*	20,678	20,678	20,678
Total	22,078	22,028	22,028

* FAO estimates (output assumed to be unchanged since 1994).

Source: FAO.

SAWNWOOD PRODUCTION
('000 cubic metres, incl. railway sleepers)

	2003	2004	2005
Total (all broadleaved)	496	480	460

Source: FAO.

Fishing

('000 metric tons, live weight)

	2003	2004	2005
Capture	390.8	399.4*	392.3*
Freshwater fishes	75.0	75.0*	75.0*
Bigeye grunt	7.7	26.5	16.8
Round sardinella	78.8	82.4	64.4
Madeiran sardinella	15.6	27.0	14.2
European anchovy	82.9	52.6	36.4
Skipjack tuna	32.8	33.6	54.3
Yellowfin tuna	19.0	15.1	19.8
Aquaculture	0.9	1.0	1.2
Total catch	391.7	400.3*	393.4*

* FAO estimate.

Source: FAO.

Mining

('000 metric tons, unless otherwise indicated)

	2003	2004	2005
Crude petroleum ('000 barrels)*	3,000	3,000	2,190
Natural gas (million cu m)	112	112*	100*
Bauxite	495	498	726
Manganese ore: gross weight	1,509	1,597	1,715
Manganese ore: metal content	528	559	600*
Silver (kilograms)†	3,379	3,329	3,300*
Gold (kilograms)‡	70,749	63,139	66,852
Salt (unrefined)*	250	265	300
Diamonds ('000 carats)§	904	905	1,063

* Estimated production.
† Silver content of exported doré.
‡ Gold content of ores and concentrates, excluding smuggled or undocumented output.
§ Of the total, the estimated production of gemstones (in '000 carats) was: 724 in 2003; 725 in 2004; 850 in 2005.

Source: US Geological Survey.

Industry

SELECTED PRODUCTS

('000 metric tons, unless otherwise indicated)

	2002	2003	2004
Groundnut oil*	98.9	76.4	61.5
Coconut oil	6.5*	7.0†	7.0†
Palm oil†	108.0	108.4	114.0
Palm kernel oil*	10.8	13.4	13.4
Butter of karité nuts (shea butter)*	8.4	9.8	18.3
Beer of barley*	100.0	100.0	100.0
Beer of millet*	66.6	73.8	60.2
Beer of sorghum*	234.6	258.3	340.7
Gasoline (petrol)	5,850	5,580	5,580†
Jet fuel	625	625	625†
Kerosene	1,950	1,950	1,950†
Distillate fuel oil	4,450	4,450	4,450†
Residual fuel oil	1,250	1,250	1,250†
Cement	1,900	1,900	1,900†
Aluminium (unwrought)‡	117	16	n.a.
Electric energy ('000 million kWh)	7,296	5,901	n.a.

* FAO estimate(s).

† Provisional or estimated figure(s).

‡ Primary metal only.

2005: Groundnut oil 7.0 (unofficial figure); Coconut oil 46.0 (FAO estimate); Palm oil 117.0 (unofficial figure); Palm kernel oil 14.6 (unofficial figure).

Sources: FAO; US Geological Survey; Energy Commission of Ghana.

Finance

CURRENCY AND EXCHANGE RATES

Monetary Units

100 pesewas = 1 new cedi.

Sterling, Dollar and Euro Equivalents (30 April 2007)

£1 sterling = 18,498.85 cedis;
US $1 = 9,274.47 cedis;
€1 = 12,617.91 cedis;
100,000 cedis = £5.41 = $10.78 = €7.93.

Average Exchange Rate (cedis per US $)

2004 9,004.63
2005 9,072.54
2006 9,174.38

Note: A new currency, the Ghana cedi, equivalent to 10,000 old cedis, was to be introduced over a six-month period beginning in July 2007.

GENERAL BUDGET

('000 million new cedis)

Revenue*	2004	2005	2006
Tax revenue	17,861.7	21,302.1	24,646.1
Income and property	5,344.0	6,615.1	7,183.3
Personal (PAYE)	1,908.2	2,435.1	3,111.5
Company tax	2,340.3	3,108.3	3,013.3
Domestic goods and services	3,734.6	4,429.3	4,776.8
Petroleum tax	3,119.4	3,751.0	4,071.3
International trade	3,988.0	4,114.0	5,418.4
Import duties	3,002.2	3,795.7	4,169.8
Cocoa export duty	931.1	615.1	1,248.6
Non-tax revenue	1,136.3	1,854.1	923.0
Total	18,998.0	23,156.2	25,569.1

Expenditure†	2004	2005	2006
Recurrent expenditure	16,278.0	18,032.8	24,734.9
Wages and salaries	6,946.7	8,920.8	11,069.5
Goods and services	2,360.3	3,305.9	4,049.1
Transfers to households	3,498.6	3,332.4	5,682.6
Interest payments	3,472.4	3,473.8	3,933.7
Domestic (accrual)	2,545.0	2,622.5	3,030.9
External (accrual)	927.4	851.3	902.8
Capital expenditure	8,081.9	9,726.8	10,961.8
Domestic	3,470.8	3,780.8	5,683.2
External	4,611.1	5,946.1	5,278.6
HIPC-financed expenditure	1,869.6	1,946.6	1,791.6
Adjustment	—	—	1,246.4
Total	26,229.5	29,706.2	38,734.7

* Excluding grants received ('000 million new cedis): 4,940.3 in 2004; 5,100.2 in 2005; 6,348.6 in 2006.

† Including net lending ('000 million new cedis): 182.9 in 2004; 72.8 in 2005; 7.62 in 2006.

Source: Bank of Ghana.

INTERNATIONAL RESERVES

(US $ million at 31 December)

	2004	2005	2006
Gold (national valuation)	122.6	144.5	177.9
IMF special drawing rights	20.7	1.1	1.2
Foreign exchange	1,605.9	1,751.8	2,089.1
Total	1,749.2	1,897.4	2,268.2

Source: IMF, *International Financial Statistics*.

MONEY SUPPLY

('000 million new cedis at 31 December)

	2004	2005	2006
Currency outside banks	7,306.5	8,032.3	10,207.8
Demand deposits at deposit money banks	6,358.0	6,614.3	9,781.1
Total money (incl. others)	13,745.3	14,707.5	20,045.2

Source: IMF, *International Financial Statistics*.

COST OF LIVING

(Consumer Price Index; prices at December; base: 1997 = 100)

	2004	2005	2006
Food and beverages	317.1	364.6	387.8
Clothing and footwear	341.5	372.1	389.9
Housing and utilities	756.5	883.7	1,030.4
Medical care and health expenses	257.0	314.9	342.6
Transport and communications	516.1	691.4	916.8
All items	360.7	414.2	457.9

Source: Bank of Ghana.

NATIONAL ACCOUNTS

National Income and Product

('000 million new cedis at current prices)

	2002	2003	2004
GDP at market prices	48,862	66,158	79,865
Net primary income from abroad	–797	–774	–872
Gross national income	48,065	65,384	78,993
Less Consumption of fixed capital	1,917	1,918	1,919
Net national income	46,148	63,466	77,074
Net transfers from abroad	3,528	6,197	7,158
Net national disposable income	49,676	69,663	84,232

Expenditure on the Gross Domestic Product
('000 million new cedis at current prices, estimates)

	2002	2003	2004
Government final consumption expenditure	8,595	11,722	12,780
Private final consumption expenditure	36,677	47,234	61,304
Increase in stocks	244	0	0
Gross fixed capital formation	9,391	15,175	22,278
Total domestic expenditure	54,907	74,131	96,362
Exports of goods and services	20,758	26,922	29,574
Less Imports of goods and services	26,803	34,895	46,071
GDP in purchasers' values	48,862	66,158	79,865
GDP at constant 1993 prices	5,601	5,895	6,236

Gross Domestic Product by Economic Activity
('000 million new cedis at constant 1993 prices)

	2004	2005*	2006*
Agriculture and livestock	1,533.1	1,625.1	1,662.7
Cocoa	265.0	300.0	326.1
Forestry and logging	225.0	237.6	240.0
Fishing	265.4	275.0	278.9
Mining and quarrying	321.7	331.4	347.3
Manufacturing	560.8	591.7	613.6
Electricity and water	155.1	165.4	214.4
Construction	504.6	539.9	600.5
Transport, storage and communications	305.1	323.4	351.6
Wholesale and retail trade, restaurants and hotels	429.7	455.9	513.4
Finance, insurance, real estate and business services	267.4	282.4	309.6
Government services	667.1	700.5	740.4
Community, social and personal services	117.3	122.3	127.5
Private non-profit services	53.2	55.1	54.6
Sub-total	5,670.3	6,005.5	6,383.5
Indirect taxes, *less* subsidies	565.5	590.6	617.0
GDP at market prices	6,235.8	6,596.1	7,000.5

* Preliminary.

Source: Bank of Ghana.

BALANCE OF PAYMENTS
(US $ million)

	2003	2004	2005
Exports of goods f.o.b.	2,562.4	2,704.5	2,802.2
Imports of goods f.o.b.	–3,232.8	–4,297.3	–5,345.4
Trade balance	–670.4	–1,592.8	–2,543.1
Exports of services	630.0	702.3	1,066.4
Imports of services	–899.8	–1,058.5	–1,264.4
Balance on goods and services	–940.2	–1,949.0	–2,741.2
Other income received	21.4	44.5	43.3
Other income paid	–178.1	–242.4	–230.4
Balance on goods, services and income	–1,096.9	–2,146.8	–2,928.3
Current transfers received	1,408.4	1,831.0	2,125.4
Current transfers paid	–9.2	—	–8.7
Current balance	302.3	–315.8	–811.6
Direct investment from abroad	136.8	139.3	106.5
Other investment assets	68.0	–88.3	106.6
Other investment liabilities	135.6	150.6	582.9
Net errors and omissions	–139.1	37.3	25.6
Overall balance	503.6	–77.0	10.0

Source: IMF, *International Financial Statistics*.

2006 (US $ million, preliminary): Exports f.o.b. 3,735.1; Imports f.o.b. –6,523.6; *Trade balance* –2,788.5; Services (net) –255.3; *Balance on goods and services* –3,043.8; Other income (net) –127.4; *Balance on goods, services and income* –3,171.2; Transfers (net) 2,615.2; *Current balance* –555.9; Direct investment 334.5; Other investment 517.3; Net errors and omissions 119.3; *Overall balance* 415.1 (Source: Bank of Ghana).

External Trade

PRINCIPAL COMMODITIES
(distribution by SITC, US $ million)

Imports c.i.f.	2002	2003	2004
Food and live animals	491.7	468.5	793.4
Fish, crustaceans and molluscs, and preparations thereof	115.4	56.2	116.7
Fish, fresh, chilled or frozen	102.2	49.5	105.4
Fish, frozen, excluding fillets	82.5	15.3	21.4
Cereals and cereal preparations	193.1	190.4	350.0
Rice	104.0	117.3	185.2
Sugar and honey	70.8	88.5	137.0
Crude materials (inedible), except fuels	109.2	65.7	68.4
Mineral fuels, lubricants, etc.	233.6	596.7	65.2
Petroleum, petroleum products, etc.	206.0	596.1	65.1
Crude petroleum and oils obtained from bituminous materials	151.1	576.5	0.0
Petroleum products, refined	35.3	8.6	49.6
Chemicals and related products	331.4	404.7	548.3
Basic manufactures	485.4	491.1	679.3
Non-metallic mineral manufactures	96.5	83.9	143.9
Iron and steel	70.4	89.2	113.3
Machinery and transport equipment	865.0	947.3	1,601.4
Power-generating machinery and equipment	38.7	47.5	76.0
Machinery specialized for particular industries	126.9	151.9	239.1
General industrial machinery and equipment, and parts thereof	108.8	122.0	194.4
Telecommunications, sound recording and reproducing equipment	49.2	74.3	169.3
Other electric machinery, apparatus and appliances, and parts thereof	88.7	100.0	178.5
Road vehicles and parts*	413.1	397.3	675.4
Passenger motor vehicles (excluding buses)	234.7	222.3	0.0
Motor vehicles for the transport of goods or materials	122.7	111.3	242.7
Miscellaneous manufactured articles	148.7	187.7	264.7
Total (incl. others)	2,720.1	3,210.2	4,073.9

* Data on parts exclude tyres, engines and electrical parts.

Exports f.o.b.	2003	2004
Food and live animals	1,046.2	1,246.9
Fish, crustaceans and molluscs, and preparations thereof	120.2	93.8
Fish, prepared or preserved	100.6	70.3
Vegetables and fruit	61.4	65.5
Fruit and nuts, fresh, dried	43.8	43.2
Fruit, fresh or dried	37.9	33.2
Pineapples, fresh or dried	33.4	0.0
Coffee, tea, cocoa, spices and manufactures thereof	846.6	1,074.3
Cocoa	838.0	1,070.3
Cocoa beans, raw, roasted	676.1	1,003.5
Cocoa butter and paste	126.1	34.4
Cocoa butter (fat or oil)	25.4	28.4
Crude materials (inedible) except fuels	215.3	130.1
Cork and wood	97.9	55.8
Wood, non-coniferous species, sawn, planed, tongued, grooved, etc.	93.8	55.3
Wood, non-coniferous species, sawn lengthwise, sliced or peeled	87.9	42.1

Exports f.o.b.—*continued*	2003	2004
Mineral fuels, lubricants, etc.	1.1	55.4
Basic manufactures	150.6	108.9
Cork and wood manufactures (excl. furniture)	81.6	84.6
Veneers, plywood, 'improved' wood and other wood, worked	76.9	75.4
Wood sawn lengthwise, veneer sheets, etc., up to 5 mm in thickness	60.5	35.1
Aluminium and aluminium alloys, unwrought	10.2	2.3
Machinery and transport equipment	17.7	38.4
Gold, non-monetary, unwrought or semi-manufactured	829.6	125.3
Total (incl. others)	2,324.3	1,779.1

Source: UN, *International Trade Statistics Yearbook*.

Imports f.o.b. (US $ million): Total 5,345.4 (Petroleum 1,127.5, Non-petroleum 4,217.9) in 2005; Total 6,523.6 (Petroleum 1,416.1, Non-petroleum 5,107.5) in 2006 (preliminary) (Source: Bank of Ghana).

Exports f.o.b. (US $ million): Total 2,802.2 (Cocoa beans and products thereof 908.4, Gold 945.8, Timber and products thereof 226.5, Other 721.5) in 2005; Total 3,735.1 (Cocoa beans and products thereof 1,187.4, Gold 1,277.3, Timber and products thereof 199.5, Other 1,070.9) in 2006 (preliminary) (Source: Bank of Ghana).

PRINCIPAL TRADING PARTNERS
(US $ million)

Imports c.i.f.	2002	2003	2004
Belgium	143.2	145.8	251.6
Brazil	46.8	78.2	156.3
Burkina Faso	89.5	0.3	0.0
Canada	57.1	66.5	119.5
China, People's Republic	128.9	179.6	364.8
Côte d'Ivoire	41.8	13.4	31.3
France (incl. Monaco)	104.7	118.4	164.0
Germany	190.0	218.8	314.8
India	69.9	99.4	150.1
Italy (incl. San Marino)	124.2	98.1	155.0
Japan	66.4	99.5	150.5
Korea, Republic	61.0	51.5	98.7
Nigeria	194.9	599.7	35.2
Netherlands	137.9	161.9	206.5
South Africa	101.6	145.8	224.1
Spain	56.0	67.6	94.6
Thailand	47.0	81.8	135.2
United Kingdom	239.3	218.9	234.0
USA	202.4	225.8	362.7
Total (incl. others)	2,720.1	3,210.2	4,073.9

Exports f.o.b.	2003	2004
Belgium	113.9	130.5
Benin	42.4	14.6
China, People's Republic	32.3	20.1
Côte d'Ivoire	18.9	2.5
France (incl. Monaco)	109.7	109.7
Germany	113.3	37.7
Ireland	5.6	14.1
Italy (incl. San Marino)	110.7	62.9
Japan	58.3	59.5
Netherlands	274.1	452.4
Nigeria	24.4	11.7
South Africa	87.8	106.4
Spain	49.4	44.0
Switzerland-Liechtenstein	587.9	34.9
Togo	30.0	0.0
Turkey	0.0	52.5
United Kingdom	464.7	239.5
USA	67.7	66.7
Total (incl. others)	2,324.3	1,779.1

Source: UN, *International Trade Statistics Yearbook*.

Transport

RAILWAYS
(traffic)

	2001	2002	2003
Passenger-km (million)	238	242	245
Net ton-km (million)	168	170	173

Source: UN, *Statistical Yearbook*.

ROAD TRAFFIC
(motor vehicles in use at 31 December)

	2001	2002	2003
Passenger cars	90,800	91,200	91,000
Lorries and vans	121,100	123,500	124,300

Source: UN, *Statistical Yearbook*.

SHIPPING

Merchant Fleet
(registered at 31 December)

	2004	2005	2006
Number of vessels	210	211	224
Total displacement ('000 grt)	116.7	115.2	116.3

Source: Lloyd's Register-Fairplay, *World Fleet Statistics*.

International Sea-borne Freight Traffic
(estimates, '000 metric tons)

	1991	1992	1993
Goods loaded	2,083	2,279	2,424
Goods unloaded	2,866	2,876	2,904

Source: UN Economic Commission for Africa, *African Statistical Yearbook*.

CIVIL AVIATION
(traffic on scheduled services)

	2001	2002	2003
Kilometres flown (million)	18	12	12
Passengers carried ('000)	301	256	241
Passenger-km (million)	1,233	912	906
Total ton-km (million)	157	107	101

Source: UN, *Statistical Yearbook*.

Tourism

ARRIVALS BY NATIONALITY

	2003	2004	2005
Côte d'Ivoire	25,521	28,069	25,155
France	19,181	21,096	10,089
Germany	25,611	28,168	14,094
Liberia	13,920	15,310	14,472
Netherlands	12,850	14,133	13,663
Nigeria	72,857	80,131	74,983
Togo	15,886	17,472	11,888
United Kingdom	45,959	50,547	36,747
USA	35,013	38,508	50,475
Total (incl. others)*	530,827	583,819	428,533

* Includes Ghanaian nationals resident abroad: 144,492 in 2003; 158,917 in 2004; 59,821 in 2005.

Receipts from tourism (US $ million, incl. passenger transport): 441 in 2003; 495 in 2004; n.a. in 2005.

Source: World Tourism Organization.

Communications Media

	2003	2004	2005
Telephones ('000 main lines in use)	291.0	313.3	313.3
Mobile cellular telephones ('000 subscribers)	795.5	1,695.0	1,765.0
Personal computers ('000 in use)	96	112	112
Internet users ('000)	250	368	401

Source: International Telecommunication Union.

Radio receivers ('000 in use): 4,400 in 1997.

Television receivers ('000 in use): 2,390 in 2000.

Facsimile machines (number in use, estimate): 5,000 in 1995.

Daily newspapers: 4 titles in 1998 (average circulation 260,000).

Book production (titles, 1998): 7.

Sources: UNESCO Institute for Statistics; UNESCO, *Statistical Yearbook*; UN, *Statistical Yearbook*.

Education

(2003/04, unless otherwise indicated)

	Institutions	Teachers	Students ('000)		
			Males	Females	Total
Pre-primary	n.a.	29,335	413.0	394.1	807.1
Primary	13,115*	82,833	1,408.6	1,270.5	2,678.9
Junior secondary	6,394*	51,419	498.8	420.5	919.3
Senior secondary	512*	16,527	209.6	147.7	357.3
Tertiary	n.a.	3,933	47.6	22.1	69.7

* 1998/99 figure.

1998/99: *Teacher training* 38 institutions; *Technical institutes* 61 institutions; *Polytechnics* 8 institutions; *Universities* 7 institutions.

Source: UNESCO and former Ministry of Education, Accra.

Adult literacy rate (UNESCO estimates): 57.9% (males 66.4%; females 49.8%) in 2004 (Source: UN Development Programme, *Human Development Report*).

Directory

The Constitution

Under the terms of the Constitution of the Fourth Republic, which was approved by national referendum on 28 April 1992, Ghana has a multi-party political system. Executive power is vested in the President, who is Head of State and Commander-in-Chief of the Armed Forces. The President is elected by universal adult suffrage for a term of four years, and designates a Vice-President (prior to election). The duration of the President's tenure of office is limited to two four-year terms. It is also stipulated that, in the event that no presidential candidate receives more than 50% of votes cast, a new election between the two candidates with the highest number of votes is to take place within 21 days. Legislative power is vested in a 230-member unicameral Parliament, which is elected by direct adult suffrage for a four-year term. (This number was increased from 200 at the general election of December 2004.) The Council of Ministers is appointed by the President, subject to approval by the Parliament. The Constitution also provides for a 25-member Council of State, principally comprising presidential nominees and regional representatives, and a 20-member National Security Council (chaired by the Vice-President), both of which act as advisory bodies to the President.

The Government

HEAD OF STATE

President and Commander-in-Chief of the Armed Forces: JOHN AGYEKUM KUFUOR (inaugurated 7 January 2001; re-elected 7 December 2004 and inaugurated 7 January 2005).

Vice-President: Alhaji ALIU MAHAMA.

CABINET
(August 2007)

Minister of Defence: ALBERT KAN DAPAAH.

Minister of the Interior: KWAMENA BARTELS.

Minister of Education, Science and Sports: Prof. DOMINIC FOBIH.

Minister of Water Resources, Works and Housing: Alhaji ABUBAKAR SADDIQUE BONIFACE.

Minister of Lands, Forestry and Mines: ESTHER OBENG DAPAAH.

Minister of Tourism and Diasporan Relations: STEPHEN ASAMOAH-BOATENG.

Minister of Local Government, Rural Development and the Environment: KWADWO ADJEI-DARKO.

Minister of Finance and Economic Planning: KWADWO BAAH-WIREDU.

Minister of National Security: FRANCIS POKU.

Minister of Health: Maj. (retd) COURAGE QUASHIGAH.

Attorney-General, Minister of Justice: JOSEPH GHARTEY.

Minister of Food and Agriculture: ERNEST AKUBOUR DEBRAH.

Minister of Energy: JOSEPH KOFI ADDA.

Minister of Foreign Affairs, Regional Integration and NEPAD: AKWASI OSEI-ADJAI.

Minister of Fisheries: GLADYS ASMAH.

Minister of Parliamentary Affairs: ABRAHAM OSEI-AIDOOH.

Minister of Trade and Industry: JOE BAIDOO-ANSAH.

Minister of Manpower, Youth and Employment: NANA AKOMEA.

Minister of Information and National Orientation: OBOSHIE SAI-COFIE.

Minister of Communication: Dr BENJAMIN AGGREY-NTIM.

Minister of Women's and Children's Affairs: Hajia ALIMA MAHAMA.

Minister of Ports, Harbours and Railways: Prof. CHRISTOPHER AMEYAW-AKUMFI.

MINISTERS OF STATE
(August 2007)

Minister of State for Finance and Economic Planning: Dr ANTHONY AKOTO OSEI.

Minister of State for Justice and the Attorney-General: AMBROSE DERY.

Minister of State for Culture and Chieftaincy: SAMPSON KWAKU BOAFO.

Minister of State for Aviation: GLORIA AKUFFO.

Minister of State for Public Sector Reform: SAMUEL OWUSU-ADJEI.

Minister of State for Education: ELIZABETH OHENE.

Minister of State for the Interior: NANA OBIRI BOAHEN.

Minister of State for Water Resources, Works and Housing: CECILIA ABENA DAPAAH.

Minister of State for Transportation: GODFRED T. BONYON.

Ministers of State at the Presidency: CHARLES BINTIMYAW BARIMAH.

REGIONAL MINISTERS
(August 2007)

Ashanti: EMMANUEL OWUSU-ANSAH.

Brong Ahafo: IGNATIUS BAFFOUR AWUAH.

Central: NANA ATO ARTHUR.

Eastern: KWADWO AFRAM ASIEDU.

Greater Accra: Sheikh IBRAHIM CUDJOE QUAYE.

Northern: Alhaji MUSTAPHA ALI IDRIS.

Upper East: ALHASSAN SAMARI.

Upper West: GEORGE HIKAH BENSON.

Volta: KOFI DZAMESI.

Western: EVANS A. AMOAH.

MINISTRIES

Office of the President: POB 1627, Osu, Accra; tel. (21) 665415; internet www.ghanacastle.gov.gh.

Ministry of Aviation: POB M232, Accra.

Ministry of Communication: POB M38, Accra; tel. (21) 666465; fax (21) 667114; e-mail info@moc.gov.gh; internet www.moc.gov.gh.

Ministry of Culture and Chieftaincy: Accra.

Ministry of Defence: Burma Camp, Accra; tel. (21) 777611; fax (21) 778549; e-mail kaddok@internetghana.com.

Ministry of Education, Science and Sports: POB M45, Accra; tel. (21) 666070; fax (21) 664067.

Ministry of Energy: FREMA House, Spintex Rd, POB T40 (Stadium Post Office), Stadium, Accra; tel. (21) 667152; fax (21) 668262; e-mail moen@energymin.gov.gh; internet www.energymin.gov.gh.

Ministry of Finance and Economic Planning: POB M40, Accra; tel. (21) 686204; fax (21) 668879.

Ministry of Fisheries: State House, POB 1627, Accra; tel. (21) 776005; fax (21) 785670.

Ministry of Food and Agriculture: POB M37, Accra; tel. (21) 663036; fax (21) 668245; e-mail info@mofa.gov.gh; internet www.mofa.gov.gh.

Ministry of Foreign Affairs: Treasury Rd, POB M53, Accra; tel. (21) 664951; fax (21) 680017; e-mail ghmaf00@ghana.com.

Ministry of Health: POB M44, Accra; tel. (21) 666151; fax (21) 666810; internet www.moh-ghana.org.

Ministry of Information and National Orientation: POB M41, Accra; tel. (21) 228059; fax (21) 235800; e-mail webmaster@moi.gov.gh; internet www.ghana.gov.gh.

Ministry of the Interior: POB M42, Accra; tel. (21) 684400; fax (21) 684408.

Ministry of Justice and Attorney General's Department: POB M60, Accra; tel. (21) 665051; fax (21) 667609; e-mail info@mjag.gov.gh.

Ministry of Lands, Forestry and Mines: POB M212, Accra; tel. (21) 687314; fax (21) 666801; e-mail motgov@hotmail.com.

Ministry of Local Government, Rural Development and the Environment: POB M50, Accra; tel. (21) 664763; fax (21) 661015.

Ministry of Manpower, Youth and Employment: State House, POB M84, Accra; tel. (21) 684532; fax (21) 667251; e-mail info@mmde.gov.gh; internet www.mmde.gov.gh.

Ministry of National Security: Accra.

Ministry of Parliamentary Affairs: State House, POB 1627, Accra; tel. (21) 665349; fax (21) 667251.

Ministry of Ports, Harbours and Railways: Ministries Post Office, PMB M, Accra; tel. (21) 681780; fax (21) 681781; e-mail poharail@yahoo.com; internet www.mphrgh.org.

Ministry of Public-Sector Reform: State House, POB 1627, Accra; tel. (21) 684086.

Ministry of Tourism and Diasporan Relations: POB 4386, Accra; tel. (21) 666701; fax (21) 666182; e-mail motgov@hotmail.com; internet www.ghanatourism.gov.gh.

Ministry of Trade and Industry: POB M47, Accra; tel. (21) 679283; fax (21) 665663; e-mail info@moti.gov.gh; internet www.moti-ghana.com.

Ministry of Transportation: POB M38, Accra; tel. (21) 661577; fax (21) 667114; e-mail info@mrt.gov.gh; internet www.mrt.gov.gh.

Ministry of Water Resources, Works and Housing: POB M43, Accra; tel. (21) 665940; fax (21) 667689; e-mail mwh@ighmail.com.

Ministry of Women's and Children's Affairs: POB M186, Accra; tel. (21) 255411; fax (21) 688182; e-mail barnes@africaonline.com.gh.

President and Legislature

PRESIDENT

Presidential Election, 7 December 2004

Candidate	Valid votes	% of valid votes
John Agyekum Kufuor (NPP)	4,524,074	52.45
John Evans Atta Mills (NDC)	3,850,368	44.64
Edward Nasigre Mahama (PNC)	165,375	1.92
George Aggudey (CPP)	85,968	1.00
Total	8,625,785*	100.00

* Excluding 188,213 spoilt papers.

PARLIAMENT

Parliament: Parliament House, Accra; tel. (21) 664042; fax (21) 665957; e-mail clerk@parliament.gh; internet www.parliament.gh.

Speaker: EBENEZER BEGYINA SEKI HUGHES.

Legislative Elections, 7 December 2004

Party	% of votes	Seats
New Patriotic Party (NPP)	55.6	128
National Democratic Congress (NDC)	40.9	94
People's National Convention (PNC)	1.7	4
Convention People's Party (CPP)	1.3	3
Independents	0.4	1
Total	100.0	230

COUNCIL OF STATE

Chairman: Prof. DANIEL ADZEI BEKOE.

Election Commission

Electoral Commission (EC): Accra; internet www.ec.gov.gh; f. 1993; appointed by the President; Chair. Dr KWADWO AFARI-GYAN.

Political Organizations

Convention People's Party (CPP): 825/3 Mango Tree Ave, Asylum Down, POB 10939, Accra-North; tel. (21) 221773; f. 1998 as Convention Party by merger of the National Convention Party (f. 1992) and the People's Convention Party (f. 1993); present name adopted in 2000; Nkrumahist; Chair. Dr EDMUND DELLE; Sec.-Gen. Dr NII NOI DOWUONA.

Democratic Freedom Party (DFP): Accra; f. 2006; Leader Dr OBED YAO ASAMOAH.

Democratic People's Party (DPP): 698/4 Star Ave, Kokomlemle, Accra; tel. (21) 221671; f. 1992; Chair. THOMAS WARD-BREW; Gen. Sec. G. M. TETTEY.

Ghana National Party (GNP): Accra; f. 2006; Chair. VICTOR OFORI AMPOFO.

Grand Coalition: Accra; f. 2004 to contest general election; Chair. DAN LARTEY.

EGLE (Every Ghanaian Living Everywhere) Party: Kokomlemle, POB 1859, Accra; tel. (21) 231873; f. 1992 as the Eagle Party; Chair. DANIEL OFFORI-ATTA.

Great Consolidated People's Party (GCPP): Citadel House, POB 3077, Accra; tel. (21) 311498; f. 1996; Nkrumahist; Chair. DAN LARTEY; Sec.-Gen. NICHOLAS MENSAH.

People's National Convention (PNC): Kokomlemle, near Sadisco, POB 7795, Accra; tel. (21) 236389; f. 1992; Nkrumahist; Leader Dr EDWARD MAHAMA; Chair. Dr MIKE MENSAH; Gen.-Sec. GABRIEL PWAMANG.

National Democratic Congress (NDC): 641/4 Ringway Close, POB 5825, Kokomlemle, Accra-North; tel. and fax (21) 230761; e-mail ndc2004@hotmail.com; internet www.ndc.org.gh; f. 1992; party of fmr Pres. Jerry Rawlings; Chair. Dr KWABENA ADJEI; Gen. Sec. JOHNSON ASEIDU NKETIAH.

National Reform Party (NRP): 31 Mango Tree Ave, Asylum Down, POB 19403, Accra-North; tel. (21) 228578; f. 1999 by a breakaway group from the NDC; Sec.-Gen. OPOKU KYERETWIE.

New Patriotic Party (NPP): C912/2 Duade St, Kokomlemle, POB 3456, Accra-North; tel. (21) 227951; fax (21) 224418; e-mail npp@africanonline.com.gh; internet www.nppghana.org; f. 1992; Chair. PETER MAC MANU; Sec.-Gen. NANA OHENE NTOW.

United Ghana Movement (UGM): 1 North Ridge Cres., POB C2611, Cantonments, Accra; tel. (21) 225581; fax (21) 231390; e-mail info@ugmghana.org; f. 1996 by a breakaway group from the NPP; Chair. WEREKO BROBBY.

United Renaissance Party (URP): Accra; f. 2006; Chair. KOFI WAYO; Gen. Sec. ALHASSAN SAEED.

Diplomatic Representation

EMBASSIES AND HIGH COMMISSIONS IN GHANA

Algeria: 22 Josif Broz Tito Ave, POB 2747, Cantonments, Accra; tel. (21) 776719; fax (21) 776828; e-mail embdzacc@africaonline.com.gh; Ambassador LAKHAL BENKELAI.

Angola: Accra; Ambassador EARISTO D. KIMBA.

Benin: 19 Volta St, Second Close, Airport Residential Area, POB 7871, Accra; tel. (21) 774860; fax (21) 774889; Ambassador PIERRE SADELER.

Brazil: Millennium Heights Bldg 2A, 14 Liberation Link, Airport Commercial Area, POB CT3859, Accra; tel. (21) 774908; fax (21) 778566; e-mail brasemb@brasilghana.org; Ambassador LOUIS FERNANDO DE ANDRADI SERRA.

Bulgaria: 3 Kakramadu Rd, POB 3193, East Cantonments, Accra; tel. (21) 772404; fax (21) 774231; e-mail bulembgh@ghana.com; Chargé d'affaires a.i. GEORGE MITEV.

Burkina Faso: 772 Asylum Down, off Farrar Ave, POB 65, Accra; tel. (21) 221988; fax (21) 777490; e-mail ambafaso@ghana.com; Ambassador PIERRE SEM SANOU.

Canada: 42 Independence Ave, Sankara Interchange, POB 1639, Accra; tel. (21) 211521; fax (21) 211523; e-mail accra@international.gc.ca; internet www.accra.gc.ca; High Commissioner (vacant).

China, People's Republic: 6 Agostino Neto Rd, Airport Residential Area, POB 3356, Accra; tel. (21) 777073; fax (21) 774527; e-mail chinaemb_gh@mfa.gov.cn; internet gh.china-embassy.org; Ambassador YU WENZHE.

Côte d'Ivoire: 9 18th Lane, off Cantonments Rd, POB 3445, Christiansborg, Accra; tel. (21) 774611; fax (21) 773516; e-mail acigh@ambaci-ghana.org; Ambassador (vacant).

Cuba: 20 Amilcar Cabral Rd, Airport Residential Area, POB 9163 Airport, Accra; tel. (21) 775868; fax 774998; e-mail embghana@africaonline.com.gh; Ambassador MIGUEL PEREZ GRUZ.

Czech Republic: C260/5, 2 Kanda High Rd, POB 5226, Accra-North; tel. (21) 223540; fax (21) 225337; e-mail accra@embassy.mzv.cz; internet www.mzv.cz/accra; Ambassador MIROSLAV KŘENEK.

Denmark: 67 Dr Isert Rd, North Ridge, POB CT 596, Accra; tel. (21) 253473; fax (21) 228061; e-mail accamb@um.dk; internet www.ambaccra.um.dk; Ambassador FLEMMING BJØRK PEDERSEN.

Egypt: 38 Senchi St, Airport Residential Area, Accra; tel. (21) 776795; fax (21) 777579; e-mail boustaneaccra@hotmail.com; Ambassador SEIF ALLAH MOSTAFA ABDUL MAGUID NOSEIR.

Ethiopia: 2 Milne Close, Airport Residential Area, POB 1646, Accra; tel. (21) 775928; fax (21) 776807; e-mail ethioemb@ghana.com; Ambassador Ato CHAM UGALA URIAT.

France: 12th Rd, off Liberation Ave, POB 187, Accra; tel. (21) 214550; fax (21) 214589; e-mail ambaccra@africaonline.com.gh; internet www.ambafrance-gh.org; Ambassador PIERRE JACQUEMOT.

Germany: 6 Ridge St, North Ridge, POB 1757, Accra; tel. (21) 211000; fax (21) 221347; e-mail info@accra.diplo.de; internet www.accra.diplo.de; Ambassador Dr MARIUS HAAS.

Guinea: 11 Osu Badu St, Dzorwulu, POB 5497, Accra-North; tel. (21) 777921; fax (21) 760961; e-mail embagui@ghana.com; Ambassador MAMADOU FALILOU BAH.

Holy See: 8 Drake Ave, Airport Residential Area, POB 9675, Accra; tel. (21) 777759; fax (21) 774019; e-mail nuncio@ghana.com; Apostolic Nuncio Most Rev. GEORGE KOCHERRY (Titular Archbishop of Othona).

India: 9 Ridge Rd, Roman Ridge, POB 5708, Cantonments, Accra; tel. (21) 775601; fax (21) 772176; e-mail indiahc@ncs.com.gh; internet www.indiahc-ghana.com; High Commissioner RAJESH N. PRASAD.

Iran: 12 Arkusah St, Airport Residential Area, POB 12673, Accra-North; tel. (21) 774474; fax (21) 777043; Ambassador VALIOLLAH MOHAMMADI NASRABADI.

Italy: Jawaharlal Nehru Rd, POB 140, Accra; tel. (21) 775621; fax (21) 777301; e-mail ambasciata.accra@esteri.it; internet www.ambaccra.esteri.it; Ambassador FABRIZIO DE AGOSTINI.

Japan: Fifth Ave, POB 1637, West Cantonments, Accra; tel. (21) 765060; fax (21) 762553; Ambassador MASSAMICHI ISHIKAWA.

Korea, Democratic People's Republic: 139 Nortei Ababio Loop, Ambassadorial Estate, Roman Ridge, POB 13874, Accra; tel. (21) 777825; Ambassador KIM PYONG GI.

Korea, Republic: 3 Abokobi Rd, POB GP13700, East Cantonments, Accra-North; tel. (21) 776157; fax (21) 772313; e-mail koreaadm@africaonline.com.gh; Ambassador WI KEYEI-CHUI.

Lebanon: F864/1, off Cantonments Rd, Osu, POB 562, Accra; tel. (21) 776727; fax (21) 764290; e-mail lebanon@its.com.gh; Ambassador JAWDAT EL-HAJJAR.

Liberia: 10 Odoi Kwao St, Airport Residential Area, POB 895, Accra; tel. (21) 775641; fax (21) 775987; Ambassador RUDOLPH P. VON BALLMOOS.

Libya: 14 Sixth St, Airport Residential Area, POB 9665, Accra; tel. (21) 774819; fax (21) 774953; Secretary of People's Bureau MUHAMMAD AL-GAMUDI.

Malaysia: 18 Templesi Lane, Airport Residential Area, POB 16033, Accra; tel. (21) 763691; fax (21) 764910; e-mail mwaccra@africaonline.com.gh; Chargé d'affaires YAACOB AWANG CHIK.

Mali: 1st Bungalow, Liberia Rd, Airport Residential Area, POB 1121, Accra; tel. and fax (21) 666942; Ambassador MUPHTAH AG HAIRY.

Netherlands: 89 Liberation Rd, Ako Adjei Interchange, POB CT1647, Accra; tel. (21) 214350; fax (21) 773655; e-mail acc@minbuza.nl; internet www.ambaccra.nl; Ambassador LIDI REMMELZWAAL.

Niger: E104/3 Independence Ave, POB 2685, Accra; tel. (21) 224962; fax (21) 229011; Ambassador ABDOULKARIMOU SEINI.

Nigeria: 5 Tito Ave, POB 1548, Accra; tel. (21) 776158; fax (21) 774395; e-mail nighicom@africaonline.com.gh; High Commissioner OLUTUNGI KOLAPO.

Russia: 856/1 Ring Rd East, 13 Lane, POB 1634, Accra; tel. (21) 775611; fax (21) 772699; e-mail russia@4u.com.gh; internet www.ghana.mid.ru; Ambassador ANDREY V. POKROVSKIY.

Sierra Leone: 83A Senchi St, Airport Residential Area, POB 55, Cantonments, Accra; tel. (21) 769190; fax (21) 769189; e-mail slhc@ighmail.com; High Commissioner MOKOWA ADU- GYAMFI.

South Africa: 10 Klotey Cres., Labone North, POB 298, Accra; tel. (21) 762380; fax (21) 762381; e-mail sahcgh@africaonline.com.gh; High Commissioner Dr R. S. MOLEKANE.

Spain: Drake Ave Extension, Airport Residential Area, PMB KA44, Accra; tel. (21) 774004; fax (21) 776217; e-mail emb.accra@mae.es; Ambassador JORGE MONTEALEGRE BUIRE.

Switzerland: Kanda Highway, North Ridge, POB 359, Accra; tel. (21) 228125; fax (21) 223583; e-mail acc.vertretung@eda.admin.ch; internet www.eda.admin.ch/accra; Ambassador GEORG ZUBLER.

Togo: Togo House, near Cantonments Circle, POB C120, Accra; tel. (21) 777950; fax (21) 765659; e-mail togamba@ighmail.com; Ambassador JEAN-PIERRE GBIKPI-BENISSAN.

United Kingdom: Osu Link, off Gamel Abdul Nasser Ave, POB 296, Accra; tel. and fax (21) 7010655; e-mail high.commission.accra@fco.gov.uk; internet www.britishhighcommission.gov.uk/ghana; High Commissioner GORDON WETHERELL.

USA: Ring Rd East, POB 194, Accra; tel. (21) 775348; fax (21) 776008; e-mail prsaccra@pd.state.gov; internet accra.usembassy.gov; Ambassador PAMELA ETHEL BRIDGEWATER.

Judicial System

The civil law in force in Ghana is based on the Common Law, doctrines of equity and general statutes which were in force in England in 1874, as modified by subsequent Ordinances. Ghanaian customary law is, however, the basis of most personal, domestic and contractual relationships. Criminal Law is based on the Criminal Procedure Code, 1960, derived from English Criminal Law, and since amended. The Superior Court of Judicature comprises a Supreme Court, a Court of Appeal, a High Court and a Regional Tribunal; Inferior Courts include Circuit Courts, Circuit Tribunals, Community Tribunals and such other Courts as may be designated by law. In 2001 'fast-track' court procedures were established to accelerate the delivery of justice.

Supreme Court

Consists of the Chief Justice and not fewer than nine other Justices. It is the final court of appeal in Ghana and has jurisdiction in matters relating to the enforcement or interpretation of the Constitution.

Chief Justice: GEORGINA WOOD.

Court of Appeal: Consists of the Chief Justice and not fewer than five Judges of the Court of Appeal. It has jurisdiction to hear and determine appeals from any judgment, decree or order of the High Court.

High Court: Comprises the Chief Justice and not fewer than 12 Justices of the High Court. It exercises original jurisdiction in all matters, civil and criminal, other than those for offences involving treason. Trial by jury is practised in criminal cases in Ghana and the Criminal Procedure Code, 1960, provides that all trials on indictment shall be by a jury or with the aid of Assessors.

Circuit Courts: Exercise original jurisdiction in civil matters where the amount involved does not exceed 100,000 cedis. They also have jurisdiction with regard to the guardianship and custody of infants, and original jurisdiction in all criminal cases, except offences where the maximum punishment is death or the offence of treason. They have appellate jurisdiction from decisions of any District Court situated within their respective circuits.

District Courts: To each magisterial district is assigned at least one District Magistrate who has original jurisdiction to try civil suits in which the amount involved does not exceed 50,000 cedis. District Magistrates also have jurisdiction to deal with all criminal cases, except first-degree felonies, and commit cases of a more serious nature to either the Circuit Court or the High Court. A Grade I District Court can impose a fine not exceeding 1,000 cedis and sentences of imprisonment of up to two years and a Grade II District Court may impose a fine not exceeding 500 cedis and a sentence of imprisonment of up to 12 months. A District Court has no appellate jurisdiction, except in rent matters under the Rent Act.

Juvenile Courts: Jurisdiction in cases involving persons under 17 years of age, except where the juvenile is charged jointly with an adult. The Courts comprise a Chairman, who must be either the District Magistrate or a lawyer, and not fewer than two other members appointed by the Chief Justice in consultation with the Judicial Council. The Juvenile Courts can make orders as to the protection and supervision of a neglected child and can negotiate with parents to secure the good behaviour of a child.

National Public Tribunal: Considers appeals from the Regional Public Tribunals. Its decisions are final and are not subject to any further appeal. The Tribunal consists of at least three members and not more than five, one of whom acts as Chairman.

Regional Public Tribunals: Hears criminal cases relating to prices, rent or exchange control, theft, fraud, forgery, corruption or any offence which may be referred to them by the Provisional National Defence Council.

Special Military Tribunal: Hears criminal cases involving members of the armed forces. It consists of between five and seven members.

Attorney-General: JOSEPH GHARTEY.

Religion

According to the 2000 census, 69% of the population were Christians and 15.6% Muslims, while 6.9% followed indigenious beliefs.

CHRISTIANITY

Christian Council of Ghana: POB GP919, Accra; tel. (21) 776678; fax (21) 776725; e-mail christiancouncil@4u.com.gh; f. 1929; advisory body comprising 16 mem. churches and 2 affiliate Christian orgs (2005); Gen. Sec. Rev. Dr FRED DEEGBE.

The Anglican Communion

Anglicans in Ghana are adherents of the Church of the Province of West Africa, comprising 13 dioceses and a missionary region, of which nine are in Ghana.

Archbishop of the Province of West Africa and Bishop of Ho: Most Rev. ROBERT GARSHONG ALLOTEY OKINE, Bishop's Lodge, BT A167, Betom, POB 980, Koforidua; tel. (81) 22329; fax (21) 669125; e-mail archbishopwa@yahoo.com.

Bishop of Accra: Rt Rev. JUSTICE OFEI AKROFI, Bishopscourt, POB 8, Accra; tel. (21) 662292; fax (21) 669125; e-mail cpwa@ghana.com.

Bishop of Cape Coast: Rt Rev. DANIEL ALLOTEY, Bishopscourt, POB A233, Adisadel Estates, Cape Coast; tel. (42) 32502; fax (42) 32637.

Bishop of Koforidua: Rt Rev. FRANCIS QUASHIE, POB 980, Koforidua; tel. (81) 22329; fax (81) 22060; e-mail cpwa_gh@yahoo.com; internet koforidua.org.

Bishop of Kumasi: Rt Rev. DANIEL YINKAH SAFO, Bishop's Office, St Cyprian's Ave, POB 144, Kumasi; tel. and fax (51) 24117; e-mail kumangli@africaonline.com.gh.

Bishop of Sekondi: Rt Rev. JOHN KWAMINA OTOO, POB 85, Sekondi; tel. (31) 669125.

Bishop of Sunyani: Rt Rev. THOMAS AMPAH BRIENT, Bishop's House, POB 23, Sunyani, BA; tel. (61) 27213; fax (61) 27203; e-mail deegyab@ighmail.com.

Bishop of Tamale: Rt Rev. EMMANUEL ARONGO, POB 110, Tamale NR; tel. (71) 22906; fax (71) 22849.

The Roman Catholic Church

Ghana comprises four archdioceses and 14 dioceses. At 31 December 2004 there were 2,652,380 adherents in the country, equivalent to 12.8% of the total population.

Ghana Bishops' Conference

National Catholic Secretariat, POB 9712, Airport, Accra; tel. (21) 500491; fax (21) 500493; e-mail dscncs@africaonline.com.gh.

f. 1960; Pres. Rt Rev. LUCAS ABADAMLOORA APPIAH-TURKSON (Archbishop of Cape Coast).

Archbishop of Accra: Most Rev. GABRIEL CHARLES PALMER-BUCKLE, Chancery Office, POB 247, Accra; tel. (21) 222728; fax (21) 231619.

Archbishop of Cape Coast: Cardinal PETER KODWO APPIAH-TURKSON, Archbishop's House, POB 112, Cape Coast; tel. (42) 33471; fax (42) 33473; e-mail archcape@ghanacbc.com.

Archbishop of Kumasi: Most Rev. PETER KWASI SARPONG, POB 99, Kumasi; tel. (51) 24012; fax (51) 29395; e-mail cadiokum@ghana.com.

Archbishop of Tamale: Most Rev. GREGORY EBO KPIEBAYA, Archbishop's House, Gumbehini Rd, POB 42, Tamale; tel. and fax (71) 22425; e-mail tamdio2@yahoo.co.uk.

Other Christian Churches

African Methodist Episcopal Zion Church: POB MP522, Mamprobi, Accra; tel. (21) 669200; e-mail amezion@africaonline.com.gh; f. 1898; Pres. Rt Rev. WARREN M. BROWN.

Christian Methodist Episcopal Church: POB 3906, Accra; Pres. Rev. YENN BATA.

Church of Pentecost: POB 2194 Accra; tel. and fax (21) 772193; e-mail cophq@ghana.com; internet www1.thechurchofpentecost.com; Chair. Apostle M. K. NTUMY; Gen.-Sec. Apostle ALFRED KODUAH; 1,021,856 mems (July 2002).

Evangelical-Lutheran Church of Ghana: POB KN197, Kaneshie, Accra; tel. (21) 223487; fax (21) 220947; e-mail elcga@africaonline.com.gh; Pres. Rt Rev. Dr PAUL KOFI FYNN; 26,000 mems.

Evangelical-Presbyterian Church of Ghana: 19 Main St, Tesano, PMB, Accra-North; tel. (21) 220381; fax (21) 233173; f. 1847; Moderator Rev. Dr LIVINGSTON BUAMA; 295,000 mems.

Ghana Baptist Convention: PMB, Kumasi; tel. (51) 25215; fax (51) 28592; e-mail mail@gbconvention.org; internet www.gbconvention.org; f. 1963; Pres. Rev. Dr KOJO OSEI-WUSUH; Sec. Rev. KOJO AMO; 65,000 mems.

Ghana Mennonite Church: POB 5485, Accra; fax (21) 220589; f. 1957; Moderator Rev. THEOPHILUS TETTEH; Sec. JOHN ADETA; 5,000 mems.

Ghana Union Conference of Seventh-day Adventists: POB GP1016, Accra; tel. (21) 223720; fax (21) 227024; e-mail salarmie@compuserve.com; f. 1943; Pres. Pastor P. O. MENSAH; Sec. Pastor SAMUEL A. LARMIE; 23,700 mems.

Methodist Church of Ghana: E252/2, Liberia Rd, POB 403, Accra; tel. (21) 228120; fax (21) 227008; e-mail mcghqs@africaonline.com.gh; Pres. Rt Rev. Dr SAMUEL ASANTE ANTWI; Sec. Rev. MACLEAN AGYIRI KUMI; 341,000 mems.

Presbyterian Church of Ghana: POB 106, Accra; tel. (21) 662511; fax (21) 665594; f. 1828; Moderator Rt Rev. YAW FRIMPONG-MANSON; Sec. Rev. Dr D. N. A. KPOBI; 422,500 mems.

The African Methodist Episcopal Church, the Christ Reformed Church, the F'Eden Church, the Gospel Revival Church of God and the Religious Society of Friends (Quakers) are also active in Ghana.

ISLAM

In 2000 some 15.6% of the population of Ghana were Muslims, with a particularly large concentration in the Northern Region. The majority are Malikees.

Coalition of Muslim Organizations (COMOG): Accra; Pres. Alhaji Maj. MOHAMMED EASAH.

Ghana Muslim Representative Council: Accra.

Chief Imam: Sheikh USMAN NUHU SHARABUTU.

BAHÁ'Í FAITH

National Spiritual Assembly: POB 7098, Accra-North; tel. (21) 222127; e-mail bahaigh@africaonline.com.gh; Sec. KOBINA AMISSAH FYNN.

The Press

DAILY NEWSPAPERS

Accra Daily Mail: POB CT4910, Cantonments, Accra; e-mail mike@accra-mail.com; internet www.accra-mail.com; Man. Editor A.R. HARUNA ATTAH.

The Daily Dispatch: 1 Dade Walk, North Labone, POB C1945, Cantonments, Accra; tel. (21) 763339; e-mail ephson@usa.net; Editor BEN EPHSON.

Daily Graphic: Graphic Communications Group Ltd, POB 742, Accra; tel. (21) 684001; fax (21) 234754; e-mail info@graphicghana

.com; internet www.graphicghana.com; f. 1950; state-owned; Editor YAW BOADU AYEBOAFO; circ. 100,000.

Daily Guide: Accra; owned by Western Publications Ltd; Editor GINA BLAY.

The Ghanaian Times: New Times Corpn, Ring Rd West, POB 2638, Accra; tel. (21) 228282; fax (21) 229398; e-mail newtimes@ghana .com; f. 1958; state-owned; Editor AJOA YEBOAH-AFARI (acting); circ. 45,000.

The Telescope: Takoradi; f. 2005; Editor LOUIS HENRY DANSO.

PERIODICALS

Thrice Weekly

Ghanaian Chronicle: PMB, Accra-North; tel. (21) 222319; fax (21) 232608; e-mail chronicl@africaonline.com.gh; internet www .ghanaian-chronicle.com; Acting Editor JONATHAN ATO KOBBIE; circ. 60,000.

The Independent: Clear Type Press Bldg Complex, off Graphic Rd, POB 4031, Accra; tel. and fax (21) 661091; f. 1989; Editor ANDREW ARTHUR.

Network Herald: NBS Multimedia, PMB, OSU, Accra; tel. (21) 701184; fax (21) 762173; e-mail support@ghana.com; internet www .networkherald.gh; f. 2001; Editor ELVIS QUARSHIE.

Bi-Weekly

Ghana Palaver: Palaver Publications, POB WJ317, Wejia, Accra; tel. (21) 850495; e-mail palaver@ghana-palaver.com; internet www .ghana-palaver.com; f. 1994; Editor JOJO BRUCE QUANSAH.

The Ghanaian Lens: Accra; Editor KOBBY FIAGBE.

The Ghanaian Voice: Newstop Publications, POB 514, Mamprobi, Accra; tel. (21) 324644; fax (21) 314939; Editor CHRISTIANA ANSAH; circ. 100,000.

Weekly

Business and Financial Times: POB CT16, Cantonments, Accra; tel. and fax (21) 223334; f. 1989; Editor JOHN HANSON; circ. 20,000.

The Crusading Guide: POB 8523, Accra-North; tel. (21) 763339; fax (21) 761541; Editor KWEKU BAAKO, Jr.

Free Press: Tommy Thompson Books Ltd, POB 6492, Accra; tel. (21) 225994; independent; Editor FRANK BOAHENE.

Ghana Life: Ghana Life Publications, POB 11337, Accra; tel. (21) 229835; Editor NIKKI BOA-AMPONSEM.

Ghana Market Watch: Accra; internet www.ghanamarketwatch .com; f. 2006; financial; CEO AMOS DOTSE.

Graphic Showbiz: Graphic Communications Group Ltd, POB 742, Accra; tel. (21) 228911; fax (21) 234754; e-mail info@graphicghana .com; internet www.graphicghana.info; state-owned; Editor NANA-BANYIN DADSON.

Graphic Sports: Graphic Communications Group Ltd, POB 742, Accra; tel. (21) 228911; fax (21) 234754; e-mail info@graphicghana .com; state-owned; Editor FELIX ABAYATEYE; circ. 60,000.

The Guide: Western Publications Ltd, POB 8253, Accra-North; tel. (21) 232760; Editor KWEKU BAAKO, Jr.

Gye Nyame Concord: Accra; internet www.ghanaweb.com/ concord.

The Heritage: POB AC503, Arts Center, Accra; tel. (21) 258820; fax (21) 258823; e-mail heritage@africaonline.gh; internet www .theheritagenews.com; Chair. STEPHEN OWUSU; Editor NII NOI VANDERPUYE.

High Street Journal: POB 7974, Accra-North; tel. (21) 239835; fax (21) 239837; e-mail hsjaccra@ghana.com; Editor SHEIKH ABUTIATE.

The Mirror: Graphic Communications Group Ltd, POB 742, Accra; tel. (21) 228911; fax (21) 234754; e-mail info@graphicghana.com; internet www.graphicghana.info; f. 1953; state-owned; Sat.; Editor E. N. O. PROVENCAL; circ. 90,000.

The National Democrat: Democrat Publications, POB 13605, Accra; Editor ELLIOT FELIX OHENE.

Public Agenda: P. A. Communications, POB 5564, Accra-North; tel. (21) 238821; fax (21) 231687; e-mail isodec@ghana.com; f. 1994; Editor YAO GRAHAM; circ. 12,000.

The Standard: Standard Newspapers & Magazines Ltd, POB KA 9712, Accra; tel. (21) 513537; fax (21) 500493; e-mail snam.ncs@ ghanacbc.org; internet www.ghanacbc.org; Roman Catholic; Editor ISAAC FRITZ ANDOH; circ. 10,000.

Statesman: Kinesic Communications, POB 846, Accra; tel. and fax (21) 233242; official publ. of the New Patriotic Party; Editor GABBY ASARE OTCHERE-DARKO.

The Vanguard: Accra; Editor OSBERT LARTEY.

The Weekend: Newstop Publications, POB 514, Mamprobi, Accra; tel. (21) 324644; fax (21) 314939; Editor EMMANUEL YARTEY; circ. 40,000.

Weekly Insight: Militant Publications Ltd, POB K272, Accra New Town, Accra; tel. (21) 660148; fax (21) 774338; e-mail insight93@ yahoo.com; f. 1993; independent; English; Editor KWESI PRATT, Jr.

Weekly Spectator: New Times Corpn, Ring Rd West, POB 2638, Accra; tel. (21) 228282; fax (21) 229398; state-owned; f. 1963; Sun.; Editor WILLIE DONKOR; circ. 165,000.

Other

African Observer: POB 1171, Kaneshie, Accra; tel. (21) 231459; bi-monthly; Editor STEVE MALLORY.

African Woman: Ring Rd West, POB 1496, Accra; monthly.

AGI Newsletter: c/o Asscn of Ghana Industries, POB 8624, Accra-North; tel. (21) 779023; e-mail agi@agighana.org; internet www .agighana.org; f. 1974; monthly; Editor CARLO HEY; circ. 1,500.

AGOO: Newstop Publications, POB 514, Mamprobi, Accra; tel. (21) 324644; fax (21) 314939; monthly; lifestyle magazine; Publr KOJO BONSU.

Akwansosem: Ghana Information Services, POB 745, Accra; tel. (21) 228011; quarterly; in Akuapim Twi, Asanti Twi and Fante; Editor KATHLEEN OFOSU-APPIAH.

Armed Forces News: General Headquarters, Directorate of Public Relations, Burma Camp, Accra; tel. (21) 776111; f. 1966; quarterly; Editor ADOTEY ANKRAH-HOFFMAN; circ. 4,000.

Boxing and Football Illustrated: POB 8392, Accra; f. 1976; monthly; Editor NANA O. AMPOMAH; circ. 10,000.

Business and Financial Concord: Sammy Tech Consult Enterprise, POB 5677, Accra-North; tel. (21) 232446; fortnightly; Editor KWABENA RICHARDSON.

Business Watch: Sulton Bridge Co. Ltd, POB C3447, Cantonments, Accra; tel. (21) 233293; monthly.

Chit Chat: POB 7043, Accra; monthly; Editor ROSEMOND ADU.

Christian Messenger: Presbyterian Book Depot Bldg, POB 3075, Accra; tel. and fax (21) 663124; e-mail danbentil@yahoo.com; f. 1883; English-language; every two weeks; quarterly; Editor GEORGE MARTINSON; circ. 40,000.

Drum: POB 1197, Accra; monthly; general interest.

Ghana Journal of Science: Ghana Science Asscn, POB 7, Legon; tel. (21) 500253; monthly; Editor Dr A. K. AHAFIA.

Ghana Official News Bulletin: Information Services Dept, POB 745, Accra; English; political, economic, investment and cultural affairs.

Ghana Review International (GRi): POB GP14307, Accra; tel. (21) 677437; fax (21) 677438; e-mail accra@ghanareview.com; internet www.ghanareview.com; publishes in Accra, London and New York; CEO NANA OTUO ACHEAMPONG; print circ. 100,000.

Ideal Woman (Obaa Sima): POB 5737, Accra; tel. (21) 221399; f. 1971; fortnightly; Editor KATE ABBAM.

Insight and Opinion: POB 5446, Accra; quarterly; Editorial Sec. W. B. OHENE.

Legon Observer: POB 11, Legon, Accra; fax (21) 774338; f. 1966; publ. by Legon Society on National Affairs; fortnightly; Chair. J. A. DADSON; Editor EBOW DANIEL.

Police News: Police HQ, Accra; monthly; Editor S. S. APPIAH; circ. 20,000.

The Post: Ghana Information Services, POB 745, Accra; tel. (21) 228011; f. 1980; monthly; current affairs and analysis; circ. 25,000.

Radio and TV Times: Ghana Broadcasting Corpn, Broadcasting House, POB 18167, Accra; tel. (21) 508927; fax (21) 773612; f. 1960; quarterly; Editor SAM THOMPSON; circ. 5,000.

The Scope: POB 8162, Tema; monthly; Editor EMMANUEL DOE ZIORKLUI; circ. 10,000.

Students World: POB M18, Accra; tel. (21) 774248; fax (21) 778715; e-mail afram@wwwplus.co.za; f. 1974; monthly; educational; Man. Editor ERIC OFEI; circ. 10,000.

The Teacher: Ghana National Asscn of Teachers, POB 209, Accra; tel. (21) 221515; fax (21) 226286; f. 1931; quarterly; circ. 30,000.

Truth and Life: Gift Publications, POB 11337, Accra-North; monthly; Editor Pastor KOBENA CHARM.

Uneek: POB 230, Achimota, Accra; tel. (21) 543853; fax (21) 231355; e-mail info@uneekmagazine.com; internet www.uneekmagazine .com; f. 1998; monthly; leisure, culture; CEO and Editor FRANCIS ADAMS.

The Watchman: Watchman Gospel Ministry, POB GP4521, Accra; tel. and fax (21) 500631; e-mail watchmannewspaper@yahoo.com; f. 1986; Christian news; fortnightly; Pres. and CEO DIVINE P. KUMAH; Chair. Dr E. K. OPUNI; circ. 5,000.

Other newspapers include **The Catalyst**, **The Crystal Clear Lens**, **The Enquirer** and **Searchlight**. There are also internet-based news sites, including **Ghana Today**, at www.ghanatoday.com and **ThisWeekGhana**, at www.thisweekghana.com.

NEWS AGENCY

Ghana News Agency: POB 2118, Accra; tel. (21) 215135; fax (21) 669841; e-mail ghnews@ncs.com.gh; f. 1957; Gen. Man. Sam B. Quaicoe; 10 regional offices and 110 district offices.

PRESS ASSOCIATION

Ghana Journalists' Association: POB 4636, Accra; tel. (21) 234692; fax (21) 234694; e-mail info@ghanamedia.com; internet www.ghanamedia.com/gja; Pres. Ransford Tetteh.

Publishers

Advent Press: Osu La Rd, POB 0102, Osu, Accra; tel. (21) 777861; fax (21) 775327; e-mail eaokpoti@ghana.com; f. 1937; publishing arm of the Ghana Union Conference of Seventh-day Adventists; Gen. Man. Emmanuel C. Tetteh.

Adwinsa Publications (Ghana) Ltd: Advance Press Bldg, 3rd Floor, School Rd, POB 92, Legoh Accra; tel. (21) 221654; f. 1977; general, educational; Man. Dir Kwabena Amponsah.

Afram Publications: C 184/22 Midway Lane, Abofu-Achimota, POB M18, Accra; tel. (21) 412561; e-mail aframpub@pubchgh.com; internet www.aframpublications.com.gh; f. 1973; textbooks and general; Man. Dir Eric Ofei.

Africa Christian Press: POB 30, Achimota, Accra; tel. (21) 244147; fax (21) 220271; e-mail acpbooks@ghana.com; f. 1964; religious, fiction, theology, children's, leadership; Gen. Man. Richard A. B. Crabbe.

Allgoodbooks Ltd: POB AN10416, Accra-North; tel. (21) 664294; fax (21) 665629; e-mail allgoodbooks@hotmail.com; f. 1968; children's; Man. Dir Mary Asirifi.

Asempa Publishers: POB GP919, Accra; tel. (21) 233084; fax (21) 235140; e-mail asempa@ghana.com; f. 1970; religion, social issues, African music, fiction, children's; Gen. Man. Sarah O. Apronti.

Benibengor Book Agency: POB 40, Aboso; fiction, biography, children's and paperbacks; Man. Dir J. Benibengor Blay.

Black Mask Ltd: POB CT770, Cantonments, Accra; tel. (21) 234577; f. 1979; textbooks, plays, novels, handicrafts; Man. Dir Yaw Owusu Asante.

Catholic Book Centre: North Liberia Rd, POB 3285, Accra; tel. (21) 226651; fax (21) 237727.

Editorial and Publishing Services: POB 5743, Accra; general, reference; Man. Dir M. Danquah.

Educational Press and Manufacturers Ltd: POB 9184, Airport-Accra; tel. (21) 220395; f. 1975; textbooks, children's; Man. G. K. Kodua.

Encyclopaedia Africana Project: POB 2797, Accra; tel. (21) 776939; fax (21) 779228; e-mail eap@africaonline.com.gh; internet encyclopaediaafricana.org; f. 1962; reference; Dir Grace Bansa.

Frank Publishing Ltd: POB MB414, Accra; tel. (21) 240711; f. 1976; secondary school textbooks; Man. Dir Francis K. Dzokoto.

Ghana Publishing Corpn: POB 124, Greater Accra.

Ghana Publishing Corpn—Assembly Press Ltd: POB 124, Accra; tel. (21) 664338; fax (21) 664330; e-mail asspcom@africaonline.com.gh; f. 1965; state-owned; textbooks and general fiction and non-fiction; Man. Dir F. K. Nyarko.

Ghana Universities Press: POB GP4219, Accra; tel. (21) 513401; fax (21) 513402; f. 1962; scholarly, academic and general and textbooks; CEO Dr K. M. Ganu.

Golden Wings Publications: 26 Mantse Kwao St, POB 1337, Accra; educational and children's; Man. Editor Gregory Ankrah.

Sam-Woode Ltd: A.979/15 Dansoman High St, POB 12719, Accra-North; tel. (21) 305287; fax (21) 310482; e-mail samwoode@ghana.com; f. 1984; educational and children's; Chair. Kwesi Sam-Woode.

Sedco Publishing Ltd: Sedco House, 5 Tabon St, North Ridge, POB 2051, Accra; tel. (21) 221332; fax (21) 220107; e-mail sedco@africaonline.com.gh; f. 1975; educational; Chair. Courage K. Segbawu; Man. Dir Frank Segbawu.

Sub-Saharan Publishers: PO Box 358, Legon, Accra; tel. and fax (21) 233371; e-mail sub-saharan@ighmail.com; Man. Dir Akoss Ofori-Mensah.

Unimax Macmillan Ltd: 42 Ring Rd South Industrial Area, POB 10722, Accra-North; tel. (21) 227443; fax (21) 225215; e-mail info@unimacmillan.com; internet www.unimacmillan.com; representative of Macmillan UK; atlases, educational and children's; Man. Dir Edward Addo.

Waterville Publishing House: 4 Thorpe Rd, POB 195, Accra; tel. (21) 663124; f. 1963; general fiction and non-fiction, textbooks, paperbacks, Africana; Man. Dir E. Anim-Ansah.

Woeli Publishing Services: POB NT601, Accra New Town; tel. and fax (21) 229294; e-mail woeli@libr.ug.edu.gh; f. 1984; children's, fiction, academic; Dir W. A. Dekutsey.

PUBLISHERS' ASSOCIATIONS

Ghana Book Development Council: POB M430, Accra; tel. (21) 229178; f. 1975; govt-financed agency; promotes and co-ordinates writing, production and distribution of books; Exec. Dir D. A. Nimako.

Ghana Book Publishers' Association (GBPA): POB LT471, Laterbiokorshie, Accra; tel. (21) 229178; fax (21) 810641; e-mail stevebrob@yahoo.co.uk; f. 1976; Exec. Sec. Stephen Brobbey.

Private Newspaper Publishers' Association of Ghana (PRINPAG): POB 125, Darkuman, Accra; Chair. Nana Kofi Koomson; Gen. Sec. K. Agyemang Duah.

Broadcasting and Communications

TELECOMMUNICATIONS

Regulatory Authority

National Communication Authority (NCA): 1 Rangoon Close, POB 1568, Cantonments, Accra; tel. (21) 776621; fax (21) 763449; e-mail nca@nca.org.gh; internet www.nca.org.gh; f. 1996; regulatory body; Chair. Jude Arthur; Dir-Gen. Maj. (retd) J. R. K. Tandoh.

Major Telecommunications Companies

Ghana Telecom (GT): Telecom House, nr Kwame Nkrumah Circle, Accra-North; tel. (21) 200200; fax (21) 221002; e-mail info@ghanatel.net; internet www.ghanatelecom.com.gh; f. 1995; govt-owned; operates mobile cellular, fixed line networks and data services; Chair. Nana Antwi Boasiako; CEO Dickson Oduro-Nyaning.

Millicom Ghana Ltd: Millicom Place, Barnes Rd, PMB 100, Accra; tel. (27) 7551000; fax (27) 7503999; e-mail info@tigo.com.gh; internet www.tigo.com.gh; f. 1990; mobile cellular telephone services through the network Tigo; Man. Dir Gareth Townley.

Scancom Ltd: Auto Parts Bldg, 41A Graphic Rd, South Industrial Area, POB 281, International Trade Fair Lane, Accra; tel. (24) 4300000; fax (21) 231974; internet www.areeba.com.gh; f. 1994; Ghana's largest mobile cellular telephone provider, through the network Areeba (formerly Spacefon); CEO Brett Goschen.

Western Telesystems Co (WESTEL): Accra; f. 1997; state-owned; fixed line operator.

Kasapa Telecommunication Ltd and GT-Onetouch also offer mobile cellular services.

BROADCASTING

There are internal radio broadcasts in English, Akan, Dagbani, Ewe, Ga, Hausa and Nzema, and an external service in English and French. There are three transmitting stations, with a number of relay stations. The Ghana Broadcasting Corporation operates two national networks, Radio 1 and Radio 2, which broadcast from Accra, and four regional FM stations. In late 2004 128 radio stations and 24 television stations were registered in Ghana.

Ghana Broadcasting Corpn (GBC): Broadcasting House, Ring Rd Central, Kanda, POB 1633, Accra; tel. and fax (21) 768975; e-mail gbc@ghana.com; internet www.gbcghana.com; f. 1935; Acting Dir-Gen. Yaw Owusu-Addo; Dir of TV Kofi Bucknor; Dir of Radio Theo Agbam.

CitiFM: 11 Tettey Loop, Adabraka, Accra; tel. (21) 226171; fax (21) 224043; e-mail info@citifmonline.com; internet www.citifmonline.com; Man. Dir Samuel Atta Mensah.

Joy FM: 355 Faanofa St, Kokomlemle, POB 17202, Accra; tel. (21) 701199; fax (21) 224405; e-mail info@myjoyonline.com; internet www.myjoyonline.com; f. 1995; news, information and music broadcasts; Dir Kwesi Twum.

Metro TV: POB C1609, Cantonments, Accra; tel. (21) 765701; fax (21) 765702; e-mail webdesign@metrotv.com.gh; internet www.metrotv.com.gh.

Radio Ada: POB KA9482, Accra; tel. (21) 500907; fax (21) 516442; e-mail radioada@kalssinn.net; f. 1998; community broadcasts in Dangme; Dirs Alex Quarmyne, Wilna Quarmyne.

Radio Gold FM: POB 17298, Accra; tel. (22) 779404; fax (22) 300284; Man. Dir Baffoe Bonnie.

Sky Broadcasting Co, Ltd: 45 Water Rd, Kanda Overpass, North Ridge, POB CT3850, Cantonments, Accra; tel. (21) 225716; fax (21)

221983; e-mail vayiku@yahoo.com; internet www.spirit.fm; f. 2000; Chief Operations Officer VERONICA AYIKU; Gen. Man. ANDY GLOVER.

TV3: 12th Rd, Kanda, (opposite French embassy), Accra; tel. (21) 228679; fax (21) 763450; e-mail cbo@tv3.com.gh; internet www.tv3.com.gh; f. 1997; private television station; progamming in English and local languages; Man. Dir MUSNI BINMOHAMAD.

Vibe FM: Pyramid House, 3rd Floor, Ring Rd Central, Accra; internet www.vibefm.com.gh; educational; CEO MIKE COOKE.

Finance

(cap. = capital; res = reserves; dep. = deposits; m. = million; br(s). = branch(es); amounts in cedis)

BANKING

The commercial banking sector comprised 10 commercial banks, three development banks, five merchant banks and five foreign banks in 2004. There were also 115 rural banks and several non-banking financial institutions.

Central Bank

Bank of Ghana: 1 Thorpe Rd, POB 2674, Accra; tel. (21) 666902; fax (21) 662996; e-mail bogsecretary@bog.gov.gh; internet www.bog.gov.gh; f. 1957; bank of issue; cap. 100,000m., res 706,657m., dep. 16,642,274m. (Dec. 2004); Gov. PAUL A. ACQUAH.

Commercial Banks

Amalgamated Bank Ltd: 131–3 Farrar Ave, Cantonments, POB CT1541, Accra; tel. (21) 249690; fax (21) 249697; e-mail amalbank@amalbank.com.gh; internet www.amalbank.com.gh; f. 1999; Man. Dir WELBECK ABRA-APPIAH.

Ghana Commercial Bank Ltd: Thorpe Rd, POB 134, Accra; tel. (21) 664914; fax (21) 662168; e-mail gcbmail@gcb.com.gh; internet www.gcb.com.gh; f. 1953; 46.8% state-owned; cap. 20,000m., res 5,607,047m., dep. 4,265,733m. (Dec. 2004); Chair. K. G. OSEI-BONSU; Man. Dir LAWRENCE NEWTON ADU-MANTE; 131 brs.

NTHC Ltd: Martco House, Okai Mensah Link, off Kwame Nkrumah Ave, POB 9563, Adabraka, Accra; tel. (21) 238492; fax (21) 229975; e-mail nthc@ghana.com; internet www.nthcghana.com; fmrly National Trust Holding Co Ltd; f. 1976 to provide stockbrokerage services, asset management and financial advisory services; cap. 9,000m. (2001); Chair. BENJAMIN ADU-AMANKWA; Man. Dir Dr A. W. Q. BARNOR.

Prudential Bank Ltd: 8 Nima Ave, Ring Rd Central, PMB GPO, Accra; tel. (21) 781201; fax (21) 781210; e-mail prudential@ghana.com; internet www.prudentialbank-ghana.com; f. 1996; Exec. Chair. JOHN SACKAH ADDO; Man. Dir STEPHEN SEKYERE-ABANKWA; 9 brs.

The Trust Bank Ltd: Re-insurance House, 68 Kwame Nkrumah Ave, POB 1862, Accra; tel. (21) 240049; fax (21) 240059; e-mail trust@ttbgh.com; internet www.ttbgh.net; f. 1996; 35% owned by Banque Belgolaise (Belgium), 33% owned by the Social Security and National Insurance Trust; cap. 10,000m., res 61,469m., dep. 692,266m. (Dec. 2004); Chair. ALBERT OSEI; Man. Dir PAUL CARDOEN; 6 brs.

uniBank (Ghana) Ltd: Royal Castle Rd, POB AN15367, Kokomlemle, Accra; tel. (21) 253696; fax (21) 253695; e-mail info@unibankghana.com; internet www.unibankghana.com; f. 2001; Man. Dir JOSEPH N. B. TETTEH.

Development Banks

Agricultural Development Bank (ADB): Cedi House, Liberia Rd, POB 4191, Accra; tel. (21) 662758; fax (21) 662846; e-mail adbweb@agricbank.com; internet www.agricbank.com; f. 1965; 51.8% state-owned, 48.2% owned by Bank of Ghana; credit facilities for farmers and commercial banking; cap. and res 390,064.5m., dep. 968,713.0m. (Dec. 2002); Chair. PAUL S. M. KORANTENG; Man. Dir EDWARD BOAKYE-AGYEMANG; 32 brs.

National Investment Bank Ltd (NIB): 37 Kwame Nkrumah Ave, POB 3726, Accra; tel. (21) 661701; fax (21) 661730; e-mail info@nib-ghana.com; internet www.nib-ghana.com; f. 1963; 86.4% state-owned; provides long-term investment capital, jt venture promotion, consortium finance man. and commercial banking services; cap. 3,260m., surplus & res 166,598m., dep. 446,703m. (Dec. 2004); Man. Dir DANIEL CHARLES GYIMAH; 23 brs.

Merchant Banks

CAL Bank Ltd: 23 Independence Ave, POB 14596, Accra; tel. (21) 680068; fax (21) 680081; e-mail calbank@calbank-gh.com; internet www.calbank-gh.com; f. 1990; cap. 70,588m., res 88,474m., dep. 542,687m. (Dec. 2004); Chair. GEORGE VICTOR OKOH; Man. Dir FRANK BRAKO ADU, Jr.

Databank: 61 Barnse Rd, Adabraka, PMB, Ministries Post Office, Accra; tel. (21) 681389; fax (21) 681443; e-mail info@databankgroup.com; internet www.databankgroup.com; f. 1990; Exec. Chair. KEN OFORI-ATTA; Exec. Dir YOFI GRANT; 3 brs.

Ecobank Ghana Ltd (EBG): 19 7th Ave, Ridge West, PMB-GPO, Accra; tel. (21) 681148; fax (21) 680428; e-mail ecobankgh@ecobank.com; internet www.ecobank.com; f. 1989; 92.2% owned by Ecobank Transnational Inc (Togo, operating under the auspices of the Economic Community of West African States); cap. 70,000m., res 168,958m., dep. 1,959,689m. (Dec. 2004); Chair. EDWARD PATRICK LARBI GYAMPOH; 7 brs.

First Atlantic Merchant Bank Ltd: Atlantic Pl., 1 Seventh Ave, Ridge West, POB C1620, Cantonments, Accra; tel. (21) 682203; fax (21) 479245; e-mail info@firstatlanticbank.com.gh; internet www.firstatlanticbank.com.gh; f. 1994; cap. 50,000.0m., res 18,167.1m., dep. 692,675.0m. (Dec. 2005); Chair. PHILIP OWUSU; Man. Dir JUDE ARTHUR.

Merchant Bank (Ghana) Ltd: Merban House, 44 Kwame Nkrumah Ave, POB 401, Accra; tel. (21) 666331; fax (21) 667305; e-mail merban_services@merbangh.com; internet www.merbankgh.com; f. 1972; cap. 70,000m., res 107,616m., dep. 1,490,187m. (Dec. 2005); Chair. SOLOMON KWAMI TETTEH; Man. Dir B. O. MANKWA; 9 brs.

Foreign Banks

Barclays Bank of Ghana Ltd (UK): Barclays House, High St, POB 2949, Accra; tel. (21) 664901; fax (21) 669254; e-mail barclays.ghana@barclays.com; internet www.africa.barclays.com/ghana.htm; f. 1971; 90% owned by Barclays Bank Plc; 10% owned by Government of Ghana; res 389,484m., dep. 9,810m. (Dec. 2003); Chair. NANA WEREKO AMPEM II; Man. Dir K. QUANSAH; 26 brs.

Guaranty Trust Bank (Ghana) Ltd: 25A Castle Rd, Ambassadorial Area Ridge, Accra; tel. (21) 680662; fax (21) 662727; e-mail corporateaffairs@gtbghana.com; internet www.gtbghana.com; f. 2004; 15% owned by Netherlands Development Finance Company (FMO), 15% owned by Alhaji Yusif Ibrahim; Man. Dir. DOLAPO OGUNDIMU.

International Commercial Bank (Ghana) Ltd (Taiwan): Meridian House, Ring Rd Central, PMB 16, Accra; tel. (21) 236133; fax (21) 238228; e-mail icb@icbank-gh.com; internet www.icbank-gh.com; f. 1996; cap. and res 31,205m., total assets 218,318m. (Dec. 2003); CEO LALGUDI KRISHNAMURTHY GANAPATHIRAMAN; 6 brs.

SG-SSB Bank Ltd: Ring Rd Central, POB 13119, Accra; tel. (21) 202001; fax (21) 248920; e-mail enquiries@socgen.com; internet www.sg-ssb.com.gh; f. 1976 as Social Security Bank; 51.0% owned by Société Générale, France; cap. 70,000m., surplus and res 438,262m., dep. 2,367,711m. (Dec. 2006); Chair. GÉRALD LACAZE; Man. Dir ALAIN BELLISSARD; 37 brs.

Stanbic Bank Ghana: Valco Trust House, Castle Rd Ridge, POB CT2344, Cantonments, Accra; tel. (21) 234683; fax (21) 234685; e-mail stanbic@ghana.com; internet www.stanbic.com.gh; f. 1999; subsidiary of the Standard Bank of South Africa Ltd; cap. and res 14,981m., total assets 97,253m. (Dec. 2001); Chair. DENNIS W. KENNEDY; Man. Dir W. A. THOMAS; 1 br.

Standard Chartered Bank Ghana Ltd (UK): High St, POB 768, Accra; tel. (21) 664591; fax (21) 667751; internet www.standardchartered.com/gh; f. 1896 as Bank of British West Africa; cap. 131,313m., res 517,024m., dep. 3,718,469m. (Dec. 2005); Chair. PETER SULLIVAN; CEO VISHNU MOHAN; 18 brs.

Zenith Bank Ghana (Nigeria): Premier Towers, Liberia Rd, PMB CT393, Accra; tel. (21) 660075; fax (21) 660087; internet www.zenithbank.com.

Other banks include Fidelity Bank (www.fidelitybankplc.com).

STOCK EXCHANGE

Ghana Stock Exchange (GSE): Cedi House, 5th Floor, Liberia Rd, POB 1849, Accra; tel. (21) 669908; fax (21) 669913; e-mail info@gse.com.gh; internet www.gse.com.gh; f. 1990; 29 listed cos in early 2006; Chair. NORBERT KUDJAWU; Man. Dir KOFI YAMOAH.

INSURANCE

In 2004 there were 19 insurance companies.

Donewell Insurance Co Ltd: POB 2136, Accra; tel. (21) 760483; fax (21) 760484; e-mail donewell@africaonline.com.gh; internet www.donewellinsurance.com; f. 1992; Chair. JOHN S. ADDO.

Enterprise Insurance Co Ltd: Enterprise House, 11 Hight St, POB GP50, Accra; tel. (21) 666847; fax (21) 666186; e-mail quotes@eicghana.com; internet www.eicghana.net; f. 1972; Chair. TREVOR TREFGARNE; Man. Dir GEORGE OTOO.

Ghana Union Assurance Co Ltd: F828/1 Ring Rd East, POB 1322, Accra; tel. (21) 780627; fax (21) 780647; e-mail gua@ghanaunionassurancecompany.com; f. 1973; insurance underwriting; Man. Dir NANA AGYEI DUKU.

Metropolitan Insurance Co Ltd: Caledonian House, Kojo Thompson Rd, POB GP20084, Accra; tel. (21) 220966; fax (21) 237872; e-mail met@metinsurance.com; internet www.metinsurance.com; f. 1991; Chair. ROBERT AHOMKA-LINDSAY; CEO KWAME-GAZO AGBENYADZIE.

Social Security and National Insurance Trust (SSNIT): Pension House, POB M149, Accra; tel. (21) 667731; e-mail infodesk@ssnit.org.gh; internet www.ssnit.com; f. 1972; covers over 650,000 contributors; Dir-Gen. KWASI OSEI.

Starlife Assurance Co Ltd: Accra; f. 2005; CEO Dr KWABENA DUFFUOR.

State Insurance Corpn of Ghana Ltd: 6 Kinbu Rd, POB 2363, Accra; tel. (21) 666961; fax (21) 662205; e-mail sic.info@ighmail.com; f. 1962; state-owned; privatization pending; all classes of insurance; Chair. LARRY ADJETEY; Man. Dir L. K. MOBILA.

Vanguard Assurance Co Ltd: Derby House, POB 1869, Accra; tel. (21) 666485; fax (21) 668610; e-mail vanguard@ghana.com; f. 1974; general accident, marine, motor and life insurance; Man. Dir A. E. B. DANQUAH; 7 brs.

Trade and Industry

GOVERNMENT AGENCIES

Divestiture Implementation Committee: F35, 5 Ring Rd East, North Labone, POB CT102, Cantonments, Accra; tel. (21) 772049; fax (21) 773126; e-mail dic@dic.com.gh; internet www.dic.com.gh; f. 1988; Chair. C. O. NYANOR; Exec. Sec. BENSON POKU-ADJEI.

Environmental Protection Agency (EPA): 91 Starlets Rd, POB M326, Accra; tel. (21) 664697; fax (21) 662690; e-mail epaed@africaonline.com.gh; internet www.epa.gov.gh; f. 1974; Exec. Dir JONATHAN A. ALLOTEY.

Export Development and Investment Fund (EDIF): POB M493, Accra; tel. (21) 570532; fax (21) 670536; e-mail info@edif.com.gh; f. 2000; part of Ministry of Trade, Industry, the Private Sector and Special Presidential Initiatives.

Forestry Commission of Ghana (FC): 4 3rd Ave Ridge, PMB 434, Accra; tel. (21) 221315; fax (21) 220818; e-mail info@hq.fcghana.com; internet www.fcghana.com; subsidiary of Ministry of Lands, Forestry and Mines; CEO JOHN OTOO.

Ghana Export Promotion Council (GEPC): Republic House, Tudu Rd, POB M146, Accra; tel. (21) 683153; fax (21) 677256; e-mail gepc@gepcghana.com; internet www.gepcghana.com; f. 1974; part of Ministry of Trade, Industry, the Private Sector and Special Presidential Initiatives; Exec. Sec. EDWARD BOATENG.

Ghana Free Zones Board: POB M626, Accra; tel. (21) 780534; fax (21) 785036; e-mail info@gfzb.com; internet www.gfzb.com; f. 1996; part of Ministry of Trade, Industry, the Private Sector and Special Presidential Initiatives; approves establishment of cos in export-processing zones; Exec.-Sec. E. DWOMOH APPIAH.

Ghana Heavy Equipment Ltd (GHEL): POB 1524, Accra; tel. (21) 680118; fax (21) 660276; e-mail ghelops@africaonline.com; fmrly subsidiary of Ghana National Trading Corpn; part of Ministry of Trade, Industry, the Private Sector and Special Presidential Initiatives; organizes exports, imports and production of heavy equipment; Chair. KOFI ASARE DARKWA POKU.

Ghana Investment Promotion Centre (GIPC): POB M193, Accra; tel. (21) 665125; fax (21) 663801; e-mail info@gipc.org.gh; internet www.gipc.org.gh; f. 1994; negotiates new investments, approves projects, registers foreign capital and decides extent of govt participation; Chair. PAUL VICTOR OBENG; Dir PETER ANKRAH.

Ghana Minerals Commission (MINCOM): 9 Switchback Rd Residential Area, POB M248, Cantonments, Accra; tel. (21) 772783; fax (21) 773324; e-mail mincom@mincomgh.org; internet www.mincomgh.org; f. 1986 to regulate and promote Ghana's mineral industry; CEO BENJAMIN NII AYI ARYEE.

Ghana National Petroleum Agency (NPA): Accra; f. 2005; oversees petroleum sector; Chair. Prof. IVAN ADDAE-MENSAH.

Ghana National Procurement Agency (GNPA): POB 15331, Accra; tel. (21) 228321; fax (21) 221049; e-mail info@gnpa-ghana.com; internet www.gnpa-ghana.com; f. 1976; part of Ministry of Trade, Industry, the Private Sector and Special Presidential Initiatives; imports essential commodities.

Ghana Standards Board: POB MB245, Accra; tel. (21) 500065; fax (21) 500092; e-mail gsbdir@ghanastandards.org; internet ghanastandards.org; f. 1967; establishes and promulgates standards; promotes standardization, industrial efficiency and development and industrial welfare, health and safety; operates certification mark scheme; 402 mems; Chair. Prof. EMMANUEL KENNETH AGYEI; Exec. Dir ADU G. DARKWA.

Ghana Trade Fairs Co Ltd: Trade Fair Centre, POB 111, Accra; tel. (21) 776611; fax (21) 772012; e-mail gftc@ghana.com; f. 1989; part of Ministry of Trade, Industry, the Private Sector and Special Presidential Initiatives.

Ghana Trade and Investment Gateway Project (GHATIG): POB M47, Accra; tel. 663439; fax 773134; e-mail gateway1@ghana.com; promotes private investment and trade, infrastructural development of free-trade zones and export-processing zones.

National Board for Small-scale Industries (NBSSI): POB M85, Accra; tel. (21) 668641; fax (21) 661394; e-mail nbssided@ghana.com; f. 1985; part of Ministry of Trade, Industry, the Private Sector and Special Presidential Initiatives; promotes small and medium-scale industrial and commercial enterprises by providing credit, advisory services and training; Exec. Dir Dr NANA BAAH BOAKYE.

In late 2004 the Ghana Trade Centre and the Ghana ECOWAS Trading Co were launched to facilitate trade by small and medium-sized enterprises.

DEVELOPMENT ORGANIZATIONS

Agence Française de Développement (AFD): 8th Rangoon Close, Ring Rd Central, POB 9592, Airport, Accra; tel. (21) 778755; fax (21) 778757; e-mail afdaccra@gh.groupe-afd.org; internet www.afd.fr; f. 1985; fmrly Caisse Française de Développement; Resident Man. JEAN-FRANÇOIS ARNAL.

Private Enterprise Foundation (PEF): POB C1671, Cantonments, Accra; tel. (21) 771504; fax (21) 771500; e-mail pet@ighmail.com; internet www.pefghana.org; promotes development of private sector; Pres. WILSON ATTA KROFAH.

CHAMBER OF COMMERCE

Ghana National Chamber of Commerce and Industry (GNCCI): 1st Floor, Tudu, 65 Kojo Thompson Rd, POB 2325, Accra; tel. (21) 662427; fax (21) 662210; e-mail gncc@ghana.com; internet www.ghanachamber.org; f. 1961; promotes and protects industry and commerce, organizes trade fairs; 2,500 individual mems and 10 mem. chambers; Pres. WILSON ATTA KROFAH; CEO SALATHIEL DOE AMEGAVIE.

INDUSTRIAL AND TRADE ORGANIZATIONS

Federation of Associations of Ghanaian Exporters (FAGE): POB M124, Accra; tel. (21) 232554; fax (21) 222038; e-mail fage@ighmail.com; internet www.ghana-exporter.org; non-governmental, not-for-profit organization for exporters of non-traditional exports; over 2,500 mems.

Forestry Commission of Ghana, Timber Industry Development Division (TIDD): 4 Third Ave, Ridge, POB MB434, Accra; tel. (31) 221315; fax (31) 220818; e-mail info@hq.fcghana.com; internet www.ghanatimber.org; f. 1985; promotes the development of the timber industry and the sale and export of timber.

Ghana Cocoa Board (COCOBOD): Cocoa House, Kwame Nkrumah Ave, POB 933, Accra; tel. (21) 661872; fax (21) 667104; e-mail cocobod@africaonline.com.gh; internet www.cocobod.gh; f. 1985; monopoly purchaser of cocoa until 1993; responsible for purchase, grading and export of cocoa, coffee and shea nuts; also encourages production and scientific research aimed at improving quality and yield of these crops; controls all exports of cocoa; subsidiaries include the Cocoa Marketing Co (Ghana) Ltd and the Cocoa Research Institute of Ghana; CEO ISAAC OSEI.

Grains and Legumes Development Board: POB 4000, Kumasi; e-mail gldb@africaonline.com.gh; f. 1970; subsidiary of Ministry of Food and Agriculture; produces, processes and stores seeds and seedlings, and manages national seed security stocks.

EMPLOYERS' ORGANIZATION

Ghana Employers' Association (GEA): State Enterprises Commission Bldg, POB GP2616, Accra; tel. (21) 678455; fax (21) 678405; e-mail gea@ghanaemployers.com; internet www.ghanaemployers.com; f. 1959; 550 mems (2006); Pres. CHARLES ALEXANDER COFIE; Vice-Pres. JOYCE R. ARYEE.

Affiliated Bodies

Association of Ghana Industries (AGI): Trade Fair Centre, POB AN8624, Accra-North; tel. (21) 779023; fax (21) 773143; e-mail agi@agighana.org; internet www.agighana.org; f. 1957; Pres. Prince KOFI KLUDJESON; Exec. Dir ANDREW LAWSON; c. 500 mems.

Ghana Booksellers' Association: POB 10367, Accra-North; tel. (21) 773002; fax (21) 773242; e-mail minerva@ghana.com; Pres. FERD J. REIMMER; Gen. Sec. ADAMS AHIMAH.

Ghana Chamber of Mines: Minerals House 10, Sixth St, Airport Residential Area, POB 991, Accra; tel. (21) 760652; fax (21) 760653; e-mail ingo@ghanachamberofmines.org; internet ghanachamberofmines.org; f. 1928; Pres. JURGEN EIJGENDAAL; CEO JOYCE R. ARYEE.

Ghana Timber Association (GTA): POB 1020, Kumasi; tel. and fax (51) 25153; f. 1952; promotes, protects and develops timber industry; Chair. TETTEH NANOR.

UTILITIES

Regulatory Bodies

Energy Commission (EC): FREMA House, Plot 40, Spintex Rd, PMB Ministries, Accra; tel. (21) 813756; fax (21) 813764; e-mail info@energycom.gov.gh; internet www.energycom.gov.gh; f. 2001; Chair. DAASEBRE OSEI BONSU; Exec. Sec. (vacant).

Public Utilities Regulatory Commission (PURC): 51 Liberation Rd, African Liberation Circle, POB CT3095, Cantonments, Accra; tel. (21) 244181; fax (21) 224188; e-mail info@purcghana.com; internet www.purcghana.com; f. 1997; Exec. Sec. STEPHEN N. ADU.

Electricity

Electricity Co of Ghana (ECG): Electro-Volta House, POB 521, Accra; tel. (21) 676727; fax (21) 666262; e-mail ecgho@ghana.com; internet www.electricitygh.com; Chair. KWAME SAARAH MENSAH; Man. Dir Chief MUSA B. ADAM.

Volta River Authority (VRA): Electro-Volta House, 28th February Rd, POB M77, Accra; tel. (21) 664941; fax (21) 662610; e-mail paffairs@vra.com; f. 1961; controls the generation and distribution of electricity; Northern Electricity Department of VRA f. 1997 to distribute electricity in northern Ghana; CEO JOSHUA OFEDIE.

Water

In mid-2006 the Volta Basin Authority (VBA) was created by Ghana, Benin, Burkina Faso, Côte d'Ivoire, Mali and Togo to manage the resources of the Volta River basin.

Ghana Water Co Ltd (GWCL): POB M194, Accra; tel. (21) 666781; fax (21) 663552; e-mail gwsc@africaonline.com.gh; f. 1965 to provide, distribute and conserve water supplies for public, domestic and industrial use, and to establish, operate and control sewerage systems; jointly managed by Aqua Vitens (the Netherlands) and Rand Water (South Africa); Chair. A. R. MUSSAH; Man. Dir COBBIE KESSIE, Jr.

MAJOR COMPANIES

The following are among the largest companies in terms of capital investment or of employment.

AngloGold Ashanti: Gold House, Patrice Lumumba Rd, Roman Ridge, POB 2665, Accra; tel. (21) 722190; fax (21) 775947; e-mail investors@anglogold.com; internet www.anglogold.com; f. 1897 as Ashanti Goldfields; merged 2004 with AngloGold; gold-mining at the Obuasi, Iduapriem and Bibiani mines; leases mining and timber concessions from the Govt, which holds a 17% interest; Pres. RUSSELL EDEY; CEO ROBERT GODSELL; 8,924 employees (2004).

British American Tobacco Ghana Ltd: Tobacco House, Kwame Nkrumah Ave, POB 5211, Accra; tel. (21) 221111; fax (21) 221705; f. 1952; fmrly Pioneer Tobacco Company Ltd; manufacture and sale of tobacco products; Man. Dir JOHN K. RICHARDSON.

Cocoa Processing Co Ltd: PMB, Tema; tel. and fax (22) 212153; fax (22) 206657; e-mail info@cpc-goldentree.com; f. 1992; produces high-grade cocoa products for export and domestic consumption; wholly-owned subsidiary of COCOBOD; two factories divested to WAMCO Ltd in 1992 and 1993; Man. Dir RICHARD AMARH TETTEH; 600 employees (2005).

Equatorial Coca-Cola Bottling Co (ECCBC) (Coca-Cola Bottling Co of Ghana Ltd): Accra–Tema Motorway, Industrial Area, Spintex Rd, POB C1607, Accra; internet www.ghana.coca-cola.com; bottling plants in Accra and Kumasi.

Ghana Bauxite Co Ltd: 10 Sixth St, Airport Residential Area, POB 1, Accra; tel. (21) 664287; fax (21) 669497; e-mail gblacc@ghana.com; f. 1940; 20% state-owned, 80% owned by Alcan Inc (Canada); fmrly British Aluminium Co Ltd; mining of bauxite at Awaso with loading facilities at Takoradi; Man. Dir YVAN TRENBLAY.

Ghana Breweries Ltd: POB 3829, Accra; tel. (21) 400649; fax (21) 400673; e-mail gblacc@ghana.com; f. 1955; Chair. ISHMAEL YAMSON; Man. Dir MARTIN ESON-BENJAMIN; 473 employees.

Ghana Consolidated Diamonds Ltd: 10 3rd Roman Close, off North Roman Road, POB GP2978, Accra; tel. (21) 664577; fax (21) 664635; f. 1986; grades, values and processes diamonds, buys all locally won, produced or processed diamonds; engages in purchasing, grading, valuing, export and sale of local diamonds; owned by Sappers and Associates (UK); privatized in 2003; Chair. KOFI AGYEMAN; Man. Dir MAXWELL KUSI MANSAH.

Ghana Manganese Co Ltd (GMC): POB 2, Nsuta-Wassaw, Western Region; tel. (362) 20225; fax (362) 20443; e-mail headoffice@ghaman.com; internet www.ghanamanganese.com; transferred to private ownership in 1995; Chair. B. WINKLER; Gen. Mines Man. F. W. K. ANANI.

Ghana National Petroleum Corpn (GNPC): Harbour Rd, PMB, Tema, Accra; tel. (22) 206020; fax (22) 206592; e-mail info@gnpcghana.com; internet gnpcghana.com; f. 1983; exploration, development, production and disposal of petroleum; Chair. STEPHEN SEKYERE-ABANKWA; Man. Dir MOSES ODURO BOATENG.

Goldfields Ghana Ltd: Plot 53, North Ridge, POB 16160, Accra; tel. (21) 225812; fax (21) 228448; f. 1995; operates a gold mine, Tarkwa, and one at Damang, through its subsidiary Abosso Goldfields Ltd; 70% owned by Gold Fields Ltd, South Africa; Man. Dir RICHARD ROBINSON.

Nestlé Ghana Ltd: Plot 33, South Legon Commercial Area, Motorway Extension, PMB KIA, Accra; tel. (21) 517020; fax (21) 401195; e-mail consumerservices@gh.nestle.com; internet www.nestleghana.com; f. 1957; Man. Dir ANDRÉ PORCHET; 556 employees.

Phyto-Riker Pharmaceuticals Ltd: Mile 7, off Nsawam Rd, POB AN5266, Dome, Accra-North; tel. (21) 400482; e-mail info@phyto-riker.com; internet www.phyto-riker.com; fmrly Ghana Industrial Holding Corporation Pharmaceuticals Ltd; CEO A. MICHAEL VAN VLECK; 200 employees.

Precious Minerals Marketing Co Ltd (PMMC): Diamond House, POB M108, Accra; tel. (21) 664931; fax (21) 662586; e-mail pmmc@ghana.com; internet www.pmmcghana.com; f. 1963; govt-owned; Chair. STEPHEN ADUBOFOUR; Man. Dir ARISTOTLE KOTEY (acting).

Tema Oil Refinery Ltd (TOR): POB 599, Tema; tel. (21) 302881; fax (22) 302884; e-mail tor@tor.com.gh; internet www.tor.com.gh; f. 1963; sole oil refinery in Ghana; state-controlled since 1977; undergoing privatization in 2006; Chair. Dr JOHN KOBINA RICHARDSON; Man. Dir KOFI KODUA SARPONG; 350 employees (2001).

Total Ghana Ltd: 95 Kojo Thompson Rd, Adabraka, POB 553, Accra; tel. (21) 221445; e-mail totalgha@ghana.com; f. 1960; subsidiary of Total (France); distribution of petroleum products, incl. liquefied petroleum gas; Man. Dir JEAN-JACQUES CESTARI.

Unilever Ghana Ltd: POB 721, Tema; tel. (22) 218100; fax (22) 210352; e-mail vicky.wireko@unilever.com; internet www.unileverghana.com; f. 1955 as United Africa Co of Ghana Ltd; comprises 6 divisions and assoc. cos; subsidiary of Unilever plc (United Kingdom); agricultural, industrial, specialized merchandising, distributive and service enterprises; cap. 9.9m. cedi (Dec. 1999); Chair. ISHMAEL YAMSON; 900 employees (2001).

Volta Aluminium Co Ltd (Valco): POB 625, Tema; tel. (21) 231004; fax (21) 231423; 90% owned by the Ghanaian Government; Alcoa (10%); operates an aluminium smelter at Tema (annual capacity 200,000 metric tons); Chair. JAMES L. CHAPMAN; Man. Dir WINTON RON HELTON; 1,265 employees (2002).

West Africa Mills Co Ltd (WAMCO): Wamco Rd, Takoradi; cocoa processing for export; Man. Dir MICHAEL HOZAEPFEL; c. 800 employees (2003).

CO-OPERATIVES

Department of Co-operatives: POB M150, Accra; tel. (21) 666212; fax (21) 772789; f. 1944; govt-supervised body, responsible for registration, auditing and supervision of co-operative socs; Registrar R. BUACHIE-APHRAM.

Ghana Co-operatives Council Ltd (GACOCO): POB 4034, Accra; tel. (21) 686253; fax (21) 672014; e-mail ghacoco@ghana.com; f. 1951; co-ordinates activities of all co-operative socs and plays advocacy role for co-operative movement; comprises 11 active nat. asscns and two central organizations; Sec.-Gen. ALBERT AGYEMAN PREMPEH.

The national associations and central organizations include the Ghana Co-operative Marketing Asscn Ltd, the Ghana Co-operative Credit Unions Asscn Ltd, the Ghana Co-operative Distillers and Retailers Asscn Ltd, and the Ghana Co-operative Poultry Farmers Asscn Ltd.

TRADE UNIONS

Ghana Federation of Labour: POB 209, Accra; tel. (27) 552433; Sec.-Gen. ABRAHAM KOOMSON; 10,540 mems.

Ghana National Association of Teachers (GNAT): POB 209, Accra; tel. (21) 221515; fax (21) 226286; e-mail info@ghanateachers.org; internet www.ghanateachers.org; f. 1962; Pres. JOSEPH KWEKU ADJEI; Gen. Sec. IRENE DUNCAN ADANUSA; 178,000 mems (2003).

Trades Union Congress (Ghana) (TUC): Hall of Trade Unions, POB 701, Accra; tel. (21) 662568; fax (21) 667161; e-mail tuc@ighmail.com; f. 1945; 17 affiliated unions; Chair. ALEX K. BONNEY; Sec.-Gen. KWASI ADU-AMANKWAH.

General Agricultural Workers' Union (GAWU): Accra; e-mail gawu@ighmail.com; affiliated to the TUC; Gen. Sec. SAMUEL KANGAH.

Teachers and Educational Workers' Union (TEWU): Hall of Trade Unions, Liberia Road, POB 701, Accra; tel. (21) 663050; fax

(21) 662766; e-mail tewu@ghana.com; mem. of TUC; Chair. MICHAEL NYAME; Sec.-Gen. DANIEL AYIM ANTWI.

Transport

RAILWAYS

Ghana has a railway network of 947 km, which connects Accra, Kumasi and Takoradi. In late 2004 OPEC provided a loan of US $5m. to upgrade the Accra–Tema railway. In 2006 the Government was undertaking negotiations to contract out the upgrading and operation of the rail network, and plans were underway regarding the construction of a rail link with Burkina Faso.

Ghana Railway Co Ltd (GRC): POB 251, Takoradi; f. 1901; responsible for the operation and maintenance of all railways; to be run under private concession from April 2004; 947 km of track in use in 2003; Chair HENRY BENYA; Acting Man. Dir RUFUS OKAI QUAYE.

Ghana Railway Development Authority (GRDA): Ministry of Ports and Railways, PMB, Accra; tel. (21) 681780; fax (21) 681781; f. 2005; regulatory and development authority.

ROADS

In 2005 Ghana had a total road network of approximately 57,6134 km, of which just 15% was paved. Construction work on 36 bridges nation-wide, funded by the Japanese Government, commenced in 2003. In 2006 a comprehensive upgrade of the road network was underway; in 2005 €11m. was pledged by the European Union for upgrading the road network in key cocoa-producing areas.

Ghana Highway Authority: POB 1641, Accra; tel. (21) 666591; fax (21) 665571; e-mail eokonadu@highways.mrt.gov.gh; f. 1974 to plan, develop, administer and maintain trunk roads and related facilities; CEO E. ODURO-KONADI.

Vanef STC: POB 7384, 1 Adjuma Cres., Ring Rd West Industrial Area, Accra; tel. (21) 221912; fax (21) 221945; e-mail stc@ghana.com; f. 1965; fmrly State Transport Company, transferred to private-sector ownership in 2000; regional and international coach services; CEO JAMES OWUSU BONSU.

SHIPPING

The two main ports are Tema (near Accra) and Takoradi, both of which are linked with Kumasi by rail. There are also important inland ports on the Volta, Ankobra and Tano rivers. At 31 December 2005 the merchant fleet comprised 211 vesels, totalling 115,239 grt.

Ghana Maritime Authority (GMA): PMB 34, Ministries, Accra; tel. (21) 662122; fax (21) 677702; e-mail info@ghanamaritime.org; internet www.ghanamaritime.org; f. 2002; part of Ministry of Port and Railways; regulates shipping industry; Dir-Gen. ISSAKA PETER AZUMA.

Ghana Ports and Harbour Authority: POB 150, Tema; tel. (22) 202631; fax (22) 202812; e-mail ghpa@ghana.com; holding co for the ports of Tema and Takoradi; Dir-Gen. BEN OWUSU-MENSAH.

Alpha (West Africa) Line Ltd: POB 451, Tema; operates regular cargo services to West Africa, the United Kingom, the USA, the Far East and northern Europe; shipping agents; Man. Dir AHMED EDGAR COLLINGWOOD WILLIAMS.

Liner Agencies and Trading (Ghana) Ltd: POB 214, Tema; tel. (22) 202987; fax (22) 202989; e-mail enquiries@liner-agencies.com; international freight services; shipping agents; Dir J. OSSEI-YAW.

Maersk Ghana Ltd: Obourwe Bldg, Torman Rd, Fishing Harbour Area, POB 8800, Community 7, Tema; tel. (22) 206740; fax (22) 204114; e-mail gnamkt@maersk.com; internet www.maerskline.com/ghana; f. 2001; owned by Maersk Line(Denmark); offices in Tema, Takoradi and Kumasi; Man. Dir JEFF GOSCINIAK.

Scanship (Ghana) Ltd: CFAO Bldg, High St, POB 1705, Accra; tel. (21) 664314; shipping agents.

Shipping Association

Ghana Shippers' Council: Enterprise House, 5th Floor, High St, POB 1321, Accra; tel. (21) 666915; fax (21) 668768; e-mail scouncil@shippers-gh.com; internet www.ghanashipperscouncil.org; f. 1974; represents interests of 28,000 registered Ghanaian shippers; also provides cargo-handling and allied services; Chief Exec. KOFI MBIAH.

CIVIL AVIATION

The main international airport is at Kotoka (Accra). There are also airports at Kumasi, Takoradi, Sunyani, Tamale and Wa. The construction of a dedicated freight terminal at Kotoka Airport was completed in 1994. In 2001 622,525 passengers and 44,779 metric tons of freight passed through Kotoka Airport. The rehabilitation of Kumasi Airport was under way in 2006, while there were also plans to construct a further international airport at Kumasi.

Ghana Civil Aviation Authority (GCAA): PMB, Kotoka International Airport, Accra; tel. (21) 776171; fax (21) 773293; e-mail info@gcaagh.com; internet www.gcaa.com.gh; f. 1986; Chair. S. AKUFFO; Dir-Gen. NII ADUMASA BADDOO.

Afra Airlines Ltd: 7 Nortei St, Airport Residential Area, Accra; tel. (244) 932488; e-mail lukebutler@afraairlines.com; f. 2005; CEO LUKE BUTLER.

Gemini Airlines Ltd (Aero Gem Cargo): America House, POB 7238, Accra-North; tel. (21) 771921; fax (21) 761939; e-mail aerogemcargo@hotmail.com; f. 1974; operates weekly cargo flight between Accra and London; Gen. Man. ENOCH ANAN-TABURY.

Ghana International Airlines, Ltd (GIA): Silver Star Tower, PMB 78, Kotoka International Airport, Accra; tel. (21) 213555; fax (21) 767744; e-mail media@fly-ghana.com; internet www.fly-ghana.com; f. 2005 to replace Ghana Airways; owned by Government of Ghana and GIA-USA, Llc (US); flies to destinations in Africa and Europe; Pres. AZU MATE; CEO Dr CHARLES WEREKO.

Tourism

Ghana's attractions include fine beaches, game reserves, traditional festivals, and old trading forts and castles. In 2005 some 428,533 tourists visited Ghana, with revenue from tourism totalling US $495m. in 2004.

Ghana Tourist Board: POB GP3106, Accra-North; tel. (21) 222153; fax (21) 244611; e-mail gtb@africaonline.com.gh; internet www.ghanatourism.gov.gh; f. 1968; Exec. Dir CHARLES OSEI-BONSU (acting).

Ghana Association of Tourist and Travel Agencies (GATTA): Swamp Grove, Asylum Down, POB 7140, Accra-North; tel. (21) 222398; fax (21) 231102; e-mail info@gattagh.com; internet www.gattagh.com; Pres. GODWIN PINTO; Exec. Sec. GIFTY KORANTENG-ADDO.

Ghana Tourist Development Co Ltd: POB 8710, Accra; tel. (21) 257244; fax (21) 772093; f. 1974; develops tourist infrastructure, incl. hotels, restaurants and casinos; operates duty-free shops; Man. Dir ALFRED KOMLADZEI.

Defence

As assessed at November 2006, Ghana's total armed forces numbered 13,500 (army 10,000, navy 2,000 and air force 1,500). In March 2000 the Government restructured the armed forces; the army was subsequently organized into north and south commands, and the navy into western and eastern commands.

Defence Expenditure: Estimated at 671,000m. cedis in 2006.

Commander-in-Chief of the Armed Forces: PRES. JOHN AGYEKUM KUFUOR.

Chief of Defence Staff: Maj.-Gen. J. B. DANQUAH.

Commander of the Navy: Rear-Adm. A. R. S. NUNOO.

Commander of the Air Force: Air Vice-Marshall J. O. BOATENG.

Commander of the Army: Maj.-Gen. SAMUEL A. ODOTEI.

Education

Education is officially compulsory for eight years, between the ages of six and 14. Primary education begins at the age of six and lasts for six years. Secondary education begins at the age of 12 and lasts for a further six years, comprising two cycles of three years. Following three years of junior secondary education, pupils are examined to determine admission to senior secondary school courses, or to technical and vocational courses. In 2004/05, according to UNESCO, primary enrolment included 65% of children in the relevant age-group (boys 65%; girls 65%), while the comparable ratio for secondary enrolment in that year was estimated at 37% (boys 39%; girls 35%). Some 82,346 students were enrolled in higher education in 1996/97, with 23,126 students attending the country's five universities. By 1998/99 the number of universities in Ghana had increased to seven. Tertiary institutions also included 38 teacher-training colleges, eight polytechnics and 61 technical colleges. In late 2003 the Government was granted US $23m. by donor agencies for the improvement of the education system. In early 2004 the World Bank granted credit of $78m. for educational development.

Bibliography

Adjei, M. *Death and Pain: Rawlings' Ghana, The Inside Story.* London, Black Line Publishing Ltd, 1994.

Agbodeka, F. *An Economic History of Ghana from the Earliest Times.* Accra, Ghana Universities Press, 1992.

Allman, J. M. *The Quills of the Porcupine: Asante Nationalism in an Emergent Ghana.* Madison, University of Wisconsin Press, 1993.

Allman, J. M., and Tashjian, V. *I Will Not Eat Stone: A Women's History of Colonial Asante.* Oxford, James Currey, 2001.

Amenumey, D. E. K. *The Ewe Unification Movement: A Political History.* Accra, Ghana Universities Press, 1989.

Amoah, M. *Reconstructing the Nation in Africa: The Politics of Nationalism in Ghana.* London, I. B. Tauris, 2007.

Ankama, S. K. *The Westminster Model in Africa and a Search for African Democracy.* London, Silkan Books, 1996.

Aryeetey, E., Harrigan, J., and Nissanke, M. (Eds). *Economic Reforms in Ghana: The Miracle and the Mirage.* Oxford, James Currey, 1999.

Ayensu, K. B., and Darkwa, S. N. *The Evolution of Parliament in Ghana.* Accra, Sub-Saharan Publishers, 2006.

Babatope, E. *The Ghana Revolution from Nkrumah to Jerry Rawlings.* Enugu, Fourth Dimension Publishers, 1984.

Baynham, S. *The Military and Politics in Nkrumah's Ghana.* Boulder, CO, Westview Press, 1988.

Berry, S. *Chiefs Know Their Boundaries: Essays on Property, Power and the Past in Asante, 1896–1996.* Oxford, James Currey, 2000.

Cruise O'Brien, D. B., Dunn, J., and Rathbone, R. (Eds). *West African States.* Cambridge, Cambridge University Press, 1989.

Davidson, B. *Black Star. A View of the Life and Times of Kwame Nkrumah.* London, Panaf Books, 1974.

Dickson, K. B. *A Historical Geography of Ghana.* Cambridge, Cambridge University Press, 1969.

Donkor, K. *Structural Adjustment and Mass Poverty in Ghana.* Aldershot, Ashgate, 1997.

Eisenstadt, T. A. 'Institutionalizing Credible Elections in Ghana', in Schedler, A., *et al.* (Eds). *The Self-Restraining State: Power and Accountability in New Democracies.* Boulder, CO, Lynne Rienner Publishers, 1999.

English, P. *Recovery is Not Enough: The Case of Ghana.* New York, World Bank, 1999.

Frimpong, J. H. *The Vampire State in Africa: The Political Economy of Decline in Ghana.* London, James Currey, 1991.

Gocking, R. S. *The History of Ghana.* Westport, CT, Greenwood Press, 2005.

Goodall, H. B. *Beloved Imperialist: Sir Gordon Guggisberg, Governor of the Gold Coast.* Durham, Pentland Press, 1998.

Greenhalgh, P. *West African Diamonds: An Economic History 1919–83.* Manchester, Manchester University Press, 1985.

Gyimah-Boardi, E. (Ed.). *Ghana under PNDC Rule.* Dakar, CODESRIA, 1993.

Hansen, E. *Ghana under Rawlings: Early Years.* Oxford, ABC and Malthouse Press, 1991.

Hasty, J. *The Press and Political Culture in Ghana.* Bloomington, IN, Indiana University Press, 2005

Herbst, J. *The Politics of Reform in Ghana, 1982–1991.* Berkeley, University of California Press, 1993.

Huq, M. M. *The Economy of Ghana: The First 25 Years since Independence.* London, Macmillan, 1988.

Hutchful, E. *Ghana's Adjustment Experience: The Paradox of Reform.* Oxford, James Currey, 2002.

Jackson, K. A. *When Gun Rules: A Soldier's Testimony of the Events Leading to June 4 Uprising in Ghana and its Aftermath.* Accra, Woeli Publishing Services, 1999.

Jones, T. *Ghana's First Republic.* London, Methuen, 1976.

Kay, G. (Ed.). *The Political Economy of Colonialism in Ghana: A Collection of Documents and Statistics 1900–60.* Cambridge, Cambridge University Press, 1972.

Killick, A. *Development Economics in Action: A Study of Economic Policies in Ghana.* London, Heinemann, 1978.

Kuada, J. (Ed.). *Internationalisation and Enterprise Development in Ghana.* London, Adonis & Abbey, 2005.

Manuh, T. (Ed.). *At Home in the World? International Migration and Development in Contemporary Ghana and West Africa.* Accra, Sub-Saharan Publishers, 2006.

Milne, J. *Kwame Nkrumah—A Biography.* London, PANAF Books, 2000.

Ninsin, K. A. (Ed.). *Ghana: Transition to Democracy.* Dakar, CODESRIA, 1998.

Ninsin, K. A., and Drah, F. K. (Eds). *The Search for Democracy in Ghana: A Case Study in Political Instability in Africa.* Accra, Asempa Publishers, 1987.

Ghana's Transition to Constitutional Rule. Accra, Ghana University Press, and Oxford, ABC, 1991.

Political Parties and Democracy in Ghana's Fourth Republic. Accra, Woeli Publishing Services, 1993.

Nugent, P. *Big Men, Small Boys and Politics in Ghana: Power, Ideology and the Burden of History, 1982–1994.* London, Pinter, 1995.

The Flight-Lieutenant Rides (To Power) Again: National Delusions, Local Fixations and the 1996 Ghanaian Elections. Edinburgh, Centre of African Studies, Edinburgh University (Occasional Papers, no. 76), 1998.

Ofori, S. *Regional Policy and Regional Planning in Ghana.* Brookfield, VT, Ashgate Publishing, 1997.

Okafor, G. M. *Christianity and Islam in West Africa; the Ghana Experience: A Study of the Forces and Influence of Christianity and Islam in Modern Ghana.* Würzburg, Oros, 1997.

Okeke, B. E. *4 June: A Revolution Betrayed.* Enugu, Ikenga Publishers, 1982.

Osei, A. P. *Ghana: Recurrence and Change in a Post-Independence African State.* New York, P. Lang, 1999.

Owusu-Ansah, D., and McFarland, M. D. *Historical Dictionary of Ghana.* 2nd Edn. Lanham, MD, Scarecrow Press, 1995.

Perbi, A. A. *A History of Indigenous Slavery in Ghana, From the 15th to the 19th Century.* Accra, Sub-Saharan Publishers, 2004.

Pinkney, R. *Ghana under Military Rule 1966–1969.* London, Methuen, 1972.

Democracy and Dictatorship in Ghana and Tanzania. New York, St. Martin's Press, 1997.

Quay, R. *Underdevelopment and Health Care in Africa: The Ghanaian Experience.* Lewiston, Edwin Mellen Press, 1996.

Rathbone, R. J. A. R. *Nkrumah and the Chiefs: The Politics of Chieftaincy in Ghana, 1951–60.* Oxford, James Currey, 2000.

Rimmer, D. *Staying Poor: Ghana's Political Economy, 1950–1990.* Oxford, Pergamon, 1992.

Sarris, A., and Shams, H. *Ghana under Structural Adjustment: The Impact on Agriculture and the Rural Poor.* New York, New York University Press (IFAD Studies in Rural Poverty), 1991.

Stockwell, S. E. *The Business of Decolonization: British Business Strategies in the Gold Coast.* Oxford, Clarendon Press, 2000.

Thompson, N., and Thompson, S. *The Baobab and the Mango Tree; Lessons about Development: African and Asian Contrasts.* London, Zed Books, 2001.

Tsikata, D. *Living in the Shadow of the Large Dams: Long Term Responses of Downstream and Lakeside Communities of Ghana's Volta River Project.* Leiden, Brill Academic Publishers, 2006.

Yeebo, Z. *Ghana: The Struggle for Popular Power—Rawlings: Saviour or Demagogue?* Accra, New Beacon Books, 1992.

GUINEA

Physical and Social Geography

R. J. HARRISON CHURCH

The Republic of Guinea covers an area of 245,857 sq km (94,926 sq miles), containing exceptionally varied landscapes, peoples and economic conditions. The census of 31 December 1996 recorded a population of 7,156,406, which had increased to 9,181,000 by mid-2006, according to UN estimates (giving an average density of 37.3 inhabitants per sq km). The population is concentrated in the plateau area of central Guinea: about one-quarter of the population is estimated to be living in Conakry and its environs; Conakry itself had a population of 1,092,936 in 1996.

Guinea's coast is part of the extremely wet south-western sector of west Africa, which has a monsoonal climate. Thus Conakry, the capital, has five to six months with almost no rain, while 4,300 mm fall in the remaining months. The coastline has shallow drowned rivers and estuaries with much mangrove growing on alluvium eroded from the nearby Fouta Djallon mountains. Much of the mangrove has been removed, and the land bunded for rice cultivation. Only at two places, Cape Verga and Conakry, do ancient hard rocks reach the sea. At the latter they have facilitated the development of the port, while the weathering of these rocks has produced exploitable deposits of bauxite on the offshore Los Islands.

Behind the swamps a gravelly coastal plain, some 65 km wide, is backed by the steep, often sheer, edges of the Fouta Djallon, which occupies the west-centre of Guinea. Much is over 900 m high, and consists of level Primary sandstones (possibly of Devonian age) which cover Pre-Cambrian rocks to a depth of 750 m. The level plateaux, with many bare lateritic surfaces, are the realm of Fulani (Peul) herders. Rivers are deeply incised in the sandstone. These more fertile valleys were earlier cultivated with food crops by slaves of the Fulani, and then with bananas, coffee, citrus fruits and pineapples on plantations under the French. Falls and gorges of the incised rivers have great hydroelectric potential. This is significant in view of huge deposits of high-grade bauxite located at Fria and Boké. The climate is still monsoonal but, although the total rainfall is lower—about 1,800 mm annually—it is more evenly distributed than on the coasts, as the rainy season is longer. In such a mountainous area there are sharp variations in climatic conditions over a short distance, and from year to year.

On the Liberian border the Guinea highlands rise to 1,752 m at Mt Nimba, where substantial deposits of haematite iron ore are eventually to be developed. These rounded mountains contrast greatly with the level plateaux and deep narrow valleys of the Fouta Djallon. Rainfall is heavier than in the latter, but is again more evenly distributed, so that only two or three months are without significant rain. Coffee, kola and other crops are grown in the forest of this remote area. Diamonds are mined north of Macenta and west of Beyla, and gold at Siguiri and Léro.

Recent History

RICHARD SYNGE

Based on an earlier article by PIERRE ENGLEBERT

THE SEKOU TOURÉ PERIOD

On 2 October 1958, having rejected membership of a proposed community of self-governing French overseas territories, French Guinea became the independent Republic of Guinea. Ahmed Sekou Touré, the Secretary-General of the Parti démocratique de Guinée—Rassemblement démocratique africain (PDG—RDA), which had led the campaign for independence, became the Republic's first President, and the PDG—RDA the sole political party. Punitive economic reprisals were taken by the departing French authorities, and French aid and investment were suspended. Sekou Touré's Government initially obtained assistance from the USSR and withdrew from the Franc Zone in 1960, but after 1961 the USA became a more significant source of aid.

Radical socialist policies were applied to Guinea's internal economy. In 1975 all private trading was forbidden, and financial transactions were supervised by an 'economic police', who were widely suspected of extortion and smuggling. Resentment against their activities culminated in August 1977 in widespread demonstrations and rioting, as a so-called 'women's revolt' in Conakry quickly extended to other towns. In response, Sekou Touré disbanded the 'economic police' and permitted the resumption (from July 1979) of small-scale private trading. In 1978 it was decided to merge the PDG—RDA and the State, and in January 1979 the country was renamed the People's Revolutionary Republic of Guinea.

Diplomatic relations with France were resumed in 1976, and in the following year the two countries reached an agreement on economic co-operation. In 1978 Sekou Touré declared a policy of 'co-operation with capitalist as well as socialist states'. The Government sought also to improve relations with Côte d'Ivoire and Senegal, and increased its participation in regional organizations.

CONTÉ AND THE MILITARY COMMITTEE

Sekou Touré died suddenly in March 1984. Before a successor could be chosen, the army staged a *coup d'état* in April, and a Comité militaire de redressement national (CMRN) seized power. Its principal leaders Col (later Gen.) Lansana Conté and Col Diarra Traoré, who became President and Prime Minister, respectively, had both held senior positions for some years. A semi-civilian Government was appointed, and efforts were furthered to improve regional relations and links with potential sources of economic aid (most notably France). In May the country resumed the designation of Republic of Guinea. The PDG—RDA and organs of Sekou Touré's 'party state' were dismantled under this Second Republic, which was initially greeted with great enthusiasm. State surveillance and control were ended, and many political detainees were freed. In the first months of his presidency Conté adopted an open style of government, inviting constructive advice and criticism from all sectors of society.

Undercurrents of Opposition

In December 1984 Conté abolished the office of Prime Minister, demoting Traoré to a lesser cabinet post. In July 1985, while Conté was attending a regional summit meeting in Togo, Traoré attempted a *coup d'état*, supported mainly by members of the police force. Troops loyal to Conté swiftly regained control, and the President returned two days later. Traoré and many of his family were among more than 200 people arrested, and the armed forces conducted a purge of his suspected sympathizers. Traoré and a half-brother of Sekou Touré were executed in the immediate aftermath of the coup attempt and about 60 other military officers were later sentenced to death.

The coup attempt effectively strengthened Conté's position, allowing him to pursue the extensive economic reforms demanded by the World Bank and the IMF as a prerequisite for the disbursement of new funds. The national currency, the syli, was devalued and replaced in January 1986 by a revived Guinean franc. Civil service reform entailed numerous redundancies; many state-owned enterprises were dissolved or offered for sale, and the banking system was overhauled. In December 1985 Conté reorganized the Council of Ministers, introducing a majority of civilians for the first time since he took power and creating resident 'regional' ministries.

In October 1988, commemorating the 30th anniversary of the country's independence, Conté declared an amnesty for 39 political prisoners, including some of those implicated in the 1985 coup attempt. At the same time he announced the establishment of a committee to draft a new constitution, which would be submitted for approval in a national referendum. In October 1989 Conté revealed plans whereby a Comité transitoire de redressement national (CTRN) would succeed the CMRN and oversee a five-year transitional period prior to the establishment of a two-party political system under an elected president and legislature. In February 1990 an amnesty was announced for all remaining political detainees and exiled dissidents.

Conté appealed in November 1990 for the return to Guinea of political exiles. However, three members of an illegal opposition movement, the Rassemblement populaire guinéen (RPG), were imprisoned later in the month. Rejecting widespread demands for an accelerated programme of political reform, the Government proceeded with its plan for a gradual transition to a two-party political system. The draft Constitution was submitted to a national referendum in December, and was declared to have been approved by 98.7% of those who voted (some 97.4% of the registered electorate). In February 1991 the 36-member CTRN was inaugurated, under the chairmanship of Conté. Military officers continued to hold the most sensitive posts in a new Government, implying that the President intended to ensure the continued loyalty of the armed forces.

Contrary to the earlier scheme for political change, in October 1991 Conté announced that the registration of an unlimited number of political parties would come into effect on 3 April 1992, and that legislative elections would take place before the end of 1992 in the context of a full multi-party political system.

CONTÉ AND THE THIRD REPUBLIC

The Constitution of the Third Republic was promulgated on 23 December 1991. In January 1992 Conté ceded the presidency of the CTRN, in accordance with constitutional provision for the separation of the powers of the executive and legislature. In the following month most military officers and all *Guinéens de l'extérieur* (former dissidents who had returned from exile after the 1984 coup) were removed from the Government: it later became apparent that some of these long-serving ministers had left public office in order to establish a pro-Conté political party, the Parti de l'unité et du progrès (PUP).

The RPG was among the first opposition parties to be legalized in April 1992. Other than the RPG, the most prominent challengers to the PUP were the Parti pour le renouveau et le progrès (PRP), led by a well-known journalist, Siradiou Diallo, and the Union pour la nouvelle République (UNR), led by Mamadou Boye Bâ. However, the fragmented nature of the opposition undermined attempts to persuade the Government to convene a national political conference. The opposition alleged that the PUP was benefiting from state funds, and that the Government was coercing civil servants into joining the party. Clashes between pro- and anti-Conté activists (seemingly fuelled by ethnic rivalries) occurred frequently from mid-1992, and in October the Government again banned all unauthorized public gatherings. In that month Conté was reported to have escaped an assassination attempt when gunmen opened fire on the vehicle in which he was travelling.

In December 1992 the Government announced the indefinite postponement of the legislative elections, which had been scheduled for the end of the month, citing technical and financial difficulties. It was later indicated that the elections would be organized in late 1993, and that they would be preceded by the presidential election. The principal opposition parties failed in their attempts to form an electoral alliance. Thus, there were eight candidates for the presidential election, which was scheduled for 5 December 1993. Conté's main challengers were the leader of the RPG, Alpha Condé, Diallo and Bâ. In September the Government banned all political gatherings and marches, following violent incidents in Conakry when police opened fire on demonstrators, as a result of which, according to official figures, some 18 people were killed (unofficial reports claimed as many as 63 deaths). In October, at an unprecedented meeting between Conté and representatives of 43 political organizations, it was agreed to establish an independent electoral commission. However, controversy immediately arose regarding its composition and also the Government's decision to place it under the jurisdiction of the Ministry of the Interior and Security. Opposition candidates demanded that the presidential election be postponed, citing technical and procedural irregularities and delays. In late November the Government announced a two-week postponement of the presidential poll, admitting that technical preparations for voting were incomplete.

At least four deaths resulted from outbreaks of violence prior to the presidential election. A further six people were reported to have been killed as voting proceeded on 19 December 1993. Despite confused reports of opposition appeals for a boycott of the poll (and the absence of voters' lists in some polling centres), the rate of participation was, officially, 78.5% of the registered electorate. Conté was elected at the first round of voting, having secured an absolute majority (51.7%) of the votes cast. Condé, his nearest rival, took 19.6% of the votes; however, the Supreme Court's invalidation (having found evidence of malpractice) of the results of voting in the Kankan and Siguiri prefectures, in both of which Condé had won more than 90% of the votes, fuelled opposition claims that the poll had been manipulated in favour of Conté.

Conté (who had, as required by the Constitution, resigned from the armed forces in order to contest the presidency) was inaugurated as President on 29 January 1994. His stated priorities were to strengthen national security and unity and to promote economic growth.

In May 1994 Bâ, asserting his lack of confidence in the Guinean opposition movement, expressed the UNR's willingness to recognize Conté as the country's legitimately elected Head of State. Relations between the Government and opposition otherwise remained generally poor, and the RPG in particular protested that its activists were being harassed by members of the armed forces. The brief detention, in June, of eight senior armed forces officers, including the Deputy Chief of Staff of the air force, prompted rumours of a coup plot; the Government confirmed that certain members of the armed forces had participated in a 'political' meeting, in contravention of their terms of service, but denied the existence of any conspiracy. In September the authorities refuted RPG assertions that attempts had been made to assassinate Condé. The ban on political gatherings ended in November, but the Government emphasized that rallies should not be confused with street demonstrations. The UNR condemned the decision, announced by the Government in November, that no provision would be made for expatriate Guineans to vote in the forthcoming legislative elections (following violent disturbances at polling stations outside Guinea at the 1993 presidential election), and withdrew its support for Conté. In February 1995 it was announced that the President was to readopt his military rank.

In March 1995 it was announced that elections to the new Assemblée nationale would take place on 11 June. Parties of the so-called 'radical' opposition (principally the RPG, the PRP and the UNR) frequently alleged harassment of their activists by the security forces, claiming that efforts were being made to prevent campaigning in areas where support for the opposition was likely to be strong. As preliminary results indicated that the PUP had won an overwhelming majority in the 114-seat legislature, the radical opposition protested that voting had been conducted fraudulently, stating that they would take no further part in the electoral process and that they would boycott the Assemblée nationale. According to the official results, the PUP won 71 seats—having taken 30 of the country's 38 single-member constituencies, together with 41 of the 76 seats allocated by proportional representation. Eight other parties won representation, among them the RPG, which took 19 seats, the PRP and the UNR, both of which won nine seats. Some 63% of the electorate were reported to have voted. The results were confirmed by the Supreme Court in July, whereupon the new legislature formally superseded the CTRN.

In July 1995 the three radical opposition parties joined forces with nine other organizations in a new opposition front, the Coordination de l'opposition démocratique (Codem), which indicated its willingness to enter into a dialogue with the authorities. At a subsequent meeting with a representative of Codem, the Minister of the Interior, Alsény René Gomez, declared that any purported fraud did not affect the overall credibility of the results.

Military Unrest

In early February 1996 Conté was reportedly seized as he attempted to flee the presidential palace during a mutiny by disaffected elements of the military. He was released after making concessions including a doubling of salaries and immunity from prosecution for those involved in the uprising. (Conté had already agreed to the demand that the Minister of Defence, Col Abdourahmane Diallo, be dismissed, assuming personal responsibility for defence.) About 50 people were killed and 100 injured as rebels clashed with forces loyal to the Conté regime. In all, as many as 2,000 soldiers, including members of the presidential guard, were believed to have joined the rebellion. Several officers were arrested shortly afterwards, and both Conté and Gomez stated that any legal proceedings would be a matter for the judiciary. Members of Codem subsequently withdrew from a parliamentary commission that had been established to investigate the circumstances surrounding the rebellion, apparently in protest at Conté's allusions to opposition links with anti-Government elements within the military.

Among the initial recommendations of the parliamentary commission was a complete depoliticization of the military, accompanied by the demilitarization of political life. In late March 1996 it was announced that eight members of the military had been charged with undermining state security in connection with the recent coup attempt. A reinforcement of security measures followed the assassination of the commander (a close associate of Conté) of the Alpha Yaya military barracks, where the February rebellion had begun, apparently in reprisal against the charges. By June some 42 members of the armed forces had reportedly been charged in connection with the coup plot.

The replacement, in April 1996, of two close associates of Conté, the armed forces Chief of Staff and the governor of Conakry (also a military officer), was regarded as an indication of the President's commitment to a restructuring of both the civilian and military administration. An armed forces conference was convened in June to consider the reorganization of the military, at which there was consensus regarding several of the parliamentary commission's recommendations for reform. In July Conté announced (for the first time under the Third Republic) the appointment of a Prime Minister. The premiership was assigned to a non-partisan economist, Sidya Touré. A comprehensive reorganization of the Government included the departure of Gomez and the division of the Ministry of the Interior into two separate departments (one responsible for territorial administration and decentralization, the other for security); Conté retained the defence portfolio. Touré stated that his Government's priorities were to be economic recovery and the combating of institutionalized corruption, with the aim of securing renewed assistance from the international donor community, and of attracting increased foreign investment; the new Prime Minister, who assumed personal responsibility for the economy, finance and planning, announced immediate measures to reduce public expenditure by one-third—although the salary increases for the military conceded by Conté in February were to be honoured.

In February 1997, following the conclusion of a new financing arrangement with the IMF, Touré relinquished control of the economy portfolio to two ministers-delegate, including Ibrahima Kassory Fofana, who became Minister of the Economy and Finance. The issue of the premiership (for which position there was no explicit constitutional provision) remained controversial, and in May, in response to parliamentary appeals for the establishment of a post of constitutional Prime Minister, the Government stated that for the Constitution to vest powers directly in an office of Prime Minister would result in political instability and confusion.

Meanwhile, in August 1996 some 40 of those detained in connection with the February mutiny were released from custody; charges remained against three suspects. The announcement, in June 1997, that a State Security Court was to be established to deal with matters of exceptional jurisdiction, and that its first task would be to try the alleged leaders of the previous year's mutiny, provoked outrage among opposition parties and prompted strong protests by the national lawyers' association. Particular concerns were that there was no constitutional provision for such a court, that its members were to be personally appointed by Conté, and that the trial of the alleged mutineers would be held in camera. The opposition again warned of the potential consequences should Conté renege on his pledge that there would be no reprisals for those involved in the rebellion.

Trials and Tensions

A total of 96 defendants were brought before the State Security Court in mid-February 1998, to answer charges related to the attempted coup two years earlier; hearings commenced in March, but defence lawyers refused to represent their clients, on the grounds that their rights were being infringed by the State Security Court. The Court did not reconvene until mid-September. At the end of the month 38 of the accused received custodial sentences ranging from seven months to 15 years, some with hard labour; 51 defendants were acquitted.

Codem was critical of the Government's preparations for the forthcoming presidential election, notably proposals for the establishment of a new body, the Haut conseil aux affaires électorales (HCE), to act in conjunction with the Ministry of the Interior and Decentralization in preparing and supervising the poll. The 68-member HCE was to be composed of representatives of the presidential majority, together with opposition delegates, ministerial representatives and members of civil society. A ban on public demonstrations was imposed by the HCE in early November 1998. The opposition again asserted that the PUP was abusing the state apparatus in support of Conté's re-election campaign. Conté was challenged by four candidates, including Bâ, representing the Union pour le progrès et le renouveau (UPR—formed in September by a merger of the UNR and the PRP) and Alpha Condé (who had been resident abroad since early 1997, owing to fears for his personal safety) for the RPG. Voting proceeded on 14 December 1998, despite several violent incidents during the election campaign. Further violence followed the arrest, two days after the poll, of Condé, who was accused of seeking to leave the country illegally (Guinea's borders had been sealed prior to the election) and of seeking to recruit troops to destabilize Guinea. By the end of December at least 12 people were reported to have been killed as a result of violence in Conakry, Kankan, Siguiri and Baro. Condé was formally charged in late December with having recruited mercenaries with the aim of overthrowing the Conté regime. Some 100 other opposition activists remained in detention. Meanwhile, the opposition withdrew its representatives from the HCE, denouncing the conduct of the election as fraudulent. The official results, issued by the HCE on 17 December and confirmed by the Supreme Court two weeks later, showed a decisive victory for Conté, with 56.1% of the valid votes cast. Bâ took 24.6% and Condé 16.6%. The electoral turn-out was recorded at 71.4% of the registered electorate.

At his inauguration, on 30 January 1999, President Conté proclaimed that all abuses, including those committed by the security forces, would be severely punished. In early March Sidya Touré was dismissed as premier and replaced by Lamine Sidimé, hitherto the Chief Justice of the Supreme Court and of no party-political affiliation. Fofana, widely credited with Guinea's recent economic successes, was reappointed Minister of the Economy and Finance, while Dorank Assifat Diassény, redesignated Minister at the Presidency, retained the national defence portfolio. An effective purge of the military high command took place in mid-March: 18 officers were dismissed, accused of high treason, and a further 13 retired early, on the grounds of what were termed serious faults arising from the 1996 mutiny.

From 1999 opposition groups and human rights organizations urged the release from detention of Alpha Condé and other activists arrested at the time of the presidential election. Condé's lawyers protested that neither the defence nor the prosecution had received any documentation relating to his trial and in February 2000 members of the Assemblée nationale, including members of the PUP, urged the President to release Condé. The deputies noted that Condé possessed parliamentary immunity from prosecution, and suggested that his release would encourage democracy in Guinea. Nevertheless, in April, some 16 months after the initial arrests, the trial began of Condé and his 47 co-defendants on charges that included plotting to kill Conté, hiring mercenaries and threatening state security. Following several delays and interruptions to the trial, in mid-September Condé was sentenced to five years' imprisonment, while six other defendants also received prison terms.

On 25 June 2000 local elections (postponed from 1999) were held to elect some 660 council members in 38 constituencies, although legislative elections scheduled for the same date were postponed, reportedly for financial reasons. Eight parties presented candidates at the elections, and observers reported that, with the exception of a few clashes between members of the opposition and of the PUP in central Conakry, voting had taken place in an atmosphere of calm. Observers noted, however, that there had been little enthusiasm for the elections in those districts where the Government had invalidated the opposition's list of candidates. The elections were followed by a series of clashes between members of the security forces and UPR members, who claimed that the delayed announcement of the election results indicated the determination of the authorities to falsify the results in favour of the PUP. It was reported that at least five people had been killed and many more injured during demonstrations. It was subsequently announced that the PUP and its allies had won control of 33 of the 38 constituencies.

Regional Upheavals

In early September 2000 an armed rebellion in south-east Guinea reportedly resulted in at least 40 deaths. Instability subsequently intensified in regions near the borders with Sierra Leone and Liberia, with incidences of cross-border attacks on Guinean civilians and the military. Fighting between armed groups and Guinean soldiers was reported to have led to some 360 deaths between early September and mid-October. The Government attributed the upsurge in violence to forces supported by the Governments of Liberia and Burkina Faso, and to members of the Sierra Leonean rebel group, the Revolutionary United Front (RUF, see the Recent History of Sierra Leone), who, the Government alleged, were acting in alliance with Guinean dissidents. In October 2000 a previously unknown organization, the Rassemblement des forces démocratiques de Guinée (RFDG), claimed responsibility for the armed attacks, which, it stated, were intended to overthrow President Conté. In October, in a speech that was widely regarded as inflammatory, Conté accused refugees from Sierra Leone and Liberia of forming alliances with rebel groups seeking to destabilize Guinea. Meanwhile, some 32,000 refugees were expelled from Forécariah, following an attack on the town. In November 2000 a number of cross-border attacks were attributed to forces associated with the RUF, and to former members of a faction of a dissolved Liberian dissident group, the United Liberation Movement of Liberia for Democracy (ULIMO), ULIMO—K (see the Recent History of Liberia), which President Conté had previously supported. The President cited the state of insecurity in the country as the reason for further postponement of Guinea's legislative elections.

Rebel attacks around Guéckédou continued throughout January 2001. In that month Conté dismissed Diassény from his defence portfolio, which henceforth became the direct responsibility of the President; Diassény was redesignated Minister, Special Adviser at the Presidency. In late January and early February a series of attacks around Macenta were reported to have resulted in more than 130 deaths. Allegations persisted that an unofficial alliance between former ULIMO—K rebels and Guinean government forces had broken down, with the result that ULIMO—K forces were now attacking Guinean military and civilian targets. Renewed clashes around Guéckédou delayed the proposed deployment by the Economic Community of West African States (ECOWAS) of an ECOMOG (ECOWAS Cease-fire Monitoring Group) force, which had been intended to monitor stability and border security in the region from mid-February, and in the event no such force was deployed.

During 2001 the dynamics of the cross-border conflict changed dramatically as a result of the success of the UN-assisted peace process in Sierra Leone and the growth of an armed rebellion in Liberia against the regime of President Charles Taylor, which was co-ordinated by a new group, Liberians United for Reconciliation and Democracy (LURD). Sierra Leonean RUF fighters, who were associated with Guinean rebels and supplied much of their weaponry, were defeated by Kamajor militias loyal to the Sierra Leonean Government; under forceful pressure from the Guinean military, they subsequently retreated across the border to participate in Sierra Leone's demobilization process. The Guinean rebels thereby lost their means of challenging their own government forces and began to disperse, although one group, the Union des forces pour une Guinée nouvelle, led by Dr N'Faly Kaba, claimed in several statements that its armed wing, supported by Taylor, was planning a nation-wide armed uprising to remove Conté from power. Despite such threats, made from neighbouring capital cities, there was a reduction in rebel activity, and government forces were able to reinforce their authority in the border regions, often with scant regard for the needs of refugees in these areas. In June 2001 Human Rights Watch alleged that security forces and vigilante groups in Guinea had frequently detained, tortured and assaulted Sierra Leonean and Liberian refugees, notably at roadside checkpoints. The organization also stated that RUF- and Liberian-backed forces had repeatedly attacked and set fire to refugee camps in border regions. Taylor, meanwhile, persistently accused Guinea of providing military support to the LURD rebellion in Liberia.

Conté Extends his Rule

In mid-May 2001 Alpha Condé and two of his co-defendants were released from prison, following the granting of a presidential pardon. Condé, none the less, was prohibited from participating in political activities for a period of unspecified duration. In mid-June President Conté announced his intention to hold a national referendum on a proposed constitutional amendment that would permit the President of the Republic to seek longer and limitless terms of office. Although opposition and human rights groups condemned the proposal, Conté justified it by reference to the ongoing instability in border regions. In late June gendarmes enforced the closure of the headquarters of the Union des forces républicaines (UFR), the party led by former Prime Minister Sidya Touré, who had announced the formation of a group to oppose Conté's proposed constitutional amendment.

The referendum was held on 11 November 2001. According to official results, 98.4% of voters endorsed the constitutional revisions, with a turn-out of 87.2% recorded, although opposition and media sources claimed that the turn-out was lower than 20%. The presidential term of office was thus extended from five years to seven, with effect from the presidential election due in 2003, and the constitutional provision restricting the President to two terms of office was rescinded. Moreover, the President was to be permitted to appoint local government officials, who were hitherto elected. Despite the overwhelming official result in favour of the amendments, opposition to the referendum was expressed very strongly, in particular by Boubacar Biro Diallo (who remained Speaker of the reconvened Assemblée nationale, the mandate of which had, officially, expired in July 2000), who deplored the lack of involvement of the legislature in deciding such a major constitutional change. Meanwhile, Bâ urged the international community to assist the opposition in removing Conté.

In mid-April 2002 President Conté issued a decree scheduling the repeatedly postponed elections to the Assemblée nationale for 30 June. However, concern was expressed that transparency in the conduct of the polls would not be guaranteed, and in late May four opposition parties, which had announced their intention to boycott the legislative elections, including the RPG and the UFR, announced the formation of a political alliance, the Front de l'alternance démocratique (FRAD). Notably, Boubacar Biro Diallo, who was not affiliated to any party, and Bâ, the honorary President of the UPR, pledged allegiance to the FRAD, and a split in the UPR became increasingly apparent between those, led by Siradiou Diallo, the President of the party, who sought to engage with the electoral process, and those, led by Bâ, who rejected any such engagement. In early June Conté appointed François Lonseny Fall, previously the representative of Guinea to the UN, as Minister at the Presidency, responsible for Foreign Affairs.

Legislative elections were held on 30 June 2002, and a turnout of 71.6% was recorded; the PUP increased its majority in the legislature, winning all 38 single-member constituency seats and 47 of the 76 seats allocated by proportional representation, giving it a total of 85 seats. The UPR became the second largest party in the Assemblée, securing 20 seats, while four other parties shared the remaining nine seats. In late September the Secretary-General of the PUP, Aboubacar Sompare, was chosen as Speaker of the Assemblée nationale. In mid-October 2002 Bâ was elected as President of a new party, the Union des forces démocratiques de Guinée (UFDG), which largely comprised the faction of the UPR that had boycotted the elections to the Assemblée nationale. The UFDG was affiliated to the FRAD, which announced its intention of nominating a common opposition candidate at the presidential election scheduled to be held in December 2003.

The absence of an obvious successor to Conté, who was known to be suffering ill health, caused widespread concern from 2002–03, with fears that a destabilizing 'power vacuum' could arise in the event of his death. The FRAD opposition alliance boycotted the December 2003 presidential election, owing to a perceived lack of independence on the part of the electoral commission and the alliance's lack of access to the state-controlled media. The election was preceded by numerous arrests of junior army officers. The only rival to Conté was the leader of a minor political party, Mamadou Bhoye Barry, and Conté was declared the winner with 95.25% of the vote. The Government claimed that voter turn-out was 82%. The European Union declined to send observers on the grounds that the conditions under which the vote was conducted were neither free nor fair.

Following the election, President Conté was rarely seen in public, prompting renewed concerns about his apparent ill health. In February 2004 Conté dismissed Sidimé as Prime Minister, and appointed Fall in his place. In March a new Minister of the Economy and Finance, Mady Kaba Camara, was appointed; the Governor of the central bank, Ibrahim Chérif Bah, was also dismissed, amid increasing concern at the country's economic performance. In mid-March Siradiou Diallo died; he was replaced as President of the UPR by Ousmane Bah. In late March three senior members of the UFR were detained on suspicion of involvement in an alleged plot to assassinate President Conté; although all three were provisionally released in mid-April, it was reported that they were to be charged with breaching national security, and were to remain under judicial control. In late April it was announced that Fall had resigned as Prime Minister and had fled the country; Fall claimed that he had been obstructed in trying to implement economic reforms. The atmosphere of government suspicion of its political opponents intensified in 2004 following a sustained round of public protests in Conakry against increases in the cost of living. The post of Prime Minister remained vacant until early December, when the hitherto Minister of Fishing and Aquaculture, Cellou Dalein Diallo, was appointed to that position. Diallo's first attempt to initiate dialogue with the opposition was undermined when a leading figure in Alpha Condé's RPG, Antoine Soromou, was arrested in January 2005, shortly after he had met Diallo.

Following an alleged assassination attempt against the President on 19 January 2005, when shots were fired on a presidential convoy, thousands of suspects were rounded up for questioning. An elderly Muslim cleric, Mohamed Touré, died in detention, and other supporters of the opposition were still being held in detention several months later. Tension mounted on 15 May when detainees being held in the main prison in Conakry managed to break free before being rounded up by armed forces. In an atmosphere of increasing anarchy, the opposition parties in the FRAD alliance called for Conté's resignation, and in July Alpha Condé returned from exile, encouraging a boycott of the municipal and local elections scheduled to be held in December. In the period leading up to the elections several senior members of the armed forces, including the army Chief of Staff, and several hundred less high ranking figures, were forced into retirement, around 1,000 officers and non-commissioned officers being promoted in their place. The PUP claimed an overwhelming victory in the local and municipal elections, held on 18 December, although all of the opposition parties rejected the legitimacy of the officially declared results. The UPR, the only opposition party in parliament, denounced the results as 'electoral robbery' and withdrew all of its parliamentary representatives in protest. In a further extension of ongoing social unrest sparked by high inflation, the principal trade unions staged a week-long strike in February 2006 to support their call for wage increases.

The political crisis deepened in March 2006 following the President's return from medical treatment in Switzerland, whereupon he retreated to his home village of Wawa, 100 km east of Conakry. On 4 April it appeared that Prime Minister Diallo had won the President's support for increased powers and an extensive government reshuffle, including the appointment of deputy prime ministers in charge of the economy and foreign aid, was approved. However, before the radio announcement of the presidential decree authorizing these changes was completed, troops invaded the radio and television headquarters to stop the broadcast. On the following day another presidential decree was issued, cancelling the previous decree (thereby restoring the previous members of the Government to office) and dismissing Diallo for having committed a 'grave error'. Those perceived to have been responsible for the Prime Minister's sudden removal were the Chief of Staff of the Armed Forces, Gen. Kerfalla Camara, and the hitherto Minister, Secretary-General to the Presidency, Fodé Bangoura, who was, immediately following the dismissal of Diallo, promoted to the position of Minister of State for Presidential Affairs, in which capacity he held effective control of defence, security and economic and financial affairs, and was the most senior member of the Government other than the President.

Mounting Political Crisis

The sudden dismissal of Cellou Diallo, who had won widespread respect for his commitment to reform, sparked a new political crisis. Diallo's fall was widely seen to be linked to his efforts to expose corrupt dealings between the central bank and Conté's close business associate Mamadou Sylla, who was alleged to have withdrawn US $22m. in cash from the bank in recompense for arms he had delivered to the Government in 2000–01. With Conté undergoing frequent medical examination and treatment, the vacuum at the head of the administration was filled by Bangoura who was elevated to Minister-Secretary General to the Presidency while also remaining Minister of State for the Presidency. The country's trade unions planned a round of protests demanding better economic management and lower prices of essential goods and the first of these strikes occurred in early June 2006; however, when the action was joined on 12 June by school students, who were protesting at the postponement of their exams, the security forces reacted brutally, firing at groups of students in Conakry, Labé and Nzérékoré. Between 10 and 20 students were killed and hundreds more wounded. The trade unions continued their strike throughout much of June, only suspending their action after prices were nominally cut by up to 30% and after the Assemblée nationale agreed to set up an inquiry into the shootings. Investigations were also launched into the case against Sylla, who was eventually detained later in the year along with a former Deputy Governor of the central bank, Fodé Soumah. There were clear signs of tensions in the barracks as Conté continued to remove some officers and promote others.

On 27 December 2006 Conté, whose declining health prevented him from managing government affairs in any detail, again increased the powers of Bangoura, without naming a premier, and reinstated the transport minister Alpha Ibrahima Keita, who had previously been dismissed. Shortly afterwards he ordered the release from detention of both Sylla and Soumah, precipitating a larger wave of protests, which were led most visibly by the Confédération Nationale des Travailleurs de Guinée and the Union Syndicale des Travailleurs de Guinée. They called for a general strike to commence on 10 January 2007. As protestors marched in Conakry and other major towns, they demanded the return to jail of Syllah and Soumah, but the unions were quick to add more far-reaching demands such as the appointment of a new prime minister, lower fuel prices and the enforcement of heavier taxation on foreign mining companies. The unions' platform successfully won the support of the political opposition parties, whose previous inability to forge a common front was attributed to their largely parochial and ethnic appeal. The new round of nation-wide protests was again met by violence from the security forces and, as the strike continued, it quickly led to an economic shutdown with the suspension of activity at mining operations, railways and ports and the closure of many businesses.

Over the last three weeks of January 2007 some 60 people lost their lives, prompting increasing international concern that the situation could further deteriorate much more sharply still. The security forces often overreacted to minor provocations and at times singled out the Peulh minority for especially harsh treatment. Many foreign companies and organizations suspended operations and began to evacuate staff. After the Chairman of the African Union (AU) Commission, Alpha Oumar Konare, urged a spirit of co-operation and dialogue, on 19 January Conté raised expectations that he was considering appointing a Prime Minister when he removed Bangoura from the position of Minister of State. The unions declared their support for premiership candidates such as Cellou Diallo, Kabinet Kamara and Aboubacar Sylla, but another potential nominee appeared in the person of former ECOWAS Executive Secretary Lansana Kouyaté, who visited the country to offer his services. A negotiation process was also initiated by the Assemblée Speaker, Aboubacar Sompare, focusing on the powers that might be granted to a new premier. On 22 January there was a huge march through Conakry in which demonstrators demanded change. The crowds blocked off all three roads leading to the Samory Touré barracks in the city, while members of the Presidential Guard retaliated with physical assaults on union organizers, many of whom were detained.

Sompare's negotiations resulted in an agreement on the prime ministerial role that was signed on 27 January 2007 by the Minister of State for the Economy, Madikaba Camara, as well as by representatives of employers and unions. It declared that the Prime Minister should head and appoint the Council of Ministers and senior officials and hold responsibility for public finance and economic policy. Following this, the trade unions' spokesman, Dr Ibrahim Fofana, ordered the suspension of the general strike and urged Guineans to return to work. However, on 9 February, when Conté named his close associate Eugène Camara, a former planning minister, as his choice for Prime Minister, the protests erupted again and were met with yet more shootings of demonstrators in the following days. Around 20 died in Conakry, Nzérékoré and other towns, and more than 100 were injured. In Conakry looters pillaged offices and homes of ministers and senior officials and, in one incident, an official vehicle carrying Conté himself was surrounded by protesters, some of whom were shot on the spot while bodyguards safely removed the President to another vehicle. On 12 February Conté declared a state of emergency and visited military camps to offer pay increases to the troops.

A resolution to the crisis was by this stage urgently sought both by ECOWAS and by individual West African Governments. Nigeria's President Olusegun Obasanjo supported an initiative whereby former Nigerian Head of State, Gen. Ibrahim Babangida, would assume the role of mediator. Babangida arrived in Conakry with ECOWAS Executive Secretary Mohamed Ibn Chambas in mid-February 2007. In their discussions with the unions they found support for the candidacy of Kouyaté, who also had significant experience in the search for solutions during the Liberia and Sierra Leone crises, and whose candidacy was strongly supported by Côte d'Ivoire's President Laurent Gbagbo. On 27 February Conté agreed to the appointment of Kouyaté as Prime Minister and negotiations began regarding the appointment of a new government. Most of the principal posts in the new administration, which was unveiled in late March, were awarded to those chosen by Kouyaté, but some key Conté loyalists were retained, including Gen. Arafan Camara as Minister of National Defence (marking the first time in 13 years that the President had agreed to relinquish this key position), while further pay rises were awarded to the military. In addition, an IMF official, Ousmane Doré, was appointed Minister of Economy, Finance and Planning and a new panel was set up to look at the possibility of creating an independent judicial mechanism to investigate and prosecute those responsible for abuses during the events of January and February.

EXTERNAL AFFAIRS

Of particular concern to the Guinean authorities since the early 1990s has been the internal instability of neighbouring Liberia, Sierra Leone and Guinea-Bissau. The conflicts in Guinea's neighbouring states have, in particular, led to a large influx of refugees, who in the late 1990s were estimated to number some 5%–10% of the total population of Guinea.

In August 1990 Guinean armed forces were stationed along the border with Liberia, following a series of incursions by deserters from the Liberian army. Guinean army units also participated in the ECOMOG cease-fire monitoring group that was dispatched to Liberia in that month, and in April 1991 it was announced that a Guinean contingent was to be deployed in Sierra Leone to assist that country in repelling violations of its territory by the National Patriotic Front of Liberia (NPFL), led by Charles Taylor. Following the *coup d'état* in Sierra Leone in April 1992, ex-President Maj-Gen. Joseph Saidu Momoh of that country took asylum in Guinea, although the Conté Government expressed its wish to establish 'normal' relations with the new regime, led by Capt. Valentine Strasser, and announced that Guinean forces would remain in Sierra Leone.

In October 1992 the Guinean Government confirmed that it was providing training facilities for Liberian forces; however, assurances were given that those receiving military instruction were not, as had been widely rumoured, members of the anti-Taylor ULIMO, but that they were to constitute the first Liberian government forces following the eventual restoration of peace. In March 1993 the NPFL protested to the UN that ULIMO had launched an armed attack on NPFL-held territory from Guinea, and threatened reprisals should further offensives occur. Although Guinea continued to deny support for ULIMO, it was admitted that, contrary to earlier indications, Liberian forces trained in Guinea (at the request of the Liberian interim Government) had already returned to Liberia. Efforts were undertaken from early 1994 to reinforce security along Guinea's borders, following recent incursions by both ULIMO and NPFL fighters.

A resurgence of violence in Liberia in September 1994, following a coup attempt in that country, caused as many as 50,000 refugees to cross into Guinea. Moreover, an intensification of hostilities involving government and rebel forces in Sierra Leone in January 1995 resulted in a further influx.

Although Strasser took refuge in Guinea after he was deposed in January 1996, close co-operation developed with subsequent governments in Sierra Leone, and President Ahmed Tejan Kabbah made several visits to Guinea both before and after his election to the presidency in March of that year. Kabbah in turn fled to Guinea in May 1997, and established a Government-in-exile, following the seizure of power in Sierra Leone by forces led by Maj. Johnny Paul Koroma. Military reinforcements were deployed to protect Guinea's border, and 1,500 Guinean troops were dispatched in support of the Nigerian-led ECOMOG force in Sierra Leone. Guinea joined other members of the international community in condemning the subversion of constitutional order in Sierra Leone; following an ad hoc conference of ECOWAS ministers responsible for foreign affairs, which was convened in Conakry in June, Guinea became a member of the 'committee of four' (with Côte d'Ivoire, Ghana and Nigeria) charged with ensuring the implementation of decisions and recommendations pertaining to the situation in Sierra Leone. The total number of Sierra Leonean refugees in Guinea was estimated at 192,200 at the end of 1997; however, the operation leading to the return of Kabbah from Conakry to Sierra Leone in March 1998 to resume the presidency again led to an influx of thousands of refugees from Sierra Leone, while fighting in April in eastern Sierra Leone between ECOMOG forces and soldiers supporting Koroma caused a further influx of refugees and the closure of parts of the border. By the end of 1998 the number of Sierra Leonean refugees in Guinea had increased to 297,200.

Relations between Guinea and Liberia deteriorated further following the beginning of an insurgency in the border regions of southern Guinea in September 2000 (see above), in which the Guinean Government implicated rebel groups from Liberia and Sierra Leone. In early 2001 Liberia claimed that LURD rebels were launching attacks on Liberia from within Guinea.

In May 2001 Guinean troops fired artillery shells at the town of Rokupr, in northern Sierra Leone, as a UN-backed disarmament process got under way, precipitating fears that the peace process in that country would be disrupted. In June Kabbah and Conté met in Kambia, in northern Sierra Leone, to discuss regional tensions; following the discussions, it was announced that the commercial highway between Conakry and Freetown, closed since 1998, was to reopen. Guinea's border regions were largely cleared of rebel activity in the course of 2001, although the advances made by LURD within Liberia resulted in a fresh influx of Liberian refugees into Guinean territory. After the return of relative peace to Sierra Leone from 2002, Guinea continued to keep military control of the strategic Sierra Leonean border town of Yenga, provoking strong criticism from Sierra Leonean opposition politicians.

Although regional tensions were aggravated by the outbreak of civil conflict in Côte d'Ivoire in September 2002, the reported involvement of Liberian rebels in the conflict in western regions of Côte d'Ivoire had the effect of reducing instability at the Liberia–Guinea border. Guinea was also reported to have increased its support for LURD, whose leader, Sekou Konneh, was based in Conakry. Following the exiling of Liberia's former President, Charles Taylor, relations with subsequent administrations in Liberia have improved.

In general, the Conté administration has maintained good relations with the French Government, which is Guinea's primary source of financial and technical assistance. However, the progress of the trial of opposition leader Alpha Condé remained a source of concern to the French authorities, and during his visit to Guinea in July 1999 President Jacques Chirac of France sought assurances from the Government that the trial would be 'transparent'. A meeting of the joint commission for Franco-Guinean co-operation took place in Conakry in November. However, in mid-2000 a meeting of francophone parliamentarians called on Guinea's donor countries to suspend assistance in protest at the conduct of the Condé trial. Guinea, a member of the Organization of the Islamic Conference, has also forged links with the governments of other predominantly Islamic countries, notably signing several co-operation agreements with Iran in the mid-1990s. Guinea has also received significant material assistance from Libya and from the People's Republic of China. In May 2006 France awarded the Guinean Chief of Staff of the Armed Forces, Gen. Kerfalla Camara, the *Légion d'honneur*, that country's premier order; in that month France also agreed to release some €100m. of budgetary support for the Guinean Government for the period 2006–10 that had hitherto been suspended.

Economy

RICHARD SYNGE

Based on an earlier article by EDITH HODGKINSON

With successful management of its substantial mineral deposits and excellent agricultural potential, Guinea could eventually be one of the richest countries in West Africa. However, the country's economic record since independence has been significantly below expectations. The country's gross domestic product (GDP) expanded, in real terms, at an average rate of 3.0% per year in 1970–80, reflecting the rapid development of the bauxite sector during that decade, but declined by an average of 1.4% per year in 1980–85. The causes of Guinea's relatively poor performance during this period were largely political. First, there was the abrupt severance of the country's links with France in 1958, which was followed by the withdrawal of French officials and the discontinuation of aid, as well as the loss of the leading traditional market for Guinea's exports. Second, the newly independent Guinea immediately sought to set up a socialist economy, with direct state control of production and consumption in virtually every sector—an objective demanding managerial input that Guinea lacked, and which resulted in great inefficiency and waste. Mining, the one economic sector where state control was diluted, developed as an enclave, with admittedly major benefits for Guinea's export earnings but little linkage and feedback into the rest of the economy, which remained essentially based on agriculture and which suffered from Ahmed Sekou Touré's system of highly centralized management. The economy consequently became highly dualistic, with the development of a large informal sector in response to the near monopoly of the state over formal economic activity.

During the 1990s, in an attempt to remove at least the domestic constraints on growth, the Lansana Conté regime introduced a series of policy reforms, agreed with the IMF and the World Bank. These included the transfer to private interests, or elimination, of parastatal organizations, the liberalization of foreign trade and the abolition of price controls, together with monetary and banking reforms and a reduction in the number of civil-service personnel. The recovery programme initially received substantial international support, in the form of debt relief and new funds from bilateral and multilateral sources. Such reforms enjoyed considerable success, and real GDP growth in 1998–2005 averaged 3.1% per year. However, the reform process collapsed in 2002 as the country began to build up budget deficits in an inflationary environment. Most financial assistance from the international community was suspended until more rational economic management could be imposed. Average inflation rose from 3.0% in 2002 to 17.5% in 2004, before rising even more sharply to 31.1% in 2005 and to an estimated 250% in 2006, coinciding with the collapse of economic reform during a long round of political upheavals. Continuing growth in real GDP, at 2.7% in 2004, 3.0% in 2005 and an estimated 2.0% in 2006, was attributed principally to an expansion in mineral exports and some modest investment in infrastructure projects. In 2004 the economic situation began to deteriorate seriously, without effective political management, even as mineral revenues began to increase as a consequence of increasing world prices and demand. Rising inflation provoked widespread social unrest, and there was a widening differential between the official and unofficial exchange rates of the Guinean franc. Credible economic statistics were, however, increasingly difficult to find.

POPULATION AND EMPLOYMENT

Population growth has been relatively slow, following a high level of emigration during the Sekou Touré regime. Therefore, while the population was stated to be 4.5m. (excluding adjustment for underenumeration) at the 1983 census, a further 2m. Guineans (some of whom returned following the 1984 coup) were estimated to be living abroad. The census conducted in December 1996 enumerated a population of 7,156,406, including an estimated 640,000 refugees. The urban population numbered 2.1m. In mid-2006 the total population was estimated at 9,370,000 by the UN.

The active labour force in 2004 was estimated at 4,248,000. Although agriculture remained the principal sector of employment in the mid-2000s, an increasing proportion of the population have been engaged in industrial and service activities since the 1980s. The Conté Government succeeded in reducing the number of employees in the public sector from 90,000 in 1986 to about 48,000 in 1995. The diminution in job opportunities in the public sector, previously guaranteed to all university graduates, has caused a rapid increase in urban unemployment and fuelled student unrest.

AGRICULTURE, FORESTRY AND FISHING

Despite the rapid development and potential of the mining sector, agriculture remains an important economic activity in terms of value of output (contributing 25.6% of GDP in 2005) and the most significant in terms of employment (engaging some 82.3% of the labour force in 2004). Under the Sekou Touré regime, agricultural production was depressed by the demands and inefficiencies of the collectivist regime, and, in consequence, smuggling of produce by peasant farmers was widespread. On taking power, the Conté Government immediately abolished collectives, increased producer prices and ended the production tax. Improvements to the infrastructure (notably to the road network) and the easier availability of farm credits began to stimulate an increase in production by small-scale farmers.

Production of foods has thus recovered in recent years, with production in the late 1990s and early 2000s some 20% more than the average output recorded in 1979–81. In 2004 output of paddy rice (cultivated mainly in the south-eastern Guinée forestière region) was an estimated 900,000 metric tons, while production of cassava was 1.4m. tons, sweet potatoes an estimated 60,000 tons and maize 90,000 tons. The rise in output has, in the long term, failed to keep pace with population growth, so that Guinea—a net exporter of food in the past—now imports large quantities, representing about double the value of its agricultural exports. The staple crops are supplemented by the substantial livestock herd (raised by traditional methods), which FAO estimated at 3.4m. cattle, 1.1m sheep and 1.4m. goats in 2005.

The major commercial crops are bananas, coffee, pineapples, oil palm, groundnuts and citrus fruit. The banana plantations, which suffered in the late 1950s from disease and, with independence, from the withdrawal of European planters and the closing of the protected French market, have shown a good recovery, with estimated output averaging about 150,000 metric tons per year in the late 1990s and early 2000s. Officially recorded coffee output fluctuated widely in the Sekou Touré era—in some years net imports were recorded—because of smuggling to neighbouring countries, where higher prices were obtainable. Before independence Guinea exported about 20,000 tons of coffee annually. The reforms of the late 1980s prompted more output to be sold on the official domestic market: production rose strongly, from 6,500 tons (according to unofficial figures) in 1986, to peak at 30,000 tons in 1994, before stabilizing at an average of more than 20,000 tons per year in the late 1990s and early 2000s. Similarly pineapple production, which measured approximately 16,000 tons per year in the late 1970s, had increased to more than 70,000 tons per year by the late 1990s. FAO estimated output of 105,000 tons in 2003 and 107,000 tons in 2004. An export trade in fruit and vegetables for the European market has been developed, as quality control and transportation links have improved. In 1986 a nine-year project was launched to plant 13,000 ha with rubber and oil palm in Guinée forestière, with the aim of re-establishing, in a modified form, the plantation agriculture that was characteristic of the colonial period, and of attracting foreign investment to this sector. Meanwhile, a cotton development scheme, aided by France, was inaugurated in 1985, aiming to produce a total of 43,000–50,000 tons from plantations in Haute Guinée (where it is the largest single development project) and Moyenne Guinée. However, progress was slow, with output of seed cotton reaching 19,350 tons (according to unofficial figures) in 1993, before decreasing again owing to unfavourable weather and a reduction in the area planted, as farmers transferred to other economic activities, notably gold mining. The sector exhibited marked growth after 1998, largely as a result of an increase in the area of the crop cultivated. In that year output amounted to 37,504 tons, increasing to some 65,700 tons in 2000, according to unofficial figures. Output was estimated at 40,000 tons in 2004.

There is considerable potential for timber production, with forests covering more than two-thirds of the land area. Timber resources are currently used mainly for fuel, with production of roundwood totalling an estimated 12.3m. cu m in 2005.

The fishing sector remains relatively undeveloped. Only a small proportion of the total catch from Guinean waters—92,600 metric tons in 2004—has been accounted for by indigenous fleets, the rest having been taken by factory ships and industrial trawlers. Since 1983 the Guinean Government has concluded a series of fishing accords with the European Community (EC, now European Union—EU). It has since been agreed to award foreign licences exclusively to EU fleets, in an effort to preserve the viability of fish stocks on the continental shelf. The African Development Bank has helped to finance the establishment of onshore facilities and the supply of equipment for small-scale fishermen. In addition, the rehabilitation of the port of Conakry, implemented in the mid-1990s, included the installation of deep-freeze equipment to serve the fishing industry, while further improvements to facilities were expected to include an enlargement of the port, which had been one of several regional ports to receive increased trade following the onset of civil rebellion in Côte d'Ivoire in late 2002.

MINING AND POWER

Mining has long been Guinea's most dynamic sector and the country's most important source of foreign exchange, providing more than 90% of recorded export revenues for much of the 1980s and around 80% in the 1990s. It has been contributing around one-fifth of GDP each year since the end of the 1980s, accounting for 17.2% of GDP (at 1996 prices) in 2003. Minerals again accounted for over 90% of export earnings in 2003, when the value of bauxite exports was US $290m., alumina $148m., gold $139m. and diamonds $49m. In 1995 the Government introduced revisions to the mining code, which were intended to encourage foreign investment and to define the state's new non-participatory role in the mining sector. The Government also announced the foundation of the Centre de Promotion et de Développement Miniers (CPDM), which was to act as the advisory and regulatory body for the mining sector. Foreign investment was further encouraged by the completion in 1998 of a comprehensive evaluation of Guinea's mineral resources by the German Federal Institute for Geosciences and Natural Resources. In the late 1990s some 128 exploration licences were issued, and it was hoped that increased production in subsequent years would, to a large extent, offset the effects of depressed world commodity prices. Currently bauxite, diamonds and gold are commercially exploited, but it is also anticipated that deposits of iron ore and nickel may prove viable. The further development of the sector is, however, dependent on improvements in infrastructure and power supply.

Bauxite and Alumina

The country possesses 30% of the world's known bauxite reserves, with a very high-grade ore. Guinea ranks second only to Australia in terms of ore production, and is the world's largest exporter of bauxite. After the mid-1980s, however, bauxite revenues were affected by a weakening in world demand for aluminium and the considerable surplus in world production capacity. Annual output has been running at around the 12m.–17m. metric tons level since the early 1980s, reaching a high of 18.39m. tons in 1996. Output was 16.37m. tons in 2004 and was estimated to have been maintained at close to the same level in 2005. Current expansion and rehabilitation programmes at the country's mines were projected to increase annual output to 20m. tons, and it was expected that a restructuring of the sector, through the reduction in the state interest to 15% of equity, would enhance both investment and efficiency. In 2006–07, however, although there were some advances in negotiations with foreign investors, the deteriorating political situation eventually brought many mining operations to a halt for a sustained period of time.

The exploitation of bauxite reserves at Fria, by the Cie internationale pour la production de l'alumine Fria (an international consortium that included Pechiney of France—now Alcan), began in the 1930s. Processing into alumina began in 1960, at what remains the country's only refinery. Following independence, the Government took a 49% share in the company, which was renamed Friguia. The refinery's output eased from a peak of 692,000 metric tons (recorded in 1980, and close to the plant's total capacity of 700,000 tons annually) to some 550,000 tons (calcined equivalent) in 2000. In October 1998 the international consortium ceded its 51% stake in Friguia to the Guinean Government. In late 1999 the Government formed a controlling company, the Alumina Company of Guinea Ltd (ACG-Guinea), and concluded a management and technical assistance agreement with the Reynolds Metal Company of the USA (which subsequently merged with Alcoa Inc, also of the USA), by which it was hoped to achieve significant improvements in production efficiency. However, in 2002 Russian Aluminium (RusAl) took a majority stake in ACG as part of a plan to increase Friguia's production capacity to 1.2m. tons per year; subsequently in 2006 RusAl increased its stake in ACG to 100% at the same time as it developed plans for the expansion of the Kindia mine (see below).

The country's principal bauxite mine is at Boké-Sangaredi, in the north-west, which was commissioned in 1973 by the Cie des bauxites de Guinée (CBG), a joint venture between the Government and the Halco group (an international consortium of Canadian, US, French, German and Australian aluminium companies). The Government holds 49% of the capital and receives 65% of the mine's net profits. The scheme involved considerable infrastructural development—142 km of railway and a port at Kamsar. Output increased from around 900,000 metric tons per year to the complex's full capacity (at that time) of 10m. tons in 1981, eased subsequently, and then rose to 13.6m. tons in 1999. Plans were advanced during the early 2000s for the construction of an alumina refinery, with an annual capacity of 2.8m. tons and at a cost estimated at US $2,100m. The investors were initially grouped in Guinea Aluminium Products Corporation (GAPCO), a combination of Japanese and US interests. Following international trends of increasing demand for aluminium (and consequent higher prices), the investors took an increasing interest in the development of the proposed refinery and in November 2005 Halco and the Guinean Government signed an agreement to provide the Canadian-based Global Alumina Corporation with access to CBG resources for the new refinery. Global Alumina announced in 2006 that it would commence mining in 2008 and that it would bring its refinery into production in 2009 with a capacity of 3.0m. tons a year. In return for sharing and managing Global Alumina's access to its infrastructure, CBG was due to receive additional mining titles for a further 2,000m. tons of bauxite. Halco has also considered investing in a smaller refinery project at Kamsar, with a cost of $1,500m. and a projected annual production capacity of 1.5m. tons.

A similar agreement to that signed with Halco was concluded in 1969 by Guinea and the USSR for the working of bauxite deposits at Debélé, near Kindia. Production by the Office des bauxites de Kindia began in 1974 and averaged about 3m. metric tons per year, compared with design capacity of 5m. tons, in the late 1980s. Following the dissolution of the USSR in December 1991, the company suffered severe financial difficulties, and output has fluctuated around the 1m.–2m. metric tons level since the company was reorganized as the Société des bauxites de Kindia (SBK) in 1992: production was 1.3m. tons in 1999. A majority stake was subsequently acquired by RusAl, which in May 2001 announced a US $40m. investment programme to modernize equipment in order to ensure the continued productivity of SBK. Further agreement was reached with RusAl in 2006 that bauxite production would soon double from its scheduled rate of 2.8m. tons.

The Société des bauxites de Dabola-Tougué, established as a joint venture with Iran, planned to develop reserves at Dabola and Tougué and eventually to operate an alumina-processing plant. Initial output was expected to amount to 3.5m. tons a year, and was projected to increase to an eventual 10m. tons annually, although the facilitation of exports from the reserves would necessitate the upgrading of the rail link to Conakry.

Diamonds

Production of diamonds reached 80,000 carats per year in the early 1970s: the official figure did not include substantial illicit production, and mining was suspended in the late 1970s to prevent smuggling and theft. In 1980 the Government allowed the resumption of diamond mining by private companies, and AREDOR-Guinée was founded in 1981 with Australian, Swiss, British and—for the first time in Guinea—International Finance Corpn participation. The Government had a 50% holding and was to take 65% of net profits. AREDOR-Guinée began production in 1984, and output reached a peak of 204,000 carats in 1986. However, mining was suspended in 1994. AREDOR has since been restructured, with Canada's Trivalence Mining taking a majority stake with a view to developing new kimberlite resources within the concession. In 1992 the Government revoked the ban (imposed in 1985) on small-scale prospecting. Of a recorded 379,639 carats exported in 1997, 342,187 were from artisanal producers. In 2003 some 666,000 carats of diamonds were mined, including those from artisanal producers; output in 2004 was 627,900 carats. In 2006 South Africa's De Beers negotiated a resumption of activities and was awarded permits for exploration in the Macenta area.

Gold

Gold is mined both industrially and by individuals (the latter smuggle much of their output abroad). A joint venture with Belgian interests, the Société Aurifère de Guinée (SAG), was established in 1985 to develop gold mining in the Siguiri and Mandiana districts. Alluvial production began in 1988, and reached 2,000 kg in the following year; however, extraction ceased in 1992, owing to financial and technical difficulties and conflicts with artisanal miners. Golden Shamrock of Australia took a 70% interest in the project, which was in turn taken over by Ghana's Ashanti Goldfields in 1996; production by SAG (renamed Société Ashanti Goldfields de Guinée—now AngloGold Ashanti Guinea) resumed in early 1998, with output in its first year estimated at 160,000 oz. The Société minière de Dinguiraye (a joint venture with Norwegian, Australian and French interests) began production at the Léro site in 1995; output in 1998 was in the region of 52,000 oz. The Norwegian-based Kenor has developed an extension of the mine east of the Karta river. A project to develop the Jean Gobele mine, with the potential to produce 60,000 oz per year, was initiated by a Moroccan mining company in 2001. Several other foreign enterprises are also actively prospecting for gold. In 2005, according to the US Geological Survey, 15,300 kg of gold were mined in Guinea.

Iron Ore

Working of the iron-ore deposits on the Kaloum peninsula (near Conakry) was begun in 1953 by an Anglo-French group, and provided a stable output of about 700,000 metric tons per year in 1960–69, when operations were abandoned. An ambitious project for the exploitation of the far superior deposits at Mt Nimba has been discussed for many years. The original proposals failed to attract sufficient capital, since commitments by potential customers for the ore were far below the planned level of output (an eventual 15m. tons per year). A scaled-down version of the project was to be undertaken by

Nimba International Mining Co (Nimco), a joint venture of the Governments of Guinea and Liberia (each with a stake of 20%) and the Euronimba consortium of international mining interests. This US $500m. scheme envisaged transport via an 18-km rail spur for processing in Liberia, with export through that country's port of Buchanan. The conflict in Liberia during the early and mid-1990s prevented any progress on the proposal, however, and Nimco was dissolved in 1999. An existing study into the viability of the Transguinean Railway was being updated in 2006 by Euronimba and Simfer, a subsidiary of Rio Tinto (of Australia and the United Kingdom), the groups still potentially interested in developing the Nimba project.

Energy

Installed electricity generation capacity is currently estimated at 245 MW, of which one-half is privately operated, notably by mining companies. Supplies of energy outside the mining and industrial sector are vastly inadequate, with less than one-10th of the population receiving electricity from the national grid; even Conakry is subject to frequent and prolonged power-cuts during dry periods. None the less, the country has a very large, as yet unexploited, hydroelectric potential, estimated at some 6,000 MW. Several ambitious projects for the development of hydroelectric facilities on the Konkouré river finally came to fruition—in a much reduced form—in 1999, with the commissioning of a 75-MW plant at Garafiri. This, together with a planned station at Kaléta, 100 km downstream (scheduled for completion in 2007), was to increase total generating capacity by 155 MW. As part of the economic reform programme the national power corporation has been restructured, to allow the participation of Canadian and French companies.

MANUFACTURING

The principal aim of Guinea's small manufacturing sector, which accounted for only 4.1% of GDP in 2005, has been import-substitution, but the experience of the state-run projects that were established under Sekou Touré was disappointing. Lack of foreign exchange for raw materials, of skilled workers and of technical expertise, combined with poor management and low domestic purchasing power, meant that most of the plants were operating substantially below capacity. The sector has been rationalized under the Conté administration, with the former state-run textile and fruit-processing companies closed and no new factories established. Manufacturing is now largely limited to food, drinks and cigarettes, and basic inputs such as cement, metal manufactures and fuel products, all geared to the domestic market.

TRANSPORT AND INFRASTRUCTURE

The inadequacy of Guinea's transport infrastructure has been cited by the World Bank as the 'single most severe impediment to output recovery'. None the less, some improvements have been made since the mid-1980s. The road network is being almost entirely reconstructed, to restore links between Conakry and the country's interior, while road tracks have been built to open up rural areas. The network comprised 21,215 km of roads (of which 1,959 km were paved) in 1999. In 2001 work commenced on an EU-financed road link from Kankan to the Malian capital, Bamako. The rail network is better developed, but is entirely geared to serving the bauxite sector: a 135-km heavy-gauge railway links the Boké bauxite deposits with the deep-water port at Kamsar, which handles around 9m. metric tons per year and is thus the country's major export outlet in tonnage terms. The 662-km public rail line from Conakry to Kankan has ceased to function despite the signing of a contract for the upgrading of the line with a Slovak company in 1997. The port of Conakry, which handled 3.9m. tons of foreign trade in 1999, has been extended and modernized as part of a programme that envisages the construction of naval-repair and deep-water port facilities; further improvements were under consideration in the early 2000s. A petroleum terminal is also planned for Conakry. The international airport at Conakry-Gbessia handled some 300,000 passengers in 1999; there are several smaller airfields in the interior. Several major donors, including the World Bank, have made funds available for both rural and urban water-supply networks; in 2001 the Government invited bids for private-sector management of water-supply companies.

FINANCE

Government revenue remains heavily reliant on income from the mining sector, but this contribution declined sharply from a peak of 60% in 1987 to about 25% in the late 1990s. Although mining revenue rose strongly in the mid- and late 1970s, reflecting the growth of the bauxite sector, current expenditure exceeded revenue, owing to the Government's policy of providing jobs in the public sector to all graduates, combined with the rising losses of the state enterprises and the growing burden of servicing the foreign debt. Thus, by 1981 the deficit of the public sector was equivalent to around one-fifth of GDP, with parastatal enterprises alone accounting for some three-quarters of the deficit.

As part of Guinea's programme for economic stabilization, inaugurated in 1986 with support from the IMF, consumer subsidies were reduced or eliminated, while the activities of state enterprises were curtailed and employment in the civil service was to be reduced by more than one-half. This severe fiscal austerity proved difficult to implement, and the Government was obliged to rescind some of the price increases resulting from the devaluation of the currency in 1986, while the intended reduction in civil-service personnel was finally achieved only in 1995. None the less, the budget balance improved as the Government succeeded in raising its revenue from non-mining activities 10-fold in 1987–95, through changes in the tax system and improvements in collection. This was particularly significant, as mining revenue fell in every year from 1990 to 1994. The liquidation or sale of the state's industrial and commercial enterprises has also been of economic benefit. The overall budget (i.e. taking into account both grants and capital expenditure) remained in deficit, but as a proportion of GDP this declined to 2.5% in 2000. Attempts to improve budgetary management were made in 2001 but were not pursued in 2002 because of a combination of poor tax collection and overspending by the Government. State finances were also thrown into confusion by a dispute with mining companies over the Government's failure to reimburse their value-added tax payments. The budget deficit rose to 6.0% of GDP in 2003 (compared with 4.4% in 2002), but thanks to sharply increasing mining revenue the deficit is estimated to have narrowed in subsequent years. The IMF has recently expressed concern that mining companies have been providing interest-free tax advances to the Government to pay external creditors. In 2004 the budget deficit was 436,800m. Guinean francs, equivalent to 4.9% of GDP.

In 1999 the IMF expressed concern at weaknesses, particularly in fiscal revenue collection, and the annual funding under the Enhanced Structural Adjustment Facility (ESAF) originally agreed in early 1997 was delayed until the end of 1999, when support under the Poverty Reduction and Growth Facility (PRGF—the successor to the ESAF) was granted in three yearly instalments. In May 2001 the IMF approved a further three-year arrangement for Guinea, worth a total of US $82m. over three years, under the PRGF; the programme aimed, initially, to generate annual GDP growth of 6.5% in 2004. Non-compliance with agreed fiscal targets led to the IMF's suspension of disbursements under the PRGF in late 2002 and prevented the adoption of a staff-monitored programme in early 2003; as a result, budgetary assistance from donors also virtually ceased.

An important element of the economic liberalization initiated in the final years of the Sekou Touré regime and pursued with vigour by the Conté administration was the reform of the banking sector, ending the state monopoly by allowing the establishment of private commercial banks and then closing down the six state-controlled institutions. Government plans fully to privatize the Banque internationale pour le commerce et l'industrie de la Guinée (BICIGUI) have not materialized; however, by 2005 the Government had reduced its shareholding in the bank from 51% of the total to 38%; BICIGUI accounts for 45% of the country's banking resources and for about one-third of credits to the private sector.

FOREIGN TRADE AND PAYMENTS

With the development of bauxite resources from the early 1970s, the country's external trade position greatly improved. The sharp rise in bauxite exports resulted in strong growth in export earnings after 1975, and sales of bauxite and alumina contributed more than 90% of recorded earnings in the early 1980s. Export earnings were subsequently bolstered by contributions from sales of diamonds and gold, which accounted for 15% of the total in 1990. The sustained growth in exports throughout this period allowed a similarly strong rise in spending on imports, in large part reflecting capital investment in the mining sector. However, as earnings from bauxite and alumina declined from 1991 onwards, and spending on imports was relatively little changed, the trade account moved into deficit, reaching a peak of US $169.7m. in 1994. By the mid-1990s, with bauxite and alumina earnings recovering from their trough of 1994, the trade account had moved back into surplus by 1996; a surplus of $40.1m. was recorded in 2002. Although the balance of trade recorded a deficit, of $35.0m., in 2003, a surplus, of $37.2m., was recorded in 2004. The current account remained in deficit because of high outflows on services (including interest payments and profit remittances), with deficits of $199.8m., $187.5m. and $174.8m. in 2002, 2003 and 2004, respectively. The deficit began to fall in 2004, however, from 5.5% of GDP for the year to 3.8% in 2005, owing to an improvement in the trade surplus. Foreign exchange reserves were nevertheless uncomfortably low, and were estimated by the IMF at only $107.7 m. at the end of 2005, equivalent to only 1.3 months of imports.

A formerly important and positive item on the current account was the inflows of official aid to Guinea. The country's rapprochement with France and adherence to successive aid and trade agreements with the EU (the Lomé Conventions and, subsequently, the Cotonou Agreement), in conjunction with the change of political regime in 1984, resulted in a rapid increase in the flow of official development assistance (both grants and loans) from non-Eastern bloc countries and agencies. Most such assistance has been suspended since 2002.

Guinea's foreign debt rose very sharply, from US $137m. in 1960 to $1,387m. at the end of 1981—equivalent to 86% of the country's gross national income (GNI) in that year—a level that was broadly maintained in the following four years. Although the burden of servicing the debt was alleviated by concessionary interest rates on most of the borrowing and by the buoyancy of Guinean exports, it remained at a high level throughout this period, fluctuating within the range of 14%–24% of exports of goods and services, and obligations were not discharged in full. Arrears on both repayment and interest had apparently reached $300m. at the time of the 1984 coup. In early 1986, following final agreement between the IMF and the Conté administration on the terms of the economic stabilization programme (which included a 93% devaluation of the currency), the country's Western creditors agreed to a rescheduling of debt, covering arrears and debt-service due up to early 1987. However, with the external debt and debt-service continuing to rise, the 'Paris Club' of official creditors rescheduled debt in every year from 1990 to 1992. With a rising share of concessionary loans, this meant that, while total foreign debt remained close to 100% of GNI (at $3,110m. at the end of 1994, it was equivalent to 94% in that year), the debt-service ratio was kept at a manageable 11%–14% in 1992–94. Another round of rescheduling, in January 1995, was under the highly concessionary 'Naples terms', and included the cancellation of one-half of debt-servicing liabilities due in 1994 and 1995 to France, Germany, Norway and the USA. The award of the new ESAF in 1997 generated another round of 'Paris Club' restructuring, again under 'Naples terms', and Guinea was also permitted to convert up to 20% of its outstanding debt (double the usual limit) into local-currency equity in the form of investment in development projects. Total debt at the end of 2004 was $3,538m. (equivalent to 92.4% of GNI), while the cost of debt-servicing was equivalent to 19.9% of the value of exports of goods and services. Further debt relief under the initiative for heavily indebted poor countries (HIPC) was not granted, as a consequence of the collapse of the IMF's PRGF programme in 2002. The country qualified for the HIPC 'decision point' in 2000 but by mid-2005 the criteria to reach 'completion point' had not been met. Guinea was one of nine 'second wave' countries deemed eligible for the cancellation of its obligations to the World Bank, the IMF and the African Development Bank under the terms of the agreement reached by the Group of Eight industrialized nations (G-8), but no further progress was made in 2006. Some foreign aid for humanitarian and social infrastructure projects was announced in 2006. The World Bank pledged $228m. for 11 educational and health projects and the EU announced that it was working to unfreeze its development funds to Guinea, but actual spending remained at a low level.

Statistical Survey

Source (unless otherwise stated): Direction Nationale de la Statistique, BP 221, Conakry; tel. 21-33-12; e-mail dnstat@biasy.net; internet www.afristat.org/ins-guinee.

Area and Population

AREA, POPULATION AND DENSITY

Area (sq km)	245,857*
Population (census results)	
4–17 February 1983	4,533,240†
31 December 1996‡	
Males	3,497,551
Females	3,658,855
Total	7,156,406
Population (UN estimates at mid-year)§	
2004	8,833,000
2005	9,003,000
2006	9,181,000
Density (per sq km) at mid-2006	37.3

* 94,926 sq miles.
† Excluding adjustment for underenumeration.
‡ Including refugees from Liberia and Sierra Leone (estimated at 640,000).
§ Source: UN, *World Population Prospects: The 2006 Revision*.

ETHNIC GROUPS

1995 (percentages): Peul 38.7; Malinké 23.3; Soussou 11.1; Kissi 5.9; Kpellé 4.5; Others 16.5 (Source: La Francophonie).

ADMINISTRATIVE DIVISIONS

(1996 census)

Region	Area (sq km)	Population	Density (per sq km)	Principal city
Conakry	450	1,092,936	2,428.7	Conakry
Basse-Guinée	47,063	1,460,577	31.0	Kindia
Moyenne-Guinée	52,939	1,639,617	31.0	Labé
Haute-Guinée	99,437	1,407,734	14.2	Kankan
Guinée Forestière	45,968	1,555,542	33.8	N'Zérékoré
Total	245,857	7,156,406	29.1	

Note: The regions were subsequently reorganized. The new regions (which in each case share their name with the regional capital) are: Boké; Conakry; Faranah; Kankan; Kindia; Labé; Mamou; and N'Zérékoré.

PRINCIPAL TOWNS
(population at 1996 census)

Conakry (capital)	1,092,936	Kindia	96,074
N'Zérékoré	107,329	Guéckédou	79,140
Kankan	100,192	Kamsar	61,526

Mid-2005 ('000, incl. suburbs, UN estimate): Conakry 1,425 (Source: UN, *World Urbanization Prospects: The 2005 Revision*).

BIRTHS AND DEATHS
(annual averages, UN estimates)

	1990–95	1995–2000	2000–05
Birth rate (per 1,000)	45.6	43.7	42.0
Death rate (per 1,000)	17.4	15.2	13.5

Source: UN, *World Population Prospects: The 2006 Revision*.

Expectation of life (years at birth, WHO estimates): 53 (males 52; females 55) in 2004 (Source: WHO, *World Health Report*).

ECONOMICALLY ACTIVE POPULATION
('000 persons at 1996 census)

	Males	Females	Total
Agriculture, hunting and forestry	1,140,775	1,281,847	2,422,622
Fishing	9,969	889	10,858
Mining and quarrying	26,599	8,376	34,975
Manufacturing	84,974	5,911	90,885
Electricity, gas and water supply	4,366	324	4,690
Construction	59,802	724	60,526
Wholesale and retail trade; repair of motor vehicles and motorcycles and personal and household goods	176,527	191,230	367,757
Restaurants and hotels	3,162	2,790	5,952
Transport, storage and communications	75,374	1,696	77,070
Financial intermediation	1,728	626	2,354
Real estate, renting and business activities	877	209	1,086
Public administration and defence; compulsory social security	50,401	12,791	63,192
Education	15,044	3,773	18,817
Health and social work	4,762	3,522	8,284
Other community, social and personal service activities	44,897	48,292	93,189
Private households with employed persons	5,553	6,202	11,755
Extra-territorial organizations and bodies	3,723	1,099	4,822
Total employed	1,708,533	1,570,301	3,278,834

Mid-2005 ('000 persons): Agriculture, etc. 3,788; Total labour force 4,631 (Source: FAO).

Health and Welfare

KEY INDICATORS

Total fertility rate (children per woman, 2005)	5.7
Under-5 mortality rate (per 1,000 live births, 2005)	150
HIV/AIDS (% of persons aged 15–49, 2005)	1.5
Physicians (per 1,000 head, 2004)	0.11
Hospital beds (per 1,000 head, 1990)	0.55
Health expenditure (2004): US $ per head (PPP)	95.6
Health expenditure (2004): % of GDP	5.3
Health expenditure (2004): public (% of total)	13.2
Access to water (% of persons, 2004)	50
Access to sanitation (% of persons, 2004)	18
Human Development Index (2004): ranking	160
Human Development Index (2004): value	0.445

For sources and definitions, see explanatory note on p. vi.

Agriculture

PRINCIPAL CROPS
('000 metric tons)

	2003	2004	2005
Rice (paddy)	1,146.8	1,208.0	1,272.4
Maize	423.3	461.0	502.1
Fonio	197.9	208.4	219.4
Sweet potatoes	182.7	187.7	201.0
Cassava (Manioc)	922.5	968.8	1,017.4
Taro (Coco Yam)*	30	30	30
Yams*	40.0	57.1	61.6
Sugar cane*	280	280	280
Pulses*	60	60	60
Groundnuts (in shell)	240.4	257.2	275.2
Coconuts†	28.1	28.1	28.1
Oil palm fruit*	830.0	872.8	896.3
Bananas*	150.0	158.0	162.3
Plantains*	430.0	440.7	446.5
Guavas, mangoes and mangosteens*	160.0	147.0	145.0
Pineapples*	105.0	102.1	103.1
Cotton (lint)*	15	15	15
Cottonseed*	15.0	19.3	21.5
Coffee (green)*	20.9	20.2	21.4

* FAO estimates.
† Unofficial figures.

Source: FAO.

LIVESTOCK
('000 head, year ending September)

	2003	2004	2005
Cattle	3,376	3,561	3,756
Sheep	1,027	1,096	1,169
Goats	1,226	1,308	1,396
Pigs	67.9	71.3	74.8
Chickens	14,120	14,967	15,865

Source: FAO.

LIVESTOCK PRODUCTS
('000 metric tons, FAO estimates)

	2003	2004	2005
Cattle meat	33.9	35.5	36.8
Chicken meat	4.5	4.7	5.1
Sheep meat	4.0	4.3	4.5
Goat meat	5.3	5.6	6.0
Other meat	5.8	5.9	6.0
Cows' milk	79.0	81.8	84.6
Goats' milk	6.7	7.2	7.6
Hen eggs	16.7	17.3	18.6

Source: FAO.

Forestry

ROUNDWOOD REMOVALS
('000 cubic metres, excl. bark, FAO estimates)

	2003	2004	2005
Sawlogs, veneer logs and logs for sleepers	138	138	138
Other industrial wood	513	513	513
Fuel wood	11,585	11,635	11,687
Total	12,236	12,286	12,338

Source: FAO.

SAWNWOOD PRODUCTION
('000 cubic metres, incl. railway sleepers)

	1998	1999	2000
Total (all broadleaved)	26	26*	26*

* FAO estimate.

2001–05: Figures assumed to be unchanged from 2000 (FAO estimates).

Source: FAO.

Fishing

('000 metric tons, live weight)

	2003	2004	2005*
Freshwater fishes*	4.0	4.0	4.0
Sea catfishes	11.8	6.0	6.0
Bobo croaker	9.8	7.7	8.0
West African croakers	3.2	2.5	2.5
Sardinellas	3.7	1.4	1.5
Bonga shad	52.8	32.4	34.0
Total catch (incl. others)*	120.2	93.9	96.6

* FAO estimates.

Source: FAO.

Mining

('000 metric tons, unless otherwise indicated)

	2003	2004	2005*
Bauxite (dry basis)†	15,000	15,254	15,200
Gold (kilograms)‡	16,622	11,100	15,300
Salt (unrefined)*	15	15	15
Diamonds ('000 carats)‡	666	740	550

* Estimates.
† Estimated to be 3% water.
‡ Including artisanal production.

Source: US Geological Survey.

Industry

SELECTED PRODUCTS
('000 metric tons, unless otherwise indicated)

	2000	2001	2002
Salted, dried or smoked fish*	11.0	11.0	11.0
Palm oil (unrefined)*†	50	50	50
Beer of barley*†	11.5	7.8	7.8
Raw sugar*	25‡	25†	25†
Alumina (calcined equivalent)§	571	644	680
Electric energy (million kWh)†	569	796	798

* Data from FAO.
† Estimate(s).
‡ Unofficial figure.
§ Data from the US Geological Survey.

Alumina ('000 metric tons, calcined equivalent): 730 in 2003; 877 in 2004; 730 in 2005 (estimate) (Source: US Geological Survey).

Electric energy (million kWh): 801 in 2003; 801 in 2004.

Source: mainly FAO; UN, *Industrial Commodity Statistics Yearbook*.

Finance

CURRENCY AND EXCHANGE RATES

Monetary Units
100 centimes = 1 franc guinéen (FG or Guinean franc).

Sterling, Dollar and Euro Equivalents (29 September 2006)
£1 sterling = 10,465.643 Guinean francs;
US $1 = 5,596.000 Guinean francs;
€1 = 7,084.540 Guinean francs;
100,000 Guinean francs = £9.55 = $17.87 = €14.12.

Average Exchange Rate (Guinean francs per US $)
2003 1,984.9
2004 2,225.0
2005 3,644.3

BUDGET
('000 million Guinean francs)

Revenue*	2004	2005†	2006†
Mining-sector revenue	171.0	348.8	495.8
Other revenue	765.0	1,086.8	1,302.6
Tax revenue	702.3	1,002.2	1,202.3
Taxes on income and profits	117.6	168.6	199.8
Taxes on domestic production and trade	402.8	557.9	660.6
Value-added tax (VAT)‡	268.8	n.a.	n.a.
Excise surcharge	14.9	n.a.	n.a.
Petroleum excise tax	88.8	n.a.	n.a.
Taxes on international trade	181.9	275.7	341.9
Import duties	144.2	n.a.	n.a.
Total	936.0	1,435.6	1,798.4

Expenditure§	2004	2005†	2006†
Current expenditure	1,015.9	1,183.1	1,382.3
Wages and salaries	274.8	337.6	381.3
Other goods and services	255.7	320.6	380.0
Subsidies and transfers	260.4	237.3	288.3
Interest due on external debt	120.6	160.4	192.7
Interest due on domestic debt	104.3	127.3	140.0
Capital expenditure	444.0	484.7	578.6
Domestically financed	181.1	183.8	227.9
Externally financed	262.9	300.9	350.6
Restructuring of banking system	3.6	2.1	2.2
Total	1,463.5	1,669.9	1,963.1

* Excluding grants received ('000 million Guinean francs): 91.4 in 2004; 95.8 in 2005 (projection); 103.2 in 2006 (projection).
† Projections.
‡ Includes value-added tax on imports.
§ Excluding lending minus repayments ('000 million Guinean francs): 0.7 in 2004; 2.8 in 2005 (projection); 3.4 in 2006 (projection).

Source: mostly IMF, *Guinea: Selected Issues and Statistical Appendix* (January 2006).

INTERNATIONAL RESERVES
(US $ million at 31 December)

	2004	2005
Gold (national valuation)	1.29	1.27
IMF special drawing rights	—	0.02
Reserve position in IMF	0.12	0.11
Foreign exchange	110.37	94.93
Total	111.78	96.33

2003 (US $ million at 31 December): IMF special drawing rights 0.22; Reserve position in IMF 0.11.

Source: IMF, *International Financial Statistics*.

MONEY SUPPLY
(million Guinean francs at 31 December)

	2003	2004	2005
Currency outside banks	478,133	536,169	786,587
Demand deposits at commercial banks	386,359	518,469	590,420
Total (incl. others)	893,055	1,143,312	1,394,203

Source: IMF, *International Financial Statistics*.

COST OF LIVING
(Consumer Price Index for Conakry; base: 2002 = 100)

	2003	2004
Foodstuffs, beverages and tobacco	116.1	147.1
Clothing and shoes	108.0	109.8
Housing, water, electricity and gas	104.5	114.0
All items (incl. others)	109.1	115.0

Source: IMF, *Guinea: Selected Issues and Statistical Appendix* (January 2006).

NATIONAL ACCOUNTS

Expenditure on the Gross Domestic Product
('000 million Guinean francs at current prices)

	2004	2005*	2006*
Government final consumption expenditure	566.8	689.5	799.3
Private final consumption expenditure	7,827.0	10,128.0	11,903.5
Gross fixed capital formation	976.2	1,435.0	1,874.8
Change in stocks	1.1	0.9	0.5
Total domestic expenditure	9,371.1	12,253.4	14,578.1
Exports of goods and services	1,868.5	3,219.3	3,919.8
Less Imports of goods and services	2,235.7	3,534.2	4,307.1
GDP at market prices	9,004.1	11,938.5	14,190.8

* Projections.

Gross Domestic Product by Economic Activity
('000 million Guinean francs at constant 1996 prices)

	2004	2005*	2006*
Agriculture, livestock, forestry and fishing	956.5	987.6	1,034.5
Mining	834.3	856.0	884.2
Manufacturing	198.5	201.5	211.5
Electricity and water	27.8	28.1	29.3
Construction	527.5	560.8	608.1
Trade	1,302.5	1,319.5	1,353.1
Transport	288.4	292.5	302.8
Administration	267.4	270.4	278.5
Other services	514.6	528.0	546.2
GDP at factor cost	4,917.7	5,044.2	5,248.2
Indirect taxes	199.1	225.4	282.4
GDP at constant prices	5,116.8	5,269.6	5,530.6

* Projections.

Source: IMF, *Guinea: Selected Issues and Statistical Appendix* (January 2006).

BALANCE OF PAYMENTS
(US $ million)

	2002	2003	2004
Exports of goods f.o.b.	708.6	609.3	725.6
Imports of goods f.o.b.	−668.5	−644.3	−688.4
Trade balance	40.1	−35.0	37.2
Exports of services	90.5	133.7	85.4
Imports of services	−330.6	−307.3	−275.2
Balance on goods and services	−200.1	−208.6	−152.7
Other income received	6.1	12.6	9.8
Other income paid	−51.6	−124.3	−37.1
Balance on goods, services and income	−245.6	−320.3	−180.0
Current transfers received	70.5	194.6	55.1
Current transfers paid	−24.8	−61.7	−49.9
Current balance	−199.8	−187.5	−174.8
Capital account (net)	91.9	57.6	−30.2
Direct investment from abroad	30.0	79.0	—
Portfolio investment assets	5.1	−4.6	14.8
Other investment assets	−71.0	−4.4	49.5
Other investment liabilities	−79.2	−11.4	13.4
Net errors and omissions	143.1	−157.1	68.6
Overall balance	−79.8	−228.5	−58.6

Source: IMF, *International Financial Statistics*.

External Trade

PRINCIPAL COMMODITIES
(US $ million)

Imports c.i.f.	2000	2001	2002
Food and live animals	110.0	110.9	115.1
Cereals and cereal preparations	55.9	61.2	63.0
Rice	28.8	33.2	43.0
Rice, semi-milled or wholly milled	28.5	32.7	42.9
Rice, semi-milled or milled (unbroken)	17.0	20.3	16.2
Rice, broken	11.5	12.3	26.7
Sugar, sugar preparations and honey	15.5	18.1	21.3
Sugar and honey	13.8	17.1	19.9
Refined sugar, etc.	13.5	16.8	19.3
Beverages and tobacco	26.3	22.1	25.3
Tobacco and tobacco manufactures	23.6	19.2	22.3
Cigarettes	23.0	18.7	21.8
Mineral fuels, lubricants, etc.	152.8	112.0	144.3
Petroleum products, refined	151.6	111.1	139.9
Chemicals and related products	51.6	65.7	82.3
Inorganic chemicals	6.2	25.5	24.0
Inorganic chemical elements, oxides and halogen salts	4.1	17.2	16.7
Medicinal and pharmaceutical products	23.3	15.7	34.2
Medicaments (incl. veterinary medicaments)	21.6	14.2	33.6
Medicaments (incl. veterinary medicaments) containing other substances	21.5	14.0	29.1
Basic manufactures	81.5	83.4	102.8

Imports c.i.f.—*continued*	2000	2001	2002
Non-metallic mineral manufactures	19.0	28.4	37.0
Lime, cement and fabricated construction materials	13.7	22.4	30.7
Cement	12.7	19.2	27.9
Iron and steel	19.3	16.1	21.6
Machinery and transport equipment	116.2	149.7	127.2
General industrial machinery, equipment and parts	22.8	37.1	31.7
Road vehicles	53.1	61.8	49.8
Passenger motor vehicles (excl. buses)	26.3	36.6	32.1
Miscellaneous manufactured articles	51.0	39.2	42.5
Total (incl. others)	612.4	600.8	666.5

Exports f.o.b.	2000	2001	2002
Crude materials (inedible) except fuels	283.5	310.8	277.6
Aluminium ore and concentrate	269.9	309.8	257.3
Chemicals and related products	56.9	98.6	90.0
Aluminium hydroxide	56.9	98.4	89.9
Miscellaneous manufactured articles	61.9	15.5	8.4
Unused postage; stamp-impressed papers; stock; cheque books, etc.	61.3	14.7	8.1
Gold, non-monetary, (excl. gold ores and concentrates) unwrought or semi-manufactured	96.3	118.6	129.9
Total (incl. others)	522.4	574.9	525.4

Source: UN, *International Trade Statistics Yearbook*.

PRINCIPAL TRADING PARTNERS
(US $ million)

Imports c.i.f.	2000	2001	2002
Australia	7.2	11.9	18.0
Belgium	47.4	78.9	42.6
Brazil	2.7	2.3	9.5
China, People's Republic	28.4	32.4	43.7
Côte d'Ivoire	130.9	76.4	96.9
Cyprus	9.6	0.3	n.a.
Denmark	4.1	9.5	1.3
France (incl. Monaco)	121.2	104.8	107.7
Gabon	7.3	3.6	9.6
Germany	19.2	13.6	21.8
Hong Kong	6.1	6.0	8.9
India	11.4	9.3	20.9
Indonesia	5.6	6.5	9.0
Italy	21.0	20.6	29.5
Japan	34.2	23.2	36.3
Netherlands	14.3	28.7	11.8
Senegal	4.0	6.8	2.8
South Africa	3.9	9.9	8.1
Spain	11.5	17.8	12.6
Switzerland-Liechtenstein	4.5	9.6	8.9
Thailand	5.8	11.4	7.5
Ukraine	4.6	3.7	10.0
United Arab Emirates	4.2	6.1	7.9
United Kingdom	9.2	15.8	15.7
USA	48.4	42.8	55.3
Total (incl. others)	612.4	600.8	666.5

Exports f.o.b.	2000	2001	2002
Australia	—	—	9.2
Belgium	2.7	16.0	20.5
Cameroon	9.6	15.5	4.2
Canada	17.2	15.8	21.6
China, People's Republic	—	—	9.8
France (incl. Monaco)	172.6	149.7	127.9
Germany	32.1	37.6	42.1
Hungary	5.8	—	—
Ireland	47.5	65.1	53.5
Malta	6.3	—	—
Morocco	7.3	5.6	1.7
Netherlands	0.3	7.3	6.6
Romania	1.8	—	7.0
Russia	21.6	44.6	33.8
Seychelles	5.8	0.3	—
Spain	50.1	54.6	53.4
Sudan	6.5	—	—
Switzerland-Liechtenstein	26.5	5.5	30.9
Ukraine	15.5	1.6	7.3
United Kingdom	17.4	32.3	29.1
USA	66.7	96.9	46.3
Total (incl. others)	522.4	574.9	525.4

Source: UN, *International Trade Statistics Yearbook*.

Transport

RAILWAYS
(estimated traffic)

	1991	1992	1993
Freight ton-km (million)	660	680	710

Source: UN Economic Commission for Africa, *African Statistical Yearbook*.

ROAD TRAFFIC
('000, motor vehicles in use, estimates)

	2001	2002	2003
Passenger cars	41.6	43.1	47.5
Buses and coaches	24.8	20.5	20.9
Lorries and vans	11.1	10.5	15.7

SHIPPING

Merchant Fleet
(registered at 31 December)

	2004	2005	2006
Number of vessels	38	41	40
Total displacement ('000 grt)	13.4	14.7	18.5

Source: Lloyd's Register-Fairplay, *World Fleet Statistics*.

International Sea-borne Freight Traffic
('000 metric tons)

	2001	2002	2003
Goods loaded	2,424	2,595	2,828
Goods unloaded	2,043	2,178	2,453

CIVIL AVIATION
(traffic on scheduled services)

	1997	1998	1999
Kilometres flown (million)	1	1	1
Passengers carried ('000)	36	36	59
Passenger-km (million)	55	55	94
Total ton-km (million)	6	6	10

Source: UN, *Statistical Yearbook*.

Tourism

FOREIGN VISITOR ARRIVALS*

Country of origin	2003	2004	2005
Belgium	1,067	973	1,353
Canada	914	969	1,144
China, People's Repub.	1,002	1,515	1,562
Côte d'Ivoire	4,504	3,397	3,434
France	10,654	9,168	9,783
Germany	879	920	1,160
Mali	1,659	1,287	1,382
Senegal	4,358	4,993	5,536
Sierra Leone	3,345	2,714	848
USA	2,987	3,121	3,925
Total (incl. others)	43,966	42,041	45,334

* Arrivals of non-resident tourists at national borders, by country of residence.

Receipts from tourism (US $ million, incl. passenger transport): n.a. in 2004; n.a. in 2005.

Source: World Tourism Organization.

Communications Media

	2002	2003	2004
Telephones ('000 main lines in use)	26.0	26.2	26.2
Mobile cellular telephones ('000 subscribers)	90.8	111.5	154.9
Personal computers ('000 in use)	42	43	44
Internet users ('000)	35	40	46

2005: Mobile cellular telephones ('000 subscribers) 189.0.

Source: International Telecommunication Union.

Television receivers ('000 in use): 351 in 2000 (Source: UNESCO, *Statistical Yearbook*).

Radio receivers ('000 in use): 380 in 1999 (Source: UNESCO, *Statistical Yearbook*).

Facsimile machines (number in use, estimate): 3,186 in 1999 (Source: UNESCO, *Statistical Yearbook*).

Non-daily newspapers: 1 title in 1996 (average circulation 20,000) (Source: UNESCO, *Statistical Yearbook*).

Education

(2003/04, unless otherwise indicated)

	Institutions	Teachers	Students ('000) Males	Females	Total
Pre-primary	202*	1,895	34.5	33.4	67.9
Primary	5,765	25,361	650.3	497.1	1,147.4
Secondary	557	10,465	239.5	109.2	348.7
Technical	41	n.a.	3.3	3.9	7.2
University	7	860	13.5	2.7	16.4

* 1996/97.

Source: partly UNESCO Institute for Statistics.

Adult literacy rate (UNESCO estimate): 53.9% in 2004 (males 60.8%; females 38.6%) in 2004 (Source: UN Development Programme, *Human Development Report*).

Directory

The Constitution

The Constitution (*Loi fondamentale*) of the Third Republic of Guinea was adopted in a national referendum on 23 December 1990 and promulgated on 23 December 1991. An 'organic law' of 3 April 1992, providing for the immediate establishment of an unlimited number of political parties, countermanded the Constitution's provision for the eventual establishment of a two-party political system. There was to be a five-year period of transition, overseen by a Comité transitoire de redressement national (CTRN), to civilian rule, at the end of which executive and legislative authority would be vested in organs of state elected by universal adult suffrage in the context of a multi-party political system. The CTRN was dissolved following the legislative elections of June 1995. Amendments to provisions concerning the President were approved by referendum in November 2001.

The Constitution defines the clear separation of the powers of the executive, the legislature and the judiciary. The President of the Republic, who is Head of State, must be elected by an absolute majority of the votes cast, and a second round of voting is held should no candidate obtain such a majority at a first round. The duration of the presidential mandate is seven years, and elections are by universal adult suffrage. Any candidate for the presidency must be more than 40 years old, must not be a serving member of the armed forces, and must be proposed by a political party. There are no restrictions on the number of terms of office the President may serve. The President is Head of Government, and is empowered to appoint ministers and to delegate certain functions. The legislature is the 114-member Assemblée nationale. One-third of the Assemblée's members are elected as representatives of single-member constituencies, the remainder being appointed from national lists, according to a system of proportional representation. The legislature is elected, by universal suffrage, with a five-year mandate.

The Government

HEAD OF STATE

President: Gen. LANSANA CONTÉ (took office 4 April 1984; elected 19 December 1993; re-elected 14 December 1998 and 21 December 2003).

COUNCIL OF MINISTERS
(August 2007)

Prime Minister: LANSANA KOUYATÉ.

Minister of the Economy, Finance and Planning: OUSMANE DORÉ.

Minister of Foreign Affairs, Co-operation, African Integration and Guineans Abroad: ABDOUL KABÈLÈ CAMARA.

Minister of National Defence: Gen. BAILO DIALLO.

Minister of the Interior and Security: MAMADOU M'BOH KEÏTA.

Minister of Justice and Human Rights: PAULETTE KOUROUMA.

Minister of Economic and Financial Control, Ethics and Transparency: SAIDOU DIALLO.

Minister of Mines and Geology: AHMED KANTÉ.

Minister of Energy and Water Resources: GOMOU GNANGA KOUMATA.

Minister of Agriculture, Livestock, the Environment, Water and Forests: Dr MAMADOU CAMARA.

Minister of Fishing and Aquaculture: MOHAMED YOULA.

Minister of Trade, Industry, Tourism and Handicrafts: MAMADI TRAORÉ.

Minister of Public Works, Town Planning and Housing: THIERNO OUMAR BAH.

Minister of Transport: BOUBACAR SOW.

Minister of Communication and Information Technology: JUSTIN MOREL JUNIOR.

Minister of National Education and Scientific Research: Dr OUSMANE SOUARÉ.

Minister of Youth, Culture and Sports: BAIDI ARIBOT.

Minister of Public Health: SANGARÉ MAÏMOUNA BAH.

Minister of Social Affairs and the Promotion of Women and Children: HADJA TETE NABE.

Minister of Employment, Public Service and Administrative Reform: AMADOU DIALLO.

Secretary-General at the Presidency: SAM MAMADOU SOUMAH.

Secretary-General of the Government: El Hadj OURY BAILO BAH.

Secretary-General of Religious Affairs: MAHMOUD CHÉRIF NABANIOU.

MINISTRIES

Office of the President: BP 1000, Boulbinet, Conakry; tel. 30-41-10-16; fax 30-41-16-73.

Office of the Prime Minister: BP 5141, Conakry; tel. 30-41-51-19; fax 30-41-52-82.

Office of the Secretary-General of the Government: Boulbinet, Conakry; tel. 30-41-11-27.

Office of the Secretary-General at the Presidency: Conakry.

Office of the Secretary-General of Religious Affairs: BP 386, Conakry; tel. 30-41-23-38.

Ministry of Agriculture, Livestock, the Environment, Water and Forests: face à la Cité du Port, BP 576, Conakry; tel. 30-41-11-81; fax 30-41-11-69.

Ministry of Communication and Information Technology: Conakry.

Ministry of Economic and Financial Control, Ethics and Transparency: Conakry.

Ministry of the Economy, Finance and Planning: Boulbinet, BP 221, Conakry; tel. 30-45-17-95; fax 30-41-30-59.

Ministry of Employment, Public Service and Administrative Reform: Boulbinet, Conakry; tel. 30-45-20-01.

Ministry of Energy and Water Resources: Conakry; tel. 30-41-31-90.

Ministry of Fishing and Aquaculture: face à la Cité du Port, BP 307, Conakry; tel. 30-41-35-23; fax 30-41-35-28.

Ministry of Foreign Affairs, Co-operation, African Integration and Guineans Abroad: face au Port, ex-Primature, BP 2519, Conakry; tel. 30-45-12-70; fax 30-41-16-21.

Ministry of the Interior and Security: Coléah-Domino, Conakry; tel. 30-41-45-50.

Ministry of Justice and Human Rights: face à l'Immeuble 'La Paternelle', Almamya, Conakry; tel. 30-41-29-60.

Ministry of Mines and Geology: BP 295, Conakry; tel. 30-41-38-33; fax 30-41-49-13.

Ministry of National Defence: Camp Samory-Touré, Conakry; tel. 41-11-54.

Ministry of National Education and Scientific Research: face à la Cathédrale Sainte-Marie, BP 964, Conakry; tel. 30-45-12-17; fax 30-41-20-12.

Ministry of Public Health: blvd du Commerce, BP 585, Conakry; tel. 30-41-20-32; fax 30-41-41-38.

Ministry of Public Works, Town Planning and Housing: Conakry; tel. 30-41-35-60.

Ministry of Social Affairs and the Promotion of Women and Children: Corniche-Ouest, face au Terminal Conteneurs du Port de Conakry, BP 527, Conakry; tel. 30-41-20-15; fax 30-41-46-60.

Ministry of Trade, Industry, Tourism and Handicrafts: BP 468, Conakry; tel. 30-44-26-06; fax 30-44-49-90.

Ministry of Transport: BP 715, Conakry; tel. 30-41-36-39; fax 30-41-35-77.

Ministry of Youth, Sports and Culture: ave du Port Secrétariat, BP 262, Conakry; tel. 30-41-19-59; fax 30-41-19-26.

President and Legislature

PRESIDENT

Election, 21 December 2003

Candidate	Votes	% of votes
Lansana Conté (PUP)	3,884,594	95.25
Mamadou Bhoye Barry (UPN—PUD)	193,579	4.75
Total	4,078,173	100.00

LEGISLATURE

Assemblée nationale

Palais du Peuple, BP 414, Conakry; tel. 30-41-28-04; fax 30-45-17-00; e-mail s.general@assemblee.gov.gn; internet www.assemblee.gov.gn.

Speaker: ABOUBACAR SOMPARÉ.

General Election, 30 June 2002

Party	% of votes	Seats
Parti de l'unité et du progrès (PUP)	61.57	85
Union pour le progrès et le renouveau (UPR)	26.63	20
Union pour le progrès de la Guinée (UPG)	4.11	3
Parti démocratique de Guinée—Rassemblement démocratique africain (PDG—RDA)	3.40	3
Alliance nationale pour le progrès (ANP)	1.98	2
Union pour le progrès national—Parti pour l'unité et le développement (UPN—PUD)	0.69	1
Others	1.61	—
Total	100.00	114*

* Comprising 76 seats allocated by proportional representation from national party lists and 38 seats filled by voting in single-member constituencies, all of which were won by the PUP.

Election Commission

Commission électorale nationale autonome (CENA): Villa 17, Cité des Nations, Conakry; f. 2005; comprises seven representatives of the parliamentary majority, seven representatives of the parliamentary opposition, five representatives of the state administration and three representatives of civil society; Pres. Dr RACHID TOURÉ.

Advisory Council

Conseil Économique et Social: Immeuble FAWAZ, Corniche Sud, Coléah, Matam, BP 2947, Conakry; tel. 30-45-31-23; fax 30-45-31-24; e-mail ces@sotelgui.net.gn; f. 1997; 45 mems; Pres. MICHEL KAMANO; Sec.-Gen. MAMADOU BOBO CAMARA.

Political Organizations

There were 46 officially registered parties in mid-2003, of which the following are the most important:

Alliance nationale pour le progrès (ANP): Conakry; opposes Govt of Pres. Conté; Leader Dr SAGNO MOUSSA.

Front de l'alternance démocratique (FRAD): Conakry; f. 2002; opposes Govt of Pres. Conté; boycotted legislative elections in 2002 and presidential election in 2003; Pres. MAMADOU BOYE BÂ; affiliated parties include:

- **Alliance nationale pour le developpement:** Conakry; Sec.-Gen. ANTOINE GBOKOLO SOROMOU.
- **Parti démocratique africain (PDA):** Conakry; Pres. MARCEL CROS.
- **Parti Dyama:** Conakry; moderate Islamist party; Leader MOHAMED MANSOUR KABA.
- **Rassemblement du peuple de Guinée (RPG):** Conakry; e-mail admin@rpgguinee.org; internet www.rpgguinee.org; socialist; Pres. ALPHA CONDÉ.
- **Union des forces démocratiques (UFD):** Conakry; Pres. MAMADOU BAADIKKO BAH.

Union des forces démocratiques de Guinée (UFDG): Conakry; f. 2002 by faction of UPR (q.v.) in protest at that party's participation in elections to Assemblée nationale; Pres. MAMADOU BOYE BÂ; Sec.-Gen. AMADOU OURY BAH.

Union des forces républicaines (UFR): Immeuble 'Le Golfe', 4e étage, BP 6080, Conakry; tel. 30-45-42-38; fax 30-45-42-31; e-mail ufrguinee@yahoo.fr; internet www.ufrguinee.net; f. 1992; liberal-conservative; Pres. SIDYA TOURÉ; Sec.-Gen. BAKARY G. ZOUMANIGUI.

Union pour le progrès de la Guinée (UPG): Conakry; opposes Govt of Pres. Conté; Leader JEAN-MARIE DORÉ.

Parti démocratique de Guinée—Rassemblement démocratique africain (PDG—RDA): Conakry; f. 1946; revived 1992; supports Govt of Pres. Conté; Sec.-Gen. El Hadj ISMAËL MOHAMED GASSIM GHUSSEIN.

Parti écologiste de Guinée (PEG—Les Verts): BP 3018, Quartier Boulbinet, 5e blvd, angle 2e ave, Commune de Kaloum, Conakry; tel. 30-44-37-01; supports Govt of Pres. Conté; Leader OUMAR SYLLA.

Parti du peuple de Guinée (PPG): BP 1147, Conakry; socialist; opposes Govt of Pres. Conté; boycotted presidential election in 2003, following the Supreme Court's rejection of its nominated candidate; Leader CHARLES-PASCAL TOLNO.

Parti de l'unité et du progrès (PUP): Camayenne, Conakry; Pres. Gen. LANSANA CONTÉ; Sec.-Gen. El Hadj Dr SÉKOU KONATÉ.

Union pour le progrès et le renouveau (UPR): BP 690, Conakry; tel. 30-25-26-01; e-mail basusmane@mirinet.net.gn; internet www.uprguinee.org; f. 1998 by merger of the Parti pour le renouveau et le progrès and the Union pour la nouvelle République; opposes Govt of Pres. Conté; boycotted presidential election in 2003; Pres. OUSMANE BAH.

Union pour le progrès national—Parti pour l'unité et le développement (UPN—PUD): Conakry; Leader MAMADOU BHOYE BARRY.

Diplomatic Representation

EMBASSIES IN GUINEA

Algeria: Cité des Nations, Quartiers Kaloum, BP 1004, Conakry; tel. 30-44-15-05; fax 30-41-15-35.

China, People's Republic: Quartier Donka, Cité Ministérielle, Commune de Dixinn, BP 714, Conakry; tel. 30-41-48-35; fax 30-45-15-26; e-mail chinaemb_gn@mfa.gov.cn; internet gn.chineseembassy.org; Ambassador HUO ZHENGDE.

Congo, Democratic Republic: Quartier Almamya, ave de la Gare, Commune du Kaloum, BP 880, Conakry; tel. 30-45-15-01.

Côte d'Ivoire: blvd du Commerce, BP 5228, Conakry; tel. 30-45-10-82; fax 30-45-10-79; Ambassador JEANNOT ZORO BI BAH.

Cuba: rue DI 256, Corniche Nord, Conakry; tel. 30-46-95-25; fax 30-46-95-28; e-mail embagcon@sotelgui.net.gn; Ambassador MARCELLO CABALLERO TORRES.

Egypt: Corniche Sud, BP 389, Conakry; tel. and fax 30-41-23-94; e-mail ambconakry@hotmail.com; Ambassador MOHAMED ABD ELHAY HASSOUNA.

France: ave du Commerce, BP 373, Conakry; tel. 30-47-10-00; fax 30-47-10-15; e-mail amb.fr.conakry@biasy.net; internet www.ambafrance-gn.org; Ambassador JEAN-MICHEL BERRIT.

Germany: 2e blvd, Kaloum, BP 540, Conakry; tel. 30-41-15-06; fax 30-45-22-17; e-mail amball@sotelgui.net.gn; internet www.conakry.diplo.de; Ambassador KARL PRINZ.

Ghana: Immeuble Ex-Urbaine et la Seine, BP 732, Conakry; tel. 30-44-15-10; Ambassador LAMISI MBILAH.

Guinea-Bissau: Quartier Bellevue, Commune de Dixinn, BP 298, Conakry; Ambassador MALAM CAMARA.

Holy See: La Minière, BP 2016, Conakry; tel. 30-42-26-76; fax 30-46-36-71; e-mail nonce@biasy.net; Apostolic Nuncio Most Rev. GEORGE ANTONYSAMY (Titular Archbishop of Sulci).

Iran: Donka, Cité Ministerielle, Commune de Dixinn, BP 310, Conakry; tel. 30-22-01-97; fax 30-46-56-38; e-mail ambiran_guinea@yahoo.com; Ambassador BAKHTIAR ASADZADEH SHEIKHJANI.

Japan: Lanseboundji, Corniche Sud, Commune de Matam, BP 895, Conakry; tel. 30-46-85-10; fax 30-46-85-09; Ambassador KEIICHI KITABAN.

Korea, Democratic People's Republic: BP 723, Conakry; Ambassador KIM PONG HUI.

Liberia: Cité Ministérielle, Donka, Commune de Dixinn, BP 18, Conakry; tel. 30-42-26-71; Chargé d'affaires a. i. SIAKA FAHNBULLEH.

Libya: Commune de Kaloum, BP 1183, Conakry; tel. 30-41-41-72; Ambassador B. AHMED.

Malaysia: Quartier Mafanco, Corniche Sud, BP 5460, Conakry; tel. 30-22-17-54; e-mail mwcky@sotelgui.net.gn; Ambassador (vacant).

Mali: rue D1–15, Camayenne, Corniche Nord, BP 299, Conakry; tel. 30-46-14-18; fax 30-46-37-03; e-mail ambamaliguinee@yahoo.fr; Ambassador HAMADOUN IBRAHIMA ISSEBERE.

Morocco: Cité des Nations, Villa 12, Commune du Kaloum, BP 193, Conakry; tel. 30-41-36-86; fax 30-41-38-16; e-mail ambargu@sotelgui.net.gn; Ambassador MOHAMED LASFAR.

Nigeria: Corniche Sud, Quartier de Matam, BP 54, Conakry; tel. 30-46-13-41; fax 30-46-27-75; Ambassador ABDULKADIR SANI.

Russia: Matam-Port, km 9, BP 329, Conakry; tel. 30-40-52-22; fax 30-46-57-81; e-mail ambrus@biasy.net; Ambassador DMITRII V. MALEV.

Saudi Arabia: Quartier Camayenne, Commune de Dixinn, BP 611, Conakry; tel. 30-46-24-87; fax 30-46-58-84; e-mail gnemb@mofa.gov.sa; Chargé d'affaires a.i. MOHAMMAD MAHMOUD HILAL.

Senegal: bâtiment 142, Coleah, Corniche Che Sud, BP 842, Conakry; tel. 30-44-61-32; fax 30-46-28-34; Ambassador Gen. CHARLES ANDRÉ NELSON.

Sierra Leone: Quartier Bellevue, face aux cases présidentielles, Commune de Dixinn, BP 625, Conakry; tel. 30-46-40-84; fax 30-41-23-64; Ambassador Dr SHEKU B. SACCOH.

Ukraine: Commune de Calum, Corniche Nord, Quartier Camayenne, BP 1350, Conakry; tel. 30-45-37-56; fax 30-45-37-95; e-mail ambgv@sotelgui.net.gn; Ambassador OLEKSANDR O. SHULHA.

United Kingdom: BP 6729, Conakry; tel. 30-45-58-07; fax 30-45-60-20; e-mail britcon.oury@biasy.net; Ambassador JOHN MCMANUS.

USA: Koloma, Ratoma, BP 603, Conakry; tel. 30-42-08-61; fax 30-42-08-73; e-mail Consularconkr@state.gov; internet conakry.usembassy.gov; Chargé d'affaires a.i. DAVID H. KAEUPER.

Judicial System

The Constitution of the Third Republic embodies the principle of the independence of the judiciary, and delineates the competences of each component of the judicial system, including the Higher Magistrates' Council, the Supreme Court, the High Court of Justice and the Magistrature.

Supreme Court

Corniche-Sud, Camayenne, Conakry; tel. 30-41-29-28; Pres. Me LAMINE SIDIMÉ

Director of Public Prosecutions: ANTOINE IBRAHIM DIALLO.

Note: A State Security Court was established in June 1997, with exceptional jurisdiction to try, 'in times of peace and war', crimes against the internal and external security of the State. Members of the court are appointed by the President of the Republic. There is no constitutional provision for the existence of such a tribunal.

President of the State Security Court: Commdr SAMA PANNIVAL BANGOURA.

Religion

It is estimated that 85% of the population are Muslims and 8% Christians, while 7% follow animist beliefs.

ISLAM

National Islamic League: BP 386, Conakry; tel. 30-41-23-38; f. 1988; Sec.-Gen. (vacant).

CHRISTIANITY

The Roman Catholic Church

Guinea comprises one archdiocese and two dioceses. At 31 December 2004 there were an estimated 233,255 Roman Catholics in Guinea, comprising about 3.5% of the total population.

Bishops' Conference

Conférence Episcopale de la Guinée, BP 1006 bis, Conakry; tel. and fax 30-41-32-70; e-mail dhewara@eti.met.gn; Pres. Most Rev. PHILIPPE KOUROUMA (Bishop of N'Zérékoré).

Archbishop of Conakry: Most Rev. VINCENT COULIBALY, Archevêché, BP 2016, Conakry; tel. and fax 30-41-32-70; e-mail arnaky@sotelgui.gn.

The Anglican Communion

Anglicans in Guinea are adherents of the Church of the Province of West Africa, comprising 12 dioceses. The diocese of Guinea was established in 1985 as the first French-speaking diocese in the

Province. The Archbishop and Primate of the Province is the Bishop of Koforidua, Ghana.

Bishop of Guinea: Rt Rev. ALBERT D. GÓMEZ, Cathédrale Toussaint, BP 105, Conakry; tel. 30-45-13-23.

BAHÁ'Í FAITH

Assemblée spirituelle nationale: BP 2010, Conakry 1; e-mail kouchek@sotelgui.net.gn.

The Press

REGULATORY AUTHORITY

Conseil National de la Communication (CNC): en face Primature, BP 2955, Conakry; tel. 30-45-54-82; fax 30-41-23-85; f. 1991; regulates the operations of the press, and of radio and television; regulates political access to the media; nine mems; Pres. BOUBACAR YACINE DIALLO.

NEWSPAPERS AND PERIODICALS

In early 2004 there were more than 200 periodicals and newspapers officially registered with the National Council of Communication, although only around 60 were believed to be in operation at that time.

Le Démocrate: Quartier Manquepas, 4e ave, axe Soguidip-Ministère des finances, près du restaurant 'Relaxe', Commune de Kaloum, BP 2427, Conakry; tel. 30-45-54-34; fax 30-41-43-19; e-mail mamadoudianb@yahoo.fr; weekly; Editor-in-Chief THIERNO DAYEDIO BARRY.

Le Diplomate: BP 2427, Conakry; tel. and fax 30-41-23-85; f. 2002; weekly; Dir SANOU KERFALLAH CISSÉ.

L'Enquêteur: Conakry; e-mail habib@boubah.com; internet enqueteur.boubah.com; f. 2001; two a month; Editor HABIB YAMBERING DIALLO.

L'Evénement de Guinée: BP 796, Conakry; tel. 30-44-33-91; monthly; independent; f. 1993; Dir BOUBACAR SANKARELA DIALLO.

Fonike: BP 341, Conakry; sport and general; Dir IBRAHIMA KALIL DIARE.

La Guinée Actuelle: Sans Fils, près Le Makity, BP 3618, Conakry; tel. 30-69-36-20.

Le Guinéen: Conakry; f. 2002; Dir JEAN-MARIE MORGAN.

Horoya (Liberty): Coléah, BP 341, Conakry; tel. 30-41-34-75; fax 30-45-10-16; govt daily; Dir OUSMANE CAMARA.

L'Indépendant: Quartier Manquepas, 4e ave, axe Soguidip-Ministère des finances, près du restaurant 'Relaxe', Commune de Kaloum, BP 2427, Conakry; tel. 30-41-57-62; fax 30-41-43-19; e-mail lindependant@afribone.net.gn; weekly; also *L'Indépendant Plus*; Publr ABOUBACAR SYLLA; Editor-in-Chief HASSANE KABA; Editor-in-Chief, *L'Indépendant Plus* ALADJI CELLOU.

Journal Officiel de Guinée: BP 156, Conakry; fortnightly; organ of the Govt.

La Lance: route du Palais du Peuple, BP 4968, Conakry; tel. and fax 30-41-23-85; weekly; general information; Dir SOULEYMANE E. DIALLO.

Le Lynx: Immeuble Baldé Zaïre Sandervalia, BP 4968, Conakry; tel. 30-41-23-85; fax 30-45-36-96; e-mail le-lynx@mirinet.net.gn; internet www.mirinet.net.gn/lynx; f. 1992; weekly; satirical; Editor SOULEYMANE DIALLO.

La Nouvelle Tribune: blvd Diallo Tally entre 5e et 6e ave, BP 35, Conakry; tel. 30-22-33-02; e-mail abdcond@yahoo.fr; weekly, Tuesdays; independent; general information and analysis; Dir of Publication and Editing ABDOULAYE CONDÉ.

L'Observateur: Immeuble Baldé, Conakry; tel. 30-40-05-24; independent; Dir EL-BÉCHIR DIALLO.

L'Oeil du Peuple: BP 3064, Conakry; tel. 30-67-23-78; weekly; independent; Dir of Publishing ISMAËL BANGOURA.

Sanakou: Labé, Foutah Djallon, Moyenne-Guinée; tel. 30-51-13-19; e-mail sanakoulabe@yahoo.fr; f. 2000; monthly; general news; Publr IDRISSA SAMPIRING DIALLO; Editor-in-Chief YAMOUSSA SOUMAH; circ. 1,000.

3-P Plus (Parole-Plume-Papier) Magazine: 7e ave Bis Almamyah, BP 5122, Conakry; tel. 30-45-22-32; fax 30-45-29-31; e-mail 3p-plus@mirinet.net.gn; internet www.mirinet.net.gn/3p_plus; f. 1995; journal of arts and letters; supplements *Le Cahier de l'Economie* and *Mag-Plus: Le Magazine de la Culture*; monthly; Pres. MOHAMED SALIFOU KEÏTA; Editor-in-Chief SAMBA TOURÉ.

NEWS AGENCY

Agence Guinéenne de Presse: BP 1535, Conakry; tel. 30-46-54-14; f. 1960; Man. Dir MOHAMED CONDÉ.

PRESS ASSOCIATION

Association Guinéenne des Editeurs de la Presse Indépendante (AGEPI): Conakry; f. 1991; an asscn of independent newspaper publishers; Chair. BOUBACAR SANKARELA DIALLO.

Publishers

Les Classiques Guinéens (SEDIS sarl): 545 rue KA020, Mauquepas, BP 3697, Conakry; tel. 11-21-18-57; fax 13-40-92-62; e-mail cheick.sedis@mirinet.net.gn; f. 1999; art, history, youth literature; Dir CHEICK ABDOUL KABA.

Editions du Ministère de l'Education Nationale: Direction nationale de la recherche scientifique, BP 561, Conakry; tel. 30-45-43-06; f. 1959; general and educational; Deputy Dir Dr TAMBA TAGBINO.

Editions Ganndal (Knowledge): BP 542, Conakry; tel. and fax 30-46-35-07; e-mail ganndal@mirinet.net.gn; f. 1992; educational, youth and children, general literature and books in Pular; Dir MAMADOU ALIOU SOW.

Société Africaine d'Edition et de Communication (SEAC): Belle-Vue, Commune de Dixinn, BP 6826, Conakry; tel. 30-29-71-41; e-mail dtniane@yahoo.fr; social sciences, reference, literary fiction; Editorial Assistant OUMAR TALL.

Broadcasting and Communications

TELECOMMUNICATIONS

Regulatory Bodies

Comité National de Coordination des Télécommunications (CNCT): BP 5000, Conakry; tel. 30-41-40-79; fax 30-45-31-16; Exec. Sec. SEKOU BANGOURA.

Direction Nationale des Postes et Télécommunications (DNPT): BP 5000, Conakry; tel. 30-41-13-31; fax 30-45-31-16; e-mail dnpt.dnr@biasy.net; f. 1997; regulates transport, postal and telecommunications services; Dir KOLY CAMARA.

Service Providers

Intercel: Quartier Coleah Larseboundji, près du pont du 8 Novembre, Immeuble le Golfe, BP 965, Conakry; tel. 30-45-57-44; fax 30-40-92-92; e-mail info@gn.intercel.net; mobile cellular telephone operator; fmrly Telecel Guinée; Dir FRANÇOIS DICK.

Société des Télécommunications de Guinée (SOTELGUI): 4e blvd, BP 2066, Conakry; tel. 30-41-12-12; fax 30-45-02-01; e-mail marzuki@sotelgui.net.gn; f. 1993; privatized 1995; 60% owned by Telekom Malaysia; 40% state-owned; also provides mobile cellular services (as Lagui); 161,800 subscribers (Sept. 2005); Dir El Hadj MARZUKI ABDULLAH.

Spacetel Guinée SA (Mobilis Guinée): BP 835, Conakry; tel. and fax 12-66-00-11; e-mail info@spacetelguinee.com; f. 1994; mobile cellular telephone operator; operates with a range of 70km around Conakry; 35,000 subscribers (2002); also operates GSM satellite telephone network; Chair. K. ABOU KHALIL.

BROADCASTING

Regulatory Authority

Conseil National de la Communication (CNC): see The Press.

In mid-2005 a presidential decree permitted the creation of private radio and television stations in Guinea, subject to certain conditions. Political parties and religious organizations were to be prohibited from creating broadcast media, however, while restrictions were to be placed on foreign ownership of radio and television stations.

Radio

Radiodiffusion-Télévision Guinéenne (RTG): BP 391, Conakry; tel. 30-44-22-01; fax 30-41-50-01; broadcasts in French, English, Créole-English, Portuguese, Arabic and local languages; Dir-Gen. AISSATOU BELLA DIALLO; Dir of Radio ISSA CONDÉ.

Radio Rurale de Guinée: BP 391, Conakry; tel. 30-42-11-09; fax 30-41-47-97; e-mail ruralgui@mirinet.net.gn; network of rural radio stations.

Television

Radiodiffusion-Télévision Guinéenne (RTG): see Radio; transmissions in French and local languages; one channel; f. 1977.

Finance

(cap. = capital; res = reserves; m. = million; brs = branches; amounts in Guinean francs)

BANKING

Central Bank

Banque Centrale de la République de Guinée (BCRG): 12 blvd du Commerce, BP 692, Kaloum, Conakry; tel. 30-41-26-51; fax 30-41-48-98; e-mail gouv.bcrg@eti-bull.net; internet www.bcrg.gov.gn; f. 1960; bank of issue; Gov. ALKALY MOHAMED DAFFE; Dep. Gov. DAOUDA BANGOURA.

Commercial Banks

Banque Internationale pour le Commerce et l'Industrie de la Guinée (BICIGUI): ave de la République, BP 1484, Conakry; tel. 30-41-45-15; fax 30-41-39-62; e-mail dg.bicigui@biasy.net; internet www.bicigui.com; f. 1985; 38.1% state-owned, 18.8% by BNP Paribas BDDI Participations (France); cap. and res 37,989.3m., total assets 315,689.5m. (Dec. 2003); Pres. IBRAHIMA SOUMAH; Dir-Gen. BERNARD DELEUZE; 11 brs.

Banque Populaire Maroco-Guinéenne (BPMG): Immeuble BPMG, blvd du Commerce, Kaloum, BP 4400, Conakry 01; tel. 30-41-36-93; fax 30-41-32-61; e-mail bpmg@sotelgui.net.gn; f. 1991; 55% owned by Crédit Populaire du Maroc, 42% state-owned; cap. and res 9,936m., total assets 65,549m. (Dec. 2004); Pres. EMMANUEL GNAN; Dir-Gen. AHMED IRAQUI HOUSSAINI; 3 brs.

Ecobank Guinée: Immeuble Al Iman, ave de la République, BP 5687, Conakry; tel. 30-45-58-77; fax 30-45-42-41; e-mail ecobankgn@ecobank.com; internet www.ecobank.com; f. 1999; wholly owned by Ecobank Transnational Inc. (Togo—operating under the auspices of the Economic Community of West African States); cap. and res 6,474.2m., total assets 70,602.9m. (Dec. 2001); Pres. SANGARE N'FALY; Man. Dir KUMLAN ADJARHO OWEH; 2 brs.

First American Bank of Guinea: blvd du Commerce, angle 9e ave, BP 4540, Conakry; tel. 30-41-34-32; fax 30-41-35-29; f. 1994; jointly owned by Mitan Capital Ltd, Grand Cayman and El Hadj Haidara Abdourahmane Chérif, Mali.

International Commercial Bank: 4e ave Boulbinet, Bâtiment 346, BP 3547, Conakry; tel. 30-41-25-89; fax 30-41-25-92; f. 1997; total assets 19.6m. (Dec. 1999); Pres. JOSÉPHINE PREMLA; Man. Dir HAMZA BIN ALIAS.

Société Générale de Banques en Guinée (SGBG): Immeuble Boffa, Cité du Chemin de Fer, BP 1514, Conakry; tel. 30-45-60-00; fax 30-41-25-65; e-mail contact@sgbg.net.gn; internet www.sgbg.net.gn; f. 1985; 53% owned by Société Générale (France); cap. and res 13,074m., total assets 228,196m. (Dec. 2003); Pres. GÉRALD LACAZE; 5 brs.

Union Internationale de Banques en Guinée (UIBG): 6e ave de la République, angle 5e blvd, BP 324, Conakry; tel. 30-41-43-09; fax 30-97-26-30; e-mail uibg@financial-bank.com; f. 1988; cap. and res 5,700m., total assets 104,000m. (Dec. 2004); Pres. ALPHA AMADOU DIALLO; Dir-Gen. JACQUES DE VIGNAUD.

Islamic Bank

Banque Islamique de Guinée: Immeuble Nafaya, 6 ave de la République, BP 1247, Conakry; tel. 30-41-50-86; fax 30-41-50-71; e-mail bigdmiconakry@biasy.net; f. 1983; 51% owned by Dar al-Maal al-Islami Trust (Switzerland); cap. and res 2,368.5m., total assets 26,932.1m. (Dec. 2003); Pres. ADERRAOUF BENESSAIAH; Dir-Gen. AZHAR SALEEM KHAN.

INSURANCE

Gras Savoye Guinée: 4e ave, angle 4e blvd, Quartier Boulbinet, Commune de Kaloum, Conakry; tel. 30-45-58-43; fax 30-45-58-42; e-mail grasavoye@biasy.net; affiliated to Gras Savoye (France); Man. CHÉRIF BAH.

Société Guinéenne d'Assurance Mutuelle (SOGAM): Immeuble Sonia, BP 434, Conakry; tel. 30-44-50-58; fax 30-41-25-57; f. 1990; Chair. Dr M. K. BAH; Man. Dir P. I. NDAO.

Société Nouvelle d'Assurance de Guinée (SONAG): BP 3363, Conakry; tel. 30-41-49-77; fax 30-41-43-03.

Union Guinéenne d'Assurances et de Réassurances (UGAR): pl. des Martyrs, BP 179, Conakry; tel. 30-41-48-41; fax 30-41-17-11; e-mail ugar@ugar.com.gn; f. 1989; 40% owned by AXA (France), 35% state-owned; cap. 2,000m.; Man. Dir RAPHAËL Y. TOURÉ.

Trade and Industry

GOVERNMENT AGENCIES

Centre de Promotion et de Développement Miniers (CPDM): BP 295, Conakry; tel. 30-41-15-44; fax 30-41-49-13; e-mail cpdm@mirinet.net.gn; f. 1995; promotes investment and co-ordinates devt strategy in mining sector; Dir MOCIRÉ SYLLA.

Entreprise Nationale Import-Export (IMPORTEX): BP 152, Conakry; tel. 30-44-28-13; state-owned import and export agency; Dir MAMADOU BOBO DIENG.

Office de Développement de la Pêche Artisanale et de l'Aquaculture en Guinée (ODEPAG): 6 ave de la République, BP 1581; Conakry; tel. 30-44-19-48; development of fisheries and fish-processing.

Office de Promotion des Investissements Privés-Guichet Unique (OPIP): Conakry; tel. 30-41-49-85; fax 30-41-39-90; e-mail dg@opip.org.gn; f. 1992; promotes private investment; Dir-Gen. DIANKA KOEVOGUI.

DEVELOPMENT ORGANIZATIONS

Agence Française de Développement (AFD): 5e ave, KA022, BP 283, Conakry; tel. 30-41-25-69; fax 30-41-28-74; e-mail afdconakry@groupe-afd.org; internet www.afd.fr; Country Dir MARC DUBERNET.

Association Française des Volontaires du Progrès (AFVP): BP 570, Conakry; tel. 30-35-08-60; e-mail afvp-gui@biasy.net; internet www.afvp.org; f. 1987; development and research projects; Nat. Delegate FRANCK DAGOIS.

Mission Française de Coopération et d'Action Culturelle: BP 373, Conakry; tel. 30-41-23-45; fax 30-41-43-56; administers bilateral aid; Dir in Guinea ANDRÉ BAILLEUL.

CHAMBERS OF COMMERCE

Chambre de Commerce, d'Industrie et de l'Artisanat de la Guinée (CCIAG): BP 545, Conakry; tel. 30-45-45-16; fax 30-45-45-17; f. 1985; Pres. El Hadj MAMADOU SYLLA.

Chambre Economique de Guinée: BP 609, Conakry.

TRADE AND EMPLOYERS' ASSOCIATIONS

Association des Commerçants de Guinée: BP 2468, Conakry; tel. 30-41-30-37; fax 30-45-31-66; Sec.-Gen. OUMAR CAMARA.

Association des Femmes Entrepreneurs de Guinée (AFEG): BP 104, Conakry; tel. 60-28-02-95; e-mail afeguine@yahoo.fr; f. 1987; Pres. HADJA RAMATOULAYE SOW.

Conseil National du Patronat Guinéen (CNPG): Dixinn Bora, BP 6403, Conakry; tel. and fax 30-41-24-70; e-mail msylla@leland-gn.org; f. 1992; Pres. El Hadj MAMADOU SYLLA.

Fédération Patronale de l'Agriculture et de l'Elevage (FEPAE): BP 5684, Conakry; tel. 30-22-95-56; fax 30-41-54-36; Pres. El Hadj MAMDOU SYLLA; Sec.-Gen. MAMADY CAMARA.

Groupement des Importateurs Guinéens (GIG): BP 970, Conakry; tel. 30-42-18-18; fax 30-42-19-19; Pres. FERNAND BANGOURA.

UTILITIES

Electricity

Barrage Hydroélectrique de Garafiri: BP 1770, Conakry; tel. 30-41-50-91; inaugurated 1999.

Electricité de Guinée (EDG): BP 1463, Conakry; tel. 30-45-18-56; fax 30-45-18-53; e-mail di.sogel@biasy.net; f. 2001 to replace Société Guinéenne d'Electricité; majority state-owned; production, transport and distribution of electricity; Dir-Gen. NOUCTAR BARRY.

Water

Service National d'Aménagement des Points d'Eau (SNAPE): BP 2064, Conakry; tel. 30-41-18-93; fax 30-41-50-58; e-mail snape@mirinet.net.gn; supplies water in rural areas.

Société Nationale des Eaux de Guinée (SONEG): Belle-vue, BP 150, Conakry; tel. 30-45-44-77; e-mail oaubot@seg.org.gn; f. 1988; national water co; Dir-Gen. Dr OUSMANE ARIBOT; Sec.-Gen. MAMADOU DIOP.

MAJOR COMPANIES

The following are among the largest companies in terms either of capital investment or employment.

Alumina Company of Guinea (Friguia/ACG): BP 554, Conakry; f. 1999 to control Friguia (f. 1957); majority owned by Russian Aluminium (RusAl), 15% state-owned; mining of bauxite and production of alumina; technical and management agreement with Alcoa (USA); Dir-Gen. ANATOLII PANCHENKO.

AngloGold Ashanti Guinea (SAG): BP 1006, Conakry; tel. 30-41-58-09; fax 30-41-15-80; e-mail ashanti@sotelgui.net.gn; f. 1985 as Société Aurifère de Guinée; name changed 1997; cap. US $20m.; sales US $67.3m. (1999); 85% owned by AngloGold Ashanti Goldfields (Ghana/South Africa); gold prospecting and exploitation at Siguiri; Man. Dir BRENT HOROCHUK; 1,978 employees (2005).

AREDOR: BP 1218, Conakry; tel. 30-44-31-12; internet www.trivalence.com/guinea.html; f. 1981 as Association pour la recherche et l'exploitation de diamants et de l'or; operations suspended 1994, restructured 1996; cap. US $8m.; 85% owned by Trivalence Mining Corpn (Canada); diamond mining.

BONAGUI: Z.I. Matoto, BP 3009, Conakry; tel. 30-47-28-52; fax 30-40-34-53; e-mail esmeli@mininet.com; f. 1986; privately owned; drinks bottling factory; Man. EMMANUEL ESMEL ESSIS; 180 employees (2001).

Ciments de Guinée: BP 3621, Conakry; tel. 30-41-45-12; fax 30-41-45-13; e-mail webmaster-trading@holcim.com; one cement plant (Sinfonia); annual production 400,000 metric tons (2000); 58.7% owned by Holcim (Switzerland), 38.7% state owned; cap. 6,393m. FG; sales US $25m. (2000); Man. Dir PATRICE CHANTON.

Compagnie des Bauxites de Guinée: BP 523, Conakry; tel. 30-44-18-01; fax 30-41-28-14; f. 1964; cap. US $2m.; 51% owned by Halco (Mining) Inc (a consortium of interests from USA, Canada, France, Germany and Australia), 49% state-owned; bauxite mining at Boké; Pres. JOHN L. PERVOLA; Vice-Pres. G. COKER; 3,000 employees (2001).

Compagnie des Eaux Minérales de Guinée (CEG): BP 3023 Conakry; tel. 30-46-16-19; fax 30-41-28-66; e-mail cegcoyah@leland-gn.org; f. 1987; mineral water bottling plant.

Compagnie Shell de Guinée: BP 312, Conakry; tel. 30-46-37-37; fax 30-46-49-12; e-mail corporate@csgcky.simis.com; distribution of petroleum products; owned by Royal Dutch/Shell (Netherlands/United Kingdom); Dir-Gen. CHRISTOPHE BOULANGER.

Mobil Oil Guinea: autoroute Fidel Castro, Commune de Matam, BP 305, Conakry; tel. 30-46-52-74; fax 30-40-92-06; petroleum and gas exploration and distribution; owned by ExxonMobil Corpn (USA); Gen. Man. AYITE AMOUZOU KODJO.

La Nouvelle Soguipêche: Port de pêche, BP 1414, Conakry; tel. 30-44-35-85; f. 1999 to replace Société Guinéenne de Pêche; fishing and processing of fish products.

Société d'Aquaculture de Koba (SAKOBA): BP 4834, Conakry; tel. 30-44-24-75; fax 30-41-46-43; f. 1991; 49% state-owned, 51% owned by private Guinean and French interests; prawn-farming venture; 700 employees.

Société Arabe Libyo-Guinéenne pour le Développement Agricole et Agro-industrielle (SALGUIDIA): BP 622, Conakry; tel. 30-44-46-54; fax 30-41-13-09; e-mail salgdia@sotelgui.net.gn; cap. 15m. FG; f. 1997; fmrly Société Industrielle des Fruits Africains; fruit growing (pineapples, grapefruit, oranges and mangoes); fruit canning and juice extracting; marketing; Pres. FALILOU BARRY; Man. Dir SHARIF TELLISSY.

Société des Bauxites de Dabola-Tougué (SBDT): BP 2859, Conakry; tel. and fax 30-41-47-21; f. 1992; owned jtly by Govts of Guinea and Iran; bauxite mining at Dabola and Tougué; Dir-Gen. A. SAADATI.

Société des Bauxites de Kindia (SBK): BP 613, Conakry; tel. 30-41-38-28; fax 30-41-38-29; e-mail sbk@mirinet.net.gn; internet www.rusal.com/business/geography/alumina/kindii; f. 1969 as Office des Bauxites de Kindia, a jt venture with the USSR; production began 1974; name changed 1992; managed by Russian Aluminium (RusAl) for 25-year (2001–26) contract; bauxite mining at Debélé; Man. Dir ANATOLII PANCHENKO; 1,750 employees (2001).

Société Guinéenne des Hydrocarbures (SGH): BP 892, Conakry; tel. 30-46-12-56; f. 1980; 50% state-owned; research into and exploitation of offshore petroleum reserves; Gen. Man. F. WALSH.

Société Guinéenne de Lubrifiants et d'Emballages (SOGUILUBE): BP 4340, Conakry; tel. 30-44-50-58; fax 30-44-49-92; blends lubricants; 50% owned by Royal Dutch/Shell (Netherlands/United Kingdom, 50% by Govt of Guinea).

Société Minière de Dinguiraye (SMD): BP 2162, Conakry; tel. 30-46-36-81; fax 30-46-35-73; e-mail smd.gui@eti-bull.net; 85% owned by Crew Gold Corpn (Canada), 15% state-owned; exploitation of gold deposits in the Lefa corridor and devt of other areas of Dinguiraye concession; Man. Dir PETER CONNERY.

Société Minière et de Participation Guinée-Alusuisse: Conakry; f. 1971; owned by Guinean Govt and Alusuisse (Switzerland); to establish bauxite mine and aluminium smelter at Tougué; estimated production of bauxite 8m. metric tons annually.

Société de Pêche de Kamsar (SOPEKAM): Kamsar Free Zone; f. 1984; 40% state-owned, 40% Universal Marine & Shark Products (USA); fishing and processing of fish products; fleet of 18 fishing vessels.

TGH Plus: BP 1562, Conakry; tel. 30-46-40-01; fax 30-46-19-83; e-mail tgh.plus@eti-bull.net; f. 1993; natural gas distribution; private co; Pres. and Man. Dir BAH ALIMOU YALI; 54 employees (2001).

Total Guinée: Route du Niger, Coleah Km 4, BP 306, Conakry; tel. 30-35-29-50; f. 1988; storage of petroleum products.

TRADE UNIONS

Confédération Nationale des Travailleurs de Guinée (CNTG): Bourse du Travail, Corniche Sud 004, BP 237, Conakry; tel. and fax 30-41-50-44; f. 1984; Sec.-Gen. RABIATOU SERAH DIALLO.

Organisation Nationale des Syndicats Libres de Guinée (ONSLG): BP 559, Conakry; tel. 30-41-52-17; fax 30-43-02-83; 27,000 mems (1996); Sec.-Gen. YAMOUDOU TOURÉ.

Union Syndicale des Travailleurs de Guinée (USTG): BP 1514, Conakry; tel. 30-41-25-65; fax 30-41-25-58; independent; 64,000 mems (2001); Sec.-Gen. IBRAHIMA FOFANA.

Transport

RAILWAYS

There are 1,086 km of railways in Guinea, including 662 km of 1-m gauge track from Conakry to Kankan in the east of the country, crossing the Niger at Kouroussa. The contract for the first phase of the upgrading of this line was awarded to a Slovak company in early 1997. Three lines for the transport of bauxite link Sangaredi with the port of Kamsar in the west, via Boké, and Conakry with Kindia and Fria, a total of 383 km.

Office National des Chemins de Fer de Guinée (ONCFG): BP 589, Conakry; tel. 30-44-46-13; fax 30-41-35-77; f. 1905; Man. Dir MOREL MARGUERITE CAMARA.

Chemin de Fer de Boké: BP 523, Boké; operations commenced 1973.

Chemin de Fer Conakry–Fria: BP 334, Conakry; operations commenced 1960; Gen. Man. A. CAMARA.

Chemin de Fer de la Société des Bauxites de Kindia: BP 613, Conakry; tel. 30-41-38-28; operations commenced 1974; Gen. Man. K. KEITA.

ROADS

The road network comprised 44,348 km of roads (of which 4,342 km were paved) in 2003. An 895-km cross-country road links Conakry to Bamako, in Mali, and the main highway connecting Dakar (Senegal) to Abidjan (Côte d'Ivoire) also crosses Guinea. The road linking Conakry to Freetown (Sierra Leone) forms part of the Trans West African Highway, extending from Morocco to Nigeria.

La Guinéenne-Marocaine des Transports (GUIMAT): Conakry; f. 1989; owned jtly by Govt of Guinea and Hakkam (Morocco); operates national and regional transport services.

Société Générale des Transports de Guinée (SOGETRAG): Conakry; f. 1985; 63% state-owned; bus operator.

SHIPPING

Conakry and Kamsar are the international seaports. Conakry handled 3.9m. metric tons of foreign trade in 1999.

Getma Guinée: Immeuble KASSA, Cité des Chemins de Fer, BP 1648, Conakry; tel. 30-41-32-05; fax 30-41-42-73; e-mail info@getmaguinee.com.gn; internet www.getma.com; f. 1979; fmrly Société Guinéenne d'Entreprises de Transports Maritimes et Aeriens; marine transportation; cap. 1,100m. FG; Chair. JEAN-JACQUES GRENIER; 135 employees.

Port Autonome de Conakry (PAC): BP 805, Conakry; tel. 30-41-27-28; fax 30-41-26-04; e-mail pac@eti-bull.net; internet www.biasy.net/~pac; haulage, porterage; Gen. Man. ALIOU DIALLO.

Société Navale Guinéenne (SNG): BP 522, Conakry; tel. 30-44-29-55; fax 30-41-39-70; f. 1968; state-owned; shipping agents; Dir-Gen. NOUNKÉ KEITA.

SOAEM: BP 3177, Conakry; tel. 30-41-25-90; fax 30-41-20-25; e-mail soaem.gn@mirinet.net.gn.

SOTRAMAR: Kamsar; e-mail sotramar@sotramar.com; f. 1971; exports bauxite from mines at Boké through port of Kamsar.

Transmar: 33 blvd du Commerce, Kaloum, BP 3917, Conakry; tel. 30-43-05-41; fax 30-43-05-42; e-mail transmar@eti.net.gn; shipping, stevedoring, inland transport.

CIVIL AVIATION

There is an international airport at Conakry-Gbessia, and smaller airfields at Labé, Kankan and Faranah. Facilities at Conakry have been upgraded, at a cost of US $42.6m.; the airport handled some 300,000 passengers in 1999.

Air Guinée Express: 6 ave de la République, BP 12, Conakry; tel. 30-44-46-02; fax 30-41-29-07; e-mail air-guinee@mirinet.net.gn; f. 2002 to replace Air Guinée (f. 1960); regional and internal services; Dir-Gen. ANTOINE CROS.

Guinée Air Service: Aéroport Conakry-Gbessia; tel. 30-41-27-61.

Guinée Inter Air: Aéroport Conakry-Gbessia; tel. 30-41-37-08.

Société de Gestion et d'Exploitation de l'Aéroport de Conakry (SOGEAC): BP 3126, Conakry; tel. 30-46-48-03; f. 1987; manages Conakry-Gbessia international airport; 51% state-owned.

Union des Transports Aériens de Guinée (UTA): scheduled and charter flights to regional and international destinations.

Tourism

Some 45,334 tourists visited Guinea in 2005; receipts from tourism in 2003 totalled US $32m., an increase from $14m. in 2001.

Office National du Tourisme: Immeuble al-Iman, 6e ave de la République, BP 1275, Conakry; tel. 30-45-51-63; fax 30-45-51-64; e-mail ontour@leland-gn.org; internet www.mirinet.net.gn/ont; f. 1997; Dir-Gen. IBRAHIM A. DIALLO.

Defence

As assessed at November 2006, Guinea's active armed forces numbered 9,700, comprising an army of 8,500, a navy of 400 and an air force of 800. Paramilitary forces comprised a republican guard of 1,600 and a 1,000-strong gendarmerie, as well as a reserve 'people's militia' of 7,000. Military service is compulsory (conscripts were estimated at some 7,500 in 2001) and lasts for two years.

Defence Expenditure: Estimated at 200,000m. Guinean francs in 2006.

Chief of Staff of the Armed Forces: Brig.-Gen. DIARRA CAMARA.

Education

Education is provided free of charge at every level in state institutions. Primary education, which begins at seven years of age and lasts for six years, is officially compulsory. According to UNESCO estimates, in 2003/04 enrolment at primary schools included 64% of children in the relevant age-group (males 69%; females 58%), while enrolment at secondary schools in that year included 21% of children in the appropriate age-group (boys 28%; girls 14%). Secondary education, from the age of 13, lasts for seven years, comprising a first cycle (collège) of four years and a second (lycée) of three years. There are universities at Conakry and Kankan, and other tertiary institutions at Manéyah, Boké and Faranah. Independent schools, which had been banned for 23 years under the Sekou Touré regime, were legalized in 1984. Budget estimates for 1999 allocated 62,300m. FG to education (equivalent to 8.1% of total budgetary expenditure).

Bibliography

Adamolekun, L. *Sekou Touré's Guinea: An Experiment in Nation Building.* London, Methuen, 1976.

Arulpragasam, J., and Sahn, D. E. *Economic Transition in Guinea: Implications for Growth and Poverty.* New York, NY, New York University Press, 1997.

Bangoura, D. (Ed.). *Guinée: L'alternance politique à l'issue des élections présidentielles de décembre 2003; actes des colloques des 21 novembre 2003 et 17 mars 2004.* Paris, L'Harmattan, 2004.

Barry, A. O. *Parole futée, peuple dupé: discours et révolution chez Seékou Touré.* Paris, L'Harmattan, 2003.

Les racines du mal guinéen. Paris, Editions Karthala, 2004.

Binns, M. *Guinea.* Oxford, Clio Press, 1996.

Camara, D. K. *La diaspora Guinéenne.* Paris, L'Harmattan, 2003.

Camara, S. S. *La Guinée sans la France.* Paris, Presses de la Fondation Nationale des Sciences Politiques, 1976.

Condé, A. *La décentralisation en Guinée: une expérience réussie.* Paris, L'Harmattan, 2003.

Devey, M. *La Guinée.* Paris, Editions Karthala, 1997.

Diallo, A. *La mort de Diallo Telli.* Paris, Editions Karthala, 1983.

Diallo, El Hadj M. *Histoire du Fouta Djallon.* Paris, L'Harmattan, 2002.

Dicko, A. A. *Journal d'une défaite: autour du référendum du 28 septembre 1958 en Afrique noire.* Paris, L'Harmattan, 1992.

Goerg, O. *Commerce et colonisation en Guinée, 1850–1913.* Paris, L'Harmattan, 1986.

Jeanjean, M. *Sékou Touré: un totalitarisme africain.* Paris, L'Harmattan, 2004.

Kaba, L. *Le "non" de la Guinée à de Gaulle.* Paris, Chaka, 1990.

Kake, I. B. *Sekou Touré, le héros et le tyran.* Paris, Jeune Afrique Livres, 1987.

Keita, S. K. *Ahmed Sekou Touré, l'homme et son combat anticolonial (1922–58).* Conakry, Editions SKK, 1998.

Des complots contre la Guinée de Sékou Touré 1958–84. Boulbinet, Les Classiques Guinéens—SOGUIDIP, 2002.

Larrue, J. *Fria en Guinée: première usine d'alumine en terre d'Afrique.* Paris, Editions Karthala, 1997.

O'Toole, T. E. *Historical Dictionary of Guinea.* Metuchen, NJ, Scarecrow Press, 1988.

Rivière, C. *Guinea: The Mobilization of a People* (trans. by Thompson, V., and Adloff, R.). Ithaca, NY, Cornell University Press, 1977.

Ruë, O. *L'aménagement du littoral de Guinée (1945–1995): mémoires de mangroves: des mémoires de développement pour de nouvelles initiatives.* Paris, L'Harmattan, 1998.

Soumah, M. *Guinée: de Sékou Touré à Lansana Conté.* Paris, L'Harmattan, 2004.

Guinée: la démocratie sans le peuple. Paris, L'Harmattan, 2006.

Touré, S. *L'expérience guinéenne et l'unité africaine.* Paris, Présence africaine, 1959.

Vieira, G. *L'Eglise catholique en Guinée à l'épreuve de Sékou Touré (1958–1984).* Paris, Editions Karthala, 2005.

Yansané, A. Y. *Decolonization in West African States, with French Colonial Legacy: Comparison and Contrast: Development in Guinea, the Ivory Coast, and Senegal, 1945–1980.* Cambridge, MA, Schenkman Publishing Co, 1984.

GUINEA-BISSAU

Physical and Social Geography

RENÉ PÉLISSIER

The Republic of Guinea-Bissau is bounded on the north by Senegal and on the east and south by the Republic of Guinea. Its territory includes a number of coastal islets, together with the offshore Bissagos or Bijagós archipelago, which comprises 18 main islands. The capital is Bissau.

The country covers an area of 36,125 sq km (13,948 sq miles), including some low-lying ground which is periodically submerged at high tide. Except for some higher terrain (rising to about 300 m above sea-level), close to the border with Guinea, the relief consists of a coastal plain deeply indented by *rias*, which facilitate internal communications, and a transition plateau, forming the Planalto de Bafatá in the centre, and the Planalto de Gabú, which abuts on the Fouta Djallon.

The country's main physical features are its meandering rivers and wide estuaries, where it is difficult to distinguish mud, mangrove and water from solid land. The principal rivers are the Cacheu, also known as Farim on part of its course, the Mansôa, the Geba and Corubal complex, the Rio Grande and, close to the Guinean southern border, the Cacine. Ocean-going vessels of shallow draught can reach most of the main population centres, and there is access by flat-bottomed vessels to nearly all significant outposts except in the north-eastern sector.

The climate is tropical, hot and wet with two seasons. The rainy season lasts from mid-May to November and the dry season from December to April. April and May are the hottest months, with temperatures ranging from 20°C to 38°C, and December and January are the coldest, with temperatures ranging from 15°C to 33°C. Rainfall is abundant (1,000–2,000 mm per year in the north), and excessive on the coast. The interior is savannah or light savannah woodland, while coastal reaches are covered with mangrove swamps, rain forest and tangled forest.

The first official census since independence, conducted in April 1979, recorded a population of 753,313. At the census of December 1991 the National Census and Statistics Institute enumerated the population at 983,367. According to UN estimates, the total was 1,646,000 at mid-2005, giving a population density of 45.6 inhabitants per sq km. The main population centre is Bissau, which had an estimated 367,000 inhabitants in 2005. Bafatá, Bolama, Farim, Cantchungo, Mansôa, Gabú, Catió and Bissorã are the other important towns. Prior to the war of independence, the main indigenous groups were the Balante (about 32% of the population), the Fulani or Fula (22%), the Mandyako or Mandjak (14.5%), the Malinké, Mandingo or Mandinka (13%) and the Papel (7%). The non-Africans were mainly Portuguese civil servants and traders, and Syrian and Lebanese traders. Although Portuguese is the official language, a Guinean *crioulo* is the lingua franca. In 2004, according to WHO, the average life expectancy at birth was 47 years.

Recent History

LUISA HANDEM PEITTE

Revised by EDWARD GEORGE

The campaign for independence in Portuguese Guinea (now the Republic of Guinea-Bissau) began in the 1950s with the formation of the Partido Africano da Independência da Guiné e Cabo Verde (PAIGC), under the leadership of Amílcar Cabral. In January 1973 Cabral was assassinated by PAIGC dissidents. The subsequent escalation of hostilities prompted the deployment of some 40,000 Portuguese troops. Guinea-Bissau unilaterally declared its independence from Portugal on 24 September 1973 under the presidency of Luís Cabral, the brother of Amílcar Cabral. The heavy losses sustained by the Portuguese in 1973–74 have been cited as a contributory factor in the military *coup d'état* in Portugal in April 1974. In August Portugal withdrew its forces from Guinea-Bissau and on 10 September it recognized the country's independence. Guinea-Bissau became a single-party state governed by the PAIGC. The party introduced measures to lay the foundations for a socialist state. However, the Government adopted a non-aligned stance in its foreign relations, receiving military aid from the Eastern bloc and economic assistance from Western countries and Arab states. Friendly relations with Portugal were renewed.

Until 1980 the PAIGC supervised both Cape Verde and Guinea-Bissau, the two Constitutions remaining separate, but with a view to eventual unification. These arrangements were abruptly terminated by Cape Verde in November 1980, when Cabral was overthrown by the Prime Minister, João Bernardo Vieira, and a military-dominated revolutionary council took control of government.

VIEIRA AND THE PAIGC, 1980–99

The period following the 1980 coup was one of considerable political ferment, with major shifts in the leadership, although President Vieira remained the dominant force. The unrest was attended by economic decline, which prompted Vieira to bring some former opponents of the regime into the Government, and to recruit Portuguese-trained civil servants into the bureaucracy. In May 1982 Vieira postponed forthcoming elections and Vítor Saúde Maria, Vice-Chairman of the ruling Council of the Revolution and former Minister of Foreign Affairs, was appointed Prime Minister. A struggle for primacy ensued between Vieira and Saúde Maria, the issue eventually being decided in Vieira's favour.

A new Constitution was introduced in May 1984, following elections to a new legislative assembly. Changes to the Government consolidated the position of Vieira as Head of State, Chief of Government, Commander-in-Chief of the armed forces and head of the PAIGC, and assembled a Government in which the emphasis was placed on economic competence.

Economic liberalization was accelerated in the late 1980s. In 1986 the Government abolished trading restrictions and Vieira introduced further proposals to reduce state controls over trade and the economy, and to increase foreign investment. In 1987 the Government and the World Bank agreed on a structural adjustment programme which included further liberalization measures for the economy. Concerns surrounding the Government's new economic policies led to an increase in political tension.

In early 1989 it was announced that the PAIGC had set up a six-member constitutional revision commission. Regional elections were held in early June, at which all candidates were nominated by the PAIGC. In mid-June the Regional Councils elected the legislature, the Assembléia Nacional Popular (ANP), which in turn elected the Conselho de Estado from among its members. Vieira was confirmed as President for a second five-year term.

Constitutional Transition

In April 1990, from its base in Lisbon, Portugal, an *émigré* opposition group, the Resistência da Guiné-Bissau—Movimento Bafatá (RGB—MB), proposed political negotiations with the PAIGC, with the implied threat that civil war might ensue should its demands for reform not be met. Shortly afterwards, in the wake of mounting international pressure for political democratization, Vieira gave approval in principle to the introduction of a multi-party political system. In June 1990 another external opposition movement, the Frente para a Libertação e Independência da Guiné (FLING), demanded an immediate conference of all political parties. In August Vieira informed a meeting of the PAIGC Central Committee that members of the ANP would in future be elected by universal adult suffrage. At a national conference on the transition to democracy, held in October, representatives of the Government, the ruling party and private organizations voted in favour of the holding of a national referendum on the nature of political reforms to be introduced. At an extraordinary conference of the PAIGC, which opened in January 1991, Vieira confirmed that the transition to a multi-party system would be completed by 1993, when a presidential election would be held. During the transitional period, the armed forces would become independent of the PAIGC, and the party would cease to be the country's dominant social and political force.

Constitutional amendments, formally terminating single-party rule, were approved unanimously by the ANP in May 1991. The reforms terminated the PAIGC's role as the leading political force, severed the link between the party and the armed forces, and guaranteed the operation of a free-market economy. A number of opposition parties were subsequently created. In mid-1991 two factions broke away from the Frente Democrática Social (FDS) (which had been set up clandestinely in 1990) to form the Frente Democrática (FD) and the Partido Unido Social Democrático (PUSD). In November the FD became the first party to be legalized by the Supreme Court, formally ending 17 years of one-party politics. The PAIGC met in December to discuss its strategy for the first democratic elections. As part of this process, the post of Prime Minister, which had been abolished in May 1984, was revived with the appointment of Carlos Correia to the position.

Three further opposition parties were registered in December 1991 and January 1992: the Resistência da Guiné-Bissau—Movimento Bah-Fatah (RGB—MB) (the party changed its name prior to legalization, from Resistência da Guiné-Bissau—Movimento Bafatá, owing to a constitutional ban on parties with names connoting regional or tribal affiliation), the FDS, and the PUSD. Three other parties had yet to achieve recognition and another was formed in January, following a further split in the FDS: the Partido para a Renovação Social (PRS), led by former FDS Vice-Chairman Kumba Yalá. In late January four opposition parties, the RGB—MB, FDS, PUSD and the Partido da Convergência Democrática (PCD), agreed to set up a 'democratic forum' for consultations. They demanded that the Government dissolve the political police and cease using state facilities for political purposes. They also called for a revision of press law, free access to media, the creation of an electoral commission and the declaration of election dates in consultation with all the opposition parties.

An opposition demonstration, the first to be permitted by the Government, was held in Bissau in March 1992, attended by an estimated 30,000 people. It was subsequently announced that presidential and legislative elections would take place in November and December, respectively. The FLING was legalized in May. In that month a dissident group known as the 'Group of 121' broke away from the PAIGC to form a new party, the Partido da Renovação e Desenvolvimento (PRD), led by João da Costa, a former Minister of Health. In mid-May the leader of the RGB—MB, Domingos Fernandes, returned from exile in Portugal. Following his return, Fernandes and the leaders of the FD, PCD, FDS and the PUSD met Vieira to discuss the political reform programme. As a result of the talks it was decided that commissions would be set up to oversee and facilitate the organization of the forthcoming elections.

In August 1992, in response to opposition demands for the establishment of a national conference to oversee the transition to multi-party democracy, Vieira inaugurated the Comissão Multipartidária de Transição (Multi-party Transition Commission), charged with drafting legislation in preparation for democratic elections. All officially recognized parties were to be represented on the commission. Several other political parties were given legal status during the second half of 1992; these included the PRD, the Movimento para a Unidade e a Democracia (MUDE) and the PRS.

Legislation preparing for the transition to a pluralist democracy was approved by the ANP in February 1993, and in the following month a commission was appointed to supervise the elections. However, reports in mid-March of a coup attempt against the Government threatened to disrupt the progress of democratic transition. Initial reports indicated that Maj. Robalo de Pina, commander of the élite guard responsible for protecting the President, had been assassinated in what appeared to be an army mutiny. About 50 people were arrested in connection with the mutiny, including the leader of the PRD, João da Costa. Opposition politicians, however, alleged that the incident had been contrived by the Government in an effort to discredit its political opponents and to maintain its hold on power. Da Costa and nine other members of the PRD in detention were released in June, but banned from political activity. In July Vieira announced that simultaneous presidential and legislative multi-party elections would be held in March 1994.

Multi-Party Elections

One week before the designated election date, set for 27 March 1994, Vieira announced a further postponement of the elections owing to financial and technical difficulties. Voter registration for the postponed elections was conducted between 11 and 23 April. On 11 May it was announced that the elections would be held on 3 July. In early May six opposition parties, the FD, FDS, MUDE, Partido Democrático do Progresso (PDP), PRD and the Liga para a Protecção da Ecologia, formed an electoral coalition, the União para a Mudança (UM). Later in May a further five opposition parties, the FLING, PRS, PUSD, RGB—MB and the Foro Cívico da Guiné, announced the establishment of an informal alliance under which each party reserved the right to present its own candidates in the elections.

The elections took place on 3 July 1994, although voting was extended for two days owing to logistical problems. The PAIGC secured a clear majority in the ANP, winning 62 seats, but the results of the presidential election were inconclusive, with Vieira winning 46.3% of the votes, while his nearest rival, Kumba Yalá of the PRS, secured 21.9% of the votes. As no candidate had obtained an absolute majority, a second round presidential election between the two leading candidates was conducted on 7 August. Despite receiving the combined support of all the opposition parties, Yalá was narrowly defeated, securing 48.0% of the votes to Vieira's 52.0%. International observers later declared the elections to have been free and fair. Vieira was inaugurated as President on 29 September 1994 and appointed Manuel Saturnino da Costa as Prime Minister in late October. The Council of Ministers, comprising solely members of the PAIGC, was appointed in November.

Post-Election Politics

In April 1995 the FD, FDS, MUDE, PDP and the PRD reconsolidated themselves within the UM coalition and elected João da Costa as President and Amine Michel Saad as its Secretary-General. In August registration was granted to a new party, the Partido Social Democrático (PSD), which was formed by dissidents from the RGB—MB.

In early November 1996 government plans to join the Union économique et monétaire ouest-africaine (UEMOA) were rejected by the ANP. However, in late November, on receiving a plea from Vieira, the legislature approved a constitutional amendment authorizing the Government to seek membership of the UEMOA, which it duly attained in March 1997. Guinea-Bissau subsequently entered the Franc Zone on 17 April, the national currency was replaced by the franc CFA, and the Banque Centrale des Etats de l'Afrique de l'Ouest (BCEAO) assumed central banking functions.

In May 1997, in light of what Vieira described as a serious political crisis, da Costa was dismissed. Carlos Correia was subsequently appointed Prime Minister and a new Council of Ministers was inaugurated. On 11 October Correia was dismissed, bringing to an end an institutional crisis that began with his inauguration as Prime Minister. The legislative process had been obstructed by opposition deputies who claimed that, by omitting to consult those parties represented in the legislature on Correia's appointment, Vieira had acted unconstitutionally. In August the matter was referred to the Supreme Court, which ruled, in early October, that Vieira had indeed contravened the Constitution. Following consultations with party leaders, Vieira reappointed Correia on 13 October, with the full support of the main opposition parties.

In March 1998, following protests by opposition parties at delays in the organization of legislative elections, an independent national elections commission was established. Elections were due to be held in July. In April a new political party, the União Nacional para a Democracia e o Progresso (UNDP), led by former Minister of the Interior Abubacar Baldé, was established.

Army Rebellion

In June 1998 rebel troops, led by the recently dismissed Chief of Staff of the Armed Forces, Brig. Ansumane Mané, seized control of the Bra military barracks in the capital and the international airport. Mané subsequently formed a 'military junta for the consolidation of democracy, peace and justice' and demanded the resignation of Vieira and his administration and the conduct of free and democratic elections in July. With the support of Senegalese and Guinean soldiers, troops loyal to the Government attempted unsuccessfully to regain control of rebel-held areas of the city, and heavy fighting ensued. In the following days an estimated 200,000 residents of Bissau fled the city, prompting fears of a humanitarian disaster. Fighting continued into July, with many members of the Guinea-Bissau armed forces reportedly defecting to the side of the rebels. On 26 July, following mediation by a delegation from the lusophone commonwealth body, the Comunidade dos Países de Língua Portuguesa (CPLP, see below), the Government and the rebels agreed to implement a truce. On 25 August representatives of the Government and the rebels met, under the auspices of the CPLP and the Economic Community of West African States (ECOWAS), on Sal island, Cape Verde, where agreement was reached to transform the existing truce into a cease-fire. The accord provided for the reopening of the international airport and for the deployment of international forces to maintain and supervise the cease-fire.

In September 1998 talks between the Government and the rebels resumed in Abidjan, Côte d'Ivoire. In October the rebels agreed to a government proposal for the creation of a demilitarized zone separating the opposing forces in the capital. However, before the proposal could be formally endorsed, the cease-fire collapsed as fighting erupted in the capital and several other towns. On 20 October the Government imposed a nation-wide curfew, and on the following day Vieira declared a unilateral cease-fire. By that time almost all of the government troops had defected to the rebel forces, which were believed to control most of the country. On 23 October Brig. Mané agreed to observe a 48-hour truce to allow Vieira time to clarify his proposals for a negotiated peace settlement, and agreement was subsequently reached for direct talks to be held in Banjul, The Gambia. At the talks the rebels confirmed that they would not seek Vieira's resignation. Further talks, held under the aegis of ECOWAS, in Abuja, Nigeria, resulted in the signing of a peace accord on 1 November. Under the terms of the accord, the two sides reaffirmed the cease-fire of 25 August, and resolved that the withdrawal of Senegalese and Guinean troops from Guinea-Bissau be conducted simultaneously with the deployment of an ECOMOG (ECOWAS Cease-fire Monitoring Group) interposition force, which would guarantee security on the border with Senegal. It was also agreed that a government of national unity would be established, to include representatives of the rebel junta, and that presidential and legislative elections would be held no later than March 1999. In early November 1998 agreement was reached on the composition of a Joint Executive Commission to implement the peace accord. In late November the commission approved the structure of the new Government, which was to comprise 10 ministers and seven secretaries of state. On 3 December Francisco José Fadul was appointed Prime Minister, and later that month Vieira and Mané reached agreement on the allocation of portfolios to the two sides.

In January 1999 Fadul announced that presidential and legislative elections would not take place in March as envisaged in the Abuja accord, but would be conducted at the end of the year. Also in January agreement was reached between the Government, the rebel military junta and ECOWAS on the strength of the ECOMOG interposition force, which was to comprise some 710 troops, and on a timetable for the withdrawal of Senegalese and Guinean troops from the country. However, at the end of January hostilities resumed in the capital, resulting in numerous fatalities and the displacement of some 250,000 residents. On 9 February talks between the Government and the rebels produced agreement on a cease-fire and provided for the immediate withdrawal of Senegalese and Guinean troops. At a meeting held in Lomé, Togo, on 17 February, Vieira and Mané pledged never again to resort to armed conflict. On 20 February the new Government of National Unity was announced. The disarmament of rebel troops and those loyal to the President, as provided for under the Abuja accord, began in early March and the withdrawal of Senegalese and Guinean troops was completed that month.

TRANSITIONAL GOVERNMENT

In early May 1999 Vieira announced that legislative and presidential elections would take place on 28 December. However, on 7 May, to widespread condemnation by the international community, Vieira was overthrown by the rebel military junta. Fighting had erupted in Bissau on the previous day when rebel troops seized stockpiles of weapons that had been held at Bissau airport since the disarmament of the rival forces in March. The rebels, who claimed that their actions had been prompted by Vieira's refusal to allow his presidential guard to be disarmed, surrounded the presidential palace and forced its surrender. Vieira subsequently took refuge at the Portuguese embassy, where on 10 May he signed an unconditional surrender. The President of the ANP, Malam Bacai Sanhá, was appointed acting President of the Republic pending a presidential election. The Government of National Unity, including the ministers appointed by Vieira, remained in office. At a meeting of the ruling bodies of the PAIGC that month, Manuel Saturnino da Costa was appointed to replace Vieira as party President. At a meeting conducted in late May by representatives of the Government, the military junta and the political parties, agreement was reached that Vieira should stand trial for his involvement in the trafficking of arms to separatists from the Senegalese region of Casamance and for political and economic crimes relating to his terms in office. Vieira subsequently agreed to stand trial, but only after receiving medical treatment abroad, after which, he pledged, he would return to Guinea-Bissau. At a meeting of ECOWAS foreign ministers held in Togo that month Vieira's overthrow was condemned and demands were made for him to be permitted to leave Guinea-Bissau. It was also decided that ECOMOG forces would be withdrawn from the country; the last ECOMOG troops left in early June. In that month Vieira was permitted to leave Guinea-Bissau to seek medical treatment in France. Sanhá cited humanitarian reasons for allowing Vieira's departure, but stressed that he would return to stand trial. In the same month Sanhá asserted that presidential and legislative elections would take place by 28 November. In July constitutional amendments were introduced limiting the tenure of presidential office to two terms and abolishing the death penalty. It was also stipulated that the country's principal offices of state could only be held by Guinea-Bissau nationals born of Guinea-Bissau parents. In September an extraordinary congress of the PAIGC voted to expel Vieira from the party. The incumbent Minister of Defence and Freedom Fighters, Francisco Benante, was appointed President of the party. Later in October the Attorney-General announced that he had sufficient evidence to prosecute Vieira for crimes against humanity and expressed his intention to seek Vieira's extradition from Portugal.

THE YALÁ PRESIDENCY

Presidential and legislative elections were conducted on 28 November 1999, with voting extended for a further day owing to logistical problems. As no candidate received the necessary 50% of the votes to win the presidential election outright, the leading candidates, Kumba Yalá of the PRS and Malam Bacai Sanhá of the PAIGC, contested a second round of voting on 16 January 2000. Of the 102 seats in the legislature (enlarged from 100) the PRS secured 38, the RGB—MB 28, the PAIGC 24, the Aliança Democrática four, the UM three, the PSD three, and the FDS and the UNDP obtained one each. In that month former President Luís Cabral returned from Portugal to Guinea-Bissau for the first time since he was exiled following his removal from power by Vieira in 1980. At the second round of the presidential election Yalá secured victory, with 72% of the votes cast, and took office on 17 February, installing a new Council of Ministers, which included members of several former opposition parties. Later that month Caetano N'Tchama of the PRS was appointed Prime Minister. The election was judged by international observers to have been free and fair. In May it was reported that tensions were increasing between Yalá and certain elements in the army, who viewed the head of the military junta, Gen. Ansumane Mané, as the rightful leader of the country, on the grounds that it was he who had ousted Vieira from power.

Poor relations between civilians and the military remained a major obstacle to political stability, despite the approval, in August 2000, by the ANP, of a measure formally making the Head of State the Supreme Commander of the armed forces. The conflict between the Government and the military junta worsened in mid-November 2000, following the promotion by Yalá of a number of high-ranking officers. Gen. Mané rejected the promotions and appointed himself Commander-in-Chief of the armed forces. The conflict came to an end on 23 November when forces loyal to the Government defeated a rebellion led by Mané, who was killed a few days later by the security forces.

Following the November 2000 insurgency, the PAIGC divided into various factions, the two most significant of which incorporated hard-liners and young moderate reformers, respectively. Another outcome of the crisis was the increasing dominance of the Balante ethnic group over state institutions. In mid-December, a thorough overhaul of the military leadership and command structure brought Balante into most positions of authority. The dissolution of the junta did not lead to political and social stability. President Yalá used his new political strength to change the composition of the Government. A minor reshuffle in January 2001 was followed by the withdrawal from the Government of the junior coalition party, the RGB—MB, whose members accused Yalá of not respecting the coalition agreement, which stated that the Council of Ministers could not be extensively reshuffled without all parties being consulted. Lacking a parliamentary majority, the new PRS-led Government was reliant on the support of one of the two larger opposition parties.

The main liability of the new Government continued to be the unpopularity of the Prime Minister. As friction increased between Yalá and his own party, the PRS, the President dismissed N'Tchama in March 2001. Faustino Fudut Imbali was appointed to replace him. Imbali formed a broad-based Council of Ministers, including a substantial number of members of opposition parties.

In early May 2001 the process of demobilizing and reintegrating war veterans commenced. Some 150 volunteers were involved in the pilot phase, the first of 5,000 veterans who were to be demobilized in the first phase of the process. A census concluded in November 2000 had estimated the total number of veterans to be 28,000. Political instability increased in late 2001, much of it caused by the increasingly erratic, autocratic and unpredictable behaviour of President Yalá.

In August 2001 the Judges' Association complained about the President's interference in the judicial system and Yalá escalated the crisis in the following month, when he replaced the Attorney-General, Rui Sanhá, with N'Tchama. Shortly afterwards the President replaced three Supreme Court judges, prompting a lawsuit and a strike organized by the Judges' Association. When it ended, the Government agreed to reinstate the judges only on a case-by-case basis, pending an evaluation by a commission appointed by the new Supreme Court. The recently dismissed President and Vice-President of the Supreme Court were arrested on corruption charges, which they denied, but were released on bail in February 2002. Two unsuccessful attempts were made to mediate between the President and the judiciary. In August and September 2001 a National Civil Society Movement met with both sides and proposed terms for a settlement that were rejected by Yalá. In October the ANP rejected the dismissal of the Supreme Court judges as unconstitutional and withdrew its political confidence in the President. Yalá responded on 1 November by threatening to dissolve the legislature and to initiate a 10-year transition period in which Guinea-Bissau's politicians would gain maturity.

On 3 December 2001, following months of rumours, a group comprising mainly Mandinka officers, led by Lt-Col Almani Camara, attempted a military coup. A few days later Imbali, having been accused of abuse of power by the President, was replaced as Prime Minister by the Minister of Internal Administration, Alamara Nhassé. At the same time, a new Council of Ministers was appointed, in which the PRS held 20 of the 24 posts.

Political tension appeared to decline after the appointment of Nhassé as Prime Minister, as Yalá had successfully increased control over the capacity of national institutions to criticize the Government. In January 2002 the President appointed five more Supreme Court judges. Another source of conflict was resolved to the President's satisfaction when Samuel Nana-Sinkam, the controversial head of the UN Peace-building Support Office in Guinea-Bissau (UNOGBIS), was replaced by David Stephens. Nana-Sinkam's reports to the UN Secretary-General had displeased the Government, particularly that of December 2001, in which Yalá was advised to take steps to resolve the country's political problems. In mid-January 2002 the armed forces revealed that 29 of those suspected of involvement in the December coup attempt had been detained, and that evidence had been gathered against them and presented to the judicial system. The governing PRS held its congress in that month, electing the Prime Minister as its new President, further reinforcing his standing. At the end of January 2002 the fourth extraordinary congress of the PAIGC commenced under the banner of 'reconciliation, restructuring and unity'. The PAIGC elected Carlos Gomes Júnior as its new leader. The extraordinary congress took the controversial measure of pardoning and reintegrating former members who had either abandoned or been expelled from the party. The inclusion in this pardon of former President Vieira provoked an angry reaction from President Yalá.

In March 2002 the Government and the opposition signed a 10-point stability pact that had been proposed by the Prime Minister. The signing of the pact was followed by the unanimous approval of the Government's programme for 2002. However, the stability pact was weakened by the opposition's obstruction of discussion and adoption of the 2002 budget, and by the Government's failure to hold local elections. In mid-April UNOGBIS sponsored a National Reconciliation Forum, at which, *inter alia*, the Government, political parties and civil organizations discussed national dialogue, governance and the role of institutions.

In July 2002 N'Tchama ordered the arrest of Imbali and several of his advisers on corruption charges, drawing an angry response from Prime Minister Nhassé, who threatened to resign unless Imbali was released. The dispute escalated into an international affair, when the UN Security Council called for its peaceful resolution, and the police refused to arrest the former Prime Minister. Eventually Imbali was freed on the orders of President Yalá. Also in July the first phase of the veteran demobilization and reintegration programme commenced. This phase, which ended in September, involved the demobilization of 90% of the planned total of 4,392 men. Of these, 1,376 were active soldiers, 737 civilians who fought for Vieira in the civil war and 556 civilians who fought for the junta.

Relations between President Yalá and Prime Minister Nhassé deteriorated in August 2002 after the President was accused of violating the Constitution by reshuffling the Council of Ministers and crediting the changes to Nhassé. Artur Sanhá, hitherto the Minister of Fisheries and the Sea, was appointed President of the Supreme Court. N'Tchama was replaced as Attorney-General by the previous Supreme Court President, António Sedja Man, after N'Tchama had filed a case against Nhassé for abuse of power. Sanhá and N'Tchama, who was appointed ambassador to Cuba, rejected their new posts. The institutional conflict led to an attempt by Yalá to dismiss the Prime Minister, a move blocked by the military during a crisis meeting. The military also protested at the frequent changes in the Government and the ensuing instability. Nevertheless, further government changes were made when new Ministers of Fisheries and the Sea and of Justice were appointed. Mamadou Djaló became the new Attorney-General.

In August 2002, at the Government's request, the UN Security Council extended to December 2003 the mandate of UNOGBIS, which had been due to expire in December 2002. Both the authorities and the UN, despite frequent disagreements, recognized the valuable contribution of the organization to maintaining a semblance of peace and stability. However, during a speech to the ANP in September Yalá subjected the opposition leader Victor Mandinga to such public abuse that many opposition deputies abandoned the room. The attack, which shocked representatives of the international community, was followed a few days later by the firing of shots at Mandinga's house in what Mandinga claimed was an assassination attempt. Demands for the resignation of President Yalá increased. In October the RGB—MB and the PAIGC signed the 'Declaration of Bissau', naming Yalá as the main obstacle to stability and development. More controversially, the declaration questioned the President's mental capacity, suggesting that he be subject to a medical evaluation.

Political instability intensified in November 2002, when President Yalá dissolved the ANP and dismissed the Council of Ministers, accusing both bodies of creating the political stalemate and economic crisis. Yalá appointed Mário Pires, a founding member of the PRS, at the head of a transitional Government. It became clear that the elections could not be held in February 2003 as scheduled, given the severe financial and organizational difficulties of the authorities, and President Yalá postponed them until 20 April. However, doubts about the appropriateness of the new date arose immediately, as it was increasingly obvious that the Government lacked the financial and technical capacity to stage the elections.

The announcement of early elections precipitated a profound realignment of political forces. A faction of the RGB—MB led by Domingos Fernandes and Helder Vaz, formed the Grupo de Democratas Independentes, which then participated in the creation of a coalition, the Plataforma Unida—Mufunessa Larga Guiné (PU—MLG), together with the PCD and four other smaller political forces. In February 2003 several political groups were legalized: the Manifesto do Povo, the Partido Democrático Guineense (PDG) and the Movimento Democrático Guineense. In March a second coalition was registered, the União Eleitoral (UE), which united four small parties. That month also marked the return from exile in Portugal of former Prime Minister Fadul, who became leader of the PUSD. Fadul and his party immediately became the main targets of harassment by the authorities.

In March 2003, yielding to international and domestic pressure, Yalá postponed the legislative elections to 6 July. The main difficulty with preparations continued to be financial. Further government changes were effected in April and later that month and in early May the Ministers of Defence and of the Presidency of the Council of Ministers, Marcelino Cabral and José de Pina, respectively, were dismissed and arrested shortly afterwards without explanation. The two men were not freed until June, and their detention created serious friction between the Government and the military.

In April 2003 the PU—MLG selected Helder Vaz as its candidate for Prime Minister. In the same month most opposition parties, with the exception of the UE, signed an open letter to Yalá, urging him to postpone the polls, as it was increasingly obvious that they could not be held on 6 July. The UE dissented, considering that elections should take place as soon as possible to end the lack of a legitimate government and an elected parliament. The opposition also proposed the formation of a government of national unity.

In June 2003 there was a change in strategy on the part of the authorities regarding the Council of Ministers. Five new ministers, linked to opposition circles, were appointed to the Government, with the clear intention of broadening its appeal. In July Yalá replaced the Minister of Foreign Affairs, Joãozinho Vieira Có, with Fatumata Djau Baldé, and abolished the Secretary of State for Information, replacing it with the Ministry of Social Communication. Its new head, Juliano Augusto Fernandes, was dismissed after only two months, however, after failing to restrain the press in its criticism of the President. In late June Yalá announced that legislative elections would be held on 12 October.

MILITARY INTERVENTION AND ELECTIONS

Following a further postponement of the elections, on 14 September 2003 Yalá was detained by soldiers acting on the orders of the Chief of Staff of the Armed Forces, Gen. Veríssimo Correia Seabra, who declared himself interim President, and his second-in-command, Emílio Costa. Both belonged to the army faction which led the rebellion under the late Gen. Ansumane Mané, which ousted Vieira in 1999. On the following day Seabra and a newly appointed Military Committee for the Restoration of Constitutional Order and Democracy held talks with representatives of civil society and political organizations, apparently aimed at forming a transitional, civilian-led government. A 16-member commission was charged with appointing the transitional government and preparing for general elections. Meanwhile, the UN, the African Union and several African countries condemned the coup, and ECOWAS dispatched a mission to Bissau to mediate between the military authorities and Yalá. The ECOWAS mission withdrew its demand that Yalá be reinstated, however, once the scale of his unpopularity became clear. National support for the new Government was strong, and all political parties (including Yalá's PRS) signed a declaration supporting the coup. Yalá formally resigned on 17 September after it emerged that he had approached army officers from his own Balante ethnic group and offered them posts in a future government if they helped him to launch his own counter-coup.

On 22 September 2003 the military announced the appointment of Henrique Pereira Rosa, a respected businessman and former head of the national electoral commission, as President. Gen. Seabra declined to take the presidency himself as he would have been required to give up his position as Chief of Staff of the Armed Forces. The appointment as Prime Minister of Artur Sanhá, the Secretary-General of the PRS, aroused controversy, however, after 15 of the 17 parties consulted about the new Government protested that they had been promised a new premier without political affiliations. Their objections were nevertheless overruled by the coup leaders, apparently in an attempt to ensure that the Balante ethnic group was fully represented in the Government.

In October 2003 a 56-member Comissão Nacional de Transição (CNT) was formed, comprising military officials, politicians and representatives of civil society, to oversee the preparations for legislative elections which were set for 28 March 2004. The interim President, Henrique Rosa, pledged to continue in his post until presidential elections in March 2005 completed the democratization process. Responding positively to the CNT's rapid moves towards elections, the international community granted the transitional Government recognition and agreed to provide US $20m. towards the cost of the elections. Although banned from further political activity, Yalá continued to increase political tensions with inflammatory public statements in the months following his ousting and, as a result, was placed under house arrest.

In early 2004 divisions began to appear in the transitional Government as campaigning for the elections commenced. A total of 15 political parties (including three coalitions) fielded candidates, although most were overshadowed by the three largest parties: the PAIGC, now led by Carlos Gomes Júnior, the PRS and the RGB (which had removed the Movimento Bah-Fatah suffix in 2003). Seeking to distance itself from the ousted President, in early 2004 the PRS replaced Yalá with Alberto Nambeia as party leader, although Prime Minister Sanhá continued to be the public face of the party.

Legislative elections were held on 28 March 2004, although voting was extended for a second day after a number of polling stations failed to open in the capital as a result of organizational problems. According to the Comissão Nacional de Eleições (CNE—National Election Commission), some 75% of Guinea-Bissau's 603,000 registered voters cast ballots in the elections, which were declared 'free, fair and transparent' by a team of more than 100 international observers. The PAIGC secured 45 of the 100 seats in the ANP, narrowly failing to attain an overall majority. The PRS obtained 35 seats, the PUSD 17, the UE two seats and the Aliança Popular Unida (APU) one seat. Pledging to form a broadly based coalition Government, Gomes Júnior attempted to form an alliance with the PUSD. However, negotiations between the two parties proved unsuccessful and the PAIGC signed a formal agreement with the PRS under which it pledged to support the Government's legislative plan. In return, the PRS would not receive any ministerial posts but would instead be awarded two senior posts in the ANP's governing body, and a number of prominent positions in government departments and parastatal organizations.

A new Government, led by Gomes Júnior, was appointed in May 2004 following the completion of the six-month term of the Comissão Nacional de Transição. Gomes Júnior promised that his Government would focus on restoring the basic social services which had collapsed under Yalá's administration, and also on promoting agriculture and improving conditions in the military. The new Government faced a crisis in October when soldiers from an army contingent recently returned from a UN peace-keeping mission in Liberia mutinied, demanding the payment of overdue salaries. The mutiny resulted in the deaths of Seabra, and the army's information officer, Lt-Col Domingos de Barros. The new Chief of Staff appointed in the wake of the mutiny, Maj. Gen. Baptista Tagmé Na Wai, vowed to work to unify the army and respect the authority of the future head of state, regardless of his political affiliation. Given the continuing political instability and increased tensions, on 22 December the UN Security Council extended UNOGBIS's mandate for a further year.

In March 2005 the Government announced that a presidential election would take place on 19 June, despite objections from the opposition which protested that it violated the timetable set out in the Transitional Charter drafted in October 2003. The delay was due to a number of disrupting factors, including the need to compile a new voter register, the army mutiny in October 2004 and a general lack of resources. To help the Government accelerate the election process, in February the European Union (EU) granted €9.5m. (US $12m.) to pay overdue civil-service salaries and to finance electoral preparations. In March both the UN Office for West Africa and the UN Security Council expressed deep concern over political developments in Guinea-Bissau, particularly over the probable participation in the election of Yalá.

These fears were confirmed in March 2005 when the PRS nominated Yalá as its candidate for the presidential election. In April former President Vieira returned to Guinea-Bissau from exile in Portugal with the intention of contesting the election as an independent candidate. The participation of both men in the election contravened the terms of the Transitional Charter, which barred them from political activity for five years, and raised concerns that they could reignite ethnic tensions. Yalá relied upon strong support from the largest ethnic group, the Balante (representing 30% of the population) while Vieira claimed support from the Papel ethnic group (representing 13%). Statements by Yalá in early 2005 that he would seize the presidency by force if he were barred from running, and that he still considered himself legally to be President, also raised fears of a fresh coup attempt. In April the Supreme Court overturned legal obstacles to the candidacies of Vieira and Yalá on grounds which were unclear.

The PAIGC nominated Malam Bacai Sanhá as its presidential candidate. Sanhá had been defeated by Yalá in the 2000 presidential elections, but was viewed as the favourite to secure victory over his two discredited predecessors. Other candidates included Fadul and Cirilo Augusto Rodrigues de Oliveira of the Partido Socialista Guineense. The interim President, Henrique Rosa, confirmed that he would not stand as a candidate. In May 2005 the PAIGC central committee suspended 37 party members after they publicly voiced their support for Vieira's candidacy.

Meanwhile, in April 2005 Gomes Júnior effected a major reorganization of the Council of Ministers. Most notably, Daniel Gomes, previously Minister of Defence, became Minister of the Presidency of the Council of Ministers, Social Communication and Parliamentary Affairs, while Martinho N'Dafa Cabi, hitherto Deputy Prime Minister and Minister of Energy and Natural Resources, assumed the national defence portfolio. Furthermore, the Ministry of the Economy and Finance was separated; Issufo Sanhá was appointed Minister of the Economy, while João Mamadu Fadiah retained the finance portfolio.

The presidential election was held as scheduled on 19 June 2005 and was contested by 13 candidates. The vote was monitored by 200 observers from the USA, the EU, the CPLP and ECOWAS—including Joaquim Chissano, the former President of Mozambique, who was appointed the UN Secretary-General's special envoy to Guinea-Bissau—and was subsequently declared to have been free and fair. Sanhá secured 35.5% of the votes cast, while Vieira won 28.9% and Yalá received 25.0%. The rate of voter participation was recorded at 87.6%. As none of the candidates achieved an outright majority, a second round of voting to be contested by Sanhá and Vieira was scheduled for 24 July. Yalá subsequently announced his support for Vieira in the second ballot. Final results of the second round, released on 10 August by the CNE, revealed that Vieira had won 216,167 votes (or 52.35% of valid votes cast), while Sanhá received 196,759. Voter turn-out was 78.6%. Sanhá, who alleged widespread electoral fraud, declared that he would contest the legitimacy of the election; however, the result was upheld by the Supreme Court on 19 August.

VIEIRA RETURNS TO POWER

On 1 October 2005 Vieira was sworn in as President of Guinea-Bissau, ending months of political uncertainty. In his inauguration speech to the ANP, Vieira promised to respect the constitutional separation of powers and to work with the Government of Prime Minister Carlos Gomes Júnior. However, less than two weeks later 14 of the PAIGC's 45 deputies defected to join the two largest opposition parties, the PRS and PUSD, in a new coalition—the Fórum de Convergência para o Desenvolvimento (FCD)—with the aim of removing the Prime Minister from power. Gomes Júnior responded by requesting a vote of confidence, but before the ANP could be convened he and his Government were dismissed by Vieira. Gomes Júnior protested against his dismissal, insisting that the PAIGC, which had won the largest number of seats in the legislative election, had the right to form the Government. Nevertheless, on 2 November Vieira appointed a new Prime Minister, the former PAIGC Vice-President, Aristides Gomes, who had been suspended from the PAIGC in May for openly supporting Vieira. One week later Gomes unveiled his new multi-party Government, comprising 19 ministers and nine secretaries of state drawn from the PRS, the PUSD, the PCD, the UE, several independents and eight dissident members of the PAIGC. The Minister of the Economy, Issufo Sanhá, a member of the PAIGC, was the only member of the previous Government to retain his portfolio. Fierce disagreement between the coalition members over which party would be given the interior ministry ensued, and it was not until 16 November that Ernesto de

Carvalho, a previous director of state security, was appointed as Minister of the Interior.

On 25 January 2006 the Supreme Court rejected a legal challenge by the PAIGC disputing the appointment of Gomes as Prime Minister, thus removing the last obstacle to the Government's full instatement. Despite determined opposition from the PAIGC, in mid-March the ANP approved the Government's programme by 53 votes to 36. However, a disagreement immediately broke out between Gomes and the leader of the PUSD, Francisco Fadul, over the Minister of Justice, Namuano Dias Gomes, who Fadul accused of involvement in a corruption scandal at the Empresa de Electricidade e Águas da Guiné-Bissau. After the Prime Minister refused to replace Dias, Fadul suspended his party's participation in the Government in protest. However, only one PUSD deputy complied with Fadul's orders, prompting his resignation from the leadership of the party in April. In late May the Government sent an open letter to the PAIGC demanding the reinstatement of 30 of its members, including the Prime Minister and the Minister of National Defence, who had been suspended in May 2005. However, the PAIGC leadership refused to comply with the ruling.

In July 2006 Artur Sanhá resigned as Secretary-General of the PRS, citing disagreements with the party leadership over political strategy. Later that month he formed a dissident movement, the Grupo de Iniciativa para o Congresso (GIC), which demanded that the PRS congress be brought forward to elect a new leader, but the party's leadership insisted the congress would proceed in November as planned. On 28 October Yalá, the PRS President, returned to Guinea-Bissau after one year in exile in Morocco; he immediately raised tensions by declaring the FCD Government illegitimate and demanding new legislative elections. In mid-November the PRS held its third party congress during which Yalá was comfortably re-elected as party leader, receiving more than three times as many votes as his closest rival and former party leader, Nambeia. Following the congress, Yala again departed to Rabat, although he promised to return to Guinea-Bissau permanently before the end of 2006 (a promise he failed to keep). In late November President Vieira dismissed Minister of the Interior de Carvalho, in a move widely interpreted as retaliation against Yalá's inflammatory comments (Carvalho had previously been Yalá's personal adviser). He was replaced by Dionísio Kabi, a former Minister of Justice and Public Works.

In January 2007 political tensions flared after the former Navy Chief of Staff, Mohamed Lamine Sanhá, was shot dead in Bissau. Sanhá was a member of the junta formed after the overthrow of Vieira in 1999, and was the third of its members to be killed, following the deaths of Gen. Mané in November 2001 and Seabra in October 2004. Sanhá's death sparked violent protests by angry youths who erected barricades in central Bissau and burned down several houses, leaving one person dead and many injured. In response to the Government's denials of involvement in the assassination, the leader of the PAIGC, Gomes Júnior, claimed in an interview with a Portuguese news agency that Vieira had masterminded the murders of former members of the junta that overthrew him. Angered by the allegation, Vieira's Government issued an arrest warrant against Gomes Júnior, who took refuge within a UNOGBIS building where he remained under UN protection for 17 days. Eventually the UN brokered an agreement under which the Government withdrew the arrest warrant and guaranteed the safety of Gomes Júnior and his family, in return for which Gomes Júnior agreed to testify in the Sanhá murder investigation.

In March 2007 a political crisis erupted when the PRS and PUSD withdrew from the FCD ruling coalition and signed a political stability pact with the PAIGC, pledging to form a government of national unity. On 19 March the Government lost a vote of 'no confidence' in the ANP by 54 votes to 28. Initially, Vieira refused to make a public statement concerning the vote, but public protests intensified in Bissau and on 28 March Gomes tendered his resignation as Prime Minister, forcing Vieira to respond. Eventually, after three weeks of political uncertainty, Vieira acquiesced and on 10 April he appointed Cabi as Prime Minister. Cabi held the national defence portfolio in 2005, and was one of the PAIGC's Vice-Presidents. On 17 April Cabi announced his new cabinet, with only two of the 20 members remaining from the previous administration. The new Government was heavily weighted in favour of the PAIGC and the PRS, with those parties holding nine and six cabinet posts, respectively. However, at Vieira's insistence the key portfolios of interior, finance and foreign affairs were awarded to his supporters, notably Vieira's former security adviser, Baciro Dabó, who became Minister of the Interior, and Issufo Sanhá, who relinquished the economy portfolio to become Minister of Finance. However, these appointments were unpopular with the PRS, which previously controlled the Ministry of the Interior and had lost influence over the electoral process as a result.

Cabi's Government immediately implemented measures to address the acute fiscal crisis and regain the confidence of donors, whose assistance the country desperately needed. These measures included a moratorium on unauthorized government spending, and a pledge to settle outstanding public-sector salary arrears and to provide assistance to the struggling cashew nut sector. During its first months in office the Government was judged to have performed competently, prompting donors, led by the World Bank and the IMF, to re-engage fully in Guinea-Bissau and release large inflows of aid. However, despite Cabi's reportedly good relationship with Vieira, deep-seated animosity between the PAIGC's old guard and Vieira threatened to revive political deadlock.

FOREIGN AFFAIRS

In its foreign relations, Guinea-Bissau is motivated primarily by the need to solicit aid, and secondly by a sense of vulnerability to the economic interests of its larger and more prosperous francophone neighbours, Senegal and Guinea. As a result, the country has actively promoted co-operation with Portugal. As a sign of further commitment to rapprochement between the two countries, the Portuguese Prime Minister, Cavaco Silva, visited Guinea-Bissau in March 1989, when both Governments promised increased bilateral co-operation, and agreed to continue to promote relations between African lusophone states. In July 1996 Vieira paid an official visit to Portugal, during which agreement was reached on improved bilateral relations, particularly in the area of defence. In the same month Guinea-Bissau was among the five lusophone African nations which, together with Brazil and Portugal, formally established the CPLP, a lusophone commonwealth intended to benefit each member state by means of joint co-operation on technical, cultural and social matters. Relations with Angola were strengthened following a visit by President Vieira to Luanda in February 2007, during which a number of economic and technical co-operation agreements were signed; this led to Angola opening its first embassy in Guinea-Bissau in May 2007.

Diplomatic relations were established with Taiwan in May 1990, causing the People's Republic of China to cease diplomatic relations with Guinea-Bissau. However, relations with China were restored in April 1998, and have improved in recent years as the Government has given its support to the 'one China' policy. Following a visit by President Vieira to China in November 2006 to attend the Forum on China-Africa Cooperation (FOCAC), the Chinese Government pledged to finance several projects in Guinea-Bissau, including a new military hospital, a Palace of Justice and a Government Palace in Bissau, as well as other infrastructure projects and the construction of some 1,000 new homes. China also offered to finance the construction of a dam at Saltinho on the Corubal river, and a deepwater port in Buba.

Guinea-Bissau's generally very cordial relations with Portugal have recently been punctuated by minor contretemps. This was inevitable, considering that among the large number of Guinean immigrants in Portugal are many members of the political élite that fled during the civil war and many opposition leaders. President Yalá threatened to sever ties with Portugal unless it prevented allowing his political opponents to operate freely, but this incident was defused by correspondence between Yalá and the Portuguese Government. As the 12 October elections approached in 2003, President Yalá increasingly employed a populist 'nationalist' discourse, accusing the opposition of trying to recolonize the country. Following Yalá's overthrow in September 2003 relations with Portugal improved, and only two weeks later Portugal made a donation of 45 metric tons of humanitarian aid (including food, seeds and medical supplies). Portugal's bilateral co-operation programme expired at the end of 2003, and in 2004 Portugal announced a new aid package worth €42m. (US $55m.) covering the years 2005–07. In February 2006 Portugal agreed to pay Guinea-Bissau's $100,000 membership fee for the World Bank's Multilateral Investment Guarantee Agency, enabling potential investors in the country to mitigate against future risks.

Relations with neighbouring countries have been improving in recent years and those between Guinea-Bissau and Cape Verde, which had deteriorated following the coup in 1980, have gradually become closer. The two countries signed a bilateral co-operation agreement in February 1988. A boundary dispute with the Republic of Guinea was resolved in Guinea-Bissau's favour by the International Court of Justice (ICJ) in February 1985. In August 1989 a dispute arose between Guinea-Bissau and Senegal over the demarcation of maritime borders, which had been based on a 1960 agreement between the former colonial powers, France and Portugal. Guinea-Bissau brought proceedings against Senegal in the ICJ after rejecting an international tribunal's ruling in favour of Senegal. In April 1990 Guinea-Bissau accused Senegal of repeated territorial violations and in early May Guinea-Bissau and Senegal appeared close to military conflict after a reconnaissance platoon of the Senegalese army entered Guinea-Bissau territory. However, the detachment was withdrawn, and military confrontation was avoided. A meeting of the two countries' joint commission in July resulted in an agreement to establish a commission to monitor security on the common land border (a response to claims by Senegal that Guinea-Bissau had supported separatists in Senegal's Casamance region). Action by the Senegalese armed forces against the separatists of the Mouvement des forces démocratiques de la Casamance (MFDC) led to the flight of several hundred refugees to Guinea-Bissau in late 1990.

In November 1991 the ICJ ruled that the agreement concluded between France and Portugal in 1960 regarding the demarcation of maritime borders between Guinea-Bissau and Senegal remained valid. In October 1993 the Presidents of Guinea-Bissau and Senegal signed an agreement providing for the joint management and exploitation of the countries' maritime zones (see Economy). The agreement, which was for a renewable 20-year period, was expected to put a definitive end to the countries' dispute over the demarcation of their common maritime borders. In December 1995 the legislature authorized the ratification of the October 1993 accord. In November 1995 the ICJ announced that Guinea-Bissau had abandoned all proceedings regarding the border dispute with Senegal.

Relations with Senegal have, however, continued to be strained by separatist violence in the Casamance region. In December 1992, following an attack by separatists that resulted in the deaths of two Senegalese soldiers, Senegalese aircraft bombarded border villages in Guinea-Bissau. Vieira protested to the Senegalese authorities and denied Senegalese claims that the Government was providing support for the rebels. The Senegalese Government apologized and offered assurances that there would be no repetition of the incident. In March 1993, in an apparent attempt to convince Senegal that it did not support the rebels, the Government handed over one of the exiled leaders of the Casamance separatists, to the Senegalese authorities. In February 1995 the Senegalese air force bombarded the village of Ponta Rosa in Guinea-Bissau, close to the border with Senegal. Despite an acknowledgement by the Senegalese authorities that the bombing had occurred as the result of an error, the Senegalese military conducted a similar attack later in the same month, when the border village of Ingorezinho came under artillery fire. In March, in an attempt to forge a rapprochement between the two countries, President Diouf visited Guinea-Bissau to provide a personal apology for the two recent incidents and to offer the commitment that Senegal would respect Guinea-Bissau's sovereignty. In September, following a meeting at Gabú, in Guinea-Bissau, between representatives of both Governments, agreement was reached to strengthen co-operation and establish regular dialogue concerning security on the countries' joint border. However, a further attack by the Senegalese air force in October, which resulted in injuries to several Guinea-Bissau nationals, prompted the legislature to establish a commission of inquiry to investigate such border incidents. In June 1996 a meeting held at Kolda, in Senegal, between ministerial delegations from Guinea-Bissau and Senegal resulted in renewed commitments to improved collaboration on security.

Relations with Senegal reached a low point following the intervention of Senegalese military forces in support of President Vieira in the 1998–99 military conflict. After the junta's victory, incidents continued in the border area, despite diplomatic efforts to resolve the crisis. In May 2000 calls by the Senegalese President, Abdoulaye Wade, for the presence of UN military observers along the border between the two countries, were rejected by Yalá. However, in July Yalá agreed to provide assistance to Senegal, in the hope of finding a rapid solution to the separatist conflict in that country. In August, during a visit to Dakar, Yalá and Wade signed an agreement allowing for the joint surveillance of the border. Guinea-Bissau radically changed its stance on the Casamance rebellion after the defeat of the military junta in November, as several members of the MFDC were arrested in Bissau with junta supporters. President Yalá accused veteran PAIGC leaders of supporting and supplying the separatists. He ordered the military to expel the rebels from the northern border area. Not surprisingly, relations with Senegal improved substantially in 2001. In July the military withdrew a contingent of 1,500 men from the border, ostensibly for want of funds, leaving it guarded only by the border police. Officials from both countries have continued to meet regularly, even though peace in the area remains a distant achievement, largely because of the division of the MFDC into several factions. In March 2002 the authorities arrested Alexandre Djiba, a prominent leader of the Sidy Badji faction—the most militarily assertive. In May Djiba was delivered to the Senegalese authorities after they promised to release him. Fishing disputes have also impaired relations between the two countries. In March and April dozens of small fishing boats and more than 100 Senegalese fishermen were apprehended for fishing illegally in Guinea-Bissau's waters in incidents that resulted in the death of two coastguards. The fishermen were released in early June after the Senegalese Government accepted responsibility for the death of the coastguards. As the Government in Guinea-Bissau maintained its policy of denying sanctuary to the MFDC, bilateral relations continued to improve. Fewer and fewer violent incidents have been registered and even cattle-rustling has been curtailed. In May 2003 the Senegalese Minister of the Interior visited Yalá to propose Bissau as the venue for an MFDC conference to try to unify the faction-ridden group and to negotiate a ceasefire. Fighting continued in the northern border region, however, and in February 2004 the Guinea-Bissau army was involved in skirmishes with a radical faction of the MFDC. On 30 December 2004 a general peace accord was signed between the Senegalese Government and the MFDC. Since the rebellion began in 1982, an estimated 3,500 people have been killed in Casamance. The accord promised to greatly improve security in the region, and could have positive repercussions for relations between Senegal and Guinea-Bissau. However, in June 2005 a dissident faction of the MFDC, led by Salif Sadio, which was opposed to the peace deal, launched a series of attacks in Casamance, prompting fears that the ceasefire might collapse. Responding to the growing instability in the border region, on 16 March 2006 the army launched a large operation, involving more than 2,500 soldiers and heavy weaponry, targeting bases of Sadio's dissident rebels in the area around São Domingos. By the time military operations ended on 27 April, over 100 soldiers and an unknown number of rebels had been killed, with at least twice as many injured. Following the attacks Sadio was reported to have fled with 50 guerrillas towards the border with The Gambia. As a result of the fighting, the UN estimated that 10,000 refugees fled the area around São Domingos to nearby villages and towns, while a further 2,500 fled across the border into Senegal. In addition, the UN estimated that 20,000 Guineans were facing severe food shortages after being cut off from their main sources of supply. In mid-May the UN launched an appeal to raise US $3.6m. to provide emergency food aid and to clear land-mines along the region's main arterial roads. Responding to the appeal, in June the EU donated €1m. to assist refugees affected by the conflict; this was followed in July by a donation from the UN Central Emergency Response Fund (CERF), which gave $1.3m. However, tensions continued in the border area. In September the army intercepted a boat at Bandim carrying weapons to be delivered to rebels in Casamance, including machine-guns, rocket-launchers, mortars, grenades and anti-tank mines.

The UN played a significant, if quiet, role in the political stabilization of Guinea-Bissau. On 30 April 1999 the UN Secretary-General established UNOGBIS, with a mandate to aid peace-building efforts, support the consolidation of democracy and the rule of law, encourage friendly relations with its neighbours and assist in the electoral process. The UNOGBIS mandate, scheduled to end on 31 December 1999, was first extended by three months to 31 March 2000, and later by a year to 31 March 2001, at the Government's request. The mandate was repeatedly extended. The successive extensions are an acknowledgement of UNOGBIS' success (especially in assisting the electoral process) and also of the fragility of Guinea-Bissau's political system. Relations with UNOGBIS had deteriorated as a result of the reports to the UN Secretary-General produced by Samuel Nana-Sinkam. In his December 2001 report he blamed the Government for the country's political and economic crisis and was replaced by David Stephens in February 2002. Guinea-Bissau's standing in the UN was diminished by the withdrawal of its right to vote at the UN General Assembly for not having paid its membership dues. In March 2003 UNOGBIS presented a 'National Plan for Human Rights' for 2003–04, part of the UN programme to assist countries in improving their implementation of international agreements. In June 2003 it presented a bleak report to the UN Secretary-General, stating that the country was in a downward spiral of political, economic and social crisis, and threatening to withdraw its support for the electoral process if Yalá's Government did not improve its performance. UNOGBIS's mandate was repeatedly extended, most recently until 31 December 2007.

The UN deepened its commitment to assisting Guinea-Bissau through its political, economic and social crisis when, in October 2002, the UN Economic and Social Council (ECOSOC) created an ad hoc advisory group to study the country's needs in these areas. A delegation of the group first visited Bissau in November for talks with all the interested parties—Government, opposition, civil society and international partners. From this trip an action plan was presented to the UN system and Bretton Woods institutions. However, the group also recommended specific immediate actions, as the country's situation was increasingly liable to collapse.

A number of other international and regional organizations have played an important role in assisting Guinea-Bissau in overcoming its problems. Among them are lusophone organizations, namely the CPLP and the Países Africanos de Língua Oficial Portuguesa (PALOP), and regional ones, such as ECOWAS.

Economy

MILES SMITH-MORRIS

Revised by EDWARD GEORGE

INTRODUCTION

According to the World Bank, Guinea-Bissau was one of the poorest countries in the world in 2005, ranking 200th of 208 countries in terms of gross national income (GNI) per head. In 2005 the country's GNI totalled US $289m., equivalent to $180 per head (or $790 on an international purchasing-power parity basis). During 1995–2005 Guinea-Bissau's gross domestic product (GDP) decreased, in real terms, at an average annual rate of 0.2%. Over the same period the population increased at an average annual rate of 2.9%, while GDP per head declined at an average annual rate of 3.0%. Real GDP fell by an estimated 28.1% in 1998, owing to the military conflict, but resumed its growth in 1999, rising by 7.8%, and increasing again in 2000, by 8.7%. Growth in 2001 was only 0.2%, owing to a decline in the international price of cashew nuts. As a result of a continuing fall in both prices and production of cashews, a reduction in foreign aid, and political instability caused by the Yalá regime, GDP contracted by an estimated 7.1% in 2002 and a further 0.6% in 2003. However, in 2004 GDP returned to positive growth, registering 2.2%, and 3.5% in 2005, due to a strong cashew crop and a return to political stability. The UN Development Programme (UNDP) ranked Guinea-Bissau 173rd of 177 countries in 2004 under its Human Development Index, which measures GDP per head, adult literacy and life expectancy.

Following independence in 1974, the Government established a centrally planned economy, and an ambitious investment programme—financed mainly by foreign borrowing—was initiated, with emphasis on the industrial sector. However, the economy, which had been adversely affected by the campaign for independence, continued to deteriorate, partly as a result of the Government's policies, and by the late 1970s Guinea-Bissau had an underdeveloped agricultural sector, a growing external debt, dwindling exports and escalating inflation.

In the 1980s the Government initiated a policy of economic liberalization. In 1983 measures were initiated to liberalize the trading sector, to increase producer prices and to encourage private enterprise. Although agricultural production and exports increased in 1984, the momentum behind the reforms slowed in 1985–86. By the end of 1986 export earnings had fallen, and the production of many goods had been halted, as the depletion of the country's reserves of foreign exchange made it difficult to import fuel or spare parts. In response to the deteriorating economic situation, the Government adopted a structural adjustment programme (SAP) for 1987–90 (see below), which aimed to strengthen the role of the private sector. In 1990 the Government began the reform of the country's public enterprises and initiated the first phase of its programme of privatization. By mid-1995 the process of removing subsidies from public enterprises, which had begun in 1991, had been virtually completed.

AGRICULTURE AND FISHING

Agriculture is the principal economic activity. The agricultural sector (including forestry and fishing) engaged an estimated 82% of the working population and accounted for an estimated 60.3% of GDP in 2005. The main cash crop is cashew nuts, of which an estimated 97,277 metric tons were produced in 2005, accounting for some 92.8% of total merchandise exports that year. In addition, rice, roots and tubers, maize, millet, sorghum, fruits, sugar cane, cotton, coconuts and groundnuts are produced. Livestock and timber production are also important, while the sale of fishing licences now represents the country's second largest source of export revenue (US $14.2m. in 2005, representing 27% of total government revenue).

Among food crops, rice constitutes the staple fare of the population. The southern region of Tombali accounts for about 70% of the country's rice production. Production of paddy rice expanded in the pre-war period, and some rice was exported in years of good harvests, such as 1995, when there was production of 133,266 metric tons. According to FAO, production of paddy rice fell to an estimated 66,424 tons in 2003, before recovering to 89,192 tons in 2004 and 98,340 tons in 2005. However, heavy flooding in late 2005 which damaged paddy fields and disrupted planting was expected to reduce the rice crop by 25% in 2006. Imports of rice have risen sharply in recent years; increasing salination in mangrove areas has reduced local production, while unfavourable dollar prices for cashews have encouraged producers to barter the commodity directly for imported rice. In the late 1990s imports accounted for some 40% of domestic rice consumption, thus depressing the market for domestic produce. In 2001 rice imports accounted for 6.6% of all merchandise imports, the single largest item. In May 2003 a US $4.35m. loan from the Kuwaiti Development Fund was announced for the development of the rice industry in 2003–08. Production of cereals (excluding rice) totalled 55,031 tons in 2003, before rising to 82,183 tons in 2004 and 114,198 tons in 2005. In 2002 food security was threatened by drought, particularly in the east of the country. Consequently, FAO estimated that Guinea-Bissau would need to import 70,000 tons of cereals (imports were some 79,953 tons in 2001). As a result of a second poor harvest in 2003 the UN World Food Programme (WFP) provided 39,000 tons of food aid, in addition to a donation of 4,500 tons of food aid from the Japanese Government (of which 2,035 tons were rice). For the 2004 agricultural season the Government requested assistance from FAO, including 900 tons of seed rice, 515 tons of groundnuts, and $80,000 worth of farming tools. Following a poor harvest in the southern rice-growing region, in May 2006 the Government appealed for $2.35m. in emergency assistance to feed up to 130,000 citizens who were facing severe food shortages. In May 2007 FAO reported ongoing localized food insecurity due to market disruptions, and estimated that the country would need to import 85,700 tons of cereal in 2007. Maize, beans, cassava, sorghum and sweet potatoes are important subsistence crops.

Among Guinea-Bissau's traditional exports during the colonial period were groundnuts, grown in the interior as an extension of the Senegalese cultivation, oil-palm products on the islands and the coast, and coconuts. In 1977 groundnut exports, totalling 16,335 metric tons, accounted for 60% of total export earnings. However, by 1993, according to the IMF, exports of groundnuts had ceased altogether and had not resumed in the early 2000s. According to FAO estimates, production of groundnuts (in shell) totalled 20,000 tons in 2005. The Government is working to develop the production of groundnuts in their traditional areas by distributing seeds to peasants. Cashew nuts are a relatively recent crop, and output is expanding. The value of cashew-nut exports was US $93.5m. in 2005, when production was estimated at 97,277 tons. The country's trade in cashew nuts had been hampered by a rift between producers and buyers regarding prices and export taxes. In early 2006 a buyers' dispute over government-fixed prices led to a sharp decline in the cashew nut trade, cutting annual production to an estimated 85,200 tons. In April 2007 the new Government set a lower reference price for cashew nuts which, along with other measures, has helped revive cashew sales, although capacity constraints at Bissau's port are restraining export growth. The majority of Guinea-Bissau's cashew nuts are purchased by India for processing; however, in the early 2000s Indian processors were increasingly turning to domestic producers, and it was hoped that the establishment of two processing firms in Guinea-Bissau would open new markets for direct sales to Europe (with a higher potential revenue from processed nuts).

In the Government's development plans, priority has been given to agriculture, with the aim of achieving self-sufficiency in food. A sugar refinery (with an annual capacity of 10,000 metric tons), capable of satisfying domestic needs, was to be built at Gambiel and will be supplied from new, irrigated plantations covering an area of 6,000 ha. An agro-industrial complex at Cumeré is capable of processing 50,000 tons of rice and 70,000 tons of groundnuts annually. It is estimated that these schemes, together with the projected construction of a thermoelectric power station, will require investment of US $200m., mainly from external sources. The Government has nationalized most of the land but does grant private concessions to work it and has maintained the rights of those tilling their fields. The post-independence regime confiscated the property of former pro-Portuguese Guineans and introduced state control over foreign trade and domestic retail trade through 'people's shops', the inefficiency and corruption of which led to serious shortages of consumer goods and contributed to the downfall of the Cabral regime in 1980. In 1983/84 the Government partially privatized the state-controlled trading companies, and raised producer prices by about 70%, in an attempt to accelerate agricultural output. Despite the introduction of these measures, Guinea-Bissau continued to operate a 'war economy', superimposed upon a rudimentary peasant economy where most products are bought and sold by the state. Since 1987, however, plans have been accelerated for the removal of price controls on most agricultural products, except essential goods, and for the liberalization of internal marketing systems. A Land Act was approved in 1998, but further efforts at reform were stalled two months later by the outbreak of civil war. The approval of long-awaited legislation on land reform, which would allow the allocation of land for private ownership and provide a delimitation of communal land, was still pending in mid-2007.

The fishing industry has expanded rapidly since the late 1970s, and it has been estimated that the potential annual catch in Guinea-Bissau's waters could total some 300,000 metric tons. However, the total catch was estimated at just 6,200 tons in 2005. In 2000 Guinea-Bissau recorded its largest ever fish exports totalling US $807,000, but with overfishing and the deterioration of the national fleet this declined to $508,000 in 2001 (all of which was shrimp), $200,000 in 2003 and less than $100,000 in 2004. However, new investment in the sector boosted fishing exports to an estimated $700,000 in 2005. The local fishing sector is principally artisanal, while industrial fishing is conducted largely by foreign vessels operating under licence, depriving Guinea-Bissau of a potential revenue source in processing. Revenues from fishing licences have risen steadily from $13m. in 1999 to $14.2m. in 2005, with 193 foreign vessels registered. If illegal fishing could be effectively prevented, fishing could become Guinea-Bissau's main source of revenue, as the country's maritime zone is potentially among the richest in West Africa. In 2006 40 trawlers and dozens of pirogues were impounded after being caught fishing illegally. In 1980 Guinea-Bissau entered into an agreement with the European Community (EC, now the European Union—EU), under the terms of which EC vessels were allowed to fish in Guinea-Bissau's waters in return for aid. The arrangement has since been renewed and updated on nine occasions. In May 2007 the EU renewed its fishing agreement with Guinea-Bissau, agreeing to pay annual compensation of €7m. over the period 2007–11 for licences for 60 ships to fish shrimp in its territorial waters, roughly the same amount in compensation offered under the 2004 accord. However, the number of tuna licences was reduced from 70 to 37, reflecting the reduction in tuna stocks. In addition, the EU agreed to grant €500,000 to improve the patrolling of the country's maritime waters to deter pirates and to improve sanitation facilities in the fishing sector. Securing access to West Africa's rich stocks of fish is a priority for the EU, which has, in recent years, been forced to cut back quotas in its own waters as a result of overfishing. In 1993 an agreement was signed with Senegal providing for the joint management of the countries' maritime zones, with fishing resources to be divided according to the determination of a joint management agency, formally established in 1995 (see below).

Cattle-breeding is a very important activity among Balante and Muslim tribes of the interior. In 2005 there were 530,000 head of cattle, 370,000 pigs, 335,000 goats and 300,000 sheep, according to FAO estimates. Meat consumption is significant, and some hides and skins are exported. Timber exports resumed in 1986, after a full assessment of resources, reaching US $898,000m. in that year, and production totalled 592,000 cu m in 2005, according to FAO estimates. Earnings from the export of rough and processed timber totalled $1.5m. in 1995, but declined to an estimated $600,000 in 1997 and ceased entirely in 1999.

INDUSTRY, MINING, TRANSPORT AND TELECOMMUNICATIONS

There is little industrial activity other than food-processing, brewing and wood- and cotton-processing. Industry (including mining, manufacturing, construction and power) employed 4.1% of the economically active population in 1994 and provided 11.7% of GDP in 2005. According to the World Bank, industrial GDP declined, in real terms, at an average annual rate of 1.9% in 1995–2005; however, growth of 2.4% was recorded in 2003, and this improved to 4.6% in 2005. Energy is derived principally from thermal and hydroelectric power. In 2003 domestic electricity production totalled 15.8m. kWh, a significant decline compared with 1997, when it amounted to 48.2m. kWh. The state electricity company, Empresa de Electricidade e Águas da Guiné-Bissau (EAGB), performs poorly, but attempts by the Government to restructure the company and attract private-sector investment have so far proved unsuccessful. Only 12% of households in Guinea-Bissau have regular access to electricity, the lowest electrification rate recorded in West Africa. Energy production since 1999 has been insufficient to supply demand in Bissau, the centre of non-agricultural economic activity, which suffers from regular black-outs. As a result, most energy is currently supplied by private generators. The supply deficit is due mainly to fuel shortages caused by government-set low prices, and equipment failures that result from poor maintenance. In 2004 imports of petroleum and petroleum products comprised an estimated 15.6% of the value of total imports. In December 2006 the Chinese Government agreed to finance the construction of the 18-MW Saltinho Rapids dam on the Corubal River, 100 km south-east of Bissau, at an estimated cost of US $87m. The Government plans to import electricity from the Sambangalo dam in Senegal and from the Kaleta dam in Guinea by 2009. The mining sector has still to be developed, and prospecting for bauxite, petroleum and phosphates is in progress. In 2006 an international consortium—GB Phosphates Mining—announced that it would invest $105m. over 25 years in developing phosphate reserves at Farim, with mining due to start in late 2008. Eventual production of 2.1m. tons per year was expected, generating an estimated $50m.–$100m. in annual export earnings. In 2007 Angolan companies were evaluating plans to develop bauxite discoveries in the Boé area.

Petroleum exploration has resumed in two offshore areas contested with neighbouring countries. In October 1993 an agreement was signed with Senegal, providing for the joint management of the countries' maritime zones. The agreement, which was to operate for an initial 20-year period, provided for an 85%:15% division of petroleum resources between Senegal and Guinea-Bissau, respectively, altered to 80%:20% in August 2000. Guinea-Bissau formally ratified the agreement in December 1995, and the Agence de Gestion et Coopération was created to administer petroleum and fishing activity in the 100,000 sq km joint area. This area has been divided into two zones, one denominated Cheval Marin (6,500 sq km), operated by an Italian company, Agip (now owned by Eni of Spain), the other called Croix du Sud, operated by an Australian firm, Fusion Oil. In June 2002 Fusion Oil sold its interests in this section to a US company, Amerada Hess, which has not yet commenced drilling. The southern section of the joint exploration area, on the border with Guinea, which may contain significant deposits, was contested until 1985, when a joint commission was formed with Guinea to facilitate exploration in the two countries' maritime border area. A US petroleum company, Pecten, began exploratory drilling in its offshore concession area in 1990. In July of that year the Government announced that a new exploration programme was to begin in 1991. In 1996 a Canadian petroleum company, Petrobank, agreed terms for a joint venture with the state petroleum company of Guinea-Bissau, PetroGuin, to explore an offshore block covering some 280,000 ha. Petrobank's initial investment was to total $1m., but the company subsequently sold its interest to a British company, Premier Oil. Premier Oil signed an agreement with PetroGuin to explore two adjacent blocks, and by mid-2003 had drilled 11 wells in the three blocks without finding viable deposits. Premier Oil holds production rights on the 10 southern exploration blocks and in 2004 drilled two more exploration wells, Sanapa-2 and Esperança-1, on Blocks 2, 4A and 5A, discovering oil in Sanapa-2. In May 2001 a US company, First Exchange Corpn, delivered data on seismic surveys conducted on the remaining blocks, revealing that there might be reserves of petroleum totalling 20m.–40m. barrels in the offshore area. By late 2003 estimates of recoverable reserves had risen to 2,000m. barrels. A three-year concession for the exploration of Dome Flore was signed by Fusion Oil in May 2003. In September 2004 a French petroleum company, Maurel and Prom, signed an agreement with PetroGuin for an onshore concession and for Block 3, which covers over one-half of Guinea-Bissau's shallow offshore acreage. Maurel & Prom took a 90% stake in both concessions, with PetroGuin retaining the remaining 10%. In late 2004 the US oil company, ExxonMobil, acquired a 37% stake in the Cheval Marin concession. In June 2006 the ministerial council awarded four exploration licences for Blocks 2, 4A, 5A and 7B, but gave no details of the companies or the contractual terms. This raised fresh concerns over the lack of transparency in the Government's management of the licensing process and the award of exploration blocks. In August it was announced that studies had revealed oil reserves around the Bijagós archipelago, which could produce 120,000 barrels per year. In October PetroGuin announced that it would auction nine offshore blocks through public tender in early 2007, including two blocks that were relinquished by Premier Oil in early 2006. In February 2007 Premier Oil sold an 11.4% stake in its Esperança 4A and 5A, and its Sinapa concessions in Block 2, to an Israeli oil company, Delek Energy Systems. In March Premier Oil announced that it would abandon development of its Espinafre-1 well due to technical difficulties, but would restart drilling at its Eirozes-1 well in late 2007. In May PetroGuin awarded three more exploration licences: Block 1 to Ser Petrolium (Qatar), Block 7A to Sociedade Angolana de Hidrocarbonetos (Angola) and Block 7B Super Nova (Netherlands). Sinopec (China), PETROBRÁS (Brazil) and Sonangol (Angola) have also expressed interest in exploring for oil in Guinea-Bissau's offshore area.

For strategic reasons, an impressive network of 3,500 km of roads was built from Bissau to the north and north-east in 1972. The road system is poor, however, especially during the rainy season. In 2002, according to International Road Federation estimates, there were some 3,455 km of roads, of which 964 km were paved. The EU has financed the extension and upgrade of the road between the capital, Bissau, and the northern border with Senegal. In 2004 the EU provided €35m. for the repair and maintenance of roads in Bambadinca, Bafatá and Gabú. That year the African Development Bank (ADB) also granted 2,900m. francs CFA for the reconstruction of the Jugudul–Bambadinca road. ECOWAS has pledged to fund the rehabilitation of the motorway connecting Senegal, Guinea-Bissau and Guinea through Dakar, Bissau and Conakry. In February 2006 Portugal, France and the EU agreed to fund a US $10.9m. programme to rehabilitate 350 km of roads in the north and centre of the country. In 2006 the World Bank funded $4m. of road rehabilitation, and in 2007 the Chinese Government agreed to finance the rehabilitation of roads from Buba to Catio, and from Quebo to Cacine. In December 2003 Guinea-Bissau's largest civil engineering project, the 750m-long Ponte Amílcar Cabral over the Mansoa river at João Landim, was completed. The bridge, which links the north and south of the country, was financed by the EU. In 2006 work began on a new bridge over the Cacheu river, at São Domingos, with €28.8m. of EU funding and €4.5m. from the Union économique et monétaire ouest-africaine (UEMOA). The bridge will open a transport link between Bissau and the border with Senegal, and is due for completion in April 2009. Water transport could be greatly developed, as 85% of the population live within 20 km of a navigable waterway. The country's main commercial port is Bissau, and the Chinese Government is considering financing the construction of a deepwater port in Buba which could provide an outlet for future bauxite exports from the Boé deposits.

Guinea-Bissau's national airline, Transportes Aéreos da Guiné-Bissau, was liquidated in 1997 following an unsuccessful privatization. A weekly service was provided by the Portuguese national airline, TAP, to Lisbon. In July 2003 a twice-weekly service to Lisbon was introduced by the Portuguese carrier Air Luxor, which created a subsidiary, Air Luxor GB (renamed Hifly in 2005), with 49% capital owned by Air Luxor and 51% by local investors, to operate the service, with an initial investment of €4m. Also in July 2003 Air Luxor agreed to provide $2.5m. towards the rehabilitation of Guinea-Bissau's Osvaldo Vieira International Airport, which will be carried out by a Portuguese company, Aeroportos e Navegação Aérea. Flights to Dakar, Senegal, are provided by Air Senegal International and Transportes Aéreos de Cabo Verde, from where there are daily connections to Europe and elsewhere. The collapse of Air Luxor in late 2006 led to the suspension of its flights from Bissau to Lisbon, leaving just one weekly flight operated by TAP. In 2007 the Government was in negotiations with Angola's national airline, TAAG, to create a Luanda–Bissau–Lisbon route which would be served by a new national airline, Air Bissau Internacional.

Guinea-Bissau's telecommunications infrastructure is poorly developed. In 2005 the fixed-line network was estimated to have 10,600 functioning lines, 500 less than in 2000, of which only 500 had international access. Fax, internet and data transmission services are limited to Bissau city, Bafatá and Gabú. In August 2003 the Government opened bids for a licence to operate cellular services, but take-up by investors was poor given the Government's track record. In November 2003 the Government established a mobile telecoms company, Guiné Tel, and in December three companies submitted bids: Canelux (Portugal), Dataport Enterprises (Morocco), and Investcom Holdings (a Lebanese-Luxembourg venture). However, only two mobile phone companies subsequently started operating in Guinea-Bissau: Guiné Tel and Spacetel Guinea-Bissau (Areeba), which is owned by MTN (South Africa). In March 2007 the Government awarded a third mobile-phone licence to a Senegalese company, Société nationale des télécommunications du Sénégal (Sonatel). The new operator, Orange Bissau, started operations in June, initially only in Bissau and the north of the country. In 2004 Portugal Telecom signed a new 10-year concession, following the revocation of its 20-year concession in 2003. This reduced its 51% stake in Guiné Telecom to 40%, and committed Portugal Telecom to providing universal access to the fixed line network, investing in public telephone booths and ensuring the availability of telephone lines in rural areas. In 2005 there were an estimated 26,000 internet users in Guinea-Bissau. Eguitel Comunicações was the only company providing broadband services.

EXTERNAL TRADE AND FINANCE

The value of exports has increased consistently during the 2000s from US $50.0m. in 2001 to an estimated $100.8m. in 2005. In that year India, a major importer of cashew nuts, was by far the largest market for exports (67.4%), followed by Nigeria (19.0%), Senegal (1.5%) and Portugal (1.1%). Cashew nuts were Guinea-Bissau's most important export commodity, accounting for 92.8% of total export earnings in 2005.

Before the adoption of the CFA franc to replace the peso in 1997, demand for manufactured goods, machinery, fuel and food had ensured a high level of imports, which averaged US $60m. per year in the 1980s. However, foreign-exchange controls and the closure of some state enterprises caused a large decline in imports of industrial raw materials. Imports reached $88.6m. in 1997 and have fluctuated since 1998, reaching $83m. in 2004 and $119.1m. in 2005. The largest categories in 2005 were petroleum products ($15.8m.), foodstuffs ($15.1m.) and consumer goods ($15.0m.). In 2005 the principal sources of imports were Senegal (34.6%), Italy (20.4%) and Portugal (12.7%).

In 2005 revenues and grants of the central Government totalled 41,378m. francs CFA, of which around two-thirds, (27,978m. francs CFA) originated from revenues (tax and non-tax). This was lower than in 2004, when total revenues reached 49,029m. francs CFA, but was more than offset by the fall in total expenditure from 70,418m. francs CFA in 2004 to 60,524m. francs CFA in 2005. As a result, the budget deficit (including grants from abroad and net lending) fell from 21,389m. francs CFA in 2004 to 19,146 francs CFA in 2005, equivalent to 12.1% of GDP. According to the IMF, the deficit on the current account of the balance of payments (including official transfers) fell from a peak of $44m. in 2001 to a surplus of $8.2m. in 2004, before returning to a deficit of $21.4m. in 2005. In 1990–2000 the average annual rate of inflation was 32.8%. The consumer price index declined by an average of 2.1% in 1999, and in 2001–2006 increased at a modest average of 2.6% per year, averaging 3.3% in 2001 and 2002, 1.6% in 2003, 0.8% in 2004, 3.4% in 2005 and 2.0% in 2006. Bilateral aid forms the major source of international assistance, and in 2005 it accounted for $39.4m. of total official aid of $79.1m., while multilateral aid accounted for $39.6m. Guinea-Bissau also received generous amounts of balance-of-payments and food aid. The country has attended various Franco-African summit conferences and has been a signatory to successive Lomé Conventions and to their successor, the Cotonou Agreement, signed in Cotonou, Benin, in 2000 and ratified by Guinea-Bissau in April 2003.

An extensive reorganization of Guinea-Bissau's banking system has been under way since 1989, involving the replacement of Banco Nacional da Guiné-Bissau by three institutions: a central bank, a commercial bank (Banco Internacional da Guiné-Bissau, which began operations in March 1990), and a national credit bank, established in September 1990, to channel investment. A fourth financial institution, responsible for managing aid receipts, was subsequently created with assistance from the EC, the US Agency for International Development, Sweden and Portugal. In 1991 the Government authorized the establishment of privately operated foreign-exchange bureaux. However, unpaid loans placed the Banco Internacional da Guiné-Bissau on the brink of bankruptcy. Since its closure would have been a severe blow to the fragile private sector, the central bank promised in late 2001 to grant it US $9m. in order to offset $8m.-worth of debts. However, this recapitalization was not forthcoming, obliging the Government to announce the bank's closure in March 2002. This was followed by the closure of the branch of a Portuguese bank, the Banco Totta e Açores. However, the sector has since recovered and in 2006 there were four commercial banks active in the country. In December 2005 a branch of the Banco Regional de Solidariedade opened in Guinea-Bissau, focusing on micro-credit projects. However, banking usage is extremely low and in 2006 there were only seven bank accounts per 1,000 inhabitants.

In November 1987 Guinea-Bissau applied to join the Franc Zone, but withdrew its application in January 1990 following the formulation of an exchange-rate agreement with Portugal linking the Guinea peso rate to that of the Portuguese escudo. This accord was considered to form the initial stage in the creation of an 'escudo zone'. However, in August 1993 Guinea-Bissau renewed its application to join the Franc Zone. Guinea-Bissau joined the UEMOA in March 1997 and was admitted to the Franc Zone on 17 April. The Guinea peso and the franc CFA co-existed for a period of three months to allow for the gradual replacement, at foreign-exchange offices, of the national currency at a rate of 1 franc CFA = 65 Guinea pesos. With the entry of Guinea-Bissau into the Franc Zone, the Banco Central da Guiné-Bissau ceased to operate as the country's central bank and its functions were assumed by the Banque centrale des états de l'Afrique de l'ouest (BCEAO), which has its headquarters in Dakar, Senegal.

DEVELOPMENT AND AID

The Government, led by President Vieira, which came to power in 1980, aimed to downgrade many of the prestigious projects that had been initiated by Cabral's administration, and to emphasize rural development. A programme of economic stabilization in the early 1980s hoped to liberalize trade and to increase activity in the private sector. In 1986 trading restrictions were lifted, allowing private traders to import and export goods, although the two state-owned enterprises retained their monopolies in rice, petroleum products and various other commodities. After consultations with the World Bank, the IMF and other external donors, Guinea-Bissau initiated a SAP covering the period 1987–90. The programme was to be wholly financed by external aid totalling US $46.4m. In May 1987 the peso was devalued by about 60%, with the official rate set at 650 pesos = $1, and new taxes and higher tariffs were introduced. The Development Plan (1989–92) aimed to consolidate the progress made under the SAP in the reduction of the state's role in the economy and the growth of private investment.

In January 1989 the Government announced the adoption of a US $104.6m. investment programme, to be funded entirely by external donors, which was to supplement development projects already proceeding under the SAP. Customs duties and general taxes on imported goods were reduced in April. In the following month international donor countries pledged allocations of $120m., of which 40% was to assist in financing the balance-of-payments deficit, and the remainder to meet general financing requirements. In accordance with these agreements, the World Bank approved a $23.4m. loan to support the second stage of the SAP. The Government undertook to extend the aims of its economic liberalization programme.

In June 1990 President Vieira initiated new measures to attract domestic and foreign private investment. It was stated that most of the 50 public enterprises were to be restructured and made more efficient although some strategic sectors, such as telecommunications, electricity and infrastructure, were expected to remain under state control. A decree on privatization was adopted in March 1991, defining areas of state intervention in the economy and outlining the rules for transferring state holdings in public enterprises to the private sector. The second phase of privatization began in early 1994. In January 1995 the IMF approved a series of loans totalling US $13.6m. under an enhanced structural adjustment facility (ESAF) in support of the Government's economic reform programme. According to the World Bank, by the end of 2001 total external debt was $668.3m., down from $965.6m. in 1998, which was equivalent to 1,177.6% of the value of exports of goods and services. Of this total, $364.7m. was owed to multilateral institutions, and $262.4m. was bilateral debt. In that year the cost of debt servicing was equivalent to 41.1% of the total value of exports of goods and services. Before the military conflict, efforts to renegotiate the country's external debt were being made with the assistance of UNDP. In March 1998 the IMF announced its approval of the Government's execution of its SAP for 1995–98, thus improving Guinea-Bissau's eligibility for debt relief under the initiative for heavily indebted poor countries (HIPCs). After the war, efforts for debt reduction continued. In November 2000 the IMF found Guinea-Bissau to be, on a preliminary basis, eligible for debt relief under the HIPC initiative. The country gained entry to the programme (which commenced on 15 December), from which it was to receive $790m. in debt-service relief. In January 2001 the 'Paris Club' of international creditors agreed to reschedule 90% of Guinea-Bissau's debt ($141m.) under the HIPC initiative.

In February 1998 the Government announced a further stage in its privatization programme. This programme was interrupted by the military conflict and associated political instability and resumed only in May 2001. With support from the World Bank, more than 24 public and parastatal companies in the sectors of telecommunications, utilities, tourism, agro-industry, fishing and port and airport management were to be divested by the Ministry of the Economy by 2006. It was hoped that these measures would significantly boost the private sector, which had been adversely affected by the military conflict.

As part of the ESAF agreed in 1995, the IMF provided US $6.5m. in support of the Government's programme for 1997–98. However, the economy suffered a serious reversal following the military uprising of June 1998. Several months of intense fighting in the capital resulted in extensive destruction of public buildings, causing severe disruption to government and services, and of private business premises. In addition, as many as 400,000 people were displaced by the conflict, imposing a serious burden on the country's underdeveloped infrastructure and necessitating appeals for high levels of humanitarian aid. Following the overthrow of President Vieira in May 1999, the Prime Minister, Francisco José Fadul, urged the international community to continue with economic aid, in particular with the $200m. funding awarded earlier that month at a Geneva (Switzerland) round table meeting on Guinea-Bissau that had been organized by the UN and Guinea-Bissau's development partners. In July the EU granted Guinea-Bissau emergency aid worth 580m. escudos to assist those affected by the armed conflict. In September the IMF awarded $3m. in emergency aid in support of the Government's reconstruction and economic recovery programme. The programme, which, it was estimated, would cost some $138m., focused on the reconstruction of housing and basic infrastructure, the demobilization of former combatants and the strengthening of private-sector operations.

In January 2000 the IMF approved a US $2m. loan in emergency assistance. The funds were expected to be used to accelerate demobilization, decrease military spending and improve health and education facilities, which had been damaged during the 1998–99 conflict. In April 2000 the ADB agreed to provide $500m. in funding for the improvement of Guinea-Bissau's health system.

Praising the Government's economic performance, the IMF approved a three-year poverty reduction and growth facility (PRGF), worth some US $18m., in December 2000. As a prerequisite, the Government had previously submitted an interim poverty reduction and strategy paper to the IMF outlining its strategy for 2000–03. The strategy was based on four points: rapid and sustained economic growth; increased access to social goods; a reduction in poverty; and good governance. However, the Government appeared to be struggling to achieve its commitments, as indicated by a statement made by the IMF and the World Bank in May 2001, in which they stated their intention to suspend the aid programme for a period of four months, pending an investigation. The suspension was in response to the disappearance of $15m. in donor assistance, which the Government was unable to explain. Although Guinea-Bissau was still able to resort to bilateral aid, the suspension represented a reversal for the Government's economic policy, as 80% of the recently approved budget was to be financed by foreign aid. The suspension of the PRGF was extended indefinitely until the Government's compliance with its commitments was demonstrated. A short-term macroeconomic programme (STMP) was set up in its stead, originally for the August–November 2001 period. The final STMP evaluation mission, in March 2002, found the performance of the Government disappointing, particularly with regard to the increase in the fiscal deficit. As the likelihood of complying with the PRGF was low, with an infrastructure still recovering from civil war, an extended staff-monitored programme was posited, which would co-ordinate donor aid, but not provide direct IMF funding. In February 2003 a report by the Ad Hoc Advisory Group on Guinea-Bissau from the UN Economic and Social Council recommended the establishment of an Emergency Economic Management Fund to address Guinea-Bissau's short-term requirements, including the financing of elections in 2003–04. After international fears that further postponement of legislative elections would threaten the democratic process in the country, some $1.3m. was granted by the EU in July 2003 and 1,600m. francs CFA ($2.5m.) by UEMOA, to help cover electoral expenses. Despite the political and economic unrest caused by President Yalá's administration, Guinea-Bissau continued to receive international donor support.

The World Bank and the IMF had decided to delay negotiations on resuming assistance to Guinea-Bissau until after the legislative elections, recognizing that there was little prospect of meaningful reforms before then. However, following the overthrow of President Yalá in September 2003, the IMF raised the prospect that aid totalling US $458m., pledged by donors in May 1999 following the civil war, could be disbursed soon. In December 2003 UNDP established an Emergency Economic Management Fund (EEMF) to assist Guinea-Bissau through its transition process. The fund was to be managed jointly by the Government, the IMF and the World Bank, UNDP and the ADB.

In January 2004 an 'emergency budget' for 2004 was drawn up with expenditure totalling US $108m. (the bulk of which would pay for salary arrears), producing a financing gap of $18.3m. However, by June 2004 only $4m. had been pledged by donors to meet this shortfall, principally from the Netherlands, Portugal and Angola. In February 2005 the Portuguese Government hosted a mini-donor conference, attended by more than 24 countries and international organizations, including Brazil, the EU, France, the Netherlands, Sweden, the USA, the World Bank, the IMF and the ADB. The conference secured financing to cover a shortfall in the 2005 budget, and extended the EEMF until June 2005. A full round table conference was scheduled for December 2005, but was postponed due to prolonged disputes over the re-election of President Vieira. The roundtable was rescheduled for November 2006, provided the Government succeeded in passing the 2006 budget.

In March 2005 the IMF published its Article IV consultation report, highlighting the dangers of Guinea-Bissau's continuing political instability, deepening fiscal crisis and dependence on external financing to pay civil-service salaries. However, in April the Minister of the Economy and Finance announced that the Government was on the verge of obtaining a staff-monitored programme with the IMF. A full PRGF programme could follow by 2007. In May 2005 the World Bank agreed to provide US $10m. to cover budget and balance-of-payments deficits. In July the Group of Eight leading industrialized nations (G-8) announced that Guinea-Bissau was one of nine 'second wave' countries that would qualify for the cancellation of its entire debt to the IMF, the World Bank and the ADB by the end of 2006, subject to the country fulfilling a number of criteria. In June 2005 the IMF awarded Guinea-Bissau a six-month Staff-Monitored Programme (SMP) to help the country return to macroeconomic stability, with the expectation that this would be followed by a two-year emergency post-conflict assistance (EPCA) programme. However, in October the IMF was forced to postpone its negotiations following the dismissal of the Government by President Vieira.

Following the completion of the first SMP in December and further negotiations, in March 2006 the IMF awarded Guinea-Bissau a second SMP, running from April to December. The SMP focused on restraining public expenditure and boosting revenue mobilization, while preventing the build-up of public-sector salary arrears. In October an IMF mission visited Bissau to evaluate the country's performance under the SMP, noting encouraging progress, although several revenue and financing targets had been missed. In November the Government finally held a donor conference in Geneva, attended by the IMF, World Bank, the UNDP and donors, during which it submitted a national poverty-reduction strategy, worth US $400m., and a security forces reform programme, worth $184m. Donors pledged a total of $262.5m. in budget support and development aid, plus a further $178.5m. in 2007 provided that certain governance criteria were met. However, these pledges were again put in jeopardy by the collapse of the Government in March 2007. In late May another IMF mission visited Bissau, and after discussions with the new Government the Fund indicated that it was likely to grant an EPCA arrangement later in the year. This was expected to yield additional funds for development projects as well as providing conditions for a debt write-off within the following three years.

The Government's financial problems and its difficulties in paying civil servants' wages on time has generated an almost permanent state of labour unrest. Strikes continued in 2002–03, despite a decision, criticized by the IMF, to increase public-sector wages from September 2002, as by August 2003 many civil servants had not been paid for nine months. Teachers' arrears were to be paid by the World Bank by June 2003, while five months of arrears owed to military personnel were cleared in August. In November workers at the state water and electricity utility, Electricidade e Agua da Guiné-Bissau, held a one-week strike in Bissau, Gabú and Bafatá, demanding payment of 12 months of salary arrears and 20 months of bonuses. The strike ended on 19 November after the Government began paying salaries from October. The interim administration has had some success in clearing the wage arrears inherited from the Yalá administration (which in some cases dated back one year), and in early 2004 drew US $2.5m. from the emergency budget to pay January to April 2004 salaries for 11,000 civil servants. However, the lack of resources and the huge accumulation of wage arrears led to further strikes, by hospital staff in January 2004, and by the national television station, Televisão Guiné-Bissau, in February. Paying wage arrears remains a serious problem for the new Government and has been identified by the IMF and the World Bank as one of its top priorities. In February 2005 the European Commission agreed that €9.5m. ($12.3m.) previously approved by the EU could be reallocated to pay public-sector salaries and to finance the June elections. In February 2006 Guinea-Bissau's 20,000 schoolteachers held a 10-day strike, demanding unpaid salaries dating back to 2001. In the same month the public-sector unions held a three-day strike, protesting at the introduction of new working hours. In March UEMOA and Brazil agreed to pay public-sector salaries for February and March. In May the Prime Minister, Aristides Gomes, promised to pay public-sector workers two months of salary arrears by the end of the month, but when the money failed to materialize the public-sector unions held another national strike on 20 June. In an effort to defuse the tension, ECOWAS offered to finance three months of public-sector salary arrears. Labour unrest continued in late 2006 as the Government struggled to pay salaries, and by the time of its collapse in late March 2007 they were five months in arrears. The resumption of donor funding in May enabled the new Government to pay the first two months of salary arrears, which temporarily eased tensions.

Statistical Survey

Area and Population

AREA, POPULATION AND DENSITY

Area (sq km)	36,125*
Population (census results)	
16–30 April 1979	753,313
1 December 1991	
Males	476,210
Females	507,157
Total	983,367
Population (UN estimates at mid-year)†	
2004	1,549,000
2005	1,597,000
2006	1,646,000
Density (per sq km) at mid-2006	45.6

* 13,948 sq miles.

† Source: UN, *World Population Prospects: The 2006 Revision*.

ETHNIC GROUPS

1996 (percentages): Balante 30; Fulani 20; Mandjak 14; Mandinka 12; Papel 7; Other 16 (Source: Comunidade dos Países de Língua Portuguesa).

POPULATION BY REGION

(1991 census)

Bafatá	143,377	Gabú	134,971
Biombo	60,420	Oio	156,084
Bissau	197,610	Quinara	44,793
Bolama/Bijagos	26,691	Tombali	72,441
Cacheu	146,980	**Total**	983,367

PRINCIPAL TOWNS
(population at 1979 census)

Bissau (capital)	109,214	Catió	5,170
Bafatá	13,429	Cantchungo†	4,965
Gabú*	7,803	Farim	4,468
Mansôa	5,390		

* Formerly Nova Lamego.
† Formerly Teixeira Pinto.

Mid-2005 (incl. suburbs, UN estimate): Bissau 367,000 (Source: UN, *World Urbanization Prospects: The 2005 Revision*).

BIRTHS AND DEATHS

	2004	2005	2006
Birth rate (per 1,000)	49.6	49.6	49.5
Death rate (per 1,000)	19.6	19.4	19.2

Source: African Development Bank.

Expectation of life (years at birth, WHO estimates): 47 (males 45; females 48) in 2004 (Source: WHO, *World Health Report*).

ECONOMICALLY ACTIVE POPULATION
('000 persons at mid-1994)

	Males	Females	Total
Agriculture, etc.	195	175	370
Industry	15	5	20
Services	80	14	94
Total	290	194	484

Source: UN Economic Commission for Africa, *African Statistical Yearbook*.

Mid-2005 (estimates in '000): Agriculture, etc. 551; Total labour force 676 (Source: FAO).

Health and Welfare

KEY INDICATORS

Total fertility rate (children per woman, 2005)	7.1
Under-5 mortality rate (per 1,000 live births, 2005)	200
HIV/AIDS (% of persons aged 15–49, 2005)	3.8
Physicians (per 1,000 head, 2004)	0.12
Hospital beds (per 1,000 head, 1990)	1.48
Health expenditure (2004): US $ per head (PPP)	28.4
Health expenditure (2004): % of GDP	4.8
Health expenditure (2004): public (% of total)	27.3
Access to water (% of persons, 2004)	59
Access to sanitation (% of persons, 2004)	35
Human Development Index (2004): ranking	173
Human Development Index (2004): value	0.349

For sources and definitions, see explanatory note on p. vi.

Agriculture

PRINCIPAL CROPS
('000 metric tons)

	2003	2004	2005
Rice (paddy)	66.4	89.2	98.3
Maize	20.6	31.9	39.8
Millet	22.7	31.5	47.2
Sorghum	10.0	15.5	23.4
Cassava*	38.0	39.9	42.3
Other roots and tubers*	68.0	68.0	68.0
Sugar cane*	5.5	5.5	5.5
Cashew nuts*	81.0	90.9	97.3
Groundnuts (in shell)*	20.0	19.9	20.1
Coconuts†	45.5	45.5	45.5
Oil palm fruit*	80.0	82.4	83.9
Vegetables*	25.5	25.5	25.5
Plantains*	39.0	39.8	40.6
Oranges*	5.0	5.1	5.1
Other fruits*	71.6	72.2	73.0

* FAO estimates.
† Unofficial figures.

Source: FAO.

LIVESTOCK
('000 head, year ending September, FAO estimates)

	2003	2004	2005
Cattle	520	520	530
Pigs	360	360	370
Sheep	290	290	300
Goats	330	330	335
Chickens	1,500	1,550	1,600

Source: FAO.

LIVESTOCK PRODUCTS
('000 metric tons, FAO estimates)

	2003	2004	2005
Cattle meat	5.1	5.1	5.2
Pig meat	11.2	11.2	11.5
Cows' milk	14.1	14.3	14.5
Goats' milk	3.0	3.0	3.1

Source: FAO.

Forestry

ROUNDWOOD REMOVALS
('000 cubic metres, excluding bark)

	1997	1998	1999
Sawlogs, veneer logs and logs for sleepers*	40	40	40
Other industrial wood	124	127	130
Fuel wood†	422	422	422
Total	586	589	592

* Assumed to be unchanged since 1971.
† Assumed to be unchanged since 1979.

2000–05: Production as in 1999 (FAO estimates).

Source: FAO.

SAWNWOOD PRODUCTION
('000 cubic metres, including railway sleepers, FAO estimates)

	1970	1971	1972
Total	10	16	16

1973–2005: Production assumed to be unchanged since 1972 (FAO estimates).

Source: FAO.

Fishing

(metric tons, live weight)

	2003	2004*	2005*
Freshwater fishes*	150	150	150
Sea catfishes	315	320	320
Meagre	337	340	340
Mullets*	1,500	1,500	1,500
Sompat grunt	202	200	200
Lesser African threadfin	498	500	500
Total catch (incl. others)*	6,153	6,200	6,200

* FAO estimates.

Source: FAO.

Industry

SELECTED PRODUCTS
('000 metric tons, unless otherwise indicated)

	2001	2002	2003
Hulled rice	69.1	68.4	67.7
Groundnuts (processed)	6.8	6.7	6.6
Bakery products	7.6	7.7	7.9
Frozen fish	1.7	1.7	1.7
Dry and smoked fish	3.6	3.7	3.8
Vegetable oils (million litres)	3.6	3.6	3.7
Beverages (million litres)	3.5	0.0	0.0
Dairy products (million litres)	1.1	0.9	0.9
Wood products	4.7	4.5	4.4
Soap	2.6	2.5	2.4
Electric energy (million kWh)	18.9	19.4	15.8

Source: IMF, *Guinea-Bissau: Selected Issues and Statistical Appendix* (March 2005).

Finance

CURRENCY AND EXCHANGE RATES

Monetary Units

100 centimes = 1 franc de la Communauté financière africaine (CFA).

Sterling, Dollar and Euro Equivalents (31 May 2007)

£1 sterling = 964.116 francs CFA;
US $1 = 487.592 francs CFA;
€1 = 655.957 francs CFA;
10,000 francs CFA = £10.37 = $20.51 = €15.24.

Average Exchange Rate (francs CFA per US $)

2004 528.285
2005 527.468
2006 522.890

Note: An exchange rate of 1 French franc = 50 francs CFA, established in 1948, remained in force until January 1994, when the CFA franc was devalued by 50%, with the exchange rate adjusted to 1 French franc = 100 francs CFA. This relationship to French currency remained in effect with the introduction of the euro on 1 January 1999. From that date, accordingly, a fixed exchange rate of €1 = 655.957 francs CFA has been in operation. Following Guinea-Bissau's admission in March 1997 to the Union économique et monétaire ouest-africaine, the country entered the Franc Zone on 17 April. As a result, the Guinea peso was replaced by the CFA franc, although the peso remained legal tender until 31 July. The new currency was introduced at an exchange rate of 1 franc CFA = 65 Guinea pesos. At 31 March 1997 the exchange rate in relation to US currency was $1 = 36,793.3 Guinea pesos.

BUDGET
(million francs CFA)

Revenue*	2003	2004	2005
Tax revenue	11,941	11,830	18,334
Income taxes	2,907	2,838	4,074
Corporate tax	2,139	1,596	1,973
Individual taxes	587	605	1,338
Consumption taxes	1,437	1,420	2,148
General sales tax	3,568	3,192	5,649
Taxes on international trade and transactions	3,745	4,047	6,429
Import duties	2,583	2,347	3,754
Export duties	1,171	1,699	2,010
Port service charges	—	—	662
Other taxes	—	50	77
Non-tax revenue	8,903	12,699	9,644
Fees and duties	8,142	9,101	7,558
Fishing licences	7,977	8,988	7,515
Other non-tax revenues	760	3,597	2,087
Total	20,844	24,529	27,978

Expenditure	2003	2004	2005
Current expenditure	34,899	42,075	44,032
Wages and salaries	13,645	16,168	21,257
Goods and services	3,922	4,496	7,606
Transfers	5,137	5,018	6,083
Other current expenditures	4,487	7,666	2,372
Scheduled interest payments	7,709	8,728	6,716
Capital expenditure	17,930	28,342	16,491
Total	52,830	70,418	60,524

* Excluding grants received (million francs CFA): 10,600 in 2003; 24,500 in 2004; 13,400 in 2005.

Source: IMF, *Guinea-Bissau: Selected Issues and Statistical Appendix* (August 2006).

CENTRAL BANK RESERVES
(US $ million at 31 December)

	2004	2005	2006
IMF special drawing rights	0.68	0.57	0.50
Foreign exchange	72.41	79.24	81.52
Total	73.09	79.81	82.02

Source: IMF, *International Financial Statistics*.

MONEY SUPPLY
(million francs CFA at 31 December)

	2004	2005	2006
Currency outside banks	32,570	40,661	39,679
Demand deposits at deposit money banks	10,277	10,868	13,436
Total money (incl. others)	42,964	51,679	53,260

Source: IMF, *International Financial Statistics*.

COST OF LIVING
(Consumer Price Index; base: 2003 = 100)

	2004	2005	2006
Food, beverages and tobacco	101.1	104.7	105.2
Clothing	98.9	99.0	n.a.
Rent, water, electricity, gas and other fuels	101.7	101.9	n.a.
All items (incl. others)	100.9	104.3	106.4

Source: ILO.

NATIONAL ACCOUNTS

Expenditure on the Gross Domestic Product
('000 million francs CFA at current prices)

	2003	2004	2005*
Government final consumption expenditure	22.5	24.8	22.4
Private final consumption expenditure	110.1	119.9	152.9
Increase in stocks Gross fixed capital formation	23.9	22.8	14.4
Total domestic expenditure	156.5	167.5	189.7
Exports of goods and services	41.3	44.1	57.2
Less Imports of goods and services	58.9	67.2	86.1
GDP in purchasers' values	138.8	144.4	160.8

* Estimates.

Source: Banque de France, *Rapport Zone franc 2005*.

Gross Domestic Product by Economic Activity
(million francs CFA at current prices)

	2003	2004	2005
Agriculture, hunting, forestry and fishing	82,763	84,009	94,193
Manufacturing, electricity and water	12,186	12,515	13,605
Construction	4,039	4,190	4,647
Trade, restaurants and hotels	21,578	23,352	26,274
Transport, storage and communications	3,656	3,888	4,270
Finance, insurance, real estate, etc. Community, social and personal services (excl. government)	484	504	559
Government services	10,485	11,849	12,757
GDP at factor cost	135,191	140,307	156,305
Indirect taxes	1,927	2,269	2,522
GDP at market prices	137,118	142,576	158,827

Source: IMF, *Guinea-Bissau: Selected Issues and Statistical Appendix* (August 2006).

BALANCE OF PAYMENTS

(US $ million)

	2003	2004	2005
Exports of goods f.o.b.	62.2	75.8	100.8
Imports of goods f.o.b.	–70.8	–83.0	–119.1
Trade balance	–8.6	–7.2	–18.2
Exports of services	8.6	7.8	12.7
Imports of services	–33.4	–44.4	–47.1
Balance on goods and services	–33.4	–43.8	–52.6
Other income (net)	–12.5	–11.4	–12.0
Balance on goods, services and income	–45.9	–55.2	–64.6
Official current transfers	21.8	39.8	23.9
Private current transfers	17.5	23.7	19.3
Current balance	–6.6	8.2	–21.4
Capital account (net)	16.3	29.2	19.6
Financial account (net)	–123.8	–47.1	–21.3
Overall balance	–114.2	–9.6	–23.1

Source: IMF, *Guinea-Bissau: Selected Issues and Statistical Appendix* (August 2006).

External Trade

PRINCIPAL COMMODITIES

(US $ million)

Imports c.i.f.	2003	2004	2005*
Foodstuffs	25.8	19.1	15.1
Rice	18.2	12.7	10.8
Wheat flour	2.5	1.8	0.9
Oil	2.1	1.0	1.2
Beverages and tobacco	5.5	4.9	6.0
Other consumer goods	5.0	9.8	15.0
Petroleum and petroleum products	8.7	12.4	15.8
Diesel fuel and gasoline	7.7	8.8	13.7
Construction materials	7.2	12.5	20.6
Transport equipment	4.9	10.2	13.2
Passenger vehicles	3.4	7.5	8.2
Freight vehicles	1.1	2.1	3.5
Electrical equipment and machinery	6.0	10.6	12.0
Non-registered trade	6.1	3.3	15.7
Total (incl. others)	70.8	83.0	119.1

* Estimates.

Exports f.o.b.	2003	2004	2005
Agricultural products	56.7	73.2	94.4
Cashew nuts	55.7	72.8	93.5
Total (incl. others)	62.2	75.8	100.8

Source: IMF, *Guinea-Bissau: Selected Issues and Statistical Appendix* (August 2006).

PRINCIPAL TRADING PARTNERS

(percentage of trade)

Imports	2003	2004	2005
France	2.7	2.2	2.5
India	2.0	0.8	0.6
Italy	8.0	3.7	20.4
Netherlands	2.9	4.0	3.0
Pakistan	0.3	1.9	1.4
Portugal	13.3	13.8	12.7
Senegal	36.2	44.5	34.6
Spain	4.4	2.3	1.2

Exports	2003	2004	2005
Guinea	1.9	0.2	0.3
India	62.3	52.2	67.4
Nigeria	15.7	13.2	19.0
Portugal	2.6	0.8	1.1
Senegal	0.9	1.1	1.5
USA	2.6	22.2	0.2

Source: IMF, *Guinea-Bissau: Selected Issues and Statistical Appendix* (August 2006).

Transport

ROAD TRAFFIC

(motor vehicles in use, estimates)

	1994	1995	1996
Passenger cars	5,940	6,300	7,120
Commercial vehicles	4,650	4,900	5,640

Source: International Road Federation, *World Road Statistics*.

SHIPPING

Merchant Fleet
(registered at 31 December)

	2004	2005	2006
Number of vessels	23	25	25
Total displacement (grt)	5,943	6,627	6,627

Source: Lloyd's Register-Fairplay, *World Fleet Statistics*.

International Sea-Borne Freight Traffic
(UN estimates, '000 metric tons)

	1991	1992	1993
Goods loaded	40	45	46
Goods unloaded	272	277	283

Source: UN Economic Commission for Africa, *African Statistical Yearbook*.

CIVIL AVIATION
(traffic on scheduled services)

	1996	1997	1998
Kilometres flown (million)	1	0	0
Passengers carried ('000)	21	21	20
Passenger-km (million)	10	10	10
Total ton-km (million)	1	1	1

Source: UN, *Statistical Yearbook*.

Tourism

TOURIST ARRIVALS BY NATIONALITY

	2005
Cape Verde	159
France	599
Italy	213
Libya	12
Portugal	1,552
Senegal	235
Spain	324
USA	57
Total (incl. others)	4,978

Receipts from tourism (US $ million, excl. passenger transport): 3 in 2001; 2 in 2002; 3 in 2003.

Source: World Tourism Organization.

Communications Media

	2003	2004	2005
Telephones ('000 main lines in use)	10.6	10.6.	10.6
Mobile cellular telephones ('000 subscribers)	1.3	41.7	67.0
Internet users ('000)	19	26	26

Facsimile machines (number in use): 550 in 2000.

Radio receivers ('000 in use): 49 in 1997.

Daily newspapers: 1 (average circulation 6,200 copies) in 1998.

Sources: UNESCO Institute for Statistics; UNESCO, *Statistical Yearbook*; UN, *Statistical Yearbook*; International Telecommunication Union.

Education

(1999)

	Teachers	Students		
		Males	Females	Total
Pre-primary	194	2,027	2,132	4,159
Primary	4,306	89,401	60,129	149,530
Secondary: general	1,913*	16,109	8,925	25,034
Secondary: technical and vocational		208	72	280
Tertiary	n.a.	n.a.	n.a.	463

* UNESCO estimate.

Institutions (1999): Pre-primary 54; Primary 759.

Source: UNESCO Institute for Statistics.

Adult literacy rate (UNESCO estimates): 39.6% (males 55.2%; females 24.7%) in 2003 (Source: UN Development Programme, *Human Development Report*).

Directory

The Constitution

A new Constitution for the Republic of Guinea-Bissau was approved by the Assembléia Nacional Popular on 16 May 1984 and amended in May 1991, November 1996 and July 1999 (see below). The main provisions of the 1984 Constitution were:

Guinea-Bissau is an anti-colonialist and anti-imperialist Republic and a State of revolutionary national democracy, based on the people's participation in undertaking, controlling and directing public activities. The Partido Africano da Independência da Guiné e Cabo Verde (PAIGC) shall be the leading political force in society and in the State. The PAIGC shall define the general bases for policy in all fields.

The economy of Guinea-Bissau shall be organized on the principles of state direction and planning. The State shall control the country's foreign trade.

The representative bodies in the country are the Assembléia Nacional Popular and the regional councils. Other state bodies draw their powers from these. The members of the regional councils shall be directly elected. Members of the councils must be more than 18 years of age. The Assembléia Nacional Popular shall have 150 members, who are to be elected by the regional councils from among their own members. All members of the Assembléia Nacional Popular must be over 21 years of age.

The Assembléia Nacional Popular shall elect a 15-member Council of State (Conselho de Estado), to which its powers are delegated between sessions of the Assembléia. The Assembléia also elects the President of the Conselho de Estado, who is also automatically Head of the Government and Commander-in-Chief of the Armed Forces. The Conselho de Estado will later elect two Vice-Presidents and a Secretary. The President and Vice-Presidents of the Conselho de Estado form part of the Government, as do Ministers, Secretaries of State and the Governor of the National Bank.

The Constitution can be revised at any time by the Assembléia Nacional Popular on the initiative of the deputies themselves, or of the Conselho de Estado or the Government.

Note: Constitutional amendments providing for the operation of a multi-party political system were approved unanimously by the Assembléia Nacional Popular in May 1991. The amendments stipulated that new parties seeking registration must obtain a minimum of 2,000 signatures, with at least 100 signatures from each of the nine provinces. (These provisions were adjusted in August to 1,000 and 50 signatures, respectively.) In addition, the amendments provided for the Assembléia Nacional Popular (reduced to 100 members) to be elected by universal adult suffrage, for the termination of official links between the PAIGC and the armed forces, and for the operation of a free-market economy. Multi-party elections took place in July 1994.

In November 1996 the legislature approved a constitutional amendment providing for Guinea-Bissau to seek membership of the Union économique et monétaire ouest-africaine and of the Franc Zone.

In July 1999 constitutional amendments were introduced limiting the tenure of presidential office to two terms and abolishing the death penalty. It was also stipulated that the country's principal offices of state could only be held by Guinea-Bissau nationals born of Guinea-Bissau parents.

The Government

HEAD OF STATE

President: JOÃO BERNARDO VIEIRA (took office 1 October 2005).

COUNCIL OF MINISTERS
(August 2007)

Prime Minister: MARTINHO N'DAFA CABI.

Minister of the Presidency of the Council of Ministers and Parliamentary Affairs: PEDRO DA COSTA.

Minister of National Defence: MARCIANO SILVA BARBEIRO.

Minister of Foreign Affairs, International Co-operation and Communities: MARIA DE CONCEIÇÃO NOBRE CABRAL.

Minister of Internal Administration: MAIOR BACIRO DABO.

Minister of the Economy and Regional Integration: ABUBACAR DEMBA DAHABA.

Minister of Finance: ISSUFO SANHÁ.

Minister of Justice: CARMELITA BABOSA RODRIGUES PIRES.

Minister of Administrative Reform, the Civil Service and Labour: PEDRO MORATO MILACO.

Minister of Transport and Communications: JOSÉ GASPAR GOMES FERNANDES.

Minister of Culture, Youth and Sports: ADJA DJALÓ NANDINGA.

Minister of Natural Resources: SOARES SAMBÚ.

Minister of Trade and Handicrafts: HENRI MANÉ.

Minister of Social Solidarity, the Family and the Fight against Poverty: ALFREDO ANTÓNIO DA SILVA.

Minister of Public Health: EUGENIA SALDANHA.

Minister of National and Higher Education: BRUNO SIDNA NA MON.

Minister of Agriculture and Rural Development: DANIEL SULEMANE EMBALO.

Minister of Fisheries: DANIEL GOMES.

Minister of Public Works and Urbanization: RUI ARAÚJO GOMES.

Minister of Energy and Industry: VENÇA MENDES NA LUAC.

Minister of the Fight for the Freedom of the Homeland: ISABEL BUSCARDINE.

There are, in addition, nine Secretaries of State.

MINISTRIES

Office of the Prime Minister: Av. Unidade Africana, CP 137, Bissau; tel. 211308; fax 201671.

Ministry of Administrative Reform, the Civil Service and Labour: Bissau.

Ministry of Agriculture and Rural Development: Av. Amílcar Cabral, CP 102, Bissau; tel. 221200; fax 222483.

Ministry of Culture, Youth and Sports: Bissau.

Ministry of the Economy and Regional Integration: Rua Justino Lopes 74A, CP 67, Bissau; tel. 203670; fax 203496; e-mail info@mail.guine-bissau.org; internet www.guine-bissau.org.

Ministry of Energy and Industry: Bissau.

Ministry of the Fight for the Freedom of the Homeland: Bissau.

Ministry of Finance: Rua Justino Lopes 74A, CP 67, Bissau; tel. 203670; fax 203496; e-mail info@mail.guine-bissau.org; internet www.guine-bissau.org.

Ministry of Fisheries: Av. Amílcar Cabral, CP 102, Bissau; tel. 201699; fax 202580.

Ministry of Foreign Affairs, International Co-operation and Communities: Rua Gen. Omar Torrijo, Bissau; tel. 204301; fax 202378.

Ministry of Internal Administration: Av. Unidade Africana, Bissau; tel. 203781.

Ministry of Justice: Av. Amílcar Cabral, CP 17, Bissau; tel. 202185.

Ministry of National Defence: Amura, Bissau; tel. 223646.

Ministry of National and Higher Education: Rua Areolino Cruz, Bissau; tel. 202244.

Ministry of Natural Resources: CP 311, Bissau; tel. 215659; fax 223149.

Ministry of the Presidency of the Council of Ministers and Parliamentary Affairs: Bissau.

Ministry of Public Health: CP 50, Bissau; tel. 204438; fax 201701.

Ministry of Public Works and Urbanization: Bissau.

Ministry of Social Solidarity, the Family and the Fight against Poverty: Bissau; tel. 204785.

Ministry of Territorial Administration: Bissau.

Ministry of Trade and Handicrafts: Av. 3 de Agosto, CP 67, Bissau; tel. 202172; fax 202171.

Ministry of Transport and Communications: Bissau; fax 201137.

President and Legislature

PRESIDENT

Presidential Election, First Round, 19 June 2005

Candidate	Votes	% of votes
Malam Bacai Sanhá (PAIGC)	158,276	35.45
João Bernardo Vieira (Independent)	128,918	28.87
Kumba Yalá (PRS)	111,606	25.00
Francisco José Fadul (PUSD)	12,733	2.85
Aregado Mantenque Té (PT)	9,000	2.02
Mamadú Yaya Djaló (Independent)	7,112	1.59
Mário Lopes da Rosa (Independent)	4,863	1.09
Others	13,985	3.13
Total	446,493	100.00

Second Round, 24 July 2005

Candidate	Votes	% of votes
João Bernardo Vieira (Independent)	216,167	52.35
Malam Bacai Sanhá (PAIGC)	196,759	47.65
Total	412,926	100.00

LEGISLATURE

Assembléia Nacional Popular: Palácio Colinas de Boé, Bissau; tel. 201991; fax 206725.

President: FRANCISCO BENANTE.

General Election, 28 and 30 March 2004

Party	Votes	% of votes	Seats
Partido Africano da Independência da Guiné e Cabo Verde (PAIGC)	141,455	31.45	45
Partido para a Renovação Social (PRS)	111,354	24.76	35
Partido Unido Social Democrático (PUSD)	72,362	16.09	17
União Eleitoral (UE)	18,253	4.06	2
Aliança Popular Unida (APU)	5,776	1.28	1
Total (incl. others)	449,755	100.00	100

Election Commission

Comissão Nacional de Eleições (CNE): Av. 3 de Agosto 44, CP 359, Bissau; tel. 203600; fax 203601; e-mail cne-info@guinetel.com; Pres. Alhaji MALAM MANÉ.

Political Organizations

The legislative elections of March 2004 were contested by 12 parties and three coalitions or alliances. In mid-2006 a total of 31 political organizations were registered.

Aliança Popular Unida (APU): Bissau; f. 2003 as coalition to contest the legislative elections of March 2004; Leader FERNANDO GOMES.

Aliança Socialista da Guiné-Bissau (ASG): Bissau; f. 2000; Leader FERNANDO GOMES.

Partido Popular Guineense (PPG): Bissau; Leader JOÃO TÁTIS SÁ.

Foro Cívico da Guiné/Social Democracia (FCG/SD): Bissau; Pres. ANTONIETA ROSA GOMES; Sec.-Gen. CARLOS VAIMAN.

Forúm de Convergência para o Desenvolvimento (FCD): Bissau; f. 2005; alliance comprising the PRS, the PUSD, dissident, pro-Vieira, mems of the PAIGC and other parties; the PRS and the PUSD announced their withdrawal from the movement in March 2007; Leader FRANCISCO FADUL.

Frente Republicana Ampla (FRA): Bissau; f. 2006; anti-Vieira alliance comprising 11 parties, including the PAIGC, the FSG/SD, the LIPE, the PDG, the PP, the PRP, the PST, the UM and the UPG.

Manifesto do Povo: Bissau; f. 2003 to contest legislative elections; Leader FAUSTINO FUTUT IMBALI.

Movimento Democrático da Guiné-Bissau: Bissau; f. 2002; Leader SILVESTRE ALVES.

Partido Africano da Independência da Guiné e Cabo Verde (PAIGC): CP 106, Bissau; internet www.paigc.org; f. 1956; fmrly the ruling party in both Guinea-Bissau and Cape Verde; although Cape Verde withdrew from the PAIGC following the coup in Guinea-Bissau in Nov. 1980, Guinea-Bissau has retained the party name and initials; Pres. CARLOS DOMINGOS GOMES JÚNIOR.

Partido Democrático Guineense (PDG): Lisbon, Portugal; f. 2002; Leader MANUEL CÁ.

Partido Democrático Socialista da Salvação Guineense (PDSSG): Bissau; Leader SERIFO BALDÉ.

Partido para a Nova Democracia (PND): Bissau; f. 2006; Pres. IBRAIMA DJALÓ.

Partido da Reconciliação Nacional (PRN): Bissau; f. 2004; Leader ALMARA NHASSÉ; Sec.-Gen. OLUNDO MENDES.

Partido para a Renovação Social (PRS): c/o Assembléia Nacional Popular, Bissau; f. 1992; Pres. KUMBA YALÁ.

Partido de Solidariedade e Trabalho (PST): Bissau; f. 2002; Leader IANCUBA INDJAI; Sec.-Gen. ZACARIAS BALDÉ.

Partido dos Trabalhadores da Guiné-Bissau (PT): Bissau; e-mail contact@nodjuntamon.org; internet www.nodjuntamon.org; f. 2002; left-wing; Pres. AREGADO MANTENQUE TÉ.

Partido da Unidade Nacional (PUN): Bissau; f. 2002; Leader IDRISSA DJALÓ.

Partido Unido Social Democrático (PUSD): Bissau; f. 1991; officially registered in Jan. 1992; Interim Pres. AUGUSTO BARAI MANGO FERNANDES.

Plataforma Unida—Mufunessa Larga Guiné: f. 2003 as coalition to contest legislative elections; comprises the following parties:

Aliança Democrática (AD): c/o Assembléia Nacional Popular, Bissau; Leader VICTOR MANDINGA.

Frente Democrática (FD): Bissau; f. 1991; officially registered in Nov. 1991; Pres. CANJURA INJAI; Sec.-Gen. MARCELINO BATISTA.

Partido da Convergência Democrática (PCD): Bissau; Leader VÍTOR MANDINGA.

Frente Democrática Social (FDS): c/o Assembléia Nacional Popular, Bissau; f. 1991; legalized in Dec. 1991; Leader RAFAEL BARBOSA.

Frente para a Libertação e Independência da Guiné (FLING): Bissau; f. 1962 as an external opposition movement; legally registered in May 1992; Leader KATENGUL MENDY.

Grupo de Democratas Independentes (GDI): Bissau; f. 2003 by fmr mems of the RGB; Leader HELDER VAZ.

Resistência da Guiné-Bissau (RGB): Bissau; f. 1986 in Lisbon, Portugal, as Resistência da Guiné-Bissau—Movimento Bafatá; adopted present name prior to official registration in Dec. 1991; changed name as above in 2003; maintains offices in Paris (France), Dakar (Senegal) and Praia (Cape Verde); Pres. Lic. SALVADOR TCHONGO; Sec.-Gen. MÁRIO USSUMANE BALDÉ.

União Eleitoral (UE): f. 2002; coalition; supported the PAIGC candidate, Malam Bacai Sanhá, in the 2005 presidential election; Leader JOAQUIM BALDÉ; comprises a group of RGB dissidents, and the following parties:

Liga Guineense de Protecção Ecológica (LIPE): Bairro Missirá 102, CP 1290, Bissau; tel. and fax 252309; f. 1991; ecology party; Pres. Alhaji BUBACAR DJALÓ.

Partido da Renovação e Progresso (PRP): Bissau; Leader MAMADÚ URI DJALÓ.

Partido Social Democrático (PSD): c/o Assembléia Nacional Popular, Bissau; f. 1995 by breakaway faction of the RGB—MB; Leader JOAQUIM BALDÉ; Sec.-Gen. GASPAR FERNANDES.

Partido Socialista Guineense (PSG): Bissau; Leader CIRÍLO VIEIRA.

União para a Mudança (UM): Bissau; f. 1994 as coalition to contest presidential and legislative elections; re-formed April 1995; Leader AMINE MICHEL SAAD; comprises the following parties:

Movimento para a Unidade e a Democracia (MUDE): Bissau; officially registered in Aug. 1992; Leader FILINTO VAZ MARTINS.

Partido Democrático do Progresso (PDP): Bissau; f. 1991; officially registered in Aug. 1992; Pres. of Nat. Council AMINE MICHEL SAAD.

Partido de Renovação e Desenvolvimento (PRD): Bissau; f. 1992 as the 'Group of 121' by PAIGC dissidents; officially registered in Oct. 1992; Leaders MANUEL RAMBOUT BARCELOS, AGNELO REGALA.

União Nacional para a Democracia e o Progresso (UNDP): c/o Assembléia Nacional Popular, Bissau; f. 1998; Leader ABUBACAR BALDÉ.

União Patriótica Guineense (UPG): Bissau; f. 2004 by dissident members of the RGB; Pres. FRANCISCA VAZ TURPIN.

Other parties included the **Partido Democrático Socialista (PDS)** and the **Partido para o Progresso (PP)**, led by IBRAHIMA SOW. The **Centro Democrático** was founded in late 2005 by PAULINO IMPOSSA IÉ.

Diplomatic Representation

EMBASSIES IN GUINEA-BISSAU

Brazil: Rua São Tomé, Esquina Rua Moçambique, CP 29, Bissau; tel. 201327; fax 201317; e-mail embaixada-brasil@bissau.net; internet www.guine.org; Ambassador JOÃO BATISTA CRUZ.

China, People's Republic: Av. Francisco João Mendes, Bissau; tel. 203637; fax 203590; e-mail chinaemb_gw@mail.mfa.gov.cn; Ambassador YAN BANGHUA.

Cuba: Rua Joaquim N'Com 1, y Victorino Costa, CP 258, Bissau; tel. 213579; fax 201301; e-mail embcuba@sol.gtelecom.gw; Ambassador PEDRO FÉLIZ DOÑA SANTANA.

France: Av. Immeuble des 8 logements, ave Francisco Mendez, Bissau; tel. 201312; fax 205094; e-mail chancellerie@ambafrance-gw.org; internet www.ambafrance-gw.org; Ambassador JEAN-FRANÇOIS PAROT.

The Gambia: 47 Victorino Costa, Chao de Papel, CP 529, 1037 Bissau; tel. 203928; fax 251099; Ambassador (vacant).

Guinea: Rua 14, no. 9, CP 396, Bissau; tel. 212681; Ambassador TAMBA TIENDO MILLIMONO.

Korea, Democratic People's Republic: Bissau; Ambassador KIM KYONG SIN.

Libya: Rua 16, CP 362, Bissau; tel. 212006; Representative DOKALI ALI MUSTAFA.

Portugal: Av. Cidade de Lisboa, CP 76, 1021 Bissau; tel. 201261; fax 201269; e-mail embaixada@bissau.dgaccp.pt; Ambassador JOSÉ MANUEL SOARES B. PAIS MOREIRA.

Russia: Av. 14 de Novembro, CP 308, Bissau; tel. 251036; fax 251028; Chargé d'affaires a.i. VIACHELAV ROZHNOV.

Senegal: Rua Omar Torrijos 43A, Bissau; tel. 212944; fax 201748; Ambassador Gen. ABDOULAYE DIENG.

Judicial System

The Supreme Court is the final court of appeal in criminal and civil cases and consists of nine judges. Nine Regional Courts serve as the final court of appeal for the 24 Sectoral Courts, and deal with felony cases and major civil cases. The Sectoral Courts hear minor civil cases.

President of the Supreme Court: MARIA DO CEU SILVA MONTEIRO.

Religion

According to the 1991 census, 45.9% of the population are Muslims, 39.7% are animists and 14.4% are Christians, mainly Roman Catholics.

ISLAM

Associação Islâmica Nacional: Bissau; Sec.-Gen. Alhaji Abdú Baio.

Conselho Superior dos Assuntos Islâmicos da Guiné-Bissau (CSAI-GB): Bissau; Exec. Sec. Mustafa Rachid Djaló.

CHRISTIANITY

The Roman Catholic Church

Guinea-Bissau comprises two dioceses, directly responsible to the Holy See. The Bishops participate in the Episcopal Conference of Senegal, Mauritania, Cape Verde and Guinea-Bissau, currently based in Senegal. At 31 December 2004 there were an estimated 122,000 adherents in the country, equivalent to 9.1% of the total population.

Bishop of Bafatá: Rev. Carlos Pedro Zilli, CP 17, Bafatá; tel. 411507; e-mail diocesebafata@mail.bissau.net.

Bishop of Bissau: José Câmnate na Bissign, Av. 14 de Novembro, CP 20, 1001 Bissau; tel. 251057; fax 251058; e-mail diocesebissau@hotmail.com.

The Press

REGULATORY AUTHORITY

Conselho Nacional de Comunicação Social (CNCS): Bissau; f. 1994; dissolved in 2003, recreated in November 2004; Pres. Augusto Mendes.

NEWSPAPERS AND PERIODICALS

Banobero: Rua José Carlos Schwarz, CP 760, Bissau; tel. 230702; fax 230705; e-mail banobero@netscape.net; weekly; Dir Fernando Jorge Pereira.

Comdev Negócios (Community Development Business): Av. Domingos Ramos 21, 1° andar, Bissau; tel. 215596; f. 2006; weekly; independent; business; Editor Francelino Cunha.

Correio-Bissau: Bissau; weekly; f. 1992; Editor-in-Chief João de Barros; circ. 9,000.

Diário de Bissau: Rua Vitorino Costa 29, Bissau; tel. 203049; daily; Owner João de Barros.

Fraskera: Bairro da Ajuda, 1ª fase, CP 698, Bissau; tel. 253060; fax 253070.

Gazeta de Notícias: Av. Caetano Semeao, CP 1433, Bissau; tel. 254733; e-mail gn@mail.eguitel.com; f. 1997; weekly; Dir Humberto Monteiro.

Journal Nô Pintcha: Av. do Brasil, CP 154, Bissau; tel. 213713; Dir Sra Cabral; circ. 6,000.

Kansaré: Edifico Sitec, Rua José Carlos Schwazz, Bissau; tel. 4906547; e-mail kansare@eguitel.com; internet www.kansare.com; f. 2003; Editor Fafali Koudawo.

Voz de Bissau: Rua Eduardo Mondlane, Apdo 155, Bissau; tel. 202546; twice weekly.

Wandan: Rua António M'Bana 6, CP 760, Bissau; tel. 201789.

NEWS AGENCIES

Agência Bissau Media e Publicações: Rua Eduardo Mondlane 52, CP 1069, Bissau; tel. 206147; e-mail agenciabissau@agenciabissau.com; internet www.agenciabissau.com.

Agência Noticiosa da Guiné-Bissau (ANG): Av. Domingos Ramos, CP 248, Bissau; tel. 212151; fax 202155.

Foreign Bureau

Lusa (Agência de Notícias de Portugal, SA): Bissau; Bureau Chief Ricardo Bordalo.

Broadcasting and Communications

TELECOMMUNICATIONS

In June 2004 a 10-year agreement was signed by Guiné Telecom and Portugal Telecom to develop the telecommunications sector.

Instituto das Comunicações da Guiné-Bissau (ICGB): Av. Domingos Ramos 53, CP 1372, Bissau; tel. 204873; fax 204876; e-mail icgb@mail.bissau.net; internet www.icgb.org; regulatory authority; Pres. Anésimo da Silva Cardoso.

Guiné Telecom (GT): Bissau; tel. 202427; internet www.gtelecom.gw; f. 2003 to replace the Companhia de Telecomunicações da Guiné-Bissau (Guiné Telecom—f. 1989); 40% owned by Portugal Telecom

Guiné Tel: Bissau; f. 2003; 55% owned by Portugal Telecom; mobile operator; not yet operational as of mid-2006; CEO João Frederico de Barros.

Two further mobile networks, Spacetel and Orange Bissau, began operating in 2004 and 2007, respectively.

RADIO AND TELEVISION

An experimental television service began transmissions in 1989. Regional radio stations were to be established at Bafatá, Cantchungo and Catió in 1990. In 1990 Radio Freedom, which broadcast on behalf of the PAIGC during Portuguese rule and had ceased operations in 1974, resumed transmissions. Other radio stations included Radio Televisão Portuguesa Africa (RTP/Africa), which broadcasts from Bissau, and Rádio Sintchã Oco.

Radiodifusão Nacional da República da Guiné-Bissau (RDN): Av. Domingos Ramos, Praça dos Martires de Pindjiguiti, CP 191, Bissau; tel. 212426; fax 253070; e-mail rdn@eguitel.com; f. 1974; govt-owned; broadcasts in Portuguese on short-wave, MW and FM; Dir-Gen. Lamine Djata.

Rádio Bafatá: CP 57, Bafatá; tel. 411185.

Rádio Bombolom: Bairro Cupelon, CP 877, Bissau; tel. 201095; f. 1996; independent; Dir Agnelo Regala.

Rádio Mavegro: Rua Eduardo Mondlane, CP 100, Bissau; tel. 201216; fax 201265.

Rádio Pindjiguiti: Bairro da Ajuda, 1ª fase, CP 698; tel. 253070; f. 1995; independent.

Televisão da Guiné-Bissau (TGB): Bairro de Luanda, CP 178, Bissau; tel. 221920; fax 221941; Dir-Gen. Eusébio Nunes.

Finance

(cap. = capital; res = reserves; m. = million; amounts in francs CFA)

BANKING

Central Bank

Banque centrale des états de l'Afrique de l'ouest (BCEAO): Av. Amílcar Cabral 124, CP 38, Bissau; tel. 215548; fax 201305; internet www.bceao.int; HQ in Dakar, Senegal; f. 1955; bank of issue for the mem. states of the Union économique et monétaire ouest-africaine (UEMOA, comprising Benin, Burkina Faso, Côte d'Ivoire, Guinea-Bissau, Mali, Niger, Senegal and Togo); cap. and res 859,313m., total assets 5,671,675m. (Dec. 2002); Gov. Damo Justin Baro (acting); Dir in Guinea-Bissau Luís Cândido Lopes Ribeiro.

Other Banks

Banco da África Ocidental, SARL: Rua Guerra Mendes 18, CP 1360, Bissau; tel. 203418; fax 203412; e-mail bao-info@eguitel.com; f. 2000; International Finance Corporation 15%, Grupo Montepio Geral (Portugal) 15%, Carlos Gomes Júnior 15%; cap. and res 1,883m. (Dec. 2003); Chair. Abdool Vakil; Man. Dir Luis Almeida.

Banco da União (BDU): Bissau; f. 2005; CEO Hugo Borges.

Caixa de Crédito da Guiné: Bissau; govt savings and loan institution.

Caixa Económica Postal: Av. Amílcar Cabral, Bissau; tel. 212999; postal savings institution.

STOCK EXCHANGE

In 1998 a regional stock exchange, the Bourse Régionale des Valeurs Mobilières, was established in Abidjan, Côte d'Ivoire, to serve the member states of the UEMOA.

INSURANCE

Instituto Nacional de Seguros e Previdência Social: CP 62, Bissau; tel. and fax 201665; state-owned; Gen. Man. A. Mondes.

Trade and Industry

CHAMBER OF COMMERCE

Câmara de Comércio, Indústria e Agricultura da Guiné-Bissau (CCIA): Av. Amílcar Cabral 7, CP 361, Bissau; tel. 212844; fax 201602; f. 1987; Pres. Macária Barai; Sec.-Gen. Saliu Ba.

INDUSTRIAL AND TRADE ASSOCIATIONS

Associação Comercial, Industrial e Agricola (ACIA): CP 88, Bissau; tel. 222276.

Direcção de Promoção do Investimento Privado (DPIP): Rua 12 de Setembro, Bissau Velho, CP 1276, Bissau; tel. 205156; fax 203181; e-mail dpip@mail.bissau.net.

Fundaçao Guineense para o Desenvolvimento Empresarial Industrial (FUNDEI): Rua Gen. Omar Torrijos 49, Bissau; tel. 202470; fax 202209; e-mail fundei@fundei.bissau.net; internet www .fundei.net; f. 1994; industrial development org.; Pres. MACÁRIA BARAI.

Procajú: Bissau; private-sector association of cashew producers.

UTILITIES

Electricity and Water

Empresa de Electricidade e Águas da Guiné-Bissau (EAGB): CP 6, EAGB E.P., Bissau; tel. 215191; fax 202716; operated under contract by private management co; Dir-Gen. WASNA PAPAI DAFNA.

Gas

Empresa Nacional de Importação e Distribuição de Gás Butano: CP 269, Bissau; state gas distributor.

MAJOR COMPANIES

The Government has actively pursued a policy of small-scale industrialization to compensate for the almost total lack of manufacturing capacity. Following independence, it adopted a comprehensive programme of state control, and in 1976 acquired 80% of the capital of a Portuguese company, Ultramarina, a large firm specializing in a wide range of trading activities, including ship-repairing and agricultural processing. The Government also held a major interest in the CICER brewery (until its privatization in 1996) and created a joint-venture company with the Portuguese concern SACOR to sell petroleum products. Since 1975 three fishing companies have been formed with foreign participation: GUIALP (with Algeria), Estrela do Mar (with Russia) and SEMAPESCA (with France), all of which were awaiting divestment. In December 1976 SOCOTRAM, an enterprise for the sale and processing of timber, was inaugurated. It operates a factory in Bissau for the production of wooden tiles and co-ordinates sawmills and carpentry shops throughout the country. SOCOTRAM was partially divested through separate sales of its regional operational divisions. The restructuring of several further public enterprises was proceeding in the late 1990s, as part of the Government's programme to attract private investment. In 2003 a list of 30 state-owned companies to be privatized or placed under private management was presented as part of an attempt to rehabilitate the private sector.

PetroGuin: Rua Eduardo Mondlane 20, CP 387, Bissau; tel. and fax 221155; e-mail dg.petroguin@yahoo.com.br; internet www .petroguin.com; state-owned; fmrly Empresa Nacional de Pesquisas e Exploração Petrolíferas e Mineiras (PETROMINAS); exploration for and production of petroleum and natural gas; Dir-Gen. LEONARDO CARDOSO.

Petromar—Sociedade de Abastecimentos Petrolíferos Lda: Rua 7, CP 838, Bissau; tel. 214281; fax 201557; e-mail castro@sol .gtelecom.gw; f. 1990; 65% owned by Petrogal GB and 35% by Grucar; import and distribution of petroleum, gas and lubricants; CEO Eng. JOSÉ CASTRO.

TRADE UNIONS

Sindicato Nacional dos Marinheiros (SINAMAR): Bissau.

Sindicato Nacional dos Professores (SINAPROF): CP 765, Bissau; tel. and fax 204070; e-mail ict@mail.bissau.net; Pres. VINÇA MENDES.

União Nacional dos Trabalhadores da Guiné (UNTG): 13 Av. Ovai di Vievra, CP 98, Bissau; tel. 212094; Pres. DESEJADO LIMA DA COSTA; Sec.-Gen. MÁRIO MENDES CORREIA.

Legislation permitting the formation of other trade unions was approved by the Assembléia Nacional Popular in 1991.

Transport

RAILWAYS

There are no railways in Guinea-Bissau. In March 1998 Guinea-Bissau and Portugal signed an agreement providing for the construction of a railway linking Guinea-Bissau with Guinea.

ROADS

In 2002, according to International Road Federation estimates, there were about 3,455 km of roads, of which 964 km were paved. A major road rehabilitation scheme is proceeding, and an international road, linking Guinea-Bissau with The Gambia and Senegal, is planned. In early 2006 the European Union announced that it would provide financing for the rehabilitation of 350 km of the road network.

SHIPPING

Under a major port modernization project, the main port at Bissau was to be renovated and expanded, and four river ports were to be upgraded to enable barges to load and unload at low tide. The total cost of the project was estimated at US $47.4m., and finance was provided by the World Bank and Arab funds. At 31 December 2005 the merchant fleet comprised 25 vessels, totalling 6,627 grt. In mid-2004 plans were announced to improve links with the Bijagós islands, by providing a regular ferry service.

Empresa Nacional de Agências e Transportes Marítimos: Rua Guerva Mendes 4–4A, CP 244, Bissau; tel. 212675; fax 213023; state shipping agency; Dir-Gen. M. LOPES.

CIVIL AVIATION

There is an international airport at Bissau, which there are plans to expand, and 10 smaller airports serving the interior.

Halcyon Air/Bissau Airways: Bissau; f. 2006; flights to Dakar, Senegal; Chair. BALTASAR CARDOSO.

Hifly: Av. 24 de Setembro, CP 665, Bissau; tel. 206422; fax 206433; e-mail hiflygb@hifly.aero; internet www.hifly.aero; f. 2003 as Air Luxor; name changed as above in 2005.

Air Sénégal International, TAP Portugal and Transportes Aéreos de Cabo Verde (TACV) also fly to Bissau.

Tourism

There were 4,978 tourist arrivals in 2005.

Central de Informação e Turismo: CP 294, Bissau; tel. 213905; state tourism and information service.

Direcção Geral do Turismo: CP 1024, Bissau; tel. 202195; fax 204441.

Defence

As assessed at November 2006, the armed forces officially totalled an estimated 9,250 men: army 6,800, navy an estimated 350, air force 100, and the paramilitary gendarmerie 2,000.

Defence Expenditure: Budgeted at 7,000,000m. francs CFA in 2006.

Chief of Staff of the Armed Forces: Maj. Gen. BAPTISTA TAGMÉ NA WAI.

Army Chief of Staff: Brig. Gen. ARMANDO GOMES.

Navy Chief of Staff: Commdr JOSÉ AMERICO BUBO NA TCHUTO.

Chief of Staff of the Air Force: Brig. Gen. ANTÓNIO GOMES.

Education

Education is officially compulsory only for the period of primary schooling, which begins at six years of age and lasts for seven years. Secondary education, beginning at the age of 13, lasts for up to five years (a first cycle of three years and a second of two years). According to UNESCO estimates, in 2000/01 enrolment at primary schools included 45% of children in the relevant age-group (males 53%; females 37%), while enrolment at secondary schools was equivalent to only 9% of children in the relevant age-group (males 11%; females 6%). In 1999/2000 463 students were enrolled in tertiary education. Some 200 students completed their studies in Havana, Cuba, in 2002, while a further 186 had scholarships to study in Paris, France, and Dakar, Senegal. In November 2003 the country's first public university, the Amílcar Cabral University, opened; a private university had also opened in September. In June 2005 the African Development Bank agreed a loan of US $11m. to upgrade the education system. According to the 2005 budget, expenditure on education was forecast at 15.0% of total spending.

Bibliography

Andreini, J.-C., and Lambert, M.-L. *La Guinée-Bissau*. Paris, 1978.

Cabral, A. *Unity and Struggle* (collected writings) (trans. by M. Wolfers). London, Heinemann Educational, 1979.

Cabral, L. *Crónica da Libertação*. Lisbon, O Jornal, 1984.

Cann, J. P. *Counter-insurgency in Africa: The Portuguese Way of War 1961–1974*. Westport, CT, Greenwood Press, 1997.

Chabal, P. *Amílcar Cabral: Revolutionary Leadership and People's War*. 2nd Edn. London, C. Hurst & Co (Publishers) Ltd, 2001.

No Fist is Big Enough to Hide the Sky: The Liberation of Guinea-Bissau and Cape Verde. 2nd Edn. London, Zed Press, 1984.

Fisas Armengol, V. *Amílcar Cabral y la Independencia de Guinea-Bissau*. Barcelona, Nova Terra, 1974.

Forrest, J. B. *Lineages of State Fragility: Rural Civil Society in Guinea-Bissau*. Athens, OH, University of Ohio Press, 2003.

Galli, R., and Jones, D. *Guinea-Bissau: Politics, Economics and Society*. New York, NY, and London, Pinter Publishers, 1987.

Henry, C. *Les Iles où dansent les enfants défunts: age, sexe et pouvoir chez les Bijagós de Guinée-Bissau*. Paris, CNRS, 1994.

Lobban, R. A., and Mendy, P. K. *Historical Dictionary of Guinea-Bissau*. 2nd Edn. Lanham, MD, Scarecrow Press, 1997.

Lopes, C. *Guinea-Bissau: From Liberation Struggle to Independent Statehood*. Boulder, CO, Westview Press, 1987.

Mettas, J. *La Guinée portugaise au vingtième siècle*. Paris, Académie des Sciences d'Outre-mer, 1984.

Monteiro, A. I. *O Programa de Ajustamento Estrutural na Guiné-Bissau*. INEP, Bissau, 1996.

da Mota Teixeira, A. *Guiné Portuguesa*. 2 vols. Lisbon, 1964.

Núñez, B. *Dictionary of Portuguese-African Civilization*. Vol. I. London, Hans Zell, 1995.

Paulini, T. *Guinea-Bissau, Nachkoloniale Entwicklung eines Agrarstaates*. Göttingen, 1984.

Pereira, L. T., and Moita, L. *Guiné-Bissau: Três Anos de Independência*. Lisbon, CIDAC, 1976.

Proença, C. S. *Os efeitos da política de estabilização e ajustamento estrutural no bem-estar das famílias urbanas: o caso de Bissau 1986–93*. ISEG, Lisbon, 1998.

Rimmer, D. *The Economies of West Africa*. London, Weidenfeld and Nicolson, 1984.

Rudebeck, L. *Guinea-Bissau*. Uppsala, 1974.

Problèmes de pouvoir populaire et de développement. Uppsala, Scandinavian Institute of African Studies, Research Report 63.

Vigh, H. E. *Navigating Terrains of War: Youth and Soldiering in Guinea-Bissau*. Oxford, Berghahn Books, 2006.

World Bank. *Guinea-Bissau: A Prescription for Comprehensive Adjustment*. Washington, DC, 1988.

KENYA

Physical and Social Geography

W. T. W. MORGAN

PHYSICAL FEATURES

The total area of the Republic of Kenya is 582,646 sq km (224,961 sq miles) or 571,416 sq km (220,625 sq miles) excluding inland waters (mostly Lake Turkana and part of Lake Victoria). Kenya is bisected by the Equator and extends from approximately 4°N to 4°S and 34°E to 41°E.

The physical basis of the country is composed of extensive erosional plains, cut across ancient crystalline rocks of Pre-Cambrian age. These are very gently warped—giving an imperceptible rise from sea level towards the highlands of the interior which have their base at about 1,500 m above sea-level. The highlands are dominated by isolated extinct volcanoes, including Mt Kenya (5,200 m) and Mt Elgon (4,321 m), while outpourings of Tertiary lavas have created plateaux at 2,500–3,000 m. The Great Rift Valley bisects the country from north to south and is at its most spectacular in the highlands, where it is some 65 km across and bounded by escarpments 600–900 m high. The trough is dotted with lakes and volcanoes which are inactive but generally associated with steam vents and hot springs. Westwards the plains incline beneath the waters of Lake Victoria, and eastwards they have been down-warped beneath a sediment-filled basin, which may hold deposits of petroleum.

CLIMATE AND NATURAL RESOURCES

Although Kenya lies on the Equator, its range of altitude results in temperate conditions in the highlands above 1,500 m, with temperatures which become limiting to cultivation at about 2,750 m, while Mt Kenya supports small glaciers. Average temperatures may be roughly calculated by taking a sea-level mean of 26°C and deducting 1.7°C for each 300 m of altitude. For most of the country, however, rainfall is more critical than temperature. Only 15% of the area of Kenya can be expected to receive a reliable rainfall adequate for cultivation (750 mm in four years out of five). Rainfall is greatest at the coast and in the west of the country, near Lake Victoria and in the highlands, but the extensive plains below 1,200 m are arid or semi-arid. In the region of Lake Victoria and in the highlands west of the Rift Valley, rain falls in one long rainy season. East of the Rift Valley there are two distinct seasons: the long rains (March–May) and the short rains (September–October).

The high rainfall areas tend to be intensively cultivated on a small-scale semi-subsistence basis with varying amounts of cash cropping. Food crops are in great variety, but most important and widespread are maize, sorghum, cassava and bananas. The principal cash crops, which provide the majority of exports, are tea, coffee (mainly *Coffea arabica*), pyrethrum and sisal. The first three are particularly suited to the highlands and their introduction was associated with the large-scale farming on the alienated lands of the former 'White Highlands'. Horticultural produce (in particular, cut flowers) is an increasingly significant export. The dairy industry is important both for domestic consumption and for export. The herds of cattle, goats, sheep and camels of the dry plains support a low density of mainly subsistence farmers.

Fisheries are of local importance around Lake Victoria and are of great potential at Lake Turkana.

Soda ash is mined at Lake Magadi in the Rift Valley. Deposits of fluorspar, rubies, gold, salt, vermiculite, iron ore and limestone are also exploited. However, mineral resources make a negligible contribution to Kenya's economy.

POPULATION AND CULTURE

A total population of 28,686,607, excluding adjustment for underenumeration, was recorded at the census of August 1999. At mid-2006 the population was officially estimated at 33,947,066. The resultant overall density of 58.3 inhabitants per sq km is extremely unevenly distributed, with a large proportion of the population contained in only 10% of the area; densities approach 400 per sq km on the small proportion of the land that is cultivable. None the less, by 2001 about 33% of the population resided in urban areas, principally in Nairobi (population estimated to be 2,143,020 at the 1999 census) and Mombasa (660,800 at the 1999 census). The towns also contain the majority of the non-African minorities of some 89,185 Asians, 41,595 Arabs and 34,560 Europeans (1989 census).

Kenya has been a point of convergence of major population movements in the past, and, on a linguistic and cultural basis, the people have been divided into Bantu, Nilotic, Nilo-Hamitic (Paranilotic) and Cushitic groups. Persian and Arab influence at the coast is reflected in the Islamic culture. Kiswahili is the official language, although English, Kikuyu and Luo are widely understood.

Recent History

ALAN RAKE

Revised by MICHAEL JENNINGS

COLONIAL RULE TO THE KENYATTA ERA

Kenya, formerly known as British East Africa, was declared a British protectorate in 1895. Subsequent white settlement met with significant African armed resistance by 1914, and by the early 1920s some African political activity had begun to be organized. In 1944 the Kenya African Union (KAU), an African nationalist organization, was formed, demanding African access to white-owned land. Leadership of the movement, which drew its main support from the Kikuyu, passed in 1947 to Jomo Kenyatta, himself a Kikuyu. During 1952–56 a campaign of terrorism was conducted by the Mau Mau, a predominantly Kikuyu secret society. A state of emergency was declared by the British authorities, Kenyatta was detained and a ban on all political activity remained in force until 1955. During this period, two Luo political activists, Tom Mboya and Oginga Odinga, came to prominence. Following the removal of the state of emergency in January 1960, a transitional Constitution was introduced, legalizing political parties and according Africans a large majority in the legislative council. The KAU was reorganized as the Kenya African National Union (KANU), and Mboya and Odinga were elected to the party's leadership. Following his release in August 1961, Kenyatta assumed the presidency of KANU, which won a decisive victory at the general election of May 1963. Kenyatta became Prime Minister in June, and independence followed on 12 December. The country was declared a republic (with Kenyatta as President) exactly one year later.

By 1965 KANU had become divided into a 'conservative' wing, led by Mboya, and a 'radical' group, led by Odinga, who left KANU to form the Kenya People's Union (KPU). Kenyatta moved swiftly to curtail the activities of the KPU, introducing legislation giving the Government powers of censorship and the right to hold suspects in detention without trial. Following the assassination of Mboya in July 1969, the KPU was banned and Odinga was placed in detention, where he remained for 15 months. During the early 1970s President Kenyatta became increasingly reclusive and autocratic. He was elected, unopposed, for a third five-year term in September 1974, but died in August 1978.

THE MOI PRESIDENCY

Daniel arap Moi succeeded to the presidency in October 1978, with the support of Charles Njonjo, the Attorney-General. Political detainees were released and the Government sought to bring greater regional representation into government. By the early 1980s, however, Moi grew increasingly intolerant of criticism, and in June 1982 Kenya's Constitution was amended to create a one-party state. Criticism continued to increase, however. In August a section of the Kenya air force dominated by the Luo attempted a coup. It was swiftly put down, 3,000 arrests were made and the air force was disbanded. The Government had sufficiently recovered in strength by March 1983 to suspend death sentences and release detainees. From mid-1983 the Mwakenya (a Swahili acronym for the Union of Nationalists to Liberate Kenya) 'conspiracy' dominated Kenyan politics. It included a wide spectrum of opposition to the Moi presidency, and was not confined to any particular region. It opposed in particular the decision, in August 1986, to adopt a 'queue-voting' system to replace the secret ballot, and the announcement in December that the power of the presidency was to be increased by transferring control over the civil service to the Office of the President and by granting the Head of State the power to dismiss the Attorney-General and Auditor-General. By early 1987 over 100 people had been arrested in connection with Mwakenya.

Political Retrenchment

Despite increasing international criticism over human rights abuses in Kenya, Moi was returned unopposed for a third term in office prior to a general election to the National Assembly in March 1988. The open-air 'queue-voting' technique of candidate selection effectively excluded candidates critical of the administration from seeking election. The National Assembly approved constitutional amendments in July that allowed the President to dismiss judges at will (thus ending the independence of the judiciary) and to increase detention periods for those suspected of capital offences from 24 hours to 14 days. In September Joseph Karanja took over from Mwai Kibaki as Vice-President. The following April, he resigned following allegations of conspiring against the Government (which he denied) and was expelled from KANU. The Minister of Finance, Prof. George Saitoti, succeeded Karanja as Vice-President.

In May 1990 a broad alliance of intellectuals, lawyers and church leaders was established (under the leadership of a former cabinet minister, Kenneth Matiba) which sought to legalize political opposition. Several leaders of the movement were arrested, and serious rioting in Nairobi and unrest in the Kikuyu-dominated Central province followed. The KANU leadership denounced the advocates of multi-party political reform as 'tribalists' in the pay of 'foreign masters'. In November Amnesty International reported that several hundreds of people detained at the time of the July riots remained in custody, and accused the Kenyan authorities of torturing some prisoners.

In December 1990 KANU abolished the system of 'queue-voting'. In August 1991 six opposition leaders, including Oginga Odinga, established the Forum for the Restoration of Democracy (FORD). It was immediately outlawed, but continued to operate. In November several members of FORD were arrested prior to a planned pro-democracy rally in Nairobi; protesters at the rally (which took place despite a government ban) were dispersed by the security forces. The Kenyan authorities were condemned internationally for suppressing the demonstration, and most of the opposition activists who had been detained were subsequently released. During that month bilateral and multilateral creditors suspended aid to Kenya for 1992, pending the acceleration of both economic and political reforms.

Political Pluralism and Ethnic Tensions

In early December 1991 Moi submitted to domestic and international pressure to reform, and introduced a multi-party political system. Several new parties were registered in early 1992, including the Democratic Party (DP) established by Kibaki, who resigned as Minister of Health. Nevertheless, the opposition to KANU remained weak and divided. FORD was riven by internal divisions, and in August 1992 split into two factions. The split was formalized in October when both registered as separate parties: FORD—Asili, led by Kenneth Matiba, and FORD—Kenya, led by Odinga. The absence of an effective opposition led to Moi being elected for his fourth term as President in December. In January 1994 Odinga died and was succeeded as Chairman of FORD—Kenya by Michael Kijana Wamalwa. In May 1995 several opposition leaders, including Gitobu Imanyara, a former secretary-general of FORD—Kenya, and Paul Muite, a human-rights lawyer and supporter of FORD—Kenya, formed a new political grouping called Safina (the Swahili term for 'Noah's Ark'). The former Kenya Wildlife Service Director, Dr Richard Leakey, who had resigned the previous year after being attacked by several government ministers, was appointed as Secretary-General. Safina's application for registration was refused, and attacks on Safina officials (including Leakey) were led by members of the KANU youth wing. The opposition remained fragmented and unable effectively to challenge KANU's political dominance. By the end of 1995, 11 opposition National Assembly delegates had defected to KANU, and leadership struggles paralysed FORD—Kenya and FORD—Asili. In December 1996 Raila Odinga was reportedly expelled from FORD—Kenya and joined the National Development Party (NDP), becoming its leader in 1997.

During this period, the Government was accused of inciting ethnic tensions and violence to undermine the opposition. Clashes in 1992 killed over 2,000 people and left over 20,000 homeless. The following year, tribal clashes continued, particularly in the Rift Valley. By November 1993 at least 1,500 people had been killed and over 300,000 displaced in the violence. Continued clashes in April 1994 between Kikuyu and Kalenjin were similarly blamed on the Government.

In May 1996 the opposition-dominated public accounts committee accused a number of senior members of the Government of withholding information vital to its investigation into the collapse of a number of Kenyan banks. This was linked to the loss of an estimated US $430m. in public funds from fraudulent claims for export-tax rebates (the affair was to become known as the Goldenberg scandal).

During the mid-1990s, human rights organizations became increasingly concerned with the record of the Government. In 1995 Kenya's Roman Catholic bishops published a pastoral letter accusing the Government of seeking to erode judicial independence, of condoning police brutality and of endemic corruption. Under increased international pressure, the Government signed the UN Convention Against Torture and Other Cruel, Inhuman and Degrading Treatment or Punishment in February 1997.

In April 1997 the National Convention Executive Council (NCEC) was established to lobby for constitutional reform. In early July illegal rallies were held across the country in support of reform. In dispersing the crowds, security forces were accused of using excessive force, and a number of people were killed during several days of violent demonstration. In order to lessen tensions KANU's executive council recommended establishing a constitutional review commission, and in September 1997 amendments were passed by the National Assembly. Detention without trial was ended; greater freedom to hold rallies was granted; opposition members were appointed to the electoral commission; and rules on registering political parties were eased.

Elections and Internal Concerns

The presidential and legislative elections took place concurrently on 29 December 1997, and were characterized by poor organization, logistical difficulties and violence, as well as by allegations of electoral fraud. Moi was declared the winner of the presidential poll, obtaining 40.6% of the valid votes cast. KANU was the only major party that drew support from all ethnic groups, although voting was, as in 1992, predominantly conducted in accordance with ethnic allegiances.

During early 1998 KANU set about building links with key opposition parties. Raila Odinga appeared to have formed an unofficial alliance with KANU and Moi also won the co-operation of FORD—Kenya, assuring KANU of a comfortable legislative majority.

In early August 1998 a car bomb exploded at the US embassy in Nairobi (concurrently with a similar attack on the US mission to Dar es Salaam, Tanzania). Some 254 people were killed in Nairobi and more than 5,000 suffered injuries. The attacks were believed to have been co-ordinated by international Islamist fundamentalist terrorists, led by a Saudi-born dissident, Osama bin Laden. The Government banned five local Islamic aid organizations, provoking deep resentment among Kenyan Muslims. Nation-wide protest demonstrations were held in October. Subsequently, the Government permitted two of the organizations to resume operations. In February 2001 the trial of four men accused of involvement in the bombings began in New York, USA. All four were convicted at the end of May that year and were later sentenced to life imprisonment.

In early April 1999 Prof. Saitoti was reappointed to the position of Vice-President (vacant since January 1998), despite his rumoured implication in the Goldenberg scandal. In late July 1999 Dr Leakey was nominated head of the civil service and secretary to the Cabinet, responsible for combating the corruption that was allegedly widespread in the public services.

In early 1999 KANU was accused by the opposition of seeking to dominate representation on the constitutional review commission. In late May Moi stated that the constitutional review process should be conducted by the National Assembly. The NCEC, fearing the ruling party would use its parliamentary majority to sabotage the reform process, strongly opposed this. A protest march organized by the NCEC in early June was dispersed by the security forces. The establishment of the commission was suspended throughout the second half of 1999. In December the National Assembly voted in favour of appointing a parliamentary select commission to review the situation.

An IMF team visited Kenya in mid-February 2000 and expressed its satisfaction at the reforms initiated since Leakey's appointment; however, it noted that efforts to investigate corruption at the highest levels were being blocked by senior politicians, and the Kenya Anti-Corruption Authority (KACA—established in 1987) had made no prosecutions. The IMF team left Kenya without approving the expected credits or balance-of-payments support. In response Moi declared that he would personally take charge of all future negotiations with the IMF.

Raila Odinga was chosen to head the parliamentary select commission charged with reviewing constitutional reform; however, the opposition boycotted the commission's inaugural meeting in January 2000. Odinga completed his review in the first four months of 2000, and on 27 April introduced the Kenya Constitutional Amendment Report to the National Assembly. The main opposition parties boycotted the debate, allowing a sizable parliamentary majority to approve the amendment. Discussion of the constitutional process was confined to 15 commissioners, appointed by Moi and advised by the National Assembly.

In December 2000 the KACA was effectively dismantled after the Constitutional Court ruled that its powers of prosecution were illegal. In January 2001 the IMF and the World Bank expressed concern over the set-backs in the reforms and suspended aid to Kenya until the situation could be resolved. In March Leakey resigned as head of the civil service. Proposed legislation to provide for the establishment of a new anti-corruption authority was narrowly defeated in the National Assembly in August 2001. Following the result, the IMF confirmed that its suspension of aid to Kenya would continue, prompting fears for the weakening economy. On the following day Moi announced the creation of a new police unit to tackle corruption, which would investigate all of the 132 cases that the KACA had been formerly handling.

Electoral Campaigning

In January 2001 Raila Odinga signed a memorandum of understanding with KANU, which allowed Moi to appoint ministers from the NDP. In June 2001 Moi reshuffled the Cabinet and appointed Odinga as Minister of Energy, thereby creating the first coalition Government in Kenya's history. In mid-March 2002 the NDP was dissolved and absorbed into KANU, despite opposition from elements within both parties; Moi was elected as party Chairman, while Odinga was elected as Secretary-General.

In July 2002 some 12 opposition parties, including the DP, FORD—Kenya and the National Party of Kenya, formed an electoral alliance, the National Alliance Party of Kenya (NAPK). Meanwhile, divisions emerged within KANU over Moi's support for Uhuru Kenyatta as the party's presidential candidate.

In August 2002 Odinga established the Rainbow Alliance faction within KANU in an attempt to pressure Moi into accepting the will of the party in selecting a presidential candidate. Vice-President Saitoti was dismissed at the end of August for disloyalty, having refused to back the choice of Uhuru Kenyatta (son of the late President Jomo Kenyatta) as the KANU presidential candidate. In September the NAPK announced that Mwai Kibaki, the leader of the DP, was to be its candidate in the forthcoming election and in October Kenyatta was unveiled as the official KANU candidate. In response, six government ministers, including Odinga, and 30 KANU deputies resigned from the party and joined the opposition. In mid-October negotiations between the ex-KANU politicians (who had formed the Liberal Democratic Party—LDP) and the NAPK culminated in the establishment of the National Rainbow Coalition (NARC), an alliance of 14 opposition parties, headed by Kibaki. FORD—People and the SDP refused to join the alliance, with both parties nominating their own presidential candidates in early November.

On 28 November 2002 three suicide bombers attacked the Paradise Hotel, used mainly by Israeli tourists, just outside Mombasa. The attack killed 16 people, including 12 Kenyans and three Israeli tourists, and injured 80 people. At almost the same time two surface-to-air missiles were fired at an Israeli charter aircraft as it took off from Mombasa airport. Both missiles narrowly missed their target. The militant Islamist al-Qa'ida (Base) organization later claimed responsibility for the attacks; however, US and Israeli officials, who were assisting investigations into the attacks, suspected that a Somali militant Islamist group—al-Ittihad al-Islam—had carried out the attacks with support from al-Qa'ida. Four Kenyans were charged with murder in connection with the attacks in June 2003, and their trial began in Nairobi in February 2004. A further three Kenyans were tried separately for their alleged involvement in the Mombasa attacks, the 1998 bombing of the US embassy and an alleged plot to target the new US embassy between November 2002 and June 2003.

THE KIBAKI ADMINISTRATION

Presidential and legislative elections took place on 27 December 2002. The opposition secured an emphatic victory, with Kibaki taking 62.3% of the votes cast in the presidential election and NARC securing 125 of the 210 elected seats in the National Assembly. Kenyatta received 31.2% of votes and KANU won 64 seats. FORD—People, Sisi Kwa Sisi, Safina and FORD—Asili each won two seats, and Shirikisho Party of Kenya won one. In his first Cabinet, Kibaki appointed Wamalwa as Vice-President and Raila Odinga Minister of Roads, Public Works and Housing. Despite its victory, the new Government was almost immediately subject to infighting between the coalition members. The LDP, led by Raila Odinga, accused Kibaki of breaking a power-sharing agreement and demanded a reshuffle. By April 2003 suggestions had surfaced that KANU could replace the LDP as the key partner in the NARC Government. In August Vice-President Wamalwa died while undergoing hospital treatment in the United Kingdom. Following a month of bitter infighting over who should succeed him, Moody Awori was appointed as Vice-President. In December, in a bid to strengthen his position within the coalition, Kibaki announced that the 14 parties making up NARC were to be dissolved, and a single unified political party established. Leaders of the constituent elements of NARC reacted against the suggestion, and the LDP announced it would continue to function as a distinct political party. Kibaki was forced to back down, but offered four cabinet positions to KANU politicians in order to increase support for his faction. A cabinet reshuffle in June 2004 included KANU and FORD—People members in the new Government in a further effort to shift the balance of power and undermine the LDP in particular. Meanwhile, now in opposition, KANU began a process of rehabilitation. Moi resigned as Chairman of KANU in September 2003, leaving Uhuru Kenyatta as acting Chairman. In September 2004 Kenyatta called on the party to apologize for its abuses of power in a bid to undermine the popularity of NARC. Kenyatta was elected as Chairman of KANU in February 2005.

In December 2004 the Minister for Lands and Housing, Amos Kimunya, unveiled a government campaign to repossess illegally held land; plots owned by 60 individuals were repossessed. An official report suggested millions of hectares had been illegally acquired since independence. Pressure mounted on the Government to institute a reform of land policy. In April 2005 the National Assembly approved a motion requesting that the Government set limits on the amount of land an individual could possess, and to distribute unused land to landless people.

In January 2006 aid agencies had announced that 2.5m. people were facing severe food shortages in northern Kenya as a result of serious drought. More than 3,000 pastoralists, with over 20,000 head of cattle, were reported to be moving into Uganda in search of water sources. In Kenya there was widespread criticism that the Government was taking insufficient action and had no long-term strategy for dealing with the underlying problems of food shortages. In March the United Kingdom announced it was providing an additional £15m. in humanitarian assistance to Kenya for food aid.

In early March 2006, following the publication of an article stating that Kibaki had secretly met with opposition politician, Kalonzo Musyoka, the police raided the offices of the *East African Standard* newspaper (commonly known as *The Standard*). Thousands of copies of the paper were destroyed, and television broadcasts by the Standard Group were halted. Raids also took place at the Kenya Television News station. The Orange Democratic Movement—a coalition of opposition parties—organized demonstrations in protest at the raids, and thousands of protesters marched through Nairobi, demanding the resignation of the Minister of Information and Communications, Mutahi Kagwe. Relations between the Government and the media continued to worsen, and in April 2007 *The Standard* published allegations that the minister responsible for national security, John Michuki, had hired two hitmen to assassinate Gideon Moi, the son of former President Moi. In response the Government withdrew all advertising from the publication.

In October and November 2006 flooding in North-eastern, Coast and Western provinces left at least 60,000 homeless. Key bridges on roads linking Nairobi and Mombasa, and road links to Tanzania, were destroyed in the floods. In December 2006 an epidemic of Rift Valley fever (RVF) broke out, centred on North-Eastern, Coast, Eastern, and Central provinces. Over 400 human cases were reported, with 120 deaths. By March 2007 over 400,000 cattle had been vaccinated in efforts to control the epidemic, livestock markets in affected areas were closed, and the slaughtering of cattle banned. The disease impacted on neighbouring countries, with Tanzania and Uganda imposing restrictions on livestock movements from Kenya. Cattle trade with Somalia, usually accounting for around 10,000 head of cattle each month, collapsed, and Somalia also reported cases of RVF.

Constitutional Reform

The issue of constitutional reform, which had been supported by the opposition before the December 2002 elections, became another focus for political rivalries within NARC. At the end of April 2003 the constitutional review conference opened. Odinga and his supporters within NARC advocated a constitution limiting presidential powers through the creation of a strong prime ministerial position, whereas Kibaki and his supporters sought to maintain a strong presidency with a weaker Prime Minister, answerable to the President.

The wrangling over the proposed constitution became the first major political crisis that the NARC Government had to confront. The struggle between the Odinga-led LDP and Kibaki and his supporters over the issue of the post of executive Prime Minister continued to dominate proceedings. Other contentious issues included the proposal for an upper age-limit for presidential candidates: Kibaki regarded this as a direct challenge to himself, as it would have prevented the 72-year-old from seeking re-election. The proposal to widen the jurisdiction of the Islamic Kadhi courts, granted limited powers over largely domestic and family issues in the 1963 Constitution, gave rise to opposition outside the political arena, with the General Secretary of the National Council of Churches declaring the proposal to be discriminatory.

In November 2003 the Minister of Justice and Constitutional Affairs, Kiraitu Murungi, postponed negotiations on the draft constitution until January 2004; however, the Chairman of the Constitution of Kenya Review Commission (CKRC), Prof. Yash Pall Ghai, rejected this decision and continued to hold talks. In response, the Government threatened to remove Ghai from his post.

In February 2004 the factions within NARC agreed on a proposal that sought to end their infighting and restore progress to the stalled review process. Under the proposal, executive power was to remain with the President, with the prime ministerial position functioning more as a chief minister. However, in March most of the 629 delegates at the constitutional review conference, including three cabinet ministers, voted to reduce the powers vested in the presidency and to create the new post of executive Prime Minister following the next elections, scheduled for 2007. The Prime Minister was to be appointed by the elected President, and would in turn appoint and lead the Government. Under the recommendations adopted by the National Constitutional Conference, more power was to be accorded to the National Assembly. The Government withdrew from the Conference in protest and attempted to block the process, but the draft constitution was successfully presented to the Attorney-General, after which it was to be considered by the National Assembly. The High Court subsequently ruled that before the draft constitution could enter into force it had also to be approved in a referendum. However, the Government introduced two bills to the National Assembly that, if adopted, would allow the legislature to amend the draft constitution, contrary to the Constitutional Review Act.

Tensions within the Government came to a head in late March 2004, with certain members of the LDP alleging a Cabinet-supported conspiracy to murder Odinga. Kibaki's supporters demanded Odinga's resignation, accusing him of deliberately sabotaging the Government's attempt to secure approval for its proposals for amending the constitution and of engineering the crisis in order to pursue his own ambitions. Although Kibaki opened the National Assembly later that month with a commitment to completing the constitutional reform process as soon as possible, little further progress was made. Moreover, a new debate appeared to be emerging within the Government over when any new constitution should take effect. Some members insisted that it should take effect from its ratification in the National Assembly, while others supported a delay until after the next elections.

After months of arguments over the proposed new constitution, the Government announced in June 2004 that the deadline for its implementation would be missed. Kibaki blamed the failure to meet the deadline on continued divisions over key points, indicating that the controversial idea of an executive prime ministerial post remained the stumbling block. Violent demonstrations continued throughout mid-2004, as the Government promised that a constitutional referendum would be held in October 2005.

By mid-2005 a draft constitution was finally prepared and submitted to the National Assembly. It included measures to reform land ownership and distribution, increased women's rights and introduced political reforms over the devolution of power. However, the most controversial aspect was the creation of a weak prime ministerial position subordinate to the President. Despite strong opposition, the draft—reflecting the views of Kibaki's faction in the Government—was passed in July but was still subject to approval at a referendum. The Kenyan Electoral Commission created symbols for the referendum campaign: the 'Yes' campaign was represented by a banana; and the 'No' with a picture of an orange. The opposition 'No' campaign was led by Raila Odinga, and the 'Yes' campaign by Kibaki, creating serious divisions within the Government.

The referendum took place on 21 November 2005 amid relative calm. The draft constitution was rejected by 57% of voters. Following the failed referendum, Kibaki dismissed the entire Cabinet, and banned opposition rallies and demonstrations calling for national elections. In the first week of December a new Cabinet was announced, largely comprising those close to Kibaki; however, within an hour of the announcement 16 ministers and deputy ministers refused to take up their positions (including the Minister of Environment and Natural Resources, Orwa Ojode, the Minister of Local Government, Musikari Kombo, and the Minister of Health, Charity Ngulu).

Political Fragmentation and Crisis

During the summer of 2006 the ruling NARC coalition collapsed as the political fallout from the constitutional crisis continued. In June, after a succession of attempts to secure control over NARC, Kibaki established a new governing party, NARC—Kenya, in an effort to reimpose his authority. Meanwhile the LDP, led by Raila Odinga, had left NARC to establish the Orange Democratic Movement. This move was contested by former NARC members, not least Kibaki's own former party, the DP, which decided to run its own members in July's by-elections. During the campaigning Kibaki in effect campaigned against his own former party in calling for voters to endorse NARC—Kenya. The new party won three of the five seats being contested, taking two from KANU.

In mid-November 2006 Kenyatta announced that he would lead KANU into an alliance with the new Orange Democratic Movement, now officially titled the Orange Democratic Movement—Kenya (ODM—Kenya). The move infuriated senior KANU members, and after intervention by former President Moi, Kenyatta and the KANU Secretary-General, William Ruto, were expelled from the party. Biwott was elected as leader of New—KANU, while Kenyatta vowed to challenge the decision. In December supporters of Kenyatta clashed with police as they attempted to hold a rally to protest against his ousting. Biwott's return to political power completed the split within the former governing party as Kenyan politics continued to fragment in the aftermath of the draft constitution row. In an effort to secure his own authority, Kibaki established links with the Biwott- and Moi-dominated New—KANU. The fragmentation of Kenya's political parties continued with FORD—Kenya (a member of the NARC—Kenya government) splitting as Soita Shitanda ousted Musikari Kombo as Chairman.

By early 2007 political manoeuvring for candidatures for the presidential and parliamentary elections due at the end of the year had begun in earnest. Within ODM—Kenya the three main leaders, Odinga, Kenyatta and Kalonzo Musyoka, each sought the nomination, threatening further to undermine the alliance's already shaky unity. NARC—Kenya, FORD—People and the DP announced they would support Kibaki for the presidency. Opinion polls early in the year suggested that Kibaki had a strong lead, and that Musyoka would present the greatest challenge to a Kibaki campaign. At the end of January Vice-President Awori, implicated in several corruption scandals, announced that he would run alongside Kibaki.

Corruption

Despite a pre-election pledge to work towards combating the endemic corruption in public life, the issue continued to dominate Kenya's politics and its relations with foreign donors in the mid-2000s. In January 2003 the Government nullified all illegal allocation of public property to individuals and businessmen who had links with the former KANU Government. In the same month Chief Justice Bernard Chunga was suspended while he was investigated for alleged corrupt practices under the former Government. In May the National Assembly passed legislation obliging all civil servants to declare and account for their income and assets. John Githongo was appointed Permanent Secretary for Governance and Ethics in the Office of the President to lead the anti-corruption campaign.

In February 2003 the Government launched a special commission of inquiry into the Goldenberg financial scandal (uncovered in 1996—see above). The inquiry heard repeated allegations of Moi's personal involvement: a former head of the civil service, Prof. Phillip Mbithi, testified that he had been asked by Moi to arrange for US $76m. to be transferred to Goldenberg International and a second witness also alleged that Moi had personally ordered the payments. The inquiry was suspended for a week in January 2004 following allegations that senior investigators had been offered bribes to influence the outcome and it was adjourned in November 2004, following a High Court ruling that a further 1,500 witnesses, including Moi, should appear before it. The inquiry's Chairman, Justice Samuel Bosire, suggested that at least five more years would be required as a result, and questioned whether resources would be made available. The cost of the inquiry was such that it had already been blamed for shortfalls in the Treasury, and it was widely believed that the inquiry would never be concluded.

In October 2003 one-half of Kenya's senior judges were suspended over allegations of corruption, and tribunals were established to investigate the charges against them. The first of the 24 senior judges suspended appeared before a tribunal in October 2004; he was cleared of seven counts of corruption and reinstated.

In July 2004 the British High Commissioner, Sir Edward Clay, criticized the Government for failing to tackle corruption which, he claimed, had cost Kenya some Ks. 15,000m. since Kibaki's inauguration. Clay was summoned to appear before the Minister of Foreign Affairs, Chirau Mwakwere, and substantiate his claims. Clay reiterated his criticisms and subsequently produced a dossier of some 20 allegedly dubious contracts involving corruption in four ministries. The diplomatic tension threatened to spread into a wider political crisis as international donors responded by demanding tougher action. The European Union (EU) announced it was suspending aid, citing concerns over the level of corruption within the Kenyan Government. Responding to the criticisms, Kibaki announced the launch of the Kenya Anti-Corruption Commission (KACC), consisting of representatives from civil society, faith-based groups and expert monitors, with five commissioners given responsibility for investigating and prosecuting corrupt officials. Within a month the KACC had secured the conviction of two prominent Kenyan businessmen for corruption amounting to US $1,400m. during the 1990s.

The Government faced renewed questions about its commitment to combating corruption in early 2005 when a World Bank survey noted that graft remained the biggest obstacle to business in Kenya. Githongo accused officials of undermining efforts to prosecute those accused of corruption and his frustration at this lack of co-operation, and the absence of any real reform, culminated with his resignation in February. Four members of the National Anti-Corruption Campaign also resigned citing lack of co-operation from the Government. In February Clay again spoke out on the issue, accusing the Government of 'massive looting'. Much of the independent print media appeared to support his allegations.

The response of the donor community was immediate: the USA suspended aid worth US $2.5m. for 2005 and 2006; Germany suspended $6.5m. of aid until ministers found to be corrupt were dismissed; and Canada, Germany, Japan, Sweden, the United Kingdom and the USA urged the Government to force ministers to resign while they were being investigated. The Government responded by defending its record, and launched a further inquiry into corruption. A cabinet reshuffle in February 2005 was widely condemned for failing to make any serious changes or remove several ministers implicated in allegedly corrupt transactions. The World Bank refused to make funding pledges during its subsequent visit and exhorted the Government to undertake serious and significant reforms to eradicate corruption. A two-year plan was presented which included proposals to grant greater power to magistrates' courts and other organizations fighting corruption. By mid-2005 donors remained wary of the Government's commitment to fighting corruption, and were withholding judgement (and renewed aid pledges) until they saw signs of real progress.

Despite the Government's assurances that it was taking the issue of corruption seriously, little progress appeared to be made. In July 2005 the Kenya branch of the African Peer Review Mechanism announced that it had stopped work following a disagreement with the Government over spending accountability. In December a police recruitment drive was ended following allegations that it was subject to widespread corruption. A report by the KACC suggested that up to 80% of candidates had paid bribes or used connections to gain a position.

In 2006 reports into two long-running scandals troubled the Government. Githongo fled to the United Kingdom claiming that threats had been made against his life and from exile he claimed to have a taped recording of the Minister of Justice at the time (Kiraitu Murungi, subsequently the Minister of Energy) attempting to impede a corruption inquiry. Githongo stated that he had informed Kibaki, who had failed to take action. The Government responded by asking for the tape to be made available, and sent officials to interview Githongo in London, United Kingdom. In late January Githongo's report on the Anglo Leasing affair (the scandal over the contract for replacing Kenya's passport system in 2002) was leaked, implicating several leading politicians. Murungi and the Minister of Finance, David Mwiraria, subsequently resigned and a delegation of 80 deputies demanded the dismissal of Vice-President Awori, who had also been named in the report. Awori initially denied any knowledge or role in the scandal to the Parliamentary Accounts Committee, but was further implicated in a report published in mid-April, along with several other leading politicians and officials.

In February 2006 a report on the long-running Goldenberg affair was presented to Kibaki. The Minister of Education, Science and Technology (and former Vice-President), George Saitoti, was ordered to hand in his passport, and resigned from the Government. However, under the terms of a previous court order, he could not be prosecuted in connection with the scandal. In March six people were charged in connection with the Goldenberg affair, including the former head of the intelligence service, the former treasury secretary and the former Governor of the central bank. In response to the corruption scandals and resignations of three ministers, Kibaki reshuffled his Cabinet in mid-February. However, he faced international criticism for not undertaking a radical transformation of the Government. The Minister of Lands and Housing, Amos Kimunya, was promoted to Minister of Finance, but no other ministerial appointments were made. In mid-March the Governor of the central bank was charged with abuse of office by an anti-corruption court, but could not be dismissed due to provisions in the Constitution. Following on from this, an investigation by the office of the Auditor-General into 18 government tenders for military and security equipment in April found that the Government had paid inflated prices and in seven cases had awarded contracts to non-existent firms. The report recommended that future contracts be subject to parliamentary scrutiny.

In June 2006 a commission of inquiry was launched following an incident at Kenyatta Airport. Two Armenian nationals were asked by security staff to open their luggage for inspection and responded by brandishing firearms. The two men were subsequently deported without being charged. Amidst allegations that the two were being protected by high level officials, the head of the Criminal Investigations Department, Joseph Kamau, was suspended along with 11 other officials. President Kibaki appeared on television in an effort to distance himself from the allegations. A search at the residence of the Armenians discovered a weapons cache containing similar items to those used in the raid on the *The Standard*, as well as government-issued vehicle number plates. The incident took on international dimensions, with diplomats questioning the Government over security at the airport.

International donors continued to focus on the issue of corruption throughout 2005 and the first half of 2006. In July 2005 the British Government prevented the Minister of Transport, Chris Murungaru, from entering the United Kingdom following allegations of corruption. In October the USA imposed a similar ban on Murungaru. In January 2006 the World Bank called upon Kibaki to suspend and prosecute officials suspected of corruption, and approved a US $25m. loan to help fight corruption. The loan was condemned by some donors as simply adding to the problem. In late April the Dutch Government suspended $148m. in aid, citing concern over levels of corruption in the country.

In August 2006 the High Court ruled that Saitoti could not be prosecuted for his role in the Goldenberg affair. The Government announced its intention to challenge this ruling. However, in mid-November, Kibaki risked provoking renewed donor anger at the Government's poor record in tackling graft by reappointing Saitoti and Kiraitu Murungi, another former minister implicated in a corruption scandal, to his Cabinet. In October the KACC recommended that four former ministers be prosecuted over the Anglo Leasing scandal. The following month an inquiry uncovered evidence of tax evasion and money laundering at the Charterhouse Bank, worth some US $1,500m. (around 10% of Kenya's national income). The Government was accused of not taking action and of moving investigators off the case.

Crime and Violence

Fears over a worsening crime rate, in Nairobi in particular, were heightened in mid-2006, when a Russian diplomat was stabbed during a robbery in August. In November clashes between rival Mungiki and Taliban gangs in Nairobi's Kibera slum left at least eight people dead and caused thousands to flee their homes. Politicians were accused of encouraging the gangs in pursuit of their own political interests. Police imposed a night-time curfew and riot police increased patrols of the area. The following month, when a former leader of the Mungiki gang attempted to hold a rally, police and demonstrators clashed. Four people died as a result.

In early 2007 the level of crime in Nairobi raised widespread concern following a number of violent robberies. In January alone, around US $1.5m. was stolen during robberies in Nairobi and other urban centres. Following orders from President Kibaki to 'shoot to kill', one of Kenya's most notorious criminals, Simon Matheri, was killed during a raid on his house in February. Matheri was believed to have been responsible for a number of murders and armed robberies (including the killing of two US diplomats during a robbery). In a further effort to curb armed crime, in March the Government destroyed more than 8,000 guns recovered by authorities in a crack-down on illegal firearms.

In mid-2007 tensions in Kibera rose again. In late May six headless corpses were discovered. Mungiki members were suspected of murdering the individuals as part of a struggle to force transport operators to pay protection money. In early June police and paramilitaries launched a security operation designed to destroy the Mungiki gang. This operation resulted in 30 deaths and 250 arrests, and police were accused by human rights organizations of operating a policy of executions of suspected Mungiki and other gang members. Later that month John Kamunya, a former leader of Mungiki, was jailed for possession weapons and narcotics. Apparently in response, 11 people were murdered in attacks in and around Nairobi, including eight deaths caused when gunmen opened fire in a bar.

In late 2006 raiders from the Pokot tribe targeted Samburu communities in cattle-raiding missions. Fighting between Pokot and Samburu appeared to increase over the 2005–06 period, linked to the drought that seriously depleted water sources and pasture land. By September 2006 over 22,000 people had been displaced as a result of the latest fighting. The allocation of land by the Government to squatters in the Mount Elgon District in western Kenya led to clashes over land rights which left 45,000 displaced and at least 137 dead by March 2007. The Sabaot Lands Defence Force claimed responsibility for the clashes, and Kenyan security forces were deployed to the region to end the violence.

EXTERNAL RELATIONS

During Jomo Kenyatta's presidency, Kenya remained ambivalent towards the East African Common Services Organization, and its successor, the East African Community (EAC). By 1977, as tensions peaked between EAC member states, the Community ceased to function. Following Dr Milton Obote's accession to Uganda's presidency, Kenya's relations with both Uganda and Tanzania improved. When the National Resistance Army seized power in Uganda in January 1986, President Moi offered full co-operation to the new Ugandan President, Yoweri Museveni. However, relations became less cordial as Moi became increasingly distrustful of the radical nature of the new regime in Uganda.

In November 1994 the Presidents of Kenya, Uganda and Tanzania met at Arusha, Tanzania, and established a permanent tripartite commission for co-operation, with a view to reviving the defunct EAC. In March 1996 Moi, Museveni and Tanzanian President Benjamin Mkapa, meeting in Nairobi, formally inaugurated the Secretariat of the Permanent Tripartite Commission for East African Co-operation, and the new EAC was officially inaugurated in Arusha in January 2001. In March 2004 a protocol was signed to establish the East African Customs Union (EACU), although its full establishment was delayed by Tanzania's decision to delay ratification until late 2004. On 1 January 2005 the EACU came into effect, creating a common market within the EAC. Under the terms of the EACU, Kenya would continue to pay duty on certain goods entering Tanzania and Uganda for a period of five years.

In December 2006 Rwanda and Burundi were accepted as members of the EAC, expanding the block to include around 90m. people. In March 2007 the East African Court of Justice in Arusha rejected Kenya's nominees for the East African Legislative Assembly (EALA), after a case was filed by Kenyan opposition activists. The Court demanded that the three EAC members harmonise election procedures to the EALA, and the ruling further delayed the establishment of the Assembly, already delayed since November 2006.

During the 1980s Kenya and Ethiopia signed a treaty of friendship and co-operation, and a mutual defence pact. Relations with the Government of Meles Zenawi in Ethiopia came under strain in 1997, following an increased incidence of cross-border cattle-rustling, including an attack in March in which 16 members of the Kenyan security forces were killed. A number of communiqués were subsequently signed by representatives of the two countries, agreeing to tighten border security, to take measures to prevent arms and drugs-smuggling and to enhance trade. In November 1998 some 189 people (mainly Somalis) were found to have been massacred in north-eastern Kenya; Ethiopian guerrillas belonging to the Oromo Liberation Front (OLF) were widely believed to be responsible. In January 1999 the Kenyan Government protested to the Ethiopian authorities, following an incursion into Kenya by Ethiopian security forces, who were reported to be in pursuit of OLF rebels. In May Kenya deployed additional troops at the two countries' common frontier, following a series of landmine explosions in the region, which had resulted in several fatalities. Ethiopian troops allegedly made a further incursion into Kenyan territory in early July. In December Kenya claimed that Ethiopian militiamen had killed 12 civilians on the Wajir North frontier. In January 2001 border officials of Ethiopia and Kenya met and pledged to increase border controls and resolve their disputes diplomatically. In April 2006 troops were deployed along the Ethiopian border after a series of cross-border cattle raids left 10 people dead and caused some 10,000 people to leave their homes.

Friction between ethnic Somali and Kenyan communities in north-eastern Kenya has been an endemic problem, with frequent outbreaks of violent conflict. In mid-1999 conflict broke out again, as regional problems spread across Kenya's borders. Somali militia overwhelmed the Ammuma border post in June and seized arms, a number of Kenyan army trucks and other military equipment. In July the Kenyan navy was, for the first time, placed on alert and ordered to guard the maritime borders and intercept any hostile craft from Somalia. On land, the Kenyan Government reported frequent penetration of its borders, an influx of outlaws and a strong increase of incidents of smuggling. Violent clashes along the border between Kenya and Somalia recurred in February 2000. When unrest spread across the Kenyan frontier, Kenya's north-eastern provincial commissioner sealed the border with heavily armed security personnel. The following week Merille bandits from Ethiopia attacked Turkana homesteads north of Marsabit. Security forces killed 35 raiders. In May more than 70 people were reported to have been killed in a major clash between Somalis and Boran tribesmen. Moi agreed in 2000 to mediate between the interim Government and opposing rebel factions in Somalia and in November 2002 hosted US-supported peace talks between rival factions. By January 2003 the warring factions had agreed to a temporary truce while talks continued, but little else had been achieved. In July President Kibaki appointed Mohammed Affey as Kenya's first ambassador to Somalia for 13 years. Nevertheless, clashes continued throughout 2004 and 2005. In March 2005 violence between rival clans left 30 dead, and over 5,000 members of the Garre clan fled their homes. The Kenyan Government was accused of doing little to end the violence.

Meanwhile, in August 2004 the members of Somalia's new National Assembly, based in Kenya, were sworn in. The transitional parliament held its inaugural session in Nairobi in September, when it elected Shariff Hassan Sheikh Adan as speaker. The following month, Abdullahi Yussuf Ahmed was elected President, and appointed Ali Mohammed Ghedi as Prime Minister. In January 2005 the Somali legislature, still based in Kenya, approved the new Somali Cabinet.

In September 2006 Kenya, Ethiopia and Somalia's Transitional National Government agreed to plans for an international peace force to be based in Somalia. In October 2006 a UN report pointed to a large increase in the numbers of Somali refugees crossing into Kenya; around 30,000 had entered Kenya since the start of 2006. With 150,000 Somali refugees already based in camps in northern Kenya, requests were made for new resources amid warnings of increased tensions between Somali refugees and local Kenyan pastoralist groups. In November 2006 Kenya banned flights to Somalia following warnings from the USA that Islamist militants were planning suicide attacks. In January 2007, as the USA-backed action by Ethiopia against the Union of Islamic Courts in Somalia continued, Kenya closed its border with Somalia. Tanks and helicopters were deployed to the border area to enforce the closure and assist with the capture of Islamist forces trying to escape into Kenya. The wife and children of one of al-Qa'ida's operatives in Somalia, Fazul Abdullah Mohammed (implicated in the 1998 embassy bombings and the 2002 Mombasa attacks), were arrested crossing into Kenya, although Mohammed himself was not found.

Relations between Kenya and Sudan deteriorated in June 1988, as they exchanged mutual accusations of aiding rebel factions. In early 1989 Sudan rekindled a long-standing dispute with Kenya over the sovereignty of territory on the Kenyan side of the Kenya–Sudan border. From the late 1990s Kenya hosted a series of peace talks between the Sudanese Government and opposition leaders, under the auspices of the Intergovernmental Authority on Development (IGAD), in an attempt to resolve the conflict in southern Sudan. Further negotiations were held in Nairobi between September 2000 and mid-2004, and in May 2004 a peace accord was signed between the two parties at Naivasha, Kenya. In January 2005 the Sudanese Government and southern rebels signed a peace accord in Nairobi at a ceremony attended by US Secretary of State Colin Powell, which officially ended the 21-year civil war.

In February 2004 the Government announced it was to be a contributory member of a new Eastern African Standby Brigade, part of the African Union's African Standby Force (ASF), which was intended to play a leading role in peace-keeping and conflict resolution in the continent. The ASF, which established its planning headquarters in Nairobi, was expected to have up to 16,000 troops spread across five regional brigades at its disposal.

In July 2002 the British Government agreed to pay a total of £4.5m. in compensation to 228 Masai and Samburu pastoralists who had been bereaved or injured by unexploded ordnance left on their herding grounds by the British armed forces, which had used the land for firing practice and military manoeuvres for more than 50 years. In June 2003 650 Masai women won British legal aid to take the British Ministry of Defence to court following allegations of systematic rape by British soldiers training in Kenya over the previous 30 years. The British Royal Military Police began investigations into the claims, despite calls from the women and their lawyer for an independent inquiry. The British High Commission announced in September that no evidence had been found to corroborate the allegations, and suggested that records of rape in police files had been forged at a later date. In October several hundred women protested outside a camp established by the Royal Military Police against the refusal of the British to set up an independent commission. The British army announced that month that individual soldiers might face charges over specific instances of rape, admitting that some rape claims appeared to be genuine. Relations with the United Kingdom, already tense following the British High Commissioner's criticism of the Government (see above), were further strained in March 2005 when the Minister of Justice, Kiraitu Murungi, demanded an apology from the United Kingdom for atrocities committed during the Emergency in the 1950s.

With Moi leaving power in December 2002, one of the major concerns of bilateral and multilateral donors was removed, and international relations subsequently improved considerably. In January 2003 the IMF met with government officials to discuss the resumption of aid. The EU promised to grant Kenya US $200m. in aid over five years for development projects, and announced that it would consider increasing that amount if good progress continued to be made. The USA, however, cut its development aid from $13.5m. in 2002 to $3.8m. in 2003. Nevertheless, in view of concerns for security in Kenya, the USA committed itself to providing military training for the Kenyan armed forces and $6.5m. for military equipment. In November 2003 the IMF approved a three-year Poverty Reduction and Growth Facility for Kenya, and a $252.2m. loan. The World Bank Consultative Group meeting that month also gave a positive welcome to the policy and direction of the NARC Government. International donors followed suit pledging $4,100m. over 2004–06. In late June 2004 the World Bank announced that it had granted Kenya $200m. in grants and loans, having been satisfied that the Government was acting to combat corruption.

The speech attacking corrupt officials by the British High Commissioner in July 2004 led to a sharp decline in relations between Kenya and the donor community and the EU announced a suspension of aid. In September the crisis appeared to have been weathered, with the IMF backing a US $35m. loan as part of a three-year deal. The resignation of Githongo in February 2005 and concerns that the Government was blocking reforms and prosecutions renewed the impression that too little was being done. The USA and Germany immediately suspended aid, and a succession of donor countries demanded that the Government fully commit to eradicating poverty. International concern that the cabinet reshuffle that month had left in place several ministers allegedly involved in corruption did little to ease tensions. A World Bank visit in April found no indications of strong government action, and the Bank refused to make new funding pledges.

In November 2006 an official from the British Foreign and Commonwealth Office claimed that Kenya's continued refusal to seriously tackle graft was increasing security risks to the United Kingdom, in particular from drug trafficking and international terrorism. In late March 2007 the World Bank announced it was renewing lending to Kenya after an 18-month break, approving US $154.5m. for livelihood protection and natural resource management programmes. The decision reflected revised anti-corruption measures for Bank-funded projects introduced in an effort to circumvent high-level corruption.

Security Concerns

Warnings of potential terrorist attacks, and instability in Somalia, led to continued security concerns in Kenya. In 2004 the Suppression of Terrorism Bill was passed as part of the Government's attempts to boost its security structure. It also created a new Anti-Terrorism Unit within the police force, and a National Counter-Terrorism centre controlled by Kenya's National Security and Intelligence Services. It also worked closely with IGAD countries to tackle regional terrorist activities. Security in public places was enhanced, and travel restrictions on Somalia were periodically imposed. A substantial number of arrests were made between 2002 and 2004.

International concern over Kenya's record on security was further raised in June 2006 after an incident between security services and two Armenian nationals (see above). In July five Pakistani nationals were arrested in Mombassa on suspicion of activities linked to terrorism. Officers from the USA were sent to the country to participate in their interrogation. In mid-June 2007 an explosion in central Nairobi, near the former location of the US embassy, killed one person and injured 30 others. Police made arrests but refused to comment on whether this incident was linked to international terrorism.

Economy

LINDA VAN BUREN

INTRODUCTION

Kenya recovered from a failure of the 'short rains' in October–December 2005 to record impressive real gross domestic product (GDP) growth of 6.1% in 2006, with growth of 6.5% forecast for 2007. The 'long rains' of April–June 2006 were described as 'good' throughout most of the country, although the pastoralists of the dry north-east whose herds had died would continue to be affected for many more months. Despite the drought and high global petroleum prices, growth boosted in part by a tourism boom, exceeded the forecast of 5.5% and represented Kenya's best economic performance in a decade. Nevertheless, in April and May 2007, the 'long rains' in the northern Rift Valley region were reported as 'erratic', leading to low germination rates for newly planted maize in this region, the breadbasket of Kenya, and raising the prospect of a reduced harvest and a lower economic growth rate than the 6.5% forecast. Reflecting higher food prices owing to reduced supply in the marketplace, overall inflation rose from 10.3% in 2005 to 14.5% in 2006, while underlying inflation (which excludes food prices) fell from 7.4% in 2005 to 5.5% in 2006, despite the global price rises for imported oil.

Kenya's National Rainbow Coalition (NARC) Government continued to win the approval of the IMF, even though a May 2006 IMF mission to Nairobi expressed 'deep concern' over the drought and also expressed the hope that more would be done to deal with corruption. In November 2003 the IMF granted a three-year US $252.8m. Poverty Reduction and Growth Facility (PRGF) arrangement for Kenya, of which $36.1m. was made available to be drawn immediately. A further tranche, of $76.9m., was approved in December 2004, followed by a $56.8m. tranche in April 2007.

When presenting its first budget, in June 2003, the NARC Government lamented that it was having to devote much of its revenue to paying off the rapidly accumulated domestic debt inherited from the Moi administration. Yet the budget called for a 2003/04 deficit equivalent to 6.5% of GDP, well outside the IMF/World Bank preferred limit, which, observers feared, would deter donors from providing funding and would have to be financed by adding to the domestic debt burden. The last budget of the Moi tenure (2002/03) carried a deficit equivalent to 4.6% of GDP, which 'compared unfavourably' with the 3.1% shortfall recorded in 2001/02, the NARC Government noted. The 2003/04 budget introduced a reduction in the rate of value-added tax (VAT) from 18% to 16%; this measure was undoubtedly popular, but did little to strengthen the revenue base. The new Government had campaigned on a promise to create 500,000 new jobs per year; the budget speech reported that the number of persons employed outside small-scale agriculture and pastoralism had, during the Moi era, risen from 6.4m. in 2001 to 6.9m. in 2002—an increase of 484,700 new jobs. The administration of President Mwai Kibaki also took office in a climate of severe depression in the tourism sector, the country's largest contributor of foreign exchange before the economic slowdown. Tourism's foreign-exchange contribution fell to third place, behind tea and horticultural exports, in that year. In the event, the figures projected in the 2003/04 budget had to be augmented by a Supplementary Estimates bill, and the resulting 2003/04 budget found that total expenditure in that year had risen to Ks. 333,900m. The 2004/05 budget proposed a budgetary deficit of Ks. 57,900m., after taking account of various external grants and aid already committed. To finance this deficit the Government planned to borrow Ks. 22,000m. on the domestic market and to seek the remaining Ks. 35,900m. through further negotiations with development partners and through privatization proceeds. The 2007/08 budget called for total expenditure of Ks. 580,400m. in 2007/08 and forecast total revenue of Ks. 428,800m., leaving, after grants, a deficit of Ks 109,800m., equivalent to 5.3% of GDP. Targets set out in this budget included real GDP growth of between 6.5% and 7% and gross international reserves sufficient to cover 3.9 months' worth of imports.

Kenya's record in the first 15 years or so after independence placed it, in terms of the growth of output, among the most successful of African developing countries. From independence until 1980, the economy progressed at a cumulative annual rate of growth of 6.8% in real terms, with growth in the industrial sector reaching 9.7% per year during the 1970s. This expansion was financed by a substantial inflow of capital as well as by domestic sources.

Throughout the 1980s the economy was characterized by a boom-and-bust pattern, depending on the global prices of coffee and tea and the presence or absence of drought in food-growing areas. Even though agriculture still predominates, in the more than four decades since independence in 1963 Kenya has seen the rise of a substantial middle class encompassing all ethnic groups in the country. This middle class, engaged primarily in the services and manufacturing sectors, accounts for both the production and the consumption that are necessary to sustain these sectors, which are substantially more important to this economy than would normally be expected in a country of Kenya's income level. Before independence, the disproportionate development of manufacturing, processing and service industries was bound up with the early presence in Kenya of a substantial number of non-African settlers, whose high incomes generated demand. Since independence, the demand necessary to sustain these sectors has come primarily from the growing African middle class, as well as from the presence of large numbers of non-Kenyans, both as residents (expatriate staff of non-governmental organizations and multinational companies) and as visitors (tourists and business travellers).

Most of Kenya's estimated 34m. people are concentrated in the central highlands, along the coastal strip and in the Lake Victoria area. According to official estimates, about one-third of the population lived in urban areas in 2001. The average rate of population increase had been 3.5% per year in 1985–90 but fell to 2.3% per year by 1995–2005, according to the World Bank. In 1985–90 the country's average annual birth rate, at 46.2 per 1,000, was one of the highest in the world, but by 2000–05 the rate stood at 39.1 per 1,000, one of the lowest in sub-Saharan Africa. The rate of mortality among children under the age of five was 120 per 1,000 live births in 2004, compared with 96 per 1,000 in 1970. In 2005 6.1% of all Kenyans aged between 15 and 49 years were living with HIV/AIDS, and about 500,000 Kenyan children had been orphaned by AIDS. It was estimated that HIV-related illnesses were killing some 500 Kenyans every day in 2002 and contributed in large measure to the decline in Kenyans' average life expectancy to 50.9 years in that year and to 48.3 years in 2004. The UN World Food Programme estimates that 25% of all Kenyans live below the poverty line. Despite these challenges, more than 80% of all female Kenyans aged 15–24 years were literate.

AGRICULTURE

At independence in 1963, formal-sector agriculture in Kenya was export-orientated and was based upon large-scale commercial agriculture of the settled 'White Highlands' and on European- and Asian-owned plantations. Much of the Government's agricultural effort in the early years of independence was devoted to a land-reform programme designed to transfer land from the European settlers and to resettle Africans upon it. Later, the Government turned its attention to the 'Kenyanization' of commerce, which at that time was dominated by non-African and frequently non-citizen businesses. Although the agricultural sector's direct contribution to GDP has declined slightly in recent years as the share contributed by tourism rose, it remains significant, accounting, with forestry and fishing, for an estimated 30% of GDP in 2006. The sector's indirect contribution to GDP is also very important: the World Bank estimates that agriculture-based subsectors of the manufacturing and services sectors provide about 30% of GDP annually. The principal cash crops are tea, horticultural produce and coffee. In 2006 some 80% of the working population made their living on the land, the same percentage as in 1980. More than one-half of total agricultural output is subsistence production. During 1995–2005, according to the World Bank, agricultural GDP increased at an average annual rate of 2.6%. Agricultural GDP increased by an estimated 0.7% in 2005. The main growth subsectors in 2005 were sugar, coffee and horticultural products. Prospects for coffee subsequently declined, however.

Agricultural output is greatly dependent upon the weather, since only about 20% of Kenya's irrigation potential has been harnessed. The Kenya National Water Master Plan, announced in the 2003/04 budget, identified an irrigation potential of some 180,000 ha, with only 6,000 ha then under irrigation. The plan had two main targets: 140 small-scale irrigation schemes of some 7,000 ha, each costing about US $7m., at a unit cost of $1,000 per ha; and 160 larger-scale schemes at a cost of $5,730 per ha, of which 18 have been shortlisted for further study.

The Agriculture Ministry's response to the poor performance in the maize sector was to introduce a 10-year 'Blue Print Code' called the Strategy for the Revitalization of Agriculture (SRA). Within the SRA context is a sector-wide Kenya Agricultural Productivity Project (KAPP), in support of research, extension and 'farmer or client empowerment'. Phase I of the KAPP, covering 2004–07, received the backing of the World Bank, which approved $40m. worth of funding, of which $13m. is in the form of a grant.

Kenya has some 1.7m. smallholders in the monetary sector and 3,200 large farms, ranches and plantations. There is an acute shortage of arable land, and only 7% of the country is classified as first-class land. The majority of smallholders have plots of less than 2 ha, and successive subdivision of plots among farmers' heirs impels large numbers of people to travel to towns in search of employment.

Kenya's leading visible earner of foreign exchange is tea. High-quality tea has been grown in Kenya since 1903. In the year to 31 March 2003 tea earned US $402m., more than four times as much as coffee. In volume terms, early 2004 saw a significant increase in tea output, of 88,140 metric tons in January–March 2004, an increase of 23.3% from the 71,450 tons produced in January–March 2003. In 1998 Kenya ranked as the world's second largest exporter of tea, behind Sri Lanka, and ahead of China and India. In the 1990s Kenya replaced India as the United Kingdom's principal tea supplier, providing about 40% of British tea imports. Pakistan was also an important customer. The total area planted with tea rose from 87,473 ha in 1989 to 141,315 ha in 2005, of which 67% was controlled by about 200,000 smallholders.

The share of small farms in the total area under tea expanded rapidly under the high-density settlement schemes of the Kenya Tea Development Authority (KTDA), distinguished itself as one of the most successful parastatals in Africa. In July 1992 the Government announced the forthcoming transfer of tea factories to the private sector, and in 1998 details of the privatization were made public. Each tea factory was to become an independent company, while the KTDA was converted to a management company, now known as the Kenya Tea Development Agency. Of the remaining assets of the former KTDA, a 50% share was to be retained by the new KTDA, 25% was to be divided evenly among the then 45 tea factory companies, and the remaining 25% was to be distributed among the companies in accordance with the proportion of management fees that they had paid to the old KTDA between 1983 and 1998. In 2007 the KTDA managed 65 tea factories, including the showpiece Tirgaga factory, commissioned in May of that year. The country's large tea estates, grouped in the Kenya Tea Growers' Association, cover about 31,017 ha. Kenya produced 324,600 tons of tea leaves in 2004, an increase of 30.9% on the 293,700 tons produced in 2003; output rose to 328,500 tons in 2005. The proportion of the 2006 crop that was produced by smallholders was 64%.

Kenya's high elevation favours the cultivation of a variety of fruits and vegetables, and by March 2003 horticulture earnings had eclipsed coffee revenue. Kenya is the second largest horticultural exporter in sub-Saharan Africa, after South Africa. Fresh flowers, fruits and vegetables are air-freighted to Europe and the Middle East. Production increased from 1,500 tons in 1968 to 548,000 tons in 1993. Output of fresh vegetables alone reached 648,000 tons in 2000, a drought year. Kenya's horticultural produce ranges from lettuce to cucumbers, tomatoes, onions, garlic, leeks, carrots, cabbages, green beans, broad beans, peas, pimentos and peppercorns. The range of fruits includes papayas, coconuts, pineapples, avocados, mangoes, passion fruits, citrus fruits and, most recently, currants and guavas. It was estimated in 2001 that as much as 40% of Kenya's horticultural crop is lost to post-harvest waste. In the same year, with Ks. 1,400m. in funding from the Japanese Bank for International Co-operation, it was announced that six pre-cooling and handling centres were to be built. Small-scale producers were to be able to deliver their horticultural crops into these centres promptly after harvesting, and the produce was to be kept fresh there until it could be transferred for loading aboard aircraft. According to the Kenya Flower Council, Kenya accounts for 60% of African cut-flower exports, in terms of value, and is the world's second largest exporter of cut flowers, after Colombia. Two large companies account for most of the production, which is concentrated mainly on large-scale farms in the Naivasha region of Central province. The Kenya Flower Council joined the quality-certification scheme operated by Milieu Programma Sierteelt of the Netherlands in 2003, whereby Kenyan growers who measure up to the high quality standards receive certification and boost their market access. The 2003/04 budget removed the 20% withholding tax on commissions paid to non-resident agents in overseas (mainly Dutch) flower auctions. In 2004 Kenya exported 40 varieties of flowers, and 98% of these flowers supplied the European market. Kenya began exporting fresh pineapples in 1988. The United Kingdom imports 44% of the vegetables and fruit.

The rise of the tea and horticultural sectors coincided with a decline in coffee production. Until October 1992, the Coffee Board of Kenya (CBK) controlled coffee production and handled much of its marketing. Since then, the marketing of coffee was liberalized, and the role of the CBK was nominally confined to licensing, regulation and research. However, even in the 2007/08 budget, an allocation of Ks. 641m. was made towards the payment of debts which the CBK owed to coffee growers. Smallholders accounted for 117,677 ha of the total 156,304 ha planted with coffee in 1986, when they produced about 60% of the crop. Until the abandonment of coffee quotas by the International Coffee Organization (ICO) in July 1989, Kenya's production consistently exceeded its quota allocations, with the result that buyers were sought on the open market, mainly in the Middle East. Although Kenya's premium arabica coffee has long commanded a high price, the instability of the coffee market (in April 1992 world coffee prices were, in nominal terms, at a 22-year 'low', and overall 1992 prices were only one-third of their 1980 level) acted as a disincentive to Kenyan producers, many of whom decided to abandon coffee-growing in favour of more profitable crops. With the deregulation of coffee marketing in 1992, official production figures declined even further, to just 75,100 metric tons in 1993, before recovering steadily to peak at 103,192 tons in 1996. From a low of 40,380 tons in 2003, production rose to 48,000 tons in 2005 and to 52,000 tons in 2006. In March 1997 the Coffee Millers' Forum (subsequently renamed the Coffee Millers' Association) was founded to advocate further liberalization of the coffee marketing sector, which remained dominated by the still-powerful CBK. Although the CBK was instructed to issue marketing licences to all suitable applicants, a deposit of Ks. 1,000m. was required as security, which, it was argued, few applicants could afford. The European Union (EU), under its Stabilization of Exports (Stabex) scheme, extended compensation to Kenya in respect of lower coffee revenues; but the Government's decision to offer these funds to farmers only in the form of 'soft' loans, at 5% interest, rather than as outright grants led to an outcry among growers, who set up a new pressure group, the Kenya Federation of Coffee Co-operative Societies, and called for 75% of the Stabex compensation to be granted to them in the form of agricultural inputs and for the other 25% to be advanced to them in cash with which they could pay labourers. That all coffee produced in Kenya still has to be sold at auction at Waikulima House in Nairobi remains contentious. Coffee growers, who still produce some of the best arabica coffee in the world, argue that they are regularly offered higher prices than they can obtain at the Nairobi coffee auction, and they are lobbying the NARC Government to allow them to sell independently, on the open market.

Kenya's sugar industry experienced a revival in 2005, when output increased by 10%. The sugar sector had fallen into a deep decline in the late 1990s, brought on in large part by price distortions. The Kenya Sugar Authority was established in 1971 to develop the growing and processing of sugar cane. By 1990 domestic consumption (which may have included an undetermined amount of demand for sugar intended for illegal export to neighbouring countries) had increased to 537,999 tons, against production of 431,836 tons. Cheap imported sugar meant that Kenyan producers were unable to sell their output at a profit, and large stockpiles accumulated. The Government reacted by raising the duty on imported sugar from 20% to 40%. The Government challenged the country's sugar producers in 1999, pledging that it would ban imports of sugar into Kenya if they, in turn, would terminate illegal exports to neighbouring countries. A number of Kenyan sugar factories underwent restructuring in 2003, and consequently, they have improved their performance, have moved into profitability and have been able to make prompter payments to cane growers. The Kenya Sugar Industry Strategic Plan 2004–2009 was approved in 2004. Pressing for development in the industry is the Sugar Campaign for Change (SUCAM), which has listed the industry's main problems as outdated technology, low-yielding cane varieties, ineffective and unco-ordinated institutions, poor roads, a weak regulatory regime and lack of credit for small-scale farmers. All these factors increase the cost of growing sugar in Kenya; to produce an equal amount of sugar costs Malawi US $120 compared with $300 in Kenya. SUCAM estimates that the industry needs Ks. 20,000m. just to clear the sugar factories' debts and that a further Ks. 30,000m. is needed for 'co-generation', ethanol production and sugar refining. Kenya is more exposed to global sugar price fluctuations than it need be, according to SUCAM; it could cushion itself by offering a variety of sugar products and not just raw sugar alone. Cane is sold to the sugar companies by smallholders and co-operatives; it has been argued that the sugar companies' need to compensate these growers prevents them from achieving the profitability that overseas competitors can attain by growing all their cane on huge estates. Of the seven sugar companies, the largest company by far is Mumias, whose privatization has been the subject of lengthy debate. The Government remains the majority shareholder in Mumias, but in June 2003 Mumias was one of five sugar companies designated for privatization, the others being Chemelil Sugar,

East African Sugar, Nzoia Sugar and South Nyanza Sugar. It was announced in 2001 that sugar exports to the EU were to resume in July of that year, after a 15-year hiatus; Kenya enjoys a 10,026-ton quota. The sugar sector provides an income for 35,000 direct employees and for about 100,000 outgrowers; the outgrowers contribute 88% of the cane, a much higher proportion than in many other sugar-producing countries. In 2007, several of Kenya's sugar companies expressed concern at the prospect of duty-free sugar imports from other countries in the Common Market (formerly the Preferential Trade Area) for Eastern and Southern Africa (COMESA) region starting in 2008; Mumias, however, indicated that it welcomed and would be able to withstand the competition.

Production of cotton increased steadily in the 1970s, but subsequently entered a prolonged decline, to a low of 4m. metric tons in 1995. Although production had recovered to 6.5m. tons by 1997/98, Kenya still imported about 8.7m. tons in that year. Nevertheless, potential output of lint is estimated at more than 47m. tons. The reasons for the poor performance include low prices, an erratic payments system, inefficient marketing and drought. Output of seed cotton recovered from about 15,000 tons in 1999 to about 20,000 tons in 2004. The Cotton Board of Kenya was radically reorganized during the early 1990s, to be succeeded by the Cotton Development Authority. The transfer to private-sector ownership of the country's 15 cotton ginneries commenced in 1995. The Government unveiled a Ks. 250m. cotton reform plan in 2006 that included re-establishing the cotton board, clearing outstanding debts, expanding irrigation schemes, reviewing the outdated Cotton Act and encouraging small-scale ginning.

Kenya became self-sufficient in tobacco in 1983, with production at about 6,600 metric tons. Output of tobacco leaves amounted to about 20,000 tons in 2004. About 75% of the crop is flue-cured, with fire-cured accounting for nearly all of the remainder. A small amount of burley tobacco is also produced.

In the 1990s Kenya was the world's third largest producer of sisal. However, output of sisal, which reached a peak of 86,526 metric tons in 1974, had dwindled to 16,607 tons by 2000, although output recovered to some 25,000 tons in 2004. Revenue from the crop averaged an estimated US $11m. per year in the early 1990s. The number of large estates fell from about 60 in 1954 to 19 in the mid-1990s. Kenya exports only sisal fibre, having no processing industry. Small amounts of abaca (Manila hemp) are also produced.

Kenya supplies 65%–70% of the world market for pyrethrum, a daisy-like flower that yields pyrethrin, a natural insecticide. In the early 1990s there were about 30,000 ha under pyrethrum, its output being mainly linked to co-operatives. The Pyrethrum Board of Kenya allocates quotas and works to improve production and its quality. By the early 1990s the increasing use of biological insecticides (particularly in the USA, the mainstay of Kenyan pyrethrum exports), had led to declining levels of demand for this commodity. Nevertheless, growing environmental concern in developed countries over the use of synthetic pesticides contributed to a modest upturn in demand for Kenya's output in the late 1990s. Kenya produced about 8,000 tons of dried pyrethrum flowers in 2004, earning Ks. 305.7m., less than one-half of the Ks. 781.9m. earned in 2003. The 2007/08 budget allocated Ks. 664m. to clear remaining arrears owed to pyrethrum growers.

Two agricultural crops with growth potential for export are cashew nuts and macadamia nuts. The former have been well established in Kenya for decades; large, graceful cashew-nut trees are a feature of the southern coastal area, between Mombasa and the Tanzanian border. Macadamia nuts, also known as Queensland nuts, are native to Australia and are regarded as a relatively new, expansion crop in Kenya. To encourage the production of these two types of high-value nuts, the NARC Government's 2003/04 budget removed the export duty on them.

Kenya's principal food crop is maize. Output levels depend heavily on weather conditions and tend to follow a boom-or-bust cycle. Good weather in the main growing regions of Kenya, despite drought in the north-east and an infestation of army worms, boosted the maize crop from 2.61m. metric tons in 2004/05 to 2.91m. in 2005/06. Maize contaminated with a poisonous aflotoxin killed 80 people who consumed it in Kitui in 2004, and a further 10 people died in Eastern province after eating maize brought into the area. Kenya has a high consumer demand for wheat yet normally provides less than 50% of its requirements. A major wheat expansion programme increased the area under wheat to 155,000 ha in 1994. Output reached a record 313,000 metric tons in 1995; the 2005/06 crop, estimated at 128,700 tons, was almost 50% larger than the previous year's harvest. In 1990 production costs for wheat were reported to have a foreign-exchange component of about 80%, compared with 50% for maize production.

Livestock and dairy production are important both for domestic consumption and for export. The country had an estimated 11.5m. cattle in 2005. The national dairy herd produced an estimated 3,100m. litres of milk in 2004/05, but relatively little of it—274m. litres—was delivered into the formal economy. Even so, this figure was a 39% increase on the 197m. litres delivered the previous year. A substantial proportion of dairy cattle are in small herds of up to 10 animals. Kenya has traditionally exported butter, cheese and skimmed milk powder, and maintains strategic stocks of these products. In 2005 FAO reported that Kenya had an estimated 14m. goats, 10m. sheep, 320,000 pigs, 931,300 camels and 29m. chickens. Kenya, which has a reputation for high-quality honey, also had 2.49m. beehives in 2004. Ironically, in the drought period of late 2005 and early 2006, while pastoralists of the north-east saw many of their herds and flocks die, the dairy sector of the rest of the country experienced a good year.

INDUSTRY

Kenya is the most industrially developed country in East Africa, with a relatively good infrastructure, extensive transport facilities and considerable private-sector activity. The manufacturing sector contributed an estimated 11.1% of GDP in 2005, although it employed only some 200,000 people in that year. The annual increase in the output of the sector averaged 10.5% in 1965–80, but had virtually stagnated by the late 1990s. During 1995–2005, according to the World Bank, manufacturing GDP increased at an average annual rate of only 1.1%. Manufacturing GDP, exhibiting an upward trend, grew by 0.1% in 2002, by 1.4% in 2003, by 2.7% in 2004, by 5.0% in 2005 and by 6.9% in 2006. In May 2005 manufacturers called for the Government to remove administrative and legal barriers that were hindering the sector. The Government responded with a review of business licensing and a temporary reduction in import paperwork at ports until the end of 2006. In mid-June 2007 the Government proposed the elimination of 205 of the 1,325 licences required by businesses. A total of 110 had already been removed and some 400 licences were also to be simplified. The Government's Regulatory Reform Strategy sought to reduce government 'red tape' in priority areas by 25% by mid-2010.

Manufacturing is, in practice, based on import-substitution, although the Moi Government in its last few years placed great emphasis on developing export-orientated industries, and the NARC Government in its first year reconfirmed its endorsement of an export development strategy. In 1990 imports of goods intended for the manufacture of exports were exempted from import duty and value-added tax (VAT). Kenyan manufacturers hoped to find new markets among the member countries of COMESA. Subsectors exhibiting the best performance in 2005 were dairy processing, brewing, cigarette production, cement production, the manufacture of galvanized sheets and motor-vehicle assembly. Changes in customs duties, VAT and income taxes were to be investor-based. However, the reduction in tax came with a warning from the Minister of Finance that where tax reductions were granted to producers to reduce costs yet the producers did not pass the benefits to consumers, the Ministry of Finance would not consider any further requests from the industries concerned.

The textile industry performed relatively well following independence, and diversification was encouraged in the clothing and leather industries. By 1993 some 65 textile factories were operating in the country, of which about 40 were engaged in manufacturing under bond for export. The expansion in the sector was mostly induced by Kenya's unrestricted access to the US market, which encouraged manufacturers in Asian countries to use Kenya as a conduit for their goods and, thus, to bypass US-imposed quotas. However, in 1994 the US authorities imposed a quota on Kenyan textile imports, quantities of which had increased suspiciously. The industry swiftly collapsed: by the late 1990s only a few factories remained in operation, and those at a much-reduced rate of production. In 1998 it was estimated that 10,000 Kenyans had lost jobs in the textiles sector as a consequence of the quota. From 2001 onwards, the African Growth and Opportunity Act (AGOA) spurred a recovery by allowing qualifying African textile producers preferential access to the US market. This was reinforced by the Multi-Fibre Arrangement (MFA), which placed quotas on Chinese and Indian textiles in a bid to give a boost to African producers. Textile producers soon mushroomed in Kenya's Export Processing Zones (EPZs) as a result, creating some 39,000 jobs. Kenya exported US $261m. worth of clothing to the USA in 2004 under the AGOA provisions. However, the MFA expired in January 2005, ending restrictions on Chinese and Indian products, with the result that large quantities of Chinese textiles entered the US market at a low price, creating difficult trading conditions for African producers such as Kenya. Even before the MFA expired, allowing major cotton producers including China and India direct access to the US market, Kenya's cotton sector was struggling, buoyed up only by favourable quotas. Without those quotas, the sector was in danger of collapse. Kenya, Lesotho and other African textile producers requested that the US Government amend AGOA to increase its effectiveness. As a result, the US in November 2005 entered into the US-China Memorandum of Understanding (MoU), which placed restrictions on 34 categories of textile and clothing imports into the USA from China for the period from 1 January 2006 to 31 December 2008. This MoU did potentially provide some much needed relief to Kenyan textile exporters, but the sector was too weak to take advantage of the new opportunities. Six investors pulled out of Kenya's EPZs in late 2004. It has been claimed that Kenya's EPZs could compete with China on cost and productivity if it were not for the abundance of regulations imposed by the Kenyan Government.

Kenya's vehicle-assembly plants produce trucks, commercial vehicles, pickups, minibuses, four-wheel-drive vehicles and passenger cars from kits supplied from abroad. About 30% of components are produced locally. The Government has announced plans to reduce its 35% interest in Leyland Kenya and its 51% interest in the other two assembly firms. Tyres are manufactured by Firestone East Africa, with the capacity to produce 700,000 tyres per year. The NARC Government's 2003/04 budget removed the excise duty on locally assembled motor vehicles to encourage the local manufacture of vehicle components and spare parts.

Cement, produced by Bamburi Cement and East African Portland Cement, was one of the most successful industries during the 1980s, and by the early 2000s the country was producing about 1.5m. metric tons of cement per year. The domestic use of cement declined by 16.5% in 2000 and by a further 9.6% in 2001. There are three glassware factories, two owned by the Madhvani Group and one by Kenya Breweries Ltd, and a sheet-glass factory at Mombasa. Charcoal is produced from coffee husks by Kenya Planters' Co-operative Union at Nairobi and is exported to the Middle East, as well as being used locally to replace some of the wood charcoal. A machine-tool manufacturing plant is being set up at Nairobi, in a joint venture with an Indian firm, and will include a training centre. Kenya Breweries Ltd, part of the East African Breweries Group, has four brewing plants, and exports a small percentage of its beer. In May 2004 East African Breweries became the first ever company to reach a capitalization of US $1,000m. on the Nairobi Stock Exchange.

Kenya Petroleum Refinery Limited (KPRL) is a joint venture that owns the Mombasa petroleum refinery, which is both operated and 70%-owned by Shell. The refinery entered production in 1963. It is capable of handling 4.2m. metric tons of crude petroleum annually, although it does not always work at full capacity. Refined petroleum products were, until relatively recently, Kenya's largest source of foreign exchange, but the refinery has been in need of modernizing. A spokesman for Shell indicated in June 2004 that the move to cleaner fuels in Africa would require significant investment in the refinery. The volume of crude-petroleum imports rose by 47.8% in 2004, while the cost of these imports rose from Ks. 25,410m. in 2003 to Ks. 45,950m. in 2004. Plans to extend the Mombasa–Nairobi petroleum pipeline as far as the Ugandan border were pledged financing of US $120m. in 1990. Construction of the pipeline from Eldoret in west-central Kenya to Kampala in Uganda was due to reach completion by the end of 2008, after several delays.

In 2000 the Investment Promotion Centre identified several subsectors of manufacturing in which incoming private-sector foreign investment would be especially welcome. They included paper products (especially coated white-lined chipboard and newsprint), textile equipment and inputs such as dyes, metallurgy, electrical equipment, electronics, pharmaceuticals, gelatin capsules, ink for ballpoint pens, PVC granules made from ethyl alcohol, ceramics and sheet glass.

MINERALS

Mining activity in Kenya is as yet limited, but prospecting is continuing. Soda ash, Kenya's principal mineral product for export, is extracted at Lake Magadi, in the Rift Valley; output was estimated at 355,400 metric tons in 2004. In 1997 a Canadian company, Tiomin Resources, announced the discovery of mineral sands at Kwale, 105 km south of Mombasa, containing reserves of 200m. tons of titanium- and zirconium-bearing sands. These discoveries followed earlier discoveries at Kwale of rutile, zircon and ilmenite. Tiomin Resources announced the results of a positive feasibility study by an Australian firm and a South African company in May 2000. The study found that the Kwale titanium-bearing sands presented 'robust economics', with a projected lifespan of at least 14 years (later estimated at 16 years) and an expected capital repayment period of not more than 3.5 years. The project was expected to produce 300,000 tons of ilmenite, 75,000 tons of rutile and 37,000 tons of premium zircon annually during its first six years of operation. The company expected to have won all the necessary permits from the Kenyan Government, to have signed long-term sales contracts and to have secured project financing for the US $137m. scheme by the end of December 2000; however, environmentalists lodged objections in a court case that postponed approval until 2003.

Kenya's other principal mineral products are gold, salt, vermiculite and limestone. A fluorspar ore deposit in the Kerio valley in Rift Valley province has been mined since 1975: it produced 85,000 metric tons in 2002 and had remaining estimated reserves of 4.5m. tons. In 2002 the Kenya Fluorspar Co employed 531 workers at its nearby processing plant. The extraction of extensive deposits of rubies began in 1974; gems of up to 30 kg have been reported. President Moi announced in 2002 that the Government was to market rubies and pink sapphires that had been discovered in Baringo district. By February 2005 350 such gemstones had been faceted in Kenya, at Eldoret. Deposits of tsavorite, a green grossularite garnet discovered at Tsavo in the 1970s, have received high valuations and have been exploited at the Lualani mine in the Taita Hills since 1981. In the 1990s a new tsavorite source was discovered at Lokirima, in the north-west, and is exploited at the Scorpion mine. Other minerals identified in Kenya include apatite, graphite, kaolin, kyanite, topazes and green tourmalines. Searches for chromite, nickel, fluorspar and vermiculite in Central province, and for chromite, nickel and copper in the Kerio valley are being undertaken. In April 2003 the Kibaki Government announced plans to review the Mining Act and designated gold and coal as potential revenue earners. Kansai Mining Corporation of Canada, through the wholly owned Mid-Migori Mining Co Ltd, holds an annually renewable gold-mining concession covering 310.5 sq km of the Migori Greenstone Belt in Nyanza, western Kenya. The area was previously mined as early as the 1910s and was subsequently mined out, but later advancements in technology made it economically viable to extract gold from the old mine tailings. Prospecting for petroleum and natural gas has continued intermittently on and off shore, but so far without significant results.

POWER

Kenya has 937 MW of installed electricity-generating capacity, of which 677.3 MW, or 72.3%, is hydroelectric. The country supplies about 80% of its national requirement domestically. Electricity, apart from small local stations, is supplied by hydroelectric plants in the Tana river basin and the Turkwel Gorge, by the geothermal station at Olkaria, and by the diesel-fired Kipevu plant on the south coast. The five Seven Forks hydrostations lie on the Tana river and have a combined installed capacity of 543.2 MW: Gitaru (225 MW), Kiambere (144 MW), Kamburu (94.2 MW), Kindaruma (40 MW) and Masinga (40 MW). Another station, with a capacity of 106 MW, operates at Turkwel Gorge in Turkana district. In May 2007 France extended a €40m. credit to upgrade Kipevu 1 from 60 MW to 90 MW; work was to begin in July 2007, with completion due in April 2009. The 74-MW Kipevu 2 was formally inaugurated in March 2002, at a cost of US $86m. Kenya's energy demand is supplemented by a bulk supply of 30 MW from Owen Falls in Uganda under a 50-year agreement signed in 1958. However, the revival of Uganda's economy in the 1990s led to increased demand for electricity there; an agreement was reached in 1997 that Kenya would pay a higher rate for electricity imported from Uganda. Kenya was the first African country to harness geothermal potential for electricity generation, in the form of the Olkaria scheme in the Rift Valley. Olkaria I has three 15-MW generators, Olkaria II has two 32-MW generators, and Olkaria III has one 12 MW binary generator; further developments in the form of Olkaria IV are planned. Construction of the 60 MW Japanese-funded and Japanese-built Sondu-Miriu hydropower project began in 1999; Phase 1 was commissioned in 2005, and Phase 2 is expected to come on stream by the end of 2007. Sondu-Miriu is to deliver an annual energy output of 331 gigawatt-hours.

With power demand exceeding power supply and with high electricity tariffs, lack of adequate electricity supply is often cited as a deterrent to manufacturing development in Kenya. In a bid to address this problem, the Government sought in 2005 to 'fast-track' projects such as Sondu-Miriu and Olkaria IV. Two further 'fast-track' units, to be situated at Kakuru and Eldoret, were also planned. In 1997 the Kenya Power Co (now the Kenya Electricity Generating Co Ltd—KenGen) was established, to deal exclusively with the generation of electricity; the Kenya Power and Lighting Co (KPLC) continued to be responsible for electricity transmission and distribution. A 30% stake of the Government's equity in KenGen was privatized in 2005 in a share flotation that was significantly oversubscribed. Unrest precipitated by the severe rationing of power in 2000 compelled the KPLC to bring in additional capacity, and within days it had arranged for delivery of two 55-MW diesel-powered generators for Lanet and Eldoret. It also sought to increase the 30 MW of power it had been importing from Uganda to 50 MW, following the completion of that country's $230m. Kiyira hydroelectric power station near Jinja. This emergency capacity carried a high cost, which the KPLC passed on to consumers in the form of a Ks. 2.50-per-kWh fuel surcharge. The 2007/08 budget called for 460 market centres, 110 secondary schools, 38 health centres and 17 water projects to be connected to the national electricity grid by May 2008.

COMMUNICATIONS

This sector experienced phenomenal growth in 2000–06, owing to the proliferation of mobile cellular telephones. The number of mobile cellular telephone subscribers in Kenya increased from 24,000 in 1999 to 1.6m. in 2003, to 2.2m. in August 2004 and to 7.3m. in October 2006. This growth may have been rapid, but it was largely unstructured, leading to wide variations in airtime costs across international borders, which operators sought to exploit. In 2003 the NARC Government reached an agreement with Tanzania and Uganda to harmonize the taxation of mobile telephone airtime. Kenya had 282,000 fixed telephone lines in use in 2005, compared with 106,000 in 1984. In August 1992 a Ks. 2,380m. radio transmitter, in the Ngong Hills near Nairobi, was inaugurated, reportedly bringing 95% of the population within range of radio transmissions. During 1999 Kenya Posts and Telecommunications Corpn was divided, pending privatization, into three entities: Telkom Kenya, the Postal Corpn of Kenya and the Communications Commission of Kenya (a regulatory body). It was reported in 2005 that Telkom Kenya was to be further split before privatization, with the Kenya Telecommunication Training Centre and the Gilgil Telecommunications Industries due to become separate entities. The Government declared 12,000 Telkom staff redundant in April 2005. The Telkom flotation was to have taken place in 2006 but was subsequently postponed and was still pending in mid-2007.

Kenya's extensive transport system includes road, rail, air, and coastal and inland waterways. Full container-handling facilities were built at Mombasa, the chief port, to deal with the volume of containers, which expanded from 50,000 20-ft (6-m) equivalent units (TEU) in 1982 to nearly 103,000 TEU in 1985. The modern container-handling terminal was opened in 1983, and the country's first inland clearance depot for containers, at Embakasi on the outskirts of Nairobi, began operating in 1984, followed by other inland container ports at Kisumu and Eldoret. In 1993 it was announced that Mombasa's Kilindini port was to be expanded by 1,200 ha. Mombasa provides access to the sea for Uganda, Burundi, Rwanda and the eastern part of the Democratic Republic of the Congo. In April 1998 the World Bank's International Finance Corpn (IFC) pledged US $10m. to the private-sector Kenyan company Grain Bulk Handlers Ltd towards the building of the first modern bulk handling and storage terminal for unloading grain and fertilizer at Mombasa port. The $32m. facility's rated capacity was the unloading of 10,000 metric tons per day, and it was expected to handle about one-half of the East African region's food imports in its first year. Although faced with competition from Dar es Salaam, in Tanzania, which was undergoing modernization, Mombasa handled 10.6m. dead-weight tons in 2002, of which about 70% was private-sector cargo, compared with 7.1m. tons in 1991. Transit cargo passing through the port to neighbouring states (including northern Tanzania) increased sharply from 527,418 metric tons in 1991 to 1.2m. tons in 1992 and to 2.5m. tons by 2003. Of total transit traffic, 77% by volume was for Uganda. The Kenya Ports Authority (KPA), undergoing restructuring during the late 1990s in preparation for privatization, introduced a $70 surcharge per container and prepared to reduce its work-force. It was announced in 2000 that local interests would be given preference over foreign bidders when KPA's components were offered for privatization. Cargo handled by KPA in the year to July 2005 was 8% up on the previous year's volume. In total, 19 shipping lines called at the port of Mombasa in 2006, and the average turnaround time per vessel was just two days. The KPA had increased the number of container crane moves from five to 10 per hour and hoped to boost it even further, to 15 moves per hour; in order to achieve this target, however, the KPA would need to replace some of its equipment. This equipment rehabilitation and replacement programme was well under way by 2003 and encompassed the acquisition of two more pilot boats (in addition to the four existing ones), three berthing tugs, two ship-to-shore gantry cranes, four rubber-tyred gantry cranes, three reach stackers and five terminal tractors. KPA acquired three new Dutch-built tugs in 2004, at a cost of $19m. In the longer term, KPA is seeking private-sector investors to construct, operate and transfer two additional container terminals. In mid-2005, after a series of computer failures led to delays, importers complained that they were being charged storage fees on containers left for more than 21 days, even though the only reason that the containers had not been removed before 21 days was the malfunctioning of the KPA computers, which meant that KPA staff were unable to complete the paperwork necessary to allow the release of the containers. Nevertheless, KPA has the capacity to tranship significantly more cargo than can be evacuated inland, placing Kenya's rail and road systems in the critical path inhibiting further port expansion. In May 2007 KPA engaged two companies to decongest the port by removing 6,000 containers per month to other locations; the port had been offloading some 15,000 containers per month, more than double its rated capacity of 7,000. The limiting factor is not an inability to handle 15,000 containers but instead a lack of space to store them.

Kenya Airways (KQ) has operated its own international services since the break-up of East African Airways. In April 1989 the airline inaugurated a freighter service to Europe: fresh flowers and vegetables were the main outward cargo. In 1992 KQ underwent a major reorganization in preparation for partial privatization, which took place in 1996, when KLM Royal Dutch Airlines paid US $24m. for a 26% stake. KQ carried 536,191 passengers in the January–March 2005 quarter, a 24% increase over passenger levels a year earlier. The carrier flies to Hong Kong and Guangzhou in China, to Mumbai in India, to Bangkok in Thailand and to Amsterdam, London and Paris in Europe, as well as to 28 cities in Africa. It also serves four Kenyan destinations. In the domestic market, KQ faces competition from three low-cost airlines: Fly 540, East African Airlines and Jetlink Express. Construction of the country's third international airport, at Eldoret in central Kenya (President Moi's home town), was completed in 1996, at an estimated cost of $49m. Critics, including international donors, considered the facility to be an unnecessary waste of resources. It was reported in May 2004 that no flights had landed at Eldoret International for three months. After the Government reduced the landing and navigational fees in May 2004, KQ announced that it would begin using Eldoret International; however, as of May 2007 KQ had yet to commence services to Eldoret. The only carrier serving Eldoret in May 2007 was Aero Kenya, linking the costly airport to Nairobi's Wilson Airport twice daily. Meanwhile, Jomo Kenyatta International and Moi International Airports were modernized during the mid-1990s. In May 2004 Kenya Wildlife Services sought a licence to operate non-scheduled air services for passengers and freight, as a means of earning revenue from its aircraft when they are not needed for their wildlife operations. Also that month KQ announced that it was to invest $2.6m. to expand and upgrade Kenyatta International Airport. KQ embarked on a $700m. fleet-modernization programme, which included the purchase of three new Boeing 767-300ER aircraft in 2001. Another two Boeing 767-300ER aircraft were leased. In 2003 the carrier also purchased a new long-haul Boeing 777-200ER aircraft, with financing from the IFC, the PTA Bank, Rand Merchant Bank, Standard Bank and IMIC Bank. This 320-seat aircraft was to serve long-haul destinations. The full fleet comprises 15 aircraft.

A 590-km road between Kitale and Juba, in southern Sudan, provides an all-weather road link between the two countries. A senior government official estimated in May 2000 that only about 57% of Kenya's road system was in 'usable condition' and that to bring the entire network up to standard would cost US $631m. In 1999 the IFC approved a $1m. loan to the Kenyan private-sector company Multiple Hauliers (EA) Ltd, which is the largest cross-border road transporter in the region and the largest transporter of fuel to Uganda. The funds were to go towards the purchase of 16 new prime movers with tanker trailers, costing $2.8m. The 2005/06 budget allocated a 44% funding rise for road construction in Kenya, giving priority to those unfinished projects it had inherited from the Moi administration that were at least 75% complete. The 2007/08 national budget allocated a further Ks. 62,100m. to roads construction, 46% more than the previous year.

The railway in Kenya runs from the coast at Mombasa, through Nairobi, to western Kenya, and on to points in Tanzania and Uganda. Kenya Railways Corpn handled 7.2% more freight in 2000 than in 1999, but the increase was negated by a 7.9% decline in cargo carried in 2001. The joint Kenyan-Ugandan bid to privatize the railway line drew substantial interest despite the fact that one of the conditions of the privatization would be that the new owner would be required to retain the 9,000 employees. Other requirements are that the new owner must meet stringent safety and performance criteria, with fewer derailments and a doubling within five years of the volume of cargo carried. Seven companies or consortia had entered the bidding by mid-2005, and in October it was announced that the Rift Valley Railways Consortium (RVRC), led by Sheltam Rail Company (Pty) Ltd of South Africa, had secured the tender. RVRC was to pay an initial fee of $3m. for the Kenyan portion of the railway line and $2m. for the Ugandan portion. Thereafter, an annual concession fee was payable, equivalent to 11.1% of gross revenue in each of the two countries. In addition, the consortium was to pay $1m. per year to Kenya for passenger services. RVRC would also invest $28m. in rehabilitation and a further $42m. in new rolling stock and operating equipment.

TOURISM

Kenya's tourism sector has generally exhibited steady and strong growth in most years since independence, and by the 1990s the sector had become the country's largest source of foreign exchange. An important exception occurred in the first half of 2003, when a high-level security alert led to the suspension of British Airways flights to Kenya and to the sudden cancellation of a number of holiday visits. Kenya's tourism sector has, however, shown itself to be resilient. Even though the outlook for 2004 was bleak, owing to negative travel advisories from both the USA and the United Kingdom, the Kenyan tourism sector saw its earnings soar from Ks. 25,800m. in 2003 to Ks. 56,000m. in 2006. International visitor arrivals increased from 1.1m. in 2003 to 2.6m. in 2006. Germany and the United Kingdom provide the largest number of tourists. The tourism sector contributed 16% of GDP in 2006.

BALANCE OF PAYMENTS AND DEBT

Kenya typically has a substantial deficit in visible trade with countries outside Africa. Its terms of trade have fluctuated quite widely since the mid-1970s, but, overall, there has been a general decline. Imports, on a cost, insurance and freight basis, increased from US $3,394m. in 2002 to $3,769m. in 2003, largely because of more expensive fuel imports during a time of higher global petroleum prices. Exports rose from $2,198m. in 2002 to $2,411m. in 2003, boosted by tea, horticultural produce, manufactured goods and re-exports. Export revenue covered 64% of import costs in 2003, compared to about 60% of import costs in 2001 and just 33% in 2002. The services account, boosted by tourism, consistently showed a surplus from the late 1990s onwards; the surplus in 2002/03 was $649m. In 2004 Kenya's import costs exceeded export earnings by Ks. 149,400m., the largest ever gap. By volume, imports increased by 29.2% in the same year, while exports grew by 17.3%. Import costs surged by 31.4% in 2004/05, overshadowing the 16.8% rise in export revenue; a January 2006 forecast indicated that both imports and exports would increase by 19% in 2005/06.

The current account of the balance of payments has shown a deficit in most years; the smallest current-account shortfall of the late 1990s was US $74m. in 1996, while the largest was $475m. in 1998. The deficit widened sharply from $147m. in 2003/04 to $917m. in 2004/05. The overall balance of payments has fluctuated in recent years: a surplus of $10m. in 2001 was followed by a deficit of $16m. in 2002. In the year to 31 March 2003 a surplus of $141m. was recorded, followed by a surplus of $291m. in the year to January 2004. Gross international reserves stood at $2,500m. at 31 December 2006, the highest-ever level for Kenya.

According to the Central Bank of Kenya, Kenya's total debt at 31 March 2003 stood at Ks. 635,600m., equivalent to 64.6% of GDP; of this total, Ks. 364,900m. was external debt, over one-half of which was owed to multilateral institutions. As of 28 May 2004 the Kenyan Government's debt owed on the domestic market was Ks. 249,200m., equivalent to about $3,120m. and amounting to about 25% of GDP. A Government assessment put Kenya's total stock of debt at 39.1% of GDP in June 2005 and forecast that it would remain at about 40% through to 30 June 2006.

FOREIGN TRADE AND AID

In an attempt to reduce dependence on fluctuating world prices for its main agricultural commodities, the Government has made efforts to stimulate non-traditional exports including horticultural produce, canned pineapple products, handicrafts, clothing, leather, cement, soda ash, fluorspar and, most recently, titanium, cashew nuts and macadamia nuts. The stimulation of exports of manufactured goods, including textiles, paper and vehicles, has also been a priority. After crude petroleum and petroleum products, the largest import bill is usually for industrial machinery and transport equipment. Consumer goods generally account for only about 15% of the total.

The main source of Kenya's imports in 2004 was the United Arab Emirates, Kenya's main supplier of crude petroleum; other principal suppliers were South Africa, Saudi Arabia the United Kingdom and Japan. Kenya's main export client was Uganda; other important purchasers were the United Kingdom, Tanzania and the Netherlands. Regional trade is important to Kenya, which has consistently had a favourable trade balance with its neighbours, to which it exports petroleum products, food and basic manufactures in particular. After the reopening of the Kenya–Tanzania border (closed in 1977–83), trade with Tanzania was limited by that country's lack of foreign exchange. However, exports to Tanzania advanced and accounted for some 8.4% of Kenya's total exports in 2004. A treaty for the re-establishment of the East African Community (EAC) providing for the promotion of free trade between the member states (envisaging the eventual introduction of a single currency), and for the development of infrastructure, tourism and agriculture within the Community, was finally ratified by the Kenyan, Tanzanian and Ugandan Heads of State in June 2000. The new EAC was officially inaugurated in January 2001. In March 2004 the Presidents of Kenya, Tanzania and Uganda signed a protocol on the creation of a customs union (see below).

Aid

Since independence, Kenya has received substantial amounts of development aid. The World Bank-sponsored Consultative Group of aid donors to Kenya meets regularly to pledge financing for the country's development strategy. The sources of aid have diversified considerably in recent years. The share provided by the United Kingdom has fallen, while multilateral agencies, particularly the World Bank and the European Development Fund, have increased their share. Shortly after the NARC Government came to power in January 2003, an IMF team visited Nairobi to meet the country's new financial planners. The Fund's satisfaction with the NARC Government's structural reforms was marked by its approval, in November 2003, of a three-year US $252.75m. PRGF arrangement. A further tranche, of $76.9m., was agreed in December 2004, followed by a $56.8m. tranche in April 2007. These reforms are aimed at restoring debt sustainability and at providing increased resources for priority poverty-reduction spending.

PUBLIC FINANCE AND DEVELOPMENT PLANNING

Development policy in Kenya emphasizes the role of private enterprise in industry and commerce, and foreign investment is actively encouraged. This was true during the Kenyatta years and during the Moi years, and it is true now during the post-Moi era. Direct participation by the state in productive enterprises is limited, and in recent years the Government has been withdrawing from unprofitable joint ventures. The NARC Government emphasized that it intended to continue in this vein. In 1991 the Moi Government announced that all remaining unproductive, 'non-strategic' state-owned companies were to be transferred to private-sector ownership. By June 1997 148 of these companies had been either privatized or dissolved. However, concerns were raised from 1997 onwards over the slow pace of the privatization process; this could in part be attributed to the poor performance of some parastatals, but there were also suspicions that the Government was unwilling to divest itself of some lucrative assets. The National Bank of Kenya, Telkom Kenya and the Kenya Ports Authority were all scheduled for privatization in 2007/08. The IMF urged the Government to allow very weak financial institutions to close and to take decisive measures for the full privatization of its interests in the remaining banks. More than 40 financial institutions were operating in Kenya in 2002. The 2007/08 budget proposed a four-fold increase of the minimum capital for banks over the next three years, raising the threshold from Ks. 250m. to Ks.1,000m. The aim of this move was to encourage the large number of 'small unviable institutions' to merge, thereby creating indigenous banks with enough resources to invest in modern technology so as to become competitive with the foreign banks, which have dominated the sector. In 2003 the NARC Government promised to formulate a privatization policy with greater transparency. The 2004/05 budget called for a tax amnesty, pointing out that 'a number of Kenyans, while willing to comply, remain outside the tax net for fear of being heavily penalized on undisclosed amounts should they reveal themselves'. The six-month tax amnesty ran from 11 June 2004 to 31 December 2004. Kenya's first Development Plan, revised in 1966, covered the period 1964–70. Important objectives of the plan included the 'Kenyanization' of the economy, until then largely in expatriate hands. Subsequent five-year plans stressed rural development and were aimed at achieving a better incomes balance between urban and rural areas.

The eighth Development Plan (1997–2001) differed from previous plans in that it aimed primarily to foster an enabling environment for the private sector, rather than emphasizing the state's role in raising and sustaining growth. However, the Plan was jeopardized by the suspension of IMF assistance in August 1997. It also failed to meet its GDP growth targets. The World Bank's most high-profile initiative in Kenya in the late 1990s, the Kenya Urban Transport Infrastructure Project, was halted in 2001, when details of a bribery scandal emerged, prompting the Bank to suspend funding. In 2003 the NARC Government published its Economic Recovery Strategy for Wealth and Employment Creation 2003–07. Broadly, this strategy called for: reversing declines in per-head income growth; increasing investments in both the private and the public sectors, while raising the productivity of capital; developing a foreign-aid policy that targeted poverty reduction and involved the participation of the private sector (a key component of this aim was the transfer of technology); channelling more budgetary resources towards growth and poverty reduction; maintaining a stable macroeconomic situation, a sustainable balance of payments and a sustainable level of public debt, both domestic and external; creating an enabling environment, not least through investment incentives; promoting exports; and restoring and maintaining sound relations with development partners. The successor to this programme was Vision 2030, unveiled in 2007 and due to be launched in 2008 (see below).

REGIONAL ARRANGEMENTS AND PROBLEMS

In 1967 Kenya, Tanzania and Uganda founded the EAC, which comprised a customs union and a range of public services, including the East African Development Bank, operated on a collectively managed basis. During the early 1970s, however, major economic and political tensions developed between the EAC's member countries. By July 1977 the railways had effectively become national enterprises, East African Airways had broken up and Kenya had launched its own Kenya Airways, Tanzania had closed its border with Kenya, and official trade between the two countries was suspended: for all practical purposes, the EAC had ceased to exist. The East African Development Bank, however, continued to function.

Negotiations concerning the distribution of the EAC's assets and liabilities among the former member states continued intermittently for six years, under the chairmanship of a World Bank-appointed mediator. Agreement was eventually reached in 1983, and a new era of improved relations between the three countries seemed possible. Kenya was allocated a 42.5% share of the assets, whose value was put at US $898m., while Tanzania received 32.5% and Uganda 25.0%. In addition, Uganda was to be paid compensation of $191m. by the other two partners, because their shares of the assets were calculated as greater than the equity shares which they held in the former community corporations. Kenya started to pay this compensation by transferring some of its railway rolling stock to Uganda. An immediate result of the settlement was the reopening of the Kenya–Tanzania border, which provided some limited opportunities for Kenyan exporters. The two countries' airlines resumed inter-state flights in 1984 and agreed arrangements covering overland transport, the cross-border transport of tourists, an expanded air service and co-operation in shipping and port services. In November 1994 the leaders of Kenya, Tanzania and Uganda established a permanent tripartite commission for East African co-operation, and in March 1996 the commission's secretariat was formally inaugurated. A treaty for the re-establishment of the EAC, providing for the promotion of free trade between the member states, the development of the region's infrastructure and economy, and the creation of a regional legislative assembly and court, was approved by Kenya and Uganda in November 1999 and was finally ratified by Tanzania in June 2000 (see Recent History). The new EAC was officially inaugurated in Arusha, Tanzania, in January 2001. Talks on integrating the economies of the three EAC members followed, and in March 2004 the Presidents of Kenya, Uganda and Tanzania signed a protocol on the creation of a customs union, eliminating most duties on goods traded within the EAC. The level of cross-border co-operation during the new EAC era has been much lower than that achieved during the old EAC era, with fewer joint-venture capital investments; nevertheless, the potential exists for better trade co-operation, with a view to creating a larger three-country market that can offer better economies of scale to the region's manufacturers. The East African Customs Union came into force in January 2005. The concessioning of the Kenya–Uganda railway line in October 2005 (see above) by a single consortium operating both countries' sections was also seen as a significant step forward in cross-border co-operation.

PROBLEMS AND PROSPECTS

Kenya's high rate of population growth has imposed major strains upon the economy, in terms of public expenditure, as well as threatening social stability. However, government initiatives to encourage family planning have had significant success in reducing the rate in recent years. The average fertility rate fell from 7.8 children per adult female in 1980 to 5.0 in 2004, and the population growth rate declined from an average of 3.5% per year in 1985–90 to 2.3% in 1995–2005. Although the rate of population growth has declined significantly in recent years, it remains a problem, as nearly one-half of the population are under 14 years of age. Another major constraint to growth has been the balance-of-payments problem. External factors contributing to the sharp slowdown included deteriorating terms of trade, with rising prices for petroleum and other imports and generally low world prices for Kenya's commodities. Internal factors included lack of incentives and slow payments to agricultural producers in some sectors; shortages of imported inputs for manufacturers; high government spending; low wages, which have declined in real terms, and consequent poor productivity; and too much stress on industries relying heavily on expensive imported materials and equipment.

Following the collapse of a number of financial institutions, owing to the malpractice and mismanagement of their directors, the Government formed a committee in 1996 to investigate the scandal and to restore public confidence in Kenya's financial system. The IFC supported two Kenyan banks with loans, providing, in June 1998, US $10m. to the Development Bank of Kenya (one of the few long-established private-sector lending institutions in Africa) and, in January 1999, $30m. to the Kenya Commercial Bank (KCB), thereby signalling the World Bank's approval of the privatization of the oldest and largest financial institution in the country (see above). The KCB was to lend the proceeds of the loan to small and medium-sized export-orientated enterprises in the agricultural, manufacturing and tourism sectors.

During the 1990s progress was made towards solving some of Kenya's economic problems. Liberalization made imported inputs more freely available and eased currency distortions, and government expenditure was more restrained. In addition, productivity levels improved, with gross output per employee increasing by 135% between 1980 and 1991. Privatization of unprofitable state-owned companies took place, albeit more slowly than the IMF would have liked. However, there remained many serious flaws in the economy's basic structure, and pressure on land and the lack of alternative employment for the growing numbers of landless people represented serious long-term difficulties. By 1993, the introduction of foreign-exchange retention accounts had clearly facilitated the importation of raw materials by manufacturers. The effects on the economy of widespread corruption became increasingly manifest during the late 1990s and contributed in no small measure to the economic crisis of 2000. In March 2002 the IMF emphasized the importance of approving appropriate legislation to establish a code of ethics for civil servants, legislators and the judiciary, as well as to strengthen and safeguard the legal status of the anti-corruption police unit.

In 2002 the IMF commended a High Court decision to declare null and void the Central Bank of Kenya (Amendment) Act, also known as the Donde Act, adding that the independence of the Central Bank was vital to the creation of a stable environment for the country's financial markets and also to the formulation and execution of monetary policy. Interest rates, it was stressed, were to be determined not by government policy but by market forces. Meanwhile, the IMF awaits clear results from the new NARC Government's anti-corruption strategy. The 2003/04 budget hinted at some of the innovations that the NARC Government may have in mind. A number of tax-relief incentives sought to create a more enabling environment in which to do business in Kenya, and some tax changes were clearly aimed at alleviating the tax burden on the poorest citizens. Nevertheless, the disadvantage of these tax cuts is that they erode the revenue base. Although the 2003/04 budget did not address a clear strategy for strengthening that revenue base, measures to strengthen the Kenya Revenue Authority were swiftly put into place. By May 2004 the Central Bank of Kenya was able to report that total tax revenue collection was 25.4% above target. In 2004 the greatest cause for concern was the continuing high level of government domestic borrowing; the latest figures confirm that this problem has not yet been addressed. The 2007/08 budget acknowledged that excessive domestic borrowing distorts capital markets and addressed this by preventing the central Government's domestic borrowing from rising further, but it stopped short of making a significant reduction. Nevertheless, the Kenya shilling's exchange rate remains stable, and inflation remains relatively low.

A UN report released in 2005 found that one out of every two Kenyans either had bribed an official or knew someone who had bribed an official to obtain basic services. Many Kenyans expressed the belief that corruption was the underlying cause of excessive bureaucracy and that both the corruption and the resultant 'red tape' acted as deterrents to investment, both local and foreign. The NARC Government has acknowledged this verbally, but action against it is slow. A number of high-level corruption scandals continued to adversely affect the NARC Government in 2006, despite its expressed intention of stamping out corruption. Both Kenya's citizens and Kenya's donors will want to see significant and tangible achievements to that end.

The Government's Integrated Household Budget Survey showed that overall poverty in Kenya declined from 56.8% in 2000 to 46% in 2006; the greatest gains were made in rural areas, where the number of people living below the poverty line declined from 51.5% in 2000 to 33.7% in 2006. According to an independent survey by the Steadman Group in March 2007, 19% of Kenyans surveyed believed that their living conditions had worsened in the past year, 41% believed that they were neither better off nor worse off, and 40% believed that they were better off. Looking ahead, 60% of Kenyans surveyed believed that their living conditions would improve in the year to come. The Government's strategy for development and poverty reduction was set out in its Vision 2030 programme, unveiled in 2007 and due to be launched in January 2008. With an investment of US $7,500m., Vision 2030 seeks to transform Kenya into a globally competitive and prosperous nation with a high quality of life by the year 2030.

Statistical Survey

Source (unless otherwise stated): Central Bureau of Statistics, Ministry of Finance and Planning, POB 30266, Nairobi; tel. (20) 333971; fax (20) 333030; internet www.cbs.go.ke.

Area and Population

AREA, POPULATION AND DENSITY

Area (sq km)	
Land area	571,416
Inland water	11,230
Total	582,646*
Population (census results)†	
24 August 1989	21,443,636
24 August 1999	
Males	14,205,589
Females	14,481,018
Total	28,686,607
Population (official projected estimates at mid-year)	
2004	32,751,523
2005	33,368,802
2006	33,947,066
Density (per sq km) at mid-2006	58.3

* 224,961 sq miles.

† Excluding adjustment for underenumeration.

PRINCIPAL ETHNIC GROUPS
(census of August 1989)

African	21,163,076	European	34,560
Arab	41,595	Other*	115,220
Asian	89,185	**Total**	21,443,636

* Includes persons who did not state 'tribe' or 'race'.

POPULATION BY PROVINCE
(2006, projected estimates)

Nairobi	2,845,353	Nyanza	4,984,935
Central	3,923,946	Rift Valley	8,418,073
Coast	2,975,387	Western	4,150,964
Eastern	5,322,404	**Total**	33,947,066
North-Eastern	1,326,004		

PRINCIPAL TOWNS
(estimated population at census of August 1999)

Nairobi (capital)	2,143,020	Meru	78,100
Mombasa	660,800	Kitale	63,245
Nakuru	219,366	Malindi*	53,805
Kisumu*	194,390	Nyeri*	46,969
Eldoret*	167,016	Kericho	30,023
Thika	82,665	Kisii	29,634

* Boundaries extended between 1979 and 1989.

Mid-2005 ('000, incl. suburbs, UN estimates): Nairobi 2,773; Mombasa 817 (Source: UN, *World Urbanization Prospects: The 2005 Revision*).

BIRTHS AND DEATHS
(annual averages, UN estimates)

	1990–95	1995–2000	2000–05
Birth rate (per 1,000)	38.6	38.0	39.1
Death rate (per 1,000)	9.4	11.4	13.2

Source: UN, *World Population Prospects: The 2006 Revision*.

Expectation of life (years at birth, WHO estimates): 51 (males 51; females 50) in 2004 (Source: WHO, *World Health Report*).

EMPLOYMENT
(labour force survey, selected urban and rural settlements, '000s)*

	2003	2004	2005†
Agriculture and forestry	316.1	320.6	327.5
Mining and quarrying	5.4	5.6	5.8
Manufacturing	239.7	242.0	247.5
Electricity and water	21.1	20.8	20.2
Construction	76.6	77.4	78.4
Wholesale and retail trade	162.8	168.0	175.8
Transport and communications	86.8	100.8	117.3
Finance, insurance, real estate and business services	83.8	83.6	85.7
Community, social and personal services	734.9	744.9	749.5
Total	1,727.3	1,763.7	1,807.7

* Data are for salaried employees in the formal sector only, and therefore exclude 66,800 self-employed and unpaid family workers and 6,407,200 workers in the informal sector. According to ILO, the 1999 census recorded an employed population of 14,474,200.

† Provisional figures.

Mid-2005 (estimates in '000): Agriculture, etc. 12,714; Total labour force 17,395 (Source: FAO).

Health and Welfare

KEY INDICATORS

Total fertility rate (children per woman, 2005)	5.0
Under-5 mortality rate (per 1,000 live births, 2005)	120
HIV/AIDS (% of persons aged 15–49, 2005)	6.1
Physicians (per 1,000 head, 2004)	0.14
Hospital beds (per 1,000 head, 2003)	1.97
Health expenditure (2004): US $ per head (PPP)	85.6
Health expenditure (2004): % of GDP	4.1
Health expenditure (2004): public (% of total)	42.7
Access to water (% of persons, 2004)	61
Access to sanitation (% of persons, 2004)	43
Human Development Index (2004): ranking	152
Human Development Index (2004): value	0.491

For sources and definitions, see explanatory note on p. vi.

Agriculture

PRINCIPAL CROPS
('000 metric tons)

	2003	2004	2005
Wheat	378.7	379.4	368.9
Barley	26.6	39.2	41.2
Maize	2,710.8	2,607.1	2,905.6
Millet	63.6	50.5	53.1
Sorghum	127.2	69.5	149.7
Potatoes	1,223.5	1,084.4	980.2
Sweet potatoes	615.5	571.3	230.7
Cassava (Manioc)	423.8	642.9	347.8
Sugar cane	4,204.1	4,661.0	4,800.8
Dry beans	428.8	277.5	382.3
Dry cow peas	47.0	29.3	36.2
Pigeon peas	98.3	105.6	96.1
Cashew nuts*	10.0	10.0	11.2
Coconuts*	60.0	60.0	66.1
Seed cotton*	20.0	20.0	n.a.
Cottonseed*	13.0	13.0	13.0
Cabbages	709.0	676.3*	689.6*
Tomatoes	318.6	330.0	330.0
Dry onions	65.8	68.0	68.0
Carrots	44.3	44.8*	42.9*

—continued	2003	2004	2005
Bananas	509.7	600.0	600.0
Plantains	509.7	600.0	600.0
Guavas, mangoes and mangosteens	129.5	118.0	149.3*
Avocados	70.9	70.0*	72.0*
Pineapples	399.1	600.0	600.0
Papayas	86.5	86.0*	87.7*
Coffee (green)	55.4	48.4	45.2
Tea (made)	293.7	324.6	328.5
Tobacco (leaves)*	20.0	20.0	n.a.
Sisal	24.4	25.0*	n.a.

* FAO estimate(s).

Source: FAO.

LIVESTOCK
('000 head, year ending September)

	2003	2004	2005
Cattle	12,531.3	13,022.4	13,019.0
Sheep	8,195.1	10,298.5	10,033.9
Goats	11,945.5	13,390.5	13,882.6
Pigs	415.2	379.8	320.0
Camels	895.1	1,193.6	931.3
Chickens	29,901	25,906	28,657

Source: FAO.

LIVESTOCK PRODUCTS
('000 metric tons)

	2003	2004	2005
Cattle meat	342.7	350.2	396.2
Sheep meat	35.5	35.5	36.7
Goats' meat	38.9	38.9	38.9
Pig meat	15.3	14.5	12.8
Chicken meat	20.8	19.2	18.2
Game meat*	14.0	14.0	n.a.
Camel meat*	19.8	19.8	19.8
Cows' milk	2,819.5	2,829.9	2,650.0
Sheep's milk*	31.0	31.0	31.0
Goats' milk	107.2	118.5	129.0
Camels' milk*	25.2	25.2	25.2
Hen eggs*	60.7	60.7	60.7
Honey	22.0*	21.5	22.0

* FAO estimate(s).

Source: FAO.

Forestry

ROUNDWOOD REMOVALS
('000 cubic metres, excluding bark)

	2003	2004	2005
Sawlogs, veneer logs and logs for sleepers	251.0	241.0	241.0
Pulpwood	349.0	391.0	391.0
Other industrial wood*	1,160.0	1,160.0	1,160.0
Fuel wood*	20,182.4	20,369.6	20,563.6
Total	21,942.4	22,161.6	22,355.6

* FAO estimates.

Source: FAO.

SAWNWOOD PRODUCTION
('000 cubic metres, including railway sleepers)

	2000*	2001	2002
Coniferous (softwood)	184	74	70
Broadleaved (hardwood)	1	10	8
Total	185	84	78

* FAO estimates.

2003–05: Production as in 2002.

Source: FAO.

Fishing

('000 metric tons, live weight)

	2003	2004	2005
Capture	124.1	130.9	152.1
Silver cyprinid	31.7	34.7	56.5
Nile tilapia	16.0	17.5	18.7
Other tilapias	4.5	3.9	4.0
Nile perch	55.2	57.2	53.1
Other freshwater fishes	5.9	5.7	8.7
Aquaculture	1.0	1.0	1.0
Total catch	125.1	131.9	153.2

Note: Figures exclude crocodiles, recorded by number rather than by weight. The number of Nile crocodiles caught was: 3,811 in 2003; 3,862 in 2004; 3,794 in 2005.

Source: FAO.

Mining

('000 metric tons, estimates)

	2003	2004	2005
Soda ash	352.6	353.8	360.2
Fluorspar	95.3	118.0	109.6
Salt	48.0	60.0	52.0
Limestone flux	33.0	34.0	35.0

Source: US Geological Survey.

Industry

SELECTED PRODUCTS
('000 metric tons, unless otherwise indicated)

	2003	2004	2005*
Wheat flour	248.6	262.3	271.6
Raw sugar	448.0	516.8	489.0
Beer ('000 hectolitres)	222.3	237.5	266.3
Cigarettes (million)	4,753.0	5,351.0	7,324.2
Cement	1,659.5	1,873.3	2,123.2
Electric energy (million kWh)	4,851.6	5,194.5	5,547.0

* Preliminary data.

2002: Kerosene and jet fuels 273; Motor spirit (petrol) 253; Gas-diesel (distillate fuel) oils 405; Residual fuel oils 533.

Finance

CURRENCY AND EXCHANGE RATES

Monetary Units

100 cents = 1 Kenya shilling (Ks.).
Ks. 20 = 1 Kenya pound (K£).

Sterling, Dollar and Euro Equivalents (30 April 2007)

£1 sterling = Ks. 136.24;
US $1 = Ks. 68.31;
€1 = Ks. 92.93;
Ks. 1,000 = £7.34 sterling = $14.64 = €10.76.

Average Exchange Rate (Ks. per US $)

2004 79.174
2005 75.554
2006 72.101

Note: The foregoing information refers to the Central Bank's mid-point exchange rate. However, with the introduction of a foreign exchange bearer certificate (FEBC) scheme in October 1991, a dual exchange rate system is in effect. In May 1994 foreign exchange transactions were liberalized and the Kenya shilling became fully convertible against other currencies.

BUDGET

(Ks. million, year ending 30 June)

Revenue	1999/2000	2000/01	2001/02*
Tax revenue	151,359.5	160,771.6	160,394.2
Taxes on income and profits	53,317.0	53,428.9	55,861.9
Taxes on goods and services	69,437.3	78,538.9	82,948.6
Value-added tax	40,944.2	50,220.9	50,871.7
Excise duties	28,493.1	28,317.9	32,076.9
Taxes on international trade	28,605.2	28,803.7	21,583.7
Import duties	28,605.2	28,803.7	21,583.7
Non-tax revenue	27,585.1	26,306.1	25,399.4
Property income	6,482.4	4,786.1	4,105.5
Administrative fees and charges	21,538.1	21,538.1	21,293.9
Total (incl. others)	184,550.9	192,221.0	187,863.8

Expenditure	1999/2000	2000/01	2001/02*
General administration	44,080.7	62,943.3	57,584.5
Defence	10,427.2	14,202.8	16,268.2
Social services	59,670.4	67,611.1	71,953.1
Education	47,726.8	49,611.3	54,653.0
Health	9,188.6	15,629.3	14,336.5
Economic services	28,481.1	39,362.3	38,069.4
General administration	5,101.3	14,085.6	12,696.2
Agriculture, forestry and fishing	8,115.4	8,269.6	7,850.1
Roads	8,848.5	9,458.4	8,856.7
Interest on public debt	28,917.8	24,425.5	29,850.9
Total	171,577.2	208,545.7	213,726.2

* Forecasts.

2004/05 (year ending 30 June, Ks. '000 million, estimates): Revenue 342.3 (Direct taxes 140.5; Customs and excise 81.3; VAT and other indirect taxes 93.1); Expenditure 492.2 (General public services 70.8; Defence 27.0; Social services 158.0; Economic affairs 77.1; Other services 116.2).

INTERNATIONAL RESERVES

(excl. gold, US $ million at 31 December)

	2004	2005	2006
IMF special drawing rights	0.6	0.0	0.5
Reserve position in IMF	19.7	18.2	19.2
Foreign exchange	1,499.0	1,780.6	2,395.3
Total	1,519.3	1,798.8	2,415.0

Source: IMF, *International Financial Statistics*.

MONEY SUPPLY

(Ks. million at 31 December)

	2004	2005	2006
Currency outside banks	62,728	66,327	76,479
Demand deposits at commercial banks	136,729	157,460	206,583
Total money (incl. others)	209,368	230,845	291,741

Source: IMF, *International Financial Statistics*.

COST OF LIVING

(Consumer Price Index at December; base: October 1997 = 100)

	2000	2001	2002
Food and non-alcoholic beverages	136.3	134.8	142.5
Alcohol and tobacco	120.8	136.3	137.1
Clothing and footwear	109.9	109.8	110.7
Housing	121.6	129.3	133.9
Fuel and power	143.1	154.1	165.8
Household goods and services	117.6	119.0	120.8
Medical goods and services	134.1	152.6	158.8
Transport and communications	128.4	127.7	130.8
Recreation and education	120.2	129.6	132.8
Personal goods and services	118.2	120.5	122.8
All items (incl. others)	129.0	131.1	136.7

Source: IMF, *Kenya: Statistical Appendix* (July 2003).

All items (Consumer Price Index, annual averages; base 2000 = 100): 118.4 in 2003; 132.2 in 2004; 145.8 in 2005; 166.9 in 2006 (Source: IMF, *International Financial Statistics*).

NATIONAL ACCOUNTS

Expenditure on the Gross Domestic Product

(Ks. million at current prices)

	2003	2004	2005
Government final consumption expenditure	205,140	226,016	242,409
Private final consumption expenditure	875,154	965,528	1,077,071
Changes in inventories	7,288	10,546	−25,311
Gross fixed capital formation	179,282	206,634	263,063
Total domestic expenditure	1,266,865	1,408,724	1,557,231
Exports of goods and services	270,118	336,360	378,068
Less Imports of goods and services	338,394	434,234	529,749
Statistical discrepancy	−60,614	−28,345	9,605
GDP at market prices	1,137,975	1,282,504	1,415,155

Gross Domestic Product by Economic Activity

(Ks. million at current prices)

	2003	2004	2005
Agriculture, forestry and fishing	293,028	318,409	348,797
Mining and quarrying	6,217	6,491	7,173
Manufacturing	109,959	127,502	148,188
Electricity, gas and water	23,330	24,877	27,823
Construction	37,680	46,429	56,298
Wholesale and retail trade, repairs	104,074	126,986	153,528
Restaurants and hotels	10,713	16,214	19,533
Transport, storage and communication	104,411	127,271	154,412
Financial services	48,921	44,343	44,489
Real estate, renting and business services	67,316	72,702	79,015
Government services	167,040	186,346	204,614
Private households	4,561	5,224	5,787
Community, social and personal service activities	45,488	49,058	52,981
Sub-total	1,022,738	1,151,852	1,302,638
Less Imputed bank service charge	10,111	9,052	11,412
Indirect taxes, less subsidies	125,348	139,705	123,928
GDP in market prices	1,137,975	1,282,504	1,415,155

BALANCE OF PAYMENTS
(US $ million)

	2003	2004	2005
Exports of goods f.o.b.	2,412.2	2,720.7	3,239.8
Imports of goods f.o.b.	−3,554.8	−4,350.6	−5,408.1
Trade balance	−1,142.6	−1,629.9	−2,168.3
Exports of services	1,197.6	1,556.5	1,885.9
Imports of services	−690.6	−938.8	−1,132.4
Balance on goods and services	−635.6	−1,012.2	−1,414.7
Other income received	59.6	45.0	73.3
Other income paid	−148.2	−171.5	−181.7
Balance on goods, services and income	−724.2	−1,138.7	−1,523.2
Current transfers received	884.5	828.4	1,094.7
Current transfers paid	−14.1	−42.6	−66.6
Current balance	146.2	−352.9	−495.0
Capital account	163.0	145.2	103.3
Direct investment abroad	−2.1	−4.4	−9.7
Direct investment from abroad	81.7	46.1	21.2
Portfolio investment assets	−38.6	−71.7	−45.9
Portfolio investment liabilities	0.9	5.4	15.4
Other investment assets	−67.4	−307.1	−200.6
Other investment liabilities	431.7	372.0	730.8
Net errors and omissions	−290.3	154.4	−2.6
Overall balance	425.2	−13.1	117.0

Source: IMF, *International Financial Statistics*.

External Trade

PRINCIPAL COMMODITIES
(distribution by SITC,US $ million)

Imports c.i.f.	2002	2003	2004
Food and live animals	182.1	241.6	314.1
Cereals and cereal preparations	99.8	140.4	195.6
Crude materials (inedible) except fuels	75.7	80.2	116.4
Mineral fuels, lubricants, etc.	513.1	802.4	1,107.9
Petroleum, petroleum products, etc.	501.7	788.2	1,086.0
Crude petroleum oils	191.6	316.6	545.1
Refined petroleum products	305.2	465.4	531.6
Animal and vegetable oils, fats and waxes	163.5	164.7	112.4
Chemicals and related products	497.7	531.8	715.8
Medicinal and pharmaceutical products	104.2	117.4	135.6
Artificial resins, plastic materials, etc.	17.7	23.2	26.8
Basic manufactures	430.5	475.5	655.2
Iron and steel	142.7	168.6	277.6
Machinery and transport equipment	976.7	948.3	1,107.8
Power-generating machinery and equipment	62.1	36.7	71.0
Machinery specialized for particular industries	62.9	96.1	123.5
General industrial machinery, equipment and parts	87.0	103.9	115.7
Electrical machinery, apparatus, etc.	18.1	18.8	21.1
Road vehicles and parts*	235.3	263.7	337.2
Passenger motor cars (excl. buses)	84.3	105.3	125.2
Motor vehicles for goods transport and special purposes	62.7	71.3	95.3
Aircraft, associated equipment and parts*	255.9	216.8	107.4
Miscellaneous manufactured articles	205.8	213.8	389.9
Total (incl. others)	3,074.6	3,475.0	4,563.5

* Data on parts exclude tyres, engines and electrical parts.

Exports f.o.b.*	2002	2003	2004
Food and live animals	388.9	987.1	983.2
Vegetables and fruit	146.3	260.9	290.0
Fresh or simply preserved vegetables	74.9	153.3	160.9
Coffee, tea, cocoa and spices	178.1	583.7	570.8
Tea	140.9	481.2	462.1
Crude materials (inedible) except fuels	177.1	337.7	421.7
Cut flowers and foliage	101.4	179.4	234.8
Mineral fuels, lubricants, etc.	430.1	488.7	614.7
Petroleum, petroleum products, etc.	429.1	487.4	612.5
Refined petroleum products	427.8	483.9	609.1
Chemicals and related products	39.3	123.5	113.6
Basic manufactures	133.6	253.7	309.9
Iron and steel	31.2	61.8	96.7
Miscellaneous manufactured articles	90.5	173.8	113.9
Total (incl. others)	1,400.4	2,551.1	2,683.2

* Excluding re-exports.

PRINCIPAL TRADING PARTNERS
(Ks. million)

Imports c.i.f.	2003	2004	2005*
Belgium	6,757	9,689	8,000
China, People's Repub.	8,023	12,795	19,764
France	8,957	12,209	13,883
Germany	10,962	13,183	15,761
India	14,811	22,660	24,236
Indonesia	12,497	7,691	9,749
Italy	5,840	7,154	7,857
Japan	18,611	24,151	23,021
Korea, Repub.	2,966	3,289	3,386
Netherlands	6,256	7,310	9,629
Pakistan	4,456	3,247	2,532
Saudi Arabia	24,305	31,368	27,580
Singapore	2,352	4,452	7,574
South Africa	23,309	34,654	42,305
Spain	2,154	1,989	2,951
Sweden	1,615	2,007	2,404
United Arab Emirates	31,918	45,044	62,130
United Kingdom	19,621	27,124	26,134
USA	14,388	14,425	42,493
Total (incl. others)	281,844	364,557	430,740

Exports f.o.b.	2003	2004	2005*
Belgium	2,332	2,474	2,920
Egypt	5,453	6,918	8,839
France	3,100	3,592	5,086
Germany	5,330	4,574	5,221
India	2,498	4,147	4,000
Italy	1,671	1,764	2,170
Japan	1,215	1,593	1,855
Netherlands	14,139	17,094	18,316
Pakistan	9,153	11,359	14,072
Rwanda	6,012	6,190	7,273
Tanzania	14,588	17,921	19,887
Uganda	30,668	37,059	42,545
United Arab Emirates	2,108	2,396	3,923
United Kingdom	21,525	22,404	23,371
USA	2,796	4,502	4,518
Total (incl. others)	183,154	214,793	244,198

* Provisional.

Transport

RAILWAYS
(traffic)

	2000	2001	2002*
Passenger-km (million)	302	216	288
Freight ton-km (million)	1,557	1,603	1,538

* Provisional figures.

ROAD TRAFFIC
(motor vehicles in use)

	2000	2001	2002*
Motor cars	244,836	255,379	269,925
Light vans	159,450	162,603	166,811
Lorries, trucks and heavy vans	57,796	58,501	59,835
Buses and mini-buses	38,930	42,629	46,606
Motorcycles and autocycles	44,894	46,004	47,451
Other motor vehicles	31,820	32,255	32,724

* Provisional figures.

2004: Motor cars 307,772; Buses 55,705; Lorries and vans 243,612; Motorcycles 53,508.

SHIPPING

Merchant Fleet
(registered at 31 December)

	2004	2005	2006
Number of vessels	41	41	38
Total displacement ('000 grt)	18.7	19.9	17.6

Source: Lloyd's Register-Fairplay, *World Fleet Statistics*.

International Sea-borne Freight Traffic
('000 metric tons)

	1999	2000	2001*
Goods loaded	1,845	1,722	1,998
Goods unloaded	6,200	7,209	8,299

* Provisional figures.

Freight handled ('000 metric tons at Kenyan ports): 11,931 in 2003; 12,920 in 2004; 13,282 in 2005.

CIVIL AVIATION
(traffic on scheduled services)

	2001	2002	2003
Kilometres flown (million)	32	36	41
Passengers carried ('000)	1,418	1,600	1,732
Passenger-km (million)	3,706	3,939	4,245
Total ton-km (million)	427	465	527

Source: UN, *Statistical Yearbook*.

Passengers carried ('000): 4,747 in 2003; 5,450 in 2004; 5,905 in 2005 (estimate).

Tourism

FOREIGN TOURIST ARRIVALS
(number of visitors by country of origin)

	2001	2002	2003
Austria	19,929	20,054	22,954
France	47,802	48,101	55,057
Germany	156,414	157,394	180,156
India	23,858	24,007	27,479
Italy	53,328	53,662	61,428
Sweden	34,376	34,591	39,593
Switzerland	39,081	39,326	45,013
Tanzania	111,735	112,435	128,695
Uganda	69,781	70,218	80,373
United Kingdom	153,968	154,933	177,339
USA	65,191	65,599	75,086
Total (incl. others)	993,600	1,001,297	1,146,099

Tourism receipts (US $ million, incl. passenger transport): 513 in 2002; 611 in 2003; 808 in 2004.

Source: World Tourism Organization.

Total arrivals ('000): 1,361 in 2004; 1,479 in 2005.

Communications Media

	2003	2004	2005
Telephones ('000 main lines in use)	328	299	282
Mobile cellular telephones ('000 subscribers)	1,591	2,546	4,612
Personal computers ('000 in use)	204	441	300
Internet users ('000)	400	1,500	3,050

Source: International Telecommunication Union.

Television receivers ('000 in use, 2000): 768.

Radio receivers ('000 in use, 1999): 6,383.

Facsimile machines (number in use, year ending 30 June 1995): 3,800.

Daily newspapers (2000): 4 titles (average circulation 310,000 copies).

Book production (titles, 1994): 300 first editions (excl. pamphlets).

Sources: UNESCO, *Statistical Yearbook*; UN, *Statistical Yearbook*.

Education

(2003/04, unless otherwise indicated)

	Institutions	Teachers	Pupils
Pre-primary	23,977[1]	70,058	1,627,721
Primary	17,611[1]	149,893	5,926,078
Secondary:			
general secondary	3,057[1]	75,875	2,405,259
technical	36[2]	834[3]	14,597[3]
teacher training	26[4]	808[5]	18,992[6]
Higher	n.a.[7]	n.a.[7]	106,407

[1] 1998/99 figures.
[2] 1988 figure.
[3] UNESCO estimate.
[4] 1995 figure.
[5] 1985 figure.
[6] 1992 figure.
[7] In 1990 there were four universities, with 4,392 teachers.

Sources: Ministry of Education, Nairobi; UNESCO Institute for Statistics.

2005 ('000, estimates): Enrolment in primary schools 7,592; Enrolment in secondary schools 928; Enrolment in universities 90.

Adult literacy rate (UNESCO estimates): 73.6% (males 77.7%; females 70.2%) in 2003 (Source: UN Development Programme, *Human Development Report*).

Directory

The Constitution

The Constitution was introduced at independence on 12 December 1963. Subsequent amendments, including the adoption of republican status on 12 December 1964, were consolidated in 1969. A further amendment in December 1991 permitted the establishment of a multi-party system. In September 1997 the National Assembly approved legislation which amended the Constitution with a view to ensuring free and fair democratic elections. All political parties were granted equal access to the media, and detention without trial was prohibited. In addition, the opposition was to participate in selecting the 12 nominated members of the National Assembly and 10 of the 12 members of the supervisory Electoral Commission. An amendment to the Constitution, approved by the National Assembly in November 1999, reduced the level of presidential control over the legislative process. The Constitution can be amended by the affirmative vote on Second and Third Reading of 65% of the membership of the National Assembly (excluding the Speaker and Attorney-General).

The central legislative authority is the unicameral National Assembly, in which there are 210 directly elected Representatives, 12 nominated members and two ex officio members, the Attorney-General and the Speaker. The maximum term of the National Assembly is five years from its first meeting (except in wartime). It can be dissolved by the President at any time, and the National Assembly may force its own dissolution by a vote of 'no confidence', whereupon presidential and Assembly elections have to be held within 90 days.

Executive power is vested in the President, Vice-President and Cabinet. Both the Vice-President and the Cabinet are appointed by the President, who must be a member of the Assembly and at least 35 years of age. Election of the President, for a five-year term, is by direct popular vote; the winning candidate at a presidential election must receive no less than 25% of the votes in at least five of Kenya's eight provinces. If a President dies, or a vacancy otherwise occurs during a President's period of office, the Vice-President becomes interim President for up to 90 days while a successor is elected.

The Government

HEAD OF STATE

President: MWAI KIBAKI (took office 30 December 2002).

CABINET
(August 2007)

Vice-President and Minister of Home Affairs: ARTHUR MOODY AWORI.

Minister of Finance: AMOS KIMUNYA.

Minister of Planning and National Development: HENRY ONYANCHA OBWOCHA.

Minister of Energy: KIRAITU MURUNGI.

Minister of Foreign Affairs: RAPHAEL TUJU.

Minister of East African and Regional Co-operation: JOHN KOECH.

Minister of Roads and Public Works: SIMEON NYACHAE.

Minister of Science and Technology: Dr NOAH WEKESA.

Minister of Education: Prof. GEORGE SAITOTI.

Minister of Agriculture: KIPRUTO RONO ARAP KIRWA.

Minister of Livestock and Fisheries Development: JOSEPH KONZOLO MUNYAO.

Minister of Health: CHARITY KALUKI NGILU.

Minister of Tourism and Wildlife: MORRIS DZORO.

Minister of Information and Communications: MUTAHI KAGWE.

Minister of Transport: CHIRAU ALI MAKWERE.

Minister of Local Government: MUSIKARI N. KOMBO.

Minister of Gender, Sports, Culture and Social Services: MAINA KAMANDA.

Minister of Water and Irrigation: MUTUA KATUKU.

Minister of Regional Development Authorities: ABDI M. MOHAMED.

Minister of the Environment and Natural Resources: DAVID MWIRARIA.

Minister of Lands: Prof. KIVUTHA KIBWANA.

Minister of Labour and Human Resource Development: Dr NEWTON W. KULUNDU.

Minister of Co-operative Development and Marketing: PETER N. NDWIGA.

Minister of Justice and Constitutional Affairs: MARTHA KARUA.

Minister of Housing: SOITA SHITANDA.

Minister of Trade and Industry: Dr MUKHISA KITUYI.

Ministers of State in the Office of the President: JOHN NJOROGE MICHUKI (Provincial Administration and National Security), NJENGA KRUME (Defence), MOSES AKARANGA (Public Service), JOHN MUNYES (Special Programmes), GIDEON KONCHELAH (Immigration and Registration of Persons).

Ministers of State in the Office of the Vice-President: SULEIMAN SHAKOMBO (National Heritage), MOHAMMED ABDI KUTI (Youth Affairs).

The Attorney-General and the Solicitor-General are also members of the Cabinet.

MINISTRIES

Office of the President: Harambee House, Harambee Ave, POB 30510, Nairobi; tel. (20) 227411; internet www.officeofthepresident.go.ke.

Office of the Vice-President and Ministry of Home Affairs: Jogoo House 'A', Taifa Rd, POB 30520, Nairobi; tel. (20) 228411; internet www.homeaffairs.go.ke.

Ministry of Agriculture: Kilimo House, Cathedral Rd, POB 30028, Nairobi; tel. (20) 718870; fax (20) 720586; internet www.agriculture.go.ke.

Ministry of Co-operative Development and Marketing: Reinsurance Plaza, Taifa Rd, POB 30547, 00100 Nairobi; tel. (20) 339650; internet www.co-operative.go.ke.

Ministry of East African and Regional Co-operation: Old Treasury Bldg, 1st Floor, Harambee Ave, POB 30551, Nairobi; tel. (20) 310310; fax (20) 310365.

Ministry of Education, Science and Technology: Jogoo House 'B', Harambee Ave, POB 30040, Nairobi; tel. (20) 334411; e-mail info@education.go.ke; internet www.education.go.ke.

Ministry of Energy: Nyayo House, Kenyatta Ave, POB 30582, 00100 Nairobi; tel. (20) 310112; fax (20) 240910; internet www.energy.go.ke.

Ministry of the Environment and Natural Resources: Maji House, Ngong Rd, POB 30521, Nairobi; tel. (20) 2716103; e-mail mec@nbnet.co.ke; internet www.environment.go.ke.

Ministry of Finance: Treasury Bldg, Harambee Ave, POB 30007, Nairobi; tel. (20) 338111; fax (20) 330426; e-mail info@treasury.go.ke; internet www.treasury.go.ke.

Ministry of Foreign Affairs: Old Treasury Bldg, Harambee Ave, POB 30551, Nairobi; tel. (20) 334433; e-mail mfapress@nbnet.co.ke; internet www.mfa.go.ke.

Ministry of Gender, Sports, Culture and Social Services: Jogoo House 'A', Taifa Rd, POB 30520, Nairobi; tel. (20) 228411; internet www.kenya.go.ke/gender.

Ministry of Health: Medical HQ, Afya House, Cathedral Rd, POB 30016, Nairobi; tel. (20) 2717077; fax (20) 2725902; internet www.health.go.ke.

Ministry of Information and Communications: Utalii House, off Uhuru Highway, POB 30027, Nairobi; tel. (20) 333555; fax (20) 318045.

Ministry of Justice and Constitutional Affairs: Cooperative Bank House, POB 56057-00200, Nairobi; tel. (20) 224025; internet www.justice.go.ke.

Ministry of Labour and Human Resource Development: Social Security House, Block 'C', Bishop Rd, POB 40326, Nairobi; tel. (20) 2729800; fax (20) 2726497; internet www.labour.go.ke.

Ministry of Lands and Housing: Ardhi House, Ngong Rd, POB 30450, Nairobi; tel. (20) 2718050; internet www.ardhi.go.ke.

Ministry of Livestock and Fisheries Development: Kilimo House, Cathedral Rd, POB 34188, 00100 Nairobi; tel. (20) 2718870; fax (20) 316731; internet www.livestock.go.ke.

Ministry of Local Government: Jogoo House 'A', Taifa Rd, POB 30004, Nairobi; tel. (20) 217475; e-mail mlog@form-net.com; internet www.localgovernment.go.ke.

Ministry of Planning and National Development: Treasury Bldg, Harambee Ave, POB 30007, Nairobi; tel. (20) 338111; internet www.planning.go.ke.

Ministry of Regional Development Authorities: Harambee Ave, POB 62345, Nairobi; tel. (20) 227411; internet www.regional-dev.go.ke.

Ministry of Roads and Public Works: Ministry of Works Bldg, Ngong Rd, POB 30260, Nairobi; tel. (20) 723101; fax (20) 720044; e-mail ps@roadsnet.go.ke; internet www.publicworks.go.ke.

Ministry of Trade and Industry: Teleposta Towers, Kenyatta Ave, POB 30430, Nairobi; tel. (20) 331030; internet www.tradeandindustry.go.ke.

Ministry of Transport: Transcom House, Ngong Rd, POB 52692, Nairobi; tel. (20) 729200; fax (20) 726362; internet www.transport.go.ke.

Ministry of Water: Maji House, Ngong Rd, POB 49720, Nairobi; tel. (20) 2716103; internet www.kenya.go.ke/water.

President and Legislature

PRESIDENT

Election, 27 December 2002

Candidates	Votes	%
Mwai Kibaki (NARC)	3,646,409	62.3
Uhuru Kenyatta (KANU)	1,828,914	31.2
Simeon Nyachae (Ford—People)	345,378	5.9
James Orengo (SDP)	24,537	0.4
David Ng'ethe (CCU)	10,038	0.2
Total	5,855,276	100.0

NATIONAL ASSEMBLY

Speaker: FRANCIS XAVIER OLE KAPARO.

General Election, 27 December 2002

Party	Seats
NARC	125
KANU	64
FORD—People	14
FORD—Asili	2
Safina	2
SKS	2
SPK	1
Total	210*

* In addition to the 210 directly elected seats, 12 are held by nominees (NARC 7; KANU 4; FORD—People 1). The Attorney-General and the Speaker are, ex officio, members of the National Assembly.

Election Commission

Electoral Commission of Kenya: Anniversary Towers, University Way, POB 45371, Nairobi; tel. (20) 222072; e-mail eck@eck.or.ke; internet www.eck.or.ke; independent; Chair. SAMUEL KIVUITU.

Political Organizations

Chama Cha Uma (CCU): Nairobi; DAVID NG'ETHE.

Dawa Ya Wakenya (Remedy for Kenya): f. 2007 by politicians from the North-Eastern region and the north of the Rift Valley to defend the rights of the inhabitants of those areas and to campaign for improved infrastructure, social services and security; Chair. HASSAN HAJI; Gen. Sec. MORU SHAMBARU.

Democratic Party of Kenya (DP): Continental House, POB 56396, Nairobi; tel. (20) 340044; f. 1991; Chair. MWAI KIBAKI; Sec. JOSEPH MUNYAO; rival faction led by NGENGI MUIGAI.

Forum for the Restoration of Democracy—Asili (FORD—Asili): Anyany Estate, POB 72595, Nairobi; f. 1992; Chair. GEORGE NTHENGE; Sec. MARTIN J. SHIKUKU.

Forum for the Restoration of Democracy—Kenya (FORD—Kenya): Odinga House, POB 57449, Nairobi; tel. (20) 570361; f. 1992; predominantly Luo support; Chair. SOITA SHITANDA; Sec. GITOBU IMANYARA.

Forum for the Restoration of Democracy for the People (FORD—People): Nairobi; f. 1997 by fmr mems of FORD—Asili; Chair. KIPKALIA KONES.

Growth and Development Party of Kenya (GDP): Nairobi; e-mail info@gdp.co.ke; internet www.gdp.co.ke; f. 2007; Chair. AURELIO REBELO.

New Kenya African National Union (New—KANU): KICC POB 72394, Nairobi; tel. (20) 332383; f. 1960 as KANU; sole legal party 1982–91; absorbed the National Development Party (f. 1994) in 2002; became known as New—KANU in 2006 after the expulsion of hitherto party President Uhuru Kenyatta; Pres. NICHOLAS BIWOTT.

Kenya National Congress (KNC): POB 9474, Nairobi; f. 1992; Chair. Prof. KATANA MKANGI; Sec.-Gen. ONESMUS MUSYOKA MBALI.

Kenya National Democratic Alliance (KENDA): Wetithe House, Nkrumah St, POB 1851, Thika; tel. (151) 562304; f. 1991; Chair. KAMLESH PATTNI (acting); Sec.-Gen. BERNARD KALOVE.

Kenya Social Congress (KSC): POB 55318, Nairobi; f. 1992; Chair. GEORGE MOSETI ANYONA; Sec.-Gen. KASHINI MALOBA FAFNA.

Liberal Democratic Party (LDP): Nairobi; f. 2002 by fmr mems of KANU; Chair. DAVID MUSHA; Sec.-Gen. J. J. KAMOTHO.

Labour Party Democracy: POB 7905, Nairobi; Chair. GEOFFREY MBURU; Sec. DAVID MBURI NGACHURA.

Liberal Party: Chair. WANGARI MAATHAI.

Mazingira Party of Kenya (MPK): f. 2007; campaigns for the equitable sharing of wealth, sustainable use of natural resources, women's rights and the defence of Kenyan cultural values; Leader WANGARI MAATHAI; Chair. MWANGI MAKANGA.

National Alliance Party of Kenya (NAPK): Nairobi; f. 2002; alliance of some 12 parties, including the DP, FORD—Kenya and the NPK.

National Party of Kenya (NPK): f. 2001; Chair. CHARITY KALUKI NGILU; Sec.-Gen. FIDELIS MWEKE.

National Rainbow Coalition—Kenya (NARC—Kenya): Woodland Rd, off Lenana Rd, Kilimani; POB 34200-00100, Nairobi; tel. (20) 2726783; fax (20) 2726786; e-mail info@narckenya.co.ke; internet www.narckenya.or.ke; f. 2005 by former mems of NARC; Chair. RAPHAEL TUJU; Sec.-Gen. Dr MUKHISA KITUYI.

New Kanu Alliance: Sec. IMANYARA MUGAMBI.

Party of Independent Candidates of Kenya (PICK): Plot No 299/096 Kenyatta Ave, POB 21821, Nairobi; Chair. G. N. MUSYIMI; Sec. F. NGUGI.

Patriotic Pastoralist Alliance of Kenya: f. 1997; represents the interests of northern Kenyan pastoralist communities; Leaders KHALIF ABDULLAHI, IBRAHIM WOCHE, JACKSON LAISAGOR.

People's Alliance for Change in Kenya (PACK): Nairobi; f. 1999; aims to unite diverse ethnic groups; Sec.-Gen. OLANG SANA.

Safina ('Noah's Ark'): POB 135, Nairobi; f. 1995; aims to combat corruption and human rights abuses and to introduce proportional representation; Chair. CLEMENT MUTURI KIGANO; Sec.-Gen. MWANDAWIRO MGHANGA.

Shirikisho Party of Kenya (SPK): POB 70421, Nairobi; Chair. HAMISI SAIDI JEFFAH; Sec. OMARA ABAE KALASINGHA.

Sisi Kwa Sisi (SKS): Nairobi; f. 2001; Leader JOHN RUKENYA KABUGUA.

Social Democratic Party of Kenya (SDP): POB 55845, Nairobi; tel. (20) 260309; f. 1992; Chair. JUSTUS NYAGAYA; Sec.-Gen. Dr APOLLO LUGANO NJONJO.

United Agri Party of Kenya: f. 2001; Chair. GEORGE KINYUA; Sec.-Gen. SIMON MITOBIO.

United Democratic Movement: Nairobi; Chair. KIPRUTO RONO ARAP KIRWA; Sec.-Gen. STEPHEN TARUS.

United Patriotic Party of Kenya: POB 115, Athi River; Chair. JOSEPHAT GATHUA GATHIGA; Sec. MICHAEL NJUGUNA KIGANYA.

The following organizations are banned:

February Eighteen Resistance Army: believed to operate from Uganda; Leader Brig. JOHN ODONGO (also known as Stephen Amoke).

Islamic Party of Kenya (IPK): Mombasa; f. 1992; Islamic fundamentalist; Chair. Sheikh KHALIFA MUHAMMAD (acting); Sec.-Gen. ABDULRAHMAN WANDATI.

Diplomatic Representation

EMBASSIES AND HIGH COMMISSIONS IN KENYA

Algeria: 37 Muthaiga Rd, POB 53902, Nairobi; tel. (20) 310440; fax (20) 310450; e-mail algerianembassy@mitsuminett.com; Ambassador MUHAMMAD-HACENE ECHARIF.

Argentina: Posta Sacco, 6th Floor, University Way, POB 30283, 00100 Nairobi; tel. (20) 339949; fax (20) 217693; e-mail argentina@form-net.com; Ambassador DANIEL CHUBURU.

Australia: ICIPE House, Riverside Dr., off Chiromo Rd, POB 39341, Nairobi; tel. (20) 445034; fax (20) 444718; internet www.kenya.embassy.gov.au; High Commissioner LISA FILIPETTO.

Austria: City House, 2nd Floor, Wabera St, POB 30560, 00100 Nairobi; tel. (20) 319076; fax (20) 342290; e-mail nairobi-ob@bmeia

.gv.at; internet www.aussenministerium.at/nairobi; Ambassador ROLAND HAUSER.

Bangladesh: Lenana Rd, POB 41645, Nairobi; tel. (20) 562816; fax (20) 562817; e-mail bdken@iconnect.co.ke; High Commissioner YAKUB ALI.

Belgium: Muthaiga, Limuru Rd, POB 30461, Nairobi; tel. (20) 741564; fax (20) 442701; e-mail nairobi@diplobel.be; internet www.diplomatie.be/nairobi; Ambassador LEO WILLEMS.

Brazil: Tanar Center, UN Crescent Rd, UN Close, Gigiri, Nairobi; tel. (20) 7125765; fax (20) 7125767; Ambassador JOAQUIM AUGUSTO WHITAKER SALLES.

Burundi: Development House, 14th Floor, Moi Ave, POB 44439, Nairobi; tel. (20) 575113; fax (20) 219005; Ambassador JEREMIE NGENDAKUMANA.

Canada: Limuru Rd, POB 1013, 00621 Gigiri, Nairobi; tel. (20) 3663000; fax (20) 3663900; e-mail nrobi@international.gc.ca; High Commissioner ROSS HYNES.

Chile: Riverside Dr. 66, Riverside, POB 45554, 00100 Nairobi; tel. (20) 4452950; fax (20) 4443209; e-mail echile@echile.co.ke; Ambassador GAETE VIDAL PABLO RODRIGO.

China, People's Republic: Woodlands Rd, Kilimani District, POB 30508, Nairobi; tel. (20) 2722559; fax (20) 2726402; e-mail chinaemb_ke@mfa.gov.cn; internet ke.china-embassy.org; Ambassador ZHANG MING.

Colombia: International House, 6th Floor, Mam Ngina St, POB 48494, 00100 Nairobi; tel. (20) 246770; fax (20) 246771; e-mail enairobi@cancilleria.gov.co; Ambassador MARIA VICTORIA DIAZ DE SUAREZ.

Congo, Democratic Republic: Electricity House, Harambee Ave, POB 48106, Nairobi; tel. (20) 229771; fax (20) 334539; Ambassador (vacant).

Cuba: International House, Mama Ngina St, 13th Floor, POB 41931, Nairobi; tel. (20) 241003; fax (20) 241023; e-mail embacuba@swiftkenya.com; Ambassador JULIO CÉSAR GONZÁLEZ MARCHANTE.

Cyprus: Eagle House, 5th Floor, Kimathi St, POB 30739, 00100 Nairobi; tel. (20) 220881; fax (20) 312202; e-mail cyphc@nbnet.co.ke; High Commissioner VASSOS CHAMBERLEN.

Czech Republic: Jumia Pl., Lenana Rd, POB 48785, 00100 Nairobi; tel. (20) 2731010; fax (20) 2731013; e-mail nairobi@embassy.mzv.cz; internet www.mzv.cz/nairobi; Ambassador PETER KOPØIVA.

Denmark: Cassia House, Westlands Office Park, POB 40412, 00100 Nairobi; tel. (20) 4451460; fax (20) 4451474; e-mail nboamb@um.dk; internet www.ambnairobi.um.dk; Ambassador BO JENSEN.

Djibouti: Comcraft House, 2nd Floor, Haile Selassie Ave, POB 59528, Nairobi; tel. (20) 339640; Ambassador ADEN HOUSSEIN ABDILLAHI.

Egypt: Kingara Rd, Lavington, POB 30285, Nairobi; tel. (20) 570360; fax (20) 570383; Ambassador SAHER HASANEEN TAWFEEK HAMZA.

Eritrea: New Rehema House, 2nd Floor, Westlands, POB 38651, Nairobi; tel. (20) 443164; fax (20) 443165; e-mail eriembk@africaonline.co.ke; Ambassador SALIH OMAR ABDU.

Ethiopia: State House Ave, POB 45198, Nairobi; tel. (20) 2732054; fax (20) 2732054; e-mail ethioemb@kenyaweb.com; Ambassador DISSASA DIRBISSA WINSA.

Finland: International House, 2nd Floor, Mama Ngina St, POB 30379, 00100 Nairobi; tel. (20) 334777; fax (20) 335986; e-mail finland@form-net.com; Ambassador HELI SIRVE (designate).

France: Barclays Plaza, 9th Floor, Loita St, POB 41784, Nairobi; tel. (20) 2778000; fax (20) 2778180; e-mail ambafrance.nairobi@diplomatie.gouv.fr; internet www.ambafrance-ke.org; Ambassador ELIZABETH BARBIER.

Germany: Ludwig Krapf House, Riverside Dr. 113, POB 30180, Nairobi; tel. (20) 4262100; fax (20) 4262129; e-mail info@nairobi.diplo.de; internet www.nairobi.diplo.de; Ambassador WALTER JOHANNES LINDNER.

Greece: Nation Centre, 13th Floor, Kimathi St, POB 30543, Nairobi; tel. (20) 340722; fax (20) 216044; e-mail embgr@kenyaweb.com; Ambassador IOANNIS KORINTHIOS.

Holy See: Apostolic Nunciature, Manyani Rd West, Waiyaki Way, POB 14326, 00800 Nairobi; tel. (20) 4442975; fax (20) 4446789; e-mail nunciokenya@nunciokenya.org; Apostolic Nuncio Most Rev. ALAIN PAUL CHARLES LEBEAUPIN (Titular Archbishop of Vico Equense).

Hungary: Kabarsiran Ave, off James Gichuru Rd, Lavington, POB 61146, Nairobi; tel. (20) 560060; fax (20) 560114; e-mail huembnai@africaonline.co.ke; internet www.mfa.gov.hu/kulkepviselet/KE/en/; Ambassador GÁBOR SÁGI.

India: Jeevan Bharati Bldg, 2nd Floor, Harambee Ave, POB 30074, Nairobi; tel. (20) 225104; fax (20) 316242; e-mail hcindia@kenyaweb.com; internet www.hcinairobi.co.ke; High Commissioner PARAMPREET SINGH RANDHAWA.

Indonesia: Menengai Rd, Upper Hill, POB 48868, Nairobi; tel. (20) 2714196; fax (20) 2713475; e-mail indonbi@indonesia.or.ke; internet www.indonesia.or.ke; Ambassador DJISMUN KASRI.

Iran: Dennis Pritt Rd, POB 49170, Nairobi; tel. (20) 711257; fax (20) 339936; Ambassador MOHAMMAD RAESI.

Israel: Bishop's Rd, POB 30354, Nairobi; tel. (20) 2722182; fax (20) 2715966; e-mail info@nairobi.mfa.gov.il; internet nairobi.mfa.gov.il; Ambassador EMMANUEL SERI.

Italy: International House, 9th Floor, Mama Ngina St, POB 30107, Nairobi; tel. (20) 247750; fax (20) 247086; e-mail ambasciata.nairobi@esteri.it; internet www.ambnairobi.esteri.it; Ambassador PIERANDREA MAGISTRATI.

Japan: Mara Rd, Upper Hill, POB 60202, Nairobi; tel. (20) 2898000; fax (20) 2898220; e-mail jinfocul@eojkenya.org; internet www.ke.emb-japan.go.jp; Ambassador SATORU MIYAMURA.

Korea, Republic: Anniversary Towers, 15th Floor, University Way, POB 30455, Nairobi; tel. (20) 333581; fax (20) 217772; e-mail emb-ke@mofat.go.kr; Ambassador YUM KI-SYUB.

Kuwait: Muthaiga Rd, POB 42353, Nairobi; tel. (20) 761614; fax (20) 762837; e-mail kuwaitembassy@form-net.com; Chargé d'affaires a.i. JABER SALEM HUSSAIN EBRAHEEM.

Lesotho: Nairobi; tel. (20) 224876; fax (20) 337493; High Commissioner (vacant).

Mexico: Kibagare Way, off Loresho Ridge, POB 14145, Nairobi; tel. (20) 4182593; fax (20) 4181500; e-mail mexico@embamexken.com; Ambassador JUAN CARLOS CUE VEGA.

Morocco: Diamond Trust House, 3rd Floor, Moi Ave, POB 61098, Nairobi; tel. (20) 710647; fax (20) 222364; e-mail embassymorocco@form-net.com; Ambassador ABDELILAH BENRYANE.

Mozambique: Bruce House, 3rd Floor, Standard St, POB 66923, Nairobi; tel. (20) 221979; fax (20) 222446; High Commissioner PAULO ELIAS CIGARRO.

Netherlands: Riverside Lane, off Riverside Dr., POB 41537, Nairobi; tel. (20) 4288000; fax (20) 4447416; e-mail nlgovnai@africaonline.co.ke; internet www.netherlands-embassy.or.ke; Ambassador MARIA ALICE CRISPINA VAN DEN ASSUM.

Nigeria: Lenana Rd, Hurlingham, POB 30516, Nairobi; tel. (20) 564116; fax (20) 564117; e-mail nigken@todays.co.ke; High Commissioner N. TAPGUN.

Norway: Lion Pl., 1st Floor, Wayiaki Way, POB 46363, 00100 Nairobi; tel. (20) 4251000; fax (20) 4451517; e-mail emb.nairobi@mfa.no; internet www.norway.or.ke; Ambassador ELISABETH JACOBSEN.

Pakistan: St Michel Rd, Westlands Ave, POB 30045, 00100 Nairobi; tel. (20) 4443911; fax (20) 4446507; e-mail parepnairobi@iwayafrica.com; internet www.pakistanafrica.org; High Commissioner IFTIKHAR A. ARIAN.

Poland: Kabarnet Rd, off Ngong Rd, Woodley, POB 30086, 00100 Nairobi; tel. (20) 3872811; fax (20) 3872814; e-mail ambnairo@kenyaweb.com; internet www.nairobi.polemb.net; Ambassador WOJCIECH JASINSKI.

Portugal: Reinsurance Plaza, 10th Floor, Aga Khan Walk, POB 34020, 00100 Nairobi; tel. (20) 313203; fax (20) 214711; e-mail embassy.nairobi@portugal.co.ke; Ambassador LUIS LORUÁO.

Romania: Gardenia Rd, Gigiri, POB 63240, Nairobi; tel. (20) 7123109; fax (20) 7122061; e-mail secretariat@romanianembassy.co.ke; Ambassador MIHAIL CONSTANTIN COMAN.

Russia: Lenana Rd, POB 30049, Nairobi; tel. (20) 728700; fax (20) 721888; e-mail russemb@swiftkenya.com; Ambassador VALERY YEGOSHKIN.

Rwanda: International House, 12th Floor, Mama Ngina St, POB 48579, Nairobi; tel. (20) 560178; fax (20) 561932; Ambassador GEORGE WILLIAM KAYONGA.

Saudi Arabia: Muthaiga Rd, POB 58297, Nairobi; tel. (20) 762781; fax (20) 760939; Ambassador NBEEL KHALAF A. ASHOUR.

Slovakia: Milimani Rd, POB 30204, Nairobi; tel. (20) 721896; fax (20) 721898; Ambassador STEFAN MORAVEK.

Somalia: POB 30769, Nairobi; tel. (20) 580165; fax (20) 581683; Ambassador MOHAMMED ALI NUR.

South Africa: Roshanmaer Place, Lenana Rd, POB 42441, Nairobi; tel. (20) 2827100; fax (20) 2827219; e-mail sahc@africaonline.co.ke; High Commissioner TONY MSIMANGA.

Spain: International House, 3rd Floor, Mama Ngina St, POB 45503, 00100 Nairobi; tel. (20) 226568; fax (20) 332858; Ambassador NICOLÁS MARTÍN CINTO.

Sri Lanka: Lenana Rd, POB 48145 GPO, Nairobi; tel. (20) 572627; fax (20) 572141; e-mail slhckeny@africaonline.co.ke; internet www.lk/dipmissionf.html; High Commissioner HABEEB MOHAMMED FAROOK.

Sudan: Minet-ICDC Bldg, 7th Floor, Mamlaka Rd, POB 48784, Nairobi; tel. (20) 720853; fax (20) 721015; Ambassador OMER EL-SHEIKH.

Swaziland: Transnational Plaza, 3rd Floor, Mama Ngina St, POB 41887, Nairobi; tel. (20) 339231; fax (20) 330540; High Commissioner Prince SOLOMON MBILINI N. DLAMINI.

Sweden: Lion Pl., 3rd Floor, Waiyaki Way, Westlands, POB 30600, 00100 Nairobi; tel. (20) 4234000; fax (20) 4452008; e-mail ambassaden.nairobi@sida.se; internet www.swedenabroad.com/nairobi; Ambassador ANNA BRANDT.

Switzerland: International House, 7th Floor, Mama Ngina St, POB 30752, Nairobi; tel. (20) 228735; fax (20) 217388; e-mail nai.vertretung@eda.admin.ch; Ambassador GEORGE MARTIN.

Tanzania: Continental House, Uhuru Highway, POB 47790, Nairobi; tel. (20) 331056; fax (20) 218269; e-mail tanzania@user.africaonline.co.ke; High Commissioner Maj.-Gen. MIRISHO SAM HAGGAI SARAKIKYA.

Thailand: Ambassador House, Rose Ave, POB 58349, Nairobi; tel. (20) 715243; fax (20) 715801; e-mail thainbi@form-net.com; internet www.thaiembassy.org/nairobi; Ambassador AOPICHITY ASATTHAWASI.

Turkey: Gigiri Rd, off Limuru Rd, POB 64748, 00620 Nairobi; tel. and fax (20) 522562; e-mail tcbenair@wananchi.com; Ambassador OSMAN M. BUYUKDAVRAS.

Uganda: Uganda House, 5th Floor, Kenyatta Ave, POB 60853, Nairobi; tel. (20) 4449096; fax (20) 4443772; High Commissioner Brig. (retd) MATAYO KYALIGONZA.

United Kingdom: Upper Hill Rd, POB 30465, 00100 Nairobi; tel. (20) 2844000; fax (20) 2844033; e-mail nairobi-chancery@fco.gov.uk; internet www.britishhighcommission.gov.uk/kenya; High Commissioner ADAM WOOD.

USA: United Nations Ave, POB 606, Village Market, 00621 Nairobi; tel. (20) 3636000; fax (20) 537810; e-mail ircnairobi@state.gov; internet nairobi.usembassy.gov; Ambassador MICHAEL E. RANNEBERGER.

Venezuela: Ngong/Kabarnet Rd, POB 34477, Nairobi; tel. (20) 574646; fax (20) 337487; e-mail embavene@africaonline.co.ke; Ambassador MARIA JACQUELINE MENDOZA.

Yemen: cnr Ngong and Kabarnet Rds, POB 44642, Nairobi; tel. (20) 564379; fax (20) 564394; Ambassador AHMAD MAYSARI.

Zambia: Nyerere Rd, POB 48741, Nairobi; tel. (20) 724850; fax (20) 718494; High Commissioner ENESS CHISHALA CHIYENGE.

Zimbabwe: Minet-ICDC Bldg, 6th Floor, Mamlaka Rd, POB 30806, Nairobi; tel. (20) 721071; fax (20) 726503; e-mail kenhicom@africaonline.co.zw; Ambassador KELEBERT NKOMANI.

Judicial System

The Kenya Court of Appeal

POB 30187, Nairobi.

The final court of appeal for Kenya in civil and criminal process; sits at Nairobi, Mombasa, Kisumu, Nakuru and Nyeri.

Chief Justice: JOHNSON EVANS GICHERU.

Justices of Appeal: MATHEW MULI, J. M. GACHUHI, J. R. O. MASIME, SAMUEL BOSIRE, R. O. KWACH, EFFIE OWUOR.

The High Court of Kenya: Between Taifa Rd and City Hall Way, POB 30041, Nairobi; tel. (20) 221221; e-mail hck-lib@nbnet.co.ke; has unlimited criminal and civil jurisdiction at first instance, and sits as a court of appeal from subordinate courts in both criminal and civil cases. The High Court is also a court of admiralty. There are three resident puisne judges at Mombasa and at Nakuru, two resident puisne judge at Eldoret, Kisumu and Meru and one resident puisne judge at Bungoma, Embu, Kakamega, Kissi, Kitale, Machakos, Malindi and Nyeri.

Resident Magistrates' Courts: have country-wide jurisdiction, with powers of punishment by imprisonment for up to five years or by fines of up to K£500. If presided over by a chief magistrate or senior resident magistrate the court is empowered to pass any sentence authorized by law. For certain offences, a resident magistrate may pass minimum sentences authorized by law.

District Magistrates' Courts: of first, second and third class; have jurisdiction within districts and powers of punishment by imprisonment for up to five years, or by fines of up to K£500.

Kadhi's Courts: have jurisdiction within districts, to determine questions of Islamic law.

Religion

According to official government figures, Protestants, the largest religious group, represent approximately 38% of the population. Approximately 25% of the population is Roman Catholic, 7% of the population practices Islam, 1% practices Hinduism and the remainder follows various traditional indigenous religions or offshoots of Christian religions. There are very few atheists. Muslim groups dispute government estimates; most often they claim to represent 15% to 20% of the population, sometimes higher. Members of most religious groups are active throughout the country, although certain religions dominate particular regions. Muslims dominate North-Eastern Province, where the population is chiefly Somali. Muslims also dominate Coast Province, except for the western areas of the province, which are predominantly Christian. Eastern Province is approximately 50% Muslim (mostly in the north) and 50% Christian (mostly in the south). The rest of the country is largely Christian, with some persons following traditional indigenous religions. Many foreign missionary groups operate in the country, the largest of which are the African Inland Mission (Evangelical Protestant), the Southern Baptist Church, the Pentecostal Assembly of Kenya, and the Church Missionary Society of Britain (Anglican). The Government generally has permitted these missionary groups to assist the poor and to operate schools and hospitals. The missionaries openly promote their religious beliefs and have encountered little resistance.

CHRISTIANITY

National Council of Churches of Kenya: Church House, Moi Ave, POB 45009, Nairobi; tel. (20) 242278; fax (20) 224463; f. 1943 as Christian Council of Kenya; 35 full mems and eight assoc. mems; Chair. Rev. JOSEPH WAITHONGA; Sec.-Gen. Rev. MUTAVA MUSYIMI.

The Anglican Communion

Anglicans are adherents of the Church of the Province of Kenya, which was established in 1970. It comprises 28 dioceses, and has about 2.5m. members.

Archbishop of Kenya and Bishop of Nairobi: Most Rev. Dr DAVID M. GITARI, POB 40502, Nairobi; tel. (20) 2714755; fax (20) 2718442; e-mail davidgitari@insightkenya.com.

Greek Orthodox Church

Archbishop of East Africa: NICADEMUS OF IRINOUPOULIS, Nairobi; jurisdiction covers Kenya, Tanzania and Uganda.

The Roman Catholic Church

Kenya comprises four archdioceses, 20 dioceses and one Apostolic Vicariate. At 31 December 2004 an estimated 24.6% of the total population were adherents of the Roman Catholic Church.

Kenya Episcopal Conference

Kenya Catholic Secretariat, POB 13475, Nairobi; tel. (20) 443133; fax (20) 442910; e-mail secgeneral@catholicchurch.or.ke; internet www.catholicchurch.or.ke.

f. 1976; Pres. Rt Rev. CORNELIUS K. ARAP KORIR (Bishop of Eldoret).

Archbishop of Kisumu: Most Rev. ZACCHAEUS OKOTH, POB 1728, Kisumu; tel. (57) 43950; fax (57) 42415; e-mail archdiocese-ksm@net2000ke.com.

Archbishop of Mombasa: Most Rev. JOHN NJENGA, Catholic Secretariat, Nyerere Ave, POB 83131, Mombasa; tel. (43) 311526; fax (43) 228217; e-mail devmsa@africaonline.co.ke.

Archbishop of Nairobi: Most Rev. RAPHAEL NDINGI MWANA'A NZEKI, Archbishop's House, POB 14231, 00800 Nairobi; tel. (20) 241391; fax (20) 223799; e-mail arch-nbo@wananchi.com.

Archbishop of Nyeri: Most Rev. NICODEMUS KIRIMA, POB 288, 10100 Nyeri; tel. (61) 2030446; fax (61) 2030435; e-mail adn@wananchi.com.

Other Christian Churches

Africa Inland Church in Kenya: Bishop Rev. Dr TITUS M. KIVUNZI.

African Christian Church and Schools: POB 1365, Thika; e-mail accsheadoffice@yahoo.com; f. 1948; Moderator Rt Rev. JOHN NJUNGUNA; Gen. Sec. Rev. SAMUEL MWANGI; 50,000 mems.

African Church of the Holy Spirit: POB 183, Kakamega; f. 1927; 20,000 mems.

African Israel Nineveh Church: Nineveh HQ, POB 701, Kisumu; f. 1942; High Priest Rt Rev. JOHN KIVULI, II; Gen. Sec. Rev. JOHN ARAP TONUI; 350,000 mems.

Baptist Convention of Kenya: POB 14907, Nairobi; Pres. Rev. ELIUD MUNGAI.

Church of God in East Africa: Pres. Rev. Dr BYRUM MAKOKHA.

Evangelical Fellowship of Kenya: Co-ordinator Rt Rev. ARTHUR GITONGA; Sec.-Gen. Dr WASHINGTON NG'ENG'I.

Evangelical Lutheran Church in Kenya: POB 874, Kisii; tel. (40) 31231; fax (40) 30475; e-mail elok@africaonline.co.ke; Bishop Rev. FRANCIS NYAMWARO ONDERI; 65,000 mems.

Methodist Church in Kenya: POB 47633, 00100 Nairobi; tel. (20) 2724828; fax (20) 2729790; e-mail mckconf@wananchi.com; f. 1862; autonomous since 1967; Presiding Bishop Rev. Dr STEPHEN KANYARU M'IMPWII; 900,000 mems (2005).

Presbyterian Church of East Africa: POB 27573-00506, Nairobi; tel. (20) 608848; fax (20) 609102; e-mail info@pcea.or.ke; internet www.pcea.or.ke; Moderator Rt Rev. Dr DAVID GITHI; Sec.-Gen. Rev. SAMUEL MURIGYH.

Other denominations active in Kenya include the Africa Gospel Church, the African Brotherhood Church, the African Independent Pentecostal Church, the African Interior Church, the Episcopal Church of Kenya, the Free Pentecostal Fellowship of Kenya, the Full Gospel Churches of Kenya, the Lutheran Church in Kenya, the National Independent Church of Africa, the Pentecostal Assemblies of God, the Pentecostal Evangelistic Fellowship of God and the Reformed Church of East Africa.

BAHÁ'Í FAITH

National Spiritual Assembly: POB 47562, Nairobi; tel. (20) 725447; mems resident in 9,654 localities.

ISLAM

Supreme Council of Kenyan Muslims (SUPKEM)
POB 45163, Nairobi; tel. and fax (20) 243109; Nat. Chair. Prof. ABD AL-GHAFUR AL-BUSAIDY; Sec.-Gen. MOHAMMED KHALIF.

Chief Kadhi: NASSOR NAHDI.

The Press

PRINCIPAL DAILIES

Daily Nation: POB 49010, Nairobi; tel. (20) 2221222; fax (20) 2337710; e-mail nation@africaonline.co.ke; internet www .nationaudio.com; f. 1960; English; owned by Nation Media Group; Editor-in-Chief WANGETHI MWANGI; Man. Editor JOSEPH ODINDO; circ. 195,000.

East African Standard: POB 30080, Nairobi; tel. (20) 2540280; fax (20) 2553939; e-mail online@eastandard.net; internet www .eastandard.net; f. 1902; Editor MUTUMA MATHIY; circ. 59,000.

Kenya Leo: POB 30958, Nairobi; tel. (20) 332390; f. 1983; Kiswahili; KANU party newspaper; Group Editor-in-Chief AMBOKA ANDERE; circ. 6,000.

Kenya Times: POB 30958, Nairobi; tel. (20) 2336611; fax (20) 2927348; internet www.timesnews.co.uk; f. 1983; evening; English; KANU party newspaper; Group Editor-in-Chief AMBOKA ANDERE; circ. 10,000.

The People: POB 10296, 00100 Nairobi; tel. (20) 249686; fax (20) 253344; e-mail info@people.co.ke; internet www.people.co.ke; f. 1993; Man. Editor MUGO THEURI; circ. 40,000.

Taifa Leo: POB 49010, Nairobi; tel. (20) 337691; Kiswahili; f. 1960; daily and weekly edns; owned by Nation Media Group; Editor ROBERT MWANGI; circ. 57,000.

Kenya has a thriving vernacular press, but titles are often short-lived. Newspapers in African languages include:

Kihooto (The Truth): Kikuyu; satirical.

Mwaria Ma (Honest Speaker): Nyeri; f. 1997; Publr Canon JAMLICK M. MIANO.

Mwihoko (Hope): POB 734, Muranga; f. 1997; Roman Catholic.

Nam Dar: Luo.

Otit Mach (Firefly): Luo.

SELECTED PERIODICALS

Weeklies and Fortnightlies

The Business Chronicle: POB 53328, Nairobi; tel. (20) 544283; fax (20) 532736; f. 1994; weekly; Man. Editor MUSYOKA KYENDO.

Coastweek: Oriental Bldg, 2nd Floor, Nkrumah Rd, POB 87270, Mombasa; tel. (41) 2230125; fax (41) 2225003; e-mail coastwk@africaonline.co.ke; internet www.coastweek.com; f. 1978; English, with German section; Friday; Editor ADRIAN GRIMWOOD; Man. Dir SHIRAZ D. ALIBHAI; circ. 54,000.

The East African: POB 49010, Nairobi; tel. (20) 221222; fax (20) 2213946; e-mail nation@africaonline.co.ke; internet www .nationaudio.com/news/eastafrican/current; f. 1994; weekly; English; owned by Nation Media Group; Editor-in-Chief JOE ODINDO; Man. Editor MBATAU WA NGAI.

The Herald: POB 30958, Nairobi; tel. (20) 332390; English; sponsored by KANU; Editor JOB MUTUNGI; circ. 8,000.

Kenrail: POB 30121, Nairobi; tel. (20) 2221211; fax (20) 2340049; quarterly; English and Kiswahili; publ. by Kenya Railways Corpn; Editor J. N. LUSENO; circ. 20,000.

Kenya Gazette: POB 30746, Nairobi; tel. (20) 334075; f. 1898; official notices; weekly; circ. 8,000.

Post on Sunday: Nairobi; weekly; independent; Editor-in-Chief TONY GACHOKA.

Sunday Nation: POB 49010, Nairobi; f. 1960; English; owned by Nation Media Group; Man. Editor BERNARD NDERITU; circ. 170,000.

Sunday Standard: POB 30080, Nairobi; tel. (20) 552510; fax (20) 553939; English; Man. Editor DAVID MAKALI; circ. 90,000.

Sunday Times: POB 30958, Nairobi; tel. (20) 337798; Group Editor AMBOKA ANDERE.

Taifa Jumapili: POB 49010, Nairobi; f. 1987; Kiswahili; owned by Nation Media Group; Editor ROBERT K. MWANGI; circ. 56,000.

Taifa Weekly: POB 49010, Nairobi; tel. (20) 337691; f. 1960; Kiswahili; Editor ROBERT K. MWANGI; circ. 68,000.

Trans Nzoia Post: POB 34, Kitale; weekly.

The Weekly Review: Stellacom House, POB 42271, Nairobi; tel. (20) 2251473; fax (20) 2222555; f. 1975; English; Man. Dir JAINDI KISERO; circ. 16,000.

What's On: Rehema House, Nairobi; tel. (20) 27651; Editor NANCY KAIRO; circ. 10,000.

Monthlies

Africa Law Review: Tumaini House, 4th Floor, Nkrumah Ave, POB 53234, Nairobi; tel. (20) 330480; fax (20) 230173; e-mail alr@africalaw.org; f. 1987; English; Editor-in-Chief GITOBU IMANYARA.

East African Medical Journal: POB 41632, 00100 Nairobi; tel. (20) 2712010; fax (20) 2724617; e-mail eamj@ken.healthnet.org; English; f. 1923; Editor-in-Chief Prof. WILLIAM LORE; circ. 4,500.

East African Report on Trade and Industry: POB 30339, Nairobi; journal of Kenya Asscn of Mfrs; Editor GORDON BOY; circ. 3,000.

Executive: POB 47186, Nairobi; tel. (20) 530598; fax (20) 557815; e-mail spacesellers@wananchi.com; f. 1980; business; Publr SYLVIA KING; circ. 25,000.

Kenya Farmer (Journal of the Agricultural Society of Kenya): c/o English Press, POB 30127, Nairobi; tel. (20) 20377; f. 1954; English and Kiswahili; Editor ROBERT IRUNGU; circ. 20,000.

Kenya Yetu: POB 8053, Nairobi; tel. (20) 250083; fax (20) 340659; f. 1965; Kiswahili; publ. by Ministry of Information and Communications; Editor M. NDAVI; circ. 10,000.

Nairobi Handbook: POB 30127, Accra Rd, Nairobi; Editor R. OUMA; circ. 20,000.

News from Kenya: POB 8053, Nairobi; tel. (20) 253083; fax (20) 340659; publ. by Ministry of Information and Communications.

PC World (East Africa): Gilgil House, Monrovia St, Nairobi; tel. (20) 246808; fax (20) 215643; f. 1996; Editor ANDREW KARANJA.

Presence: POB 10988, 00400 Nairobi; tel. (20) 577708; fax (20) 4948840; f. 1984; economics, law, women's issues, fiction.

Sparkle: POB 47186, Nairobi; tel. (20) 530598; fax (20) 557815; e-mail spacesellers@wananchi.com; f. 1990; children's; Editor ANNA NDILA NDUTO.

Today in Africa: POB 60, Kijabe; tel. (25) 64210; English; Man. Editor MWAURA NJOROGE; circ. 13,000.

Other Periodicals

African Ecclesiastical Review: POB 4002, 30100 Eldoret; tel. (53) 2061218; fax (53) 2062570; e-mail gabapubs@africaonline.co.ke; internet www.gabapublications.org; f. 1969; scripture, religion and development; 4 a year; Editor and Dir Sister JUSTIN C. NABUSHAWO; circ. 2,500.

Afya: POB 30125, Nairobi; tel. (20) 501301; fax (20) 506112; e-mail amrefkco@africaonline.co.ke; journal for medical and health workers; quarterly.

Azania: POB 30710-00100, Nairobi; tel. (20) 4343190; fax (20) 4343365; f. 1966; annual (Dec.); English and French; history, archaeology, ethnography and linguistics of East African region; circ. 650.

Busara: Nairobi; literary; 2 a year; Editor KIMANI GECAU; circ. 3,000.

Defender: AMREF, POB 30125, Nairobi; tel. (20) 201301; f. 1968; quarterly; English; health and fitness; Editor WILLIAM OKEDI; circ. 100,000.

East African Agricultural and Forestry Journal: POB 30148, Nairobi; f. 1935; English; quarterly; Editor J. O. MUGAH; circ. 1,000.

Eastern African Economic Review: POB 30022, Nairobi; f. 1954; 2 a year; Editor J. K. MAITHA.

Economic Review of Agriculture: POB 30028, Nairobi; tel. (20) 728370; f. 1968; publ. by Ministry of Agriculture; quarterly; last issue 1999; Editor OKIYA OKOITI.

Education in Eastern Africa: Nairobi; f. 1970; 2 a year; Editor JOHN C. B. BIGALA; circ. 2,000.

Finance: Nairobi; monthly; Editor-in-Chief NJEHU GATABAKI.

Inside Kenya Today: POB 8053, Nairobi; tel. (20) 340010; fax (20) 340659; English; publ. by Ministry of Tourism; quarterly; Editor M. NDAVI; circ. 10,000.

Kenya Education Journal: Nairobi; f. 1958; English; 3 a year; Editor W. G. BOWMAN; circ. 5,500.

Kenya Statistical Digest: POB 30007, Nairobi; tel. (20) 338111; fax (20) 330426; publ. by Ministry of Finance; quarterly.

Safari: Norwich Bldg, 4th Floor, Mama Ngina St, POB 30339, Nairobi; tel. (20) 2246612; fax (20) 2215127; 6 a year; English.

Target: POB 72839, Nairobi; f. 1964; English; 6 a year; religious; Editor FRANCIS MWANIKI; circ. 17,000.

NEWS AGENCIES

Kenya News Agency (KNA): Information House, POB 8053, Nairobi; tel. (20) 223201; f. 1963; Dir S. MUSANDU.

Foreign Bureaux

Agence France-Presse (AFP): International Life House, Mama Ngina St, POB 30671, 00100 Nairobi; tel. (20) 230613; fax (20) 230649; e-mail afpnai@swiftkenya.com; Bureau Chief GERARD VANDENBERGHE.

Agenzia Nazionale Stampa Associata (ANSA) (Italy): 12 Kyuna Rd, Spring Valley, Morningside, POB 479, 00220 Nairobi; tel. (20) 4183565; fax (20) 4182358; e-mail ansake@africaonline.co.ke; Rep. Dr LUCIANO CAUSA.

Associated Press (AP) (USA): CVS Plaza, Lenana Rd, Nairobi; tel. (20) 2859000; fax (20) 2724726; e-mail naiburo@ap.org; Bureau Chief CHRIS TOMLINSON.

Deutsche Presse-Agentur (dpa) (Germany): CVS Plaza, POB 48546, 00100 Nairobi; tel. (0) 733633379; e-mail dpa@swiftkenya.com; Bureau Chief Dr ULRIKE KOLTERMANN.

ITAR—TASS (Information Telegraphic Agency of Russia—Telegraphic Agency of the Sovereign Countries): Likoni Lane, POB 49602, Nairobi; tel. and fax (20) 721978; e-mail itartass@swiftkenya.com; Correspondent ANDREI K. POLYAKOV.

Inter Press Service (IPS) (Italy): Chester House, 1st Floor, Room 3, Koinange St, POB 42005; tel. (20) 240951; e-mail ipsnrb@iconnect.co.ke; Correspondent JOYCE MULAMA.

Kyodo Tsushin (Japan): Koinange St, POB 58281, Nairobi; tel. (20) 243250; fax (20) 230448; e-mail kyodonew@africaonline.co.ke; Bureau Chief OHNO KEIICHIRO.

Newslink Africa (United Kingdom): POB 3325, Nairobi; tel. (20) 241339; Correspondent PAMPHIL KWEYUH.

Reuters (United Kingdom): Finance House, 12th Floor, Loita St, POB 34043, Nairobi; tel. (20) 330261; fax (20) 338860; e-mail nairobi.newsroom@reuters.com; Bureau Chief DAVID FOX.

United Press International (UPI) (USA): POB 76282, Nairobi; tel. (20) 337349; fax (20) 213625; Correspondent JOE KHAMISI.

Xinhua (New China) News Agency (People's Republic of China): Ngong Rd at Rose Ave, POB 30728, Nairobi; tel. and fax (20) 711685; Pres. and Editor-in-Chief Prof. FLAMINGO Q. M. CHEN.

Publishers

Academy Science Publishers: POB 24916, Nairobi; tel. (20) 884401; fax (20) 884406; e-mail asp@africaonline.co.ke; f. 1989; part of the African Academy of Sciences; Editor-in-Chief Prof. KETO E. MSHIGENI.

Amecea Gaba Publications: Amecea Pastoral Institute, POB 4002, 30100 Eldoret; tel. (53) 2061218; fax (53) 2062570; e-mail gabapubs@africaonline.co.ke; internet www.gabapublications.org; f. 1989; anthropology, religious; Editor and Dir Sister JUSTIN C. NABUSHAWO.

Camerapix Publishers International: POB 45048, GPO 00100, Nairobi; tel. (20) 4448923; fax (20) 4448818; e-mail rukhsana@camerapix.co.ke; internet www.camerapix.com; f. 1960; travel, topography, natural history; Man. Dir RUKHSANA HAQ.

East African Educational Publishers: cnr Mpaka Rd and Woodvale Grove, Westlands, POB 45314, Nairobi; tel. (20) 222057; fax (20) 448753; e-mail eaep@africaonline.co.ke; internet www.eastafricanpublishers.com; f. 1965 as Heinemann Kenya Ltd; present name adopted 1992; academic, educational, creative writing; some books in Kenyan languages; Man. Dir and Chief Exec. HENRY CHAKAVA.

Evangel Publishing House: Lumumba Drive, off Kamiti Rd, Thika Rd, Private Bag 28963, 00200 Nairobi; tel. (20) 8560839; fax (20) 8562050; e-mail info@evangelpublishing.org; internet www.evangelpublishing.org; f. 1952; Christian literature; current backlist of about 300 titles; marriage and family, leadership, Theological Education by Extension (TEE); Gen. Man. BARINE A. KIRIMI.

Foundation Books: Nairobi; tel. (20) 765485; f. 1974; biography, poetry; Man. Dir F. O. OKWANYA.

Kenway Publications Ltd: POB 45314, Nairobi; tel. (20) 444700; fax (20) 4451532; e-mail sales@eastafricanpublishers.com; internet www.eastafricanpublishers.com/kenway/defult.htm; f. 1981; general, regional interests; Chair. HENRY CHAKAVA.

Kenya Literature Bureau: Bellevue Area, off Mombasa Rd, POB 30022, 00100 Nairobi; tel. (20) 600839; fax (20) 601474; e-mail customer@kenyaliteraturebureau.com; f. 1947; educational and general books; CEO M. A. KARAURI.

Jomo Kenyatta Foundation: Industrial Area, Enterprise Rd, POB 30533, 00100 Nairobi; tel. (20) 557222; fax (20) 531966; e-mail publish@jomokenyattaf.com; internet www.jkf.co.ke; f. 1966; primary, secondary, university textbooks; Man. Dir NANCY W. KARIMI.

Longman Kenya Ltd: Banda School, Magadi Rd, POB 24722, Nairobi; tel. (20) 891220; fax (20) 890004; f. 1966.

Macmillan Kenya Publishers Ltd: Kijabe St, POB 30797, Nairobi; tel. (20) 220012; fax (20) 212179; e-mail dmuita@macken.co.ke; f. 1970; atlases, children's educational, guide books, literature; Man. Dir DAVID MUITA.

Newspread International: POB 46854, Nairobi; tel. (20) 331402; fax (20) 607252; f. 1971; reference, economic development; Exec. Editor KUL BHUSHAN.

Oxford University Press (Eastern Africa): Waiyaki Way, ABC Place, POB 72532, Nairobi; tel. (20) 440555; fax (20) 443972; f. 1954; children's, educational and general; Regional Man. ABDULLAH ISMAILY.

Paulines Publications-Africa: POB 49026, 00100 Nairobi; tel. (20) 447202; fax (20) 442097; e-mail publications@paulinesafrica.org; internet www.paulinesafrica.org; f. 1985; children's, educational; religious; Pres. Sister MARIA PEZZINI; Dir Sister MARIA ROSA.

Transafrica Press: Kenwood House, Kimathi St, POB 48239, Nairobi; tel. (20) 331762; f. 1976; general, educational and children's; Man. Dir JOHN NOTTINGHAM.

GOVERNMENT PUBLISHING HOUSE

Government Printing Press: POB 30128, Nairobi; tel. (20) 317840.

PUBLISHERS' ORGANIZATION

Kenya Publishers' Association: POB 42767, 00100 Nairobi; tel. (20) 3752344; fax (20) 3754076; e-mail kenyapublishers@wananchi.com; internet www.kenyabooks.org; f. 1971; organizes Nairobi International Book Fair each Sept; Chair. DAVID MUITA.

Broadcasting and Communications

TELECOMMUNICATIONS

Celtel: Parkside Towers, Mombasa Rd, Nairobi; tel. (20) 6910000; e-mail customercare@ke.celtel.com; internet www.ke.celtel.com; f. 2004; mobile cellular telephone network provider; subsidiary of Celtel International; CEO DAVID MURRAY.

KenCell Communications Ltd: Parkside Towers, City Sq., Mombasa Rd, POB 73146, 00200 Nairobi; e-mail info@kencell.co.ke; internet www.kencell.co.ke; f. 2000; operates a national mobile cellular telephone network; Man. Dir and CEO PHILLIPE VANDEBROUCK.

Telkom Kenya Ltd: Telposta Towers, Kenyatta Ave, POB 30301, Nairobi; tel. (20) 227401; fax (20) 251071; e-mail mdtelkom@kenyaeafix.net; f. 1999; operates a national fixed telephone network; privatization pending; Man. Dir AUGUSTINE CHESEREM.

Safaricom Ltd: Safaricom House, Waiyaki Way, Westlands, POB 46350, Nairobi; e-mail info@safaricom.co.ke; internet www.safaricom.co.ke; f. 1999; owned by Telkom Kenya Ltd and Vodafone Airtouch (UK); operates a national mobile telephone network; Gen. Man. and CEO MICHAEL JOSEPH.

Regulatory Authority

Communications Commission of Kenya (CCK): Kijabe St, Longonot Place, POB 14448, Nairobi; tel. (20) 240165; fax (20) 252547;

e-mail info@cck.go.ke; internet www.cck.go.ke; f. 1999; Dir-Gen. and Chief Exec. SAMUEL K. CHEPKONG'A.

BROADCASTING

Radio

Kenya Broadcasting Corpn (KBC): Broadcasting House, Harry Thuku Rd, POB 30456, Nairobi; tel. (20) 334567; fax (20) 220675; e-mail kbc@swiftkenya.com; internet www.kbc.co.ke; f. 1989; state corpn responsible for radio and television services; Chair. Dr JULIUS KIANO; Man. Dir JOE M. KHAMISI.

Radio: National service (Kiswahili); General service (English); Vernacular services (Borana, Burji, Hindustani, Kalenjin, Kikamba, Kikuyu, Kimasai, Kimeru, Kisii, Kuria, Luo, Luhya, Rendile, Somali, Suba, Teso and Turkana).

Capital FM: Lonrho House, Standard St, POB 74933, Nairobi; tel. (20) 210020; fax (20) 332349; e-mail info@capitalfm.co.ke; internet www.capitalfm.co.ke; f. 1999; commercial station broadcasting to Nairobi and environs; Man. Dir LYNDA HOLT.

Citizen Radio: Ambank House, University Way, POB 45897, Nairobi; tel. (20) 249122; fax (20) 249126; commercial radio station broadcasting in Nairobi and its environs; Man. Dir S. K. MACHARIA.

IQRA Broadcasting Network: Bandari Plaza, 7th Floor, Woodvale Grove, Westlands, POB 45163 GPO, Nairobi; tel. (20) 4447624; fax (20) 4443978; e-mail iqrafm@swiftkenya.com; Islamic radio station broadcasting religious programmes in Nairobi; Man. Dir SHARIF HUSSEIN OMAR.

Kameme FM: Longonot Pl., Kijabe St, POB 49640, 00100 Nairobi; tel. (20) 217963; fax (20) 338129; e-mail rroach@kenyaweb.com; commercial radio station broadcasting in Kikuyu in Nairobi and its environs; Man. Dir ROSE KIMOTHO.

Kitambo Communications Ltd: NSSF Bldg, POB 56155, Nairobi; tel. (20) 331770; fax (20) 212847; commercial radio and television station broadcasting Christian programmes in Mombasa and Nairobi; Man. Dir Dr R. AYAH.

Nation FM: Nation Centre, Kimathi St, POB 49010, Nairobi; tel. (20) 32088801; fax (20) 241892; e-mail philmatthews@nation.co.ke; internet www.nationmedia.com; f. 1999; commercial radio station broadcasting in English and Swahili; owned by Nation Media Group; Man. Dir IAN FERNANDES.

Radio Africa Ltd (KISS FM): Safina Towers, 16th Floor, University of Nairobi, POB 45897, Nairobi; tel. (20) 245368; fax (20) 245565; Man. Dir KIPRONO KITTONY.

Sauti ya Raheme RTV Network: POB 4139, Eldoret; Christian, broadcasts in Eldoret and its environs; Man. Dir Rev. ELI ROP.

Television

Kenya Broadcasting Corpn (KBC): see Radio

Television: KBC–TV, financed by licence fees and commercial advertisements; services in Kiswahili and English; operates on five channels for c. 50 hours per week. KBC–II: private subscription service.

Citizen TV: POB 45897, Nairobi; tel. (20) 249122; fax (20) 249126; commercial station broadcasting in Nairobi and its environs.

Family TV: NSSF Bldg, POB 56155, Nairobi; tel. (20) 331770; fax (20) 212847.

Kenya Television Network (KTN–TV): Nyayo House, 22nd Floor, POB 56985, Nairobi; tel. (20) 227122; fax (20) 214467; e-mail ktn@form-net.com; f. 1990; commercial station operating in Nairobi and Mombasa; Man. Dir D. J. DAVIES.

Nation TV: POB 49010, Nairobi; e-mail nation@users.co.ke; f. 1999; commercial station; owned by Nation Media Group; Man. Dir CYRILLE NABUTOLA.

Stellagraphics TV (STV): NSSF Bldg, 22nd Floor, POB 42271, Nairobi; tel. (20) 218043; fax (20) 222555; f. 1998; commercial station broadcasting in Nairobi; Gen. Man. KANJA WARURU.

Finance

(cap. = capital; res = reserves; dep. = deposits; m. = million; brs = branches; amounts in Kenya shillings)

BANKING

Central Bank

Central Bank of Kenya (Banki Kuu Ya Kenya): Haile Selassie Ave, POB 60000, 00200 Nairobi; tel. (20) 226431; fax (20) 217940; e-mail info@centralbank.go.ke; internet www.centralbank.go.ke; f. 1966; bank of issue; cap. 1,500m., res 5,398m., dep. 79,897m. (March 2005); Gov. Prof. NJUGUNA S. NDUNG'U.

Commercial Banks

African Banking Corpn Ltd: ABC-Bank House, Mezzanine Floor, Koinange St, POB 46452, Nairobi; tel. (20) 223922; fax (20) 222437; e-mail ho@abcthebank.co.ke; internet www.abcthebank.com; f. 1984 as Consolidated Finance Co; converted to commercial bank and adopted present name 1995; cap. 350m., dep. 4,433m. (Dec. 2005); Man. Dir ASHRAF SAVANI; 7 brs.

Barclays Bank of Kenya Ltd: Barclays Plaza, Loita St, POB 30120, 00100 Nairobi; tel. (20) 332230; fax (20) 213915; e-mail barclays.kenya@barclays.com; f. 1978; cap. 2,037m., res 1,630m., dep. 77,417m. (Dec. 2003); Chair. SAMUEL O. J. AMBUNDO; Man. Dir ADAN MOHAMMED; 87 brs.

CFC Bank Ltd: CFC Centre, Chiromo Rd, POB 72833, 00200 Nairobi; tel. (20) 3752900; fax (20) 3752905; e-mail cfcbank@cfcgroup.co.ke; internet www.cfcbank.co.ke; f. 1955 as Credit Finance Corpn Ltd; became commercial bank and adopted present name 1995; cap. 720m., res 1,802m., dep. 14,137m. (Dec. 2004); Chair. P. K. JANI; Man. Dir R. J. BARRY.

Chase Bank (Kenya) Ltd: Prudential Assurance Bldg, Wabera St, POB 28987, Nairobi; tel. (20) 244035; fax (20) 246334; e-mail info@chasebank.co.ke; cap. 520m. (Dec. 2004); Chair. OSMAN MURGIAN; Man. Dir ZAFRULLAH KHAN.

Commercial Bank of Africa Ltd: Commercial Bank Bldg, cnr Wabera and Standard Sts, POB 30437, Nairobi; tel. (20) 228881; fax (20) 335827; e-mail cba@cba.co.ke; internet www.cba.co.ke; f. 1962; owned by Kenyan shareholders; cap. 1,000m., res 962m., dep. 167,788m. (Dec. 2004); Chair. M. H. DA GAMA-ROSE; Pres. and Man. Dir ISAAC O. AWUONDO; 9 brs.

Consolidated Bank of Kenya Ltd: Consolidated Bank House, Koinange St, POB 51133, Nairobi; tel. (20) 340551; fax (20) 340213; e-mail headoffice@consolidated-bank.com; internet www.consolidated-bank.com; f. 1989; state-owned; cap. 1,120m., res 102m., dep. 2,189m. (Dec. 2004); Chair. PHILIP J. NJUKI; Man. Dir DAVID K. WACHIRA.

Dubai Bank Kenya Ltd: ICEA Bldg, Kenyatta Ave, POB 11129, Nairobi; tel. (20) 330562; fax (20) 245242; e-mail info@dubaibank.co.ke; internet www.dubaibank.co.ke; 25% owned by World of Marble and Granite, Dubai (United Arab Emirates), 25% owned by Abdul Hassan Ahmed, 16% owned by Hassan Bin Hassan Trading Co LLC, Dubai (United Arab Emirates), 15% owned by Ahmed Mohamed Zubeidi; cap. 323m., res 39m., dep. 479m. (Dec. 2004); Chair. HASSAN AHMED ZUBEIDI; Man. Dir VIJU CHERIAN.

EABS Bank Ltd: Fedha Towers, 5th Floor, Muindi Mbingu St, POB 49584, 00100 Nairobi; tel. (20) 2883000; fax (20) 2883815; e-mail akiba.ho@akibabank.com; internet www.eabsbank.com; f. 1972; as Akiba Bank Ltd, present name adopted 2005; cap. 1,663m., res –376m., dep. 7,019m. (Dec. 2005); Chair. N. P. G. WARREN; CEO R. L. PANDIT; 3 brs.

Equatorial Commercial Bank Ltd: Sasini House, Loita St, POB 52467, Nairobi; tel. (20) 331122; fax (20) 331606; e-mail customerservice@ecb.co.ke; internet www.equatorialbank.co.ke; cap. 306m. (Dec. 2001); Chair. EDGAR I. MANASSEH; Man. Dir TAHIR N. KHWAJA.

Fidelity Commercial Bank Ltd: IPS Bldg, 7th Floor, Kimathi St, POB 34886, Nairobi; tel. (20) 242348; fax (20) 243389; e-mail customerservice@fidelitybankkenya.com; f. 1993 as Fidelity Finance; present name adopted 1996; CEO SULTAN KHIMJI.

Gulf African Bank (GAB): Nairobi; e-mail info@gulfafricanbank.com; internet www.gulfafricanbank.com; f. 2007; 20% owned by Bank Muscat International (BMI); 10% owned by the International Finance Corpn (IFC); Chair. SULEIMAN SHAHBAL; CEO YUSUF ABDULRAHMAN NZIBO.

Kenya Commercial Bank Ltd: Kencom House, Moi Ave, POB 48400, Nairobi; tel. (20) 223846; fax (20) 215565; e-mail kcbhq@kcb.co.ke; internet www.kcb.co.ke; f. 1970; 26.2% state-owned; cap. 1,996m., res 3,236m., dep. 64,639m. (Dec. 2005); CEO and Man. Dir TERRY DAVIDSON; 105 brs and sub-brs.

Middle East Bank Kenya Ltd: Mebank Tower, Milimani Rd, POB 47387-00100, Nairobi; tel. (20) 2723120; fax (20) 343776; e-mail ho@mebkenya.com; internet www.mebkenya.com; f. 1981; 25% owned by Banque Belgolaise SA (Belgium), 75% owned by Kenyan shareholders; cap. 506m., res 302m., dep. 2,334m. (Dec. 2006); Man. Dir PETER HARRIS; Exec. Dir. B. S. PAI; 2 brs.

National Bank of Kenya Ltd (Banki ya Taifa La Kenya Ltd): National Bank Bldg, Harambee Ave, POB 72866, Nairobi; tel. (20) 339690; fax (20) 330784; e-mail nbkops@nbnet.co.ke; internet www.nationalbank.co.ke; f. 1968; 64.5% state-owned; cap. 6,675m., res –4,050m., dep. 25,470m. (Dec. 2004); Exec. Chair. JOHN P. N. SIMBA; Gen. Man. A. H. AHMED; 25 brs.

Stanbic Bank Kenya Ltd: Stanbic Bank Bldg, Kenyatta Ave, POB 30550, Nairobi; tel. (20) 335888; fax (20) 330227; e-mail stanbickenya@stanbic.com; internet www.stanbic.co.ke; f. 1992; 89.5% owned by Stanbic Africa Holdings Ltd (London), 10.5%

state-owned; cap. 1,260m., res 128m., dep. 5,526m. (Dec. 2001); Chair. J. B. WANJUI; Man. Dir M. L. DU TOIT; 3 brs.

Standard Chartered Bank Kenya Ltd: Stanbank House, Moi Ave, POB 30003, Nairobi; tel. (20) 330200; fax (20) 214086; e-mail mds.office@ke.standardchartered.com; internet www.standardchartered.com/ke; f. 1987; 74.5% owned by Standard Chartered Holdings (Africa) BV (Netherlands); cap. 1,236m., res 4,191m., dep. 54,358m. (Dec. 2003); Chair. HARRINGTON AWORI; CEO RICHARD ETEMESI; 43 brs.

Trans-National Bank Ltd: Transnational Plaza, 2nd Floor, Mama Ngina St, POB 34352, 00100 Nairobi; tel. (20) 224234; fax (20) 339227; e-mail tnbl@form-net.com; f. 1985; cap. 584m., res 589m., dep. 1,196m. (Dec. 2004); Chair. MWAKAI SIO; CEO DHIRENDRA RANA; 5 brs.

Merchant Banks

Diamond Trust Bank of Kenya Ltd: Nation Centre, 8th Floor, Kimathi St, POB 61711, 00200 Nairobi; tel. (20) 210988; fax (20) 336836; e-mail user@dtbkenya.co.ke; f. 1945; cap. 398m., res 201m., dep. 9,304m. (Dec. 2004); Chair. ROBERT A. BIRD; Man. Dir NASIM DEVJI.

National Industrial Credit Bank Ltd (NIC): NIC House, Masaba Rd, POB 44599, Nairobi; tel. (20) 718200; fax (20) 718232; e-mail info@nic-bank.com; internet www.nic-bank.com; cap. 412m. (Dec. 2001); Chair. J. P. M. NDEGWA; Man. Dir JAMES MACHARIA.

Foreign Banks

Bank of Baroda (Kenya) Ltd (India): Bank of Baroda Bldg, cnr Mandlane St and Tom Mboya St, POB 30033, Nairobi; tel. (20) 2337611; fax (20) 2333089; e-mail barodabk-ho@kenyaweb.com; cap. 600m., res 126m., dep. 7,183m. (Dec. 2004); Chair. RAMA KRISHNAN; Man. Dir GIRIDHAR GOVINDRAO JOSHI; 6 brs.

Bank of India: Kenyatta Ave, POB 30246, 00100 Nairobi; tel. (20) 221414; fax (20) 229462; e-mail boinrb@futurenet.co.ke; internet www.bankofindiake.com; CEO A. K. JALOTA.

Citibank NA (USA): Citibank House, Upperhill Rd, POB 30711, 00100 Nairobi; tel. (20) 2711221; fax (20) 2714811; internet www.citibank.co.ke; f. 1974; Gen. Man. ADE AYAYEMI.

Habib Bank AG Zurich (Switzerland): Nagina House, Koinange St, POB 30584, 00100 Nairobi; tel. (20) 334984; fax (20) 218699; e-mail habibbank@form-net.com; Country Man. IQBAL A. ALLAWALA.

Co-operative Bank

Co-operative Bank of Kenya Ltd: Co-operative Bank House, POB 48231, Nairobi; tel. (20) 32076000; fax (20) 249474; e-mail md@co-opbank.co.ke; internet www.co-opbank.co.ke; f. 1968; cap. 1,211m., res 589m., dep. 25,084m. (Dec. 2002); Chair. STANLEY C. MUCHIRI; Man. Dir GIDEON MURIUKI; 30 brs.

Development Banks

Development Bank of Kenya Ltd: Finance House, Loita St, POB 30483, 00100 Nairobi; tel. (20) 340401; fax (20) 338426; e-mail dbk@africaonline.co.ke; f. 1963 as Development Finance Co of Kenya; current name adopted 1996; owned by Industrial and Commercial Devt Corpn (30.5%), govt agencies of Germany and the Netherlands (28.8% and 22.8%, respectively), the Commonwealth Development Corpn (10.7%) and the International Finance Corpn (7.2%); cap. 348m., res 625m., dep. 586m. (Dec. 2004); Chair. Prof. HAROUN NGENY KIPKEMBOI MENGECH; Man. Dir SAJAL RAKHIT.

East African Development Bank: Rahimtulla Tower, 2nd Floor, Upper Hill Rd, Nairobi; tel. (20) 340642; fax (20) 2731590; e-mail cok@eadb.org; Dirs J. KINYUA, F. KARUIRU.

Industrial Development Bank Ltd (IDB): National Bank Bldg, 18th Floor, Harambee Ave, POB 44036, Nairobi; tel. (20) 337079; fax (20) 334594; e-mail bizcare@idbkenya.com; f. 1973; 49% state-owned; cap. 272m., res 83m., dep. 190m. (Dec. 2002); Chair. DAVID LANGAT; Man. Dir L. A. MASAVIRU.

STOCK EXCHANGE

Nairobi Stock Exchange (NSE): Nation Centre, 1st Floor, Kimathi St, POB 43633, 00100 Nairobi; tel. (20) 230692; fax (20) 224200; e-mail info@nse.co.ke; internet www.nse.co.ke; f. 1954; Chair. JIMNAH MBARU; CEO CHRIS MWEBESA.

INSURANCE

American Life Insurance Co (Kenya) Ltd: POB 30364, 00100 Nairobi; tel. (20) 2711242; fax (20) 2711378; e-mail alicolife@alico-kenya.com; internet www.alico-kenya.com; f. 1964; life and general; Man. Dir ERWIN BREWSTER.

Apollo Insurance Co Ltd: POB 30389, Nairobi; tel. (20) 223562; fax (20) 339260; e-mail insurance@apollo.co.ke; f. 1977; life and general; Chair. B. M. SHAH.

Blue Shield Insurance Co Ltd: POB 49610, Nairobi; tel. (20) 219592; fax (20) 337808; f. 1983; life and general.

Cannon Assurance (Kenya) Ltd: Haile Selassie Ave, POB 30216, Nairobi; tel. (20) 335478; fax (20) 331235; e-mail info@cannon.co.ke; internet www.cannon.co.ke; f. 1964; life and general; Man. Dir I. J. TALWAR.

Fidelity Shield Insurance Ltd: POB 47435, Nairobi; tel. (20) 430635; fax (20) 445699.

Heritage Insurance Co Ltd: CFC House, Mamlaka Rd, POB 30390–00100, Nairobi; tel. (20) 2783000; fax (20) 2727800; e-mail info@heriaii.com; internet www.heritageinsurance.co.ke; f. 1976; general; Man. Dir JOHN H. D. MILNE.

Insurance Co of East Africa Ltd (ICEA): ICEA Bldg, Kenyatta Ave, POB 46143, Nairobi; tel. (20) 221652; fax (20) 338089; e-mail hof@icea.co.ke; internet www.icea.co.ke; life and general; Man. Dir J. K. NDUNGU.

Jubilee Insurance Co Ltd: POB 30376, Nairobi; tel. (20) 340343; fax (20) 216882; f. 1937; life and general; Chair. ABDUL JAFFER.

Kenindia Assurance Co Ltd: Kenindia House, Loita St, POB 44372, Nairobi; tel. (20) 333100; fax (20) 218380; e-mail kenindia@users.africaonline.co.ke; f. 1978; life and general; Exec. Dir R. S. BEDI.

Kenya Reinsurance Corpn Ltd (KenyaRe): Reinsurance Plaza, Taifa Rd, POB 30271, Nairobi; tel. (20) 240188; fax (20) 339161; e-mail kenyare@kenyare.co.ke; internet www.kenyare.co.ke; f. 1970; Man. Dir JOHNSON GITHAKA.

Lion of Kenya Insurance Co Ltd: POB 30190, Nairobi; tel. (20) 710400; fax (20) 711177; e-mail insurance@lionofkenya.com; f. 1978; general; CEO J. P. M. NDEGWA.

Mercantile Insurance Co Ltd: Nairobi; tel. (20) 218244; fax (20) 215528; e-mail mercantile@mercantile.co.ke; internet www.mercantile.co.ke; Man. Dir SUDHIR SATHE.

Monarch Insurance Co Ltd: Chester House, 2nd Floor, Koinange St, POB 44003, Nairobi; tel. (20) 330042; fax (20) 340691; e-mail monarch@form-net.com; f. 1975; general; Exec. Dir R. A. VADGAMA.

Pan Africa Insurance Co Ltd: POB 30065, Nairobi; tel. (20) 252168; fax (20) 217675; e-mail insure@pan-africa.com; f. 1946; life and general; Man. Dir WILLIAM OLOTCH.

Phoenix of East Africa Assurance Co Ltd: Ambank House, University Way, POB 30129, Nairobi; tel. (20) 338784; fax (20) 211848; general; Man. Dir D. K. SHARMA.

Prudential Assurance Co of Kenya Ltd: Yaya Centre, Argwings Kodhek Rd, POB 76190, Nairobi; tel. (20) 567374; fax (20) 567433; f. 1979; general; Man. Dir JOSEPH MURAGE.

PTA Reinsurance Co (ZEP-RE): Zep-Re Pl., Longonot Rd, Upper Hill, POB 42769, Nairobi; tel. (20) 212792; fax (20) 224102; e-mail mail@zep-re.com; internet www.zep-re.com; f. 1992; Man. Dir S. M. LUBASI.

Royal Insurance Co of East Africa Ltd: Mama Ngina St, POB 40001, Nairobi; tel. (20) 717888; fax (20) 712620; f. 1979; general; CEO S. K. KAMAU.

Standard Assurance (Kenya) Ltd: POB 42996, Nairobi; tel. (20) 224721; fax (20) 224862; Man. Dir WILSON K. KAPKOTI.

UAP Provincial Insurance Co of East Africa Ltd: Old Mutual Bldg, Kimathi St, POB 43013, Nairobi; tel. (20) 330173; fax (20) 340483; f. 1980; general; CEO E. C. BATES.

United Insurance Co Ltd: POB 30961, Nairobi; tel. (20) 227345; fax (20) 215609; Man. Dir G. KARRUIKI.

Trade and Industry

GOVERNMENT AGENCIES

Export Processing Zones Authority: POB 50563, Nairobi; tel. (20) 712800; fax (20) 713704; e-mail epzahq@africaonline.co.ke; established by the Govt to promote investment in Export Processing Zones; CEO SILAS ITA.

Export Promotion Council: Anniversary Towers, 1st and 16th Floors, University Way, POB 40247, Nairobi; tel. (20) 228534; fax (20) 218013; e-mail chiefexe@epc.or.ke; internet www.cbik.or.ke; f. 1992; promotes exports; CEO MATANDA WABUYELE.

Investment Promotion Centre: National Bank Bldg, 8th Floor, Harambee Ave, POB 55704, 00200 Nairobi; tel. (20) 221401; fax (20) 336663; e-mail info@investmentkenya.com; internet www.investmentkenya.com; f. 1986; promotes and facilitates local and foreign investment; CEO LUKA E. OBBANDA.

Kenya National Trading Corpn Ltd: Yarrow Rd, off Nanyuki Rd, POB 30587, Nairobi; tel. (20) 543121; fax (20) 532800; f. 1965;

promotes national control of trade in both locally produced and imported items; exports coffee and sugar; CEO S. W. O. OGESSA.

Settlement Fund Trustees: POB 30449, Nairobi; administers a land purchase programme involving over 1.2m. ha for resettlement of African farmers.

DEVELOPMENT ORGANIZATIONS

Agricultural Development Corpn: POB 47101, Nairobi; tel. (20) 250695; fax (20) 243571; f. 1965 to promote agricultural development and reconstruction; CEO WILLIAM K. KIRWA.

Agricultural Finance Corpn: POB 30367, Nairobi; tel. (20) 317199; fax (20) 219390; e-mail afc@wananchi.com; a statutory organization providing agricultural loans; Man. Dir OMUREMBE IYADI.

Horticultural Crops Development Authority: POB 42601, Nairobi; tel. (20) 8272601; fax (20) 827264; e-mail hcdamd@wananchi.com; internet www.hcda.or.ke; f. 1968; invests in production, dehydration, processing and freezing of fruit and vegetables; exports of fresh fruit and vegetables; Chair. Prof. ROSALIND W. MUTUA; Man. Dir S. P. GACHANJA.

Housing Finance Co of Kenya Ltd: Rehani House, cnr Kenyatta Ave and Koinange St, POB 30088, 00100 Nairobi; tel. (20) 333910; fax (20) 334670; e-mail hfck@hfck.co.ke; internet www.hfck.co.ke; f. 1965; Chair. RICHARD KEMOLI; Man. Dir PETER LEWIS-JONES.

Industrial and Commercial Development Corpn: Uchumi House, Aga Khan Walk, POB 45519, Nairobi; tel. (20) 229213; fax (20) 333880; e-mail icdcexe@africaonline.co.ke; f. 1954; govt-financed; assists industrial and commercial development; Chair. JOHN NGUTHU MUTIO; Exec. Dir K. ETICH ARAP BETT.

Kenya Fishing Industries Ltd: Nairobi; Man. Dir ABDALLA MBWANA.

Kenya Industrial Estates Ltd: Nairobi Industrial Estate, Likoni Rd, POB 78029, Nairobi; tel. (20) 530551; fax (20) 534625; f. 1967 to finance and develop small-scale industries.

Kenya Industrial Research and Development Institute: POB 30650, Nairobi; tel. (20) 603842; fax (20) 607023; e-mail info@kirdi.go.ke; internet www.kirdi.go.ke; f. 1942; reorg. 1979; restructured 1995; research and development in industrial and allied technologies including engineering, agro-industrial, mining and environmental technologies; Dir Dr TOM OGADA.

Kenya Tea Development Agency: POB 30213, Nairobi; tel. (20) 221441; fax (20) 211240; e-mail info@ktdateas.com; internet www.ktdateas.com; f. 1964 as Kenya Tea Development Authority; to develop tea growing, manufacturing and marketing among African smallholders; operates 51 factories; privatized in 2000; Chair. STEPHEN M. IMANYARA; Man. Dir ERIC KIMANI.

CHAMBER OF COMMERCE

Kenya National Chamber of Commerce and Industry: Ufanisi House, Haile Selassie Ave, POB 47024, Nairobi; tel. (20) 220867; fax (20) 334293; f. 1965; 69 brs; Nat. Chair. DAVID M. GITHERE; Chief Exec. TITUS G. RUHIU.

INDUSTRIAL AND TRADE ASSOCIATIONS

Central Province Marketing Board: POB 189, Nyeri.

Coffee Board of Kenya: POB 30566, Nairobi; tel. (20) 332896; fax (20) 330546; f. 1947; Chair. JOHN NGARI ZACHARIAH; Gen. Man. AGGREY MURUNGA.

East African Tea Trade Association: Tea Trade Centre, Nyerere Ave, POB 85174, 80100 Mombasa; tel. (41) 2220093; fax (41) 2225823; e-mail info@eatta.co.ke; internet www.eatta.com; f. 1957; organizes Mombasa weekly tea auctions; Exec. Officer HADIJA SHAKOMBO; 264 mems in 11 countries.

Fresh Produce Exporters' Association of Kenya: Nairobi; Chair. JAMES MATHENGE.

Kenya Association of Manufacturers: POB 30225, Nairobi; tel. (20) 746005; fax (20) 746028; e-mail kam@users.africaonline.co.ke; Chair. MANU CHANDARIA; Exec. Sec. LUCY MICHENI; 200 mems.

Kenya Dairy Board: POB 30406, Nairobi.

Kenya Flower Council: POB 24856, Nairobi; tel. and fax (20) 883041; e-mail kfc@africaonline.co.ke; internet www.kenyaflowers.co.ke; regulates production of cut flowers; Exec. Dir MICHAEL MORLAND.

Kenya Meat Corpn: POB 30414, Nairobi; tel. (20) 340750; f. 1953; purchasing, processing and marketing of beef livestock; Chair. H. P. BARCLAY.

Kenya Planters' Co-operative Union Ltd: Nairobi; e-mail gm@kpcu.co.ke; coffee processing and marketing; Chair. J. M. MACHARIA; Gen. Man. RUTH MWANIKI.

Kenya Sisal Board: Mutual Bldg, Kimathi St, POB 41179, Nairobi; tel. (20) 248919; f. 1946; CEO J. H. WAIRAGU; Man. Dir CHARLES K. KAGWIMI (acting).

Kenya Sugar Authority: NSSF Complex, 9th Floor, Bishops Rd, POB 51500, Nairobi; tel. (20) 710600; fax (20) 723903; e-mail ksa@users.africaonline.co.ke; Chair. LUKE R. OBOK; CEO F. M. CHAHONYO.

Mild Coffee Trade Association of Eastern Africa (MCTA): Nairobi; Chair. F. J. MWANGI.

National Cereals and Produce Board (NCPB): POB 30586, Nairobi; tel. (20) 536028; fax (20) 542024; e-mail cereals@africaonline.co.ke; f. 1995; grain marketing and handling, provides drying, weighing, storage and fumigation services to farmers and traders, stores and manages strategic national food reserves, distributes famine relief; Chair. JAMES MUTUA; Man. Dir NAFTALI MOGERE.

Pyrethrum Board of Kenya: POB 420, Nakuru; tel. (37) 211567; fax (37) 45274; e-mail pbk@pyrethrum.co.ke; internet www.kenya-pyrethrum.com; f. 1935; 14 mems; Chair. J. O. MARIARIA; CEO J. C. KIPTOON.

Tea Board of Kenya: Naivasha Rd, off Ngong Rd, POB 20064, 00200 Nairobi; tel. (20) 3875554; fax (20) 3872120; e-mail info@teaboard.or.ke; internet www.teaboard.or.ke; f. 1950; regulates tea industry on all matters of policy, licenses tea processing, carries out research on tea through **Tea Research Foundation of Kenya**, monitors tea planting and trade through registration, promotes Kenyan tea internationally; 16 mems; Chair. DUNSTAN M. NGUMO; Man. Dir SICILY K. KARIUKI.

EMPLOYERS' ORGANIZATIONS

Federation of Kenya Employers: Waajiri House, Argwings Kodhek Rd, POB 48311, Nairobi; tel. (20) 721929; fax (20) 721990; Chair. J. P. N. SIMBA; Exec. Dir TOM DIJU OWUOR.

Association of Local Government Employers: POB 52, Muranga; Chair. S. K. ITONGU.

Distributive and Allied Industries Employers' Association: POB 30587, Nairobi; Chair. P. J. MWAURA.

Engineering and Allied Industries Employers' Association: POB 48311, Nairobi; tel. (20) 721929; Chair. D. M. NJOROGE.

Kenya Association of Building and Civil Engineering Contractors: Nairobi; Chair. G. S. HIRANI.

Kenya Association of Hotelkeepers and Caterers: Heidelberg House, Mombasa Rd, POB 9977, 00100 Nairobi; tel. (20) 604419; fax (20) 602539; e-mail info@kahc.co.ke; internet www.kahc.co.ke; f. 1944; CEO KABANDO WA KABANDO.

Kenya Bankers' Association: POB 73100, Nairobi; tel. (20) 221792; e-mail kba@kenyaweb.com; Chair. RICHARD ETEMESI.

Kenya Sugar Employers' Union: Kisumu; Chair. L. OKECH.

Kenya Tea Growers' Association: POB 320, Kericho; tel. (20) 21010; fax (20) 32172; Chair. M. K. A. SANG.

Kenya Vehicle Manufacturers' Association: POB 1436, Thika; Chair. C. PETERSON.

Motor Trade and Allied Industries Employers' Association: POB 48311, Nairobi; tel. (20) 721929; fax (20) 721990; Exec. Sec. G. N. KONDITI.

Sisal Growers' and Employers' Association: POB 47523, Nairobi; tel. (20) 720170; fax (20) 721990; Chair. A. G. COMBOS.

Timber Industries Employers' Association: POB 18070, Nairobi; Chair. H. S. BAMBRAH.

UTILITIES

Electricity

Energy Regulatory Commission: Integrity Centre, Milimani Rd, POB 42681–00100, Nairobi; tel. (20) 2847000; fax (20) 2717603; e-mail info@erb.go.ke; internet www.erb.go.ke; f. 1997; govt-owned; regulates the generation, distribution, supply and use of electric power; Chair. HINDPAL SINGH JABBAL.

Kenya Electricity Generating Co Ltd (KenGen): Stima Plaza, Phase 3, Kolobot Rd, Parklands, POB 47936, Nairobi; tel. (20) 3666000; fax (20) 248848; e-mail comms@kengen.co.ke; internet www.kengen.co.ke; f. 1997 as Kenya Power Co; present name adopted 1998; generates 82% of Kenya's electricity requirements; partially privatized in 2006; CEO EDWARD NJOROGE.

Kenya Power and Lighting Co (KPLC): Stima Plaza, Kolobot Rd, POB 30099, Nairobi; tel. (20) 243366; fax (20) 337351; e-mail isd@form-net.com; partially privatized in 2006; 4% owned by Transcentury Group; co-ordinates electricity transmission and distribution; Man. Dir SAMUEL GICHURU.

MAJOR COMPANIES

The following are among the largest companies in terms either of capital investment or employment.

Athi River Mining (Kenya) Ltd (ARM): POB 41908, 00100 Nairobi; tel. (20) 3744620; fax (20) 3753676; internet www.armkenya.com; f. 1974; mines and processes industrial minerals and chemicals; ISO certified manufacturer of cement and lime; manufactures cement, quick and hydrated lime, sodium silicate, industrial minerals, special cements and building products and fertilizers; sales Ks. 1,240m. (2003); Chair. B. ROGERS; 700 employees.

Bamburi Cement Ltd: POB 10921, 00100 Nairobi; tel. (20) 2710487; fax (20) 2710581; e-mail corp.info@bamburi.lafarge.com; internet www.bamburicement.com; f. 1951; 73.3% owned by Bamcem Holdings Ltd; produces portland cement; sales Ks. 7,710m. (2000); Man. Dir MICHEL PUCHERCOS; 850 employees.

BAT (Kenya) Ltd: Likoni Rd, Industrial Area, POB 30000, Nairobi; tel. (20) 535555; fax (20) 531717; e-mail batkenya@bat.com; f. 1956; subsidiary of British American Tobacco Co Ltd, UK; mfrs of tobacco products; sales Ks. 10,896m. (2000); Chair. E. MWANIKI; 700 employees.

Bedi Investments Ltd: Lower Factory Rd, Industrial Area, POB 230, Nakuru; tel. (51) 2212320; fax (51) 2216214; e-mail info@bedi.com; internet www.bedi.com; f. 1972; manufactures finished fabrics, yarns and garments; Dir J. S. BEDI; 745 employees.

Brooke Bond Kenya Ltd: POB 42011, Nairobi; tel. (20) 532520; fax (20) 532521; e-mail richard.fairburn@unilever.com; f. 1825; 88.2% owned by Unilever PLC; growth, production and sale of tea; sales Ks. 4,2595m. (2002); Man. Dir R. A. FAIRBURN; 18,000 employees.

Brookside Dairy Ltd: POB 236, 00232 Ruiru; tel. (67) 25044; fax (67) 54101; e-mail maziwa@brookside.co.ke; internet www.brookside.co.ke; manufacture of dairy products; sales US $4.5m. (2004); Gen. Man. DAVID HEATH; 1,000 employees.

Chemelil Sugar Co Ltd: POB 1649, Kisumu; tel. (57) 41406; fax (57) 44530; e-mail chemelil@swiftkisumu.com; f. 1965; production and processing of sugar; sales Ks. 1,495.1m. (2000); Man. Dir A. THULKONG; 1,244 employees.

CMC Holdings Ltd: POB 30060, Nairobi; tel. (20) 511470; fax (20) 543793; e-mail md@cmcmotors.com; f. 1948; investment co, with interests in motor, aviation, engineering, and agricultural machinery and equipment; sales Ks. 4,112.4m. (2000); Man. Dir JAN THOENES; 1,100 employees.

East African Breweries Ltd: Thika Rd, Ruaraka, POB 30161, Nairobi; tel. (20) 864000; fax (20) 8561090; e-mail eabl.info@eabl.com; internet www.eabrew.com; f. 1922; brews Tusker, Pilsner, Whitecap, Allsopps, Bell Lager and Kibo Gold; Group Chair. J. G. KIEREINI; Group Man. Dir G. K. MAHINDA.

East African Packing Industries Ltd (EAPI): Kitui Rd, off Kampala Rd, POB 30146, Nairobi; tel. (20) 3955000; fax (20) 3955500; e-mail sales@eapi.co.ke; internet www.eapi.co.ke; f. 1959; produces multiwall paper bags, corrugated cardboard containers and toilet tissue; sales Ks. 1,299.3m. (1999); Chair. A. P. HAMILTON; Man. Dir RON FASOL; 400 employees.

East African Portland Cement Co Ltd: Namanga Rd, off Mombasa Rd, Athi River, Nairobi; tel. (45) 22777; fax (45) 20406; e-mail info@eapcc.co.ke; internet www.eastafricanportland.com; f. 1932; cement mfrs; sales Ks. 2,000m. (1998); Chair. BENSON SANDE NDETA; Man. Dir NDEGWA KAGIO.

Eastern Produce Kenya Ltd: POB 45560, Nairobi; tel. (20) 440115; fax (20) 449635; e-mail mail@easternproduce.co.ke; f. 1951; 81.6% owned by Linton Park PLC; growth and processing of tea; sales Ks. 36m. (1998); Chair. M. C. PERKINS; 3,200 employees.

Eldoret Steel Mills Ltd: POB 142, Eldoret; tel. (32) 32644; fax (32) 62475; e-mail factory@kenknit.com; f. 1989; steel production; Chair. H. S. LOCHAB; 550 employees.

Insteel Ltd: POB 78161, 00507 Nairobi; tel. (20) 555099; fax (20) 533944; e-mail insteel@insteellimited.com; internet www.insteellimited.com; f. 1983; manufactures steel water pipes and hollow sections; sales Ks. 1,345m. (2004); COO and Dir H. P. MODI; 300 employees.

Kakuzi Ltd: Punda Milia Rd, Makuyu, POB 24, Thika; tel. (15) 64620; fax (15) 64240; e-mail mail@kakuzi.co.ke; f. 1927; 26.1% owned by Bordure Ltd, 24.6% by Lintak Investments Ltd, 5.0% by Kenya Reinsurance Corpn; tea and coffee growing, livestock farming, horticulture, forestry development; sales Ks. 1,250.9m. (2001); Chair. Dr T. R. FOWKES.

Kaluworks Ltd: POB 90421, Mombasa; tel. (41) 2491401; fax (41) 2495099; e-mail corporate@kaluworks.com; mfr of aluminium kitchenware and catering equipment for export, mfrs of aluminium sheets, coils and circles; sales US $28.7m. (2003); Gen. Man. V. NAIR; Man. Dir R. R. TEWARY; Exec. Dir R. C. SHARMA; 800 employees.

Kapa Oil Refineries Ltd: Main Mombasa Rd, POB 18492, 00500 Nairobi; tel. (20) 6420000; fax (20) 6420642; e-mail info@kapa-oil.com; internet www.kapa-oil.com; produces cooking fats and edible oils, margarines, baking powder, detergents powder and glycerine; Dir MILAN SHAH; 1,000 employees.

KCC Holdings Ltd: Creamery House, Dakar Rd, POB 30131, Nairobi; tel. (20) 532535; fax (20) 544879; f. 1925 as Kenya Co-operative Creameries Ltd; processes and markets the bulk of dairy produce; Chair. K. KOROSS; Man. Dir J. P. L. NYABERI; 5,000 employees.

Kenya Oil Co Ltd: POB 44202, Nairobi; tel. (20) 249333; fax (20) 230967; e-mail kenkob@kenkob.co.ke; internet www.kenolkobil.com; f. 1959; import of crude petroleum; marketing of fuel and lubricants; sales Ks. 10,959.2m. (2001); Chair. JACOB I. SEGMAN; 190 employees.

Kenya Seed Co Ltd: POB 553, Kitale; tel. (39) 20942; fax (39) 20458; f. 1956; 52.88% owned by Agricultural Development Corpn; seed growers and merchants; sales Ks. 2,393.5m. (2000); Man. Dir N. K. TUM; 392 employees.

Kenya Tea Packers Ltd: POB 413, Kericho; tel. (52) 20530; fax (52) 20536; e-mail ketepa@africaonline.co.ke; production of packed tea; sales US $25m. (2000); Gen. Man. SAMUEL LERLONKA TIAMPATI; 500 employees.

Mowlem Construction Co (East Africa) Ltd: POB 30079, Nairobi; tel. (20) 441158; fax (20) 440805; e-mail mowlem@africaonline.co.ke; f. 1822; owned by John Mowlem and Co PLC; civil engineering and construction, geotechnical and water-well drilling; Chair. K. J. MINTON; 12,285 employees.

Mumias Sugar Co Ltd: Private Bag, Mumias; tel. (33) 41620; fax (33) 41234; e-mail msc@africaonline.co.ke; f. 1971; state-owned; designated for privatization in mid-2003; sugar production; Chair. M. K. SANG; 3,000 employees.

Njoro Canning Factory (Kenya) Ltd: POB 7076, Nakuru; tel. (37) 211736; fax (37) 43830; e-mail info@njorocanning.com; internet www.njorocanning.com; f. 1978; produces canned, dried and frozen vegetables; Chair. and Man. Dir T. K. PATEL; 1,000 employees.

Orbit Chemical Industries Ltd: POB 48870, Nairobi; tel. (20) 543210; fax (20) 542850; f. 1972; manufacture of chemicals, soaps and detergents; Chair. V. D. CHANDARIA; 600 employees.

Pan African Paper Mills (East Africa) Ltd: Kenindia House, Loita St, POB 30221, 00100 Nairobi; tel. (20) 227942; fax (20) 215692; e-mail vsaboo@panpaperkenya.com; f. 1969; mfrs of paper, paperboard and pulp; sales Ks. 5,700m. (2004); Chair. C. K. BIRLA; Exec. Dir V. D. SABOO; 1,589 employees.

Sameer Africa Ltd: POB 30429, 00100 Nairobi; tel. and fax (20) 554910; e-mail info@firestone.co.ke; f. 1969; formerly Firestone East Africa (1969) Ltd; tyre and tube mfrs; sales Ks. 3,400m. (2004); Chair. N. N. MERALI; Man. Dir Dr S. K. CHATHERJI; 686 employees.

Sasini Tea and Coffee Ltd: POB 30151, 00100 Nairobi; tel. (20) 342166; fax (20) 316573; e-mail infi@sasini.co.ke; f. 1952; owned by Sameer Investments Ltd; tea and coffee farming and production; turnover Ks. 1.3m. (2006); Chair. A. P. HAMILTON; 5,000 employees.

Spin-Knit Ltd: POB 1478, 20100 Nakuru; tel. (51) 2211517; fax (51) 2217155; e-mail spinknit@africaonline.co.ke; f. 1982; manufacture of hand-knitted clothing, yarn, blankets, towels; Man. Dir SHASHI SHAH; 750 employees.

Spinners & Spinners Ltd: Agip House, 6th Floor, Haile Selassie Ave, POB 46206, Nairobi; tel. (20) 226178; fax (20) 218154; e-mail spinners@kenyaweb.com; internet www.spinnersandspinners.com; f. 1981; mfrs of blankets, knitting yarns, ethnic fabrics and baby shawls and blankets; sales US $15.2m. (2000); Chair. D. M. DHANANI; 1,800 employees.

Steelmakers Ltd: POB 44574, 00100 Nairobi; tel. (20) 821790; fax (20) 821796; e-mail nbo@steelmakers.com; f. 1986; production of foundry products and hot rolled steel profiles and sections; Chair. RASIK PATEL; Man. Dir KALPESH PATEL; 1,200 employees.

Unga Group Ltd: Ngano House, Commercial St, POB 30096, Nairobi; tel. (20) 532471; fax (20) 545448; e-mail information@unga.com; f. 1928; 51% owned by Victus Ltd; mfrs of flour, maize meal, porridges, animal feed and animal minerals; sales Ks. 7,306m. (2006); Chair. R. KEMOLI; Man. Dir NICHOLAS HUTCHINSON; 400 employees.

Williamson Tea Kenya Ltd: Williamson House, 4th Ngong Ave, POB 42281, Nairobi; tel. (20) 710740; fax (20) 718737; e-mail gwkenya@Williamson.co.ke; f. 1952; fmrly George Williamson Kenya Ltd; 50.41% owned by Williamson Tea Holdings PLC (United Kingdom); tea cultivation and production; sales Ks. 1,255.5m. (2001); Chair. and Man. Dir N. G. SANDYS-LUMSDAINE; 5,910 employees.

TRADE UNIONS

Central Organization of Trade Unions (Kenya) (COTU): Solidarity Bldg, Digo Rd, POB 13000, Nairobi; tel. (20) 761375; fax (20) 762695; f. 1965 as the sole trade union fed.; Chair. PETER G. MUTHEE; Sec.-Gen. JOSEPH J. MUGALLA.

Amalgamated Union of Kenya Metalworkers: POB 73651, Nairobi; tel. (20) 211060; Gen. Sec. F. E. OMIDO.

Bakers', Confectionary Manufacturing and Allied Workers' Union (Kenya): POB 57751, 00200 Nairobi; Lengo House, 3rd Floor, Room 20, Tom Mboya St, opposite Gill House, Nairobi; tel. (20) 330275; fax (20) 222735; e-mail bakers@form-net.com.

Communication Workers' Union of Kenya: POB 48155, Nairobi; tel. (20) 219345; e-mail cowuk@clubinternet.com.

Dockworkers' Union: POB 98207, Mombasa; tel. (11) 491427; f. 1954; Gen. Sec. J. KHAMIS.

Kenya Airline Pilots' Association: POB 57505, Nairobi; tel. (20) 716986.

Kenya Building, Construction, Timber, Furniture and Allied Industries Employees' Union: POB 49628, 00100 Nairobi; tel. (20) 223434; Gen. Sec. FRANCIS KARIMI MURAGE.

Kenya Chemical and Allied Workers' Union: POB 73820, Nairobi; tel. (20) 338815; Gen. Sec. WERE DIBI OGUTO.

Kenya Electrical Trades Allied Workers' Union: POB 47060, Nairobi; tel. (20) 334655.

Kenya Engineering Workers' Union: POB 73987, Nairobi; tel. (20) 333745; Gen. Sec. JUSTUS MULEI.

Kenya Game Hunting and Safari Workers' Union: Nairobi; tel. (20) 25049; Gen. Sec. J. M. NDOLO.

Kenya Jockey and Betting Workers' Union: POB 55094, Nairobi; tel. (20) 332120.

Kenya Local Government Workers' Union: POB 55827, Nairobi; tel. (20) 217213; Gen. Sec. WASIKE NDOMBI.

Kenya National Union of Fishermen: POB 83322, Nairobi; tel. (20) 227899.

Kenya Petroleum Oil Workers' Union: POB 48125, Nairobi; tel. (20) 338756; Gen. Sec. JACOB OCHINO.

Kenya Plantation and Agricultural Workers' Union: POB 1161, 20100 Nakuru; tel. and fax (51) 2212310; e-mail kpawu@africaonline.co.ke; Gen. Sec. FRANCIS ATWOLI.

Kenya Quarry and Mine Workers' Union: POB 332120, Nairobi; f. 1961; Gen. Sec. WAFULA WA MUSAMIA.

Kenya Railway Workers' Union: RAHU House, Mfangano St, POB 72029, Nairobi; tel. (20) 340302; f. 1952; Nat. Chair. FRANCIS O'LORE; Sec.-Gen. JOHN T. CHUMO.

Kenya Scientific Research, International Technical and Allied Institutions Workers' Union: Ngumba House, Tom Mboya St, POB 55094, Nairobi; tel. (20) 215713; Sec.-Gen. FRANCIS D. KIRUBI.

Kenya Shipping, Clearing and Warehouse Workers' Union: POB 84067, Mombasa; tel. (11) 312000.

Kenya Shoe and Leather Workers' Union: POB 49629, Nairobi; tel. (20) 533827; Gen. Sec. JAMES AWICH.

Kenya Union of Commercial, Food and Allied Workers: POB 2628-00100, Nairobi; tel. (20) 245054; fax (20) 313118; e-mail kucfaw@yahoo.com.

Kenya Union of Domestic, Hotel, Educational Institutions, Hospitals and Allied Workers: POB 41763, 00100 Nairobi; tel. (20) 241509; fax (20) 243806; e-mail kudheihaworkers@hotmail.com.

Kenyan Union of Entertainment and Music Industry Employees: Nairobi; tel. (20) 333745.

Kenya Union of Journalists: POB 47035, 00100 Nairobi; tel. (20) 250888; fax (20) 250880; e-mail info@kujkenya.org; f. 1962; Gen. Sec. and CEO EZEKIEL MUTUA; Chair. TERVIL OKOKO.

Kenya Union of Printing, Publishing, Paper Manufacturers and Allied Workers: POB 72358, Nairobi; tel. (20) 331387; Gen. Sec. JOHN BOSCO.

Kenya Union of Sugar Plantation Workers: POB 36, Kisumu; tel. (35) 22221; Gen. Sec. ONYANGO MIDIKA.

National Seamen's Union of Kenya: Mombasa; tel. (11) 312106; Gen. Sec. I. S. ABDALLAH MWARUA.

Tailors' and Textile Workers' Union: POB 72076, Nairobi; tel. (20) 338836.

Transport and Allied Workers' Union: POB 45171, Nairobi; tel. (20) 545317; Gen. Sec. JULIAS MALII.

Independent Unions

Academic Staff Association: Nairobi; e-mail dorata@uonbi.ac.ke; Interim Chair. Dr KORWA ADAR.

Kenya Medical Practitioners' and Dentists' Union: not officially registered; Nat. Chair. GIBBON ATEKA.

Kenya National Union of Teachers: POB 30407, Nairobi; f. 1957; Sec.-Gen. AMBROSE ADEYA ADONGO.

Transport

RAILWAYS

In 1999 there were some 2,700 km of track open for traffic.

Kenya Railways Corpn: POB 30121, Nairobi; tel. (20) 221211; fax (20) 224156; f. 1977; management of operations assumed by Rift Valley Railways consortium in November 2006; Man. Dir A. HARIZ.

ROADS

At the end of 2004 there were an estimated 63,265 km of classified roads, of which 6,527 km were main roads and 18,885 km were secondary roads. Only an estimated 14.1% of road surfaces were paved. An all-weather road links Nairobi to Addis Ababa, in Ethiopia, and there is a 590-km road link between Kitale (Kenya) and Juba (Sudan). The rehabilitation of the important internal road link between Nairobi and Mombasa (funded by a US $165m. loan from the World Bank) was undertaken during the late 1990s.

Abamba Public Road Services: POB 40322, Nairobi; tel. (20) 556062; fax (20) 559884; operates bus services from Nairobi to all major towns in Kenya and to Kampala in Uganda.

East African Road Services Ltd: Nairobi; tel. (20) 764622; f. 1947; operates bus services from Nairobi to all major towns in Kenya; Chair. S. H. NATHOO.

Kenya Roads Board: Nairobi; tel. (20) 722865; f. 2000 to co-ordinate maintenance, rehabilitation and development of the road network; Chair. ALFRED JUMA.

Nyayo Bus Service Corpn: Nairobi; tel. (20) 803588; f. 1986; operates bus services within and between major towns in Kenya.

Speedways Trans-Africa Freighters: POB 75755, Nairobi; tel. (20) 544267; private road haulier; CEO HASSAN KANYARE.

SHIPPING

The major international seaport of Mombasa has 16 deep-water berths, with a total length of 3,044 m, and facilities for the off-loading of bulk carriers, tankers and container vessels. Mombasa port handled more than 8.5m. metric tons of cargo in 1998. An inland container depot with a potential full capacity of 120,000 20-ft (6-m) equivalent units was opened in Nairobi in 1984.

Kenya Ports Authority: POB 95009, Mombasa; tel. (41) 312211; fax (41) 311867; e-mail md@kpa.co.ke; internet www.kenya.ports.com; f. 1978; sole operator of coastal port facilities, and operates two inland container depots at Nairobi and Kisimu; Chair. Gen. (Retd) JOSEPH KIBWANA; Man. Dir ABDALLAH HEMED MWARURA.

Inchcape Shipping Services Kenya Ltd: POB 90194, Mombasa; tel. (11) 314245; fax (11) 314224; Man. Dir DAVID MACKAY.

Mackenzie Maritime Ltd: Maritime Centre, Archbishop Makarios Close, POB 90120, Mombasa; tel. (11) 221273; fax (11) 316260; e-mail mml@africaonline.co.ke; shipping agents; Man. Dir M. M. BROWN.

Marship Ltd: Mombasa; tel. (11) 314705; fax (11) 316654; f. 1986; shipbrokers, ship management and chartering agents; Man. Dir MICHELE ESPOSITO.

Mitchell Cotts Kenya Ltd: Cotts House, Wabera St, POB 30182, Nairobi; tel. (20) 221273; fax (20) 214228.

Motaku Shipping Agencies Ltd: Motaku House, Tangana Rd, POB 80419, 80100 Mombasa; tel. (41) 2229065; fax (41) 2220777; e-mail motaku@motakushipping.com; f. 1977; ship managers and shipping agents, freight broker and charter; Man. Dir KARIM KUDRATI.

PIL (Kenya) Ltd: POB 43050, Mombasa; tel. (11) 225361; fax (11) 312296.

Shipmarc Ltd: POB 99553, Mombasa; tel. (11) 229241; fax (11) 315673; e-mail shipmarc@form-net.com.

Southern Line Ltd: POB 90102, Mombasa 80107; tel. (11) 229241; fax (11) 221390; e-mail shipmarc@africaonline.co.ke; operating dry cargo and tanker vessels between East African ports, Red Sea ports, the Persian (Arabian) Gulf and Indian Ocean islands.

Spanfreight Shipping Ltd: Cannon Towers, Moi Ave, POB 99760, Mombasa; tel. (11) 315623; fax (11) 312092; e-mail a23ke464@gncomtext.com; Exec. Dir DILIPKUMAR AMRITLAL SHAH.

Star East Africa Co: POB 86725, Mombasa; tel. (11) 314060; fax (11) 312818; shipping agents and brokers; Man. Dir YEUDA FISHER.

CIVIL AVIATION

Jomo Kenyatta International Airport (JKIA), in south-eastern Nairobi, and Moi International Airport, at Mombasa both service international flights. Wilson Airport, in south-western Nairobi, Eldoret Airport (which opened in 1997) and airports at Malindi and Kisumu handle internal flights. Kenya has about 150 smaller airfields. The rehabilitation and expansion of JKIA and Moi International Airport was undertaken during the late 1990s. A new cargo handling facility,

The Nairobi Cargo Centre, opened at JKIA in June 1999, increasing the airport's capacity for storing horticultural exports.

Kenya Airports Authority: Jomo Kenyatta International Airport, POB 19001, Nairobi; tel. (20) 825400; fax (20) 822078; e-mail info@kenyaairports.co.ke; f. 1991; state-owned; responsible for the provision, management and operation of all airports and private airstrips; Man. Dir GEORGE MUHOHO.

African Airlines International: POB 74772, Nairobi; tel. (20) 824333; fax (20) 823999; placed under receivership mid-1999; CEO Capt. MUSA BULHAN.

Airkenya Aviation: Wilson Airport, POB 30357, Nairobi; tel. (20) 605730; fax (20) 500845; e-mail info@airkenya.com; internet www.airkenya.com; f. 1985; operates internal scheduled and charter passenger services; Man. Dir JOHN BUCKLEY.

Blue Bird Aviation Ltd: Wilson Airport, Langata Rd, POB 52382, Nairobi; tel. (20) 506004; fax (20) 602337; e-mail bbal@form-net.com.

Eagle Aviation (African Eagle): POB 93926, Mombasa; tel. (11) 434502; fax (11) 434249; e-mail eaglemsa@africaonline.co.ke; f. 1986; scheduled regional and domestic passenger and cargo services; Chair. RAJA TANUJ; CEO Capt. KIRAN PATEL.

East African Safari Air: Mombasa; operates charter service.

Kenya Airways Ltd (KQ): Jomo Kenyatta International Airport, POB 19002, Nairobi; tel. (20) 823000; fax (20) 823757; e-mail gmurira@kenya-airways.com; internet www.kenya-airways.com; f. 1977; in private-sector ownership since 1996; passenger services to Africa, Asia, Europe and Middle East; freight services to Europe; internal services from Nairobi to Kisumu, Mombasa and Malindi; also operates a freight subsidiary; Chair. EVANSON MWANIKI; Man. Dir and CEO TITUS NAIKUNI.

CIVIL AVIATION AUTHORITY

Kenya Directorate of Civil Aviation: Jomo Kenyatta International Airport, POB 30163, Nairobi; tel. (20) 822950; f. 1948; under Kenya govt control since 1977; responsible for the conduct of civil aviation; advises the Govt on civil aviation policy; Dir J. P. AYUGA.

Kenya Civil Aviation Authority: POB 30163, 00100 Nairobi; tel. (20) 824557; fax (20) 824716; e-mail cav@insightkenya.com; f. 2002; regulatory and advisory services for air navigation; Dir Gen. C. A. KUTO.

Tourism

Kenya's main attractions for visitors are its wildlife, with 25 National Parks and 23 game reserves, the Indian Ocean coast and an equable year-round climate. In 2005 there were 1,479,000 foreign visitors. Earnings from the sector totalled US $808m. in 2004.

Kenya Tourism Board: Kenya-Re Towers, Ragati Rd, POB 30630, 00100 Nairobi; tel. (20) 271126; fax (20) 2719925; e-mail info@kenyatourism.org; internet www.magicalkenya.com; f. 1997; promotes Kenya as a tourist destination, monitors the standard of tourist facilities.

Kenya Tourist Development Corpn: Utalii House, 11th Floor, Uhuru Highway, POB 42013, Nairobi; tel. (20) 330820; fax (20) 227815; e-mail info@ktdc.co.ke; internet www.ktdc.co.ke; f. 1965; Chair. PAUL KITOLOLO; Man. Dir JOHN A. M. MALITI.

Defence

As assessed at November 2006, Kenya's armed forces numbered 24,120, comprising an army of 20,000, an air force of 2,500 and a navy of 1,620. Military service is voluntary. The paramilitary police general service unit was 5,000 strong in 2006. Military assistance is received from the United Kingdom, and from the USA, whose Rapid Deployment Force uses port and onshore facilities in Kenya.

Defence Expenditure: Budgeted at Ks. 33,000m. for 2006.

Commander-in-Chief of the Armed Forces: Pres. MWAI KIBAKI.

Chief of Armed Forces General Staff: Gen. JOSEPH KIBWANA.

Education

The Government provides, or assists in the provision of, schools. In 2002/03 enrolment at pre-primary level was 33% (32% of boys; 33% of girls). Primary education, which is compulsory, is provided free of charge. The education system involves eight years of primary education (beginning at six years of age), four years at secondary school and four years of university education. According to UNESCO estimates, in 2003/04 enrolment at primary schools included 76% of pupils in the relevant age group (males 76%; females 77%), while enrolment at secondary schools included 40% of children in the relevant age-group (males 40%; females 40%). Tertiary enrolment in 2001/02 included just 3% of those in the relevant age group (4% males; 2% females), according to UNESCO estimates. There are five state universities and five chartered private universities. The education sector was allocated Ks. 54,653m. in the budget for 2001/02 (equivalent to 25.6% of total budgetary expenditure by the central Government).

Bibliography

Anguka, J. *Absolute Power: The Ouko Murder Mystery*. London, Pen Press Publishers Ltd, 1998.

arap Moi, D. T. *Kenya African Nationalism: Nyayo Philosophy and Principles*. London, Macmillan, 1986.

Azam, J.-P., and Daubrée, C. *Bypassing the State: Economic Growth in Kenya, 1964–1990*. Paris, OECD, 1997.

Bailey, J. *Kenya: The National Epic*. Nairobi, East African Education Publishers, 1993 (Pictorial history).

Bates, R. H. *Beyond the Miracle of the Market: The Political Economy of Agrarian Development in Kenya*. (2nd Edn) Cambridge, Cambridge University Press, 2005.

Booth, K. M. *Local Women, Global Science: Fighting AIDS in Kenya*. Bloomington, IN, Indiana University Press, 2003.

Central Bank of Kenya. *Kenya: Land of Opportunity*. Nairobi, Central Bank of Kenya, 1991.

Clough, M. S. *Mau Mau Memoirs: History, Memory and Politics*. Boulder, CO, Lynne Rienner Publishers, 1998.

Cohen, D. W., and Odhiambo, E. S. A. *Burying SM: The Politics of Knowledge and the Sociology of Power in Africa*. London, James Currey, 1992.

Coughlin, P., and Gerrishon, K. I. (Eds). *Kenya's Industrialization Dilemma*. (Contains industrial studies carried out under the Industrial Research Project.) Nairobi, Kenyan Heinemann, 1991.

Eshiwani, G. S. *Education in Kenya since Independence*. Nairobi, East African Educational Publishers, 1993.

Faulkner, C. *A Two Year Wonder: The Kenya Police 1953–1955*. Elgin, Librario Publishing Ltd, 2005.

Fogken, D., and Tellegen, W. *Tied to the Land: Living Conditions of Labourers on Large Farms in Trans-Nzoia District, Kenya*. Leiden, African Studies Centre, 1995.

Gibbon, P. (Ed.). *Markets, Civil Society and Democracy in Kenya*. Uppsala, Nordic Africa Institute, 1995.

Govt of Kenya. *Economic Reforms for 1996–1998: The Policy Framework Paper*. Nairobi, Govt Printing Press, 1996.

Haugerud, A. *The Culture of Politics in Modern Kenya*. Cambridge, Cambridge University Press, 1995.

Himbara, D. *Kenyan Capitalists, the State and Development*. Boulder, CO, Lynne Rienner Publishers, 1993.

Hoorweg, J., Fogken, D., and Klaver, W. *Seasons and Nutrition at the Kenya Coast*. Brookfield, VT, Ashgate Publishing, 1996.

Hughes, L. *Moving the Maasai: A Colonial Misadventure*. Basingstoke, Palgrave Macmillan, 2006.

Karp, I. *Fields of Change Among the Iteso of Kenya* (Routledge Library Editions: Anthropology and Ethnography). London, Routledge, 2004.

Kenyatta, J. *Facing Mount Kenya*. London, Heinemann, 1979.

Kimenyi, M. S. (Ed.), *et al. Restarting and Sustaining Economic Growth and Development in Africa: The Case of Kenya* (Contemporary Perspectives on Developing Societies). Brookfield, VT, Ashgate Publishing, 2003.

King, K. *Jua Kali Kenya: Change and Development in an Informal Economy, 1970–1995*. Athens, OH, Ohio University Press, 1996.

Kyle, K. *The Politics of the Independence of Kenya*. London and Basingstoke, Palgrave, 1999.

Leakey, L. *Defeating Mau Mau* (Routledge Library Editions: Anthropology & Ethnography). London, Routledge, 2004.

Lewis, J. *Empire State-Building: War and Welfare in Kenya, 1925–52*. Athens, OH, Ohio University Press, 2001.

Little, P. D. *The Elusive Granary: Herder, Farmer and State in Northern Kenya*. Cambridge, Cambridge University Press, 1992.

Lovatt Smith, D. *Kenya, the Kikuyu and Mau Mau*. Mawenzi Books, 2005.

Malobe, W. O. *Mau Mau and Kenya: An Analysis of a Peasant Revolt*. Bloomington, IN, Indiana University Press, 1993.

Miller, N., and Yeager, R. *Kenya: The Quest for Prosperity*. Boulder, CO, Westview Press, 1994.

Morton, A. *Moi: The Making of an African Statesman*. London, Michael O'Mara Books, 1998.

Murunga, G. R., and Nasong'o, S. W. (Eds). *Kenya: The Struggle for Democracy*. London, Zed Books, 2007.

Mwau, G., and Handa, J. *Rational Economic Decisions and the Current Account in Kenya*. Aldershot, Avebury, 1995.

Ndegwa, P. *Development and Employment in Kenya: A Strategy for the Transformation of the Economy; Report of the Presidential Committee on Employment*. Southwell, Leishman and Taussig, 1991.

Nowrojee, B. *Divide and Rule: State-Sponsored Ethnic Violence in Kenya*. Washington, DC, Human Rights Watch and Africa Watch, 1993.

Ochieng, W. R., and Maxon, R. M. *An Economic History of Kenya*. Nairobi, East African Educational Publishers, 1992.

Odhiambo, E. S. *Mau Mau and Nationhood*. Athens, OH, Ohio University Press, 2003.

Ogot, B. A., and Ochieng, W. R. (Eds). *Decolonization and Independence in Kenya, 1940–1993*. London, James Currey, 1995.

Otiende, J. E., Wamahiu, S. P., and Karugu, A. M. *Education and Development in Kenya: An Historical Perspective*. Nairobi, Oxford University Press, 1992.

Owino, J. *Kenya into the 21st Century*. London, Minerva Press, 2001.

Paarlberg, R. L. *The Politics of Precaution*. Baltimore, MD, Johns Hopkins University Press, 2001.

Pearson, S., *et al. Agricultural Policy in Kenya*. Ithaca, NY, Cornell University Press, 1995.

Presley, C. A. *Kikuyu Women and Social Change in Kenya*. Boulder, CO, Westview Press, 1992.

Rotberg, R. I. (Ed.). *Kenya (Africa: Continent in the Balance Series)*. Broomall, PA, Mason Crest Publishers, 2005.

Sabar, G. *Church, State and Society in Kenya*. London, Frank Cass Publishers, 2001.

Somjee, S. *Material Culture of Kenya*. Nairobi, East African Educational Publications, 1993.

Spencer, P. *The Maasai of Matapato: A Study of Rituals of Rebellion*. London, Routledge, 2003.

The Samburu: A Study in Geocentracy. London, Routledge, 2003.

Thomas-Slayter, B., and Rocheleau, D. *Gender, Environment and Development in Kenya: A Grassroots Perspective*. Boulder, CO, Lynne Rienner, 1995.

Trench, C. C. *Men Who Ruled Kenya: The Kenya Administration 1892–1963*. London, Radcliffe Press, 1993.

wa Wamwere, K. *The People's Representative and the Tyrants: or, Kenya, Independence without Freedom*. Nairobi, New Concept Typesetters, 1993.

I Refuse to Die. New York, NY, Seven Stories Press, 2004.

Widner, J. A. *The Rise of a Party State in Kenya: From 'Harambee' to 'Nyayo'*. Berkeley, CA, University of California Press, 1992.

Willis, J. *Mombasa, the Swahili and the Making of the Mijikenda*. New York, Oxford University Press, 1993.

LESOTHO

Physical and Social Geography

A. MacGREGOR HUTCHESON

PHYSICAL FEATURES

The Kingdom of Lesotho, a small, land-locked country of 30,355 sq km (11,720 sq miles), is enclosed on all sides by South Africa. It is situated at the highest part of the Drakensberg escarpment on the eastern rim of the South African plateau. About two-thirds of Lesotho is very mountainous. Elevations in the eastern half of the country are generally more than 2,440 m above sea-level, and in the north-east and along the eastern border they exceed 3,350 m. This is a region of very rugged relief, bleak climate and heavy annual rainfall (averaging 1,905 mm), where the headstreams of the Orange river have incised deep valleys. Westwards the land descends through a foothill zone of rolling country, at an altitude of 1,830–2,135 m, to Lesotho's main lowland area. This strip of land along the western border, part of the Highveld, averages 40 km in width and lies at an altitude of about 1,525 m. Annual rainfall averages in this region are 650–750 mm, and climatic conditions are generally more pleasant. However, frost may occur throughout the country in winter, and hail is a summer hazard in all regions. The light, sandy soils which have developed on the Karoo sedimentaries of the western lowland compare unfavourably with the fertile black soils of the Stormberg basalt in the uplands. The temperate grasslands of the west also tend to be less fertile than the montane grasslands of the east.

POPULATION AND NATURAL RESOURCES

At the census of April 2006 the population was 1,872,721 (excluding absentee workers in South Africa), giving an average density of 61.7 inhabitants per sq km. The noticeable physical contrasts between east and west Lesotho are reflected in the distribution and density of the population. While large parts of the mountainous east (except for valleys) are sparsely populated, most of the fertile western strip, which carries some 70% of the population, has densities in excess of 200 inhabitants per sq km. Such population pressure, further aggravated by steady population growth, has resulted in: (i) the permanent settlement being pushed to higher levels (in places to 2,440 m) formerly used for summer grazing, and on to steep slopes, thus adding to the already serious national problem of soil erosion; (ii) an acute shortage of cultivable land and increased soil exhaustion, particularly in the west; (iii) land holdings which are too small to maintain the rural population; and (iv) the country's inability, in its current stage of development, to support all its population, thus necessitating the migration of large numbers of workers to seek paid employment in South Africa. It was estimated in 1995 that some 25% of the adult male labour force were employed in South Africa, mainly in the mines. The number of Basotho employed in South Africa declined somewhat in the late 1990s, however, reaching about 17% of the male labour force in 2000. Lesotho's economy depends heavily on their remitted earnings, and a migratory labour system on this scale has grave social, economic and political implications for the country.

Lesotho's long-term development prospects largely rely upon the achievement of optimum use of its soil and water resources. About 11% of the country is cultivable and, since virtually all of this is already cultivated, only more productive use of the land can make Lesotho self-sufficient in food (20% of domestic needs are currently imported from South Africa). The high relief produces natural grasslands, well suited for a viable livestock industry, but this has been hindered through inadequate pasture management, excessive numbers of low-quality animals and disease. Lesotho and South Africa are jointly implementing the Lesotho Highlands Water Project (see Economy), which will provide employment for thousands of Basotho and greatly improve Lesotho's infrastructure. Reserves of diamonds have been identified in the mountainous north-east, and there are small surface workings at Lemphane, Liquobong and Kao. Uranium deposits have been located near Teyateyaneng in the north-west, but their exploitation must await a sustained improvement in world prices. The search for other minerals continues.

Recent History

CHRISTOPHER SAUNDERS

Based on an earlier article by RICHARD BROWN

Lesotho, formerly known as Basutoland, became a British protectorate in 1868, at the request of the Basotho paramount chief, Moshoeshoe I, in the face of Boer expansionism. Basutoland was annexed to Cape Colony (now part of South Africa) in 1871, but became a separate British colony in 1884, and was administered as one of the high commission territories in southern Africa. Unlike the other territories—Bechuanaland (now Botswana) and the protectorate of Swaziland—Basutoland was entirely surrounded by South African territory.

Modern party politics began in 1952 with the founding of the Basutoland Congress Party (BCP, renamed the Basotho Congress Party in 1966) by Dr Ntsu Mokhehle. Basutoland's first general election, held on the basis of universal adult suffrage, took place in April 1965. The majority of seats in the new Legislative Assembly were won by the Basutoland National Party (BNP, renamed the Basotho National Party at independence), a conservative group that had the support of the South African Government. Following the election, Moshoeshoe II, the paramount chief, was recognized as King. The BNP's leader, Chief Leabua Jonathan, became Prime Minister. Basutoland became independent, as the Kingdom of Lesotho, on 4 October 1966.

JONATHAN AND THE BNP, 1966–86

In January 1967 executive power was transferred from the King to the Prime Minister. In the general election held in January 1970, the BCP appeared to have won a majority of seats in the National Assembly. Chief Jonathan declared a state of emergency, suspended the Constitution and arrested Mokhehle and other leaders of the BCP. The election was annulled, and the country effectively passed under the Prime Minister's control. King Moshoeshoe went briefly into exile, but returned in December after agreeing to take no part in politics. The BCP split into an 'internal' faction, whose members were willing to accept the political status quo, and an 'external' faction, whose members demanded a return to normal political life: the latter group was led by Mokhehle, who fled the country in 1974, following a coup attempt.

Despite Lesotho's economic dependence on South Africa and the Government's official policy during the 1970s of 'dialogue' with its neighbour, Jonathan repeatedly criticized the South African Government's policy of apartheid, and declared his support for the prohibited African National Congress of South Africa (ANC). During the late 1970s Jonathan accused the South African Government of supporting the Lesotho Liberation Army (LLA), the military wing of the 'external' faction of the BCP, which was conducting a campaign of violence. The cancellation by Jonathan of elections promised for 1985 increased the hostility of the LLA, which launched a number of attacks on BNP targets late in that year.

Lesotho's reluctance to sign a joint non-aggression pact with South Africa was a persistent cause of friction during the mid-1980s and on 1 January 1986 South Africa blockaded its border with Lesotho, impeding access to vital supplies of food and fuel. On 15 January troops of the Lesotho paramilitary force, led by Maj.-Gen. Justin Lekhanya, surrounded government buildings. Five days later Lekhanya, having returned from 'security consultations' in South Africa, together with Maj.-Gen. S. K. Molapo, the commander of the security forces, and S. R. Matela, the chief of police, deposed the Jonathan Government.

MILITARY RULE, 1986–93

The new regime established a Military Council, headed by Lekhanya and including senior officers of the paramilitary force (which subsequently became the Royal Lesotho Defence Force—RLDF). The National Assembly was dissolved, and all executive and legislative powers were vested in the King, who acted on the advice of the Military Council. One week after the coup, some 60 members of the ANC were deported from Lesotho, and the South African blockade was lifted. The main opposition groups initially welcomed the military takeover, although Mokhehle's wing of the BCP demanded the immediate restoration of the 1966 Constitution, the integration of the LLA into Lesotho's armed forces and the holding of free elections within six months. All formal political activity was, however, suspended by the Military Council in March 1986.

In April 1988 the five main opposition parties appealed to the Organization of African Unity (OAU, now the African Union—AU), the Commonwealth and the South African Government to restore civilian rule. In the following month, after 14 years of exile, Mokhehle was allowed to return to Lesotho for peace talks, together with other members of the BCP. It was widely believed that the South African Government had played a part in promoting this reconciliation. In 1989 the LLA was reported to have been disbanded, and by 1990 the two factions of the BCP had apparently reunited under the leadership of Mokhehle.

In early 1990 conflict developed between Lekhanya and King Moshoeshoe. Following the King's refusal to approve changes made by Lekhanya to the Military Council, Lekhanya suspended his executive and legislative powers. Lekhanya promised that a return to civilian government would take place in 1992, and, to reassure business interests, a programme for privatizing state enterprises was announced. In March 1990 the Military Council assumed the executive and legislative powers that were previously vested in the King, and Moshoeshoe (who remained Head of State) went into exile, in the United Kingdom. In June the National Constituent Assembly was inaugurated to draft a new constitution acceptable to the majority of Basotho; its members included Lekhanya, together with members of the Council of Ministers, traditional chiefs, local councillors, businessmen and representatives of banned political parties.

When Lekhanya invited King Moshoeshoe to return from exile in October 1990, the King announced that his return would be conditional upon the lifting of military rule and the formation, by representatives of all political parties, of an interim government, pending the restoration of the 1966 Constitution and the holding of an internationally supervised general election. On 6 November Lekhanya promulgated an order deposing the King with immediate effect, and Lesotho's 22 principal chiefs elected Moshoeshoe's eldest son, Prince Bereng Seeisa, as the new King. He succeeded to the throne on 12 November, as King Letsie III, having undertaken not to involve himself in the political life of the country.

On 30 April 1991 Lekhanya was removed as Chairman of the Military Council in a coup led by Col (later Maj.-Gen.) Elias Phitsoane Ramaema, a member of the Military Council. Ramaema soon announced the repeal of the law that had banned party political activity in 1986, and by July the National Constituent Assembly had drafted a new Constitution. Following talks in the United Kingdom with Ramaema, under the auspices of the Secretary-General of the Commonwealth, former King Moshoeshoe returned to Lesotho in July 1992, and the general election, returning Lesotho to democracy, finally took place on 27 March 1993.

THE MOKHEHLE GOVERNMENT AND THE 'ROYAL COUP'

The BCP swept to power in the election, winning all 65 seats in the new National Assembly. On 2 April 1993 Mokhehle was sworn in as Prime Minister, and King Letsie swore allegiance to the new Constitution. Although independent local and international observers pronounced the election to be broadly free and fair, the BNP, which had the support of members of the former military regime, alleged widespread irregularities and refused to accept the results; the BNP also subsequently declined the BCP Government's offer of two seats in the newly established Senate.

In July 1994 Mokhehle appointed a commission of inquiry into the circumstances surrounding the dethronement of former King Moshoeshoe II in 1990. In the following month, however, having petitioned the High Court to abolish the commission on the grounds of bias on the part of its members, King Letsie dissolved Parliament, dismissed the Mokhehle Government and suspended sections of the Constitution, citing 'popular dissatisfaction' with the BCP administration. A provisional government was to be established, pending a general election, which was to be organized by an independent commission. A prominent human rights lawyer, Hae Phoofolo, was appointed Chairman of the transitional Council of Ministers, and announced that his primary concern was to amend the Constitution to enable the restoration of Moshoeshoe as monarch. In the mean time, Letsie acted as legislative and executive Head of State.

The suspension of constitutional government was widely condemned outside Lesotho. Several countries threatened economic sanctions against Lesotho, and the USA withdrew financial assistance. King Letsie and Mokhehle attended negotiations in Pretoria, South Africa, in late August 1994, at which Letsie was urged to reinstate all elected institutions. In September King Letsie and Mokhehle signed an agreement, guaranteed by Botswana, South Africa and Zimbabwe, providing for the restoration of Moshoeshoe as reigning monarch, and for the immediate restitution of the elected organs of government; the commission of inquiry into Moshoeshoe's dethronement was to be abandoned; persons involved in the 'royal coup' were to be immune from prosecution; the political neutrality of the armed forces and public service was to be guaranteed; and consultations were to be undertaken with the expressed aim of broadening the democratic process.

On 25 January 1995 Moshoeshoe II, who undertook not to intervene in politics, was restored to the throne, following the voluntary abdication of Letsie III, who took the title of Crown Prince. When Moshoeshoe was killed in a motor accident in January 1996, the Crown Prince was formally elected by the College of Chiefs to succeed his father and returned to the throne, resuming the title King Letsie III, in February. Like his father, Letsie undertook not to involve the monarchy in any aspect of political life. His coronation took place on 31 October 1997 at a ceremony in the capital, Maseru.

In March 1997 Mokhehle announced his intention to retire from politics prior to the 1998 elections, citing ill health and old age. However, in June 1997, following a protracted struggle between rival factions for control of the party, Mokhehle resigned from the BCP and, with the support of a majority of BCP members in the National Assembly, formed a new political party, the Lesotho Congress for Democracy (LCD), to which he transferred executive power. Opposition leaders denounced the move as a political coup, declaring that Mokhehle should have resigned as Prime Minister, sought a dissolution of the National Assembly and held new elections. The LCD denied that Mokhehle had contravened the Constitution, as he was supported by a majority in the National Assembly. At the LCD's annual conference, held in January 1998, Mokhehle resigned as leader, and was made honorary Life President of the party. (He died in January 1999.) In February 1998 Bethuel Pakalitha Mosisili, the Deputy Prime Minister, was elected to replace him as party leader.

THE 1998 GENERAL ELECTION AND SUBSEQUENT UNREST

Elections to an expanded National Assembly took place on 23 May 1998. The LCD secured 78 of the 80 seats, while the BNP won only one seat. Voting in the remaining constituency was postponed, owing to the death of a candidate. Prior to the election, opposition parties had unsuccessfully submitted an application to the High Court for a postponement, on the grounds that the Independent Electoral Commission (IEC) had not allowed sufficient time for parties to examine the electoral roll. Despite the pronouncement of regional and international observers that the election had been fair, it was reported that several hundred people demonstrated in Maseru, protesting against the results and accusing both the LCD and the IEC of irregularities. Mosisili was elected Prime Minister by the National Assembly, and a new Cabinet was appointed at the beginning of June. At the end of that month more than 200 defeated opposition candidates filed petitions in the High Court calling for the annulment of the election results and a re-examination of the ballot papers. In July, after the Court granted the complainants access to the relevant documentation, and evidence of irregularities began to emerge, anti-Government protests broke out in the capital. In early August crowds besieged the royal palace and demanded that the King exercise his power to annul the elections and appoint a government of national unity. Letsie, however, declined to act.

As protests escalated in Maseru, the Southern African Development Community (SADC), under South African leadership, intervened. A commission was appointed under Pius Langa, the Deputy President of South Africa's Constitutional Court, to investigate the allegations of electoral fraud. When the report was eventually released, in mid-September 1998, it stated that, while voting irregularities had occurred, they were insufficient to invalidate the results of the election. Meanwhile, influential elements within the Lesotho Defence Force (LDF, as the RLDF had been redesignated) had openly declared their support for the opposition, and junior officers forced a number of senior commanders to flee into South Africa. Prime Minister Mosisili, fearing a possible collapse of law and order and an imminent military coup, sought assistance from other SADC countries.

South African troops arrived in late September 1998, followed by a military contingent from Botswana. 'Operation Boleas', as the intervention was named, caused outrage in Lesotho, and on its entry into Maseru, the South African contingent met considerably fiercer resistance from the LDF than it had expected, resulting in the deaths of some 68 soldiers. Extensive looting spread rapidly from Maseru to other towns, causing serious damage to the economy. Thousands of people fled into the countryside and to South Africa. With the gradual restoration of calm and with South African mediation, an Interim Political Authority (IPA), representing the various parties, was formed to prepare for a new general election, which was to be held within 18 months. The remaining SADC troops were withdrawn in May 1999, although a small number of advisers remained behind until May 2000 to continue training the LDF, with the aim of making it a more professional and less politicized body.

The multi-party IPA, which was inaugurated in December 1998, rapidly became embroiled in controversy over electoral arrangements for the proposed elections. The Government wished the existing voting system to remain, but the BNP (under the leadership of Lekhanya) demanded a system of full proportional representation, on the South African model. Following protracted negotiations, the issue was eventually referred to arbitration. In October 1999 a tribunal appointed to resolve the divisions proposed a system combining both simple majority voting (for 80 seats) and proportional representation (for 50 new seats), which was accepted by the IPA. An agreement to this effect was signed by the Government and the IPA in December. However, when the draft legislation on the new electoral system was introduced to Parliament in February 2000, the LCD-dominated National Assembly rejected it, prompting the IPA to accuse the Government of reneging on its undertaking to abide by the tribunal's decision and the December accord.

The LCD subsequently proposed to the legislature that the country should retain the existing simple majority system, which had led to the 1998 violence, and which the opposition had rejected. The LCD-sponsored legislation was endorsed by the National Assembly, but rejected by the Senate, on the grounds that it differed from the electoral model approved by the IPA. Several weeks of political stalemate ensued, and, as the end of the 18-month period during which fresh elections were to have been held approached, a sense of crisis developed. Opposition parties urged the IPA to demand the dissolution of Parliament and the replacement of the LCD Government with one of national unity. Intense diplomatic efforts were made by SADC, Scandinavian diplomats and the Commonwealth to broker an agreement between Lesotho's political parties. The opposition accepted that a postponement of the elections was inevitable, but blamed the LCD and the National Assembly for stalling the process. Following mediation, the opposition parties agreed to the LCD remaining in office, in return for assurances that the electoral system would be changed as soon as possible.

In mid-May 2000 the IPA and the Government adopted a provisional electoral timetable; Mosisili announced that a general election would be held between March and May 2001, on the grounds that there was insufficient time to prepare for a poll in 2000. The IPA was to remain in existence until the results of the election were announced. In July 2000 the election date was provisionally set for 26 May 2001, although legislation pertaining to a new voting system had still to be finalized and approved by Parliament. Political leaders remained divided over the proposed expansion of the National Assembly and the number of seats to be decided by simple majority voting and by proportional representation. The LCD now favoured 40 seats elected by proportional representation, and 80 by constituencies; this arrangement for the new 120-seat National Assembly was finally agreed by all parties and approved by Parliament in January 2002. Meanwhile, in September 2001 internal strife within the LCD prompted a group of party deputies, led by Kelebone Maope, hitherto Deputy Prime Minister, to split from the LCD and establish a new party, the Lesotho People's Congress (LPC), which was subsequently declared the main opposition party.

THE 2002 GENERAL ELECTION AND BEYOND

The general election took place on 25 May 2002 and was contested by 19 parties. Each signed a code of conduct, promising to accept the results. Voting was conducted peacefully, although there were a number of logistical problems, and polling had to be extended to a second day in a number of constituencies. The voting process was generally accepted as being free and fair by observers and a turn-out of some 68% of the 831,315 registered voters was recorded. The ruling LCD won 54.9% of the valid votes cast and 77 of the 78 contested constituency seats (voting was postponed in two constituencies, owing to the deaths of candidates). The LPC gained the remaining contested seat, and four of the 40 seats allocated by proportional representation. The BNP won 22.4% of the vote and secured 21 of the seats allocated by proportional representation.

The BNP leader, Lekhanya, demanded a forensic audit of the results, claiming that they had been manipulated, refused to attend the ceremony at which Mosisili was sworn in as Prime Minister for another five-year term, and threatened to boycott the new National Assembly. However, there was no widespread support for his legal challenges regarding the election results, and he was persuaded that the BNP should participate in Parliament. Though Mosisili's Government enjoyed greater legitimacy than its predecessor, there remained many weaknesses in the democratic process. Parliament sat for brief periods only, and with few effective deputies, and no portfolio committee system in place, opposition parties found it difficult to play a constructive political role. Mosisili himself was criticized for appointing relatives to his Cabinet.

Mosisili identified three main challenges facing his new Government when it took office in June 2002. First, almost one-third of the adult population of Lesotho was estimated to be living with HIV/AIDS. Second, over 50% of the population was unemployed. Finally, there was a major food crisis, precipitated in part by the failure to keep sufficient reserves of grain. In response to a poor harvest and the high cost of importing maize, the Government declared a state of famine in April, hoping to attract foreign aid. By June the World Food Programme (WFP) and FAO estimated that some 500,000 people, almost one-quarter of the kingdom's population, needed emergency food aid. All three crises intensified in the following years.

In March 2004 Mosisili and the Roman Catholic Archbishop of Lesotho took public HIV tests to try to increase awareness of the disease and encourage others to be tested. On World AIDS Day in 2005 the King launched a 'Know Your Status' campaign. It offered confidential and voluntary HIV testing and counselling, and aimed to reach all households by the end of 2007. With an adult prevalence rate of 23.2% in a total population of 1.8m., an estimated 265,000 people were living with HIV, 50,000 of whom needed antiretroviral treatment. Although free testing and treatment was available at hospitals, by mid-2006 only 80,000 people had been tested, and fewer than 10,000 were receiving antiretrovirals. Nurses and doctors were in very short supply, and efforts to import medical staff were largely unsuccessful. By 2006 the country had about 100,000 AIDS orphans, and a growing number of street children were to be seen in urban areas. With most of those infected with HIV also having tuberculosis, there was fear of the spread of multidrug-resistant tuberculosis from the neighbouring South African province KwaZulu/Natal after it emerged there in 2006.

Following the death of the Minister of Public Works and Transport in late September 2004, the Prime Minister reshuffled the Cabinet in November. The most significant change was the demotion of Tom Thabane, who as Minister of Home Affairs had launched vigorous campaigns against crime and corruption, and had been seen as a potential successor to Mosisili. He became Minister of Communications, Science and Technology, while the home affairs portfolio was assumed by the Deputy Prime Minister, Lesao Lehohola. It appeared that the Prime Minister wished to indicate through the changes that he was in full control prior to the annual party congress early in 2005. When in October 2004 the LCD won over 93% of the vote in a by-election, with only one-quarter of the registered voters voting, some observers claimed that the proportional representation system encouraged complacency among the fragmented opposition. That month Mosisili announced that the first country-wide democratic local government elections would be held before the end of March 2005.

After further delays, the elections took place on 30 April 2005. More than 1,000 new councillors were elected to 129 councils, replacing previous councils comprising traditional leaders and government officials. In the local government elections the first-past-the-post voting system was used and one-third of the seats were reserved for women, in line with SADC guide-lines. Prior to the elections the main opposition parties had declared their dissatisfaction with the use of military helicopters to deliver and collect ballot papers from isolated rural areas, the quota of seats reserved for women and the Government's method of drawing constituency boundaries. In the event, the ruling LCD won over three-quarters of the seats at the elections, although the rate of voter participation, recorded by the IEC at less than 30%, was officially attributed to the fact that it was the first such election to be held. While LCD supporters could credit the Government with providing free primary education and improving social grants, the ongoing food crisis and the rising levels of unemployment were all too apparent.

In mid-October 2006 Thabane resigned from the Cabinet and the LCD, accusing the party of rampant corruption, and along with 17 other dissident LCD deputies formed a new party, the All Basotho Convention (ABC). This new party began attracting large crowds of supporters, particularly among younger people, at rallies in the urban areas. In response to this challenge the Government announced that the parliamentary elections would be brought forward by three months, giving the electoral authorities little time to register new voters and preventing the ABC from organizing effectively. Fewer than 1m. people were registered in time for the elections. Wary of its now fragile legislative majority, the LCD proposed an electoral alliance with the National Independent Party (NIP), and while the NIP leader, Anthony Manyeli, strongly opposed the idea, the LCD made an agreement with his deputy, Tsibiso Motikoe.

Controversy arose prior to the elections, when it emerged that cabinet ministers had awarded themselves an 84% pay rise, while Lesotho's main weekly newspaper revealed that ministers and senior civil servants were subsidizing their purchases of imported Mercedes Benz cars out of government funds and reselling them at vast profit. One of the smaller parties that contested the elections, the Popular Front for Democracy, campaigned on the platform of merging Lesotho into South Africa, but gained little support for such an idea. Mosisili based his election campaign on his party's achievements thus far, boasting that his Government had provided free primary education, controlled inflation and brought peace and stability to the country.

The legislative elections took place on 17 February 2007 with fewer than one-half of the registered voters casting their ballots. The LCD was re-elected for a third term, winning 61 of the 80 contested constituency seats. The ABC won in 17 constituencies, primarily in Maseru and the lowland towns, while the LCD dominated the rural constituencies and the southern districts. The final constituency seat was won by the Alliance of Congress Parties, with voting in one further constituency being postponed, owing to the death of a candidate. Of the 40 seats allocated by proportional representation, the NIP won 21, giving the LCD-NIP alliance control over 82 seats in the 120-member assembly. In the mean time Manyeli had obtained an order from the High Court overturning his ouster and the LCD-NIP alliance. Had he and 20 of his supporters been able to replace the elected NIP candidates in Parliament, the LCD majority would have fallen to only one seat; however, the Court of Appeal upheld the alliance. Following this judgment and with increasing discontent at the allocation of proportional representation seats, a coalition of opposition parties, including the ABC, called a national strike which commenced on 12 March and which paralysed much of the country. The Government reacted by emphasising that SADC and other observers had agreed that the election had been free and fair and that the courts had upheld the alliance. The opposition parties continued to claim that the IEC's allocation of proportional representation seats had been unfair and appealed unsuccessfully to SADC to intervene.

RELATIONS WITH SOUTH AFRICA

The Jonathan regime was initially supported by South Africa, but as Jonathan's support among the Basotho, most of whom disliked his pro-South African policies, declined, he became increasingly critical of the South African Government. In November 1974 he revived Lesotho's claim to 'conquered territory' in South Africa's Orange Free State (OFS—now the Free State Province). The vigorous anti-South African stance that Lesotho took at the UN and OAU in the first half of 1975 increased tensions between the two countries, as did Lesotho's refusal to recognize South Africa's proclamation of an 'independent' Transkei in October 1976. However, Jonathan met P. W. Botha in August 1980, the first meeting of the leaders of Lesotho and South Africa since 1967, and the two leaders accepted a preliminary agreement on the Lesotho Highlands Water Project (LHWP—see Economy), providing for Lesotho to supply water to South Africa.

During 1982–83 relations with South Africa deteriorated sharply, following allegations of South African armed raids against ANC sympathizers in Lesotho. In April 1983 Jonathan announced that Lesotho was effectively in a state of war with South Africa. South Africa responded by applying strict border controls on its main frontier with Lesotho, resulting in food shortages. The border controls were eased in June, after a meeting between both countries in which they agreed to curb cross-border guerrilla infiltration, but were reimposed in July. Further talks with South Africa followed, and, soon afterwards, Lesotho declared that it had received an ultimatum from the republic, either to expel (or repatriate) some 3,000 refugees or to face the economic consequences. In September two groups of refugees left the country.

Relations with South Africa remained at a low ebb for most of 1984. South Africa attempted to coerce Lesotho into signing a joint non-aggression pact, similar to the Nkomati Accord, agreed in March 1984 with Mozambique. Lesotho's continued refusal to sign such a pact led South Africa to impound consignments of armaments destined for Lesotho, and to threaten further economic sanctions in August, including the suspension of the LHWP. However, after talks between the two countries in the following month, and an announcement by Lesotho that the ANC had agreed to withdraw completely from its territory, relations improved slightly in October, when South Africa released the arms that it had impounded and resumed talks on the LHWP.

Following the military coup of January 1986, the new Government was much more amenable to South Africa's policy on regional security. It was agreed that neither country would allow its territory to be used for attacks on the other; South African refugees began to be flown out, and South Africa withdrew its special border checks. In March Lekhanya travelled to Pretoria to meet President Botha, and the two leaders reiterated the principles of mutual respect and non-interference. In October the treaty for the LHWP was signed by Lesotho and South Africa, to generate hydro-electric power for Lesotho and, more importantly, to increase the supply of the Vaal river, which provided water to South Africa's industrial heartland. Mohale and Katse dams, the first phase of the LHWP, were then built at a cost of US $4,000m. In April 1987 the two countries signed an agreement to establish a joint trade mission. Lesotho and South Africa concluded 'friendly and successful' negotiations on issues relating to their common border in March 1988. As South Africa moved towards democratic governance, it agreed to establish diplomatic relations with Lesotho, at ambassadorial level, in May 1992.

Following the election of the ANC-dominated Government in 1994, relations became even more cordial. On an official visit to Lesotho in July 1995, President Nelson Mandela stressed the importance of good relations between the two countries, and their mutual interest in the success of the LHWP. Friction continued, however, over the persistent problem of cross-border cattle thefts and the still unresolved claim by Lesotho to 'conquered territory' in the former OFS. Following the SADC intervention of September 1998 (see above), South African influence on the affairs of Lesotho increased further, as a large number of South African officials attempted to help bring stability to the kingdom. An intergovernmental liaison committee was established, headed by the South African Director-General of Foreign Affairs and Lesotho's Permanent Secretary for Foreign Affairs. In April 2001, during a state visit by President Thabo Mbeki of South Africa, it was agreed to replace this committee with a joint bi-national commission at ministerial level.

Relations between the Mbeki Government and the ruling LCD were further strengthened in May 2002, with the signing of the Joint Bilateral Commission of Co-operation Programme by the South African and Lesotho ministers of foreign affairs, which aimed to raise Lesotho from its current status as a 'least developed country' by 2007. The programme envisaged a number of joint projects, including the establishment of a Maloti-Drakensberg Trans-Frontier Conservation and Development area. Prevention of cross-border crime remained an issue for the joint commission, but after the South African legislative elections of April 2004, an agreement was reached between the two countries easing travel between them—thenceforth no visa was needed, only a passport. By far the largest joint project was the LHWP. Sections of Phase 1B become operational in 1998, with the transfer of water from a network of reservoirs at Mohale's Hoek, Katse and Mulela in the Lesotho highlands. The project was extended in 2003 to include the construction of another tunnel from the Katse reservoir. In mid-March 2004 South African President Thabo Mbeki and King Letsie III held a ceremony to mark the completion of Phase 1B of what had become the world's largest water transfer operation. The more than R200m. (US $30m.) that Lesotho received annually in royalties from South Africa for the LHWP represented the country's largest source of foreign exchange and amounted to 75% of its budget.

The kingdom gained international credit from the way it pursued the corruption that had taken place in the building of the LHWP. Masupha Sole, the former Chief Executive of the LHWP, was found guilty in May 2002 of accepting bribes totalling some US $2m. over a 10-year period, and sentenced to a 15-year jail term. The severity of his sentence seemed designed to show that Lesotho was determined to prosecute individuals and companies involved in corrupt practices. In September that year a Canadian construction company was found guilty of paying bribes to Sole in return for a contract to work on the LHWP and was fined $2.5m. Further convictions followed. Germany's largest engineering consultancy, Lahmeyer International, was fined $1.9m. in early 2004, and appeared in court again in November that year to face further charges of making payments to senior LHWP officials. After heavy rain in February 2006 caused a crack in the wall of the Mohale dam, fears were expressed that standards for constructing the dam might have been compromised. The Transformation Resource Centre (TRC), a local non-governmental organization representing the communities displaced by the LHWP, called for an audit of all the tenders allocated in the LHWP before Phase 2 was approved. The TRC pointed out that compensation had yet to be paid to some of those displaced by construction of the dams.

South Africa welcomed the successful conduct of the general election in Lesotho in May 2002 as a boost for the New Partnership for Africa's Development, a long-term strategy for socio-economic recovery in Africa. Some political observers considered that Lesotho's new mixed electoral system (see above), similar to those in Germany and New Zealand but the first of its kind in an African country, might serve as a model for other African countries, including South Africa itself, even despite the renewed political instability after the February 2007 election (see above).

Economy

LINDA VAN BUREN

Stability is the priority for the Lesotho economy, according to the IMF. Despite high global price rises for imported petroleum, Lesotho saw inflation decline to 3.6% in 2005/06. Increased inflows due to Lesotho's higher share of Southern African Customs Union (SACU) revenues, helped to offset contraction of 2.0% in 2006 in the nation's already small manufacturing sector, which is heavily reliant on textiles for export to the USA. The full effects of the ending of the World Trade Organization's (WTO) Multi-fibre Agreement on Textiles and Clothing (MFA) in January 2005 on the Lesotho economy became apparent in the 2005/06 fiscal year. During much of 2004, the textile sector had been aided by favourable access to the US market under the provisions of two US initiatives, the African Growth and Opportunity Act (AGOA—see below) and the MFA. Without the MFA, the People's Republic of China and India were no longer limited by export quotas. China, in particular, was able to flood the US market with inexpensive textile goods that cost 30%–40% less to produce than those made in Lesotho. Furthermore, the earnings from Lesotho's textile exports to the USA were denominated in US dollars, which meant that the loti (plural: maloti—M) equivalent of these proceeds was lower, as the loti is tied to the South African rand (R) at par, and during 2004 the dollar endured a period of weakness against the rand. At the same time, the costs of production, paid in maloti, remained static, making Lesotho's exports less competitive than they previously had been. Some textile producers found themselves in a cash-flow crisis. Overall, according to the African Development Bank (ADB), the economy grew by just 1.6% in 2006, down from the 5.0% registered in 2005.

As the kingdom of Lesotho is completely surrounded by South Africa geographically, its economic and political fortunes are inextricably linked to those of its much larger neighbour. Both prior to and since independence in 1966, Lesotho has relied heavily on remittances from Basotho citizens working in South Africa, primarily in the gold mines; by treaty, a share of their earnings has automatically accrued to the Lesotho Government. In the late 1990s the economic fragility of this arrangement became sharply apparent, following the fall in the world price of gold to below US $300 per troy oz in December 1997; it subsequently declined further, although it has since recovered to $660 per oz in June 2007. Gold-mining companies hastened to reduce their costs and their work-forces as the gold price continued to decline in the 1990s. Thousands of miners lost their jobs, and priority for employment was given to South African citizens. Between 1989 and April 2001 some 61,000 unemployed Basotho returned to the kingdom, where few jobs were available, while the Government lost the significant revenues generated by these workers' remittances. Whereas these remittances were equivalent to about two-thirds of gross national income (GNI) in 1990, they had fallen to one-third by 1997 and to less than one-quarter by 2004.

The proportion of revenue from remittances reflected both severe pressure on agricultural land and a continuing lack of opportunities in the domestic formal sector, despite government attempts to develop manufacturing and services. About 70% of the resident population live in rural areas, compared with 86% a decade earlier. The number of Basuto migrant workers fell from 126,000 in 1987 to just 52,000 in January 2007, and the share of revenue from remittances accruing to the Lesotho Government from this source continued to decline. A trend from 1999 onwards has been the increased wage employment of Basotho women, primarily in the textile sector. In 2004 37% of the national labour force of 736,000 were women. However, many of these women joined the ranks of the unemployed during the time when US textile import policy favoured China at the expense of less competitive African textile exporters (see below). In all, 46,424 workers were employed in the textile sector in March 2007.

The population of Lesotho was an estimated 1.9m. in February 2007. During 1995–2005 it was estimated that the population increased at an average annual rate of 0.6%. The pressure on productive land is reflected in the wide disparity of population density. In the lowlands of the west, where virtually all arable land and 57% of the population are concentrated, the population density reaches 160 inhabitants per sq km, compared with a national average density of an estimated 94 per sq km in March 2007.

AGRICULTURE

Although only about 11% of the total land area of 30,355 sq km can support arable cultivation, a further 66% is suitable for pasture. Subsistence agriculture is the primary occupation for the great majority of Basotho (an estimated 70% of the internal labour force in March 2007) and accounts for about one-fifth of export earnings. The sector's contribution to gross domestic product (GDP) fluctuates with changes in yields caused by soil erosion, the prevalence of poor agricultural practices and the impact of drought and other adverse weather conditions, but the overall trend is downward. Agriculture accounted for 47% of GDP in 1970 but for only 25% in 1980 and for just an estimated 16.6% in 2005. Apart from increases in the use of fertilizers and tractors since 1970, the sector remains largely unmodernized. Most crops continue to be produced using traditional methods, by peasant farmers who have little security of tenure under existing laws. Most of the sector's decline is accounted for by the crop sector; the livestock sector's downturn has been less pronounced.

Excessive rainfall in late 2001 meant that planting was delayed in some areas and had to be abandoned altogether in others. Frosts in early 2002 shortened the growing season, with devastating effects, and in April the Government proclaimed a state of famine. In December 2002 the IMF estimated Lesotho's requirement for emergency cereal food assistance at 36,000 metric tons, needed to feed 30% of the population. Drought continued into 2003 and 2004. In the year to March 2004 Lesotho's cereal import requirement was 245,000 tons, of which 223,000 tons was covered by commercial imports, leaving a shortfall of 22,000 tons which needed to be covered in the form of food aid. That month Prime Minister Pakalitha Mosisili declared a national food emergency, and 650,000 Basotho were reported to be in need of food aid. Early 2004 saw the return of good rains, but they arrived too late to save the 2004 maize crop, which, according to the UN World Food Programme (WFP), was 68% below average. WFP indicated that the number of people in Lesotho in need of food aid had diminished in 2005, and made favourable assessments of the January–February 2006 rains, even though flooding and the possible risk of frost would reduce the yield by as much as 3%. However, 2007 saw the onset of the worst drought in 30 years, leading WFP to issue a stark warning of food insecurity for the mountain kingdom. Food shortages were forecast to begin in the third quarter of 2007, and the crisis was predicted to peak in the first quarter of 2008, when an estimated 400,000 Basutho would require food aid. Lesotho's total cereal production for 2007 was projected at just 72,000 tons, compared with an annual cereal requirement of 360,000 tons. In comparison, maize output in 2005, a relatively good year, was 247,550 tons. WFP also observed that, while drought reduced yields dramatically, the situation was exacerbated by the fact that 20% less area had been planted with food crops in 2007. The Government has for some time been preaching the merits of developing irrigation potential and planting high-value cash crops; however, the decline in the area planted is attributed not to a change of use but to a lack of use. Fields have been left uncultivated owing to a lack of cash for inputs and for paying farm labourers.

Maize is the staple crop, accounting for 60% of the total planted area in most years, followed by sorghum with 30%. Despite the government's claim that the planting of high-value export cash crops is the answer to Lesotho's agricultural woes, summer wheat is so far the only crop to have been exported in significant quantities, with most exports sold to South Africa. Small quantities of barley and oats are also grown. Other crops include beans, peas, melons and vegetables. The considerable potential of the livestock sector has been little exploited, although cattle exports have traditionally accounted for about one-third of agricultural exports, with wool and mohair providing a further 30% each. In 2005 the national herd was estimated at 530,000 cattle, 850,000 sheep and 650,000 goats. An export-orientated abattoir in Maseru, along with associated fattening pens, is aimed at satisfying domestic demand and at exporting to regional and European Union (EU) markets. Milk production is also being promoted.

The Government has promoted the development of small-scale irrigated agricultural schemes and the general improvement of rural water supplies. The Central Bank of Lesotho (CBL) launched the Rural Savings and Credit Scheme in April 2005. Under the scheme, the CBL backs loans by commercial banks to qualifying groups for amounts ranging from M5,000 to M50,000. Two horticultural outgrower pilot schemes were allocated funding in the 2007/08 budget. A 21-hectare block farm undertook to supply fruit, first to the Lesotho market, then to South Africa, the Southern African Development Community (SADC) market and eventually to the United Kingdom.

MANUFACTURING AND MINING

Confronted by the chronic problems of agriculture and by the need to create jobs for a rapidly expanding resident population, Lesotho has promoted development in other sectors, with varying degrees of success. Its main assets are proximity and duty-free access to the South African market. An additional asset has been the abundance of labour. Lesotho also enjoys one of the lowest average rates of adult illiteracy in Africa (18.6% in 2003, according to UNESCO estimates), and immigrant Basotho workers command an excellent reputation in South Africa. Until the mid-1990s South Africa actively discouraged the development of competing industries in Lesotho. During 1995–2005 Lesotho's manufacturing GDP increased by an average of 2.9% per year.

The Lesotho National Development Corpn (LNDC), founded in 1967, and the Basotho Enterprises Development Corpn (BEDCO), which provides finance to local entrepreneurs, have been the main bodies stimulating manufacturing development, promoting a wide variety of small industries, including tyre retreading, tapestry weaving, shoemaking and the production of clothing (particularly denim jeans), food-processing and beverages, candles, ceramics, explosives, fertilizers, furniture, electric-lamp assembly, television sets, diamond-cutting and -polishing and jewellery. Inducements to foreign companies have included a low corporate income-tax rate (15% in 2004, reduced to zero in 2006, as against the general company tax rate of 25%, reduced from 35%) and free repatriation of profits; and there is no withholding tax on dividends paid by manufacturing companies to shareholders, domestic or foreign. In addition, there are generous allowances and tax 'holidays', duty-free access to EU and SACU markets, the provision of industrial infrastructure and the construction of industrial estates in Maseru and Maputsoe, with further estates planned elsewhere in the country. The 2007/08 budget pledged to boost manufacturing by providing a Minimum Infrastructure Platform (MIP) for production and exports, comprising the removal of 'investment impediments', the provision of skilled labour, and investment in infrastructure and support services. Tangible components of the MIP strategy included the commencement of the construction phase of the Metolong water-supply project, a US $30m. Chinese-backed expansion of Telecom Lesotho, the expansion of electricity supply, and improvements to cross-border immigration and customs facilities, to urban water and sewerage systems and to urban roads.

In recent years the growth engine of Lesotho's economy has been the textile industry, which not only has spearheaded most of the job creation in the mountain kingdom but also contributes the greatest proportion of the country's export revenue. The sector benefited from the provisions of AGOA, for which Lesotho was first declared eligible in April 2001, and especially from the MFA, until its demise at the beginning of 2005. Under AGOA terms, textiles and clothing made in Lesotho have preferential quota-free and duty-free access to the US market. By early 2002 exports of these products to the USA had increased by nearly 40%, at a time when the MFA limited access to the US market by large producers such as China and India, in order to favour African producers. However, while in theory AGOA allows unlimited access to the US market, in practice, without the protective quotas of the MFA restricting access from China and India, Lesotho's textile output is simply not competitive. In 2004 Lesotho was the largest textile exporter to the USA under the AGOA programme, and the textile industry was the largest employer in the country (at its peak, creating more than 55,000 jobs in around 60 enterprises). However, more than 80% of companies in the sector were foreign affiliates, including Indian and Chinese manufacturers, and were set up specifically to gain access to the US market through Lesotho's preferential status. When the quota barriers against India and especially China were removed in January 2005, investors from these countries pulled out of Lesotho; some of them formally withdrew, while others simply abandoned their factories, leaving the country during the Christmas break, not to return.

Lesotho's textile sector contracted rapidly, with an estimated 10,000 textile jobs lost between January 2005 and February 2006. The 2005/06 and 2006/07 Lesotho national budgets sought to revitalize the sector through such measures as tax incentives and refund allowances on value-added tax (VAT) introduced in 2003 (see below). However, even the reduction of the preferential company tax rate from 15% to zero could not address the fact that the cost of making textile products in Lesotho was much higher than the cost of making them in China. Lesotho must import its raw material, as it does not grow cotton or flax and makes no silk or synthetic fabrics. Lesotho does produce wool and mohair, and Lesotho Wool and Mohair seeks to add value locally by manufacturing garments before export. However, wool accounts for just 5% of the global fibre industry, and the primary textile demand in the USA is not for wool. Essentially, the wool sector in Lesotho is in need of reform if it is to reach its full potential. The Government owns 98 of the 132 shearing sheds. Private licensed wool traders cater mainly to small-scale wool farmers. To gain a licence, they are required to pay into the national dipping fund, maintain the 34 shearing sheds they use and comply with demanding proof-of-stock-ownership regulations. As a result, unlicensed wool traders abound, circumventing the system entirely and smuggling wool out of the country. Lesotho, Kenya and other African textile producers requested that the US Government amend AGOA to increase its effectiveness, and as a result, in November 2005 the USA entered into the Memorandum of Understanding (MoU) with China, which placed restrictions on 34 categories of textile and clothing imports into the USA from China for the period from 1 January 2006 to 31 December 2008. This MoU did provide some much-needed relief to the Lesotho textile-export sector, and the sector did experience a recovery, but only a modest one.

Diamond mining was limited to small artisanal diggings, exploited by primitive methods, until 1977, when a small modern mine began production at Lets'eng-la-Terae, developed and administered by De Beers Consolidated Mines of South Africa. Most of the diamonds were of industrial quality, although a few unusually large gemstones were also reportedly found. Recovery rates, at only 2.8 carats per 100 metric tons, proved to be the lowest of any mine in the De Beers group, and operations ceased in 1982. In the late 1990s, however, the Government explored the feasibility of reopening the mine, forming Lets'eng Diamonds (Pty) Ltd, a joint venture with a South African company, in which the Government held a 24% share. A mining licence was issued in 1999, and small-scale production began in 2003 with a work-force of some 291 people. Production is estimated at 65,000 carats per year over an 18-year period.

Co-operatives using labour-intensive methods still recover a small quantity of diamonds from the low-grade kimberlite pipes, and the mine is known for the large size of the stones. An estimated 15% of its diamond production is of diamonds of more than 10 carats, and some have been found of over 100 carats. In addition to the Lets'eng-la-Terae site, in 2001 the Lesotho Government awarded a 25-year licence for the exploration of a 390-ha site containing two kimberlite pipes to the Liqhobong Mining Development Company (LMDC), a subsidiary of European Diamonds PLC of the United Kingdom; the Lesotho Government owns a 25% share of LMDC. Production began in early 2006 with output forecast at 250,000 to 290,000 carats per year from the satellite pipe, with a stone value estimated at US $40 per carat. A positive pre-scoping study of the main pipe found that a 4m. ton per year operation over a life of 10 or more years would yield up to 700,000 carats each year. Garnets and other semi-precious gemstones have been discovered at Lets'eng-la-Terae, but the potential for commercial exploitation has not been confirmed. Lets'eng-la-Terae has a reputation for both quality and size, and it was reported that four large gem-quality diamonds found in January 2005 were valued at $6m.

TOURISM

Tourism has seen significant development since independence. In 2002 the Government identified the development of the tourism sector as a priority, aimed at reducing the deficit on the current account of the balance of payments: tourism receipts for 2004 were US $34m., declining to an estimated $30m. in 2005. Tourist arrivals recovered from 186,000 in 1999, reaching 329,301 in 2003, and totalling 303,578 in 2005. The Lesotho Tourist Board was closed in 2000 and was succeeded by the Lesotho Tourism Development Corpn. Eco-tourism is seen as a niche market offering potential for Lesotho, and there is even a winter-sports development. A consortium of four companies joined with the Lesotho Government to develop a ski resort on a 500-ha site in the Mahlasela Valley in the Lesotho Highlands, which boasts the highest annual snowfall in southern Africa; the resort opened 1 March 2007. It also offers summer-season recreational activities, including an 18-hole golf course. Lesotho has 3,064 tourist beds and an occupancy rate of 17.9%.

POWER AND WATER

Lesotho's major exploitable natural resource is running water. After much uncertainty over economic and technical feasibility, the Governments of Lesotho and South Africa signed a treaty in October 1986 to create the Lesotho Highlands Water Project (LHWP). The agreement for this huge and controversial scheme was reconfirmed in the mid-1990s, after the change of government in South Africa. Parastatal bodies in each country were assigned responsibility for the implementation of the project; in Lesotho this fell to the Lesotho Highlands Development Authority (LHDA). A massive undertaking for any country (particularly for one as small as Lesotho), with costs originally estimated at US $3,770m., the LHWP proposed the diversion of water from Lesotho's rivers for export to South Africa, with self-sufficiency in hydro-generated electricity as the major by-product. About 75% of the cost of the $2,500m. Phase 1A was raised in southern Africa (including some 57% from banks), with diversified external sources providing the balance, including $110m. from the World Bank in 1989. The commercial segment of the debt was to be met from royalty payments received on water sales to South Africa. Phase 1B, the total cost of which was projected to be $1,100m., was also to be funded largely from South African capital and money markets and from the water users themselves.

Construction of Phase 1A, which included Katse dam, was not completed until 1998 but was sufficiently advanced for water delivery to have already begun in the previous year. However, in mid-1997, as the first delivery of water to South Africa and the first M110m. annual royalty payment to Lesotho were about to be made, rumours became widespread that the troubled scheme was far too ambitious and was about to be downsized. The World Bank had observed that the scheme had been under poor management, and there were even suggestions that it might not fund the remaining four phases. After several months of deliberation, the World Bank finally announced in June 1998 that it would lend US $45m. in support of Phase 1B. This phase involves the construction of the 145-m-high Mohale dam on the Senqunyane river, a 15-m weir on the Matsoku river, and water tunnels from both these sites to the Katse dam, linking up with the facilities built there in Phase 1A to transfer the water to South Africa. Water spilled over Mohale dam for the first time in February 2006, signalling that its reservoir had reached capacity.

Phase 1A was beset by dismissals, strikes and opposition from environmental, trade-union and other groups. A further problem was that many of the 1,750 families who had been displaced by Phase 1A had received little or none of the compensation they had been promised. The World Bank acknowledged that the scheme's 'social targets' had not been achieved, suggesting a reluctance to proceed with the displacement of upwards of 8,000 more families to allow the construction of a further five dams. Nevertheless, the continuation of Phase 1B was to contribute more than 5% of Lesotho's GDP in 1998 and was said to have created the equivalent of 40,000 full-time jobs. The Lesotho Government had to meet M61.1m. in debt-service payments in that year in respect of the project. In November 1999 the Lesotho Government announced that a number of foreign companies (from countries including Canada, France, Italy, South Africa and the United Kingdom) had offered bribes in order to win LHWP construction contracts. The World Bank pledged financial support for an investigation into bribery and corruption in connection with the scheme, and in May 2002 the former Chief Executive of the LHDA, Masupha Sole, was found guilty of having accepted about US $2m. in bribes from the contractors; he was sentenced to 15 years' imprisonment. With the completion of Phase 1B, the whole of Phase 1 was officially inaugurated with a ceremony at Mohale in March 2004, attended by King Letsie III of Lesotho and President Thabo Mbeki of South Africa. A feasibility study to help South Africa and Lesotho decide whether to implement Phase 2 was due for completion in December 2007.

As of September 2006, less than one Basotho in 10 was connected to the national electricity grid. The World Bank estimated that the cost of bringing mains electricity to the remaining 90% of the population was about US $1,000 per household, in a country whose gross national income (GNI) per head was $950. In an attempt to improve the situation, the World Bank provided a grant of $129,530 towards a project to use innovative solar micro-generator technology to provide affordable electricity and hot water in rural areas.

The demand for water in Lesotho exceeds supply. In 2003 the Government sought to boost the water supply by raising the level of the Maqalika dam so that more water could be stored behind it. This, however, would flood a larger area of land, in what is known as the Maqalika Selective Development Area. The original occupants were compensated, but squatters moved into the area and also demanded compensation through the courts. As a result, while the Maqalika scheme remained in abeyance pending the outcome of legal action, the Government made alternative arrangements to boost the water supply. The result was the fast-tracking, in 2004, of the Lesotho Lowlands Water Supply Scheme, established in April 2002. This scheme centred on the Metolong dam on the Phuthiatsana river south-east of Maseru, which, it was envisaged, could be on stream by 2012. The dam would also supply water to Maseru and to the communities of Roma, Morija and Matsieng and would potentially provide year-round irrigation in the valley of the Phuthiatsana river. A mid-2005 roundtable discussion regarding the financing of the project included the World Bank, the Arab Bank for Economic Development in Africa, the ADB and the European Development Bank. However, concerns over the escalating cost meant that the project was on hold in 2006 as the estimated cost escalated from $154m., after the feasibility study in 2003, to $192m. in 2006. Nevertheless, the March 2007 budget speech established the commencement of construction of the Metolong scheme during the 2007/08 fiscal year as a priority.

TRANSPORT AND COMMUNICATIONS

Owing to its mountainous terrain, much of Lesotho was previously virtually inaccessible except by horse or light aircraft. However, a substantial network of nearly 6,000 km of tracks, passable by four-wheel-drive vehicles, has now been built up, largely by 'food for work' road builders in the mountain areas, and by 1996 some 887 km of tarred roads had been constructed. Lesotho's economic development has relied heavily on South African road and rail outlets, a dependence which was graphically illustrated in 1983–86, when the South African Government instituted roadblocks and checks, as a form of economic sanctions, which had debilitating effects on the Lesotho economy. A greater degree of independence in international communications was reached after the Maseru international airport became operational in 1986. In 2006 Lesotho had four airports with paved runways and 24 with unpaved runways. Lesotho has 2.6 km of railway line, which is operated as part of South Africa's railway system.

The Lesotho Telecommunications Corpn was privatized in 2000 as Telecom Lesotho, when a 70% majority shareholding was sold to the Mountain Kingdom Communications consortium, comprising the Electricity Supply Commission of South Africa (ESKOM) and Econet Wireless Group (EWG); the Lesotho Government retained the remaining 30%. Under the terms of the consortium agreement, ESKOM and EWG each gave the other a first-refusal, should either decide to sell their share. In February 2007, ESKOM agreed to sell its share to EWG for an undisclosed sum, giving EWG 100% of the consortium and a 70% interest in Telecom Lesotho.

EMPLOYMENT, WAGES AND MIGRANT LABOUR

Industrial diversity still eludes Lesotho in 2007, and the country's dependence on a single source for job creation continues. The exodus of Basotho workers to the South African mines was caused by land shortage, by the depressed state of agriculture, by the lack of employment opportunities inside the kingdom and by low wages in the formal sectors. Unemployment in Lesotho was officially estimated at 40% in 2001 and at 45% in 2002, and more than one-half of the population were thought to be either unemployed or underemployed in 2007. Only the finite labour demands of the construction phases of the LHWP have prevented it from reaching an even higher level, and this source of job creation was rapidly declining. The LHWP's contribution to Lesotho's GDP fell from 12.1% in 1999/2000, to 6.8% in 2001/02 and to 6.6% in 2002/03. Manufacturing, especially the textile sector, created the most new jobs. In his budget speech following the end of the MFA the Minister of Finance and Development Planning announced that retention of investors was a priority. Cash-flow relief was to be provided in two forms: first, through accelerated VAT refund procedures, allowing refunds to be claimed in advance; and secondly, by the resuscitation of the Duty Credit Certificate scheme, for which 28 firms had registered as of February 2005. The 2006/07 budget reduced the preferential company tax rate from 15% to zero in a bid to shore up the textile subsector, but without quota protection from cheaper competitors for the US market, the Lesotho textile subsector's outlook seemed bleak. In November 2005 the US-China MoU (see above) provided African textile exporters a return to a protected status. Lesotho's textile sector began to recover, but as of mid-2007 this recovery was still of moderate proportions.

The Lesotho economy's dependence on receipts from services and transfers, in the form of migrants' remittances (see above), has traditionally been reflected in the fact that the country's GNI is generally more than double its GDP. (In most other African states the net outflow of remittances means that GDP is greater than GNI.) Apart from their obvious role in financing the large trade gap, the remittances are central to the income of up to 60% of families and are also used by the Government to finance development. The Lesotho Deferred Payment Scheme was set up in 1974, at the instigation of the Lesotho Government, and, as it was compulsory, it was widely criticized by labour-relations groups. It also served as an impetus to encourage Basotho to conceal their employment from the authorities in the hope of retaining more of their wage. Under the scheme, the South African employer of a Lesotho national was required to deposit 60% of his wage into a special account at Lesotho Bank every month; this proportion was reduced to 30% in 1990. Although the employee was permitted to make two withdrawals during the contract period, of up to a total of 50% of the accumulated balance, the remainder was available to the Lesotho Government. The National Union of Miners for years called for the abolition of the scheme, and a commission established in South Africa to investigate migrant labour in that country recommended that the scheme be phased out over a period of five years. In any case, South Africa's policy (announced in late 1995) of granting permanent residency rights to migrant workers further weakened the scheme. It was decided that migrant workers who had voted in the 1994 South African election, and who were in South Africa before 30 June 1996, would be eligible for 'permanent status'. By March 1996 some 37,000 applications had been approved, although it was not specified how many of these were from Lesotho nationals.

The decline in the number of migrant workers from 1990 presented potentially serious implications for Lesotho's economy. In 1996 the Government announced incentives for South African manufacturing companies, particularly those in labour-intensive industries, relocating to Lesotho. However, once South Africa entered the post-sanctions era, interest in Lesotho as a gateway into that lucrative market rapidly dwindled.

SACU AND OTHER AGREEMENTS

Together with Botswana, Namibia, South Africa and Swaziland, Lesotho is a member of SACU, which dates formally from 1910, when the Union (now the Republic) of South Africa was established. The 1969 SACU agreement provided for payments to Botswana, Lesotho and Swaziland (the BLS countries, later BLNS after Namibia gained independence in 1990 and joined) to be made on the basis of their share of goods imported by SACU countries, multiplied by an 'enhancement' factor of 1.42 as a form of compensation for the BLS countries' loss of freedom to conduct a completely independent economic policy, and for the costs that this restriction involved in trade diversion and loss of investment. SACU revenue was paid two years in arrears and earned no interest, but even so, for Lesotho it formed up to 70% of government recurrent revenues in some years. Lesotho resisted attempts by South Africa to renegotiate the terms governing SACU. However, pressure on SACU grew after the Mandela Government came to power in South Africa. The longer-term role of SACU in southern Africa's changed environment was made unclear by the October 1999 Trade, Development and Co-operation Agreement between South Africa and the EU, which allowed South Africa's exports to enter the EU on the same preferential terms as Lesotho's. Under the terms of the agreement, South Africa was compelled to reciprocate the EU's trade preferences by 2005, thereby allowing improved access to the South African market for EU goods and reducing SACU customs revenues.

Although Lesotho's statutory share of these revenues is the smallest of any member state's, Lesotho is the most heavily dependent on this income as a source of government revenue. In 2001/02 Lesotho received 7.9% of the SACU revenue pool, and this sum accounted for 51% of the country's total revenue. Lesotho receives a share of the Union's customs receipts, which accounted for 52.2% of non-grant budgetary revenue in 2004/05 and for 23.3% of GDP. A new SACU agreement was signed in October 2002. Under this new agreement, the BLNS countries were to receive a share of the SACU revenue pool in inverse proportion to their level of economic development. From May 2004 Lesotho was to receive 13% of the total customs pool. Receipts from this source amounted to M2,306m. in 2005/06; the 2006/07 budget forecast SACU revenue of M3,087.8m. In the event this target was exceeded. To strengthen other revenue sources, the Government successfully launched a treasury bill auction in September 2001, which was followed by the establishment of the new Lesotho Revenue Authority (LRA) in January 2003. The LRA was immediately charged with the task of introducing VAT on 1 July 2003, levied initially at 14%. Imported goods valued at more than M150 are subject to the tax. Most imported goods come from South Africa, where VAT is also levied at 14%. VAT revenue amounted to M672.6m. in 2004/05 and contributed 16% of non-grant budgetary revenue.

SADC plans to establish a 14-nation free-trade area, which would include all the members of SACU including Lesotho, although criticism has been directed at just how free such trade will be. A commodity that illustrates the dilemma well is beef. The European beef protocol permitted qualifying African developing countries (the four small SACU members qualify as developing countries, but South Africa does not) to sell beef to the EU at a price well above the going market rate. The EU then sold some of the excess beef it acquired in this manner to South Africa at a much-reduced price, in an arrangement not bearing much resemblance to 'free trade'. Negotiations began in June 2003 towards a US-SACU free-trade agreement.

In December 1974 the Governments of Lesotho, Swaziland and South Africa concluded the Rand Monetary Agreement (RMA). Under this agreement, Lesotho received interest on rand currency circulating in Lesotho, at a rate of two-thirds of the current yield to redemption of the most recent issues of long-dated South African government stock offered the previous year. In January 1980, however, Lesotho followed Botswana and Swaziland in their moves towards monetary independence by introducing its own currency, the loti, replacing the South African rand at par. This measure was designed to give Lesotho greater control over factors influencing its development and over cash outflows by Basotho visiting South Africa. In July 1986 the RMA was superseded by a new agreement, establishing the Tripartite Monetary Area (TMA, now the Common Monetary Area—CMA), comprising Lesotho, Swaziland and South Africa (and later including Namibia, which became independent of South Africa in 1990), the terms of which allowed Lesotho to determine the exchange rate of its own currency.

During a brief period in 2000/01, the loti was allowed to float. Despite an IMF statement in March 2001 referring to Lesotho's monetary policy of a one-to-one exchange rate peg between the loti and the rand, by June the exchange rate had drifted to M1.29 = R1. The loti was again fixed at par with the rand, on the recommendation of the IMF, which observed that the fixed monetary regime with South Africa had served Lesotho well and kept inflation relatively low. When the rand—and therefore the loti—depreciated in 2002 by 18.5% against the US dollar, Lesotho's textile exports became significantly more competitive in the US market; however, the rand subsequently appreciated by the same amount, bringing the loti rate in June 2006 to M6.75 = US $1, compared to M8.02 = $1 three years earlier. Fluctuations of this type are an unavoidable side effect of the fixed loti-rand exchange rate. The result is that, based on loti-denominated costs, Lesotho's textile products became less competitive in the US market. By June 2007 the rate was M7.19 = $1.

EXTERNAL TRADE AND PAYMENTS

Until the 1980s Lesotho was largely able to ignore its balance of payments; owing to its membership of the South African-dominated RMA, situations that in other countries would have shown up as a balance-of-payments problem would, in Lesotho, have appeared as a general credit shortage. In fact, this happened only rarely until the 1980s, as Lesotho's chronic trade deficit, resulting from a limited export base and large requirements of food imports, was more than offset by current transfers, migrant remittances and surpluses on the capital account of the balance of payments. As a result of a sharp decline in export earnings from 1980, combined with a reduction in aid receipts and an increase in imports, deficits on the current account of the balance of payments were incurred. In 2005/06 Lesotho's total export revenue on a free-on-board (f.o.b.) basis was US $606.5m., of which income from the export of garments was $416.1m., or 68.6%. Export earnings covered less than one-half of the cost of total imports f.o.b., which were $1,267.7m. The resultant trade deficit of $661.2m. was larger than the 2004/05 shortfall of $586.5m. The current-account deficit in 2005/06 was projected at $366.6m. before, or $84.9m. after, official transfers. The overall balance of payments was also in deficit, at $8.2m, in 2004/05. Gross international reserves at 31 December 2005 stood at $474.4m., enough to cover 4.1 months' worth of imports. This was projected to lengthen to 4.8 months' worth, or $626.2m., by 31 December 2007.

GDP increased, in real terms, by an average of 2.5% per year in 1995–2005, according to the IMF. GDP grew by 3.2% in 2003/04 but fell back to 2.6% in 2004/05 and to just 1.7% in 2005/06, owing to the depressed state of the textile subsector. A recovery to 2.5% was estimated to have occurred in 2006/07, largely as a consequence of the US-China MoU (see above).

In March 2001 the IMF approved a three-year Poverty Reduction and Growth Facility (PRGF) loan worth US $32m., of which $5m. was made available immediately. After a review, the IMF allowed Lesotho to draw a further $4m. in March 2002; the Fund estimated that about 40% of Lesotho's population was living in poverty in 2002. A further tranche of the PRGF, of $5.2m., was disbursed in January 2004. The sixth and final tranche of the PRGF arrangement amounted to $5m. and was released in September.

South Africa is Lesotho's main trading partner. In 2005 SACU countries were the main source of Lesotho's imports, supplying 83.9% of the total. The USA was the principal market for exports in that year (61.5%, primarily finished textile manufactures), while SACU countries were the destination for 17.2% of Lesotho's exports in 2005, down from 22.9% in 2002. The principal imports in 2003 were maize, other foodstuffs, petroleum products, machinery, medicines and vehicles. The principal exports in that year were clothing and footwear.

PUBLIC FINANCE

In 1995 the Mokhehle Government unveiled its plans for a five-year privatization programme. A government Privatisation Unit was established to decide the future of 31 public enterprises, including: BEDCO (see above); the Drug Service Organization; the LEC; the Lesotho Water and Sewerage Authority; Radio Lesotho; the Lesotho Housing and Development Corpn; the Lesotho National Abattoir and Feedlot Complex; the Lesotho Handknits Project; Lesotho Airways; Lesotho Flour Mills; Lesotho Pharmaceutical Corpn; the Lesotho Telecommunications Corpn; and tourism installations, such as a car-hire firm and the Marakabei Lodge at Ha Marakabei, on the Senqunyane river. Critics of the privatization programme, led by trade-union organizations, argued that selling off these enterprises would only make Lesotho more dependent on South Africa. Despite maintaining that Lesotho Flour Mills in particular should not be privatized for reasons of food security it was sold to US buyers in 1998. In 2007 many of these enterprises were still to be privatized.

Lesotho's gross government debt was equivalent to 87.5% of GDP in 2002/03, but the proportion gradually declined, significantly, to an estimated 53% of GDP in February 2006; almost all of the decrease resulted from the appreciation of the loti against the US dollar. The trend since 2000 has been to avoid foreign financing in favour of domestic sources. Lesotho's total foreign debt stood at US $716m. at 31 December 2005, and the 2005/06 debt-service ratio as a percentage of exports was 6.8%. Lesotho is not eligible for the provisions of the IMF's enhanced Heavily Indebted Poor Countries (HIPC) initiative. The IMF commended Lesotho for using a substantial proportion of its SACU revenue windfall in 2006 to retire non-concessional debt, with the result that the net value of the country's public external debt was 'significantly below' the sustainability threshold. Lesotho pledged to continue to use its SACU revenue for this purpose in 2007, a year in which this revenue was expected to reach a record level. The 2007/08 budget called for total expenditure of M7,239.7m., of which M5,315.5m. was recurrent and M1,924.2m. was capital. Total government revenue was forecast at M6,393.1m., which, when donor assistance was factored in, resulted in a budgetary deficit of M346.7m.

CONCLUSION

Lesotho continues to face formidable economic challenges. The acute shortage of fertile land, the problem of soil erosion, and the backward state of agriculture make it highly unlikely that this sector can absorb the increase in population that is now resulting from returning migrants. Much will depend on the attitudes of the Government in South Africa and on the Lesotho Government's ability to find alternative sources of revenue to the Lesotho Deferred Payment Scheme (see above), SACU receipts and the LHWP. The Government has targeted manufacturing as the sector most likely to generate new jobs and has introduced policies to stimulate output, especially in the textiles subsector. Efforts here did bear fruit during the MFA era, with manufacturing GDP growing by 7.9% in 2001/02, by an estimated 10.0% in 2002/03 and by 5.0% in 2003/04. The Government in 2007 was still pinning its job-creation hopes on the textile industry, while acknowledging that agriculture will also need to absorb excess labour. The Government is aware that if the gains made in this sector are to be sustained, it will have to work with the private sector to make textile production in Lesotho more cost effective despite the necessity of importing the raw material from a qualifying source under the terms of the third-country fabric provisions of AGOA. The Government also recognized that agricultural problems were only partly the result of natural phenomena such as drought and climate change and that some of the difficulties had been man-made. The 2007 budget speech cited a World Bank ranking of 175 countries in the world in terms of ease of doing business in which Lesotho occupied 114th position. This compared unfavourably with Swaziland (76th), Botswana (48th), Namibia (42nd) and South Africa (28th).

There is concern that foreign inward investment has been concentrated on the textile industry—a narrow, low-technology base—and that there has been little development beyond this sector; the Government acknowledges that diversification is an important priority, but the challenge will be to translate these good intentions into actions. The fact also remains that 40,000 new jobs need to be created every year to keep up with demand, and Lesotho's work-force is, like those of its neighbours, seriously affected by the HIV/AIDS pandemic: an estimated 30% of all Basotho adults of working age were living with HIV/AIDS in March 2007, the fourth highest incidence of HIV in the world. In June 2006 Lesotho became the first nation in Africa—and the second nation in the world, after Brazil—to embark on an ambitious Universal Voluntary Counselling and Testing (UVCT) plan, which involves carrying out door-to-door on-the-spot HIV tests for the entire population. The US $12.5m. 'Know Your Status' campaign, implemented by the Lesotho Government and the World Health Organization, was to run until the end of 2007.

Statistical Survey

Sources (unless otherwise stated): Bureau of Statistics, POB 455, Maseru 100; tel. 22323852; fax 22310177; internet www.bos.gov.ls; Central Bank of Lesotho, POB 1184, Maseru 100; tel. 22314281; fax 22310051; e-mail cbl@centralbank.org.ls; internet www.centralbank.org.ls.

Area and Population

AREA, POPULATION AND DENSITY

Area (sq km)	30,355*
Population (*de jure* census results)	
14 April 1996	1,841,967
9 April 2006	
Males	911,848
Females	960,873
Total	1,872,721
Density (per sq km) at April 2006	61.7

* 11,720 sq miles.

DISTRICTS

(*de jure* population at 2006 census, preliminary figures)

District	Population
Berea	248,225
Butha-Buthe	109,139
Leribe	296,673
Mafeteng	192,795
Maseru	436,399
Mohale's Hoek	173,706
Mokhotlong	95,332
Qacha's Nek	71,756
Quthing	119,811
Thaba-Tseka	128,885
Total	**1,872,721**

PRINCIPAL TOWNS

(population at 1986 census)

Maseru (capital)	109,400	Hlotse	9,600
Maputsoa	20,000	Mohale's Hoek	8,500
Teyateyaneng	14,300	Quthing	6,000
Mafeteng	12,700		

Source: Stefan Helders, *World Gazetteer* (www.world-gazetteer.com).

Mid-2005 (including suburbs, UN estimate): Maseru 172,000 (Source: UN, *World Urbanization Prospects: The 2005 Revision*).

BIRTHS AND DEATHS

(annual averages, UN estimates)

	1990–95	1995–2000	2000–05
Birth rate (per 1,000)	35.0	34.0	31.3
Death rate (per 1,000)	10.3	11.9	17.7

Source: UN, *World Population Prospects: The 2006 Revision*.

Expectation of life (years at birth, WHO estimates): 41 (males 39; females 44) in 2004 (Source: WHO, *World Health Report*).

ECONOMICALLY ACTIVE POPULATION

('000 persons at mid-1990, ILO estimates)

	Males	Females	Total
Agriculture, etc.	130	150	280
Industry	183	13	196
Manufacturing	8	7	15
Services	134	91	225
Total	**447**	**254**	**701**

1997 (household survey, '000 persons aged 15 years and over): Total employed 353.1 (males 197.3, females 155.8); Unemployed 215.9 (males 80.2, females 135.7).

Source: ILO.

Mid-2005 (estimates in '000): Agriculture, etc. 684; Total 725 (Source: FAO).

Health and Welfare

KEY INDICATORS

Total fertility rate (children per woman, 2005)	3.4
Under-5 mortality rate (per 1,000 live births, 2005)	132
HIV/AIDS (% of persons aged 15–49, 2005)	23.2
Physicians (per 1,000 head, 2003)	0.05
Health expenditure (2004): US $ per head (PPP)	138.5
Health expenditure (2004): % of GDP	6.5
Health expenditure (2004): public (% of total)	84.2
Access to water (% of persons, 2004)	79
Access to sanitation (% of persons, 2004)	37
Human Development Index (2004): ranking	149
Human Development Index (2004): value	0.494

For sources and definitions, see explanatory note on p. vi.

Agriculture

PRINCIPAL CROPS
('000 metric tons)

	2003	2004	2005
Wheat	13.1	11.6	2.1
Maize	84.8	81.0	76.1
Sorghum	12.0	10.3	15.8
Potatoes*	90	90	90
Dry beans	3.7	4.8	1.0
Dry peas	1.3	1.5	0.9
Vegetables*	18	18	18
Fruit*	13	13	13

* FAO estimates.

Source: FAO.

LIVESTOCK
('000 head, year ending September)

	2003	2004*	2005*
Cattle	644.6	650	650
Sheep	1,030.8	1,000	1,000
Goats	789.6	790	790
Pigs	79.0	65	65
Horses	37.7	100	100
Asses, mules or hinnies	76.3	155.2	155.2
Poultry	1,800*	1,800	1,800

* FAO estimate(s).

Source: FAO.

LIVESTOCK PRODUCTS
('000 metric tons, FAO estimates)

	2002	2003	2004
Cows' milk	23.8	23.8	23.8
Pig meat	2.8	2.8	2.8
Chicken meat	1.8	1.8	1.8
Game meat	3.9	3.9	3.9
Other meat	16.8	15.9	16.1
Hen eggs	30.2	30.2	30.2
Wool (greasy)	2.6	2.6	2.6

2005: Production assumed to be unchanged from 2004 (FAO estimates).

Source: FAO.

Forestry

ROUNDWOOD REMOVALS
('000 cubic metres, excluding bark, FAO estimates)

	2003	2004	2005
Total (all fuel wood)	2,040.4	2,046.6	2,052.8

Source: FAO.

Fishing

(metric tons, live weight)

	2003	2004	2005
Capture	42	45	45
Common carp	12	15	15
North African catfish	5	5	5
Other freshwater fishes	25	25	25
Aquaculture	4	2	2
Common carp	4	2	1
Total catch	46	47	46

Source: FAO.

Mining

(cubic metres, unless otherwise indicated)

	2003	2004	2005*
Fire clay	14,470	15,000*	15,000
Diamond (carats)	2,099	14,000	37,000
Gravel and crushed rock	389,695	300,000*	300,000

* Estimate(s).

Source: US Geological Survey.

Finance

CURRENCY AND EXCHANGE RATES

Monetary Units
100 lisente (singular: sente) = 1 loti (plural: maloti).

Sterling, Dollar and Euro Equivalents (31 May 2007)
£1 sterling = 14.207 maloti;
US $1 = 7.185 maloti;
€1 = 9.666 maloti;
100 maloti = £7.04 = $13.92 = €10.35.

Average Exchange Rate (maloti per US $)
2004 6.4597
2005 6.3593
2006 6.7716

Note: The loti is fixed at par with the South African rand.

BUDGET
(million maloti, year ending 31 March)

Revenue*	2003/04	2004/05	2005/06
Tax revenue	2,887.5	3,376.3	4,000.3
Taxes on net income and profits	852.5	729.2	924.6
Company tax	236.5	219.1	192.0
Individual income tax	493.8	452.4	615.0
Other income and profit taxes	122.2	57.7	117.6
Taxes on goods and services	602.9	579.6	735.2
Sales tax	519.3	541.7	655.7
Petrol levy	80.6	35.8	77.0
Customs duties	1,421.6	2,012.4	2,305.9
Other taxes	10.5	57.2	34.6
Non-tax revenue	551.8	479.7	489.5
Property and other income	431.3	368.6	382.3
Water royalties	193.1	194.5	236.0
Adjustment for underrecording	—	470.1	—
Total	3,439.3	4,326.1	4,489.8

Expenditure and net lending	2003/04	2004/05	2005/06
Wages and salaries	1,123.2	1,176.9	1,275.8
Goods and services	958.4	985.5	1,103.8
Subsidies and transfers	631.3	779.1	976.0
Pensions	118.9	194.5	296.1
Subventions and transfers	512.4	584.6	679.9
Interest payments	216.4	156.2	120.6
Capital expenditure (incl. lending minus repayments)	625.4	664.6	741.1
Total	3,554.7	3,762.3	4,217.3

* Excluding grants received (million maloti): 177.8 in 2003/04; 224.3 in 2004/05; 95.3 in 2005/06.

Source: IMF, *Kingdom of Lesotho: Selected Issues and Statistical Appendix* (November 2006).

INTERNATIONAL RESERVES
(US $ million at 31 December)

	2004	2005	2006
IMF special drawing rights	0.62	0.44	0.22
Reserve position in IMF	5.53	5.15	5.45
Foreign exchange	495.35	513.42	652.74
Total	501.50	519.01	658.41

Source: IMF, *International Financial Statistics*.

MONEY SUPPLY
(million maloti at 31 December)

	2004	2005	2006
Currency outside banks	204.54	212.78	309.42
Demand deposits at commercial banks	1,197.50	1,427.86	2,187.20
Total money (incl. others)	1,589.42	1,829.48	2,688.81

Source: IMF, *International Financial Statistics*.

COST OF LIVING
(Consumer Price Index; base: April 1997 = 100)

	2004	2005	2006
Food (incl. non-alcoholic beverages)	179.8	184.3	195.2
Alcoholic beverages and tobacco	188.2	198.0	210.2
Housing, water, electricity, and other fuels	162.0	172.8	188.0
Clothing (incl. footwear)	148.0	152.5	158.1
All items (incl. others)	167.9	173.7	182.5

Source: IMF, *Kingdom of Lesotho: Selected Issues and Statistical Appendix* (November 2006).

NATIONAL ACCOUNTS
(million maloti at current prices)

National Income and Product
(fiscal year ending 31 march)

	2003/04	2004/05*	2005/06*
GDP in market prices	8,248.5	8,930.4	9,405.0
Net factor income from abroad	1,932.8	2,031.1	2,043.9
Gross national product (GNP)	10,181.3	10,961.5	11,448.9
Net current transfers from abroad	1,290.8	1,741.3	2,014.9
Gross national disposable income	11,472.2	12,702.8	13,463.8

* Estimates.

Expenditure on the Gross Domestic Product

	2003	2004	2005
Government final consumption expenditure	1,238.2	1,250.5	1,400.1
Private final consumption expenditure	7,801.0	8,260.7	9,271.0
Increase in stocks	49.9	8.7	—
Gross fixed capital formation	3,558.0	3,620.1	3,743.2
Statistical discrepancy	—	—	–1,495.6
Total domestic expenditure	12,647.1	13,140.0	12,918.7
Exports of goods and services	3,932.7	4,928.1	4,419.6
Less Imports of goods and services	8,526.1	9,235.3	8,115.6
GDP in purchasers' values	8,053.8	8,833.0	9,222.7
GDP at constant 1995 prices	4,291.4	4,426.5	4,479.9

Source: IMF, *International Financial Statistics*.

Gross Domestic Product by Economic Activity

	2003	2004	2005*
Agriculture	1,304.5	1,368.8	1,439.1
Mining and quarrying	13.0	183.4	208.6
Manufacturing and handicraft	1,432.0	1,623.7	1,539.6
Electricity and water	350.3	375.6	402.0
Construction	1,214.5	1,261.6	1,330.6
Wholesale and retail trade	770.8	861.7	913.3
Restaurants and hotels	146.7	160.4	177.6
Transport and storage	164.7	174.6	186.7
Post and telecommunications	170.0	169.1	192.7
Financial intermediation and insurance	383.4	401.9	457.1
Real estate and business services	124.6	136.5	144.0
Ownership of dwellings	262.1	267.3	281.9
Public administration	511.8	532.3	565.8
Education	548.3	559.0	595.3
Health and social work	117.2	123.4	130.5
Other services	83.8	89.2	93.5
Sub-total	7,597.7	8,288.5	8,658.3
Less Imputed bank service charge	322.3	293.4	321.0
GDP at factor cost	7,275.5	7,995.1	8,337.3
Indirect taxes, less subsidies	778.2	837.9	885.4
GDP at market prices	8,053.7	8,833.0	9,222.7

* Estimates.

Source: IMF, *Kingdom of Lesotho: Selected Issues and Statistical Appendix* (November 2006).

BALANCE OF PAYMENTS
(million maloti)

	2003/04	2004/05	2005/06*
Exports of goods f.o.b.	3,610.4	4,305.6	4,171.0
Imports of goods f.o.b.	–7,440.0	–8,152.7	–8,157.2
Trade balance	–3,829.6	–3,847.2	–3,986.2
Services (net)	–281.3	–195.6	–245.1
Balance on goods and services	–4,110.9	–4,042.7	–4,231.3
Income (net)	1,932.8	2,031.1	2,043.9
Balance on goods, services and income	–2,178.1	–2,011.6	–2,187.4
Current transfers (net)	1,290.8	1,741.3	2,014.9
Current balance	–887.2	–270.4	–172.6
Capital account (net)	118.5	154.7	71.5
Financial account (net)	313.2	–148.6	57.9
Net errors and omissions	134.0	194.8	143.7
Overall balance	–321.5	–69.5	100.5

* Estimates.

Source: IMF, *Kingdom of Lesotho: Selected Issues and Statistical Appendix* (November 2006).

External Trade

PRINCIPAL COMMODITIES
(distribution by SITC, million maloti)

Imports c.i.f.*	1999	2000	2001
Food and live animals	787.8	928.7	768.7
Beverages and tobacco	33.7	115.6	386.6
Crude materials, inedible except fuels	177.7	228.6	167.7
Mineral fuels and lubricants	323.7	840.8	317.0
Animal and vegetable oils, fats and waxes	54.2	104.2	67.0
Chemicals and related products	309.4	254.6	525.1
Manufactured goods	715.6	558.7	1,026.5
Machinery and transport equipment	674.6	426.4	620.0
Miscellaneous manufactured articles	458.5	486.7	797.3
Total (incl. others)	3,888.5	4,236.2	5,119.1

* Unrevised figures.

Exports	2002	2003	2004
Foodstuffs, etc.	197.6	194.0	180.8
Cereals	75.7	71.2	55.2
Beverages and tobacco	94.9	96.5	98.5
Live animals	20.4	20.4	16.8
Livestock materials	64.6	90.3	3.3
Wool	56.1	80.6	1.8
Manufactures	3,439.8	3,238.1	4,433.3
Chemicals and petroleum	45.5	49.3	21.0
Telecommunication equipment	291.7	289.7	153.6
Machinery	50.0	53.9	55.1
Furniture and parts	37.4	33.1	2.9
Clothing, etc.	2,745.2	2,555.6	3,462.0
Footwear	135.1	130.5	128.7
Other manufactures	39.8	35.2	566.8
Total (incl. others)	3,739.9	3,557.4	4,652.2

Source: IMF, *Kingdom of Lesotho: Selected Issues and Statistical Appendix* (December 2005).

Exports (million maloti, 2005): Foodstuffs 227.3 (Cereals 65.0; Beverages and tobacco 134.6); Diamonds 637.7; Manufactures 3,214.1 (Telecommunication equipment 143.6; Machinery 158.9; Clothing, etc. 2,704.8; Footwear 95.8); Total 4,134.6. Source: IMF, *Kingdom of Lesotho: Selected Issues and Statistical Appendix* (November 2006).

PRINCIPAL TRADING PARTNERS
(million maloti)

Imports c.i.f.*	2003	2004	2005
Africa	7,242.7	6,628.7	6,641.8
SACU†	7,234.1	6,584.0	6,603.3
Asia	1,141.7	2,183.5	1,133.1
China, People's Repub.	241.8	457.4	205.8
Hong Kong	401.3	623.9	332.8
Taiwan	367.6	670.4	386.3
European Union	8.9	70.3	53.0
North America	15.1	97.5	32.8
USA	14.5	97.5	27.4
Total (incl. others)	8,411.6	9,036.5	7,870.1

Exports f.o.b.	2003	2004	2005
Africa	695.6	657.5	812.6
SACU†	689.7	622.2	713.6
European Union	3.7	692.0	710.4
North America	2,849.1	3,168.6	2,597.8
Canada	19.7	48.3	56.1
USA	2,829.4	3,120.3	2,541.7
Total (incl. others)	3,557.4	4,533.3	4,134.6

* Valuation exclusive of import duties. Figures also exclude donated food.
† Southern African Customs Union, of which Lesotho is a member; also including Botswana, Namibia, South Africa and Swaziland.

Source: IMF, *Kingdom of Lesotho: Selected Issues and Statistical Appendix* (November 2006).

Transport

ROAD TRAFFIC
(motor vehicles in use at 31 December, estimates)

	1994	1995	1996
Passenger cars	9,900	11,160	12,610
Lorries and vans	20,790	22,310	25,000

Source: International Road Federation, *World Road Statistics*.

CIVIL AVIATION
(traffic on scheduled services)

	1997	1998	1999
Kilometres flown (million)	0	1	0
Passengers carried ('000)	10	28	1
Passenger-km (million)	3	9	0
Total ton-km (million)	0	1	0

Source: UN, *Statistical Yearbook*.

Tourism

FOREIGN TOURIST ARRIVALS BY COUNTRY OF RESIDENCE

	2003	2004	2005
Botswana	3,970	1,973	2,129
Germany	2,878	1,687	1,775
South Africa	286,349	282,070	280,399
Swaziland	2,380	1,408	1,481
United Kingdom	2,005	1,970	1,950
USA	2,196	955	1,054
Zimbabwe	3,590	1,963	2,088
Total (incl. others)	329,301	303,530	303,578

Tourism receipts (US $ million, excl. passenger transport): 28 in 2003; 34 in 2004; n.a. in 2005.

Source: World Tourism Organization.

Communications Media

	2003	2004	2005
Telephones ('000 main lines in use)	35.1	37.2	48.0
Mobile cellular telephones ('000 subscribers)	101.5	159.0	245.1
Internet users ('000)	30	43	n.a.

Facsimile machines (number in use, year ending 31 March 1996): 569.

Radio receivers ('000 in use): 104 in 1997.

Television receivers ('000 in use): 70 in 2001.

Daily newspapers (1998): 2 (estimated average circulation 15,750 copies).

Non-daily newspapers (1996): 7 (average circulation 74,000 copies).

Sources: UNESCO Institute for Statistics; International Telecommunication Union.

Education

(2002)

	Institutions	Teachers	Students		
			Males	Females	Total
Primary	1,333	8,908	209,024	209,644	418,668
Secondary:					
general	224	3,384	35,467	45,663	81,130
technical and vocational	8	172	1,040	818	1,859
teacher training	1	108	1,206	533	1,739
University	1	n.a.	1,567	1,699	3,266

Adult literacy rate (UNESCO estimates): 81.4% (males 73.7%; females 90.3%) in 2004 (Source: UN Development Programme, *Human Development Report*).

Directory

The Constitution

The Constitution of the Kingdom of Lesotho, which took effect at independence in October 1966, was suspended in January 1970. A new Constitution was promulgated following the March 1993 general election. Its main provisions, with subsequent amendments, are summarized below:

Lesotho is an hereditary monarchy. The King, who is Head of State, has no executive or legislative powers. Executive authority is vested in the Cabinet, which is headed by the Prime Minister, while legislative power is exercised by the 120-member National Assembly, which comprises 80 members elected on a single-member constituency basis and 40 selected by a system of proportional representation. The National Assembly is elected, at intervals of no more than five years, by universal adult suffrage in the context of a multi-party political system. There is also a Senate, comprising 22 traditional chiefs and 11 nominated members. The Prime Minister is the official head of the armed forces.

The Government

HEAD OF STATE

King: HM King LETSIE III (acceded to the throne 7 February 1996).

CABINET
(August 2007)

Prime Minister and Minister of Defence and National Security: BETHUEL PAKALITHA MOSISILI.

Deputy Prime Minister and Minister of Home Affairs and Public Safety and Parliamentary Affairs: ARCHIBALD LESAO LEHOHLA.

Minister of Education and Training: Dr 'MAMPHONO KHAKETLA.

Minister of Local Government and Chieftainship: Dr PONTŠO SUZAN 'MATUMELO SEKATLE.

Minister of Tourism, Environment and Culture: LEBOHANG NTŠINYI.

Minister of Natural Resources (Water, Lesotho Water Highlands Project, Energy, Mining and Technology): MONYANE MOLELEKI.

Minister of Foreign Affairs and International Relations: MOHLABI TSEKOA.

Minister of Trade, Industry, Co-operatives and Marketing: POPANE LEBESA.

Minister of Agriculture and Food Security: Dr LESOLE MOKOMA.

Minister of Forestry and Land Reclamation: LINCOLN RALECHATE 'MOKOSE.

Minister of Communications, Science and Technology: MOTHEJOA METSING.

Minister of Public Works and Transport: TS'ELE CHAKELA.

Minister of Gender, Youth, Sports and Recreation: 'MATHABISO LEPONO.

Minister of Finance and Development Planning: Dr TIMOTHY THAHANE.

Minister of Health and Social Welfare: Dr MPHU RAMATLAPENG.

Minister of Employment and Labour: REFILOE MASAMENE.

Minister of Justice, Human Rights and Correctional Services, Law and Constitutional Affairs: MPEO MAHASE-MOILOA.

Minister of Public Service: SEMANO SEKATLE.

Minister in the Prime Minister's Office: MOTLOHELOA PHHOKO.

There were also six assistant ministers.

MINISTRIES

Office of the Prime Minister: POB 527, Maseru 100; tel. 22311000; fax 22310578; internet www.lesotho.gov.ls.

Ministry of Agriculture and Food Security: POB 24, Maseru 100; tel. 22316407; fax 22310906.

Ministry of Communications, Science and Technology: POB 36, Maseru 100; tel. 22323561; fax 22310264.

Ministry of Defence and National Security: POB 527, Maseru 100; tel. 22316570; fax 22310518.

Ministry of Education and Training: POB 47, Maseru 100; tel. 22323956; fax 22310206; e-mail kokomen@education.gov.ls.

Ministry of Employment and Labour: Private Bag A116, Maseru 100; tel. 22322602; fax 22310374.

Ministry of Finance and Development Planning: POB 395, Maseru 100; tel. 22311101; fax 22310964.

Ministry of Foreign Affairs and International Relations: POB 1387, Maseru 100; tel. 22311150; fax 22310642.

Ministry of Forestry and Land Reclamation: POB 24, Maseru 100; tel. 22316407; fax 22310146.

Ministry of Gender, Youth, Sports and Recreation: POB 10993, Maseru 100; tel. 22311006; fax 22310506.

Ministry of Health and Social Welfare: POB 514, Maseru 100; tel. 22314404; fax 22310467.

Ministry of Home Affairs and Public Safety: POB 174, Maseru 100; tel. 22323771; fax 22310319.

Ministry of Law and Constitutional Affairs: POB 402, Maseru 100; tel. 22322683; fax 22311092; e-mail dps@justice.gov.ls.

Ministry of Local Government and Chieftainship: POB 174, Maseru 100; tel. 22323771; fax 22310587.

Ministry of Natural Resources: POB 772, Maseru 100; tel. 22323163; fax 22310520.

Ministry of Public Service: POB 527, Maseru 100; tel. 22311000; internet www.publicservice.gov.ls.

Ministry of Public Works and Transport: POB 20, Maseru 100; tel. 22311362; fax 22310125.

Ministry of Tourism, Environment and Culture: POB 52, Maseru 100; tel. 22313034; fax 22310194.

Ministry of Trade, Industry, Co-operatives and Marketing: POB 747, Maseru 100; tel. 22312938; fax 22310644.

Legislature

PARLIAMENT

National Assembly

POB 190, Maseru; tel. 22323035.

Speaker: NTLHOI MOTSAMAI.

General Election, 17 February 2007

Party	Constituency seats	Compensatory seats*	Total seats
Lesotho Congress for Democracy	61	—	61
National Independent Party	—	21	21
All Basotho Convention	17	—	17
Lesotho Workers' Party	—	10	10
Basotho National Party	—	3	3
Alliance of Congress Parties	1	1	2
Basotho Batho Democratic Party	—	1	1
Basotho Congress Party	—	1	1
Basotho Democratic National Party	—	1	1
Marematlou Freedom Party	—	1	1
Popular Front for Democracy	—	1	1
Total	79†	40	119†

* Allocated by proportional representation.

† Voting in one constituency was postponed, owing to the death of a candidate.

Senate

POB 190, Maseru; tel. 22315338.

Speaker: Chief SEMPE LEJAHA.

The Senate is an advisory chamber, comprising 22 traditional chiefs and 11 members appointed by the monarch.

Election Commission

Independent Electoral Commission (IEC): POB 12698, Kingsway 100, Maseru; tel. 314991; fax 310398; internet www.iec.org.ls; f. 1997 as successor to the Constituency Delimitation Commission; Chair. LESHELE THOAHLANE.

Political Organizations

All Basotho Convention (ABC): Maseru; f. 2006 by fmr mems of the Lesotho Congress for Democracy; Pres. MOTSOAHAE TOM THABANE.

Basotho Batho Democratic Party: f. 2006.

Basotho Congress Party (BCP): POB 111, Maseru 100; tel. 8737076; f. 1952; Leader NTSUKUNYANE MPHANYA.

Basotho Democratic Alliance (BDA): Maseru; f. 1984; Pres. S. C. NKOJANE.

Basotho Democratic National Party: internet bdnp.blogspot.com; f. 2006; Leader THABANG NYEOE.

Basotho National Party (BNP): POB 124, Maseru 100; f. 1958; Leader Maj.-Gen. JUSTIN METSING LEKHANYA; Sec.-Gen. RANTHOMENG MATETE; 280,000 mems.

Basutoland African Congress (BAC): Maseru; f. 2002 following split in the BCP; Leader Dr KHAUHELO RADITAPOLE; Sec.-Gen. MAHOLELA MANDORO.

Khokanyana-Phiri Democratic Alliance: Maseru; f. 1999; alliance of opposition parties comprising:

Christian Democratic Party: Maseru.

Communist Party of Lesotho (CPL): Maseru; f. 1962; banned 1970–91; supported mainly by migrant workers employed in South Africa; Sec.-Gen. MOKHAFISI KENA.

Kopanang Basotho Party (KBP): Maseru; f. 1992; campaigns for women's rights; Leader LIMAKATSO NTAKATSANE.

National Independent Party (NIP): Maseru; f. 1984; Pres. ANTHONY CLOVIS MANYELI.

National Progressive Party (NPP): Maseru; f. 1995 following split in the BNP; Leader Chief PEETE NKOEBE PEETE.

Popular Front for Democracy (PFD): Maseru; f. 1991; left-wing; Leader LEKHETHO RAKUOANE.

Social Democratic Party: Maseru; Leader MASITISE SELESO.

Lesotho Congress for Democracy (LCD): Maseru; f. 1997 as a result of divisions within the BCP; Leader BETHUEL PAKALITHA MOSISILI; Chair. MOEKETSI MOLETSANE; Sec.-Gen. MPHO MALIE; 200,000 mems.

Lesotho Labour Party (LLP): Maseru; f. 1991; Leader MUTHUTHULEZI TYHALI.

Lesotho People's Congress (LPC): f. 2001 following split in the LCD; Leader KELEBONE ALBERT MAOPE; Sec.-Gen. SHAKHANE MOKHEHLE.

Lesotho Workers' Party (LWP): f. 2001; Leader MACAEFA BILLY.

Marematlou Freedom Party (MFP): POB 0443, Maseru 105; tel. 315804; f. 1962 following merger between the Marema Tlou Party and Basutoland Freedom Party; Leader (vacant); Dep. Leader THABO LEANYA; 300,000 mems.

Sefate Democratic Union (SDU): Maseru; Leader BOFIHLA NKUEBE.

United Democratic Party (UDP): POB 776, Maseru 100; f. 1967; Chair. BEN L. SHEA; Leader CHARLES DABENDE MOFELI; Sec.-Gen. MOLOMO NKUEBE; 26,000 mems.

United Party (UP): Maseru; Pres. MAKARA SEKAUTU.

Diplomatic Representation

EMBASSIES AND HIGH COMMISSIONS IN LESOTHO

China, People's Republic: POB 380, Maseru 100; tel. 22316521; fax 22310489; e-mail chinaemb_ls@mfa.gov.cn; internet ls.china-embassy.org; Ambassador QIU BOHUA.

Korea, Republic: Maseru; Ambassador KIM EUN SOO.

South Africa: Lesotho Bank Tower, 10th Floor, Kingsway, Private Bag A266, Maseru 100; tel. 22325758; fax 22310128; e-mail sahcmas@leo.co.ls; High Commissioner WILLIAM LESLIE.

USA: 254 Kingsway, POB 333, Maseru 100; tel. 22312666; fax 22310116; e-mail infomaseru@state.gov; internet maseru.usembassy.gov; Ambassador ROBERT NOLAN.

Judicial System

HIGH COURT

The High Court is a superior court of record, and in addition to any other jurisdiction conferred by statute it is vested with unlimited original jurisdiction to determine any civil or criminal matter. It also has appellate jurisdiction to hear appeals and reviews from the subordinate courts. Appeals may be made to the Court of Appeal.

POB 90, Maseru; tel. 22312188; internet www.justice.gov.ls/judiciary/high_court.html.

Chief Justice: MAHAPELA LEHOHLA.

Judges: T. NOMNGCONGO, W. C. M. MAQUTU, B. K. MOLAI, T. E. MONAPATHI, K. MAFOSO-GUNI, G. MOFOLO, S. PEETE, M. HLAJOANE, N. MAJARA.

COURT OF APPEAL

POB 90, Maseru; tel. 22312188; internet www.justice.gov.ls/judiciary/appeal.html.

President: J. H. STEYN.

Judges: M. M. RAMODIBEDI, M. E. KUMBLEBEN, H. GROSSKOPF, C. PLEWMAN, J. J. GAUNTLETT, L. S. MELUNSKY (acting).

SUBORDINATE COURTS

Each of the 10 districts possesses subordinate courts, presided over by magistrates.

Chief Magistrate: MOLEFI MAKARA.

JUDICIAL COMMISSIONERS' COURTS

These courts hear civil and criminal appeals from central and local courts. Further appeal may be made to the High Court and finally to the Court of Appeal.

CENTRAL AND LOCAL COURTS

There are 71 such courts, of which 58 are local courts and 13 are central courts which also serve as courts of appeal from the local courts. They have limited civil and criminal jurisdiction.

Religion

About 90% of the population profess Christianity.

CHRISTIANITY

African Federal Church Council (AFCC): POB 70, Peka 340; f. 1927; co-ordinating org. for 48 African independent churches.

Christian Council of Lesotho (CCL): POB 547, Maseru 100; tel. 22313639; fax 22310310; f. 1833; 112 congregations; 261,350 mems (2003); Chair. Rev. M. MOKHOSI; Sec. CATHERINE RAMOKHELE.

The Anglican Communion

Anglicans in Lesotho are adherents of the Church of the Province of Southern Africa. The Metropolitan of the Province is the Archbishop of Cape Town, South Africa. Lesotho forms a single diocese, with an estimated 200,000 members.

Bishop of Lesotho: Rt Rev. PHILIP STANLEY MOKUKU, Bishop's House, POB 87, Maseru 100; tel. 22311974; fax 22310161; e-mail diocese@ilesotho.com.

The Roman Catholic Church

Lesotho comprises one archdiocese and three dioceses. At 31 December 2004 there were some 1,092,517 adherents of the Roman Catholic Church, equivalent to an estimated 50.8% of the total population.

Lesotho Catholic Bishops' Conference

Catholic Secretariat, POB 200, Maseru 100; tel. 22312525; fax 22310294.

f. 1972; Pres. Rt Rev. EVARISTUS THATHO BITSOANE (Bishop of Qacha's Nek).

Archbishop of Maseru: Most Rev. BERNARD MOHLALISI, Archbishop's House, 19 Orpen Rd, POB 267, Maseru 100; tel. 22312565; fax 22310425; e-mail archmase@lesoff.co.za.

Other Christian Churches

At mid-2000 there were an estimated 279,000 Protestants and 257,000 adherents professing other forms of Christianity.

African Methodist Episcopal Church: POB 223, Maseru 100; tel. 22311801; fax 22310416; f. 1903; Presiding Prelate Rev. DANIEL RANTLE; 11,295 mems.

Lesotho Evangelical Church: POB 260, Maseru 100; tel. 22323942; f. 1833; independent since 1964; Pres. Rev. JOHN RAPELANG MOKHAHLANE; Exec. Sec. Rev. A. M. THEBE; 230,000 mems (2003).

Other denominations active in Lesotho include the Apostolic Faith Mission, the Assemblies of God, the Dutch Reformed Church in Africa, the Full Gospel Church of God, Methodist Church of Southern Africa and the Seventh-day Adventists. There are also numerous African independent churches.

BAHÁ'Í FAITH

National Spiritual Assembly: POB 508, Maseru 100; tel. 22312346; fax 22310092; mems resident in 444 localities.

The Press

Lesotho does not have a daily newspaper.

Leseli ka Sepolesa (The Police Witness): Press Dept, Police Headquarters, Maseru CBD, POB 13, Maseru 100; tel. 22317262; fax 22310045; fortnightly; Sesotho; publ. by the Lesotho Mounted Police Services.

Leselinyana la Lesotho (Light of Lesotho): Morija Printing Works, POB 7, Morija 190; tel. 22360205; fax 22360005; f. 1863; fortnightly; Sesotho, with occasional articles in English; publ. by the Lesotho Evangelical Church; Editor SELBORNE MOTLATSI MOHLALISI; circ. 10,000.

Lesotho Today/Lentsoe la Basotho (Voice of the Lesotho Nation): Lesotho News Agency Complex, Lerotholi St, opp. Royal Palace, POB 36, Maseru 100; tel. 22323561; fax 22322764; f. 1974; weekly; Sesotho; publ. by Ministry of Communications, Science and Technology; Editor KAHLISO LESENYANE; circ. 14,000.

Makatolle: POB 111, Maseru 100; tel. 22850990; f. 1963; weekly; Sesotho; Editor M. RAMANGOEI; circ. 2,000.

The Mirror/Setsomi sa Litaba: Mothamo House, 1st Floor, POB 903, Maseru 100; tel. 22323208; fax 22320941; f. 1986; weekly; English and Sesotho; Owner TEBELLO PITSO-HLOHLONGOANE; Editor NAT MOLOMO; circ. 4,000.

MoAfrika: MoAfrika Broadcasting and Publishing Services, Carlton Centre Bldg, 1st Floor, POB 7234, Maseru 100; tel. 22321854; fax 22321956; f. 1990 as *The African*; weekly; Sesotho and English; Editor-in-Chief Prof. SEBONONOLA R. K. RAMAINOANE; circ. 5,000.

Moeletsi oa Basotho: Mazenod Institute, POB 18, Mazenod 160; tel. 22350465; fax 22350010; e-mail mzpwrks@lesoff.co.za; f. 1933; weekly; Sesotho; publ. by the Roman Catholic Church; Editor FRANCIS KHOARIPE; circ. 20,000.

Mohahlaula: Allied Bldg, 1st Floor, Manonyane Centre, POB 14430, Maseru 100; tel. 22312777; fax 22320941; e-mail medinles@lesoff.co.za; weekly; Sesotho; publ. by Makaung Printers and Publrs; Editor WILLY MOLLUNGOA.

Mololi: Cooperatives Bldg, Main North 1 Rd, POB 9933, Maseru 100; tel. 22312287; fax 22327912; 1997; publ. suspended in 2000; Sesotho; organ of the Lesotho Congress for Democracy; Editor MONYANE MOLELEKI.

Mopheme (The Survivor): Allied Bldg, 1st Floor, Manonyane Centre, POB 14184, Maseru; tel. and fax 22311670; e-mail mopheme@lesoff.co.za; weekly; English and Sesotho; publ. by Newsshare Foundation; Owner and Editor LAWRENCE KEKETSO; circ. 2,500.

Public Eye/Mosotho: House No. 14A3, Princess Margaret Rd, POB 14129, Old Europa, Maseru 100; tel. 22321414; fax 22310614; e-mail editor@publiceye.co.ls; internet www.publiceye.co.ls; f. 1997; weekly; 80% English, 20% Sesotho; publ. by Voice Multimedia; also publ. *Eye on Tourism* and *Family Mirror* magazines; Editor-in-Chief BETHUEL THAI; circ. 20,000 (Lesotho and South Africa).

Southern Star: POB 7590, Maseru; tel. 22312269; fax 22310167; e-mail ba-holdings@ilesotho.com; weekly; English; Editor FRANK BOFFOE; circ. 1,500.

PERIODICALS

Justice and Peace: Catholic Bishops' Conference, Our Lady of Victories Cathedral Catholic Centre, POB 200, Maseru 100; tel. 22312750; fax 22312751; quarterly; publ. by the Roman Catholic Church.

Moqolotsi (The Journalist): House No. 1B, Happy Villa, POB 14139, Maseru 100; tel. and fax 22320941; e-mail medinles@lesoff.co.za; monthly newsletter; English; publ. by the Media Institute of Lesotho (MILES).

NGO Web: 544 Hoohlo Extension, Florida, Maseru 100; tel. 22325798; fax 22317205; e-mail lecongo@lecongo.org.ls; quarterly; English and Sesotho; publ. of the Lesotho Council of NGOs; circ. 2,000.

Review of Southern African Studies: Institute of Southern African Studies, National University of Lesotho, PO Roma 180; tel. 22340247; fax 22340601; 2 a year; arts, social and behavioural sciences; Editor TANKIE KHALANYANE.

Shoeshoe: POB 36, Maseru 100; tel. 22323561; fax 22310003; quarterly; women's interest; publ. by Ministry of Communications, Science and Technology.

Other publications include *Mara LDF Airwing/Airsquadron* and *The Sun/Thebe*.

NEWS AGENCIES

Lesotho News Agency (LENA): Lesotho News Agency Complex, Lerotholi St, opp. Royal Palace, POB 36, Maseru 100; tel. 22325317; fax 22324608; e-mail l_lenanews@hotmail.com; internet www.lena.gov.ls; f. 1985; Dir NKOE THAKALI; Editor VIOLET MARAISANE.

Foreign Bureau

Inter Press Service (IPS) (Italy): c/o Lesotho News Agency, POB 36, Maseru 100; Correspondent LEBOHANG LEJAKANE.

Publishers

Longman Lesotho (Pty) Ltd: 104 Christie House, 1st Floor, Orpen Rd, Old Europa, POB 1174, Maseru 100; tel. 22314254; fax 22310118; Man. Dir SEYMOUR R. KIKINE.

Macmillan Boleswa Publishers Lesotho (Pty) Ltd: 523 Sun Cabanas Hotel, POB 7545, Maseru 100; tel. 22317340; fax 22310047; e-mail macmillan@lesoff.co.ls; Man. Dir PAUL MOROLONG.

Mazenod Institute: POB 39, Mazenod 160; tel. 22350224; f. 1933; Roman Catholic; Man. Fr B. MOHLALISI.

Morija Sesuto Book Depot: POB 4, Morija 190; tel. and fax 22360204; f. 1862; owned by the Lesotho Evangelical Church; religious, educational and Sesotho language and literature.

St Michael's Mission: The Social Centre, POB 25, Roma; tel. 22316234; f. 1968; religious and educational; Man. Dir Fr M. FERRANGE.

GOVERNMENT PUBLISHING HOUSE

Government Printer: POB 268, Maseru; tel. 22313023.

Broadcasting and Communications

TELECOMMUNICATIONS

Lesotho Telecommunications Authority (LTA): Moposo House, 6th Floor, Kingsway Rd, POB 15896, Maseru 100; tel. 22325595; fax 22310984; e-mail lta@lta.org.ls; internet www.lta.org.ls; f. 2000; regulates telecommunications and broadcasting.

Telecom Lesotho: POB 1037, Maseru 100; tel. 22211100; fax 22310183; internet www.telecom.co.ls; 70% holding acquired by the Mountain Kingdom Communications consortium in 2000; 30% state-owned; Chair. JOHN BAYLEY; CEO ADRI VAN DER VEER.

Vodacom Lesotho (Pty) Ltd: Block B, Development House, Kingsway Rd, POB 7387, Maseru 100; tel. 52212201; fax 22311079; internet www.vodacom.co.ls; f. 1996; jt venture between Telecom Lesotho and Vodacom (Pty) Ltd; fmrly VCL Communications; mobile cellular telecommunications provider; Man. Dir MERVYN VISAGIE.

BROADCASTING

RADIO

The first licences for private radio stations were issued in 1998. Licences are issued by the Lesotho Telecommunications Authority. Radio Lesotho is the only station to broadcast nationwide; all the other stations are restricted to urban areas and their peripheries.

Catholic Radio FM: Our Lady of Victories Cathedral, Catholic Centre POB 200, Maseru 100; tel. 22323247; fax 22310294; f. 1999.

Joy FM: Lesotho Sun Hotel, Suites 2204–2206, Private Bag A457, Maseru 100; tel. 22310920; fax 22310104; internet www.joyfm.co.ls; f. 2001; Sesotho and English; relays Voice of America broadcasts.

Khotso FM: Institute of Extramural Studies, National University of Lesotho POB 180, Roma; Private Bag A47, Maseru 100; tel. 22322038; fax 22340000; community radio station; sister station of DOPE FM (f. 2004).

MoAfrika FM: Carlton Centre, 2nd Floor, Kingsway, POB 7234, Maseru 100; tel. 22321956; fax 22321956; e-mail info@moafrika.co.ls; internet www.moafrika.co.ls; affiliated to the *MoAfrika* newspaper; Sesotho, Xhosa and Mandarin; news and entertainment; Man. and Editor-in-Chief Prof. SEBONONOLA R. K. RAMAINOANE.

People's Choice Radio (PCFM): LNDC Centre, Development House, Level 9, Block D, POB 8800, Maseru 100; tel. 22322122; fax 22310888; e-mail pcfm@pcfm.co.ls; internet www.pcfm.co.ls; f. 1998; news and entertainment; Man. Dir MOTLATSI MAJARA.

Radio Lesotho: Lesotho News Agency Complex, Lerotholi St, opp. Royal Palace, POB 552, Maseru 100; tel. and fax 22323371; e-mail enquiries@africanextension.com; internet www.radiolesotho.co.ls; f. 1964; state-owned; part of Lesotho Nat. Broadcasting Services; Sesotho and English; Dir of Broadcasting LEBOHANG DADA MOQASA.

TELEVISION

Lesotho Television (LTV): Lesotho News Agency Complex, Lerotholi St, opp. Royal Palace, POB 36, Maseru 100; tel. 22324735; fax 22310149; e-mail mfalatsa@yahoo.com; f. 1988 in association with M-Net, South Africa; state-owned; part of Lesotho Nat. Broadcasting Services; Sesotho and English.

Finance

(cap. = capital; res = reserves; dep. = deposits; m. = million; brs = branches; amounts in maloti)

BANKING

Central Bank

Central Bank of Lesotho: cnr Airport and Moshoeshoe Rds, POB 1184, Maseru 100; tel. 22314281; fax 22310051; e-mail cbl@centralbank.org.ls; internet www.centralbank.org.ls; f. 1978 as the Lesotho Monetary Authority; present name adopted in 1982; bank of issue; cap. 25.0m., res 1,676.2m., dep. 1,544.7m. (Dec. 2002); Gov. and Chair. ESSELEN MOTLATSI MATEKANE.

Commercial Banks

Nedbank Lesotho: Nedbank Building, 361 Kingsway, POB 1001, Maseru 100; tel. 22312696; fax 22310025; f. 1997; fmrly Standard Chartered Bank Lesotho Ltd; 100% owned by Nedcor Group (South Africa); cap. 20m., res 21.5m., dep. 704.2m. (Dec. 2002); Chair. WILLEM P. FROST; Man. Dir PHILIP D. OPPERMAN; 3 brs and 7 agencies.

Standard Lesotho Bank: Banking Bldg, 1st Floor, Kingsway Rd, Kingsway Town Centre, POB 115, Maseru 100; tel. 22312423; fax 22310235; internet www.standardbank.co.ls; f. 2006 following merger between Lesotho Bank (1999) Ltd (f. 1972) and Standard Bank Lesotho Ltd (fmrly Stanbic Bank Lesotho Ltd); Chair. THABO MAKEBA; Man. Dir COLIN ADDIS; 6 brs.

INSURANCE

Alliance Insurance Co Ltd: Alliance House, 4 Bowker Rd, POB 01118, Maseru West 105; tel. 22312357; fax 22310313; e-mail alliance@alliance.co.ls; internet www.alliance.co.ls; f. 1993; life and short-term insurance; Man. Dir JOHANN PIENAAR; Gen. Mans MOK'HAPHEK'HA LAZARO, THABISO MADIBA.

Customer Protection Insurance Co Ltd: POB 201, Maseru 100; tel. 22312643; e-mail craigb@relyant.co.za; wholly owned subsidiary of Ellerine Holdings Ltd, South Africa; general short-term insurance; Chair. DENZIL MCGLASHAN.

Lesotho National Insurance Group (LNIG): Lesotho Insurance House, Kingsway, Private Bag A65, Maseru 100; tel. 22313031; fax 22310008; f. 1977; 50% state-owned; part-privatized in 1995; incorporating subsidiaries specializing in life and short-term insurance; Chair. Dr M. SENAOANA; CEO M. MOLELEKOA.

Metropolitan Lesotho Ltd: POB 645, Maseru; tel. 22323970; fax 22317126; f. 2003; subsidiary of Metropolitan Holdings Ltd, South Africa; Man. Dir TSOANE MPHAHLELE.

Trade and Industry

GOVERNMENT AGENCIES

Privatisation Unit: Privatisation Project, Lesotho Utilities Sector Reform Project, Ministry of Finance and Development Planning, Lesotho Bank Mortgage Division Bldg, 2nd Floor, Kingsway St, Private Bag A249, Maseru 100; tel. 22317902; fax 22317551; e-mail mntsasa@privatisation.gov.ls; internet www.privatisation.gov.ls; CEO MOSITO KHETHISA.

Trade Promotion Unit: c/o Ministry of Trade, Industry, Co-operatives and Marketing, POB 747, Maseru 100; tel. 322138; fax 310121.

DEVELOPMENT ORGANIZATIONS

Basotho Enterprises Development Corpn (BEDCO): POB 1216, Maseru 100; tel. 22312094; fax 22310455; e-mail admin@bedco.org.ls; f. 1980; promotes and assists in the establishment and devt of Basotho-owned enterprises, with emphasis on small- and medium-scale; CEO VICTOR R. LECHESA.

Lesotho Council of Non-Governmental Organizations: House 544, Hoohlo Extension, Private Bag A445, Maseru 100; tel. 22317205; fax 22310412; e-mail seabatam@lecongo.org.ls; internet www.lecongo.org.ls; f. 1990; promotes sustainable management of natural resources, socio-economic devt and social justice; Exec. Dir SEABATA MOTSAMAI.

Lesotho Highlands Development Authority (LHDA): Bank Tower, 3rd Floor, Kingsway, POB 7332, Maseru 100; tel. 22311280; fax 22310060; internet www.lhda.org.ls; f. 1986 to supervise the Lesotho Highlands Water Project, being undertaken jtly with South Africa; Chair. JOHN J. EAGER (acting); CEO MASILO PHAKOE (acting).

Lesotho National Development Corpn (LNDC): Development House, Block A, Kingsway, Private Bag A96, Maseru 100; tel. 22312012; fax 22310038; e-mail info@lndc.org.ls; internet www.lndc.org.ls; f. 1967; state-owned; total assets M477.5m. (March 2006); interests in manufacturing, mining, food-processing and leisure; Chair. MOHLOMI RANTEKOA; CEO PEETE MOLAPO.

Lesotho Co-operative Handicrafts: Basotho Hat Bldg, Kingsway, PO Box 148, Maseru; tel. 22322523; e-mail ich@ilesotho.com; f. 1978; marketing and distribution of handicrafts; Gen. Man. KHOTSO MATLA.

CHAMBER OF COMMERCE

Lesotho Chamber of Commerce and Industry: Kingsway Ave, POB 79, Maseru 100; tel. 22316937; fax 22322794; Pres. SIMON PHAFANE.

INDUSTRIAL AND TRADE ASSOCIATIONS

Livestock Marketing Corpn: POB 800, Maseru 100; tel. 22322444; f. 1973; sole org. for marketing livestock and livestock products; liaises with marketing boards in South Africa; projects incl. an abattoir, tannery, poultry and wool and mohair scouring plants; Gen. Man. S. R. MATLANYANE.

EMPLOYERS' ORGANIZATION

Association of Lesotho Employers: 8 Bowker Rd, POB 1509, Maseru 100; tel. 22315736; fax 22325384; f. 1961; represents mems in industrial relations and on govt bodies, and advises the Govt on employers' concerns; Treas. R. LEBOELA; Exec. Dir THABO MAKEKA.

UTILITIES

Lesotho Electricity Corpn (LEC): POB 423, Maseru 100; tel. 22312236; fax 22310093; internet www.lec.co.ls; f. 1969; bids for transfer to the private sector were under consideration in mid-2004; Man. Dir S. L. MHAVILLE.

Lesotho Water and Sewerage Authority (WASA): POB 426, Maseru 100; tel. 22312449; fax 22312006; Chair. REFILOE TLALI.

MAJOR COMPANIES

Kingsway Construction (Pty) Ltd: Private Bag A53, Maseru 100; tel. 22313181; fax 22310137; f. 1986; Chair. T. HENDRY; 220 employees.

Lesotho Brewing Co (Pty) Ltd: Maseru; tel. 22311111; fax 22310020; e-mail njmatete@lbc.co.ls; f. 1981; 39% owned by SABMiller Africa BV, Netherlands; beer and carbonated soft drinks; Chair. PEETE MOLAPO; Man. Dir GREG UYS; 315 employees.

Lesotho Flour Mills: Private Bag A62, Maseru 100; tel. 22313498; fax 22310037; f. 1979; 51% owned by Seaboard USA; mfrs of maize and wheat products and animal feed; incorporates Lesotho Maize Mills, Lesotho Farm Feed Mills, and Lesotho Sugar Packers; privatized in 1998; Man. Dir JAN H. VAN DER MOLEN; 334 employees.

Lesotho Milling Co Pty Ltd: POB 39, Maputsoe; tel. 22430622; fax 22430010; e-mail lescoit@yebo.co.za; f. 1980; subsidiary of Tiger Group, South Africa; milling and export of maize; Man. Dir GRAHAM GATCKE; 235 employees (2004).

Lesotho Pharmaceutical Corpn (LPC): POB 256, Mafeteng 900; tel. 22700326; fax 22700002; e-mail gertie@lpc.co.ls; pharmaceutical products; CEO GERTRUDE MOTHIBE; 110 employees.

Lesotho Sandstone Co (Pty) Ltd (LESACO): POB 43522, Heuwelsig 9332; tel. 826513229; fax 514363668; e-mail lesaco@xsinet.co.za; internet www.sandstoneales.co.za; f. 1989; import, export and mfrs of natural sandstone products; CEO R. FACTA; 120 employees.

Between 1986 and 2003 the Lesotho National Development Corpn provided assistance to 49 foreign shoe and garment manufacturers; of these 29 were Taiwanese. Some 26 of these companies were established after the declaration of the US African Growth and Opportunity Act (AGOA) in 2000. In 2004, collectively, they employed some 42,000 people.

TRADE UNIONS

Congress of Lesotho Trade Unions (COLETU): POB 13282, Maseru 100; tel. 22320958; fax 22310081; f. 1998; Sec.-Gen. JUSTICE TSÍUKULU; 15,587 mems.

Construction and Allied Workers' Union of Lesotho (CAWULE): Manonyana Centre, 2nd Floor, Room 24, POB 132282, Maseru 100; tel. 63023484; fax 22321951; f. 1967; affiliated to the Building and Wood Workers International; Pres. L. PUTSOANE; Sec. T. TLALE.

Factory Workers' Union (FAWU): Maseru; f. 2003 following split from the Lesotho Clothing and Allied Workers' Union; Pres. KHABILE TSILO; Sec.-Gen. MACAEFA BILLY.

Lesotho Association of Teachers (LAT): POB 12528, Maseru 100; tel. and fax 22317463; affiliated to the Education International; Exec. Sec. PAUL P. SEMATLANE.

Lesotho Clothing and Allied Workers' Union (LECAWU): LNDC Centre, 2nd Floor, Rm 12–14, Kingsway Rd, POB 11767, Maseru 100; tel. 22324296; fax 22320958; e-mail lecawu@lesoff.co.ls; affiliated to the Int. Textile, Garment and Leather Workers' Fed.; Sec.-Gen. DANIEL MARAISANE; 6,000 mems.

Lesotho General Workers' Union: POB 322, Maseru 100; f. 1954; Chair. J. M. RAMAROTHOLE; Sec. T. MOTLOHI.

Lesotho Congress of Democratic Unions (LECODU): Maseru; Sec.-Gen. E. T. RAMOCHELA; 15,279 mems.

Lesotho Teachers' Trade Union (LTTU): POB 0509, Maseru West 105; tel. 22322774; fax 22321951; e-mail lecawu@lesoff.co.ls; affiliated to the Education International; Pres. CHEFANE JOSEPH CHEFANE; Gen. Sec. MALIMABE JOAKIM MOTOPELA.

Lesotho Transport and Allied Workers' Union: Maseru 100; f. 1959; Pres. M. BERENG; Gen. Sec. TSEKO KAPA.

Lesotho University Teachers' and Researchers' Union (LUTARU): Maseru; Pres. Dr FRANCIS MAKOA.

Transport

RAILWAYS

Lesotho is linked with the South African railway system by a short line (2.6 km in length) from Maseru to Marseilles, on the Bloemfontein–Natal main line.

ROADS

In 1999 Lesotho's road network totalled 5,940 km, of which 1,084 km were main roads and 1,950 km were secondary roads. About 18.3% of roads were paved. In 1996 the International Development Association granted US $40m. towards the Government's rolling five-year road programme. From 1996/97 an extra-budgetary Road Fund was to finance road maintenance. In March 2000 a major road network was opened, linking Maseru with the Mohale Dam.

CIVIL AVIATION

King Moshoeshoe I International Airport is at Thota-Moli, some 20 km from Maseru; in January 2002 the Government announced plans for its expansion. International services between Maseru and Johannesburg are operated by South African Airlink. The national airline company, Lesotho Airways, was sold to a South African company in 1997 as part of the Government's ongoing privatization programme; however, after two years of losses the company was liquidated in 1999.

Tourism

Spectacular mountain scenery is the principal tourist attraction, and a new ski resort was opened in 2003. Tourist arrivals totalled 303,578 in 2005. In 2004 receipts from tourism amounted to an estimated US $34m.

Lesotho Tourism Development Corpn (LTDC): cnr Linare and Parliament Rds, POB 1378, Maseru 100; tel. 22312238; fax 22310189; e-mail ltdc@ltdc.org.ls; internet www.ltdc.org.ls; f. 2000; successor to the Lesotho Tourist Board; CEO MTHWALO MTHWALO.

Defence

Military service is voluntary. As assessed at November 2006, the Lesotho Defence Force (LDF, formerly the Royal Lesotho Defence Force) comprised 2,000 men, including an air wing of 110 men. The creation of a new commando force unit, the first professional unit in the LDF, was announced in October 2001, as part of ongoing efforts to restructure the armed forces.

Defence Expenditure: Estimated at M220m. for 2006.

Commander of the Lesotho Defence Force: Lt-Gen. THUSO MOTANYANE.

Education

All primary education is available free of charge, and is provided mainly by the three main Christian missions (Lesotho Evangelical, Roman Catholic and Anglican), under the direction of the Ministry of Education. Education at primary schools is officially compulsory for seven years between six and 13 years of age. Secondary education, beginning at the age of 13, lasts for up to five years, comprising a first cycle of three years and a second of two years. According to UNESCO estimates, of children in the relevant age-groups in 2003/04, 86% (males 83%; females 88%) were enrolled at primary schools, while only 23% (males 18%; females 28%) were enrolled at secondary schools. Some 3,266 students were enrolled at the National University of Lesotho, at Roma, in 2002. Proposed expenditure on education under the 2006/07 budget was M927.4m. (representing more than 20% of total government expenditure). In January 2006 17 new schools constructed with the assistance of the Government of Japan were opened; they were expected to accommodate some 14,000 pupils.

Bibliography

Akindele, F., and Senyane, R. (Eds). *The Irony of the 'White Gold'.* Morija, Transformation Resource Centre, 2004.

Chaka-Makhooane, L., *et al. Sexual Violence in Lesotho: the Realities of Justice for Women.* Morija, Women and Law in Southern Africa Research and Education Trust, 2002.

Ferguson, J. (Ed.). *The Anti-Politics Machine: Development, Depoliticization and Bureaucratic State Power in Lesotho.* Cambridge, Cambridge University Press; Cape Town, David Philip, 1990.

Franklin, A. S. *Land Law in Lesotho: The Politics of the 1979 Land Act.* Aldershot, Avebury; Brookfield, VT, Ashgate Publishing, 1995.

Gary, J., *et al* (Eds). *Lesotho's Long Journey: Hard Choices at the Crossroads: A Comprehensive Overview of Lesotho's Historical, Social, Economic and Political Development With a View to the Future.* (Commissioned and funded by Irish Aid.) Maseru, Sechaba Consultants, 1995.

Gary, J., and Hall, D. *Poverty in Lesotho.* Maseru, Sechaba Consultants, 1994.

Gill, S. J. *A Short History of Lesotho, From the Late Stone Age Until the 1993 Elections.* Morija, Morija Museum and Archives, 1993.

Kabemba, C. (Ed.), *et al. From Military Rule to Multiparty Democracy: Political Reforms and Challenges in Lesotho.* Johannesburg, Electoral Institute of Southern Africa (EISA), 2003.

Kimyaro, S. S. (Ed.), *et al. Turning a Crisis into an Opportunity: Strategies for Scaling up the National Response to the HIV/AIDS Pandemic in Lesotho.* New York, NY, New Rochelle, 2004.

Leduka, R. C. *Informal Land Delivery Processes and Access to Land for the Poor in Maseru, Lesotho.* Birmingham, International Development Department, School of Public Policy, University of Birmingham, 2004.

Letuka, P., Mapetla, M., and Matashane-Marite, K. *Gender and Elections in Lesotho: Perspectives on the 2002 Elections.* Johannesburg, Electoral Institute of Southern Africa (EISA), 2004.

Lundahl, M., McCarthy, C., and Petersson, L. *In the Shadow of South Africa: Lesotho's Economic Future.* Aldershot; Burlington, VT, Ashgate, 2003.

Lundahl, M., and Petersson, L. *The Dependent Economy: Lesotho and the Southern Africa Customs Union.* Boulder, CO, Westview Press, 1991.

Machobane, L. B. B. J. *Government and Change in Lesotho, 1800–1966: A Study of Political Institutions.* Maseru, Macmillan Lesotho, 1990.

The King's Knights: Military Governance in the Kingdom of Lesotho, 1986–1993. Roma, Institute of Southern African Studies, National University of Lesotho, 2001.

Machobane, L. B. B. J., and Manyeli, T. L. *Essays on Religion and Culture among Basotho, 1800–1900.* Mazenod, Mazenod Publrs, 2001.

Makoa, F. K. *Elections, Election Outcomes and Electoral Politics in Lesotho.* Pretoria, Africa Institute of South Africa, 2002.

Maloka, E. T. *Basotho and the Mines: A Social History of Labour Migrancy in Lesotho and South Africa, c. 1890–1940.* Dakar, Council for the Development of Social Science Research in Africa, 2004.

Maqutu, W. C. M. *Contemporary Constitutional History of Lesotho.* Mazenod, Mazenod Institute, 1990.

McCall Theal, G. *Basutoland Records: Vols 4–6, 1868–1872.* Roma, Institute of Southern African Studies, National University of Lesotho, 2002.

Mochebelele, M. T., *et al. Agricultural Marketing in Lesotho.* Ottawa, International Development Research Centre, 1992.

Mohapeloa, J. M. *Tentative British Imperialism in Lesotho, 1884–1910: a Study in Basotho-colonial Office Interaction, and South Africa's Influence on it.* Morija, Morija Museum and Archives, 2002.

Mphanya, N. *A Brief History of the Basutoland Congress Party: Lekhotla la Mahatammoho, 1952-2002.* Morija, 2004.

Murray, C., and Sanders, P. *Medicine Murder in Colonial Lesotho: the Anatomy of a Moral Crisis.* Edinburgh, Edinburgh University Press for the International African Institute, London, 2005

Olaleye, W. *Democratic Consolidation and Political Parties in Lesotho.* Johannesburg, Electoral Institute of Southern Africa (EISA), 2004.

Pherudi, M. L. *Storm in the Mountain.* Maluti, Hochland Printers, 2004.

Pule, N. W., and Thabane, M. (Eds). *Essays on Aspects of the Political Economy of Lesotho, 1500–2000.* Roma, Department of History, National University of Lesotho, 2002.

Rosenberg, S., Weisfelder, R. F., and Frisbie-Fulton, M. *Historical Dictionary of Lesotho.* Lanham, MD, Scarecrow Press, 2004.

Rule, S., and Mapetla, N. *Lesotho 2000: Public Perceptions and Perspectives.* Pretoria, Institute of Southern African Studies, 2001.

Rwelamira, M. *Refugees in a Chess Game: Reflections on Botswana, Lesotho and Swaziland Refugee Policies.* Trenton, NJ, Red Sea Press, 1990.

Southall, R., and Petlane, T. (Eds). *Democratisation and Demilitarisation in Lesotho: The General Election of 1993 and its Aftermath.* Pretoria, Africa Institution of South Africa, 1996.

Van der Wiel, A. C. A. *Migratory Wage Labour: Its Role in the Economy of Lesotho.* Maseru, Mazenod Book Centre, 1977.

Witzsch, G. *Lesotho Environment and Environmental Law.* Roma, National University of Lesotho, 1992.

LIBERIA

Physical and Social Geography

CHRISTOPHER CLAPHAM

The Republic of Liberia was founded in 1847 by freed black slaves from the USA who were resettled from 1821 onwards along the western Guinea coast between Cape Mount (11° 20′ W) and Cape Palmas (7° 40′ W). Liberia extends from 4° 20′ N to 8° 30′ N with a maximum breadth of 280 km between Buchanan and Nimba. The country occupies an area of 97,754 sq km (37,743 sq miles) between Sierra Leone to the west, the Republic of Guinea to the north and Côte d'Ivoire to the east.

PHYSICAL FEATURES AND POPULATION

An even coastline of 570 km, characterized by powerful surf, rocky cliffs and lagoons, makes access from the Atlantic Ocean difficult, except at the modern ports. The flat coastal plain, which is 15–55 km wide, consists of forest and savannah. The interior hills and mountain ranges, with altitudes of 180–360 m, form part of an extended peneplain, covered by evergreen (in the south) or semi-deciduous (in the north) rainforests. The northern highlands contain Liberia's greatest elevations, which include the Nimba mountains, reaching 1,752 m above sea-level, and the Wologisi range, reaching 1,381 m. The descent from the higher to the lower belts of the highlands is characterized by rapids and waterfalls.

Liberia has two rainy seasons near Harper, in the south, and one rainy season (from May to October) in the rest of the country. From Monrovia, on the coast in north-west Liberia, with an average of 4,650 mm per year, rainfall decreases towards the south-east and the hinterland, reaching 2,240 mm per year at Ganta. Average temperatures are more extreme in the interior than at the coast. Monrovia has an annual average of 26°C, with absolute limits at 33°C and 14°C respectively. At Tappita temperatures may rise to 44°C in March and fall to 9°C during cool harmattan nights in December or January. Mean water temperature on the coast is 27°C.

The drainage system consists of 15 principal river basins, of which those of the Cavalla river, with an area of 30,225 sq km (including 13,730 sq km in Liberia), and of the St Paul river, with an area of 21,910 sq km (11,325 sq km in Liberia), are the largest. The water flow varies considerably and may reach over 100,000 cubic feet per second (cfs) at the Mt Coffee gauge of the St Paul river in August or decrease to 2,000 cfs during the dry season in March.

The first Liberian census enumerated a population of 1,016,443 in April 1962. According to the second census, in February 1974, an increase of 47.9%, to 1,503,368, had taken place, indicating an average annual growth rate of 3.4%, one of the highest in Africa. A third census, held in February 1984, enumerated a total population of 2,101,628. The population was estimated by the UN to have increased to 3,750,000 at mid-2006.

The 1984 census officially recognized 16 principal ethnic groups in the Liberian population, comprising 96% of the population. The remaining population consisted of non-Liberian Africans (2%) and 'non-ethnic' Liberians (principally descendants of the original settlers—2%). The main ethnic groups were the Kpelle (numbering 408,176 in 1984), living in Bong County and other central areas of the country, and the Bassa (291,106), in the Buchanan region. Other prominent ethnic groups were the Krahn (79,352), living mainly in Grand Gedeh County, the Mandingo (107,186), a predominantly Muslim group widely distributed throughout the country, and the Gio and Mano of Nimba County (164,823 and 149,277, respectively).

The demographic pattern of Liberia is characterized by a number of features typical of developing countries: a high birth rate (estimated at 49.8 per 1,000 in 2000–05); a high proportion of children under 15 years of age (estimated at 45.1% of the total population in 1996); and a low expectation of life at birth (estimated at 42 years in 2004). The average population density is low (33.6 inhabitants per sq km at mid-2005), but urbanization has been rapid, resulting in an estimated 45.6% of the population living in urban areas in 1996. The population of Monrovia increased from 80,992 in 1962 to 208,629 in 1978, and to 421,058 in 1984; influxes of people displaced by the fighting may have taken the population above 1.3m. during the 1989–96 war. In 2003 the population of Monrovia was estimated at 550,200.

The war of 1989–96 caused massive displacements of population: at many times during the conflict one-third of the population fled to neighbouring countries, and a further one-third were internally displaced. The mass repatriation of Liberian refugees commenced in 1997. In the late 1990s large numbers of Sierra Leoneans fled to Liberia, after the intensification of civil conflict in that country. Following further rebel activity in Liberia from early 2001, some 119,293 Liberian refugees were in Guinea and about 43,000 in Côte d'Ivoire at 1 January 2003, according to the office of the UN High Commissioner for Refugees (UNHCR). The advance of hostilities to Monrovia in mid-2003 precipitated a further humanitarian crisis. Following the signing of a comprehensive peace agreement in August, the security situation improved significantly, with the deployment of UN peace-keeping troops and the initiation of a disarmament programme for former combatants. During 2004 more than 50,000 refugees returned to Liberia, while UNHCR completed the voluntary repatriation programme for some 13,000 Sierra Leonean refugees. At the end of 2006 an estimated 33,345 Liberian refugees remained in Sierra Leone, 25,612 in Côte d'Ivoire, and 21,816 in Guinea; at that time 12,590 refugees from Côte d'Ivoire were in Liberia.

Recent History

QUENTIN OUTRAM

Liberia traces its origins to liberated US slaves, who were resettled along the western Guinean coast by US philanthropic organizations from 1821 onwards. The country declared itself an independent sovereign state in 1847 and has remained an independent republic ever since. The new state adopted a Constitution modelled on that of the USA, although citizenship was confined to the settlers, known as 'Americo-Liberians' or 'Americos', who were then, and have always remained, a small proportion of the Liberian population, never exceeding a few tens of thousands. In 1878 the True Whig Party (TWP) regained the presidency and remained in continuous control of the polity from that year until 1980. During the 19th century a number of serious armed conflicts between the 'Americo' settlers and the indigenous peoples of Liberia occurred; the final revolt of the indigenous population was not suppressed until the early 1930s. By this time Liberia was taking the first steps towards establishing a modern economy. In 1926 agreements were made with the Firestone Tire and Rubber Co of the USA, under which the company leased land for the development of rubber plantations and constructed the necessary infrastructure for their operation. In 1929, however, the USA accused Liberia of running a system of forced labour within the country and supplying labour to the island of Fernando Póo in Spanish Guinea (now Equatorial Guinea) and the French colony of Gabon, in a system considered to be barely distinguishable from an organized slave trade. The resulting League of Nations inquiry substantially confirmed these charges. The subsequent reforms, together with the Firestone agreement, represented a transition from pre-modern to modern labour practices in Liberia. However, the issue of Fernando Póo has been mainly remembered in Liberia as a humiliation by the international community, and continues to be deployed with this meaning in Liberian political rhetoric.

The modernization of Liberia progressed significantly with the election of President William V. S. Tubman in 1943. Tubman's 1944 inaugural address initiated two policies ('unification' and 'open door') which were to guide Liberian politics until 1980. The 'unification' policy sought to assimilate indigenous Liberians to the established 'Americo' society and polity. The indigenous population gained the right to vote in 1946, although this was limited by a property qualification. The three hinterland provinces were replaced by four counties in 1963, thus extending the reach of statutory law to the entire country and putting the representation of the hinterland in the legislature onto the same basis as that of the coastal counties. The 'open door' policy reaffirmed Liberia's openness to foreign investment and its commitment to a capitalist economy. Less publicized by the Government was a conservative foreign policy, and during the period of the Cold War Liberia maintained its traditionally close relations with the USA. Liberia took a significant role in the establishment of the Organization of African Unity (OAU, now the African Union—AU) in 1961, and in ensuring that it remained only an association of independent states. Liberia's relations with its immediate neighbours followed a similarly conservative stance. In 1973 Liberia and Sierra Leone established the Mano River Union (MRU), originally conceived as a customs union. In 1975 Liberia signed the Treaty of Lagos establishing the Economic Community of West African States (ECOWAS).

In the early 1970s Liberia presented a picture of remarkable political stability, emphasized by the peaceful succession of Tubman's Vice-President, William Tolbert, to the presidency in 1971 and symbolized by the continuing power of the TWP, the oldest political party in Africa. However, the country was effectively a one-party state, which showed little respect for freedom of speech and where the judiciary and the legislature demonstrated little independence of the executive. Despite the US-style Constitution, the 'Americo' élite maintained a political culture based on a presidency with largely unrestricted powers, secured by practices of co-option, incorporation and an extensive, centralized network of patronage. In the 1970s internal discontent and dissent emerged rapidly, generated by the failure of the 'unification' policy to eliminate substantial economic, social and political disparities between the 'Americo' élite and indigenous Liberians, increasing economic difficulties, and encouraged by Tolbert's experiments with liberalism and the rising expectations of an increasingly educated class of technocrats and functionaries. In 1973 Togba Nah Roberts (later Togba Nah Tipoteh), a US-educated professor of economics at the University of Liberia, formed the Movement for Justice in Africa (MOJA), dedicated to radical change in Liberia and throughout Africa. Among its leading members was the US-educated Amos Sawyer, an assistant professor of political science (later to be President of the Interim Government of National Unity). In 1975 the Progressive Alliance of Liberia (PAL) was established among the Liberian diaspora in the USA, with an openly revolutionary programme. Its Chairman was Gabriel Baccus Matthews, a Liberian educated in the USA. Liberia's economic difficulties culminated in 1979, when PAL and a number of other groups organized a demonstration in April against a proposed 36% increase in the government-controlled price of rice, the staple food. The demonstration was suppressed by the armed forces, resulting in a number of deaths. Although an amnesty was soon granted to those arrested, the episode exposed the weakness of Tolbert's administration. In January 1980 PAL was reconstituted as a registered political party, the People's Progressive Party (PPP), and in March the PPP urged a national strike to force Tolbert's resignation. Tolbert ordered the arrest of Matthews and the rest of the PPP leadership on treason charges, and the PPP was prohibited. The political atmosphere became increasingly tense and in April 17 non-commissioned officers and soldiers of the Armed Forces of Liberia (AFL) assassinated Tolbert.

THE DOE REGIME

All of the 17 who seized power were indigenous Liberians. They declared a junta, the People's Redemption Council (PRC), and elected Master Sgt (later Gen.) Samuel Doe, a Krahn, as Chairman. Thomas Quiwonkpa, a Gio, became Commanding General of the AFL. The Constitution was suspended and political parties were prohibited. The new regime had no clear programme. The 1980 Council of Ministers, appointed to advise the PRC, contained an incoherent spectrum of political opinion, including Matthews and other leaders of the PPP and Togba Nah Tipoteh of MOJA. A power struggle soon developed, resulting in a defeat for the radicals. Individuals associated with the Tolbert regime and other members of the former 'Americo' élite became increasingly prominent in Doe's Government; among these were Charles Taylor, who became de facto director of the state General Services Agency. At lower levels, the regime became increasingly staffed by Krahn and Gio, as both Doe and Quiwonkpa sought to gain support within their own ethnic groups.

Domestic and international pressure for a return to democracy resulted in the formation in April 1981 of a commission to draft a new constitution. The new draft remained modelled on the US Constitution and was approved by a referendum in July 1984; the ban on political activity ended in the same month and a date was announced for presidential and legislative elections. Nevertheless, seven political parties, including Sawyer's Liberian People's Party and Matthews's new United People's Party (UPP), were prevented from contesting the elections, which took place in October 1985. According to the official result, now universally acknowledged as fraudulent, Samuel Doe won 50.9% of the vote; most observers consider that Jackson F. Doe (a former Minister of Education under Tolbert, later an adviser to Doe—no relation of the President) was the rightful victor. Jackson Doe's defeat increased the resentment towards Samuel Doe's regime, especially in Nimba County, from which Jackson Doe, a Gio, originated. The USA urged that Samuel Doe's election should be accepted. A nominally civilian administration, with Samuel Doe as President, was installed in January 1986.

The malpractice of the 1985 election encouraged political violence. In late 1983 military supporters of Quiwonkpa had already launched an unsuccessful raid on Nimba County from Côte d'Ivoire. Quiwonkpa fled to the USA and a number of his supporters, including Charles Taylor, left the country at about the same time. Taylor took refuge in the USA; Doe demanded his extradition, accusing him of embezzlement, and he was arrested in May 1984 in Massachusetts and imprisoned. In November 1985 Quiwonkpa launched another unsuccessful coup attempt, this time prompting Doe to conduct a bloody and, in part, ethnically targeted purge. Virtually all prominent opposition politicians were arrested and held without charge. After pressure from the USA, Doe granted a general amnesty in June 1986. The human rights abuses perpetrated in 1985–86 brought considerable international attention to Liberia and a previously unknown salience to ethnic identity for Krahn, for Gio, and for a group closely associated with the latter, the Mano.

By the time of the June 1986 amnesty, Doe's victory over his rivals appeared complete and Krahn domination of the AFL, especially of its élite units, was heavy. Quiwonkpa's coup attempt was followed by a period of political repression, during which many of Liberia's prominent opposition politicians and intellectuals fled abroad, and diaspora politics became increasingly important. In 1987 a group of Liberian exiles, including Prince Yormie Johnson, a former aide to Quiwonkpa and later the leader of one of the warring factions in the 1989–96 Liberian civil war, assisted Capt. Blaise Compaoré's successful coup in Burkina Faso. Another group gradually came under the leadership of Charles Taylor, who had escaped from prison in Massachusetts in September 1985. Compaoré introduced him to Col Muammar al-Qaddafi of Libya and Taylor gained Qaddafi's support. Dissidents under various leaderships, including that of Taylor, undertook military training in Libya and Burkina Faso in the late 1980s. In mid-1989 Taylor formed an alliance with another group of Libyan-trained dissidents, the Revolutionary United Front of Sierra Leone (RUF), led by a former corporal, Foday Sankoh. By this time Taylor's group had become known as the National Patriotic Front of Liberia (NPFL). On 24 December 1989 some 100 armed members of the NPFL launched an attack on Liberia, entering the country near Butuo, in Nimba County, from Côte d'Ivoire.

THE 1989–96 CIVIL WAR

The civil war initiated by the NPFL incursion followed a highly complex course. Starting as an insurrection against the Doe regime in late 1989, the hostilities degenerated rapidly into a predominantly inter-ethnic conflict, and then gradually transformed into a war between powerful rebel leaders, a transformation completed by about 1993. In this last stage several factions fought not only for control over the state, but also for control over easily exploitable resources. The war became notable for the exceptionally brutal maltreatment of civilians, with numerous incidents of looting, forced labour, arbitrary arrest and detention, torture, rape and murder. In response, civilians often fled, and displacements of refugees were often extraordinarily large in relation to the size of the population. Mass displacement, the destruction wrought by the fighting, and the inability of aid agencies to operate in insecure areas resulted in under-nutrition and intermittent episodes of starvation. While there is no reliable estimate of the numbers killed during the conflict, the figure of 200,000 is most quoted.

Four phases of heavy fighting can be distinguished during the 1989–96 war: December 1989–December 1990; October 1992–July 1993; September 1994–August 1995; and April–June 1996. The first phase began with the NPFL's initial offensive in December 1989. The incursion into Nimba County was initially welcomed by the local population of Gios and Manos and the NPFL rapidly gained supporters. Counter-insurgency operations by AFL units in early 1990 involved gross abuses of human rights. NPFL forces retaliated by hunting down and killing Krahns. By May 1990 an estimated 160,000 Gios, Manos and others had fled to Guinea and Côte d'Ivoire; a further 135,000 were displaced within Liberia. The human rights advocacy group Africa Watch described this phase of the civil war as 'near-genocidal', with Krahn and, to a lesser extent, Mandingo on the one side and Gio and Mano on the other. Africa Watch also reported the use of child combatants by the NPFL at this time, a practice which continued to be reported until the end of the civil war and one with which all the factions, except the AFL, were associated. The NPFL made rapid progress and in July 1990 it launched its attack on Monrovia. Prince Yormie Johnson broke away from the NPFL, forming the Independent National Patriotic Front of Liberia (INPFL), and occupied Monrovia Free Port and some of the outlying areas of the capital. On 30 July, in one of the most notorious incidents of the war, an AFL unit massacred some 185 unarmed displaced civilians who had sought refuge in St Peter's Lutheran Church in Monrovia.

In August 1990 forces provided by the ECOWAS Cease-Fire Monitoring Group (ECOMOG), arrived in Monrovia. ECOMOG came under fire from NPFL combatants almost immediately on landing. A few weeks later ECOMOG, in alliance with the INPFL, began an offensive against the NPFL and rapidly gained control of the port area of Monrovia. The joint action with the INPFL compromised ECOMOG's neutrality and established a pattern of ECOMOG collaboration with anti-NPFL factions which continued for the rest of the war. In September 1990, with the aid (witting or unwitting) of ECOMOG, Samuel Doe was captured by the INPFL, tortured and finally murdered. ECOMOG advanced to create a neutral zone, separating the forces of the AFL (already considered as little more than another faction), the INPFL and the NPFL, and in November 1990 a cease-fire was signed in Bamako, Mali, under which the warring parties agreed to progress towards a civilian government and democratic elections. An Interim Government of National Unity (IGNU) was installed by ECOWAS, with Amos Sawyer, elected at a national conference of representatives prominent in Liberian politics and civil society, as its President. The IGNU excluded the heads of the warring factions and their representatives, and was wholly dependent on ECOMOG for its survival. The NPFL refused to recognize the new Government and established its headquarters in Gbarnga, the capital of Bong County. Taylor, despite Prince Johnson's defection, remained in undisputed control of the NPFL, having allegedly ordered the killing of a number of potential rivals, including Jackson Doe and Gabriel Kpolleh (another candidate in the 1985 presidential election). At the end of this first phase of the conflict the number of Liberian refugees and internally displaced civilians was estimated to total nearly 2m.

The cease-fire continued uneasily for nearly two years. In January 1991 the UN Security Council supported the diplomatic and military initiatives pursued by ECOWAS and largely transferred its functions to the organization for the rest of the war. In April a new IGNU, again with Sawyer at its head, was installed. Peace negotiations conducted at Yamoussoukro, Côte d'Ivoire, in 1991 achieved little progress. The peace agreements of this period gave no incentive to the NPFL to demobilize, and its participation in disarmament was perfunctorily performed and continually delayed.

During 1991 Mandingo Liberian refugees in Sierra Leone joined with another exile group, the Liberian United Defense Force, comprising both Mandingo and Krahn, and including former members of the AFL, to form the United Liberation Movement of Liberia for Democracy (ULIMO). ULIMO's leadership was poorly defined. Alhaji G. V. Kromah, a Mandingo, who had served in the Tolbert and Doe administrations, presented himself as ULIMO's leader with increasing success. ULIMO, which received the support of President Joseph Saidu Momoh's Government in Sierra Leone, opposed Taylor's attempts to destabilize Sierra Leone through the RUF, and joined counter-attacks by the Sierra Leonean army against the RUF soon after its formation. ULIMO incursions into NPFL territory in north-west and south-west Liberia from late 1991 escalated into serious inter-factional armed conflict in August 1992, with ULIMO gaining control of large areas of Lofa and Cape Mount Counties, including their diamond fields.

In October 1992 the NPFL launched an unexpected attack on Monrovia, known as 'Operation Octopus'. This introduced the second phase of heavy fighting, which was to continue until July 1993. ECOMOG fought back to defend the capital and, to this end, rearmed the local remnants of the AFL. An estimated

200,000 people fled from the outskirts of Monrovia towards its centre. In late October five US nuns based in Gardnersville, a suburb of Monrovia, were killed, almost certainly by NPFL combatants, in an atrocity that brought renewed international attention to the country. In November 1992 the UN Security Council responded to the upsurge in fighting by imposing a mandatory armaments embargo against the factions, under Resolution 788, and ECOWAS imposed economic sanctions against NPFL territory. However, ECOMOG was unable to deploy to Liberia's land borders, and the sanctions were never effectively enforced. In late 1992 Johnson's INPFL collapsed, and he took no further part in the war. In January 1993 ULIMO launched attacks against the NPFL and the RUF from the Sierra Leonean border. ULIMO consolidated its hold on Lofa and Cape Mount Counties and expelled the NPFL from Bomi County. ULIMO's position prevented the NPFL from receiving RUF support and gave it sole control over the land routes between Liberia and Sierra Leone. In early 1993 ECOMOG regained control of the outskirts of Monrovia and advanced south-eastwards along the coast, eventually capturing the port of Buchanan, the capital of Grand Bassa County. In June nearly 600 unarmed displaced civilians sheltering at Carter Camp on the Firestone plantation at Harbel, Margibi County, were massacred. A UN investigation concluded that AFL members were responsible for the atrocity.

Following its military successes, ULIMO was included in the peace negotiations, and in July 1993 Kromah, together with representatives of the UN Secretary-General, the OAU, ECOWAS, the IGNU and the NPFL, signed a cease-fire agreement at Cotonou, Benin. The aim of the Cotonou Agreement was to secure peace by yielding a share in a still supposedly civilian interim government to those warring factions sufficiently powerful to insist on representation at the negotiations. The accord provided for the establishment of the Liberia National Transitional Government (LNTG), headed by a five-person Council of State, or collective presidency. The Council of State was to comprise two eminent Liberians, indirectly appointed by the factions, and one direct nominee of each of the IGNU, the NPFL and ULIMO. The ECOWAS Chairman requested greater support from the UN, and from late 1993 the UN Military Observer Group in Liberia (UNOMIL) was deployed in the country. In November 1993 a new faction, the self-styled Liberian Peace Council (LPC), led by George Saigbe Boley, attacked resource-rich areas under NPFL control in the south-east. The LPC's attacks provided Taylor with an excuse to halt NPFL participation in the disarmament process; other factions followed suit, and the peace process was suspended. Nevertheless, Sawyer, in accordance with the Cotonou Agreement, transferred power to David Kpomakor, the Chairman of the Council of State, in March 1994.

After more than a year of violent dissension among its leadership, ULIMO divided at about the end of 1993, resulting in repeated armed clashes in and around Tubmanburg, in Bomi County, between the rival groups within the faction. The two groups became known as ULIMO—K, under Kromah, which operated from Guinea in the north, and ULIMO—J, under Roosevelt Johnson, with headquarters at Tubmanburg. A new faction, the Lofa Defence Force (LDF), led by François Massaquoi, emerged in early 1994 and attacked ULIMO—K positions. Discord emerged between Taylor and the NPFL's Central Revolutionary Committee (CRC) and resulted in the creation of an NPFL breakaway group, the NPFL—CRC, led by Thomas Woewiyu. In August the UN Secretary-General admitted that the disarmament process had 'largely come to a halt'.

In August 1994 a coalition of the LPC, the AFL, ULIMO—J and the LDF, with the political support of the NPFL—CRC, began assembling forces for an attack on Gbarnga, the NPFL stronghold. In September, however, the coalition offensive was pre-empted by ULIMO—K forces, which succeeded in taking Gbarnga. Coalition forces immediately launched attacks against NPFL fighters in the north and east of Liberia. This marked the beginning of the third phase of heavy fighting in the civil war, which continued until August 1995. At the end of 1994 forces loyal to Taylor regained control of Gbarnga. Meanwhile, in Monrovia, a coup attempt was staged by elements in the AFL loyal to Doe, led by Gen. Charles Julu. Julu's coup was defeated by ECOMOG, which proceeded to a partial disarming of the AFL; reportedly some AFL elements then joined the LPC and ULIMO—J. Julu was captured and, in 1995, sentenced to seven years' imprisonment, but was later pardoned and released. About 200,000 people fled the fighting in late 1994. In total, there were estimated to be nearly 800,000 refugees in neighbouring countries and a large number of internally displaced persons at the end of 1994; the population of Monrovia, estimated at 400,000 before the start of the civil war, increased dramatically, reaching 1.3m. in January 1995, as civilians sought the relative security of the ECOMOG zone.

On the diplomatic front, a further series of peace negotiations began, under ECOWAS auspices, in September 1994. The new Chairman of ECOWAS, Flt-Lt Jerry Rawlings of Ghana, appeared to have added a new pragmatism to ECOWAS deliberations. The principle of a civilian transitional government was abandoned, and Taylor and the other principal faction leaders were allowed representation on the Council of State. In September the first agreement in this new round of diplomacy was signed in Akosombo, Ghana. It provided for a five-member Council of State; one representative was to be appointed by each of the AFL, the NPFL and ULIMO—K, one by the Liberia National Conference (LNC—a consortium of Liberian political parties and civil society groups) and one, supposedly also representing civil society, was to be nominated jointly by the NPFL and ULIMO—K, which eventually agreed to appoint a traditional chief, Tamba Taylor, to this position. The Akosombo Agreement also sought to discourage the formation of new factions by a declaration that they would not be recognized, and that their members would be prosecuted as criminals. In this respect, the Akosombo Agreement was successful, and the proliferation of factions came to a halt. A cease-fire was implemented in December. However, armed clashes between the factions continued. In August a further peace agreement, signed at Abuja, Nigeria, provided for the establishment of a new LNTG, headed by a six-member Council of State: Charles Taylor of the NPFL; Alhaji Kromah of ULIMO—K; George Boley representing a coalition of the LPC, NPFL—CRC and the LDF; Oscar Quiah and Wilton Sankawulo representing the LNC; and Chief Tamba Taylor. Sankawulo was appointed Chairman, assuming, in September, the position occupied by David Kpomakpor. With the formation of the Council of State, Taylor was finally installed in the Executive Mansion.

Despite the cease-fire provisions of the Abuja Agreement, intermittent fighting between ULIMO—J and ULIMO—K continued. In November 1995 a further cease-fire agreement was signed (but not consistently implemented) by the leaders of the NPFL and ULIMO—K. The return of refugees and displaced persons remained slow, and some 768,000 refugees remained in neighbouring countries. In December 1995 and January 1996 ULIMO—J forces, possibly assisted by the LDF, attacked ECOMOG positions in Tubmanburg, causing significant ECOMOG and civilian casualties. The fighting was brought to a halt, but the situation remained tense, and, after this, the peace process never recovered. In early 1996 a renewed leadership struggle erupted in ULIMO—J. Johnson's rivals issued a statement claiming that he had been replaced, and in February he was suspended from his ministerial post by the Council of State. In April 1996 Taylor and Kromah launched a military assault on Johnson and his supporters in the capital, and, for the first time since 1990, hostilities spread to central Monrovia. This marked the beginning of the fourth phase of heavy fighting in the civil war.

In May 1996 a cease-fire was agreed. ECOMOG was redeployed throughout Monrovia, and armed combatants withdrew from the capital. However, fighting continued in the south-east and the west, especially between the ULIMO factions. By mid-1996 ECOMOG had regained control of the outskirts of Monrovia and a zone extending from the Po river in the west, to Kakata, in Margibi County, in the north, and to Buchanan in the east. In August a revised form of the Abuja Agreement was signed, replacing the ineffective Sankawulo with Ruth Sando Perry. ECOWAS threatened that violators of the Agreement would face charges at a war crimes tribunal, and that other sanctions targeted specifically at the factional leaderships would be imposed. In September a local cease-fire was finally agreed between the ULIMO—J and ULIMO—K factions, which had been engaged in hostilities around Tubmanburg. The agreement allowed aid agencies access to the area for the first time in seven months; the levels of starvation discovered among the estimated 25,000 civilians there were among the worst ever to have been reliably reported.

Progress towards demobilization, in accordance with the second Abuja Agreement, was achieved in early 1997. At the end of February the three faction leaders on the Council of State, Taylor, Kromah and Boley, resigned from their posts in order to contest the presidential election stipulated by the Abuja Agreement. Each formed a political party as a vehicle for their candidacy: Taylor established the National Patriotic Party (NPP), Kromah the All Liberian Coalition Party (ALCOP), and Boley the National Democratic Party of Liberia (NDPL). Several political parties that had become inactive during the civil conflict re-emerged to present candidates. Ellen Johnson-Sirleaf represented the Unity Party (UP), Gabriel Baccus Matthews the UPP, while Togba Nah Tipoteh, rather than Amos Sawyer, became the candidate of the Liberian People's Party (LPP). Chea Cheapoo headed a revived PPP, of which he had been a leader in the late 1970s. Henry Boima Fahnbulleh, Jr, a MOJA leader in the 1970s and a prominent opponent of Doe in the late 1980s, represented a new association, the Reformation Alliance Party. Henry Moniba, Doe's last Vice-President, submitted his candidacy on behalf of another new party, the Liberian National Union (LINU). Cletus Wotorson, a minister in Tolbert's last Cabinet and a leader of the Liberian Action Party (LAP), became the candidate for an alliance of the LAP and the Liberian Unification Party (LUP). Voting. More than 500 international observers, who monitored the election, which took place on 19 July 1997, declared that no serious irregularities had occurred. Taylor secured an outright victory in the presidential poll, with 75% of the votes cast. Johnson-Sirleaf obtained 10% of the votes, while Kromah won 4%, Wotorson and Matthews 3% each and Tipoteh 2%; no other candidate secured more than 10,000 votes. In the legislative elections the NPP won 49 of the 64 seats in the House of Representatives and 21 of the 26 seats in the Senate. Taylor was duly inaugurated as President on 2 August. ECOWAS ended the economic sanctions that had been imposed against Liberia, although the UN armaments embargo remained in force. UNOMIL was dissolved, following the expiry of its final mandate at the end of September 1997. Refugees began to return to Liberia in significant numbers; by January 1998 the refugees remaining in neighbouring countries had declined to 480,000.

DOMESTIC POLITICS UNDER TAYLOR, 1997–2003

The new legislature confirmed the 1984 Constitution. The state remained highly centralized; the counties had no independent revenue-raising powers and were governed by superintendents appointed by the President. Two new counties were created in 2000: River Gee, formed from Lower Grand Gedeh County, with its capital at Fish Town, and Gbarpolu, created from southern Lofa County, with its capital at Bopolu. The legislature was largely inactive under Taylor's administration. The judiciary remained weakened by inadequate funding and shortages of qualified personnel and subject to political, social and financial pressures limiting its independence.

Shortly after his election, Taylor appointed a number of opposition politicians and the former faction leaders, Johnson and Kromah, to the Government, allegedly as a gesture of reconciliation. Within a year, however, prominent opposition politicians came under attack from Taylor's regime. In March 1998 Johnson accused Taylor's security agents of arresting and assaulting his bodyguards and claimed that his own life was under threat. Johnson was subsequently removed from the Cabinet, and he left Liberia, supposedly for medical treatment. Also in that month Kromah, who, like Johnson, had expressed fears for his safety, was removed from his position as head of the Reconciliation Commission, and he also left the country. In August Johnson unexpectedly returned to Liberia and in September Taylor's security forces attempted to capture Johnson and close down his base in Monrovia. During the ensuing fighting Johnson and about 23 of his supporters took refuge in the US embassy compound. Under an agreement reached with the US embassy, Johnson was allowed to leave the country for Sierra Leone. Some 18,000 Krahn fled to Côte d'Ivoire, following the attack.

In October 1998 32 civilians (several, including Johnson, Kromah, George Boley and Ellen Johnson-Sirleaf, *in absentia*) were charged with treason; of these, 18 were arrested. Nine AFL officers, all Krahn, were also arrested and charged with sedition. In April 1999 12 of the civilians, all of them Krahn, were convicted and each sentenced to 10 years' imprisonment. Four of the nine AFL officers were convicted in February 2000, and each was sentenced to 10 years' imprisonment with hard labour. (Taylor, exercising powers of clemency, released three of the 12 civilians in July 2001 and the remaining civilian and military prisoners in March 2002. Both Kromah and Johnson refused to return to Liberia, despite Taylor's declaration of a general amnesty for all treason suspects living abroad. Johnson was reported to have died of natural causes in Nigeria in October 2004.)

Party political activity was limited under Taylor's regime and the strongest civil political opposition to Taylor's policies came from within the NPP itself. In March 1999 the President of the Senate, Charles Brumskine, who was considered to be a moderate figure in the NPP, fled the country, expressing fears for his personal security. More active opposition may have been discouraged by the deaths of two prominent former associates of Taylor. Samuel Dokie and members of his family were killed, following an order for their arrest issued by the head of the Special Security Service in November 1997. Dokie was a former supporter of Taylor during the war, but had joined the group of NPFL dissidents, the NPFL—CRC, in 1994. Enoch Dogolea, the Vice-President and a long-standing ally of Taylor, died in June 2000. Rumours emerged that he had been murdered at Taylor's stronghold.

Under the terms of the 1991 Yamoussoukro Accords and subsequent agreements, ECOMOG was to supervise the disarmament process and participate in the restructuring of the AFL to create a national army. However, shortly after his election, Taylor stated that reorganization of the armed forces was solely a matter for the elected Government and failed to implement the agreed restructuring. In January 1999 it was announced that most of the remaining ECOMOG troops in Liberia were to be relocated to Sierra Leone and they finally withdrew in October.

Security agencies proliferated under Taylor's administration; their identities, command structures and financing were often unclear. Two élite paramilitary security forces, the Anti-Terrorist Unit (ATU) or Anti-Terrorist Brigade and the Special Security Service (SSS), were created in 1997. Both reported directly to the President; the ATU was headed by the President's son, Charles Taylor, Jr. The AFL, in contrast, was significantly reduced in size. During 2000 a paramilitary police unit, the Special Operations Division (SOD) emerged. In addition to these security forces, almost every large organization, including government ministries, parastatals and private businesses, and some prominent individuals, employed private security forces. Those hired by logging companies became well-known after the international scrutiny of the industry began in 2001. Reports of harassment by security forces, often unidentified, were frequent during Taylor's administration.

INTERNATIONAL RELATIONS UNDER TAYLOR

Liberia's international relations during Taylor's regime were dominated by Taylor's role in fomenting regional instability, particularly in Sierra Leone. In the first months of his administration Taylor remained critical of ECOWAS policy towards Sierra Leone and sought to obstruct ECOMOG efforts to reinstate the elected Sierra Leonean President, Ahmad Tejan Kabbah. Although for some time after the reinstatement of President Kabbah in March 1998, Liberia's relations with Sierra Leone and its rebels appeared to conform to ECOWAS policy, the international community made increasingly strong accusations during 1998 and 1999 that Taylor continued to support the RUF covertly. The collapse of the Lomé Agreement, following the RUF attacks on UNAMSIL peace-keeping troops in late April and early May 2000, raised the issue of

Taylor's involvement in the Sierra Leone conflict once again. Press reports suggested that Taylor was training RUF combatants under the control of Sam Bockarie, who had left Sierra Leone for Liberia in December 1999. In August 2000 the UN Security Council resolved to establish a Special Court to prosecute war crimes perpetrated in the Sierra Leonean civil war, and it became evident that Taylor could face trial for war crimes committed by the RUF in Sierra Leone.

From late 1999 the issue of 'conflict diamonds' (diamonds illicitly mined and exported by rebel forces) had become increasingly prominent. In June 2000 the British Government once more referred to links between the RUF and 'supporters in Liberia' and urged a UN boycott of unlicensed diamonds from Sierra Leone. In July the UN Security Council adopted Resolution 1306, prohibiting the international sale of diamonds originating with the RUF, and demanded that the Liberian Government comply with the ban. A Panel of Experts established by the UN reported in December 2000 that there was substantial evidence that the Government of Liberia was supporting the RUF in providing training, armaments and logistical support, and in allowing its territory to be used as a base for attacks and as a refuge. The Panel made extensive recommendations, many of which were incorporated in Resolution 1343, adopted by the UN Security Council in March 2001. Resolution 1343 demanded that the Liberian Government immediately cease its support for the RUF and other armed rebels in the region. In particular, it demanded that Liberia expel all RUF members from its territory, end direct or indirect import of unlicensed rough diamonds from Sierra Leone, and ground all aircraft on the Liberian registry within its jurisdiction, until such time as it could operate a registry in accordance with international conventions. The Resolution replaced the 1992 armaments embargo on Liberia, which had never been rescinded, with a revised embargo, with immediate effect. The UN Security Council further threatened to impose an embargo on the direct or indirect import of all rough diamonds from Liberia, whatever their origin, and to place an international travel ban on senior members of the Liberian Government and armed forces if Liberia did not demonstrably cease its support of the RUF within two months.

In May 2001 the UN determined that Liberia had failed to take sufficient measures to comply with its demands and, in particular, expressed dissatisfaction with Liberia's inability to provide evidence of Bockarie's departure from the country. Accordingly, the diamond embargo and the travel ban were imposed. The list of those affected by the travel ban included not only senior government figures and their immediate families, as expected, but also businessmen, arms dealers and figures from the logging industry.

The armament and diamond embargoes and the travel ban were reviewed in early 2002. By this time, as the Liberian Government emphasized repeatedly, the war in Sierra Leone had officially ended. However, the UN again concluded that Liberia had failed to comply fully with the Security Council's demands, the crucial evidence being that Liberian armed forces were clearly in possession of new armaments and ammunition, indicating a breach of the arms embargo. The Security Council reimposed the armaments and diamond embargoes and the travel ban for a further 12 months, from May 2002, under Resolution 1408. The Resolution also indicated that, should preparation of an effective certificate-of-origin scheme be completed, Liberian diamonds proven to be legally mined would be exempted from the embargo, and it urged Liberia to establish transparent and internationally verifiable audit regimes to ensure that revenue derived from the maritime registry and the timber industry were used only for legitimate purposes. The measures concerning Liberia's air registry were allowed to lapse.

In October the UN Panel of Experts reported that some 1,250–1,500 former RUF combatants continued to operate in élite Liberian military units, under the command of Liberian Gen. Benjamin Yeaten, but with continuing loyalty to Bockarie. In March 2003 the Liberian Minister of Foreign Affairs confirmed in a letter to the President of the UN Security Council that it had breached the armaments embargo, citing Liberia's right to self-defence as justification. Also in March the Sierra Leone Special Court issued indictments against seven former leaders of armed factions in Sierra Leone, including Sankoh, Bockarie and Koroma. The indictments alleged that Sankoh, Bockarie and Koroma had acted in co-operation with Taylor, and the possibility that Taylor himself might be indicted for war crimes began to be taken more seriously. The Special Court further claimed that Bockarie was supported by the Liberian Government and threatened to indict Taylor if he did not transfer him to the Sierra Leonean authorities, later also demanding the arrest of Koroma, who was reported to have fled to Liberia. In April the Panel of Experts for the first time accused Guinea of supporting the rebel group Liberians United for Reconciliation and Democracy (LURD—see below) and violating the armaments embargo. The UN Security Council adopted Resolution 1478, renewing sanctions for a further 12 months in May 2003, and also imposed a 10-month ban on imports of round logs and timber products from Liberia, effective from July.

Almost simultaneously with the renewal and extension of UN sanctions came the announcement of the death of Bockarie, who, together with a group of supporters, had joined rebels in Côte d'Ivoire in November 2002. Liberian government sources claimed that he was killed by Liberian troops as he and his followers attempted to enter Liberia from Côte d'Ivoire. Other sources claimed that Bockarie was killed in Monrovia by Taylor's bodyguards, after threatening to give evidence against Taylor at the Sierra Leone Special Court. In May 2003 Alan White, the chief of investigations for the Special Court, announced that he had evidence that Bockarie's immediate family had also been killed on Taylor's orders. On 4 June, while Taylor was attending peace talks in Accra, Ghana (see below), the Special Court unsealed its indictment of Taylor for war crimes, crimes against humanity and serious violations of international law, and issued an international warrant for his arrest. However, the Ghanaian authorities failed to take any action to arrest Taylor and he returned to Monrovia on the following day. In mid-June the Special Court announced that it was investigating claims that Koroma had been killed early that month in Lofa County, where he had been reportedly training troops for Taylor.

RESURGENCE OF CIVIL CONFLICT, 1999–2003

A series of security incidents, beginning in Lofa County in 1999, developed into renewed civil conflict, which finally resulted in the ousting of Taylor's Government in mid-2003. In April 1999 an unidentified armed militia attacked the town of Voinjama, in Lofa County. In August an initially unidentified group, later named as the Joint Forces for the Liberation of Liberia (JFLL), captured five towns in the Foya and Kolahun districts of Lofa County. In both cases AFL troops rapidly regained control.

There was a renewed outbreak of fighting in upper Lofa County in July and August 2000. Armed rebels took control of several towns, causing the displacement of an initial 30,000 civilians. The dissidents identified themselves as LURD, a previously unknown grouping, under the leadership of Mohammed S. K. Jumandy, with 'Gen.' Joe Wylie as their military spokesman. Its political programme was limited to the removal of the Taylor regime. (In 2003 it was reported that approximately 90% of the LURD command and 60% of its combatants were former ULIMO supporters, although the movement also included former members of the NPFL, INPFL, AFL, Sierra Leonean Kamajors and RUF, and a few remnants of the Sierra Leonean 'West Side Boys'.) Taylor at various times accused both Alhaji Kromah and Roosevelt Johnson of involvement with the rebels, but LURD appears to have remained distant from the faction leaders of the 1989–96 conflict. With greater credibility, Charles Julu, the Doe loyalist, was also accused of involvement. In September 2000 Taylor, who had accused Guinea of responsibility for the August 1999 attack, staged an offensive, with the RUF supporting Liberian government troops, on Guinean towns near the border with northern Liberia. Guinea retaliated by bombarding the Liberian town of Zorzor with long-range-artillery. From this time it became widely accepted that LURD was receiving support and assistance from Guinea.

Renewed attacks near Zorzor in October 2000 prompted the flight of a further 15,000 civilians. In late November and early December fighting erupted in northern Nimba County. In April 2001 François Massaquoi, the Liberian Minister of Youth and Sport (and former leader of the LDF, the anti-ULIMO—K faction), was killed, apparently after insurgents opened fire on his helicopter as it prepared to land at Voinjama, in Lofa County. At the end of that month the fighting was reported to have advanced in Lofa County, reaching Salayea district. The human rights organization Amnesty International accused government forces of torturing, raping and killing civilians suspected of supporting the rebels and also publicized reports that the rebels were committing atrocities. Some 80,000 persons were reported to have been internally displaced by the conflict and another 162,000 had become refugees in neighbouring countries. At the end of May UN intelligence sources considered that Lofa was under LURD control. In late 2001 fighting advanced increasingly near to Monrovia. In February 2002, in response to deeper incursions into Liberia by the rebel forces, Taylor declared a state of emergency.

In March 2002 peace negotiations were arranged by ECOWAS in Abuja; LURD representatives failed to attend. Taylor failed to attend a further conference in Ouagadougou, Burkina Faso, in July. The Ougadougou conference urged greater international involvement and an International Contact Group on Liberia (ICGL), comprising delegations from the UN, the AU, ECOWAS, Morocco, Nigeria, Senegal (later replaced by Ghana), the European Union (EU), France, the United Kingdom and the USA, was established and held its inaugural meeting in New York, USA, in September.

The fighting continued while these discussions took place. By March 2002 Bopolu, in Gbarpolu County, was increasingly referred to as a LURD base area. In April there were reports of a split in the leadership of LURD between Joe Wylie and Sekou Damate Conneh who had replaced Jumandy as the national Chairman of LURD in December 2001. Conneh had served in former President Samuel Doe's administration; he was believed to have gone into exile after Taylor's Government was installed. Conneh was reported to head a Mandingo faction within LURD, while Wylie led a predominantly Krahn faction. Julu was believed to support Wylie's faction. Human rights abuses perpetrated during the conflict were further documented in a May 2002 report by a New York-based advocacy group, Human Rights Watch (HRW), which accused government forces of systematically committing atrocities against civilians and also accused LURD of gross abuses.

LURD occupied Tubmanburg in May 2002, and claimed to be in control of Lofa, Gbarpolu and Bomi Counties and significant regions in central Liberia at the end of that month. Government forces regained control of Tubmanburg and the surrounding towns in July. In August the Government announced it had recaptured Voinjama, the capital of Lofa County, and, in September, Bopolu, allowing Taylor to end the seven-month state of emergency, despite an admission that Voinjama and Zorzor remained under LURD control.

During the first half of 2003 hostilities spread into Côte d'Ivoire, with LURD regaining the initiative, and a new armed faction emerged in south-eastern Liberia. In early January Côte d'Ivoire accused Liberian mercenaries of attacking the village of Neka and later that month Côte d'Ivoire announced that Liberian government troops had participated in Ivorian rebel attacks on Toulépleu, close to the Liberian border. Further south, unidentified forces crossed into Liberia from Côte d'Ivoire and captured the town of Beam, in Grand Gedeh County. At the end of February heavy fighting was reported from Toe Town, north-west of Zwedru, near the Ivorian border, during which three aid workers, including a Norwegian national, were killed, attracting condemnation from the UN. Meanwhile, in the west, LURD regained control of Bopolu, Sawmill and Tubmanburg in February. Renewed accusations of Liberian government involvement with Ivorian rebel groups, notably the Mouvement pour la justice et la paix (MJP) and the Mouvement populaire ivoirien du grand ouest (MPIGO), were made by Global Witness and the International Crisis Group. In late March reports began to emerge of a new armed group, the Movement for Democracy in Liberia (MODEL), which attacked and held Zwedru in Grand Geddeh County. MODEL was reported to comprise principally Krahn former members of the AFL and Doe loyalists, who were predominantly based in Côte d'Ivoire. Some observers alleged that the Ivorian Government provided it with armaments and financial assistance, while financial support from the US Krahn diaspora was also suspected.

Further meetings of the ICGL had been held in December 2002 and February 2003. The ICGL urged both LURD and the Liberian Government to negotiate a cease-fire. By this time members of the Ivorian MJP and MPIGO had clashed with Liberian rebels and RUF members formerly allied with them. In the course of this conflict, Felix Doh, the leader of MPIGO, was killed in April, possibly by Bockarie, who had been leading former RUF elements fighting with the Ivorian rebels. At this point, according to a report by the UN Secretary-General, about 60% of Liberian territory was under rebel control. On 7 May the death of Bockarie was announced (see above). In mid-May Taylor announced his intention to attend peace discussions, which were convened for early June by the ICGL in Accra, Ghana. MODEL captured Harper and Pleebo, both timber exporting harbour towns near the Ivorian border, and began to advance towards Buchanan, Liberia's second largest city, later that month. By this time only Margibi and Grand Bassa Counties were unaffected by the fighting. In response to demands from the USA, LURD and MODEL halted their advances on Monrovia and Buchanan on 29 May and pledged to observe a cease-fire, provided that their positions were not attacked.

Peace discussions began in Accra on 4 June 2003, with Taylor and LURD in attendance, but were thrown into chaos by the announcement of Taylor's indictment for war crimes by the Sierra Leone Special Court (see above). Taylor returned to Monrovia on 5 June, where he immediately announced that he had suppressed an attempted coup, involving some of his senior officials and an unnamed foreign embassy. On the same day LURD launched a major attack on Monrovia, rapidly reached Monrovia's western suburbs, and caused an exodus from refugee camps on the outskirts of Monrovia towards the city centre and the eastern suburbs. The US embassy urged Taylor to resign from office. On 7 June a government counter-offensive forced the rebels to withdraw back over the St Paul's Bridge over the Mesurado river, which separated the western suburbs from the city centre. The peace discussions in Ghana were suspended, pending a cease-fire and the arrival of the MODEL delegation. On 11 June the Ghanaian Minister of Foreign Affairs and the ECOWAS Executive Secretary arrived in Monrovia to mediate a truce and there was a lull in the fighting, as LURD withdrew to the Po river, 20 km west of Monrovia. The Liberian authorities estimated that about 400 civilians and military personnel had been killed in the fighting around Monrovia at that time. About 50,000 internally displaced civilians were living in temporary conditions in the national sports stadium and other buildings in central and eastern Monrovia, and the humanitarian situation caused grave concern. Peace talks resumed on 12 June and a new cease-fire agreement was signed on 17 June. The accord required the deployment of a multinational stabilization force and a 30-day period of consultation, prior to the adoption of a comprehensive peace agreement, the main provision of which would be the departure of Taylor from the presidency.

Less than a week after the cease-fire was signed, LURD attacked Monrovia again, seizing Bushrod Island and the Free Port. About 300 civilians were killed before LURD withdrew once more, in early July 2003. At the end of June US President George W. Bush had urged Taylor to resign and the UN Secretary-General had recommended to the Security Council that a multinational intervention force be deployed in Liberia. On 6 July Taylor announced that he had accepted, in principle, an offer of asylum from the Nigerian President, Olusegun Obasanjo, but stipulated that he would not leave the country until a peace-keeping force arrived. Despite increasing international support for US intervention, President Bush indicated that he would only deploy peace-keeping troops in Liberia after Taylor had left the country and a West African mission had restored order. On 17 July a third attack on Monrovia by LURD forces prompted the USA to order a naval task force to Liberia. On 22 July a summit meeting of ECOWAS

Heads of State was convened in the Senegalese capital, Dakar. Following pressure from the UN Secretary-General, the West African delegates agreed the following day to dispatch an initial 1,300 Nigerian peace-keeping troops to Liberia. On 1 August, following a proposal by the US Administration, the UN Security Council adopted Resolution 1497, authorizing the establishment of a multinational force in Liberia. The deployment of the ECOWAS Mission in Liberia (ECOMIL) began on 4 August when an advanced party of troops arrived in Monrovia. The fighting in Monrovia came to an end on their arrival without ECOMIL having to engage in combat.

On 11 August 2003, following continued pressure from West African governments and the international community, Taylor relinquished power to his Vice-President, Moses Zeh Blah, before leaving Liberia for exile in Calabar, south-eastern Nigeria. Blah was inaugurated as interim Head of State, pending the installation of a government of national unity. Taylor's departure fulfilled the main demand of the rebel leadership, and was received with celebrations in Monrovia. On the following day the US naval task force reached the Liberian coast. The Government and LURD rebels withdrew their forces from the Monrovia Free Port and the city centre, ceding control of the area to ECOMIL, which was assisted by about 200 US marines. On 18 August the Government of Liberia signed a comprehensive peace agreement (CPA), with leaders of the LURD and MODEL factions in Accra. The CPA provided for an immediate cease-fire, a disarmament, demobilization, rehabilitation and reintegration (DDRR) programme, a restructuring of the national army to include former rebel combatants, the disbanding of all irregular forces, Blah's departure from office by 14 October—by which time he was to transfer power to a transitional power-sharing administration, which was to govern Liberia until January 2006—and elections, to be held not later than October 2005. On 21 August 2003 the delegations elected Charles Gyude Bryant, a businessman and founder member of the LAP, as Chairman of the transitional administration, later known as the National Transitional Government of Liberia (NTGL). Despite the cease-fire, skirmishes, and some instances of more extensive fighting, continued to occur. In mid-September the strength of the ECOMIL contingent reached 3,500 personnel, with contributions from The Gambia, Ghana, Guinea-Bissau, Mali, Nigeria, Senegal and Togo. At this time LURD was estimated to number some 5,000 combatants, MODEL some 1,500–3,000 and government forces some 20,000–30,000. There were an estimated 500,000 internally displaced Liberians, about 300,000 Liberian refugees in neighbouring countries and about 50,000 refugees from Sierra Leone and Côte d'Ivoire in Liberia at that time. On 19 September the UN Security Council adopted Resolution 1509, establishing the UN Mission in Liberia (UNMIL), designed to take over the functions of ECOMIL, and with an authorized strength of 15,000 military personnel and 1,115 civilian police-officers in a component known as CIVPOL. At the end of September 2003 the US Department of Defense announced the withdrawal of the naval task force. On 1 October ECOMIL transferred its troops, role and authority to UNMIL. On 14 October, in accordance with the peace agreement, President Blah transferred power to Chairman Gyude Bryant and the NTGL was formally installed.

THE NATIONAL TRANSITIONAL GOVERNMENT, 2003–06

Despite Taylor's departure, fears continued to be expressed that his influence on Liberian politics persisted. In December 2003 the Security Council reaffirmed the travel ban on Taylor and his associates and in March 2004, under Resolution 1532, the UN Security Council imposed a freeze on the assets of Taylor, his family and his associates. In March 2005 the UN Secretary-General reported continuing concerns that some of Taylor's former commanders and business associates were planning to undermine the peace process. Also in March, Taylor's associate, Guus van Kouwenhoven (see Economy), was arrested by Dutch police and charged with war crimes and violating UN sanctions (he was convicted of the latter charge in June 2006 and sentenced to eight years' imprisonment). In May 2005 the Chief Prosecutor of the Sierra Leone Special Court, referring to an assassination attempt made on President Lansana Conté of Guinea in January, stated that he had information from 'multiple sources' that Taylor had orchestrated the coup attempt in Guinea. Demands for the Nigerian Government to extradite Taylor to the Special Court in Sierra Leone gathered strength in 2005. However, Nigeria indicated that it would hand over Taylor only at the request of the new administration, to be elected in October.

The first six months of the NTGL were marked by continuous disputes over the allocation of posts within the Government. At the end of November 2003 representatives of LURD, MODEL and the former Government jointly demanded a postponement of the DDRR programme until their objections to the allocation of posts had been satisfied. This threat was condemned by the peace agreement Implementation Monitoring Committee, comprising representatives of UNMIL, ECOWAS, the AU, the EU and the ICGL, which effectively ended the impasse by demanding that appropriate measures (including prosecution under international law) be taken against parties responsible for the continuing violations of the cease-fire. (Eventually, in January 2004 Bryant reached an agreement with LURD, MODEL and the former government grouping that each would receive 17 of the 86 assistant ministerial positions available, a resolution effected by reducing the numbers allocated to civil society representatives.)

UNMIL's troop strength was augmented only by the arrival of various specialist units before mid-December 2003. Violations of the cease-fire continued to occur and numerous incidents of abuse of civilians by faction members to be reported, including apparently ethnically targeted atrocities against Gio and Mano perpetrated by Krahn elements associated with MODEL. The arrival of UNMIL contingents from Pakistan and Ethiopia in December together with other contributions raised UNMIL strength to about 10,000 by mid-January 2004, thereby enabling an extension of UNMIL's deployment early that year. UNMIL first reached a figure approximating its authorized strength and completed its deployment in late July. UNMIL's largest military contingents at this time were from Bangladesh, Pakistan, Ethiopia, Nigeria and other West African states.

Cease-fire violations became less frequent with the deployment of UNMIL troops, and after June 2004 were limited to incidents involving opposing elements within LURD; none was reported after September. However, a large-scale riot occurred in Monrovia at the end of October and rapidly assumed ethnic and religious dimensions focused on the predominantly Muslim Mandingo ethnic group. These disturbances resulted in 19 deaths and injuries to 208 people. Further incidents of violent unrest, including some involving former combatants, occurred in early 2005. While violent disputes between LURD factions subsided thereafter, incidents involving ex-combatants and AFL personnel continued. Organized groups of former combatants began an illegal occupation of the Guthrie rubber plantation in August 2004 and others occupied the Sapo National Park. (UNMIL assisted with the evacuation of Sapo National Park in late August and early September 2005, but did not end the Guthrie occupation until August 2006, despite reports of assaults and forced labour at the plantation.) Inter-ethnic clashes, mainly in Lofa and Nimba Counties, also continued to be reported in 2005. Despite these incidents, there was a notable improvement in the observance of human rights in Liberia after the inauguration of the NTGL and the disarmament of the factions. However, high levels of violent crime, especially rape and other sexual violence, continued to cause concern. Incidents of 'mob justice' and the formation of vigilante groups have been continually reported since the signing of the CPA. The incapacity of the judicial and prison systems also became the focus of increasing attention during 2005. In December 2005 the legislature approved a new law on rape, which significantly strengthened previous legislation. The involvement of members of UNMIL and of national and international non-governmental organizations in cases of sexual abuse and exploitation of children was revealed in May 2006.

The formal disarmament programme began in December 2003, but was immediately suspended after violent disturbances and was not relaunched until mid-April 2004. Apart from a riot of former government forces in Monrovia, during which one protester was killed in May, the programme then proceeded smoothly and was formally terminated on 31 October, although disarmament operations continued in some areas after that date. The armed factions were formally dissolved in early November. By March 2005 101,000 combatants had been disarmed and demobilized since December 2003, and some 28,000 weapons had been collected. The disparity between the number of combatants and the number of weapons may have been owing to fraudulent claimants, who qualified for benefits under the DDRR by obtaining and then surrendering ammunition rather than weapons. The other possibility, that weapons were retained by genuine former combatants, caused widespread concern and suspicions that armaments had been concealed within Liberia or removed to areas just beyond Liberia's borders. The illegal occupation of the Guthrie rubber plantation by ex-combatants, apparently still armed and with commanding officers still present, and of the Sapo National Park by former MODEL combatants, again apparently in possession of weapons, also raised doubts about the effectiveness of the disarmament programme. In March 2005 the UN Secretary-General announced that only some 26,000 disarmed and demobilized former combatants had been absorbed into projects funded by UN and other agencies; he reported that projects had been planned for a further 45,000, but implied that there was no provision, actual or planned, for some 30,000 former combatants, owing to funding shortfalls. From 2005 there have been persistent reports that former child soldiers from Liberia were being recruited into armed groups in Côte d'Ivoire. The demobilization and retirement process for the AFL began at the end of May. By September some 9,400 irregular personnel had been successfully demobilized. A retirement programme for regular personnel began shortly afterwards, but was delayed by funding shortages and was not completed until December.

UN sanctions continued. At the end of December 2003 the UN Security Council adopted Resolution 1521, which authorized the renewal of the armaments, diamond and logging embargoes imposed on Liberia and extended the travel ban on Taylor and his associates for a further year, while revising the basis for these sanctions. Although the previous concern over Taylor's support for the RUF was no longer relevant, the UN Security Council noted that the cease-fire and peace agreement were not being universally implemented, particularly in areas to which UNMIL troops were not yet deployed, that the NTGL had yet to extend its authority to much of the country and that illicit trade in diamonds and logs remained a potential threat to peace and stability. The sanctions were renewed in December 2004 under Resolution 1579, which extended the armaments, logging and travel embargoes for 12 months and the diamond embargo for a further six months. In June 2005 the diamond embargo was extended for a further six months under Resolution 1607.

In early 2005 the international community became increasingly concerned by the levels of financial malpractice and the poor economic governance in the NTGL. In May representatives of the UN, the EU, ECOWAS, the World Bank, the IMF and the USA met in Copenhagen, Denmark, and concluded that the NTGL had demonstrated an unwillingness to institute reforms and that corruption, misappropriation and a lack of transparency and accountability were undermining the implementation of the CPA. They agreed to formulate an action plan, later known as the Governance and Economic Management Assistance Programme (GEMAP), to be presented to the NTGL for implementation. In response, the NTGL did take some action against corruption. In July J. D. Slanger, formerly of MODEL, the Commissioner of the Bureau of Maritime Affairs, and Morris (or Mohammed) Dukuly, Liberia's representative at the International Maritime Organization (IMO), were suspended indefinitely by Bryant. The men were accused, with two others, of misappropriating more than US $4m. After prolonged negotiation with the NTGL, during which the demand that international judges should preside in the Liberian courts was abandoned, the GEMAP document was finally signed by Bryant in September. The signing was intended to signal to candidates in the forthcoming elections that illicit opportunities to acquire wealth from office would come to an end. GEMAP provided for detailed international oversight of Liberia's public revenue, spending, contracts and concessions and for capacity-building in anti-corruption activities (see Economy).

Following the settlement of disputes over the allocation of government posts, domestic politics under the NTGL were dominated by three interconnected issues: the continued dissension within the LURD leadership; preparations for the 2005 elections; and the position of the Speaker of the National Transitional Legislative Assembly (NTLA), George Dweh. In January 2004 a split was reported in the LURD leadership, with Aisha Keita Conneh, the estranged wife of Sekou Damate Conneh, supported by 40 of LURD's military commanders, contesting the leadership with Sekou Conneh and his supporters. (Aisha Conneh's influence within LURD was believed to derive from her close relationship with President Lansana Conté of Guinea.) It later emerged that Aisha Conneh's faction sought the removal of the LURD-nominated Minister of Finance, Lusine Kamara. Both factions asserted their commitment to the peace agreement, but the dispute reportedly caused armed clashes in Gbarnga, Tubmanburg and Voinjama.

In June 2004 LURD's national executive council announced the 'indefinite suspension' of Sekou Conneh and his replacement by Chayee Z. Doe, a younger brother of the former President. Conneh rejected the suspension and refused to concede to demands for the removal of Kamara. Matters were thrown into further confusion by the death in that month of Doe after surgery in the USA. In July Kabineh Ja'neh, the LURD-nominated Minister of Justice in the NTGL, was declared the Chairman of LURD following a ballot conducted by some LURD elements. However, Conneh refused to accept Ja'neh's election as legitimate and continued to present himself as LURD Chairman. In December the UN Secretary-General stated that UNMIL had received reports that Aisha Conneh's faction was planning to oust Chairman Bryant and halt the peace process. At this time divisions emerged between Sekou Conneh and George Dweh, the Speaker of the NTLA and a member of LURD. Conneh accused Dweh of attempting to garner international support for the removal of Bryant. In late October Dweh led an anti-Conneh faction in a further election, held by some members of the LURD executive committee, which again resulted in a vote for the removal of Conneh and his replacement by Ja'neh. The situation was regarded as sufficiently serious to prompt a reconciliatory meeting in Freetown, Sierra Leone, hosted by that country's President, Ahmad Tejan Kabbah, in November.

In January 2005 NPP members of the NTLA led the first moves to suspend Dweh from the post of Speaker for corruption. A report by a special parliamentary committee accused him and three associates of misappropriating US $92,000. In March the NTLA voted to suspend all four indefinitely. Armed UNMIL troops were deployed around the Assembly building at the installation of Dweh's successor, George Koukou, on 17 March. In the following month Dweh's name was added to the UN's travel ban list for activities undermining the CPA. The split within LURD resulted in the emergence in early 2005 of a grouping known as the LURD-Freedom Alliance, led by Ja'neh, and the registration of the Sekou Conneh faction as a political party, the Progressive Democratic Party (PRODEM), and the contentions between the two factions subsided. In April Conneh announced his intention to contest the presidency later that year. Ja'neh did not register as a political candidate.

Elections to the presidency, Senate and House of Representatives were scheduled for October 2005. Of the 22 presidential candidates approved by the National Elections Commission, by far the best known was George Manneh Weah, a Liberian footballer, who became internationally famous in the 1990s. Other leading contenders included Winston A. Tubman, a former UN envoy to Somalia and nephew of the former President, Harry Varney Gboto-Nambi Sherman, an adviser to Chairman Bryant, as well as candidates from the 1997 election, notably Ellen Johnson-Sirleaf and Togba-Nah Tipoteh. Taylor's party, the NPP, was represented by his former Minister of Agriculture, Roland Chris Yarkpah Massaquoi;

Alhaji G. V. Kromah was the only faction leader from the 1989–96 conflict and Conneh the only rebel leader from the 1999–2003 conflict to contest the presidency. Bryant and other members of the NTGL were not eligible to participate under the terms of the CPA.

Legislative and presidential elections were held, as scheduled, on 11 October 2005, and international and local observers agreed that the elections were generally free and fair. In the presidential ballot no candidate secured more than one-half of the votes cast. Weah, representing the Congress for Democratic Change (CDC), came first with 28.3% of the votes, followed by Johnson-Sirleaf of the UP with 19.8%, Charles Brumskine (Liberty Party—LP) with 13.9%, Tubman (NDPL—the party formerly led by George Boley) with 9.2% and Sherman (Coalition for the Transformation of Liberia—COTOL) with 7.8%. No other candidate secured more than 5% of votes cast. In the concurrently held elections for the 30-seat Senate, nine parties secured at least one seat. The largest parties were COTOL, which won nine seats, the UP with four seats, and the CDC, the Alliance for Peace and Democracy (led by Togba-Nah Tipoteh), the LP and the NPP, all with three seats each. In elections to the 64-seat House of Representatives, 11 parties secured at least one seat. The CDC became the largest single party in the lower house, with 15 seats; the LP secured nine seats while the UP won eight seats. The legislature consequently became politically fragmented and neither of the two leading presidential candidates could command a majority of supporters in either house. Associates or former associates of Taylor to secure legislative seats included Jewel Howard-Taylor, Taylor's then recently divorced wife, and Adolphus Dolo and Saah Richard Gbollie, both former Taylor commanders. All three were on the UN's travel ban list. A remarkable instance of political survival was presented by Prince Yormie Johnson, the former leader of the INFPL, who returned to Liberia in 2004 after an 11-year period of exile, as a self-proclaimed evangelical Christian; he won a Senate seat in his native Nimba County. In January 2006 the House of Representatives elected Edwin Snowe as Speaker of the chamber, a post usually regarded as the third most senior political position in Liberia, after the President and Vice-President. Snowe, a former director of the Liberian Petroleum and Refining Corporation, where he was alleged to have amassed much wealth, is also a former son-in-law of Taylor and has been accused of facilitating money transfers to Taylor during his exile in Nigeria; he also featured on the UN travel ban list. (Snowe resigned in February 2007 to be replaced initially by his deputy Tokpah Mulbah and then, after an election in April, by Alex Janekai Tyler of the LAP.)

In accordance with the Constitution, a second round ballot between the two leading presidential candidates was held on 8 November 2005. Observers again declared the election to have been free and fair. Johnson-Sirleaf won 59.4% of the votes cast, compared with 40.6% secured by Weah. A clear regional split emerged in the run-off ballot, with Weah performing well in the south-eastern counties and Johnson-Sirleaf attracting the most votes in central and western areas. Weah strongly contested the results, alleging 'massive and systematic' fraud, and protests were staged in Monrovia on 11 and 14 November after the provisional results were released. Nevertheless, on 21 December, following considerable pressure from regional leaders, Weah announced that he would not persist in his challenge to the results and Johnson-Sirleaf was sworn into office on 16 January 2006.

THE JOHNSON-SIRLEAF ADMINISTRATION

Johnson-Sirleaf's inaugural address stressed national reconciliation, political inclusion, sustainable development and economic governance reform. Despite her emphasis on inclusion, her nominations for government appointments failed to provide a position for Weah and the only opposition politicians (Joseph Korto, Walter Gwenigale and Jeremiah Sulunteh) to receive posts were those who had transferred their support to her in the second round of the presidential elections. The majority of nominees were 'technocrats', most importantly Antoinette Sayeh, a former World Bank official, as Minister of Finance, an appointment widely welcomed by the international community. The nominations of Samuel Kofi Woods, a human rights activist who had fled Liberia in 1999 citing threats to his life, and Tiawan Gongloe, a prominent human rights activist imprisoned by Taylor, as Minister of Labour and Solicitor-General, respectively, indicated a welcome commitment to human rights. Amos Sawyer, the former President of the IGNU, was nominated to head the Governance Reform Commission. However, some nominations caused controversy. Morris Dukuly, who organized Johnson-Sirleaf's campaign and who was proposed as Chief of Staff to the presidency, had been a ULIMO—K parliamentary deputy in the mid-1990s, and had been dismissed as Liberia's representative at the IMO in 2005, allegedly in connection with the misappropriation of funds. (Dukuly resigned his post in 2006.) The nomination of Kabineh Ja'neh, formerly of LURD (see above), as an Associate Justice of the Supreme Court also provoked opposition from a number of local human rights organizations, which alleged his participation in human rights abuses. Furthermore, the nomination of Frances Johnson-Morris, Chairwoman of the National Elections Commission, as Minister of Justice prompted protests from the CDC, which alleged that the appointment was a reward for ensuring Johnson-Sirleaf's victory. However, only the nominations of Ja'neh and of Jonathan Sagbe as Deputy Minister of Youth and Sports were vetoed by the Senate.

The first political problem confronting Johnson-Sirleaf on taking office was what decision to take regarding former President Taylor. Although the new President initially described Taylor's fate as a 'secondary issue', in March 2006 she ceded to pressure from a number of governments, intergovernmental organizations and human rights groups demanding the transfer of Taylor from Nigeria to the Special Court in Sierra Leone. Liberia formally requested Taylor's extradition on 17 March. Two days later Taylor disappeared from his residence in Calabar; he was recaptured shortly afterwards attempting to cross the Nigeria–Cameroon border. Taylor was immediately flown to Monrovia, from where he was transferred to Sierra Leone. At his first appearance before the Special Court on 3 April he pleaded not guilty to 11 charges of war crimes and crimes against humanity. On 30 April the Court requested that the Netherlands allow Taylor's trial be heard at the International Criminal Court (ICC) in The Hague, an arrangement that would also require a UN Security Council Resolution. The Dutch Government stated that it would accede to the request only if any ensuing prison sentence was served in another country. In June the United Kingdom agreed that Taylor could serve any custodial term in a British prison and Taylor was transferred to the custody of the ICC with the assent of the UN Security Council the same month. In December Taylor's son, Charles McArthur Emmanuel, commonly known as 'Chuckie' Taylor and the former head of the ATU, was charged in the USA with committing torture in Liberia. He denied the charge and the trial had yet to begin at mid-2007. The trial of former President Taylor began at The Hague in June 2007. Taylor announced he would boycott the trial. A verdict was not expected until mid-2009.

In January 2006 President Johnson-Sirleaf began measures to address state corruption. In her inaugural address, she emphasized acceptance of GEMAP and announced that all those appointed to high office would be required to reveal their assets. On 28 January she ordered all political appointees of the former NTGL to resign with immediate effect and two days later she ordered an audit of the NTGL and announced measures to curb overseas travel. A review of all concessions and contracts signed by the NTGL was initiated; all existing forestry concessions were rescinded. In December 2006 the former Minister of Finance in the NTGL, Lusine Kamara, his deputy, Tugbeh Doe, and the former Minister of Commerce, Samuel Wlue, were arrested and charged with misappropriating over US $9m. In February 2007 Gyude Bryant was charged with embezzling more than US $1m. during his period as Chairman of the NTGL.

Programmes to address human rights issues, initiated under the NTGL, were progressed slowly. The Truth and Reconciliation Commission (TRC), originally constituted under the NTGL, was formally relaunched in February 2006, under the chairmanship of Jerome Verdier, a human rights activist;

other commissioners included Bishop Arthur Kulah and Sheikh Kafumba F. Konneh, a Muslim leader. The TRC reported little activity in the first few months of its existence, however. The Independent National Commission on Human Rights (INHCR), also originally constituted under the NTGL under the chairmanship of a human rights lawyer once arrested by Taylor's regime, T. Dempster Brown, began the process of reappointing members in early 2006. However, neither the TRC not the INCHR made much further progress. The TRC was due to hold its first hearings in January 2007 but these were suspended indefinitely and had not begun by mid-2007. Concern at the inactivity of the TRC and the INCHR was voiced by Charlotte Abaka, the UN Independent Expert on the Promotion and Protection of Human Rights in Liberia in November 2006, and echoed by the UN Secretary-General in late 2006 and early 2007. The improved observance of human rights in Liberia visible under the NTGL has continued under the Johnson-Sirleaf administration, however, and has encouraged the resettlement of internally displaced persons and the return of refugees. The formal resettlement programme for internally displaced persons (IDPs) was officially completed in April 2006 and the remaining official IDP camps closed. Some 312,000 IDPs were assisted to return during the course of this programme. Nevertheless, it emerged shortly after the official closure of the IDP camps that some 29,000 people were still living on the former campsites. Many were assisted to return home during the remainder of 2006 and their numbers declined substantially. However, there appeared to be substantial numbers of IDPs remaining in unofficial camps or squats in the Monrovia area in late 2006. Over 160,000 Liberian refugees remained at the end of 2006 according to the UN High Commissioner for Refugees, a large majority in Ghana, the USA, Sierra Leone, Côte d'Ivoire and Guinea.

UN sanctions continued in the early stages of the Johnson-Sirleaf administration. The arms embargo and the travel bans were renewed for a further 12 months and the logging and diamond embargoes for a further 6 months by Resolution 1647 of December 2005. In June 2006 the logging ban was finally rescinded by Resolution 1689 but the diamond ban continued. In December 2006 Resolution 1731 renewed the arms embargo for 12 months but for the first time non-lethal military equipment, including non-lethal weapons and ammunition, intended for the use of Liberian government police and security forces, were excluded. Travel bans were renewed for a further 12-month period and the diamond ban for a further six months. In April 2007 the diamond ban was finally lifted by Resolution 1753.

Johnson-Sirleaf inherited an incomplete DDRR programme and incomplete restructuring programmes for the Liberian National Police and the AFL; reform of the justice and prison systems had barely begun. Concerns regarding high levels of violent crime. including rape. had been voiced since 2005 and continued during the Johnson-Sirleaf administration. In April 2006 a detailed report by the International Crisis Group drew attention to major defects in the justice system, including illiteracy among Justices of the Peace, dysfunctional circuit courts, a widespread lack of confidence in the system resulting in incidents of 'mob justice', corruption, impunity and illegal practices by Chiefs applying traditional law. In September 2006 the Ministry of Justice issued a statement admitting that the Liberian National Police, despite the assistance of the CIVPOL unit of UNMIL, were unable to cope with the rising levels of crime in Monrovia and its environs, and requested that citizens form vigilante groups to protect themselves. An additional UN police unit arrived in January 2007 bringing CIVPOL's strength up to 1,201 officers. Nevertheless, some progress in reforming the justice system was made, particularly in revising the legal framework, including the adoption of legislation to provide for the financial autonomy of the judiciary.

At March 2007 approximately 24,000 former combatants were still to be placed in reintegration programmes, the delay owing to funding shortfalls. A lack of finance was also impeding the redeployment of officers ineligible to join the restructured Liberian National Police. Following the demobilization of the AFL in December 2005, recruitment and training of soldiers for the new national army began in January 2006. The new force originally was intended to have a strength of 4,000; however, funding shortfalls reduced this target to 2,000.

Although the UN had formulated plans for a reduction in the size of UNMIL and one infantry battalion had been withdrawn from UNMIL in December 2006, the expectation that the mission would remain in Liberia throughout a 'consolidation phase' remained and UNMIL's mandate was repeatedly extended, most recently by Resolution 1750 until 30 September 2007. At 1 March 2007 the number of UNMIL troops was estimated at 14,832. The security situation remained generally calm though fragile, with the major threats to stability thought to arise from unemployed ex-combatants internally and, externally, from the unstable situations in Côte d'Ivoire and Guinea. In July 2007 Julu, the former AFL General, Doe loyalist, and leader of the 1994 coup attempt (see above) and Koukou, formerly an NPP Senator during the Taylor administration and Speaker of the National Transitional Assembly under the NTGL, were arrested on charges of treason. Julu was accused of attempting to smuggle weapons into the country from Côte d'Ivoire.

In summary, the election of Johnson-Sirleaf to the presidency was widely welcomed by the international community and Liberia's relations with the USA and other major aid donors undoubtedly improved. The main achievements of her first 18 months in office have been to construct a largely technocratic administration, to resolve the problem posed by former President Taylor's exile, to take steps to combat corruption and to secure the lifting of the UN embargoes on timber and diamond exports. Nevertheless, the challenges confronting her administration remained immense.

Economy

QUENTIN OUTRAM

Prior to the 1989–96 civil conflict, the Liberian economy was divided between a largely foreign-owned, export-orientated sector producing plantation crops, minerals and timber, and a traditional, subsistence agricultural sector. Revenues derived from exports supported the state, and allowed its leaders and functionaries to enjoy relatively high standards of living. In contrast, the agricultural sector, which employed a high proportion of the population, was of low productivity and here poverty was endemic. In the late 1970s and 1980s crises in the world economy caused economic decline; the 1989–96 civil war and the renewed conflict during 1999–2003 devastated the economy.

During 1980–88 Liberia's real gross domestic product (GDP) declined at an average annual rate of 1.8%. The subsequent civil conflict brought a dramatic further decline and real GDP may have fallen to as low as 10% of the 1987 level during the war. After the end of the conflict in 1996, the economy initially recovered rapidly, with real GDP doubling in 1997 and growing by over 20% per year in the following three years. (Much of this recovery was simply owing to the return of refugees, however, and real GDP per head grew much more slowly than total output.) Real GDP growth decelerated to an estimated 4.9% in 2001 and 3.7% in 2002, and real GDP in 2002 was still less than one-half of the level achieved before the 1989–96 war. The conflict with the rebels of the Liberians United for Reconciliation and Democracy (LURD) and the Movement for Democracy in Liberia (MODEL), and the UN sanctions in force against Liberia between 2001 and 2007 (see Recent History), had a significant impact on the economy, and real GDP contracted by more than 30% in 2003. Following the end of the conflict the economy recovered, although at a slower pace than during 1997–2000; real GDP grew by an estimated 2.6% in 2004, by 5.3% in 2005, and by 7.8% in 2006, according to the African Development Bank.

Charles Taylor's regime was marked by large-scale economic misappropriation by Taylor and his associates. In May 2005 the US-based advocacy group Coalition for International Justice published a detailed report which concluded that Taylor had derived an income of at least US $105m. each year during his presidency. Corrupt practices were given a semblance of legality by the strategic commodities law of 2000, which granted the presidency sole powers to negotiate, conclude and sign all contracts concerning Liberia's 'strategic' natural resources. (Gold, diamonds, iron ore, logs, rice and rubber were included under the 'strategic' designation.) State corruption continued under the National Transitional Government of Liberia (NTGL) and the Ellen Johnson-Sirleaf administration has charged Gyude Bryant, the Chairman of the NTGL and other former ministers with the misappropriation and embezzlement of substantial sums.

In 2007 agricultural activity continued to provide a subsistence living for the majority of the population, although many recently returned refugees and others including a large proportion of the internally displaced, were reliant on international humanitarian aid. Unemployment was believed to be widespread, particularly in urban areas, but frequently reiterated estimates that 80%–85% of Liberians are unemployed apply only to the small formal sector, not to the economy as a whole. Liberia's GDP per head, estimated at US $163 in 2005, has become one of the lowest in the world. According to a UN Survey conducted in 2000, 76% of the population subsisted in poverty, with incomes of less than US $1 per day; of these, about two-thirds had daily incomes of less than US $0.5. The health status of many Liberians remains extremely poor.

AGRICULTURE

Agriculture (including forestry and fishing) employed more than 70% of the labour force in the 1980s and, in 1980, contributed 36.7% of the country's GDP. By 2005 it was estimated by FAO that agriculture employed for 65% of the economically active population. The main cash crop was rubber. The principal food crops were, and continue to be, rice and cassava (manioc), and these crops, together with palm oil and some fish or meat, form the basis of the national diet. Agricultural production fell dramatically during the 1989–96 conflict, by about one-half, according to FAO. By 2000, however, the recovery of agricultural production was virtually complete. Owing to the failure of other economic activities to revive as quickly or completely, the agricultural sector has become relatively more significant, accounting for an estimated 63.6% (including forestry and fishing) of GDP in 2005.

Paddy rice production averaged more than 290,000 metric tons per year in the late 1980s; there were also substantial imports of rice, averaging 96,000 tons annually during the same period, largely to satisfy urban markets. Following the outbreak of war in 1989, production of paddy rice was estimated to have declined to only 50,000 tons in 1994, and much of the population became dependent on emergency relief grain. With the end of the fighting, and the return of refugees and displaced civilians, rice production recovered to about 209,400 tons in 1998. Renewed insecurity in Lofa County, one of the main rice-producing areas, from 1999 and the more widespread war of 2000–03 resulted in falls in production, which reached only an estimated 100,000 tons in 2003. Production was believed to have increased in 2004, to 110,000 tons, but fell again to 96,000 tons in 2005, limited by the slow return of refugees and the internally displaced to rural areas. Imports of milled rice gradually recovered after the 1989–96 war, reaching about 90,000 tons in 2002, despite the disruption caused by the 1999–2003 conflict, and rising to over 130,000 tons in 2005, according to FAO estimates. Nevertheless, the UN World Food Programme (WFP), the major provider of food aid in Liberia, planned to assist over 700,000 people in the first half of 2007.

Production of cassava increased rapidly in the late 1980s, from 280,000 metric tons in 1985 to 446,000 tons in 1989. Since cassava requires less consistent attention than rice, production of cassava was not as badly disrupted by the 1989–96 or 1999–2003 wars as rice-growing. During the 1989–96 conflict production declined to a low of 175,000 tons in 1995, according to FAO estimates. By 2000 cassava was reported to be a much more significant component of the national diet than before the civil war, and the area under cultivation was increasing rapidly. Production rose from an estimated 282,200 tons in 1997 to an estimated 480,000 tons in 2005.

Before the 1989–96 war the rubber sector was divided about equally in terms of land area between a domestically owned sector, comprising both smallholders and commercially operated plantations, and a small number of large, foreign-owned concessions. Rubber plantations covered an estimated 110,000 ha in 1990. Employment in rubber production was about 15,000 in the concession sector and perhaps 28,000 in the domestically owned sector, and accounted for about 15% of total employment in the economy. The concessions produced about 70% of total annual production, which amounted to about 100,000 metric tons in the late 1980s. Crude rubber and latex, together, were Liberia's second largest export earner in the 1980s, generating US $110m. in 1988 (28% of total export earnings). The largest of the concessions, Firestone, had long been Liberia's largest private-sector employer, with about 7,000 workers at its 53,000-ha Harbel plantation east of Monrovia before the 1989–96 war. Firestone sold its Liberian interests to the Japanese tyre company Bridgestone in 1988, and the company is now known as Bridgestone/Firestone; the Firestone Natural Rubber Company continues to be responsible for local management of the plantation. There are now three other foreign-owned plantations: one owned by the Liberian Agricultural Co (LAC), another by Kumpulan Guthrie, and the Cavalla Plantation. There is also one major Liberian-owned plantation, the Sinoe Rubber Plantation.

The Firestone plantation was seriously affected by the 1989–96 war. Production was suspended in 1990 and over-tapping by illegal producers and the cutting down of trees for firewood and charcoal subsequently damaged up to one-half of the plantation. Operations at the plantation resumed in mid-1997, and in 2002 it was reported to be producing at the limits of its then capacity (about 90% of its pre-war capacity). During the 1999–2003 conflict the plantation, located in an area affected by the war only in its very final stages, was able to continue production almost without interruption. In February 2005 Firestone signed an agreement with the NTGL, which extended its lease, formerly due to expire in 2025, until 2042. In February 2007 President Johnson-Sirleaf announced that she had started the renegotiation of Firestone's lease; no further details were available at mid-2007.

The LAC plantation comprises 13,800 ha of a 125,000-ha concession 45 km north-west of Buchanan, in Grand Bassa County, and employed 3,000 before the 1989–96 war. Owned by the US rubber company Uniroyal between 1961 and 1980, LAC is now wholly owned by the Compagnie Internationale de Cultures (Intercultures), a subsidiary of the Luxembourg-registered but Belgium-based Société Financière des Caoutchoucs Luxembourg (SOCFINAL). Intercultures is also the majority shareholder of the Weala Rubber Co, which operates a rubber factory, processing smallholder rubber, near Salala, north-east of Monrovia. LAC commenced a US $7m. programme to rehabilitate the plantation in February 2000. In 2006 it produced 21,000 metric tons of rubber from its own plantation and smallholder plantations under its supervision. Yields from the plantation were low, owing to the increasing age of the trees. It directly employs some 1,500 workers. The company became involved in controversy in late 2004 after it issued eviction notices to residents to vacate some 120 ha of land in order to extend the plantation; in September 2006 after intervention by Johnson-Sirleaf the company agreed to suspend its expansion programme.

The Kumpulan Guthrie concession comprises 200,000 ha, located north of Monrovia, in Bomi County; 8,000 ha were planted with rubber. Its new Malaysian owners completed the rehabilitation of the plantation in 2001, but almost immediately announced that they were ceasing operations in view of the continuing instability in the country. The plantation, which was attacked by LURD in May 2002, appears to have been under LURD control from early 2003. The plantation was not repossessed until August 2006 when the Government granted a temporary management permit to the Liberian Rubber Planters' Association (LPRA).

Part of the original Firestone concession area became the Cavalla Rubber Plantation in Maryland County. Control of the plantation was ceded to the Government of Samuel Doe in 1981, and in 1983 the Government granted 50% ownership to SIPEF, a Belgian company, in exchange for its management of the whole. The plantation ceased operations between 1992 and 1998, owing to the civil conflict, and in 2003 it was occupied by MODEL forces. After a complex series of disputes, the plantation was initially put under the management of the LPRA in 2006. Press reports in mid-2007 indicated that the Ministry of Agriculture was preparing to put the plantation into the possession of Salala Rubber Investments, a Liberian company. The concession area is approximately 8,000 ha, of which 3,910 ha are developed; it employed 1,350 workers in 2006.

The Sinoe Rubber Plantation, originally owned by a German company, was acquired by the family of President William Tolbert in 1973. The concession area, which is located in Sinoe County, is 240,000 ha, of which 20,000 ha are developed. After the Tolberts fled the country in the 1980s, the plantation was controlled by a variety of management companies. It was seized by MODEL forces in March 2003, and appeared to remain under MODEL occupation and control in mid-2006. Its status in mid-2007 was unclear.

The recovery of the rubber sector after the 1989–96 war was fairly rapid. Output reached 115,000 metric tons in 2004 but has since fallen back slightly to 112,000 tons in 2005 according to FAO figures. Export revenues have risen rapidly since 2003, buoyed by rising international rubber prices, to an estimated US $93.4m. in 2004, US $126.7m. in 2005, and US $172.3m. in 2006. The more recent of these figures have, for the first time, exceeded (although only in monetary terms) the 1988 export revenue of US $107m.

Other agricultural products include sugar cane (with an output of 255,000 metric tons in 2006, according to FAO), bananas (115,000 tons), plantains (42,000 tons), palm oil (34,800 tons), yams (20,000 tons), taro or cocoyams (25,500 tons), and sweet potatoes (20,000 tons). None of these are exported in significant quantities. Small quantities of cocoa beans, coconuts, coffee, oranges, and pineapples are also produced.

Little information is available on livestock. FAO estimates, little revised since 1990, indicated that there were some 210,000 sheep, 220,000 goats, 130,000 pigs and 36,000 head of cattle in Liberia in 2005. In the same year FAO estimated that the country produced some 22,000 metric tons of meat, of which about one-quarter was game meat ('bushmeat'), a significant food source in rural areas. Other estimates of bushmeat production were substantially higher and reports of the commercial production and export of bushmeat have raised conservation issues.

Marine and freshwater fishing provided a livelihood and a source of nutrition in some areas. In 1999 marine catches regained the levels recorded prior to the 1989–96 war, though catches have since fallen back. In 2005, according to FAO estimates, the marine catch amounted to about 10,000 tons, while the freshwater catch provided a further 4,000 tons.

FORESTRY

Liberia possesses substantial forest reserves: forest covers 3.2m. ha (32.7% of the total land area of Liberia). The forests are almost entirely lowland tropical moist forests, but savannah woodlands occur on the coast and in the north-west. Some 240 different timber species occur in Liberia, of which about 40 are traded commercially. The most valuable species are mahagonies and African walnut. Ten National Forests, with a limited degree of protection, were designated under legislation enacted in 1953. The Sapo National Park, in Sinoe County, designated in 1983, is the one major protected area of rainforest. In October 2003 the Sapo National Park Act extended the park from 130,845 ha to 180,500 ha and the Nimba Nature Reserve Act created a forest nature reserve contiguous to similar reserves in Guinea and Côte d'Ivoire. In 2004 it emerged that former members of MODEL, who continued to be armed, were occupying the Sapo Park and were engaged in illicit mining and hunting; although they were evicted with the assistance of the UN Mission in Liberia (UNMIL) in September 2005, illicit miners and hunters were reported to have returned to Sapo Park in December 2006.

Historically, smallholder agriculture, where land clearing by slash and burn is common, has been responsible for 95% of all deforestation, and the use of trees for domestic fuel has dwarfed the activities of commercial timber producers. Before the 1989–96 war commercial logging practices were selective, focusing on the extraction of high-value species, and the rate of deforestation resulting directly from logging was slow. The mass population displacement during the 1989–96 war slowed the rate of deforestation arising from agricultural activities and the insecurity of that time inhibited large-scale logging operations. After 1996 commercial logging greatly increased deforestation, before UN timber sanctions resulted in the suspension of the commercial industry in 2003–04. FAO estimates that, despite very low rates of deforestation in the early 1990s, an annual average of 1.6% of Liberian forestland was lost during 1990–2000 and that deforestation continued at this same rate during 2000–05.

The major use of wood from Liberia's forests has always been for fuel. Of the estimated 4.5m. cu m of roundwood production in 1988, 3.3m. cu m was used as fuel. Additionally, about 0.1m. cu m of charcoal was produced. The demand for fuel wood was estimated to be growing at 5%–6% annually during 1983–93 by a UNDP-World Bank study. The destruction of electricity-generating capacity during the 1989–96 war was assumed to have increased demand for fuel wood and charcoal further, despite the difficulties of production in wartime conditions. Charcoal dominates the urban household energy market and is a major item in retail trade. Recent reports suggest that a significant export trade with neighbouring countries is emerging. Wood is the usual domestic fuel in rural areas and remains an important energy source for small-scale industry.

Production of saw logs and veneer logs reached more than 1m. cu m in 1988, with other industrial roundwood contributing 154,000 cu m in the same year. Exports of roundwood reached 681,000 cu m in 1988, with a value of US $88m. Reliable data on output and exports since that time are not available; figures compiled by the IMF indicated that the recovery of the industry after the 1989–96 war was initially slow, with output of logs and timber standing at only 157,000 cu m in 1998, but accelerated rapidly in 1999, with output rising to 336,000 cu m in that year, followed by a dramatic increase to 934,000 cu m in 2000 and 982,000 cu m in 2001, and another surge, to 1.3m. cu m, in 2002. The IMF estimated that about 80% of the output of the industrial roundwood production was exported, yielding some US $85m. in 2002. By 2002, the last full year before UN sanctions were introduced, output from the forestry sector overall had increased to almost 290% of the pre-war (1987) level in real value terms, and forestry represented about 23.9% of total GDP.

Liberia has never possessed a major wood-processing industry. Before the outbreak of the civil war in 1989, there were 18 sawmills, three veneer and plywood factories, six dry kilns and three wood-processing factories in the country, but much of this capacity was destroyed during the war. Some rebuilding of timber-processing capacity took place after 1997 and, according to a UN Panel of Experts, sawnwood production showed a rapid increase from negligible levels in 1998 to 225,000 cu m in 2000. Some 12 sawmills were operational in 2001. A US $10m. plywood factory and sawmill, owned by Maryland Wood Processing Inc, commenced production in River Gee County in 2001 and a US $40m. plywood factory was opened in Buchanan by the Oriental Timber Co (OTC) in January 2002. It appeared that these facilities survived the 1999–2003 conflict undamaged.

Forest exploitation is based on leased concessions supervised by the Forestry Development Authority (FDA). By the late 1980s virtually all significant national forestland was under concessionary arrangements with commercial logging companies. By the mid-point of Taylor's regime, the industry was dominated by 11 companies, each producing over 10,000 cu m per year and together accounting for more than 90% of output. Of these, the OTC was the largest, with an output, according to the FDA, of 385,000 cu m, or 57% of total production in 2000. From that year the activities of the OTC attracted widespread attention, both domestically and abroad. The OTC gained a forestry concession in Grand Bassa, Grand Gedeh, Rivercess and Sinoe Counties in 1999–2000 of 1.6m. ha, or 42% of Liberia's productive forest area, according to FDA figures. The project, supported by an investment of US $110m. from companies associated with the OTC, was by far the largest in Liberia's post-1997 history. Protests against the activities of the OTC reached their peak in Sinoe County in April 2001. Armed militia working for the OTC were accused of serious and widespread abuses of the local population. The company's extraction rates were estimated to have been at exceptionally high and unsustainable levels, raising conservation concerns.

In December 2000 a UN report concluded that the Chairman of the OTC since 1999, Guus or 'Gus' van Kouwenhoven, a Dutch national, was responsible for the logistics of arms transfers through Liberia into Sierra Leone, utilizing the position and resources of the OTC. In view of this and evidence of other connections between the Liberian timber trade and regional instability, Global Witness urged the UN Security Council to impose a total embargo on Liberian timber exports in January 2001. A draft UN resolution, supported by the USA and the United Kingdom in early 2001, aimed to impose a timber trade ban, but failed in March. The October report of the UN Panel of Experts on Liberia noted a payment for armaments made directly from the Singapore accounts of one of the OTC holding companies. Other logging companies, including the Exotic Tropical Timber Enterprise, once managed by Leonid Minin, who was described by UN officials as an 'arms dealer', were believed to be involved in similar activities. The objections to a timber trade ban were overcome and in May 2003 the UN Security Council announced that it would impose a 10-month ban on exports of round logs and timber products from Liberia, to take effect in July 2003. Following successive renewals, timber sanctions remained in place until 2006 (see Recent History). (Kouwenhoven was arrested in the Netherlands and in March 2005 was convicted of violating UN sanctions and sentenced to eight years' imprisonment. He, and Minin, remained subject to an international travel ban and an assets 'freeze' under UN Resolutions.)

The renewed conflict emerging from early 1999 impeded timber production in Lofa County. However, the major logging areas in the south and east of the country were largely unaffected until the 2003 incursions by MODEL (see Recent History). Major companies in the area, including the OTC and the Inland Logging Company, then suspended operations, repatriated staff and withdrew equipment. In late May the OTC announced that it was ending its operations in Liberia. The UN Panel of Experts found no evidence of industrial logging or timber exports in investigations during 2004–06 and concluded that industrial logging had come to a halt. IMF estimates indicated that the total value of the output of logs and timber fell from US $86.7m. in 2002 to US $2.2m. in 2005. (Output of charcoal and wood, however, has increased from an estimated US $47.2m. in 2002 to US $56.1m. in 2004 and US $62.0m. in 2005.) These estimates were consistent with the December 2004 and December 2005 reports of the Panel of Experts, which noted that pit-sawing (the processing of logs using chain saws) was increasing as the domestic market grew and had become widespread. This was despite a ban on pit-sawing from November 2004, announced by the FDA, made partly because commanders of the former factions were controlling the operations. The Panel was strongly critical in its assessment of FDA financial practices and of its progress in making the reforms necessary for sanctions to be lifted during the period of the NTGL. Estimates of output for 2006 were not yet available in mid-2007.

In February 2006 the newly elected President, Ellen Johnson-Sirleaf, declared by decree that all existing forestry concessions were null and void. She also established a Forest Reform Monitoring Committee (FRMC) to develop forestry policy. The FRMC included representatives of Liberian civil society and the international community, as well as representatives of the Liberian Government. In June the UN Panel of Experts reported a 'dramatic' improvement in FDA operations, particularly in revenue collection. In view of these developments, in the same month the UN Security Council suspended the timber sanctions under Resolution 1689 for a period of 90 days. Permanent removal of the sanctions was made dependent on the adoption of forestry legislation in accordance with FRMC proposals. A reformed Forestry Law was duly brought into effect in October 2006. However no new forestry concessions were created under this law and commercial logging remained at a standstill. For 2008 the FDA projects approximately US $25m. of production. In the long term the UN Panel of Experts thought it unlikely that an annual gross revenue of more than $100m. would be sustainable.

MINING AND PETROLEUM EXPLORATION

The mining sector was once a major sector of the economy, accounting for 10.9% of GDP in 1989. In 2005 the sector contributed under 0.1% of GDP. Iron ore was the principal product of the sector prior to the 1989–96 civil war. In the 1980s, however, the reduction in international demand for iron ore severely depressed production and during the 1989–96 civil war the industry closed down completely. The most well-known extraction site was the Mount Nimba site, near the Guinean border. The mine was formerly worked by the Liberian-American Minerals Company (LAMCO), which constructed the 267-km Buchanan–Yekepa railway line to enable the export of the ore. LAMCO's assets were transferred to a government-owned holding company, the Liberian Mining Company (LIMINCO), in September 1989. LIMINCO continued production until 1993, at which point the mine was believed to be exhausted. The industry is supervised by the Ministry of Lands, Mines and Energy. Agreements between the Ministry and mining companies are referred to as Mineral Development Agreements. In early 2005 bids to reopen the mine and rehabilitate the railway were received from Rio Tinto, BHP Billiton, Mittal Steel and Global Infrastructure Holdings Ltd (GIHL—the overseas investment arm of two privately owned Indian steel companies, Ispat and Esser). Industry analysts speculated that the applicants were primarily interested in the railway, since it would allow exploitation of iron ore deposits in Guinea, near to Mount Nimba. A contract was finally signed with Mittal Steel, now known as Arcelor Mittal, in September 2005. The contract was renegotiated by the Johnson-Sirleaf administration during 2006 and received approval from the legislature in 2007. The new concession agreement left the railway and the port of Buchanan in government hands and revised provisions concerning taxation and royalties in Liberia's favour. In February 2005 it was reported that BHP Billiton had acquired exploration licences in various regions of western Liberia, and in June Mano River Resources, a Canadian company previously active in the gold and diamond sector, announced that it had been awarded a three-year mineral exploration agreement for iron ore in the Putu range in Grand Gedeh County. In July 2007 it was reported that 13 companies had expressed an interest in the western region iron ore deposits at the Mano River and Bomi Hills, both previously exploited, and at the Bea Mountains.

Diamond deposits were first discovered in the lower Lofa river area in 1957, and continue westwards to the border with Sierra Leone at the Mano River. These deposits consist of both alluvial deposits, and kimberlites and kimberlite dykes, and yield both industrial and gem diamonds. Alluvial diamond occurrences have also been located in the Cavalia and Ya Creek drainage systems in Nimba County, in Grand Bassa and Montserrado Counties, and there have been reports of discoveries near Greenville. Reserves are estimated at about 10m. carats. Official data on production and exports are believed to be distorted by illicit production and smuggling. However, according to the US Geological Survey (USGS), 263,000 carats of industrial diamonds and 67,000 carats of gem diamonds were produced in 1988. The warring factions became heavily involved in diamond production during the 1989–96 civil conflict and may have produced 40,000–60,000 carats of gem diamonds and 60,000–90,000 carats of industrial diamonds annually in the later years of the war. The annual value of diamond exports during the 1989–96 war, estimated from Belgian data on diamond imports en route to Antwerp, was believed to be US $300m.–$500m. (These included diamonds originating from elsewhere in Africa.)

Much of the mining for diamonds in Liberia, both by the warring factions and by civilians, has been illicit and the Taylor Government admitted its inability to control the artisanal sector. Estimates of the numbers employed in the industry in rural areas in early 2002 varied from the Government's claim of 60,000 to industry estimates of 20,000–30,000. Output collapsed in 2002, as UN sanctions took hold, to about 48,000 carats (gem) and 32,000 carats (industrial) in 2002 and continued to fall, to no more than 36,000 carats (gem) and 24,000 carats (industrial) in 2003 and 10,000 carats (gem and industrial) in 2004 and 2005. In 2006 an artisanal diamond rush near the site of the Butaw Oil Palm Corporation's plantation and other artisanal mining along the Lofa River and in parts of Nimba produced at a rate of between 130,000 and 150,000 carats per annum according to the UN Panel of Experts.

Recent formal diamond exploration activity in Liberia has been limited, and has involved only a few junior mining companies. Mano River Resources acquired rights from the Taylor administration to more than 8,000 sq km in the diamond fields of western Liberia. A diamond exploration programme commenced in 2000, and the discovery of six kimberlite deposits in the Wuesua area of the Kpo Range was announced in May 2002. A 200 sq km Mineral Development Agreement with the Government was signed in early 2002 and the company formed a joint venture in 2002 with the Trans Hex Group of South Africa to advance this project. The company's diamond exploration activities were brought to a halt by the 1999–2003 conflict and only began to resume after the official completion of the disarmament programme at the end of October 2004. Nevertheless, in May 2004 the company announced that it had signed a mineral co-operation agreement with the NTGL, which allowed it to explore a 15,000 sq km area adjacent to Sierra Leone. In June 2007 it was announced that the company's diamond interests throughout West Africa had been re-organized into a single subsidiary called Stellar Diamonds; exploration work was continuing. In April 2004 Diamond Fields International, then a Canadian public company listed on the Toronto stock exchange, the principal activity of which was a marine diamond mining project in Namibian waters, also announced that it had obtained two mineral reconnaissance licences, in one of which prospecting would be for gold (see below) and in the other of which, covering 2,000 sq km in the Ya Creek area of Nimba County, prospecting would be for diamonds. In 2006 Diamond Fields relocated to Cape Town, South Africa, and announced plans, subsequently aborted, to merge with Moydow Mines International, a mineral exploration and development company based in Dublin, Ireland. Exploration work in Liberia continued in 2006.

The export of rough diamonds from Liberia was banned under UN resolutions in May 2001 (see Recent History). The UN Panel of Experts reported in 2002 that the embargo had not been fully successful; while rough diamonds categorized as 'Liberian' had disappeared from official international markets, there was evidence that diamonds continued to be smuggled out of Liberia via Sierra Leone, Côte d'Ivoire and Guinea. However, by September 2004 the Panel of Experts was convinced that diamond production and export levels were negligible, with activity discouraged not only by the sanctions regime but also by the insecurity in the main diamond producing areas and shortages of equipment. With the improving security situation towards the end of 2004 the Panel noted a steady increase in mining activity and indications that diamonds were once again being smuggled onto international markets. In June 2006 the Panel noted with alarm the resumption of industrial-scale diamond mining by American Mining Associates at a site in Lofa County; mining at this site was stopped later in the year, although preparatory work continued. Two other sites, one owned by Italgems, the other by Jungle Waters were reported to be inactive at mid-2007 except for preparatory work. Progress towards achieving Kimberley Process compliancy and the removal of UN diamond sanctions was slow under the Taylor regime and under the NTGL, but accelerated rapidly under the Johnson-Sirleaf administration and the diamond sanctions were removed in April 2007 by UN Security Council Resolution 1753. As a direct consequence Liberia was granted membership of the Kimberley Process Certification Scheme in May. A government moratorium on diamond mining remained in place until the end of July 2007 when the Government announced it was ready to consider applications for diamond mining and brokering licences.

Alluvial gold has been exploited since the 1940s in an area near Zwedru in Grand Gedeh County and exploration for primary (lode) gold in the 1970s rapidly focused on this area. Further exploration and exploitation have been focused on alluvial gold. Reserves are distributed throughout the country, but the most significant occurrences are in western Liberia between the Lofa and Mano rivers, in Bong and Nimba Counties along the St John river and Ya Creek, and in the south-east of the country. Liberia's total reserves of gold are estimated at 3m. troy oz. Prior to the 1989–96 civil conflict, production was small-scale, with some 6,000–14,000 diggings for gold and diamonds believed to exist. The prevalence of illicit production renders output estimates highly uncertain, but, according to official figures, annual gold production increased from 359 kg in 1982 to 677 kg in 1988, indicating a small-scale industry by world standards. Production continued throughout the 1989–96 war, organized by the various rebel factions. The USGS, which recently dramatically reduced its estimates of recent Liberian gold production, estimated that production reached its highest post-war level of 57 kg in 2001, falling to 16 kg in 2005. The Central Bank of Liberia estimated production in 2006 at less than 10 kg.

Corporate involvement in gold exploration is now limited to four companies: Mano River Resources, Diamond Fields International, Freedom Gold and America-Liberian United Minerals (AmLib). The western concessions belonging to Mano River Resources have already been mentioned in the context of diamond exploration. The company's exploration for gold has advanced furthest at its Bea Mountains concession. Resources at the Weaju and New Liberty properties in the Bea Mountains have been estimated to be capable of yielding 233,000 oz and 535,000 oz of gold respectively. The company obtained a Mineral Development Agreement from Liberia to cover the Bea Mountains properties, but government and LURD forces were in conflict over control of the company's concession area in January 2003 and activities were in abeyance until the end of 2004. Exploration work resumed in 2005 and was still continuing in mid-2007. Diamond Fields International secured an exploration licence over 1,300 sq km in River Cess and Sinoe Counties in April 2004. Freedom Gold's operations were seized by MODEL forces in April 2003 and the enterprise has been inactive since then. AmLib was reported to be preparing to resume its activities during 2005 and let a drilling contract for a project in the Kokoya district of Bong County in 2007. Artisanal gold mining was reported to have experienced an upsurge in activity after the end of the 1999–2003 conflict, particularly in eastern areas formerly under MODEL control.

Offshore deposits of hydrocarbons were first discovered during explorations carried out in 1968–73, but remained unexploited. President Taylor referred to petroleum as 'our salvation' in 1998 and the Government established the National Oil Co of Liberia (NOCAL) in 1999 to develop Liberia's petroleum resources. In 2000 the Liberian Government employed the Norwegian contractors TGS-Nopec to carry out a seismic survey of practically all of Liberia's offshore waters. The survey was completed in February 2001 and Taylor referred to a 'huge deposit' of oil at the Liberia–Sierra Leone offshore border in September that year. The deteriorating security position prevented progress until February 2004, however, when NOCAL announced a bidding round for 17 exploration blocks, covering 55,000 sq km, of which six blocks would be awarded. The bidding round was regarded as unsuccessful, attracting applications from only six companies. In April, before the bidding round was closed, it was announced that two blocks had already been leased, one to Oranto Petroleum and another to Repsol (now Repsol YPF) of Spain. Oranto is believed to be affiliated to Atlas Petroleum owned by Prince Arthur Eze, the Nigerian businessman and a former campaigner for ex-President Gen. Sani Abacha. Repsol already held neighbouring concessions in Sierra Leonean waters. In January 2005 it was announced that Repsol had won rights to another block and that Woodside West Africa Pty Ltd, wholly owned by Woodside Petroleum of Australia, and a partner of Repsol in its operations off shore of Sierra Leone, had secured exploration rights in another block. In June it was announced that NOCAL had signed three production-sharing contracts: one with Oranto Petroleum, one with a US company, Broadway Consolidated, and one with a consortium comprising Regal Liberia of the United Kingdom and European Hydrocarbons. Of these three, only Oranto is an established oil producer. The agreements provided for an exploration phase prior to production and the three companies were not expected to commence production in the short term. In September 2006 two of these contracts, those with Oranto and Broadway, were submitted by President Johnson-Sirleaf for ratification by the legislature; that with Broadway was approved in March 2007.

MANUFACTURING

The significance of the manufacturing sector to the Liberian economy has always been limited. It contributed only 7.4% to the country's GDP in 1989, and employed only about 6% of the labour force in 1990. Prior to the 1989–96 war, the manufacturing sector had few companies of any size, and many firms were owned and operated by only one person. Large-scale industry included a 125,000-ton capacity cement factory, initially owned by the Liberian Cement Corpn (CEMENCO), which commenced operations in 1968, and is now owned by the Norwegian firm Scancem International, a subsidiary of HeidelbergCement of Germany. The only other large-scale manufacturing plant was a 15,000 barrels per day (b/d) petroleum refinery, which was initially largely owned by US oil interests but was acquired by the Doe regime's Liberia Petroleum Refining Corpn (LPRC) in the early 1980s. After it ceased refining operations in 1982, Liberia again became dependent on imports of refined petroleum products. The LPRC maintained a monopoly over the import of petroleum products, which continued following the collapse of its refining operations. The Taylor Government resisted pressure from the IMF to liberalize the market in petroleum products but the NTGL took some measures towards ending LPRC's monopoly by granting import franchises to a number of companies in April 2004; President Johnson-Sirleaf stated that these companies' share of the market had risen from 11% in 2005 to 40% in 2007. Nevertheless, petrol prices remain state controlled. Consumption of petroleum has declined from about 8,000 b/d in 1988 to an estimated 4,000 b/d in 2005.

The reconstruction and development of the rest of the manufacturing sector since the 1989–1996 civil conflict has been limited and the almost total lack of large-scale industry has continued; a 2001 report indicated that the 11 largest manufacturing firms together employed no more than 500 people. Since the end of the 1999–2003 war the manufacturing sector has experienced a partial recovery and it was estimated by the IMF to have contributed 7% of GDP in 2005. The largest sub-sector by value of output in 2005 was beverages and beer (US $40.6m.), followed by cement (US $20.2m.). The remainder of the sector consists of paint and domestic chemical manufacturing and the production of mattresses.

THE TERTIARY SECTOR

The tertiary sector (transport, utilities, construction, commerce, private services and public administration) produced an estimated 45.1% of GDP in 1989. The sector collapsed during the 1989–96 war, with the value of output declining from an estimated US $504m. in 1989 to about US $9m. in 1996. Output recovered to an estimated US $133.3m. in 2005, equivalent to 20.4% of GDP. Construction, commerce, road transport and private services are dominated by informal employment, while public administration is the major sector of formal employment in the Liberian economy. There were estimated to be 58,500 public employees in 2006, about double the number of 1991.

Transport and Telecommunications

Liberia's road network is inadequate and mostly in very poor repair. A main road between Monrovia and Freetown, Sierra Leone, completed in 1988, reduced the distance between the two capitals from 1,014 km to 544 km. The bridge over the River Mano, at the Liberia–Sierra Leone border on this route, was officially reopened in June 2007. Another major road links Monrovia to Ganta in Nimba County. Road connections between Monrovia and the south-east of the country are very poor and coastal shipping remains a significant mode of transport on this route. Logging companies were allowed to offset the cost of road-building against tax liabilities under the Taylor administration and a substantial network of forest roads was constructed after 1999, including an upgrading by the OTC of the 174-km dirt road connecting Buchanan and Greenville. Analysis of satellite images indicated that the road network has grown substantially since 1999, largely owing to the opening of forest roads, and totalled 13,585 km in 2005.

The railways from Monrovia to Mano River via Bomi Hills (145 route-km), from Monrovia to the Bong Mines (78 route-km) and from Buchanan to Yekepa (267 route-km) were constructed for the transport of iron ore. The closure of Liberia's iron ore industry resulted in the cessation of all traffic on these lines. Arcelor Mittal's planned investment programme includes the restoration of the Buchanan–Yekepa line.

At the end of 2005 the Liberian-registered merchant fleet comprised 1,653 vessels of 1,000 or more gross registered tons (grt), with a total displacement of 59.6m. grt. None of this fleet is owned by Liberian nationals. Although it remained the second largest open-registry fleet in the world in terms of tonnage in 2005, the registry has experienced a long-term decline from a 1982 peak of 81.5m. grt, reflecting the fall in the number of oil tankers, competition from other 'open registry' (or 'flag of convenience') states and growing international opposition to 'open registry' shipping. The Liberian registry is, however, regarded as one of the more reputable open registries, with below average casualty and detention rates. Although the political responsibility of the Bureau of Maritime Affairs in Liberia, the management of the Liberian registry was, from its inception in 1949, conducted by the International Trust Co (ITC), an associate company of International Registries Incorporated (IRI) of New York, USA. Since the registry was, for all intents and purposes, managed from the USA, it was little affected by the 1989–96 civil conflict. In February 1997 Liberia instituted legal proceedings against the IRI, alleging that it had diverted business from the Liberian registry to the Marshall Islands registry, also controlled by the IRI. An out of court settlement was reached under which the management of the registry was transferred to the newly created Liberia International Ship and Corporate Registry (LISCR), based in Virginia, USA, from January 2000. The UN Panel of Experts discovered that payments for arms and transportation had been made directly from LISCR accounts during 2000; however, the shipping registry was not included in the UN's sanctions. The contributions of the ship registry, under both IRI and LISCR management, to official Liberian budget revenue have been substantial. In 2004 the registry contributed some US $13.5m. of revenue, equivalent to about 20% of all official government revenue in that year, according to IMF sources. Contributions were considerably less in 2005 and were less again in 2006 prompting President Johnson-Sirleaf to announce a review of the agreement with LISCR in her annual address in February 2007.

Liberia's principal ports are Monrovia Freeport, Buchanan, Greenville and Harper. Before the 1989–96 war these ports handled about 200,000 metric tons of general cargo and about 400,000 tons of petroleum products per year. The 1989–96 war resulted in extensive damage to dock and warehouse facilities; siltation and uncleared wrecks also impeded a quick return to normal operations. In 2006 nearly all the dry-bulk and container traffic was handled by the Freeport, which also handled all oil imports. The Freeport has four piers and one main wharf. The latter provides four berths, one of which remains obstructed by the wreck of the 4,160 ton MV *Torm Alexandra*. The last six months of 2006 saw 171 vessels docking at the Freeport and 676,000 metric tons of cargo handled according to the National Port Authority. At the end of 2006 the World Bank approved a grant for rehabilitation projects at the Freeport including dredging, upgrading of the oil jetty, and providing a fire fighting capacity. The other three ports were barely operational in 2006. The port at Buchanan was managed by the OTC until the company's withdrawal from Liberia in 2003; Arcelor Mittal's planned investment programme includes the restoration of the port. Greenville and Harper are shallow-water ports, which were used mainly for the export of logs before UN sanctions resulted in the trade's suspension in 2003–04.

Liberia's principal airports are Robertsfield International Airport (RIA), at Harbel, 56 km east of Monrovia, and the smaller James Spriggs Payne Airport, at Monrovia. In 1990 the civil conflict in Monrovia resulted in severe damage to RIA, and it was finally reopened to civilian airlines only in December 1997. The UN Panel of Experts, appointed in 2000 under Resolution 1306, described how irregularities and failures in the Liberian registry of civil aircraft contributed to violations of the armaments embargo against Sierra Leone. The UN Security Council grounded all Liberian-registered aircraft by Resolution 1343 of 2001. A new aviation registry was subsequently established in conformity with international procedures and the UN grounding order lapsed in May 2002. The new registry has remained largely inactive, however. In 2001 Liberia unilaterally opted out of the joint air traffic control regime established by Guinea, Liberia and Sierra Leone in 1975, possibly in order to conceal arms flights arriving at RIA. Liberia began to re-establish co-operative relations with the civil aviation authorities in Guinea and Sierra Leone in September 2003. In late 2006 the World Bank approved a grant to further rehabilitate the airport. In 2007 services into RIA were operated by SN Brussels Airlines, with services from Brussels, Belgium, via Freetown, Sierra Leone, and Dakar, Senegal. The Nigerian Bellview Airlines operated services from Abidjan, Accra, Freetown and Lagos, while Kenya Airways operated a service to Nairobi. The Spriggs Payne Airport was under UNMIL control and closed to commercial civilian traffic at mid-2007.

Almost all of the installations of the parastatal Liberia Telecommunications Corpn (LTC) were damaged during the 1989–96 war. Under the Taylor administration, some progress was made in rehabilitating LTC's facilities. Total capacity was estimated at 6,700 fixed lines in 2002, compared with 9,380 in 1990. The fighting in Monrovia in 2003 resulted in renewed damage to the telecommunications infrastructure. The fixed-line telephone system was unreliable and operated only in parts of Monrovia. The most recent estimates of telephone density in Liberia, of two main telephone lines per 1,000 inhabitants and 49 mobile cellular telephone subscribers per 1,000 inhabitants in 2005, are among the lowest in Africa. The LTC's monopoly of telecommunications services was rescinded by the Taylor administration. The LTC considered rival bids to revitalize its facilities in early 2005, but continuing disputes over the bidding process prevented progress before the end of the NTGL, and the process was suspended. Growth in mobile telephone ownership and use is believed to have been rapid since 2001. In 2006 there were four licenced GSM (Global System for Mobile Communications) mobile operators: Lonestar Communications Corpn (LCC), operating since 2000; LiberCell (Atlantic Wireless) and Cellcom, both operating since 2004; and Comium, a Lebanese company, which acquired a GSM licence in December 2004. Cellcom, LiberCell and Comium provide internet services.

Power and Utilities

The government-owned Liberia Electricity Corpn (LEC) produced about one-half of the total output of electricity in the mid-1980s, most of the rest being produced by the iron-ore mining companies then operating in the country. The LEC operated two systems, the Monrovia Grid and the Rural Electrification Network, serving the remainder of the country through 11 isolated grids supplied by diesel generators. Total net electricity production declined from an estimated 790m. kWh in 1989 to an estimated 301m. kWh in 1990. The Monrovia Grid, with a total installed capacity of 182 MW, was powered by the Mt Coffee hydroelectric dam (64 MW), gas turbine power plants (68 MW) and diesel generators (50 MW). The rural diesel stations had an installed capacity of 20 MW. During the 1989–96 conflict all the power generating plant was looted or destroyed, including the Mt Coffee hydroelectric dam, which was wrecked in December 1990. Damage to the rural networks was as complete. Since then businesses and other organizations have depended on privately owned generators for electricity; there were thought to be 45,000 generators in the country in 2003. Despite aid from the USA and Taiwan, little progress in restoring electricity supplies was made under the Taylor administration or under the NTGL. The LEC installed a diesel generating set rated at 7 MW in 2000 and this was the only functioning public generating plant in Liberia until 2006. Total net electricity production rose from an estimated 310m. kWh in 1998 to 490m. kWh in 2002 but fell to 320m. kWh in 2003, almost all from privately owned diesel generators (later data were unavailable). In April 2003 Liberia signed an aid agreement with Taiwan for the repair of the Mt Coffee hydroelectric plant. However, Liberia severed its diplomatic relations with Taiwan and restored its relations with the People's Republic of China in October; it hoped China would take over the Mt Coffee project. Some progress in this direction was reported in June 2004 and in June 2006 a Chinese government delegation announced it was finalizing plans to restore the Mt Coffee plant. In her inaugural address in January 2006, President Johnson-Sirleaf reiterated campaign promises to restore electric light to Monrovia within six months. To this end, in March it was announced that the LEC had leased four generators with a combined power rating of 2,665 kVA. At a keenly awaited event, electric light was restored to parts of Monrovia on 26 July, Independence Day, an event described by the President as symbolizing Liberia's journey from darkness to illumination.

The provision of piped water was limited to urban areas before the 1989–96 war, and rural areas are still normally dependent on supplies collected from wells, bore holes, ponds and streams. It was estimated that 61% of the population had access to improved drinking water sources in 2004. In Monrovia, the parastatal Liberia Water and Sewer Corpn (LWSC) provided 273m.–365m. litres of water per day before the war. The central water supply and sewage disposal system in Monrovia was damaged during the 1992 offensive on the capital and a shortage of safe water has continued in Monrovia since that time, alleviated by donor-operated distribution systems and the partial restoration of piped water supplies in July 2006. In August it was announced that the World Bank would provide funds to rehabilitate and redesign the piped water supply network to further areas of Monrovia, including New Kru Town and Clara Town. Water shortages have been common during the dry season, enabling street vendors to charge L $10–$15 per gallon in Monrovia. Incidences of disease linked to unsafe water supplies remain a major public health problem. Serious outbreaks of cholera affected Monrovia during the rebel offensive on the capital in mid-2003, and again in June 2005; another outbreak affected various areas of south-west Liberia in August 2006. Only 27% of the population were estimated to have had access to adequate sanitation facilities in 2004.

THE MACROECONOMY

The rapid expansion of the Liberian economy in the 1950s and 1960s was largely generated by exports of rubber, iron ore and timber and by infrastructural projects financed by foreign aid. After the first major decline in international prices in 1974, rubber and iron ore exports stagnated. It is from this period that Liberia's macroeconomic difficulties originate. Public-sector deficits increased from negligible levels in 1975 to 13% of GDP in 1979; external debt nearly quadrupled. The Doe regime borrowed massively, almost entirely from abroad and mainly at commercial rates, and used the funds obtained to finance unproductive public investments and maintain domestic consumption. Export demand failed to recover in the 1980s, and by 1988 external public debt had risen to US $1,800m., equivalent to 164% of GDP, while scheduled debt-servicing payments would have taken 40% of export earnings.

Currency, Banking, Exchange Rate and Consumer Prices

Before 1981 the US dollar was the principal currency in Liberia; it remained legal tender in mid-2007 and is the main currency for trade and financial transactions and for larger cash payments. In December 2006 US dollar deposits accounted for 81% of all deposits in the Liberian commercial banking system. Doe issued a L $5 coin from 1981 and a L $5 banknote, later known as the 'JJ Roberts', from 1989. In early 1992 the interim administration introduced new banknotes, known as 'Liberty' dollars. The resulting threefold currency system (US dollars, JJ Roberts and Liberty dollars) continued until 2000, when the banking authorities introduced a new Liberian dollar.

In November 1999 a new central bank, the Central Bank of Liberia (CBL), was established. With IMF assistance, the CBL has introduced measures to supervise the commercial banking sector effectively, and the inter-bank clearing system was also restored during 2000. However, the commercial banking system has remained 'fragile', hindered by substantial difficulties resulting from an uncertain legal environment and the collapse of the Liberian economy since 1989. Banks were reluctant to lend to the private sector and processing fees continued to be the main source of banking income.

From 1940 the Liberian dollar was maintained nominally at par with the US dollar. The official 1:1 exchange rate became increasingly unrealistic during the 1989–96 war. After the 1997 elections, Liberty dollars traded at 40–45 to the US dollar, and the JJ Roberts at 20–22 to the US dollar on unofficial markets. The official 1:1 exchange rate was abandoned at the end of August 1998, and the rate was allowed to float. The exchange rate remained stable until the end of 2000, at about 41 Liberty dollars to the US dollar. In December 2000, however, in response to an upsurge in government spending financed by a recourse to the banking system, to the deteriorating security situation and to fears of UN sanctions, the new Liberian dollar started to weaken and reached L $70 = US $1 in mid-2002, and, after a partial recovery, again sank to this level in mid-2003. Following the end of the 1999–2003 conflict, there was an immediate strengthening of the Liberian dollar and the rate has fluctuated between about L $50 and L $60 to the US dollar since that time.

A new Consumer Price Index (CPI) was compiled in May 1998. The main threat to price stability in Monrovia is presented by government monetary policy and currency depreciation. The CPI remained fairly stable in the first few years after 1996, but currency depreciations after 2001 led to rapidly rising prices, with the CPI increasing by 10%–14% annually during 2001–03. Price stability was restored in early 2004 and has been below 10% per year since that time.

INTERNATIONAL TRADE AND DEBT

International trade has generated Liberia's growth. Merchandise exports increased from negligible levels before the Second World War to US $400.2m. in 1974, stimulated by strong demand in the world economy for iron ore and supported by continuing exports of rubber and other primary commodities. In 1974 exports were equivalent in value to 87% of GDP. Exports stagnated, in volume terms, in the 1970s, as a result of international recession. In the 1980s the volume of exports broadly declined and stagnating, or falling, export unit values exacerbated the effects on the economy. Nevertheless, the dominance of the export sector continued: exports were equivalent to 58% of GDP in 1980 and 50% in 1989.

After the 1989–96 civil conflict, identified exports, according to IMF estimates, recovered to US $166.5m. in 2002, The impact of the war with LURD and MODEL was severe in 2003, with the value of timber and rubber exports declining to US $54.6m. and US $43.9m., respectively, and total exports falling to US $108.9m. Timber exports collapsed to a negligible level in 2004 as UN sanctions took effect, although rubber exports recovered to US $93.4m., so that total exports fell only marginally, to US $103.8m. Net private remittances from abroad have become a significant element in the balance of payments in recent years, amounting to an estimated US $23m. in 2005.

Liberia's external debt problem originated in the 1970s, but the majority of the debt now owing was arranged under the Doe regime. Borrowings in the early and mid-1970s were conservative, and consisted mainly of loans at concessional interest rates over long repayment periods. From 1977, however, the earlier caution disappeared as the Government sought funds for the hosting of the 1979 summit meeting of the Organization of African Unity and loans were arranged with commercial banks at high interest rates. In 1980 requirements for finance to cover rice imports and substantial public-sector pay increases became urgent, and Doe's regime made recourse to borrowing abroad, establishing a pattern that persisted through the decade. Despite several debt-relief agreements in the early 1980s, Liberia fell into arrears to the IMF in 1984, a position it has remained in ever since. In January 1986 Liberia was declared ineligible for further drawings on the IMF and later that year the World Bank suspended disbursements. By the end of 1988 arrears on the external public debt had risen from the US $50m. of 1984 to US $863m. In March 1990 the IMF declared Liberia a 'non-co-operating' country and threatened Liberia with expulsion from the Fund owing to the Government's failure to pay outstanding arrears. By this time Liberia's total external debt had climbed to US $1,849m. The 1989–96 conflict resulted in the suspension of debt-servicing payments and the arrears accumulated at a rapid rate. By 1997 accumulated arrears and penalties had increased Liberia's total external debt to some US $2,012m. and further, to US $2,706m. (equivalent to more than US $750 per head) by 2004, of which most was in arrears.

Relations between the international financial institutions and Liberia registered some improvement immediately after the 1997 elections. However, the IMF, together with the World Bank, voiced continuing concerns over a range of issues. The Taylor administration offered only token co-operation with the IMF, including monthly payments of US $50,000 in respect of long overdue arrears. During 2001 delays in Liberia's monthly payments became frequent and lengthy, and in March 2003 the IMF finally suspended Liberia's voting rights at the IMF. The NTGL early expressed its commitment to normalizing relations with the Fund and resumed the $50,000 token payments in January 2004; the IMF responded by offering technical assistance. In 2005 the IMF voiced renewed concerns over the lack of transparency in government transactions and budgetary control. Progress towards the normalization of relations came to a halt and international activity focused on the formulation of the Governance and Economic Management Assistance Programme (GEMAP—see Recent History). The GEMAP consisted of six components: financial management and accountability; budgeting and expenditure management; procurement and concession-granting practices; corruption; assistance for key institutions such as the General Auditing Office; and capacity-building. The most notable feature of the Programme was its provision for the deployment of 'international experts' to state institutions and enterprises with binding co-signatory powers. It also provided for the control through international management contracts of the National Ports Authority, the RIA, the Liberia Petroleum Refining Corporation, the Forestry Development Authority, the Bureau of Maritime Affairs and the Bureau of Customs and Excise. Johnson-Sirleaf pledged her administration's commitment to the GEMAP on her inauguration.

In May 2006 the IMF pronounced itself 'encouraged' by developments in economic management in Liberia, and, for the first time in many years, progress towards debt relief was mentioned, if only as a distant objective. In October, the IMF lifted the declaration of non-co-operation that had been in force since 1990 and decided that it could consider lifting the suspension of Liberia's voting rights. In February 2007 the USA promised to write off US $391m. of Liberia's debt and in the same month China cancelled debts of US $10m.

PUBLIC FINANCE AND AID

A new tax code, developed in accordance with IMF advice, was introduced in July 2001, replacing the emergency tax regulations that had been in force since 1997. The new tax code was based on a personal income tax, a business income tax and a new flat-rate general sales tax. A new tariff structure, bringing Liberian tariffs into closer accordance with Economic Community of West African States rates, was also announced in 2000. Taxes on incomes and profits yielded US $25.1m. in 2005–06, or 30% of total revenue; the general sales tax yielded $4.4m. (5%); import duties yielded $35.1m. (42%) and revenue from the maritime registry yielded $12.1m. (14%). The Government's receipts from international aid programmes remained low throughout Taylor's administration and the NTGL, as almost all donors preferred to channel their assistance through UN agencies, other multilateral agencies and non-governmental organizations.

Johnson-Sirleaf's first budget, submitted to the legislature at the end of June 2006, was for US $120m., an expenditure to be covered by taxation receipts without recourse to borrowing. Expenditure allocations were shifted towards education and health, and away from defence: education accounted for 8% of budgeted expenditure, health 6%, security and justice 6% and defence only 1%. However, the state apparatus (the legislature and the Ministries of State, Internal Affairs and Foreign Affairs) was expected to consume 17% of the budget, indicating the low priority still accorded to service delivery. The 2007/08 budget, signed into law in July 2007, was for US $199m.

The willingness of the USA to increase its aid, from some US $10m. in 1979 to US $64m. in 1985, undoubtedly encouraged the Doe Government to maintain Liberia's traditional alignment with Western countries. However, US aid was sharply reduced, to $43m., in 1986, and further cuts followed US federal agency reports of misappropriations. From 1990, however, the USA provided emergency assistance to counteract the effects of the civil conflict. Total US government assistance over the 1989–96 war period amounted to more than US $450m. Total net official development assistance (ODA) from the development assistance committee countries of the Organisation for Economic Co-operation and Development and other multilateral organizations over the same period exceeded US $900m., almost all of which was humanitarian aid. After the 1989–96 war Liberia's net ODA receipts declined from US $173m. in 1997 to US $68m. in 2000, as peace reduced the necessity for humanitarian aid. The USA has been Liberia's largest donor in the period since 1996, followed by the agencies of the UN and the European Union.

Following the re-emergence of armed conflict in Liberia, humanitarian aid was again provided. Net ODA receipts rose from US $39m. in 2001 to US $52m. in 2002 and to US $107m. in 2003. The US Agency for International Development provided small amounts of assistance in 2002, US $29.0m. in 2003–04 and US $95.8m. in 2004–05. However, responses to the UN's Consolidated Inter-Agency Appeals for 2001–03 were poor. Aid has been more forthcoming since the departure of Taylor. In February 2004 an International Reconstruction Conference for Liberia, held in New York, under UN auspices, received offers of funds totalling US $520m. Disbursements of this aid were slow, however, totalling only US $189m. in 2004 and US $270m. in 2005, with donors citing concerns about Liberian financial management practices as the cause of the delays. As was the case with reconstruction aid after the 1989–96 conflict, very little of the aid received was channelled through the NTGL and virtually no aid was provided for general support of the government budget. Donor disbursements were estimated at US $245m. in 2006 and were expected to continue at about this level in 2007. The cost of UNMIL, estimated at about US $1,000m. per year, but little of which is spent in-country, was in addition to these figures. As before, none of this aid was to be given for general budgetary support and international aid was not, therefore, expected to ameliorate the Johnson-Sirleaf administration's fiscal difficulties.

GROWTH AND ECONOMIC PROSPECTS

Reconstruction of the country's economy, especially its infrastructure, was far from complete before the conflict with the LURD and MODEL rebels which wrought further damage in 1999–2003. However, slow progress under the NTGL has been superseded by renewed progress and hope under the Johnson-Sirleaf administration. The removal of the timber and diamond sanctions and the restoration of electricity and piped water to parts of Monrovia have been significant achievements. Relations with the international financial institutions have improved substantially and the prospect of substantial international debt relief, although still very distant, now appears real. However, poverty remains widespread and severe. The renewed interest in iron ore and offshore oil exploration has yet to yield tangible results. The recovery of the timber and diamond sectors awaits foreign investment which, in these as in other sectors, remains restricted by the devastated infrastructure. Even sustained and rapid growth will not return the economy to the position it achieved in the 1980s for many years. The outlook for the economy consequently remains difficult.

Statistical Survey

Sources (unless otherwise stated): the former Ministry of Planning and Economic Affairs, POB 9016, Broad St, Monrovia.

Area and Population

AREA, POPULATION AND DENSITY

Area (sq km)	97,754*
Population (census results)	
1 February 1974	1,503,368
1 February 1984 (provisional)	
Males	1,063,127
Females	1,038,501
Total	2,101,628
Population (UN estimates at mid-year)†	
2004	3,348,000
2005	3,442,000
2006	3,579,000
Density (per sq km) at mid-2006	36.6

* 37,743 sq miles.

† Source: UN, *World Population Prospects: The 2006 Revision*.

ADMINISTRATIVE DIVISIONS

(population at 1984 census)

Counties:		Nimba	313,050
Bomi	66,420	Rivercess	37,849
Bong	255,813	Sinoe	64,147
Grand Bassa	159,648	*Territories:*	
Grand Cape Mount	79,322	Gibi	66,802
Grand Gedeh	102,810	Kru Coast	35,267
Lofa	247,641	Marshall	31,190
Maryland	85,267	Sasstown	11,524
Montserrado	544,878	**Total**	2,101,628

Note: The counties of Grand Kru and Margibi were subsequently established. Two further counties, River Gee and Gbarpolu, were created in 1998 and 2001, respectively.

PRINCIPAL TOWNS
(2003)

Monrovia (capital)	550,200	Harbel	17,700
Zwedru	35,300	Tubmanburg	16,700
Buchanan	27,300	Gbarnga	14,200
Yekepa	22,900	Greenville	13,500
Harper	20,000	Ganta	11,200
Bensonville	19,600		

Source: Stefan Helders, *World Gazetteer* (internet www.world-gazetteer.com).

BIRTHS AND DEATHS
(annual averages, UN estimates)

	1990–95	1995–2000	2000–05
Birth rate (per 1,000)	50.0	49.7	49.9
Death rate (per 1,000)	23.0	21.2	19.8

Source: UN, *World Population Prospects: The 2006 Revision*.

Expectation of life (years at birth, WHO estimates): 42 (males 39; females 44) in 2004 (Source: WHO, *World Health Report*).

ECONOMICALLY ACTIVE POPULATION

	1978	1979	1980
Agriculture, forestry, hunting and fishing	355,467	366,834	392,926
Mining	25,374	26,184	28,047
Manufacturing	6,427	6,631	7,102
Construction	4,701	4,852	5,198
Electricity, gas and water	245	246	263
Commerce	18,668	19,266	20,636
Transport and communications	7,314	7,549	8,086
Services	49,567	51,154	54,783
Others	28,555	29,477	31,571
Total	496,318	512,193	548,615

Mid-2005 (estimates in '000): Agriculture, etc. 796; Total labour force 1,225 (Source: FAO).

Health and Welfare

KEY INDICATORS

Total fertility rate (children per woman, 2005)	6.8
Under-5 mortality rate (per 1,000 live births, 2005)	235
HIV/AIDS (% of persons aged 15–49, 2003)	5.9
Physicians (per 1,000 head, 2004)	0.03
Health expenditure (2004): US $ per head (PPP)	22.2
Health expenditure (2004): % of GDP	5.6
Health expenditure (2004): public (% of total)	63.9
Access to water (% of persons, 2004)	61
Access to sanitation (% of persons, 2004)	27

For sources and definitions, see explanatory note on p. vi.

Agriculture

PRINCIPAL CROPS
('000 metric tons)

	2003	2004	2005
Rice (paddy)	100*	110*	110†
Sweet potatoes†	19	19	19
Cassava (Manioc)†	490	490	490
Taro (Coco yam)†	26	26	26
Yams†	20	20	20
Sugar cane†	255	255	255
Oil palm fruit†	174	174	174
Vegetables†	61	61	61
Bananas†	110	110	110
Plantains†	42	42	42
Other fresh fruit (excl. melons)†	17	17	17
Natural rubber (dry weight)*	110	115	112

* Unofficial figure(s).
† FAO estimate(s).

Source: FAO.

LIVESTOCK
('000 head, year ending September, FAO estimates)

	2003	2004	2005
Cattle	36	36	36
Pigs	130	130	130
Sheep	210	210	210
Goats	220	220	220
Chickens	4,800	5,000	5,300
Ducks	200	200	200

Source: FAO.

LIVESTOCK PRODUCTS
(metric tons, FAO estimates)

	2003	2004	2005
Pig meat	4,400	4,400	4,400
Chicken meat	7,880	8,200	8,680
Other meat	8,816	8,816	8,816
Cows' milk	715	715	715
Hen eggs	4,320	4,320	4,320

Source: FAO.

Forestry

ROUNDWOOD REMOVALS
('000 cubic metres, excluding bark)

	2003	2004	2005
Sawlogs, veneer logs and logs for sleepers	800	250	150
Other industrial wood*	180	180	180
Fuel wood*	5,350	5,576	5,811
Total	6,330	6,006	6,141

* FAO estimates.

Source: FAO.

SAWNWOOD PRODUCTION
('000 cubic metres, including railway sleepers, unofficial figures)

	2003	2004	2005
Total (all broadleaved)	25	20	20

Source: FAO.

Fishing

(metric tons, live weight, capture)

	2003*	2004	2005*
Freshwater fishes	4,000	4,000	4,000
Dentex	250	4	4
Sardinellas	1,000	643	620
Sharks, rays, skates, etc.	440	60	40
Total catch (incl. others)	10,700	10,359	10,000

* FAO estimates.

Source: FAO.

Mining

	2003	2004	2005
Diamonds ('000 carats)*	25	40	40
Gold (kilograms)*	40	10	10

* Estimates.

Note: In addition to the commodities listed, Liberia produced significant quantities of a variety of industrial minerals and construction materials (clays, gypsum, sand and gravel, and stone), but insufficient information is available to make reliable estimates of output levels.

Source: US Geological Survey.

Industry

SELECTED PRODUCTS

('000 metric tons unless otherwise indicated)

	2002	2003	2004
Beer (metric tons)*	6,150	6,420	n.a.
Palm oil†	42	42	42
Cement	54	25‡	40‡
Electric energy (million kWh)	540‡	n.a.	n.a.

* FAO estimates.

† Unofficial figures; annual output assumed to be unchanged since 1997.

‡ Estimate.

Sources: FAO; US Geological Survey; UN, *Industrial Commodity Statistics Yearbook*.

Finance

CURRENCY AND EXCHANGE RATES

Monetary Units

100 cents = 1 Liberian dollar (L $).

Sterling, Dollar and Euro Equivalents (29 December 2006)

£1 sterling = L $116.799;
US $1 = L $59.500;
€1 = L $78.361;
L $1,000 = £8.56 = US $16.81 = €12.76.

Average Exchange Rate (L $ per US $)

2004 54.9058
2005 57.0958
2006 57.0133

Note: The aforementioned data are based on market-determined rates of exchange. Prior to January 1998 the exchange rate was a fixed parity with the US dollar (L $1 = US $1).

BUDGET

(US $ million)

Revenue*	2004/05	2005/06	2006/07
Tax revenue	75.7	81.0	116.8
Taxes on income and profits	28.4	25.1	33.7
Taxes on goods and services	16.9	20.3	12.2
Maritime revenue	10.1	12.1	11.0
Stumpage fees and land rental	0.0	0.0	4.8
Taxes on international trade	30.2	35.3	56.4
Other revenue	3.6	3.6	4.1
Total	79.3	84.6	120.9

Expenditure	2003/04	2004/05	2005/06
Current expenditure	66.3	64.5	119.1
Wages and salaries	42.3	30.7	48.5
Other goods and services	16.0	15.4	46.8
Subsidies, transfers and net lending	6.0	9.8	16.4
Interest payments	2.0	2.4	2.2
Domestic arrears clearance	—	6.2	5.3
Capital expenditure†	10.6	7.7	33.4
Total	77.0	72.5	152.5

* Excluding grants received (US $ million): 1.0 in 2004/05; 5.0 in 2005/06; 14.2 in 2006/07.

† Includes expenditure related to national security.

Source: IMF, *Liberia: Second Review of Performance Under the Staff-Monitored Program and New Program for 2007* (February 2007).

INTERNATIONAL RESERVES

(US $ million at 31 December)

	2004	2005	2006
Reserve position in IMF	0.05	0.04	0.05
Foreign exchange	18.69	25.35	71.94
Total	18.74	25.40	71.99

Source: IMF, *International Financial Statistics*.

MONEY SUPPLY

(L $ million at 31 December)

	2004	2005	2006
Currency outside banks*	1,754.9	2,168.9	2,647.6
Demand deposits at commercial banks	1,971.9	2,701.9	3,973.2
Total money (incl. others)	3,727.5	4,871.6	6,663.5

* Figures refer only to amounts of Liberian coin in circulation. US notes and coin also circulate, but the amount of these in private holdings is unknown. The amount of Liberian coin in circulation is small in comparison to US currency.

Source: IMF, *International Financial Statistics*.

COST OF LIVING

(Consumer Price Index; base: May 1998 = 100)

	2003	2004	2005
Food	140.9	153.8	167.0
Fuel and light	154.4	217.6	342.1
Clothing	121.2	128.7	137.3
Rent	131.8	156.1	180.9
All items (incl. others)	157.0	169.3	187.6

Source: IMF, *Liberia: Selected Issues and Statistical Appendix* (May 2006).

All items (Consumer Price Index; base 2000 = 100): 160.8 in 2004; 171.9 in 2005; 185.7 in 2006 (Source: African Development Bank).

NATIONAL ACCOUNTS
(at current prices)

Expenditure on the Gross Domestic Product
(L $ million)

	1987	1988	1989
Government final consumption expenditure	143.9	136.3	141.6
Private final consumption expenditure	713.9	733.3	656.8
Increase in stocks*	7.0	3.5	4.0
Gross fixed capital formation	120.4	115.3	96.8
Statistical discrepancy	22.9	39.1	48.2
Total domestic expenditure	1,008.1	1,027.5	947.4
Exports of goods and services	438.2	452.3	521.4
Less Imports of goods and services	356.8	321.5	275.2
GDP in purchasers' values	1,089.5	1,158.3	1,193.6
GDP at constant 1981 prices	1,015.0	1,043.7	1,072.8

* Figures refer only to stocks of iron ore and rubber.

Source: UN, *National Accounts Statistics*.

Gross Domestic Product by Economic Activity
(US $ million, estimates)

	2003	2004	2005
Agriculture, hunting, forestry and fishing	293.9	319.3	349.0
Mining and quarrying	0.3	0.4	0.4
Manufacturing	29.9	58.8	65.7
Electricity, gas and water	3.5	3.7	4.0
Construction	9.9	10.0	13.4
Trade, restaurants and hotels	24.1	25.8	30.5
Transport, storage and communications	31.9	33.2	36.3
Finance, insurance, real estate and business services	13.1	13.8	14.9
Government services	11.6	13.2	14.4
Other services	17.1	18.4	19.7
GDP in purchasers' values	435.3	496.8	548.4

Source: IMF, *Liberia: Selected Issues and Statistical Appendix* (May 2006).

BALANCE OF PAYMENTS
(US $ million, estimates)

	2004	2005	2006
Exports of goods f.o.b.	104	112	158
Imports of goods c.i.f.	–236	–272	–366
Trade balance	–132	–160	–209
Services (net)	–37	–47	–70
Balance on goods and services	–169	–207	–279
Income (net)	–87	–113	–137
Balance on goods, services and income	–256	–320	–416
Current transfers (net)	243	311	342
Current balance	–13	–9	–74
Capital and financial account (net)	–39	–43	–51
Net errors and omissions	–27	–64	–1
Overall balance	–79	–115	–126

Source: IMF, *Liberia: Second Review of Performance Under the Staff-Monitored Program and New Program for 2007* (February 2007).

External Trade

PRINCIPAL COMMODITIES
(US $ million, estimates)

Imports c.i.f.	2003	2004	2005
Food and live animals	40.6	61.9	51.2
Rice	39.2	27.5	24.5
Beverages and tobacco	4.4	9.2	6.8
Mineral fuels and lubricants	30.7	70.6	92.2
Petroleum	29.7	66.2	90.8
Chemicals and related products	5.5	7.1	7.3
Basic manufactures	11.9	25.4	21.8
Machinery and transport equipment	11.9	50.6	44.9
Miscellaneous manufactured articles	30.3	38.3	40.9
Total (incl. others)	140.0	268.1	273.6

Exports f.o.b.	2003	2004	2005
Rubber	43.9	93.4	98.7
Timber	54.6	—	—
Cocoa	0.9	3.5	5.7
Total (incl. others)	108.9	103.8	112.2

Source: IMF, *Liberia: Selected Issues and Statistical Appendix* (May 2005).

PRINCIPAL TRADING PARTNERS
(US $ million)

Imports c.i.f.	1986	1987	1988
Belgium-Luxembourg	8.5	11.2	15.0
China, People's Repub.	7.1	14.7	4.8
Denmark	10.6	7.6	5.9
France (incl. Monaco)	6.5	6.4	4.7
Germany, Fed. Repub.	32.7	52.3	39.5
Italy	2.5	2.2	7.3
Japan	20.1	15.0	12.0
Netherlands	20.6	26.8	14.4
Spain	2.5	6.6	3.1
Sweden	2.4	0.6	4.6
United Kingdom	24.2	18.4	12.7
USA	42.5	58.0	57.7
Total (incl. others)	259.0	307.6	272.3

Source: UN, *International Trade Statistics Yearbook*.

Exports f.o.b.	2003	2004	2005
Belgium	—	30.6	28.5
China, People's Repub.	—	5.5	1.2
France	16.3	1.7	—
Hong Kong	41.2	—	—
USA	34.1	63.7	96.8
Total (incl. others)	108.9	103.8	131.8

Source: Ministry of Commerce and Industry, Monrovia.

Transport

RAILWAYS
(estimated traffic)

	1991	1992	1993
Passenger-km (million)	406	417	421
Freight ton-km (million)	200	200	200

Source: UN Economic Commission for Africa, *African Statistical Yearbook*.

ROAD TRAFFIC
(estimates, vehicles in use at 31 December)

	1999	2000	2001
Passenger cars	15.3	17.1	17.1
Commercial vehicles	11.9	12.8	12.8

2002: Figures assumed to be unchanged from 2001.

Source: UN, *Statistical Yearbook*.

SHIPPING

Merchant Fleet
(registered at 31 December)

	2004	2005	2006
Number of vessels	1,538	1,653	1,907
Displacement ('000 gross registered tons)	53,898.8	59,600.2	68,405.1

Source: Lloyd's Register-Fairplay, *World Fleet Statistics*.

International Sea-borne Freight Traffic
(estimates, '000 metric tons)

	1991	1992	1993
Goods loaded	16,706	17,338	21,653
Goods unloaded	1,570	1,597	1,608

Source: UN Economic Commission for Africa, *African Statistical Yearbook*.

CIVIL AVIATION
(traffic on scheduled services)

	1990	1991	1992
Passengers carried ('000)	32	32	32
Passenger-km (million)	7	7	7
Total ton-km (million)	1	1	1

Source: UN, *Statistical Yearbook*.

Communications Media

	1995	1996	1997
Radio receivers ('000 in use)	675	715	790
Television receivers ('000 in use)	56	60	70
Telephones ('000 main lines in use)	5	5	6
Daily newspapers:			
number	8	6	6
average circulation ('000 copies, estimates)	35	35	36

Sources: UNESCO Institute for Statistics; UN, *Statistical Yearbook*.

Telephones ('000 main lines in use): 6.7 in 2000; 6.8 in 2001; 6.9 in 2002 (Source: International Telecommunication Union).

Mobile cellular telephones ('000 subscribers): 47.2 in 2003; 94.4 in 2004; 160.0 in 2005 (Source: International Telecommunication Union).

Internet users ('000): 0.3 in 1999; 0.5 in 2000; 1.0 in 2001 (Source: UN, *Statistical Yearbook*).

Daily newspapers: 6 in 1998 (estimated average circulation 36,600) (Source: UNESCO Institute for Statistics).

Education

(1999/2000)

	Teachers	Students		
		Males	Females	Total
Pre-primary	4,322	82,215	72,908	155,123
Primary	12,966	288,227	208,026	496,253
Secondary:				
general	4,529	52,072	38,370	90,442
technical and vocational	603	26,988	18,079	45,067
Post-secondary technical and vocational	430	8,842	6,789	15,631
University	723	25,236	18,871	44,107

Source: UNESCO Institute for Statistics.

Adult literacy rate (UNESCO estimates): 55.9% (males 72.3%; females 39.3%) in 2003 (Source: UN, *Human Development Report*).

Directory

The Constitution

The Constitution of the Republic of Liberia entered into effect on 6 January 1986, following its approval by national referendum in July 1984. Its main provisions are summarized below:

PREAMBLE

The Republic of Liberia is a unitary sovereign state, which is divided into counties for administrative purposes. There are three separate branches of government: the legislative, the executive and the judiciary. No person is permitted to hold office or executive power in more than one branch of government. The fundamental human rights of the individual are guaranteed.

LEGISLATURE

Legislative power is vested in the bicameral National Assembly, comprising a Senate and a House of Representatives. Deputies of both chambers are elected by universal adult suffrage. Each county elects two members of the Senate (one for a term of nine years and one for six years), while members of the House of Representatives are elected by legislative constituency for a term of six years. Legislation requires the approval of two-thirds of the members of both chambers, and is subsequently submitted to the President for endorsement. The Constitution may be amended by two-thirds of the members of both chambers.

EXECUTIVE

Executive power is vested in the President, who is Head of State and Commander-in-Chief of the armed forces. The President is elected by universal adult suffrage for a term of six years, and is restricted to a maximum of two terms in office. A Vice-President is elected at the same time as the President. The President appoints a Cabinet, and members of the judiciary and armed forces, with the approval of the Senate. The President is empowered to declare a state of emergency.

JUDICIARY

Judicial power is vested in the Supreme Court and any subordinate courts, which apply both statutory and customary laws in accordance with standards enacted by the legislature. The judgments of the Supreme Court are final and not subject to appeal or review by any other branch of government. The Supreme Court comprises one Chief Justice and five Associate Justices. Justices are appointed by the President, with the approval of the Senate.

POLITICAL PARTIES AND ELECTIONS

Political associations are obliged to comply with the minimum registration requirements imposed by the Elections Commission. Organizations that endanger free democratic society, or that organize, train or equip groups of supporters, are to be denied registration. Prior to elections, each political party and independent candidate is required to submit statements of assets and liabilities to the Elections Commission. All elections of public officials are determined by an absolute majority of the votes cast. If no candidate obtains an absolute majority in the first ballot, a second ballot is conducted between the two candidates with the highest number of votes. Complaints by parties or candidates must be submitted to the Elections Commission within seven days of the announcement of election results. The Supreme Court has final jurisdiction over challenges to election results.

The Government

HEAD OF STATE

President: ELLEN JOHNSON-SIRLEAF (inaugurated 16 January 2006).

THE CABINET
(March 2007)

Vice-President: JOSEPH NYUMAH BOAKAI.

Minister of Agriculture: J. CHRISTOPHER TOE.

Minister of Commerce and Industry: BANKIE KING AKERELE.

Minister of Defence: BROWNIE SAMUKAI.

Minister of Education: JOSEPH KORTO.

Minister of Finance: ANTOINETTE SAYEH.

Minister of Foreign Affairs: GEORGE W. WALLACE.

Minister of Gender Development: VARBAH GAYFLOR.

Minister of Health and Social Welfare: WALTER GWENIGALE.

Minister of Information, Culture and Tourism: Rev. Dr LAWRENCE K. BROPLEH.

Minister of Internal Affairs: AMBULLAI JOHNSON.

Minister of Justice: FRANCES JOHNSON-MORRIS.

Minister of Labour: SAMUEL KOFI WOODS.

Minister of Lands, Mines and Energy: EUGENE SHANNON.

Minister of Planning and Economic Affairs: TOGA G. MCINTOSH.

Minister of Posts and Telecommunications: JACKSON E. DOE.

Minister of Public Works: LUSENI DONZO.

Minister of National Security: ANTHONY B. KROMAH.

Minister of Transport: JEREMIAH SULUNTEH.

Minister of Youth and Sport: ETMONIA TARPEH.

Minister of State for Presidential Affairs: Dr EDWARD MCCLAIN (acting).

MINISTRIES

All ministries are based in Monrovia.

Office of the President: Executive Mansion, POB 10-9001, Capitol Hill, 1000 Monrovia 10; e-mail emansion@liberia.net.

Ministry of Agriculture: Tubman Blvd, POB 10-9010, 1000 Monrovia 10; tel. 226399.

Ministry of Commerce and Industry: Ashmun St, POB 10-9014, 1000 Monrovia 10; tel. 226283.

Ministry of Defence: Benson St, POB 10-9007, 1000 Monrovia 10; tel. 226077.

Ministry of Education: E. G. N. King Plaza, Broad St, POB 10-1545, 1000 Monrovia 10; tel. and fax 226216.

Ministry of Finance: Broad St, POB 10-9013, 1000 Monrovia 10; tel. 47510680; internet www.finance.gov.lr.

Ministry of Foreign Affairs: Mamba Point, POB 10-9002, 1000 Monrovia 10; tel. 226763; internet www.mofa.gov.lr.

Ministry of Health and Social Welfare: Sinkor, POB 10-9004, 1000 Monrovia 10; tel. 226317.

Ministry of Information, Culture and Tourism: Capitol Hill, POB 10-9021, 1000 Monrovia 10; tel. and fax 226269.

Ministry of Internal Affairs: cnr Warren and Benson Sts, POB 10-9008, 1000 Monrovia 10; tel. 226346.

Ministry of Justice: Ashmun St, POB 10-9006, 1000 Monrovia 10; tel. 227872.

Ministry of Labour: Mechlin St, POB 10-9040, 1000 Monrovia 10; tel. 226291.

Ministry of Lands, Mines and Energy: Capitol Hill, POB 10-9024, 1000 Monrovia 10; tel. 226281.

Ministry of Planning and Economic Affairs: Broad St, POB 10-9016, 1000 Monrovia 10; tel. 226962.

Ministry of Posts and Telecommunications: Carey St, 1000 Monrovia 10; tel. 226079.

Ministry of Presidential Affairs: Executive Mansion, Capitol Hill, 1000 Monrovia 10; tel. 228026.

Ministry of Public Works: Lynch St, POB 10-9011, 1000 Monrovia 10; tel. 227972.

President and Legislature

PRESIDENT

Presidential Election, First Round, 11 October 2005

Candidate	Votes	% of votes
George Manneh Weah (Congress for Democratic Change)	275,265	28.26
Ellen Johnson-Sirleaf (Unity Party)	192,326	19.75
Charles Walker Brumskine (Liberty Party)	135,093	13.87
Winston A. Tubman (National Democratic Party of Liberia)	89,623	9.20
Harry Varney Gboto-Nambi Sherman (Coalition for the Transformation of Liberia)	76,403	7.85
Roland Chris Yarkpah Massaquoi (National Patriotic Party)	40,361	4.14
Joseph D. Z. Korto (Liberia Equal Rights Party)	31,814	3.27
Alhaji G. V. Kromah (All Liberian Coalition Party)	27,141	2.79
Togba-Nah Tipoteh (Alliance for Peace and Democracy)	22,766	2.34
William Vacanarat Shadrach Tubman (Reformed United Liberia Party)	15,115	1.55
John Sembe Morlu (United Democratic Alliance)	12,068	1.24
Milton Nathaniel Barnes (Liberia Destiny Party)	9,325	0.96
Margaret J. Tor-Thompson (Freedom Alliance Party of Liberia)	8,418	0.84
Joseph Mamadee Woah-Tee (Labour Party of Liberia)	5,948	0.61
Sekou Damate Conneh (Progressive Democratic Party)	5,499	0.56
David M. Farhat (Free Democratic Party)	4,497	0.46
George Klay Kieh, Jr (New Deal Movement)	4,476	0.46
Armah Zolu Jallah (National Party of Liberia)	3,837	0.39
Robert Momo Kpoto (Union of Liberian Democrats)	3,825	0.39
George Momodu Kiadii (National Vision Party of Liberia)	3,646	0.37
Samuel Raymond Divine, Sr (Independent)	3,188	0.33
Alfred Reeves (National Reformation Party)	3,156	0.32
Total	973,790	100.00

Presidential Election, Second Round, 8 November 2005

Candidate	Votes	% of votes
Ellen Johnson-Sirleaf (Unity Party)	478,526	59.40
George Manneh Weah (Congress for Democratic Change)	327,046	40.60
Total	805,572	100.00

LEGISLATURE

House of Representatives

Speaker: ALEX JANEKAI TYLER.

General Election, 11 October 2005

Party	% of votes	Seats
Congress for Democratic Change	23.4	15
Liberty Party	14.1	9
Unity Party	12.5	8
Coalition for the Transformation of Liberia	12.5	8
Independents	10.9	7
Alliance for Peace and Democracy	7.8	5
National Patriotic Party	6.3	4
New Deal Movement	4.7	3
All Liberian Coalition Party	3.1	2
National Democratic Party of Liberia	1.6	1
United Democratic Alliance	1.6	1
National Reformation Party	1.6	1
Total	100.0	64

Senate

President: ISAAC NYENABO.

General Election, 11 October 2005

	% of votes	Seats
Coalition for the Transformation of Liberia	23.3	7
Congress for Democratic Change	10.0	3
Unity Party	10.0	3
Liberty Party	10.0	3
Alliance for Peace and Democracy	10.0	3
National Patriotic Party	10.0	3
Independents	10.0	3
National Democratic Party of Liberia	6.7	2
National Reformation Party	3.3	1
All Liberian Coalition Party	3.3	1
United Democratic Alliance	3.3	1
Total	100.0	30

Election Commission

National Elections Commission: Tubman Blvd, 16th St, Sinkor, Monrovia; internet www.necliberia.org; independent; Chair. JAMES FLOMOYAN.

Political Organizations

At the end of January 1997 the armed factions in Liberia officially ceased to exist as military organizations; a number of them were reconstituted as political parties, while long-standing political organizations re-emerged. In August 2003 the two main rebel movements in conflict with government forces, Liberians United for Reconciliation and Democracy and the Movement for Democracy in Liberia, signed a peace agreement, which provided for their inclusion in a power-sharing administration. Following the completion of the disarmament process in November 2004, these were officially dissolved. A total of 30 political parties had been granted registration prior to presidential and legislative elections in October and November 2005.

Alliance for Peace and Democracy (APD): Benson St, Monrovia; tel. (6) 547710; internet www.members.tripod.com/tipoteh12/index.html; f. 2005; Leader TOGBA-NAH TIPOTEH; Chair. DUSTY WOLOKOLIE.

Liberian People's Party (LPP): Monrovia; f. 1984 by fmr mems of the Movement for Justice in Africa; Leader DUSTY WOLOKOLLIE.

United People's Party (UPP): Monrovia; f. 1984 by fmr mems of the Progressive People's Party, which led opposition prior to April 1980 coup; Leader WESLEY JOHNSON.

All Liberian Coalition Party (ALCOP): Broad St, Monrovia; tel. (6) 524735; f. 1997 from elements of fmr armed faction the United Liberation Movement of Liberia for Democracy; Leader Alhaji G. V. KROMAH; Chair. JOHNSTON P. FANNEBRDE.

Coalition for the Transformation of Liberia (COTOL): Monrovia; f. 2005; Leader HARRY VARNEY GBOTO-NAMBI SHERMAN.

Liberian Action Party (LAP): Monrovia; f. 1984; Leader GYUDE BRYANT.

Liberian Unification Party (LUP): Monrovia; f. 1984; Leader LAVELI SUPUWOOD.

People's Democratic Party of Liberia (PDPL): Monrovia; Leader FIYAH GBOLIE.

True Whig Party (TWP): Monrovia; Leader RUDOLPH SHERMAN.

Congress for Democratic Change: Bernard Beach Compound, Monrovia; tel. (6) 513469; f. 2004; Leader GEORGE MANNEH WEAH; Chair. J. BANGULA COLE.

Free Democratic Party (FDP): Center St, Monrovia; tel. (6) 582291; Leader DAVID M. FARHAT; Chair. S. CIAPHA GBOLLIE.

Liberia Equal Rights Party (LERP): Duala Gas Station, Bushrod Island, Opposite Duala Market, Monrovia; f. 2005; Leader JOSEPH D. Z. KORTO; Chair. SOLOMON KING.

Liberia Destiny Party (LDP): Congo Town Back Rd, Monrovia; tel. (6) 511531; f. 2005; Leader MILTON NATHANIEL BARNES; Sec.-Gen. BORBOR B. KROMAH.

Liberty Party (LP): Old Rd, Sinkor Opposite Haywood Mission, POB 1340, Monrovia; tel. (6) 547921; f. 2005; Leader CHARLES WALKER BRUMSKINE; Chair. LARRY P. YOUQUOI.

National Democratic Party of Liberia (NDPL): Capital Bye Pass, Monrovia; f. 1997 from the fmr armed faction the Liberia Peace Council; Leader WINSTON A. TUBMAN; Chair. NYANDEH SIEH.

National Patriotic Party (NPP): Sinkor, Tubman Bldg, Monrovia; tel. (6) 515312; f. 1997 from the fmr armed faction the National Patriotic Front of Liberia; won the majority of seats in legislative elections in July 1997; Leader ROLAND CHRIS YARKPAH MASSAQUOI; Chair. LAWRENCE A. GEORGE.

National Reformation Party (NRP): Duala Market, Monrovia; tel. (6) 511531; Leader Bishop ALFRED GARPEE REEVES; Chair. Rev. SAMUEL TORMETIEE.

New Deal Movement (NDM): Randall St, Monrovia; tel. (6) 567470; f. 2003; Leader Prof. GEORGE KLAY KIEH, Jr; Chair. T. WILSON GAYE.

Progressive Democratic Party (PRODEM): McDonald St, Monrovia; tel. (6) 521091; f. early 2005 by mems of fmr rebel movement, Liberians United for Reconciliation and Democracy (emerged 1999); Leader SEKOU DAMATE CONNEH.

Reformed United Liberia Party (RULP): 70 Ashmun St, POB 1000, Monrovia; tel. (6) 571212; f. 2005; Leader WILLIAM VACANARAT SHADRACH TUBMAN.

United Democratic Alliance (UDA): Monrovia; f. 2005 by the **Liberia National Union (LINU)**; led by HENRY MONIBA; the **Liberia Education and Development Party (LEAD)**; and the **Reformation Alliance Party (RAP)**, led by HENRY BOIMAH FAHNBULLEH; Leader JOHN SEMBE MORLU.

Unity Party (UP): 86 Broad St, Monrovia; tel. (6) 512528; e-mail info@theunityparty.org; internet www.theunityparty.org; f. 1984; Leader ELLEN JOHNSON-SIRLEAF; Chair. Dr CHARLES CLARKE.

Diplomatic Representation

EMBASSIES IN LIBERIA

Algeria: Capitol By-Pass, POB 2032, Monrovia; tel. 224311; Chargé d'affaires a.i. MUHAMMAD AZZEDINE AZZOUZ.

Cameroon: 18th St and Payne Ave, Sinkor, POB 414, Monrovia; tel. 261374; Ambassador VICTOR E. NDIBA.

China, People's Republic: Tubman Blvd, Congotown, POB 5970, Monrovia; tel. 228024; fax 226740; e-mail Chinaemb_lr@mfa.gov.cn; internet lr.china-embassy.org; Ambassador LIN SONGTIAN.

Congo, Democratic Republic: Spriggs Payne Airport, Sinkor, POB 1038, Monrovia; tel. 261326; Ambassador (vacant).

Côte d'Ivoire: Tubman Blvd, Sinkor, POB 126, Monrovia; tel. 261123; Ambassador CLÉMENT KAUL MELEDJE.

Cuba: 17 Kennedy Ave, Congotown, POB 3579, Monrovia; tel. 262600; Ambassador Dr MIGUEL GUSTAVO PÉREZ CRUZ.

Egypt: Coconut Plantation, Randal St, Mamba Point, POB 462, Monrovia; tel. 226226; fax 226122; Ambassador OMAR ABD EL AZIZ EL SHEEMY.

Ghana: cnr 11th St and Gardiner Ave, Sinkor, POB 471, Monrovia; tel. 261477; Ambassador Maj.-Gen. FRANCIS ADU-AMANFOH.

Guinea: Monrovia; Ambassador ABDOULAYE DORÉ.

Lebanon: 12th St, Monrovia; tel. 262537; Ambassador MANSOUR ABDALLAH.

Libya: Monrovia; Ambassador MUHAMMAD UMARAT-TABI.

Morocco: Tubman Blvd, Congotown, Monrovia; tel. 262767; Ambassador MOHAMED LASFAR.

Nigeria: Congotown, POB 366, Monrovia; tel. 227345; fax 226135; Ambassador EINEJE ONOBU.

Russia: Payne Ave, Sinkor, POB 2010, Monrovia; tel. 261304; Ambassador ANDREY V. POKROVSKII.

Senegal: Monrovia; Ambassador MOCTAR TRAORÉ.

Sierra Leone: Tubman Blvd, POB 575, Monrovia; tel. 261301; Ambassador PATRICK J. FOYAH.

USA: 111 United Nations Dr., Mamba Point, POB 10-0098, Monrovia; tel. 054826; fax 10370; e-mail ConsularMonrovia@state.gov; internet monrovia.usembassy.gov; Ambassador DONALD E. BOOTH.

Judicial System

In February 1982 the People's Supreme Tribunal (which had been established following the April 1980 coup) was renamed the People's Supreme Court, and its Chairman and members became the Chief Justice and Associate Justices of the People's Supreme Court. The judicial system also comprised People's Circuit and Magistrate Courts. The five-member Supreme Court was established in January 1992 to adjudicate in electoral disputes.

Chief Justice of the Supreme Court of Liberia: JOHNNIE LEWIS.

Justices: KABINEH JA'NEH, FRANCIS KORPKPOR, GLADYS JOHNSON.

Religion

Liberia is officially a Christian state, although complete religious freedom is guaranteed. Christianity and Islam are the two main religions. There are numerous religious sects, and many Liberians hold traditional beliefs.

CHRISTIANITY

Liberian Council of Churches: 16 St, Sinkor, POB 10-2191, 1000 Monrovia; tel. 226630; fax 226132; f. 1982; 11 mems, two assoc. mems, one fraternal mem.; Pres. Rt Rev. Dr W. NAH DIXON; Gen. Sec. Rev. STEVEN W. MUIN.

The Anglican Communion

The diocese of Liberia forms part of the Church of the Province of West Africa, incorporating the local Episcopal Church. Anglicanism was established in Liberia in 1836, and the diocese of Liberia was admitted into full membership of the Province in 1982. In 1985 the Church had 125 congregations, 39 clergy, 26 schools and about 20,000 adherents in the country. The Metropolitan of the Province is the Bishop of Koforidua, Ghana.

Bishop of Liberia: Rt Rev. EDWARD NEUFVILLE, POB 10-0277, 1000 Monrovia 10; tel. 224760; fax 227519.

The Roman Catholic Church

Liberia comprises the archdiocese of Monrovia and the dioceses of Cape Palmas and Gbarnga. At 31 December 2004 there were an estimated 172,362 adherents in the country, equivalent to 5.4% of the total population.

Catholic Bishops' Conference of Liberia
POB 10-2078, 1000 Monrovia 10; tel. 227245; fax 226175.

f. 1998; Pres. Rt Rev. LEWIS ZEIGLER (Bishop of Gbarnga).

Archbishop of Monrovia: Most Rev. MICHAEL KPAKALA FRANCIS, Archbishop's Office, POB 10-2078, 1000 Monrovia 10; tel. 227245; fax 226411; e-mail kpakala1936@hotmail.com.

Other Christian Churches

Assemblies of God in Liberia: POB 1297, Monrovia; f. 1908; 14,578 adherents, 287 churches; Gen. Supt JIMMIE K. DUGBE, Sr.

Lutheran Church in Liberia: POB 1046, Monrovia; tel. 226633; fax 226262; e-mail lwfliberia@compuserve.com; 35,600 adherents; Pres. Bishop SUMOWARD E. HARRIS.

Providence Baptist Church: cnr Broad and Center Sts, Monrovia; f. 1821; 2,500 adherents, 300 congregations, 6 ministers, 8 schools; Pastor Rev. A. MOMOLUE DIGGS.

Liberia Baptist Missionary and Educational Convention, Inc: POB 390, Monrovia; tel. 222661; f. 1880; Pres. Rev. J. K. LEVEE MOULTON; Nat. Vice-Pres. Rev. J. GBANA HALL; Gen. Sec. CHARLES W. BLAKE.

United Methodist Church in Liberia: cnr 12th St and Tubman Blvd, POB 1010, 1000 Monrovia 10; tel. 223343; f. 1833; c. 68,300 adherents, 600 congregations, 700 ministers, 394 lay pastors, 121 schools, one university; Resident Bishop Rev. Dr JOHN G. INNIS; Sec. Rev. Dr SAMUEL J. QUIRE, Jr.

Other active denominations include the National Baptist Mission, the Pentecostal Church, the Presbyterian Church in Liberia, the Prayer Band and the Church of the Lord Aladura.

ISLAM

The total community numbers about 670,000.

National Muslim Council of Liberia: Monrovia; Leader Shaykh KAFUMBA KONNAH.

The Press

NEWSPAPERS

The Inquirer: Benson St, POB 20-4209, Monrovia; tel. and fax 227105; independent; Man. Editor PHILIP WESSEH.

Monrovia Guardian: Monrovia; independent; Editor SAM O. DEAN.

News: ACDB Bldg, POB 10-3137, Carey Warren St, Monrovia; tel. 227820; e-mail imms@afrlink.com; independent; weekly; Chair. WILSON TARPEH; Editor-in-Chief JEROME DALIEH.

PERIODICALS

The Kpelle Messenger: Kpelle Literacy Center, Lutheran Church, POB 1046, Monrovia; Kpelle-English; monthly; Editor Rev. JOHN J. MANAWU.

Liberia Orbit: Voinjama; e-mail orbit@tekmail.com; internet www.liberiaorbit.org; national current affairs; Editor LLOYD SCOTT.

Liberian Post: e-mail info@liberian.org; internet www.liberian.org; f. 1998; independent internet magazine; tourist information; Publr WILLEM TIJSSEN.

New Democrat: Monrovia; e-mail newdemnews@yahoo.com; internet www.newdemocrat.org; national news and current affairs.

Patriot: Congotown 1000, Monrovia; internet www.allaboutliberia.com/patriot.htm.

The People Magazine: Bank of Liberia Bldg, Suite 214, Carey and Warren Sts, POB 3501, Monrovia; tel. 222743; f. 1985; monthly; Editor and Publr CHARLES A. SNETTER.

PRESS ORGANIZATIONS

Liberia Institute of Journalism: Kashour Bldg, 2nd Floor, cnr Broad and Johnson Sts, POB 2314, Monrovia; tel. 227327; e-mail lij@kabissa.org; internet www.kabissa.org/lij; Dir VINICIUS HODGES.

Press Union of Liberia: Benson St, POB 20-4209, Monrovia; tel. and fax 227105; e-mail pul@kabissa.org; internet www.kabissa.org/pul; f. 1985; Pres. ELIZABETH HOFF.

NEWS AGENCIES

Liberian News Agency (LINA): POB 9021, Capitol Hill, Monrovia; tel. and fax 226269; e-mail lina@afrlink.com; Dir-Gen. ERNEST KIAZOLY (acting).

Foreign Bureaux

Agence France-Presse (AFP): Monrovia; Rep. JAMES DORBOR.

United Press International (UPI) (USA): Monrovia; Correspondent T. K. SANNAH.

Xinhua (New China) News Agency (People's Republic of China): Adams St, Old Rd, Congotown, POB 3001, Monrovia; tel. 262821; Correspondent SUN BAOYU.

Reuters (United Kingdom) is also represented in Liberia.

Broadcasting and Communications

TELECOMMUNICATIONS

Liberia Telecommunications Corpn: Monrovia; tel. 227523; Man. Dir JOE GBALAH.

BROADCASTING

Radio

Liberia Communications Network: Congotown 1000, Monrovia; govt-operated; broadcasts information, education and entertainment 24 hours daily in English, French and several African languages; short-wave service.

Liberia Rural Communications Network: POB 10-02176, 1000 Monrovia 10; tel. 271368; f. 1981; govt-operated; rural development and entertainment programmes; Dir J. RUFUS KAINE (acting).

Radio Veritas: Monrovia; Catholic; independent; nation-wide shortwave broadcasts.

Star Radio: Sekou Toure Ave, Mamba Point, Monrovia; tel. 226820; fax 227360; e-mail star@liberia.net; independent news and information station; f. July 1997 by Fondation Hirondelle, Switzerland, with funds from the US Agency for International Development; broadcasts in English, French and 14 African languages; operations suspended by the Govt in March 2000; ban on transmissions ended Nov. 2003; Dir GEORGE BENNETT.

Television

Liberia Broadcasting System: POB 594, Monrovia; tel. 224984; govt-owned; Dir-Gen. CHARLES SNETTER.

Finance

(cap. = capital; res = reserves; dep. = deposits; m. = million; br. = branch; amounts in Liberian dollars, unless otherwise indicated)

BANKING

Following intensive fighting between government and rebel forces in the capital in mid-2003, it was reported that commercial banks had resumed operations at the end of August. At that time, however, only four (of a total of 18 deposit banks established since 1954) were active, the remainder having been closed as a result of poor bank management or the 1989–96 civil conflict. The Liberian Bank for Development and Investment is the only locally owned bank.

Central Bank

Central Bank of Liberia: cnr Warren and Carey Sts, POB 2048, Monrovia; tel. 226144; fax 227685; e-mail webmaster@cbl.org.lr; internet www.cbl.org.lr; f. 1974 as National Bank of Liberia; name changed March 1999; bank of issue; cap. 7,240.8m., res 2,995.4m., dep. 1,093.6m. (Dec. 2004); Gov. JOSEPH MILLS JONES.

Other Banks

Ecobank Liberia Ltd: Ashmun and Randall Sts, POB 4825, Monrovia; tel. 226428; fax 227029; e-mail ecobanklr@ecobank.com; internet www.ecobank.com; commenced operations Aug. 1999; cap. and res US $2.1m., total assets US $10.2m. (Dec. 2001); Chair. EUGENE H. COOPER; Man. Dir ESIJOLONE OKORODUDU.

First International Bank (Liberia) Ltd: Luke Bldg, Broad St, Monrovia; tel. 77026241; fax 8981286; e-mail info@fib-lib.com; internet www.fib-lib.com; f. April 2005; Chair. FRANCIS L. M. HORTON; Exec. Dir. ARISA AWA.

Global Bank Liberia Ltd (GBLL): Ashmun and Mechlin Sts, POB 2053, Monrovia; tel. 425760; fax 443802; e-mail mail@globalbankliberia.com; internet www.globalbankliberia.com; f. 2005; Italian-owned; Pres. RICCARDO SEMBIANTE.

International Bank (Liberia) Ltd: 64 Broad St, POB 292, Monrovia; tel. 226092; fax 226505; e-mail tjeffrey@ibliberia.com; internet www.ibliberia.com; f. 1948 as International Trust Co of Liberia; name changed April 2000; cap. 2m. (1989), dep. 96.4m. (Dec. 1996); Pres. F. A. GUIDA; Gen. Man. THOMAS S. JEFFREY; 1 br.

Liberian Bank for Development and Investment (LBDI): Ashmun and Randall Sts, POB 547, Monrovia; tel. 226366; fax 226359; e-mail lbdi@lbdi.net; internet www.lbdi.net; f. 1961; 18.6% govt-owned; cap. and res US $12.5m., total assets US $26.8m. (Dec. 2001); Chair. NATHANIEL BARNES; Pres. FRANCIS A. DENNIS.

Banking Association

Liberia Bankers' Association: POB 292, Monrovia; mems include commercial and development banks; Pres. LEN MAESTRE.

INSURANCE

American International Underwriters, Inc: Carter Bldg, 39 Broad St, POB 180, Monrovia; tel. 224921; general; Gen. Man. S. B. MENSAH.

American Life Insurance Co: Carter Bldg, 39 Broad St, POB 60, Monrovia; f. 1969; life and general; Vice-Pres. ALLEN BROWN.

Insurance Co of Africa: 64 Broad St, POB 292, Monrovia; f. 1969; life and general; Pres. SAMUEL OWAREE MINTAH.

National Insurance Corpn of Liberia (NICOL): LBDI Bldg Complex, POB 1528, Sinkor, Monrovia; tel. 262429; f. 1983; state-owned; sole insurer for Govt and parastatal bodies; also provides insurance for the Liberian-registered merchant shipping fleet; Man. Dir MIATTA EDITH SHERMAN.

Royal Exchange Assurance: Ashmun and Randall Sts, POB 666, Monrovia; all types of insurance; Man. RONALD WOODS.

United Security Insurance Agencies Inc: Randall St, POB 2071, Monrovia; life, personal accident and medical; Dir EPHRAIM O. OKORO.

Trade and Industry

GOVERNMENT AGENCIES

Budget Bureau: Capitol Hill, POB 1518, Monrovia; tel. 226340; Dir-Gen. AUGUSTINE K. NGAFUAN.

General Services Agency (GSA): Sinkor, Monrovia; tel. 226745; Dir-Gen. WILLIARD RUSSELL.

DEVELOPMENT ORGANIZATIONS

Forestry Development Authority: POB 3010, 1000 Monrovia; tel. 224940; fax 226000; f. 1976; responsible for forest management and conservation; Chair. EDWIN ZELEE; Man. Dir JOHN T. WOODS.

Liberia Industrial Free Zone Authority (LIFZA): One Free Zone, Monrovia; tel. 533671; e-mail mskromah@lifza.com; internet www.lifza.com; f. 1975; 98 mems; Man. Dir MOHAMMED S. KROMAH.

National Investment Commission (NIC): Fmr Executive Mansion Bldg, POB 9043, Monrovia; tel. 226685; internet www.nic.gov.lr; f. 1979; autonomous body negotiating investment incentives agreements on behalf of Govt; promotes agro-based and industrial development; Chair. RICHARD TOLBERT.

CHAMBER OF COMMERCE

Liberia Chamber of Commerce: Warren St, POB 92, Monrovia; tel. 223738; e-mail liberiachamber2006@yahoo.com; f. 1951; Pres. HENRY REED COOPER; Sec.-Gen. EMMETT C. A. GOODING.

INDUSTRIAL AND TRADE ASSOCIATIONS

Liberian Produce Marketing Corpn: POB 662, Monrovia; tel. 222447; f. 1961; govt-owned; exports Liberian produce, provides industrial facilities for processing of agricultural products and participates in agricultural development programmes; Man. Dir NYAH MARTEIN.

Liberian Resources Corpn (LIBRESCO): controls Liberia's mineral resources; 60% govt-owned; 40% owned by South African co, Amalia Gold.

EMPLOYERS' ASSOCIATION

National Enterprises Corpn: POB 518, Monrovia; tel. 261370; importer, wholesaler and distributor of foodstuffs, and wire and metal products for local industries; Pres. EMMANUEL SHAW, Sr.

UTILITIES

Electricity

Liberia Electricity Corpn (LEC): Waterside, POB 165, Monrovia; tel. 226133; Chair. DUNSTAN MACAULEY; Man. Dir HARRY YUAN.

National Oil Co of Liberia (NOCL): Episcopal Church Plaza, Ashmun and Randall Sts, Monrovia; Chair. CLEMENCEAU B. UREY.

MAJOR COMPANIES

The following are among the largest companies in terms either of capital investment or employment. In 1990 the majority of industrial companies were forced to suspend activity, owing to the disruption caused by the civil war. Commercial activity normalized following a peace agreement, which was reached in August 1996.

Bong Mining Co Ltd: POB 538, Monrovia; tel. 225222; fax 225770; f. 1958; iron ore mining, upgrading of crude ore and transportation of concentrate and pellets to Monrovia Free Port for shipment abroad; capacity: 4.5m. tons of concentrate and 3m. tons of pellets annually; Pres. HANSJOERG RIETZSCH; Gen. Man. HANS-GEORG SCHNEIDER; 2,200 employees.

Bridgestone Firestone Co: POB 140, Harbel; f. 1926 by Firestone Rubber Co (USA); acquired by Japanese co, Bridgestone, in 1988, although Firestone retained control of local management; operations severely disrupted during 1990–92 and 1993–97; Man. Dir CLYDE TABOR; c. 3,000 employees.

Liberia Cement Corpn (CEMENCO): POB 150, Monrovia; tel. 222650; fax 226219; mfrs of Portland cement; Gen. Man. H. WALLWITZ.

The Liberia Co: POB 45, Broad St, Monrovia; f. 1947; shipping agents Delta Steamship Lines; owns COCOPA rubber plantations; Pres. J. T. TRIPPE (New York); Vice-Pres. J. M. LIJNKAMP (Monrovia); 850 employees.

Liberian Mining Co (LIMINCO): Monrovia; govt-owned; mining of iron ore; assumed control of LAMCO JV Operating Co in 1989; operations suspended in 1993.

Liberia Petroleum Refining Corpn (LPRC): POB 90, Monrovia; tel. 222600; sole producer of domestically produced fuels, with designed capacity of 15,000 b/d; products include diesel fuel, fuel oils, liquid petroleum gas; supplies domestic market and has limited export facilities for surplus products; Man. Dir HARRY GREAVES.

National Iron Ore Co Ltd: POB 548, Monrovia; f. 1958; 85% govt-owned co mining iron ore at Mano river; Gen. Man. S. K. DATTA RAY.

Royal Stationery Stores: 128 Broad St, POB 346, Monrovia; tel. and fax 227513; e-mail rssmon@yahoo.com; Chair. G. BHARWANEY.

Shell Liberia Ltd: Bushrod Island, POB 360, Monrovia; f. 1920; distributors of petroleum products; Man. M. Y. KUENYEDZI; 15 employees.

Texaco Exploration Belize Inc: ULRC Bldg, Randall St and United Nations, Monrovia; oil and gas exploration; Pres. C. R. BLACK.

TRADE UNIONS

Congress of Industrial Organizations: 29 Ashmun St, POB 415, Monrovia; Pres. Gen. J. T. PRATT; Sec.-Gen. AMOS N. GRAY; 5 affiliated unions.

Labor Congress of Liberia: 71 Gurley St, Monrovia; Sec.-Gen. P. C. T. SONPON; 8 affiliated unions.

Liberian Federation of Labor Unions: J. B. McGill Labor Center, Gardnersville Freeway, POB 415, Monrovia; f. 1980; Sec.-Gen. AMOS GRAY; 10,000 mems (1983).

Transport

RAILWAYS

Railway operations were suspended in 1990, owing to the civil conflict. Large sections of the 480-km rail network were subsequently dismantled.

Bong Mining Co Ltd: POB 538, Monrovia; tel. 225222; fax 225770; f. 1965; Gen. Man. HANS-GEORG SCHNEIDER.

Liberian Mining Co: Monrovia; tel. 221190; govt-owned; assumed control of LAMCO JV Operating Co in 1989.

National Iron Ore Co Ltd: POB 548, Monrovia; f. 1951; Gen. Man. S. K. DATTA RAY.

ROADS

In 1999 the road network in Liberia totalled an estimated 10,600 km, of which about 657 km were paved. The main trunk road is the Monrovia–Sanniquellie motor road, extending north-east from the capital to the border with Guinea, near Ganta, and eastward through the hinterland to the border with Côte d'Ivoire. Trunk roads run through Tapita, in Nimba County, to Grand Gedeh County and from Monrovia to Buchanan. A bridge over the Mano river connects with the Sierra Leone road network, while a main road links Monrovia and Freetown (Sierra Leone). Although principal roads were officially reopened to commercial traffic in early 1997, following the 1989–96 armed conflict, much of the infrastructure remained severely damaged. In late 2003 the Liberian authorities announced plans for the extensive rehabilitation of the road network, including a highway linking Monrovia with Harper, which was to be funded by the People's Republic of China.

SHIPPING

In December 2005 Liberia's open-registry fleet (1,653 vessels), the second largest in the world (after Panama) in terms of gross tonnage, had a total displacement of 59.6m. grt. Commercial port activity in Liberia was frequently suspended from 1990, as a result of hostilities. At September 2004 only Monrovia Freeport had fully resumed operations and (compared with the corresponding period in 2003) experienced a rise in vessel traffic of 95.2%, owing to increasing commercial and humanitarian activities.

Bureau of Maritime Affairs: Tubman Blvd, POB 10-9042, 1000 Monrovia 10; tel. and fax 226069; e-mail maritime@liberia.net; internet www.maritime.gov.lr; Commissioner JOHN S. MORLU.

Liberia National Shipping Line (LNSL): Monrovia; f. 1987; jt venture by the Liberian Govt and private German interests; routes to Europe, incl. the United Kingdom and Scandinavia.

National Port Authority: POB 1849, Monrovia; tel. 226646; fax 226180; e-mail natport@liberia.net; f. 1967; administers Monrovia Freeport and the ports of Buchanan, Greenville and Harper; Chair. TOGBA NAH TIPOTEH; Man. Dir JOE T. GBALA.

CIVIL AVIATION

Liberia's principal airports are Robertsfield International Airport, at Harbel, 56 km east of Monrovia, and James Spriggs Payne Airport, at Monrovia.

ADC Liberia Inc: Monrovia; f. 1993; services to the United Kingdom, the USA and destinations in West Africa.

Air Liberia: POB 2076, Monrovia; f. 1974; state-owned; scheduled passenger and cargo services; Man. Dir JAMES K. KOFA.

Defence

Following a major rebel offensive against the capital in June 2003, the UN Security Council on 1 August authorized the establishment of a Economic Community of West African States (ECOWAS) peace-keeping contingent, the ECOWAS Mission in Liberia (ECOMIL), which was to restore security and prepare for the deployment of a longer-term UN stabilization force. The UN Mission in Liberia (UNMIL), which was officially established on 19 September and replaced ECOMIL on 1 October, was mandated to support the implementation of a comprehensive peace agreement, and a two-year transitional administration. With a total authorized strength of up to 15,000, at the end of December 2006 UNMIL numbered 13,613 troops, 188 military observers, 1,097 civilian police; supported by 504 international civilian police and 941 local staff. Following the completion of the disarmament programme, in January 2005 a US military commission arrived in Liberia to assist in the restructuring of the armed forces, which was scheduled to be completed by December 2007. A 3,500-member police force trained by UNMIL was also to be established. As assessed at November 2006, the total strength of the Liberian armed forces was 2,400.

Defence Expenditure: Estimated at US $50m. (equivalent to 8.2% of GDP) in 2005.

Chief of Staff of the Armed Forces of Liberia: Maj.-Gen. SURAJ ALAO ABDURRAHMAN.

Education

Education is provided by a mixture of government, private, church and mosque schools. The civil conflicts of 1989-1996 and 1999-2003 devastated the education system as buildings and equipment were damaged and looted, and teachers, parents and children became refugees or internally displaced. By September 2005 3,817 of the country's 4,500 schools were reported to be functioning again. Education in Liberia is officially compulsory for 10 years, between six and 16 years of age. Primary education begins theoretically at six years of age and lasts for six years (grades 1–6). Secondary education, beginning theoretically at 12 years of age, lasts for a further six years, and is divided into two three-year cycles, known in Liberia as 'junior high school' (grades 7–9) and 'senior high school' (grades 10-12). Pre-primary education is undertaken from the age of five or younger and is important for those students whose mother language is not English, since English is the language of instruction throughout the school system. School attendance is not enforced and in 2000 an estimated 34% of primary school age children were out of school (26% of boys and 42% of girls). Although the 1984 Liberian Constitution includes the aspiration to provide universal free education, school attendance is discouraged by the poor quality of education offered and by official and unofficial school fees, charges and the cost of uniforms and travel. In 2004 UNESCO estimated the adult literacy rate at 52% (58% male and 46% female). The higher education sector consists of the University of Liberia in Monrovia, Cuttington University College in Bong County, the Booker Washington Institute in Kakata, Margibi County, and the William V. S. Tubman College in Maryland County. According to UNESCO, a total of 44,107 students were enrolled in tertiary education in 2000.

Bibliography

Aboagye, F. B., and Bah, Alhaji M. S. *A Tortuous Road to Peace: The Dynamics of Regional, UN and International Humanitarian Interventions in Liberia*. Pretoria, Institute for Security Studies, 2005.

Adebajo, A. *Liberia's Civil War: Nigeria, Ecomog and Regional Security in West Africa*. Boulder, CO, Lynne Rienner Publishers, 2002.

Alao, A. *The Burden of Collective Goodwill: The International Involvement in the Liberian Civil War*. Aldershot, Ashgate, 1998.

Peacekeepers, Politicians and Warlords: The Liberian Peace Process (Foundations of Peace). UN Publications, 2000.

Cruise O'Brien, D. B., Dunn, J., and Rathbone, R. (Eds). *Contemporary West African States*. Cambridge, Cambridge University Press, 1989.

Deme, M. *Law, Morality, and International Armed Intervention: The United Nations and Ecowas (African Studies: History, Politics, Economics and Culture)*. Abingdon, Routledge, 2005.

Dolo, E. *Democracy versus Dictatorship: The Quest for Freedom and Justice in Africa's Oldest Republic, Liberia*. Lanham, MD, University Press of America, 1996.

Dunn, D. E., and Holsoe, S. E. *Historical Dictionary of Liberia*. Metuchen, NJ, Scarecrow Press, 1986.

Dunn, D. E., and Tarr, S. B. *Liberia: A National Polity in Transition*. Metuchen, NJ, Scarecrow Press, 1988.

Ellis, S. *The Mask of Anarchy: The Destruction of Liberia and the Religious Dimension of an African Civil War*. London, C. Hurst, 1999.

Fahnbulleh, B. H. *Voices of Protest: Liberia on the Edge, 1974–1980*. Macquarie Park, NSW, Universal Publishers, 2005.

Gifford, P. *Christianity and Politics in Doe's Liberia*. Cambridge, Cambridge University Press, 2003.

Givens, W. *Liberia: The Road to Democracy under the Leadership of Samuel Kanyon Doe*. London, Kensal Press, 1986.

Hall, R. *On Africa's Shore: A History of Maryland in Liberia, 1834–1857.* Baltimore, MD, Maryland Historical Society, 2003.

Harris, J. *Mother Liberia.* New York, Vantage Press, 2004.

Horton A. P., *Liberia's Underdevelopment.* Lanham, MD, University Press of America, 1994.

Huband, M. *The Liberian Civil War.* London, Frank Cass, 1998.

Huffman, A. *Mississippi in Africa: The Saga of the Slaves of Prospect Hill Plantation and their Legacy in Liberia Today.* New York, Gotham Books, 2004.

Hyman, L. S. *United States Policy Towards Liberia, 1822 to 2003: Unintended Consequences.* New Jersey, NJ, Africana Homestead Legacy Publications, 2003.

Jaye, T. *Issues of Sovereignty, Strategy and Security in the Economic Community of West African States (Ecowas) Intervention in the Liberian Civil War.* Lewiston, NY, Edwin Mellen Press, 2003.

Keih, G. K., Jr. *Dependency and the Foreign Policy of a Small Power.* Lewiston, NY, Edwin Mellen Press, 1992.

Kulah, A. F. *Liberia Will Rise Again: Reflections on the Liberian Civil Crisis.* London, Abingdon Press, 1999.

Levitt, J. *The Evolution of Deadly Conflict in Liberia: From 'Paternaltarianism' to State Collapse.* Durham, NC, Carolina Academic Press, 2005.

Liebenow, J. G. *Liberia: The Quest for Democracy.* Bloomington, IN, Indiana University Press, 1987.

Lyons, T. *Voting for Peace: Postconflict Elections in Liberia* (Studies in Foreign Policy). Washington, DC, Brookings Institution Press, 1999.

Magyar, K. P., and Conteh-Morgan, E. (Eds). *Peace-keeping in Africa: ECOMOG in Liberia.* Basingstoke, Macmillan, 1998.

McDaniel, A. *Swing Low, Sweet Chariot: The Mortality Cost of Colonizing Liberia in the Nineteenth Century* (Population and Development). Chicago, IL, University of Chicago Press, 1995.

Mgbeoji, I. *Collective Insecurity: The Liberian Crisis, Unilateralism and Global Order.* Vancouver, BC, University of British Columbia Press, 2003.

Moran, M. H. *Liberia: The Violence of Democracy (Ethnography of Political Violence).* Philadelphia, PA, University of Pennsylvania Press, 2005.

Morse, K., and Sawyer, A. *Beyond Plunder: Toward Democratic Governance in Liberia.* Boulder, CO, Lynne Rienner Publishers, 2005.

Moses, W. J. (Ed.), *Liberian Dreams: Back-to-Africa Narratives from the 1850s.* Philadelphia, PA, University of Pennsylvania Press, 1998.

Nass, I. A. *A Study in Internal Conflicts: The Liberian Crisis and the West African Peace Initiative.* Enugu, Fourth Dimension Publishing, 2001.

Pham, J.-P. *Liberia: Portrait of a Failed State.* New York, Reed Press, 2004.

Rimmer, D. *The Economies of West Africa.* London, Weidenfeld and Nicolson, 1984.

Sawyer, A. *The Emergence of Autocracy in Liberia: Tragedy and Challenge.* San Francisco, CA, ICS Press, 1992.

Sirleaf, A. M. *The Role of the Economic Community of the West African States: Ecowas—Conflict Management in Liberia.* New York, 1stBooks Library, 2003.

Stryker, R. L. *Forged from Chaos: Stories and Reflections from Liberia at War.* New York, 1stBooks Library, 2003.

Tellewoyan, J. *The Years the Locusts have Eaten: Liberia 1816-2004.* Philadelphia, PA, Xlibris Corporation, 2005.

US Library of Congress. *Liberia during the Tolbert Era: A Guide.* Washington, DC, 1984.

Vogt, M. A. (Ed.). *Liberian Crisis and ECOMOG: A Bold Attempt at Regional Peace-keeping.* Lagos, Gabumo Publishing Co, 1992.

Williams, G. I. H. *Liberia: The Heart of Darkness.* New Bern, NC, Trafford, 2002.

Yumi Ng, Neo, M., and Guntl, J. D. *Welcome to Liberia* (Welcome to My Country). Milwaukee, WI, Gareth Stevens Publishing, 2004.

MADAGASCAR

Physical and Social Geography

VIRGINIA THOMPSON

PHYSICAL FEATURES

The Democratic Republic of Madagascar comprises the island of Madagascar, the fourth largest island in the world, and several much smaller offshore islands. Madagascar lies 390 km from the east African mainland across the Mozambique Channel. It extends 1,600 km from north to south and is up to 570 km wide. The whole territory covers an area of 587,041 sq km (226,658 sq miles). Geologically, the main island is basically composed of crystalline rock, which forms the central highlands that rise abruptly from the narrow eastern coastal strip and descend gradually to the wide plains of the west coast.

Topographically, Madagascar can be divided into six fairly distinct regions. Antsiranana province, in the north, is virtually isolated by the island's highest peak, Mt Tsaratanana, rising to 2,800 m above sea level. Tropical crops can be grown in its fertile valleys, and the natural harbour of Antsiranana is an important naval base. Another rich agricultural region lies in the north-west, where a series of valleys converge on the port of Mahajanga. To the south-west along the coastal plains lies a well-watered region where there are large animal herds and crops of rice, cotton, tobacco and manioc. The southernmost province, Toliary (Tuléar), contains most of Madagascar's known mineral deposits, as well as extensive cattle herds, despite the almost total lack of rainfall. In contrast, the hot and humid climate of the east coast favours the cultivation of the island's most valuable tropical crops—coffee, vanilla, cloves, and sugar cane. Although this coast lacks sheltered anchorages, it is the site of Madagascar's most important commercial port, Toamasina. Behind its coral beaches a continuous chain of lagoons, some of which are connected by the Pangalanes Canal, provides a partially navigable internal waterway. The island's mountainous hinterland is a densely populated region of extensive rice culture and stock raising. Despite its relative inaccessibility, this region is Madagascar's administrative and cultural centre, the focal point being the capital city of Antananarivo.

Climatic conditions vary from tropical conditions on the east and north-west coasts to the hotness and dryness of the west coast, the extreme aridity of the south and the temperate zone in the central highlands. Forests have survived only in some areas of abundant rainfall, and elsewhere the land has been eroded by over-grazing and slash-and-burn farming methods. Most of the island is savannah-steppe, and much of the interior is covered with laterite. Except in the drought-ridden south, rivers are numerous and flow generally westward, but many are interspersed by rapids and waterfalls, and few are navigable except for short distances.

POPULATION AND CULTURE

Geography and history account for the diversity and distribution of the population, which was enumerated at 12,092,157 at the census of August 1993. By mid-2006 the population had increased to 19,159,000, according to official estimates. The island's 18 principal ethnic groups are the descendants of successive waves of immigrants from such diverse areas as South-East Asia, continental Africa and Arab countries. The dominant ethnic groups, the Merina (estimated at 1,993,000 in 1974) and the Betsileo (920,600), who inhabit the most densely populated central provinces of Antananarivo and Fianarantsoa, are of Asian-Pacific origin. In the peripheral areas live the tribes collectively known as *côtiers*, of whom the most numerous are the Betsimisaraka (1,134,000) on the east coast, the Tsimihety (558,100) in the north, and the Antandroy (412,500) in the south. Population density ranges from 30 inhabitants per sq km on the central plateaux to 2 per sq km along much of the west coast. At the 1993 census the average density was 20.6 inhabitants per sq km. Population density had increased to 32.6 inhabitants per sq km by mid-2006, according to official estimates. Although continuous migrations, improved means of communication and a marked cultural unity have, to some extent, broken down geographical and tribal barriers, traditional ethnic antagonisms—notably between the Merina and the *côtiers*—remain close to the surface.

Increasing at an average annual rate of 2.9% during 1995–2005, the Malagasy are fast exceeding the island's capacity to feed and employ them. The World Bank estimated that 44.8% of the population was under 15 years of age in 2001, and that the urban component was steadily growing. French nationals, who numbered some 50,000 before 1972, dwindled to fewer than 15,000 by 1986. In 1981 there were some 5,000 Indians holding French nationality and an equal number of creoles. The Comorans, who were formerly the second largest non-indigenous population group and were concentrated in the Mahajanga area (60,000 in 1976), have become an almost negligible element there, owing to the repatriation of about 16,000 after clashes with the Malagasy in December 1976. Also inhabiting the west coast are the 10,000 or so Indian nationals, who are also unpopular with the Malagasy because of their social clannishness and their wealth, acquired through control of the textile and jewellery trades and of urban real estate. Administratively, the Asians are organized into *congrégations*, each headed by a representative chosen by them but appointed by and responsible to the Government. A Chinese community, numbering about 10,000, is dispersed throughout the east-coast region, where they are principally employed as grocers, small-scale bankers and traders in agricultural produce.

Up to 60% of the Malagasy still live in rural areas, but the towns are attracting an increasing percentage of the fast-growing youthful population, thus aggravating urban socio-economic problems. Antananarivo, the capital, is by far the largest city (with a population of 1,585,000 in mid-2005) and continues to expand, as do all the six provincial capitals.

Recent History

MERVYN BROWN

Revised for this edition by JULIAN COOKE

Madagascar was annexed by France in 1896. The imposition of colonial rule did not, however, resolve the basic ethnic conflict between the dominant Merina tribe, based on the central plateau, and the coastal peoples (*côtiers*). The introduction in 1946 of elected deputies from Madagascar to the French parliament brought two opposing parties to the fore: the Mouvement démocratique pour la rénovation malgache, a predominantly Merina group favouring immediate independence, and the Parti des déshérités de Madagascar (PADESM), a *côtier* party opposed to rapid constitutional change. Following violent ethnic and partisan confrontations during 1947, in which about 80,000 people were killed, the French authorities suspended all political activity.

INDEPENDENCE

New constitutional arrangements introduced by France in 1956 opened the way to a resumption of political activity. The predominantly *côtier*-supported Parti social démocrate (PSD), formed from progressive elements of PADESM and led by a schoolteacher, Philibert Tsiranana, emerged as the principal party. In October 1958 Madagascar became a self-governing republic within the French Community. In 1959 Tsiranana was elected President. Full independence as the Malagasy Republic followed on 26 June 1960.

Following Tsiranana's accession to power, the PSD, which practised a moderate, pragmatic socialism, was joined by nearly all of its early rivals. The only significant opposition was the left-wing Parti du congrès de l'indépendance de Madagascar (AKFM), led by Richard Andriamanjato, a Merina Protestant pastor and Mayor of Antananarivo. The rivalry between the two parties reflected the continuing antagonism between Merina and *côtiers*.

Following a period of economic decline in the late 1960s, a serious agrarian uprising, accompanied by student unrest, broke out in 1971. A new radical opposition group, the Mouvement national pour l'indépendance de Madagascar (MONIMA), led by Monja Jaona and based in the agricultural south-west of the island, became a significant opposition movement, also attracting urban and student support. As the sole candidate in the presidential election of January 1972, Tsiranana was re-elected with 99.9% of the votes cast, but this result bore little relation to the true state of political opinion. In May, following a resurgence of violent protest, Tsiranana relinquished power to Gen. Gabriel Ramanantsoa, the Merina Chief of Staff of Madagascar's armed forces.

MILITARY GOVERNMENT

Ramanantsoa moved swiftly to restore public order. A referendum conducted in October 1972 obtained the endorsement of 96% of the voters for Ramanantsoa to govern for a transitional period of five years, while a new constitutional structure was established.

The promotion of Malagasy as the official language and the 'Malagasization' of education was welcomed by student and nationalist opinion, but revived fears among *côtiers* of Merina domination. Nationalists and radicals, including the extreme left-wing Mouvement pour le pouvoir prolétarien (MFM), led by Rakotonirina Manandafy, supported the major changes in foreign policy: the establishment of diplomatic relations with the People's Republic of China, the Soviet bloc countries and Arab nations; the withdrawal from the Franc Zone and the Organisation commune africaine et mauricienne (OCAM); and, in particular, the renegotiation of the co-operation agreements with France, which resulted in the evacuation of French air and naval bases.

However, Ramanantsoa's authority was undermined by the country's worsening trade and financial position, disunity in the armed forces and the Government, and continuing discord between *côtiers* and Merina. Contention arose in the Council of Ministers where a radical faction led by Col Richard Ratsimandrava demanded administrative and political reform, based on a revival of the traditional communities, known as *fokonolona*.

On 31 December 1974 the mobile police, a mainly *côtier* force, staged an attempted coup in protest at Merina domination of the armed forces. In February 1975 Ramanantsoa transferred power to Ratsimandrava, who was, however, assassinated six days later. Gen. Gilles Andriamahazo immediately assumed power. Martial law and press censorship were imposed, and political parties suspended. In June 1975 Andriamahazo was succeeded as Head of State by Lt-Commdr Didier Ratsiraka, a *côtier* and a former Minister of Foreign Affairs. Ratsiraka established a Supreme Revolutionary Council (CSR), originally entirely military, to supervise a Government that principally comprised civilians. Ratsiraka declared his intention to carry out administrative and agrarian reforms based on the *fokonolona*, to reorganize the armed forces as an 'army of development' and to pursue a non-aligned foreign policy. At a referendum held in December, Ratsiraka's proposals were endorsed by 94.7% of voters. Ratsiraka was elected to a seven-year term as President, the country was renamed the Democratic Republic of Madagascar and the Second Republic was proclaimed.

THE SECOND REPUBLIC

Having reorganized the CSR with a predominantly civilian base, in March 1975 Ratsiraka formed the Avant-garde de la révolution malgache (AREMA) as the nucleus of the Front national pour la défense de la révolution socialiste malgache (FNDR), the only political organization permitted by the Constitution. Several existing parties subsequently joined the FNDR, including the MONIMA, the MFM and the Elan populaire pour l'unité nationale (known as the Vonjy), which comprised left-wing elements of the former PSD. Local government elections, which took place in 1977, led to divisions within the FNDR. MONIMA withdrew from the FNDR and was subsequently banned. Strains within AREMA also became apparent within the National Assembly.

At a presidential election held in November 1982, Ratsiraka was re-elected with 80% of the vote, while his opponent Jaona won only 20%. Jaona denounced the result as fraudulent and called for a general strike in support of demands for a new poll. Following rioting in December, Jaona was arrested and expelled from the CSR. In August 1983 elections to the National Assembly took place, with AREMA securing 117 of the 137 seats.

Social Unrest

In 1987 opposition within the FNDR to Ratsiraka appeared to be increasing. The MSM and the Vonjy, joined later by the Parti socialiste monima (VSM), began to co-operate openly with MONIMA in opposing government policies and, from May 1987, in demands for the resignation of the Government and the holding of new elections. Ratsiraka subsequently announced that the legislative and local government elections scheduled for 1988 would be postponed until May and September 1989, respectively. In February 1988 the Prime Minister, Gen. Désiré Rakotoarijaona, resigned, ostensibly on grounds of ill health, and was succeeded by the Minister of Public Works, Lt-Col Victor Ramahatra. In January 1989 the Constitution was amended to allow Ratsiraka to bring forward the presidential election from November to March. In February the MFM, the Vonjy and the VSM announced the formation of an opposition alliance, the Alliance démocratique de Madagascar (ADM), but retained separate presidential candidates. In the same month restrictions on the freedom of the press were relaxed and the abolition of press censorship was announced.

At the presidential election, which took place in March 1989, Ratsiraka was elected to a third term of office, receiving 62% of the total votes cast (compared with 80% at the previous election). Manandafy, the candidate of the MFM (which had now moved from the extreme left to a market-orientated liberalism), obtained 20% of the votes, while the Vonjy candidate, Dr Jérôme Razanabahiny, secured 15%. Later in March a new political movement, the AKFM/Fanavaozana, was formed by Richard Andriamanjato, in response to the refusal of the AKFM to support his presidential candidature. Allegations by the ADM of electoral fraud led to subsequent rioting. At the legislative elections in May AREMA increased its previously substantial parliamentary majority by a further three seats, winning 120 of the 137 parliamentary seats. The MFM, which obtained seven seats, rejected the results, alleging fraud. The Vonjy secured four seats, the AKFM/Fanavaozana three seats, the original AKFM two seats and MONIMA only one. The abstention rate was high, averaging 25% of registered voters and reaching almost 35% in some urban constituencies.

Political Reform

Despite AREMA's electoral success, widespread discontent with the Government continued among the intellectual and urban classes. In August 1989 Ratsiraka reorganized both the CSR and the Government, removing members of doubtful loyalty and replacing them with strong supporters. The fragile opposition alliance was divided by the reappointment of Jaona to the CSR, together with the Vice-President of the Vonjy and some minor opposition figures, while several economic and technical specialists were appointed to the Government. Shortly before the government reshuffle, Ratsiraka convened a meeting of the FNDR, the first to be held since 1982, at which the constituent parties were invited to submit proposals for the future of the FNDR and a possible revision of the 1975 Constitution. He also consulted privately with leaders of the churches and other opinion groups. However, demands by the Christian Council of Churches in Madagascar (FFKM) for the abolition of the FNDR's monopoly on political activity, as well as the elimination of socialist references in the Constitution, received wide support.

In the first round of local government elections (to the *fokontany*) in September 1989, AREMA again gained the majority of votes, except in Antananarivo, but the average abstention rate was 30%. AREMA's electoral strength and a divided opposition enabled Ratsiraka to limit constitutional changes. The amendments adopted by parliament in December abolished the requirement for political parties to be members of the FNDR, thus effectively dissolving the FNDR itself, but the privileged status of socialism in the Constitution was retained. Nevertheless, provisions were made for a multiparty system, backed by economic liberalism imposed by the IMF and the new freedom of the press, which opposition newspapers were using increasingly to criticize the Government. In the early months of 1990 a number of new parties were formed. Two former PSD ministers established a centre-right party, the Mouvement des démocrates chrétiens malgaches (MDCM), while the Vonjy was seriously weakened by the departure of André Resampa and nine other leading members to relaunch the PSD, with Resampa as Secretary-General.

In March 1990 the Government formally assented to the resumption of multi-party politics. Numerous organizations subsequently emerged, some of them small left-wing parties supporting the President that joined with AREMA, the old AKFM and elements of the Vonjy and MONIMA to form a new coalition, the Mouvement militant pour le socialisme malagasy (MMSM). Other new parties, notably the Union nationale pour le développement et la démocratie (UNDD), led by a medical professor, Albert Zafy, joined the MFM, AKFM/Fanavaozana and the newly formed MDC and PSD in opposition to the Government. The MFM now changed its name to Mouvement pour le progrès de Madagascar, while retaining the same Malagasy initials, MFM.

The withdrawal of Soviet support following the collapse of communism in the USSR compelled Ratsiraka to look to Western countries, particularly France, for economic aid. These improved relations were demonstrated by a state visit by President François Mitterrand in June 1990, during which it was announced that Madagascar's US $750m. debt to France had been cancelled and that France would be permitted to resume use of the facilities at the naval base at Antsiranana.

In mid-1990 the FFKM invited all political associations to attend conferences, which were to take place in August and December, to discuss a programme of reform. At the conference, held in December, 16 opposition factions, together with trade unions and other groups, established an informal alliance, under the name Forces vives (FV), to co-ordinate proposals for constitutional reform. The leading figures of the FV were Zafy (UNDD), Manandafy (MFM) and Andriamanjato (AKFM/Fanavaozana). In the same month the National People's Assembly adopted legislation that abolished press censorship, ended the state monopoly of radio and television and permitted the establishment of private broadcasting stations in partnership with the Government. In January 1991 Ratsiraka announced that further constitutional amendments would be adopted by the Assembly at its next meeting in May. It was later indicated that the main change would be the replacement of the CSR by an elected Senate.

Confrontation and General Strike

At the session of the National People's Assembly in May 1991, FV supporters forced their way into the chamber to submit their alliance's proposals for amending the Constitution, including the elimination of references to socialism, a reduction in the powers of the President and a limit on the number of terms he could serve. However, the only amendments considered were those presented by the Government, which, although numerous, did not meet the FV's basic demands. In early June the FV leadership demanded that a constitutional conference be convened. When the Government failed to respond, the FV called a general strike from 10 June and began a series of peaceful demonstrations in support of demands for the resignation of the President and the appointment of a new 'provisional government', which would include opposition leaders. The army and police did not intervene in the demonstrations, and similar gatherings took place in the provincial capitals.

The strike was widely supported in the civil service, banks, major firms and transport and, together with the daily demonstrations, resulted in the suspension of economic activity in the capital. In July 1991 various negotiations between the FV and the MMSM, with the mediation of the FFKM or the French embassy, failed, owing to the FV's insistence on the resignation of the President. Ratsiraka refused to resign, on the grounds that he had been democratically elected. In response, the FV maintained that the 1989 elections were not democratic, since only political parties adhering to the FNDR were allowed to operate, and denounced abuses of human rights and widespread corruption in the Government and in the President's family. In mid-July the FV appointed its own 'Provisional Government', with a retired general, Jean Rakotoharison, as President and Zafy as Prime Minister. 'Ministers' of the 'Provisional Government' then began to occupy various ministry buildings, with the assistance of civil servants observing the strike. Later in July Ratsiraka announced a state of emergency, reimposed censorship and prohibited mass meetings. This had little effect, however, as the army and police took no action to enforce it. In the next few days Zafy and three other FV 'ministers' were abducted and held in various army camps. There were also murders of several FV leaders in Toamasina and Antsiranana.

On 28 July 1991 Ratsiraka dissolved his Government and pledged to organize a referendum on a new constitution by the end of the year. At a demonstration on the following day, however, the FV insisted on the President's resignation, the lifting of the state of emergency and the release of their 'ministers'. They were freed unharmed on the following day. On 8 August Ratsiraka nominated a new Prime Minister, Guy Razanamasy, hitherto the Mayor of Antananarivo, who invited the FV to join the Government. The offer was rejected, and on 10 August the FV organized a large but peaceful protest march on the President's residence to demand his resignation. The President's bodyguard fired into the crowd, killing 100 and wounding many more. On the same day a further 20 people were killed in the suppression of a similar demonstration in

Mahajanga. The French Government subsequently suspended military aid and advised Ratsiraka to resign, offering him asylum in France. The Roman Catholic Archbishop of Antananarivo joined those calling for the President's resignation, and the FFKM announced that it was abandoning its role as mediator and would henceforth support the FV. Later that month Ratsiraka declared Madagascar to be a federation of six states, under his presidency, and claimed to command the support of five provinces, where AREMA held the majority of seats in regional councils. On 26 August Razanamasy formed a Government, which contained some defectors from the FV, including Resampa. The state of emergency was modified, but Razanamasy warned that civil servants would be dismissed unless they returned to work by 4 September. On that day, however, the FV, which had denounced the new Government as 'puppets' of Ratsiraka, organized a massive demonstration and all economic activity in Antananarivo was halted.

Interim Settlement

Following an ultimatum from the army, an interim agreement was signed on 31 October 1991 by Razanamasy and representatives of the FV, MMSM and FFKM, providing for the suspension of the Constitution and the creation of a transitional Government, which was to remain in office for a maximum period of 18 months, pending the adoption of a new constitution and the holding of elections. Under the agreement, Ratsiraka remained as President with the ceremonial duties of Head of State and titular Head of the Armed Forces, but relinquished all executive powers. A 31-member Haute autorité de l'état (HAE), under Zafy, and a 130-member advisory Conseil de redressement économique et social (CRES), headed jointly by Andriamanjato and Manandafy, replaced the CSR and the National People's Assembly, while Razanamasy's Government was to be expanded to include members of the FV.

In February 1992 the interim authorities suspended the elected bodies (nearly all controlled by AREMA and supporting Ratsiraka) at the various levels of local government and replaced them with special delegations. In the same month proposals for a new constitution and electoral code were compiled at a series of regional forums, and delegates were elected to attend a national forum, which was convened in Antananarivo in late March. After attacks against the conference hall and an attempt to assassinate Zafy, the forum was moved to a military camp. At the end of March security forces fired at supporters of Ratsiraka, led by Jaona, who had marched on the camp; eight people were killed.

Ratsiraka reasserted his intention to stand for re-election, and called for a federalist draft constitution to be submitted to a referendum as an alternative to the unitary draft being considered by the forum. After much debate, a clause was included in the electoral code excluding the candidature of anyone who had been elected President twice under the Second Republic. The Constitution adopted by the forum, subject to approval by the transitional authorities and at a national referendum, was of a parliamentary type, with a constitutional President, a Senate and a National Assembly elected by proportional representation, and with executive power vested in a Prime Minister elected by the National Assembly. The referendum on the Constitution was scheduled for 21 June 1992, and was to be followed by a presidential election in August and legislative elections in October. However, continuing lack of agreement within the Government and the HAE regarding the exclusion of Ratsiraka from the presidential election and the extent of the future President's powers delayed the publication of the draft Constitution and therefore caused the referendum to be postponed. Despite attempts by federalist supporters of Ratsiraka to disrupt the referendum, the new Constitution was approved on 19 August by 73% of the votes cast.

The federalists subsequently intensified pressure for Ratsiraka's right to stand for re-election. After a number of violent incidents involving federalists, including the temporary seizure of the airport at Antsiranana and the bombing of the railway track linking Toamasina and the capital, the transitional authorities agreed to allow Ratsiraka to contest the presidential election. A further seven candidates, including Zafy and Manandafy, were also to participate. In the first round, which was conducted peacefully under international supervision on 25 November 1992, Zafy secured 45% of votes cast, while Ratsiraka obtained 29% and Manandafy 10% of the vote. The second round, which was contested by the two leading candidates, took place on 10 February 1993. Most of the other candidates transferred their support to Zafy, who obtained a substantial majority of 67% of the vote, against 33% for Ratsiraka. Zafy was formally invested as President in late March, amid violent clashes between security forces and federalists in northern Madagascar. However, the transitional authorities continued to function, pending the formation of a new government after the legislative elections. In accordance with the constitution, Zafy resigned as President of the UNDD in May.

In early June 1993 two people were killed and a further 40, including Jaona, were arrested after security forces attacked federalists who had seized the prefecture building in Toliary. On 16 June the elections to the National Assembly were contested under a system of proportional representation. Several elements of the FV coalition presented separate lists of candidates; however, the remaining parties in the alliance, known as the Cartel HVR, proved the most successful group, securing 45 of the 138 seats; Manandafy's MFM obtained 16 seats, while a new pro-Ratsiraka movement, FAMIMA, won only 11. Intensive inter-party negotiations prior to the first meeting of the National Assembly resulted in some shifting in party support for the various candidates contesting the post of Prime Minister. At the election on 9 August, Manandafy obtained 32 votes and Roger Ralison (the candidate of the Cartel) 45 votes. The winner, with 55 votes, was Francisque Ravony, who was the favoured candidate both of Zafy and of the business community. Ravony, a respected lawyer and a son-in-law of former President Tsiranana, had served as Deputy Prime Minister in the transitional Government. The leader of the AKFM/Fanavaozana, Richard Andriamanjato, was elected Speaker of the National Assembly.

THE THIRD REPUBLIC

At the end of August 1993 Ravony formed a new Council of Ministers, which was endorsed by 72% of deputies in the National Assembly, as was his programme which emphasized economic recovery based on free-market policies and measures to eradicate corruption. Effective action regarding economic recovery subsequently proved difficult, however, owing in part to the fragmented nature of the National Assembly, which comprised some 25 separate parties; these became largely two informal coalitions of equal size, known respectively as the HVR group, which included supporters of Zafy and Andriamanjato, and the G6. However, neither was specifically a government or opposition organization, and ministers were appointed from both alliances and also from independent members. Despite the immediate necessity for substantial assistance to sustain the economy, a number of deputies opposed the acceptance of structural adjustment measures, required by the World Bank and IMF as a precondition to the approval of financial credit, owing to the additional widespread hardship that would ensue. A strike by civil servants in January 1994 opposed IMF demands for substantial retrenchment in the civil service and a 'freeze' of public-sector salaries.

Ravony's position was undermined by public opposition from Zafy and Andriamanjato, who rejected the IMF and World Bank demands as an affront to national sovereignty and favoured financial arrangements with private enterprises (known as 'parallel financing'). In July 1994 31 deputies belonging to the G6 coalition proposed a motion of censure against Ravony for failing to conclude an agreement with the Bretton Woods institutions, which was, however, defeated with the assistance of the HVR group. In August Ravony reorganized the Council of Ministers to reflect the HVR's support; the President of the LEADER/Fanilo party, Herizo Razafimahaleo, subsequently resigned, after his portfolio was divided.

In January 1995, at the insistence of the Bretton Woods institutions, Ravony dismissed the Governor of the central bank. In a balancing move to appease the HVR group, the

Minister of Finance also resigned, with Ravony assuming the portfolio himself. The Government subsequently pledged to undertake further austerity measures, while the IMF and World Bank approved the doubling of the minimum wage and additional expenditure on health and education to counteract the effect of the structural adjustment reforms.

In June 1995 members of the G6 group staged a demonstration urging the impeachment of Zafy, on the grounds that he had exceeded his constitutional powers and supported Andriamanjato's demands for 'parallel financing'. At the same time Ravony strengthened his parliamentary position by recruiting additional deputies to his hitherto single-member party, the Committee for the Support of Democracy and Development in Madagascar (CSDDM). The CSDDM then joined the G6, which became the G7, and had a clear majority in the National Assembly. In July Zafy publicly criticized Ravony and, at his instigation, the HVR group in the National Assembly proposed a motion of censure against the Prime Minister, which was, however, rejected by a large majority.

Zafy subsequently announced that he could not co-operate with Ravony and called a referendum for 17 September 1995 to endorse a constitutional amendment, whereby the President, rather than the National Assembly, would select the Prime Minister. Ravony, who had reorganized the Council of Ministers to reflect changes in the composition of his support in the National Assembly, announced that he would resign when the result of the referendum was formally announced in October. He also declined to campaign against the referendum, and many of his supporters decided to express their disapproval by abstaining from voting. In the referendum, notable for a high degree of abstention, the constitutional amendment was approved by 63.5% of the valid votes.

Ravony and his Government duly resigned and President Zafy appointed as Prime Minister Emmanuel Rakotovahiny, the leader of his own party, the UNDD. The new Government contained no members of the G7 majority group and was heavily weighted in favour of the UNDD at the expense of other groups from the former HVF.

The Government was further weakened by public disagreement between the Prime Minister and the finance minister over the 1996 budget, and could make no progress in negotiations with the IMF and the World Bank. Public discontent was expressed by strikes of university students and railway workers and an unprecedented strike by officials of the finance ministry, joined by customs officials at the ports, calling for the resignation of their minister who, it was later revealed, had been convicted of corruption in 1982. Under increasing pressure to change the Government, Zafy offered a reshuffle but insisted on retaining Rakotovahiny as Prime Minister. In April most of the parties that previously supported Zafy joined in a new group, the Rassemblement pour la Troisième République (RP3R), to oppose him. At the same time, the FFKM returned to the public stage to appeal for a new government, an agreement with the IMF and World Bank and the elimination of corruption in the Government. The Managing Director of the IMF, Michel Camdessus, stressed during a visit to Madagascar that the IMF could negotiate only with a cohesive government united in favour of agreements with the Bretton Woods institutions.

When Zafy failed to carry out even the government reshuffle that he had promised, the G7 and RP3R joined on 16 May 1996 in a motion of censure against the Government, which required a two-thirds' majority and was carried by 109 votes to 15. Rakotovahiny resigned and Zafy appointed a non-political Prime Minister, Norbert Ratsirahonana, hitherto the President of the High Constitutional Court (HCC) and a leading member of the Protestant Reformed Church. Ratsirahonana's programme, emphasizing economic reform in the context of agreements with the IMF and World Bank and action on poverty, corruption and crime, won general approval. He proposed a government including a number of members of the G7 majority group and only one UNDD member. However, Zafy vetoed all but one G7 minister and insisted on the retention of five UNDD members and other ministers from the previous Government. Most G7 and RP3R deputies therefore walked out when Ratsirahonana presented his Government and programme to the National Assembly on 10 June. However, in July Ratsirahonana obtained a vote of confidence by linking it with legislation necessary for the agreements with the IMF and World Bank.

On 26 July 1996 the National Assembly voted by 99 votes to 34 to impeach the President for various violations of the Constitution. After granting Zafy a month to contest the charges, the HCC endorsed the impeachment and removed him from office; on the same day Zafy resigned. The Court appointed the Prime Minister, Ratsirahonana, to act as interim President pending the outcome of a new presidential election, to be held within two months. He formed a new Government, excluding those ministers whom Zafy had forced him to accept. Despite the impeachment, Zafy immediately declared himself a candidate for the presidential election and was joined by ex-President Ratsiraka, acting President Ratsirahonana and 12 other candidates, including most of the leaders of the main political parties.

The Return of Ratsiraka

In the first round of the presidential election on 3 November 1996, marked by a high abstention rate, Ratsiraka came first with 37% of the valid votes, followed by Zafy with 23%. In the run-off on 29 December Ratsiraka won narrowly with 51% of the valid votes to Zafy's 49%, but abstentions and spoilt votes comprised 52% of the electorate. In February 1997 Ratsiraka appointed as Prime Minister Pascal Rakotomavo, who formed a Government consisting largely of technocrats.

During the election campaign Ratsirahonana had successfully completed negotiations with the IMF, leading in due course to a resumption of international aid and debt-relief arrangements. Ratsiraka's first act was to visit Washington, DC, and New York (USA), Paris (France) and Brussels (Belgium) to reassure the donor community of his intention to adhere to the reform programme approved by the IMF. He announced his intention to fulfil an electoral promise to submit to a national referendum two alternative new constitutions. The legislative elections due in August 1997 were postponed for 10 months so that they could be held under whatever new constitutional arrangements emerged from the referendum; the National Assembly's mandate was subsequently extended, with the approval of the HCC. The opposition, led by Zafy, condemned the delay (which was officially to allow time for the distribution of newly compulsory identity cards for voters) and declared it to be a violation of the Constitution.

The Government decided that the referendum would concern amendments to the existing Constitution rather than two alternative new constitutions. These revisions were so extensive that they amounted to an almost totally new Constitution reverting to a presidential regime, greatly increasing the President's powers at the expense of the legislature and weakening the independence of the judiciary. They also provided for a considerable degree of decentralization of government to the provinces. Most opposition parties decided not to campaign actively for a 'No' vote in the referendum. Despite this, the amendments were only narrowly adopted on 15 March 1998, by 51% of the valid votes, cast by 66% of the electorate. The amended Constitution provided for President Ratsiraka to complete his term of office and allowed him to be re-elected twice rather than only once.

Elections to an enlarged 150-member National Assembly took place on 17 May 1998 under a new electoral law, which favoured the larger parties: the previous system of proportional representation using party lists was replaced by 82 single-member constituencies and a form of proportional representation for 34 two-member constituencies. Ratsiraka's party, AREMA, received only 25% of the votes, but won 63 of the 150 seats. The 19 seats won by its government coalition partners, LEADER/Fanilo and AKFM/Fanavaozana, assured the Government of a majority in the National Assembly. Independent candidates received 27% of the votes and 32 seats. The parties of Andriamanjato (AKFM/Fanavaozana) and Manandafy (MFM) won only three seats each, and neither party leader was re-elected. In July Ratsiraka appointed as Prime Minister Tantely Andrianarivo, who formed a coalition Government dominated by AREMA, but including members of other parties and some independents.

Subsequently the Government was strengthened by the support of the Rassemblement pour le socialisme et la démocratie (RPSD) and 24 independent deputies. However, disillusionment with the Government's economic performance, notably the long delay in obtaining the release of additional structural adjustment funds from the World Bank and the IMF, led to a loss of support. The opposition divided into two groups: the radicals, including Zafy's Asa, fahamarinana, fampandrosoana, arinda (AFFA) and Manandafy's MFM, which called for the overthrow of the Government and a new constitution; and the moderates, led by Ratsirahonana's Ny asa vita no ifampitsara (AVI), who engaged in more constructive opposition.

Local government elections, originally scheduled for October 1993, were repeatedly postponed for various reasons, thus delaying the establishment of the Senate, two-thirds of which was to be elected by local government councillors. Elections to the rural and municipal communes were held in November 1995 and again in November 1999, when AREMA was confirmed as the largest party, although, with 41% of the vote, it was some way short of an overall majority. In the mayoral elections, popular disillusionment with politicians resulted in the widespread rejection of candidates from political parties in favour of independent candidates, who were mostly businessmen. The new Mayor of Antananarivo, Marc Ravalomanana, a self-made millionaire, reinforced his popularity by succeeding in cleaning up the shabby, polluted capital.

Under the decentralization arrangements of the 1998 Constitution, elections for provincial councillors in the new autonomous provinces were held on 3 December 2000 and were marked by a high abstention rate, averaging 55% throughout the country, but reaching higher rates in the towns. With the opposition vote split among a number of parties, some of them advocating a boycott of the elections, AREMA attained the most votes in all six provinces, with an absolute majority in all except Antananarivo. Thus, all the governors, now elected by provincial councillors rather than being appointed by the central Government, were members of AREMA. On 18 March 2001 the provincial councillors joined with the mayors of the communes to elect two-thirds of the Senate (the remaining one-third was nominated by the President). AREMA was again victorious, winning 49 of the 60 seats, thus completing the presidential party's domination at all levels of both government and legislature.

Disputed Presidential Election

A presidential election was held on 16 December 2001. In the first round the results issued by the Government, and confirmed by a newly appointed HCC, gave Ravalomanana 46% of the votes cast and Ratsiraka 40%, thereby necessitating a second round of voting. However, Ravalomanana, supported by a consortium of observers, claimed that he had won 52% of the vote and therefore should be proclaimed President. After massive demonstrations by his supporters failed to persuade the HCC to take into account his own and the observers' evidence, he declared himself President and appointed a Government, headed by Jacques Sylla, which subsequently took over government offices in the capital. Ratsiraka withdrew his Government to the port of Toamasina and his supporters erected road-blocks and destroyed bridges on all roads leading to the capital, creating an effective blockade of the plateau area. In the coastal towns supporters of Ravalomanana and people of plateau origin were subjected to violent intimidation by armed militias recruited from AREMA. The violence resulted in a number of deaths and the blockade began to cause serious damage to the economy.

At a meeting in Dakar, Senegal, called by the Organization of African Unity (OAU), the two contenders agreed in mid-April 2002 to a recount (followed by a second round if necessary) and a cessation of the blockade and the violence. Meanwhile, the Supreme Court in Madagascar ruled that the recent appointment of the HCC had been irregular and accordingly reinstated the former HCC. Thus, the former members of the body carried out the recount and declared Ravalomanana the winner, with 51.5% of the votes cast to Ratsiraka's 35.9%. Ravalomanana was duly inaugurated as President on 6 May. However, Ratsiraka refused to accept the recount. He persisted in demanding a second round of voting, and the blockade and the violence in coastal towns continued. Lack of fuel and other essential supplies caused increasing hardship in the capital and surrounding areas.

The OAU and France supported Ratsiraka by continuing to call for the establishment of a government of national reconciliation and for new elections. Other Western countries followed the French lead in withholding recognition from Ravalomanana. The Malagasy armed forces were initially divided, and both 'Presidents' appointed new ministers of defence as well as army and gendarmerie chiefs of staff. Following the formal transfer of power to Ravalomanana's appointees, the majority of the armed forces accepted Ravalomanana as Commander-in-Chief.

Further OAU attempts at mediation and reconciliation were given renewed urgency when Ravalomanana's troops, in the face of armed opposition, successfully occupied the area around Sambava in the north-east. In June 2002 Ravalomanana agreed to advance the legislative elections and made a gesture towards a government of national reconciliation by reshuffling the Government to include two former supporters of Ratsiraka, but this did not satisfy France and the OAU. Later that month a special meeting of the OAU Central Organ declared the Malagasy seat at the OAU vacant until new elections under international supervision had clarified the leadership question. The exclusion of Madagascar was maintained in July at the summit of the OAU in Durban, South Africa, where it was transformed into the African Union (AU).

Meanwhile, the armed forces had begun their threatened operation to lift the blockade by force, and in mid-June 2002 they occupied Toliary and Mahajanga without resistance. In the northern province of Antsiranana they encountered stubborn resistance from hard-line Ratsiraka supporters, and it was not until early July that the provincial capital was taken, leaving only Toamasina under Ratsiraka's control.

On 26 June 2002 (Madagascar's Independence Day) the USA recognized Ravalomanana as President and released Malagasy assets in the USA. Recognition quickly followed from Australia, Germany and Japan. France continued to call for reconciliation, but limited its demands to the inclusion of two more AREMA members in the Government. When Ravalomanana complied in early July, the French immediately released Malagasy assets in France and signed new aid agreements with Ravalomanana. French recognition, followed by that of the other EU Governments, effectively ended Ratsiraka's resistance. On 5 July he and most of his ministers flew into exile in France, and on the same day government troops peacefully occupied Toamasina.

Peace and Reconciliation

President Ravalomanana proclaimed a policy of national reconciliation, but it proved difficult to resist the widespread demand for the punishment of those responsible for the suffering and damage caused by the blockade and the brutal behaviour of the pro-Ratsiraka militia. Over 200 leading supporters of Ratsiraka, both civilian and military, were arrested and imprisoned for sometimes lengthy periods before being either condemned to heavy fines and imprisonment or released for lack of evidence. Ravalomanana also set up a National Council to tackle the corruption in government that had become endemic during the Second and Third Republics.

In fulfilment of his promise, Ravalomanana brought forward the legislative elections due in May 2003 to 15 December 2002, having amended the electoral rules to abolish the limited element of proportional representation. The President's party, Tiako I Madagasikara (TIM—I Love Madagascar), won 104 of the 160 seats, and allies from AVI and elements of the RPSD joined in a Front patriotique (FP) that gained a further 22 seats. AREMA, which had been split by a demand to boycott the elections, came second in many constituencies, but the 'first-past-the-post' system limited its seats to three. There were 23 independent deputies.

The new Government formed by Prime Minister Jacques Sylla in January 2003 was reduced from 30 to 20 ministers and was dominated by TIM. Several smaller parties that had supported Ravalomanana in the presidential election as members of the Committee for Support of Marc Ravalomanana

(KMMR), and had hoped to be rewarded with ministerial posts, set up an opposition group, KMMR Nouveau. A Committee of National Reconciliation, established by ex-President Zafy in 2002, also became a focus of opposition. Nevertheless, there was little threat to the dominance of TIM and the popularity of the President. In August 2003 Ratsiraka was sentenced, *in absentia*, to 10 years of hard labour for embezzling public funds and in December former Prime Minister Tantely Andrianarivo was sentenced to 12 years' hard labour and fined heavily for embezzling public funds and endangering state security; this was mitigated, however, by the subsequent permission for his departure overseas in order to seek medical treatment. Following expressions of international concern, President Ravalomanana granted pardons to former Ratsiraka loyalists who had been sentenced to less than three years' imprisonment.

The four-month blockade of the capital had inflicted severe damage on the economy, which recovered only slowly in 2003. In August the President suspended all taxes on a wide range of imported goods in the hope of stimulating the economy and facilitating exports. The immediate result was a flood of imports but no significant increase in exports. The resulting imbalance, exacerbated by two severe cyclones in 2004, led the currency to collapse to less than two-thirds of its value and to a steep rise in inflation. While the President retained much of his popularity, support for his party declined. In communal and municipal elections in November 2003 TIM candidates received little more than 50% of the national vote, an unusually low figure for a governing party. In January 2004 Ravalomanana effected a restructuring of the Council of Ministers, further reducing its size and appointing several former supporters of Ratsiraka in order to diversify its ethnic composition. From January army reservists, who had supported Ravalomanana in 2002, expressed their discontent with the Government for failing to pay their demobilization bonuses as promised through various demonstrations (including barricading the parliament in May) and more generalized public protests began to take place in response to the strong increases in consumer prices. A spate of unattributed grenade attacks on political and business associates of President Ravalomanana from the end of June, however, signalled a more worrying development (although no injuries were sustained).

Unrest continued to build up as the price of rice increased by 150% between March and November 2004; an increase of 50% in one week of November brought hundreds of people on to the streets of the capital in protest. Declining purchasing power was a factor in a series of strikes in early 2005 by magistrates, university lecturers and students. There were violent clashes between police and students in Antananarivo, while in Toamasina students set up a road-block. In March 2005 there was a minor reshuffle of the Government involving the abolition of the post of Deputy Prime Minister. Further minor reshuffles followed in October and in December, when Gen. Charles Rabemananjara replaced Gen. Soja as the Minister of the Interior and Administrative Reform, following an alleged attempt on the President's life.

The steep increase in the international petroleum price in 2005 was a setback to the Government's hopes of reducing inflation and improving living standards. The Government's position was further weakened by dissent within TIM, manifested in the dismissal by the National Assembly of its President, Jean Lahiniriko in May 2006. The radical opposition, including ex-President Zafy, formed a new grouping, 3FN (Trois forces nationales), which organized street demonstrations, resulting in violent clashes with the police and government supporters. During a visit in March 2006 the UN Secretary-General Kofi Annan recommended a national dialogue between Government and opposition. However, when the Government organized such a dialogue in May, it was boycotted by most of the opposition on the basis that the Government had made it clear that it was not prepared to accept the main opposition proposals, especially revision of the Electoral Law. Nevertheless, further consultative talks were held in August. In the same month the former Prime Minister, Pierrot Rajaonarivelo, was sentenced, *in absentia*, to 15 years' imprisonment after being convicted of the embezzlement of public funds.

Ravalomanana Re-elected

The Government brought forward the date of the presidential election to 3 December 2006. This appeared to be contrary to the Constitution but was approved by the HCC, which barred four of the possible 18 candidates, including Rajaonarivelo whose attempts to return from exile in France in October were thwarted at airports in Mauritius and Madagascar. AREMA failed to provide an alternative candidate and this, together with the fragmented nature of the opposition, resulted in Ravalomanana facing no notable challengers. His campaign was widespread and efficiently run, and concentrated on the continuation of reforms. The final results, announced by the HCC, awarded Ravalomanana 54.79% of the vote, well ahead of Lahiniriko who took 11.65%, Roland Ratsiraka with 10.14% and Herizo Razafimahaleo with 9.03%, and enough to avoid a second round of voting. Voter turn-out was 62% and international observers commented favourably on the way the election was held. Lahiriniko sought to build on his relative success by forming a new political party, the Parti socialiste et démocratique pour l'union de Madagascar. During the election campaign there was an attempted coup by Gen. Randrianafidisoa, commonly known as 'Fidy', and one soldier was killed in a clash between his supporters and government troops at the military air base at Ivato, to which Ravalomanana was returning from a trip to Europe. The attempt was suppressed and Gen. 'Fidy' was sentenced to four years' imprisonment in February 2007.

Meanwhile, in January 2007 the President appointed Rabemananjara as the new Prime Minister. Rabemananjara also retained the interior portfolio. The new Government announced later that month included Gen. Marcel Ranjeva as Minister of Foreign Affairs and Benjamin Andriamparany Radavidson as Minister of Finance; however, the key area of the Ministry of Decentralization was retained in the Presidency and awarded to Yvan Randriasandratriniony, who ranked in precedence after the Prime Minister.

A referendum was held on 4 March 2007 at which 75.3% of voters approved amendments to the Constitution. They were asked 'Do you accept these constitutional changes for rapid and sustainable regional development to improve the lives of the Malagasy?' Voter turn-out was reported at just 44%. The amendments covered a range of modifications that generally increased the power of the President, granting him, for example, full powers in times of emergency and catastrophe and the right to terminate his appointments to the Senate, which despite earlier suggestions remained in place but had its term reduced from seven to five years. The six autonomous provinces were suppressed and instead the 22 regions took on more powers while the *fokonolona*, organised in *fokontany*, were introduced as the base of development. A further change was the introduction of English as a third official language alongside French and Malagasy (which remains the national language), in an effort to boost links with English-speaking trading partners such as the Southern African Development Community (SADC). Concerns were expressed over the change to no longer describe the country as lay, which the Roman Catholic Church believed could lead to government interference in religious affairs, and over the new requirement for presidential candidates to be Malagasy and of Malagasy parents (and to have lived in the country for the previous six months), which was seen as an attack on the métis or mixed-blood population.

While TIM suffered from some internal tension in 2007, the opposition parties fared much worse. AREMA in particular was divided between supporters of ex-President Ratsiraka and Rajaonarivelo, while Roland Ratsiraka, who had emerged as a possible consensus leader, was first dismissed as mayor of Toamasina in late January then arrested in April and charged with corruption. Another opposition leader, Pety Rakotoniaina, who was mayor of Fianarantsoa and who secured less than 2% of the votes in the presidential election, was sought and finally arrested in July on suspicion of corruption and possible links to Gen. Fidy's coup attempt. The opposition seemed to have provoked unrest in various cities in April and May, which was prompted in part by serious power cuts, but which also reflected renewed tension between the Merina and *côtiers*. Political rivalries also intensified after the President's decision in July to dissolve the National Assembly and set 23 September as the date for legislative elections.

A devastating succession of cyclones and tropical storms between late 2006 and May 2007 severely damaged the country's infrastructure and crops, and the worst, Cyclone Indlala in March, killed at least 150 people. The Government's appeal for emergency aid met with little response, although the country did continue to benefit from support from donors such as the IMF and the European Commission, as well as from a growing level of investment into promising mineral and energy projects.

FOREIGN AFFAIRS

In a complete reversal of Ratsiraka's foreign policies, in the early 1990s Ravony's Government established relations with Israel, South Africa, the Republic of Korea and (for trade and economic purposes only) Taiwan. These arrangements were not altered after Ratsiraka's return as President in 1997, but by 2000, under pressure from the People's Republic of China, the Taiwan office had been closed. However, relations with the People's Republic of China were somewhat strained by popular resentment at a large influx of Chinese small traders undercutting Malagasy shopkeepers. Successive foreign ministers made the promotion of the economy the main focus of foreign policy and moved to strengthen relations with South Africa, the newly industrialized countries of South-East Asia and the Far East. France remained the principal trading partner and supplier of bilateral aid. Political relations with France became even closer after the settlement, in October 1998, of the long-standing dispute over compensation for nationalized French assets. Disagreement remained over the sovereignty of the Iles Glorieuses and three other uninhabited islets in the Mozambique Channel, which are claimed by France, but in February 2000 it was agreed that the islands would be co-administered by France, Madagascar and Mauritius, without prejudice to the question of sovereignty. In 2002 the new Malagasy Government's relations with France were soured by French support for Ratsiraka, but France declared its intention of remaining the leading donor of aid, and relations soon recovered their traditional closeness.

Relations with African countries were also adversely affected by the support of the OAU (now the AU) for the outgoing President and Madagascar's exclusion from that organization. It was not until July 2003 that Madagascar was formally readmitted. In April 2004 Prime Minster Paul Bérenger of Mauritius made an official visit to Madagascar, during which political and economic agreements between the two countries were signed.

President Jacques Chirac of France made a brief visit in July 2005, in which he announced the cancellation of debts owed to that country. The USA had announced in June that Madagascar was to be the first country to qualify for its new and significant Millennium Challenge Account supplementary aid scheme, an endorsement as qualification was based on a demonstrable record of reform. The opening of new embassies by Norway, Senegal, South Africa and Thailand was also seen as an endorsement of Ravalomanana. In sharp contrast the British Government closed its embassy in August 2005, for reasons of economy.

An official visit to Morocco by Ravalomanana in April 2005 ended a long period of strained relations following Ratsiraka's recognition of the Sahrawi Arab Democratic Republic (SADR), and was accompanied by the closure of the SADR mission in Antananarivo. In the same month Ravalomanana visited Réunion and signed an agreement delimiting the maritime zones between the two islands. In November 2005 a visit by a delegation from the People's Republic of China, headed by the Deputy Prime Minister, highlighted the extent of Chinese involvement and investment in many areas of the Malagasy economy. The closer links were confirmed in further visits to Madagascar in 2006 and Ravalomanana's visit to Beijing in April 2007 to attend the Forum on China-Africa Co-operation summit. The President also visited Germany, the holder of the European Union Presidency in the first six months of 2007, to seek financial support for his Madagascar Action Plan. Madagascar also hosted a meeting of SADC, with which it is also developing closer links.

Economy

JULIAN COOKE

Based on an earlier article by GILL TUDOR

In 2005 Madagascar's gross national income (GNI) at current prices was US $5,371m., equivalent to $290 per capita for the population of some 18.6m., according to estimates by the World Bank. Between 1995 and 2005 the country's population increased by an estimated annual average of 2.9%, while Madagascar's gross domestic product (GDP) per head decreased in real terms by an average of 0.1% per year, even though overall GDP increased at an average annual rate of 3.0% in 1998–2005. The economy has grown at improved rates in recent years, with growth of 9.8% recorded in 2003, 5.3% in 2004, 4.6% in 2005 and an estimated 4.9% in 2006. In 2005, according to the IMF, the incidence of poverty was 68.7% (comprising 75.3% in rural areas and 52.0% in urban areas), with the worst levels on the eastern coast. Madagascar was ranked 143rd out of 177 countries on the UN Human Development Index in 2006.

AGRICULTURE, FORESTRY AND FISHING

The agricultural sector (including forestry and fishing) accounted for a provisional 27.6% of GDP in 2006, and engaged an estimated 80.9% of the country's active labour force in 2005. The rural economy also accounted for 80% of Madagascar's export revenues prior to the development of export-processing zones (EPZs) and manufacturing industry. The production of food and of export crops (except cotton) either stagnated or declined after President Didier Ratsiraka first took power in 1975, mainly as a result of natural disasters and the imposition of doctrinaire socialist principles. The island's agricultural sector also suffered from adverse climatic conditions, from a lack of insecticides, spare parts and fertilizers, and from the poor maintenance of rural roads. The introduction of higher producer prices during the 1980s aimed to increase the output of food crops in particular to achieve self-sufficiency in food, but Madagascar continues to import rice for consumption. A further major policy objective was to improve the quality of export crops, while limiting the expansion in output, and the government continues to encourage reform and investment in various areas. Continued pressures meant that agricultural GDP only increased at an average annual rate of 2.0% in 1995–2005, according to the World Bank.

Paddy rice is the main crop, grown by 70% of the population whose basic food is rice—the average annual consumption per head is about 135 kg, the highest of any country in the world—and it occupies about 1.2m ha, or approximately one-half of the area under cultivation. Following extensive damage to rice fields caused by consistent cyclones from 1982 to 1990, the area planted to rice was reduced, while output of potatoes and maize was increased. The country suffered extensive crop damage again in early 1997, when cyclones struck both the south-east and the north-east. Heavy rains brought by the cyclones led also to an increase in the number of locusts, which destroyed rice fields and maize plantations in the south and covered 5m. ha by June 1998. Rice production declined to 2.4m. metric tons in 1998, which constituted only some 60% of domestic consumption. Further cyclones in 2000 caused the loss of 150,000 tons of rice, and production totalled just 2.5m. tons. In 2002 the economic blockades resulting from the political crisis exacerbated the situation, and caused rice prices to escalate more than three-fold. Production improved in 2003 to some 2.8m. tons, but in 2004 severe rice shortages were again experienced, owing to cyclone activity, the flooding of paddy fields and a two-year drought in the south of the country. However, production, with a yield of 2.6 tons per ha, reached some 3.4m. tons in 2005, according to the IMF, and a 14% increase on the previous year was recorded. Stronger land tenure and the allocation of many more land titles has increased productivity, as have higher-yielding varieties, although again there was severe damage from cyclones and floods in 2006–07. Other important staple crops are maize, cassava, bananas and sweet potatoes.

Madagascar's main cash crops are vanilla and cloves. Madagascar is the world's largest producer of natural vanilla, produced from approximately 25,000 ha of beans grown in the north-east of the country. The USA and France are the main purchasers, taking 51% and 25%, respectively, in 2006. Output has fluctuated widely in recent years, between 600 metric tons and 4,400 tons per year, and is very sensitive to damage to the crop from cyclones and tropical storms, as experienced in 2000, 2003 and again in 2007, when an estimated 20% of the crop was lost. Prices rose dramatically in 2003 to a record level of US $400 per kg when production almost halved to 2,650 tons. The price rise stimulated competition from cheap synthetic substitutes, which contributed to a collapse in prices, to $20 per kg, by 2006, from which they have since recovered slightly to $30 per kg. The Government and producer confederations follow a policy of limited exports and managed prices. As reform of the vanilla sector was a key prerequisite for further funding from the Bretton Woods institutions, in 1994 the Government implemented a number of changes, which included the abolition of the guaranteed producer price; the fall in free-market prices discouraged production but the abolition of the 25% export tax in 1997 aided a recovery. Exports of vanilla in 2006 were 2,000 tons, and this accounted for about two-thirds of world demand. Export prices have stabilized, but at approximately $30 per kg the proceeds remain well below previous levels, and the country will face continued competition from other producers. To help production in 2006 the UN Development Programme sponsored a $17m. partnership between three large electricity companies—France's EDF, Germany's RWE, and Canada's Hydro-Electric Quebec—to provide affordable electricity in the main vanilla-growing area of Sava. Cyclone damage is, nevertheless, likely to limit exports.

The production of cloves rose from the late 1980s as farmers responded to the liberalization of controls. In 1998, however, export revenue from cloves fell by 25%, to US $9.2m., as production and prices declined, owing to continued competition from Indonesia. Export revenue recovered to an estimated $28.8m. in 2003, and production appeared to have stabilized at an estimated 15,500 metric tons. The world price of cloves increased from $2 per kg in 2004 to $4.3 per kg in 2005, when Madagascar exported 6,182 tons, earning an estimated $17m.

Coffee formerly occupied an important place in agricultural production and exports but consistently low international prices have led to lower production. Domestic consumption has risen steadily in recent years, to about 15,000 metric tons per year, but in 2004 coffee represented only an estimated 0.5% of the value of total exports. In 2000 there was a relaunch of the sector, led by the National Coffee Marketing Committee and financed by the European Union (EU), with one aim: to encourage a shift from robusta beans to the more highly-valued arabica, which has been a partial success. Coffee production was 65,000 tons in 2004, a small decrease from 70,315 tons in 2003 and in 2006 exports increased, even though overall production declined slightly.

Among other products litchis (or lychees), ylang ylang and geranium flowers (for essential oils used in the perfume industry) are exported, with the production and export of litchis doubling towards the end of the 1990s as a result of EU support. In 2005–06 exports reached a record 22,400 tons, but a sharp fall in prices in the main market of France reduced the returns to producers. From 2000 production of cinnamon (canella) and pepper decreased, and production of seed cotton also declined from a peak of around 50,000 metric tons in 1986 to 12,500 tons in 2004. Sisal is a minor export crop, which was adversely affected for a number of years by synthetic substitutes and is particularly vulnerable to the continued drought in the south, which in 1988 caused the closure of three major sisal estates. Annual production has ranged widely between 10,000 and 20,000 tons, and production was 17,000 tons in 2004. There are five sugar factories, four of which were rehabilitated in the late 1980s with French aid, and the fifth, built with Chinese assistance, began operating in 1987. The state-owned company Société Siramamy Malagasy managed all the factories, but the sugar estates have suffered from under-investment and several have been threatened with closure because of debts. Production of sugar cane averaged about 2m. tons per year in the 1990s and was 2.5m. tons in 2003 and 2004. Imports of sugar are necessary to meet domestic requirements. There are two current developments to use extensive sugar cane plantations for the production of ethanol, which are due to commence by the end of 2007. Groundnuts, pineapples, coconuts, butter beans and tobacco are also grown on a small scale.

There is little in the way of a forestry sector, even though FAO estimated that in 2005 the country's 28.9m. ha of forest and other wooded land made up just over one-half of the total area of the country. The majority of forest products are the wood and charcoal that generate 84% of domestic fuel consumption, and contribute heavily to deforestation. Only about 20% of the land area is covered by primary forests, which remain under threat despite an increase in reforestation and despite recent research that suggests a stabilization. Debt-conversion schemes for environmental projects have helped, as has President Marc Ravalomanana's commitment in 2003 to triple the country's total protected territory to 6m. ha by 2008. Good progress has already been made, with 1.1m. ha added to protected schemes in 2006, following a similar total in 2005. The development of the country's national parks was also closely associated with potential for the eco-tourism sector, and should be assisted by the inclusion in June 2007 of some of Madagascar's eastern forests on UNESCO's World Heritage list.

Madagascar has sizeable potential in its coastal resources. Sea fishing by coastal fishermen has been industrialized, with assistance from Japan and France. Shrimp fishing has expanded considerably and has become an important source of export revenue; the catch of shrimps and prawns reached 9,900 metric tons by 1995, and grew to 13,223 tons in 2002, yielding an estimated US $68m. Fisheries was the one sector relatively unaffected by the economic crisis and blockades of 2002. Exports of fish and fish products provided 22.1% of total export earnings in 2003, when the total catch was an estimated 150,345 tons, decreasing slightly to 137,701 tons in 2004. In 2005 fees and royalties collected increased by nearly two-thirds, according to the IMF. However, concerns regarding overfishing and environmental damage intensified as the sector reached a maximum sustainable level. While exports of prawns alone reached 11,380 tons in 2006 and could now benefit from the granting of US certification in January 2007, the pressure on stocks may make it difficult to profit from the potential. Fish farming is a possible solution to this problem and is a rapidly growing industry, with some 50,000 ha of suitable territory in swamps along the western coast. Vessels from EU countries, Japan and Russia fish by agreement for tuna and prawns in Madagascar's exclusive maritime zone, which extends 370 km (200 nautical miles) off the coast. However, illegal fishing in Malagasy waters is increasingly problematic and the country lacks sufficient resources to police the area. An $18m. tuna-canning complex was established as a joint venture with a French company at Antsiranana, financed predominantly by France and the European Investment Bank (EIB). The EIB, the International Finance Corporation (IFC) and France also provided funds for Pêcheries de Nosy Bé to replace three trawlers and to modernize the shrimp-processing plant at Hellville in the north-west.

Madagascar had some 10.5m. head of cattle in 2005 but they are generally regarded as an indication of wealth rather than as a source of income, making the development of a commercial beef sector difficult. Nevertheless, there is some ranching and an estimated 146,625 metric tons of beef and veal were produced commercially in 2004, with a similar amount produced in 2005, according to FAO. Some beef is exported but volumes have declined in recent years to about 800 tons per year, despite an EU quota of 11,000 tons. There is a pressing need to revive veterinary services, to improve marketing and to rehabilitate abattoirs, partly to meet EU import standards. Live animals and some canned corned beef are exported to African countries, the Gulf states and Indian Ocean islands. There are increasing numbers of dairy cattle, estimated at some 500,000 in 2004. FAO also estimated that in 2005 there were 1.2m. goats and 650,000 sheep, and some 1.6m. pigs in 2004, with about 70,000 tons of pig meat produced, equivalent to one-quarter of total meat production.

INDUSTRY

Industry accounted for a preliminary 15.4% of Madagascar's GDP in 2006 and employed about 3.4% of the engaged labour force in 2005. Industrial GDP increased at an average annual rate of 3.2% in 1995–2005. The sector's GDP grew by 7.6% in 2001, but declined drastically by 25.1% in 2002, owing to the political and economic crisis, recovering to increase by 14.5% in 2003, by 6.6% in 2004, and by 6.1% in 2005. The island's major industrial centres, other than mines, are located in the High Plateaux or near the port of Toamasina. Food processing accounts for a significant portion of all industrial value added while brewing, paper and soap are also important sectors. Textile production declined by one-half between 1990 and 2000, largely owing to illegal imports, but textile production from the export-processing zones became increasingly successful under the preferential terms of the USA's African Growth and Opportunity Act (AGOA). The ending of the international Multi-fibre Agreement (MFA) in January 2005 led to a surge of Chinese goods into the US market, although increased sales to the EU limited the decline in exports in that year to 4%. Textile exports have since been stagnant, a trend that continued in the first nine months of 2006.

There are cement plants at Mahajanga and Toamasina; production of cement reached 51,882 metric tons in 2001. The Chinese Government has also provided funding for a new cement factory. A fertilizer plant at Toamasina, which began operations in 1985, produces some 90,000 tons per year of urea- and ammonia-based fertilizers. Other industries include the manufacture of wood products and furniture, agricultural machinery, and the processing of agricultural products, especially tobacco.

In 1986 the Government introduced a new investment code, which provided incentives for domestic and foreign private investment in activities outside the public sector (and areas seen as strategic), particularly in manufacturing for the export market. Rules on foreign exchange and the number of expatriate employees were relaxed and private investors were granted tax incentives. For small and medium-sized enterprises, profits are exempt from corporation tax for the first five years, after which there is tax relief for a further five years. A number of EPZs were established and attracted foreign investors, particularly from South-East Asia, Mauritius and France. In 2004 1,276 companies employed an estimated 115,000 people in the EPZs, although textile companies were a significant part and their number of employees was initially reduced by an estimated 10,000 in 2005. Development of the manufacturing sector overall has been hampered by poor infrastructure and high transportation costs. In mid-2003 new legislation was introduced that allowed foreign investors to acquire property for tourism or industrial development (they had only been able to do so under a long-term lease until that time) and reduced taxes on consumer goods and industrial items, in order to encourage both national and foreign investment. Increased investment remains a priority of the Madagascar Action Plan (MAP).

MINING

Madagascar has sizeable deposits of a wide range of minerals and their exploitation is on the increase, with higher commodity prices helping to offset the expense of reaching their remote location. Chromite, graphite and mica are all exported, as are small quantities of semi-precious stones such as topaz, garnet and amethyst. The main deposits of chromium ore at Andriamena contributed to a chromite output of 131,293 metric tons in 2000, which decreased to only 10,700 tons in 2002, before recovering to 42,156 tons in 2003, 82,839 in 2004 and over 100,000 tons in 2005, as the reopening of the Bemanevika pit (with its reserves of 2.2m. tons) offset declines at Andriamena; this was expected to underpin production in future years. Graphite output reached 40,328 tons in 2000 before drastically declining to 2,000 tons in 2002 and then recovering to 15,000 tons in 2004. Production of mica, which had reached 1,138 tons in 1997, remained at only 90 tons annually in 2002–04.

One major project is Rio Tinto's ilmenite (titanium ore) mine in an area of coastal rainforest and sand-dunes near to Fort Dauphin (Tolagnaro) in the south-east, operated through its subsidiary QIT Madagascar Minerals Ltd (QMM). Construction of the mining facilities together with a deep-sea, multi-purpose port facility at Ehoala commenced in 2006, and will cost an estimated US $585m. Production at the new facility is scheduled to commence in late 2008, with an initial capacity of some 750,000 metric tons, which could equate to 10% of global output per annum. The project is expected to bring substantial revenues to the Malagasy Government and will stimulate economic development in that part of the country. However, there are considerable concerns over the social impact of the development, and over the environmental impact on such a fragile landscape. A separate $150m. ilmenite project near Toliara is being studied by Madagascar Resources, a company backed by three South African companies, including Anglo-American.

The other major current project is the exploitation of nickel deposits in the Moramanga area, where Dynatec Corpn of Canada expect to start production from the nickel mine at Ambatovy in early 2008, with anticipated full production of 60,000 metric tons of nickel and 5,600 tons of cobalt per year, and with operating costs expected to be among the lowest in the world. A consortium led by Korea Resources Corpn took a 27.5% stake in the mine through the provision of US $1,200m. of finance and will receive one-half of the planned output of the mine for the first 15 years (the Republic of Korea is the world's fourth largest consumer of nickel). Sumitomo also has a 27.5% stake, while Dynatec, acquired in 2007 by another Canadian company, Sherritt, retains 40%. The project is expected to employ 8,500 people, contribute some $85m. per year to Madagascar's GNP, and to have a life of 28 years.

Other mineral projects include the eventual exploitation of an estimated 100m. metric tons of bauxite at Manantenina in the south-east of the country, in which Alcan is involved, and coal deposits, also estimated at 100m. tons, with Pan African Mining among the companies involved. A number of companies are developing platinum projects, including Jubilee Platinum which has 100,000 ha of concessions in north-central and south-eastern Madagascar. There is also potential in diamonds, in gold (for which minimal official production has been recorded, but which unofficially provided an estimated 2–3 tons annually), and uranium.

The discovery of sapphires in early 1997 in the north of the island prompted the arrival of thousands of unofficial miners, who caused serious damage to the Ankarana nature reserve. A further discovery in the south in 1998 prompted a further influx and aroused the interest of foreign investors. Sapphires worth some US $100m. were reported to have been mined by early 1999 although little tax income came to the country, and the Government ordered the suspension of sapphire mining, pending the results of studies into the effects of exploitation on the environment. However, unauthorized mining continued on a wide scale and one-half of the world's sapphires are now estimated to come from Madagascar.

In early 2000 a new mining code came into force, setting out the legal and environmental framework for the sector. According to the IMF, mining investments in the country increased by 53% in 2005, to US $542m. Royalties and fees have increased but will amount to only $200,000 and $1.6m., respectively, in 2007 according to the MAP, although as production increases they should rise and could reach the Government's target of

$15m. and $45m., respectively, in 2012 if mineral exports rise to $300m.

ENERGY

Madagascar's prospects for reducing fuel imports were improved by the development of hydroelectric power. The Andekaleka hydroelectric scheme, which began operations in 1982, supplies the regions of Antananarivo and Antsirabe, as well as the Andriamena chromite mine. There are seven hydroelectric stations, which provided an estimated 64% of electricity production in 2005, while the remainder came from thermal installations. However, fuel wood and charcoal are estimated still to provide 84% of the country's total energy needs. Petroleum products account for 11% of energy consumption and the remaining 5% is provided by electricity. Many mines and factories have their own small diesel- or steam-powered generators. Fuel imports accounted for 10.1% of total merchandise imports in 2004.

Madagascar has sizeable potential onshore and offshore petroleum reserves, which will vastly improve the country's economic position. For some years the USSR provided about two-thirds of Madagascar's imports of petroleum, some on a concessionary financing basis, but in 1988 the USSR suspended deliveries of petroleum, owing to unpaid bills totalling some US $240m. Madagascar subsequently bought crude petroleum at market prices from Iran, Libya and Gabon, and suffered from the 70% increase in petroleum prices in 1999–2000, when transport charges doubled.

In the 1980s several foreign companies signed concession agreements with the Government to prospect in a number of areas, particularly in the Morandava basin in western Madagascar. The war in the Persian (Arabian) Gulf in 1990–91 stimulated interest among Western petroleum companies in locating deposits of petroleum outside the Gulf region, although only deposits of oil and natural gas regarded as non-commercial were found. Contracts for further exploration were granted in 1997, in 1999 and in mid-2004, while work continued on deposits of heavy petroleum at Tsimororo and on the Bemolanga oil sands. Madagascar Oil, which has financed these and other projects, has raised $85m. to date. High international petroleum prices in 2006 and advances in deep-sea technology improved the potential profitability of reserves, which helped the Government's auction for drilling rights. Official estimates of offshore basin reserves were 500m. barrels, although exact amounts remain unknown. Initial projections estimated that Madagascar could produce 60,000 barrels per day by 2010. By July 2006 the Government had awarded nine prospecting licenses to companies from the People's Republic of China, France, Norway, the Republic of Korea, the United Kingdom and the USA; a further auction in November was less successful, yet still brought new entrants. The proposed tax of 30% on profits from the industry, to be spent on infrastructure and education, was expected to increase the country's incomes, although there are concerns about transparency.

In 1995, under pressure from the World Bank, the Government relinquished the state monopoly on retail sales of petroleum products. The privatization of Solitany Malagasy, the state petroleum company, was completed by October 2000 following a long delay, and included the sale of the country's only refinery in Toamasina to Galana, a Mauritian company. Production at the plant had for many years been below capacity, and production eventually ceased in 2004.

In 2005 the Government awarded a two-year contract for the management of the national electricity and water utility Jiro sy rano Malagasy (JIRAMA) to the German company Lahmeyer International. However, the management company faced extensive financial problems, exacerbated by high rates of inflation and petroleum prices and by the depreciation of the Malagasy currency. The World Bank offered emergency funding of US $5m. for JIRAMA to maintain operations and a further $10m. in 2006, to help restore a minimum level of operational and financial performance, and to reflect support for the Government's decision to increase prices ahead of the presidential election. (In 2005 two tariff increases were implemented, raising electricity prices by 76%. This was consolidated in 2006 with a further increase of 15%, and an increase of 20% in water charges.) The Lahmeyer contract was not extended after its two-year term, although the German chief executive remained to ensure continuity. JIRAMA's problems continued in the first half of 2007 when power shortages and cuts disrupted industrial production and contributed to unrest in several cities. Reforms are still needed to meet growing demand (the number of subscribers increased on average by 8% per annum between 1996 and 2005) and to widen access to electricity, still limited to 24% of the population in 2005 and to barely 5% of those living outside the major cities. As part of a government proposal to double rural access to electricity to 10% by 2010, a new agency was created to encourage private investment and the use of new sources of energy, such as solar and wind, as well as further development of hydroelectricity. For 2007–12 the MAP also envisaged the need for further supplies of 2,000 MW–3,000 MW to cover growth, especially in the energy-intensive mining sector

TRANSPORT

Madagascar's mountainous topography has hindered the development of adequate communications and the infrastructure is also prone to cyclone damage, making even major routes impassable in bad weather. In June 2000 the Government started a motorway and road development programme funded by the World Bank and the EU. In 2002 the EU pledged US $10m. for the reconstruction of 11 bridges destroyed during the political crisis, and in 2003 Japan committed to assistance in building several bridges and a bypass road in the capital, which was opened in early 2007. The African Development Fund approved a large-scale loan and grant in mid-2004 aimed at improving the transport infrastructure in Toliary province, with a long-term goal of helping to alleviate poverty in the region. Improving and integrating the transport infrastructure is a major feature of the Government's MAP, which has targeted increasing regularly maintained national roads from 5,700 km in 2005 to 12,000 km by 2012, and rural roads from 1,300 km to 13,000 km over the same period, and which would give two-thirds of communes permanent access to all-weather roads.

In 2001 there were 893 km of railway. Three lines in the north of the country primarily served the capital, while the fourth in the south linked Fianarantsoa to the east coast. A 72-km extension to a line on the northern system was opened in 1986. In 1994 Cyclone Geralda damaged the line from Antananarivo to Toamasina so extensively that the World Bank recommended its replacement by a road link. However, Comazar of South Africa was awarded the operating concession for the Madarail Ltd northern railway network in 2001, including access to the port at Toamasina. Comazar committed to invest 150m. French francs over five years to upgrade the network, and in 2003 the EIB granted a €11m. loan towards its rehabilitation, completing the privatization process. Insufficient bids at the end of 2005 for the concession to operate the smaller southern network between Fianarantsoa and the neglected port of Manankara led instead to Madarail taking a two-year management contract.

Domestic air services are important to Madagascar, on account of its size, difficult terrain and the poor quality of road and rail networks. There are 211 airfields, two-thirds of which are privately owned. The main international airport is at Antananarivo, where there are plans to increase its capacity to 3m. passengers per year by 2012 through the construction of a new terminal and an additional runway. The Government owns 90% of the national airline, Air Madagascar, which lost its monopoly on domestic services in 1995; few competitors subsequently emerged, although Air Transport et Transit Régional has started a regional operation. On international routes, Air Madagascar in effect operates a duopoly with Air France; it has improved its finances, despite the high level of fuel prices, and has introduced new flights on international routes while also reducing its domestic network. The possible privatization of Air Madagascar was delayed owing to outstanding debts and other issues, and the present Government has stated it will retain ownership of the company. The lack of competition and subsequent high prices for flights remain a constraint on tourism growth.

Toamasina and Mahajanga, the principal seaports, have suffered from a lack of storage space and equipment, but are receiving new investment in part financed by a tax on the importing of containers that was introduced in 2000. Toamasina port handles about 70% of Madagascar's foreign trade and was in the process of being enlarged when it was destroyed by a cyclone in 1986; it suffered further serious damage from cyclones in 1994, in 2003 and in 2007, which also damaged Mahajanga. Toamasina port is independently managed by the Philippine company International Container Terminal Services, Inc., which in July 2007 completed the US $30m. first phase of its modernization programme. Other ports are operated by the Malagasy Ports Authority, which in 2006 upgraded three of the country's other significant ports (Mahajanga, Toliary and Antsiranana/Nosy-Bé) to prepare them for similar private concessions and investment. Coastal shipping is conducted mainly by private companies. The Government announced plans in 2007 to rehabilitate the Pangalanes canal, which runs for 600 km near the east coast from Toamasina to Farafangana.

TOURISM

In 1989 the Government introduced a tourism investment programme, which aimed to achieve 100,000 tourist arrivals by 1995 by exploiting specialist markets attracted by Madagascar's unusual varieties of wildlife, and in the early 1990s a number of state-owned hotels were transferred to private-sector ownership. Tourist arrivals of 74,619 in 1995 were less than the target, although numbers increased consistently thereafter, reaching 160,071 in 2000, when tourism receipts totalled US $116m. and made the sector the country's second most important source of foreign currency earnings. Activity in the sector was seriously affected in 2002 by the political and economic turmoil following the disputed presidential election of December 2001, although it was judged to have recovered well in 2003, to 139,000 arrivals and further in 2004, to 228,785 arrivals. Revenue from tourism totalled $231m. in 2006, when the number of tourists was 311,000, an increase of 14% on the 277,000 arrivals in 2005, and helped by marketing efforts in France and Italy, the leading sources of visitors. With its unique biodiversity and strikingly varied scenery, Madagascar has considerable potential for the development of eco-tourism, which should be helped by the commitment to expand the country's protected areas, while improving infrastructure. One difficult area is the necessary expansion of hotels, as foreign investors are deterred to some extent by the difficulty in acquiring full ownership of land, but various new openings have been announced.

EXTERNAL TRADE AND BALANCE OF PAYMENTS

Imports increased at an unhealthy rate for the economy in the 1980s, owing to the official policy of industrialization and an overriding emphasis on investment. As the balance of payments became increasingly unfavourable, the Government was obliged to yield to pressure from the IMF, the World Bank and Western aid donors and creditors to liberalize trade and to adjust the Malagasy franc exchange rate. The reforms succeeded in reducing the external current-account deficit, as a result of improved export earnings. However, the deficit continued to fluctuate and increased again to reach US $291m. in 1996. The Government moved to reduce import restrictions and to introduce comprehensive tariff reforms. In 1988 the Government simplified import procedures and also announced the removal of export duties from all goods except those, such as coffee, handled by state marketing boards, which helped to give a trade surplus of $1m. in 1989, although this had become a deficit the next year of $249m. The deficit continued to fluctuate and in 2000 it stood at $174m. In 2001 it was only $27m., but increased again to $117m. in 2002 and to $258m. in 2003. In 2004 and 2005, it increased again, to $437m. and to $592m., respectively.

In 2000 there was a deficit of US $283m. on the current account of the balance of payments, which was reduced to $170m. in 2001, before increasing to $298m. in 2002 and to $458m. in 2003. It continued to increase in 2004 and 2005, to $541m. and $626m., respectively. The principal exports in 2004 were from the EPZs (totalling $497m.), while the export of vanilla totalled $120m. and shellfish $50m. in the same year, according to the EIU. The principal imports in 2004 were capital goods, raw materials, consumer goods and fuel products. Receipts from merchandise exports declined in 2005, owing to the sharp fall in vanilla prices and lower shrimp exports from overfishing. Import volumes also declined, owing to reduced economic activity and because of the termination of a duty exemption scheme on capital goods. The IMF reported that the current account balance (including official transfers) improved from 10.9% of GDP in 2005 to an estimated 8.8% in 2006.

According to the EIU, the principal sources of imports in 2004 were China (17.6%), France (16.3%), Iran, South Africa and India. The principal markets for exports were the USA (35.4%) and France (30.4%). In an effort to boost the country's economic recovery, the Government authorized from August 2003 a suspension of import taxes and tariffs for two years on capital goods and selected commodities, which caused a surge in imports in 2004 and incurred the disapproval of the Bretton Woods institutions; the Government revoked the suspension in 2005, although much damage had already been done.

ECONOMIC POLICY, PLANNING AND AID

There was a noticeable rise in the cost of living in the 1980s when successive devaluations of the Malagasy franc and the lack of any appreciable increase in the wages of non-agricultural workers put the cost of basic necessities beyond the means of the average Malagasy. Even though Madagascar's overall economic condition improved, lower levels of production, especially in export crops, caused an increasing dependence on costly imports, particularly fuel and rice, and on foreign aid.

After significant rescheduling and cancellation of debt by the 'Paris Club', debt-servicing costs were reduced, although debt servicing still represented 33.1% of the value of exports of goods and services in 1991; the ratio had declined to 9.6% by 1994, but largely because much of the debt service due went unpaid, leading to a steep accumulation of arrears. External debt at the end of 2004 totalled US $3,462m., of which $3,232m. was long-term public debt; the cost of debt servicing in the previous year was estimated to be equivalent to 6.0% of the value of exports of goods and services. Madagascar has benefited from further cancellation of debt, with the IMF cancelling $197m. in 2005. The Fund estimated in June 2006 that debt relief had left Madagascar's external debt on a broadly sustainable basis. External public debt was equivalent to 69.9% of GDP in 2005, but estimated at just 28.8% in 2006.

From an annual average inflation rate of just over 11% per year in 1990–93, consumer prices increased in 1994 and 1995 by 39% and 49% respectively, as a result of the devaluation of the currency, a less disciplined monetary policy and the effects of the boom in world coffee prices. The rate of inflation slowed to 19.8% in 1996 and to just 4.5% in 1997, before gradually increasing to reach 15.9% in 2002, giving an average of 15.7% per year in 1990–2001. In 2003 there was deflation of 1.2% owing to the effect on the economy of the political crisis and blockade, but inflation increased to 27.1% in 2004, and was 11.4% in 2005, according to the IMF. The sharp rise in energy prices was a major factor in the high level of inflation, which was estimated at 10.9% in 2006. The Government's tight monetary policy has helped to keep inflation under control in the mid-2000s, but the continued high prices of fuel worldwide, and of food due to cyclone damage, will make its target of maintaining the rate of inflation below 10% difficult to achieve in 2007.

A general strike in 1991 severely affected the country's finances and, despite a substantial decline in capital expenditure, the ensuing fall in tax revenue together with increased other expenditure caused a rise in the budget deficit in 1991 to 5.5% of GDP. Reserves of foreign exchange declined to US $89m. Economic conditions failed to improve in 1992, owing to continued political instability. In 1993 the new Government initiated negotiations with the Bretton Woods institutions to obtain funding through a further economic reform programme (agreed in early 1994 on condition of a number of economic reforms), which political opposition made difficult to enact (see Recent History). Severe cyclones in early 1994 resulted in a further deterioration in the economy. In May the Government accepted the conditions imposed by the World Bank and the IMF, notably the 'floating' of the Malagasy franc, which resulted in an immediate devaluation; the removal of price controls; further privatization; and measures to reduce expenditure, including substantial retrenchment in the civil service. In February 1995 the Government accepted a number of economic measures similar to those agreed to in June 1994, including the imposition of a new tax on petroleum products and restrictions on loans by the central bank to private enterprises, while the World Bank and IMF agreed to a doubling of the minimum wage and some increased expenditure.

Continued political tension in early 1996 stalled the necessary reforms, and the IMF assessed that no new deal with the Fund would be possible without a cohesive government. The appointment of Norbert Ratsirahonana as Prime Minister in May 1996, followed by a successful vote of confidence in July on the reforms, opened the way for the IMF in August to agree to the Government's economic policy framework document for 1996–99, which set out the measures needed to satisfy the aid donors, mainly controlling inflation, promoting growth and investment, and improving the working of the foreign-exchange market. Discussions continued during the presidential elections and in November 1996 the IMF approved a three-year loan of US $118m., and subsequent negotiations with the 'Paris Club' of official creditors resulted in yet another reduction of Madagascar's debt, by 67%.

The economy progressed well in 1997–98, with real GDP growth exceeding population growth and a reduction in the rate of inflation, but slow progress with structural reforms and a deterioration in fiscal performance prompted the IMF to delay the disbursement of a second structural-adjustment credit. Privatization policies in particular advanced little due to a strike by civil servants in early 1998 and demands by French petroleum companies for compensation for assets nationalized by the first Ratsiraka Government, which was agreed in late 1998; by May 1999 a settlement had been agreed on compensation for all French businesses nationalized in the 1970s.

In late 1998 the Government announced measures to widen the tax base and to improve customs and tax administration, including the removal of exemptions and an extension of value-added tax. Following the sale of the state-owned Banky Fampandrosoana ny Varotra in December, the Government pledged to complete by June 2000 the first phase of its privatization programme, involving 46 companies, but several major enterprises remained under state control, which delayed the release of recently agreed World Bank and IMF funding. Proceeds from the privatization programme totalled only US $7.2m. in 1999, compared with a forecast of $83m. that year. However, tax receipts improved in 1999 to reach the IMF target of 11.3% of GNI. Investment was equivalent to only 12.3% of GNI in 1999, the low level attributed largely to investors' reluctance to commit finance pending the resolution of the Government's problems with the Bretton Woods institutions.

The serious damage caused by three cyclones in February to April 2000, which killed more than 100 people and which destroyed crops and infrastructure, led to significant international aid of US $20.1m. An IMF review in June 2000 concluded that economic growth had been sustained, export performance had improved, the external current-account deficit had narrowed and international reserves had increased. These factors and progress in the privatization of the banking sector led the IMF to disburse $41m. and to extend until November the Poverty Reduction and Growth Facility (PRGF—the former Enhanced Structural Adjustment Facility), while advising the continuation of the privatization process and the reform of the legal system. In November Madagascar participated in the formation of a free trade area between nine (and subsequently 11) of the 20 countries of the Common Market for Eastern and Southern Africa (COMESA), which eliminated all tariff barriers. In December the International Development Association (IDA) and the IMF agreed to support a comprehensive debt-reduction package under the enhanced initiative for heavily indebted poor countries (HIPC), amounting to $1,500m. or 40% of total debt outstanding.

The country's economic performance in 2000 was again affected by cyclones, which destroyed crops and reduced tourism receipts, owing to damage to infrastructure and a cholera outbreak. Inflation rose to 11.9%, GNI growth was only 4.5%, and the budget deficit increased to US $200m. The franc remained relatively stable, however, while exports increased and currency reserves reached their highest ever level, at $350m. In September the World Bank's investment portfolio in the country included 18 projects, accounting for $629m.

In March 2001 the IMF approved a new three-year loan of US $103m. under the PRGF, with $15m. available immediately, following the successful completion of the first three-year programme in December 2000. The 'Paris Club' consequently agreed an interim settlement that directly cancelled $161m. of debt and rescheduled $93m. over a period of 23 years, with a six-year period of grace. Textile exports, particularly to the USA, had increased substantially during the period of an IMF-supported programme, and Madagascar's eligibility for the textile provisions of AGOA, also approved in March 2001, allowed duty-free access to the US market until 2004, leading to further rises. The establishment within the EPZs of information technology firms (processing archives and data for large foreign firms) was also a positive development.

In mid-2001 a World Trade Organization report commended economic reforms in the country since 1998, which had contributed to significant GDP growth, of 4.8% in 2000 and 6.7% in 2001. Foreign investment had also increased, as had taxation revenue (equivalent to 12% of GDP in 2000). In December 2001 the IMF reiterated the analysis of strong growth, increased exports and reduced inflation for that year, but expressed concern at the continuing high level of poverty in Madagascar. The overall budget deficit for 2001 was estimated at 4.4% of GDP.

However, in response to the political and economic disruption that followed the disputed presidential election in late 2001 (see Recent History), international financial organizations 'froze' the nation's assets and the central bank was closed, rendering the country unable to service its debts. The six months of economic blockades, destruction of infrastructure and general strikes meant that the economy had largely ceased to function. It was estimated that between 150,000 and 500,000 jobs were lost in the economic crisis, and the loss of foreign investment was sizeable if hard to quantify.

In July 2002 a 'Friends of Madagascar' meeting of donors took place in Paris, at which some US $2,300m. of aid over four years was pledged; the IMF and World Bank accounted for one-half of this figure and France and the USA granted aid of $150m. and $100m., respectively. In its economic programme the new Government emphasized its commitment to good governance and its plans for private-sector development, including encouraging the return of foreign investment with long-awaited legislation on foreign investment in mining accelerated through the National Assembly. The international aid allowed the country to repay the arrears that had accumulated on its external payments during the crisis, and from August the foreign-exchange markets reopened, with the currency settling to a relatively stable level following an initial depreciation. In November the Government confirmed that it had applied for membership of the Southern African Development Community (SADC), and was officially admitted as a member in August 2004. The IMF disbursed a $100m. Structural Adjustment Credit in October and a $50m. Emergency Economic Recovery Credit in November 2002, as well as loans towards reforming public-sector management and developing the private sector. Following legislative elections in December 2002, the Fund approved the disbursement of $15m. under the PRGF, extending the arrangement until November 2004, and granted a further $4m. in interim assistance under the HIPC initiative. According to the IMF, real GDP declined by 12.7% in 2002, due to the crisis and poor weather, and with government expenditure significantly reduced owing to lower external aid and privatization receipts.

In early 2003, despite comparative political stability, the social and economic situation in Madagascar declined further, owing to a long drought and some cyclone damage. However, France, Germany and the United Kingdom cancelled further significant amounts of Malagasy debt, and in June the IMF granted an additional US $15.9m. under the PRGF. From the end of July the country replaced the Malagasy franc with its former currency, the ariary; the two currencies circulated simultaneously until November 2004 (subsequently extended to 2006); accounts were changed on 1 January 2005, at a rate of 1 ariary to 5 francs. Real GDP was estimated by the IMF to have increased by 9.8% in 2003, which while impressive was not a full recovery from the previous year.

A depreciation of the currency in 2004, together with further severe cyclone damage and high international petroleum prices, had an inflationary effect on the economy, leading to national discontent and international concern. However, the performance of the EPZs, the busy construction sector and the improving agricultural industry all supported the rate of real GDP growth. In response to the severe cyclones in March, the IMF immediately released US $35m. in funds and extended the PRGF until March 2005. In July 2004 the World Bank granted a Poverty Reduction Support Credit of $88m. and a credit of $37m. under the Poverty Reduction Strategy Paper programme. In August the EU approved two grants to the country amounting to €165m. for development programmes in the southern provinces in 2005–11. In mid-2004 President Jacques Chirac of France announced, during an informal visit to the country, that France would forgive the remaining public debt owed to it by Madagascar, which amounted to some €70m., once the country had met the conditions of the IMF's HIPC initiative. As a member of COMESA, Madagascar started to participate in a customs union operational from December 2004. In November, following the successful fulfilment of the criteria of the HIPC initiative in the preceding month, the 'Paris Club' of creditors once more restructured the country's debt, with many participants joining France in cancelling the whole amount owed to them. The overall debt was scheduled to decrease by some $836m. and the ratio of debt service to exports of goods and services was estimated to have decreased to 6% in 2004 compared with 32% in 1990. Subsequently, Madagascar also successfully completed the PRGF. The economy had withstood challenging factors in 2004 and grown at a rate of 5.3%.

In April 2005 Madagascar was the first country to negotiate a compact with the USA under the Millennium Challenge Account programme, whereby some US $110m. was to be disbursed over four years. In July following a summit of the Group of Eight leading industrialized countries (G-8) held in Gleneagles, Scotland, in July, Madagascar qualified as a primary candidate for debt cancellation, owing to its success in the HIPC schedule, and received a second Poverty Reduction Support Credit, of $80m., from the World Bank; a grant of $129m. under an IDA 'integrated growth poles' project, to stimulate economic growth in the three export processing zones; and a further IDA credit of $30m. for health sector projects to combat HIV/AIDS (which remains at a low level of incidence). In 2005 the economic growth rate was 4.6%, which was lower than forecast owing to substantial fuel price increases exacerbated by inconsistencies in power supply from JIRAMA. The ending of the textile industry's international MFA had a negative impact on the industrial sector, particularly the EPZs. However, tourism recorded consistent growth, contributing 3.0% of GDP in 2005, and agriculture performed better than in preceding years as the country escaped severe cyclones, with the primary sector accounting for 27.9% of GDP. Foreign direct investment doubled in 2005 from the previous year.

In 2006 the Government formulated the MAP for 2007–12, to succeed the PRSP and to pursue the World Bank's Millennium Development Goals of halving poverty by 2015. In mid-2006 the World Bank approved a new PRGF arrangement of US $81m. over three years, in support of the Government's own economic programme for 2006–08. Also in mid-2006 the French telecommunications company Alcatel was awarded the tender to construct the $205m. East African Submarine Cable System, linking countries including Madagascar via 9,900 km of high-performance fibre-optic cable along the seabed between South Africa and Sudan. The project was originally scheduled to be completed by the end of 2007 but has been delayed until 2008 and will greatly reduce communication costs in the region, providing a strong advantage to the information technologies business park planned under the 'integrated growth poles' scheme.

Madagascar has one of the lowest tax revenue-to-GDP ratios in the world, at around 10%, although there was an increase in 2005 and 2006, to 10.5% and 11.5%, respectively; further increases in revenue remain a strong priority and necessary to reduce dependency on aid, which was estimated to be US $929m. in 2005. The combination of higher duties in some areas (such as on petroleum and diesel in 2006), measures to improve the administration of value-added tax and a simplified tax structure should help to raise the figure to nearer 15%. GDP increased by an estimated 4.7% in 2006, which continues a positive recent trend but was lower than earlier forecasts and still not sufficient to make a substantial impact on poverty in the country, especially in rural areas, and particularly if the rate of population growth continues at around 3%. Necessary reductions in expenditure were in part offset by the benefits of the Multilateral Debt Relief Initiative, which amounted to 0.6% of GDP. A government overspend of 60,000m. ariary (US $ 29m.) was largely due to one-off factors, as the IMF accepted in its review in December 2006, which commended the Government but demanded, *inter alia*, tax reform and reform of JIRAMA. The EU's approval of the Malagasy Government's policies prompted an increased allocation of funds under the ninth programme of the Fonds Européens de développement (FED) and a commitment of €462m. under the tenth FED. The budget deficit stayed at around 5% of GDP.

In 2007 the World Bank and the IMF confirmed their support for the country and its prudent macroeconomic policies, agreeing a further US $140m. per annum for 2007–11 under the Strategic Country Assistance programme and $69m. of finance for investment in health, mines, transport, telecommunications and governance. The ariary moved in line with the euro and strengthened against a weak US dollar, which prompted the central bank to intervene on a small scale to help exporters. Continued problems of power supply in cities such as Antsiranana and Toliara affected industry and prompted civil unrest. The Government's constitutional reforms included plans to increase the role of the communes in economic development, with a target of trebling local tax collection and giving the communes 10% of the total budget by 2012, compared with 1.5% in 2005. The severe cyclone season caused extensive damage to infrastructure and crops, especially rice and vanilla, and the Government appealed for $243m. in aid, although it received little of that. The economy was forecast to grow in the region of 5% in 2007.

Statistical Survey

Source (unless otherwise stated): Institut National de la Statistique Malagache, BP 485, Anosy Tana, 101 Antananarivo; tel. (20) 2227418; e-mail dridnstat@wanadoo.mg; internet www.instat.mg; Ministry of Economy, Finance and Budget, BP 61, 101 Antananarivo; internet www.mefb.gov.mg.

Area and Population

AREA, POPULATION AND DENSITY

Area (sq km)	587,041*
Population (census results)	
1974–75†	7,603,790
1–19 August 1993	
Males	5,991,171
Females	6,100,986
Total	12,092,157
Population (UN estimates at mid-year)‡	
2004	18,135,000
2005	18,643,000
2006	19,159,000
Density (per sq km) at mid-2006	32.6

* 226,658 sq miles.

† The census took place in three stages: in provincial capitals on 1 December 1974; in Antananarivo and remaining urban areas on 17 February 1975; and in rural areas on 1 June 1975.

‡ Source: UN, *World Population Prospects: The 2006 Revision*.

PRINCIPAL ETHNIC GROUPS
(estimated population, 1974)

Merina (Hova)	1,993,000	Sakalava	470,156*
Betsimisaraka	1,134,000	Antandroy	412,500
Betsileo	920,600	Antaisaka	406,468*
Tsimihety	558,100		

* 1972 figure.

PRINCIPAL TOWNS
(population at 1993 census)

Antananarivo (capital)	1,103,304	Mahajanga (Majunga)	106,780
Toamasina (Tamatave)	137,782	Toliary (Tuléar)	80,826
Antsirabé	126,062	Antsiranana (Diégo-Suarez)	59,040
Fianarantsoa	109,248		

2001 (estimated population, incl. Renivohitra and Avaradrano): Antananarivo 1,111,392.

Mid-2005 ('000, incl. suburbs, UN estimate): Antananarivo 1,585 (Source: UN, *World Urbanization prospects: The 2005 Revision*).

BIRTHS AND DEATHS

	2004	2005	2006
Birth rate (per 1,000)	38.6	38.0	37.4
Death rate (per 1,000)	11.7	11.5	11.4

Source: African Development Bank.

Expectation of life (years at birth, WHO estimates): 55.8 (males 54.6; females 57.1) in 2005 (Source: African Development Bank).

ECONOMICALLY ACTIVE POPULATION
(labour force survey, '000 persons)

	2005
Agriculture, hunting and forestry	7,745.3
Fishing	99.0
Mining and quarrying	18.8
Manufacturing	267.5
Electricity, gas and water	27.5
Construction	13.0
Wholesale and retail trade; repair of motor vehicles, motor cycles and personal and household goods	470.5
Hotels and restaurants	63.9
Transport, storage and communications	86.3
Financial intermediation	4.1
Public administration and defence; compulsory social security	202.4
Education	44.5
Health and social work	9.9
Other community, social and personal service activities	517.7
Total employed	9,570.4
Unemployed	274.3
Total labour force	9,844.7
Males	4,942.2
Females	4,902.4

Source: ILO.

Health and Welfare

KEY INDICATORS

Total fertility rate (children per woman, 2005)	5.1
Under-5 mortality rate (per 1,000 live births, 2005)	119
HIV/AIDS (% of persons aged 15–49, 2005)	0.5
Physicians (per 1,000 head, 2004)	0.29
Hospital beds (per 1,000 head, 2002)	0.42
Health expenditure (2004): US $ per head (PPP)	28.9
Health expenditure (2004): % of GDP	3.0
Health expenditure (2004): public (% of total)	59.1
Access to water (% of persons, 2004)	50
Access to sanitation (% of persons, 2004)	34
Human Development Index (2004): ranking	143
Human Development Index (2004): value	0.509

For sources and definitions, see explanatory note on p. vi.

Agriculture

PRINCIPAL CROPS
('000 metric tons)

	2003	2004	2005
Rice (paddy)	2,800	3,030	3,400
Maize	318	350	n.a.
Potatoes	255	281	n.a.
Sweet potatoes	493	542	n.a.
Cassava (Manioc)	1,992	2,191	n.a.
Taro (Coco yam)*	200	200	214
Sugar cane	2,236	2,224	2,284*
Dry beans	75	83	n.a.
Groundnuts (in shell)	36	39	n.a.
Coconuts*	85	85	85
Oil palm fruit*	21	21	21
Cottonseed†	8	10	20
Tomatoes*	22	22	23
Bananas*	290	290	303
Oranges*	83	83	83
Mangoes*	210	210	210

—continued	2003	2004	2005
Avocados*	23	23	24
Pineapples*	51	51	51
Cashewapple*	68	68	68
Coffee (green)	70	65	n.a.
Vanilla	3	3	6
Cinnamon (Canella)*	2	2	1
Cloves*	16	16	16
Cotton (lint)†	5	7	6
Sisal	17	17	17*
Tobacco (leaves)	1	2	2

* FAO estimate(s).
† Unofficial figures.

Source: FAO.

LIVESTOCK
('000 head, year ending September)

	2003	2004	2005
Cattle	8,020	8,105	9,687
Pigs*	1,600	1,600	1,600
Sheep	843	650*	703
Goats	1,252	1,249	1,200*
Chickens*	24,000	24,000	24,000
Ducks*	3,800	3,800	3,800
Geese*	3,000	3,000	3,000
Turkeys*	2,000	2,000	2,000

* FAO estimate(s).

Source: FAO.

LIVESTOCK PRODUCTS
('000 metric tons, FAO estimates)

	2002	2003	2004
Cattle meat	111.6	114.8	146.6
Sheep meat	2.5	3.2	2.5
Goat meat	6.1	6.1	6.1
Pig meat	70	70	70
Chicken meat	35.5	35.5	35.5
Duck meat	10.6	10.6	10.6
Goose meat	12.6	12.6	12.6
Turkey meat	8.4	8.4	8.4
Cows' milk	535	535	535
Hen eggs	14.9	14.9	14.9
Other eggs	4.5	4.5	4.5
Honey	3.9	3.9	3.9

2005: Production assumed to be unchanged from 2004 (FAO estimates).

Source: FAO.

Forestry

ROUNDWOOD REMOVALS
('000 cubic metres, excl. bark)

	2003	2004	2005
Sawlogs, veneer logs and logs for sleepers	185	160	160
Pulpwood	23	23	23
Fuel wood*	10,486	10,770	11,055
Total	10,694	10,953	11,238

* FAO estimates.

Source: FAO.

SAWNWOOD PRODUCTION
('000 cubic metres, incl. railway sleepers)

	2002	2003	2004
Coniferous (softwood)	4*	8	8
Broadleaved (hardwood)	91	485	886
Total	95	493	894

* FAO estimate.

2005: Production assumed to be unchanged from 2004 (FAO estimates).

Source: FAO.

Fishing

('000 metric tons, live weight)

	2003	2004	2005
Capture	140.8	146.8	136.4
Cichlids	21.5	21.5	21.5
Other freshwater fishes	4.5	4.5	4.5
Narrow-barred Spanish mackerel	12.0	12.0	12.0
Other marine fishes	82.1	89.9	80.0
Shrimps and prawns	13.3	11.3	10.9
Aquaculture	9.5	8.7	8.5*
Giant tiger prawn	7.0	6.2	6.0*
Total catch	150.3	155.5	144.9*

* FAO estimate.

Note: Figures exclude aquatic plants ('000 metric tons, capture only): 1.7 in 2003; n.a. in 2004; n.a. in 2005. Also excluded are crocodiles, recorded by number rather than weight, and shells. The number of Nile crocodiles caught was: 7,300 in 2003; 4,760 in 2004; 4,850 in 2005. The catch of marine shells (in metric tons) was: 194 in 2003; n.a. in 2004; n.a. in 2005.

Source: FAO.

Mining

(metric tons, estimates)

	2003	2004	2005
Chromite*	45,040	77,386	140,000
Salt	26,000	26,000	26,000
Graphite (natural)	15,000	15,000	15,000
Mica	90	90	90

* Figures refer to gross weight. The estimated chromium content is 27%.

Source: US Geological Survey.

Industry

SELECTED PRODUCTS
(metric tons, unless otherwise indicated)

	1999	2000	2001
Raw sugar	61,370	62,487	67,917
Beer ('000 hectolitres)	610.1	645.5	691.7
Cigarettes	3,839	4,139	4,441
Woven cotton fabrics (million sq metres)	20.4	23.3	29.6
Leather footwear ('000 pairs)	460	570	568
Plastic footwear ('000 pairs)	375	303	291
Paints	1,918	1,487	1,554
Soap	15,884	15,385	15,915
Motor spirit—petrol ('000 cu metres)	98.0	122.6	128.3
Kerosene ('000 cu metres)	65.0	65.2	75.1
Gas-diesel (distillate fuel) oil ('000 cu metres)	119.0	150.4	150.2
Residual fuel oils ('000 cu metres)	198.8	225.7	247.2
Cement	45,701	50,938	51,882
Electric energy (million kWh)*	721.3	779.8	833.9

* Production by the state-owned utility only, excluding electricity generated by industries for their own use.

2002: Raw sugar 35,000 metric tons; Beer 439,000 hectolitres; Woven cotton fabrics 20m. sq metres; Soap 14,100 metric tons; Motor spirit—petrol 112,000 metric tons (estimate); Kerosene 66,000 metric tons (estimate); Gas-diesel (distillate fuel) oil 57,000 metric tons (estimate); Residual fuel oils 77,000 metric tons (estimate); Electric energy 840m. kWh (Source: mostly UN, *Industrial Commodity Statistics Yearbook*).

Cement ('000 metric tons, estimates): 80 in 2003; 130 in 2004; 180 in 2005 (: US Geological Survey).

Finance

CURRENCY AND EXCHANGE RATES

Monetary Units
5 iraimbilanja = 1 ariary.

Sterling, Dollar and Euro Equivalents (30 March 2007)
£1 sterling = 3,821.57 ariary;
US $1 = 1,951.67 ariary;
€1 = 2,599.24 ariary;
100,000 ariary = £2.62 = $5.12 = €3.85.

Average Exchange Rate (ariary per US $)
2004 1,868.9
2005 2,003.0
2006 2,142.3

Note: A new currency, the ariary, was introduced on 31 July 2003 to replace the franc malgache (franc MG). The old currency was to remain legal tender until 30 November. Some figures in this survey are still given in terms of francs MG.

BUDGET

('000 million ariary, central government operations)

Revenue and grants	2005	2006*	2007†
Tax revenue	1,020.0	1,259.2	1,523.8
Non-tax revenue	82.8	80.8	28.3
Grants	579.5	5,580.0	699.3
Total	1,682.3	6,920.0	2,251.4

Expenditure	2005	2006*	2007†
Current expenditure	1,107.2	1,240.6	1,411.1
Budgetary expenditure	1,021.5	1,226.2	1,397.5
Wages and salaries	456.4	596.9	721.0
Other non-interest expenditure	298.5	375.9	455.3
Interest payments	266.6	253.4	221.1
Treasury operations (net)	84.2	12.5	13.7
Counterpart funds-financed operations	1.5	1.9	—
Capital expenditure	1,038.3	1,290.3	1,406.8
Total	2,145.5	2,530.9	2,817.9

* Provisional.
† Forecasts.

INTERNATIONAL RESERVES

(US $ million at 31 December)

	2004	2005	2006
IMF special drawing rights	0.2	0.0	0.0
Foreign exchange	503.3	481.2	583.1
Total	503.5	481.2	583.1

Source: IMF, *International Financial Statistics*.

MONEY SUPPLY

('000 million ariary at 31 December)

	2004	2005	2006
Currency outside banks	591.38	599.12	715.05
Demand deposits at deposit money banks	808.05	815.57	1,035.75
Total money	1,399.43	1,414.69	1,750.81

Source: IMF, *International Financial Statistics*.

COST OF LIVING

(Consumer Price Index for Madagascans in Antananarivo; base: 2000 = 100)

	2003	2004	2005
Food	112.9	135.1	170.1
Clothing*	115.4	119.3	122.0
Rent	132.0	150.8	174.8
All items (incl. others)	123.0	140.0	152.6

* Including household linen.

2006: All items 183.7.

Source: ILO.

NATIONAL ACCOUNTS

Expenditure on the Gross Domestic Product
('000 million ariary at current prices)

	2004	2005	2006*
Government final consumption expenditure	778.0	849.1	993.4
Private final consumption expenditure	6,725.1	8,349.2	9,739.2
Increase in stocks; Gross fixed capital formation	1,980.8	2,276.3	2,563.5
Total domestic expenditure	9,483.9	11,474.6	13,296.1
Exports of goods and services	2,650.7	2,674.8	3,230.6
Less Imports of goods and services	3,979.0	4,052.0	4,766.0
Statistical discrepancy†	—	461.7	33.0
GDP in purchasers' values	8,155.7	10,559.1	11,793.7
GDP at constant 1984 prices	498.8	521.7	546.4

* Provisional.
† Representing the difference between the expenditure and production approaches.

Gross Domestic Product by Economic Activity
('000 million francs MG at current prices)

	2002	2003	2004
Agriculture, hunting, forestry and fishing	8,963	9,073	9,857
Mining and quarrying; Manufacturing; Electricity, gas and water	4,078	4,777	5,456
Construction	552	652	794
Trade, restaurants and hotels	3,555	3,909	4,316
Transport, storage and communications	4,817	5,154	5,796
Financial intermediation	246	293	324
Administration	1,641	2,140	2,281
Other services	4,610	5,289	5,644
Sub-total	28,462	31,287	34,468
Less imputed bank charges	196	226	251
GDP at factor cost	28,265	31,061	34,217
Indirect taxes, less subsidies	1,777	2,803	3,435
GDP in purchasers' values	30,042	33,863	37,651

Source: Ministry of the Economy, Finance and Budget.

2004 ('000 million ariary at current prices): Agriculture, hunting, forestry and fishing 2,135.2; Industry 1,182.6; Services 4,148.8; *Sub-total* 7,466.6; Imputed bank charges –52.4; *GDP at factor cost* 7,414.2; Indirect taxes, less subsidies 741.5; *GDP in purchasers' values* 8,155.7.

2005 ('000 million ariary at current prices): Agriculture, hunting, forestry and fishing 2,668.8; Industry 1,476.6; Services 5,519.2; *Sub-total* 9,664.6; Imputed bank charges –70.2; *GDP at factor cost* 9,574.4; Indirect taxes, less subsidies 981.6; *GDP in purchasers' values* 10,559.1.

2006 ('000 million ariary at current prices, provisional): Agriculture, hunting, forestry and fishing 2,967.5; Industry 1,656.7; Services 6,143.1; *Sub-total* 10,767.3; Imputed bank charges –79.6; *GDP at factor cost* 10,688.0; Indirect taxes, less subsidies 1,105.6; *GDP in purchasers' values* 11,793.7.

BALANCE OF PAYMENTS
(US $ million)

	2003	2004	2005
Exports of goods f.o.b.	854	990	834
Imports of goods f.o.b.	–1,111	–1,427	–1,427
Trade balance	–258	–437	–592
Exports of services	322	425	498
Imports of services	–619	–637	–615
Balance on goods and services	–555	–649	–710
Other income received	16	15	24
Other income paid	–94	–89	–104
Balance on goods, services and income	–632	–723	–790
Current transfers received	357	245	208
Current transfers paid	–183	–62	–45
Current balance	–458	–541	–626
Capital account (net)	143	182	192
Direct investment from abroad	13	53	85
Other investment assets	–29	295	11
Other investment liabilities	–110	–97	–102
Net errors and omissions	67	–35	91
Overall balance	–374	–143	–349

Source: IMF, *International Financial Statistics*.

External Trade

PRINCIPAL COMMODITIES
(US $ million)

Imports c.i.f.	2002	2003	2004
Food and live animals	60.3	123.7	117.8
Cereals and cereal preparations	23.7	79.0	67.4
Rice	10.3	50.2	34.4
Mineral fuels, lubricants and related materials	219.2	233.4	280.3
Petroleum, petroleum products and related materials	216.9	231.6	275.5
Crude petroleum and oils obtained from bituminous materials	77.8	84.1	0.0
Residual petroleum products	2.5	3.8	7.8
Gas oils	136.6	143.7	267.7
Chemicals and related products	61.9	107.0	103.2
Medicinal and pharmaceutical products	27.0	35.8	36.6
Basic manufactures	71.9	162.3	196.5
Textile yarn and related products	11.5	31.0	45.1
Woven cotton fabrics	2.7	4.8	6.0
Machinery and transport equipment	92.9	218.8	369.3
Electric machinery, apparatus and appliances	16.8	36.8	42.2
Road vehicles	28.8	69.3	121.3
Miscellaneous manufactures	34.6	86.9	78.3
Total (incl. others)	566.1	992.9	1,204.2

Exports f.o.b.	2002	2003	2004
Food and live animals	390.2	366.2	258.2
Fish, crustaceans and molluscs and preparations thereof	162.3	69.1	61.7
Crustaceans and molluscs	130.5	66.5	59.3
Vegetables and fruit	22.5	16.8	26.5
Coffee, tea, cocoa, spices	203.6	275.9	158.4
Spices	191.1	263.1	147.7
Vanilla	165.5	231.5	118.6
Cloves	23.2	29.4	26.9
Crude materials, inedible, except fuels	35.4	38.4	47.1
Basic manufactures	33.5	28.6	31.8
Miscellaneous manufactures	145.9	10.4	53.4
Articles of apparel and clothing accessories	113.2	1.7	1.6
Men's and boys' outerwear	32.0	0.2	0.1
Women's, girls' and infants' outerwear	17.4	0.5	0.6
Knitted or crocheted outerwear	46.2	0.0	0.0
Total (incl. others)	639.7	494.5	426.6

Source: UN, *International Trade Statistics Yearbook*.

PRINCIPAL TRADING PARTNERS
(US $ million)

Imports	2002	2003	2004
Bahrain	57.2	19.0	107.7
Belgium	8.8	20.0	38.7
China, People's Repub.	33.2	96.9	123.6
France	85.6	162.5	184.5
Germany	14.9	36.8	50.1
Hong Kong	1.3	1.1	2.6
India	21.0	48.7	52.2
Indonesia	12.3	23.7	20.3
Italy	8.8	17.8	22.3
Japan	10.3	26.8	51.1
Korea, Republic	6.4	13.3	15.5
Malaysia	8.4	16.9	21.2
Mauritius	18.0	26.0	19.0
Pakistan	3.5	23.9	15.4
Qatar	17.6	0.5	0.5
South Africa	29.7	85.6	87.6
Thailand	2.9	13.6	30.6
United Arab Emirates	79.1	27.4	17.7
United Kingdom	4.2	11.4	19.3
USA	14.3	28.6	38.6
Total (incl. others)	566.1	992.9	1,204.2

Exports	2002	2003	2004
Belgium	8.6	5.2	4.0
Canada	13.8	9.4	8.8
France	267.4	152.2	152.6
Germany	31.0	20.6	13.2
Hong Kong	7.4	7.7	7.6
Italy	19.4	8.0	12.7
Japan	23.9	13.5	10.2
Mauritius	19.9	43.3	24.5
Netherlands	8.4	3.8	5.0
Singapore	20.9	25.2	23.9
South Africa	1.2	4.2	1.6
Spain	13.7	5.1	9.6
Thailand	6.8	7.9	3.2
United Kingdom	21.7	7.6	3.1
USA	128.9	129.5	87.9
Total (incl. others)	639.7	494.5	426.6

Source: UN, *International Trade Statistics Yearbook*.

Transport

RAILWAYS
(traffic)

	1997	1998	1999
Passengers carried ('000)	359	293	273
Passenger-km (million)	37	35	31
Freight carried ('000 metric tons)	227	213	141
Ton-km (million)	81	71	46

Source: Réseau National des Chemins de Fer Malagasy.

2000: Passenger-km (million) 19; Ton-km (million) 26 (Source: UN, *Statistical Yearbook*).

ROAD TRAFFIC
(vehicles in use)

	1994	1995	1996*
Passenger cars	54,821	58,097	60,480
Buses and coaches	3,797	4,332	4,850
Lorries and vans	35,931	37,232	37,972
Road tractors	488	560	619

* Estimates.

Source: IRF, *World Road Statistics*.

1998 ('000): Passenger cars 64.0; Commercial vehicles 9.1 (Source: UN, *Statistical Yearbook*).

SHIPPING

Merchant Fleet
(registered at 31 December)

	2003	2004	2005
Number of vessels	103	103	103
Displacement ('000 gross registered tons)	34.8	32.9	33.2

Source: Lloyd's Register-Fairplay, *World Fleet Statistics*.

International Sea-borne Freight Traffic
('000 metric tons)

	1987	1988	1989
Goods loaded:			
Mahajanga	17	18	29.4
Toamasina	252	350	360.6
other ports	79	100	137.4
Total	348	468	527.4
Goods unloaded:			
Mahajanga	37	32	30.8
Toamasina	748	778	708.9
other ports	48	53	52.0
Total	833	863	791.7

1990 ('000 metric tons): Goods loaded 540; Goods unloaded 984 (Source: UN, *Monthly Bulletin of Statistics*).

CIVIL AVIATION
(traffic on scheduled services)

	2001	2002	2003
Kilometres flown (million)	7	2	4
Passengers carried ('000)	146	241	140
Passenger-km (million)	654	266	562
Total ton-km (million)	86	42	60

Source: UN, *Statistical Yearbook*.

Tourism

TOURIST ARRIVALS BY NATIONALITY

	2000	2001	2002
Canada and USA	6,402	6,808	1,880
France	88,039	95,316	32,070
Germany	6,403	6,808	3,084
Italy	8,004	8,510	3,084
Japan	2,055	3,404	617
Mauritius	4,526	8,510	3,134
Réunion	14,406	17,021	3,084
Switzerland	3,201	3,404	2,467
United Kingdom	4,802	5,106	2,467
Total (incl. others)	160,071	170,208	61,674

2003: Total arrivals 139,000.

2004: Canada and USA 9,151; France 129,263; Germany 9,609; Italy 17,159; Mauritius 9,609; Réunion 22,878; United Kingdom 6,864; Total (incl. others) 228,785.

Tourism receipts (US $ million, incl. passenger transport): 62 in 2002; 118 in 2003; 265 in 2004.

Source: World Tourism Organization.

Communications Media

	2003	2004	2005
Telephones ('000 main lines in use)	59.6	58.7	66.9
Mobile cellular telephones ('000 subscribers)	283.7	333.9	504.7
Personal computers ('000 in use)	80	91	91
Internet users ('000)	71	90	90

Source: International Telecommunication Union.

1995: Radio receivers ('000 in use) 2,850; Book production (incl. pamphlets): titles 131, copies ('000) 292; Daily newspapers: number 6, circulation ('000 copies) 59 (Source: UNESCO, *Statistical Yearbook*).

1996: Radio receivers ('000 in use) 2,950; Book production (incl. pamphlets): titles 119, copies ('000) 296; Daily newspapers: number 5, circulation ('000 copies) 66 (Source: UNESCO, *Statistical Yearbook*).

1997: Radio receivers ('000 in use) 3,050 (Source: UNESCO, *Statistical Yearbook*).

2000: Television receivers ('000 in use) 375.

Education

(2003/04, UNESCO estimates, public and private schools)

		Pupils ('000)		
	Teachers	Males	Females	Total
Pre-primary (all programmes)	3,520	n.a.	n.a.	170.6
Primary (all programmes)	64,270	1,718.7	1,647.8	3,366.5
Secondary:				
Lower secondary (general programmes)*	17,850	211.8	208.8	420.6
Upper secondary (general programmes)	5,930	45.3	43.1	88.4
Total secondary (general programmes)	23,780	258.1	251.8	509.9
Tertiary	1,560	22.2	19.9	42.1

* Lower secondary, all programmes: 431.0 (males 218.1, females 212.9).

Source: UNESCO, Institute for Statistics.

2003/04: Primary schools 19,961 (3,556,042 pupils) (Source: IMF, *Republic of Madagascar: Poverty Reduction Strategy Paper Progress Report*, December 2004).

2005/06: 6 universities; 14 private institutes of higher education.

Adult literacy rate (UNESCO estimates): 70.7% (males 76.5%; females 65.3%) in 2004 (Source: UN Development Programme, *Human Development Report*).

Directory

The Constitution

The Constitution of the Third Republic of Madagascar was endorsed by national referendum on 19 August 1992, but was substantially altered by amendments that were endorsed in a national referendum on 15 March 1998. The amended Constitution enshrines a 'federal-style' state, composed of six autonomous provinces—each with a governor and up to 12 general commissioners (holding executive power) and a provincial council (holding legislative power). It provides for a government delegate to each province, who is charged with supervising the division of functions between the state and the province. The bicameral legislature consists of the National Assembly (the lower house), which is elected by universal adult suffrage in single-seat constituencies for a five-year term of office. The Constitution also provides for a Senate (the upper house), of which one-third of the members are presidential nominees and two-thirds are elected in equal numbers by the provincial councillors and mayors of each of the six autonomous provinces, for a term of six years. The constitutional Head of State is the President. If no candidate obtains an overall majority in the presidential election, a second round of voting is to take place a maximum of 30 days after the publication of the results of the first ballot. Any one candidate can be elected for a maximum of three five-year terms. The powers of the President were greatly increased by constitutional amendments of March 1998: he has the power to determine general state policy in the Council of Ministers, to call referendums on all matters of national importance, and to dissolve the National Assembly not less than one year after a general election. Executive power is vested in a Prime Minister, who is appointed by the President. The President appoints the Council of Ministers, on the recommendation of the Prime Minister. In a national referendum held on 4 April 2007 a number of constitutional reforms were endorsed, including the abolition of autonomous powers for the six provinces. The amended Constitution conferred on the President new powers, including the right to legislate by decree in the event of a state of emergency. English was also adopted as the country's third official language.

The Government

HEAD OF STATE

President: MARC RAVALOMANANA (inaugurated 6 May 2002, re-elected 3 December 2006).

COUNCIL OF MINISTERS

(August 2007)

Prime Minister and Minister of the Interior: CHARLES RABEMANANJARA.

Minister of Finance and the Budget: BENJAMIN ANDRIAMPARANY RADAVIDSON.

Minister of Justice and Keeper of the Seals: LALA HENRIETTE RATSIHAROVALA.

Minister of Foreign Affairs: Gen. MARCEL RANJEVA.

Minister of Defence: Maj.-Gen. PETERA BEHAJAINA.

Minister of National Education and Scientific Research: HAJA NIRINA RAZAFINJATOVO.

Minister of Health and Family Planning: JEAN-LOUIS ROBINSON.

Minister of the Economy, Planning, the Private Sector and Commerce: HARISON EDMOND RANDRIARIMANANA.

Minister of the Civil Service, Labour and Social Legislation: JACKY TSIANDOPY MAHAFALY.

Minister of the Environment, Water and Forests: KOTO BERNARD.

Minister of Mines: OLIVIER DONAT ANDRIAMAHEFAMPARANY.

Minister of Agriculture, Livestock and Fisheries: MARIUS RATOLONJANAHARY.

Minister of Telecommunications, Post and Communications: BRUNO RAMAROSON ANDRIATAVISON.

Minister of Public Works and Meteorology: ROLAND RANDRIAMAMPIONONA.

Minister of Sports: RABARISON PHILÉMON MICHEL.

Minister of Transport and Tourism: JULIEN VELONARIVO LAPORTE.

Minister of Decentralization and Territorial Development: YVAN RANDRIASANDRATRINIONY.

Secretary of State for Public Security at the Ministry of the Interior and Administrative Reform: DÉSIRÉ RASOLOFOMANANA.

General Secretary with responsibility for Culture and Leisure: HERMANN RAZAFINDRAVELO.

MINISTRIES

Office of the President: Antananarivo; internet www.madagascar-presidency.gov.mg.

Office of the Prime Minister: BP 248, Palais d'Etat Mahazoarivo, 101 Antananarivo; tel. (20) 2264498; fax (20) 2233116; e-mail dircom@primature.gov.mg; internet www.primature.gov.mg.

Ministry of Agriculture, Livestock and Fisheries: BP 301, Anosy, 101 Antananarivo; tel. (20) 2261002; fax (20) 2226561; e-mail info@maep.gov.mg; internet www.maep.gov.mg.

Ministry of the Civil Service, Labour and Social Legislation: BP 207, Cité des 67 Hectares, 101 Antananarivo; tel. (20) 2224209; fax (20) 2233856; e-mail ministre@mfptls.gov.mg; internet www.mfptls.gov.mg.

Ministry of Decentralization and Territorial Development: BP 24 bis, 101 Antananarivo; tel. (20) 2235881; fax (20) 2237516; internet www.mprdat.gov.mg.

Ministry of Defence: BP 08, Ampahibe, 101 Antananarivo; tel. (20) 2222211; fax (20) 2235420; e-mail mdn@wanadoo.fr; internet 196.192.32.105/MDN.

Ministry of the Economy, Planning, the Private Sector and Commerce: Bâtiment Commerce, Ambohidahy, 101 Antananarivo; tel. (20) 2264681; fax (20) 2234530; e-mail sg@mepspc.gov.mg; internet www.mepspc.gov.mg.

Ministry of Energy: BP 527, Immeuble de l'Industrie, Antaninarenina, 101 Antananarivo; tel. (20) 2228928; fax (20) 2232554; internet www.mem.gov.mg.

Ministry of the Environment, Water and Forests: rue Farafaty, BP 571 Ampandrianomby, 101 Antananarivo; tel. (20) 2261359; fax (20) 2241919; e-mail minenv@wanadoo.mg; internet www.minenvef.gov.mg.

Ministry of Finance and the Budget: BP 61, Antaninarenina, Antananarivo; tel. (20) 2230173; fax (20) 2264680; internet www.mefb.gov.mg.

Ministry of Foreign Affairs: BP 836, Anosy, 101 Antananarivo; tel. (20) 2221198; fax (20) 2234484; e-mail contact@madagascar-diplomatie.net; internet www.madagascar-diplomatie.net.

Ministry of Health and Family Planning: BP 88, Ambohidahy, 101 Antananarivo; tel. (20) 2263121; fax (20) 2264228; e-mail cabminsan@wanadoo.mg; internet www.sante.gov.mg.

Ministry of the Interior: BP 833, Anosy, 101 Antananarivo; tel. (20) 2223084; fax (20) 2235579; internet www.mira.gov.mg.

Ministry of Justice: rue Joel Rakotomalala, BP 231, Faravohitra, 101 Antananarivo; tel. (20) 2237684; fax (20) 2264458; e-mail presse.justice@justice.gov.mg; internet www.justice.gov.mg.

Ministry of Mining: BP 527,101 Antananarivo; tel. (20) 2228928; fax (20) 2232554; internet www.mem.gov.mg.

Ministry of National Education and Scientific Research: BP 247, Anosy, 101 Antananarivo; tel. (20) 2224308; fax (20) 2223897; e-mail mlraharimalala@yahoo.fr; internet 196.192.32.105/menrs/.

Ministry of Public Works and Meteorology: BP 295, 101 Antananarivo; tel. (20) 2228715; fax (20) 2220890; e-mail secreab@mtpm.gov.mg.

Ministry of Telecommunications, Post and Communications: pl. de l'Indépendance, Antaninarenina, 101 Antananarivo; tel. (20) 2222902; fax (20) 2234115; internet www.mtpc.gov.mg.

Ministry of Transport and Tourism: BP 610, rue Fernand Kasanga Tsimbazaza, 101 Antananarivo; tel. (20) 2262816; fax (20) 2235410; e-mail mintourdadi@wanadoo.mg; internet www.tourisme.gov.mg.

Ministry of Sports: Ambohijatovo, pl. Goulette, BP 681, 101 Antananarivo; tel. (20) 2227780; fax (20) 2234275; e-mail mjs_101@yahoo.fr; internet www.mjs.gov.mg.

General Secretariat for Culture and Leisure: 101 Antananarivo.

State Secretariat for Public Security: BP 23 bis, 101 Antananarivo; tel. (20) 2221029; fax (20) 2231861.

President and Legislature

PRESIDENT

Presidential Election, 3 December 2006

Candidate	Votes	% of votes
Marc Ravalomanana	2,435,199	54.79
Jean Lahiniriko	517,994	11.65
Iarovana Roland Ratsiraka	450,717	10.14
Herizo J. Razafimahaleo	401,473	9.03
Norbert Lala Ratsirahonana	187,552	4.22
Ny Hasina Andriamanjato	185,624	4.18
Others	266,191	5.99
Total	4,444,750*	100.00

* Excluding 87,196 invalid votes.

LEGISLATURE

Senate

President: GUY RAJEMISON RAKOTOMAHARO.

Senatorial Election, 18 March 2001

Party	Seats
AREMA	49
LEADER/Fanilo	5
Independents	3
AVI	2
AFFA	1
Total	60*

* Elected by a 1,727-member electoral college of provincial councillors and mayors. An additional 30 seats were appointed by the President.

National Assembly

President: MAHAFARITSY SAMUEL RAZAKANIRINA.

General Election, 15 December 2002

Party	Seats
TIM	104
Front Patriotique	22
AVI	20
RPSD	2
RPSD	5
AREMA	3
MFM	2
LEADER/Fanilo	1
Independents	23
Total	160

Election Commission

Conseil national électoral (CNE): Immeuble Microréalisation, 4 étage, 67 ha, 101 Antananarivo; tel. (20) 2225179; fax (20) 2225881; e-mail cne@wanadoo.mg; internet www.cne.mg; Pres. THÉODORE RANDREZASON.

Political Organizations

Following the restoration of multi-party politics in March 1990, more than 120 political associations emerged, of which six secured representation in the National Assembly in 2002. The following were among the more influential political organizations in 2007:

Association pour la renaissance de Madagascar (Andry sy riana enti-manavotra an'i Madigasikara) (AREMA): f. 1975 as Avant-garde de la révolution malgache; adopted present name 1997; party of fmr Pres. Adm. (retd) Ratsiraka (now in exile); control disputed between two factions, headed by Gen. Sec. PIERROT RAJAONARIVELO (in exile), and Asst. Gen. Sec. PIERRE RAHARIJAONA.

Comité pour la Réconciliation Nationale (CRN): Antananarivo; f. 2002 by fmr President Zafy; radical opposition; does not recognize the presidency of Marc Ravalomanana; formed part of the 3FN (Trois Forces Nationales) group of opposition parties, established in Sept. 2005; Leader ALBERT ZAFY.

Herim-Bahoaka Mitambatra (HBM) (Union of Popular Forces): formed part of the coalition supporting Pres. Ravalomanana prior to the presidential election; Leader TOVONANAHARY RABETSITONTA.

Libéralisme économique et action démocratique pour la reconstruction nationale (LEADER/Fanilo) (Torch): f. 1993 by Herizo Razafimahaleo; Leader Prof. MANASSE ESOAVELOMANDROSO.

Mouvement pour le progrès de Madagascar (Mpitolona ho amin'ny Fandrosoan'ny Madagasikara) (MFM): 42 & 44 Cité Ampefiloha Bldg, 101 Antananarivo; tel. (20) 2437560; e-mail servasia@wanadoo.mg; internet www.votemfm.com; f. 1972 as Mouvement pour le pouvoir prolétarien (MFM); adopted present name in 1990; advocates liberal and market-orientated policies; Leader RAKOTONIRINA MANANDAFY; Sec.-Gen. OLIVIER RAKOTOVAZAHA.

Ny asa vita no ifampitsara (AVI) (People are judged by the work they do): f. 1997 to promote human rights, hard work and development; Leader NORBERT RATSIRAHONANA.

Parti socialiste et démocratique pour l'union de Madagascar (PSDUM): f. 2006; Pres. JEAN LAHINIRIKO.

Rassemblement des forces nationales (RFN): f. 2005; a coalition of parties comprising the AKFM, LEADER/Fanilo and Fihavanantsika (led by Pasteur Daniel Rajakoba); formed part of the 3FN (Trois Forces Nationales) group of opposition parties, established in Sept. 2005; Leader Pasteur EDMOND RAZAFIMAHEFA.

Rassemblement pour le socialisme et la démocratie (RPSD): f. 1993 by fmr mems of PSD; also known as Renaissance du parti social-démocratique; Jean-Eugène Voninahitsy formed a breakaway party known as the RPSD Nouveau in 2003; Leader EVARISTE MARSON.

Tiako i Madagasikara (TIM) (I Love Madagascar): internet www .tim-madagascar.org; f. 2002; supports Pres. Ravalomanana; Pres. RAZOHARIMIHAJA SOLOFONANTENAINA.

Diplomatic Representation

EMBASSIES IN MADAGASCAR

China, People's Republic: Ancien Hôtel Panorama, BP 1658, 101 Antananarivo; tel. (20) 2240129; fax (20) 2240215; e-mail chinaemb_mg@mfa.gov.cn; internet mg.china-embassy.org; Ambassador LI SHULI.

Comoros: Antananarivo; tel. (20) 2265819; Ambassador Col HALIDI CHARIF.

Egypt: Lot MD 378 Ambalatokana Mandrosoa Ivato, BP 4082, 101 Antananarivo; tel. (20) 2245497; fax (20) 2245379; Ambassador MAGID FOAD SALEH FOAD.

France: 3 rue Jean Jaurès, BP 204, 101 Antananarivo; tel. (20) 2239898; fax (20) 2239927; e-mail ambatana@wanadoo.mg; internet www.ambafrance-mada.org; Ambassador ALAIN LE ROY.

Germany: 101 rue du Pasteur Rabeony Hans, BP 516, Ambodirotra, 101 Antananarivo; tel. (20) 2223802; fax (20) 2226627; e-mail amballem@wanadoo.mg; internet www.antananarivo.diplo.de; Ambassador Dr WOLFGANG MOSER.

Holy See: Amboniloha Ivandry, BP 650, 101 Antananarivo; tel. (20) 2242376; fax (20) 2242384; e-mail nuntiusantana@wanadoo.mg; Apostolic Nuncio Most Rev. AUGUSTINE KASUJJA (Titular Archbishop of Caesarea de Numidia).

India: 4 Làlana Emile Rajaonson, Tsaralalana, BP 1787, 101 Antananarivo; tel. (20) 2223334; fax (20) 2233790; e-mail indembmd@wanadoo.mg; Ambassador DILJIT SINGH PANNUN.

Indonesia: 26–28 rue Patrice Lumumba, BP 3969, 101 Antananarivo; tel. (20) 2224915; fax (20) 2232857; Chargé d'affaires a.i. SLAMET SUYATA SASTRAMIHARDZA.

Iran: route Circulaire, Lot II L43 ter, Ankadivato, 101 Antananarivo; tel. (20) 2228639; fax (20) 2222298; Ambassador ABDOL RAHIM HOMATASH.

Japan: 8 rue du Dr Villette, BP 3863, Isoraka, 101 Antananarivo; tel. (20) 2226102; fax (20) 2221769; Ambassador TADAHARU CHICHII.

Korea, Democratic People's Republic: 101 Antananarivo; tel. (20) 2244442; Ambassador RI YONG HAK.

Libya: Lot IIB, 37A route Circulaire Ampandrana-Ouest, 101 Antananarivo; tel. (20) 2221892; Chargé d'affaires a.i. Dr MOHAMED ALI SHARFEDIN AL-FITURI.

Mauritius: Anjaharay, route Circulaire, BP 6040, Ambanidia, 101 Antananarivo; tel. (20) 2221864; fax (20) 2221939; Ambassador ERNEST GÉRARD LEMAIRE.

Morocco: Bâtiment D1, Rez-de-chaussée, Ankorondrano, BP 12, 104 Antananarivo; tel. (20) 2221347; fax (20) 2221124; e-mail amar_med@hotmail.com; Ambassador MUHAMMAD AMAR.

Norway: Explorer Business Park, Bâtiment 2D, Antananarivo; tel. (20) 2230507; fax (20) 2237799; e-mail emb.antananarivo@mfa.no; internet www.amb-norvege.mg; Ambassador HANS FREDERIK LEHNE.

Russia: BP 4006, Ivandry-Ambohijatovo, 101 Antananarivo; tel. (20) 2242827; fax (20) 2242642; e-mail ambrusmad@wanadoo.mg; Ambassador VLADIMIR B. GONCHARENKO.

Senegal: Lot II R, 179B Ambohirakely, Betongolo, Antananarivo; tel. (20) 2252186; fax (20) 2252186; Ambassador CÉSAR COLY.

South Africa: Villa Chandella, Lot Bonnet 38, Ivandry, BP 12101-05, 101 Antananarivo; tel. (20) 2243350; fax (20) 2243386; e-mail antananarivo@foreign.gov.za; Ambassador WALTER THEMBA THABETHE.

Switzerland: Immeuble ARO, Solombavambahoaka, Frantsay 77, BP 118, 101 Antananarivo; tel. (20) 2262997; fax (20) 2228940; e-mail ant.vertretung@eda.admin.ch; internet www.eda.admin.ch/antananarivo; Chargé d'affaires a.i. BENOÎT GIRARDIN.

USA: 14–16 rue Rainitovo, Antsahavola, BP 620, 101 Antananarivo; tel. (20) 2221257; fax (20) 2234539; internet www.usmission.mg; Ambassador R. NIELS MARQUARDT.

Judicial System

HIGH CONSTITUTIONAL COURT

Haute Cour Constitutionnelle: POB 835, Ambohidahy, 101 Antananarivo; tel. (20) 2266061; e-mail hcc@simicro.mg; internet www.simicro.mg/hcc; interprets the Constitution and rules on constitutional issues; nine mems; Pres. JEAN-MICHEL RAJAONARIVONY.

HIGH COURT OF JUSTICE

Haute Cour de Justice: 101 Antananarivo; nine mems.

SUPREME COURT

Cour Suprême: Palais de Justice, Anosy, 101 Antananarivo; Pres. ALICE RAJAONAH (acting); Attorney-General COLOMBE RAMANANTSOA (acting); Chamber Pres YOLANDE RAMANGASOAVINA, FRANÇOIS RAMANANDRAIBE.

COURT OF APPEAL

Cour d'Appel: Palais de Justice, Anosy, 101 Antananarivo; Pres. AIMÉE RAKOTONIRINA; Pres of Chamber CHARLES RABETOKOTANY, PÉTRONILLE ANDRIAMIHAJA, BAKOLALAO RANAIVOHARIVONY, BERTHOLIER RAVELONTSALAMA, LUCIEN RABARIJHON, NELLY RAKOTOBE, ARLETTE RAMAROSON, CLÉMENTINE RAVANDISON, GISÈLE RABOTOVAO, JEAN-JACQUES RAJAONA.

OTHER COURTS

Tribunaux de Première Instance: at Antananarivo, Toamasina, Antsiranana, Mahajanga, Fianarantsoa, Toliary, Antsirabé, Ambatondrazaka, Antalaha, Farafangana and Maintirano; for civil, commercial and social matters, and for registration.

Cours Criminelles Ordinaires: tries crimes of common law; attached to the Cour d'Appel in Antananarivo but may sit in any other large town. There are also 31 Cours Criminelles Spéciales dealing with cases concerning cattle.

Tribunaux Spéciaux Economiques: at Antananarivo, Toamasina, Mahajanga, Fianarantsoa, Antsiranana and Toliary; tries crimes specifically relating to economic matters.

Tribunaux Criminels Spéciaux: judges cases of banditry and looting; 31 courts.

Religion

It is estimated that more than 50% of the population follow traditional animist beliefs, some 41% are Christians (about one-half of whom are Roman Catholics) and some 7% are Muslims.

CHRISTIANITY

Fiombonan'ny Fiangonana Kristiana eto Madagasikara (FFKM)/Conseil Chrétien des Eglises de Madagascar (Christian Council of Churches in Madagascar): Vohipiraisama, Ambohijatovo-Atsimo, BP 798, 101 Antananarivo; tel. (20) 2229052; f. 1980; four mems and one assoc. mem.; Pres. Pastor EDMOND RAZAFIMAHALEO; Gen. Sec. Rev. RÉMY RALIBERA.

Fiombonan'ny Fiangonana Protestanta eto Madagasikara (FFPM)/Fédération des Eglises Protestantes à Madagascar (Federation of the Protestant Churches in Madagascar): VK 3 Vohipiraisana, Ambohijatovo-Atsimo, BP 4226, 101 Antananarivo; tel. (20) 2415888; e-mail edrazafi@wanadoo.mg; f. 1958; two mem. churches; Pres Rev. Dr ENDOR MODESTE RAKOTO; Gen. Sec. Rev. Dr EDMOND RAZAFIMANANTSOA.

The Anglican Communion

Anglicans are adherents of the Church of the Province of the Indian Ocean, comprising six dioceses (four in Madagascar, one in Mauritius and one in Seychelles). The Archbishop of the Province is the Bishop of Antananarivo. The Church has about 160,000 adherents in Madagascar, including the membership of the Eklesia Episkopaly Malagasy (Malagasy Episcopal Church), founded in 1874.

Bishop of Antananarivo (also Archbishop of the Province of the Indian Ocean): Most Rev. RÉMI JOSEPH RABENIRINA, Evêché anglican, Lot VK57 ter, Ambohimanoro, 101 Antananarivo; tel. (20) 2220827; fax (20) 2261331; e-mail eemdanta@wanadoo.mg.

Bishop of Antsiranana: Rt Rev. ROGER CHUNG PO CHEN, Evêché anglican, 4 rue Grandidier, BP 278, 201 Antsiranana; tel. (20) 8222650; e-mail eemdants@wanadoo.mg.

Bishop of Fianarantsoa: Rt Rev. GILBERT RATELOSON RAKOTONDRAVELO, Evêché anglican, BP 1418, 531 Fianarantsoa.

Bishop of Mahajanga: Rt Rev. JEAN-CLAUDE ANDRIANJAFIMANANA, Evêché anglican, BP 169, 401 Mahajanga; e-mail eemdmaha@wanadoo.mg.

Bishop of Toamasina: Rt Rev. JEAN PAUL SOLO, Evêché anglican, rue James Seth, BP 531, 501 Toamasina; tel. (20) 5332163; fax (20) 5331689.

The Roman Catholic Church

Madagascar comprises four archdioceses and 16 dioceses. At 31 December 2004 the number of adherents in the country represented about 24.5% of the total population.

Bishops' Conference

Conférence episcopale de Madagascar, 102 bis, rue Cardinal Jerôme Rakotomalala, BP 667, 101 Antananarivo; tel. (20) 2220478; fax (20) 2224854; e-mail ecar@vitelcom.mg.

f. 1969; Pres. Most Rev. FULGENCE RABEONY (Archbishop of Toliary).

Archbishop of Antananarivo: ODON ARSÈNE RAZANAKOLONA, Archevêché, Andohalo, BP 3030, 101 Antananarivo; tel. (20) 2220726; fax (20) 2264181; e-mail didih@simicro.org.

Archbishop of Antsiranana: Most Rev. MICHEL MALO, Archevêché, blvd le Myre de Villers, BP 415, 201 Antsiranana; tel. (82) 21605; e-mail archevediego@blueline.mg.

Archbishop of Fianarantsoa: Most Rev. FULGENCE RABEMAHAFALY, Archevêché, pl. Mgr Givelet, BP 1440, Ambozontany, 301 Fianarantsoa; tel. (20) 7550027; fax (20) 7551436; e-mail ecarfianar@vitelcom.mg.

Archbishop of Toliary: Most Rev. FULGENCE RABEONY, Archevêché, Maison Saint Jean, BP 30, 601 Toliary; tel. (20) 9442416; e-mail diocesetulear@wanadoo.mg.

Other Christian Churches

Fiangonan'i Jesoa Kristy eto Madagasikara/Eglise de Jésus-Christ à Madagascar (FJKM): Lot 11 B18, Tohatohabato Ranavalona 1, Trano 'Ifanomezantsoa', BP 623, 101 Antananarivo; tel. (20) 2226845; fax (20) 2226372; e-mail fjkm@dts.mg; f. 1968; Pres. LALA HAJA RASENDRAHASINA; Gen. Sec. Rev. RÉMY RALIBERA; 2m. mems.

Fiangonana Loterana Malagasy (Malagasy Lutheran Church): BP 1741, 101 Antananarivo; tel. (20) 2422703; fax (20) 2423856; e-mail flm@wanadoo.mg; f. 1867; Pres. Rev. Dr ENDOR MODESTE RAKOTO; 600,000 mems.

The Press

In December 1990 the National People's Assembly adopted legislation guaranteeing the freedom of the press and the right of newspapers to be established without prior authorization.

PRINCIPAL DAILIES

Bulletin de l'Agence Nationale d'Information 'TARATRA' (ANTA): 8/10 Làlana Rainizanabololona, Antanimena, BP 194, 101 Antananarivo; tel. (20) 2234308; e-mail taratramada@blueline.mg; internet www.taratramada.com; f. 1977; Malagasy; Editor-in-Chief HANITRA RABETOKOTANY.

L'Express de Madagascar: BP 3893, 101 Antananarivo; tel. (20) 2221934; fax (20) 2262894; e-mail lexpress@malagasy.com; internet www.lexpressmada.com; f. 1995; French and Malagasy; Editor (vacant); circ. 10,000.

Gazetiko: BP 1414 Ankorondrano, 101 Antananarivo; tel. (20) 2269779; fax (20) 2227351; e-mail gazetikom@yahoo.fr; Malagasy; circ. 50,000.

La Gazette de la Grande Ile: Lot II, W 23 L Ankorahotra, route de l'Université, Antananarivo; tel. (20) 2261377; fax (20) 2265188; e-mail admin@lagazette-dgi.com; internet www.lagazette-dgi.com; French; 24 pages; Pres. LOLA RASOAMAHARO; circ. 15,000–30,000.

Imongo Vaovao: 11K 4 bis Andravoahangy, BP 7014, 101 Antananarivo; tel. (20) 2221053; f. 1955; Malagasy; Dir CLÉMENT RAMAMONJISOA; circ. 10,000.

Madagascar Tribune: Immeuble SME, rue Ravoninahitriniarivo, BP 659, Ankorondrano, 101 Antananarivo; tel. (20) 2222635; fax (20) 2222254; e-mail tribune@wanadoo.mg; internet www.madagascar-tribune.com; f. 1988; independent; French and Malagasy; Editor RAHAGA RAMAHOLIMIHASO; circ. 12,000.

Maresaka: Cité Logt. 288, Analamahitsy, 101 Antananarivo; tel. (20) 2231665; f. 1953; independent; Malagasy; Editor R. RABEFANANINA; circ. 5,000.

Midi Madagasikara: Làlana Ravoninahitriniarivo, BP 1414, Ankorondrano, 101 Antananarivo; tel. (20) 2269779; fax (20) 2227351; e-mail infos@midi-madagasikara.mg; internet www.midi-madagasikara.mg; f. 1983; French and Malagasy; Dir MAMY RAKOTOARIVELO; circ. 21,000 (Mon.–Fri.), 35,000 (Sat.).

Les Nouvelles: BP 194, 101 Antananarivo; tel. (20) 2235433; fax (20) 2229993; e-mail administration@les-nouvelles.com; internet www.les-nouvelles.com; in French and Taratra; f. 2003; Editors-in-Chief RENAUD RAHARIJAONA, ANDRY TSILEFERINTSOA.

Ny Vaovaontsika: BP 11137, MBS Anosipatrana; tel. (20) 2227717; e-mail nyvaovaontsika@mbs.mg; f. 2004; re-estd as a daily; Malagasy; Malagasy Broadcasting System; Editor-in-Chief ROLAND ANDRIAMAHENINA; circ. 10,000.

Le Quotidien: BP 11 097, 101 Antananarivo; tel. (20) 2227717; fax (20) 2265447; e-mail lequotidien@mbs.mg; internet www.lequotidien.mg; f. 2003; owned by the Tiko Group plc; French.

PRINCIPAL PERIODICALS

Basy Vava: Lot III E 96, Mahamasina Atsimo, 101 Antananarivo; tel. (20) 2220448; f. 1959; Malagasy; Dir GABRIEL RAMANANJATO; circ. 3,000.

Bulletin de la Société du Corps Médical Malgache: Imprimerie Volamahitsy, 101 Antananarivo; Malagasy; monthly; Dir Dr RAKOTOMALALA.

Dans les Médias Demain (DMD): Immeuble Jeune Afrique, 58 rue Tsiombikibo, BP 1734, Ambatovinaky, 101 Antananarivo; tel. (20) 2230755; fax (20) 2230754; e-mail dmd@wanadoo.mg; internet www.dmd.mg; f. 1986; independent; economic information and analysis; weekly; Editorial Dir JEAN ERIC RAKOTOARISOA; circ. 4,000.

Feon'ny Mpiasa: Lot M8, Isotry, 101 Antananarivo; trade union affairs; Malagasy; monthly; Dir M. RAZAKANAIVO; circ. 2,000.

Fiaraha-Miasa: BP 1216, 101 Antananarivo; Malagasy; weekly; Dir SOLO NORBERT ANDRIAMORASATA; circ. 5,000.

Gazetinao: Lot IPA 37, BP 1758, Anosimasina, 101 Antananarivo; tel. (33) 1198161; e-mail jamesdigne@caramail.com; f. 1976; French and Malagasy; monthly; Editors-in-Chief ANDRIANIAINA RAKOTOMAHANINA, JAMES FRANKLIN; circ. 3,000.

L'Hebdo: BP 3893, 101 Antananarivo; tel. (20) 2221934; f. 2005; French and Malagasy; weekly; Editor-in-Chief NASOLO VALIAVO ANDRIAMIHAJA.

Isika Mianakavy: Ambatomena, 301 Fianarantsoa; f. 1958; Roman Catholic; Malagasy; monthly; Dir J. RANAIVOMANANA; circ. 21,000.

Journal Officiel de la République de Madagascar/Gazetim-Panjakan' Ny Repoblika Malagasy: BP 248, 101 Antananarivo; tel. (20) 2265010; fax (20) 2225319; e-mail segma.gvt@wanadoo.mg; f. 1883; official announcements; Malagasy and French; weekly; Dir HONORÉE ELIANNE RALALAHARISON; circ. 1,545.

Journal Scientifique de Madagascar: BP 3855, Antananarivo; f. 1985; Dir Prof. MANAMBELONA; circ. 3,000.

Jureco: BP 6318, Lot IVD 48 bis, rue Razanamaniraka, Behoririka, 101 Antananarivo; tel. (20) 2255271; e-mail jureco@malagasy.com; internet www.jureco.com; law and economics; monthly; French; Dir MBOARA ANDRIANARIMANANA.

Lakroan'i Madagasikara/La Croix de Madagascar: BP 7524, CNPC Antanimena, 101 Antananarivo; tel. (20) 2266128; fax (20) 2224020; e-mail info@lakroa.org; internet www.geocities.com/lakroam; f. 1927; Roman Catholic; French and Malagasy; weekly; Dir Fr VINCENT RABEMAHAFALY; circ. 25,000.

La Lettre de Madagascar (LLM): Antananarivo; f. 2003; 2 a month; in French and English; economic; Editor-in-Chief DANIEL LAMY.

Mada—Economie: 15 rue Ratsimilaho, BP 3464, 101 Antananarivo; tel. (20) 2225634; f. 1977; reports events in south-east Africa; monthly; Editor RICHARD-CLAUDE RATOVONARIVO; circ. 5,000.

Mpanolotsaina: BP 623, 101 Antananarivo; tel. (20) 2226845; fax (20) 2226372; e-mail fjkm@wanadoo.mg; religious, educational; Malagasy; quarterly; Dir RAYMOND RAJOELISOL.

New Magazine: BP 7581, Newprint, Route des Hydrocarbures, 101 Antananarivo; tel. (20) 2233335; fax (20) 2236471; e-mail newmag@wanadoo.mg; internet www.newmagazine.mg; monthly; in French; Dir CLARA RAVOAVAHY.

Ny Mpamangy-FLM: 9 rue Grandidier Isoraka, BP 538, Antsahamanitra, 101 Antananarivo; tel. (20) 2232446; f. 1882; monthly; Dir Pastor JEAN RABENANDRASANA; circ. 3,000.

Ny Sakaizan'ny Tanora: BP 538, Antsahaminitra, 101 Antananarivo; tel. (20) 2232446; f. 1878; monthly; Editor-in-Chief DANIEL PROSPER ANDRIAMANJAKA; circ. 5,000.

PME Madagascar: rue Hugues Rabesahala, BP 953, Antsakaviro, 101 Antananarivo; tel. (20) 2222536; fax (20) 2234534; f. 1989; French; monthly; economic review; Dir ROMAIN ANDRIANARISOA; circ. 3,500.

Recherche et Culture: BP 907, 101 Antananarivo; tel. (20) 2226600; f. 1985; publ. by French dept of the University of Antananarivo; 2 a year; Dir GINETTE RAMAROSON; circ. 1,000.

Revue Ita: BP 681, 101 Antananarivo; tel. (20) 2230507; f. 1985; controlled by the Ministry of Population, Social Protection and Leisure; monthly; Dir FILS RAMALANJAONA; circ. 1,000.

Revue de l'Océan Indien: Communication et Médias Océan Indien, rue H. Rabesahala, BP 46, Antsakaviro, 101 Antananarivo; tel. (20) 2222536; fax (20) 2234534; e-mail roi@dts.mg; internet www.madatours.com/roi; f. 1980; monthly; French; Man. Dir GEORGES RANAIVOSOA; Sec.-Gen. HERY M. A. RANAIVOSOA; circ. 5,000.

Sahy: Lot VD 42, Ambanidia, 101 Antananarivo; tel. (20) 2222715; f. 1957; political; Malagasy; weekly; Editor ALINE RAKOTO; circ. 9,000.

Sosialisma Mpiasa: BP 1128, 101 Antananarivo; tel. (20) 2221989; f. 1979; trade union affairs; Malagasy; monthly; Dir PAUL RABEMANANJARA; circ. 5,000.

Vaovao: BP 271, 101 Antananarivo; tel. (20) 2221193; f. 1985; French and Malagasy; weekly; Dir MARC RAKOTONOELY; circ. 5,000.

NEWS AGENCIES

Agence Nationale d'Information 'TARATRA' (ANTA): 7 rue Jean Ralaimongo, Ambohiday, BP 386, 101 Antananarivo; tel. and fax (20) 2236047; e-mail taratra.mtpc@mtpc.gov.mg; f. 1977; Man. Dir JOÉ ANACLET RAKOTOARISON.

Mada: Villa Joëlle, Lot II J 161 R, Ivandry, 101 Antananarivo; tel. (20) 2242428; e-mail communication@mada.mg; internet www.mada.mg; f. 2003; independent information agency; Dir RICHARD CLAUDE RATOVONARIVO.

Foreign Bureaux

Associated Press (AP) (USA): BP 73, 101 Antananarivo; tel. (20) 2241944; e-mail zadefo@malagasy.com; Correspondent (vacant).

Korean Central News Agency (KCNA) (Democratic People's Republic of Korea): 101 Antananarivo; tel. (20) 2244795; Dir KIM YEUNG KYEUN.

Xinhua (New China) News Agency (People's Republic of China): BP 1656, 101 Antananarivo; tel. (20) 2229927; Chief of Bureau WU HAIYUN.

Reuters (United Kingdom) is also represented in Madagascar.

Publishers

Edisiona Salohy: BP 4226, 101 Antananarivo; Dir MIRANA VOLOLOARISOA RANDRIANARISON.

Editions Ambozontany Analamalintsy: BP 7553, 101 Antananarivo; tel. (20) 2243111; fax (20) 2243111; e-mail editionsj@wanadoo.mg; f. 1962; religious, educational, historical, cultural and technical textbooks; Dir Fr GUILLAUME DE SAINT PIERRE RAKOTONANDRATONIARIVO.

Foibe Filankevitry Ny Mpampianatra (FOFIPA): BP 202, 101 Antananarivo; tel. (20) 2227500; f. 1971; textbooks; Dir Frère RAZAFINDRAKOTO.

Imprimerie Nouvelle: PK 2, Andranomahery, route de Majunga, BP 4330, 101 Antananarivo; tel. (20) 2221036; fax (20) 2269225; e-mail nouvelle@wanadoo.mg; Dir EUGÈNE RAHARIFIDY.

Imprimerie Takariva: 4 rue Radley, BP 1029, Antanimena, 101 Antananarivo; tel. (20) 2222128; f. 1933; fiction, languages, school textbooks; Man. Dir PAUL RAPATSALAHY.

Madagascar Print and Press Co (MADPRINT): rue Rabesahala, Antsakaviro, BP 953, 101 Antananarivo; tel. (20) 2222536; fax (20) 2234534; f. 1969; literary, technical and historical; Dir GEORGES RANAIVOSOA.

Maison d'Edition Protestante Antso: 19 rue Venance Manifatra, Imarivolanitra, BP 660, 101 Antananarivo; tel. (20) 2220886; fax (20) 2226372; e-mail fjkm@dts.mg; f. 1972; religious, school, social, political and general; Dir HANS ANDRIAMAMPIANINA.

Nouvelle Société de Presse et d'Edition (NSPE): Immeuble Jeune Afrique, 58 rue Tsiombikibo, BP 1734, Ambatorinaky, 101 Antananarivo; tel. (20) 2227788; fax (20) 2230629.

Office du Livre Malgache: Lot 111 H29, Andrefan' Ambohijanahary, BP 617, 101 Antananarivo; tel. (20) 2224449; f. 1970; children's and general; Sec.-Gen. JULIETTE RATSIMANDRAVA.

Société Malgache d'Edition (SME): BP 659, Ankorondrano, 101 Antananarivo; tel. (20) 2222635; fax (20) 2222254; e-mail tribune@wanadoo.mg; f. 1943; general fiction, university and secondary textbooks; Man. Dir RAHAGA RAMAHOLIMIHASO.

Société Nouvelle de l'Imprimerie Centrale (SNIC): Làlana Ravoninahitriniarivo, BP 1414, 101 Antananarivo; tel. (20) 2221118; e-mail mrakotoa@wanadoo.mg; f. 1959; science, school textbooks; Man. Dir MAMY RAKOTOARIVELO.

Société de Presse et d'Edition de Madagascar: Antananarivo; non-fiction, reference, science, university textbooks; Man. Dir RAJAOFERA ANDRIAMBELO.

Trano Printy Fiangonana Loterana Malagasy (TPFLM): BP 538, 9 ave Général Gabriel Ramanantsoa, 101 Antananarivo; tel. (20) 2223340; fax (20) 2262643; e-mail impluth@wanadoo.mg; f. 1877; religious, educational and fiction; Man. RAYMOND RANDRIANATOANDRO.

GOVERNMENT PUBLISHING HOUSE

Imprimerie Nationale: BP 38, 101 Antananarivo; tel. (20) 2223675; e-mail dinm@wanadoo.mg; all official publs; Dir JEAN DENIS RANDRIANIRINA.

Broadcasting and Communications

TELECOMMUNICATIONS

Mobile cellular telephone networks are operated by Antaris, Sacel and Telecel.

Office Malagasy d'Etudes et de Régulation des Télécommunications (OMERT): BP 99991, Route des Hydrocarbures-Alarobia, 101 Antananarivo; tel. (20) 2242119; fax (20) 2321516; e-mail omert@wanadoo.mg; internet www.omert.mg; f. 1997; Gen. Man. GILBERT ANDRIANIRINA RAJAONASY.

Madacom SA: BP 763, Bâtiments B1-B2, Explorer Business Park, Ankorondrano, 101 Antananarivo; tel. (22) 66055; fax (20) 66056; e-mail madacom@madacom.mg; internet www.madacom.com; f. 1997; mobile telecommunications GSM network provider; partly owned by Celtel International B. V. (Netherlands); Dir EMILIENNE MACAULEY.

Orange Madagascar: Antananarivo; internet www.orange.mg; f. 1998; fmrly Antaris, la Société Malgache de Mobiles; name changed as above 2003; mobile telecommunication GSM network provider; market leader; Dir-Gen. PATRICE PEZAT.

Télécom Malagasy SA (TELMA): BP 763, 101 Antananarivo; tel. (20) 2242705; fax (20) 2242654; e-mail telmacorporate@telma.mg; internet www.telma.mg; 68% owned by Distacom (Hong Kong); owns DTS Wanadoo internet service provider; Chair. DAVID WHITE; Dir-Gen. RON ALLARD.

BROADCASTING

Radio

In 2001 there were an estimated 127 radio stations.

Radio MBS (Malagasy Broadcasting System): BP 11137, Anosipatrana, Antananarivo; tel. (20) 2266702; fax (20) 2268941; e-mail marketing@mbs.mg; internet www.mbs.mg; broadcasts by satellite; Man. SARAH RAVALOMANANA.

Radio Nationale Malagasy: BP 442, Anosy, 101 Antananarivo; tel. (20) 2221745; fax (20) 2232715; e-mail radmad@wanadoo.mg; internet www.takelaka.dts/radmad; state-controlled; part of the Office de Radiodiffusion et de Télévision de Madagascar (ORTM); broadcasts in French and Malagasy; Dir ALAIN RAJAONA.

Le Messager Radio Evangélique: BP 1374, 101 Antananarivo; tel. (20) 2234495; broadcasts in French, English and Malagasy; Dir JOCELYN RANJARISON.

Radio Antsiva: BP 632, Enceinte STEDIC, Village des Jeux, Zone Industrielle Nord, Route des Hydrocarbures, 101 Antananarivo; tel. (20) 2254849; e-mail antsiva@freenet.mg; internet www.antsiva.mg; f. 1994; broadcasts in French and Malagasy; Dir LALATIONE RAKOTONDRAZAFY.

Radio Don Bosco: BP 60, 105 Ivato; tel. (20) 2244387; fax (20) 2244511; e-mail rdb@wanadoo.mg; internet www.radiodonbosco.mg; f. 1996; Catholic, educational and cultural; Chair. Fr GIUSEPPE MIELE.

Radio Feon'ny Vahoaka (RFV): 103 Immeuble Ramaroson, 8e étage, 101 Antananarivo; tel. (20) 2233820; broadcasts in French and Malagasy; Dir ALAIN RAMAROSON.

Radio Lazan'iarivo (RLI): Lot V A49, Andafiavaratra, 101 Antananarivo; tel. (20) 2229016; fax (20) 2267559; e-mail rli@simicro.mg; broadcasts in French, English and Malagasy; privately owned; specializes in jazz music; Dir IHOBY RABARIJOHN.

Radio Tsioka Vao (RTV): Tana; tel. (20) 2221749; f. 1992; broadcasts in French, English and Malagasy; Dir DETKOU DEDONNAIS.

Television

MA TV: BP 1414 Ankorondrano, 101 Antananarivo; tel. (20) 2220897; fax (20) 2234421; e-mail matv@wanadoo.mg; internet www.matvonline.tv.

MBS Television (Malagasy Broadcasting System): BP 11137, Anosipatrana, Antananarivo; tel. (20) 2266702; fax (20) 2268941; e-mail journaltv@mbs.mg; internet www.mbs.mg; broadcasts in French and Malagasy.

Radio Télévision Analamanga (RTA): Immeuble Fiaro, 101 Antananarivo; e-mail rta@rta.mg; internet www.rta.mg; including four provincial radio stations; Gen. Man. PATRICK COTTRELLE.

Télévision Nasionaly Malagasy: BP 1202, Anosy, 101 Antananarivo; tel. (20) 2222381; state-controlled; part of the Office de Radiodiffusion et de Télévision de Madagascar (ORTM); broadcasts in French and Malagasy; Dir-Gen. RAZAFIMAHEFA HERINIRINA LALA.

Finance

(cap. = capital; res = reserves; dep. = deposits; m. = million; brs = branches; amounts in Malagasy francs)

BANKING

Central Bank

Banque Centrale de Madagascar: rue de la Révolution Socialiste Malgache, BP 550, 101 Antananarivo; tel. (20) 2221751; fax (20) 2234532; e-mail banque-centrale@banque-centrale.mg; internet www.banque-centrale.mg; f. 1973; bank of issue; cap. 1,000m., res –87,555.6m., dep. 3,842,281.0m. (Dec. 2004); Gov. FRÉDÉRIC RASAMOELY.

Other Banks

Bank of Africa (BOA)—Madagascar: 2 pl. de l'Indépendance, BP 183, 101 Antananarivo; tel. (20) 2239100; fax (20) 2229408; e-mail boamg.dg@bkofafrica.com; internet www.bkofafrica.net; f. 1976 as Bankin'ny Tantsaha Mpamokatra; name changed as above 1999; 35.1% owned by African Financial Holding, 15% state-owned; commercial bank, specializes in micro-finance; cap. 40.0m., res 17.4m., dep. 2,075.7m. (Dec. 2004); Pres. PAUL DERREUMAUX; Gen. Man. ALAIN LEPATRE LAMONTAGNE; 51 brs.

Banque Industrielle et Commerciale de Madagascar (BICM): 2 rue du Dr Raseta Andraharo, BP 889, 101 Antananarivo; tel. (20) 2356568; fax (20) 2356656; e-mail bicm@bicm.mg; internet www.bicm.mg; f. 2002; successor of the Banque Internationale Chine Madagascar, fmrly Compagnie Malgache de Banque; cap. 21,167.0m., res –5,377.9m., dep. 51,656.3m. (Dec. 2004); Dir Gen. DELMOTTE NICOLAS.

Banque Malgache de l'Océan Indien (BMOI) (Indian Ocean Malagasy Bank): pl. de l'Indépendance, BP 25 bis, Antaninarenina, 101 Antananarivo; tel. (20) 2234609; fax (20) 2234610; e-mail karine.rabefaritra@africa.bnpparibas.com; internet www.bmoi.mg; f. 1990; 75% owned by BNP Paribas SA (France); cap. 30,000m., res 121,700m., dep. 1,942,000m. (Dec. 2004); Pres. GASTON RAMENASON; Dir-Gen. JEAN-CLAUDE HERIDE; 8 brs.

Banque SBM Madagascar (SBM): rue Andrianary Ratianarivo Antsahavola 1, 101 Antananarivo; tel. (20) 2266607; fax (20) 2266608; e-mail sbmm@wanadoo.mg; f. 1998; 79.99% owned by SBM Global Investments Ltd (Mauritius), 20.01% owned by Nedbank Africa Investments Ltd (South Africa); cap. and res 20,873.4m., dep. 186,682.8m. (Dec. 2002); Chair. CHAITLALL GUNNESS; Gen. Man. KRISHNADUTT RAMBOJUN.

BFV—Société Générale: 14 Làlana Jeneraly Rabehevitra, BP 196, Antananarivo 101; tel. (20) 2220691; fax (20) 2237140; internet www.bfvsg.mg; f. 1977 as Banky Fampandrosoana ny Varotra; changed name in 1998; 70% owned by Société Générale (France) and 28.5%

state-owned; cap. 70,000m., res 24,300.3m., dep. 1,114,111.4m. (Dec. 2004); Chief Exec. MARCEL LENGUIN; 30 brs.

BNI—Crédit Lyonnais Madagascar: 74 rue du 26 Juin 1960, BP 174, 101 Antananarivo; tel. (20) 2223951; fax (20) 2233749; e-mail info@bni.mg; internet www.bni.mg; f. 1976 as Bankin 'ny Indostria; 51% owned by Crédit Lyonnais Global Banking (France), 32.58% state-owned; cap. and res 232,489.0m., dep. 2,374,632.0m. (Dec. 2004); Pres. and Chair. EVARISTO MARSON; Dir-Gen. PASCAL FALL; 22 brs.

Union Commercial Bank SA (UCB): 77 rue Solombavambahoaka Frantsay, Antsahavola, BP 197, 101 Antananarivo; tel. (20) 2227262; fax (20) 2228740; e-mail ucb.int@wanadoo.mg; f. 1992; 70% owned by Mauritius Commercial Bank Ltd; cap. 6,000m., res 60,087.6m., dep. 327,141.9m. (Dec. 2002); Pres. RAYMOND HEIN; Gen. Man. MARC MARIE JOSEPH DE BOLLIVIER; 3 brs.

INSURANCE

ARO (Assurances Réassurances Omnibranches): Antsahavola, BP 42, 101 Antananarivo; tel. (20) 2220154; fax (20) 2234464; e-mail arol@wanadoo.mg; state-owned; Pres. GUY ROLLAND RASOANAIVO; Dir-Gen. JIMMY RAMIANDRISON.

Compagnie Malgache d'Assurances et de Réassurances 'Ny Havana': Immeuble 'Ny Havana', Zone des 67 Ha, BP 3881, 101 Antananarivo; tel. (20) 2226760; fax (20) 2224303; e-mail nyhavana@wanadoo.mg; f. 1968; state-owned; cap. 5,435.6m. (2006); Dir-Gen. BERA RAZANAKOLONA.

Mutuelle d'Assurances Malagasy (MAMA): Lot 1F, 12 bis, rue Rainibetsimisaraka, Ambalavao-Isotry, BP 185, 101 Antananarivo; tel. (20) 2261882; fax (20) 2261883; f. 1965; Pres. FRÉDÉRIC RABARISON.

Société Malgache d'Assurances (SMA—ASCOMA): 13 rue Patrice Lumumba, BP 673, 101 Antananarivo; tel. (20) 2223162; fax (20) 2222785; e-mail ascoma@simicro.mg; f. 1952; Dir VIVIANE RAMANITRA.

Trade and Industry

DEVELOPMENT ORGANIZATIONS

Bureau d'Information pour les Entreprises (BIPE): Nouvel Immeuble ARO, Ampefiloha, 101 Antananarivo; tel. (20) 2230512; e-mail micdsp@wanadoo.mg; internet www.bipe.mg; part of the Ministry of Industry, Trade and the Development of the Private Sector.

Economic Development Board of Madagascar (EDBM): Nouvel Immeuble Aro Ampefiloha, Antananarivo; tel. (20) 2268121; fax (20) 2266105; e-mail edbm@edbm.mg; internet www.edbm.mg; f. 2006; advisory service for starting a business, obtaining visas and land acquisition; attracts and promotes foreign investment; Gen. Dir PREGA RAMSAMY.

La maison de l'entreprise: rue Samuel Ramahefy Ambatonakanga, BP 74, 101 Antananarivo; tel. (20) 2225386; fax (20) 2233669; e-mail cite@cite.mg; internet www.cite.mg; f. 1967; supports and promotes Malagasy businesses; Dir-Gen. ISABELLE GACHIE.

Office des Mines Nationales et des Industries Stratégiques (OMNIS): 21 Làlana Razanakombana, BP 1 bis, 101 Antananarivo; tel. (20) 2224439; fax (20) 2222985; e-mail omnis@simicro.mg; f. 1976; promotes the exploration and exploitation of mining resources, in particular oil resources; Dir-Gen. ELISE ALITERA RAZAKA.

Société d'Etude et de Réalisation pour le Développement Industriel (SERDI): BP 3180, 101 Antananarivo; tel. (20) 2225204; fax (20) 2229669; e-mail serdi@wanadoo.mg; f. 1966; Dir-Gen. RAOILISON RAJAONARY.

CHAMBER OF COMMERCE

Fédération des Chambres de Commerce, d'Industrie et d'Agriculture de Madagascar: 20 rue Paul Dussac, BP 166, 101 Antananarivo; tel. (20) 2221567; 12 mem. chambers; Pres. JEAN RAMAROMISA; Chair. HENRI RAZANATSEHENO; Sec.-Gen. HUBERT RATSIANDAVANA.

Chambre de Commerce, d'Industrie, d'Artisanat et d'Agriculture—Antananarivo (CCIAA): BP 166, 20 rue Henri Razanatseheno, Antaninarenina, 101 Antananarivo; tel. (20) 2220211; fax (20) 2220213; e-mail cciaa@tana-cciaa.org; internet www.tana-cciaa.org; f. 1993.

TRADE ASSOCIATION

Société d'Intérêt National des Produits Agricoles (SINPA): BP 754, rue Fernand-Kasanga, Tsimbazaza, Antananarivo; tel. (20) 2220558; fax (20) 2220665; f. 1973; monopoly purchaser and distributor of agricultural produce; Chair. GUALBERT RAZANAJATOVO; Gen. Man. JEAN CLOVIS RALIJESY.

EMPLOYERS' ORGANIZATIONS

Groupement des Entreprises de Madagascar (GEM): Kianja MDRM sy Tia Tanindrazana, Ambohijatovo, BP 1338, 101 Antananarivo; tel. (20) 2223841; fax (20) 2221965; e-mail gem@simicro.mg; internet www.gem-madagascar.com; f. 1976; 10 nat. syndicates and five regional syndicates comprising 700 cos and 47 directly affiliated cos; Pres. NAINA ANDRIANTSITOHAINA; Sec.-Gen. ZINAH RASAMUEL RAVALOSON.

Groupement National des Exportateurs de Vanille de Madagascar (GNEV): BP 21, Antalaha; tel. (13) 20714532; fax (13) 20816017; e-mail rama.anta@sat.blueline.mg; 18 mems; Pres. JEAN GEORGES RANDRIAMIHARISOA.

Malagasy Entrepreneurs' Association (FIV.MPA.MA): Lot II, 2e étage, Immeuble Santa Antaninarenina; tel. (20) 2229292; fax (20) 2229290; e-mail fivmpama@simicro.mg; comprises 10 trade assocs, representing 200 mems, and 250 direct business mems; Chair. HERINTSALAMA RAJAONARIVELO.

Syndicat Professionel des Producteurs d'eExtraits Aromatiques, Alimentaires et Medicinaux de Madagascar (SYPEAM): Lot II M 80 bis, Antsakaviro, BP 8530, 101 Antananarivo; tel. (20) 2226934; fax (20) 2261317.

Syndicat des Industries de Madagascar (SIM): Immeuble Holcim, Lot 1 bis, Tsaralalàna; BP 1695, 101 Antananarivo; tel. (20) 2224007; fax (20) 2222518; e-mail syndusmad@wanadoo.mg; internet www.syndusmad.com; f. 1958; Chair. SAMUEL RAVELOSON; 82 mems (2006).

Syndicat des Planteurs de Café: 37 Làlana Razafimahandry, BP 173, 101 Antananarivo.

Syndicat Professionnel des Agents Généraux d'Assurances: Antananarivo; f. 1949; Pres. SOLO RATSIMBAZAFY; Sec. IHANTA RANDRIAMANDRANTO.

UTILITIES

Electricity and Water

Office de Regulation de l'Électricité (ORE): Antananarivo; f. 2004; Dir MAMY RAKOTOMIZAO.

Jiro sy Rano Malagasy (JIRAMA): BP 200, 149 rue Rainandriamampandry, Faravohitra, 101 Antananarivo; tel. (20) 2220031; fax (20) 2233806; e-mail dgjirama@wanadoo.mg; f. 1975; controls production and distribution of electricity and water; managed by Lahmeyer International (Germany) from April 2005; Chair. PATRICK RAMIARAMANANA; Dir-Gen. BERNARD ROMAHN.

MAJOR COMPANIES

The following are some of the largest in terms either of capital investment or employment.

Brasseries STAR Madagascar: BP 3806, 101 Antananarivo; tel. (20) 2227711; fax (20) 2234682; f. 1953; cap. 10,090.9m. FMG; mfrs of beer and carbonated drinks; Pres. H. FRAISE; Gen. Man. YVAN COUDERC.

Compagnie Salinière de Madagascar: rue Béniowsky, BP 29, 201 Antsiranana; tel. (20) 8221373; fax (20) 8229394; e-mail consalmag@wanadoo.mg; f. 1895; cap. 1,312m. FMG; exploitation of salt marshes (60,000 tons a year); Pres. PANAYOTIS TALOUMIS; Dir-Gen. JEAN-YVES MORVAN; 200 employees (2007).

Coralma: Immeuble ARO Antsahavola, BP 1083, 101 Antananarivo; tel. (20) 2225189; fax (20) 2228037; e-mail coralmad@wanadoo.mg; f. 1989; production and distribution of tobacco; Administrator ERIC DAHLSTRÖM.

COTONA: route d'Ambositra, BP 45, Antsirabé; tel. (20) 4449422; fax (20) 4449222; e-mail sag@cotona.com; f. 1952; owned by Socota Textile Mills Ltd; cap. 8,000m. FMG; spinning, weaving, printing and dyeing of textiles; Chair. SALIM ISMAIL; Dir-Gen. HAKIM FAKIRA; 959 employees.

DINIKA International SA (Entreprise d'Etudes Pluridisciplinaires): BP 3359, 101 Antananarivo; tel. (20) 2222233; fax (20) 2221324; e-mail dinika@wanadoo.mg; f. 1979; civil engineering, architecture.

Dynatec Madagascar SARL: BP 4254, Bâtiment C2, Explorer Business Park, Ankorondrano,101 Antananarivo; tel. (20) 2254030; fax (20) 2254412; f. 2003; nickel and cobalt mining at Ambatovy.

Etablissements Gallois: BP 159, Antananarivo; tel. (20) 2222951; fax (20) 2234452; cap. 220m. FMG; leading producer of graphite and sisal; Pres. and Dir-Gen. HENRY GALLOIS.

Galana Distribution Petrolière SA: Immeuble Ikopa Centre, BP 60, 118 Antananarivo; tel. (20) 2246803; fax (20) 2246797; e-mail info@galana.com; internet www.galana.com; subsidiary of Galana,

Kenya; owns the national petroleum refinery at Toamasina: Galana Raffinerie Terminale SA.

Hasy Malagasy SA (HASYMA): BP 692, Antananarivo; tel. (20) 2264239; fax (20) 2234958; e-mail hasyma@wanadoo.mg; f. 1973; 51.98% owned by Développement des Agro-industries du Sud—Dagris (France); accounts for 75% of national cotton production; Gen. Dir YANNICK DAVENEL.

Holcim (Madagascar) SA: BP 332, 1 bis, rue Patrice Lumumba, Tsaralalana; tel. (20) 2232908; fax (20) 2233277; part of Holcim Overseas Group companies (Holcim (Outre-Mer)); fmrly Matériaux de Constructions Malgaches—MACOMA, renamed as above 2002; annual production capacity is 0.4m. metric tons; operates a cement plant in Antsirabe and three concrete plants; Chief Exec. ANDREAS ROGENMOSER; Dir-Gen JEAN PIERRE BISIAUX.

Jovenna: BP 12087, Antananarivo; tel. (20) 2269470; fax (20) 2269453; e-mail office@jovenna.mg; subsidiary of Jovenna, South Africa; one of three petroleum distributors to purchase the assets of the state company Solitany Malagasy.

Kraomita Malagasy (KRAOMA): BP 936, Ampefihola, 101 Antananarivo; tel. (20) 2224304; fax (20) 2224654; e-mail kraoma@dts.mg; internet takelaka.dts.mg/kraoma; f. 1966 as Cie Minière d'Andriamena (COMINA); cap. 1,540m. FMG; 100% state-owned; chrome mining and concentration; Gen. Man. CHRISTIAN RANAIVO; 450 employees (2000).

Laboratoires Pharmaceutiques Malgaches (FARMAD): BP 828, 101 Antananarivo; tel. (20) 2246622; fax (20) 2244775; pharmaceutical mfrs.

Madagascar Oil: Villa La Pervenche, Lotissement Bonnet, Ivandry, Antananarivo 101; e-mail info@madagascaroil.com; internet www.madagascaroil.com; f. 2004; CEO ALEX ARCHILA.

Marbres et Granits de Madagascar (MAGRAMA): 8 rue de la Réunion, 101 Antananarivo; tel. (20) 2230042; fax (20) 2228578; mines labradorite from Ambatofinandrahana and Bekily.

QIT Madagascar Minerals Ltd (QMM SA): BP 4003, Villa 3H, Lot II J-169 Ivandry, 101 Antananarivo; tel. (20) 2242559; fax (20) 2242506; f. 2001; 20% state owned; 80% owned by Rio Tinto plc (United Kingdom/Australia); construction of an ilmenite mine and deep-sea port in the Fort Dauphin region.

Societé Alubat/NACM Service: 352 route Circulaire Anjahana, BP 1073, 101 Antananarivo; tel. (20) 2223126; fax (20) 2233744; e-mail alubat@simicro.mg; internet www.lk-oi.com/alubat; f. 1960; mfrs of cutlery, tools, implements and metal parts; Dir-Gen. PATRICIA KWAN HUA; 40 employees (2004).

Omnium Industriel de Madagascar (OIM JB): BP 207, 24 rue Radama, 101 Antananarivo; tel. (20) 2222373; fax (20) 2228064; e-mail oim@oimjb.com; f. 1929; cap. 1,300m. FMG; mfrs of shoes and luggage; operates a tannery; Pres. and Dir-Gen. A. BARDAY; 174 employees (2004).

Pan-African Mining Madagascar Sarl (PAM): Lot II N 174 PA Analamahitsy, 101 Antananarivo; tel. (20) 2201961; fax (20) 2201960; e-mail pammsarl@wanadoo.mg; internet www.panafrican.com; f. 2003; mining exploration, particularly for gold, nickel, precious stones and uranium; a subsidiary of Pan-African Mining Corpn (Canada); Assoc. Man. OLIVIER RAKOTMALALA.

Papeteries de Madagascar SA (PAPMAD): BP 1756, 101 Antananarivo; Ambohimanambola 103; tel. and fax (20) 2220674; e-mail papmad@malagasy.com; f. 1963; cap. 6,364m. FMG (2000); paper-making; Chair. P. RAJAONARY; 472 employees (2003).

Société Bonnetière Malagasy (SOBOMA): BP 3789, 101 Antananarivo; tel. (20) 2244354; fax (20) 2244891; f. 1968; produces knitwear; Pres. RÉNÉ TARDY; Dir-Gen. JEAN-PIERRE TARDY; 300 employees.

Société Commerciale Laitière (SOCOLAIT): BP 4126; 101 Antananarivo; tel. (20) 2222282; fax (20) 2222279; cap. 2,800m. FMG; dairy products; Pres. SOCOTALY KARMALY.

Société des Cigarettes Melia de Madagascar (SACIMEM): route d'Ambositra, BP 128, Antsirabé 110; tel. (20) 4448241; e-mail sacimem@wanadoo.mg; f. 1956; cap. 881m. FMG; mfrs of cigarettes; Pres. and Dir-Gen. PHILIPPE DE VESINNE LARUE; Dir LAURENT TABELLION.

Société d'Etudes de Constructions et Réparations Navales SA (SECREN): 201 Diego Suarez, POB 135, Antsiranana; tel. (20) 29321; fax (20) 29326; e-mail secren@wanadoo.mg; 37.5% state-owned; f. 1975; transfer to the private sector pending; cap. 400m. ariary; ship-building and repairs; Gen. Man. CHARLES HILAIRE SOLOHERY; 1,000 employees (2007).

Société d'Exploitation des Sources d'Eaux Minérales Naturelles d'Andranovelona SA (Sema Eau Vive): BP 22, 101 Antananarivo; tel. (20) 2227711; fax (20) 2234692; produces mineral water.

Société de Filature et de Tissage de Madagascar (FITIM): BP 127, Mahajanga; tel. (20) 6222127; fax (20) 6229345; e-mail fitim@malagasy.com; f. 1930; cap. 1,444m. FMG; spinning and weaving of jute; Pres. C. A. WILLIAM RAVONINJATOVO; Dir-Gen. AZIZ HOUSSEN; 113 employees.

Société Malgache de Collecte et de Distribution: BP 188, 101 Antananarivo; tel. (20) 2224871; fax (20) 2225024; f. 1972; Chair. HENRI RASAMOELINA; Gen. Man. NORBERT RAZANAKOTO.

Société Malgache de Cosmetiques et de Parfumerie (SOMALCO): Tanjombato, BP 852, 101 Antananarivo; tel. (20) 2246537; fax (20) 2247079; e-mail somalco@sicob.mg; perfumery, cosmetics and toothpaste; Pres. GOULSENBANOU BARDAY; Dir-Gen. NIGAR BARDAY; 56 employees (1999).

Société Malgache d'Exploitations Minières (SOMEM): BP 266, Antananarivo; f. 1926; cap. 130m. FMG; mining of graphite and mica; Pres. JEAN SCHNEIDER; Dir-Gen. LUCIEN DUMAS.

Société Malgache de Pêcherie (SOMAPECHE): BP 324, Mahanga; 33% state-owned; cap. 200m. FMG; sea fishing; Pres. J. RABEMANANJARA; Dir-Gen. J. BRUNOT; 1,200 employees (1996).

Société des Produits Chimiques de Madagascar SA (PROCHIMAD): BP 3145, 101 Antananarivo; tel. (20) 2244140; fax (20) 2244726; e-mail pest-vr@dts.mg; manufactures chemicals and fertilizers; Pres. and Dir-Gen. CHARLES ANDRIANTSITOHAINA.

Société Siramamy Malagasy SA (SIRAMA): BP 1633, Impasse, rue de Belgique Isoraka, 101 Antananarivo; tel. (20) 2225235; fax (20) 2227231; e-mail sirama@wanadoo.mg; f. 1949; 74.4% state-owned; scheduled for privatization; undergoing restructuring; cap. 2,500m. FMG; sugar refinery at St Louis; accounts for 85% of national sugar production; cap. 1,874.8m.; Pres. and Dir-Gen. ZAKA HARISON RAKOTONIRAINY; 4,691 employees (2005).

Société Verrerie Malagasy (SOVEMA): BP 84, Toamasina; f. 1970; 31.2% state-owned; cap. 235.6m. FMG; bottles and glass articles; Pres. and Dir-Gen. A. SIBILLE.

Tiko Group: BP 3877, Antananarivo; tel. (20) 2246877; fax (20) 2247859; e-mail carina_sdg@tiko.mg; internet www.tiko.mg; f. 1979; includes agro-alimentary (dairy), commercial, construction, media and transport interests; Pres. LALAO RAVALOMANANA; Gen. Man. BRUNO RANDRIARISON.

Total: Immeuble Titaratra, Ankolondrano, 101 Antananarivo; tel. (20) 2239040; fax (20) 2237545; e-mail philippe.bourgeois@total.com.mg; subsidiary of Total, France; one of four petroleum distributors to purchase the assets of the state company Solitany Malagasy; Dir PIERRE-AIMÉE CLERC.

TRADE UNIONS

Cartel National des Organisations Syndicales de Madagascar (CARNOSYMA): BP 1035, 101 Antananarivo.

Confédération des Travailleurs Malagasy Révolutionnaires (FISEMARE): Lot IV N 76-A, Ankadifotsy, BP 1128, Befelatanana-Antananarivo 101; tel. (20) 2221989; fax (20) 2267712; f. 1985; Pres. PAUL RABEMANANJARA.

Confédération des Travailleurs Malgaches (Fivomdronamben'ny Mpiasa Malagasy—FMM): Lot IVM 133 A Antetezanafovoany I, BP 846, 101 Antananarivo; tel. (20) 2224565; f. 1957; Sec.-Gen. JEANNOT RAMANARIVO; 30,000 mems.

Fédération des Syndicats des Travailleurs de Madagascar (Firaisan'ny Sendika eran'i Madagaskara—FISEMA): Lot III, rue Pasteur Isotry, 101 Antananarivo; f. 1956; Pres. DESIRÉ RALAMBOTAHINA; Sec.-Gen. M. RAZAKANAIVO; 8 affiliated unions representing 60,000 mems.

Sendika Kristianina Malagasy (SEKRIMA) (Christian Confederation of Malagasy Trade Unions): Soarano, route de Mahajanga, BP 1035, 101 Antananarivo; tel. (20) 2223174; f. 1937; Pres. MARIE RAKOTOANOSY; Gen. Sec. RAYMOND RAKOTOARISAONA; 158 affiliated unions representing 40,000 mems.

Union des Syndicats Autonomes de Madagascar (USAM): Ampasadratsarahoby, Lot 11 H67, Faravohitra, BP 1038, 101 Antananarivo; tel. (20) 2227485; fax (20) 2222203; e-mail usam@wanadoo.mg; Pres. NORBERT RAKOTOMANANA; Sec.-Gen. VICTOR RAHAGA; 46 affiliated unions representing 30,000 mems.

Transport

RAILWAYS

In 2001 there were 893 km of railway, including four railway lines, all 1-m gauge track. The northern system, which comprised 720 km of track, links the east coast with Antsirabé, in the interior, via Moramanga and Antananarivo, with a branch line from Moramanga to Lake Alaotra and was privatized in 2001. The southern system, which comprised 163 km of track, links Manakara, on the east coast, with Fianarantsoa.

Réseau National des Chemins de Fer Malagasy (RNCFM): 1 ave de l'Indépendance, BP 259, Soarano, 101 Antananarivo; tel. (20) 2220521; fax (20) 2222288; f. 1909; in the process of transfer to private sector; Administrator DANIEL RAZAFINDRABE.

Fianarantsoa-Côte Est (FCE): FCE Gare, Fianarantsoa; tel. (20) 7551354; e-mail fce@blueline.mg; internet www.fce-madagascar.com; f. 1936; southern network, 163 km.

Madarail: Gare de Soarano, 1 ave de l'Indépendance, BP 1175, 101 Antananarivo; tel. (20) 2234599; fax (20) 2221883; e-mail madarail@wanadoo.mg; internet www.comazar.com/madarail.htm; f. 2001; joint venture, operated by Comazar, South Africa; 45% of Comazar is owned by Sheltam Locomotive and Rail Services, South Africa; 31.6% is owned by Spoornet, South Africa; operates the northern network of the Madagascan railway (650 km); Chair. ERIC PEIFFER; Gen. Dir PATRICK CLAES; 878 employees.

ROADS

In 2001 there were an estimated 49,837 km of classified roads; about 11.6% of the road network was paved. In 1987 there were 39,500 km of unclassified roads, used only in favourable weather. A road and motorway redevelopment programme, funded by the World Bank (€300m.) and the European Union (EU—€61m.), began in June 2000. In August 2002 the EU undertook to disburse US $10m. for the reconstruction of 11 bridges destroyed during the political crisis in that year. In 2003 Japan pledged $28m. to build several bridges and a 15-km bypass. The Government planned to have restored and upgraded 14,000 km of highways and 8,000 km of rural roads to an operational status by 2015. In 2005, according to the IMF, 8,982 km of roads had been maintained or rehabilitated.

INLAND WATERWAYS

The Pangalanes canal runs for 600 km near the east coast from Toamasina to Farafangana. In 1990 432 km of the canal between Toamasina and Mananjary were navigable.

SHIPPING

There are 18 ports, the largest being at Toamasina, which handles about 70% of total traffic, and Mahajanga; several of the smaller ports are prone to silting problems. A new deep-sea port was to be constructed at Ehoala, near Fort Dauphin, in order to accommodate the activity of an ilmenite mining development by 2008.

CMA—CGM Madagascar: BP 12042, Village des jeux, Bat. C1 Ankorondrano, 101 Antananarivo; tel. (20) 2235949; fax (20) 2266120; e-mail tnr@cma-cgm.mg; internet www.cma-cgm.com; maritime transport; Gen. Man. PHILIPPE MURCIA.

Compagnie Générale Maritime Sud (CGM): BP 1185, lot II U 31 bis, Ampahibe, 101 Antananarivo; tel. (20) 2220113; fax (20) 2226530.

Compagnie Malgache de Navigation (CMN): rue Rabearivelo, BP 1621, 101 Antananarivo; tel. (20) 2225516; fax (20) 2230358; f. 1960; coasters; 13,784 grt; 97.5% state-owned; privatization pending; Pres. ELINAH BAKOLY RAJAONSON; Dir-Gen. ARISTIDE EMMANUEL.

SCAC-SDV Shipping Madagascar: rue Rabearivelo Antsahavola, BP 514, 102 Antananarivo; tel. (20) 2220631; fax (20) 2247862; operates the harbour in Antananarivo Port.

Société Malgache des Transports Maritimes (SMTM): 6 rue Indira Gandhi, BP 4077, 101 Antananarivo; tel. (20) 2227342; fax (20) 2233327; f. 1963; 59% state-owned; privatization pending; services to Europe; Chair. ALEXIS RAZAFINDRATSIRA; Dir-Gen. JEAN RANJEVA.

CIVIL AVIATION

The Ivato international airport is at Antananarivo, while the airports at Mahajanga, Toamasina and Nossi-Bé can also accommodate large jet aircraft. There are 211 airfields, two-thirds of which are privately owned. In 1996 the Government authorized private French airlines to operate scheduled and charter flights between Madagascar and Western Europe.

Air Madagascar (Société Nationale Malgache des Transports Aériens): 31 ave de l'Indépendance, Analakely, BP 437, 101 Antananarivo; tel. (20) 2222222; fax (20) 2233760; e-mail commercial@airmadagascar.com; internet www.airmadagascar.com; f. 1962; 90.60% state-owned; 3.17% owned by Air France (France); transfer to the private sector pending; restructured and managed by Lufthansa Consulting since 2002; extensive internal routes connecting all the principal towns; external services to France, Italy, the Comoros, Kenya, Mauritius, Réunion, South Africa and Thailand; Chair. HERINIAINA RAZAFIMAHEFA; Chief Exec. ULRICH LINK.

Air Transport et Transit Régional (ATTR): tel. (32) 0518811; fax (32) 3205218; e-mail attr.reservation@blueline.mg; internet www.attrmada.com; f. 2006; private; regular local and regional services; Dir Gen. FRÉDÉRIC RABESAHALA.

Aviation Civile de Madagascar (ACM): BP 4414, 101 Tsimbazaza-Antananarivo; tel. (20) 2222438; fax (20) 2224726; e-mail acm@acm.mg; f. 2000; Chair. MAXIME RAVELOJAOMA; Dir-Gen. FRANÇOIS XAVIER RANDRIAMAHANDRY.

Transports et Travaux Aériens de Madagascar (TAM): 17 ave de l'Indépendance, Analakely, Antananarivo; tel. (20) 2222222; fax (20) 2224340; e-mail tamdg@wanadoo.mg; f. 1951; provides airline services; Administrators LALA RAZAFINDRAKOTO, FRANÇOIS DANE.

Tourism

Madagascar's attractions include unspoiled scenery, many unusual varieties of flora and fauna, and the rich cultural diversity of Malagasy life. In 2004 some 228,785 tourists visited Madagascar, the majority were from France (56.5%). Revenue from tourism in that year was estimated at US $265m. The number of hotel rooms increased from some 3,040 in 1991 to an estimated 8,435 in 2001.

Direction d'Appui aux Investissements Publiques: Ministry of Culture and Tourism, BP 610, rue Fernand Kasanga Tsimbazaza, 101 Antananarivo; tel. (20) 2262816; fax (20) 2235410; e-mail mintourdati@wandaoo.mg; internet www.tourisme.gov.mg.

La Maison du Tourisme de Madagascar: pl. de l'Indépendance, BP 3224, 101 Antananarivo; tel. (20) 2235178; fax (20) 2269522; e-mail mtm@simicro.mg; internet www.tourisme.madagascar.com; Exec. Dir ANDRÉ ANDRIAMBOAVONJY.

Defence

As assessed at November 2006, total armed forces numbered 13,500 men: army 12,500, navy 500 and air force 500. There is a paramilitary gendarmerie of 8,100.

Defence Expenditure: Budgeted at an estimated 639,000m. Malagasy francs in 2006.

Chief of Armed Forces General Staff: Comm. MAMY SOLOFONIAINA.

Education

Education is officially compulsory between six and 13 years of age. Madagascar has both public and private schools, although legislation that was enacted in 1978 envisaged the progressive elimination of private education. Primary education generally begins at the age of six and lasts for five years. Secondary education, beginning at 11 years of age, lasts for a further seven years, comprising a first cycle of four years and a second of three years. In 2005/06 primary net enrolment included 98% of children in the relevant age-group, while, according to UNESCO estimates, in 1998/99 secondary enrolment included 11% of children in the relevant age-group (males 11%; females 12%). In 2003/04 42,100 students attended institutions providing tertiary education. In 1999 the OPEC Fund granted a loan worth US $10m. to support a government programme to improve literary standards and to increase access to education. In 2001 the Arab Bank for Economic Development in Africa granted a loan of $8m. to finance general education-related projects. The budget for 2004 allocated 205,4000m. ariary (22.9% of budgetary expenditure) to education.

Bibliography

Allen, P. M. *Madagascar: Conflicts of Authority in the Great Island.* Boulder, CO, Westview Press, 1995.

Archer, R. *Madagascar depuis 1972, la marche d'une révolution.* Paris, L'Harmattan, 1976.

Bastian, G. *Madagascar, étude géographique et économique.* Nathan, 1967.

Bradt, H., and Brown, M. *Madagascar.* Oxford, Clio Press, 1993.

Brown, Sir M. *Madagascar Rediscovered.* London, Damien Tunnacliffe, 1978.

A History of Madagascar. London, Damien Tunnacliffe, 1995.

Cadoux, C. *La République malgache.* Paris, Berger-Levrault, 1970.

Chaigneau, P. *Rivalités politiques et socialisme à Madagascar.* Paris, Centre des Hautes Etudes sur l'Afrique et l'Asie Modernes, 1985.

Covell, M. *Madagascar. Politics, Economics and Society.* London, Frances Pinter, 1987.

Historical Dictionary of Madagascar. Lanham, MD, Scarecrow Press, 1995.

Deleris, F. *Ratsiraka: socialisme et misère à Madagascar.* Paris, L'Harmattan, 1986.

Deschamps, H. *Histoire de Madagascar.* 4th Edn. Paris, Berger-Levrault, 1972.

Dodwell, C. *Madagascar Travels.* London, Hodder & Stoughton, 1995.

Drysdale, H. *Dancing with the Dead: A Journey through Zanzibar and Madagascar.* London, Hamish Hamilton, 1991.

Duruflé, G. *L'Ajustement structurel en Afrique (Sénégal, Côte d'Ivoire, Madagascar).* Paris, Editions Karthala, 1987.

Feeley-Harnick, G. *A Green Estate: Restoring Independence in Madagascar.* Washington, DC, Smithsonian Institution Press, 1991.

de Gaudusson, J. *L'Administration malgache.* Paris, Berger-Levrault, 1976.

Heseltine, N. *Madagascar.* London, Pall Mall, 1971.

Hugon, P. *Economie et enseignement à Madagascar.* Paris, Institut International de Planification de l'Education, 1976.

Litalien, R. *Madagascar 1956–1960. Etape vers la décolonisation.* Paris, Ecole Pratique des Hautes Etudes, 1975.

Massiot, M. *L'organisation politique, administrative, financière et judiciaire de la République malgache.* Antananarivo, Librairie de Madagascar, 1970.

Mutibwa, P. *The Malagasy and the Europeans: Madagascar's Foreign Relations 1861–95.* London, Longman, 1974.

Pascal, R. *La République malgache: Pacifique indépendance.* Paris, Berger-Levrault, 1965.

Pezzotta, F. *Madagascar, a Mineral and Gemstone Paradise.* East Hampton, CT, Lapis International LLC, 2001.

Pryor, F. L. *Malawi and Madagascar: The Political Economy of Poverty, Equity and Growth.* New York, NY, Oxford University Press, 1991.

Rabemananjara, J. *Nationalisme et problèmes malgaches.* Paris, 1958.

Rabenoro, C. *Les relations extérieures de Madagascar, de 1960 à 1972.* Paris, L'Harmattan, 1986.

Raison-Jourde, F. *Les souverains de Madagascar.* Paris, Editions Karthala, 1983.

Rajoelina, P. *Quarante années de la vie politique de Madagascar, 1947–1987.* Paris, L'Harmattan, 1988.

Rajoelina, P., and Ramelet, A. *Madagascar, la grande île.* Paris, L'Harmattan, 1989.

Ralaimihoatra, E. *Histoire de Madagascar.* 2 vols. Antananarivo, Société Malgache d'Editions, 1966–67.

Ramahatra, O. *Madagascar: une économie en phase d'ajustement.* Paris, L'Harmattan, 1989.

Roubaud, F. *Identités et transition démocratique: l'exception malgache.* Paris, L'Harmattan, 2001.

Schuurman, D., and Ravelojoana, N. *Madagascar.* London, New Holland, 1997.

Sharp, L. A. *The Possessed and the Dispossessed.* Berkeley, CA, University of California Press, 1993.

Spacensky, A. *Madagascar: cinquante ans de vie politique (de Ralaimongo à Tsiranana).* Paris, Nouvelles Editions Latines, 1970.

Thompson, V., and Adloff, R. *The Malagasy Republic.* Stanford, CA, Stanford University Press, 1965.

Tronchon, J. *L'insurrection malgache de 1947.* Paris, Editions Karthala, 1986.

Tyson, P. *The Eighth Continent: Life, Death and Discovery in the Lost World of Madagascar.* New York, NY, William Morrow & Co, 2000.

Vérin, P. *Madagascar.* Paris, Editions Karthala, 1990.

Vindard, G. R., and Battistini, R. *Bio-geography and Ecology of Madagascar.* The Hague, 1972.

Wilson, J. *Lemurs of the Lost World.* 2nd Edn. London, Impact Books, 1995.

MALAWI

Physical and Social Geography

A. MacGREGOR HUTCHESON

The land-locked Republic of Malawi extends some 840 km from north to south, varying in width from 80 to 160 km. It has a total area of 118,484 sq km (45,747 sq miles), including 24,208 sq km (9,347 sq miles) of inland water, and is aligned along the southern continuation of the east African rift valley system. There are land borders with Tanzania to the north, with Zambia to the west, and with Mozambique to the south and east. Frontiers with Mozambique and Tanzania continue to the east, along the shores of Lake Malawi.

Malawi occupies a plateau of varying height, bordering the deep rift valley trench, which averages 80 km in width. The northern two-thirds of the rift valley floor are almost entirely occupied by Lake Malawi, which is 568 km in length and varies in width from 16 km to 80 km. The lake covers an area of 23,310 sq km, and has a mean surface of 472 m above sea-level. The southern third of the rift valley is traversed by the Shire river, draining Lake Malawi, via the shallow Lake Malombe, to the Zambezi river. The plateau surfaces on either side of the rift valley lie mainly at 760–1,370 m, but elevations up to 3,002 m are attained; above the highlands west of Lake Malawi are the Nyika and Viphya plateaux (at 2,606 m and 1,954 m, respectively) and the Dedza mountains and Kirk Range, which rise to between 1,524 m and 2,440 m in places. South of Lake Malawi are the Shire highlands and the Zomba and Mulanje mountain ranges; the Zomba plateau rises to 2,087 m, and Mt Mulanje, the highest mountain in central Africa, to 3,050 m above sea-level.

The great variations in altitude and latitudinal extent are responsible for a wide range of climatic, soil and vegetational conditions within Malawi. There are three climatic seasons. During the cool season, from May to August, there is very little cloud, and mean temperatures in the plateau areas are 15.5°C–18°C, and in the rift valley 20°C–24.5°C. The coldest month is July, when the maximum temperature is 22.2°C and the minimum 11.7°C. In September and October, before the rains, a short hot season occurs when humidity increases: mean temperatures range from 27°C–30°C in the rift valley, and from 22°C–24.5°C on the plateaux at this time. During October–November temperatures exceeding 37°C may be registered in the low-lying areas. The rainy season lasts from November to April, and over 90% of the total annual rainfall occurs during this period. Most of Malawi receives an annual rainfall of 760–1,015 mm, but some areas in the higher plateaux experience over 1,525 mm.

Malawi possesses some of the most fertile soils in south-central Africa. Of particular importance are those in the lake-shore plains, the Lake Chilwa-Palombe plain and the upper and lower Shire valley. Good plateau soils occur in the Lilongwe-Kasungu high plains and in the tea-producing areas of Thyolo, Mulanje and Nkhata Bay districts. Although just over one-half of the land area of Malawi is considered suitable for cultivation, rather less than 50% of this area is cultivated at present; this is an indication of the agricultural potential yet to be realized. The lakes and rivers have been exploited for their considerable hydroelectric and irrigation potential.

Malawi is one of the more densely populated countries of Africa, with 9,933,868 inhabitants (an average density of 105.4 per sq km) at the 1998 census. The UN estimated the population at 13,571,000 in mid-2006. Population patterns are expected to be affected by the high rate of incidence of HIV/AIDS, which is particularly prevalent in urban areas. Labour has been a Malawian resource for many years, and thousands of migratory workers seek employment in neighbouring countries, particularly in South Africa.

As a result of physical, historical and economic factors, Malawi's population is unevenly distributed. At the 1998 census the Southern Region, the most developed of the three regions, contained 47% of the population, while the Central Region had 41% and the Northern Region only 12%.

Recent History

CHRISTOPHER SAUNDERS

Based on an earlier article by RICHARD BROWN

On 6 July 1964 the previously British colony of Nyasaland became the independent state of Malawi. Two years later Malawi became a republic and one-party state, with Dr Hastings Kamuzu Banda, who had led the struggle against British rule, as its President, and his party, the Malawi Congress Party (MCP), the only legal political organization. In 1971 Banda was awarded the title President-for-life. No political opposition was tolerated, and human rights organizations, including Amnesty International, repeatedly criticized the treatment of political detainees. In 1983 rivalry developed between Dick Matenje, the Secretary-General of the MCP and a Minister without Portfolio, and John Tembo, the Governor of the Reserve Bank of Malawi, concerning the eventual succession to the presidency. When Matenje and three other senior politicians died in May that year, apparently in a road accident, Banda's opponents-in-exile claimed that they had been murdered while trying to leave the country (see below).

TRANSITION TO DEMOCRACY

In March 1992 the Government was exposed to unprecedented criticism from the influential Roman Catholic Church in Malawi, whose bishops published an open letter condemning the state's alleged abuses of human rights. Pressure on the Government intensified later that month, when some 80 Malawian political exiles gathered in Lusaka, Zambia, to devise a strategy to precipitate political reforms. In April Chakufwa Chihana, a prominent trade union leader who had demanded multi-party elections, returned to Malawi from exile, only to be immediately arrested. In the following month industrial unrest in the southern city of Blantyre escalated into violent anti-Government riots, which spread to the capital, Lilongwe, and resulted in at least 40 deaths. Shortly afterwards international donors suspended all non-humanitarian aid to Malawi, pending an improvement in the Government's observance of human rights.

Elections to an enlarged legislature took place in June 1992. A total of 675 MCP candidates contested 141 elective seats in the National Assembly: 45 candidates were returned unopposed, five seats remained vacant, owing to the disqualification of some candidates, and 62 former members of the National Assembly lost their seats. Opposition groups challenged the Government's claim of a turn-out of about 80% of the electorate. In September a group of opposition politicians formed the

Alliance for Democracy (AFORD), a pressure group operating within Malawi under the chairmanship of Chihana, which aimed to campaign for democratic political reform. Another opposition organization, the United Democratic Front (UDF), was formed in the same month. In October Banda reluctantly conceded to demands for a national referendum by secret ballot on the introduction of multi-party democracy.

In the referendum, held in mid-June 1993, turn-out was recorded at 67% of the electorate, with 63.2% of those who voted supporting the reintroduction of multi-party politics, despite the Government's efforts to disrupt the opposition. Banda agreed to establish a National Executive Council, to oversee the transition to a multi-party system, and a National Consultative Council to draft a new constitution. Both councils were to comprise members of the Government and the opposition. Banda announced a general amnesty for thousands of political exiles, and stated that a general election would be held, on a multi-party basis, within a year. In late June the Constitution was amended to allow the registration of political parties other than the MCP: by mid-August five organizations, including AFORD and the UDF, had been accorded legal status.

In October 1993 Banda became seriously ill and underwent neurological surgery in South Africa. Having rejected opposition demands for the election of an apolitical interim Head of State, the office of the President announced the formation of a three-member Presidential Council to assume executive power in Banda's absence. In mid-November the National Assembly adopted constitutional amendments that included the repeal of the institution of life presidency, the reduction of the qualifying age for a presidential candidate from 40 to 35 years, the repeal of the requirement that election candidates be members of the MCP, the repeal of the right of the President to nominate members of the legislature exclusively from the MCP and the lowering of the minimum voting age from 21 to 18 years.

Having made an unexpected recovery, Banda resumed full presidential powers on 7 December 1993 and the Presidential Council was dissolved. Shortly afterwards, in response to increasing pressure from the opposition, the Government amended the Constitution to provide for the appointment of an acting President in the event of the incumbent being incapacitated. In February 1994 the MCP announced that Banda was to be the party's presidential candidate in the forthcoming general election, which was scheduled to take place on 17 May. In the same month the National Assembly approved an increase in the number of elected legislative members in the approaching general election from 141 to 177. On 16 May a provisional Constitution was adopted by the National Assembly. The new document provided for the appointment of a Constitutional Committee and of a human rights commission, and abolished the system of 'traditional' courts. Banda's domination of the country finally ended with the multi-party elections held on the following day. In the four-candidate presidential contest, Bakili Muluzi, the leader of the UDF, obtained 47.3% of the votes, Banda 33.6% and Chihana (of AFORD) 18.6%. The UDF won 84 of the 177 parliamentary seats, the MCP 55 seats and AFORD 36 seats. (The results of voting in two constituencies were invalidated.)

THE MULUZI GOVERNMENT

President Muluzi and his Vice-President, Justin Malewezi, were inaugurated later in May 1994. The principal aims of the new administration were defined as being to alleviate poverty and ensure food security, and to combat corruption and the mismanagement of resources. Three prisons where abuses of human rights were known to have taken place were closed, an amnesty was granted to the country's remaining political prisoners and all death sentences were commuted to terms of life imprisonment. Although the new Government was dominated by the UDF, it included members of the Malawi National Democratic Party and the United Front for Multiparty Democracy. Attempts to recruit members of AFORD into a coalition administration initially failed, owing to disagreements regarding the allocation of senior portfolios, and in June AFORD and the MCP signed what was termed a 'memorandum of understanding' whereby they would function as an opposition front. The Muluzi Government was thus deprived of a majority in the National Assembly, which was inaugurated at the end of June. In August it was announced that Banda, while remaining honorary Life President of the MCP, was to retire from active involvement in politics. Gwandaguluwe Chakuamba, Vice-President of the MCP, effectively succeeded to the party leadership.

Although Chihana was appointed Second Vice-President and Minister of Irrigation and Water Development in September 1994, and AFORD members were allocated responsibility for agriculture, transport, research and the environment, the AFORD-MCP 'memorandum of understanding' remained in force until January 1995, when AFORD, acknowledging that the new Government had made significant progress in the restoration of political stability and the establishment of democracy, announced an end to its co-operation with the MCP. The creation of the post of Second Vice-President necessitated a constitutional amendment and provoked severe criticism from the MCP. In March the National Assembly approved the establishment—although not before May 1999—of a second chamber of parliament, the Senate.

Meanwhile, Muluzi had, in June 1994, established an independent commission of inquiry to investigate the deaths of Matenje and his associates in May 1983. In January 1995, in accordance with the findings of the commission, Banda was placed under house arrest, Tembo and two former police-officers were arrested and detained, and the four were charged with murder and conspiracy to murder. A former inspector-general of the police, who was alleged, *inter alia*, to have destroyed evidence relating to the deaths, was later also charged with conspiracy to murder. In December, however, Banda and the other defendants were acquitted of conspiracy to murder and to pervert the course of justice. The Director of Public Prosecutions subsequently appealed against the verdict, complaining that the presiding judge had effectively instructed the jury to acquit the defendants. In July 1997 the Supreme Court dismissed an appeal against the acquittal of Banda and Tembo on murder charges, shortly after Muluzi reportedly requested that all criminal cases against Banda be discontinued. In the same month Banda announced his intention to resign as President of the MCP. In November Banda died in South Africa, where he had been undergoing emergency medical treatment.

In May 1996 Chihana resigned from the Government, expressing his intention to devote himself more fully to the work of his party, and the following month AFORD withdrew from its coalition with the UDF (which meant that the Government lost its parliamentary majority) and declared that its ministers still in the Cabinet should resign. Dr Mponda Mkandawire, the Minister of Natural Resources, did step down, and became a member of AFORD's 'shadow cabinet', but five ministers who refused to relinquish their ministerial posts were dismissed from AFORD's National Executive. Another AFORD member was included in the Cabinet in July. AFORD and the MCP insisted that AFORD ministers who had disobeyed instructions to resign should be regarded as members of the UDF, as they were effectively maintaining that party's parliamentary majority. When this demand was rejected, the opposition parties boycotted Parliament and appealed to the High Court to declare the previous parliamentary session illegal and unconstitutional, but the case was dismissed. In April 1997 the MCP ended its parliamentary boycott, following a meeting between Muluzi and Chakuamba, at which Muluzi allegedly promised to amend the Constitution to prevent parliamentary delegates from changing their political affiliation without standing for re-election.

In June 1998 the National Assembly approved legislation that provided for the replacement of the current multiple-ballot electoral system with the use of a single ballot, and for a reinforcement of the authority and independence of the electoral commission. In November legislation was adopted to allow presidential and parliamentary elections to run concurrently and the elections were subsequently scheduled for 18 May 1999. An electoral alliance between the MCP and AFORD—officially announced in February 1999—created serious divisions within the MCP, when the party's leader and presidential candidate, Chakuamba, selected AFORD leader

Chakufwa Chihana as the candidate for the vice-presidency, in preference to the MCP's Tembo. Thousands of Tembo's supporters mounted protests to demand Chakuamba's resignation. The Chakuamba-Chihana alliance also provoked a wider dispute with the UDF and the Malawi Electoral Commission (MEC), which claimed that the arrangement was unconstitutional, but in April the High Court rejected their petition. In February the National Assembly adopted a report by the MEC, which had caused considerable controversy by recommending the creation of a further 72 parliamentary seats, including an additional 42 in the Southern Region, a UDF stronghold. After widespread opposition to the proposals, only 16 of the 72 seats were approved.

After two postponements, the presidential and legislative elections were held on 15 June 1999. The turn-out was high, with some 93.8% of registered voters reported to have participated. Muluzi was re-elected to the presidency, securing 51.4% of the votes cast, while Chakuamba obtained 43.3% and Kamulepo Kalua of the MDP 1.4%. At the elections to the expanded National Assembly, 658 candidates and 11 parties contested the 193 seats. The ruling UDF won 93 seats, while the MCP secured 66, AFORD 29 and independent candidates four. (Voting in the remaining constituency was later postponed until October, owing to the death of a candidate.)

Despite declarations from international observers that the elections were largely free and fair, the MCP-AFORD alliance filed two petitions with the High Court, challenging Muluzi's victory and the results in 16 districts. The opposition alleged irregularities in the voter registration process and claimed that Muluzi's win was unconstitutional, as he had failed to gain the support of 50% of all registered voters. None the less, Muluzi was inaugurated in late June 1999 and a new Cabinet was appointed. In July the High Court ordered the MEC to allow opposition lawyers access to voting materials from the disputed districts, but the commission subsequently appealed against the order. In August the UDF regained a parliamentary majority when the four independent deputies decided to ally themselves with the UDF, of which they had all previously been members.

In December 1999 a report published by the electoral commissions forum of the Southern African Development Community (SADC) emphasized the failings of the MEC and recommended that in future it consist solely of members with no party political affiliation. A recount of votes cast in the presidential election began and later in December lawyers representing the MCP-AFORD alliance claimed to have discovered evidence of electoral fraud carried out to the benefit of the UDF. Meanwhile, in October by-elections were held in three constituencies, with UDF candidates winning all of the three available seats, thus increasing the number of deputies supporting the UDF to 100. In early March 2000 Muluzi appointed Mathews Chikoanda, hitherto Governor of the Central Bank, as Minister of Finance and Economic Planning to replace Cassim Chilumpha, who was given responsibility for the Ministry of Education, Sports and Culture. Chilumpha had come under investigation by the Anti-Corruption Bureau, following media reports questioning the legality of circumstances surrounding the awarding of a pre-shipment contract. In May the High Court dismissed the opposition's case disputing Muluzi's victory in June 1999 and declared his election to the presidency lawful.

Ongoing divisions within the leadership of the MCP prompted the defection of two of the party's deputies to the UDF in May 2000. In June Tembo, the Vice-President of the MCP, was designated as the new leader of the opposition in the National Assembly, after deputies voted to suspend Chakuamba, the incumbent, from the chamber for a period of one year, on the grounds that he had persistently boycotted legislative proceedings. In early August the two factions of the MCP held separate conventions in Blantyre and Lilongwe, which elected Chakuamba and Tembo, respectively, as Presidents of the party. The High Court annulled the results of both leadership elections, pending a full hearing on the legitimacy of the two conventions. Chakuamba regained his position as leader of the party in September and went on to lead the challenge against the Muluzi Government. Meanwhile, in June, at a party rally, 37 of the 41 MCP district chairmen publicly endorsed Tembo as their new leader, claiming that they had lost confidence in Chakuamba; however, the latter dismissed the significance of the rally and vowed to fight on for the leadership. In November, following allegations of corruption, Muluzi dismissed three ministers, including Brown Mpinganjira, the Minister of Transport and Public Works. Mpinganjira was acquitted of the corruption charges in January 2001 and subsequently formed the National Democratic Alliance (NDA).

From early 2001 the possibility that Muluzi might seek a third five-year term as President dominated Malawian politics. Senior members of the UDF campaigned for the Constitution to be amended to make this possible. In January 2002 Muluzi dismissed Chikaonda, the popular Minister of Finance and Economic Planning, from the Cabinet; it was widely believed that Chikaonda had been regarded as a possible successor to Muluzi. Following the rejection of the idea of a third term by opposition parties and leaders of both the Protestant and Roman Catholic churches, Muluzi banned assemblies or demonstrations that either supported or condemned the proposal, on the grounds of security, and militant youth members of the UDF were reported to have attacked opposition supporters.

By May 2002 the worsening food crisis, in what remained one of the poorest countries in the world, was eclipsing other domestic issues. In February the President had declared a state of famine, in the hope of securing large amounts of aid. Donor countries held the Government partly responsible for failing to manage the crisis properly and initially aid was not forthcoming. It was revealed that emergency stores of maize, amounting to more than 160,000 metric tons, had been sold during the previous two years, primarily to Kenya. The authorities claimed that this sale had taken place on the advice of the IMF, a charge the IMF denied, stating that it had recommended that only a fraction of the reserves be sold. In August the Minister of Poverty Alleviation, Leonard Mangulama, was dismissed from the Government and charged with abuse of office for selling off the grain stores during his term in office as Minister of Agriculture. By mid-2002 an estimated 3m. people needed food aid, which began to arrive in large quantities from the USA, the European Union and the United Kingdom. The situation was compounded by the effects of an outbreak of cholera and the AIDS crisis: by the end of 2003 an estimated 14% of the adult population (aged between 15 and 49 years) was living with HIV/AIDS and, despite measures taken to deal with the pandemic, the rate of infection continued to increase. However, from December 2002 the food situation began to improve, as rain, together with millions of seed and fertilizer packs, supplied mainly by the British Government, enabled new crops to be planted.

Although the UDF was clearly the dominant party in 2003, it nevertheless abandoned its efforts to secure a third term for Muluzi. In April Muluzi dissolved the Cabinet, without prior warning, and named Bingu wa Mutharika, who had recently been appointed Minister of Economic Planning and Development, as the UDF candidate for the 2004 presidential election. On the eve of the third democratic election, civil society appeared stronger than ever, having successfully opposed an open term for the President and a third five-year term, but corruption was widespread and the economy was in severe difficulties. Malawi ranked 162 out of 175 countries on the UN Development Programme's 2003 Human Development Index, with 85% of the population living below the poverty line and 65% illiterate. An estimated 85,000 people per year were dying of AIDS and average life expectancy had fallen to as low as 36 years. With the assistance of the Global Fund, free antiretroviral drug treatment was started in May 2004, but initially only reached 6,000 of the estimated 150,000 people with HIV/AIDS.

THE 2004 ELECTIONS AND AFTER

Following a short postponement to allow for additional checks to be carried out on the updated electoral roll, the presidential and legislative elections took place on 20 May 2004. The MEC initially claimed that it had registered 6.6m. voters, but this was widely considered to be an inflated figure. After complaints from opposition parties, the MEC revised the voters' roll and removed almost 1m. people from the register. The MEC blamed incorrect information given to its officials by those registering, but opposition parties held the MEC responsible for failing properly to manage the process. Under the Constitution, voters had 21 days to scrutinize the roll, and the opposition coalition argued that the MEC had not allotted sufficient time for this to occur, and that vote-rigging was possible. The Supreme Court ordered the election to proceed, stating that it was impractical to recall all the surplus ballot papers, which the coalition feared might be misused by the UDF.

Polling itself proceeded peacefully although upon the release of the results opposition parties alleged electoral malpractice and threatened legal challenges to the polls. Mutharika was declared the winner of the presidential election, with 35.89% of the vote. Tembo and Chakuamba received 27.13% and 25.72%, respectively. In the parliamentary election, the UDF won only 49 seats in the 193-seat legislature, which necessitated the forging of alliances with other parties in order to govern. The MCP won the largest number of seats, taking 56, while the newly formed Republican Party (RP—led by Chakuamba, who had left the MCP) secured 15, the NDA eight and AFORD six. Results were disputed in three constituencies, while voting in a further six constituencies was not conducted owing to irregularities.

On 24 May 2004 Mutharika was sworn in as the country's new President. Most election observer groups stated that while the poll had been free, it had not been fair, owing to the inadequacies in the registration process and the bias of the public media in favour of the UDF. The MEC was blamed for failing to ensure fair media coverage for all parties and candidates, and for failing to update the voters' roll satisfactorily. Both the MCP and the Mgwirizano (Unity) Coalition of smaller parties, headed by Chakuamba, sought the nullification of the presidential election. There were widespread calls for the MEC to be disbanded owing to its chaotic handling of the election, and fears that the international community might again decide to suspend aid to the impoverished country if indeed the election was deemed not to have been free or fair.

The UDF quickly secured a working majority, as Muluzi, who remained as National Chairman of the party, was able to attract opposition support for the new Government. For a time it appeared that Muluzi would retain influence over his successor, but Mutharika commenced investigations into associates of Muluzi on suspicion of corruption. Relations between Muluzi and Mutharika became increasingly strained and in February 2005 Mutharika resigned from the leadership of the UDF, accusing Muluzi of being power-hungry and of having plundered the economy. After announcing his resignation at a meeting in Lilongwe, organized by the Anti-Corruption Bureau, Mutharika dismissed three members of the Government loyal to Muluzi and appointed Chakuamba to head the Ministry of Agriculture, Irrigation and Food Security. Mutharika also announced his intention to form a new political party and began to create a parliamentary support base from small parties, independents and disaffected UDF members.

Mutharika formally launched the Democratic Progressive Party (DPP) in May 2005 and by July 18 UDF deputies had joined the new party. The President pledged that it would promote good governance and transparency, and he promised to make improvements to the country's economy. Mutharika admitted that 1.7m. of the country's 11m. people required food aid after the recurrence of drought in the early months of 2005.

In late May 2005 the Minister of Education and Human Resources, Yusuf Mwawa, was arrested on charges of corruption and misuse of public funds, and the infighting among the political élite grew more intense. In late July the President provoked criticism after increasing the size of his Cabinet from 27 to 33. Chakuamba, who had been appointed Minister of Irrigation and Water Development, was dismissed in September and detained for questioning over allegations that he had purchased a luxury car with World Bank funds. While he was accused of acting dictatorially, Mutharika in turn accused the UDF of seeking to slow the pace of his clampdown on corruption and of undermining his moves to modernize the economy; moreover, he accused Muluzi of plotting to assassinate him.

Following an agreement between the UDF and Tembo, in mid-October 2005 the National Assembly voted in favour of beginning proceedings to impeach Mutharika. Envoys from several donor countries (including the United Kingdom, the USA and South Africa) were signatories to a letter to the opposition requesting them to reconsider their decision in the interests of the country at large. Despite their appeal Mutharika was summoned to face an indictment before the National Assembly later that month. However, the impeachment process was halted by the High Court after concern was expressed over the constitutionality of the process, and the impeachment motion was eventually withdrawn in late January 2006, after which some UDF members crossed the floor to join the DPP. Following a judgment of the Constitutional Court in November which placed restrictions on deputies who changed party allegiance, Mutharika's political opponents requested a court ruling on whether the Speaker of Parliament should declare a seat vacant when parliamentarian crossed the floor. This would have a potentially serious impact on the DPP in particular, as most of the 80 deputies affected were from the President's party. The Supreme Court of Appeal was expected to issue its ruling on the matter in mid-2007.

Meanwhile, in February 2006 the President accepted Chilumpha's 'constructive resignation', asserting that he had abandoned his duties and thus led the Cabinet to conclude that he had resigned. Chilumpha denied the allegations, and claimed before the High Court that as an elected minister he could only be dismissed by Parliament. In March the High Court ordered his reinstatement; however, the following month he was arrested and brought before a court in Lilongwe on charges of treason and conspiring to assassinate the President. Lawyers for Chilumpha argued that he was immune from prosecution while in office, but for a time he remained in custody, then was placed under house arrest. In January 2007 Chilumpha was finally brought to trial. He continued to deny the charges against him, and claimed that his treatment was a result of his refusal to join the DPP. Later that month, the Secretary-General of the UDF, Kennedy Makwangwala, and his deputy, Hophmally Makande, were charged with sedition over a recording that allegedly revealed Mutharika ordering the arrest of former President Muluzi.

Meanwhile, after returning from the United Kingdom, where he had been recuperating from a spinal cord operation, Muluzi was arrested in July 2006 on charges of corruption, but soon released. In March 2007 he announced at a rally that he would stand as the UDF candidate in the 2009 presidential election. The following month, however, a set of constitutional revisions were approved at a constitutional review conference held in Lilongwe, which stated that a President would be limited to serving a maximum of two terms, and laid down a minimum requirement of a first degree in order to stand for President. Muluzi had not only already served two terms, but did not have a university degree. Whether the new rule, if approved by Parliament, could be applied to him retrospectively was not clear. As Tembo, the MCP's presidential candidate, possessed a degree it was believed that the MCP might side with the DPP when the matter came before Parliament; however, the fact that MCP and UDF MPs were re-elected to chair key parliamentary committees in May demonstrated that the two parties were working together against the DPP. After Mutharika dismissed two of his cabinet ministers for not joining the DPP, another minister, a former Secretary-General of the MCP, declared her support for the DPP; however, it seemed likely to remain a minority party in Parliament.

EXTERNAL RELATIONS

Banda's establishment of diplomatic relations with South Africa in 1967 alienated him for a time from most other African leaders, as did his promotion of friendly relations with Portugal under the pre-1974 right-wing regime. Following independence, Malawi's relations with Tanzania and Zambia were strained by disputes over territorial boundaries: during the late 1960s Malawi claimed that its natural boundaries included the whole of the northern half of Lake Malawi, and extended at least 160 km north of Tanzania's Songwo river, as well as east and west into Mozambique and Zambia. Full diplomatic relations with Zambia were established in 1971, but it was not until 1985 that diplomatic relations were established with Tanzania. Malawi became a member of the Southern African Development Co-ordination Conference in 1980, and in 1993 was a founder member of its successor organization, SADC. Following talks in April 1994, the Presidents of Tanzania and Malawi agreed that social and economic relations between the two countries should be improved, and that the joint commission on co-operation (which had last met in 1983) should be re-established. An agreement formalizing cross-border trade was signed in August 1996.

Relations with Mozambique in the 1980s were complicated by allegations by the Mozambique Government that its opponents, members of the Resistência Nacional Moçambicana (Renamo), were operating from bases in Malawi. However, in 1988 President Chissano of Mozambique made a state visit to Malawi and later that year the two countries signed an agreement to promote the voluntary repatriation of an estimated 650,000 Mozambican refugees who had fled into Malawi over the previous two years. In mid-1994 an estimated 600,000 Mozambican refugees still remained in Malawi, but by early 1996 the majority of the refugees had been repatriated in an operation organized by the UN High Commissioner for Refugees (UNHCR).

Malawi's relations with Zimbabwe improved during the 1980s, despite the Banda regime's hostility to the Patriotic Front during its struggle for independence in Zimbabwe, and absence from the country's independence celebrations in 1980. Diplomatic relations were subsequently established and in 1986 a joint permanent commission was formed. In April 1990 Banda was a guest of honour at celebrations for Zimbabwe's 10th anniversary of independence. Relations cooled a decade later, as Zimbabwean President Robert Mugabe's anti-democratic actions threatened the stability of the region. As Chairman of SADC in 2002–03, Muluzi led missions to Zimbabwe in an attempt to persuade Mugabe to enter into dialogue with the opposition Movement for Democratic Change. President Mutharika was less experienced in international affairs and less active in the region than his predecessor. However, as Zimbabwe's economic crisis grew worse, he invited Mugabe to make a state visit to Malawi in May 2006. During the visit Mugabe opened a new road, named after him, between Blantyre and the tea-growing region of Mulanje in the south-east, and Mutharika praised Mugabe as a true African hero. Concerns that this would impact negatively on Malawi's reputation among donors appeared to be ill founded. In September the IMF and the World Bank announced that, having met the requirements of the enhanced initiative for heavily indebted poor countries, Malawi was eligible for the cancellation of US $2,900m. worth of debt. This would eliminate more than 90% of the country's total debt and result in a saving of $110m.per year. In February 2007 the British Government, the country's largest donor, pledged a further £280m. in aid over four years and praised Malawi for good economic management, tackling corruption, and providing HIV/AIDS treatment for over 80,000 people.

Economy

LINDA VAN BUREN

Buoyed by a good harvest, Malawi recorded gross domestic product (GDP) growth of 8.5% in 2006, with 6% expected for 2007; these figures are a significant improvement over the 2.1% growth of 2005. Improved supply of food in marketplaces reduced inflation from 17.1% in February 2006 to 8.2% at 31 March 2007. None the less, Malawi remains among the 10 poorest countries in the world, with a per head income in 2006 of just US $170. More than 65% of the population live below the benchmark extreme poverty indicator of $1 per day, and, in many areas, the population is coping with less than one-quarter of that figure.

In March 2007 the IMF found Malawi's economic policy implementation to be 'broadly satisfactory', granted Malawi's request for a waiver of its non-observance of the performance criterion concerning government domestic borrowing, and released a further US $10m. tranche of its $57.4m. three-year Poverty Reduction and Growth Facility (PRGF), covering the period 2005–2007. In May 2005 the IMF had credited the Government of President Bingu wa Mutharika with a 'noteworthy turnaround from the experience in previous years'. Following his election to the presidency in May 2004, President Mutharika, himself an economist, appointed a former IMF Director for Africa, Goodall Gondwe, as Minister of Finance. The 'previous years' reference was to the last years of the Bakili Muluzi administration, when overspending triggered a suspension of assistance from the Fund.

The principal subject of discord from 2000 onwards was agricultural policy. Under IMF pressure, in 2000 the Muluzi Government agreed to a range of agricultural reforms, which included an end to wholesale subsidization by the Agricultural Development and Marketing Corporation (ADMARC) and instead targeted specific food subsidies towards the poorest citizens. To carry out the latter plan, the National Food Reserve Agency (NFRA) was established in 1999; its objective was to administer disaster relief by managing a Strategic Grain Reserve (SGR). Market forces would have dictated that the plentiful harvest of 1999 would lead to an excess of supply over demand and therefore a drop in maize prices, in the absence of ADMARC intervention. However, the NFRA did not confine its activities to its stated objective; instead, it began engaging in what the IMF termed 'substantial price-stabilization operations, thus taking over the price-support function relinquished by ADMARC'. By the end of 1999 the government-held maize stocks had risen to 167,000 metric tons, far in excess of the recommended strategic maize reserve of between 30,000 and 60,000 tons. A study commissioned in 2000 by the Malawi Government, and financed by the European Commission, found that a buffer stock of maize of not more than 60,000 tons was sufficient to address a localized disaster and that maintaining stocks at this lower level would allow government resources to increase international monetary reserves for the purchase of additional grain, if necessary. This strategy, it was concluded, was more cost-effective than physically holding large stores of grain, as the cost of maintaining 167,000 tons of maize was equivalent to 20% of the value of the stocks themselves. The IMF stated that the NFRA was likely to become a burden on the budget, as ADMARC had been before it. The IMF, in conjunction with the World Bank, therefore recommended a transparent, rule-based and cost-effective food-security policy and, in particular, the formulation of new operational guidelines for the NFRA. However, it emerged that the NFRA had sold not only the excess but virtually the entire maize stock by the beginning of 2002, instead of maintaining reserves at the recommended level of 60,000 tons. This unfortunate turn of events coincided with a poor harvest in 2000/01, which meant that the NFRA was unable to replenish the SGR: in February 2002 Malawi ran out of food and declared a national disaster, in what was described as the worst food shortage in Malawi for 50 years. The Government had placed orders for 150,000 tons of food imports in late 2001, but they did not arrive in time.

When the harvest began in April 2002 the crisis was alleviated, but only temporarily, as in May UN food agencies predicted a 485,000-metric ton maize deficit for the period August 2002–March 2003. Assistance to cover this shortfall was forthcoming from donors, including the World Bank, which in November 2002 approved US $50m. for the Malawi Emergency Drought-Recovery Project. Meanwhile, the Auditor-General and the Anti-Corruption Bureau began an investigation into how the situation had arisen. The Government also agreed to an external audit, at the request of donors. By May 2003 the situation had improved, with maize more readily available in most parts of the country. In June 2004 after another disappointing maize harvest and prolonged drought, the NFRA requested tenders for the purchase of 28,000 tons of maize with which to replenish the SGR. The Malawi Vulnerability Assessment Committee reported a shortfall in maize production of over 600,000 tons, with the SGR standing at 15,000 tons and imports (including 'informal' cross-border trade) comprising an estimated 104,000 tons. Of the overall cereal shortage of 481,000 tons, 271,000 tons was covered by food aid, leaving another 210,000 tons to be found from other sources. The 2005/06 budget, presented in June 2005, allocated $45m. for the procurement and distribution of 300,000 tons of maize, a quantity described as the largest amount ever imported. Fortunes took a favourable turn in 2006, when Malawi produced what the UN World Food Programme described as a 'bumper harvest', amounting to 2.4m. metric tons. As a result, Malawi found itself in possession of a surplus of 250,000 tons of cereals.

The budget deficit in the mid-1990s during the Muluzi years grew far beyond any lender's acceptable level, in relation to GDP. The resulting 2001/02 shortfall was equivalent to 8% of GDP according to the 2002 budget, but was equivalent to 16% of GDP according to the IMF. Overspending by the Muluzi Government during the period of the 2003/04 budget, which coincided with the run-up to the 2004 elections, was so severe that a 'supplementary' K11,000m. budget had to be announced three-quarters of the way through the period. The Minister of Finance declared that the supplementary budget was needed to service Malawi's debt and to run the country in the absence of anticipated donor funds, which had been suspended in 2002.

The Mutharika Government made rapid progress in repairing relations with the IMF in 2004 and 2005, and increasing donor confidence was signalled by a US $5.5m. pledge from Sweden under the Common Approach to Budget Support (CABS) facility. In May 2005 the World Bank also approved a $37m. loan to establish new irrigation schemes, as well as to rehabilitate four existing ones. However, the country's economic advancement is impeded by problems of subsistence agriculture and its overdependence on one principal export crop. Low educational levels and the effects of HIV/AIDS have resulted in a shortage of skilled personnel. The country has few mineral resources, and industry is dependent on imports and hampered by inadequate infrastructure; the problem is compounded by the limitations of the country's landlocked position and small domestic market.

AGRICULTURE

Agriculture is the most important sector of the economy; including forestry and fishing, it accounted for 40% of GDP and for about 90% of export revenue in 2005. An estimated 85% of the working population were engaged in agriculture in mid-2005. The vast majority of these people work in the smallholder sector, which accounts for nearly 80% of the cultivated area and for nearly 83% of agricultural output, which is mostly on a subsistence basis. About two-thirds of the raw materials for Malawi's manufacturing industry are agricultural products grown locally. Agricultural GDP grew at an average annual rate of 4.4% in 1995–2005, but the sector is at the mercy of unreliable weather patterns and exhibits pronounced swings between crop failure in some years and crop excess in others. Lack of availability of credit to small-scale farmers remains a significant hindrance to agricultural growth. The liberalization of agricultural marketing and production arrangements undertaken by the Muluzi Government in the mid-1990s contributed, together with favourable weather conditions, to substantial increases in smallholder production, estimated by the IMF to amount to 34% in 1995 and 40% in 1996. Nevertheless, in 1998 fertilizer prices rose by an average 56% for the three most commonly used types, owing to the sharp depreciation of the kwacha. The Government's Fertilizer Subsidy Programme made available 147,000 metric tons in 2005/06, and a coupon system was being implemented in order to 'track down those who might want to beat the system'. Malawi's principal agricultural exports are tobacco, sugar, tea, coffee and large, hand-shelled, confectionery-grade groundnuts.

Maize is the principal food crop and is grown almost entirely by smallholders. It has been exported in some years and imported in others, depending on weather conditions. The NFRA in June 2004 urged farmers to plant a second crop, of winter maize, which was to produce a further 250,000 metric tons. In this drought-prone country, overdependence on maize, a crop not resistant to drought, is seen as a factor contributing to food shortages; therefore, diversification away from maize and towards other food crops has been recommended. One such alternative crop is sorghum, which was grown in Malawi for centuries before the British planted maize. The sorghum harvest fluctuates between about 35,000 metric tons in poor years and about 45,000 tons in good years. The Government is also trying to encourage cultivation of the more drought-resistant cassava. Cassava production peaked in 2001, at 3.3m. tons, and in 2003 amounted to only 1.7m. tons. However, cassava is not as nutritional as maize, and supplies are erratic: the crop is harvested as it is needed, and there are poor transfer rates of surplus stocks to areas where they are required. Potatoes, pulses and plantains are also important food crops. The potato crop also varies; the largest crop was 2001's 2.9m. tons.

In cash crops, there was a marked improvement in Malawi's groundnut sector from the mid-1990s onwards. Production had declined to 31,000 metric tons of groundnuts in shells in 1994 and 1995, but output reached 190,112 tons in 2003 before falling to 161,162 tons in 2004 and to 102,000 tons in 2005. The output of green coffee beans, mostly arabica grown on steep slopes, also fluctuates; 2001 was a bumper year, with a crop of 4,320 tons, whereas 2004 was a poor year, with a harvest of just 1,590 tons. According to the International Coffee Organization, exports through that organization fell from 45,663 60-kg bags in 2003/04 to just 19,226 bags in 2004/05; they recovered to 21,292 bags in 2005/06 but then declined to 16,444 bags in the year to 30 April 2007. The Smallholder Coffee Farmers Trust was set up in 1999 as a transitional organization, aimed at capacity-building and the training of 4,000 smallholder growers in five co-operatives in northern Malawi to run their own businesses. The trust estimated in 2004 that output could potentially rise to over 20,000 tons per year. Most of Malawi's coffee is arabica, grown on steep slopes.

The leading export crop, tobacco, was grown on an estimated 96,083 ha in 2003. In that year 2003 output amounted to 69,500 metric tons. Malawi is the only significant African producer of burley, which is the most important of the six types of tobacco cultivated in Malawi. Output of this variety achieved record levels in several consecutive years after 1991, the first year in which its cultivation on smallholdings was permitted (the production of burley had previously been confined to estates), and quotas for burley production on smallholdings were eliminated. The importance of burley increased greatly in the early 1980s, when strong world demand encouraged a major expansion in output. Output of flue-cured tobacco, which traditionally has been grown only on estates, and of the four types of tobacco traditionally cultivated by smallholders (dark-fire-cured, southern-dark-fired, sun/air-cured and oriental) is declining. President Mutharika has openly encouraged Malawi's tobacco growers to turn to other crops instead. According to Malawi's Tobacco Control Commission, in 2004 there were some 133,871 registered tobacco growers working on 82,482 estates; there were also 51,389 clubs that largely produce burley. The Government is trying to improve smallholder production and output of flue-cured tobacco through instructional and training programmes aimed at improving yields. However, with millions of people in the developed world trying to give up smoking, the long-term prospects for the global crop, as well as for Malawi's tobacco industry, are not good; some 34,400 farmers left the sector between 2000 and 2004, but it was hoped that output would be boosted by the arrival of dispossessed white tobacco farmers from Zimbabwe. Malawi's tobacco output declined from 181m. kg in 2003/04 to 155.5m. kg in 2004/05.

Livestock improvements have made the country self-sufficient in meat and liquid milk. In 2005 the national herd comprised 1.9m. goats, 750,000 cattle, 450,000 pigs and 115,000 sheep. Traditionally, almost all livestock has been kept by smallholders.

Fish provides about 70% of animal protein consumption, and the fisheries sector is thought to employ about 250,000 people, but the annual catch has on the whole been in decline since 1990, when a peak of 74,100 metric tons was achieved. By 2003 the annual catch amounted to 54,194 tons, although it increased to more than 57,000 tons in 2004. Much of the commercial fishing activity centres on Nkhotakota, on the western shore of Lake Malawi. The lake has more than 500 species of fish, including several species of tilapia; the tilapia catch in 2004 amounted to 6,000 tons. Fish stocks in some of Malawi's lakes have been almost obliterated by a combination of overfishing (as drought reduces crops and impels more people to fish in order to survive), declining water levels and pollution.

Timber and pulpwood plantations have been developed since the early 1970s, with the area under state plantations totalling 20,800 ha in 1985. In addition, 54,000 ha of pine and eucalyptus were planted on the Viphya plateau, in the north, to supply a pulp and paper project. The project focused on development of part of the Viphya plantation, and the construction of processing facilities. The scheme aimed eventually to provide employment for several thousand people, not only in forestry but also in infrastructural development, which includes the construction of a port on the lake at Chintheche and a new town. The total area under forests in 1990 was 35,000 sq km. Acacia, conifers and baobab trees grow in the highlands. Malawi holds the responsibility for the Southern African Development Community (SADC) Forestry Sector Co-ordinating Unit and has the highest rate of deforestation of all the SADC states, at 1.6% per year. Malawi annually produces about 520,000 cubic metres of industrial roundwood. Out of the 5.5m. cu m of roundwood felled per year, 5.1m. cu m, or almost 93%, is burned as wood fuel.

MAJOR EXPORTS

Tobacco alone contributes about 60% of export volume and up to 75% of export revenue. In 2003 Malawi became the largest exporter of tobacco in Africa, overtaking Zimbabwe, exports from which fell dramatically from 2001 onwards owing to the severe disruption of the Zimbabwe economy. Tobacco is sold at auction from April to October each year. As the 2005 auction season opened in April, prices were well below expectations, so much so that trading was suspended within a few days as farmers refused to trade. This situation was repeated in 2006, when an 'indefinite' suspension of auction trading turned out to be of one week's duration. The 2006 crop amounted to 158,000 tons, and with an abundant supply headed for the auction floor in April of that year, the market pressure on prices was decidedly downward. President Mutharika had in March 2006 proclaimed a recommended floor price of US $1.10 per kg for lower-quality leaf and of $1.70 for higher-quality leaf. These guide prices raised growers' expectations, and when buyers' bids were significantly lower, at $0.70 per kg, growers were deeply disappointed, and some buyers were ordered to leave the country. The low prices were attributed to three factors: continued declining global demand, high inventory levels among the tobacco purchasers and accusations that some unscrupulous traders were placing stones and pieces of plastic in bales of tobacco to increase their weight. The smuggling of Malawi-grown tobacco into neighbouring countries was reported in 2006. The 2007 crop was significantly smaller than the previous year, at 141,000 tons, and with less supply, the 2007 auction season opened in April with much better prices, of the order of US $1.60 and $1.70 per kg. It reportedly costs a Malawian grower an average of $1.00 to produce 1 kg of leaf.

Much of Malawi's sugar production, amounting to some 130,000 metric tons per year, is consumed locally. The principal foreign customer is the European Union (EU), followed by the USA. Illovo Sugar (Malawi) Ltd (formerly the Sugar Corpn of Malawi—SUCOMA) is the sole sugar producer in Malawi; the company has two sugar mills at Dwangwa and Nchalo. The Dwangwa sugar project covers some 5,250 ha of the Central Region. Illovo reported a record sugarcane harvest in 2005/06 in Malawi, and in that year, Illovo's Malawi operations made the largest contribution to profits of any of the company's holdings, at 39%.

Malawi is, after Kenya, Africa's second largest producer and exporter of tea, accounting for about 15% of all African tea exports in 2003. Tea provided 6.7% of Malawi's total export earnings in that year. In 2005 Malawi had about 18,000 ha planted with tea and harvested about 50,000 metric tons. More than four-fifths of the land under cultivation was controlled by large estates and 5,200 smallholders worked the remainder. The United Kingdom is by far the most important foreign purchaser.

Cassava, rice, sunflower seed, and medium-staple cotton are also exported. Malawi produced over 50,000 metric tons of cottonseed in 1996, but output declined to 34,000 tons in 2004 and to 24,000 tons in 2005. A growing horticultural sector is expanding into a variety of export crops, from the more traditional cabbages, tomatoes and onions to such items as chestnuts, nutmeg, fennel and vanilla. Malawi also produces about 2,000 tons of tung nuts per year, the oil from which is used in paints and varnishes as a drying agent and to provide a water-resistant finish. Paprika is being promoted as an alternative crop to tobacco; output is about 6,000 tons per year of a variety called Papri Queen. Most of the crop is exported to South Africa where it is processed into powdered form for export to Europe.

INDUSTRY

The manufacturing sector contributed 9% of GDP in 2006. Government encouragement of private enterprise initially attracted foreign private direct investment and management expertise, especially in collaboration with the state-owned Malawi Development Corpn (MDC), established in 1964. In common with other major parastatal bodies, however, the MDC became subject to major reorganization and management restructuring in 1985. Small-scale industrial development has been promoted by the Small Enterprise Development Organization of Malawi (SEDOM). The single largest industrial sector concern during the period when Dr Banda held power was the Press Corpn. Nominally a private company, but indirectly controlled by Banda, Press had interests throughout the modern sector of the economy. Often in joint-venture arrangements with foreign companies, these interests included tobacco and sugar estates, cattle ranching, ethanol production, civil engineering, transport, retail and wholesale trade, property development, banking and insurance.

Malawi, like other African countries, came under pressure to privatize loss-making government-owned companies, and the Privatisation Commission of Malawi was established in 1996. Between 1996 and 2004 about one-half of the country's parastatals were privatized; they employed some 500,000 people and generated around 20% of GDP. The pace of privatization has been slow; by May 2007 45 entities had been wholly or partially privatized. In several cases, entities offered for privatization failed to attract buyers. Companies for which privatization has been completed include the Brick and Tile Company, Chemicals and Marketing Ltd, Chillington Agrimal Ltd (now Agrimal Ltd), Optichem (Malawi) Ltd, Packaging Industries (MW) Ltd, the Portland Cement Co (1974) Ltd, a plywood company and three sugar companies. Those industrial companies the privatization of which was still pending in mid-2007 included ADMARC, Air Malawi, Auction Holdings, Lilongwe International Airport, Chileka International Airport (Blantyre), several financial institutions and several tourism entities. In 2004 most potential buyers for Malawi Telecommunications Ltd (MTL) had withdrawn, stating that the company was overvalued, and in mid-2005 talks again stalled again, after the directors of MTL maintained that, at US $30.7m., the company had been undervalued; the current price was based on a valuation made in 1999–2000 and did not take into account the value of assets or projects undertaken since then. Future proposed privatizations include the Electricity Supply Commission of Malawi (ESCOM, see below) and the Malawi Development Corpn.

Malawi has provided a range of incentives for potential investors, including low-cost estate sites, tariff protection, exclusive licensing where justified, generous investment allowances and unrestricted repatriation of capital, profits and dividends. However, the rate of new investment has been inhibited by the small size of the local market and the limited possibilities for exports. Although new investment has not created as many new jobs as the Government had hoped, owing to the capital-intensive nature of some operations, employment in industry more than doubled between 1980 and 1992. The value of exports of unknitted apparel increased four-fold in 2001 and earned more than 50 times as much revenue in 2001 as in 1996. The Government's package of investment incentives seeks to attract foreign investment in such sectors as manufacturing, agriculture, agribusiness, tourism and mining. These incentives include tax allowances of 40% on new buildings and machinery, of 15% on investments in certain designated areas, of 50% on training expenditure and of 20% on used buildings and machinery. In addition, an Export Processing Zone (EPZ) was established in 1995, which is free from withholding tax on dividends, duties on the import of capital equipment and raw materials, and value-added tax. Companies established in the EPZ are allowed free access to foreign exchange in Malawi and full repatriation of profits, dividends, investment capital and interest and principal payments for international loans. By 2000 21 companies had received approval for EPZ status, but by 2006, four of them had ceased trading.

Mining

Deposits of a number of minerals have been discovered—including bauxite, asbestos, coal, phosphates, gemstones, uranium, vermiculite, granite, glass sands, graphite and several types of construction stone—but only a few industrial minerals have so far been exploited to any extent, notably limestone by the Portland Cement Co (1974) Ltd. Limestone production was an estimated 190,000 metric tons in 2003. There has been some exploitation of Malawi's coal reserves; the Mchenga mine, privatized in 1999, is estimated to contain some 2.3m. tons of bituminous coal, with a further 20m. tons in the vicinity. At full capacity, Mchenga can produce 8,000 tons per month, supplying a regional demand of about 12,500 tons per month; its target is to achieve 5,000 tons per month. Further coal deposits, of poorer quality, lie at Ngana and Mwabvi. Clays suitable for use in the production of ceramics have also been identified. Surveys have also found deposits of marble and granite, while reserves of vermiculite exist at Fereme. Semi-precious stones are mined, mostly on an artisanal basis. Natural (as opposed to heat-treated) gem-quality corundum is mined at Chimwadzulu Hill and is marketed as Nyala rubies and sapphires. Finds of up to seven carats have been recorded. Aquamarines and blue agates have also been found. Other gemstones, found in small quantities, include amethysts, garnets and yellow tourmaline.

In 1997 the Geological Survey Department reported that deposits of gold had been found at Mwanza and on the outskirts of Lilongwe and that there were indications of diamond reserves at Livingstonia, in the north. Cost factors have prevented the exploitation of Malawi's most important mineral discovery so far, the bauxite reserves in the Mulanje area, which have been assessed at almost 29m. metric tons of ore, containing an average of 43.9% alumina. Their development would involve heavy transport costs, owing to the remote location of the area, supplemented by further transport costs to the coast, making their exploitation uneconomic in present world market conditions. The feasibility of the project could improve if development of Malawi's hydroelectric capacity were to result in sufficient low-cost power to meet the substantial requirements of alumina smelting. Indeed, a major restraint on the entire mining sector's expansion is that current levels of electricity generation are insufficient for most heavy industrial mining.

Power

A shortage of reliable electricity supply is often cited as a factor hindering growth in the manufacturing and mining sectors. Blackouts are a continual occurrence. ESCOM operates both thermal and hydroelectric power stations in its grid; the latter supply 85% of the central grid generating capacity of 190 MW. Three plants on the middle Shire river account for 76% of hydroelectric capacity: Tedzani (40 MW), Nkula A (24 MW) and Nkula B (80 MW). Outside the grid, ESCOM operates four small diesel sets in remote areas in the north. Some companies, for example sugar estates, generate their own electricity supply. Although the central grid is currently operating at below capacity, ESCOM has invested in new capacity in an attempt to satisfy projected future demand, as well as to reinforce the existing grid. In 2000 ESCOM announced the completion of a seven-year hydroelectric power scheme, at a cost of K5,900m. At present, fewer than 5% of the population have access to electricity, most of whom live in urban areas. The majority of Malawi's domestic energy requirements are supplied by fuel wood, which has accounted for more than 90% of energy needs (compared with 3% for hydropower, 4% for petroleum products and 1% for coal) in the 2000s.

In 1998 the Muluzi Government increased electricity tariffs by 35% in a bid to place ESCOM, 100% state-owned, on a firmer financial footing in preparation for its privatization. ESCOM was to be unbundled before privatization into three entities: generation, transmission and distribution. Its privatization was still pending as of mid-2007. In 2003 ESCOM finalized a deal with Hidroelectrica de Cahora Bassa (HCB) of Mozambique, whereby HCB would supply the Malawian national grid with power from the Cahora Bassa dam, starting with 100 MW in 2004 and rising to 300 MW during the 20-year term of the contract. Under the agreement, ESCOM was to build the transmission lines, at an estimated cost of US $80m. In May 2004 the Ministry of Energy and Mining estimated that power blackouts cost Malawi $338m. a year. The reason given for the frequent power cuts was soil erosion and siltation along the Shire river, causing blockages and flooding at the river's four hydroelectric power stations.

Petroleum and diesel fuel constitute Malawi's principal imports. In the 1980s a factory producing ethyl alcohol (ethanol) from molasses commenced operations, and in its first five years of service it produced 6.8m. litres of ethanol annually, for 20% blending with petroleum, equivalent to 10% of Malawi's petroleum needs. Full design capacity of 8.5m. litres per year was reached in 1988. Serious shortfalls in the supply of petroleum products occurred in the mid-1990s, prompting research (funded by the World Bank) that was to produce contingency plans, and to evaluate a minimum level below which rationing of petroleum products should automatically take effect. In 2005 Energem of Canada built and commissioned a 1,400-metric ton refined-product storage and distribution facility at Chirimba, in Blantyre at a cost of US $1.2m. The company commissioned a second, smaller storage facility in Lilongwe in 2006, to supply the tobacco industry.

Transport and Tourism

Malawi Railways developed an internal rail network covering 797 km, extending to Mehinji on the Zambian border. It also operated 465 km of the 830-km single-line rail link from Salima, on the central lake shore, to Mozambique's Indian Ocean port of Beira. Another rail link provided access to the Mozambican port of Nacala, north of Beira. The railway was privatized in 1999, when it was transferred to CFM/SDCN, a consortium owned by Mozambique's Empresa Nacional dos Portos e Caminhos de Ferro de Moçambique (CFM) and the USA's Railroad Development Corpn, and also including Portugal's Tertir and South Africa's Rennies. The new owners pledged to invest US $26m. in the Malawian railway system. The railway was subsequently renamed the Central East African Railways Co Ltd (CEAR). At the time of transfer, only about 10% of the rolling stock was operational, but by June 2000 the consortium reported that it had returned nearly 90% to active service. The Government continued to own the land and essential buildings. The US company Railroad Development Corpn operates CEAR under a 20-year contract agreed in 2000. In January 2005 the same consortium that owns CEAR purchased Mozambique's Nacala port and railway. In 2004 CEAR carried 273,000 metric tons of freight along the 797-km corridor with 24 locomotives and 439 wagons; the main cargo was maize, containers, fuel, fertilizers, cement, tobacco and sugar.

Malawi's road network is being gradually upgraded, in particular the lake-shore Kamuzu Highway, which provides the main land link between the remote Northern Region and the Central and Southern Regions. Feeder and crop-extraction roads are also being extended. Road transport grew steadily during the 1980s, when Malawi's rail outlets were closed.

Malawi has two international airports: one at Lilongwe and one (Chileka) at Blantyre. There are also three domestic airports. Lilongwe is regularly served by a number of international and regional airlines, as well as by the national carrier, Air Malawi. Lilongwe International Airport, Chileka International Airport and Air Malawi Limited have all been long earmarked for privatization, but progress is slow. A study to assess private-sector participation options for all the country's airports was undertaken in 2005, and results released in 2006 indicated that the three busiest airports required an investment of US $23.5m. to upgrade them. The privatization of the state-owned Air Malawi Ltd was postponed in 2005 until market conditions in the depressed global airline industry improve. The airline has expressed a preference for seeking a 'strategic partner' as opposed to a change of equity ownership.

The Government is currently aiming to expand the tourism sector, which has grown substantially since Malawi began to develop its considerable tourism potential in the mid-1970s. Malawi, like other tourism destinations in the region, has been affected by the destabilization in Zimbabwe. Tourism receipts in 2003 totalled US $43m. The number of visitors reached 470,640 in 2004, according to provisional figures, increasing from 228,100 in 2000. In 2001 the Government was actively seeking foreign-investment partners in such tourism projects as hotels and lodges around Lake Malawi and in game-viewing areas, time-share developments, hotels and restaurants in the main cities and in lakeside resorts, cruise boats on Lake Malawi and casinos. Government holdings in Blantyre Rest House, Government Hostel (now Hotel Masongola), Kasungu Inn, Likhubula Lodge, Chigumukire Lodge, Kachere Lodge, Dzalanyama Lodge, Ntchisi Lodge, Limbe Rest House and Mangochi Lodge were all privatized by 2003. Malawi also promotes its five national parks, including Nyika National Park, with its high escarpment providing views of the north shore of Lake Malawi; Kasungu National Park, with its rolling woodlands, grassy river channels and elephant herds; and Liwonde National Park, with its reed swamps, floodplains and tropical birds. In May 2006 it was announced that tourism consultants from VisitScotland of the United Kingdom were to work with Malawi's tourism managers to draw up a tourism development plan.

EXTERNAL TRADE AND PAYMENTS

Malawi's prospects for sustained development depend upon the achievement of improved export performance. Although private investment in industry is encouraged, it is agriculture that the IMF identifies as the 'engine of the Government's growth strategy'. Agricultural products still account for about 90% of domestic export receipts, with tobacco providing about two-thirds of total foreign-exchange earnings at a time when global demand for the controversial crop is weakening (see above). Exports of manufactured goods, mainly clothing, natural rubber, cotton fabrics, wood products and beverages, provided less than 10% of all export earnings in 2005. The principal imports in 2006 were diesel fuel and petroleum (by far the largest item), fertilizers (principally for tobacco), machinery and transport equipment, piece goods, and medical and pharmaceutical goods. In many years, maize also has to be imported. Exports, on a free-on-board basis, earned an estimated US $466.5m. in 2006, down from $507.4m. in 2005. Meanwhile, imports, on a cost, insurance and freight basis, also declined, from $1,069.6m. in 2005 to $889.3m. in 2006. The resulting trade deficit, at a worrying $562.2m. in 2005, narrowed to $422.8m. in 2006.

Malawi has sustained a deficit on the current account of its balance of payments in every year since 1966. The deficit on the current account, excluding transfers, narrowed from US $38.9m. in 2005 to $29.4m. in 2006. The overall balance is also regularly in deficit; the shortfall was estimated at $87.7m. in 2006 and was projected at $122m. in 2007.

PUBLIC FINANCE AND BANKING

In 2003/04, the Muluzi Government indulged in a serious overspend in the election year of 2004, to the extent that the 2003/04 annual budget had been fully utilized after just nine months, and the Muluzi Government had to introduce a supplementary budget in March 2004. As a result, the incoming Government of President Mutharika faced a major exercise in damage control. By the time of the 2005/06 budget, signs had appeared that the Mutharika Government had done enough to regain the approval of the IMF and the World Bank. Nevertheless, total expenditure in the 2005/06 budget was equivalent to 32.2% of GDP. The 2006/07 budget sought to reduce this to 28.7% of GDP, and the out-turn showed that this target was exceeded; the overall balance excluding grants was equivalent to 19.3% of GDP, and even this level is regarded as unsustainable.

The Malawi Stock Exchange was established in March 1995, under guidance from a Zimbabwean company, although once launched it was managed by Malawians. In 2007 11 companies were listed, of which 10 were Malawian and one was foreign. In April 2000, affected by problems on Malawi's tobacco auction floors (see above), the kwacha lost 17% of its value in six weeks. Its value subsequently declined to K72.46 = $1 in June 2002, to K90.40 = $1 in June 2003 and to K106.50 = $1 in June 2004. In April 2005, concurrent with the commencement of the tobacco auctions, the kwacha underwent an unwelcome appreciation, from K113.00 = $1 to K110.00 = $1; thus, tobacco receipts, denominated in US dollars, yielded fewer kwacha. By June 2006 the currency was trading at K136.46 = $1, and in June 2007 it was still trading at a similar level, at K137.29 = $1. The overvaluation of the kwacha came in for particular criticism in a February 2006 IMF review.

FOREIGN AND GOVERNMENT DEBT

Prior to its significant debt-relief package in August 2006, Malawi had the highest debt-to-GDP ratio in the world. Malawi began to undertake significant commercial borrowing in the mid-1970s, initially to finance development programmes. International organizations replaced bilateral donors as the main source of foreign funding, granting 78.8% of foreign aid given in 1994, with IDA as the leading multilateral creditor. As a proportion of outstanding debt, commercial borrowing increased from less than 2% in 1976 to more than 24% in 1980. After 1979 non-concessionary borrowing rose sharply, as the Banda Government resorted to the banks to help finance its budget deficits. This led to a substantial increase in total public debt-service payments and the repeated rescheduling of 'Paris Club' debt. World Bank figures for 1994 indicated that the Muluzi Government inherited a total external debt of US $2,025m., equivalent to 163.2% of Malawi's gross national income in that year. By the end of 2000 total debt had grown, albeit at a considerably slower rate, to $2,706m. The 2001/02 budget identified debt-servicing as the largest single expenditure item, requiring 25% of total revenue, greater than spending on education or health. This was the case even after debt-servicing charges were reduced by 40% relief under the initiative for heavily indebted poor countries (HIPC—see below). Malawi's total public-sector external debt was $2,900m. as of February 2006. Subsequent debt relief, agreed in August 2006, brought this figure down from 143% of GDP in 2005 to 50.6% in 2006. The debt-service ratio as a percentage of export revenue was 22.1% in 2005 and 30.7% in 2006. The IMF stressed the 'critical' importance of channelling the benefits of debt relief into a sustainable poverty-reduction strategy. Also of great concern to the IMF was Malawi's 'domestic debt spiral'; in June 2004 the country's domestic debt was equivalent to almost 25% of GDP, and interest payments on domestic debt consumed almost 25% of the budget. In 2005/06, domestic borrowing—although higher than had been programmed—had been reduced to below 20% of GDP. In May 2007 the IMF indicated that reducing domestic borrowing to below 10% of GDP was a 'key objective'. To help achieve this goal, the IMF agreed that debt relief under the Multilateral Debt Relief Initiative would be used to reduce domestic debt.

The United Kingdom was Malawi's major aid donor in the years after independence and has remained an important source of funding. Similarly, the apartheid Government of South Africa was a significant source of donor aid, particularly in providing finance for the purpose-built capital, Lilongwe, where construction of government buildings began in 1968. Other major donors are the EU (currently the main donor overall), France, Canada, the USA, Germany, Denmark, Japan, the African Development Bank, IDA and the World Bank.

According to the IMF, Malawi's 2005 three-year PRGF (see above) set targets of sustainable GDP growth of 4.5% per year, a significant decline in the inflation rate to 'low levels' and a reduction in the number of people below the poverty line. Malawi's economic planners were to achieve these goals by reducing monetary growth, achieving a balanced fiscal position, improving spending control, deepening structural reform, strengthening governance and prioritizing expenditure to benefit the poor. Although the GDP growth target was met and exceeded, the monetary growth goal was not. M2 money supply had grown by 29.8% in 2004, the year before the PRGF, and was reduced to growth of 14.3% in 2005, the year of implementation; however, 2006 saw M2 money supply growth rise to 22%. More specifically, the IMF insisted that intervention in maize marketing and the subsidization of petroleum should not be resumed and that the 'surtax' be extended to wholesale and retail transactions, making it equivalent to a value-added tax.

The Mutharika Government afforded high priority to the rebuilding of relations with Malawi's donors and creditors. By mid-2005 it was clear that much of the damage inflicted by the Muluzi Government had been repaired and that the Mutharika Government had regained the confidence of donors and creditors. Once in office, the Government took a sharp turn in its own direction, and away from that taken by the Muluzi Government, in economic terms, as well as in political terms. A crackdown on corruption was warmly greeted by the Malawian people and donors alike. The successful introduction of the fertilizer subsidy programme in 2005 (see above) was also very popular with the people, if not with the IMF.

PROSPECTS AND PROBLEMS

The 2006/07 budget, unveiled in mid-June 2006, allocated the largest sectoral expenditure to agriculture and water and irrigation. After a year in which one-third of the country's farmers had no food crops of their own, 2006 appeared promising, with fields full of maize ears. The abundant crop boosted the forecast for 2006/07 GDP growth to 8.5%. The Mutharika Government was seeking to capitalize on this growth by proceeding with a major construction project, the Shire-Zambezi canal, which will account for about one-half of all capital expenditure. In the longer term, the Government faced the challenge of reducing Malawi's very heavy dependence on a single cash crop, especially since that cash crop is tobacco. Signs that tobacco's fortunes are on the wane have been evident for many years now, and the low prices that characterize each year's opening auctions have become painfully predictable. The negative repercussions are felt across the spectrum, from the worsening national balance of payments to the declining incomes of smallholder tobacco-growing families. Even in 2007, when tobacco prices were higher than the average of the decade, confidence that the crop can provide growers with a living in the longer term was eroding.

A Poverty and Vulnerability Assessment, compiled by the Malawi Government and the World Bank, was released in June 2006. It compared figures from the Integrated Household Surveys of 1998 and 2005 and concluded that there had been little or no progress in reducing poverty and inequality in that time. It found that more than one-half of the country's population continued to live below the poverty line on around US $0.32 per day. Over one-fifth of Malawians, mostly in rural areas in the south and north of the country, lived on $0.20 per day and were not able to meet the daily recommended food requirements. With 60% of Malawi's 12.3m. people under the age of 20 years, more than one-half of the poor were children, and an estimated 44% of pre-school children were 'stunted' because of malnutrition. Despite the bumper maize harvest of 2006, aid agencies warned that pockets of vulnerable people remained, especially in the north.

Statistical Survey

Sources (unless otherwise indicated): National Statistical Office of Malawi, POB 333, Zomba; tel. 1524377; fax 1525130; e-mail enquiries@statistics.gov.mw; internet www.nso.malawi.net; Reserve Bank of Malawi, POB 30063, Capital City, Lilongwe 3; tel. 1770600; fax 1772752; e-mail webmaster@rbm.mw; internet www.rbm.mw.

Area and Population

AREA, POPULATION AND DENSITY

Area (sq km)	118,484*
Population (census results)	
1–21 September 1987	7,988,507
1–21 September 1998	
Males	4,867,563
Females	5,066,305
Total	9,933,868
Population (UN estimates at mid-year)†	
2004	12,894,000
2005	13,226,000
2006	13,571,000
Density (per sq km) at mid-2006	114.5

* 45,747 sq miles. The area includes 24,208 sq km (9,347 sq miles) of inland water.

† Source: UN, *World Population Prospects: The 2006 Revision*.

REGIONS
(census of September 1998)

Region	Area (sq km)*	Population	Density (per sq km)	Regional capital
Southern	31,753	4,633,968	145.9	Blantyre
Central	35,592	4,066,340	114.2	Lilongwe
Northern	26,931	1,233,560	45.8	Mzuzu
Total	94,276	9,933,868	105.4	

* Excluding inland waters, totalling 24,208 sq km.

PRINCIPAL TOWNS
(population at census of September 1998)

Blantyre	502,053	Karonga	27,811
Lilongwe (capital)	440,471	Kasungu	27,754
Mzuzu	86,890	Mangochi	26,570
Zomba	65,915	Salima	20,355

Mid-2005 (incl. suburbs, UN estimate): Lilongwe 676,000 (Source: UN, *World Urbanization Prospects: The 2005 Revision*).

BIRTHS AND DEATHS
(annual averages, UN estimates)

	1990–95	1995–2000	2000–05
Birth rate (per 1,000)	49.1	47.0	43.8
Death rate (per 1,000)	17.1	17.2	17.5

Source: UN, *World Population Prospects: The 2006 Revision*.

Expectation of Life (years at birth, WHO estimates): 41 (males 41; females 41) in 2004 (Source: WHO, *World Health Report*).

ECONOMICALLY ACTIVE POPULATION*
(persons aged 10 years and over, 1998 census)

	Males	Females	Total
Agriculture, hunting, forestry and fishing	1,683,006	2,082,821	3,765,827
Mining and quarrying	2,206	293	2,499
Manufacturing	94,545	23,938	118,483
Electricity, gas and water	6,656	663	7,319
Construction	70,196	3,206	73,402
Trade, restaurants and hotels	176,466	80,923	257,389
Transport, storage and communications	29,438	3,185	32,623
Financing, insurance, real estate and business services	10,473	3,484	13,957
Public administration	82,973	18,460	101,433
Community, social and personal services	52,980	33,016	85,996
Total employed	2,208,940	2,249,989	4,458,929
Unemployed	34,697	15,664	50,361
Total labour force	2,243,637	2,265,653	4,509,290

* Excluding armed forces.

Mid-2005 (estimates in '000): Agriculture, etc. 4,903; Total labour force 6,068 (Source: FAO).

Health and Welfare

KEY INDICATORS

Total fertility rate (children per woman, 2005)	5.9
Under-5 mortality rate (per 1,000 live births, 2005)	125
HIV/AIDS (% of persons aged 15–49, 2005)	14.1
Physicians (per 1,000 head, 2004)	0.02
Hospital beds (per 1,000 head, 1998)	1.34
Health expenditure (2004): US $ per head (PPP)	57.8
Health expenditure (2004): % of GDP	12.9
Health expenditure (2004): public (% of total)	74.7
Access to water (% of persons, 2004)	73
Access to sanitation (% of persons, 2004)	61
Human Development Index (2004): ranking	166
Human Development Index (2004): value	0.400

For sources and definitions, see explanatory note on p. vi.

Agriculture

PRINCIPAL CROPS
('000 metric tons)

	2003	2004	2005
Rice (paddy)	88.2	49.7	50.0*
Maize	1,983.4	1,733.1	1,253.0†
Millet	24.6	17.3	17.5*
Sorghum	45.0†	40.9	41.0*
Potatoes	1,100.0*	1,784.7	1,800.0*
Cassava (Manioc)	1,735.1	2,559.3	2,075.0†
Dry beans	109.8	79.4	80.0*
Chick-peas*	35.0	34.4	34.1
Cow peas (dry)*	54.0	54.0	n.a.
Pigeon peas*	79.0	79.0	n.a.
Groundnuts (in shell)	190.1	161.2	92.0†
Cottonseed	27.0†	34.8	24.0†
Cabbages and other brassicas	28.0*	50.0	37.5*
Tomatoes*	35.0	35.0	34.9
Onions (dry)	35.0*	50.0	50.0*
Guavas, mangoes and mangosteens	60.0	33.0*	44.5*
Bananas	2.1*	360.0	54.2*
Plantains	200*	300.0	247.6*
Sugar cane	2,100	2,100	n.a.
Coffee (green)	2.6	1.6	1.5†
Tea	41.7	50.1	38.0
Tobacco (leaves)*	69.5	69.5	n.a.
Cotton (lint)	14.0	18.8	19.0*

* FAO estimate(s).
† Unofficial figure.

Source: FAO.

LIVESTOCK
('000 head, year ending September)

	2003	2004	2005
Cattle	750*	765	750*
Pigs*	456.3	456.3	n.a.
Sheep*	115	115	n.a.
Goats	1,700*	1,900	1,900*
Chickens*	15,200	15,200	15,200

* FAO estimate(s).

Source: FAO.

LIVESTOCK PRODUCTS
('000 metric tons, FAO estimates)

	2003	2004	2005
Cattle meat	15.9	15.7	16.0
Goat meat	6.0	6.6	6.6
Pig meat	21.0	23.1	24.5
Chicken meat	15.3	16.0	16.4
Cows' milk	35.0	35.0	n.a.
Hen eggs	19.5	19.5	n.a.

Source: FAO.

Forestry

ROUNDWOOD REMOVALS
('000 cubic metres, excluding bark)

	2003	2004	2005
Sawlogs, veneer logs and logs for sleepers*	130	130	130
Other industrial wood*	390	390	390
Fuel wood	5,064.4	5,101.7	5,140.7
Total*	5,584.4	5,621.7	5,660.7

* FAO estimates.

Source: FAO.

SAWNWOOD PRODUCTION
('000 cubic metres, including railway sleepers)

	1991*	1992†	1993
Coniferous (softwood)	28	28	30
Broadleaved (hardwood)	15	15	15†
Total	43	43	45

* Unofficial figures.
† FAO estimate(s).

1994–2005: Annual production as in 1993 (FAO estimates).

Source: FAO.

Fishing

('000 metric tons, live weight)

	2003	2004	2005
Capture	53.8	56.5	59.4
Cyprinids	6.7	7.1	7.2
Tilapias	5.7	6.0	6.0
Cichlids	29.8	31.4	33.6
Torpedo-shaped catfishes	8.2	8.7	8.7
Other freshwater fishes	3.1	3.3	3.3
Aquaculture	0.7	0.7	0.8
Total catch	54.5	57.2	60.2

Note: Figures exclude aquatic mammals, recorded by number rather than weight. The number of Nile crocodiles caught was: 301 in 2003; 20 in 2004; 637 in 2005.

Source: FAO.

Mining

('000 metric tons, unless otherwise indicated)

	2003	2004	2005*
Bituminous coal	47.0	40.9	49.0
Lime	18.9	23.1	29.0
Gemstones (kilograms)	2,297	1,820	1,400
Aggregate	159.9	168.6	175.0
Limestone	24.0	21.2	28.0

* Estimates.

Source: US Geological Survey.

Industry

SELECTED PRODUCTS

('000 metric tons, unless otherwise indicated)

	2000	2001	2002
Raw sugar	96	107	260*
Beer ('000 hectolitres)	739	1,033	n.a.
Blankets ('000)	574	281	n.a.
Cement	198	111	174

* Natural sodium carbonate (Na_2Co_3).

2003 ('000 metric tons): Raw sugar (Na_2Co_3) 257; Cement 190 (Source: US Geological Survey).

Electric energy (million kWh): 1,129 in 2002; 1,177 in 2003; 1,270 in 2004.

Source (unless otherwise indicated): UN, *Industrial Commodity Statistics Yearbook*.

Cement ('000 metric tons, hydraulic): 119.5 in 2004; 120.0 in 2005 (estimate) (Source: US Geological Survey).

Finance

CURRENCY AND EXCHANGE RATES

Monetary Units

100 tambala = 1 Malawi kwacha (K).

Sterling, Dollar and Euro Equivalents (30 April 2007)

£1 sterling = 280.303 kwacha;
US $1 = 140.531 kwacha;
€1 = 191.192 kwacha;
1,000 Malawi kwacha = £3.57 = $7.12 = €5.23.

Average Exchange Rate (kwacha per US $)

2004	108.898
2005	118.420
2006	136.014

BUDGET

(K million, year ending 30 June)

Revenue	2001/02	2002/03	2003/04*
Tax revenue	22,899.8	27,684.4	40,436.0
Taxes on income and profits	10,053.8	12,206.4	15,919.6
Companies	3,792.9	3,848.3	4,589.2
Individuals	6,260.9	8,358.1	11,379.0
Fringe benefits	651.1	509.9	556.1
Taxes on goods and services	9,353.1	12,170.0	15,949.0
Surtax	7,214.0	9,086.0	11,092.7
Excise duties	2,139.1	3,084.1	4,856.3
Taxes on international trade	3,492.9	3,307.9	8,567.4
Less Tax refunds	555.6	508.1	840.0
Non-tax revenue	2,161.2	5,297.0	1,675.9
Departmental receipts	2,092.9	1,600.2	—
Total	24,505.4	32,473.3	41,271.8

Expenditure	2001/02	2002/03	2003/04*
General public services	10,333.4	9,171.8	17,594.0
General administration	8,022.9	6,118.0	14,213.2
Defence	890.1	1,122.5	1,461.4
Public order and safety	1,420.3	1,931.3	1,919.3
Social and community services	12,430.7	11,521.1	13,985.2
Education	4,300.2	5,968.3	7,379.8
Health	3,365.6	3,589.2	3,591.4
Social security and welfare	4,363.0	1,466.1	1,815.4
Housing and community amenities	247.21	376.3	973.3
Recreational, cultural and other social services	86.4	55.0	79.0
Broadcasting and publishing	68.3	66.1	146.3
Economic affairs and services	2,614.6	3,338.9	3,869.4
Energy and mining	24.8	47.1	108.6
Agriculture and natural resources	1,768.7	2,262.7	2,638.7
Tourism	25.1	143.7	152.2
Physical planning and development	22.1	92.3	119.7
Transport and communications	445.5	437.4	383.3
Industry and commerce	203.4	103.0	205.7
Labour relations and employment	45.7	237.2	242.3
Environmental protection and conservation	9.3	—	—
Scientific and technological services	36.5	—	—
Other economic services	15.4	15.4	18.9
Unallocable expenditure	6,820.6	1,005.1	—
Total recurrent expenditure	32,199.2	25,036.7	35,448.6
Debt amortization	4,383.7	14,717.9	18,139.9
Total	36,582.9	39,754.6	53,588.6

* Estimates.

INTERNATIONAL RESERVES

(US $ million at 31 December)

	2004	2005	2006
Gold (national valuation)	0.54	0.54	0.54
IMF special drawing rights	1.20	1.05	0.68
Reserve position in IMF	3.56	3.27	3.48
Foreign exchange	123.30	154.59	129.61
Total	128.60	159.45	134.31

Source: IMF, *International Financial Statistics*.

MONEY SUPPLY

(K million at 31 December)

	2004	2005	2006
Currency outside banks	10,992.8	11,947.0	15,470.9
Demand deposits at commercial banks	14,730.2	19,356.1	20,217.8
Total money (incl. others)	25,723.0	31,303.1	35,688.7

Source: IMF, *International Financial Statistics*.

COST OF LIVING

(Consumer Price Index; base: 2000 = 100)

	2004	2005	2006
Food (incl. beverages)	154.4	181.0	209.1
Clothing (incl. footwear)	179.5	192.8	n.a.
Rent	211.7	236.9	n.a.
All items (incl. others)	172.0	198.5	226.1

Source: ILO.

NATIONAL ACCOUNTS

Expenditure on the Gross Domestic Product

(K million at current prices)

	2004	2005	2006*
Government final consumption expenditure	34,990.1	41,344.5	49,124.8
Private final consumption expenditure	324,697.4	395,671.5	435,651.9
Gross capital formation	25,091.9	29,106.9	32,783.5
Total domestic expenditure	384,779.4	466,122.9	517,560.2
Exports of goods and services	58,914.3	61,785.8	84,188.8
Less Imports of goods and services	135,181.6	164,387.6	166,523.9
GDP in purchasers' values	308,512.1	363,521.1	435,225.0
GDP at 2002 factor cost	271,050.6	276,801.2	300,123.6

Gross Domestic Product by Economic Activity

(K million at current prices)

	2004	2005	2006*
Agriculture, forestry and fishing	88,955.7	81,395.9	91,814.5
Mining and quarrying	1,450.5	2,177.2	2,386.2
Manufacturing	52,040.1	55,786.9	59,022.6
Electricity and water	3,434.4	3,740.0	4,016.8
Building and construction	3,904.4	4,189.5	4,759.2
Wholesale and retail trade services	53,418.1	58,118.9	62,826.6
Hotels and restaurants	10,804.3	11,470.0	12,341.3
Transport and communication	14,584.4	15,926.2	16,802.1
Financial intermediation and insurance	8,405.0	9,069.0	9,540.6
Business activities and real estate	9,815.1	10,050.6	10,362.2
Ownership of dwellings	2,407.2	2,457.8	2,583.1
Private social services	7,984.7	8,240.2	8,808.8
Government services	13,846.7	14,179.0	14,859.6
Sub-total	271,050.6	276,801.2	300,123.6
Net indirect taxes	25,706.2	31,813.3	40,000.0
Adjustment to current prices	11,755.2	54,906.6	95,101.4
GDP in market prices	308,512.0	363,521.1	435,225.0

* Projected figures.

BALANCE OF PAYMENTS

(K million)

	2004	2005	2006
Exports of goods f.o.b.	54,464.3	59,592.5	62,530.0
Imports of goods f.o.b.	–73,406.7	–104,639.0	–133,634.5
Trade balance	–18,942.5	–45,046.4	–71,104.5
Net services	–14,813.5	–21,229.6	–11,246.8
Balance on goods and services	–33,756.0	–66,276.0	–82,351.3
Net other income	–4,321.0	–5,162.4	–4,560.9
Balance on goods, services and income	–38,077.0	–71,438.4	–89,912.2
Net transfers	1,292.3	5,562.6	7,583.9
Statistical discrepancy	–6,762.1	—	—
Current balance	–43,546.8	–65,875.8	–79,328.3
Government transfers (net)	17,029.3	26,858.4	21,330.5
Government drawings on loans	4,865.1	6,426.9	7,811.8
Public enterprises (net)	1,180.7	1,319.2	1,376.0
Private sector (net)	391.9	425.7	444.1
Short-term capital (net)	10,103.2	70.6	73.6
Errors and omissions	9,896.8	25,130.9	30,069.3
Statistical discrepancy	—	—	9,000.0
Overall balance*	–79.8	–5,644.1	–9,223.0

* Excluding debt relief (K million): 4,614.0 in 2004; 5,644.1 in 2005; 9,223.0 in 2005.

External Trade

PRINCIPAL COMMODITIES

(distribution by SITC, US $ million)

Imports c.i.f.	2002	2003	2004
Food and live animals	128.3	56.9	40.2
Cereals and cereal preparations	104.6	30.9	15.5
Beverages and tobacco	16.9	46.0	11.9
Tobacco and tobacco products	14.3	43.8	10.1
Mineral fuels, lubricants, etc.	77.1	86.3	13.0
Petroleum, petroleum products, etc.	73.8	85.2	11.7
Refined petroleum products	71.1	82.0	9.1
Chemicals and related products	120.1	121.5	80.7
Medicinal and pharmaceutical products	23.1	26.2	22.6
Manufactured fertilizers	49.2	43.3	13.8
Basic manufactures	106.6	130.9	106.1
Paper, paperboard, etc.	16.1	22.6	15.8
Textile yarn, fabrics, etc.	29.3	33.7	31.7
Iron and steel	19.5	21.9	16.5
Machinery and transport equipment	163.6	188.5	152.5
Machinery specialized for particular industries	21.1	32.6	26.4
General industrial machinery, equipment and parts	17.0	23.8	19.3
Office machinery and automatic data processing equipment	13.9	12.2	15.3
Electrical machinery, apparatus, etc.	17.0	26.3	21.1
Road vehicles	73.8	76.2	49.1
Goods vehicles (lorries and trucks)	29.9	32.4	14.6
Miscellaneous manufactured articles	52.4	58.6	55.2
Total (incl. others)	695.0	723.5	477.6

Exports f.o.b.	2002	2003	2004
Food and live animals	87.1	162.6	145.7
Sugar and honey	34.8	105.4	75.6
Raw beet and cane sugars	27.5	92.5	72.4
Coffee, tea, cocoa and spices	42.2	36.3	50.9
Tea	36.7	32.8	47.2
Beverages and tobacco	232.1	225.0	221.4
Tobacco and tobacco products	232.0	224.9	221.4
Unstripped tobacco	143.9	123.7	130.3
Stripped or partly stripped tobacco	88.1	101.3	91.1
Crude materials (inedible) except fuels	12.1	15.3	35.5
Textile fibres	7.4	5.8	21.0
Basic manufactures	34.7	40.8	57.9
Clothing and accessories	32.0	34.2	44.3
Total (incl. others)	377.4	457.0	483.3

Source: UN, *International Trade Statistics Yearbook*.

PRINCIPAL TRADING PARTNERS
(K million)

Imports	2002	2003	2004
France	1,379	530	2,680
Germany	504	1,099	1,116
Japan	1,597	3,202	3,924
Mozambique	1,576	4,061	13,705
Netherlands	431	429	579
South Africa	22,272	30,621	32,221
United Kingdom	2,806	4,079	5,193
USA	2,264	2,874	2,795
Zambia	968	2,172	3,915
Zimbabwe	3,118	4,996	4,800
Total (incl. others)	53,657	76,650	101,554

Exports	2002	2003	2004
France	451	1,726	385
Germany	3,321	3,655	3,974
Japan	1,238	2,681	1,052
Mozambique	548	1,873	3,050
Netherlands	863	3,174	2,319
South Africa	4,246	7,865	7,706
United Kingdom	2,905	3,822	5,197
USA	4,659	6,394	5,934
Zambia	255	884	1,114
Zimbabwe	485	851	1,002
Total (incl. others)	31,416	51,672	52,627

Transport

RAILWAYS
(traffic)

	2002	2003	2004
Passengers carried ('000)	402	488	394
Passenger-kilometres ('000)	23,845	30,311	29,523
Net freight ton-kilometres ('000)	86,018	26,009	26,055

ROAD TRAFFIC
(estimates, motor vehicles in use at 31 December)

	1994	1995	1996
Passenger cars	23,520	25,480	27,000
Lorries and vans	26,000	29,000	29,700

Source: International Road Federation, *World Road Statistics*.

SHIPPING

Inland Waterways
(lake transport)

	2002	2003	2004
Passengers carried ('000)	78	68	55
Passenger-km ('000)	6,955	5,659	4,299
Net freight-ton km	392	1,438	316

CIVIL AVIATION
(traffic on scheduled services)

	2001	2002	2003
Kilometres flown (million)	3	3	4
Passengers carried ('000)	113	105	109
Passenger-km (million)	221	140	147
Total ton-km (million)	23	14	16

Source: UN, *Statistical Yearbook*.

Freight carried (metric tons): 3,468 in 2002; 2,768 in 2003; 4,011 in 2004.

Passengers carried ('000): 431 in 2002; 239 in 2003; 335 in 2004.

Tourism

FOREIGN TOURIST ARRIVALS BY COUNTRY OF RESIDENCE

	2003	2004	2005
Mozambique	92,200	104,698	95,019
North America	17,210	19,431	17,278
Southern Africa*	49,200	54,230	48,155
United Kingdom and Ireland	31,220	17,030	28,157
Zambia	50,540	45,817	43,855
Zimbabwe	63,910	57,518	60,807
Total (incl. others)	424,000	427,360	437,718

* Comprising South Africa, Botswana, Lesotho and Swaziland.

Tourism receipts (US $ million, excl. passenger transport): 33 in 2003; 24 in 2004; n.a. in 2005.

Source: World Tourism Organization.

Communications Media

	2003	2004	2005
Telephones ('000 main lines in use)	85.0	93.0	102.7
Mobile cellular telephones ('000 subscribers)	135.1	222.1	429.3
Personal computers ('000 in use)	16	20	—
Internet users ('000)	36.0	46.1	—

Radio receivers ('000 in use): 4,929 in 1998.

Television receivers ('000 in use): 40 in 2001.

Facsimile machines (number in use): 1,250 in 1997.

Book production (first editions only): 120 titles in 1996.

Daily newspapers: 5 in 1998 (estimated average circulation 26,000 copies).

Non-daily newspapers: 4 in 1996 (estimated average circulation 120,000 copies).

Sources: UNESCO Institute for Statistics; UN, *Statistical Yearbook*; International Telecommunication Union.

Education

(2003)

	Institutions	Teachers	Students
Primary	3,160*	45,100	3,112,513
Secondary	n.a.	7,076	131,100
Universities	6	654	4,757

* 1997 figure. Source: UNESCO Institute for Statistics.

Primary education (2004): Schools 5,103; Students 3,166,786; Teachers 43,952 (Source: partly Ministry of Education, Science and Technology).

Adult literacy rate (UNESCO estimates): 64.1% (males 74.9%; females 54.0%) in 1995–99 (Source: UN Development Programme, *Human Development Report*).

Directory

The Constitution

A new Constitution, replacing the (amended) 1966 Constitution, was approved by the National Assembly on 16 May 1994, and took provisional effect for one year from 18 May. During this time the Constitution was to be subject to review, and the final document was promulgated on 18 May 1995. The main provisions (with subsequent amendments) are summarized below:

THE PRESIDENT

The President is both Head of State and Head of Government. The President is elected for five years, by universal adult suffrage, in the context of a multi-party political system. The Constitution provides for up to two Vice-Presidents.

PARLIAMENT

Parliament comprises the President, the Vice-President(s) and the National Assembly. The National Assembly has 193 elective seats, elections being by universal adult suffrage, in the context of a multi-party system. Cabinet ministers who are not elected members of parliament also sit in the National Assembly. The Speaker is appointed from among the ordinary members of the Assembly. The parliamentary term is normally five years. The President has power to prorogue or dissolve Parliament.

In 1995 the National Assembly approved proposals for the establishment of a second chamber, the Senate, to be implemented in 1999. The chamber was not established by that date, however, and in January 2001 the National Assembly approved a proposal to abandon plans for its creation.

EXECUTIVE POWER

Executive power is exercised by the President, who appoints members of the Cabinet.

The Government

HEAD OF STATE

President: Dr BINGU WA MUTHARIKA (took office 24 May 2004).

Vice-President: Dr CASSIM CHILUMPHA.

CABINET

(August 2007)

President and Commander-in-Chief of the Malawi Defence Force and Police Service, Minister of Agriculture and Food Security and Minister of Education, Science and Technology: Dr BINGU WA MUTHARIKA.

Minister for Presidential and Parliamentary Affairs: DAVIES KATSONGA.

Minister of Finance: Dr GOODALL E. GONDWE.

Minister of Foreign Affairs: JOYCE BANDA.

Minister of Industry and Trade: Dr KENNETH LIPENGA.

Minister of Energy and Mines: HENRY CHIMUNTHU BANDA.

Minister of Local Government and Rural Development: Dr GEORGE CHAPONDA.

Minister of Transport, Public Works and Housing: HENRY MUSSA.

Minister of Economic Planning and Development: TEDSON KALEBE.

Minister of Irrigation and Water Development: SIDIK MIA.

Minister of National Defence: BOB KHAMISA.

Minister of Information and Civic Education: PATRICIA KALIATI.

Minister of Lands and Natural Resources: KHUMBO CHIRWA.

Minister of Home Affairs and Internal Security: ERNEST MALENGA.

Minister of Justice: HENRY DAMA PHOYA.

Attorney-General: JANE ANSAH.

Minister of Labour and Social Development: ANNA KACHIKO.

Minister of Health: MAJORIE NGAUNJE.

Minister of Women and Child Development: KATE KAINJA KALULUMA.

Minister of Youth Development and Sports: KHUMBO KACHALI.

Minister of Persons with Disabilities and the Elderly: CLEMENT KHEMBO.

Minister of Tourism, Wildlife and Culture: CALLISTA CHIMOMBO.

There were also 20 Deputy Ministers.

MINISTRIES

Office of the President and Cabinet: Private Bag 301, Capital City, Lilongwe 3; tel. 1789311; fax 1788456; internet www.malawi.gov.mw/opc/opc.htm.

Ministry of Defence: Private Bag 339, Lilongwe 3; tel. 1789600; fax 1789176; e-mail defence@malawi.gov.mw; internet www.malawi.gov.mw/defence/defence.htm.

Ministry of Economic Planning and Development: POB 30136, Capital City, Lilongwe 3; tel. 1788390; fax 1788131; e-mail epd@malawi.net; internet www.malawi.gov.mw/nec/nec.htm.

Ministry of Education and Vocational Training: Private Bag 328, Capital City, Lilongwe 3; tel. 1789422; fax 1788064; e-mail secretaryforeducation@sdnp.org.mw; internet www.malawi.gov.mw/educ/educ.htm.

Ministry of Finance: Capital Hill, POB 30049, Lilongwe 3; tel. 1789355; fax 1789173; internet www.finance.malawi.gov.mw.

Ministry of Foreign Affairs and International Co-operation: POB 30315, Capital City, Lilongwe 3; tel. 1789323; fax 1788482; e-mail foreign@malawi.net; internet www.malawi.gov.mw/foreign/foreign.htm.

Ministry of Gender, Child Welfare and Community Services: Private Bag 330, Capital City, Lilongwe 3; tel. 1770411; fax 1770826; internet www.malawi.gov.mw/gender/gender.htm.

Ministry of Health: POB 30377, Capital City, Lilongwe 3; tel. 1789400; fax 1789431; e-mail doccentre@malawi.net; internet www.malawi.gov.mw/health/health.htm.

Ministry of Home Affairs and Internal Security: Private Bag 331, Lilongwe 3; tel. 1789177; fax 1789509; internet www.malawi.gov.mw/homeaff/homeaffairs.htm; comprises the Immigration Dept, Prison and Police Services.

Ministry of Information and Tourism: Private Bag 326, Capital City, Lilongwe 3; tel. 1775499; fax 1770650; e-mail psinfo@sdnp.org.mw; internet www.information.gov.mw.

Ministry of Irrigation and Water Development: Tikwere House, Private Bag 390, Capital City, Lilongwe 3; tel. 1770238; fax 1773737; internet www.malawi.gov.mw/water/water.htm.

Ministry of Justice and Constitutional Affairs: Private Bag 333, Capital City, Lilongwe 3; tel. 1788411; fax 1788332; e-mail justice@malawi.gov.mw; internet www.malawi.gov.mw/mojca/mojca.htm; also comprises the Attorney-General's Chambers and the Directorate of Public Prosecutions.

Ministry of Labour and Social Development: Private Bag 344, Capital City, Lilongwe 3; tel. 1783277; fax 1783805.

Ministry of Lands, Housing and Surveys: POB 30548, Lilongwe 3; tel. 1774766; fax 1773990; internet www.malawi.gov.mw/lands/lands.htm.

Ministry of Local Government and Rural Development: POB 30312, Lilongwe 3; tel. 1784500; fax 1782130.

Ministry of Mines, Energy and Natural Resources: Private Bag 350, Lilongwe 3; tel. 1789488; fax 1773379; internet www.malawi.gov.mw/natres/natres.htm.

Ministry of Persons with Disabilities and the Elderly: Lilongwe 3.

Ministry of Statutory Corporations: Gemini House, 7th Floor, City Centre, POB 30061, Lilongwe 3; tel. 1774266; fax 1774110; internet www.malawi.gov.mw/statcoorp/statcohome.htm; manages parastatal cos.

Ministry of Trade, Industry and Private-Sector Development: POB 30366, Capital City, Lilongwe 3; tel. 1770244; fax 1770680; internet www.malawi.gov.mw/commerce/commerce.htm.

Ministry of Transport and Public Works: Private Bag 322, Capital City, Lilongwe 3; tel. 1789377; fax 1789328; internet www.malawi.gov.mw/transport/transhq.htm.

Ministry of Youth, Sports and Culture: Lingadzi House, Private Bag 384, Lilongwe 3; tel. 1774999; fax 1771018; internet www.malawi.gov.mw/sports/sports.htm.

President and Legislature

PRESIDENT

Presidential Election, 20 May 2004

Candidate	Votes	% of votes
Bingu wa Mutharika (UDF)	1,119,738	35.89
John Tembo (MCP)	846,457	27.13
Gwandaguluwe Chakuamba (Mgwirizano Coalition*)	802,386	25.72
Brown Mpinganjira (NDA)	272,172	8.72
Justin Malewezi (Independent)	78,892	2.53
Total	3,119,645	100.00

* Comprising the Malawi Democratic Party, the Malawi Forum for Unity and Development, the Movement for Genuine Democratic Change (MGODE), the National Unity Party, the People's Progressive Movement, the People's Transformation Party and Chakuamba's Republican Party (RP); in early June 2004 MGODE and the RP signed a memorandum of understanding on co-operation with the UDF.

NATIONAL ASSEMBLY

National Assembly: Parliament Bldg, Private Bag B362, Lilongwe 3; tel. 1773566; fax 1774196; internet www.malawi.gov.mw/parliament/parliament.htm.

Speaker: Louis Joseph Chimango.

General Election, 20 May 2004*

Party	Seats
Malawi Congress Party (MCP)	56
United Democratic Front (UDF)	49
Republican Party (RP)†	15
National Democratic Alliance (NDA)	8
Alliance for Democracy (AFORD)	6
People's Progressive Movement (PPM)†	6
Movement for Genuine Democratic Change (MGODE)†	3
Congress for National Unity (CONU)	1
People's Transformation Party (PETRA)†	1
Independents	39
Total	193‡

* Provisional results.

† Contested the election as part of the Mgwirizano Coalition, which also comprised the Malawi Democratic Party, the Malawi Forum for Unity and Development and the National Unity Party; in early June 2004 MGODE and the RP signed a memorandum of understanding on co-operation with the UDF.

‡ Disputed results in three constituencies remained under investigation in early June 2004, while voting in a further six constituencies was not conducted owing to irregularities.

Election Commission

Malawi Electoral Commission (MEC): Development House, Private Bag 113, Blantyre; tel. 1822033; fax 1823960; internet www.sdnp.org.mw/~solomon/mec/index.htm; f. 1998; Chair. James Kalaile; Chief Elections Officer David Kambauwa (acting).

Political Organizations

Alliance for Democracy (AFORD): Private Bag 28, Lilongwe; f. 1992; in March 1993 absorbed membership of fmr Malawi Freedom Movement; Pres. Chakufwa Chihana; First Vice-Pres. Kalundi Chirwa; Sec.-Gen. Wallace Chiume.

Congress for National Unity (CONU): Lilongwe; f. 1999; Pres. Bishop Daniel Kamfosi Nkhumbwa.

Democratic Progressive Party (DPP): Lilongwe 3; f. 2005 following Bingu wa Mutharika's resignation from the UDF; Leader Dr Bingu wa Mutharika; Sec.-Gen. Joyce Banda.

Malawi Congress Party (MCP): Private Bag 388, Lilongwe 3; tel. 1730388; f. 1959; sole legal party 1966–93; Pres. John Tembo.

Malawi Democratic Party (MDP): Pres. Kamlepo Kalua.

Malawi Forum for Unity and Development (MAFUNDE): f. 2002; aims to combat corruption and food shortages; Pres. George Mnesa.

Movement for Genuine Democratic Change (MGODE): Lilongwe; f. 2003 by fmr mems of AFORD; Pres. Egbert Chibambo (acting); Nat. Chair. Greene Lulilo Mwamondwe; Sec.-Gen. Rogers Nkhwazi.

National Democratic Alliance (NDA): POB 994, Blantyre; tel. 1842593; f. 2001 by fmr mems of the UDF; officially merged with the UDF in June 2004 but maintained independent structure; Pres. Brown James Mpinganjira; Nat. Chair. James Makhumula Nkhoma.

National Solidarity Movement: Leader Ngwazi Kazuni Kumwenda.

National Unity Party (NUP): Blantyre; Pres. Harry Chiume; Sec.-Gen. Harry Muyenza.

New Congress for Democracy (NCD): Lilongwe; f. 2004 by fmr mems of the MCP; Pres. Hetherwick Ntaba.

New Dawn for Africa (NDA): Lilongwe; f. 2003; associated with the UDF; Pres. Thom Chiumia; Sec.-Gen. Chikumbutso Mtumodzi.

Pamodzi Freedom Party (PFP): Lilongwe; f. 2002; Pres. Rainsford Chigadula Ndiwo.

People's Progressive Movement (PPM): f. 2003 by fmr mems of the UDF; Pres. Aleke Kadonaphani Banda; Sec.-Gen. Knox Varela.

People's Transformation Party (PETRA): POB 31964, Chichiri, Blantyre 3; tel. 1671577; fax 1671573; e-mail president@petra.mw; internet www.petra.mw; f. 2002; Pres. Kamuzu Chibambo.

Republican Party (RP): f. 2004; Leader (vacant).

Social Democratic Party (SDP): Pres. Ison Kakome.

United Democratic Front (UDF): POB 5446, Limbe; internet www.udf.malawi.net; f. 1992; officially merged with the NDA in June 2004 but maintained independent structure; Nat. Chair. Dr Bakili Muluzi; Sec.-Gen. Kennedy Makwangwala.

United Front for Multi-party Democracy (UFMD): f. 1992 by three exiled political groups: the Socialist League of Malawi, the Malawi Freedom Party and the Malawi Dem. Union; Pres. Edmond Jika.

United Party (UP): f. 1997.

The Movement for the Restoration of Democracy in Malawi (f. 1996) is based in Mozambique and consists of fmr Malawi Young Pioneers; it conducts occasional acts of insurgency.

Diplomatic Representation

EMBASSIES AND HIGH COMMISSIONS IN MALAWI

China (Taiwan): Area 40, Plot No. 9, POB 30221, Capital City, Lilongwe 3; tel. 1773611; fax 1774812; e-mail mwi@mofa.gov.tw; Ambassador Chuang Shyan-Kai.

Egypt: 10/247 Tsoka Rd, POB 30451, Lilongwe 3; tel. 1780668; fax 1780691; Ambassador Adel el-Hamid Ahmed Marzouk.

Germany: Convention Dr., POB 30046, Lilongwe 3; tel. 1772555; fax 1770250; e-mail info@lilongwe.diplo.de; internet www.lilongwe.diplo.de; Ambassador Albert Josef Gisy.

Ireland: Gomani Rd, POB 1582, Blantyre; Ambassador Anne Barrington (designate).

Mozambique: POB 30579, Lilongwe 3; tel. 1784100; fax 1781342; High Commissioner Jorge de Sousa Mateus.

Norway: Plot 13–14 Arwa House, City Centre, Private Bag B323, Lilongwe 3; tel. 1774211; fax 1772845; e-mail emb.lilongwe@mfa.no; Ambassador Gunnar Føreland.

South Africa: Kang'ombe House, 3rd Floor, City Centre, POB 30043, Lilongwe 3; tel. 1773722; fax 1772571; e-mail sahc@malawi.net; High Commissioner N. M. Tsheole.

Tanzania: POB 922, Capital City, Lilongwe 3; tel. 1770150; fax 1770148; e-mail tanzanianhighcomm@tz.lilongwe.mw; High Commissioner Maj.-Gen. (retd) Makame Rashid.

United Kingdom: British High Commission Bldg, Capital Hill, POB 30042, Lilongwe 3; tel. 1772400; fax 1772657; e-mail bhclilongwe@fco.gov.uk; internet www.britishhighcommission.gov.uk/malawi; High Commissioner Richard Wildash.

USA: Area 40, Plot No. 18, 16 Jomo Kenyatta Rd, POB 30016, Lilongwe 3; tel. 1773166; fax 1770471; e-mail ConsularLilongwe@state.gov; internet lilongwe.usembassy.gov; Ambassador Alan W. Eastham.

Zambia: POB 30138, Lilongwe 3; tel. 1782635; fax 1784349; High Commissioner Ian Sikazwe.

Zimbabwe: POB 30187, Lilongwe 3; tel. 1774988; fax 1772382; e-mail zimhighcomllw@malawi.net; High Commissioner Thandiwe S. Dumbutshena.

Judicial System

The courts administering justice are the Supreme Court of Appeal, High Court and Magistrates' Courts.

The High Court, which has unlimited jurisdiction in civil and criminal matters, consists of the Chief Justice and five puisne judges. Traditional Courts were abolished under the 1994 Constitution. Appeals from the High Court are heard by the Supreme Court of Appeal in Blantyre.

High Court of Malawi

POB 30244, Chichiri, Blantyre 3; tel. 1670255; fax 1670213; e-mail highcourt@sdnp.org.mw; internet www.judiciary.mw; Registrar SYLVESTER KALEMBERA.

Chief Justice: LOVEMORE MUNLO.

Justices of Appeal: J. B. KALAILE, D. G. TAMBALA, H. M. MTEGHA, A. S. E. MSOSA, I. J. MTAMBO, A. K. TEMBO.

High Court Judges: D. F. MWAUNGULU, A. K. C. NYIRENDA, G. M. CHIMASULA PHIRI, B. S. CHIUDZA BANDA, E. B. TWEA, R. R. MZIKAMANDA, Dr J. M. ANSAH, R. R. CHINANGWA, A. C. CHIPETA, F. E. KAPANDA, L. P. CHIKOPA, H. S. B. POTANI, E. CHOMBO, J. N. KATSALA, J. S. MANYUNGWA, M. L. KAMWAMBE, M. C. C. MKANDAWIRE, I. C. KAMANGA.

Religion

More than 70% of the population profess Christianity. Islam, the fastest growing religion, is practised by about 20% of the population. Traditional beliefs are followed by about 10% of the population. The Asian community includes Hindus.

CHRISTIANITY

Malawi Council of Churches (MCC): POB 30068, Capital City, Lilongwe 3; tel. 1783499; fax 1783106; f. 1939; Chair. Rev. HOWARD MATIYA NKHOMA; Gen. Sec. Rev. Dr A. C. MUSOPOLE; 22 mem. churches.

The Anglican Communion

Anglicans are adherents of the Church of the Province of Central Africa, covering Botswana, Malawi, Zambia and Zimbabwe. The Church comprises 15 dioceses, including four in Malawi. There were about 230,000 adherents in Malawi at mid-2000.

Archbishop of the Province of Central Africa and Bishop of Upper Shire: Most Rev. BERNARD AMOSI MALANGO, Private Bag 1, Chilema, Zomba; tel. and fax 1539203; e-mail esjopembamoyo@malawi.net.

Bishop of Lake Malawi: (vacant), POB 30349, Capital City, Lilongwe 3; tel. 1797858; fax 1797548; e-mail anglama@eomw.net.

Bishop of Northern Malawi: Rt Rev. CHRISTOPHER JOHN BOYLE, POB 120, Mzuzu; tel. 1331486; fax 1333805; e-mail angdioofnm@sdnp.org.mw.

Bishop of Southern Malawi: Rt Rev. JAMES TENGATENGA, POB 30220, Chichiri, Blantyre 3; tel. 1641218; fax 1641235; e-mail angsoma@sdnp.org.mw.

Protestant Churches

At mid-2001 there were an estimated 2.1m. Protestants in Malawi.

Assemblies of God in Malawi: POB 1220, Lilongwe; tel. 1761057; fax 1762056; 639,088 mems in 3,114 churches (2005).

Baptist Convention of Malawi (BACOMA): POB 51083, Limbe; tel. 1643224; Gen. Sec. Rev. FLETCHER KAIYA.

Church of Central Africa (Presbyterian) (CCAP): Blantyre Synod: POB 413, Blantyre; tel. and fax 1633942; comprises three synods in Malawi (Blantyre, Livingstonia and Nkhoma); Co-ordinator Rev. J. J. MPHATSE; Gen. Sec. DANIEL GUNYA; Exec. Dir ROBSON CHITENGO; more than 1m. adherents in Malawi.

Evangelical Association of Malawi: Lilongwe; tel. and fax 1730373; Chair. Rev. Dr LAZARUS CHAKWERA; Gen. Sec. FRANCIS MKANDAWIRE.

Lutheran Church of Central Africa—Malawi Conference: POB 748, Blantyre; tel. and fax 1630821; e-mail pwegner@africa-online.net; f. 1963; Pres. FRACKSON B. CHINYAMA; Co-ordinator PAUL WENGER; 30,000 mems.

Seventh-day Adventist Church: Robins Rd, Kabula Hill, POB 951, Blantyre; tel. 1620264; fax 1620528; e-mail musda@malawi.net; Pres. SAUSTIN K. MFUNE; Exec. Sec. BAXTER D. CHILUNGA; 200,000 mems.

The African Methodist Episcopal Church, the Churches of Christ, the Free Methodist Church, the New Apostolic Church and the United Evangelical Church in Malawi are also active. At mid-2000 there were an estimated 2m. adherents professing other forms of Christianity.

The Roman Catholic Church

Malawi comprises one archdiocese and six dioceses. At 31 December 2004 there were some 3.3m. adherents of the Roman Catholic Church (equivalent to approximately 22.8% of the total population).

Episcopal Conference of Malawi

Catholic Secretariat of Malawi, Chimutu Rd, POB 30384, Capital City, Lilongwe 3; tel. 1772066; fax 1772019; e-mail ecm@malawi.net.

f. 1969; Pres. Most Rev. TARCISIUS GERVAZIO ZIYAYE (Archbishop of Blantyre).

Archbishop of Blantyre: Most Rev. TARCISIUS GERVAZIO ZIYAYE, Archbishop House, POB 385, Blantyre; tel. and fax 1637905.

ISLAM

Muslim Association of Malawi (MAM): POB 497, Blantyre; tel. 1622060; fax 1623581; f. 1946 as the Nyasaland Muslim Asscn; umbrella body for Muslim orgs; provides secular and Islamic education; Sec.-Gen. MOHAMMED IMRAN SHAREEF.

BAHÁ'Í FAITH

National Spiritual Assembly: POB 30922, Lilongwe 3; tel. 1771177; fax 1771713; e-mail bahaimalawi@africa-online.net; f. 1970; mems resident in over 1,200 localities.

The Press

The Chronicle: Private Bag 77, Lilongwe; tel. 1756530; e-mail thechronicle@africa-online.net; f. 1993; publ. by Jamieson Publications; Mon. and Thurs.; English; ceased publ. in Dec. 2006; Owner and Editor-in-Chief ROBERT JAMIESON; circ. c. 5,000 (2006).

The Daily Times: Private Bag 39, Blantyre; tel. 1670115; fax 1671114; e-mail bnl@sdnp.org.mw; f. 1895; fmrly the *Nyasaland Times*; Mon.–Fri., Sun.; English; publ. by Blantyre Newspapers Ltd (Chayamba Trust); affiliated to the MCP; Editor-in-Chief JIKA NKOLOKOSA; circ. Mon.–Fri. c. 20,000, Sun. c. 40,000 (2006).

The Democratus: Aquarius House, Convention Dr., City Centre, Box 1100, Lilongwe 3; tel. 1770033; internet democratusmalawi.blogspot.com; f. 2004; publ. by Democratus Ltd; Wed. and Sun.; Chair. ZIKHALE NG'OMA.

The Dispatch: The Dispatch Publications Ltd, POB 30353, Capital City, Lilongwe 3; tel. 1751639; fax 9510120; e-mail thedispatchmw@sdnp.org.mw; Thurs. and Sun.; Publr and Man. Editor MARTINES NAMINGAH; circ. Thurs. 5,000, Sun. 7,000.

The Enquirer: POB 1745, Blantyre; tel. 1670022; e-mail pillycolette@yahoo.co.uk; English and Nyanja; affiliated to the UDF; Owner LUCIOUS CHIKUNI.

The Guardian: Area 47, Lilongwe; Man. Dir DUWA MUTHARIKA-KAFOTEKA; circ. c. 5,000 (2006).

The Lamp: Montfort Media, POB 280, Balaka, Zomba; tel. 1545267; e-mail montfortmedia@malawi.net; f. 1995; fortnightly; Roman Catholic and ecumenical; Editor Fr GAMBA PIERGIORGIO; circ. 5,500.

Malawi Government Gazette: Government Printer, POB 37, Zomba; tel. 1523155; fax 1522301; f. 1894; weekly.

Malawi News: Private Bag 39, Blantyre; tel. 1671679; fax 1671233; f. 1959; weekly; English and Chichewa; publ. by Blantyre Newspapers Ltd (Chayamba Trust); Gen. Man. JIKA NKOLOKOSA; Man. Editor EDWARD CHISAMBO; Editor FREDERICK NDALA, Jr; circ. c. 40,000 (2006).

The Malawi Standard: POB 31781, Blantyre 3; tel. 1674013; e-mail bligomeka@yahoo.co.uk; fortnightly; Editor BRIAN LIGOMEKA.

The Mirror: POB 30721, Blantyre; tel. 1675043; f. 1994; weekly; English and Nyanja; affiliated to the UDF; Owner and Publr BROWN MPINGANJIRA; circ. 10,000.

The Nation: POB 30408, Chichiri, Blantyre 3; tel. 1673611; fax 1674343; e-mail nation@nationmalawi.com; internet www.nationmalawi.com; f. 1993; daily; publ. by Nation Publs Ltd; weekly edn of *The Weekend Nation* (circ. 30,000); English and Nyanja; Owner ALEKE BANDA; Editor-in-Chief ALFRED NTONGA; circ. 15,000.

Odini: POB 133, Lilongwe; tel. 1721135; fax 1721141; f. 1949; fortnightly; Chichewa and English; Roman Catholic; Dir P. I. AKOMENJI; circ. 12,000.

UDF News: POB 3052, Blantyre; tel. 1645314; fax 1645725; e-mail echapusa@yahoo.co.uk; organ of the UDF; fortnightly; English and Nyanja.

The Weekly News: Dept of Information, POB 494, Blantyre; tel. 1642600; fax 1642364; f. 1996; English and Nyanja; publ. by the Ministry of Information; Editor-in-Chief GEORGE TUKHUWA.

Weekly Courier: Lilongwe 3; affiliated to the Democratic Progressive Party; Man. Editor DENIS MZEMBE; circ. c. 3,000 (2006).

PERIODICALS

Boma Lathu: POB 494, Blantyre; tel. 1620266; fax 1620039; internet www.maform.com/bomalathu.htm; f. 1973; quarterly; Chichewa; publ. by the Ministry of Information; circ. 100,000.

Business Monthly: POB 906646, Blantyre 9; tel. 16301114; fax 1620039; f. 1995; English; economic, financial and business news; Editor ANTHONY LIVUZA; circ. 10,000.

Fairlane Magazine: POB 1745, Blantyre; tel. 1880205; e-mail fairlane@sndp.org.mw; internet www.fairlane.emalawi.com; f. 2006; 6 a year; lifestyle magazine; English and Chichewa; Man. Dir MARIE FRANCE CHIKUNI; Editor AGNES DUMISANI MIZERE.

Journal of Humanities: Faculty of Humanities, Univ. of Malawi, Chancellor College, POB 280, Zomba; tel. (1) 522622; fax (1) 524046; e-mail publications@chanco.unima.mw; annually; focus on east, central and southern Africa; Chief Editor PASCAL KASHINDO; circ. 250.

Kuunika (The Light): POB 17, Nkhoma, Lilongwe; tel. 1722807; e-mail nkhomasynod@globemw.net; f. 1909; monthly; Chichewa; publ. by the Church of Central Africa (Presbyterian) Nkhoma Synod; Presbyterian; Editor Rev. M. C. NKHALAMBAYAUSI; circ. 6,000.

Malawi Journal of Science and Technology: The Research Coordinator, University Office, POB 278, Zomba; tel. (1) 522622; fax (1) 522760; e-mail publications@chanco.unima.mw; annually; applied and natural sciences; Editor Dr M. W. MFITILODZE.

Malawi Medical Journal: College of Medicine and Medical Asscn of Malawi, Private Bag 360, Blantyre 3; tel. 1676444; fax 1675774; e-mail mchilongo@mlw.medcol.mw; f. 1980; replaced *Medical Quarterly*; quarterly; Chair. Prof. ERIC BORGSTEIN; Editor-in-Chief Prof. MALCOLM E. MOLYNEUX.

Moni Magazine: POB 5592, Limbe; tel. 1651833; fax 1651171; f. 1964; monthly; Chichewa and English; Editor PRINCE SHONGA; circ. 40,000.

Moyo Magazine: Health Education Unit, POB 30377, Lilongwe 3; 6 a year; English; publ. by the Ministry of Health; Editor-in-Chief JONATHAN NKHOMA.

Pride: POB 51668, Limbe; tel. 1640569; f. 1999; quarterly; Publr JOHN SAINI.

This is Malawi: POB 494, Blantyre; tel. 1620266; fax 1620807; f. 1964; monthly; English and Chichewa edns; publ. by the Dept of Information; Editor ANTHONY LIVUZA; circ. 12,000.

Together: Montfort Media, POB 280, Balaka, Zomba; tel. 1545267; e-mail together@sdnp.org.mw; f. 1995; quarterly; Roman Catholic and ecumenical, youth; Editor LUIGI GRITTI; circ. 6,000.

Other publications include *Dzukani*, *Inspiration* and *Msilikali*.

NEWS AGENCIES

Malawi News Agency (MANA): POB 20284 Luwinga, Mzuzu 2; tel. 1332390; fax 1332063; f. 1966.

Foreign Bureau

Newslink Africa (United Kingdom): POB 2688, Blantyre; Correspondent HOBBS GAMA.

Publishers

Christian Literature Association in Malawi (CLAIM): POB 503, Blantyre; tel. 1620839; f. 1968; Chichewa and English; general and religious; Gen. Man. J. T. MATENJE.

Likuni Press and Publishing House: POB 133, Lilongwe; tel. 1721388; fax 1721141; f. 1949; English and Chichewa; general and religious.

Macmillan Malawi Ltd: Private Bag 140, Kenyatta Dr., Chitawira, Blantyre; tel. 1676499; fax 1675751; e-mail macmillan@macmillanmw.net; Gen. Man. HASTINGS MATEWERE.

Montfort Press and Popular Publications: POB 5592, Limbe; tel. 1651833; fax 1641126; f. 1961; general and religious; Gen. Man. VALES MACHILA.

GOVERNMENT PUBLISHING HOUSE

Government Press: Government Printer, POB 37, Zomba; tel. 1525515; fax 1525175.

Broadcasting and Communications

TELECOMMUNICATIONS

Celtel Malawi: Celtel House, Raynor Ave, Limbe, Blantyre; tel. 1644022; internet www.mw.celtel.com; f. 1999; 80% owned by Mobile Systems Int. Cellular Investments Holding B.V., 10% owned each by Malawi Devt Corpn and Investment and Devt Bank of Malawi Ltd; Man. Dir TIM BAHRANI.

Malawi Telecommunications Ltd (MTL): Lamya House, Masauko Chipembere Highway, POB 537, Blantyre; tel. 1620977; fax 1624445; e-mail mtlceo@malawi.net; f. 2000 following division of Malawi Posts and Telecommunications Corpn into two separate entities; privatized in 2006; 80% owned by Telecom Holdings Ltd, 20% state-owned; CEO EMMANUEL MAHUKA.

Telekom Networks Malawi (TNM): POB 3039, Munif House, Livingstone Ave, Limbe, Blantyre; tel. 1641088; fax 1642805; e-mail nasirbah@malawi.net; internet www.telekom.co.mw; f. 1995; 60% owned by Telekom Malaysia Berhad; operates mobile cellular telephone network; CEO GHAZALI HASHIM.

BROADCASTING

Radio

An estimated 85% of the population regularly listens to radio programmes.

Malawi Broadcasting Corpn: POB 30133, Chichiri, Blantyre 3; tel. 1671222; fax 1671257; e-mail dgmbc@malawi.net; internet www.mbcradios.com; f. 1964; statutory body; semi-commercial, partly state-financed; two channels: MBC 1 and Radio 2 (MBC 2); programmes in English, Chichewa, Chitonga, Chitumbuka, Kyangonde, Lomwe, Sena and Yao; Chair. LEONARD NAMWERA; Dir-Gen. OWEN MAUNDE.

Private commercial and religious radio stations include:

African Bible College Radio (Radio ABC): POB 1028, Lilongwe; tel. 1761965; e-mail radioabc@malawi.net; f. 1995; regional Christian religious programming; Asst Station Man. MCLEOD MUNTHALI.

Calvary Family Radio: POB 30239, Blantyre 3; tel. 1671627; fax 1671642; e-mail calvaryministries@hotmail.com; operated by the Calvary Family Church; religious community radio station.

Capital Radio 102.5 FM: Plot 475, cnr Victoria Ave and Juachim Chissano Rd, Sunnyside; Private Bag 437, Chichiri, Blantyre 3; tel. 1620858; fax 1623282; e-mail stationmanager@capitalradiomalawi.com; internet www.capitalradiomalawi.com; f. 1999; commercial radio station; music and entertainment; Man. Dir and Editor-in-Chief ALAUDIN OSMAN.

Channel for All Nations (CAN): POB 1220, Lilongwe; tel. 1761763; fax 1762056; e-mail assemblies@malawi.net; f. 2004; operated by the Assemblies of God church; regional Christian religious programming.

Dzimwe Community Radio (DCR): POB 425, Chichiri, Blantyre; tel. 1672288; fax 1624330; e-mail mamwa@yahoo.com; f. 1997; operated by the Malawi Media Women's Asscn; focus on rural women's issues; Station Man. JANET KARIM.

Joy FM: Private Bag 17, Limbe, Blantyre; tel. 1638330; fax 1638329; e-mail joyradio@globemalawi.net; commercial radio station; Owner BAKILI MULUZI.

MIJ FM: POB 30165, Chichiri, Blantyre 3; tel. 1675087; fax 1675649; e-mail mij@clcom.net; f. 1996; operated by students of the Malawi Institute of Journalism; community radio station; closed by the Govt during May 2004.

Nkhota Kota Community Radio: Nkhota Kota; f. 2003 with assistance from UNESCO; focus on social and devt issues.

Power 101 FM: POB 761, Blantyre; tel. 1844101; fax 1841387; e-mail fm101@malawi.net; f. 1998; commercial radio station; music and entertainment; Dir and Station Man. OSCAR THOMSON.

Radio Alinafe: Maula Cathedral, POB 631, Lilongwe; tel. 1759971; fax 1752767; e-mail radioalinafe@sdnp.org.mw; f. 2002; Chichewa and English; operated by the Archdiocese of Lilongwe; regional Roman Catholic religious programming; Dir GABRIEL JANA; Editor MOSES KAUFA.

Radio Islam: PO Box 5400, Limbe; tel. 1641408; e-mail zakaat@malawi.net; f. 2001; operated by the Islamic Zakaat Fund; religious programming; Dir MAHMUD SARDAR ISSA.

Radio Maria Malawi: POB 408, Mangochi; tel. 1599626; fax 1599691; e-mail radiomaria@malawi.net; internet www.radiomaria.mw; f. 2003; operated by Asscn of Radio Maria Malawi as part of the World Family of Radio Maria, Italy; Roman Catholic religious programming; Chichewa, Chiyao and English; Gen. Man. JOSEPH KIMU; Dir of Programmes HENRY SAINDI.

Radio Tigawane: Bishop's House, POB 252, Mzuzu; tel. 1332271; e-mail tigawane@sndp.org.mw; f. 2005; operated by the Diocese of Mzuzu; regional Roman Catholic religious programming; Tumbuka, Chichewa and English; Project Co-ordinator EUGENE NGOMA.

Star FM: Everest House, Lower Sclatter Rd, Blantyre; f. 2006; commercial radio station; Station Man. PATRICK KAMKWATIRA.

Trans World Radio Malawi (TWR): POB 52, Lilongwe; tel. and fax 1751763; e-mail twr@malawi.net; f. 2000; part of Trans World Radio-

Africa, South Africa; Christian religious programming; Dir PATRICK SEMPHERE.

Zodiak Broadcasting Station (ZBS): Private Bag 312, Lilongwe 3; f. 2005; operated by Zodiak Broadcasting Services; programmes in Chichewa and English; Man. Dir GOSPEL KAZAKO.

Television

Television Malawi (TVM): Private Bag 268, Blantyre; tel. 1675033; fax 1762627; e-mail tvmalawi@sdnp.org.mw; f. 1999; broadcasts 55 hours per week, of which 10 hours are produced locally; relays programmes from France, Germany, South Africa and the United Kingdom; Chair. MOHAMMED KULESI; Dir-Gen. KENSON M'BWANA.

Finance

(cap. = capital; res = reserves; dep. = deposits; m. = million; br(s). = branch(es); amounts in kwacha)

BANKING

Central Bank

Reserve Bank of Malawi: Convention Dr., POB 30063, Capital City, Lilongwe 3; tel. 1770600; fax 1772752; internet www.rbm.malawi.net; f. 1965; bank of issue; cap. 306m., res –1,361m., dep. 17,388m. (Dec. 2004); Gov. and Chair. VICTOR MBEWE; br. in Blantyre.

Commercial Banks

Finance Bank Malawi Ltd: Finance House, Victoria Ave, POB 421, Blantyre; tel. 1624232; fax 1622957; e-mail finbank@malawi.net; internet www.financebank.co.mw; f. 1995; 93.6% owned by Finance Holdings Corpn Ltd (International), 6.4% owned by Finance Bank Zambia Ltd; cap. and res 439.2m., total assets 4,152m. (Dec. 2003); Chair. Dr RAJAN L. MAHTANI; CEO A. S. PILLAI; 5 brs, 1 agency.

INDEBank Ltd: INDEBank House, Kaohsiung Rd, Top Mandala, POB 358, Blantyre; tel. 1820055; fax 1823353; e-mail enquiriesho@indebank.com; f. 1972 as Investment and Devt Bank of Malawi Ltd; total assets 2,162.6m. (Dec. 2003); 41.38% owned by TransAfrica Holdings Ltd, 30% owned by Press Trust, 25.67% owned by ADMARC Investments Holding, 2.95% owned by Employee Ownership Scheme; commercial and devt banking; provides loans to statutory corpns and to private enterprises in the agricultural, industrial, tourism, transport and commercial sectors; Chair. FRANKLIN KENNEDY; CEO KEITH STEWART.

Loita Investment Bank Ltd: Loita House, cnr Victoria Ave and Henderson St, Private Bag 389, Chichiri, Blantyre 3; tel. 1620099; fax 1622683; internet www.loita.com; total assets 3,100.3m. (Dec. 2003); 100% owned by Loita Capital Partners Int.; Chair. N. JUSTIN CHIMYANTA; CEO AUBERY CHALERA (acting); 2 brs.

National Bank of Malawi: Victoria Ave, POB 945, Blantyre; tel. 1620622; fax 1620321; e-mail natbank@malawi.net; internet www.natbank.mw.com; f. 1971; 51.8% owned by Press Corpn Ltd, 20.7% owned by ADMARC (Investments Holding Co), 11.2% owned by Old Mutual Life Assurance; cap. 456m., res 895m., dep. 24,254m. (Dec. 2005); Chair. Dr M. A. P. CHIKAONDA; CEO ISAAC K. NSAMALA; 13 brs; 10 agencies.

NBS Bank Ltd: Ginnery Cnr, Chipembere Highway, off Masajico, POB 32251 Chichiri, Blantyre; tel. 1876222; fax 1875041; e-mail nbs@nbsmw.com; internet www.nbsmw.com; f. 2003; 74% owned by NICO, 16% owned by the Govt, 10% owned by the Nat. Investment Trust 10%; fmrly New Building Society; 10,978m. (Mar. 2007); Chair. FELIX L. MLUSU; Gen. Man. JOHN S. BIZIWICK.

Nedbank (Malawi) Ltd: Development House, cnr Henderson St and Victoria Ave, POB 750, Blantyre; tel. 1620477; fax 1620102; e-mail office@mw.nedcor.com; f. 1999; fmrly Fincom Bank of Malawi Ltd; 68.8% owned by Nedbank Africa Investments Ltd, 28.4% owned by SBM Nedcor Holdings Ltd; 1,426.9m. (Dec. 2003); Chair. C. DREW; Man. Dir PAUL TUBB.

Stanbic Bank Ltd: Kaomba Centre, cnr Sir Glyn Jones Rd and Victoria Ave, POB 1111, Blantyre; tel. 1620144; fax 1620360; e-mail malawi@stanbic.com; internet www.stanbicbank.co.mw; f. 1970 as Commercial Bank of Malawi; present name adopted June 2003; 60% owned by Stanbic Africa Holdings Ltd, 20% owned by Nat. Insurance Co; cap. 200m., res 1,818m., dep. 13,774m. (Dec. 2005); Chair. ALEX CHITSIME; Man. Dir PHILIP ODERA; 8 brs.

Development Bank

Opportunity International Bank of Malawi Ltd (OIBM): Kamuzu Procession Rd, Plot No. 4/044, Private Bag A71, Lilongwe; tel. 1758403; fax 1758400; e-mail oibm@oibm.mw; internet www.oibm.mw; f. 2003; 63.7% owned by Opportunity Transformation Investments, USA, 25.3% owned by Opportunity Micro Investments (UK) Ltd, United Kingdom, 11% owned by Trust for Transformation; total assets 967.4m. (Dec. 2005); Chair. FRANCIS PELEKAMOYO; CEO RODGER VOORHIES.

Discount Houses

Continental Discount House: Unit House, 5th Floor, Victoria Ave, POB 1444, Blantyre; tel. 1821300; fax 1822826; e-mail discount@cdh-malawi.com; internet www.cdh-malawi.com; f. 1998; 84% owned by Trans-Africa Holdings; 6,728.8m. (Dec. 2005); Chair. ROBERT SEKOH ABBEY; CEO JOSEPH MWANAMVEKHA.

First Discount House Ltd: Umoyo House, Upper Ground Floor, 8 Victoria Ave North, POB 512, Blantyre; tel. 1820219; fax 1523044; e-mail fdh@fdh.co.mw; internet www.fdh.co.mw; f. 2000; 40.16% owned by Kingdom Financial Holdings Ltd, 39.84% owned by Thomson F. Mpinganjira Trust, 20% owned by Old Mutual Life Assurance Co (Malawi) Ltd; total assets 5,960.7m. (Dec. 2004); CEO THOMSON FRANK MPINGANJIRA; Chair. NIGEL CHAKANIRA.

Merchant Banks

First Merchant Bank Ltd: Livingstone Towers, Glyn Jones Rd, Private Bag 122, Blantyre; tel. 1821955; fax 1821978; e-mail fmb.headoffice@fmbmalawi.com; internet www.fmbmalawi.com; f. 1994; cap. 100.0m., res 411.8m., dep. 6,015.4m. (Dec. 2005); 44.9% owned by Zambezi Investments Ltd, 22.5% owned by Simsbury Holdings Ltd, 11.2% owned each by Prime Capital and Credit Ltd, Kenya, and Prime Bank Ltd, Kenya; Chair. RASIKBHAI C. KANTARIA; Man. Dir KASHINATH N. CHATURVEDI; 7 brs.

Leasing and Finance Co of Malawi Ltd: Livingstone Towers, Glyn Jones Rd, POB 1963, Blantyre; tel. 1820233; fax 1820275; e-mail lfc@malawi.net; f. 1986; subsidiary of First Merchant Bank Ltd since June 2002; total assets 2,087.4m. (Dec. 2006); Chair. HITESH ANADKAT; Gen. Man. MBACHAZWA LUNGU.

National Finance Co Ltd: Plantation House, POB 821, Blantyre; tel. 1623670; fax 1620549; e-mail natfin@malawi.net; internet www.natbank.mw.com; f. 1958; 69.8% owned by Nat. Bank of Malawi, 12% owned by each Lincoln Investments and Mbabzi Estates; cap. and res 148.0m., total assets 475.0m. (Dec. 2004); Chair. I. K. NSAMALA; Gen. Man. M. T. BAMFORD.

Savings Bank

Malawi Savings Bank: Umoyo House, Victoria Ave, POB 521, Blantyre; tel. 1625111; fax 1621929; 99.9% state-owned; total assets 1,191.7m. (Dec. 2003); Sec.-Treas. P. E. CHILAMBE; Gen. Man. IAN C. BONONGWE.

STOCK EXCHANGE

Malawi Stock Exchange: Old Reserve Bank Bldg, 17 Victoria Ave, Private Bag 270, Blantyre; tel. 1824233; fax 1823636; e-mail mse@mse-mw.com; internet www.mse.co.mw; f. 1996; Chair. KRISHNA SAVJANI; CEO SYMON W. MSEFULA; 11 cos listed in 2007.

INSURANCE

In 2005 the insurance sector comprised 10 local companies and one foreign company; there was also one reinsurance company. Of these, eight companies dealt in non-life insurance.

NICO Holdings Ltd: NICO House, 3 Stewart St, POB 501, Blantyre; tel. 1822699; fax 1822364; e-mail info@nicomw.com; internet www.nicomw.com; f. 1970; fmrly National Insurance Co Ltd; transferred to private sector in 1996; incorporates NICO Gen. Insurance Co Ltd, NICO Life Insurance Co Ltd and NICO Technologies Ltd; cap. and res 104.7m. (Sept. 1997); offices at Blantyre, Lilongwe, Mzuzu and Zomba; agencies country-wide; CEO and Man. Dir FELIX L. MLUSU.

Old Mutual Malawi: Trust Finance Ltd, Michiru House, Ground Floor, Victoria Ave, POB 1396, Blantyre; tel. 0623856; f. 1845; subsidiary of Old Mutual PLC, United Kingdom; Chair. MIKE LEVETT; Man. Dir JEAN DU PLESSIS.

Royal Insurance Co of Malawi Ltd: Hannover House, Independence Dr., POB 442, Blantyre; tel. 1824044; fax 1823862; e-mail royalbt@royal.mw; internet www.royalinsure.com/malawi.htm; associate of Royal and SunAlliance PLC, United Kingdom; Man. Dir ROBERT G. NDUNGU; Gen. Man. DAMIANO K. PHIRI.

United General Insurance Co Ltd (UGI): Michiru House, Victoria Ave, POB 383, Blantyre; tel. 1621770; fax 1621980; e-mail ugi@malawi.net; internet www.ugimalawi.com; f. 1986 as Pearl Assurance Co Ltd; latterly Property and Gen. Insurance Co Ltd; present name adopted following merger with Fide Insurance Co Ltd in July 1998; subsidiary of ZimRE Holdings, Zimbabwe; Chair. ALBERT NDUNA; Man. Dir IAN K. KUMWENDA.

Vanguard Life Assurance Co (Pvt) Ltd: MDC House, 2nd Floor, Sir Glyn Jones Rd, POB 1625, Blantyre; tel. 1623356; fax 1623506;

f. 1999; 90% owned by Fidelity Life Assurance Ltd, Zimbabwe; Man. Dir THEMBA MPALA.

Trade and Industry

GOVERNMENT AGENCIES

Agricultural Development and Marketing Corpn (ADMARC): POB 5052, Limbe; tel. 1640500; fax 1640486; f. 1971; involved in cultivation, processing, marketing and export of grain and other crops; Chair. Prof. KANYAMA PHIRI; CEO Dr CHARLES J. MATABWA.

Malawi Export Promotion Council (MEPC): Kanabar House, 2nd Floor, Victoria Ave, POB 1299, Blantyre; tel. 1820499; fax 1820995; e-mail mepco@malawi.net; internet www.malawiepc.com; f. 1971; promotes and facilitates export and investment, and provides technical assistance and training to exporters; Gen. Man. LAWRENCE M. CHALULUKA.

Malawi Investment Promotion Agency (MIPA): Aquarius House, Private Bag 302, Lilongwe 3; tel. 1770800; fax 1771781; e-mail mipall@malawi.net; f. 1993; promotes and facilitates local and foreign investment; CEO JAMES R. KAPHWELEZA BANDA.

Petroleum Control Commission: POB 2827, Blantyre; e-mail sichioko@pccmalawi.com; state-owned; held monopoly on fuel imports until 2000; also serves regulatory role; Chair. Rev Dr LAZARUS CHAKWERA; Gen. Man. ISHMAEL CHIOKO.

Privatisation Commission of Malawi: Livingstone Towers, 2nd Floor, Glyn Jones Rd, POB 937, Blantyre; tel. 1823655; fax 1821248; e-mail info@pcmalawi.org; internet www.pcmalawi.org; f. 1996; has sole authority to oversee divestiture of Govt interests in public enterprises; Chair. EDWARD SAWERENGERA; Exec. Dir JIMMY LIPUNGA (acting); 66 privatizations completed by January 2006.

Tobacco Control Commission: POB 40045, Kanengo, Lilongwe 4, Malawi; tel. 1712777; fax 1712632; regulates tobacco production and marketing; Chair Dr ANDREW MZUMACHARO IV; Gen. Man. Dr GODFREY M. CHAPOLA; brs in Mzuzu and Limbe.

DEVELOPMENT ORGANIZATIONS

Council for Non-Governmental Organizations in Malawi (CONGOMA): Chitawira, Waya Bldg, POB 480, Blantyre; tel. 1676459; fax 1677908; e-mail info@congoma.org; internet www.congoma.org; f. 1992; promotes social and economic devt; Chair. TADEYO SHABA; Exec. Dir EMMANUEL TED NANDOLO; 86 mem. orgs (2004).

Human Rights Consultative Committee (HRCC): c/o Centre for Human Rights and Rehabilitation, POB 2340 Lilongwe; tel. 1761700; fax 1761122; e-mail chrr@sdnp.org.mw; f. 1995; umbrella body comprising 40 mem orgs; promotes human rights and the rule of law; Chair. ROGERS NEWA.

Small Enterprise Development Organization of Malawi (SEDOM): POB 525, Blantyre; tel. 1622555; fax 1622781; e-mail sedom@sdnp.org.mw; f. 1982; financial services and accommodation for indigenous small- and medium-scale businesses; Chair. STELLA NDAU.

CHAMBER OF COMMERCE

Malawi Confederation of Chambers of Commerce and Industry (MCCCI): Masauko Chipembere Highway, Chichiri Trade Fair Grounds, POB 258, Blantyre; tel. 1671988; fax 1671147; e-mail ckaferapanjira@mccci.org; internet www.mccci.org; f. 1892; promotes trade and encourages competition in the economy; Pres. MARTIN KANSICHI; CEO CHANCELLOR L. KAFERAPANJIRA; 400 mems.

INDUSTRIAL AND TRADE ASSOCIATIONS

Dwangwa Cane Growers Trust (DCGT): POB 156, Dwangwa; tel. 1295111; fax 1295164; e-mail dcgt@malawi.net; f. 1999; fmrly Smallholder Sugar Authority; Chair (vacant).

National Hawkers and Informal Business Association (NAHIBA): POB 60544, Ndirande, Blantyre; tel. 1935415; Exec. Dir EVA JOACHIM.

Smallholder Coffee Farmers Trust: POB 20133, Luwinga, Mzuzu 2; tel. 1332899; fax 1333902; e-mail mzuzucoffee@malawi.net; f. 1971; successor to the Small Holder Coffee Authority, disbanded in 1999; producers and exporters of arabica coffee; Gen. Man. HARRISON KARUA; 4,000 mems.

Smallholder Tea Co (STECO): POB 135, Mulanje; f. 2002 by the merger of the Smallholder Tea Authority and Malawi Tea Factory Co Ltd.

Tea Association of Malawi Ltd (TAML): Kidney Cres., POB 930, Blantyre; tel. 1671182; fax 1671427; f. 1936; Exec. Dir G.T. BANDA; 20 mems.

Tobacco Association of Malawi (TAMA): 13/69 Independence Dr., TAMA House, POB 31360, Lilongwe 3; tel. 1773099; fax 1773493; e-mail tama@eomw.net; f. 1929; Pres. CHARLES A. KAMULAGA; Chief Exec. FELIX MKUMBA; brs in Mzuzu, Limbe and Chinkhoma; 60,000 mems.

Tobacco Exporters' Association of Malawi Ltd (TEAM): Private Bag 403, Kanengo, Lilongwe 4; tel. 1775839; fax 1774069; f. 1930; Chair. CHARLES A. M. GRAHAM; Gen. Man. H. M. MBALE; 9 mems.

EMPLOYERS' ORGANIZATIONS

Employers' Consultative Association of Malawi (ECAM): POB 2134, Blantyre; tel. and fax 1830151; e-mail ecam@malawi.net; f. 1963; Pres. DICKENS CHAULA; Exec. Dir Dr VINCENT SINJANI; 250 mem. asscns and six affiliates representing 80,000 employees.

Master Printers' Association of Malawi: POB 2460, Blantyre; tel. 1632948; fax 1632220; f. 1963; Chair. PAUL FREDERICK; 21 mems.

Motor Traders' Association: POB 311, Blantyre; tel. and fax 1624754; f. 1954; Chair. A. R. OSMAN; 24 mems (2003).

UTILITY

Electricity

Electricity Supply Commission of Malawi (ESCOM): ESCOM House, Haile Selassie Rd, POB 2047, Blantyre; tel. and fax 1622008; f. 1966; controls electricity distribution; Chair. ABDUL WAHAB MIA; CEO Dr ALLEXON CHIWAYA.

MAJOR COMPANIES

The following are among the largest companies in terms of capital investment or employment.

Agrimal Ltd: POB 143, Blantyre; tel. 1670933; fax 1670651; f. 2001, fmrly Chillington Agrimal (Malawi) Ltd; 44% owned by Plantation and Gen. Investments PLC; mfrs of agricultural hand tools, hoes and implements; Gen. Man. MANUEL PILLAI.

Alliance One Tobacco (Malawi) Ltd: POB 30522, Lilongwe 3; tel. 1710044; fax 1710312; f. 2005 through merger of Standard Commercial Tobacco (Malawi) Ltd and Dimon (Malawi) Ltd; tobacco merchants; Man. Dir ALASTAIR CRAIK.

Auction Holdings Ltd: POB 40035, Kanengo, Lilongwe 4; tel. 1710377; fax 1710384; e-mail ahll@globemw.net; f. 1962; privatized 1997; cap. K914.0m. (2004); tobacco and tobacco products; auction floor operators; 88% state-owned, 5% owned by the Nat. Investment Trust Ltd; Chair. Dr C. J. MATABA; Group Gen. Man. G. C. MSONTHI; 3,000 employees.

Bakhresa Grain Milling (Malawi) Ltd: Charterland Rd, POB 5847, Limbe; tel. 1643272; fax 1643342; e-mail mahesh@bakhresagroup.com; fmrly Grain and Milling Co Ltd (GRAMIL), acquired by Said Salim Bakhresa Co Ltd, Tanzania in 2003; 100% owned by Bakhresa Family; grain millers; Gen. Man. MAHESH JOSYABHATLA; 150 employees.

BATA Shoe Company (Malawi) Ltd: POB 936, Blantyre; tel. 1670511; fax 1670519; e-mail bata@africa-online.net; mfrs of shoes; Man. Dir A. T. MUZONDIWA.

BP Malawi Ltd: 8 Independence Dr., POB 469, Blantyre; f. 1963; 50% owned by BP PLC, United Kingdom, 50% owned by Press Corpn Ltd; fuel and oil distributor.

British American Tobacco Malawi Ltd: Chipembere Highway, POB 428, Blantyre; tel. 1670033; fax 1670808; e-mail bat@malawi.net; f. 1942; mfrs and distributors of cigarettes; Chair. and Man. Dir KEITH GRETTON; 185 employees.

Blantyre Netting Co Ltd (Blanet): POB 30575, Chichiri, Blantyre 3; tel. 1677398; fax 1671227; polypropylene woven sacks, ropes, bristles, strapping tapes, nylon twines, nets; Admin. Man. DIVERSON LIVATA; 400 employees.

Chemical Manufacturers Ltd: POB 30242, Chichiri, Blantyre 3; tel. 1671536; fax 1671915; f. 1981; mfrs and distributors of industrial chemical products; Man. Dir ATHOL ESTMENT; 22 employees.

Illovo Sugar (Malawi) Ltd: Private Bag 580, Limbe; tel. 1643988; fax 1640135; f. 1965; fmrly Sugar Corpn of Malawi Ltd (SUCOMA); present name adopted 2004; 76% owned by Illovo Sugar Group, South Africa, 10% owned by Old Mutual Life Assurance Co; sugar mills at Dwangwa and Nchalo; cap. K488.9m. (2001); sugar production and processing; Group Chair. ROBBIE WILLIAMS; Man. Dir BRETT M. STEWARDSON; 8,000 permanent employees, 5,000 seasonal employees.

Packaging Industries (Malawi) Ltd: POB 30533, Chichiri, Blantyre 3; tel. 1870533; fax 1871283; e-mail pim@malawi.net; f. 1969; 60% owned by Transmar; cap. K13.5m. (2006); mfrs of cardboard boxes, paper sacks and liquid packaging containers; Man. Dir SIMON A. ITAYE; 163 employees (Sept. 2006).

Petroleum Importers Ltd (PIL): Unit House, 6th Floor, Victoria Ave, Private Bag 200, Blantyre; tel. 1822886; fax 1821876; e-mail petroleum@pilmalawi.mw; f. 2000 following liberalization of the petroleum industry; industry consortium incl. national and international oil cos; imports 80% of the country's fuel requirements; Gen. Man. ROBERT MDEZA.

Plastic Products Ltd: POB 907, Blantyre; tel. 1670455; fax 1670664; 100% owned by the Malawi Devt Corpn; mfrs of polythene bags; Gen. Man. ROBERT KAPYEPYE.

Portland Cement Co (Malawi) Ltd: POB 523, Heavy Industrial Area, Blantyre; tel. 1671933; fax 1671026; f. 1974; part of the Pan Africa Cement Group, subsidiary of Lafarge Group; mfrs and distributors of cement; projected annual capacity: 140,000 metric tons; Snr Man. TONY RIX; 650 employees.

Press Corpn Ltd: Chayamba Bldg, Victoria Ave, POB 1227, Blantyre; tel. 1633569; fax 1633318; e-mail companysec@presscorp.com; internet www.presscorp.com; f. 1983 as Press Group Ltd; revenue 10,978m. (Dec. 2003); holding co operating through 19 subsidiaries and four assoc. cos in distribution, banking, insurance, manufacturing and processing; Chair. DEAN C. LUNGU; Group CEO Dr MATHEWS A. P. CHIKAONDA; 9,500 employees.

Subsidiaries incl. The Foods Co Ltd, Hardware and Gen. Dealers Ltd, People's Trading Centre Ltd, Presscane Ltd and also:

Ethanol Co Ltd (ETHCO): POB 469, Blantyre; tel. 1295200; f. 1982; producer and distributor of ethanol fuel; 58.9% owned by Press Corpn Ltd, 42% owned by Illovo Sugar (Malawi) Ltd; distillery at Dwangwa; Man. Dir S. DANIEL LIWIMBI.

Limbe Leaf Tobacco Co Ltd: Plot 29/125–126, Area 29, POB 40044, Kanengo, Lilongwe 4; tel. 1710355; fax 1710763; e-mail lltc@malawi.net; 58% owned by Universal Leaf Corpn,USA, 42% owned by Press Corpn Ltd; Group Chair. Dr M. A. P. CHIKAONDA; Man. Dir K. R. STAINTON.

Macsteel (Malawi) Ltd: Raynor Ave, POB 5651, Limbe, Blantyre; tel. 1641677; fax 1645871; fmrly Press Steel and Wire Ltd; present name adopted in 2003; 50% owned by Press Corpn Ltd, 50% owned by Macsteel Africa, South Africa; steel processors.

Malawi Pharmacies Ltd: POB 51041, Limbe; tel. 1642293; fax 1677784; e-mail mpl@mpl.com.mw; 90% owned by Press Corpn Ltd; mfrs and distributors of pharmaceuticals.

Maldeco Aquaculture Ltd: POB 45, Mangochi; tel. 1584300; fax 1584724; e-mail maldeco@malawi.net; 100% subsidiary of Press Corpn Ltd; Operations Man. J. H. MGASA.

PROMAT Ltd: POB 30041, Lilongwe 3; tel. 1710388; fax 1711653; e-mail promat@eomw.net; mfrs of polyvinylchloride (PVC)-U pipes, high-density polyethylene pipes, PVC hosepipes.

Raiply Malawi Ltd: Private Bag 1, Chikangawa, Mzimba; tel. 1333944; fax 1333642; e-mail raiplymalawi@malawi.net; fmrly Viphya Plywoods and Allied Industries (Viply); acquired by T. S. Rai Ltd, Kenya in 1999; mfrs of plywood, blockboard, timber and furniture; CEO THOMAS OOMMEN (acting); 900 employees.

Toyota Malawi Ltd: Queens Cnr, Masauko Chipembere Highway, POB 430, Blantyre; tel. 1641933; fax 1645369; f. 1964; cap. K122m. (1999); import and distribution of motor vehicles and parts; Man. Dir JOHN J. CONNELL; 156 employees.

Unilever Malawi Ltd: cnr Tsiranana Rd and Citron Ave, POB 5151, Limbe; tel. 1641100; fax 1645720; e-mail charles.cofie@unilever.com; f. 1963; fmrly Lever Brothers (Malawi) Ltd until 2003; subsidiary of Unilever PLC, United Kingdom; mfrs of soaps, detergents, cooking oils, foods, beverages and chemicals; Chair. MALCOLM HUGHES; Man. Dir TUYI EHINDERO.

Universal Industries Ltd: Ginnery Cnr, Masauko Chipembere Highway, POB 507, Blantyre; tel. 1670055; fax 1677408; e-mail unibisco@malawi.net; mfrs of confectionery; Chair. and Man. Dir D. K. AMIN; 1,000 employees.

TRADE UNIONS

According to the Malawi Congress of Trade Unions, in 2005 some 18% of the workforce was unionized.

Congress of Malawi Trade Unions (COMATU): POB 1443 Lilongwe; tel. 1757255; fax 1770885; Pres. THOMAS L. BANDA; Gen. Sec. PHILLMON E. CHIMBALU.

Malawi Congress of Trade Unions (MCTU): POB 1271, Lilongwe; tel. 1754581; fax 1755614; e-mail mctu@malawi.net; f. 1994 as successor to the Trade Union Congress of Malawi (f. 1964); affiliated to the Int. Trade Union Confed.; Pres. LUTHER MAMBALA (acting); Gen. Sec. AUSTIN KALIMANJIRA; 93,973 paid-up mems (2006).

Affiliated unions incl.:

Building Construction, Civil Engineering and Allied Workers' Union (BCCEAWU): c/o MCTU, POB 5094, Limbe; tel. 1620381; fax 1622304; e-mail johnmwafulirwa@yahoo.com; f. 1961; Pres. LAWRENCE KAFERE; Gen. Sec. JOHN O. MWAFULIRWA; 6,401 mems (2006).

Commercial Industrial and Allied Workers' Union (CIAWU): c/o MCTU, POB 5094, Limbe; tel. 1820716; fax 1622303; e-mail mareydzinyemba@yahoo.com; affiliated to the Int. Textile, Garment and Leather Workers' Fed. and Union Network Int.; Pres. TRYSON KALANDA; Gen. Sec. MARY DZINYEMBA; 3,075 mems (2006).

Communications Workers' Union of Malawi: Armarsi Odvarji Plaza, 1st Floor, Chipembere Highway, Private Bag 186, Blantyre; tel. 1820716; fax 1830830; e-mail cowuma@yahoo.co.uk; f. 1997; Pres. BATWELL KULEMERO; Gen. Sec. ROBERT JAMES DANIEL MKWEZALAMBA; 2,854 mems (2006).

Electronic Media Workers' Union: POB 30133, Chichiri, Blantyre 3; tel. 1871343; e-mail mmsowoya@hotmail.com; Pres. LASTEN KUNKEYANI; Gen. Sec. MALANI MSOWOYA; 243 mems (2006).

ESCOM Staff Union: POB 2047, Blantyre; tel. 1773447; Pres. OSCAR CHIMWEZI; affiliated to the Int. Fed. of Chemical, Energy, Mine and General Workers' Unions; Gen. Sec. RACHEL CHASWEKA; 1,899 mems (2006).

Hotels, Food and Catering Service Union: c/o MCTU 5094, Limbe; tel. 1820314; e-mail hfpcwu@sdnp.org.mw; affiliated to the Int. Union of Food, Agricultural, Hotel, Restaurant, Catering, Tobacco and Allied Workers' Asscns; Pres. AUSTIN KALIMANJIRA; Gen. Sec. DOROTHEA MAKHASU; 3,565 mems (2006).

Malawi Housing Co-operation Workers' Union: c/o MHC, POB 84, Mzuzu; tel. 1332655; Pres. GREY SADIKI; Gen. Sec. ROOSEVELT MSISKA; 236 mems (2006).

Plantation and Agriculture Workers' Union: Nchima Tea Estate, POB 52, Thyolo; tel. 1473300; Pres. PATRICK KADYANJI; Gen. Sec. DENNIS BANDA; 2,086 mems (2006).

Private Schools Employees' Union of Malawi (PSEUM): c/o MCTU, Kepell Compton Cres., Area 3/089, POB 1271, Lilongwe; tel. 1755614; fax 1752162; e-mail hendrixbanda@yahoo.com; Pres. SAMUEL NJIWA; Gen. Sec. HENDRIX S. BANDA; 1,713 mems (2006).

Railway Workers' Union of Malawi (Central East African Railway Workers' Union—CEARWU): POB 5393, Limbe; tel. 1640844; e-mail cear@cearcdn.mw; f. 1954; affiliated to the Int. Transport Workers' Fed.; Pres. DINA M'MERA; Gen. Sec. LUTHER MAMBALA; 485 mems (2006).

Sugar Plantation and Allied Workers' Union (SPAWUM): c/o Illovo Sugar (Malawi) Ltd, Private Bag 50, Blantyre; tel. 1425200; e-mail spawum@illovo.co.za; Pres. KEEPER GUMBO; Gen. Sec. STEPHEN MKWAPATIRA; 8,598 mems (2006).

Teachers' Union of Malawi: Aphunzitsi Centre, Private Bag 11, Lilongwe; tel. 1724224; fax 1755614; e-mail tum@sdnp.org.mw; Pres. BERNARD MANDA; Gen. Sec. LUCIEN CHIKADZA; 46,207 mems (2006).

Textile, Garment, Leather and Security Services Workers' Union: POB 5094, Limbe; tel. 8345576; e-mail textilegarmentunion@yahoo.com; f. 1995; affiliated to the Int. Textile, Garment and Leather Workers' Fed.; Gen. Sec. GRACE NYIRENDA; 5,514 mems (2006).

Tobacco Tenants Workers' Union: POB 477, Nkhotakota; tel. 1292288; e-mail totawum@malawi.net; affiliated to the Int. Union of Food, Agricultural, Hotel, Restaurant, Catering, Tobacco and Allied Workers' Asscns; Pres. LUTHER MAMBALA; Gen. Sec. RAPHAEL SANDRAM; 5,579 mems (2006).

Transport and General Workers' Union: POB 2778, Blantyre; tel. 8877795; fax 1830219; e-mail ronaldmbewe2002@yahoo.com; f. 1945; affiliated to the Int. Transport Workers' Fed.; Pres. FRANCIS ANTONIO; Gen. Sec. RONALD MBEWE; 3,257 mems (2006).

Water Employees' Trade Union of Malawi (WETUM): c/o Lilongwe Water Board, Madzi House, off Likuni Rd, POB 96, Lilongwe; tel. 1750366; fax 1752294; affiliated to the Public Services Int.; Pres. ANTHONY A. CHIMPHEPO; Gen. Sec. OLIVIA KUNJE; 1,195 mems (2006).

Transport

RAILWAYS

The Central East African Railways Co (fmrly Malawi Railways) operates between Nsanje (near the southern border with Mozambique) and Mchinji (near the border with Zambia) via Blantyre, Salima and Lilongwe, and between Nkaya and Nayuchi on the eastern border with Mozambique, covering a total of 797 km. The Central East African Railways Co and Mozambique State Railways connect Malawi with the Mozambican ports of Beira and Nacala. These links, which traditionally form Malawi's principal trade routes, were effectively closed during 1983–85, owing to insurgent activity in Mozambique. The rail link to Nacala was reopened in October 1989;

however, continued unrest and flooding in Mozambique prevented full use of the route until the completion of a programme of improvements in September 2000; the service was temporarily suspended in 2002 while safety was improved. There is a rail/lake interchange station at Chipoka on Lake Malawi, from where vessels operate services to other lake ports in Malawi.

Central East African Railways Co Ltd (CEAR): Station Rd, POB 5144, Limbe; tel. 1640844; fax 1643496; f. 1994 as Malawi Railways Ltd; sold to a consortium owned by Mozambique's Empresa Nacional dos Portos e Caminhos de Ferro de Moçambique and the USA's Railroad Corpn in mid-1999 and subsequently renamed as above; ceased passenger services in Oct. 2005; Dir RUSSELL NEELY.

ROADS

In 2004 Malawi had a total road network of some 15,500 km, of which 3,600 km was paved. In addition, unclassified community roads total an estimated 10,000 km. All main roads, and most secondary roads, are all-weather roads. Major routes link Lilongwe and Blantyre with Harare (Zimbabwe), Lusaka (Zambia) and Mbeya and Dar es Salaam (Tanzania). A 480-km highway along the western shore of Lake Malawi links the remote Northern Region with the Central and Southern Regions. A project to create a new trade route, or 'Northern Corridor', through Tanzania, involving road construction and improvements in Malawi, was completed in 1992.

Department of Road Traffic: c/o Ministry of Transport and Public Works, Private Bag 257, Capital City, Lilongwe 3; tel. 1756138; fax 1752592; comprises the Nat. Road Authority.

Road Transport Operators' Association: Chitawira Light Industrial Site, POB 30740, Chichiri, Blantyre 3; tel. 1870422; fax 1871423; e-mail rtoa@sdnp.org.mw; f. 1956; Chair. P. CHAKHUMBIRA; Exec. Dir SHADRECK MATSIMBE; 200 mems (2004).

Shire Bus Lines Ltd: POB 176, Blantyre; tel. 1671388; fax 1670038; 100% state-owned; operates local and long-distance bus services between Mzuzu, Lilongwe, and Blantyre; services to Harare (Zimbabwe) and Johannesburg (South Africa); Chair. Al-haj Sheik ALIDI LIKONDE.

SHIPPING

There are 23 ports and landing points on Lake Malawi. The four main ports are at Chilumba, Nkhata Bay, Chipoka and Monkey Bay. Ferry services carry around 60,000 passengers annually; the principal cargoes transported are sugar, fertilizer, dried fish and maize. The amount of cargo transported was expected to rise from August 2005 with the inclusion of a new landing point at Ngala, near Dwangwa, to carry sugar to Chipoka. Smaller vessels are registered for other activities including fishing and tourism. Lake Malawi is at the centre of the Mtwara Development Corridor transport initiative agreed between Zambia, Malawi, Tanzania and Mozambique in mid-December 2004.

Department of Marine Services: c/o Department of Transport and Public Works, Private Bag A-81; tel. 1751531; fax 1756290; e-mail marinedepartment@malawi.net; responsible for vessel safety and control, ports services, and maritime pollution control.

Malawi Lake Services (MLS): POB 15, Monkey Bay; tel. and fax 1587221; e-mail ilala@malawi.net; f. 1994; privatized in 2001; 20-year operating concession granted to Glens Waterways Ltd; operates passenger and freight services to Mozambique, and freight services to Tanzania; Gen. Man. ANTON BOTES; 9 vessels, incl. 3 passenger and 4 cargo vessels; carried 14,000 metric tons of cargo in 2005/06.

CIVIL AVIATION

Kamuzu (formerly Lilongwe) International Airport was opened in 1982. There are also international airports at Chileka, and at Mzuzu and Karonga in the Northern region. There is one domestic airport, Club Makokola, at Mangochi.

Department of Civil Aviation: c/o Ministry of Transport and Public Works, Private Bag B311, Lilongwe 3; tel. 1770577; fax 1774986; e-mail aviationhq@malawi.net; Dir L. Z. PHESELE.

Air Malawi Ltd: 4 Robins Rd, POB 84, Blantyre; tel. 1820811; fax 1820042; e-mail cd@airmalawi.net; internet www.airmalawi.net; f. 1967; privatization, begun in 1999, was postponed in 2003; scheduled domestic and regional services; Chair. JIMMY KOREIA-MPATSA; CEO Capt. A. B. W. MCHUNGULA.

Tourism

Fine scenery, beaches on Lake Malawi, big game and an excellent climate form the basis of the country's tourist potential. According to official figures, the number of foreign visitor arrivals was 437,718 in 2005. Receipts from tourism totalled US $24m. in that year.

Department of Tourism: POB 402, Blantyre; tel. 1620300; fax 1620947; f. 1969; responsible for tourism policy; inspects and licenses tourist facilities, sponsors training of hotel staff and publishes tourist literature; Dir of Tourism Services ISAAC K. MSISKA.

Malawi Tourism Association (MTA): POB 1044, Lilongwe; tel. 1770010; fax 1770131; e-mail mta@malawi.net; internet www.malawi-tourism-association.org.mw; f. 1998; Exec. Dir SAM BOTOMANI.

Defence

As assessed at November 2006, Malawi's defence forces comprised a land army of 5,300, a marine force of 220 and an air force of 200; all form part of the army. There was also a paramilitary police force of 1,500. In 2006 some 173 Malawian troops were stationed abroad, attached to UN missions in Africa and Europe; of these, 60 were serving as observers.

Defence Expenditure: Estimated at K2,700m. in 2006.

Commander-in-Chief of the Armed Forces: Gen. MARK DAITON CHIZIKO.

Education

Primary education, which is officially compulsory, begins at six years of age and lasts for eight years. Secondary education, which begins at 14 years of age, lasts for four years, comprising two cycles of two years. According to UNESCO estimates, in 2003/04 primary enrolment included 95% of children in the relevant age-group (males 93%; females 98%), while in 2003/04 secondary enrolment included 25% of children in the relevant age-group (males 27%; females 23%). A programme to expand education at all levels has been undertaken; however, the introduction of free primary education in September 1994 led to the influx of more than 1m. additional pupils, resulting in severe overcrowding in schools. In January 1996 the International Development Association granted US $22.5m. for the training of 20,000 new teachers, appointed in response to the influx. In 2004 there were some 45,300 primary school teachers, of whom 17,300 were female. In mid-1997 additional funding was provided by the African Development Bank for the construction of primary and secondary schools. The University of Malawi had 3,565 students in 1999. Some students attend institutions in the United Kingdom and the USA. A small number of students attended the Marine College at Monkey Bay, established in 1998, and in 2005 a proposal to merge the college with Malawi Lake Services was under consideration. Expenditure on education in 2003/04 was estimated at 8,714m. kwacha (equivalent to 19.6% of total expenditure).

Bibliography

Baker, C. *Seeds of Trouble: Government Policy and Land Rights in Nyasaland, 1946–1964*. London, British Academic Press, 1993.

Bone, D. (Ed.). *Malawi's Muslims: Historical Perspectives*. Blantyre, Kachere Series, 2001.

Burton, P., Pelser, E., and Gondwe, L. *Understanding Offending: Prisoners and Rehabilitation in Malawi*. Pretoria, Institute for Security Studies, 2005.

Catholic Institute for International Relations (CIIR). *Malawi: Moment of Truth*. London, CIIR, 1993.

Chikago, J. J. *Crossing Cultural Frontiers: Analysis and Solutions to Poverty Reduction, Japanese Parallels*. Limbe, Montfort Press, 2003.

Conroy, A. C. (Ed.), *et al. Poverty, AIDS and Hunger: Breaking the Poverty Trap in Malawi*. Basingstoke, Palgrave Macmillan, 2006.

Crosby, C. A. *Historical Dictionary of Malawi* 2nd Edn. Metuchen, NJ, Scarecrow Press, 1993.

Cullen, T. *Malawi: A Turning Point*. Edinburgh, Pentland Press, 1994.

De Kok, B. *Christianity and African Traditional Religion: Two Realities of a Different Kind*. Zomba, Kachere Series, 2005.

Englund, H. (Ed.). *A Democracy of Chameleons: Politics and Culture in the New Malawi*. Uppsala, Nordic African Institute; London, Global, 2002.

Harrigan, J. *From Dictatorship to Democracy*. Aldershot, Ashgate Publishing Ltd, 2000.

Immink, B., Lembani, S., Ott, M., and Peters Berries, C. (Eds). *From Democracy to Empowerment: Ten Years of Democratisation in Malawi*. Maputo, Konrad-Adenauer-Stiftung, 2003.

Kay, L. *And Then I Came Here: Expatriate Women Talk About Living in Malawi and Other Parts of the World*. Cambridge, Cirrus Books, 2005.

Langwe, K. J. *Impact of Structural Adjustment and Stabilisation Programmes in Malawi*. Manchester, University of Manchester, 2005.

Levy, S. *Starter Packs: A Strategy to Fight Hunger in Developing Countries?: Lessons from the Malawi Experience 1998–2003*. Cambridge, MA, CABI Publishing, 2005.

Lwanda, J. L. C. *Kamazu Banda of Malawi: A Study in Promise, Power and Paralysis: Malawi under Dr Banda, 1961 to 1993*. Glasgow, Dudu Nsomba Publrs, 1993.

Promises, Power Politics and Poverty: Democratic Transition in Malawi, 1961–1996. Glasgow, Dudu Ngemba Publrs, 1996.

Politics, Culture and Medicine in Malawi: Historical Continuities and Ruptures with Special Reference to HIV/AIDS. Zomba, University of Malawi, Religious and Theological Studies Dept.; East Lansing, MI, Michigan State University Press, 2005.

Maliyamkono, T.L., and Kanyongolo F.E. *When Political Parties Clash*. Dar es Salaam, TEMA Publrs, 2003

Manda, M. A. Z. *State and Labour in Malawi*. Glasgow, Dudu Nsomba Publications, 2000.

Mandala, E. C. *The End of Chidyerano: A History of Food and Everyday Life in Malawi, 1860-2004*. Portsmouth, NH, Heinemann, c. 2005.

McCracken, J. (Ed.). *Twentieth Century Malawi: Perspectives on History and Culture*. Stirling, University of Stirling, 2001.

Mchenga, R. G. *Macroeconomic Stabilisation and Structural Adjustment Programmes: Policy Objectives and Outcomes. A Case Study of Malawi*. Manchester, University of Manchester, 2005.

Meinhardt, H., and Patel, N. *Malawi's Process of Democratic Transition: An Analysis of Political Developments between 1990 and 2003*. Maputo, Konrad-Adenauer-Stiftung, 2003.

Mhone, G. C. Z. (Ed.). *Malawi at the Crossroads: The Post-Colonial Political Economy*. Harare, SAPES Books, 1992.

Mkamanga, E. *Suffering in Silence: Malawi Women's Thrity-Year Dance with Dr Banda*. Glasgow, Dudu Nsomba Publications, 2000.

Moto, F. *Trends in Malawian Literature*. Zomba, Chancellor College Publications, 1999.

Muula, A., and Cahnika, E. T. *Malawi's Lost Decade: 1994–2004*. Limbe, Montfort Press, 2005.

Ndalama, J. S. *Impact of Economic Reform Programmes on Economic Growth of Malawi*. Manchester, University of Manchester, 2005.

Nzunda, M. S., and Ross, K. R. (Eds). *Church, Law and Political Transition in Malawi 1992–1994*. Gweru, Mambo, 1995.

Pfeffer Engels, J. *Chewa*. New York, NY, Rosen Publishing Group, Inc., 1996.

Phiri, D. D. *History of Malawi: From Earliest Times to the Year 1915*. Blantyre, Christian Literature Asscn of Malawi (CLAIM), 2004.

History of the Tumbuka. Blantyre, Dzuka Publishing Co Ltd, 2000.

Sindima, H. J. *Malawi's First Republic: An Economic and Political Analysis*. Lanham, MD, University Press of America, 2002

Spring, A. *Agricultural Development and Gender Issues in Malawi*. Lanham, MD, University Press of America, 1995.

Takame, T. (Ed.). *Africa Research Series (Ajia Keizai Kenkyujo—Japan): Macro and Micro Perspectives*. Chiba, Institute of Developing Economies, 2005.

Africa Research Series (Ajia Keizai Kenkyujo—Japan): Current Issues of Rural Development in Malawi. Chiba, Institute of Developing Economies, 2006.

Van Breugel, J. W. M. *Chewa Traditional Religion*. Blantyre, Kachere Series, 2001.

Wendland, E. R. *Sewero! Christian Drama and the Drama of Christianity in Africa: On the Genesis and Genius of Chinyanja Radio Plays in Malawi*. Zomba, Kachere Series, 2005.

White, S. V., Kachika, T., and Chipasula Banda, M. *Women in Malawi: A Profile of Women in Malawi*. Limbe, Women and Law in Southern Africa, Research and Education Trust; Harare, Southern African Research and Documentation Centre, Women in Development Southern Africa Awareness, 2005.

MALI

Physical and Social Geography

R. J. HARRISON CHURCH

With an area of 1.24m. sq km (478,841 sq miles), the Republic of Mali is only slightly smaller than Niger, West Africa's largest state. Like Niger and Burkina Faso, Mali is land-locked. Bordering on seven countries, it extends about 1,600 km from north to south, and roughly the same distance from east to west, with a narrowing at the centre. The *de jure* population was 9,790,492 at the census of April 1998, and was estimated by the UN at 11,968,000 in mid-2006 (giving an average density of 9.7 inhabitants per sq km). The only large city is the capital, Bamako, which had a population of 1,016,167 at the 1998 census, according to provisional figures.

The ancient Basement Complex rocks of Africa have been uplifted in the mountainous Adrar des Iforas of the north-east, whose dry valleys bear witness to formerly wetter conditions. Otherwise the Pre-Cambrian rocks are often covered by Primary sandstones, which have bold erosion escarpments at, for example, Bamako and east of Bandiagara. At the base of the latter live the Dogon people, made famous by Marcel Griaule's study. Where the River Niger crosses a sandstone outcrop below Bamako, rapids obstruct river navigation, giving an upper navigable reach above Bamako, and another one below it from Koulikoro to Ansongo, near the border with Niger.

Loose sands cover most of the rest of the country and, as in Senegal and Niger, are a relic of drier climatic conditions. They are very extensive on the long border with Mauritania and Algeria.

Across the heart of the country flows the River Niger, a vital waterway and source of fish. As the seasonal floods retreat, they leave pasture for thousands of livestock desperate for food and water after a dry season of at least eight months. The retreating floods also leave damp areas for man, equally desperate for cultivable land in an arid environment. Flood water is sometimes retained for swamp rice cultivation, and has been made available for irrigation, particularly in the 'dead' south-western section of the inland Niger delta.

The delta is the remnant of an inland lake, in which the upper River Niger once terminated. In a more rainy era this overflowed to join the then mighty Tilemsi river, once the drainage focus of the now arid Adrar des Iforas. The middle and lower courses of the Tilemsi now comprise the Niger below Bourem, at the eastern end of the consequential elbow turn of the Niger. The eastern part of the delta, which was formed in the earlier lake, is intersected by 'live' flood-water branches of the river, while the relic channels of the very slightly higher western part of the delta are never occupied naturally by flood water and so are 'dead'. However, these are used in part for irrigation water retained by the Sansanding barrage, which has raised the level of the Niger by an average of 4.3 m.

Mali is mainly dry throughout, with a rainy season of four to five months and a total rainfall of 1,120 mm at Bamako, and of only seven weeks and an average fall of 236 mm at Gao. North of this there is no rain-fed cultivation, but only semi-desert or true desert, which occupies nearly one-half of Mali. The exploitation of gold reserves, most of which are located near the borders with Senegal and Guinea, is becoming an increasingly important activity. Modest quantities of diamonds are mined near the border with Senegal.

Distances to the nearest foreign port from most places in Mali are at least 1,300 km, and, not surprisingly, there is much seasonal and permanent emigration.

Recent History

PIERRE ENGLEBERT

Revised by KATHARINE MURISON

The former French colony of Soudan merged with Senegal in April 1959 to form the Federation of Mali, which became independent on 20 June 1960. Senegal seceded two months later, and the Republic of Mali was proclaimed on 22 September. President Modibo Keita declared the country a one-party state, under his Union soudanaise—Rassemblement démocratique africain (US—RDA). Keita's Marxist regime severed links with France and developed close relations with the Eastern bloc. In November 1968 Keita was deposed in an army *coup d'état*, and a Comité militaire pour la libération nationale was formed, with Lt (later Gen.) Moussa Traoré as President.

THE TRAORÉ PERIOD

The new regime promised a return to civilian rule when Mali's economic problems had been overcome. Relations with France improved, and French budgetary aid ensued. In 1976 a new ruling party, the Union démocratique du peuple malien (UDPM), was established. Traoré, as sole candidate for the presidency, received 99% of the votes cast at elections in 1979, and a single list of UDPM candidates was elected to the legislature. From 1981 the Traoré regime undertook a programme of economic reform and, following his unopposed re-election to the presidency in 1985, Traoré vigorously pursued measures to suppress public corruption.

At elections to the Assemblée nationale in June 1988, provision was made for up to three UDPM-nominated candidates to contest each of the 82 seats. Doubtlessly influenced by political events elsewhere in the region, in March 1990 Traoré initiated a nation-wide series of conferences to consider the exercise of democracy within and by the ruling party. Mali's first cohesive opposition movements began to emerge in the second half of 1990: among the most prominent were the Comité national d'initiative démocratique (CNID) and the Alliance pour la démocratie au Mali (ADEMA), which organized mass pro-democracy demonstrations in December. In January 1991 Traoré relinquished the defence portfolio to Brig.-Gen. Mamadou Coulibaly, the air force Chief of Staff. Gen. Sékou Ly, Minister of the Interior and Basic Development, warned opposition groups that their political activities must cease.

ARMY INTERVENTION AND POLITICAL REFORM

The security forces harshly repressed violent pro-democracy demonstrations in March 1991: official figures later revealed that 106 people were killed and 708 injured, during three days of unrest. On 26 March it was announced that Traoré had been arrested. A military Conseil de réconciliation nationale (CRN), led by Lt-Col (later Lt-Gen.) Amadou Toumani Touré, assumed power, and the Constitution, Government, legislature and the

UDPM were dissolved. Following negotiations with ADEMA, the CNID and other reformist political groups, the CRN was swiftly succeeded by a 25-member Comité de transition pour le salut du peuple (CTSP), chaired by Touré, whose function was to oversee a transition to a democratic, civilian political system. It was announced that municipal, legislative and presidential elections would be organized by the end of the year, and that the armed forces would withdraw from political life in early 1992. In April 1991 Soumana Sacko, working in the Central African Republic (CAR) as a UN development official, and briefly Minister of Finance and Trade in 1987, accepted an invitation to return to Mali to head a transitional, civilian-dominated government.

The CTSP affirmed its commitment to the policies of economic adjustment that had been adopted by the Traoré administration and initiated efforts to recover funds allegedly embezzled by Traoré and his associates. Sékou Ly, Mamadou Coulibaly and Ousmane Coulibaly, the army Chief of Staff, were among the senior officials arrested in connection with the brutal repression of the unrest prior to Traoré's overthrow.

An amnesty was proclaimed for most political prisoners detained under Traoré, and provision was made for the registration of political parties. The CNID was legalized as the Congrès national d'initiative démocratique (led by a prominent lawyer, Mountaga Tall), while ADEMA (chaired by Alpha Oumar Konaré) adopted the additional title of Parti panafricain pour la liberté, la solidarité et la justice, and the US—RDA was revived.

A national conference was convened in Bamako in July 1991, during which some 1,800 delegates prepared a draft Constitution for what was to be designated the Third Republic of Mali, together with an electoral code and a charter governing political parties. In August seven government ministers and about one-half of the members of the CTSP were replaced, following reports implicating them in the repression prior to the coup. In November it was announced that the period of transition to civilian rule was to be extended until 26 March 1992. (The delay was attributed principally to the CTSP's desire first to secure an agreement with Tuareg groups in the north—see below.) The Constitution was approved by 99.8% of those who voted (about 43% of the electorate) in a referendum on 12 January 1992. Municipal elections followed one week later, contested by 23 of the country's 48 authorized parties. ADEMA enjoyed the greatest success, winning 214 of the 751 local seats, while the US—RDA took 130 seats and the CNID 96. The rate of abstention by voters was, however, almost 70%. Legislative elections were held on 23 February and 8 March, amid allegations that the electoral system was unduly favourable to ADEMA. Of the 21 parties that submitted candidates, 10 secured seats in the 129-member Assemblée nationale: ADEMA won 76 seats, the CNID nine and the US—RDA eight. Overall, only about one-fifth of the electorate voted.

Nine candidates contested the first round of the presidential election, on 12 April 1992 (the date for the transition to civilian rule having again been postponed). The largest share of the votes (some 45%) was won by Konaré. A second round of voting, contested by the ADEMA leader and his nearest rival, Tiéoulé Mamadou Konaté of the US—RDA, followed two weeks later, at which Konaré won 69% of the votes cast. Again, participation by voters was little more than 20%.

THE KONARÉ PRESIDENCY

Konaré was sworn in as President of the Third Republic on 8 June 1992. Younoussi Touré, formerly the director in Mali of the Banque centrale des états de l'Afrique de l'ouest, was designated Prime Minister. While most strategic posts in Touré's Government were allocated to members of ADEMA, the US—RDA and the Parti pour la démocratie et le progrès (PDP) were also represented.

In February 1993 Traoré, Sékou Ly, Mamadou Coulibaly and Ousmane Coulibaly were sentenced to death, having been convicted of 'premeditated murder, battery and voluntary manslaughter' at the time of the March 1991 disturbances. Although the Supreme Court rejected appeals against the death sentences, no execution was known to have been carried out since 1980. Charges relating to 'economic crimes' remained against Traoré, his wife and other members of the discredited regime.

Younoussi Touré resigned the premiership in April 1993, following several weeks of student protests against austerity measures. The new Prime Minister, Abdoulaye Sekou Sow, who was not affiliated to any political party, appointed a Council of Ministers dominated by ADEMA and its supporters. A reorganization of the Government in November was prompted by the resignation of ADEMA's Vice-President, Mohamed Lamine Traoré, from his ministerial post. ADEMA remained the majority party in the Government, which also included representatives of the CNID, the PDP and the Rassemblement pour la démocratie et le progrès (RDP). The US—RDA withdrew from the coalition shortly afterwards.

Political and social tensions were exacerbated by the 50% devaluation, in January 1994, of the CFA franc. Sow resigned in February, and was replaced as Prime Minister by Ibrahim Boubacar Kéita—since November 1993 the Minister of Foreign Affairs, Malians Abroad and African Integration, a close associate of Konaré and regarded as a member of ADEMA's 'radical' wing. The CNID and the RDP withdrew from the government coalition, protesting that they had not been consulted about the changes; a new, ADEMA-dominated Government was appointed, from which the PDP in turn withdrew.

In September 1994 the election of Kéita to the presidency of ADEMA precipitated the resignation of prominent party members, including Mohamed Lamine Traoré. Disaffected members of ADEMA formed the Mouvement pour l'indépendance, la renaissance et l'intégration africaine (MIRIA) in December. In January 1995 an application for legalization by a revived UDPM was rejected by the Supreme Court. However, the Mouvement patriotique pour le renouveau (MPR), established by several of those who had sought to revive the UDPM, was granted official status later in the month. A 'breakaway' movement from the CNID was registered in September 1995 as the Parti pour la renaissance nationale (PARENA); ADEMA and PARENA established a political alliance in February 1996, and the Chairman and Secretary-General of PARENA were appointed to the Government in July.

The Assemblée nationale approved a new electoral code in January 1997. Under the new code, the electoral commission, the Commission électorale nationale indépendante (CENI), was to comprise 14 representatives of political parties (seven for the majority party and seven for the opposition parties), together with eight representatives of the Government and eight non-political members. The number of parliamentary seats was to be increased from 129 to 147.

Having been postponed for logistical reasons, the first round of the legislative elections was held on 13 April 1997, contested by more than 1,500 candidates. As early results indicated a clear victory for ADEMA, the main opposition parties condemned the results as fraudulent. Independent national and international monitors recognized that the conduct of the poll had been flawed but not fraudulent. However, the opposition parties announced that they would boycott the second round, and also withdrew their candidates from the presidential and municipal elections. In late April the Constitutional Court annulled the first round of voting on the grounds of irregularities.

The first round of the presidential election was postponed, by one week, until 11 May 1997. Konaré emphasized that he had no wish to be the sole candidate. In early May Mamadou Maribatrou Diaby, the leader of the Parti pour l'unité, la démocratie et le progrès, announced that he was prepared to contest the presidency. However, the so-called 'radical' opposition collective adhered to its demands for the cancellation of the ongoing electoral process, for the complete revision of the voters' register, and, in the mean time, for the resignation of the Government and the appointment of a transitional administration. The Constitutional Court rejected an opposition petition seeking the cancellation of the presidential poll. The final results of voting allocated 95.9% of the valid votes cast to Konaré. Claiming success for its campaign for a boycott of the election, the radical opposition stated that the low rate of participation by voters, 28.4% of the registered electorate, effectively invalidated Konaré's victory. (The turn-out was, none the less, higher than that recorded at the 1992 election.)

Political tensions escalated following the presidential election, as the radical opposition refused to recognize the legitimacy of Konaré's mandate. In late May 1997 the municipal elections were postponed indefinitely. On 8 June, the day of Konaré's investiture, there were violent disturbances in Bamako, and Tall, Almamy Sylla (the RDP President and leader of the opposition collective) and Sogal Maïga (the MPR Secretary-General) were among five opposition leaders arrested and charged with 'non-recognition of the results of the presidential election' and with opposition to state authority, as well as with arson and incitement to violence. They were released on bail in mid-June, shortly after the first round of the legislative elections, due on 6 July, had been postponed by two weeks. Meanwhile, several opposition activists were sentenced to three months' imprisonment for their part in recent disturbances. While some opposition parties announced their intention to present candidates for the Assemblée nationale, 18 others, including the US—RDA, the MPR and the CNID, grouped in a Collectif des partis politiques de l'opposition (COPPO), reiterated their refusal to re-enter the electoral process unless their demands were met in full.

Legislative voting took place on 20 July 1997, preceded by violent disturbances in Bamako and elsewhere, in which two people were reported to have been killed: a total of 17 parties (including five 'moderate' opposition parties), as well as a small number of independent candidates, contested seats in the Assemblée nationale. As at the presidential election, COPPO claimed that its appeal for a boycott of the poll had been successful, and that the low rate of participation by voters (about 12% of the registered electorate in Bamako, and 22% elsewhere) would render the assembly illegitimate. The official results confirmed a large majority for ADEMA. A second round of voting was held for eight seats on 3 August. The final results allocated 130 seats to ADEMA (including one seat won in alliance with the Convention patriotique pour le progrès), eight to PARENA, four to the Convention démocratique et sociale (CDS), three to the Union pour la démocratie et le développement (UDD) and two to the PDP. International monitors stated that both rounds of voting had been conducted fairly.

Konaré undertook a series of consultations with representatives of the political majority and opposition, and there were indications that he was prepared to concede the allocation of public funds to opposition parties, acknowledging that ADEMA was disproportionately advantaged by the prevailing system. However, the political climate deteriorated further with the lynching of a police officer at an opposition rally in Bamako following the second round of legislative voting. Several opposition leaders, among them Tall, Sylla and the MIRIA leader, Mohamed Lamine Traoré, were subsequently arrested, and 10 activists were charged with violence, assault and battery. (All 10 were acquitted in April 1998.)

In September 1997 Konaré held a meeting with some 20 opposition leaders, including representatives of COPPO, at which he proposed the formation of a broadly based coalition government. A new Government was appointed in mid-September, again with Kéita as Prime Minister: the new administration included a number of representatives of the moderate opposition parties (among them the PDP and the UDD). In October a presidential pardon was granted to all political activists charged during the election period and its aftermath. In December Konaré formally commuted some 21 death sentences, most notably those imposed on ex-President Traoré and his associates.

Although several parties had withdrawn from COPPO by early 1998, little progress had been made towards full political reconciliation. In February 13 parties confirmed their intention to boycott the forthcoming municipal elections. The elections, scheduled for 19 April, were subsequently cancelled, and in mid-April the radical opposition announced that it was prepared to accept a mediation initiative by former US President Jimmy Carter. (Since his withdrawal from Malian political life the leader of the 1991 coup, Amadou Toumani Touré, had become involved in the crisis-management work of the US-based Carter Center.) During a recent visit to Mali Carter had proposed that all parties recognize the legitimacy of Konaré's presidential mandate, and recommended the dissolution and recomposition of the CENI, a 'consensual' revision of voters' lists, and the holding of communal elections before the end of June. While accepting mediation, COPPO continued to reject the legitimacy of the Government and warned of an imminent campaign of nation-wide civil disobedience. During May, however, the opposition's strength was undermined by a split in the US—RDA, as 29 members of the party's political bureau announced their recognition of Konaré's election; in response, the party leader, Mamadou Bamou Touré, suspended these members.

Municipal voting commenced in June 1998, when voting took place in the 19 mayoralties, although violence was reported in Bamako prior to the poll. The remaining COPPO parties boycotted the elections, at which ADEMA won control of 16 councils. Voting in 682 municipalities was scheduled to take place in November, but was subsequently postponed until April 1999.

In October 1998 the trial for 'economic crimes' began in Bamako of ex-President Traoré, his wife Mariam, her brother, Abraham Douah Cissoko (the former head of customs), together with a former finance minister under the Traoré regime, Tiena Coulibaly, and the former representative in France of the Banque de développement du Mali, Moussa Koné. All five were accused of embezzlement of public funds and illegal enrichment while in office. In January 1999 Traoré, his wife and brother-in-law were sentenced to death, having been convicted of 'economic crimes' to the value of some US $350,000; the original claims had cited embezzled funds amounting to $4m. Coulibaly and Koné were acquitted. In September Konaré commuted the death sentences to terms of life imprisonment.

ADEMA won an overwhelming majority of seats in municipal elections held in May–June 1999, and retained control of 16 of the 19 mayoralities; many of the radical opposition parties, however, boycotted these polls.

In February 2000 Kéita submitted his Government's resignation. An extensively reorganized Council of Ministers was subsequently appointed, with Mandé Sidibé as Prime Minister. Sidibé was widely considered to be a supporter of economic reform and of an anti-corruption campaign being undertaken by Konaré. The establishment, in June, of a discussion forum on electoral issues between the administration and political parties was regarded as signifying an improvement in relations between the Government and opposition parties.

New legislation approved by the Assemblée nationale in mid-2000 included measures designed to ensure the provision of state funding for political parties, and to encourage greater freedom of the press. The legislature also approved a major revision of the Constitution proposed by President Konaré, although a national referendum on the amendments would be required before their implementation. Notably, under the proposed changes, the electoral system at legislative elections would be reformed to incorporate an element of proportional representation, people of dual nationality would be authorized to contest presidential elections, certain powers of the Supreme Court would be divested to new autonomous judicial institutions and a new press regulatory body would be created. In July COPPO, which now comprised 15 parties and was led by Almamy Sylla of the RDP, announced that it would henceforth participate in the political process. In August the Assemblée nationale approved electoral legislation, which reportedly envisaged a chamber comprising 150 members, 40 of whom would be elected by a system of proportional representation. However, this legislation was rejected by the Constitutional Court in October.

In October 2000 Kéita resigned as leader of ADEMA; a significant faction within the party opposed the proposed nomination of Kéita as the party's candidate at the presidential election scheduled to be held in 2002. At an extraordinary congress of the party, held in November, Dioncounda Traoré was elected as the new Chairman. In February 2001 a number of leading members of ADEMA loyal to Kéita, including some 21 deputies and four former ministers, formed a new movement, Alternative-2002, in an attempt to distance themselves from the leadership and policies of the party. A minor ministerial reshuffle was effected in June. In July a new party led by

Kéita, the Rassemblement pour le Mali (RPM), was officially registered.

In November 2001 Konaré indefinitely postponed a referendum (due to take place in the following month) on the constitutional amendments adopted by the Assemblée nationale in July 2000. In January 2002 Soumaïla Cissé, the Minister of Facilities, National Development, the Environment and Town Planning, was elected as the presidential candidate of ADEMA; Cissé consequently stepped down from his ministerial position. In March Sidibé resigned as Prime Minister in order to contest the presidency; Modibo Kéita, hitherto Secretary-General at the presidency, was appointed to the premiership. Ahmed El Madani Diallo, the Minister of Rural Development, also resigned from the Government later that month and announced his presidential candidacy. In early April it was reported that 15 opposition parties, including the CNID, the RPM and the MPR, had formed an electoral alliance, Espoir 2002, agreeing to support a single opposition candidate in the event of a second round of voting. Meanwhile, an alliance of 23 political parties announced its support for the presidential candidacy of Amadou Toumani Touré, the leader of the 1991 coup and subsequent transitional regime, while the RPM formally announced the candidacy of Ibrahim Boubacar Kéita.

AMADOU TOUMANI TOURÉ ELECTED PRESIDENT

At the first round of the presidential election, which was held, as scheduled, on 28 April 2002, and contested by 24 candidates, Touré secured the largest share of the votes cast, with 28.7%, followed by Cissé, with 21.3%, and Kéita, with 21.0%. As no candidate had secured an overall majority, Touré and Cissé contested a second round of voting on 12 May. Touré, supported by more than 40 parties (including those of Espoir 2002), won 65.0% of the valid votes cast, defeating Cissé. The electoral process was marred by allegations of fraud and incompetence, which led the Constitutional Court to annul around one-quarter of the votes cast in the first ballot, and reports indicated that the turn-out was very low, particularly in the second round, when the rate of participation was approximately 25%. In late May Konaré announced the granting of a pardon to former President Moussa Traoré; however, Traoré rejected this pardon, demanding his rehabilitation prior to his acceptance of any pardon. (He finally left prison in July, after Konaré had left office.) Touré was inaugurated as President on 8 June and subsequently formed a new Government, appointing Ahmed Mohamed Ag Hamani as Prime Minister and Minister of African Integration, the first Tuareg to hold the Malian premiership.

Legislative elections, which were held in two rounds on 14 and 28 July 2002, were also marked by a low rate of participation and demonstrated the clear absence of any one dominant political grouping in Mali. After the second round, the RPM emerged as the single largest party in the new Assemblée nationale, with 46 of the 147 seats (although 20 of its seats had been won in local electoral alliances with other parties of the Espoir 2002 grouping), closely followed by ADEMA, which secured 45 seats. Other parties of Espoir 2002 obtained a further 21 seats, giving a total of 66 to supporters of the RPM, while other constituent parties of the pro-ADEMA Alliance pour la République et la démocratie won an additional six seats, giving a total of 51. The CNID received 13 seats, while parties belonging to an informal alliance supportive of President Touré, the Convergence pour l'alternance et le changement (ACC), including PARENA and the US—RDA, won a total of 10 seats. As had been the case in the presidential election, the Constitutional Court annulled a significant number of votes prior to the publication of the definitive results of the elections, amid further allegations of electoral fraud. The results of voting in eight constituencies were declared void, as a result of administrative flaws. President Touré announced his willingness to govern in co-operation with any party that could establish command of the legislature. In early September 19 deputies, comprising those of the ACC parties, several independent deputies and other declared supporters of Touré, formed a grouping, the Bloc présidentiel, within the legislature. Later in the month Ibrahim Boubakar Kéita was elected President of the Assemblée nationale.

On 16 October 2002 Touré announced the formation of a Government of National Unity, comprising 21 ministers and seven minister-delegates. The new Government stated that improvements to the health and education systems were among its priorities, as was the introduction of measures to alleviate the consequences of recent price rises. ADEMA increased its representation in the Assemblée nationale to 53 deputies, becoming the single largest party, following its victory in by-elections in all eight constituencies where elections were rerun on 20 October, although the RPM-led Espoir 2002 grouping continued to hold a majority of seats. A minor government reorganization was announced in November.

In mid-2003 a split in ADEMA resulted in the formation, by Cissé, of a new party, the Union pour la République et la démocratie (URD). However, as Cissé's position as a commissioner of the Union économique et monétaire ouest-africaine prohibited him from engaging in political activity, former Prime Minister Younoussi Touré was elected as the interim Chairman of the party. In August clashes between adherents of rival Islamic groups, apparently provoked by a dispute over land, resulted in 13 deaths in the west of the country. (In April 2005 84 people were found guilty of participating in the violence; five of the defendants were sentenced to death.) In October the principal trade union federation, the Union nationale des travailleurs du Mali (UNTM), called a two-day strike in protest at what it described as the Government's failure to improve workers' conditions, or to reduce utility charges, since the 2002 elections.

In April 2004 Ag Hamani tendered his resignation as premier, apparently in response to a request by President Touré. A new administration, headed by Prime Minister Ousmane Issoufi Maïga, hitherto Minister of Equipment and Transport (and not affiliated to any political party), was formed in May. ADEMA was the most successful party at municipal elections held at the end of May, winning 28% of the seats contested, followed by the URD, which secured 14%, and the RPM, with 13%; the rate of participation by the electorate was relatively high, at 43.6%.

The death of a student in clashes between two rival student groups provoked violent unrest at the University of Bamako in December 2004, during which a further two students were killed. A number of arrests were made in connection with the deaths. In March 2005 severe rioting and looting erupted in Bamako after the national football team lost a match against Togo. The violence was attributed by the media to youths angered by high unemployment, increasing poverty and a resulting lack of prospects. The security forces were widely criticized for failing to suppress the disturbances. Labour unrest also appeared to be increasing. Cotton workers held a two-day strike in June in support of demands for social assistance, following the privatization of a cottonseed oil plant, and the payment of salary arrears, and in September a one-day general strike was organized by the UNTM after negotiations broke down with the Government on a list of 14 grievances submitted by the trade union federation in May. In October the UNTM and the Government signed a memorandum of understanding on the federation's demands, although subsequent negotiations on the implementation of the agreement, particularly over an increase in the minimum wage, proved difficult.

From mid-2004 there was considerable speculation regarding potential realignments of political organizations ahead of the presidential and legislative elections due in 2007. In February and March 2005 the President conducted a series of consultations with the leaders of various political organizations. However, there were signs that the political consensus that had existed since Touré's election in 2002 was likely to come to an end before the elections, as parties began to distance themselves from the President. Notably, in April 2005 the RPM, the URD and a faction of ADEMA refused to attend a meeting of support for the President, which was organized in response to the rioting of late March. Touré effected a minor government reshuffle in June. In July a group of supporters of Touré formed a new political organization, the Parti citoyen pour le renouveau, although other followers of the President opposed its establishment, and Touré himself remained unaffiliated to any particular party.

In October 2005 the RPM refused to join a pro-presidential majority group being formed by ADEMA and most of the other parties represented in the Assemblée nationale, having deemed insufficient the two posts that it had been allocated in the renewal of the legislature's board. The party claimed that its marginalization within the ruling coalition had forced it to enter into parliamentary opposition, although the party's representatives in the Council of Ministers did not resign their positions. In November the Secretary-General of the RPM, Dr Bocary Treta, claimed that Kadari Bamba, the Chairman of the party's parliamentary group and also one of its Vice-Presidents, had been assassinated for political reasons, following the deputy's death in a road accident involving the car of a presidential aide. The unexpected victory of an RPM candidate in the second round of a by-election in mid-November indicated continued support for the party, despite its parliamentary isolation, and represented a set-back for ADEMA and its pro-presidential allies, whose candidate had secured a majority of votes in the first round of voting in October. Meanwhile, the national conference of ADEMA adopted a resolution pledging the party's support for Touré in the presidential election, although several senior officials, notably the party's First Vice-President, Soumeylou Boubèye Maïga, opposed this decision and favoured fielding an internal candidate.

The RPM chose not to contest the by-election to fill Bamba's seat in the Assemblée nationale, instead opting to support the candidate of the URD. However, the URD candidate was defeated by ADEMA's representative, who had the backing of some 21 political parties and associations, in a second round of voting in April 2006; the turn-out was extremely low, at around 9.5%. The URD had succeeded in securing a vacant seat in the legislature in a by-election in March, defeating the RPM's candidate with the support of the pro-presidential coalition. Observers speculated that uncertainty over party alliances was alienating voters. In June it was reported that the executive secretariat of the URD had unanimously decided to support the candidacy of Touré in the 2007 presidential election.

In November 2006 it was announced that the first rounds of the presidential and legislative elections would be held on 29 April and 1 July, respectively, with second rounds to take place on 13 May and 22 July if required. State funding of 1,700m. francs CFA was to be distributed among 46 eligible political parties. Later that month Maïga was expelled from ADEMA, together with three other members of the party's executive committee, after he suggested that he might stand in the presidential election for a newly formed political movement, Convergence 2007; Maïga subsequently announced his candidature and was formally expelled from ADEMA, which confirmed its support for Touré. Kéita was nominated as the RPM's presidential candidate in January 2007. In the following month Kéita, Maïga and two other presidential candidates, Mamadou Bakary Sangaré and Tiébilé Dramé, representing the CDS and PARENA, respectively, formed an electoral coalition, the Front pour la démocratie et la République (FDR), pledging to support each other in the event of a second round of presidential voting. By the end of February a total of 16 parties and associations had joined the FDR. Touré finally declared his candidature at the end of March.

TOURÉ SECURES SECOND TERM

A total of eight candidates contested the presidential election on 29 April 2007, six of whom had stood in the 2002 election. Touré was re-elected to the presidency with a clear majority of 71.20% of the votes cast, according to final results, thus avoiding the need for a second round of voting. Kéita, his nearest rival, secured 19.15%, while a turn-out of 36.2% was recorded. Although officially an independent, Touré had been reportedly supported by more than 40 parties, as well as the former Tuareg rebels who had recently signed peace accords with the Government following an uprising in May 2006 (see below). The FDR refused to recognize the results, alleging that state assets had been used to fund Touré's campaign, that the electoral register had been manipulated to favour the incumbent and that voters had been intimidated, but international observers (some 1,000 of whom had monitored polling) declared the election to have been largely free and fair. Touré was inaugurated to serve his second and final term on 8 June.

ETHNIC TENSIONS

Ethnic violence emerged in the north in mid-1990, as large numbers of light-skinned Tuaregs, who had migrated to Algeria and Libya during periods of drought, began to return to Mali and Niger (q.v.). In July of that year the Traoré Government, claiming that Tuareg rebels were attempting to establish a secessionist state, imposed a state of emergency in the Gao and Tombouctou regions, and the armed forces began a repressive campaign against the nomads. In January 1991 representatives of the Government and of two Tuareg groups, the Mouvement populaire de l'Azaouad (MPA) and the Front islamique-arabe de l'Azaouad (FIAA), meeting in Tamanrasset, Algeria, signed a peace accord: there was to be an immediate cease-fire, and the state of emergency was revoked. Tuareg military prisoners were released in March. Following the overthrow of the Traoré regime, the transitional administration affirmed its commitment to the Tamanrasset accord, and Tuareg representatives were included in the CTSP. However, unrest continued, and in June Amnesty International reported instances of the repression of Tuaregs by the armed forces. Thousands of Tuaregs, Moors and Bella (the descendants of the Tuaregs' black slaves, some of whom remained with the nomads) had fled to neighbouring countries to escape retaliatory attacks by the armed forces and the sedentary black population; there were also many casualties in the Malian armed forces.

During the second half of 1991 the MPA was reported to have lost the support of more militant Tuaregs, and a further group, the Front populaire de libération de l'Azaouad (FPLA), emerged to claim responsibility for several attacks. In December a 'special conference on the north' was convened in Mopti. With Algerian mediation, representatives of the transitional Government and of the MPA, the FIAA, the FPLA and the Armée révolutionnaire de libération de l'Azaouad (ARLA) agreed in principle to a peace settlement. Negotiations resumed in Algiers, the Algerian capital, in January 1992, at which the Malian authorities and the MPA, the FIAA and the ARLA (now negotiating together as the Mouvements et fronts unifiés de l'Azaouad—MFUA) formally agreed to implement the Mopti accord; the FPLA was reported not to have attended the Algiers sessions. A truce entered into force in February, and, following further talks in Algiers, a 'national pact' was signed in April in Bamako by the Malian authorities and the MFUA. In addition to the provisions of the Mopti accord, the pact envisaged special administrative structures for the country's three northern regions (a new administrative region of Kidal having been established in May 1991), the incorporation of Tuareg fighters into the Malian armed forces, the demilitarization of the north and the instigation of efforts more fully to integrate Tuaregs in the economic and political fields.

Despite sporadic attacks occurring, the implementation of the 'national pact' was pursued: joint patrols were established, and new administrative structures were inaugurated in November 1992. In February 1993 the Malian Government and the MFUA signed a preliminary accord facilitating the integration of Tuaregs into the national army. In May the FPLA's Secretary-General, Rhissa Ag Sidi Mohamed, declared the rebellion at an end and returned to Mali from Burkina Faso. However, in February 1994 the assassination of the MPA's military leader (a principal architect of the peace process, who had recently joined the Malian army) was allegedly perpetrated by the ARLA, and clashes between the MPA and the ARLA continued for several weeks.

In May 1994, at a meeting in Algiers, agreement was reached by the Malian Government and the MFUA regarding the integration of 1,500 former rebels into the regular army and of a further 4,860 Tuaregs into civilian sectors; the MFUA agreed to dismantle its military bases, while the Government reaffirmed its commitment to the pursuit of development projects. The agreement was, however, undermined by an intensification of violence, and tensions between 'integrated' Tuareg fighters and regular members of the Malian armed forces periodically escalated into violence. Meanwhile, the Mouvement patriotique malien Ghanda Koy ('Masters of the Land'), a resistance movement dominated by the majority ethnic group in the north, the Songhai, emerged amid rumours of official complicity in its actions against the Tuaregs. Meeting in Tamanrasset in June, the Malian authorities and the MFUA agreed on the need for the reinforcement of the army presence in areas affected by the violence, and for the more effective integration of Tuareg fighters.

In August 1994 agreement was reached by Mali, Algeria, representatives of the UN High Commissioner for Refugees (UNHCR) and the International Fund for Agricultural Development regarding the voluntary repatriation from Algeria of Malian refugees. The accord was welcomed by the Tuaregs: the MFUA pledged the reconciliation of the Tuareg movements and reiterated its commitment to the 'national pact'. However, the FIAA did not attend the talks, and unrest continued. Hostilities intensified, and in October, following an attack by the FIAA on Gao and retaliatory action, as a result of which, according to official figures, 66 people were killed, both the Government and the MFUA appealed for an end to the violence.

The Government subsequently appeared to adopt a less conciliatory approach towards the Tuareg rebels; the army announced the capture of several rebel bases. In January 1995 representatives of the FPLA and Ghanda Koy issued a joint statement urging an end to hostilities. Shortly afterwards the FIAA leader asserted that his organization was willing to co-operate in the restoration of peace. Discussions involving Tuareg groups, Ghanda Koy and representatives of local communities took place in subsequent weeks, and in April an agreement was signed providing for co-operation in resolving hitherto contentious issues. Ministerial delegations, incorporating representatives of the MFUA and Ghanda Koy, toured the north of Mali, as well as refugee areas in Algeria, Burkina Faso and Mauritania, with the aim of promoting reconciliation and awareness of the peace programme. Konaré also visited those countries, and made direct appeals to refugees to return. In June the FIAA announced an end to its armed struggle. In July representatives of the Government and of Mali's creditors met at Tombouctou, where they agreed development strategies for the northern regions.

By February 1996 some 3,000 MFUA fighters and Ghanda Koy militiamen had registered and surrendered their weapons at designated centres, under an encampment programme initiated in November 1995 in preparation for the eventual integration of former rebels into the regular army or civilian structures. The MFUA and Ghanda Koy subsequently affirmed their adherence to Mali's Constitution, national unity and territorial integrity, and advocated the full implementation of the 'national pact' and associated accords. They further proclaimed the 'irreversible dissolution' of their respective movements. In September 1997 the graduation of MFUA and Ghanda Koy contingents in the gendarmerie was reported as marking the accomplishment of the integration of all Malian fighters within the regular armed and security forces.

From 1995 significant numbers of refugees were reported to be returning voluntarily to Mali. Smaller quantities of refugees were also repatriated from Algeria and Mauritania under UNHCR supervision. The process of repatriating some 42,000 Malian refugees from Mauritania was completed in July 1997. The remaining refugee camps in Burkina (where, in all, 160,000 Malians were reported to have sought shelter at some time during the conflict) were closed in December 1997. In November 1996, meanwhile, Mali, Niger and UNHCR signed an agreement for the repatriation of 25,000 Malian Tuaregs from Niger. In June 1998 the last groups of refugees returned from Algeria.

In July 1999 clashes were reported in Gao and Kidal between members of the Arab and Kounta communities. The conflict had been provoked by disagreements between the two communities following the municipal elections in Tarkint. Despite mediation efforts, 10 people were reportedly killed in the violence. Meanwhile, ethnic violence was also reported in the Kayes region, where eight people were killed in a dispute between Soninké farmers and Fulani (Peul) herders over access to water and pasture. Numerous such disputes between the two ethnic groups had been reported in the area since early 1999, and at the end of July the Malian authorities brokered a peace agreement, which was signed by representatives of both communities. In October, however, clashes over the division of territory and control again led to an outbreak between the two sides, in which up to 40 people were estimated to have been killed. In November 2000 it was reported that Malian government forces had been dispatched to end widespread banditry by an armed group, led by Ibrahim Bahanga, a former Tuareg rebel, in the Kidal area, near to the border with Algeria. In September 2001 Bahanga reportedly announced that his forces were to cease hostilities, following talks with a state official.

There were reports of increased banditry and violence in north-eastern Mali from mid-2004. In September 13 people were killed in fighting between the Kounta and Arab communities near Bamba, some 220 km west of Gao. A few days earlier 16 Arabs and Kountas who had been imprisoned in connection with previous clashes had escaped from a gaol in Gao.

In February 2006 it was reported that Lt-Col Hassan Fagaga, a former member of the MPA, had deserted from the army and was leading a group of young armed Tuaregs in Kidal. His demands included the creation of an autonomous commune in Kidal and an improvement in conditions for former rebels integrated into the army. Fagaga returned to ranks in March, after the Government agreed not to punish him and to examine his grievances; his followers also disbanded. In late May, however, Fagaga was believed to have orchestrated a more serious uprising, when former Tuareg rebels raided weapons depots and attacked three military bases in the north, two in Kidal and one in the town of Menaka, further south. The armed forces swiftly regained control of the bases as the rebels withdrew, demanding negotiations with the Government on the development of the region. In the days following the attacks, in which six people (including three civilians) were killed, an estimated 4,500 residents of Kidal fled the town, while reports of further desertions of Tuareg soldiers from the regular army raised fears of renewed conflict in the region. None the less, both the Tuareg rebels and the Government stated their intention to seek a peaceful resolution to the crisis through international mediation. In early July both sides signed an agreement in Algiers, following talks mediated by Algerian officials, in which the Tuareg rebels pledged to desist from demanding autonomy in return for a special investment programme for northern regions, increased powers for local governments, particularly on development issues, and the reintegration into the army of Tuareg soldiers who had deserted. Later that month the Government launched a US $21m. economic development programme for the regions of Kidal, Gao and Tombouctou, supported by the European Union (EU). Further accords signed by the Malian Government and the Tuaregs in Algiers in February 2007 outlined measures required to facilitate the implementation of the July 2006 agreement and the disarmament and reintegration into society of the Tuaregs. In addition, special security units were to be established in the Kidal region. A two-day international forum on the development of Kidal, Gao and Tombouctou, which was held in March, resulted in a 10-year plan to undertake 39 projects at an estimated cost of 560,660m. francs CFA. In May at least 10 people, including two soldiers, were killed during an attack on a security post near the Algerian border by a group of armed men reportedly led by Bahanga; the attack was believed to have been prompted by a leadership dispute within the Tuareg movement ahead of the legislative elections scheduled for July.

EXTERNAL RELATIONS

In the 1990s the presence in neighbouring countries of large numbers of refugees from the conflict in northern Mali, and the attendant issue of border security, dominated Mali's regional relations. Although the process of repatriation of refugees was completed by mid-1998, the north of the country remains vulnerable to continuing insecurity and, particularly, to cross-border banditry. In May 1998 the interior ministers of Mali, Senegal and Mauritania met to strengthen co-operation and border controls, and in December Mali and Senegal decided to reinforce border security. Following a visit by

Konaré to Algiers in February 1999 Mali and Algeria also agreed to revive their joint border committee to promote development and stability in the region. In March Konaré visited Mauritania to discuss border security; however, in June a dispute over watering rights escalated into an armed conflict between neighbouring Malian and Mauritanian communities, in which 13 people were killed. The two Governments responded to the disturbances by increasing border patrols, and by sending a joint delegation to the villages involved. In August, at a meeting in Dakar, Senegal, the Malian, Mauritanian and Senegalese interior ministers agreed to establish an operational unit drawn from the police forces of the three countries in order to ensure security in the area of their joint border.

Renewed concerns about insecurity in the region arose in mid-2003, following reports, in July, that some 15 German, Swiss and Dutch tourists, who had purportedly been kidnapped in February in southern Algeria by Islamist militants belonging to the Groupe salafiste pour la prédication et le combat (GSPC), had been smuggled into Mali. Following negotiations with the kidnappers, conducted by a former rebel Tuareg leader, Iyad Ag Agaly, 14 hostages were released in August (the remaining hostage had reportedly died earlier from heatstroke). It was later reported that the German Government had paid a large ransom to secure their release. In October the Malian Minister of the Armed Forces and War Veterans, Mahamane Kalil Maïga, visited Algeria and met the Chief of Staff of the Algerian Army, Lt-Gen. Muhammad Lamari, to discuss security in the region. Some 30 US military instructors were dispatched to Mali in early 2004 to train troops in techniques to combat banditry and international terrorism. In March Mali announced that it was to increase anti-terrorism co-operation with the authorities in Algeria, Chad and Niger. Four Malian soldiers were reportedly injured in the north of Mali during clashes with the GSPC in April. The armed forces subsequently increased patrols in the area, and further fighting between the army and the GSPC, near the northern town of Enchay, was reported in late 2004. In December two aides to a member of the Qatari royal family were abducted by an armed gang near the Malian town of Lerneb, some 26 km from the border with Mauritania. The Malian armed forces succeeded in freeing the hostages after nine days, capturing five of the kidnappers and killing two others. A faction of the GSPC was thought to have been responsible for the kidnapping. Two Malians were subsequently convicted of abducting the Qatari nationals and sentenced, respectively, to 10 years' and life imprisonment.

In January 2005 the Presidents of Mali and Mauritania signed an agreement on military co-operation aimed at strengthening border security. Mali dispatched troops to the common border in June, in response to a request from the Mauritanian authorities for assistance in detaining the perpetrators of an attack on one of its military bases in which 15 soldiers had been killed. The GSPC claimed responsibility for the incident. Meanwhile, Mali was one of nine north and west African countries that participated in US-led military exercises aimed at increasing co-operation in combating cross-border banditry and terrorism in the region. In July the army chiefs of Mali, Algeria, Mauritania and Niger discussed security issues with a US military delegation at a meeting in Mauritania. In February 2006, during an official visit to Mauritania, President Touré held talks with Col Ely Ould Mohamed Vall, who had assumed the leadership of Mauritania, as President of a self-styled Military Council for Justice and Democracy, in August 2005. Touré expressed support for Vall's plans for democratic transition, and the two Presidents agreed to revive the process of demarcating the common border between their countries. In late 2006 some 300–350 Malian soldiers underwent training by the US military in northern Mali in counter-terrorism techniques and peace-keeping operations.

Mali was a founder member, with Libya, of the Community of Sahel-Saharan States, established in the Libyan capital, Tripoli, in 1997. In January 2005 more than 240 Malians were repatriated from Libya, mostly voluntarily. Apparently disillusioned with immigrant life, around 1,000 were reported to have registered with the Malian embassy in Tripoli for a voluntary repatriation programme. The Libyan Government was under increasing pressure from European governments to deter African migrants attempting to reach Europe. Nevertheless, relations between Mali and Libya remained close, and in April, during a visit to Tripoli, the Malian Minister of the Economy and Finance, Aboubacar Traoré, signed an agreement on co-operation with his Libyan counterpart.

In October 2005 more than 600 illegal migrants were repatriated to Mali from Morocco after attempting to enter Europe through the Spanish exclaves of Ceuta and Melilla. Following the reinforcement of security measures by the Moroccan authorities, hundreds of Malians sought a new route to Europe, by boat from Mauritania to Spain's Canary Islands, and around 350 were returned to Mali during March and April 2006. In January 2007 the EU announced plans to open a job centre in Mali as part of a new initiative aimed at promoting legal and temporary immigration from Africa; it was envisaged that the centre would provide training for would-be migrants and co-ordinate potential offers of employment from European countries.

The Government of France granted financial support for the recovery efforts that were necessary after March 1991, and promised continued aid for Mali's programme of economic adjustment. French financial assistance was also forthcoming for the implementation of the 'national pact' between the Malian Government and Tuareg movements. From mid-1996 a series of much-publicized expulsions from France of illegal immigrants, including Malians, was generally criticized in Mali. During a visit to Mali in December 1997 the French Prime Minister, Lionel Jospin, gave assurances that the mass expulsions by chartered aircraft would cease. Further progress was achieved in September 1998, with the establishment of a Franco-Malian joint committee on immigration, intended to promote co-operation on the repatriation of migrants and their reintegration into Malian society. Illegal immigration and the related issues of poverty and youth unemployment were the principal topics of discussion at the 23rd France-Africa summit, which was held in Mali in December 2005. A visit to Mali by the French Minister of State, Minister of the Interior and Land Management, Nicolas Sarkozy, in May 2006 proved controversial, as it followed immediately after the approval by the French Assemblée nationale of legislation proposed by Sarkozy on 'selective' immigration, which generally introduced stricter conditions for immigrants to France and favoured skilled migrants. A group of 21 Malian deputies issued a statement urging Sarkozy to cancel his visit, describing it as a provocation, and several hundred people marched in Bamako in protest against the new legislation and Sarkozy's arrival. According to the French Ministry of the Interior and Land Management, there were some 45,000 legal immigrants from Mali living in France, and a similar number of illegal Malian immigrants. The legislation was approved by the French Sénat in June. France continued to be Mali's principal source of bilateral economic assistance, and in July 2006 agreed to provide 200,000m. francs CFA for the period 2006–10.

Mali has, notably, contributed actively to UN peace-keeping forces, and has been prominent in efforts to establish an African military crisis-response force. In late 1996 and early 1997, moreover, Amadou Toumani Touré led a regional mediation effort to resolve the crisis in the CAR, and in February 1997 a Malian military contingent was dispatched to the CAR as part of a regional surveillance mission. Malian troops remained in the CAR, until February 2000, as part of the UN peace-keeping mission that succeeded the regional force in April 1998. In February 1999 488 Malian troops joined the ECOMOG peace-keeping forces of the Economic Community of West African States (ECOWAS) in Sierra Leone. In response to domestic criticism of this intervention, the Malian authorities emphasized that the troops would take on a purely peace-keeping role. In May, however, seven members of the Malian contingent were killed in fighting with rebel forces, provoking widespread indignation in Bamako, and demands for the withdrawal of Malian troops. In August 150 soldiers withdrew from Sierra Leone, and further withdrawals followed. As Chairman of ECOWAS, in March 2001 Konaré hosted a mini-summit, attended by the leaders of the three countries of the Mano River Union (Sierra Leone, Liberia and Guinea), in

Bamako on the subject of the peace process in Sierra Leone. In mid-2007 Malian military personnel were participating in UN peace-keeping missions in the Democratic Republic of the Congo, Liberia and Sudan.

Economy

CHARLOTTE VAILLANT

Based on an earlier article by EDITH HODGKINSON

Mali, the second largest country in francophone West Africa, is sparsely populated (with an estimated population of 12.3m. at mid-2007, representing an average density of 9.9 inhabitants per sq km) and land-locked, and most parts are desert or semi-desert, with the economically viable area confined to the Sahelian-Sudanese regions irrigated by the River Niger, which comprise about one-fifth of the total land area. The rate of economic growth in the three decades that followed independence was largely affected by drought, changes in the terms of international trade, as well as political instability. There were thus wide fluctuations in trends in real gross domestic product (GDP) from year to year. Overall, GDP increased at an annual rate of only 2.8% in the 1980s.

After a period of erratic progress in the early 1990s, stability and growth resumed. The stimulus to the agricultural sector that resulted from the 50% devaluation of the currency in January 1994 coincided with a marked increase in world commodity prices in that year. With the prospect of further expansion in exports of cotton (which accounted for about two-fifths of total export earnings in the mid-1990s) and gold (as new capacity came into production), Mali's immediate prospects for sustained economic growth were good. GDP grew, in real terms, by an annual average of 5.7% in 1996–99, as the agricultural sector prospered and public investment resumed. Nevertheless, in 2000 a decline of 3.2% was recorded, owing to a drought-induced fall in cereal production, an increase in the world price of petroleum, and the farmers' decision to boycott the cotton-growing season. In contrast with previous years, this growth figure was compiled using a new accounting methodology, under which agricultural production in the 2000/01 season was included in GDP for 2000 instead of GDP for 2001. In 2001 GDP increased, in real terms, by 12.1%, following a particularly abundant cotton harvest in the 2001/02 season. In 2002 buoyant activity in mining and cotton ginning helped to compensate for falling agricultural production and the impact of the crisis in Côte d'Ivoire on all sectors, especially services, with growth attaining 4.3%. Bumper cereal and cotton harvests increased growth to an exceptional 7.2% in 2003, according to the IMF. Growth declined to 2.4% in 2004, because of a decline in agricultural production resulting from below average rainfalls and the worst locust attack in 15 years. Growth recovered significantly in 2005, to 6.1%, and remained strong in 2006, at an estimated 4.6% (according to the IMF), as a result of improved agricultural performance and increased gold production. Despite improved policy performance in the last decade, Mali remains both highly vulnerable to external shocks and dependent on external funds. The country ranks among the world's poorest, with gross national income (GNI) per head equivalent to only some US $380 in 2005 according to the World Bank—less than that of Ghana and Nigeria, and considerably less than other West African countries such as Guinea and Senegal.

Mali adopted a very ambitious capital spending programme at independence, and state companies were established to operate the main sectors of the economy (including foreign trade, transport and mineral exploration). Most state enterprises were operating at a loss, however, and the simultaneous, and related, deterioration in the balance-of-payments situation led Mali, in 1967, to seek to rejoin the Franc Zone and the Union monétaire ouest-africaine (UMOA), from which it had withdrawn in 1962. This forced the regime of President Modibo Keita to adopt stringent austerity measures, one year before the regime was overthrown in 1968. The final stage in the return to financial integration with other francophone countries of the region came under Moussa Traoré in 1984, when Mali rejoined UMOA and readopted the CFA franc as its currency.

Beginning in 1981, the Government of Moussa Traoré, under pressure from the IMF, the World Bank and bilateral donors, undertook successive programmes of market liberalization and civil service reforms. The unpopularity of the austerity programme contributed to the downfall of Traoré in March 1991. Negotiations with the Bretton Woods institutions resumed following the 50% devaluation, in January 1994, of the CFA franc. The institutions agreed to provide some 207,000m. francs CFA in budgetary support for 1994–96. Continued financial support was subsequently secured under the Enhanced Structural Adjustment Facility (ESAF) of the IMF for 1996–99. Under the supervision of the World Bank and the IMF, Mali adjustment policies largely concentrated on macro-economic stabilization; fiscal consolidation and tax reform; the liberalization of price and trade policies; regulatory reform; and the reform of public enterprises and the agricultural sector. In August 1999 Mali was declared eligible for a further three-year ESAF arrangement (for the period 1999–2002), and qualified for concessionary debt relief under the Bretton Woods institutions' initiative for heavily indebted poor countries (HIPC). As a result of economic difficulties experienced by the Malian Government, particularly the problems in the cotton sector, the consequences of a drought in 2000 and the increase in petroleum prices, the duration of the Poverty Reduction and Growth Facility (PRGF, as the ESAF had been renamed) was extended until August 2003. The new Government formed following the election of Amadou Toumani Touré as President in June 2002 confirmed that it would continue to implement the requirements of the PRGF-supported programme, in addition to the demands of a poverty reduction strategy paper adopted by the former Government in the previous month. In June 2004 the IMF approved a new three-year PRGF, worth some US $13.7m., for Mali, with the three-year programme setting out new measures towards fiscal consolidation, privatization, and reforms in the cotton sector. In February 2007 the IMF announced an extension of Mali's PRGF from June 2007 to the end of October 2007.

Employment patterns have changed little since independence. Subsistence agriculture and livestock remain the dominant economic activity. There is still significant seasonal migration (during the agricultural off-season) to Côte d'Ivoire and Senegal, and some 3m. Malians are thought to work abroad, with France also an important host country. Wage employment is very low, and is concentrated in the state sector and in formal-sector businesses in Bamako. In 2003 the Government launched an employment action plan, with special attention to the youth.

AGRICULTURE

Agriculture and livestock dominate Mali's economy. In 2001 the primary sector engaged an estimated 79.9% of the total labour force. The primary sector contibuted 34.8% of GDP in 2004 and an estimated 35.3% in 2005, according to local sources, although its contribution to growth varies greatly from year to year. Rural development has long become one of the Government's main priorities, with aims to modernize activity in agriculture, livestock-rearing and fishing and bring more land under cultivation.

Agricultural exports, including processed crops (notably cotton) and livestock, account for about a third of Mali's total exports value, a share that has declined since the 1990s, as gold production picked up to become Mali's leading export. Further development is constrained by the inadequacy of the country's transport infrastructure for the movement of perishable goods over long distances. Pending the improvement of that infrastructure, the Government aims to promote the development of agro-industry in order to increase the proportion of processed goods among agricultural exports.

Millet and sorghum—two basic food crops—are essentially produced at subsistence level, although the output of cereals has recovered since the drought years of the early 1980s, and exportable surpluses were occasionally recorded in some years. In 1999 cereal output reached a record 2.9m. metric tons. However, largely as a result of inadequate rainfall, production declined to 2.3m. tons in 2000, before increasing to 2.6m. tons in 2001. A similar level, of 2.5m. tons, was recorded in 2002; in 2003 cereal production increased to reach some 2.9m. tons, owing to excellent growing conditions. Although cereal production remained above the last five years' average in 2004, at 2.8m. tons, despite the impact of lower rainfalls and the locust attack, the cereal import requirement (mostly wheat and rice) in that year was relatively high, at 257,000 tons. Favourable weather conditions contributed to a further recovery in cereal production, to 3.40m. tons in 2005 and an estimated 3,42m. tons in 2006.

Production of rice has increased steadily since the mid-1980s, partially because the area harvested has also increased markedly, from 135,275 ha in 1980 to 468,239 ha in 2001. Rice output totalled an estimated 907,000 metric tons in 2005, and is estimated to have increased by a further 8% in 2006, according to local sources. An important factor in the improvement in rice production has been the reform of the parastatal Office du Niger. This agency was originally established by the French colonial authorities to irrigate the Niger delta, mainly for the cultivation of cotton. For many years the agency operated at a substantial financial loss, with about one-third of its irrigated area remaining uncultivated. In 1986 a rehabilitation programme was initiated which aimed to rationalize the organization's management and to increase the total cultivable area to more than 100,000 ha, of which 46,730 ha were to be planted with rice. In 1988 a programme was inaugurated to improve the irrigation network for the cultivation of rice both on the Office du Niger land and in the inland delta of the Niger in the Ségou region. By 2002 the Office du Niger produced 427,807 tons of rice on 74,500 ha of cultivated land. In 2004 it is estimated to have harvested 458,240 tons of rice on 81,222 ha of cultivated land. There is considerable potential for the export of rice to regional markets, now that self-sufficiency has been achieved. According to FAO figures, 20,000 tons were exported in the marketing year 2005/06.

By far the most important cash crop is cotton. Mali was formerly the leading cotton producer in the Franc Zone but has latterly been replaced in this position by Burkina Faso. Mostly exported, cotton provides a livelihood for over 3m. people. Cultivation is in the southern region, by means of village co-operatives co-ordinated by the parastatal Compagnie Malienne pour le Développement des Textiles (CMDT), in which the French company Dagris holds a 40% interest. Following the 47% rise in the producer price that accompanied the 1994 devaluation of the CFA franc, output increased further, as strong international prices encouraged an expansion in the area cultivated, and a record seed cotton crop of 522,903 metric tons was recorded in 1997. Production declined subsequently, as lower world prices of cotton prompted some producers to plant cereal crops rather than cottonseed. Farmers boycotted cotton production in 2000, in protest against falling producer prices and the proposed restructuring of the CMDT. As a result, the recorded crop in that year fell to 242,772 tons—its lowest level for more than a decade. However, good climatic conditions and an increase in producer prices resulted in a significant recovery in 2001, when output increased to 571,335 tons, representing a new record. Cotton production fell to 439,800 tons in 2002, but rebounded to an exceptional 620,700 tons in 2003, as a result of higher world and farm-gate cotton prices and improved growing conditions. Cotton production fell back to 590,000 tons in 2004 and 534,100 tons in 2005, owing to less favourable growing conditions as well as declining world prices for cotton. It is estimated to have fallen to 428,000 tons in 2006, according to local sources, owing to unfavourable weather conditions. The Government has worked closely with the World Bank on reforms to liberalize the cotton sector. The privatization of the CMDT has been postponed repeatedly, however, and in 2005 the Government announced that the full liberalization of the sector—in particular the division of the CMDT into four regional companies—would not be implemented until 2008. In the mean time, the CMDT has successfully reduced its workforce, and has started to refocus on its core activities, by notably finding a domestic private-sector buyer for a majority stake in its cottonseed oil plant, the Huilerie Cotonnière du Mali (HUICOMA) in 2005. However, the CMDT continues to face financial difficulties, aggravated by the fall in cotton production, and in early 2007 the Government estimated the company's recapitalization needs at 44,000m. francs CFA. Mali, in association with Benin, Burkina Faso and Chad, lodged an official complaint with the World Trade Organization in September 2003, regarding the use of cotton subsidies by the US and by the European Union and the consequent dampening effect on world prices. The WTO has ruled in their favour and asked the US to eliminate its cotton subsidies, a measure that, if implemented, could be expected to result in a marked increase in world prices for cotton. Cotton exports in Mali contributed an estimated 150,000m. francs CFA in export earnings in 2005, equivalent to 25.7% of total exports.

Groundnut production, which reached 230,000 metric tons in 1976, declined sharply in the early 1980s, but recovered over the following decade, reaching 215,160 tons in 1994. However, production declined to just 134,129 tons in 1996 before increasing again, to a new record level, of 278,058 tons in 1999. Output thereafter fluctuated, averaging around 197,000 tons per year in 2000–2005. Groundnut production is estimated to have totalled 171,500 tons in 2006. Production is mainly for domestic consumption.

Livestock-raising accounts for about one third of the primary sector's contribution to GDP, and is the principal economic activity in the north. After cotton, livestock traditionally represented Mali's second highest recorded export, although gold has supplanted both agricultural exports since 2001; in the late 1990s livestock exports accounted for around 10% of all exports. Since 2002, however, earnings from livestock products (including leather and hides) have been affected by the crisis in Côte d'Ivoire, Mali's main export outlet for livestock. Livestock exports fell to 24,000m. francs CFA in 2003, representing 4.4% of all exports, and further declined to 22,900m. francs (4.7% of all exports) in 2004. Livestock numbers fell significantly during the droughts of the 1970s and early 1980s. Nevertheless, at 7.8m. cattle and 20.4m. sheep and goats (according to unofficial figures) in 2004, Mali's herd remained by far the largest in francophone West Africa. The droughts also tended to move livestock-rearing from the north to the south, where it is geared towards export to Côte d'Ivoire and Ghana.

In the early 1990s fishing on the River Niger produced an annual catch of about 65,000 metric tons, although this was more than doubled in 1995, and in each of the seven following years a catch in the region of 100,000 tons was landed. None the less, the sector remains very vulnerable to drought, to the effects of large-scale dam building on the upper reaches of the river, and to pollution from urban centres.

MINING AND POWER

Mining accounted for 7.2% of GDP in 2004 (compared with 8.6% in 2003) and an estimated 8.0% of GDP in 2005, according to local sources. Deposits of bauxite, copper, iron ore, manganese and uranium have been located but not yet exploited, largely because of the country's land-locked position and lack of infrastructure. Marble is mined at Bafoulabé, and phosphate rock at Gao, but by far the most important mineral currently being exploited is gold. In 2001 Mali became the third largest African producer of gold, after South Africa and Ghana, following the opening of the Morila field in late 2000 and the Yatela field in mid-2001 (see below). In 2001 gold production increased to some 53,658 kg, compared with production of 28,717 kg reported in 2000. Production increased further to

66,068 kg in 2002, before declining to 53,998 kg in 2003 and 44,585 kg in 2004, according to the Banque centrale des états de l'Afrique de l'ouest (BCEAO). Production recovered to 49,121 kg in 2005, largely as a result of accelerated production at Morila and the start of production at a new mine, Loulo, in November of that year. Gold output increased further in 2006, to 61,882 kg. In 2000, for the first time, gold was the principal source of Mali's export earnings, supplanting cotton; by 2002 gold accounted for 67.1% of exports, and has continued to represent an absolute majority of Mali's export trade in recent years.

Gold is generally exploited in open-cast mines, where production costs are extremely low; this has allowed most (but not all) foreign operators to withstand the decline in the world price of gold that occurred in the late 1990s. The Government has also begun to implement a programme for the development of the gold sector elaborated by the World Bank; a comprehensive topographical survey of potential gold reserves is also envisaged. In August 1999 a new mining code was adopted by the Malian Government, which it was hoped would increase foreign investment in the sector. The code limits the Government to a 20% stake in mining companies, and provides an improved legal framework for investment. Taxation of the sector was, however, increased, and new taxes were imposed on the sale, transfer and renewal of mining licences, while new requirements were also introduced in the areas of employment conditions, environmental protection, and worker safety.

An open-pit gold mine at Syama, in the south, was established in 1992 by a consortium led by BHP-Utah (which took 65% of the shares). Although gold production reached 6,200 kg in 1995, BHP sold its interest to Randgold of South Africa in mid-1996, citing operational difficulties and Syama's incompatibility with BHP's global corporate strategy. Randgold subsequently increased its stake to 80%. Lower international prices for gold and increased operating costs at the mine led Randgold to terminate operations at Syama in early 2001, although it was estimated that some 160,000 kg of gold remained at the mine. In 2004 Randgold sold its stake in the Syama gold mine to Resolute Mining of Australia; the redevelopment of this facility commenced in April 2007. One of Mali's largest gold-mining projects, Sadiola Hill, in the Kayes region—a joint venture between the Canadian operator IAMGOLD Corpn and AngloGold of South Africa—started operation in 1997. The mine enjoys relatively low operating costs; output peaked at 20,800 kg in 2001 before declining to 16,200 kg in 2002, 15,700 kg in 2003, 15,600 kg in 2004 and 12,600 kg in 2005. In 2006, however, gold output at Sadiola recovered to 14,200 kg.

Operations commenced at the Morila field, in the south-east, in November 2000, with an initial production of 3,500 kg; Morila is now Mali's largest operating gold mine and enjoys some of the lowest operating costs in the world. The mine is operated by a company jointly owned by Randgold, AngloGold (each of which owned a 40% share) and the Malian Government (with the remaining 20%). The mine was expected to yield an annual average output of 14,000 kg in 2002–12, but production of some 23,400 kg and 38,900 kg were recorded in 2001 and 2002, respectively. Production fell, however, to 28,600 kg in 2003 and 17,600 kg in 2004 owing to technical difficulties and a management dispute between AngloGold and Randgold. It recovered to 18,600 kg in 2005, before falling back to 14,700 kg in 2006, owing to a fall in ore grades and a reduction in the ore process capacity.

The first output of gold from a further mine, at Yatela, a joint venture between AngloGold and IAMGOLD, was reported in May 2001, with commercial production commencing two months later; total production of 43,500 kg was expected over a period of six years, with output of 5,000 kg and 8,600 kg reported in the years 2001 and 2002, respectively. Yatela's gold output remained stable at 8,600 kg in 2003 before declining to 8,100 kg in 2004 and 7,000 kg in 2005. It recovered, to 10,000 kg, in 2006. Operations at Randgold's Loulo deposit began in late 1999, while a new company, Société des Mines de Loulo (SOMILO), in which the Malian Government was to have a 20% share, was formed to exploit the Kodieran deposit. Production at Loulo mine started in November 2005 and production totalled around 6,900 kg in 2006. Other Australian, French, British, South African, Japanese, US and Canadian companies are active in both gold exploration and production. A Malian company, Wassoul'Or, is also planning to start production at the Yanfolia mine by the end of 2007. Prospecting for other mineral resources has also been conducted. In the mid-2000s a joint venture between Canada's Mink Minerals and Ashton Pty of Australia was investigating kimberlite pipes in the Kéniéba area of the south-west, in the hope of locating exploitable deposits of diamonds. By that time, however, petroleum had become by far the most promising mining activity in Mali. Prospecting activity increased in Mali, following the discovery of commercially viable petroleum reserves in neighbouring Mauritania in 2001. The petroleum code was revised in 2004 and in 2005, and, as of mid-2007, 15 prospecting licences have been awarded by the Government for the 25 designated petroleum blocks. Mali currently imports all of the petroleum it requires.

Mali suffers from a serious shortage of energy. According to the World Bank, only 7.6% of the population had access to electricity in 2004; in many areas there is no supply of electricity, and in others quantities were insufficient to meet the requirements of agriculture and the mining sector. The Government aims to expand electricity supply, notably in rural areas, while reducing the country's reliance on fuel wood. In November 2000 a 39% stake in the electricity utility, Electricité du Mali (EdM) was sold to SAUR International, a consortium of the French companies Bouygues and Energie de France; another 21% being owned by Industrial Promotion Services-West Africa (IPS) and 40% by the Malian Government. There were pledges to rehabilitate and expand the company's facilities and the Government ensured that EdM reduced electricity tariffs in 2003 and 2004. However, in October 2005 SAUR International announced it was withdrawing from EdM owing to an unresolved dispute with the Government. SAUR International's 39% share was subsequently divided between IPS and the Government, which became the majority stakeholder with a 66% share. The country generated an estimated 415 kWh of electricity in 2001, compared with 276 kWh in 1994. Roughly one-half of the electricity generated in 2001 was hydroelectric in origin, mostly provided by the Selingué facility on the Sankarani river, making it subject to drought. Nonetheless, the energy situation in Mali has improved since the Manantali project on the Senegal river began production in 2001. The operation of the Manantali dam (constructed at a cost of some US $600m.) was supervised by the Organisation pour la mise en valeur du fleuve Sénégal, in which both Mauritania and Senegal also participate. Mali has rights to receive 55% of the annual output of the hydroelectric plant (estimated at 800m. kWh). Construction of the dam was completed in 1988, but the installation of generating equipment was delayed by disagreements over supply routes, as well as the deterioration in relations between Mauritania and Senegal in 1989–90, so that the dam was not formally inaugurated until 1992. After further problems with funding and cross-border arrangements, Mali finally began to receive electricity generated at Manantali in December 2001. Manantali could eventually increase Mali's total installed capacity in electricity—which in 2005 comprised 31.4 MW held by EdM, and 19 MW held by various other plants, including CMDT and HUICOMA—by an additional 104 MW.

MANUFACTURING

Manufacturing activity is concentrated in Bamako, mainly taking the form of agricultural processing —according to the Organisation for Economic Co-operation and Development, the agro-industry represents around 45% of Mali's industrial activity and is dominated by HUICOMA—and the manufacture of construction materials and basic consumer goods. Manufacturing contributed 7.0% of GDP in 2003, according to the BCEAO, 11.0% of GDP in 2004 and an estimated 10.3% in 2005, according to local sources. According to the World Bank, manufacturing GDP declined at an average annual rate of 0.8% in 1995–2005. During the mid-1980s more than 75% of industrial turnover was accounted for by state companies, which operated nine of the 12 major food-sector plants—a legacy of the Keita era. The 40 parastatal bodies generally proved to be inefficient and unprofitable. Following the failure of successive governments to improve its performance, the sector has been substantially reorganized, under pressure from the IMF and other foreign creditors. The growth of the manufacturing sector has, however, been hindered by frequent energy shortage in recent years. Trends in manufacturing vary greatly from year to year, and in large part reflect activity in the cotton ginning sector. Prospects in manufacturing have nonetheless increased in recent years. The textile industry has started to expand following Mali's qualification to the US-sponsored African Growth Opportunity Act in December 2003; a new spinning factory, Fils et tissus naturels d'Afrique, was subsequently opened near Bamako, and the Industrie Textile du Mali, now renamed Bakary Textile Commerce et Industrie, re-opened under private ownership in 2005. The Chinese company, Covec, which already owned the formerly state-owned Compagnie Malienne des Textiles (COMATEX), expressed the intention of opening a further textile plant in the country. Other manufacturing activities in Mali include cement, sugar processing, and beverages production.

TRANSPORT

The early 1960s saw very substantial investment (one-fifth of total planned investment spending) in road-building, in particular after Mali's withdrawal from the Franc Zone in 1962 disrupted traditional trading outlets. Some 40 years later, road communications remain poor: of some 18,709 km of classified roads in 2004, only 3,370 km were paved. Mali's main access to the sea has historically been via the Bamako–Abidjan (Côte d'Ivoire) road, although, as a result of heightened instability in Côte d'Ivoire from late 2002, an increasing proportion of freight was diverted to other regional ports, including Tema (Ghana), Lomé (Togo) and Nouakchott (Mauritania). A number of construction and maintenance road projects have received significant funding from the European Development Fund (EDF), the World Bank, and the African Development Bank to help restore some of the vital links in the sub-region, notably Bamako–Dakar (Senegal) and Bamako–Accra (Ghana). An announced increase in the EU's development assistance for 2008–13, through the EDF, will benefit the transport sector, in particular road development. Some road sections, such as the Kayes–Kidira road in the west, have been completed. The donor-funded programme for the modernization of the transport infrastructure in Mali also aimed to rehabilitate a section of the very dilapidated 1,286-km rail link from Bamako to Dakar. In October 2003, a Franco-Canadian consortium, Canac-Getma, took over the concession to operate the railway from the state-owned Régie du chemin de fer du Mali. The Bamako–Dakar rail link is a particularly important one, as, even prior to the onset of conflict in Côte d'Ivoire, some 500,000 metric tons of Mali's freight had been transported by this route annually. Transrail, the company formed by Canac-Getma, has prioritized freight over passenger traffic in its first stage of development. As a result, freight carried increased from around 25,000 tons per month at late 2003 to around 55,000 tons per month at late 2004. Railway freight averaged an estimated 30,975 tons per month in the first eight months of 2006, according to local sources. Owing to the inadequacy of the road and rail facilities, the country's inland waterways are of great importance to the transport infrastructure. The River Niger is used for bulk transport during the rainy season, while traffic on the River Senegal was expected to improve as a result of the completion of measures associated with the Manantali hydro project. There is an international airport in Bamako, which is expected to be renovated through funding from the US Millennium Challenge Account (MCA)

FINANCE

In 1991 the new administration acknowledged that there was no feasible alternative to complete acceptance of IMF-prescribed policies, and further cuts in expenditure prevented any significant increase in the budget deficit (which had been equivalent to around 3.8% of GDP in 1991) in 1992 and 1993. However, in October 1993 the IMF and the World Bank qualified the Government's overall fiscal performance as unacceptable, and temporarily suspended all assistance to Mali until the CFA franc was devalued in January 1994. Under the 1996–99 ESAF, the fiscal deficit (excluding grants) was targeted to narrow to 7.7% of GDP by 1999; in the event, fiscal deficits (on a commitment basis, excluding grants) rose from 7.2% of GDP in 1997–98 to 8.1% of GDP in 1999. Including grants, the 1999 deficit was 61,500m. francs CFA, equivalent to 3.4% of GDP. The Government consolidated its fiscal position by introducing a single-rate value-added tax at 18%, and expanding the tax base in order to compensate for possible losses of revenue following the introduction of a common external tariff within UMOA on 1 January 2000.

In 2001 the overall budget deficit of Mali was 88,000m. francs CFA, equivalent to 4.0% of GDP, if grants, net lending and HIPC initiative spending were included, or 165,400m. francs CFA (7.5% of GDP) if these factors were excluded. In 2002 the budget deficit (including grants, net lending and HIPC initiative spending) was 114,700m. francs CFA (5.0% of GDP), or 174,500m. francs CFA (7.6% of GDP) if those factors were excluded. Fiscal consolidation continued under the new regime. Focus also turned towards improving the management and prioritization of public expenditures, as the country started to receive HIPC-related debt relief funds, to be allocated towards priority social sectors. The Government exceeded its fiscal target in 2003, with the deficit (excluding grants) falling to 147,200m. francs CFA, (5.7% of GDP), or 32,500. francs CFA, equivalent to 1.3% of GDP if these factors were included. This was largely explained by an improvement in tax collection and higher taxes in the mining sector; in addition, the rise in investment outlays was lower than envisaged, as a result of administrative bottlenecks. In 2004 overall fiscal performance remained good. The budget deficit (excluding grants) rose to 171,200. francs CFA (6.6% of GDP), or 67,900. francs CFA (2.6% of GDP), including grants, in that year, as a result of increased spending in priority sectors and a 14.6% rise in civil servants' salaries, higher public investment and lending to the CMDT. Tax on petroleum products was meanwhile reduced to cushion the impact of rising fuel prices on consumers. The bulk of the deficit was financed through grants and concessionary lending. Preliminary estimates from the IMF showed an increased budget deficit of 7.3% of GDP (excluding grants) in 2005, resulting mainly from a higher wage bill and the Government's decision to increase cotton producer prices. In 2006 continued efforts by the Government to widen the tax base, improve fiscal administration and reduce tax exemptions were expected to contribute to an increase in revenue; however, increased social and election-related expenditure (in preparation for the 2007 presidential and legislative elections) were estimated to have contributed to an increase of the fiscal deficit, to 8.7% of GDP.

FOREIGN TRADE AND PAYMENTS

Mali's trade deficit has been greatly reduced since the early 1970s, when exports typically represented only six months of imports. Significantly lower deficits were recorded annually in 1986–91, as rising sales of gold and an increase in the volume of cotton exports helped to offset weaknesses in international prices for these commodities while imports showed only modest growth. Devaluation also had a beneficial impact on the trade balance in 1994. Export earnings were boosted in the late 1990s by the sharp increase in cotton production (in response to much higher local prices), by higher demand from Côte d'Ivoire for Malian livestock, and by enhanced gold production. Import spending, meanwhile, remained contained as a result of higher prices, tight management of demand and improved domestic food supply. In 1997 Mali recorded a visible trade surplus of US $9.1m. owing, largely, to the tripling of gold exports in that year. The trade balance returned to a small deficit in 1999 and 2000, owing to falling terms of trade. In 2001 a very substantial increase in gold export earnings helped to compensate for a smaller decline in those from cotton with the trade deficit reduced to $9.6m. The trade balance turned positive in 2002, at $162.7m., as cotton exports were boosted by a recovery in the international price and bumper harvests, which helped to compensate for lower exports to other countries of the region associated with the onset of conflict in Côte d'Ivoire. Rising international prices for gold and cotton, combined with the strengthening of the franc CFA against the US dollar, helped to finance the petroleum-import bill in 2003. None the less, the trade balance recorded a deficit of $60.5m. in 2003, because of lower gold exports in volume terms and higher imports in capital goods. Similar trends were recorded in 2004, with the trade deficit widening to 62,000m. francs CFA (equivalent to $89m.), according to the IMF. Despite increased gold exports in 2005, higher oil-related imports contributed to a widening of the trade deficit, to an estimated 65,000m. francs CFA francs (equivalent to $132.2m.). In 2006, although imports remained strong, a dramatic increase in gold exports—reflecting rising gold production and high international prices—resulted in the trade balance moving to a surplus, projected by the IMF at 28,000m. CFA francs (equivalent to $53.5m.).

Mali's services balance has traditionally recorded a structural deficit, as a result of high transport costs and interest repayments on external debt. Grant inflows, but also emigrants' remittances have helped to fill the financing gap in most years. In 2003 net private and official transfers amounted to 53,200m. francs CFA and 67,400m. francs CFA, respectively, according to IMF sources. They declined to 50,600m. francs CFA and 51,400m. francs CFA, respectively, in 2004, before recovering in 2005, to an estimated 58,000m. francs CFA and 60,000m. francs CFA, respectively. Net private and official transfers were projected to fall back slight to 55,000m. francs CFA and 53,000m. francs CFA in 2006, respectively, according to the IMF. Workers' remittances often go unrecorded; although evidence points to a decline since the onset of unrest in Côte d'Ivoire in 2002, where, prior to that time an estimated 2m. Malians worked. The current account deficit (including official transfers) in 2003 was 156,800m. francs CFA (6.1% of GDP) and 216,200m. francs CFA in 2004 (8.3% of GDP). The deficit narrowed to 199,000m. francs CFA (7% of GDP) in 2005 and was projected by the IMF to narrow further in 2006, to 185,000m. francs CFA (5.9% of GDP), owing mainly to an improvement in the trade balance. This was more than financed by concessionary lending and debt relief.

Overseas development assistance inflows peaked at US $541.3m. in 1995 and averaged $389.2m. per year in 1996–2001. All donors disbursed a total of $542.8m. in 2003 and $567.4m. in 2004. France, in particular, has maintained a high level of support for the structural adjustment programme, in the form of budgetary grants as well as loans and debt relief. Total aid from France amounted to $81.5m. in 2004, up from $69.9m. in 2003.

In October 1988, following agreement with the IMF on a programme of economic adjustment, Mali became the first debtor country to benefit from a system of exceptional debt relief that had been agreed in principle at that year's summit meeting of industrialized nations, held in Toronto, Canada. In addition, Mali was one of 35 countries whose official debt to France (equivalent to US $240m.) was cancelled at the beginning of 1990. None the less, external debt, which reached $2,468m. by the end of 1990, continued to represent a substantial burden. The debt-service ratio in that year was reduced to a tolerable level—12.3%—only because of the non-payment of some obligations. The 'Paris Club' of Western official creditors agreed in November 1992 to a further round of rescheduling. However, with debt at the end of 1993 equivalent to 108% of GNI, Mali was a prime candidate for the special measures of debt relief that followed the 50% devaluation of the CFA franc in January 1994. Major bilateral aid sources, led by France, cancelled a proportion of debt and rescheduled repayments. Following the approval of a further three-year ESAF allowance in April 1996, further debt relief was granted by Mali's external creditors in May of that year, under the 'Naples terms', although only a small proportion of Mali's debt was deemed eligible, and the net benefit to Mali was estimated to have been around $50m.

In September 2000 the IMF and the World Bank announced that Mali was to receive some US $220m. in debt-service relief under their original HIPC initiative (for which Mali had been deemed eligible in 1998) and a further $650m. under an enhanced framework. Mali reached completion point in March 2003, when full debt relief started. According to the World Bank, Mali's total external debt amounted to $3,320m. at the end of 2004, which was equivalent to 71% of GNI. Mali's total external debt stock fell to $2,969m. at the end of 2005, represented 58.5% of GNI. The annual cost of servicing the debt was equivalent to 5.8% of the value of exports of goods and services in 2003 and 7.3% in 2004. In the medium term, Mali will remain highly dependent on inflows of aid to underpin the budget and to compensate the funding shortfall on the current account. In June 2005 Mali was among 18 countries to be granted 100% debt relief under the Multilateral Debt Relief Initiative agreed by the Group of Eight leading industrialized nations (G-8). The IMF, the African Development Bank and the World Bank subsequently announced debt write-offs worth around 2,000m., contributing to a significant fall in Mali's external debt stock.

Statistical Survey

Source (unless otherwise stated): Direction Nationale de la Statistique et de l'Informatique, rue Archinard, porte 233, BP 12, Bamako; tel. 222-24-55; fax 222-71-45; e-mail cnpe.mali@afribonemali.net; internet www.dnsi.gov.ml.

Area and Population

AREA, POPULATION AND DENSITY

Area (sq km)	1,240,192*
Population (census results)†	
1–30 April 1987	7,696,348
17 April 1998	
Males	4,847,436
Females	4,943,056
Total	9,790,492
Population (UN estimates at mid-year)‡	
2004	11,265,000
2005	11,611,000
2006	11,968,000
Density (per sq km) at mid-2006	9.7

* 478,841 sq miles.

† Figures are provisional and refer to the *de jure* population.

‡ Source: UN, *World Population Prospects: The 2006 Revision*.

Ethnic Groups (percentage of total, 1995): Bambara 36.5; Peul 13.9; Sénoufo 9.0; Soninké 8.8; Dogon 8.0; Songhaï 7.2; Malinké 6.6; Diola 2.9; Bobo and Oulé 2.4; Tuareg 1.7; Moor 1.2; Others 1.8 (Source: La Francophonie).

ADMINISTRATIVE DIVISIONS

(*de jure* population at 1998 census, provisional figures)

District		Mopti	1,475,274
Bamako	1,016,167	Kayes	1,372,019
Regions		Tombouctou	461,956
Sikasso	1,780,042	Gao	397,516
Ségou	1,679,201	Kidal	42,479
Koulikoro	1,565,838		

PRINCIPAL TOWNS*
(*de jure* population at 1998 census, provisional figures)

Bamako (capital)	1,016,167	Koutiala	74,153
Sikasso	113,813	Kayes	67,262
Ségou	90,898	Gao	54,903
Mopti	79,840	Kati	49,756

* With the exception of Bamako, figures refer to the population of communes (municipalities).

Mid-2005 ('000, incl. suburbs, UN estimate): Bamako 1,368 (Source: UN, *World Urbanization Prospects: The 2005 revision*).

BIRTHS AND DEATHS
(annual averages, UN estimates)

	1990–95	1995–2000	2000–05
Birth rate (per 1,000)	51.6	51.2	48.6
Death rate (per 1,000)	19.3	18.1	16.4

Source: UN, *World Population Prospects: The 2006 Revision*.

Expectation of life (years at birth, WHO estimates): 46 (males 44; females 47) in 2004 (Source: WHO, *World Health Report*).

ECONOMICALLY ACTIVE POPULATION
('000 persons, 2004, estimates)

	Males	Females	Total
Agriculture, hunting and forestry	657.7	291.7	949.4
Fishing	33.3	2.0	35.2
Mining	8.4	3.0	11.4
Manufacturing	136.1	136.4	272.5
Electricity, gas and water	5.1	—	5.1
Construction	97.5	4.7	102.1
Wholesale and retail trade; repair of motor vehicles, motorcycles and personal household goods	266.1	402.1	668.1
Hotels and restaurants	1.4	6.3	7.6
Transport, storage and communications	51.8	3.5	55.3
Financial Intermediation	4.4	—	4.4
Real estate	3.5	0.6	4.0
Public administration	33.3	6.6	39.9
Education	35.6	18.3	53.9
Health and social work	11.4	9.5	20.9
Other social services	42.6	97.5	140.1
Total employed	1,388.3	982.5	2,370.8
Unemployed	107.0	120.5	227.4
Total labour force	1,495.3	1,103.0	2,598.2

Source: ILO.

Mid-2005 (estimates in '000): Agriculture, etc. 4,978; Total labour force 6,378 (Source: FAO).

Health and Welfare

KEY INDICATORS

Total fertility rate (children per woman, 2005)	6.8
Under-5 mortality rate (per 1,000 live births, 2005)	218
HIV/AIDS (% of persons aged 15–49, 2005)	1.7
Physicians (per 1,000 head, 2004)	0.08
Hospital beds (per 1,000 head, 1998)	0.24
Health expenditure (2004): US $ per head (PPP)	54.0
Health expenditure (2004): % of GDP	6.6
Health expenditure (2004): public (% of total)	49.2
Access to water (% of persons, 2004)	50
Access to sanitation (% of persons, 2004)	46
Human Development Index (2004): ranking	175
Human Development Index (2004): value	0.338

For sources and definitions, see explanatory note on p. vi.

Agriculture

PRINCIPAL CROPS
('000 metric tons)

	2003	2004	2005
Rice (paddy)	931.9	718.1	945.8
Maize	451.0	459.5	634.5
Millet	1,260.5	974.7	1,157.8
Sorghum	728.7	664.1	629.1
Fonio	22.4	19.7	26.6
Sweet potatoes	103.9	49.2	133.1
Cassava (Manioc)	24.2*	13.5	56.1
Yams	31.0	12.4	47.8
Sugar cane	336.0	348.0	348.0
Groundnuts (in shell)	214.7	161.0	279.5
Karité nuts (Sheanuts)*	85	85	n.a.
Cottonseed	311.1	309.2	311.0
Tomatoes	52.0	47.9	64.6
Dry onions	24.9	23.1	34.9
Guavas, mangoes and mangosteens	60.4	54.8*	61.4
Cotton (lint)	259.7	239.7	250.4†

* FAO estimate(s).
† Unofficial figure.

Source: FAO.

LIVESTOCK
('000 head, year ending September)

	2003	2004	2005
Cattle	7,312	7,500	7,682
Sheep	7,967*	8,364*	8,403
Goats	11,464*	12,036*	12,000
Pigs	68	68	69
Horses†	170	172	172
Asses, mules or hinnies†	700	720	720
Camels†	470	472	472
Chickens	29,000	30,000	31,000†

* Unofficial figure.
† FAO estimate(s).

Source: FAO.

LIVESTOCK PRODUCTS
('000 metric tons, FAO estimates)

	2003	2004	2005
Cattle meat	113.0	97.8	97.8
Sheep meat	33.8	36.0	36.0
Goat meat	46.0	48.5	48.5
Chicken meat	33.6	34.8	36.0
Game meat	18.0	18.0	18.0
Pig meat	2.2	2.2	2.2
Cows' milk	179.3	183.8	188.7
Sheep's milk	117.0	124.5	126.0
Goats' milk	227.0	238.3	238.6
Camels' milk	54.9	55.2	55.2

Source: FAO.

Forestry

ROUNDWOOD REMOVALS
('000 cubic metres, excl. bark, FAO estimates)

	2003	2004	2005
Sawlogs, veneer logs and logs for sleepers	4	4	4
Other industrial wood	409	409	409
Fuel wood	4,905	4,965	5,027
Total	5,318	5,378	5,440

Source: FAO.

SAWNWOOD PRODUCTION
('000 cubic metres, incl. railway sleepers)

	1987	1988	1989
Total (all broadleaved)	11	13	13*

* FAO estimate.

1990–2005: Annual production as in 1989 (FAO estimates).

Source: FAO.

Fishing

('000 metric tons, live weight)

	2000	2001*	2002*
Capture	109.9	100.0	100.0
Nile tilapia	33.0	30.0	30.0
Elephantsnout fishes	7.7	7.0	7.0
Characins	5.5	5.0	5.0
Black catfishes	4.4	4.0	4.0
North African catfish	27.5	25.0	25.0
Nile perch	6.6	6.0	6.0
Other freshwater fishes	25.3	23.0	23.0
Aquaculture	0.0	0.5	1.0
Total catch	109.9	100.5	101.0

* FAO estimates.

2003–05 (FAO estimates): Data assumed to be unchanged from 2002.

Source: FAO.

Mining

(metric tons, unless otherwise indicated, estimates)

	2003	2004	2005
Gold (kg)	45,535	37,911	44,230
Gypsum	500	300	300
Salt	6,000	6,000	6,000

Source: US Geological Survey.

Industry

SELECTED PRODUCTS
('000 metric tons, unless otherwise indicated)

	1999	2000	2001
Raw sugar*	31.2†	29.1	28.0
Salted, dried or smoked fish*	6.4	8.0	7.9
Cigarettes ('000 packets)	51.4	n.a.	n.a.
Cement‡	10	10	n.a.
Electric energy (million kWh)§	404	412	415

* Data from FAO.
† Unofficial figure.
‡ Data from the US Geological Survey.
§ Provisional or estimated figures.

2002: Electric energy 417m. kWh (estimate); Raw sugar ('000 metric tons) 32.0 (Data from FAO).

Source: mainly UN, *Industrial Commodity Statistics Yearbook*.

Finance

CURRENCY AND EXCHANGE RATES

Monetary Units
100 centimes = 1 franc de la Communauté financière africaine (CFA).

Sterling, Dollar and Euro Equivalents (31 May 2007)
£1 sterling = 964.116 francs CFA;
US $1 = 487.592 francs CFA;
€1 = 655.957 francs CFA;
10,000 francs CFA = £10.37 = $20.51 = €15.24.

Average Exchange Rate (francs CFA per US $)
2004 528.29
2005 527.47
2006 522.89

Note: An exchange rate of 1 French franc = 50 francs CFA, established in 1948, remained in force until January 1994, when the CFA franc was devalued by 50%, with the exchange rate adjusted to 1 French franc = 100 francs CFA. This relationship to French currency remained in effect with the introduction of the euro on 1 January 1999. From that date, accordingly, a fixed exchange rate of €1 = 655.957 francs CFA has been in operation.

BUDGET
('000 million francs CFA)*

Revenue†	2002	2003	2004
Budgetary revenue	354.7	397.6	422.3
Tax revenue	323.5	362.4	403.6
Taxes on net income and profits	45.1	63.0	68.6
Enterprises	13.8	31.9	32.2
Individuals	28.4	29.3	34.5
Payroll tax	6.5	9.7	7.9
Taxes on goods and services	72.0	70.0	89.3
Value-added tax	42.9	48.1	66.8
Taxes on international trade	180.4	194.1	218.2
Customs duties	42.8	45.0	51.5
Value-added tax on imports	83.8	91.3	111.5
Petroleum import duties	30.2	33.7	30.3
Other tax revenue	19.3	25.0	19.4
Stamp duties	9.9	11.9	12.4
Other current revenue	31.2	35.2	18.7
Special funds and annexed budgets	33.7	37.4	42.6
Total	388.4	435.0	464.9

Expenditure‡	2002	2003	2004
Budgetary expenditure	511.7	535.5	592.2
Current expenditure	308.7	316.3	350.0
Wages and salaries	93.5	106.2	121.7
Goods and services	109.0	107.6	136.5
Transfers and subsidies	87.8	83.8	74.5
Interest payments (scheduled)	18.4	18.8	17.2
Capital expenditure	203.1	219.2	242.2
Externally financed	140.3	140.9	152.8
Special funds and annexed budgets	33.7	37.4	42.6
Total	545.4	572.9	634.8

* Figures represent a consolidation of the central government budget, special funds and annexed budgets.
† Excluding grants received ('000 million francs CFA): 85.8 in 2002; 114.8 in 2003; 103.3 in 2004.
‡ Excluding net lending ('000 million francs CFA): –4.9 in 2002; –3.9 in 2003; –9.0 in 2004.

Source: IMF, *Mali: Statistical Appendix* (March 2006).

INTERNATIONAL RESERVES
(excluding gold, US $ million at 31 December)

	2004	2005	2006
IMF special drawing rights	0.6	0.3	0.1
Reserve position in IMF	13.9	13.1	14.1
Foreign exchange	846.2	841.2	955.4
Total	860.7	854.6	969.5

Source: IMF, *International Financial Statistics*.

MONEY SUPPLY
('000 million francs CFA at 31 December)

	2004	2005	2006
Currency outside banks	275.4	344.9	344.4
Demand deposits	294.1	297.1	349.8
Total money (incl. others)	569.7	642.4	694.5

Source: IMF, *International Financial Statistics*.

COST OF LIVING
(Consumer Price Index for Bamako: base: 2000 = 100)

	2004	2005	2006
Food, beverages and tobacco	103.3	115.1	114.6
Clothing	99.5	96.3	n.a.
Housing, water, electricity and gas	110.1	107.5	n.a.
All items (incl. others)	105.6	112.3	114.1

Source: ILO.

NATIONAL ACCOUNTS
('000 million francs CFA at current prices)

Expenditure on the Gross Domestic Product

	2001	2002	2003
Final consumption expenditure	1,887.8	1,916.2	2,038.8
Households; Non-profit institutions serving households	1,541.5	1,548.1	1,654.9
General government	346.3	368.1	383.9
Gross capital formation	540.2	425.0	614.1
Gross fixed capital formation	420.6	439.5	446.8
Changes in inventories; Acquisitions, less disposals, of valuables	119.6	−14.5	167.3
Total domestic expenditure	2,428.0	2,341.2	2,652.9
Exports of goods and services	642.3	727.9	674.8
Less Imports of goods and services	847.4	766.2	833.6
GDP in market prices	2,222.9	2,302.9	2,494.1

GDP in market prices ('000 million francs CFA at current prices): 2,517.1 in 2004; 2,699.3 in 2005.

Source: IMF, *International Financial Statistics*.

Gross Domestic Product by Economic Activity

	2001	2002	2003
Agriculture, livestock-rearing, forestry and fishing	774.1	740.3	924.9
Mining	206.4	238.8	196.1
Manufacturing	127.3	171.0	158.1
Electricity, gas and water	30.2	36.6	42.8
Construction and public works	110.8	118.5	119.7
Trade	92.4	96.6	111.0
Transport, storage and communications	153.8	161.8	168.0
Non-market services	232.4	249.1	259.6
Other services	301.6	273.6	290.5
Sub-total	2,029.0	2,086.3	2,270.7
Import duties	183.0	211.2	223.7
GDP in purchasers' values	2,212.0	2,297.5	2,494.4

Source: Banque centrale des états de l'Afrique de l'ouest.

BALANCE OF PAYMENTS
(US $ million)

	2003	2004	2005
Exports of goods f.o.b.	927.8	976.4	1,100.9
Imports of goods f.o.b.	−988.3	−1,092.9	−1,245.5
Trade balance	−60.5	−116.4	−144.6
Exports of services	224.3	241.1	274.3
Imports of services	−482.2	−531.8	−588.0
Balance on goods and services	−318.5	−407.1	−458.3
Other income received	21.3	24.0	67.7
Other income paid	−181.2	−218.8	−274.7
Balance on goods, services and income	−478.4	−601.9	−665.3
Current transfers received	265.5	251.3	286.0
Current transfers paid	−58.1	−58.3	−58.5
Current balance	−271.0	−409.0	−437.7
Capital account (net)	113.7	151.4	148.9
Direct investment abroad	−1.4	−0.8	−34.7
Direct investment from abroad	132.3	101.0	223.8
Portfolio investment assets	−27.1	−3.2	−18.0
Portfolio investment liabilities	27.6	0.6	2.9
Other investment assets	3.7	−130.9	−109.2
Other investment liabilities	153.7	133.5	232.9
Net errors and omissions	45.2	−26.3	6.6
Overall balance	176.5	−184.0	15.5

Source: IMF, *International Financial Statistics*.

External Trade

PRINCIPAL COMMODITIES
('000 million francs CFA)

Imports c.i.f.	2002	2003	2004*
Foodstuffs	82.7	86.8	114.6
Cereals	27.1	28.7	17.1
Sugar	19.9	20.7	10.2
Petroleum products	112.9	108.6	224.2
Construction materials	79.7	85.5	101.2
Chemical products	129.2	122.2	116.7
Textiles and leather	19.3	20.2	12.1
Total (incl. others)	640.0	564.3	823.8

Exports f.o.b.	2002	2003	2004*
Cotton	158.0	144.3	184.2
Cotton fibre	155.4	140.9	181.4
Livestock	27.3	24.0	22.9
Gold	400.0	326.8	270.4
Total (incl. others)	596.5	503.8	484.7

* Estimates.

Source: IMF, *Mali: Statistical Appendix* (March 2006).

SELECTED TRADING PARTNERS
(US $ million)

Imports	2002	2003	2004
Belgium	32.4	32.0	49.2
China, People's Repub.	37.1	31.6	34.5
Côte d'Ivoire	197.5	107.6	141.3
France	192.1	234.1	268.8
Germany	54.4	54.9	73.7
India	27.7	42.4	29.6
Senegal	92.5	117.8	182.4
South Africa	19.3	25.6	63.0
USA	12.2	34.3	47.4
Total (incl. others)	1,382.7	1,523.1	1,857.6

Exports	2002	2003	2004
Belgium	5.1	n.a.	n.a.
China, People's Repub.	1.7	25.8	103.3
Côte d'Ivoire	1.8	0.1	0.1
France	6.5	7.7	7.4
Germany	8.5	7.3	16.5
India	14.0	25.8	15.5
Indonesia	3.8	4.1	7.3
Italy	16.9	16.1	22.4
Korea, Repub.	3.6	2.2	1.2
Spain	8.4	n.a.	n.a.
Thailand	23.9	30.0	22.7
Tunisia	3.2	4.8	2.3
United Kingdom	4.8	n.a.	n.a.
Total (incl. others)	162.3	214.5	326.7

Source: mostly IMF, *Mali: Statistical Appendix* (March 2006).

Transport

RAILWAYS
(traffic)

	1999	2000	2001
Passengers ('000)	778.7	682.3	649.0
Freight carried ('000 metric tons)	535	438	358

Passenger-km (million): 210 in 1999.

Freight ton-km (million): 241 in 1999.

ROAD TRAFFIC
(motor vehicles in use, estimates)

	1994	1995	1996
Passenger cars	24,250	24,750	26,190
Lorries and vans	16,000	17,100	18,240

1998 (motor vehicles in use): Passenger cars 29,374; Total road vehicles 47,374.

Source: IRF, *World Road Statistics*.

CIVIL AVIATION
(traffic on scheduled services)*

	1999	2000	2001
Kilometres flown (million)	3	3	1
Passengers carried ('000)	84	77	46
Passenger-km (million)	235	216	130
Total ton-km (million)	36	32	19

* Including an apportionment of the traffic of Air Afrique.

Source: UN, *Statistical Yearbook*.

Communications Media

	2003	2004	2005
Telephones ('000 main lines in use)	60.9	74.9	75.0
Mobile cellular telephones ('000 subscribers)	244.9	400.0	869.6
Personal computers ('000 in use)	25	42	45
Internet users ('000)	35	50	60

Source: International Telecommunication Union.

Television receivers ('000 in use): 160 in 2000 (Source: UNESCO, *Statistical Yearbook*).

Radio receivers ('000 in use): 570 in 1997 (Source: UNESCO, *Statistical Yearbook*).

Daily newspapers (national estimates): 3 (total circulation 12,350 copies) in 1997; 3 (total circulation 12,600) in 1998 (Source: UNESCO Institute for Statistics).

Book production: 14 titles (28,000 copies) in 1995 (first editions only, excluding pamphlets); 33 in 1998 (Sources: UNESCO, *Statistical Yearbook*, UNESCO Institute for Statistics).

Tourism

FOREIGN VISITORS BY NATIONALITY*

	2003	2004	2005
Austria	636	1,167	2,175
Belgium, Luxembourg and the Netherlands	9,046	6,591	9,002
Canada	3,280	3,543	3,646
France	27,047	37,971	37,851
Germany	3,200	3,676	5,885
Italy	11,570	6,087	7,066
Japan	1,200	3,117	2,090
Middle Eastern states	2,712	1,524	1,064
Scandinavian states	2,728	800	1,964
Spain	4,692	4,322	7,069
Switzerland	1,345	1,236	2,384
United Kingdom	1,752	560	5,180
USA	6,113	8,951	9,641
West African states	19,000	21,993	23,972
Total (incl. others)	110,365	112,654	142,814

* Arrivals at hotels and similar establishments.

Receipts from tourism (US $ million, incl. passenger transport): 136 in 2003; 148 in 2004; n.a. in 2005.

Source: World Tourism Organization.

Education

(2003/04, unless otherwise indicated)

			Students ('000)		
	Institutions*	Teachers	Males	Females	Total
Pre-primary	212	1,503†	16.1†	15.7†	31.8†
Primary	2,871	26,737	794.5	602.3	1,396.8
Secondary	n.a.	8,274‡	251.0	146.6	397.6
Tertiary	n.a.	975	17.7	8.1	25.8

* 1998/99.

† 2002/03.

‡ 1999/2000.

Source: mainly UNESCO Institute for Statistics.

2004/05: *University of Bamako*: 32,609 students (Source: Office of the Secretary-General of the Government, Bamako).

2005/06: *Pre-primary*: 412 institutions; 1,510 teachers; 51,071 students; *Primary and Secondary (lower)*: 8,079 institutions; 39,109 teachers; 1,990,765 students (1,137,787 males, 852,978 females); *Secondary (higher)*: 121 institutions; 1,904 teachers; 47,279 students (31,724 males, 15,555 females—estimates); *Secondary (technical and vocational)*: 119 institutions; 41,137 students; *Secondary (teacher training)*: 10,467 students (Source: Office of the Secretary-General of the Government, Bamako).

Adult literacy rate (UNESCO estimates): 19.0% (males 26.7%; females 11.9%) in 1995–99 (Source: UN Development Programme, *Human Development Report*).

Directory

The Constitution

The Constitution of the Third Republic of Mali was approved in a national referendum on 12 January 1992. The document upholds the principles of national sovereignty and the rule of law in a secular, multi-party state, and provides for the separation of the powers of the executive, legislative and judicial organs of state.

Executive power is vested in the President of the Republic, who is Head of State and is elected for five years by universal adult suffrage. The President appoints the Prime Minister, who, in turn, appoints other members of the Council of Ministers.

Legislative authority is exercised by the unicameral 147-member Assemblée nationale, which is elected for five years by universal adult suffrage.

The Constitution guarantees the independence of the judiciary. Final jurisdiction in constitutional matters is vested in a Constitutional Court.

The rights, freedoms and obligations of Malian citizens are enshrined in the Constitution. Freedom of the press and of association are guaranteed.

The Government

HEAD OF STATE

President: Gen. (retd) AMADOU TOUMANI TOURÉ (took office 8 June 2002; re-elected 29 April 2007).

COUNCIL OF MINISTERS
(August 2007)

Prime Minister: OUSMANE ISSOUFI MAÏGA.

Minister of the Environment and Decontamination: NANCOUMA KÉITA.

Minister of Planning and Territorial Development: MARIMATIA DIARRA.

Minister of Stockbreeding and Fisheries: OUMAR IBRAHIMA TOURÉ.

Minister of Crafts and Tourism: BAH N'DIAYE.

Minister of National Education: MAMADOU LAMINE TRAORÉ.

Minister of Industry and Trade: CHOGUEL KOKALA MAÏGA.

Minister of Territorial Administration and Local Communities: Gen. KAFOUGOUNA KONÉ.

Minister of Foreign Affairs and International Co-operation: MOKTAR OUANE.

Minister of Malians Abroad and African Integration: OUMAR HAMADOUN DICKO.

Minister of Agriculture: SEYDOU TRAORÉ.

Minister of Communication and New Information Technologies: GAOUSSOU DRABO.

Minister of Mining, Energy and Water Resources: AHMED DIANE SEMEGA.

Minister of Culture: CHEICK OUMAR SISSOKO.

Minister of Social Development, Solidarity and the Elderly: DJIBRIL TANGARA.

Minister of the Economy and Finance: ABOUBACAR TRAORÉ.

Minister of the Civil Service, the Reform of the State and Relations with the Institutions: BADI OULD GANFOUD.

Minister of Employment and Professional Training: BÂ AWA KÉÏTA.

Minister of the Promotion of Investment and of Small and Medium-sized Enterprises, Government Spokesperson: OUSMANE THIAM.

Minister for the Promotion of Women, Children and the Family: DIALLO M'BODJI SÈNE.

Minister of Defence and Veterans: MAMADOU CLAZIÉ SISSOUMA.

Minister of Justice, Keeper of the Seals: FANTA SYLLA.

Minister of State-Administered Estates and Housing Affairs: SOUMARÉ AMINATA SIDIBÉ.

Minister of Health: MAÏGA ZEINAB MINT YOUBA.

Minister of Capital Works and Transport: ABDOULAYE KOÏTA.

Minister of Internal Security and Civil Protection: Col SADJO GASSAMA.

Minister of Youth and Sports: NATHIÉ PLÉA.

Minister of Housing and Town Planning: MODIBO SYLLA.

Minister, Secretary-General of the Government: FOUSSEYNI SAMAKE.

MINISTRIES

Office of the President: BP 1463, Koulouba, Bamako; tel. 222-25-72; fax 223-00-26; e-mail presidence@koulouba.pr.ml; internet www.koulouba.pr.ml.

Office of the Prime Minister: Quartier du Fleuve, BP 790, Bamako; tel. 223-06-80; fax 222-85-83.

Office of the Secretary-General of the Government: BP 14, Koulouba, Bamako; tel. 222-25-52; fax 222-70-50; e-mail sgg@sgg.gov.ml; internet www.sgg.gov.ml.

Ministry of Agriculture: BP 1676, Bamako; tel. 222-27-85.

Ministry of Capital Works and Transport: Bamako; tel. 222-39-37.

Ministry of the Civil Service, the Reform of the State and Relations with the Institutions: Bamako; tel. 222-31-80.

Ministry of Communication and New Information Technologies: Quartier du Fleuve, BP 116, Bamako; tel. 222-26-47; fax 223-20-54.

Ministry of Crafts and Tourism: Badalabougou, Semagesco, BP 2211, Bamako; tel. 223-64-50; fax 223-82-01; e-mail malitourisme@afribone.net.ml; internet www.malitourisme.com.

Ministry of Culture: Korofina, BP 4075, Bamako; tel. 224-66-63; fax 224-57-27; e-mail info@culture.gov.ml; internet w3.culture.gov.ml.

Ministry of Defence and Veterans: route de Koulouba, BP 2083, Bamako; tel. 222-50-21; fax 223-23-18.

Ministry of the Economy and Finance: BP 234, Koulouba, Bamako; tel. 222-51-56; fax 222-01-92.

Ministry of Employment and Professional Training: Bamako; tel. 222-34-31.

Ministry of the Environment and Decontamination: Bamako; tel. 223-05-39.

Ministry of Foreign Affairs and International Co-operation: Koulouba, Bamako; tel. 222-83-14; fax 222-52-26.

Ministry of Health: BP 232, Koulouba, Bamako; tel. 222-53-02; fax 223-02-03.

Ministry of Housing and Town Planning: Bamako; tel. 223-05-39.

Ministry of Industry and Trade: Quartier du Fleuve, BP 234, Koulouba, Bamako; tel. 222-43-87; fax 222-88-53.

Ministry of Internal Security and Civil Protection: BP E 4771, Bamako; tel. 222-00-82.

Ministry of Justice: Quartier du Fleuve, BP 97, Bamako; tel. 222-26-42; fax 223-00-63; e-mail ucprodej@afribone.net.ml; internet www.justicemali.org.

Ministry of Malians Abroad and African Integration: Bamako; e-mail info@maliensdelexterieur.gov.ml; internet www.maliensdelexterieur.gov.ml.

Ministry of Mining, Energy and Water Resources: BP 238, Bamako; tel. 222-41-84; fax 222-21-60.

Ministry of National Education: BP 71, Bamako; tel. 222-57-80; fax 222-21-26; e-mail info@education.gov.ml; internet www.education.gov.ml.

Ministry of Planning and Territorial Development: Bamako; tel. 223-20-02.

Ministry of the Promotion of Investment and of Small and Medium-sized Enterprises: Bamako.

Ministry for the Promotion of Women, Children and the Family: Porte G9, rue 109, Badalabougou, BP 2688, Bamako; tel. 222-66-59; fax 223-66-60; e-mail mpfef@mpfef.gov.ml; internet www.mpfef.gov.ml.

Ministry of Social Development, Solidarity and the Elderly: Bamako; tel. 223-23-01.

Ministry of State-Administered Estates and Housing Affairs: Bamako; tel. 223-63-44.

Ministry of Stockbreeding and Fisheries: Bamako; tel. 223-36-96.

Ministry of Territorial Administration and Local Communities: face Direction de la RCFM, BP 78, Bamako; tel. 222-42-12; fax 223-02-47; internet www.matcl.gov.ml.

Ministry of Youth and Sports: route de Koulouba, BP 91, Bamako; tel. 222-31-53; fax 223-90-67; e-mail mjsports@mjsports.gov.ml; internet www.mjsports.gov.ml.

President and Legislature

PRESIDENT

Presidential Election, 29 April 2007

Candidates	Votes	% of votes
Gen. (retd) Amadou Toumani Touré (Independent)	1,612,912	71.20
Ibrahim Boubacar Kéita (RPM)	433,897	19.15
Tiébilé Dramé (PARENA)	68,956	3.04
Oumar Mariko (SADI)	61,670	2.72
Others	88,048	3.89
Total	2,265,483	100.00

LEGISLATURE

Assemblée nationale

BP 284, Bamako; tel. 221-57-24; fax 221-03-74; e-mail mamou@blonba.malinet.ml.

President: IBRAHIM BOUBACAR KÉITA.

General Election, 14 and 28 July 2002*

Parties and alliances	Seats
Alliance pour la démocratie au Mali—Parti pan-africain pour la liberté, la solidarité et la justice (ADEMA)	53
Rassemblement pour le Mali (RPM)	46†
Congrès national d'initiative démocratique—Faso Yiriwa Ton (CNID)	13
Rassemblement pour la démocratie et le travail (RDT)	7
Parti de la solidarité africaine pour la démocratie et l'indépendance (SADI)	6
Convention démocratique et sociale (CDS)	4
Bloc pour la démocratie et l'intégration africaine—Faso Jigi (BDIA)	3
Union soudanaise—Rassemblement démocratique africaine (US—RDA)/Rassemblement national pour la démocratie (RND)	3
Mouvement patriotique pour le renouveau (MPR)	2
Rassemblement malien pour le travail (RAMAT)	2
Parti pour la démocratie et le renouveau—Dounkafa Ton (PDR)	1
Parti pour la renaissance nationale (PARENA)	1
Independents	6
Total	147

* These figures include the results of voting in eight constituencies where the elections were rerun on 20 October 2002.

† Including 20 seats won in coalitions with other parties.

Election Commission

Commission électorale nationale indépendante (CENI): Bamako; Pres. FODIÉ TOURÉ.

Advisory Councils

Economic, Social and Cultural Council: Koulouba, Bamako; tel. 222-43-68; fax 222-84-52; e-mail cesc@cefib.com; f. 1987; Pres. MOUSSA BALLA COULIBALY.

High Council of Communities: Bamako; compulsorily advises the Govt on issues relating to local and regional devt; comprises national councillors, elected indirectly for a term of five years; Sec.-Gen. MAMANI NASSIRE.

Political Organizations

In 2004 there were some 96 political parties officially registered in Mali, of which 51 received funding from the state authorities. In early 2007 the most active parties and political groupings included:

Alliance pour la démocratie au Mali—Parti pan-africain pour la liberté, la solidarité et la justice (ADEMA): rue Fankélé, porte 145, BP 1791, Bamako-Coura; tel. 222-03-68; f. 1990 as Alliance pour la démocratie au Mali; Pres. DIONCOUNDA TRAORÉ; Sec.-Gen. MARIMATIA DIARRA.

Bloc pour la démocratie et l'intégration africaine—Faso Jigi (BDIA): Bolibana, rue 376, porte 83, BP E 2833, Bamako-Coura; tel. 223-82-02; f. 1993; liberal, democratic; mem. of informal alliance supportive of Pres. Touré, the Convergence pour l'alternance et le changement (ACC), during 2002 legislative elections; Leader SOULEYMANE MAKAMBA DOUMBIA.

Congrès national d'initiative démocratique—Faso Yiriwa Ton (CNID): rue 426, porte 58, Niarela, BP 2572, Bamako; tel. 221-42-75; fax 222-83-21; e-mail cnid@cefib.com; f. 1991; Chair. Me MOUNTAGA TALL; Sec.-Gen. N'DIAYE BA.

Convention démocratique et sociale (CDS): Ouolofobougou-Bolibana, rue 417, porte 46, Bamako; tel. 229-26-25; f. 1996; Chair. MAMADOU BAKARY SANGARÉ.

Convention parti du peuple (COPP): Korofina nord, BP 9012, Bamako; fax 221-35-91; e-mail lawyergakou@datatech.toolnet.org; f. 1996; Pres. Me MAMADOU GACKOU.

Mouvement patriotique pour le renouveau (MPR): Quinzambougou, BP E 1108, Bamako; tel. 221-55-46; fax 221-55-43; f. 1995; Pres. Dr CHOGUEL KOKALA MAÏGA.

Mouvement pour l'indépendance, la renaissance et l'intégration africaine (MIRIA): Dravéla, Bolibana, rue 417, porte 66, Bamako; tel. 229-29-81; fax 229-29-79; e-mail miria12002@yahoo.fr; f. 1994 following split in ADEMA; Pres. MOHAMED LAMINE TRAORÉ.

Parti citoyen pour le renouveau (PCR): Bamako; f. 2005; supports administration of Pres. Touré; Pres. OUSMANE BEN FANA TRAORÉ.

Parti de la solidarité africaine pour la démocratie et l'indépendance (SADI): Djélibougou, rue 246, porte 559, BP 3140, Bamako; tel. 224-10-04; f. 2002; Leader CHEICK OUMAR SISSOKO.

Parti malien pour le développement et le renouveau (PMDR): Sema I, rue 76, porte 62, BP 553, Badalabougou, Bamako; tel. 222-25-58; f. 1991; social democratic; Pres. Me ABDOUL WAHAB BERTHE.

Parti pour la démocratie et le progrès (PDP): Korofina sud, rue 96, porte 437, Bamako; tel. 224-16-75; fax 220-23-14; f. 1991; Leader MADY KONATÉ.

Parti pour la démocratie et le renouveau—Dounkafa Ton (PDR): Bamako; f. 1998; mem. of informal alliance supportive of Pres. Touré, the Convergence pour l'alternance et le changement (ACC), during 2002 legislative elections; Pres. ADAMA KONÉ; Leader KALILOU SAMAKE.

Parti pour la renaissance nationale (PARENA): rue Soundiata, porte 1397, BP E 2235, Ouolofobougou, Bamako; tel. 223-49-54; fax 222-29-08; e-mail info@parena.org.ml; internet www.parena.org.ml; f. 1995 following split in CNID; mem. of informal alliance supportive of Pres. Touré, the Convergence pour l'alternance et le changement (ACC), during 2002 legislative elections; Pres. TIÉBILÉ DRAMÉ; Sec.-Gen. AMIDOU DIABATÉ.

Parti pour l'indépendance, la démocratie et la solidarité (PIDS): Hippodrome, rue 250, porte 1183, BP E 1515, Bamako; tel. 277-45-75; f. 2001 by dissidents from US—RDA; Pres. DABA DIAWARA.

Rassemblement malien pour le travail (RAMAT): Marché, Hippodrome, rue 224, porte 1393, BP E 2281, Bamako; tel. 674-46-03; f. 1991; mem. of informal alliance supportive of Pres. Touré, the Convergence pour l'alternance et le changement (ACC), during 2002 legislative elections; Leader ABDOULAYE MACKO.

Rassemblement national pour la démocratie (RND): Niaréla, route Sotuba, porte 1892, Hamdallaye, Bamako; tel. 229-18-49; fax 229-09-39; f. 1997 by 'moderate' breakaway group from RDP; mem. of informal alliance supportive of Pres. Touré, the Convergence pour l'alternance et le changement (ACC), during 2002 legislative elections; Pres. ABDOULAYE GARBA TAPO.

Rassemblement pour la démocratie et le progrès (RDP): Niarela, rue 485, porte 11, BP 2110, Bamako; tel. 221-30-92; fax 224-67-95; f. 1991; Sec.-Gen. IBRAHIM DIAKITE (acting).

Rassemblement pour la démocratie et le travail (RDT): Bamako; tel. 222-25-58; f. 1991; Leader AMADOU ALI NIANGADOU.

Rassemblement pour le Mali (RPM): Hippodrome, rue 232, porte 130, BP 9057, Bamako; tel. 221-14-33; fax 221-13-36; e-mail siegerpmbko@yahoo.fr; internet www.rpm.org.ml; f. 2001; Pres. IBRAHIM BOUBACAR KÉITA; Sec.-Gen. Dr BOCARY TRETA.

Union des forces démocratiques pour le progrès—Sama-ton (UFDP): Quartier Mali, BP E 37, Bamako; tel. 223-17-66; f. 1991; mem. of informal alliance supportive of Pres. Touré, the Convergence pour l'alternance et le changement (ACC), during 2002 legislative elections; Sec.-Gen. Col YOUSSOUF TRAORÉ.

Union pour la démocratie et le développement (UDD): ave OUA, porte 3626, Sogoniko, BP 2969, Bamako; tel. 220-39-71; f. 1991 by supporters of ex-Pres. Traoré; Leader Me HASSANE BARRY.

Union pour la République et la démocratie (URD): Niaréla, rue 268, porte 41, Bamako; tel. 221-86-40; e-mail urd@timbagga.com.ml;

f. 2003 by fmr mems of ADEMA (q.v.) allied to 2002 presidential candidate Soumaïla Cissé; Pres. YOUNOUSSI TOURÉ.

Union soudanaise—Rassemblement démocratique africain (US—RDA): Hippodrome, porte 41, BP E 1413, Bamako; tel. and fax 221-45-22; f. 1946; sole party 1960–68, banned 1968–1991; 'moderate' faction split from party in 1998; mem. of informal alliance supportive of Pres. Touré, the Convergence pour l'alternance et le changement (ACC), during 2002 legislative elections; Leader Dr BADARA ALIOU MACALOU.

Diplomatic Representation

EMBASSIES IN MALI

Algeria: Daoudabougou, BP 02, Bamako; tel. 220-51-76; fax 222-93-74; Ambassador ABDELKREM GHRAIEB.

Burkina Faso: ACI-2000, Commune III, BP 9022, Bamako; tel. 223-31-71; fax 221-92-66; e-mail ambafaso@experco.net; Ambassador Prof. SANNÉ MOHAMED TOPAN.

Canada: route de Koulikoro, Immeuble Séméga, Hippodrome, BP 198, Bamako; tel. 221-22-36; fax 221-43-62; e-mail bmako@international.gc.ca; internet www.dfait-maeci.gc.ca/world/embassies/mali; Ambassador ISABELLE ROY.

China, People's Republic: route de Koulikoro, Hippodrome, BP 112, Bamako; tel. 221-35-97; fax 222-34-43; e-mail chinaemb_ml@mfa.gov.cn; Ambassador ZHANG GUOQING.

Côte d'Ivoire: square Patrice Lumumba, Immeuble CNAR, BP E 3644, Bamako; tel. 222-03-89; fax 222-13-76; Ambassador ABOUBACAR SIRIKI DIABATÉ.

Cuba: porte 31, rue 328, Niarela, Bamako; tel. 221-02-89; fax 221-02-93; e-mail emcuba.mali@malinet.ml; Ambassador ALBERTO MIGUEL OTERO LÓPEZ.

Egypt: Badalabougou-est, BP 44, Bamako; tel. 222-35-65; fax 222-08-91; e-mail mostafa@datatech.net.ml; Ambassador MOSTAFA ABDEL HAMID GENDY.

France: square Patrice Lumumba, BP 17, Bamako; tel. 221-31-41; fax 222-31-36; e-mail ambassade@france-mali.org.ml; internet www.ambafrance-ml.org; Ambassador MICHEL REVEYRAND-DE MENTHON.

Germany: Badalabougou-est, rue 14, porte 334, BP 100, Bamako; tel. 222-32-99; fax 222-96-50; e-mail allemagne.presse@afribone.net.ml; Ambassador Dr REINHARD SCHWARZER.

Ghana: BP 3161, Bamako; Ambassador Maj.-Gen. C. B. YAACHIE.

Guinea: Immeuble Saybou Maïga, Quartier du Fleuve, BP 118, Bamako; tel. 222-30-07; fax 221-08-06; Ambassador (vacant).

Iran: ave al-Quds, Hippodrome, BP 2136, Bamako; tel. 221-76-38; fax 221-07-31; Ambassador MOHAMMED SOLEIMANI.

Korea, Democratic People's Republic: Bamako; Ambassador KIM PONG HUI.

Libya: Badalabougou-ouest, face Palais de la Culture, BP 1670, Bamako; tel. 222-34-96; fax 222-66-97; Ambassador Dr SALAHEDDIN AHMED ZAREM.

Mauritania: route de Koulikoro, Hippodrome, BP 135, Bamako; tel. 221-48-15; fax 222-49-08; Ambassador SIDAMINE OULD AHMED CHALLA.

Morocco: Badalabougou-est, rue 25, porte 80, BP 2013, Bamako; tel. 222-21-23; fax 222-77-87; e-mail sifamali@afribone.net.ml; Ambassador MOULAY DRISS FADHILL.

Netherlands: rue 437, BP 2220, Hippodrome, Bamako; tel. 221-56-11; fax 221-36-17; e-mail bam@minbuza.nl; internet www.mfa.nl/bam; Ambassador ELLEN VAN DER LAAN.

Nigeria: Badalabougou-est, BP 57, Bamako; tel. 221-53-28; fax 222-39-74; e-mail ngrbko@malinet.ml; Ambassador MOHAMMED SANI KANGIWA.

Russia: BP 300, Niarela, Bamako; tel. 221-55-92; fax 221-99-26; e-mail ambrusse_mali@datatech.toolnet.org; Ambassador ANATOLII P. SMIRNOV.

Saudi Arabia: Villa Bal Harbour, 28 Cité du Niger, BP 81, Bamako; tel. 221-25-28; fax 221-50-64; e-mail mlemb@mofa.gov.sa; Chargé d'affaires a.i. IMAD BIN AMEEN ELIAS.

Senegal: porte 341, rue 287, angle ave Nelson Mandela, BP 42, Bamako; tel. 221-08-59; fax 216-92-68; Ambassador SAOUDATOU NDIAYE SECK.

South Africa: bât. Diarra, Hamdallaye, ACI-2000, BP 2015, Bamako; tel. 229-29-25; fax 229-29-26; e-mail bamako@foreign.gov.za; Ambassador W. T. THABETHE.

Spain: porte 81, rue 13, Badalabougou Est, BP 3230, Bamako; tel. 223-65-27; fax 223-65-24; e-mail emb.bamako@mae.es; Ambassador Dr MARTA BETANZOS ROIG.

Tunisia: Quartier du Fleuve, Bamako; tel. 223-28-91; fax 222-17-55; Ambassador FARHAT CHEOUR.

USA: ACI 2000, Rue 243, Porte 297, Bamako; tel. 270-23-00; fax 270-24-79; e-mail webmaster@usa.org.ml; internet mali.usembassy.gov; Ambassador TERENCE PATRICK MCCULLEY.

Judicial System

The 1992 Constitution guarantees the independence of the judiciary.

High Court of Justice: Bamako; competent to try the President of the Republic and ministers of the Government for high treason and for crimes committed in the course of their duties, and their accomplices in any case where state security is threatened; mems designated by the mems of the Assemblée nationale, and renewed annually.

Supreme Court: BP 7, Bamako; tel. 222-24-06; e-mail csupreme@afribone.net.ml; f. 1969; comprises judicial, administrative and auditing sections; judicial section comprises five chambers, administrative section comprises two chambers, auditing section comprises three chambers; Pres. ASKIA M'BARAKOU TOURÉ; Sec.-Gen. ALKAÏDY SANIBIÉ TOURÉ.

President of the Bar: Me MAGATTÉ SÈYE.

Constitutional Court: BP E 213, Bamako; tel. 222-56-09; fax 223-42-41; e-mail tawatybouba@yahoo.fr; f. 1994; Pres. SALIF KANOUTÉ; Sec.-Gen. BOUBACAR TAWATY.

There are three Courts of Appeal, seven Tribunaux de première instance (Magistrates' Courts) and also courts for labour disputes.

Religion

According to the UN Development Programme's *Human Development Report*, around 80% of the population are Muslims, while 18% follow traditional animist beliefs and under 2% are Christians.

ISLAM

Association Malienne pour l'Unité et le Progrès de l'Islam (AMUPI): Bamako; state-endorsed Islamic governing body.

Chief Mosque: pl. de la République, Bagadadji, Bamako; tel. 221-21-90.

Haut Conseil Islamique: Bamako; f. 2002; responsible for management of relations between the Muslim communities and the State; Pres. MODY SYLLA (acting).

CHRISTIANITY

The Roman Catholic Church

Mali comprises one archdiocese and five dioceses. At 31 December 2004 there were an estimated 232,182 Roman Catholics, comprising about 1.5% of the total population.

Bishops' Conference

Conférence Episcopale du Mali, Archevêché, BP 298, Bamako; tel. 222-67-84; fax 222-67-00; e-mail cemali@afribone.net.ml.

f. 1973; Pres. Most Rev. JEAN-GABRIEL DIARRA (Bishop of San).

Archbishop of Bamako: JEAN ZERBO, Archevêché, BP 298, Bamako; tel. 222-54-99; fax 222-52-14; e-mail mgrjeanzerbo@afribone.net.ml.

Other Christian Churches

There are several Protestant mission centres, mainly administered by US societies.

BAHÁ'Í FAITH

National Spiritual Assembly: BP 1657, Bamako; e-mail ntirandaz@aol.com.

The Press

The 1992 Constitution guarantees the freedom of the press. In 2000 there were six daily newspapers, 18 weekly or twice-weekly publications and six monthly or twice-monthly publications.

DAILY NEWSPAPERS

Les Echos: Hamdallaye, ave Cheick Zayed, porte 2694, BP 2043, Bamako; tel. 229-62-89; fax 226-76-39; e-mail jamana@malinet.ml; f. 1989; publ. by Jamana cultural co-operative; circ. 30,000; Dir ALEXIS KALAMBRY; Editor-in-Chief ABOUBACAR SALIPH DIARRA.

L'Essor: square Patrice Lumumba, BP 141, Bamako; tel. 222-36-83; fax 222-47-74; e-mail info@essor.gov.ml; internet www.essor.gov.ml; f. 1949; pro-Govt newspaper; Editor SOULEYMANE DRABO; circ. 3,500.

Info Matin: rue 56/350, Bamako Coura, BP E 4020, Bamako; tel. 223-82-09; fax 223-82-27; e-mail redaction@info-matin.com; internet www.info-matin.com; independent; Dir SAMBI TOURÉ; Editor-in-Chief MOHAMED SACKO.

Le Républicain: 116 rue 400, Dravéla-Bolibana, BP 1484, Bamako; tel. 229-09-00; fax 229-09-33; e-mail republicain@cefib.com; f. 1992; independent; Dir SALIF KONÉ.

PERIODICALS

26 Mars: Badalabougou-Sema Gesco, Lot S13, BP MA 174, Bamako; tel. 229-04-59; f. 1998; weekly; independent; Dir BOUBACAR SANGARÉ.

L'Aurore: Niarela 298, rue 438, BP 3150, Bamako; tel. and fax 221-69-22; e-mail aurore@timbagga.com.ml; f. 1990; 2 a week; independent; Dir KARAMOKO N'DIAYE.

Le Canard Déchaîné: Immeuble Koumara, bloc 104, Centre Commercial, Bamako; tel. 621-26-86; fax 222-86-86; e-mail maison.presse@afribone.net.ml; weekly; satirical; Dir OUMAR BABI; circ. 3,000 (2006).

Le Carrefour: ave Cheick Zayed, Hamdallaye, Bamako; tel. 223-98-08; e-mail journalcarrefour@yahoo.fr; f. 1997; Dir MAHAMANE IMRANE COULIBALY.

Citoyen: Bamako; f. 1992; fortnightly; independent.

Le Continent: AA 16, Banankabougou, BP E 4338, Bamako; tel. and fax 229-57-39; e-mail le_continent@yahoo.fr; f. 2000; weekly; Dir IBRAHIMA TRAORÉ.

Le Courrier: 230 ave Cheick Zayed, Lafiabougou Marché, BP 1258, Bamako; tel. and fax 229-18-62; e-mail journalcourrier@webmails.com; f. 1996; weekly; Dir SADOU A. YATTARA; also *Le Courrier Magazine*, monthly.

L'Indépendant: Immeuble ABK, Hamdallaye ACI, BP E 1040, Bamako; tel. and fax 223-27-27; e-mail independant@cefib.com; 2 a week; Dir SAOUTI HAÏDARA.

L'Inspecteur: Immeuble Nimagala, bloc 262, BP E 4534, Bamako; tel. 672-47-11; e-mail inspecteurmali@yahoo.fr; f. 1992; weekly; Dir ALY DIARRA.

Jamana—Revue Culturelle Malienne: BP 2043, Bamako; BP E 1040; e-mail jamana@malinet.ml; f. 1983; quarterly; organ of Jamana cultural co-operative.

Journal Officiel de la République du Mali: Koulouba, BP 14, Bamako; tel. 222-59-86; fax 222-70-50; official gazette.

Kabaaru: Village Kibaru, Bozola, Bamako; f. 1983; state-owned; monthly; Fulbé (Peul) language; rural interest; Editor BADAMA DOUCOURÉ; circ. 5,000.

Kabako: Bamako; tel. 221-29-12; f. 1991; weekly; general; Dir DIABY MACORO CAMARA.

Kibaru: Village Kibaru, Bozola, BP 1463, Bamako; f. 1972; monthly; state-owned; Bambara and three other languages; rural interest; Editor NIANZÉ SAMAKÉ; circ. 5,000.

Liberté: Immeuble Sanago, Hamdallaye Marché, BP E 24, Bamako; tel. 228-18-98; e-mail ladji.guindo@cefib.com; f. 1999; weekly; Dir ABDOULAYE LADJI GUINDO.

Le Malien: rue 497, porte 277, Badialan III, BP E 1558, Bamako; tel. 223-57-29; fax 229-13-39; e-mail lemalien2000@yahoo.fr; f. 1993; weekly; Dir SIDI KEITA.

Match: 97 rue 498, Lafiabougou, BP E 3776, Bamako; tel. 229-18-82; e-mail bcissouma@yahoo.fr; f. 1997; 2 a month; sports; Dir BABA CISSOUMA.

Musow: Bamako; e-mail musow@musow.com; internet www.musow.com; women's interest.

Nyéléni Magazine: Niarela 298, rue 348, BP 13150, Bamako; tel. 229-24-01; f. 1991; monthly; women's interest; Dir MAÏMOUNA TRAORÉ.

L'Observateur: Galérie Djigué, rue du 18 juin, BP E 1002, Bamako; tel. and fax 223-06-89; e-mail belcotamboura@hotmail.com; f. 1992; 2 a week; Dir BELCO TAMBOURA.

Le Reflet: Immeuble Kanadjigui, Route de Koulikoro, Boulkassoumbougou, BP E 1688, Bamako; tel. 224-39-52; fax 223-23-08; e-mail lereflet@afribone.malinet.ml; weekly; fmrly Le Carcan; present name adopted Jan. 2001; Dir ABDOUL KARIM DRAMÉ.

Royal Sports: BP 98, Sikasso; tel. 672-49-88; weekly; also *Tatou Sports*, published monthly; Pres. and Dir-Gen. ALY TOURÉ.

Le Scorpion: 230 ave Cheick Zayed, Lafiabougou Marché, BP 1258, Bamako; tel. and fax 229-18-62; f. 1991; weekly; Dir MAHAMANE HAMÈYE CISSÉ.

Le Tambour: rue 497, porte 295, Badialan III, BP E 289, Bamako; tel. and fax 222-75-68; e-mail tambourj@yahoo.fr; f. 1994; 2 a week; Dir YÉRO DIALLO.

NEWS AGENCIES

Agence Malienne de Presse et Publicité (AMAP): square Patrice Lumumba, BP 141, Bamako; tel. 222-36-83; fax 222-47-74; e-mail amap@afribone.net.ml; f. 1977; Dir SOULEYMANE DRABO.

Foreign Bureau

Agence France-Presse (AFP): BP 778, Bamako; tel. 222-07-77.

IPS (Italy) and Xinhua (New China) News Agency (People's Republic of China) are also represented in Mali.

PRESS ASSOCIATIONS

Association des Editeurs de la Presse Privée (ASSEP): BP E 1002, Bamako; tel. 671-31-33; e-mail belcotamboura@hotmail.com; Pres. BELCO TAMBOURA.

Association des Femmes de la Presse Privée: Porte 474, rue 428, BP E 731, Bamako; tel. 221-29-12; Pres. FANTA DIALLO.

Association des Journalistes Professionels des Médias Privés du Mali (AJPM): BP E 2456, Bamako; tel. 222-19-15; fax 223-54-78; Pres. MOMADOU FOFANA.

Association des Professionnelles Africaines de la Communication (APAC MALI): Porte 474, rue 428, BP E 731, Bamako; tel. 221-29-12; Pres. MASSIRÉ YATTASSAYE.

Maison de la Presse de Mali: 17 rue 619, Darsalam, BP E 2456, Bamako; tel. 222-19-15; fax 223-54-78; e-mail maison.presse@afribone.net.ml; internet www.mediamali.org; independent media asscn; Pres. SADOU A. YATTARA.

Union Interprofessionnelle des Journalistes et de la Presse de Langue Française (UIJPLF): rue 42, Hamdallaye Marché, BP 1258, Bamako; tel. 229-98-35; Pres. MAHAMANE HAMÈYE CISSÉ.

Union Nationale des Journalistes Maliens (UNAJOM): BP 141, Bamako; tel. 222-36-83; fax 223-43-13; e-mail amap@afribone.net.ml; Pres. OUSMANE MAÏGA.

Publishers

EDIM SA: ave Kassé Keïta, BP 21, Bamako; tel. 222-40-41; f. 1972 as Editions Imprimeries du Mali; general fiction and non-fiction, textbooks; Chair. and Man. Dir ALOU TOMOTA.

Editions Donniya: Cité du Niger, BP 1273, Bamako; tel. 221-46-46; fax 221-90-31; e-mail imprimcolor@cefib.com; internet www.imprimcolor.cefib.com; f. 1996; general fiction, history, reference and children's books in French and Bambara.

Le Figuier: 151 rue 56, Semal, BP 2605, Bamako; tel. and fax 223-32-11; e-mail lefiguier@afribone.net.ml; f. 1997; fiction and non-fiction.

Editions Jamana: BP 2043, Bamako; tel. 229-62-89; fax 229-76-39; e-mail jamana@timbagga.com.ml; f. 1988; literary fiction, poetry, reference; Dir BA MAÏRA SOW.

Editions Teriya: BP 1677, Bamako; tel. 224-11-42; theatre, literary fiction; Dir GAOUSSOU DIAWARA.

Broadcasting and Communications

TELECOMMUNICATIONS

Orange Mali SA: Immeuble Orange Mali ACI-2000, BP E 3991, Bamako; tel. 499-90-00; fax 499-90-01; e-mail orange@orangemali.com; internet www.orangemali.com; f. 2003 as Ikatel; GETESA (Equatorial Guinea), Sonatel (Senegal) and Ikatel (Mali) were repackaged under brand name Orange in 2007; fixed-line and mobile cellular telecommunications; jtly owned by France Télécom and Société Nationale des Télécommunications du Sénégal; Dir-Gen. ALIOUME N'DIAYE; 100,000 subscribers (2003).

Société des Télécommunications du Mali—Malitel (SOTELMA): route de Koulikoro, Hippodrome, BP 740, Bamako; tel. 221-52-80; fax 221-30-22; e-mail segal@sotelma.ml; internet www.sotelma.ml; f. 1990; state-owned; 49% privatization proposed; operates fixed-line telephone services, also mobile and cellular telecommunications in Bamako, Kayes, Mopti, Ségou and Sikasso; 47,000 subscribers to mobile cellular telecommunications services (2003); Pres. and Dir-Gen. SIDIKI KONATE.

BROADCASTING

Radio

Office de Radiodiffusion-Télévision Malienne (ORTM): BP 171, Bamako; tel. 221-20-19; fax 221-42-05; e-mail ortm@afribone.net.ml; internet www.ortm.net; Dir-Gen. SIDIKI KONATÉ; Dir of Radio OUMAR TOURÉ.

Radio Mali–Chaîne Nationale: BP 171, Bamako; tel. 221-20-19; fax 221-42-05; e-mail ortm@spider.toolnet.org; f. 1957; state-owned; radio programmes in French, Bambara, Peulh, Sarakolé, Tamachek, Sonrai, Moorish, Wolof, English.

Chaîne 2: Bamako; f. 1993; radio broadcasts to Bamako.

In late 2003 there were an estimated 130 community, commercial and religious radio stations broadcasting in Mali.

Fréquence 3: Bamako; f. 1992; commercial.

Radio Balanzan: BP 419, Ségou; tel. 232-02-88; commercial.

Radio Bamakan: Marché de Médine, BP E 100, Bamako; tel. and fax 221-27-60; e-mail radio.bamakan@ifrance.com; f. 1991; community station; 104 hours of FM broadcasts weekly; Man. MODIBO DIALLO.

Radio Espoir—La Voix du Salut: Sogoniko, rue 130, porte 71, BP E 1399, Bamako; tel. 220-67-08; e-mail accm@mali.maf.net; f. 1998; broadcasts 16 hours of radio programming daily on topics including Christianity, devt and culture; Dir DAOUDA COULIBALY.

Radio Foko de Ségou Jamana: BP 2043, Bamako; tel. 232-00-48; fax 222-76-39; e-mail radiofoko@cefib.com.

Radio Guintan: Magnambougou, BP 2546, Bamako; tel. 220-09-38; f. 1994; community radio station; Dir RAMATA DIA.

Radio Jamana: BP 2043, Bamako; tel. 229-62-89; fax 229-76-39; e-mail jamana@malinet.net.

Radio Kayira: Djélibougou Doumanzana, BP 3140, Bamako; tel. 224-87-82; fax 222-75-68; f. 1992; community station; Dir OUMAR MARIKO.

Radio Klédu: Cité du Niger, BP 2322, Bamako; tel. 221-00-18; f. 1992; commercial; Dir FADIALA DEMBÉLÉ.

Radio Liberté: BP 5015, Bamako; tel. 223-05-81; f. 1991; commercial station broadcasting 24 hours daily; Dir ALMANY TOURÉ.

Radio Patriote: Korofina-Sud, BP E 1406, Bamako; tel. 224-22-92; f. 1995; commercial station; Dir MOUSSA KEÏTA.

Radio Rurale: Plateau, BP 94, Kayes; tel. 253-14-76; e-mail rrk@afribone.net.ml; f. 1988; community stations established by the Agence de coopération culturelle et technique (ACTT); transmitters in Niono, Kadiolo, Bandiagara and Kidal; Dir FILY KEÏTA.

Radio Sahel: BP 394, Kayes; tel. 252-21-87; f. 1991; commercial; Dir ALMAMY S. TOURÉ.

Radio Tabalé: Bamako-Coura, BP 697, Bamako; tel. and fax 222-78-70; f. 1992; independent public-service station; broadcasting 57 hours weekly; Dir TIÉMOKO KONÉ.

La Voix du Coran et du Hadit: Grande Mosquée, BP 2531, Bamako; tel. 221-63-44; f. 1993; Islamic station broadcasting on FM in Bamako; Dir El Hadj MAHMOUD DICKO.

Radio Wassoulou: BP 24, Yanfolila; tel. 265-10-97; commercial.

Radio France International, the Voix de l'Islam and the Gabonese-based Africa No. 1 began FM broadcasts in Mali in 1993; broadcasts by Voice of America and the World Service of the British Broadcasting Corpn are also transmitted via private radio stations.

Television

Office de Radiodiffusion-Télévision Malienne (ORTM): see Radio; Dir of Television BALY IDRISSA SISSOKO.

Multicanal SA: Quinzambougou, BP E 1506, Bamako; tel. 221-49-64; e-mail sandrine@multi-canal.com; internet www.multi-canal.com; private subscription broadcaster; relays international broadcasts; Pres. ISMAÏLA SIDIBÉ.

TV Klédu: 600 ave Modibo Keïta, BP E 1172, Bamako; tel. 223-90-00; fax 223-70-50; e-mail info@tvkledu.com; private cable TV operator; relays international broadcasts; Pres. MAMADOU COULIBALY.

Finance

(cap. = capital; res = reserves; dep. = deposits; m. = million; br(s). = branch(es); amounts in francs CFA)

BANKING

Central Bank

Banque centrale des états de l'Afrique de l'ouest (BCEAO): BP 206, Bamako; tel. 222-37-56; fax 222-47-86; internet www.bceao.int; f. 1962; HQ in Dakar, Senegal; bank of issue for the mem. states of Union économique et monétaire ouest-africaine (UEMOA, comprising Benin, Burkina Faso, Côte d'Ivoire, Guinea-Bissau, Mali, Niger, Senegal and Togo); cap. and res 859,313m., total assets 5,671,675m. (Dec. 2002); Gov. DAMO JUSTIN BARO (acting); Dir in Mali IDRISSA TRAORÉ; brs at Mopti and Sikasso.

Commercial Banks

Bank of Africa—Mali (BOA—MALI): 418 ave de la Marné, Bozola, BP 2249, Bamako; tel. 270-05-00; fax 270-05-60; e-mail information@boamali.net; internet www.bank-of-africa.net; f. 1983; cap. 3,000m., res 1,666m., dep. 82,402m. (March 2007); Pres. BOUREIMA SYLLA; Dir-Gen. CHRISTOPHE LASSUS-LALANNE; 7 brs.

Banque Commerciale du Sahel (BCS–SA): ave Kassé Keïta, BP 2372, Bamako; tel. 221-01-95; fax 221-97-82; e-mail bcs@cefib.com; f. 1980; fmrly Banque Arabe Libyo-Malienne pour le Commerce Extérieur et le Développement; 50% owned by Libyan-Arab Foreign Bank, 49.5% state-owned; cap. 1,100m., total assets. 22,555m. (Dec. 2000); Pres. FANGATIGUI DOUMBIA; Dir-Gen. MOHAMED SAED EL ATRACH; 1 br.

Banque de l'Habitat du Mali (BHM): ACI 2000, ave Kwamé N'Krumah, BP 2614, Bamako; tel. 222-91-90; fax 222-93-50; e-mail bhm@bhm.malinet.ml; f. 1990; present name adopted 1996; 37.1% owned by Institut National de Prévoyance Social, 25.9% by Agence Cession Immobilière; cap. and res 5,414.7m., total assets 98,237.5m. (Dec. 2003); Pres. and Dir-Gen. MAMADOU BABA DIAWARA; 1 br.

Banque International pour le Commerce et l'Industrie au Mali (BICI–Mali): Immeuble Nimagala, blvd du Peuple, BP 72, Bamako; tel. 223-33-70; fax 223-33-73; e-mail secretariatdirection@bicim.com; f. 1998; 50% owned by SFOM Interafrica (Switzerland), 35% by BNP Paribas BDDI Participations (France); cap. and res 3,678m., total assets 40,076m. (Dec. 2003); Pres. and Dir-Gen. LUC-MARIE VIDAL; 1 br.

Banque Internationale pour le Mali (BIM): ave de l'Indépendance, BP 15, Bamako; tel. 222-51-11; fax 222-45-66; e-mail bim@bim.com.ml; f. 1980; present name adopted 1995; 61.5% state-owned; privatization pending; cap. 4,255m., res 1,099m., dep. 78,806m. (Dec. 2002); total assets 91,725m. (Dec. 2003); Pres. and Dir-Gen. DIAKARIDIA KEITA; 7 brs.

Banque Malienne de Crédit et de Dépôts: ave Mobido Keita, BP 45, Bamako; tel. 222-53-36; fax 222-79-50; e-mail bmcd@malinet.ml; 100% state-owned; transfer to private-sector ownership proposed.

Ecobank Mali: pl. de la Nation, Quartier du Fleuve, BP E 1272, Bamako; tel. 223-33-00; fax 223-33-05; e-mail ecobank@cefib.com; f. 1998; 49.5% owned by Ecobank Transnational Inc., 17.8% by Ecobank Bénin, 14.9% by Ecobank Togo, 9.9% by Ecobank Burkina; cap. and res 2,973.9m., total assets 46,222.7m. (Dec. 2003); Pres. SEYDOU DJIM SYLLA; Dir-Gen. KASSIM ABOU KABASSI; 2 brs.

Development Banks

Banque de Développement du Mali (BDM-SA): ave Modibo Keita, Quartier du Fleuve, BP 94, Bamako; tel. 222-20-50; fax 222-50-85; e-mail info@bdm-sa.com; internet www.bdm-sa.com; f. 1968; absorbed Banque Malienne de Crédit et de Dépôts in 2001; 22.1% state-owned, 20.7% owned by Banque Marocaine du Commerce Extérieur (Morocco), 16.0% by by BCEAO, 16% by Banque ouest-africaine de développement; cap. and res 15,658m., total assets 276,148m. (Dec. 2002); Pres. and Dir-Gen. ABDOULAYE DAFFÉ; 14 brs.

Banque Malienne de Solidarité (BMS): ave du Fleuve, Immeuble Dette Publique, 2e étage, BP 1280, Bamako; tel. and fax 223-50-43; e-mail bms-sa@bms-sa.com; f. 2002; cap. 2.4m.; 1 br.

Banque Nationale de Développement Agricole—Mali (BNDA—Mali): Immeuble BNDA, blvd du Mali, ACI 2000, BP 2424, Bamako; tel. 229-64-64; fax 229-25-75; e-mail bnda@bndamali.com; f. 1981; 36.8% state-owned, 22.5% owned by Agence française de développement (France), 21.3% owned by Deutsche Entwicklungs Gesellschaft (Germany), 19.3% owned by BCEAO; cap. 10,988m., res 2,188m., dep. 107,896m. (Dec. 2004); Chair., Pres. and Gen. Man. MOUSSA ALASSAME DIALLO; Dir-Gen. ARNAUD BELLAMY BROWN; 22 brs.

Financial Institutions

Direction Générale de la Dette Publique: Immeuble ex-Caisse Autonome d'Amortissement, Quartier du Fleuve, BP 1617, Bamako; tel. 222-29-35; fax 222-07-93; management of the public debt; Dir NAMALA KONÉ.

Equibail Mali: rue 376, porte 1319, Niarela, BP E 566, Bamako; tel. 21-37-77; fax 21-37-78; e-mail equip.ma@bkofafrica.com; internet www.bkofafrica.net/jeux_de_cadres/equibail/equibail_mali/equibail_mali.htm; f. 1999; 50.2% owned by African Financial Holding, 17.5% by Bank of Africa—Benin; cap. 300m. (Dec. 2002); Mems of Administrative Council RAMATOULAYE TRAORÉ, PAUL DERREUMAUX, LÉON NAKA.

Société Malienne de Financement (SOMAFI): Immeuble Air Afrique, blvd du 22 octobre 1946, BP E 3643, Bamako; tel. 222-18-66; fax 222-18-69; e-mail somafi@malinet.ml; f. 1997; cap. and res 96.9m., total assets 3,844.9m. (Dec. 2002); Man. Dir ERIC LECLÈRE.

STOCK EXCHANGE

Bourse Régionale des Valeurs Mobilières (BRVM): Chambre de Commerce et de l'Industrie du Mali, pl. de la Liberté, BP E 1398, Bamako; tel. 223-23-54; fax 223-23-59; e-mail abocoum@brvm.org; f. 1998; national branch of BRVM (regional stock exchange based in Abidjan, Côte d'Ivoire, serving the mem. states of UEMOA); Man. AMADOU DJÉRI BOCOUM.

INSURANCE

Les Assurances Générales de France (AGF): ave du Fleuve, BP 190, Bamako; tel. 222-58-18.

Assurance Colina Mali SA: BP E 154, Bamako; tel. 222-57-75; fax 223-24-23; e-mail c-mali@colina-sa.com; f. 1990; cap. 1,000m.; Dir-Gen. MARYUONNE SIDIRE.

Caisse Nationale d'Assurance et de Réassurance du Mali (CNAR): BP 568, Bamako; tel. 222-64-54; fax 222-23-29; f. 1969; state-owned; cap. 50m.; Dir-Gen. F. KEITA; 10 brs.

Compagnie d'Assurance Privée—La Soutra: BP 52, Bamako; tel. 222-36-81; fax 222-55-23; f. 1979; cap. 150m.; Chair. AMADOU NIONO.

Compagnie d'Assurance et de Réassurance de Mali: BP 1822, Bamako; tel. 222-60-29.

Compagnie d'Assurance Sabu Nyuman: Bamako Coura 135–136, BP 1822, Bamako; tel. 222-60-29; fax 222-57-50; f. 1984; cap. 250m.; Dir-Gen. MOMADOU SANOGO.

Gras Savoye Mali: Immeuble SOGEFIH, 3me Etage, Quartier du Fleuve, ave Moussa Travele, Bamako; tel. 222-64-75; fax 222-64-70; e-mail moussa.hiam@ml.grassavoye.com; affiliated to Gras Savoye (France); Man. FAYEZ SAMB.

Lafía Assurances: ave de la Nation, BP 1542, Bamako; tel. 222-35-51; fax 222-52-24; f. 1983; cap. 50m.; Dir-Gen. ABDOULAYE TOURÉ.

Trade and Industry

GOVERNMENT AGENCIES

Centre d'Etudes et de Promotion Industrielle (CEPI): BP 1980, Bamako; tel. 222-22-79; fax 222-80-85.

Direction Nationale des Affaires Economiques (DNAE): Bamako; tel. 222-23-14; fax 222-22-56; involved in economic and social affairs.

Direction Nationale des Travaux Publics (DNTP): ave de la Liberté, BP 1758, Bamako; tel. and fax 222-29-02; administers public works.

Guichet Unique–Direction Nationale des Industries: rue Titi Niare, Quinzambougou, BP 96, Bamako; tel. and fax 222-31-66.

Office National des Produits Pétroliers (ONAP): Quartier du Fleuve, rue 315, porte 141, BP 2070, Bamako; tel. 222-28-27; fax 222-44-83; e-mail onap@datatech.toolnet.org; Dir-Gen. TAPA NOUGA NADIO.

Office du Niger: BP 106, Ségou; tel. 232-02-92; fax 232-01-43; f. 1932; taken over from the French authorities in 1958; restructured in mid-1990s; cap. 7,139m. francs CFA; principally involved in cultivation of food crops, particularly rice; Pres. and Man. Dir NANCOMA KEÏTA.

Office des Produits Agricoles du Mali (OPAM): BP 132, Bamako; tel. 222-37-55; fax 221-04-06; e-mail opam@datatech.toolnet.org; f. 1965; state-owned; manages National (Cereals) Security Stock, administers food aid, responsible for sales of cereals and distribution to deficit areas; cap. 5,800m. francs CFA; Pres. and Dir-Gen. YOUSSOUF MAHAMANE TOURÉ.

DEVELOPMENT ORGANIZATIONS

Agence Française de Développement (AFD): Quinzambougou, Route de Sotuba, BP 32, Bamako; tel. 221-28-42; fax 221-86-46; e-mail afdbamako@ml.groupe-afd.org; internet www.afd.fr; Country Dir JEAN-FRANÇOIS VAVASSEUR.

Agence pour le Développement du Nord-Mali (ADN): Gao; f. 2005 to replace l'Autorité pour le Développement Intégré du Nord-Mali (ADIN); govt agency with financial autonomy; promotes devt of regions of Tombouctou, Gao and Kidal; br. in Bamako.

Office de Développement Intégré du Mali-Ouest (ODIMO): square Patrice Lumumba, Bamako; tel. 222-57-59; f. 1991 to succeed Office de Développement Intégré des Productions Arachidières et Céréalières; devt of diversified forms of agricultural production; Man. Dir ZANA SANOGO.

Service de Coopération et d'Action Culturelle: square Patrice Lumumba, BP 84, Bamako; tel. 221-83-38; fax 221-83-39; administers bilateral aid from France; Dir BERTRAND COMMELIN.

CHAMBER OF COMMERCE

Chambre de Commerce et d'Industrie du Mali (CCIM): pl. de la Liberté, BP 46, Bamako; tel. 222-50-36; fax 222-21-20; e-mail ccim@cimmali.org; f. 1906; Pres. JEAMILLE BITTAR; Sec.-Gen. DABA TRAORÉ.

EMPLOYERS' ASSOCIATIONS

Association Malienne des Exportateurs de Légumes (AMELEF): Bamako; f. 1984; Pres. BADARA FAGANDA TRAORÉ; Sec.-Gen. BIRAMA TRAORÉ.

Association Malienne des Exportateurs de Ressources Animales (AMERA): Bamako; tel. 222-56-83; f. 1985; Pres. AMBARKÉ YERMANGORE; Admin. Sec. ALI HACKO.

Fédération Nationale des Employeurs du Mali (FNEM): BP 2445, Bamako; tel. 221-63-11; fax 221-90-77; f. 1980; Pres. MOUSSA MARY BALLA COULIBALY; Permanent Sec. LASSINA TRAORÉ.

UTILITIES

Electricity

Energie du Mali (EdM): square Patrice Lumumba, BP 69, Bamako; tel. 222-30-20; fax 222-84-30; e-mail sekou.edm@cefib.com; f. 1960; 66% state-owned, 34% owned by Industrial Promotion Services (West-Africa); planning, construction and operation of power-sector facilities; cap. 7,880m. francs CFA.

Enertech GSA: marché de Lafiabougou, BP 1949, Bamako; tel. 222-37-63; fax 222-51-36; f. 1994; cap. 20m. francs CFA; solar energy producer; Dir MOCTAR DIAKITÉ.

Société de Gestion de l'Energie de Manantali (SOGEM): Parcelle 2501, ACI 2000, BP-E 4015, Bamako; tel. 223-32-86; fax 223-83-50; to generate and distribute electricity from the Manantali HEP project, under the auspices of the Organisation pour la mise en valeur du fleuve Sénégal; Dir-Gen. SALOUM CISSÉ.

Gas

Maligaz: route de Sotuba, BP 5, Bamako; tel. 222-23-94; gas distribution.

MAJOR COMPANIES

The following are among the major private and state-owned companies in terms of capital investment or employment.

Abattoir Frigorifique de Bamako (AFB): Zone Industrielle, BP 356, Bamako; tel. 222-24-67; fax 222-99-03; f. 1965; cap. 339m. francs CFA; transferred to 80% private ownership in 2002; Man. Dir El Hadj YOUSSOUF CAMARA.

Bakary Textile Commerce et Industrie (BATEX-CI): Zone Industrielle, BP 299, Bamako; tel. 222-46-47; f. 2005 following purchase of liquidated textile co Industrie Textile du Mali (ITEMA); Pres. and Dir-Gen. BAKARY CISSÉ.

Compagnie Malienne pour le Développement des Textiles (CMDT): BP 487, Bozola; tel. 222-24-62; fax 222-81-41; f. 1975; 60% state-owned, 40% owned by Dagris (France); restructured in 2001–03; privatization proposed; cotton cultivation, ginning and marketing; Chair. BAKARY TRAORÉ.

Compagnie Malienne des Textiles (COMATEX): route de Markala, BP 52, Ségou; tel. 232-01-83; fax 232-01-23; f. 1994; production of unbleached fibre and textiles; owned by Covec (People's Republic of China); cap. 1,500m. francs CFA; sales US $9.4m. (2001); Dir-Gen. LIU ZHEN SHAN; 1,300 employees (2002).

Ets Peyrissac–Mali: Bamako; tel. 222-20-62; f. 1963; cap. 300m. francs CFA; distributors of motor vehicles; Dir FRANÇOIS GRULOIS.

Fils et tissus naturels d'Afrique (Fitina): Bamako; f. 2004; cotton products; Pres. PATRICE COSTA.

Grands Moulins du Mali (GMM): BP 324, Bamako; tel. 221-36-64; fax 222-58-74; e-mail groupeami@groupeami.com; internet www.groupeami.com/GMM.html; f. 1979; mfrs of flour and animal feed; cap. 2,500m. francs CFA; sales US $52.2m. (2006); Pres. GÉRARD ACHCAR; Man. and Dir-Gen. CYRIL ACHCAR.

Huilerie Cotonnière du Mali (HUICOMA): Immeuble Graphique Industrie, ave Cheick Zayed, BP 2474, Bamako; tel. 223-42-61; fax 223-60-32; e-mail dc@huicoma.net; f. 1979; cap. 1,500m. francs CFA; majority stake transferred to ownership of Groupe Alou Tomota in 2005; processing of oilseeds; Dir-Gen. ABEL KEITA; 800 employees (2004).

Pharmacie Populaire du Mali (PPM): ave Houssa Travele, BP 277, Bamako; tel. 222-50-59; fax 222-90-34; f. 1960; majority state-owned; import and marketing of medicines and pharmaceutical products; cap. 400m. francs CFA; sales US $6.8m. (2000); Pres. and Dir-Gen. HAMA CISSÉ; 157 employees (2002).

Shell Mali: BP 199, Bamako; tel. 221-24-52; fax 221-76-15; f. 1963; subsidiary of Royal Dutch Shell (Netherlands); distribution of petroleum; cap. 549m. francs CFA (Dec. 1999); Gen. Man. IBRA DIENG.

Société des Brasseries du Mali (BRAMALI/BGI): BP 442, Bamako; f. 1981; owned by Groupe Castel (France); cap. 500m. francs CFA; mfrs of beer and soft drinks; Chair. and Man. Dir SEYDOU DJIM SYLLA.

Société d'Equipement du Mali (SEMA): Face Ecole Cathédrale, BP 163, Bamako; tel. 222-50-71; fax 223-06-47; f. 1961; construction and public works; cap. 140m. francs CFA; Dir MAMADOU DIAKITE; 51 employees.

Société d'Exploitation des Mines d'Or de Sadiola (SEMOS): Sadiola; e-mail Rdagenais@semos-sadiola.com; f. 1994; 38% owned by AngloGold Ashanti (South Africa), 38% by IAMGOLD (Canada); devt of gold deposits at Sadiola Hill.

Société Industrielle de Karité (SIKA-MALI): Bamako; f. 1980; cap. 938m. francs CFA; processors of sheanuts (karité nuts); Dir DRISSA SANGARÉ.

Société Karamoko Traoré et Frères (SOKATRAF): BP 88, Mopti; f. 1975; cap. 318m. francs CFA; import/export; Chair. and Man. Dir DRAMANE TRAORÉ.

Société Malienne de Piles Electriques (SOMAPIL): route de Sotuba, Zone Industrielle, BP 1546, Bamako; tel. 222-46-87; fax 222-29-80; f. 1975; cap. 500m. francs CFA; mfrs of batteries; Chair. KOUMAN DOUMBIA; Man. Dir GÉRARD HELIX.

Société Malienne de Profilage et de Transformation des Métaux (TOLMALI): Zone Industrielle, TSF, BP 68, Bamako; tel. 221-33-35; fax 221-53-77; e-mail info@tolmali.com; internet www.ips-wa.org/anglais/tolmali.htm; f. 1978; majority-owned by Aga Khan Fund for Development; mfrs of iron and steel construction materials and aluminium utensils; sales US $6m. (2001); Pres. and Dir-Gen. MOCTAR TGIAM; 30 employees (2002).

Société Malienne de Sacherie (SOMASAC): BP 74, Bamako; tel. 222-49-41; f. 1971; cap. 462.5m. francs CFA; production of sacking from dah and kenaf fibre and manufacture of sacks; Chair. DOSSOLO TRAORÉ; Man. Dir ERNEST RICHARD.

Société des Mines d'or de Loulo (SOMILO): Loulo; fax 222-81-87; f. 1987; cap. 2,133m. francs CFA; 51% owned by Randgold Resources (South Africa); exploration and development of gold deposits at Loulo; Chair. MAMADOU TOURÉ; Man. Dir ROBERT KRUH.

Société des Mines de Morila: Morila, près de Sanso; f. 2000; exploration and development of gold deposits at Morila; 40% owned by Randgold Resources (South Africa), 40% by AngloGold Ashanti (South Africa), 20% owned by Govt of Mali; Chair. MAMADOU TOURÉ; Dir-Gen. JOHAN BOTHA.

Société Nationale des Tabacs et Allumettes du Mali (SONATAM): route de Sotuba, Zone Industrielle, BP 59, Bamako; tel. 222-49-65; fax 222-23-72; f. 1968; cap. 2,177m. francs CFA; 35% owned by Lafico (Libya); 35% state-owned; further transfer to private ownership proposed for 2003; production of cigarettes and matches; Chair. MOUSSA BABA DIARRA; Man. Dir BOUBACAR DEMBÉLÉ; 820 employees.

Société pour le Développement des Investissements en Afrique (SODINAF): Quartier du Fleuve, ave de l'Yser, porte 345, BP 8012, Bamako; tel. 222-37-86; devt of gold deposits at Kodieran; Pres. and Dir-Gen. ALIOU BOUBACAR DIALLO.

Star Oil Mali: Quartier TSF, Zone Industrielle, Niarela, BP 145, Bamako; tel. 222-25-98; fax 222-68-82; f. 2004 by purchase of Mobil Oil Mali; distribution of petroleum products; Dir-Gen. TIDIANI BEN HOUSSEIN.

Tannerie de l'Afrique de l'Ouest (TAO): Zone Industrielle, Commune II, Bamako; tel. 221-44-70; fax 221-40-65; f. 1994; jt venture by private Malian interests and Curtidos Corderroura (Spain); processing of skins and hides; 150 employees.

Total Mali: ave Kasse Keita, BP 13, Bamako; tel. 222-29-71; fax 222-80-27; fmrly Elf Oil Mali, subsequently renamed TotalFinaElf Mali; present name adopted 2003; production and distribution of petroleum; sales US $45.2m. (2000); Dir-Gen. FRANC PAILLERE.

Usine Malienne de Produits Pharmaceutiques (UMPP): Zone Industrielle, BP 2286, Bamako; tel. 222-51-61; fax 222-51-69; e-mail umpp1@datatech.toolnet.org; f. 1983; 100% state-owned; 51% transfer to private ownership proposed in late 2006; producer of pharmaceutical products; cap. 2,551m. francs CFA (2006); Gen. Man. OUSMANE DOUMBIA; 187 employees (2003).

TRADE UNION FEDERATION

Union nationale des travailleurs du Mali (UNTM): Bourse du Travail, blvd de l'Indépendance, BP 169, Bamako; tel. 222-36-99; fax 223-59-45; f. 1963; 13 national and 8 regional unions, and 52 local orgs; Sec.-Gen. SIAKA DIAKITÉ.

There are, in addition, several non-affiliated trade unions.

Transport

RAILWAYS

Mali's only railway runs from Koulikoro, via Bamako, to the Senegal border. The line continues to Dakar, a total distance of 1,286 km, of which 729 km is in Mali. The track is in very poor condition, and is frequently closed during the rainy season. In 1995 the Governments of Mali and Senegal agreed to establish a joint company to operate the Bamako–Dakar line, and the line passed fully into private ownership in 2003. Some 358,000 metric tons of freight were handled on the Malian railway in 2001. Plans exist for the construction of a new rail line linking Bamako with Kouroussa and Kankan, in Guinea.

Transrail: Ouolofabougou, BP 4150, Bamako; tel. 222-67-77; fax 222-54-33; f. 2003 on transfer to private management of fmr Régie du Chemin de Fer du Mali; jt venture of Canac (Canada) and Getma (France); Pres. REJEAN BELANGER.

ROADS

The Malian road network in 2004 comprised 18,709 km, of which about 3,370 km were paved. A bituminized road between Bamako and Abidjan (Côte d'Ivoire) provides Mali's main economic link to the coast; construction of a road linking Bamako and Dakar (Senegal) is to be financed by the European Development Fund. The African Development Bank also awarded a US $31.66m. loan to fund the Kankan–Kouremale–Bamako road between Mali and Guinea. A road across the Sahara to link Mali with Algeria is also planned.

Compagnie Malienne de Transports Routiers (CMTR): BP 208, Bamako; tel. 222-33-64; f. 1970; state-owned; Man. Dir MAMADOU TOURÉ.

INLAND WATERWAYS

The River Niger is navigable in parts of its course through Mali (1,693 km) during the rainy season from July to late December. The River Senegal was, until the early 1990s, navigable from Kayes to Saint-Louis (Senegal) only between August and November, but its navigability was expected to improve following the inauguration, in 1992, of the Manantali dam, and the completion of works to deepen the river-bed.

Compagnie Malienne de Navigation (COMANAV): BP 10, Koulikoro; tel. 226-20-94; fax 226-20-09; f. 1968; 100% state-owned; river transport; Pres. and Dir-Gen. DEMBÉLÉ GOUNDO DIALLO.

Conseil Malien des Chargeurs (CMC): Dar-salam, Bamako; f. 1999; Pres. AMADOU DJIGUÉ.

Société Navale Malienne (SONAM): Bamako; tel. 222-60-52; fax 222-60-66; f. 1981; transferred to private ownership in 1986; Chair. ALIOUNE KEÏTA.

Société Ouest-Africaine d'Entreprise Maritime (SOAEM): rue Mohamed V, BP 2428, Bamako; tel. 222-58-32; fax 222-40-24; maritime transport co.

CIVIL AVIATION

The principal airport is at Bamako-Senou. The other major airports are at Bourem, Gao, Goundam, Kayes, Kita, Mopti, Nioro, Ségou, Tessalit and Tombouctou. There are about 40 small airfields. Mali's airports are being modernized with external financial assistance. In early 2005 the Malian Government announced its intention to establish a new national airline, in partnership with the Aga Khan Fund for Economic Development and Industrial Promotion Services.

Agence Nationale de l'Aéronautique Civile (ANAC): Ministère de l'Equipement et des Transports, BP 227, Bamako; tel. 229-55-24; fax 228-61-77; e-mail anacmali@hotmail.com; f. 2005 to replace Direction Nationale de l'Aéronautique Civile (f. 1990); Dir-Gen. ADAMA KONE.

Air Affaires Mali: BP E 3759, Badalabougou, Bamako; tel. 222-61-36.

Compagnie Aérienne du Mali (CAM): Bamako; f. 2005; 51% owned by Fonds Aga Khan pour le Développement Economique (AKAFED), 20% state-owned; domestic and international flights.

STA Trans African Airlines: Quartier du Fleuve, BP 775, Bamako; tel. 222-44-44; fax 221-09-81; e-mail sta-airlines@sta-airlines.com; internet www.sta-airlines.com; f. 1984 as Société des Transports Aériens; privately owned; local, regional and international services; Man. Dir MELHEM ELIE SABBAGUE.

Tourism

Mali's rich cultural heritage is promoted as a tourist attraction. In 1999 the Government launched a three-year cultural and tourism development programme centred on Tombouctou, Gao and Kidal. In

2005 142,814 tourists visited Mali, while receipts from tourism in 2004 totalled some US $148m.

Ministry of Crafts and Tourism: see section on The Government.

Defence

As assessed at November 2006, the active Malian army numbered some 7,350 men. Paramilitary forces numbered 4,800 and there was an inactive militia of 3,000 men. Military service is by selective conscription and lasts for two years.

Defence Expenditure: Estimated at 70,000m. francs CFA in 2006.

Chief of Staff of the Armed Forces: Col SEYDOU TRAORÉ.

Chief of Staff of the Air Force: Col YOUSSOUF BAMBA.

Chief of Staff of the Land Army: Col GABRIEL POUDIOUGOU.

Chief of Staff of the National Guard: Col BROULAYE KONÉ.

Education

Education is provided free of charge and is officially compulsory for nine years between seven and 16 years of age. Primary education begins at the age of seven and lasts for six years. Secondary education, from 13 years of age, lasts for a further six years, generally comprising two cycles of three years. The rate of school enrolment in Mali is among the lowest in the world: in 1997 total enrolment at primary and secondary schools excluding Medersas (Islamic schools) was equivalent to only 32% of the school-age population (males 39%; females 25%). According to UNESCO estimates, in 2003/04 primary enrolment included 47% of the appropriate age-group (males 46%; females 43%), while secondary enrolment was equivalent to only 22% (males 28%; females 17%). Tertiary education facilities include the national university, developed in the mid-1990s. Hitherto many students have received higher education abroad, mainly in France and Senegal. Estimated budgetary expenditure on education in 2000 was 64,930m. francs CFA, equivalent to 15.6% of total government expenditure in that year.

Bibliography

Bastian, D. E., Myers, R. A., and Stamm, A. L. *Mali*. Oxford, ABC-Clio, 1994.

Bertrand, M. *Transition malienne, décentralisation, gestion communale bamakoise: Rapport de recherche, ministère de la coopération, villes et décentralisation en Afrique, novembre 1997*. Paris, Pôle de recherche pour l'organisation et la diffusion de l'information géographique, 1999.

Bingen, R. J., Staatz, J. M., and Robinson, D. (Eds). *Democracy and Development in Mali*. East Lancing, MI, The Michigan State University Press, 2000.

Bocquier, P., and Diarra, T. *Population et société au Mali*. Paris, L'Harmattan, 1999.

Boilley, P. *Les Touaregs Kel Adagh: dépendances et révoltes: du Soudan français au Mali contemporain*. Paris, Editions Karthala, 1999.

Bonneval, P., Kuper, M., Tonneau, J.-P. *et al. L'Office du Niger, grenier à riz du Mali: succès économiques, transitions culturelles et politiques de développement*. Paris, Editions Karthala, 2002.

Brenner, L. *Controlling Knowledge: Religion, Power, and Schooling in a West African Muslim Society*. Bloomington, IN, Indiana University Press, 2001.

Camara, M. M. *Questions brûlantes pour démocratie naissante*. Dakar, Nouvelles éditions africaines du Sénégal, 1998.

Cissé, A. *Mali: Une Démocratie à Refonder*. Paris, L'Harmattan, 2006.

Cissé, Y. T., and Kamissoko, W. *La grande geste du Mali, des origines à la fondation de l'empire*. Paris, Editions Karthala, 1988.

Couloubaly, P. B. *Le Mali d'Alpha Oumar Konaré: ombres et lumières d'une démocratie en gestation*. Paris, L'Harmattan, 2004.

Davies, S. *Adaptable Livelihoods: Coping with Food Insecurity in the Malian Sahel*. New York, St Martin's Press, 1995.

Dayak, M. *Touareg, la tragédie*. Paris, J.-C. Lattès, 1992.

Diakite, Y. *La Fédération du Mali: sa création et les causes de son éclatement*. Bamako, Ecole Normale Supérieure de Bamako, 1985.

Diarrah, C. O. *Le Mali de Modibo Keita*. Paris, L'Harmattan, 1986.

Mali: Bilan d'une gestion désastreuse. Paris, L'Harmattan, 2000.

Foltz, W. J. *From French West Africa to the Mali Federation*. New Haven, CT, Yale University Press, 1965.

Gaudio, A. *Le Mali*. Paris, Editions Karthala, 1988.

Gibbal, J. M. *Genii of the River Niger*. Chicago, IL, University of Chicago Press, 1994.

Grevoz, D. *Les canonnières de Tombouctou: les français à la conquête de la cité mythique 1870–1894*. Paris, L'Harmattan, 1992.

Harrison Church, R. J. *West Africa*. 8th Edn. London, Longman, 1979.

Imperato, P. J. *Historical Dictionary of Mali*. 3rd Edn. Lanham, MD, Scarecrow Press, 1996.

Jenkins, M. *To Timbuktu: A Journey down the Niger*. New York, NY, William Morrow & Co Inc, 1997.

Jus, C. *Soudan français-Mauritanie: Une géopolitique coloniale (1880–1963)*. Paris, L'Harmattan, 2003.

Klein, M. A. *Slavery and Colonial Rule in French West Africa*. Cambridge, Cambridge University Press, 1998.

Konaré B. A. *Ces mots que je partage: discours d'une Première Dame d'Afrique, avec une introduction sur la parole*. Bamako, Editions Jamana, 1998.

Lucke, L. *Waiting for Rain: Life and Development in Mali, West Africa*. Hanover, MS, Christopher Publishing House, 1998.

Maharaux, A. *L'Industrie au Mali*. Paris, L'Harmattan, 2000.

Maïga, A. B. C. *La politique africaine du Mali de 1960 à 1980*. Bamako, Ecole Normale Supérieure de Bamako, 1983.

Maïga, M. T.-F. *Le Mali: De la secheresse à la rebellion nomade: Chronique et analyse d'un double phénomène du contre-développement en Afrique Sahélienne*. Paris, L'Harmattan, 1997.

Mariko, K. *Les Touaregs Ouelleminden*. Paris, Editions Karthala, 1984.

Roberts, R. L. *Two Worlds of Cotton: Colonialism and the Regional Economy in the French Soudan, 1800–1946*. Stanford, CA, Stanford University Press, 1996.

Snyder, F. G. *One-Party Government in Mali: Transition towards Control*. New Haven, CT, and London, Yale University Press, 1965.

Tag, S. *Paysans, état et démocratisation au Mali: enquête en milieu rural*. Hamburg, Institut für Afrika-Kunde, 1994.

Toulmin, C. *Cattle, Women, and Wells: Managing Household Survival in the Sahel*. Oxford, Clarendon, 1992.

MAURITANIA

Physical and Social Geography

DAVID HILLING

Covering an area of 1,030,700 sq km (397,950 sq miles), the Islamic Republic of Mauritania forms a geographical link between the Arab Maghreb and black West Africa. Moors, heterogeneous groups of Arab/Berber stock, form about two-thirds of the population, which totalled 2,508,159 at the November 2000 census. In mid-2006 the population totalled 3,162,338, according to official estimates, giving an average population density of 3.1 persons per sq km.

The Moors are divided on social and descent criteria, rather than skin colour, into a dominant group, the Bidan or 'white' Moors, and a group, probably of servile origin, known as the Harratin or 'black' Moors. All were traditionally nomadic pastoralists. The country's black African inhabitants traditionally form about one-third of the total population, the principal groups being the Wolof, the Toucouleur and the Fulani (Peul). They are mainly sedentary cultivators and are concentrated in a relatively narrow zone in the south of the country.

During the drought of the 1970s and early 1980s, there was mass migration to the towns, and the urban population increased from 18% of the total in 1972 to as much as 35% in 1984. The population of Nouakchott was 393,300 at the time of the 1988 census, but had risen to 588,195 by the census of 2000. The populations of towns such as Nouadhibou (59,200 in 1988) and Rosso (27,783 in 1988) had increased to 72,337 and 48,922, respectively, by 2000. There has been a general exodus from rural areas and an associated growth of informal peri-urban encampments. In 1963 about 83% of the population was nomadic, and 17% sedentary, but by 1988 only 12% remained nomadic, while 88% were settled, mainly in the larger towns. By 2001 the nomadic population numbered only 128,063, equivalent to less than 5% of the population.

Two-thirds of the country may be classed as 'Saharan', with rainfall absent or negligible in most years and always less than 100 mm. In parts vegetation is inadequate to graze even the camel, which is the main support of the nomadic peoples of the northern and central area. Traditionally this harsh area has produced some salt, and dates and millet are cultivated at oases such as Atar. Southwards, in the 'Sahelian' zone, the rainfall increases to about 600 mm per year; in good years vegetation will support sheep, goats and cattle, and adequate crops of millet and sorghum can be grown. There is evidence that the 250 mm precipitation line has moved 200 km further south since the early 1960s, as Saharan conditions encroach on Sahelian areas. In 1983 rainfall over the whole country reached an average of only 27% of that for the period 1941–70, and was only 13% in the pasturelands of the Hodh Ech Chargui (Hodh Oriental) region. Average annual rainfall in the capital in the 1990s was 131 mm. In the early 1990s the Senegal river was at record low levels, and riverine cultivation in the seasonally inundated *chemama* lands was greatly reduced, although larger areas of more systematic irrigation could be made possible by dams that have been constructed for the control of the river.

Geologically, Mauritania is a part of the vast western Saharan 'shield' of crystalline rocks, but these are overlain in parts with sedimentary rocks, and some 40% of the country has a superficial cover of unconsolidated sand. Relief has a general north-east–south-west trend, and a series of westward-facing scarps separate monotonous plateaux, which only in western Adrar rise above 500 m. Locally these plateaux have been eroded, so that only isolated peaks remain, the larger of these being known as kedias and the smaller as guelbs. These are often minerally enriched; however, reserves of high-grade iron ore in the *djbel le-hadid* ('iron mountains') of the Kédia d'Idjil were nearing exhaustion in the late 1980s, and production ceased in 1992. Mining at a neighbouring guelb, El Rhein (some 40 km to the north), began in 1984, while the exploitation of the important M'Haoudat deposit (55 km to the north of Zouïrât) began in 1994. Gypsum is currently mined on a small scale, and reserves of gold, phosphates, sulphur and rock salt have been identified.

In 1991 Arabic was declared to be the official language. The principal vernacular languages, Pular, Wolof and Solinké, were, with Arabic, recognized as 'national languages'. French is still widely used, particularly in the commercial sector.

Recent History

PIERRE ENGLEBERT

Revised by KATHARINE MURISON

OULD DADDAH AND THE MPP

Mauritania achieved independence from France on 28 November 1960. Moktar Ould Daddah, whose Mauritanian Assembly Party (MAP) had won all the seats in the previous year's general election, became Head of State. All parties subsequently merged with the MAP to form the Mauritanian People's Party (MPP), and Mauritania was declared a one-party state in 1964. A highly centralized and tightly controlled political system was imposed on a diverse political spectrum. Some elements among the Moorish population favoured union with Morocco and, although each Government included a small minority of black Mauritanians, the southern population feared Arab domination.

In the early 1970s the Ould Daddah Government undertook a series of measures to assert Mauritania's political, cultural and economic independence. In 1973 the country joined the League of Arab States (more generally known as the Arab League), and in 1974 withdrew from the Franc Zone. In that year the foreign-owned iron-ore mines were nationalized. The period of reform culminated in the adoption, in 1975, of a charter for an Islamic, national, centralized and socialist democracy.

For the next four years Mauritanian political life was dominated by the question of the Spanish-controlled territory of the Western Sahara, sovereignty of which was claimed by both Morocco and Mauritania. In October 1975 the International Court of Justice ruled that the territory's people were entitled to self-determination. In November Spain agreed to cede the territory in February 1976 for division between Mauritania and Morocco. However, the occupation of the territory by Mauritania and Morocco met with fierce resistance from guerrillas of the Frente Popular para la Liberación de Saguia el-Hamra y Río de Oro (the Polisario Front), which had, with Algerian support, proclaimed a 'Sahrawi Arab Democratic Republic' (SADR). With the assistance of Moroccan troops, Mauritania occupied Tiris el Gharbia, the province it had been allocated, but resistance by Polisario forces continued. Despite a rapid expansion of its army, Mauritania became increasingly dependent on support from Moroccan troops and on financial assistance from France and conservative Arab states. Mauritania was unable to defend itself militarily and its economy was in ruins.

SALEK AND OULD HAIDALLA

In July 1978 Ould Daddah was overthrown in a bloodless military coup. (He was detained until 1979, when he went into exile in France.) Power was assumed by a Military Committee for National Recovery (MCNR), headed by the Chief of Staff, Lt-Col (later Col) Moustapha Ould Mohamed Salek, which suspended the Constitution and dissolved the National Assembly and MPP. Two days after the coup Polisario declared a cease-fire with Mauritania. Salek assumed absolute power in March, replacing the MCNR with a Military Committee for National Salvation (MCNS). In May Lt-Col Mohamed Khouna Ould Haidalla was appointed Prime Minister, and in the following month Salek resigned and was succeeded as President by Lt-Col Mohamed Mahmoud Ould Ahmed Louly. In July Polisario announced an end to the cease-fire. Later in the month the Organization of African Unity (OAU, now the African Union—AU) appealed for a referendum to be held in Western Sahara. These events provided the impetus for Mauritania's withdrawal from the war: Ould Haidalla declared that Mauritania had no territorial claims in Western Sahara, a decision that was formalized in the Algiers Agreement, signed with Polisario in August. King Hassan of Morocco then announced that his country had taken over Tiris el Gharbia 'in response to local wishes'.

Ould Haidalla displaced Louly as President in January 1980 and dismissed several members of the MCNS. Ould Haidalla formed a civilian Government in December and published a draft constitution with provision for a multi-party system. In April 1981, however, the army Chief of Staff, Lt-Col (later Col) Maawiya Ould Sid'Ahmed Taya, became Prime Minister of a new military Government, and the draft constitution was abandoned.

TAYA ASSUMES POWER

Popular discontent with Ould Haidalla's rule led to a bloodless *coup d'état* in December 1984, led by Col Taya. The new Government introduced major economic reforms, which attracted support from foreign donors, and sought a political rapprochement with supporters of Ould Daddah by appointing three members of the ex-President's Government to ministerial posts. Ould Daddah was himself officially pardoned, but chose to remain in exile.

The second half of the 1980s witnessed growing unrest among the black Mauritanian population—resentful at what they perceived as the increasing Arabicization of the country. The distribution of a document entitled the *Oppressed Black African Manifesto* in April 1986 provoked the arrest, in September, on charges of 'undermining national unity', of a number of prominent black Mauritanians, and further civil disturbance ensued. Inter-ethnic tensions were again highlighted by the arrest, in October 1987, of 51 members of the black Toucouleur ethnic group, following the discovery of a coup plot. Three military officers were sentenced to death and 41 others were imprisoned.

CONSTITUTIONAL REFORM

At a national referendum on 12 July 1991, 97.9% of those who voted (85.3% of the registered electorate) endorsed a new Constitution, which provided for the introduction of a multi-party political system, although opposition movements claimed as few as 8% of registered voters had participated. The new Constitution accorded extensive powers to the President of the Republic, who was to be elected, by universal suffrage, for a period of six years, with no limitation placed on further terms of office. Provision was made for a bicameral legislature—comprising a National Assembly (al Jamiya al-Wataniyah), to be elected by universal suffrage every five years, and a Senate (Majlis al-Shuyukh), to be indirectly elected by municipal leaders. Arabic was designated as the sole official language. Following the adoption of the Constitution, legislation permitting registration of political parties took effect. Among the first parties to be accorded official status was the pro-Government Democratic and Social Republican Party (DSRP).

The presidential election took place on 17 January 1992. According to official results, Taya obtained 62.7% of the poll (51.7% of the registered electorate voted); his nearest rival, Ahmed Ould Daddah (the half-brother of the country's first President), received 32.8% of the votes cast. The defeated candidates denounced Taya's victory as fraudulent.

At the legislative elections, which took place on 6 and 13 March 1992, the DSRP won 67 of the National Assembly's 79 seats, with all but two of the remaining seats being secured by independent candidates. Six opposition parties had previously withdrawn their candidates, claiming that the electoral process favoured the DSRP. The rate of participation by voters was reportedly low. Other than the DSRP, only one party presented candidates for the Senate (indirect elections to which followed on 3 and 10 April). The DSRP consequently obtained some 36 of the 54 seats.

At his inauguration, on 18 April 1992, President Taya designated Sidi Mohamed Ould Boubacar, hitherto Minister of Finance, as Prime Minister, to lead a civilian Government, in which the sole military officer was the Minister of Defence. Ahmed Ould Daddah and his supporters formally joined the principal opposition to Taya's administration, the Union of Democratic Forces (UDF, which was renamed the UDF—New Era, UDF—NE), in June.

Mauritania's first multi-party municipal elections took place in January and February 1994, the DSRP winning control of 172 of the country's 208 districts. Opposition groups, including the UDF—NE (the only other party to win control of any districts, with 17), protested that the elections had been fraudulently conducted. The DSRP's control of the political process was confirmed at elections to renew one-third of the Senate's membership in April and May.

In March 1995 the Movement of Independent Democrats, which until 1994 had been a member of the UDF—NE, announced that it was to join the DSRP. Internal tensions within the UDF—NE threatened to undermine the influence of the party, as dissident groups complained of excessive centralization around Ould Daddah's leadership. In July several UDF—NE members were reported to have defected to the Union for Democracy and Progress (UDP).

A series of arrests followed reports of a foiled coup, allegedly supported by the Iraqi Government, in October 1995. Among those arrested were several journalists, two parliamentarians, the Secretary-General of the National Assembly, army officers and a police commissioner. In December 52 defendants stood trial on charges of forming an illegal organization, but all 52 were discharged on appeal in January 1996.

In January 1996 Taya appointed Cheikh el Avia Ould Mohamed Khouna (hitherto Minister of Fisheries and Marine Economy) as Prime Minister, and a new Council of Ministers was formed. At the elections to the National Assembly, held on 11 and 18 October, the DSRP won 71 of the 79 seats. The Rally for Democracy and Unity (RDU), closely allied with the administration, also secured a seat. The Action for Change (AC), which largely represented Harratin ('black' Moors who had formerly been slaves) was the only opposition party to win a seat, and six independent candidates were also elected. Later in October the Prime Minister named a new Council of Ministers.

In January 1997 several opposition leaders, including Messaoud Ould Boulkheir, the AC Chairman, were arrested on charges of maintaining 'suspicious relations' with Libya. Boulkheir and several others were later released, although five opposition members were sentenced to short terms of imprisonment for conspiring to break the law. (However, in April four of the convicted were acquitted on appeal.) In February five prominent opposition parties, including the AC and the UDF—NE, formed a coalition Forum of Opposition Parties (FOP).

At the presidential election, held on 12 December 1997, Taya was returned to office with 90.9% of the valid votes cast; his nearest rival, Mohamed Lemine Ch'bih Ould Cheikh Melainine (who had resigned from the DSRP in 1996), obtained 7.0% of the vote. Opposition parties alleged that there had been widespread electoral fraud and claimed that the official rate of voter participation (73.8% of the registered electorate) was unrealistically high. Taya subsequently appointed Mohamed Lemine Ould Guig, a university academic, as Prime Minister, and a new Council of Ministers was installed.

In March 1998 serious internal divisions in the UDF—NE caused a split in the party, with two rival factions (led by Ahmed Ould Daddah and Moustapha Ould Bedreddine) claiming leadership of the party. The DSRP won 17 of the 18 contested seats in partial elections to the Senate in April. In November Khouna, premier in 1996–97, replaced Guig as Prime Minister. In December Ould Daddah and two other members of his faction were placed under house arrest, after they demanded that a public inquiry be held into allegations that the Government had agreed to allow Israeli nuclear waste to be stored underground in Mauritanian territory. They were acquitted of charges of threatening public order in March 1999. In November the pro-Iraqi Baathist National Vanguard Party (Taliaa), a constituent member of the FOP, was banned by the Government for 'attempted subversion and public order violation', following its criticism of the Mauritanian Government's decision to establish full diplomatic relations with Israel in the previous month. In November Mauritania severed diplomatic relations with Iraq.

Partial elections to the Senate took place on 7 and 14 April 2000. The DSRP secured 13 of the 18 contested seats, although the UDP and the National Union for Democracy and Development each won one seat, while three seats were gained by independent candidates. Later that month Ould Daddah was detained two days prior to a meeting of the UDF—NE at which he was expected to address the purportedly illicit acquisition of wealth by associates of President Taya. He was released after five days, although a ban on public gatherings implemented following his arrest remained in force.

In October 2000, following violent anti-Israeli protests organized by the UDF—NE in response to renewed violence in the Palestinian Autonomous Areas, the Council of Ministers held an extraordinary session at which the party was officially dissolved, on the grounds that it had incited violence and sought to damage Mauritanian national interests. Several senior members of the UDF—NE were detained in November, while a demonstration in Nouadhibou by supporters of the party reportedly attracted 15,000 protesters. Ould Daddah refused to recognize the dissolution of the party, and the UDF—NE's partners in the FOP condemned the Government's action as unconstitutional. The faction of the UDF—NE led by Ould Bedreddine, which remained authorized, restyled itself as the Union of Progressive Forces (UPF). In December Ould Daddah was detained for three days on his return to Nouakchott from Paris, France, apparently in connection with allegations that he had met with terrorist groups while in France.

In January 2001 the National Assembly approved several electoral reforms, according to which an element of proportional representation would apply in subsequent legislative elections, with all registered parties to be granted equal funding and access to the media by the State; moreover, independent candidates were to be prohibited and the number of deputies was to be increased from 79 to 81. Although the FOP continued to demand the establishment of an independent electoral commission and the reregistration of Taliaa and the UDF—NE, in mid-January the Popular Front (PF) was the first party of the radical opposition to announce its participation in the electoral process.

In January 2001 a government reshuffle included the appointment of a new Minister of Foreign Affairs and Co-operation, Dah Ould Abdi. In April Ould Cheikh Melainine, who was now leader of the PF, was arrested on charges of 'directing a conspiracy against the State'. In June Melainine was sentenced to five years' imprisonment on charges of 'associating with criminals in order to commit acts of sabotage and terrorism in concert with Libya'.

LEGISLATIVE ELECTIONS

Some 15 political parties contested elections to the National Assembly, held on 19 and 26 October 2001, when an electoral turn-out of 54.5% was recorded. The DSRP won 64 of the 81 seats in the National Assembly. The AC took four seats, while the UDP, the RDU, the UPF and the newly formed Rally of Democratic Forces (RDF—which replaced the banned UDF—NE) each won three seats, and the PF secured one seat. At concurrent municipal elections the DSRP secured control of 184 of the 216 districts. In November Khouna was reappointed as Prime Minister, and a new Council of Ministers was announced.

In January 2002 the Government officially dissolved the AC, accusing the party of racism and extremism, and of attempting to undermine national unity and Mauritania's relations with Senegal. At partial senatorial elections, held on 12 and 19 April, the DSRP won 17 of the 18 contested seats. The remaining seat was won by the RDF, as a result of which part of the radical opposition gained representation in the Senate for the first time. In August the Convention for Change (CC), an organization including many former members of the AC, and led by Ould Boulkheir, was denied the right to register as a political party.

In October 2002 the UPF announced that it was to organize a series of meetings intended to promote a 'national dialogue' between the authorities and the opposition parties. However, later that month seven other opposition parties, including the banned CC, the PF and the RDF, formed a new grouping, the United Opposition Framework (UOF), which also stated as its purpose the co-ordination of dialogue between the opposition and the Government; the UPF was excluded from the UOF. Expressing discontent at the situation, in November the UPF withdrew its three deputies from the National Assembly. As a result, the group of opposition deputies was dissolved, as it was now reduced to eight members, less than the 10 required for the formation of a parliamentary group. Meanwhile, a government reorganization was effected in October.

HEIGHTENED TENSIONS

In March 2003 the commencement of full-scale military operations aimed at ousting the Baathist Iraqi regime of Saddam Hussain by a US-led coalition prompted protests in Mauritania, with widespread demonstrations held to demand that the Government break off diplomatic relations with Israel and with the two principal nations involved in the conflict, the United Kingdom and the USA. As opposition to the Government's broadly pro-US stance intensified in May, police raided the headquarters of a tolerated—although not officially authorized—Baathist party, the National Renaissance Party (Nouhoudh), arresting three of its leaders on unspecified charges; 13 other Baathists were also arrested over a period of four days. Ten of the detainees were subsequently charged with attempting to re-establish Taliaa. The Government's increasing intolerance of radical opposition movements targeted not only secularist Arab nationalist groupings, but also Islamist activists: a senior member of the RDF, Mohamed Jemil Ould Mansour, the leader of an extremist committee opposed to the normalization of relations between Mauritania and Israel, was one of several prominent Islamists and religious leaders, including at least eight imams, arrested in early May. The Government also stated that it would close any mosques that were being used for political purposes or that incited hatred against Jews. Meanwhile, in late March the registration of a new party, the Alliance for Democracy in Mauritania (ADEMA), was refused by the authorities, which stated that the party represented an attempt to re-establish the banned AC.

In May 2003 Taya implemented a minor government reorganization, dismissing Cheyakh Ould Ely, the Minister of Communication and Relations with Parliament, who, although a member of the DSRP, was considered a pan-Arab nationalist. A new Minister of Culture and Islamic Affairs, Lembrabott Ould Mohamed Lemine, was also appointed, apparently in an attempt to reduce tensions between the Government and Islamic communities. However, throughout May the arrest of Baathist and Islamist activists continued. At the end of the month a pro-Islamist weekly journal, *Ar-Rayah*, was closed, and nine Baathists were given suspended prison sentences by a Nouakchott court on charges of illegal political activity. In early June four Islamic cultural associations were closed down, and, according to opposition reports, more than 100 alleged Islamists were detained, 36 of whom (including Ould Mansour) were charged with plotting against the constitutional order.

The tensions that had been building throughout the first half of 2003 culminated in an attempted *coup d'état*, which commenced in the early hours of 8 June. Exchanges of fire were reported near the presidential palace and at other strategic locations in Nouakchott. Fighting in the capital resulted in the deaths of 15 people (including six civilians and the Chief of Staff of the Armed Forces, Col Mohamed Lamine Ould Ndiayane), according to official reports, with a further 68 people injured. Although the exact identity and motives of the rebels were unclear, reports named the leaders of the coup as Saleh Ould Hnana, a former colonel and Baathist sympathizer, who had been expelled from the Mauritanian armed forces in 2002, and Mohamed Ould Sheikhna, a squadron leader in the national air force; Taya subsequently stated, however, that Islamists had been responsible for the rebellion. (Other sources claimed that the attempted coup had been prompted by tribal rivalries.)

In the days following the restoration of order, at least 12 alleged rebel leaders were arrested, including Ould Sheikhna, although the whereabouts of Ould Hnana remained unknown. Meanwhile, more than 30 detained Islamists, who had been freed during the disorder, were reported to have surrendered themselves to the authorities, although Ould Mansour fled to Senegal, before later being granted political asylum in Belgium. In mid-June 2003 several senior officials, including the Chief of Staff of the National Gendarmerie, the President of the High Court of Justice (who was subsequently arrested) and the Mayor of Nouakchott, were dismissed and replaced by new appointees regarded as loyal to the President. In July another suspected coup leader, Lt Didi Ould M'Hamed, who had fled to Senegal, was extradited to Mauritania.

In early July 2003 President Taya announced the appointment of a new Prime Minister: Sghaïr Ould M'Barek, a Harratin, was regarded as a close ally of the President. A new Government was subsequently formed. Although several of the high-ranking officials who had been arrested in mid-June had been released by mid-July, it was reported that former Prime Minister Khouna had been detained, apparently after having sought political asylum in Spain. Further arrests of Islamists were reported throughout the month. In early August more than 80 members of the military, who had been arrested immediately after the restoration of order in June, were released, although many more reportedly remained in detention. At the end of the month Ould Cheikh Melainine was released from prison, having been granted a presidential pardon. Some 41 Islamists had also been released from detention by the end of the month, although others continued to face charges. In September it was announced that some 30 members of the military, including 20 senior officers, were to be tried in connection with the June coup attempt.

In mid-October 2003 the Constitutional Council announced that six candidates, including Taya, Ahmed Ould Daddah, Ould Boulkheir and former President Ould Haidalla, were to be permitted to contest the forthcoming presidential election. Ould Haidalla was widely regarded as the most credible challenger to Taya, and the former President's campaign attracted the support of several prominent Islamists and secular Arab nationalists, as well as a number of proponents of liberal reform. On 6 November Ould Haidalla and four of his close associates were detained; the State Prosecutor announced that all five were to be charged with planning a *coup d'état* and endangering national security, although they were released without charge later that day. Voting in the presidential election proceeded on 7 November, in largely calm conditions. According to official results, Taya won 66.7% of the votes cast, followed by Ould Haidalla, with 18.7%. Some 60.8% of the electorate participated in the election. Opposition candidates accused the Government of perpetrating fraud at the election, which international observers had not been permitted to monitor. On 13 November Taya announced the formation of a new Government, which included eight new appointees, although most of the principal posts remained unchanged.

In mid-November 2003 the trial of Ould Haidalla (who had again been arrested on 9 November) and 14 of his supporters, on charges of seeking to obtain power by force and by threatening the strategic interests of Mauritania, commenced in Nouakchott; one of Ould Haidalla's sons was additionally accused of having accepted US $1m. from Libya as an inducement to destabilize Mauritania. (In December the Government claimed that the Libyan authorities had provided significant financial support for Ould Haidalla's election campaign.) At the end of December Ould Haidalla and four of his co-defendants, including his son, were convicted of plotting to overthrow the Head of State; they received five-year suspended sentences, during which time they were forbidden to engage in political activity, and were fined the equivalent of $1,600 each. Four others received lesser sentences and fines. Ould Haidalla's conviction and sentence were upheld on appeal in April 2004.

In January 2004 Ould Mansour was arrested following his return to Mauritania, although he was released, subject to certain conditions, later in the month. In April the Government refused to consider an application for the registration of a new political party, the Party for Democratic Convergence (PDC), filed by supporters of Ould Haidalla, on the grounds that the party leadership comprised Islamist radicals, a number of individuals who were being sought by the courts and others who had recently received suspended prison sentences.

The DSRP won 15 of the 18 seats contested at partial elections to the Senate, held on 9 and 16 April 2004, while its ally, the RDU, secured its first senatorial representation. The opposition Popular Progressive Alliance (PPA) also obtained legislative representation for the first time, winning two seats; Ould Boulkheir was elected President of the party in August. In July a new political party opposed to the Taya regime, and apparently supportive of Ould Haidalla, Reward (Sawab), was officially registered. Later that month Taya effected a major government reshuffle, notably replacing the ministers responsible for finance, economic affairs and trade, following a sharp rise in consumer prices and a decline in the value of the national currency.

In August 2004 the Government announced that the security forces had discovered a plot to overthrow President Taya. The Minister of National Defence, Baba Ould Sidi, claimed that the conspirators belonged to a group known as the Knights of Change (Fursan al-Taghyir), which had been formed by those who had escaped capture following the coup attempt of June 2003. Thirty-one members of the Mauritanian armed forces were arrested following the foiled coup, and Ould Mansour was detained briefly. Later that month the Chief of Staff of the National Gendarmerie, Col Sidi Ould Riha, alleged that Ould Hnana and Ould Sheikhna had organized the coup with assistance from Libya and Burkina Faso (where they were said to be based). The Governments of both countries vehemently denied any involvement in the alleged plot, while opposition leaders suggested that the Mauritanian Government had invented the conspiracy as a pretext to purge the military of opponents.

The Government announced that it had averted a further attempted coup in September 2004. Among those arrested in connection with the latest plot was Capt. Abderahmane Ould Mini, who was also believed to have been one of the leaders of the June 2003 uprising. The Government accused Burkina Faso and Libya of providing logistical and financial support to the rebels through Sidi Mohamed Mustapha Ould Limam Chavi, a Mauritanian-born adviser to President Blaise Compaoré of Burkina Faso. In October Ould Hnana was arrested on the border with Senegal. Also that month Ould Mansour and two other Islamist leaders, Mohamed El Hacen Ould Dedew and Moktar Ould Mohamed Moussa, were detained for several days for questioning regarding the September coup plot. In November the three were arrested again and charged with falsifying photographs that had appeared on the internet and an Arabic television station, purportedly depicting detainees at a Mauritanian prison being tortured by prison warders. Meanwhile, Ould Haidallah, Ahmed Ould Daddah and Ould

Horma, the President of the PDC, were arrested on suspicion of having given financial assistance to the coup plotters.

In November 2004 the trial of 195 soldiers and civilians accused of participating in the coup attempt of June 2003 and the two more recent plots commenced at a military barracks in Ouad Naga, some 50 km east of Nouakchott. Ould Hnana and Ould Mini were the only defendants to admit to conspiring to overthrow the President, stating that they had been motivated by a desire to bring an end to tribalism, corruption, discrimination against black Mauritanians, and poor pay and mismanagement within the army. Ould Sheikhna and Chavi were among 19 defendants who were tried *in absentia*. At the conclusion of the trial in early February 2005, Ould Hnana, Ould Mini, Ould Sheikhna and a fourth army officer, Capt. Mohamed Ould Salek, were sentenced to life imprisonment with hard labour. The court acquitted 111 of the defendants, including Ould Haidallah, Ould Daddah and Ould Horma, while the remainder received prison sentences ranging from 18 months to 15 years. Chavi was sentenced to a 15-year term. In mid-February the three Islamist leaders arrested in November were released pending trial, shortly after two of them commenced a hunger strike in protest against their continued detention.

Taya effected a government reshuffle in March 2005, notably creating a new Ministry of Petroleum and Energy, headed by Zeidane Ould H'Maeyda, hitherto Minister of Mines and Industry. A day earlier it had emerged that government ministers had been awarded a large pay increase in an attempt to curb high-level corruption, with monthly salaries rising from UM 150,000 to UM 950,000.

In late April 2005 police arrested some 20 prominent Islamists (among them Ould Dedew and Ould Mohamed Moussa), who were accused of preparing 'terrorist acts'. At the same time the Government revealed that earlier that month seven Mauritanians had been intercepted on their return from Algeria, where they had allegedly received military training from a radical Islamist militant group, the Groupe salafiste pour la prédication et le combat (GSPC); it was claimed that others remained in training camps in southern Algeria. The seven men were reportedly charged with establishing a criminal association in May. In mid-May further arrests were made during police raids on several mosques in Nouakchott. The Government claimed that weapons had been discovered in the mosques, together with plans to carry out terrorist and subversive acts to destabilize the country. Islamist groups dismissed these claims and condemned the detentions, claiming that the crackdown on religious leaders was an effort to stifle opposition to Taya's regime. In late May 14 Islamists were released without charge, while some 40 others appeared in court, variously charged with leading or belonging to an unauthorized group, fomenting unrest and distributing propaganda in mosques.

In early June 2005 15 soldiers were killed, and a further 17 injured, in an attack by some 150 assailants on a military post in Lemgheity, in north-eastern Mauritania. The Government blamed the raid on the GSPC, which claimed responsibility shortly afterwards in a statement posted on its website, describing the attack as revenge for the imprisonment of Islamists in Mauritania. The Mauritanian Islamist movement condemned the attack. Meanwhile, an 'anti-terrorism' march organized by the ruling DSRP in Nouakchott was attended by an estimated 60,000 people, according to the party. Later in June it was reported that a government inquiry had discovered the existence of a radical Islamist group in Mauritania with links to the GSPC, known as the Mauritanian Group for Preaching and Jihad. The Government subsequently released documents that it claimed had been seized from detained Islamist leaders, listing potential targets of bombings and detailing plans to manufacture explosives. At the end of the month the Senate adopted legislation aimed at countering terrorism and money-laundering.

TAYA OVERTHROWN

On 3 August 2005, while President Taya was absent from Mauritania, attending the funeral of King Fahd ibn Abd al-Aziz as-Sa'ud of Saudi Arabia, a group of army officers seized control of state broadcasting services and the presidential palace in a bloodless *coup d'état*. A 17-member self-styled Military Council for Justice and Democracy (MCJD) under the leadership of Col Ely Ould Mohamed Vall, the Director of National Security, who had hitherto been regarded as a close ally of Taya, announced that it had assumed power. The Council stated that it would preside over the country for a transitional period of up to two years, at the end of which democratic elections, in which members of the MCJD and the Government would be prohibited from participating, would be held; the dissolution of the National Assembly was subsequently announced, although the 1991 Constitution, supplemented and amended by the Council's own charter, was to be retained, as were most of the institutions provided for by the Constitution, including the Constitutional Council and judicial bodies. Taya was prevented from re-entering the country and was flown initially to the Nigerien capital, Niamey; after a subsequent two-week stay in The Gambia, he took up residence in Qatar, where he had been offered political asylum.

On 7 August 2005 Vall appointed Sidi Mohamed Ould Boubacar, hitherto ambassador to France, as Prime Minister, a position that he had previously held in 1992–96; a new, civilian Government was named on 10 August. None of the ministers in the outgoing Government were reappointed, although Ahmed Ould Sid'Ahmed, who, in his former capacity as Minister of Foreign Affairs and Co-operation, had been largely responsible for Mauritania's rapprochement with Israel in 1999, was, notably, reappointed to that position. In the immediate aftermath of the coup, which was initially widely condemned internationally, the AU announced the suspension of Mauritania's membership. However, the overthrow of Taya's regime was reported to have widespread domestic support, including that of several prominent members of opposition parties and the DSRP. In mid-August a delegation from the AU met members of the MCJD, subsequently announcing the willingness of the Union to co-operate with the new leadership of Mauritania, although the country was to remain suspended from the organization pending democratic elections, in accordance with the Constitutive Act of the Union.

Having already released 21 Islamist leaders from prison a few days after seizing power, in early September 2005 Vall announced a general amnesty for political prisoners; Ould Hnana and Ould Mini were among the first to be freed. Some 20 detainees alleged to have links with the GSPC were excluded from the pardon. Later that month a number of exiled opponents of Taya's regime, including Ould Sheikhna, returned to Mauritania. In mid-October, however, the Ministry of the Interior, Posts and Telecommunications refused to register the PDC, led by Ould Horma and Ould Mansour, on the grounds that legislation on political organizations stipulated that Islam could not be the exclusive ideology of a party. (However, Ould Horma subsequently formed a new party, the Rally for Mauritania—TEMAM (RM—TEMAM), that was authorized.)

TRANSITION TO CIVILIAN RULE

In November 2005, following broad-based consultations with politicians and members of civil society, the MCJD issued a timetable for the transition to democratic rule: a constitutional referendum was to be held in June 2006, followed by elections to municipal councils and to the National Assembly in November, elections to the Senate in January 2007 and, finally, a presidential election in March 2007. A 15-member National Independent Electoral Commission was inaugurated at the end of November 2005. Meanwhile, the former ruling DSRP, which had changed its name to the Republican Party for Democracy and Renewal (RPDR), elected Ethmane Ould Cheikh Ebi el Maali, hitherto ambassador to Kuwait, as its new President. In December the MCJD replaced 12 of the country's regional governors, as well as most prefects and district administrators. A few days later Vall announced a 50% increase in civil servants' salaries aimed at reducing corruption within the public sector. In January 2006 the Knights of Change movement transformed itself into a political party, the

Mauritanian Party for Union and Change, led by Ould Hnana, as President, and Ould Mini, as Secretary-General.

An electoral census was conducted in February–April 2006. In March the MCJD approved proposals presented by the transitional Government on constitutional amendments to be put to a national referendum on 25 June. The principal changes envisaged included: limiting the presidential term of office to five years, renewable only once; stipulating a maximum age of 75 years for presidential candidates; and prohibiting a President from holding any other official post, particularly the leadership of a political party. The proposed reforms were generally supported by most major political parties, including the RPDR. In May the European Union (EU) announced the resumption of co-operation with Mauritania, which had been suspended following the coup in August 2005.

An independent human rights commission was established in May 2006. In June the MCJD approved new legislation liberalizing the media, notably abolishing the previous requirement that newspapers obtain government permits prior to publishing. The reforms were based on the recommendations of a national consultative commission on media reforms established six months earlier. In March the transitional Government had announced that it would allow the creation of private radio and television stations before the end of its term.

In late May and early June 2006 around 25 Islamists were arrested on suspicion of belonging to the GSPC; six of the detainees were released in mid-June, having reportedly agreed to break any links with extremist organizations. Meanwhile, 18 of the Islamists excluded from the amnesty granted after Vall seized power remained in prison awaiting trial; three others had escaped in April.

The constitutional referendum was held, as scheduled, on 25 June 2006. Several days earlier five associates of former President Taya had been arrested on suspicion of planning to sabotage the plebiscite, while a coalition of four parties critical of the Vall administration, the Bloc of Parties for Change, encouraged their supporters to boycott the referendum. None the less, observers from the AU and the Arab League declared their satisfaction with the conduct of the poll. According to official results, 96.9% of the valid votes cast were in favour of the amendments to the Constitution and a turn-out of 76.5% of the registered electorate was recorded. In late June 11 political parties, including the RDF, the PF, the PPA, the UPF and the RM—TEMAM, announced the formation of the Coalition of Forces for Democratic Change (CFDC), chaired by Ould Cheikh Melainine, to contest the forthcoming legislative and local elections.

The elections to the National Assembly and to municipal councils took place on 19 November 2006, with a second round of legislative voting held on 3 December. At least 28 parties and numerous independent candidates contested the polls, which were monitored by some 200 foreign observers from organizations including the EU, the Arab League and the AU. Turn-outs of 73.4% and 69.5% were recorded at the first and second rounds, respectively. The RDF became the largest single party in the National Assembly, winning 15 of the 95 seats, followed by the UPF, which took nine, the former ruling RPDR, with seven, and the PPA and the Centre Reformists, with five each. Parties belonging to the CFDC secured a total of 41 seats, while 41 independent candidates also secured legislative representation. In the months preceding the elections non-governmental organizations and the CFDC had accused the MCJD of encouraging independent candidacies with the aim of undermining political parties. In the concurrent local elections, it was reported that parties that had opposed Taya's regime had won 63% of the municipal posts. Independent candidates secured 34 seats in the 56-member Senate at indirect elections held on 21 January and 4 February 2007, while 15 seats were taken by constituent parties of the CFDC.

The first round of the presidential election, which was held on 11 March 2007, was contested by 20 candidates, eight of whom were representing political parties. Sidi Mohamed Ould Cheikh Abdellahi, who had served in the Governments of both Moktar Ould Daddah and Taya, won 24.8% of the votes cast, while the RDF's Ahmed Ould Daddah secured 20.7%, Zeine Ould Zeidane, the former Governor of the central bank, received 15.3% and Ould Boulkheir, of the PPA, took 9.8%. Some 70.1% of the electorate participated in the poll. As none of the candidates had achieved the 50% threshold required for an outright victory, Ould Cheikh Abdellahi and Ould Daddah proceeded to a second round of voting.

Although nominally an independent, Ould Cheikh Abdellahi was believed to be the candidate favoured by the MCJD and was also supported by The Charter (Al-Mithaq), an alliance formed in January 2007 by 18 political parties and movements that had formerly been loyal to Taya. Dominated by the RPDR and also including 39 of the 41 independent deputies, The Charter held a majority in the legislature. In addition, following the first round of voting, Ould Zeidane and, more surprisingly, Ould Boulkheir (a member of the CFDC, like Ould Daddah) also announced their support for Ould Cheikh Abdellahi. At the second round, which was held on 25 March, Ould Cheikh Abdellahi defeated Ould Daddah, with 52.9% of the votes cast, securing a majority in 10 of the country's 13 regions. A turn-out of 67.5% was recorded. International observers declared their satisfaction with the conduct of the election, and in April the AU restored full membership rights to Mauritania.

Ould Cheikh Abdellahi was inaugurated on 19 April 2007, marking the formal transfer of power from the MCJD. On the following day the President appointed Ould Zeidane as Prime Minister, and later that month the formation was announced of a new 28-member Council of Ministers, mainly comprising technocrats with no ministerial experience. The stated priorities of the new administration included the eradication of slavery, the promotion of national unity, the encouragement of job creation, the improvement of the health and education sectors, and the repatriation of Mauritanian refugees from Senegal and Mali (see below). In late April Ould Boulkheir was elected President of the National Assembly, becoming the first Harratin to hold this position. At its first meeting, in early May, the Government decided that all senior officials would be required to declare their assets with the aim of curbing corruption. Lower than expected petroleum revenues, which had resulted in a budget deficit of US $112m., prompted a 25% reduction in the salaries of the President and government ministers in early June. Later that month the Government adopted draft legislation on criminalizing and penalizing slavery. Although the practice had been officially abolished by presidential decree in 1981, criminal legislation to enforce the ban had not been introduced.

In late May 2007 the trial of 25 suspected Islamist militants commenced in Nouakchott; several of the accused were being tried *in absentia*. Some of the defendants were charged in connection with the attack on a military post in Lemgheity in June 2005 (see above), while others were accused of having received training from the GSPC (which had reportedly restyled itself as the al-Qa'ida Organization in the Islamic Maghreb). Their trial had been delayed by the MCJD until the transfer of power to a democratically elected Government had been completed. In early June 24 of the defendants were acquitted owing to lack of evidence, and one defendant, who had escaped from prison in April 2006, was sentenced, *in absentia*, to two years' imprisonment for falsifying identity papers. The trial of a second group of 14 alleged militants began in late June 2007. Three were charged with participating in the attack at Lemgheity, while 11 were charged with having links to the GSPC.

EXTERNAL RELATIONS

The persistence of inter-ethnic tensions within Mauritania was exemplified by the country's border dispute with Senegal. The deaths, in April 1989, of two Senegalese, following a disagreement over grazing rights with Mauritanian livestock-breeders, provoked a crisis that was exacerbated by long-standing ethnic and economic rivalries. In the aftermath of this incident Mauritanian nationals residing in Senegal were attacked, and their businesses ransacked. Senegalese nationals in Mauritania, together with black Mauritanians, suffered similar attacks, and it was believed that by early May several hundred people had been killed. Operations to repatriate nationals of both countries commenced, with international assistance. Many black Mauritanians fled, or were expelled, to

Mali. Mauritania and Senegal suspended diplomatic relations in August 1989. Hopes of a rapprochement were further undermined in late 1990, when the Mauritanian authorities accused Senegal of complicity in an alleged attempt to overthrow Taya. In December several sources reported the arrests of large numbers of Halpulaars (Toucouleurs) in Mauritania. The Government confirmed that many arrests had been made in connection with a foiled coup conspiracy, but denied suggestions that detainees had been tortured.

In July 1991 the foreign ministers of Mauritania and Senegal, meeting in Guinea-Bissau, agreed in principle to the reopening of the Mauritania–Senegal border and the resumption of diplomatic relations between the two countries. Full diplomatic links were restored in April 1992, and the process of reopening the border began in May. In late 1994 the Governments of Mauritania and Senegal agreed measures to facilitate the free movement of goods and people between the two countries, and in early 1995 it was reported that diplomatic initiatives with a view to the repatriation of Afro-Mauritanians from Senegal were in progress. According to provisional figures published by the office of the UN High Commissioner for Refugees (UNHCR), 19,630 Mauritanian refugees remained in Senegal at the end of 2006, compared with the population of 65,500 recorded in 1995. After taking office in April 2007, President Ould Cheikh Abdellahi urged Mauritanian refugees in Senegal and Mali to return, requesting assistance from UNHCR to facilitate their repatriation.

Meanwhile, in early June 2000 relations between Mauritania and Senegal deteriorated after Mauritania accused the new Senegalese administration of relaunching an irrigation project that involved the use of joint waters from the Senegal river, in contravention of the Organisation pour la mise en valeur du fleuve Sénégal project. The dispute escalated when the Mauritanian authorities requested that all of its citizens living in Senegal return home and issued the estimated 100,000 Senegalese nationals living in Mauritania with a 15-day deadline by which to leave the country. Tension was further heightened when the Mauritanian Minister of Communication and Relations with Parliament accused the Senegalese Government of supporting groups hostile to the Mauritanian Government. In mid-June, following mediation by Morocco, The Gambia and Mali, the Mauritanian Minister of the Interior announced that the decision to expel Senegalese citizens had been withdrawn and that Mauritanians living in Senegal could remain there. President Abdoulaye Wade of Senegal visited Mauritania later that month and announced that the irrigation project had been abandoned. In April President Taya's presence as guest of honour at a ceremony in Dakar to commemorate the 41st anniversary of the independence of Senegal was widely regarded as indicating an improvement in relations between the countries. Presidents Taya and Wade met again in July 2003, when negotiations were conducted on a range of bilateral and international issues; Wade reiterated his support for Taya's administration, following the attempted coup in Nouakchott in the previous month. The extradition of one of the suspected coup plotters, Lt Didi Ould M'Hamed, from Senegal to Mauritania was also regarded as evidence of a strengthening of relations.

In January 2006 Wade became the first foreign Head of State to visit Mauritania since Vall seized power in August 2005. Both leaders pledged to enhance co-operation in a number of areas, announcing that their Governments would henceforth hold regular joint committee meetings, and Wade expressed his support for the transitional process under way in Mauritania. In March 2006 Vall paid a reciprocal visit to Senegal. In the following month the two countries signed an agreement regulating the seasonal migration of Mauritanian cattle into Senegal, an issue that had caused significant disputes in the past, notably in 1989. In July 2007 Ould Cheikh Abdellahi held talks with Wade during his first official visit to Senegal since his election as President of Mauritania; both leaders affirmed their commitment to strengthening bilateral relations.

Relations with Mali were also dominated in the 1990s by the issue of refugees, which was the subject of senior-level bilateral negotiations. The problem of Mauritanian refugees in Mali was compounded by the presence in Mauritania of light-skinned Malian Tuaregs and Moors and also Bella (for further details, see the Recent History of Mali), who, the Malian authorities asserted, were launching raids on Malian territory from bases in Mauritania. Following reports that Malian troops had, in turn, crossed into Mauritania in pursuit of rebels, the two countries agreed in early 1993 to establish the precise demarcation of their joint border, which was concluded in September 1993. In April 1994 Mauritania, Mali and UNHCR representatives signed an agreement for the eventual voluntary repatriation of Malian refugees from Mauritania. The Tuareg refugee camp in Mauritania closed in mid-1997, following the repatriation of some 42,000 Malians. According to UNHCR provisional figures, there were some 6,165 Mauritanian refugees in Mali at the end of 2006. In January 2005 the Presidents of Mali and Mauritania signed an agreement on military co-operation intended to strengthen border security. In response to a request from the Mauritanian authorities following the attack on the military post at Lemgheity (see above), Mali dispatched troops to the common border in June. Meanwhile, both countries joined seven other North and West African countries in participating in US-led military exercises aimed at increasing co-operation in combating cross-border banditry and terrorism in the region. In July the army chiefs of Mauritania, Mali, Niger and Algeria discussed security issues with a US military delegation at a meeting in Nouakchott. Although the USA initially condemned the overthrow of Taya's regime in August 2005, US-Mauritanian military co-operation continued. In February 2006, during an official visit to Mauritania by the President of Mali, Gen. (retd) Amadou Toumani Touré, plans were announced to revive the process of demarcating the common border.

Although France has remained an important source of aid and technical assistance, the Taya regime sought increasingly to enhance links with the other countries of the Maghreb and with the wider Arab world. In February 1989 Mauritania became a founder member, with Algeria, Libya, Morocco and Tunisia, of a new regional economic organization, the Union du Maghreb arabe (UMA). The member states subsequently formulated 15 regional co-operation conventions. In February 1993, however, it was announced that, given the differing economic orientations of each signatory, no convention had actually been implemented, and the organization's activities were to be 'frozen'. None the less, meetings of UMA leaders continued to be convened annually. There was speculation that, during his visits to both Mauritania and Burkina Faso in March 2005, King Muhammad VI of Morocco attempted to mediate informally between the two countries' Presidents (whose relations remained strained following Mauritania's accusation that Burkina Faso and Libya had supported an attempt to overthrow Taya—see below), but without apparent success. Having earlier expressed a desire to strengthen Mauritania's ties with Morocco, Vall paid an official two-day visit to that country in November 2005, at the invitation of King Muhammad. During the visit, Vall's first outside Mauritania since assuming power in August, agreements were signed on co-operation in the fields of drinking water, maritime fishing and agricultural development. Vall also sought to improve relations with Algeria and Saudi Arabia.

Mauritania formerly enjoyed cordial relations with Iraq. In early 1990 the Mauritanian Government denied persistent rumours that it was allowing Iraq to test long-range missiles on national territory. Following Iraq's invasion of Kuwait, in August of that year, Mauritania condemned the deployment of troops in the region of the Persian (Arabian) Gulf by those countries that opposed the Iraqi action, and demonstrations in protest against what was regarded as a US-led offensive took place in Nouakchott. Mauritanian support for Iraq during the 1990–91 crisis resulted in the loss of financial assistance from other countries of the Gulf region. During 1993, however, Mauritania sought to improve its relations with Kuwait and its allies, and there was a perceived loss of influence for Iraqi sympathizers. In April 1994 Kuwait's First Deputy Prime Minister and Minister of Foreign Affairs visited Mauritania, and the two countries issued a joint communiqué in which the Taya Government emphasized its recognition of Kuwait's borders, as defined by the UN in 1993. Relations with Iraq deteriorated following the establishment, in 1999, of full diplomatic relations between Mauritania and Israel, and the proscription of the Baathist National Vanguard (Taliaa) Party late that year. Mauritania broke off diplomatic relations with Iraq in November 1999, following allegations that Iraq was seeking to undermine the stability of the Mauritanian regime. Despite widespread public opposition to the US-led military campaign against Iraq, which intensified in March 2003, the authorities in Nouakchott refused to support the Saddam Hussain regime.

Mauritania's relations with France improved significantly in the 1990s. Bilateral relations were consolidated in September 1997 and in February 1998 as a result of reciprocal official visits made by President Jacques Chirac of France and Taya, respectively. However, relations deteriorated abruptly in 1999, following the arrest by the French authorities in July of Ely Ould Dah, a captain in the Mauritanian army, who was attending a training course in France. Ould Dah was charged with torturing, in 1991, fellow Mauritanian soldiers suspected of participating in the unsuccessful attempt to overthrow the Taya administration in 1990. The charges were brought at the request of human rights organizations under the 1984 International Convention against Torture and Other Cruel, Inhuman or Degrading Treatment or Punishment, to which France is a signatory. The Mauritanian Government responded by suspending military co-operation with France (expelling French military advisers from Mauritania and recalling army officers receiving training in French institutions) and introducing visas for French nationals visiting Mauritania. In late September a court in Montpellier, France, ordered Ould Dah's release from custody, although he was required to remain in France until the end of legal proceedings. By April 2000, however, Ould Dah had illicitly returned to Mauritania. Relations with France appeared to improve following the election of a new, centre-right Government there in 2002, and in September of that year the French Minister of Defence, Michèle Alliot-Marie, met Taya in Nouakchott, and affirmed that co-operation between the two countries was to be strengthened. The French Minister of Foreign Affairs, Dominique de Villepin, visited Mauritania in June 2003, shortly after the attempted *coup d'état* had been suppressed, when he expressed renewed support for the Taya administration; it was announced that French military co-operation with Mauritania was to recommence later in the year. In July 2005 a French court found Ould Dah guilty of torture, sentencing him *in absentia* to 10 years' imprisonment.

In March 2006 Mauritania and Spain reached agreement on a plan to counter illegal migration in response to a significant increase in the number of West African migrants attempting to enter Europe by sailing to Spain's Canary Islands from Mauritania. In November it was reported that almost 10,000 would-be migrants had been detained and expelled by the Mauritanian security forces since May, when Spain had begun providing assistance to patrol the coast.

In November 1995, during a European-Mediterranean conference in Barcelona, Spain, Mauritania signed an agreement to recognize and re-establish relations with Israel. (The Libyan Government denounced these measures, closed its embassy in Mauritania and severed all economic assistance to the country, although diplomatic relations with Libya were restored in March 1997.) In October 1998 Mauritania's Minister of Foreign Affairs and Co-operation visited Israel and held talks with the Prime Minister, Binyamin Netanyahu. The visit was strongly criticized by the Arab League, which argued that it contravened the League's resolutions on the suspension of the normalization of relations with Israel. Shortly afterwards the Taya administration denied reports that it had agreed to store Israeli nuclear waste in Mauritania. Widespread controversy was provoked by the establishment of full diplomatic relations between Mauritania and Israel in October 1999. (Of Arab countries, only Egypt and Jordan, under their respective peace treaties with Israel, had taken such a step.) The announcement was widely criticized by other Arab nations, particularly Iraq (see above), as well as by opposition groups within Mauritania. Following the resumption of the Palestinian uprising in late September 2000, the Mauritanian Government came under renewed pressure to suspend diplomatic relations with Israel. However, although Taya's Government strongly condemned the use of excessive force by Israeli forces in the Palestinian territories, it did not accede to these demands, and in March 2001 Syria reduced its diplomatic representation in Nouakchott to the level of a chargé d'affaires and closed its cultural centre in Mauritania. A visit by the Mauritanian Minister of Foreign Affairs and Co-operation, Dah Ould Abdi, to Israel in May 2001, when he met the Israeli Prime Minister, Ariel Sharon, and the Minister of Foreign Affairs, Shimon Peres, provoked further controversy, particularly as it followed a violent escalation in the Israeli–Palestinian conflict and an appeal by the Arab League for all member countries to cease political contacts with Israel. A further meeting between Peres, Taya and Ould Abdi, in Nouakchott, in October 2002, also proved controversial. A visit to Mauritania by the Israeli Deputy Prime Minister and Minister of Foreign Affairs, Silvan Shalom, in early May 2005 was preceded, and followed, by the detention of several Islamists, although the Government denied that the arrests were linked to Shalom's presence. His visit was accompanied by a number of anti-Israeli protests in Nouakchott. Although some concern was initially expressed, following the *coup d'état* of August 2005, that diplomatic relations between the two countries might be terminated, the appointment as Minister of Foreign Affairs and Co-operation of Ahmed Ould Sid'Ahmed (who had held that position when Mauritania re-established full diplomatic relations with Israel in 1999) appeared to indicate that the new regime intended to maintain amicable relations with Israel. The transitional Government subsequently affirmed its commitment in this regard.

Mauritania's relations with Libya and Burkina Faso were severely strained in August 2004, after the Government accused both countries of supporting a plot to seize power from President Taya (see above). The Government claimed that Burkina Faso and Libya had supplied the insurgents with weapons and funding, while Burkina Faso was also accused of having provided refuge and training to Ould Hnana and Ould Sheikhna after the failed coup attempt of June 2003. Both countries vigorously rejected the allegations, and Burkina Faso requested that the AU establish a commission of inquiry into the charges. In December 2004, during the trial of those accused of participating in the plots to overthrow Taya, Ould Hnana denied receiving assistance from Burkina Faso or Libya. In March 2005 a ministerial committee appointed by the UMA to investigate the accusations made against Libya concluded that the Libyan leader, Col Muammar al-Qaddafi, had not been involved in the events in Mauritania. In December Vall's attendance at the inauguration of President Blaise Compaoré of Burkina Faso, following the latter's re-election in the previous month, appeared to indicate a willingness on both sides to improve bilateral relations, and the two leaders held talks after the ceremony. A few days later Vall led an official delegation to Libya, where he held talks with Col Muammar al-Qaddafi.

In December 2000 Mauritania withdrew from the Economic Community of West African States, owing to decisions adopted by the organization at its summit in December 1999, including the integration of the armed forces of member states and the removal of internal border controls and tariffs.

Economy

EDITH HODGKINSON

Revised by the editorial staff

Mauritania has few natural resources other than minerals and its rich marine fisheries, which benefit from the Canary Current large marine ecosystem. There are hopes that the development of offshore petroleum resources will strengthen the economy in the medium to long term. The commercial part of the economy that contributes to foreign-exchange earnings is based on the exploitation of its fishery and mineral resources, while the traditional rural economy is based mainly on livestock and agriculture, which is continually exposed to the problems of drought and desertification.

Overall gross domestic product (GDP) growth has remained solid, averaging 3.9% per year during 1995–2006, according to the African Development Bank (ADB). During 1995–2005 GDP per head increased at an average annual rate of 1.9%, according to the World Bank, while in 2005, Mauritania's gross national income (GNI), measured at 2003–2005 prices, was US $1,715.1m., equivalent to $560 per head (or $2,150 on an international purchasing-power parity basis). GDP increased by 13.9% in 2006.

Mauritania has undergone a series of economic reform programmes sponsored by the World Bank and the IMF since the early 1980s. A 1985–88 programme, agreed with the IMF, aimed to reduce budget and balance-of-payments deficits by means of more stringent criteria for selecting public investment projects. Emphasis was given to immediately productive schemes in fishing and agriculture, and to the rehabilitation of existing capacity and infrastructure in mining and transport. The achievements of the programme were to be consolidated under the terms of the 1989–91 economic support and revival programme, aided by an Enhanced Structural Adjustment Facility (ESAF) from the IMF.

In the late 1990s donors sought a greater commitment from the Government to create an expanded economic role for the private sector. The private sector contributed more than 60% of GDP in 1996, and its share in total investment increased from 10.0% in 1996 to 15.5% in 1997. However, donors claimed that government investment practice continued to inhibit the diffusion of wealth and the creation of domestic markets; consequently, foreign investment remained low. Nevertheless, since 1990 the Government had ceded control in 19 of some 41 parastatal companies and, in the agreement concluded with the World Bank in late 1998 (see below), it undertook to privatize the state telecommunications and public utility companies, and the national airline. The state telecommunications company, the Société Mauritanienne des Télécommunications was transferred to majority private ownership in 2001 and was renamed Mauritel. In late 2002, the hitherto majority owner, Maroc Télécom, reduced its stake in the company, and the state again became the owner with the largest proportion of share equity in the company, with 46%. The electricity company, the Société Mauritanienne d'Electricité (SOMELEC), was initially scheduled to be transferred to majority private ownership in 2004; however, in mid-2004, the Government announced that the privatization process was being temporarily suspended, owing to a global recession in the electricity sector, while the overthrow of the regime of President Maawiya Ould Sid'Ahmed Taya in 2005 further delayed progress towards privatization, although the new administration announced the intention of pursuing liberal economic policies.

In May 1999 Mauritania concluded a further agreement with the World Bank and the IMF, in accordance with which Mauritania was to receive US $450m. in support. In July the IMF approved a loan equivalent to some $56.5m., under the terms of a further three-year ESAF (subsequently known as the Poverty Reduction and Growth Facility—PRGF) to support the Government's 1999–2002 economic programme. A further PRGF arrangement was agreed with the IMF in June 2003. This arrangement was to provide access to funds equivalent to $8.8m. in 2003–06, and the principal aims of the programme included reforms of the banking sector, and of fiscal arrangements, and annual growth rates in excess of 5%. Following a sharp depreciation in the value of the national currency in mid-2004, and a related increase in consumer prices, the ministers responsible for finance, economic affairs and trade were replaced in July, together with the Governor of the central bank. The new authorities took measures to ensure fiscal and monetary stability, although inflation continued to increase, to an estimated annual average of 10.4% in 2004. However, in November the Mauritanian authorities requested the cancellation of the PRGF arrangement, following the publication of revised figures that revealed substantial (and previously unreported) extrabudgetary spending. In early 2006 the IMF determined that Mauritania should repay two non-complying disbursements issued under the 1999–2002 PRGF; the first of these repayments was made to the Fund in April 2006.

The severe drought of the early 1970s, with its destruction of livestock, and the growth of the modern sector caused a significant diminution in numbers of those living a nomadic or semi-nomadic way of life. In 1965 these were estimated to total 83% of the population, but by 1988 the proportion had declined to 12%, and by 2000 to less than 5%. A trend towards settlement in urban areas has been apparent, with an average annual growth rate of the population of Nouakchott, by far the largest urban settlement, of 5.2% estimated in 1988–2000. About 53% of the population was urban in 1996, compared with 14% in 1970. More than 50% of Mauritania's population is affected by poverty. Mauritania's first Poverty Reduction Strategy Paper (PRSP), prepared in conjunction with the IMF and the World Bank, was finalized in 2001, to cover the period 2001–15. The paper envisaged an acceleration of private-sector growth and increased infrastructural and institutional development. The Mauritanian economy remains vulnerable because of its dependence on the mining and fisheries sectors, both of which are liable to changes in world market prices. Moreover, these two sectors are relatively poorly integrated with the local, predominantly rural economy, which remains liable to droughts and desertification.

AGRICULTURE

As mining has developed, the contribution of agriculture and livestock-rearing to GDP has declined—from about 44% in 1960 to 23.7% in 2005, according to preliminary figures. In 2005 an estimated 51.6.1% of the economically active population were employed in the sector, according to FAO. Less than 1% of the land receives sufficient rainfall to sustain crop cultivation, which is largely confined to the riverine area in the extreme south. During 1995–2006, according to the ADB, agricultural GDP (including fishing) contracted by an average of 2.7% per year. Agricultural GDP increased by 4.0% in 2006.

As a result of considerable investment in irrigation and extension services by the Government and foreign donors, the area planted with cereals increased dramatically in 1993 and 1994, by 60.7% and 56.0%, respectively, which, combined with good rains, produced a bumper harvest of 234,314 tons in 1996. Output of cereals fluctuated thereafter: output reach 152,600 tons in 2003, partially reflecting an increase in the area of the crop harvested, but declined in 2004 to 124,600 tons. Improvements in irrigation led to a rise in rice production from 41,678 tons in 1991 to a record crop of 101,900 tons in 1998. Output declined subsequently and totalled 95,500 tons in 2005, according to FAO estimates. Mauritania's total production of cereals in 2004 was estimated at 176,891 tons in 2005, compared with an estimated 152,600 tons in 2003. In addition to the rice crop, the 2005 total included 88,900 tons of millet and sorghum and an estimated 14,400 tons of maize. Other crops produced included cow peas, dates, fresh fruit, tubers and vegetables. In mid-2004 Mauritania was one of several West African countries to suffer a severe invasion of locusts. The authorities estimated that 1m. ha had been infested by mid-August, with up to 80m. locusts per sq km. It was feared that the country, which had completed most of its planting for the year, could lose much of its harvest. FAO provided 90,000 litres of pesticide in response to a Mauritanian appeal for international assistance to combat the locusts.

Herding is the main occupation of the rural population and its contribution to GDP is more than three times that of crop cultivation. In 2004 the estimated number of cattle stood at 1.7m., while sheep and goats numbered 14.5m.

The Gorgol valley irrigation scheme, funded by the World Bank, the European Community (EC, now European Union—EU), Saudi Arabia, Libya and France, provided irrigation for 3,600 ha of rice, sugar, wheat and maize from the inauguration of the dam in 1985. Two similar projects were in progress: one at Boghé, on the Senegal river, and the other based on a number of small dams in the centre and west of the country. In total, the three schemes were projected to bring some 30,000 ha into cultivation. The construction of dams at Djama, in Senegal (completed in 1985) and at Manantali in Mali (completed in 1988), under the auspices of the Organisation pour la mise en valeur du fleuve Sénégal (OMVS) has increased the amount of land available for irrigation as well as generating power, some of which goes to the capital, Nouakchott. In 1996 Mauritania won funding of some US $76.5m. from various donors for a major five-year irrigation project along the Senegal river. In late 1999 the World Bank granted funding worth $102m. to support irrigated agricultural projects in Mauritania. In addition, Mauritania has signed a water management agreement with Mali and Senegal concerning water and pollution management within the Senegal river valley.

FISHING

The fisheries sector became increasingly important to the Mauritanian economy during the 1990s, and in 2005 it contributed more than 6% of national GDP, 29% of government receipts and around 29% of foreign-exchange receipts. The sector is increasingly regarded as an important potential contributor to national food security. It is also the second most important source of exports, and employed about 25,000 people in 1998. The Société Mauritanienne de Commercialisation de Poissons (SMCP), the marketing organization responsible for all exports of frozen fish, was transferred to majority private-sector ownership in the late 1990s. Virtually all the Mauritanian industrial fishing fleet is concentrated in Nouadhibou, in the north, which has both industrial and artisanal fishing ports, the latter constructed with Arab finance and Japanese aid. Artisanal fishing fleets are based along the coast and also in Nouakchott.

A series of three-year fishing agreements was signed with the EC in 1987, 1990 and 1993, granting defined fishing rights to certain vessels of EC countries. In 1996 a five-year accord was signed with the EU. The new accord increased substantially Mauritania's annual compensation entitlement (including licence fees), from around US $10.7m. in the previous three-year treaty, to $75.4m. The annual catch quota was raised from 76,050 metric tons to 183,392 tons. For the first time EU vessels were allowed to trawl the deep-water (pelagic) species. As part of the accord, the EU agreed to increase local employment in the industry from around 400 workers to 1,000 and to observe an annual two-month rest period (September and October) to protect species during their peak reproductive season. After prolonged negotiations, Mauritania signed a new fishing agreement with the EU for 2001–06, despite increasing fears that Mauritanian waters were being overfished, and subsequent concerns that the annual rest period was being neither observed nor effectively policed. The 2001 agreement with the EU provided for annual financial compensation of €86m., including support for surveillance and the management of fishing licences. In addition, EU vessels were to pay licence fees in accordance with the tonnage captured. A further accord, valid for six years, was concluded by the Mauritanian authorities and the EU in mid-2006; the fishing of sensitive species was to be significantly reduced under the terms of the new agreement. Mauritania was to receive €86m. annually, equivalent to the sum provided for by the 2001–06 agreement.

The value of fish exports generally declined during the late 1990s and 2000s, partially because of the poor state of the Mauritanian fleet, only 60% of which was considered operational at that time, while the potential for fishing to contribute to the national economy has also been challenged by the extent to which catches by EU and other distant-water fleet-fishing vessels from Mauritanian waters are landed outside the country, in centres such as Las Palmas (in Spain's Canary Islands—a major regional entrepôt) or Vigo (Spain). High-value species that are targeted by distant-water fleets and local fishing vessels include octopus, squid, hake and crustaceans. Lower-value small pelagic species (sardines and mackerel) are mainly targeted by vessels from Eastern Europe (the Baltic states, Poland and Russia), the Netherlands and Ireland. Substantial external assistance has been made available for the reform of the fishing sector.

Effective management of Mauritania's fisheries resources will require closer regional co-ordination, given the importance of migratory species and stocks that straddle national boundaries. Mauritania is a member of regional organizations concerned with fisheries management and surveillance and collaborates with neighbouring maritime states. Notably, in March 2002 Mauritania signed a fisheries pact with Senegal, which was aimed at co-operation in the management of marine resources, fisheries surveillance, bilateral economic ventures and enhanced collaboration in other fields such as scientific research and education.

MINING AND POWER

While over one-half of the population depends on agriculture and livestock for its livelihood, the country's economic growth prospects were transformed during the 1960s by the discovery and exploitation of reserves of iron ore and copper, which made Mauritania one of West Africa's wealthier countries in terms of per-head income. Moreover, the commencement of petroleum production, in early 2006, was expected to lead to significant economic growth. Mining and quarrying contributed 15.9% of GDP in 2005, according to preliminary figures. In the early 2000s iron ore still accounted for about 11% of Mauritania's GNI and for 50%–60% of the country's exports, although higher international prices for the commodity increased the share of exports accounted for by iron ore to 64.5% in 2005, compared with 52.4% in 2004, despite a small decline (from 11.0m. metric tons to 10.6m. tons) of the quantity exported. The Guelbs region has workable reserves of iron ore estimated at 5,000m.–6,000m. tons. These were being developed by the 80% state-owned Société Nationale Industrielle et Minière (SNIM), the successor to a private company established by the French Government in 1959. Production of ore, which began in 1963, reached 11.7m. tons (gross weight) in 1974, but by 1978 had fallen to 7.3m. tons, owing in part to attacks on the supply line by the Polisario Front. Following the cease-fire of 1978, production began to recover. However, by the late 1980s the Kédia d'Idjil mines were nearing exhaustion, production ceasing in 1992. Meanwhile, SNIM began exploitation of the lower-grade (36%) iron-ore deposits at El Rhein. Production began in 1984, increasing total national output to 11.5m. tons in 1990. However, production declined to 8.3m. tons in 1992, as technical problems at El Rhein meant that the deposit yielded little more than 2m. tons per year, thus rendering the site unprofitable. The company's main interest has now been transferred to the deposits at M'Haoudat, near Zouîrât (estimated to contain recoverable reserves of 100m. tons), which revealed potential for annual production of about 5.6m. tons of high-grade ore. The mine was inaugurated in 1994. As part of the project the mineral port at Point-Central, 10 km south of Nouadhibou, has been modernized and expanded. With the entry into production of the M'Haoudat scheme, the Government hoped to sustain overall output averaging 12m. tons of ore annually, over at least 25 years. Although the Government hoped to raise output to 15.5m. tons of ore per year, annual production in 1999–2005 averaged 10.5m. tons, with output of 10.8m. recorded in 2005, the highest annual output recorded since 2000.

In June 1995 the Government granted General Gold Resources Ltd (Australia—subsequently renamed Yilgarn Gold Ltd) exclusive rights to explore and exploit minerals in the south of the country. In November 1996 General Gold Resources applied for a new mining permit covering a region close to the northern border with Western Sahara. In June 1995 France awarded a substantial grant to aid gold prospecting in the Inchiri region, and in 1998 new exploration permits (mainly for gold and diamonds) were granted for sites in several regions to a joint venture between SNIM and the Office Mauritanien de Recherches Géologiques (OMRG), to General Gold Resources and to a joint venture between OMRG, the French Bureau de Recherches Géologiques and General Gold Resources. In 2001 a project at Akjoujt, which was being developed by Guelb Moghrein Mines d'Akjoujt, SA, and which contained an estimated 2,600 metric tons of cobalt, 328,000 tons of copper and about 25,700 kg of gold, was put up for sale. In July 2004 First Quantum Minerals Ltd of Canada announced that the Mauritanian Government had approved its involvement in the development of the copper and gold deposits at Akjoujt. A new company, the Société des Mines du Cuivre de Mauritanie, was duly formed, 80% owned by First Quantum. Production of some copper and gold at the site commenced in late 2005, with annual output anticipated to reach 30,000 tons of copper and 1,600 kg of gold. In March 1999 it was reported that geologists had discovered diamond deposits in northern Mauritania. By late 1999 two companies had reported progress with their diamond exploration projects, and in March 2000 the Mauritanian Government granted the US company Brick Capital Corpn a licence to prospect for diamonds in the Tiris Zemmour region. In January 2001 Ashton Mining announced the first discovery of diamond-bearing kimberlite in Mauritania, at Maqetir in the north. In that year BHP Billiton PLC of Australia, De Beers Consolidated Mines Ltd of South Africa, Rex Diamond Mining Corpn of Canada, and Rio Tinto PLC of the United Kingdom were all involved in prospecting for diamonds in the north of the country. However, Rex Diamond Mining Corpn ended diamond exploration activities in Mauritania in mid-2004.

SNIM is involved in prospecting for tungsten (wolfram), iron, petroleum, phosphates and uranium. Phosphate reserves estimated at more than 135m. metric tons have been located at Bofal, near the Senegal river. In October 1998 the Société Arabe des Industries Métallurgiques (SAMIA) was granted a permit to begin exploiting these reserves in co-operation with foreign partners. In October 1999 highly valuable blue granite deposits were discovered in the north of the country.

Exploratory drilling for petroleum began at the offshore Autruche field in 1989. A consortium led by two Australian companies, Hardman Resources and Woodside Petroleum, and Agip (of Italy) was also seeking financial partners to develop the Shafr el Khanjar field, where potential reserves are estimated at 290m.–850m. barrels. In May 2001 it was announced that exploratory drilling at the offshore Chinguetti field had discovered petroleum-bearing sands; it was subsequently estimated that reserves at the field amounted to 120m. barrels. In June 2004 it was announced that the Government and Woodside Petroleum had reached a final agreement on the development of the Chinguetti oilfield. The company was to invest US $600m. in the field and commenced production in February 2006, with initial output forecast at 75,000 barrels per day (b/d). The company signed a revised contract, which *inter alia*, would result in a greater share of petroleum revenue being payable to the Government when petroleum prices were high, with the new authorities in early 2006, thereby resolving a dispute between the company and the former Taya regime. However, in mid-2006 Woodside stated that initial output from Chinguetti was somewhat lower than expected, with around 37,000 b/d recorded at that time. Meanwhile, exploration and seismic testing for offshore petroleum and gas were continuing, with reports of further discoveries, including significant levels of both petroleum and gas at the offshore Tiof field in November 2003, although outstanding concerns regarding the protection of the marine environment and the avoidance of conflict between the petroleum sector and marine fisheries remained unresolved.

Reflecting the needs of mineral development, electricity generation has expanded rapidly since the late 1960s, from 38m. kWh in 1967 to 165m. kWh in 2001. About one-half of the electricity is now generated by hydroelectric installations built on the Senegal river under the OMVS scheme (see above). SNIM generates electrical power for its production centres from two diesel-powered plants at Zouïrât, and from the Point-Central plant in Nouadhibou. Mauritania receives 15% of the output from the Manantali dam. Additionally, it was intended to connect the dam under construction at Boghé (see above) to the Manantali electricity grid, in a project funded by the Arab Fund for Economic and Social Development. A new power station that was intended to generate 35% of the power needed in the capital was inaugurated in Nouakchott in May 2003.

MANUFACTURING

There is, as yet, no significant industrial development outside the mining and the fish-processing sectors, although some development has occurred in areas such as construction materials and food processing. Initially, development concentrated on import substitution. However, as income from iron mining rose during the early 1970s, the Government promoted the development of large-scale, capital-intensive manufacturing projects, in which it participated directly. These included the petroleum refinery at Nouadhibou, which entered production in 1978, with an annual capacity of 1m. metric tons. In the event, this wholly government-financed project was closed by the new regime. After reopening in 1982 (with Algerian assistance), the refinery closed again after only six months. However, an agreement on rehabilitation was reached with Algeria in 1985, and operations resumed in mid-1987. More than three-quarters of its total annual output of 1.5m. tons are exported.

The development of fish-processing units at Nouadhibou, as a result of the Government's fisheries policy, made this subsector into the single most important manufacturing activity, accounting for as much as 3.9% of GDP in 2002. However, several plants have closed, mainly because of high utility costs, a lack of skilled labour and inadequate port facilities. In 2005 the manufacturing sector contributed 5.1% of GDP, according to preliminary figures. According to the ADB, in 1995–2006 manufacturing GDP grew at an average annual rate of just 0.9%. The sector grew by 5.0% in 2006.

TRANSPORT INFRASTRUCTURE

Transport and communications in Mauritania are difficult, with sparse coverage and a lack of maintenance, although infrastructure related to mineral development is of a high standard. The iron-ore port of Point-Central can accommodate 150,000-ton bulk carriers (a 740-km railway line links the port with the iron-ore deposits at Zouïrât, the El Rhein deposit and M'Haoudat), while Nouakchott's capacity was expanded to 950,000 metric tons with the completion, in 1986, of a 500,000-ton deep-water facility, financed and constructed by the People's Republic of China. This development reduced the country's dependence on transportation through Senegal, and the excess capacity that the port currently represents could be used for gypsum and copper exports, and for traffic to Mali. Outside the mineral shipment network, communications are at present still poor: in 1999 there were some 7,891 km of roads and tracks, of which only 2,090 km were tarred. In early 2004 the construction of a 470-km road linking Nouakchott and Nouadhibou was completed; the new highway was expected to improve prospects for both tourism and external trade. The Senegal river is navigable for 210 km throughout the year, and there are three major river ports, at Rosso, Kaédi and Gouraye. There are international airports at Nouakchott, Nouadhibou and Néma, 13 small regional airports and a number of other airstrips. Meanwhile, a new Mauritanian airline was created in early 2007. Mauritanian Airlines was established following an agreement signed between TunisAir of Tunisia and the Mauritanian private group Bouamatou.

FINANCE

Mauritania's budget situation was transformed by mineral development. In the late 1970s, until the withdrawal from Western Sahara in 1979, spending increased as a result of the guerrilla war and the administrative costs associated with the annexed territory. Even after this time, the budget remained in deficit. In return for IMF stand-by credits, successive Mauritanian Governments have since 1980 attempted to restrain the level of budgetary spending and to raise current revenue. The 1985–88 recovery programme aimed to balance the current budget in 1986 and to generate a surplus by 1988. Despite initial difficulties, the current budget did achieve the intended balance, and the overall deficit eased to about UM 900m. in 1986, before widening to UM 2,000m. in 1987 and to UM 6,300m. in 1989. Improvements in revenue from taxes, in conjunction with strict controls on expenditure, reduced the deficit to an average of UM 3,930m. per year in 1990–92 (equivalent to 4.4% of GDP).

In 2000 a budgetary deficit of UM 7,400m. (equivalent to 3.3% of GDP) was recorded, and in 2001 the deficit increased to UM 9,800m. (equivalent to 4.0% of GDP). A budget surplus of UM 20,900m., equivalent to 7.8% of GDP, was recorded in 2002. The 2003 budget concentrated on increased spending on poverty reduction, income-tax reform and the monitoring of tax revenues, and a substantial reorganization and simplification of the taxation system was implemented in that year. None the less, a budgetary deficit of some UM 39,900m. (equivalent to 13.0% of GDP) was recorded in that year. In 2004 the deficit was reduced to UM 19,100m., equivalent to 5.3% of GDP, but increased in 2005 to UM 35,000m. (7.9% of GDP), according to preliminary figures. According to the IMF, in 2006 revenue totalled UM 153,500m., while expenditure was UM 206,400m.

FOREIGN TRADE AND PAYMENTS

Foreign trade has been transformed by the development, first, of the mineral sector and, second, of fishing. The balance of trade remained positive from 1983 until 1992 when a sharp fall in earnings from iron ore (resulting from both lower volumes and international prices) and a large increase in capital imports caused a deficit of some US $55m. Following a small surplus in 1993, a trade surplus of $184m. was recorded in 1995. Official estimates indicated a reduced trade surplus, of $96m., in 1996, owing to a substantial increase in imports. The balance of trade remained in surplus until 2001, when a deficit of $33.7m. was recorded. The deficit widened in 2002, to an estimated $87.7m., further increasing, in 2003 to $223.8m., in 2004 to $483.8m. and in 2005 to $783.3m. (according to provisional data). The IMF estimated a provisional deficit of $199.6m. in 2006. The sharp increase in the deficit during this period was principally the consequence of the import of petroleum-related machinery and equipment prior to the coming on-stream of various facilities. Such fluctuations in the trade balance were largely responsible for changes in the deficit on the current account of the balance of payments, although this remained substantial into the 2000s. In 1999 the current account registered a surplus of $24.0m., but a deficit of $26.0m. was recorded in 2000, which widened to $104.5m. in 2001. The current-account deficit increased to $51.2m. in 2002, to $175.3m. in 2003, $517.1m. in 2004 and to $934.0m. in 2005. According to the IMF, it had been significantly reduced in 2006, to $35.6m. In 2002 the principal source of imports (20.8%) was France; other major suppliers were Belgium-Luxembourg, Spain and Germany. The principal markets for exports in that year were Italy (14.8%), France (14.4%), Spain and Belgium-Luxembourg. The principal exports in 2005 were iron ore and fish. The principal imports in that year were petroleum exploration-related machinery and equipment (accounting for 43.2% of the total, according to preliminary data), non-petroleum mining-related machinery and equipment and petroleum products.

The substantial trade surpluses that occurred every year during 1965–74 enabled Mauritania to service its extensive foreign borrowing, while reaching a payments surplus in 1971–74. This allowed Mauritania to leave the West African Monetary Union in 1973 and establish its own currency, the ouguiya (UM), not linked to the franc. In subsequent years continued capital borrowing was necessary to sustain Mauritania's reserves. Despite a rescheduling of debt obtained by the regime that came to power in 1978, indebtedness continued to rise, totalling US $1,342m. at the end of 1984, which was almost double the level of GNI in that year. Against the background of the economic stabilization programme agreed with the IMF, the Taya Government secured rescheduling of its debt to official creditors in 1985, 1986 and 1987, on the latter occasion obtaining a 15-year rescheduling (including five years' grace) on repayment. Moreover, Mauritania continued to receive substantial aid, of which more than one-half was in grant form: such funding averaged $242m. per year in 1985–88.

The debt rose inexorably, to US $2,054m. at the end of 1987 (equivalent to 247% of GNI), and arrears on interest payments had doubled by 1988, to $52m. Mauritania was classified by the World Bank as 'debt-distressed' and was thus eligible for the system of exceptional debt-relief that was agreed in principle at the summit meeting of industrialized nations, held in Toronto, Canada, in June 1988. Accordingly, in June 1989 the 'Paris Club' of Western official creditors agreed to reschedule $52m. of the country's external debt. While the foreign debt continued to rise, to $2,233m. by the end of 1991, debt-rescheduling agreements meant that the debt-service ratio was reduced to 20.4% of the value of exports of goods and services in that year. Mauritania's failure to pay off debt arrears or to achieve the fiscal targets agreed with the IMF for 1989–91 meant that no further debt relief was accorded until early 1993, when the 'Paris Club' agreed to cancel one-half of the interest due on non-concessional debt and to reschedule the remainder over 23 years, with a 10-year grace period. Nevertheless, debt had risen to $2,396m. by the end of 1995, equivalent to 235.9% of GNI. In early 1995 the IMF approved a $63m. loan, extending an ESAF to support the Government's financial and economic reform programme for 1995–97.

Towards the end of 1996 almost the entire stock of foreign privately contracted commercial debt (of US $92m.) was retired through a discounted buy-back operation funded by the World Bank and other donors. A further ESAF for the period 1999–2002 was agreed in July 1999. At the end of 1998 total external debt stood at $2,391m., while the cost of debt-servicing was equivalent to 27.7% of the value of exports of goods and services. Total external debt was equivalent to 250.8% of GNI at that time. Debt relief increased considerably, totalling UM 11,603m. in 2001. At the end of 2003 total external debt amounted to $2,297m. (of which 89.1% was long-term public debt), equivalent to some 141.9% of GNI.

In late 1998 Mauritania concluded a three-year (1999–2001) arrangement that would allow it to reduce its multilateral debt substantially under the initiative of the World Bank and the IMF for heavily indebted poor countries (HIPCs). In return, Mauritania undertook to privatize the posts and telecommunications sectors, public utilities (water and electricity) and the national air carrier, Air Mauritanie. A second phase of the agreement, to be implemented in its final year, related to Mauritania's monetary policies and the control of the exchange market. The agreement was to be complemented by measures to protect fish stocks and reform the country's tax regime. In February 2000 Mauritania became one of the first countries to receive assistance under the HIPC initiative, amounting to a reduction of Mauritania's debt by US $622m. in net present value terms, representing savings of an estimated 40% of annual debt-service obligations. Agreement under the enhanced HIPC initiative was reached in 2002. Additionally, the 'Paris Club' of official creditors agreed in March 2000 to cancel $80m. of Mauritania's external debt; a further sum, equivalent to $188m., was cancelled by the 'Paris Club' in July 2002. In June 2003 a further PRGF arrangement was agreed with the IMF. The PRGF was cancelled in late 2004, following the provision of inaccurate information to the Fund (see above), and the IMF emphasized that full disclosure of the mis-stated official reserves for 2000–02, as well as independent verification of the central bank's financial statements would be required before any further requests for funding would be considered. Following the assumption of power by a new, transitional Government in August 2005, a significant revision of economic and financial data was undertaken, as a result of which marked discrepancies were found between economic data provided to the IMF during much of the 1990s and early 2000s. However, following the repayment of two disbursements issued during 1999–2002 deemed to be non-complying, the authorities entered into a new PRGF-supported programme later in 2006. After completion of the first review under the PRGF, the IMF commended Mauritania's progress. The country had met all criteria under the programme, with significant structural reforms carried out, including the adoption of legislation granting greater autonomy to the central bank. The new law also made it more difficult for the Government to interfere in banking affairs. Another positive structural reform noted by the Fund was the new foreign exchange market, which was introduced in early 2007.

The support of foreign donors remains essential to stimulate the key sectors of the economy. It was estimated that Mauritania would require some US $44m. in foreign aid to finance the programmes envisaged in its PRSP for 2004/05. Net official development assistance was $355m. in 2002 (compared with $212m. in 2000 and $268m. in 2001), with a number of multilateral (principally the EU and the World Bank, but also the ADB, the Islamic Development Bank (IDB) and the International Fund for Agricultural Development) and bilateral (notably France, Japan, Germany and the Netherlands) sources of support. In June 2005 Mauritania was among 18 countries to be granted 100% debt relief on multilateral debt agreed by the Group of Eight leading industrialized nations (G-8), subject to the approval of the lenders. In December 2006 the IMF offered Mauritania a loan of $24.2m. (to be dispersed over three years) to combat poverty. More recently, in April 2007 the IDB granted the Government $18m. in the form of two loans. The money has been set aside for road-building and the agricultural sector.

Statistical Survey

Source (unless otherwise stated): Office National de la Statistique, BP 240, Nouakchott; tel. 525-28-80; fax 525-51-70; e-mail webmaster@ons.mr; internet www.ons.mr.

Area and Population

AREA, POPULATION AND DENSITY

Area (sq km)	1,030,700*
Population (census results)	
5–20 April 1988	1,864,236†
1–15 November 2000‡	
Males	1,241,712
Females	1,266,447
Total	2,508,159
Population (official estimates)	
2004	2,823,062
2005	2,905,727
2006	3,162,338
Density (per sq km) at mid-2006	3.1

* 397,950 sq miles.

† Including an estimate of 224,095 for the nomad population.

‡ Figures include nomads, totalling 128,163 (males 66,007, females 62,156), enumerated during 10 March–20 April 2001.

Ethnic Groups (percentage of total, 1995): Moor 81.5; Wolof 6.8; Toucouleur 5.3; Sarakholé 2.8; Peul 1.1; Others 2.5 (Source: La Francophonie).

REGIONS
(census of November 2000)

Region	Area ('000 sq km)	Population*	Chief town
Hodh Ech Chargui	183	281,600	Néma
Hodh el Gharbi	53	212,156	Aïoun el Atrous
Assaba	37	242,265	Kiffa
Gorgol	14	242,711	Kaédi
Brakna	33	247,006	Aleg
Trarza	68	268,220	Rosso
Adrar	215	69,542	Atâr
Dakhlet-Nouadhibou	22	79,516	Nouadhibou
Tagant	95	76,620	Tidjikja
Guidimagha	10	177,707	Sélibaby
Tiris Zemmour	253	41,121	Zouïrât
Inchiri	47	11,500	Akjoujt
Nouakchott (district)	1	558,195	Nouakchott
Total	1,030	2,580,159	

* Including nomad population, enumerated during 10 March–20 April 2001.

PRINCIPAL TOWNS
(population at census of 2000*)

Nouakchott (capital)	558,195	Kiffa	32,716
Nouadhibou	72,337	Bougadoum	29,045
Rosso	48,922	Atâr	24,021
Boghé	37,531	Boutilimit	22,257
Adel Bagrou	36,007	Theiekane	22,041
Kaédi	34,227	Ghabou	21,700
Zouïrât	33,929	Mal	20,488

* With the exception of Nouakchott, figures refer to the population of communes (municipalities), and include nomads.

Mid-2005 (incl. suburbs, UN estimate): Nouakchott 637,000 (Source: UN, *World Urbanization Prospects: The 2005 Revision*).

BIRTHS AND DEATHS
(annual averages, UN estimates)

	1990–95	1995–2000	2000–05
Birth rate (per 1,000)	39.0	37.2	35.3
Death rate (per 1,000)	10.7	9.6	8.7

Source: UN, *World Population Prospects: The 2006 Revision*.

Expectation of life (years at birth, WHO estimates): 58 (males 55; females 60) in 2004 (Source: WHO, *World Health Report*).

ECONOMICALLY ACTIVE POPULATION
(census of 2000, persons aged 10 years and over, including nomads)

	Males	Females	Total
Agriculture, hunting, forestry and fishing	219,771	94,535	314,306
Mining and quarrying	5,520	249	5,769
Manufacturing	18,301	11,855	30,156
Electricity, gas and water	2,655	182	2,837
Construction	15,251	311	15,562
Trade, restaurants and hotels	83,733	24,799	108,532
Transport, storage and communications	17,225	691	17,916
Financing, insurance, real estate and business services	1,557	454	2,011
Community, social and personal services	72,137	26,583	98,720
Other and unspecified	33,350	22,608	55,958
Total	469,500	182,267	651,767

Mid-2005 (estimates in '000): Agriculture, etc. 705; Total labour force 1,367 (Source FAO).

Health and Welfare

KEY INDICATORS

Total fertility rate (children per woman, 2005)	5.6
Under-5 mortality rate (per 1,000 live births, 2005)	125
HIV/AIDS (% of persons aged 15–49, 2005)	0.7
Physicians (per 1,000 head, 2004)	0.11
Hospital beds (per 1,000 head, 2006)	0.60
Health expenditure (2004): US $ per head (PPP)	42.9
Health expenditure (2004): % of GDP	2.9
Health expenditure (2004): public (% of total)	69.4
Access to water (% of persons, 2004)	53
Access to sanitation (% of persons, 2004)	34
Human Development Index (2004): ranking	153
Human Development Index (2004): value	0.486

For sources and definitions, see explanatory note on p. vi.

Agriculture

PRINCIPAL CROPS
('000 metric tons)

	2003	2004	2005
Rice (paddy)	79.0	85.5	72.0
Maize*	6.0	5.2	14.4
Sorghum	68.0†	22.6*	88.0*
Roots and tubers	6.7	6.5	6.5
Peas, dry†	10.0	11.0	11.7
Cow peas†	7.5	7.5	7.5
Beans, dry†	10.0	10.0	10.0
Other pulses†	17.0	17.0	17.0
Vegetables†	3.9	3.9	3.9
Dates	20.0*	24.0*	22.0
Other fruit†	3.1	3.1	3.1

* Unofficial figure(s).
† FAO estimate(s).

Source: FAO.

LIVESTOCK
('000 head, year ending September, FAO estimates)

	2003	2004	2005
Cattle	1,600	1,600	1,692
Goats	5,600	5,600	5,600
Sheep	8,800	8,850	8,850
Asses, mules or hinnies	158	158	158
Horses	20	20	20
Camels	1,300	1,300	1,397
Chickens	4,200	4,200	4,200

Source: FAO.

LIVESTOCK PRODUCTS
('000 metric tons, FAO estimates)

	2003	2004	2005
Goat meat	13.8	13.8	13.8
Camel meat	23.0	23.0	23.0
Chicken meat	4.4	4.3	4.3
Camel milk	22.0	22.0	22.0
Cows' milk	120.8	120.8	120.8
Sheep's milk	96.3	96.3	96.3
Goats' milk	109.8	109.8	109.8
Hen eggs	5.3	5.3	5.3

Source: FAO.

Forestry

ROUNDWOOD REMOVALS
('000 cubic metres, excl. bark, FAO estimates)

	2003	2004	2005
Sawlogs, veneer logs and logs for sleepers	1	1	1
Other industrial wood	5	5	5
Fuel wood	1,541	1,581	1,623
Total	1,547	1,587	1,629

Source: FAO.

Fishing

('000 metric tons, live weight)

	2003	2004	2005
Freshwater fishes*	5.0	5.0	5.0
Sardinellas	15.0*	19.2	30.5
European pilchard (sardine)	4.0	8.1	14.8
European anchovy	20.0	33.4	37.4
Jack and horse mackerels	33.5*	51.5	79.4
Chub mackerel	16.0*	23.7	14.3
Octopuses	12.0*	12.1	14.6
Total catch (incl. others)*	141.9	199.4	247.6

* FAO estimate(s).

Source: FAO.

Mining

('000 metric tons)

	2003	2004	2005
Gypsum	34.3	38.9	39.0
Iron ore: gross weight	10,377	11,000	11,000
Iron ore: metal content*	6,890	7,200	7,200

* Estimates.

Source: US Geological Survey.

Industry

SELECTED PRODUCTS
('000 metric tons, unless otherwise indicated)

	2003	2004	2005
Cement*	200	300	300
Crude steel*	5	5	5
Electric energy (million kWh)	312.0	336.0	375.5

* Data from US Geological Survey.

Finance

CURRENCY AND EXCHANGE RATES

Monetary Units
5 khoums = 1 ouguiya (UM).

Sterling, Dollar and Euro Equivalents (30 June 2006)
£1 sterling = 496.407 ouguiyas;
US $1 = 270.610 ouguiyas;
€1 = 344.027 ouguiyas;
1,000 ouguiyas = £2.01 = $3.70 = €2.91.

Average Exchange Rate (ouguiyas per US $)

2003	263.030
2004	257.190
2005	265.528

BUDGET

('000 million ouguiyas)

Revenue*	2003	2004	2005†
Tax revenue	44.9	59.2	76.0
Taxes on income and profits	12.0	16.3	26.6
Tax on business profits	6.6	9.3	15.7
Tax on wages and salaries	4.8	6.3	9.9
Taxes on goods and services	24.7	30.8	36.2
Value-added tax	16.6	21.8	26.7
Turnover taxes	3.3	2.7	2.8
Tax on petroleum products	2.4	2.8	2.5
Other excises	1.6	2.7	3.3
Taxes on international trade	7.3	11.1	10.8
Other current revenue	42.9	47.4	38.8
Fishing royalties and penalties	32.6	36.6	35.3
Revenue from public enterprises	2.1	4.2	0.6
Capital revenue	16.1	11.3	6.2
Other revenue (incl. special accounts)	8.3	6.6	2.8
Total	103.9	117.9	121.0

Expenditure‡	2003	2004	2005†
Current expenditure	105.0	96.7	126.7
Wages and salaries	16.0	17.2	22.4
Goods and services	35.3	36.9	60.6
Transfers and subsidies	26.3	9.6	8.7
Military expenditure	16.4	18.6	17.7
Interest on public debt	9.3	11.9	16.1
Capital expenditure	44.0	43.1	36.7
Domestically financed	25.4	24.6	21.4
Financed from abroad	18.6	18.5	15.2
Unidentified	9.2	9.6	0.0
Total	158.1	149.3	163.4

* Excluding grants received ('000 million ouguiyas): 15.7 in 2003; 12.5 in 2004; 10.3 (preliminary) in 2005.

† Preliminary figures.

‡ Excluding restructuring and net lending ('000 million ouguiyas): 1.4 in 2003; 0.2 in 2004; 2.9 in 2005 (preliminary).

Source: IMF, *Islamic Republic of Mauritania: Statistical Appendix* (July 2006).

2006 ('000 million ouguiyas): Total revenue 153.5; Total expenditure 206.4 (Source: IMF, *Islamic Republic of Mauritania: First Review Under the Three-Year Arrangement Under the Poverty Reduction and Growth Facility - Staff Report; Press Release on the Executive Board Discussion; and Statement by the Executive Director for the Islamic Republic of Mauritania* (July 2007)).

INTERNATIONAL RESERVES

(US $ million at 31 December)

	2001	2002	2003
Gold*	3.1	3.1	4.0
IMF special drawing rights	0.2	0.2	0.1
Foreign exchange	284.3	396.0	415.2
Total	287.6	399.3	419.3

* Valued at market-related prices.

2004 (US $ million at 31 December): IMF special drawing rights 0.0.

2005 (US $ million at 31 December): IMF special drawing rights 0.1.

Source: IMF, *International Financial Statistics*.

MONEY SUPPLY

(million ouguiyas at 31 December)

	2001	2002	2003
Currency outside banks	6,688	6,282	6,412
Demand deposits at deposit money banks	21,033	22,628	25,790
Total money (incl. others)	27,721	28,910	32,202

Source: IMF, *International Financial Statistics*.

COST OF LIVING

(Consumer Price Index in Nouakchott; base: April 2002–March 2003 = 100)

	2003	2004	2005
Food (incl. beverages)	117.9	131.2	149.3
Clothing (incl. footwear)	105.4	121.2	131.1
Rent	114.1	123.3	134.7
All items (incl. others)	114.4	124.2	139.3

Source: ILO.

NATIONAL ACCOUNTS

Expenditure on the Gross Domestic Product
(US $ million at current prices)

	2004	2005	2006
Government final consumption expenditure	408.30	420.84	483.86
Private final consumption expenditure	1,097.37	1,729.61	1,646.01
Gross capital formation	693.15	832.46	802.88
Total domestic expenditure	2,198.82	2,982.91	2,932.75
Exports of goods and services	462.67	666.89	1,520.55
Less Imports of goods and services	1,167.56	1,778.04	1,683.94
GDP in purchasers' values	1,493.92	1,871.75	2,769.37
GDP at constant 2000 prices	1,139.59	1,189.78	1,355.16

Source: African Development Bank.

Gross Domestic Product by Economic Activity
('000 million ouguiyas at current prices)

	2003	2004	2005*
Agriculture, hunting, forestry and fishing	84.7	91.6	105.4
Mining and quarrying	28.1	45.5	70.6
Manufacturing	18.5	21.3	22.5
Electricity, gas and water } Construction }	26.0	33.9	37.3
Trade, restaurants and hotels	43.9	50.2	60.9
Transport and communications	19.8	22.5	23.8
Public administration	41.5	44.4	65.4
Other services	45.3	48.6	59.3
GDP at factor cost	307.8	358.2	445.3
Indirect taxes, *less* subsidies	30.2	38.4	51.7
GDP in purchasers' values	338.0	396.6	497.0

* Preliminary figures.

Source: IMF, *Islamic Republic of Mauritania: Statistical Appendix* (July 2006).

BALANCE OF PAYMENTS
(US $ million)

	2004	2005	2006*
Exports of goods f.o.b.	439.6	625.1	1,366.6
Imports of goods f.o.b.	−923.4	−1,428.3	−1,167.0
Trade balance	−483.8	−803.2	199.6
Exports of services	52.0	79.6	86.7
Imports of services	−259.6	−378.7	−406.3
Balance on goods and services	−691.4	−1,102.3	−120.0
Other income received	104.5	108.6	119.0
Other income paid	−38.9	−44.0	−193.3
Balance on goods, services and income	−625.8	−1,037.7	−194.3
Private unrequited transfers (net)	47.7	60.0	66.5
Official transfers	61.0	101.0	92.1
Current balance	−517.1	−876.8	−35.6
Capital account (net)	15.5	0.0	1,107.2
Direct investment (net)	391.6	814.1	154.6
Official medium- and long-term loans	19.9	−28.0	−835.7
Other capital	0.1	−22.5	−168.3
Net errors and omissions	−19.2	39.4	60.2
Overall balance	−109.7	−73.8	282.3

* Preliminary figures.

Source: IMF, *Islamic Republic of Mauritania: First Review Under the Three-Year Arrangement Under the Poverty Reduction and Growth Facility - Staff Report; Press Release on the Executive Board Discussion; and Statement by the Executive Director for the Islamic Republic of Mauritania* (July 2007).

External Trade

PRINCIPAL COMMODITIES
(US $ million)

Imports c.i.f.	1999	2000	2001
Food and live animals	160.3	112.1	77.6
Live animals chiefly for food	80.2	56.1	38.8
Cereals and cereal preparations	39.8	32.2	20.6
Sugar and honey	30.1	17.3	12.6
Mineral fuels, lubricants, etc.	41.5	35.4	94.7
Petroleum products, refined	41.5	35.4	94.7
Animal and vegetable oils, fats and waxes	18.7	8.0	5.9
Animal oils and fats	18.6	7.9	5.9
Basic manufactures	14.6	17.2	35.1
Non-metallic mineral manufactures	13.4	15.6	34.4
Machinery and transport equipment	34.9	33.0	34.9
Road vehicles	34.9	33.0	34.9
Total (incl. others)	342.8	310.2	353.0

Source: UN, *International Trade Statistics Yearbook*.

2002 (US $ million): Petroleum exploration-related machinery and equipment 48.3, Petroleum products 85.2; Total imports f.o.b. (incl. others) 431.2 (Source: IMF, *Islamic Republic of Mauritania: Statistical Appendix*—July 2006).

2003 (US $ million): Petroleum exploration-related machinery and equipment 74.5, Petroleum products 100.3; Total imports f.o.b. (incl. others) 542.1 (Source: IMF, *Islamic Republic of Mauritania: Statistical Appendix*—July 2006).

2004 (US $ million): Petroleum exploration-related machinery and equipment 298.0, Petroleum products 145.0; Total imports f.o.b. (incl. others) 923.4 (Source: IMF, *Islamic Republic of Mauritania: Statistical Appendix*—July 2006).

2005 (US $ million, provisional figures): Petroleum-exploration-related machinery and equipment 600.0, Non-petroleum mining-related machinery and equipment 69.8, Petroleum products 196.4; Total imports f.o.b. (incl. others) 1,387.4 (Source: IMF, *Islamic Republic of Mauritania: Statistical Appendix* —July 2006).

Exports f.o.b.	2003	2004	2005*
Iron ore	163.9	230.2	389.4
Fish	131.5	172.6	172.7
Total (incl. others)	318.2	439.6	604.1

* Preliminary figures.

Source: IMF, *Islamic Republic of Mauritania: Statistical Appendix* (July 2006).

PRINCIPAL TRADING PARTNERS
(US $ million)*

Imports c.i.f.	2000	2001	2002
Belgium-Luxembourg	32.9	31.4	36.8
France	94.5	89.2	86.9
Germany	17.2	21.3	23.2
Italy	21.9	22.1	17.6
Japan	9.2	9.8	16.2
Netherlands	10.0	10.7	14.0
Spain	21.8	21.5	27.9
United Kingdom	8.5	7.2	14.0
USA	9.6	16.0	14.4
Total (incl. others)	336.2	372.3	418.0

Exports c.i.f.	2000	2001	2002
Belgium-Luxembourg	30.8	28.9	33.9
France	63.5	50.7	47.6
Germany	13.2	20.8	35.7
Italy	47.4	51.0	48.8
Japan	53.0	27.1	21.0
Portugal	7.6	7.0	7.8
Spain	38.1	42.2	39.9
United Kingdom	5.4	5.4	1.5
Total (incl. others)	344.7	338.6	330.3

* Data are compiled on the basis of reporting by Mauritania's trading partners. Data detailing imports and exports of trade with developing and emerging countries were not available.

Source: IMF, *Islamic Republic of Mauritania: Statistical Appendix* (October 2003).

Transport

RAILWAYS

1984: Passengers carried 19,353; Passenger-km 7m.; Freight carried 9.1m. metric tons; Freight ton-km 6,142m.

Freight ton-km (million): 6,365 in 1985; 6,411 in 1986; 6,473 in 1987; 6,535 in 1988; 6,610 in 1989; 6,690 in 1990; 6,720 in 1991; 6,810 in 1992; 6,890 in 1993 (figures for 1988–93 are estimates) (Source: UN Economic Commission for Africa, *African Statistical Yearbook*).

ROAD TRAFFIC
('000 motor vehicles in use)

	1998	1999	2000
Passenger cars	8.6	9.9	12.2
Commercial vehicles	16.7	17.3	18.2

2001–02 ('000 motor vehicles in use): Figures assumed to be unchanged from 2000.

Source: UN, *Statistical Yearbook*.

SHIPPING

Merchant Fleet
(registered at 31 December)

	2004	2005	2006
Number of vessels	146	152	153
Total displacement ('000 grt)	49.3	51.9	51.9

Source: Lloyd's Register-Fairplay, *World Fleet Statistics*.

International Sea-borne Freight Traffic
(Port of Nouakchott, '000 metric tons)

	2003	2004	2005
Goods loaded	47.5	77.4	113.2
Goods unloaded	1,399.9	1,434.9	1,712.9

Source: Port Autonome de Nouakchott.

CIVIL AVIATION
(traffic on scheduled services)*

	2001	2002	2003
Kilometres flown (million)	2	1	1
Passengers carried ('000)	156	106	116
Passenger-km (million)	174	45	49
Total ton-km (million)	23	4	5

* Including an apportionment of the traffic of Air Afrique.

Source: UN, *Statistical Yearbook*.

Tourism

Tourist arrivals (estimates, '000): 24 in 1999.

Receipts from tourism (US $ million, excl. passenger transport): 28 in 1999 (Source: World Tourism Organization).

Communications Media

	2003	2004	2005
Telephones ('000 main lines in use)	38.2	39.0	41.0
Mobile cellular telephones ('000 subscribers)	351.0	522.4	745.6
Personal computers ('000 in use)	35	42	42
Internet users ('000)	12	14	14

Television receivers ('000 in use): 247 in 1999.

Radio receivers ('000 in use): 570 in 1997.

Facsimile machines (number in use): 3,300 in 1999.

Daily newspapers: Number 2; Estimated average circulation ('000 copies) 12 in 1996.

Sources: UNESCO, *Statistical Yearbook*; UN, *Statistical Yearbook*; International Telecommunication Union.

Education

(2003/04, unless otherwise indicated)

			Students		
	Institutions	Teachers	Males	Females	Total
Pre-primary	n.a.	243	n.a.	n.a.	4,709
Primary	2,676*	9,753	219,581	214,600	434,181
Secondary	n.a.	3,126	48,636	40,290	88,926
Tertiary	4†	331	7,092	2,200	9,292

* 1998/99.

† 1995/96.

Adult literacy rate (UNESCO estimates): 51.2% (males 51.5%; females 43.4%) in 2004 (Source: UN Development Programme, *Human Development Report*).

Sources: mainly UNESCO Institute for Statistics and Ministry of National Education, Nouakchott.

Directory

While no longer an official language under the terms of the 1991 Constitution (see below), French is still widely used in Mauritania, especially in the commercial sector. Many organizations are therefore listed under their French names, by which they are generally known.

The Constitution

Following the *coup d'état* of 3 August 2005, the self-styled Military Council for Justice and Democracy (MCJD) introduced a Constitutional Charter that was intended to supplement and partially replace the Constitution approved by referendum in 1991 for a transitional period for up to two years, following which time democratic elections were to be held. Those provisions of the Constitution pertaining to the role of Islam, individual and collective freedoms and the prerogatives of the State were to remain in force, while certain judicial organs (namely: the High Council of Magistrates; courts and tribunals; the High Council of Islam; the Audit Court; and the Constitutional Council) were to continue to function. A number of the legislative powers previously held by a bicameral legislature (which was abolished) were transferred to the MCJD, which was also to assume executive powers. The President of the MCJD was empowered to appoint a Prime Minister and other Ministers, who were to be responsible to the MCJD and its President. The MCJD was permitted to consult with the Constitutional Council with regard to any constitutional question. A referendum held on 25 June 2006 approved various amendments to the Constitution: notably, the presidential term of office was to be reduced to five years, renewable only once, a maximum age of 75 years was to be stipulated for presidential candidates, and the President was to be prohibited from holding any other official post, including the leadership of a political party. Elections to a new bicameral legislature were held during November 2006–February 2007, while a presidential election was held over two rounds in March. Sidi Mohamed Ould Cheikh Abdellahi was inaugurated as President on 19 April, assuming executive powers in place of the MCJD, which was disbanded, and a new Government was unveiled on 28 April.

The Constitution states that the official language is Arabic, and that the national languages are Arabic, Pular, Wolof and Solinké.

The Government

HEAD OF STATE

President: SIDI MOHAMED OULD CHEIKH ABDELLAHI (inaugurated 19 April 2007).

COUNCIL OF MINISTERS
(August 2007)

Prime Minister: ZEINE OULD ZEIDANE.

Minister of Justice: LIMAM OULD TEGUEDI.

Minister of Foreign Affairs and Co-operation: MOHAMED SALECK OULD MOHAMED LEMINE.

Minister of National Defence: MOHAMED MAHMOUD OULD MOHAMED LEMINE.

Minister of the Interior: YALL ZAKARIA.

Minister of the Economy and Finance: ABDERRAHMANE OULD HAMMA VEZZAZ.

Minister of National Education: NEGGHOUHA MINT MOHAMED VALL.

Minister of Islamic Affairs and Original Education: AHMED VALL OULD SALEH.

Minister of Labour, Integration and Vocational Training: CHEIKH EL KÉBIR OULD CHBIH.

Minister of Health: MOHAMED LEMINE OULD RAGHANI.

Minister Petroleum and Mines: MOHAMED EL MOKTAR OULD MOHAMED EL HACEN.

Minister of Fisheries: ASSANE SOUMARÉ.

Minister of Trade and Industry: SID AHMED OULD RAISS.

Minister of Handicrafts and Tourism: BA MADINE.

Minister of Decentralization and Land Development: YAHYA OULD KEBD.

Minister of Agriculture and Animal Resources: CORRÉRA ISSAGHA.

Minister of Equipment, Urban Development and Housing: MOHAMED OULD BILAL.

Minister of Transport: AHMED OULD MOHAMEDEN.

Minister of Water Resources, Energy and Information and Communication Technologies: OUMAR OULD YALI.

Minister of Culture and Communication: MOHAMED VALL OULD CHEIKH.

Minister of the Civil Service and the Modernization of Administration: AZIZ OULD DAHI.

Minister in charge of Relations with Parliament and Civil Society: MOHAMED MAHMOUD OULD BRAHIM KHLIL.

Minister in charge of Women's, Childhood and Family Development: FATIMETOU MINT KHATTRI.

Minister in charge of Youth and Sports: MOHAMED OULD AHMED OULD YERG.

Minister-delegate to the Prime Minister, in charge of the Environment: AICHA MINT SIDI BOUNA.

Minister-delegate to the Ministry of Foreign Affairs and Co-operation, in charge of the Union of the Arab Maghreb: MOHAMED EL HAFEDH OULD ISMAEL.

Secretary-General of the Government: ABDELLAHI OULD LIMAM MALECK.

Commissioner in charge of Social Security: MOHAMED OULD MOHAMEDOU.

General Commissioner for the Promotion of Private Investment: MOHAMED ABDELLAHI OULD YAHA.

MINISTRIES

Office of the President: BP 184, Nouakchott; tel. and fax 525-26-36.

Office of the Prime Minister: BP 237, Nouakchott; tel. 525-33-37.

Ministry of Capital Works and Transport: BP 237, Nouakchott; tel. 525-33-37.

Ministry of the Civil Service and Employment: BP 193, Nouakchott; tel. and fax 525-84-10.

Ministry of Communication: Nouakchott.

Ministry of Culture, Youth and Sports: BP 223, Nouakchott; tel. 525-11-30.

Ministry of Economic Affairs and Development: 303 Ilot C, BP 5150, Nouakchott; tel. 525-16-12; fax 525-51-10; e-mail nfomaed@mauritania.mr; internet www.maed.gov.mr.

Ministry of Energy and Petroleum: Nouakchott; tel. 525-71-40.

Ministry of Finance: BP 181, Nouakchott; tel. 525-20-20.

Ministry of Fisheries and the Maritime Economy: BP 137, Nouakchott; tel. 525-46-07; fax 525-31-46; e-mail ministre@mpem.mr; internet www.mpem.mr.

Ministry of Foreign Affairs and Co-operation: BP 230, Nouakchott; tel. 525-26-82; fax 525-28-60.

Ministry of Fundamental and Secondary Education: BP 387, Nouakchott; tel. 525-12-37; fax 525-12-22.

Ministry of Health and Social Affairs: BP 177, Nouakchott; tel. 525-20-52; fax 525-22-68.

Ministry of Higher Education and Scientific Research: Nouakchott.

Ministry of the Interior, Posts and Telecommunications: BP 195, Nouakchott; tel. 525-36-61; fax 525-36-40; e-mail paddec@mauritania.mr.

Ministry of Justice: BP 350, Nouakchott; tel. 525-10-83; fax 525-70-02.

Ministry of Mines and Industry: BP 199, Nouakchott; tel. 525-30-83; fax 525-69-37; e-mail mmi@mauritania.mr.

Ministry of Rural Development and the Environment: BP 366, Nouakchott; tel. 525-15-00; fax 525-74-75.

Ministry of Trade, Crafts and Tourism: BP 182, Nouakchott; tel. 525-35-72; fax 525-76-71.

Ministry of Water Resources: BP 4913, Nouakchott; tel. 525-71-44; fax 529-42-87; e-mail saadouebih@yahoo.fr.

Office of the Secretary-General of the Government: BP 184, Nouakchott.

President and Legislature

PRESIDENT

Presidential Election, First Round, 11 March 2007

Candidate	Votes	% of votes
Sidi Mohamed Ould Cheikh Abdellahi	183,743	24.79
Ahmed Ould Daddah	153,242	20.68
Zeine Ould Zeidane	113,194	15.27
Messaoud Ould Boulkheir	72,611	9.80
Ibrahim Moctar Sarr	58,818	7.94
Saleh Ould Mohamedou Ould Hanana	56,718	7.65
Mohamed Ould Maouloud	30,265	4.08
Dahane Ould Ahmed Mahmoud	15,316	2.07
Others	57,159	7.71
Total	741,066	100.00

Presidential Election, Second Round, 25 March 2007

	Votes	% of votes
Sidi Mohamed Ould Cheikh Abdellahi	373,519	52.85
Ahmed Ould Daddah	333,184	47.15
Total	706,703	100.00

Al Jamiya al-Wataniyah (National Assembly)

ave de l'Indépendance, BP 185, Nouakchott; tel. 525-11-30; fax 525-70-78; internet www.mauritania.mr/assemblee.

President: MESSOUD OULD BOULKHEIR.

General Election, 19 November and 3 December 2006

Party	Constituency seats	National list seats	Total seats
Rally of Democratic Forces	12	3	15
Union of Progressive Forces	7	1	9
Republican Party for Democracy and Renewal	5	2	7
Popular Progressive Alliance	4	1	5
Centrist Reformists	2	2	5
Mauritanian Party for Union and Change—Hatem	3	1	4
Union for Democracy and Progress	2	1	3
Rally for Democracy and Unity	2	1	3
Democratic Renewal	1	1	2
Alternative	1	—	1
Union of the Democratic Centre	1	—	1
Popular Front	—	1	1
Independents	41	—	41
Total	81	14	95

Majlis al-Shuyukh (Senate)

ave de l'Indépendance, BP 5838, Nouakchott; tel. 525-68-77; fax 525-73-73; internet www.senat.mr.

President: BÂ MAMADOU DIT M'BARÉ.

Election, 21 January and 4 February 2007

Party	Seats
Independents	34
Coalition of Forces for Democratic Change	15
Republican Party for Democracy and Renewal	3
Total*	52

* The total number of seats in the Senate is 56. The result from one constituency was annulled by the Constitutional Council and the remaining three seats, reserved for representatives of the Mauritanina diaspora, were yet to be allocated.

Election Commission

National Independent Electoral Commission: Nouakchott; 15 mems; Pres. Col (retd) Cheikh Sid'Ahmed Ould Babamine.

Advisory Council

Economic and Social Council: Nouakchott.

Political Organizations

Following the *coup d'état* of August 2005, and in advance of the election of a new legislature and president, several new political parties were formed, and a number of politicians hitherto in exile returned to Mauritania. At the time of the legislative elections held in November–December 2006 some 35 political parties were legally recognized in Mauritania. The organizations listed below were among the most significant to operate at that time.

Alliance for Justice and Democracy (AJD): Nouakchott; Leader Cissé Amadou Chiekhou.

Alternative (Al-Badil): Nouakchott; f. 2006; Leader Mohamed Yehdhih Ould Moktar El Hassen.

Centrist Reformists: Nouakchott; f. 2006; mem. of Coalition of Forces for Democratic Change, formed in advance of legislative and local elections in 2006; moderate Islamist grouping; Co-ordinator Mohamed Jemil Ould Mansour.

Democratic Renewal: Nouakchott; f. 2005; mem. of Coalition of Forces for Democratic Change, formed in advance of legislative and local elections in 2006; Pres. Moustapha Ould Abeiderrahmane.

Mauritanian African Liberation Forces—Renovation (MALF—Renovation): Nouakchott; tel. 228-77-40; internet www.flam-renovation.org; f. 2006 in split from clandestine, exiled, Mauritanian African Liberation Forces; represents interests of Afro- (Black) Mauritanians; mem. of Coalition of Forces for Democratic Change, formed in advance of legislative and local elections in 2006; Leader Mamadou Bocar Bâ.

Mauritanian Labour Party: Nouakchott; f. 2001; Leader Mohamed El Hafedh Ould Denna.

Mauritanian Party for Renewal and Agreement: Nouakchott; f. 2001; Leader Moulay el-Hassen Ould Jiyid.

Mauritanian Party for the Defence of the Environment (MPDE—The Greens): Nouakchott; internet pmde.hautetfort.com; ecologist; mem. of Bloc of Parties for Change, formed in advance of planned legislative and local elections in 2006; Pres. Mohamed Ould Sidi Ould Dellahi.

Mauritanian Party for Union and Change—Hatem: Nouakchott; f. 2005 by leadership of the fmr prohibited Knights of Change militia and reformist elements of the fmr ruling Democratic and Social Republican Party; mem. of Coalition of Forces for Democratic Change, formed in advance of legislative and local elections in 2006; Pres. Saleh Ould Hnana; Sec.-Gen. Abderahmane Ould Mini.

Party for Liberty, Equality and Justice (PLEJ): Nouakchott; mem. of Bloc of Parties for Change, formed in advance of legislative and local elections in 2006; Pres. Mamadou Alassane Bâ.

Popular Front (FP): Nouakchott; f. 1998; social-liberal; mem. of Coalition of Forces for Democratic Change, formed in advance of legislative and local elections in 2006; Leader Mohamed Lemine Ch'Bih Ould Cheikh Melainine.

Popular Progressive Alliance (APP): Nouakchott; internet www.app-mauritanie.org; f. 1991; absorbed Convention for Change (the successor to the banned Action for Change, which sought to represent the interests of Harratin—black Moors who had frmly been slaves) in 2003; mem. of Coalition of Forces for Democratic Change, formed in advance of legislative and local elections in 2006; Pres. Messaoud Ould Boulkhar.

Rally for Democracy and Unity (RDU): Nouakchott; f. 1991; supported regime of fmr Pres. Taya; Chair. Ahmed Ould Sidi Baba.

Rally for Mauritania (RPM—Temam): Nouakchott; f. 2005; Islamist; mem. of Coalition of Forces for Democratic Change, formed in advance of legislative and local elections in 2006; Pres. Dr Cheikh Ould Horma.

Rally of Democratic Forces (RDF): Ilot K, 120, BP 4986, Nouakchott; tel. 525-67-46; fax 525-65-70; e-mail info@rfd-mauritanie.org; internet www.rfd-mauritanie.org; f. 2001 by fmr mems of the officially dissolved Union of Democratic Forces—New Era (f. 1991); mem. of Coalition of Forces for Democratic Change, formed in advance of legislative and local elections in 2006; Pres. Ahmed Ould Daddah.

Republican Party for Democracy and Renewal (RPDR): ZRB, Tevragh Zeina, Nouakchott; tel. 529-18-36; fax 529-18-00; e-mail info@prdr.mr; internet www.prdr.mr; f. 2006 to replace Democratic and Social Republican Party, the fmr ruling party, prior to *coup d'état* of August 2005; Leader Sidi Mohamed Ould Med Vall dit Ghriny.

Reward (Sawab): Nouakchott; f. 2004; social democratic; Chair. of Central Council Mohamed Mahmoud Ould Ghoulma; Pres. Dr Cheikh Ould Sidi Ould Hanena.

Social Democratic Union: Nouakchott; Pres. Isselmou Ould Hannefi.

Union for Democracy and Progress (UDP): Ilot V, 70, Tevragh Zeina, BP 816, Nouakchott; tel. 525-52-89; fax 525-29-95; f. 1993; Pres. Naha Hamdi Mint.

Union of the Democratic Centre (UDC): Nouakchott; f. 2005 by fmr mems of the Democratic and Social Republican Party, the fmr ruling party; Pres. Cheikh Sid'Ahmed Ould Baba.

Union of Progressive Forces (UPF) (Ittihad Quwa al-Taqaddum): Nouakchott; e-mail ufpweb2@yahoo.fr; internet www.ufpweb.org; tel. 529-32-66; fax 524-35-86; e-mail infos@ufpweb.org; f. 2000, following the enforced dissolution of the fmr Union of Democratic Forces—New Era, which it had existed as a faction thereof since 1998; mem. of Coalition of Forces for Democratic Change, formed in advance of legislative and local elections in 2006; Pres. Mohamed Ould Maouloud; Sec.-Gen. Mohamed El Moustapha Ould Bedreddine.

Unauthorized, but influential, is the Islamic **Ummah Party** (the Constitution prohibits the operation of religious political organizations), founded in 1991 and led by Imam Sidi Yahya, and the Baathist **National Vanguard Party (Taliaa)**, which was officially dissolved by the Government in 1999 and is led by Ahmedou Ould Babana. The clandestine **Mauritanian African Liberation Forces (MALF)** was founded in 1983 in Senegal to represent Afro-Mauritanians (; Point d'ébullition, BP 5811, Dakar-Fann, Senegal; tel. +221 822-80-77; e-mail ba_demba@yahoo .fr; internet members .lycos .co .uk/flamnetPres. Samba Thiam); a faction broke away from this organization and returned to Mauritania in early 2006, forming the Mauritanian African Liberation Forces—Renovation. A further group based in exile is the **Arab-African Salvation Front against Slavery, Racism and Tribalism—AASF** (e-mail faas@caramail.com; internet membres .lycos .fr/faas). In August 2007 a further 18 new parties were registered: included were an Islamist party, the **National Rally for Reform and Development**, and two parties led by women, the **National Party for Development**, led by Sahla Bint Ahmad Zayid, and the **Mauritanian Hope Party**, led by Tahi Bint Lahbib.

Diplomatic Representation

EMBASSIES IN MAURITANIA

Algeria: Ilot A, Tevragh Zeina, BP 625, Nouakchott; tel. 525-35-69; fax 525-47-77; Ambassador Abdelkrim ben Hocine.

China, People's Republic: rue 42-133, Tevragh Zeina, BP 257, Nouakchott; tel. 525-20-70; fax 525-24-62; e-mail chinaemb_mr@mfa.gov.cn; internet mr.china-embassy.org; Ambassador Zhang Xun.

Congo, Democratic Republic: Tevragh Zeina, BP 5714, Nouakchott; tel. 525-46-12; fax 525-50-53; e-mail ambardc.rim@caramail.com; Chargé d'affaires a.i. Tshibasu Mfuad.

Egypt: Villa no. 468, Tevragh Zeina, BP 176, Nouakchott; tel. 525-21-92; fax 525-33-84; Ambassador Bahaa Eddin Mokhtar Mowafi.

France: rue Ahmed Ould Hamed, Tevragh Zeina, BP 231, Nouakchott; tel. 529-96-99; fax 529-69-38; e-mail ambafrance.nouakchott-amba@diplomatie.gouv.fr; internet www.france-mauritanie.mr; Ambassador Patrick Nicoloso.

Germany: Tevragh Zeina, BP 372, Nouakchott; tel. 525-17-29; fax 525-17-22; e-mail amb-allemagne@toptechnology.mr; Ambassador Eberhard Schanze.

Israel: Ilot A516, Tevragh Zeina, BP 5714, Nouakchott; tel. 525-82-35; fax 525-46-12; e-mail info@nouakchott.mfa.gov.il; Ambassador Boaz Besmuth Bismuth.

Korea, Democratic People's Republic: Nouakchott; Ambassador Pak Ho Il.

Kuwait: Tevragh Zeina, BP 345, Nouakchott; tel. 525-33-05; fax 525-41-45.

Libya: BP 673, Nouakchott; tel. 525-52-02; fax 525-50-53.

Mali: Tevragh Zeina, BP 5371, Nouakchott; tel. 525-40-81; fax 525-40-83; e-mail ambmali@hotmail.com; Ambassador Moussa Kalilou Coulibaly.

Morocco: 569 ave de Gaulle, Tevragh Zeina, BP 621, Nouakchott; tel. 525-14-11; fax 529-72-80; e-mail sifmanktt@mauritel.mr; Ambassador Abderrahmane Benomar.

Nigeria: Ilot P9, BP 367, Nouakchott; tel. 525-23-04; fax 525-23-14; Ambassador Alhaji BALA MOHAMED SANI.

Qatar: BP 609, Nouakchott; tel. 525-23-99; fax 525-68-87; e-mail nouakchoti@mofa.gov.qa; Ambassador MOHAMMED KURDI TALEB AL-MERRI.

Russia: rue Abu Bakr, BP 221, Nouakchott; tel. 525-19-73; fax 525-52-96; e-mail ambruss@opt.mr; Ambassador LEONID V. ROGOV.

Saudi Arabia: Las Balmas, Zinat, BP 498, Nouakchott; tel. 525-26-33; fax 525-29-49; e-mail mremb@mofa.gov.sa; Ambassador MOHAMED AL FADH EL ISSA.

Senegal: Villa 500, Tevragh Zeina, BP 2511, Nouakchott; tel. 525-72-90; fax 525-72-91; Ambassador MAHMOUDOU CHEIKH KANE.

Spain: BP 232, Nouakchott; tel. 525-20-80; fax 525-40-88; e-mail emb.nouakchott@mae.es; Ambassador ALEJANDRO POLANCO MATA.

Syria: Tevragh Zeina, BP 288, Nouakchott; tel. 525-27-54; fax 525-45-00.

Tunisia: BP 681, Nouakchott; tel. 525-28-71; fax 525-18-27; Ambassador ABDEL WEHAB JEMAL.

United Arab Emirates: BP 6824, Nouakchott; tel. 525-10-98; fax 525-09-92.

USA: rue Abdallaye, BP 222, Nouakchott; tel. 525-26-60; fax 525-15-92; e-mail tayebho@state.gov; internet mauritania.usembassy.gov; Chargé d'affaires a.i. STEVEN C. KOUTSIS.

Yemen: Tevragh Zeina, BP 4689, Nouakchott; tel. 525-55-91; fax 525-56-39.

Judicial System

The Code of Law was promulgated in 1961 and subsequently modified to incorporate Islamic institutions and practices. The main courts comprise three courts of appeal, 10 regional tribunals, two labour tribunals and 53 departmental civil courts. A revenue court has jurisdiction in financial matters. The members of the High Court of Justice are elected by the National Assembly and the Senate.

Shari'a (Islamic) law was introduced in February 1980. A special Islamic court was established in March of that year, presided over by a magistrate of Islamic law, assisted by two counsellors and two *ulemas* (Muslim jurists and interpreters of the Koran). A five-member High Council of Islam, appointed by the President, advises upon the conformity of national legislation to religious precepts, at the request of the President.

Audit Court (Cour des Comptes): Nouakchott; audits all govt institutions; Pres. SOW ADAMA SAMBA.

Constitutional Council: f. 1992; includes six mems, three nominated by the Head of State and three designated by the Presidents of the Senate and National Assembly; Pres. ABDOULLAH OULD ELY SALEM; Sec.-Gen. MOHAMED OULD M'REIZIG.

High Council of Islam (al-Majlis al-Islamiya al-A'la'): Nouakchott; f. 1992; Pres. AHMED OULD NEINI.

High Court of Justice: Nouakchott; f. 1961; comprises an equal number of appointees elected from their membership by the National Assembly and the Senate, following each partial or general renewal of those legislative bodies; competent to try the President of the Republic in case of high treason, and the Prime Minister and members of the Government in case of conspiracy against the state.

Supreme Court: BP 201, Palais de Justice, Nouakchott; tel. 525-21-63; f. 1961; comprises an administrative chamber, a civil and commercial chamber, a social and employment chamber and a criminal chamber; also functions as the highest court of appeal; Pres. KABR OULD ELEWA.

Religion

ISLAM

Islam is the official religion, and the population are almost entirely Muslims of the Malekite rite. The major religious groups are the Tijaniya and the Qadiriya. Chinguetti, in the region of Adrar, is the seventh Holy Place in Islam. A High Council of Islam supervises the conformity of legislation to Muslim orthodoxy.

CHRISTIANITY

Roman Catholic Church

Mauritania comprises the single diocese of Nouakchott, directly responsible to the Holy See. The Bishop participates in the Bishops' Conference of Senegal, Mauritania, Cape Verde and Guinea-Bissau, based in Dakar, Senegal. At 31 December 2004 there were an estimated 4,500 adherents, mainly non-nationals, in the country.

Bishop of Nouakchott: Most Rev. MARTIN ALBERT HAPPE, Evêché, BP 5377, Nouakchott; tel. 525-04-27; fax 525-37-51; e-mail mgr-martin-happe@mauritel.mr.

The Press

Of some 400 journals officially registered in Mauritania in mid-2004, some 30 were regular, widely available publications, of which the following were among the most important:

Al-Akhbar: BP 5346, Nouakchott; tel. 525-08-94; fax 525-37-57; f. 1995; weekly; Arabic.

Al-Qalam/Le Calame: BP 1059, Nouakchott; tel. 529-02-34; fax 525-75-55; e-mail calame@compunet.mr; internet www.calame.8k.com; f. 1994; weekly; Arabic and French; independent; Editors-in-Chief RIYAD OULD AHMED EL-HADI (Arabic edn), HINDOU MINT AININA (French edn).

Le Carrefour: Nouakchott; Dir MOUSSA OULD SAMBA SY.

Châab: BP 371, Nouakchott; tel. 525-29-40; fax 525-85-47; daily; Arabic; also publ. in French *Horizons*; publ. by Agence Mauritanienne de l'Information; Dir-Gen. MOHAMED EL-HAFED OULD MAHAM.

Challenge: BP 1346, Nouakchott; tel. and fax 529-06-26.

Ech-tary: BP 1059, Nouakchott; tel. 525-50-65; fortnightly; Arabic; satirical.

L'Essor: BP 5310, Nouakchott; tel. 630-21-68; fax 525-88-90; e-mail sidiel2000@yahoo.fr; monthly; the environment and the economy; Dir SIDI EL-MOCTAR CHEÏGUER; circ. 2,500.

El-Anba: BP 3901, Nouakchott; tel. and fax 525-99-27.

L'Eveil-Hebdo: BP 587, Nouakchott; tel. 525-67-14; fax 525-87-54; e-mail symoudou@yahoo.fr; f. 1991; weekly; independent; Dir of Publication SY MAMADOU.

Inimich al-Watan: Nouakchott; independent; Arabic; Dir of Publication MOHAMED OULD ELKORY.

Journal Officel: BP 188, Nouakchott; tel. 525-33-37; fax 525-34-74; fortnightly.

Maghreb Hebdo: BP 5266, Nouakchott; tel. 525-98-10; fax 525-98-11; f. 1994; weekly; Dir KHATTRI OULD DIÈ.

Nouakchott-Info: Immeuble Abbas, Tevragh Zeina, BP 1905, Nouakchott; tel. 525-02-71; fax 525-54-84; e-mail jedna@mapeci.com; internet www.akhbarnouakchott.com; f. 1995; daily; independent; Arabic and French; Dir of Publication and Editor-in-Chief CHEIKHNA OULD NENNI.

L'Opinion Libre: Nouakchott; weekly; Editor ELY OULD NAFA.

Rajoul Echarée: Nouakchott; e-mail rajoul_echaree@toptechnology.mr; weekly; independent; Arabic; Dir SIDI MOHAMED OULD YOUNÈS.

Ar-Rayah (The Banner): Nouakchott; e-mail team@rayah.info; internet www.rayah.info; f. 1997; independent; weekly; pro-Islamist; publication prohibited in May 2003; Editor AHMED OULD WEDIAA.

Le Rénovateur: Nouakchott; every 2 months; f. 2001; Editor Chiekh TIDIANE DIA.

La Tribune: BP 6227, Nouakchott; tel. 525-44-92; fax 525-02-09; Editor-in-Chief MOHAMMED FALL OULD OUMÈRE.

NEWS AGENCIES

Agence Mauritanienne de l'Information (AMI): BP 371, Nouakchott; tel. 525-29-40; fax 525-45-87; e-mail ami@mauritania.mr; internet www.ami.mr; fmrly Agence Mauritanienne de Presse; state-controlled; news and information services in Arabic and French; Dir MOHAMED CHEIKH OULD SIDI MOHAMED.

Foreign Bureaux

Foreign bureaux represented in Mauritania include Agence France-Presse, Reuters (United Kingdom) and Xinhua (New China) News Agency (People's Republic of China).

Publishers

Imprimerie Commerciale et Administrative de Mauritanie: BP 164, Nouakchott; textbooks, educational.

Imprimerie Nationale: BP 618, Nouakchott; tel. 525-44-38; fax 525-44-37; f. 1978; state-owned; Pres. RACHID OULD SALEH; Man. Dir ISSIMOU MAHJOUB.

GOVERNMENT PUBLISHING HOUSE

Société Nationale d'Impression: BP 618, Nouakchott; Pres. MOUSTAPHA SALECK OULD AHMED BRIHIM.

Broadcasting and Communications

TELECOMMUNICATIONS

Mauritel: BP 7000, Nouakchott; tel. 525-23-40; fax 525-17-00; e-mail webmaster@mauritel.mr; internet www.mauritel.mr; fmrly Société Mauritanienne des Télécommunications; 46% state-owned, 34% owned by Maroc Télécom (Morocco), 20% owned by Abdallahi Ould Noueigued group; Dir Col Ahmedoul Ould Mohamed el Kory

El-Jawel Mauritel Mobiles: ave du Roi Fayçal, BP 5920, Nouakchott; tel. 529-80-80; fax 529-81-81; e-mail mminfos@mauritel.mr; internet www.mauritelmobiles.mr; f. 2000; operates a mobile cellular telephone network (El Jawal) in Nouakchott and more than 27 other locations and three highways nation-wide; more than 350,000 subscribers (2005).

Société Mauritano-Tunisienne de Télécommunications (Mattel): BP 3668, Nouakchott; tel. 529-53-54; fax 529-81-03; e-mail mattel@mattel.mr; internet www.mattel.mr; f. 2000; privately owned Mauritanian-Tunisian co; operates mobile cellular communications network in Nouakchott and more than 10 other locations nation-wide.

BROADCASTING

Radio

Radio de Mauritanie (RM): ave Nasser, BP 200, Nouakchott; tel. and fax 525-21-64; e-mail rm@mauritania.mr; f. 1958; state-controlled; five transmitters; radio broadcasts in Arabic, French, Sarakolé, Toucouleur and Wolof; Dir Sid Brahim Ould Hamdinou.

Television

Télévision de Mauritanie (TVM): BP 5522, Nouakchott; tel. 525-40-67; fax 525-40-69; Dir-Gen. Hamoud Ould M'hamed.

Finance

(cap. = capital; res = reserves; dep. = deposits; m. = million; br(s).= branch(es); amounts in ouguiyas, unless otherwise stated)

BANKING

Central Bank

Banque Centrale de Mauritanie (BCM): ave de l'Indépendance, BP 623, Nouakchott; tel. 525-22-06; fax 525-27-59; e-mail info@bcm.mr; internet www.bcm.mr; f. 1973; bank of issue; total assets 200m. (2001); Gov. Kane Ousmane; 4 brs.

Commercial Banks

Banque El Amana pour le développement et l'Habitat (BADH): BP 5559, Nouakchott; tel. 525-34-90; fax 525-34-95; e-mail badh@opt.mr; f. 1997; 73% privately owned, 27% owned by Société Nationale Industrielle et Minière; cap. and res 1,297.4m., total assets 7,248.4m. (Dec. 2001); cap. 1,500m. (Dec. 2005); Pres. Ahamed Salem Ould Bouna Mokhtar; Dir-Gen. Mohammed Ould Oumarou; 6 brs.

Banque Internationale d'Investissement (BII): Nouakchott; tel. 529-70-00; fax 524-53-00; e-mail contact@bii.mr; f. 2005; cap. 4,000m. (Jan. 2006); Pres. and Dir-Gen. Jean-Phillipe Equilbecq; 1 br.

Banque pour le Commerce et l'Industrie (BCI): ave Nasser, BP 5050, Nouakchott; tel. 529-28-76; fax 529-28-77; e-mail bci@bci-banque.com; internet www.bci-banque.com; f. 1999; privately owned; cap. 2,040m. (Dec. 2005); Pres. and Dir-Gen. Isselmou Ould Didi Ould Tajedine; 9 brs.

Banque pour le Commerce et l'Investissement en Mauritanie (Bacim-Bank): BP 1268, Nouakchott; tel. 529-19-00; fax 529-13-60; e-mail bacim-bank@mauritel.mr; internet www.bacim.mr; f. 2002; privately owned; cap. 1,500m. (Dec. 2005); Pres. and Dir-Gen. Ahmed Ould el Wafi; 6 brs.

Banque Mauritanienne pour le Commerce International (BMCI): Immeuble Afarco, ave Nasser, BP 622, Nouakchott; tel. 525-28-26; fax 525-20-45; e-mail info@bmci.mr; internet www.bmci.mr; f. 1974; privately owned; cap. 3,000m. (Dec. 2005); res 801m., dep. 19,066m. (Dec. 2003); Pres. and Dir-Gen. Moulay Sidi Ould Hacen Ould Abass; 24 brs.

Banque Nationale de Mauritanie (BNM): ave Nasser, BP 614, Nouakchott; tel. 525-26-02; fax 525-33-97; e-mail bnm10@bnm.mr; f. 1989; privately owned; cap. 2,500m., res 977m., dep. 20,659m. (Dec. 2003); cap. 6,000m. (Dec. 2005); Pres. and Dir-Gen. Mohamed Ould Noueigued; 14 brs.

Chinguitty Bank: ave Nasser, BP 626, Nouakchott; tel. 525-21-42; fax 525-23-82; e-mail chinguittybank@mauritel.mr; f. 1972; 51% owned by Libyan Arab Foreign Bank, 49% state-owned; cap. and res 2,434.3m., total assets 13,832.4m. (Dec. 2002); cap. 3,500m. (Dec. 2005); Pres. M. el Hassen Ould Saleh; Gen. Man. Daw Amar Abdalla; 2 brs.

Générale de Banque de Mauritanie pour l'Investissement et le Commerce SA (GBM): ave de l'Indépendance, BP 5558, Nouakchott; tel. 525-36-36; fax 525-46-47; e-mail gbm@gbm.mr.com; f. 1995; 70% privately owned; cap. 5,100m., res. 2,941.6m., dep. 12,989.1m. (Dec. 2003); cap. 7,200m. (Dec. 2005); Pres. and Dir-Gen. Mohamed Hmayen Ould Bouamatou; 2 brs.

Islamic Bank

Banque al-Wava Mauritanienne Islamique (BAMIS): 758, rue 22–018, ave du Roi Fayçal, BP 650, Nouakchott; tel. 525-14-24; fax 525-16-21; e-mail bamis@bamis.mr; internet www.bamis.mr; f. 1985; fmrly Banque al-Baraka Mauritannienne Islamique; majority share privately owned; cap. 2,000m., res 2,821m., dep. 13,778m. (Dec. 2005); Pres. Mohamed Abdellahi Ould Abdellahi; Dir-Gen. Mohamed Abdellahi Ould Sidi; Exec. Dir Mohamed Ould Taya; 2 brs.

INSURANCE

Assurances Générales de Mauritanie: BP 2141, ave de Gaulle, TZA Ilot A 667, Nouakchott; tel. 529-29-00; fax 529-29-11; Man. Moulaye Ely Bouamatou.

Compagnie Nationale d'Assurance et de Réassurance (NASR): 12 ave Nasser, BP 163, Nouakchott; tel. 525-26-50; fax 525-18-18; e-mail nasr@nasr.mr; internet www.nasr.mr; f. 1994; state-owned; Pres. Mohamed Abdallahi Ould Sidi; Dir-Gen. Ahmed Ould Sidi Baba.

Société Anonyme d'Assurance et de Réassurance (SAAR): ave J. F. Kennedy, Immeuble El-Mamy, BP 2841, Nouakchott; tel. 525-30-56; fax 525-25-36; e-mail saar@infotel.mr; f. 1999; Pres. and Dir-Gen. Ahmed Bezeid Ould Med Lemine.

TAAMIN: BP 5164, Nouakchott; tel. 529-40-00; fax 529-40-02; e-mail taamin@toptechnology.mr; Pres. and Dir-Gen. Moulaye el Hassen Ould Moctar el Hassen.

Trade and Industry

DEVELOPMENT ORGANIZATIONS

Agence Française de Développement (AFD): rue Mamadou Kouaté prolongée, BP 5211, Nouakchott; tel. 525-25-25; fax 525-49-10; e-mail afdnouakchott@groupe-afd.org; internet www.afd.fr; Country Dir Gilles Chausse.

Mission Française de Coopération et d'Action Culturelle: BP 203, Nouakchott; tel. 525-21-21; fax 525-20-50; e-mail mcap.coop.france@opt.mr; administers bilateral aid from France; Dir Maurice Dadouche.

Société Nationale pour le Développement Rural (SONADER): BP 321, Nouakchott; tel. 521-18-00; fax 525-32-86; e-mail sonader@toptechnology.mr; f. 1975; Dir Ahmed Ould Bah Ould Cheikh Sidia.

CHAMBER OF COMMERCE

Chambre de Commerce, d'Industrie et d'Agriculture de Mauritanie: BP 215, Nouakchott; tel. 525-22-14; fax 525-38-95; f. 1954; Pres. Mahmoud Ould Ahmedou; Dir Habib Ould Ely.

EMPLOYERS' ORGANIZATION

National Confederation of Mauritanian Employers (CNPM): 824 ave de Roi Fayçal, Ksar, BP 383, Nouakchott; tel. 525-33-01; fax 525-91-08; e-mail germe@opt.mr; f. 1960; professional asscn for all employers active in Mauritania; Pres. Mohamed Ould Bouamatou; Sec.-Gen. Seyid Ould Abdallahi.

UTILITIES

Electricity

Société Mauritanienne d'Electricité (SOMELEC): BP 355, Nouakchott; tel. 525-23-08; fax 525-39-95; f. 2001; state-owned; transfer to majority private-sector ownership proposed; production and distribution of electricity; Dir-Gen. Col Ahmedou Ould Mohamed el-Kori.

Gas

Société Mauritanienne des Gaz (SOMAGAZ): POB 5089, Nouakchott; tel. 525-18-71; fax 529-47-86; e-mail somagaz@compunet.mr; production and distribution of butane gas; Dir-Gen. Mohamed Yahya Ould Mohamed el-Moctar.

Water

Société Nationale d'Eau (SNDE): ave 42-096, no. 106, Tevragh Zeina, BP 796, Nouakchott; tel. 525-52-73; fax 525-19-52; e-mail mfoudail@infotel.mr; f. 2001; Dir-Gen. THIAM SAMBA.

MAJOR COMPANIES

The following are some of the largest companies in terms of either capital investment or employment:

Compagnie Mauritano-Coréenne de Pêche (COMACOP): BP 527, Nouakchott; tel. 525-37-47; fax 525-20-34; f. 1977; cap. UM 230m.; fishing and freezer complex; Pres. and Dir-Gen. ABDOU OULD AL HACHEME.

Naftal, SA Mauritanie: BP 73, Nouadhibou; tel. 574-52-40; f. 1981 as Société Mauritanienne des Industries de Raffinage (SOMIR); affiliate of Naftec(Algeria); cap. UM 4,600m.; operates a petroleum refinery and negotiates overseas transactions; Chair. ABDELMADJID KAZI TANI; Man. Dir MOHAMED OTHMANI.

Naftec, SA Mauritanie: ave Abdellahi, BP 679, Nouakchott; tel. 525-26-51; fax 525-25-42; e-mail naftec@toptechnology.mr; internet www.naftec.mr; f. 1980; cap. UM 120m.; majority-owned by Naftec (Algeria), Mauritanian Govt is a minority shareholder; import and distribution of petroleum products; fmrly Société Mauritanienne de Commercialisation des Produits Pétroliers; Dir-Gen. A. GHIMOOZ.

Société Algéro-Mauritanienne des Pêches (ALMAP): BP 321, Nouadhibou; tel. 574-51-48; f. 1974; cap. UM 180m.; 51% state-owned, 49% owned by Govt of Algeria; fishing, processing of fishery products; Dir BRAHIM OULD BOIDAHA; 500 employees.

Société Arabe du Fer et de l'Acier en Mauritanie (SAFA): BP 114, Nouadhibou; tel. 574-53-89; fax 574-61-28; e-mail safa@snim.com; f. 1985; cap. UM 450m.; 75% owned by SNIM; steel-rolling mill; Chair. MOHAMED ALI OULD SIDI MOHAMED; Man. Dir MOHAMED YARBANA OULD MOHAMED EL MAMY; 142 employees (2001).

Société Arabe des Industries Métallurgiques (SAMIA): BP 1248, Nouakchott; tel. 525-44-55; fax 529-05-85; e-mail samia@mauritel.mr; f. 1974; cap. UM 762m.; 50% owned by SNIM, 50% owned by Kuwait Real Estate Investment Consortium; extraction of gypsum and production of plaster of Paris; Man. Dir MOHAMED SALEM OULD CHEIKH; 56 employees (2001).

Société Arabe Libyenne-Mauritanienne des Ressources Maritimes (SALIMAUREM): BP 75, Nouadhibou; tel. 574-52-41; f. 1978; cap. UM 2,300m.; 50% state-owned, 50% owned by Libyan-Arab Finance Co; fishing and fish-processing; freezer factory; Chair. AHMED OULD GHNAHALLA; Dir-Gen. SALA MOHAMED ARIBI.

Société Arabe des Mines de l'Inchiri (SAMIN): Akjoujt; tel. 576-71-04; f. 1981; cap. UM 3,276m.; 75% owned by Wadi Al Rawda Mining (United Arab Emirates); Chair. TAHER TABET; Man. Dir SIDI MALEK.

Société de Construction et de Gestion Immobilière de la Mauritanie (SOCOGIM): BP 28, Nouakchott; tel. 525-42-13; e-mail socogim@mauritel.mr; f. 1974; cap. UM 1,088.2m.; 89% state-owned; Chair. DIALLO MAMADOU BATHIA; Dir-Gen. MOHAMED LEMINE OULD KHATTRI.

Société des Mines du Cuivre de Mauritanie (MCM): BP 5576, Nouakchott; tel. 525-64-23; fax 525-63-20; f. 2005 to acquire operations of Guelb Moghrein Mines d'Akjoujt (GEMAK); exploitation of copper and other ores at Akjoujt; 80% owned by First Quantum Minerals (Canada).

Société Mauritanienne de Commercialisation de Poissons, SA (SMCP): blvd Median, BP 250, Nouadhibou; tel. 574-52-81; fax 524-55-66; internet www.smcpsa.com; f. 1984; cap. UM 500m.; Govt is a minority shareholder; until 1992 monopoly exporter of demersal fish and crustaceans; Pres. MOHAMED SALEM OULD LEKHAL; Dir-Gen. BOIJEL OULD HEMEID.

Société Nationale d'Importation et d'Exportation (SONIMEX): BP 290, Nouakchott; tel. 525-14-72; fax 525-30-14; f. 1966; cap. UM 914m.; 74% state-owned; import of foodstuffs and textiles, distribution of essential consumer goods, export of gum arabic; Pres. HAMOUD OULD AHMEDOU; Dir-Gen. Col N'DIAGA DIENG.

Société Nationale Industrielle et Minière (SNIM): BP 42, Nouadhibou; tel. 574-51-74; fax 574-53-96; e-mail snim@snim.com; internet www.snim.com; f. 1972; cap. UM 9,059.5m.; 78.4% state-owned; balance held by Islamic Development Bank (Saudi Arabia) and private Kuwaiti and Jordanian interests; operates mining centre at Zouerate, three open pit cast iron mines, port facilities, and 700-km railway line; Man. Dir MOHAMED SALECK OULD HEYINE; 3,764 employees (2005).

Total Mauritanie: E Nord, Lot no 110, BP 4973, Nouakchott; tel. 529-00-19; distribution of petroleum.

TRADE UNIONS

Confédération Générale des Travailleurs de Mauritanie: BP 6164, Nouakchott; tel. 525-80-57; e-mail admin@cgtm.org; internet cgtm.org; f. 1992; obtained official recognition in 1994; Sec.-Gen. ABDALLAHI OULD MOHAMED, dit NANA.

Confédération Libre des Travailleurs de Mauritanie: Nouakchott; f. 1995; Sec.-Gen. SAMORI OULD BEYI.

Union des Travailleurs de Mauritanie (UTM): Bourse du Travail, BP 630, Nouakchott; f. 1961; Sec.-Gen. ABDERAHMANE OULD BOUBOU; 45,000 mems.

Transport

RAILWAYS

A 670-km railway connects the iron-ore deposits at Zouérate with Nouadhibou; a 40-km extension services the reserves at El Rhein, and a 30-km extension those at M'Haoudat. Motive power is diesel-electric. The Société Nationale Industrielle et Minière (SNIM) operates one of the longest (2.4 km) and heaviest (22,000 metric tons) trains in the world.

SNIM—Direction du Chemin de Fer et du Port: BP 42, Nouadhibou; tel. 574-51-74; fax 574-53-96; e-mail m.khalifa.beyah@zrt.snim.com; internet www.snim.com; f. 1963; Gen. Man. MOHAMED SALECK OULD HEYINE.

ROADS

In 1999 there were about 7,891 km of roads and tracks, of which only 2,090 km were paved. The 1,100-km Trans-Mauritania highway, completed in 1985, links Nouakchott with Néma in the east of the country. Plans exist for the construction of a 7,400-km highway, linking Nouakchott with the Libyan port of Tubruq (Tobruk). In August 1999 the Islamic Development Bank granted Mauritania a loan worth US $9.4m. to help finance the rebuilding of the Chouk–Kiffa road. The construction of a 470-km highway between Nouakchott and Nouadhibou was completed in 2004.

Société Mauritanienne des Transports (SOMATRA): Nouakchott; tel. 525-29-53; f. 1975; Pres. CHEIKH MALAININE ROBERT; Dir-Gen. MAMADOU SOULEYMANE KANE.

INLAND WATERWAYS

The River Senegal is navigable in the wet season by small coastal vessels as far as Kayes (Mali) and by river vessels as far as Kaédi; in the dry season as far as Rosso and Boghé, respectively. The major river ports are at Rosso, Kaédi and Gouraye.

SHIPPING

The principal port, at Point-Central, 10 km south of Nouadhibou, is almost wholly occupied with mineral exports. In 1998 the port handled 11.6m. metric tons of cargo and cleared 3,804 vessels. There is also a commercial and fishing port at Nouadhibou. The deep-water Port de l'Amitié at Nouakchott, built and maintained with assistance from the People's Republic of China, was inaugurated in 1986. The port, which has a total capacity of about 1.5m. tons annually, handled 843,000 tons in 1998 (compared with 479,791 tons in 1990); the port cleared 453 vessels in 1998 (compared with 244 in 1990). In 2005 Mauritania's merchant fleet consisted of 152 vessels and had a total displacement of 51,866 grt.

Port Autonome de Nouakchott (Port de l'Amitié): BP 267/5103, El Mina, Nouakchott; tel. 525-14-53; fax 525-16-15; f. 1986; deep-water port; Dir-Gen. Col WALLAD OULD HAIMDOUNE.

Port Autonome de Nouadhibou: BP 236, Nouadhibou; tel. 574-51-34; f. 1973; state-owned; Pres. BAL MOHAMEDED EL HABIB; Dir-Gen. BÉBAHA OULD AHMED YOURA.

Shipping Companies

Cie Mauritanienne de Navigation Maritime (COMAUNAM): 119 ave Nasser, BP 799, Nouakchott; tel. 525-36-34; fax 525-25-04; f. 1973; 51% state-owned, 49% owned by Govt of Algeria; nat. shipping co; forwarding agent, stevedoring; Chair. MOHAND TIGHILT; Dir-Gen. KAMIL ABDELKADER.

Société d'Acconage et de Manutention en Mauritanie (SAMMA): BP 258, Nouadhibou; tel. 574-52-63; fax 574-52-37; e-mail didi.samma@snim.com; internet www.samma.mr; f. 1960; freight and handling, shipping agent, forwarding agent, stevedoring; Dir-Gen. DIDI OULD BIHA.

Société Générale de Consignation et d'Entreprises Maritimes (SOGECO): 1765 rue 22-002, Commune du Ksar, BP 351, Nouakchott; tel. 525-22-02; fax 525-39-03; e-mail sogeco@sogeco.sa.mr; internet www.sogecosa.com; f. 1973; shipping agent, forwarding, stevedoring; Man. Dir SID'AHMED ABEIDNA.

Société Mauritanienne pour la Pêche et la Navigation (SMPN): BP 40254, Nouakchott; tel. 525-36-38; fax 525-37-87; e-mail smpn@toptechnology.mr; Dir-Gen. ABDALLAHI OULD ISMAIL.

VOTRA: Route de l'Aéroport, BP 454, Nouakchott; tel. 525-24-10; fax 525-31-41; e-mail votra@mauritel.mr; internet www.votra.net; Dir-Gen. MOHAMED MAHMOUD OULD MAYE.

CIVIL AVIATION

There are international airports at Nouakchott, Nouadhibou and Néma, and 23 smaller airstrips.

Air Mauritanie (Société Mixte Air Mauritanie): BP 41, Nouakchott; tel. 525-22-11; fax 525-38-15; e-mail reservation@airmauritanie.mr; internet www.airmauritanie.mr; f. 1974; 11% state-owned; domestic, regional and international passenger and cargo services; Dir-Gen. SIDI ZEIN.

Tourism

Mauritania's principal tourist attractions are its historical sites, several of which have been listed by UNESCO under its World Heritage Programme, and its game reserves and national parks. Some 24,000 tourists visited Mauritania in 1999. Receipts from tourism in that year totalled an estimated US $28m.

Office National du Tourisme: BP 246, Nouakchott; tel. 525-35-72; f. 2002; Dir KHADIJÉTOU MINT BOUBOU.

SOMASERT: BP 42, Nouadhibou; tel. 574-29-91; fax 574-90-43; e-mail somasert@snim.com; subsidiary of SNIM; responsible for promoting tourism, managing hotels and organizing tours; Dir-Gen. MOHAMED OULD BIYAH.

Defence

As assessed at November 2006, the total armed forces numbered an estimated 15,870 men: army 15,000, navy about 620, air force 250. Full-time membership of paramilitary forces totalled about 5,000. Military service is by authorized conscription, and lasts for two years.

Defence Expenditure: Estimated at UM 4,800m. in 2006.

Chief of Staff of the Armed Forces: Brig. AL-HADI OULD AL-SADIK.

Chief of Staff of the Navy: Col CHEIKH OULD BAYE .

Chief of Staff of the National Gendarmerie: Col MOHAMED MAHMOUD OULD DEH.

Education

Primary education, which is officially compulsory, begins at six years of age and lasts for six years. In 2000/01 total enrolment at primary schools included 64% of children in the relevant age-group (66% of boys; 62% of girls), according to UNESCO estimates. Secondary education begins at 12 years of age and lasts for six years, comprising two cycles of three years each. Total enrolment at public secondary schools in 2000/01 included only 14% of children in the appropriate age-group (16% of boys; 13% of girls), according to UNESCO estimates. In 1998/99 a total of 12,912 students were enrolled at Mauritania's four higher education institutions (including the Université de Nouakchott, which was opened in 1983). In 2001 a UN project was initiated to address sexual inequality in the Mauritanian education system, which was particularly evident at higher education institutions, where only 16.6% of students were female in 1998. Total expenditure on education in 1998 was UM 6,197.8m. (equivalent to 27.5% of total government expenditure). In 1999 total expenditure on education amounted to UM 6,557.6m.

Bibliography

Abdoul, M., *et al. Regards sur la Mauritanie.* L'ouest saharien: cahiers d'études pluridisciplinaires; vol. 4. Paris, L'Harmattan, 2004.

Audibert, J. *MIFERMA: Une aventure humaine et industrielle en Mauritanie.* Paris, L'Harmattan, 1991.

Bader, C., and Lefort, F. *Mauritanie, la vie réconciliée.* Paris, Fayard, 1990.

Balta, P., and Rulleau, C. *Le Grand Maghreb, des indépendances à l'an 2000.* Paris, Découverte, 1990.

Belvaude, C. *La Mauritanie.* Paris, Editions Karthala, 1989.

Bonte, P. *La montagne de fer: la SNIM, Mauritanie: une entreprise minière saharienne à l'heure de la mondialisation.* Paris, Editions Karthala, 2001.

Boye, A. H., and Thiam, S. *J'étais à Oualata: le racisme d'Etat en Mauritanie.* Paris, L'Harmattan, 1999.

Calderini, S., Cortese, D., and Webb, J. L. A. *Mauritania.* Oxford, ABC Clio, 1992.

Clausen, U. *Demokratisierung in Mauritanien: Einfuehrung und Dokumente.* Hamburg, Deutsches Orient-Institut, 1993.

de Chassey, C. *Mauritanie 1900–1975: de l'ordre colonial à l'ordre néo-colonial entre Maghreb et Afrique noire.* Paris, Anthropos, 1978.

Désiré-Vuillemin, G. *Histoire de la Mauritanie: des origines à l'indépendance.* Paris, Editions Karthala, 1997.

Devey, M. *La Mauritanie.* Paris, Editions Karthala, 2005.

Diaw, M. *La politique étrangère de la Mauritanie.* Paris, L'Harmattan, 1999.

Garnier, C., and Ermont, P. *Désert fertile: un nouvel état, la Mauritanie.* Paris, Hachette, 1960.

Human Rights Watch, Africa. *Mauritania's Campaign of Terror: State-Sponsored Repression of Black Africans.* New York, Human Rights Watch, 1994.

Jus, C. *Soudan français–Mauritanie, une géopolitique coloniale (1880–1963): tracer une ligne dans le désert.* Paris, L'Harmattan, 2003.

Marchesin, P. *Tribus, ethnies et pouvoir en Mauritanie.* Paris, Editions Karthala, 1992.

Ould Ahmed Salem, M. *L'économie mauritanienne: le bilan de la planification économique depuis l'indépendance* (trans. from Arabic by Ould Moulaye Ahmed, A.). Nouakchott, Imprimerie Atlas, 1994.

Ould Daddah, M. *La Mauritanie contre vents et marées.* Paris, Editions Karthala, 2003.

Ould-May, M. *Global Restructuring and Peripheral States: The Carrot and the Stick in Mauritania.* Lanham, MD, Littlefield Adams, 1996.

Ould Saleck, El-A. *Les Haratins: La paysage politique mauritanien.* Paris, L'Harmattan, 2003.

Pazzanika, A. G. *Historical Dictionary of Mauritania.* Lanham, MD, Scarecrow Press, 1996.

Robinson, D. *Sociétés musulmanes et pouvoir colonial français au Sénégal et en Mauritanie 1880–1920.* Paris, Editions Karthala, 2004.

Sy, A. A. *L'Enfer d'Inal: Mauritanie—l'horreur des camps.* Paris, L'Harmattan, 2000.

Vandermotten, C. *Géopolitique de la vallée du Sénégal: les flots de la discorde.* Paris, L'Harmattan, 2004.

Wolff, W. J., van der Land, J., Nienhuis, P. H., and de Wilde, P. A. W. J. (Eds). *Ecological Studies in the Coastal Waters of Mauritania.* London, Kluwer Academic Publishers, 1993.

MAURITIUS

Physical and Social Geography

The Republic of Mauritius, comprising the islands of Mauritius and Rodrigues, together with the Agalega Islands and the Cargados Carajos Shoals, lies in the Indian Ocean 800 km east of Madagascar. The island of Mauritius covers 1,865 sq km (720 sq miles) in area. It is a volcanic island, consisting of a plain rising from the north-east to the highest point on the island, Piton de la Rivière Noire (827 m above sea-level) in the south-west, interspersed by abrupt volcanic peaks and gorges, and is almost completely surrounded by a coral reef. Including Rodrigues and its other islands, the republic occupies a land area of 2,040 sq km (788 sq miles).

The climate is sub-tropical maritime, but with two distinct seasons; additionally, the warm dry coastal areas contrast with the cool rainy interior. Mauritius and Rodrigues are vulnerable to cyclones, particularly between September and May.

Rodrigues, a volcanic island of 104 sq km (40 sq miles) surrounded by a coral reef, lies 585 km east of the island of Mauritius. Its population was enumerated at 35,779 in the 2000 census, and was estimated to number 36,995 at December 2005. Mauritius has two dependencies (together covering 71 sq km, with 289 inhabitants at the 2000 census): Agalega, two islands 935 km north of Mauritius; and the Cargados Carajos Shoals (or St Brandon Islands), 22 islets without permanent inhabitants but used as a fishing station, 370 km north-north-east of Mauritius.

Mauritius claims sovereignty over Tromelin, a small island without permanent inhabitants, 556 km to the north-west. This claim is disputed by Madagascar and France. Mauritius also seeks the return of the Chagos Archipelago (notably the coral atoll of Diego Garcia), about 2,000 km to the north-east. The archipelago was formerly administered by Mauritius but in 1965 became part (and in 1976 all) of the British Indian Ocean Territory.

The population of the Republic of Mauritius was enumerated at 1,179,137 at the July 2000 census and (excluding Agalega and the Cargados Carajos Shoals) was officially estimated at 1,256,739 in December 2006, giving a density of 616.0 inhabitants per sq km. During 1995–2005 the population increased at an average annual rate of only 1.1%, owing, in part, to higher emigration and a decline in the birth rate. Almost 42% of the population reside in the urban area extending from Port Louis (the capital and business centre) on the north-west coast, to Curepipe in the island's centre. The population is of mixed origin, including people of European, African, Indian and Chinese descent. English is the official language, and Creole (Kreol), derived from French, the lingua franca. The most widely spoken languages at the 2000 census were Creole (38.6%) and Bhojpuri (30.6%), a Hindi dialect.

Recent History

Revised by KATHARINE MURISON

The islands of Mauritius and Rodrigues passed from French into British control in 1810. Subsequent settlement came mainly from East Africa and India, and the European population has remained predominantly francophone.

The Indian community in Mauritius took little part in politics until 1947, when the franchise was extended to adults over the age of 21 years who could establish simple literacy in any language. This expansion of the electorate deprived the Franco-Mauritian and Creole communities of their political dominance, and the Mauritius Labour Party (MLP), led by Dr (later Sir) Seewoosagur Ramgoolam, consolidated the new political role of the Indian community. The Parti Mauricien Social Démocrate (PMSD) emerged to represent traditional Franco-Mauritian and Creole interests, under the leadership of Gaëtan (later Sir Gaëtan) Duval. With impetus from Ramgoolam's MLP, Mauritius proceeded to independence, within the Commonwealth, on 12 March 1968, with Ramgoolam as Prime Minister of a coalition Government that was subsequently extended to include the PMSD.

In November 1965 the United Kingdom transferred the Chagos Archipelago (including the atoll of Diego Garcia), a Mauritian dependency about 2,000 km (1,250 miles) north-east of the main island, to the newly created British Indian Ocean Territory (BIOT, q.v.). Mauritius has subsequently campaigned for the return of the islands, which have been developed as a major US military base.

From 1970 the strongest opposition to the Ramgoolam coalition came from a newly formed left-wing group, the Mouvement Militant Mauricien (MMM), led by Paul Bérenger. Having attracted considerable public support during a period of labour unrest, the MMM emerged as the largest single party in the Legislative Assembly at elections in December 1976, although with insufficient seats to form a government. Ramgoolam was able to form a new coalition with the PMSD, which, despite resurgences of public disorder, retained power for its full legislative term.

THE JUGNAUTH COALITIONS, 1982–95

At elections to the Legislative Assembly in June 1982, an alliance of the MMM and the Parti Socialiste Mauricien (PSM) won all 60 elective seats on the main island. Anerood (later Sir Anerood) Jugnauth became Prime Minister and appointed Bérenger as Minister of Finance. In March 1983, however, following discord within the cabinet over Bérenger's stringent economic policies and his attempts to make Creole (Kreol) the official language (despite the Indian descent of the majority of the population), Bérenger and his supporters resigned. Jugnauth formed a new Government, and in April formed a new party, the Mouvement Socialiste Militant (MSM), which subsequently merged with the PSM. However, the new Government lacked a legislative majority, and Jugnauth was obliged to dissolve the Assembly in June. At a general election in August, an alliance comprising the MSM, the MLP and the PMSD, obtained a decisive majority. Jugnauth remained as Prime Minister, with Duval as Deputy Prime Minister.

In December 1983 Sir Seewoosagur Ramgoolam was appointed Governor-General. The new leader of the MLP, Satcam (later Sir Satcam) Boolell, was dismissed from the cabinet in February 1984, prompting the party to withdraw from the coalition. During 1985 the Jugnauth Government began to incur public dissatisfaction, which was increased by the introduction in April of legislation banning material that was judged to be damaging to the administration. Serious public disquiet arose in December, when four members of the Legislative Assembly were arrested in the Netherlands on charges of drugs-smuggling. In January 1986, following Jugnauth's refusal to comment on allegations that other deputies were involved in the affair, four cabinet ministers resigned. A new Government formed by Jugnauth retained the political balance of the previous administration. In March five MSM deputies, including three who had resigned as ministers in January, withdrew their support from the coalition.

In June 1986, in response to pressure from within the MSM, Jugnauth appointed a commission of inquiry to investigate the drugs scandal. In the following month, however, three ministers resigned, citing lack of confidence in Jugnauth's leadership. The Government retaliated by expelling 11 MSM dissidents from the party. In November, following a report by the commission of inquiry into the drugs affair, four MSM deputies resigned from the Legislative Assembly, thus reducing the MSM/PMSD coalition's strength in the legislature to only 30 of the 62 elective seats. In the subsequent political realignment, the MMM gained the support of several deputies who had previously left the coalition.

In March 1987 the commission of inquiry issued a further report alleging that six deputies of the MSM/PMSD alliance had been involved in drugs-trafficking. In the same month further allegations associated Sir Gaëtan Duval, a Deputy Prime Minister, with the affair. However, Duval's subsequent offer of resignation was rejected by Jugnauth. In May Diwakar Bundhun, the Minister of Industry, was dismissed, after openly criticizing Jugnauth. Having lost majority support in the Legislative Assembly, Jugnauth announced that a general election would take place in August.

At the general election held on 30 August 1987, an electoral alliance comprising the MSM, the PMSD and the MLP won 39 of the 60 elective seats on the main island, although it received only 49.8% of total votes cast. The MMM, which campaigned in alliance with two smaller parties, won 21 seats, obtaining 48.1% of votes cast. Dr Paramhansa (Prem) Nababsingh subsequently became the leader of the MMM and of the opposition in the Assembly, replacing Bérenger, who had failed to secure a seat. In September Jugnauth appointed a new Council of Ministers.

In August 1988, following a disagreement over employment policies, Sir Gaëtan Duval, the leader of the PMSD, left the Government, together with his brother, Hervé Duval, the Minister of Industry. Two attempts on Jugnauth's life (in November 1988 and March 1989) were attributed by him to criminals involved in drugs-trafficking.

In July 1990 the MMM and MSM agreed to form an alliance to contest the next general election, and to proceed with constitutional measures that would allow Mauritius to become a republic within the Commonwealth. Under the proposed new constitution, Bérenger would assume the presidency, while Jugnauth would remain as executive Prime Minister, with Nababsingh as Deputy Prime Minister. However, the draft amendments, which were submitted to the Legislative Assembly in August, were opposed by members of the MLP (in alliance with the PMSD) and Jugnauth failed to secure the necessary parliamentary majority. He subsequently dismissed Boolell, as well as two ministers belonging to the MSM, who had refused to support the proposed amendments. A further three ministers representing the MLP also resigned, leaving only one MLP member in the Government. Boolell subsequently relinquished the leadership of the MLP to Dr Navinchandra (Navin) Ramgoolam (the son of Sir Seewoosagur Ramgoolam, who died in December 1985). In September 1990 Jugnauth announced the formation of a new coalition Government, in which the six vacant ministerial posts were awarded to the MMM, while Nababsingh became one of the three Deputy Prime Ministers.

At a general election on 15 September 1991, an alliance of the MSM, the MMM and the Mouvement des Travaillistes Démocrates (MTD) won 57 of the 62 elective seats, while the alliance of the MLP and the PMSD secured only three seats. Members of the Organisation du Peuple Rodriguais (OPR) were returned to the remaining two seats. However, members of the opposition, including Dr Ramgoolam and Sir Gaëtan Duval, alleged electoral malpractice. Jugnauth subsequently formed a new Government, to which nine representatives of the MMM (including Bérenger) and one representative of the MTD were appointed. Later in September Sir Gaëtan Duval resigned from the Legislative Assembly. In the following month the MLP/PMSD alliance refused to participate in municipal elections, in which the MSM/MMM/MTD alliance won 125 of the 126 contested seats.

In December 1991 the Legislative Assembly approved constitutional amendments providing for Mauritius to become a republic within the Commonwealth on 12 March 1992. Under the terms of the revised Constitution, the Governor-General, Sir Veerasamy Ringadoo, who had been nominated by Jugnauth, was to assume the presidency for an interim period, pending the election of a President and Vice-President, for a five-year term, by a simple majority of the Legislative Assembly (which would be renamed the National Assembly). The Constitution vested executive power in the Prime Minister, who would be appointed by the President, and would be the parliamentary member best able to command a majority in the National Assembly. On 12 March 1992 Ringadoo officially became interim President, replacing the British monarch, Queen Elizabeth II, as Head of State. Later that month the Government announced that Cassam Uteem, the Minister of Industry and Industrial Technology and a member of the MMM, was to be nominated to the presidency after a period of three months. (Under the terms of the alliance between the MSM and the MMM, members of the MMM were to be appointed to the presidency and vice-presidency, while Jugnauth was to remain as Prime Minister.) Uteem was duly elected President by the National Assembly in June, with Sir Rabindrah Ghurburrun as Vice-President.

Following a number of disagreements between the MMM and MSM, the government coalition was further weakened in August 1993, when candidates of the PMSD secured the three vacant seats in a municipal by-election (in a constituency where the MMM traditionally attracted most support). Later in August a meeting between Bérenger and Ramgoolam prompted speculation that an alliance between the MMM and MLP was contemplated. Shortly afterwards, Jugnauth dismissed Bérenger from the Council of Ministers, on the grounds that he had repeatedly criticized government policy.

The removal of Bérenger precipitated a serious crisis within the MMM, the political bureau of which decided that the other nine members of the party who held ministerial portfolios should remain in the coalition Government. Led by Nababsingh, the Deputy Prime Minister, and the Minister of Industry and Industrial Technology, Jean-Claude de l'Estrac, supporters of the pro-coalition faction announced in October 1993 that Bérenger had been suspended as Secretary-General of the MMM. Bérenger and his supporters responded by expelling 11 MMM officials from the party, and subsequently obtaining a legal ban on Nababsingh and de l'Estrac using the party name. The split in the MMM led in November to a government reshuffle, in which the remaining two MMM ministers supporting Bérenger were replaced by members of the party's pro-coalition faction.

In April 1994 the MLP and the MMM announced that they had agreed terms for an alliance to contest the next general elections. Under its provisions, Ramgoolam was to be Prime Minister and Bérenger Deputy Prime Minister, with cabinet portfolios allocated on the basis of 12 ministries to the MLP and nine to the MMM. In the same month three deputies from the MSM withdrew their support from the Government.

Nababsingh and the dissident faction of the MMM, having lost Bérenger's legal challenge for the use of the party name, formed a new party, the Renouveau Militant Mauricien (RMM), which formally commenced political activity in June 1994. In the same month Jugnauth declared that the Government would remain in office until the conclusion of its mandate in September 1996.

In November 1994, during the course of a parliamentary debate on electoral issues, Bérenger and de l'Estrac accepted a mutual challenge to resign their seats in the National Assembly and to contest by-elections. In the following month the MSM indicated that it would not oppose RMM candidates in the two polls. In January 1995, however, Jugnauth unsuccessfully sought to undermine the MLP/MMM alliance by offering electoral support to the MLP. The by-elections, held in February, were both won by MLP/MMM candidates, and Bérenger was returned to the National Assembly. Following these results, Jugnauth opened political negotiations with the PMSD, whose leader, Charles Gaëtan Xavier-Luc Duval (the son of Sir Gaëtan Duval), agreed to enter the coalition as Minister of Industry and Industrial Technology and Minister of Tourism. The cabinet post of Attorney-General and Minister of Justice, previously held by Jugnauth, was also allocated to the PMSD, and Sir Gaëtan Duval accepted an appointment as an economic adviser to the Prime Minister. As a result, however, of widespread opposition within the PMSD to participation in the coalition, Xavier-Luc Duval left the Government in October, and Sir Gaëtan Duval subsequently resumed the leadership of the party. The Minister for Rodrigues, representing the OPR, also resigned from the cabinet.

MLP/MMM COALITION

At a general election in December 1995 the MLP/MMM alliance won a decisive victory: of the 62 elected seats, the MLP secured 35 seats, the MMM obtained 25 seats and the OPR two seats. Under constitutional arrangements providing representation for unsuccessful candidates attracting the largest number of votes, Sir Gaëtan Duval re-entered the National Assembly, together with two members of the Mouvement Rodriguais and a representative of Hizbullah, an Islamist fundamentalist group. Ramgoolam became Prime Minister of the new MLP/MMM coalition, with Bérenger as Deputy Prime Minister with responsibility for foreign and regional relations. Sir Gaëtan Duval died in May 1996 and was succeeded in the National Assembly and as leader of the PMSD by his brother, Hervé Duval, although Xavier-Luc Duval continued to command a significant personal following within the party.

Evidence of strains within the MLP/MMM coalition began to emerge in June 1996, when austerity proposals, put forward by Rundheersing Bheenick, the Minister of Finance, aroused considerable opposition from the MMM. Bheenick subsequently resigned, and the finance portfolio was taken over by Ramgoolam until November, when an extensive reallocation of ministerial responsibilities was carried out.

THE MLP IN POWER

More serious divisions within the coalition Government emerged in late 1996, when differences were reported between Ramgoolam and Bérenger over the allocation of ministerial responsibilities, and the perception by the MMM of delays in the implementation of social and economic reforms. In January 1997 rumours had begun to circulate of a possible political alliance between the MMM and the MSM. Bérenger's criticism of the coalition's performance intensified in the following months, and culminated in June in his dismissal from the Government and the consequent withdrawal of the MMM from the coalition. Following unsuccessful efforts to draw the PMSD into a new administration, Ramgoolam formed an MLP cabinet, assuming personal responsibility for foreign affairs. Bheenick returned to the Government as Minister of Economic Development and Regional Co-operation. Ahmed Rashid Beebeejaun, Minister of Land Transport, Shipping and Public Safety in the former coalition, left the MMM and retained his former portfolio as an independent. Ramgoolam emphasized his determination to remain in office for the full legislative term to December 2000. In June 1997 the National Assembly re-elected Cassam Uteem to a second five-year term as President. A prominent supporter of the MLP, Angidi Verriah Chettiar, was elected Vice-President.

Following the dissolution of the MLP/MMM alliance, Bérenger sought to assume the leadership of a consolidated political opposition to the Government. In August 1997 two small parties, the Mouvement Militant Socialiste Mauricien (MMSM) and the Rassemblement pour la Réforme (RPR), agreed to support Bérenger in this aim. The alliance was extended to include a breakaway faction of the PMSD, known as the 'Vrais Bleus', under the leadership of Hervé Duval, who had been replaced as party leader by his nephew, Xavier-Luc Duval, an opponent of co-operation with the MMM. In April 1998 the MMM, the MMSM, the RPR and the 'Vrais Bleus' parties formed an electoral coalition, the Alliance Nationale, to contest a by-election for a vacant seat in the National Assembly. The seat, which was retained by the MLP, had also been sought by Jugnauth on behalf of the MSM, which remained unrepresented in the National Assembly. Jugnauth subsequently opened negotiations with Bérenger for an MSM/MMM electoral alliance, and in December both parties agreed terms for a joint list of candidates.

In February 1999 Jugnauth assumed the leadership of the informal MSM/MMM alliance. An agreement creating a federation of the two parties stipulated that Jugnauth would serve as Prime Minister in any future government formed by the alliance. Bérenger was appointed deputy leader of the alliance, and was to be Deputy Prime Minister in the event of the alliance winning the legislative elections (due to be held in late 2000). However, the appointment of Jugnauth's son, Pravind, as deputy leader of the MSM later that year caused divisions within the alliance, with members of the MMM claiming that Jugnauth was attempting to establish a political dynasty.

A reorganization of the Council of Ministers was carried out in October 1999, following the victory of Xavier-Luc Duval in a by-election the preceding month; the MLP had endorsed the candidature of Duval, who had formed his own party, the Parti Mauricien Xavier-Luc Duval (PMXD), in 1998. Duval was appointed Minister of Industry, Commerce, Corporate Affairs and Financial Services.

THE 2000 GENERAL ELECTION

A general election was held on 11 September 2000. There was a high rate of participation, with 81% of the 790,000 registered electors casting their ballots. The result was a significant victory for the opposition MSM/MMM alliance, also comprising the PMSD, which had remained united despite apparent signs of division earlier in the year. The alliance won a total of 54 of the 62 directly elective seats in the National Assembly, while the MLP/PMXD alliance took six seats and the OPR two. As agreed, Sir Anerood Jugnauth became Prime Minister again, while Paul Bérenger was appointed Deputy Prime Minister and Minister of Finance. A new Council of Ministers was sworn in on 20 September.

In November 2000 the British High Court of Justice ruled that the eviction of several thousand inhabitants of the Chagos Archipelago between 1967 and 1973, to allow the construction of a US military base on the atoll of Diego Garcia, had been unlawful. The Court overturned a 1971 ordinance preventing the islanders from returning to the Archipelago. (The majority of the displaced islanders had been resettled in Mauritius, which had administered the Chagos Archipelago until its transfer to BIOT in 1965.) Following the ruling, the Mauritian Government declared its right to sovereignty over the islands to be indisputable and sought international recognition of this. Jugnauth stated that he would be prepared to negotiate with the USA over the continued presence of the military base. The United Kingdom reiterated that it would return the islands if, as had been maintained for many years, the USA was prepared to move out of the base on Diego Garcia. India declared its support for the Mauritian Government's claim to sovereignty, as part of the close relationship being encouraged between the two countries. In May 2002 legislation allowing the displaced islanders to apply for British citizenship came into effect.

In May 2001 the Mouvement Républicain (MR) withdrew its support from the ruling alliance owing to an alleged lack of communication between party leaders. At municipal elections, held on 7 October, the governing alliance won control of all five municipalities with 115 of 226 council seats, although the rate of voter participation was only an estimated 40%. In November legislation providing for the creation of an 18-member Regional Assembly for Rodrigues received the President's assent. At the first elections to the new Assembly, which were held in September 2002, the OPR won 10 seats and the Mouvement Rodriguais took eight.

PRESIDENTIAL CHANGE

In February 2002 President Uteem resigned in protest at controversial anti-terrorism legislation (drawn up in response to the attacks in New York and Washington, DC, USA, on 11 September 2001), which he felt surrendered too great a part of the nation's sovereignty to Western powers and ascribed excessive powers to the authorities, at the expense of the rights of the citizen. Vice-President Chettiar also resigned as his successor when called on to sanction the legislation, which was widely opposed. The bill was finally promulgated by the Chief Justice of the Supreme Court, Arianga Pillay, acting as interim President, as it had already been passed twice by the National Assembly. On 25 February Karl Offman of the MSM was elected President at an extraordinary session of the National Assembly, which was boycotted by opposition deputies. Offman was not to remain in office for the full five-year term, but to relinquish the presidency to Jugnauth in October 2003, as already agreed by his party. In April 2003 Sir Anerood Jugnauth resigned from the leadership of the MSM in favour of his son, Pravind.

In August 2003, in preparation for the transfer of governing roles, a constitutional amendment was approved by the National Assembly to increase the powers of the President, giving the incumbent the right to refuse a request from the Prime Minister to dissolve the legislature following a vote of 'no confidence'. Sir Anerood Jugnauth resigned as premier on 30 September and was immediately replaced by Paul Bérenger, the first non-Hindu Prime Minister, who appointed a new Council of Ministers. On 1 October, as agreed, Offman resigned from the presidency and Jugnauth was elected as his successor by the National Assembly one week later. Bérenger conducted a premiership that concentrated on international relations and assumed the rotating presidency of the Southern African Development Community in mid-2004. The Government threatened to pursue its claim of sovereignty over the Chagos Archipelago at the International Court of Justice, on the basis that the separation of the Archipelago from Mauritian territory prior to independence was contrary to international law. In June 2004 the British authorities issued two decrees (known as Orders in Council) effectively prohibiting the islanders and their descendants from returning to live on the Chagos Archipelago, despite the High Court ruling in their favour in 2000. The Chagossians subsequently challenged the validity of these Orders in Council.

In early 2005 Anil Bachoo, the Minister of Public Infrastructure, Land Transport and Shipping, and Mookhesswur Choonee, the Minister of Local Government and Solid Waste Management, resigned from the Government and from the MSM, before founding a new party, the Mouvement Social Démocrate (MSD). The politicians reportedly disapproved of an implicit arrangement between the ruling parties that Bérenger would resign from the premiership at mid-term, in order for Pravind Jugnauth to assume power, just as Jugnauth's father (the incumbent President) had done for Bérenger. The MSD subsequently joined the MLP-led Alliance Sociale (AS), also comprising the MMSM, the MR and the PMXD, which had been established to contest forthcoming elections to the National Assembly.

THE AS IN GOVERNMENT

At the legislative elections, which were held on 3 July 2005, the AS defeated the incumbent coalition of the MSM/MMM/PMSD, winning 38 of the 62 directly elected mandates. The MSM/MMM/PMSD alliance secured 22 seats, and the remaining two were taken by the OPR. The rate of voter participation was 81.5%. Navin Ramgoolam was appointed as Prime Minister, and a new 19-member Council of Ministers was sworn into office on 7 July. Xavier-Luc Duval became one of three Deputy Prime Ministers and was also allocated the tourism, leisure and external communications portfolio. The new premier pledged to revive the economy, focusing particularly on the beleaguered textiles and sugar sectors, to address rising unemployment and inflation, and to improve standards of living. Electoral reform, including the introduction of a system of proportional representation in legislative elections, was also envisaged. Friction was apparent between the politically opposed President and Prime Minister during the new Government's first few weeks in office, notably as a result of Sir Anerood Jugnauth's rejection of a number of Ramgoolam's public-service appointments, although tensions later eased.

The AS won an overwhelming victory at municipal elections held in October 2005, taking 122 of the 126 seats contested and securing control of all five municipalities. The opposition MSM/MMM/PMSD alliance only managed to retain four seats, all in the town of Beau Bassin/Rose Hill (where a total of 24 seats were available), traditionally an MMM stronghold. Following the elections the PMSD withdrew from the alliance, in which it had, in any case, been a very minor partner. The AS also performed well at village elections in December.

In October 2005 Ramgoolam paid a week-long state visit to India, a major source of direct investment in Mauritius, aimed at further strengthening the already close bilateral relationship; eight agreements on economic co-operation were signed during the visit. In March 2006 the Indian President, Aavul Pakkiri Jainulabidin Abdul Kalam, attended celebrations to mark National Day during a three-day visit to Mauritius. Meanwhile, the AS Government also sought to enhance bilateral relations with other island nations in the Indian Ocean. In November 2005 the President of Madagascar, Marc Ravalomanana, held talks with Ramgoolam in Mauritius, while a wide-ranging agreement on co-operation between Mauritius and Seychelles was signed in the following month.

The AS Government continued with efforts to regain sovereignty over the Chagos Archipelago. A group of 102 Chagossians was permitted to visit the Archipelago in March 2006, accompanied by Deputy Prime Minister Duval and two other government ministers, principally in order to visit the graves of relatives. In May the British High Court of Justice overturned the Orders in Council issued by the British Government under the royal prerogative in June 2004, ruling them to be unlawful, and confirmed the right of the islanders to return to the Archipelago without any conditions. In May 2007 the British High Court of Appeal rejected an appeal lodged by the British Government against the High Court's decision. In the following month the British Government appealed to the House of Lords.

In April 2006 the opposition was further weakened when the PMSD announced that it was joining the government coalition and the MSM/MMM alliance collapsed following weeks of increasing tension between Pravind Jugnauth and Bérenger. The MSM withdrew its support from Bérenger as official leader of the opposition. Bérenger was succeeded by Nando Bodha, the Secretary-General of the MSM and a close ally of Pravind Jugnauth (who had failed to retain his seat in the legislature in July 2005), since the MSM held 11 seats in the National Assembly to the MMM's 10. Bodha's nomination was rejected by Ashock Jugnauth, a senior member of the MSM (and uncle of Pravind), who resigned from the party and established a new opposition party, the Union Nationale.

The budget for 2006/07, announced in June 2006 by the Deputy Prime Minister and Minister of Finance and Economic Development, Rama Sithanen, included a number of liberalizing reforms aimed at promoting growth, attracting foreign investment, diversifying the economic base and restoring fiscal stability. However, there were divisions within the Government over economic policy, and in February 2007 Sithanen threatened to resign following the appointment as Governor of the central bank of Rundheersing Bheenick, who was believed to oppose the former's ambitious reform programme. Nevertheless, Sithanen's budget for 2007/08, presented in June 2007, indicated that he intended to continue to pursue radical reform.

Meanwhile, elections to the Rodrigues Regional Assembly were held in December 2006. The Mouvement Rodriguais secured 10 of the Assembly's 18 seats, while the OPR took eight.

Enhancing bilateral economic relations remained a priority for the AS Government in 2006–07. In September 2006 Mauritius and the USA signed a trade and investment framework agreement, and in January 2007 Mauritius concluded discussions on a preferential trade agreement with Pakistan. Moreover, an Indian-Mauritian Comprehensive Economic Co-operation and Partnership Agreement was under negotiation in mid-2007. The Government also sought closer ties with the People's Republic of China. Ramgoolam attended a summit meeting of the Forum on China-Africa Co-operation in the Chinese capital, Beijing, in November 2006, and in the following month China granted Mauritius an interest-free loan of some Rs 135m. in support of the Government's economic restructuring plans. Ramgoolam returned to China in July 2007 on a six-day official visit, during which he held talks with the Chinese President, Hu Jintao, and Premier, Wen Jiabao.

Economy

DONALD L. SPARKS

The Republic of Mauritius is a small island state, with only 2,040 sq km in land area, and a population of 1,250,882. Unlike most other members of the African Union Mauritius is classified by the World Bank as an 'upper middle-income' economy. In 2006 the UNDP's Human Development Report gave Mauritius the highest rank in sub-Saharan Africa on its human development index (HDI). This index combines life expectancy, school enrolment and gross domestic product (GDP) per head. With a score of 0.8, it was well above the region's average of 0.47. Mauritius also ranked higher than India or Pakistan. In fact, the score places Mauritius in the category of the world's wealthiest nations. Unlike many other countries in the sub-Saharan region, Mauritius has achieved good rates of economic growth during the past two decades. Between 1985 and 1995 the economy grew at an annual average rate of 15.5%, one of the highest rates in the region, and in 1995–2005 it averaged 10.3%. The Government's Central Statistics Office recorded GDP growth of 4.7% in 2006, up from 2.3% in 2005. The export promotion zone (EPZ) showed a strong performance, due principally to growth in the seafood sector. This was accompanied by growth in the tourism, transportation and communications sectors. Tourism increased by 6.2%, while transport and communications expanded by 7.8% in 2006. Manufacturing and construction, stagnant in 2005 showed signs of growth in 2006.

Mauritius, in the past a 'mono-culture' economy, was traditionally dependent on sugar production, and economic growth was therefore vulnerable to adverse climatic conditions and variations in international prices for sugar. However, the dominance of sugar in the economy has been eclipsed by steadily expanding manufactured exports, activity in the financial services sectors and by tourism. The contribution of revenue from agriculture, fisheries and forestry to GDP declined from 25% in 1979 to 5.2% in 2006. Nonetheless, sugar remains important to the economy, earning an estimated 16.2% of export revenues in 2006. In 2005 manufacturing accounted for 19.8% of GDP, followed by transport and communications (12.7%), wholesale and retail trade (11.2%), and the financial and business services sector (20.5%). Mauritius' gross national income (GNI) per head was an estimated by the World Bank at US $5,260 in 2006. From 1999 until 2006 the average annual rate of inflation was 4.9%, according to the IMF. The inflation rate averaged 4.7% in 2004, 4.9% in 2005 and 8.9% in 2006, the highest in 13 years. While the new Alliance Sociale (AS) Government initially restricted price increases in important household items such as medicines, transportation and certain food stuffs, in early 2006 the Government relaxed those restrictions and reduced or removed some food subsidies (including those on imported rice and flour, soft drinks and cigarettes). The other major source of upward price pressures came from increased petroleum prices, with diesel prices increasing by 78%, while petrol rose by 40%.

INDUSTRY

Until the 1970s the industrial sector was effectively limited to the import substitution of basic consumer products, such as food, beverages, tobacco, footwear, clothing, metal products, paints and board for furniture. Since then there has been a rapid expansion in manufacturing, with the sector accounting for an estimated 19.0% of GDP in 2006 and 42.1% of total exports. The manufacturing sector declined by 2.4%, in real terms, in 2002, compared with an increase of 4.4% in 2001, but remained static in 2003, before recovering again by 0.3% in 2004. However, it declined by 5.0% in 2005, according to preliminary estimates.

In view of the limited domestic market, the high level of unemployment and the emphasis on reducing dependence on the sugar sector, the Government adopted a policy of export promotion by developing the EPZ, concentrating on labour-intensive processing of imported goods for the export market. Within the EPZ, the Government offers both local and foreign investors attractive incentives, including tax 'holidays', exemption from import duties on most raw materials and capital goods, free repatriation of capital, profits and dividends, low-price electricity, etc. In 1993 there were 554 enterprises in the EPZ (down from 586 in 1988), employing about 83,500 workers, the lowest level since 1987. The decline both in new enterprises and employment continued in the mid-1990s, when a total of 494 businesses were employing 82,220 workers. By December 2005 506 companies were employing 66,931 workers and investment stood at MRs 2,355m. The fastest-growing EPZ sectors have been textiles and clothing, which account for about 71% of total EPZ exports, more than 52% of EPZ enterprises, and 82% of EPZ labour. The EPZ's performance in 2005 was down from the previous year. EPZ exports amounted to MRs 29,187m., according to provisional figures, equal to 46% of export earnings, declining from 58% in the preceding year.

Other rapidly growing sectors include electronics components and diamond processing, and emphasis has been put on the development of precision engineering (electronics, watch and instrument making, etc.) and skilled crafts (diamond cutting and polishing, furniture, quality goods, etc.). Other items produced include toys, razor blades, nails, industrial chemicals, detergents, rattan furniture, plastic goods, tyres and recording cassettes.

As a result of increasing labour costs, many firms in the EPZ are using more capital-intensive technologies; this will affect employment in the next few years. The demand for skilled personnel in various business sectors, including marketing, management, accounting and computing, has also exceeded the number of suitable candidates, and the Government began to address this problem in 1999 by expediting the granting of labour permits to non-nationals possessing relevant professional qualifications. Emphasis on the potential of the textiles sector prompted the creation of a MRs 200m. fund to modernize textile equipment, and a centre of textile technology was also established by the University of Mauritius. In 2003 the Government established the Textile Emergency Support Team (TEST) to review the entire industry and offer help to individual businesses. By late 2004 42 textile companies had participated and were eligible for debt restructuring. The debt relief comes from the Corporate Debt Restructuring Committee (CDRC), an agency of TEST.

Following changes in the General Agreement on Tariffs and Trade and the subsequent implementation of the world-wide Multi-fibre Arrangement under the World Trade Organization (WTO), Mauritius' EPZ faced considerable challenges, particularly in relation to increased international competition in its principal export sectors. The WTO's Agreement on Textiles and Clothing ended in 2005, and the Minister of Finance and Economic Development suggested that the results will be 7,000 jobs lost and a revenue loss of MRs 400m. by 2010. Also, India's and the People's Republic of China's membership of the WTO will no doubt increase international competition and put Mauritius at a disadvantage. Mauritius qualified to export duty-free textiles and manufactures to the USA under the African Growth and Opportunity Act (AGOA). It was hoped that this would prove to be a major advantage in the early 2000s, in contrast to the quotas that had been imposed in the past by the USA. Indeed, Mauritian exports to the USA increased, from US $275m. in 2001 to $298m. in 2003. However, with the enactment of the third version of the Act in 2004, Mauritius, together with South Africa, was not classified as a 'least developed country' because of its high income levels, and was therefore not eligible for the Third Country Fibre benefit, which allows the sourcing of fabrics from any country. Mauritius and South Africa were obliged to source their fabrics regionally or from the USA in order to qualify for duty-free access to North American markets. Thus, other regional states such as Lesotho, Madagascar and Swaziland, which are classified as less-developed countries, began to erode Mauritian textile exports. At least two textile companies made severe retrenchments to their operations in Mauritius following these developments.

Mauritius has a large, and growing, informal sector. Women comprise almost one-third of the economically active population, although they represent up to 65% of the workforce in the EPZ. Unemployment, in the past hardly a major issue, increased from 1991, owing to a structural shift in the economy, whereby rising incomes reduce the number of low-wage jobs. The rate of unemployment was 9.3% of the labour force in 2005 and 8.9% in 2006. The labour force amounted to 559,100 in 2005 (of whom 35.9% were female and 3.0% foreign workers). The percentage of children in the labour force declined from 5.8% in 1970 to less than 2% in 2001 (compared to a regional average of 29.9%). In 2006 agriculture engaged 9.3% of the employed labour force, while industry employed 33.5% and services 57.2% of the total. (In 2003 14,400 new jobs were created against 9,400 jobs lost, according to the Central Statistics Office.)

TOURISM

Tourism is one of the most important sources of foreign exchange, and has become increasingly important with the decline of contributions from sugar and textiles. Arrivals of foreign tourists increased from 27,650 visitors in 1970 to 788,276 in 2006. Despite this growth, however, the industry has yet to meet the Government's long-term targets. The 2015 target is 2m. tourist arrivals annually. If this target was to be met, the number of arrivals will have to increase by about 8% annually until then (which would be about twice the average of 3.7% recorded in 2002–06).

Tourism was dampened in 2006 by the outbreak of Chikungunya (a rare form of mosquito borne fever which reached the Indian Ocean), although it did not actually affect Mauritius. Nonetheless, arrivals from the traditionally leading sources of tourists were lower: France (by 18%) and Reunion (by 10%). In 2005 66% of the visitors were from Europe (43.8% of those were from France, 19% from the United Kingdom, 11% from Germany and 8.6% from Italy). South Africans comprised 7.7% of all tourists in 2005 and visitors from Réunion 13%. In 2006 Italian tourists arrivals grew by 60%, emerging as the fourth largest source, while British visitors grew by 7.3%, surpassing Réunion as the second most important market after France.

Traditionally Air Mauritius has maintained an arrangement allowing a monopoly of service with French and British routes (via Air France and British Airways), resulting in higher fares and inflexible rates. In an effort to end this monopoly, the Government allowed Virgin Atlantic to operate two flights a week from the United Kingdom to Mauritius, in addition to British Airways flights. By 2006 new flights by Corsair (French) and Virgin Atlantic (United Kingdom) have added additional competition. To safeguard the natural amenities of the island, the Government is implementing measures to curtail and, where possible, reverse environmental damage that has been caused by the uncontrolled expansion of tourism in the recent past. In an effort to harmonize environmental considerations with higher rates of hotel-room occupancy, the Government has, since 1990, largely ceased issuing permits to construct new hotels. The Hilton Group built a hotel at a cost of US $33m. in 2000, and a Saudi Arabian-owned group, Kingdom Hotel Investment, announced it was to develop a $230m. luxury resort in 2006. The overall room-occupancy rate for 2005 was 63%, with 10,497 rooms. Tourism provided employment directly for 25,377 people in March 2005. This sector, however, also contributes to the demand for costly imports, especially foodstuffs.

AGRICULTURE AND FISHERIES

Historically, agriculture formed the backbone of the Mauritian economy and sugar dominated the sector. However, the agricultural sector's contribution to GDP decreased to 6% in 2005, compared with 20% in 1970. Agricultural activity currently faces a number of difficulties unrelated to adverse weather conditions. Labour costs have been rising sharply, as have the prices of agricultural inputs and land. Producer prices have not kept pace with these factors, and the Government has not allocated sufficient resources to agricultural expansion and other services.

Sugar remains the dominant crop, accounting for just over one-half of agricultural output, but contributing some 3% of GDP. Sugar cane is grown on a total of 68,333 ha, accounting for more than three-quarters of the islands' arable land; food crops account for only 6,971 ha There are several large privately-owned estates, and 11 factories for processing the estate sugar and the cane grown by planters in the surrounding areas. The other land under sugar cane, producing more than 50% of the total crop, is owned by planters; in 2004 there were 27,942 owner and tenant planters. Plans for the rationalization of the sector (the US $100m. Sugar Sector Strategic Plan—SSSP), implemented from 2001, were to reduce the number of sugar factories from 14 to no more than eight by 2005, in order to centralize, increase efficiency and improve unit costs. In addition, in 2005 the Government announced its 10-Year Accelerated Action Plan (2005–15). This programme aims to retain a strong sugar industry, with annual output of 400,000 metric tons by the large producers in addition to helping the 30,000 small-scale producers. The National Assembly passed the Sugar Industry Efficiency (Amendment) Bill in February 2007, intended to restructure and modernize the industry. In addition, the Multi-Annual Adaptation Strategy Action Plan 2006–15, approved in April 2006, aimed to consolidate output at 520,000 metric tons per year.

Many of the 'small' sugar planters, who are mostly Indo-Mauritian and who cultivate about one-quarter of the total land under cane, have grouped themselves into co-operatives to facilitate the consignment of cane to the factories on the estates. Some 18,600 workers (3.7% of the employed labour force) were employed in the sugar industry in 2005, representing 37.1% of those employed in agriculture. A bulk sugar terminal, opened in 1980 with an annual capacity of 350,000 metric tons, is the third largest in the world. The Mauritius Sugar Syndicate markets all manufactured sugar, while the main estates are grouped into the Mauritius Sugar Producers' Association. Cyclones, however, periodically cause severe damage to the crop. This problem beset the industry in the early 1990s, when raw sugar production was about 540,000 tons. Sugar output decreased by 9.2% in 2005 due to bad weather and low productivity. It was estimated that sugar production fell again to 504,857 tons in 2006, a 3% decline, and the lowest amount recorded since 1994. This means that sugar production has fallen by 12% since 2004 (itself a bad year affected by Cyclone Hollanda). From 1990 until 2002 sugar exports declined by an annual average of 0.8%. Sugar exports amounted to $355m. in 2004. Sugar prices averaged an estimated £148 per ton in 2001, but declined to £116 per ton in 2002, remaining at a similar level in both 2003 (£115) and 2004 (£116). The Global Alliance for Sugar Trade Reform (backed by South Africa) was lobbying for the reduction of sugar export subsidies under WTO trade liberalization rounds.

In 1975 Mauritius acceded to the sugar protocol of the first Lomé Convention, which was signed in that year by the European Community (EC, now the EU) and 46 developing countries. Under this protocol and its successors, Mauritius received a basic annual export quota of 507,000 metric tons of raw cane sugar and is the principal exporter of sugar to the EU, which comprises the main market for Mauritian sugar. Other important customers are the USA, Canada and New Zealand. Local consumption is not significant, estimated at some 400 tons in 2003/04, down from 25,600 tons in 2001/02. Until recently, Mauritius has benefited from the EU quota arrangement in that, for these exports, the guaranteed price has been three times higher than the 'spot' price on the world market. Sugar import quotas, operated from 1982 by the USA, have been extremely detrimental to Mauritius. In 1995 the EU signed, in addition, the Special Preferential Sugar Agreement (SPSA), allowing Mauritius a quota well above its production capacity for five years, also with significantly beneficial price guarantees. This was renewed in 2001, but Mauritius' allocation was drastically reduced to 38,000 tons for the initial year and was scheduled to be gradually eliminated over the following five years. In July 2004 the EU ratified a proposal for the reform of its sugar regime whereby sugar prices paid to African, Caribbean and Pacific (ACP) countries would decrease by 37% over four years from July 2005. The complaint of unfair competition in the sugar trade brought against the EU by Australia, Brazil and Thailand was upheld by the WTO in the same period. In 2005 the EU was to continue negotiating with the ACP countries to investigate ways in which to mitigate the impact of the price reductions. In early 2006 the EU confirmed its guaranteed price reduction in stages: the regime will be cut by 36% in stages between 2006–10 (5% annually from 2006–08 and larger reductions of 15% in later years). The EU made this decision after the WTO (under pressure from Australia, Brazil and Thailand) ruled against it. The EU agreed a €47m. compensation package to the ACP countries, of which Mauritius should receive 19.4% of the total. None the less, Mauritius' share is unlikely to be sufficient to make the changes the sector needed to remain competitive in the long term.

Tea production, once a significant component of the islands' economy, has been adversely affected over recent decades by rising production costs and the low level of prices on world markets. Exports of tea in 2004 were 50,700 metric tons (up from 39,700 tons in 2000). In 2004 production of green tea was estimated at 7,229 tons and black tea at 1,482 tons. Most tea-growing is carried out by about 1,400 smallholders, grouped into co-operatives. The supervision of the sector is carried out by the Mauritius Tea Factories Co (TeaFac), owned jointly by several state bodies and by tea producer co-operatives. TeaFac currently operates four factories, which account for about 75% of tea exports, and is responsible for export sales. The tea industry receives support from state subsidies. Following the conversion of tea plots into sugar-cane plantations, the area under tea plantation was 674 ha in 2004, compared with 3,000 ha in 1999.

Tobacco is the other main cash crop, after sugar and tea. Production has been expanded to the point where locally manufactured cigarettes are composed entirely of local tobacco, apart from certain luxury grades. Practically all tobacco is grown and processed by British American Tobacco (BAT—Mauritius). Output during the late 1990s averaged about 700 metric tons per year but had declined to an estimated 357 tons by 2005. The effective area under cultivation in that year was 348 ha.

Subsistence farming is conducted on a small scale, although the cultivation of food crops is becoming more widespread in view of the need to diversify the economy and reduce food imports. Food accounted for an estimated 15.6% of the total cost of imports in 2004. The expansion of vegetable cultivation and experiments in intercropping with sugar have resulted in self-sufficiency in potatoes and nearly all other vegetables. Other crops now being experimentally intercropped with sugar are maize, rice, vanilla and groundnuts. The production of food crops was estimated to have decreased by 10.7% in 2005 to 99,738 tons.

Mauritius produces only 8% of its total beef requirements and about 20% of its total consumption of dairy products, the remainder having to be imported, mainly from New Zealand, Australia and South Africa. Mauritius is, however, self-sufficient in pork, eggs and poultry. Most cattle fodder has to be imported, in particular maize from South Africa, at considerable cost. Studies have been conducted on the possible production of high-protein feeding-stuffs, as by-products of sugar cane.

Mauritius sees the fishing sector as an important part of its economic diversification agenda. In 2005 exports of fish (and fish preparations) made up 27.8% of its food and live animal exports. The value of fish exports increased by 39%, representing 7.7% of total exports. In early 2006 Mauritius joined FAO's South West Indian Ocean Fisheries Commission scheme to increase its oceanic bank fisheries. The programme will provide technical assistance for boat repair and maintenance. Vessels from Japan, Taiwan and the Republic of Korea fish in offshore waters and tranship 15,000–16,000 metric tons of fish, mostly tuna, every year.

TRANSPORTATION, COMMUNICATIONS AND INFORMATION TECHNOLOGY

Mauritius has a very good transportation infrastructure. In 2005 there were 2,020 km of classified roads, of which 75 km were motorways, 950 km were other main roads and 592 km were secondary roads. The road network is good, considering the mountainous terrain, and about 98% of the roads are paved. A motorway connects Port Louis with the Plaisance international airport. There are a number of road projects planned or under way, including a new road from Pamplemousses to Grande Baie, and the reconstruction of the Nouvelle France–Mahébourg road. Port Louis, the major commercial port, underwent modernization and expansion during the 1990s, with loan finance from the World Bank. Mauritius was keen to establish itself as a shipping hub—as a possible alternative to Durban, South Africa—for both cargo and cruise shipping; in 2003 the Mauritius Ports Authority formed a long-term regeneration plan for its facilities and development, which had already undergone a decade of investment. The volume of cargo handled at Port Louis was forecast to increase steadily from some 5.2m. metric tons in 2003, with several major shipping and shipping support services companies having established transhipment operations there. The number of containers handled in the port increased from a reported 44,226 in 2001 to 102,394 in 2002. The Ports Authority is improving security under the International Ship and Port Facility Service Code to better access US ports.

The international airport at Plaisance is served by 15 airlines. In 2005 the airport handled about 49,100 metric tons of freight and more than 1m. passengers. Proposals for the construction of a second airport, at Plaine-les-Roches, in the north of the island, were rejected in favour of modernizing and extending the existing airport. Air Mauritius, which is 51% state-owned, generates about one-half of total passenger traffic.

Mauritius has made the most significant advances in the region in developing the usage of computers, telephones and the internet. The number of telephones per 1,000 people increased from 132.1 in 1995 to 288.4 in 2005 and in that year there were 572.9 mobile phone subscribers per 1,000 people (one of the region's highest, behind Seychelles and South Africa). In 2004 personal computers per 1,000 people amounted to 162 and internet hosts per 10,000 people increased from virtually nil to 34.4. The number of internet hosts reached a record of 4,997 in 2006, and there were 180,000 internet users in 2005. Indeed, Mauritius regards information technology (IT) as an area in which it can establish a comparative advantage. The Government announced its intentions to transform the island into an IT free-zone (a so-called 'cyber island') and to establish subsidized IT digital parks. One such park, Cyber City, created 173 new jobs during late 2004, and the number of firms increased from 60 to 72 (see below). At January 2006 there were 107 companies operating in the sector and demand had exceeded supply for occupancy of the facility. Construction on a second park was to conclude in mid-2006, and Business Parks of Mauritius Ltd was conducting a feasibility study for a third, with a projected cost of MRs 750m. The Infocom Development Authority was established, combining the National Computer Board with the Telecommunications Authority and known as the Information and Communication Technologies Authority (ICTA). The National Education Qualifications Act introduced a new curriculum including additional emphasis on computer studies. India awarded Mauritius a US $100m. credit for the purchase of computer equipment and software. In 2000 the South Africa-Far East (SAFE) underwater fibreoptic cable was laid, linking Port Louis to both regions, which was to become the key to the internet infrastructure. Mauritius Telecom undertook an investment programme of $21m. into new technology, and a second cellular telephone provider, Emtel, invested MRs 250m. in its Global System for Mobile Communications (GSM) network. The construction of the Cyber City at Ebène was estimated to cost MRs 1,500m. ($50m.) and had attracted several high profile companies at mid-2004 (some establishing disaster recovery centres there as back-up for their main operations); investors are offered a low corporate taxation rate (15%), free repatriation of profits and exemption from customs duties on raw materials and equipment. Mauritius hoped to capitalize on the bilingual nature of its workforce in providing IT services on to francophone Africa, in co-operation with Indian expertise. From the beginning of 2003 the telecommunications market was opened to competition, and in August the ICTA approved 14 licences (including 10 international licences, one fixed-line licence, one payphone licence, one internet service licence and one mobile communication licence). In early 2006 the ICTA reduced the prices of international private leased circuits and direct dialing charges. Also, Mauritius Telecom's (MT, 40% owned by the state, 40% owned by France Télécom and 20% owned by the State Bank of Mauritius) monopoly over fixed phone lines ended when an Indian company, MTN, began operations. MTN is investing $25m. in its efforts to service 100,000 wireless subscribers by 2007. Mauritius also hopes to utilize the bilingual skills of its population to attract call-centre businesses.

POWER AND WATER

Mauritius relies on imports for most of its energy needs (although, as noted above, it is trying to diversify using sugar by-products). The sugar estates generate electricity from bagasse. Bagasse accounted for as much as 93% of the indigenous production of electricity in 2005 (19.0% of the country's total energy requirement), when Mauritius generated an estimated 20% of its own energy (the rest deriving from imported fuels). Owing to the normally abundant rainfall and precipitous water courses, 4%–6% of electricity is generated from hydro sources (5.1% in 2005). Most of the supply, however, is provided by diesel-powered thermal stations (estimated at 94.9% in 2005). Final energy consumption increased by 1.0% in 2005, with the transport (49.5%) and manufacturing (29.4%) sectors accounting for the greatest proportion of consumption. An estimated 1,062.6m. GWh were purchased from sugar and other factories (independent power producers) in 2005 (energy from this source increased by 75% in 2000). There is a 21.7-MW bagasse-fuelled station attached to the Flacq United Estates sugar factory and a French-financed bagasse pelletization pilot plant, Bagapel, operates at the nearby Deep River–Beau Champ sugar estate. The objective is to establish bagasse as a year-round fuel; currently it is available only in the harvesting season. Two 15-MW bagasse-fired power stations are planned. Studies on wave power and wind power are also being carried out. Water supply and distribution are well developed, with only 0.75% of the population without piped provision. Subterranean reserves are tapped to supply industry, the principal consumer. Imports of mineral fuels comprised an estimated 16.4% of the value of merchandise imports in 2005. In 2004 the Indian Oil Company (IOC) opened its 15,000-ton petroleum storage terminal, increasing the island's storage capacity by 20%. The IOC planned to build a network of 25 petrol stations at an investment of US $18m. However, increased international petroleum prices posed a significant threat to Mauritius in the mid-2000s.

BALANCE OF PAYMENTS, FINANCE, FOREIGN INVESTMENT AND AID

The consistent trade deficits recorded in the 2000s have been caused by increases in EPZ imports for manufacturing inputs, and increases in imported fuel costs, disappointing sugar harvests and the fixed price for sugar exports to the EU. In 2006 exports amounted to MRs 74,171m. and imports MRs 115,612m., resulting in a deficit of MRs 41,441m. (equal to 20% of GDP). The 2006 deficit was a record, exceeding the 2005 figure of MRs 30,000m., itself a record. EPZ exports declined by 15.1% in 2005, despite the rupee's depreciation against the major international currencies. As most of the country's import bills are denominated in US dollars, and its export receipts in euros, the strengthening value of the euro was beneficial for the external account. Imports continued to grow in 2005 and 2006 (reversing the trend of small import growth during the previous few years). Imports grew by 22.1% in 2005 and 23.9% in 2006, due primarily to high petroleum prices and the 7.5% depreciation of the rupee. Domestic exports grew by only 13.4%. It should be noted, however, that if the purchase of the new Airbus were taken into account (MRs 6,700m.), the 2006 deficit would have been similar to that recorded in 2005.

In 2005 the principal domestic exports were manufactured articles, mainly EPZ products (clothing and textiles), valued at MRs 22,494m., and the principal imports were machinery and transportation equipment (MRs 26,250m.), manufactured goods (MRs 19,300m.), and mineral fuels (MRs 15,327m.). In that year the principal sources of imports were the People's Republic of China and South Africa (at 9.8% and 8.6%, respectively) and other major suppliers were France (7.5%) and India (6.9%). The principal market for exports (taking 32.0% of exports in that year) was the United Kingdom; other significant purchasers were France (14.2%) and the USA (9.6%). The importance of South Africa in Mauritius' trade with southern Africa was expected to increase significantly when the Common Market for Eastern and Southern Africa (COMESA) became fully operational. China has recently become a major supplier to Mauritius, with sales in 2006 of US $197m., an 85% increase since 2004.

Mauritius has actively promoted economic initiatives to advance the trading interests of countries on the Indian Ocean rim, and in 1998 joined the Government of Mozambique in establishing a 100,000-ha special economic zone on the Mozambique mainland. Proposals to establish a second such zone were announced in November. Mauritius maintains an active commitment to the Indian Ocean Commission, the Indian Ocean Rim Association for Regional Co-operation (IOR–ARC) and the South African Development Community (SADC). Indeed, Mauritius was involved in the negotiations with the EU that could lead to a free-trade zone with SADC before the EU's Cotonou Agreement with ACP countries expired in 2005. Negotiations were underway in mid-2007 to extend that agreement until 2020. Mauritius would like to have strengthened the AGAO, which gives Mauritius preferential access to America's markets for certain goods (see above).

From 2001 until 2004 Mauritius maintained a surplus in the current account. In 2001 the surplus amounted to US $276.0m., in 2002 $249.4m. and in 2003 $93.1m. In 2004 the current accounts went into deficit by $107.5m. and the deficit increased to $152.8m. in 2005 and $610m. in 2006 (equal to 8.9% of GDP). Mauritius' external debt amounted to approximately $3,000m. at the end of 2005. Its total public debt has increased from 63.9% of GDP in 2000 to 71.8% in 2005. Nonetheless, Mauritius has an excellent international credit rating. Its debt service ratio has remained between 6-7% for the past five years.

Mauritius' economic advances in the mid-1980s, precipitated by the growth of the EPZ sector, enabled the Government to introduce far-reaching measures to encourage economic expansion. Additional finance was to be obtained from the privatization of state enterprises, and the imposition of a value-added tax (VAT) from September 1998 to replace the previous sales tax. The budget for 2005/06 continued to support economic diversity and encourage investment and employment, as well as the reduction of poverty and of the budgetary deficit, proposing an extended duty-free zone for the island. This scheme would eliminate or reduce several duties over the following four years, and transform Mauritius into a duty-free nation; 80% of all tariff lines eventually were to become duty free. The initiative also presented favourable tax incentives for foreign and local investors, and more simplified procedures for the acquisition of land and other assets. The duty-free project was to benefit the tourism sector by making Mauritius an attractive shopping destination, instead of merely a location with excellent beaches. The overall plan is based on a similar model to Dubai. The 2006/07 budget projected a deficit of MRs 8,600m., or 4% of GDP. This compared with a deficit of 5.5% the previous year. The reduction is projected to be the result of decreasing expenditure.

As part of a long-term strategy to establish Mauritius as an international financial centre, controls on the movement of foreign exchange were relaxed in 1986. However, the Bank of Mauritius (the nation's central bank) intervened in the foreign exchange market in order to help maintain the value of the rupee against the US dollar. The rupee continued to decline in the late 1990s, falling from MRs 25.19 to the US dollar in 1999 to MRs 26.25 in 2000. In 2001 the rate was MRs 29.13 to the US dollar and declined even further, to MRs 29.96, in 2002, rebounding slightly to MRs 27.9 in 2003. The Bank of Mauritius sought to continue to allow the rupee to appreciate against the dollar to stem increases in fuel import prices (mostly denominated in dollars). However, such an appreciation damaged Mauritius' textile exports to the US, and by late 2004 the authorities aimed to devalue the rupee against the dollar. During 2006 the rupee depreciated 11.9% against the US dollar, despite strong intervention by the central bank. It depreciated even more against the euro, by 25%, and against the pound sterling, by 19.5%. Such depreciation has been attributed to the worsening trade and budget deficits. By mid-2007 the exchange rate was US $1 = MRs 31.71.

From July 1988 commercial banks were allowed to settle all import payments without having to refer to the central bank. An offshore banking facility was established in 1989. By 1997 a total of seven offshore banks were in operation. The updated Companies Act and Financial Services Act of 2001 were intended to encourage the country's development as a business and financial centre. Mauritius has strengthened trade and investment relations with South Africa since the early 1990s. The Mauritius financial services sector has sought actively to attract capital from Hong Kong, following that territory's reversion to Chinese sovereignty in 1997. In addition, the island has become a significant provider of offshore banking and investment services for a number of South Asian countries (particularly India), as well as for countries in the SADC and IOR–ARC groupings. However, in 2003 the Indian authorities began investigating a number of companies claiming residence in Mauritius in order to qualify for the Double Tax Avoidance Treaty between the two countries, exempting them from paying capital gains tax; any threat to the treaty would undermine the Mauritian offshore financial industry. In late 2005 the central bank created the Mauritius Credit Information Bureau to provide credit information to most of the commercial banks; by mid-2006 the programme was operational, and was to help households from succumbing to over-indebtedness.

Aid per head declined from US $36 in 1999 to $20 in 2002. Net aid from all donors totalled $24m. in 2002 and $38m. in 2004. In late 2005 the World Bank approved a US $30m. Trade and Competitive Policy Loan to help the Government's restructuring plans. Soon thereafter, France announced it would resume aid with a €24m. loan. In March 2006 the EU made a new four-year loan, of €127.5m. also for economic reforms. China provided a US $3.3m. loan at the end of 2005 directed at the textile sector.

The Mauritius stock market's all-share index performed remarkably well in 2004, increasing from an index of 581.6 in January to 710.8 in December. The largest share of capitalization was from the banking and insurance sectors (34% of the total), followed by hotels (14%) and sugar (10%). It continued its growth in 2005, with the index increasing by 13.1%. Servicing transactions worth MRs 4,500m., in 2005 the Stock Exchange of Mauritius (SEM) had its highest levels of transactions since it was established in 1898. The SEM has 43 companies listed, with a total market capitalization of MRs 82,000m. at the beginning of 2006.

ECONOMIC PROSPECTS

Despite its relatively favourable economic performance in recent years, Mauritius faces a number of problems and uncertainties. Prominent among these is the rate of population growth (an estimated 0.8% in 2006), which projects a population of more than 1.5m. people by the year 2010, exclusive of the numbers of émigré Mauritians, estimated at about 50,000, who are expected to return to the islands following retirement. In addition, Mauritius has the region's longest life expectancy at birth (in 2007) of 72.8 years, considerably higher than the region's average of 46 years. This demographic trend is expected to pose considerable economic challenges, especially with employment. For the past three years the official unemployment rate has been slightly beneath 10%.

The EPZ sector, which has led the islands' industrial expansion in recent years, slowed in growth in the late 1990s. As the base of export diversification was unlikely to be widened in the short term, a sharper decline in this sector could be expected. Mauritius' infrastructure continues to require heavy investment in projects such as roads, telecommunications and public utilities. Mauritius is faced by increased competition in the international textile market, and any future alteration in its privileged access to the EU markets would necessitate the industry's becoming more competitive, with the use of newer, costly technology. A more long-term cause for concern was the gradual decline of foreign direct investment during the 1990s. The main reason for this decline had been that Mauritius was no longer competitive with regard to its labour costs, which averaged about US $1.41 per hour—much higher than those in some competing countries, such as Indonesia at $0.24 and Madagascar at $0.41. Between 1995 and 2005 average compensation increased by 8.0%, whilst labour productivity increased by 3.8% annually. Unit labour cost declined, in dollar terms, however, as a result of annual depreciation of the Mauritian rupee to the dollar during that period (in spite of an increase in unit labour cost in rupees). Mauritius is moving away, slowly perhaps, from the labour-intensive parts of its economy. None the less, increasing costs and logistical problems also reduce the country's competitiveness.

In the short term, Mauritius should expect at least moderate economic growth, based on recovering Asian and European economies (especially with regard to tourism). Government investment in IT should also reap benefits. In 2001 India granted a US $110m. credit to Mauritius for the further development of the IT sector and the creation of the Cyber City at Ebène. India continues to provide support for the expansion of IT education through its Indian Technical and Economic Co-operation programme at the University of Technology of Mauritius. In 2005 the Indian Prime Minister visited Mauritius and signed four agreements to strengthen co-operation. The two states committed themselves to establishing a bilateral free-trade zone. The country's expertise in sugar production has resulted in increased technical consulting in a number of nearby sub-Saharan African states. Mauritius continues to strengthen its regional relationships. For example, in 2005 and 2006 it signed a number of bilateral agreements on tourism, fisheries, textiles and tourism with Madagascar, and similar (although more limited) agreements with Seychelles. Air Mauritius and Air Seychelles also began to co-operate more closely.

The Mauritius Offshore Business Activities Authority is keen to promote a better climate to ensure the country's development as a centre for international business. Mauritius will be among the first group of African nations to participate in the New Partnership for African Development (NEPAD) initiative. Along with Ghana and perhaps Kenya, it will take part in the peer review mechanism. This procedure will evaluate the country's performance in a wide range of activities including political stability, governance and democracy, in addition to overall macroeconomic performance. As Mauritius has a good reputation in most of these areas, it is likely to be given an excellent evaluation, thereby boosting further its international reputation. Indeed, the Government is particularly concerned about its international financial standing and has made efforts to counter the impression of corporate and official corruption. Mauritius' international reputation for financial integrity is not as strong as it once was. In mid-2000 the Swiss-based Forum on Financial Stability placed Mauritius on a list of 25 suspected tax haven or money-laundering sites. In 2005 the non-governmental organization Transparency International ranked Mauritius as the 54th least corrupt nation out of 158. The World Bank's most recent study of governance standards of 209 countries ranks Mauritius among only four African nations with positive scores (the others were South Africa, Namibia and Botswana). In 2007 the Hertiage Foundation gave Mauritius the highest ranking of sub-Saharan African countries in its economic freedom index. That index included 10 variables, from property rights to the level of corruption, and attempted to rank how friendly a country is toward business (foreign and domestic). Interestingly, Mauritius just missed entering the category 'mostly free'. There were only five other regional states in its category of 'moderately free'.

The Government forecast real GDP growth of 5.1% in 2006, driven primarily by a recovery of the sugar sector and strong growth in financial services. None the less, the IMF was concerned that the new Government faced serious challenges.

In late 2005 it published its Article IV Consultation and noted the problems of high debt levels and the risk of higher inflation, suggesting a new comprehensive economic strategy, including a review of the role of the public sector in commercial enterprises. The IMF report came just before Moody's Investment Services downgraded Mauritius' risk assessment from stable to negative. In September 2006 the IMF generally approved of the reform measures being implemented, but noted work still remained regarding the large fiscal deficit. According to the IMF, GDP growth for 2006 missed the Government forecast, although was still positive at 3.7%. A slightly improved figure of 4.1% was projected for 2007. The issue of economic reform was controversial during 2006. The Government was somewhat divided over the extent to which economic reforms should be carried out. A new central bank governor, Rundheersing Bheenick, was appointed and he was believed to oppose the reform measures promoted by the finance minister, Rama Sithanen. In fact, Sithanen threatened to resign from the AS coalition in February. Such controversy will not adversely affect the generally favourable impression that Mauritius has developed in recent years with the international business community.

As Mauritius is a small, open economy, it is vulnerable to external shocks. However, its economy showed remarkable strength in 2002, after being adversely affected by a major cyclone and the world-wide tourism downturn associated with the terrorist attacks of 11 September 2001 in the USA, and continued to maintain growth thereafter. Certainly, in comparison with any neighbouring country (excluding South Africa), Mauritius' economy has diversified very successfully. In addition, the country has achieved an unusually high level of economic growth and stability. With increased returns from tourism, the financial and IT sectors, Mauritius can reasonably expect to achieve sustained growth through the end of the first decade of the 21st century.

Statistical Survey

Source (unless otherwise stated): Central Statistics Office, LIC Bldg, President John F. Kennedy St, Port Louis; tel. 212-2316; fax 211-4150; e-mail cso@mail.gov.mu; internet statsmauritius.gov.mu.

Area and Population

AREA, POPULATION AND DENSITY

Area (sq km)	2,040*
Population (census results)	
1 July 1990	1,058,942†
2 July 2000‡	
Males	583,949
Females	595,188
Total	1,179,137
Population (official estimates at 31 December)	
2004	1,238,061
2005	1,248,592
2006	1,256,739
Density (per sq km) at 31 December 2006	616.0

* 788 sq miles.

† Including an adjustment of 2,115 for underenumeration.

‡ Excluding an adjustment for underenumeration.

ISLANDS

		Population	
	Area (sq km)	2000 census	Official estimates 31 December 2006
Mauritius	1,865	1,143,069	1,219,220
Rodrigues	104	35,779	37,230
Other islands	71	289	289

Ethnic Groups: Island of Mauritius, mid-1982: 664,480 Indo-Mauritians (507,985 Hindus, 156,495 Muslims), 264,537 general population (incl. Creole and Franco-Mauritian communities), 20,669 Chinese.

LANGUAGE GROUPS

(census of 2 July 2000)*

Arabic	806	Marathi	16,587
Bhojpuri	361,250	Tamil	44,731
Chinese	16,972	Telegu	18,802
Creole	454,763	Urdu	34,120
English	1,075	Other languages	169,619
French	21,171	Not stated	3,170
Hindi	35,782	**Total**	1,178,848

* Figures refer to the languages of cultural origin of the population of the islands of Mauritius and Rodrigues only. The data exclude an adjustment for underenumeration.

POPULATION BY DISTRICT

(estimates at 31 December 2005)

Plaine Wilhems	376,418	Riv du Rempart	105,593
Flacq	135,648	Moka	79,435
Port Louis	130,420	Savanne	69,391
Pamplemousses	131,990	Black River	69,574
Grand Port	112,833	Rodrigues	36,994

PRINCIPAL TOWNS

(2005, estimates)

Port Louis (capital)	148,780	Curepipe	82,904
Beau Bassin/Rose Hill	108,685	Quatre Bornes	79,857
Vacoas/Phoenix	105,602		

BIRTHS, MARRIAGES AND DEATHS*

	Registered live births		Registered marriages		Registered deaths	
	Number	Rate (per 1,000)	Number	Rate (per 1,000)	Number	Rate (per 1,000)
1999	20,311	17.3	11,295	9.6	7,944	6.8
2000	20,205	17.0	10,963	9.2	7,982	6.7
2001	19,696	16.4	10,635	8.9	7,983	6.7
2002	19,983	16.5	10,484	8.6	8,310	6.9
2003	19,343	15.8	10,812	8.8	8,520	7.0
2004	19,230	15.5	11,385	9.2	8,475	6.8
2005	18,829	15.1	11,294	n.a.	8,648	7.0
2006	17,605	14.1	11,471	n.a.	9,151	7.3

* Figures refer to the islands of Mauritius and Rodrigues only. The data are tabulated by year of registration, rather than by year of occurrence.

Expectation of life (WHO estimates, years at birth, WHO estimates): 72 (males 69; females 75) in 2004 (Source: WHO, *World Health Report*).

ECONOMICALLY ACTIVE POPULATION
('000 persons aged 15 years and over, incl. foreign workers)

	2004	2005	2006
Agriculture, forestry and fishing	49.0	48.7	48.1
Sugar cane	19.1	18.6	18.2
Mining and quarrying	0.3	0.3	0.3
Manufacturing	125.2	120.1	121.0
EPZ	71.6	65.5	65.0
Electricity and water	3.0	3.0	3.0
Construction	49.1	47.0	48.4
Wholesale and retail trade, repair of motor vehicles and household goods	74.8	76.5	78.8
Hotels and restaurants	28.4	31.1	31.8
Transport, storage and communications	35.9	36.4	36.9
Financial intermediation	7.9	8.8	9.4
Real estate, renting and business activities	18.1	20.0	21.1
Public administration and defence	39.0	39.4	39.6
Education	26.2	27.1	28.4
Health and social work	14.5	15.0	15.0
Other services	33.1	33.6	34.0
Total employed	504.5	507.0	515.8
Males	336.9	338.2	340.8
Females	167.6	168.8	175.0
Unemployed	45.1	52.1	50.1
Total labour force	549.6	559.1	565.9

Health and Welfare

KEY INDICATORS

Total fertility rate (children per woman, 2005)	2.0
Under-5 mortality rate (per 1,000 live births, 2005)	15
HIV/AIDS (% of persons aged 15–49, 2005)	0.6
Physicians (per 1,000 head, 2004)	1.06
Hospital beds (per 1,000 head, 2005)	3.0
Health expenditure (2004): US $ per head (PPP)	516.1
Health expenditure (2004): % of GDP	4.3
Health expenditure (2004): public (% of total)	54.7
Access to sanitation (% of persons, 2004)	94
Human Development Index (2004): ranking	63
Human Development Index (2004): value	0.800

For sources and definitions, see explanatory note on p. vi.

Agriculture

PRINCIPAL CROPS
('000 metric tons)

	2003	2004	2005
Potatoes	12.4	11.2	12.8
Sugar cane	5,199.4	5,280.4	4,984.1
Coconuts*	1.9	1.9	1.9
Cabbages	6.3	6.5	4.8
Lettuce	2.0	1.9	1.7
Tomatoes	13.2	14.4	12.8
Cauliflower	1.9	3.0	2.0
Pumpkins, squash and gourds	16.0	17.8	14.1
Cucumbers and gherkins	11.8	12.6	8.7
Aubergines (Eggplants)*	2.1	2.8	2.1
Dry onions	4.2	4.7	5.6
Carrots	5.0	5.8	3.9
Bananas	12.1	12.0	11.6
Pineapples	4.6	4.5	4.9
Tea (made)	1.4	1.5	1.4
Tobacco (leaves)	0.4	0.4	0.3

* FAO estimates.

Source: FAO.

LIVESTOCK
('000 head, year ending September)

	2001	2002	2003
Cattle*	28	28	28
Pigs	14*	12*	13
Sheep*	12	12	12
Goats*	95	93	93
Poultry*	8,900	9,800	9,800

* FAO estimate(s).

2004–05: Production as in 2003 (FAO estimates).

Source: FAO.

LIVESTOCK PRODUCTS
('000 metric tons)

	2002	2003	2004
Cattle meat	2	3	2
Chicken meat	29	30	33
Cows' milk	4	4	4
Hen eggs*	5	5	5

* FAO estimates.

2005: Figures assumed to be unchanged from 2004 (FAO estimates).

Source: FAO.

Forestry

ROUNDWOOD REMOVALS
('000 cubic metres, excl. bark)

	2003	2004	2005
Sawlogs, veneer logs and logs for sleepers	5	5	6
Other industrial wood	3	3	2
Fuel wood	6	6	5
Total	14	14	13

Source: FAO.

SAWNWOOD PRODUCTION
('000 cubic metres, incl. railway sleepers)

	2002*	2003	2004
Coniferous (softwood)	2	2	2
Broadleaved (hardwood)	1	1	1
Total	3	3	3

* FAO estimates.

2005: Figures assumed to be unchanged from 2004 (FAO estimates).

Source: FAO.

Fishing

(metric tons, live weight)

	2003	2004	2005
Capture	11,136	10,627	10,168
Groupers and seabasses	879	794	633
Snappers and jobfishes	1,806	1,595	2,584
Emperors (Scavengers)	3,955	3,374	2,534
Goatfishes	537	425	456
Spinefeet (Rabbitfishes)	404	319	345
Swordfish	601	1,011	1,001
Tuna-like fishes	745	736	730
Octopuses	327	307	293
Aquaculture	33	350	400
Red drum	n.a.	326	368
Total catch	11,169	10,977	10,568

Source: FAO.

Industry

SELECTED PRODUCTS
('000 metric tons, unless otherwise indicated)

	2003	2004	2005*
Fish	37.5	40.7	46.0
Frozen	6.3	5.7	5.9
Canned	30.5	34.2	38.9
Raw sugar	537.2	572.3	519.8
Molasses	160.0	155.8	145.4
Beer and stout (hectolitres)	400.8	363.7	339.0
Cigarettes (million)	938	918	900
Iron bars and steel tubes	58.7	59.9	60.5
Fertilizers	89.4	89.4	85.0
Electric energy (million kWh)	2,057	2,138	2,242

* Estimates.

Finance

CURRENCY AND EXCHANGE RATES

Monetary Units
100 cents = 1 Mauritian rupee.

Sterling, Dollar and Euro Equivalents (30 March 2007)
£1 sterling = 63.40 rupees;
US $1 = 32.38 rupees;
€1 = 43.12 rupees;
1,000 Mauritian rupees = £15.77 = $30.88 = €23.19.

Average Exchange Rate (Mauritian rupees per US $)
2004 29.499
2005 29.496
2006 31.708

BUDGET
(million rupees, year ending 30 June)

Revenue*

	2004/05	2005/06	2006/07†
Current revenue	35,192.4	38,508.7	42,193.0
Tax revenue	32,718.6	35,381.5	38,562.0
Taxes on income, profits and capital gains	5,829.0	7,468.9	7,800.0
Individual income tax	2,553.2	2,767.9	2,525.0
Corporate tax	3,275.8	4,701.0	5,275.0
Taxes on property	1,680.2	1,939.5	2,509.0
Domestic taxes on goods and services	17,464.7	18,762.0	21,473.0
Excise duties	2,838.4	2,467.8	3,360.0
Taxes on services	1,235.1	n.a.	n.a.
Value-added tax	12,529.3	13,709.5	15,000.0
Taxes on international trade	7,730.5	7,195.4	6,745.0
Other tax revenue	14.2	15.7	35.0
Non-tax revenue	2,473.8	3,127.2	3,631.0
Property income	1,234.7	1,804.8	2,036.0
Other non-tax revenue	1,239.1	1,322.4	1,595.0
Capital revenue	383.2	221.7	110.0
Total	35,575.6	38,730.4	42,303.0

Expense/outlays

Expense by economic type	2004/05	2005/06	2006/07†
Current expenditure	38,042.3	41,915.3	44,089.7
Wages and salaries	11,670.3	12,298.7	12,278.8
Other purchases of goods and services	3,658.0	4,593.6	3,958.7
Interest payments	7,184.4	7,354.7	9,409.9
Subsidies and other current transfers	15,529.6	17,668.3	18,442.3
Transfer to non-profit institutions and households	12,776.1	14,130.9	15,491.9
Capital expenditure	6,344.8	6,959.9	7,663.1
Acquisition of fixed capital assets	5,354.6	5,159.2	5,445.6
Capital transfers	940.6	1,653.0	2,147.5
Total	44,387.1	48,875.2	51,752.8

Outlays by function of government	2004/05	2005/06	2006/07†
General government services	6,755.5	7,419.0	7,608.3
General public services	3,105.5	3,439.3	3,532.8
Defence	292.3	345.4	385.5
Public order and safety	3,357.7	3,634.3	3,690.0
Community and Social Services	19,225.5	21,110.7	21,767.1
Education	5,834.3	6,127.7	6,291.1
Health	3,597.0	4,049.0	3,817.0
Social security and welfare	8,568.7	9,578.8	10,293.2
Housing and community amenities	771.0	869.6	875.5
Recreational, cultural and religious services	454.5	485.6	490.3
Economic services	2,828.1	3,884.8	3,211.6
Agriculture, forestry, fishing and hunting	1,212.4	1,187.6	1,238.0
Transportation and communications	357.3	822.3	954.1
Other economic services	1,098.4	1,714.4	811.9
Other current expenditure	9,233.2	9,500.8	11,502.7
Public debt interest	7,184.4	7,354.7	9,409.9
Capital expenditure	6,344.8	6,959.9	7,663.1
Total expenditure	44,387.1	48,875.2	51,752.8

* Excluding grants received (million rupees): 444.0 in 2004/05; 489.2 in 2005/06; 790.0 in 2006/07 (estimate).
† Budget estimates.

INTERNATIONAL RESERVES

(US $ million at 31 December)

	2004	2005	2006
Gold (market prices)	23.9	25.9	31.3
IMF special drawing rights	27.2	25.7	27.5
Reserve position in IMF	34.0	25.0	15.8
Foreign exchange	1,544.7	1,298.2	1,226.3
Total	1,629.8	1,374.8	1,300.9

Source: IMF, *International Financial Statistics*.

MONEY SUPPLY

(million rupees at 31 December)

	2004	2005	2006
Currency outside banks	10,651.5	11,664.1	13,028.3
Demand deposits at deposit money banks	22,588.5	24,711.2	26,780.5
Total money (incl. others)	33,330.3	36,702.8	40,206.6

Source: IMF, *International Financial Statistics*.

COST OF LIVING

(Consumer Price Index; base: July 2001–June 2002 = 100)

	2003	2004	2005
Food and non-alcoholic beverages	105.9	112.5	119.1
Alcoholic beverages and tobacco	109.7	119.8	127.0
Clothing and footwear	103.3	105.0	106.3
Housing, fuel and electricity	105.0	107.1	110.8
Household operations	105.5	107.6	112.8
All items (incl. others)	107.0	112.1	117.6

2006: All items 128.1.

NATIONAL ACCOUNTS

(million rupees in current prices, revised estimates)

National Income and Product

	2004	2005	2006
Compensation of employees	64,378	68,843	74,512
Operating surplus Consumption of fixed capital	86,486	91,580	105,251
Gross domestic product (GDP) at factor cost	150,864	160,423	179,763
Taxes on production and imports *Less* Subsidies	24,733	24,781	26,061
GDP in purchasers' values	175,597	185,204	205,824
Primary incomes received from abroad *Less* Primary incomes paid abroad	−390	−239	118
Gross national income	175,207	184,965	205,942
Current transfers from abroad *Less* Current transfers paid abroad	1,374	1,797	2,264
Gross national disposable income	176,581	186,762	208,206

Expenditure on the Gross Domestic Product

	2004	2005	2006
Private final consumption expenditure	111,837	127,349	145,481
Government final consumption expenditure	25,043	27,368	29,355
Gross fixed capital formation	38,003	39,531	49,375
Increase in stocks	4,879	2,083	5,122
Total domestic expenditure	179,762	196,331	229,333
Exports of goods and services	94,859	110,940	127,252
Less Imports of goods and services	99,024	122,067	150,761
GDP in purchasers' values	175,597	185,204	205,824

Gross Domestic Product by Economic Activity

	2004	2005	2006
Agriculture, hunting, forestry, and fishing	9,830	9,790	9,988
Mining and quarrying	87	88	101
Manufacturing	31,942	32,187	36,313
Electricity, gas and water	3,546	3,355	3,591
Construction	8,835	9,023	10,109
Wholesale and retail trade, repair of motor vehicles and personal goods	17,327	19,503	22,156
Hotels and restaurants	11,296	12,423	15,431
Transport, storage and communications	19,682	20,447	22,427
Financial intermediation	14,875	16,766	18,850
Real estate, renting and business activities	14,679	16,609	19,015
Public administration and defence; compulsory social security	10,580	11,460	12,199
Education	7,087	7,780	8,390
Health and social work	5,087	5,580	6,267
Other services	5,390	6,007	6,785
Sub-total	160,243	171,018	191,622
Less Financial intermediation services indirectly measured	7,818	8,991	10,117
Gross value added in basic prices	152,425	162,027	181,505
Taxes, less subsidies, on products	23,172	23,177	24,319
GDP in market prices	175,597	185,204	205,824

BALANCE OF PAYMENTS

(US $ million)

	2003	2004	2005
Exports of goods f.o.b.	1,898.1	1,993.1	2,143.7
Imports of goods f.o.b.	−2,201.1	−2,572.6	−2,938.4
Trade balance	−303.0	−579.5	−794.6
Exports of services	1,280.1	1,455.6	1,618.1
Imports of services	−906.3	−1,023.3	−1,216.1
Balance on goods and services	70.8	−147.2	−392.6
Other income received	47.0	51.7	142.8
Other income paid	−77.1	−65.7	−151.2
Balance on goods, services and income	40.8	−161.1	−401.0
Current transfers received	163.0	168.1	162.3
Current transfers paid	−110.6	−118.7	−101.3
Current balance	93.2	−111.8	−339.9
Capital account (net)	−0.9	−1.6	−1.8
Direct investment abroad	6.0	−31.8	−47.0
Direct investment from abroad	62.6	13.9	39.2
Portfolio investment assets	−27.1	−52.4	−41.6
Portfolio investment liabilities	8.9	15.3	25.4
Other investment assets	−22.8	−49.4	−283.7
Other investment liabilities	62.0	112.4	358.0
Net errors and omissions	40.4	77.9	126.3
Overall balance	222.4	−27.5	−165.0

Source: IMF, *International Financial Statistics*.

External Trade

PRINCIPAL COMMODITIES
(million rupees)

Imports c.i.f.	2004	2005	2006*
Food and live animals	11,947	13,820	17,312
Fish and fish preparations	3,170	4,266	6,722
Mineral fuels, lubricants, etc.	10,020	15,394	19,367
Refined petroleum products	8,791	13,471	17,018
Chemicals	6,412	7,386	8,156
Basic manufactures	19,297	21,825	21,825
Textile yarn, fabrics, etc	4,189	4,096	747
Cotton fabrics	2,210	1,751	1,878
Machinery and transport equipment	17,916	26,110	35,945
Machinery specialized for particular industries	3,451	3,046	3,351
General industrial machinery, equipment and parts	2,368	2,795	3,051
Telecommunications and sound equipment	2,666	9,739	10,677
Other electrical machinery, apparatus, etc.	2,796	2,996	2,929
Road motor vehicles	4,028	4,216	4,507
Miscellaneous manufactured articles	6,624	7,257	8,206
Total (incl. others)	76,387	93,281	115,612

Exports f.o.b.†	2004	2005	2006*
Food and live animals	13,277	17,248	20,201
Sugar	9,631	10,536	11,165
Fish and fish preparations	2,250	4,785	7,120
Basic manufactures	3,371	5,002	5,536
Textile yarn, fabrics, etc.	1,453	2,197	2,482
Pearls, precious and semi-precious stones	1,252	1,431	1,514
Miscellaneous manufactured articles	26,136	25,757	29,073
Clothing and accessories (excl. footwear)	23,386	21,843	24,531
Total (incl. others)	43,676	59,095	69,099

* Provisional figures.

† Excl. re-exports (million rupees): 9,028 in 2004; 16,991 in 2005; 21,362 in 2006 (provisional). Also excluded are stores and bunkers for ships and aircraft (million rupees): 2,201 in 2004; 4,124 in 2005; 5,072 in 2006 (provisional).

PRINCIPAL TRADING PARTNERS
(million rupees)*

Imports c.i.f.	2004	2005	2006†
Argentina	910	1,137	994
Australia	2,845	2,699	3,106
Bahrain	4,021	5,086	1,349
Belgium	1,368	1,488	1,749
China, People's Repub.	7,068	9,166	9,986
Denmark	196	1,010	240
Finland	822	4,485	2,785
France	6,818	6,958	16,437
Germany	2,852	3,794	4,614
Hong Kong	771	652	596
Hungary	226	2,141	4,008
India	6,989	6,461	15,694
Indonesia	1,558	2,112	2,345
Italy	2,431	2,402	2,952
Japan	3,083	3,333	3,254
Korea, Repub.	797	906	1,082
Madagascar	932	436	478
Malaysia	2,285	2,670	2,979
Pakistan	1,182	1,011	1,239
Saudi Arabia	1,418	3,409	3,996
Singapore	1,175	1,586	1,103
South Africa	8,562	8,066	8,489
Spain	1,475	2,091	2,343
Switzerland	1,444	1,121	1,296
Taiwan	1,246	1,718	2,340
Thailand	1,168	1,532	1,677
United Arab Emirates	1,737	3,588	3,310
United Kingdom	2,377	2,589	2,894
USA	1,651	1,972	2,337
Total (incl. others)	76,387	93,282	115,612

Exports f.o.b.	2004	2005	2006†
Belgium	1,363	1,559	1,845
France	9,084	8,391	8,736
Germany	1,268	1,070	1,293
Italy	2,156	3,308	2,748
Madagascar	2,689	3,373	3,294
Netherlands	914	723	874
Portugal	732	558	187
Réunion	1,485	1,561	1,657
South Africa	775	788	1,487
Spain	860	1,589	2,487
Switzerland	640	644	647
United Arab Emirates	778	4,903	7,881
United Kingdom	17,356	19,215	22,406
USA	7,768	5,640	5,761
Total (incl. others)	52,704	59,095	69,099

* Imports by country of origin; exports by country of destination (including re-exports, excluding ships' stores and bunkers).

† Provisional figures.

Transport

ROAD TRAFFIC
(motor vehicles registered at 31 December)

	2004	2005	2006
Private vehicles: cars	111,527	120,046	128,272
Private vehicles: motorcycles and mopeds	129,500	133,430	138,174
Commercial vehicles: buses	2,457	2,560	2,612
Commercial vehicles: taxis	6,482	6,798	6,860
Commercial vehicles: goods vehicles	35,100	36,036	36,794

SHIPPING

Merchant Fleet
(registered at 31 December)

	2004	2005	2006
Number of vessels	50	47	45
Total displacement ('000 grt)	79.0	70.6	68.6

Source: Lloyd's Register-Fairplay, *World Fleet Statistics*.

Sea-borne Freight Traffic
('000 metric tons)

	2003	2004	2005
Goods unloaded	4,076	4,696	4,709
Goods loaded*	1,165	1,773	1,197

* Excluding ships' bunkers.

CIVIL AVIATION
(traffic)

	2003	2004	2005
Aircraft landings*	9,455	9,316	9,705
Freight unloaded (metric tons)†	20,000	22,400	23,900
Freight loaded (metric tons)†	24,300	26,000	25,200

* Commercial aircraft only.
† Figures are rounded.

Tourism

FOREIGN TOURIST ARRIVALS

Country of residence	2004	2005	2006*
France	210,411	220,421	182,295
Germany	52,277	55,983	57,251
India	24,716	29,755	37,498
Italy	41,277	43,458	69,407
Réunion	96,510	99,036	89,127
South Africa	52,609	58,446	70,796
Switzerland	16,110	15,773	16,161
United Kingdom	92,652	95,407	102,333
Total (incl. others)	718,861	761,063	788,276

* Provisional figures.

Tourism earnings (gross, million rupees): 23,448 in 2004; 25,704 in 2005; 31,942 in 2006.

Communications Media

	2003	2004	2005
Telephones ('000 main lines in use)	348.2	353.8	359.0
Mobile cellular telephones ('000 subscribers)	326	510	713
Personal computers ('000 in use)	190	200	200
Internet users ('000)	150	180	180
Television sets licensed ('000)	259.4	260.3	277.9
Daily newspapers	7	7	9
Non-daily newspapers	35	35	37

1996: Book production: titles 80, copies ('000) 163.

1997: Facsimile machines (number in use) 28,000.

Sources: partly UNESCO, *Statistical Yearbook*; UN, *Statistical Yearbook*; International Telecommunication Union.

Education

(March 2006)

	Institutions	Personnel	Students*
Pre-primary	1,087	2,527	37,129
Primary	290	5,349†	121,387
Secondary	189	7,079	114,657
Technical and vocational	152	682	10,424

* By enrolment.
† Excluding instruction in oriental language.

Adult literacy rate (official estimates): 84.4% (males 88.4%; females 80.5%) in 2004 (Source: UN Development Programme, *Human Development Report*).

Directory

The Constitution

The Mauritius Independence Order, which established a self-governing state, came into force on 12 March 1968, and was subsequently amended. Constitutional amendments providing for the adoption of republican status were approved by the Legislative Assembly (henceforth known as the National Assembly) on 10 December 1991, and came into effect on 12 March 1992. The main provisions of the revised Constitution are listed below:

HEAD OF STATE

The Head of State is the President of the Republic, who is elected by a simple majority of the National Assembly for a five-year term of office. The President appoints the Prime Minister (in whom executive power is vested) and, on the latter's recommendation, other ministers.

COUNCIL OF MINISTERS

The Council of Ministers, which is headed by the Prime Minister, is appointed by the President and is responsible to the National Assembly.

THE NATIONAL ASSEMBLY

The National Assembly, which has a term of five years, comprises the Speaker, 62 members elected by universal adult suffrage, a maximum of eight additional members and the Attorney-General (if not an elected member). The island of Mauritius is divided into 20 three-member constituencies for legislative elections. Rodrigues returns two members to the National Assembly. The official language of the National Assembly is English, but any member may address the Speaker in French.

The Government

HEAD OF STATE

President: Sir Anerood Jugnauth (took office 7 October 2003).

Vice-President: Raouf Bundhun.

COUNCIL OF MINISTERS
(August 2007)

Prime Minister and Minister of Defence and Home Affairs, Civil Service and Administrative Reforms and Rodrigues and Outer Islands: Navinchandra Ramgoolam.

Deputy Prime Minister and Minister of Public Infrastructure, Land Transport and Shipping: Ahmed Rashid Beebeejaun.

Deputy Prime Minister and Minister of Tourism, Leisure and External Communications: Charles Gaëtan Xavier-Luc Duval.

Deputy Prime Minister and Minister of Finance and Economic Development: Rama Krishna Sithanen.

Minister of Foreign Affairs, International Trade and Co-operation: Madan Murlidhar Dulloo.

Minister of the Environment and the National Development Unit: Anil Kumar Bachoo.

Minister of Education and Human Resources: Dharambeer Gokhool.

Minister of Public Utilities: Abu Twalib Kasenally.

Minister of Local Government: James Burty David.

Minister of Agro-industry and Fisheries: Arvin Boolell.

Minister of Labour, Industrial Relations and Employment: Vasant Kumar Bunwaree.

Minister of Social Security, National Solidarity and Senior Citizens' Welfare and Reform Institutions: Sheilabai Bappoo.

Minister of Women's Rights, Child Development, Family Welfare and Consumer Protection: Indranee Seebun.

Minister of Labour, Industrial Relations and Employment: Vasant Kumar Bunwaree.

Attorney-General and Minister of Justice and Human Rights: Jayarama Valayden.

Minister of Health and Quality of Life: Satya Veyash Faugoo.

Minister of Industry, Small and Medium Enterprises, Commerce and Co-operatives: Rajeshwar Jeetah.

Minister of Arts and Culture: Mahendra Gowressoo.

Minister of Housing and Land: Mohammed Asraf Ally Dulull.

Minister of Information Technology and Telecommunications: JOSEPH NOËL-ETIENNE GHISLAIN SINATAMBOU.

Minister of Youth and Sports: SYLVIO HOCK SHEEN TANG WAH HING.

MINISTRIES

President's Office: State House, Le Réduit, Port Louis; tel. 454-3021; fax 464-5370; e-mail statehouse@mail.gov.mu; internet president.gov.mu.

Prime Minister's Office: New Treasury Bldg, Port Louis; tel. 201-1003; fax 208-8619; e-mail primeminister@mail.gov.mu; internet pmo.gov.mu.

Ministry of Agro-industry and Fisheries: Renganaden Seeneevassen Bldg, 8th and 9th Floor, cnr Jules Koenig and Maillard Sts, Port Louis; tel. 212-2335; fax 212-4427; e-mail moa-headoffice@mail.gov.mu; internet agriculture.gov.mu.

Ministry of Arts and Culture: Renganaden Seeneevassen Bldg, 7th Floor, cnr Pope Hennessy and Maillard Sts, Port Louis; tel. 212-9993; fax 208-0315; e-mail minoac@intnet.mu; internet culture.gov.mu.

Ministry of Civil Service Affairs and Administrative Reform: New Government Centre, 7th Floor, Port Louis; tel. 201-2886; fax 212-9528; e-mail civser@mail.gov.mu; internet www.civilservice.gov.mu.

Ministry of Defence and Home Affairs: New Government Centre, 4th Floor, Port Louis; e-mail pmo@mail.gov.mu; internet pmo.gov.mu/dha.

Ministry of Education and Human Resources: IVTB House, Pont Fer, Phoenix; tel. 601-5200; fax 698-2550; e-mail moeps@mail.gov.mu; internet ministry-education.gov.mu.

Ministry of the Environment and the National Development Unit: Ken Lee Tower, Barracks St, Port Louis; tel. 212-3363; fax 212-8324; e-mail admenv@internet.mu; internet environment.gov.mu.

Ministry of Finance and Economic Development: Government House, Ground Floor, Port Louis; tel. 201-2557; fax 208-9823; e-mail mof@bow.intnet.mu; internet mof.gov.mu.

Ministry of Foreign Affairs, International Trade and Co-operation: New Government Centre, 5th Floor, Port Louis; tel. 201-1648; fax 208-8087; e-mail mfa@mail.gov.mu; internet foreign.gov.mu.

Ministry of Health and Quality of Life: Emmanuel Anquetil Bldg, Sir Seewoosagur Ramgoolam St, Port Louis; tel. 201-1912; fax 208-0376; e-mail mohql@intnet.mu; internet health.gov.mu.

Ministry of Housing and Land: Moorgate House, Port Louis; tel. 212-6022; fax 212-7482; internet housing.gov.mu.

Ministry of Industry, Small and Medium Enterprises, Commerce and Co-operatives: Air Mauritius Centre, 7th Floor, John F. Kennedy St, Port Louis; tel. 210-7100; fax 212-8201; e-mail mind@mail.gov.mu; internet industry.gov.mu.

Ministry of Information Technology and Telecommunications: Air Mauritius Centre, Level 9, John F. Kennedy St, Port Louis; tel. 210-0201; fax 212-1673; e-mail mtel@mail.gov.mu; internet telecomit.gov.mu.

Ministry of Justice and Human Rights: Renganaden Seeneevassen Bldg, 2nd Floor, Port Louis; tel. 212-2139; fax 212-6742; e-mail ago@intnet.mu; internet attorneygeneral.gov.mu.

Ministry of Labour, Industrial Relations and Employment: Victoria House, cnr St Louis and Barracks Sts, Port Louis; tel. 207-2600; fax 212-3070; e-mail mol@mail.gov.mu; internet labour.gov.mu.

Ministry of Local Government: Emmanuel Anquetil Bldg, 3rd Floor, cnr Sir Seewoosagur Ramgoolam and Jules Koenig Sts, Port Louis; tel. 201-1216; fax 208-9729; e-mail mlg@mail.gov.mu; internet localgovernment.gov.mu.

Ministry of Public Infrastructure, Land Transport and Shipping: Moorgate House, 9th Floor, Sir William Newton St, Port Louis; tel. 210-7270; fax 212-8373; internet publicinfrastructure.gov.mu.

Ministry of Public Utilities: Medcor Bldg, 10th Floor, John F. Kennedy St, Port Louis; tel. 210-3994; fax 208-6497; e-mail minpuuti@intnet.mu; internet publicutilities.gov.mu.

Ministry of Rodrigues and Outer Islands: Fon Sing Bldg, 1st floor, Edith Cavell St, Port Louis; tel. 208-8472; fax 212-6329; internet shipping.gov.mu.

Ministry of Social Security, National Solidarity and Senior Citizens' Welfare and Reform Institutions: Renganaden Seeneevassen Bldg, Jules Koenig St, Port Louis; tel. 212-9813; fax 212-8190; e-mail mssns@intnet.mu; internet socialsecurity.gov.mu.

Ministry of Tourism, Leisure and External Communications: Air Mauritius Centre, Level 12, John F. Kennedy St, Port Louis; tel. 211-7930; fax 208-6776; e-mail mot@intnet.mu; internet tourism.gov.mu.

Ministry of Women's Rights, Child Development, Family Welfare and Consumer Protection: CSK Bldg, cnr Remy Ollier and Emmanuel Anquetil Sts, Port Louis; tel. 240-1377; fax 240-7717; e-mail mwfwcd@bow.intnet.mu; internet women.gov.mu.

Ministry of Youth and Sports: Emmanuel Anquetil Bldg, 3rd Floor, Sir Seewoosagur Ramgoolam St, Port Louis; tel. 201-2543; fax 210-7554; e-mail mys@mail.gov.mu; internet youthsport.gov.mu.

Legislature

National Assembly

Port Louis; tel. 201-1414; fax 212-8364; e-mail themace@intnet.mu; internet mauritiusassembly.gov.mu.

Speaker: KAILASH PURRYAG.

General Election, 3 July 2005

Party	Seats		
	Directly elected	Additional*	Total
Social Alliance†	38	4	42
Mouvement Socialiste Militant (MSM)/Mouvement Militant Mauricien (MMM)	22	2	24
Organisation du Peuple Rodriguais (OPR)	2	2	4
Total	62	8	70

* Awarded to those among the unsuccessful candidates who attracted the largest number of votes, in order to ensure that a balance of ethnic groups are represented in the Assembly.

† Alliance primarily comprising the Mauritius Labour Party, the Parti Mauricien Xavier-Luc Duval, the Mouvement Républicain and the Mouvement Militant Socialiste Mauricien.

Election Commission

Electoral Commissioner's Office (ECO): 4th Floor, Max City Bldg, cnr Louis Pasteur and Remy Ollier Sts, Port Louis; tel. 241-7000; fax 241-0967; e-mail elec@mail.gov.mu; internet www.gov.mu/portal/site/eco; under the aegis of the Prime Minister's Office; Commissioner appointed by the Judicial and Legal Service Commission; Electoral Commissioner M. I. ABDOOL RAHMAN.

Political Organizations

Mauritius Labour Party (MLP) (Parti Travailliste): 7 Guy Rozemont Sq., Port Louis; tel. 212-6691; fax 210-0189; e-mail labour@intnet.mu; internet labour.intnet.mu; f. 1936; formed part of the Social Alliance for the 2005 election and subsequently a govt; Leader Dr NAVINCHANDRA RAMGOOLAM; Chair. ETIENNE SINATAMBOU; Sec.-Gen. DEVENAND VIRAHSAWMY.

Mouvement Militant Mauricien (MMM): 21 Poudrière St, Port Louis; tel. 212-6553; fax 208-9939; internet mmm.mmmonline.org; f. 1969; socialist; formed an alliance with the Mouvement Socialiste Militant for both the 2000 and the 2005 elections; Pres. SAM LAUTHAN; Leader PAUL BÉRENGER; Sec.-Gen. STEVEN OBEEGADOO, RAJESH BHAGWAN.

Mouvement Militant Socialiste Mauricien (MMSM): Port Louis; forms part of the incumbent Social Alliance, elected in 2005; Leader MADUN DULLOO.

Mouvement Rodriguais: Port Mathurin, Rodrigues; tel. 831-1876 (Port Mathurin); tel. and fax 686-8859 (Port Louis); f. 1992; represents the interests of Rodrigues; Leader JOSEPH (NICHOLAS) VON-MALLY.

Mouvement Sociale Démocrate (MSD) (Social Democratic Movement): Port Louis; f. 2005; Leader ANIL BACHOO.

Mouvement Socialiste Militant (MSM): Sun Trust Bldg, 31 Edith Cavell St, Port Louis; tel. 212-8787; fax 208-9517; e-mail request@msmsun.com; internet www.msmsun.com; f. 1983; by fmr mems of the MMM; dominant party in subsequent coalition govts until Dec. 1995 and again from 2000–05; Leader PRAVIND JUGNAUTH; Chair. JOE LESJONGARD; Sec.-Gen. VISHWANATH SAJADAH.

Organisation du Peuple Rodriguais (OPR): Port Mathurin, Rodrigues; represents the interests of Rodrigues; Leader LOUIS SERGE CLAIR.

Parti Mauricien Social Démocrate (PMSD): Melville, Grand Gaube; centre-right; participated in an alliance with the MSM and

MMM for the 2005 legislative and municipal elections; Leader MAURICE ALLET; Sec.-Gen. JACQUES PANGLOSE.

Parti Mauricien Xavier-Luc Duval (PMXD): Port Louis; f. 1998; forms part of the Social Alliance; Leader CHARLES GAËTAN XAVIER-LUC DUVAL.

Union Nationale (Mauritian National Union): Port Louis; f. 2006; Chair. ASHOCK JUGNAUTH.

Some of the blocs and parties that participated in the 2005 election include the **Front Solidarité Mauricienne (FSM)**, **Les Verts Fraternels/The Greens** (Leader SYLVIO MICHEL), the **Mouvement Républicain** (Leader RAMA VALAYDEV), the **Parti du Peuple Mauricien (PPM)**, the **Mouvement Démocratique National Raj Dayal (MDN Raj Dayal)**, the **Rezistans ek Alternativ** (Secretary ASHOK SUBRON), **Lalit** (lalitmauritius.com) and the **Tamil Council**.

Diplomatic Representation

EMBASSIES AND HIGH COMMISSIONS IN MAURITIUS

Australia: Rogers House, 2nd Floor, John F. Kennedy St, POB 541, Port Louis; tel. 202-0160; fax 208-8878; e-mail ahc.portlouis@dfat.gov.au; internet www.mauritius.embassy.gov.au; High Commissioner CATHERINE JOHNSTONE.

China, People's Republic: Royal Rd, Belle Rose, Rose Hill; tel. 454-9111; fax 464-6012; e-mail chinaemb_mu@mfa.gov.cn; internet www.ambchine.mu; Ambassador GAO YUCHEN.

Egypt: Sun Trust Bldg, 2nd floor, Edith Cavell St, Port Louis; tel. 213-1765; fax 213-1768; e-mail egyemb@intnet.mu; Ambassador BAKRY ROSHDY EL-AMARY.

France: 14 St George St, Port Louis; tel. 202-0100; fax 202-0110; e-mail ambafr@intnet.mu; internet www.ambafrance-mu.org; Ambassador JACQUES MAILLARD.

India: Life Insurance Corpn of India Bldg, 6th Floor, John F. Kennedy St, POB 162, Port Louis; tel. 208-3775; fax 208-6859; e-mail hicom.ss@intnet.mu; internet indiahighcom.intnet.mu; High Commissioner BONDAL JAISHANKAR.

Madagascar: Guiot Pasceau St, Floreal, POB 3, Port Louis; tel. 686-5015; fax 686-7040; e-mail madmail@intnet.mu; Ambassador BRUNO RANARIVELO.

Pakistan: 9A Queen Mary Ave, Floreal, Port Louis; tel. 698-8501; fax 698-8405; e-mail pareportlouis@hotmail.com; High Commissioner SYED HASAN JAVED.

Russia: Queen Mary Ave, POB 10, Floreal, Port Louis; tel. 696-1545; fax 696-5027; e-mail rusemb.mu@intnet.mu; Ambassador OLGA IVANOVA.

South Africa: BAI Bldg, 4th Floor, 25 Pope Hennessy St, POB 908, Port Louis; tel. 212-6925; fax 212-6936; e-mail sahc@intnet.mu; High Commissioner AJAY KUMAR BRAMDEO.

United Kingdom: Les Cascades Bldg, 7th Floor, Edith Cavell St, POB 1063, Port Louis; tel. 202-9400; fax 202-9408; e-mail bhc@intnet.mu; High Commissioner Dr JOHN MURTON.

USA: Rogers House, 4th Floor, John F. Kennedy St, POB 544, Port Louis; tel. 208-4400; fax 208-9534; e-mail usembass@intnet.mu; internet mauritius.usembassy.gov; Ambassador CESAR BENITO CABRERA.

Judicial System

The laws of Mauritius are derived both from the French Code Napoléon and from English Law. The Judicial Department consists of the Supreme Court, presided over by the Chief Justice and such number of Puisne Judges as may be prescribed by Parliament (currently nine), who are also Judges of the Court of Criminal Appeal and the Court of Civil Appeal. These courts hear appeals from the Intermediate Court, the Industrial Court and 10 District Courts (including that of Rodrigues). The Industrial Court has special jurisdiction to protect the constitutional rights of the citizen. There is a right of appeal in certain cases from the Supreme Court to the Judicial Committee of the Privy Council in the United Kingdom.

Supreme Court: Jules Koenig St, Port Louis; tel. 212-0275; tel. 212-9946; internet supremecourt.intnet.mu.

Chief Justice: ARIANGA PILLAY.

Senior Puisne Judge: B. YEUNG SIK YUEN.

Puisne Judges: B. DOMAH, K. P. MATADEEN, N. MATADEEN, A. F. CHUI YEW CHEONG, M. F. E. BALANCY, P. LAM SHANG LEEN, P. BALGOBIN, S. PEEROO, A. A. CAUNHYE.

Religion

Hindus are estimated to comprise more than 50% of the population, with Christians accounting for some 30% and Muslims 17%. There is also a small Buddhist community.

CHRISTIANITY

The Anglican Communion

Anglicans in Mauritius are within the Church of the Province of the Indian Ocean, comprising six dioceses (four in Madagascar, one in Mauritius and one in Seychelles). The Archbishop of the Province is the Bishop of Antananarivo, Madagascar. In 1983 the Church had 5,438 members in Mauritius.

Bishop of Mauritius: Rt Rev. IAN ERNEST, Bishop's House, Phoenix; tel. 686-5158; fax 697-1096; e-mail dioang@intnet.mu.

The Presbyterian Church of Mauritius

Minister: Pasteur ANDRÉ DE RÉLAND, cnr Farquhar and Royal Rds, Coignet, Rose Hill; tel. 464-5265; fax 395-2068; e-mail embrau@bow.intnet.mu; f. 1814.

The Roman Catholic Church

Mauritius comprises a single diocese, directly responsible to the Holy See, and an apostolic vicariate on Rodrigues. At 31 December 2004 there were an estimated 281,000 adherents in the country, representing about 24.3% of the total population.

Bishop of Port Louis: Rt Rev. MAURICE PIAT, Evêché, 13 Mgr Gonin St, Port Louis; tel. 208-3068; fax 208-6607; e-mail eveche@intnet.mu.

BAHÁ'Í FAITH

National Spiritual Assembly: Port Louis; tel. 212-2179; mems resident in 190 localities.

ISLAM

Mauritius Islamic Mission: Noor-e-Islam Mosque, Port Louis; Imam S. M. BEEHARRY.

The Press

DAILIES

China Times: 24 Emmanuel Anquetil St, POB 325, Port Louis; tel. 240-3067; f. 1953; Chinese; Editor-in-Chief LONG SIONG AH KENG; circ. 3,000.

Chinese Daily News: 32 Rémy Ollier St, POB 316, Port Louis; tel. 240-0472; f. 1932; Chinese; Editor-in-Chief WONG YUEN MOY; circ. 5,000.

L'Express: 3 Brown Sequard St, POB 247, Port Louis; tel. 202-8200; fax 208-8174; e-mail sentinelle@bow.intnet.mu; internet www.lexpress-net.com; f. 1963; owned by La Sentinelle Ltd; English and French; Editor-in-Chief RAJ MEETARBHAN; circ. 35,000.

Maurice Soir: Port Louis; f. 1996; Editor SYDNEY SELVON; circ. 2,000.

Le Matinal: AAPCA House, 6 La Poudrière St, Port Louis; tel. 207-0909; fax 213-4069; e-mail editorial@lematinal.com; internet www.lematinal.com; f. 2003; in French and English; AAPCA (Mauritius) Ltd; Dir SIDHARTH BHATIA.

Le Mauricien: 8 St George St, POB 7, Port Louis; tel. 208-3251; fax 208-7059; e-mail redaction@lemauricien.com; internet www.lemauricien.com; f. 1907; English and French; Editor-in-Chief GILBERT AHNEE; circ. 35,000.

Le Quotidien: Pearl House, 4th Floor, 16 Sir Virgile Naz St, Port Louis; tel. 208-2631; fax 211-7479; e-mail quotidien@bow.intnet.mu; f. 1996; English and French; Dirs JACQUES DAVID, PATRICK MICHEL; circ. 30,000.

Le Socialiste: Manilall Bldg, 3rd Floor, Brabant St, Port Louis; tel. 208-8003; fax 211-3890; English and French; Editor-in-Chief VEDI BALLAH; circ. 7,000.

The Tribune: Port Louis; f. 1999; Publr HARISH CHUNDUNSING.

WEEKLIES AND FORTNIGHTLIES

5-Plus Dimanche: 3 Brown Sequard St, Port Louis; tel. 213-5500; fax 213-5551; e-mail comments@5plusltd.com; internet www.5plusltd.com; f. 1994; English and French; Editor-in-Chief FINLAY SALESSE; circ. 30,000.

5-Plus Magazine: 3 Brown Sequard St, Port Louis; tel. 213-5500; fax 213-5551; e-mail comments@5plusltd.com; f. 1990; English and French; Editor-in-Chief PIERRE BENOÎT; circ. 10,000.

Business Magazine: TN Tower, 2nd Floor, 13 St George St, Port Louis; tel. 211-1925; fax 211-1926; e-mail businessmag@intnet.mu;

internet www.businessmag.mu; f. 1993; owned by La Sentinelle Ltd; English and French; Editor-in-Chief LINDSAY RIVIÈRE; circ. 6,000.

Le Croissant: cnr Velore and Noor Essan Mosque Sts, Port Louis; tel. 240-7105; English and French; Editor-in-Chief RAYMOND RICHARD NAUVEL; circ. 25,000.

Le Défi-Plus: Royal Rd, G.R.N.W., Port Louis; tel. 211-7766; Saturdays.

Le Dimanche: 5 Jemmapes St, Port Louis; tel. 212-5887; fax 212-1177; e-mail ledmer@intnet.mu; f. 1961; English and French; Editor RAYMOND RICHARD NAUVEL; circ. 25,000.

Impact News: 10 Dr Yves Cantin St, Port Louis; tel. 211-5284; fax 211-7821; e-mail farhadr@wanadoo.mu; internet www.impactnews.info; English and French; Editor-in-Chief FARHAD RAMJAUN.

Lalit de Klas: 153B Royal Rd, G.R.N.W., Port Louis; tel. 208-2132; e-mail lalitmail@intnet.mu; internet www.lalitmauritius.org; English, French and Mauritian Creole; Editor RADA KISTNASAMY.

Le Mag: Industrial Zone, Tombeay Bay; tel. 247-1005; fax 247-1061; f. 1993; English and French; Editor (vacant); circ. 8,000.

Mauritius Times: 23 Bourbon St, Port Louis; tel. and fax 212-1313; e-mail mtimes@intnet.mu; internet mauritiustimes.com; f. 1954; English and French; Editor-in-Chief MADHUKAR RAMLALLAH; circ. 15,000.

Mirror: 39 Emmanuel Anquetil St, Port Louis; tel. 240-3298; Chinese; Editor-in-Chief NG KEE SIONG; circ. 4,000.

News on Sunday: Dr Eugen Laurent St, POB 230, Port Louis; tel. 211-5902; fax 211-7302; e-mail newsonsunday@news.intnet.mu; internet newsonsunday.150m.com; f. 1996; owned by Le Défi Group; weekly; in English; Editor NAGUIB LALLMAHOMED; circ. 10,000.

Le Nouveau Militant: 21 Poudrière St, Port Louis; tel. 212-6553; fax 208-2291; f. 1979; publ. by the Mouvement Militant Mauricien; English and French; Editor-in-Chief J. RAUMIAH.

Le Rodriguais: Saint Gabriel, Rodrigues; tel. 831-1613; fax 831-1484; f. 1989; Creole, English and French; Editor JACQUES EDOUARD; circ. 2,000.

Star: 38 Labourdonnais St, Port Louis; tel. 212-2736; fax 211-7781; e-mail starpress@intnet.mu; internet www.mauriweb.com/star; English and French; Editor-in-Chief REZA ISSACK.

Sunday: Port Louis; tel. 208-9516; fax 208-7059; f. 1966; English and French; Editor-in-Chief SUBASH GOBIN.

Turf Magazine: 8 George St, POB 7, Port Louis; tel. 207-8200; fax 208-7059; e-mail bdlm@intnet.mu; internet www.lemauricien.com/turfmag; owned by Le Mauricien Ltd.

La Vie Catholique: 28 Nicolay Rd, Port Louis; tel. 242-0975; fax 242-3114; e-mail viecatho@intnet.mu; internet pages.intnet.mu/lavie; f. 1930; weekly; English, French and Creole; Editor-in-Chief Fr GEORGES CHEUNG; circ. 8,000.

Week-End: 8 St George St, POB 7, Port Louis; tel. 207-8200; fax 208-3248; e-mail redaction@lemauricien.com; internet www.lemauricien.com/weekend; f. 1966; owned by Le Mauricien Ltd; French and English; Editor-in-Chief GÉRARD CATEAUX; circ. 80,000.

Week-End Scope: 8 St George St, POB 7, Port Louis; tel. 207-8200; fax 208-7059; e-mail wes@lemauricien.com; internet www.lemauricien.com/wes; owned by Le Mauricien Ltd; English and French; Editor-in-Chief JACQUES ACHILLE.

OTHER SELECTED PERIODICALS

CCI–INFO: 3 Royal St, Port Louis; tel. 208-3301; fax 208-0076; e-mail mcci@intnet.mu; internet www.mcci.org; English and French; f. 1995; publ. of the Mauritius Chamber of Commerce and Industry.

Ciné Star Magazine: 64 Sir Seewoosagur Ramgoolam St, Port Louis; tel. 240-1447; English and French; Editor-in-Chief ABDOOL RAWOOF SOOBRATTY.

Education News: Edith Cavell St, Port Louis; tel. 212-1303; English and French; monthly; Editor-in-Chief GIAN AUBEELUCK.

Le Message de L'Ahmadiyyat: c/o Ahmadiyya Muslim Assen, POB 6, Rose Hill; tel. 464-1747; fax 454-2223; e-mail darussalaam@intnet.mu; French; monthly; Editor-in-Chief MOHAMMAD AMEEN JOWAHIR; circ. 3,000.

Le Progrès Islamique: 51B Solferino St, Rose Hill; tel. 467-1697; fax 467-1696; f. 1948; English and French; monthly; Editor DEVINA SOOKIA.

La Voix d'Islam: Parisot Rd, Mesnil, Phoenix; f. 1951; English and French; monthly.

NEWS AGENCIES

The following foreign bureaux are represented in Mauritius: Agence France Presse, Associated Press (United Kingdom), International News Service (USA), Reuters (United Kingdom).

Publishers

Boukié Banané (The Flame Tree): 5 Edwin Ythier St, Rose Hill; tel. 454-2327; fax 465-4312; e-mail limem@intnet.mu; internet pages.intnet.mu/develog; f. 1979; Morisien literature, poetry and drama; Man. Dir DEV VIRAHSAWMY.

Business Publications Ltd: TN Tower, 1st Floor, St George St, Port Louis; tel. 211-1925; fax 211-1926; f. 1993; English and French; Dir LYNDSAY RIVIÈRE.

Editions du Dattier: 82 Goyavier Ave, Quatre Bornes; tel. 466-4854; fax 446-3105; e-mail dattier@intnet.mu; English and French; Dir JEAN-PHILIPPE LAGESSE.

Editions de l'Océan Indien: Stanley, Rose Hill; tel. 464-6761; fax 464-3445; e-mail eoibooks@intnet.mu; internet www.eoi-info.com; f. 1977; general, textbooks, dictionaries, literature; English, French and Asian languages; Gen. Man. DEVANAND DEWKURUN.

Editions Le Printemps: 4 Club Rd, Vacoas; tel. 696-1017; fax 686-7302; e-mail elp@bow.intnet.mu; Man. Dir A. I. SULLIMAN.

Editions Vizavi: 9 St George St, Port Louis; tel. 211-3047; e-mail vizavi@intnet.mu; Dir PASCALE SIEW.

Broadcasting and Communications

TELECOMMUNICATIONS

Information and Communication Technologies Authority (ICTA): The Celicourt, 12th Floor, 6 Sir Celicourt Antelme St, Port Louis; tel. 211-5333; fax 211-9444; e-mail icta@intnet.mu; internet www.icta.mu; f. 1999; regulatory authority; Chair. TRILOK DWARKA.

Mauritius Telecom Ltd: Telecom Tower, Edith Cavell St, Port Louis; tel. 203-7000; fax 208-1070; e-mail ceo@mauritiustelecom.com.mu; internet www.mauritiustelecom.com; f. 1992; 60% owned by Govt of Mauritius, State Bank of Mauritius and National Pensions Fund, 40% owned by France Télécom through RIMCOM; privatized in 2000; provides all telecommunications services, including internet and digital mobile cellular services; Chair. APPALSAMY (DASS) THOMAS; CEO SARAT LALLAH.

Cellplus Mobile Communications Ltd: Telecom Tower, 9th Floor, Edith Cavell St, Port Louis; tel. 203-7500; fax 211-6996; e-mail cellplus@intnet.mu; internet www.cellplus.mu; f. 1996; introduced the first GSM cellular network in Mauritius and recently in Rodrigues (Cell-Oh); a wholly owned subsidiary of Mauritius Telecom.

Emtel: 1 Boundary Road, Rose Hill; tel. 454-5400; fax 454-1010; e-mail emtel@emtelnet.com; internet www.emtel-ltd.com; f. 1989; CEO SHYAM ROY.

BROADCASTING

In 1997 the Supreme Court invalidated the broadcasting monopoly held by the Mauritius Broadcasting Corporation.

Independent Broadcasting Authority: 5 de Courson St, Curepipe Rd, Curepipe; tel. 670-4621; fax 670-2335; e-mail iba@intnet.mu; internet iba.gov.mu; Dir PIERRE AH-FAT.

Radio

Mauritius Broadcasting Corpn: Broadcasting House, Louis Pasteur St, Forest Side; tel. 602-1200; fax 674-0488; e-mail mbc@intnet.mu; internet www.mbcradio.tv; f. 1964; independent corpn operating eight national radio services and nine television channels; Chair. FAREED JANGEER-KHAN; Dir-Gen. BIJAYE COOMAR MADHOU.

Radio One: Port Louis; tel. 211-4555; fax 211-4142; e-mail sales@r1.mu; internet www.r1.mu; f. 2002; owned by Sentinelle media group; news and entertainment; Dir-Gen. JEAN-MICHEL FONTAINE.

Top FM: The Peninsula, Caudan Bldg, 7th Floor, 2A Falcon ST, Caudan, Port Louis; tel. 213-2121; fax 213-2222; e-mail topfm@intnet.mu; internet www.topfmradio.com; f. 2003; part of the International Broadcasting Group, in partnership with the Sunrise Group; Chair. BALKRISHNA KAUNHYE.

A further two private stations, Radio Plus and Sunrise Radio, were issued licences in early 2002.

Television

Independent television stations were to commence broadcasting from 2002, as part of the liberalization of the sector.

Mauritius Broadcasting Corpn: see Radio.

Finance

(cap. = capital; res = reserves; dep. = deposits; m. = million; brs = branches; amounts in Mauritian rupees, unless otherwise stated)

BANKING

Central Bank

Bank of Mauritius: Sir William Newton St, POB 29, Port Louis; tel. 208-4164; fax 208-9204; e-mail bomrd@bow.intnet.mu; internet bom.intnet.mu; f. 1966; bank of issue; cap. 1,000.0m., res 16,653.5m., dep. 8,867.2m. (June 2005); Gov. RUNDHEERSING BHEENICK.

Principal Commercial Banks

Bank of Baroda: 32 Sir William Newton St, POB 553, Port Louis; tel. 208-1504; fax 208-3892; e-mail info@bankofbaroda-mu.com; internet www.bankofbaroda-mu.com; f. 1962; total assets 2,655,000m. (June 2007); Vice-President (Mauritius Operations) PRABHAT AGARWAL; 7 brs.

Barclays Bank PLC, Mauritius: Harbour Front Bldg, 8th Floor, John F. Kennedy St, POB 284, Port Louis; tel. 208-2685; fax 208-2720; e-mail barclays.mauritius@barclays.com; f. 1919; absorbed Banque Nationale de Paris Intercontinentale in 2002; cap. 100.0m., res 616.1m., dep. 6,886.7m. (Dec. 2001); Dir Gen. KARL STUMKE; 16 brs.

First City Bank Ltd: 16 Sir William Newton St, POB 485, Port Louis; tel. 208-5061; fax 208-5388; e-mail info@firstcitybank-mauritius.com; f. 1991 as the Delphis Bank Ltd; merged with Union International Bank in 1997; private bank; taken over by consortium in 2002; 51.6% owned by the Development Bank of Mauritius Ltd; cap. 450.0m., res 98.9m., dep. 4,361.0m. (June 2005); Chair. B. CHOORAMUN; Chief Exec. ROHIT AUKLE.

Hongkong and Shanghai Banking Corpn Ltd (HSBC): pl. d'Armes, POB 50, Port Louis; tel. 208-1801; fax 210-0400; e-mail hsbcmauritius@hsbc.co.mu; internet www.hsbc.co.mu; f. 1916; CEO PHILLIP DAWE.

Indian Ocean International Bank Ltd (IOIB): 34 Sir William Newton St, POB 863, Port Louis; tel. 208-0121; fax 208-0127; e-mail ioibltd@intnet.mu; internet www.ioib.intnet.mu; f. 1978; 51% owned by the State Bank of India; cap. 100.5m., res 305.7m., dep. 2,934.4m. (June 2005); Pres. VISWANATHEN VALAYDON; Chief Exec. A. K. SINGH; 8 brs.

Mauritius Commercial Bank Ltd: MCB Centre, 9–15 Sir William Newton St, POB 52, Port Louis; tel. 202-5000; fax 208-7054; e-mail mcb@mcb.mu; internet www.mcb.mu; f. 1838; cap. 2,821.1m., res 2,295.0m., dep. 68,257.1m. (June 2005); Pres. GERARD J. HARDY; Gen. Man. JOSEPH-ALAIN SAUZIER; 41 brs.

Mauritius Post and Co-operative Bank Ltd: 1 Sir William Newton St, Port Louis; tel. 207-9999; fax 208-7270; e-mail mpcb@mpcb.mu; internet www.mpcb.mu; f. 2003; 44.3% owned by The Mauritius Post Ltd, 35.7% state owned, 10% owned by the Sugar Investment Trust; cap. 384.0m., res 39.5m., dep. 4,516.1m. (Dec. 2005); CEO RAJIV KUMAR BEEHARRY; Gen. Man. PAVADAY THONDRAYON.

South East Asian Bank Ltd (SEAB): Max City Bldg, 2nd Floor, cnr Rémy Ollier and Louis Pasteur Sts, POB 13, Port Louis; tel. 208-8826; fax 211-4900; e-mail seab@intnet.mu; internet www.seabmu.com; f. 1989; 60% owned by Bumiputra-Commerce Bank Berhad (Malaysia); cap. 200.0m., res 16.4m., dep. 2,423.4m. (Dec. 2005); Chair. Tan Sri Dato' MOHD DESA PACHI; 5 brs.

Standard Chartered Bank (Mauritius) Ltd: Happy World House, Level 8, 37 Sir William Newton St, Port Louis; tel. 213-9000; fax 208-5992; e-mail scbmauritius@intnet.mu; internet www.standardchartered.com/mu; wholly owned subsidiary of Standard Chartered Bank Plc; offshore banking unit.

State Bank of Mauritius Ltd: State Bank Tower, 1 Queen Elizabeth II Ave, POB 152, Port Louis; tel. 202-1111; fax 202-1234; e-mail sbm@sbm.intnet.mu; internet www.sbmonline.com; f. 1973; cap. 325.1m., surplus and res 7,857.8m., dep. 32,930.9m. (June 2005); Chair. RAJA RAMDAURSING; Chief Exec. CHAITLALL GUNNESS; 43 brs.

Development Bank

Development Bank of Mauritius Ltd: La Chaussée, POB 157, Port Louis; tel. 208-0241; fax 208-8498; e-mail dbm@intnet.mu; internet www.dbm.mu; f. 1964; name changed as above in 1991; 65% govt-owned; cap. 125m., res 1,507.6m., dep. 3,240.8m. (June 2004); Chair. CHANDAN KHESWAR JANKEE; Man. Dir B. CHOORAMUN; 6 brs.

Principal 'Offshore' Banks

Mascareignes International Bank Ltd: 1 Cathedral Square, Level 8, 16 Jules Koenig St, POB 489, Port Louis; tel. 207-8700; fax 212-4983; e-mail mib@mib.mu; internet www.mib.mu; f. 1991; name changed as above 2004; 65% owned by Banque de la Réunion (65%), 35% owned by Financière Océor (France); cap. 423.7m., res 43.3m., dep. 6,546.2m. (Dec. 2005); Chair. BERNARD BOBROWSKI; CEO CHRISTIAN MONTAGARD.

SBI International (Mauritius) Ltd: Harbour Front Bldg, 7th Floor, John F. Kennedy St, POB 376, Port Louis; tel. 212-2054; fax 212-2050; e-mail sbilmaur@intnet.mu; f. 1989; 98% owned by the State Bank of India; cap. US $10.0m., res $13.3m., dep. $120.0m. (June 2007); Chair. S. K. HARIHARAN; Man. Dir V. SRINIVASAN.

Bank of Baroda, Barclays Bank PLC, African Asian Bank, PT Bank International Indonesia, Investec Bank (Mauritius) and HSBC Bank PLC also operate 'offshore' banking units.

STOCK EXCHANGE

Financial Services Commission: Harbour Front Bldg, 4th Floor, John F. Kennedy St, Port Louis; tel. 210-7000; fax 208-7172; e-mail fscmauritius@intnet.mu; internet www.fscmauritius.org; f. 2001; regulatory authority for securities, insurance and global business activities; Chief Exec. MILAN MEETARBHAN.

Stock Exchange of Mauritius Ltd: 1 Cathedral Sq. Bldg, 4th Floor, 16 Jules Koenig St, Port Louis; tel. 212-9541; fax 208-8409; e-mail stockex@intnet.mu; internet www.semdex.com; f. 1989; 11 mems; Chair. JEAN DE FONDAUMIÈRE; CEO SUNIL BENIMADHU.

INSURANCE

Albatross Insurance Co Ltd: 22 St George St, POB 116, Port Louis; tel. 207-9007; fax 208-4800; e-mail headoffice@albatross-insurance.mu; internet www.albatross-insurance.com; f. 1975; Chair. TIMOTHY TAYLOR.

Anglo-Mauritius Assurance Society Ltd: Swan Group Centre, 10 Intendance St, POB 837, Port Louis; tel. 202-8600; fax 208-8956; e-mail anglomtius@intnet.mu; internet www.groupswan.com; f. 1951; Chair. CYRIL MAYER; CEO LOUIS RIVALLAND.

British American Insurance Co (Mauritius) Ltd: BAI Bldg, 25 Pope Hennessy St, POB 331, Port Louis; tel. 202-3600; fax 208-3713; e-mail bai@intnet.mu; f. 1920; Chair. DAWOOD RAWAT; Man. Dir HEINRICH K. DE KOCK.

Ceylinco Stella Insurance Co Ltd: 36 Sir Seewoosagur Ramgoolam St, POB 852, Port Louis; tel. 208-0056; fax 208-1639; e-mail stellain@intnet.mu; internet www.stellain.com; f. 1977; Chair. and Man. Dir R. KRESHAN JHOBOO.

Indian Ocean General Assurance Ltd: 35 Corderie St, POB 865, Port Louis; tel. 212-4125; fax 212-5850; e-mail iogaltd@intnet.mu; f. 1971; Chair. SAM M. CUNDEN; Man. Dir SHRIVANA CUNDEN.

Island Insurance Co Ltd: Labourdonnais Court, 5th Floor, cnr Labourdonnais and St George Sts, Port Louis; tel. 212-4860; fax 208-8762; e-mail island.ins@intnet.mu; f. 1998; Chair. CARRIM A. CURRIMJEE; Man. Dir OLIVIER LAGESSE.

Jubilee Insurance (Mauritius) Ltd: PCL Bldg, 4th Floor, 43 Sir William Newton St, POB 301, Port Louis; tel. 210-3678; fax 212-7970; e-mail jubilee@intnet.mu; f. 1998; Chair. and CEO AUGUSTINE J. HATCH.

Lamco International Insurance Ltd: 12 Barracks St, Port Louis; tel. 212-4494; fax 208-0630; e-mail lamco@intnet.mu; internet www.lamcoinsurance.com; f. 1978; Chair. A. B. ATCHIA; Gen. Man. N. C. ADIA.

Life Insurance Corpn of India: LIC Centre, John F. Kennedy St, Port Louis; tel. 212-5316; fax 208-6392; e-mail liccmm@intnet.mu; f. 1956; Chief Man. HEMANT BHARGAVA.

Mauritian Eagle Insurance Co Ltd: 1st Floor, IBL House, Caudan Waterfront, POB 854, Port Louis; tel. 203-2200; fax 203-2299; e-mail caudan@mauritianeagle.com; internet www.mauritianeagle.com; f. 1973; Chair. P. D'HOTMAN DE VILLIERS; Man. Dir ERIC A. VENPIN.

Mauritius Union Assurance Co Ltd: 4 Léoville L'Homme St, POB 233, Port Louis; tel. 208-4185; fax 212-2962; e-mail mua@mua.mu; internet www.muaco.com; f. 1948; Chair. Sir MAURICE LATOUR-ADRIEN; Gen. Man. JEAN-NÖEL LAM CHUN.

The New India Assurance Co Ltd: Bank of Baroda Bldg, 3rd Floor, 15 Sir William Newton St, POB 398, Port Louis; tel. 208-1442; fax 208-2160; e-mail niasurance@intnet.mu; internet www.niacl.com; f. 1935; general insurance; Chief Man. A. K. JAIN.

La Prudence Mauricienne Assurances Ltée: Le Caudan Waterfront, 2nd Floor, Barkly Wharf, POB 882, Port Louis; tel. 207-2500; fax 208-8936; e-mail prudence@intnet.mu; Chair. ROBERT DE FROBERVILLE; Man. Dir FÉLIX MAUREL.

Rainbow Insurance Co Ltd: 23 Edith Cavell St, POB 389, Port Louis; tel. 212-5767; fax 208-8750; f. 1976; Chair. B. GOKULSING; Man. Dir PREVIN RENBURG.

State Insurance Co of Mauritius Ltd (SICOM): SICOM Bldg, Sir Célicourt Antelme St, Port Louis; tel. 203-8400; fax 208-7662; e-mail email@sicom.intnet.mu; internet www.sicom.mu; f. 1975; Chair. A. F. HO CHAN FONG; Man. Dir K. BHOOJEDHUR-OBEEGADOO.

Sun Insurance Co Ltd: 2 St George St, Port Louis; tel. 208-0769; fax 208-2052; f. 1981; Chair. Sir KAILASH RAMDANEE; Man. Dir A. MUSBALLY.

Swan Insurance Co Ltd: Swan Group Centre, 10 Intendance St, POB 364, Port Louis; tel. 211-2001; fax 208-6898; e-mail swan@intnet.mu; f. 1955; Chair. J. M. ANTOINE HAREL; CEO LOUIS RIVALLAND.

L. and H. Vigier de Latour Ltd: Les Jamalacs Bldg, Old Council St, Port Louis; tel. 212-2034; fax 212-6056; Chair. and Man. Dir L. J. D. HENRI VIGIER DE LATOUR.

Trade and Industry

GOVERNMENT AGENCIES

Agricultural Marketing Board (AMB): Dr G. Leclézio Ave, Moka; tel. 433-4025; fax 433-4837; e-mail agbd@intnet.mu; internet amb.intnet.mu; f. 1964; operates under the aegis of the Ministry of Agro-industry and Fisheries; markets certain locally produced and imported food products (such as potatoes, onions, garlic, spices and seeds); also collects raw milk and distributes pasteurized milk; provides storage facilities to importers and exporters; Gen. Man. PARMANAND RAMNAWAZ.

Mauritius Meat Authority: Abattoir Rd, Roche Bois, POB 612, Port Louis; tel. 242-5884; fax 217-1077; e-mail mauritiusmeat@intnet.mu; licensing authority; controls and regulates sale of meat and meat products; also purchases and imports livestock and markets meat products; Gen. Man. A. BALGOBIN.

Mauritius Sugar Authority: Ken Lee Bldg, 2nd Floor, Edith Cavell St, Port Louis; tel. 208-7466; fax 208-7470; e-mail msa@intnet.mu; regulatory body for the sugar industry; Chair. S. HANOOMANJEE; Exec. Dir Dr G. RAJPATI.

Mauritius Tea Board: Wooton St, Curepipe Rd, Curepipe; POB 28, Eau Coulée; tel. 675-3497; fax 676-1445; e-mail teaboard@intnet.mu; internet www.gov.mu/portal/site/teaboard; f. 1975; regulates and controls the activities of the tea industry; Gen. Man. A. SEEPERGAUTH.

Mauritius Tobacco Board: Plaine Lauzun, Port Louis; tel. 212-2323; fax 208-6426; e-mail tobaco@intnet.mu; internet agriculture.gov.mu/tobacco; Chair. N. MAUDARBACCUS.

DEVELOPMENT ORGANIZATIONS

Board of Investment—Mauritius (BOI): Cathedral Square Bldg 1, 10th Floor, 16 Jules Koenig St, Port Louis; tel. 211-4190; fax 208-2924; e-mail invest@boi.intnet.mu; internet www.boimauritius.com; f. 2001 to promote international investment, business and services; Chair. of Bd MAURICE LAM; Gen. Man. RAJU JADDOO.

Enterprise Mauritius: 7th Floor, Saint James Court, Saint Denis St, Port-Louis; tel. 212-9760; fax 212-9767; e-mail info@em.intnet.mu; internet www.enterprisemauritius.biz; f. 2004 from parts of the Mauritius Industrial Development Authority, the Export Processing Zones Development Authority and the Sub-contracting and Partnership Exchange—Mauritius; comprises a Corporate Services Unit, a Strategic Direction Unit, a Business Development Unit, a Client-Services Unit and a Special Support Unit (estd from the former Clothing and Textile Centre); Chair. AMÉDÉE DARGA; CEO PRAKESH BEEHARRY.

Joint Economic Council (JEC): Plantation House, 3rd Floor, pl. d'Armes, Port Louis; tel. 211-2980; fax 211-3141; e-mail jec@intnet.mu; internet www.jec-mauritius.org; f. 1970; the co-ordinating body of the private sector of Mauritius, including the main business organisations of the country; Pres. ARIF CURRIMJEE; Dir RAJ MAKOOND.

Mauritius Freeport Authority (MFA): Trade and Marketing Centre, 1st Floor, Freeport Zone 6, Mer Rouge; tel. 206-2500; fax 206-2600; e-mail mfa@freeport.gov.mu; internet www.efreeport.com; f. 1990; Chair. KAVYDASS RAMANO; Dir-Gen. RAJAKRISHNA CHELLAPERMAL.

National Productivity and Competitiveness Council (NPCC): Alexander House, 4th Floor, Cybercity, Reduit; tel. 467-7700; fax 467-3838; e-mail natpro@intnet.mu; internet www.npccmauritius.com; f. 2000; represents the Government, the private sector and trade unions; Exec. Dir Dr KRISHNA COONJAN.

Small and Medium Industries Development Organization (SMIDO): Industrial Zone Coromandel; tel. 233-0500; fax 233-5545; e-mail smido@intnet.mu; internet smido.gov.mu; f. 1993.

State Investment Corpn Ltd (SIC): Air Mauritius Centre, 15th Floor, John F. Kennedy St, Port Louis; tel. 202-8900; fax 208-8948; e-mail contactsic@stateinvestment.com; internet www.stateinvestment.com; f. 1984; provides support for new investment and transfer of technology, in agriculture, industry and tourism; Man. Dir IDBAL MALLAM-HASHAM; Chair. RAJ RINGADOO.

CHAMBERS OF COMMERCE

Chinese Chamber of Commerce: Port Louis; tel. 208-0946; fax 242-1193; Pres. JEAN KOK SHUN.

Mauritius Chamber of Commerce and Industry: 3 Royal St, Port Louis; tel. 208-3301; fax 208-0076; e-mail mcci@intnet.mu; internet www.mcci.org; f. 1850; 400 mems; Pres. AZIM CURRIMJEE; Sec.-Gen. MAHMOOD CHEEROO.

INDUSTRIAL ASSOCIATIONS

Association of Mauritian Manufacturers (AMM): c/o The Mauritius Chamber of Commerce and Insdustry, 3 Royal St, Port Louis; tel. 208-3301; e-mail mcci@intnet.mu; Dir JACQUES LI WAN PO.

Mauritius Export Processing Zone Association (MEPZA): Unicorn House, 6th Floor, 5 Royal St, Port Louis; tel. 208-5216; fax 212-1853; internet www.mepza.org; f. 1976; consultative and advisory body; Chair. LOUIS LAI FAT FUR.

Mauritius Sugar Producers' Association (MSPA): Plantation House, 2nd Floor, pl. d'Armes, Port Louis; tel. 212-0295; fax 212-5727; e-mail mspa@intnet.mu; Chair. ARNAUD LAGESSE; Dir PATRICE LEGRIS.

EMPLOYERS' ORGANIZATION

Mauritius Employers' Federation: Cernée House, 1st Floor, Chaussée St, Port Louis; tel. 212-1599; fax 212-6725; e-mail info@mef-online.org; internet www.mef-online.org; f. 1962; Chair. MOOKHESHWARSING GOPAL; Dir Dr AZAD JEETUN.

UTILITIES

Electricity

Central Electricity Board: Royal Rd, POB 40, Curepipe; tel. 601-1100; fax 675-7958; e-mail ceb@intnet.mu; internet ceb.intnet.mu; f. 1952; state-operated; Chair. PATRICK ASSIRVADEN; Gen. Man. KRISHNANAND GUPTAR.

Water

Central Water Authority: Royal Rd, St Paul-Phoenix; tel. 601-5000; fax 686-6264; e-mail cwa@intnet.mu; internet ncb.intnet.mu/putil/cwa; corporate body; scheduled for privatization; f. 1973; Gen. Man. H. K. BOOLUCK; Chair. Prof. ANWAN HUSSEIN SUBRATTY.

Waste Water Management Authority: Sir Celicourt Antelme St, Port Louis; tel. 206-3000; fax 211-7007; e-mail wma@intnet.mu; internet wma.gov.mu; f. 2000; Chair. KHUSHAL LOBINE.

MAJOR COMPANIES

British American Tobacco Mauritius PLC: POB 101, Nicolay Rd, Port Louis; tel. 242-2821; fax 241-8552; e-mail batmtius@intnet.mu; f. 1926; mfrs of tobacco products; Gen. Man. JIM MCCORMICK.

Business Parks of Mauritius Ltd (BPML): NPF Bldg, 10th Floor, Route Moka, Rose Hill; tel. 467-6900; fax 467-6907; e-mail bpml@bpmlmauritius.mu; internet www.e-cybercity.mu; f. 2001 by the Government as a private company; develops, constructs and manages high technology business parks, including Ebène Cyber-City; Exec. Chair. DHARAM HAUGAH.

Compagnie Mauricienne de Textile International Ltée (CMT): c/o CMT Spinnning Mills Ltd, La Tour Koenig, Pointe aux Sables; tel. 234-2898; fax 234-2842; e-mail info@cmt-intl.com; internet www.cmt-intl.com; f. 1983; textiles and pharmaceuticals; subsidiaries in Hong Kong, China, Madagascar and Zimbabwe; Man. Dir KRIS POONOOSAMY; 3,000 employees.

Compagnie sucrière de St Antoine Ltée: Cerné House, 6th Floor, La Chaussée, Port Louis; tel. 283-9545; fax 283-9551; mfrs of sugar products; Dir BERNARD MAYER.

Consolidated Investments and Enterprises Group (CIEL): Swan Group Centre, 12th Floor, Intendance St, Port Louis; tel. 202-2200; fax 208-8680; e-mail info@cielgroup.com; internet www.cielgroup.com; f. 1977; comprises CIEL Agro-Industry (Deep River—Beau Champ sugar estate), CIEL Corporate Services Ltd, CIEL Investment Ltd and CIEL Textile Ltd (incl. Floreal Knitwear); Chief Exec. P. A. DALAIS; Chair. J. C. LAGESSE.

Currimjee Jeewanjee and Co Ltd: 38 Royal St, POB 49, Port Louis; tel. 206-6200; fax 240-8133; e-mail webmaster@currimjee.intnet.mu; internet www.currimjee.com; f. 1890; media and communications, food and beverages, financial services, real estate, textiles, trading, travel and freight; Chair. BASHIRALI A. CURRIMJEE; 4,500 employees.

Espitalier Noël Ltd (ENL): Swan Group Centre, 7th Floor, Intendance St, Port Louis; tel. 213-3800; fax 208-0968; e-mail enlgroup@intnet.mu; internet www.enlgroup.biz; f. 1944; holding co; agriculture, manufacturing and services; comprises more than 20 companies; notable subsidiaries include Mon Désert Alma Ltd, Savannah Sugar Estate Co Ltd and General Investment & Development Co Ltd (GIDC); Chair. GUY RIVALLAND; Chief Exec. HECTOR ESPITALIER-NOËL; 5,000 employees.

General Construction Co Ltd: POB 503, Port Louis; tel. 202-2000; fax 208-8249; e-mail gcc@gcc.mu; f. 1958; civil engineering and construction; Chair. J. C. MAINGARD; Man Dir D. ADAM; 4,300 employees.

Groupe Mon Loisir (GML): Swan Group Centre, 11th Floor, 10 Intendance St, Port Louis; tel. 211-1714; fax 208-0134; e-mail corporate@gmlmail.com; internet www.groupemonloisir.com; tourism, manufacturing, financial services and real estate interests; 117 subsidiaries and affiliates; Chief Exec. ARNAUD LAGESSE; 12,500 employees.

Flacq United Estates Ltd (FUEL): Swan Group Centre, 11th Floor, 10 Intendance St, Port Louis; tel. 211-1713; fax 210-1300; e-mail ceo@fuelmru.com; internet www.groupemonloisir.com; f. 1948; investment co; owned by Groupe Mon Loisir; cultivates 8,000 ha of sugar cane plantation; operates the largest sugar factory on the island; supplies electricity derived from bagasse to the national grid; Chair. THIERRY LAGESSE; Chief Exec. JOSEPH VAUDIN.

Harel Frères Ltd: 18 Edith Cavell St, POB 317, Port Louis; tel. 208-0808; fax 208-8798; e-mail harelfreres@harelfreres.com; internet www.harelfreres.com; f. 1960; multiple activities, incl. financial and beverage supplies; Pres. J. HUGUES MAIGROT; Man.Dir M. E. CYRIL MAYER.

Harel Mallac and Co Ltd: 18 Edith Cavell St, Port Louis; tel. 207-3000; fax 207-3030; e-mail ho@harelmallac.com; internet www.harelmallac.com; f. 1830; multiple activities, incl. 6 divisions: technologies; office equipment; travel, tourism and retail; reprographics; engineering and outsourcing; Chair. of Bd ANTOINE L. HAREL; Chief Exec. CHRISTOPHER BOLAND; 740 employees.

IndianOil (Mauritius) Ltd (IOML): Terminal, Mer Rouge; tel. 217-2714; fax 217-2712; e-mail indianoil@intnet.mu; internet www.ioml.mu; wholly owned by IndianOil Corpn (India); Man. Dir RAJESH AHUJA.

Innodis Ltd: Innodis Bldg, Caudan; tel. 206-0800; fax 286-3058; e-mail info@innodis.mu; internet www.innodis.mu; operates a frozen foods unit, a consumer goods unit of branded food, an ice cream and dairy unit, a poultry unit, Peninsula Rice Milling Ltd and Supercash retail outlets; f. 1973 as Happy World Foods Ltd; present name assumed in 2006; owned by Altima Group; Chief Operating Officer JEAN HOW HONG; more than 800 employees.

International Distillers (Mauritius) Ltd: POB 661, Plaine Lauzun; tel. 212-6896; fax 208-6076; e-mail idmltd@intnet.mu; f. 1972; mfrs, importers and distributors of wines and spirits; Chief Exec. JACQUES T. LI WAN PO; Man. Dir W. L. SHEPHERD.

Ireland Blyth Ltd (IBL): IBL House, 5th Floor, Caudan, POB 56, Port Louis; tel. 203-2000; fax 203-2001; e-mail iblinfo@iblgroup.com; internet www.iblgroup.com; f. 1972; marketing and distribution of consumer goods and durables, pharmaceuticals, fertilizers and pesticides, mechanical and electrical engineering and cold storage operations; Chair. THIERRY LAGESSE; Chief Exec. PATRICE D'HOTMAN DE VILLIERS; 1,500 employees.

Mauritius Chemical and Fertilizer Industry Ltd: Chaussée Tromelin, POB 344, Port Louis; tel. 261-3965; fax 240-9969; e-mail mcficontact@mfci.intnet.mu; f. 1975; mfrs of agricultural chemicals and fertilizers; Chair. F. MONTOCCHIO.

Mauritius Oil Refineries Ltd: Quay Rd, POB 602, Port Louis; tel. 240-2147; fax 240-8320; e-mail moroil@bow.intnet.mu; f. 1968; edible oil; Chair. PAUL DE CHASTEIGNER DU MÉE; Man. Dir R. J. PAUL CLARENC.

Mauritius Sugar Terminal Corporation (MSTC): 17 Kwan Tee St, Caudan, Port Louis; tel. 208-1451; fax 208-3225; f. 1979; provides, operates and maintains facilities for storage, sampling, bagging, packing, loading and unloading of sugar and advises on the provisions of adequate means of inland or sea access to the terminal; Gen. Man. R. M. HURDOWAR.

Mon Trésor et Mon Désert Ltd: Anglo-Mauritius House, 7th Floor, A. de Plevitz St, Port Louis; tel. 212-3252; fax 208-8263; e-mail bm@socrdc.com; internet www.montresor.mu; f. 1926; sugar-cane and energy production; Chair. CYRIL MAYER; Man. Dir GEORGES LEUNG SHING; 4,000 employees.

Phoenix Beverages Ltd: Phoenix House, Pont-Fer, Phoenix; tel. 601-2000; fax 696-0455; e-mail pbg@pbg.mu; internet www.phoenixbeveragesgroup.com; f. 1960; formerly Mauritius Breweries Ltd, now part of the Phoenix Beverages Group; name changed as above 2004; brews, bottles and distributes alcoholic and soft drinks; Chief Exec. RICHARD WOODING.

Prince's Tuna (Mauritius) Ltd: New Trunk Rd, Riche Terre, POB 313, Port Louis; tel. 206-9000; fax 249-2300; e-mail ptm@princestuna.com; f. 1970; processors of tuna fish; Chair. J. MUTCH; 2,400 employees.

Robert Le Maire Group (RLM): Old Moka Rd, POB 161, Belle Village, Port Louis; tel. 212-1865; fax 208-0112; e-mail headoffice.rlm@rlmgroup.mu; internet www.rlmgroup.mu; importers and merchants, general agents and providers of engineering and contracting services; CEO ROGER KOENIG.

Rogers & Co Ltd: 5 John F. Kennedy St, POB 60, Port Louis; tel. 208-6801; fax 208-5045; e-mail info@rogers.mu; internet www.rogers.mu; f. 1948; aviation, chemicals and pharmaceuticals, construction materials, engineering, food, financial services, property development, shipping, tourism; Chair. ROGER HECTOR ESPITALIER-NOËL; CEO TIMOTHY TAYLOR; 3 vessels.

Shell Mauritius Ltd: 5 St Georges St, POB 85, Port Louis; tel. 212-2222; fax 208-8347; internet www.shell.com/home/content2/mu-en; f. 1905; marketing and distribution of petroleum products; Chair. PAWAN K. JUWAHEER.

State Trading Corporation (STC): Fon Sing Bldg, 3rd Floor, 12 Edith Cavell St, Port Louis; tel. 208-5440; fax 208-8359; e-mail stcfin@intnet.mu; internet stc.intnet.mu; f. 1982; responsible for the importation of essential commodities, such as petroleum products, cement, rice and wheat flour and liquefied petroleum gas; Gen. Man. RANJIT SINGH SOOMAROOAH.

Sugar Investment Trust (SIT): Alexander House, 3rd Floor, 35 Cybercity, Ebene; tel. 465-4747; fax 466-6566; e-mail sitrust@intnet.mu; internet www.sit.intnet.mu; f. 1994; largest shareholder-based public company in Mauritius, with more than 40,000 membs; subsidiaries include SIT Leisure Ltd, SIT Land Holdings Ltd, SIT Property Development Ltd, Sir Seewoosagur Ramgoolam Botanical Garden Investment Company Limited (SSRBG), SIT Corporate and Secretarial Services Ltd; Chair. RITESH SUMPUTH.

Sun Resorts Ltd (SRL): Regional Office, Poste de Flacq; tel. 401-1688; fax 415-1935; e-mail Ingrid.Dyson@sunresorts.mu; internet www.sunresort.com; f. 1983; holding co, with interests in the hotel business; Chair. G. CHRISTIAN DALAIS; 2,900 employees.

United Basalt Products Ltd (UBP): Trianon, Quatre Bornes; tel. 454-1964; fax 454-8043; e-mail ubp@intnet.mu; internet www.ubp.mu; f. 1953; mfrs of building materials; Chair. JACQUES LAGESSE; Gen. Man. JEAN-MICHEL GIRAUD; 720 employees.

TRADE UNIONS

Federations

Federation of Civil Service and Other Unions (FCSOU): Jade Court, Rm 308, 3rd Floor, 33 Jummah Mosque St, Port Louis; tel. 216-1977; fax 216-1475; e-mail f.c.s.u@intnet.mu; internet www.fcsu.org; f. 1957; 72 affiliated unions with 30,000 mems (2006); Pres. TOOLSYRAJ BENYDIN; Sec. AWADHKOOMARSINGH BALLUCK.

General Workers' Federation: 13 Brabant St, Port Louis; tel. 212-3338; Pres. FAROOK AUCHOYBUR; Sec.-Gen. DEVANAND RAMJUTTUN.

Mauritius Federation of Trade Unions: Arc Bldg, 3rd Floor, cnr Sir William Newton and Sir Seewoosagur Ramgoolam Sts, Port Louis; tel. 208-9426; f. 1958; four affiliated unions; Pres. FAROOK HOSSENBUX; Sec.-Gen. R. MAREEMOOTOO.

Mauritius Labour Congress (MLC): 8 Louis Victor de la Faye St, Port Louis; tel. 212-4343; fax 208-8945; e-mail mlcongress@intnet.mu; f. 1963; 55 affiliated unions with 70,000 mems (1992); Pres. NURDEO LUCHMUN ROY; Gen. Sec. JUGDISH LOLLBEEHARRY.

Mauritius Trade Union Congress (MTUC): Emmanuel Anquetil Labour Centre, James Smith St, Port Louis; tel. 210-8567; internet www.mtucmauritius.org; f. 1946.

Trade Union Trust Fund: Richard House, 2nd Floor, cnr Jummah Mosque and Remy Ollier Sts, Port Louis; tel. and fax 217-2073; internet www.gov.mu/portal/site/tradeuniontf; f. 1997 to receive and manage funds and other property obtained from the Govt and other sources; to promote workers' education and provide assistance to workers' orgs; Chair. RADHAKRISNA SADIEN.

Principal Unions

Government Servants' Association: 107A Royal Rd, Beau Bassin; tel. 464-4242; fax 465-3220; e-mail gsa@intnet.mu; internet www.gsa.mauritius.org; f. 1945; Pres. R. SADIEN; Sec.-Gen. P. RAMJUG.

Government Teachers' Union: 3 Mgr Gonin St, POB 1111, Port Louis; tel. 208-0047; fax 208-4943; f. 1945; Pres. JUGDUTH SEEGUM; Sec. MOHAMMAD SALEEM CHOOLUN; 4,550 mems (2005).

Nursing Association: Royal Rd, Beau Bassin; tel. 464-5850; f. 1955; Pres. CASSAM KUREEMAN; Sec.-Gen. FRANCIS SUPPARAYEN.

Organization of Artisans' Unity: 42 Sir William Newton St, Port Louis; tel. and fax 212-4557; f. 1973; Pres. AUGUSTE FOLLET; Sec. ROY RAMCHURN; 2,874 mems (1994).

Plantation Workers' Union: 8 Louis Victor de la Faye St, Port Louis; tel. 212-1735; f. 1955; Pres. C. Bhagirutty; Sec. N. L. Roy; 13,726 mems (1990).

Port Louis Harbour and Docks Workers' Union: Port Louis; tel. 208-2276; Pres. M. Veerabadren; Sec.-Gen. Gerard Bertrand.

Sugar Industry Staff Employees' Association: 1 Rémy Ollier St, Port Louis; tel. 212-1947; f. 1947; Chair. T. Bellerose; Sec.-Gen. G. Chung Kwan Fang; 1,450 mems (1997).

Textile, Clothes and Other Manufactures Workers' Union: Thomy d'Arifat St, Curepipe; tel. 676-5280; Pres. Padmatee Teeluck; Sec.-Gen. Désiré Guildaree.

Union of Bus Industry Workers: Port Louis; tel. 212-3338; f. 1970; Pres. M. Babooa; Sec.-Gen. F. Auchoybur.

Union of Employees of the Ministry of Agriculture and other Ministries: 28 Hennessy Ave, Quatre-Bornes; tel. 465-1935; e-mail bruno5@intnet.mu; f. 1989; Sec. Bruneau Dorasami; 2,500 mems (Dec. 2003).

Union of Labourers of the Sugar and Tea Industry: Royal Rd, Curepipe; f. 1969; Sec. P. Ramchurn.

Transport

RAILWAYS

There are no operational railways in Mauritius.

ROADS

In 2004 there were 2,015 km of paved roads, of which 70 km were motorways, 950 km were other main roads, and 592 km were secondary roads. An urban highway links the motorways approaching Port Louis. A motorway connects Port Louis with Plaisance airport.

SHIPPING

Mauritius is served by numerous foreign shipping lines. In 1990 Port Louis was established as a free port to expedite the development of Mauritius as an entrepôt centre. In 1995 the World Bank approved a loan of US $30.5m. for a programme to develop the port. At 31 December 2005 Mauritius had a merchant fleet of 47 vessels, with a combined displacement of 70.6 grt.

Mauritius Ports Authority: Port Administration Bldg, POB 379, Mer Rouge, Port Louis; tel. 206-5400; fax 240-0856; e-mail mauport@intnet.mu; internet www.mauport.com; f. 1976; Chair. Eddy Boisssézon; Dir-Gen. Capt. Jean Wong Chung Toi.

Ireland Blyth Ltd: IBL House, Caudan, Port Louis; tel. 203-2000; fax 203-2001; e-mail iblinfo@iblgroup.com; internet www.iblgroup.com; Chair. Thierry Lagesse; CEO P. d'Hotman de Villiers; 2 vessels.

Islands Services Ltd: Rogers House, 5 John F. Kennedy St, POB 60, Port Louis; tel. 208-6801; fax 208-5045; services to Indian Ocean islands; Chair. Sir René Maingard; Exec. Dir Capt. René Sanson.

Mauritius Freeport Development Co Ltd: Freeport Zone 5, Mer Rouge; tel. 206-2000; fax 206-2025; e-mail info@mfd.mu; internet www.mfd.mu; f. 1997; manages and operates Freeport Zone 5, more than 40,000 sq m of storage facility; facilities include dry warehouses, cold warehouses, processing and transformation units, open storage container parks and a container freight station; largest logistics centre in the Indian Ocean region; CEO Dominique De Froberville.

Mauritius Shipping Corpn Ltd: St James Court, Suite 417/418, St Denis St, Port Louis; tel. 208-5900; fax 210-5176; e-mail info@mscl.mu; internet www.mauritiusshipping.mu; f. 1985; state-owned; operates two passenger-cargo vessels between Mauritius, Rodrigues, Reunion and Madagascar; Man. Dir Capt. J. Patrick Rault.

Société Mauricienne de Navigation Ltée: 1 rue de la Reine, POB 53, Port Louis; tel. 208-3241; fax 208-8931; e-mail iblsh@bow.intnet.mu; Man. Dir Capt. François de Gersigny.

CIVIL AVIATION

Sir Seewoosagur Ramgoolam International Airport is at Plaisance, 4 km from Mahébourg. From 2006 air routes with France and the United Kingdom were to be liberalized, allowing new carriers to operate on the routes.

Civil Aviation Department: Sir Seewoosagur Ramgoolam International Airport, Plaine Magnien; tel. 603-2000; fax 637-3164; e-mail civa@mail.gov.mu; internet civil-aviation.gov.mu; overseen by the Ministry of Training, Skills Development, Productivity and External Communications; Dir Sarupanand Kinnoo.

Air Mauritius: Air Mauritius Centre, John F. Kennedy St, POB 441, Port Louis; tel. 207-7070; fax 208-8331; e-mail mkcare@airmauritius.intnet.mu; internet www.airmauritius.com; f. 1967; 51% state-owned; services to 28 destinations in Europe, Asia, Australia and Africa; Chair. Sanjay Buckhory; Man. Dir Manoj R. K. Ujoodha.

Tourism

Tourists are attracted to Mauritius by its scenery and beaches, the pleasant climate and the blend of cultures. Accommodation capacity totalled 21,072 beds in 2005. The number of visitors increased from 300,670 in 1990 to 788,276 in 2006, when the greatest numbers of visitors were from France (23.1%), the United Kingdom (13.0%) and Réunion (11.3%). Gross revenue from tourism in 2006 was estimated at Rs 31,942m. The Government sought to increase the volume of tourists visiting the country (to some 2m. people by 2015) by improving the jetty facilities in the port in order to welcome cruise ships and by liberalizing air transit routes.

Mauritius Tourism Promotion Authority: Air Mauritius Centre, 11th Floor, John F. Kennedy St, Port Louis; tel. 210-1545; fax 212-5142; e-mail info@mtpa.mauritius.net; internet www.mauritius.net; Chair. Robert Desvaux.

Tourism Authority (TA): Fon Sing Bldg, 5th Floor, Port Louis; tel. 213-1740; fax 213-1745; e-mail tourism.authority@intnet.mu; f. 2004; issues licences for and monitors compliance of the regulation of the tourism industry; Pres. Joël Rault.

Defence

The country has no standing defence forces, although as assessed at November 2006 paramilitary forces were estimated to number 2,000, comprising a special 1,500-strong mobile police unit, to ensure internal security, and a coastguard of 500.

Defence Expenditure: Budgeted at Rs 575m. in 2006.

Education

Education is officially compulsory for seven years between the ages of five and 12. Primary education begins at five years of age and lasts for six years. Secondary education, beginning at the age of 11, lasts for up to seven years, comprising a first cycle of three years and a second of four years. At March 2005 up to 77% of pre-primary schools were privately run institutions. Primary and secondary education are available free of charge and became compulsory in 2005. According to UNESCO estimates, in 2004/05 enrolment at primary schools included 95% of pupils in the relevant age group (males 94%; females 95%), while the comparable ratio for secondary schools was 83% (males 82%; females 83%). The Government exercises indirect control of the large private sector in secondary education (in 2005 only 70 of 188 schools were state administered). The University of Mauritius, founded in 1965, had 6,602 students in 2005/06 (35% of whom were part-time students), out of a total of 16,852 students in higher education; in addition, many students receive further education abroad. Of total expenditure by the central Government in 2005/06, MR 7,378.7m. (equivalent to 14.3% of total government spending) was allocated to education, according to provisional figures.

Other Islands

RODRIGUES

The island of Rodrigues covers an area of 104 sq km. Its population, which was enumerated at 35,779 at the 2000 census, was officially estimated to number 36,995 at December 2005. Formerly also known as Diego Ruys, Rodrigues is located 585 km east of the island of Mauritius, and is administered by a resident commissioner. Rodrigues is currently represented in the National Assembly by four members. Fishing and farming are the principal activities, while the main exports are cattle, salt fish, sheep, goats, pigs and onions. The island is linked to Mauritius by thrice-weekly air and monthly boat services.

THE LESSER DEPENDENCIES

The Lesser Dependencies (area 71 sq km, population enumerated at 289 at the 2000 census) are the Agalega Islands, two islands about 935 km north of Mauritius, and the Cargados Carajos Shoals (St Brandon Islands), 22 islets without permanent inhabitants, lying 370 km north-north-east. Mauritius also claims sovereignty over Tromelin Island, 556 km to the north-west. This claim is disputed by Madagascar, and also by France, which maintains an airstrip and weather station on the island.

Bibliography

Addison, J., and Hazareesingh, K. *A New History of Mauritius*. Oxford, ABC; Rose Hill, Editions de l'Océan Indien, 1991.

Alladin, I. *Economic Miracle in the Indian Ocean: Can Mauritius Show the Way?* Port Louis, Editions de l'Océan Indien, 1993.

Baker, P. *Kreol: A Description of Mauritian Creole*. London, Hurst, 1972.

Benedict, B. *Indians in a Plural Society: A Report on Mauritius*. London, HMSO, 1961.

Mauritius, A Plural Society. London, 1965.

Bissoonoyal, B. *A Concise History of Mauritius*. Bombay, Bharatiya Vidya, 1963.

Bowman, L. W. *Mauritius: Democracy and Development in the Indian Ocean*. Boulder, CO, Westview Press, 1991.

Cohen, R. *African Islands and Enclaves*. London, Sage Publications, 1983.

Dukhira, C. D. *Mauritius and Local Government Management*. Oxford, ABC; Port Louis, Editions de l'Océan Indien; Bombay, LSG Press, 1992.

Favoreu, L. *L'Île Maurice*. Paris, Berger-Levrault, 1970.

Ingrams, W. H. *A Short History of Mauritius*. London, Macmillan, 1931.

International Monetary Fund. *Mauritius: Recent Economic Developments and Selected Issues*. Washington, DC, 1997.

Jones, P., and Andrews, B. *A Taste of Mauritius*. London, Macmillan, 1982.

Lehembre, B. *L'Île Maurice*. Paris, Editions Karthala, 1984.

Mahadeo, T. *Mauritian Cultural Heritage*. Port Louis, Editions de l'Océan Indien, 1995.

Mathur, H. *Parliament in Mauritius*. Oxford, ABC; Rose Hill, Editions de l'Océan Indien, 1991.

Ramgoolam, Sir S. *Our Struggle: 20th Century Mauritius*. New Delhi, Vision Books, 1982.

Selvon, S. *Historical Dictionary of Mauritius*. 2nd Edn. Metuchen, NJ, Scarecrow Press, 1991.

Simmons, A. S. *Modern Mauritius: The Politics of Decolonization*. Bloomington, IN, Indiana University Press, 1982.

Titmuss, R. M., and Abel-Smith, B. *Social Policies and Population Growth in Mauritius*. Sessional Paper No. 6, 1960. London, Methuen, reprinted by Frank Cass, 1968.

Toussaint, A. *Port Louis, deux siècles d'histoire (1735–1935)*. Port Louis, 1946.

Bibliography of Mauritius 1501–1954. Port Louis, 1956.

Histoire des Îles Mascareignes. Paris, Berger-Levrault, 1972.

World Bank. *Mauritius: Economic Memorandum: Recent Developments and Prospects*. Washington, DC, 1983.

Mauritius: Managing Success. Washington DC, 1989.

Mauritius: Expanding Horizons. Washington, DC, 1992.

Wright, C. *Mauritius*. Newton Abbot, David and Charles, 1974.

MOZAMBIQUE

Physical and Social Geography

RENÉ PÉLISSIER

The Republic of Mozambique covers a total area of 799,380 sq km (308,641 sq miles). This includes 13,000 sq km of inland water, mainly comprising Lake Niassa, the Mozambican section of Lake Malawi. Mozambique is bounded to the north by Tanzania, to the west by Malawi, Zambia and Zimbabwe, and to the south by South Africa and Swaziland.

With some exceptions towards the Zambia, Malawi and Zimbabwe borders, Mozambique is generally a low-lying plateau of moderate height, descending through a sub-plateau zone to the Indian Ocean. The main reliefs are Monte Binga (2,436 m above sea-level), the highest point of Mozambique, on the Zimbabwe border in Manica province, Monte Namúli (2,419 m) in Zambézia province, the Serra Zuira (2,227 m) in Manica province and several massifs that are a continuation into northern Mozambique of the Shire highlands of Malawi. The coastal lowland is narrower in the north but widens considerably towards the south, so that terrain less than 1,000 m high comprises about 45% of the total Mozambican area. The shore-line is 2,470 km long and generally sandy and bordered by lagoons, shoals and strings of coastal islets in the north.

Mozambique is divided by at least 25 main rivers, all of which flow to the Indian Ocean. The largest and most historically significant is the Zambezi, whose 820-km Mozambican section is navigable for 460 km. Flowing from eastern Angola, the Zambezi provides access to the interior of Africa from the eastern coast.

Two main seasons, wet and dry, divide the climatic year. The wet season has monthly averages of 26.7°–29.4°C, with cooler temperatures in the interior uplands. The dry season has June and July temperatures of 18.3°–20.0°C at Maputo. Mozambique is vulnerable to drought and attendant famine, which severely affected much of the country during the 1980s, particularly during the period 1982–84 and again during 1986–87. In 2000 serious flooding affected the centre and south of Mozambique, displacing an estimated 500,000 people and causing severe damage to the country's infrastructure.

The census taken by the Portuguese authorities in December 1970 recorded a total population of 8,168,933, and the population increased to 11,673,725, excluding underenumeration (estimated at 3.8%), by the census of 1 August 1980. At the census of 1 August 1997 the population stood at 16,099,246, and in 2007, according to official projections, it was 20,366,795. The population density was 25.5 per sq km at mid-2007. Mozambique's population increased by an annual average of 2.2% during 1995–2005, according to World Bank figures.

North of the Zambezi, the main ethnic groupings among the African population, which belongs to the cultural division of Central Bantu, are the Makua-Lomwe groups, who form the principal ethno-linguistic subdivision of Mozambique and are believed to comprise about 40% of the population. South of the Zambezi, the main group is the Thonga, who feature prominently as Mozambican mine labourers in South Africa. North of the Thonga area lies the Shona group, numbering more than 1m. Southern ethnic groups have tended to enjoy greater educational opportunities than those of other regions. The Government has sought to balance the ethnic composition of its leadership, but the executive is still largely of southern and central origin.

Mozambique is divided into 11 administrative provinces, one of which comprises the capital, Maputo, a modern seaport whose population was estimated at 1,244,227 in 2006. The second seaport of the country is Beira. Other towns of importance include Nampula, on the railway line to Niassa province and Malawi, and Matola.

Recent History

JOÃO GOMES CRAVINHO

Revised by EDWARD GEORGE

The territory now comprising the Republic of Mozambique came under Portuguese control in the 19th century and became a Portuguese 'overseas province' in 1951. Nationalist groups began to form in the early 1960s, eventually uniting in the Frente de Libertação de Moçambique (Frelimo), under the leadership of Eduardo Mondlane, in 1962. In 1964 Frelimo launched a military campaign for independence that subsequently developed into a serious conflict, engaging thousands of Portuguese troops by the early 1970s. Following the assassination of Mondlane in 1969, Samora Machel was elected leader. After the military coup in Portugal in April 1974, the Portuguese authorities agreed to hand over power to a transitional Frelimo-dominated Government, and full independence followed on 25 June 1975, when the People's Republic of Mozambique was declared, with Machel as its President.

The new Frelimo Government implemented a centrally planned economy and one-party state, and in 1977 Frelimo declared itself to be a 'Marxist-Leninist vanguard party'. Despite impressive advances in the fields of public health, social welfare and education, Frelimo's policy of *socialização do campo* (socialization of the countryside) succeeded in antagonizing most of the country's peasantry (which accounted for 80% of the population); collective agriculture was promoted, traditional beliefs and ceremonies were prohibited, *regulos* (tribal kings) were stripped of their powers and church-run social projects were closed.

CIVIL WAR AND CONFLICT WITH SOUTH AFRICA

In its foreign policy Frelimo embraced international activism during the late 1970s, implementing sanctions against the white regime in Rhodesia (now Zimbabwe) by cutting off its main transport route via the Mozambican port of Beira. It also allowed Robert Mugabe's Zimbabwe African National Union (ZANU) forces to set up bases on its territory and mount cross-border raids. The Rhodesian authorities responded by arming and providing support to the dissident Movimento Nacional de Resistência de Moçambique (MNR).

After 1980, following the emergence of an independent Zimbabwe, South Africa became the MNR's main supporter; the MNR, now renamed Resistência Nacional Moçambicana (Renamo), rapidly expanded from some 500 to a force of an estimated 8,000 guerrillas. Renamo concentrated its attacks on the symbols of Frelimo achievements, such as schools, health centres, social projects and transport infrastructure, and acquired a reputation for brutality, including mass murders of civilians as well as mutilations.

The high economic cost of the conflict with Renamo prompted Mozambique to enter into discussions with the South African Government in late 1983. Negotiations culminated in the Nkomati Accord, a non-aggression treaty signed in 1984, in which both sides bound themselves not to give material aid to opposition movements in each other's countries, and to establish a joint security commission. Effectively, this meant that Mozambique would prevent the African National Congress of South Africa (ANC) from conducting military operations from its territory, while South Africa would cease to support Renamo. However, the South African Government effectively ignored the Accord, and by August 1984 Renamo forces were active in all of Mozambique's provinces, with the capital increasingly under threat.

The escalating internal conflict led the Frelimo Government to warn South Africa in August 1984 that the Accord was under threat unless Renamo activity was halted. South Africa responded by convening a number of separate but parallel talks with Renamo and Frelimo government representatives, which culminated, in October, in the so-called 'Pretoria Declaration' in which a cease-fire was agreed in principle between the Frelimo Government and the rebels, and a tripartite commission, comprising Frelimo, Renamo and South African representatives, was established to implement the truce. In November, however, Renamo withdrew from the peace negotiations, citing the Frelimo Government's refusal to recognize its legitimacy. In March 1985 the two countries reiterated their continued commitment to the Nkomati Accord, and South Africa announced that a restricted air space, partly aimed at preventing support from reaching Renamo guerrillas from South African territory, would be established in the border area with Mozambique. In April a joint operational centre dealing with security and other matters relating to the Nkomati Accord was also established on the border between Mozambique and South Africa. However, in the same month, Renamo guerrilla activity effectively severed rail links between the two countries.

The worsening security situation precipitated a meeting in June 1985 in Harare, Zimbabwe, between President Machel, the Prime Minister of Zimbabwe, Robert Mugabe, and President Julius Nyerere of Tanzania, at which it was agreed that Tanzania and Zimbabwe would support Mozambique, and, in particular, that Zimbabwe would augment its military presence in Mozambique. This arrangement resulted in the capture, in August, of the largest Renamo base, the so-called 'Casa Banana' in Sofala province, and of other major rebel bases in the area. Not only were large quantities of weapons captured, but also incriminating documentation concerning South African support for Renamo since the signing of the Nkomati Accord, although the South African Government claimed that its continued contacts with Renamo were designed to promote peace negotiations between the guerrillas and the Frelimo Government. In October Mozambique unilaterally suspended the joint security commission.

In early 1986 the Mozambique Government's military situation deteriorated sharply, illustrated by the temporary recapture in February of the 'Casa Banana' base by Renamo forces. In October a Soviet civilian aircraft carrying Machel, on his return from a meeting in Zambia of leaders of the 'front-line' states, crashed just inside South African territory, killing the President. Machel was succeeded as President by Joaquim Chissano, the Minister of Foreign Affairs. Controversy has continued to surround the causes of the crash, especially over the strong possibility of South African involvement. In January 1987 a joint report, compiled by Mozambican, Soviet and South African experts, was presented to an international board of inquiry established to investigate the crash. The board concluded that pilot error, and not sabotage, had caused the accident. In 1998 South Africa's Truth and Reconciliation Commission opened another inquiry, but although it raised the possibility that a false beacon had caused the crash, its findings were inconclusive. In February 2006 the South African Government reopened the inquiry into the crash.

In February 1987 Zimbabwean and Mozambican troops recaptured five towns in northern Mozambique that Renamo had seized in late 1986. This signified a general shift in the balance of power, with Renamo increasing its operations in the south, while government troops registered important successes in the north and along the coastline. Following the death of Machel, Mozambique had applied intense pressure on Malawi, including threats of military action, to induce its neighbour to cease accommodating Renamo, and in December 1987 a joint security agreement was signed between the two states.

An open raid in May 1987 by South African security forces on alleged ANC bases in metropolitan Maputo effectively signalled the demise of the Nkomati Accord. In December President Chissano announced a 'law of pardon', offering to release on parole or shorten the sentences of repentant convicted prisoners; he also offered amnesty for members of Renamo willing to surrender their weapons.

POLITICAL LIBERALIZATION

Fundamental changes in Frelimo's political and economic philosophy began to emerge in 1987, when an economic recovery programme, the Programa de Reabilitação Econômica (PRE), was launched; it included wide-ranging policy reforms designed to move the country away from socialist central planning towards a free-market economy (see Economy). In 1989 the party renounced its Marxist-Leninist orientation, embracing social democracy and opening its membership to all. In January 1990 draft proposals for a new constitution were published, providing for the direct election of the President and Assembléia Popular by universal suffrage. The draft constitution, which was submitted to public debate during 1990, provided for the separation of Frelimo and the state and the independence of the judiciary. The process of political change was further advanced in August, when Frelimo announced that the country's name was to be changed from the People's Republic of Mozambique to the Republic of Mozambique.

The new Constitution was formally approved by the Assembléia Popular (renamed Assembléia da República) in November 1990. Provisions outlawing censorship and enshrining freedom of expression had been added and the death penalty was abolished. The new Constitution was welcomed by Western aid donors but rejected by Renamo as the product of an unrepresentative, unelected body. One of the first acts of the new legislature, in December, was to pass legislation allowing the formation of new political parties.

After President Chissano had announced in March 1991 that general elections would be held in 1992, new political parties continued to organize. In March 1993 the Government published a draft electoral law proposing the establishment of a 21-member national electoral commission, chaired by a member of the Supreme Court, to organize and supervise the elections.

PEACE INITIATIVES

In June 1989 the Government launched a peace initiative based on a number of principles, which demanded the cessation of acts of terrorism, guaranteed the right of political participation to all 'individuals' who renounced violence, recognized the principle that no group should impose its will on another by force and demanded that all parties respect the legitimacy of the state and of the Constitution. In mid-1989 Presidents Daniel arap Moi of Kenya and Robert Mugabe of Zimbabwe agreed to mediate between Renamo and the Mozambique Government. Renamo rejected the plan, demanding its recognition as a political entity, the introduction of multi-party elections and the withdrawal of Zimbabwean troops from Mozambique. However, in July 1990 the first direct talks between the two sides were held in Rome, Italy, after which Renamo demanded the withdrawal of all foreign troops from the country and the abandonment of the new Constitution. The talks culminated in the signing on 1 December of a partial cease-fire agreement, which provided for the withdrawal of Zimbabwean forces to within 3 km of the Beira and Limpopo transport 'corridors'. In exchange, Renamo agreed to cease hostilities and refrain from attacking the 'corridors'. The withdrawal of Zimbabwean troops to the 'corridors' was completed by the end of December.

Although attacks by Renamo resumed in the early months of 1991, peace talks nevertheless continued in Rome, and in October 1991 the two sides signed a protocol that was said to represent a recognition by Renamo of the Government's legitimacy. The establishment of a commission to oversee the eventual cease-fire was also agreed. In the following month it was agreed that Renamo would function as a political party immediately after a cease-fire. The role of Mugabe as a mediator resumed in mid-January 1992, when Mugabe and President Hastings Kamuzu Banda of Malawi held direct discussions with the Renamo leader, Afonso Dhlakama, in Malawi, in an effort to expedite the peace talks. In March 1992 a protocol was signed in Rome, establishing the principles for the country's future electoral system. The protocol provided for a system of proportional representation for the legislature, with legislative and presidential elections to take place simultaneously within one year of the signing of a cease-fire. A national electoral commission was to be established to oversee the elections, with one-third of its members appointed by Renamo. The protocol also guaranteed freedom of the press and media as well as of association, expression and movement.

Rebel activity within Mozambique, with attacks on the fringes of major cities, including Maputo, Beira and Chimoio, continued in 1992, but in early August Chissano and Dhlakama signed a joint declaration in Rome, committing the two sides to a total cease-fire by 1 October 1992, as part of a general peace agreement that would provide for presidential and legislative elections within one year. The two leaders agreed to guarantee the political rights and freedoms and personal security of all Mozambican citizens and political parties, and to accept the role of the international community, particularly the UN, in monitoring and guaranteeing the peace agreement.

THE PEACE AGREEMENT

The peace agreement, known as the Acordo Geral de Paz (AGP), was eventually signed on 4 October 1992. It provided for a general cease-fire to come into force immediately after ratification of the treaty by the Assembléia da República. Both Renamo and government forces were to withdraw to assembly points within seven days of ratification. A new 30,000-strong national defence force, the Forças Armadas de Defesa de Moçambique (FADM), would then be created, drawing on equal numbers from each side, with the remaining troops surrendering their weapons to a UN peace-keeping force within six months. A cease-fire commission, incorporating representatives from the Government, Renamo and the UN, would be established to assume responsibility for supervising the implementation of the truce regulations. In overall political control of the peace process would be the Comissão de Supervisão e Controle (CSC—Supervision and Control Commission), comprising representatives of the Government, Renamo and the UN, with responsibilities including the supervision of the Cease-fire Commission and other commissions charged with establishing the joint armed forces and reintegrating demobilized soldiers into society, as well as verifying the withdrawal of foreign troops from Mozambique. Presidential and legislative elections were to take place, under UN supervision, one year after the signing of the AGP, provided that it had been fully implemented and the demobilization process completed.

In October 1992 the UN Security Council agreed to appoint a special representative for Mozambique, and to dispatch 25 military observers. In December the UN Security Council approved a plan for the establishment of the UN Operation in Mozambique (ONUMOZ), providing for the deployment of some 7,500 troops, police and civilian observers to oversee the process of demobilization and formation of the new national armed forces, and to supervise the forthcoming elections. There were continued delays in the deployment of the peace-keeping force. Renamo, in turn, refused to begin demobilizing its forces until the UN force was in place. Renamo withdrew from the CSC and the Cease-fire Commission in March, protesting that its officials had not been provided with necessary accommodation, transport and food. The first UN troops became operational in the Beira corridor on 1 April, prompting the withdrawal of the Zimbabwean troops guarding the Beira and Limpopo corridors.

Renamo, however, continued to use demands for finance to delay the demobilization process, claiming, in late May 1993, that it needed US $100m. from the international community to transform itself into a political party. In June a meeting in Maputo of the CSC announced a formal postponement of the election date to October 1994 (one year behind the original schedule) and called for immediate action on establishing assembly points and commencing the formation of the new national armed forces. The CSC meeting was followed by a meeting of aid donors, which revealed growing impatience among the international community with the repeated delays in implementing the peace agreement and with Renamo's escalating demands for funds. The meeting produced additional promises of support for the peace process, bringing the total pledged by donors to $520m., including support for the repatriation of 1.5m. refugees from neighbouring countries, the resettlement of 4m.–5m. displaced people and the reintegration of some 80,000 former combatants into civilian life, as well as for emergency relief and reconstruction. The UN also agreed to establish a trust fund of $10m. to finance Renamo's transformation into a political party.

In September 1993, following direct talks between Chissano and Dhlakama, an agreement was signed, whereby Renamo was to appoint three advisers to each of the incumbent provincial governors to advise on all issues relating to the reintegration of areas under Renamo control into a single state administration. It was also agreed that the UN be requested to provide a police corps to supervise the activities of the national police and ensure neutrality in areas under Renamo control. In response, the UN Security Council authorized the deployment of 1,144 police observers.

In addition, an agreement was signed at a meeting of the CSC in November 1993, which provided for the confinement of troops to begin at the end of that month, and in January 1994 540 military instructors (comprising government and Renamo troops who had been trained by British instructors in Zimbabwe) arrived in Mozambique to begin training the FADM. However, only a fraction of the originally planned numbers was eventually trained. In March, in an effort to expedite the confinement process, the Government announced its decision to begin the unilateral demobilization of its troops. Renamo responded by beginning the demobilization of its troops. In April Lt-Gen. Lagos Lidimo, the nominee of the Government, and the former Renamo guerrilla commander, Lt-Gen. Mateus Ngonhamo, were inaugurated as the high command of the FADM. The demobilization processes continued to make slow progress, however, and the deadline for troop confinement was continuously extended. On 16 August, in accordance with the provisions of the AGP, the government Forças Armadas de Moçambique were formally dissolved and their functions transferred to the FADM.

In October 1993 the CSC approved a new timetable covering all aspects of the peace process, including the elections in October 1994, and in November consensus was finally reached on the text of the electoral law. The Comissão Nacional de Eleições (CNE—National Elections Commission) was inaugurated in early February 1994. It included 10 members from the Government, seven from Renamo, three from the other opposition parties and an independent chairperson. In April 1994 Chissano issued a decree establishing the date of the general election as 27–28 October. Voter registration for the elections took place in mid-1994, with the total potential electorate estimated at some 7.9m. people. In August Renamo formally registered as a political party. In the same month three other opposition parties formed an electoral coalition, the União Democrática (UD).

THE 1994 ELECTIONS

Presidential and legislative elections were held on 27–28 October 1994. Hours before the beginning of the poll Renamo withdrew, claiming that conditions were not conducive to free and fair elections. Following intense international pressure, Renamo abandoned its boycott in the early hours of 28 October, necessitating the extension of the voting by a day. The official election results were issued by the CNE on 19 November. In the presidential election Chissano secured an outright majority (53.3%) of the votes, thus avoiding the need for a second round of voting. His closest rival was Dhlakama, who received 33.7% of the votes. In the legislative election Frelimo also secured an overall majority, winning 129 of the 250 seats, while Renamo obtained 112 and the UD the remaining nine seats. The level of participation by the electorate was considerable, with some 80% of all registered voters exercising their right to vote. The UN recognized the occurrence of irregularities, but asserted that these were insufficient to have affected the overall credibility of the poll, which it declared to have been free and fair.

In December 1994 the Cease-fire Commission issued its final report, according to which ONUMOZ had registered a combined total of 91,691 government and Renamo troops during the confinement process, of whom 11,579 had enlisted in the FADM (compared with the 30,000 envisaged in the AGP). In practice, demobilization had continued until 15 September, with special cases still being processed the day before the elections. Furthermore, an estimated 3m. internally displaced Mozambicans had been successfully resettled since the signing of the AGP, according to the office of the United Nations High Commissioner for Refugees (UNHCR). In May 1995 UNHCR also reported that a total of 1.7m. refugees had returned to Mozambique from six southern African countries. Expenditure on the repatriation process then totalled some US $152m. In November the process was reported to have been completed.

Chissano was inaugurated as President on 9 December 1994, and the new Government was sworn in on 23 December. All the portfolios were assigned to members of Frelimo. At the second national conference of opposition parties, held in May 1995 in Inhambane province, an extra-parliamentary forum was established through which parties without representation in the legislature intended to convey their concerns to the executive and legislative bodies.

In February 1996 the Government proposed that municipal elections, which the Constitution stipulated must be conducted no later than October 1996, be held in 1997. Delays had resulted from a dispute between the Government and the opposition regarding the scope of the elections: the opposition demanded simultaneous local elections throughout Mozambique, while the Government sought to hold elections only in those areas that had attained municipal status, which would have excluded almost 60% of the population. In October 1996 the Assembléia da República approved a constitutional amendment differentiating between municipalities (including 23 cities and 116 other district capitals) and administrative posts (numbering 394). Each of these units would have its own elected council and mayor.

In June 1997 the Government announced that the municipal elections would be conducted in December. However, the elections were further postponed, owing to delays in the disbursement by international donors of funding for the voter registration process. In January 1998 Renamo claimed that the registration process had been fraudulent, although the CNE claimed that errors had only affected a minor percentage of the electorate. In April Renamo and 15 other opposition parties officially announced their withdrawal from the elections, and Renamo subsequently began a vigorous campaign to dissuade the electorate from voting. In the event, very few opposition parties contested the elections, which took place on 30 June, and Frelimo's main opposition came from independent candidates. Frelimo secured all the mayoral posts and took control of all the municipal authorities contested. However, the rate of voter participation was just 14.6%.

In October 1998 the Government published draft constitutional amendments that envisaged substantial changes to the country's political system, including a reduction in presidential powers and a concomitant increase in those of the Prime Minister, as well as the separation of the jurisdictions of central government and local administration. The amendments would confer the status of Head of Government on the Prime Minister, transferring this from the President—who would remain Head of State. The President would no longer be able to appoint the Prime Minister without first consulting the Assembléia da República, and would dismiss and appoint ministers only on the proposal of the Prime Minister. In addition, a Council of State would be formed as a consultative body to advise the President. The underlying aim of the proposed changes was to make provision for a situation in which a President and government could be drawn from different parties.

THE 1999 ELECTIONS

Under the Constitution, the five-year term of the President and the Assembléia was to end in November 1999. However, political disputes and administrative delays made it increasingly unlikely that elections would be held in that year. The delay was caused by Renamo's insistence on the need to re-register the entire electorate and by the late appointment of the CNE. In May the Government announced that voter registration would take place between July and September, thus allowing for elections to take place in November, but Renamo protested that a longer period would be necessary in order to ensure that the majority of the population would be able to register in time. In June Frelimo announced that Chissano would stand as its presidential candidate. In the following month 11 opposition parties, led by Renamo, signed an agreement to contest the forthcoming elections as a coalition, styled Renamo—União Eleitoral (Renamo—UE), presenting a single list of legislative candidates, with Dhlakama as its presidential candidate.

Presidential and legislative elections took place on 3–5 December 1999. In the presidential contest Chissano defeated Dhlakama (his sole challenger), taking 52.3% of the valid votes cast. Frelimo increased its outright majority in the legislative elections, winning 133 of the 250 seats in the Assembléia da República; Renamo—UE obtained the remaining seats. International monitors declared the elections to have been free and fair. In January 2000, following the Supreme Court's rejection of an appeal by Renamo against the results of the elections, Dhlakama publicly accused the judges of being manipulated by Frelimo. On 15 January Chissano was sworn in for a further five-year presidential term and subsequently effected a substantial reshuffle of the Council of Ministers. However, Renamo continued to dispute the legitimacy of the newly elected Government.

In February 2000 Mozambique suffered massive flooding in southern and central areas, following the heaviest rainfall recorded in the country for some 50 years. Large sections of the country's transport infrastructure were destroyed, and many villages were washed away. The catastrophe left an estimated 2m. people seriously affected by the flooding, of whom some 1m. were in need of assistance and 500,000 were reported to have been displaced. The number of confirmed deaths was put at 699.

In May 2000 an attack on a police station in the northern province of Nampula, in which five people were killed, was believed to have been carried out by members of Renamo. At the same time, Dhlakama threatened to regroup demobilized Renamo soldiers and seize control of the country. Tensions worsened in November, when more than 100 people died in riots in the northern parts of the country. While 41 people were killed in the riots themselves, more than 83 died after being arrested and detained in an overcrowded jail in Montepuez, Cabo Delgado. A parliamentary inquiry, dominated by Frelimo, eventually blamed Renamo for the riots. In January 2002 several Renamo members were found guilty of armed rebellion, but the human rights organization Amnesty International criticized the judicial process for lacking transparency.

The riots brought an abrupt end to the negotiations that had been taking place between Chissano and Renamo since June 2000. Renamo had announced in July that it was to boycott the election of the new CNE, while denouncing the appointment of new provincial governors, all of whom were Frelimo appointees, on the grounds that it did not recognize the Government's legitimacy. In late December Dhlakama and Chissano held talks in an attempt to resolve the growing political tension between their two parties. Dhlakama stated that he was prepared to accept the results of the 1999 elections, and Chissano pledged to discuss the appointment of Renamo governors in the provinces where the latter had won a majority of the votes. Negotiations resumed in January 2001. Chissano rejected Dhlakama's demand for an early election and the appointment of Renamo governors. Moreover, at another meeting in March Chissano referred the latter issue to the Assembléia da República, whose Frelimo representatives were strongly opposed to accommodating Renamo demands. Consequently, in protest, Dhlakama ceased negotiations in April.

At the Renamo party congress held in October–November 2001 Dhlakama was re-elected as party President, while the party's representative in Portugal, Joaquim Vaz, was elected as the new Secretary-General. Vaz subsequently attempted to promote greater internal transparency and proposed policies that were less obstructive than those that led to confrontation with Frelimo. However, in July 2002 Dhlakama announced the dismissal of Vaz and the dissolution of the party's national political commission, assuming the position of Secretary-General himself.

President Joaquim Chissano announced in May 2001 that he would not stand for re-election on the expiry of his term in 2004, although he would remain President of Frelimo after the presidential election. The announcement formally opened the succession battle between conservatives, who held the upper hand in the party, and modernizers, who were dominant in the Government. The latter had the apparent support of Chissano, who was also keen to open the leadership to a successor from the central or northern regions. At the eighth party congress, held in mid-June 2002, Armando Guebuza was elected as Frelimo's new Secretary-General, thereby becoming Frelimo's presidential candidate for the 2004 election.

Frelimo was weakened in 2002–03 by the revelations that emerged during the trial of those accused of involvement in the murder, in November 2000, of Carlos Cardoso, the editor of an influential journal, *Metical*. Cardoso had been investigating a major corruption scandal at the Banco Comercial de Moçambique, dating back to 1996. In January 2003 six people were sentenced to prison terms exceeding 20 years for their roles in the incident. The leader of the group that assassinated Cardoso, Aníbal dos Santos, had escaped from custody in September 2002 and was tried *in absentia*; his escape was widely considered to have been orchestrated to prevent him from testifying. He was, however, recaptured by South African police in January 2003 and extradited to Mozambique. The trial of seven prison officers implicated in his escape began in August but collapsed one month later when the judge ruled that they were low-level figures taking the blame for the escape, which had been ordered by senior figures, among them the Minister of the Interior, Almerino da Cruz Marcos Manhenje. Dos Santos escaped again in May 2004 and was subsequently arrested in Canada. In January 2005 he was extradited from Canada to Mozambique, and the following month the Supreme Court ordered a retrial of his case. In January 2006 dos Santos was again found guilty by a Mozambican court and sentenced to 30 years in gaol.

On 19 November 2003, following a postponement of one month owing to administrative and logistical delays, municipal elections were held in 33 of Mozambique's cities and towns. The governing party, Frelimo, was the outright victor, winning a majority on 29 of the 33 municipal councils, and the mayorship in 28 municipalities. Renamo, which had boycotted Mozambique's first municipal elections in 1998, gained control of five urban centres, including the third largest city, Beira, but failed to win a majority on the councils located in its northern and central heartlands. Accusations of electoral fraud were inevitably made by Renamo, in particular in Beira where electoral officials allegedly altered results in favour of Frelimo; however, in January 2004 the Constitutional Council formally ruled that the elections had been free and fair, and upheld the results. In the wake of the elections all political parties began campaigning in earnest for the legislative and presidential elections due to take place in December 2004.

In February 2004 Pascoal Mocumbi, who had been Prime Minister since 1994, resigned his post to take up an international appointment. In his place Luísa Dias Diogo was appointed as Mozambique's first female Prime Minister, combining the role with her existing finance portfolio.

THE 2004 ELECTIONS

The legislative and presidential elections, which were held on 1–2 December 2004, were the most controversial since multiparty democracy was established in 1994, and Frelimo was accused of widespread electoral fraud. Voter turnout was a record low of 36.3%, reflecting disillusionment with and apathy towards the political system among the population. The results, which were announced on 21 December 2004 by the CNE, handed Frelimo a decisive victory, and were in sharp contrast to the closely fought 1999 elections. Guebuza won 63.7% of the votes in the presidential election and Frelimo took 62.0% in the parliamentary election, while Renamo managed just 29.7% of the votes in the parliamentary election, and Afonso Dhlakhama secured 31.7% of the presidential votes. The smaller parties failed to reach the threshold of 5% of votes and did not gain any seats in the Assembléia da República. Although international observers subsequently endorsed the election results as 'generally free', there were widespread accusations of irregularities, fraud and intimidation of opposition parties during the elections, and both the European Union and the US Carter Center expressed concerns over the results.

Despite the controversy, on 17 January 2005 the Constitutional Council validated the results, and on 2 February Armando Guebuza was sworn in as Mozambique's new President in a ceremony that was boycotted by Renamo. On the same day Joaquim Chissano formally stood down as President after 18 years in power, and one month later he also relinquished his role as President of Frelimo.

THE GUEBUZA PRESIDENCY

Following his inauguration in February 2005, Guebuza unveiled a new Council of Ministers, replacing 18 of the 22 members of the previous Government. Diogo retained the post of Prime Minister, but relinquished the role as Minister of Finance to her deputy, Manuel Chang. Other new appointments included Alcinda Abreu, previously the head of Frelimo's youth organization, as the Minister of Foreign Affairs and Co-operation and José Pacheco as Minister of the Interior. The most significant change came at the Ministry of Planning and Finance which was divided into two ministries, with the new Ministry of Development and Planning, headed by Aiuba Cuereneia, taking on the development functions previously held by the Ministry of Agriculture and Rural Development. However, donors expressed concerns about the changes, which they feared could weaken the management of the economy, and there was criticism that many of the new government appointees lacked the experience of their predecessors. Guebuza identified as the priorities of his presidency an overhaul of the justice system and a campaign against corruption in the police force. He also pledged that his Government would focus strongly on measures to reduce poverty.

In May 2005 controversy over the transparency of the electoral process was reignited when Frelimo's candidate in the mayoral by-election for the northern city of Mocímboa da Praia, Amadeu Pedro, defeated his Renamo rival, Saide Assane, by only 602 votes. An investigation by the CNE revealed an unusually high proportion of invalid votes, which Renamo claimed was the decisive factor in Pedro's victory. However, the CNE subsequently validated the poll, precipitating protests in Mocímboa da Praia in September, and prompting Assane to hold a mock swearing-in ceremony in the city centre, which was dispersed by the security forces. In ensuing clashes at least eight Renamo supporters were killed and 47 others were injured, after which the army intervened to restore order. In an effort to restore faith in the electoral process, Frelimo proposed amending the system for appointing members to the CNE, reducing the allocation of political parties to the body to one-third, with the remaining two-thirds to be split between appointees from the Government, the judiciary and civil society. However, given Frelimo's strong influence in Government and over the judiciary, the changes were not expected to have any significant effect.

As part of efforts to make the Government more responsive to divergent views and to promote national unity, on 23 December 2005 President Guebuza swore into office the Council of State, a consultative body the creation of which had been authorized by the Assembléia da República in November. In late December, during his New Year's address to the nation, Guebuza pledged to refocus his Government's energies on reducing poverty, improving justice and policing, and combating corruption. He was expected to be supported in this endeavour by Cuereneia, who quickly emerged as the most influential figure in Guebuza's Council of Ministers. In February 2006 Renamo announced that it would hold its party congress in November—only its second since the end of the civil war in 1992—during which it would elect a new leader. In the same month, Dhlakama announced that he would seek re-election as party leader and as Renamo's candidate in the presidential election scheduled for 2009. Dhlakama's announcement provoked disappointment among reformist elements in Renamo, however, who sought a clean break with the previous leadership. In a related development, Frelimo voted to bring forward its own party congress, originally scheduled to take place in 2007, to 2006, in order to reorganize the party prior to provincial assembly elections in 2007.

In May 2006 Nyimpine Chissano, the son of the former President, Joachim Chissano, was charged with involvement in the murder of Carlos Cardoso in 2000 (see above), following years of allegations in the Mozambican press that he had been the assassination's paymaster. However, it remained unclear in mid-2007 whether the case would go to trial, or whether dos Santos would testify against Chissano.

In June 2006 the South African President, Thabo Mbeki, visited Mozambique at the head of a delegation including six cabinet ministers, to discuss improving co-operation in investment, trade, transport and tourism. That same month Frelimo announced that it would hold its ninth party congress in Quelimane, the capital of Zambézia province, from 10–14 November, with the goal of electing a new central committee and debating the party's political strategy for the upcoming provincial, municipal and national elections. In late September Frelimo held district conferences to elect delegates who would attend the congress. Angered by Frelimo's choice to hold its congress in Quelimane, as the area is a Renamo stronghold, Renamo announced that it would hold a special conference of war veterans in Quelimane shortly before Frelimo's congress. However, Renamo was forced to postpone its own party congress, which had been due to take place in late 2006 in Nampula province, until 2007. The party was expected to use the congress to address rising internal divisions and draw up a strategy for the elections in 2007–09. In November 2006 Frelimo's party congress went ahead as planned in Quelimane, unanimously re-electing Guebuza as President and further consolidating his control over the party. Guebuza did, however, cede the party's secretary-generalship to the Governor of Nampula province, Filipe Paúnde. The congress also elected a new and enlarged political commission which included five new members, notably the Minister of Development and Planning, Aiuba Cuereneia, and the Minister of Education and Culture, Aires Bonifácio Ali. A new central committee, which was expanded from 160 to 180 members, was also elected, with the remit to meet twice per year to discuss party matters.

In late November 2006 the Assembléia da República passed legislation creating directly-elected provincial assemblies, a demand which had been pursued by Renamo since negotiations on constitutional changes started in 2004. The new law established ten provincial assemblies, each with a minimum of 50 elected members, which were to have responsibility for approving and monitoring provincial governments' official programmes. On 20 December the Assembléia da República passed three revised electoral laws: on the composition of the CNE, voter registration and electoral procedures. The new legislation reduced the CNE's membership from 18 to 13 members, five of whom were to be parliamentary deputies, with the remaining eight coming from civil society, subject to approval by the legislature. A key change in the electoral code was the removal of the 5% threshold required for parties to win seats in the Assembléia; this was expected to benefit the many small parties that failed to gain seats in previous elections. In January 2007 the Government announced plans to appoint a civil service representative to oversee Mozambique's 33 municipal governments, a measure criticized by the opposition, which accused the Government of trying to recentralize authority in Maputo.

In February 2007 the Chinese President, Hu Jintao, made his first official visit to Mozambique as part of a ten-day tour of Africa. The visit followed Guebuza's attendance at the Forum on China-Africa Co-operation in Beijing in November 2006, during which several co-operation agreements were signed. During Hu's visit new agreements worth US $234m. were signed, including a $20m. debt cancellation arrangement, a $40m. loan for infrastructure development, and a $195m. interest-free loan for projects in the agriculture, health and education sectors.

During the first three months of 2007 over 400,000 Mozambicans were affected by heavy flooding in central Mozambique and a cyclone in Inhambane and Sofala provinces. Heavy rains in January resulted in extensive flooding in the Zambeze Valley, causing 45 deaths and the evacuation of 163,000 people from low-lying areas. In late February Cyclone Flavio struck the northern coast of Inhambane province, causing 10 deaths, 70 injuries and widespread damage to Vilanculos, forcing a further 150,000 people to flee their homes. The country's national relief agency, Instituto Nacional de Gestão de Calamidades, housed 140,000 displaced people in emergency camps, and in June it launched food-for-work programmes across the country. A total of US $10.8m. was disbursed in emergency relief by Mozambique's donors, and the Government appealed internationally for a further $71m. to fund the rebuilding of public infrastructure.

After months of bitter wrangling between Frelimo and Renamo, in mid-March 2007 the Assembléia da República passed legislation relating to the election of provincial assemblies. One week later, legislation was also adopted governing municipal elections, which were due to be held in 2008. The main change to the code was the provision that voters could still vote if they lost their voting card, provided that their name appeared on the register and that they produced photographic identification.

In late March 2007 the suburb of Malhazine in the capital was severely damaged by a series of explosions at a military arsenal which fired rockets and artillery shells into surrounding residential areas. At least 105 people were killed and more than 500 treated for injuries, while around 1,000 homes were severely damaged or destroyed. The explosions provoked angry demonstrations against the military and the Minister of Defence, Tobias Dai. In response, the Government set up a commission of inquiry which reported in April that the disaster had been caused by several factors, including obsolete explosives, poor storage conditions and human error. The Government promised to compensate the victims of the blasts and to rebuild damaged or destroyed houses, and in late March it launched a programme to relocate 17 army arsenals away from urban areas.

Meanwhile, in late February 2007 Guebuza dismissed the Minister of Agriculture, Tomás Mandlate, and replaced him with Erasmo Muhate, the former head of Mozambique's cotton institute, the Instituto do Algodão de Moçambique. The new minister promised to give greater support to commercially-marketed food production and to smallholders.

In early May 2007 the CNE's five parliamentary members were appointed by the Assembléia da República, three from Frelimo and two from Renamo, and in mid-June Guebuza swore into office the eight other members from civil society. The same month Guebuza issued a presidential decree confirming that the country's first provincial elections would take place on 20 December. According to the Constitution, the elections had to take place before February 2008. However, there were widespread concerns that the CNE would not be able to arrange the elections in time, especially as the rainy season was due to start in October and last until March 2008, greatly hampering voting in the country's many remote rural communities. It was also unclear whether the Government had sufficient resources to fund the estimated US $45m. cost of holding the election.

Economy

JOÃO GOMES CRAVINHO

Revised by EDWARD GEORGE

INTRODUCTION

Mozambique's post-independence economy has suffered the damaging effects of a guerrilla war, drought, floods, famine, the displacement of population and a severe scarcity of skilled workers and foreign exchange. These difficulties have been compounded by a large visible trade deficit, with export earnings covering less than one-third of import costs, and high levels of debt repayments. As a result, Mozambique has remained heavily reliant on foreign credits. In recent years, however, substantial debt relief has reduced servicing to a more sustainable level, while exports have increased sharply. Following the signing of the Nkomati Accord with South Africa in March 1984 (see Recent History), the USA lifted its ban on aid to Mozambique. In the same year Mozambique acceded to the third Lomé Convention, thus becoming eligible for assistance from the European Community (now the European Union—EU), and also became a member of the IMF and of the World Bank.

In January 1987 the Government initiated an economic recovery programme (Programa de Reabilitação Econômica—PRE), which was supported by the IMF, and which aimed to increase economic efficiency and to reduce internal and external deficits by a 'liberalization' of the economy. Signs of economic recovery began to emerge with real growth in gross domestic product (GDP) averaging 5.4% per year in 1987–89. Economic growth averaged only 0.8% per year in 1990–92, owing to drought, the effects of the war on production and reduced foreign support. With an end to the drought and prospects for sustained peace after 1993, the Mozambican economy became one of the fastest growing in the world, with annual real GDP growth averaging 8.3% in 1997–2006, according to estimates by the World Bank. GDP growth slowed to an estimated 1.9% in 2000, as a result of massive flooding in the early part of that year. However, real GDP growth rebounded to 13.1% in 2001, the highest increase ever recorded, and averaged 8.2% in 2002, 7.8% in 2003, 7.2% in 2004, 7.5% in 2005 and an estimated 7.9% in 2006. In 2006 Mozambique's gross national income (GNI), was estimated by the World Bank at US $6,294m., equivalent to $310 per head (or $1,160 on an international purchasing-power parity basis).

With the impact of economic reforms after 1987, the average annual rate of inflation fell from 160.0% in 1987 to 35.2% in 1991. During 1993–96 it averaged 26.5% per year, before declining to some 4.2% during 1997–99. However, owing partly to economic disruption caused by flooding, the average rate of inflation has been uneven since 2000, when it increased to 12.7%. In 2001 it fell to 9.1% before accelerating again to 16.8% in 2002. Thereafter inflation declined, falling to 7.2% by 2005, aided by the strengthening of the currency—the metical—against the US dollar, strong monetary discipline and lower food prices. However, after an inflationary spike in late 2005 and early 2006, caused by seasonal price increases and higher fuel import costs, the overall rate of inflation rose again in 2006, averaging 13.2% for the year.

The implementation of the PRE in 1987 also began with two substantial devaluations of the metical, from US $1 = 40 meticais in January 1987 to $1 = 400 meticais in June of that year. Subsequent devaluations brought the official exchange rate to $1 = 11,300 meticais by December 1996; the currency then depreciated more slowly to $1 = 13,200 meticais in December 1999. As a result, there was a marked appreciation of the metical against the currencies of its major trading partners, in particular the South African rand. Owing to floods, the exchange rate fell to $1 = 23,700 meticais in June 2002. The downward trend has been encouraged by the central bank, following concerns that the strength of the metical in 1997–99 had a negative impact on the country's export performance, although in late 2004 the central bank was suspected of having intervened to sustain the value of the currency. After June 2002 the metical began to stabilize, strengthening considerably against both the rand and the US dollar in 2004, to average $1 = 22,581 meticais. However, the introduction of a new foreign-exchange auction system in early 2005 led to sharp periods of volatility, particularly in late 2005, which forced the central bank to introduce a temporary trading band. This helped stabilize the metical, which depreciated in real terms against the US dollar by only 0.3% during 2006. On 1 July 2006 the currency was once again devalued, with one new currency unit becoming equivalent to 1,000 of the former units. Most old currency was withdrawn from circulation by the end of 2006, but old notes were to be accepted at banks until the end of 2007 and at the central bank until the end of 2012. At 3 July 2007 the currency stood at $1 = 25.7 meticais.

ECONOMIC POLICY

Major components of the PRE included fiscal measures to reduce the budget deficit, which included an increase in income taxes, a reduction in government wage costs and subsidies, as well as monetary measures, including the maintenance of stringent control on the rate of credit growth and the increased linkage of wages to productivity. Other measures under the programme included a deregulation of some prices previously controlled by the Government, the stimulation of the private sector in industry and agriculture, the focusing of resources on activities of import-substitution or those yielding a high level of value added, the stimulation of exports, and a review of procedures for the allocation of foreign exchange. Price rises were duly introduced in 1988, during the second phase of the PRE.

In March 1992 the Government unveiled a three-year plan for significant cuts in public expenditure, which provided for reductions in investment in agriculture, mining and manufacturing, accompanied by a programme of privatizations in these areas. Plans to sell a number of major state-owned enterprises were announced in early 1992 and a new investment code was approved by the legislature in 1993, providing identical fiscal and customs benefits to both local and foreign investors. By the end of 1999 over 1,000 state-owned enterprises had been privatized in what was considered to be one of the world's most successful privatization programmes.

In 1993 the Government introduced a national reconstruction plan to account for post-war reconstruction needs. Donors pledged a total of US $3,334m. over the next four years. Following the floods in February 2000, in March the IMF authorized the release of $50m. under the Poverty Reduction and Growth Facility (PRGF); in June international aid donors pledged an estimated $530m. for 2000. A further $560m. was pledged for 2001. In June 2002 the IMF authorized the release of a further tranche worth $11m., noting that Mozambique had resumed rapid rates of growth, which had been interrupted by the floods of 2000, and that most performance benchmarks under the PRGF had been met.

In June 2003 the IMF completed its review of Mozambique's performance under the PRGF and approved the drawing of a further US $11.8m. from the total fund of $122.9m. In November the IMF completed its Article IV consultations with the Government, concluding that it had achieved higher than expected economic growth, had met the agreed macroeconomic benchmarks and had made satisfactory progress in implementing the policies and measures of its Poverty Reduction Strategy Paper (PRSP). In July 2004 the Government concluded its PRSP with the IMF. The PRSP's main objectives were to ensure macroeconomic stability, maintain high and sustainable rates of poverty-reducing growth and improve social services. That month the IMF approved a new PRGF programme for 2004–06 worth $17.1m. In February 2005 the IMF confirmed that the country could draw its first $2.4m.

tranche of the PRGF, and commended Mozambique's strong economic performance in 2004.

In June 2005 the IMF completed its second PRGF review, giving a broadly positive assessment of Mozambique's economic performance and releasing a further US $2.4m. However, the IMF urged the Government to improve revenue collection and to press ahead with a second wave of structural reforms to improve the adverse business environment and boost private-sector employment. In December the IMF completed its third PRGF review, commending the Government for maintaining macroeconomic stability and strong economic growth, despite high petroleum prices and drought, and released a further $2.3m. In April 2006 an IMF team reported stronger GDP growth than expected in 2005, estimated at 7.5%, and the lowest inflation rate in a decade, of 6.5%. Although tax collection improved strongly, the IMF urged more progress with structural reforms to the judiciary, civil service and business environment. During the talks the Government discussed moving to a new programme, the Policy Support Instrument (PSI), on the completion of the PRGF in July 2007. A PSI would guarantee Mozambique advice, monitoring and policy endorsement from the IMF, but not its financial assistance, which would be provided by donors. In June 2006 the fourth PRGF review was completed, releasing a further $2.4m., and the IMF praised the Government's improved revenue collection. In the same month the Government launched a new four-year poverty reduction strategy, the Plano de Acção para a Redução da Pobreza Absoluta (PARPA II), covering 2006–09. PARPA II's overall target was to reduce poverty from 54% of the population in 2003 to 45% by 2009, through improving governance, investing in human capital and supporting private-sector growth.

In January 2007 the IMF completed its fifth PRGF review, judging that policy performance had been positive and that the economy was becoming increasingly diversified, with growth across all sectors. The Fund reported that revenue collection was equivalent to 0.4% of GDP above target, whereas spending was as programmed, leading to a lower domestic deficit. In June the IMF completed its sixth and final PRGF review, releasing a final US $2.4m, and praising the Government for its strong performance over the three years of the arrangement. The Fund awarded a three-year PSI, which was aimed at maintaining macroeconomic stability as foreign aid was scaled up, implementing a second wave of economic and structural reforms and continuing implementation of the poverty reduction programme outlined in PARPA II.

Government finances improved considerably in the years following the signing of the Acordo Geral de Paz (AGP—General Peace Agreement) in 1992, owing to improvements in economic opportunities and performance, favourable weather conditions (except in 2000) and reduced expenditure on defence and security. The 2004 budget focused on establishing greater transparency in government expenditure and accountability in order to enable donors to channel more funding directly into government spending programmes. With donor help the Government set up a Performance Assessment Framework to monitor prioritized spending on social sectors and the implementation of policy reforms. The Government boosted spending substantially in 2005 and 2006, in particular on public-sector wages and priority social sectors, the bulk of which was financed by donor inflows. In December 2006 the Assembléia da República approved the 2007 budget, which was also highly expansionary, with large increases in revenue and expenditure. Total revenue was forecast to rise by 17.2%, to 31,300m. meticais (US $1,300m.), and expenditure by 31.4%, to 66,100m. meticais, increasing the domestic primary balance from 4,600m. meticais in 2006 to 6,000m. meticais in 2007. In line with PARPA II, 68% of spending was to be on priority sectors, with education (22%), infrastructure (20.5%) and health (12.4%) receiving the next largest allocations. The large rise in current expenditure reflected the recruitment of 18,000 additional public-sector workers, one-half of whom were teachers, in line with government pledges to improve education, health and police services. Mozambique's 19 main donors, which provided direct budget support as part of the Programme Aid Partnership (PAP), pledged $369m. for the 2007 budget and $385.8m. for the 2008 budget.

The Government pursued further reforms, having already introduced value-added tax in June 1999, as a condition to the implementation of debt reduction under the IMF and World Bank's initiative for heavily indebted poor countries (HIPC). In November 2001 the Assembléia da República approved legislation prohibiting the process of 'money laundering' and, in April 2002, adopted legislation that aimed to overhaul the country's tax system. Further revision of income tax was announced in December 2002. These changes were expected to increase fiscal revenues, reflecting the need for greater mobilization of domestic resources at a time when Mozambique's level of aid dependency was extremely high. In December 2005 a centralized tax service, the Autoridade Tributária de Moçambique (ATM), was created, combining the tax directorate and the customs service, in an attempt to streamline tax collection and increase revenue collection. In 2007 the Government was due to complete the roll-out of an integrated payroll database for the civil service (e-SISTAFE), which was intended to improve the management of public expenditure.

AGRICULTURE

Before independence large-scale modern agriculture was mainly under Portuguese control. About 3,000 farms and plantations existed on more than 1.6m. ha, while African plots covered some 2.8m. ha. More than 80% of the total working population were engaged in agriculture. Since independence agricultural production has been adversely affected by the scarcity of skilled labour following the post-independence exodus by the Portuguese, the internal conflict which prevented nearly 3m. Mozambicans from farming the land, and drought, flooding, cyclones and insect pests, which have combined to destroy food crops in large areas of the country (notably in the south and the Zambézia region). The sector was seriously damaged by the floods of 2000, which affected an estimated 2m. people. Some 127,000 ha of crops (10% of the country's cultivated land) were destroyed, and much livestock, including more than 20,000 head of cattle, lost. The World Bank later estimated the cost of losses at between US $270m. and $430m. However, since 2000 the sector has recovered strongly, averaging annual growth estimated at 8.1% in 2001–05, which contributed to strong GDP growth during this period.

At present only 5% of arable lands are cultivated, but agriculture (including fishing) has recovered considerably from the conflict and the floods, accounting for an estimated 19.7% of Mozambique's GDP in 2005. Agricultural GDP increased by an average of 5.9% per year during 1996–2005. Before the resumption of electricity supplies to South Africa in 1998 and the start of aluminium exports in 2000, agricultural exports represented Mozambique's major source of export revenue. The major cash crops are tobacco, sugar, cotton and cashew nuts. Prawns remain the principal agricultural export earner, with revenue totalling US $91.8m. in 2004, which accounted for some 6.1% of export earnings. Maize, bananas, rice, tea, sisal and coconuts are also grown, and the main subsistence crop is cassava.

After independence the Government sought to establish communal agriculture at village level. Until 1985 the state sector accounted for one-half of marketed production, but the state farms proved to be uneconomic, and since 1983 the Government has given increased priority to improving production from small farms in the family sector. With the advent of the PRE, subsidies have been reduced, and the prices of several agricultural products have been deregulated, while private producers and traders were encouraged with higher prices.

During 1996–97 a major programme for the promotion of Mozambican agriculture, Proagri, was drawn up by the Government. The five-year programme, which aimed to increase state capacity and co-ordination in all areas of agricultural production, began in 1999 with the support of all major donors, at a total cost of US $202m. At the same time, donors strongly urged the introduction of new land legislation and made their approval of the Proagri programme conditional upon certain guarantees for peasant land-tenure rights. Existing legislation placed all land in the hands of the state. Various levels of state authority had the capacity to offer land concessions, giving rise to multiple claims for the same area of land. Moreover, the law did not adequately address matters relating to disputes over land use. In December 2003 the Ministry of Agriculture announced that the Proagri programme had fallen behind schedule and that the second phase of implementation would not begin until 2005. However, it was not until February 2007 that donors agreed to fund the second, €45m. phase of Proagri, covering 2007–09. The programme's main objectives were to help small farmers increase marketed output and diversify into high-value crops, with the goal of improving food security, to develop agro-industries and to manage better the country's natural resources.

Following the implementation of the policy of land seizures in Zimbabwe from 1998, more than 150 white Zimbabwean farmers have resettled in Mozambique's sparsely populated central province of Manica. The farmers have revived the cultivation of previously defunct crops, in particular tobacco, tea and edible oils (in particular, from sunflowers). As a result, tobacco production grew by 360% in 2001–05, earning US $41m. in export revenues in 2004. In May 2006 Mozambique Leaf Tobacco (MLT) opened a $55m. tobacco processing plant, with a capacity of 50,000 metric tons per year, in Tete; tobacco had previously been sent to Malawi for processing. In 2006 tobacco production rose by 11.8%, to 72,704 metric tons, with exports reaching a value of $37.2m. during the first six months of 2006.

Major Crops

The development of the cultivation of cashew nuts is a relatively recent occurrence. Production of cashew nuts was 204,000 metric tons in 1974. Output decreased sharply after independence and declined to 20,000 tons in 1984, owing to inefficient marketing practices by state enterprises, lack of transportation and the effects of drought. In an attempt to increase production levels, the Government doubled producer prices for the crop that year. Production increased subsequently, but fluctuated according to weather conditions. Output of cashew nuts rose from 65,500 tons in 2001 to an unusally high 105,337 tons in 2005 (as a result of exceptional climactic conditions), before falling back to 62,821 tons in 2006 owing to drought.

In 1991 the Government authorized the export of cashews in unprocessed form, mainly to India, for the first time since 1976, because of the inability of processing plants to cope with increased output. Following demands by the World Bank that the industry be privatized, in 1994–95 the Government sold the processing factories to six Mozambican trading companies for US $9m. In response to a further request by the World Bank, the Government agreed to impose an export tax of 20% for unprocessed cashew nuts, which would gradually be phased out by 2000. However, by February 1999 all but three of the country's 14 principal cashew processing plants had closed. Facing a growing demand for an outright ban on the export of unprocessed cashews, in September 1999 the Government increased the existing tax (which had declined to 14%) to between 18% and 22%. However, by the end of 2000 cashew prices had declined to just over one-half of the 1999 price, and by early April 2001 some 8,500 out of an estimated 10,000 cashew processing workers were unemployed. The decline in prices was thought principally to be the result of a collapse in the demand for cashews in India, although it has also been suggested that the liberalization of the cashew processing industry, as requested by the World Bank, had adversely affected the sector. Since 2003 there has been a revival in the cashew-processing industry with the opening of small plants using labour-intensive methods. By 2006 a total of 23 processing factories were operating in northern Mozambique, processing 33,000 tons of nuts. Two more factories were due to open in Sofala and Zambézia provinces in 2007, employing 3,000 workers and processing 4,000–5,000 tons each year.

Cotton has traditionally been the main cash crop of northern Mozambique, with more than 500,000 growers in the Cabo Delgado, Niassa, Nampula and Zambézia provinces. Nearly all cotton is cultivated by peasant producers working in concession areas where large companies have sole right of purchase. Production of seed (unginned) cotton was an estimated 107,000 metric tons in 1999, the highest level since independence. According to Mozambique's cotton institute, in 2006 production of seed cotton reached 123,000 tons, up from 78,000 tons in 2005.

Before independence, sugar was produced by large cane-growing companies. This formerly monopolistic system produced 227,800 metric tons of sugar in 1975. After independence, all the companies were nationalized and entrusted to Cuban experts. Climatic conditions, combined with production difficulties, reduced raw sugar production to 17,000 tons by 1986. Production has increased dramatically since the peace agreement, from 234,000 tons in 1994 to 517,560 tons in 2005. In June 1999 the Maragra sugar company, near Maputo, which had been purchased in 1996 by Illovo Sugar of South Africa, reopened. However, in February 2000 the mill, as well as its adjoining plantation, were affected by the floods, destroying a substantial portion of the investment. In the aftermath of the flooding, Illovo Sugar, Tongaat-Hulett and a consortium of Mauritian investors committed US $300m. for four sugar refineries at Maragra, Xinavane, Mafambisse and Marromeu, turning Mozambique into a net sugar exporter in 2002. In November 2004 Illovo Sugar agreed to purchase the abandoned Buzi plantation, south-west of Beira, for $1.2m. The plantation was the last sugar company in state hands, and Illovo was carrying out feasibility studies with a view to resuming production in 2009. In 2006 a French agro-industrial group, Tereos, purchased a 50% stake in Mozambique's largest sugar refinery, Sena Sugar, pledging to invest $30m. in the sugar sector. In June 2007 the South African sugar company, Tongaat-Hulett, announced that it would invest $177m. in expanding production at its sugar factories in Xinavane and Mafambisse, with the aim of raising production from 124,000 tons to 296,000 tons. In 2007 the director of the agriculture promotion centre (CEPAGRI), Roberto Albino, announced that the Government would invest $250m. in the sugar sector over the next seven years, with the aim of improving productivity and competition in the sector.

The Zambézia hills and mountains, close to the Malawi border, are the main producing area for tea. The principal markets for Mozambican tea are the United Kingdom and the USA. The country produced 18,800 metric tons of made tea in 1973, but output fell to an estimated 1,500 tons in 1988. Production was estimated at 10,500 tons in 2005. Copra is produced mainly on immense coconut plantations on the coastal belt of the Zambézia and Nampula provinces. It is also a popular crop among Mozambicans who use the oil and other copra products in daily life. In 1972 copra exports totalled 44,000 metric tons. Production levels declined to 5,200 tons in 1989, owing largely to a fall in prices. Since then output has increased significantly, reaching an estimated 75,000 tons in 2005. About 120,000 tons of rice were produced in the irrigated lowlands in 1974, falling to an estimated 33,300 tons in 1992. In the late 1990s significant efforts were made to rehabilitate the vast rice fields between Massingir and Chokwe, in the Limpopo valley, and by 1999 production had risen to 186,000 tons. However, the rice fields were almost entirely destroyed by the floods in early 2000, although production fell less dramatically, to 151,000 tons. The rice harvest has steadily risen since then, reaching 174,000 tons in 2005 and an estimated 183,000 tons in 2006. Oil seeds, such as sesame and sunflower, and, above all, groundnuts (production of which was estimated at 146,000 metric tons in 2006) are exported in limited quantities to Portugal. The processing of vegetable oils produced 87,500 tons in 2005. Bananas (production estimated at 90,000 tons in 2005) and citrus fruits (estimated at 115,000 tons) are exported, as well as potatoes (estimated at 80,000 tons) and kenaf (a jute-like fibre—production estimated at 3,300 tons in 2005).

Mozambique has to import fresh and prepared meat. Livestock is still of secondary importance, owing partly to the prevalence of the tsetse fly over about two-thirds of the country. Most of the cattle are raised south of the Save river, notably in Gaza province, which has about 500,000 head. There were an estimated 1.32m. head of cattle, 125,000 sheep, 392,000 goats and 180,000 pigs in 2005.

Mozambique has 19m. hectares of productive forest and, according to government estimates, can annually produce 500,000 cubic metres of logs. Forestry has developed chiefly along the Beira railway and in the wetter Zambézia province. Some eucalyptus plantations have been established in the south of the country to produce wood for paper; in July 2006 work began on two plantation projects in Niassa province, worth US $80m., which will plant 210,000 ha with eucalyptus and pines—local government forecast that $100m.–$150m. would be invested in the forestry sector over the next decade. The majority of exports are sawn timber and construction timber, with South Africa being the principal market. However, the forestry sector is affected by widespread corruption, with numerous small companies, including Chinese ones, felling hardwood trees indiscriminately, particularly in the central provinces of Zambézia, Manica and Sofala. Between 2002 and 2006 commercial logging production averaged 135,000 cu m per year, although the figure may be much higher as a result of the increase in unregulated logging. In 2002 the Government banned the export of unprocessed logs, which led to growth in the number of sawmills, from 139 in 2000 to 178 in 2005, increasing annual production of sawn wood, from 28,121 cu m in 2004 to 40,000 cu m in 2006.

Fishing is a relatively recent development along Mozambique's extensive coastline. Shrimp and prawn exports totalled 19,500 metric tons in 2002, a 40% increase on 2001. However, the collapse in the international price for prawns meant that export revenue declined, dropping from US $138.3m. in 2000 to $91.8m. in 2004. In 2005 the total catch was estimated at 43,751 tons (of which 6,135 tons was shrimp). Although Mozambique is still not self-sufficient in fish, domestic catches cover about 34% of consumption at present, compared with 6% in 1979. The potential annual catch is estimated at 500,000 tons of fish and 14,000 tons of shrimp. The country has potential to develop aquaculture, and from 1998 a French company invested €30m. in a shrimp-farming project at Quelimane where it planned to harvest 1,500 tons of shrimp per year by 2007. A Chinese company, WIETC, invested more than €10m. in aquaculture in Beira, producing 450 tons of prawns per year. In December 2006 Mozambique signed a five-year fishing agreement with the EU, which came into effect on 1 January 2007. In exchange for an annual payment of €1.2m., the EU was granted a 10,000-ton quota for tuna and other species, excluding deep-water prawns, which had been included in previous agreements.

Food Shortages and Security

In 2002 Mozambique experienced a serious drought, and it was estimated that 500,000 people would require food aid. Although total production of cereals in 2001/02 was estimated at 1.8m. metric tons, (an increase on the 1.7m. tons produced in 2000/01), surpluses from the north and centre of the country traditionally reached the areas in deficit in the south at greatly inflated prices, owing to high transport costs, making it more cost-effective to import maize from South Africa and to export surpluses to Tanzania and Malawi. As a result, total cereal import requirements were estimated at 642,000 tons for 2002. Rehabilitation of the commercial networks that link the areas with surplus maize to neighbouring countries and to the ports of Nacala and Beira was an urgent requirement. In 2003 cumulative rainfall in the Maputo area was the lowest in 50 years, and 156,000 tons of emergency food aid was required to feed an estimated 949,000 people. Total cereal import requirements in 2003 were estimated at 744,000 tons, in addition to 90,000 tons of maize. Despite the drought in the south, agricultural production grew by 4.2% in 2003, fuelled by strong investment in sugar, tobacco, tea and citrus plantations in the north of the country. A severe drought in the south during 2005 reduced the cereal harvest by 5.2%, to 1.9m. tons, compared with 2004, and by October 2005 it was estimated that 500,000 Mozambicans were facing food shortages. However, following improved rains in late 2005, cereal production increased by 10.5% in 2006, reaching 2.1m. tons. Further droughts and flooding in late 2006 were expected to reduce agricultural output by up to 60% in 2007, and the Government planned to import 280,000 tons of cereals. In May 2007 FAO estimated that 800,000 Mozambicans required food aid.

MINING

Mozambique has considerable mineral resources, although exploitation has been limited by internal unrest. As a result, mining was estimated to have contributed less than 1.6% of GDP in 2006. Until recently, mining production has been small-scale and consisted mainly of marble, granite, gold and bauxite. Exports reached only US $35m. in 2006 (excluding the Sasol pipeline—see below), but they are set to grow strongly over the coming years. Investment in the sector grew from $40m. in 2004 to $160m. in 2005 and an estimated $250m. in 2006. In 2006 the Government issued 900 mining licences, with 25% covering base metals, 25% tantalite, 10% coal and 8% gold. Unofficial artisanal production, mainly of gold and precious stones is estimated to be worth around $40m.–$60m. The Government has sought to develop the mining sector and increase its share of the economy to 10% of GDP. To that effect, the Assembléia da República adopted a new mining investment code in May 2002, which was drafted with World Bank assistance. However, the IMF recommended that the Government review the package of tax exemptions offered to companies investing in Mozambique, and in May 2007 legislation was passed establishing new tax regimes for the mining and petroleum sectors, which ought to increase their contribution to tax revenues. In addition, the Government supported a $33m. project to establish a geological survey of the country.

There are confirmed coal reserves of some 10,000m. metric tons, but so far output remained relatively low. The Moatize coal mine, near Tete, has an annual production capacity of 600,000 tons, but output declined from 574,800 tons in 1975 to only 84,500 tons in 1989, owing to rebel attacks against the railway to Beira and a lack of other facilities for transporting the coal to the port. Moreover, exports of coal from Moatize declined from pre-independence levels of some 100,000 tons per year to only 19,000 tons in 1990. The majority of coal exports are to neighbouring Malawi. Production was an estimated 36,742 tons in 2003 and 16,525 tons in 2004. There have been plans to revive the industry, with a new deep-water coal-handling terminal at Beira increasing annual capacity from 400,000 tons to 1.2m. tons. The plans envisaged foreign investment in mining projects of more than US $700m., and in railway and port infrastructural work of almost $500m., to be repaid in coal. Brazil's Companhia do Vale do Rio Doce (CVRD) and American Metals and Coal International (AMCI) completed feasibility studies for this project in November 2006; construction work at the mine started in May 2007. The consortium expected to start exporting coal from Moatize by May 2010, with forecast annual production of 12m. tons. The 550-km Moatize–Beira railway line was being rebuilt along with a coal-loading terminal on the coast, near the port of Beira, while there were plans to build a 1,500-MW coal-fired power station at Moatize. In February 2006 the Government awarded a licence to Aquila Coal (Australia) to prospect for coal in the Moatize area, and in April another Australian company, Riversdale Mining, acquired two coal concessions in the Zambezi valley, where it intended to complete a feasibility study by the end of 2008.

Mozambique has significant reserves of tantalite, with annual production estimated at 712,095 metric tons in 2004. However, only small quantities are exported. In May 2005 South Africa's TAN Mining and Exploration announced that it would invest US $11m. to restart production at the Muiane tantalite mine, in Zambézia province, which closed during the civil war. Annual production is expected to reach 420,000 tons. There are deposits of ilmenite in the area north of the mouth of the Zambezi river. In January 2002 the Government and the Anglo-Irish company Kenmare Resources signed an agreement to develop the Moma Titanium Minerals Project (MTMP) in Nampula province, with estimated heavy mineral reserves of 163m. tons. Development costs were estimated at over US $400m., and the site was projected to produce exports of ilmenite worth up to $150m. per year by 2009. Construction work on the site started in October 2004; the mine started producing titanium ore in late 2006 and expected to make its first exports in July 2007. Kenmare planned to implement a $6.5m. expansion of the mine's capacity during the second half of 2007, boosting annual production to 800,000 tons of ilmenite, 56,000 tons of zircon and 21,000 tons of rutile. The company expected the mine to account for 6.5% of world titanium production by the end of 2007. The MTMP is the largest single mining project in Mozambique since independence, and in 2004 the mining sector expanded by 130% as a result of this project. Investigations have also been proceeding along the coast to confirm other deposits of ilmenite, zircon and titano-magnetite, and smaller reserves of rutile and monazite. Preliminary assessments estimated the heavy mineral content at some 2m.–5m. tons.

In 1999 the largest reserve of titanium in the world (estimated at 100m. metric tons), known as Corridor Sands, was discovered in the district of Chibuto in the province of Gaza. The development costs were estimated at US $495m. initially, rising to $1,000m. if the building of a smelter and transport connections were taken into account. A South African company, Southern Mining Corpn (SMC), was considering developing the site, particularly following the decision by Western Mining Corpn (WMC, bought by BHP Billiton, a South African-Australian mining group, in 2005) of Australia to purchase a 20% stake in 2000 (which was later increased to a possible 54% stake). After a feasibility study was completed, the Government and SMC finally signed a project implementation agreement in May 2002. In December 2002 SMC's share in the venture was bought out by WMC, which increased its stake to 90%. Production was forecast to start in 2010; however, in February 2007 BHP Billiton announced that it was reducing the size of the project due to increased mining costs, and planned to carry out a new feasibility study in 2008. The mine had been expected to export up to 370,000 tons per year, either through Maputo port or through a new terminal north of Xai Xai, but it is now likely to be transformed at the Mozal smelter in Matola, in which BHP Billiton is a also shareholder. The project was expected to be connected to the new power line that already supplies the Mozal aluminium smelter (see below).

The mining of iron ore began in the mid-1950s, and production of ore averaged about 6m. metric tons (60%–65% iron) annually in the early 1970s. Production was disrupted by the civil war and ceased altogether between 1975 and 1984. At present, output is stockpiled and the resumption of exports of iron ore depends upon the eventual rehabilitation of the rail link between the mines at Cassinga and the coast. Bauxite is mined in the Manica area; in the early 1990s several thousand tons annually were exported directly to Zimbabwe. New deposits of manganese, graphite, fluorite, platinum, nickel, radioactive minerals (e.g. uranium), asbestos, iron, diamonds and natural gas (of which there are confirmed reserves of about 60,000m. cu m) have been found. In July 2006 Kenmare Resources acquired three uranium exploration licences in the Zambezi valley, Tete province, which it intended to develop. Australia's Omega Corpn is also exploring for uranium on the Mavuzi project, Tete province, where there was previously a uranium mine.

In October 1987 Lonrho, a multinational conglomerate, signed a 25-year agreement for rights to prospect for gold in five blocks on a seam in Manica province. In 1990 the company announced the formation of a joint venture with Aluviões de Manica. Despite estimated reserves of 50 metric tons, total national official extraction of gold was just an estimated 63 kg in 2005, although artisanal production by 20,000 *garimpeiros* (gold panners) was estimated at an average of 600–900 kg per year, worth US $10m.–$20m. In January 2006 the United Kingdom's Pan African Resources gained control of a gold prospecting licence in Manica province after acquiring a Mozambican company, Explorator Limitada, and, in early 2007, it completed a feasibility study for an opencast gold mine. Also in early 2006 the United Kingdom's African Eagle Resources started exploration on two gold-mining permits at Majele and Muazua in Nampula province. In September 2006 Pan African Mining acquired an 85% stake in the Fingoe and Casula gold prospects in Tete province and pledged to invest at least $150,000 in exploration in 2007–08. In May 2007 a Portuguese-Angolan consortium, Agrupamento Mineiro, started mining for gold in Manica after four years of prospecting at a cost of $15m.; the mine was expected to produce 60 kg of gold per month.

Annual production from the Montepuez marble quarry in Cabo Delgado province was projected at 8,100 cu m, with Portugal and South Africa identified as potential export markets. An Israeli company is mining emeralds and garnets in Zambézia province.

PETROLEUM AND GAS

Mozambique imports all its petroleum supplies. In recent years lack of foreign exchange has resulted in severe shortages of fuel. As a result, the Government has aimed to encourage foreign investment in the minerals sector. Petroleum prospecting has been carried out by US, French, German and South African companies, both off shore near the Rovuma river basin and Beira and on the mainland, but so far only gas has been found. In 1998 the National Iranian Oil Co and the Malaysian state energy company, Petronas, indicated their interest in constructing a refinery in Beira, to produce 100,000 barrels per day (b/d), at a cost of US $1,200m. In 2000 the French company TotalFinaElf commenced a technical evaluation of a new, deep-water concession, 300 km east of Beira, while the state energy company Empresa Nacional de Hidrocarbonetos de Moçambique (ENH) commenced the sale of 14 offshore energy exploration licences to foreign companies. However, the response was poor. Finally, in 2002 an agreement was signed with Petronas for exploration rights on the 29,000-sq km Zambezi block, opposite the river delta. The new agreement involved an investment of $60m. over eight years, with a 15% stake for ENH, to prospect for oil and natural gas.

In July 2005 the Instituto Nacional de Petróleo (INP—National Petroleum Institute) launched a licensing round for five exploration blocks in the 60,000-km Rovuma basin, attracting bids from seven oil companies. In March 2006 the INP announced the results, awarding the 15,000-km onshore area to Canada's Artumas, Block 1 to the USA's Anadarko Petroleum Corpn, Blocks 3 and 6 to Malaysia's Petronas and Block 4 to Italy's ENI. In addition, in February Norway's Norsk Hydro was awarded Blocks 2 and 5 as a result of separate negotiations. The winning companies were expected to invest US $300m. in exploration and to drill at least eight exploratory wells. In addition they have committed themselves to funding $1.3m. of social projects and a $1.5m. training programme for locals. The Government planned to issue more licences for petroleum and gas exploration in the Rovuma basin in 2008, following the completion of environmental assessment reports.

In May 1998 the Government signed a production-sharing agreement with an international consortium, led by the state-owned South African fuel procurement company, Sasol, under the terms of which the consortium was to invest at least US $30m. over a seven-year period in gas exploration in the Temane region of southern Inhambane province. In October 2000 ENH signed another contract with Sasol for the development of the Pande and Temane gas fields, in which Sasol was to hold 70% of the equity and ENH the remainder. The field's reserves were estimated at 55,000m. cu m. Construction of an 895-km pipeline was completed in February 2004. While the pipeline will primarily supply the South African market, a branch was also extended to Maputo. The first exports of gas began in February 2004, and Sasol expected to export 85m. gigajoules of gas per year during 2004–05, rising to 120m. gigajoules by 2008. The exploitation of the sites could yield between 23m. and 50m. cu ft (8m.–18m. cu m) of gas per day for 50 years. Sales of the gas domestically and in South Africa (and potentially in Zimbabwe) may exceed $100m. per year. In February 2004 the International Finance Corpn announced that it was acquiring a 5% stake in the project from ENH, valued at $18.5m., leaving ENH and Sasol with 25% and 70% stakes, respectively. In 2004 Sasol planned to drill three exploration wells in fields adjoining Pande and Temane and, if successful, these will be followed with three appraisal wells. In 2006 production from Sasol's gas fields in Inhambane accounted for 64% of national mining output.

POWER

Mozambique has hydroelectric potential of 12,500 MW, four-fifths of which is concentrated in the Zambezi basin. The main component of the Mozambican power-generating industry is the Cahora Bassa dam, built and operated by the Portuguese authorities. In April 1984 tripartite talks between Mozambique, Portugal and South Africa resulted in an agreement whereby Mozambique was to receive a share of the revenues, which had previously been paid exclusively to Portugal. Under the agreement, Mozambique acquired an 18% stake in the company managing the dam, Hidroelétrica de Cahora Bassa (HCB), with Portugal owning the remainder. However, frequent sabotage of power lines by Renamo subsequently halted supplies from the dam to the South African grid. In June 1988 Mozambique, Portugal and South Africa signed an agreement to restore operations at the dam. Under the agreement, 1,400 km of power lines (of which 900 km traversed areas under Renamo control) were to undergo rehabilitation. However, rehabilitation was continually delayed as a result of the security situation.

After the peace agreement a programme to rehabilitate the lines, at an estimated cost of US $130m., began in July 1995, with funding from South Africa, Portugal, the EU, the European Investment Bank and the Caisse Française de Développement. However, a dispute concerning the price that South Africa should pay for electricity from Cahora Bassa delayed the resumption of exports. Transmission commenced in July 1998, but was suspended in September when South Africa reneged on an agreement to increase payments. Supplies resumed in March 1999 at the original tariff pending international arbitration. A temporary agreement was reached between HCB and the state-owned South African electricity provider, the Electricity Supply Commission (ESKOM), in late 2000. The two sides agreed to suspend arbitration hearings in return for a payment by ESKOM of R165m. ESKOM agreed to a one-year contract for 2001, pending further negotiations, but talks on a final agreement broke down at the end of 2001. At the same time, negotiations between Portugal and Mozambique to allow Mozambique to have a majority control in HCB stalled. Eventually, in February 2004 a final agreement was reached under which ESKOM agreed to increase the tariff it pays from $0.05 per kWh to $0.10 per kWh, with a commitment to increase it again to $0.16 per kWh in 2007.

The issue of ownership of HCB remained unresolved, however, as the Mozambican authorities, which had repeatedly stated their intention of taking over ownership of the company, were keen to avoid taking on the company's debt. Nevertheless, under a 1975 agreement the Government could legally assume ownership of HCB once it has paid off its debts, estimated in 2005 at US $2,300m., which built up during the civil war when it was unable to export power to South Africa. In early 2004 Portugal announced it was willing to sell its shares in HCB to the Mozambican Government, but the sale could not go ahead until HCB's debts to Portugal had been settled. Following the election of President Guebuza, negotiations moved forward quickly and, during a visit to Portugal in November 2005, Guebuza signed a memorandum of understanding with the Portuguese Government transferring ownership of HCB to Mozambique. Under the deal, Mozambique would acquire an 85% stake in HCB while Portugal would retain a 15% stake, in return for a payment of $950m. from the Government and $250m. from HCB's cash reserves and revenue from electricity sales to South Africa. In addition, Portugal would write off an estimated $1,500m. in HCB debt. In October 2006 the Government signed a final agreement with Portugal, agreeing to pay the outstanding $700m. by the end of 2007, with an extension to 30 June 2008 in exceptional circumstances. In May 2007 the government appointed two banks, France's Calyon and Portugal's BPI, to arrange the $700m. commercial loan, and the repayment to Portugal was expected to be completed before the end of 2007.

An agreement for Zimbabwe, which was experiencing power shortages, to buy electricity from Cahora Bassa was signed in April 1992. The project involved the construction, at a cost of US $45m., of a 350-km transmission line to Harare, which was completed in January 1998. The new line allowed Zimbabwe to draw 500 MW from Cahora Bassa—about 25% of the dam's installed capacity. In May 2000 it was reported that the Zimbabwe Electricity Supply Authority (ZESA) had defaulted on its payments to HCB, eventually offering food and agricultural products in a barter arrangement. By early 2004 ZESA had amassed arrears of $30m. to HCB, with little prospect of these being paid, given the catastrophic collapse of Zimbabwe's economy. Plans for the construction of further lines to supply Malawi and Swaziland were also being pursued following the signing of agreements between Mozambique and those countries in 1994.

Other main hydroelectric plants are on the Revue river, west of Beira at Chicamba Real and Mavúzi. Further south, on the Limpopo, is the dam that helps to irrigate the *colonato* (a former Portuguese settler scheme). In 1991 an agreement was signed with South Africa and Swaziland to build three dams for power generation and irrigation in the joint Komati river basin. Plans were under review in the mid-1990s for the construction of the Mepandua Ncua hydroelectric power station at a site in the Zambezi valley, some 70 km downstream of Cahora Bassa. The plant, which was expected to have a generating capacity of 2,300 MW, was projected to cost some US $1,800m., with a further $500m. for the construction of transmission lines linking it to the South African grid. In April 2006 the Export-Import Bank of China (Eximbank) announced it would finance the construction of the dam, with production expected to start in 2010 or 2011. Eximbank has also pledged to finance the $300m. construction of the Moamba-Major dam in Maputo province. There is also a coal-fired power station in Maputo with a capacity of 60 MW, which is supplied by importing coal from South Africa. Brazil's CVRD plans to construct a 1,500-MW plant at Moatize as part of its coal-mining project. In 2007 the Government was seeking foreign investment for eight major power-generation projects in Mozambique, at an estimated cost of $6,000m., which would have a combined generating capacity of 6,500 MW. These include existing projects, as well as new hydroelectric dams on the Zambezi and Lúrio rivers.

By 1997, in the absence of regular power supplies from Cahora Bassa, electricity production had dwindled to 570m. kWh. Mozambique was importing an estimated 1,500m. kWh annually from South Africa, which cost the equivalent of almost 10% of the country's annual export earnings. In 1996 the state electricity company announced that it was to invest US $60m. over a period of three years in the rehabilitation and expansion of the country's electricity grid. Combined with the rehabilitation of the Cahora Bassa dam, this has allowed imports to fall to around 500m. kWh per year. Electricity production increased to 6,974m. kWh in 2000. In April 2002 the electricity grid supplied by the Cahora Bassa dam was extended to Inhambane. In early 2004 the grid was extended to Manica and Sofala provinces, and to Cabo Delgado and Niassa in 2006. Electricity production increased to 14,737m. kWh in 2006, nearly all of which was hydroelectric. That year exports reached 11,177m. kWh, worth $184m., while imports (mostly re-imports from Cahora Bassa via South Africa) were 8,171m. kWh, worth $84m. Domestic demand for electricity grew from 118 MW in 1977 to 235 MW in 1998 and, by 2006, had more than doubled to 577 MW, while the number of households connected to the grid increased from 62,000 to 414,471 over the same period. The state-owned electricity utility, Electricidade de Moçambique (EDM), has pledged to connect an additional 210,000 homes to the grid in 2007–09. The percentage of the population with access to electricity has risen from 5.3% in 2002 to 9.4% in 2006. In 2005 the Government set up the INP to regulate the energy sector, a role which had previously been carried out by ENH, which was to continue to manage the state's joint ventures with foreign companies.

INDUSTRY

Industries are mainly devoted to the processing of primary materials, and Mozambique remains dependent on South African industrial products. About one-half of Mozambican manufacturers are located in and around Maputo, although the Government is encouraging decentralization towards Beira and northern Mozambique. Under the colonial administration, investments from Portugal, South Africa, Italy and the United Kingdom established export-orientated industries. Food processing formed the traditional basis of this sector, with sugar refining, cashew- and wheat-processing predominating.

Other industries include the manufacture of cement, fertilizers and agricultural implements. Textile production and brewing gained in importance during the 1980s. Cotton spinning and weaving are undertaken at Chimoio, at Maputo and in Nampula province. Other secondary industries produce glass, ceramics, paper, tyres and railway carriages. Official sources estimated that industrial output increased by 6% per year in 1987–89, owing partly to the restructuring of the sector under the PRE and partly to increased imports of raw materials. Under the PRE, resources were to be focused on industries with high domestic added value, and on import-substitution products. Government control of prices was relaxed in several industrial sectors in 1987. In 1995–2004 industrial GDP, according to the World Bank, increased by an estimated annual average of 17.2%.

In July 1998 construction began on the Mozal aluminium smelter at Beloluane, near Maputo. Of the total cost of US $1,300m., $800m. was raised in loans, from sources including the World Bank. Mozal is majority owned by BHP Billiton, with a 3% stake held by the Mozambique state. An electricity consortium, Motraco, consisting of the state electricity company EDM and its counterparts in South Africa and Swaziland, was also created in November 1998 to provide 435 MW of electricity to Mozal. The construction of a 300-km 149-MW power line from South Africa to Beloluane was completed in November 1999. The smelter began production in June 2000, with an initial output capacity of 250,000 metric tons per year, which was expected to double following the completion of the second phase of the project, making it one of the largest smelters world-wide. Full production was reached in March 2001, when aluminium was expected to have become the country's largest export. In June 2001 Mozal announced its decision to undertake an $860m. expansion, which was expected to double production to 506,000 tons per year. Mozal II became operational in October 2003. Mozal's impact on the Mozambican economy has been huge: in 2003 its aluminium exports provided 55% of total export earnings and accounted for one-quarter of Mozambique's GDP growth. In 2004 Mozal II doubled its production capacity to 506,000 tons of aluminium ingots per year, leading to dramatic growth in the mining sector of 129.8% in the first half of 2005. Plans to implement a third expansion, Mozal III, have been postponed until the company can guarantee a sufficient supply of electricity. In early 2005 CVRD commenced a feasibility study on constructing an aluminium smelter in Beira, using the 1,500-MW power station at Moatize for power.

Cement output increased from 179,000 metric tons in 1996 to 800,000 tons in 2006. A programme to rehabilitate the cement plant at Matola, near Maputo, enabling it to produce 400,000 tons per year, was completed by the end of 1993. In 2007 an Anglo-Mozambican consortium started construction of a new cement plant at Boane, near Maputo, at a cost of US $99m. A $4m. ammoniac plant in Sofala province, a joint venture between the ENH, Scimitar Production (Canada) and Zarara Petroleum Resources (UAE) started production in late 1997. In May 2007 the computer manufacturer, Sahara, announced plans to build an assembly plant in Maputo, at an estimated cost of $3m., which was intended to produce 3,000 computers per month.

TRANSPORT

Mozambique's transport system was based around 'transport corridors', which included rail, road and energy infrastructure, and linked the interior and neighbouring countries with the Mozambican ports, and were undergoing development. There were four main corridors: the 'Beira Corridor' from the Zimbabwean border to the port of Beira, the 'Limpopo Corridor' and the 'Maputo Corridor' from South Africa to Maputo, and the 'Nacala Corridor' from Nacala to Malawi. Further corridors were planned.

Railways

Prior to independence Mozambique derived much of its income from transit charges on goods carried between Zimbabwe, Zambia, Malawi, Swaziland and South Africa and its ports. The main lines are: from Maputo, the Ressano Garcia line to the South African border, the Goba line to the Swaziland border and the Chicualacuala line to the Zimbabwe border (the Limpopo rail link) in the south; from Beira, the Beira–Mutare line to the Zimbabwe border, the Trans-Zambézia line to the Malawi border and the Tete line. In the north the main route is the Nacala–Malawi line, with a branch-line to Lichinga. All of these lines are intended primarily to export the products of land-locked countries, and secondarily to transport Mozambican goods.

Before independence Mozambique had 3,131 km of track, excluding the Sena Sugar Estates railway (90 km), which served only the company's properties. By 2003 the total length of track was 3,114 km, of which 2,072 km was operational. Most of the international lines are controlled by international conventions, since their effective functioning is vital to Mozambique's neighbours. However, during the war the whole of Mozambique's rail network was subject to frequent disruption by Renamo guerrilla sabotage. The end of the war precipitated a rapid increase in rail traffic. Passenger traffic escalated from 26m. passenger-km in 1992 to 403m. passenger-km in 1997, before falling back to 169m. passenger-km in 2005 as a result of deterioration of the network and rolling stock. Freight traffic also increased, to a lesser extent, from 616m. ton-km in 1992 to 899m. ton-km in 1997. By 2005 freight traffic had increased to 2,212m. ton-km, of which 769m. ton-km was on the railways.

In 1987 a programme to reinstate the 'Beira Corridor', linking Zimbabwe to Beira harbour, was initiated, at a cost of more than US $300m., while the rehabilitation of the Limpopo railway was completed in early 1993, at a cost of some $200m. In 2004 an Indian company, Rites, won the tender to operate the rail line from Beira to Zimbabwe, and in 2006 it took over management of the line. In June 1997 the Government had invited contractors to tender for private concessions to operate Maputo port and the three railways linking it with South Africa, Swaziland and Zimbabwe. The state ports and railway company, Empresa Nacional dos Portos e Caminhos de Ferro de Moçambique (CFM), was to retain a 33% stake in the companies. The operators were to have a 51% stake, while the remaining 16% was to be open to other investors. However, excessive financial terms were demanded by the Government, and negotiations were slow. In December 2002 South Africa's state-owned railway operator, Spoornet, signed an agreement, under which it paid $67m. for a 15-year concession and a 51% stake in a new company, the Ressano Garcia Rail Consortium. However, disagreements between Spoornet and its partner, New Limpopo Bridge Project Investments (NLPI), led to no work being carried out on the line and, in late 2005, CFM withdrew the concession. CFM immediately started rehabilitation work, with the first $12m. upgrade scheduled for completion by mid-2006, and the line's full rehabilitation by October. In 2002 the CFM had been privatized as the Empresa Portos e Caminhos de Ferro de Moçambique and restructured into divisions overseeing four lines and their connected ports. As a result of privatization, CFM's work-force was reduced from nearly 20,000 in 1998 to 1,863 in 2005.

In May 1999 a consortium headed by CFM was given approval to purchase the privatized Malawi Railways. CFM was partnered by the Sociedade de Desenvolvimento do Corredor de Nacala (SDCN—Nacala Corridor Development Co), which consisted of US, French and Mozambican private companies. Payment, of some US $20m., was to be made over a period of 20 years. The assets of the rail company were to belong to the consortium, although the task of upgrading the infrastructure was to remain the duty of the Malawian Government, with World Bank funding. In late February 2000 an agreement was signed providing for the transfer to SDCN the management of the port of Nacala and the 800-km railway line to Malawi. However, management of the port and railway line was only assumed by SDCN in 2005. Work began on rehabilitating the line in late 2005, but in mid-2006 disputes arose with the Mozambican authorities over interference in the concession's management. At mid-2007 SDCN was still seeking $50m. in financing to operate the railway line and the port of Nacala. In May 2004 an Indian consortium won the tender to reconstruct the 500-km Beira railway line running from Dondo to the Moatize coal mines in Tete, and in December of that year the World Bank agreed to lend $110m. to upgrade the railway system. In early 2006 CFM completed rehabilitation of the first

32-km section of the Beira–Tete line, estimating the project's total cost at $200m. CFM planned to complete work on the line as far as Inhaminga, in addition to a new a branch line to Marromeu, by mid-2007.

Roads

Railway-dominated Mozambique suffers from a lack of good roads. In 1999 there were only an estimated 30,400 km of roads and tracks, of which 5,685 km were tarred. Furthermore, the main roads are penetration lines toward bordering countries and are grossly insufficient for Mozambique's purposes. Most of the northern provinces are lacking in roads, although attempts are being made to construct a paved road from the Tanzanian border to the south. There is a bridge across the Zambezi river at Tete, on the Zimbabwe–Malawi route, and a tarred road links Malawi to Maputo via Tete. Prior to the end of hostilities in 1992 the poor security situation all but halted normal road transport to and from most cities, and it was necessary to organize military guards for convoys. A major programme, supervised by the Southern African Development Co-ordination Conference (now the Southern African Development Community), began in 1989 to improve the road links between Mozambique and neighbouring countries. Mozambique's only privately operated toll road, the Maputo–Witbank, South Africa, highway, opened in 2000. In June 2001 a US $1,700m. wide-ranging programme to maintain or rehabilitate up to 28,000 km of roads per year was announced by the Government. In June 2003 upgrade work was completed on the road from Inchope (in the 'Beira Corridor' in Sofala province) to Caia (on the Zambezi river). The 315-km tarmac road was rehabilitated with $50m. of funding from the US Agency for International Development (USAID) and has raised Mozambique's main national road connecting the north and south, the Estrada Nacional 1, to an all-weather standard. In 2006 a total of 822 km of roads were constructed or rehabilitated and 7,700 km were maintained, far short of the Government's target of 28,000 km of roads per year. In June 2007 the Government announced the next phase of the national road programme, PRISE, covering 2007–11. The programme was to cost $1,140m., over one-half of which to be provided by donors. Priority projects included further upgrades to the north–south national highway, the construction of 15 new bridges, the rehabilitation of the Beira–Zimbabwe road and improvements to the Lichinga–Pemba and Milange–Mocuba roads.

In 2006 work began on a bridge over the Zambezi river at Caia to replace the ferry service. The US $90m., three-year project was funded by the EU, Sweden, Italy and Japan. During 2004 the Government had set as its priority improvements to the Nampula to Nacala road and to the Oasse to Mocímboa da Praia road. In October 2005 work began on a bridge over the Rovuma river, which forms the border between Mozambique and Tanzania. The Unity Bridge, which was to be constructed by a Chinese company, would cost an estimated $25m.–$35m. However, the project was criticized by donors, which instead suggested upgrading the existing ferry service at far less cost; as a result, the two Governments were to bear the full cost. In December 2005 work had also begun on a $14.4m. bridge over the Limpopo river, in Gaza province, funded by the Nordic Development Fund and the Mozambican Government. The bridge was expected to open by the end of 2007.

Ports

The main ports are Maputo (the second largest port in Africa, with its annex at Matola), Beira, Nacala and Quelimane. Maputo and Beira ports exist chiefly as outlets for South Africa, Swaziland, Zimbabwe, Zambia, Malawi and the Democratic Republic of the Congo. The total freight traffic handled by Maputo was an estimated 6.4m. metric tons in 2005. Maputo has an excellent, multi-purpose harbour and rehabilitation of its facilities, which aimed to increase the port's annual handling capacity to 12m. tons, was completed in 1989. In 2003 the management of the port of Maputo was transferred to the private sector. The Maputo Port Development Co (MPDC), a consortium led by a British company, Merseyside Docks and Harbour, and including Sweden's Skanska and some Portuguese investors, as well as a local company, Gestores de Moçambique, acquired a 15-year lease of the facility. The company invested US $45m. in priority works, including the dredging of the harbour and the purchase of new tugs and equipment. However, a proposed $170m. expansion, which would have increased the port's capacity to 17m. tons per year by 2010, was put on hold as a result of the company's non-payment of $10m. in annual fixed fees to the Government, which it withheld until rehabilitation work on the Ressano Garcia railway had been completed. In April 2006 a special committee was established, with members from MPDC, CFM and the Ministry of Finance, to find a resolution to the dispute. Also in that month a South African shipping company, Grindrod, acquired a 12.2% equity stake in MPDC.

CFM was also planning a new deep-water port at Ponto Dobela, 70 km south of Maputo, in partnership with a company based in the Isle of Man, Porto Dobela Developments, which will have a 60% stake. The US $515m. development was considered controversial as it was located within the limits of a nature reserve and only 20 km north of the tourist resort at Ponto do Ouro, and might also be regarded as competing for trade with the port of Maputo. Although in mid-2003 it was announced that construction would begin within 18 months, by mid-2006 no further progress had been made with the project.

The coal terminal at Maputo port, which has a handling capacity of 6m. metric tons per year, has been rented for a period of 15 years to the South African company CMR Engineers and Project Managers. The sugar terminal reopened in June 1995, following four years of inactivity. In February 1996 the terminal was leased to a private consortium, Mozambique International Port Services (MIPS), which, by the end of 1998, had renovated most of its facilities in a US $7.5m. investment programme. CFM and Mozal also planned to spend $70m. on the expansion of Matola mineral port, situated outside Maputo. In October 2006 Grindrod started work on a $25m. expansion of its Matola Coal Terminal, which would boost its capacity from 1.7m. tons per year to 8m. tons per year by 2008. The company was due to complete work on a new car terminal in December 2007, as part of $80m. of investments in Maputo port during 2007–09.

The first phase of the rehabilitation of Beira port, which included a joint terminal for petroleum and 'roll on, roll off' traffic, as well as an increase in the capacity of the coal terminal, was completed in 1987. In 2005 Denmark financed a second US $53m. rehabilitation of the port, expanding its storage facilities and dredging the harbour to enable large-draught ships to moor permanently. In 2005 cargo traffic totalled 1.5m. tons, a 12.3% increase on 2004, and this was expected to rise substantially once the second phase of rehabilitation was complete. In July 2007 work was due to start on a $19m. project to rehabilitate Beira's fishing port (which had closed in 2001), intended to enable it to export up to $90m. worth of fish each year.

In 2006 the company that manages the port of Nacala, CDN, announced plans to expand the port's facilities to handle Panamax-size vessels weighing up to 200,000 tons. The project, which would cost $150m., could start in 2009, if investors were found, and would increase the port's capacity to 3m. metric tons per year in 2010. In 2007 work began on an $8m. interim project to increase the port's capacity to handle containers.

Air

International air transport is operated by the state-owned Linhas Aéreas de Moçambique (LAM), and domestic and regional routes by Sociedade de Transporte e Trabalho Aéreo (TTA). There are 18 airports, of which eight are international—Beira, Maputo, Nampula, Pemba, Ponto Douro, Quelimane, Tete and Vilankulos. During 1983–93 most provincial capitals were accessible from Maputo only by air; however, the restoration of civil order and the rehabilitation of the road network considerably lessened dependence on internal air transport. Despite opposition from within the ruling party, sustained pressure from the World Bank led the Government to agree to transfer LAM and TTA to private-sector ownership. The latter was privatized in May 1997. Efforts to privatize LAM suffered a reverse when the restricted tender, apparently won by a consortium led by the Portuguese airline TAP, was cancelled following renewed opposition from within the ruling party. At the same time the government strategy of preserving LAM's monopoly on lucrative routes until 2003 was challenged in court by TTA. In November 2000 TTA was authorized to begin regional flights. However, TTA was unable to raise enough funding to operate on these routes, which covered the largest cities, such as Maputo and Beira. The Government announced in May 2002 that the domestic airline market had been fully liberalized, in the hope that other companies would be attracted to the Mozambique market, at a time when LAM was struggling financially. In 2004 a local company, Air Corridor, started the first domestic services in competition with LAM, flying from its base in Nampula to Maputo, Quelimane, Beira, Pemba and Lichinga. In September 2006 the airport authority, Aeroportos de Moçambique (ADM), announced a two-year project, worth $136m., to rehabilitate and expand the country's main airports. This would include the expansion of Maputo's Mavalane airport, to more than double handling capacity from 495,000 to 1m. passengers per year. The Government was also seeking to lease the management of the airport to a private operator. In early 2005 the Government announced it was again preparing LAM for privatization, but by mid-2007 no further progress had been made.

TELECOMMUNICATIONS

The telecommunications sector in Mozambique is underdeveloped. In 2006 the state monopoly Telecomunicações de Moçambique (TDM) operated a network of 69,700 fixed lines. A mobile cellular telephone company, Moçambique Celular (mCel), a joint venture between TDM and Germany's Deutsche Telekom, was launched in 1997, and by the end of 2006 had 1.7m. subscribers. In June 2002 Vodacom Moçambique (VM), a subsidiary of Vodafone South Africa, paid US $15m. for a second mobile phone operating licence. However, it was unable to launch services until late 2003 due to a protracted dispute over interconnection fees to other networks operated by TDM and mCel. In 2004 VM launched a $567m. investment programme covering Maputo, the main towns of the south, the road routes to South Africa and Swaziland, and the city of Nampula, before extending its service to other parts of the country. By the end of 2006 the company claimed to have 490,000 subscribers. In 2006 there were an estimated 2.2m. mobile telephone users in Mozambique. Internet usage is low, although it has expanded in recent years. According to the UN's International Telecommunications Union, there were 138,000 internet users at the end of 2005, compared with 50,000 in 2002.

TOURISM

A highly profitable activity during the pre-independence period, tourism relied on the influx of Rhodesians and South Africans to Beira and the southern beaches. However, by 1978 organized tourist travel had ceased and, except on coastal islands and in the immediate vicinity of Maputo, the security situation hampered any improvement in this sector. Some hotels were rehabilitated during the late 1980s, and since the 1992 peace agreement South African tourism has increased rapidly. By the end of the 1990s tourism was the fastest growing sector of the Mozambique economy. Recognizing the importance of the industry, a Minister of Tourism was appointed in 1999, and a comprehensive tourist development plan was prepared. In 2004, according to official figures, there were 711,000 tourist arrivals in Mozambique, not including returning nationals, a sharp increase on 1995 when there were only 150,000 tourists, suggesting annual growth of 17%. According to official figures, over 700,000 tourists visited Mozambique in 2005, and the Government expected this to increase to 1m. in 2007. The central bank estimated receipts from tourism at US $108m. in 2005 and $134m. in 2006, and expected this to rise to $157m. in 2007; however, the true figure could be five times higher, as most tourist transactions are in cash and go unrecorded. By December 2006 there were 5,030 hotels in the country and around 35,000 Mozambicans employed in tourism. During 2006 the Ministry of Tourism planned to regrade all hotels in Mozambique to bring them into line with international standards. According to the World Tourism Organization, in 2005 Mozambique's tourism sector grew by 37%, the fastest rate of growth in the world, with nearly $500m. of projects being approved. According to the tourism ministry, investment in the sector reached $604m. in 2006, most of which financed the construction of new hotels and related tourism infrastructure.

The Government hopes that nature and game reserves will develop into a major tourist attraction. In April 1998 the Government announced plans for the development of the 22,000-sq km Niassa reserve in the far north of the country; the core area was further protected by a 20,000-sq km buffer area. The most significant development, however, is the extension of South Africa's Kruger National Park into Mozambique. This forms part of a programme, supported by the World Bank, the EU, South Africa's Peace Parks Foundation, and the US and German Governments, to develop five trans-frontier conservation areas (TFCAs). A cross-border park linking territories in Mozambique with the Kruger Park and Gonarezhou park in Zimbabwe, the Great Limpopo Transfrontier Park, will create a single conservation area. Under a first phase, the Mozambique section of the park will reach 35,000 sq km, eventually expanding to 100,000 sq km, creating one of the world's largest wildlife reserves. During 2002 the first elephants were transferred from South Africa to Mozambique and sections of the border fence between the two countries were dismantled. In December 2002 an international treaty establishing the park was signed, and in 2004 the Government invited tenders for licences to operate hiking trails on the Mozambique side of the park. In November 2005 a border post was opened within the park at Giriyondo, and the park was expected to formally open in late 2006. By the end of 2006 the Government estimated that the elephant population in all national parks had grown to 20,000. The other TFCA parks are Libombo, which is on the border with Swaziland, Chimanimani on the Zimbabwean border, Niassa/Selous on the Tanzanian border and Zimoza, which joins Mozambique, Zambia and Zimbabwe.

In March 1998 Mozambique, South Africa and Swaziland announced the creation of the US $121m. Libombo Spatial Development Initiative, with the purpose of attracting tourists to the sparsely inhabited area of their common borders. In 2001 the Ministry of Tourism sought to attract investment for a large tourism complex at Ponta do Ouro, 117 km south of Maputo. A road from Maputo to Ponta do Ouro was being extended, providing a transportation route between Maputo and Durban in South Africa. The tourist investment the Government hoped to attract would be the largest in Mozambique, including a 200-room beach resort, yacht marina and golf course. In February 2004 a British company, Echo Delta, purchased the Magaruque Island tourist resort near Vilanculos in Inhambane province for $1m. The company planned to invest $10m. in developing the site, which includes Magaruque, the smallest of four islands in the Bazaruto archipelago, and Santa Carolina Island, where a hotel and luxury villa complex was to be built. In mid-2006 USAID launched a $5.5m. project, covering 2006–08, which aimed to attract investors and tourists to the northern region, with an emphasis on sustainable development.

TRADE AND DEBT

Prior to the advent of peace, Mozambique's severe balance-of-payments problem was accentuated by high defence spending, much of it in already scarce foreign exchange, and by the drastic decline in tourism. Mozambique also suffered from adverse movements in the terms of trade. Exports traditionally covered only a small proportion of the country's imports. However, the beginning of aluminium production at the Mozal smelter almost doubled exports, from US $364m. in 2000 to $726m. in 2001, and they have since risen strongly, reaching $1,043.9m. in 2003. Exports again rose sharply to $1,503.9m. in 2004 as a result of the expansion of the Mozal aluminium smelter and the construction of the Sasol gas pipeline to South Africa; buoyed by high aluminium prices they reached $1,745.3m. in 2005 and an estimated $2,381.1m. in 2006. Imports also rose, but at a slower pace than exports, from $997.3m. in 2001 to $2,648.8m. in 2006. As a result, the trade deficit dropped from a peak of $666.6m. in 2002 to an estimated $267.7m. in 2006. In 2002 the current-account deficit stood at

$869.1m., but by 2006 had grown to $1,087.4m. Mozambique has a diversified set of trading partners. In 2006 the principal source of imports was South Africa (56.3%), followed by Australia (14.7%), the People's Republic of China (7.9%) and India (6.1%). In that year Belgium was the principal market for exports (21.6%), primarily of steel, followed by Italy (16.2%), Spain (9.4%) and the People's Republic of China (3.0%). In December 2001 the USA first declared Mozambique eligible for the African Growth and Opportunity Act, which would allow Mozambique duty-free access to the US market for most of its products; its eligibility was renewed in December 2002.

Agreements on the rescheduling of Mozambique's debts, covering more than US $400m. of repayments and arrears, were signed in May–June 1987 with Western official and commercial creditors, in order to reduce repayments on the country's external debt. In June 1990 Western official and commercial creditors agreed a further rescheduling of the country's debts. In March 1993 a restructuring of bilateral debt resulted in $180m. being written off. In November 1996 the 'Paris Club' of official creditors agreed to cancel or reschedule debt-servicing obligations of some $600m.

The prospect of reducing Mozambique's debt burden improved following the decision by the 'Paris Club' to admit Russia as a member in 1997. Since Mozambique owed substantial debts to Russia, this cleared the way for Mozambique to benefit from the IMF and World Bank's HIPC debt-reduction initiative. A programme under HIPC terms was approved in April 1998 and took effect in June 1999. Mozambique was to receive US $3,700m. in debt relief under the HIPC initiative, reducing the country's external debt by almost two-thirds.

Following massive flooding in the southern and central regions of the country in February 2000, in mid-March the 'Paris Club' agreed to defer all payments due on the country's external debt, valued at US $73m., for a period of one year. However, a number of conditions were attached to the debt-relief package, including the maintenance of a stable economic environment and the implementation of the poverty reduction strategy in the areas of social development and public-sector reform. In April the IMF agreed to grant Mozambique a further $600m. in debt relief under the enhanced terms of the HIPC initiative. The value of the country's debt-stock was reduced to $7,052m. at the end of 2000, and the debt-servicing ratio was reduced to the equivalent of 11.7% of exports in that year.

In 2002 Mozambique attracted US $406m. in foreign direct investment (FDI), making it the fifth highest destination for FDI in sub-Saharan Africa, according to a report by the UN Conference on Trade and Development. Between 1998 and 2002 total FDI reached $1,420m., much of it related to the expansion of the Mozal project (see above). In October 2003 Mozambique held its annual Consultative Group conference with foreign donors in Paris, France, resulting in pledges of $709m. for 2004, exceeding the amount the Government requested. Three-quarters was to be in the form of grants, with the balance made up by highly concessional loans with a grant element. In March 2004 a Joint Donor Review was convened by the 12 bilateral donors that provide budgetary support to the Mozambican Government. The two-week review discussed Mozambique's macroeconomic stability, the progress of its poverty reduction programme and the state of its health and education sectors. In 2003 $200m. was provided in budgetary support to Mozambique, up from $118m. in 2002.

In May 2004 Mozambique was one of 16 countries selected for access to the US Government's Millennium Challenge Corpn (MCC), the body set up to disburse additional development funding. The Mozambican Government established a working group to draw up funding proposals, which had to be presented to the MCC for approval before any funding could be disbursed. In January 2005 the United Kingdom cancelled its US $150m. bilateral debt with Mozambique, as part of a plan to encourage debt forgiveness among the Group of Eight leading industrialized nations (G-8), prior to hosting the G-8 summit in July. The United Kingdom also committed to paying 10% of Mozambique's debt service owed to the World Bank, on the condition that any funds freed must be spent on the social sector. In July Mozambique was one of 19 countries deemed eligible by the G-8 for immediate, full debt relief under the Multilateral Debt Relief Initiative (MDRI). In January 2006, as part of the MDRI, the IMF wrote off Mozambique's entire debt to the Fund, an amount worth $153m. It was followed by the African Development Bank, which wrote off $370.4m. in debt, and in July by the World Bank, which wrote off $1,359m. in International Development Assistance loans. In October 2006 the Romanian Government agreed to write off more than $140m. of Mozambique's external debt. In April 2007 France agreed to extend its debt relief programme, C2D, for a further two years, freeing up an additional €8.8m., which would fund health projects in Mozambique. In May 2007 Mozambique completed a buy-back operation for commercial debt nominally worth $176m. at less than one-10th of its value; the $16.1m. operation was funded by the Norwegian Government and the World Bank.

Statistical Survey

Source (unless otherwise stated): Instituto Nacional de Estatística, Comissão Nacional do Plano, Av. Ahmed Sekou Touré 21, CP 493, Maputo; tel. 21491054; fax 21490384; e-mail webmaster@ine.gov.mz; internet www.ine.gov.mz.

Area and Population

AREA, POPULATION AND DENSITY

Area (sq km)	799,380*
Population (census results)	
1 August 1980	11,673,725†
1 August 1997	
Males	7,714,306
Females	8,384,940
Total	16,099,246
Population (official projections)	
2005	19,420,036
2006	19,888,701
2007	20,366,795
Density (per sq km) at 2007	25.5

* 308,641 sq miles. The area includes 13,000 sq km (5,019 sq miles) of inland water.

† Excluding an adjustment for underenumeration. This was estimated to have been 3.8%, and the adjusted total was 12,130,000.

PROVINCES

(official projections, 2007)

Province	Area (sq km)	Population	Density (per sq km)
Cabo Delgado	82,625	1,683,681	20.4
Gaza	75,709	1,362,174	18.0
Inhambane	68,615	1,444,282	21.0
Manica	61,661	1,400,415	22.7
City of Maputo	300	1,271,569	4,238.6
Maputo Province	26,058	1,098,846	42.2
Nampula	81,606	3,861,347	47.3
Niassa	129,056	1,055,482	8.2
Sofala	68,018	1,715,557	25.2
Tete	100,724	1,593,258	15.8
Zambézia	105,008	3,880,184	37.0
Total	799,380	20,366,795	25.5

PRINCIPAL TOWNS
(population at 1997 census)

Maputo (capital)	966,837	Nacala-Porto	158,248
Matola	424,662	Quelimane	150,116
Beira	397,368	Tete	101,984
Nampula	303,346	Xai-Xai	99,442
Chimoio	171,056	Gurue	99,335

Mid-2005 (incl. suburbs, UN estimate): Maputo 1,320,000 (Source: UN, *World Urbanization Prospects: The 2005 Revision*).

BIRTHS AND DEATHS

	2004	2005	2006
Crude birth rate (per 1,000)	39.3	38.8	38.2
Crude death rate (per 1,000)	20.1	20.0	19.9

Source: African Development Bank.

Expectation of life (years at birth, WHO estimates): 45 (males 44; females 46) in 2004 (Source: WHO, *World Health Report*).

ECONOMICALLY ACTIVE POPULATION
(persons aged 12 years and over, 1980 census)

	Males	Females	Total
Agriculture, forestry, hunting and fishing	1,887,779	2,867,052	4,754,831
Mining and quarrying Manufacturing	323,730	23,064	346,794
Construction	41,611	510	42,121
Commerce	90,654	21,590	112,244
Transport, storage and communications	74,817	2,208	77,025
Other services*	203,629	39,820	243,449
Total employed	2,622,220	2,954,244	5,576,464
Unemployed	75,505	19,321	94,826
Total labour force	2,697,725	2,973,565	5,671,290

* Including electricity, gas and water.

Source: ILO, *Yearbook of Labour Statistics*.

1997 (percentage distribution of economically active population at census of 1 August): Agriculture, forestry and hunting: 91.3% of females, 69.6% of males; Mining: 0.0% of females, 1.0% of males; Manufacturing: 0.8% of females, 5.5% of males; Energy: 0.0% of females, 0.3% of males; Construction: 0.3% of females, 3.9% of males; Transport and communications: 0.1% of females, 2.3% of males; Commerce and finance: 4.3% of females, 9.7% of males; Services: 2.2% of females, 3.4% of males; Unknown: 0.9% of females, 1.4% of males.

Mid-2005 (estimates in '000): Agriculture, etc. 8,250; Total labour force 10,321 (Source: FAO).

Health and Welfare

KEY INDICATORS

Total fertility rate (children per woman, 2005)	5.3
Under-5 mortality rate (per 1,000 live births, 2005)	145
HIV/AIDS (% of persons aged 15–49, 2005)	16.1
Physicians (per 1,000 head, 2004)	0.03
Hospital beds (per 1,000 head, 1990)	0.87
Health expenditure (2004): US $ per head (PPP)	42.0
Health expenditure (2004): % of GDP	4.0
Health expenditure (2004): public (% of total)	68.4
Access to water (% of persons, 2004)	43
Access to sanitation (% of persons, 2004)	32
Human Development Index (2004): ranking	168
Human Development Index (2004): value	0.390

For sources and definitions, see explanatory note on p. vi.

Agriculture

PRINCIPAL CROPS
('000 metric tons)

	2003	2004	2005
Rice (paddy)*	200	177	174
Maize*	1,248	1,437	1,403
Millet*	48	53	36
Sorghum*	315	337	307
Potatoes†	80	80	80
Sweet potatoes†	66	66	66
Cassava (Manioc)	6,150*	6,413†	11,458†
Cashew nuts†	58	58	58
Groundnuts (in shell)*	110	127	132
Coconuts†	265	265	265
Copra*	72	75	75
Sunflower seed†	11	11	11
Cottonseed*	47	47	45
Tomatoes†	9	9	9
Other vegetables†	105	105	105
Bananas†	90	90	90
Oranges†	14	14	14
Grapefruits and pomelos†	13	13	13
Guavas, mangoes and mangosteens†	24	24	24
Pineapples†	13	13	13
Papayas†	43	43	43
Other fruits†	115	105	105
Cotton (lint)	19†	26†	26*
Tobacco†	12	12	12

* Unofficial figure(s).
† FAO estimate(s).

Source: FAO.

LIVESTOCK
('000 head, year ending September, FAO estimates)

	1998	1999	2000
Asses, mules or hinnies	22	23	23
Cattle	1,300	1,310	1,320
Pigs	176	178	180
Sheep	123	124	125
Goats	388	390	392
Chickens	26,000	27,000	28,000

2001–05: Figures assumed to be unchanged from 2000 (FAO estimates).

Source: FAO.

LIVESTOCK PRODUCTS
('000 metric tons, FAO estimates)

	2001	2002	2003
Cattle meat	38	38	38
Goat meat	2	2	2
Pig meat	13	13	13
Chicken meat	37	40	36
Cows' milk	60	60	60
Goats' milk	8	8	8
Hen eggs	14	14	14

2004–05: Figures assumed to be unchanged from 2003 (FAO estimates).

Source: FAO.

Forestry

ROUNDWOOD REMOVALS
('000 cubic metres, excl. bark)

	2003	2004	2005
Sawlogs, veneer logs and logs for sleepers	128	123	113
Other industrial wood	1,191	1,191	1,191
Fuel wood	16,724	16,724	16,724
Total	18,043	18,038	18,028

Source: FAO.

SAWNWOOD PRODUCTION
('000 cubic metres, incl. railway sleepers)

	2003	2004	2005
Total	28	32	38

Source: FAO.

Fishing

(metric tons, live weight)

	2003	2004	2005
Dagaas	10,948	18,759	13,007
Tuna-like fishes	1,728	n.a.	n.a.
Penaeus shrimps	13,551	12,403	13,005
Knife shrimp	1,413	992	1,774
Total catch (incl. others)	44,342*	45,129*	45,018

* FAO estimate.

Note: Figures exclude crocodiles, recorded by number rather than by weight. The number of Nile crocodiles caught was: 5,130 in 2003; n.a. in 2004; 1,323 in 2005.

Source: FAO.

Mining

('000 metric tons, unless otherwise indicated)

	2003	2004	2005
Bauxite	11.8	6.7	9.5
Coal	36.7	16.5	3.4
Gold (kilograms)*	63	56	63
Quartz (metric tons)	31.0	173.5	n.a.
Gravel and crushed rock ('000 cubic metres)†	800.0	800.0	800.0
Marble (slab) ('000 square metres)	10.2	13.4	12.3
Salt (marine)†	80	80	80
Natural gas (million cu m)	1.0	1,295	2,316

* Figures exclude artisanal gold production; total gold output is estimated at 360 kg–480 kg per year.

† Estimates.

Source: US Geological Survey.

Industry

SELECTED PRODUCTS
('000 metric tons, unless otherwise indicated)

	2002	2003	2004
Flour (cereals other than wheat)	1	1	n.a.
Wheat flour	145	163	160
Raw sugar	35	225	199
Groundnut oil ('000 metric tons)*	13.8	15.8	20.2
Beer ('000 hl)	779	1,044	1,025
Soft drinks ('000 hl)	547	30	1,224
Cigarettes (million)	1,255	1,390	n.a.
Footwear (excl. rubber, '000 pairs)	12†	17†	n.a.
Cement	274	582	484
Electric energy (million kWh)	12,713	10,602	11,714

* FAO estimates.

† Estimate.

Sources: FAO; UN, *Industrial Commodity Statistics Yearbook*.

2005 ('000 metric tons): Groundnut oil 16.9 (FAO estimate) (Source: FAO).

Finance

CURRENCY AND EXCHANGE RATES

Monetary Units

100 centavos = 1 metical (plural: meticais).

Sterling, Dollar and Euro Equivalents (30 April 2007)

£1 sterling = 52.36 meticais;
US $1 = 26.25 meticais;
€1 = 35.71 meticais;
1,000 meticais = £1.91 = $3.81 = €2.80.

Average Exchange Rate (meticais per US $)

2004 22.58
2005 23.06
2006 25.40

Note: Between April 1992 and October 2000 the market exchange rate was the rate at which commercial banks purchased from and sold to the public. Since October 2000 it has been the weighted average of buying and selling rates of all transactions of commercial banks and stock exchanges with the public. A devaluation of the metical, with 1 new currency unit becoming equivalent to 1,000 of the former currency, was implemented on 1 July 2006.

BUDGET
('000 million meticais)

Revenue*	2003	2004	2005
Taxation	13,695	18,993	16,721
Taxes on income	3,235	4,445	4,469
Domestic taxes on goods and services	7,799	11,522	8,936
Customs duties	2,229	2,398	2,816
Other taxes	432	627	500
Non-tax revenue	1,019	1,476	3,662
Total	14,714	20,469	20,383

Expenditure†	2003	2004	2005
Current expenditure	16,342	21,890	20,365
Compensation of employees	7,734	11,045	10,358
Goods and services	2,991	4,908	4,407
Interest on public debt	1,319	1,244	1,248
Transfer payments	3,075	3,778	3,730
Other	1,223	915	622
Capital expenditure	13,369	17,026	13,101
Unallocated	252	—	170
Total	29,963	38,917	33,636

* Excluding grants received ('000 million meticais): 10,590 in 2003; 9,992 in 2004; 9,937 in 2005.

† Excluding net lending ('000 million meticais): 481 in 2003; 1,826 in 2004; 2,171 in 2005.

Source: Banco de Moçambique.

INTERNATIONAL RESERVES

(US $ million at 31 December)

	2004	2005	2006
IMF special drawing rights	0.08	0.23	0.23
Reserve position in IMF	0.01	0.01	0.01
Foreign exchange	1,130.86	1,053.58	1,155.49
Total	1,130.96	1,053.82	1,155.73

Source: IMF, *International Financial Statistics*.

MONEY SUPPLY

('000 million meticais at 31 December)

	2004	2005	2006
Currency outside banks	5,487.8	6,417.9	7,152.0
Demand deposits at commercial banks	10,240.9	12,809.4	17,095.4
Total money (incl. others)	15,728.7	19,227.4	24,247.5

Source: IMF, *International Financial Statistics*.

COST OF LIVING

(Consumer Price Index; base: 1998 = 100)

	2002	2003	2004
Food, beverages and tobacco	151	175	187
Clothing and footwear	126	122	125
Firewood and furniture	190	215	263
Health	119	133	134
Transportation and communications	205	232	234
Education, recreation and culture	145	150	151
Other goods and services	136	154	159
All items	157	179	195

Source: IMF, *Republic of Mozambique: Selected Issues and Statistical Appendix* (August 2005).

NATIONAL ACCOUNTS

('000 million meticais at current prices)

National Income and Product

	2001	2002	2003
Compensation of employees	20,446.5	27,012.5	36,346.7
Net operating surplus	11,059.2	11,282.6	11,239.4
Net mixed income	31,949.0	42,114.9	47,406.5
Domestic primary incomes	63,454.8	80,410.1	94,992.6
Consumption of fixed capital	10,401.4	13,865.7	15,079.6
Gross domestic product (GDP) at factor cost	73,856.1	94,275.8	110,072.2
Taxes on production and imports	4,634.2	5,050.1	6,145.3
Less Subsidies	1,945.5	2,442.4	2,314.9
GDP in market prices	76,544.9	96,883.5	113,902.5

Expenditure on the Gross Domestic Product

	2003	2004*	2005*
Government final consumption expenditure	14,236.2	16,737.7	20,298.4
Private final consumption expenditure	77,338.0	94,825.0	108,695.9
Increase in stocks	1,346.2	2,570.1	2,805.6
Gross capital formation	29,903.6	33,224.3	44,291.3
Total domestic expenditure	122,824.0	147,357.1	176,091.3
Exports of goods and services	28,927.6	39,729.3	48,679.2
Less Imports of goods and services	37,849.1	53,767.4	67,425.1
GDP in purchasers' values	113,902.5	133,318.9	157,345.4
GDP at constant 1996 prices	59,238.2	63,677.3	67,648.8

* Preliminary estimates.

Gross Domestic Product by Economic Activity

	2003	2004*	2005*
Agriculture, livestock and forestry	23,517.5	26,727.6	29,217.8
Fishing	1,707.0	1,577.0	1,846.5
Mining	379.9	1,142.3	1,416.3
Manufacturing	14,391.6	17,992.0	20,118.4
Electricity and water	5,053.7	7,030.7	9,349.8
Construction	9,207.4	9,365.1	10,090.4
Wholesale and retail trade	24,702.8	28,342.9	33,420.4
Repairs	980.3	987.2	1,091.9
Restaurants and hotels	1,412.9	1,691.4	1,824.0
Transport and communications	14,202.1	18,501.6	25,835.1
Financial services	4,211.0	4,326.7	5,205.7
Real estate and business services	1,879.5	1,993.3	2,125.2
Public administration and defence	3,839.1	4,303.9	5,176.0
Education	2,761.6	3,274.9	3,877.8
Health	1,088.2	1,278.9	1,393.1
Other services	4,697.2	4,709.6	5,111.4
Sub-total	114,031.7	133,245.0	157,100.0
Less Financial services indirectly measured	2,223.1	2,346.8	2,570.8
Gross value added in basic prices	111,808.6	130,898.2	154,529.2
Taxes on products *Less* Subsidies on products	2,093.9	2,420.8	2,816.2
GDP in market prices	113,902.5	133,318.9	157,345.4

* Preliminary estimates.

BALANCE OF PAYMENTS

(US $ million)

	2004	2005	2006
Exports of goods f.o.b.	1,503.9	1,745.3	2,381.1
Imports of goods f.o.b.	–1,849.7	–2,242.3	–2,648.8
Trade balance	–345.8	–497.1	–267.7
Exports of services	255.6	341.9	386.4
Imports of services	–531.4	–648.6	–758.1
Balance on goods and services	–621.7	–803.8	–639.5
Other income received	74.5	98.9	159.8
Other income paid	–374.0	–458.8	–655.4
Balance on goods, services and income	–921.2	–1,163.6	–1,135.0
Current transfers received	370.5	479.0	121.4
Current transfers paid	–56.7	–76.0	–73.8
Current balance	–607.4	–760.7	–1,807.4
Capital account (net)	578.1	187.9	488.5
Direct investment (net)	244.7	107.9	153.7
Portfolio investment assets	–25.4	–88.8	–124.2
Other investment assets	–88.7	–78.5	–13.8
Other investment liabilities	–177.1	154.3	–1,656.4
Errors and omissions (net)	216.4	281.0	143.8
Overall balance	140.7	–196.9	–2,095.7

Source: IMF, *International Financial Statistics*.

External Trade

PRINCIPAL COMMODITIES
(US $ million)

Imports c.i.f.	2002	2003
Food and live animals	187.4	215.7
Cereals	113.1	126.7
Mineral fuels, lubricants etc.	159.6	288.5
Chemicals and related products	86.6	117.1
Plastic and related products	56.9	21.6
Metals and related products	107.6	87.6
Iron and steel	20.7	22.9
Wood pulp and related products	28.1	50.5
Books, magazines, etc.	12.0	27.6
Textiles and related products	29.2	35.7
Machinery and transport equipment	405.6	476.7
General industrial machinery, equipment and parts	89.4	140.4
Electrical machinery, apparatus, etc.	85.4	144.2
Road vehicles and parts	194.9	157.7
General optical and photographic material, etc.	18.4	26.4
Miscellaneous manufactured articles	24.2	27.4
Commodities and transactions not classified elsewhere	402.2	318.5
Total (incl. others)	1,543.0	1,753.0

Exports f.o.b.	2002	2003
Food, live animals and tobacco	204.1	179.8
Fish, crustaceans, molluscs and other seafood	122.4	95.9
Textiles	25.2	45.4
Cotton	16.0	30.8
Mineral fuels, lubricants, etc.	136.0	136.1
Basic manufactures	367.1	574.2
Aluminium and alloys, unwrought	361.4	568.1
Machinery and transport equipment	32.5	44.8
Total (incl. others)	809.8	1,043.9

PRINCIPAL TRADING PARTNERS
(US $ million)

Imports c.i.f.	2002	2003	2004
Australia	7.5	211.3	2.7
France-Monaco	22.5	35.3	34.5
Germany	10.2	36.6	18.9
India	53.6	72.9	62.8
Japan	42.4	29.8	16.6
Malawi	2.3	19.2	n.a.
Pakistan	6.8	14.3	n.a.
Portugal	77.5	62.4	67.0
Saudi Arabia	25.0	18.4	n.a.
South Africa	342.2	654.4	842.0
Spain	5.8	27.6	24.6
Taiwan	16.9	40.6	n.a.
United Kingdom	12.5	19.9	n.a.
USA	55.6	104.3	48.3
Total (incl. others)	1,262.9	1,753.0	2,034.7

Exports f.o.b.	2002	2003	2004
Belgium	282.6	454.5	8.6
Italy	1.5	30.4	0.8
Malawi	10.4	32.8	49.9
Netherlands	1.9	29.6	916.6
Portugal	29.8	38.9	42.0
South Africa	120.4	169.6	211.4
Spain	19.0	70.0	38.0
Swaziland	0.5	17.4	2.7
United Kingdom	0.7	30.6	2.9
USA	10.7	15.7	n.a.
Zimbabwe	39.2	29.5	35.0
Total (incl. others)	682.0	1,043.9	1,503.9

Transport

RAILWAYS
(traffic)

	2002	2003	2004
Freight ton-km (million)	808	778	794
Passenger-km (million)	138	82	106

Source: UN, *Statistical Yearbook*.

ROAD TRAFFIC
(motor vehicles in use at 31 December)

	1999	2000	2001
Passenger cars	78,600	81,600	81,600
Lorries and vans	46,900	76,000	76,000

Source: UN, *Statistical Yearbook*.

SHIPPING

Merchant Fleet
(registered at 31 December)

	2004	2005	2006
Number of vessels	128	126	129
Total displacement ('000 grt)	36.1	35.4	36.5

Source: Lloyd's Register-Fairplay, *World Fleet Statistics*.

Freight Handled
('000 metric tons)

	2001	2002	2003
Goods loaded and unloaded	7,423	8,201	8,421

International Sea-borne Freight Traffic
('000 metric tons)

	2001	2002	2003
Goods loaded	2,962	2,780	2,982
Goods unloaded	3,144	4,062	3,837

CIVIL AVIATION
(traffic on scheduled services)

	2001	2002	2003
Kilometres flown (million)	7.5	6.6	6.5
Passengers carried ('000)	266.5	284.2	285.3
Passenger-km (million)	354.7	402.4	410.8

Tourism

TOURIST ARRIVALS BY COUNTRY OF RESIDENCE

Country	2003	2004	2005
Malawi	121,267	74,933	100,580
Portugal	25,392	11,898	15,970
South Africa	335,426	288,104	306,177
Swaziland	20,018	17,773	23,856
United Kingdom	5,798	6,700	8,993
USA	5,035	5,647	7,878
Zimbabwe	114,936	65,896	88,450
Total (incl. others)	726,099	711,060	954,433

Tourism receipts (US $ million, excl. passenger transport): 98 in 2003; 96 in 2004; n.a. in 2005.

Source: World Tourism Organization.

Communications Media

	2003	2004	2005
Telephones ('000 main lines in use)	77.6	69.7	69.7
Mobile cellular telephones ('000 subscribers)	435.8	708.0	1,220.0
Personal computers ('000 in use)	83	138	138
Internet users ('000)	96	112	112

1998: Daily newspapers 12 (average circulation 43,099); Non-daily newspapers 40 (estimated average circulation 205,800); Periodicals 32 (average circulation 83,000).

Television receivers ('000 in use): 230 in 2001.

Radio receivers ('000 in use): 730 in 1997.

Facsimile machines ('000 in use): 7.2 in 1996.

Sources: International Telecommunication Union; UN, *Statistical Yearbook*; UNESCO Institute for Statistics.

Education

(2003)

	Institutions	Teachers	Students
Pre-primary*†	5,689	28,705	1,745,049
Primary	9,027	51,912	3,177,586
Secondary	154	4,112	160,093
Technical	36	924	20,086
Teacher training‡	18	n.a.	9,314

* Public education only.

† 1997 figures.

‡ 2002 figures.

Source: mainly Ministry of Education.

Adult literacy rate (UNESCO estimates): 46.5% (males 62.3%; females 31.4%) in 2002 (Source: UN Development Programme, *Human Development Report*).

Directory

The Constitution

The Constitution came into force on 30 November 1990, replacing the previous version, introduced at independence on 25 June 1975 and revised in 1978. Its main provisions, as amended in 1996 and 2004, are summarized below. There are 306 articles in the Constitution.

GENERAL PRINCIPLES

The Republic of Mozambique is an independent, sovereign, unitary and democratic state of social justice. Sovereignty resides in the people, who exercise it according to the forms laid down in the Constitution. The fundamental objectives of the Republic include:

the defence of independence and sovereignty;

the defence and promotion of human rights and of the equality of citizens before the law; and

the strengthening of democracy, of freedom and of social and individual stability.

POLITICAL PARTICIPATION

The people exercise power through universal, direct, equal, secret, personal and periodic suffrage to elect their representatives, by referendums and through permanent democratic participation. Political parties are prohibited from advocating or resorting to violence.

FUNDAMENTAL RIGHTS AND DUTIES OF CITIZENS

All citizens enjoy the same rights and are subject to the same duties, irrespective of colour, race, sex, ethnic origin, place of birth, religion, level of education, social position or occupation. In realizing the objectives of the Constitution, all citizens enjoy freedom of opinion, assembly and association. All citizens over 18 years of age are entitled to vote and be elected. Active participation in the defence of the country is the duty of every citizen. Individual freedoms are guaranteed by the State, including freedom of expression, of the press, of assembly, of association and of religion. The State guarantees accused persons the right to a legal defence. No Court or Tribunal has the power to impose a sentence of death upon any person.

STATE ORGANS

Public elective officers are chosen by elections through universal, direct, secret, personal and periodic vote. Legally recognized political parties may participate in elections.

THE PRESIDENT

The President is the Head of State and of the Government, and Commander-in-Chief of the armed forces. The President is elected by direct, equal, secret and personal universal suffrage on a majority vote, and must be proposed by at least 10,000 voters, of whom at least 200 must reside in each province. The term of office is five years. A candidate may be re-elected on only two consecutive occasions, or again after an interval of five years between terms. The President is advised by a Council of State, but is not obliged to follow its advice.

THE ASSEMBLY OF THE REPUBLIC

Legislative power is vested in the Assembléia da República (Assembly of the Republic). The Assembléia is elected by universal direct adult suffrage on a secret ballot, and is composed of 250 Deputies. The Assembléia is elected for a maximum term of five years, but may be dissolved by the President before the expiry of its term. The Assembléia holds two ordinary sessions each year. The Assembléia, with a two-thirds majority, may impeach the President.

THE COUNCIL OF MINISTERS

The Council of Ministers is the Government of the Republic. The Prime Minister assists and advises the President in the leadership of the Government and presents the Government's programme, budget and policies to the Assembléia da República, assisted by other ministers.

LOCAL STATE ORGANS

The Republic is administered in provinces, municipalities and administrative posts. The highest state organ in a province is the provincial government, presided over by a governor, who is answerable to the central Government. There shall be assemblies at each administrative level.

THE JUDICIARY

Judicial functions shall be exercised through the Supreme Court and other courts provided for in the law on the judiciary, which also subordinates them to the Assembléia da República. Courts must safeguard the principles of the Constitution and defend the rights and legitimate interests of citizens. Judges are independent, subject only to the law.

The Government

HEAD OF STATE

President of the Republic and Commander-in-Chief of the Armed Forces: ARMANDO EMÍLIO GUEBUZA (took office 2 February 2005).

COUNCIL OF MINISTERS

(August 2007)

Prime Minister: LUÍSA DIAS DIOGO.

Minister of Foreign Affairs and Co-operation: ALCINDA ABREU.

Minister of National Defence: Gen. (retd) TOBIAS JOAQUIM DAI.

Minister of Finance: MANUEL CHANG.

Minister of Justice: ESPERANÇA ALFREDO MACHAVELA.

Minister of the Interior: JOSÉ PACHECO.

Minister of Development and Planning: AIUBA CUERENEIA.

Minister of State Administration: LUCAS CHOMERA.

Minister of Agriculture: ERASMO MUHATE.

Minister of Fisheries: CADMIEL FILIANE MUTHEMBA.

Minister of Industry and Trade: ANTÓNIO FERNANDO.

Minister of Energy: SALVADOR NAMBURETE.

Minister of Mineral Resources: ESPERANÇA BIAS.

Minister of Transport and Communications: ANTÓNIO FRANCISCO MUNGUAMBE.

Minister of Education and Culture: AIRES BONIFÁCIO ALI.

Minister of Health: PAULO IVO GARRIDO.

Minister of Environmental Co-ordination: LUCIANO ANDRE DE CASTRO.

Minister of Labour: MARIA HELENA TAIPO.

Minister of Public Works and Housing: FELÍCIO ZACARIAS.

Minister of Youth and Sport: DAVID SIMANGO.

Minister of Women's Affairs and Social Welfare Co-ordination: VIRGÍLIA BERNARDA NETO ALEXANDRE SANTOS MATABELE.

Minister of Tourism: FERNANDO SUMBANA, Jr.

Minister of Veterans' Affairs: FELICIANO SALOMÃO GUNDANA.

Minister of Science and Technology: VENÂNCIO MASSINGUE.

Minister in the Presidency with responsibility for Parliamentary Affairs: ISABEL MANUEL NKAVANDEKA.

Minister in the Presidency with responsibility for Diplomatic Affairs: FRANCISCO CAETANO MADEIRA.

MINISTRIES

Office of the President: Av. Julius Nyerere 1780, Maputo; tel. 21491121; fax 21492065; e-mail gabimprensa@teldata.mz; internet www.presidencia.gov.mz.

Office of the Prime Minster: Praça da Marinha Popular, Maputo; tel. 21426861; fax 21426881; e-mail dgpm.gov@teledata.mz; internet www.govmoz.gov.mz.

Ministry of Agriculture: Praça dos Heróis Moçambicanos, CP 1406, Maputo; tel. 21460011; fax 21460055.

Ministry of Development and Planning: Av. Ahmed Sekou Touré 21, CP 4087, Maputo; tel. 21490006; fax 21495477.

Ministry of Education and Culture: Av. 24 de Julho 167, CP 34, Maputo; tel. 21490677; fax 21492196.

Ministry of Energy: Av. 25 de Setembro, CP 1218, Maputo; e-mail asi@me.gov.mz.

Ministry of Environmental Co-ordination: Av. Acordos de Lusaka 2115, CP 2020, Maputo; tel. 21466245; fax 21465849; e-mail jwkacha@virconn.com; internet www.micoa.gov.mz.

Ministry of Finance: Maputo.

Ministry of Fisheries: Rua Consiglieri Pedroso 347, CP 1723, Maputo; tel. 21431266; fax 21425087.

Ministry of Foreign Affairs and Co-operation: Av. Julius Nyerere 4, CP 2787, Maputo; tel. 21490222; fax 21494070; e-mail minec@zebra.uem.mz.

Ministry of Health: Avs Eduardo Mondlane e Salvador Allende 1008, CP 264, Maputo; tel. 21427131; fax 21427133.

Ministry of Industry and Trade: Praça 25 de Junho 300, CP 1831, Maputo; tel. 21426093; fax 214262301; e-mail infomic@mic.gov.mz; internet www.mic.gov.mz.

Ministry of the Interior: Av. Olof Palme 46/48, CP 290, Maputo; tel. 21420131; fax 21420084.

Ministry of Justice: Av. Julius Nyerere 33, Maputo; tel. 21491613; fax 21494264.

Ministry of Labour: Av. 24 de Julho 2351–2365, CP 258, Maputo; tel. 21427051; fax 21421881.

Ministry of Mineral Resources: Av. Fernão de Magalhães 34, CP 2904, Maputo; tel. 21425682; fax 21427103.

Ministry of National Defence: Av. Mártires de Mueda 280, CP 3216, Maputo; tel. 21492081; fax 21491619.

Ministry of Public Works and Housing: Av. Karl Marx 268, CP 268, Maputo; tel. 21420543; fax 21421369.

Ministry of Science and Technology: Av. Patrice Lumumba 770, Maputo; tel. 21352800; fax 21352860; e-mail secretariado@mct.gov.mz; internet www.mct.gov.mz.

Ministry of State Administration: Rua da Rádio Moçambique 112, CP 4116, Maputo; tel. 21426666; fax 21428565.

Ministry of Tourism: Av. 25 de Setembro 1018, CP 4101, Maputo; tel. 21313755; fax 21306212; e-mail tourism@mitur.gov.mz; internet www.moztourism.gov.mz.

Ministry of Transport and Communications: Rua Mártires de Inhaminga 336, Maputo; tel. 21420152; fax 21431028.

Ministry of Veterans' Affairs: Rua General Pereira d'Eça 35, CP 3697, Maputo; tel. 21490601.

Ministry of Women's Affairs and Social Welfare Co-ordination: Rua de Tchamba 86, CP 516, Maputo; tel. 21490921; fax 21492757.

Ministry of Youth and Sport: Av. 25 de Setembro 529, CP 2080, Maputo; tel. 21312172; fax 21300040; e-mail mjd@tvcabo.co.mz; internet www.mjd.gov.mz.

PROVINCIAL GOVERNORS

(August 2007)

Cabo Delgado Province: LÁZARO MATHE.

Gaza Province: DJALMA LOURENÇO.

Inhambane Province: FRANCISCO MEQUE.

Manica Province: RAIMUNDO DIOMBO.

Maputo Province: TELMINA PEREIRA.

Nampula Province: FELISMINO ERNESTO TOCOLE.

Niassa Province: ARNALDO VICENTE BIMBE.

Sofala Province: ALBERTO CLEMENTINO VAQUINA.

Tete Province: ILDEFONSO MUANANTAPHA.

Zambézia Province: CARVALHO MUÁRIA.

City of Maputo: ROSA MANUEL DA SILVA.

President and Legislature

PRESIDENT

Presidential Election, 1–2 December 2004

Candidate	Votes	% of votes
Armando Guebuza (Frelimo)	2,004,226	63.74
Afonso Macacho Marceta Dhlakama (Renamo—União Eleitoral)	998,059	31.74
Raul Domingos (PPDD)	85,815	2.73
Yaqub Sabindy (PIMO)	28,656	0.91
Carlos Alexandre dos Reis (FMBG)	27,412	0.87
Total*	3,144,168	100.00

* Excluding 96,684 blank votes and 81,315 spoilt votes.

LEGISLATURE

Assembléia da República: CP 1516, Maputo; tel. 21400826; fax 21400711; e-mail cdi@sortmoz.com.

Chair.: EDUARDO MULÉMBUE.

General Election, 1–2 December 2004

Party	Votes	% of votes	Seats*
Frente de Libertação de Moçambique (Frelimo)	1,889,054	62.03	160
Resistência Nacional Moçambicana—União Eleitoral (Renamo—UE)	905,289	29.73	90
Partido para a Paz, Democracia e Desenvolvimento (PPDD)	60,758	2.00	—
Partido para a Liberdade e Solidariedade (PAZS)	20,686	0.68	—
Partido de Reconciliação Nacional (PARENA)	18,220	0.60	—
Partido Independente de Moçambique (PIMO)	17,960	0.59	—
Partido Social de Moçambique (PASOMO)	15,740	0.52	—
Others	117,722	3.87	—
Total (incl. others)†	3,045,429	100.00	250

* Parties must obtain a minimum of 5% of the vote in order to gain representation in the Assembléia da República.

† Excluding 166,540 blank votes and 109,957 spoilt votes.

Election Commission

Comissão Nacional de Eleições (CNE): Maputo; f. 1997; 13 mems; Chair. ARAO LITSURE.

Political Organizations

In mid-2004 there were five coalitions and 42 parties registered with the Comissão Nacional de Eleiçoes. The parties listed below secured votes in the December 2004 legislative elections.

Congresso dos Democratas Unidos (CDU): Maputo; f. 2001; Leader ANTÓNIO PALANGE.

Frente de Libertação de Moçambique (Frelimo): Rua Pereira do Lago 10, Bairro de Sommerschield, Maputo; tel. 21490181; fax 21490008; e-mail info@frelimo.org.mz; internet www.frelimo.org.mz; f. 1962 by merger of three nationalist parties; reorg. 1977 as a 'Marxist-Leninist vanguard movement'; in 1989 abandoned its exclusive Marxist-Leninist orientation; Pres. ARMANDO GUEBUZA.

Frente de Mudança e Boa Governa (FMBG): f. 2004; comprises:

Partido de Todos os Nativos Moçambicanos (Partonamo): f. 1996; Pres. MUSSAGY ABDUL REMANE.

União Nacional Moçambicana (Unamo): f. 1987; breakaway faction of Renamo; social democratic; obtained legal status 1992; fmr mem. of União Eleitoral; Pres. CARLOS ALEXANDRE DOS REIS; Sec.-Gen. FLORENCIA JOÃO DA SILVA.

Partido Democrático de Libertação de Moçambique (Padelimo): based in Kenya; Pres. JOAQUIM JOSÉ NHOTA.

Partido Independente de Moçambique (PIMO): f. 1993; Islamist; Leader YAQUB SABINDY; Sec.-Gen. MAGALHÃES BRAMUGY.

Partido Liberal e Democrático de Moçambique (Palmo): f. 1991; obtained legal status 1993; Pres. ANTÓNIO MUEDO.

Partido para a Paz, Democracia e Desenvolvimento (PPDD): Quelimane; f. 2003; liberal; Leader RAUL DOMINGOS.

Partido Popular Democrático (PPD): f. 2004; Leader MARCIANO FIJAMA.

Partido de Reconciliação Nacional (PARENA): Maputo; f. August 2004; Leader ANDRÉ BALATE.

Partido Social, Liberal e Democrático (Sol): breakaway faction of Palmo; Leader CASIMIRO MIGUEL NHAMITHAMBO.

Partido Social de Moçambique (Pasomo): Maputo; Leader FRANCISCO CAMPIRA.

Partido do Trabalho (PT): f. 1993; breakaway faction of PPPM; Pres. MIGUEL MABOTE; Sec.-Gen. LUÍS MUCHANGA.

Partido Verde de Moçambique (PVM): Leader BRUNO SAPEMBA.

Resistência Nacional Moçambicana-União Eleitoral (Renamo-UE): f. 1999; coalition comprising Renamo and the União Eleitoral which, in late 2004, consisted of 10 minor parties. Constituent members include:

Resistência Nacional Moçambicana (Renamo): Av. Julius Nyerere 2541, Maputo; tel. 21493107; also known as Movimento Nacional da Resistência de Moçambique (MNR); f. 1976; fmr guerrilla group, in conflict with the Govt between 1976 and Oct. 1992; obtained legal status in 1994; Pres. AFONSO MACACHO MARCETA DHLAKAMA; Sec.-Gen. OSSUFO MOMADE.

Aliança Independente de Moçambique (Alimo): Maputo; f. 1998; Sec.-Gen. ERNESTO SERGIO.

Frente de Ação Patriótica (FAP): Maputo; f. 1991; Pres. JOSÉ CARLOS PALAÇO.

Frente Democrática Unida—United Democratic Front (UDF): Maputo; Pres. JANEIRO MARIANO.

Frente Unida de Moçambique (Fumo): Av. Mao Tse Tung 230, 1° andar, Maputo; tel. 21494044; in early 2005 the party was reported to have split, with the faction led by Simeão Cuamba and Pedro Loforte supporting a withdrawal from the UE; Sec.-Gen. JOSÉ SAMO GUDO.

Partido de Convenção Nacional (PCN): Av. de 25 Setembro 1123, 3° andar, Maputo; tel. 21426891; obtained legal status in 1992; Chair. LUTERO CHIMBIRIMBIRI SIMANGO; Sec.-Gen. Dr GABRIEL MABUNDA.

Partido Ecologista de Moçambique (PEMO): Maputo.

Partido do Progresso do Povo de Moçambique (PPPM): Av. de 25 Setembro, 1123, 4° andar, Maputo; tel. 21426925; f. 1991; obtained legal status 1992; Pres. Dr PADIMBE MAHOSE KAMATI; Sec.-Gen. CHE ABDALA.

Partido Renovador Democrático (PRD): obtained legal status 1994; Pres. MANECA DANIEL.

Partido de Unidade Nacional (PUN): TV Sado 9, Maputo; tel. 21419204; Pres. HIPOLITO COUTO.

União para a Salvação de Moçambique (Usamo): f. 2004; coalition comprising the União para a Mudança (UM), PADRES, PSDM, and the PSM; Chair. JULIO NIMUIRE.

Partido Socialista de Moçambique (PSM): Leader JOÃO NKALAMBA.

Other parties obtaining votes at the December 2004 legislative elections were the **Frente do Amplo Oposicão (FAO)** (f. 2004), the **Partido Ecologista—Movimento da Terra** (f. 2002), the **Partido para a Liberdade e Solidariedade (PAZS)** (f. 2004), the **Partido para a Reconciliação Democrática (PAREDE)**, and the **União Democrática (UD)** (f. 1994, coalition). In 2005 a coalition comprising 18 small parties, including the **Partido Popular Democrático (PPD)**, the **Partido Nacional de Moçambique (Panamo)** and the **Partido Progressivo e Liberal de Moçambique (PPLM)**, was formed.

Diplomatic Representation

EMBASSIES AND HIGH COMMISSIONS IN MOZAMBIQUE

Algeria: Rua de Mukumbura 121–125, CP 1709, Maputo; tel. 21492070; fax 21490582; e-mail ab220261@virconn.com; Ambassador FOUAD BOUTTOURA.

Angola: Av. Kenneth Kaunda 783, CP 2954, Maputo; tel. 21493139; fax 21493930; Ambassador JOÃO GARCIA BIRES.

Brazil: Av. Kenneth Kaunda 296, CP 1167, Maputo; tel. 21484800; fax 21484806; e-mail ebrasil@teledata.mz; Ambassador LEDA CAMARGO.

China, People's Republic: Av. Julius Nyerere 3142, CP 4668, Maputo; tel. 21491560; fax 21491196; e-mail emb.chi@tvcabo.co.mz; Ambassador TIAN GUANGFENG.

Congo, Democratic Republic: Av. Kenneth Kaunda 127, CP 2407, Maputo; tel. 21497154; fax 21494929; Chargé d'affaires a.i. MULUMBA TSHIDIMBA MARCEL.

Congo, Republic: Av. Kenneth Kaunda 783, CP 4743, Maputo; tel. 21490142; Chargé d'affaires a.i. MONSEGNO BASHA OSHEFWA.

Cuba: Av. Kenneth Kaunda 492, CP 387, Maputo; tel. 21492444; fax 21491905; e-mail residcuba.mozambique@tvcabo.co.mz; Ambassador MARCELINA EVANGELINA SEOANE DOMÍNGUEZ.

Denmark: Av. Julius Nyerere 1162, CP 4588, Maputo; tel. 21480000; fax 21480010; e-mail mpmamb@um.dk; internet www.ambmaputo.um.dk; Ambassador MADS SANDAU-JENSEN.

Egypt: Av. Mao Tse Tung 851, CP 4662, Maputo; tel. 21491118; fax 21491489; e-mail egypt2@tropical.co.mz; Ambassador HAMDY ABD ELWAHAB SALEH.

Finland: Av. Julius Nyerere 1128, CP 1663, Maputo; tel. 21482400; fax 21491662; e-mail sanomat.map@formin.fi; Ambassador KARI ALANKO.

France: Av. Julius Nyerere 2361, CP 4781, Maputo; tel. 21484600; fax 21484680; e-mail ambafrancemz@tvcabo.co.mz; internet www.ambafrance-mz.org; Ambassador THIERRY VITEAU.

Germany: Rua Damião de Góis 506, CP 1595, Maputo; tel. 21492700; fax 21492888; e-mail germaemb@tvcabo.co.mz; internet www.maputo.diplo.de; Ambassador KLAUS-CHRISTIAN KRAEMER.

Holy See: Av. Kwame Nkrumah 224, CP 2738, Maputo; tel. 21491144; fax 21492217; e-mail namoz.secret@teledata.mz; Apostolic Nuncio Most Rev. GEORGE PANIKULAM (Titular Archbishop of Caudium).

Iceland: Av. Zimbabwe 1694, Maputo; tel. 21483509; fax 21483511; e-mail mozambique@iceida.is; internet www.iceland.org/mo; Chargé d'affaires a.i. JÓHANN PÁLSSON.

India: Av. Kenneth Kaunda 167, CP 4751, Maputo; tel. 21492437; fax 21492364; e-mail hicomind@tvcabo.co.mz; internet www.hicomind-maputo.org; High Commissioner RAJINDER BHAGAT.

Ireland: Av. Julius Nyerere 3332, Maputo; tel. 21491440; fax 21493023; e-mail maputo@dfa.ie; Ambassador FRANK SHERIDAN.

Italy: Av. Kenneth Kaunda 387, CP 976, Maputo; tel. 21492229; fax 21492046; e-mail ambasciata.maputo@esteri.it; internet www.ambmaputo.esteri.it; Ambassador GUIDO LARCHER.

Japan: Av. Julius Nyerere 2832, CP 2494, Maputo; tel. 21499819; fax 21498957; Ambassador TATSUYA MIKI.

Korea, Democratic People's Republic: Rua da Kaswende 167, Maputo; tel. 21491482; Ambassador PAK KUN GWANG.

Malawi: Av. Kenneth Kaunda 75, CP 4148, Maputo; tel. 21491468; fax 21490224; High Commissioner SAM KANDODO BANDA.

Mauritius: Rua Dom Carlos 42, Av. de Zimbabwe, Sommerscheid, Maputo; tel. 21494624; fax 21494729; e-mail mhcmoz@intra.co.mz; High Commissioner ALAIN LARIDON.

Netherlands: Av. Kwame Nkrumah 324, CP 1163, Maputo; tel. 21484200; fax 21484248; e-mail map@minbuza.nl; internet www.hollandinmozambique.org; Ambassador FRANS BIJVOET.

Nigeria: Av. Kenneth Kaunda 821, CP 4693, Maputo; tel. and fax 21490991; High Commissioner ALBERT G. PIUS OMOTAIO.

Norway: Av. Julius Nyerere 1162, CP 828, Maputo; tel. 21480100; fax 21480107; e-mail emb.maputo@mfa.no; internet www.norway.org.mz; Ambassador THORBJØRN GAUSTADSÆTHER.

Portugal: Av. Julius Nyerere 720, CP 4696, Maputo; tel. 21490316; fax 21491172; e-mail embaixada@embpormaputo.org.mz; Ambassador JOSÉ JOAQUIM ESTEVES DOS SANTOS DE FREITAS FERRAZ.

Russia: Av. Vladimir I. Lénine 2445, CP 4666, Maputo; tel. 21417372; fax 21417515; e-mail embrus@tvcabo.co.mz; internet www.mozambique.mid.ru; Ambassador IGOR V. POPOV.

South Africa: Av. Eduardo Mondlane 41, CP 1120, Maputo; tel. 21493030; fax 21493029; e-mail sahc@tropical.co.mz; High Commissioner THANDI LUJABE-RANKOE.

Spain: Rua Damião de Góis 347, CP 1331, Maputo; tel. 21492048; fax 21494769; e-mail emb.maputo@mae.es; Ambassador JUAN MANUEL MOLINA LAMOTHE.

Swaziland: Av. Kwame Nkrumah, CP 4711, Maputo; tel. 21491601; fax 21492117; High Commissioner Prince TSHEKEDI.

Sweden: Av. Julius Nyerere 1128, CP 338, Maputo; tel. 21480300; fax 21480390; e-mail ambasseden.maputo@foreign.ministry.se; internet www.swedenabroad.com/maputo; Ambassador TORVALD ÅKESSON.

Switzerland: Av. Ahmed Sekou Touré 637, CP 135, Maputo; tel. 21315275; fax 21315276; e-mail map.vertretung@eda.admin.ch; internet www.eda.admin.ch/maputo; Ambassador RUDOLF BAERFUSS.

Tanzania: Ujamaa House, Av. dos Mártires da Machava 852, CP 4515, Maputo; tel. 21490110; fax 21494782; e-mail ujamaa@zebra.eum.mz; High Commissioner ISSA MOHAMED ISSA.

Timor-Leste: Maputo; Chargé d'affaires a.i. MARINA ALKATIRI.

United Kingdom: Av. Vladimir I. Lénine 310, CP 55, Maputo; tel. 21356000; fax 21356060; e-mail bhc.consular@tvcabo.co.mz; internet www.britishhighcommission.gov.uk/mozambique; High Commissioner ANDREW SOPER.

USA: Av. Kenneth Kaunda 193, CP 783, Maputo; tel. 21492797; fax 21490114; e-mail consularmaputo@state.gov; internet www.usembassy-maputo.gov.mz; Ambassador WILLIAM R. STEIGER (designate).

Zambia: Av. Kenneth Kaunda 1286, CP 4655, Maputo; tel. 21492452; fax 21491893; e-mail zhcmmap@zebra.uem.mz; High Commissioner SIMON GABRIEL MWILA.

Zimbabwe: Av. Kenneth Kaunda 816, CP 743, Maputo; tel. 21490404; fax 21492237; e-mail maro@isl.co.mz; Ambassador GODFREY DZVAIRO.

Judicial System

The Constitution of November 1990 provides for a Supreme Court and other judicial courts, an Administrative Court, courts-martial, customs courts, maritime courts and labour courts. The Supreme Court consists of professional judges, appointed by the President of the Republic, and judges elected by the Assembléia da República. It acts in sections, as a trial court of primary and appellate jurisdiction, and in plenary session, as a court of final appeal. The Administrative Court controls the legality of administrative acts and supervises public expenditure.

President of the Supreme Court: MÁRIO MANGAZE.

Attorney-General: AUGUSTO PAULINO.

Religion

There are an estimated 5m. Christians and 4m. Muslims, as well as small Hindu, Jewish and Bahá'í communities. In 2004 over 100 religious groups were officially registered.

CHRISTIANITY

There are many Christian organizations registered in Mozambique.

Conselho Cristão de Moçambique (CCM) (Christian Council of Mozambique): Av. Agostino Neto 1584, CP 108, Maputo; tel. 21322836; fax 21321968; f. 1948; 22 mems; Pres. Rt Rev. ARÃO MATSOLO; Gen. Sec. Rev. DINIS MATSOLO.

The Roman Catholic Church

Mozambique comprises three archdioceses and nine dioceses. At 31 December 2004 it was estimated that there were some 4,976,302 adherents, representing some 24.2% of the total population.

Bishops' Conference

Conferência Episcopal de Moçambique (CEM), Secretariado Geral da CEM, Av. Paulo Samuel Kankhomba 188/RC, CP 286, Maputo; tel. 21490766; fax 21492174.

f. 1982; Pres. Most Rev. JAIME PEDRO GONÇALVES (Archbishop of Beira).

Archbishop of Beira: Most Rev. JAIME PEDRO GONÇALVES, Cúria Arquiepiscopal, Rua Correia de Brito 613, CP 544, Beira; tel. 23322313; fax 23327639; e-mail arquidbeira@teledata.mz.

Archbishop of Maputo: Most Rev. FRANCISCO CHIMOIO, Paço Arquiepiscopal, Avda Eduardo Mondlane 1448, CP 258, Maputo; tel. 21426240; fax 21421873.

Archbishop of Nampula: Most Rev. TOMÉ MAKHWELIHA, Paço Arquiepiscopal, CP 84, 70100 Nampula; tel. 26213024; fax 26214194; e-mail arquidioce.npl@teledata.mz.

The Anglican Communion

Anglicans in Mozambique are adherents of the Church of the Province of Southern Africa. There are two dioceses in Mozambique. The Metropolitan of the Province is the Archbishop of Cape Town, South Africa.

Bishop of Lebombo: Rt Rev. DINIS SALOMÃO SENGULANE, CP 120, Maputo; tel. 21734364; fax 21401093; e-mail libombo@zebra.uem.mz.

Bishop of Niassa: Rev. MARK VAN KOEVERING, CP 264, Lichinga, Niassa; tel. 27112735; fax 27112336; e-mail anglican-niassa@maf.org.

Other Churches

Baptist Convention of Mozambique: Av. Maguiguane 386, CP 852, Maputo; tel. 2126852; Pres. Rev. BENTO BARTOLOMEU MATUSSE; 78 churches, 25,000 adherents.

The Church of Jesus Christ of the Latter-Day Saints: Maputo; 9 congregations, 1,975 mems.

Free Methodist Church: Pres. Rev. FRANISSE SANDO MUVILE; 214 churches, 21,231 mems.

Igreja Congregational Unida de Moçambique: Rua 4 Bairro 25 de Junho, CP 930, Maputo; tel. 21475820; Pres., Sec. of the Synod A. A. LITSURE.

Igreja Maná: Rua Francisco Orlando Magumbwe 528, Maputo; tel. 21491760; fax 21490896; e-mail adm_mocambique@igrejamana.com; Bishop DOMINGOS COSTA.

Igreja Reformada em Moçambique (IRM) (Reformed Church in Mozambique): CP 3, Vila Ulongue, Anogonia-Tete; f. 1908; Gen. Sec. Rev. SAMUEL M. BESSITALA; 60,000 mems.

Presbyterian Church of Mozambique: Av. Ahmed Sekou Touré 1822, CP 21, Maputo; tel. 21421790; fax 21428623; e-mail ipmoc@

zebra.uem.mz; 100,000 adherents; Pres. of Synodal Council Rev. MÁRIO NYAMUXWE.

Seventh-Day Adventist Church: Av. Maguiguana 300, CP 1468, Maputo; tel. and fax 21427200; e-mail victormiconde@teledata.co.mz; 937 churches, 186,724 mems (2004).

Other denominations active in Mozambique include the Church of Christ, the Church of the Nazarene, the Greek Orthodox Church, the United Methodist Church of Mozambique, the Wesleyan Methodist Church, the Zion Christian Church, and Jehovah's Witnesses.

ISLAM

Comunidade Mahometana: Av. Albert Luthuli 291, Maputo; tel. 21425181; fax 21300880; e-mail toranias@zebra.uem.mz; internet www.paginaislamica.8m.com/pg1.htm; Pres. ABDUL ASSIZ OSMAN LATIF.

Congresso Islâmico de Moçambique (Islamic Congress of Mozambique): represents Sunni Muslims; Chair. ASSANE ISMAEL MAQBUL.

Conselho Islâmico de Moçambique (Islamic Council of Mozambique): Leader Sheikh AMINUDDIN MOHAMAD.

The Press

DAILIES

Correio da Manha: Av. Filipe Samuel Magaia 528, CP 1756, Maputo; tel. 21305322; fax 21305321; e-mail refi@virconn.com; f. 1997; published by Sojornal, Lda; also publishes weekly Correio Semanal; Dir REFINALDO CHILENGUE.

Diário de Moçambique: Av. 25 de Setembro 1509, 2° andar, CP 2491, Beira; tel. and fax 23427312; f. 1981; under state management since 1991; Dir EZEQUIEL AMBRÓSIO; Editor FARUCO SADIQUE; circ. 5,000 (2003).

Expresso da Tarde: Av. Patrice Lumumba 511, 1° andar, Maputo; tel. 21314912; e-mail expresso@teledata.mz; subscription only; distribution by fax; Dir SALVADOR RAIMUNDO HONWANA.

Mediafax: Av. Amílcar Cabral 1049, CP 73, Maputo; tel. 21301737; fax 21302402; e-mail mediafax@tvcabo.co.mz; f. 1992 by co-operative of independent journalists Mediacoop; news-sheet by subscription only, distribution by fax and internet; Editor BENEDITO NGOMANE.

Notícias de Moçambique: Rua Joaquim Lapa 55, CP 327, Maputo; tel. 21420119; fax 21420575; f. 1926; morning; f. 1906; under state management since 1991; Dir BERNARDO MAVANGA; Editor HILÁRIO COSSA; circ. 12,793 (2003).

Further newspapers available solely in email or fax format include Diário de Notícias and Matinal.

WEEKLIES

Campeão: Av. 24 de Julho 3706, CP 2610, Maputo; tel. and fax 21401810; sports newspaper; Dir RENATO CALDÉIRA; Editor ALEXANDRE ZANDAMELA.

Correio Semanal: Av. Filipe Samuel Magaia 528, CP 1756, Maputo; tel. 21305322; fax 21305312; Dir REFINALDO CHILENGUE.

Desafio: Rua Joaquim Lapa 55, Maputo; tel. 21305437; fax 21305431; Dir ALMIRO SANTOS; Editor BOAVIDA FUNJUA; circ. 3,890 (2003).

Domingo: Rua Joaquim Lapa 55, CP 327, Maputo; tel. 21431026; fax 21431027; f. 1981; Sun.; Dir JORGE MATINE; Editor MOISES MABUNDA; circ. 10,421 (2003).

Fim de Semana: Rua da Resistência 1642, 1° andar, Maputo; tel. and fax 21417012; e-mail fimdomes@tvcabo.co.mz; internet www.fimdesemana.co.mz; f. 1997; independent.

Savana: Av. Amílcar Cabral 1049, CP 73, Maputo; tel. 21301737; fax 21302402; e-mail savana@mediacoop.co.mz; internet www.mediacoop.odline.com; f. 1994; Dir KOK NAM; Editor FERNANDO GONÇALVES; circ. 15,000 (2006).

Tempo: Av. Ahmed Sekou Touré 1078, CP 2917, Maputo; tel. 21426191; f. 1970; magazine; under state management since 1991; Dir ROBERTO UAENE; Editor ARLINDO LANGA; circ. 40,000.

Zambeze: Rua José Sidumo, Maputo; tel. 21302019; Dir SALOMÃO MOYANE; circ. 2,000 (2003).

PERIODICALS

Agora: Afrisurvey, Lda, Rua General Pereira d'Eça 200, 1° andar, CP 1335, Maputo; tel. 21494147; fax 21494204; e-mail agora@agora.co.mz; internet www.agora.co.mz; f. 2000; monthly; economics, politics, society; Pres. MARIA DE LOURDES TORCATO; Dir JOVITO NUNES; Editor-in-Chief ERCÍLIA SANTOS; circ. 5,000.

Agricultura: Instituto Nacional de Investigação Agronómica, CP 3658, Maputo; tel. 2130091; f. 1982; quarterly; publ. by Centro de Documentação de Agricultura, Silvicultura, Pecuária e Pescas.

Aro: Av. 24 de Julho 1420, CP 4187, Maputo; f. 1995; monthly; Dir POLICARTO TAMELE; Editor BRUNO MACAME, Jr.

Arquivo Histórico: Av. Filipe Samuel Magaia 715, CP 2033, Maputo; tel. 21421177; fax 21423428; e-mail jneves@zebra.uem.mz; f. 1934; Editor JOEL DAS NEVES TEMBE.

Boletim da República: Av. Vladimir I. Lénine, CP 275, Maputo; govt and official notices; publ. by Imprensa Nacional da Moçambique.

Maderazinco: Maputo; e-mail maderazinco@yahoo.com; f. 2002; quarterly; literature.

Moçambique–Novos Tempos: Av. Ahmed Sekou Touré 657, Maputo; tel. 21493564; fax 21493590; f. 1992; Dir J. MASCARENHAS.

Mozambiquefile: c/o AIM, Rua da Radio Moçambique, CP 896, Maputo; tel. 21313225; fax 21313196; e-mail aim@aim.org.mz; internet www.sortmoz.com/aimnews; monthly; Dir GUSTAVO MAVIZ; Editor PAUL FAUVET.

Mozambique Inview: c/o Mediacoop, Av. Amílcar Cabral 1049, CP 73, Maputo; tel. 21430722; fax 21302402; e-mail inview@mediacoop.co.mz; internet www.mediacoop.odline.com; f. 1994; 2 a month; economic bulletin in English; Editor FRANCES CHRISTIE.

Portos e Caminhos de Ferro: CP 276, Maputo; English and Portuguese; ports and railways; quarterly.

Revista Médica de Moçambique: Instituto Nacional de Saúde, Ministério da Saúde e Faculdade de Medicina, Universidade Eduardo Mondlane, CP 264, Maputo; tel. 21420368; fax 21431103; e-mail mdgedge@malarins.uem.mz; f. 1982; 4 a year; medical journal; Editor MARTINHO DGEDGE.

NEWS AGENCIES

Agência de Informação de Moçambique (AIM): Rua da Rádio Moçambique, CP 896, Maputo; tel. 21313225; fax 21313196; e-mail aim@aim.org.mz; internet www.sortmoz.com/aimnews; f. 1975; daily reports in Portuguese and English; Dir GUSTAVO LISSETIANE MAVIE.

Foreign Bureaux

Agence France-Presse (AFP): CP 4650, Maputo; tel. and fax 21422940; fax 21422940; Correspondent RACHEL WATERHOUSE.

Agenzia Nazionale Stampa Associata (ANSA) (Italy): Maputo; tel. 21430723; fax 21421906; Correspondent PAUL FAUVET.

Lusa (Agência de Notícias de Portugal, SA): Av. Ho Chi Minh 111, Maputo; tel. 21427591; fax 21421690; e-mail lsa@lusa.pt; Bureau Chief LUÍS ANDRAD DE SÁ.

Xinhua (New China) News Agency (People's Republic of China): Rua Coimbra 258, Maputo; tel. 21414445.

Reuters (UK) is also represented in Mozambique.

Publishers

There are an estimated 30 printing and publishing companies in Mozambique.

Arquivo Histórico de Moçambique (AHM): Av. Filipe Samuel Magaia 715, CP 2033, Maputo; tel. 21421177; fax 21423428; e-mail jneves@zebra.uem.mz; internet www.ahm.uem.mz; Dir JOEL DAS NEVES TEMBE.

Central Impressora: c/o Ministério da Saúde, Avs Eduardo Mondlane e Salvador Allende 1008, CP 264, Maputo; tel. 21427131; fax 21427133; owned by the Ministry of Health.

Centro de Estudos Africanos: Universidade Eduardo Mondlane, CP 1993, Maputo; tel. 21490828; fax 21491896; f. 1976; social and political science, regional history, economics; Dir Col SERGIO VIEIRA.

Editora Minerva Central: Rua Consiglieri Pedroso 84, CP 212, Maputo; tel. 2122092; f. 1908; stationers and printers, educational, technical and medical textbooks; Man. Dir J. F. CARVALHO.

Editorial Ndjira, Lda: Av. Ho Chi Minh 85, Maputo; tel. 21300180; fax 21308745; f. 1996.

Empresa Moderna Lda: Av. 25 de Setembro, CP 473, Maputo; tel. 21424594; f. 1937; fiction, history, textbooks; Man. Dir LOUIS GALLOTI.

Fundo Bibliográfico de Língua Portuguesa: Av. 25 de Setembro 1230, 7° andar, Maputo; tel. 21429531; fax 21429530; e-mail palop@zebra.uem.mz; f. 1990; state owned; Pres. LOURENÇO ROSÁRIO.

Imprensa Universitária: Universidade Eduardo Mondlane, Praça 19 de Maio, Maputo; internet www.uem.mz/imprensa_universitaris; university press.

Instituto Nacional do Livro e do Disco: Av. 24 de Julho 1921, CP 4030, Maputo; tel. 21434870; govt publishing and purchasing agency; Dir ARMÉNIO CORREIA.

Moçambique Editora: Rua Armando Tivane 1430, Bairro de Polana, Maputo; tel. 21495017; fax 21499071; e-mail info@me.co.mz; internet www.me.co.mz; f. 1996; educational textbooks, dictionaries.

Plural Editores: Av. 24 de Julho 414, Maputo; tel. 21486828; fax 21486829; e-mail plural@pluraleditores.co.mz; internet www.pluraleditores.co.mz; f. 2003; educational textbooks; part of the Porto Editora Group.

GOVERNMENT PUBLISHING HOUSE

Imprensa Nacional de Moçambique: Rua da Imprensa, CP 275, Maputo; tel. 21427021; fax 21424858; internet www.imprensanac.gov.mz; part of Ministry of State Administration; Dir VENÂNCIO T. MANJATE.

Broadcasting and Communications

TELECOMMUNICATIONS

Regulatory Authority

Instituto Nacional das Comunicações de Moçambique (INCM): Av. Eduardo Mondlane 123–127, CP 848, Maputo; tel. 21490131; fax 21494435; e-mail info@incm.gov.mz; internet www.incm.gov.mz; regulates post and telecommunications systems.

Major Telecommunications Companies

TDM currently has a monopoly on fixed lines; however, plans were announced in 2004 to open this sector to competition by 2007.

Telecomunicações de Moçambique, SARL (TDM): Rua da Sé 2, CP 25, Maputo; tel. 21431921; fax 21431944; e-mail jcarvalho@tdm.mz; internet www.tdm.mz; f. 1993; Chair. JOAQUIM RIBEIRO PEREIRA DE CARVALHO; Man. Dir SALVADOR ADRIANO.

Moçambique Celular (mCel): Edif. Mcel, Esquina Av. 25 de Setembro e Rua Belmiro Obede Muianga, CP 1463, Maputo; tel. 21351111; fax 21351119; e-mail mcel@mcel.co.mz; internet www.mcel.co.mz; f. 1997 as a subsidiary of TDM; separated from TDM in 2003; mobile cellular telephone provider.

Vodacom Moçambique: Time Square Complex, Bloco 3, Av. 25 de Setembro, Maputo; tel. 21084111; internet www.vm.co.mz; f. 2002; owned by Vodacom (South Africa); Chair. HERMENGILDO GAMITO; Man. Dir CLIVE TARR.

BROADCASTING

Radio

Rádio Encontro: Av. Francisco Manyanga, CP 366, Nampula; tel. 26215588.

Rádio Feba Moçambique: Av. Julius Nyerere 441, Maputo; tel. 21440002.

Rádio Maria: Rua Igreja 156A, Machava Sede, Matola, Maputo; tel. 21750505; fax 21752124; e-mail ramamo@virconn.com; f. 1995; evangelical radio broadcasts; Dir Fr JOÃO CARLOS H. NUNES.

Rádio Miramar: Rede de Comunicação, Av. Julius Nyerere 1555, Maputo; tel. and fax 21488613; e-mail jose.guerra@tvcabo.co.mz; owned by Brazilian religious sect, the Universal Church of the Kingdom of God.

Rádio Moçambique: Rua da Rádio 2, CP 2000, Maputo; tel. 21431687; fax 21321816; e-mail sepca_mz@yahoo.com.br; internet www.teledata.mz/radiomocambique; f. 1975; programmes in Portuguese, English and vernacular languages; Chair. MANUEL FERNANDO VETERANO.

Rádio Terra Verde: fmrly Voz da Renamo; owned by former rebel movement Renamo; transmitters in Maputo and Gorongosa, Sofala province.

Rádio Trans Mundial Moçambique: Av. Eduardo Mondlane 2998, Maputo; tel. 21407358; fax 21407357.

Television

The Portuguese station RTP-Africa also broadcasts in Mozambique.

Rádio Televisão Klint (RTK): Av. Agostinho Neto 946, Maputo; tel. 21422956; fax 21493306; Dir CARLOS KLINT.

Televisão Miramar: Rua Pereira Lago 221, Maputo; owned by Brazilian religious sect, the Igrega Universal do Reino de Deus (Universal Church of the Kingdom of God).

Televisão de Moçambique, EP (TVM): Av. 25 de Setembro 154, CP 2675, Maputo; tel. 21308117; fax 21308122; e-mail tvm@tvm.co.mz; internet www.tvm.co.mz; f. 1981; Chair. and CEO SIMÃO JORDÃO ANGUILAZE.

TV Cabo Moçambique: Av. dos Presidentes 68, CP 1750, Maputo; tel. 21480500; fax 21480501; e-mail tvcabo@tvcabo.co.mz; internet www.tvcabo.co.mz; cable television and internet services in Maputo.

Finance

(cap. = capital; res = reserves; dep. = deposits; m. = million; brs = branches; amounts in meticais, unless otherwise stated)

BANKING

Central Bank

Banco de Moçambique: Av. 25 de Setembro 1679, CP 423, Maputo; tel. 21318000; fax 21323247; e-mail cdi@bancomoc.mz; internet www.bancomoc.mz; f. 1975; bank of issue; cap. 248,952m., res 532,697m., dep. 17,360m. (Dec. 2006); Gov. ERNESTO GOUVEIA GOVE; 4 brs.

National Banks

Banco Austral: Av. 25 de Setembro 1184, CP 757, Maputo; tel. 21308800; fax 21301094; internet www.bancoaustral.co.mz; f. 1977; fmrly Banco Popular de Desenvolvimento (BPD); renationalized in 2001; 80% owned by Amalgamated Banks of South Africa, 20% owned by União, Sociedade e Participacões, SARL, which represents employees of the bank; cap. 315,000m., res –550m., dep. 2,047,081m. (Dec. 2003); Chair. CASIMIRO FRANCISCO; Man. Dir GERALD JORDAAN; 52 brs and agencies.

BCI Fomento (BCI) (Banco Comercial e de Investimentos, SARL): Edif. John Orr's, Av. 25 de Setembro 1465, CP 4745, Maputo; tel. 21307777; fax 21307762; e-mail bci@bci.co.mz; internet www.bci.co.mz; f. 1996; renamed as above following 2003 merger between Banco Comercial e de Investimentos and Banco de Fomento; 42% owned by Caixa Geral de Depósitos (Portugal); 30% Banco Português de Investimento; dep. 360.0m. (US $, Dec. 2004); Chair. ABDUL MAGID OSMAN; 34 brs.

Banco de Desenvolvimento e de Comércio de Moçambique, SARL (BDCM): Av. 25 de Setembro 420, 1° andar, sala 8, Maputo; tel. 21313040; fax 21313047; f. 2000; 42% owned by Montepio Geral (Portugal).

BIM—Investimento (Banco Internacional de Moçambique—Investimento): Av. Kim Il Sung 961, Maputo; tel. 21354896; fax 21354897; e-mail mpinto@bim.co.mz; internet www.bimnet.co.mz; f. 1998; 50% owned by Millennium bim, 25% by BCP Investimento and 15% by International Finance Corpn; total assets US $2.7m. (Dec. 2003); Chair. Dr MÁRIO FERNANDES DA GRAÇA MACHUNGO; Gen. Dir Dr JOSÉ A. FERREIRA GOMES.

Banco Mercantil e de Investimento, SARL (BMI): Av. 24 de Julho 3549, Maputo; tel. 21407979; fax 21408887; e-mail bmibanco@teledata.mz.

ICB-Banco Internacional de Comércio, SARL: Av. 25 de Setembro 1915, Maputo; tel. 21311111; fax 21314797; e-mail icbm@teledata.mz; internet www.icbank-mz.com; f. 1998; cap. and res 44,923,748m., total assets 164,773,569m. (Dec. 2003); Chair. JOSEPHINE SIVARETNAM; CEO LEE SANG HUAT.

Millennium bim: Av. 25 de Setembro 1800, CP 865, Maputo; tel. 21351500; fax 21354808; internet www.bimnet.co.mz; f. 1995; name changed from Banco Internacional de Moçambique in 2005; 66.7% owned by Banco Comercial Português, 23.1% by the state; cap. 741,000m., res 634,158m., dep. 14,772,502m. (Dec. 2004); Pres. ANTÓNIO DE ALMEIDA; 76 brs.

Novo Banco, SARL: Av. do Trabalho 750, Maputo; tel. and fax 21407705; e-mail novobanco@teledata.mz; f. 2000; cap. and res 51,995m., total assets 108,847m. (Dec. 2003).

Standard Bank, SARL (Moçambique): Praça 25 de Junho 1, CP 2086, Maputo; tel. 21352500; fax 21426967; e-mail camal.daude@standardbank.co.mz; internet www.standardbank.co.mz; f. 1966 as Banco Standard Totta de Mozambique; 96.0% owned by Stanbic Africa Holdings, UK; cap. 174,000m., res 173,295m., dep. 6,080,437m. (Dec. 2003); Man. Dir ANTONIO COUTINHO; 24 brs.

Foreign Banks

African Banking Corporation (Moçambique), SARL: ABC House, Av. Julius Nyerere 999, Polana, CP 1445, Maputo; tel. 21482100; fax 21487474; e-mail abcmoz@africanbankingcorp.com; internet www.africanbankingcorp.com; f. 1999; 100% owned by African Banking Corpn Holdings Ltd (Botswana); fmrly BNP Nedbank (Moçambique), SARL; changed name as above after acquisition in 2002; cap. 65,000m., res 8,642m., dep. 675,833m. (Dec. 2003); Chair. BENJAMIN ALFREDO; Man. Dir ZANDILE CHIRESHE.

African Banking Corporation Leasing, SARL: Rua da Imprensa 256, 7° andar, CP 4447, Maputo; tel. 21300451; fax 21431290; e-mail ulcmoz@mail.tropical.co.mz; 66% owned by African Banking Corpn Holdings Ltd (Botswana); fmrly ULC (Moçambique); changed name as above in 2002; total assets US $1.8m. (Dec. 1998); Chair. ANTÓNIO BRANCO; Gen. Man. VICTOR VISEU.

União Comercial de Bancos (Moçambique), SARL: Av. Friedrich Engels 400, Maputo; tel. 21481900; fax 21498675; e-mail contact@mcbmozambique.com; f. 1999; 81.24% owned by Mauritius Commercial Bank Group; total assets US $46,777m. (Dec. 2006); Chair. PIERRE GUY NOEL; Gen. Man. ROBERT CANTIN.

DEVELOPMENT FUND

Fundo de Desenvolvimento Agrícola e Rural: CP 1406, Maputo; tel. 21460349; fax 21460157; f. 1987; to provide credit for small farmers and rural co-operatives; promotes agricultural and rural development; Sec. EDUARDO OLIVEIRA.

STOCK EXCHANGE

Bolsa de Valores de Moçambique: Av. 25 de Setembro 1230, Prédio 33, 5° andar, Maputo; tel. 21308826; fax 21310559; e-mail jussub@bvm.com; Chair. Dr JUSSUB NURMAMAD.

INSURANCE

In December 1991 the Assembléia da República approved legislation terminating the state monopoly of insurance and reinsurance activities. In 2005 five insurance companies were operating in Mozambique.

Companhia de Seguros de Moçambique, IMPAR: Rua da Imprensa 625, Prédio 33, Maputo; tel. 21429695; fax 21430640; e-mail impar@zebra.uem.mz; f. 1992; Pres. INOCÊNCIO A. MATAVEL; Gen. Man. MANUEL BALANCHO.

Empresa Moçambicana de Seguros, EE (EMOSE): Av. 25 de Setembro 1383, CP 1165, Maputo; tel. 21356300; fax 21424526; f. 1977 as state insurance monopoly; took over business of 24 fmr cos; 80% govt–owned, 20% private; cap. 150m.; Chair. VENÂNCIO MONDLANE.

Seguradora Internacional de Moçambique: Maputo; tel. 21430959; fax 21430241; e-mail simseg@zebra.uem.mz; Pres. MÁRIO FERNANDES DA GRAÇA MACHUNGO.

Trade and Industry

GOVERNMENT AGENCIES

Centro de Promoção de Investimentos (CPI) (Investment Promotion Centre): Rua da Imprensa 332, CP 4635, Maputo; tel. 21313295; fax 21313325; e-mail cpi@cpi.co.mz; internet www.cpi.co.mz; f. 1987; encourages domestic and foreign investment and IT ventures with foreign firms; evaluates and negotiates investment proposals; Dir MAHOMED RAFIQUE JUSOB MAHOMED.

Instituto de Algodão de Moçambique (IAM): Av. Eduardo Mondlane 2221, 1° andar, CP 806, Maputo; tel. 21424264; fax 21430679; e-mail iampab@zebra.uem.mz; responsible for promotion of and development of the cotton industry; Dir (vacant).

Instituto do Fomento do Cajú (INCAJU): Maputo; national cashew institute; Dir CLEMENTINA MACHUNGO.

Instituto Nacional de Açúcar (INA): Rua da Gávea 33, CP 1772, Maputo; tel. 21326550; fax 21427436; e-mail gpsca.ina@tvcabo.co.mz; Chair. ARNALDO RIBEIRO.

Instituto Nacional de Petróleo (INP): Av. Fernão de Magalhães 34, CP 4724, Maputo; tel. 21320935; fax 21430850; e-mail info@inp.gov.mz; internet www.inp.gov.mz; f. 2005; regulates energy sector; Dir ARSÉNIO MABOTE.

Instituto para a Promoção de Exportações (IPEX): Av. 25 de Setembro 1008, 3° andar, CP 4487, Maputo; tel. 21307257; fax 21307256; e-mail ipex@tvcabo.co.mz; internet www.ipex.gov.mz; f. 1990 to promote and co-ordinate national exports abroad; Pres. Dr FELISBERTO FERRÃO.

Unidade Técnica para a Reestruturação de Empresas (UTRE): Rua da Imprensa 256, 7° andar, CP 4350, Maputo; tel. 21426514; fax 21421541; e-mail utre@teledata.mz; implements restructuring of state enterprises; Dir MOMADE JUMAS.

CHAMBERS OF COMMERCE

Câmara de Comércio de Moçambique (CCM): Rua Mateus Sansão Muthemba 452, CP 1836, Maputo; tel. 21491970; fax 21490428; e-mail cacomo@teledata.nz; internet www.teledata.mz/cacomo; f. 1980; Pres. JACINTO VELOSO; Sec.-Gen. MANUEL NOTIÇO.

Mozambique-USA Chamber of Commerce: Rua Matheus Sansão Muthemba 452, Maputo; tel. 21492904; fax 21492739; e-mail ccmusa@tvcabo.co.mx; internet www.ccmusa.co.mz; f. 1993; Sec. PETER VAN AS.

South Africa-Mozambique Chamber of Commerce (SAMOZACC): e-mail info@samozacc.co.za; internet www.samozacc.co.za; f. 2005; Chair. (Mozambique) ANTÓNIO MATOS.

TRADE ASSOCIATIONS

Associação das Indústrias do Cajú (AICAJU): Maputo; cashew processing industry asscn; Chair. CARLOS COSTA; 12 mem. cos.

Confederação das Associações Económicas (CTA): Av. 10 de Novembro, CP 2975, Maputo; tel. 21311734; fax 21311732; e-mail info@cta.org.mz; internet www.cta.org.mz; Pres. SALIMO ABDULA; Exec. Dir SÉRGIO CHITARÁ; 46 mem. cos.

STATE INDUSTRIAL ENTERPRISES

Empresa Nacional de Carvão de Moçambique (CARBOMOC): Rua Joaquim Lapa 108, CP 1773, Maputo; tel. 21427625; fax 21424714; f. 1948; mineral extraction and export; transfer to private ownership pending; Dir JAIME RIBEIRO.

Empresa Nacional de Hidrocarbonetos de Moçambique (ENH): Av. Fernão de Magalhães 34, CP 4787, Maputo; tel. 21429456; fax 21421608; controls concessions for petroleum exploration and production; Dir MÁRIO MARQUES.

Petróleos de Moçambique (PETROMOC): Praça dos Trabalhadores 9, CP 417, Maputo; tel. 21427191; fax 21430181; internet www.petromoc.co.mz; f. 1977 to take over the Sonarep oil refinery and its associated distribution co; formerly Empresa Nacional de Petróleos de Moçambique; state directorate for liquid fuels within Mozambique, incl. petroleum products passing through Mozambique to inland countries; CEO CASIMIR FRANCISCO.

UTILITIES

Electricity

Electricidade de Moçambique (EDM): Av. Agostinho Neto 70, CP 2447, Maputo; tel. 21490636; fax 21491048; e-mail ligacaoexpresso@edm.co.mz; internet www.edm.co.mz; f. 1977; 100% state-owned; production and distribution of electric energy; in 2004 plans were announced to extend EDM grid to entire country by 2020, at an estimated cost of US $700m; Pres. MANUEL JOÃO CUAMBE; Dir PASCOAL BACELA; 2,700 employees.

Companhia de Transmissão de Moçambique, SARL (MOTRACO) (Mozambique Transmission Co): Prédio JAT, 4° andar, Av. 25 de Setembro 420, Maputo; tel. 21313427; fax 21313447; e-mail asimao@motraco.co.mz; internet www.motraco.co.mz; f. 1998; jt venture between power utilities of Mozambique, South Africa and Swaziland; electricity distribution; Gen. Man. FRANCIS MASAWI.

Water

Direcção Nacional de Águas: Av. 25 de Setembro 942, 9° andar, CP 1611, Maputo; tel. 21420469; fax 21421403; e-mail watco@zebra.uem.mz; internet www.dna.mz; Dir AMÉRICO MUIANGA.

MAJOR COMPANIES

British American Tobacco (BAT) (Sociedade Agricola de Tabacos Lda): CP 713, Maputo; tel. 21496011; fax 21491397; internet www.bat.com; production of cigarettes; Gen. Man. LUIZ RIBEIRO.

BP Moçambique Lda: Av. dos Mártires da Inhaminga 170, CP 854, Maputo; tel. 21325025; fax 21326042; internet www.bp.com; f. 1981; distribution of petroleum products; Gen. Man. JOSEPH F. M. SCHERRENBERG; 306 employees.

Cervejas de Moçambique, SARL (CDM): Rua do Jardim 1329, CP 3555, Maputo; tel. 21475007; fax 21475120; brewery.

Cimentos de Moçambique, SARL (CM): Av. 24 de Julho 7, 9° andar, Maputo; tel. 214870; fax 21487868; e-mail cmocambique@mz.cimpor.com; owned by Cimentos de Portugal; cement; Admin. Dir JOSE ALFINAR; 506 employees.

Coca Cola Sabco (Moçambique), SARL: Av. OUA 270, Maputo; tel. 21400190; fax 21400375; internet www.ccsabco.co.za; bottling co; Man. SOREN HANSEN.

Comércio Grossista de Produtos Alimentares (COGROPA): Av. 25 de Setembro 916, CP 308, Maputo; tel. and fax 21420153; food supplies; transfer pending to private ownership; Dir ANTÓNIO BAPTISTA DO AMARAL.

Companhia de Desenvolvimento Mineiro, SARL (CDM): Av. 24 de Julho 1895, CP 1152, Maputo; tel. 214205889; fax 21428921; e-mail ljossene@teledata.mz; f. 1989; mineral exploration and mineral trade; Pres. LUÍS JOSSENE.

Companhia Industrial do Monapo, SARL: Av. do Trabalho 2106, CP 1248, Maputo; tel. 21400290; fax 21401164; animal and vegetable oils and soap; CEO CARMEN RAMOS.

Construtora do Tâmega: Rua da Tâmega, Machava, CP 1238, Maputo; tel. 21750012; fax 21750174; e-mail tamega@tamega.co.mz;

f. 1946; civil engineering and construction; Chair. JOAQUÍM DA MOTA; Man. Dir JOAQUÍM CORDEIRO; 1,450 employees.

Custódio e Irmão, Lda (CIL): Av. de Angola 2351, CP 2495, Maputo; tel. 21465225; fax 21465677; f. 1972; concrete, wood and steel construction materials; Chair. LEONEL CUSTÓDIO.

Embalagens Mondipak, Lda: CP 303, Maputo; tel. 21750372; fax 21750044; e-mail mondipak@teledata.mz; f. 1969 as Embalagens Holdains, Lda; present name adopted in 2006; packaging materials; Gen. Man. NURO MOMEDE MULÁ.

Empresa de Construções Metálicas (ECOME): Av. das Indústrias-Machava, CP 1358, Maputo; tel. 214020114; fax 21417176; agricultural equipment; Dir JUSTINO LUCAS.

ENACOMO, SARL (Empresa Nacional de Comércio): Av. Samora Machel 285, 1° andar, CP 698, Maputo; tel. 21427471; fax 21427754; e-mail enacomo-sede@virconn.net; f. 1976; imports, exports, acquisition, investment, tourism; Man. Dir CARLOS PACHECO FARIA.

Forjadora, SARL (Fábrica de Equipamentos Industriais): Av. de Angola 2850, CP 3078, Maputo; tel. 21465537; fax 21465211; motor vehicle and truck bodies; Chair. CARLOS SIMBINE; Man. Dir JORGE MORGADO.

Hidroeléctrica de Cahora Bassa, SARL (HCB): tel. 25282223; fax 25282364; Mozambican Govt (18%), Portuguese Govt (82%); Portuguese stake of 67% to be purchased by Mozambican Govmt; production and transmission of electricity.

Indústria Moçambicana de Aço, SARL (IMA): Av. 24 de Julho 2373, 12° andar, CP 2566, Maputo; tel. 21421141; fax 21420087; f. 1970; steel; Dir MANUEL JOSÉ SEREJO.

Lojas Francas de Moçambique (INTERFRANCA): Rua Timor Leste 106, CP 1206, Maputo; tel. 21425199; fax 21431044; music equipment, motor cars, handicrafts, furniture; Gen. Dir CARLOS E. N. RIBEIRO.

Mabor de Moçambique: CP 2341, Maputo; tel. 21470551; fax 21470227; e-mail mabormoc@virconn.com; f. 1979; manufacture of tyres; Chair. Dr H. GAMITO; Dir LUIS F. RODRIGUES; 610 employees.

MEDIMOC SA: Av. Julius Nyerere 500, 1° andar, CP 600, Maputo; tel. 21491211; fax 21490168; e-mail rro nda@medimoc.co.mz; f. 1977 as Empresa Estatal de Importação e Exportação de Medicamentos (MEDIMOC); pharmaceuticals, medical equipment and supplies; Gen. Dir RENATO RONDA; 230 employees.

Mozal: Parque Industrial Beluluane, Boane, CP 1235, Maputo; tel. 21735000; fax 21735082; e-mail mozal.site@bhpbilliton.com; internet www.mozal.com; in 2004 Mozal II reached full production level; aluminium smelting and production; 47% owned by BHP Billiton; Gen. Man. CARLOS MESQUITA; 1,150 employees.

Riopele Têxteis de Moçambique, SARL: Rua Joaquim Lapa 21, CP 1658, Maputo; tel. 21331331; fax 21422902; textiles; Dir CARLOS RIBEIRO.

Sociedade de Pesca de Mariscos Lda (PESCAMAR): Rua Joaquim Lapa 192, Maputo; tel. 21424568; fax 21306801; fishing trawlers; subisidiary of Pescanova SA, Spain; 608 employees.

Vidreira de Moçambique, SARL: Talhão 77, Av. das Indústrias, Machava, Maputo; tel. 21750353; fax 21750371; e-mail vidreira@teledata.mz; 45% govt-owned; production of glass; Chair. CARLOS MOREIRA DA SILVA; Gen. Man. CARLOS NEVES; 525 employees.

TRADE UNIONS

Freedom to form trade unions, and the right to strike, are guaranteed under the 1990 Constitution.

Confederação de Sindicatos Livres e Independentes de Moçambique (CONSILMO): Sec.-Gen. JEREMIAS TIMANE.

Organização dos Trabalhadores de Moçambique—Central Sindical (OTM—CS) (Mozambique Workers' Organization—Trade Union Headquarters): Rua Manuel António de Sousa 36, Maputo; tel. 21426786; fax 21421671; e-mail otmdis@teledata.mz; internet www.otm.org.mz; f. 1983; Pres. AMÓS JÚNIOR MATSIUHE; Sec.-Gen. (vacant); 15 affiliated unions with over 94,000 mems including:

Sindicato Nacional dos Empregadores Bancários (SNEB): Av. Fernão de Magalhães 785, 1° andar, CP 1230, Maputo; tel. 21428627; fax 21303274; e-mail snebmoz@tvcabo.co.mz; internet www.snebmoz.co.mz; f. 1992; Sec.-Gen. CARLOS MELO.

Sindicato Nacional da Função Pública (SNAPF): Av. Ho Chi Min 365, Maputo; Sec.-Gen. MANUEL ABUDO MOMAD.

Sindicato Nacional dos Profissionais da Estiva e Ofícios Correlativos (SINPEOC): Av. Paulo Samuel Kakhomba 1568, Maputo; tel. and fax 21309535; Sec.-Gen. BENTO MADALA MAUNGUE.

Sindicato Nacional dos Trabalhadores Agro-Pecuários e Florestais (SINTAF): Av. 25 de Setembro 1676, 1° andar, CP 4202, Maputo; tel. 21306284; f. 1987; Sec.-Gen. EUSÉBIO LUÍS CHIVULELE.

Sindicato Nacional dos Trabalhadores da Aviação Civil, Correios e Comunicações (SINTAC): Rua de Silves 24, Maputo; tel. 21309574; Sec.-Gen. LUCAS LUCAZE.

Sindicato Nacional dos Trabalhadores do Comércio, Seguros e Serviços (SINECOSSE): Av. Ho Chi Minh 365, 1° andar, CP 2142, Maputo; tel. 21428561; Sec.-Gen. AMÓS JÚNIOR MATSINHE.

Sindicato Nacional dos Trabalhadores da Indústria do Açúcar (SINTIA): Av. das FPLM 1912, Maputo; tel. 21461772; fax 21461975; f. 1989; Sec.-Gen. ALEXANDRE CÂNDIDO MUNGUAMBE.

Sindicato Nacional dos Trabalhadores da Indústria Alimentar e Bebidas (SINTIAB): Av. Eduardo Mondlane 1267, CP 394, Maputo; tel. 21324709; fax 21324123; f. 1986; Gen. Sec. SAMUEL FENIAS MATSINHE.

Sindicato Nacional dos Trabalhadores da Indústria de Cajú (SINTIC): Rua do Jardim 574, 4° andar, Maputo; tel. 21477732; Sec.-Gen. BOAVENTURA MONDLANE.

Sindicato Nacional dos Trabalhadores da Indústria Metalúrgica, Metalomecânica e Energia (SINTIME): Av. Samora Machel 30, 6°, Maputo; Sec.-Gen. SIMIÃO NHATUMBO.

Sindicato Nacional dos Trabalhadores da Indústria Química, Borracha, Papel e Gráfica (SINTIQUIGRA): Av. Olof Palme 255, CP 4439, Maputo; tel. 21320288; fax 21321096; f. 1987; chemical, rubber, paper and print workers' union; due to merge with SINTEVEC in 2007; Co-ordinator JESSICA GUNE; 4,970 mems.

Sindicato Nacional dos Trabalhadores da Indústria Têxtil Vestuário, Couro e Calçado (SINTEVEC): Av. do Trabalho 1276, 1° andar, CP 2613, Maputo; tel. 21404669; fax 21409295; clothing, leather and footwear workers' union; due to merge with SINTIQUIGRA in 2007; Sec.-Gen. MARIO RAIMUNDO SITOE; 1,700 mems.

Sindicato Nacional dos Trabalhadores da Marinha Mercante e Pesca (SINTMAP): Rua Joaquim Lapa 22, 5° andar, No. 6, Maputo; tel. 21305593; Sec.-Gen. DANIEL MANUEL NGOQUE.

Sindicato Nacional dos Trabalhadores dos Portos e Caminhos de Ferro (SINPOCAF): Av. Guerra Popular, esquina 24 de Setembro, CP 2158, Maputo; tel. 21403912; fax 21303839; Sec.-Gen. SAMUEL ALFREDO CHEUANE.

Sindicato Nacional de Jornalistas (SNJ): Av. 24 de Julho 231, Maputo; tel. 21492031; fax 823015912; f. 1978; Sec.-Gen. EDUARDO CONSTANTINO.

Transport

Improvements to the transport infrastructure since the signing of the Acordo Geral de Paz (General Peace Agreement) in 1992 have focused on the development of 'transport corridors', which include both rail and road links and promote industrial development in their environs. The Beira Corridor, with rail and road links and a petroleum pipeline, runs from Manica, on the Zimbabwean border, to the Mozambican port of Beira, while the Limpopo Corridor joins southern Zimbabwe and Maputo. Both corridors form a vital outlet for the land-locked southern African countries, particularly Zimbabwe. The Maputo Corridor links Ressano Garcia in South Africa to the port at Maputo, and the Nacala Corridor runs from Malawi to the port of Nacala. Two further corridors were planned: the Mtwara Development Corridor was to link Mozambique, Malawi, Tanzania and Zambia, while the Zambezi Corridor was to link Zambézia province with Malawi. In February 2000 much of the country's infrastructure in the southern and central provinces was devastated as the result of massive flooding. Railway lines, roads and bridges suffered considerable damage.

RAILWAYS

In 2003 the total length of track was 3,114 km, of which 2,072 km was operational. There are both internal routes and rail links between Mozambican ports and South Africa, Swaziland, Zimbabwe and Malawi. During the hostilities many lines and services were disrupted. Improvement work on most of the principal railway lines began in the early 1980s. In the early 2000s work began on upgrading the railway system and private companies were granted non-permanent concessions to upgrade and run the railways.

Empresa Portos e Caminhos de Ferro de Moçambique (CFM): Praça dos Trabalhadores, CP 2158, Maputo; tel. 21327173; fax 21427746; e-mail cfmnet@cfmnet.co.mz; internet www.cfmnet.co.mz; fmrly Empresa Nacional dos Portos e Caminhos de Ferro de Moçambique; privatized and restructured in 2002; Chair. RUI FONSECA; comprises four separate systems linking Mozambican ports with the country's hinterland, and with other southern African countries, including South Africa, Swaziland, Zimbabwe and Malawi:

CFM—Centro (CFM—C): Largo dos CFM, CP 236, Beira; tel. 23321000; fax 23329290; lines totalling 994 km linking Beira with Zimbabwe and Malawi, as well as link to Moatize (undergoing rehabilitation); Exec. Dir JOAQUIM VERÍSSIMO.

CFM—Norte: Av. do Trabalho, CP 16, Nampula; tel. 26214320; fax 26212034; lines totalling 872 km, including link between port of Nacala with Malawi; management concession awarded to Nacala Corridor Development Co (a consortium 67% owned by South African, Portuguese and US cos) in January 2000; Dir FILIPE NHUSSI; Dir of Railways MANUEL MANICA.

CFM—Sul: Praça dos Trabalhadores, CP 2158, Maputo; tel. and fax 21430894; lines totalling 1,070 km linking Maputo with South Africa, Swaziland and Zimbabwe, as well as Inhambane–Inharrime and Xai-Xai systems; Exec. Dir JOAQUIM ZUCULE.

CFM—Zambézia: CP 73, Quelimane; tel. 24212502; fax 24213123; 145-km line linking Quelimane and Mocuba; Dir ORLANDO J. JAIME.

Beira Railway Co: Dondo; f. 2004; 51% owned by Rites & Ircon (India), 49% owned by CFM; rehabilitating and managing Sena and Zimbabwe railway lines.

ROADS

In 1999 there were an estimated 30,400 km of roads in Mozambique, of which 5,685 km were paved. Although the road network was improved in the 1990s, the severe floods in February 2000 meant that much of the construction would have to be repeated. In 2001 the Government announced plans to invest US $1,700m. in upgrading and maintaining the road network. In 2003 827 km of road were built or upgraded. Road and bridge construction projects were ongoing in the mid-2000s.

Administraçao Nacional de Estradas (ANE): Av. de Moçambique 1225, CP 1294, Maputo; tel. 21475157; fax 21475290; e-mail pce.ane@teledata.mz; internet www.dnep.gov.mz; f. 1999 to replace the Direcção Nacional de Estradas e Pontes; implements government road policy through the Direcção de Estradas Nacionais (DEN) and the Direcção de Estradas Regionais (DER); Pres. Eng. CARLOS FRAGOSO; Dir-Gen. IBRAIMO REMANE.

SHIPPING

Mozambique has three main sea ports, at Nacala, Beira and Maputo, while inland shipping on Lake Niassa and the river system was underdeveloped. At December 2005 Mozambique's registered merchant fleet consisted of 126 vessels, totalling 35,419 grt.

Empresa Portos e Caminhos de Ferro de Moçambique (CFM-EP): Praça dos Trabalhadores, CP 2158, Maputo; tel. 21427173; fax 21427746; e-mail cfmnet@cfmnet.co.mz; internet www.cfmnet.co.mz; fmrly Empresa Nacional dos Portos e Caminhos de Ferro de Moçambique; privatized and restructured in 2002; Port Dir CFM-Sul BOAVENTURA CHAMBAL; Port Dir CFM-Norte AGOSTINHO LANGA, Jr; Port Dir CFM-Centro CHINGUANE MABOTE.

Agência Nacional de Frete e Navegação (ANFRENA): Rua Consiglieri Pedroso 396, CP 492, Maputo; tel. 21427064; fax 21427822; Dir FERDINAND WILSON.

Empresa Moçambicana de Cargas, SARL (MOCARGO): Rua Consiglieri Pedroso 430, 1°–4° andares, CP 888, Maputo; tel. 21421440; fax 21302067; e-mail mocargo1@teledata.mz; internet www.mocargo.co.mz; f. 1982; shipping, chartering and road transport; Man. Dir MANUEL DE SOUSA AMARAL.

Manica Freight Services, SARL: Praça dos Trabalhadores 51, CP 557, Maputo; tel. 21356500; fax 21431084; e-mail fdimande@manica.co.mz; internet www.manica.co.mz; international shipping agents; Man. Dir A. Y. CHOTHIA.

Maputo Port Development Co, SARL (MPDC): Port Director's Building, Porto de Maputo, CP 2841, Maputo; tel. 21313920; fax 21313921; e-mail info@portmaputo.com; internet www.portmaputo.com; f. 2002; private-sector international consortium with concession (awarded 2003) to develop and run port of Maputo until 2018; CEO PETER LOWE.

Mozline, SARL: Av. Karl Marx 478, 2° andar, Maputo; tel. 21303078; fax 21303073; e-mail mozline1@virconn.com; shipping and road freight services.

Navique, SARL: Av. Mártires de Inhaminga 125, CP 145, Maputo; tel. 21312705; fax 21426310; e-mail smazoi@navique.co.mz; internet www.navique.com; f. 1985; Chair. J. A. CARVALHO; Man. Dir PEDRO VIRTUOSO.

CIVIL AVIATION

In 2006 there were five international airports.

Instituto de Aviação Civil de Moçambique (IACM): Maputo; civil aviation institute; Dir ANÍBAL SAMUEL.

Air Corridor, SARL: Av. Eduardo Mondlane 945, Nampula; tel. 26213333; fax 26213355; e-mail fagadit@aircorridor.com.mz; internet www.aircorridor.co.mz; f. 2004; domestic carrier and cargo transport; Chair. MOMADE AQUI RAJAHUSSEN; Commercial Dir FARUK ALY GADIT.

Linhas Aéreas de Moçambique, SARL (LAM): Aeroporto Internacional de Maputo, CP 2060, Maputo; tel. 21465137; fax 21422936; e-mail flamingoclub@lam.co.mz; internet www.lam.co.mz; f. 1980; 80% state-owned; operates domestic services and international services to South Africa, Tanzania, Mayotte, Zimbabwe and Portugal; Chair. and Dir-Gen. JOSÉ RICARDO ZUZARTE VIEGAS.

Sociedade de Transportes Aéreos/Sociedade de Transporte e Trabalho Aéreo, SARL (STA/TTA): CP 665, Maputo; tel. 21742366; fax 21491763; e-mail dido@mail.tropical.co.mz; internet www.sta.co.mz; f. 1991; domestic airline and aircraft charter transport services; acquired Empresa Nacional de Transporte e Trabalho Aéreo in 1997; Chair. ROGÉRIO WALTER CARREIRA; Man. Dir JOSÉ CARVALHEIRA.

Other airlines operating in Mozambique include Serviço Aéreo Regional, South African Airlines, Moçambique Expresso, SA—Airlink International, Transairways (owned by LAM) and TAP Air Portugal.

Tourism

Tourism, formerly a significant source of foreign exchange, ceased completely following independence, and was resumed on a limited scale in 1980. There were 1,000 visitors in 1981 (compared with 292,000 in 1972 and 69,000 in 1974). With the successful conduct of multi-party elections in 1994 and the prospect of continued peace, there was considerable scope for development of this sector. By the late 1990s tourism was the fastest growing sector of the Mozambique economy, and in 2000 it was announced that a comprehensive tourism development plan was to be devised, assisted by funding from the European Union. In 2005 there were 5,030 hotels in Mozambique. The opening of the Great Limpopo Transfrontier Park, linking territories in Mozambique with South Africa and Zimbabwe, was expected to attract additional tourists. Further national parks were planned. Foreign tourist arrivals in 2005 were 954,433; tourism receipts totalled US $96m. in 2004.

Fundo Nacional do Turismo: Av. 25 de Setembro 1203, CP 4758, Maputo; tel. 21307320; fax 21307324; e-mail info@futur.org.mz; internet www.futur.org.mz; f. 1993; hotels and tourism; CEO ZACARIAS SUMBANA.

Defence

According to the final report, issued in December 1994, of the Ceasefire Commission, which was established under the Acordo Geral de Paz (AGP—General Peace Agreement) to supervise the implementation of truce regulations, a combined total of only 11,579 government and Renamo troops (from a total of 91,691 troops registered at assembly points) had enlisted in the Forças Armadas de Defesa de Moçambique (FADM). In November 1997 legislation was approved providing for the reintroduction of compulsory military service, which had been suspended under the AGP. It was envisaged that the strength of the FADM, which stood at less than 11,000 in late 1996, would be increased to 15,000. In late 1998 the Ministry of National Defence announced plans to recruit an additional 3,000 conscripts into the armed forces in 1999; however, only 1,000 recruits were conscripted in that year. The total strength of the FADM was to be defined by government policy, and the figure of 30,000 envisaged in the AGP would not necessarily be observed. As assessed at November 2006, total active armed forces were estimated at 11,200 (army 10,000, navy 200, air force 1,000).

Defence Expenditure: Budgeted at an estimated 1,500,000m. meticais in 2006.

Commander-in-Chief of the Armed Forces: Pres. ARMANDO EMÍLIO GUEBUZA.

Chief of General Staff: Gen. LAGOS LIDIMO.

Deputy Chief of General Staff: Lt-Gen. MATEUS NGONHAMO.

Education

Education is officially compulsory for seven years from the age of six. Primary schooling comprises a first cycle of five years and a further cycle of two years. Secondary schooling, which begins at 13 years of age, lasts for six years and comprises a first cycle of three years and a further cycle of three years. As a proportion of the school-age population, the total enrolment at primary and secondary schools was equivalent to 49% in 2000/01 (males 56%; females 42%). According to UNESCO estimates, in 2003/04 71% of children in the relevant age-group were enrolled at primary schools (males 75%; females 67%), while secondary enrolment included only 4% of children in the relevant age-group (males 5%; females 4%). In 2003 some 3,177,586 children attended primary school, while 160,093 were undertaking secondary education. In 2003 it was announced that education would now take place in some Mozambican languages, as well as Portuguese. In 2006 some US $39m. was granted by international donors to develop educational resources. Education was allocated 20.2% of total current expenditure in that year.

Bibliography

Abrahamsson, H., and Nilsson, A. *Mozambique: The Troubled Transition from Socialist Construction to Free Market Capitalism.* London, Zed Books, 1995.

Alden, C. *Mozambique and the Construction of the New African State: From Negotiations to Nation Building.* Basingstoke, Palgrave Publishers, 2001.

Armon, J., *et al.* (Eds). *Accord: The Mozambique Peace Process in Perspective.* London, Conciliation Resources, 1998.

Azevedo, M. *Historical Dictionary of Mozambique.* Metuchen, NJ, Scarecrow Press, 1991.

Tragedy and Triumph: Mozambique Refugees in Southern Africa, 1977–2001. Westport, CT, Greenwood Publishing Group, 2002.

Berman, E. *Managing Arms in Peace Processes: Mozambique.* New York, United Nations, 1996.

Bowen, M. L. *The State Against the Peasantry (Rural Struggles in Colonial and Postcolonial Mozambique).* Charlottesville, VA, University Press of Virginia, 2000.

Cabrita, J. *Mozambique (The Tortuous Road to Democracy).* Basingstoke, Palgrave Publishers, 2001.

Cann, J. P. *Counter-insurgency in Africa: The Portuguese Way of War 1961–1974.* Westport, CT, Greenwood Press, 1997.

Chan, S. *War and Peace in Mozambique.* Basingstoke, Macmillan, 1998.

Chingono, M. F. *Conspicuous Destruction: War, Famine and the Reform Process in Mozambique.* New York, NY, Human Rights Watch, 1992.

The State, Violence and Development: The Political Economy of War in Mozambique, 1975–1992. Aldershot, Avebury, 1996.

Chissano, J. A. *Peace and Reconstruction.* Harare, Southern African Research and Documentation Centre, 1997.

Englund, H. *From War to Peace on the Mozambique–Malawi Borderlands.* New York, NY, Columbia University Press, 2002.

Finnegan, W. A. *A Complicated War: The Harrowing of Mozambique.* Berkeley, CA, University of California Press, 1992.

Geffray, C. *La Cause des Armes au Mozambique—Anthropologie d'une guerre civile.* Paris, Editions Karthala, 1990.

Hanlon, J. *Apartheid's Second Front: South Africa's War Against its Neighbours.* Harmondsworth, Penguin, 1986.

Harrison, G. *The Politics of Democratisation in Rural Mozambique (Grassroots Governance in Mecufi)—African Studies, 55.* Lampeter, Edwin Mellen Press, 2000.

Henriksen, T. H. *Mozambique: A History.* London, Rex Collings; Cape Town, David Philips, 1978.

Revolution and Counterrevolution: Mozambique's War of Independence 1964–74. Westport, CT, Greenwood Press, 1983.

Hoile, D. *Mozambique: A Nation in Crisis.* London, Claridge Press, 1989.

Mozambique: Propaganda, Myth and Reality. London, Mozambique Institute, 1991.

Mozambique: Resistance and Freedom: A Case for Reassessment. London, Mozambique Institute, 1994.

Hoile, D. (Ed.). *Mozambique 1962–1993: A Political Chronology.* London, Mozambique Institute, 1994.

Isaacman, A., and Isaacman, B. *Mozambique from Colonialism to Revolution, 1900–82.* Boulder, CO, Westview Press, 1983.

Ishemo, S. L. *The Lower Zambezi Basin in Mozambique (A Study in Economy and Society, 1850–1920)—The Making of Modern Africa.* Aldershot, Avebury, 1995.

Knauder, S. *Globalization, Urban Progress, Urban Problems, Rural Disadvantages (Evidence from Mozambique).* Aldershot, Ashgate Publishing Ltd, 2000.

Macqueen, N. *The Decolonization of Portuguese Africa: Metropolitan Revolution and the Dissolution of Empire.* Harlow, Longman, 1997.

Manning, C. *The Politics of Peace in Mozambique.* Westport, CT, Praeger Publishers, 2002.

Mazula, B. *Mozambique: Elections, Democracy and Development.* Maputo, Manila, 1996.

Miech-Chatenay, M. *Mozambique: The Key Sectors of the Economy.* Paris, BIDOI, 1986.

Mozambique 1991: The New Phase. Montréal, CIDMAA, 1991.

Minter, W. *Apartheid's Contras: An Inquiry into the Roots of War in Angola and Mozambique.* London, Zed Press, 1994.

Newitt, M. *A History of Mozambique.* Bloomington, IN, Indiana University Press; London, Hurst, 1993.

Pélissier, R. *Naissance du Mozambique.* 2 vols. France, Editions Pélissier, 1984.

Pitcher, A. *Transforming Mozambique: The Politics of Privatization, 1975–2000.* Cambridge, Cambridge University Press, 2002.

Rafael, S. D. *Dicionário Toponímico, Histórico, Geográfico e Etnográfico de Moçambique.* Maputo, Arquivo Histórico de Moçambique, 2002.

Saul, J. (Ed.). *A Difficult Road: The Transition to Socialism in Mozambique.* New York, Monthly Review Press, 1985.

Sheldon, K. *Pounders of Grain: A History of Women, Work, and Politics in Mozambique.* Westport, CT, Greenwood Publishing Group, 2002.

Torp, J. E. *Mozambique: Politics, Economics, Society.* London, Pinter, 1989.

Vail, L., and White, L. *Capitalism and Colonialism in Mozambique.* London, Heinemann Educational, 1995.

Vines, A. *No Democracy Without Money: The Road to Peace in Mozambique (1981–1992).* London, Catholic Institute for International Relations, 1994.

Renamo Mozambique. London, James Currey; Bloomington, IN, Indiana University Press, 1994.

Renamo: From Terrorism to Democracy in Mozambique. USA and Canada, World Press, 1995.

Renamo: Terrorism in Mozambique. 2nd Edn. London, James Currey, 1996.

Young, T., and Hall, M. *Confronting Leviathan: Mozambique Since Independence.* London, Hurst, 1997.

NAMIBIA

Physical and Social Geography

A. MacGREGOR HUTCHESON

The Republic of Namibia, lying across the Tropic of Capricorn, covers an area of 824,292 sq km (318,261 sq miles). It is bordered by South Africa on the south and south-east, by Botswana on the east and Angola on the north, while the narrow Caprivi Strip, between the two latter countries, extends Namibia's boundaries to the Zambezi river and a short border with Zambia.

The Namib Desert, a narrow plain 65–160 km wide and extending 1,600 km along the entire Atlantic seaboard, has a mean annual rainfall of less than 100 mm; long lines of huge sand dunes are common and it is almost devoid of vegetation. Behind the coastal plain the Great Escarpment rises to the plateau, which forms the rest of the country. Part of the Southern African plateau, it has an average elevation of 1,100 m above sea-level, but towards the centre of the country it rises to altitudes of 1,525–2,440 m. A number of mountain masses rise above the general surface throughout the plateau. Eastwards the surface slopes to the Kalahari Basin and northwards to the Etosha Pan. Much of Namibia's drainage is interior to the Kalahari. There are no perennial rivers apart from the Okavango and the Cuando, which cross the Caprivi Strip, and the Orange, Kunene and Zambezi, which form parts of the southern and northern borders.

Temperatures in the coastal areas are modified by the cool Benguela Current, while altitude modifies plateau temperatures (Walvis Bay, sea level: January 19°C, July 14.5°C; and Windhoek,1,707 m: January 24°C, July 14°C). Average annual rainfall varies from some 50 mm on the coast to 550 mm in the north. Most rain falls during the summer (September–March), but is unreliable and there are years of drought. Grasslands cover most of the plateau; they are richer in the wetter north, but merge into poor scrub in the south and east.

Most of the population (estimated at 2,047,000 at mid-2006) reside on the plateau. Figures for the density of population (2.5 inhabitants per sq km at mid-2006) are misleading, as the better-watered northern one-third of the plateau contains more than one-half of the total population and about two-thirds of the African population, including the Ovambo (the largest single ethnic group), Kavango, East Caprivians and Kaokovelders. Almost the entire European population (80,000 in 1988, including the European population of Walvis Bay, an exclave of South Africa that was ceded to Namibia in March 1994) are concentrated in the southern two-thirds of the plateau, chiefly in the central highlands around Windhoek, the capital, together with the other main ethnic groups, the Damara, Herero, Nama, Rehoboth and Coloured. Excluding ports and mining centres in the Namib, and apart from small numbers of Bushmen (San) in the Kalahari, the desert regions are largely uninhabited.

Namibia possesses scattered deposits of valuable minerals, and its economy is dominated by the mining sector. Of particular importance are the rich deposits of alluvial diamonds, which are exploited by surface mining, notably in the area between Oranjemund and Lüderitz. Operations at the Oranjemund mine are, however, expected to decline progressively in the years after 2003, although new diamond fields off shore have been developed with much success. Uranium ore (although of a low grade) is mined open-cast at Rössing, 39 km north-east of Swakopmund, which is the world's largest open-pit uranium oxide complex. There is another, smaller uranium deposit, thought to be of a higher grade, about 80 km south of Rössing. Tin, copper, rock salt, lead and zinc are also mined, and Namibia is believed to have significant reserves of coal, iron ore and platinum, although these have yet to be assessed. Other minerals currently produced or awaiting exploitation include vanadium, manganese, gold, silver, tungsten (wolfram), cadmium and limestone. There are also considerable reserves of offshore natural gas.

Despite the limitations imposed by frequent drought, agriculture is a significant economic activity. With the help of water from boreholes, large areas are given over to extensive ranching. Rivers, notably the Orange, Kunene and Okavango, are potential water resources for irrigation and hydroelectric power, while swamps, such as those situated in the Caprivi Strip, could be drained to enhance arable output.

Namibia possesses potentially the richest inshore and deepwater fishing zones in tropical Africa as a consequence of the rich feeding provided by the Benguela Current. Measures are being taken to counter the effects of decades of overfishing by both domestic and foreign fleets.

Recent History

CHRISTOPHER SAUNDERS

HISTORICAL BACKGROUND

The origins of the modern territory of Namibia lie in the protectorate established by the German Government in 1884. The present boundaries were demarcated in the late 19th and early 20th centuries, with Walvis Bay initially under the rule of the United Kingdom, then of Cape Colony and subsequently of the Union of South Africa. Following the outbreak of the First World War, South African forces occupied the German colony of South West Africa (SWA). After the war the League of Nations awarded South Africa a mandate to administer the territory. No trusteeship agreement was concluded with the UN after the Second World War, and the refusal of that organization in 1946 to agree to South Africa's request to annex SWA marked the beginning of a protracted legal dispute about the status of the territory. In 1950 the International Court of Justice (ICJ) ruled that South Africa did not have to place the territory under the UN trusteeship system, but could not alter the legal status of the territory unilaterally. In 1966, after the ICJ had failed to make a substantive ruling on whether South Africa's rule of the territory was illegal, the UN General Assembly voted to terminate South Africa's mandate and to assume responsibility for the territory; a 'Council for South West Africa' was appointed in 1967, and in the following year the UN resolved that the territory should be renamed Namibia. This had no immediate practical effect, however, as South Africa remained in firm occupation of the territory. Another result of the ICJ's 'non-decision' was that the South West Africa People's Organization (SWAPO), which had been founded in 1960 under the leadership of Sam Nujoma, began an armed insurgency in the north of the territory.

A turning point came in 1971 when the ICJ issued an advisory opinion that South Africa's presence in Namibia was illegal and that it should withdraw. In December 1973 the UN General Assembly recognized SWAPO as the 'authentic representative of the people of Namibia', and appointed the first UN Commissioner for Namibia to undertake 'executive and administrative tasks'. South Africa's unsuccessful intervention in Angola in the second half of 1975 set the scene for the escalation of the Namibian armed struggle. With support from the new pro-SWAPO Government in Angola, the military wing of SWAPO, the People's Liberation Army of Namibia (PLAN), was able to establish bases close to the borders of Namibia. South Africa reacted to this threat by greatly expanding counter-insurgency forces in the territory and taking initiatives on the political front. In September 1975 a constitutional conference was convened to discuss the territory's future. The Turnhalle Conference, as it became known (after a historic building in the Namibian capital, Windhoek, that was badly damaged by fire in 2007), designated 31 December 1978 as the target date for Namibian independence, and in March 1977 it produced a draft constitution for a pre-independence interim government. This constitution, providing for 11 ethnic administrations, was denounced by the UN and SWAPO, which issued its own constitutional proposals based on a parliamentary system with universal adult suffrage.

THE WESTERN 'CONTACT GROUP'

In order to persuade South Africa to reject the Turnhalle proposals in favour of a plan that would be acceptable to the UN, a 'contact group' comprising the five Western members of the UN Security Council was established in 1977. In September South Africa appointed an Administrator-General for Namibia, and the territory's representation in the South African Parliament was terminated. By April 1978 the 'contact group' was able to present proposals for a settlement providing for UN-supervised elections, a reduction in the numbers of South African troops from Namibia and the release of political prisoners. These proposals were accepted by South Africa in late April and by SWAPO in July. The proposals were then incorporated into UN Security Council Resolution 435 of 28 September 1978. South Africa insisted on holding its own election for a Namibian Constituent Assembly in the territory in December; with SWAPO boycotting the election, 41 of the 50 seats were won by the Democratic Turnhalle Alliance (DTA), a conservative coalition of the ethnic groups involved in the conference. Its leader, Dirk Mudge, became Chairman of a Ministerial Council, which was granted limited executive powers.

In January 1981 the UN convened a conference in Geneva, Switzerland, which was attended by SWAPO, South Africa, the DTA and other internal parties. The UN 'contact group' and the 'front-line' states (Angola, Botswana, Mozambique, Tanzania, Zambia and Zimbabwe) were present as observers. South Africa and the internal parties would not agree on a cease-fire date and the implementation of the UN plan. Under US chairmanship, the Western 'contact group' resumed consultations with South Africa and SWAPO during 1981. In July 1982 constitutional guide-lines were agreed by the two parties, which provided that the constitution for an independent Namibia should include a bill of rights and be approved by two-thirds of the members of a constituent assembly. Although South Africa and SWAPO were unable to agree on whether the election should be conducted wholly on the basis of proportional representation, the UN Secretary-General was able to report that all other points at issue had been resolved.

By then, however, a more formidable obstacle to the implementation of the UN plan had arisen. South Africa now insisted that the Cuban troops withdraw from Angola. This concept, known as 'linkage', was initiated in 1981 by the US Government, which viewed the war in Namibia and southern Angola as a buffer against Soviet expansionism. The other members of the 'contact group', particularly France, which left the group in December 1983, did not share this view. The USA then continued the negotiations alone. Within the territory, the DTA was weakened in early 1982 by losing support among the Ovambo, the largest ethnic group in Namibia. After several months of disputes with the South African Government over the future role of the DTA, Mudge resigned as Chairman of the Ministerial Council in January 1983, and the Council itself was automatically dissolved. The Administrator-General, in turn, dissolved the National Assembly, and assumed direct rule of Namibia on behalf of the South African Government.

In February 1984 a cease-fire agreement was concluded in Lusaka, Zambia, following talks between South African and US government officials. Under the terms of the agreement, a joint commission was established to monitor the withdrawal of South African troops from Angola, and Angola undertook to permit neither SWAPO nor Cuban forces to move into the areas vacated by South African troops. SWAPO declared that it would abide by the agreement, but made it clear that it would continue PLAN operations until a cease-fire was established in Namibia as the first stage in the implementation of UN Resolution 435. In November 1984, in response to US proposals, President dos Santos of Angola suggested a timetable for the withdrawal of Cuban troops from the south of Angola, but in the mid-1980s the possibility of a settlement involving implementation of UN Resolution 435 seemed remote.

TRANSITIONAL GOVERNMENT

After the dissolution of the DTA Ministerial Council in January 1983, there was a political hiatus until an informally constituted Multi-Party Conference (MPC) began to meet in November of that year. At that time, its membership extended beyond the DTA to include the Damara Council, the Rehoboth Liberation Front, the SWAPO—Democrats (SWAPO—D, a breakaway faction of SWAPO), the right-wing National Party of South West Africa (SWANP) and the Herero-dominated South West African National Union (SWANU). In October 1984 the MPC called for an all-party meeting by 31 December of that year, failing which it would negotiate unilaterally with South Africa for independence. The credibility of the MPC was not high, owing to the past history of the DTA, the corruption and mismanagement of ethnic authorities under the control of MPC member parties, its failure to attract any Ovambo party, and its readiness to deal with South Africa. Aware of the lack of support for the MPC, the South African Government sought to involve at least part of SWAPO in an internal settlement. In March 1984 it released Toivo ya Toivo, a SWAPO activist who had been imprisoned in South Africa since 1968, together with a number of activists who had been detained since 1978.

On 17 June 1985 the South African Government formally installed a 'Transitional Government of National Unity' (TGNU) in Windhoek, which consisted of a Cabinet and a National Assembly. Neither was elected; appointments were made from among the constituent parties of the MPC. A 'bill of rights', drawn up by the MPC, prohibited racial discrimination, and a Constitutional Council was established, under a South African judge, to prepare a constitution for an independent Namibia. South Africa retained responsibility for foreign affairs, defence and internal security.

As the Cold War appeared to be coming to an end, in January 1988 Angola and Cuba accepted, in principle, US demands for a complete withdrawal of Cuban troops from Angola. In March proposals for the withdrawal of all Cuban troops were rejected by South Africa as 'insufficiently detailed'; but with South African troops unable to gain the upper hand outside Cuito Cunavale, in southern Angola, and given the increasing proximity of Cuban forces to the Namibian border, South Africa agreed to participate in tripartite negotiations with Angola and Cuba, with the USA acting as mediator. These began in May 1988. South Africa agreed to implement Resolution 435, providing that a timetable for the withdrawal of Cuban troops could be agreed. By mid-July the participants in the negotiations had accepted a document containing 14 'essential principles' for a peaceful settlement, and in early August it was agreed that the implementation of Resolution 435 would begin on 1 November. South African troops were withdrawn from southern Angola by the end of August. The November deadline was not met, however, owing to disagreement on an exact schedule for the evacuation of Cuban troops. In mid-November these arrangements were agreed in principle, although their formal ratification was delayed until mid-December, owing to South African dissatisfaction with verification procedures.

On 22 December 1988 South Africa, Angola and Cuba signed an agreement designating 1 April 1989 as the implementation date for Resolution 435. Another treaty, signed by Angola and Cuba, required the evacuation of all Cuban troops from Angola by July 1991. A joint commission was established to monitor the implementation of the trilateral treaty. Under the terms of Resolution 435, South African forces in Namibia were to be confined to their bases, and their numbers reduced to 1,500 by 1 July 1989; all South African troops were to have been withdrawn from Namibia one week after the election. A multinational UN observer force, the UN Transition Assistance Group (UNTAG), was to monitor the South African withdrawal and supervise the election.

IMPLEMENTATION OF THE UN INDEPENDENCE PLAN

The first UNTAG forces (which were eventually to comprise 4,650 troops, with a further 500 police and about 1,000 civilian observers) arrived in February 1989. At the end of that month the TGNU was formally disbanded, and on 1 March the National Assembly voted to dissolve itself. From then until independence the territory was governed by the Administrator-General, Louis Pienaar, in consultation, from 1 April, with the special representative of the UN Secretary-General, Martti Ahtisaari.

The scheduled implementation of Resolution 435 was disrupted by large-scale movements, beginning on 1 April 1989, of PLAN troops into Ovamboland. The South African Government obtained Ahtisaari's agreement to the release from base of its forces, and more than 300 PLAN troops were killed in the subsequent fighting. The origins of the sudden and unanticipated conflict apparently lay in differing interpretations of the terms of the UN peace plan; SWAPO, excluded from the 1988 negotiations, relied on provisions under Resolution 435 for the confinement to base of PLAN combatants located within the territory on 1 April 1989, and it was claimed that the insurgents had intended to report to UNTAG officials. On 9 April the joint commission produced conditions for an evacuation of the PLAN forces, after Sam Nujoma, President of SWAPO, had ordered their withdrawal to Angola. At a meeting of the joint commission on 19 May, the cease-fire was certified to be in force. In June most racially discriminatory legislation was repealed, and an amnesty was granted to Namibian refugees and exiles. By late September nearly 42,000 refugees, including Nujoma, had returned to Namibia.

The pre-independence election was conducted peacefully in the second week of November 1989; more than 95% of the electorate voted. The 72 seats in the Constituent Assembly were contested by candidates from 10 political parties and alliances: representatives of seven parties and fronts were elected. SWAPO received 57.3% of all votes cast and won 41 seats, thus obtaining a majority of the seats in the assembly but failing to achieve the two-thirds' majority that would have allowed SWAPO to draft the constitution without recourse to wider consultation. The DTA, with 28.6% of the votes, won 21 seats. The election was pronounced 'free and fair' by the special representative of the UN Secretary-General. Following the election, the remaining South African troops left Namibia, and SWAPO bases in Angola were disbanded.

In February 1990 the Constituent Assembly unanimously adopted a draft Constitution, which provided for a multi-party political system, based on universal adult suffrage, with an independent judiciary and a 'bill of rights'. Executive power was to be vested in a President who was permitted to serve a maximum of two five-year terms, while a 72-member National Assembly was to have legislative power. The Constituent Assembly subsequently elected Nujoma as Namibia's first President. On 21 March 1990 Namibia became independent: the Constituent Assembly became the National Assembly, and the President and his Cabinet (headed by Hage Geingob, hitherto Chairman of the Constituent Assembly) took office.

SWAPO IN GOVERNMENT

Following independence, Namibia became a member of the UN, the Organization of African Unity (now the African Union—AU) and the Commonwealth. Full diplomatic relations were established with many states, and partial diplomatic relations with South Africa. In May 1990 Angola and Namibia agreed to form a joint commission to monitor their common border. However, relations became strained in February 1991 when Angolan aircraft bombed a northern Namibian village; the Angolan Government claimed that it had attacked covert destabilization bases sponsored by South Africa, and promised to pay compensation to the Namibian Government. With the resumption of the civil war in Angola in late 1992, the Namibian Government remained concerned about the security of its northern border. Instability in South Africa also threatened to affect Namibia; the Government was, therefore, much relieved when South Africa's first democratic election took place peacefully in April 1994.

In March 1990 Namibia became a full member of the Southern African Customs Union (having previously been a de facto member of that organization) and a member of the South African Development Co-ordination Conference (SADCC), which sought to reduce the dependence of southern African states on South Africa. In August 1992 Namibia joined the other SADCC members in recreating the organization as the Southern African Development Community (SADC), to which South Africa was admitted in August 1994.

The disclosure by the South African Government in July 1991 that it had provided some R100m. in funding to the DTA and other anti-SWAPO political parties during the 1989 election campaign added to the DTA's post-independence problems. In November 1991 the DTA, formerly a coalition of ethnically based interests, reorganized itself as a single party, but its support continued to dwindle. In late November and early December 1992 the first elections were held for the country's 13 regional councils and 48 local authorities. SWAPO won nine regional councils, while the DTA won only three (in the remaining council there was no clear majority). SWAPO thus secured control of the newly established second house of parliament, the National Council, which comprised two members from each regional council; it began work in May 1993.

Namibia's first post-independence presidential and legislative elections took place on 7–8 December 1994, and resulted in overwhelming victories for Nujoma and SWAPO. Nujoma was elected for a second term as President, securing 76.3% of the votes cast; his only challenger was Mudge's successor as President of the DTA, Mishake Muyongo. SWAPO secured 53 of the elective seats in the National Assembly, obtaining 73.9% of the valid votes cast. The DTA retained 15 seats (with 20.8% of the votes), and the United Democratic Front (UDF) two. The remaining two seats were won by the Democratic Coalition of Namibia (DCN—an alliance of the National Patriotic Front and the German Union) and the Monitor Action Group. SWANU, which had been a founder member of the DCN in August, but subsequently withdrew to contest the elections in its own right, failed to secure representation in the legislature. Although SWAPO thus had a two-thirds' majority in the National Assembly, Nujoma gave assurances that no amendments would be made to the Constitution without prior approval by national referendum. The success of Nujoma and SWAPO was, in part, attributed to the popularity of land reform legislation recently approved by the National Assembly.

Nujoma was sworn in for his second presidential term on 21 March 1995. The previous day, as part of a major reorganization of cabinet portfolios, he assumed personal responsibility for home affairs and the police, in what was interpreted as an attempt to curb an increase in crime and discontent within the police force. Geingob remained as Prime Minister, with Hendrik Witbooi, previously Minister of Labour, Public Services and Manpower Development, as his deputy.

In May 1997, at SWAPO's second party congress since independence, the most intensive debate was on land reform, with the congress urging the Government to expedite measures in that area. A resolution endorsing the proposal that Nujoma should seek re-election for a third term as President was justified on the grounds that Nujoma had initially been chosen by the Constituent Assembly, and had only once been elected President on a popular mandate. Witbooi, who had been Vice-President of the party since 1983, was re-elected to the post, defeating a challenge by Geingob. The Minister of Fisheries and Marine Resources, Hifikepunye Pohamba, one of

Nujoma's closest associates in the years of exile, replaced Moses Garoëb as Secretary-General of the party. In a minor reshuffle of the Cabinet in December, Pohamba was appointed Minister without portfolio.

REGIONAL CONCERNS

In March 1993 the Angolan insurgent movement, União Nacional para a Independência Total de Angola (UNITA), alleged that members of the Namibian Defence Force had crossed the border into southern Angola to assist Angolan government forces in offensives against UNITA. The Namibian authorities denied any involvement in the Angolan civil conflict, but a section of the border with Angola was closed from September 1994, following an attack, attributed by the Namibian authorities to UNITA, in which Namibian nationals were killed. In 1996 it was announced that some 1,000 members of a special field force of the Namibia police, created in 1995 to provide employment for former PLAN troops, were to be deployed along the Okavango river on the Angolan border to deter possible UNITA attacks. In August 1996 Namibian and Angolan officials agreed on further measures to increase border security.

In 1996 Namibia and Botswana referred their dispute over the demarcation of their joint border on the Chobe river (specifically, the issue of the sovereignty of the sparsely inhabited island of Kasikili-Sedudu) for adjudication by the ICJ. In December 1997 a new dispute began concerning two further islands, Situngu and Luyondo, when Botswanan soldiers allegedly harvested crops planted on the islands by Namibian villagers. In May 1998 the two countries signed an accord establishing a joint technical commission to demarcate their joint border on the Chobe river.

In August 1998 President Nujoma ordered the dispatch of Namibian troops in support of President Laurent-Désiré Kabila of the Democratic Republic of the Congo (DRC) against rebel forces supported by Uganda and Rwanda. Within weeks almost 2,000 Namibian troops were fighting in the DRC alongside troops from Angola and Zimbabwe (at that time, also from Chad), helping to secure the Matadi corridor from Kinshasa to the sea. Although Nujoma asserted that Namibian involvement was an act of solidarity and support for the territorial integrity of the DRC in the face of external aggression, many observers considered that he hoped participation in the war might mean that Namibia would be well placed to benefit from future mineral exploitation in the DRC. Nujoma played a prominent role in efforts towards a negotiated settlement, undertaking numerous visits to other countries of the region, helping persuade Kabila to enter talks with the rebels and Uganda to withdraw from the DRC. He continued to deny that there were any Namibian troops supporting the Angolan Government against UNITA, but stated that, if requested, Namibia would assist its neighbour under the auspices of SADC. In April Namibia signed a regional defence pact with Angola, the DRC and Zimbabwe, providing for mutual assistance in the event of aggression against any of the signatories.

Efforts to resolve the conflict in the DRC were accelerated in early 2001, following the assassination of Laurent-Désiré Kabila and the succession to the presidency of his son, Maj.-Gen. Joseph Kabila. Proposals for the withdrawal of the foreign troops stationed in the DRC, including the Namibian contingent, were subsequently approved by the participating countries, under the aegis of the UN Security Council, and the withdrawal of Namibian forces from the DRC was completed in September.

Relations with Botswana were further complicated from late 1998, when refugees began entering that country from Caprivi (the Caprivi Strip, a thin section of Namibian territory extending from the north-eastern corner of that country and bordering Angola, Zambia and Botswana). Beginning in October a stream of refugees fled to Botswana, citing police harassment, after a man was reportedly killed at a secret military training base that the Namibian Government alleged was being used by the secessionist Caprivi Liberation Movement (CLM). The people of Caprivi had long sought closer links with their neighbours to the east, believing that the Government in Windhoek was ignoring the development of their region because they did not support SWAPO. It emerged that the leading refugee figure was Muyongo, who had been forced out of SWAPO in 1980 because of disagreement regarding the Caprivi issue, and had later become leader of the DTA. In August 1998 the DTA's executive had in turn announced the suspension of Muyongo as party President, and dissociated the party from Muyongo's overt support for the secession of the Caprivi Strip. With 14 other members of the CLM, he sought, and was granted, asylum by the Botswana Government in February 1999. Nujoma, who had at first sought the extradition of the refugees so that they could be tried as terrorists, made a state visit to Botswana in March 1999, during which he agreed with President Mogae that the secessionist leaders could be accorded refugee status, on condition that they be resettled in a third country; the remaining refugees, who by then numbered some 2,500 (including many San Bushmen), would be able to return without fear of punishment or persecution. This agreement was subsequently ratified by the two countries and the office of the UN High Commissioner for Refugees (UNHCR). Muyongo and another leader of the movement, Boniface Mamili (a chief of the Mafwe), were granted political asylum in Denmark.

In early August 1999, however, an unanticipated attack by members of what was styled the Caprivi Liberation Army (CLA) on the regional capital of Caprivi, Katima Mulilo, resulted in 12 deaths. The Namibian Government imposed a state of emergency in Caprivi, and was offered support by Zimbabwe and Zambia against the separatists. The CLA, which had bases in western Zambia, was said to have close links with the separatist Barotse Patriotic Front in that country. It was widely suspected that UNITA had given the CLA military training and supported the attack because of the Namibian Government's close ties with the Angolan Government. Although the state of emergency was revoked in late August, human rights groups in Namibia produced evidence that Namibian troops had committed acts of brutality against those believed to support the rebels. More than 120 of those arrested appeared in court in 2001, charged with high treason, murder and sedition, but their trial was postponed, initially because of controversy over whether the state should pay for their defence. A number of defendants died waiting for the trial to begin. One of the reasons for the delay was that the Supreme Court was asked to rule on whether or not the High Court had jurisdiction to try 13 of the accused, including the alleged commander of the CLA, who claimed that they had been abducted illegally from Zambia or Botswana. Human rights groups criticized the recurrent delays in bringing the case to trial, and the violation of defendants' rights.

Tensions in the region of the Namibia–Angola border escalated from late 1999, after the two countries began joint patrols targeting UNITA, and the Namibian Government authorized the Angolan armed forces to launch attacks against UNITA from Namibian territory. UNITA responded by launching sporadic attacks in the Caprivi Strip. By June 2000, when a curfew was imposed along the Kavango river on the north-eastern border with Angola, more than 50 Namibians had been killed in cross-border raids by the Angolan rebels. However, following the death of Jonas Savimbi, the UNITA leader, and the signing of a cease-fire between the Angolan Government and UNITA in April 2002, the situation in the north-east of Namibia improved considerably. In June the military suspended the escorts that had been required on the Trans-Caprivi Highway since 2000, and some tourists began to return to Kavango and Caprivi. As Angola became more peaceful, trade with Namibia increased, and in August 2002 Namibian refugees in Botswana began to be repatriated. In that month the return of Angolan refugees in Namibia to their country began; the majority of them, estimated at around 20,000, were due to return home in the second half of 2003, under the auspices of UNHCR.

At a March 1999 meeting, Presidents Nujoma and Mogae confirmed that Namibia and Botswana would each respect the judgment of the ICJ regarding sovereignty of Kasikili-Sedudu. In December 1999 the judgment was finally made in Botswana's favour. The two countries then established a joint commission to settle the remaining disputes in the Chobe river area, and agreed that its decisions would be binding on both

Governments. In March 2003 the two Governments accepted the commission's demarcation of their joint border along the Kwando, Linyanti and Chobe rivers. The issue of Namibia's border with South Africa remained unresolved: Namibia claimed that its southern border extended to the middle of the Orange river, while South Africa claimed its territory stretched to the northern bank; how the boundary ran out to sea (and thus to diamond deposits) was also disputed.

One of the most significant developments on the country's borders occurred in 2004 when President Nujoma and his Zambian counterpart, Levy Mwanawasa, opened the Sesheke bridge across the Zambezi river. This linked the Trans-Caprivi Highway to the Zambian copperbelt, creating the possibility of exports being sent from Zambia and the southern DRC to the Namibian port of Walvis Bay.

NUJOMA'S THIRD TERM

In October 1998 an exceptional amendment to the Constitution, allowing Nujoma to seek a third presidential term, was approved by the requisite two-thirds' majority in the National Assembly; in the following month it was endorsed by the National Council. The regional council elections held in December revealed increased apathy among voters, as the turn-out was only about 30%. SWAPO won a majority in 11 of the 13 regional councils, thereby increasing its representation in the National Council from 19 to 22 seats.

The first real challenge to SWAPO's dominance emerged with the establishment in March 1999 of a new political party under a former senior SWAPO official, Ben Ulenga. A member of the PLAN who had served a long prison sentence on Robben Island under the apartheid regime, and later become Namibia's best-known trade union leader, Ulenga resigned from his post as Namibia's High Commissioner to the United Kingdom in August 1998, in protest against SWAPO's decision to alter the Constitution to allow Nujoma to seek a third term as President. Ulenga also opposed Namibia's involvement in the conflict in the DRC, and was critical of the SWAPO Government's failure adequately to address the issue of unemployed former combatants. Ulenga did not initially resign from SWAPO, although he was suspended from its central committee; in October he formed a 'consultative forum', with a view to establishing a new party, eventually forming the Congress of Democrats (CoD). Unlike the DTA, it was not tainted with a history of collaboration with South Africa under apartheid. Apparently concerned as to the CoD's prospects in the presidential and general elections due in late 1999, Nujoma swiftly appointed two key figures from the labour movement as deputy ministers, and the Government set aside N $255m. in the 1999/2000 budget for the social integration of about 9,000 former combatants, who were to be offered employment in the public service. A number were given posts in the police, and a national youth service scheme was also proposed.

The elections, which were held on 30 November and 1 December 1999, resulted in an overwhelming victory for Nujoma and SWAPO, with Ulenga and the CoD apparently winning support at the expense of the DTA. In the presidential election Nujoma was returned for a third (and final) term of office, with 76.8% of the votes cast, while Ulenga took 10.5% and Katuutire Kaura (Muyongo's successor as President of the DTA) 9.6%. SWAPO won 55 of the elective seats in the National Assembly, with 76.1% of the votes cast (thus ensuring that it retained the two-thirds' majority enabling it to amend the Constitution); the CoD and the DTA each won seven seats (taking, respectively, 9.9% and 9.5% of the total votes cast), but the DTA was able to retain its status as the official opposition by forming an alliance with the Damara-based UDF, which secured two seats. Geingob was reappointed Prime Minister in a reorganization of the Cabinet announced by Nujoma in mid-March 2000. Pohamba relinquished his post as Minister without Portfolio, but remained Secretary-General of SWAPO until the party's congress in 2002 when he was elevated to the position of party Vice-President. In January 2001 he had been appointed Minister of Lands, Resettlement and Rehabilitation. In what was widely seen as a move by Nujoma to remove a potential successor, in August 2002 he suddenly dismissed Geingob as Prime Minister and replaced him with the long-serving Minister of Foreign Affairs, Theo Ben-Gurirab.

As Namibia entered the new millennium, many thought that the most serious problem confronting the country was HIV/AIDS; 21.3% of Namibia's adult population (aged between 15 and 49 years) were estimated to be living with HIV/AIDS in 2003. It was widely believed that government measures to deal with the pandemic were inadequate. In 2002 the effect of AIDS in reducing the agricultural labour force and production was cited as one of the reasons for the serious food crisis that had developed by the middle of that year, when an estimated 70,000 people in the north-eastern Caprivi region needed urgent food aid. In late August UN agencies, government officials and other organizations undertook a joint assessment of food supplies throughout the country. Severe flooding in the Caprivi region in May 2003 necessitated further food aid, this time supplied by the International Committee of the Red Cross. The decision by the Namibian Government to allocate more than N $80m. in the 2003/04 budget for the purchase of antiretroviral drugs for people infected with HIV was widely welcomed, as was the announcement in May 2003 that the Government was to support the manufacture of generic medication for the treatment of HIV/AIDS.

After Zimbabwean President Robert Mugabe allowed the forcible seizure of land from white farmers and its redistribution to the black population, the issue of land reform gained more prominence on the Namibian Government's agenda. The Government remained firm that it would not permit land invasions, and by 2000 only 35,000 black farmers had been settled on land obtained from white farmers. However, during a visit to Germany in mid-2002, Nujoma sought financial aid for the purchase of land from white commercial farmers for landless blacks. In late August that year Nujoma warned white farmers to co-operate with the Government's scheme for land redistribution. Representatives of the Herero people, meanwhile, proceeded with cases against the German Government, Deutsche Bank AG and Woermann Line (a shipping firm), from which they demanded compensation of some US $4,000m. for their involvement in the dispossession of the Herero and the atrocities committed against them under German colonial rule. The Namibian Government refused to support this claim, declaring that it was in Namibia's interests to continue to work harmoniously with the German Government and industry.

The parliamentary opposition fragmented further when in November 2003 the Herero-based National Unity Democratic Organisation (NUDO) withdrew from the DTA and in December registered as a separate party. Under the leadership of the Herero paramount chief, Kuaima Riruako, the new party began to campaign on a platform of establishing a federal state in which minorities would be protected.

In April 2004 at a special meeting of SWAPO's central committee Nujoma confirmed he would not seek a fourth term as President. That body recommended three candidates for the post: Nahas Angula, the Minister of Higher Education, Training and Employment Creation; Hidipo Hamutenya, the Minister of Foreign Affairs; and Pohamba, the Minister of Lands, Resettlement and Rehabilitation.

The Namibian Government had long maintained that it would target farms owned by foreigners for expropriation, and in 2003 a list of 192 farms owned by foreigners, mostly South Africans and Germans, had been compiled. As Hamutenya and Pohamba began to emerge as the two main candidates to succeed Nujoma, the Government announced in February 2004 that it had lost patience with the slow pace of land reform under the 'willing buyer, willing seller' programme and would now use compulsory expropriation to speed up the process of redistributing land to the estimated 240,000 landless people. This announcement came soon after the South African Government had taken similar measures.

By 2004 some 700 farms had been sold to the Government for land-reform purposes over a decade, and some 4,000 white commercial farmers owned about 30m. ha of land, although much of that was arid and unsuitable for peasant agriculture. In March Pohamba wrote to 15 landowners informing them that they were required to sell their property to the state, and giving them 14 days to respond. The Namibia Agricultural Union stated that it would accept expropriation providing it was carried out within the country's legal and constitutional framework, which required that compensation should be paid at market value and that those targeted should have the right to have recourse to the law to contest expropriation. Expropriation with compensation meant that budgetary constraints would determine the rate of redistribution, and some Namibians spoke out against paying for land that had been seized in the process of colonial settlement. Many farmers feared that their land would be forcibly seized, as in Zimbabwe, and Nujoma's continued support for Mugabe added to the farmers' concerns. In May Nujoma confirmed that his Government was not only targeting underused land, but would expropriate land as a punitive step against whites who did not treat their labourers properly. The CoD pointed out that those who most deserved to benefit from land reform were San and Herero, not wealthy SWAPO members, and that the expropriation process would create uncertainty and dissuade potential foreign investors.

On the eve of the extraordinary SWAPO congress held to choose his successor in May 2004, Nujoma dismissed Hamutenya and the Deputy Minister for Foreign Affairs, Kaire Mbuende. It was alleged that they had involved themselves in SWAPO primary elections in the Omaheke region; however, it was apparent that Nujoma wished to improve the chances of his preferred successor, Pohamba, who conducted a low-profile campaign. Pohamba attempted to reassure white farmers, stating that expropriations would only occur as a last resort, and that the 'willing buyer, willing seller' policy would continue. He was duly selected as SWAPO's candidate, after receiving 341 votes to Hamutenya's 167 in the second round of voting.

THE POHAMBA PRESIDENCY

In its election manifesto for the parliamentary and presidential elections, SWAPO pledged to expedite the settlement of landless people on commercial farmland, and promised to expropriate 192 farms owned by foreign absentee landlords. At the legislative elections held on 15–16 November 2004, SWAPO won 76.1% of the national vote and retained its 55 seats in the 72-seat National Assembly. The opposition remained fragmented and weak. Although the CoD became the largest opposition party in parliament, with five seats, the DTA (which took four seats) was able to remain the official opposition by concluding an agreement with the UDF, which gained an additional seat, securing three in total. Pohamba overwhelmingly defeated his opponents in the presidential election, in which there was a turn-out of 85% of registered voters, taking 76.4% of the votes cast.

Following the elections the CoD and the Republican Party, which won a seat for the first time, alleged widespread voting irregularities and instigated proceedings at the High Court. Although the court would not declare the elections null and void, it ordered the Electoral Commission to make available the reports of returning officers for each of the 1,168 polling stations and all of the 107 constituencies. In March 2005 the High Court ordered a recount of the results. However, although the recount resulted in all parties, with the exception of the CoD, receiving a smaller number of votes, the allocation of seats remained unchanged.

Meanwhile, in late November 2004 regional elections were held. The 54% turnout was much lower than in the general election, but considerably higher than at the previous regional elections held in 1998. SWAPO won 96 of the 107 constituencies, and gained control of 12 of the 13 regional authorities. The CoD failed to win a single seat, and the DTA was able to win seats only in Kunene, which was the only region not in SWAPO hands. As each regional authority nominated two members to the 26-member National Council (the upper house of the legislature), SWAPO's majority in that house was now greater than before. Parliament as a whole was increasingly marginalized, and unable to provide any effective check on executive power.

On 21 March 2005, at celebrations to mark the 15th anniversary of independence, Pohamba was inaugurated as President. He appointed Nahas Angula, the former Minister of Higher Education, Training and Employment Creation, as the new Prime Minister, and Dr Libertina Amathila as Deputy Prime Minister. Both were veterans of the liberation struggle, and Angula, one of the country's leading intellectuals, had been influential in securing support for Pohamba.

Implementation of the Government's land-reform programme continued to be slow and frustrating both for the Government itself and for those seeking land. Those targeted were members of the San ethnic group, former liberation war combatants, people who lived in exile during apartheid, displaced persons and those living in overcrowded communal areas, and over 240,000 applications were received. By mid-2006, however, only 10,000 people had been resettled, on some 150 commercial farms. In many cases of resettlement the new owners were not able to operate the farms commercially, and valuable equipment was stolen or lay idle. The Government made available about US $7.7m. annually to buy commercial farms, and all farms for sale had to be offered to the state in the first instance. In the year to March 2006 one-half of the money allocated was spent on resettling 150 families on 19 farms, three of which were expropriated. The first farmer to have a farm expropriated appealed to the Land Tribunal against the compensation offered her, which she claimed was only one-third of the farm's real value, and three absentee farmers who had land expropriated appealed to the High Court against the expropriations. Although an Affirmative Action Loan Scheme (see Economy) allowed individual black Namibians to buy commercial farms on preferential terms, in many cases those who bought under this scheme were not able to keep up their loan repayments.

Namibia remained among the most unequal societies in the world. During President Pohamba's visit to the USA in June 2005, he argued to the administrators of the Millennium Challenge Account (a development assistance fund set up by US President George W. Bush in 2002) that the country's classification as a middle income country was misleading because of the skewed per capita income. In 2007 it emerged that his appeal had been successful and that the country would qualify for a large grant from that fund. While the country had moved up to 125th place out of the 177 countries in the 2005 UN Human Development Report, with over 90% of children of primary school age attending school, and water and electricity reaching over 80% of the population, 35% of the country's 2m. people still lived on less than US $1 per day, and nearly 56% on less than US $2 per day. The Government claimed it could not afford to introduce the Basic Income Grant for which many in the non-governmental sector called. HIV prevalence was estimated at 19.6% among adults nationally, but among antenatal clinic attendees it was 42% in Katima Mulilo, the main town in the Caprivi Strip, and it ranged between 22% and 28% in the port cities of Lüderitz, Swakopmund and Walvis Bay. Of the estimated 230,000 Namibians who were HIV-positive in early 2007, it was believed that 50,000 required antiretroviral medication, but that only 22,000 were receiving such treatment.

While President Pohama spoke of 'zero tolerance' for corruption soon after taking up office, and appointed an Anti-Corruption Commission which began work in 2006, the latter had very limited resources and in its first year produced no significant results. No prosecutions followed from the report into the N $30m. that the Social Security Commission had lost by investing in Avid Investment Corporation, and an investigation into the loss of the N $3.1m. paid by the Ministry of Defence to an overseas military hardware supplier for mortar bombs and primers, none of which arrived, continued without apparent progress. The state-owned Namibia Development Corporation admitted to a parliamentary committee hearing in April 2007 that tens of millions of Namibian dollars given as credits to black empowerment initiatives would never be repaid.

The presidential succession was the chief divisive issue within SWAPO in 2007. A faction led by Justice Minister Pendukeni Ithana-Iivula, along with the Minister of Lands, Resettlement and Rehabilitation, Jerry Ekandjo, argued that the Constitution did not prevent Nujoma from returning to power as the country's President after Pohama's five-year term. Nujoma, who would then be 81 years old, remained President of SWAPO. and as the party's constitution provided that its President should be its national presidential candidate,

Nujoma would, if re-elected as SWAPO President at that party's annual congress in November, be a presidential candidate in the 2009 election. SWAPO's regional branches began to declare themselves in favour of retaining him as party President, and Nujoma tried to replace those party members who did not support his re-election. Nujoma's supporters blamed the media for criticizing the 'founder of the nation', and, after some callers had demanded that Nujoma explain his past links with a US diamond trader and others with alleged CIA connections, stated that the radio call-in programmes of the Namibian Broadcasting Corpn should be shut down. When this occurred in early May it aroused a torrent of public criticism, and three days later they were restored, allegedly after the direct instructions of President Pohamba. There followed a noticeable reduction in suggestions from within SWAPO that Nujoma be retained as the party's President, although intense speculation remained regarding proceedings at the conference.

In June 2007 a group claiming to be war veterans began a protest outside the Ministry of Veteran Affairs in Windhoek, claiming that their contribution to the nation's liberation struggle had not been recognized, and demanding monetary compensation and employment. The Prime Minister admitted in the National Assembly that the Government's programmes to integrate the former combatants into the life of the country had not been wholly successful. He revealed that of the 20,825 ex-combatants and 1,165 war orphans registered by 2000, 17,395 had been employed and 2,325 put on the War Veterans Subvention Fund, while 1,105 remained unemployed.

Economy

DONALD L. SPARKS

INTRODUCTION

Namibia is relatively prosperous in African terms: in 2006 the IMF estimated its gross domestic product (GDP) per head at US $3,022. This compared favourably to the sub-Saharan African regional average, which was US $837 in 2004. Indeed, Namibia recorded the seventh highest in income per head in the region. The World Bank classifies Namibia as a lower middle income country. It should be noted, however, that Namibia has one of the world's most unequal income distributions, with a Gini coefficient of 0.7 (Gini coefficients measure income inequalities with zero indicating perfect equality. In developed countries it is usually about 0.3). The reason for this imbalance principally lies in the economic structure that was imposed in colonial times. Ranches were established as settlers displaced Africans on two-thirds of the viable farmland. From the African 'reserves' came a stream of migrant workers, on whose low wages the development of the early mines and ranches depended. In the diamond and uranium mines, where profits have been high and the wage bill a small proportion of costs, the situation has changed, and these enterprises now pay the highest wages in the country. Elsewhere, particularly on the ranches, wages remain extremely low.

The latest UN Development Programme (UNDP) Human Development Index, a compilation of life expectancy, adult literacy, education and GDP per head gave Namibia a score of 0.626, a ranking just behind South Africa. Namibia also compared well in some indicators of health and welfare. For example, 80% of its population had access to improved water sources in 2002 (compared to a regional average of 55%) and currently the Government spends US $189 per head on health care, compared with, the average for sub-Saharan Africa of US $45. However, HIV/AIDS has had a devastating effect on the nation's economy, inhibiting its chances for growth; 19.6% of its adult population were living with HIV/AIDS at the end of 2005. Owing to this pandemic, life expectancy at birth declined from 54 years in 1982 to 48 years in 2005, according to UNDP. The problem is so acute that the IMF warned in 2005 in its consultation with the Government that unless a programme to combat the disease was immediately implemented, Namibia's medium-term economic prospects were in question.

Namibia's comparative wealth reflects a large and fairly diversified mining sector, producing diamonds, uranium and base metals for export. Despite frequent drought, large ranches generally provide significant exports of beef and karakul sheepskins. Yet the economy is highly extractive and poorly integrated. About 80% of the goods that Namibia produces are exported, and about 70% of the goods that are used in the country, including about one-half of the food, are imported.

During the early 1980s Namibia experienced a deep economic recession, intensified by the liberation war, severe drought and low world prices for the country's mineral products and for karakul pelts. In real terms, output per head declined by more than 20% over the period 1977–84, representing a fall of about one-third in real purchasing power. The impact of the recession was partly masked by a rapid expansion in state expenditure in the early 1980s, as South Africa tried to buy support for an internal political settlement. The economic growth rate during this period was hampered by a number of factors, including depressed international prices for Namibia's mineral exports, a corresponding decline in mining production, and the poor performance of the South African economy (in the period prior to and since independence the Namibian and South African economies have remained closely linked). The economy has made significant strides since independence. Overall GDP increased, in real terms, at an average annual rate of 4.1% from 1998–2005. Real GDP increased by 3.5% in 2003, 6.6% in 2004, 4.2% in 2005 and, according to the Central Bureau of Statistics, by an estimated 4.6% in 2006. The Finance Ministry projected growth of 4.9% during 2007.

Namibia's economy has become more diversified in recent years. In 2005 government services made the largest contribution to Namibia's economy, accounting for 19% of GDP, followed by financial services and real estate (13.3%), agriculture and fishing (11.2%) and manufacturing (10.7%), wholesale and retail trade (10.5%), mining and quarrying (8.6%). In late 2005 Namibia became one of only three countries in sub-Saharan Africa with an investment-grade credit rating from the Fitch Ratings international ratings agency, with foreign currency bonds and local currency bonds receiving rating BBB– and BBB, respectively.

FINANCE

Before Namibia's independence, South Africa was an important source of public finance for Namibia. South Africa made its final contribution, of R83m., at independence in 1990 and ceased acting as guarantor of Namibian loans. In addition, revenue from the Southern African Customs Union (SACU) has remained an important source of revenue for the Government. The Customs Union was renegotiated in 2002 and a new SACU secretariat was established in Windhoek. The new agreement, which came into effect in mid-July 2004, guarantees a duty rate of 17%, reducing the yearly fluctuations of the past. In addition, each country will now receive customs revenues based on its relative share of SACU GDP, of which Namibia has 2.4%. Namibia received a record US $600m. from SACU customs receipts in 2004. The increase was due to adjustments to compensate for the switch from a two-year lag in payments. Receipts for 2006 were expected to be even higher, at a projected US $1,000m. The conclusion of a debt-cancellation agreement with South Africa reduced Namibia's outstanding external public debt by 85%, to some N $200m., which represented less than 2% of Namibia's GDP. However, Namibia's external debt situation may not be as favourable as in the past. The Government has undertaken increased foreign borrowing in recent years. By the end of 2004 Namibia's total outstanding debt amounted to a record N $13,799, equivalent to 31.1% of GDP. Of that debt N $10,9444 was domestic and N $2,855 was external. The debt-service ratio to exports reached 14.4% in 2004, 19.3% in 2005 and 11.6% in 2006. Compared to most of its neighbours, Namibia's overall debt situation is reasonable. About one-quarter of its debt is denominated in South African rand (thus avoiding exchange rate risk), about one-half in euros and only 7% in US dollars. As Namibia's GDP per capita is higher than the qualifying threshold, it does not receive loans (denominated in dollars) from the International Development Association and currently has no outstanding World Bank loans.

Namibia's economic policy is based on the second five-year development plan to be launched in 2007. Its major goals will include poverty reduction, increased private sector employment, more income equalities, economic diversification and fighting HIV/AIDS. The Government's budget for 2006/07 projected a first ever surplus of N $921m. (2.1% of GDP), followed by a surplus of N $559m. for the fiscal year 2007/08. Much of this surplus was attributed to the larger-than-expected revenues gained from the SACU revenue-sharing scheme (see above). Defence spending grew most, with an increase over 2006/07 of 21.8% (N $1,683m.). Education received the largest amount of revenue, N $3,700m., an increase of 13.6% compared with the previous year's budget. Other sectors included health, up 20.6% (N $1,683m.), police, up 16.6% (N $976m. and labour/social welfare, increasing by 11.3% at N $787m. The Government plans to spend N $450m. fighting HIV/AIDS over the next three years. The national airline was to receive N $137m. in 2007/08 and N $108m. was allocated to completing the presidential complex in Windhoek. It should be noted, however, that the Government projected a deficit for 2008/09 due to an expected lowering of SACU revenues and the expanded SACU free-trade agreements beginning in 2008.

The relatively new Namibian Stock Exchange (NSX) continues to expand, although perhaps more slowly than many anticipated. The market value of shares traded on the exchange increased substantially in the late 1990s, establishing NSX as sub-Saharan Africa's second largest stock exchange in capital value, although 98% of it was provided by dual-listed shares in South African firms, and trading volumes, while on the increase, remained relatively modest. From April 1998 dual-listing was permitted with all other stock exchanges of the Southern African Development Community (SADC). Namibia is continuing its efforts to establish itself as a leading offshore financial centre in the region. The new investment regime will allow investors to bypass some restrictions on foreign-exchange transactions imposed by the South African Reserve Bank with which Namibia had hitherto been obliged to comply, as a member of the Common Monetary Area. Both the Namibian dollar linked at parity to the South African rand (one of the world's most volatile currencies), declined in value by some 20% in 1998 and further depreciation occurred in 2000–01, but the currency strengthened during 2001–02, with the exchange rate at US $1 = N $6.67 at June 2006, and US $1 = N $7.17 at June 2007. Namibia's foreign exchange reserves rose to N $2,900m. in 2006, compared with N $1,900m. the year before. This reserve is equal to about two months' worth of imports. The large increase was due in large part to the higher SACU revenues and the revenues from the part-privatization of the national mobile cellular telephone company Mobile Telecommunications Ltd.

The annual rate of inflation has improved in recent years. Consumer prices increased by an average of 11.3% in 2002. With the appreciation of the rand, inflation fell to 7.3% in 2003, and continued to decline to 4.1% in 2004 (principally owing to lower utility and fuel costs and a slowdown in housing price increases), although it was estimated at 6.3% in 2007, its highest level since 2002. The South African central bank's sustained policy of monetary restraint curbs inflation in Namibia (as Namibia's monetary policies are effectively controlled by South Africa).

Unemployment remains a serious problem for Namibia, both in the light industrial sector and in urban areas, and there are serious concerns as to how jobs will be found for recent school-leavers. By 2001 unemployment in the formal sector stood at 35%, with many observers estimating the figure to be even higher by 2005. The formal labour force has grown from 429,000 workers in 1980 to 753,000 in 2002 (of whom 41% were female). The services sector was the largest employer, with 47% of total workers, followed by agriculture (38%) and industry (14%). A new labour bill was introduced in 2006, which was likely to include an increase in the minimum wage, a new 45-hour working week and provide all workers with 20 days of annual leave each year.

Following independence, Namibia began to receive financial assistance from the international donor community. Germany, the USA and Scandinavian countries are the principal bilateral donors. Total official development assistance (ODA) declined from US $192m. in 1995 to US $135m. in 2002. As a percentage of GDP, ODA declined from 5.5% in 1995 to 4.7% in 2002. On a per-capita basis Namibia receives more than double the average for sub-Saharan Africa: in 2003 aid per capita amounted to US $73, compared with US $34 for the region. In May the World Bank announced a US $7.5m. loan to use toward the five-year, US $357m. Education and Training Sector Improvement Program, Also in 2007 the People's Republic of China announced a N $1,000m. loan, and a N $720m. line of credit to purchase Chinese goods and services. China had extended a N $18m. interest-free loan in 2006 and a N $45m. interest-free loan for Namibia's small scale farming sector.

MINERALS AND MINING

By almost any standards Namibia is mineral-rich. In 1980 mining accounted for about one-half of Namibia's GDP, but had declined to 8.6% by 2005. However, in that year diamonds accounted for 41% of total export earnings. Indeed, Namibia is the world's leading producer of gem-quality diamonds, traditionally accounting for some 30% of total world output. In addition, Namibia has the world's largest uranium mine (see below) and is the world's fifth largest producer of uranium. Namibia is Africa's second largest producer of zinc, its third largest producer of lead and fourth largest source of copper. Other important minerals include hydrocarbons, tungsten, vanadium, silver, gold, columbite-tantalite (coltan), germanium and beryl; there are also significant reserves of tin, lithium and cadmium. Under the Minerals (Prospecting and Mining) Act, which came into operation in early 1994, the Government has taken action to diversify the mining sector. There was a general increase in mining exploration in recent years.

Diamonds form a key component of Namibia's economy. Diamond mining generally contributes approximately 70% of the sector's GDP and some 10% of national GDP. The ownership of Namibia's most important diamond mine, centred on Oranjemund, underwent a significant reorganization in late 1994, when a new operating company, Namdeb Diamond Corpn (owned in equal shares by the Namibian Government and the Switzerland-based De Beers Centenary AG), acquired the diamond assets of Consolidated Diamond Mines (CDM), the De Beers subsidiary that had previously held sole exploitation rights to Namibian alluvial diamond deposits. Namdeb accounted for 97% of the country's total output of 1.9m. carats in 2004. About 98% of the diamonds recovered in Namibia are of gem quality, and under the new arrangements these stones continue to be marketed by De Beers through the Central Selling Organisation (CSO). Total production was 2.1m. carats in 2006, an increase of 17.5% compared with 2005. Of that amount, 1.0m. carats was onshore production, with 1.1m. carats produced offshore.

In early 2004 the Sakawe Mining Corpn (Samicor) announced a three-year US $46m. investment in offshore production. It will spend US $7m. on a third mining vessel, and US $10m. on the refurbishment of its two other vessels. A new Diamond Act, to succeed legislation in force since 1939, was approved by the Namibian parliament in mid-1999; the Act allows individuals to apply for licences to trade in, import or export diamonds, subject to criminal penalties for unauthorized dealing. Namibia is co-operating in international efforts to ensure that diamonds from conflict areas are not used to support continued warfare (so-called 'conflict diamonds'). However, in 2000 the Government admitted that it had obtained a diamond concession in the Democratic Republic of Congo to help pay for Namibia's military operations in that country. In March 2004 DFI and Samicor entered into a joint venture agreement to explore the Lüderitz Bay concession, formerly owned by Namco. In June Lev Leviev Group of Israel (of which Samicor forms a part), opened Namibia's first diamond-cutting and -polishing factory in Windhoek, LLD Diamonds Namibia (Pty) Ltd. The factory was constructed at a cost of some N $40m. During 2004 the facility was producing some 4,000 carats per month, significantly below its capacity of 30,000 carats. The Government announced a new marketing agreement in January to allow firms to buy uncut stones directly from Namdeb. This new arrangement should allow local firms to cut more locally mined stones: N $2,000m. worth of local rough diamonds will be available by the end of 2009, equal to about 13% of total diamond production. In addition, a new 50:50 joint venture between the Government and De Beers, the Namibian Diamond Trading Company, will be responsible for sorting, establishing value and marketing Namdeb's output to the local firms as well as to the world market. The Government also placed a moratorium on new licences for cutting and polishing diamonds in 2007.

The huge, although low-grade, Rössing uranium mine, came into production in 1976. After an initial period of profitability for its owner, the Rio Tinto-Zinc group, the mine suffered from the depression in the uranium market. The Rössing mine's uranium is sold by means of long-term contracts to European Union (EU) countries, Japan and Taiwan, but the persistently weak 'spot' price of uranium has forced renegotiations of the contract prices. Rössing's output in 2003 declined by 13%, from 1,887 metric tons to 1,647 tons. This reduction was due to the closure of the main plant in the first quarter of 2003 during which time a new tailings disposal facility was built. Although the spot market for uranium had recovered by 2003, most of its sales were under long-term contracts made when the market price was lower; it was anticipated that the mine would close before 2007. None the less, Rössing recorded a 13-year record output of 3,600 tons of uranium oxide in 2004, owing in part to new equipment coming online and additional contracts. This was a 49% increase over 2003 output, and was equivalent to US $124m. Production declined to 3,617 tons in 2006. The mines has a 4,000-ton capacity, and the company has stated it wants to meet that capacity in 2007. However, Rössing showed a net profit of US $39m. in 2006, compared to earnings of US $3m. in 2005. Given that Namibia's reserves are far from exhausted, there is exploration ongoing in 2007. In 2003 an Australian company, Paladin Resources, began developing a uranium operation south of Rössing at Langer Heinrich. Construction began in September 2005 at a cost of US $92m. The mine was officially opened in March 2007, and production in the first year was projected at 1,180 tons. When the Langer Heinrich and Rössing mines are producing at full capacity, Namibia will export some 5,200 tons annually, placing Namibia as Africa's largest uranium producer, and fifth in the world, behind Canada, Australia, Kazakhstan and Russia. Furthermore, a third mine, at Trejjopje-Klein, 20 km. north of Rössing, was expected to start operation in 2008 and the Valencia project, 35 km east of Rössing, is at the feasibility study stage of development.

Namibia's principal metals producer, Tsumeb Corpn Ltd, which operated three base-metal mines and a major copper smelter and lead refinery, was placed in provisional liquidation by the owner, Gold Fields Namibia, in August 1998. Subsequent bids to acquire Tsumeb, whose assets were valued at N $180m., failed to prevent a liquidation order, issued by the High Court in March 1999, and Tsumeb's mineral rights reverted to the Namibian Government. Imcor Zinc (Pty) Ltd, a subsidiary of South Africa's state-controlled Iron and Steel Corpn (ISCOR), has been one of the very few companies to have undertaken significant prospecting for base metals in recent years, increasing capacity at the Uis tin mine by 30% and at the Rosh Pinah zinc-lead mine by 25%. Output at Rosh Pinah increased by 4% in 1998, to 55,600 metric tons of concentrates. A new company, Rosh Pinah Zinc Corpn, was established in May 1999 as a joint venture between ISCOR and PE Minerals, which holds the mineral rights to the mine. Zinc is on the way to becoming Namibia's second largest source of export revenues (after diamonds). The Skorpion Zinc mine, opened in 2000 at a cost of US $454m., produced 47,000 tons in 2003, all of which was exported. Production of zinc concentrates increased by nearly 40% in 2003, to a record 108,000 tons, the majority of which was sent for processing by Skorpion's South African facility.

Namibia is believed to have considerable offshore reserves of natural gas, estimated at as much as 560,000m. cu m of natural gas in the Kudu field off Lüderitz. Exploration rights for the offshore Kudu gas fields were held by a consortium led by Shell, which planned to pipe gas to power stations to be constructed in Namibia and South Africa. However, following initial surveys Shell withdrew from the consortium in August 2002, later to be followed by ChevronTexaco in December 2003. Energy Africa was left as the sole permit holder until the state-owned National Petroleum Corpn of Namibia (NAMCOR) acquired a 10% stake later that month. (The Irish petroleum company Tullow bought Energy Africa in May 2004.) In July 2004 Energy Africa and South Africa's Electricity Supply Commission (ESKOM) reached a joint development agreement with NAMCOR and NamPower (Namibia Power Corpn—see below) to develop a N $6,400m. gas-fired power plant that would make Namibia self-sufficient in energy. Tullow Oil, the owner of the Kudu 'gas-to-power' facility, announced the completion of its financial study in early 2005. The construction costs were estimated at US $1,000m., which would be financed in co-operation with the Namibian Government. In addition to natural gas, there is also vast petroleum potential. In 2001 Australia's Eagle Bay Resources was awarded an exploration permit for an area off shore from the mouth of the Orange river, and had expectations of finding reserves in excess of 1,300m. barrels. Finally, in early 2005 the Chinese oil firm China Shine acquired a majority stake in the inland Etosha concession, with plans to spend US $50m. on exploration.

AGRICULTURE AND FISHING

Drought, overgrazing and unscientific farming methods have had an adverse effect on the agricultural sector. The contribution of agriculture and fisheries to GDP, however, increased from 7.3% in 1986 to 10.8% in 2003, and to 11.2% in 2005. Agricultural GDP increased at an average annual rate of 2.5% in 1995–2005, with growth in the fishing sector generally offsetting poorer performances in other areas of agriculture. An estimated 38% of Namibia's labour force were employed in the agricultural sector in 2004 (a fall from 52% in 1980).

Namibia has a fragile, desert ecology, and most of the land can support only livestock. The major agricultural activities are the processing of meat and other livestock products, and more than 90% of commercial agricultural output comprises livestock production. The most important agricultural product is beef, beef production representing some 87% of Namibia's gross non-fishing agricultural income. Ostrich farming was an expanding sector in the early 1990s, mainly in the south of the country. In early 2000 flooding caused extensive damage to ostrich farms and during the 2001–02 breeding season a funding shortage resulted in the deaths of some 2,500 ostriches on communal farms, effectively collapsing the sector. The only large-scale commercial arable farming is in the karstveld around Tsumeb, and on the Hardap irrigation scheme in the south. Subsistence crops include beans, potatoes and maize. The country usually imports about one-half of its cereals requirement, but in the drought-free years it is able to provide some 70% of local demand. In an effort to diversify agricultural production, seedless-grape plantations are being developed on the banks of the Orange river bordering South Africa. Exports of the grapes to the EU have increased remarkably in recent years. In 2002 some 200,000 cartons were exported, increasing to 310,000 cartons in 2003, making them the second largest source of agricultural export earnings, after beef.

Colonial history bequeathed Namibia three different agricultural sectors: about 4,000 large commercial ranches, almost all white-owned; 20,000 African stock-raising households, compressed into central and southern reserves; and 120,000 black families practicing mixed farming on just 5% of the viable farmland in the far north. The planted area is currently estimated at 241,000 ha.

The Government has plans to transfer some communal lands (mostly in the north) to private ownership, although there is considerable opposition from traditional leaders. At the time of Namibia's independence about 50% of the country's commercial farms were owned by absentee landlords, and the possible redistribution of such land was an important political issue. In 1992 the Government initiated the National Resettlement Policy (NRP), which was designed to redistribute 7.3m. ha of farmland owned by absentee landowners or otherwise underutilized, representing almost one-quarter of the 32m. ha owned by commercial (mostly white) farmers at independence. The Namibian Government, through Agribank, began to grant low-interest loans (under the Affirmative Action Loan Scheme—AALS) to farmers in 1994. By 1999 very little farmland had been purchased by the Government for redistribution, primarily because the allocated budget, totalling N $20m., had proved inadequate; the budget allocation was raised to N $50m. in 2003. However, that year a parliamentary committee found that the land reform programme had spent only N $3.8m. of its annual N $20m. allocation in 2000. By the end of 2003 the Government had acquired some 829,500 ha of land and had redistributed about 1% annually since the beginning of the NRP; by contrast, in the same period more than 3.1m. ha of land had been bought with individual AALS loans.

The Government was facing increasing pressure to take possession of commercial farmland without paying full compensation, a development that would require an amendment of the Constitution, which stipulates that market prices be paid for land. None the less, in 2001 President Nujoma warned the National Farmers' Union that its 'willing buyer, willing seller' programme (see Recent History) might change, if white commercial farmers remained hesitant to sell. In early 2004 the Prime Minister announced that the Government would expand the programme to include domestically owned commercial farms. The Government's declared target was to resettle more than 243,000 people within the next five years; at that time some 37,000 people had been given land since 1990. Namibia is mindful of the negative consequences Zimbabwe has experienced from such actions and in mid-2004 there were calls to revise the AALS to concentrate on building new farms. In early 2005 the Government adopted a new land tenure law covering reforms in urban areas, communal resettlement and compensation policies, although no changes to previous policies have yet been made. In July 2004 the European Commission set aside funds amounting to €91m. for projects in Namibia, of which some €52m. were earmarked for projects including land reform and rural development.

The Namibia Early Warning and Food Information Unit estimated the grain harvest (white maize, pearl millet and sorghum) for 2006/07 at 119,300 tons, a decrease of 34% from the previous year. The most affected areas are in the north-central regions of Namibia. This reduced output will mean more cereal imports, mainly from South Africa. However, as the South African harvest was also likely to be reduced, prices were predicted to rise sharply.

Owing to the cold, nutrient-rich Benguela Current, Namibia has one of the richest fisheries in the world. Prior to independence, however, Namibia received no tax or licence fees from fishing because the illegal occupation of the territory deprived it of an internationally recognized fishing zone within the usual limit of 200 nautical miles (370 km). There are, in fact, two separate fisheries off Namibia: in shore and off shore. The inshore fishery, for pilchard, anchovy and rock lobster, is controlled by Namibian and South African companies, based at Lüderitz and Walvis Bay. During the mid-1980s, however, persistent overfishing left stocks severely depleted, and in March 1990 the new Namibian Government requested foreign fleets cease fishing Namibia's coastal waters, pending an assessment of fish stocks. Following independence the Namibian authorities enforced a 370-km exclusive economic zone (EEZ), thereby achieving considerable success in restocking its waters. Under licensing arrangements implemented in 1992 25 deep-sea trawlers were authorized to fish within Namibian coastal waters. Fish stocks have recovered substantially since independence, and many foreign commercial companies are pressing the Government to increase the annual 30,000-ton interim catch limit. Onshore fish-processing has increased the sector's added value: thus, landings declined by 4% in 1997, to 488,100 tons, but export earnings increased by some 24%, to N $1,564m. In 1997 scientific surveys indicated a recovery in the pilchard stock, and the Government approved a small catch quota for that year's season. The 25,000-ton total allowable catch (TAC), announced by the Minister of Fisheries and Marine Resources, was 5,000 tons more than that of 1996. The marked recovery in stocks of pilchard, hake and horse mackerel prompted the Government to increase TACs for the major species. The TAC for hake, the most valuable of species landed, increased from 165,000 tons in 1998 to 210,000 tons in 2000. The Minister of Fisheries and Marines Resources maintained that the one-month moratorium on hake fishing in 2006 was successful, as the catch levels had increased, and the value of fish landings had risen from N $3,700m. in 2005 to N $3,900m. in 2006. However, some in the industry claimed that the moratorium had resulted in numerous job losses.

The fishing industry is an important source of employment, and there is considerable scope for job creation in the sector, particularly in fish-processing. Indeed, since independence the number of workers in this industry has increased from 6,000 to 9,000, and the fishing industry could soon replace mining as the largest source of private-sector employment. None the less, the fishing sector has suffered during the past few years. The sector is faced with increased operational costs, a strengthening Namibian dollar (making exports less attractive), poor catches and smaller sized fish being caught.

OTHER ECONOMIC SECTORS

Namibia's manufacturing sector is small. It provided an estimated 10.7% of GDP in 2005, and consists mainly of processing fish, minerals and meat for export, and production of basic consumer products, such as beer and bread. Food products account for about 70% of all goods produced in Namibia. During 1995–2005 manufacturing GDP increased, in real terms, by an estimated annual average of 3.7%. The development of the manufacturing sector has been limited by fluctuations in the supply of cattle and fish, by the small domestic market, by the high cost of energy and transport, and by the lack of an educated entrepreneurial class. Furthermore, Namibia's traditional dependence on South Africa for most manufactured goods has resulted in the underdevelopment of the sector. There are 278 manufacturing firms, mostly located in or near the main urban centres.

The Export Processing Zone Act was approved in 1995, establishing an export processing zone (EPZ) in Walvis Bay and allowing others to follow. Seven companies were approved for EPZ status in 1995. The largest of these, Purity Manganese, announced plans to construct a N $30m. industrial pipe-manufacturing facility. Although the Government has banned strikes in the EPZ, all other labour legislation was in force from 1996. In 1997 the European Commission granted N $32m. (US $7.2m.) to develop the EPZ project and to strengthen Namibia's capacity to attract investment and expand foreign trade. Funding was reserved for EPZ infrastructure and services, investment promotion and the establishment of a Namibian Exporters' Association. However, the EPZ's incentives have failed to attract substantial investment in non-traditional manufacturing capacity. While some factories in Oshikango's EPZ, near the Angolan border, are advancing, in Walvis Bay, along the coast, several factories have closed and other EPZ projects have been postponed. In fact, only three EPZ factories were operating there in 1999. Namtex, the first EPZ operation, which began in 1996, reduced its operations and now produces garments only for the domestic market, while Global Textiles and the Italian-backed MN Construction have actually closed down. During 2005 a number of firms in the EPZ closed, including Rhino Garments Namibia, resulting in a loss of 1,700 jobs. In 2004 there were 32 firms, and only 25 by the end of 2005. Employment likewise declined, from 10,057 workers to 6,967. Investment declined slightly, from N $5,558m. in 2004 to N $5,234m. in 2005. Total investment in the EPZ reached US $785m. by mid-2005, according to the Offshore Development Company.

A Malaysian company, Ramatex, established a N $900m. integrated textile and garment facility in Windhoek in 2002. Exports were to be primarily to the USA, owing to the US African Growth and Opportunity Act (AGOA), which allows duty-free access for certain textiles from sub-Saharan Africa. Owing to the high demand for cotton inputs, the Government hoped to be able to stimulate the country's small cotton industry and envisaged the creation of some 20,000 jobs in the textile industry by 2005. The textile industry faces challenges as the World Trade Organization's Multi-fibre Agreement quota system expired at the beginning of 2005. Namibia, like many of its neighbours, will face stiff competition from China and other lower cost producers. Under AGOA, from 2007 African firms will have to obtain raw materials such as cotton from within Africa.

Construction contributed only 2.2% of GDP in 2002. Following the 1993–94 expansion in commercial and residential property developments, growth in the GDP of the construction sector slowed to 2.8% in 1995. The GDP contribution of the sector declined by 11.6% in 1999, before increasing by 25.4% in 2000. New employment opportunities in the construction sector were to be provided in 2001 by the new Skorpion Zinc mine (see above) and government-financed infrastructure projects in the southern part of the country. The country's major new construction project was an expansion of a shopping mall outside Windhoek at a cost of US $28m.

The electricity, gas and water sectors (which represented 2.4% of GDP in 2003) are somewhat more integrated and extensive than might be expected. The principal mines and towns are linked in a national grid, which can be fed by the 120-MW Van Eck power station outside Windhoek, the hydroelectric station at Ruacana (which has a generating capacity of up to 320 MW) on the Kunene river, and the 45-MW Paratus scheme at Walvis Bay. There is a link to the system operated by South Africa's ESKOM, and the Zambia Electricity Supply Corpn provides electricity to the Caprivi region. ESKOM was expected to cease exports to Namibia in the late 2000s, due to increased demands in the South African market.

In 1991 Namibia and Angola signed an agreement on the further development of the Kunene river as a source of energy. The planned Epupa hydroelectric scheme, on the Kunene river, continues to attract controversy. Fears have been expressed that the dam will disrupt the area's ecology and displace the Himba people. In 1999 the Namang consortium of consultants submitted its final report, concluding that there would be significant environmental consequences, but that the dam would none the less be the most efficient, and least expensive, method of increasing Namibia's electricity generating capacity. There is, however, a significant difference in approach between the two Governments, which may delay the project indefinitely. While Namibia prefers the construction of a reservoir at Epupa Falls, at an estimated cost of N $539m., Angola favours a smaller, slightly more costly, but less ecologically damaging site at Baynes Mountains. Work began in 1999 on a second power interconnector to the South African grid, at a cost of N $870m.; this was to be Namibia's largest post-independence construction project. In late August 2002 it was also announced that NamPower would collaborate with Zambia on the construction of a power interconnector between the two countries. An agreement was finalized in late July 2004 and the project was expected to be completed by November 2005. Between 1992 and 2003 electricity demand in Namibia rose from 225 MW to 378 MW; in 2003 the national generation capacity was 393 MW. In 2006 Russia offered to help Namibia build a nuclear power plant, as the Government has pledged to become self-sufficient in energy within three years.

Mines and towns in Namibia's white-inhabited areas are also the main places served by the long-distance water supply. Windhoek and its surrounding mines are supplied from a number of dams. Rössing, Walvis Bay and Swakopmund draw their water from boreholes in a series of dry riverbeds. Both the Tsumeb and coastal underground reserves are under strain, and the long-term plan is to connect the two systems together, and to draw water from the Okavango river in the extreme north of the country.

Tourism is playing an increasingly important role in the economy. Some 282,000 tourists visited Namibia in 1991, contributing N $32m. to the economy. By 2003 tourist numbers had increased to 695,221; receipts totalled US $333m. that year. The Government has also promoted the development of 'eco-tourism' in Namibia. The Namibian Government appears to intend to introduce a liberalized air policy, with the minister responsible for transport deciding not to object to a proposal by Kalahari Express Airlines that services operate between Windhoek, Cape Town and Johannesburg, despite strong criticism from Air Namibia, the state airline. In 1998 Air Namibia signed a co-operation agreement with a German airline, LTU, under which joint flights were to be operated to Frankfurt, Düsseldorf and Munich. In mid-2005 Air Namibia was scheduled to resume its Windhoek–London direct flights, after a three-year suspension. As the United Kingdom is Namibia's second major source of European visitors (after Germany), this service should prove successful, especially as there is no competition on this route. In 2006 a N $550m. joint venture between Namibian-, Kuwait- and Swiss-based hotel firms was formed to construct three five-star hotels in Namibia. They will be operated under the Kempinski name and were scheduled for completion in 2010.

The newly completed Trans-Kalahari Highway is an important development for regional trade and economic integration. The Highway provides a link between Walvis Bay and South Africa's important Gauteng industrial area. However, until Walvis Bay's harbour development programme is completed the port is likely to remain underutilized. Currently Walvis Bay attracts only a 1% share of container traffic to southern Africa, because it is too shallow. A project to deepen the port to 12.8 m began in February 2000. When completed, it should enable Walvis Bay to receive container vessels with a capacity of 2,200–2,400 metric tons, allowing the port to attract at least some of the business currently using the South African ports of Cape Town and Durban. In late 2003 the Government announced plans to examine a new harbour at Cape Fria, 120 km south of the Angolan border. This area could be a base for the northern fishing industry, as well as provide a more direct routing to regional neighbours. However, there are no roads or other infrastructure there presently, and such an undertaking would be costly.

Access to telephones, computers and the internet has increased more rapidly in Namibia than in most neighbouring countries. In 2005 Namibia had 101.4 telephones per 1,000 people (up from 50.5 in 1995), 16.4 internet hosts per 10,000 people (up from 0.1 in 1995) and 99.3 personal computers per 1,000 people (up from 24.1 in 1998).

FOREIGN TRADE AND BALANCE OF PAYMENTS

Namibia's principal trading partners traditionally include South Africa, the United Kingdom, Germany, Japan and the USA. In 2006 exports amounted to US $2,655m., an increase of 37% compared with 2005, while imports were US $2,558. resulting in a trade surplus of US $97m. In 2004 Namibia sold 28% of its exports South Africa, 15% to the UK, 14% to Angola and 11% to the USA. Diamond exports contributed 41% of the total value of Namibia's exports in 2006, an increase of 36% over the previous year. By far its largest supplier in 2004 was South Africa (which accounted for 86% of all imports). Principal exports in 2005 were diamonds (41% of all exports), manufacturing goods (24%), food and live animals (15%) and other minerals (13%). Namibia's principal imports in 2005 were vehicles and transport equipment (17% of the total imports), refined petroleum products (14%.), chemicals and related products (12%), food (9%), machinery electrical goods (8%). The current account balance remained in surplus in 2006 at a record US $1,158m., a large increase from the surplus of US $432m. recorded the previous year. Namibia's overall balance of payments posted a surplus of US $159m. in 2006, compared with US $2m. in 2005. Namibia's foreign-exchange reserves reached US $323m. in 2002 and US $325m. in 2003, US $345m. in 2004, US $312m. in 2005 and a record US $450m. in 2006. At independence Namibia became a member of the Southern African Development Co-ordination Conference (SADCC—reorganized as SADC in 1992). Namibia has been a consistent supporter of Zimbabwe's president, Robert Mugabe, and extended that country a US $40m. loan to the

Zimbabwe Electricity Supply Authority to rehabilitate four thermal power generators. The agreement was signed during President Mugabe's state visit to Namibia in March 2007.

ECONOMIC PROSPECTS

Namibia will continue to be dominated economically by its large neighbour, South Africa, for the foreseeable future. South Africa is the source of some 90% of Namibia's imports; in addition, South Africa has significant control over Namibia's transport infrastructure, as Namibia's only external rail links are with South Africa. In 1993 Namibia and South Africa agreed to establish joint customs control over Walvis Bay, which handles about 90% of Namibia's sea-borne trade. Although the enclave of Walvis Bay was transferred to Namibia in 1994, the port facilities (owned by Portnet of South Africa) were not ceded. In late 1995, however, the harbour assets at Walvis Bay were formally transferred to Namibia, after the Government paid N $30m. for the facilities (considerably below the N $66m. asked for by Portnet).

The SWAPO Government has committed the nation to a mixed-market economy and is trying to encourage private-sector investment and export-orientated manufacturing industries. In 1990 Namibia joined the IMF, and that year liberal legislation on foreign investment was introduced. In 1993 a programme of incentives for private-sector investment in manufacturing was announced. The incentives include tax relief, cash grants and low-interest loans for export promotion. In 2000 the National Assembly approved a plan from the Ministry of Finance and the Ministry of Trade and Industry to begin a privatization programme. The Government has established a council for state-owned enterprises, with a divestiture sub-committee that will work on privatization details. In late 2005 the Prime Minister sponsored legislation that would give the Government full responsibility over parastatals. The State-Owned Governance Act will apply to all of the nation's 52 parastatals and could provide stronger oversight over their management. However, during the past two years the Government has backed away from privatization, but has focused on attempting to ensure the parastatals perform more efficiently with improved management.

Namibia's abundant mineral reserves and rich fisheries are expected to form the basis of the nation's potential economic prosperity. However, this narrow base—accounting for well more than one-half of export value—can be viewed as a liability. The economic development of the impoverished northern region of the country remains a priority. Economic advance has hitherto been accomplished primarily by the extractive industries and has not yet filtered through to the wider economy in terms of increased employment, more equitable income distribution or higher incomes per head. Indeed, the second five-year national development plan (for 2002–06) called for reducing poverty and income inequality, stimulating economic growth, creating employment, promoting economic empowerment and a renewed effort to prevent the spread of HIV/AIDS. The third development plan (NDP3), to be launched in 2007, is expected to retain those objectives. Namibia has moved from colonial rule to independence with relatively little social or economic upheaval, and with relatively sound public economic policies and a physical infrastructure that should eventually lead to long-term development and growth.

Statistical Survey

Source (unless otherwise indicated): Central Bureau of Statistics, National Planning Commission, Government Office Park, Block D2, Luther St, Windhoek; Private Bag 13356, Windhoek; tel. (61) 2834056; fax (61) 237620; e-mail info@npc.gov.na; internet www.npc.gov.na.

Area and Population

AREA, POPULATION AND DENSITY*

Area (sq km)	824,292†
Population (census results)	
21 October 1991	1,409,920
28 August 2001	
Males	936,718
Females	890,136
Total	1,826,854
Population (UN estimates at mid-year)‡	
2004	1,994,000
2005	2,020,000
2006	2,047,000
Density (per sq km) at mid-2006	2.5

* Including data for Walvis Bay, sovereignty over which was transferred from South Africa to Namibia with effect from March 1994. Walvis Bay has an area of 1,124 sq km (434 sq miles) and had a population of 22,999 in 1991.

† 318,261 sq miles.

‡ Source: UN, *World Population Prospects: The 2006 Revision*.

ETHNIC GROUPS
(population, 1988 estimate)

Ovambo	623,000	Caprivian	47,000
Kavango	117,000	Bushmen	36,000
Damara	94,000	Baster	31,000
Herero	94,000	Tswana	7,000
White	80,000	Others	12,000
Nama	60,000	**Total**	1,252,000
Coloured	51,000		

PRINCIPAL TOWNS
(population at 2001 census)

Windhoek	233,529	Rehoboth	21,300
Rundu	44,413	Otjiwarongo	19,614
Walvis Bay	42,015	Keetmanshoop	15,543
Oshakati	28,255	Gobabis	13,856
Katima Mulilo	22,694	Tsumeb	13,108

Mid-2005 (including suburbs, UN estimate): Windhoek (capital) 289,000 (Source: UN, *World Urbanization Prospects: The 2005 Revision*).

BIRTHS AND DEATHS
(annual averages, UN estimates)

	1990–95	1995–2000	2000–05
Birth rate (per 1,000)	39.2	32.7	27.4
Death rate (per 1,000)	8.5	9.4	12.9

Source: UN, *World Population Prospects: The 2006 Revision*.

Expectation of life (WHO estimates, years at birth): 54 (males 52; females 55) in 2004 (Source: WHO, *World Health Report*).

ECONOMICALLY ACTIVE POPULATION
(persons aged 15 to 69 years, 2000 labour force survey)

	Males	Females	Total
Agriculture, hunting, and forestry	69,782	56,677	126,459
Fishing	4,725	3,075	7,800
Mining and quarrying	3,154	713	3,868
Manufacturing	11,375	11,548	22,922
Electricity, gas and water	3,709	484	4,193
Construction	20,740	1,048	21,788
Wholesale and retail trade, repair of motor vehicles, motorcycles and personal and household goods	17,220	21,683	38,902
Restaurants and hotels	3,006	4,671	7,677
Transport, storage and communications	12,243	2,065	14,308
Financial intermediation	2,489	2,444	4,933
Real estate, renting and business activities	17,880	21,437	39,318
Public administration and defence; compulsory social security	15,372	9,047	24,419
Education	11,742	18,797	30,538
Health and social work	2,993	10,143	13,135
Other community, social and personal services	24,324	21,965	46,289
Private households with employed persons	4,754	17,456	22,210
Extra-territorial organizations and bodies	155	172	327
Not classifiable by economic activity	1,166	1,599	2,765
Total employed	226,828	205,021	431,849
Unemployed	89,350	131,284	220,634
Total labour force	316,178	336,305	652,483

Source: ILO.

Mid-2005 ('000 persons, FAO estimates): Agriculture, etc. 311; Total labour force 832 (Source: FAO).

Health and Welfare

KEY INDICATORS

Total fertility rate (children per woman, 2005)	3.7
Under-5 mortality rate (per 1,000 live births, 2005)	62
HIV/AIDS (% of persons aged 15–49, 2005)	19.60
Physicians (per 1,000 head, 2004)	0.30
Health expenditure (2004): US $ per head (PPP)	407.4
Health expenditure (2004): % of GDP	6.8
Health expenditure (2004): public (% of total)	69.0
Access to water (% of persons, 2004)	87
Access to sanitation (% of persons, 2004)	25
Human Development Index (2004): ranking	125
Human Development Index (2004): value	0.626

For sources and definitions, see explanatory note on p. vi.

Agriculture

PRINCIPAL CROPS
('000 metric tons)

	2003	2004	2005
Wheat	10.3	8.3	11.0
Maize	28.9	28.2	40.7
Millet	52.2	74.4	47.9
Sorghum	6.0	6.0*	5.8
Roots and tubers*	295	295	295
Pulses*	9	9	9
Cottonseed*	3.4	4.1	4.5
Vegetables (incl. melons)*	14.8	14.8	14.9
Grapes*	8.5	8.9	9.5

* FAO estimate(s).

Source: FAO.

LIVESTOCK
('000 head, year ending September)

	2003	2004	2005
Horses	50.0*	62.7	47.4
Asses, mules or hinnies*	136.7	141.7	147.0
Cattle	2,336.1	2,309.4	3,133.9
Sheep	2,955.5	2,619.4	2,663.8
Goats	2,086.8	1,997.2	2,043.5
Chickens*	3,500	3,500	3,500

* FAO estimate(s).

Source: FAO.

LIVESTOCK PRODUCTS
('000 metric tons)

	2003	2004	2005
Cattle meat	45.0*	42.9	38.6
Sheep meat	6.3*	6.6	6.7*
Chicken meat*	5.0	5.8	6.2
Cows' milk*	109	109	109
Hen eggs*	1.9	1.9	1.9
Wool (greasy)*	2.2	2.2	2.2

* FAO estimate(s).

Source: FAO.

Forestry

Separate figures are not yet available. Data for Namibia are included in those for South Africa.

Fishing

('000 metric tons, live weight)*

	2003	2004	2005
Capture†	671.6	605.7	588.1
Cape hakes (Stokvisse)	192.3	173.9	158.1
Kingklip	7.2	7.5	5.6
Devil anglerfish	12.9	9.0	11.1
Southern African pilchard	22.3	28.6	27.3
Cape horse mackerel (Maasbanker)	366.9	314.5	324.5
Aquaculture†	0.0	0.0	0.0
Total catch†	671.7	605.8	588.1

* Figures include quantities caught by licensed foreign vessels in Namibian waters and processed in Lüderitz and Walvis Bay. The data exclude aquatic mammals (whales, seals, etc.). The number of South African fur seals caught was: 35,000 in 2003–05 (FAO estimates). The number of Nile crocodiles caught was: 400 in 2005.

† FAO estimate(s).

Source: FAO.

Mining

(metric tons, unless otherwise indicated)

	2003	2004	2005
Copper ore*	16,175	11,174	10,157
Lead concentrates*	18,782	14,338	14,320
Zinc concentrates*	60,500	66,028	68,000†
Silver ore (kilograms)*	45,100	27,153	30,003
Uranium oxide	2,401	3,583	3,711
Gold ore (kilograms)*	2,508	2,205	2,703
Fluorspar (Fluorite)‡	79,349	104,785	84,211
Salt (unrefined)	697,914	754,351	573,248
Diamonds ('000 metric carats)	1,481	2,004	1,902

* Figures refer to the metal content of ores and concentrates.
† Estimate.
‡ Figures (on a wet-weight basis) refer to acid-grade material.

Source: US Geological Survey.

Industry

SELECTED PRODUCTS

(metric tons)

	2003	2004	2005
Unrefined (blister) copper (unwrought)	26,036	24,704	23,551

Source: US Geological Survey.

Finance

CURRENCY AND EXCHANGE RATES

Monetary Units

100 cents = 1 Namibian dollar (N $).

Sterling, US Dollar and Euro Equivalents (31 May 2007)

£1 sterling = N $14.207;
US $1 = N $7.185;
€1 = N $9.666;
N $100 = £7.04 = US $13.92 = €10.35.

Average Exchange Rate (N $ per US $)

2004 6.4597
2005 6.3593
2006 6.7716

Note: The Namibian dollar was introduced in September 1993, replacing (at par) the South African rand. The rand remained legal tender in Namibia.

CENTRAL GOVERNMENT BUDGET

(N $ million, year ending 31 March)

Revenue*	2004/05	2005/06	2006/07†
Taxation	10,468.2	11,354.8	14,270.4
Taxes on income and profits	4,024.2	4,385.9	4,688.0
Taxes on property	85.9	100.1	122.0
Domestic taxes on goods and services	2,057.3	3,041.9	3,187.8
Taxes on international trade and transactions	4,206.8	3,728.8	6,149.6
Other taxes	94.1	98.1	123.0
Non-tax revenue	885.8	846.4	935.3
Entrepreneurial and property income	490.0	396.6	467.2
Fines and forfeitures	17.0	22.0	23.5
Administrative fees and charges	342.1	397.9	410.7
Return on capital from lending and equity	36.8	29.9	33.9
Total	11,354.0	12,201.1	15,205.7

Expenditure‡	2004/05	2005/06	2006/07†
Current expenditure	10,786.0	10,993.2	12,405.3
Personnel expenditure	5,527.1	5,534.1	6,129.7
Expenditure on goods and other services	1,921.9	1,883.0	2,167.7
Interest payments	1,040.2	1,146.8	1,478.1
Subsidies and other current transfers	2,296.9	2,479.3	2,629.8
Capital expenditure	1,618.5	1,568.3	2,097.5
Capital investment	1,401.1	1,435.1	1,849.1
Capital transfers	217.4	133.2	248.4
Total	12,404.6	12,561.5	14,502.8

* Excluding grants received from abroad (N $ million): 70.4 in 2004/05; 153.2 in 2005/06; 72.0 in 2006/07.
† Estimates.
‡ Excluding total lending and equity participation (N $ million): 365.9 in 2004/05; 207.5 in 2005/06; 652.4 in 2006/07.

Source: Bank of Namibia, *Quarterly Bulletin* (June 2006).

INTERNATIONAL RESERVES

(US $ million at 31 December, excl. gold)

	2004	2005	2006
IMF special drawing rights	0.03	0.03	0.03
Reserve position in IMF	0.09	0.10	0.11
Foreign exchange	344.94	311.98	449.44
Total	345.06	312.10	449.58

Source: IMF, *International Financial Statistics*.

MONEY SUPPLY

(N $ million at 31 December)

	2004	2005	2006
Currency outside banks	632.7	680.0	763.4
Demand deposits at deposit money banks	8,898.0	8,728.8	12,915.6
Total money	9,530.7	9,408.8	13,678.9

Source: IMF, *International Financial Statistics*.

COST OF LIVING

(Consumer Price Index; base: December 2001 = 100)

	2003	2004	2005
Food and non-alcoholic beverages	121.6	122.6	124.4
Alcoholic beverages and tobacco	110.9	121.2	130.1
Housing, fuel and power	114.6	122.4	124.3
Clothing and footwear	108.8	109.3	108.2
All items (incl. others)	115.4	120.2	122.9

NATIONAL ACCOUNTS

(N $ million at current prices, preliminary figures)

National Income and Product

	2004	2005	2006
Compensation of employees	13,903	14,937	16,361
Operating surplus	12,863	13,969	17,204
Domestic factor incomes	26,766	28,906	33,565
Consumption of fixed capital	5,913	6,585	6,298
Gross domestic product (GDP) at factor cost	32,680	35,491	39,863
Indirect taxes	4,030	4,367	4,847
Less Subsidies	213	238	244
GDP in purchasers' values	36,496	39,621	44,467
Factor income received from abroad	1,483	955	1,185
Less Factor income paid abroad	944	1,670	1,674
Gross national income	37,035	38,906	43,978
Less Consumption of fixed capital	5,913	6,585	6,298
National income in market prices	31,122	32,321	37,680
Other current transfers from abroad	4,529	4,711	6,956
Less Other current transfers paid abroad	225	286	306
National disposable income	35,426	36,746	44,330

Expenditure on the Gross Domestic Product

	2004	2005	2006
Government final consumption expenditure	9,027	9,734	10,554
Private final consumption expenditure	21,031	20,973	22,585
Increase in stocks	175	537	519
Gross fixed capital formation	9,190	9,727	12,235
Total domestic expenditure	39,423	40,970	45,893
Exports of goods and services	16,757	18,867	24,222
Less Imports of goods and services	18,992	20,261	24,676
Statistical discrepancy	–693	44	–973
GDP in purchasers' values	36,496	39,621	44,467
GDP in constant 1995 prices	18,201	19,058	19,611

Gross Domestic Product by Economic Activity

	2004	2005	2006
Agriculture and forestry	1,873	2,399	2,530
Fishing	1,547	1,916	1,870
Mining and quarrying	3,489	3,391	3,694
Diamond mining	3,048	2,782	2,231
Manufacturing	4,001	4,055	5,596
Electricity and water	1,197	1,344	1,250
Construction	1,100	1,247	1,743
Wholesale and retail trade, repairs, etc.	3,985	4,235	5,146
Hotels and restaurants	653	670	724
Transport, storage and communications	2,671	2,948	3,237
Financial intermediation	1,213	1,465	1,575
Real estate and business services	3,542	3,737	4,034
Government services	7,124	7,752	8,269
Other community, social and personal services	282	320	354
Other services	647	673	721
Sub-total	33,324	36,153	40,744
Less Financial services indirectly measured	394	445	550
GDP at basic prices	32,930	35,708	40,194
Taxes, less subsidies, on products	3,567	3,913	4,273
GDP in purchasers' values	36,496	39,621	44,467

BALANCE OF PAYMENTS

(US $ million)

	2002	2003	2004
Exports of goods f.o.b.	1,071.6	1,262.0	1,827.5
Imports of goods f.o.b.	–1,282.5	–1,726.0	–2,110.3
Trade balance	–210.9	–464.0	–282.8
Exports of services	283.2	420.2	482.4
Imports of services	–223.8	–249.4	–385.1
Balance on goods and services	–151.5	–293.2	–185.4
Other income received	172.6	283.9	368.5
Other income paid	–133.9	–54.0	–217.6
Balance on goods, services and income	–112.8	–63.4	–34.6
Current transfers received	270.4	426.2	642.1
Current transfers paid	–29.9	–27.2	–34.9
Current balance	127.7	335.7	572.6
Capital account (net)	40.7	68.3	77.2
Direct investment abroad	4.7	10.8	21.6
Direct investment from abroad	51.2	33.3	88.2
Portfolio investment assets	–144.1	–217.4	–249.9
Portfolio investment liabilities	8.2	3.9	4.5
Other investment assets	–247.2	–452.8	–467.8
Other investment liabilities	–19.7	–41.5	–113.6
Net errors and omissions	–31.8	–69.3	–69.7
Overall balance	–210.3	–329.1	–136.9

Source: IMF, *International Financial Statistics*.

External Trade

PRINCIPAL COMMODITIES

(US $ million)

Imports c.i.f.	2001	2002	2003
Food and live animals	172.4	138.6	163.7
Mineral fuels and lubricants	160.4	158.8	147.0
Petroleum and petroleum products	158.5	149.4	142.6
Chemicals and related products	166.4	116.3	113.7
Basic manufactures	267.5	224.0	268.3
Non-metallic mineral manufactures	51.0	41.0	52.0
Metal products	86.2	75.9	68.5
Machinery and transport equipment	533.5	447.4	460.0
Machinery specialized for particular industries	89.9	60.6	57.7
General industrial machinery, equipment and parts	51.3	60.9	57.4
Telecommunications and sound equipment	38.2	27.0	44.0
Telecommunications equipment, parts and accessories	28.1	17.4	27.9
Electrical machinery, apparatus, etc.	71.1	62.0	69.8
Road vehicles	180.9	132.2	163.3
Passenger motor vehicles (excl. buses)	119.7	83.2	103.1
Other transport equipment	44.4	51.8	14.9
Miscellaneous manufactured articles	185.5	154.1	164.2
Clothing and accessories	46.0	37.1	35.5
Total (incl. others)	1,552.9	1,310.1	1,427.9

Exports f.o.b.	2001	2002	2003
Food and live animals	438.0	391.4	479.8
Fish, shellfish and preparations thereof	315.9	270.8	318.9
Fresh or frozen fish	293.8	253.6	305.2
Beverages and tobacco	67.2	77.7	139.7
Beverages	65.5	74.3	136.9
Alcoholic beverages	49.0	52.4	68.0
Beer made from malt	43.5	41.0	55.2
Crude materials (inedible) except fuels	132.5	146.7	84.2
Metal ores and scrap	103.6	116.8	49.3
Ores and concentrates of uranium and thorium	102.2	115.8	47.1
Basic manufactures	485.2	471.3	229.4
Non-metallic mineral manufactures	450.3	430.5	151.6
Pearl, precious and semi-precious stones	448.1	425.4	141.3
Diamonds	447.8	424.3	141.0
Machinery and transport equipment	54.6	74.5	112.3
Miscellaneous manufactured articles	176.8	66.4	197.2
Printed matter	154.8	31.0	147.8
Total (incl. others)	1,404.5	1,282.9	1,303.7

Source: UN, *International Trade Statistics Yearbook*.

PRINCIPAL TRADING PARTNERS
(US $ million)

Imports c.i.f.	2001	2002	2003
China, People's Repub.	16.9	11.7	18.2
Germany	30.6	41.1	33.4
South Africa	1,335.9	1,013.3	1,148.9
Spain	13.0	16.3	19.4
United Kingdom	18.2	34.3	17.5
USA	14.0	26.3	14.2
Total (incl. others)	1,552.9	1,310.1	1,427.9

Exports f.o.b.	2001	2002	2003
Angola	82.1	186.5	324.8
Belgium	7.7	7.5	7.1
Canada	0.5	4.1	12.9
Congo, Republic	5.0	9.1	33.8
France	25.2	82.4	23.4
Germany	12.2	14.7	14.5
Italy	24.5	23.3	23.0
Netherlands	19.4	17.3	13.9
South Africa	433.5	326.1	410.6
Spain	184.5	155.8	167.0
United Kingdom	495.5	315.1	135.7
USA	41.6	40.4	35.2
Total (incl. others)	1,404.5	1,282.9	1,303.7

Source: UN, *International Trade Statistics Yearbook*.

Transport

RAILWAYS

	2002/03	2003/04
Freight (million net ton-km)	1,244.6	1,247.4
Passengers carried	125,656	112,033

Source: TransNamib Holdings Ltd, *2004 Annual Report*.

ROAD TRAFFIC
(motor vehicles in use at 31 December)

	1994*	1995*	1996
Passenger cars	61,269	62,500	74,875
Buses and coaches	5,098	5,200	10,175
Lorries and vans	60,041	61,300	59,352
Motorcycles and mopeds	1,450	1,480	1,520

* Estimate(s).

Total vehicles in use (excl. motorcycles and mopeds): 146,999 in 2000; 152,794 in 2001; 166,998 in 2002.

2002: Passenger cars 82,580; Buses and coaches 4,922; Lorries and vans 79,496; Motorcycles and mopeds 3,416.

Source: International Road Federation, *World Road Statistics*.

SHIPPING

Merchant Fleet
(at 31 December)

	2004	2005	2006
Number of vessels	157	178	173
Displacement (gross registered tons)	92,299	106,350	102,901

Source: Lloyd's Register-Fairplay, *World Fleet Statistics*.

Sea-borne Freight Traffic
('000 freight tons†, year ending 30 August, unless otherwise indicated)

	1999/2000*	2000/01	2001/02
Port of Lüderitz:			
Goods loaded	93.6	143.3	171.2
Goods unloaded	39.5	105.1	101.7
Goods transhipped	14.1	10.0	4.6
Containers handled (total TEUs)	2,311	2,320	2,480
Port of Walvis Bay:			
Goods loaded	723.4	720.7	915.8
Goods unloaded	1,460.3	1,452.1	1,443.1
Goods transhipped	40.0	56.6	60.3
Containers handled (total TEUs)	24,859	25,768	31,569

* Year ending 30 September 2000.
† One freight ton = 40 cu ft (1.133 cu m) of cargo capacity.

Source: Namibian Ports Authority.

CIVIL AVIATION
(traffic on scheduled services)

	2001	2002	2003
Kilometres flown (million)	9	9	11
Passengers carried ('000)	215	222	266
Passenger-km (million)	754	760	930
Total ton-km (million)	151	98	139

Source: UN, *Statistical Yearbook*.

Tourism

FOREIGN TOURIST ARRIVALS*

Country of origin	2002	2003	2005†
Angola	278,816	222,752	281,365
Botswana	29,328	22,679	22,333
Germany	61,236	58,036	61,222
South Africa	243,894	222,009	230,949
United Kingdom	19,560	19,291	20,978
Zimbabwe	19,145	17,795	22,765
Total (incl. others)	757,201	695,221	777,890

* Excluding same-day visitors: 947,778 in 2002; 917,000 in 2003; 973,168 in 2005.

† Figures for 2004 were not available.

Tourism receipts (US $ million, excl. passenger transport): 218 in 2002; 333 in 2003; n.a. in 2004; n.a. in 2005.

Source: World Tourism Organization.

Communications Media

	2003	2004	2005
Telephones ('000 main lines in use)	127.4	127.9	127.9*
Mobile cellular telephones ('000 subscribers)	223.7	286.1	495
Personal computers ('000 in use)	191	220	n.a.
Internet users ('000)	65.0	75.0	n.a.

* Estimate.

Television receivers ('000 in use): 67 in 2000.

Source: International Telecommunication Union.

Radio receivers ('000 in use): 232 in 1997 (Source: UNESCO, *Statistical Yearbook*).

Daily newspapers (1997): 4; average circulation ('000 copies) 10 (Source: UNESCO, *Statistical Yearbook*).

Non-daily newspapers (1997): 5; average circulation ('000 copies) 9 (Source: UNESCO, *Statistical Yearbook*).

Education

(2002/03, unless otherwise indicated)

	Teachers	Students		
		Males	Females	Total
Pre-primary	1,314*	23,442†	25,740†	49,182†
Primary	14,442†	204,794	204,118	408,912
Secondary	5,989†	66,455	74,521	140,976
Tertiary	898	5,517	6,271	11,788

* Estimate for 1999/2000.

† Estimate.

Institutions (1998/99): Primary 1,362.

Source: UNESCO, Institute for Statistics.

Adult literacy rate (UNESCO estimates): 85.0% (males 83.5%; females 86.8%) in 2004 (Source: UN Development Programme, *Human Development Report*).

Directory

The Constitution

The Constitution of the Republic of Namibia took effect at independence on 21 March 1990. Its principal provisions are summarized below:

THE REPUBLIC

The Republic of Namibia is a sovereign, secular, democratic and unitary State and the Constitution is the supreme law.

FUNDAMENTAL HUMAN RIGHTS AND FREEDOMS

The fundamental rights and freedoms of the individual are guaranteed regardless of sex, race, colour, ethnic origin, religion, creed or social or economic status. All citizens shall have the right to form and join political parties. The practice of racial discrimination shall be prohibited.

THE PRESIDENT

Executive power shall be vested in the President and the Cabinet. The President shall be the Head of State and of the Government and the Commander-in-Chief of the Defence Force. The President shall be directly elected by universal and equal adult suffrage, and must receive more than 50% of the votes cast. The term of office shall be five years; one person may not hold the office of President for more than two terms.*

THE CABINET

The Cabinet shall consist of the President, the Prime Minister and such other ministers as the President may appoint from members of the National Assembly. The President may also appoint a Deputy Prime Minister. The functions of the members of the Cabinet shall include directing the activities of ministries and government departments, initiating bills for submission to the National Assembly, formulating, explaining and assessing for the National Assembly the budget of the State and its economic development plans, formulating, explaining and analysing for the National Assembly Namibia's foreign policy and foreign trade policy and advising the President on the state of national defence.

THE NATIONAL ASSEMBLY

Legislative power shall be vested in the National Assembly, which shall be composed of 72 members elected by general, direct and secret ballots and not more than six non-voting members appointed by the President by virtue of their special expertise, status, skill or experience. Every National Assembly shall continue for a maximum period of five years, but it may be dissolved by the President before the expiry of its term.

THE NATIONAL COUNCIL

The National Council shall consist of two members from each region (elected by regional councils from among their members) and shall have a life of six years. The functions of the National Council shall include considering all bills passed by the National Assembly, investigating any subordinate legislation referred to it by the National Assembly for advice, and recommending legislation to the National Assembly on matters of regional concern.

OTHER PROVISIONS

Other provisions relate to the administration of justice (see under Judicial System), regional and local government, the public service commission, the security commission, the police, defence forces and prison service, finance, and the central bank and national planning commission. The repeal of, or amendments to, the Constitution require the approval of two-thirds of the members of the National Assembly and two-thirds of the members of the National Council; if the proposed repeal or amendment secures a majority of two-thirds of the members of the National Assembly, but not a majority of two-thirds of the members of the National Council, the President may make the proposals the subject of a national referendum, in which a two-thirds' majority is needed for approval of the legislation.

* In late 1998 the National Assembly and National Council approved legislation whereby the Constitution was to be exceptionally amended to allow the incumbent President to seek a third term of office.

The Government

HEAD OF STATE

President and Commander-in-Chief of the Defence Force: HIFIKEPUNYE POHAMBA (elected by direct suffrage 15–16 November 2004; took office 21 March 2005).

THE CABINET
(August 2007)

President: HIFIKEPUNYE POHAMBA.

Prime Minister: NAHAS ANGULA.

Deputy Prime Minister: Dr LIBERTINA AMATHILA.

Minister of Presidential Affairs: ALBERT KAWANA.

Minister of Home Affairs and Immigration: ROSALIA NGHIDINWA.

Minister of Safety and Security: PETER TSHIRUMBU-TSHEEHAMA.

Minister of Defence: Maj.-Gen. (retd) CHARLES NAMOLOH.

Minister of Foreign Affairs: MARCO HAUSIKU.

Minister of Information and Broadcasting: NETUMBO NANDI-NDAITWAH.

Minister of Education: NANGOLO MBUMBA.

Minister of Mines and Energy: ERRKI NGHIMTINA.

Minister of Justice and Attorney-General: PENDUKENI IVULA-ITHANA.

Minister of Trade and Industry: IMMANUEL NGATJIZEKO.

Minister of Agriculture, Water and Forestry: Dr NICKEY IYAMBO.

Minister of Finance: SAARAH KUUGONGELWA-AMADHILA.

Minister of Health and Social Services: RICHARD KAMWI.

Minister of Labour and Social Welfare: ALPHEUS NARUSEB.

Minister of Regional and Local Government and Housing: JOHN PANDENI.

Minister of Environment and Tourism: WILLEM KONJORE.

Minister of Works, Transport and Communications: JOEL NATANGWE KAAPANDA.

Minister of Lands, Resettlement and Rehabilitation: JERRY EKANDJO.

Minister of Fisheries and Marine Resources: ABRAHAM IYAMBO.

Minister of Gender Equality and Child Welfare: MARLENE MUNGUNDA.

Minister of Youth, National Service, Sport and Culture: JOHN MUTORWA.

Minister of War Veterans: Dr NGARIKUTUKE TJIRIANGE.

Also attending Cabinet

Dir-Gen. of the Namibia Central Intelligence Agency: Lt-Gen. LUCAS HANGULA.

Dir-Gen. of the National Planning Commission: HELMUT ANGULA.

MINISTRIES

Office of the President: State House, Robert Mugabe Ave, PMB 13339, Windhoek; tel. (61) 2707111; fax (61) 221780; e-mail angolo@op.gov.na; internet www.op.gov.na.

Office of the Prime Minister: Robert Mugabe Ave, PMB 13338, Windhoek; tel. (61) 2879111; fax (61) 230648; internet www.opm.gov.na.

Ministry of Agriculture, Water and Forestry: cnr Robert Mugabe Ave and Peter Muller St, PMB 13184, Windhoek; tel. (61) 2087111; fax (61) 229961.

Ministry of Defence: PMB 13307, Windhoek; tel. (61) 2049111; fax (61) 232518.

Ministry of Education: Troskie House, Uhland St, PMB 13186, Windhoek; tel. (61) 2933111; fax (61) 224277.

Ministry of Environment and Tourism: Swabou Bldg, Post St Mall, PMB 13346, Windhoek; tel. (61) 2842111; fax (61) 221930; internet www.tourism.com.na.

Ministry of Finance: Fiscus Bldg, John Meinert St, PMB 13295, Windhoek; tel. (61) 2099111; fax (61) 230179.

Ministry of Fisheries and Marine Resources: Uhland and Goethe Sts, Private Bag X13355, Windhoek; tel. (61) 2059111; fax (61) 233286; e-mail mfmr@mfmr.gov.na; internet www.mfmr.gov.na.

Ministry of Foreign Affairs: Govt Bldgs, Robert Mugabe Ave, PMB 13347, Windhoek; tel. (61) 2829111; fax (61) 223937; internet www.mfa.gov.na.

Ministry of Gender Equality and Child Welfare: Windhoek.

Ministry of Health and Social Services: Old State Hospital, Harvey St, PMB 13198, Windhoek; tel. (61) 2039111; fax (61) 227607.

Ministry of Home Affairs and Immigration: Cohen Bldg, Kasino St, PMB 13200, Windhoek; tel. (61) 2922111; fax (61) 2922185.

Ministry of Information and Broadcasting: Windhoek.

Ministry of Justice: Justitia Bldg, Independence Ave, PMB 13248, Windhoek; tel. (61) 2805111; fax (61) 221615; includes the office of the Attorney-General.

Ministry of Labour and Social Welfare: 32 Mercedes St, Khomasdal, PMB 19005, Windhoek; tel. (61) 2066111; fax (61) 212323.

Ministry of Lands, Resettlement and Rehabilitation: Brendan Simbwaye Bldg, Goethe St, PMB 13343, Windhoek; tel. (61) 2852111; fax (61) 254240.

Ministry of Mines and Energy: 1st Aviation Rd, PMB 13297, Windhoek; tel. (61) 2848111; fax (61) 238643; e-mail info@mme.gov.na; internet www.mme.gov.na.

Ministry of Presidential Affairs: Windhoek.

Ministry of Regional and Local Government and Housing: PMB 13289, Windhoek; tel. (61) 2975111; fax (61) 226049.

Ministry of Safety and Security: Brendan Simbwaye Bldg, Goethe St, PMB 13323; tel. (61) 2846111; fax (61) 233879.

Ministry of Trade and Industry: Uhland St, cnr Goethe St, Private Bag 13340, Windhoek; tel. (61) 2837111; fax (61) 220227; internet www.mti.gov.na.

Ministry of War Veterans: Windhoek.

Ministry of Works, Transport and Communications: PMB 13341, Windhoek; tel. (61) 2088111; fax (61) 228560.

Ministry of Youth, National Service, Sport and Culture: Windhoek.

President and Legislature

PRESIDENT

Presidential Election, 15–16 November 2004

Candidate	Votes	% of votes
Hifikepunye Pohamba (SWAPO)	625,605	76.44
Ben Ulenga (CoD)	59,547	7.28
Katuutire Kaura (DTA)	41,905	5.12
Kuaima Riruako (NUDO)	34,616	4.23
Justus Garoeb (UDF)	31,354	3.83
Henk Mudge (RP)	15,955	1.95
Kosie Pretorius (MAG)	9,738	1.15
Total	818,360	100.00

NATIONAL ASSEMBLY*

Speaker: THEO-BEN GURIRAB.

General Election, 15–16 November 2004

Party	Votes	% of votes	Seats
South West Africa People's Organisation of Namibia (SWAPO)	620,787	76.11	55
Congress of Democrats (CoD)	59,465	7.29	5
Democratic Turnhalle Alliance of Namibia (DTA)	41,714	5.11	4
National Unity Democratic Organisation (NUDO)	33,874	4.15	3
United Democratic Front (UDF)	29,336	3.60	3
Republican Party	15,965	1.96	1
Monitor Action Group (MAG)	6,920	0.85	1
Namibia Movement for Democratic Change (NMDC)	4,138	0.51	—
South West African National Union (SWANU)	3,438	0.42	—
Total	815,637	100.00	72

* In addition to the 72 directly elected members, the President of the Republic is empowered to nominate as many as six non-voting members.

NATIONAL COUNCIL

Chairman: ASSER KUVERI KAPERE.

The second chamber of parliament is the advisory National Council, comprising two representatives from each of the country's 13 Regional Councils, elected for a period of six years.

Election Commission

Electoral Commission of Namibia (ECN): Daniel Munamava St, POB 13352 Windhoek; tel. (61) 220337; fax (61) 224174; internet www.ecn.gov.na; f. 1992; independent; Chair. VICTOR L. TONCHI; Dir of Elections and CEO PHILEMON H. KANIME.

Political Organizations

Congress of Democrats (CoD): 8 Storch St, POB 40905, Windhoek; tel. (61) 256954; fax (61) 256980; internet www.cod.org.na; f. 1999 after split from SWAPO; Leader BEN ULENGA; Nat. Chair. TSUDAO GURIRAB; Sec.-Gen. KALA GERTZE.

Democratic Turnhalle Alliance of Namibia (DTA): POB 173, Windhoek 9000; tel. 238530; fax 226494; e-mail m.venaani@parliament.gov.na; f. 1977 as a coalition of 11 ethnically based political groupings; reorg. in 1991 to allow dual membership of coalition groupings and the main party; Pres. KATUUTIRE KAURA; Chair. JOHAN DE WAAL; Sec.-Gen. ALOIS GENDE.

Monitor Action Group (MAG): POB 80808, Olympia, Windhoek; tel. (61) 252008; fax (61) 229242; e-mail monitor@cyberhost.com.na; f. 1991 by mems of the National Party of South West Africa alliance; Leader and Chair. J. W. F. (KOSIE) PRETORIUS.

Namibia Democratic Movement for Change (NDMC): POB 60043, Katutura; tel. and fax (61) 297795; f. 2004; Pres. FRANS GOAGOSEB; Sec.-Gen. CLAUDIA NAMISES.

National Unity Democratic Organisation (NUDO): POB 60043, Katutura; tel. and fax 297795; f. 1964 by the Herero Chiefs' Council; joined the DTA in 1977; broke away from the DTA in 2003; Pres. Chief KUAIMA RIRUAKO; Sec.-Gen. JOSEPH KAUANDENGE.

Republican Party: 6 Hügel St, POB 20020, Windhoek; tel. (61) 225632; fax (61) 225636; f. 1977 after breaking away from the National Party; joined the DTA later in 1977; dissolved in 1991; reactivated in 2003 after breaking away from the DTA; Pres. HENK MUDGE; Sec.-Gen. CAROLA ENGELBRECHT.

SWAPO Party of Namibia (SWAPO): POB 1071, Windhoek; tel. (61) 238364; fax (61) 232368; f. 1957 as the Ovamboland People's Congress; renamed South West Africa People's Organisation in 1960; adopted present name in 1997; Pres. Dr SAMUEL DANIEL NUJOMA; Vice-Pres. HIFIKEPUNYE POHAMBA; Sec.-Gen. NGARIKUTUKE TJIRIANGE.

South West African National Union (SWANU): Windhoek; f. 1959 by mems of the Herero Chiefs' Council; formed alliance with the Workers' Revolutionary Party in 1999; Pres. RIHUPISA KANDANDO.

United Democratic Front (UDF): POB 20037, Windhoek; tel. (61) 230683; fax (61) 237175; f. 1989 as a centrist coalition of eight parties; reorg. as a single party in 1999; Nat. Chair. ERIC BIWA; Pres. JUSTUS GAROEB.

Workers' Revolutionary Party: Windhoek; f. 1989; Trotskyist; Leaders WERNER MAMUGWE, HEWAT BEUKES.

The **Caprivi Liberation Army (CLA)**, f. 1998 as the Caprivi Liberation Movement, seeks secession of the Caprivi Strip; conducts military operations from bases in Zambia and Angola; political wing operates from Denmark as the **Caprivi National Union**, led by MISHAKE MUYONGO and BONIFACE MAMILI.

Diplomatic Representation

EMBASSIES AND HIGH COMMISSIONS IN NAMIBIA

Algeria: 111A Gloudina St, Ludwigsdorf, POB 3079, Windhoek; tel. (61) 221507; fax (61) 236376; Chargé d'affaires a.i. YOUCEF DELILECHE.

Angola: Angola House, 3 Dr Agostinho Neto St, Ausspannplatz, PMB 12020, Windhoek; tel. (61) 227535; fax (61) 221498; Ambassador MANUEL A. D. RODRIGUEZ.

Botswana: 101 Nelson Mandela Ave, POB 20359, Windhoek; tel. (61) 221942; fax (61) 221948; High Commissioner NORMAN MOLEBOGE.

Brazil: 52 Bismarck St, POB 24166, Windhoek; tel. (61) 237368; fax (61) 233389; e-mail brasemb@mweb.com.na; Ambassador CHRISTIANO WINDHOEK.

China, People's Republic: 13 Wecka St, POB 22777, Windhoek; tel. (61) 222089; fax (61) 225544; e-mail chinaemb@iafrica.com.na; internet na.chineseembassy.org; Ambassador LIANG YINZHU.

Congo, Republic: 9 Korner St, POB 22970, Windhoek; tel. (61) 257517; fax (61) 240796; Ambassador PATRICE NDOUNGA.

Cuba: 31 Omuramba Rd, Eros, POB 23866, Windhoek; tel. (61) 227072; fax (61) 231584; e-mail embacuba@iafrica.com.na; Ambassador ANA VILMA VALLEJERA RODRÍGUEZ.

Egypt: 10 Berg St, POB 11853, Windhoek; tel. (61) 221501; fax (61) 228856; Ambassador MOHAMED HADI MOSTAFA EL-TONSI.

Finland: 2 Crohn St (cnr Bahnhof St), POB 3649, Windhoek; tel. (61) 221355; fax (61) 221349; e-mail sanomat.win@formin.fi; internet www.finland.org.na; Chargé d'affaires a.i. SEIJA KINNI-HUTTUNEN.

France: 1 Goethe St, POB 20484, Windhoek; tel. (61) 2276700; fax (61) 231436; e-mail frambwdk@iafrica.com.na; internet www.ambafrance-na.org; Ambassador PHILIPPE BOSSIÈRE.

Germany: Sanlam Centre, 6th Floor, 154 Independence Ave, POB 231, Windhoek; tel. (61) 273100; fax (61) 222981; e-mail germany@iway.na; internet www.windhuk.diplo.de; Ambassador ARNE FREIHERR VON KITTLITZ UND OTTENDORF.

Ghana: 5 Nelson Mandela Ave, POB 24165, Windhoek; tel. (61) 221341; fax (61) 221343; High Commissioner MAUREEN A. AMEMATEKPOR.

India: 97 Nelson Mandela Ave, POB 1209, Windhoek; tel. (61) 226037; fax (61) 237320; e-mail hicomind@mweb.com.na; internet www.highcommissionofindia.web.na; High Commissioner TSEWANG TOPDEN.

Indonesia: 103 Nelson Mandela Ave, POB 20691, Windhoek; tel. (61) 2851000; fax (61) 2851231; e-mail kbri@iafrica.com.na; internet www.indonesiawindhoek.org; Ambassador (vacant).

Kenya: Kenya House, 5th Floor, 134 Robert Mugabe Ave, POB 2889, Windhoek; tel. (61) 226836; fax (61) 221409; e-mail rboit@mfa.go.ke; High Commissioner ROSE BOIT.

Libya: 69 Burg St, Luxury Hill, POB 124, Windhoek; tel. (61) 234454; fax (61) 234471; Ambassador SALAM MOHAMMED KRAYEM; (designate).

Malawi: 56 Bismarck St, POB 13254, Windhoek 9000; tel. (61) 221391; fax (61) 227056; e-mail mhc@mweb.co.na; High Commissioner F. CHIKUTA.

Malaysia: 12 Babs Street, Ludwigsdorf, POB 312, Windhoek; tel. (61) 259344; fax (61) 259343; e-mail malwdhoek@kln.gov.my; High Commissioner HAYATI BT ISMAIL.

Mexico: Southern Life Tower, 3rd Floor, 39 Post St Mall, POB 13220, Windhoek; tel. (61) 229082; fax (61) 229180; Ambassador MAURICIO DE MARÍA Y CAMPOS.

Nigeria: 4 Omuramba Rd, Eros Park, POB 23547, Windhoek; tel. (61) 232103; fax (61) 221639; High Commissioner OKUN AYODEJI.

Russia: 4 Christian St, POB 3826, Windhoek; tel. (61) 228671; fax (61) 229061; Ambassador NIKOLAI M. GRIBKOV.

South Africa: RSA House, cnr Jan Jonker and Nelson Mandela Aves, POB 23100, Windhoek; tel. (61) 229765; fax (61) 224140; Chargé d'affairs a.i. P. J. COETZEE.

Spain: 58 Bismarck St, POB 21811, Windhoek-West; tel. (61) 223066; fax (61) 223046; e-mail emb.windhoek@mae.es; Ambassador MARÍA VICTORIA SCOLA PLIEGO.

Sweden: Sanlam Centre, 9th Floor, POB 23087, Windhoek; tel. (61) 2859111; fax (61) 2859222; e-mail ambassaden.windhoek@sida.se; Chargé d'affaires a.i. LENA JOHANSSON BLOMSTRAND.

United Kingdom: 116 Robert Mugabe Ave, POB 22202, Windhoek; tel. (61) 274800; fax (61) 228895; e-mail bhc@mweb.com.na; High Commissioner ALASDAIR MACDERMOTT.

USA: 14 Lossen St, Ausspannplatz, PMB 12029, Windhoek 9000; tel. (61) 221601; fax (61) 229792; internet windhoek.usembassy.gov; Ambassador JOYCE A. BARR.

Venezuela: Southern Life Tower, 3rd Floor, 39 Post St Mall, PMB 13353, Windhoek; tel. (61) 227905; fax (61) 227804; Chargé d'affaires a.i. JORGE JIMÉNEZ.

Zambia: 22 Sam Nujoma Dr., cnr Mandume Ndemufayo Rd, POB 22882, Windhoek; tel. (61) 237610; fax (61) 228162; e-mail zahico@iway.na; internet www.zahico.iway.na; High Commissioner GRIFFIN NYIRONGO.

Zimbabwe: cnr Independence Ave and Grimm St, POB 23056, Windhoek; tel. (61) 228134; fax (61) 226859; Ambassador CHIPO ZINDOGA.

Judicial System

Judicial power is exercised by the Supreme Court, the High Court and a number of Magistrate and Lower Courts. The Constitution provides for the appointment of an Ombudsman.

Chief Justice: PETER SHIVUTE.

Religion

It is estimated that about 90% of the population are Christians.

CHRISTIANITY

Council of Churches in Namibia: 8 Mont Blanc St, POB 41, Windhoek; tel. (61) 217621; fax (61) 62786; e-mail ccn.windhoek@iafrica.com.na; f. 1978; eight mem. churches; Pres. Bishop HENDRIK FREDERIK; Gen. Sec. NANGULA KATHINDI.

The Anglican Communion

Namibia comprises a single diocese in the Church of the Province of Southern Africa. The Metropolitan of the Province is the Archbishop of Cape Town, South Africa. In 2006 there were an estimated 110,000 Anglicans in the country.

Bishop of Namibia: Rt Rev. NATHANIEL NDAXUMA NAKWATUMBAH, POB 57, Windhoek; tel. (61) 238920; fax (61) 225903; e-mail bishop@anglicanchurchnamibia.com.

Dutch Reformed Church

Dutch Reformed Church in Namibia (Nederduitse Gereformeerde Kerk): 34 Feldstreet, POB 389, Windhoek; tel. (61) 374350; fax (61) 227287; e-mail clem@ngkn.com.na; internet www.ngkn.com.na; f. 1898; Sec. Rev. CLEM MARAIS; 22,500 mems in 44 congregations (2006).

Evangelical Lutheran

Evangelical Lutheran Church in Namibia (ELCIN): PMB 2018, Ondangwa; tel. (65) 240241; fax (65) 240472; e-mail head.office@elcin.org.na; f. 1870; became autonomous in 1954; Presiding Bishop Dr THOMAS SHIVUTE; Gen. Sec. Rev. ELIKAIM N. K. SHAANIKA; 663,338 mems (2005).

Evangelical Lutheran Church in the Republic of Namibia (ELCRN) (Rhenish Mission Church): POB 5069, Windhoek; tel. (61) 224531; fax (61) 226775; f. 1957; became autonomous in 1972; Pres. Bishop Dr ZEPHANIA KAMEETA; 250,000 mems in 55 congregations.

German Evangelical-Lutheran Church in Namibia (ELCIN—GELC): POB 233, Windhoek; tel. (61) 224294; fax (61) 221470; e-mail delk@namibnet.com; Pres. Bishop REINHARD KEDING; 5,000 mems.

Methodist

African Methodist Episcopal Church: POB 798, Keetmanshoop; tel. (63) 222347; fax (63) 223026; e-mail erikke5@hotmail.com; bishop resident in Cape Town, South Africa; Rep. Rev. Dr ANDREAS BIWA; c. 8,000 mems in 33 churches.

Methodist Church of Southern Africa: POB 143, Windhoek; tel. (61) 228921; fax (61) 229202; e-mail central@iway.na; Rep. Rev. EDGAR LUKEN.

The Roman Catholic Church

Namibia comprises one archdiocese, one diocese and one apostolic vicariate. At 31 December 2004 there were 391,530 adherents of the Roman Catholic Church, representing some 17.2% of the total population.

Bishops' Conference

Namibian Catholic Bishops' Conference, POB 11525, Windhoek 9000; tel. (61) 224798; fax (61) 228126.

f. 1996; Pres. (vacant).

Archbishop of Windhoek: LIBORIUS NDUMBUKUTI NASHENDA, POB 272, Windhoek 9000; tel. (61) 227595; fax (61) 229836; e-mail rcarch@iafrica.com.na; internet www.rcchurch.na.

Other Christian Churches

Among other denominations active in Namibia are the Evangelical Reformed Church in Africa, the Presbyterian Church of Southern Africa, Seventh Day Adventists and the United Congregational Church of Southern Africa. At mid-2000 there were an estimated 820,000 Protestants and 192,000 adherents professing other forms of Christianity.

JUDAISM

Windhoek Hebrew Congregation: POB 563, Windhoek; tel. (61) 221990; fax (61) 226444.

BAHÁ'Í FAITH

National Spiritual Assembly: POB 20372, Windhoek; tel. (61) 250890; fax (61) 272745; e-mail zayanih@potentia.com.na; Sec. ZAYANIH DENNIS; mems resident in 215 localities.

The Press

The African Magazine: NCCI, 2 Jenner St, POB 1770, Windhoek; tel. and fax (61) 255018; e-mail info@theafricanmagazin.org; internet www.theafricanmagazin.org.

AgriForum: 114 Robert Mugabe Ave, POB 86641, Windhoek; tel. (61) 256023; fax (61) 256035; quarterly; Afrikaans and English; publ. by the Namibia Agricultural Union; Editor RICHTER ERASMUS; circ. 5,000.

Allgemeine Zeitung: Omurambaweg 11, POB 86695, Eros, Windhoek; tel. (61) 225822; fax (61) 220225; e-mail azinfo@az.com.na; internet www.az.com.na; f. 1916; publ. by Newsprint Namibia; daily; German; Editor-in-Chief STEFAN FISCHER; circ. 5,300 (Mon.–Thurs.), 6,500 (Fri.).

The Big Issue Namibia: 37 Bahnhof St, POB 97140 Maerua Park, Windhoek; tel. (61) 242216; fax (61) 242232; e-mail jo@bigissue.com.na; internet www.bigissuenamibia.org; f. 2002; monthly; Man. Dir JO ROGGE; Editor CATHERINE SASMAN.

Insight Namibia: 34 Sam Nujoma Dr., POB 86058, Windhoek; tel. (61) 301437; fax (61) 240385; e-mail editor@insight.com.na; internet www.insight.com.na; f. 2004; monthly; business and current affairs; Editor ROBIN SHERBOURNE.

Namib Times: Sam Nujoma Ave, POB 706, Walvis Bay; tel. (64) 205854; fax (64) 204813; e-mail ntimes@iway.na; 2 a week; Afrikaans, English, German and Portuguese; Editor FLORIS STEENKAMP; circ. 4,300.

Namibia Brief: Independence Ave, POB 2123, Windhoek; tel. and fax (61) 251044; quarterly; English; Editor CATHY BLATT; circ. 7,500.

Namibia Economist: 7 Schuster St, POB 49, Windhoek 9000; tel. (61) 221925; fax (61) 220615; e-mail daniel@economist.com.na; internet www.economist.com.na; f. 1986; weekly; English; business, finance and economics; Editor DANIEL STEINMANN; circ. 7,000.

Namibia Magazin: POB 6870, Windhoek; tel. and fax (61) 224929; e-mail evonwiet@iafrica.com.na; publ. by Klaus Hess Verlag; German; politics, tourism and culture; Rep. ERIKA VON WIETERSHEIM.

Namibia Review: Directorate Print Media and Regional Offices, Regular Publications, Turnhalle Bldg, Bahnhof St, PMB 13344, Windhoek; tel. (61) 222246; fax (61) 224937; e-mail bupe@webmail.co.za; f. 1992; publ. by the Ministry of Information and Broadcasting; monthly; information on govt policy and developmental issues; Editor ELIZABETH KALAMBO-M'ULE; circ. 5,000.

Namibia Sport: POB 1246, Windhoek; tel. (61) 224132; fax (61) 224613; e-mail editor@namibiasport.com.na; internet www.namibiasport.com.na; f. 2002; monthly; Editor HELGE SCHUTZ; circ. 2,500.

Namibia Today: 21 Johan Albrecht St, POB 24669, Windhoek; tel. (61) 276730; fax (61) 276381; 2 a week; Afrikaans, English, Oshiherero and Oshiwambo; publ. by SWAPO; Editor KAOMO-VIJINDA TJOMBE; circ. 5,000.

The Namibian: 42 John Meinert St, POB 20783, Windhoek; tel. (61) 279600; fax (61) 279602; e-mail editor@namibian.com.na; internet www.namibian.com.na; daily; English; Editor GWEN LISTER; circ. 23,000 (Mon.–Thurs.), 32,000 (Fri.).

The Namibian Worker: POB 50034, Bachbrecht, Windhoek; tel. (61) 215037; fax (61) 215589; e-mail nunw@mweb.com.na; newsletter publ. by National Union of Namibian Workers; revived in 2003; Afrikaans, English and Oshiwambo; Editor-in-Chief C. RANGA HAIKALI; circ. 1,000.

NCCI Namibia Business Journal: NCCI Head Office, 2 Jenner St, POB 9355, Windhoek; tel. (61) 228809; fax (61) 228009; publ.by the Namibia Chamber of Commerce and Industry; 6 a year; English; CEO TARAH SHAANIKA; Editor CHARITY MWIYA; circ. 4,000.

New Era: Daniel Tjongarero House, cnr Kerby and W. Kulz Sts, Private Mail Bag 13364, Windhoek; tel. (61) 273300; fax (61) 220583; internet www.newera.com.na; e-mail editor@newera.com.na; f. 1991; daily; publ. by the Ministry of Information and Broadcasting; English; Chair. VILBARD USIKU; CEO SYLVESTER BLACK; Editor RAJAH MUNAMAVA; circ. 10,000.

Plus Weekly: POB 21506, Windhoek; tel. (61) 233635; fax (61) 230478; e-mail info@namibiaplus.com; internet www.namibiaplus.com; publ. by Federsen Publications; Afrikaans, English and German.

Republikein: 11 Omuramba Rd, POB 3436, Eros, Windhoek; tel. (61) 2972000; fax (61) 223721; e-mail republkn@republikein.com.na; internet www.republikein.com.na; f. 1977; daily; Afrikaans and English; publ. by Newsprint Namibia; Group Gen. Man. CHRIS JACOBIE; circ. 17,500 (Mon.–Wed.), 21,000 (Thur.–Fri.).

Sister Namibia: POB 40092, Ausspanplatz, Windhoek; tel. (61) 230618; fax (61) 236371; e-mail sister@iafrica.com.na; 6 a year; publ. by Sister Namibia human rights org.; women's issues; Editor LIZ FRANK.

The Southern Times: Maerua Mall, POB 31413, Windhoek; tel. (61) 301094; fax (61) 301095; e-mail tst@newera.com.na; internet www.southerntimesafrica.com; f. 2004; weekly (Sun.); owned by New Era and Zimpapers, Zimbabwe; printed in Zimbabwe; regional; Chair. V. T. USIKU; Editor MOSES E. D. MAGADZA.

Space Magazine: Sanlam Centre, 3rd Floor, POB 3717, Windhoek; tel. (61) 225155; e-mail space@mweb.com.na; monthly; English; family life; Publr ESTER SMITH; Editor YANNA SMITH.

Windhoek Observer: 6 Schuster St, POB 2255, Windhoek; tel. (61) 221737; fax (61) 226098; e-mail whkob@africaonline.com.na; f. 1978; weekly; English; Editor HANNES SMITH; circ. 14,000.

NEWS AGENCIES

Namibia Press Agency (Nampa): cnr Keller and Eugene Marais Sts, POB 61354, Windhoek 9000; tel. (61) 374000; fax (61) 221713; e-mail admin@nampa.org; internet www.nampa.org; f. 1990; Chair. MAUREEN HINDA; CEO NGHIDINUA HAMUNIME; Editor TOMMY KATAMILA.

Foreign Bureaux

Agence France Presse (AFP): POB 20893,Windhoek; tel. 238568; e-mail weidlich@mweb.com.na; Correspondent BRIGITTE WEIDLICH.

ITAR—TASS (Information Telegraphic Agency of Russia—Telegraphic Agency of the Sovereign Countries): POB 24821, Windhoek; tel. and fax (61) 232909; Correspondent PAVE MYLTSEV.

Inter Press Service (IPS) (Italy): POB 20783, Windhoek; tel. (61) 226645; Correspondent MARK VERBAAN.

South African Press Association (SAPA): POB 2032, Windhoek; tel. (61) 231565; fax (61) 220783; Representative CARMEN HONEY.

Xinhua (New China) News Agency (People's Republic of China): POB 22130, Windhoek; tel. and fax (61) 226484; Bureau Chief TENG WENYI.

Reuters (UK) is also represented in Namibia.

PRESS ASSOCIATION

Press Club Windhoek: POB 2032, Windhoek; tel. (61) 231565; fax (61) 220783; Chair. CARMEN HONEY.

Publishers

ELOC Printing Press: PMB 2013, Oniipa, Ondangwa; tel. and fax (6756) 40211; f. 1901; Rev. Dr KLEOPAS DUMENI.

Gamsberg Macmillan Publishers (Pty) Ltd: 19 Faraday St, POB 22830, Windhoek; tel. (61) 232165; fax (61) 233538; e-mail gmp@iafrica.com.na; internet www.macmillan-africa.com; imprints incl. New Namibia Books and Out of Africa; Man. Dir HERMAN VAN WYK.

Longman Namibia: POB 9251, Eros, Windhoek; tel. (61) 231124; fax (61) 224019; Publr LINDA BREDENKAMP.

National Archives of Namibia: 1–9 Eugène Marais St, PMB 13250, Windhoek; tel. (61) 2935213; fax (61) 2935217; e-mail natarch@mec.gov.na; f. 1939; Chief Archivist WERNER HILLEBRECHT.

PUBLISHERS' ASSOCIATION

Association of Namibian Publishers: POB 21601, Windhoek; tel. (61) 235796; fax (61) 235279; f. 1991; Sec. PETER REINER.

Broadcasting and Communications

TELECOMMUNICATIONS

Telecom Namibia Ltd (Telecom): POB 297, Windhoek; tel. (61) 2019211; fax (61) 248723; internet www.telecom.na; f. 1992; state-owned; Chair. T. HAIMBILI; Man. Dir FRANS NDOROMA.

Mobile Telecommunications Ltd (MTC): cnr Malcolm Spence and Reginald Walker Sts, Olympia, Windhoek; POB 23051, Windhoek; tel. (61) 249570; fax (61) 249571; e-mail aaochamub@mtc.com.na; f. 1994; 1995 as jt venture between Namibia Post and Telecommunications Holdings (NPTH), Telia and Swedfund; 34% owned by Portugal Telecom, 64% by NPTH; Chair. STEVE MOTINGA; Man. Dir JOSE A. FERREIRA.

BROADCASTING

Radio

In 2004 there were a total of 19 radio stations broadcasting from Windhoek including:

Namibian Broadcasting Corpn (NBC): POB 321, Windhoek; tel. (61) 2913133; fax (61) 215767; e-mail tnandjaa@nbc.com.na; internet www.nbc.com.na; f. 1990; runs 10 radio stations, broadcasting daily to 90% of the population in English (24 hours), Afrikaans, German and eight indigenous languages (10 hours); Chair. PONHELE YA FRANCE; Dir-Gen. VEZERA BOB KANDETU.

Channel 7/Kanaal 7: POB 20500, Windhoek; tel. (61) 235815; fax (61) 240190; e-mail channel7@k7.com.na; internet www.k7.com.na; Christian community radio station; English and Afrikaans; Man. NEAL VAN DEN BERGH.

Katutura Community Radio: POB 22355, Windhoek; tel. (61) 263768; fax (61) 262786; f. 1995 by non-governmental orgs; Dir FREDERICK GOWASEB.

Kudu FM: 158 Jan Jonker St, POB 5369, Windhoek; tel. (61) 247262; fax (61) 247259; e-mail radiokudu@radiokudu.com.na; internet www.radiokudu.com.na; f. 1998; commercial station affiliated to Omulunga Radio; English, Afrikaans and German.

Omulunga Radio: POB 40789, Windhoek; tel. (61) 239706; fax (61) 247259; e-mail omulunga@omulunga.com.na; internet www.omulunga.com.na; f. 2002; Ovambo interest station affiliated to Kudu FM; Oshiwambo and English.

Radio Antenna Namibia (Pty) Ltd (Namibia FM 99): 6 Teinert St, POB 11849, Windhoek; tel. (61) 223634; fax (61) 230964; e-mail radio99@namfm99.com; f. 1994; Man. Dir GERT JACOBIE.

Radio Energy (Radio 100): 17 Bismarck St, Windhoek West; POB 676, Windhoek; tel. (61) 256380; fax (61) 256379; internet www.energy100fm.com; commercial radio station; Man. Dir MARIO AITA.

Other radio stations included: Kosmos Radio, Radio France International (via relay), Radio 99, and Radio Wave. There were six community radio stations including: Radio Ecclesia (Catholic), Live FM (in Rehoboth), Ohangwenga Community Radio, and UNAM Radio (University of Namibia). A further four community stations were planned in 2005 at Oshakti, Gobabis, Keetmanshoop and Swakopmund.

Television

Namibian Broadcasting Corpn (NBC): POB 321, Windhoek; tel. (61) 2913111; fax (61) 216209; internet www.nbc.com.na; f. 1990; broadcasts television programmes in English to 45% of the population, 18 hours daily; Chair. UAZUVA KAUMBI; Dir-Gen. GERRY MUNYAMA.

Multi-Choice Namibia: POB 1752, Windhoek; tel. (61) 222222; fax (61) 227605; commercial television channels; Gen. Man. HARRY AUCAMP.

Finance

(cap. = capital; res = reserves; dep. = deposits; m. = million; brs = branches; amounts in Namibian dollars)

BANKING

Central Bank

Bank of Namibia: 71 Robert Mugabe Ave, POB 2882, Windhoek; tel. (61) 2835111; fax (61) 2835228; internet www.bon.com.na; f. 1990; cap. 40.0m., res 1,048.7m., dep. 1,270.5m. (Dec. 2002); Gov. TOM K. ALWEENDO; Dep. Gov. P. HARTMAN.

Commercial Banks

Bank Windhoek Ltd: Bank Windhoek Bldg, 262 Independence Ave, POB 15, Windhoek; tel. (61) 2991122; fax (61) 2991620; e-mail info@bankwindhoek.com.na; internet www.bankwindhoek.com.na; f. 1982; cap. 4.7m., res 283.2m., dep. 2,939.0m. (March 2002); Chair. J. C. 'KOOS' BRANDT; Man. Dir J. J. SWANEPOEL; 22 brs.

First National Bank of Namibia Ltd: 209–211 Independence Ave, POB 195, Windhoek; tel. (61) 2992016; fax (61) 2220979; e-mail info@fnbnamibia.com.na; internet www.fnbnamibia.com.na; f. 1987 as First Nat. Bank of Southern Africa Ltd; present name adopted 1990; total assets 4,731.9m. (June 2003); Chair. H. DIETER VOIGTS; CEO VEKUII RUKORO; 28 brs and 12 agencies.

Namibian Banking Corpn: Carl List Haus, Independence Ave, POB 370, Windhoek; tel. (61) 225946; fax (61) 223741; Chair. J. C. WESTRAAT; Man. Dir P. P. NIEHAUS; 3 brs.

Nedbank Namibia: 12–20 Dr Frans Indongo St, POB 1, Windhoek; tel. (61) 2959111; fax (61) 2952120; e-mail serviceplus@nedbank.com; internet www.nedbank.com.na; f. 1973; fmrly Commercial Bank of Namibia Ltd; subsidiary of Nedbank Ltd, South Africa; total assets 3,000.0m. (June 2005); Chair. T. J. FRANK; Man. Dir BILL TURTON; 17 brs and 4 agencies.

Standard Bank Namibia Ltd: Standard Bank Centre, cnr Werner List St and Post St Mall, POB 3327, Windhoek; tel. (61) 2942126; fax (61) 2942583; e-mail info@standardbank.com.na; internet www.standardbank.com.na; f. 1915; controlled by Standard Bank Africa; total assets 10,400.2m. (Dec. 2006); Chair. LEAKE S. HANGALA; Man. Dir MPUMZI PUPUMA; 23 brs.

Agricultural Bank

Agricultural Bank of Namibia (AgriBank): 10 Post St Mall, POB 13208, Windhoek; tel. (61) 2074200; fax (61) 2074289; e-mail agribank@iafrica.com.na; f. 1922; total assets 739.1m. (March 2001); Chair. HANS-GUENTHER STIER; CEO IIPUMBU LEONARD NANGOLO.

Development Bank

Development Bank of Namibia (DBN): POB 235, Windhoek; tel. (61) 2908000; fax (61) 2908071; e-mail info@dbn.com.na; internet www.dbn.com.na; f. 2004; Chair. SVEN THIEME; CEO DAVID NUYOMA.

STOCK EXCHANGE

Namibian Stock Exchange (NSX): Kaiser Krone Centre, Shop 8, Post St Mall, POB 2401, Windhoek; tel. (61) 227647; fax (61) 248531; e-mail loiden@nsx.com.na; internet www.nsx.com.na; f. 1992; Chair. Exec. Cttee P. HANGO; Gen. Man. HEIKO NIEDERMEIER.

INSURANCE

Corporate Guarantee and Insurance Co of Namibia Ltd (CGI): Corporate House, Ground Floor, 17 Lüderitz St, POB 416, Windhoek; tel. (61) 259525; fax (61) 255213; e-mail info@corporateguarantee.com; internet www.corporateguarantee.com; f. 1996; wholly owned subsidiary of Nictus Group Ltd since 2001; Chair. J. L. OLIVER; Man. Dir and Principal Officer F. R. VAN STADEN.

Insurance Co of Namibia (INSCON): POB 2877, Windhoek; tel. (61) 275900; fax (61) 233808; f. 1990; short-term insurance; Chair. CHARLES KAURAISA; Man. Dir FERDINAND OTTO.

Legal Shield: 140–142 Robert Mugabe Ave, POB 11363, Windhoek; tel. (61) 2754200; fax (61) 2754090; internet www.legalshield.com.na; f. 2000; legal, funeral and medical insurance; Man. Dir QUINTON VAN ROOYEN.

Metropolitan Namibia: Metropolitan Pl., 1st Floor, cnr Bülow and Stubel Sts, POB 3785, Windhoek; tel. (61) 2973000; fax (61) 248191; internet www.metropolitan.com.na; f. 1996; subsidiary of Metropolitan Group, South Africa; acquired Channel Life in 2004; Chair. M. L. SMITH; Man. Dir LEEBA FOUCHÉ.

Mutual and Federal Insurance Co Ltd: Mutual and Federal Centre, 5th–7th Floors, 227 Independence Ave, POB 151, Windhoek; tel. (61) 2077111; fax (61) 2077205; f. 1990; subsidiary of Mutual and Federal, South Africa; acquired CGU Holdings Ltd in 2000 and FGI Namibia Ltd in 2001; Man. Dir G. KATJIMUNE; Gen. Man. J. W. B. LE ROUX.

Namibia National Reinsurance Corpn Ltd (NamibRE): Capital Centre, 2nd Floor, Levinson Arcade, POB 716 Windhoek; tel. (61) 256905; fax (61) 256904; e-mail administrator@namibre.com; f. 2001; 100% state-owned; Man. Dir ANNA NAKALE-KAWANA.

Old Mutual Life Assurance Co (Namibia) Ltd: Mutual Platz, 5th Floor, Post St Mall, POB 165, Windhoek; tel. (61) 2993999; fax (61) 2993520; e-mail nambusdev@oldmutual.com; internet www.oldmutual.com.na; Chair. G. S. VAN NIEKERK; Chief Exec. BERTIE VAN DER WALT.

Sanlam Namibia: 154 Independence Ave, POB 317, Windhoek; tel. (61) 2947418; fax (61) 2947416; e-mail marketing@sanlam.com.na; internet www.sanlam.com.na; f. 1928; subsidiary of Sanlam Ltd, South Africa; merged with Regent Life Namibia, Capricorn Investments and Nam-Mic Financial Services in Dec. 2004; Chair. ROY ANDERSEN; CEO Dr JOHAN VAN ZYL.

Santam Namibia Ltd: Ausspanplaza Complex, Ausspanplatz POB 204, Windhoek; tel. (61) 2928000; fax (61) 235225; 60% owned by Santam, South Africa; 33.3% owned by Bank Windhoek Holdings Ltd; acquired Allianz Insurance of Namibia Ltd in 2001; Chief Exec. NAMA SIMON GOABAB.

Swabou Insurance Co Ltd: Swabou Bldg, Post St Mall, POB 79, Windhoek; tel. (61) 2997528; fax (61) 2997551; internet www.swabouinsurance.com.na; f. 1990; acquired by FNB Namibia Holdings Ltd in 2004; short-term insurance; Man. Dir RENIER TALJAARD.

Swabou Life Assurance Co Ltd: 209–211 Independence Ave, POB 79, Windhoek; tel. (61) 2997502; fax (61) 2997550; e-mail tgurirab@fnbnamibia.com.na; internet www.swaboulife.com.na; f. 1990; acquired by FNB Namibia Holdings Ltd in 2004; life assurance; CEO GERHARD MANS.

Trade and Industry

GOVERNMENT AGENCIES

Karakul Board of Namibia—Swakara Fur Producers and Exporters: Private Bag 13300, Windhoek; tel. (61) 235168; fax (61) 2909300; e-mail swakara@agra.com.na; internet www.swakara.net; Chair. H. J. VAN WYK; Man. W. H. VISSER.

Meat Board of Namibia: POB 38, Windhoek; tel. (61) 275830; fax (61) 228310; f. 1935; Chair. JOHN LE ROUX; Gen. Man. PAUL STRYDOM.

Meat Corpn of Namibia (Meatco Namibia): POB 3881, Windhoek; tel. (61) 3216400; fax (61) 3216401; e-mail hoffice@meatco.com.na; internet www.meatco.com.na; processors of meat and meat products at four abattoirs and one tannery; f. 1986; CEO KOBUS DU PLESSIS.

Namibian Agronomic Board: 30 Hochland Rd, POB 5096, Ausspannplatz, Windhoek; tel. (61) 379500; fax (61) 225371; internet www.nab.com.na; e-mail christof@nammic.com.na; f. 1985; CEO CHRISTOF BROCK.

National Petroleum Corpn of Namibia (NAMCOR): Petroleum House, 1 Aviation Rd, Private Bag 13196, Windhoek; tel. (61) 2045000; fax (61) 221785; internet www.namcor.com.na; f. 1965 as Southern Oil Exploration Corpn (South-West Africa) (Pty) Ltd—SWAKOR; present name adopted 1990; state petroleum co; responsible for importing 50% of national oil requirements; Chair. F. KISTING; Man. Dir SAM BEUKES (acting).

DEVELOPMENT ORGANIZATIONS

Namibia Investment Centre (NIC): Ministry of Trade and Industry, Brendan Simbwaye Sq., Block B, 6th Floor, Goethe St, Private Bag 13340, Windhoek; tel. (61) 2837335; fax (61) 220278; e-mail nic@mti.gov.na; f. 1990; promotes foreign and domestic investment; Exec. Dir BERNADETTE ARTIVOR.

Namibia Non-Governmental Organisation Forum (NANGOF): 18 Axalie Doeseb St, POB 70433 Khomasdal, Windhoek; tel. (61) 239469; fax (61) 239471; e-mail nangof@iafrica.com.na; f. 1991; umbrella body representing 95 community-based orgs; Chair. SANDY TJARONDA.

National Housing Enterprise: 7 Omuramba Rd, Eros, POB 20192, Windhoek; tel. (61) 2927111; fax (61) 2927271; internet www.nhe.com.na; f. 1983; replaced Nat. Building and Investment Corpn; provides low-cost housing; manages Housing Trust Fund; 100% state-owned; total assets N $496.4m. (Dec. 2001); Chair. V. R. RUKORO; CEO VINCENT HAILULU.

CHAMBERS OF COMMERCE

Chamber of Mines of Namibia (CoM): Channel Life Tower, 4th Floor, Post St Mall, 2895, Windhoek; tel. (61) 237925; fax (61) 222638; e-mail malango@iway.na; f. 1979; Pres. OTTO SHILOONGO; Gen. Man. VESTON MALANGO; 59 mems (2005).

Namibia National Chamber of Commerce and Industry (NNCCI): 2 Jenner St, cnr Simpson and Jenner Sts, POB 9355, Windhoek; tel. (61) 228809; fax (61) 228009; e-mail info@ncci.org.na; internet www.ncci.org.na; f. 1990; Chair. Dr ESTHER HOVEKA; CEO TARAH SHAANIKA; *c.* 2,000 mems (2005).

Windhoek Chamber of Commerce and Industries: SWA Building Society Bldg, 3rd Floor, POB 191, Windhoek; tel. (61) 222000; fax (61) 233690; f. 1920; Pres. H. SCHMIDT; Gen. Man. T. D. PARKHOUSE; 230 mems.

EMPLOYERS' ORGANIZATIONS

Construction Industries Federation of Namibia: 22 Stein St, POB 1479, Klein Windhoek; tel. (61) 230028; fax (61) 224534; e-mail info@cif.namibia.na; internet www.cif.namibia.na; Pres. RENATE SCHMIDT; Sec. RICKI WILSON; 60 contracting mems, 12 trade mems, 5 affiliated mems.

Namibia Agricultural Union (NAU): PMB 13255, Windhoek; tel. (61) 237838; fax (61) 220193; e-mail nau@agrinamibia.com.na; internet www.agrinamibia.com.na; f. 1947; represents commercial farmers; Pres. RAIMAR VON HASE; Exec. Man. SAKKIE COETZEE.

Namibia National Farmers' Union (NNFU): 4 Axalie Doeseb St, Windhoek West; POB 3117, Windhoek; tel. (61) 271117; fax (61) 271115; e-mail info@nnfu.org.na; represents communal farmers; Pres. MANFRED RUKORO.

Namibia Professional Hunting Association (NAPHA): 318 Sam Nujoma Dr., Klein WindhoekPOB 11291, Windhoek; tel. (61) 234455; fax (61) 222567; internet www.natron.net/napha; f. 1974; represents hunting guides and professional hunters; Pres. FRANK HEGER; c. 400 mems.

Retail Motor Industry of Namibia (RMI Namibia): POB 2110, Windhoek; tel. (61) 240280; fax (61) 240276; fmrly Motor Industries Federation of Namibia; present name adopted 2002; affiliated to RMI South Africa; Chair. HAROLD PUPKEWITZ; Pres. NEELS SWIEGERS; 40 mems (2003).

UTILITIES

Namibia Power Corpn (Pty) Ltd (NamPower): NamPower Centre, 15 Luther St, POB 2864, Windhoek; tel. (61) 2054111; fax (61) 232805; e-mail register@nampower.com.na; internet www.nampower.com.na; Chair. ANDRIES LEEVI HUNGAMO; Man. Dir Dr LEAKE S. HANGALA.

Northern Electricity: POB 891, Tsumeb; tel. (67) 222243; fax (67) 222245; private electricity supply co; Man. Dir C. G. N. HUYSEN.

MAJOR COMPANIES

CIC Holdings Ltd: United House, cnr Solingen and Iscor Sts, Northern Industrial Area, POB 98, Windhoek; tel. (61) 219670; fax (61) 234489; f. 1946 as J.J. van Zyl (Pty) Ltd; 30% owned by Super Group Ltd, South Africa; provides logistical and administrative services to consumer goods industry; Chair. RON BAC; CEO TREVOR P. ROGERS.

Namdeb Diamond Corpn Ltd: POB 35, Oranjemund; tel. (63) 235493; fax (63) 235401; f. 1994; 50% state-owned, 50% owned by De Beers Centenary AG, Switzerland; operates alluvial diamond mine at Oranjemund; also recovers marine diamonds; Chair. NICHOLAS F. OPPENHEIMER; Man. Dir I. ZAAMWANI; 2,953 employees.

Namibia Breweries Ltd (Nambrew): Iscor St, Northern Industrial Area, Windhoek; tel. (61) 320499; fax (61) 263327; internet www.nambrew.com; f. 1920 as South West Breweries Ltd; present name adopted 1990; 56% owned by Olfitra, 29% jtly owned by Diageo PLC, United Kingdom, and Heineken NV, the Netherlands; producers and distributors of beer, spirits and soft drinks; sales N $509.2m. (2000); Chair. SVEN THIEME; Man. Dir O. ADEBANJI; 700 employees.

Namibia Fishing Industries Ltd (Namfish): Ben Amathila Ave, POB 2932, Walvis Bay; tel. (64) 218200; fax (64) 206617; f. 1947 as South West Africa Fishing Industries; present name adopted 1990; went into provisional liquidation June 2005; fishery; Man. Dir JOHAN BLEEKER; Sec. SAM ALFHEIM; 500 employees.

Namibia Sea Products (NamSea): POB 2715, Walvis Bay; tel. (64) 203497; fax (64) 203498; e-mail namsea@iafrica.com.na; 35% owned by Namibia Fishing Industries, 28.6% Standard Bank Nominees, 2.3% NamSea Share Trust; fishery, cannery, and producers of fish meal and fish oil; sales N $91.8m. (2004); Chair. C. L. R. HAIKALI; Sec. P. A. SCHWIEGER.

Nictus Group: POB 13231, Windhoek; tel. (61) 229558; fax (61) 227320; e-mail ncs@nictus.com.na; f. 1964; furniture carpet and motor retail, and financial services; Chair. J. L. OLIVIER; CEO NICO TROMP.

Rosh Pinah Zinc Corpn (RPZC): Rosh Pinah Mine, Rosh Pinah; tel. (63) 274201; e-mail deon.garbers@kumbaresources.com; f. 1999 to succeed Imcor Zinc (Pty) Ltd; owned and operated by Kumba Resources, South Africa (fmrly Iscor Mining); Chair. R. MYBURGH; Mine Man. M. DEON GARBERS; lead and zinc producers; 493 employees.

Rössing Uranium Ltd: Private Bag 5005, Swakopmund; tel. (64) 5202382; fax (64) 5202286; e-mail yourcontact@rossing.com.na; internet www.rossing.com; f. 1970; began production in 1976; operates world's largest open-pit uranium mine in the Namib desert; Chair. CHARLES V. KAURAISA; Man. Dir MIKE LEECH; 930 employees (2006).

Skorpion Zinc: Skorpion Zinc Mine, Private Bag 2003, Rosh Pinah; tel. (63) 2712100; fax (63) 2712331; e-mail Recruitment@skorpionzinc.com.na; internet www.skorpionzinc.com.na; f. 2000; entered commercial production 2004; owned and operated by Anglo Base Metals (Anglo American PLC—UK); producers of zinc; Mine Man. GERALD BOTING; 615 employees.

TRADE UNIONS

In 2004 there were 27 unions representing more than 100,000 workers.

Trade Union Federations

National Union of Namibian Workers (NUNW): Mungunda St, Katutura; POB 50034, Windhoek; tel. (61) 215037; fax (61) 215589; f. 1972; affiliated to the SWAPO party; Pres. RISTO KAPENDA; Sec.-Gen. EVILASTUS KAARONDA; c. 70,000 mems.

The NUNW has 10 affiliates which include:

Metal and Allied Namibian Workers' Union (MANWU): Mingunda St, POB 22771, Windhoek 9000; tel. (61) 263100; fax (61) 264300; e-mail jeffrey_naobeb@mpsa.co.za; f. 1987; affiliated to the Building and Wood Workers Int. and Int. Metalworkers' Fed.; Pres. J. NAOBEB; Gen. Sec. MOSES SHIIKWA (acting); 5,500 mems.

Mineworkers' Union of Namibia (MUN): POB 1566, Windhoek; tel. (61) 261723; fax (61) 217684; f. 1986; Pres. ANDRIES EISEB; 12,500 mems.

Namibia Farm Workers' Union (NAFWU): POB 21007, Windhoek; tel. (61) 218653; f. 1994; Sec.-Gen. ALFRED ANGULA.

Namibia Financial Institutions Union (NAFINU): POB 61791, Windhoek; tel. (61) 239917; fax (61) 215589; f. 2000; Pres. ALEX KAMAUNDJU.

Namibia Food and Allied Workers' Union (NAFAU): Mungunda St, Katutura; POB 1553, Windhoek; tel. (61) 218213; fax (61) 263714; e-mail nafau@mweb.com.na; f. 1986; affiliated to the Int. Textile, Garment and Leather Workers' Fed. and Int. Union of Food, Agricultural, Hotel, Restaurant, Catering, Tobacco and Allied Workers' Asscns; Pres. DAVID NAMALENGA; Gen. Sec. KIROS SACARIAS; 12,000 mems.

Namibia National Teachers' Union (NANTU): POB 61009, Windhoek; tel. (61) 262247; fax (61) 261926; e-mail nantu@nantu.org.na; f. 1989; affiliated to Education Int.; Pres. NDAPEWA NGHIPANDULWA; Gen. Sec. MIRIAM HAMUTENYA-KATONYALA; 13,000 mems (2002).

Namibia Public Workers' Union (NAPWU): POB 50035, Bachbrecht, Windhoek; tel. (61) 261961; fax (61) 263100; e-mail napwu@namibnet.com; f. 1987; affiliated to the Public Services Int.; Pres. ELIPHAS NDINGARA; Sec.-Gen PETRUS NEVONGA; 11,000 mems.

Namibia Transport and Allied Workers' Union (NATAU): POB 7516, Katutura, Windhoek; tel. (61) 218514; fax (61) 263767; f. 1988; affiliated to the Int. Transport Workers' Fed.; Pres. DAWID TJOMBE; Gen. Sec. JOHN KWEDHI; 7,500 mems.

Trade Union Congress of Namibia (TUCNA): POB 2111, Windhoek; tel. (61) 246143; fax (61) 212828; f. 2002 following the merger of the Namibia People's Social Movement (f. 1992 as the Namibia Christian Social Trade Unions) and the Namibia Fed. of Trade Unions (f. 1998); Pres. PAULUS HANGO; c. 45,000 mems (2005).

TUCNA has 14 affiliates including:

Local Authorities Union of Namibia (LAUN): Frans Indongo St, Windhoek; POB 22060, Windhoek; tel. (61) 234625; fax (61) 230035; Pres. FRANCOIS ADONIS.

Namibia Building Workers' Union (NABWU): 3930 Verbena St, Khomasdal; POB 22679, Windhoek; tel. (61) 212828.

Namibia Seamen and Allied Workers Union (NASAWU): Nataniel Maxuilli St, Walvis Bay; POB 1341, Walvis Bay; tel. (64) 204237; fax (64) 205957; Pres. PAULUS HANGO.

Namibia Wholesale and Retail Workers Union (NWRWU): 19 Verbena St, Khomasdal; POB 22769, Windhoek; tel. (61) 212378; fax (61) 212828; Sec.-Gen. JOSHUA MABUKU.

Public Service Union of Namibia (PSUN): 45–51 Kroon Rd, Khomasdal; POB 21662, Windhoek; tel. (61) 213083; fax (61) 213047; e-mail psun@namibnet.com; f. 1991; successor to the

Govt Service Staff Asscn; Pres. AWEBAHE HOESEB; Sec.-Gen. VICTOR KAZONJATI.

Teachers Union of Namibia (TUN): POB 30800, Windhoek; tel. (61) 229115; fax (61) 246360; Pres. GERT JANSEN.

Transport

RAILWAYS

The main line runs from Nakop, at the border with South Africa, via Keetmanshoop to Windhoek, Kranzberg, Tsumeb, Swakopmund and Walvis Bay. There are three branch lines, from Windhoek to Gobabis, Otavi to Grootfontein and Keetmanshoop to Lüderitz. The total rail network covers 2,382 route-km. There are plans for a railway line connecting Namibia with Zambia, as part of a programme to improve transport links among the members of the Common Market for Eastern and Southern Africa; plans to extend the northern railway line by 248 km, from Tsumeb to Ondangwa, were announced in 2001. In 2006 the Namibian and Botswana Governments commenced discussions regarding a proposed railway linking the two countries.

TransNamib Holdings Ltd: TransNamib Bldg, cnr Independence Ave and Bahnhof St, PMB 13204, Windhoek; tel. (61) 2981111; fax (61) 227984; e-mail pubrelation@transnamib.com.na; internet www.transnamib.com.na; state-owned; Chair. FOIBE JACOBS; CEO JOHN M. SHAETONHODI.

ROADS

Between 2000 and 2002 the total road network decreased from 66,467 km to 42,237 km of roads, of which 12.8% was paved in 2002. A major road link from Walvis Bay to Jwaneng, northern Botswana, the Trans-Kalahari Highway, was completed in 1998, along with the Trans-Caprivi Highway, linking Namibia with northern Botswana, Zambia and Zimbabwe. The Government is also upgrading and expanding the road network in northern Namibia. In 2001 total spending on the road network was equivalent to US $17.7m.

SHIPPING

The ports of Walvis Bay and Lüderitz are linked to the main overseas shipping routes and handle almost one-half of Namibia's external trade. Walvis Bay has a container terminal, built in 1999, and eight berths; it is a hub port for the region, serving land-locked countries such as Botswana, Zambia and Zimbabwe. In 2005 NAMPORT added a N $30m. floating dock to the Walvis Bay facilities with a view to servicing vessels used in the region's expanding petroleum industry. Traditionally a fishing port, a new quay was completed at Lüderitz in 2000, with two berths, in response to growing demand from the offshore diamond industry. At the end of 2005 Namibia's merchant fleet comprised 178 vessels, with a combined displacement of 106,350 gross registered tons.

African Portland Industrial Holdings (APIH): Huvest Bldg, 1st Floor, AE/Gams Centre, Sam Nujoma Dr., POB 40047, Windhoek; tel. (61) 248744; fax (61) 239485; e-mail jacques@apiholdings.com; f. 1994; 80% owned by Grindrod (South Africa); bulk port terminal operator; Man. Dir ATHOL EMERTON; Sec. JACQUES CONRADIE.

Namibian Ports Authority (NAMPORT): 17 Rikumbi Kandanga Rd, POB 361, Walvis Bay; tel. (64) 2082207; fax (64) 2082320; e-mail jerome@namport.com.na; internet www.namport.com; f. 1994; Chair. SHAKESPEARE MASIZA; Man. Dir SEBBY KANKONDI.

Pan-Ocean Shipping Services Ltd: POB 2613, Walvis Bay; tel. (64) 203959; fax (64) 204199; f. 1995; Man. Dir JÜRGEN HEYNEMANN; Gen. Man. GEORGE KIROV.

CIVIL AVIATION

There are international airports at Windhoek (Hosea Kutako) and Walvis Bay (Rooikop), as well as a number of other airports throughout Namibia, and numerous landing strips.

Air Namibia: TransNamib Bldg, cnr Independence Ave and Bahnhof St, POB 731, Windhoek; tel. (61) 2996000; fax (61) 2996101; e-mail aarickerts@airnamibia.com.na; internet www.airnamibia.com.na; f. 1946 as South West Air Transport; present name adopted in 1991; state-owned; part-privatization postponed indefinitely in 2003; services to Angola, Botswana, South Africa and Zimbabwe, Germany and the United Kingdom; Chair. H. PIUS ASHEEKE; Man. Dir KOSMOS EGUMBO.

Kalahari Express Airlines (KEA): POB 40179, Windhoek; tel. (61) 245665; fax (61) 245612; f. 1995; domestic and regional flights; Exec. Dir PEINGONDJABI SHIPOH.

Tourism

Namibia's principal tourist attractions are its game parks and nature reserves, and the development of 'eco-tourism' is being promoted. Tourist arrivals in Namibia in 2005 totalled 777,890. In 2003 tourism receipts amounted to US $333m.

Namibia Tourism Board: Suite 22, Sanlam Centre, Ground Floor, 272 Independence Ave, Windhoek; tel. (61) 2906000; fax (61) 254848; e-mail info@namibiatourism.com.na; internet www.namibiatourism.com.na; Chair. Dr RUKEE TJINGAETE; CEO DIGU NAOBEB (acting).

Defence

As assessed at November 2006, the Namibian Defence Force numbered an estimated 9,000 men; there was also a 200-strong navy, operating as part of the Ministry of Fisheries and Marine Resources, and a paramilitary force of 6,000. In 2006 some 644 Namibian troops were stationed abroad, attached to UN missions in Africa; of these, 29 were serving as observers.

Defence Expenditure: Budgeted at N $1,300m. for 2006.

Commander-in-Chief of the Defence Force: Pres. HIFIKEPUNYE POHAMBA.

Chief of Staff of the Defence Force: Lt-Gen. MARTIN SHALLI.

Commander of the Army: Maj.-Gen. PETER NAMBUNDUNGA.

Education

Education is officially compulsory for 10 years between the ages of six and 16 years, or until primary education has been completed (whichever is the sooner). Primary education consists of seven grades, and secondary education of five. According to UNESCO estimates, in 2002/03 enrolment at primary schools included 74% of children in the relevant age-group (males 71%; females 76%), while the comparable ratio for secondary enrolment in that year was 38% (males 32%; females 44%). In that year there were some 455,077 children enrolled in pre-primary and primary education, and 138,099 in secondary education.Higher education is provided by the University of Namibia, the Technicon of Namibia, a vocational college and four teacher-training colleges. In 2002/03 13,536 students were enrolled in tertiary education. Various schemes for informal adult education are also in operation in an effort to combat illiteracy. Under the 2004/05 budget N $2,613.2m. was allocated to education (20.6% of total government expenditure).

Bibliography

Afro-Asian Peoples' Solidarity Organization. *Namibia: Road to Independence*. Cairo, 1990.

Allison, C., and Green, R. H. *Political Economy and Structural Change: Namibia at Independence*. Brighton, University of Sussex, Institute of Development Studies, 1989.

Amukugo, E. M. *Education and Politics in Namibia: Past Trends and Future Prospects*. Windhoek, Gamsberg Macmillan, 1995.

Arcadi de Saint-Paul, M. *Namibie: Une Siècle d'Histoire*. Paris, Albatron, 1984.

Bley, H. *Namibia under German Rule*. Uppsala, Nordiska Afrikainstitutet, 1997.

Catholic Institute for International Relations. *Land Reform in Namibia*. London, 1995.

Cros, G. *Chroniques Namibiennes: La Dernière Colonie*. Paris, Présence Africaine, 1983.

La Namibie. Paris, Presses Universitaires de France, 1983.

Dale, R. *The UN and the Independence of Namibia: The Longest Decolonization, 1946–1990*. 1994.

Diescho, J. *The Namibian Constitution in Perspective*. Windhoek, Gamsberg Macmillan, 1994.

Du Pisani, A. *SWA/Namibia: The Politics of Continuity and Change*. Johannesburg, Jonathan Ball, 1986.

Du Pisani, A., and Otaala, B. *UNAM HIV/AIDS Policy*. Windhoek, University of Namibia Press, 2002.

Duggal, N. K. (Ed.). *Namibia: Perspectives for National Reconstruction and Development*. Lusaka, UN Institute for Namibia, 1986.

Frayne, B. *Urbanisation in Post-Independence Windhoek (With Special Emphasis on Katutura)*. Windhoek, University of Namibia, 1992.

Gewald, J. *Herero Heroes: A Socio-Political History of the Herero of Namibia, 1890–1923*. London, James Currey Publishers, 1999.

Good, K. *Realizing Democracy in Botswana, Namibia and South Africa*. Pretoria, Africa Institute, 1997.

Green, R. H. *From Sudwesafrika to Namibia: The Political Economy of Transition*. Uppsala, Scandinavian Institute for African Studies, 1981.

Groth, S. *Namibia: the Wall of Silence*. Wiepperthal, Peter Hammer Verlag, 1995.

Grotpeter, J. J. *Historical Dictionary of Namibia*. Metuchen, NJ, Scarecrow Press, 1994.

Harvey, C., and Isaksen, J. (Eds). *Monetary Independence for Namibia*. Windhoek, NEPRU, 1990.

Hayes, P., Silvester, J., Wallace, M., and Hartmann, W. *Namibia under South African Rule*. London, James Currey Publishers, 1998.

Heribert, W., and Matthew, B. (Eds). *The Namibian Peace Process: Implications and Lessons for the Future*. Freiburg, Arnold-Bergstraesser-Institut, 1994.

Hishongwa, N. *The Contract Labour System and its Effects on Social and Family Life in Namibia*. Windhoek, Gamsberg Macmillan, 1992.

Hofnie, K., Friedman, S., and Iipinge, S. *The Relationship Between Gender Roles and HIV Infection in Namibia*. Windhoek, University of Namibia, 2004.

Jezkova, P. *Namibia: New Avenue of Industrial Development*. Vienna, UNIDO, 1994.

Karase, C., and Gutto, S. (Eds). *Namibia: The Conspiracy of Silence*. Harare, Nehanda, 1989.

Katjavivi, P. H. *A History of Resistance in Namibia*. London, James Currey Publishers, 2004.

LeBeau, D. *Namibia: Ethnic Stereotyping in a Post-Apartheid State*. Windhoek, University of Namibia, 1991.

Leys, C., and Saul, J. S. *Namibia's Liberation Struggle: The Two-Edged Sword*. London, James Currey Publishers, 1995.

Lister, S. (Ed.) *Aid, Donors and Development Management*. Windhoek, NEPRU, 1991.

Lush, D. *Last Steps to Uhuru: An Eye-Witness Account of Namibia's Transition to Independence (1988–1992)*. Ibadan, Spectrum Books, 1993.

McKittrick, M. *To Dwell Secure: Generation, Christianity, and Colonialism in Ovamboland*. London, James Currey Publishers, 2002.

Mans, M. *Music as Instrument of Diversity and Unity: Notes On A Namibian Landscape*. Uppsala, Nordic Africa Institute, 2003.

Mbuende, K. *Namibia: The Broken Shield: Anatomy of Imperialism and Revolution*. Uppsala, Scandinavian Institute for African Studies, 1986.

Melber, H. *Cross-examining Transition in Namibia: Socio-economic and Ideological Transformation since Independence*. Uppsala, Nordiska Afrikainstitutet, 2006.

Namuhuja, H. D. *Ondonga Royal Kings*. Windhoek, Out of Africa, 2002.

Omar, G., *et al. Introduction to Namibia's Political Economy*. Cape Town, Southern Africa Labour and Development Research Unit, 1990.

Otaala, B. *HIV/AIDS: The Challenge for Tertiary Institutions in Namibia*. Windhoek, University of Namibia, 2000.

Otaala, B. (Ed.) *Government Leaders in Namibia Responding to HIV/AIDS Epidemic*. Windhoek, University of Namibia, 2003.

Peltola, P. *The Lost May Day: Namibian Workers' Struggle for Independence*. Uppsala, Finnish Anthropological Society and Nordiske Afrikainstitutet, 1995.

Saunders, C. (Ed.). *Perspectives on Namibia: Past and Present*. Cape Town, Centre for African Studies, 1983.

Silvester, J., and Gewald, J. *Words Cannot Be Found: German Colonial Rule in Namibia, An Annotated Reprint of the 1918 Blue Book*. Leiden, E. J. Brill, 2004.

Singham, A. W. *Namibian Independence: A Global Responsibility*. Westport, CT, Hill, 1985.

Soggot, D. *Namibia: The Violent Heritage*. London, Collings, 1986.

Soiri, I. *Radical Motherhood: Namibian Women's Independence Struggle*. Uppsala, Nordiske Afrikainstitutet, 1996.

Sparks, D. L., and Green, D. *Namibia: The Nation after Independence*. Boulder, CO, Westview Press, 1992.

Talavera, P. *Challenging the Namibian Perception of Sexuality*. Windhoek, Gamsberg Macmillan, 2002.

Thornberry, C. *A Nation is Born: The Inside Story of Namibia's Independence*. Windhoek, Gamsberg Macmillan, 2004.

Totemeyer, G. *The Reconstruction of the Namibian National, Regional and Local State*. Windhoek, University of Namibia, 1992.

Totemeyer, G., *et al.* (Eds). *Namibia in Perspective*. Windhoek, Council of Churches in Namibia, 1987.

Udechukwu, A. *Herero*. New York, NY, Rosen Publishing Group Inc., 1996.

Walther, D. J. *Creating Germans Abroad: Cultural Policies and National Identity in Namibia*. Athens, OH, Ohio University Press, 2002.

Werner, W. *Land Reform in Namibia: The First Seven Years*. Windhoek, NEPRU, 1997.

Wilmsen, E. N. *Land Filled with Flies: A Political Economy of the Kalahari*. Chicago, IL, University of Chicago Press, 1989.

Winterfeldt, V., Fox, T., and Mufune, P. (Eds) *Namibia: Society, Sociology*. Windhoek, University of Namibia, 2002.

NIGER

Physical and Social Geography

R. J. HARRISON CHURCH

The land-locked Republic of Niger is the largest state in West Africa. With an area of 1,267,000 sq km (489,191 sq miles), it is larger than Nigeria, its immensely richer southern neighbour, which is Africa's most populous country. The relatively small size of Niger's population, 11,060,291 at the census of May 2001, rising to 13,737,000 by mid-2006, according to UN estimates, is largely explained by the country's aridity and remoteness. Population density in 2005 averaged 10.8 persons per sq km. Two-thirds of Niger consists of desert, and most of the north-eastern region is uninhabitable. The only large city is Niamey, which had a population of 707,951 in 2001. Hausa tribespeople are the most numerous (representing some 55.4% of Nigerien citizens in 2001), followed by the Djerma and Sonraï (together amounting for a total of 21.0%), Tuareg (9.3%) and Peulh (8.5%).

In the north-centre is the partly volcanic Aïr massif, with many dry watercourses remaining from earlier wetter conditions. Agadez, in Aïr, receives an average annual rainfall of no more than about 180 mm. None the less, the Tuaregs keep considerable numbers of livestock by moving them seasonally to areas further south, where underground well-water is usually available. Further south, along the Niger–Nigerian border, are sandy areas where annual rainfall is just sufficient for the cultivation of groundnuts and millet by Hausa farmers. Cotton is also grown in small, seasonally flooded valleys and depressions.

In the south-west is the far larger, seasonally flooded Niger valley, the pastures of which nourish livestock that have to contend with nine months of drought for the rest of the year. Rice and other crops are grown by the Djerma and Sonraï peoples as the Niger flood declines.

Niger thus has three very disparate physical and cultural focuses. Unity has been encouraged by French aid and by economic advance, but the attraction of the more prosperous neighbouring state of Nigeria is considerable. Distances to the nearest ports (Cotonou, in Benin, and Lagos, in Nigeria) are at least 1,370 km, both routes requiring breaks of bulk.

Recent History

PIERRE ENGLEBERT

Revised by KATHARINE MURISON

Formerly a part of French West Africa, Niger became a self-governing republic within the French Community in December 1958, and proceeded to full independence on 3 August 1960. Control of government passed to the Parti progressiste nigérien (PPN), whose leader, Hamani Diori, favoured the maintenance of traditional social structures and the retention of close economic links with France. Organized opposition, principally by the left-wing nationalist Union nigérienne démocratique (UND, or Sawaba party), had been suppressed since 1959 and the UND leader, Djibo Bakary, was forced into exile.

The period 1968–74 was overshadowed by the Sahelian drought. Widespread civil disorder followed allegations that some government ministers were misappropriating stocks of food aid, and in April 1974 Diori was overthrown by the Chief of Staff of the Armed Forces, Lt-Col (later Maj.-Gen.) Seyni Kountché. A Conseil militaire suprême (CMS) was established, and the legislature was replaced by a consultative Conseil national de développement (CND). Although political parties were outlawed, Bakary and other opposition activists were permitted to return to the country.

THE KOUNTCHÉ REGIME

The military Government's major preoccupation was planning an economic recovery. Generally amicable relations were maintained with France, and new links were formed with Arab states. Domestically, there was a renewal of political activism following Bakary's return from exile, and plots to remove Kountché were thwarted in 1975 and 1976. In January 1983 a civilian Prime Minister, Oumarou Mamane, was appointed, although he was removed from that post in November of that year. Economic adjustment efforts were impeded by the recurrence of drought in 1984–85 and by the closure of the land border with Nigeria in 1984–86, with the result that Niger's dependence on external financial assistance was increased.

A draft 'national charter' was overwhelmingly approved (by some 99.6% of voters) at a national referendum in June 1987. The charter provided for the establishment of non-elective, consultative institutions at both national and local levels.

SAÏBOU AND THE SECOND REPUBLIC

Kountché died in November 1987, after a year of ill health. The Chief of Staff of the Armed Forces, Col (later Brig.) Ali Saïbou, was inaugurated as Chairman of the CMS and Head of State on 14 November. Both Diori and Bakary were received by Saïbou, an appeal was made to exiled Nigeriens to return, and an amnesty was announced for political prisoners. Although the military continued to play a prominent role in government, Oumarou Mamane was reappointed as Prime Minister in July 1988.

In August 1988 Saïbou announced an end to the 14-year ban on all political organizations, with the formation of a new ruling party, the Mouvement national pour une société de développement (MNSD). In May 1989 the constituent congress of the MNSD elected a Conseil supérieur d'orientation nationale (CSON) to replace the CMS. A constitutional document, drafted by the CND, which provided for the continued role of the armed forces in what was to be designated the Second Republic, was endorsed by 99.3% of voters in a national referendum in September. As President of the CSON, Saïbou was the sole candidate at a presidential election in December, when he was confirmed as Head of State, for a seven-year term, by 99.6% of voters. At the same time a single list of 93 CSON-approved deputies to a new Assemblée nationale (to succeed the CND) was endorsed by a similar margin. The post of Prime Minister was abolished later in December, but was restored in March 1990, when it was allocated to a prominent industrialist, Aliou Mahamidou, in an extensive government reorganization.

In November 1990 Saïbou announced that a multi-party political system would be established. Interim provision was made for the registration of political parties (the Constitution was amended to this effect in April 1991).

THE TRANSITION PERIOD

In March 1991 it was announced that the armed forces were to withdraw from political life, and serving military officers were, accordingly, removed from the Council of Ministers. In July Saïbou resigned as Chairman of the MNSD—Nassara (as the MNSD had been restyled), in order to distance himself from party politics in preparation for a national conference, which was to determine the country's political evolution. He was succeeded as party leader by Col (retd) Mamadou Tandja.

The National Conference, convened on 29 July 1991, was attended by about 1,200 delegates, including representatives of the organs of state, 24 political organizations, professional, women's and students' groups. Declaring the Conference sovereign, delegates voted to suspend the Constitution and to dissolve its organs of state: Saïbou was to remain in office as interim Head of State. The Government was deprived of its authority to make financial transactions, and in October the Conference voted to suspend adherence to the country's IMF- and World Bank-sponsored programme of economic adjustment. The Conference assumed control of the armed forces and the police, appointing a new armed forces Chief of Staff. The Government was dissolved, and in October the Conference appointed Amadou Cheiffou (a regional official of the International Civil Aviation Organization) to head a transitional Government pending the installation (scheduled for early 1993) of elected democratic institutions. The Conference ended in November 1991; its Chairman, André Salifou (a dean of the University of Niamey), was designated Chairman of a 15-member Haut conseil de la République (HCR), which was to function as an interim legislature.

In February 1992 junior-ranking members of the armed forces staged a mutiny, demanding the payment of salary arrears, the release of an army captain found responsible by the National Conference for the violent suppression of a Tuareg attack on Tchin-Tabaraden in May 1990 (see below), and the dismissal of senior armed forces officers. The mutineers detained Salifou and the Minister of the Interior, Mohamed Moussa (himself of Tuareg extraction), and took control of the offices of the broadcasting media in Niamey, the capital. Order was restored when the Government agreed to consider the mutineers' demands. The Council of Ministers was reorganized in March, with four ministers dismissed and Moussa transferred to a lesser government post.

A constitutional referendum took place on 26 December 1992, when the new document was approved by 89.8% of those who voted (56.6% of the electorate). At elections to the new 83-member Assemblée nationale, which were held on 14 February 1993 and contested by 12 political parties, the MNSD—Nassara won the greatest number of seats (29), but was prevented from resuming power by the rapid formation of the Alliance des forces de changement (AFC), which grouped six parliamentary parties with a total of 50 seats. Principal members of the AFC were the Convention démocratique et sociale—Rahama (CDS), the Parti nigérien pour la démocratie et le socialisme—Tarayya (PNDS) and the Alliance nigérienne pour la démocratie et le progrès social—Zaman Lahiya (ANDP).

The MNSD—Nassara, which denounced opposition tactics in the legislative elections, was similarly frustrated at the presidential election. At the first round, on 27 February 1993, Tandja won the greatest proportion of the votes cast (34.2%). He and his nearest rival, Mahamane Ousmane (the leader of the CDS, who took 26.6% of the first-round votes), proceeded to a second round on 27 March, at which Ousmane was elected President by 55.4% of those who voted (just over 35% of the electorate), aided by the support of four of the six other candidates at the first round, who were members of the AFC.

OUSMANE AND THE THIRD REPUBLIC

Mahamane Ousmane, a devout Muslim and the country's first Hausa Head of State (his predecessors having been members of the Djerma community), who had consistently expressed his commitment to the principle of a secular state, was inaugurated as President of the Third Republic on 16 April 1993. Ousmane appointed a presidential candidate, Mahamadou Issoufou of the PNDS, to the post of Prime Minister, and in May, despite MNSD—Nassara attempts to prevent his election, Moumouni Amadou Djermakoye (the leader of the ANDP and another presidential candidate) was elected Speaker of the Assemblée nationale.

A 48-hour strike by members of the independent Union des syndicats des travailleurs du Niger (USTN) in July 1993 was followed by unrest in the army, as soldiers at Zinder, Tahoua, Agadez and Maradi took local officials hostage and demanded the payment of salary arrears. The USTN organized a 72-hour strike in September, in protest at the Government's austerity budget. Social tensions were exacerbated following the 50% devaluation, in January 1994, of the CFA franc. Following further strikes, in July the USTN agreed to halt industrial action, pending efforts to achieve a negotiated settlement on salary increases with the Government.

In September 1994 the PNDS withdrew from the AFC, and Issoufou resigned as Prime Minister, in protest against the perceived transfer of some of the premier's powers to the President. A new minority Government, led by Souley Abdoulaye of the CDS, failed to withstand a parliamentary motion of 'no confidence' proposed by the MNSD—Nassara and the PNDS in October. Ousmane dissolved the Assemblée nationale.

Legislative elections were held on 12 January 1995. The results indicated that the MNSD—Nassara, combining its 29 seats with those of its allies, would be able to form a 43-strong majority group in the legislature. While Ousmane's CDS increased its representation to 24 seats, the AFC (having lost the support of the PNDS and also that of the PPN) held 40 seats. However, Ousmane declined to accept the new majority's nominee as Prime Minister, Hama Amadou (the Secretary-General of the MNSD—Nassara); he appointed instead another member of that party, Amadou Aboubacar Cissé, a former official of the World Bank. Cissé was expelled from the MNSD—Nassara, and the party and its allies announced that they would not co-operate with his administration. His position was further undermined by continuing strike action, and by the election of Issoufou to the post of Speaker of the Assemblée nationale. A parliamentary motion of censure against Cissé was narrowly approved, and Ousmane was obliged to accept Amadou as Prime Minister.

Political and Institutional Conflict

The new Government, appointed in February 1995, swiftly ended several months of labour unrest, agreeing to cancel controversial legislation restricting the right of workers to strike, and to pay two months' salary arrears. Relations between the Government and the presidency were, however, less conciliatory. Difficulties of 'cohabitation' precipitated an institutional crisis from July, when Ousmane apparently refused to chair a session of the Council of Ministers at which Amadou's nominations for new senior executives of state-owned organizations were to have been adopted. The Government ordered the deployment of security forces at the premises of state enterprises, thereby preventing the incumbent executives from performing their duties. The crisis over the delineation of responsibilities between the President and Prime Minister deepened in subsequent weeks and was compounded by uncertainty as to Amadou's competence to sign an amnesty decree for all those involved in the Tuareg conflict (see below). Ousmane's rejection, in January 1996, of the Government's draft budget precipitated a severe decline in institutional relations.

MILITARY TAKE-OVER

On 27 January 1996 the elected organs of state were overthrown by the military, under the command of Col (later Brig.-Gen.) Ibrahim Baré Maïnassara (Chief of Staff of the Armed Forces since March 1995 and a former aide-de-camp to the late President Kountché). The coup leaders, who formed a 12-member Conseil de salut national (CSN), chaired by Maïnassara, asserted that their seizure of power had been necessitated by Niger's descent into political chaos. The CSN suspended the Constitution, dissolving the Assemblée nationale and other institutions; political parties were suspended, and a state of emergency was imposed.

The coup was generally condemned internationally; Western donors withdrew all non-humanitarian assistance, and negotiations with the IMF were stalled. The CSN appointed Boukary Adji, the Deputy Governor of the Banque centrale des états de l'Afrique de l'ouest (BCEAO) and a former finance minister, as Prime Minister. Adji's transitional Government was composed entirely of civilians. The appointment, in early February 1996, of military officers to the governorships of Niger's administrative regions was attributed by the CSN to the need to ensure neutrality in the organization of elections. In mid-February Ousmane, Amadou and Issoufou signed a joint text, in Maïnassara's presence, which effectively endorsed the legitimacy of the CSN and recognized that the assumption of power by the military had been necessitated by the prolonged administrative difficulties that had preceded the coup.

Two independent consultative bodies were established in late February 1996: the advisory Conseil des sages (which elected Saïbou as its Chairman); and the Co-ordinating Committee of the National Forum. The National Forum for Democratic Renewal was convened in April. Other than the members of the Co-ordinating Committee and the Conseil des sages, its 700 members included representatives of the dissolved parliament and of workers' and employers' organizations. The Forum adopted constitutional revisions that aimed to guarantee greater institutional stability, essentially by conferring executive power solely on the President of the Republic and requiring the Prime Minister to implement a programme stipulated by the Head of State.

Despite Maïnassara's earlier assurances that he and his associates in the CSN had no personal political ambitions, by May 1996 he had confirmed reports of his intention to seek election to the presidency. Adji's transitional Government was reshuffled shortly afterwards. The revised Constitution was approved by 92.3% of voters on 12 May; only 35% of the electorate were reported to have voted, however. The ban on activities by political organizations was revoked shortly afterwards. Ousmane, Issoufou, Tandja and Djermakoye swiftly announced their intention to contest the presidential election, scheduled for July. The end to the political consensus of recent months was compounded by tensions between the authorities and the electoral supervisory body, the Commission électorale nationale indépendante (CENI), as the Government disregarded the latter's recommendations that the presidential election be postponed owing to logistical difficulties.

Voting in the presidential election commenced, as scheduled, on 7 July 1996, but was quickly halted in Niamey and in other areas where preparations were incomplete: polling took place in these areas the following day. Controversy arose when, shortly before the end of voting, the authorities announced the dissolution of the CENI, in response to what they termed its 'obvious and deliberate' obstruction of the electoral process. A new commission was appointed to collate the election results. The democratic credentials of the CSN were further brought into doubt after Maïnassara's four rivals for the presidency were placed under house arrest. The provisional results of voting showed an outright victory for Maïnassara, with some 52.2% of the votes cast; Ousmane had won 19.8%, and Tandja 15.7%. The Supreme Court validated the election results on 21 July, and the release from house arrest of the defeated presidential candidates (excepting Issoufou) was announced the following day.

THE FOURTH REPUBLIC

Maïnassara was installed as President of the Fourth Republic on 7 August 1996. Issoufou was released from house arrest in mid-August. The new Government, under Adji, included former Prime Ministers Abdoulaye and Cissé. Members of the CDS, the MNSD—Nassara and the PNDS who accepted government posts were subsequently expelled from their parties.

In September 1996 a group of eight opposition parties (including the CDS, the MNSD—Nassara and the PNDS) stipulated several preconditions for their participation in the forthcoming legislative elections, foremost among them the annulment of the presidential election and the restitution of the CENI. These parties subsequently formed a Front pour la restauration et la défense de la démocratie (FRDD). At inter-party negotiations, convened at Maïnassara's request, the Government agreed to concede opposition access to the state media and an end to the ban (in force since the presidential election) on public meetings and demonstrations. The Government announced the restoration of the CENI, with the same composition as that which had overseen the 1995 elections, and agreed to a postponement of the elections. The commission's prerogatives were, however, amended, and the FRDD reiterated that it would not participate in the forthcoming poll unless the CENI was reinstated with its original powers and the presidential election was annulled.

The legislative elections, held on 23 November 1996, were contested by 11 parties and movements, as well as by independent candidates. The FRDD claimed that its appeal to supporters to boycott the vote had been successful. According to official results, the pro-Maïnassara Union nationale des indépendants pour le renouveau démocratique (UNIRD) took 52 of the 83 seats in the Assemblée nationale. International observers pronounced themselves satisfied with the organization and conduct of the elections. (The Supreme Court later upheld complaints of fraud in three constituencies won by the UNIRD, annulling the results there.)

The CSN was formally dissolved on 12 December 1996. A new Government was appointed shortly afterwards, with Cissé as Prime Minister. The FRDD leaders had rejected an invitation by Maïnassara to join the Government, and the deputy leader of the CDS, Sanoussi Jackou, was expelled from the party after accepting a ministerial post.

In January 1997 an unauthorized demonstration in Niamey by supporters of the opposition degenerated into clashes with the security forces. Some 62 people were arrested, among them Ousmane, Tandja and Issoufou, who were to be tried by the State Security Court, which had been restored in the aftermath of the demonstration. Considerable controversy ensued regarding the validity of the Court's revival. Neither the Constitution nor the penal code made provision for the Court, which had been in existence under the Kountché regime; however, the Government invoked constitutional provisions whereby, unless specifically repealed, laws in force at the time of the promulgation of the Constitution remained valid. The opposition leaders were released later in the month, following further protests, reportedly on Maïnassara's direct order. The FRDD rejected an invitation from the President to participate in forming a government of national unity, continuing to demand the dissolution of the Assemblée nationale and the holding of free and fair elections.

In November 1997 Maïnassara dismissed the Government; by this time a resumption of hostilities in the north had been compounded by chronic food insecurity as a result of poor harvests, by further labour unrest, and by ongoing political agitation. Maïnassara appointed Ibrahim Hassane Maiyaki, hitherto Minister of Foreign Affairs and Co-operation, as Prime Minister and named a new Council of Ministers in December.

In January 1998 it was announced that members of a commando unit had been arrested and charged with attempting to overthrow Maïnassara and other senior officials. Four of the accused made a televised confession, stating that they had been operating on the direct orders of Amadou, who was himself arrested. Two other former ministers were also arrested. Although all three denied involvement in any conspiracy, Maïnassara stated that Amadou had admitted to having been associated with the alleged commandos. The two former ministers were released within a week; Amadou was released on bail shortly afterwards, on charges that included forming a militia and criminal conspiracy.

In February 1998 the Parti nigérien pour l'autogestion—al Umat, the Parti pour l'unité nationale et le développement—Salama and the ANDP formed the Alliance des forces démocratiques et sociales (AFDS). However, the AFDS subsequently protested that it was being marginalized in the political process and by the state media; the alliance subsequently became increasingly associated with the opposition.

Political tensions escalated from April, as clashes in Tahoua between the security forces and FRDD activists, who were demanding Maïnassara's resignation, were followed by violent protests in Maradi and in Zinder, where opposition activists allegedly attacked vehicles and property belonging to the pro-Maïnassara Rassemblement pour la démocratie et le progrès—Djamaa (RDP).

In July 1998 it was reported that the Government and the opposition parties of the FRDD and the AFDS had signed an agreement aimed at ending two years of political crisis. Revisions were outlined to electoral procedures and institutions, as well as to the manner in which senior appointments were made to the Supreme Court and to the presidency of the CENI. It was agreed that all political groups should have equal access to the state media. However, the opposition challenged the appointment by Maïnassara of Lawali Mahamane Danda to head the electoral body. The remaining members of the CENI were appointed by presidential decree in September. Preparations were inadequate to allow local elections to proceed in November as scheduled, however, and the CENI announced a postponement of voting.

Voting in the regional, district and municipal elections took place on 7 February 1999, one day after the Minister of the Interior had presented a document purportedly giving evidence of an opposition plot aimed at the 'total conquest of power' by July. Following the discovery of overt irregularities, including the absence and destruction of voting equipment, the CENI emphasized that it favoured by-elections in affected areas. Full results, which were not released by the Supreme Court until 7 April, gave the 11 opposition parties a marginal overall majority of seats in those municipal, district and regional assemblies where the elections were deemed valid. Voting was to be rerun at 4,000 polling stations in 21 regional wards and 17 of the country's 72 districts. The FRDD and AFDS denounced Maïnassara as personally responsible for the disruption to votes in those areas, and demanded the President's resignation.

DEATH OF MAÏNASSARA

On 9 April 1999 Maiyaki made a broadcast to the nation, announcing the death of Maïnassara in an 'unfortunate accident' at a military airbase in Niamey. The Prime Minister stated that the defence and security forces would continue to be the guarantors of republican order and national unity. A one-month period of national mourning was decreed. Maiyaki announced the dissolution of the Assemblée nationale, as well as the temporary suspension of all party political activity. Despite the official explanation for his death, it was generally perceived that Maïnassara had been assassinated by members of his presidential guard in a *coup d'état*. On 11 April the Constitution was suspended, and its institutions dissolved. The February local elections were annulled. A military Conseil de réconciliation nationale (CRN), under the chairmanship of Maj. Daouda Mallam Wanké (hitherto head of the presidential guard), was to exercise executive and legislative authority during a nine-month transitional period. A new constitution was to be prepared, for submission to a national referendum, prior to the restoration of civilian rule and the installation of elected organs of state on 31 December. Maiyaki was reappointed as Prime Minister on 12 April, and a new transitional Council of Ministers was named shortly afterwards. New appointees notably included the former CENI Chairman, Danda, as Minister of Justice, and Moussa Moumouni Djermakoye, a former Chief of Staff of the Armed Forces who had reputedly rejected the post of CRN Chairman, as Minister of National Defence. In July, in a minor government reshuffle, the Minister of the Interior and Territorial Administration, Lt-Col Boureima Moumouni, was appointed Chief of General Staff of the Armed Forces.

Although the military take-over was condemned by the parties that had supported Maïnassara, the incoming regime was broadly welcomed, in its initial stages, by the FRDD and the AFDS. Niger's creditors, however, strongly denounced the events of 9 April 1999: France announced the immediate suspension of all non-humanitarian assistance, while the European Union (EU) announced that it was to review its co-operation with Niger. In subsequent weeks the EU appeared to make the maintenance of assistance conditional upon the commissioning of an independent inquiry into Maïnassara's death. (The CRN confirmed in June that such an inquiry would be commissioned.) Other West African Governments also denounced the apparent coup, and Wanké embarked on a tour of the region in an effort to explain and secure support for the CRN's actions. In May a meeting of ministers responsible for foreign affairs of the Economic Community of West African States (ECOWAS) strongly condemned the military take-over; however, ministers noted the CRN's expressed commitment to implementing the transition programme, and recognized the need to assist Niger in its efforts towards the restoration of constitutional democracy. The CRN subsequently stated that a report on the circumstances of Maïnassara's death had been lodged with those organizations concerned.

THE FIFTH REPUBLIC

The draft Constitution of what was to be designated the Fifth Republic envisaged a balance of powers between the President, Government and legislature, although the President was to be politically liable only in the case of high treason. The Government, under an appointed Prime Minister, was to be responsible to the Assemblée nationale, which would be competent to remove the Prime Minister by vote of censure. The draft document was submitted to a referendum on 18 July 1999, when it was approved by 89.6% of those who voted (about one-third of the registered electorate). Wanké promulgated the new Constitution on 9 August. In mid-August it was announced that the first round of presidential voting would take place on 17 October; a second round would take place, concurrently with legislative voting, on 24 November. There were seven candidates for the presidency, including Moumouni Amadou Djermakoye (of the ANDP), Issoufou (PNDS), Tandja (MNSD—Nassara) and former President Ousmane (CDS).

Voting proceeded as scheduled, and was considered both by the CENI and by independent observers to have been largely transparent and peaceful. Tandja won 32.3% of the votes cast in the first round of the presidential election, followed by Issoufou, with 22.8%, and Ousmane, with 22.5%. The rate of participation by voters was 43.7%. Tandja and Issoufou thus proceeded to a second round. Having secured the support of Ousmane, Tandja was elected President, with 59.9% of the votes cast. The rate of participation was about 39% of the registered electorate. The MNSD—Nassara was similarly successful in the concurrent elections to the new Assemblée nationale, winning 38 of the 83 seats; the CDS took 17, the PNDS 16, the RDP eight and the ANDP four.

Tandja was inaugurated as President on 22 December 1999. Amadou was subsequently appointed Prime Minister, and a new Council of Ministers was announced in January 2000. Tandja urged the Government to act to address the problem of outstanding salaries, grants and scholarships, and to adopt an emergency financial programme so as to allow the rapid resumption of international assistance. In January the Assemblée nationale adopted draft amnesty legislation, as provided for in the Constitution. The amnesty was opposed by the RDP, and many activists of the party joined a demonstration in February to denounce the legislation and to demand an international inquiry into the death of Maïnassara.

President Tandja undertook a state visit to France in January 2000, meeting President Jacques Chirac and Prime Minister Lionel Jospin; the resumption of French co-operation was subsequently formalized. Niger's new Minister of Foreign Affairs, Co-operation and African Integration visited Washington, DC, USA, in February, and in March the USA announced an end to the sanctions imposed after Maïnassara's death; however, the US Administration subsequently stated that its former aid programmes in Niger would not be resumed.

In March 2000 12 opposition parties, led by the PNDS, formed the Coordination des forces démocratiques (CFD) coalition. Similarly, 17 parties loyal to the President, chief among them the MNSD—Nassara and CDS, formed the Alliance des forces démocratiques (AFD) in July. In May a new armed forces Chief of Staff was appointed, although rumours persisted of dissent within the army. In June 10 soldiers were arrested in connection with the kidnapping of Maj. Djibrilla Hima, a spokesman for the former Wanké regime. In July 2005 a military court sentenced three soldiers to prison terms ranging from one year to five years for their involvement in the kidnapping; a further 11 soldiers were each sentenced *in absentia* to nine years' imprisonment.

In July 2002 the ANDP withdrew from the opposition CFD alliance and joined the pro-Government AFD alliance, thereby increasing the Government's parliamentary majority by four seats.

At the end of July 2002 a mutiny broke out at a barracks in Diffa (the home town of President Tandja), and a number of officers were taken hostage. Several officers, in addition to the mayor of Diffa and the regional governor, were arrested by the mutinous soldiers, who also took control of a radio station to broadcast their demands for improved pay and conditions. The Government declared a state of emergency in Diffa, where the rebels had already imposed a dusk-to-dawn curfew, and dispatched troops to bring the rebellion, which continued for 10 days, to a halt. Six soldiers, including three officers, were arrested in connection with the rebellion, but other rebel soldiers were reported to have fled, while a further uprising, at a barracks in Nguigmi, was rapidly quashed. In early August, before the rebellion in Diffa had been conclusively suppressed, a military uprising broke out in Niamey, although government forces quickly restored order in the capital. Some 217 soldiers were arrested in connection with the mutinies (of these, 52 were released from custody in May 2003). By mid-September 2002 special security measures in the Diffa region had been relaxed.

In late August 2002 Amadou announced that the rebellion in Diffa had been intended to serve as a distraction while a *coup d'état* was being prepared in Niamey. At the end of December the Assemblée nationale approved legislation providing for the creation of a special military tribunal to try those accused of involvement in the rebellion; elements within the opposition alleged that the legislation violated several articles of the Constitution. However, many soldiers were reportedly released during 2003, owing to a lack of evidence, and the three highest ranking officers arrested were provisionally freed in February 2004. In March 2006 a special military tribunal established in Kollo, near Niamey, sentenced six soldiers to prison terms ranging from three to seven years for their involvement in the mutiny, while a further 57 were acquitted. Human rights organizations criticized the fact that the accused had been detained for more than three years without trial. In mid-June it was reported that 31 of the acquitted soldiers had been dismissed from the army.

Meanwhile, in September 2002 the President and Vice-President of the Constitutional Court resigned, following a ruling by the Court, earlier in the month, that two decrees announced by President Tandja in relation to the suppression of the rebellion were unconstitutional; in particular, the imposition of emergency measures by the Head of State without consulting the Prime Minister, the Assemblée nationale and the Constitutional Court was deemed a breach of constitutional requirements, while a further decree, which restricted media coverage of the uprising, was also determined to be illegal.

Tandja implemented a major government reshuffle in November 2002, as a result of which the position of allies of Amadou was reportedly strengthened. Among the 13 new ministerial appointments was Moumouni Adamou Djermakoye as Minister of State, responsible for African Integration and the NEPAD (New Partnership for Africa's Development) Programmes, while seven ministers left the Government.

In June 2003 the Assemblée nationale approved legislation, proposed by President Tandja, amending the electoral code. Henceforth, ministers seeking elected office would no longer be obliged to resign from their government posts, while the requirement that the CENI be chaired by a judge was to be abolished. Opposition parties boycotted the vote, stating that reforms to electoral law had hitherto been decided by consensus. Following an attempt by the opposition to introduce a vote of censure against the Government, Tandja closed the parliamentary session. However, by August tensions regarding the CENI had abated, and a Chairman was appointed to the commission. In October the Council of Ministers announced proposals to increase the number of deputies in the Assemblée nationale in order to reflect the growth in the population recorded between the national censuses of 1988 and 2001. A minor government reshuffle was effected in October 2003.

During the second half of 2003 increasing concern was expressed, both nationally and internationally, at apparent attempts to restrict the freedom of the press and broadcast media in Niger. In September the editor of the weekly newspaper *L'Enquêteur*, Ibrahim Souley, was arrested and charged with inciting ethnic hatred, following the publication of an article alleging that the Government had acted improperly in the awarding of business contracts. In the following month Souley received a one-year suspended sentence and was prohibited from living in Niamey for a period of six months. Meanwhile, in late September the Conseil supérieur de la communication (CSC) withdrew the broadcasting licences of 15 independent radio stations; although official sources stated that they had been closed because their licences had been issued illegally, it was reported that the stations had broadcast programmes that had been critical of the Government immediately prior to their closure. In November Mamane Abou, the director of the weekly newspaper *Le Républicain*, was arrested, reportedly in response to the publication of allegations of corrupt practice by the Government with regard to the issuing of contracts; later in the month Abou was sentenced to six months' imprisonment, having been convicted of libelling the Head of Government. In December Abou's sentence was reportedly reduced, on appeal, to a suspended term of four months; fines of 300,000 francs CFA for costs and 10m. francs CFA in damages were also reduced to 100,000 francs CFA and 2m. francs CFA, respectively. He was provisionally released in January 2004, pending the outcome of a further case relating to charges of theft and receiving confidential documents.

In early February 2004 it was announced that municipal elections, initially scheduled to be held on 28 March, had been postponed until 29 May, owing to logistical difficulties experienced by several political parties. In mid-February Rhissa Ag Boula, the Minister of Tourism and Crafts, and a former Tuareg rebel leader (see below), was dismissed, following allegations that he was implicated in the murder of an MNSD—Nassara activist earlier in the year; he was subsequently arrested and charged with complicity in the murder.

In May 2004 the municipal elections were further postponed; the Constitutional Court had earlier ruled that 264 potential candidates had not complied with the conditions of the electoral code and were therefore not eligible to stand. The municipal elections finally took place on 24 July. According to provisional results, pro-presidential parties won a total of 2,335 of the 3,747 seats in the country's 265 communes (the MNSD—Nassara 1,388, the CDS 748 and the ANDP 199), while, of the opposition parties, the PNDS secured 821 seats, coming second overall, and the RDP 217. The non-aligned Rassemblement social-démocratique, which had been formed following a split in the CDS, also unexpectedly won 217 seats; the turn-out was 43.6%.

Tandja Re-elected

The first round of the presidential election, which was held on 16 November 2004, was contested by six candidates, four of whom (Djermakoye, Issoufou, Ousmane and Tandja) were standing for a fourth time. Tandja won 40.7% of the votes cast, followed by Issoufou, with 24.6%, and Ousmane, with 17.4%. The rate of voter participation was 48.2%. Tandja succeeded in securing the support of all four eliminated candidates ahead of the second round, which took place on 4 December. As in 1999, Tandja comfortably defeated Issoufou, with 65.5% of the votes cast, winning an unprecedented second term in office. Turn-out at the second round declined slightly, to 45.0%. The ruling MNSD—Nassara also performed well at concurrent elections to the enlarged 113-member Assemblée nationale, winning 47 seats, while five other parties loyal to Tandja secured a further 41 seats, including 22 taken by the CDS. The opposition PNDS and its allies won a total of 25 seats. The elections were deemed to have been 'free and fair' by international observers.

Amadou was reappointed to the premiership in late December 2004, and the formation of a new Council of Ministers, composed of members of the MNSD—Nassara and its allies, was announced. Although the 27-member Government included 17 new appointees, the most significant positions were allocated to ministers who had served in the previous administration.

Public Discontent and Food Insecurity

In mid-March 2005 up to 20,000 people protested in Niamey against rising prices, following the recent introduction of a 19% value-added tax on basic commodities. The demonstration, which ended in isolated violent incidents, as shops were looted and buildings damaged, was organized by a coalition of some 30 groups, including trade unions, human rights organizations and consumer movements, known as the Coalition contre la vie chère (CCVC). In the following week, after the Government refused to authorize a second protest march, the Coalition staged a one-day strike, which halted most activity in the capital. The authorities subsequently agreed to hold talks with the Coalition, although they ruled out withdrawing the tax, insisting that it was required to reduce the budget deficit and to bring Niger into line with the other member states of the Union économique et monétaire ouest-africaine. However, before a meeting could take place, five leaders of the CCVC were arrested and accused of establishing an unauthorized association and plotting against state security. Several of them had appeared on private radio and television stations, appealing to religious leaders to hold prayers in order to save Niger from misery, in what the Minister responsible for Relations with Institutions and Government Spokesman, Mohamed Ben Omar, described as a 'veiled call to rebellion'. The radio station *Alternative FM*, the director of which, Moussa Tchangari, was one of those charged, was also closed by police, prompting protests from international press freedom groups. During a further one-day strike, held a few days later, protesters erected barricades and burned tyres in Maradi and Tahoua, leading to further arrests. A third strike was suspended by the CCVC in early April in the hope that a compromise could be reached with the Government. Two days later the five leaders of the CCVC were released, shortly after President Tandja intervened in an attempt to ease tensions, urging the Coalition to negotiate with his Government and acknowledging that the tax had been imposed at a particularly difficult time. (The Government estimated that food shortages would affect some 3.6m. people in 2005, owing to a poor harvest in 2004, resulting from poor rainfall combined with an invasion of locusts.) Following four days of talks, the Government and the Coalition reached an agreement exempting flour and milk from the 19% tax and limiting its effect on water and electricity prices.

None the less, public discontent with the Government arose again in mid-2005 over severe food shortages. According to the Ministry of Agricultural Development, there was a shortfall of more than 223,000 metric tons of grain, representing the country's largest deficit for more than 20 years. In early June up to 2,000 people marched through Niamey in protest at the Government's failure to respond adequately to the crisis and in support of opposition-backed demands for the distribution of free food. The march was organized by a group of civil society organizations, which accused the authorities of being ill-prepared despite having had sufficient warning of the shortages. Meanwhile, in early May 11 people were killed in Dosso, some 140 km south-east of Niamey, when clashes broke out between nomadic herdsmen and local landowners in a dispute over scarce grazing land. In mid-May, as national food stocks neared depletion, the UN appealed to donors to provide US $16.2m. in emergency aid to assist the estimated 3.6m. people suffering food insecurity; by late August the sum required had been raised to $81m. The Government, which had been supplying cereals at subsidized prices in the most stricken areas, also appealed for international assistance, but insisted that it did not have the resources to distribute free food and instead announced plans to 'loan' grain to farmers most at risk until they could reimburse the Government after the harvest later in the year. As people reportedly began fleeing to Nigeria, government ministers and officials contributed financially to efforts to alleviate the crisis. In mid-July the UN World Food Programme appealed for further international aid for Niger, noting that its ability to assist those in need had been hampered by a slow response from donors. Following widespread international media coverage of the food shortages later that month, donors substantially increased their contributions to the appeal and the Government agreed to distribute free food to those worst affected. In September the Government announced that it had allocated 5,000m. francs CFA for the establishment of food reserves of 100,000 tons and planned to modernize farming methods in an attempt to increase agricultural production and reduce vulnerability to drought in the longer term. Despite a relatively good harvest in late 2005, food insecurity remained a problem in 2006, owing in large part to high levels of personal indebtedness resulting from the previous year's shortages.

In February 2006 government and media representatives commenced discussions on the reform of the media sector. During 2005 domestic and international press freedom groups had continued to protest against the imprisonment of journalists convicted of defamation, urging the swift adoption of planned legislation decriminalizing press offences. In May 2006 privately owned media organizations criticized new legislation approved by the Assemblée nationale on the composition and functioning of the CSC, claiming to be under-represented in the 11-member regulatory body.

At the beginning of June 2006 some 60 people were injured when university students who were protesting against poor living conditions and non-payment of grants clashed with police. Around 20 students were arrested and the Abdou Moumouni University was closed. Later that month an estimated 3,000 students and teachers demonstrated in Niamey, alleging that funding allocated to the university had been misappropriated by officials. In mid 2006 the CCVC organized a series of protest marches and strikes in support of demands for reductions in the cost of social services such as health and education, as well as fuel, water and electricity prices. In response, the President appointed a panel to negotiate with the Coalition. The 2006/07 academic year was disrupted by a series of strikes by school teachers demanding higher salaries and by demonstrations by students demanding improved learning conditions. University students also staged several large protests, some of which led to violence.

The Minister of Basic Education and Literacy, Hamani Harouna, and his predecessor in that post, Ari Ibrahim (currently Minister of Public Health and the Fight against Epidemics), were dismissed in late June 2006, following their implication in an EU investigation into the embezzlement of funds intended for the education sector. In October the National Assembly decided that Harouna and Ibrahim should be tried by the High Court of Justice. They were subsequently imprisoned pending trial, but were provisionally released in June 2007.

At the beginning of September 2006 Mamane Abou, the director of *Le Républicain*, and Oumarou Keita, a journalist at the newspaper, were convicted of 'spreading false news' and defamation following the publication of an article accusing the Prime Minister of jeopardizing relations with Western countries by pursuing closer ties with Iran. The newspaper had also published several articles on the corruption scandal surrounding education funding. They were sentenced to 18 months' imprisonment and each ordered to pay 300,000 francs CFA in fines and 5m. francs CFA in damages. Later that month the editor-in-chief of *L'Enquêteur*, Salif Dago, was sentenced to six months' imprisonment and fined 100,000 francs CFA, again for 'spreading false news'. Both rulings were condemned by press freedom groups. Abou and Keita were provisionally released in November by the Court of Appeal, and their convictions were overturned in February 2007.

President Tandja effected a government reshuffle in March 2007, creating a number of new ministries, although most of the key portfolios remained unchanged. At the end of May a parliamentary motion of censure against Amadou's Government was approved. The opposition had proposed the vote in protest at Amadou's refusal to testify before an inquiry into the misappropriation of education funds. A number of deputies representing movements hitherto loyal to the ruling MNSD—Nassara voted against the Government. Three days later

Tandja appointed a new Prime Minister, Seyni Oumarou, who had been Minister of State and Minister of Infrastructure in the outgoing administration. Despite complaints from opposition members that Oumarou was too closely associated with his predecessor, the new Prime Minister was officially sworn into office on 7 June and a new Council of Ministers was named two days later. Several senior ministers retained their positions in the new Government, including those responsible for the interior, foreign affairs, and the economy and finance, although new Ministers of National Defence and of Justice were appointed.

ETHNIC CONFLICT

As in neighbouring Mali, ethnic unrest was precipitated by the return to Niger, beginning in the late 1980s, of large numbers of Tuareg nomads, who had migrated to Libya and Algeria earlier in the decade to escape the drought. In May 1985, following an armed incident near the Niger–Libya border, all non-Nigerien Tuaregs were expelled from the country. In May 1990 Tuaregs launched a violent attack on the prison and gendarmerie at Tchin-Tabaraden, in north-eastern Niger. Reports suggested that the incident reflected Tuareg dissatisfaction that promises, made by Saïbou following his accession to power in 1987, regarding assistance for the rehabilitation of returnees to Niger had not been fulfilled. The alleged brutality of the armed forces in quelling the raid was to provoke considerable disquiet, both within Niger and internationally. In April 1991 44 Tuaregs were acquitted of involvement in the attack on Tchin-Tabaraden. Rebels mounted a renewed offensive in October, and in the months that followed numerous violent attacks were directed at official targets in the north, and clashes took place between Tuareg rebels and the security forces. Many arrests were reported, while Tuareg groups were known to have kidnapped several armed forces members. In early 1992 the transitional Government intensified security measures in northern Niger, formally recognizing, for the first time, that there was a rebellion in that area and acknowledging the existence of a Tuareg movement, the Front de libération de l'Aïr et l'Azaouad (FLAA). The leader of the FLAA, Rhissa Ag Boula, stated that the Tuareg rebels were seeking the establishment of a federal system, in which each ethnic group would have its own administrative entity.

A two-week truce, agreed in May 1992 by the Government and FLAA, failed. Tuareg attacks subsequently resumed, precipitating a major offensive, in August, against the rebellion. Among some 186 Tuaregs arrested, according to official figures, by September, were Mohamed Moussa (who, as Minister of the Interior, had initiated contacts with Tuareg leaders) and the prefect of Agadez. Military authority was intensified by the appointment, in October, of senior members of the security forces to northern administrative posts. In November a commission appointed by the transitional Government to consider the Tuareg issue recommended a far-reaching programme of decentralization, according legal status and financial autonomy to local communities.

In January 1993 five people were killed in a Tuareg attack on an MNSD—Nassara meeting in the northern town of Abala. Although he escaped injury, the principal target of the attack was said to have been Mamadou Tandja, who had been Minister of the Interior at the time of the suppression of the Tchin-Tabaraden raid. Although Tuareg attacks and acts of sabotage persisted, later in January 81 Tuaregs, including Mohamed Moussa, were released from detention (57 others had been released in December 1992), and a Minister of State for National Reconciliation, whose main responsibility would be to seek a resolution of the dispute, was appointed to the Government. In February 1993 30 people were reported to have been killed in raids by Tuaregs (for which the FLAA denied responsibility) around Tchin-Tabaraden.

The Ousmane administration identified the resolution of the Tuareg dispute as a major priority, and, in June 1993 a formal, three-month truce agreement, providing for the demilitarization of the north and envisaging negotiations on the Tuaregs' political demands, was signed in Paris, France. Financial assistance was promised to facilitate the return of Tuareg refugees from Algeria, and for the development of northern areas. However, a new Tuareg group, the Armée révolutionnaire de libération du nord-Niger (ARLN), emerged to denounce the accord, and by July a further split was evident between supporters of the truce (led by Mano Dayak, the Tuareg signatory to the agreement), who broke away from the FLAA to form the Front de libération de Tamoust (FLT), and its opponents (led by Ag Boula), who stated that they could not support any agreement that contained no specific commitment to discussion of federalism. In September the FLT and the Government agreed to extend the truce for a further three months. Although the FLAA and the ARLN refused to sign the accord, in October they joined the FLT in a Coordination de la résistance armée (CRA), with the aim of presenting a cohesive programme in future negotiations.

There was an escalation of violence during May 1994, as a result of which as many as 40 deaths were recorded. Negotiations reopened in Paris in June, but there was renewed unrest in August and September, including attempts by Tuaregs to disrupt power supplies to uranium mines. A grenade attack on a meeting in Agadez of the mainly Tuareg Union pour la démocratie et le progrès social—Amana (UDPS), which Tuareg groups attributed to government forces, resulted in six deaths. At a meeting in Ouagadougou, Burkina Faso, in late September, none the less, the CRA presented Nigerien government negotiators with what it termed a 'comprehensive and final' plan for a restoration of peace. Formal negotiations resumed in Ouagadougou in October, with mediation by the Burkinabè President, Blaise Compaoré, as well as representatives of France and Algeria. A new peace accord was signed on 9 October, which, while emphasizing that Niger was 'unitary and indivisible', proposed the establishment of elected assemblies or councils for territorial communities, to which would be delegated responsibility for the implementation of economic, social and cultural policies. The Government was to take immediate measures to ensure the rehabilitation and security of areas affected by the conflict. Provisions were also to be made to facilitate the return and resettlement of refugees. A renewable three-month truce was to take immediate effect, to be monitored by French and Burkinabè military units. By the time of the conclusion of the Ouagadougou agreement the number of deaths since the escalation of the Tuareg rebellion in late 1991 was officially put at 150.

In January 1995 a commission was established to consider the administrative reorganization of the country. Shortly afterwards representatives of the Nigerien Government, the CRA, Algeria, Burkina Faso and France agreed to a three-month renewal of the truce, which observers confirmed was being generally adhered to, and a further round of negotiations was scheduled to take place in Ouagadougou in March. The opening of these talks was, however, briefly delayed by a split in the Tuareg movement. Ag Boula, who in January had withdrawn from the CRA (having repeatedly criticized Dayak's negotiating stance) and refused to participate in the decentralization committee, emerged as the leader of the Tuareg delegation (now renamed the Organisation de la résistance armée, ORA) in Ouagadougou. In April it was announced that a lasting peace agreement had been reached. The accord, which essentially confirmed the provisions of the October 1994 agreement, provided for the establishment of a special peace committee, to be overseen by representatives of the three mediating countries, whose task would be to ensure the practical implementation of the accord. Demobilized rebels were to be integrated into the Nigerien military and civil sectors, and special military units were to be accorded responsibility for the security of the northern regions; particular emphasis was to be placed on the economic, social and cultural development of the north, and the Government undertook to support the decentralization process. There was to be a general amnesty for all parties involved in the Tuareg rebellion and its suppression, and a day of national reconciliation was to be instituted in memory of the victims of the conflict. The peace agreement, which envisaged the implementation of its provisions within a period of six months, was formally signed by Ag Boula and the Nigerien Government negotiator, Mai Maigana, in Niamey on 24 April 1995. A cease-fire took effect the following day.

Meanwhile, there was increasing evidence in late 1994 and early 1995 of ethnic unrest in the Lake Chad region of south-east Niger, where several thousand (mainly Toubou) Chadian refugees had settled since the overthrow of President Hissène Habré in late 1990. Clashes between settled Toubous and nomadic Peuls resulted in numerous deaths. The Front démocratique du renouveau (FDR), which emerged in October 1994 to demand increased autonomy for south-eastern regions, was believed to be responsible for many of the deaths. It was from the Lake Chad region, regarded as a major centre for weapons-trading, that one of the greatest potential obstacles to national reconciliation seemed to emerge in subsequent months.

Although the ORA expressed concern at the slow implementation of the April 1995 peace agreement, its provisions were gradually enacted: the Comité spécial de la paix (CSP) was inaugurated in May, under the chairmanship of Maigana, and a military observer group, comprising representatives of Burkina Faso and France, was deployed in the north in July. The amnesty decree was signed by Hama Amadou in July, and all Tuareg prisoners were reported to have been released shortly afterwards. The peace process was undermined following a clash in the north between Tuaregs and an Arab militia unit, as a result of which a Tuareg leader and at least 12 others were killed. Moreover, there was evidence that Dayak and other Tuareg groups in a revived CRA were making common cause with the FDR in demanding autonomy for their regions. Talks between representatives of the Tuareg movements and the FDR, which took place in northern Niger in September–October, failed either to reunite the CRA and the ORA, or to establish the principle of the FDR's adherence to the April peace accord. In October clashes in the north-east involving rebel Tuaregs and the armed forces were attributed to elements of the CRA. Dayak subsequently stated that the fragmentation of the Tuareg movement represented a major obstacle to a lasting peace, but stipulated that the CRA would not join the peace process until the authorities and the ORA recognized all groups within the CRA. In November a clash in the Tchin-Tabaraden region between government forces and a security unit of the ORA provoked tensions between the signatories to the peace agreement. In December Dayak was killed, together with two other leading CRA members, in an air crash. In January 1996 the new leader of the FLT (and acting leader of the CRA), Mohamed Akotai, indicated that his movement favoured inter-Tuareg reconciliation and a dialogue with the Government.

Following the *coup d'état* of January 1996, the CSN quickly expressed its commitment to the peace process. Maïnassara had previously been involved in the work of the CSP, and the Government, the ORA and the CRA all expressed the view that direct contacts between the military authorities and the Tuareg movements would expedite the peace process. The FDR also expressed its willingness to co-operate with the new authorities; in February, none the less, an armed assault on Dirkou by members of that movement, and an army counter-attack, resulted in 12 deaths. In March agreements were signed by the Nigerien authorities, the office of the UN High Commissioner for Refugees (UNHCR) and the Governments of Algeria and Burkina Faso regarding the repatriation of Tuareg refugees. Shortly afterwards the CRA, including the FDR, affirmed its recognition of the April 1995 agreement, and announced that it would observe a unilateral truce for one month, pending the outcome of negotiations with the authorities, and in April 1996 the Government and the CRA signed an agreement formalizing the latter's adherence to the 1995 accord. In May 1996 the ORA and the CRA agreed to establish a joint committee to co-ordinate their activities and represent their interests in negotiations with the authorities.

In July 1996 preliminary agreement was reached between the CSP and the resistance movements regarding the integration of demobilized fighters into regular military and civilian sectors, although Tuareg leaders expressed some disappointment that the number of fighters to be integrated into the army and paramilitary forces (1,400) was not greater. In September joint peace-keeping patrols of the Nigerien armed forces and former rebels were inaugurated in the north. In late September, however, Ag Boula, denouncing the inadequacy of arrangements for the reintegration of demobilized fighters, announced that the ORA was no longer bound by the peace treaty. The authorities asserted that this abandonment of the 1995 accord was linked primarily to the arrest of ORA members in connection with the diversion, some months previously, of a large consignment of cigarettes bound for the north. In an apparent gesture of reconciliation, however, the detainees were released at the end of October 1996 and the ORA surrendered the consignment to the authorities. In November it was reported that a new group had emerged from among the ORA and the CRA; led by Mohamed Anako, the Union des forces de la résistance armée (UFRA) affirmed its commitment to the peace accord. A meeting between the High Commissioner for the Restoration of Peace and 10 of the reported 12 resistance groups was followed in December by the signing of a protocol for the encampment of some 5,900 former fighters, prior to their disarmament and reintegration into regular armed forces and civilian structures. The ORA, however, remained excluded from this process.

Following a meeting in Niamey between Maïnassara and Ag Boula in early January 1997, and assurances regarding the implementation of provisions of the 1995 accord, the ORA declared its renewed support; it was announced, moreover, that the FLAA and FLT would establish a joint patrol aimed at combating insecurity and banditry. In February 1997 the UFRA joined members of the regular armed forces, the CRA and the Comité de vigilance de Tassara (CVT) in a peace-keeping patrol in Agadez. In April Maïnassara signed a decree establishing a commission, under his direct jurisdiction, charged with overseeing the process of encampment and reintegration of former fighters. Chaired by the Minister of National Defence, the commission was to include representatives of other ministries, the military and paramilitary, the High Commissioner for the Restoration of Peace, all signatories to the 1995 accord and the CVT.

Insecurity persisted in early 1997, however, particularly in the east. In June it was announced that Toubous and Arabs of the Forces armées révolutionnaires du Sahara (FARS) had, following negotiations in Chad, agreed to join the peace process. It was reported that large numbers of armed Toubous had fled to north-eastern Nigeria following the defeat of the FARS. In July the FDR announced its withdrawal from the peace process, stating that Nigerien and Chadian military units had attacked one of its bases in the Lake Chad region, although the Nigerien authorities denied that any engagement had taken place.

A further meeting of the parties to the peace process took place in September 1997, at which agreement was reached on several areas regarding the integration of former fighters into the armed and security forces. At this time, however, elements of the UFRA, apparently frustrated at the slow progress of the implementation of the peace process, had taken up arms again. Meanwhile, the FARS was held responsible by the authorities for a number of violent incidents in the east of Niger. A total of 27 deaths resulted from an armed attack on Aderbissanat, in Agadez province.

The conclusion of the disarmament process was officially celebrated in Tchin-Tabaraden in October 1997. The armed forces subsequently undertook an offensive against positions held by dissident fronts. In November, following two weeks of talks, a peace accord, incorporating an immediate cease-fire, was signed in Algeria between the Nigerien Government, the UFRA and the FARS. In March 1998 the ORA and CRA surrendered their weapons stocks at Agadez. The handover of armaments was attended by Ag Boula (who had been appointed Minister-delegate responsible for Tourism in the Government named in late 1997) and, on behalf of the CRA, Mohamed Akotai. In his new ministerial capacity, the ORA leader gave assurances of the restoration of security in the north. Voluntary repatriations of Nigerien refugees from Algeria, under the supervision of UNHCR and the Algerian Red Crescent, began in March 1998.

In April 1998 Maiyaki chaired a meeting in Niamey of the peace monitoring and implementation committee, now charged with overseeing the implementation of the April 1995 peace agreement and what was termed the November 1997 Algiers addendum protocol. In June 1998 it was reported that the last units of the UFRA had disarmed at a ceremony near Agadez. Negotiations in Chad resulted in the signing of a peace agreement in August by the Government of Niger and the FDR.

Following the death of President Maïnassara, in April 1999, the military CRN gave assurances that the peace process would be continued. Ag Boula was promoted to the rank of minister in the transitional Government, while Mohamed Anako was appointed as special adviser to Wanké. Ag Boula retained his post in the new Government of Hama Amadou, formed in January 2000. In June the final groups of fighters from the UFRA and other resistance movements participating in the peace process were disarmed near Agadez, prior to their intended integration into the national forces. In September more than 1,200 guns, surrendered by the disarmed factions, were ceremoniously burned in Agadez, in the presence of President Tandja, leaders of other West African countries and representatives of the UN. At the ceremony, Anako announced the dissolution of several of the rebel groups and militias.

In June 2001 ethnic violence between Toubou and Haussa groups in Dirkou led to two deaths and the destruction, by fire, of the market in the city. In September Chahayi Barkaye, the leader of the FARS, the only ethnic rebel group to have refused disarmament, was killed in heavy fighting with Nigerien soldiers near the Libyan border.

Ag Boula retained his ministerial post until February 2004, when he was dismissed and charged with complicity in the murder of a MNSD—Nassara activist; in order to maintain Tuareg representation in the Government, Anako was appointed as a Minister-delegate at the Ministry of the Economy and Finance. In June of that year concerns emerged of a renewed rebellion in northern Niger, following reports of attacks on vehicles in the region, the desertion of former Tuareg rebels who had been integrated into the national security forces and the declaration by some former combatants that they had reconstituted the FLAA and planned to resume hostilities. The UN imposed restrictions on the movements of its staff in the area in response to increasing insecurity, although the Nigerien Minister of the Interior and Decentralization, Albade Aboura, dismissed suggestions that a Tuareg rebellion had recommenced and rejected reports of mass desertions of former Tuareg rebels from the army, stating that the absence without leave of five soldiers had been registered. None the less, in mid-August armed men attacked three buses on the Agadez–Arlit road, killing three passengers and injuring a further 11, and in October five people died in clashes in northern Niger between government forces and apparent Tuareg rebels, who also took four soldiers hostage. Mohamed Ag Boula, the brother of Rhissa Ag Boula, claimed responsibility for the attacks, stating that he was leading an insurgent force of 200 Tuareg, Toubou and Semori nomads, who were seeking the full implementation of the 1995 peace agreement and the release of all former rebels. However, the Government insisted that the perpetrators were not rebels, describing them rather as bandits. The four soldiers were freed in late January 2005, following Libyan mediation. In early March Rhissa Ag Boula was released from prison, where he had been awaiting trial. The authorities reportedly denied Ag Boula's release was linked to that of the hostages, although Mohamed Ag Boula had previously refused to free the kidnapped soldiers while his brother remained in detention. According to reports, in July Mohamed Ag Boula surrendered weapons to the Libyan leader, Col Muammar al-Qaddafi, and around 500 former combatants of the FLAA joined the Libyan army; however, Libya denied having enlisted the former rebels. In August Rhissa Ag Boula was elected Chairman of the UDPS. An economic assistance programme for more than 3,000 former Tuareg rebels was launched in northern Niger in October. France, Libya and the USA provided funding for the project, which was to be conducted jointly by the Government and the UN Development Programme.

Following an uprising by former Tuareg rebels in Mali in May 2006, President Tandja held talks with Rhissa Ag Boula and other leading Tuaregs in June in an attempt to prevent any such unrest extending to Niger. None the less, there was evidence of continued activity by ethnic rebel groups in Niger in 2006–07. The Toubou-dominated FARS claimed responsibility for the kidnapping of more than 20 foreign tourists in south-east Niger, near the border with Chad, in August 2006. Most of the tourists were released shortly afterwards, but two were held hostage until October, when they were finally freed following Libyan mediation. A new Tuareg militia group, the Mouvement des Nigériens pour la justice (MNJ), emerged in February 2007, when it claimed responsibility for an attack on an army base near Iferouane, some 1,000 km north of Niamey, in which three soldiers were killed and two kidnapped. As with previous incidents, the Government sought to minimize the significance of the attack, blaming it on bandits rather than rebels. It was reported that the MNJ, led by Agaly Alambo, was demanding an increased role for Tuaregs in Niger's institutions and in the mining sector and a more equitable distribution of revenue from mineral resources. Meanwhile, the FARS was reported to have demanded the expulsion of a group of Chinese petroleum prospectors from the north-east of the country. In April a security guard at a French-owned uranium exploration site was killed in an attack by heavily armed men claiming to belong to the MNJ. Insecurity in northern Niger intensified in June. After mounting a largely unsuccessful raid on the airport in Agadez, the MNJ attacked a military base in Tanzerzait, claiming to have killed 15 government soldiers and captured 72 others (although the Government later stated that 13 soldiers had died and 47 been kidnapped). Meanwhile, President Tandja refused to recognize the MNJ as a rebel group, continuing to attribute the growing unrest in the north to acts of banditry perpetrated by arms- and drugs-traffickers. The International Committee of the Red Cross subsequently dispatched a team to an MNJ camp to treat wounded troops being held captive, and shortly afterwards the MNJ released some 30 injured soldiers. In late June the Government dispatched additional troops to northern Niger, while political parties, human rights groups and former Tuareg rebels urged Tandja to negotiate with the MNJ. In early July an employee of a Chinese mining company was abducted by the MNJ in Ingall, around 100 km south of Agadez, prompting the company to cease its operations in the area; the worker was released a few days later.

FOREIGN RELATIONS

Relations with the USA, which had deteriorated markedly following the 1996 presidential election and the death of Maïnassara in early 1999, appeared to improve after the reinstallation of an elected Government in January 2000, and in March the USA announced an end to the sanctions imposed after Maïnassara's death. In August President Tandja met President Bill Clinton and other US representatives in Abuja, Nigeria. In January 2003 US President George W. Bush, during the annual State of the Union address, stated that the Iraqi regime of Saddam Hussain had sought to obtain illicit supplies of uranium, for an alleged nuclear weapons programme, from an unnamed African state, which was subsequently revealed to be Niger. The Nigerien Government denied having providing any such assistance to the Iraqi authorities, and in June the Assistant to the President for National Security Affairs, Condoleezza Rice, stated that the evidence for Nigerien association with the regime of Saddam Hussain lacked credibility. In July an Italian newspaper, *La Repubblica*, published fascimilies of the documents that had apparently provided the basis for the allegations made in the State of the Union address; these documents, which contained several flaws and inaccuracies, were widely considered to be forgeries by this time.

Countries of the region with which Maïnassara had forged close relations also condemned the military take-over of April 1999: Libya notably denounced the new regime; it was reported in mid-April that Maiyaki had been made to leave a summit meeting in Libya of the Community of Sahel-Saharan States, of which Niger had been a founder member in 1997. In January 2000 President Tandja undertook an official visit to Libya and held talks Qaddafi. Qaddafi made a reciprocal visit to Agadez in July, where he pledged support for the peace process involving the Tuaregs. In January 2006 the Governments of Libya and Niger signed an agreement to co-operate in security matters.

In May 2000 a long-term dispute between Niger and Benin regarding the ownership of a number of small islands along their common border at the Niger river escalated, reportedly following the sabotage of a Beninois administrative building on the island of Lété, apparently by Nigerien soldiers. A meeting between representatives of the two Governments failed to resolve the dispute, which was subsequently referred to the Organization of African Unity (now the African Union) for arbitration. Further clashes between rival groups of farmers were reported on Lété in late August. In April 2002 the two Governments ratified an agreement (signed in June 2001) to refer the issue of ownership of the islands to the International Court of Justice (ICJ) at The Hague, Netherlands. Benin and Niger filed confidential written arguments with the Court, and in November 2003 a five-member Chamber formed to consider the case held its first public sitting. Both countries subsequently submitted counter-arguments, and each filed a third pleading in December 2004. Final submissions were presented by the two Governments at public hearings before the Chamber in March 2005. In July the Chamber of the ICJ issued its judgment on the delineation of the border between Benin and Niger, ruling that 16 of the 25 disputed islands, including Lété, belonged to Niger. Niger officially took ownership of Lété in February 2007, in a ceremony held on the island. Meanwhile, in November 2004 Nigerien traders and haulage contractors commenced a boycott of the Beninois port of Cotonou in response to the fatal shooting in the city of two Nigeriens by Beninois gendarmes in September. The boycott was ended in January 2005 following a meeting in Niamey between President Tandja and the Beninois Minister of Foreign Affairs and African Integration, Rogatien Biaou, during which Biaou announced that the Beninois Government would pay compensation to the families of the victims.

In June 2001 Niger and Nigeria announced that joint patrols of their common frontier would be instigated, in order to combat increasing cross-border crime and smuggling in the region. It was reported that the introduction of Islamic *Shari'a* law in several northern Nigerian states had been instrumental in encouraging Nigerian criminal gangs to operate from within Niger. Further concerns regarding regional security were raised in early 2004, when Islamist militants belonging to the Algerian-based Groupe salafiste pour la prédication et le combat (GSPC) reportedly attacked a group of tourists in northern Niger. In March clashes between the militants and Chadian and Nigerien troops reportedly resulted in the deaths of some 43 GSPC fighters in northern Niger. It was reported in that month that the Governments of Algeria, Chad, Mali and Niger were to reinforce security co-operation in the regions of their common borders. A further four GSPC members were reportedly killed by Nigerien troops near the Malian border in mid-April. In June the Nigerian police force announced that it had established a committee to co-ordinate joint border patrols with the security forces of Cameroon, Chad and Niger. In June 2005 Niger, Algeria, Chad, Mali and Nigeria were among nine North and West African countries that participated in US-led military exercises aimed at increasing co-operation in combating cross-border banditry and militancy in the region. At a meeting in March 2006 government officials from Mali and Niger agreed on the need to increase security at their common border. In the following month Niger's Minister of the Interior and Decentralization, Moukaïla Modi, visited Algeria to attend a two-day session of the bilateral Algeria–Niger border committee, which had first met in January 2004. In June 2006 government ministers and officials responsible for security from Benin, Burkina Faso and Niger agreed to establish border patrols in an attempt to curb cross-border crime. In early 2007 it was reported that Niger and Burkina Faso had agreed to refer a border dispute to the ICJ for arbitration.

The Government provoked controversy in October 2006 when it announced its intention to expel Mahamid Arabs from Niger and return them to Chad. The Mahamids, believed to number up to 150,000, had first crossed into Niger in large numbers in 1974 to escape severe drought conditions, and more had followed in the 1980s, fleeing conflict. Most had settled in the Diffa region, where the Government claimed they now posed a threat to security owing to their possession of firearms and poor relations with the local population. Amid protests from Chad and within Niger, most notably from legislative deputies of Arab origin, the Government insisted that only those without the correct documentation would be removed, estimating that at most 4,000 people would be affected, and subsequently suspended the expulsions altogether, stating that the Mahamids would instead be moved to regions where water and grazing land were more plentiful. However, this reversal of policy prompted demonstrations in Diffa by several thousand people opposed to the continued presence in Niger of the Mahamids.

Economy

CHARLOTTE VAILLANT

Based on an earlier article by EDITH HODGKINSON

The UN's Human Development Index, which takes into account life expectancy and conditions in health and education, has continuously ranked Niger last or second from last of all the countries surveyed. This was confirmed in the 2006 UN *Human Development Report*. Poverty is widespread and gross domestic product (GDP), at only US $240 per head (according to estimates by the World Bank) in 2005, was among the lowest in the world. The country is greatly influenced by its economic relations with its southern neighbour, Nigeria and substantial unrecorded trade, particularly the smuggling of fuel from Nigeria into Niger, flourishes across the 2,000-km border. The informal, or 'grey', economy is unusually large in Niger, and the World Bank estimates that it represents about 70% of all economic activity.

Niger's economy has lost the earlier momentum towards growth and modernization that had resulted from the development of the uranium-mining industry in the 1970s. The economy contracted in almost every year of the 1980s, owing to a combination of weakening earnings from uranium, drought and economic turmoil in neighbouring Nigeria. There was a long-term decline in international demand and prices for uranium, while the traditional rural economy remained subject to the vagaries of the Sahelian climate. It was hoped that the enhanced flows of aid and measures of debt relief that followed the devaluation of the CFA franc in January 1994 would help achieve the objectives of the development programme for 1994–96. This aimed at economic growth of 4% in 1994 and of more than 5% annually thereafter. In the event, these targets were not met, with growth in GDP averaging 3.4% per year in 1994–96. The potentially very damaging boycott by aid donors after the military coup in January 1996 came to an end relatively rapidly: the signing of an Enhanced Structural Adjustment Facility (ESAF) agreement with the IMF in June of that year was followed by pledges of funding from the World Bank, the African Development Bank (ADB), the European Union (EU), France and Japan. The programme, supported by the ESAF, aimed to achieve average annual GDP growth of 4.5% in 1997–98. Economic performance was slightly below this level (at 3.4%) in 1997, but the target was exceeded in 1998, when exceptional growth, of 10.4%, was recorded, following a recovery in agriculture. Meanwhile, the disposal of state assets accelerated, with the privatization of three state enterprises in 1998: the textiles company, Société nigérienne des textiles (SONITEXTIL); the dairy, Office du lait du Niger (OLANI); and the cement plant, Société nigérienne de cimenterie (SNC).

In March 1999 a joint mission of the World Bank and IMF reported 'significant progress' in Niger's meeting of commitments under the ESAF (which was due to expire at the end of June), raising the prospect that another such facility would be accorded, and that Niger would be declared eligible for debt reduction under the initiative for heavily indebted poor countries (HIPC). This progress was jeopardized by the presumed assassination of President Ibrahim Baré Maïnassara in April 1999 and his replacement by another military Head of State, Maj. Daouda Mallam Wanké. Niger's most important donors—France, the IMF and World Bank, and the EU—all suspended aid, and GDP declined by 0.6% in 1999. The conduct of presidential and legislative elections in October–November of that year, in polls that were deemed both fair and transparent, facilitated the resumption of aid in 2000. The new administration of President Mamadou Tandja committed itself to reinstating the programme of public-sector reform and privatization, and was successful, in December 2000, in securing a Poverty Reduction and Growth Facility (PRGF—the successor to the ESAF) equivalent to US $78m. for 2001–03. The programme had foreseen respective growth rates of 3.0% in 2000 and 3.7% in 2001. In the event, GDP declined by 1.4% in 2000, as a result of a drought in the second half of the year. In 2001 economic growth increased beyond expectations, largely as a result of a recovery in agricultural output, and as a consequence of lower fuel prices, to reach 7.1%. However, popular opposition, particularly from the trade unions, to privatization remained a significant constraint on the rapid implementation of the structural adjustment programme. Although progress in the proposed privatizations of the national electricity and petroleum distribution companies was slow, the water and telecommunications companies were transferred to private ownership by the end of 2001. Improved agricultural production and sustained activity in construction and trade supported growth of 3.0% in 2002 and 4.0% in 2003. Economic performance weakened in 2004, as a result of drought, a locust attack and higher energy prices, and the rate of growth was reduced to 0.9%. In February 2005 the IMF approved a new three-year PRGF, worth $10m., in view of the Government's overall strong policy performance. Following difficulties early in that year, when inflation surged as a result of the 2004 drought, growth in 2005 rebounded, with a good harvest recorded in the last quarter of the year. As a result, average growth accelerated to 7.0%. Growth in 2006 was still strong, at 4.8%, while inflationary pressures decreased as a result of satisfactory harvests for the second consecutive year. Growth prospects were also favourable for 2007. According to the ADB, GDP increased at an average annual rate of 3.3% in 1995–2006.

THE TRADITIONAL ECONOMY

Although only a small proportion of Niger's land is capable of supporting settled farming, agriculture, livestock, forestry and fishing contributed 44.3% of GDP in 2005, according to preliminary figures, and employed an estimated 86.5% of the working population in 2005, according to FAO. According to the ADB, the agriculture sector grew at an average annual rate of 5.2% in 1995–2006. It grew by 2.3% in 2006. Principal staple products are millet, sorghum, and cassava, all grown mainly for household consumption. Rice is also produced, on the small area that is under modern irrigation, while cow-peas, cotton, groundnuts, and onions are the principal cash crops. In 1997 cereal production was only 1.7m. metric tons, far below the national requirement (of about 2.3m. tons), because of poor weather and a desert locust invasion. Production recovered to 3.0m. tons in 1998 and 2.9m. tons in 1999, allowing stocks to replenish. A severe drought in the second half of 2000 brought output in the crop year down to 2.1m. tons. The drought continued throughout the first half of 2001, making the country critically dependent on imports and food aid. Following the return of regular rainfall later in that year, a record cereals crop, of 3.2m. tons, was recorded in 2001. Cereal output subsequently rose to a new record, of 3.3m. tons, in 2002, before declining slightly, to 3.1m. tons, in 2003, the harvests in both years reflecting improved climatic conditions. A food crisis re-emerged in 2004–05, as a result of drought and a locust invasion in 2004. Commercial purchases and food aid totalled 454,600 tons of cereals for the 2004/05 marketing year, with both the Government and the UN World Food Programme appealing for food aid. Production consequently recovered from 2.7m. tons in 2004 to 3.7m. tons in 2005. In 2006 cereal production was officially estimated at 4.1m. tons, creating a cereal surplus in the country of over 450,000 tons.

Niger's cash crops include groundnuts, cotton, cow-peas and onions. After a period of prosperity in the years following independence, cotton output fell to around 2,000–4,000 metric tons per year in the early 1990s. Production has recovered in recent years, ranging between 8,000 tons and 10,000 tons per year. In 2006 cotton output reached a record 10,700 tons. After a bumper harvest of 209,369 tons in 2003/04 (according to unofficial figures), groundnut production declined to 159,100 tons in 2004/05. Production was estimated at 126,800 tons in 2005/06. Cow-peas and onions have become profitable regional export crops, after benefiting from the impact of the 1994 devaluation. In 2003 cow-pea and onion output reached an estimated 549,035 tons and 270,000 tons, respectively. In recent years onions have become a principal export crop and source of foreign exchange, after uranium and livestock.

The most important traditional activity in Niger after crop farming is livestock-rearing, which typically accounts for more than 10% of GDP. Cattle are the second most significant export, in terms of foreign-exchange earnings, after uranium, with a significant—if largely unrecorded—trade across the border with Nigeria. In 2005 cattle accounted for an estimated 8.9% of export earnings (including re-exports), with hides and skins contributing another 11.6%. As in the rest of the region, extensive stock-rearing made appreciable progress in the years following independence, stimulated by demand from the highly-populated coastal region and Nigeria. The droughts of the 1970s and early 1980s, however, caused a sharp fall in numbers, either because of death or because of the removal of livestock to neighbouring countries, although the sector did benefit from the strong rise in foreign demand after the 1994 currency devaluation. Despite the return of better rains from the late 1980s, allowing the partial restoration of the herd, cattle stocks remain significantly below pre-drought levels. In 2004 there were an estimated 2.3m. cattle in Niger and an estimated 11.4m. sheep and goats. The 2004 drought brought new losses in stocks, however. The Government has been unable to promote either intensive commercial livestock operations or dairy farming, in part owing to Niger's ecological conditions. Like several other states in West Africa, Niger was affected by an outbreak of avian influenza in 2006.

With about 90% of cultivable land believed to have been lost to drought in the 20th century, and losses recently averaging 200,000 ha per year, the anti-desertification campaign is a priority for the Nigerien Government, and a programme of afforestation and environmental protection is proceeding. A new forestry code was adopted in June 2004. Better conservation through behavioural changes has also led to some success in recovering hundreds of thousands of hectares of forest.

MINING AND POWER

There has been renewed foreign interest in Niger's mineral resources in recent years and the mining code was updated in August 2006. The mining and export of uranium has played a very significant role in Niger's formal economy and until recently, represented a steady source of budgetary revenue and foreign-exchange earnings. In the mid-2000s Niger ranked fourth, after Canada, Australia, and Kazakhstan of the world's principal producers of uranium. Niger's uranium industry has witnessed a renaissance in recent years, owing to rising demand from the People's Republic of China. Prospecting and exploitation in the country's other mineral resources, including gold, petroleum, iron ore, copper, phosphates, coal, and salt, have been slow to pick up. Petroleum and gold have nonetheless received increased attention from foreign prospectors in recent years and gold was produced on a commercial scale for the first time in late 2004.

The mining of uranium began in 1971 at Arlit, in the desolate Aïr mountains. The Compagnie générale des matières nucléaires (COGEMA—a subsidiary of the French Government's Commissariat à l'énergie atomique) and French private interests hold a majority share in the mining company, Société des mines de l'Aïr (SOMAÏR), with the Nigerien Government's Office nationale des ressources minières du Niger (ONAREM) holding a 36.6% share. Production at the country's second uranium mine, at Akouta, was begun in 1978 by a consortium—the Compagnie minière d'Akouta (COMINAK)—of the Government, COGEMA, the Japanese Overseas Uranium Resources Development and the Spanish Empresa Nacional del Uranio. Operating costs at the mine are high, owing to the remoteness of the sites. Total uranium production by Niger reached its peak in 1981, at 4,366 metric tons. With international demand plummeting following the end of the 'Cold War' and the scaling down of nuclear-power programmes, annual production in Niger fell to an average 3,070 tons in 1990–98. Plans to increase capacity, which had hitherto been postponed indefinitely, have been revived as a result of a recovery in the world price of uranium since late 2002. The recovery in world uranium prices reflects a renewed interest in nuclear energy, not only because of concerns over CO_2 emission, but also because of electricity shortage in fast growing Asian countries, which has prompted the construction of new nuclear power plants. Production in Niger only recovered slightly to an average of 3,114 tons in 2002–05, which is roughly in line with the present capacity of COMINAK and SOMAÏR. The Government has actively awarded new uranium mining concessions to Canadian and Chinese interests since 2006, with discoveries first being announced in 2007.

In 2003 the uranium sector contributed 4.2% to government revenue (excluding grants), 45.8% of which was from royalties; compared with 40.0% in 1979. Exceptional uranium receipts totalled an estimated 30,400m. francs CFA in 2006, following the sale of prospecting licenses. Meanwhile, an increase in export prices was being renegotiated between the Government and mining companies. In 2004 export earnings from uranium totalled 78,500m. francs CFA, equivalent to 28% of total exports.

Niger's gold reserves, most of which are located in the Liptako region, near the border with Burkina Faso, have been exploited on a small scale since the early 1980s. Gold reserves are estimated at 50,000 metric tons. Canadian, Ghanaian and South African interests are all active in this sector. Production at the Samira Hill gold mine, in which Etruscan Resources and SEMAFO, of Canada, have an interest, started in September 2004. The country's gold production subsequently increased from 1,531 kg in 2004, the first year in which gold was produced commercially, to an estimated 5,300 kg in 2005. The Government expected production to increase further in the late 2000s, as other exploration projects came on line.

Coal deposits, estimated at 6m. metric tons, have been located at Anou-Anaren, to the north-west of Agadez. Annual production, which began in 1981, has generally been in the region of 160,000–200,000 tons, most of which is used for uranium processing in Arlit and Akokan. Reserves of some 30m. tons of coal deposits were discovered at Salkadamna, 600 km north-east of Niamey, in early 2006.

Deposits of petroleum, located in the south-west, were for a long time not deemed commercially exploitable. Elf Aquitaine (now Total), of France, and the US Exxon Corpn (now ExxonMobil) began seismic work in 1992 in the previously unexplored Agadem region north of Lake Chad. Reserves there have been estimated at 1m. tons. Elf Aquitaine subsequently withdrew from the project. There was a marked increase in petroleum-exploration activity in the late 1990s, with TG World Energy (of Canada) taking on a concession in the central region of Ténéré in 1997 and Hunt Oil (of the USA) starting exploratory drilling near the border with Libya in late 1999. The China National Petroleum Corporation (of the People's Republic of China) also owns an exploration permit in the Ténéré region. In January 2005 a consortium led by ExxonMobil and Petronas (of Malaysia) announced its first discovery of petroleum in Niger, less than one year after it drilled three exploratory wells in the Agadem region.

According to the most recent estimates, electricity production in Niger, which is entirely thermal, totalled 201,600 MW in 2005. As a result, a total of 339,000 MW had to be imported from hydroelectric supplies from Nigeria to cover the country's consumption needs, the major consumers being uranium companies. Access to electricity was estimated at a low 7% in 2005. Because of the unreliability of the Nigerian supply, there are long-standing plans to build a facility at Kandadji, on the Niger river. The 165-MW facility (originally proposed to be 230 MW) was expected to cost US $270m. A regional project to enhance the electricity grid connection between Burkina Faso, Niger and Nigeria, was envisaged in the medium-term. Long-standing plans to privatize the national electricity company, the Société Nigérienne d'Electricité (NIGELEC) and the petroleum distribution parastatal, Société Nigérienne des produits pétroliers (SONIDEP), were abandoned in early 2007, ostensibly owing to the lack of foreign interest. This came as a surprise, given the Government's commitment to accelerate its programme of privatization under the PRGF programme agreed for 2005–08.

MANUFACTURING

As in most other West African countries, manufacturing takes the form of the processing of agricultural commodities and import substitution. The sector contributed 6.1% of GDP in 2005, according to provisional figures. According to the ADB, the manufacturing sector grew at an average annual rate of 1.8% in 1995–2006. It grew by 3.6% in 2006. There is a groundnut oil extraction plant, as well as a brewery, cotton ginneries, rice mills, flour mills and tanneries. Import substitution has been stimulated by the very high cost of transport. A textile plant, the Entreprise Nigérienne de Textile, with output of 5.6m. metres in 2003 and a cement works, the Société Nigérienne de Cimenterie (annual capacity 60,000 metric tons), are in operation; both were transferred from state to majority private ownership in the late 1990s. There are also light industries serving the very limited local market. Activity in the sector remains predominantly small-scale and artisanal, and, in that it draws on local inputs, will have been stimulated by the currency devaluation, which made foreign manufactures correspondingly expensive. The modern sector, which is more dependent on imports, was severely affected by devaluation: several businesses closed down in 1994, with the loss of about 3,000 jobs. Similarly, the flour milling company, Les Moulins du Sahel (MDS), closed down in 1999, but resumed its operations under new ownership in 2005. The Société nigérienne des cuirs et peaux closed down in 2001, leading to a sharp contraction in hides and leather output.

TRANSPORT, TOURISM AND TELECOMMUNICATION

The transport system is still poorly developed. Road rehabilitation heavily depends on funding from the World Bank, the European Development Fund, the ADB, but also the Islamic Development Bank as well as bilaterals, including Libya, Saudi Arabia, and more recently, Algeria. In 2004 there were an estimated 14,565 km of classified roads, of which some 25% was paved. There is, at present, no railway. Long-mooted plans to extend the Cotonou–Parakou line from Benin has nonetheless recently elicited some renewed interest from India, which pledged US $500m for the 10-year construction project in 2006. Most foreign trade is shipped through Cotonou, via the Organisation Commune Bénin-Niger des Chemins de Fer et des Transports (OCBN). The emphasis in transport development is on diversifying and improving access to the seaports of Lomé, Togo, via Burkina Faso, as well as extending the Trans-Sahara Highway. There are international airports at Niamey, Agadez and Zinder, and three major domestic airports.

The development of tourism was impeded, during the 1990s, by insecurity in the north and east of the country. Tourist arrivals, however, increased from 39,190 in 1997 to 45,700 in 2000. In 2003 around 55,000 tourist arrivals were recorded in Niger, and the sector (including passenger transport) generated receipts of US $29m. Tourist arrivals increased to 63,451 in 2005, when Niger hosted the Games of La Francophonie (comprising both sporting and other cultural events).

Telecommunication in Niger has expanded with the arrival of three mobile phone and two internet service providers. The Société Nigérienne des Télécommunications (SONITEL), the national telecommunications operator established in March 1997 following the merger of telecommunication and post office parastatals, was privatized in 2001, with a majority stake being sold to Chinese and Libyan interests.

FINANCE

The fundamental problem in Nigerien public finances is the gross inadequacy of tax revenue, as successive governments have failed to bring most of the economy into the tax 'net'. Total revenues accounted for 10.5% of GDP in 2005, against a target of 17%.

The Maïnassara regime installed in early 1996 brought with it the prospect of tax increases and enforced cuts in public-sector salaries, although union opposition prevented the implementation of a planned 40% reduction in civil service pay. The programme for 1996–98, supported by ESAF funding, aimed to increase tax receipts to more than 10% of GDP in 1997. The 1997 budget envisaged a one-third reduction in the public-sector wage bill, largely through redundancies, while fiscal stability was to be improved through privatization of public utilities and divestment of some other government corporate assets. The budget deficit (on a cash basis) was reduced in 1998, to 3.2% of GDP, by accumulating arrears (notably on wages to public-sector workers), while the 1999 budget envisaged no increase in the Government's wage bill, by means of a freeze on both salaries and recruitment, and in that year the budget deficit was reduced to 15,500m. francs CFA, equivalent to only 1.2% of GDP.

The new Government of Hama Amadou, from January 2000, was confronted with a severe financial crisis, partly as a result of trade union pressure having forced the transitional Government to abandon the scheduled reduction in public-sector employment, and partly as a result of frozen foreign assistance. All payments on its domestic and external debt were suspended, pending the preparation of a new budget. Emergency funding was raised from donors in February to help meet some wage arrears. The new administration meanwhile recommitted Niger to a wide-ranging privatization programme and in March 2000, civil service reforms were pushed through, resulting in the early retirement of some 2,400 public servants. As relations with external creditors were regularized and external debt payment arrears settled, the budget deficit (on a cash basis) increased to 156,800m. francs CFA by the end of 2000, equivalent to 12.2% of GDP. The deficit narrowed in 2001, to 53,400m. francs CFA, equivalent to 4.1% of GDP, as resumed external assistance and tax reforms—notably the introduction of value-added tax—helped boost revenue. Public finances remained sound in 2002, as a result of the divestiture of the telecommunications and water utilities. In that year the budgetary deficit was 58,700m. francs CFA, equivalent to 4.1% of GDP. Tight control over spending was maintained in 2003, after the Government took some measures to compensate for a loss in revenue related to lower transfers from the Union économique et monétaire ouest-africaine and the repeated closure, during the course of the year, of the border with Nigeria. None the less, the budget deficit reduced slightly, to 51,000m. francs CFA, equivalent to 3.6% of GDP.

While fiscal performance in 2004 (a year in which both presidential and legislative elections were held) was in line with expectations, budgetary performance in 2005 was revised to account for a shortfall in domestic revenues as a result of the drought. According to the Banque centrale des états de l'Afrique de l'ouest estimates, the budget deficit (including grants) increased from 54,800m. francs CFA (3.7% of GDP) in 2004 to 69,100m. francs CFA (4.7% of GDP) in 2005, before falling to 47,000m. francs CFA in 2006 (2.7% of GDP). Continued progress was made in reducing domestic payment arrears in 2006.

Capital spending has increased significantly since 2002. In that year it amounted to 116,500m. francs CFA (41.9% of total budgetary expenditure), compared with 89,000m. francs CFA (36.1% of budgetary expenditure) in the previous year. In 2003 capital expenditure declined slightly (to 115,500m. francs CFA), but its proportion of budgetary spending increased, to 42.4%. In 2005 capital expenditure amounted to 175,400m. francs CFA. This increase is largely explained by rising external support, mostly grants and debt relief, as well as a shift from recurrent to capital expenditures, as a result of priority spending in health and education. At the same time, spending frequently remains lower than expectations, because of delays in the disbursement of external budget support and low implementation capacity at government level.

FOREIGN TRADE AND PAYMENTS

Uranium earnings were responsible for the rapid rise in export receipts in the late 1970s, and reached a peak of 100,804m. francs CFA in 1980—three times the level of 1977. The rise in uranium earnings was matched by the rise in import spending, reflecting higher petroleum prices and investment in capital equipment for the mining industry. Since 1980 the trade balance has fluctuated widely, but deficits have tended to rise over time, owing to the persistent depression in the uranium market and the severe grain shortfall in the drought years. The devaluation of the CFA franc had a very limited impact on officially recorded exports (although unrecorded earnings, from sales of livestock in particular, were thought to have risen very strongly in 1994), while the contraction in imports, because of their doubling in local-cost terms, was brief. Rising oil prices, food needs and the rising demand for capital equipment have put pressure on the import bill since 2002. This was in part compensated by the depreciation of the US dollar against the franc CFA. On the export side, the onset of armed conflict in Côte d'Ivoire in September 2002 put a temporary halt to Niger's exports in livestock and onions, until other alternative trade routes were found. Since then, stronger international prices for gold and uranium—and the beginning of commercial gold production in 2004—have improved Niger's prospects. None the less, uranium export prices have remained substantially below world prices, which, combined with upward pressures on the oil import bill, led to an increase in the trade deficit each year from 2002 to 2005; in the latter year the deficit stood at 94,800m. francs CFA, equivalent to 5.5% of GDP.

With merchandise trade normally in deficit, and the high transportation costs arising from the country's land-locked position, the current account of the balance of payments has been in persistent deficit, restricted to manageable levels only by inflows of official aid. Statistics on the current account balance vary greatly from one source to another, however. Grants from members of the Organisation for Economic Co-operation and Development and of the Organization of the Petroleum Exporting Countries averaged US $273m. per year in 1994–98, roughly equivalent to Niger's average annual export earnings. This still left the current account in deficit by an annual average of $167m. over the same period. The current-account deficit as a percentage of GDP was roughly stable in 1998–2000, at about 6.5%, despite a fall in unrequited official transfers after the 1999 coup. External assistance resumed by the end of 2000, with all donors' Overseas Development Assistance inflows totalling $257.1m. in 2001. This helped to reduce the current account deficit to 5.2% of GDP in that year. Levels of external assistance continued to rise in the ensuing years, to $298m. in 2002, $453m. in 2003 and $536m. in 2004. This has helped to compensate for higher transport costs arising from the crisis in Côte d'Ivoire and strong international petroleum prices. In 2003 the current account deficit was 98,700m. francs CFA, equivalent to 7.0% of GDP. In 2005 a current-account deficit (including grants) of 124,100m. francs CFA was recorded, equivalent to 6.3% of GDP.

External borrowing to compensate for the chronic deficit on the current account resulted in a sharp escalation in Niger's foreign debt in the late 1970s and 1980s. Meanwhile, export earnings declined, with the result that in 1982 Niger's debt service was equivalent to more than one-half of the country's foreign earnings—an unsustainable burden. Subsequent restructuring and rescheduling arrangements ensured that the debt-service ratio remained below its 1982 peak, despite the continued sharp rise in the foreign debt. However, with a debt-service ratio of 41% in 1988, Niger was classified as 'debt-distressed' by the World Bank, and hence at the December rescheduling of debt by the 'Paris Club' of official creditors, the highly concessionary 'Toronto terms' for debt relief were applied. The cancellation by France of debts of US $320m. in 1990, further 'Paris Club' rescheduling and a 'buy-back', supported by the World Bank, of $108m. in commercial debt reduced the debt-service ratio to 12% of foreign earnings by 1992.

After the devaluation of the CFA franc in January 1994 doubled the cost in local currency terms of repayment of and interest on debt, exceptional measures of debt relief were required. In March a new agreement with the 'Paris Club' rescheduled 85,000m. francs CFA in debt, and France cancelled one-half of Niger's liabilities. Another round of rescheduling on the more concessionary 'Naples terms' (which effectively allow two-thirds of eligible debt to be written off) followed agreement of the ESAF in 1996. Niger's debt remained in the region of US $1,600m. in 1995–2001. Interim debt relief under the HIPC initiative also started in 2001, following the negotiation of a PRGF, which took effect from December 2000, and the declaration of Niger's eligibility for the initiative. Under the HIPC Niger's foreign debt was to be reduced by $1,200m. in nominal terms, with $680.2m. being provided by multilateral creditors. Total debt relief was achieved in April 2004, when the country reached completion point. As a result, the 'Paris Club' agreed to cancel $160m. of Niger's debt and reschedule the remaining $90m. In June 2005 Niger was among 18 countries to be granted 100% debt relief on multilateral debt agreed by the Group of Eight leading industrialized nations (G-8), subject to the approval of the lenders. According to 2005 figures published by the World Bank, Niger's foreign debt remained broadly unchanged at $1,970m. in 2005, equivalent to 58.1% of gross national income. The country is expected to remain highly dependent on external support for the foreseeable future.

Statistical Survey

Source (unless otherwise stated): Institut national de la Statistique, Immeuble sis à la Rue Sirba, derrière la Présidence de la république, BP 720, Niamey; tel. 20-72-35-60; fax 20-72-21-74; e-mail insniger@ins.ne; internet www.stat-niger.org.

Area and Population

AREA, POPULATION AND DENSITY

Area (sq km)	1,267,000*
Population (census results)	
20 May 1988	7,248,100
20 May 2001	
Males	5,516,588
Females	5,543,703
Total	11,060,291
Population (UN estimates at mid-year)†	
2004	12,808,000
2005	13,264,000
2006	13,737,000
Density (per sq km) at mid-2006	10.8

* 489,191 sq miles.

† Source: UN, *World Population Prospects: The 2006 Revision*.

ETHNIC GROUPS
(2001 census, Nigerien citizens only)

	Population	%
Hausa	6,069,731	55.36
Djerma-Sonraï	2,300,874	20.99
Tuareg	1,016,883	9.27
Peulh	935,517	8.53
Kanouri-Manga	513,116	4.68
Toubou	42,172	0.38
Arab	40,085	0.37
Gourmantché	39,797	0.36
Others	5,951	0.05
Total	10,964,126	100.00

ADMINISTRATIVE DIVISIONS
(population at 2001 census)

Agadez	321,639	Niamey (city)	707,951
Diffa	346,595	Tahoua	1,972,729
Dosso	1,505,864	Tillabéri	1,889,515
Maradi	2,235,748	Zinder	2,080,250

PRINCIPAL TOWNS
(population at 2001 census)

Niamey (capital)	707,951	Agadez	78,289
Zinder	170,575	Tahoua	73,002
Maradi	148,017	Arlit	69,435

Mid-2005 (incl. suburbs, UN estimate): Niamey 850,000 (Source: UN, *World Urbanization Prospects: The 2005 Revision*).

BIRTHS AND DEATHS
(annual averages, UN estimates)

	1990–95	1995–2000	2000–05
Birth rate (per 1,000)	55.4	53.8	51.2
Death rate (per 1,000)	21.1	18.3	15.6

Source: UN, *World Population Prospects: The 2006 Revision*.

Expectation of life (years at birth, WHO estimates): 41 (males 42; females 41) in 2004 (Source: WHO, *World Health Report*).

EMPLOYMENT
('000 persons aged 10 years and over, 2002, official estimates)

	Males	Females	Total
Agriculture, hunting, forestry and fishing	2,366	401	2,767
Mining and quarrying	8	2	10
Manufacturing	48	64	112
Electricity, gas and water	3	0	3
Construction	20	0	20
Trade, restaurants and hotels	149	197	346
Transport, storage and communications	21	0	21
Financing, insurance, real estate and business services	2	0	2
Community, social and personal services	149	46	195
Total	2,766	710	3,476

2001 census (persons aged 10 years and over): Total employed 4,015,951 (males 2,706,910, females 1,309,041), Unemployed 64,987 (males 49,437, females 15,550); Economically active population 4,080,938 (males 2,756,347, females 1,324,591).

Mid-2005 (estimates in '000): Agriculture, etc. 5,635; Total labour force 6,515 (Source: FAO).

Health and Welfare

KEY INDICATORS

Total fertility rate (children per woman, 2005)	7.7
Under-5 mortality rate (per 1,000 live births, 2005)	256
HIV/AIDS (% of persons aged 15–49, 2005)	1.1
Physicians (per 1,000 head, 2004)	0.03
Hospital beds (per 1,000 head, 1998)	0.12
Health expenditure (2004): US $ per head (PPP)	25.9
Health expenditure (2004): % of GDP	4.2
Health expenditure (2004): public (% of total)	52.5
Access to water (% of persons, 2004)	47
Access to sanitation (% of persons, 2004)	13
Human Development Index (2004): ranking	177
Human Development Index (2004): value	0.311

For sources and definitions, see explanatory note on p. vi.

Agriculture

PRINCIPAL CROPS
('000 metric tons)

	2003	2004	2005
Wheat	3.5	9.0*	9.0*
Rice (paddy)	69.3	80.0	60.0
Maize†	2	4	1
Millet	2,745	2,038	2,652
Sorghum	758	600	944
Potatoes†	4.2	4.2	4.2
Sweet potatoes†	30	30	30
Cassava (Manioc)†	100	100	100
Sugar cane†	220	220	220
Dry cow-peas	549.0*	339.5	586.1
Other pulses†	22.2	22.3	22.2
Groundnuts (in shell)	385.6	159.0	139.1
Sesame seed†	22	22	22
Cottonseed†	10	10	10
Cabbages†	120	120	120
Lettuce and chicory†	40	40	40
Tomatoes†	132	100	100
Chillies and green peppers†	17	17	17
Dry onions†	359	270	322
Garlic†	8	8	8
Green beans†	23	23	23
Carrots†	18	18	18
Dates†	7.8	7.8	7.8
Tobacco (leaves)	1.0†	0.9*	1.0†

* Unofficial figure.
† FAO estimate(s).

Source: FAO.

LIVESTOCK
('000 head, year ending September, FAO estimates)

	2001	2002	2003
Cattle	2,260	2,260	2,260
Sheep	4,500	4,500	4,500
Goats	6,900	6,900	6,900
Pigs	39	40	40
Horses	105	105	106
Asses	580	580	580
Camels	415	415	420
Chickens	24,000	24,500	25,000

2004–05: Figures assumed to be unchanged from 2003 (FAO estimates).

Source: FAO.

LIVESTOCK PRODUCTS
('000 metric tons, FAO estimates)

	2002	2003	2004
Game meat	15	15	15
Horse meat	0.6	0.7	0.7
Other equine meat	1.6	1.8	1.8
Chicken meat	28.4	29.0	29.0
Hen eggs	10.6	10.6	10.6

2005: Figures assumed to be unchanged from 2004 (FAO estimates).

Source: FAO.

Forestry

ROUNDWOOD REMOVALS
('000 cubic metres, excl. bark, FAO estimates)

	2003	2004	2005
Industrial wood	411	411	411
Fuel wood	8,391	8,596	8,806
Total	8,802	9,007	9,217

Source: FAO.

SAWNWOOD PRODUCTION
('000 cubic metres, incl. railway sleepers, FAO estimates)

	1991	1992	1993
Total (all broadleaved)	0	1	4

1994–2005: Figures assumed to be unchanged from 1993 (FAO estimates).

Source: FAO.

Fishing

(metric tons, live weight)

	2003	2004	2005
Capture (freshwater fishes)	55,860	51,466	50,018
Aquaculture	40	40	40
Total catch	55,900	51,506	50,058

Source: FAO.

Mining

('000 metric tons, unless otherwise indicated)

	2003	2004	2005
Hard coal	188.9	200.4	182.1
Tin (metric tons)*†	5	4	14
Uranium (metric tons)*	3,143	3,273	3,093
Gold (kg)	34.0†	1,531.3	4,922
Gypsum	17.8†	34.9	17.4

* Data refer to the metal content of ore.
† Artisanal production only.

Industry

SELECTED PRODUCTS

('000 metric tons, unless otherwise indicated)

	2003	2004	2005
Raw sugar ('000 metric tons)*	22.0	n.a.	n.a.
Cement	63.7	59.2	83.4
Soap	10.4	10.2	9.4
Textile fabrics (million metres)	5.6	4.0	2.0
Beer ('000 bottles)	116.5	103.5	94.9
Electric energy (million kWh)	45.8	n.a.	n.a.

* FAO estimates.

Source: mostly IMF, *Niger: Selected Issues and Statistical Appendix* (January 2007).

Finance

CURRENCY AND EXCHANGE RATES

Monetary Units

100 centimes = 1 franc de la Communauté financière africaine (CFA).

Sterling, Dollar and Euro Equivalents (31 May 2007)

£1 sterling = 964.116 francs CFA;
US $1 = 487.592 francs CFA;
€1 = 655.957 francs CFA;
10,000 francs CFA = £10.37 = $20.51 = €15.24.

Average Exchange Rate (francs CFA per US $)

2004 528.285
2005 527.468
2006 522.890

Note: An exchange rate of 1 French franc = 50 francs CFA, established in 1948, remained in force until January 1994, when the CFA franc was devalued by 50%, with the exchange rate adjusted to 1 French franc = 100 francs CFA. This relationship to French currency remained in effect with the introduction of the euro on 1 January 1999. From that date, accordingly, a fixed exchange rate of €1 = 655.957 francs CFA has been in operation.

BUDGET

('000 million francs CFA, estimates)

Revenue*	2004	2005	2006
Tax revenue	167.6	181.3	203.8
Non-tax revenue	1.4	4.9	38.5
Annexed budgets and special accounts	3.9	2.8	4.9
Statistical discrepancy	1.1	—	—
Total	173.8	189.0	247.2

Expenditure†	2004	2005	2006
Current expenditure	172.7	165.3	174.2
Wages and salaries	59.2	63.0	68.0
Materials and supplies	50.3	43.6	47.4
Subsidies and transfers	38.2	31.9	43.5
Interest	8.1	10.1	4.9
Capital expenditure	144.0	193.3	182.6
Total	316.7	358.6	356.8

* Excluding grants received ('000 million francs CFA, estimates): 89.2 in 2004; 134.1 in 2005; 878.4 in 2006.

† Excluding net lending ('000 million francs CFA): 0.9 in 2004; –0.2 in 2005; 0.0 in 2006.

Source: IMF, *Niger: Fourth Review Under the Three-Year Arrangement Under the Poverty Reduction and Growth Facility, and Request for Waiver and Modification of Performance Criteria - Staff Report; Staff Statement and Supplements; Press Release on the Executive Board Discussion; and Statement by the Executive Director for Niger* (July 2007).

INTERNATIONAL RESERVES

(US $ million at 31 December, excl. gold)

	2004	2005	2006
IMF special drawing rights	0.9	0.3	0.1
Reserve position in IMF	13.3	12.3	13.0
Foreign exchange	243.7	236.9	357.8
Total	258.0	249.5	370.9

Source: IMF, *International Financial Statistics*.

MONEY SUPPLY

('000 million francs CFA at 31 December)

	2004	2005	2006
Currency outside banks	96.8	108.1	133.1
Demand deposits at deposit money banks*	81.8	81.4	90.0
Checking deposits at post office	3.2	2.5	1.8
Total money (incl. others)*	181.9	192.2	225.4

* Excluding the deposits of public enterprises of an administrative or social nature.

Source: IMF, *International Financial Statistics*.

COST OF LIVING

(Consumer Price Index for Niamey, annual averages; base: 2000 = 100)

	2003	2004	2005
Food	106.7	105.1	120.7
Clothing	101.1	99.4	102.6
Rent	103.9	105.3	106.2
All items (incl. others)	105.1	105.2	113.5

Source: ILO.

NATIONAL ACCOUNTS

Expenditure on the Gross Domestic Product

(US $ million at current prices)

	2004	2005	2006
Government final consumption expenditure	498.41	485.50	521.33
Household final consumption expenditure	2,193.04	2,507.15	2,656.68
Gross capital formation	409.95	608.80	592.03
Total domestic expenditure	3,101.40	3,601.45	3,770.04
Exports of goods and services	530.11	672.84	684.79
Less Imports of goods and services	851.96	1,047.65	1,051.23
GDP in market prices	2,779.55	3,226.64	3,403.60

Source: African Development Bank.

Gross Domestic Product by Economic Activity
('000 million francs CFA at current prices)

	2003	2004	2005*
Agriculture, hunting, forestry and fishing	614.3	561.9	708.7
Mining and quarrying	29.7	30.8	37.8
Manufacturing	90.5	93.6	97.8
Electricity, gas and water supply	19.2	18.0	19.2
Construction	36.3	39.3	43.7
Wholesale and retail trade; repair of motor vehicles, motorcycles and personal and household goods	174.1	180.4	192.6
Hotels and restaurants	19.9	22.0	23.6
Transport, storage and communication	79.5	87.0	95.5
Posts and telecommunications	11.2	13.9	18.1
Financial activities	12.7	15.8	22.4
Real estate, renting and business activities	137.4	151.9	169.7
Public administration and defence; compulsory social security	154.9	162.5	170.8
Sub-total	1,379.7	1,377.1	1,599.9
Less Financial intermediation services indirectly measured	11.1	12.7	16.2
Gross value added in basic prices	1,368.6	1,364.4	1,583.7
Taxes, *less* subsidies, on products	97.7	110.5	127.8
GDP at market prices	1,466.3	1,474.9	1,711.5
GDP at constant 1987 prices	1,047.1	1,040.9	1,114.9

* Provisional figures.

BALANCE OF PAYMENTS
('000 million francs CFA)

	2003	2004	2005
Exports of goods f.o.b.	204.5	230.7	304.1
Imports of goods f.o.b.	–283.9	–311.5	–398.9
Trade balance	–79.4	–80.8	–94.8
Services (net)	–75.1	–89.2	–102.9
Balance on goods and services	–154.5	–170.0	–197.7
Income (net)	–15.2	–6.8	–7.6
Balance on goods, services and income	–169.7	–176.8	–205.3
Private unrequited transfers (net)	9.7	16.2	18.0
Public unrequited transfers (net)	32.9	38.6	63.2
Current balance	–127.1	–122.0	–124.1
Capital account (net)	46.3	203.1	71.8
Direct investment (net)	6.7	7.0	7.8
Portfolio investment (net)	1.5	2.5	14.5
Other investment (net)	38.2	–91.3	50.5
Net errors and omissions	69.5	–9.6	–9.0
Overall balance	42.5	–10.3	11.5

Source: Banque centrale des états de l'Afrique de l'ouest.

External Trade

PRINCIPAL COMMODITIES
(distribution by SITC, US $ million)

Imports c.i.f.	2001	2002	2003
Food and live animals	105.8	113.7	123.9
Dairy products and birds' eggs	11.2	11.9	13.2
Milk and cream	10.8	11.6	12.8
Milk and cream, preserved, concentrated or sweetened	10.6	11.4	12.5
Cereals and cereal preparations	60.4	66.8	59.1
Rice, semi-milled or wholly milled	39.4	47.5	37.7
Rice, semi-milled or milled (unbroken)	38.2	47.5	36.5
Meal of flour of wheat or of meslin	11.2	12.7	13.0
Flour of wheat or of meslin	11.2	12.7	10.9
Sugar, sugar preparations and honey	14.1	11.3	24.8
Refined sugar, etc.	13.5	10.5	23.6
Beverages and tobacco	15.2	20.6	22.0
Cigarettes	13.3	19.2	19.5
Crude materials (inedible) except fuel	9.8	18.2	30.9
Textile fibres (not wool tops) and their wastes (not in yarn)	2.2	10.6	21.4
Bulk textile waste, old clothing, traded in bulk or in bales	1.9	10.4	20.8
Mineral fuels, lubricants, etc., (incl. electric current)	40.7	59.2	94.5
Petroleum, petroleum products, etc.	32.7	48.6	80.9
Petroleum products, refined	32.5	46.4	76.3
Animal and vegetable oils, fats and waxes	22.3	29.4	41.1
Fixed vegetable oils and fats	21.2	27.8	38.1
Palm oil	16.4	23.0	32.6
Chemicals and related products	29.5	36.9	45.2
Medicinal and pharmaceutical products	9.3	12.0	16.7
Basic manufactures	34.5	56.8	67.1
Textile yarn, fabrics, made-up articles, etc.	6.6	19.7	21.2
Cotton fabrics, woven (not incl. narrow or special fabrics)	3.1	15.0	16.5
Machinery and transport equipment	48.7	76.1	109.6
Telecommunications, sound recording and reproducing equipment	3.6	15.3	22.9
Other telecommunications equipment, parts and accessories, etc.	2.8	14.6	21.8
Electrical line telephonic and telegraphic apparatus	1.1	13.1	18.3
Road vehicles	20.9	25.1	38.0
Passenger motor vehicles (excl. buses)	12.7	13.5	17.7
Miscellaneous manufactured articles	18.0	20.1	24.1
Total (incl. others)	324.5	430.9	558.4

Exports f.o.b.	2001	2002	2003
Food and live animals	61.3	71.6	58.9
Live animals chiefly for food	43.8	39.0	40.8
Animals of the bovine species (incl. buffaloes), live	16.0	13.5	16.7
Sheep and goats, live	22.4	19.0	18.5
Fish, crustaceans and molluscs, and preparations thereof	4.3	6.3	4.1
Vegetables and fruit	12.2	24.7	12.3
Vegetables, fresh or simply preserved; roots and tubers	11.4	23.8	11.8
Other fresh or chilled vegetables	8.4	21.2	9.3
Alliaceous vegetables, fresh or chilled	5.8	18.0	7.7
Beverages and tobacco	0.1	9.8	5.2
Cigarettes	—	9.7	4.8
Crude materials (inedible) except fuels	88.2	98.8	124.0
Textile fibres (not wool tops) and their wastes (not in yarn)	0.3	6.8	7.3
Ores and concentrates of uranium and thorium	86.2	90.2	113.0
Basic manufactures	1.3	12.3	12.6
Fabrics, woven, 85% plus of cotton, bleached, dyed, etc., or otherwise finished	0.5	11.4	11.8
Total (incl. others)	154.0	200.9	209.1

Source: UN, *International Trade Statistics Yearbook*.

PRINCIPAL TRADING PARTNERS
(US $ million)

Imports c.i.f.	2001	2002	2003
Bahrain	2.9	10.7	7.2
Belgium	3.6	5.9	8.1
Benin	6.3	9.8	14.7
Brazil	2.5	8.3	17.1
Burkina Faso	7.7	4.8	11.1
China, People's Republic	20.9	39.2	52.4
Côte d'Ivoire	47.3	64.2	74.6
France	62.2	67.2	81.6
Germany	4.3	5.8	10.2
Ghana	6.4	8.1	8.1
India	1.7	17.5	18.0
Italy	4.7	7.3	6.5
Japan	15.6	20.5	25.1
Netherlands	5.3	12.2	12.2
Nigeria	33.3	30.5	40.3
South Africa	1.8	2.5	25.4
Spain	2.6	4.6	8.1
Togo	8.7	13.5	15.2
Tunisia	4.0	7.8	9.5
United Kingdom	7.1	11.5	17.5
USA	18.9	36.1	46.0
Total (incl. others)	324.5	430.9	558.4

Exports f.o.b.	2001	2002	2003
Algeria	0.3	0.6	0.5
Benin	1.7	5.1	2.2
Burkina Faso	0.8	1.0	1.5
Chad	0.6	0.1	0.1
China, People's Republic	—	0.2	0.1
Côte d'Ivoire	2.3	7.0	5.5
France (incl. Monaco)	56.2	65.1	76.3
Germany	0.1	0.1	0.2
Ghana	1.9	9.0	3.9
Japan	25.4	23.4	31.1
Libya	0.2	0.7	1.3
Mali	0.2	0.2	0.2
Netherlands	—	1.1	3.9

Exports f.o.b.—*continued*	2001	2002	2003
Nigeria	57.1	64.4	57.5
South Africa	—	—	0.7
Spain	5.8	6.1	8.4
Switzerland-Liechtenstein	0.2	0.1	0.1
Togo	0.1	1.1	0.3
United Arab Emirates	—	—	0.7
United Kingdom	—	1.5	2.6
USA	0.5	13.1	9.5
Venezuela	—	0.6	—
Total (incl. others)	154.0	200.9	209.1

Source: UN, *International Trade Statistics Yearbook*.

Transport

ROAD TRAFFIC
(estimates, motor vehicles in use)

	1994	1995	1996
Passenger cars	38,610	37,620	38,220
Lorries and vans	13,160	14,100	15,200

Source: IRF, *World Road Statistics*.

CIVIL AVIATION
(traffic on scheduled services)*

	1999	2000	2001
Kilometres flown (million)	3	3	1
Passengers carried ('000)	84	77	46
Passenger-km (million)	235	216	130
Total ton-km (million)	36	32	19

* Including an apportionment of the traffic of Air Afrique.

Source: UN, *Statistical Yearbook*.

Tourism

FOREIGN TOURIST ARRIVALS BY ORIGIN*

	2003†	2004†	2005
Africa	37,000	38,000	37,926
America	2,000	2,500	3,150
Asia	1,400	1,500	2,835
Europe	14,000	14,500	17,649
France	11,000	12,000	14,588
Total (incl. others)	55,000	57,000	63,451

* Figures refer to arrivals at national borders.
† Rounded figures.

Receipts from tourism (US $ million, incl. passenger transport): 29 in 2003.

Source: World Tourism Organization.

Communications Media

	2003	2004	2005
Telephones ('000 main lines in use)	23.0	24.1	24.0
Mobile cellular telephones ('000 subscribers)	59.3	148.3	299.9
Personal computers ('000 in use)*	8	9	10
Internet users ('000)*	19.0	24.0	24.0

* Estimates.

Television receivers ('000 in use): 395 in 2000.

Radio receivers ('000 in use): 680 in 1997.

Facsimile machines (number in use): 327 in 1995.

Daily newspapers: 1 (average circulation 2,000 copies) in 1996; 1 (average circulation 2,000 copies) in 1997; 1 (average circulation 2,000 copies) in 1998.

Non-daily newspapers: 5 (average circulation 14,000 copies) in 1996.

Books published (first editions): titles 5; copies ('000) 11 in 1991.

Sources: UNESCO, *Statistical Yearbook*; UNESCO Institute for Statistics; UN, *Statistical Yearbook*; International Telecommunication Union.

Education

(2004/05)

	Institutions	Teachers	Students
Pre-primary	307	839	19,597
Primary	8,301	24,091	1,064,056
Secondary	410	6,144	177,033
Tertiary	7	278	4,953
University	1	287	7,374

Adult literacy rate (UNESCO estimates): 14.4% (males 19.6%; females 9.4%) in 2003 (Source: UN Development Programme, *Human Development Report*).

Directory

The Constitution

Following the death of President Ibrahim Baré Maïnassara, on 9 April 1999, a military Conseil de réconciliation nationale (CRN) was formed to exercise executive and legislative authority during a transitional period prior to the restoration of elected organs of government. A new Constitution, of what was to be designated the Fifth Republic, was approved by national referendum on 18 July 1999. The Constitution of the Fifth Republic, promulgated on 9 August, envisages a balance of powers between the President, Government and legislative Assemblée nationale. The President, who is elected by universal adult suffrage, is Head of State, and is accorded 'broad ordinary and arbitral powers'. The Government, under a Prime Minister appointed by the President, is responsible to the Assemblée nationale, which is competent to remove the Prime Minister by vote of censure. The Assemblée nationale is similarly elected by direct adult suffrage. The new President and legislature were inaugurated in December 1999.

Enshrined in the Constitution is a clause granting immunity from prosecution for all those involved in the *coups d'état* of January 1996 and April 1999. Legislation to this effect was adopted by the Assemblée nationale in January 2000.

Among regulatory bodies provided for in the Constitution are the Conseil supérieur de la communication, responsible for the broadcasting and communications sector, and the Conseil supérieur de la défense nationale, which advises the Head of State on defence matters.

The Government

HEAD OF STATE

President: Col (retd) Mamadou Tandja (inaugurated 22 December 1999, re-elected 4 December 2004).

COUNCIL OF MINISTERS

(August 2007)

Prime Minister: Seyni Oumarou.

Minister of State, Minister of the Interior: Albadé Abouba.

Minister of Foreign Affairs, Co-operation and African Integration: Aïchatou Mindaoudou.

Minister of the Economy and Finance: Ali Mahamane Lamine Zeine.

Minister of Agricultural Development: Mahaman Moussa.

Minister of Youth and Sports: Moussa Abdourahamane Seydou.

Minister of Town Planning, Living Conditions and the Land Register: Aïssa Diallo Abdoulaye.

Minister of Mines and Energy: Mohamed Abdoulahi.

Minister of Secondary and Higher Education, Research and Technology: Prof. Sidikou Oumarou.

Minister of Communication, Spokesperson for the Government: Mohamed Ben Omar.

Minister of the Civil Service and Labour: Kanda Siptey.

Minister of Culture, the Arts and Leisure, responsible for the Promotion of Entrepreneurship in the Arts: Oumarou Hadary.

Minister of Population and Social Reform: Boukari Zila Mahamadou.

Minister of National Education: Dr Ousmane Samba Mamadou.

Minister responsible for Relations with State Institutions: Salifou Madou Kelzou.

Minister of the Environment and Anti-desertification: Mohamed Akotey.

Minister of National Competitiveness and the Reduction of the High Cost of Living: Abdou Daouda.

Minister responsible for Religious Affairs and Humanitarian Action: Labo Issaka.

Minister of Infrastructure: Lamido Moumouni Harouna.

Minister of Trade, Industry and Normalization: Halidou Badje.

Minister of National Defence: Jidda Hamadou.

Minister of Justice, Attorney-General: Dagra Mahamadou.

Minister of Transport: Kindo Hamani.

Minister of Tourism and Crafts: Amadou Aissa Siddo.

Minister of Land Management and Community Development: Sadé Souley.

Minister of Public Health: Issa Lamine.

Minister of Animal Resources: Issiah Kato.

Minister for the Promotion of Young Entrepreneurs and the Reform of Public Enterprises: Salou Gobi.

Minister of Vocational and Technical Training: Maizama Hadiza.

Minister for the Promotion of Women and the Protection of Children: Barry Bibata Niandou.

Minister of African Integration and Nationals Living Abroad: Seydou Hachimou.

Minister of Water Resources: Aminou Tassiou.

MINISTRIES

Office of the President: BP 550, Niamey; tel. 20-72-23-80; fax 20-72-33-96; internet www.delgi.ne/presidence.

Office of the Prime Minister: BP 893, Niamey; tel. 20-72-26-99; fax 20-73-58-59.

Ministry of Agricultural Development: BP 12091, Niamey; tel. 20-73-35-41; fax 20-73-20-08.

Ministry of Animal Resources: BP 12091, Niamey; tel. 20-73-79-59; fax 20-73-31-86.

Ministry of Basic Education and Literacy: BP 557, Niamey; tel. 20-72-28-33; fax 20-72-21-05; e-mail scdameb@intnet.ne.

Ministry of Capital Works: BP 403, Niamey; tel. 20-73-53-57; fax 20-72-21-71.

Ministry of the Civil Service and Labour: BP 11107, Niamey; tel. 20-73-22-31; fax 20-73-61-69; e-mail sani.yakouba@caramail.com.

Ministry of Culture, the Arts and Communication: BP 452, Niamey; tel. 20-72-28-74; fax 20-73-36-85.

Ministry of the Economy and Finance: BP 389, Niamey; tel. 20-72-23-74; fax 20-73-59-34.

Ministry of Foreign Affairs, Co-operation and African Integration: BP 396, Niamey; tel. 20-72-29-07; fax 20-73-52-31.

Ministry of the Interior and Decentralization: BP 622, Niamey; tel. 20-72-32-62; fax 20-72-21-76.

Ministry of Justice: BP 466, Niamey; tel. 20-72-31-31; fax 20-72-37-77.

Ministry of Land Management and Community Development: BP 403, Niamey; tel. 20-73-53-57; fax 20-72-21-71.

Ministry of Mines and Energy: BP 11700, Niamey; tel. 20-73-45-82; fax 20-73-28-12.

Ministry of National Defence: BP 626, Niamey; tel. 20-72-20-76; fax 20-72-40-78.

Ministry of Population and Social Reform: BP 11286, Niamey; tel. 20-72-23-30; fax 20-73-61-65.

Ministry of Privatization and the Restructuring of Enterprises: Immeuble CCCP, BP 862, Niamey; tel. 20-73-27-50; fax 20-73-59-91; e-mail ccpp@intnet.ne.

Ministry of Professional and Technical Training: BP 628, Niamey; tel. 20-72-26-20; fax 20-72-40-40.

Ministry for the Promotion of Women and the Protection of Children: BP 11286, Niamey; tel. 20-72-23-30; fax 20-73-61-65.

Ministry of Public Health and the Fight against Epidemics: BP 623, Niamey; tel. 20-72-28-08; fax 20-73-35-70.

Ministry of Secondary and Higher Education, Research and Technology: BP 628, Niamey; tel. 20-72-26-20; fax 20-72-40-40; e-mail mesnt@intnet.ne.

Ministry of Tourism and Crafts: BP 480, Niamey; tel. 20-73-65-22; fax 20-72-23-87.

Ministry of Town Planning, Living Conditions and the Land Register: BP 403, Niamey; tel. 20-73-53-57; fax 20-72-21-71.

Ministry of Trade, Industry and the Promotion of the Private Sector: BP 480, Niamey; tel. 20-73-29-74; fax 20-73-21-50; e-mail nicom@intnet.ne.

Ministry of Transport: BP 12130, Niamey; tel. 20-72-28-21; fax 20-73-36-85.

Ministry of Water Resources, the Environment and Anti-desertification: BP 257, Niamey; tel. 20-73-47-22; fax 20-72-40-15.

Ministry of Youth, Sports and the Games of La Francophonie: BP 215, Niamey; tel. 20-72-32-35; fax 20-72-23-36.

President and Legislature

PRESIDENT

Presidential Election, First Round, 16 November 2004

Candidate	Votes	% of votes
Mamadou Tandja (MNSD—Nassara)	991,764	40.67
Mahamadou Issoufou (PNDS)	599,792	24.60
Mahamane Ousmane (CDS)	425,052	17.43
Cheiffou Amadou (RSD)	154,732	6.34
Moumouni Adamou Djermakoye (ANDP)	147,957	6.07
Hamid Algabid (RDP)	119,153	4.89
Total	2,438,450	100.00

Second Round, 4 December 2004

Candidate	Votes	% of votes
Mamadou Tandja (MNSD—Nassara)	1,509,905	65.53
Mahamadou Issoufou (PNDS)	794,397	34.47
Total	2,304,302	100.00

LEGISLATURE

Assemblée nationale

pl. de la Concertation, BP 12234, Niamey; tel. 20-72-27-38; fax 20-72-43-08; e-mail webmestre@assemblee.ne; internet www.assemblee.ne.

President: El Hadj MAHAMANE OUSMANE.

General Election, 4 December 2004

Party	Seats
Mouvement national pour la société de développement—Nassara (MNSD—Nassara)	47
Parti nigérien pour la démocratie et le socialisme—Tarayya (PNDS)	25*
Convention démocratique et social—Rahama (CDS)	22
Rassemblement social-démocratique—Gaskiya (RSD)	7
Rassemblement pour la démocratie et le progrès—Jama'a (RDP)	6
Alliance nigérienne pour la démocratie et le progrès social—Zaman Lahiya (ANDP)	5
Parti Social Démocrate du Niger—Alheri	1
Total	113

* Including eight seats won by parties running in coalition with the PNDS, namely the Parti nigérien pour l'autogestion (PNA), the Parti progressiste nigérien pour le rassemblement démocratique africain (PPN—RDA), the Union pour la démocratie et la République (UDR) and the Union nigérienne des indépendants (UNI).

Election Commission

Commission électorale nationale indépendante (CENI): Niamey; Chair. HAMIDOU SALIFOU KANE.

Political Organizations

In mid-2007 there were some 24 political parties registered in Niger, of which the following were among the most prominent:

Alliance nigérienne pour la démocratie et le progrès social—Zaman Lahiya (ANDP): Quartier Abidjan, Niamey; tel. 20-74-07-50; fmrly mem. of opposition Coordination des forces démocratiques (CFD); joined pro-Govt Alliance des forces démocratiques (AFD) in 2002; Leader Col (retd) MOUMOUNI ADAMOU DJERMAKOYE.

Alliance pour la démocratie et le progrès—Zuminci (ADP): Niamey; Chair. ISSOUFOU BACHAR.

Convention démocratique et social—Rahama (CDS): BP 11973, Niamey; tel. 20-74-19-85; f. 1991; supports Govt of Hama Amadou; mem. of Alliance des forces démocratiques (AFD); Pres. MAHAMANE OUSMANE.

Mouvement national pour la société de développement—Nassara (MNSD—Nassara): rue Issa Beri 30, cnr blvd de Zarmaganda, porte 72, BP 881, Niamey; tel. 20-73-39-07; fax 20-72-41-74; e-mail presi@mnsd-nassara.org; internet www.mnsd.ne; f. 1988; sole party 1988–90; restyled as MNSD—Nassara in 1991; Chair. Col (retd) MAMADOU TANDJA; Pres. HAMA AMADOU.

Parti nigérien pour l'autogestion—al Umat (PNA): Quartier Zabarkian, Niamey; tel. 20-72-33-05; f. 1997; contested legislative elections in Dec. 2004 in coalition with the PNDS; Leader SANOUSSI JACKOU.

Parti nigérien pour la démocratie et le socialisme—Tarayya (PNDS): pl. Toumo, Niamey; tel. 20-74-48-78; f. 1990; mem. of Coordination des forces démocratiques (CFD); Sec.-Gen. MAHAMADOU ISSOUFOU.

Parti progressiste nigérien—Rassemblement démocratique africain (PPN—RDA): Quartier Sonni, Niamey; tel. 20-74-16-70; associated with the late Pres. Diori; mem. of Coordination des forces démocratiques (CFD); contested legislative elections in Dec. 2004 in coalition with the PNDS; Chair. ABDOULAYE DIORI.

Parti social-démocrate nigérien—Alheri (PSDN): Leader KAZELMA OUMAR TAYA.

Rassemblement pour la démocratie et le progrès—Djamaa (RDP): pl. Toumo, Niamey; tel. 20-74-23-82; party of late Pres. Maïnassara; Chair. HAMID ALGABID; Sec.-Gen. MAHAMANE SOULEY LABI.

Rassemblement social-démocratique—Gaskiya (RSD): Quartier Poudrière, Niamey; tel. 20-74-00-90; f. 2004 following split in the CDS; Pres. CHEIFFOU AMADOU.

Rassemblement pour un Sahel vert—Ni'ima (RSV): BP 12515, Niamey; tel. and fax 20-74-11-25; e-mail agarba_99@yahoo.com; f. 1991; Pres. ADAMOU GARBA.

Union pour la démocratie et le progrès—Amici (UDP): supports Govt of Hama Amadou; mem. of Alliance des forces démocratiques (AFD); Leader ABDOULAYE TONDI.

Union pour la démocratie et le progrès social—Amana (UDPS): represents interests of Tuaregs; mem. of Coordination des forces démocratiques (CFD); Chair. RHISSA AG BOULA.

Union pour la démocratie et la République—Tabbat (UDR): Quartier Plateau, Niamey; f. 2002; contested legislative elections in Dec. 2004 in coalition with the PNDS; Pres. AMADOU BOUABACAR CISSÉ.

Union des forces populaires pour la démocratie et le progrès—Sawaba (UFPDP): Niamey.

Union des Nigeriens indépendants (UNI): Quartier Zabarkan, Niamey; tel. 20-74-23-81; contested legislative elections in Dec. 2004 in coalition with the PNDS; Leader AMADOU DJIBO.

Union des patriotes démocratiques et progressistes—Shamuwa (UPDP): Niamey; tel. 20-74-12-59; Chair. Prof. ANDRÉ SALIFOU.

Union des socialistes nigériens—Talaka (USN): f. 2001 by mems of the UFPDP; Leader ISSOUFOU ASSOUMANE.

In March 2001 12 opposition parties, led by the PNDS, formed the **Coordination des forces démocratiques (CFD)** (Zabarkan, rue du SNEN, BP 5005, Niamey; tel. 20-74-05-69), while 17 parties loyal to Prime Minister Hama Amadou, headed by the MNSD, formed the **Alliance des forces démocratiques (AFD)**. In July 2002 the ANDP withdrew from the CFD and joined the AFD.

Diplomatic Representation

EMBASSIES IN NIGER

Algeria: route des Ambassades-Goudel, BP 142, Niamey; tel. 20-72-35-83; fax 20-72-35-93; Ambassador HAMID BOUKRIF.

Benin: BP 11544, Niamey; tel. 20-72-28-60; Ambassador TAÏROU MAMADOU DJAOUGA.

Chad: Niamey; tel. 20-77-34-64; fax 20-72-43-61; Ambassador ALI ABDOULAYE SABRE.

China, People's Republic: BP 873, Niamey; tel. 20-72-32-83; fax 20-72-32-85; e-mail embchina@intnet.ne; Ambassador CHEN GONGLAI.

Cuba: rue Tillaberi, angle rue de la Cure Salée, face lycée Franco-Arabe, Plateau, BP 13886, Niamey; tel. 20-72-46-00; fax 20-72-39-32; e-mail embacuba@niger.cubaminrex.cu; Ambassador SERAFIN GIL RODRÍGUEZ VALDÉS.

Egypt: Terminus Rond-Point Grand Hôtel, BP 254, Niamey; tel. 20-73-33-55; fax 20-73-38-91; Ambassador MOHAMED MAHMOUD MOUSTAFA EL-ASHMAWI.

France: route de Tondibia, Quartier Yantala, BP 10660, Niamey; tel. 20-72-24-32; fax 20-72-25-18; e-mail webmestre@mail.com; internet www.ambafrance-ne.org; Ambassador FRANÇOIS PONGE.

Germany: 71 ave du Général de Gaulle, BP 629, Niamey; tel. 20-72-35-10; fax 20-72-39-85; e-mail amballny@intnet.ne; Ambassador HEIKE THIELE.

Iran: 11 rue de la Présidence, BP 10543, Niamey; tel. 20-72-21-98; fax 20-72-28-10; Ambassador MOHAMMAD AMIN NEJAD.

Korea, Democratic People's Republic: Niamey; Ambassador PAK SONG IL.

Libya: route de Goudel, BP 683, Niamey; tel. 20-72-40-19; fax 20-72-40-97; e-mail boukhari@intnet.ne; Ambassador BOUKHARI SALEM HODA.

Morocco: ave du Président Lubke, face Clinique Kaba, BP 12403, Niamey; tel. 20-73-40-84; fax 20-73-80-27; e-mail ambmang@intnet.ne; Ambassador MOHAMED JABER.

Nigeria: rue Goudel, BP 11130, Niamey; tel. 20-73-24-10; fax 20-73-35-00; e-mail embnig@intnet.ne; Ambassador Dr YAKUBU KWARI.

Pakistan: 90 rue YN 001, ave des Zarmakoye, Yantala Plateau, BP 10426, Niamey; tel. 20-75-32-57; fax 20-75-32-55; e-mail parepniamey@yahoo.com; internet www.brain.net.pk/~farata; Ambassador (vacant).

Saudi Arabia: route de Tillabery, BP 339, Niamey; tel. 20-75-32-15; fax 20-75-24-42; e-mail neemb@mofa.gov.sa; Ambassador ABDUL KAREEM MOHAMMAD AL MALIKI.

USA: rue des Ambassades, BP 11201, Niamey; tel. 20-73-31-69; fax 20-73-55-60; e-mail NiameyPASN@state.gov; internet niamey.usembassy.gov; Ambassador BERNADETTE MARY ALLEN.

Judicial System

The Supreme Court was dissolved following the death of President Ibrahim Baré Maïnassara in April 1999, but was re-established following the return to constitutional order later in that year. In accordance with the Constitution of the Fifth Republic, promulgated in August 1999, a Constitutional Court was established to replace the former Constitutional Chamber of the Supreme Court.

High Court of Justice: Niamey; internet www.assemblee.ne/organes/hjc.htm; competent to indict the President of the Republic and all other state officials (past and present) in relation to all matters of state, including high treason; comprises seven perm. mems and three rotating mems; Pres. OUMAROU CISSE.

Supreme Court: Niamey; tel. 20-74-26-36; comprises three chambers; in 2002 the Government announced proposals to replace the Supreme Court with three separate courts: a Court of Cassation, a Council of State and an Audit Court; Pres. MAMADOU MALLAM AOUMI; Vice-Pres. SALIFOU FATIMATA BAZEYE; Pres. of the Administrative Chamber DILLE RABO; Pres. of the Judicial Chamber (vacant); Pres. of the Chamber of Audit and Budgetary Discipline SIKKOSO MORY OUSMANE; Prosecutor-Gen. MAHAMANE BOUKARY.

Constitutional Court: BP 10779, Niamey; tel. 20-72-30-81; fax 20-72-35-40; e-mail cconstit@intnet.ne; f. 1999; comprises a President, a Vice-President and five Councillors; Pres. SANI KOUTOUBI; Vice-Pres. ABDOU HASSAN.

Courts of First Instance: located at Niamey (with sub-divisions at Dosso and Tillabéri), Maradi, Tahoua (sub-divisions at Agadez, Arlit and Birni N'Konni) and Diffa (sub-division at Diffa).

Labour Courts: function at each Court of the First Instance and sub-division thereof.

Religion

It is estimated that some 95% of the population are Muslims, 0.5% are Christians and the remainder follow traditional beliefs.

ISLAM

The most influential Islamic groups in Niger are the Tijaniyya, the Senoussi and the Hamallists.

Association Islamique du Niger: Niamey; Dir CHEIKH OUMAROU ISMAEL.

CHRISTIANITY

Various Protestant missions maintain 13 centres, with a personnel of 90.

The Roman Catholic Church

Niger comprises two dioceses, directly responsible to the Holy See. The Bishops participate in the Bishops' Conference of Burkina Faso and Niger (based in Ouagadougou, Burkina Faso). At 31 December 2004 there were an estimated 16,490 adherents in Niger.

Bishop of Maradi: Rt Rev. AMBROISE OUÉDRAOGO, Evêché, BP 447, Maradi; tel. and fax 20-41-03-30; e-mail ambroiseoued@yahoo.fr.

Bishop of Niamey: Rt Rev. MICHEL CHRISTIAN CARTATÊGUY, Evêché, BP 10270, Niamey; tel. 20-73-32-59; fax 20-73-80-01; e-mail cartateguymi@voila.fr; internet www.multimania.com/cathoniger.

The Press

The published press expanded considerably in Niger after 1993, when the requirement to obtain prior authorization for each edition was lifted, although legislation continued to require that a copy of each publication be deposited at the office of the Procurator of the Republic. For the most part, however, economic difficulties have ensured that few publications have maintained a regular, sustained appearance. The following were among those newspapers and periodicals believed to be appearing regularly in early 2005:

L'Action: Quartier Yantala, Niamey; tel. 96-96-92-22; e-mail action_ne@yahoo.fr; internet www.tamtaminfo.com/action.pdf; f. 2003; fortnightly; popular newspaper intended for youth audience; Dir of Publication BOUSSADA BEN ALI; circ. 2,000 (2003).

L'Alternative: BP 10948, Niamey; tel. 20-74-24-39; fax 20-74-24-82; e-mail alter@intnet.ne; internet www.alternative.ne; f. 1994; weekly; in French and Hausa; Dir MOUSSA TCHANGARI; Editor-in-Chief ABDRAMANE OUSMANE.

Anfani: Immeuble DMK, rue du Damagaram, BP 2096, Niamey; tel. 20-74-08-80; fax 20-74-00-52; e-mail anfani@intnet.ne; f. 1992; 2 a month; Editor-in-Chief IBBO DADDY ABDOULAYE; circ. 3,000.

As-Salam: BP 451, Niamey; tel. 20-74-29-12; e-mail assa_lam@yahoo.fr; monthly; Dir IBBO DADDY ABDOULAYE.

Le Canard Déchainé: BP 383, Niamey; tel. 93-92-66-64; satirical; weekly; Dir of Publication ABDOULAYE TIÉMOGO; Editor-in-Chief IBRAHIM MANZO.

Le Canard Libéré: BP 11631, Niamey; tel. 20-75-43-52; fax 20-75-39-89; e-mail canardlibere@caramail.com; satirical; weekly; Dir of Publication TRAORÉ DAOUDA AMADOU; Editorial Dir OUMAROU NALAN MOUSSA.

Le Démocrate: 21 rue 067, NB Terminus, BP 11064, Niamey; tel. 20-73-24-25; e-mail le_democrate@caramail.com; internet www.tamtaminfo.com/democrate.pdf; weekly; independent; f. 1992; Dir of Publication ALBERT CHAÏBOU; Editor-in-Chief OUSSEINI ISSA.

Les Echos du Sahel: Villa 4012, 105 Logements, BP 12750, Niamey; tel. and fax 20-74-32-17; e-mail ecosahel@intnet.ne; f. 1999; rural issues and devt; quarterly; Dir IBBO DADDY ABDOULAYE.

L'Enquêteur: BP 172, Niamey; tel. 93-90-18-74; e-mail lenqueteur@yahoo.fr; fortnightly; Publr TAHIROU GOURO; Editor IBRAHIM SOULEY.

Haské: BP 297, Niamey; tel. 20-74-18-44; fax 20-73-20-06; e-mail webmaster@planetafrique.com; internet www.haske.uni.cc; f. 1990; weekly; also Haské Magazine, quarterly; Dir CHEIKH IBRAHIM DIOP.

La Jeune Académie: BP 11989, Niamey; tel. 20-73-38-71; e-mail jeune.academie@caramail.com; monthly; Dir ABDOULAYE HASSOUMI GARBA.

Journal Officiel de la République du Niger: BP 116, Niamey; tel. 20-72-39-30; fax 20-72-39-43; f. 1960; fortnightly; govt bulletin; Man. Editor BONKOULA AMINATOU MAYAKI; circ. 800.

Libération: BP 10483, Niamey; tel. 96-97-96-22; f. 1995; weekly; Dir BOUBACAR DIALLO; circ. 1,000 (2003).

Matinfo: BP 11631, Niamey; tel. 20-75-43-52; fax 20-75-39-89; e-mail matinfo@caramail.com; daily; independent; Dir DAOUDA AMADOU TRAORÉ.

Nigerama: BP 11158, Niamey; tel. 20-74-08-09; e-mail anpniger@intnet.ne; quarterly; publ. by the Agence Nigérienne de Presse.

L'Opinion: BP 11116, Niamey; tel. 20-74-09-84; e-mail lopinion@dounia.ne; Dir ALZOUMA ZAKARI.

Le Regard: Niamey; tel. 20-73-84-07; e-mail le_regard@usa.net; Dir MAHAMADOU TOURÉ.

Le Républicain: Nouvelle Imprimerie du Niger, place du Petit Marché, BP 12015, Niamey; tel. 20-73-47-98; fax 20-73-41-42; e-mail webmasters@republicain-niger.com; internet www.republicain-niger.com; f. 1991; weekly; independent; Dir of Publication MAMANE ABOU; circ. 2,500.

La Roue de l'Histoire: Zabarkan, rue du SNEN, BP 5005, Niamey; tel. 20-74-05-69; internet www.tamtaminfo.com/roue.pdf; weekly; Propr SANOUSSI JACKOU; Dir ABARAD MOUDOUR ZAKARA.

Le Sahel Quotidien: BP 13182, ONEP, Niamey; tel. 20-73-34-87; fax 20-73-30-90; f. 1960; publ. by Office National d'Edition et de Presse; daily; Dir IBRAHIM MAMANE TANTAN; Editor-in-Chief ALASSANE ASOKOFARE; circ. 5,000; also Sahel-Dimanche, Sundays; circ. 3,000.

Sauyi: BP 10948, Niamey; tel. 20-74-24-39; fax 20-74-24-82; e-mail sarji@alternative.ne; fortnightly; Hausa; publ. by Groupe Alternative; Hausa; rural interest; Dir SAÏDOU ARJI.

Stadium: BP 10948, Niamey; tel. 20-74-08-80; e-mail kiabba@yahoo.fr; sports; 2 a month; Dir ABDOU TIKIRÉ.

Le Témoin: BP 10483, Niamey; tel. 96-96-58-51; e-mail istemoin@yahoo.fr; internet www.tamtaminfo.com/temoin.pdf; 2 a month; Dir of Publication IBRAHIM SOUMANA GAOH; Editors AMADOU TIÉMOGO, MOUSSA DAN TCHOUKOU, I. S. GAOH; circ. 1,000 (2005).

Ténéré Express: BP 13600, Niamey; tel. 20-73-35-76; fax 20-73-77-75; e-mail tenerefm@intnet.ne; daily; independent; current affairs; Dir ABDOULAYE MOUSSA MASSALATCHI.

La Tribune du Peuple: Niamey; tel. 20-73-34-28; e-mail tribune@intnet.ne; f. 1993; weekly; Man. Editor IBRAHIM HAMIDOU.

Le Trophée: BP 2000, Niamey; tel. 20-74-12-79; e-mail strophee@caramail.com; sports; 2 a month; Dir ISSA HAMIDOU MAYAKI.

NEWS AGENCIES

Agence Nigérienne de Presse (ANP): BP 11158, Niamey; tel. 20-74-08-09; e-mail anpniger@intnet.ne; f. 1987; state-owned; Dir YAYE HASSANE.

Sahel—Office National d'Edition et de Presse (ONEP): BP 13182, Niamey; tel. 20-73-34-86; f. 1989; Dir ALI OUSSEÏNI.

Publishers

La Nouvelle Imprimerie du Niger (NIN): pl. du Petit Marché, BP 61, Niamey; tel. 20-73-47-98; fax 20-73-41-42; e-mail nin@intnet.ne; f. 1962 as Imprimerie Nationale du Niger; govt publishing house; brs in Agadez and Maradi; Dir E. WOHLRAB.

Réseau Sahélien de Recherche et de Publication: Niamey; tel. 20-73-36-90; fax 20-73-39-43; e-mail resadep@ilimi.uam.ne; press of the Université Abdou Moumouni; Co-ordinator BOUREIMA DIADIE.

Broadcasting and Communications

REGULATORY AUTHORITY

Conseil Supérieur de la Communication (CSC): Plateau, Niamey; tel. 20-72-23-56; comprises 15 mems; Pres. MARIAMA KEÏTA.

TELECOMMUNICATIONS

Celtel Niger: Route de l'Aéroport, BP 11922, Niamey; tel. 20-73-23-46; fax 20-73-23-85; e-mail b-sghir@intnet.ne; internet www.ne.celtel.com; f. 2001 to operate mobile cellular telecommunications network in Niamey and Maradi; 70% owned by Celtel International (United Kingdom), 30% owned by Caren Assurance; Dir-Gen. COLIN CAMPBELL.

Société Nigérienne des Télécommunications (SONITEL): BP 208, Niamey; tel. 20-72-20-00; fax 20-73-58-12; e-mail sonitel@intnet.ne; internet www.intnet.ne; f. 1998; 51% jtly owned by ZTE Corpn (People's Republic of China) and Laaico (Libya), 46% state-owned; Dir-Gen. MOUSSA BOUBACAR.

Sahel Com: BP 208, Niamey; f. 2002; mobile cellular telecommunications in Niamey.

Telecel Niger: Niamey; tel. 20-74-44-44; e-mail telecel@telecelniger.com; internet www.telecelniger.com; f. 2001 to operate mobile cellular telecommunications network, initially in Niamey and western regions, expanding to cover Maradi and Zinder by 2003, and Tahoua and Agadez by 2004; 68% owned by Orascom Telecom (Egypt); Dir HIMA SOULEY.

BROADCASTING

Radio

Independent radio stations have been permitted to operate since 1994, although the majority are concentrated in the capital, Niamey. In 2000 the first of a network of rural stations, RURANET, which were to broadcast mainly programmes concerned with development issues, mostly in national languages, was established. Several local radio stations, funded by the Agence intergouvernementale de la francophonie, were expected to commence operations in the early 2000s.

Anfani FM: blvd Nali-Béro, BP 2096, Wadata, Niamey; tel. 20-74-08-80; fax 20-74-00-52; e-mail anfani@intnet.ne; private radio station, broadcasting to Niamey, Zinder, Maradi and Diffa; Dir ISMAËL MOUTARI.

Office de Radiodiffusion-Télévision du Niger (ORTN): BP 309, Niamey; tel. 20-72-31-63; fax 20-72-35-48; state broadcasting authority; Dir-Gen. YAYÉ HAROUNA.

La Voix du Sahel: BP 361, Niamey; tel. 20-72-22-02; fax 72-35-48; e-mail ortny@intnet.ne; f. 1958; govt-controlled radio service; programmes in French, Hausa, Djerma, Kanuri, Fulfuldé, Tamajak, Toubou, Gourmantché, Boudouma and Arabic; Dir IBRO NA-ALLAH AMADOU.

Ténéré FM: BP 13600, Niamey; tel. 20-73-65-76; fax 20-73-46-94; e-mail tenerefm@intnet.ne; f. 1998; Dir ABIBOU GARBA; Editor-in-Chief SOULEYMANE ISSA MAÏGA.

Ruranet: Niamey; internet membres.lycos.fr/nigeradio; f. 2000; network of rural radio stations, broadcasting 80% in national languages, with 80% of programmes concerned with devt issues; 31 stations operative in April 2002.

La Voix de l'Hémicycle: BP 12234, Niamey; f. 2002 as the radio station of the Assemblée nationale; broadcasts parliamentary debates and analysis for 15 hours daily in French and national languages to Niamey and environs.

Sudan FM: Dosso; auth. 2000; private radio station; Dir HIMA ADAMOU.

Television

Office de Radiodiffusion-Télévision du Niger (ORTN): see Radio

Télé-Sahel: BP 309, Niamey; tel. 20-72-31-55; fax 20-72-35-48; govt-controlled television service; broadcasts daily from 13 transmission posts and six retransmission posts, covering most of Niger; Dir-Gen. ABDOU SOULEY.

Télévision Ténéré (TTV): BP 13600, Niamey; tel. 20-73-65-76; fax 20-73-77-75; e-mail tenerefm@intnet.ne; f. 2000; independent broadcaster in Niamey; Dir ABIBOU GARBA.

The independent operator, Télé Star, broadcasts several international or foreign channels in Niamey and environs, including TV5 Monde, Canal Horizon, CFI, RTL9, CNN and Euro News.

Finance

(cap. = capital; res = reserves; dep. = deposits; m. = million; brs = branches; amounts in francs CFA)

BANKING

Central Bank

Banque centrale des états de l'Afrique de l'ouest (BCEAO): BP 487, Niamey; tel. 20-72-24-91; fax 20-73-47-43; HQ in Dakar, Senegal; f. 1962; bank of issue for the mem. states of the Union économique et monétaire ouest-africaine (UEMOA, comprising Benin, Burkina Faso, Côte d'Ivoire, Guinea-Bissau, Mali, Niger, Senegal and Togo); cap. and res 859,313m., total assets 5,671,675m. (Dec. 2002); Gov. DAMO JUSTIN BARO (acting); Dir in Niger ABDOULAYE SOUMANA; brs at Maradi and Zinder.

Commercial Banks

Bank of Africa—Niger (BOA-Niger): Immeuble BOA, rue du Gaureye, BP 10973, Niamey; tel. 20-73-36-20; fax 20-73-38-18; e-mail information@boaniger.com; internet www.bank-of-africa.net; f. 1994 to acquire assets of Nigeria International Bank Niamey; 42.6% owned by African Financial Holding; cap. 1,500m., res 1,097m., total assets 39,755m. (Dec. 2005); Pres. PAUL DERREUMAUX; Dir-Gen. MAMADOU SÉNÉ; 2 brs.

Banque Commerciale du Niger (BCN): Rond-Point Maourey, BP 11363, Niamey; tel. 20-73-39-15; fax 20-73-21-63; f. 1978; 83.15% owned by Libyan Arab Foreign Bank, 16.85% state-owned; cap. and res 1,477m., total assets 14,618m. (Dec. 2003); Administrator IBRAHIM MAJDOUB NAJI (acting).

Banque Internationale pour l'Afrique au Niger (BIA—Niger): ave de la Mairie, BP 10350, Niamey; tel. 20-73-31-01; fax 20-73-35-95; e-mail bia@intnet.ne; internet www.bianiger.com; f. 1980; 35% owned by Groupe Belgolaise (Belgium); cap. 2,800m., res 1,905m., dep. 58,108m. (Dec. 2005); Pres. AMADOU HIMA SOULEY; Dir-Gen. DANIEL HASSER; 11 brs.

Banque Islamique du Niger pour le Commerce et l'Investissement (BINCI): Immeuble El Nasr, BP 12754, Niamey; tel. 20-73-27-30; fax 20-73-47-35; e-mail binci@intnet.ne; f. 1983; fmrly Banque Masraf Faisal Islami; 33% owned by Dar al-Maal al-Islami (Switzerland), 33% by Islamic Development Bank (Saudi Arabia); cap. 1,810m., total assets 7,453m. (Dec. 2003); Pres. ABDERRAOUF BENESSAÏAH; Dir-Gen. AISSANI OMAR.

Ecobank Niger: blvd de la Liberté, angle rue des Bâtisseurs, BP 13804, Niamey; tel. 20-73-71-81; fax 20-73-72-04; e-mail ecobankni@ecobank.com; internet www.ecobank.com; f. 1999; 59.4% owned by Ecobank Transnational Inc. (Togo, operating under the auspices of the Economic Community of West African States), 28.6% by Ecobank Benin, 11.9% by Ecobank Togo; total assets 38,256m. (Dec. 2005); Chair. MAHAMADOU OUHOUMOUDOU; Dir-Gen. FELIX BIKPO.

Société Nigérienne de Banque (SONIBANK): ave de la Mairie, BP 891, Niamey; tel. 20-73-45-69; fax 20-73-46-93; e-mail sonibank@intnet.ne; f. 1990; 25% owned by Société Tunisienne de Banque; cap. 2,000m., res 5,124m., dep. 43,216m. (Dec. 2005); Pres. ILLA KANÉ; 6 brs.

Development Banks

Caisse de Prêts aux Collectivités Territoriales (CPCT): route Torodi, BP 730, Niamey; tel. 20-72-34-12; fax 20-72-30-80; f. 1970; 100% state-owned (94% by organs of local govt); cap. and res 744m., total assets 2,541m. (Dec. 2003); Administrator ABDOU DJIBO (acting).

Crédit du Niger (CDN): 11 blvd de la République, BP 213, Niger; tel. 20-72-27-01; fax 20-72-23-90; e-mail cdb-nig@intnet.ne; f. 1958; 54% state-owned, 20% owned by Caisse Nationale de Sécurité Sociale; transfer to full private ownership pending; cap. and res 1,058m., total assets 3,602m. (Dec. 2003); Administrator ABDOU DJIBO (acting).

Fonds d'Intervention en Faveur des Petites et Moyennes Entreprises Nigériennes (FIPMEN): Immeuble Sonara II, BP 252, Niamey; tel. 20-73-20-98; f. 1990; state-owned; cap. and res 124m. (Dec. 1991); Chair. AMADOU SALLA HASSANE; Man. Dir IBRAHIM BEIDARI.

Savings Bank

Office National de la Poste et de l'Epargne: BP 11778, Niamey; tel. 20-73-24-98; fax 20-73-35-69; fmrly Caisse Nationale d'Epargne; Chair. Mme PALFI; Man. Dir HASSOUME MATA.

STOCK EXCHANGE

Bourse Régionale des Valeurs Mobilières (BRVM): c/o Chambre de Commerce et d'Industrie du Niger, Place de la Concertation, BP 13299, Niamey; tel. 20-73-66-92; fax 20-73-69-47; e-mail imagagi@brvm.org; internet www.brvm.org; f. 1998; national branch of BRVM (regional stock exchange based in Abidjan, Côte d'Ivoire, serving the member states of UEMOA); Man. IDRISSA S. MAGAGI.

INSURANCE

Agence d'Assurance du Sahel: BP 10661, Niamey; tel. 20-74-05-47.

Agence Nigérienne d'Assurances (ANA): pl. de la Mairie, BP 423, Niamey; tel. 20-72-20-71; f. 1959; cap. 1.5m.; owned by L'Union des Assurances de Paris; Dir JEAN LASCAUD.

Caren Assurance: BP 733, Niamey; tel. 20-73-34-70; fax 20-73-24-93; e-mail carenas@intnet.ne; insurance and reinsurance; Dir-Gen. IBRAHIM IDI ANGO.

Leyma—Société Nigérienne d'Assurances et de Réassurances (SNAR—Leyma): BP 426, Niamey; tel. 20-73-57-72; fax 20-73-40-44; f. 1973; restructured 2001; Pres. AMADOU HIMA SOULEY; Dir-Gen. GARBA ABDOURAHAMANE.

La Nigérienne d'Assurance et de Réassurance: BP 13300, Niamey; tel. 20-73-63-36; fax 20-73-73-37.

Union Générale des Assurances du Niger (UGAN): rue de Kalley, BP 11935, Niamey; tel. 20-73-54-06; fax 20-73-41-85; f. 1985; cap. 500m.; Pres. PATHÉ DIONE; Dir-Gen. MAMADOU TALATA; 7 brs.

Trade and Industry

GOVERNMENT AGENCIES

Cellule de Coordination de la Programme de Privatisation: Immeuble Sonibanque, BP 862, Niamey; tel. 20-73-29-10; fax 20-73-29-58; responsible for co-ordination of privatization programme; Coordinator IDÉ ISSOUFOU.

Office des Eaux du Sous-Sol (OFEDES): BP 734, Niamey; tel. 20-74-01-19; fax 20-74-16-68; govt agency for the maintenance and devt of wells and boreholes; Pres. DJIBO HAMANI.

Office du Lait du Niger (OLANI): BP 404, Niamey; tel. 20-73-23-69; fax 20-73-36-74; f. 1971; devt and marketing of milk products; transferred to majority private ownership in 1998; Dir-Gen. M. DIENG.

Office National de l'Energie Solaire (ONERSOL): BP 621, Niamey; tel. 20-73-45-05; govt agency for research and devt, commercial production and exploitation of solar devices; Dir ALBERT WRIGHT.

Office National des Ressources Minières du Niger (ONAREM): Rond-Point Kennedy, BP 12716, Niamey; tel. 20-73-59-28; fax 20-73-28-12; f. 1976; govt agency for exploration, exploitation and marketing of all minerals; Pres. MOUDY MOHAMED; Dir-Gen. A. A. ASKIA.

Office des Produits Vivriers du Niger (OPVN): BP 474, Niamey; tel. 20-73-44-43; fax 20-74-27-18; govt agency for developing agricultural and food production; Dir-Gen. M. ISSAKA.

Riz du Niger (RINI): BP 476, Niamey; tel. 20-71-13-29; fax 20-73-42-04; f. 1967; cap. 825m. francs CFA; 30% state-owned; transfer to 100% private ownership proposed; production and marketing of rice; Pres. YAYA MADOUGOU; Dir-Gen. M. HAROUNA.

DEVELOPMENT ORGANIZATIONS

Agence Française de Développement (AFD): 203 ave du Gountou-Yéna, BP 212, Niamey; tel. 20-72-33-93; fax 20-72-26-05; e-mail afdniamey@groupe-afd.org; internet www.afd.fr; Country Dir FRANÇOIS GIOVALUCCHI.

Mission Française de Coopération et d'Action Culturelle: BP 494, Niamey; tel. 20-72-20-66; administers bilateral aid from France; Dir JEAN BOULOGNE.

SNV (Société Néerlandais de Développement): ave des Zarmakoye, BP 10110, Niamey; tel. 20-75-36-33; fax 20-75-35-06; e-mail snvniger@snv.ne; internet www.snv.ne; present in Niger since 1978; projects concerning food security, agriculture, the environment, savings and credit, marketing, water and communications; operations in Tillabéri, Zinder and Tahoua provinces.

CHAMBERS OF COMMERCE

Chambre de Commerce d'Agriculture, d'Industrie et d'Artisanat du Niger: BP 209, Niamey; tel. 20-73-22-10; fax 20-73-46-68; e-mail cham209n@intnet.ne; internet www.ccaian.org; BP 201, Agadez; tel. 20-44-01-61; BP 91, Diffa; tel. 20-54-03-92; BP 79,

Maradi; tel. 20-41-03-76; BP 172, Tahoua; tel. 20-61-03-84; BP 83, Zinder; tel. 20-51-00-78; f. 1954; comprises 80 full mems and 40 dep. mems; Pres. IBRAHIM IDI ANGO; Sec.-Gen. SADOU AISSATA.

INDUSTRIAL AND TRADE ORGANIZATIONS

Centre Nigérien du Commerce Extérieur (CNCE): pl. de la Concertation, BP 12480, Niamey; tel. 20-73-22-88; fax 20-73-46-68; f. 1984; promotes and co-ordinates all aspects of foreign trade; Dir AÏSSA DIALLO.

Société Nationale de Commerce et de Production du Niger (COPRO-Niger): Niamey; tel. 20-73-28-41; fax 20-73-57-71; f. 1962; monopoly importer of foodstuffs; cap. 1,000m. francs CFA; 47% state-owned; Man. Dir DJIBRILLA HIMA.

EMPLOYERS' ORGANIZATIONS

Syndicat des Commerçants Importateurs et Exportateurs du Niger (SCIMPEXNI): Chambre de Commerce, d'Agriculture, d'Industrie et d'Artisanat du Niger, Niamey; tel. 20-73-33-17; Pres. M. SILVA; Sec.-Gen. INOUSSA MAÏGA.

Syndicat National des Petites et Moyennes Entreprises et Industries Nigériennes (SYNAPEMEIN): Chambre de Commerce, d'Agriculture, d'Industrie et d'Artisanat du Niger, Niamey; Pres. SEYBOU SLAEY; Sec.-Gen. ADOLPHE SAGBO.

Syndicat Patronal des Entreprises et Industries du Niger (SPEIN): BP 415, Niamey; tel. 20-73-24-01; fax 20-73-47-07; f. 1994; Pres. AMADOU OUSMANE; Sec.-Gen. NOUHOU TARI.

UTILITIES

Electricity

Société Nigérienne d'Electricité (NIGELEC): 46 ave du Gen. de Gaulle, BP 11202, Niamey; tel. 20-72-26-92; fax 20-72-32-88; e-mail nigelec@intnet.ne; f. 1968; 95% state-owned; 51% transfer to private ownership proposed; production and distribution of electricity; Dir-Gen. IBRAHIM FOUKORI.

Water

Société d'Exploitation des Eaux du Niger (SEEN): blvd Zarmaganda, BP 12209, Niamey; tel. 20-72-25-00; fax 20-73-46-40; fmrly Société Nationale des Eaux; 51% owned by Veolia Environnement (France); production and distribution of drinking water; Pres. ABARY DAN BOUZOUA SOULEYMENE; Dir-Gen. SEYNI SALOU.

MAJOR COMPANIES

The following are among the largest companies in terms of either capital investment or employment.

Compagnie Minière d'Akouta (COMINAK): Immeuble Sonora, rond-point Kennedy, BP 10545, Niamey; tel. 20-73-45-86; fax 20-73-28-55; f. 1974; 34% owned by Areva NC (France), 31% by ONAREM (Niger govt), 25% by Overseas Uranium Resources Development (Japan), 10% by Enusa Industrias Avanzadas (Spain); mining and processing of uranium at Akouta; cap. 3,500m. francs CFA; sales €66.3m. (2000); Chair. El Hadj ALLELE HABIBOU; 1,054 employees (2002).

Entreprise Nigérienne de Textile (ENITEX): route de Kolo, BP 10735, Niamey; tel. 20-73-25-11; f. 1997; cap. 1,000m. francs CFA; textile complex at Niamey; fmrly Société Nouvelle Nigérienne des Textiles (SONITEXTIL); 80% owned by China Worldbest Group (People's Rep. of China), 20% by Nigerien interests; sales 2,300m. francs CFA (2005); Chair. SAIDOU MAMANE; Man. Dir ROGER HUBER; 920 employees (2002).

Les Moulins du Sahel (MDS): Route de Kalmaharo, BP 12710, Niamey; tel. 20-74-26-07; fax 20-74-26-19; milling of flour; operations (suspended in 1999) resumed in 2005; Dir-Gen. IBRAHIM BOLHO; 25 employees (2005).

Office National des Produits Pharmaceutiques et Chimiques (ONPPC): BP 11585, Niamey; tel. 20-74-27-92; fax 20-74-26-34; e-mail onppc@intnet.ne; f. 1962; cap. 440m. francs CFA; state-owned; Dir HAMIDOU HAROUNDA.

Société des Brasseries et Boissons Gazeuses du Niger (BRANIGER): BP 11245, Niamey; tel. 20-74-26-83; fax 20-74-29-48; e-mail braniger@intnet.ne; f. 1967; cap. 1,428m. francs CFA; mfrs of beer and other soft drinks; Chair. JEAN-CLAUDE PALU; Dir XAVIER DE BRABANDÈRE; 125 employees (2005).

Société des Mines de l'Aïr (SOMAÏR): BP 10545, Niamey; tel. 20-72-29-70; fax 20-72-51-13; f. 1971; cap. 4,349m. francs CFA; 56.9% owned by Areva NC (France), 36.6% by ONAREM (Niger govt); uranium mining at Arlit; Chair. FREDERIC TONA; Dir-Gen. SERGE MARTINEZ; 571 employees (2003).

Société des Mines du Liptako (SML): BP 11583, Niamey; tel. 20-75-30-32; fax 20-75-30-40; e-mail smlniger@hotmail.com; internet www.etruscan.com/s/SamiraHill.asp; f. 2004; 80% owned by African GeoMin Mining Development Corpn (jtly owned by Etruscan Resources—Canada and Semafo—Canada), 20% by Nigerian Govt; operates gold mine at Samira Hill.

Société Minière du Niger (SMDN): Niamey; tel. 20-73-45-82; f. 1941; cap. 36m. francs CFA; 71% state-owned, 10% owned by Benin govt; cassiterite mining at El Mecki and Tarrouadji; Chair. AMANI ISSAKA; Man. Dir MAMADOU SAADOU.

Société Minière de Tassa N'Taghalgué (SMTT): Niamey; tel. 20-73-36-66; f. 1979; cap. 10,500m. francs CFA; 33% owned by ONAREM (Niger Govt), 33% by Areva NS (France), 33% by Kuwait Foreign Trading, Contracting and Investment Co; owns uranium-mining rights at Taza (leased to SOMAÏR in 1986); Chair. Minister of Mines and Energy; Man. Dir MICHEL HAREL.

Société Nigérienne du Charbon (SONICHAR): BP 51, Agadez; tel. 20-44-02-48; fax 20-44-03-49; e-mail sonichar@intnet.ne; internet www.sonichar.com; f. 1975; cap. 19,730m. francs CFA; 69.3% state-owned, 10.1% owned by the Islamic Development Bank (Saudi Arabia), 15.8% by COMINAK and SOMAÏR; exploitation of coal reserves at Anou Araren and generation of electricity; Chair. MALEMI HASSANE CHETIMA; Man. ASSANE SEYDOU; 290 employees (2003).

Société Nigérienne de Cimenterie (SNC): BP 03, Malbaza; tel. 20-64-04-49; fax 20-64-04-50; e-mail snc_dfc@intnet.ne; f. 1963; privatized 1998; cap. 582m. francs CFA; 93% owned by SCANLEM International SNC (Heidelberg Cement Group); production and marketing of cement at Malbaza; Chair. IDI ANGO IBRAHIM; Dir-Gen. BO WALLANDER; 125 employees (2004).

Société Nigerienne de Distribution des Produits Pétroliers (SONIDEP): BP 11702, Niamey; tel. 20-73-33-34; fax 20-73-43-28; e-mail sonidep@intnet.ne; internet www.sonidep.com; f. 1977; 100% state-owned; transfer to 51% private ownership proposed; distribution of petroleum products; cap. 1,000m.; sales 45,018m. (2001); Dir-Gen. AMADOU DIOFFO; 160 employees (2001).

Société Nigérienne d'Exploitation des Ressources Animales (SONERAN): Niamey; tel. 20-73-23-75; f. 1968; cap. 270m. francs CFA; 99.9% state-owned; production and export of fresh and processed meat; ranch of 110,000 ha; Man. Dir MOUCTARI MAHAMANE FALALOU.

Total Niger: Route de l'Aéroport, BP 10349, Niamey; tel. 20-38-28-81; distribution of petroleum.

Unimo-Industrie et Chimie: BP 71, Maradi; tel. 20-41-00-56; f. 1978; cap. 710m. francs CFA; mfrs of foam rubber; Dir ASSAD GHASSAN.

TRADE UNION FEDERATIONS

Confédération des Travailleurs du Niger (CTN): Niamey; Sec.-Gen. ISSOUFOU SEYBOU.

Entente des Travailleurs du Niger (ETN): Bourse du Travail, BP 388, Niamey; tel. and fax 20-73-52-56; f. 2005 by merger of Confédération Nigérienne du Travail, Union Generale des Travailleurs du Niger and Union des Syndicats des Travailleurs du Niger.

Transport

ROADS

Niger is crossed by highways running from east to west and from north to south, giving access to neighbouring countries. A road is under construction to Lomé, Togo, via Burkina Faso, and the 428-km Zinder–Agadez road, scheduled to form part of the Trans-Sahara Highway, has been upgraded. Niger and Algeria appealed jointly in mid-1998 for international aid to fund construction of the Trans-Sahara Highway, development of which was suspended in the mid-1990s because of the conflict in northern Niger. Some 2,100m. francs CFA of the budget for 2001 was allocated to road maintenance. In 2004 there were 14,565 km of classified roads, of which 3,641 km were paved.

Société Nationale des Transports Nigériens (SNTN): BP 135, Niamey; tel. 20-72-24-55; fax 20-74-47-07; e-mail stratech@intnet.ne; f. 1963; operates passenger and freight road-transport services; 49% state-owned; Chair. MOHAMED ABDOULAHI; Man. Dir BARKE M. MOUSTAPHA.

RAILWAYS

There are as yet no railways in Niger.

Organisation Commune Bénin-Niger des Chemins de Fer et des Transports (OCBN): BP 38, Niamey; tel. 20-73-27-90; f. 1959; 50% owned by Govt of Niger, 50% by Govt of Benin; manages the Benin-Niger railway project (begun in 1978); also operates more than 500 km within Benin (q.v.); extension to Niger proposed; transfer to private ownership proposed; Dir-Gen. FLAVIEN BALOGOUN.

INLAND WATERWAYS

The River Niger is navigable for 300 km within the country. Access to the sea is available by a river route from Gaya, in south-western Niger, to the coast at Port Harcourt, Nigeria, between September and March. Port facilities at Lomé, Togo, are used as a commercial outlet for land-locked Niger: some 126,000 metric tons of goods imported by Niger pass through Lomé annually. An agreement providing import facilities at the port of Tema was signed with Ghana in November 1986.

Niger-Transit (NITRA): Zone Industrielle, BP 560, Niamey; tel. 20-73-22-53; fax 20-73-26-38; f. 1974; 48% owned by SNTN; customs agent, freight-handling, warehousing, etc.; manages Nigerien port facilities at Lomé, Togo; Pres. OUMAROU ALI BEÏOLI; Man. Dir SADE FATIMATA.

Société Nigérienne des Transports Fluviaux et Maritimes (SNTFM): Niamey; tel. 20-73-39-69; river and sea transport; cap. 64.6m. francs CFA; 99% state-owned; Man. Dir BERTRAND DEJEAN.

CIVIL AVIATION

There are international airports at Niamey (Hamani Diori), Agadez (Mano Dayak) and Zinder, and major domestic airports at Diffa, Maradi and Tahoua.

Air Continental: Niamey; f. 2003 to replace Air Niger International (f. 2002); 60% owned by private Nigerian interests, 20% by private Nigerien interests, 5% by Govt of Niger; regional and international services.

Air Inter Afrique: Niamey; tel. 20-73-85-85; fax 20-73-69-73; f. 2001; operates services within West Africa; CEO CHEIKH OUSMANE DIALLO.

Air Inter Niger: Agadez; f. 1997 to operate services to Tamanrasset (Algeria).

Niger Air Continental: Niamey; e-mail info@nigeraircontinental.com; f. 2003.

Nigeravia: BP 10454, Niamey; tel. 20-73-30-64; fax 20-74-18-42; e-mail nigavia@intnet.ne; internet www.nigeravia.com; f. 1991; operates domestic, regional and international services; Pres. and Dir-Gen. JEAN SYLVESTRE.

Société Nigérienne des Transports Aériens (SONITA): Niamey; f. 1991; owned by private Nigerien (81%) and Cypriot (19%) interests; operates domestic and regional services; Man. Dir ABDOULAYE MAIGA GOUDOUBABA.

Tourism

The Aïr and Ténéré Nature Reserve, covering an area of 77,000 sq km, was established in 1988. Tourism was hampered by insecurity in the north and east during the 1990s. However, the number of foreign arrivals at hotels and similar establishments increased from 39,190 in 1997 to 42,433 in 1999, when tourism receipts amounted to US $24m. In 2005 some 63,451 tourists entered Niger, while receipts from tourism totalled $34m. in 2003.

Centre Nigerien de Promotion Touristique (CNPT): ave de Président H. Luebke, BP 612, Niamey; tel. 20-73-24-47; fax 20-73-28-07; e-mail CNPT2@yahoo.fr; internet www.maisontourism-niger.com; Dirs BOULOU AKANO, IBRAHIM HALIDOU, KIEPIW TOYÉ FANTA.

Defence

As assessed at November 2006, Niger's armed forces totalled 5,300 men (army 5,200; air force 100). Paramilitary forces numbered 5,400 men, comprising the gendarmerie (1,400 men), the republican guard (2,500) and the national police force (1,500). Conscription is selective and lasts for two years.

Defence Expenditure: Estimated at 22,000m. francs CFA in 2005.

Chief of General Staff of the Armed Forces: Brig.-Gen. BOUREIMA MOUMOUNI.

Chief of General Staff of the Land Army: Col MAMADOU OUSSEINI.

Chief of General Staff of the Air Force: Col SALOU SOULEYMANE.

Education

Education is available free of charge, and is officially compulsory for eight years between the ages of seven and 15 years. Primary education begins at the age of seven and lasts for six years. Secondary education begins at the age of 13 years, and comprises a four-year cycle followed by a three-year cycle. According to UNESCO estimates, primary enrolment in 2003/04 included 39% of children in the appropriate age-group (boys 46%; girls 32%). Secondary enrolment in that year included only 7% of the relevant age-group (boys 8%; girls 5%). The Abdou Moumouni University (formerly the University of Niamey) was inaugurated in 1973, and the Islamic University of Niger, at Say (to the south of the capital), was opened in 1987. In December 2001 the Assemblée nationale approved legislation providing for the introduction of teaching in all local languages, with the aim of improving the literacy rate—one of the lowest in the world. Expenditure on education in 2000 was 32,500m. francs CFA, representing 15.5% of total spending.

Bibliography

Abdourhame, B. *Crise institutionnelle et démocratisation au Niger*. Talance, Université de Bordeaux IV, 1997.

Adji, B. *Dans les méandres d'une transition politique*. Paris, Editions Karthala, 1998.

Asiwaju, A. I., *et al.*, and Barkindo, B. M. *The Nigerian-Niger Transborder Co-operation*. Lagos, Malthouse Press, 1993.

Azam, J.-P. *Le Niger: la pauvreté en période d'ajustement*. Paris, L'Harmattan, 1993.

Bernus, E. *Touaregs, un peuple du désert*. Paris, Robert Laffont, 1996.

Carlier, M. *Meharistes au Niger*. Paris, L'Harmattan, 2001.

Charlick, R. B. *Niger: Personal Rule and Survival in the Sahel*. Boulder, CO, Westview Press, 1991.

Decalo, S. *Historical Dictionary of Niger*. 3rd Edn. Metuchen, NJ, Scarecrow Press, 1996.

Decoudras, P.-M., and Souleymane, A. *La rébellion touarègue au Niger: actes des négociations avec le Gouvernement*. Bordeaux, Centre d'Etude d'Afrique Noire, Institut d'Etudes Politiques de Bordeaux, 1995.

Deschamps, A. *Niger 1995: Révolte touaregue: Du cessez-le-feu provisoire à la "paix définitive"*. Paris, L'Harmattan, 2000.

Fluchard, C. *Le PPN/RDA et la décolonisation du Niger 1946–1960*. Paris, L'Harmattan, 1996.

Frère, M.-S. *Presse et démocratie en Afrique francophone: les mots et les maux de la transition au Bénin et au Niger*. Paris, Editions Karthala, 2000.

Gilliard, P. *L'extrême pauvreté au Niger:mendier ou mourir?*. Paris, Editions Karthala, 2005.

Grégoire, E. *Touaregs du Niger: Le Destin d'un mythe*. Paris, Editions Karthala, 2000.

Hamani, A. *Les femmes et la politique au Niger*. Paris, L'Harmattan, 2001.

Harrison Church, R. J. *West Africa*. 8th Edn, London, Longman, 1979.

Idrissa, K. (Ed.). *Le Niger: Etat et démocratie*. Paris, L'Harmattan, 2001.

Lund, C. *Law, Power and Politics in Niger: Land Struggles and the Rural Code*. Uppsala, Nordiska Africainstitutet, 1998.

Luxereau, A., and Roussel, B. *Changements économiques et sociaux au Niger*. Paris, L'Harmattan, 1998.

Maignan, J.-C., *et al. La difficile démocratisation du Niger*. Paris, Centre des hautes études sur l'Afrique et l'Asie modernes (CHEAM), 2000.

Mamadou, A. *A la conquête de la souveraineté populaire: les élections au Niger 1992–1999*. Niamey, Nouvelle Imprimerie de Niger, 2000.

Mayaki, I. A. *Le Caravane Passe*. Paris, Odilon Média, 1999.

Salifou, A. *La question touarègue au Niger*. Paris, Editions Karthala, 1993

Le Niger. Paris, L'Harmattan, 2002.

Séré de Rivières, E. *Histoire du Niger*. Paris, Berger-Levrault, 1966.

NIGERIA

Physical and Social Geography

AKIN L. MABOGUNJE

The Federal Republic of Nigeria covers an area of 909,890 sq km (351,310 sq miles) on the shores of the Gulf of Guinea, with Benin to the west, Niger to the north, Chad to the north-east, and Cameroon to the east and south-east. The population was enumerated at 140,003,542, according to provisional results of the census of March 2006, giving an average density of 157.2 persons per sq km.

Nigeria became independent on 1 October 1960, and in 1968 adopted a new federal structure comprising 12 states. A federal capital territory was created in 1979. The number of states was increased to 19 in 1976, to 21 in 1987, to 30 in 1991, and to 36 in 1996.

PHYSICAL FEATURES

The physical features of Nigeria are of moderate dimensions. The highest lands are along the eastern border of the country and rise to a maximum of 2,040 m above sea-level at Vogel Peak, south of the Benue river. The Jos plateau, which is located close to the centre of the country, rises to 1,780 m at Shere Hill and 1,698 m at Wadi Hill. The plateau is also a watershed, from which streams flow to Lake Chad and to the rivers Niger and Benue. The land declines steadily northwards from the plateau; this area, known as the High Plains of Hausaland, is characterized by a broad expanse of level sandy plains, interspersed by rocky dome outcrops. To the south-west, across the Niger river, similar relief is represented in the Yoruba highlands, where the rocky outcrops are surrounded by forests or tall grass and form the major watershed for rivers flowing northwards to the Niger and southwards to the sea. Elsewhere in the country, lowlands of less than 300 m stretch inland from the coast for over 250 km and continue in the trough-like basins of the Niger and Benue rivers. Lowland areas also exist in the Rima and Chad basins at the extreme north-west and north-east of the country respectively. These lowlands are dissected by innumerable streams and rivers flowing in broad sandy valleys.

The main river of Nigeria is the Niger, the third longest river of Africa. Originating in the Fouta Djallon mountains of north-east Sierra Leone, it enters Nigeria for the last one-third of its 4,200 km course. It flows first south-easterly, then due south and again south-easterly to Lokoja, where it converges with its principal tributary, the Benue. From here the river flows due south until Aboh, where it merges with the numerous interlacing distributaries of its delta. The Benue rises in Cameroon, flows in a south-westerly direction into the Niger, and receives on its course the waters of the Katsina Ala and Gongola rivers. The other main tributaries of the Niger within Nigeria are the Sokoto, Kaduna and Anambra rivers. Other important rivers in the country include the Ogun, the Oshun, the Imo and the Cross, many of which flow into the sea through a system of lagoons. The Nigerian coastline is relatively straight, with few natural indentations.

CLIMATE

Nigeria has a climate which is characterized by relatively high temperatures throughout the year. The average annual maximum varies from 35°C in the north to 31°C in the south; the average annual minimum from 23°C in the south to 18°C in the north. On the Jos plateau and the eastern highlands altitude moderates the temperatures, with the maximum no more than 28°C and the minimum sometimes as low as 14°C.

The annual rainfall total decreases from over 3,800 mm at Forcados on the coast to under 650 mm at Maiduguri in the north-east of the country. The length of the rainy season ranges from almost 12 months in the south to under five months in the north. Rain starts in January in the south and moves gradually across country. June, July, August and September are the rainiest months country-wide. In many parts of the south, however, there is a slight break in the rains for some two to three weeks in late July and early August. No such break occurs in the northern part of the country, and the rainy season continues uninterrupted for three to six months.

SOILS AND VEGETATION

The broad pattern of soil distribution in the country reflects both the climatic conditions and the geological structure; heavily leached, reddish-brown, sandy soils are found in the south, and light or moderately leached, yellowish-brown, sandy soils in the north. The difference in colour relates to the extent of leaching the soil has undergone.

The nutrient content of the soil is linked to the geological structure. Over a large part of the northern and south-western areas of the country the geological structure is that of old crystalline Basement complex rocks. These are highly mineralized and give rise to soils of high nutrient status, although variable from place to place. On the sedimentary rocks found in the south-east, north-east and north-west of the country the soils are sandy and less variable but are deficient in plant nutrient. They are highly susceptible to erosion.

The vegetation displays clear east-west zonation. In general, mangrove and rainforests are found in the south, occupying about 20% of the area of the country, while grassland of various types occupies the rest. Four belts of grassland can be identified. Close to the forest zone is a derived savannah belt, which is evidently the result of frequent fires in previously forested areas. This belt is succeeded by the Guinea, the Sudan and the Sahel savannah northwards in that order. The height of grass and density of wood vegetation decrease with each succeeding savannah belt.

RESOURCES

Although nearly 180,000 sq km of Nigeria is in the forest belt, only 23,000 sq km account for most of its timber resources. These forests are mainly in Ondo, Bendel and Cross River States. Nigeria exports a wide variety of tropical hardwoods, and internal consumption has been growing rapidly.

Cattle, goats and, to a lesser extent, sheep constitute important animal resources. Most of the cattle are found in the Sudan grassland belt in the far north. Poultry and pigs are increasing in importance.

Coastal waters are becoming important fishing grounds. Traditionally, however, major sources of fish have been Lake Chad in the extreme north-east, the lagoons along the coast, the creeks and distributaries of the Niger Delta and the various rivers in the country.

Mineral resources are varied, although considerable exploration remains to be carried out. Tin and columbite are found in alluvial deposits on the Jos plateau. Nigeria was, until 1968, Africa's main producer of tin, but output has since declined. Extensive reserves of medium-grade iron ore exist, and iron and steel production is being developed.

Fuel resources include deposits of lignite and sub-bituminous coal, exploited at Enugu since 1915; however, total reserves are small. More significant are the petroleum reserves, estimates of which alter with each new discovery in the offshore area. The oil produced, being of low sulphur content and high quality, is much in demand on the European and US markets. Since Libya restricted production in 1973, Nigeria has been Africa's leading producer of petroleum. Natural gas is also found in abundance, and has been undergoing development since the mid-1980s.

POPULATION

The Nigerian population is extremely diverse. There are more than 500 spoken languages, and well over 250 ethnic groups, some numbering fewer than 10,000 people. Ten groups, notably Hausa-Fulani, Yoruba, Ibo, Kanuri, Tiv, Edo, Nupe, Ibibio and Ijaw, account for nearly 80% of the total population. Much of the population is concentrated in the southern part of the country, as well as in the area of dense settlement around Kano in the north. Between these two areas is the sparsely populated Middle Belt.

Urban life has a long history in Nigeria, with centres of population such as Kano, Benin and Zaria dating from the Middle Ages. Recent economic development, however, has stimulated considerable rural–urban migration and led to the phenomenal growth of such cities as Lagos, Ibadan, Kaduna and Port Harcourt. In December 1991 the federal capital was formally transferred to Abuja (which then had an estimated population of 107,069); however, a number of government departments and non-government institutions have remained in the former capital, Lagos. According to UN estimates, at mid-2005 Lagos had 10,886,000, Kano 2,993,000, Ibadan 2,437,000, and Kaduna 1,375,000 inhabitants.

Recent History

RICHARD SYNGE

The territory that now comprises the Federal Republic of Nigeria (excluding the segment once part of the former German protectorate of Kamerun, see below) was colonized by the United Kingdom during the second half of the 19th century and the first decade of the 20th century. Much of the administration remained under the control of traditional rulers, supervised by the colonial authorities. In 1947 the United Kingdom introduced a new Nigerian Constitution, establishing a federal system of government, based on three regions: Eastern, Western and Northern. The federal arrangement sought to reconcile regional and religious tensions, and to accommodate the interests of Nigeria's diverse ethnic groups: mainly the Ibo (in the east), the Yoruba (in the west) and the Hausa and Fulani (in the north). The Northern Region, whose inhabitants were mainly Muslims, contained about one-half of Nigeria's total population.

Politically, the Eastern Region was dominated by the National Council for Nigeria and the Cameroons (NCNC), led by Dr Nnamdi Azikiwe, with mainly Ibo support. The leading political entity in the Western Region was the Action Group (AG), led by Obafemi Awolowo and dominated by educated Yoruba. The largest region in the country, the Northern Region, was dominated by the Northern People's Congress (NPC). The NPC represented the traditional and mercantile Hausa-Fulani élite; its nominal leader was the premier of the Northern Region, the Sardauna of Sokoto, Ahmadu (later Sir Ahmadu) Bello. The NPC's political (and subsequently parliamentary) spokesman was Abubakar (later Sir Abubakar) Tafawa Balewa, a former schoolteacher (who became the first federal Prime Minister in 1957).

In 1954 the federation became self-governing, and, following elections to a federal legislature in 1959 in which the NPC obtained the largest representation, a bicameral federal parliament was formed in January 1960.

On 1 October 1960 the Federation of Nigeria achieved independence, initially as a constitutional monarchy, with Tafawa Balewa as Prime Minister and Minister of Foreign Affairs. In June 1961 the northern section of the neighbouring UN Trust Territory of British Cameroons, formerly part of the German protectorate of Kamerun, was incorporated into Nigeria's Northern Region as the province of Sardauna. In October 1963 the country was renamed the Federal Republic of Nigeria, remaining a member of the Commonwealth. Azikiwe took office as Nigeria's first (non-executive) President.

MILITARY INTERVENTION AND CIVIL WAR, 1966–76

Nigeria's regional rivalries were reflected in the federal armed forces; most of the quota of personnel recruited from the north came from the Middle Belt of the Northern Region and were opposed to the NPC and to Hausa-Fulani dominance. Ibo from the Eastern Region formed the majority of the officer corps, and this provoked intense distrust from other ethnic groups. In January 1966 Tafawa Balewa's Government was overthrown by junior (mainly Ibo) army officers; Balewa was killed, together with a number of other ministers. Maj.-Gen. (later Gen.) Johnson Aguiyi-Ironsi, the Commander-in-Chief of the army and an Ibo, took control of the Government. The coup was followed by anti-Ibo riots, and in late May many people were killed when violence erupted in most of the major cities of the north, and in July Aguiyi-Ironsi was killed in a counter-coup by northern troops. Power was transferred to the Chief of Staff of the Army, Lt-Col (later Gen.) Yakubu Gowon, a Christian northerner. Gowon restored some degree of discipline to the armed forces, and attempted to revive the federal system, appointing a military Governor for each region.

The military Governor of the Eastern Region, Lt-Col Chukwuemeka Odumegwu-Ojukwu, under pressure from senior Ibo civil servants, announced the secession of the Eastern Region, and in May 1967 proclaimed its independence as the 'Republic of Biafra'. In July federal forces launched a massive attack and naval blockade, and in the ensuing civil war between 500,000 and 2m. 'Biafran' civilians died, mainly from starvation, before the surrender of 'Biafran' forces in January 1970.

Following the collapse of 'Biafra', Gowon implemented a strategy of reconciliation, which was seriously impeded by the failure of the national population census, conducted in 1973, to produce credible results; the census purported to show a near doubling of the population in the Northern Region, while that of the Yoruba heartland of the Western Region was reported to have declined. In October 1974 Gowon announced that the return to civilian rule, scheduled for 1976, had been indefinitely postponed, on the grounds that a government plan for socio-economic reconstruction had not been fulfilled. However, in July 1976 Gowon was forcibly 'retired' and was succeeded as Head of Government by Brig. (later Gen.) Murtala Ramat Muhammed. He proceeded to order major administrative changes, including the creation of new states, bringing the total from 12 to 19, and the instant dismissal of tens of thousands of federal civil servants (although intended to reduce corruption, the latter move was subsequently considered to have had the opposite effect).

FROM OBASANJO TO SHAGARI AND THE SECOND REPUBLIC, 1976–83

Muhammed was assassinated in February 1976 by disaffected army officers, who demanded the reinstatement of Gen. Gowon. Power was transferred to Muhammed's deputy, Lt-Gen. (later Gen.) Olusegun Obasanjo, the Chief of Staff at supreme military headquarters. As Head of State, Obasanjo pledged to fulfil his predecessor's programme for the return to civilian rule by October 1979. During 1976 legislation to reform the structure of local government was introduced, and a Constituent Assembly was created in August 1977 to draft the new Constitution. This was duly promulgated in September 1978. It envisaged an executive presidency, and a separation of powers between executive, legislative and judicial branches of government. To win the presidential election, a candidate would need to obtain an outright majority of the national vote, and also to win at least 25% of the votes in two-thirds of the states. Executive Governors were to be appointed to each state.

The ending of the state of emergency in September 1978 was accompanied by the lifting of the ban on formal activity by political parties. By November more than 50 political groupings had emerged. In the event, however, of the 19 associations that applied for registration, only five received approval by the Federal Election Commission (FEDECO).

The best prepared of the five parties was the Unity Party of Nigeria (UPN), led by Chief Obafemi Awolowo, a prominent member of Gowon's junta and of the Yoruba community. The National Party of Nigeria (NPN) included such veteran NPC politicians as Alhaji Shehu Shagari (later selected as its presidential candidate). The People's Redemption Party (PRP), the northern-based opposition to the NPN, was led by Alhaji Aminu Kano. The fourth party, the Nigerian People's Party (NPP), chose ex-President Azikiwe as its presidential candidate. The Greater Nigeria People's Party (GNPP), a breakaway faction of the NPP, was formed by Alhaji Waziri Ibrahim. At elections to the new bicameral National Assembly, and for State Assemblies and State Governors, which took place in July 1979, the NPN received the most widespread support, securing 37% of the seats in the House of Representatives, 36% in the State Assemblies, and 38% in the Senate, and winning seven of the 19 state governorships. In the presidential election, which took place in August, Shagari obtained the mandatory 25% of the vote in 12, rather than 13, of the 19 States. Following legal debate on this point, the Supreme Court upheld the election of Shagari. On 1 October military rule ended, the new Constitution came into force, and Shagari was sworn in as President of the Second Republic.

By the early 1980s it was widely believed in Nigeria that the federal democracy was a façade, which allowed NPN politicians, dominated by a powerful political community in Kaduna, to distribute contracts and rewards in order to ensure their own continuation in power. In order to reinforce its power on the federal legislature, the NPN formed an alliance with Azikiwe's NPP, which, however, was dissolved in July 1981. The NPP then established a coalition, known as the Progressive Parties' Alliance (PPA), with the UPN, the major opposition party, thereby engendering further realignments in the parties that had fought the 1979 elections. The PRP and the GNPP split, with some of their members joining the PPA, while others aligned themselves with the Government.

In 1982, in preparation for the elections of the following year, FEDECO was reconstituted and given extensive powers. FEDECO subsequently approved the National Advance Party (NAP), led by the radical Lagos lawyer Tunji Braithwaite. As campaigning began, the NPN used its entrenched position and financial influence to ensure its return to office. In May the Government granted a pardon to Odumegwu-Ojukwu, the former 'Biafran' leader, who returned to Nigeria after more than 12 years in exile, and later aligned himself with the NPN. Later that year the PPA became divided over the issue of choosing a presidential candidate; eventually, Awolowo was selected as the UPN candidate, and Azikiwe as the NPP candidate.

The elections, which were contested by the six political parties, took place in August–September 1983. In the presidential poll Shagari was returned for a second term, receiving 47% of the total votes cast. The NPN attained a decisive majority in the elections to the Senate (60 seats out of 96) and the House of Representatives (264 seats out of 450), and won 13 of the 19 state governorships. However, allegations of widespread electoral malpractice on the part of the NPN resulted in litigation and a reinforcement of the belief that the elections had been won by means of misconduct on a vast scale. On 1 October Shagari was sworn in for a second term as President.

THE RETURN OF MILITARY RULE

Buhari and the SMC, 1983–85

On 31 December 1983 Shagari was deposed in a bloodless military coup, led by Maj.-Gen. Muhammadu Buhari, a former military Governor of Borno and Federal Commissioner for Petroleum during 1976–78. All political parties were banned, FEDECO was dissolved, and all bank accounts were temporarily 'frozen'. The structure of the new regime, similar to that of the military Governments of 1975–79, comprised a reconstituted SMC, headed by Buhari. A National Council of States, with a Federal Executive Council, and State Executive Councils, presided over by military Governors, were subsequently established. The authorities subsequently stated that there was no schedule for a return to civilian rule, and prohibited all debate on the political future of Nigeria.

Babangida and the AFRC, 1985–93

In August 1985 Buhari's regime was deposed in a peaceful military coup, led by Maj.-Gen. (later Gen.) Ibrahim Babangida, the Chief of Army Staff, who was named as the new Head of State. The SMC was replaced by a 28-member armed forces ruling council (AFRC), which comprised military personnel. The post of Chief of Staff at supreme military headquarters was replaced by that of Chief of the General Staff within the AFRC, a position that carried no responsibility for actual control of the armed forces. A national Council of Ministers was formed, together with a reconstituted national Council of State. There was a redistribution of all state governorships, and Buhari's ministers were removed. In September Babangida, with the support of Maj.-Gen. Sani Abacha, the Chief of Army Staff, removed some 40 senior officers, some of whom faced military tribunals and were executed.

In October 1985 Babangida declared a state of national economic emergency and assumed extensive interventionist powers over the economy. Although formal negotiations with the IMF for financial support were suspended, preparations were made during 1986 for the introduction of a structural adjustment programme, which received strong support from the World Bank. In January Babangida announced that the armed forces would transfer power to a civilian government on 1 October 1990.

In February 1986 Babangida announced that Nigeria's application for full membership of the Organization of the Islamic Conference (OIC) had been accepted; ensuing unrest among the non-Muslim sector of the population reflected alarm at increasing 'Islamization' in the country. In May about 15 people, mostly students, were shot dead by police during demonstrations at the Ahmadu Bello University, in Zaria, and a ban was imposed on further demonstrations. Babangida subsequently established a national commission to examine the advisability of Nigeria's membership of the OIC. In March 1987 violent clashes broke out between Muslim and Christian youths at Kafanchan, in southern Kaduna State, which were reported to have resulted in some 30 deaths. A curfew was imposed, and an estimated 1,000 people were arrested. In April the AFRC formed an Advisory Council on Religious Affairs (ACRA), comprising Muslim and Christian leaders, to investigate the causes of the violence, and the authorities issued decrees banning religious organizations in schools and universities. However, sporadic outbreaks of student unrest continued in late 1987 and early 1988.

In July 1987, after receiving recommendations from the political bureau, the AFRC announced that power was to be transferred to a civilian government in 1992, two years later than envisaged. In September the number of states was increased from 19 to 21 and the AFRC proscribed all categories of former politicians and its own membership from contesting elections in 1992. In addition, the AFRC inaugurated a constitutional review committee and a National Electoral Commission (NEC) to supervise future elections. Babangida subsequently announced that the new Constitution would be promulgated in 1989, and proposed that an enlarged Constituent Assembly should debate the terms of the Constitution. Accordingly, in April 1988 newly elected local government councillors in turn elected 450 members to the Constituent Assembly. The AFRC later nominated a further 117 members, to represent various interest groups. Abuja, the future federal capital, was designated as the seat of the new Assembly. Debate over the new draft Constitution threatened to founder on the issue of religion. Muslims demanded the inclusion of *Shari'a* courts, but in November 1988 further debate on this topic was banned by Babangida, as the progress of the Assembly's work was being severely impeded. The Assembly then presented its draft Constitution the following April.

In early May 1989 the ban on political parties was lifted, and the Constitution was promulgated, with the intention that it would come into force in October 1992. Elections for the Government of the Third Republic were to be contested by only two registered political parties, which were to be selected by the AFRC from the register compiled by the NEC. A total of 13 parties succeeded in fulfilling the registration requirements by the stipulated date of 15 July. In October, following the recommendation by the NEC of six of the 13 associations to the AFRC, Babangida announced that the AFRC had decided to dissolve all 13, on the grounds that they lacked distinctive ideologies, and were allied to discredited civilian politicians. In their place the AFRC created two new political parties, the Social Democratic Party (SDP) and the National Republican Convention (NRC). There was widespread criticism of the Government's management of the political transition and the NEC admitted that delays could be expected. In December the NEC published the draft constitutions and manifestos of the SDP and the NRC. In the same month Babangida carried out a major cabinet reshuffle, in which he assumed the defence portfolio, while Abacha was appointed Chairman of the joint Chiefs of Staff. In April 1990, an abortive coup by junior officers from the Middle Belt, who attempted to seize Dodan Barracks in Lagos, was suppressed by the joint efforts of Abacha and Babangida. The coup attempt resulted in even tighter presidential control of the delayed transition to civilian rule.

The election of officials from the SDP and NRC to local government councils was held in May 1990. In July more than 44,000 delegates, representing the two political parties, elected party executives for each state. The administration of the SDP and NRC was transferred from government-appointed administrative secretaries to elected party officials in early August. In the same month Chief Tom Ikimi, a southerner, was elected Chairman of the NRC, while Baba Kingibe, a northerner, was installed as Chairman of the SDP. (It was widely believed that the NRC received most support from the north of the country, and the SDP from the south.)

Following the April 1990 coup attempt, Babangida announced that the presidency would be restructured in order to prepare for the transition to civilian rule, and that the size of the armed forces would be substantially reduced. In September, in an attempt to restrict military influence in the Government, three ministers were obliged to retire from the armed forces, leaving Abacha, the Minister of Defence, as the only serving military officer in the Cabinet. Twelve military State Governors were replaced, and 21 civilian Deputy Governors were appointed to each state, pending gubernatorial elections, scheduled for 1991. In December local government elections took place in some 440 areas, although only an estimated 20% of registered voters participated.

The electoral process was overshadowed by signs of growing ethnic discontent and religious conflict. In October 1990 the Movement for the Survival of the Ogoni People (MOSOP) was formed to co-ordinate opposition to the exploitation of petroleum reserves in the territory of the Ogoni ethnic group (Ogoniland), in Rivers State, by the Shell Petroleum Development Co of Nigeria. Following demonstrations, organized by MOSOP, in protest at alleged environmental damage caused by petroleum production, some 80 Ogonis were killed by security forces. In April 1991 a number of demonstrations by Muslims in the northern state of Katsina, in protest against the publication of an article considered to be blasphemous, culminated in violence. In the same month some 130 people, mainly Christians, were killed in riots in Bauchi and other predominantly Muslim states, where Christians proposed to slaughter pigs in a local abattoir that was also used by Muslims. It was later reported that some 120 Muslims had been killed by government troops, who had been sent to the region to suppress the riots. More than 300 people were reported to have been killed in subsequent clashes between Muslims and Christians, which were suppressed by the army. In late 1991 violence erupted in Taraba, in the east, as a result of a long-standing land dispute between the Tiv and Jukun ethnic groups. The conflict continued in subsequent months, and by March 1992 up to 5,000 people were reported to have been killed.

In September 1991 the Government created nine new states, increasing the size of the federation to 30 states, in an attempt to ease ethnic tensions prior to the elections. However, violent demonstrations took place in several states where the Government had failed to comply with demands to create a new state in the region, or where there was discontent at the relocation of the state capital. On 19 October primary elections took place to select candidates for the forthcoming gubernatorial and state assembly elections. In November, however, following allegations of electoral fraud on the part of both the NRC and the SDP, results were annulled in nine states, and 12 candidates were disqualified. Controversy over the election results led to increased divisions within both parties, especially within the SDP.

Federal Capital Moves to Abuja

In December 1991 the seat of federal government was formally transferred from Lagos to Abuja, which was to be administered by a municipal council. In the gubernatorial and state assembly elections, which took place on 14 December, the SDP gained a majority in 16 State Assemblies, while the NRC won control of 14; however, NRC candidates were elected as Governors in 16 of the 30 states, mostly in the south-east of Nigeria, where the SDP had previously received more support. Both the SDP and the NRC subsequently disputed the election results in a number of states, on the grounds of voting irregularities.

In early May 1992 widespread rioting in protest at sharp increases in transport fares (resulting from a severe fuel shortage) culminated in a number of demonstrations demanding the resignation of the Government, which were violently suppressed by the security forces; several people were reported to have been killed. An alliance of 25 organizations opposed to the Government, known as the Campaign for Democracy (CD), which had been formed six months earlier, attributed the unrest to widespread discontent at increasing economic hardship. Later in May further rioting broke out in Lagos, following the arrest of the Chairman of the CD, Dr Beko Ransome-Kuti, who had accused the Government of provoking the violence in order to delay the transition to civilian rule. The Government subsequently banned all associations with a religious or ethnic base; a security force, to be known as the national guard, was also to be established in order to reduce the role of the army in riot control.

In elections to the National Assembly, which took place on 4 July 1992, the SDP gained a majority in both chambers, securing 52 seats in the Senate and 314 seats in the House of Representatives, while the NRC won 37 seats in the Senate and 275 seats in the House of Representatives. However, the formal inauguration of the National Assembly, scheduled for 27 July, was subsequently postponed until 2 January 1993, owing to the AFRC's insistence that it retain supreme legislative power until the installation of a civilian government. Primary elections to select an NRC and an SDP presidential candidate commenced on 1 August 1992, but were suspended, owing to widespread electoral irregularities; results in states where elections had taken place were annulled. Further polls to select presidential candidates took place on 12, 19 and 26 September. By the end of the second round of voting four leading candidates had emerged: Gen. (retd) Shehu Musa Yar'Adua and Chief Olu Falae (SDP), and Alhaji Umaru Shinkafi and Adamu Ciroma (NRC). However, 10 of the original 23 aspirants (including Falae) withdrew from the third and final stage of polling, alleging fraudulent practices. Reports of irregularities were widely believed, and the participation rate in the poll was significantly low. Yar'Adua claimed to have won the SDP nomination, while Shinkafi and Ciroma were to contest a final poll for the NRC candidacy on 10 October.

On 6 October 1992 the AFRC summarily suspended the results of the presidential primaries, and when the NEC reported malpractices Babangida cancelled them. The presidential election (scheduled for 5 December) was postponed until 12 June 1993, and the transition to civilian rule until 27 August. All 23 aspirants who had contested the discredited primaries in September 1992 were disqualified as candidates. Under the new arrangements, the AFRC was to be replaced on 2 January 1993 by a National Defence and Security Council (NDSC), and the Council of Ministers by a civilian Transitional

Council. Babangida announced a new programme for the installation of an elected civilian president. In December 1992 the bicameral National Assembly was formally convened in Abuja. On 2 January 1993 the NDSC and Transitional Council were duly installed. The 14-member NDSC was chaired by Babangida, and the Transitional Council was chaired by Chief Ernest Shonekan, designated as Head of Government.

Disputed Outcome of 12 June 1993

National party congresses took place, as scheduled, during 27–29 March 1993: the NRC selected Alhaji Bashir Othman Tofa, an economist and businessman, to contest the presidential election, while Chief Moshood Kashimawo Olawale Abiola, a wealthy publisher, emerged as the SDP presidential candidate. In April Abiola chose Baba Kingibe (a former Chairman of the SDP) as his vice-presidential candidate, and Tofa selected Dr Sylvester Ugoh, who had served in the Shagari administration.

The rate of participation in the presidential election on 12 June 1993 was low but international monitors throughout Nigeria reported that it had been conducted relatively peacefully. Two days later, initial results, released by the NEC, indicated that of the 6.6m. votes cast in 14 of the 30 states, the SDP had secured 4.3m. and the NRC 2.3m. In 11 of the 14 states (including Tofa's home state of Kano), Abiola had obtained the majority of votes. Shortly afterwards, however, the NEC announced that the remaining results would not be released until further notice. Widespread confusion followed, and protests were voiced that the NDSC had deliberately sabotaged the elections. Later in June the CD promulgated election results, which indicated that Abiola had won the majority of votes in 19 states, and Tofa in 11 states.

On 23 June 1993 the NDSC declared the results of the election to be invalid, halted all court proceedings pertaining to the election, suspended the NEC, and repealed all decrees relating to the transition to civilian rule. New electoral regulations were introduced that effectively precluded Abiola and Tofa from contesting a further presidential poll. Babangida subsequently announced that the election had been marred by corruption and other irregularities, but insisted that he remained committed to the transition on 27 August; in order to meet this schedule, a reconstituted NEC was to supervise the selection of two new presidential candidates by the SDP and NRC. Abiola, however, continued to claim, with much popular agreement, that he had been legitimately elected to the presidency. The United Kingdom announced that it was to review its bilateral relations with Nigeria, and imposed a number of military sanctions, while the USA immediately suspended all assistance to the Government.

In early July 1993 a demonstration, organized by the CD, led to rioting, prompted by resentment at political developments, in conjunction with long-standing economic hardship. Order was subsequently restored, after security forces violently suppressed protests; however, sporadic unrest was reported throughout the country. The NDSC provisionally announced that a new presidential election was to take place on 14 August in order to fulfil the pledge to transfer power on 27 August, prompting general disbelief. The SDP declared that it intended to boycott an electoral process that superseded its victory on 12 June.

'Interim National Government'

At the end of July 1993 Babangida announced that an Interim National Government (ING) was to be established, on the grounds that there was insufficient time to permit the scheduled transition to civilian rule on 27 August. A committee, comprising officials of the two parties and senior military officers, headed by Aikhomu, was subsequently established to determine the composition of the ING. Abiola immediately declared his opposition to the proposed administration, and stated his intention of forming a 'parallel government'. (He subsequently fled abroad, following alleged death threats, and attempted to solicit international support for his claim to the presidency.) In August the CD continued its campaign of civil disobedience in protest at the annulment of the election, appealing for a three-day general strike (which was widely observed in the south-west of the country, where Abiola received most popular support). Several prominent members of the CD were arrested, in an attempt to prevent further protests, while additional restrictions were imposed on the press. Later in August Babangida announced his resignation, reportedly as a result of pressure from prominent members of the NDSC, notably Abacha. On 27 August a 32-member Interim Federal Executive Council, headed by Shonekan, was installed; the new administration, which included several members of the former Transitional Council, was to supervise the organization of local government elections later that year and a presidential election in early 1994, while the transitional period for the return to civilian rule was extended to 31 March 1994. (Shonekan was later designated as Head of State and Commander-in-Chief of the Armed Forces.) Supporters of democracy criticized the inclusion in the ING of several members of the former NDSC (which had been dissolved), including Abacha, who was appointed to the new post of Vice-President, and the proposed establishment of two predominantly military councils as advisory bodies to the President. Industrial action in support of Abiola resulted in a severe fuel shortage and widespread economic disruption.

As the new Head of State, Shonekan pledged his commitment to the democratic process, and, in an effort to restore order, initiated negotiations with the Nigerian Labour Congress (NLC) and effected the release of several journalists and prominent members of the CD. In early September the NLC and the National Union of Petroleum and Natural Gas Workers (NUPENG) provisionally suspended strike action, after the ING agreed to consider their demands. A series of military appointments, which included the nomination of Lt-Gen. Oladipo Diya to the office of Chief of Defence Staff, effectively removed supporters of Babangida from positions of influence within the armed forces, thereby strengthening Abacha's position. Diya, who had reportedly opposed the annulment of the presidential election, declared that military involvement in politics would cease and in the same month Abiola returned to Lagos, amid popular acclaim. Later in September the NRC and SDP agreed to a new timetable, whereby local government elections and a presidential election would take place concurrently in February 1994. The CD announced the resumption of strike action in support of demands for the installation of Abiola as President; an ensuing demonstration by supporters of the CD in Lagos was violently dispersed by security forces, and Ransome-Kuti, together with other prominent members of the CD, was arrested.

Abacha and the PRC, 1993–98

On 17 November 1993, following a meeting with senior military officials, Shonekan announced his resignation as Head of State, and immediately transferred power to Abacha (confirming speculation that Abacha had effectively assumed control of the Government following Babangida's resignation). On the following day Abacha dissolved all organs of state and bodies that had been established under the transitional process, replaced the State Governors with military administrators, prohibited political activity (thereby proscribing the NRC and the SDP), and announced the formation of a Provisional Ruling Council (PRC), which was to comprise senior military officials and the principal members of a new Federal Executive Council (FEC). He insisted, however, that he intended to relinquish power to a civilian government, and pledged to convene a conference with a mandate to determine the constitutional future of the country. On 21 November Abacha introduced legislation that formally restored the 1979 Constitution and provided for the establishment of the new government organs. In an apparent attempt to counter domestic and international criticism, several prominent supporters of Abiola, including Kingibe, and four former members of the ING were appointed to the PRC and FEC, which were installed on 24 November. Abacha subsequently removed 17 senior military officers, who were believed to be loyal to Babangida. In the same month discussions between Abacha and Abiola took place, while the NLC agreed to abandon strike action after the Government acted to limit a proposed increase in the price of petroleum products.

In April 1994 the Government announced its proposals for the establishment of the National Constitutional Conference

(NCC) to submit recommendations, including a new draft constitution, to the PRC in late October. A further stage in the transitional programme was to commence in mid-January 1995, when the ban on political activity was to end. In May 1994, however, a new pro-democracy organization, comprising former politicians, retired military officers and human rights activists, the National Democratic Coalition (NADECO), demanded that Abacha relinquish power by the end of that month and urged a boycott of the NCC. Nevertheless, later in May elections duly took place at ward, and subsequently at local government, level to select the 273 conference delegates; the boycott was widely observed in the south-west of the country, and a low level of voter participation was reported. In the same month Ken Saro-Wiwa, the leader of MOSOP, was arrested in connection with the deaths of four Ogoni electoral candidates. At the end of May Abiola announced his intention of forming a government of national unity by 12 June (the anniversary of the presidential election). Violent anti-Government protests followed the expiry of the date stipulated by NADECO for the resignation of the military administration.

In early June 1994 members of the former Senate (including its President) were detained on charges of treason, after the senators reconvened and declared the Government to be illegal. A number of prominent opposition members, including Dr Beko Ransome-Kuti, were also arrested, after the CD urged a campaign of civil disobedience, which received the support of NADECO. (Ransome-Kuti was subsequently charged with treason.) Following a symbolic ceremony, in which Abiola was publicly inaugurated as head of a parallel government, a warrant was issued for his arrest on charges of treason; the authorities alleged that he intended to organize an uprising to remove the military administration from power. Later in June security forces arrested Abiola (who had emerged from hiding to attend a rally in Lagos), prompting protests from pro-democracy organizations and criticism from the Governments of the United Kingdom and the USA. Further demonstrations in support of demands for an immediate suspension of military rule and the installation of Abiola as President ensued, while NUPENG threatened to initiate strike action unless the Government agreed to release Abiola.

In July 1994 NUPENG initiated strike action in support of dual demands for Abiola's release and installation as President, and an increase in government investment in the petroleum industry; the strike was subsequently joined by the senior petroleum workers' union, the Petroleum and Natural Gas Senior Staff Association (PENGASSAN). Government troops distributed fuel in an attempt to ease the resultant national shortage, while it was reported that senior officials of NUPENG and PENGASSAN had been arrested. In early August 1994 the trial of Abiola, who had been indicted for 'treasonable felony', was adjourned, pending a ruling regarding a defence appeal that the High Court in Abuja had no jurisdiction in the case of an offence that had allegedly been committed in Lagos. Abiola (who was reported to be in poor health) refused to accept bail, since the stipulated conditions required him to refrain from political activity. The court finally decided that it had the necessary jurisdiction, although the presiding judge withdrew from the trial. Later in August Abacha replaced the senior officials of NUPENG and PENGASSAN, and ordered petroleum workers to end strike action. Although a number of union members failed to comply, the effects of the strike soon began to recede. In September Abacha promulgated legislation that extended the period of detention without trial to three months and prohibited legal action challenging government decisions. The Minister of Justice was subsequently dismissed, after protesting that he had not been consulted regarding the new legislation. The trial of Saro-Wiwa and a further 14 MOSOP activists, on charges of complicity in the murder of the four Ogoni traditional leaders, commenced in mid-January 1995; the defendants challenged the legitimacy of the special military tribunal, which had been appointed by the Government. In February the Federal Court of Appeal dismissed Abiola's legal action challenging the jurisdiction of the High Court in Abuja.

In March 1995 some 150 military officials were arrested, apparently in response to widespread disaffection within the armed forces. The authorities subsequently confirmed reports (which had initially been denied) of a coup conspiracy. (However, opponents of the Abacha regime claimed that it had fabricated a coup attempt, with the aim of suppressing dissent within the armed forces.) Reports that about 80 members of the armed forces had been summarily executed were officially denied. However, the arrest of the former Head of State, Gen. (retd) Olusegun Obasanjo and his former deputy, Maj.-Gen. (retd) Shehu Musa Yar'Adua, together with other prominent critics of the Government, prompted international protests. In mid-March Abacha reconstituted the FEC; its 36 members included a number of civilians who were believed to favour an extended period of military rule.

In April 1995 the NCC endorsed the constitutional proposals that had been approved in late 1994. At the end of that month, however, the conference adopted a motion reversing its previous decision that a civilian government be installed on 1 January 1996, on the grounds that the requisite timetable was untenable. The NCC subsequently undertook the incorporation of the necessary amendments to the constitutional recommendations, which were to be submitted for approval by the Government. In June 1995 about 40 people, including several civilians, were arraigned before a special military tribunal in connection with the alleged coup attempt in March; it was reported that Obasanjo and Yar'Adua had also been secretly charged with conspiring to overthrow the Government. Further arrests of pro-democracy activists took place later in June, in an effort by the Government to pre-empt protests on the anniversary of the annulled presidential election; nevertheless, a one-day general strike, supported by the CD, was widely observed. At the end of June reports emerged that the military tribunal had sentenced Obasanjo to 25 years' imprisonment for his alleged involvement in the coup attempt, while Yar'Adua and a further 13 military officers had received the death penalty. Numerous international protests and appeals for clemency ensued. Despite indications that the Nigerian Government would yield to these pressures, at the end of July a military council ratified the death sentences, which were subject to confirmation by the PRC. Eventually, in early October the PRC commuted the death sentences and reduced the terms of imprisonment. The capital charges against Abiola were not withdrawn. Concurrently, Abacha announced a three-year programme for transition to civilian rule, whereby a new President was to be inaugurated on 1 October 1998, following elections at local, state and national level; the duration of the transitional period was received with international disapproval.

At the end of October 1995 Saro-Wiwa and a further eight Ogoni activists were sentenced to death by the special military tribunal; six other defendants, including the Deputy President of MOSOP, were acquitted. Although the defendants were not implicated directly in the incident, the nine convictions were based on the premise that the MOSOP activists had effectively incited the killings. An international campaign (led by Saro-Wiwa's son) against the convictions, and numerous appeals for clemency, ensued (although the Nigerian opposition criticized a number of foreign Governments, notably that of South Africa, for favouring a diplomatic approach rather than the imposition of sanctions against Nigeria). However, on 10 November (the same day as a Commonwealth summit meeting, which was to discuss, *inter alia*, events in Nigeria, was convened in Auckland, New Zealand) the nine convicted Ogonis were executed, prompting immediate condemnation by the international community. Nigeria was suspended from the Commonwealth, and threatened with expulsion if the Government failed to restore democracy within a period of two years; only The Gambia voted against the suspension. Later that month the European Union (EU) reaffirmed its commitment to existing sanctions that had been imposed in 1993 (notably an embargo on the export of armaments and military equipment to Nigeria), and extended visa restrictions to civilian members of the administration; the EU also announced the suspension of development co-operation with Nigeria. The Governments of the USA, South Africa and the EU member nations recalled their diplomatic representatives from Nigeria in protest at the executions. The Nigerian Government condemned the imposition of sanctions as an international conspiracy to overthrow the administration, and, in turn, withdrew its diplomatic representatives from the USA, South Africa and the EU member countries. Additional security forces were dispatched to Ogoniland to deter any protests against the executions, while a further 19 Ogonis were charged with complicity in the May 1994 murders.

In February 1996 the 19 Ogonis, who remained in detention pending their trial, appealed to the Commonwealth for assistance in securing their release. In the same month the South African administration denied accusations by Nigeria that it had assisted exiled opponents of the Government. In March a UN mission was dispatched to Nigeria (at the latter's request) to investigate the trial and execution of the nine Ogoni activists in 1995. (However, the Government continued to refuse to receive a Commonwealth ministerial delegation.) Also in March 1996 local government elections, which were contested on a non-party basis, took place as part of the transitional programme; although opposition leaders had urged a boycott, the National Electoral Commission of Nigeria (NECON) claimed that a high level of voter participation had been recorded. In April the UN investigative mission visited Ogoniland, where sizeable anti-Government demonstrations had taken place; it was reported that Ogoni activists and other opposition representatives were prevented from meeting the delegation.

In early June 1996 Abiola's wife, Kudirat, who had been a prominent critic of the administration, was killed by unidentified assailants. The university at Ibadan was temporarily closed, following a student demonstration in protest at the alleged assassination. Abiola's son and a number of his other immediate relatives were subsequently arrested, apparently on suspicion of complicity in the murder. Four members of NADECO were also detained in connection with the incident. Later in June Nigerian officials met the Commonwealth Ministerial Action Group (CMAG), in an attempt to avert the threatened imposition of sanctions; shortly before the discussions took place, the Government released a number of political prisoners, and promulgated legislation regarding the registration of political parties, in an apparent effort to conciliate critics. The Nigerian delegation demanded that Nigeria be readmitted to the Commonwealth in exchange for the Government's adoption of the programme for transition to civilian rule by October 1998. The Commonwealth rejected the programme as unsatisfactory, but remained divided regarding the adoption of consequent measures. It was finally agreed that the Commonwealth would suspend the adoption of sanctions, but that the situation would be reviewed at a further meeting of the CMAG, which was scheduled for September. Canada, however, announced its opposition to this decision and unilaterally imposed a number of sanctions (similar to those already adopted by the EU), including the suspension of military co-operation, the introduction of visa restrictions for members of the administration and their relatives and the cessation of sporting connections.

In October 1996 Abacha announced the creation of a further six states, increasing the total size of the federation to 36 states. At the same time he announced the establishment of a committee of economic representatives, chaired by the former Head of State, Shonekan, which was to draft the Government's future policy for economic development.

In early 1997 escalating tension between the Ijaw and Itsekiri ethnic groups in the town of Warri, in south-western Nigeria, severely disrupted Shell's petroleum-mining operations in the region. In March a demonstration by members of the Ijaw ethnic group in Warri, in protest at the relocation of local government headquarters from Ijaw to Itsekiri territory, precipitated violent clashes. Protesters seized Shell installations and took about 100 employees of the enterprise hostage, in an attempt to force the Government to accede to their demands. A curfew was subsequently imposed in the region in an attempt to restore order. By mid-April it was reported that about 90 people had been killed in the disturbances, while the disruption in petroleum production had contributed to a national fuel shortage, effectively suspending the transportation system in much of the country. The abduction and killing of two Ijaw in Warri precipitated a resumption in hostilities, and further attacks on Shell installations ensued. Later in May the authorities established a commission of inquiry, which was to investigate the cause of the clashes and submit recommendations for restoring order in the region.

In May 1997 some 22 pro-democracy and human rights organizations, including MOSOP and the CD, formed a loose alliance, the United Action for Democracy (UAD), with the aim of campaigning for the restoration of democracy in Nigeria. In July the authorities announced a new electoral timetable: elections to the State Assemblies were to take place on 6 December, followed by elections to the National Assembly on 25 April 1998, and presidential and gubernatorial elections on 1 August of that year (despite previous indications that the gubernatorial elections were to be held in late 1997). The absence from the forthcoming presidential election of any of the most prominent second- and third-republic politicians had by early 1997 been assured by NECON's failure to recognize the parties supported by these figures. The United Nigerian Congress Party (UNCP) proved to be the most successful party in the state assembly elections of 6 December, in which it won control of 29 of the 36 regional bodies, with a total of 637 of the 990 contested seats; the other four parties accused the UNCP of extensive electoral malpractice.

A CMAG report on Nigeria, which was prepared prior to a summit meeting of Commonwealth Heads of Government in October 1997, criticized the Government's record on human rights and the inadequacies of the planned transition to civilian rule. However, at the summit meeting which took place in Edinburgh, United Kingdom, the member Governments postponed for a further year the threat of more severe economic sanctions and Nigeria's expulsion from the organization, reiterating demands that democracy be restored by 1 October 1998. The Nigerian Government had succeeded in increasing its standing with Commonwealth members by pressurizing the military junta in Sierra Leone to agree to the restoration to power of the democratically elected Government of President Ahmed Tejan Kabbah.

In December 1997, following the suspicious death of Maj. Gen. Yar'Adua in prison, it was reported that an assassination attempt had been staged at Abuja airport against Abacha's deputy, Diya, who was known to favour the military's complete withdrawal from the Government. Diya was subsequently arrested and charged with planning the violent overthrow of the Government, together with several other senior officials and a number of civilians. A special military tribunal was established in Jos, and in February 1998 it commenced proceedings against some 30 defendants. At the opening session Diya claimed the charges against him had been fabricated by the military leadership. In April Diya and five others were sentenced to death; a further four defendants were sentenced to life imprisonment, while five received shorter custodial terms and 15 were acquitted. Appeals for clemency were made by foreign Governments and by prominent individuals within Nigeria.

In early March 1998 the Government's political and commercial supporters increased pressure for Abacha to be re-elected as a civilian President. A rally was staged in Abuja, in which thousands of people from around the country were transported to the capital by a group known as Youths Earnestly Ask for Abacha (YEAA); the organization's leader, Daniel Kanu, admitted that its activities were financed by the Government. The five registered political parties, having met in February 1998 to consider the adoption of Abacha as a consensus candidate, all proceeded to nominate Abacha during special government-funded conventions, which took place in mid-April. Public rejection of Abacha's rule was reflected in the boycott of the 25 April legislative elections, widely observed throughout the country; in many regions the voter turn-out was estimated to be as low as 1%. The political atmosphere became increasingly volatile from the end of April when some 10 people were killed in bomb attacks in Ife and Lagos (for which no organization claimed responsibility). In the course of anti-Government protests in early May, violent clashes between demonstrators and the security forces resulted in the deaths of at least seven people and the arrest of numerous others. Attempts at constructing a united pro-democracy alliance intensified during May with the formation of a Joint Action Committee of Nigeria (JACON), comprising a total of 45 groups which opposed the military Government.

Abubakar and Transition, 1998–99

On 8 June 1998 Abacha died unexpectedly in the presidential residence in Abuja. Senior military officers, including the Chief of Defence Staff, Maj.-Gen. Abdulsalami Abubakar and the Chief of Army Staff, Maj.-Gen. Ishaya Bamaiyi, rapidly asserted their authority, and Abubakar was designated as Abacha's successor. The regime pledged to continue the Abacha Government's transition to civilian rule. The UAD responded by urging continued protests against the military Government.

Abubakar (who was promoted to the rank of General) was formally installed as Head of State on 9 June 1998. The Secretary-General of the Commonwealth subsequently announced that the sanctions imposed against Nigeria would remain in force until democratic elections took place. In early July, following discussions with UN officials, the new authorities agreed to release Abiola from detention. Upon his release, however, Abiola, who had been met by a US government delegation, collapsed, and subsequently died. Violent rioting ensued, amid widespread speculation that the authorities were responsible for Abiola's death. Although a subsequent autopsy indicated that he had died of heart failure, it was reported that neglect of his health during his period in detention had contributed to his collapse. Later in July Abubakar, who had ordered the release of a number of political prisoners, announced that the transition to civilian rule would be completed on 29 May 1999. The Government dissolved the five political parties, NECON and other electoral bodies. In early August a new 31-member Federal Executive Council, which included a number of civilians, was appointed to remain in office pending the formal transition to civilian rule; an Independent National Electoral Commission (INEC) was also established. Later that month INEC announced that local government elections would take place on 5 December 1998 and state legislative elections on 9 January 1999, followed by elections to a bicameral national legislature on 20 February and a presidential election on 27 February. On 7 September 1998 the Government published the draft Constitution that had been submitted by the NCC in June 1995.

Abubakar also initiated a process of intensive discussions with opposition groupings, including those who had been most critical of military rule. Some prominent activists, such as leaders of JACON, refused to accept any continuation of military rule. NADECO leaders insisted on the immediate formation of a government of national unity and the holding of a sovereign national conference, but by August 1998 several prominent NADECO supporters were accepting the transition programme as proposed by the military. Abubakar continued to release political prisoners and to urge Nigerians to return from exile (an appeal that eventually prompted the return to Nigeria of Wole Soyinka and the MOSOP leader, Ledum Mitee, in October, although others chose to remain abroad).

The renewed process of transition to civilian rule progressed during August 1998, with strong indications from most northern political leaders that they would accede to demands from southern activists that the next President should be from the south of the country. When INEC commenced proceedings at the end of August numerous political groupings applied for registration. The leading party to emerge was the People's Democratic Party (PDP), which was established by a group of northern politicians who had urged Abacha not to seek re-election in March, but which also built on the political structure formerly created by Shehu Musa Yar'Adua and used funds provided by other retired generals. The All People's Party (APP) was formed by a coalition of associations that had received considerable support during Abacha's rule. By contrast, the Alliance for Democracy (AD) was formed by a grouping of politicians who had been associated with NADECO and were committed to a political restructuring of the country. Of the 29 parties that applied for registration, nine were approved by INEC in late October. Soon afterwards Obasanjo, who had been released from detention in June, announced that he was joining the PDP and that he hoped to become the party's candidate for the presidency.

After sanctions by the Commonwealth, the EU, the USA and other nations were ended (see below), Nigeria was able to secure significant international assistance for the organization of its elections. At local government elections, which took place on 5 December 1998, the PDP gained control of about 60% of local municipal councils. INEC ruled that only the PDP, APP and AD had received the requisite number of votes at these local elections to be allowed to contest the elections at state and federal level in January and February 1999. At the state legislative elections, which took place on 9 January, the PDP secured the highest number of votes, except in the south-west where the AD had its base, while the APP received most support in the Middle Belt and in various parts of the north; the PDP won 21 of the 36 governorships. After the state elections the AD and APP agreed to establish an electoral alliance to contest the federal legislative elections, and to present a joint presidential candidate.

Although the 19 detained Ogoni activists were released in September 1998, violent protests in the Niger Delta region intensified throughout the year and into 1999. The protests were most intense in areas inhabited by the Ijaw ethnic group and were staged in support of demands for compensation from the Government and the petroleum companies, while there were also clashes between the Ijaw and other ethnic groups, such as the Itsekiri and Ilaje. At times, Nigeria's daily petroleum production was seriously affected by occupations of petroleum installations, and by abductions of oil workers. Such actions intensified after the adoption by Ijaw activists in December of the 'Kaiama Declaration', which demanded the departure of all petroleum companies from the region. In January 1999 there were sharp clashes between troops and armed activists and the security situation deteriorated, particularly in the Ijaw-dominated Bayelsa State, where, as a result, the elections taking place in the rest of the country were postponed.

At the party conventions in February 1999 Obasanjo was nominated to contest the presidential election on behalf of the PDP, with Atiku Abubakar as vice-presidential candidate, while the AD–APP alliance adopted Olu Falae of the AD as its presidential candidate and the APP's Umaru Shinkafi as his running mate. There was a perceptible decline in public interest by the time of the elections to the National Assembly on 20 February, in which only 40% of the electorate participated. At the legislative elections, the PDP secured 208 seats in the 360-member House of Representatives and 60 seats in the 109-member Senate; the AD took 76 seats in the House of Representatives and 20 in the Senate, while the APP won 69 seats in the House of Representatives and 24 in the Senate. (Elections for the remaining seven seats in the House of Representatives and five in the Senate were postponed, owing to continued unrest in the Niger Delta region.) On 27 February 1999 Obasanjo was elected to the presidency, with 62.8% of votes cast. Voting irregularities were reported, and Falae submitted a legal challenge to the electoral results (which was subsequently rejected by the Court of Appeal).

RETURN TO CIVILIAN GOVERNMENT

In the transitional period prior to the installation of civilian rule on 29 May 1999, the outgoing administration approved a new constitutional framework based on the 1979 Constitution (which Obasanjo's first Government had adopted) and also issued decrees designed to reinforce economic liberalization. The new Constitution was formally promulgated on 5 May. Obasanjo was inaugurated as President on 29 May, when the Constitution came into effect; on taking office he initiated a major reorganization of military officers, appointing Rear-Adm. Ibrahim Ogohi as Chief of Defence Staff, Maj.-Gen. Victor Malu as Chief of Army Staff and Air Vice-Marshal Isaac Alfa as Chief of Air Staff. President Obasanjo's administration was subsequently formed with the aim of accommodating those with political experience and achieving full representation of the 36 states. The new federal Cabinet included several members of former military and civilian Governments, including Gen. (retd) Theophilus Danjuma as Minister of Defence, Adamu Ciroma as Minister of Finance and Bola Ige (a member of the opposition AD) as Minister of Power and Steel. Obasanjo also appointed advisers, including Gen. (retd) Aliyu Mohammed, Rilwanu Lukman (the OPEC Secretary-General) and Phillip Asiodu, who had a long-standing influence on government policy. The President ordered the removal from the armed forces of all officers who had held political positions under previous Governments, and allowed the promotion of officers from southern and Middle Belt states to create a balance with those from the northern states. Danjuma announced that troop numbers in the army would be significantly reduced.

As civilian government returned, there was an upsurge in the levels of inter-ethnic violence, first in Warri, where about 200 people were killed in early June 1999 during fighting between three rival communities, and then in the following month, with violent clashes between Hausa and Yoruba communities in the Lagos area and later in Kano. Powerful interest groups who had previously benefited from military rule appeared intent on exacerbating ethnic tension and thereby subverting the introduction of democratic rule.

A potential challenge to the new Constitution arose in late 1999 with the proposed adoption of Muslim *Shari'a* law as the state legal system for substantial parts of the north. Zamfara was the first state to take this measure with the proclamation of *Shari'a* by its Governor, Ahmed Sani Yerimah. Despite pressure for a legal challenge to the anticipated *Shari'a* proclamations, President Obasanjo did not declare it to be unconstitutional, indicating by his failure to condemn the state's action that he did not intend to alienate powerful northern interests, and particularly those strongly represented in the PDP.

In October 1999 government investigations resulted in murder charges being brought against Mohammed Abacha, the late ruler's son, and several former senior military officers. Among the murders cited was the assassination of Kudirat Abiola in 1996 and the suspected murder of Shehu Musa Yar' Adua in detention in December 1997. A series of arrests included those of two retired Generals, Ishaya Bamaiyi and Jeremiah Useni, the former Inspector-General of police, Ibrahim Coomassie, and Abacha's head of security, Hamza al-Mustapha. Also in October the Government succeeded in persuading the Swiss Government to order banks to 'freeze' the accounts of Mohammed Abacha, other members of the Abacha family and several senior officials in the former administration, and also confiscated many residences acquired by these officials during the Abacha era.

Trouble in the Niger Delta region again erupted in November 1999, when the army was sent into Bayelsa State to respond to the killing of several policemen by young Ijaw militants in the town of Odi. Armed troops burnt the town to the ground, killing large numbers of inhabitants and forcing many to flee. The Government justified the action as necessary to restore order, but the massacre was condemned by human rights groups. Later in the same month there was a further eruption of anti-Hausa violence in Lagos State, this time with the clear involvement of the militant Yoruba group, the Odua People's Congress (OPC). The killings continued for some days, and a total of about 100 people were believed to have died. The authorities took suppressive measures against the OPC, arresting a number of suspected supporters. The OPC was, nevertheless, implicated in further Yoruba violence against northerners in Lagos in October 2000. The Government subsequently banned the OPC and many other militia organizations.

In view of increasing tensions around the country, there were renewed demands for the convening of a sovereign national conference, although these were not supported in the National Assembly. The demands for a sovereign conference tended to be led by the more militant associations, such as the OPC and the Ijaw Youth Congress. Other ethnic or regional organizations, such as those representing Middle Belt and south-eastern opinion, preferred to urge the establishment of a nationwide confederation on the basis of regions. Among the new groups emerging at this time was the previously unknown Movement for the Actualization of the Sovereign State of Biafra (MASSOB), although this did not receive the support of the most prominent Ibo politicians; MASSOB leaders' declaration of Biafran independence in May 2000 was widely ignored. The Government's proposed solution to the crisis in the Niger Delta was to introduce a Niger Delta Development Commission (NDDC) and to increase the allocation to the petroleum-producing states to 13% of the federal budget. However, after disagreements between the executive and the National Assembly, the President vetoed amendments to the NDDC bill, although in May the legislature eventually overruled the veto and approved the bill.

Heightened Religious and Ethnic Divisions

The anticipated adoption of *Shari'a* law in a number of northern states, including Sokoto, Kebbi, Katsina, Kano and Yobe, caused increasing religious tensions from December 1999 onwards. In Ilorin, Kwara State, 14 churches were burnt by suspected Islamist fundamentalists, prompting Christian leaders to demand the arrest of those responsible. After news that the application of *Shari'a* had commenced in Zamfara in February 2000, Christians in the town of Kaduna staged a demonstration against the possible introduction of Islamic law in their state, but skirmishes with Muslims rapidly escalated into widespread violence, in which more than 1,000 people were killed and property was destroyed in the city from late February into early March. Revenge attacks against Muslims also occurred in southern cities, notably in Aba, Abia State. A decision at the end of February by northern State Governors to suspend the application of *Shari'a* was too late to prevent much of the violence. There was also a recurrence of the religious clashes in Kaduna in May, in which an estimated 150 people were killed. In that month state Governments that had adopted *Shari'a* law agreed to revert back to the penal code, but this proved to be only a temporary measure. By mid-2001 *Shari'a* law had been introduced in a total of 12 northern states, many of which ordered the immediate closure of establishments selling alcohol and the arrest of prostitutes. In June there was an outbreak of violent anti-*Shari'a* protests (by Christians who burned down at least one mosque in the town of Tafawa Balewa, Bauchi State). In early September violent conflict erupted between Christians and Muslims in the principal Middle Belt city of Jos, in Plateau State (a state that had not adopted *Shari'a* law and where large numbers of people had chosen to take refuge from the anticipated imposition of the Islamic code). During the violence at least 200 people were killed, while hundreds more were injured, and many houses, churches and mosques were destroyed. Fighting erupted once again in the same city two days later, after Muslim youths demonstrated in celebration of the terrorist attacks against the USA on 11 September. In subsequent days the events in Jos provoked similar violence elsewhere, including the burning of a church in Kano and attacks on Hausa traders in Onitsha. Further unrest was precipitated in Kano in October, when, in response to the first US bombardment of Afghanistan, demonstrators burned British and US flags and clashed with security forces, before rioting in the mainly Christian Sabon Gari district; rival Muslim and Christian groups of youths caused disturbances in heavily populated districts, in defiance of a night curfew.

Ethnic tension was also at a high level in several parts of the country during 2001. In June there was full-scale conflict between Tiv and Azara communities in the Middle Belt state of Nassarawa, following the assassination of a traditional Azara ruler. After violent attacks by Tiv militia groups, Azara communities retaliated, forcing the displacement of at least 35,000 Tiv villagers. In neighbouring Benue State, in October, Tiv militia killed 19 members of the armed forces, provoking brutal reprisals from government troops, who massacred at least 200 civilians and destroyed many houses. (These events were directly comparable to those in Bayelsa State two years earlier; as on that occasion, the Government endeavoured to justify the actions of the army, while human rights groups expressed outrage.) Elsewhere, there were further ethnic confrontations, notably between Itsekiri and Urhobo communities in Warri and between Yoruba and Hausa groups in Lagos. The increasing ethnic polarization of numerous communities throughout Nigeria was accompanied by a marked rise in the power of unofficial militia and vigilante groups. Some, like the OPC in the south-western states, acted in defiance of the political authorities, while others were believed to be in the direct pay of state governments, or of individual state governors, such as the 'Bakassi boys', who were employed to enforce government control in several south-eastern cities and towns. In Bayelsa the Speaker of the state House of Assembly was impeached in 2001, having allegedly employed militia to intimidate and harass members of the Assembly. A major political shock occurred in December, when a prominent AD member and Minister of Justice, Bola Ige, was assassinated at his private residence in Ibadan. Any credible motive for the killing was not immediately apparent, although Ige was believed to have had many critics and rivals within Yoruba politics, and had been actively campaigning for Yorubas to support Obasanjo in 2003.

The *Shari'a* issue not only dominated the political climate after 2001, but also complicated the relationship between the presidency and the divided National Assembly, while causing wide differences between individual states themselves and exacerbating relations between the states and the Federal Government. Although the Obasanjo administration did not attempt directly to prevent states from adopting *Shari'a* law, it repeatedly expressed its opposition to the states' actions and was active in encouraging legal challenges to *Shari'a*-based judgments. International publicity also served to restrain the courts in the implementation of the harshest penalties. In early 2002 the *Shari'a* Court of Appeal overturned death sentences that had earlier been imposed on two women. In August, however, a Court of Appeal in Katsina State upheld a sentence of death by stoning imposed against a woman on grounds of adultery, prompting strong international outrage. (A further appeal against the sentence proved successful in September 2003.)

Plans by the Minister of Defence, Gen. (retd) Theophilus Danjuma, to reduce the size of the armed forces were abandoned at the end of 2000. However, he remained committed to undertaking a major reorganization of the military, with a view to improving efficiency in maintaining national security, and in peace-keeping duties abroad. More than 250 army commanders were replaced in February 2001, and in April the senior armed forces officers were retired, including the Chief of Army Staff, Gen. Victor Malu, who had earlier expressed criticism of the planned reorganization of the services, and especially of the role of US military advisers and trainers. In response to the upsurge of religious and ethnic conflict in the second half of 2001, troops were deployed in at least six different states, although the army's reputation was damaged by a number of reported human rights violations, especially those that emerged after the government reprisals against civilians in Benue State in October 2001, for which Obasanjo eventually issued an apology.

OBASANJO'S SECOND TERM

The influence of the former military establishment on the course of Nigerian politics was again demonstrated in the political manoeuvrings that preceded the state and federal elections, held in April–May 2003. Most of the larger parties chose well-known former military figures as their presidential candidates. During 2002 the patronage of former President Babangida was also detected behind the formation of several new political parties. Three new organizations were registered by INEC in June, and a further 22 were registered at the end of the year. Within the ruling PDP, for much of 2002 there was evidence of severe division between the presidency and the party's elected representatives in the National Assembly, culminating in concerted efforts to impeach Obasanjo for alleged breaches of the Constitution. A House of Representatives vote in early August allowed the impeachment process to proceed, prompting a meeting of the PDP national executive to resolve the differences between the legislature and the President. In September former President Shagari undertook successful mediation, which concluded with a formal promise by Obasanjo to improve his office's communications system at all levels. Owing largely to the powerful influence of Vice-President Atiku Abubakar in many northern and eastern states, Obasanjo was convincingly reselected at a PDP conference in January 2003 as the party's presidential candidate. The APP, now renamed the All Nigeria People's Party (ANPP), selected Gen. (retd) Muhammadu Buhari, while the National Democratic Party (NDP) was represented by Gen. (retd) Ike Nwachukwu. Former 'Biafran' leader Ojukwu Chukwuemeka Odumegwu was to contest the election on behalf of the All Progressive Grand Alliance (APGA).

INEC's competence and independence were called into question, both prior to the elections, and subsequently, over alleged flagrant malpractice during the polls themselves. After criticism from the Catholic Episcopal Commission, INEC tried to improve the status of the electoral register, but had to plead for substantial federal funding in order to recruit and train 500,000 officials for polling station duties. During the period of federal and state elections in April–May 2003, numerous irregularities were noted, a factor that encouraged several of the opposition parties to challenge the official results later. Nevertheless, the PDP emerged with convincingly large majorities in the elections, securing 213 seats in the House of Representatives and 73 seats in the Senate. The ANPP won only 95 seats in the House of Representatives and 28 seats in the Senate, while the five other parties were very poorly represented. In the presidential election, Obasanjo won 61.9% of the votes and Buhari 32.2%. In state governorship contests, the PDP won in 28 states across the federation, the ANPP in seven northern states and the AD only in Lagos state. Most international observers endorsed the results, after allowing for margins of error. Leading representatives of the minority parties persisted in contesting the election results, claiming that widespread irregularities had been perpetrated; however, a legal challenge by Buhari was rejected by the federal Court of Appeal.

At the installation of his new Cabinet, Obasanjo pledged to transform the country, focusing on economic recovery, investment in education and poverty reduction, employment creation, improved security and a fight against corruption. The new Government incorporated some high-profile economic reformers, including Dr. Ngozi Okonjo-Iweala as Minister of Finance, Nasr El-Rufai as Minister of the Federal Capital Territory and Obiageli Ezekwesili as Minister of Education, and rapidly proved more effective than its predecessor in undertaking economic reforms and in proceeding to take action against some high-profile corruption cases. However, it still faced the challenge of maintaining security, especially in the Niger Delta and Middle Belt regions.

The most intense security problems arose in the vicinity of Warri, Delta State, and various other petroleum-producing locations in the Delta region, where an increasing state of tension continued after the 2003 elections. Militants were reported to be engaging in the regular theft and sale of substantial amounts of crude petroleum, estimated at between 15%–30% of all petroleum being produced in the Delta region, and using the proceeds to arm themselves with increasingly sophisticated weapons. Conflict between Ijaw and Itsekiri militants and communities caused more than 100 deaths in March and again in August. After the Federal Government dispatched troops in July on a mission termed 'Operation Restore Hope', Obasanjo ordered the military both to restore peace to the region and to secure oil installations in order to prevent the theft of petroleum. He also promised to find means of accommodating the interests of the warring groups, but expressed disappointment that traditional ethnic leaders had failed to intervene to quell the unrest. In February 2004 a joint Ijaw-Itsekiri peace committee succeeded in reaching a preliminary peace agreement that would allow displaced families to return to their homes, but this was followed by a further renewal of hostilities in April, accompanied by an upsurge in attacks on the petroleum installations of ChevronTexaco. Following violent incidents in Port Harcourt in September, international attention was attracted by the emergence of an Ijaw-supported movement, the Niger Delta People's Volunteer Force (NDPVF), under the leadership of Mujahid Dokubo-Asari. The NDPVF began to demand the recognition of Ijaw economic and political rights and issued a deadline for the departure of all foreign nationals. The threat of greater turmoil prompted President Obasanjo to invite Dokubo-Asari to Abuja for peace talks in October, and it was agreed that the NDPVF would disarm and demobilize its supporters. Although some weapons were relinquished, it subsequently emerged that the movement was reluctant to surrender all of them, and violent incidents against oil industry workers continued in 2005, with a sharp escalation following the arrest of Dokubo-Asari in

September and his subsequent arraignment on treason charges. A new group, the self-styled Movement for the Emancipation of the Niger Delta (MEND), claimed responsibility for a series of attacks on oil installations near Port Harcourt, starting in December, and subsequent kidnappings of foreign oil workers, usually accompanied by threats that they would be killed if the foreign enterprises employing them did not leave the Delta region. During February 2006 about 20% of oil production was suspended after new attacks near the Forcados oil terminal in Delta State. MEND allied itself with demands for the release of not only Dokubo-Asari, but also the detained Governor of Bayelsa State, Diepreye Alamieyeseigha, who had been impeached by his State Assembly in December, following an investigation into money-laundering activities which had led to his earlier arrest in the United Kingdom, from where he had returned home, forfeiting bail. The militant groups appeared to have access to more sophisticated weaponry than before and to be using more diverse tactics, including staging occasional car bomb attacks in both Port Harcourt and Warri.

A high-level political conference to examine the basis of Nigeria's federal structure and its democratic institutions opened in Abuja in February 2005, under the chairmanship of Justice Niki Tobi and Rev. Matthew Kukah. Disagreements arose over the modalities of any rotation of the presidency between different regions of the country and over oil revenue derivation issues. By the time the conference closed in July 2005, it had established little more than general principles regarding the right of oil-producing areas to be actively involved in the management of resources. It recommended an increase in the level of derivation from 13% to 17% of revenue, pending a report by an expert commission on the subject. The majority of delegates favoured the retention of the existing arrangement of two four-year terms in office for the President and State Governors; a minority group favoured the adoption of a single term of six years for the President and five years for State Governors without the possibility of re-election. Even as these issues appeared to reach resolution in the conference, supporters of President Obasanjo began to demand openly a constitutional amendment to allow him to seek a third term in office. The ruling PDP soon became deeply divided on the issue; supporters of Vice-President Atiku Abubakar's candidacy for the presidency in 2007 intensified their own campaigning, which eventually resulted in the formation of a new political party, the Advanced Congress of Democrats (ACD). The possibility of an electoral alliance between the ACD and the AD was proposed by the Governor of Lagos State, Bola Tinubu. Subsequently, in May 2006, the campaign for Obasanjo to serve a third term was abandoned, after the defeat of a motion to that effect in the Senate.

Amid much speculation about the PDP's choice of a successor to Obasanjo, the rift between President Obasanjo and Vice-President Abubakar widened to the point of mutual public recriminations. In September 2006 Obasanjo requested that the Senate commence impeachment proceedings against Abubakar on the evidence of a report by the Economic and Financial Crimes Commission (EFCC), which alleged that Abubakar had made unauthorized use of US $125m. from the Petroleum Technology Development Fund to finance the business interests of friends and close associates. (The EFCC was also conducting investigations into foreign exchange violations by at least 13 State Governors.) Following his expulsion from the PDP, although retaining the post of Vice-President, Abubakar announced that he would stand as a presidential candidate, and in November was adopted by the newly formed Action Congress (AC). The ANPP again selected Buhari as its candidate. After much manoeuvring behind the scenes, the PDP chose Katsina State Governor, Umaru Musa Yar'Adua, the younger brother of the late Shehu Musa Yar'Adua, as its candidate with the Bayelsa State Governor Goodluck Jonathan as his running mate. In January 2007 Obasanjo conducted a final reshuffle of his Government, increasing the powers of certain ministries, particularly those of Defence under Thomas I. Aguiyi-Ironsi, Energy under Dr Edmund Daukoru, Commerce and Industry under Dr Aliyu Modibbo, Mines and Steel Development under Lesley Obiora, and Agriculture and Water Resources under Alhaji Adamu Bello.

In mid-February 2007 the EFCC sent letters to all political parties, listing 130 electoral candidates for various offices who were liable to be charged with corruption; the list included Vice-President Abubakar. The PDP agreed to replace 52 of its candidates who appeared on the list, but Abubakar dismissed the move as blackmail and won a series of legal rulings permitting him to continue his campaign. As the April elections approached, the PDP emerged as one of the better organized of the parties, the only serious competition coming from the ANPP, while the AC gained only unreliable support from PDP dissidents and was hampered by INEC's repeated attempts to block Abubakar's candidature, which was eventually approved by a high court ruling on the eve of the election.

Controversial 2007 Elections

Both rounds of elections, at state level on 14 April and at federal level on 21 April, were observed as having failed to provide credible results from numerous polling stations. The EU's observer mission stated that it could not endorse the results as legitimate, while the US State Department judged that the elections were flawed, although it did not call for a rerun. Results of the presidential elections announced by INEC indicated that Yar'Adua had secured 24.8m. votes, Buhari 6.6m. and Abubakar 2.6m. Although the overall result was broadly respected and accepted, a large number of state-level and other results were subjected to legal challenges. Both sets of elections, and especially the presidential poll, were marred by a very low turn-out at polling stations, often as a result of their failure to open on time and the late arrival of election materials. Voters were also deterred by reports of violence and intimidation. Although INEC claimed a 55% turn-out, independent observers estimated that the turn-out for the presidential elections was as low as 20% and only 15% in the southern states.

In the wake of the elections, Obasanjo admitted that the elections were 'not perfect', while the head of INEC acknowledged the difficulties encountered but maintained that, overall, the elections were deemed to have been conducted freely and fairly. A second round of state-level elections was held on 28 April, including one governorship and 26 legislative polls. Election tribunals were established to examine the numerous disputes at state level.

After his inauguration on 29 May 2007, Yar'Adua appointed a transitional management team chaired by Modibbo. He also appointed Kingibe as Secretary to the Government. With a declared aim of establishing a government of national unity to include representatives of parties other than the PDP, Yar'Adua held discussions with the ANPP which produced agreement at the end of June. The appointments of high-ranking military officials, made by Obasanjo two days before he stepped down, were upheld and included Gen. Owoye Andrew Azazi as Chief of Defence Staff and Gen. Luka Nyeh Yusuf as Chief of Army Staff.

Yar'Adua also pledged to give special priority to the problems of the Niger Delta and intensive discussions commenced with the newly elected Governors from the region, on whose insistence the NDPVF leader, Dokubo-Asari, was released from detention to participate in negotiations. Over the months preceding the elections there had been an escalation of attacks on oil installations, car bombings in Port Harcourt and hostage situations affecting many groups of foreign workers. MEND claimed responsibility for the majority of these actions, although it was apparent that several groups were now active and operating autonomously.

FOREIGN RELATIONS

Nigeria has taken a leading role in African affairs and is a prominent member of the Economic Community of West African States (ECOWAS) and other regional organizations. The Nigerian Government contributed a significant number of troops to the ECOWAS Monitoring Group (ECOMOG), which was deployed in Liberia from August 1990 in response to the conflict between government forces and rebels in that country. In early 1998, following the installation of a democratically elected civilian Government in Liberia, a number of ECOMOG forces were withdrawn from the country, although some remained to assist in the reconstruction of the security forces.

Following further full-scale conflict in Liberia, some 1,500 Nigerian peace-keeping troops were deployed in the country, under an ECOWAS mandate, at the end of August 2003. The Liberian President, Charles Taylor, had accepted an offer of asylum from Obasanjo, and took up residence in Calabar, in south-eastern Nigeria, earlier that month. Nigeria subsequently contributed the largest West African contingent (numbering 1,651 at August 2004) to the UN Mission in Liberia (UNMIL—see chapter on Liberia).

In 1993 Nigerian troops were also dispatched to Sierra Leone, in response to a formal request by the Sierra Leonean Government for military assistance to repulse attacks by the rebel Revolutionary United Front in that country. Following a military coup in Sierra Leone in May 1997, the Nigerian Government increased its military strength in the Sierra Leonean capital, Freetown, and subsequently launched attacks against supporters of the new junta. In February 1998 Nigerian troops succeeded in gaining control of Freetown, and ousting the coup leaders. In March the democratically elected Sierra Leonean President, Alhaji Ahmed Tejan Kabbah, was formally reinstalled. However, the Nigerian contingent suffered heavy casualties, particularly during a concerted rebel assault on Freetown in January 1999 (in which about 800 troops were killed). Nigerian military and political leaders favoured ordering a withdrawal of Nigerian troops from Sierra Leone at the earliest possible moment; in response to the apparent subsequent progress being made in political negotiations between Sierra Leone's Government and rebels, however, it was envisaged that the Nigerian contingent (then numbering 15,000) would remain in the country until peace was restored. Following a UN Security Council decision in October to authorize the deployment of the UN Mission in Sierra Leone (UNAMSIL), ECOMOG was formally withdrawn in April 2000. In response to the taking hostage of UN troops by rebels and subsequent British military intervention to stabilize the situation in Sierra Leone, West African leaders agreed to provide renewed support, and authorized the deployment of 3,000 troops, mainly Nigerians (see chapter on Sierra Leone). A number of ECOMOG troops from Nigeria were transferred to UNAMSIL control over the years that it remained deployed in Sierra Leone.

Following Nigeria's aborted presidential election of June 1993, the United Kingdom, together with other European nations and the USA, imposed military sanctions against the country, as an immediate response to the suspension of the scheduled transition to civilian rule. Further sanctions were adopted in late 1995 (see above). In May 1997 the Nigerian Government imposed an indefinite ban on flights from the United Kingdom, after Nigerian-registered aircraft were banned from British airports on the grounds that they failed to meet safety standards. After the death of Abacha, Nigeria's relations with the United Kingdom, the USA, the EU and the Commonwealth improved rapidly. At the transition to civilian rule on 29 May 1999 Nigeria was automatically readmitted as a full member of the Commonwealth.

The return of civilian government prompted signs of strong economic, political and military support from the USA. President Bill Clinton visited Abuja in August 2000 and indicated his readiness to support a substantial reduction in Nigeria's external debt. Also during 2000 US military officers arrived in the country to train and arm Nigerian contingents for UN peace-keeping functions in Sierra Leone, and a US military advisory company, Military Professional Resources Incorporated (MPRI), began to advise the Government on means of institutionalizing civilian control of the military and restructuring the armed forces. MPRI was reported to favour the establishment of a joint land, sea and air division, to be deployed in the Niger Delta. Differences of opinion within the armed forces over the US advisory role might have reduced the involvement of MPRI, if the US Administration had not intervened with substantial financial support for Nigeria's military reform programme at the end of 2001, a decision that was taken in view of President George W. Bush's pledge to eradicate terrorism. At the same time Nigeria was in discussion with Russia and South Africa regarding military cooperation issues, and, in particular, over plans to revive its defence industries. Other forms of military co-operation were established with Israel, India and the People's Republic of China. The Chinese Government agreed in 2005 to provide new combat jets; there was also a considerable improvement in economic and business relations between Nigeria and China.

In 1991 the Nigerian Government claimed that Cameroonian security forces had annexed several Nigerian fishing settlements in Cross River State (in south-eastern Nigeria), following a long-standing border dispute, based on a 1913 agreement between Germany and the United Kingdom that ceded the Bakassi peninsula in the Gulf of Guinea (a region of strategic significance) to the German protectorate of Kamerun; Cameroon's claim to the region was upheld by an unratified agreement in 1975. Subsequent negotiations between Nigerian and Cameroonian officials in an effort to resolve the dispute achieved little progress. In December 1993 some 500 Nigerian troops were dispatched to the region, in response to a number of incidents in which Nigerian nationals had been killed by Cameroonian security forces. Later that month the two nations agreed to establish a joint patrol at the disputed area, and to investigate the cause of the incidents. In February 1994, however, the Nigerian Government increased the number of troops deployed in the region. Later in February Cameroon announced that it was to submit the dispute for adjudication by the UN, the Organization of African Unity (now the African Union), and the International Court of Justice (ICJ), and requested military assistance from France. Subsequently, owing to intensive regional and international diplomacy, the tension in the border region did not erupt into hostilities, although armed clashes occurred on various occasions between late 1994 and January 2002.

In October 2002 the ICJ issued a ruling that upheld Cameroon's claim to the Bakassi peninsula, as well as Nigeria's offshore boundary claims. The Nigerian Government did not at first reject the judgment, but later publicly criticized it, in support of the views of Nigerian inhabitants of the peninsula. At a meeting between Obasanjo and Cameroon's President, Paul Biya, arranged by the UN Secretary-General in Geneva, Switzerland, in mid-November, it was agreed to establish a joint commission to consider ways to defuse tension, including possible troop withdrawals, demilitarization of the common border and programmes of meetings between local and national officials. An agreement on the demarcation of the Cameroon border in the Lake Chad region was reached in December 2003, when Nigeria ceded 33 villages to Cameroonian control. However, Nigeria's planned withdrawal from the Bakassi peninsula under the ICJ ruling, subsequently scheduled for 15 September 2004, was opposed in the House of Representatives, which instead adopted a motion demanding that a UN-supervised referendum be conducted in the region. The Nigerian Government announced that the transfer of authority had been postponed, citing technical difficulties in the final demarcation of the maritime border. On 12 June 2006 Obasanjo and Biya signed an agreement in New York, in the presence of the UN Secretary-General, Kofi Annan, providing for the transfer of the Bakassi region to the sovereignty of Cameroon. The withdrawal of some 3,000 Nigerian troops from the region, monitored by German, British, French and US officials, began in early August. Nigeria transferred sovereignty over the Bakassi peninsula to Cameroon at an official ceremony on 14 August (although two regions—West Atabong and Akwabana—were to remain under Nigerian direct governance for a provisional period of two years, during which time the population would be expected either to opt for Cameroonian sovereignty or to move to Nigeria). Cameroon agreed not to deploy a military presence in the peninsula for five years.

Economy

LINDA VAN BUREN

The outgoing President, Olusegun Obasanjo, unveiled two highly unpopular reform measures just hours before his successor, Alhaji Umaru Musa Yar'Adua, was sworn into office on 29 May 2007. The first was an increase in the pump price of a litre of petrol from ₦65 to ₦75, and the second was a rise in the rate of value-added tax (VAT) from 5% to 10%. On 5 June the Nigeria Labour Congress (NLC) issued the new Government with a 14-day ultimatum and four demands: a reversal of the petrol-price rise, returning it to ₦65; a reversal of the VAT increase, returning it to 5%; the reinstatement of a 15% pay increase for public-sector workers, which had been previously announced and then subsequently rescinded by the Obasanjo Government; and a 'review' of the sale, announced earlier in the year during Obasanjo's tenure, of the Government's 51% share of the petroleum refineries at Port Harcourt and Kaduna. Talks continued during the 14-day period, and after intensive negotiations, the Yar'Adua Government agreed to reduce the petrol price increase to ₦70 per litre, to reverse the VAT increase completely, to reinstate the 15% public-sector pay rise effective retroactively from January 2007, and to direct the Bureau of Public Enterprises (BPE) to review the sale of the two refineries. The NLC found this to be insufficient, and when it announced that the general strike would go ahead on 20 June, reaction was swift, both internally and externally. At home, petrol prices at the pump surged, surpassing ₦200 and sometimes even ₦500 per litre, and globally, the world price of one barrel of light crude soared to US $71.20. The general strike began on 20 June and although it ended four days later, the crippling effects were felt immediately. Domestic flights were cancelled owing to a lack of aviation fuel, and some international flights were diverted to neighbouring countries for fear that fuel for the return flight would not be available in Nigeria. As oil and dock workers downed tools, the lifting of oil and the loading of oil onto tankers ground to a halt. By the time the strike ended it had cost the Nigerian economy millions of naira.

Nigeria's petroleum revenue had increased dramatically in 2005, with record prices per barrel at a time of rising volume capability, and it even increased in 2006 and 2007, despite reduced output caused by 'social unrest' in the main oil-producing areas. In June 2005 the Organization of Petroleum Exporting Countries (OPEC) had raised Nigeria's quota by 41,000 barrels per day (b/d), to 2.3m. b/d, effective from July of that year. During 2004, however, the Obasanjo Government had been confronted by the urgent need to implement economic reforms, despite domestic protests when such stringent reforms were administered. On the one hand, the administration of President Obasanjo received praise from the World Bank for its National Economic Empowerment and Development Strategy (NEEDS) programme. On the other hand, increases in the retail price of petrol, diesel and other fuels prompted popular protests, and the NLC even obtained a court injunction against the price rises. In keeping with Nigeria's three-tier system of government, NEEDS was complemented by the State Economic Empowerment and Development Strategy (SEEDS) and by the Local Economic Empowerment and Development Strategy (LEEDS); all three programmes have received funding pledges.

Despite considerable agricultural and mineral resources, Nigeria is ranked by the World Bank as a low-income country and is among the 20 poorest countries in the world on the basis of income per head. Per head assessments of one of Africa's most powerful economies have been problematic because the population of Nigeria has long been disputed. The 2006 Nigerian census (see below) found that the country's population was 140,003,542, whereas the 1991 Nigerian census had concluded that the population was 88,992,220. Either the population had been growing by 3.6% per year over the 16 years, or one or both of the censuses were inaccurate. According to World Bank estimates, Nigeria's gross national income (GNI) per head was US $280 in 2002, having declined from $300 in 2001 and from $370 in the record year of 1985; GNI per head increased to $560 in 2005; however, this 2005 figure was based on a total population of an estimated 132.8m., considerably lower than the 2006 census results indicated. In 2002 some 66% of all Nigerians were living below the national poverty level of $1 per day, compared to 43% in 1985. By 2005, the number of Nigerians living on less than $1 per day had declined to 52%. The population growth rate for 2004, according to World Bank estimates made before the 2006 census results, was 2.5%. Owing to an increase in offshore petroleum and gas production gross domestic product (GDP) grew by 10.9% in 2003, by 6.1% in 2004, by 8.2% in 2005 and by an estimated 8.9% in 2006, according to the IMF. Statistical assessments of the Nigerian economy have been subject to wide margins of error, as a result of the lack of reliable data.

After years of delays, in March 2006 Nigeria finally conducted its first census since 1991. The poll cost an estimated US $266m. and took place over a five-day period. It involved up to 1m. enumerators, together with a further 42,000 personnel to monitor the enumerators. Many Nigerians have long resisted being counted in a census, arguing that the results would be unreliable and could be used for political purposes, to favour one ethnic or religious group. Controversial subjects, such as religion and ethnic background, were removed from the list of census questions, but citizens were asked about their education level, their occupation, their income, the size of their homes, the nature of their water supply, their toilet facilities, their fuel usage and their access to radio, television and telephone services. It is claimed that the census had a coverage rate of 94%–98%. A post-enumeration survey was undertaken in June to determine public opinion about the way the census had been conducted.

The development of the petroleum industry, which began in the late 1950s and gained momentum in the late 1960s and the 1970s, radically transformed Nigeria from an agriculturally based economy to a major oil exporter. Increased earnings from petroleum exports generated high levels of real economic growth, and by the mid-1970s Nigeria ranked as the dominant economy in sub-Saharan Africa and as the continent's major exporter of petroleum. Following the decline in world petroleum prices in the early 1980s, however, successive Governments became increasingly over-extended financially, with insufficient revenue from petroleum to pay the rising cost of imports or to finance major development projects. The decline in Nigeria's earnings of foreign exchange led to an accumulation of arrears in trade debts and to import shortages, which, in turn, resulted in a sharp fall in economic activity, with most of Nigerian industry struggling to operate at a fraction of installed capacity without essential imported raw materials and spare parts. A series of poor harvests, an overvalued currency and a widening budget deficit compounded the problem. The Buhari military Government responded to the crisis by implementing further cuts in public expenditure and rigid restrictions on credit and the availability of foreign exchange in 1984 and 1985.

The Babangida military Government, which took power in August 1985, continued its predecessor's policies of austerity and monetary control. Babangida declared a state of economic emergency, under which the import of rice and maize was banned, and a national recovery fund was created. However, the dramatic fall in international prices for petroleum in 1986, together with reduced output in all sectors (except agriculture), kept the economy in the depths of recession. In 1986 the Babangida Government announced a two-year structural adjustment programme (SAP), which abolished import licences, reduced import duties and introduced a controversial dual exchange-rate system. The Government also permitted from 1991 the operation of bureaux de change, which were to sell as much as US $30,000 of foreign exchange at market rates that represented a variable premium over the official Central Bank of Nigeria (CBN) rate. Dual exchange rates continued to attract criticism from donor and creditor institutions until they were finally abolished on 1 January 1999 (see below).

In 1988 the Babangida Government issued a list of 110 state enterprises to be privatized or partially commercialized. A special technical committee was established to implement the programme, leading to the creation of the BPE to oversee the privatization process. By 1993 about 90 of the 120 enterprises scheduled for transfer to the private sector, including 12 commercial banks, had been sold, but two of the largest enterprises, National Electric Power Authority (NEPA) and Nigerian Telecommunications (NITEL), were still awaiting privatization at mid-2007. The Power Holding Company of Nigeria plc (PHCN) was established in 2005 as a temporary entity to unbundle NEPA in preparation for privatization. The NEPA conglomerate was divided into six generating companies, 11 distributing companies and one transmitting company. An attempt by the Obasanjo Government to proceed with the NITEL privatization in February 2002 had ended in failure (see below). Measures undertaken under the SAP, with the aim of attracting private capital from abroad, proved largely unsuccessful; investors were deterred by the country's reputation for corruption and by the Government's failure to control expenditure. The budget deficit began to expand rapidly, increasing to more than 12% of GDP. Economic instability was also reflected in persistently high inflation, which averaged at an annual rate of 56% in 1995, according to official figures, although at times the rate reached 72.8% in that year. Inflation was subsequently reduced to only 0.2% by December 1999 and remained in single figures, at an annual rate of 7.1%, in 2000. However, public-sector salary and petrol price increases in mid-2000 resulted in a rise in consumer prices, and the rate reached 18% in 2001. Thereafter, it declined but nevertheless remained in double figures for another four years. In mid-2006 inflation fell below 10% and was on target for the 9.4% that had been forecast for that year.

The political instability in the 1990s severely impeded the ability of successive Governments to implement economic policies and also adversely affected international confidence in the economy. The international community took punitive measures against Nigeria (see Recent History), with detrimental effects on the economy. After the transition to civilian rule on 29 May 1999 and the subsequent ending of sanctions, lending was gradually resumed. The World Bank's International Development Association (IDA) in May 2000 extended US $55m. in project aid for primary education and $20m. in programme aid for Nigeria's Economic Management Capacity Building efforts; both loans were over a period of 35 years, including 10 years' grace. The European Union (EU) in March 2000 pledged €75m. of programme aid, and Japan in December 1999 allocated $50m. to Nigeria for education, water resources and science and technology. In August 2000 the IMF approved a $1,031m., 12-month stand-by credit for Nigeria, in support of the Obasanjo Government's economic programme for 2000–01, and issued a highly favourable report, commending the Nigerian authorities for the progress made towards restoring macroeconomic stability during their first year in office. In the second half of 1999, according to the report, the federal government budget was brought to near balance from a deficit of 8% of GDP in the first five months of 1999. With the aid of higher oil prices, gross international reserves recovered to $7,100m. in 2000 and to $41,900m. at 31 March 2007. Nevertheless, while the IMF may have commended the Obasanjo Government's budgetary proposals, the National Assembly, in practice, exercised its independence by attaching amendments that substantially increased budgetary spending levels and correspondingly resulted in higher fiscal deficits (see below). From 2003 onwards, the Government came under increasing pressure from donors and creditors to exercise greater budgetary transparency. In October 2005 the IMF approved its first Policy Support Instrument (PSI) for Nigeria.

AGRICULTURE

Until Nigeria attained independence in 1960, agriculture was the most important sector of the economy, accounting for more than one-half of GDP and for more than three-quarters of export earnings. However, with the rapid expansion of the petroleum industry, agricultural development was neglected, and the sector entered a relative decline. Between the mid-1960s and the mid-1980s, Nigeria moved from a position of self-sufficiency in basic foodstuffs to one of heavy dependence on imports. Under-investment, a steady drift away from the land to urban centres, increased consumer preference for imported foodstuffs (particularly rice and wheat) and outdated farming techniques continued to keep the level of food production well behind the rate of population growth.

Agriculture contributed 24% of GDP in 2005. FAO estimated that Nigeria's principal crops performed well in 2005, and estimates for 2006 were also favourable. The staple food is cassava, and Nigeria is the world's largest producer of this root crop. Output rose steadily in the 2000s to reach 41.6m. metric tons in 2005. Traditional smallholder farmers, who use simple techniques of production and the bush-fallow system of cultivation, account for around two-thirds of Nigeria's total agricultural production. Subsistence food crops (mainly sorghum, maize, yams, cassava, rice and millet) are grown in the central and western areas of Nigeria and are traded largely outside the cash economy. Of the total cereal crop in 2005, sorghum represented the principal share of 8m. tons, followed by millet (6m. tons), maize (5m. tons) and paddy rice (5m. tons). Cash crops (mainly groundnuts, followed by oil palm, karité nuts, cotton, cashew nuts, coconuts, cocoa, rubber, kola nuts, sesame seed and coffee) are cultivated in the mid-west and north of the country. Output of cocoa beans, which had remained fairly constant at about 145,000 tons during the late 1990s, rose to an estimated 441,000 tons in 2005. Production of green coffee, nearly all of it robusta, has also risen steadily, to 4,990 tons in 2005.

Among the cash crops, only cocoa makes any significant contribution to exports, but Nigeria's share of the world cocoa market has been substantially reduced in recent years, owing to ageing trees, low producer prices, black-pod disease, smuggling and labour shortages. Moreover, the abolition of the Cocoa Marketing Board in 1987 led to poor quality control and fraudulent trading practices, which adversely affected the market reputation of Nigerian cocoa. The Government subsequently reintroduced licences for marketers of cocoa and improved inspection procedures. Recent emphasis has been placed on encouraging domestic cocoa-processing to provide higher-value products for export. The production and export of oil-palm products declined dramatically during the last several decades of the 20th century. Palm-oil production reached 965,000 metric tons in 1993, but had declined to 670,000 tons in 2001. Output of oil palm fruit rose steadily in the 2000s to 8.9m. tons in 2005. Nigeria is by far the largest producer of palm kernels and oil palm in Africa and is the third largest producer in the world (after Malaysia and Indonesia).

In 1990 Nigeria overtook Liberia as the largest rubber producer in Africa. Production reached an estimated 142,000 tons in 2005. Nigeria has about 340,000 ha of rubber plantations and more rubber plantations are planned for southern Kaduna state. Local demand from the tyre and footwear industries continued to exceed domestic supply.

Production of raw cotton fluctuates. Output declined from 420,000 bales in 2004/05 to 400,000 bales in 2005/06. The area under cotton was roughly the same in both years; the decline was attributed to poorer yields, and at 229 kg per ha, Nigeria's yield is the third-lowest in the world, with only Mozambique and Uganda lower. Incentives for local textile companies and higher tariffs on imported cotton in the early 2000s stimulated local production, but the textile manufacturers prefer the higher quality of legally or illegally imported cotton from neighbouring countries.

One crop exhibiting significant growth in production from the mid-1990s was cashew nuts; the area devoted to this crop more than doubled between 1995 and 2005, to 324,000 ha. Output of this up-market tree crop amounted to 594,000 metric tons in 2005.

According to FAO, Nigeria's output of all types of meat totalled some 1.0m. tons in 2005. In that year the national herd comprised 28m. goats, 23m. sheep, 15.9m. cattle, 6.7m. pigs and 151m. chickens. An outbreak of a lethal strain (H5NI) of highly contagious avian influenza was reported in Nigeria among wild migratory birds in 2006, but no cases were reported in humans or in domesticated poultry. The country's annual fish catch declined in the 1980s, owing to shortages of trawlers and nets and to the cancellation of industrial fishing licences. According to FAO, the total fish catch amounted to 509,201 tons in 2004, with herring, sardines and anchovies predominating.

Some 20% of the land area is forested, but exports of timber (mostly obeche, abura and mahogany) are relatively small. Deforestation, particularly in the Niger Delta area, remains a major problem. Following the removal of a ban on specific timber exports, timber production increased in the late 1980s. About 12% of the country's total land area is threatened by the encroaching Sahara desert in the north, and a National Committee on Arid Zone Afforestation was formed to lead Nigeria's anti-desertification programme. As is the case in most African countries, more trees by far are felled for fuel wood than for any other use in Nigeria. Fuel wood is still the main source of domestic energy and accounts for more than 60% of commercial primary energy consumption, in this country of huge petroleum and gas reserves.

Both the Buhari and Babangida Governments made agricultural development and food self-sufficiency key components of their overall economic strategy. Agriculture, arguably the most successful element of the SAP, exhibited sharp increases in food-crop production and a rise in commodity exports. The increase in agricultural production was attributed to three policy initiatives: the devaluation of the naira, which promoted commodity exports and discouraged cheap food imports; the abolition of the state-controlled commodity boards and removal of restrictions on agricultural pricing; and the imposition of an import ban on wheat, maize and barley. Attention was focused on the smallholder farmers, who produce some 90% of the food consumed in Nigeria.

The 1978 Land Use Decree stipulated that land be vested in the State Governors, who would hold it in trust for all Nigerians. The Government agreed to amend the Decree, in response to protests from smallholder farmers, who claimed that the Decree discriminated against them. In addition to the problem of land availability, the other key issues facing the agricultural sector are environmental degradation; inadequate storage facilities and transport, leading to massive post-harvest losses (assessed at nearly 40% of total production in 2000); lack of research and training facilities for the transfer of new technologies; and the absence of credit facilities for smallholder farmers. Nigeria's resources are not fully exploited, and many parts of the country remain very poorly developed. Inadequate provision of economic infrastructure, such as power, water supply, roads and telecommunications, especially in the rural areas, has proved an impediment to both agricultural and industrial investment. Agricultural initiatives by the Federal Government have included a tractor and fertilizer project and a buyer-of-last-resort programme, which guaranteed a minimum price during times of excess.

PETROLEUM

Nigeria is the eighth largest oil producer in the world. It has more than 3,000m. metric tons of proven petroleum reserves, and experts believe that further exploration might double that amount. The first commercial discoveries of petroleum were made in 1956 in the Niger River Delta region. Exports began in 1958, and production advanced rapidly. By the early 1970s the petroleum industry had become the dominant sector of the Nigerian economy and the major determinant of the country's economic growth. In 2005 the petroleum sector accounted for 52% of GDP, for 85% of government revenue and for 99% of exports by value. Nigeria's proven reserves rose from an estimated 22,000m. barrels in 2000 to 31,500m. barrels in 2003. The international price of petroleum has a direct and powerful effect, not only on the Nigerian economy as a whole, but on the national budget, which is based on projected earnings from petroleum exports. For example, the 2006 federal budget was based on a price of only US $35 per barrel and a production level of 2.59m. b/d. With the dramatic increase in the price of a barrel of oil, to beyond the $60 mark in June 2005, prospects for Nigeria's budgetary liquidity were extremely favourable. By using conservative forecasts of supply and price, the Government secures a cushion against unexpected unfavourable trends. If these unfavourable trends do not materialize, a windfall is generated. In recent years, this windfall has been accumulated in the Excess Crude Account, where it is saved for periods of economic disruption. Such a period occurred in the second quarter of 2006, when 'social disruptions' (see Recent History) in the Niger Delta caused an output loss of 600,000 b/d. In April 2006 the IMF commended Nigeria's economic planners for their conservative estimates of petroleum revenues when preparing national budgets, but it cautioned that additional spending in social areas and on infrastructural projects should be 'well-focused', not only at federal level but also at state level.

Nigeria is one of the 12 members of OPEC; it accounts for about 8% of the Organization's total petroleum production. Since Libya restricted output in 1973, Nigeria has been Africa's leading petroleum-producing country. Being of low sulphur content and high quality, its petroleum is much in demand on the European and North American markets. Nigeria's two main types of petroleum are Bonny Light and Forcados.

Revenues from exports of petroleum, which are shared in decreasing proportions between federal, state and local governments, have largely determined the pace of Nigeria's economic development. Successive Governments based their five-year plans on predicted earnings from petroleum. From the 1990s onwards, foreign-exchange revenue from sales of petroleum has been virtually the sole means of meeting the country's import needs and debt-servicing commitments, and the size of these earnings varies widely from year to year. Production costs for Nigerian petroleum are up to seven times as high as those in the Middle East, but the Nigerian product's low sulphur content places it at the upper end of OPEC's price scale. The Niger Delta remains Nigeria's main petroleum-producing region, containing more than 200 oilfields, the largest of which is Forcados Yorki. The USA is the major market for Nigeria's petroleum, taking, on average, about one-half of all exports. Spain, Germany, France, Portugal and the United Kingdom are also important customers. In 2005 US stocks were reported to be at a low level, and the continuing precarious nature of political relations between the USA and Iran placed upward pressure on demand, thereby contributing to the rise in the international price of petroleum. Nigeria was well placed to benefit from this, providing it could maintain regular supplies. Militant activity succeeded in suspending some output from the country's total production, but new installations came on stream in 2005 and 2006 to compensate, and more capacity was under construction.

The state-owned Nigerian National Oil Corpn (NNOC) was formed in 1971 to be the Nigerian partner in the operations of the foreign petroleum companies. In 1977 the NNOC was merged with the Ministry of Petroleum Resources to form the Nigerian National Petroleum Corpn (NNPC), which gradually increased its equity stake in most operating companies. In 1979 the NNPC nationalized the interests of British Petroleum (BP) in Nigeria, in retaliation for BP's participation in an oil-exchange agreement that led indirectly to the shipment of Nigerian petroleum to South Africa. Agreements governing the petroleum producing companies' terms of operation were not officially signed until 1984, after being effective for more than 10 years. In 1992 the Babangida Government sold the nationalized BP interests to Shell, Elf Aquitaine (now part of Total) and other private enterprises. In 1993 all major enterprises operating in Nigeria—Shell (the largest), Mobil, Chevron, Agip, Texaco and Elf Aquitaine—initiated new development programmes, while BP and Statoil, the Norwegian state-owned petroleum company, signed a new agreement with the Government. After government mismanagement of the NNPC's accounts, the company could no longer meet its financial obligations to the petroleum companies. In 1988 the NNPC was commercialized and was restructured as a holding company, with 12 subsidiaries: the National Petroleum Investment Management Services (NAPIMS), the Nigerian Petroleum Development Co (NPDC), the Nigerian Gas Co (NGC), the Products and Pipelines Marketing Co (PPMC), Integrated Data Services Limited (IDSL), Nigerian Liquefied Natural Gas (NLNG), National Engineering and Technical Co (NETCO), Hydrocarbon Services Nigeria (HYSON), Warri Refinery and Petrochemical Co (WRPC), Kaduna Refinery and Petrochemical Co (KRPC), Port Harcourt Refining Co (PHRC) and Eleme

Petrochemicals Co (EPCL). On 17 May 2007 the outgoing Obasanjo Government controversially approved the privatization of 51% of PHRC and KRPC. This sale became a major factor in the June 2007 general strike (see above) in the first month of the Yar'Adua Government. The buyer of the 51% share in these two refineries was Bluestar Oil Services Limited, a consortium comprising Sinopec of the People's Republic of China and three Nigerian firms, Dangote Oil and Gas, Transnational Corpn and Zenon Oil. In response to this unpopular sale, the Yar'Adua Government tasked the BPE with reviewing the refinery privatization, in a bid to placate the NLC and avert the general strike. On 21 June 2007 the BPE announced that 10% of the equity of the two refineries would be retained for the refinery workers and that another 10% of the equity would be reserved for the local 'host communities'.

Since 1994 security in the onshore Niger Delta has been difficult. Pipelines and manifolds have been sabotaged, spilling oil into the surrounding environment, and hostages have been regularly taken and released a few days later. In the first half of 2006 29 foreign oil workers—not only British, US and Canadian nationals, but also workers of nationalities as diverse as Bulgarian, Honduran and South Korean—were seized and then released. As security issues severely disrupted Nigeria's onshore production, the focus of attention shifted to offshore production, and construction was carried out with consideration for security. The greatest benefit to production came on 25 November 2005 with the beginning of production at the Bonga field, 120 km offshore, in water over 1,000 m deep. This 60 sq km technologically advanced field comprises 16 wells and cost US $3,600m. to develop to first production. Its designated capacity is 225,000 barrels of oil and 150m. cu ft of gas per day. The deep-water Bonga field boasts one of the world's largest Floating Production, Storage and Offloading (FPSO) vessels as well as extensive underwater operating facilities. The Erha field, 97 km offshore, in water 1,200 m deep, began production in May 2006, with a designated capacity of about 210,000 barrels of oil and about 300m. cu ft of gas per day. In February 2005 the NNPC signed a US $1,000m. contract for an FPSO vessel for the 45,000-acre Agbami deep offshore field, where reserves were estimated at more than 800m. barrels. Agbami, in which the NNPC held 50% of the equity and Chevron Texaco 32%, was expected to produce 250,000 b/d of crude oil and 450m. cu m of gas per day.

Nigeria has four petroleum refineries: Port Harcourt A, Port Harcourt B, Warri and Kaduna. Port Harcourt B, the newest, was designed to refine for export; owing to problems at the other three refineries, however, there have been times when Port Harcourt B's entire production has been for domestic consumption. The Warri refinery, Nigeria's oldest, was closed in January 2006, after militants bombed the pipeline supplying it with crude oil; at mid-2006 the refinery remained closed, as security considerations delayed repair work on the damaged pipeline.

Government subsidization of petroleum products for the domestic market reportedly amounted to US $192m. in the first quarter of 2000 alone, and these subsidies are strongly discouraged by the IMF and the World Bank. Smuggling is a continuing problem; despite popular discontent with the price increases, in neighbouring countries petrol is sold for the equivalent of ₦45 per litre and higher, providing a substantial incentive for cross-border trafficking of the commodity.

In 1996 it was announced that the Government was to divest a major part of its average 57% share in the joint-venture petroleum partnerships with Shell, Chevron, Mobil, Texaco, Elf Aquitaine and Agip, and to enter into production-sharing arrangements instead. However, subsequent diplomatic disagreements with the USA, in particular, prompted criticism over the prospect of foreign nationals owning Nigerian petroleum. In 1997 the Government announced that a committee would be set up to advise on the matter. The Deep Offshore and Inland Basin Production Sharing Contracts Decree was promulgated in March 1999, prompting a number of announcements concerning new investment in petroleum exploration and development. Shell proposed a five-year project, at an estimated cost of US $8,500m.; the enterprise planned to develop four major offshore oilfields, including the Bonga field (see above) and two large shallow-water offshore fields, which would generate $20,000m. over a 25-year period. In January 2000 Shell announced plans to drill a further two development wells and two sidetrack wells in its shallow-water Ima oilfield, near the Bonny terminal. The Ima field, discovered in 1994 and brought into production in 1996, had produced 11m. barrels by January 2000 from 10 wells and contained estimated reserves of 15m.–30m. barrels. The new wells were expected to double Ima's output by 6,000–8,000 b/d. Interest has also centred on the Nembe field. Although this area of mangrove swamps commenced petroleum production in the late 1980s, the first 'three-dimensional' seismic survey was completed only in 1998, after which 42 new wells were drilled. China National Petroleum Corpn (CNPC) International Nigeria Ltd won a contract in January 2002 to conduct a 'four-dimensional' survey of the region.

Development of an integrated petrochemicals industry has been a main priority of successive Governments since 1977. Construction of Phase I involved three plants and was completed in 1987. The three are a carbon-black plant near Warri, a polypropylene plant also near Warri and a linear alkyl benzene plant at Kaduna. The units use feedstock from the nearby refineries. Phase II comprised the construction of a larger petrochemicals complex at Alesa Eleme and methanol plants. Of this phase, only the Eleme Petrochemical Complex has been completed, and it entered production in 1996, at an estimated cost of US $1,000m. The Eleme Petrochemical Complex has a design capacity of 250,000 metric tons per year of polyethylene and 80,000 tons per year of polypropylene. By May 1999 it had generated $12,270m. in revenue from the sale of its products to the USA, the United Kingdom, the Netherlands, Egypt and Asia. Phase III, involving the production of xylenes, remained at the planning stage in 2007.

NATURAL GAS

Besides its petroleum resources, Nigeria possesses the largest deposits of natural gas in sub-Saharan Africa. Proven reserves are assessed at more than 4,500,000m. cu m, most of which is located with petroleum deposits in and around the Niger Delta. Other agas reserves were estimated at a further 1,800,000m. cu m. Production in 1990 was estimated at 27,600m. cu m, of which 77% was flared. Of the gas that was consumed, some 75% was bought by NEPA. In a bid to curtail the wasteful flaring of gas, the Government issued a decree penalizing petroleum companies for this practice. Although the decree, which came into force in 1985, affected only 69 of the 155 petroleum-producing fields, many of the large operators began to install gas reinjection facilities. Some 18,000m. cu m of gas was flared each year, at a market cost of over US $4,000m., according to petroleum companies; domestic consumption was estimated at only 3,000m. cu m per year. Utilization of gas increased substantially when the Warri associated gas project, under which 17m. cu m per day was piped from the Niger Delta to Igbin power station near Lagos, came into operation in 1990. Nevertheless, the flaring of gas was a major source of contention between the Ogoni ethnic group and Shell (see Recent History) in the 1990s. The Nigerian Government has set a target of ending all gas flaring by 2008; this objective, if achieved, not only would have positive environmental effects but would also increase the amount of gas available for export.

In 1996 the Shell Petroleum Development Co of Nigeria Limited awarded a £320m. contract for a new gas-processing plant at Soku, in Rivers State. The plant was to enable Shell to flare less gas in the Niger Delta and was to supply the liquefied natural gas (LNG) plant, which was under construction at Bonny Island (see below). The plant at Soku, when completed, was to be capable of delivering 12.7m. cu m of gas per day. The Agbami offshore field was expected to produce about 450m. cu m of gas per day, in addition to its output of crude oil (see above). In September 1995 Nigeria joined Benin, Togo and Ghana in signing an agreement to proceed with the construction of a West African Gas Pipeline (WAGP) from Nigeria. Nigeria, Benin, Togo and Ghana signed a memorandum of understanding in respect of the WAGP in 1999, and later that year a consortium comprising Chevron and Shell, led by Chevron, signed a joint-venture agreement with the national petroleum companies of the four signatory countries. In May

2003 Nigeria and partner countries signed a further agreement for the creation of the West African Pipeline Company (WAPCO) to operate the pipeline, which was expected to deliver its first methane gas in the fourth quarter of 2006. However, this pipeline came in for attack from the Niger Delta militants, whose sabotage of the Escravos segment of the pipeline caused a delay of the first delivery of gas until March 2007 and then to late 2007. Lying partly on shore in Nigeria and partly off shore in the Gulf of Guinea, the pipeline was to transport gas overland from the Escravos gasfield to Lagos, where it continues under water. The offshore part of the pipeline parallels the shoreline and carries gas westward, delivering it through to the cities of Cotonou, in Benin, Lomé, in Togo, and three Ghanaian ports, Tema (serving Accra), Takoradi and Effasu.

In 1988 the Babangida Government announced a new US $2,000m. scheme to construct a pipeline from gas fields in eastern Nigeria to the LNG plant at Bonny Island. In 1989 a joint-venture agreement was signed to implement the scheme. In March 1999 Elf Aquitaine confirmed that the expansion of the Bonny Island LNG plant was to proceed and that a long-awaited third train would be built. The first two trains, costing $3,700m., entered production in September and October 1999. Spain's Enagas was to purchase 70% of the output. Construction of the $1,800m. third train boosted output to 9m. metric tons per year of LNG and 1.3m. tons per year of liquefied petroleum gas (LPG). The fourth and fifth trains were both completed in January 2006, and a sixth train was due to begin delivery of gas in 2007. The five trains in operation in 2006 were capable of delivering 17m. cu m of LNG per year, and the sixth, upon completion, was expected to increase that total to 22m. cu m per year. The scheme was to use gas associated with oilfields in the Niger Delta, which at the time was being flared. The NLNG Co was initially owned 49% by the NNPC, 25.6% by Shell Gas Nigeria, 15% by Elf Aquitaine Gaz's affiliate, Cleag Ltd, and 10.4% by Italy's Agip International.

Meanwhile, Chevron began developing the US $1,000m. Escravos facility to manufacture liquid fuels from natural gas. This scheme would have the dual advantage of supplying fuel to the region and reducing the wasteful flaring of natural gas. Phase One of this project entered into production in 1997, supplying primarily the domestic Nigerian market, but also producing some LPG for export; a shipment of 30,000 metric tons, valued at $4.5m., was exported to the USA in September 1997. In late 1997 Escravos was producing 130m. cu ft of dry gas, more than 8,000 barrels of LPG and natural-gas liquids, and 2,000 barrels of condensate per day. In April 1998 South Africa's Sasol joined forces with Chevron for a feasibility study to assess the suitability of Sasol's gas-to-liquids (GTL) technology at Escravos, and in June 1999 Sasol and Chevron agreed to proceed with Phase Two of the Escravos scheme. The output of Phase Two is allocated for regional distribution via the WAGP. Other schemes aimed at utilizing the country's gas reserves include the National Fertilizer Co (NAFCON) gas-fed fertilizer plant at Onne, which was commissioned in 1987 and was liquidated, with the BPE looking for a buyer for its assets in 2007. Also aimed at using Nigeria's gas reserves were the Warri refinery extension and the Delta steel plant at Aladja. Gas is also planned to be used as a feedstock for the second phase of the NNPC chemicals complex near Port Harcourt. A comprehensive gas development policy, offering incentives for companies investing in gas production, distribution and consumption, was released by the NNPC in 1990. The policy provisions also supported the commercialization of LNG production for export and for domestic consumption, the establishment of gas companies distributing to domestic and industrial consumers, and viable projects, aimed at substituting gas for existing fuels.

COAL AND OTHER MINERALS

Nigeria possesses substantial deposits of lignite, but the country has yet to exploit their full potential. The Government estimates Nigeria's coal reserves at 3,000m. metric tons, situated in 17 coalfields. Nevertheless, coal accounts for only about 0.2% of Nigeria's total energy consumption. Nigerian coal is low in ash and sulphur content and so is more environmentally friendly than many other types of coal. However, in a country where attention focuses on petroleum and gas, coal takes a relatively low priority for domestic use, and export sales are hindered by the high cost of transport to countries with strict environmental criteria to meet. Deposits of bitumen near Akure were developed under the Government's Bitumen Implementation Project. Nigeria is West Africa's most important producer of coal. Coal is mined by the Nigerian Coal Corpn (NCC) and is used mainly by the railway, by traditional metal industries and for the generation of electricity. Output of bituminous coal was only 35,000 tons in 2000. There are long-term plans to exploit the Lafia/Obi coal deposits for use at the Ajaokuta steel complex. Reserves at this deposit are estimated at more than 270m. tons.

Nigeria's output of tin concentrates has been in decline since the late 1960s, and these exports have reflected the depressed conditions in world tin prices since the late 1980s. Production peaked at 357,000 tons in 1995 but then declined; output amounts to less than 130,000 tons per year. The country has two tin smelters, with a combined capacity well in excess of total ore production. Columbite is mined near Jos, but output declined steadily after the mid-1970s, to just 47 tons in 1989. In 2007 the BPE was seeking investment partners to develop several of the country's unexploited or underexploited hard minerals, including bentonite, gypsum (in Bauchi State), kaolin (in Plateau State), rock salt, barytes (at three locations in Nasarawa State), phosphates, talc, manganese, copper, bitumen, gold and tin. Gold is found mostly in south-western Nigeria and comprises both primary gold in a schist belt and alluvial gold. Nigeria also mines modest amounts of gemstones, mainly in Plateau, Bauchi and Kaduna States. The potential exists for profitable exploitation of sapphires, rubies, emeralds, aquamarines, topazes, tourmalines, amethysts, garnets and zircons.

Extensive deposits of iron ore have been discovered in Itakpe, Ajabanoko and Shokoshoko—all in Kwara State. Mining operations at Itakpe started in 1984, with the long-term aim of supplying most of the requirements of the Ajaokuta and Delta steel complexes. More than 180,000 metric tons of iron ore had been mined by early 1986. The construction of a US $250m. processing plant at Itakpe began in December 1992; the plant was projected to process 5m. tons of iron ore into a concentrated form for the Ajaokuta steel complex. In 1995 work was completed on the establishment of a river port at Ajaokuta, which was to enable the transportation of iron ore for the steel complex. An aluminium smelter at Ikot Abasi came on stream in 1991, with an installed capacity of 90,000 tons per year, but in its first seven years of operation it produced only 36,000 tons of aluminium ingots.

MANUFACTURING AND CONSTRUCTION

Industrial development has mainly taken the form of import substitution of consumer goods, although during the 1970s greater emphasis was placed on the production of capital goods and on assembly industries. Manufacturers' interests are represented by the Manufacturers' Asscn of Nigeria (MAN), which comprises more than 2,000 member companies. In 2007 manufacturing activities included 11 sectoral groups and 72 subsectoral groups. MAN's 11 sectoral groups comprised food, beverages and tobacco; chemicals and pharmaceuticals; domestic and industrial plastic, rubber and foam; basic metal, iron and steel and fabricated metal products; pulp, paper and paper products, printing, publishing and packaging; electrical and electronics; textiles, wearing apparel, carpets, leather and footwear; wood and wood products, including furniture; non-metallic mineral products; motor-vehicle and miscellaneous assembly; and manufacturing for export.

Manufacturing has traditionally been heavily reliant on imported raw materials and components. Efforts to lessen that reliance have been largely unsuccessful. According to the MAN, up to two-thirds of all the raw materials that local industry used in 2001 were imported. Manufacturing was thus extremely vulnerable to disruption if imports were restricted, as they were from 1980 onwards. Imports of raw materials declined, on average, by 10% per year during the 1980s and the 1990s. The combination of import restrictions, over-pricing and industrial disputes favoured cheaper foreign goods and encouraged smuggling and 'black-market' activities. Import licensing was abolished in 1986, and tariffs were reduced. However, the coinciding sharp devaluation of the naira increased import costs and hence production costs. Total production from the manufacturing sector declined by more than one-third between 1982 and 1985, while the level of capital expenditure fell by over 50%. The most severely affected branches of the sector were commercial vehicles, chemicals, metals, textiles, sugar, plastics and paper. Manufacturing contributed an estimated 3% of GDP in 2006. Manufacturers asserted that inadequate development funds and the Government's stringent fiscal policy had constrained the sector, which was estimated to be operating at less than one-third of its capacity in 2005. Despite successive Governments' efforts to encourage industrial dispersal, most manufacturing plants are still based in Lagos State. The Agbara industrial estate, in Ogun State, has attracted some industries away from Lagos, although most of the heavily import-based companies are reluctant to move, owing to the fact that some 70% of all industrial materials are still handled at ports in Lagos State. In June 2004 MAN estimated that 55% of all imports into Nigeria (or a total of US $6,300m.) evaded Nigerian customs. These imports, having circumvented any protective tariffs and quotas, posed formidable competition in the Nigerian market for locally produced goods.

The creation of an integrated iron and steel industry has been a high priority of successive development plans. In 1982 the Delta steel complex at Aladja was formally opened. The complex, which has a capacity of 1m. metric tons per year and operates the direct reduction system, supplies billets and wire rods to three steel-rolling mills at Oshogbo, Katsina and Jos. Each of the three mills has an initial annual capacity of 210,000 tons of steel products. The Ajaokuta Steel Co opened the first light section mill in 1983 and the rolling mill for the production of steel wire rods in 1984, but output was sporadic, owing to shortages of imported billets and to difficulties in obtaining supplies from the Delta complex. In 1996 Nigeria's steel companies were reported to be operating at just 10% of their installed capacity, owing to mismanagement and lack of foreign exchange. Delta Steel asked the civilian Obasanjo Government for a cash investment in 1999, but the 2000 budget allocated less than one-fifth of the requested amount. There were plans at least to double the capacity of the first stage of the Ajaokuta complex. Construction costs, originally estimated at US $1,400m., exceeded $3,000m. at the end of 1989, and had increased to $8,000m. by 1997. A 20-year contract with a Russian firm, Tyazhpromeksport, for the plant equipment and technology, which had been criticized by the World Bank, was terminated in December 1996. However, the 1997 federal budget allocated ₦6,600m. for the completion of the project, confirming the Government's intention to continue with the Ajaokuta project. In early 1992 a second stage of the project was initiated. In 2005 an Indian company began a $50m. rehabilitation of the Ajaokuta facility, including the sintering mill and the rolling mill, to produce steel wire rods. By mid-2006 the company claimed to have produced 128,000 tons of rolled products. Solgas of the USA is to manage and operate Ajaokuta under a 10-year contract. Ajaokuta has been designated for privatization, but at mid-2007 the BPE stated that the process was 'on hold'.

The Aluminium Smelter Co of Nigeria (ALSCON) entered into production in 1997 in Akwa Ibom State. With an installed capacity of 193,000 tons per year, ALSCON exported about 24,000 tons of aluminium per year in 1998. ALSCON (of which 70% was owned by the Nigerian Government, 20% by German interests and 10% by a Canadian firm) was fuelled by gas from Shell's plants at Alakiri and Obigbo North, and, owing in part to an inadequate supply of gas, failed ever to use more than one-fifth of its capacity. In June 1999 the enterprise suspended operations. The Federal Government intervened to prepare it for privatization, and by March 2003 the Government had increased its stake in ALSCON from 70% to 91.4%, while Ferrostaal of Germany had reduced its share from 20% to 6.8% and Alcan of Canada from 10% to 1.8%. In 2004 the Government invited investors to privatize and reopen the smelter, and indications of interest were reported to have been received from US, Russian and Swiss companies. A tripartite agreement was signed in May between the BPE, the BFIGroup Corpn (BFIG) of the USA and RUSAL of Russia. In order to demonstrate transparency, the BPE announced the opening of bids on a live national television broadcast. BFIG, based in California, USA, but with participation by businessmen of Nigerian origins, submitted the highest bid, at $410m., while RUSAL added a conditional bid of $5m. The BFIG bid was very publicly acknowledged to be the highest, but the BPE, claiming that BFIG had not met its other commitments under the agreement, subsequently reopened negotiations with RUSAL.

The assembly of motor vehicles in Nigeria is dominated by Peugeot in passenger cars and by Mercedes in commercial vehicles. Local demand remains well above supply; the cost of components and the difficulties in obtaining import licences have reduced output. The country has three tyre manufacturers. Dunlop Nigeria's US $5m. plant to produce all-steel radial truck tyres was commissioned at the end of August 2005. Various government programmes that were aimed at national self-sufficiency in food allowed for the steady growth of agri-business during the 1970s. Sugar refining, textiles, brewing, rubber, fertilizers, edible oils, footwear, paper, cigarettes and general food-processing industries were among the most significant. The large brewing industry has continued to flourish.

Activity in the construction sector fell in the second half of the 1990s, and, apart from a few major projects such as the WAGP (see above), the decline continued into the next decade. The sector suffered from serious constraints on growth, following the introduction of the structural adjustment programme in 1986 and further reductions in public sector projects. The construction of a federal capital at Abuja was formally completed in 1991. The creation of nine new states in that year necessitated several new infrastructure projects, and ongoing investment in the energy sector of some US $1,000m. a year has also benefited the sector. In 1999 the decision to construct the WAGP created expectations of new jobs in the sector. Under a 1989 decree, foreign companies are permitted to own 100% of any new venture, except for enterprises in banking, oil prospecting, insurance and mining.

The Government in 1996 stated its intention of encouraging private-sector competition in sectors such as power and telecommunications, previously monopolized by NEPA and NITEL, respectively, and pledged that, 'apart from exceptional circumstances', it would not fund these enterprises after December 1996. By late 2001 the BPE had selected three companies to bid for NITEL: Telnet, Newtel and a consortium, Investors International (London) Ltd (IILL). IILL won, and in November the consortium signed an agreement with the Federal Government to purchase the state's 51% share of NITEL for US $1,317m. Under the contract, IILL paid a non-refundable 10% deposit of $131.7m. and was to have paid the remainder by 11 February 2002. IILL then requested and was granted a six-week extension of the deadline, to 27 March. However, the consortium was unable to raise the required amount by that date, and the agreement collapsed. Meanwhile, the Government listed 25% of its remaining 49% share in NITEL on the Nigeria Stock Exchange in June. The BPE was actively seeking investors in NITEL in 2007.

The largest government agency in industrial development is the Bank of Industry Ltd (BOI), formerly the Nigerian Industrial Development Bank (NIDB). In the 1990s the NIDB centred its activities on directing multilateral funding into private-sector projects in intermediate and capital goods manufacturing, food processing and other agriculture-related industries. By December 2001 its portfolio of 101 projects included 62 small or medium-sized industries. Of these, no fewer than 53 were described as 'non-performing', and 31 of those were involved in legal disputes to prevent the bank from acquiring the assets that had secured the non-performing loans. Legislation, introduced in 1995, was aimed at stimulating foreign investment by guaranteeing the unconditional transferability of funds through an authorized dealer in freely convertible currency for debt-service payments, dividends and proceeds of sales of assets, although new investments were still required to be processed through the Nigeria Stock Exchange and new companies still had to receive the approval of the Investment Promotion Commission.

A 208,847-ha Export Processing Zone (EPZ) at the port city of Calabar, in Cross River State, has attracted investors in 14 sectors, including textiles and garments, wood processing, tyres, food processing, electrical products, light-truck assembly, packaging, carpets and rugs, iron and steel, and cocoa processing. By 1998 ₦2,500m. had been spent on the EPZ at Calabar, including the construction of an airport and improvements to the port. In 2007 the Zone was offering a streamlined one-stop approval of applications by the Nigerian Export Processing Zone Authority (NEPZA) 'to the exclusion of other government agencies'.

POWER

In a country where power blackouts are a frequent occurrence, it is estimated that a cash injection of US $12,000m. is needed to meet Nigeria's electricity needs. Plans to add 10,000 MW to the national grid through the use of national independent power producers and independent power producers (IPPs) by December 2007 were running behind schedule in mid-2007, and the new target date was postponed to the second half of 2008. The National Electricity Regulatory Commission (NERC), established in 2006, granted generating licences in June 2007 to 20 IPPs that were to add 8,237.5 MW to the national grid by 2010. Meanwhile, the Nigeria Atomic Energy Commission (NAEC) announced plans to generate a minimum of 1,000 MW of electricity using nuclear power plants by 2017. Nigeria had 6,040 MW of installed electricity-generating capacity in June 2000; therefore, if power stations were able to operate at full capacity, they would be able to meet the national demand, assessed at about 5,200 MW. Owing to 'system constraints', however, power installations were operating at only about 25% of their capacities, and consequently were able to meet less than 1,600 MW of the national power requirement. The principal supplier of electricity in Nigeria is the PHCN (see above), formerly NEPA, which was established in 1973 by the merger of the Niger Dams Authority and the Electricity Corpn of Nigeria. Although NEPA was allocated for privatization in the 1990s, it remained government owned in mid-2007. The PHCN was to oversee the distribution of NEPA assets to the six generating companies and 11 distribution companies that came into existence with the restructuring of NEPA, in preparation of its privatization. NEPA's power-generation facilities include the 1,320-MW Chinese-built thermal power station at Egbin, in Lagos State (fuelled with natural gas piped from the Escravos field); the Kainji hydroelectric installation (capacity 760 MW, using eight turbines); the gas- and oil-fuelled thermal installations at Afam, in Rivers State (742 MW, using 18 units, several of which were not producing) and at Sapele, in Delta State (696 MW); and the coal-fuelled thermal plant on the Oji River (150 MW).

In December 2001 Shell Petroleum Development Co of Nigeria acquired 15-year contracts for two gas-fuelled power projects at Afam, valued at US $540m. The first project was to refurbish, operate and transfer the Afam IV plant, and the other was to lease, operate and transfer the Afam V plant. The national grid in theory supplied electricity to 43% of all Nigerians in 1999, and NEPA then set a target of bringing mains electricity to 85% of the population by 2010 (which would require a large capital investment to fund 16 proposed new power plants and 14,500 km of new transmission lines, as well as ancillary services). Plans are under consideration for the construction of new installations at Onitsha, Kaduna, Makurdi, Oron, Katsina and Mambilla. In practice, however, it was estimated that to rehabilitate the country's thermal stations would require ₦45,000m., while the 1998 budget allocated ₦3,000m. for all electricity rehabilitation. While electricity generation was once viewed as a 'strategic' industry where foreigners were not welcome, the Obasanjo Government in 1999 invited overseas investment, particularly on 'build, own and operate' (BOO) terms. Examples of proposed BOO projects were a 350-MW gas-fuelled power station in Rivers State and a power plant in Ondo State. The West African Portland Cement Company, which operates a cement factory (with annual production of 1m. metric tons) at Ewekoro in Ogun State and has a requirement for some 20 MW of power, entered into a BOO agreement in December 2001 with the private-sector RRPV for electricity supply over a 15-year period. The country's manufacturers lose as much as two-thirds of working hours from power cuts in some years, and official sources cite unreliable electricity supplies as one of the principal factors impeding growth in the manufacturing sector. In 2002 natural gas provided 44.0% and hydroelectric power some 46.2%, of total electricity generated.

TRANSPORT

In comparison with most other West African states, Nigeria has a well-developed transport system. However, congestion, lack of maintenance, and poor planning have resulted in services that are unreliable and often dangerous. Approximately 95% of all goods and passengers travel by road, principally to and from the major ports. Road safety standards in Nigeria are virtually non-existent, and driving licences are distributed indiscriminately. On average, 30,000 accidents are reported each year, with the loss of over 8,000 lives.

The railway network covers 3,505 km. The two main narrow-gauge lines run from Lagos to Nguru and from Port Harcourt to Kaura Namoda, with extensions from Kafanchan, through Jos, to Maiduguri, and from Minna to Baro. A new 52-km railway line for iron ore traffic was constructed between the Ajaokuta steel complex and Itakpe in the 1990s. In 1997 the China Civil Engineering Co-operative Corpn was under contract to rehabilitate Nigeria's railway system, with the provision of technology, locomotives and 70 passenger carriages, which were to be built by China's Sifang Rolling Stock Plant. Nigeria's railway network accounted for 179m. passenger-km and 120,000 ton-km in 1997. In 2005 it was reported that the Nigeria Railway Corporation was operating at only 20% of its capacity. As part of a streamlining exercise to prepare it for commercialization, it was announced that the company would have to lose 50% of its workforce, reducing its 14,000 staff to 7,000. In 2007 the Nigeria Railway Corpn remained on the BPE's privatization list.

There are international airports at Ikeja (Lagos), Kano and Abuja, as well as 11 domestic airports. The Abuja airport has 10 terminals, three of which were to handle international traffic, while the other seven were to serve the domestic market. Murtala Mohammed International Airport in Lagos received new cargo-handling equipment, valued at US $4m., in May 2000. The International Air Transport Association Safety Audit Ground Operations programme sought to audit all aviation ground-handling service providers in Nigeria by 31 December 2007. Those that pass the test are to receive certificates during 2008, and any who do not pass the test will no longer be able to operate. In mid-2007 both the Federal Airports Authority of Nigeria and the Nigerian Aviation Handling Company Limited were on the BPE's privatization list. The parastatal Nigeria Airways' domestic monopoly was ended in the early 1980s, and several private charter airlines commenced operations. International traffic is dominated by foreign airlines. Successive military Governments put increasing pressure on Nigeria Airways to improve its standard of service and to reduce its costs, but the carrier continued to incur substantial financial losses. Owing to Nigeria Airways' difficulties, it was announced that private airlines would be allowed to offer international services if they satisfied safety requirements. In September 2004 Virgin Nigeria airlines was established. Despite being totally privately owned, it was to become the new national flag carrier. Its flights between Lagos and London began in June 2005, and its Lagos–Dubai service commenced in June 2006. In addition to these long-haul services, Virgin Nigeria operates regional services linking Lagos to Accra (Ghana) and Douala (Cameroon), and its domestic services link Lagos to Abuja, Kano and Port Harcourt. In May 2003 the liquidation of Nigeria Airways was announced. The winding up of the company was finalized with two court orders in February 2004. Although the demise of the carrier itself was confirmed, the BPE has identified a dozen or so former Nigeria Airways assets that could be sold to investors. They range from cargo sheds to 'the most viable subsidiary of Nigeria Airways', Skypower Aviation and Handling Company Limited.

Nigeria's principal seaports for general cargo are Apapa, Tin Can Island (both of which serve Lagos), Port Harcourt, Warri, Sapele and Calabar. The main ports for petroleum shipments are Bonny and Burutu. After steadily declining since 1982, port utilization increased in the early 1990s, as a result of the rise in import and export volumes. In 1992 a report released by the West African Shipowners Operations Committee indicated that Nigeria's ports charged disproportionately high rates to shipping lines (some 230% above the average rate for West Africa) and that their turnaround times were longer, owing to poor maintenance of equipment. In the budget for 2000, extensive reforms to Nigeria's port procedures were envisaged. In 2007 the unbundled Nigeria Ports Authority was on the BPE's privatization list, but any divestiture was on hold pending new legislation. A new national shipping line, the Nigeria Unity Line, was created in the 1990s to operate services between Europe and Nigeria. Its initial destination in Europe was Antwerp, in Belgium, with British and French ports subsequent destinations, in addition to West African ports, such as Abidjan and Dakar. CPCS Transcom was appointed in 2003 to oversee the Nigeria Ports Authority's privatization. The entity was to be dismantled into 24 concessions, and in 2005 94 companies and consortia were prequalified to bid for them.

TRADE

Nigeria, as a petroleum exporter, traditionally operates a visible trade surplus. Export revenue fluctuates according to the international price of petroleum; the volume of exports depends more on quota arrangements than on technical capacity, since Nigeria has the capacity to produce significantly more crude petroleum than it exports at present (see above). Of total export revenue of US $47,928m. in 2005, petroleum and gas accounted for $46,770m., or 97.6%. Visible imports in the same year cost $25,371m., leaving a visible trade surplus of $22,557m. The current account of the balance of payments demonstrated a surplus of $12,331m., while the overall balance of payments also showed a surplus, of $9,592m. As at 31 March 2007, Nigeria held gross external reserves of $41,900m., sufficient to cover seven months' worth of imports of goods and services. In 2005 Nigeria's main export clients were the USA, Brazil, Spain and France, while its principal import suppliers were China, the USA, the United Kingdom and the Netherlands. In the 1980s and the 1990s a series of foreign-exchange schemes were introduced, and subsequently replaced in rapid succession, with a dual exchange rate in operation most of the time. The Federal Government abolished the dual exchange rate on 1 January 1999, in favour of the Interbank Foreign Exchange Market (IFEM). However, this was soon joined by a second rate, the Autonomous Foreign Exchange Market (AFEM). In June 2001 President Obasanjo proclaimed that the Government aimed to unify the IFEM and the AFEM. At that time the IFEM rate was ₦112.55 = US $1, and the AFEM rate was ₦113.20 = US $1. One year later the IFEM rate stood at ₦115.60 = US $1, while the Nigerian Inter Bank Foreign Exchange (NIFEX) rate was ₦116.90 = US $1 and the parallel rate was about ₦139.00 = US $1. The currency continued its period of relative stability, and by June 2007 the exchange rate was ₦125.11 = US $1, changed little from the rate of ₦123.25 = US $1 one year earlier.

DEBT

After negotiations with creditors extending back over some three decades, Nigeria finally managed to reach agreement with the 'Paris Club' of public-sector creditors, and with the 'London Club' of private-sector creditors for the writing off of large amounts of debt in 2005. The World Bank was able to report in March 2007 that Nigeria had 'no major foreign debt'. However, domestic debt stocks remained above levels that were acceptable to the IMF and World Bank.

Following the sharp rise in government revenues from petroleum and the launching of several large-scale capital-intensive projects during the late 1970s, external borrowing increased dramatically. Although state borrowing was severely restricted during the 1980s, the external debt rose to ₦12,000m. by late 1983. More than one-half of the outstanding debt consisted of medium-term loans from the international capital market at 'floating' interest rates, most of which were incurred during the late 1970s. The net result was a heavy concentration of maturity dates at a time when real interest rates were high and when Nigeria's earnings of foreign currency were declining. Total debt was reduced in part through the Debt Conversion Programme, in which Nigeria repurchased some of its debt stock from third parties. In early May 1999, during the final period of the transitional Abubakar military regime, an auction summary of the Debt Conversion Programme was published which indicated that, over the 10-year duration of the programme, 406 participants had successfully redeemed their debts. Of these, 295 reportedly invested the proceeds in the Nigerian economy, including 164 in manufacturing, 67 in agriculture, 23 in construction, and others in such sectors as hotels, tourism projects, mining exploration and financial services.The Obasanjo Government budgeted ₦360,000m. for domestic and foreign debt servicing in 2004/05 and set aside $1,000m. for payments to the 'Paris Club' creditors. Total domestic debt, according to the IMF, was equivalent to 25% of GDP in April 2002, a situation exacerbated by a further series of borrowing in the form of Open Market Operations (OMO) biweekly auctions of treasury bills, introduced in June 2003, which were eventually to become daily auctions. Both the World Bank and the other creditors of the 'Paris Club' were waiting in mid-2004 for concrete signs that Nigeria's reforms would enable any debt relief to be targeted to those Nigerians who most needed poverty alleviation. In 2005 'Paris Club' member-nations negotiated and signed debt-reduction agreements with Nigeria, whereby Nigeria's debt would be reduced by $18,000m., in exchange for Nigeria's agreement to pay back the remaining $12,000m. by March 2006. Nigeria did indeed make the final payment, whereupon the debt-reduction commitments came into force on 21 April, entirely eliminating Nigeria's debt to the 'Paris Club'.

PUBLIC FINANCE

Since the early 1970s, the channelling of earnings from petroleum exports, import and excise duties and other forms of revenue from taxation through the federal, state and local governments has been the main impetus of economic activity in Nigeria. After a period in the late 1970s and early 1980s of inflationary domestic policies, the Government was faced with serious internal financial difficulties. Budgets in the early 1990s were characterized by overly ambitious targets that subsequently proved to have been unattainable. Budgetary deficits in most years were larger than those projected, and were equivalent to between 8% and 13% of GDP. Value-added tax (VAT), introduced in January 1994, increased revenue by ₦8,600m. in 1994 and by ₦21,000m. in 1995. In 2001 the Government pledged to improve its collection system, amid allegations that huge amounts of VAT receipts were failing to reach state reserves. In an attempt to avoid a repetition of the protracted dissent that had met earlier budgets, Obasanjo introduced greater transparency into the budgeting exercise, implementing the concept of 'core revenue', whereby, for 2001 and beyond, 'budget call circulars' to ministries would specify in advance the levels of current and capital expenditure to be allocated to each ministry. A lengthy procedure for adopting financial legislation began to develop, in which the World Bank and the IMF negotiated with the President and his executive team to agree a strategy for economic reform, while the legislature subsequently rejected their recommendations and followed a different course. Fiscal discipline at all levels of government, greater transparency and improved accountability were widely regarded as crucial for economic progress. There were clear indications of improved relations between Nigeria and the World Bank during a March 2004 visit to Nigeria by the Bank's President, James D. Wolfensohn, who declared that the World Bank was prepared to invest US $1,000m. over the following two years in the NEEDS economic reform and poverty-reduction programme. The strong increase in petroleum revenues in 2005 and 2006 made it possible for Nigeria to achieve the elimination of its huge 'Paris Club' debts, thereby allowing the Government henceforth to divert resources to spending on social needs, on poverty reduction and on infrastructural development. The World Bank declared that 'fiscal spending would have to leave room for the private sector to be the driver of growth in Nigeria', a principle that both the Obasanjo and Yar'Adua administrations have embraced.

ECONOMIC PROSPECTS

When Nigeria's first began to receive revenue from petroleum in the 1960s and 1970s, opportunities to utilize those earnings for economic development were notoriously and spectacularly missed. Now, Nigeria has a further opportunity to benefit from its position as Africa's major exporter of petroleum. Despite some disruption to supply by dissidents, strong global oil prices brighten the outlook for petroleum revenues, and the IMF described the prospects for Nigeria's non-oil economy as 'robust'. Reform, as the new President found out just days after he took office, will not be easy, and he will have to carefully balance policies to implement it. For his part, however, President Yar'Adua stated his intentions clearly from the moment he took the reins of power, proclaiming that the Nigerian economy remained 'the first, second and third priority'.

Statistical Survey

Source (unless otherwise stated): National Bureau of Statistics, Plot 762, Independence Avenue, Central Business District, PMB 127, Garki, Abuja; tel. (9) 2731085; fax (9) 2731084; internet www.nigerianstat.gov.ng; Central Bank of Nigeria, Central Business District, PMB 187, Garki, Abuja; tel. (9) 61639701; fax (9) 61636012; e-mail info@cenbank.org; internet www.cenbank.org.

Area and Population

AREA, POPULATION AND DENSITY

Area (sq km)	909,890*
Population (census results,)	
28–30 November 1991†	88,992,220
21–27 March 2006 (provisional)	
Males	71,709,859
Females	68,293,683
Total	140,003,542
Density (per sq km) at March 2006	157.2

* 351,310 sq miles.
† Revised 15 September 2001.

STATES
(2006 census, provisional)

	Area (sq km)	Population	Density (per sq km)	Capital
Abia	4,900	2,833,999	578	Umuahia
Adamawa	38,700	3,168,101	82	Yola
Akwa Ibom	6,900	3,920,208	568	Uyo
Anambra	4,865	4,182,032	860	Awka
Bauchi	49,119	4,676,465	95	Bauchi
Bayelsa	9,059	1,703,358	188	Yenogoa
Benue	30,800	4,219,244	137	Makurdi
Borno	72,609	4,151,193	57	Maiduguri
Cross River	21,787	2,888,966	133	Calabar
Delta	17,108	4,098,391	240	Asaba
Ebonyi	6,400	2,173,501	340	Abakaliki
Edo	19,187	3,218,332	168	Benin City
Ekiti	5,435	2,384,212	439	Ado-Ekiti
Enugu	7,534	3,257,298	432	Enugu
Gombe	17,100	2,353,879	138	Gombe
Imo	5,288	3,934,899	744	Owerri
Jigawa	23,287	4,348,649	187	Dutse
Kaduna	42,481	6,066,562	143	Kaduna
Kano	20,280	9,383,682	463	Kano
Katsina	23,561	5,792,578	246	Katsina
Kebbi	36,985	3,238,628	88	Birnin Kebbi
Kogi	27,747	3,278,487	118	Lokoja
Kwara	35,705	2,371,089	66	Ilorin
Lagos	3,671	9,013,534	2,455	Ikeja
Nassarawa	28,735	1,863,275	65	Lafia
Niger	68,925	3,950,249	57	Minna
Ogun	16,400	3,728,098	227	Abeokuta
Ondo	15,820	3,441,024	218	Akure
—continued				
Osun	9,026	3,423,535	379	Oshogbo
Oyo	26,500	5,591,589	211	Ibadan
Plateau	27,147	3,178,712	117	Jos
Rivers	10,575	5,185,400	490	Port Harcourt
Sokoto	27,825	6,696,999	241	Sokoto
Taraba	56,282	2,300,736	41	Jalingo
Yobe	46,609	2,321,591	50	Damaturu
Zamfara	37,931	3,259,846	86	Gusau
Federal Capital Territory (Abuja)	7,607	1,405,201	185	Abuja
Total	909,890	140,003,542	157	—

PRINCIPAL TOWNS
(unrevised census of November 1991)

Lagos (federal capital)*	5,195,247	Enugu	407,756
Kano	2,166,554	Oyo	369,894
Ibadan	1,835,300	Warri	363,382
Kaduna	933,642	Abeokuta	352,735
Benin City	762,719	Onitsha	350,280
Port Harcourt	703,421	Sokoto	329,639
Maiduguri	618,278	Okene	312,775
Zaria	612,257	Calabar	310,839
Ilorin	532,089	Katsina	259,315
Jos	510,300	Oshogbo	250,951
Aba	500,183	Akure	239,124
Ogbomosho	433,030	Bauchi	206,537

* Federal capital moved to Abuja (population 107,069) in December 1991.

Mid-2005 ('000 incl. suburbs, UN estimates): Lagos 10,866; Kano 2,993; Ibadan 2,437; Kaduna 1,375; Benin City 1,055; Port Harcourt 972; Ogbomosho 941; Maiduguri 854; Zaria 847 (Source: UN, *World Urbanization Prospects: The 2005 Revision*).

BIRTHS AND DEATHS
(annual averages, UN estimates)

	1990–95	1995–2000	2000–05
Birth rate (per 1,000)	46.6	44.5	42.7
Death rate (per 1,000)	17.8	17.4	17.5

Source: UN, *World Population Prospects: The 2006 Revision*.

Expectation of life (years at birth, WHO estimates): 46 (males 45; females 46) in 2004 (Source: WHO, *World Health Report*).

EMPLOYMENT
('000 persons aged 14 years and over)

	2003	2004	2005
Agriculture, hunting, forestry and fishing	27,840	28,439	37,487
Mining and quarrying	66	67	89
Manufacturing	820	836	1,173
Electricity, gas and water	410	422	551
Construction	260	267	353
Wholesale and retail trade; repairs of motor vehicles and motorcycles and personal and household articles	93	97	134
Hotels and restaurants	87	89	125
Transport, storage and communications	400	411	537
Financial intermediation	270	275	363
Real estate, renting and business activities	59	60	78
Public administration, defence and compulsory social security	4,900	5,039	6,547
Education	8,430	8,760	12,239
Health and social welfare	280	291	383
Other community, social and personal service activities	2,885	2,942	3,874
Total employed	46,800	47,993	63,932

Health and Welfare

KEY INDICATORS

Total fertility rate (children per woman, 2005)	5.6
Under-5 mortality rate (per 1,000 live births, 2005)	194
HIV/AIDS (% of persons aged 15–49, 2005)	3.9
Physicians (per 1,000 head, 2003)	0.28
Hospital beds (per 1,000 head, 2000)	1.20
Health expenditure (2004): US $ per head (PPP)	52.7
Health expenditure (2004): % of GDP	4.6
Health expenditure (2004): public (% of total)	30.4
Access to water (% of persons, 2004)	48
Access to sanitation (% of persons, 2004)	44
Human Development Index (2004): ranking	159
Human Development Index (2004): value	0.448

For sources and definitions, see explanatory note on p. vi.

Agriculture

PRINCIPAL CROPS
('000 metric tons)

	2003	2004	2005
Wheat	58	62	66
Rice (paddy)	3,116	3,334	3,567
Maize	5,203	5,567	5,957
Millet	6,260	6,699	7,168
Sorghum	8,016	8,578	9,178
Potatoes	678	726	776
Sweet potatoes	2,800	2,996	3,205
Cassava	36,304	38,845	41,565
Taro (Coco yam)	4,426	4,736	5,068
Yams	29,697	31,776	34,000
Sugar cane	798	854	914
Dry cow peas	2,459	2,631	2,815
Cashew nuts	524	555	594
Kolanuts*	85	85	n.a.
Soybeans	494	528	565
Groundnuts (in shell)	3,037	3,250	3,478
Coconuts	182	195	209
Oil palm fruit*	8,632	8,700	9,005
Sesame seed†	80	78	100
Melonseed	394	422	451
Cottonseed*	250	258	264
Tomatoes*	889	992	1,057
Green chillies and peppers*	720	730	738
Green onions and shallots*	220	220	n.a.
Dry onions*	615	615	n.a.
Carrots and turnips*	235	248	257
Okra*	730	730	n.a.
Green corn (maize)*	576	576	n.a.
Plantains	2,263	2,421	2,591
Citrus fruits*	3,250	3,436	3,546
Guavas, mangoes and mangosteens*	730	782	812
Pineapples*	889	905	917
Papayas*	755	804	834
Cocoa beans	385	412	441
Ginger	110	117	125
Cotton (lint)*	140	140	140
Tobacco (leaves)*	16	15	15
Natural rubber (dry weight)	142	142	n.a.

* FAO estimates.

† Unofficial figures.

Source: FAO.

LIVESTOCK
('000 head, year ending September)

	2003	2004	2005
Horses*	205	206	206
Asses, mules or hinnies*	1,000	1,050	n.a.
Cattle	15,164	15,700	15,875
Camels*	18	18	n.a.
Pigs	6,356	6,611*	6,650*
Sheep*	22,500	23,000	23,000
Goats*	27,000	28,000	28,000
Chickens	137,680	143,500	150,700

* FAO estimate(s).

Source: FAO.

LIVESTOCK PRODUCTS
('000 metric tons, FAO estimates)

	2003	2004	2005
Cattle meat	279.5	280.0	280.0
Sheep meat	99.0	100.7	100.7
Goat meat	142.2	147.1	147.1
Pig meat	200.2	201.2	205.6
Chicken meat	201.0	191.5	189.9
Game meat	120	120	n.a.
Cows' milk	432	432	n.a.
Hen eggs	460	n.a.	n.a.

Source: FAO.

Forestry

ROUNDWOOD REMOVALS
('000 cubic metres, excluding bark, FAO estimates)

	2003	2004	2005
Sawlogs, veneer logs and logs for sleepers	7,100	7,100	7,100
Pulpwood	39	39	39
Other industrial wood	2,279	2,279	2,279
Fuel wood	60,449	60,852	61,274
Total	69,867	70,270	70,692

Source: FAO.

SAWNWOOD PRODUCTION
('000 cubic metres, including railway sleepers)

	1995	1996	1997
Broadleaved (hardwood)	2,356	2,178	2,000

1998–2005: Broadleaved (hardwood) production as in 1997.

Source: FAO.

Fishing

('000 metric tons, live weight)

	2003	2004	2005
Capture	475.2	465.3	523.2
Tilapias	31.2	22.9	31.8
Elephant snout fishes	15.4	19.5	18.6
Torpedo-shaped catfishes	15.7	9.6	16.2
Sea catfishes	18.3	20.5	21.2
West African croakers	13.5	14.1	10.7
Sardinellas	67.4	71.4	65.8
Bonga shad	21.6	14.7	19.8
Southern pink shrimp	13.2	11.4	12.4
Other shrimps and prawns	15.0	11.5	16.2
Aquaculture	30.7	44.0	56.4
Total catch	505.8	509.2	579.5

Source: FAO.

Mining

(metric tons, unless otherwise indicated)

	2003	2004	2005
Coal, bituminous	23,089	9,000*	9,000*
Kaolin*	200,000	210,000	200,000
Gypsum*	100,000	100,0000	100,000
Crude petroleum ('000 barrels)	825,000*	900,400	923,500
Natural gas (million cu m)	53,000*	57,747	56,000*
Tin concentrates*†	1,800	1,000	790

* Estimate(s).

† Metal content.

Source: US Geological Survey.

Industry

SELECTED PRODUCTS

('000 metric tons, unless otherwise indicated)

	2001	2002	2003
Palm oil*	903	908	915
Raw sugar*†	40	40	40
Wheat flour*†	1,564	1,730	1,598
Beer of barley*†	956	1,171	1,170
Beer of sorghum*†	698	760	794
Plywood ('000 cubic metres)*†	55	55	55
Wood pulp*†	23	23	23
Paper and paperboard*†	19	19	19
Liquefied petroleum gas ('000 barrels)†	1,000	2,300	2,000
Motor spirit—petrol ('000 barrels)†	24,400	22,400	20,000
Kerosene ('000 barrels)†	12,500	11,800	12,000
Gas-diesel (distillate fuel) oil ('000 barrels)†	18,900	18,800	19,000
Residual fuel oils ('000 barrels)†	21,500	17,200	17,000
Cement†	2,400	2,100	2,100
Tin metal—unwrought (metric tons)†	25	25	25
Electric energy (million kWh)‡	15,453	21,544	20,183

* Source: FAO.

† Estimates.

‡ Source: UN, *Industrial Commodity Statistics Yearbook*.

2004 (million kWh): 20,224 (Source: UN, *Industrial Commodity Statistics Yearbook*).

Source (unless otherwise indicated): US Geological Survey.

2004 ('000 barrels, estimates): Liquefied petroleum gas 2,200; Motor spirit–petrol 22,000; Kerosene 13,000; Gas-diesel (distillate fuel) oil 21,000; Residual fuel oils 18,000 (Source: US Geological Survey).

2005 ('000 barrels, estimates): Liquefied petroleum gas 7,100; Motor spirit–petrol 14,800; Kerosene 10,100; Gas-diesel (distillate fuel) oil 15,800; Residual fuel oils 19,200 (Source: US Geological Survey).

Finance

CURRENCY AND EXCHANGE RATES

Monetary Units

100 kobo = 1 naira (₦).

Sterling, Dollar and Euro Equivalents (30 March 2007)

£1 sterling = 250.754 naira;
US $1 = 128.060 naira;
€1 = 170.550 naira;
1,000 naira = £9.99 = $7.81 = €5.86.

Average Exchange Rate (naira per US $)

2004	132.888
2005	131.274
2006	128.652

FEDERAL BUDGET

(₦ million)

Revenue	2003	2004	2005
Tax revenue	1,130,200	1,690,200	1,706,726
Income and profit	798,300	1,313,600	n.a.
Import duties	195,469	217,100	n.a.
Other duties	136,431	159,500	n.a.
Non-tax revenue	1,444,896	2,211,200	3,454,386
Total	2,575,096	3,901,400	5,161,112

Expenditure	2003	2004	2005
Recurrent expenditure	984,268	954,741	1,128,640
Administration	307,849	306,843	434,672
General	166,056	101,337	248,730
Defence	51,044	76,324	71,672
Internal security	68,352	97,800	81,950
Economic services	96,032	58,782	64,309
Social and community services	102,566	134,391	151,647
Education	64,756	76,528	82,797
Transfers	363,363	382,525	393,963
Pensions and gratuities	34,150	72,201	84,050
Other	80,309	—	—
Capital expenditure	241,689	351,260	519,510
General administration	66,706	108,964	132,610
Roads and construction	17,459	40,671	89,057
Total	1,225,957	1,306,001	1,648,150

INTERNATIONAL RESERVES

(US $ million at 31 December)

	2004	2005	2006
Total*	16,956	28,280	42,299

* Almost exclusively foreign exchange, and excluding gold reserves (687,000 troy ounces each year).

Source: IMF, *International Financial Statistics*.

MONEY SUPPLY

(₦ million at 31 December)

	2003	2004	2005
Currency outside banks	412,155	458,587	563,220
Demand deposits at commercial banks	577,664	728,552	946,640
Total money (incl. others)	1,225,559	1,330,658	1,541,650

2006 (₦ million at 31 December): Demand deposits at commercial banks 1,112,362.

Source: IMF, *International Financial Statistics*.

COST OF LIVING
(Consumer Price Index; base: May 2003 = 100)

	2004	2005	2006
Food (excl. beverages)	117.1	144.2	152.2
Alcoholic beverages, tobacco and kola	112.7	122.3	138.7
Clothing (incl. footwear)	118.3	119.1	129.3
Rent, fuel and light	140.9	158.0	184.7
Household goods and maintenance	112.7	125.7	133.0
Medical care and health	123.1	126.0	141.4
Transport	119.4	125.4	142.8
Education	134.8	144.6	150.9
All items (incl. others)	121.9	143.6	155.5

NATIONAL ACCOUNTS
(₦ '000 million at current prices)

Expenditure on the Gross Domestic Product

	2004	2005	2006*
Government final consumption expenditure	785.8	1,003.1	1,283.4
Private final consumption expenditure	8,111.1	10,258.6	12,254.3
Increase in stocks Gross fixed capital formation }	1,390.6	1,781.2	2,272.8
Total domestic expenditure	10,287.5	13,042.9	15,810.5
Exports of goods and services	3,520.9	4,664.8	6,184.6
Less Imports of goods and services	2,134.8	2,813.2	3,772.3
GDP in purchasers' values	11,673.6	14,894.5	18,222.8
GDP in constant 1990 prices	541.5	560.2	602.4

* Provisional.

Gross Domestic Product by Economic Activity

	2004	2005	2006*
Agriculture, hunting, forestry and fishing	3,903.8	4,773.2	5,794.3
Mining and quarrying	4,260.8	5,682.2	7,006.6
Crude petroleum	4,247.7	5,664.9	6,982.9
Manufacturing	349.3	412.7	548.4
Electricity, gas and water	26.8	29.4	31.6
Construction	166.1	215.8	271.5
Wholesale and retail trade	1,484.4	1,868.3	2,495.8
Hotels and restaurants	35.3	46.1	56.8
Transport, storage and communications	388.8	426.7	557.8
Finance, insurance, real estate and business services	566.2	843.6	976.7
Government services	129.9	148.1	168.8
Other community, social and personal services	99.8	126.3	159.7
Sub-total	11,411.1	14,572.2	18,067.8
Taxes, less subsidies, on products†	262.5	322.3	155.0
GDP in purchasers' values	11,673.6	14,894.5	18,222.8

* Provisional.
† Data obtained as residuals.

BALANCE OF PAYMENTS
(US $ million)

	2003	2004	2005
Exports of goods f.o.b.	23,976	34,766	48,069
Imports of goods f.o.b.	–16,152	–15,009	–17,288
Trade balance	7,824	19,757	30,781
Exports of services	3,473	3,336	4,164
Imports of services	–5,715	–5,973	–7,321
Balance on goods and services	5,582	17,120	27,624
Other income received	82	157	705
Other income paid	–3,325	–2,689	–7,437
Balance on goods, services and income	2,339	14,588	20,892
Current transfers received	1,063	2,273	3,329
Current transfers paid	–12	–21	–18
Current balance	3,391	16,840	24,202
Capital account (net)	20	36	23
Direct investment from abroad	2,005	1,874	2,013
Portfolio investment assets	183	178	2,869
Other investment assets	–5,845	–7,301	–15,786
Other investment liabilities	–6,628	–7,812	–12,682
Net errors and omissions	5,614	4,676	9,758
Overall balance	–1,260	8,491	10,397

Source: IMF, *International Financial Statistics*.

External Trade

PRINCIPAL COMMODITIES
(US $ million)

Imports c.i.f.	2001	2002	2003
Food and live animals	1,628.5	1,566.1	2,090.9
Milk and cream	168.9	171.6	197.9
Fish and fish preparations*	429.6	339.5	452.6
Cereals and cereal preparations	599.4	610.5	684.0
Wheat and meslin, unmilled	330.8	346.6	388.3
Rice	205.7	234.8	231.2
Sugar and honey	221.1	270.5	178.0
Chemicals and related products	1,393.2	1,489.3	1,531.7
Organic chemicals	198.9	221.5	257.6
Manufactured fertilizers	191.3	105.5	68.6
Basic manufactures	1,534.7	1,677.4	2,377.9
Paper and paperboard	207.5	201.2	229.9
Cement	238.8	256.3	312.0
Iron and steel	501.0	483.7	802.4
Machinery and transport equipment	2,495.4	3,232.8	5,662.8
Power-generating machinery and equipment	262.3	254.3	306.8
Machinery specialized for particular industries	529.7	513.7	523.5
General industrial machinery and parts	326.6	482.7	1,682.4
Electric machinery, apparatus and parts	203.3	405.7	550.1
Road vehicles	879.6	664.7	893.0
Passenger motor vehicles (excl. buses)	435.3	257.6	331.8
Miscellaneous manufactured articles	366.4	390.8	451.0
Total (incl. others)	7,958.0	8,758.3	14,892.5

* Including crustacea and molluscs.

Exports f.o.b.	2001	2002	2003
Crude petroleum	17,732.2	16,598.0	23,211.2
Total (incl. others)	18,046.1	18,607.1	24,078.3

Source: UN, *International Trade Statistics Yearbook*.

2004 (₦ '000 million): *Imports:* Petroleum 318.1; Non-petroleum 1,668.9 (Chemicals 451.6; Manufactured goods 584.6; Machinery and transport equipment 458.9); Total 1,987.0. *Exports:* Petroleum 4,489.5; Non-petroleum 113.3; Total 4,602.8.

2005 (₦ '000 million): *Imports:* Petroleum 182.8; Non-petroleum 2,296.6 (Chemicals 599.5; Manufactured goods 795.9; Machinery and transport equipment 543.9); Total 2,479.3. *Exports:* Petroleum 6,266.1; Non-petroleum 106.0 (Cocoa beans 13.2; Processed skins 21.7); Total 6,372.1.

2006 (₦ '000 million, provisional): *Imports:* Petroleum 221.1; Non-petroleum 2,307.0 (Chemicals 608.4; Manufactured goods 816.7; Machinery and transport equipment 552.6); Total 2,528.1. *Exports:* Petroleum 5,619.2; Non-petroleum 133.6 (Cocoa beans 18.6; Processed skins 35.5); Total 5,752.7.

PRINCIPAL TRADING PARTNERS
(US $ million)*

Imports c.i.f.	2001	2002	2003
Belgium	438.2	519.3	533.6
Brazil	174.6	519.3	533.6
China, People's Repub.	526.8	740.6	1,068.0
France (incl. Monaco)	371.7	363.8	480.0
Germany	780.7	532.1	1,088.6
Greece	43.6	32.0	45.6
Hong Kong	96.4	108.7	152.7
India	315.7	310.1	377.7
Indonesia	107.8	108.0	122.4
Italy	200.7	259.7	636.5
Japan	360.2	432.4	364.2
Korea, Repub.	216.1	300.0	415.9
Netherlands	391.7	278.1	320.4
Russia	115.7	91.0	145.6
Singapore	103.7	499.4	78.9
South Africa	231.4	189.0	290.9
Spain	108.3	84.2	142.3
Switzerland-Liechtenstein	96.5	92.9	124.8
Thailand	115.6	174.8	138.7
United Kingdom	1,069.7	1,097.0	1,420.8
USA	822.8	1,123.4	2,320.8
Total (incl. others)	7,958.0	8,758.3	14,892.5

Exports f.o.b.	2001	2002	2003
Brazil	1,051.3	1,540.9	1,636.8
Cameroon	125.0	112.7	313.1
Canada	357.3	229.7	753.7
Chile	110.2	141.2	86.1
China, People's Repub.	127.0	73.2	123.5
Côte d'Ivoire	341.5	270.1	360.3
France (incl. Monaco)	1,142.3	998.8	1,359.5
Germany	243.6	365.5	505.5
Ghana	271.2	380.2	454.8
India	2,083.3	2,160.9	2,393.4
Indonesia	537.2	963.3	770.5
Italy	854.0	722.9	688.0
Korea, Repub.	49.7	41.3	99.6
Netherlands	364.8	288.7	535.4
Portugal	461.4	491.9	589.5
Senegal	174.8	118.8	254.2
South Africa	197.7	389.0	589.8
Spain	1,175.6	1,020.7	1,484.2
USA	7,320.9	5,830.0	9,211.3
Total (incl. others)	18,046.1	18,607.1	24,078.3

* Imports by country of consignment; exports by country of destination.

Source: UN, *International Trade Statistics Yearbook*.

2004 (₦ '000 million): *Non-Petroleum imports only:* Brazil 85.4; People's Republic of China 174.9; France 156.6; Germany 104.3; India 88.7; Italy 104.2; Japan 60.1; Republic of Korea 67.1; Netherlands 124.1; Russia 74.1; South Africa 81.0; United Kingdom 131.5; USA 241.5; Total (incl. others) 1,668.9. *Petroleum exports only:* Brazil 449.8; Canada 138.1; Côte d'Ivoire 122.2; France 132.0; India 469.9; Indonesia 130.9; Italy 104.1; Japan 158.5; Spain 209.7; USA 1,940.8; Total (incl. others) 4,430.2.

2005 (₦ '000 million): *Non-Petroleum imports only:* Brazil 91.9; People's Republic of China 275.6; France 114.8; Germany 80.4; India 137.8; Italy 68.9; Japan 390.4; Republic of Korea 80.4; Netherlands 103.3; Russia 68.9; South Africa 117.1; United Kingdom 91.9; USA 459.3; Total (incl. others) 2,296.6. *Petroleum exports only:* Brazil 214.7; Canada 272.1; Côte d'Ivoire 195.2; France 226.1; India 689.2; Indonesia 118.5; Italy 166.6; Japan 112.6; Netherlands 151.5; Spain 307.2; USA 2,603.6; Total (incl. others) 6,206.1.

2006 (₦ '000 million, provisional): *Non-Petroleum imports only:* Brazil 78.4; People's Republic of China 221.5; France 176.3; Germany 100.2; India 177.6; Italy 53.5; Japan 428.1; Republic of Korea 90.0; Netherlands 47.3; Russia 64.6; South Africa 71.5; United Kingdom 43.8; USA 512.0; Total (incl. others) 2,307.0. *Petroleum exports only:* Brazil 204.2; Canada 253.8; Côte d'Ivoire 160.0; France 231.7; India 651.1; Indonesia 126.9; Italy 160.0; Japan 110.4; Netherlands 137.9; Spain 298.0; USA 2,527.1; Total (incl. others) 5,517.7.

Transport

RAILWAYS
(traffic)

	1995	1996	1997
Passenger-km (million)	161	170	179
Freight ton-km (million)	108	114	120

Source: UN, *Statistical Yearbook*.

ROAD TRAFFIC
(estimates, motor vehicles in use)

	1995	1996
Passenger cars	820,069	885,080
Buses and coaches	1,284,251	903,449
Lorries and vans	673,425	912,579
Motorcycles and mopeds	481,345	441,651

Source: IRF, *World Road Statistics*.

1997 ('000 vehicles): Passenger cars 52.3; Commercial vehicles 13.5 (Source: UN *Statistical Yearbook*).

SHIPPING

Merchant Fleet
(registered at 31 December)

	2004	2005	2006
Number of vessels	330	339	350
Displacement ('000 grt)	429.0	358.1	363.3

Source: Lloyd's Register-Fairplay, *World Fleet Statistics*.

International Sea-borne Freight Traffic
(estimates, '000 metric tons)

	1991	1992	1993
Goods loaded	82,768	84,797	86,993
Goods unloaded	10,960	11,143	11,346

Source: UN Economic Commission for Africa, *African Statistical Yearbook*.

CIVIL AVIATION
(traffic on scheduled services)

	2001	2002	2003
Kilometres flown (million)	4	6	12
Passengers carried ('000)	529	512	520
Passenger-km (million)	402	522	638
Total ton-km (million)	37	57	61

Source: UN, *Statistical Yearbook*.

Tourism

ARRIVALS BY NATIONALITY*

Country	2003	2004	2005
Benin	318,716	374,491	393,215
Cameroon	86,815	102,008	107,108
Chad	68,958	81,026	85,077
France	50,149	58,925	61,871
Germany	48,915	57,475	60,348
Ghana	16,767	19,701	20,686
Italy	53,166	62,470	65,593
Liberia	87,053	102,287	107,401
Niger	503,066	591,103	620,658
Sudan	51,101	60,044	63,046
Total (incl. others)	2,253,115	2,646,411	2,778,365

* Figures refer to arrival at frontiers of visitors from abroad, including same-day visitors (excursionists).

Tourism receipts (US $ million, incl. passenger transport): 58 in 2003; 49 in 2004; n.a. in 2005.

Source: World Tourism Organization.

Communications Media

	2003	2004	2005
Telephones ('000 main lines in use)	853.1	1,027.5	1,223.3
Mobile cellular telephones ('000 in use)	3,149.5	9,147.2	18,587.0
Personal computers ('000 in use)	860	867	867
Internet users ('000)	750	1,770	5,000

Radio receivers ('000 in use): 23,500 in 1997.

Television receivers ('000 in use): 12,000 in 2001.

Book production (titles, including pamphlets): 1,314 in 1995.

Daily newspapers: 25 (estimated average circulation 2,760,000 copies) in 1998.

Sources: International Telecommunication Union; UNESCO Institute for Statistics.

Education

(2005)

	Institutions	Teachers	Students		
			Males	Females	Total
Primary	50,741	594,192	11,712,479	9,239,339	20,951,818
Secondary	11,010	156,635	3,079,832	2,342,779	5,422,611
Poly/ Monotechnic	178	16,499	n.a.	n.a.	237,708
University	80	23,535	n.a.	n.a.	724,856

Adult literacy rate (official estimates, any language): 64.2% (males 73.0%; females 55.4%) in 2006.

Directory

The Constitution

The Constitution of the Federal Republic of Nigeria was promulgated on 5 May 1999, and entered into force on 31 May. The main provisions are summarized below:

PROVISIONS

Nigeria is one indivisible sovereign state, to be known as the Federal Republic of Nigeria. Nigeria is a Federation, comprising 36 States and a Federal Capital Territory. The Constitution includes provisions for the creation of new States and for boundary adjustments of existing States. The Government of the Federation or of a State is prohibited from adopting any religion as a state religion.

LEGISLATURE

The legislative powers of the Federation are vested in the National Assembly, comprising a Senate and a House of Representatives. The 109-member Senate consists of three Senators from each State and one from the Federal Capital Territory, who are elected for a term of four years. The House of Representatives comprises 360 members, representing constituencies of nearly equal population as far as possible, who are elected for a four-year term. The Senate and House of Representatives each have a Speaker and Deputy Speaker, who are elected by the members of the House from among themselves. Legislation may originate in either the Senate or the House of Representatives, and, having been approved by the House in which it originated by a two-thirds majority, will be submitted to the other House for approval, and subsequently presented to the President for assent. Should the President withhold his assent, and the bill be returned to the National Assembly and again approved by each House by a two-thirds majority, the bill will become law. The legislative powers of a State of the Federation will be vested in the House of Assembly of the State. The House of Assembly of a State will consist of three or four times the number of seats that the State holds in the House of Representatives (comprising not less than 24 and not more than 40 members).

EXECUTIVE

The executive powers of the Federation are vested in the President, who is the Head of State, the Chief Executive of the Federation and the Commander-in-Chief of the Armed Forces of the Federation. The President is elected for a term of four years and must receive not less than one-quarter of the votes cast at the election in at least two-thirds of the States in the Federation and the Federal Capital Territory. The President nominates a candidate as his associate from the same political party to occupy the office of Vice-President. The Ministers of the Government of the Federation are nominated by the President, subject to confirmation by the Senate. Federal executive bodies include the Council of State, which advises the President in the exercise of his powers. The executive powers of a State are vested in the Governor of that State, who is elected for a four-year term and must receive not less than one-quarter of votes cast in at least two-thirds of all local government areas in the State.

JUDICIARY

The judicial powers of the Federation are vested in the courts established for the Federation, and the judicial powers of a State in the courts established for the State. The Federation has a Supreme Court, a Court of Appeal and a Federal High Court. Each State has a High Court, a *Shari'a* Court of Appeal and a Customary Court of Appeal. Chief Judges are nominated on the recommendation of a National Judicial Council.

LOCAL GOVERNMENT

The States are divided into 768 local government areas. The system of local government by democratically elected local government councils is guaranteed, and the Government of each State will ensure their existence. Each local government council within the State will participate in the economic planning and development of the area over which it exercises authority.

Federal Government

HEAD OF STATE

President, Commander-in-Chief of the Armed Forces and Minister responsible for Petroleum Resources: Alhaji UMARU MUSA YAR'ADUA (inaugurated 29 May 2007).

Vice-President: Dr GOODLUCK EBELE JONATHAN.

CABINET
(August 2007)

Attorney-General and Minister of Justice: MICHAEL KAASE AONDOAKAA.

Minister of Agriculture and Water Resources: ABBA SAYYADI RUMA.

Minister of Commerce and Industry: CHARLES UGWU.

Minister of Culture and Tourism: ADETOKUNBO KAYODE.

Minister of Defence: MAHMUD YAYALE AHMED.

Minister of Education: IGWE AJA-NWACHUKWU.

Minister of the Environment and Housing: HALIMA TAYO ALAO.

Minister of the Federal Capital Territory: ALIYU MODIBBO UMAR.

Minister of Finance: SHAMSUDEEN USMAN.

Minister of Foreign Affairs: OJO MADUEKWE.

Minister of Health: ADENIKE GRANGE.

Minister of Information and Communications: JOHN OGAR ODEY.

Minister of the Interior: Maj. Gen. (retd) GODWIN ABBE.

Minister of Labour: HASSAN MUHAMMAD LAWAL.

Minister of Mines and Steel Development: SARAFA TUNJI ISOLA.

Minister of Transportation: DIEZANI ALISON-MADUEKE.

Minister of Science and Technology: GRACE EKPIWHRE.

Minister of Youth Development: AKINLABI OLASUNKANMI.

Minister of Women's Affairs: SAUDATU USMAN BUNGUDU.

Minister, Chairman of the National Planning Commission: MUHAMMED SANUSI DAGGASH.

Minister, Chairman of the National Sports Commission: ABDULRAHMAN HASSAN GIMBA.

There were, in addition, 18 Deputy Ministers.

MINISTRIES

Office of the Head of State: New Federal Secretariat Complex, Shehu Shagari Way, Central Area District, Abuja; tel. (9) 5233536.

Ministry of Agriculture and Water Resources: Area 11, Secretariat Complex, Garki, PMB 135, Abuja; tel. (9) 3141931; e-mail agricminister@rosecom.net.

Ministry of Commerce and Industry: Area 1, Secretariat Complex, Garki, PMB 88, Abuja; e-mail fmi@fmind.gov.ng; tel. (9) 2341662.

Ministry of Culture and Tourism: Phase II Federal Secretariat, Block A, 1st Floor, Shehu Shagari Way, Abuja; tel. (9) 2348311; fax (9) 23408297; e-mail fo@fmct-nigeria.net; internet www.fmct-nigeria.net.

Ministry of Defence: Ship House, Central Area, Abuja; tel. (9) 2340534; fax (9) 2340714.

Ministry of Education: New Federal Secretariat Complex, Shehu Shagari Way, Central Area District, PMB 146, Abuja; tel. (9) 5237487; internet www.fmegovng.org.

Ministry of Energy: Annex 3, Federal Secretariat Complex, Shehu Shagari Way, Central Area, PMB 278, Garki, Abuja; tel. (9) 5239462; fax (9) 5236652.

Ministry of the Environment and Housing: Federal Secretariat Towers, Shehu Shagari Way, Central Area, PMB 468, Garki, Abuja; tel. (9) 5234014; fax (9) 5211847; internet www.environmentnigeria.org.

Ministry of the Federal Capital Territory: Kapital St, off Obafemi Awolowo St, Garki Area 11, PMB 25, Garki, Abuja; tel. (9) 2341525; fax (9) 3143859; e-mail presunit@fct.gov.ng; internet www.fct.gov.ng.

Ministry of Finance: Ahmadu Bello Way, Central Area, PMB 14, Garki, Abuja; tel. (9) 2346290; internet www.fmf.gov.ng.

Ministry of Foreign Affairs: Maputo St, Zone 3, Wuse District, PMB 130, Abuja; tel. (9) 5230570.

Ministry of Health: New Federal Secretariat Complex, Ahmadu Bello Way, Central Business District, PMB 083, Garki, Abuja; tel. (9) 5238362.

Ministry of Information and Communications: New Federal Secretariat Complex, Shehu Shagari Way, Central Area District, PMB 1278, Abuja; tel. (9) 5237183; e-mail ceeo.adebayo@nigtel.com.

Ministry of the Interior: Area 1, Secretariat Complex, Garki, PMB 16, Abuja; tel. (9) 2341934; fax (9) 2342426.

Ministry of Justice: New Federal Secretariat Complex, Shehu Shagari Way, Central Area, PMB 192, Garki, Abuja; tel. (9) 5235208; fax (9) 5235194.

Ministry of Labour: New Federal Secretariat Complex, Shehu Shagari Way, Central Area, PMB 04, Garki, Abuja; tel. (9) 5235980.

Ministry of Mines and Steel Development: New Federal Secretariat Complex, Shehu Shagari Way, Central Area, PMB 107, Garki, Abuja; tel. (9) 5235830; fax (9) 5235831; internet www.msmdng.com.

Ministry of Science and Technology: New Federal Secretariat Complex, Shehu Shagari Way, Central Area, PMB 331, Garki, Abuja; tel. (9) 5233397; fax (9) 5235204.

Ministry of Transportation: Dipcharima House, Central Business District, off 3rd Ave, PMB 0336, Garki, Abuja; tel. (9) 2347451; fax (9) 2347453.

Ministry of Women's Affairs: New Federal Secretariat Complex, Shehu Shagari Way, Central Area, PMB 229, Garki, Abuja; tel. (9) 5237112; fax (9) 5233644.

Ministry of Youth Development: Federal Secretariat, Phase II, Shehu Shagari Way, PMB 229, Abuja; tel. (9) 5237112; fax (9) 5233644.

National Planning Commission: Old Central Bank Bldg, 4th Floor, Garki, PMB 234, Abuja; e-mail info@nigerianeconomy.com; internet www.npc.gov.ng.

National Sports Commission: New Federal Secretariat Complex, Shehu Shagari Way, Maitama, Abuja; tel. (9) 5235905; fax (9) 5235901.

President and Legislature

PRESIDENT

Election, 21 April 2007*

Candidate	Votes
Umaru Musa Yar'Adua (People's Democratic Party)	24,784,227
Muhammadu Buhari (All Nigeria People's Party)	6,607,419
Atiku Abubakar (Action Congress)	2,567,798
Orji Uzor Kalu (Progressive People's Alliance)	608,833
Attahiru Dalhatu Bafarawa (Democratic People's Party)	289,324
Dim Chukwuemeka Odumegwu-Ojukwu (All Progressive Grand Alliance)	155,947
Christopher Pere Ajuwa (Alliance for Democracy)	89,511
Chris O. Okotie (Fresh Democratic Party)	74,049
Others†	248,100

* Provisional results released by the Independent National Election Commission. The figure for the total number of votes cast at the election was not immediately made available.
† There were 16 other candidates.

NATIONAL ASSEMBLY

House of Representatives

Speaker of the House of Representatives: PATRICIA ETTEH.

Election, 12 April 2003

Party	Votes	% of votes	Seats
People's Democratic Party	15,927,807	54.49	223
All Nigeria People's Party	8,021,531	27.44	96
Alliance for Democracy	2,711,972	9.28	34
United Nigeria People's Party	803,432	2.75	2
All Progressive Grand Alliance	397,147	1.36	2
National Democratic Party	561,161	1.92	1
People's Redemption Party	185,764	0.76	1
People's Salvation Party	96,550	0.33	1
Others	527,706	1.67	—
Total	29,233,070	100.00	360

Senate

Speaker of the Senate: DAVID MARK.

Election, 12 April 2003

Party	Votes	% of votes	Seats
People's Democratic Party	15,585,538	53.69	76
All Nigeria People's Party	8,091,783	27.87	27
Alliance for Democracy	2,828,082	9.74	6
Others	2,524,704	8.70	—
Total	29,030,107	100.00	109

Election Commission

Independent National Electoral Commission (INEC): Plot 436 Zambezi Cres., Maitama District, PMB 0184, Garki, Abuja; tel. (9) 2224632; e-mail contact@inecnigeria.org; internet www.inecnigeria.org; f. 1998; Chair. MAURICE IWU.

Political Organizations

Following the death of the military Head of State in June 1998, the existing authorized political parties were dissolved. The Government established a new Independent National Electoral Commission (INEC), which officially approved three political parties to contest elections in February 1999. Prior to legislative and presidential elections in April 2003, three political associations were granted registration in June 2002, as were a further 24 in December. According to INEC, by mid-2007 51 parties were registered.

Abia Democratic Alliance (ADA): Umuahia; f. 2001; allied to the People's Democratic Party.

Action Congress (AC): Plot 779 Ona Cres., Maitama, Abuja; tel. (9) 4139999; f. 2006 by a merger of the Alliance for Democracy, the Justice Party, the Advanced Congress of Democrats and several minor parties; Chair. Alhadji HASSAN M. ZURMI.

Alliance for Democracy (AD): Plot 2096, Bumbona Close, Zone 1, Wuse, Abuja; tel. (9) 5239357; e-mail info@alliancefordemocracy.org; f. 1998; Chair. MOJISOLUWA AKINFEWA.

Justice Party (JP): 2nd Ave, Gwarimpa, Abuja; Chair. RALPH OBIOHA.

Advanced Congress of Democrats (ACD): Plot 882, Emeka Ampoku St, Area 11, Garki, Abuja; Chair. ALEXIS ANIELO.

All Nigeria People's Party (ANPP): Bassan Plaza, Plot 759, Central Business Area, Abuja; f. 1998; Chair. Alhaji Dr MODU SHERIF.

All Progressive Grand Alliance (APGA): 41b Libreville Cres., Wuse 11, Abuja; tel. 8035903910; regd June 2002; Chair. VICTOR C. UMEH.

Democratic People's Party (DPP): 1st Floor, Labour House, Central Business District, Abuja; tel. (9) 2343345; Chair. DAN NWANYANWU.

Fresh Democratic Party: 4 Park Close, Aguyi Ironsi St, Maitma, Abuja; Chair. Rev. CHRIS OKOTIE.

Movement for the Actualization of the Sovereign State of Biafra (MASSOB): Okwe, Imo; f. 1999; Leader Chief RALPH UWAZURIKE.

Movement for the Emancipation of the Niger Delta (MEND): f. 2005; main Ijaw militant group operating in the Niger Delta; Leader Maj.-Gen. GODSWILL TAMUNO.

Movement for the Survival of the Ogoni People (MOSOP): 27 Odu St, Ogbunabali, Port Harcourt; tel. (84) 230250; e-mail mosop@phca.linkserve.com; f. 1990 to organize opposition to petroleum production in Ogoni territory; Pres. LEDUM MITEE.

National Conscience Party (NCP): 18 Phase 1 Low Cost Housing Estate, Lake City Ave, Gwagwalada, Abuja; tel. (9) 4937279; e-mail info@nigeriancp.net; internet www.nigeriancp.net; Leader GANI FAWEHINMI; Chair. OSAGIE OBAYUWANA.

National Democratic Party (NDP): POB 8196, Abuja; tel. (9) 6703366; e-mail info@ndpnigeria.com; internet www.ndpnigeria.com; regd June 2002; Chair. Alhaji ALIYU HABU FARI.

Niger Delta People's Volunteer Force (NDPVF): prominent Ijaw militant group operating in the Niger Delta; Leader Alhaji MUJAHID DOKUBO-ASARI.

People's Democratic Party (PDP): Wadata Plaza, Michael Okpara Way, Zone 5, Wuse, Abuja; tel. (9) 5232589; f. 1998 by fmr opponents of the Govt of Gen. Sani Abacha; supports greater federalism; ruling party; Chair. Col. Dr AHMADU ALI.

People's Redemption Party (PRP): City Plaza, Area 11, Garki, Abuja; tel. 8033495403; regd Dec. 2002; Chair. Alhadji ABDULKADIR B. MUSA.

People's Salvation Party (PSP): 441 Oron St, Wuse Zone 1, Abuja; tel. (9) 5235359; regd Dec. 2002; Chair. Alhaji LAWAL MAITURARE.

Progressive People's Alliance (PPA): 52, Libreville St, Wuse 11, Abuja; Chair. Alhadji SULEIMAN AHMED.

United Nigeria People's Party (UNPP): Plot 1467, Safana Close, Garki 11, Abuja; tel. (9) 2340091; regd June 2002; Chair. MALLAM SALEH JAMBO.

Diplomatic Representation

EMBASSIES AND HIGH COMMISSIONS IN NIGERIA

Algeria: Plot 203, Etim Inyang Cres., POB 55238, Falomo, Lagos; tel. (1) 612092; fax (1) 2624017; Ambassador EL-MIHOUB MIHOUBI.

Angola: 5 Kasumu Ekomode St, Victoria Island, POB 50437, Falomo Ikoyi, Lagos; tel. (9) 4135121; fax (9) 4134082; Ambassador EVARISTO DOMINGOS KIMBA.

Argentina: 2 Abubakar Koko Cres., Asokoro District, Abuja; tel. (9) 3148680; fax (9) 3148683; e-mail enige@mrecic.gov.ar; Chargé d'affaires a.i. RICARDO JORGE MONTICELLI.

Australia: 5th Floor, Oakland Centre, 48 Aguiyi Ironsi St, Maitama, Abuja; PMB 5152, Abuja; tel. (9) 4135226; fax (9) 4135227; e-mail ahc.abuja@dfat.gov.au; internet www.nigeria.embassy.gov.au; High Commissioner JEFF HART.

Austria: Plot 9, Usuma St, Maitama, Abuja; tel. (9) 4130772; fax (9) 4612715; e-mail abuja-ob@bmeia.gv.at; Ambassador Dr PETER CHRISTIAN FELLNER.

Belgium: 9 Usuma St, Maitama, Abuja; tel. (9) 4131859; fax (9) 4132015; e-mail abuja@diplobel.org; internet www.belgiumvisas.org; Ambassador DIRK VAN EECKHOUT.

Benin: 4 Abudu Smith St, Victoria Island, POB 5705, Lagos; tel. (1) 2614411; fax (1) 2612385; Ambassador PATRICE HOUNGAVOU.

Brazil: Plot 324, Diplomatic Dr., Zone Central, Area District, Abuja; tel. (9) 4618688; fax (9) 4618687; e-mail nigbrem@linkserve.net; Ambassador ALBERTO FERREIRA GUIMARAES.

Bulgaria: 10 Euphrates St, cnr Aminu Kano Cres., Maitama, Abuja; tel. (9) 4130034; fax (9) 4132741; e-mail bulgarian@nigtel.com; Ambassador (vacant).

Burkina Faso: 15 Norman Williams St, Ikoyi, Lagos; tel. (1) 617985; e-mail ebfn@nova.net.ng; Ambassador DRAMANE YAMÉOGO.

Cameroon: 5 Elsie Femi Pearse St, Victoria Island, PMB 2476, Lagos; tel. (1) 2612226; fax (1) 7747510; High Commissioner ANDRÉ E. KENDECK MANDENG.

Canada: 15 Bobo St, Maitama, POB 5144, Abuja; tel. (9) 4139910; fax (9) 4139932; e-mail abuja@international.gc.ca; internet nigeria.gc.ca; High Commissioner DAVID ANGELL.

Chad: 2 Goriola St, Victoria Island, PMB 70662, Lagos; tel. (1) 2622590; fax (1) 2618314; Ambassador MAHAMAT HABIB DOUTOUM.

China, People's Republic: Plot 302–303, Central Area, Abuja; tel. (9) 4618661; fax (9) 4618660; e-mail chinaemb_ng@mfa.gov.cn; internet ng.china-embassy.org; Ambassador XU JIANGUO.

Côte d'Ivoire: 3 Abudu Smith St, Victoria Island, POB 7786, Lagos; tel. (1) 610936; fax (1) 2613822; e-mail cotedivoire@micro.com.ng; Ambassador AIKO ZIKE MARC.

Cuba: Plot 935, Idejo St, Victoria Island, POB 328, Victoria Island, Lagos; tel. (1) 2614836; fax (1) 2617036; Ambassador ELIO SAVÓN OLIVA.

Czech Republic: Plot 1223, Gnassingbé Eyadéma St, Asokoro District, POB 4628, Abuja; tel. (9) 3141245; fax (9) 3141248; e-mail abuja@embassy.mzv.cz; internet www.mzv.cz/abuja; Ambassador ALEXANDR KARYCH.

Egypt: Plot 3319, Barada Close, Abuja; tel. (9) 4136091; fax (9) 4132602; Ambassador MOHAMED ASHRAF HARBY SALAMA.

Equatorial Guinea: 7 Bank Rd, Ikoyi, POB 4162, Lagos; tel. (1) 2683717; Ambassador A. S. DOUGAN MALABO.

Ethiopia: 19 Ona Cres., Maitama, POB 2488, Abuja; tel. (1) 4131691; fax (1) 4131692; e-mail etabuja@primair.net; Ambassador YOHANESS GENDA.

Finland: Maputo St Wuse, Zone 3, PMB 5140, Abuja; tel. (9) 3147256; fax (9) 3147252; e-mail sanomat.aba@formin.fi; Ambassador ANNA-LIISA KORHONEN.

France: 37 Udi Hills St, Abuja; tel. (9) 5231055; fax (9) 5235482; e-mail ambafrance.abj@micro.com.ng; internet www.ambafrance-ng.org; Ambassador YVES GAUDEUL.

Gabon: 8 Norman Williams St, SW Ikoyi, POB 5989, Lagos; tel. (1) 2684673; fax (1) 2690692; Ambassador E. AGUEMINYA.

The Gambia: 162 Awolowo Rd, SW Ikoyi, POB 873, Lagos; tel. (1) 682192; High Commissioner OMAR SECKA.

Germany: 9 Lake Maracaibo Close, off Amazon St, Maitama, Abuja; tel. (9) 4130962; fax (9) 4130949; e-mail info@abuja.diplo.de; internet www.abuja.diplo.de; Ambassador JOACHIM CHRISTOPH SCHMILLEN.

Ghana: 21–25 King George V Rd, POB 889, Lagos; tel. (1) 2630015; fax (1) 2630338; High Commissioner Lt-Gen. JOSHUA HAMIDU.

Greece: No 6, Takum Close, Wuse II, Abuja; tel. (9) 4139433; fax (9) 4139435; e-mail grembabuja@mfa.gr; internet grembnigeria.mfa.gr; Ambassador HARALAMBOS DAFARANOS.

Guinea: 8 Abudu Smith St, Victoria Island, POB 2826, Lagos; tel. (1) 2616961; Ambassador KOMO BEAVOGUI.

Holy See: Pope John Paul II Cres., Maitama, PMB 541, Garki, Abuja; tel. (9) 4138381; fax (9) 4136653; e-mail nuntiusabj@hotmail.com; Apostolic Nuncio Most Rev. RENZO FRATINI (Titular Archbishop of Botriana).

Hungary: Plot 1685, Jose Marti Cres., Asokoro, Abuja; tel. (1) 3141180; fax (1) 3141177; e-mail huemblgs@nova.net.ng; internet www.mfa.gov.hu/emb/abuja; Ambassador Dr FERENC KATÓ.

India: 8A Walter Carrington Cres., POB 2322, Lagos; tel. (1) 2627680; fax (1) 2612660; e-mail hclag@hyperia.com; internet www.hicomindlagos.com; High Commissioner HARIHARA SUBRAMANIAM VISWANATHAN.

Indonesia: 5 Anifowoshe St, Victoria Island, POB 3473, Marina, Lagos; tel. (1) 2614601; fax (1) 2613301; e-mail indlgs@infoweb.abs.net; Ambassador SUSANTO ISMODIRDJO.

Iran: 2 Udi St, Maitama, Abuja; tel. (1) 5238048; fax (1) 5237785; e-mail irembassy_abuja@yahoo.com; Ambassador JAWAD TORKABADI.

Ireland: Plot 415, Negro Cres., Maitama District, Abuja; tel. (9) 4131751; fax (9) 4131805; e-mail abujaembassy@dfa.ie; internet www.irishembassy-nigeria.net; Ambassador LIAM CANNIFFE.

Israel: Plot 12, Mary Slessor St, Asokoro, POB 10924, Abuja; tel. (9) 3143170; fax (9) 3143177; e-mail info@abuja.mfa.gov.il; internet abuja.mfa.gov.il; Ambassador NOAM KATZ.

Italy: 21st Cres., off Constitution Ave, Central Business District, Abuja; tel. (9) 5244036; fax (9) 5244034; e-mail ambasciata.abuja@esteri.it; internet www.ambabuja.esteri.it; Ambassador MASSIMO BAISTROCCHI.

Jamaica: Plot 77, Samuel Adedoyin Ave, Victoria Island, POB 75368, Lagos; tel. (1) 2611085; fax (1) 2610047; High Commissioner ROBERT MILLER (acting).

Japan: Plot 585 Bobo St, Maitama, PMB 5070, Abuja; tel. (9) 4138898; fax (9) 4137667; Ambassador AKIO TANAKA.

Kenya: 18 Yedseram St, Maitama, PMB 5160, Abuja; tel. (9) 4139155; fax (9) 4139157; e-mail abuja@mfa.go.ke; High Commissioner DANIEL MEPUKORI KOIKAI.

Korea, Democratic People's Republic: 31 Akin Adesola St, Victoria Island, Lagos; tel. (1) 2610108; Ambassador KIM PYONG GI.

Korea, Republic: Plot 934, Idejo St, Victoria Island, POB 4668, Lagos; tel. (1) 2615353; Ambassador KIE DONG-LEE.

Lebanon: Plot 18, Walter Carrington Cres., Victoria Island, POB 651, Lagos; tel. (1) 2614511; e-mail emblebanon@hyperia.com; Ambassador IMAN YOUNES.

Liberia: 3 Idejo St, Plot 162, off Adeola Odeku St, Victoria Island, POB 70841, Lagos; tel. (1) 2618899; Ambassador Prof. JAMES TAPEH.

Libya: 46 Raymond Njoku Rd, SW Ikoyi, Lagos; tel. (1) 2680880; Chargé d'affaires a.i. IBRAHIM AL-BASHAR.

Malaysia: 2 Pechora Close, Maitama PMB 5217, Abuja; tel. (9) 4133918; fax (9) 413 3922; e-mail malabuja@kln.gov.my; Chargé d'affairs a.i MELVIN CASTELINO.

Morocco: Plot 1306, Udo Udoma Cres., Asokoro, Abuja; tel. (9) 3141961; fax (9) 3141959; Ambassador MUSTAPHA CHERAQAOUI.

Namibia: Plot 1738 T. Y., Danyuma St, Cadasdral Zone, Asokoro, Abuja; tel. (9) 3142740; fax (9) 3142743; e-mail namibiahighcomabuja@yahoo.com; Ambassador DAVID SMITH.

Netherlands: 21st Cres., Central Business District, Abuja; tel. (9) 5244024; fax (9) 5244030; Ambassador ARIE VAN DER WIEL.

Niger: 15 Adeola Odeku St, Victoria Island, PMB 2736, Lagos; tel. (1) 2612300; Ambassador MOUSSA ELHADJI IBRAHIM.

Norway: 3 Anifowoshe St, Victoria Island, PMB 2431, Lagos; tel. (1) 2618467; fax (1) 2618469; e-mail emb.lagos@mfa.no; Ambassador TORE NEDREBO.

Pakistan: 4 Molade Okoya-Thomas St, Victoria Island, POB 2450, Lagos; tel. (1) 613909; fax (1) 614822; Ambassador KHALID DURRANI.

Philippines: 16 Lake Chad Cres., cnr Kainji St, Maitama, Abuja; tel. (9) 4133649; fax (9) 4137650; e-mail abujape@dfa.gov.ph; Ambassador MASARANGA R. UMPA.

Poland: 16 Ona Cres., Maitama, Abuja; tel. (9) 4138280; fax (9) 4138281; e-mail poembabu@linkserve.com; internet www.abuja.polemb.net; Ambassador GRZEGORZ WALINSKI.

Portugal: 27B Gana St, Maitama, Abuja; tel. (9) 4137211; fax (9) 4137214; e-mail portemb@rosecom.net; Ambassador MARIA DE FÁTIMA DE PINA PERESTRELLO.

Romania: Plot 498, Nelson Mandela St, Zone A4, Asokoro, POB 10376, Abuja; tel. (9) 3142304; fax (9) 3142306; e-mail romnig@gmail.com; Ambassador MARIAN PARJOL.

Russia: 5 Walter Carrington Cres., Victoria Island, POB 2723, Lagos; tel. (1) 2613359; fax (1) 4619994; e-mail musemlagos@vgccl.net; Ambassador GENNADY V. ILYITEHEV.

Saudi Arabia: Plot 347H, off Adetokunbo Ademola Cres., Wuse 2, Abuja; tel. (9) 4131880; fax (9) 4134906; Ambassador ANWAR A. ABD-RABBUH.

Senegal: 14 Kofo Abayomi Rd, Victoria Island, PMB 2197, Lagos; tel. (1) 2611722; Ambassador AMADOU THIALAW DIOP.

Serbia: 11, Rio Negro Close, off Yedseram St, Cadastral Zone A6, Maitama District, Abuja; tel. (9) 4139492; fax (9) 4130078; e-mail mail@ambnig.com; Ambassador DRAGAN MRAOVIĆ.

Sierra Leone: 31 Waziri Ibrahim St, Victoria Island, POB 2821, Lagos; tel. (1) 2614666; High Commissioner JOSEPH BLELL.

Slovakia: POB 1290, Lagos; tel. (1) 2621585; fax (1) 2612103; e-mail obeo.sk@micro.com.ng; Ambassador VASIL HUDÁK.

Somalia: Plot 1270, off Adeola Odeka St, POB 6355, Lagos; tel. (1) 2611283; Ambassador M. S. HASSAN.

South Africa: 71 Usuma St, Maitama, Abuja,; tel. (9) 4133862; fax (9) 4133829; e-mail sahcniga@rosecom.net; High Commissioner B. SIFINGO.

Spain: Plot 611, 8 Bobo Close, Maitama, PMB 5120, Abuja; tel. (9) 4137091; fax (9) 4137095; e-mail embespng@mail.mae.es; Ambassador ÁNGEL LOSADA FERNÁNDEZ.

Sudan: 2B Kofo Abayomi St, Victoria Island, POB 2428, Lagos; tel. (1) 2615889; Ambassador AHMED ALTIGANI SALEH.

Sweden: PMB 569, Garki, Abuja; tel. (9) 3143399; fax (9) 3143398; e-mail ambassaden.abuja@foreign.ministry.se; internet www.swedenabroad.com/abuja; Ambassador Lars-Owe Persson.

Switzerland: 157 Adetokumbo Ademola Cres., Wuse II, Abuja; tel. (9) 4131081; fax (9) 4131089; e-mail abu.vertretung@eda.admin.ch; internet www.eda.admin.ch/abuja; Ambassador Pierre Helg.

Syria: 25 Kofo Abayomi St, Victoria Island, Lagos; tel. (1) 2615860; Chargé d'affaires a.i. Mustafa Haj-Ali.

Tanzania: 15 Yedseram St, Maitama, PMB 5125, Wuse, Abuja; tel. (9) 4132313; fax (9) 4132314; e-mail tanabuja@lytos.com; High Commissioner Cisco Mtiro (acting).

Thailand: Plot 766, Panama St, Cadastral Zone A6, Maitama, Abuja; e-mail thaiabj@mfa.go.th; Ambassador N. Sathaporn.

Togo: 96 Awolowo Rd, SW Ikoyi, POB 1435, Lagos; tel. (1) 2617449; Ambassador Foli-Agbenozan Tettekpoe.

Trinidad and Tobago: 3a Tiamiyu Savage St, Victoria Island, POB 6392, Marina, Lagos; tel. (1) 2612087; fax (1) 612732; High Commissioner Dr Harold Robertson.

Turkey: 3 Okunola Martins Close, Ikoyi, POB 56252, Lagos; tel. (1) 2691140; fax (1) 2693040; e-mail turkemb@infoweb.abs.net; Ambassador Ömer Sahinkaya.

United Kingdom: 19 Torren Close, off Mississippi St, Shehu Shagari Way, Maitama, Abuja; tel. (9) 4132010; fax (9) 4133552; e-mail information.abuja@fco.gov.uk; internet www.ukinnigeria.com; High Commissioner Richard Gozney.

USA: 7 Plot 1075, Diplomatic Dr., Central District Area, Abuja; tel. (9) 4614000; fax (9) 4614036; e-mail ircabuja@state.gov; internet usembassy.state.gov; Ambassador John Campbell.

Venezuela: 35b Adetokunbo Ademola St, Victoria Island, POB 3727, Lagos; tel. (1) 2611590; fax (1) 2617350; e-mail embavenez.nig@net.ng; Ambassador Alfredo Enrique Vargas.

Zambia: 11 Keffi St, SW Ikoyi, PMB 6119, Lagos; High Commissioner B. N. Nkunika (acting).

Zimbabwe: Abuja; tel. (9) 4137996; fax (9) 4137644; Ambassador Dr John Shumba Mvundura.

Judicial System

Supreme Court

Three Arms Complex, Central District, PMB 308, Abuja; tel. (9) 2346594.

Consists of a Chief Justice and up to 15 Justices, appointed by the President, on the recommendation of the National Judicial Council (subject to the approval of the Senate); has original jurisdiction in any dispute between the Federation and a State, or between States, and hears appeals from the Federal Court of Appeal.

Chief Justice: Salihu Modibbo Alpha Belgore.

Court of Appeal: consists of a President and at least 35 Justices, of whom three must be experts in Islamic (*Shari'a*) law and three experts in Customary law.

Federal High Court: consists of a Chief Judge and a number of other judges.

Each State has a **High Court**, consisting of a Chief Judge and a number of judges, appointed by the Governor of the State on the recommendation of the National Judicial Council (subject to the approval of the House of Assembly of the State). If required, a state may have a **Shari'a Court of Appeal** (dealing with Islamic civil law) and a **Customary Court of Appeal**. **Special Military Tribunals** have been established to try offenders accused of crimes such as corruption, drugs-trafficking and armed robbery; appeals against rulings of the Special Military Tribunals are referred to a **Special Appeals Tribunal**, which comprises retired judges.

Religion

ISLAM

According to the 1963 census, there were more than 26m. Muslims (47.2% of the total population) in Nigeria.

Spiritual Head: Col Muhammadu Sa'ad Abubakar (the Sultan of Sokoto).

CHRISTIANITY

The 1963 census enumerated more than 19m. Christians (34.5% of the total population).

Christian Council of Nigeria: 139 Ogunlana Dr., Surulere, POB 2838, Lagos; tel. (1) 7923495; f. 1929; 15 full mems and six assoc. mems; Pres. Rt Rev. Rogers O. Uwadi; Gen. Sec. Rev. Ikecnukwu Okorie.

The Anglican Communion

Anglicans are adherents of the Church of the Province of Nigeria, comprising 61 dioceses. Nigeria, formerly part of the Province of West Africa, became a separate Province in 1979; in 1997 it was divided into three separate provinces. The Church had an estimated 10m. members in 1990.

Archbishop of Province I and Bishop of Lagos: Most Rev. Ephraim A. Ademow, Archbishop's Palace, 29 Marina, POB 13, Lagos; tel. (1) 2635681; fax (1) 2631264.

Archbishop of Province II and Bishop of Awka: Most Rev. Maxwell Anikwenwa, Bishopscourt, Ifite Rd, POB 130, Awka.

Archbishop of Province III and Bishop of Abuja: Most Rev. Peter Jasper Akinola, Archbishop's Palace, POB 212, ADCP, Abuja; fax (9) 5230986; e-mail abuja@anglican.skannet.com.ng.

General Secretary: Ven. Samuel B. Akinola, 29 Marina, POB 78, Lagos; tel. (1) 2635681; fax (1) 2631264.

The Roman Catholic Church

Nigeria comprises nine archdioceses, 40 dioceses and two Apostolic Vicariates. At 31 December 2004 the total number of adherents represented an estimated 14% of the population.

Catholic Bishops' Conference of Nigeria

6 Force Rd, POB 951, Lagos; tel. (1) 2635849; fax (1) 2636680; e-mail cathsecl@infoweb.abs.net.

f. 1976; Pres. Most Rev. John O. Onaiyekan (Archbishop of Abuja); Sec.-Gen. of Secretariat Rev. Fr Matthew Hassan Kukah.

Archbishop of Abuja: Most Rev. John O. Onaiyekan, Archdiocesan Secretariat, POB 286, Garki, Abuja; tel. (9) 2340661; fax (9) 2340662; e-mail archbuja@infoweb.abs.net.

Archbishop of Benin City: Most Rev. Patrick E. Ekpu, Archdiocesan Secretariat, POB 35, Benin City, Edo; tel. (52) 253787; fax (52) 255763; e-mail cadobc@infoweb.abs.net.

Archbishop of Calabar: Most Rev. Joseph Edra Ukpo, Archdiocesan Secretariat, PMB 1044, Calabar, Cross River; tel. (87) 231666; fax (87) 239177.

Archbishop of Ibadan: Most Rev. Felix Alaba Job, Archdiocesan Secretariat, 8 Latosa Rd, PMB 5057, Ibadan, Oyo; tel. (22) 2413544; fax (22) 2414855; e-mail archdiocese.ibadan@skannet.com.ng.

Archbishop of Jos: Most Rev. Ignatius Ayau Kaigama, Archdiocesan Secretariat, 20 Joseph Gomwalk Rd, POB 494, Jos, Plateau; tel. (73) 451548; fax (73) 451547; e-mail josarch@hisen.org.

Archbishop of Kaduna: Most Rev. Peter Yariyok Jatau, Archbishop's House, Tafawa Balewa Way, POB 248, Kaduna; tel. (62) 246076; fax (62) 240026; e-mail catholickad@email.com.

Archbishop of Lagos: Cardinal Anthony Olubunmi Okogie, Archdiocesan Secretariat, 19 Catholic Mission St, POB 8, Lagos; tel. (1) 2635729; fax (1) 2633841; e-mail arclagos@infoweb.abs.net.

Archbishop of Onitsha: Most Rev. Valerian Okeke, Archdiocesan Secretariat, POB 411, Onitsha, Anambra; tel. (46) 413298; fax (46) 413913; e-mail secretariat@onitsha-archdiocese-org.

Archbishop of Owerri: Most Rev. Anthony John Valentine Obinna, Archdiocesan Secretariat, POB 85, Owerri, Imo; tel. (83) 230115; fax (83) 300206; e-mail owcathsec@owerriarcidiocese.org.

Other Christian Churches

Brethren Church of Nigeria: c/o Kulp Bible School, POB 1, Mubi, Adamawa; f. 1923; 100,000 mems; Gen. Sec. Rev. Abraham Wuta Tizhe.

Church of the Lord (Aladura): Anthony Village, Ikorodu Rd, POB 308, Ikeja, Lagos; tel. (1) 4964749; f. 1930; 1.1m. mems; Primate Dr E. O. A. Adejobi.

Lutheran Church of Christ in Nigeria: POB 21, Numan, Adamawa; 575,000 mems; Pres. Rt Rev. Dr David L. Windibiziri.

Lutheran Church of Nigeria: Obot Idim Ibesikpo, Uyo, Akwa Ibom; tel. and fax (85) 201848; f. 1936; 370,000 mems; Pres. Rev. S. J. Udofia.

Methodist Church Nigeria: Wesley House, 21–22 Marina, POB 2011, Lagos; tel. (1) 2702563; fax (1) 2702710; 483,500 mems; Patriarch Rev. Dr Sunday Ola Kakinde.

Nigerian Baptist Convention: Baptist Bldg, PMB 5113, Ibadan; tel. (2) 2412267; fax (2) 2413561; e-mail baptconv@skannet.com; 2.5m. mems; Pres. Rev. Emmanuel O. Bolarinwa; Gen. Sec. Dr Ademola Ishola.

Presbyterian Church of Nigeria: 26–29 Ehere Rd, Ogbor Hill, POB 2635, Aba, Imo; tel. (82) 222551; f. 1846; 130,000 mems; Moderator Rt Rev. Dr A. A. Otu; Synod Clerk Rev. Ubon B. Usung.

The Redeemed Church of Christ, the Church of the Foursquare Gospel, the Qua Iboe Church and the Salvation Army are prominent among numerous other Christian churches active in Nigeria.

AFRICAN RELIGIONS

The beliefs, rites and practices of the people of Nigeria are very diverse, varying between ethnic groups and between families in the same group.

The Press

DAILIES

Abuja Times: Daily Times of Nigeria Ltd, 2 Hasper Cres., Wuse Zone 7, PMB 115 Gaski, Abuja; tel. (1) 4900850; f. 1992; Editor CLEMENT ILOBA.

Daily Champion: Isolo Industrial Estate, Oshodi-Apapa, Lagos; fax (1) 4526011; e-mail letters@champion-newspapers.com; internet www.champion-newspapers.com; Editor AUGSTEN ADAMU.

Daily Express: Commercial Amalgamated Printers, 30 Glover St, Lagos; f. 1938; Editor Alhaji AHMED ALAO (acting); circ. 20,000.

Daily Sketch: Sketch Publishing Ltd, Oba Adebimpe Rd, PMB 5067, Ibadan; tel. (2) 414851; f. 1964; govt-owned; Chair. RONKE OKUSANYA; Editor ADEMOLA IDOWU; circ. 64,000.

Daily Star: 9 Works Rd, PMB 1139, Enugu; tel. (42) 253561; Editor JOSEF BEL-MOLOKWU.

Daily Times: Daily Times of Nigeria Ltd, New Isheri Rd, Agidingbi, PMB 21340, Ikeja, Lagos; tel. (1) 4900850; f. 1925; 60% govt-owned; Editor OGBUAGU ANIKWE; circ. 400,000.

The Democrat: 9 Ahmed Talib Ave, POB 4457, Kaduna South; tel. (62) 231907; f. 1983; Editor ABDULHAMID BABATUNDE; circ. 100,000.

Evening Times: Daily Times of Nigeria Ltd, New Isheri Rd, Agidingbi, PMB 21340, Ikeja, Lagos; tel. (1) 4900850; Man. Dir Dr ONUKA ADINOYI-OJO; Editor CLEMENT ILOBA; circ. 20,000.

The Guardian: Rutam House, Isolo Expressway, Isolo, PMB 1217, Oshodi, Lagos; tel. (1) 524111; internet www.ngrguardiannews.com; f. 1983; independent; Publr ALEX IBRU; Editor EMEKA IZEZE; circ. 80,000.

National Concord: Concord House, 42 Concord Way, POB 4483, Ikeja, Lagos; f. 1980; Editor NSIKAK ESSIEN; circ. 200,000.

New Nigerian: Ahmadu Bello Way, POB 254, Kaduna; tel. (62) 201420; f. 1965; govt-owned; Chair. Prof. TEKENA TAMUNO; Editor (vacant); circ. 80,000.

Nigerian Chronicle: Cross River State Newspaper Corpn, 17–19 Barracks Rd, POB 1074, Calabar; tel. (87) 224976; fax (87) 224979; f. 1970; Editor UNIMKE NAWA; circ. 50,000.

Nigerian Herald: Kwara State Printing and Publishing Corpn, Offa Rd, PMB 1369, Ilorin; tel. and fax (31) 220506; f. 1973; sponsored by Kwara State Govt; Editor RAZAK EL-ALAWA; circ. 25,000.

Nigerian Observer: The Bendel Newspaper Corpn, 18 Airport Rd, POB 1143, Benin City; tel. (52) 240050; f. 1968; Editor TONY IKEAKANAM; circ. 150,000.

Nigerian Standard: 5 Joseph Gomwalk Rd, POB 2112, Jos; f. 1972; govt-owned; Editor SALE ILIYA; circ. 100,000.

Nigerian Statesman: Imo Newspapers Ltd, Owerri-Egbu Rd, POB 1095, Owerri; tel. (83) 230099; f. 1978; sponsored by Imo State Govt; Editor EDUBE WADIBIA.

Nigerian Tide: Rivers State Newspaper Corpn, 4 Ikwerre Rd, POB 5072, Port Harcourt; f. 1971; Editor AUGUSTINE NJOAGWUANI; circ. 30,000.

Nigerian Tribune: African Newspapers of Nigeria Ltd, Imalefalafi St, Oke-Ado, POB 78, Ibadan; tel. (2) 2313410; fax (2) 2317573; e-mail correspondence@nigerian-tribune.com; internet www.nigerian-tribune.com; f. 1949; Editor FOLU OLAMITI; circ. 109,000.

Post Express: 7 Warehouse Rd, PMB 1186, Apapa, Lagos; tel. (1) 5453351; fax (1) 5453436; e-mail postexpress@nova.net.ng; internet www.postexpresswired.com; Publr Chief S. ODUWU; Man. Dir Dr STANLEY MACEBUH.

The Punch: Skyway Press, Kudeti St, PMB 21204, Onipetsi, Ikeja; tel. (1) 4963580; internet www.punchng.com; f. 1976; Editor GBMEIGA OGUNLEYE; circ. 150,000.

This Day: 35 Creek Rd, Apapa, Lagos; tel. (1) 5871432; fax (1) 5871436; e-mail thisday@nova.net.ng; internet www.thisdayonline.com.

Vanguard: Kirikiri Canal, PMB 1007, Apapa; e-mail vanguard@linkserve.com.ng; internet www.vanguardngr.com; f. 1984; Editor FRANK AIGBOGUN.

SUNDAY NEWSPAPERS

Sunday Chronicle: Cross River State Newspaper Corpn, PMB 1074, Calabar; f. 1977; Editor-in-Chief ETIM ANIM; circ. 163,000.

Sunday Concord: Concord House, 42 Concord Way, POB 4483, Ikeja, Lagos; f. 1980; Editor DELE ALAKE.

Sunday Herald: Kwara State Printing and Publishing Corpn, PMB 1369, Ilorin; tel. (31) 220976; f. 1981; Editor CHARLES OSAGIE (acting).

Sunday New Nigerian: Ahmadu Bello Way, POB 254, Kaduna; tel. (62) 245220; fax (62) 213778; e-mail auduson@newnigerian.com; internet www.newnigerian.com; f. 1981; weekly; Editor IBRAHIM AUDUSON; circ. 120,000.

Sunday Observer: PMB 1334, Bendel Newspapers Corpn, 18 Airport Rd, Benin City; f. 1968; Editor T. O. BORHA; circ. 60,000.

Sunday Punch: Kudeti St, PMB 21204, Ikeja, Lagos; tel. (1) 4964691; fax (1) 4960715; f. 1973; Editor DAYO WRIGHT; circ. 150,000.

Sunday Sketch: Sketch Publishing Co Ltd, PMB 5067, Ibadan; tel. (2) 414851; f. 1964; govt-owned; Editor OBAFEMI OREDEIN; circ. 125,000.

Sunday Standard: Plateau Publishing Co Ltd, Owerri-Egbu Rd, PMB 1095, Owerri; tel. (83) 230099; f. 1978; sponsored by Imo State Govt; Editor EDUBE WADIBIA.

Sunday Sun: PMB 1025, Okoro House, Factory Lane, off Upper Mission Rd, New Benin.

Sunday Tide: 4 Ikwerre Rd, POB 5072, Port Harcourt; f. 1971; Editor AUGUSTINE NJOAGWUANI.

Sunday Times: Daily Times of Nigeria Ltd, New Isheri Rd, Agidingbi, PMB 21340, Ikeja, Lagos; tel. (1) 4900850; f. 1953; 60% govt-owned; Editor DUPE AJAYI; circ. 100,000.

Sunday Tribune: Imalefalafi St, POB 78, Oke-Ado, Ibadan; tel. (2) 2310886; Editor WALE OJO.

Sunday Vanguard: Kirikiri Canal, PMB 1007, Apapa; Editor DUPE AJAYI.

WEEKLIES

Albishir: Triumph Publishing Co Ltd, Gidan Sa'adu Zungur, PMB 3155, Kano; tel. (64) 260273; f. 1981; Hausa; Editor ALIYU UMAR (acting); circ. 15,000.

Business Times: Daily Times of Nigeria Ltd, New Isheri Rd, Agidingbi, PMB 21340, Ikeja, Lagos; tel. (1) 4900850; f. 1925; 60% govt-owned; Editor GODFREY BAMAWO; circ. 22,000.

Gboungboun: Sketch Publishing Co Ltd, New Court Rd, PMB 5067, Ibadan; tel. (2) 414851; govt-owned; Yoruba; Editor A. O. ADEBANJO; circ. 80,000.

The Independent: Bodija Rd, PMB 5109, Ibadan; f. 1960; English; Roman Catholic; Editor Rev. F. B. CRONIN-COLTSMAN; circ. 13,000.

Irohin Imole: 15 Bamgbose St, POB 1495, Lagos; f. 1957; Yoruba; Editor TUNJI ADEOSUN.

Irohin Yoruba: 212 Broad St, PMB 2416, Lagos; tel. (1) 410886; f. 1945; Yoruba; Editor S. A. AJIBADE; circ. 85,000.

Lagos Life: Guardian Newspapers Ltd, Rutam House, Isolo Expressway, Isolo, PMB 1217, Oshodi, Lagos; f. 1985; Editor BISI OGUNBADEJO; circ. 100,000.

Lagos Weekend: Daily Times of Nigeria Ltd, New Isheri Rd, Agidingbi, PMB 21340, Ikeja, Lagos; tel. (1) 4900850; f. 1965; 60% govt-owned; news and pictures; Editor SAM OGWA; circ. 85,000.

The News: Lagos; independent; Editor-in-Chief JENKINS ALUMONA.

Newswatch: 3 Billingsway Rd, Oregun, Lagos; tel. (1) 4935654; fax (1) 4960950; e-mail newswatchngr@aol.com; f. 1985; English; CEO RAY EKPU; Editor-in-Chief DAN AGBESE.

Nigerian Radio/TV Times: Nigerian Broadcasting Corpn, POB 12504, Ikoyi.

Sporting Records: Daily Times of Nigeria Ltd, New Isheri Rd, Agidingbi, PMB 21340, Ikeja, Lagos; tel. (1) 4900850; f. 1961; 60% govt-owned; Editor CYRIL KAPPO; circ. 10,000.

Tempo: 26 Ijaiye Rd, PMB 21531, Ogba, Ikeja, Lagos; tel. (1) 920975; fax (1) 4924998; e-mail ijc@linkserve.com.ng; news magazine.

Times International: Daily Times of Nigeria Ltd, 3–7 Kakawa St, POB 139, Lagos; f. 1974; Editor Dr HEZY IDOWU; circ. 50,000.

Truth (The Muslim Weekly): 45 Idumagbo Ave, POB 418, Lagos; tel. (1) 2668455; f. 1951; Editor S. O. LAWAL.

ENGLISH-LANGUAGE PERIODICALS

Afriscope: 29 Salami Saibu St, PMB 1119, Yaba; monthly; African current affairs.

The Ambassador: PMB 2011, 1 peru-Remo, Ogun; tel. (39) 620115; quarterly; Roman Catholic; circ. 20,000.

Benin Review: Ethiope Publishing Corpn, PMB 1332, Benin City; f. 1974; African art and culture; 2 a year; circ. 50,000.

Headlines: Daily Times of Nigeria Ltd, New Isheri Rd, Agindingbi, PMB 21340, Ikeja, Lagos; f. 1973; monthly; Editor ADAMS ALIU; circ. 500,000.

Home Studies: Daily Times Publications, 3–7 Kakawa St, Lagos; f. 1964; 2 a month; Editor Dr ELIZABETH E. IKEM; circ. 40,000.

Insight: 3 Kakawa St, POB 139, Lagos; quarterly; contemporary issues; Editor SAM AMUKA; circ. 5,000.

Journal of the Nigerian Medical Association: 3–7 Kakawa St, POB 139, Apapa; quarterly; Editor Prof. A. O. ADESOLA.

Lagos Education Review: Faculty of Education, University of Lagos Akoka, Lagos; tel. (1) 5820396; fax (1) 4932669; f. 1978; 2 a year; African education; Editor Prof. DURO AJEYALEMI.

The Leader: 19A Assumpta Press Ave, Industrial Layout, PMB 1017, Owerri, Imo; tel. (83) 230932; fortnightly; Roman Catholic; Editor Rev. KEVIN C. AKAGHA.

Management in Nigeria: Plot 22, Idowu Taylor St, Victoria Island, POB 2557, Lagos; tel. (1) 2615105; fax (1) 614116; e-mail nim@rcl.nig.com; quarterly; journal of Nigerian Inst. of Management; Editor Rev. DEJI OLOKESUSI; circ. 25,000.

Marketing in Nigeria: Alpha Publications, Surulere, POB 1163, Lagos; f. 1977; monthly; Editor B. O. K. NWELIH; circ. 30,000.

Modern Woman: 47–49 Salami Saibu St, Marina, POB 2583, Lagos; f. 1964; monthly; Man. Editor TOUN ONABANJO.

The New Nation: 52 Iwaya Rd, Onike, Yaba, Surulere, POB 896, Lagos; tel. (1) 5863629; monthly; news magazine.

Nigeria Magazine: Federal Dept of Culture, PMB 12524, Lagos; tel. (1) 5802060; f. 1927; quarterly; travel, cultural, historical and general; Editor B. D. LEMCHI; circ. 5,000.

Nigerian Businessman's Magazine: 39 Mabo St, Surulere, Lagos; monthly; Nigerian and overseas commerce.

Nigerian Journal of Economic and Social Studies: Nigerian Economic Society, c/o Dept of Economics, University of Ibadan; tel. (2) 8700395; e-mail banayochukwu@yahoo.co.uk; internet www.nigerianeconomicsociety.org; f. 1957; 3 a year; Editor Prof. BEN AIGBOKHAN.

Nigerian Journal of Science: University of Ibadan, POB 4039, Ibadan; publ. of the Science Assen of Nigeria; f. 1966; 2 a year; Editor Prof. I. FAWOLE; circ. 1,000.

Nigerian Worker: United Labour Congress, 97 Herbert Macaulay St, Lagos; Editor LAWRENCE BORHA.

The President: New Breed Organization Ltd, Plot 14 Western Ave, 1 Rafiu Shitty St, Alaka Estate, Surulere, POB 385, Lagos; tel. (1) 5802690; fax (1) 5831175; fortnightly; management; Chief Editor CHRIS OKOLIE.

Quality: Ultimate Publications Ltd, Oregun Rd, Lagos; f. 1987; monthly; Editor BALA DAN MUSA.

Radio-Vision Times: Western Nigerian Radio-Vision Service, Television House, POB 1460, Ibadan; monthly; Editor ALTON A. ADEDEJI.

Savanna: Ahmadu Bello University Press Ltd, PMB 1094, Zaria; tel. (69) 550054; e-mail abupl@wwlkad.com; f. 1972; 2 a year; Editor Prof. J. A. ARIYO; circ. 1,000.

Spear: Daily Times of Nigeria Ltd, New Isheri Rd, Agidingbi, PMB 21340, Ikeja, Lagos; tel. (1) 4900850; f. 1962; monthly; family magazine; Editor COKER ONITA; circ. 10,000.

Technical and Commercial Message: Surulere, POB 1163, Lagos; f. 1980; 6 a year; Editor B. O. K. NWELIH; circ. 12,500.

Today's Challenge: PMB 2010, Jos; tel. (73) 52230; f. 1951; 6 a year; religious and educational; Editor JACOB SHAIBY TSADO; circ. 15,000.

Woman's World: Daily Times of Nigeria Ltd, New Isheri Rd, Agidingbi, PMB 21340, Ikeja, Lagos; monthly; Editor TOYIN JOHNSON; circ. 12,000.

VERNACULAR PERIODICALS

Abokiyar Hira: Albah International Publishers, POB 6177, Bompai, Kano; f. 1987; monthly; Hausa; cultural; Editor BASHARI F. FOUKBAH; circ. 35,000.

Gaskiya ta fi Kwabo: Ahmadu Bello Way, POB 254, Kaduna; tel. (62) 201420; f. 1939; 3 a week; Hausa; Editor ABDUL-HASSAN IBRAHIM.

NEWS AGENCIES

Independent Media Centre (IMC): POB 894, Benin City; e-mail nigeriaimc@yahoo.com; internet www.nigeria.indymedia.org.

News Agency of Nigeria (NAN): Independence Avenue, Central Business Area, PMB 7006, Garki, Abuja; tel. (9) 2349732; fax (9) 2349735; e-mail nanabujaq@rd.nig.com; internet www.newsagencyofnigeria.org; f. 1978; Man. Dir AKIN OSUNTOKUN; Editor-in-Chief SHEHU ABUI.

Foreign Bureaux

Agence France-Presse (AFP): 11 Awolowo Rd, SW Ikoyi, PMB 2448, Lagos; tel. (1) 2691336; fax (1) 2670925; e-mail afplagos@afp.com; Bureau Chief DAVID CLARKE.

ITAR—TASS (Information Telegraphic Agency of Russia—Telegraphic Agency of the Sovereign Countries): 401 St, POB 6465, Victoria Island, Lagos; tel. (1) 617119; Correspondent BORIS V. PILNIKOV.

Inter Press Service (IPS) (Italy): c/o News Agency of Nigeria, PMB 12756, Lagos; tel. (1) 5801290; Correspondent REMI OYO.

Pan-African News Agency (PANA): c/o News Agency of Nigeria, National Arts Theatre, POB 8715, Marina, Lagos; tel. (1) 5801290; f. 1979.

Xinhua (New China) News Agency (People's Republic of China): 161A Adeola Odeku St, Victoria Island, POB 70278, Lagos; tel. (1) 2612464; Bureau Chief ZHAI JINGSHENG.

Publishers

Africana First Publishers Ltd: Book House Trust, 1 Africana-First Dr., PMB 1639, Onitsha; tel. (46) 485031; f. 1973; study guides, general science, textbooks; Chair. RALPH O. EKPEH; Man. Dir J. C. ODIKE.

Ahmadu Bello University Press: PMB 1094, Zaria; tel. (69) 550054; e-mail abupl@wwlkad.com; f. 1972; history, Africana, social sciences, education, literature and arts; Man. Dir SA'IDU HASSAN ADAMU.

Albah International Publishers: 100 Kurawa, Bompai-Kano, POB 6177, Kano City; f. 1978; Africana, Islamic, educational and general, in Hausa; Chair. BASHARI F. ROUKBAH.

Alliance West African Publishers: Orindingbin Estate, New Aketan Layout, PMB 1039, Oyo; tel. (85) 230798; f. 1971; educational and general; Man. Dir Chief M. O. OGUNMOLA.

Aromolaran Publishing Co Ltd: POB 1800, Ibadan; tel. (2) 715980; f. 1968; educational and general; Man. Dir Dr ADEKUNLE AROMOLARAN.

Cross Continent Press Ltd: 25 Egbeyemi Rd, Ilupeju, POB 282, Yaba, Lagos; tel. and fax (1) 7746348; e-mail crosscontinent@yahoo.com; f. 1974; general, educational and academic; Man. Dir Dr T. C. NWOSU.

Daar Communications PLC: Daar Communications Centre, Kpaduma Hills, off Gen. T. Y. Danjuma St, Asokoro, Abuja; tel. (9) 3144802; fax (9) 3300512; broadcasting and information services; Man. Dir. LADI LAWAL.

Daystar Press: Daystar House, POB 1261, Ibadan; tel. (2) 8102670; f. 1962; religious and educational; Man. PHILLIP ADELAKUN LADOKUN.

ECWA Productions Ltd: PMB 2010, Jos; tel. (73) 52230; f. 1973; religious and educational; Gen. Man. Rev. J. K. BOLARIN.

Ethiope Publishing Corpn: Ring Rd, PMB 1332, Benin City; tel. (52) 243036; f. 1970; general fiction and non-fiction, textbooks, reference, science, arts and history; Man. Dir SUNDAY N. OLAYE.

Evans Brothers (Nigeria Publishers) Ltd: Jericho Rd, PMB 5164, Ibadan; tel. (2) 2414394; fax (2) 2410757; f. 1966; general and educational; Chair. Dr ADEKUNLE OJORA; Man. Dir GBENRO ADEGBOLE.

Fourth Dimension Publishing Co Ltd: 16 Fifth Ave, City Layout, PMB 01164, Enugu; tel. (42) 459969; fax (42) 456904; e-mail nwankwov@infoweb.abs.net; internet www.fdpbooks.com; f. 1977; periodicals, fiction, verse, educational and children's; Chair. ARTHUR NWANKWO; Man. Dir V. U. NWANKWO.

Gbabeks Publishers Ltd: POB 37252, Ibadan; tel. (62) 2315705; e-mail gbabeks@hotmail.com; f. 1982; educational and technical; Man. Dir TAYO OGUNBEKUN.

HEBN Publishers PLC: 1 Ighodaro Rd, Jericho, PMB 5205, Ibadan; tel. (2) 2412268; fax (2) 2411089; e-mail info@hebnpublishers.com; internet www.hebnpublishers.com; f. 1962; educational, law, medical and general; Chair. AIGBOJE HIGO; Man. Dir AYO OJENIYI.

Heritage Books: The Poet's Cottage, Artistes Village, Ilogbo-Eremi, Badagry Expressway, POB 610, Apapa, Lagos; tel. (1) 5871333; e-mail theendofknowledge@yahoo; internet www.theendofknowledge.com; f. 1971; general; Chair. NAIWU OSAHON.

Ibadan University Press: Publishing House, University of Ibadan, PMB 16, IU Post Office, Ibadan; tel. (2) 400550; e-mail iup-unibadan@yahoo.com; f. 1951; scholarly, science, law, general and educational; Dir F. A. ADESANOYE.

Ilesanmi Press Ltd: Akure Rd, POB 204, Ilesha; tel. 2062; f. 1955; general and educational; Man. Dir G. E. ILESANMI.

John West Publications Ltd: Plot 2, Block A, Acme Rd, Ogba Industrial Estate, PMB 21001, Ikeja, Lagos; tel. (1) 4925459; f. 1964; general; Man. Dir Alhaji L. K. JAKAUDE.

Kolasanya Publishing Enterprise: 2 Epe Rd, Oke-Owa, PMB 2099, Ijebu-Ode; general and educational; Man. Dir Chief K. OSUNSANYA.

Literamed Publications Ltd (Lantern Books): Plot 45, Alausa Bus-stop, Oregun Industrial Estate, Ikeja, PMB 21068, Lagos; tel. (1) 3450751; fax (1) 4935258; e-mail information@lantern-books.com; internet www.lantern-books.com; f. 1969; children's, medical and scientific; Chair. O. M. LAWAL-SOLARIN.

Longman Nigeria Ltd: 52 Oba Akran Ave, PMB 21036, Ikeja, Lagos; tel. (1) 4978925; fax (1) 4964370; e-mail longman@linkserve.com; f. 1961; general and educational; Man. Dir J. A. OLOWONIYI.

Macmillan Nigeria Publishers Ltd: Ilupeju Industrial Estate, 4 Industrial Ave, POB 264, Yaba, Lagos; tel. (1) 4962185; e-mail macmillan@hotmail.com; internet www.macmillan.nigeria.com; f. 1965; educational and general; Exec. Chair. J. O. EMANUEL; Man. Dir Dr A. I. ADELEKAN.

Minaj Systems Ltd: Ivie House, 4–6 Ajose Adeogun St, POB 70811, Victoria Island, Lagos; tel. (1) 2621168; fax (1) 2621167; e-mail minaj@minaj.com; broadcasting, printing and publishing; Chair. Chief MIKE NNANYE I. AJEGBO.

Nelson Publishers Ltd: 8 Ilupeju By-Pass, Ikeja, PMB 21303, Lagos; tel. (1) 4961452; general and educational; Chair. Prof. C. O. TAIWO; Man. Dir R. O. OGUNBO.

Northern Nigerian Publishing Co Ltd: Gaskiya Bldg, POB 412, Zaria; tel. (69) 332087; f. 1966; general, educational and vernacular texts; Gen. Man. JA'AFAR D. MOHAMMED.

NPS Educational Publishers Ltd: Trusthouse, Ring Rd, off Akinyemi Way, POB 62, Ibadan; tel. (2) 316006; f. 1969; academic, scholarly and educational; CEO T. D. OTESANYA.

Nwamife Publishers: 10 Ibiam St, Uwani, POB 430, Enugu; tel. (42) 338254; f. 1971; general and educational; Chair. FELIX C. ADI.

Obafemi Awolowo University Press Ltd: Obafemi Awolowo University, Ile-Ife; tel. (36) 230284; f. 1968; educational, scholarly and periodicals; Man. Dir AKIN FATOKUN.

Obobo Books: The Poet's Cottage, Artistes Village, Ilogbo-Eremi, Badagry Expressway, POB 610, Apapa, Lagos; tel. and fax (1) 5871333; e-mail theendofknowledge@yahoo.com; internet www.theendofknowledge.com; f. 1981; children's books; Editorial Dir BAKIN KUNAMA.

Ogunsanya Press Publishers and Bookstores Ltd: SW9/1133 Orita Challenge, Idiroko, POB 95, Ibadan; tel. (2) 310924; f. 1970; educational; Man. Dir Chief LUCAS JUSTUS POPO-OLA OGUNSANYA.

Onibonoje Press and Book Industries (Nigeria) Ltd: Felele Layout, Challenge, POB 3109, Ibadan; tel. (2) 313956; f. 1958; educational and general; Chair. G. ONIBONOJE; Man. Dir J. O. ONIBONOJE.

Pilgrim Books Ltd: New Oluyole Industrial Estate, Ibadan/Lagos Expressway, PMB 5617, Ibadan; tel. (2) 317218; educational and general; Man. Dir JOHN E. LEIGH.

Spectrum Books Ltd: Sunshine House, 1 Emmanuel Alayande St, Oluyole Estate, PMB 5612, Ibadan; tel. (2) 2310145; fax (2) 2318502; e-mail admin1@spectrumbooksonline.com; internet www.spectrumbooksonline.com; f. 1978; educational and fiction; Man. Dir JOOP BERKHOUT.

University of Lagos Press: University of Lagos, POB 132, Akoka, Yaba, Lagos; tel. (1) 825048; e-mail library@rcl.nig.com; university textbooks, monographs, lectures and journals; Man. Dir S. BODUNDE BANKOLE.

University Press Ltd: Three Crowns Bldg, Eleyele Rd, Jericho, PMB 5095, Ibadan; tel. (2) 2411356; fax (2) 2412056; e-mail unipress@skannet.com.ng; f. 1978; associated with Oxford University Press; educational; Man. Dir WAHEED O. OLAJIDE.

University Publishing Co: 11 Central School Rd, POB 386, Onitsha; tel. (46) 210013; f. 1959; primary, secondary and university textbooks; Chair. E. O. UGWUEGBULEM.

Vanguard Media Ltd: Vanguard Ave, off Mile 2/Apapa Expressway, Kirikiri Canal; tel. (1) 5871200; fax (1) 5872662; e-mail vanguard@linkserve.com.ng; Publr SAM AMUKA.

Vista Books Ltd: 59 Awolowo Rd, S. W. Ikoyi, POB 282, Yaba, Lagos; tel. (1) 7746348; e-mail vista-books@yahoo.com; f. 1991; general fiction and non-fiction, arts, children's and educational; Man. Dir Dr T. C. NWOSU.

West African Book Publishers Ltd: Ilupeju Industrial Estate, 28–32 Industrial Ave, POB 3445, Lagos; tel. (1) 4702757; fax (1) 5556854; e-mail w_bookafricapubl@hotmail.com; internet www.wabp.com; f. 1967; textbooks, children's, periodicals and general; Chair. B. A. IDRIS-ANIMASHAUN; Man. Dir FOLASHADE B. OMO-EBOH.

PUBLISHERS' ASSOCIATION

Nigerian Publishers Association: Book House, NPA Permanent Secretariat, Jericho G.R.A., POB 2541, Ibadan; tel. (2) 2413396; f. 1965; Pres. S. B. BANKOLE.

Broadcasting and Communications

TELECOMMUNICATIONS

Nigerian Communications Commission (NCC): Plot 19, Aguata Close, Garki 2, Abuja; tel. (9) 2340330; fax (9) 2344589; e-mail ncc@ncc.gov.ng; internet www.ncc.gov.ng; f. 1932 as an independent regulatory body for the supply of telecommunications services and facilities; Chair. Alhaji AHMED JODI; CEO ERNEST C. A. NDUKWE.

Intercellular Nigeria Ltd: UBA House, 57, Marina, PMB 80078, Victoria Island, Lagos; tel. (1) 4703010; fax (1) 2643014; e-mail hq@intercellular-ng.com; f. 1993; internet and international telephone services; Pres. BASHIR EL-RUFAI.

Motophone Ltd: C. & C. Towers, Plot 1684, Sanusi Fafumwa St, Victoria Island, Lagos; tel. (1) 2624168; fax (1) 2620079; e-mail motophone@hyperia.com; f. 1990; Man. Dir ERIC CHAMCHOUM.

Multi-Links Telecommunication Ltd: 231 Adeola Odeku St, Victoria Island, POB 3453, Marina, Lagos; tel. (1) 7740000; fax (1) 2622452; e-mail ccu@multilink.com; f. 1994; Man. Dir C. K. RAMANI.

Nigerian Mobile Telecommunications Ltd (M-TEL): 3 M-Tel St, off Mal Aminu Kano Cres., Wuse 2, Abuja; tel. (9) 5237801; fax (9) 409066; f. 1996; Man. Dir Eng. ISMAILA MOHAMMED.

Nigerian Telecommunications (NITEL): 2 Bissau St, off Herbert Macaulay Way, Wuse Zone 6, Abuja; tel. (9) 5233021; Chair. Dr MARTINS IGBOKWE.

Telnet (Nigeria) Ltd: Plot 242, Kofo Abayomi St, Victoria Island, POB 53656, Falomi Ikoyi, Lagos; tel. (1) 2611729; fax (1) 2619945; e-mail info@iteco.com; internet www.telnetng.com; f. 1985; telecommunications engineering and consultancy services; Man. Dir Dr NADU DENLOYE.

BROADCASTING

Regulatory Authority

National Broadcasting Commission: Plot 807, Ibrahim Taiwo Rd, Asokoro District, POB 5747, Garki, Abuja; tel. (9) 3147525; fax (9) 3147522; e-mail info@nbc-ng.org; internet www.nbc-ng.org; Chair. OBONG O. R. AKPAN.

Radio

Federal Radio Corpn of Nigeria (FRCN): Area 11, Garki, PMB 55, Abuja; tel. (9) 2345915; fax (9) 2345914; f. 1976; controlled by the Fed. Govt and divided into five zones: Lagos (English); Enugu (English, Igbo, Izon, Efik and Tiv); Ibadan (English, Yoruba, Edo, Urhobo and Igala); Kaduna (English, Hausa, Kanuri, Fulfulde and Nupe); Abuja (English, Hausa, Igbo and Yoruba); Chair. Y. ALABI.

Imo Broadcasting Corpn: 14 Savage Cres., Enugu, Imo; tel. (42) 250327; operates one radio station in Imo State.

Voice of Nigeria (VON): Radio House, Herbert Macaulay Way, Area 10, Garki, Abuja; tel. (9) 2344017; fax (9) 2346970; e-mail dgovon@nigol.net.ng; internet www.voiceofnigeria.org; f. 1990; controlled by the Fed. Govt; external services in English, French, Arabic, Ki-Swahili, Hausa and Fulfulde; Dir-Gen. TAIWO ALIMI.

Menage Holding's Broadcasting System Ltd: Umuahia, Imo; commenced broadcasting Jan. 1996; commercial.

Ray Power 100 Drive: Abeokuta Express Way, Ilapo, Alagbado, Lagos; tel. (1) 2644814; fax (1) 2644817; commenced broadcasting Sept. 1994; commercial; Chair. Chief RAYMOND DOKPESI.

Television

Nigerian Television Authority (NTA): Television House, Ahmadu Bello Way, Victoria Island, PMB 12036, Lagos; tel. (1) 2615949; f. 1976; controlled by the Fed. Govt; comprises 32 stations (due to be increased to 67), which broadcast local programmes; Chair. YAKUBULL HUSSAINI; Dir-Gen. Alhaji MOHAMMED IBRAHIM.

NTA Aba/Owerri: Channel 6, PMB 7126, Aba, Abia; tel. (83) 220922; Gen. Man. GODWIN DURU.

NTA Abeokuta: Channel 12, PMB 2190, Abeokuta, Ogun; tel. (39) 242971; f. 1979; broadcasts in English and local languages; Gen. Man. VICTOR FOLIVI.

NTA Abuja: PMB 55, Garki, Abuja; tel. (9) 2345915.

NTA Akure: PMB 794, Akure; tel. (34) 230351; fax (34) 243216; e-mail ntaakure2006@yahoo.com; Gen. Man. H. T. OLOWOFELA.

NTA Bauchi: PMB 0146, Bauchi; tel. (77) 42748; f. 1976; Man. MUHAMMAD AL-AMIN.

NTA Benin City: West Circular Rd, PMB 1117, Benin City; Gen. Man. J. O. N. EZEKOKA.

NTA Calabar: 105 Marion Rd, Calabar; Man. E. ETUK.

NTA Enugu: Independence Layout, PMB 01530, Enugu, Anambra; tel. (42) 335120; f. 1960; Gen. Man. G. C. MEFO.

NTA Ibadan: POB 1460, Ibadan, Oyo; tel. (2) 713238; Gen. Man. JIBOLA DEDENUOLA.

NTA Ikeja: Tejuosho Ave, Surulere.

NTA Ilorin: PMB 1478, Ilorin; tel. and fax (31) 224196; Gen. Man. VICKY OLUMUDI.

NTA Jos: PMB 2134, Jos; Gen. Man. M. J. BEWELL.

NTA Kaduna: POB 1347, Kaduna; tel. and fax (62) 246011; f. 1977; Dir MARYAM JUMMAI BEWELL.

NTA Kano: PMB 3343, Kano; tel. (64) 640072; Gen. Man. B. B. MUHAMMAD.

NTA Lagos: Ahmadu Bello Way, Victoria Island, PMB 12005, 12036, Ikaji, Lagos; tel. (1) 2622082; fax (1) 2626239; Dir-Gen. BEN MURRAY-BRUCE.

NTA Maiduguri: PMB 1487, Maiduguri; Gen. Man. M. M. MAILAFIYA.

NTA Makurdi: PMB 2044, Makurdi.

NTA Minna: TV House, PMB 79, Minna; tel. (66) 222941; fax (66) 222552; Gen. Man. VICKY OLUMUBI.

NTA Port Harcourt: PMB 5797, Port Harcourt; Gen. Man. JON EZEKOKA.

NTA Sokoto: PMB 2351, Sokoto; tel. (60) 232670; f. 1975; Gen. Man. M. B. TUNAU.

NTA Yola: PMB 2197, Yola; Gen. Man. M. M. SAIDU.

Finance

(cap. = capital; res = reserves; dep. = deposits; m. = million; brs = branches; amounts in naira)

BANKING

At the end of 2003 the Nigerian banking system included a total of 89 deposit banks (with 3,300 branches); of these, 11 were estimated by the Central Bank to be insolvent and 24 marginally solvent.

Central Bank

Central Bank of Nigeria: Central Business District, Cadastral Zone, PMB 0187, Garki, Abuja; tel. and fax (9) 6163012; e-mail info@cenbank.org; internet www.cenbank.org; f. 1958; bank of issue; cap. 3,000m., res 141,780m., dep. 2,097,234m. (Dec. 2004); Gov. Prof. CHARLES C. SOLUDO; 18 brs.

Commercial Banks

Afribank Nigeria Ltd: 51–55 Broad St, PMB 12021, Lagos; tel. (1) 2641566; fax (1) 2664890; e-mail info@afribank.com; internet www.afribank.net; f. 1969 as International Bank for West Africa Ltd; cap. 2,354.2m., res 19,032.8m., dep. 61,600.6m. (March 2005); Chair. Alhaji KOLA BELGORE; Man. Dir Chief Alhaji KASHIM M. NJIDDA; 137 brs.

Allstates Trust Bank PLC: Allstates Centre, Plot 1675, Oyin Jolayemi St, POB 73018, Victoria Island, Lagos; tel. (1) 4618445; fax (1) 2612206; e-mail enquiry@allstatesbankng.com; internet www.allstatesbankng.com; cap. 2,476.8m. (Sept. 2001); Man. Dir DUATE PATMORE IYABI.

Citizens' International Bank Ltd: 243 Ahmadu Bello Way, Victoria Island, Lagos; tel. (1) 2601030; fax (1) 2615138; e-mail info@citizensbankng.com; internet www.citizensbankng.com; f. 1990; cap. 619.8m., res 1,809.6m., dep. 31,496.3m. (March 2002); Chair. Chief JOYCE D. U. IFEGWU.

Ecobank Nigeria Ltd: 2 Ajose Adeogun St, Victoria Island, POB 72688, Lagos; tel. (1) 2626638; fax (1) 2616568; e-mail ecobank@linkserve.com.ng; internet www.ecobank.com; cap. 1,522.9m., res 1,996.0m., dep. 19,979.0m. (Dec. 2003); Chair. OMO-OBA ODIMAYO; Man. Dir FUNKE OSIBODU; 26 brs.

First Bank of Nigeria PLC: Samuel Asabia House, 35 Marina, POB 5216, Lagos; tel. (1) 2665900; fax (1) 2665934; e-mail fbn@firstbanknigeria.com; internet www.firstbanknigeria.com; f. 1894 as Bank of British West Africa; total assets 377,496.0m. (March 2005); Chair. UMAR ABDUL MUTALLAB; CEO and Man. Dir JACOBS M. AJEKIGBE; 302 brs.

Intercontinental Bank Ltd: Danmole St, Plot 999C, Adela Odeku, Victoria Island, Lagos; tel. (1) 2622940; fax (1) 2622981; e-mail info@intercontinentalbankplc.com; internet www.intercontinentalbankplc.com; cap. and res 10,181.4m., total assets 96,857.9m. (Dec. 2003); Chair. RAYMOND C. OBIERI; 42 brs.

IBTC Chartered Bank PLC (IBTC): I.B.T.C. Place, Walter Carrington Cres., POB 71707, Victoria Island, Lagos; tel. (1) 2626520; fax (1) 2626541; e-mail ibtc@ibtclagos.com; internet www.ibtc-lagos.com; f. 1989 as Investment Banking & Trust Co Ltd; name changed 2005; cap. 2,000.0m., res 3,794.4m., dep. 10,543.65m. (March 2004); Chair. Chief OLUDOLAPO IBUKUN AKINKUGBE; Man. Dir ATEDO A. PETERSIDE.

Nigeria International Bank Ltd: Commerce House, 11 Idowu Taylor St, Victoria Island, POB 6391, Lagos; tel. (1) 2622000; fax (1) 2618916; internet www.citibanknigeria.com; f. 1984; cap. 1,000.0m., res 6,791.2m., dep. 37,821.8m. (Dec. 2002); Chair. Chief CHARLES S. SANKEY; 13 brs.

Omegabank (Nigeria) PLC: 1 Engineering Close, PMB 80134, off Idowu Taylor, Victoria Island, Lagos; tel. (1) 2622580; fax (1) 2620761; e-mail omegabank@omegabankplc.com; internet www.omegabankplc.com; f. 1982 as Owena Bank plc; name changed 2001; 30% owned by Ondo State Govt; cap. 2,896.4m., res 208.0m., dep. 11,676.8m. (Dec. 2001); Chair. Chief ANTHONY ADENIYI; CEO Rev. Dr SEGUN AGBETUYI.

Sterling Bank: 20 Marina, Lagos; tel. (1) 2709550; internet www.sterlingbank.com; f. 2005 following merger of Indo-Nigerian Bank Ltd, Magnum Trust Bank, NAL Bank PLC, NBM Bank and Trust Bank of Africa Ltd; Chair. Alhaji SULAIMAN BAFFA; Man. Dir TUNDE DABIRI.

Union Bank of Nigeria Ltd: 36 Marina, PMB 2027, Lagos; tel. (1) 2665439; fax (1) 2669873; e-mail askubn@ng.com; internet www.unionbankng.com; f. 1969; as Barclays Bank of Nigeria Ltd; cap. 2,237m., res 36,892m., dep. 200,511m. (March 2005); Chair. Prof. MUSA G. YAKUBU; CEO G. A. T. OBOH; 235 brs.

United Bank for Africa (Nigeria) Ltd: UBA House, 57 Marina, PMB 12002, Lagos; tel. (1) 2644651; fax (1) 2642287; e-mail info@ubaplc.com; internet www.ubaplc.com; f. 1961; cap. 1,275m., res 16,784m., dep. 151,929m. (March 2005); Chair. HAKEEM BELO-OSAGIE; Man. Dir Mallam ABBA KYARI; 213 brs.

Wema Bank Ltd: Wema Towers, PMB 12862, 27 Nnamdi Akkzikwe St, Lagos; tel. (1) 2668043; fax (1) 2669236; e-mail info@wemabank.com; internet www.wemabank.com; f. 1945; cap. 4,451.6m., res 19,807.2m., dep. 61,284.5m. (March 2005); Chair. Alhaji OLAPADE MOHAMMED; Man. Dir and CEO Alhaji I. A. DOSUNMU; 75 brs.

Merchant Banks

FBN (Merchant Bankers) Ltd: 9/11 Macarthy St, Onikan, POB 12715, Lagos; tel. (1) 2600880; fax (1) 2633600; e-mail bisioni@fbnmb.com; internet www.fbnmb.com; cap. 1,000m. (2003); Chair. JACOBS MOYO AJEKIGBE.

Fidelity Bank PLC: Savannah House, 62-66 Broad St, Lagos; tel. (1) 2610408; fax (1) 2610414; e-mail info@fidelitybankplc.com; internet www.fidelitybankplc.com; f. 1988; cap. and res 1,189.2m., res 1,326.2m., dep. 16,888.1m. (June 2003); Chair. Chief EMMANUEL A. OKECHUKWU; CEO KENNETH O. AIGBINODE.

First City Monument Bank Ltd: Primrose Tower, 17A Tinubu St, POB 9117, Lagos; tel. (1) 2665944; fax (1) 2665126; e-mail fcmb@fcmb-ltd.com; internet www.fcmb-ltd.com; internet www.fcmb-ltd.com; f. 1983; cap. 2,226.3m., res 4,989.9m., dep. 27,123.1m. (April 2005); Chair. and CEO OTUNBA M. O. BALOGUN.

Stanbic Bank Nigeria Ltd: Plot 688, Amodu Tijani Close, off Sanusi Fafunwa St, Victoria Island, POB 54746, Lagos; tel. (1) 2709660; fax (1) 2709677; e-mail info@stanbic.com.ng; internet www.stanbic.com.ng; f. 1983 as Grindlays Merchant Bank of Nigeria; cap. 1,000.0m., res 532.9m., dep. 6,815.4m. (Dec. 2004); Chair. Dr MATTHEW TAWO MBU; Man. Dir M. A. WEEKS.

Development Banks

Bank of Industry (BOI) Ltd: BOI House, 63/71 Broad St, Lagos; tel. (1) 2663470; fax (1) 2667074; e-mail info@boi-ng.com; internet www.boi-ng.com; f. 1964 as the Nigerian Industrial Development Bank Ltd to provide medium and long-term finance to industry, manufacturing, non-petroleum mining and tourism; name changed as above Oct. 2001; cap. 400m. (Dec. 2001); Man. Dir Dr LAWRENCE OSS-AFIANA; 6 brs.

Guaranty Trust Bank PLC: The Plural House, Plot 1669, Oyin Jolayemi St, PMB 75455, Victoria Island, Lagos; tel. (1) 2622650; fax (1) 2622698; e-mail corpaff@gtbplc.com; internet www.gtbplc.com; f. 1990; cap. 2,873.2m., res 28,021.7m., dep. 95,563.6m. (Feb. 2005); Chair. Prof. MOSOBALAJE O. OYAWOYE.

Nigerian Agricultural, Co-operative and Rural Development Bank Ltd (NACB): Yakubu Gowoh, PMB 2155, Kaduna; tel. (62) 243590; fax (62) 245012; e-mail nacb@infoweb.abs.net; f. 1973; for funds to farmers and co-operatives to improve production techniques; name changed as above Oct. 2000, following merger with People's Bank of Nigeria; cap. 1,000m. (2002); Chair. Alhaji ISA TATA YUSUF; Man. Dir Alhaji UMAR BABALE GIREI; 200 brs.

Bankers' Association

Chartered Institute of Bankers of Nigeria: PC 19 Adeola Hopewell St, POB 72273, Victoria Island, Lagos; tel. (1) 2617924; fax (1) 4618930; e-mail cibn@cibnnigeria.org; internet www.cibnnigeria.org; Chair. JOHNSON O. EKUNDAYO; CEO Dr UJU M. OGUBUNKA.

STOCK EXCHANGE

Securities and Exchange Commission (SEC): Mandilas House, 96–102 Broad St, PMB 12638, Lagos; f. 1979 as govt agency to regulate and develop capital market and to supervise stock exchange operations; Dir-Gen. MUSA AL-FAKI.

Nigerian Stock Exchange: Stock Exchange House, 2–4 Customs St, POB 2457, Lagos; tel. (1) 2660287; fax (1) 2668724; e-mail nse@nigerianstockexchange.com; internet www.nigerianstockexchange.com; f. 1960; Pres. Dr OBA OTUDEKO; Dir-Gen. Dr NDI OKEREKE-ONYIUKE; 6 brs.

INSURANCE

In early 2005 more than 450 registered insurance companies were operating in Nigeria. Since 1978 they have been required to reinsure 20% of the sum insured with the Nigeria Reinsurance Corpn.

Insurance Companies

African Alliance Insurance Co Ltd: 112 Broad St, POB 2276, Lagos; tel. (1) 2664398; fax (1) 2660943; e-mail alliance@infoweb.abs.net; f. 1960; life assurance and pensions; Man. Dir OPE OREDUGBA; 30 brs.

Aiico International Insurance (AIICO): AIICO Plaza, Plot PC 12, Afribank St, Victoria Island, POB 2577, Lagos; tel. (1) 2610651; fax (1) 2617433; e-mail info@aiicoplc.com; internet www.aiicoplc.com; CEO M. E. HANSEN.

Ark Insurance Group: Glass House, 11A Karimu Kotun St, Victoria Island, POB 3771, Marina, Lagos; tel. (1) 2615826; fax (1) 2615850; e-mail ark@nova.net.ng; internet www.nigeriaweb.com/ark; Chair. F. O. AWOGBORO.

Continental Reinsurance Co Ltd: Reinsurance House, 11th Floor, 46 Marina, POB 2401, Lagos; tel. (1) 2665350; fax (1) 2665370; e-mail crcl@cyberspace.net.ng; CEO ADEYEMO ADEJUMO.

Cornerstone Insurance Co PLC: POB 75370, Victoria Island, Lagos; tel. (1) 2631832; fax (1) 2633079; e-mail marketing@cornerstone.com.ng; internet www.cornerstone.com; f. 1991; Chair. CLEMENT O. BAIYE.

Equity Indemnity Insurance Co Ltd: POB 1514, Lagos; tel. (1) 2637802; fax (1) 2637479; e-mail equity@infoweb.abs.net; f. 1991; Chair. Prof. O. A. SERIKI.

Great Nigeria Insurance Co Ltd: 8 Omo-Osaghie St, off Obafemi Awolono Rd, Ikoyi S/W, Ikoyi, Lagos; tel. (1) 2695805; fax (1) 2693483; e-mail info@greatinsure-ng.com; internet www.greatinsure-ng.com; f. 1960; all classes; Man. Dir M. A. SIYANBOLA.

Guinea Insurance Co Ltd: Guinea Insurance House, 21 Nnandi Azikiwe St, POB 1136, Lagos; tel. (1) 2665201; f. 1958; all classes; CEO AYO BAMMEKE.

Industrial and General Insurance Co Ltd: Plot 741, Adeola Hopewell St, POB 52592, Falomo, Lagos; tel. (1) 2625437; fax (1) 2621146; e-mail info@igi-insurers.com; internet www.igi-insurers.com; Chair. Y. GOWON.

Kapital Insurance Co Ltd: 116 Hadejia Rd, POB 2044, Kano; tel. (64) 645666; fax (64) 636962; CEO MOHAMMED GAMBO UMAR.

Law Union and Rock Insurance Co of Nigeria Ltd: 88–92 Broad St, POB 944, Lagos; tel. (1) 2663526; fax (1) 2664659; fire, accident and marine; 6 brs; CEO S. O. AKINYEMI.

Leadway Assurance Co Ltd: NN 28–29 Constitution Rd, POB 458, Kaduna; tel. (62) 200660; fax (62) 236838; f. 1970; all classes; Man. Dir OYEKANMI ABIODUN HASSAN-ODUKALE.

Lion of Africa Insurance Co Ltd: St Peter's House, 3 Ajele St, POB 2055, Lagos; tel. (1) 2600950; fax (1) 2636111; f. 1952; all classes; Man. Dir G. A. ALEGIEUNO.

National Insurance Corpn of Nigeria (NICON): 5 Customs St, POB 1100, Lagos; tel. (1) 2640230; fax (1) 2666556; f. 1969; all classes; cap. 200m.; Chair. JOHN IRIATA ABUHME; 28 brs.

N.E.M. Insurance Co (Nigeria) Ltd: 22A Borno Way, Ebute, POB 654, Lagos; tel. (1) 5861920; all classes; Chair. Alhaji Dr ALIYU MOHAMMED; Man. Dir J. E. UMUKORO.

Niger Insurance Co Ltd: 47 Marina, POB 2718, Lagos; tel. (1) 2664452; fax (1) 2662196; all classes; Chair. P. M. G. SOARES; 6 brs.

Nigeria Reinsurance Corpn: 46 Marina, PMB 12766, Lagos; tel. (1) 2667049; fax (1) 2668041; e-mail info@nigeriare.com; internet www.nigre.com; all classes of reinsurance; Man. Dir T. T. MIRILLA.

Nigerian General Insurance Co Ltd: 1 Nnamdi Azikiwe St, Tirubu Square, POB 2210, Lagos; tel. (1) 2662552; e-mail odua@odua.com; f. 1951; all classes; Chair. O. O. OKEYODE; Man. Dir J. A. OLANIHUN; 15 brs.

Phoenix of Nigeria Assurance Co Ltd: Mandilas House, 96–102 Broad St, POB 12798, Lagos; tel. (1) 2661160; fax (1) 2662883; e-mail phoenixassce@alpha.linkserve.com; f. 1964; all classes; cap. 10m.; Chair. A. A. OJORA; Man. Dir A. A. AKINTUNDE; 5 brs.

Prestige Assurance Co (Nigeria) Ltd: 19 Ligali Ayorinde St, Victoria Island, POB 650, Lagos; tel. (1) 3204681; fax (1) 3204684; e-mail prestigeassurance@yahoo.co.uk; f. 1952; all classes except life; Chair. Chief C. S. SANKEY; Man. Dir N. S. R. CHANDRAPRASAD.

Royal Exchange Assurance (Nigeria) Group: New Africa House, 31 Marina, POB 112, Lagos; tel. (1) 2663120; fax (1) 2664431; all classes; Chair. Alhaji MUHTAR BELLO YOLA; Man. Dir JONAH U. IKHIDERO; 6 brs.

Sun Insurance Office (Nigeria) Ltd: Unity House, 37 Marina, POB 2694, Lagos; tel. (1) 2661318; all classes except life; Man. Dir A. T. ADENIJI; 6 brs.

United Nigeria Insurance Co Ltd (UNIC): 53 Marina, POB 588, Lagos; tel. (1) 2663201; fax (1) 2664282; f. 1965; all classes except life; CEO E. O. A. ADETUNJI; 17 brs.

Unity Life and Fire Insurance Co Ltd: 25 Nnamdi Azikiwe St, POB 3681, Lagos; tel. (1) 2662517; fax (1) 2662599; all classes; Man. Dir R. A. ODINIGWE.

West African Provincial Insurance Co: WAPIC House, 119 Awolowo Rd, POB 55508, Falomo-Ikoyi, Lagos; tel. (1) 2672770; fax (1) 2693838; e-mail wapic@alpha.linkserve.com; Man. Dir D. O. AMUSAN.

Insurance Association

Nigerian Insurance Association: Nicon House, 1st Floor, 5 Customs St, POB 9551, Lagos; tel. (1) 2640825; f. 1971; Chair. J. U. IKHIDERO.

Trade and Industry

GOVERNMENT AGENCIES

Bureau of Public Enterprises: Secretariat of the National Council on Privatization, 1 Osun Cres., off Ibib Way, Maitama District, PMB 442, Garki, Abuja; tel. (9) 4134636; fax (9) 4134657; e-mail bpe@bpeng.org; internet www.bpeng.org; Dir-Gen. Mallam NASIR AHMAD EL-RUFAI.

Corporate Affairs Commission: Area 11, Garki, Abuja; tel. (9) 2342917; fax (9) 2342669; e-mail info@cac.gov.ng; internet www.cac.gov.ng; Sec. HENRIEITA O. M. TALABI.

National Council on Privatisation: Bureau of Public Enterprises, NDIC Bldg, Constitution Ave, Central Business District, PMB 442, Garki, Abuja; tel. (9) 5237405; fax (9) 5237396; e-mail bpegen@micro.com.ng; internet www.bpe.gov.ng.

Nigeria Export Processing Zones Authority: Radio House, Fourth Floor, Herbert Macaulay Way, PMB 037, Garki, Abuja; tel. (9) 2343059; fax (9) 2343061; e-mail info@nepza.com; internet www.nepza.com; Gen. Man. SINA A. AGBOLUAJE.

DEVELOPMENT ORGANIZATIONS

Benin–Owena River Basin Development Authority: 24 Benin-Sapele Rd, PMB 1381, Obayantor, Benin City; tel. (52) 254415; f. 1976 to conduct irrigation; Gen. Man. Dr G. E. OTEZE.

Chad Basin Development Authority: Dikwa Rd, PMB 1130, Maiduguri; tel. (76) 232015; f. 1973; irrigation and agriculture-allied industries; Chair. MOHAMMED ABALI; Gen. Man. Alhaji BUNU S. MUSA.

Cross River Basin Development Authority: 32 Target Rd, PMB 1249, Calabar; tel. (87) 223163; f. 1977; Gen. Man. SIXTUS ABETIANBE.

Federal Institute of Industrial Research, Oshodi (FIIRO): Murtala Muhammed Airport, Bilnd Centre St, Oshodi, Ikeja, PMB 21023, Lagos; tel. (1) 900121; fax (1) 4525880; f. 1956; plans and directs industrial research and provides tech. assistance and information to industry; specializes in foods, minerals, textiles, natural products and industrial intermediates; Dir. Prof. S. A. ODUNFA.

Industrial Training Fund: Miango Rd, PMB 2199, Jos, Plateau; tel. and fax (73) 461887; e-mail dp@itf-nigeria.com; internet www.itf-nigeria.com; f. 1971 to promote and encourage skilled workers in trade and industry; Dir-Gen. Prof. OLU E. AKEREJOLA.

Kaduna Industrial and Finance Co Ltd: Investment House, 27 Ali Akilu Rd, PMB 2230, Kaduna; tel. (62) 240751; fax (62) 240754; e-mail kifc@skannet.com; f. 1989; provides development finance; Chair. (vacant); Man. Dir Alhaji DAHIRU MOHAMMED.

Kwara State Investment Corpn: 109–112 Fate Rd, PMB 1344, Ilorin, Kwara; tel. (31) 220510.

Lagos State Development and Property Corpn: 1 Town Planning Way, Ilupeju, Lagos; tel. (1) 4972243; e-mail isdpc@isdpc.com; internet www.isdpc.com; f. 1972; planning and development of Lagos; Gen. Man. O. R. ASHAFA.

New Nigerian Development Co Ltd: 18/19 Ahmadu Bello Way, Ahmed Talib House, PMB 2120, Kaduna; tel. (62) 249355; fax (62) 245482; e-mail nndc@skannet.com.ng; f. 1949; owned by the Govts of 19 northern States; investment finance; 8 subsidiaries, 83 assoc. cos; Chair. Prof. HALIDU IBRAHIM ABUBAKAR.

Niger Delta Development Commission: 6 Olumeni St, Port Harcourt; internet www.nddconline.org; f. 1976; Man. Dir GODWIN OMENE.

Nigerian Enterprises Promotion Board: 15–19 Keffi St, S.W. Ikoyi, Lagos; tel. (1) 2680929; f. 1972 to promote indigenization; Chair. MINSO GADZAMA.

Northern Nigeria Investments Ltd: 4 Waff Rd, POB 138, Kaduna; tel. (62) 239654; fax (62) 230770; f. 1959 to identify and invest in industrial and agricultural projects in 16 northern States; cap. p.u. 20m.; Chair. Alhaji ABUBAKAR G. ADAMU; Man. Dir GIMBA H. IBRAHIM.

Odu'a Investment Co Ltd: Cocoa House, PMB 5435, Ibadan; tel. (2) 417710; fax (2) 413000; f. 1976; jtly owned by Ogun, Ondo and Oyo States; Man. Dir Alhaji R. S. ARUNA.

Plateau State Water Resources Development Board: Jos; incorporates the fmr Plateau River Basin Devt Authority and Plateau State Water Resources Devt Board.

Projects Development Institute: Emene Industrial Layout, Proda Rd, POB 01609, Enugu; tel. (42) 451593; fax (42) 457691; e-mail proda@rmrdc.nig.com; f. 1977; promotes the establishment of new industries and develops industrial projects utilizing local raw materials; Dir BASIL K. C. UGWA.

Raw Materials Research Development Council: Plot 427, Aguiyi, Ironsi St, Maitama, Abuja; tel. (9) 5237417.

Rubber Research Institute of Nigeria: PMB 1049, Benin City; tel. (52) 254792; f. 1961; conducts research into the production of rubber and other latex products; Dir Dr M. M. NADOMA.

Trans Investments Co Ltd: Bale Oyewole Rd, PMB 5085, Ibadan; tel. (2) 416000; f. 1986; initiates and finances industrial and agricultural schemes; Gen. Man. M. A. ADESIYUN.

CHAMBERS OF COMMERCE

Nigerian Association of Chambers of Commerce, Industry, Mines and Agriculture: 15A Ikorodu Rd, Maryland, PMB 12816, Lagos; tel. (1) 4964727; fax (1) 4964737; e-mail naccima@supernet300.com; Pres. CLEMENT OBINEZE MADUAKO; Dir-Gen. L. O. ADEKUNLE.

Aba Chamber of Commerce and Industry: UBA Bldg, Ikot Expene Rd/Georges St, POB 1596, Aba; tel. (82) 352084; fax (82) 352067; f. 1971; Pres. IDE J. C. UDEAGBALA.

Abeokuta Chamber of Commerce and Industry: 29 Kuto Rd, Ishabo, POB 937, Abeokuta; tel. (39) 241230; Pres. Chief S. O. AKINREMI.

Abuja Chamber of Commerce, Industry, Mines & Agriculture: International Trade Fair Complex, KM8, Airport Road, PMB 86, Garki, Abuja; tel. (9) 6707428; fax (9) 2348808; e-mail abuccima@hotmail.com; Pres. Sir PETER OKOLO.

Adamawa Chamber of Commerce and Industry: c/o Palace Hotel, POB 8, Jimeta, Yola; tel. (75) 255136; Pres. Alhaji ISA HAMMANYERO.

Akure Chamber of Commerce and Industry: 57 Oyemekun Rd, POB 866, Akure; tel. (34) 242540; f. 1984; Pres. ADEDEJI OMISAMI.

Awka Chamber of Commerce and Industry: 220 Enugu Rd, POB 780, Awka; tel. (45) 550105; Pres. Lt-Col (retd) D. ORUGBU.

Bauchi Chamber of Commerce and Industry: 96 Maiduguri Rd, POB 911, Bauchi; tel. (77) 42620; f. 1976; Pres. Alhaji MAGAJI MU'AZU.

Benin Chamber of Commerce, Industry, Mines and Agriculture: 10 Murtala Muhammed Way, POB 2087, Benin City; tel. (52) 255761; Pres. C. O. EWEKA.

Benue Chamber of Commerce, Industry, Mines and Agriculture: 71 Ankpa Qr Rd, PMB 102344, Makurdi; tel. (44) 32573; Chair. Col (retd) R. V. I. ASAM.

Borno Chamber of Commerce and Industry: Grand Stand, Ramat Sq., off Central Bank, PMB 1636, Maiduguri; tel. (76) 232832; e-mail bsumar@hotmail.com; f. 1973; Pres. Alhaji MOHAMMED RIJYA; Sec.-Gen. BABA SHEHU BUKAR.

Calabar Chamber of Commerce and Industry: Desan House Bldg, 38 Ndidem Iso Rd, POB 76, Calabar, Cross River; tel. (87) 221558; 92 mems; Pres. Chief TAM OFORIOKUMA.

Enugu Chamber of Commerce, Industry and Mines: International Trade Fair Complex, Abakaliki Rd, POB 734, Enugu; tel. (42) 250575; fax (42) 252186; e-mail eccima@infoweb.abs.net; internet www.enuguchamber.com; f. 1963; Dir EMEKA OKEREKE.

Franco-Nigerian Chamber of Commerce: Big Leaf House, 7 Oyin Jolayemi St, POB 70001, Victoria Island, Lagos; tel. (1) 2621423; fax (1) 2621422; e-mail fncci@ccife.org; internet www.ccife.org/nigeria; f. 1985; Chair. S. JEGEDE; Pres. AKIN AKINBOLA.

Gongola Chamber of Commerce and Industry: Palace Hotel, POB 8, Jimeta-Yola; tel. (75) 255136; Pres. Alhaji ALIYU IBRAHIM.

Ibadan Chamber of Commerce and Industry: Commerce House, Ring Rd, Challenge, PMB 5168, Ibadan; tel. (2) 317223; Pres. JIDE ABIMBOLA.

Ijebu Chamber of Commerce and Industry: 51 Ibadan Rd, POB 604, Ijebu Ode; tel. (37) 432880; Pres. DOYIN DEGUN.

Ikot Ekpene Chamber of Commerce and Industry: 47 Aba Rd, POB 50, Ikot Ekpene; tel. (85) 400153; Pres. G. U. EKANEM.

Kaduna Chamber of Commerce, Industry and Agriculture: 24 Waff Rd, POB 728, Kaduna; tel. (62) 211216; fax (62) 214149; Pres. Alhaji MOHAMMED SANI AMINU.

Kano Chamber of Commerce, Industry, Mines and Agriculture: Zoo Rd, POB 10, Kano City, Kano; tel. (64) 666936; fax (64) 667138; Pres. MALLAM U. J. KIRU.

Katsina Chamber of Commerce and Industry: 1 Nagogo Rd, POB 92, Katsina; tel. (65) 31014; Pres. ABBA ALI.

Kwara Chamber of Commerce, Industry, Mines and Agriculture: Kwara Hotel Premises, Ahmadu Bello Ave, POB 1634, Ilorin; tel. (31) 223069; fax (31) 224131; e-mail kwaccima@yahoo.com; internet www.kwaccima.com; Pres. Alhaji JANI IBRAHIM; Dir-Gen. ABDULSALAAM A. JIMOH.

Lagos Chamber of Commerce and Industry: Commerce House, 1 Idowu Taylor St, Victoria Island, POB 109, Lagos; tel. (1) 2705386; fax (1) 2701009; e-mail inform@micro.com.ng; f. 1888; 1,267 mems; Pres. Chief OLUSOLA FALEYE.

Niger Chamber of Commerce and Industry: Trade Fair Site, POB 370, Minna; tel. (66) 223153; Pres. Alhaji U. S. NDANUSA.

Nnewi Chamber of Commerce and Industry: 31A Nnobi Rd, POB 1471, Nnewi; tel. (46) 462258; f. 1987; Pres. AJULU UZODIKE.

Osogbo Chamber of Commerce and Industry: Obafemi Awolowo Way, Ajegunle, POB 870, Osogbo, Osun; tel. (35) 231098; Pres. Prince VICTOR ADEMLE.

Owerri Chamber of Commerce and Industry: OCCIMA Secretariat, 123 Okigwe Rd, POB 1439, Owerri; tel. (83) 234849; Pres. Chief OKEY IKORO.

Oyo Chamber of Commerce and Industry: POB 67, Oyo; Pres. Chief C. A. OGUNNIYI.

Plateau State Chambers of Commerce, Industry, Mines and Agriculture: Shama House, 32 Rwang Pam St, POB 2092, Jos; tel. (73) 53918; f. 1976; Pres. Chief M. E. JACDOMI.

Port Harcourt Chamber of Commerce, Industry, Mines and Agriculture: Alesa Eleme, POB 585, Port Harcourt; tel. (84) 239536; f. 1952; Pres. Chief S. I. ALETE.

Remo Chamber of Commerce and Industry: 7 Sho Manager Way, POB 1172, Shagamu; tel. (37) 640962; Pres. Chief S. O. ADEKOYA.

Sapele Chamber of Commerce and Industry: 144 New Ogorode Rd, POB 154, Sapele; tel. (54) 42323; Pres. P. O. FUFUYIN.

Sokoto Chamber of Commerce and Industry: 12 Racecourse Rd, POB 2234, Sokoto; tel. (60) 231805; Pres. Alhaji ALIYU WAZIRI BODINGA.

Umahia Chamber of Commerce: 44 Azikiwe Rd, Umahia; tel. (88) 223373; fax (88) 222299; Pres. GEORGE AKOMAS.

Uyo Chamber of Commerce and Industry: 141 Abak Rd, POB 2960, Uyo, Akwa Ibom; Pres. Chief DANIEL ITA-EKPOTT.

Warri Chamber of Commerce and Industry: Block 1, Edewor Shopping Centre, Warri/Sapele Rd, POB 302, Warri; tel. (53) 233731; Pres. MOSES F. OROGUN.

INDUSTRIAL AND TRADE ASSOCIATIONS

Nigerian Export Promotion Council: Zone 2, Block 312, Wuse, PMB 133, Abuja; tel. (9) 5230930; fax (9) 5230931; f. 1976; Chair. Alhaji ISIAKA ADELEKE.

Nigerian Investment Promotion Commission (NIPC): Plot 1181, Agyuiyi-Ironsi St, Maitama District, Abuja; tel. (9) 4138026; fax (9) 4138021; e-mail nipc@nipc-nigeria.org; internet www.nipc-nigeria.org; Chair. FELIX O. A. OHIWEREI; Exec. Sec. Alhaji MUSTAFA BELLO.

EMPLOYERS' ORGANIZATIONS

Association of Advertising Practitioners of Nigeria: 3 William St, off Sylvia Cres., POB 50648, Anthony Village, Lagos; tel. (1) 4970842.

Chartered Institute of Bankers: Plot PC 19, Adeola Hopewell St, POB 72273, Victoria Island, Lagos.

Institute of Chartered Accountants of Nigeria: Plot 16, Professional Layout Centre, Idowu Taylor St, Victoria Island, POB 1580, Lagos; tel. (1) 2622394; fax (1) 2610304; e-mail info.ican@ican.org.ng; f. 1965; CEO and Registrar O. OLUBUNMI SOWANDE (acting).

Nigeria Employers' Consultative Association: Commercial House, 1–11 Commercial Ave, POB 2231, Yaba, Lagos; tel. (1) 800360; fax (1) 860309; f. 1957; Pres. Chief R. F. GIWA.

Nigerian Institute of Architects: 2 Idowu Taylor St, Victoria Island, POB 178, Lagos; tel. (1) 2617940; fax (1) 2617947; f. 1960; Pres. Chief O. C. MAJOROH.

Nigerian Institute of Building: 45 Opebi Rd, Ikeja, POB 3191, Marina, Lagos; tel. (1) 4930411; f. 1970; Pres. Dr SANI HABU GUMEL.

Nigerian Institution of Estate Surveyors and Valuers: Flat 2B, Dolphin Scheme, Ikoyi, POB 2325, Lagos; tel. (1) 2673131; fax (1) 2694314; e-mail niesv@nova.net.ng; Pres. NWEKE UMEZURUIKE.

Nigerian Society of Engineers: National Engineering Centre, 1 Engineering Close, POB 72667, Victoria Island, Lagos; tel. and fax (1) 2617315; Pres. EMEKA M. EZEH.

UTILITIES

Electricity

Power Holding Company of Nigeria (PHCN): Plot 1071, Area 3, Garki, Abuja; tel. (1) 5231938; f. 1972 as National Electric Power Authority, by merger of the Electricity Corpn of Nigeria and the Niger Dams Authority; renamed as above April 2005; assets were to be diverted to six generating companies and 11 distribution companies, prior to privatization; Man. Dir JOSEPH MAKOJU.

Gas

Nigeria Liquefied Natural Gas Co Ltd (NLNG): C. & C. Towers, Plot 1684, Sanusi Fafunwa St, Victoria Island, PMB 12774, Marina, Lagos; tel. (1) 2624190; fax (1) 2616976; internet www.nigerialng.com; Man. Dir. Dr CHRIS HAYNES.

MAJOR COMPANIES

The following are some of the largest companies in terms either of capital investment or employment.

African Petroleum Ltd: AP House, 54–56 Broad St, POB 512, Lagos; tel. (1) 2600050; fax (1) 2634341; e-mail aplagos@applcng.com; cap. ₦72m.; fmrly BP Nigeria Ltd; markets lubricants, fuel oil, automotive gas oil, motor spirits, liquefied petroleum gas and kerosene; CEO PETER OLISAELOKA OKOCHA.

African Timber and Plywood (AT & P): PMB 4001, Sapele; f. 1935; a division of UAC of Nigeria Ltd and an assoc. co of UAC International Ltd, London; loggers and mfrs of plywood, particleboard, flushdoors, lumber and machined wood products; Gen. Man. L. HODGSON.

Ajaokuta Steel Co Ltd: PMB 1000, Ajaokuta, Kwara; tel. (58) 400450; fax (58) 400168; f. 1979; CEO Maj.-Gen. M. C. ALLI.

Bhn: Asogun Rd, Km 15, Badagry Expressway, POB 109, Apapa, Lagos; tel. (1) 5453057; fax (1) 5451398; e-mail bhnplc@tolaram.nig.com; cap. p.u. ₦8.1m.; fmrly Blackwood Hodge; earthmoving, construction, irrigation, mining and agricultural equipment; Chair. Chief RASHEED GBADAMOSI.

Chemical and Allied Products Co Ltd: POB 1004, 24 Commercial Rd, Apapa, Lagos; tel. (1) 803220; fax (1) 5874840; mfrs of paints, pesticides and pharmaceuticals, distributors of chemicals, dyestuffs, explosives, plastic raw materials and associated products; Chair. D. M. OMOLAYOLE.

Delta Steel Co Ltd: Ovwian-Aladja, POB 1220, Warri; tel. (53) 621001; fax (53) 621012; f. 1979; state-owned; operates direct-reduction steel complex with eventual annual capacity of 1m. tons; Chair. Gen. M. TSOHO KONTAGORA.

Guinness (Nigeria) Ltd: Oba Akran Ave, Ikeja, PMB 1071, Lagos State; tel. (1) 4971560; fax (1) 4970560; f. 1950; cap. p.u. ₦25m.; brewers; breweries in Ogba (700,000 hl) and Benin (900,000 hl); Man. Dir KEITH RICHARDS.

Henry Stephens Group: Head Office: 90 Awolowo Rd, SW Ikoyi, POB 2480, Lagos; tel. (1) 603460; subsidiary cos include:

Gilco (Nigeria) Ltd: 292 Apapa Rd, Apapa; import and export.

Henry Stephens Engineering Co Ltd: 2 Ilepeju By-Pass, Ikeja, PMB 21386, Lagos; tel. (1) 3222483; fax (1) 33489300; e-mail henrystephen@hotvoice.com; for construction machinery, motors and agricultural equipment; Chair. Chief OLADELE FAJEMIROKUN.

IBRU: 33 Creek Rd, PMB 1155, Apapa, Lagos; tel. (1) 876634; agricultural equipment, machinery and service; fishing and frozen fish distribution, civil and agricultural engineering; Man. Dir O. IBRU.

A. G. Leventis Group: Iddo House, Iddo, POB 159, Lagos; tel. (1) 800220; fax (1) 860574; activities include wholesale and retail distribution, vehicle assembly, food production and farming, manufacture of glass, plastics, beer, technical and electrical equipment, property investment and management; Chair. A. H. AHMADU; Man. Dir. J. OKE.

Lever Brothers (Nigeria) Ltd: 15 Dockyard Rd, POB 15, Apapa, Lagos; tel. (1) 5803300; fax (1) 5803711; f. 1923; cap. ₦112.0m.; mfrs of detergents, edible fats and toilet preparations; Chair. and CEO R. F. GIWA.

Mandilas Group Ltd: 96–102 Broad St, POB 35, Lagos; tel. (1) 2663220; fax (1) 2662605; e-mail mandilas@micro.com.ng; subsidiaries include Mandilas Enterprises Ltd, Mandilas Travel Ltd, Norman Industries Ltd, Electrolux-Mandilas Ltd, Phoenix of Nigeria Assurance Co Ltd, Sulzer Nigeria Ltd, Mandilas Ventures Ltd, Original Box Co Ltd; Chair. T. A. MANDILAS.

Mobil Oil Nigeria: PMB 12054, 1 Lekki Express Way, Victoria Island, Lagos; tel. (1) 2621640; fax (1) 2621733; offshore petroleum production; Chair. DUKE KEISER.

National Oil and Chemical Marketing Co Ltd: 38–39 Marina, PMB 2052, Lagos; tel. (1) 2665880; fax (1) 2662802; f. 1975; fmrly Shell Nigeria Ltd; 40% state-owned; Man. Dir O. O. OJO; 650 employees.

Nigerian Breweries Ltd: 1 Abebe Village Rd, Iganmu, POB 545, Lagos; tel. (1) 2717400; fax (1) 5852067; e-mail nbplc.info@heineken.nl; internet www.nbplc.com; f. 1946; also facilities at Aba, Kaduna, Ibadan and Enugu; Chair. and Man. Dir FELIX OHIWEREI; Man. Dir MICHIEL HERKEMIJ; 3,683 employees.

Nigerian Cement Co Ltd (NIGERCEM): Nkalugu, POB 331, Enugu; tel. and fax (42) 253829; f. 1954; Chair. Chief S. N. ANYANWU; Man. Dir Dr OZO NWEKE OZO.

Nigerian Coal Corpn: PMB 01053, Enugu; tel. (42) 335314; f. 1909; operates four mines; Chair. Dr GILBERT NWATALARI.

Nigerian Engineering and Construction Co Ltd (NECCO): Km 14, Badagry Expressway (opp. International Trade Fair Complex), PMB 12684, Lagos; tel. (1) 5880591; building, civil mechanical and electrical engineers, furniture makers and steel fabricators; Chair. EHIOZE EDIAE.

Nigerian Metal Fabricating Ltd: POB 23, Kano; tel. (64) 632427; fax (64) 634677; part of Cedar Group; mfrs of aluminium household utensils, brassware and silverware; also light engineers.

Nigerian Mining Corpn: Federal Secretariat, 7th Floor, PMB 2154, Jos; tel. (73) 465245; fax (73) 462867; f. 1972; exploration, production, processing and marketing of minerals; nine subsidiaries and eight assoc. cos; Chair. Alhaji BALA TAFIDAN YAURI.

Nigerian National Petroleum Corpn (NNPC): Herbert McCauley Way, Central Area, Abuja; tel. (9) 5234761; fax (9) 5234760; f. 1977; reorg. 1988; holding corpn for Fed. Govt's interests in petroleum cos; 11 operating subsidiaries; Man. Dir FUNSHO KUPOLUKAN.

Warri Refinery: PMB 44, Effuron, Warri; tel. (53) 254161; fax (53) 252535; e-mail wrpc@nnpc.com.na; Man. Dir W. O. AYANGBILE.

Nigerian Oil Mills Ltd: POB 342, Kano; tel. (64) 632427; fax (64) 634677; import and production of vegetable oil products.

Nigerian Textile Mills Ltd: Oba Akran Ave, Industrial Estate, PMB 21051, Ikeja; tel. (1) 4978850; fax (1) 4962011; f. 1960; cap. ₦40m.; spinners, weavers and finishers; Chair. Prof. S. O. BIOBAKU; Man. Dir Alhaji S. DANGOTE; 2,700 employees.

Nigerian Tin Mining Co Ltd: PMB 2036, Jos; tel. (73) 80634; f. 1986 by merger of Amalgamated Tin Mines of Nigeria Ltd and five other mining cos operating on the Jos plateau; owned by Nigerian Mining Corpn and fmr non-national shareholders in the above five cos; cap. p.u. ₦9.5m.; production of tin concentrate from alluvial tin ore and separation of columbite, zircon and monazite; Chair. E. A. IFATUROTI; Gen. Man. Alhaji M. ADAMU.

Nigerian Tobacco Co Ltd: POB 137, Lagos; tel. (1) 2690471; fax (1) 2690470; f. 1951; cap. ₦200m.; mfrs of tobacco products; Chair. OLUDOLAPO IBUKUN AKINKUGBE; Man. Dir PAUL KIRKHAM; 696 employees.

Oando Plc: Stallion House, 8th–10th Floor, 2 Ajose Adeogun St, Victoria Island, Lagos; tel. (1) 2601290; fax (1) 2633939; e-mail info@oandoplc.com; internet www.oandoplc.com; f. 1956 as ESSO; rebranded in 1976 as Unipetrol Nigeria Ltd; merged with Agip Nigeria Plc in 2003 and assumed present name; Chair. Maj.-Gen. (retd) M. MAGORO; CEO JUBRIL ADEWALE TINUBU.

Peugeot Automobile Nigeria Ltd: Kakuri Industrial Estate, PMB 2266, Kaduna; tel. (62) 231131; fax (62) 233860; e-mail pan_data@alpha.linksserve.com; internet www.peugeotnigeria.com; f. 1972; 40% owned by Peugeot, 30% owned by Govt of Nigeria; Man. Dir FRANÇOIS SERRE.

Phillips Oil Co (Nigeria) Ltd: Plot 853, 19 Bishop Aboyade-Cole St, Victoria Island, PMB 12612, Lagos; tel. (1) 2615656; fax (1)

2615663; petroleum exploration and production; Man. Dir M. O. TAIGA.

Port Harcourt Refining Co Ltd: Alesa Eleme, POB 585, Port Harcourt, Rivers State; tel. (84) 239536; fax (84) 239537; e-mail phrchet@linkserve.com.ng; f. 1965; Man. Dir MANSUR AHMED.

PZ Industries Ltd: Planning Office Way, Ilupeju Industrial Estate, Ikeja, PMB 21132, Lagos; tel. (1) 4973460; fax (1) 4962076; fmrly Paterson Zochonis Nigeria Ltd; soaps, detergents, toiletries, pharmaceuticals and confectionery; factories at Ikorodu, Aba and Ilupeju; Chief K. B. JAMODU; Man. Dir N. KOSMAS.

Reynolds Construction Co Nigeria Ltd: Plot 1682, Sanusi Fafunwa St, Victoria Island, Lagos; tel. (1) 2611635; fax (1) 2611635; e-mail md@rcc-nigeria.com; internet www.rcc-nigeria.com; f. 1969; Chair. Chief S. O. FADAHUNSI.

SCOA Nigeria Ltd: 67 Marina, POB 2318, Lagos; tel. (1) 2667977; fax (1) 2669642; cap. ₦44.8m.; vehicle assembly and maintenance, distribution and maintenance of heavyweight engines, industrial air-conditioning and refrigeration, home and office equipment, textiles, tanning, general consumer goods, mechanized farming; Chair. H. AGBAMU.

Shell Nigeria Oil Products: Freeman House, 21–22 Marina, PMB 2418, Lagos; tel. (1) 2765019; fax (1) 2636791; e-mail shellnigeria@shell.com; internet www.shell.com/nigeria; the largest petroleum operation in Nigeria; carries out onshore and offshore exploration and production; 55% govt-owned; Man. Dir TINU FESHITAN.

Tate Industries: 47–48 Eric Moore Rd, Iganmu Industrial Estate, POB 1240, Lagos; tel. (1) 801930; fax (1) 833488; sugar, invert syrup, PVC pipes, plastic goods, stationery; Chair. Dr A. L. CIROMA.

Texaco Nigeria Plc: 8 McCarthy St, Lagos; tel. (1) 4614500; fax (1) 2630647; internet www.texaco.com; f. 1913; petroleum marketing; Chair. M. D. FINNEGAN.

Triana Ltd: 18–20 Commercial Rd, PMB 1064, Apapa, Lagos; tel. (1) 5803040; fax (1) 5876161; e-mail triana@alpha.linkserve.com; f. 1970; shipping, clearing and forwarding, warehousing, airfreighting; Man. Dir M. P. AGUBA.

UAC of Nigeria Ltd: Niger House, 1–5 Odunlami St, POB 9, Lagos; tel. (1) 2663010; fax (1) 2662628; fmrly United Africa Co; divisions include brewing, foods, electrical materials, packaging, business equipment, plant hire, timber; Chair. Lt-Gen. M. I. WUSHISHI.

The West African Portland Cement Co Ltd: Elephant House, 237–239 Ikorodu Rd, POB 1001, Lagos; tel. (1) 4901060; fax (1) 4970704; f. 1959; production and sale of cement and decorative materials; cap. p.u. ₦60.3m.; Chair. F. ALADE; Man. Dir J. O. MAKOJU.

TRADE UNIONS

Federation

Nigerian Labour Congress (NLC): 29 Olajuwon St, off Ojuelegba Rd, Yaba, POB 620, Lagos; tel. (1) 5835582; f. 1978; comprised 29 affiliated industrial unions in 1999; Pres. ABDULLAH-WAHID IBRAHIM OMAR.

Principal Unions

Amalgamated Union of Public Corpns, Civil Service, and Technical and Recreational Services Employees: 9 Aje St, PMB 1064, Yaba, Lagos; tel. (1) 5863722; Sec.-Gen. SYLVESTER EJIOFOR.

National Union of Journalists: Lagos; Pres. LANRE OGUNDIPE; Sec. MOHAMMED KHALID.

National Union of Petroleum Workers and Natural Gas (NUPENG): Lagos; Sec.-Gen. FRANK KOKORI.

Nigerian Union of Civil Engineering, Construction, Furniture and Woodworkers: 51 Kano St, Ebute Metta, PMB 1064, Lagos; tel. (1) 5800263.

Nigerian Union of Mine Workers: 95 Enugu St, POB 763, Jos; tel. (73) 52401.

Petroleum and Gas Senior Staff Association of Nigeria (PENGASSAN): Lagos; Sec.-Gen. KENNETH NAREBOR.

Transport

RAILWAYS

There are about 3,505 km of mainly narrow-gauge railways. The two principal lines connect Lagos with Nguru and Port Harcourt with Maiduguri.

Nigerian Railway Corpn: Plot 739, Zone A6, Panama St, off IBB Way, Maitama, Abuja; tel. (9) 5231912; f. 1955; restructured in 1993 into three separate units: Nigerian Railway Track Authority; Nigerian Railways; and Nigerian Railway Engineering Ltd; Chair. Alhaji WAZIRI MOHAMMED.

ROADS

In 2004 the Nigerian road network totalled 193,200 km, including 15,688 km of highways and 18,719 km of secondary roads; some 9,660 km were paved.

Nigerian Road Federation: Ministry of Transport, National Maritime Agency Bldg, Central Area, Abuja; tel. (9) 5237053.

INLAND WATERWAYS

Inland Waterways Department: Ministry of Transport, National Maritime Agency Bldg, Central Area, Abuja; tel. (9) 5237053; responsible for all navigable waterways; Chair. Alhaji SULE ONABIYI.

SHIPPING

The principal ports are the Delta Port complex (including Warri, Koko, Burutu and Sapele ports), Port Harcourt and Calabar; other significant ports are situated at Apapa and Tin Can Island, near Lagos. The main petroleum ports are Bonny and Burutu.

National Maritime Authority: Michael Okpara St, Plot 1970, Wuse, Zone 5, Abuja; tel. (9) 5237016; fax (9) 5237015; f. 1987; Dir-Gen. Alhaji BUBA GALADIMA.

Nigerian Ports Authority: Olusegun Obasanjo Way, Plot 126, Central Business District, Garki, Abuja; tel. (9) 2347920; fax (9) 2347930; e-mail telnpo@infoweb.abs.net; internet www.nigeria-ports.com; f. 1955; CEO Chief ADEBAYO SARUMI.

Nigerian Green Lines Ltd: Unity House, 15th Floor, 37 Marina, POB 2288, Lagos; tel. (1) 2663303; 2 vessels totalling 30,751 grt; Chair. Alhaji W. L. FOLAWIYO.

Nigeria Unity Line: Maritime Complex, 34 Creek Rd, PMB 1175, Apapa, Lagos; tel. (1) 5804808; fax (1) 5804807; e-mail nul@hyperia.com; f. 1995 following the dissolution of the Nigerian National Shipping Line; govt-owned; Chair. Chief A. R. DIKIBO.

Association

Nigerian Shippers Council: 4 Park Lane, Apapa, Lagos; tel. (1) 5452307; e-mail info@shipperscouncil.com; internet www.shipperscouncil.com; Chair. Capt. A. A. BIU.

CIVIL AVIATION

The principal international airports are at Lagos (Murtala Mohammed Airport), Kano, Port Harcourt and Abuja. There are also 14 airports for domestic flights.

Federal Airport Authority of Nigeria: Murtala Mohammed Airport, PMB 21607, Ikeja, Lagos; tel. (1) 4900800; Chair. SARGEANT AWUSE.

Principal Airlines

Virgin Nigeria: 3rd Floor Ark Towers Plot 17, Ligali Ayorinde St Victoria Island Extension, Ikeja, Lagos; tel. (1) 4600505; e-mail commercial@virginnigeria.com; internet www.virginnigeria.com; f. Sept. 2004; private flag carrier; 51% owned by Nigerian institutional investors and 49% by Virgin Atlantic; scheduled domestic regional and international services; CEO CONRAD CLIFFORD.

Tourism

Potential attractions for tourists include fine coastal scenery, dense forests, and the rich diversity of Nigeria's arts. A total of 2,778,365 tourists visited Nigeria in 2005. Receipts from tourism amounted to US $49m. in 2004, compared with $263m. in 2002.

Nigerian Tourism Development Corpn: Old Federal Secretariat, Area 1, Garki, PMB 167, Abuja; tel. (9) 2342764; fax (9) 2342775; e-mail ntdc@metrong.com; internet www.nigeria.tourism.com; Chair. Prince ADESUYI HAASTRUP; CEO OMOTAYO OMOTOSHO.

Defence

As assessed at November 2006, the total strength of the armed forces was 85,000: the army totalled 67,000 men, the navy 8,000 and the air force 10,000. There was also a paramilitary force of 82,000. Military service is voluntary.

Defence Expenditure: Budgeted at ₦98,000m. in 2006.

Commander-in-Chief of the Armed Forces: Pres. Alhaji UMARU MUSA YAR'ADUA.

Chief of Defence Staff: Gen. OWOYE ANDREW AZAZI.

Chief of Army Staff: Gen. LUKA NYEH YUSUF.

Chief of Naval Staff: Vice-Adm. SAMUEL AFOLAYAN.

Chief of Air Staff: Air Marshal PAUL DIKE.

Education

Education is partly the responsibility of the state governments, although the Federal Government has played an increasingly important role since 1970. Primary education begins at six years of age and lasts for six years. Secondary education begins at 12 years of age and lasts for a further six years, comprising two three-year cycles. Education to junior secondary level (from six to 15 years of age) is free and compulsory. According to UNESCO estimates, in 2003/04 60% of children in the relevant age-group (males 64%; females 57%) were enrolled in primary education, while the comparable ratio for secondary enrolment in 1998/99 was 19% (males 19%; females 20%). In 1993 383,488 students were enrolled in 133 higher education institutions. Expenditure on education (including recurrent spending) by the Federal Government in 2002 totalled ₦109,455m., equivalent to 8.1% of total budgetary expenditure.

Bibliography

Adalemo, I. A., *et al.* (Eds). *Giant in the Tropics: A Compendium.* Lagos, Gabumo, 1993.

Adamokekun, L. *The Fall of the Second Republic.* Ibadan, Spectrum Books, 1985.

Adejumobi, S., and Momah, A. (Eds). *The Political Economy of Nigeria under Military Rule, 1984–1993.* Nigeria, Southern Africa Printing and Publishing House, 1995.

The Enigma of Military Rule in Africa. Harare, SAPES Books, 1995.

Aniagolu, A. N. *The Making of the 1989 Constitution of Nigeria.* Ibadan, Spectrum Books, 1993.

Anyanwu, U. D., and Aguwa, J. C. U. (Eds). *The Igbo and the Tradition of Politics.* Enugu, Fourth Dimension, 1993.

Apter, A. *The Pan-African Nation: Oil and the Spectacle of Culture in Nigeria.* Chicago, IL, University of Chicago Press, 2005.

Asiegbu, J. U. J. *Nigeria and its British Invaders 1851–1920.* Lagos, Nok Publishers International, 1984.

Ate, B. E., and Akinterinwa, B. A. (Eds). *Nigeria and its Immediate Neighbours: Constraints and Prospects of Sub-Regional Security in the 1990s.* Lagos, Nigerian Institute of International Affairs, 1992.

Ayeni, V., and Soremekun, K. (Eds). *Nigeria's Second Republic.* Lagos, Daily Times Publications, 1988.

Babatope, E. *Murtala Muhammed: A Leader Betrayed.* Enugu, Roy and Ezete Publishing Co, 1986.

The Abacha Regime and the 12 June Crisis. London, Beacons Books, 1995.

The Abacha Years: What Went Wrong? Lagos, Ebino Topsy, 2003.

Bakarr Bah, A. *Breakdowns and Reconstitution: Democracy, the Nation-State, and Ethnicity in Nigeria.* Lanham, MD, Lexington Books, 2005.

Bangura, Y. *Intellectuals, Economic Reform and Social Change: Constraints and Opportunities in the Formation of a Nigerian Technocracy.* Dakar, CODESRIA, 1994.

Collier, P., Soludo, C. C., and Pattillo, C. (Eds). *How Economic Choices Will Determine Nigeria's Future.* Basingstoke, Palgrave Macmillan, 2007.

Cruise O'Brien, D. B., Dunn, J., and Rathbone, R. (Eds). *Contemporary West African States.* Cambridge University Press, 1989.

Cyprian Nwagwu, E. O. *Taming the Tiger: Civil-Military Relations Reform and the Search for Political Stability in Nigeria.* Lanham, MD, University Press of America, 2003.

Diamond, L. (Ed.). *Transition Without End: Nigerian Politics and Civil Society under Babangida.* Boulder, CO, Lynne Rienner Publishers, 1997.

Dibie, R. A. *Public Management and Sustainable Development in Nigeria: Military-Bureaucracy Relationship.* London, Ashgate Publishing Company, 2003.

Dike, V. E. *The Osu Caste System in Igboland: A Challenge for Nigerian Democracy.* Kearney, NE, Morris Publishing, 2002.

Edozie, R. K. *People Power and Democracy: The Popular Movement Against Military Despotism in Nigeria, 1989–1999.* Lawrenceville, NJ, Africa World Press, 2002.

Ejobowah. J. B. *Competing Claims to Recognition in the Nigerian Public Sphere.* Lanham, MD, Rowman & Littlefield Publishing, 2002.

Elaigwu, J. I. *The Politics of Federalism in Nigeria.* London, Adonis & Abbey, 2007.

Enwerem, I. M. *Dangerous Awakening: The Politicization of Religion in Nigeria.* Ibadan, FRA, 1996.

Essien, E. *Nigeria Under Structural Adjustment.* Fountain Publications (Nigeria) Ltd, 1990.

Falola, O. O. *Mouth Sweeter Than Salt: An African Memoir.* UMP Publishing, 2004.

Forrest, T. *Politics and Economic Development in Nigeria.* Boulder, CO, Westview Press, 1993.

The Advance of African Capital: The Growth of Nigerian Private Enterprise. Charlottesville, VA, University Press of Virginia, 1994.

Forsyth, F. *The Biafra Story: the Making of an African Legend.* Barnsley, South Yorkshire, Leo Cooper, 2002.

Graf, W. D. *The Nigerian State: Political Economy, State, Class and Political System in the Post-Colonial Era.* London, James Currey, 1988.

Hayward, M. F. *Elections in Independent Africa.* Boulder, CO, Westview Press, 1987.

Honey, R., and Okafor, S. I. (Eds). *Hometown Associations: Indigenous Knowledge and Development in Nigeria.* London, Intermediate Technology Publications, 1998.

Hunt, J. T. *Politics of Bones: Dr. Owens Wiwa And The Struggle For Nigeria's Oil.* Toronto, McClelland & Stewart, 2005.

Ihonvbere, J. O. *Nigeria: The Politics of Adjustment and Democracy.* New Brunswick, NJ, Transaction, 1993.

Ihonvbere, J. O., and Shaw, T. M. (Eds). *Illusions of Power; Nigeria in Transition.* Africa World Press, 1998.

Ikoku, S. G. *Nigeria's Fourth Coup d'Etat.* Enugu, Fourth Dimension, 1985.

Ikpuk, J. S. *Militarism of Politics and Neo-colonialism: The Nigerian Experience 1966–1990.* London, Janus Publishing Co, 1995.

Iweriebor, E. E. G. *Radical Politics in Nigeria, 1945–1950: The Significance of the Zikist Movement.* Zaria, Ahmadu Bello University Press, 1996.

Jeyifo, B. (Ed.). *Perspectives on Wole Soyinka: Freedom and Complexity.* Jackson, MS, University Press of Mississippi, 2001.

Wole Soyinka: History, Politics and Colonialism. Cambridge, Cambridge University Press, 2003.

Jones, G. I. *The Trading States of the Oil Rivers: A Study of Political Development in Eastern Nigeria.* Hamburg, Lit Verlag, 2002.

Kastfelt, N. *Religion and Politics in Nigeria: A Study in Middle Belt Christianity.* London, British Academic Press, 1994.

Khan, S. A. *Nigeria: The Political Economy of Oil.* New York, Oxford University Press, 1994.

King, M. C. *Basic Currents of Nigerian Foreign Policy.* Baltimore, Harvard University Press, 1996.

Korieh, C. *Religion, History, and Politics in Nigeria: Essays in Honor of Ogbu U. Kalu.* Lanham, MD, University Press of America, 2005.

Kukah, M. H. *Religion, Politics and Power in Northern Nigeria.* Ibadan, Spectrum Books, 1993.

Mathews, M. P. (Ed.). *Nigeria: Current Issues and Historical Background.* Hauppauge, NY, Nova Science Publishers, 2002.

Mbadiwe, K. O. *Rebirth of a Nation.* Oxford ABC, Enugu, Fourth Dimension Publishing, 1991.

Maier, K. *This House Has Fallen: Midnight in Nigeria.* Public Affairs, 2000.

This House Has Fallen: Nigeria in Crisis. Boulder, CO, Westview Press, 2003.

Momah, S., and Momah, A. (Eds). *Political Economy of Nigeria under Military Rule, 1894–1993.* Harare, SAPES Books, 1995.

Na'Allah, A. R. (Ed.). *Ogoni's Agonies: Ken Saro-Wiwa and the Crisis in Nigeria.* Africa World Press, 1998.

Nnoli, O. *Ethnicity and Development in Nigeria.* Aldershot, Avebury, 1995.

(Ed.). *Dead-End to Nigerian Development: An Analysis of the Political Economy of Nigeria 1979–1989.* Dakar, CODESRIA, 1993.

Nwabueze, B. O. *Military Rule and Constitutionalism in Nigeria.* Ibadan, Spectrum Books, 1992.

Nwabueze, B. O., and Akinola, A. (Eds). *Military Rule and Social Justice in Nigeria.* Ibadan, Spectrum Books, 1993.

Nwankwo, A. A. *The Nationalities Question in Nigeria: The Class Foundation of Conflicts.* Enugu, Fourth Dimension, 1990.

Nigeria: The Political Transition and the Future of Democracy. Enugu, Fourth Dimension, 1993.

Obasanjo, O. *My Command: An Account of the Nigerian Civil War 1967–1970.* London, Heinemann, 1981.

Odole, Chief M. A. F. *Ife: The Genesis of the Yoruba Race.* Ijeka, John West, 1986.

Ogbondah, C. W. *Military Regimes and the Press in Nigeria, 1968–1993; Human Rights and National Development.* Lanham, MD, University Press of America, 1993.

Ogwu, U. J., and Olaniyan, R. O. (Eds). *Nigeria's International Economic Relations: Dimensions of Dependence and Change.* Lagos, Nigerian Institute of International Affairs, 1990.

Oje-Ade, F. *Death of a Myth: Critical Essays on Nigeria.* Lawrenceville, NJ, Africa World Press, 2002.

Okonta, I. *Where Vultures Feast: Shell, Human Rights and Oil in the Niger Delta.* Sierra Club Books, 2001.

Olaniyan, R. A. *The Amalgamation and its Enemies: An Interpretive History of Modern Nigeria.* Ile-Ife, Awolowo University Press, 2003.

Olanrewaju, S. A., and Falola, T. (Eds). *Rural Development Problems in Nigeria.* Aldershot, Avebury, 1992.

Olowu, D., and Soremekun, K. *Governance and Democratisation in Nigeria.* Ibadan, Spectrum Books, 1995.

Olowu, D., Ayo, S. B., and Akande, B. *Local Institutions and National Development in Nigeria.* Ile-Ife, Obafemi Awolowo University Press, 1991.

Olukoshi, A. O. (Ed.). *The Politics of Structural Adjustment in Nigeria.* London, James Currey, 1993.

Olupona, J. (Ed.). *Religion and Peace in Multi-Faith Nigeria.* Ile-Ife, Obafemi Awolowo University Press, 1992.

Oluwakayode Adekson, A. *The 'Civil Society' Problematique: Deconstructing Civility and Southern Nigeria's Ethnic Radicalisation.* London, Routledge, 2003.

Omoweh, D. A. *Shell Petroleum Development company, the State and Underdevelopment of Nigeria's Niger Delta: a Study in Environmental Degradation.* Lawrenceville, NJ, Africa World Press, 2005.

Osaghae, E. E. *Crippled Giant: Nigeria Since Independence.* London, Hurst, 1998.

Otobo, D. *The Trade Union Movement in Nigeria.* Lagos, Malthouse Press, 1995.

Paden, J. N. *Muslim Civic Cultures And Conflict Resolution: The Challenge Of Democratic Federalism In Nigeria.* Washington, DC, Brookings Institution Press, 2005.

Peel, J. D. Y. *Ijeshas and Nigerians: The Incorporation of a Yoruba Kingdom.* Cambridge University Press, 1983.

Religious Encounter and the Making of the Yoruba (African Systems of Thought). Bloomington, Indiana University Press, 2001.

Peters, J. *The Nigerian Military and the State.* London, Tauris, 1997.

Rotberg, R. I. *Crafting The New Nigeria: Confronting The Challenges.* Boulder, CO, Lynne Rienner Publications, 2004.

Smith, D. J. *A Culture of Corruption: Everyday Deception and Popular Discontent in Nigeria.* Princeton, NJ, Princeton University Press, 2007.

Soyinka, W. *The Open Sore of a Continent: a Personal Narrative of the Nigerian Crisis (W. E. B. Du Bois Institute Series).* Oxford University Press, 1998.

The Burden Of Memory, the Muse of Forgiveness (W. E. B. Du Bois Institute Series). Oxford University Press, 1998.

Suberu, R. T. *Federalism and Ethnic Conflict in Nigeria.* Washington, DC, United States Institute for Peace, 2002.

Synge, R. *Nigeria, the Way Forward.* London, Euromoney Books, 1993.

Tijani, H. *Britain, Leftist Nationalists and the Transfer of Power in Nigeria, 1945–1965.* Abingdon, Routledge, 2006.

Udogu, E. I. *Nigeria in the Twenty-First Century: Strategies for Political Stability and Peaceful Coexistence.* Lawrenceville, NJ, Africa World Press, 2005.

Umoren, J. A. *Democracy and Ethnic Diversity in Nigeria.* Lanham, MD, University Press of America, 1996.

Vogt, M. A., and Ekoko, A. E. (Eds). *Nigeria in International Peace Keeping, 1960–1992.* Lagos, Malthouse Press, 1993.

Watson, R. *Civil Disorder is the Disease of Ibadan: Chieftaincy and Civic Culture in a Colonial City (Western African Studies).* Columbus, OH, Ohio University Press, 2002.

West, D. L. *Governing Nigeria: Continuing Issues After the Elections.* Cambridge, MA, World Peace Foundation, 2003.

Wright, S. *Nigeria: Struggle for Stability and Status.* Boulder, CO, Westview Press, 1999.

Zwingini, J. S. *Capitalist Development in an African Economy: The Case of Nigeria.* Ibadan, UP PLC, 1992.

RÉUNION

Physical and Social Geography

Réunion is a volcanic island in the Indian Ocean lying at the southern extremity of the Mascarene Plateau. Mauritius lies some 190 km to the north-east and Madagascar about 800 km to the west. The island is roughly oval in shape, being about 65 km long and up to 50 km wide; the total area is 2,507 sq km (968 sq miles). Volcanoes have developed along a north-west to south-east angled fault; Piton de la Fournaise (2,624 m) most recently erupted in mid-August 2004, the third time in that year. The others are now extinct, although their cones rise to 3,000 m and dominate the island. The heights and the frequent summer cyclones help to create abundant rainfall, which averages 4,714 mm annually in the uplands, and 686 mm at sea-level. Temperatures vary greatly according to altitude, being tropical at sea-level, averaging between 20°C (68°F) and 28°C (82°F), but much cooler in the uplands, with average temperatures between 8°C (46°F) and 19°C (66°F), owing to frequent winter frosts.

The population of Réunion has more than doubled since the 1940s, reaching 706,300 at the March 1999 census, giving a population density of 281.7 inhabitants per sq km; the estimated population in January 2006 was 784,000. During 1990–97 the population increased at an average rate of 1.7% per year. In 1998 38.3% of Réunion's population was under 20 years of age, while 52.4% of the population was aged between 20 and 59 years. The capital is Saint-Denis, with 131,649 inhabitants at the March 1999 census; this figure was estimated to have risen to 177,648 by mid-2003. Other major towns include Saint-Paul, with 87,712 inhabitants, and Saint-Pierre and Le Tampon, with 69,009 and 60,311 inhabitants, respectively, in 1999. The population is of mixed origin, including people of European, African, Indian and Chinese descent.

Recent History

Revised by the editorial staff

Réunion (formerly known as Bourbon) was first occupied in 1642 by French settlers expelled from Madagascar, and was governed as a colony until 1946, when it received full departmental status. In 1974 it became an Overseas Department with the status of a region. Réunion administered the small and uninhabited Indian Ocean islands of Bassas da India, Juan de Nova, Europa and the Iles Glorieuses, which are also claimed by Madagascar, and Tromelin, which is also claimed by both Madagascar and Mauritius, until January 2005 when they were placed under the authority of the Prefect, Chief Administrator of the French Southern and Antarctic Territories.

In 1982 the French Government proposed a decentralization plan, envisaging the dissolution of the Conseils généraux and régionaux (Regional and General Councils) in the Overseas Departments and the creation in each department of a single assembly, to be elected on the basis of proportional representation. However, this proposal received considerable opposition in Réunion and the other Overseas Departments, and the plan was eventually abandoned. Revised legislation on decentralization in the Overseas Departments was approved by the French Assemblée nationale (National Assembly) in December.

In the elections to the French Assemblée nationale, which took place in March 1986 under a system of proportional representation, the number of deputies from Réunion was increased from three to five. The Parti Communiste Réunionnais (PCR) won two seats, while the Union pour la Démocratie Française (UDF), the Rassemblement pour la République (RPR) and a newly formed right-wing party, France-Réunion-Avenir (FRA), each secured one seat. In the concurrent elections to the Conseil régional, the centre-right RPR-UDF alliance and FRA together received 54.1% of the votes cast, winning 18 and eight of the 45 seats, respectively, while the PCR won 13 seats.

In the second round of the French presidential election, which took place in May 1988, François Mitterrand, the incumbent President and a candidate of the Parti Socialiste (PS), received 60.3% of the votes cast in Réunion. At the ensuing general election for the French Assemblée nationale in June, the system of single-member constituencies was reintroduced. As in the previous general election, the PCR won two of the Réunion seats, while the UDF, the RPR (these two parties allying to form the Union du Rassemblement du Centre) and the FRA each won one seat.

The results of the municipal elections in March 1989 represented a slight decline in support for the left-wing parties. Nevertheless, for the first time since the 1940s, a PS candidate, Gilbert Annette, became mayor of Saint-Denis. At Saint-Pierre the incumbent mayor and PCR deputy to the French Assemblée nationale, Elie Hoarau, unilaterally declared himself the winner, discounting 1,500 votes that had been secured by two minor lists. The result was therefore declared invalid by the administrative tribunal. This incident led to a rift between the PS and the PCR, and, when a fresh election in that municipality was held in September, Hoarau was unable to form an alliance. Hoarau was, however, re-elected mayor, securing just over 50% of the votes cast.

In September 1990, following the restructuring of the RPR under the new local leadership of Alain Defaud, a number of right-wing movements, including the UDF and the RPR, announced the creation of an informal alliance, known as Union pour la France (UPF), to contest the regional elections in 1992.

In March 1990 violent protests took place in support of a popular, but unlicensed, island television service, Télé Free-DOM, following a decision by the French national broadcasting commission, the Conseil supérieur de l'audiovisuel (CSA), to award a broadcasting permit to a rival company. In February 1991 the seizure by the CSA of Télé Free-DOM's broadcasting transmitters prompted further violent demonstrations in Saint-Denis. Some 11 people were killed in ensuing riots, and the French Government dispatched police reinforcements to restore order. The violence was officially ascribed to widespread discontent with the island's social and economic conditions, and a parliamentary commission was established to ascertain the background to the riots.

A visit to Réunion in March 1991 by the French Prime Minister, Michel Rocard, precipitated further rioting. In the same month the commission of inquiry attributed the riots in February to the inflammatory nature of television programmes, which had been broadcast by Télé Free-DOM in the weeks preceding the disturbances, and blamed the station's director, Dr Camille Sudre, who was also a deputy mayor of Saint-Denis. However, the commission refuted allegations by right-wing and centrist politicians that the PCR had orchestrated the violence. Later in March President Mitterrand expressed concern over the outcome of the inquiry, and appealed to the CSA to reconsider its policy towards Télé Free-

DOM. In April, however, the CSA indicated its continued opposition to Télé Free-DOM.

In March 1992 the mayor of Saint-Denis, Gilbert Annette, expelled Sudre, who was one of the deputy mayors, from the majority coalition in the municipal council, after Sudre presented a list of independent candidates to contest regional elections later that month. In the elections to the Conseil régional, which took place on 22 March, Sudre's list of candidates secured 17 seats, while the UPF obtained 14 seats, the PCR nine seats and the PS five seats. In concurrent elections to the Conseil général (which was enlarged to 47 seats), right-wing candidates secured 29 seats, the number of PCR deputies increased to 12, and the number of PS deputies to six; Boyer retained the presidency of the Conseil. Shortly after the elections, Sudre's independent candidates (known as Free-DOM) formed an alliance with the PCR, whereby members of the two groups held a majority of 26 of the 45 seats in the Conseil régional. Under the terms of the agreement, Sudre was to assume the presidency of the Conseil régional, and Paul Vergès, of the PCR, the first vice-presidency. On 27 March, with the support of the PCR, Sudre was elected as President of the Conseil régional by a majority of 27 votes. The UPF and the PS rejected Sudre's subsequent offer to join the Free-DOM-PCR coalition. The PS subsequently appealed against the results of the regional elections, on the grounds that, in contravention of regulations, Sudre's privately owned radio station, Radio Free-DOM, had campaigned on his behalf prior to the elections.

As President of the Conseil régional, Sudre announced that Télé Free-DOM was shortly to resume broadcasting. However, the CSA maintained that if transmissions were resumed Télé Free-DOM would be considered to be illegal, and would be subject to judicial proceedings. Jean-Paul Virapoullé, a deputy to the French Assemblée nationale, subsequently proposed the adoption of legislation which would legalize Télé Free-DOM and would provide for the establishment of an independent media sector outside the jurisdiction of the CSA. In April 1992 Télé Free-DOM transmitters were returned, and at the end of May broadcasting was resumed (without the permission of the CSA).

In September 1992 the French Government agreed to an economic programme that had been formulated by the Conseil régional. In the same month the PCR advocated a boycott of the French referendum on the ratification of the Treaty on European Union, which was to be conducted later that month, in protest at the alleged failure of the French Government to recognize the needs of the Overseas Departments. At the referendum only 26.3% of the registered electorate voted, of whom 74.3% approved the ratification of the treaty. Later that month Boyer and Pierre Lagourgue were elected as representatives to the French Sénat (Senate). (The RPR candidate, Paul Moreau, retained his seat.)

In March 1993 Sudre announced that he was to contest Virapoullé's seat on behalf of the Free-DOM-PCR alliance in the forthcoming elections to the French Assemblée nationale. At the elections, which took place in late March, Sudre was defeated by Virapoullé in the second round of voting, while another incumbent right-wing deputy, André Thien Ah Koon, who contested the elections on behalf of the UPF, also retained his seat. The number of PCR deputies in the Assemblée was reduced from two to one (Vergès), while the PS and RPR each secured one of the remaining seats.

In May 1993 the results of the regional elections of March 1992 were annulled, and Sudre was prohibited from engaging in political activity for one year, on the grounds that programmes broadcast by Radio Free-DOM prior to the elections constituted political propaganda. Sudre subsequently selected his wife, Margie, to assume his candidacy in fresh elections to the Conseil régional. In the elections, which took place in June 1993, the Free-DOM list of candidates, headed by Margie Sudre, secured 12 seats, while the UDF obtained 10, the RPR eight, the PCR nine and the PS six seats. Margie Sudre was subsequently elected as President of the Conseil régional, with the support of the nine PCR deputies and three dissident members of the PS, by a majority of 24 votes.

In April 1993 several prominent businessmen were arrested in connection with the acquisition of contracts by fraudulent means, while a number of members of the principal political organizations, including Boyer and Pierre Vergès, the mayor of Le Port and a member of the PCR, were also implicated in malpractice. Both Boyer and Vergès subsequently fled, following investigations into their activities, and warrants were issued for their arrest. In August Boyer, who had surrendered to the security forces, was placed in detention, pending his trial on charges of corruption. (Joseph Sinimalé, a member of the RPR, temporarily assumed the office of President of the Conseil général.) In the same month the mayor of Saint-Paul and Vice-President of the Conseil général, Cassam Moussa, was also arrested and charged with corruption.

In January 1994 Jules Raux, a deputy mayor of Saint-Denis who was also the local treasurer of the PS, was arrested on charges of financial corruption, and in February two municipal councillors from Saint-Denis were arrested on suspicion of involvement in the affair. In the same month a French citizen (who was believed to have connections with members of the Djibouti Government) was arrested on Réunion and charged with having transferred the funds that were alleged to have been illegally obtained to Djibouti. In March Annette, who was implicated in the affair, resigned as mayor of Saint-Denis, and was subsequently charged with corruption. Boyer was tried and sentenced to four years' imprisonment, while Moussa received a term of two years. In the same month Pierre Vergès (who remained in hiding) resigned as mayor of Le Port.

At elections to the Conseil général, which took place in March 1994, the PCR retained 12 seats, while the number of PS deputies increased to 12 (despite adverse publicity attached to associates of Annette within the PS). The number of seats held by the RPR and UDF declined to five and 11, respectively (compared with six and 14 in the incumbent Conseil). The RPR and UDF subsequently attempted to negotiate an alliance with the PCR; despite long-standing inter-party dissension, however, the PCR and PS established a coalition within the Conseil général, thereby securing a majority of 24 of the 47 seats. In April a member of the PS, Christophe Payet, was elected President of the Conseil général by a majority of 26 votes, defeating Sinimalé; the right-wing parties (which had held the presidency of the Conseil for more than 40 years) boycotted the poll. The PS and PCR signed an agreement, whereby they were to control the administration of the Conseil général jointly, and indicated that centrist deputies might be allowed to enter the alliance. In July Boyer's prison sentence was reduced on appeal to a term of one year.

In November 1994 an official visit to Réunion by Edouard Balladur, the French Prime Minister (and declared candidate for the presidential election in 1995), provoked strike action in protest at his opposition to the establishment of social equality between the Overseas Departments and metropolitan France. Jacques Chirac, the official presidential candidate of the RPR, visited the island in December 1994, when he was endorsed by the organ of the PCR, *Témoignages*, after declaring his commitment to the issue of social equality. In the second round of the presidential election, which took place in May 1995, the socialist candidate, Lionel Jospin, secured 56% of votes cast on Réunion, while Chirac won 44% of the votes (although Chirac obtained the highest number of votes in total); the PCR and Free-DOM had advised their supporters not to vote for Balladur, because of his opposition to the principle of social equality. In August Pierre Vergès was sentenced *in absentia* to 18 months' imprisonment; an appeal was rejected in July 1996. In September 1995 the mayor of Salazie, who was a member of the RPR, was also charged with corruption. In November Boyer lost an appeal against his 1994 conviction and was expelled from the French Sénat.

With effect from the beginning of 1996 the social security systems of the Overseas Departments were aligned with those of metropolitan France. Paul Vergès, joint candidate of the PCR and the PS, was elected to the French Sénat in April, securing 51.9% of the votes cast. Fred K/Bidy won 40.0% of the votes, failing to retain Eric Boyer's seat for the RPR. In the by-election to replace Paul Vergès, which took place in September, Claude Hoarau, the PCR candidate, was elected with 56.0% of the votes cast, while Margie Sudre obtained 44.0%. A new majority alliance between Free-DOM, the RPR and the UDF was subsequently formed in the Conseil régional, with the re-election of its 19-member permanent commission in October.

In October 1996 the trial of a number of politicians and business executives, who had been arrested in 1993–94 on charges of corruption, took place, after three years of investigations. Gilbert Annette and Jules Raux were convicted and, in December of that year, received prison sentences, although Annette's sentence was reduced on appeal in December 1997. Jacques de Châteauvieux, the Chairman of Groupe Sucreries de Bourbon, was found guilty of bribery and was also jailed. Two senior executives from the French enterprise, Compagnie Générale des Eaux, were given suspended sentences, although the public prosecutor subsequently appealed for part of the sentences to be made custodial. Some 20 others were also found guilty of corruption. Pierre Vergès surrendered to the authorities in December and appeared before a magistrate in Saint-Pierre, where he was subsequently detained; in February 1997 he was released by the Court of Appeal.

Four left-wing candidates were successful in elections to the French Assemblée nationale held in May and June 1997. Claude Hoarau (PCR) retained his seat and was joined by Huguette Bello and Elie Hoarau, also both from the PCR, and Michel Tamaya (PS), while André Thien Ah Koon, representing the RPR-UDF coalition, was re-elected.

In February 1998 the PCR (led by Paul Vergès), the PS and several right-wing mayors presented a joint list of candidates, known as the Rassemblement, to contest forthcoming elections. In the elections to the Conseil régional, which took place on 15 March, the Rassemblement secured 19 seats, while the UDF obtained nine seats and the RPR eight, with various left-wing candidates representing Free-DOM winning five. Vergès was elected President of the Conseil régional on 23 March, with the support of the deputies belonging to the Rassemblement and Free-DOM groups. In concurrent elections to an expanded 49-member Conseil général, right-wing candidates (including those on the Rassemblement's list) secured 27 seats, while left-wing candidates obtained 22 seats, the PCR and the PS each winning 10 seats. At the end of the month Jean-Luc Poudroux, of the UDF, was elected President of the Conseil général, owing to the support of two left-wing deputies.

In October 1998 Réunion's three PCR deputies to the French Assemblée nationale proposed legislation providing for the division of the island into two departments, with Saint-Pierre to gain equal status with Saint-Denis as the chief town of a department. In December 1999, whilst attending the Heads of State summit of the Indian Ocean Commission on the island, President Chirac announced that he supported the creation of a second department on Réunion, as part of a number of proposed changes to the institutional future and socio-economic development of the French Overseas Departments. In March 2000 the French Secretary of State for Overseas Departments and Territories declared that Réunion was to be divided into two departments, Réunion South and Réunion North, as of 1 January 2001. However, both the proposed date and the geographical division of the island were rejected by the PS, although it stated that it remained in favour of the creation of a second department. The President of the UDF, Jean-Paul Virapoullé, expressed his opposition to the proposals. Demonstrations both for and against the division of the island took place in March 2000. It was subsequently agreed that the proposals would not be effected until 1 January 2002, and changes were made to the initial plans regarding the geographical division of the island. However, on 15 June 2000 the creation of a second department was rejected by the French Sénat by 203 votes to 111. In November the Assemblée nationale definitively rejected the creation of a second department, but approved the changes to the institutional future of the Overseas Departments, which were finally ratified by the Constitutional Council in December. Also in that month Paul Vergès was arrested on charges of forgery and fraud in connection with his election to the Sénat in 1996.

At municipal elections, held in March 2001, the left-wing parties experienced significant losses. Notably, the PS mayor of Saint-Denis, Michel Tamaya, was defeated by the RPR candidate, René-Paul Victoria. The losses were widely interpreted as a general rejection of Jospin's proposals to create a second department on the island. At elections to the Conseil général, held concurrently, the right-wing parties also made substantial gains, obtaining 38 of the 49 seats; the UDF retained its majority and Jean-Luc Poudroux was re-elected as President. In July Elie Hoarau was obliged to resign from the French Assemblée nationale, following his conviction on charges of electoral fraud, as a result of which he received a one-year prison sentence and a three-year interdiction on holding public office.

In the first round of the presidential election, which was held on 21 April 2002, Jospin secured 39.0% of the valid votes cast in the department (although he was eliminated nationally), followed by Chirac, who received 37.1%. In the second round, on 5 May, Chirac overwhelmingly defeated the candidate of the extreme right-wing Front National, Jean-Marie Le Pen, with 91.9% of the vote. At elections to the Assemblée nationale in June, André Thien Ah Koon, allied to the new Union pour la Majorité Présidentielle (UMP, which had recently been formed by the merger of the RPR, Démocratie Libérale and elements of the UDF), and Bello were re-elected. Tamaya lost his seat to Victoria of the UMP, Claude Hoarau lost to Bertho Audifax of the UMP, while Elie Hoarau, who was declared ineligible to stand for re-election, was replaced by Christophe Payet of the PS. In November the UMP was renamed the Union pour un Mouvement Populaire.

In elections to the Conseil régional, which took place on 21 and 28 March 2004, the Alliance, a joint list of candidates led by the PCR, secured 27 seats. The UMP won 11 seats, and an alliance of the PS and Les Verts Réunion obtained seven seats. Following concurrent elections to the Conseil général, to renew 25 of the 49 seats, right-wing candidates held 30 seats, while left-wing candidates held 19. On 1 April Nassimah Dindar of the UMP was elected to succeed Poudroux as President of the Conseil général. Paul Vergès was re-elected as President of the Conseil régional on the following day. In February 2005 Gélite Hoarau replaced Paul Vergès as the PCR's representative to the Sénat.

In late May 2005 a national referendum on ratification of the proposed constitutional treaty of the European Union was held, at which 59.9% of Réunion's electorate joined with a majority of French voters in rejecting the treaty; voter turn-out on the island was around 53%.

In early 2006 an outbreak of 'chikungunya', a debilitating mosquito-borne virus, reached epidemic proportions. Chikungunya was first reported on the island in April 2005; by February 2006 some 157,000 people were believed to have been infected with the virus and it had been linked to the deaths of 77 people. Paul Vergès accused the French Government of mismanagement and of failing to react with sufficient speed to the crisis, while there were also concerns that the insecticides being used to eradicate the mosquitoes were potentially harmful to humans. In February 300 French soldiers were sent to Réunion to assist some 500 troops already deployed on the island.

In the first round of the French presidential election, held on 22 April 2007, Ségolène Royal of the PS secured 46.2% of the votes cast in Réunion, while Nicolas Sarkozy of the UMP received 25.1%. Both therefore proceeded to the second round of voting, which took place on 6 May. Sarkozy claimed victory in the second round ballot at national level; however, voting on Réunion again went in favour of Royal, who received 63.6% of the island vote. Legislative elections took place in June in which Victoria and Bello both retained their seats in the Assemblée nationale, but Audifax lost his seat to Jean-Claude Fruteau of the PS. Didier Robert of the UMP defeated Paul Vergès, while Patrick Lebreton of the PS was also elected.

In January 1986 France was admitted to the Indian Ocean Commission (IOC), owing to its sovereignty over Réunion. Réunion was given the right to host ministerial meetings of the IOC, but is not eligible to occupy the presidency, owing to its non-sovereign status.

Economy

Revised by the editorial staff

As a result of its connection with France, Réunion's economy is relatively developed, especially in comparison with its sub-Saharan African neighbours. Réunion's gross national income (GNI) in 1995 was estimated at 29,200m. French francs, equivalent to about 44,300 francs per head. In 1990–97, according to World Bank estimates, Réunion's population increased at an average annual rate of 1.7%. According to official estimates, the population at 1 January 2006 totalled 784,000, giving a population density of 312.7 per sq km. In 1997 Réunion's gross domestic product (GDP) totalled €7,228m., equivalent to €10,529 per head. In 2003 Réunion's GDP was €10,523m., equivalent to €13,988 per head. In 1990–2001 GDP increased, in real terms, at an average rate of 2.9% per year; growth in 2001 was 2.4%.

The economy has traditionally been based on agriculture, but in 2003 the sector directly contributed only 2.0% of GDP and salaried agricultural workers accounted for only 1.5% of the economically active population. (In 2003 some 10.8% of the economically active population was unsalaried.) According to FAO figures agricultural workers accounted for 5.5% of the economically active population in 2005. Agricultural GDP increased at an average annual rate of 3.9% during 1990–2000; growth in 2001 was 3.1%. At 31 December 2003 there were 7,621 farmers, compared to 14,699 in 1989; similarly, agricultural land area had decreased from 54,510 ha in 1989 to 48,233 ha in 2003. In recent years some 19.0% of the total land area has been cultivated; around a further 21% of land is classified as agricultural but remains uncultivated, mainly because of the volcanic nature of the soil, but also owing to increasing urbanization. Sugar cane is the principal crop and has formed the basis of the economy for over a century; the secondary usage of agricultural land is for fodder, and this sector is growing, with relatively high yields. In 2005 sugar accounted for 50.4% of export earnings. According to provisional figures, in 2004 some 53% of the arable land was used for sugar plantations. The cane is grown on nearly all the good cultivable land up to 800 m above sea-level on the leeward side of the island, except in the relatively dry north-west, and up to 500 m on the windward side. Sugar cane harvests entered a decline in the early 1970s, owing to drought, ageing plants, rising production costs and inefficient harvesting techniques and transport systems. By 1981, when a seven-year modernization plan came to an end, average annual production of raw sugar had risen to 247,000 metric tons. The sugar cane harvest was consistently above 1.8m. tons between 2000–02 despite the damage caused by cyclones. However, heavy rains reduced the sugar content of the cane: during the same period, raw sugar production fell from 204,000 tons to 194,313 tons; by 2003 this figure had recovered to 207,668 tons. Provisional figures for 2004 suggested a bumper cane harvest of 1.97m. tons; but while sugar production for that year was just over 221,000 tons it was perhaps lower than might have been expected, owing to heavy rains and low sunshine levels.

Geraniums, vetiver and ylang ylang are grown for the production of aromatic essences. Exporters of oil of geranium and vetiver have experienced difficulty in competing with new producers whose prices are much lower. Output of oil of geranium declined to 8.8 metric tons in 2000 and by 2003 production had fallen to 3.0 tons. Output of vetiver totalled 12.1 tons in 1987, but subsequently declined to less than one ton in 1998; output was reported to have recovered to 8.9 tons the following year but official figures continued to record levels of below 0.5 tons through to 2004. Vanilla is produced for export in the south-east; production totalled 132.8 tons in 1987, but declined to 31.2 tons in 1990. An agreement between Réunion, Madagascar and the Comoros concerning price and export quotas on vanilla ended in 1992 and production in that year reached 116.5 tons. However, between 1997 and 2003 annual production averaged just over 32 tons. Tobacco cultivation (introduced at the beginning of the century) produced a crop of 192.8 tons in 1988. Cyclone damage destroyed 115 of the island's 400 tobacco drying sheds in 1989/90 and production declined sharply, to 107.8 tons in 1990, to 73.3 tons in 1991, and to 22 tons in 1992; production between 2000–04 remained at an estimated 20 tons. A variety of tropical fruits is grown for export, including pineapples, lychees, bananas and mangoes, and the island is self-sufficient in cattle and pigs, both of which demonstrated strong growth at the end of the 1990s, and 80% self-sufficient in vegetables. Overall, however, substantial food imports are necessary to supply the dense population.

Although fish are not abundant off Réunion's coast, the commercial fishing industry is an important source of income and employment, especially in the deep-sea sector. The largest fishing vessels make voyages lasting several months, to catch spiny lobsters (langoustes) that breed in the cold waters near Antarctica. In an attempt to preserve resources, the fishing quota for 1989 was reduced, and the total catch declined to 1,725 metric tons. The total catch increased substantially thereafter, reaching 4,703 tons by 1998, before declining again; the total catch in 2005 was 4,757 tons.

In 2003 industry (including manufacturing, construction and power) contributed 13.5% of GDP and salaried workers within the sector accounted for 15.0% of the salaried population in 2005. According to the UN, industrial GDP increased at an average annual rate of 4.3% during 1990–99; growth in 2001 was 3.7%. A Law of Adjustment for Overseas Territories had a favourable effect on the overall number of enterprises in 2001, as 4,500 were created, while 2,900 were closed down. In 2003 of the 292 companies registered in the industry sector more than one-half were involved in producing intermediary goods (including metal items, construction materials, and paper, card and plastic), just under one-quarter were involved in food-processing and a slightly smaller number in the production of other consumables (including textiles and furnishings, printed materials, and pharmaceuticals).

No mineral resources have been identified in Réunion. Imports of products of cokeries, petroleum refineries and nuclear industries comprised 8.1% of the value of total imports in 2004. In 2003 the island imported 83.5% of its fuel requirements. Energy is derived principally from thermal and hydroelectric power. Power plants at Bois-Rouge and Le Gol produce around 45% of the island's total energy requirements; almost one-third of the electricity generated is produced using a mixture of coal and bagasse, a by-product of sugar cane. Total electricity production in 2005 was 2,270 kWh.

Services (including transport, communications, trade and finance) contributed 84.6% of GDP in 2003 and employed 83.6% of the salaried population in 2005. The public sector accounts for about one-half of employment in the services sector. In 2002 the 10 largest companies in terms of revenue were all from the services sector, eight of them involved in volume retail and distribution (principally of consumables but also automobiles). In terms of employment eight of the 10 largest companies provided services, while the other two were involved in construction. The development of tourism is actively promoted, and it is hoped that increased investment in this sector will lead to higher receipts and will help to reduce the trade deficit, as well as provide new jobs. The tourism sector contributed only 3%–4% of GDP in 1993. In 1988 Réunion received aid from the European Community (EC, now the European Union—EU) to stimulate the sector. Tourist arrivals subsequently increased considerably, rising by an average of 9.2% per year in 1990–97. In 2004 430,000 tourists visited Réunion and tourism receipts totalled €314.4m. in that year. In 2005 there was some decline in both the number of visitors (409,000) and receipts (€308.8m.); however, a far more dramatic decline was expected in 2006 following an epidemic of the 'chikungunya' virus (see Recent History), and hotels were reporting that reservations during the peak season were down by 60%. The figure was not as substantial as feared, although the 279,000 visitors in 2006 did represent a 31.8% decline on the previous year's results. Of the total number of visitors in 2006, more than 75% were from metropolitan France.

In 2005 Réunion recorded a trade deficit of €3,427m. The principal source of imports in 2004 was metropolitan France, providing some 57.2% of the total; other major suppliers in that year were Germany, Italy and Singapore. Metropolitan France was also the principal market for exports in 2004, taking approximately 60.4% of the total; other significant purchasers were the USA, Japan and Mayotte. The principal exports in 2004 were sugar and capital equipment. The principal imports in that year were prepared foodstuffs, road motor vehicles and parts, and chemical products. The contribution of exports to GDP declined from 12% at the beginning of the 1970s to 2% in 1992, owing partly to a decline in world sugar prices, and stood at an estimated 7.4% in 1995. In 1998 the volume of goods passing through the ports increased, exceeding 3m. metric tons for the first time, principally as a result of a rise in imports; the figure has remained consistently above 3m. tons since that time. At the ports the tonnage of goods handled increased at an average annual rate of 5.1% in 1990–98. Fuel imports were boosted by the growing number of motor vehicles and a greater number of direct flights from Réunion.

The close connection with France protects the island from the dangers inherent in the narrowness of its economic base. Nevertheless, unemployment and inflation, compounded after 1974 by a number of bankruptcies among small sugar planters, have been the cause of major social and economic problems. The annual rate of inflation averaged 2.2% in 1990–2002; consumer prices increased by 2.3% in 2005. In December 2005 an estimated 31.9% of the labour force was unemployed. Since 1980 the Government has invested significant sums in a series of public works projects in an effort to create jobs and to alleviate the high level of seasonal unemployment following the sugar cane harvest. However, large numbers of workers emigrate in search of employment each year, principally to France. In 1998 the state budgetary deficit was estimated at 8,048.9m. French francs.

The French Government has increased its infrastructural spending in Réunion, particularly on improvements to health services, housing, electricity supply and communication facilities for low-income families. In 1979 an estimated 75% of the population received welfare payments from France, and direct subsidies averaged 25% higher per recipient in Réunion than in metropolitan France. In January 1989 legislation that established a guaranteed minimum income was introduced. In November 1990 the French Government announced measures aimed at establishing parity of the four Overseas Departments with metropolitan France in social and economic programmes. The reforms included the standardization by 1992 of minimum wage levels in Réunion with those operating in the other three Overseas Departments. It was envisaged that minimum wages in the Overseas Departments would be equal with those in metropolitan France by 1995, although this was to be achieved by way of trade union negotiations with employers rather than by government wage guarantees.

In April 1991 representatives of the four Overseas Departments in the French Assemblée nationale and Sénat formed an interparliamentary group to safeguard and promote the agricultural economies of these territories. In July 1992, however, the French Government announced an increase in minimum income of 3.3%, and in family allowance of 20% (far less than required to establish parity with metropolitan France). In September the Conseil régional adopted an economic development programme, known as the emergency plan,.which provided for the creation of an export free zone (EFZ). Under the emergency plan, the French Government would subsidize wages and some employer's contributions of companies operating within the EFZ. By 1993 levels of family allowance in the Overseas Departments had reached parity with those in force in metropolitan France, as envisaged. In early 1994, however, the French Government indicated that it intended to give priority to the reduction of unemployment rather than the standardization of minimum wage levels, and announced a programme of economic and social development for the Overseas Departments, whereby approximately one-third of the unemployed population were to be involved in community projects; enterprises were to receive incentives to engage the unemployed, and a number of economic sectors that had been disadvantaged by international competition were to be exempted from certain taxes. In June the Conseil régional drafted a five-year development plan, at a projected cost of 10,000m. French francs, of which 4,900m. francs were to be financed by the EU: these funds were principally designated to support export initiatives and to improve infrastructure and the environment; allocations were also made to the tourism sector.

In 1996 a committee, established to compare incomes and prices in Réunion with those in metropolitan France, reported that the gross disposable income per inhabitant in Réunion was only 57% of the average income per inhabitant in metropolitan France. The average net salary for state employees was, however, found to be 51% higher on the island, as a result of various benefits. The disparity between prices for many consumer goods was emphasized, with minimum prices in Réunion being as much as three times the French level. The island's political organizations were united in their insistence that civil servants' salaries and benefits should be reduced, thereby releasing funds that could be used to create more employment. Reactions from trade unions were mixed, and the French Government, although willing to hold discussions, delayed making any decision on this politically sensitive issue. In March 1997, however, civil servants and their trade unions were angered by the French Government's proposal to reduce entrance-level salaries to the civil service (see Recent History).

Despite attempts to create more jobs in Réunion, its rate of unemployment remains the highest of all the French Departments. Youth unemployment is of particular concern, with 62% of those under 25 years of age unemployed in 1997. In November of that year the French Government and the authorities in Réunion signed an agreement that was designed to create nearly 3,500 jobs for young people over a period of three years. Part of Saint-Denis was designated as a 'special urban zone' in January 1997, with fiscal incentives on offer to companies establishing themselves in the area; by January 1998 some 240 companies had been attracted to the zone.

In early 1995 the minimum wage level in Réunion was about 14% below that in metropolitan France. However, by 1 January 1996 the minimum wage in Réunion was equal to that in metropolitan France, having increased on average by 23% since the end of 1993. In May 2000 the French Government announced that it had agreed to equalize the minimum taxable wage in the Overseas Departments with that of metropolitan France, within a period of three years; the current minimum taxable wage in Réunion was 20% lower than that of metropolitan France. This measure was approved by the French Sénat in June. In early 2001 the French Government announced that it was to spend €84m. on improving educational facilities in Réunion, as part of a major programme of investment in the Overseas Territories and Departments.

The year 2001 was assessed to have been positive in terms of Réunion's economic development, despite the slowdown in the world economy. Salaries in the private sector increased significantly, consequently improving domestic household consumption and benefiting local companies, and 4,000 new jobs were created. Nevertheless, in March unemployment was estimated at 33.4%. An increase in imports was mitigated by the low price of petroleum. However, the overall level of imports remained low, allowing local enterprises to supply the shortfall. Industrial investment significantly decreased following the terrorist attacks in the USA on 11 September. It was speculated that the domestic population had stimulated the economy by making many purchases in francs prior to the introduction of the euro in January 2002, in order to avoid any price increases, thus bringing savings back into circulation. However, a cyclone in January seriously damaged crops, as well as infrastructure; the French Government released €32.5m. in aid in the following month. It was hoped that a decision to allow Réunion to negotiate co-operation agreements with regional states from 2004 would enhance its trading position.

In April 2004 figures released by the French Government demonstrated that there had been a 3.7% reduction in unemployment in Réunion in 2003 and that some 4,500 new jobs had been created. However, in October 2004 official figures indicated that the rate of unemployment in Réunion remained above 33%.

Statistical Survey

Source (unless otherwise indicated): Institut National de la Statistique et des Etudes Economiques, Service Régional de la Réunion, 15 rue de l'Ecole, 97490 Sainte-Clotilde; tel. 48-81-00; fax 41-09-81; internet www.insee.fr/fr/insee_regions/reunion.

AREA AND POPULATION

Area: 2,507 sq km (968 sq miles).

Population: 597,828 (males 294,256, females 303,572) at census of 15 March 1990; 706,180 (males 347,076, females 359,104) at census of 8 March 1999. *1 January 2006* (official estimate): 784,000.

Density (1 January 2006, official estimate): 312.7 per sq km.

Principal Towns (population at census of March 1999): Saint-Denis (capital) 131,649; Saint-Paul 87,712; Saint-Pierre 69,009; Le Tampon 60,311; Saint-Louis 43,491; Saint-André 43,150. *Mid-2003* (incl. suburbs, UN estimate): Saint-Denis 177,648 (Source: UN, *World Urbanization Prospects: The 2003 Revision*).

Births, Marriages and Deaths (2004): Registered live births 14,545 (birth rate 18.9 per 1,000); Registered marriages 3,269 (marriage rate 4.3 per 1,000); Registered deaths 3,884 (death rate 5.1 per 1,000). *2005* (provisional figures): Registered live births 14,799 (birth rate 19.0 per 1,000); Registered deaths 4,357 (death rate 5.6 per 1,000). *2006* (provisional figures): Registered live births 14,495 (birth rate 18.5 per 1,000).

Expectation of Life (years at birth, 2005, provisional figures): 76.1 (males 72.3; females 80.1).

Economically Active Population (persons aged 15 years and over, 1999 census): Agriculture, hunting, forestry and fishing 9,562; Mining, manufacturing, electricity, gas and water 13,424; Construction 11,003; Wholesale and retail trade 24,658; Transport, storage and communications 5,494; Financing, insurance and real estate 4,851; Business services 11,225; Public administration 39,052; Education 23,325; Health and social work 17,376; Other services 13,707; *Total employed* 173,677 (males 100,634, females 73,043); Unemployed 124,203 (males 63,519, females 60,684); *Total labour force* 297,880 (males 164,153, females 133,727). Figures exclude 967 persons on compulsory military service (males 945, females 22). *31 December 2005* (salaried workers, preliminary): Agriculture 3,189; Industry (incl. energy) 13,692; Construction 14,176; Trade 25,992; Transport 6,745; Financial activities and real estate 5,687; Private services 17,445; Business services 16,185; Health and welfare 16,747; Education 23,731; Public administration 45,649; Total salaried 189,238; Total non-salaried 23,637; Total employed 212,875; Unemployed 86,417; Total labour force 299,292.

HEALTH AND WELFARE

Key Indicators

Total Fertility Rate (children per woman, 2004): 2.5.

Physicians (per 1,000 head, 2001): 2.2.

Hospital Beds (per 1,000 head, 2000): 3.7.

For definitions, see explanatory note on p. vi.

AGRICULTURE, ETC.

Principal Crops ('000 metric tons, 2005): Maize 12 (FAO estimate); Potatoes 3.7 (FAO estimate); Sugar cane 2,000 (FAO estimate); Cabbages 5 (FAO estimate); Lettuce 2.3 (FAO estimate); Tomatoes 4 (FAO estimate); Cauliflower 5.3 (FAO estimate); Pumpkins, squash and gourds 3 (FAO estimate); Eggplants 3.2 (FAO estimate); Onions and shallots (green) 5 (FAO estimate); Beans (green) 2.5 (FAO estimate); Carrots 4.6 (FAO estimate); Bananas 12.5 (unofficial figure); Tangerines, mandarins, clementines and satsumas 6.7 (FAO estimate); Mangoes 4.8 (official figure); Pineapples 10.5 (official estimate).

Livestock ('000 head, 2005, FAO estimates): Cattle 34.0; Pigs 88.5; Sheep 1.2; Goats 36.0; Chickens 13,500.

Livestock Products ('000 metric tons, 2005): Cattle meat 2 (FAO estimate); Pig meat 13.5 (FAO estimate); Chicken meat 19.4 (FAO estimate); Rabbit meat 2.0 (FAO estimate); Cow's milk 23.6 (official figure); Hen eggs 5.9 (FAO estimate).

Forestry ('000 cubic metres, 1991): *Roundwood Removals:* Sawlogs, veneer logs and logs for sleepers 4.2; Other industrial wood 0.9 (FAO estimate); Fuel wood 31.0 (FAO estimate); Total 36.1. *Sawnwood Production:* 2.2. *1992–2005:* Annual production assumed to be unchanged from 1991 (FAO estimates).

Fishing (metric tons, live weight, 2005, FAO estimates): Capture 4,596 (Albacore 768; Yellowfin tuna 935; Swordfish 1,205; Common dolphinfish 77; Carangids 143; Octopuses, etc. 260); Aquaculture 161; *Total catch* 4,757.

Source: FAO.

INDUSTRY

Selected Products (metric tons, 2005 unless otherwise indicated): Sugar 202,342 (provisional figure); Oil of geranium 2 (provisional figure); Oil of vetiver root 0.4 (2002); Rum (hl) 78,929; Electric energy (million kWh) 2,270.

FINANCE

Currency and Exchange Rates: The French franc was used until the end of February 2002. Euro notes and coins were introduced on 1 January 2002, and the euro became the sole legal tender from 18 February. Some of the figures in this Survey are still in terms of francs. For details of exchange rates, see Mayotte.

Budget (€ million, forecasts): *Regional Budget* (2005): Revenue 562 (Direct taxes 23, Indirect taxes 203, Transfers received 229, Loans 105, Other receipts 1); Expenditure 562 (Current expenditure 227, Capital 335). *Departmental Budget* (2006): Revenue 1,272.0 (State endowments 451.6, Direct and indirect taxes 640.8, Loans 110, Other subsidies (Europe and other bodies) 41.3, Other revenues and receipts 28.4); Expenditure 1,272.0 (Social welfare 713.0, General services 226.9, Development 98.9, Teaching 77.7, Networks and infrastructure 7.9, Security 49.0, Planning and environment 12.3, Culture, societies, youth and sports 13.2, Traffic 73.1). Source: Conseil général, *Le Budget du Département*.

Money Supply (million francs at 31 December 1996): Currency outside banks 4,050; Demand deposits at banks 7,469; Total money 11,519.

Cost of Living (Consumer Price Index for urban areas, average of monthly figures; base: 2000 = 100): All items 106.3 in 2003; 108.1 in 2004; 110.4 in 2005. Source: ILO.

Expenditure on the Gross Domestic Product (€ million at current prices, 2003): Private final consumption expenditure 6,844; Government final consumption expenditure (incl. non-profit institutions serving households) 4,431; Changes in inventories –92; Gross fixed capital formation 2,151; *Total domestic expenditure* 13,334; Exports of goods and services 612; *Less* Imports of goods and services 3,423; *GDP in market prices*10,523.

Gross Domestic Product by Economic Activity (€ million at current prices, 2003): Agriculture, forestry and fishing 188; Mining, manufacturing, electricity, gas and water 719; Construction 627; Wholesale and retail trade 949; Hotels and restaurants 164; Transport and communications 604; Finance and insurance 508; Public administration 1,243; Education, health and social work 2,454; Other services 2,486; *Sub-total* 9,941; *Less* Financial intermediation services indirectly measured 345; *Gross value added at basic prices* 9,596; Taxes on products, *less* subsidies on products 927; *GDP in market prices* 10,523.

EXTERNAL TRADE

Principal Commodities (€ million, 2005): *Imports:* Prepared foodstuffs 522.8; Road motor vehicles and parts 507.7; Chemical products 398.7; Products of cokeries, petroleum refineries and nuclear industries 314.0; Machinery and mechanical appliances 303.5; Furniture and products from miscellaneous industries 140.3; Radio, television and communications equipment 122.5; Articles of clothing and furs 127.7; Other transport equipment and parts 142.1; Total (incl. others) 3,689.2. *Exports:* Prepared foodstuffs 192.7 (Sugar 131.8); Capital goods 26.9; Intermediate goods 13.6; Road motor vehicles and parts 14.1; Consumer goods 8.1; Crops and livestock products (unprocessed) 6.2; Total (incl. others) 262.

Principal Trading Partners (€ million, 2004): *Imports:* Belgium 87.1; China, People's Republic 87.9; Germany 131.3; Italy 118.9; Singapore 111.3; South Africa 75.5; Spain 73.5; Total (incl. others) 3,299.9. *Exports f.o.b.:* Belgium 5.1; Japan 12.2; Madagascar 7.8; Mauritius 5.5; Mayotte 11.6; USA 21.7; Total (incl. others) 249.7. Note: Although trade with metropolitan France represented a significant proportion of Réunion's external trade, figures for imports from and exports to France were not available.

TRANSPORT

Road Traffic (1 January 2005): Motor vehicles in use 338,500.

Shipping: *Merchant Fleet* (total displacement at 31 December 1992): 21,000 grt (Source: UN, *Statistical Yearbook*); *Traffic 2005:* Passenger arrivals 15,330; Passenger departures 16,138; Vessels entered 712; Freight unloaded 3,233,600 metric tons; Freight loaded 531,400 metric tons; Containers unloaded 94,487 TEUs; Containers loaded 94,660 TEUs.

Civil Aviation (2005): Passenger arrivals 814,050; Passenger departures 814,139; Freight unloaded 19,969 metric tons; Freight loaded 7,910 metric tons.

TOURISM

Tourist Arrivals ('000): 430 in 2004; 409 in 2005; 279 in 2006.

Arrivals by Country of Residence (2006): France (metropolitan) 209,500; Other EU 10,500; Mauritius 20,100; Total (incl. others) 278,800.

Tourism Receipts (€ million): 314.4 in 2004; 308.8 in 2005; 224.8 in 2006.

COMMUNICATIONS MEDIA

Radio Receivers ('000 in use, 1997): 173 in use. Source: UNESCO, *Statistical Yearbook*.

Television Receivers ('000 in use, 1998): 130 in use. Source: UNESCO, *Statistical Yearbook*.

Telephones ('000 main lines in use, 2004, estimate): 300. Source: International Telecommunication Union.

Facsimile Machines (number in use, 1996): 9,164. Source: UN, *Statistical Yearbook*.

Mobile Cellular Telephones ('000 subscribers, 2005, estimate): 579.2. Source: International Telecommunication Union.

Personal Computers ('000 in use, 2004): 279. Source: International Telecommunication Union.

Internet Users ('000, 2004): 200. Source: International Telecommunication Union.

Book Production (1992): 69 titles (50 books; 19 pamphlets). Source: UNESCO, *Statistical Yearbook*.

Daily Newspapers (1996): 3 (estimated average circulation 55,000 copies). Source: UNESCO, *Statistical Yearbook*.

Non-daily Newspapers (1988, estimate): 4 (average circulation 20,000 copies). Source: UNESCO, *Statistical Yearbook*.

EDUCATION

Pre-primary and Primary (2005/06 unless otherwise indicated): Schools 532 (pre-primary 174, primary 358 in 2003/04); public-sector pupils 112,861 (pre-primary 42,647, primary 70,214); private pupils 8,999 (pre-primary 3,206, primary 5,793).

Secondary (2005/06): Schools 121 (112 public sector, 9 private); pupils 102,613 (public-sector 96,608, private 6,005).

University (2005/06): Institution 1; students 10,562.

Other Higher (2005/06): Students 4,996.

Teaching Staff (31 December 2005): Pre-primary and primary 6,540 (public-sector 6,153, private 387); Secondary 8,691 (public-sector 8,230, private 461); University 392; Other higher 587.

Directory

The Government

(August 2007)

Prefect: Pierre-Henry Maccioni, Préfecture, pl. du Barachois, 97405 Saint-Denis Cédex; tel. 262-40-77-77; fax 262-41-73-74; e-mail courrier@reunion.pref.gouv.fr; internet www.reunion.pref.gouv.fr.

President of the General Council: Nassimah Dindar (UMP), Hôtel du Département, 2 rue de la Source, 97400 Saint-Denis Cédex; tel. 262-90-30-30; fax 262-90-39-99; internet www.cg974.fr.

Deputies to the French National Assembly: Huguette Bello (PCR), Jean-Claude Fruteau (PS), Patrick Lebreton (PS), Didier Robert (UMP), René-Paul Victoria (UMP).

Representatives to the French Senate: Gélita Hoarau (PCR), Anne-Marie Payet (Union Centriste), Jean-Paul Virapoullé (UMP).

GOVERNMENT OFFICES

Direction des Actions de Solidarité et d'Intégration (DASI): ave de la Victoire, 97488 Saint-Denis Cédex; tel. 262-90-31-90; fax 262-90-39-94.

Direction de l'Aménagement et du Développement Territorial: ave de la Victoire, 97488 Saint-Denis Cédex; tel. 262-90-86-86; fax 262-90-86-70; e-mail ddees@cg974.fr.

Direction des Déplacements et de la Voirie (DDV): 6 allée Moreau, 97490 Sainte-Clotilde; tel. 262-90-04-44; fax 262-90-37-77; e-mail did-route@cg974.fr.

Direction du Développement Rural, de l'Agriculture et de la Forêt (DDRAF): ave de la Victoire, 97488 Saint-Denis Cédex; tel. 262-90-35-24; fax 262-90-39-89; e-mail ddees@cg974.fr.

Direction de l'Eau: 1A rue Charles Gounaud, 97488 Saint-Denis Cédex; tel. 262-90-04-44; fax 262-21-73-19; e-mail did-eau@cg974.fr.

Direction de l'Environnement et de l'Energie (DEE): 16 rue Jean Chatel, 97400 Saint-Denis Cédex; tel. 262-90-24-00; fax 262-90-24-19; e-mail denvironnement@cg974.fr.

Direction des Finances: ave de la Victoire, 97488 Saint-Denis Cédex; tel. 262-90-39-39; fax 262-90-39-92; e-mail dfinances@cg974.fr.

Direction Générale des Services (DGS): 2 rue de la Source, 97488 Saint-Denis Cédex; tel. 262-90-30-92; fax 262-90-30-68; e-mail dgs@cg974.fr.

Direction de l'Informatique (DI): 19 route de la Digue, 97488 Saint-Denis Cédex; tel. 262-90-32-90; fax 262-90-32-99; e-mail dinformatique@cg974.fr.

Direction de la Logistique (DL): 2 rue de la Source, 97488 Saint-Denis Cédex; tel. 262-90-31-38; fax 262-90-39-91.

Direction du Patrimoine (DP): 6 bis rue Rontaunay, 97488 Saint-Denis Cédex; tel. 262-90-86-86; fax 262-90-86-90; e-mail dpatrimoine@cg974.fr.

Direction de la Promotion Culturelle et Sportive (DPCS): 18 rue de Paris, 97488 Saint-Denis Cédex; tel. 262-94-87-00; fax 262-94-87-26; e-mail dpcs@cg974.fr.

Direction des Ressources Humaines (DRH): 2 rue de la Source, 97488 Saint-Denis Cédex; tel. 262-90-30-45; fax 262-90-30-10; e-mail drh@cg974.fr.

Direction de la Vie Educative: ave de la Victoire, 97488 Saint-Denis Cédex; tel. 262-90-32-32; fax 262-90-39-98; e-mail dvie-educative@cg974.fr.

Conseil Régional

Hôtel de Région Pierre Lagourgue, ave René Cassin, Moufia BP 7190, 97719 Saint-Denis, Cédex 9; tel. 262-48-70-00; fax 262-48-70-71; e-mail region.reunion@cr-reunion.fr; internet www.regionreunion.com.

President: Paul Vergès (PCR).

Election, 21 and 28 March 2004

Party	Seats
Alliance*	27
UMP	11
PS-Les Verts Réunion	7
Total	45

* An alliance of seven political parties and movements, dominated by the PCR, and also including Free-DOM.

Political Organizations

Front National (FN)—Fédération de la Réunion (FN): Saint-Denis; tel. 262-51-38-97; e-mail fatna@frontnational.com; internet www.frontnational.com; f. 1972; extreme right-wing; Sec. (vacant).

Mouvement pour l'Indépendance de la Réunion (MIR): f. 1981 to succeed the fmr Mouvement pour la Libération de la Réunion; grouping of parties favouring autonomy; Leader Anselme Payet.

Mouvement National Républicain (MNR)—Fédération de la Réunion: tel. 262-22-34-69; Sec. Rémi Bertin.

Parti Communiste Réunionnais (PCR): Saint-Denis; f. 1959; Pres. Paul Vergès; Sec.-Gen. Elie Hoarau.

Mouvement pour l'Egalité, la Démocratie, le Développement et la Nature: affiliated to the PCR; advocates political unity; Leader René Payet.

Parti Radical de Gauche (PRG)—Fédération de la Réunion: 18 rue des Demoiselles, Hermitage les Bains, 97434 Saint-Gilles-les-Bains; tel. 262-33-94-73; internet www.prg93.org; f. 1977; fmrly Mouvement des Radicaux de Gauche; advocates full independence and an economy separate from, but assisted by, France; Pres. Rémy Massain.

Parti Socialiste (PS)—Fédération de la Réunion (PS): 18 ave Stanislas Gimard, 97490 Saint-Denis; tel. 262-97-46-42; fax 262-28-53-03; e-mail fede974@parti-socialiste.fr; internet www.parti-socialiste.fr; left-wing; Sec. Michel Vergoz.

Union pour la Démocratie Française (UDF): Saint-Denis; internet www.udf.org; f. 1978; centrist.

Union pour un Mouvement Populaire (UMP)—Fédération de la Réunion: 6 bis blvd Vauban, BP 11, 97461 Saint-Denis Cédex; tel. 262-20-21-18; fax 262-41-73-55; f. 2002; centre-right; local branch of the metropolitan party; Departmental Sec. Jean-Luc Poudroux.

Les Verts Réunion: 8 rue des Salanganes, Plateau-Caillou, 97460 Saint Paul; tel. 262-55-73-52; fax 262-25-03-03; e-mail sr-verts-reunion@laposte.net; internet www.lesvertsreunion.com; ecologist; Regional Sec. Jean Erpeldinger.

Judicial System

Cour d'Appel: Palais de Justice, 166 rue Juliette Dodu, 97488 Saint-Denis; tel. 262-40-58-58; fax 262-20-16-37; Pres. Jean-Paul Sebileau.

There are two Tribunaux de Grande Instance, one Tribunal d'Instance, two Tribunaux pour Enfants and two Conseils de Prud'hommes.

Religion

A substantial majority of the population are adherents of the Roman Catholic Church. There is a small Muslim community.

CHRISTIANITY

The Roman Catholic Church

Réunion comprises a single diocese, directly responsible to the Holy See. At 31 December 2004 there were an estimated 620,000 adherents, equivalent to some 82.3% of the population.

Bishop of Saint-Denis de la Réunion: Mgr Gilbert Aubry, Evêché, 36 rue de Paris, BP 55, 97461 Saint-Denis Cédex; tel. 262-94-85-70; fax 262-94-85-73; e-mail eveche.lareunion@wanadoo.fr; internet www.diocese-reunion.org.

The Press

DAILIES

Journal de l'Ile de la Réunion: 357 rue du Maréchal Leclerc, BP 166, 97463 Saint-Denis Cédex; tel. 262-90-46-00; fax 262-90-46-01; f. 1956; Dir Jacques Tillier; circ. 35,000.

Quotidien de la Réunion et de l'Océan Indien: BP 303, 97712 Saint-Denis Cédex 9; tel. 262-92-15-15; fax 262-28-43-60; f. 1976; Dir Maximin Chane Ki Chune; circ. 38,900.

PERIODICALS

AGRI-MAG Réunion: Chambre d'Agriculture, 24 rue de la Source, BP 134, 97463 Saint-Denis Cédex; tel. 262-94-25-94; fax 262-21-06-17; e-mail chambagri.cda-97@wanadoo.fr; f. 2001; monthly; Dir Guy Derand; Chief Editor Hervé Cailleaux; circ. 8,000.

Al-Islam: Centre Islamique de la Réunion, BP 437, 97459 Saint-Pierre Cédex; tel. 262-25-45-43; fax 262-35-58-23; e-mail centre-islamique-reunion@wanadoo.fr; internet www.centre-islamique.com; f. 1975; 4 a year; Dir Saïd Ingar.

L'Eco Austral: Technopole de la Réunion 2, rue Emile Hugot, BP 10003, 97801 Saint-Denis Cédex 9; tel. 262-41-51-41; fax 262-41-31-14; internet www.ecoaustral.com; f. 1993; monthly; regional economic issues; Editor Alain Foulon; circ. 50,000.

L'Economie de la Réunion: c/o INSEE, Parc Technologique, 10 rue Demarne, BP 13, 97408 Saint-Denis Messag Cédex 9; tel. 262-48-89-21; fax 262-48-89-89; e-mail insee-contact@insee.fr; internet www.insee.fr/reunion; 4 a year; Dir Jean Gaillard; Editor-in-Chief Collette Berthier.

L'Eglise à la Réunion: 18 rue Montreuil, 97469 Saint-Denis; tel. 262-41-56-90; fax 262-40-92-17; e-mail eglise-reunion@wanadoo.fr; monthly; Dir Elie Cadet.

Lutte Ouvrière—Ile de la Réunion: BP 184, 97470 Saint Benoît; fax 262-48-00-98; e-mail contact@lutte-ouvriere-ile-de-la-reunion.org; internet www.lutte-ouvriere-ile-de-la-reunion.org; monthly; Communist; digital.

Le Mémento Industriel et Commercial Réunionnais: 80 rue Pasteur, BP 397, 97468 Saint-Denis; tel. 262-21-94-12; fax 262-41-10-85; e-mail memento@memento.fr; internet www.memento.fr; f. 1970; monthly; Dir Catherine Louapre-Pottier; Editor-in-Chief Georges-Guillaume Louapre-Pottier; circ. 20,000.

Témoignages: 6 rue du Général Emile Rolland, BP 1016, 97828 Le Port Cédex; tel. 262-55-21-21; e-mail temoignages@wanadoo.fr; internet www.temoignages.re; f. 1944; affiliated to the PCR; daily; Dir Jean-Marcel Courteaud; Editor-in-Chief Alain Ilan Chojnow; circ. 6,000.

Visu: 97712 Saint-Denis Cédex 9; tel. 262-90-20-60; fax 262-90-20-61; weekly; Editor-in-Chief Guy Leblond; circ. 53,000.

NEWS AGENCY

Imaz Press Réunion: 12 rue Mac Auliffe, 97400 Saint-Denis; tel. 262-20-05-65; fax 262-20-05-49; e-mail ipr@ipreunion.com; internet www.ipreunion.com; f. 2000; photojournalism and news agency; Dir Richard Bouhet.

Broadcasting and Communications

TELECOMMUNICATIONS

Orange Réunion: 35 blvd du Chaudron, BP 7431, 97743 Saint-Denis, Cédex 9; tel. 262-20-69-56; fax 262-20-67-79; f. 2000; subsidiary of Orange France; mobile cellular telephone operator.

Société Réunionnaise du Radiotéléphone (SRR): 21 rue Pierre Aubert, 97490 Sainte Clotide; BP 17, 97408 Saint-Denis, Messag Cédex 9; tel. 262-48-19-70; fax 262-48-19-80; internet www.srr.fr; f. 1995; subsidiary of SFR Cegetel, France; mobile cellular telephone operator; CEO Jean-Pierre Haggaï; 431,719 subscribers in Réunion, 46,341 in Mayotte (as Mayotte Télécom Mobile) in 2003.

BROADCASTING

Réseau France Outre-mer (RFO): 1 rue Jean Chatel, 97716 Saint-Denis Cédex; tel. 262-40-67-67; fax 262-21-64-84; internet www.rfo.fr; acquired by Groupe France Télévisions in 2004; fmrly Société Nationale de Radio-Télévision Française d'Outre-mer, present name adopted in 1998; radio and television relay services in French; broadcasts two television channels (Télé-Réunion and Tempo) and three radio channels (Radio-Réunion, France-Inter and France-Culture); Gen. Man. François Guilbeau; Regional Dir Gérald Prufer.

Radio

In 2005 there were 46 licensed private radio stations. These included:

Cherie FM Réunion: 3 rue de Kerveguen, 97400 Sainte Clotilde; tel. 262-97-32-00; fax 262-97-32-32; Editor-in-Chief Lea Berthault.

NRJ Réunion: 3 rue de Kerveguen, 97490 Sainte Clotilde; tel. 262-97-32-00; fax 262-97-32-32; e-mail acceuil@nrjreunion.com; commercial radio station; Station Man. Sylvain Peguillan.

Radio Festival: 3 rue de Kerveguen, 97490 Sainte Clotilde; tel. 262-97-32-00; fax 262-97-32-32; e-mail redaction@radiofestival.fr; f. 1995; commercial radio station; Pres. Mario Lechat; Editor-in-Chief Pierrot Dupuy.

Radio Free-DOM: BP 666, 97473 Saint-Denis Cédex; tel. 262-41-51-51; fax 262-21-68-64; e-mail freedom@freedom.fr; internet www.freedom.fr; f. 1981; commercial radio station; Dir Dr Camille Sudre.

Television

Antenne Réunion: BP 80001, 97801 Saint-Denis Cédex 9; tel. 262-48-28-28; fax 262-48-28-26; e-mail direction@antennereunion.fr; internet www.antennereunion.fr; f. 1991; broadcasts 10 hours daily; Dir Christophe Ducasse.

Canal Réunion: 35 chemin Vavangues, 97490 Sainte-Clotilde; tel. 262-29-02-02; fax 262-29-17-09; subscription television channel; broadcasts a minimum of 19 hours daily; Chair. Dominique Fagot; Dir Jean-Bernard Mourier.

TV-4: 8 chemin Fontbrune, 97400 Saint-Denis; tel. 262-52-73-73; broadcasts 19 hours daily.

TV Sud: 10 rue Aristide Briand, 97430 Le Tampon; tel. 262-57-42-42; commenced broadcasting in 1993; broadcasts 4 hours daily.

Other privately owned television services include TVB, TVE, RTV, Télé-Réunion and TV-Run.

Finance

(cap. = capital; res = reserves; dep. = deposits; m. = million; brs = branches)

BANKING

Central Bank

Institut d'Emission des Départements d'Outre-mer: 4 rue de la Compagnie, 97487 Saint-Denis Cédex; tel. 262-90-71-00; fax 262-21-41-32; Dir GUY DEBUYS.

Commercial Banks

Banque Française Commerciale Océan Indien (BFCOI): 60 rue Alexis de Villeneuve, BP 323, 97468 Saint-Denis Cédex; tel. 262-40-55-55; fax 262-20-09-07; Chair. PHILIPPE BRAULT; Dir PHILIPPE LAVIT D'HAUTEFORT; 8 brs.

Banque Nationale de Paris Intercontinentale: 67 rue Juliette Dodu, BP 113, 97463 Saint-Denis; tel. 262-40-30-02; fax 262-41-39-09; internet www.bnpgroup.com; f. 1927; 100% owned by BNP Paribas; Chair. MICHEL PEBEREAU; Man. Dir DANIEL DELANIS; 16 brs.

Banque de la Réunion (BR), SA: 27 rue Jean Chatel, 97711 Saint-Denis Cédex; tel. 262-40-01-23; fax 262-40-00-61; e-mail br@banquedelareunion.fr; internet www.banquedelareunion.fr; f. 1853; subsidiary of Financière Océor; cap. €50.0m., res €52.0m., dep. €1,120.7m. (Dec. 2001); Chair. JEAN-CLAUDE CLARAC; Gen. Man. JEAN-LOUIS FILIPPI; 20 brs.

BRED-Banque Populaire: 33 rue Victor MacAuliffe, 97461 Saint-Denis; tel. 262-90-15-60; fax 262-90-15-99.

Crédit Agricole de la Réunion: Les Camélias, Cité des Lauriers, BP 84, 97462 Saint-Denis Cédex; tel. 262-40-81-81; fax 262-40-81-40; internet www.credit-agricole.fr; f. 1949; total assets €2,564m. (Dec. 2004); Chair. CHRISTIAN DE LA GIRODAY; Gen. Man. PIERRE MARTIN.

Development Bank

Banque Populaire Fédérale de Développement: 33 rue Victor MacAuliffe, 97400 Saint-Denis; tel. 262-21-18-11; Dir OLIVIER DEVISME; 3 brs.

Société Financière pour le Développement Economique de la Réunion (SOFIDER): 3 rue Labourdonnais, BP 867, 97477 Saint-Denis Cédex; tel. 262-40-32-32; fax 262-40-32-00; part of the Agence Française de Développment; Dir-Gen. CLAUDE PÉRIOU.

INSURANCE

More than 20 major European insurance companies are represented in Saint-Denis.

AGF Vie La Réunion: 185 ave du Général de Gaulle, BP 797, 97476 Saint-Denis Cédex; tel. 262-94-72-23; fax 262-94-72-26; e-mail agfoi-vie@agfoi.com.

Capma & Capmi: 18 rue de la Cie des Indes, 97499 Saint-Denis; tel. 262-21-10-56; fax 262-20-32-67.

Groupama Océan Indien et Pacifique: 13 rue Fénelon, BP 626, 97473 Saint-Denis Cédex; tel. 262-26-12-61; fax 262-41-50-79; Chair. DIDIER FOUCQUE; Gen. Man. MAURICE FAURE (acting).

Trade and Industry

GOVERNMENT AGENCIES

Agence de Gestion des Initiatives Locales en Matière Européenne (AGILE)—Cellule Europe Réunion: 3 rue Felix Guyon, 97400 Saint-Denis; tel. 262-90-10-80; fax 262-21-90-72; e-mail celleurope@agile-reunion.org; internet www.agile-reunion.org; responsible for local application of EU structural funds; Dir SERGE JOSEPH.

Conseil Economique et Social de la Réunion (CESR): 10 rue du Béarn, BP 7191, 97719 Saint-Denis Messag Cédex; tel. 262-97-96-30; fax 262-97-96-31; e-mail cesr-reunion@cesr-reunion.fr; internet www.cesr-reunion.fr; f. 1984; Pres. JEAN-RAYMOND MONDON; Dir DIDIER LAMOTTE.

Direction Départementale de la Jeunesse, des Sports et de la Vie Associative de la Réunion (DDJS): 14 allée des Saphirs, 97487 Saint-Denis Cédex; tel. 262-20-96-40; fax 262-20-96-41; e-mail dd974@jeunesse-sports.gouv.fr; internet www.ddjs-reunion.jeunesse-sports.gouv.fr; Departmental Dir DANIEL BOILLEY.

Direction Régionale des Affaires Culturelles de la Réunion (DRAC): 23 rue Labourdonnais, BP 224, 97464 Saint-Denis Cédex; tel. 262-21-91-71; fax 262-41-61-93; e-mail drac-la.reunion@culture.gouv.fr; internet www.reunion.pref.gouv.fr; f. 1992; responsible to the French Ministry of Culture; Regional Dir LOUIS POULHÈS.

Direction Régionale des Affaires Sanitaires et Sociales de la Réunion (DRASS): 2 bis ave Georges Brassens, BP 9, 97408 Saint-Denis Messag Cédex 9; tel. 262-48-60-60; fax 262-48-60-79; internet www.reunion.pref.gouv.fr/drass.

Direction Régionale du Commerce Extérieur (DRCE): MRST, 100 route de la Rivière des Pluies, 97491 Sainte Clotilde Cédex; tel. 262-92-24-70; fax 262-92-24-76; e-mail reunion@missioneco.org; internet www.missioneco.org/reunion; Dir PHILIPPE GENIER.

Direction Régionale de l'Environnement (DIREN): 12 allée de la Forêt, Parc de la Providence, 97400 Saint-Denis; tel. 262-94-78-11; fax 262-94-72-55; e-mail estelle.loiseau@reunion.ecologie.gouv.fr; internet www.reunion.ecologie.gouv.fr.

Direction Régionale de l'Industrie, de la Recherche et de l'Environnement: 130 rue Léopold Rambaud, 97491 Sainte Clotilde Cédex; tel. 262-92-41-10; fax 262-29-37-31; internet www.reunion.drire.gouv.fr; Reg. Dir JEAN-CHARLES ARDIN; Sec.-Gen. JACQUELINE LECHEVIN.

DEVELOPMENT ORGANIZATIONS

Agence Française de Développement (AFD): 44 rue Jean Cocteau, BP 2013, 97488 Saint-Denis Cédex; tel. 262-90-00-90; fax 262-21-74-58; e-mail afdstdenis@re.groupe-afd.org; Dir PASCAL PACAUT.

Association pour le Développement Industriel de la Réunion: 8 rue Philibert, BP 327, 97466 Saint-Denis Cédex; tel. 262-94-43-00; fax 262-94-43-09; e-mail adir@adir.info; internet www.adir.info; f. 1975; Pres. MAURICE CERISOLA; Sec.-Gen. FRANÇOISE DELMONT DE PALMAS; 190 mems.

Chambre d'Agriculture de la Réunion: 24 rue de la Source, BP 134, 97463 Saint-Denis Cédex; tel. 262-94-25-94; fax 262-21-06-17; e-mail chambagri.cda-97@wanadoo.fr; Pres. GUY DERAND; Gen. Man. ALAIN TARDY.

Direction de l'Action Economique: Secrétariat Général pour les Affaires Economiques, ave de la Victoire, 97405 Saint-Denis; tel. 262-40-77-10; fax 262-40-77-01.

Jeune Chambre Economique de Saint-Denis de la Réunion: 25 rue de Paris, BP 1151, 97483 Saint-Denis; f. 1963; Chair. JEAN-CHRISTOPHE DUVAL; 30 mems.

Société de Développement Economique de la Réunion (SODERE): 26 rue Labourdonnais, 97469 Saint-Denis; tel. 262-20-01-68; fax 262-20-05-07; f. 1964; Chair. RAYMOND VIVET; Man. Dir ALBERT TRIMAILLE.

CHAMBERS OF COMMERCE

Chambre de Commerce et d'Industrie de la Réunion (CCIR): 15 route de la Balance, 97410 Saint-Pierre; tel. 262-96-96-96; fax 262-94-22-90; internet www.reunion.cci.fr; f. 1830; Pres. ERIC MAGAMOOTOO; Sec. DANIEL MOREAU.

Chambre de Métiers et de l'Artisanat: 42 rue Jean Cocteau, BP 261, 97465 Saint-Denis Cédex; tel. 262-21-04-35; fax 262-21-68-33; e-mail cdm@cm-reunion.fr; internet cm-reunion.fr; f. 1968; Pres. GIRAUD PAYET; Sec. BÉATRICE BADIN; 14 mem. orgs.

EMPLOYERS' ASSOCIATIONS

Conseil de l'Ordre des Pharmaciens: 1 bis rue Sainte Anne, Immeuble le Concorde, Appt. 26, 1er étage, 97400 Saint-Denis; tel. 262-41-85-51; fax 262-21-94-86; Pres. CHRISTIANE VAN DE WALLE.

Coopérative Agricole des Huiles Essentielles de Bourbon (CAHEB): 83 rue de Kerveguen, 97430 Le Tampon; BP 43, 97831 Le Tampon; tel. 262-27-02-27; fax 262-27-35-54; e-mail caheb@geranium-bourbon.com; f. 1963; represents producers of essential oils; Pres. ALAIN DAMBREVILLE; Sec.-Gen. LAURENT JANCI.

Mouvement des Entreprises de France Réunion (MEDEF): 14 rampes Ozoux, BP 354, 97467 Saint-Denis; tel. 262-20-01-30; fax 262-41-68-56; e-mail medef.reunion@wanadoo.fr; Pres. FRANÇOIS CAILLÉ.

Ordre National de Médecins: 2 Résidence Halley, Bât. A, 4 rue Camille-Vergoz, 97400 Saint-Denis; tel. 262-20-11-58; fax 262-21-08-02; e-mail reunion@974.medecin.fr; internet www.odmreunion.net; Pres. Dr YVAN TCHENG.

Syndicat des Fabricants de Sucre de la Réunion: 23 rue Raymond Vergès, Quartier Français, 97441 Sainte-Suzanne; tel. 262-58-82-82; fax 262-46-53-01; e-mail info@sfsrun.com; Chair. XAVIER THIEBLIN.

Syndicat des Producteurs de Rhum de la Réunion: chemin Frédéline, BP 354, 97453 Saint-Pierre Cédex; tel. 262-25-84-27; fax 262-35-60-92; Chair. OLIVIER THIEBLIN.

Union Réunionnaise des Coopératives Agricoles (URCOOPA): Z. I. Cambaie, BP 90, 97411 Saint-Paul; f. 1982; represents farmers; comprises Coop Avirons (f. 1967), Société Coopérative Agricole Nord-Est (CANE), SICA Lait (f. 1961), and CPPR; Pres. KARL TECHER.

MAJOR COMPANIES

Brasseries de Bourbon: 60 Quai Ouest, BP 420, 97468 Saint-Denis; 85.6% owned by Heineken NV, Netherlands; brewery and distributor of alcoholic beverages and soft drinks; Pres. EDWIN BOTTERMAN; Man. EUGÈNE UBALIJORO.

Caltex Oil (Reunion) Ltd: BP 103, 97823 Le Port Cédex; tel. 262-42-76-76; fax 262-43-23-11; subsidiary of ChevronTexaco Corpn, USA; retail and distribution of petroleum products; revenue c. €90m. (2002).

Coopérative d'Achats des Détaillants Réunionnais SA (CADRE): 3 rue Simone Morin, Zone Industrielle les Tamarins, 97420 Le Port; tel. 262-42-93-93; fax 262-42-92-50; retail distribution; Chair. DAVID SOUI MINE.

Compagnie Laitière des Mascareignes (CILAM): 56 Quai Ouest, 97400 Saint-Denis; f. 1965; 80% owned by mems of SICA Lait; dairy products; Pres. PAUL MARTINEL; c. 180 employees.

Distridom: 23 rue de Bordeaux, 97420 Le Port; f. 1993; supermarket retail (Leader Price); revenue €80.0m. (2003); Pres. PASCAL THIAW KINE; Man. Dir LAURENT THIAW KINE.

Établissements Jules Caillé: 1 rue Edouard Manès 97490 Sainte-Clotilde; tel. 262-21-12-30; fax 262-21-63-77; f. 1919; agent for Peugeot motor vehicles; Chair. JACQUES CAILLÉ; Dir GASTON CAILLÉ; c. 320 employees.

Grands Travaux de l'Océan Indien (GTOI): Z. I. No. 2, BP 2016, 97824 Le Port Cédex; tel. 262-42-85-85; fax 262-71-05-21; internet www.gtoi.fr; construction and civil engineering; revenue €171.1m. (2005); CEO CHRISTOPHE GUY; Gen. Man. CHRISTOPHE DA POIAN; c. 1,100 employees (2005).

Groupe Quartier Français: 23 rue Raymond Vergès, 97441 Sainte-Suzanne; tel. 262-58-82-82; fax 262-46-53-01; e-mail gqf@gqf.com; internet www.gqf.com; f. 1923; Chair. XAVIER THIÉBLIN; CEO PHILIPPE LABRO; Comprises:

Distillerie Rivière du Mât: chemin Manioc, ZI Beaufonds, 97470 Saint-Benoît; tel. 262-67-46-41; fax 262-50-27-32.

Mascarin: 1 rue Claude Chappe, ZAC 2000, BP 134, 97420 Le Port Cédex; tel. 262-55-10-20; fax 262-43-99-45; storage, packing and distribution; exports 90% of production; Chair. PHILIPPE LABRO; Man. Dir JEAN-PIERRE DANIEL SIX.

Sucrière de la Réunion: 23 rue Raymond Vergès, 97441 Sainte-Suzanne; tel. 262-58-82-82; fax 262-46-53-01; e-mail sr@gqf.com; CEO BERNARD PÉTIN; 200 permanent and 200 seasonal employees; processes c. 1.1m. metric tons of sugar cane per campaign.

Hyper Soredeco: 75 rue du Karting la Jamaique, 97490 Saint-Denis; supermarket retail (Carrefour); Chair. JACQUES CAILLÉ; c. 300 employees.

Ravate Distribution: 131 rue Maréchal Leclerc, 97400 Saint-Denis; tel. 262-21-06-63; fax 262-41-26-63; retailers of construction materials, wood, hardware; Chair. ISSOP RAVATE; Dir ADAM RAVATE; c. 440 employees.

SEMS SA: 5 impasse du Grand Prado; supermarket retail; revenue €249.0m. (2004); more than 1,000 employees.

Société Bourbonnaise de Travaux Publics et de Constructions (SBTPC): 28 rue Jules Verne, 97429 Le Port; subsidiary of Vinci Construction Filiales Int., France; construction and civil engineering; revenue €91m. (2004); Man. BERNARD LENFANT; c. 500 employees.

Société Foucque: 69 blvd du Chaudron, BP 300, 97490 Sainte-Clotilde; tel. 262-97-49-74; fax 262-48-24-61; internet www.foucque.fr; agent for Citroën motor vehicles, and farming machinery; revenue €100m. (2004); Man. Dir FRÉDÉRIC FOUCQUE; c. 300 employees.

Société Réunionnaise de Produits Pétroliers (SRPP): Zone Industrielle N1, 97420 Le Port; BP 2015, 97824 Le Port Cédex; tel. 262-42-07-11; fax 262-42-11-34; storage and retail of petroleum products; revenue €191m. (2004); Chair. ROBERT LAUROUA; CEO MOMAR NGUER; c. 100 employees.

Sodexpro: 10 rue Theodore Drouet, 97420 Le Port; supermarket retail; revenue €78.0m. (2001); Pres. FRANÇOIS CAILLÉ; c. 100 employees.

Sucrerie de Bois-Rouge: 2 chemin Bois-Rouge, BP 1017, Cambuston, 97440 Saint-André; tel. 262-58-83-30; fax 262-58-83-31; e-mail sucrerie.br@bois-rouge.fr; internet www.bois-rouge.fr; f. 1817; 51% owned by Tereos, 39% owned by Groupe Quartier Français; produces, refines and exports sugar; fmrly Groupes Sucreries de Bourbon, acquired by Tereos in 2001; Chair. JACQUES DE CHÂTEAUVIEUX; 150 permanent and 100 seasonal employees; processes c. 1m. metric tons of sugar cane per campaign; comprises:

Distillerie de Savanna: 2 chemin Bois-Rouge, Cambuston, 97440 Saint-André; tel. 262-58-03-98; fax 262-58-06-51; e-mail savanna@distilleriesavanna.com; internet www.distilleriesavanna.com; f. 1950; wholesale rum producer; produces 10m. litres of rum per year; exports 80% of production; 24 employees.

Eurocanne: La Mare, 97438 Sainte-Marie; tel. 262-43-27-79; fax 262-43-51-39; e-mail sucreriesbourbon@bois-rouge.fr; storage, packing and distribution; exports 85% of production; Dir PATRICK LORCET.

Total Réunion: 3 rue Jacques Prévert, Rivière des Galets, BP 286, 97827 Le Port Cédex; tel. 262-55-20-20; fax 262-55-20-21; e-mail total-reunion@totalreunion.fr; internet www.totalreunion.fr; retail and distribution of petroleum products; revenue €137.m. (2004); Pres. ALEXIS VOVK; Dir-Gen. PHILLIPE BODILIS; c. 30 employees.

TRADE UNIONS

CFE-CGC de la Réunion: 1 Rampes Ozoux, Résidence de la Rivière, Appt 2A, BP 873, 97477 Saint-Denis Cédex; tel. 262-90-11-95; fax 262-90-11-99; e-mail union@cfecgcreunion.com; internet www.cfecgcreunion.com; departmental br. of the Confédération Française de l'Encadrement-Confédération Générale des Cadres; represents engineers, teaching, managerial and professional staff and technicians; Pres. ALAIN IGLICKI; Sec.-Gen. DANIEL THIAW-WING-KAI.

Confédération Générale du Travail de la Réunion (CGTR): 144 rue du Général de Gaulle, BP 1132, 97482 Saint-Denis Cédex; Sec.-Gen. GEORGES MARIE LEPINAY.

Fédération Départementale des Syndicats d'Exploitants Agricoles de la Réunion (FDSEA): 105 rue Amiral Lacaze, Terre Sainte, 97410 Saint-Pierre; tel. 262-96-33-53; fax 262-96-33-90; e-mail fdsea-reunion@wanadoo.fr; affiliated to the Fédération Nationale des Syndicats d'Exploitants; Sec.-Gen. JEAN-BERNARD HOARAU.

Fedération Réunionnaise du Bâtiment et des Travaux Publics: BP 108, 97462 Saint-Denis Cédex; tel. 262-41-70-87; fax 262-21-55-07; Pres. J. M. LE BOURVELLEC.

Fédération Syndicale Unitaire Réunion (FSU): 4 rue de la Cure, BP 279, 97494 Sainte-Clotilde Cédex; tel. 262-86-29-46; fax 262-22-35-28; e-mail fsu974@fsu.fr; internet sd974.fsu.fr; f. 1993; departmental br. of the Fédération Syndicale Unitaire; represents public sector employees in sectors incl. teaching, research, and training, and also agriculture, justice, youth and sports, and culture; Sec. CHRISTIAN PICARD.

Union Départementale Confédération Française des Travailleurs Chrétiens (UD CFTC): Résidence Pointe des Jardins, 1 rue de l'Atillerie, 97400 Saint-Denis; tel. 262-41-22-85; fax 262-41-26-85; e-mail usctr@wanadoo.fr.

Union Départementale Force Ouvrière de la Réunion (FO): 81 rue Labourdonnais, BP 853, 97477 Saint-Denis Cédex; tel. 262-21-31-35; fax 262-41-33-23; e-mail emarguerite@force-ouvriere.fr; Sec.-Gen. ERIC MARGUERITE.

Union Interprofessionnelle de la Réunion (UIR-CFDT): 58 rue Fénelon, 97400 Saint-Denis; tel. 262-90-27-67; fax 262-21-03-22; e-mail uir.cfdt@wanadoo.fr; affiliated to the Confédération Française Démocratique du Travail; Regional Sec. AXEL ZETTOR.

Affiliated unions incl.:

FEP-CFDT Réunion: 58 rue Fénélon, 97400 Saint-Denis; tel. 262-90-27-67; fax 262-21-03-22; e-mail jpmarchau@uir-cfdt.org; affiliated to the Fédération Formation et Enseignement Privés; represents private-sector teaching staff.

SGEN-CFDT: 58 rue Fénélon, 97400 Saint-Denis; tel. 262-90-27-72; fax 262-21-03-22; e-mail sgen.reunion@wanadoo.fr; internet www.sgen-cfdt-reunion.org; affiliated to the Fédération des Syndicats Généraux de l'Education Nationale et de la Recherche; represents teaching staff; Sec.-Gen. JEAN-LOUIS BELHOTE.

Union Régionale UNSA-Education: BP 169, 97464 Saint-Denis Cédex; tel. 262-20-02-25; fax 262-21-58-65; e-mail hjrmtg@wanadoo.fr; represents teaching staff; Sec.-Gen. JEAN-RAYMOND MONDON.

Transport

ROADS

A route nationale circles the island, generally following the coast and linking the main towns. Another route nationale crosses the island from south-west to north-east linking Saint-Pierre and Saint-Benoît. In 1994 there were 370 km of routes nationales, 754 km of departmental roads and 1,630 km of other roads; 1,300 km of the roads were bituminized. In 2005 discussions were ongoing regarding a proposed 'tram-train' network that would link Saint-Benoît to Saint-Joseph via Saint-Denis. However, the proposals continued to face opposition from ministers who favoured a new bus service and investment in the road network.

Société d'Economie Mixte des Transports, Tourisme, Equipements et Loisirs (SEMITTEL): 24 chemin Benoite-Boulard, 97410 Saint-Pierre; tel. 262-55-40-60; fax 262-55-49-56; e-mail semittel@semittel.fr; f. 1984; bus service operator; Pres. Marrie Perianayagom.

Société des Transports Départementaux de la Réunion (SOTRADER): 2 allée Bonnier, 97400 Saint-Denis; tel. 262-94-89-40; fax 262-94-89-50; e-mail sotrader@sotrader.com; f. 1995; bus service operator; Gen. Man. Annie Philippet Fouchard.

SHIPPING

In 1986 work was completed on the expansion of the Port de la Pointe des Galets, which was divided into the former port in the west and a new port in the east (the port Ouest and the port Est), known together as Port Réunion. In 2004 some 3.3m. metric tons of freight were unloaded and 586,200 tons loaded at the two ports. The Chambre de Commerce et d'Industrie de la Réunion also manages three yachting marinas.

Port Authority (Concession Portuaire): rue Evariste de Parny, BP 18, 97821 Le Port Cédex; tel. 262-42-90-00; fax 262-42-47-90; e-mail pr.com@reunion.cci.fr; internet www.reunion.port.fr; Dir Bruno Davidsen.

CMACGM Réunion: 85 rue Jules Verne, Z.I. no 2, BP 2007, 97822 Le Port Cédex; tel. 262-55-10-10; fax 262-43-23-04; e-mail lar.genmbox@cma-cgm.com; internet www.cmacgm.com; f. 1996 by merger of Cie Générale Maritime and Cie Maritime d'Affrètement; shipping agents; Man. Dir Valérie Seveno.

Coopérative Ouvrière Réunionaise (COR): 1 voie de Liaison Portuaire, BP 119, 97823 Le Port Cédex; tel. 262-43-05-14; fax 262-43-09-44; e-mail la.cor@wanadoo.fr; stevedoring; Pres. Jaques Virin.

Mediterranean Shipping Co France, S.A. (MSC).

Réunion Ships Agency (RSA): 7 rue Ambroise Croizat, BP 186, 97825 Le Port Cédex; tel. 262-43-33-33; fax 262-42-03-10; e-mail rsa@indoceanic.com; internet www.indoceanic.com; subsidiary of Indoceanic Services; Man. Dir Harold José Thomson.

Société d'Acconage et de Manutention de la Réunionnaise (SAMR): 3 ave Théodore Drouhet, Z.A.C. 2000, BP 40, 97821 Le Port Cédex; tel. 262-55-17-55; fax 262-55-17-62; stevedoring; Pres. Dominique Lafont; Man. Michel Antonelli.

Société de Manutention et de Consignation Maritime (SOMACOM): 1 rue Evariste de Parny, BP 2007, 97420 Le Port; tel. 262-42-60-00; fax 262-42-60-10; stevedoring and shipping agents; Gen. Man. Daniel Rigat.

Société Réunionnaise de Services Maritimes (SRSM): 3 ave Théodore Drouhet, Z.A.C. 2000, BP 2006, 97822 Le Port Cédex; tel. 262-55-17-55; fax 262-55-17-62; e-mail n.hoarau@dri-reunion.com; freight only; Man. Michel Antonelli.

CIVIL AVIATION

Réunion's international airport, Roland Garros-Gillot, is situated 8 km from Saint-Denis. A programme to develop the airport was completed in 1994, and in 1997 work commenced on the extension of its terminal, at a cost of some 175m. French francs. The Pierrefonds airfield, 5 km from Saint-Pierre, commenced operating as an international airport in December 1998 following its development at an estimated cost of nearly 50m. French francs. Air France, Corsair and Air Austral operate international services.

Air Austral: 4 rue de Nice, 97400 Saint-Denis; tel. 262-90-90-91; fax 262-29-28-95; e-mail reservation@air-austral.com; internet www.airaustral.com; f. 1975; subsidiary of Air France; Dir-Gen. Gérard Etheve.

Tourism

Réunion's attractions include spectacular scenery and a pleasant climate. In January 2003 the island had some 2,910 hotel rooms. In 2006 some 279,000 tourists visited Réunion. Receipts from tourism in that year were US $224.8m.

Comité du Tourisme de la Réunion (CTR): pl. du 20 décembre 1848, BP 615, 97472 Saint-Denis Cédex; tel. 262-21-00-41; fax 262-21-00-21; e-mail ctr@la-reunion-tourisme.com; internet www.la-reunion-tourisme.com; Pres. Jocelyne Lauret.

Délégation Régionale au Commerce, à l'Artisanat et au Tourisme: Préfecture de la Réunion, 97400 Saint-Denis; tel. 262-40-77-58; fax 262-50-77-15; Dir Philippe Jean Leglise.

Office du Tourisme Intercommunal du Nord: 27 rue Amiral Lacaze, 97400 Saint-Denis; tel. 262-41-83-00; fax 262-21-37-76; e-mail otinord@wanadoo.fr; Pres. Jean-Marie Dupuis.

Defence

Réunion is the headquarters of French military forces in the Indian Ocean and French Southern and Antarctic Territories. As assessed at March 2006, there were 1,100 French troops stationed on Réunion and Mayotte, including a gendarmerie.

Education

Education is modelled on the French system, and is compulsory for 10 years between the ages of six and 16 years. Primary education begins at six years of age and lasts for five years. Secondary education, which begins at 11 years of age, lasts for up to seven years, comprising a first cycle of four years and a second of three years. For the academic year 2004/05 there were 45,457 pupils enrolled at pre-primary schools, 75,569 at primary schools, and 102,575 at secondary schools. There is a university, with several faculties, providing higher education in law, economics, politics, and French language and literature, and a teacher-training college. In 2004/05 some 10,569 students were enrolled at the university.

Bibliography

Bunge, F. M. (Ed.). *Indian Ocean: Five Island Countries*. Washington, DC, American University, 1983.

Cohen, P. *Le cari partagé: Anthropologie de l'alimentation à l'île de la Réunion*. Paris, Karthala, 2000.

Cornu, H. *Paris et Bourbon, La politique française dans l'Océan indien*. Paris, Académie des Sciences d'Outre-mer, 1984.

Defos du Rau, J. *L'île de la Réunion. Etude de géographie humaine*. Bordeaux, Institut de Géographie, 1960.

Delval, R. *Musulmans français d'origine indienne: Réunion, France métropolitaine, anciens établissements français de l'Inde*. Paris, CHEAM, 1987.

Dupont, G. *Saint-Denis de la Réunion: ville tropicale en mutation*. Paris, L'Harmattan, 1990.

Girardin, M. *Bibliographie de l'île de la Réunion, 1973–1992*. Aix en Provence, Presses Universitaires d'Aix-Marseille, 1994.

Ho, H. Q. *Contribution à l'histoire économique de l'île de la Réunion (1642-1848)*. Paris, L'Harmattan, 2000.

Leguen, M. *Histoire de l'île de la Réunion*. Paris, L'Harmattan, 1979.

Martinez, E. *Le Département français de La Réunion et la coopération internationale dans l'Océan Indien*. Paris, L'Harmattan, 1988.

Maestri, E. *Les îles du sud-ouest de l'Océan Indien et la France de 1815 à nos jours*. Paris, L'Harmattan, 1994.

Paillat-Jarousseau, H. *Une terre pour cultiver et habiter: anthropologie d'une localité de l'île de la Réunion*. Paris, L'Harmattan, 2001.

Payet, J. V. *Histoire de l'esclavage à l'île Bourbon (Réunion)*. Paris, L'Harmattan, 2000.

Prudhomme, C. *Histoire religieuse de la Réunion*. Paris, Editions Karthala, 1984.

Toussaint, A. *Histoire des Iles Mascareignes*. Paris, Berger-Levrault, 1972.

Wong-Hee-Kam, E. *La diaspora chinoise aux Mascareignes: le cas de la Réunion*. Paris, L'Harmattan, 1996.

RWANDA

Physical and Social Geography

PIERRE GOUROU

The Rwandan Republic, like the neighbouring Republic of Burundi, is distinctive both for the small size of its territory and for the density of its population. Covering an area of 26,338 sq km (10,169 sq miles), Rwanda had an enumerated population of 7,142,755 at the census of 15 August 1991, with a density of 271 inhabitants per sq km. However, political and ethnic violence during 1994 was estimated to have resulted in the death or external displacement of 35%–40% of the total population. Prior to these events, the population had been composed of Hutu (about 85%), Tutsi (about 14%) and Twa (1%). According to the preliminary results of a national census, published in December 2002, Rwanda's population had recovered to about 8.2m., indicating an increase of 12% since the 1991 census. At mid-2006, according to UN estimates, the population totalled 9,464,000, with a density of 359.3 inhabitants per sq km. The official languages are French, English (which is widely spoken by the Tutsi minority) and Kinyarwanda, a Bantu language with close similarities to Kirundi, the main vernacular language of Burundi.

It seems, at first sight, strange that Rwanda has not been absorbed into a wider political entity. Admittedly, the Rwandan nation has long been united by language and custom and was part of a state that won the respect of the east African slave-traders. However, other ethnic groups, such as the Kongo, Luba, Luo and Zande, which were well established in small territorial areas, have not been able to develop into national states. That Rwanda has been able to achieve this is partly the result of developments during the colonial period. While part of German East Africa, Rwanda (then known, with Burundi, as Ruanda-Urundi) was regarded as a peripheral colonial territory of little economic interest. After the First World War it was entrusted to Belgium under a mandate from the League of Nations. The territory was administered jointly with the Belgian Congo, but was not absorbed into the larger state. The historic separateness and national traditions of both Rwanda and Burundi have prevented their amalgamation, although both countries participate, with the Democratic Republic of the Congo, in the Economic Community of the Great Lakes Countries.

Although the land supports a high population density, physical conditions are not very favourable. Rwanda's land mass is very rugged and fragmented. It is part of a Pre-Cambrian shelf from which, through erosion, the harder rocks have obtruded, leaving the softer ones submerged. Thus very ancient folds have been raised and a relief surface carved out with steep gradients covered with a soil poor in quality because of its fineness and fragility. Rwanda's physiognomy therefore consists of a series of sharply defined hills, with steep slopes and flat ridges, which are intersected by deep valleys, the bottoms of which are often formed by marshy plains. The north is dominated by the lofty and powerful chain of volcanoes, the Virunga, whose highest peak is Karisimbi (4,519 m) and whose lava, having scarcely cooled down, has not yet produced cultivable soil.

The climate is tropical, although tempered by altitude, with a daily temperature range of as much as 14°C. Kigali, the capital (779,000 inhabitants at mid-2005, according to UN estimates), has an average temperature of 19°C and 1,000 mm of rain. Altitude is a factor that modifies the temperature (and prevents sleeping sickness above about 900 m), but such a factor is of debatable value for agriculture. Average annual rainfall (785 mm) is only barely sufficient for agricultural purposes, but two wet and two relatively dry seasons are experienced, making two harvests possible.

Recent History

THOMAS OFCANSKY

Revised by PHIL CLARK and ZACHARY KAUFMAN

HUTU ASCENDANCY

Rwanda was not an artificial creation of colonial rule. When Rwanda and Burundi were absorbed by German East Africa in 1899, they had been established kingdoms for several centuries. In 1916, during the First World War, Belgian forces occupied the region. From 1920 Rwanda formed part of Ruanda-Urundi, administered by Belgium under a League of Nations mandate and later as a UN Trust Territory. In 1961 it was decided by referendum to replace Rwanda's monarchy with a republic, to which full independence was granted on 1 July 1962. Political life in the new Republic was dominated by its first President, Grégoire Kayibanda, and the governing party, the Mouvement démocratique républicain (MDR), also known as the Parti de l'émancipation du peuple Hutu (Parmehutu). Tensions between the majority Hutu (comprising about 85% of the population) and their former Belgian-imposed overlords, the Tutsi (14%), which had sporadically erupted into serious violence during 1963–65, recurred in late 1972 and early 1973. These tensions were the seeds of the 1994 genocide, perpetrated by Hutu, of between 800,000 and 1m. people, mostly Tutsi but also some moderate Hutu.

In July 1973 the Minister of Defence and head of the National Guard, Maj.-Gen. Juvénal Habyarimana, deposed Kayibanda, proclaimed a Second Republic and established a military Government under his leadership. In 1975 a new ruling party, the Mouvement révolutionnaire national pour le développement (MRND), was formed. A referendum in December 1978 approved a new Constitution, aimed at returning the country to civil government in accordance with an undertaking by Habyarimana in 1973 to end the military regime within five years. An unsuccessful coup attempt took place in April 1980, and elections to the legislature, the Conseil national du développement (CND), were held in December 1981 and in December 1983; also in December 1983 Habyarimana was re-elected President.

From 1982 cross-border refugee problems began to affect Rwanda's relations with Uganda, and would later contribute to violence within Rwanda. In October Rwanda closed its border with Uganda after an influx of 45,000 refugees, most of whom were Rwandan exiles fleeing Ugandan persecution. A further 32,000 refugees gathered in camps on the Ugandan side of the border. In March 1983 Rwanda agreed to resettle more than 30,000 refugees, but Ugandan persecution of ethnic Rwandans continued, and in December thousands crossed into Tanzania. In November 1985 it was reported that 30,000 ethnic Rwandan refugees had been repatriated to Uganda. In 1986 the office of the UN High Commissioner for Refugees (UNHCR) reported that there were about 110,000 registered Rwandan refugees living in Uganda, while an even greater number of refugees were believed to have settled in Uganda without registering with UNHCR. In July the central committee of the MRND issued a declaration that Rwanda would not allow the return of large numbers of refugees, since the country's economy was incapable of sustaining such an influx. In the same year, President Yoweri Museveni of Uganda announced that Rwandans who had been resident in Uganda for more than 10 years would automatically be entitled to Ugandan citizenship. A resurgence of ethnic tensions in Burundi led to the flight, in August 1988, of an estimated 80,000 refugees, mainly Hutu, into Rwanda. With assistance from the international community, the Rwandan authorities were able to address their needs. By June 1989 all but approximately 1,000 of the refugees had been repatriated to Burundi.

During the December 1988 presidential election, Habyarimana, as sole candidate, reportedly secured 99.98% of the votes cast. Elections for the CND were held in the same month, and the Government was reorganized in January 1989. During 1989 economic conditions deteriorated sharply, and the introduction of an economic austerity programme in December increased public discontent. In early July 1990 Habyarimana conceded that political reform was necessary and announced that a national commission would be appointed to investigate the matter. The Commission nationale de synthèse (CNS) was duly established in September with a mandate to make recommendations for political renewal. However, these measures did little to alleviate the acute sense of political crisis.

REBEL INVASION AND POLITICAL UPHEAVAL

On 1 October 1990 an estimated force of 10,000 militia, representing the exiled, Tutsi-dominated Front patriotique rwandais (FPR), crossed the border from Uganda into north-eastern Rwanda, where they swiftly occupied several towns. The troops were primarily Tutsi refugees, but they also included significant numbers of disaffected elements of Uganda's ruling National Resistance Army (NRA, now the Uganda People's Defence Force—UPDF). The invasion force was led by Maj.-Gen. Fred Rwigyema, a former Ugandan Deputy Minister of Defence. In response to a request for assistance from Habyarimana, Belgian and French paratroopers were dispatched to the capital, Kigali, to protect foreign nationals and to secure evacuation routes. A contingent of troops sent by Zaire (now the Democratic Republic of the Congo—DRC) assisted the small Rwandan army in turning back the FPR some 70 km from Kigali.

The conflict continued throughout 1991 and into 1992, as the FPR made frequent guerrilla forays into Rwanda. Both sides of the conflict reported thousands of casualties, and many civilians resident in the border regions were killed and as many as 100,000 displaced. Increasing ethnic tensions, exacerbated by the war, resulted in a series of unprovoked attacks upon Tutsi civilians and prompted accusations of government involvement, particularly in the Bugesera region of southern Rwanda. In late July 1992 it was reported that the warring parties had negotiated a cease-fire, providing for the establishment of a 'neutral area'.

The FPR invasion accelerated the political reform process, initiated before the conflict. Following widespread public discussion of proposals put forward by the CNS in December 1990, the Commission published its report and a draft constitution in March 1991. In June the new Constitution, providing for the legalization of political parties, entered into force. Full freedom of the press was declared, leading to the establishment of a number of magazines and newspapers critical of government policy. In April 1992, following a series of unsuccessful attempts to negotiate a transitional government, the composition of a broad-based coalition Government, incorporating four opposition parties (the revived MDR, the Parti social-démocrate—PSD, the Parti libéral—PL and the Parti démocratique chrétien—PDC), together with the Mouvement républicain national pour la démocratie et le développement (MRNDD—the new party name adopted by the MRND in April 1991), was announced. The new administration was to be headed by Dismas Nsengiyaremye of the MDR as Prime Minister, a post established by the Constitution. Multi-party elections for municipalities, the legislature and the presidency were to take place before April 1993. In late April 1992, in compliance with a new constitutional prohibition of the armed forces' participation in the political process, Habyarimana relinquished his military title and functions.

The coalition Government and FPR representatives initiated a new dialogue in May 1992 and conducted formal discussions in Paris, France during June. Further negotiations, in Arusha, Tanzania, in July resulted in an agreement on the implementation of a new cease-fire, to take effect from the end of that month, and the creation of a military observer group (GOM) sponsored by the Organization of African Unity (OAU, now the African Union—AU), to comprise representatives from both sides, together with officers drawn from the armed forces of Nigeria, Senegal, Zimbabwe and Mali. However, subsequent negotiations in Tanzania, during August, September and October, failed to resolve outstanding problems concerning the creation of a 'neutral zone' between the Rwandan armed forces and the FPR (to be enforced by the GOM), the incorporation of the FPR in a Rwandan national force, the repatriation of refugees, and the demands of the FPR for full participation in the transitional Government and legislature.

A resurgence in violence followed the breakdown of negotiations in early February 1993, resulting in the deaths of hundreds on both sides. An estimated 1m. civilians fled southwards and to neighbouring Uganda and Tanzania in order to escape the fighting, as the FPR advanced as far as Ruhengeri and seemed, for a time, on the verge of capturing Kigali. Belgium, France and the USA denounced the actions of the FPR. French reinforcements were dispatched to join a small French military contingent, stationed in Kigali since October 1990, in order to protect French nationals. Meanwhile, the Commander of the GOM declared that the group possessed inadequate manpower and resources to contain the advance of the FPR and requested the deployment of an additional 400 OAU troops. In late February 1993 the Government accepted FPR terms for a cease-fire in return for an end to attacks against FPR positions and on Tutsi communities, and the withdrawal of foreign troops. Although fighting continued with varying intensity, new peace negotiations were convened in March in Arusha. Later that month France began to withdraw its troops.

Negotiations conducted during April 1993 failed to produce a solution to the crucial issue of the structure of future unitary Rwandan armed forces. In the same month the five participating parties in the ruling coalition agreed to a three-month extension of the Government's mandate in order to facilitate a peace accord. Further talks during May between the Government and the FPR in the northern town of Kinihira produced significant progress, including an agreed schedule for the demobilization of the 19,000-strong security forces. In June an agreed protocol outlined the repatriation of all Rwandan refugees resident in Uganda, Tanzania and Zaire, including recommendations that compensation be made to those forced into exile more than 12 years before. In late June the UN Security Council approved the creation of the UN Observer Mission Uganda-Rwanda (UNOMUR), to be deployed on the Ugandan side of the border for an initial period of six months, in order to block FPR military supply lines.

In July 1993, with improved prospects for a prompt resolution of the conflict, Habyarimana met representatives of the five political parties represented in the Government and sought a further extension to the mandate of the coalition Government. However, the Prime Minister's insistence that the FPR should be represented in any newly mandated government exacerbated existing divisions within the MDR, prompting Habyarimana to conclude the agreement with a conciliatory group of MDR dissidents, including the Minister of Education, Agathe Uwilingiyimana, who was elected as Rwanda's first female Prime Minister on 17 July. The Council of Ministers was reorganized to replace the disaffected MDR members.

On 4 August 1993 Habyarimana and Col Alex Kanyarengwe of the FPR formally signed a peace accord in Arusha. A new transitional Government, to be headed by a mutually approved Prime Minister (later named as the MDR moderate faction leader, Faustin Twagiramungu), was to be installed by 10 September. A multi-party general election was to take place after a 22-month period, during which the FPR would participate in a transitional government and national assembly. In mid-August the Government revoked the curfew in Kigali and removed military road-blocks from all but three northern prefectures. By the end of the month, however, the Prime Minister was forced to make a national appeal for calm, following reports of renewed outbreaks of violence in Kigali and Butare. The Government and the FPR attributed the failure to establish a transitional government and legislature by 10 September to the increasingly fragile security situation, and both sides urged the prompt dispatch of a neutral UN force to facilitate the implementation of the Arusha Accord. Meanwhile, relations between the Government and the FPR deteriorated, following the rebels' assertion that the Government had violated the Accord by attempting to dismantle and reorganize those departments assigned to the FPR under the terms of the agreement.

UN INTERVENTION

On 5 October 1993, the UN Security Council adopted Resolution 872, endorsing the recommendation of the UN Secretary-General for the creation of the UN Assistance Mission for Rwanda (UNAMIR), under the leadership of Canadian Lt-Gen. Roméo Dallaire, to be deployed in Rwanda for an initial period of six months, with a mandate to monitor observance of the cease-fire, to contribute to the security of the capital and to facilitate the repatriation of refugees. UNAMIR, incorporating UNOMUR and GOM, was formally inaugurated on 1 November, and comprised some 2,500 personnel when fully operational. In mid-December the UN declared that it was satisfied that conditions had been sufficiently fulfilled to allow for the introduction of the transitional institutions by the end of the month.

In late December 1993 UNAMIR officials escorted a 600-strong FPR battalion to Kigali (as detailed in the Arusha Accord) to ensure the safety of FPR representatives selected to participate in the transitional Government and legislature. On 5 January 1994, Juvénal Habyarimana was invested as President of a transitional Government, for a 22-month period, under the terms of the Arusha Accord. (Habyarimana's previous term of office, in accordance with the Constitution, had expired on 19 December 1993.) While government spokesmen identified the need to resolve internal differences within the MDR and the PL as the crucial expedient for the implementation of the new Government and legislature, a joint statement, issued by the PSD, the PDC and factions of the MDR and the PL, accused the President of having abused the terms of the Arusha Accord by interfering in the selection of prospective ministers and deputies. The FPR repeated this charge in late February 1994, when it rejected a list of proposed future gubernatorial and legislative representatives. During January and February Dallaire reported that the Habyarimana Government was increasing anti-Tutsi propaganda across Rwanda, stockpiling weapons and training youth militias. Dallaire insisted that anti-Tutsi sentiment was rapidly increasing and that violence against Tutsi was likely in the coming months. In March the Prime Minister-designate, Faustin Twagiramungu, declared that he had fulfilled his consultative role as established by the Arusha Accord, and announced the composition of a transitional Government, in an attempt to accelerate the installation of the transitional bodies. However, political opposition to the proposed Council of Ministers persisted, and Habyarimana insisted that the list of proposed legislative deputies, newly presented by Uwilingiyimana, should be modified to include representatives of additional political parties, including the ethnically divisive Coalition pour la défense de la république (CDR, whose participation was strongly opposed by the FPR, owing to its alleged failure to accept the code of ethics for the behaviour of political parties and its policies advocating ethnic discrimination), prompting a further postponement of the formation of a transitional administration.

In April 1994 the UN Security Council (which in February had warned that the UN presence in Rwanda might be withdrawn in the absence of swift progress in the implementation of the Arusha Accord) agreed to extend UNAMIR's mandate for four months, pending a review of progress made in implementing the accord, to be conducted after six weeks.

COLLAPSE OF CIVIL ORDER AND GENOCIDE

On 6 April 1994 the presidential aircraft, returning from a regional summit in Dar es Salaam, Tanzania, was fired upon over Kigali, and exploded on landing, killing all 10 passengers, including Habyarimana, the President of Burundi, Cyprien Ntaryamira, two Burundian cabinet ministers, and the Chief of Staff of the Rwandan armed forces. In Kigali, although it was unclear who had been responsible for the attack on the aircraft, the presidential guard obstructed UNAMIR officials attempting to investigate the crash site and immediately initiated a brutal campaign of retributive violence against political opponents of the late President. As politicians and civilians fled the capital, the brutality of the political assassinations was compounded by attacks on the clergy, UNAMIR personnel and Tutsi civilians. Hutu civilians were forced to murder their Tutsi neighbours. The mobilization of the Interahamwe, or unofficial militias (allegedly affiliated to the MRNDD and the CDR), apparently committed to the massacre of government opponents and Tutsi civilians, was encouraged by the presidential guard (with support from some factions of the armed forces) and by inflammatory broadcasts from Radio-Télévision Libre des Mille Collines in Kigali. The Prime Minister, the President of the Constitutional Court, the Ministers of Labour and Social Affairs and of Information, and the Chairman of the PSD were among the prominent politicians assassinated, or declared missing and presumed dead, within hours of Habyarimana's death.

On 8 April 1994 the Speaker of the CND, Dr Théodore Sindikubwabo, announced that he had assumed the office of interim President of the Republic, in accordance with the provisions of the 1991 Constitution. The five remaining participating political parties and factions of the Government selected a new Prime Minister, Jean Kambanda, and a new Council of Ministers (largely comprising MRNDD members). The FPR immediately challenged the legality of the new administration, claiming that the CND's constitutional right of succession to the presidency had been superseded by Habyarimana's inauguration as President in January under the terms of the Arusha Accord. The legitimacy of the new Government, which had fled to the town of Gitarama to escape escalating violence in the capital, was subsequently rejected by factions of the PL and MDR (led by Faustin Twagiramungu), and by the PDC and the PSD, which in May announced that they had allied themselves as the Democratic Forces for Change.

FPR Offensives and the Refugee Crisis

In mid-April 1994 the FPR resumed military operations from its northern stronghold, with the stated intention of relieving its beleaguered battalion in Kigali, restoring order to the capital and halting the massacre of Tutsi civilians. Grenade attacks and mortar fire intensified in the capital, prompting the UN to mediate a fragile 60-hour cease-fire, during which small evacuation forces from several countries escorted foreign nationals out of Rwanda. Belgium's UNAMIR contingent of more than 400 troops was also withdrawn, after Hutu militiamen killed 10 Belgian peace-keepers sent to protect Prime Minister Uwilingiyimana, who was also murdered.

As the political violence incited by the presidential guard and the Interahamwe gathered momentum, the militia's identification of all Tutsi as political opponents of the state promoted ethnic polarization, resulting in a pogrom against Tutsi. Reports of mass Tutsi killings and unprovoked attacks on fleeing Tutsi refugees, and on those seeking refuge in schools, hospitals and churches, elicited unqualified international condemnation and outrage, and promises of financial and logistical aid for an estimated 2m. displaced Rwandans (some 250,000 had fled across the border to Tanzania in a 24-hour period in late April 1994), many of whom were killed by famine and disease in makeshift camps. By late May attempts to assess the full scale of the humanitarian catastrophe in Rwanda were complicated by unverified reports that the FPR (which claimed to control more than one-half of the country) was carrying out retaliatory atrocities against Hutu militias and civilians. Unofficial estimates indicated that between 200,000 and 500,000 Rwandans had been killed since early April.

On 21 April 1994, in the context of intensifying violence in Kigali, and the refusal of the Rwandan armed forces to agree to the neutral policing of the capital's airport (subsequently secured by the FPR), the UN Security Council resolved to reduce its force in Rwanda to 270 personnel, a move that attracted criticism from the Rwandan Government, the FPR and international relief organizations. However, on 16 May, following intense international pressure and the disclosure of the vast scale of the humanitarian crisis in the region, the UN Security Council approved Resolution 917, providing for the eventual deployment of some 5,500 UN troops with a revised mandate, including the policing of Kigali's airport and the protection of refugees in designated 'safe areas'. In late May 1994 the UN Secretary-General criticized the failure of the UN member nations to respond to his invitation to participate in the enlarged force (only Ghana, Ethiopia and Senegal had agreed to provide small contingents). Further UN-sponsored attempts to negotiate a cease-fire failed in late May and early June, and the FPR made significant territorial gains in southern Rwanda, forcing the Government to flee Gitarama and seek refuge in the western town of Kibuye.

In early June 1994 the UN Security Council adopted Resolution 925, whereby the mandate of the revised UN mission in Rwanda (UNAMIR II) was extended until December. However, the UN Secretary-General continued to encounter considerable difficulty in securing equipment and armaments requested by the African countries that had agreed to participate. By mid-June confirmed reports of retributive murders committed by FPR members (including the massacres, in two separate incidents in early June, of 22 clergymen, among them the Roman Catholic archbishop of Kigali) and the collapse of a fragile truce, negotiated at a summit meeting of the OAU, prompted the French Government to announce its willingness to lead an armed police action, endorsed by the UN, in Rwanda. Although France insisted that its military presence (expected to total 2,000 troops) would maintain strict political neutrality and operate, from the border regions, in a purely humanitarian capacity pending the arrival of a multinational UN force, the FPR was vehemently opposed to its deployment, citing the French administration's maintenance of high-level contacts with representatives of the self-proclaimed Rwandan Government as an indication of political bias. On 23 June the first contingent of 150 French marine commandos launched 'Operation Turquoise', entering the western town of Cyangugu, in preparation for a large-scale operation to protect refugees in the area. By mid-July the French initiative had successfully relieved several beleaguered Tutsi communities and had established a temporary 'safe haven' for the displaced population in the south-west, through which a mass exodus of Hutu refugees began to flow, encouraged by reports (disseminated by supporters of the defeated interim Government) that the advancing FPR forces were seeking violent retribution against Hutu. An estimated 1m. Rwandans sought refuge in the border town of Goma, in Zaire, while a similar number attempted to cross the border elsewhere in the south-west. The FPR had swiftly secured all major cities and strategic territorial positions, but had halted its advance several kilometres from the boundaries of the French-controlled neutral zone, requesting the apprehension and return for trial of those responsible for the recent atrocities. (At the end of June the first report of the UN Special Rapporteur on human rights in Rwanda—appointed in May—confirmed that at least 500,000 Rwandans had been killed since April, and urged the establishment of an international tribunal to investigate allegations of genocide; in early July the UN announced the creation of a commission of inquiry for this purpose.)

THE FPR TAKES POWER

On 19 July 1994 Pasteur Bizimungu, a Hutu, was inaugurated as President for a five-year term. In November a multi-party protocol of understanding was concluded, providing for a number of amendments to the terms of the August 1993 Arusha Accord, relating to the establishment of a transitional legislature. The most notable of the new provisions was the exclusion from the legislative process of members of those parties implicated in alleged acts of genocide during 1994. A 70-member National Transitional Assembly was installed on 12 December. On 5 May 1995 the new legislature announced its adoption of a new Constitution based on selected articles of the 1991 Constitution, the terms of the August 1993 Arusha Accord, the FPR's victory declaration of July 1994 and the November 1994 multi-party protocol of understanding.

In July 1999 Rwanda announced the end of the five-year transitional Government and its replacement by a four-year national unity Government. The new transitional period permitted the Government to complete the national reconciliation process, restore internal security, improve the economy and social services and establish a democratic system. Critics rejected the unilateral extension of political power and claimed that the Government's action revealed its undemocratic and dictatorial nature.

The increasingly stringent policies of the Government, which by this stage was dominated by supporters of Vice-President and FPR Chairman, Paul Kagame, prompted an increasing number of prominent figures to flee Rwanda. A notable case involved the popular Speaker of the Transitional National Assembly, Kabuye Sebarenzi, who had campaigned for good governance and official accountability. After moving from the FPR to the PL and drawing attention to government ministers accused of corruption, Sebarenzi's political fortunes gradually waned. In December 1999 the PL President, Pio Mugabo, postponed the vote for a new party President, reportedly on orders from Kagame. Sebarenzi had been expected to be elected to this post, which would have strengthened his chances of winning the election for the national presidency. In early January 2000 the Transitional National Assembly forced Sebarenzi's resignation on apparently fabricated charges of official misconduct, organizing genocide survivors against the Government and supporting the 'army of the king'. Later that month Sebarenzi, who feared that the Government would assassinate him, fled to Uganda, then to Europe, and finally to the USA. On 23 March President Pasteur Bizimungu resigned and subsequently relocated to the USA. Kagame served as provisional President until 17 April, when members of the legislature and the Government elected him, by 81 votes to five, as the first Tutsi President since Rwanda gained independence from Belgium in 1962. Kagame, who was to serve for the remainder of the transition period, until legislative and presidential elections in 2003, pledged to facilitate political decentralization, expedite the trials of some 125,000 genocide suspects in prison and conduct local government elections.

Corruption pervaded all levels of government. In September 1999 a legislative commission of inquiry implicated several government ministers in cases of corruption, some of whom subsequently resigned. A further parliamentary inquiry discovered that, when he was Minister of Education in 1995, the Prime Minister, Pierre-Célestin Rwigyema, had been implicated in the diversion of funds from a World Bank education programme almost exclusively to his home town of Gitarama. Rwigyema survived a motion of censure in the Transitional National Assembly in December 1999, but he resigned, in February 2000. In March 2004 the Auditor-General, Gervais Ntaganda, informed the legislature that some 60 public institutions reported that tenders valued at US $5.8m. for 2002 had not been processed by the national tender board, as scheduled. Moreover, $7m. of government spending was unaccounted for during that year and, of 44 cases of alleged embezzlement of government funds, only nine were referred for trial and only two cases had been heard. However, the authorities did dismiss 139 police-officers in March 2004 for a series of crimes, including bribery and corruption, although allegations of corruption among senior government officials remained uninvestigated.

On 29 June 2000 the Ministry of Local Government and Social Affairs introduced legislation on decentralization, which aimed to make the district *(akarere)* the principal organ of local government. Apart from providing judicial services, the *akarere* was to assume responsibility for agriculture, extension, forestry and veterinary services. Other *akarere* duties included the stimulation of local trade and small-scale industries, education and teacher training, and the supervision of health, water, fire brigades, co-operatives, roads, land titles and tourism services. A legislative council and an executive committee, aided by an executive secretary, were to govern the *akarere*. This initiative was the most ambitious political scheme ever undertaken in post-independence Rwanda. Its success or failure depended on the availability of donor aid, the authorities' ability to collect taxes and the central Government's willingness to transfer adequate funds and power to the *akarere*. Many donors insisted that, in order to receive foreign aid, Rwanda would have to shed its authoritarian culture and near-total concentration of power in the central Government.

On 24 July 2000 former Prime Minister Rwigyema, the leader of the MDR, fled from Rwanda and sought political asylum in the USA, deeply embarrassing the Kagame regime. The Hutu-dominated MDR responded to Rwigyema's self-imposed exile by removing him from the presidency of the movement and denouncing him after he issued a statement condemning Kagame as a dictator. The MDR elected Célestin Kabanda, who enjoyed considerable support among Rwanda's Hutu population, as its interim President. However, in February 2001 an MDR committee announced that it had removed Kabanda, owing to repeated allegations that he had participated in the 1994 genocide. In an about-face, in October the MDR's political bureau confirmed Kabanda's election as the party President. Désiré Nyandwi, the influential Minister for Local Government and Social Affairs, endorsed the bureau's decision.

In October 2000 Rwanda convened a Summit on Reconciliation and Unity. However, this measure failed to convince opponents of the Government that Kagame was serious about national reconciliation. As a result, political opposition to the Kagame regime continued, particularly in Rwandan expatriate communities. In May 2001 Alexandre Kimenyi, a former senior FPR member who had relocated to the USA, announced the formation of an opposition party, the Alliance rwandaise pour la renaissance de la nation (ARENA). He maintained that membership of the organization was open to all Rwandans and denied allegations that it was pro-monarchy. Despite its increasing popularity among some expatriates, ARENA was unable to form a credible opposition to Kagame's Government.

ELECTIONS AND THE END OF THE TRANSITIONAL PERIOD

On 6 March 2001 nation-wide elections for local officials were conducted in Rwanda. A high proportion of eligible voters participated in the polls. President Kagame claimed that the elections represented a significant measure towards democratization. However, Rwandan government statistics indicated that about 45% of the districts were contested by only one candidate. Moreover, various international human rights organizations condemned the elections as unfair; according to the US-based human rights organization Human Rights Watch, irregularities marred the elections from the outset. Many voters also claimed they participated in the polls because they feared receiving fines or other penalties if they did not. In addition, local and international election monitors only received the requisite documentation late on the day before the elections, making it impossible to observe pre-election activities, such as registration, and difficult to reach distant polling stations.

On 26 May 2003 some 93.4% of the electorate approved a new Constitution. The European Union (EU) Electoral Observation Mission in Rwanda subsequently reported that the referendum had been conducted in 'satisfactory conditions'. The Constitution mandated a bicameral legislature, which would comprise an 80-member Chamber of Deputies and a 26-member Senate. Also that month the Government endorsed a parliamentary report that urged the banning of the MDR for propagating a 'divisive' ideology and the prosecution of 47 of its members and supporters for 'ethnic extremism'. Amnesty International accused the Rwandan authorities of orchestrated suppression of political opposition, and Human Rights Watch maintained that the Government was seeking to eliminate any opposition prior to Rwanda's presidential and parliamentary elections, due to be held in August and September, respectively. On 4 June the new Constitution entered into effect. However, the International Federation for Human Rights claimed that the Constitution would inhibit multi-party pluralism and freedom of expression and recommended that the Rwandan authorities guarantee such rights. Meanwhile, former Prime Minister Twagiramungu announced that he would contest the presidential election against Kagame. As most of his supporters were members of the political opposition in exile, prospects of his winning the election were minimal.

On 25 August 2003 Kagame won the first election to take place in Rwanda since the 1994 genocide, with 95.1% of the valid votes cast. Twagiramungu won 3.6% of the votes, and the only other opposition candidate, Jean-Népomuscène Nayinzira, 1.3%. Twagiramungu subsequently accused the authorities of electoral malpractice, and submitted a challenge against the official results to the Supreme Court. EU monitors confirmed that irregularities had occurred, although a South African observer mission declared that the poll had been 'free and fair'. In early September the Supreme Court rejected Twagiramungu's appeal. Kagame was officially inaugurated on 12 September. On 30 September 218 candidates (representatives submitted by eight political parties and 19 independents) contested legislative elections for 53 of 80 seats in the Chamber of Deputies. Official figures indicated that some 96% of registered voters participated in the election, although independent observers maintained that the number of voters was less than the presidential poll. The FPR won 33 seats; the PSD secured seven seats, the PL six, the Parti démocrate centriste three, the Parti démocrate idéal two, the Parti socialiste rwandais one and the Union démocratique du peuple rwandais one. The new Constitution reserved the remaining seats in the Chamber of Deputies for 'special groups' (24 women's representatives, two youth representatives and one representative of disabled persons). On 2 October some 20,000 representatives of provincial women's groups contested the 24 seats reserved for women, while local government officials and academic representatives contested 14 of the 26 Senate seats. On 9 October President Kagame appointed eight senators, as authorized by the Constitution. (A further four senators were nominated by a regulatory body, the Parties' Forum.) The EU assessed, however, that there were serious irregularities in the presidential and legislative elections.

In 2004–05 the Kagame administration accused several government officials of promoting the 'ideology of genocide'. In July 2004, the Chamber of Deputies published a report accusing several local civil society organizations, including the Ligue rwandaise pour la promotion et la défense des droits de l'homme (LIPRODHOR), one of Rwanda's largest human rights organizations, of supporting such an ideology. The report also rebuked some international non-governmental organizations (NGOs), such as CARE International and Trócaire Overseas Development Agency, for supporting these groups. The EU condemned the findings, and the Government rejected the legislature's recommendation for a ban on all suspect organizations. Nevertheless, eight LIPRODHOR officials fled to Uganda, claiming they were in danger from government agents. In September LIPRODHOR's general assembly, having been obliged by the Government to conduct an internal investigation, issued a statement denouncing some of its members for 'genocide-related acts' and seeking forgiveness from the Government and the Rwandan people. In early January 2005 the legislature renewed its accusations that LIPRODHOR was propagating a genocidal ideology and ethnic divisionism. Several senior LIPRODHOR members then fled Rwanda, while at a general meeting the organization issued an apology to the people of Rwanda. The Government again declined to close LIPRODHOR as the legislature's report had recommended, although it ordered the organization to conduct an internal investigation to expose 'divisionists'. The subsequent chaos forced LIPRODHOR to cease operations. On 28 September 2004 President Kagame dismissed three ministers (responsible for the interior, health, and youth, culture and sports) for poor performance, and accused many other officials of divisionist activities.

POST-GENOCIDE CRIMINAL JUSTICE

On 8 November 1994, the UN Security Council adopted Resolution 955, establishing the UN International Criminal Tribunal for Rwanda (ICTR) to be convened in Arusha, Tanzania, despite the negative vote of Rwanda, which held a non-permanent seat on the Council in 1994. The ICTR began formal proceedings in late November 1995 and the first trial began in January 1997. By 16 August 2006, the date of the ICTR's most recent annual report, the ICTR had imposed 22 judgments, involving 28 accused. Several of these decisions established important international criminal law precedents concerning the definition of crimes (particularly genocide and rape) and the accountability of perpetrators, regardless of their position.

In February 1996 the Rwandan Prime Minister announced the creation of special courts within the country's existing judicial system. Under these arrangements, Rwanda's Supreme Court Chief Prosecutor began investigations in each of the country's 10 districts, and established three-member judicial panels in each district to consider cases. The panels were to comprise some 250 lay magistrates, who received four months' legal training. Additionally, 320 judicial police inspectors, all of whom had attended a three-month training course, compiled dossiers on those detained for allegedly committing genocide. Newly established assessment commissions reviewed possible detentions on the basis of available evidence.

In mid-August 2004 the ICTR Chief Prosecutor, Hassan Bubacar Jallow, who had been appointed by the UN Security Council on 15 September 2003, visited Rwanda to review the Government's proposal that at least some of those convicted by the ICTR of committing atrocities should serve their sentences in Rwandan prisons. The ICTR had initially opposed this strategy as Rwanda employs the death penalty, while the maximum ICTR sentence is life imprisonment. Kagame suggested a compromise whereby Rwanda would retain the death penalty, but waive it for those convicted by the ICTR. In June 2007 legislation was adopted removing the death penalty from all national statutes. In response, the ICTR commenced proceedings to transfer five un-named suspects from Arusha to the national courts in Kigali, to be followed by further suspects in 2008.

During his 2003 visit to Rwanda, Jallow declined to answer questions about whether the ICTR intended to prosecute anyone from the FPR for crimes against humanity, prompting speculation that prosecution of FPR members would end the Rwandan Government's co-operation with the ICTR. In October 2004 unidentified assailants killed an ICTR prosecution witness in the province of Gikongoro. Many suspected that the incident had been related to the testimony that he had provided at the ICTR trial over genocide charges concerning Col Aloys Simba. In November Jallow revealed that 14 alleged *génocidaires* (perpetrators of the 1994 genocide) had taken refuge in the DRC and accused the Congolese authorities of failing to make any effort to apprehend them. In mid-December the ICTR's Appeals Chamber upheld the convictions of two defendants who had been sentenced in February 2003 to 10 and 25 years' imprisonment, respectively, for their role in the 1994 genocide in the province of Kibuye. In January 2005 Jallow announced that he was ready to proceed with 17 new genocide trials, which would be conducted at the same time as 25 ongoing trials. He also indicated that national courts would conduct some of these trials (for example, in early 2006 the ICTR announced that Norway would become the first non-African state to try a case at the ICTR's request) and that his office had completed investigations into another 16 cases, some of which he claimed concerned alleged FPR atrocities. In mid-2005 the ICTR renewed its demand for prosecutions against members of the FPR for war crimes. The alleged implication of the FPR in shooting down the aircraft of President Habyarimana in 1994 was of particular interest to the Court. In response, Aloys Mutabingwa, Rwanda's ICTR representative, demanded that the ICTR charge French government officials for their role in the events that precipitated the genocide. Despite such declarations, no prosecutions of FPR or French officials have occurred.

The Rwandan national courts, operating concurrently to the ICTR, have also played a major role in prosecuting genocide suspects. This has been a difficult undertaking, in view of the decimation of the Rwandan judiciary by the genocide, and, despite significant reconstruction of the judiciary since then, the system has had difficulties in dealing with the immense number of imprisoned genocide suspects awaiting trial. On 1 August 2003 a court in Gikondo convicted 105 people of genocide, sentencing 73 to life imprisonment and 11 to death. The remainder received custodial terms, ranging from one to 25 years, while the court acquitted 37 suspects. By late 2003 Rwandan courts had convicted approximately 6,500 suspects, of which 600–700 received death sentences. To relieve the pressure on its courts and to facilitate a communal dialogue on the root causes of the genocide as a means to reconciliation, the Rwandan Government instituted the *gacaca* community-based judicial system, based partly on a traditional model of participative justice, to deal with the majority of genocide cases. In October 2000 the Transitional National Assembly adopted legislation providing for the creation of *gacaca* courts; this was approved by the Constitutional Court on 18 January 2001. In October voters elected approximately 260,000 *gacaca* judges, who were to facilitate the community's evidence-gathering process during open-air hearings, to evaluate evidence and to impose judgments on genocide suspects. Suspects who confessed to their crimes early enough were able to benefit from the *gacaca* courts' plea-bargaining structure, which incorporated community service for certain lower-level genocide crimes. The *gacaca* system was deliberately designed to promote reconciliation, involving direct dialogue in the process of trials and employing plea-bargaining and community service as forms of punishment that would reintegrate convicted *génocidaires* into the community. The Government pledged that all court proceedings would be publicized and all court decisions subject to appeal.

On 18 June 2002 the authorities formally inaugurated the *gacaca* system. However, for the first three years of operation, *gacaca* trials involved only the community's recording of basic information related to the events of the genocide, rather than specific evidence related to particular genocide suspects. The community courts, of which 673 commenced operations throughout the country in November, followed by a further 8,258 in March 2003, were designed to expedite the trials of those accused of crimes relating to the 1994 genocide, to reveal the truth about what happened, to end the culture of impunity in Rwanda, and to promote national reconciliation through communal dialogue and the face-to-face engagement of genocide suspects and survivors.

The Government had undertaken to begin trials for 750 genocide suspects in September 2004 using the *gacaca* system, but this process was delayed until 2005. Meanwhile, in December 2004 the Gacaca Commission reported that it would use lists of genocide suspects that the Netherlands-based NGO Penal Reform International had earlier rejected as inadmissible on the grounds that they presumed guilt. Hearings of genocide suspects' cases before nearly 9,000 *gacaca* tribunals ultimately commenced on 10 March 2005. Defendants have included several current government officials, and Prime Minister Bernard Makuza and the Minister of Defence, Gen. Marcel Gatsinzi, provided testimony. It appeared that Makuza would not be liable for prosecution, but Gatsinzi, a former commander of the École des sous-officiers in Butare, was accused of providing weapons to Hutu troops to kill Tutsi. Gatsinzi admitted that some military personnel under his command had been involved in killings, but rejected allegations that he had assisted them.

As the Rwandan Government claims that up to 1m. suspects might eventually be charged with genocide during *gacaca* hearings, the Prosecutor-General has warned that the Government must change its judicial strategy as the *gacaca* system would be unable to process so many cases. *Gacaca* hearings were further complicated in early 2005 when thousands of Hutu reportedly fled to neighbouring countries to avoid possible prosecution through *gacaca*. In Burundi, for example, UNHCR initially granted refugee status to some 2,000 recently arrived Rwandans. However, after complaints from the Rwandan Government, Burundi released a statement indicating that the Rwandans would not be granted refugee status, that it would urge them to return home and that it would initiate extradition proceedings against those who refused. Additionally, it was announced in October 2006 that France, Belgium and the Netherlands had agreed to seek those who had taken up residence in those countries and bring them to trial.

In July 2006 phase two of the *gacaca* system began. The process was scheduled to be completed by December 2007, although a report by Human Rights Watch, released in January 2006, claimed that this was unlikely, and the UN later mandated the ICTR to complete the trials by 2010.

HUMAN RIGHTS AND REFUGEE ISSUES

According to the US State Department's human rights report for 2006, released on 6 March 2007, Rwanda's record remained poor, but improvements had been made even over the past year. Specifically, the report claimed that Rwandan authorities continued to commit serious abuses and to restrict the right of citizens to elect a different government. Security forces, such as the Local Defence Forces, reportedly committed unlawful killings and employed torture and excessive force. Police often mistreated suspects, and prison conditions remained life-threatening. Arbitrary arrest and detention, particularly of opposition supporters, and prolonged pre-trial detention remained serious problems. Due process or expeditious trials often did not occur and genocide trials continued to move slowly. There were restrictions on freedom of speech and of the press, and limited freedom of association, assembly and religion. Other problems cited in the report included child labour, human trafficking, social violence and discrimination against women and ethnic minorities, particularly the Batwa. Various international human rights organizations, such as Amnesty International and Human Rights Watch, expressed similar concerns.

The record of the Armée patriotique rwandaise (APR—the FPR's military wing) in eastern DRC has alarmed many international human rights organizations, owing to consistent reports of the APR's executions, rape, forcible removal of people and other abuses. An increasing number of people from the Kivu provinces of eastern DRC, especially non-Banyarwanda, strongly oppose the APR because of its harsh treatment of local populations. Many non-Banyarwanda have joined anti-Rwandan Mai-Mai militias to combat the APR and its Banyarwanda allies. In May 2000 Human Rights Watch released a report, entitled *Eastern Congo Ravaged*, which outlined the excesses committed by the APR in the DRC. Soon after, Amnesty International published *Democratic Republic of the Congo: Killing Human Decency*, which indicated that the APR had killed 'hundreds or even thousands' of unarmed civilians in Nord-Kivu province since 1998. In particular, Amnesty International cited the APR's killing of 74 civilians in a church, in the region of Kailenge.

In November 2002, the International Crisis Group (ICG) criticized Rwanda's poor human rights record, particularly regarding the country's activities in eastern DRC. In June 2003 Rwanda and Burundi agreed to co-operate in bringing stability to the Great Lakes region by supporting peace efforts in Burundi and the DRC. Kagame promised to convince armed Burundian groups to implement the cease-fire agreements that had been signed with the Government of Burundi. In October Rwanda announced that it would create a commission of inquiry to investigate two cases of alleged resource exploitation in the DRC, but the Government continued to dismiss reports of human rights violations by Rwandan troops in the DRC as uninformed and biased. In April 2004 Rwanda deployed troops along its border with Burundi and the DRC, in anticipation of possible attacks from Hutu rebels. Burundi accused Rwandan government forces of invading Ruhororo and Kaburantwa Valley, in the north-western province of Cibitoke, and demanded their withdrawal. The Burundian authorities subsequently announced that Rwanda had complied with the request.

REGIONAL CONCERNS

Rwanda's 1997 military intervention in the DRC marked a turning point in Central Africa's history. The Kagame Government justified its actions by claiming that its armed forces sought only to eliminate Hutu extremist elements there. However, it soon became evident that Rwandan troops, together with their Ugandan counterparts, had also started a systematic campaign to loot the region's resources. Efforts by the UN and the international community to prevent this illegal exploitation failed. Meanwhile, by 2004 various international human rights organizations believed that more than 4m. had died in eastern DRC as a result of warfare, disease and starvation. In June Col Jules Mutebutsi, a Congolese Tutsi rebel commander, and a number of his troops had sought refuge in Rwanda, after clashing with personnel of the UN Observer Mission in the Democratic Republic of the Congo (MONUC) in Bukavu. UNHCR refused to grant refugee status to Mutebutsi and his troops until it received proof that they were no longer combatants. In late August the Rwandan Government sought to placate the UN by moving Mutebutsi and his soldiers from a temporary camp, known as Ntendezi, near the DRC border, to a camp in the remote district of Gikongoro province, known as Coko. However, this measure failed to allay UN fears that Mutebutsi and his followers remain combatants. The UN also accused the Kagame Government of arming dissident militias in the DRC's Ituri district in Province Orientale and operating a military training camp in Kibungo province for abductees from the Kiziba and Gihembe refugee camps. Rwanda denied the allegations. On 13 August Rwanda blamed the Forces démocratiques pour la libération du Rwanda (FDLR), regarded as the successor force to the former Rwandan army and containing Interahamwe militia members who fled to the DRC after the 1994 genocide, for killing 152 Congolese Tutsi refugees in the Burundian Gatumba refugee camp, near the border with the DRC. The Rwandan Government threatened to deploy troops in the DRC unless MONUC and the Congolese authorities took action, and additionally demanded that MONUC abandon its ineffective, voluntary disarmament programme for the FDLR. MONUC responded that its efforts to disarm the FDLR had failed because Rwanda and its DRC-based allies continued to carry out military operations in eastern DRC that disrupted its operations. Additionally, MONUC accused Rwanda of using FDLR activities as justification for reintervention in the DRC.

In September 2004 the UN announced that the Rwandan and DRC Governments had agreed to launch a Joint Verification Mechanism (JVM) to enhance border security. Accordingly, both countries pledged to take reports of fighting to the JVM for verification before they were released to the media. In early November the DRC armed forces and MONUC commenced joint missions in the Walungu district of Sud-Kivu province to persuade the FDLR to disarm and return home. Shortly after, the FDLR launched a rocket attack on Rwanda's Gisenyi province from Nord-Kivu. In November 2004, Kagame warned the AU that Rwandan troops would intervene in the DRC if the armed forces and MONUC failed to disarm the FDLR. The UN, the EU, the United Kingdom, the USA, Belgium, South Africa and other countries cautioned Kagame about intervening in the DRC, while many donors, including the Swedish Government, suspended aid to the Rwandan Government. On 1 December MONUC reported that there were around 100 Rwandan troops in the Virunga mountains along the Rwanda–DRC–Uganda border. According to the DRC Government, these troops had been fighting the FDLR in Nord-Kivu for at least a week; however, the Rwandan Government denied that it had any forces in the DRC. In early December DRC armed reinforcements clashed with military units of dissidents loyal to the pro-Rwanda Rassemblement congolais pour la démocratie (RCD) in Kanyabayonga, Nord-Kivu. However, the DRC Government maintained that the incident involved its armed forces and invading Rwandan troops. The JVM investigated the matter, but was unable to confirm whether Rwandan troops had participated in the fighting. Nevertheless, MONUC suspected that Rwanda provided military aid to the RCD. On 20 December the Rwandan Government responded to growing international criticism by announcing that it would no longer intervene in the DRC. On 31 March 2005 the FDLR unexpectedly condemned the 1994 genocide, pledged to co-operate with the ICTR and announced that it was willing to end its armed struggle, begin disarmament on 5 May, and eventually return to Rwanda. These concessions resulted from secret discussions in Rome, Italy, between the rebels and the Roman Catholic Sant'Egidio community. Much of the international community welcomed this initiative. However, the FDLR has since continued its campaign of violence in the Kivus, aimed mainly at the Congolese Tutsi population.

Rwanda-Uganda relations remained tense, primarily since the Ugandan authorities believed that the Rwandan Government was aiding the self-styled People's Redemption Army (PRA), a rebel group that reportedly was linked to an opposition leader until recently in exile, Col Kizza Besigye. The Rwandan Government rejected such accusations. In November 2004 Uganda expelled a Rwandan diplomat, James Wizeye, for espionage and for co-operating with the PRA, which supposedly aimed to overthrow President Museveni's Government. Rwanda retaliated by expelling a Ugandan diplomat. Shortly afterwards Ugandan security forces arrested three UPDF soldiers for selling information to Wizeye. Rwandan officials denied these charges and accused Ugandan government elements of seeking to damage relations between the two countries. In April 2005 Rwanda announced that it had detained a UPDF officer, Capt. David Mugambe, on espionage charges. Mugambe claimed to be fleeing political persecution in Uganda, but the Ugandan Government maintained that he was sought by the authorities for providing weapons to criminals.

INTERNATIONAL RELATIONS

Despite Rwanda's alleged poor record in the areas of governance and human rights, the Government retained the support of much of the international community. However, Rwanda's relations with France and Belgium remained uneven, largely owing to the legacies of the 1994 genocide. In March 2004 the French daily newspaper *Le Monde* reported that a French magistrate's study had determined that Kagame had ordered the shooting down of President Habyarimana's plane, which had precipitated the 1994 genocide. In response, Kagame asserted that France 'supplied weapons, and, working alongside Hutu Government extremists, gave orders, to the perpetrators of the genocide'. The Rwandan Government established a commission in October 2006 to investigate France's role in the Rwandan genocide. The French Government maintained that French peace-keeping troops had saved 'several hundred thousand lives' during the killings. In November a French judge, Jean-Louis Bruguière, issued arrest warrants for Kagame and nine of his associates, alleging that they were involved in the assassination of Habyarimana. In response, Rwanda immediately severed relations with France, ordering the French ambassador and other diplomats in Rwanda to leave the country. To further demonstrate its split from France and its historic sphere of influence in Africa, in December Rwanda stated its desire to join the Commonwealth.

In May 2004 Belgium, which earlier had apologized for its failure to intervene to stop the genocide, pledged €75m. over a three-year period for Rwanda's health, education, and development sectors. The Rwandan Government planned to use the funds to improve the country's medical infrastructure, introduce universal primary education and facilitate small-scale, rural income generating activities to reduce poverty levels.

In March 2003 President Kagame met with President George W. Bush and other senior US officials to discuss bilateral relations, trade and development, the effect of HIV/AIDS and peace and security in the Great Lakes region. In December the US Secretary of Health and Human Services, Tommy Thompson, visited Rwanda to assess the impact of US aid on Rwanda's HIV/AIDS epidemic.

In mid-April 2004 156 Rwandan soldiers arrived in the Darfur region of western Sudan to protect the AU observer mission there (see the chapter on Sudan). These were the first foreign troops to arrive in Darfur, and the Rwandan Government was widely commended internationally for sending them. In his valedictory address to the contingent, Kagame announced that he expected the troops to defend Sudanese civilians as well to as protect AU observers. In November Rwanda dispatched another military contingent to Darfur, bringing its total personnel strength in the AU mission to around 400 troops. In February 2005 Kagame visited the Rwandan troops in Darfur and met with the Sudanese President, Lt-Gen. Omar Hassan Ahmad al-Bashir, for discussions. The Rwandan President maintained that he was acting in co-operation with Sudan to resolve the Darfur crisis, while Bashir declared that the two countries were linked by a 'common concern' for peace. When he returned to Rwanda, Kagame urged the AU to increase the number of troops in Darfur, claiming that, after the experiences of Rwanda in 1994, the international community could not allow another genocide to occur in Darfur. By mid-2007 six Rwandan peace-keepers had been killed during fighting in Darfur.

Economy

FRANÇOIS MISSER

With subsequent revision by PHILIP VERWIMP

Revised for this edition by the editorial staff

INTRODUCTION

Rwanda has two main physical obstacles to economic development: the extreme population density and the distance from the sea. The population problem with its concomitant effect on food resources, is aggravated by soil erosion caused by leaching and other natural factors. In 2005, according to estimates by the World Bank, Rwanda's gross national income (GNI), at average 2003–05 prices, was US $2,090m., equivalent to $230 per head (one of the lowest levels in the world). Overall gross domestic product (GDP) increased, in real terms, at an average annual rate of 7.5% in 1995–2005. In 2001 real GDP increased by 6.7%, despite the decline of coffee prices, owing to a 10-fold increase in the price of columbo-tantalite (coltan) and good tea output. External transfers, equivalent to 11.5% of GDP, stimulated manufacturing, construction, and transportation and communication activities, according to the IMF. Real GDP growth in 2002 increased to an estimated 9.4%, owing to the expansion of the construction sector and to excellent climatic conditions. Owing to late rainfall, growth slowed down to only 1.0% in 2003. The 16% rise of output in the construction sector and the 6.6% expansion of the services sector during that year partially compensated for a 5.3% recession of the manufacturing sector and a 30% decline in cash crop revenue. Real GDP growth in 2004 recovered to 4.0%, based on strong performance of the construction industry and the services sector (particularly transport, tourism and communications), and despite poor rains, which caused food production to fall for a second year (by 1%), and electricity shortages. As a result of improved export production (primarily coffee), total agricultural output (by volume, weighted for value) registered positive growth of 0.2%, after a 4.1% decline in 2003. Industrial production (excluding construction), however, suffered from the additional competition caused by entrance into the Free Trade Area of the Common Market for Eastern and Southern Africa (COMESA) in January 2004, from the energy shortages and from the high international petroleum price. According to the World Bank, Rwanda's GDP increased by 6% in 2005, reflecting good performances in the services and industrial sectors, both of which expanded by around 6%. However, the agricultural sector was adversely affected by poor weather conditions in 2005 and growth of just 4.4% was recorded as a consequence. A strengthening manufacturing sector stimulated growth in 2006 which official sources estimated at 6.2%. The commercial sector emerged in that year, and demonstrated the potential to accelerate economic growth in future years. However, rising international prices for basic foodstuffs (particularly wheat and maize) placed upward pressure on inflation, a problem exacerbated by high fuel prices. Elsewhere, cyclical weather conditions were likely to impede coffee production in 2007, leading to a loss of export earnings. In lieu of these potential difficulties, the IMF forecast relatively modest growth of 4.7% for 2007. The central bank, meanwhile, were more optimistic and projected economic growth of 6.5%.

The Government's three-year programme of rehabilitation and reconciliation for 1996–98 aimed to restore the economy to the level of its 1990 achievements by 1998. However, the Government only considered that GDP had equalized with pre-genocide levels at the end of 2001. In 1990–2001 the average annual rate of inflation was 13.2%. The estimated inflation rate was only 2.3% in 2002. However, consumer prices increased by 7.2% in 2003, owing to a sharp rise in the international price of petroleum and to a deterioration in the exchange rate of the national currency. The inflation rate was estimated at 12.0% in 2004, and a 6.0% rate was projected for 2005, although analysts feared that the target would be difficult to meet, as a result of the soaring international price of petroleum. The actual rate of inflation in 2005 was 9.1%. The value of the Rwandan franc deteriorated in 2004. At the end of May the rate was 562 Rwanda francs = US $1, compared with 521 Rwanda francs = $1 one year earlier. In 2004 the annual average exchange rate was 603 Rwanda francs = $1 and a further deterioration to 717 Rwanda francs = $1 was projected by the Banque Nationale du Rwanda. The long-term ambition of the Rwandan authorities, summarized in their 'Vision 2020' development plan, was to achieve an 8%–9% GDP annual average growth rate, which would allow a five-fold increase in GDP in 20 years. This target, combined with strengthened birth control measures aimed at reducing the population growth rate from 2.9% in 2000 to 2.2% by 2020, was expected to result in a four-fold increase in GDP per head, to $900, by the end of the period.

AGRICULTURE

Agricultural Production

Agriculture's share of GDP was estimated to have decreased to 42.2% in 2005, compared with 51.1% in 1994. Some 89.8% of the labour force were employed in the agricultural sector in 2005. The sector contributed 57.2% of total export revenue (including re-exports) in 2003. About 95% of the total value of agricultural production is provided by subsistence crops. While these have failed to meet the needs of the population, the annual increase in production of subsistence crops broadly kept pace with population growth until 1977. Since then the area of land annually made available for subsistence crops has increased only marginally and, moreover, crop yields are declining in many areas, owing to erosion and the traditional intensive cultivation methods used. (The problem of erosion was exacerbated during 1990–94 by the felling by displaced Rwandans of trees for timber and charcoal.) This resulted in the late 1980s in increasing strains on food production, and consequently in severe food shortages. Attempts to increase the yield of small farm plots have included a recent initiative to cultivate climbing beans. In late 1989 and early 1990 many parts of the country, in particular the south, were affected by famine, following drought and crop failure. The Government first did not recognize the food problem and tried to prevent it gaining attention in the media. Subsequently, the Government had recourse to emergency food aid to avert widespread starvation.

The principal food crops are bananas, sweet potatoes, potatoes, cassava, beans, sorghum, rice, maize and peas, in descending order of importance. Owing to a drought affecting the Kibungo, Gitarama, Kigali and Butare prefectures (now provinces) in the second half of 2000, banana output fell by 25.8%, to 2.2m. tons, in 2000 and further, to 2.0m., in 2001. All other crops performed well, however, and an overall 17.8% increase in agricultural output was recorded in that year. In 2000 cereals output was 240,000 tons, consisting mainly of sorghum (155,000 tons), but also of maize (63,000 tons) and rice (12,000 tons). In 2001 175,100 tons of sorghum and 92,200 tons of maize were produced. Despite an increase in both maize and rice production levels, however, domestic production was much below local demand and the discrepancy was covered by imports. Owing to increased insecurity in the north-western part of the country, output of dry beans decreased from 189,000 tons in 1996 to 150,000 tons in 1997. In 1998 the improvement of the security situation, combined with larger supplies of fertilizers, prompted a rise in bean production to 154,000 tons, and in sweet potato output, from 742,000 tons to 751,000 tons. In 1999 bean production decreased slightly, to 140,000 tons, but in 2000 it increased again, to 215,000 tons, owing to a combination of factors, including increased security, new production areas in swamps and marshes and favourable climatic conditions in the north and north-eastern parts of the country. Bean production increased to 290,700 tons in 2001. Performances were even more remarkable for sweet potatoes, of which annual output reached 863,000 tons in 1999, 1.0m. tons in 2000, 1.1m. tons in 2001 and 1.3m. tons in 2002. Potato production increased nearly six-fold, from 176,000 tons in 1999 to 954,000 tons in 2000, while cassava output rose nearly three-fold, from 317,000 tons in 1999 to 812,000 tons in 2000. The increase in cassava production was largely a result of a programme of distribution of 2m. cuttings to farmers by Rwanda's Institute of Agricultural Sciences, assisted by the US non-governmental organization (NGO) World Vision International. In 2001 potato production increased again, to 989,000 tons, but output of cassava declined to 686,000 tons. Output of potatoes and cassava both increased to more than 1m. tons in 2002, and potato production rose further to 1.1m. tons in 2003.

In total, the added value of agricultural production increased sizeably, from 176,200m. Rwanda francs in 1998 to 211,094m. Rwanda francs in 2000. In its February 2001 annual report, however, the Banque Nationale du Rwanda (the central bank) warned against the lack of maintenance of the ageing banana plantations. According to the US agency Famine Early Warning System Network, overall Rwandan crop production was estimated at 3.7m. tons at the end of 2001, compared with 2.9m. tons at the beginning of that year. Import requirements in 2001 amounted to 143,000 tons of cereal-equivalent and were expected to be fully covered by commercial imports. In 2002, for the first time, the UN World Food Programme (WFP) purchased 1,500 tons of maize and beans on the domestic market to supply the regions suffering from a deficit. At the end of June 2003 humanitarian agencies warned that a severe production shortfall in the Bugesera area might result in a rapid deterioration in food security if aid to residents was not increased. Some 70,000 civilians were already experiencing conditions of moderate food insecurity, according to WFP. By early 2004 it was apparent that the agricultural sector would not again be able to sustain the entire population, then estimated at 8.9m. (about 1m. more than in March 1994). In January some 124,000 people were entirely dependent on food aid in the Bugesera, Kibungo and Umutara provinces, which were threatened by desertification. At the same time abundant early rainfall in January disorganized agricultural activities. Moreover, the banana plantations were suffering contamination from the Banana bunchy top (BBTV) and *budusiga* viruses. The Rwandan Government was concerned that the per head food availability, which had suffered a constant decline since 1980, could decrease to even lower levels, as the population was scheduled to double by 2015, unless significant productivity gains are made. However, experts from the finance and agriculture ministries believed that the challenge could be met, provided that sufficient investments were made in disseminating the use of fertilizers, limited to 5% of the farmers in 2004, and in increasing loans to the farmers: loans to agriculture indeed represented only 1% of commercial loans. Overall, Donald Kaberuka stated that Rwanda's agricultural potential was underestimated, since the country possessed more arable land than the Nile Delta. The success of the Kabuye Sugar Works, which by the end of 2003 had doubled its 2000 output of

3,500 tons, was viewed as an example of the capacity of the Rwandan agricultural sector to improve its performance.

In 2004 poor rains caused food production to fall by 1%. Nevertheless, performances varied according to products. Outputs of sorghum, beans, soya and cassava declined by 5%, 17%, 8% and 9%, respectively. However, production of maize increased by 12% and rice output by 66%, while production of bananas registered 2.6% growth. By August of that year the outlook was critical in 31 districts of the country, where an estimated population of 250,000–400,000 was expected to rely entirely on the distribution of 25,000 metric tons of food aid between September and December. The most vulnerable districts were in the south (Bugesera, Gikongoro and Butare), owing not only to drought but also to poorer soils. As a result, by November bean prices were 87% higher than in the previous year, while those of sorghum and maize were 73% and 55% higher, respectively. However, prospects began to improve in December, owing to heavy rains, and the number of people requiring food aid decreased to 110,000. In January 2005 preliminary results recorded by the Rwandan Ministry of Agriculture and Livestock and WFP showed a 10% increase in potato production, but an 8% decrease in cassava output, mainly owing to the impact of cassava mosaic virus, in comparison with 2004.

In general terms, production of cereals is strong. Output of both maize and sorghum has been increasing over the first years of the 2000s. However, maize output is hindered by the lack of fertilizer use and soil erosion. Production of maize is estimated at 90,000 metric tons per year, compared with 160,000 tons for sorghum. Rice output remains modest (about 20,000 tons per year) but is increasing rapidly. In early 2005 the Government launched a 10-year rice development programme. Rice was selected as a 'priority crop' by the Government, since it performs well in flood-prone valleys and eases pressure on hillside land for other crops, and also because domestic demand is high. At this time it was grown on approximately 7,455 ha in Butare, Kibungo and Umutara provinces. However, it is planned to increase the cultivated area to 66,000 ha by 2016, by improved management of new areas in the marshlands, with the aim of meeting domestic requirements by 2009 and generating about US $170m. in export earnings. A sign of improving food security was that market prices of the main staple foods fell in April 2005 in Kigali, Butare and Ruhengeri, while beans were again being exported to Uganda. Confronted with adverse climatic conditions in 2004, the Government has been concentrating on improving service delivery (agricultural extension, seed availability, land conservation education). In 2004 it pursued its tree-planting and environmental awareness campaign, partly through the introduction of monthly *Umuganda* community service to plant trees and improve the environment. In 2005 the Banque Rwandaise de Développement was considering a five-fold increase in its loans to the agricultural sector, which amounted to 2,000m. Rwanda francs in 2004.

Land Reform

The Government argues that land reform, aiming at freezing the dismantlement of agricultural plots and the transformation of marshes and swamps into suitable land for agriculture, will contribute to an increase in food production. Land reforms under consideration in 2004 envisaged encouraging the development of more viable plots: the current average size of less then 0.7 ha was considered too small. Agricultural research performed at Michigan State University of the USA, however, has demonstrated that small farms in Rwanda are more productive (in yield per unit of land) than large farms. In addition, the land reform programme is not only a matter of economics, but has an important political component. Poor Hutu farmers fear that they will lose or have to sell their land to rich urban Tutsi in the process of land consolidation. In general terms, Rwanda was beset by structural problems, such as low agricultural productivity, owing to the failure to make a proper transition to intensive high-value farming. The state policy of displacing a large number of rural poor to government-designated sites, which had been initiated in 1997 and pursued until early 2000, was criticized by foreign human rights organizations in June 2001. The basic aim of the reform was to substitute the dispersed habitat and create larger landholdings in order to boost productivity. However, human rights activists, while agreeing that making agriculture more productive was imperative, considered that such reforms should not be made at the expense of the poor. The US-based organization Human Rights Watch accused military officers and businessmen with government connections of having appropriated large holdings of land from the poor.

Coffee

Revenue from coffee fluctuates considerably, and in the late 1980s it declined sharply because of the combined effects of a low level of production, declining international prices and the weakness of the US dollar in relation to the currencies of Rwanda's other major trading partners. Even prior to the catastrophic political events of 1994, it had seemed unlikely that Rwanda would benefit fully from the resurgence in world prices at the end of 1993. The volume of production has been declining for several years, partly owing to price instability. Reduced revenues have also forced farmers to abandon the purchase and introduction of pesticides and fertilizers. The impact of the political and humanitarian crisis was considerable, and production declined from 28,135 metric tons in 1992/93 to 1,994 tons in 1993/94. In 1996/97 output reached 21,051 tons. The Government prioritized agricultural diversification in its three-year investment programme of rehabilitation and reconciliation. In 1995, however, the price payable to growers for parchment coffee was increased, reflecting the Government's continuing commitment to provide incentives to producers.

The Government liberalized the processing, marketing and export of coffee, which enabled farmers to receive higher prices without resorting to subsidies. In mid-1998 the Government announced plans to remove the remaining taxes on coffee exports progressively and to sell three of its coffee factories, in order to accelerate the recovery of the sector. However, despite these efforts, coffee exports dropped to 14,459 metric tons in 1997. According to central bank statistics, coffee exports increased to 14,997 tons in 1998 and 18,532 tons in 1999, but declined again, to 16,098 tons, in 2000, owing to the drought affecting production areas in the southern part of the country, and to inadequate maintenance of the ageing plantations. Meanwhile, owing to a sharp decline in international prices, export revenue from coffee decreased by 40.7%, from 13,650m. Rwanda francs in 1997 to 8,101m. Rwanda francs in 1998. Export revenue increased to 8,875m. Rwanda francs in 1999, partly owing to a 23.5% increase in the volume exported and government efforts to encourage the trade by suppressing the tax on coffee exports. However, export figures do not entirely reflect the critical situation of the sector, owing to the prevalence of the smuggling of Burundian coffee to Rwanda, where producers are offered higher prices. One of the main problems, as the Government acknowledged, is that average yields of about 300 kg per ha are three to four times lower than in the other countries of the region. Lower production levels and a fall from US $0.84 per kg to $0.69 per kg of the average international price contributed to a slight decline in the value of coffee exports, to 8,780m. Rwanda francs, in 2000. For the first time, coffee was replaced by tea as the country's leading export product. In 2001 coffee production increased to 18,366 tons, but export revenue decreased to 8,031m. Rwanda francs, accounting for only 21.3% of the value of total exports (including re-exports), owing to a 30% decline in the international price of coffee. The trend was similar in 2002, with total output increasing to 19,426 tons and coffee export earnings falling to 6,860m. Rwanda francs, representing 22.6% of the value of Rwanda's total exports. Nevertheless, sizeable efforts were devoted to improving the quality of Rwandan coffee and promoting the products. In 2002 marketing efforts began to produce results. Small quantities from the Maraba co-operative of producers were sold in the US state of Louisiana and purchased by the British Union Coffee Roasters company. In 2003 some $400,000 was invested in 10 new washing stations; the Government planned to equip the country with a further 90 stations by 2010, with the target of attaining national output of 35,000 tons by 2010. Both the US Agency for International Development (USAID) and the Office des Cultures Industrielles du Rwanda (OCIR) were involved in the programme, while the European Union (EU) announced that it would finance the modernization of the coffee sector through its stabilization of export earnings (Stabex) scheme. However, output in 2003 was disappointing, registering, at only 13,805 tons, a 28.9% decrease compared with the 2002 crop, owing to a severe drought. However, OCIR—Café projected an increase in production in 2004 to 20,000 tons, assuming climatic conditions proved favourable, owing to the installation of 10 new washing stations financed by the EU, which would allow a rise, from 315 tons to 1,200 tons, in production of the best quality fully washed coffee, thereby generating revenue gains of $1.50 per kg. In 2003, owing to slightly higher world prices, revenue from coffee exports was estimated at $13.9m., demonstrating only a slight decline in value, compared with $14.0m. recorded for the previous year, despite the sharp decrease in volume of the production.

The long-term objective of the Government was that the coffee and tea sectors should each generate export revenue of US $100m. by 2010 and, thereby, together with projected revenues of $100m. from the services sector (in particular tourism), contribute to improving the trade balance. In 2004 output increased beyond expectation, almost doubling, to 20,017 metric tons. Increased use of fertilizers and pesticides and the increase in the area under cultivation were beginning to pay dividends. This, in conjunction with higher world prices, allowed coffee to regain its position as the leading export product, with a total of $27.5m. in export revenues (accounting for 30.5% of total exports during that year). However, sources at the Ministry of Agriculture and Livestock expected output to fall by 7.4% during 2005, owing to cyclical conditions arising from 2004's high production (since coffee trees need time to regenerate).

Tea

Prior to 1994, the Government had attempted to diversify the crops grown for export through OCIR, established in 1964. This concentrated its efforts on tobacco, cotton, pyrethrum, quinquina, forestry and, pre-eminently, tea. Production of tea declined to 10,493 tons in 1993, and export earnings decreased to US $16m. (equivalent to 23.5% of the value of total exports), following the occupation of the lucrative Mulindi plantations by forces of the Front patriotique rwandais (FPR). In 1993–94 production collapsed to just 4,902 tons, largely owing to the adverse effects of the war and to the former Government's removal to Zaire (now the Democratic Republic of the Congo—DRC) of the Cyangugu tea factory. Production in 1995 increased to 5,414 tons, still considerably below the Government's target level. In subsequent years, however, tea output increased dramatically, reaching 14,878 tons in 1998. Tea exports decreased to 12,959 tons in 1999, but increased again, to 14,481 tons, in 2000. Export revenue from tea fluctuated considerably, increasing from 5,040m. Rwanda francs in 1997 (approximately $16.8m.) to 7,154m. Rwanda francs in 1998 (approximately $22.8m.). Owing to a sharp decrease in international prices during that year and to a 16% decline in the volume of exports, revenue from tea exports dropped by 17.8% in 1999, to 5,881m. Rwanda francs. This trend eliminated the effects of an increase in the producer price in 1998, initiated by the Government, which simultaneously decided to privatize the tea estates and factories. In 2000, however, the combined effect of a 13.2% increase in tea production and an 18.5% rise in the price of Rwandan tea, from $1.51 per kg in 1999 to $1.79 per kg (well above the average world price of $1.50), contributed to an increase in the value of tea exports, to 9,277m. Rwanda francs. For the first time, tea became the country's principal source of export earnings.

In 2001 production increased again, to a record amount of 17,815 metric tons, while the Director of the Office du Thé du Rwanda expressed satisfaction at the decision by Pakistan to resume its purchases of Rwandan tea. During that year tea export earnings rose to 9,996m. Rwanda francs, accounting for 26.5% of total export revenue. Production of tea decreased to 14,893 tons in 2002. In that year, however, revenue from tea exports increased to 10,373m. Rwanda francs and accounted for 34.2% of the value of the country's total exports, owing to steady international prices. For 2004 OCIR—Thé projected that tea output would remain at the level of 2003 production of 15,483 tons, about 40% above the 1993 level. Accordingly, output could double by 2020, owing to the extension of the planted area from 12,000 ha to 15,000 ha, the creation of two new processing plants and the increase in yields from 1.5 tons per ha to 2.5 tons per ha—this last as a result of a more intensive use of fertilizers, a 20% increase in the tree population per ha, and more efficient collection techniques. In 2003 tea was a principal export product, generating $11.9m. and accounting for about 24% of the value of total exports, according to UN figures. Production was lower than expected in 2004, at some 14,493 tons. Owing to stable prices, however, tea export earnings were higher than in the previous year, at $25.6m., accounting for 28.6% of total export earnings during that year. The Ministry of Agriculture and Livestock forecast a slight increase in production in 2005, to 14,000 tons, despite a decline in production in the first quarter of the year.

Livestock

By July 1994 the livestock sector was in extreme crisis and the majority of the country's livestock had disappeared (although some cattle were introduced by refugees returning from Uganda). Limited livestock-vaccination programmes were undertaken by FAO and smaller agencies in the north-east, but the main problem remains the overstocking of cattle (and the consequent environmental strain) in this region, while livestock numbers are hopelessly insufficient elsewhere in the country. Between 1998 and 2000 livestock numbers increased from 657,137 to 732,123 head of cattle, from 192,344 to 248,345 sheep, from 481,145 to 756,522 goats and from 120,928 to 177,220 pigs, according to the Ministry of Finance and Economic Planning. In 2001 the situation deteriorated again with an epidemic of foot-and-mouth disease, which affected five of Rwanda's 11 prefectures. The Ministry of Agriculture and Livestock claimed that traders who had illicitly imported cattle from Uganda and Tanzania into Rwanda had spread the disease. Owners of large herds in Rwanda's Mutara highlands who also possessed cattle in these neighbouring countries were suspected of having contributed to the contamination of Rwanda's cattle. As a result, in March the authorities declared a quarantine on these areas and prohibited the circulation of cattle, dairy products and meat from this origin.

In an attempt to stimulate dairy production and increase household income, the Government and the UN Development Programme (UNDP) began working with communities in Mutara prefecture. Since 2000 farmers have been encouraged to produce yoghurt, cheese and cooking fat. By early 2005 some livestock numbers were approaching pre-war levels. According to government statistics, the numbers of cattle and poultry had reached 88% and 70% of the levels recorded in 1994, but the proportion was 30% for goats. In order to boost milk output, Rwanda has imported several hundred cows from Germany and South Africa; these are more productive than the local Ankole breed but more vulnerable to disease. In early 2005 an outbreak of foot-and-mouth disease in livestock herds necessitated the quarantining of six districts in four provinces.

The poultry sector is expanding rapidly. Fish production is also increasing rapidly, owing to the development of fisheries projects in Lake Kivu and in other smaller lakes throughout the country. From 1,300 metric tons in 1994, the total catch increased to 8,186 tons in 2005.

Reconstruction After Conflict

A joint FAO-WFP report estimated that food production in 1994 amounted to just 45% of the 1993 yield. It was also estimated that hundreds of hectares of natural forests had been damaged by displaced persons and that support systems for agriculture were almost completely destroyed. Food aid requirements (mainly grain and pulses) were estimated at more than 150,000 metric tons in 1994 and 116,000 tons in 1995. During the two seasons following the civil war 10,000 tons of beans, maize, vegetable and other seeds, together with 700,000 hoes, were distributed to some 690,000 households. It was estimated that 62% of farmers received seeds, while some 72% received tools. A conference of potential donors, sponsored by UNDP, was convened in Geneva, Switzerland, during January 1995, at which pledges of financial assistance totalling US $587m. were made, including a substantial share for agriculture recovery programmes. By the end of 1995 pledges amounted to $1,260m., of which $189.5m. was to be allocated to the agriculture sector. At the same time, however, disbursements amounted to just $28.6m., having been slowed, in part, by the suspension of aid channelled through the Government in the months following the April 1995 massacre of displaced persons by security forces at the Kibeho refugee camp. Disputes involving land tenure were still common in 1997, and discouraged farmers from making long-term investments. However, by the end of 1996 part of the $500m. pledged to facilitate the return of refugees had been allocated to basic rural and agricultural infrastructures. A programme of reform was also announced at this time. The Government intended to encourage a system of population regroupment called *Imidugu* (grouped habitat), which was believed to reduce social and economic costs by enabling shared use of expensive items and the maximization of water supplies. In 1997 FAO and the Government distributed seeds to approximately 2.3m. persons, including many returnees. The food deficit in that year was 179,000 tons, and the shortfall decreased slightly, to 158,000 tons, in 1998. Apart from the continuing insecurity in the north-west of the country, which particularly affected, until 1998, production of beans and potatoes, some 150,000 persons suspected to have participated in the 1994 genocide remained in prison and were therefore unable to contribute to food production. According to FAO estimates, food production in 1997 was 3.9m. tons, a decline of 14% compared with 1984, while the population had increased by 40% in the same period. By late 1999, after an 11% increase in food production, owing to the improvement of the security situation in the north-west, the authorities were again projecting an increase in the food deficit, as a result of the drought that was affecting most parts of the country. In order to avert this threat in the future and not to rely exclusively on rainwater, the Government planned to encourage the development of irrigation schemes using the country's underground water resources. The situation was also aggravated by competition from foreign imports, which undermined efforts to develop domestic rice production schemes. In March 1998 the African Development Fund disbursed $1.4m. to finance a feasibility study on the improvement of soil conservation and the utilization of marshes in order to enable the farmers to benefit from new arable land. The World Bank also planned to finance two projects (one in agriculture and one in rural irrigation), with a total value of $25m., in 2000. In 2001 USAID announced plans to use about $2.3m. to support agribusiness development; additionally, it was to disburse $3.4m. to improve data collection, policy analysis and access to financial services and also to promote technology transfers for the benefit of Rwanda's agricultural sector. In December of that year the Rwandan Government inaugurated a $165m. rural development project, of which some 95% was funded by the World Bank Group, to modernize the agricultural sector. This 14-year project aimed to establish infrastructure and finance research into developing new outlets for Rwandan agricultural products.

Regional Effects of Conflict

Before 1990 the southern provinces were much poorer compared to the northern and eastern provinces. The average income per adult equivalent in Kibungo, the richest province, was three times that in Gikongoro, the poorest province. In 2000 Kibungo was still the richest province, but the average household was only 1.5 times richer than a household in Butare, now the poorest province. Interestingly, Rwanda's high performing provinces prior to the genocide (Kibungo in the east and Ruhengeri in the north) have experienced low, even negative economic growth in the conflict decade. Provinces that were poor, prior to the war and genocide, are still poorer than the Rwandan average, but they have experienced much stronger economic growth than the other provinces. In real terms, the growth of average income was negative in the two richest provinces and was highest in the three poorest provinces. These figures suggest that income convergence has taken place in Rwanda between poor and rich provinces. The reasons behind the convergence of formerly richer and poorer provinces is that they have been differently affected by the four conflict shocks that have hit Rwanda in the course of the nineties: civil war, genocide, mass migration and counter-insurgency.

The Government's 'Vision 2020' strategy emphasized the need for Rwanda to move away from an essentially subsistence agriculture, unable to achieve its self-sufficiency objective, towards a more market-orientated agricultural sector; this would require incentives to increase the specialization of farmers and encourage diversification. The Government's objective for 2020 was to have one-half of arable land given over to modern farms. By then, production of vegetables was targeted to have increased three-fold and dairy production five-fold. A five-fold to 10-fold rise in the value of cash crops on that recorded in 2000, was also projected. Nevertheless, US agronomists emphasized that an important requirement for meeting such an ambitious target was to halt the replacement of crops providing good soil protection, such as bananas, with cassava, which could rapidly have a deleterious effect on soil fertility. Other obstacles to be removed were the lack of fertilizers and the rapid decline in fallow fields. More research was also needed on varietal improvements to increase resistance to disease and yields for selected crops.

Water shortages have become an increasing difficulty, both in rural areas of Southern Gikongoro and Bugesera prefectures, and also in the capital, where 40% of the 600,000 inhabitants had no regular access to drinking water in 2001. The Ministry of Water and Natural Resources aimed to implement plans by 2004 to divert a large volume of water from the Nyabarongo river, 8 km from Kigali, and to increase supplies from 2009 by also pumping water from the Mutobo river, in Ruhengeri province. Resources from the ninth EDF for 2002–07 were expected to finance the extension of water supply networks in the Bugesera region, which is periodically affected by drought.

INDUSTRY

The industrial sector followed the usual pattern for less developed African states, and food-based industries predominated, with the major companies prior to 1994 being BRALIRWA, the Rwandan subsidiary of a Dutch brewery, the Régie Sucrière de Kibuy (sugar-processing) and the OVIBAR factory, producing banana wine and liquors. By July 1994 the country's political turmoil had suspended economic activity in the sector. Factories and plants (where production had been virtually halted by power shortages earlier in the year) were looted, destroyed or abandoned. By early October, however, the BRALIRWA plant had resumed production. In 1994 manufacturing accounted for an estimated 3% of GDP, while industry provided 9% of GDP in the same year. In 1995, although only 40% of enterprises had resumed production, manufacturing was estimated to have recovered sufficiently to provide 14% of GDP, with industry accounting for 21%. Government officials claimed that the slow disbursement of some US $72.9m. in international donor aid, allocated to the trade and industry sectors (only $5.4m. had been released by the end of 1995), together with competition from tax-free imports of goods such as soap and plastics, had seriously hindered the recovery of the sector. By June 1997 69% of the companies existing before April 1994 had resumed their activities. Industrial output grew by 18% in 1996 and by 30% in 1997. However, sectoral growth was hampered by the lack of investment and basic infrastructure. In 1998 the sector was hindered by several factors, including excessive prices for water and energy supplies, insufficient use of installed capacity and competition from cheaper imported products; BRALIRWA and the Utexerwa textile plants, for example, reduced production by 40%. None the less, the Government resisted requests to increase customs duties or impose quotas, but instead was considering in early 1999 the provision of cheaper electricity and water for industry. By the end of 1998 prospects were improving for BRALIRWA, which obtained a contract, valued at 1,000m. Rwanda francs, for the supply of Primus beer to the neighbouring DRC. An additional difficulty for the manufacturing sector was the increase in transport costs of imported inputs as a result of the decision of Kenya and Uganda to limit the maximum weight per axle of trucks in transit on their respective road networks. The Rwandan Government was also concerned at the levels of smuggling of alcoholic beverages, petroleum products and cigarettes. In late 1999 the Government announced plans to create export-processing zones along the Congolese border in Cyangugu and other cities, which could bring added value to products imported from the DRC.

The 'Vision 2020' strategy projected growth in the industrial sector of 4.1% in both 2003 and 2004 and of 7.0% in 2005. A continued increase in construction activity was forecast by the Minister of Finance and Economic Planning to be the main contributory factor to this growth. In 2002 the Government announced plans to reintroduce a 25% import duty on cement: this had been cut from 40% in 1997 to zero in 2000, since at that time the national producer, Cimenterie du Rwanda (CIMERWA), was unable to meet the strong demand created by government and private housing projects. Between 1995 and the end of 2001 265,229 houses were constructed, under the Government's reinstallation programme for rural inhabitants. As a result of investments made by CIMERWA to increase its capacity, the Government abolished the temporary dismantling of tariffs on cement imports in order to encourage the domestic industry. (Imported cement and raw materials for use in production of cement originating from member states of COMESA were to benefit from a preferential 5% tariff.) Since 2001 CIMERWA has encountered competition from the Kenya-based East African Portland cement corporation. None the less, CIMERWA's annual output was estimated at some 100,000 metric tons in 2003, of which a small proportion of 3,922 tons was exported to the DRC and Uganda. Rwanda also became eligible in March for textile and apparel benefits under the US African Growth and Opportunity Act (AGOA), which allow less developed countries in Africa to use imported fabrics and yarns for the production of items exported to the USA. Meanwhile, in late 2001 the Rwandan Government expressed its intention to amend tax regulations in order to accommodate the parent company of BRALIRWA, Heineken of the Netherlands, which contributed some 13,000m. Rwanda francs annually to the budget and had announced plans to make new investments in the country. In 2002 manufacturing output increased by 5.9%, to a value of 52,327m. Rwanda francs. The food, beer, soft drinks and tobacco industries alone accounted for 82.8% of the total and recorded a 6.2% increase compared with 2001.

Industry as a whole (including mining, manufacturing, power and construction) accounted for 21.3% of GDP in 2003 (of which manufacturing contributed 8.9%). In that year expansion of 16% in the construction sector, to 65,031m. Rwanda francs, contributed to industrial growth of 5.3%, despite a decrease in the manufacturing sector affecting in particular the food, beer, soft drinks and tobacco industries, which declined by 6.9%, owing to the competition on the domestic market of imported products and high input costs. BRALIRWA's output declined from 562,200 hl to 433,400 hl during that year. In 2004, owing to acute energy shortages as well as the impact of foreign imports, the output of Utexerwa, the national textile manufacturer, contracted by 9%. Some important changes occurred in the course of 2005, with the Government's announcement of the privatization of the national schools printing company, Régie de l'Imprimerie Scolaire (IMPRISCO), of the pharmaceuticals manufacturer LABOPHAR and of four rice factories at Bugarama, Gikonko, Rwamagana and Kabuye.

MINING

Cassiterite (a tin-bearing ore) is Rwanda's principal mineral resource (exports of tin ore and concentrates were valued at 320m. Rwanda francs in 1991), followed by wolframite (a tungsten-bearing ore) and small, known quantities of beryl, columbo-tantalite (coltan) and gold. While tin concentrates (about 1,500 metric tons) were the third-largest export earner in 1985, high transport costs and the sharp decline in international tin prices resulted in the sector becoming virtually inactive in the late 1980s. At the end of 1985 Géomines, the Belgian company with a 51% shareholding in the Rwandan mining company SOMIRWA, went into liquidation; SOMIRWA itself was declared insolvent a few months later. Despite the insolvent state of the company, the Government's annual maintenance costs for SOMIRWA's installations had continued to exceed 70m. Rwanda francs. In 1992 the Régie d'Exploitation et de Développement des Mines (REDEMI) mining concern was established, with state involvement, and began to exploit the SOMIRWA mines in an artisanal capacity. However, the company was reported to be operating on an annual deficit of some 50m. Rwanda francs. In 1996 the Government announced its decision to privatize the company. From 1992 the SOMIRWA smelter resumed activity for six months of the year, processing cassiterite supplied by the ALICOM gold concern. Some efforts were made with EU support to stimulate the artisanal tin sector, and UNDP provided some funds towards an increase in gold production. Mining activities were resumed at a modest level in 1988 by artisans regrouped in COPIMAR, an independent co-operative offering managerial and commercial support. In May 2002 the Niobium Mining Company (NMC), owned by the German KHA international group, announced plans to invest US $4m. in order to relaunch activity at the Karuruma smelter, aiming at processing both tin from cassiterite and also niobium concentrates for the production of ferro-niobium alloys.

The IMF estimated that Rwanda's exports of gold and diamonds amounted to US $30m. for the first half of 1998, confirming (particularly in view of the fact that Rwanda has no diamond mines) suspicions that these minerals were originating from the DRC. Belgian statistics for 1998 indicated a dramatic rise in gold imports from Rwanda, from an annual average of $15m. during 1990–93 to $35m. in 1997, the first year of Rwanda's military presence in the eastern part of the DRC. In early 1997 a Belgian company established in Burundi initiated talks with the Rwandan Government in order to open a gold-refining plant in Kigali, which would process imports from the DRC. In mid-1998 the Government announced plans to revise the mining code before 2001 to attract investors. REDEMI was also included in the list of parastatals scheduled for privatization in 2001. Meanwhile, the company announced a short-term programme for the rehabilitation of several mining infrastructures, including the underground mines of Makaza, Masoro and Gasambya, and for the development of the Nyamyumba underground mines. All these projects concerned either cassiterite or coltan, or both (since often both minerals are found in the same deposits).

On 12 April 2001 a UN panel of experts on the illegal exploitation of the DRC's natural resources recommended that the UN Security Council impose an embargo against all Rwandan mineral exports. The report alleged that much of Rwanda's exported coltan, cassiterite, gold and diamonds included Congolese products, which were exploited and exported in illicit circumstances. The panel adopted this conclusion by comparing Rwandan official statistics for 1995 and 2000, which demonstrated a dramatic rise in gold exports, from 1 kg to 10 kg, in cassiterite exports, from 247 metric tons to 437 tons, and in coltan exports, from 54 tons to 87 tons. The UN report also found it suspicious that Rwanda exported up to 30,491 carats of diamonds in 2000. Furthermore, the report claimed to have obtained information that the Rwandan army had organized the shipment of coltan and cassiterite from the Sominki mine in the DRC's Sud-Kivu region to Kigali in November 1998. It was also alleged that many companies involved in the exploitation of the DRC's minerals in the territories under the control of the Rwandan army were owned by close associates of President Kagame. The Rwandan armed forces were reported to have participated directly in the illicit trade in minerals. By the time the report was published, the Armée patriotique rwandaise (APR) had shares in some of these companies and also benefited from receipts from the Rwandan-supported Rassemblement congolais pour la démocratie (RCD) rebels. Other revenue was reportedly generated by taxes collected by the APR's 'Congo desk', which had a department of mineral resources, and from payments by individuals in companies in exchange for the protection of their trade and mining activities in the DRC. The conclusions of this report were rejected both by the Rwandan Government and by the Congolese rebels, which emphasized that neither the exploitation nor the export of these minerals was illegal, on the grounds that the Economic Community of the Great Lake Countries (CEPGL), of which the DRC, Rwanda and Burundi are members, allowed the transit of goods between its member states. It was claimed that the exports were not illicit, since export taxes were paid, accordingly, to the Congolese administration of these territories, namely the RCD, which had obtained recognition by the international community as one of the signatories of the 1999 Lusaka peace agreement. The figures released by the UN panels of experts diverged from those of the Banque Nationale du Rwanda, which reported 365 tons of cassiterite exports in 2000 (compared with 308 tons in 1999), 603 tons of coltan exports (330 tons in 1999) and 144 tons of wolfram exports (84 tons in 1999). According to the central bank, these export figures matched domestic production statistics, which would indicate that the entire output was exported in that year. The increase in the volume of mineral exports and the increase in the coltan price, from US $14.00 per kg in 1999 to $18.80 per kg in 2000, contributed to a significant increase in export earnings of minerals, from $4.6m. in 1999 to $11.3m. in 2000. As a result, the share of minerals exports increased from 9.5% to 18.2% of the total. In 2001, owing to a 10-fold increase in coltan prices during the first half of the year, total mineral exports accounted for $40m., a four-fold rise compared with 2000. With new mines commencing production in both Australia and Brazil, however, the international price of coltan began to decline dramatically by the end of 2001. At that time the Rwandan Minister of Finance and Economic Planning emphasized to the international press that the coltan that was exported by Rwanda during 2001 was mined in western parts of the country, where geological properties were similar to those of eastern DRC. As expected, export revenue from coltan decreased sharply, by 62.5%, from 17,368m. Rwanda francs in 2001 to 6,521m. Rwanda francs in 2002, although the volume of coltan exports declined by only 30% during that year, from 1,488 tons to 1,042 tons. Meanwhile, cassiterite exports increased from 553 tons to 690 tons, and wolfram exports nearly doubled, from 163 tons in 2001 to 324 tons in 2002.

During 2002 mineral exports amounted to 7,440m. Rwanda francs, representing 24% of the value of total exports. In 2003 mineral exports totalled 6,307m. Rwanda francs, accounting for 18.8% of the value of total exports, as a result of lower coltan prices and lower volumes of exports. During that period coltan sales amounted to 732 metric tons, worth 3,403m. Rwanda francs. Cassiterite exports totalled 1,457 tons, valued at 2,444m. Rwanda francs, while wolfram exports amounted to 120 tons, valued at 120m. Rwanda francs. Gold exports generated 245m. Rwanda francs during this period. In early 2004 REDEMI expected to improve its performance during the year, as a result of an investment of US $420,000 provided by NMC, the Hong-Kong-based Niotan, Tradmet (Belgium) and Finmining, to purchase pumps, fuels and drilling material. The objective was to treble the 2003 cassiterite output of 182 tons, to increase coltan output from nine to 30 tons, and to treble the production of wolfram to 234 tons. Relying on higher international tin prices and the sale of some of its concessions, REDEMI envisaged the improvement of its financial situation by 2007. Meanwhile, COPIMAR was anticipating a 15% increase in its 2003 production levels, which were 60 tons of coltan, 70 tons of cassiterite and 60 tons of wolfram. Rwanda's Ministry of Finance and Economic Planning projected a 54.6% increase of the activity of the mining and quarrying sector for 2004. During that year the Rwandan Government was also seeking financial support from the ADB to finance a prospecting programme, in order to identify new reserves and thereby to compensate for the progressive exhaustion of existing small deposits. COPIMAR and REDEMI contributed about 20% of mineral exports, the rest being provided by dealing houses, which purchase the products of domestic independent miners or those sold by Congolese traders. In 2005 the Government was considering the privatization of REDEMI's concessions. The NMC smelter in Kigali, which has an installed capacity of 2,000 tons, and the Minerals Processing Company smelter in Gisenyi, with a capacity of 1,800 tons, both operate with imported Congolese minerals.

Natural Gas

Another important mineral to be exploited is natural gas, which was discovered beneath Lake Kivu on the border with the DRC. Reserves of an estimated 60,000m. cu m (about one-half of which are in the DRC) are believed to be among the largest in the world. In May 2000 Rwanda's water, electricity and gas parastatal, Electrogaz, initiated talks with the South African company Mossgas to discuss the possibility of exploiting the Lake Kivu methane and gas resources. Two pilot installations, funded by the EU, produce gas, but here again the small size of the potential market casts doubt on the likely profitability of large-scale processing. However, Electrogaz hopes to receive Belgian funding for a programme to increase its daily output of gas from 5,000 cu m to 25,000 cu m. In October 1997 the Governments of Rwanda, Uganda and the DRC agreed to finance a joint feasibility study to exploit the gas reserves of Lake Kivu. In September 1999 the Banque Rwandaise de Développement announced plans to submit a project for the establishment of a further pilot installation to process the Lake Kivu gas resources to the European Investment Bank (EIB), the Commonwealth Development Corporation, the International Finance Corporation and the Arab Bank for Economic Development in Africa (BADEA). In July 2002 the Israel Electric Corporation negotiated a 'build-own-operate' contract with the Rwandan authorities for the construction of a 25-MW methane power station. The overall electricity generation potential from natural gas resources was estimated at 200 MW by a private consultant and at 700 MW by the Rwandan Government. Speculation regarding the potential of Lake Kivu's resources to augment Rwanda's electricity supply culminated in 2006 when the British firm Dane Associates entered into a £48m. partnership with the Rwandan Government. A 30-MW power plant was expected to result, which would tap the lake's renewable methane deposit. Plans to supply natural gas to the cement and other industries were also under consideration. In February 1999 the South African oil company Engen purchased the local subsidiaries of British Petroleum and Fina (Belgium), taking control of 25% of the distribution market for petroleum products in Rwanda. In August of that year Shell Oil acquired for $2.1m. the Petrorwanda distribution company.

In 2004 the World Bank was also planning to finance consultant support for the Unité de Promotion et d'Exploitation du Gaz du Lac Kivu (UPEGAZ) parastatal, considering that the medium-term development of the power sector was 'inextricably linked' to the exploitation of Lake Kivu's methane reserves. According to Bank sources, a Strategic Social and Environmental Assessment of Power Development Options for Rwanda, Burundi and western Tanzania concluded that power generation from Kivu gas was competitive with comparable hydroelectricity options. Meanwhile, the World Bank was also considering financing the construction of a transmission link to connect potential new generation at Lake Kivu. Recent developments in the sector have included demonstrations of this methane extraction technology to the Government and potential investors by engineers from a South African firm, Murray & Roberts, at a pilot plant near Gisenyi. Cogelgaz, a joint venture between Heineken's subsidiary BRALIRWA and the Banque de Commerce, de Développement et d'Industrie (BCDI), had commissioned the South African company to undertake the technical improvement of its existing gas plant. Rwandan projects planned by Murray & Roberts included the supply of methane gas to urban areas.

ENERGY

Rwanda's electricity needs are supplied almost entirely from hydroelectric sources, as the land relief is ideal for power generation. According to studies undertaken by the CEPGL's Enérgie des Pays des Grands Lacs (EGL), the Ruzizi river alone offers potential generating capacity totalling 500 MW, of which only a fraction is currently being used. Rwanda imported more than one-half (54% in 1990) of its total electricity requirements. In April 1997 it was announced that a feasibility study would be conducted into the possibility of aligning the power grids in Rwanda and in Uganda in order to lessen Rwanda's deficit. The Ntaruka diesel power station, completed in 1998, was expected to help reduce the shortfall; in 1997 15 MW (of a total consumption of 39 MW) was provided by neighbouring countries.

Also in early 1996 the Government announced partial privatization plans for Electrogaz, which was to entrust management of network exploitation to private interests. In May 2000 the Government decided that Electrogaz should be restructured and privatized, and that its water and electricity activities should be managed separately from the methane gas sector. However, the privatization process proved more protracted than expected. In September 2001 the management of Electrogaz announced that the first stage of the privatization would only commence in the first half of 2002. The Government planned that the state should continue to own the company for the following five years, but intended to contract a private corporation to manage it. Should Electrogaz's performances be positive during that time, the Government would then sell its shares. Six foreign companies, including SAUR International of France and Manitoba Hydro Roche Ltd of Canada, expressed interest in purchasing the parastatal. One of the Government's aims in this operation was to reduce energy and water prices, in order to increase the competitiveness of the economy and alleviate the burden of charges for consumers. In June 1998 Electrogaz signed a technical co-operation agreement with the Electricity Supply Commission of South Africa (ESKOM).

In 1998 production of electricity increased to 111m. kWh. In 1999 production totalled 127.3m. kWh. In 2000, however, production was only 110.8m. kWh, and Rwanda had to import 94.1m. kWh, equivalent to 46.1% of the country's total consumption in that year. In March 2001 prospects of increasing substantially Rwanda's power-generation capacity improved following an agreement between the BCDI and BRALIRWA to finance some US $5m. of the first stage of a power station, which was to be fuelled by methane gas from Lake Kivu (see above) and operated by the Gisenyi Electric and Gas Co. The power station was to have an initial modest capacity of 2.5 MW (which might subsequently be extended to up to 10 MW). According to USAID, this improvement in power availability was expected to encourage foreign direct investment in the region. By July 2001 the management of Electrogaz estimated that the company needed US $200m. to guarantee steady supply to users in urban centres. It also expressed concern that most equipment at power stations required immediate repair to meet the demand. In 2001 electricity production declined further, to 89.3m. kWh. In December 2002 the management of the Ugandan Electricity Generation Company agreed to increase its power supplies to Electrogaz. In February 2003 the Rwandan Ministry of Finance and Economic Planning estimated that total future investments in the electricity sector, including methane power stations and the extension of the Nyabarongo and rural electricity projects, which would double the national capacity (42 MW), would amount to $400m. At the beginning of 2003 Cogelgaz contracted Murray & Roberts to carry out a feasibility study for the construction of a methane-powered electricity plant, with a projected cost of $20m. In mid-2003 the EIB was considering the extension of the oil pipeline from Eldoret, Kenya, to the Ugandan capital and, in a further stage, to Kigali and eastern DRC.

In accordance with its objective to transform the country into a centre of services and a low cost centre of production for the region, which requires regular power supply as a pre-condition, the Rwandan Government declared 2004 to be 'the year of energy'. The first priority established by Lahmeyer International, which took over the management of Electrogaz by the end of 2003, was to reduce technical losses in the transport and distribution of power. A second objective was to improve Electrogaz's performance, and thus create a favourable context for privatization. By early 2004 the ADB, the World Bank and the OPEC Fund for International Development were considering investing US $50m. in order to support the Government's energy and water programmes. Electrogaz was also seeking complementary funds in order to improve the distribution networks in Kigali and other urban areas. The state-owned company was also planning to provide Kigali with a strategic reserve of 5 MW of thermal origin. By early 2004 2-MW generators were already being rehabilitated, and Electrogaz was considering the acquisition of generators in order to enable the Gatsatsa diesel station near Kigali to produce the remaining 3 MW. Power cuts resulting from increased demand were becoming more frequent by the end of 2003. After the completion of its rehabilitation, Electrogaz was considering several options to expand its capacity. The most advanced is the project to convert into electricity the methane of Lake Kivu. Electrogaz was trying to interest local companies, which were seeking larger and more secure power supplies, in joint ventures for the construction of small pilot plants with a maximum capacity of 2 MW. Meanwhile, the Government was continuing talks with an Israeli-Norwegian independent power producer, Dane Associates, to develop a 200-MW gas-powered plant. In a first phase, an extraction unit of a 20-MW–30-MW capacity, split into four units, in order to be compatible with existent installations, was to be established. Electrogaz also planned to restore the capacity of existing hydro-power infrastructures, such as the Ruzizi 1 plant (10 MW), in the neighbouring DRC. In late 2003 the Rwandan company dispatched a team of experts, which estimated the cost of such rehabilitation work at $1.5m. Rwanda, Burundi, Tanzania and Uganda expressed interest in January 2004 in the development of the Rusumo Falls hydropower project on the Kagera river, generating capacity of which was estimated at 65–70 MW, at a ministerial meeting held in Kigali, in the framework of the Nile Basin Initiative.

Insufficient rainfall in 2004 aggravated Rwanda's chronic electricity shortfall: Electrogaz's supplies declined by 20%. As an emergency response, in June the Government provided finance for the purchase of 12.5 MW of new diesel generation capacity from Global Power System (Belgium/Germany), for the Jabana substation in Kigali (7.8 MW) and for the 4.7 MW extension of the Gatsata power station, at a total cost of €4.3m. In addition, the Government planned to add a 10–15-MW thermal capacity by 2006–07 in order to meet demand. The Rwandan authorities and Electrogaz came to the conclusion that reform was necessary to help the company reduce structural deficits. Electrogaz, which was obliged to purchase large quantities of fuel and to fund its investment programme, was already burdened by its debts to the Government and to SINELAC and World Bank experts considered that major financial restructuring was required in order to limit electricity price shocks to the economy. It was none the less estimated that in order to cover its operational costs and other expenditures, Electrogaz should increase its tariffs from 42 Rwanda francs per kWh to 131 Rwanda francs per kWh. However, the 2005 budget envisaged increasing the tariff to only 61 Rwanda francs per kWh. Long-term solutions to the problem included the revitalization of regional co-operation in the energy sector. A step in that direction was made in July 2004, when the foreign ministers of Burundi, DRC and Rwanda, meeting in Brussels, Belgium, announced their commitment to reviving the activities of the CEPGL, and, more specially, the rehabilitation of the Ruzizi 1 hydroelectric power station, of which current capacity of 28.2 MW was to be upgraded to 39.6 MW, thereby enabling Ruzizi 1 to sell electricity to Electrogaz. The upgrading of the Ruzizi 2 power station operated by SINELAC was also envisaged. The main customer of the combined Ruzizi 1/Ruzizi 2 capacity is Rwanda, which took 68% of the 187 GWh produced in 2002, followed by the DRC (31%) and Burundi (1%). In the long term, projects may include the construction of Ruzizi 3. The total potential of the river is estimated at some 200 MW. If harnessed, this would enable SINELAC not only to satisfy the needs of the CEPGL members but also to export to other countries in the region. In order to be realized, however, these projects require, on the one hand, the improvement of bilateral relations between Rwanda and the DRC and, on the other, the settlement of the debt owed by Electrogaz to SNEL, which was estimated at US $330,000 in July 2004. Another precondition for the revival of CEPGL co-operation was the restructuring of the Banque de Développement des Etats des Grands Lacs (BDEGL), which formerly arranged financing with the EIB, Italy and the World Bank for the $72m. Ruzizi 2 station. Such reform is necessary if the BDEGL is to fulfil its ambitions to become the vehicle for the implementation of the New Partnership for Africa's Development (NEPAD) projects in the region, including the interconnection between Kigoma (Rwanda) and Rwegura (Burundi), and the interconnection of the CEPGL and Tanzanian grids.

Donors also considered that the Société Commerciale et Industrielle du Gaz (SOCIGAZ), which was created in 1990 by the DRC and Rwanda to develop methane gas projects, was also badly in need of financial and technical support if it was to increase its activities. Some progress, however, was achieved in the projects to develop the Lake Kivu methane reserves for use in energy generation projects. In late 2004 the World Bank was planning to finance consultant support to UPEGAZ (see above). In March 2005 Dane Associates signed an agreement with the Government of Rwanda for a 49-year concession to extract methane gas from the central Kibuye section of Lake Kivu, to be used to generate electricity to be sold to Electrogaz. The two companies established a joint venture called Kibuye Power 1 to manage the operation, which was to require an estimated total investment of US $60m. Meanwhile, in February Cogelgas commenced negotiations for a power purchase agreement with the Government, and it was additionally looking for an operator for the development of its Gisenyi methane gas concession.

TRANSPORT AND COMMUNICATIONS

Internal communications in Rwanda are operated almost exclusively along the relatively well-developed road system (14,008 km in 2004), as there are no railways nor navigable waterways (except Lake Kivu). Asphalted highways link Rwanda with Burundi, Uganda, the DRC and Tanzania. They also connect the principal towns. Tarmac roads extend to just over 1,000 km, which, given the small size of the country, is one of the highest densities in Africa. In early 1999 works financed by IDA for the asphalting of the 91-km Gitarama–Kibuye road were completed. Moreover, the World Bank agreed to disburse an additional US $10m. by the end of 1998 for the construction of roads to connect the nearby villages to the Gitarama–Kibuye road in order to facilitate the transporting of crops.

Rwanda's external trade is heavily dependent on the ports of Mombasa (Kenya), Dar es Salaam (Tanzania) and Matadi (DRC), and about 80% of Rwandan exports and imports pass through Uganda and Kenya. Insecurity caused by the war in the north of Rwanda led to the closure of the northern transport 'corridor' through Uganda. With the Gatuna and Kagitumba roads unavailable, most traffic had to be diverted via the difficult and unreliable route through Tanzania. In 1992 several projects had been approved by the EU and the World Bank to improve road links between eastern Zaire and western Uganda, with the aim of facilitating the passage of Rwandan trade across the border with Zaire, and thereby bypassing the troubled border with Uganda. Following the FPR victory in July 1994, however, the northern transport 'corridor' was immediately reopened. By the end of 1997 some 500 army personnel were deployed permanently to protect one of the country's principal roads, between the prefectures of Gisenyi and Ruhengeri, from rebel attacks. In January of that year the EU approved funding to upgrade the main road in and around Kigali. By the end of 1997 the EU had committed a total of ECU 34.5m. to rehabilitate 200 km of roads and the national airport of Kanombe and work on the project was under way. In October 2000 the EU agreed to allocate €9.2m. towards the completion of the rehabilitation of the 111-km road between Gitarama and the Burundi border. The OPEC Fund for International Development signed a further $10m. loan agreement with Rwanda to co-finance upgrading of the Gitarama road in early 2005. Further measures to improve the road network were undertaken in 2005. In July public works companies were invited to bid for the construction of the Kicukiro–Nyamata–Nemba road, to be financed by ADB, and for the rehabilitation of tarmac roads in Kigali, financed by BADEA. In mid-2007 the World Bank reportedly agreed to disburse a grant of some US $11m. to facilitate the construction of roads in the northern provinces and to reconstruct the 83-km road connecting Kigali with Gisenyi in the DRC. The rehabilitation of these sections of road comprised part of the Government's Transport Sector Development Project, which had received an additional grant from the African Growth Catalyst fund valued at some $38m. earlier in the year.

Feasibility studies have been conducted for a railway network to link Uganda, Rwanda, Burundi and Tanzania. The Rwandan business community showed renewed interest in the sector in early 2000, dispatching a delegation to the railway terminal of Isaka (Tanzania) to discuss with the local authorities and the Tanzania Railway Corporation plans to make greater use of this central corridor, combining a road link from Kigali to Isaka (500 km) and the railway line from Isaka to the port of Dar es Salaam (1,300 km). In April 2000 Burundi, Rwanda and Tanzania expressed their renewed intention to seek funds to build the railway link between Isaka and Kigali with a possible extension to Burundi. Transport costs have increased sizeably on the northern corridor (Kigali–Kampala–Mombasa), owing to the Ugandan and Kenyan Governments' decision to limit the maximum weight per axle of the trucks passing through their territory. Furthermore, tensions arising from the military clashes between the Ugandan and the Rwandan armies in Kisangani, DRC, in June of that year contributed to a dramatic decline in traffic through the northern corridor between Uganda and Rwanda and prompted the Rwandan Government and business interests to seek alternative access routes to the Indian Ocean.

Prior to the escalation of hostilities in April 1994, a number of international airlines, most prominently Sabena of Belgium and Air France, operated services to Kigali, while the small national carrier, Air Rwanda (scheduled for privatization), operated domestic passenger and cargo services and international cargo flights to Burundi, Kenya, Tanzania, Uganda, the DRC and destinations in Europe. Only Sabena (now SN Brussels Airlines) resumed flights after the FPR took power in July 1994. However, the airport is to be upgraded to meet international standards with the aid of the EU. In early 1998 the national carrier, Air Rwanda, announced plans to buy shares in Alliance Air, a regional carrier owned jointly by the Governments of Tanzania and Uganda and by South African Airways; the creation of a new company, to be known as Air Alliance Rwanda (AAR), was announced at the same time. Jointly owned by the Rwandan Government (51%) and Alliance Air (49%), AAR was to replace Air Rwanda and offer direct flights from Kigali to Johannesburg (South Africa), Entebbe (Uganda), Nairobi (Kenya), Dar es Salaam and Lubumbashi (DRC). In 2002 Rwanda had nine airports, of which only four had paved runways. In 2003 the EIB and EDF announced contributions, of €11m. and €8.5m. respectively, to rehabilitate the runway of Kigali international airport and the supply of air navigation equipment.

By mid-1998 the Government announced it would adopt a regulatory framework to supervise the participation of private companies in the telecommunications sector and to finalize the privatization of Rwandatel. In late 1999 the Government announced that the privatization of the national telecommunications company would take place during 2000. Meanwhile, the private mobile cellular telephone corporation MTN Rwandacell announced the extension of its Global System for Mobile Communications (GSM) network, which would henceforth cover three-quarters of Rwanda's territory. Rwandatel's growth is probably the country's greatest commercial success since independence. When it was created in 1993 only 3,000 lines were operating. One year later that figure had increased to 12,000, but the disruption during the 1994 genocide resulted in the near collapse of the system. In 1996 Rwandatel had a network of 7,000 lines, and achieved a turnover of US $4m. Five years later the network had expanded to 20,000 lines and its turnover had increased five-fold, to $21m. In 2002 the management of Rwandatel expected to increase the number of lines to 40,000 and its turnover to $50m. Major innovations planned in that year included the introduction of a prepaid system to improve the recovery of bills and the construction throughout the country of public telephone facilities, including in the most remote rural areas. Meanwhile, the company invested in new technologies. By mid-2002 the country had three internet service providers (Rwandatel, the National University of Rwanda and the Kigali Institute of Science and Technology). Rwandatel's plan was to introduce high-speed and high-capacity asymmetric digital subscriber line (ADSL) connections during 2002, in order to improve services to the private sector and national institutions. Development plans included the construction of new centres, with a capacity of 20,000 lines, to provide telephone services to the inhabitants of the outskirts of Kigali, and to replace old cables outside the capital with fibre-optic ones. The long-planned privatization of the company remained the objective, but the Government took the decision to continue the expansion of the company and, after its capital reached significant proportions, to sell 51% of shares to a private operator. Plans also included the sale of Rwandatel's 26% share in Rwandacell and the creation of the government-owned company's own mobile telephone subsidiary. At the beginning of 2002 the company expanded its activities in the neighbouring DRC, signing a partnership agreement with the management of the parastatal Office Congolais des Postes et des Télécommunications in the part of the country held by the Rwandan-backed RCD, in order to improve telecommunications in both Goma and Bukavu.

The development of telecommunications was part of the national information technology policy. The Government established an Information Technology Commission, headed by the President, in 2001, and created an agency to oversee a five-year plan, with a projected cost of US $500m., to develop the sector, with the assistance of the UN Economic Commission for Africa. The mobile cellular telephone sector expanded even more rapidly. By early 2003 it was estimated that the number of mobile cellular telephones in use in the country was at least double that of fixed telephone lines. In early 2004, however, demand for telecommunication services still exceeded the capacity of the operators, as a result of lack of financing and competition in services provision. It was anticipated that the privatization of Rwandatel would improve its operational and financial performance, as well as its investment capacity. The Government was also considering the sale of its shares in Rwandacell, the market-leader (well ahead of Afritel and Artel, which operate mainly in rural areas). In early 2004 more than 300 secondary schools were provided with internet connectivity. In February 2005 President Kagame stated, at the African Information Communications Technologies conference in Accra, Ghana, that all of the country's secondary schools were to be connected to the internet by 2017. Kagame also announced that broadband infrastructure was in place in Rwanda, that there was fibre-optic infrastructure in Kigali and most others towns and that the authorities planned to extend this to other areas of the country. Rwanda, like other East and Central African countries, relies on satellite as a sole medium for international connectivity. However, the Government has, through Rwandatel, subscribed to the future East African Submarine Cable System. The number of internet centres was increasing rapidly in the country. In early 2005, for example, farmers at Maraba were using such facilities to communicate with other coffee producers from the rest of the world.

DEVELOPMENT PLANNING

The members of the CEPGL agreed in 1978 to form a joint development bank, and to co-operate in the development of a transport system and the construction of a hydroelectric power station (the Ruzizi 2 project) on the Rwanda–Congo border, the exploitation of methane gas deposits beneath Lake Kivu and the promotion of a fishing industry. The BDEGL was formerly established in 1980, with it headquarters at Goma, in what was then Zaire. Since the change of regime in the DRC, all the CEPGL states have expressed their desire for continuing regional co-operation. However, the war in the DRC between 1998 and 2003 halted CEPGL activities. It was only in July 2004 that the three countries undertook to resume co-operation within the framework of the CEPGL in the interests of promoting regional stability and economic development. Energy was given priority in the list of joint projects, more specifically the rehabilitation of the Rusizi 1 hydroelectric power station, followed by the restructuring of the BDEGL, the exploitation of the Lake Kivu methane gas reserves, and agriculture and communications projects. However, cross-border raids by Hutu rebels into Rwanda and from the Rwandan Defence Force militia into the DRC at the end of 2004 created a climate of tension, which caused delays in the implementation of these projects.

The Rwandan Government has sought unsuccessfully to limit the overall budget deficit, which reached 19.2% of GDP in 1993, compared with 9% in 1989, despite an 11% increase in tax revenue and a 25% decline in capital expenditure to 1992, and notwithstanding the Government's failure adequately to finance the social contingency fund agreed under the terms of its adjustment programme. Budget expenditure increased in order to finance the war and internal security, and to support producer prices for coffee. The situation deteriorated further in 1993, with revenue declining by an estimated 6%, while expenditure increased by an estimated 5%. By the end of October 1993 foreign reserves were estimated to be insufficient to sustain imports for one week.

The overall budget deficit amounted to 16% of GDP by the end of 1994, and to 12.5% by the end of 1995. By 1997 the budget deficit had decreased to 10% of GDP but an increase, to 13.5%, was expected in 1998, following a temporary acceleration in government investment, and the high costs of structural reforms. Although IMF projections indicated a further decrease by 2000, owing to improved savings and a stabilization of government investments, estimates for 1999 projected a budgetary deficit of 16.4% of GDP. Furthermore, the high level of military expenditure (about one-third of current expenditure in 1997, despite a demilitarization programme which commenced in that year) was a matter of concern for the donors, particularly compared with the share of the social sectors, which declined from 38% to 18% between 1985 and 1995. In November 1998 the Government pledged to limit military expenditure to 4% of GDP and civil service salaries to 3.6% of GDP. In that year the Government announced plans for some 3,600 redundancies within the civil service and for the sale of up to one-half of its vehicles in an effort to reduce expenditure. The Government also announced plans to increase substantially taxes on beer, petrol, soft drinks, cigarettes, wines and spirits, in an attempt to balance the 1999 budget.

In 1999 an overall budget deficit of 25,300m. Rwanda francs (equivalent to 3.9% of GDP) was recorded. This was attributed to a decrease in earnings from exports of coffee, pyrethrum, and hides and skins, despite the good performance of the tea sector. The 2000 budget of 168,900m. Rwanda francs (including foreign funding, which amounted to 53.7% of the total) was 2,000m. Rwanda francs lower than the budget of the previous year. In order to balance the 2000 budget, the Government decided to maximize its earnings, by introducing a value-added tax on 1 July of that year and by accelerating the privatization process. Apart from the telecommunications company Rwandatel, OCIR, tea-processing plants and plantations have been listed among the assets that are to be privatized, alongside STIR (international transport), Sodeparal (agricultural products), Soporiz (rice) and the water, electricity and gas utility, Electrogaz (see above). The state also plans divestment from three banks (Banque Commerciale du Rwanda, Banque Rwandaise de Développement and Banque de Kigali), the tobacco corporation, Tabarwanda, the flour mill, Etiru, the coffee company, Rwandex, the BRALIRWA brewery, the printing company, IMPRISCO, and the travel agency, Amirwanda. Despite the concerns expressed by donors, defence still remained a priority of the national budget in 2000, absorbing 19.8% of total expenditure. However, the Government confirmed its decision to make 3,600 redundancies and to suspend new recruitment of civil servants. In April 2000 the new Prime Minister, Bernard Makuza, expressed the Government's commitment to curb corruption, following the resignation of his predecessor and parliamentary investigations into embezzlement charges concerning several ministers of the previous administration. An overall budget deficit of 40,200m. Rwanda francs (equivalent to 5.5% of GDP) was recorded in 2001.

In May 2001 the Rwandan Government presented a 'plan of action' for the 2001–10 period at the third UN Conference on the Least Developed Countries, which took place in Brussels. The principal aims were to achieve an average annual GDP growth rate of at least 6%, restrain inflation to below 5% a year, reduce the current-account deficit (excluding official transfers) from 16.8% of GDP in 2000 to 10.7% in 2004, maintain the level of gross official reserves at a level of at least the value of six months of imports, increase the ratio of revenue to GDP by one-half of a percentage point per year, and maintain debt at sustainable levels. In order to meet those targets, the challenge was to diversify the economy, and to increase labour productivity and rural recapitalization in all sectors. To that effect, the 'plan of action' included in its strategy the creation of training opportunities for unskilled young workers and the provision of rural credit, financial services and support to small-scale enterprises. Meanwhile, the Government would also aim to increase tax collection, from 9.7% of GDP at the end of 1999 to 11% by the end of 2001. Positive results were also expected from the elimination of tariffs on regional trade consistent with the Cross-Border Initiative.

In early 2002 the Government announced its objective to increase GDP per head to US $960 by 2020, as part of the objectives of the 'Vision 2020' development strategy. Emphasis was to be placed on the development of services, which accounted for 34.4% of the country's GDP in 2001. The ambition was to transform Rwanda from an essentially agrarian economy to a knowledge-based society within 20 years, through the development of information technology. To this effect, the Kigali Institute of Science and Technology was inaugurated in July 2002. Meanwhile, efforts were being devoted to integrating the Rwandan banking system further into the global economy, as was demonstrated by the establishment, in April of the same year, by six Rwandan banks of a joint company to promote the use of credit cards and other electronic payment systems. The Government also aimed to encourage development in the tourism sector, which was undergoing a recovery, although its contribution to tertiary sector GDP had not reached pre-war levels by the end of 2001. However, by the end of 2003 the contribution of services to GDP had risen to 36.3%. The 'Vision 2020' strategy also aimed to increase the literacy rate from 48% in 2000 to 100%. By early 2004 internet connectivity was established in more than 300 schools. The long-term objective was to transform Rwanda into a regional centre for services, not least within the framework of a revived CEPGL. The expansion of the coffee and tea industries, of tourism and of new communication technologies were set as priorities of the 2004 budget. Indeed, Rwanda is endowed with considerable tourism attractions, such as its volcanos and wildlife resources such as mountain gorillas and the zebras of the Kagera National Park. South Africa's Sun Group, which acquired the Meridien Hotel in Gisenyi, together with Kenyan investors and also Rwandan private interests, has contributed significantly to the development of Rwanda's hotel capacity. The first phase of the Kigali Amusement Park (KAP) was due to open in mid-2007. The KAP project was conceived by local entrepreneurs and was to be partially funded by commercial Bank of Rwanda. A casino, botanical garden, and 15 'eco-tourist' bungalows would feature in the completed park, in addition to a series of rides to be designed by the Chinese firm SBL Co.

Of the 375,800m. Rwanda francs budget for 2005 (of which as much as 57.7% was to be foreign-financed) 27.9% was allocated to development expenditure. Health, education, defence and infrastructure accounted for most of the 9% increase in total budget spending. Some 4,000m. Rwanda francs was designated for the road fund, but total requirements for rehabilitation of the network were estimated at 12,000m. Rwanda francs. Other priorities of the budget were the need to enhance agricultural productivity and improve distribution of seeds and fertilizers, to promote better access to loans for the agricultural sector and to finance land reforms, as well as investments in information technologies. The 2006 budget increased to an estimated 399,300m. Rwanda francs, 49.8% of which was domestically financed. There has been a general trend in increasing government expenditure, which represented 28.2% of GDP in 2005. While the budget outlay increased in 2006, an improved economic performance saw expenditure decrease as a percentage of GDP (26.2%). The 2007 budget forecast expenditure of 506,700m. Rwanda francs, which included significant allocations to the agricultural and tourism sectors. Key service sectors were also scheduled to receive substantial budgetary funding, among which included the Kigali Water Project (3,300m. Rwanda francs) and the Common Development Fund (CDF) which received a bursary of 5,000m. Rwanda francs. The introduction of a 3% excise tax on a number of goods and services was expected to yield additional domestic revenue; however, around 53.3% of the budget was still expected to be financed externally, mostly in the form of grants.

Rwanda's heavy dependence on foreign assistance (equivalent to as much as 90% of public investment in recent years) has made the economy vulnerable to civil and political instability. By the end of 1995 external assistance was equivalent to 172.5% of imports, or US $56 per head. Of the $587m. pledged by donors at the UNDP-sponsored conference, convened in Geneva in January 1995, only $69m. had been disbursed by June, largely as a result of the Kibeho refugee camp massacre and the Government's failure to accept a broader political and ethnic base. In that month, however, the EU and other donors began the resumption of aid disbursements, and subsequent pledges brought the total amount to $1,260m., of which $404m. (32%) had been spent by the end of 1995. With such transfers, by the end of 1995 foreign reserves increased to the value of 3.7 months of imports, compared to that of 1.3 months in 1994. Delays to aid disbursements were not only prompted by security issues, but also by disagreements between the World Bank and the Government regarding the assignment of a procurement of commodities and technical assistance under the World Bank Emergency Recovery Credit. Other delaying factors were the Government's limited capacity to absorb aid, owing to its own limited technical and administrative staff and its unwillingness to accept foreign technical assistance. In June 1996, at a second donors' conference held in Geneva, additional funds of $617m. were pledged, although, in effect, according to some participants at the meeting, the new money made available amounted to only $240m. Indeed, the EU attached very stringent conditions for the disbursement of its funds, which were unlikely to be met by the Government in the short term. Such conditions included appropriate measures for the repatriation of refugees from Zaire and Tanzania, and the improvement of the judicial system. In late 1996 accusations were raised that external aid had been used by the Habyarimana Government to purchase weapons. It was also alleged that bank transfers, again used to purchase armaments, had been allowed, even during the genocide.

In 1995, principally as a result of external assistance funds, a surplus on the current account of the balance of payments of US $65m. was registered. In 1997, however, a deficit on the current account of the balance of payments of $62.2m. was recorded; the deficit widened to $118.2m. in 2001. Financial requirements during 1998–2001 were projected at $1,600m.; this total was expected to be met through capital grants ($465m.), project loans ($235m.) and from non-budgetary transfers (humanitarian assistance—$450m.). The remainder was expected to be covered through IMF disbursements, debt relief from the 'Paris Club' of official creditors, and refinancing and assistance from both multilateral and bilateral creditors. In July 1998 it was announced that the 'Paris Club' had agreed to restructure Rwanda's bilateral debt (then around $181m.), reducing it by up to 67%. In June of that year Rwanda obtained a $250m. quick disbursement loan from the World Bank to support the Government's 1998–2000 reform programme. This was aimed at supporting the country's efforts in the areas of health, education, national reconciliation and administrative reform, and at contributing to the fund for the survivors of the genocide. In June, furthermore, the IMF approved a three-year loan, amounting to $95m., under the Enhanced Structural Adjustment Facility (ESAF). A trust fund of $41.7m., managed by the World Bank, was established at the same time to help Rwanda manage its external debt. According to the IMF, Rwanda has made substantial progress in rebuilding its severely damaged infrastructure since 1994; most internally displaced people have been settled, macroeconomic stability has been restored and key structural reforms have been initiated. However, Rwanda's administrative and institutional capacity in the public sector remained weak. Increased amounts of concessional external assistance would, therefore, be required in the long term to finance higher social expenditure and to ensure sustained human resource development. In 2000 91.7% of Rwanda's public investment budget was to be financed by foreign aid.

In 2000, despite criticisms of Rwanda's involvement in the DRC war, donors continued to provide economic and financial support to Rwanda. In March the European Commission announced that it would allocate €110m. to Rwanda under the country's national indicative programme of the Fourth Lomé Convention. The remaining €47m. would be disbursed according to the use of the first tranche. Three-quarters of the funding under the programme was allocated to poverty alleviation projects, with the remainder being allocated to projects aimed at promoting good governance and justice. Meanwhile, the World Bank announced that it would provide assistance during 2000 through two projects, one in agriculture and one in rural water, with a total value of US $25m. The World Bank was planning to disburse an additional amount of $125m. for four projects in 2001: one in agriculture; one in human resources development; one in trade and private sector development; and a leveraged insurance facility for trade, a regional facility to guarantee investment against sovereign, but not exchange-rate, risk. In addition, in early 2000 the People's Republic of China announced a grant of 20m. yuan (approximately $2.5m.) for agriculture, road construction and education projects. In 2000 USAID assistance totalled $34.7m., supporting Economic Support Funds from the Great Lakes Justice Initiative, Development Assistance and emergency International Development Assistance from the Office of Foreign Disaster Assistance. In 2002 USAID planned to support the three priority areas: development relief and conflict prevention; global health; and economic growth. USAID also announced its intention to increase its efforts to counter HIV/AIDS by expanding awareness activities, working with other donors to prevent mother-to-child transmission and providing counselling and other support to infected persons. In that year USAID was in the early stages of implementing a three-year, multifaceted effort to stimulate agricultural production and promote broad-based economic growth, complemented by a substantial development-orientated Food for Peace programme. Components of the programme included human resource development at the principal agricultural research, training and educational institutions, policy advice to the then Ministry of Agriculture, Animal Resources and Forestry, and the expansion of agribusiness and export opportunities. In 2000 Rwanda was the main recipient of Belgian development aid on the African continent, with a loan totalling 412.5m. Belgian francs.

In January 2001 Rwanda, declared eligible to benefit from the IMF- and World Bank-sponsored initiative for heavily indebted poor countries (HIPCs) in December 2000, obtained debt relief of US $810m., which was to contribute substantially to the alleviation of the country's debt burden. Total outstanding external debt was estimated at $1,324m. by the end of 2000, equivalent to 73% of GDP. More than 87% of Rwandan external debt was owed to multilateral partners, principally the World Bank Group, with $998.4m., followed by the ADB ($208.4m.). The main bilateral creditors were France ($35.2m.), the People's Republic of China ($32.2m.), Saudi Arabia ($29.8m.), Kuwait ($29.4m.) and Japan ($13.6m.). The Government estimated that annual cash flow savings from this relief would be about $20m.–$30m. per year, equivalent to 1.5% of GDP, in 2001–10. In April 2001 Rwanda also completed an interim Poverty Strategy Reduction Paper, which was to serve as the basis for both concessional lending and debt relief under the enhanced HIPC initiative. The debt relief was expected to benefit the health, education, agriculture and infrastructure sectors.

The World Bank intensified its financial support to Rwanda in 2001, with the adoption of a US $48m. programme to revitalize the rural economy, increase rural income and reduce poverty. The project, which was financed by a credit from IDA, was to focus on the rehabilitation of farmed marshland and hillside areas, the promotion of commercial and export-orientated agriculture, support for agricultural services delivery systems, small-scale rural infrastructure development and the encouragement of off-farm productive activities. By 2005 however, only a very small amount of money in this large project had actually been spent, due to inertia at the Rwandan Ministry of Agriculture and negligence at the World Bank. The appointment of a new Minister of Agriculture and new World Bank staff in 2005 and 2006 was expected to bring about improvements. This project was part of a $165m. rural development programme, launched in December 2001, which was to be 95% financed by the World Bank. This larger programme, which was to be implemented over a 14-year period, involved the construction of infrastructure and research centres, with the aim of finding new commercial outlets for Rwanda's agricultural products.

In March 2002 the ADB, which approved a US $30m. loan in 2001, opened a permanent office in Kigali in order to intensify its co-operation with Rwanda. In January 2001 President Kagame emphasized the Rwandan Government's achievements since 1994: state revenue, negligible in 1994, reached 70,000m. Rwanda francs in 2000, while the number of Rwandan university students had increased from 3,000 to 7,000 during the same period, and 355 hospitals and health centres were rehabilitated. However, Kagame deplored Rwanda's high levels of infant mortality, low life-expectancy, which was still below 50 years, and the Rwandan population's low purchasing power. By mid-2006 health indicators remained a cause for concern. Women and children were suffering disproportionately as a result of high fertility rates, a low proportion of births attended by qualified personnel, poor nutrition and high mortality rates. HIV/AIDS remained a serious problem, with prevalence rates estimated by UNAIDS at 5.1% of persons aged 15–49 years in 2003. In that year, however, important progress was made in re-establishing health systems. The expansion in health care expenditure initiated in 2003 was consolidated, with recurrent health expenditure reaching almost 1%. Progress made in the education sector in previous years was consolidated during 2004, with important policy reforms implemented. The introduction of fee-free education led to a further improvement in primary enrolment.

FOREIGN TRADE

In 2003 exports declined by 6.0%, to US $63m., as a result of lower coffee and mineral export revenues. Coffee accounted for 27.6% of total exports, with $13.9m., ahead of tea ($11.9m., 23.6%). Coltan and other mineral products followed, ahead of re-exports, hides and manufacturing products. In 2003 imports amounted to $229m., compared with $233m. in the previous year. As a result, there was little movement in the trade deficit, which was recorded at $166m. In 2003 the main destinations of exports were Kenya (40.9%), followed by Uganda (26.6%) and the United Kingdom (6.2%), according to UN statistics. The main origins of imports in that year were Kenya (28.4%), followed by Belgium (12.2%), Uganda (7.7%), the United Arab Emirates (7.6%), Tanzania (5.6%) and South Africa (4.9%). In 2004 coffee was the leading export product, generating $27.5m. of export revenue, followed by tea ($25.6m.), cassiterite ($12.9m) and coltan ($10.6m.). At the beginning of 2004, in view of Rwanda's low underlying growth rate, the Government began to examine export promotion and broader trade issues. An export promotion strategy was adopted in the second half of the year, and a reformed Rwanda Investment and Export Promotion Agency was launched. Export performance in 2004 was promising, reversing previous negative trends. Exports increased in value by 51.4% to $98m., largely driven by coffee, cassiterite and coltan. In terms of imports, poor domestic food production and the energy crisis led to higher food and fuel imports. However, this was partly offset by lower imports of industrial goods as a result of the energy crisis and the additional competition caused by entry into the COMESA Free Trade Area. In total, imports increased by 18.9% to $276m., more than offsetting the improved export performance. As a result, the current-account deficit on the balance of payments (excluding official transfers) deteriorated marginally from 16.6% of GDP to 16.8%. Imports increased by a further 28.6% in 2005, reaching $355m. An accompanying rise in the value of exports, which increased to $128m. failed to improve the trade deficit which was reported at $227m. that year, compared with $178m. in 2004. A rise in transfer receipts, meanwhile, narrowed the current account deficit considerably, which stood at $84m. in 2005.

In March 2004 negotiations commenced between the EU and the Eastern and Southern Africa group of countries (including Rwanda) for a World Trade Organization (WTO) compatible free trade Economic Partnership Agreement, due to enter force in 2008. With the extension, until 2007, of AGOA, enacted by the USA to extend duty-free and quota-free access to the US market for nearly all textile and handicraft goods produced in eligible beneficiary countries, the Rwandan Government was keen to benefit further from this system. In the mid-2000s Rwandan small-scale cloth and textile handicraft businesses were beginning to export products to the USA.

Statistical Survey

Source (unless otherwise stated): Office rwandais d'information, BP 83, Kigali; tel. 75724.

Area and Population

AREA, POPULATION AND DENSITY

Area (sq km)	26,338*
Population (census results)	
15 August 1991	7,142,755
16 August 2002†	
Males	3,879,448
Females	4,249,105
Total	8,128,553
Population (UN estimate at mid-year)‡	
2004	9,052,000
2005	9,234,000
2006	9,464,000
Density (per sq km) at mid-2006	359.3

* 10,169 sq miles.

† Provisional results.

‡ Source: UN, *World Population Prospects: The 2006 Revision*.

PREFECTURES

(1991 census)

	Area (sq km)	Population*	Density (per sq km)
Butare	1,830	765,910	418.5
Byumba	4,987	779,365	159.2
Cyangugu	2,226	517,550	232.5
Gikongoro	2,192	462,635	211.1
Gisenyi	2,395	728,365	304.1
Gitarama	2,241	849,285	379.0
Kibungo	4,134	647,175	156.5
Kibuye	1,320	472,525	358.0
Kigali	3,251	921,050	355.2
Kigali-Ville		233,640	
Ruhengeri	1,762	765,255	434.3
Total	26,338	7,142,755	271.2

* Source: UN, *Demographic Yearbook*.

PRINCIPAL TOWNS

(population at 1978 census)

Kigali (capital)	117,749	Ruhengeri	16,025
Butare	21,691	Gisenyi	12,436

Mid-2005 (incl. suburbs, UN estimate): Kigali 779,000 (Source: UN, *World Urbanization Prospects: The 2005 Revision*).

BIRTHS AND DEATHS

(annual averages, UN estimates)

	1990–95	1995–2000	2000–05
Birth rate (per 1,000)	41.7	40.2	43.9
Death rate (per 1,000)	41.9	24.1	18.4

Source: UN, *World Population Prospects: The 2006 Revision*.

Expectation of life (years at birth, WHO estimates): 46 (males 44; females 47) in 2004 (Source: WHO, *World Health Report*).

ECONOMICALLY ACTIVE POPULATION

(persons aged 14 years and over, at census of August 2002)

	Males	Females	Total
Agriculture	1,218,181	1,731,411	2,949,592
Fishing	3,374	94	3,468
Industrial activities	3,692	1,636	5,328
Production activities	32,994	10,649	43,643
Electricity and water	2,390	277	2,667
Construction	41,641	1,244	42,885
Trade reconstruction	56,869	32,830	89,699
Restaurants and hotels	4,525	2,311	6,836
Transport and communications	29,574	1,988	31,562
Financial intermediaries	1,560	840	2,400
Administration and defence	22,479	5,585	28,064
Education	22,688	17,046	39,734
Health and social services	7,521	7,054	14,575
Activities not adequately defined	69,042	39,458	108,500
Total employed	1,516,530	1,852,423	3,368,953

Source: IMF, *Rwanda: Selected Issues and Statistical Appendix* (December 2004).

Mid-2005 (estimates in '000): Agriculture, etc. 4,376; Total labour force 4,873 (Source: FAO).

Health and Welfare

KEY INDICATORS

Total fertility rate (children per woman, 2005)	5.5
Under-5 mortality rate (per 1,000 live births, 2005)	203
HIV/AIDS (% of persons aged 15–49, 2005)	3.1
Physicians (per 1,000 head, 2004)	0.05
Hospital beds (per 1,000 head, 2004)	1.70
Health expenditure (2004): US $ per head (PPP)	125.9
Health expenditure (2004): % of GDP	7.5
Health expenditure (2004): public (% of total)	56.8
Access to water (% of persons, 2004)	74
Access to sanitation (% of persons, 2004)	42
Human Development Index (2004): ranking	158
Human Development Index (2004): value	0.448

For sources and definitions, see explanatory note on p. vi.

Agriculture

PRINCIPAL CROPS

('000 metric tons)

	2003	2004	2005
Maize	78.9	88.2	97.3
Sorghum	171.6	163.8	227.9
Potatoes	1,099.5	1,072.8	1,314.1
Sweet potatoes	868.2	908.3	885.6
Cassava (Manioc)	1,003.1	765.7	781.6
Taro (Coco yam)	138.8	136.4	136.9
Sugar cane*	70.0	70.0	70.0
Dry beans	239.4	198.2	199.6
Dry peas	17.7	16.8	18.9
Groundnuts (in shell)	10.3	10.8	10.1
Pumpkins, squash and gourds*	210.0	210.3	214.4
Plantains	2,407.8	2,469.7	2,593.1
Coffee (green)	13.8	20.0	18.6
Tea (made)	15.5	14.5	16.5

* FAO estimates.

Source: FAO.

LIVESTOCK
('000 head, year ending September)

	2003	2004	2005
Cattle	991.7	1,003.7	1,004.1
Pigs	211.9	326.7	346.9
Sheep	371.8	470.0	464.3
Goats	941.1	1,264.0	1,339.7
Rabbits	498	520	519
Chickens	1,800*	2,042	2,000*

* FAO estimate.

Source: FAO.

LIVESTOCK PRODUCTS
('000 metric tons, FAO estimates)

	2003	2004	2005
Cattle meat	23.6	23.0	23.1
Goat meat	3.3	4.5	4.7
Pig meat	3.9	6.0	6.4
Chicken meat	2.0	2.3	2.3
Game meat	11.0	11.0	11.0
Other meat	3.1	3.4	3.4
Cows' milk	112.5	121.4	120.0
Sheep's milk	1.8	1.9	1.9
Goats' milk	17.9	24.0	24.0
Poultry eggs	2.3	2.3	2.3

Source: FAO.

Forestry

ROUNDWOOD REMOVALS
('000 cubic metres, excluding bark, FAO estimates)

	2003	2004	2005
Sawlogs, veneer logs and logs for sleepers	245	245	245
Other industrial wood	250	250	250
Fuel wood	5,000	5,000	5,000
Total	5,495	5,495	5,495

Source: FAO.

SAWNWOOD PRODUCTION
('000 cubic metres, including railway sleepers)

	1997	1998	1999
Coniferous (softwood)	20	21	22
Non-coniferous (hardwood)	54	55	57
Total	74	76	79

2000–05: Figures assumed to be unchanged from 1999 (FAO estimates).

Source: FAO.

Fishing

(metric tons, live weight)

	2003	2004	2005*
Capture	7,400	7,826	7,800
Nile tilapia	2,800	3,120	3,100
Aquaculture	1,027	386	386
Nile tilapia	1,000	340	340
Total catch	8,427	8,212	8,186

* FAO estimates.

Source: FAO.

Mining

(metric tons, unless otherwise indicated)

	2003	2004*	2005*
Tin concentrates†	192	547	700
Tungsten concentrates†	78	120	200
Columbo-tantalite‡	128	200	250
Gold (kilograms)†	2	—	—
Natural gas (million cubic metres)§	314	320	320

* Estimates.

† Figures refer to the metal content of ores and concentrates.

‡ Figures refer to the estimated production of mineral concentrates. The metal content (estimates, metric tons) was: Niobium (Columbium) 40 in 2003, 63 in 2004, 80 in 2005; Tantalum 26 in 2003, 40 in 2004, 50 in 2005.

§ Figures refer to gross output.

Source: US Geological Survey.

Industry

SELECTED PRODUCTS

	2001	2002	2003
Beer ('000 hectolitres)	479	539	412
Soft drinks ('000 hectolitres)	228	n.a.	n.a.
Cigarettes (million)	278	391	402
Soap (metric tons)	7,056	5,571	4,456
Cement (metric tons)	83,024	100,568	105,105
Electric energy (million kWh)	89.3	n.a.	n.a.

Source: IMF, *Rwanda: Statistical Annex* (August 2002) and IMF, *Rwanda: Selected Issues and Statistical Appendix* (December 2004).

Finance

CURRENCY AND EXCHANGE RATES

Monetary Units
100 centimes = 1 franc rwandais (Rwanda franc).

Sterling, Dollar and Euro Equivalents (29 December 2006)
£1 sterling = 1,077.00 Rwanda francs;
US $1 = 548.65 Rwanda francs;
€1 = 722.58 Rwanda francs;
10,000 Rwanda francs = £9.29 = $18.23 = €13.84.

Average Exchange Rate (Rwanda francs per US $)
2004 574.622
2005 555.841
2006 552.555

Note: Since September 1983 the currency has been linked to the IMF special drawing right (SDR). Until November 1990 the mid-point exchange rate was SDR 1 = 102.71 Rwanda francs. In November 1990 a new rate of SDR 1 = 171.18 Rwanda francs was established. This remained in effect until June 1992, when the rate was adjusted to SDR 1 = 201.39 Rwanda francs. The latter parity was maintained until February 1994, since when the rate has been frequently adjusted. In March 1995 the Government introduced a market-determined exchange rate system.

BUDGET

('000 million Rwanda francs)

Revenue*	1999	2000	2001†
Tax revenue	60.4	65.3	79.5
Taxes on income and profits	15.2	17.9	23.9
Company profits tax	7.4	10.0	14.4
Individual income tax	6.1	7.5	9.0
Domestic taxes on goods and services	33.6	35.2	41.0
Excise taxes	17.9	18.8	14.2
Turnover tax	12.9	13.8	24.2
Road fund	2.7	2.5	2.6
Taxes on international trade	11.0	11.6	14.0
Import taxes	8.4	9.3	11.1
Non-tax revenue	3.2	3.3	6.7
Total	63.6	68.7	86.2

Expenditure‡	1999	2000	2001†
Current expenditure	86.0	89.2	107.4
General public services	31.5	35.7	53.7
Defence	27.0	25.8	28.6
Social services	21.9	30.5	36.2
Education	17.2	24.0	29.8
Health	3.3	3.8	5.1
Economic services	2.6	2.1	4.9
Energy and public works	0.7	0.4	2.3
Interest on public debt	4.0	1.8	2.8
Adjustment	−1.1	−6.7	−18.8
Capital expenditure	40.8	42.0	50.0
Sub-total	126.8	131.2	157.5
Adjustment for payment arrears§	2.0	−1.2	31.7
Total	128.8	130.0	189.2

* Excluding grants received ('000 million Rwanda francs): 38.5 in 1999; 63.7 in 2000; 63.3† in 2001.

† Estimates.

‡ Excluding lending minus repayments ('000 million Rwanda francs): −0.4 in 1999; 0.5 in 2000; 0.6 in 2001†.

§ Minus sign indicates increase in arrears.

Source: IMF, *Rwanda: Statistical Annex* (August 2002).

2002 (estimates, '000 million Rwanda francs): *Revenue:* Tax revenue 94.6; Non-tax revenue 6.6; Total 101.2, excl. grants received (70.8). *Expenditure:* Current 123.7; Capital 56.4; Total 180.1, excl. net lending (11.5) (Source: IMF, *Rwanda: First Review Under the Three-Year Arrangement Under the Poverty Reduction and Growth Facility and Request for Waiver of Performance Criteria—Staff Report; Staff Statement; Press Release on the Executive Board Discussion; and Statement by the Executive Director for Rwanda*—June 2003).

INTERNATIONAL BANK RESERVES

(US $ million at 31 December)

	2004	2005	2006
IMF special drawing rights	30.20	25.91	22.85
Foreign exchange	284.44	379.85	416.82
Total	314.64	405.76	439.67

Source: IMF, *International Financial Statistics*.

MONEY SUPPLY

(million Rwanda francs at 31 December)

	2003	2004	2005
Currency outside banks	29,246	36,512	46,277
Demand deposits at deposit money banks	52,220	62,604	82,524
Total money (incl. others)	82,305	99,941	129,326

Source: IMF, *International Financial Statistics*.

COST OF LIVING

(Consumer Price Index for Kigali; base: 2000 = 100)

	2004	2005	2006
All items	126.6	138.1	150.3

Source: IMF, *International Financial Statistics*.

NATIONAL ACCOUNTS

('000 million Rwanda francs at current prices)

Expenditure on the Gross Domestic Product

	2003	2004	2005
Government final consumption expenditure	137.1	136.1	152.6
Private final consumption expenditure Increase in stocks }	775.7	893.0	1,026.8
Gross fixed capital formation	166.8	215.8	245.5
Total domestic expenditure	1,079.6	1,244.9	1,424.9
Exports of goods and services	75.0	108.6	112.9
Less Imports of goods and services	249.4	299.2	374.9
GDP in purchasers' values	905.3	1,054.3	1,162.9
GDP at constant 1995 prices	639.1	667.0	n.a.

Source: IMF, *International Financial Statistics*.

Gross Domestic Product by Economic Activity

	2001	2002	2003
Agriculture, hunting, forestry and fishing	305.2	341.6	373.9
Mining and quarrying	14.5	9.1	5.7
Manufacturing	73.9	80.5	80.3
Electricity, gas and water	3.4	3.4	3.6
Construction	71.2	82.9	103.1
Trade, restaurants and hotels	75.2	82.0	91.7
Transport, storage and communications	55.1	60.7	61.7
Public administration	54.2	55.8	64.8
Other services	101.6	109.0	120.4
GDP at market prices	754.3	825.0	905.3

Source: IMF, *Rwanda: Selected Issues and Statistical Appendix* (December 2004).

BALANCE OF PAYMENTS

(US $ million)

	2004	2005	2006
Exports of goods f.o.b.	98	128	145
Imports of goods f.o.b.	−276	−355	−488
Trade balance	−178	−227	−343
Exports of services	103	129	131
Imports of services	−240	−304	−243
Balance on goods and services	−315	−402	−455
Other income received	6	27	27
Other income paid	−39	−44	−48
Balance on goods, services and income	−349	−418	−476
Current transfers received	169	352	319
Current transfers paid	−18	−18	−23
Current balance	−198	−84	−180
Capital account (net)	61	93	1,323
Direct investment abroad	—	—	14
Direct investment from abroad	8	8	11
Other investment assets	8	−14	−30
Other investment liabilities	−37	−52	−1,199
Net errors and omissions	23	26	87
Overall balance	−168	−23	26

Source: IMF, *International Financial Statistics*.

External Trade

PRINCIPAL COMMODITIES
(US $ million)

Imports c.i.f.	2001	2002	2003
Food and live animals	46.5	31.7	24.5
Cereals and cereal preparations	24.0	13.5	10.6
Rice	12.2	4.1	3.2
Vegetables and fruit	5.9	6.2	4.2
Sugar, sugar preparations and honey	8.6	5.9	5.0
Crude materials, inedible, except fuels	12.5	12.8	15.2
Textile fibres and their wastes	7.7	8.3	10.3
Mineral fuels, lubricants and related materials	39.7	40.7	40.6
Petroleum, petroleum products and related materials	39.5	40.6	40.5
Motor spirit, incl. aviation spirit	17.0	16.5	15.5
Gas oils	9.7	9.6	10.1
Animal and vegetable oils, fats and waxes	8.7	6.7	4.3
Chemicals and related products	23.8	33.8	30.4
Medicinal and pharmaceutical products	8.5	13.7	12.8
Basic manufactures	36.3	37.3	43.8
Iron and steel	11.3	8.9	12.9
Machinery and transport equipment	60.0	63.2	75.0
Telecommunications, sound recording and reproducing equipment	19.2	7.2	10.9
Electric machinery, apparatus and appliances, and parts	8.3	8.6	10.2
Road vehicles	18.4	24.8	31.2
Miscellaneous manufactured articles	46.2	22.4	25.7
Total (incl. others)	276.1	251.2	261.2

Exports f.o.b.	2001	2002	2003
Food and live animals	31.6	25.9	26.2
Coffee	15.0	14.0	13.9
Tea	16.6	11.8	11.9
Crude materials, inedible, except fuels	22.7	18.8	15.4
Metalliferous ores and metal scrap	20.9	16.3	11.7
Tin ores and concentrates	2.2	1.4	5.1
Ores and concentrates of other non-ferrous base metals	18.7	14.9	6.0
Ores of molybdenum, niobium and titanium	9.5	14.5	5.6
Total (incl. others)	55.5	46.0	50.4

Source: UN, *International Trade Statistics Yearbook*.

PRINCIPAL TRADING PARTNERS
(US $ million)

Imports	2001	2002	2003
Belgium	55.3	32.9	31.9
Canada	2.4	2.9	4.1
China	6.3	5.0	5.0
Denmark	1.9	5.8	2.8
France (incl. Monaco)	6.1	6.4	7.4
Germany	6.6	7.2	11.2
India	6.4	6.8	9.0
Israel	4.8	2.9	2.0
Italy	7.5	3.1	3.0
Japan	7.2	6.4	8.4
Kenya	61.9	66.7	74.1
Netherlands	7.4	5.7	4.5
Singapore	1.6	0.8	0.6
South Africa	12.5	11.0	12.9
Switzerland-Liechtenstein	1.3	1.3	1.5
Tanzania	9.6	13.2	14.7
Uganda	8.1	11.1	20.0
UAE	19.5	22.0	19.9
United Kingdom	8.0	6.5	4.3
USA	10.4	6.1	2.0
Viet Nam	4.8	0.9	0.2
Zambia	3.4	2.2	0.5
Total (incl. others)	276.1	251.2	261.2

Exports	2001	2002	2003
Belgium	2.1	2.3	0.8
Germany	2.4	0.3	0.2
Hong Kong	1.3	4.6	0.3
Kenya	24.0	18.1	20.6
Netherlands	1.2	6.5	0.0
Pakistan	0.2	1.3	0.6
Russia	1.4	0.0	0.0
South Africa	6.2	0.3	0.5
Switzerland-Liechtenstein	4.2	7.1	0.8
Tanzania	4.8	0.3	4.1
Uganda	2.5	1.0	13.4
United Kingdom	0.3	0.8	3.1
USA	3.0	1.4	0.1
Total (incl. others)	55.5	46.0	50.4

Source: UN, *International Trade Statistics Yearbook*.

Transport

ROAD TRAFFIC
(estimates, motor vehicles in use at 31 December)

	1995	1996
Passenger cars	12,000	13,000
Lorries and vans	16,000	17,100

Source: IRF, *World Road Statistics*.

CIVIL AVIATION
(traffic on scheduled services)

	1992	1993	1994
Passengers carried ('000)	9	9	9
Passenger-km (million)	2	2	2

Source: UN, *Statistical Yearbook*.

Tourism

(by country of residence)

	2000	2001*
Africa	93,058	99,928
Burundi	20,972	9,455
Congo, Democratic Republic	10,450	28,514
Kenya	2,050	2,243
Tanzania	18,320	18,697
Uganda	38,897	38,472
Americas	2,250	2,785
Europe	6,412	8,395
Belgium	1,866	2,057
Total (incl. others)	104,216	113,185

* January–November.

Tourism receipts (US $ million, excl. passenger transport): 23 in 2000; 25 in 2001; 31 in 2002; 30 in 2003; 44 in 2004.

Source: World Tourism Organization.

Communications Media

	2003	2004	2005
Telephones ('000 main lines in use)	25.6	23.0	23.0
Mobile cellular telephones ('000 subscribers)	130.7	138.7	290.0
Internet users ('000)	31	38	38

Radio receivers ('000 in use): 601 in 1997.

Facsimile machines (number in use): 900 in 1998.

Daily newspapers: 1 in 19968.

Sources: International Telecommunication Union; UN, *Statistical Yearbook*; UNESCO, *Statistical Yearbook*.

Education

(1998)

	Teachers	Students: Males	Students: Females	Students: Total
Primary	23,730	644,835	643,834	1,288,669
Secondary:				
general	3,413	39,088	38,337	77,425
technical and vocational		6,859	6,935	13,794
Tertiary	412	n.a.	n.a.	5,678

Source: mainly UNESCO Institute for Statistics.

Adult literacy rate (UNESCO estimates): 64.0% (males 70.5%; females 58.8%) in 2003 (Source: UN Development Programme, *Human Development Report*).

Directory

The Constitution

A new Constitution was approved at a national referendum on 26 May 2003 and entered into effect on 4 June. The main provisions are summarized below:

PREAMBLE

The state of Rwanda is an independent sovereign Republic. Fundamental principles are: the struggle against the ideology of genocide and all its manifestations; the eradication of all ethnic and regional divisions; the promotion of national unity; and the equal sharing of power. Human rights and personal liberties are protected. All forms of discrimination are prohibited and punishable by law. The state recognizes a multi-party political system. Political associations are established in accordance with legal requirements, and may operate freely, providing that they comply with democratic and constitutional principles, without harm to national unity, territorial integrity and state security. The formation of political associations on the basis of race, ethnicity, tribal or regional affiliation, sex, religion or any other grounds for discrimination is prohibited.

LEGISLATURE

Legislative power is vested in a bicameral Parliament, comprising a Chamber of Deputies and a Senate. The Chamber of Deputies has 80 deputies, who are elected for a five-year term. In addition to 53 directly elected deputies, 27 seats are allocated, respectively, to two youth representatives, one disabilities representative, and 24 female representatives, who are indirectly elected. The Senate comprises 26 members, of whom 12 are elected by local government councils in the 12 provinces, and two by academic institutions, while the remaining 12 are nominated (eight by the President and four by a regulatory body, the Parties' Forum). Members of the Senate serve for eight years.

PRESIDENT

The President of the Republic is the Head of State, protector of the Constitution, and guarantor of national unity. He is the Commander-in-Chief of the armed forces. Presidential candidates are required to be of Rwandan nationality and aged a minimum of 35 years. The President is elected by universal suffrage for a seven-year term, and is restricted to two mandates. He signs into law presidential decrees in consultation with the Council of Ministers.

GOVERNMENT

The President nominates the Prime Minister, who heads the Council of Ministers. Ministers are proposed by the Prime Minister and appointed by the President.

JUDICIARY

The judiciary is independent and separate from the legislative and executive organs of government. The judicial system is composed of the Supreme Court, the High Court of the Republic, and provincial, district and municipal Tribunals. In addition, there are specialized judicial organs, comprising *gacaca* and military courts. The *gacaca* courts try cases of genocide or other crimes against humanity committed between 1 October 1990 and 31 December 1994. Military courts (the Military Tribunal and the High Military Court) have jurisdiction in military cases. The President and Vice-President of the Supreme Court and the Prosecutor-General are elected by the Senate two months after its installation.

The Government

HEAD OF STATE

President: Maj.-Gen. PAUL KAGAME (took office 22 April 2000; re-elected 25 August 2003).

COUNCIL OF MINISTERS
(August 2007)

Prime Minister: BERNARD MAKUZA.

Minister of Defence: Gen. MARCEL GATSINZI.

Minister of Local Government, Rural Development and Social Affairs: PROTAIS MUSONI.

Minister of Internal Affairs: MUSSA SHEIKH HERERIMANA.

Minister of Foreign Affairs and Co-operation: Dr CHARLES MURIGANDE.

Minister of Finance and Economic Planning: JAMES MUSONI.

Minister of Agriculture and Livestock: ANASTASE MUREKEZI.

Minister of Education, Science, Technology and Research: JEANNE D'ARC MUJAWAMARIYA.

Minister of Infrastructure: STANISLAS KAMANZI.

Minister of Commerce, Industry, Investment Promotion, Tourism and Co-operatives: THARCISSE KARUGARAMA.

Minister of Lands, Environment, Forestry, Water and Natural Resources: CHRISTOPHE BAZIVAMO.

Minister of Justice: EDDA MUKABAGWIZA.

Minister of Public Services and Labour: MANASSEH NSHUTI.

Minister of Health: Dr JEAN-DAMASCÈNE NTAWUKURIRYAYO.

Minister of Youth, Sports and Culture: JOSEPH HABINEZA.

Minister in the Office of the President: SOLINA NYIRAHABIMANA.

Minister in the Office of the President, in charge of Science, Information Technology and Research: ROMAIN MURENZI.

Minister in the Office of the Prime Minister, in charge of Gender and the Promotion of Women: VALÉRIE NYIRAHABINEZA.

Minister in the Office of the Prime Minister, in charge of Information: Prof. LAURENT NKUSI.

Minister of State for Local Government, Good Governance, Rural Development and Social Affairs: CHRISTINE NYATANYI.

Minister of State for Public Services and Labour: ANGELINA MUGANZA.

Minister of State for Primary and Secondary Education: JOSEPH MUREKERAHO.

Minister of State for Lands and Environment: PATRICIA HAJABAKIGA.

Minister of State for Water and Natural Resources: Prof. BIKORO MUNYANGANIZI.

Minister of State for Economic Planning: MONIQUE NSANZABAGANWA.

Minister of State for HIV/AIDS and Other Infectious Diseases: Dr INNOCENT NYARUHIRIRA.

Minister of State for Energy and Communications: ALBERT BUTARE.

Minister of State for Agriculture: DAPHROSE GAHAKWA.

Minister of State for Regional Co-operation: ROSEMARY MUSEMINARI.

Minister of State for Industry and Industrial Promotion: VINCENT KAREGA.

MINISTRIES

Office of the President: BP 15, Kigali; tel. 59062000; fax 572431; e-mail info@presidency.gov.rw; internet www.presidency.gov.rw.

Office of the Prime Minister: Kigali; tel. 585444; fax 583714; e-mail primature@gov.rw; internet www.primature.gov.rw.

Ministry of Agriculture and Livestock: BP 621, Kigali; tel. 585008; fax 585057; internet www.minagri.gov.rw.

Ministry of Commerce, Industry, Investment Promotion, Tourism and Co-operatives: BP 2378, Kigali; tel. 574725; fax 575465; internet www.minicom.gov.rw.

Ministry of Defence: Kigali; tel. 577942; fax 576969; internet www.minadef.gov.rw.

Ministry of Education, Science, Technology and Research: BP 622, Kigali; tel. 583051; fax 582161; e-mail info@mineduc.gov.rw; internet www.mineduc.gov.rw.

Ministry of Finance and Economic Planning: BP 158, Kigali; tel. 575756; fax 577581; e-mail mfin@rwanda1.com; internet www.minecofin.gov.rw.

Ministry of Foreign Affairs and Co-operation: blvd de la Révolution, BP 179, Kigali; tel. 574522; fax 572904; internet www.minaffet.gov.rw.

Ministry of Gender and the Promotion of Women: Kigali; tel. 577626; fax 577543.

Ministry of Health: BP 84, Kigali; tel. 577458; fax 576853; e-mail info@moh.gov.rw; internet www.moh.gov.rw.

Ministry of Infrastructure: tel. 585503; fax 585755; e-mail webmaster@mininfra.gov.rw; internet www.mininfra.gov.rw.

Ministry of Internal Affairs: BP 446, Kigali; tel. 86708.

Ministry of Justice: BP 160, Kigali; tel. 586561; fax 586509; e-mail mjust@minijust.gov.rw; internet www.minijust.gov.rw.

Ministry of Lands, Environment, Forestry, Water and Natural Resources: Kigali; tel. 582628; fax 582629; internet www.minitere.gov.rw.

Ministry of Local Government, Good Governance, Rural Development and Social Affairs: BP 790, Kigali; tel. 585406; fax 582228; e-mail webmaster@minaloc.gov.rw; internet www.minaloc.gov.rw.

Ministry of Public Services and Labour: BP 403, Kigali; tel. 585714; fax 583621; e-mail mifotra@mifotra.gov.rw; internet www.mifotra.gov.rw.

Ministry of Youth, Sports and Culture: BP 1044, Kigali; tel. 583527; fax 583518; e-mail minicult@rwanda1.com; internet www.mijespoc.gov.rw.

President and Legislature

PRESIDENT

Presidential Election, 25 August 2003

Candidate	Votes	% of votes
Paul Kagame	3,544,777	95.05
Faustin Twagiramungu	134,865	3.62
Jean-Népomuscène Nayinzira	49,634	1.33
Total*	3,729,274	100.00

* Excluding 49,634 invalid votes.

CHAMBER OF DEPUTIES

Speaker: ALFRED MUKEZAMFURA.

General Election, 29 September–3 October 2003

Party	Votes	% of votes	Seats
Front patriotique rwandais*	2,774,661	73.78	40
Parti social-démocrate	463,067	12.31	7
Parti libéral	396,978	10.56	6
Others	125,896	3.35	—
Total	3,760,602	100.00	80†

* Contested the elections in alliance with the Parti démocrate centriste, Parti démocratique idéal, Union démocratique du peuple rwandais and Parti socialiste rwandais.

† In addition to the 53 directly elected deputies, 27 seats are allocated, respectively, to two youth representatives, one disabilities representative and 24 female representatives, who are indirectly elected.

SENATE

Speaker: Dr VINCENT BIRUTA.

The Senate comprises 26 members, of whom 12 are elected by local government councils in the 12 provinces and two by academic institutions, while the remaining 12 are nominated (eight by the President and four by a regulatory body, the Parties' Forum).

Election Commission

Commission électorale nationale du Rwanda: BP 6449, Kigali; tel. 515081; fax 501045; e-mail comelena@rwanda1.com; internet www.comelena.gov.rw; f. 2000; independent; Chair. Prof. CHRYSOLOGUE KARANGWA.

Political Organizations

Under legislation adopted in June 2003, the formation of any political organization based on ethnic groups, religion or sex was prohibited.

Front patriotique rwandais (FPR): f. 1990; also known as Inkotanyi; comprises mainly Tutsi exiles, but claims multi-ethnic support; commenced armed invasion of Rwanda from Uganda in Oct. 1990; took control of Rwanda in July 1994; Chair. Maj.-Gen. PAUL KAGAME; Vice-Chair. CHRISTOPHE BAZIVAMO; Sec.-Gen. CHARLES MURIGANDE.

Parti démocrate centriste (PDC): BP 2348, Kigali; tel. 576542; fax 572237; f. 1990; fmrly Parti démocrate chrétien; Leader ALFRED MUKEZAMFURA.

Parti démocratique idéal (PDI): Kigali; f. 1991; fmrly Parti démocratique islamique; Leader ANDRÉ BUMAYA HABIB.

Parti démocratique rwandais (Pader): Kigali; f. 1992; Sec. JEAN NTAGUNGIRA.

Parti libéral (PL): BP 1304, Kigali; tel. 577916; fax 577838; f. 1991; restructured 2003; Chair. PROSPER HIGORO; Sec.-Gen. Dr ODETTE NYIRAMIRIMO.

Parti du progrès et de la concorde (PPC): f. 2003; incl. fmr mems of Mouvement démocratique républicain; Leader Dr CHRISTIAN MARARA.

Parti progressiste de la jeunesse rwandaise (PPJR): Kigali; f. 1991; Leader ANDRÉ HAKIZIMANA.

Parti républicain rwandais (Parerwa): Kigali; f. 1992; Leader AUGUSTIN MUTAMBA.

Parti social-démocrate (PSD): Kigali; f. 1991 by a breakaway faction of fmr Mouvement révolutionnaire national pour le développement; Leader Dr VINCENT BIRUTA.

Parti socialiste rwandais (PSR): BP 827, Kigali; tel. 576658; fax 83975; f. 1991; workers' rights; Leader Dr MEDARD RUTIJANWA.

Rassemblement travailliste pour la démocratie (RTD): BP 1894, Kigali; tel. 575622; fax 576574; f. 1991; Leader EMMANUEL NIZEYIMANA.

Union démocratique du peuple rwandais (UDPR): Kigali; f. 1992; Leader ADRIEN RANGIRA.

Other political organizations have been formed by exiled Rwandans and operate principally from abroad; these include:

Rassemblement pour le retour des réfugiés et la démocratie au Rwanda (RDR): Postbus 3124, 2280 GC, Rijswijk, Netherlands; tel. (31) 623075674; fax (31) 847450374; e-mail info@rdrwanda.org; internet www.rdrwanda.org; f. 1995; prin. opposition party representing Hutu refugees in exile; Pres. VICTOIRE UMUHOZA INGABIRE.

Union du peuple rwandais (UPR): Brussels, Belgium; f. 1990; Hutu-led; Pres. SILAS MAJYAMBERE; Sec.-Gen. EMMANUEL TWAGILIMANA.

Diplomatic Representation

EMBASSIES IN RWANDA

Belgium: rue Nyarugenge, BP 81, Kigali; tel. 575551; fax 573995; e-mail kigali@diplobel.be; Ambassador FRANÇOIS ROUX.

Burundi: rue de Ntaruka, BP 714, Kigali; tel. 575010; Chargé d'affaires a.i. (vacant).

Egypt: BP 1069, Kigali; tel. 82686; fax 82686; e-mail egypt@rwanda1.com; Ambassador AHMED RAMI AWWAD EL HOSENI.

Germany: 8 rue de Bugarama, BP 355, Kigali; tel. 575141; fax 502087; internet www.kigali.diplo.de; Ambassador Dr CHRISTIAN CLAGES.

Holy See: 49 ave Paul VI, BP 261, Kigali (Apostolic Nunciature); tel. 575293; fax 575181; e-mail nuntrw@rwandatel1.rwanda1.com; Apostolic Nuncio Most Rev. ANSELMO GUIDO PECORARI (Titular Archbishop of Populonia).

Kenya: BP 1215, Kigali; tel. 583332; fax 510919; e-mail kigali@mfa.go.ke; Ambassador KETTER A. ALEX.

Korea, Democratic People's Republic: Kigali; Ambassador KIM PONG GI.

Libya: BP 1152, Kigali; tel. 576470; Secretary of the People's Bureau MOUSTAPHA MASAND EL-GHAILUSHI.

Russia: 19 ave de l'Armée, BP 40, Kigali; tel. 575286; fax 574818; e-mail ambruss@rwandatel1.rwanda1.com; Ambassador MIRGAYAS M. SHIRINSKII.

South Africa: 1370 blvd de l'Umuganda, POB 6563, Kacyiru-Sud, Kigali; tel. 583185; fax 511760; e-mail saemkgl@rwanda1.com; internet www.saembassy-kigali.org.rw; Ambassador Dr EZRA M. SIGWELA.

United Kingdom: Parcelle 1131, Blvd de l'Umuganda, Kacyiru, BP 576, Kigali; tel. 584098; fax 582044; e-mail embassy.kigali@fco.gov.uk; internet www.britishembassykigali.org.rw; Ambassador JEREMY MACADIE.

USA: blvd de la Révolution, BP 28, Kigali; tel. 505601; fax 507143; e-mail irckigali@state.gov; internet kigali.usembassy.gov; Ambassador MICHAEL RAY ARIETTI.

Judicial System

The judicial system is composed of the Supreme Court, the High Court of the Republic, and provincial, district and municipal Tribunals. In addition, there are specialized judicial organs, comprising *gacaca* and military courts. The *gacaca* courts were established to try cases of genocide or other crimes against humanity committed between 1 October 1990 and 31 December 1994. Trials for categories of lesser genocide crimes were to be conducted by councils in the communities in which they were committed, with the aim of alleviating pressure on the existing judicial system. Trials under the *gacaca* court system formally commenced on 25 November 2002. Military courts (the Military Tribunal and the High Military Court) have jurisdiction in military cases. The President and Vice-President of the Supreme Court and the Prosecutor-General are elected by the Senate.

Supreme Court

Kigali; tel. 87407.

The Supreme Court comprises five sections: the Department of Courts and Tribunals; the Court of Appeals; the Constitutional Court; the Council of State; and the Revenue Court.

President of the Supreme Court: ALOYSIA CYANZAIRE.

Vice-President: Prof. SAM RUGEGE.

Prosecutor-General: MARTIN NGOGAEU MUCYO.

Religion

AFRICAN RELIGIONS

About one-half of the population hold traditional beliefs.

CHRISTIANITY

Union des Eglises Rwandaises: BP 79, Kigali; tel. 85825; fax 83554; f. 1963; fmrly Conseil Protestant du Rwanda.

The Roman Catholic Church

Rwanda comprises one archdiocese and eight dioceses. At 31 December 2004 the estimated number of adherents represented about 47.8% of the total population.

Bishops' Conference

Conférence Episcopale du Rwanda, BP 357, Kigali; tel. 575439; fax 578080; e-mail cerwanda@rwanda1.com.

f. 1980; Pres. Rt Rev. ALEXIS HABIYAMBERE (Bishop of Nyundo).

Archbishop of Kigali: Most Rev. THADDÉE NTIHINYURWA, Archevêché, BP 715, Kigali; tel. 575769; fax 572274; e-mail kigarchi@yahoo.fr.

The Anglican Communion

The Church of the Province of Rwanda, established in 1992, has nine dioceses.

Archbishop of the Province and Bishop of Kigali: Most Rev. EMMANUEL MUSABA KOLINI, BP 61, Kigali; tel. and fax 573213; e-mail sonja914@compuserve.com.

Provincial Secretary: Rt Rev. JOSIAS SENDEGEYA (Bishop of Kigali), BP 2487, Kigali; tel. and fax 514160; e-mail peer@rwandatel1.rwanda1.

Protestant Churches

Eglise Baptiste: Nyantanga, BP 59, Butare; Pres. Rev. DAVID BAZIGA; Gen. Sec. ELEAZAR ZIHERAMBERE.

There are about 250,000 other Protestants, including a substantial minority of Seventh-day Adventists.

BAHÁ'Í FAITH

National Spiritual Assembly: BP 652, Kigali; tel. 575982.

ISLAM

There is a small Islamic community.

The Press

Bulletin Agricole du Rwanda: OCIR—Café, BP 104, Kigali-Gikondo; f. 1968; quarterly; French; Pres. of Editorial Bd Dr AUGUSTIN NZINDUKIYIMANA; circ. 800.

L'Ere de Liberté: BP 1755, Kigali; fortnightly.

Etudes Rwandaises: Université Nationale du Rwanda, Rectorat, BP 56, Butare; tel. 30302; f. 1977; quarterly; pure and applied science, literature, human sciences; French; Pres. of Editorial Bd CHARLES NTAKIRUTINKA; circ. 1,000.

Hobe: BP 761, Kigali; f. 1955; monthly; children's interest; circ. 95,000.

Inkingi: BP 969, Kigali; tel. 577626; fax 577543; monthly.

Inkoramutima: Union des Eglises Rwandaises, BP 79, Kigali; tel. 85825; fax 83554; quarterly; religious; circ. 5,000.

Kinyamateka: 5 blvd de l'OUA, BP 761, Kigali; tel. 576164; f. 1933; fortnightly; economics; circ. 11,000.

La Lettre du Cladho: BP 3060, Kigali; tel. 74292; monthly.

The New Times: BP 635, Kigali; tel. 573409; fax 574166; monthly.

Nouvelles du Rwanda: Université Nationale du Rwanda, BP 117, Butare; every 2 months.

Nyabarongo—Le Canard Déchaîné: BP 1585, Kigali; tel. 576674; monthly.

Le Partisan: BP 1805, Kigali; tel. 573923; fortnightly.

La Patrie—Urwatubyaye: BP 3125, Kigali; tel. 572552; monthly.

La Relève: Office Rwandais d'Information, BP 83, Kigali; tel. 75665; f. 1976; monthly; politics, economics, culture; French; Dir CHRISTOPHE MFIZI; circ. 1,700.

Revue Dialogue: BP 572, Kigali; tel. 574178; f. 1967; bi-monthly; Christian issues; Belgian-owned; circ. 2,500.

Revue Médicale Rwandaise: Ministry of Health, BP 84, Kigali; tel. 576681; f. 1968; quarterly; French.

Revue Pédagogique: Ministry of Education, Science, Technology and Research, BP 622, Kigali; tel. 85697; quarterly; French.

Rwanda Herald: Kigali; f. Oct. 2000; owned by Rwanda Independent Media Group.

Rwanda Libération: BP 398, Kigali; tel. 577710; monthly; Dir and Editor-in-Chief ANTOINE KAPITENI.

Rwanda Renaître: BP 426, Butare; fortnightly.

Rwanda Rushya: BP 83, Kigali; tel. 572276; fortnightly.

Le Tribun du Peuple: BP 1960, Kigali; tel. 82035; bi-monthly; Owner JEAN-PIERRE MUGABE.

Ukuli Gacaca: BP 3170, Kigali; tel. 585239; monthly; Dir CHARLES GAKUMBA.

Umucunguzi: Gisenyi; f. 1998; organ of Palir; Kinyarwanda and French; Chief Editor EMILE NKUMBUYE.

Umuhinzi-Mworozi: OCIR—Thé, BP 1334, Kigali; tel. 514797; fax 514796; f. 1975; monthly; circ. 1,500.

Umusemburo—Le Levain: BP 117, Butare; monthly.

Umuseso: Kigali; independent Kinyarwanda language weekly newspaper; Editor CHARLES KABONERO.

Urunana: Grand Séminaire de Nyakibanda, BP 85, Butare; tel. 530793; e-mail wellamahoro@yahoo.fr; f. 1967; 3 a year; religious; Pres. WELLAS UWAMAHORO; Editor-in-Chief DAMIEN NIYOYIREMERA.

NEWS AGENCIES

Agence Rwandaise de Presse (ARP): 27 ave du Commerce, BP 83, Kigali; tel. 576540; fax 576185; e-mail cbohizi@yahoo.fr; f. 1975.

Office Rwandais d'Information (Orinfor): BP 83, Kigali; tel. 575724; Dir JOSEPH BIDERI.

Foreign Bureau

Agence France-Presse (AFP): BP 83, Kigali; tel. 572997; Correspondent MARIE-GORETTI UWIBAMBE.

Publishers

Editions Rwandaises: Caritas Rwanda, BP 124, Kigali; tel. 5786; Man. Dir Abbé CYRIAQUE MUNYANSANGA; Editorial Dir ALBERT NAMBAJE.

Implico: BP 721, Kigali; tel. 573771.

Imprimerie de Kabgayi: BP 66, Gitarama; tel. 562252; fax 562345; e-mail imprikabgayi@yahoo.fr; f. 1932; Dir Abbé CYRILLE UWIZEYE.

Imprimerie de Kigali, SARL: 1 blvd de l'Umuganda, BP 956, Kigali; tel. 582032; fax 584047; e-mail impkig@rwandatel1.rwanda1.com; f. 1980; Dir ALEXIS RUKUNDO.

Imprimerie URWEGO: BP 762, Kigali; tel. 86027; Dir JEAN NSENGIYUNVA.

Pallotti-Presse: BP 863, Kigali; tel. 574084.

GOVERNMENT PUBLISHING HOUSES

Imprimerie Nationale du Rwanda: BP 351, Kigali; tel. 576214; fax 575820; f. 1967; Dir JUVÉNAL NDISANZE.

Régie de l'Imprimerie Scolaire (IMPRISCO): BP 1347, Kigali; tel. 85818; fax 85695; e-mail imprisco@rwandatel1.rwanda1.com; f. 1985; Dir JEAN DE DIEU GAKWANDI.

Broadcasting and Communications

TELECOMMUNICATIONS

Rwandatel: BP 1332, Kigali; tel. 576777; fax 573110; e-mail info@rwandatel.rw; internet www.rwandatel.rw; national telecommunications service; privatized mid-2005.

MTN Rwandacell: Telecom House, blvd de l'Umuganda, Kigali; f. 1998; provides mobile cellular telephone services; CEO FRANÇOIS DU PLESSIS.

BROADCASTING

Radio

Radio Rwanda: BP 83, Kigali; tel. 575665; fax 576185; f. 1961; state-controlled; daily broadcasts in Kinyarwanda, Swahili, French and English; Dir of Programmes DAVID KABUYE.

Deutsche Welle Relay Station Africa: Kigali; daily broadcasts in German, English, French, Hausa, Swahili, Portuguese and Amharic.

Television

Télévision rwandaise (TVR): Kigali; fax 575024; transmissions reach more than 60% of national territory.

Finance

(cap. = capital; res = reserves; dep. = deposits; m. = million; brs = branches; amounts in Rwanda francs)

BANKING

Central Bank

Banque Nationale du Rwanda: ave Paul VI, BP 531, Kigali; tel. 574282; fax 572551; e-mail info@bnr.rw; internet www.bnr.rw; f. 1964; bank of issue; cap. 2,000m., res 13,905.9m., dep. 157,148.0m. (Dec. 2005); Gov. FRANÇOIS KANIMBA.

Commercial Banks

Following the privatization of two commercial banks, government control of the banking section was reduced from 45% in 2003 to 22% in 2005, although the three largest banks continued to control two-thirds of the system's assets, valued at US $365m. (equivalent to 34% of GDP).

Bancor SA: 3rd Floor, UTC Bldg, 1232 ave de la Paix, BP 2059, Kigali; tel. 500091; fax 575761; e-mail bancor@rwanda1.com; internet www.bancor.co.rw; f. 1995 as Banque à la Confiance d'Or; name changed as above in 2001 when acquired by private investors; cap. and res 3,417.1m., total assets 34,549.3m. (Dec. 2005); Pres. NICHOLAS WATSON.

Banque de Commerce, de Développement et d'Industrie (BCDI): ave de la Paix, BP 3268, Kigali; tel. 574437; fax 573790; e-mail info@bcdi.co.rw; internet www.bcdi.co.rw; cap. and res 3,158.4m., total assets 45,950.9m. (Dec. 2003); Pres. and Dir-Gen. ALFRED KALISA.

Banque Commerciale du Rwanda, SA: BP 354, 11 blvd de la Revolution, Kigali; tel. 575591; fax 573395; e-mail bcr@rwandatel1.rwanda1.com; internet www.bcr-rwanda.com; f. 1963; privatized Sept. 2004; cap. and res 2,420.0m., dep. 30,564.3m. (Dec. 2003); Pres. Dr NKOSANA MOYO; Man. Dir DAVID KUWANA; 6 brs.

Banque de Kigali, SA: 63 ave du Commerce, BP 175, Kigali; tel. 593100; fax 573461; e-mail bkig10@rwanda1.com; f. 1966; cap. 1,500.0m., res 4,330.1m., dep. 59,378.6m. (Dec. 2005); Chair. FRANÇOIS NGARAMBE; Gen. Man. JAMES GATERA; 6 brs.

Caisse Hypothécaire du Rwanda (CHR): BP 1034, Kigali; tel. 576382; fax 572799; cap. 778.2m., total assets 6,966.8m. (Dec. 2003); Pres. FRANÇOIS RUTISHASHA; Dir-Gen. PIPIEN HAKIZABERA.

Compagnie Générale de Banque: blvd de l'Umuganda, BP 5230, Kigali; tel. 503343; fax 503336; e-mail cogebank@rwanda1.com; cap. and res 1,210.8m., total assets 7,297.4m. (Dec. 2003); Pres. ANDRÉ KATABARWA.

Fina Bank, SA: 20 blvd de la Révolution, BP 331, Kigali; tel. 598600; fax 573486; e-mail info@finabank.co.rw; f. 1983 as Banque Continentale Africaine (Rwanda); name changed 2005; cap. 1,650m., res 1,028.7m., dep. 22,730m. (Dec. 2006); privatized; Chair. ROBERT BINYOU; Man. Dir STEPHEN CALEY; 5 brs.

Development Banks

Banque Rwandaise de Développement, SA (BRD): blvd de la Révolution, BP 1341, Kigali; tel. 575079; fax 573569; e-mail brd@brd.com.rw; internet www.brd.com.rw; f. 1967; 56% state-owned; cap. and res 4,104.6m., total assets 13,920.7m. (Dec. 2003); Pres. GASTON MPATSWE KAGABO.

Union des Banques Populaires du Rwanda (Banki z'Abaturage mu Rwanda): BP 1348, Kigali; tel. 573559; fax 573579; e-mail ubpr@rwandatel1.rwanda1.com; f. 1975; cap. and res 1,180.5m., total assets 20,433.8m. (Dec. 2002); Pres. INNOCENT KAYITARE; 145 brs.

INSURANCE

Société Nationale d'Assurances du Rwanda (SONARWA): BP 1035, Kigali; tel. 573350; fax 572052; e-mail sonarwa@rwandatel1.rwanda1.com; f. 1975; cap. 500m.; Pres. FRANÇOIS NGARAMBE; Dir-Gen. HOPE MURERA.

Société Rwandaise d'Assurances, SA (SORAS): BP 924, Kigali; tel. 573716; fax 573362; e-mail sorasinf@rwanda1.com; f. 1984; cap. 1,002m. (2007); Pres. CHARLES MHORANYI; Dir-Gen. MARC RUGENERA.

Trade and Industry

GOVERNMENT AGENCIES

Centre for Investment Promotion: Kigali; f. 1998.

National Tender Board: ave de la Paix, POB 4276, Kigali; tel. 501403; fax 501402; e-mail ntb@rwanda1.com; internet www.ntb.gov.rw; f. 1998 to organize and manage general public procurement.

Rwanda Revenue Authority: Kigali; f. 1998 to maximize revenue collection; Commissioner-Gen. EDWARD LARBI SIAW.

DEVELOPMENT ORGANIZATIONS

Coopérative de Promotion de l'Industrie Minière et Artisanale au Rwanda (COOPIMAR): BP 1139, Kigali; tel. 82127; fax 72128; Dir DANY NZARAMBA.

Institut de Recherches Scientifiques et Technologiques (IRST): BP 227, Butare; tel. 30396; fax 30939; Dir-Gen. CHRYSOLOGUE KARANGWA.

Institut des Sciences Agronomiques du Rwanda (ISAR): BP 138, Butare; tel. 30642; fax 30644; for the devt of subsistence and export agriculture; Dir MUNYANGANIZI BIKORO; 12 centres.

Office des Cultures Industrielles du Rwanda—Café (OCIR—Café): BP 104, Kigali; tel. 575600; fax 573992; e-mail ocircafe@rwandatel1.rwanda1.com; f. 1978; devt of coffee and other new agronomic industries; operates a coffee stabilization fund; Dir ANASTASE NZIRASANAHO.

Office des Cultures Industrielles du Rwanda—Thé (OCIR—Thé): BP 1344, Kigali; tel. 514797; fax 514796; e-mail ocirthé@rwanda1.com; devt and marketing of tea; Dir CÉLESTIN KAYITARE.

Office National pour le Développement de la Commercialisation des Produits Vivriers et des Produits Animaux (OPROVIA): BP 953, Kigali; tel. 82946; fax 82945; privatization pending; Dir DISMAS SEZIBERA.

Régie d'Exploitation et de Développement des Mines (REDEMI): BP 2195, Kigali; tel. 573632; fax 573625; e-mail ruzredem@yahoo.fr; f. 1988 as Régie des Mines du Rwanda; privatized in 2000; state org. for mining tin, columbo-tantalite and wolfram; Man. Dir JEAN-RUZINDANA MUNANA.

Société de Pyrèthre au Rwanda (SOPYRWA): BP 79, Ruhengeri; tel. and fax 546364; e-mail sopyrwa@rwanda1.com; f. 1978; cultivation and processing of pyrethrum; post-war activities resumed in Oct. 1994; current production estimated at 80% prewar capacity; Dir SYLVAIN NZABAGAMBA.

CHAMBER OF COMMERCE

Chambre de Commerce et d'Industrie de Rwanda: rue de l'Umuganda, POB 319, Kigali; tel. 83534; fax 83532; Pres. T. RUJUGIRO.

INDUSTRIAL ASSOCIATIONS

Association des Industriels du Rwanda: BP 39, Kigali; tel. and fax 575430; Pres. YVES LAFAGE; Exec. Sec. MUGUNGA NDOBA.

Federation of the Rwandan Private Sector Associations: POB 319, Kigali; tel. 83538; fax 83532; e-mail frsp@rwanda1.com; f. 1999 to represent interests of private sector; Exec. Sec. EUGÈNE BITWAYIKI.

UTILITIES

Electrogaz: POB 537, Kigali; tel. 572392; fax 573802; state-owned water, electricity and gas supplier; Dir JOSEPH MUJENGA.

MAJOR COMPANIES

BP-Fina Rwanda: BP 144, Kigali; tel. 572428; fax 574998; wholesale trade in petroleum products; Man. Dir GEORGES BOSSERT.

BRALIRWA: BP 131, Kigali; tel. 82995; fax 85693; f. 1959; mfrs and bottlers of beer in Gisenyi and soft drinks in Kigali.

Cimenterie du Rwanda (CIMERWA): Kigali; f. 1984; mfrs of cement; post-war activities resumed in Aug. 1994; 1995 production estimated at 60% of pre-war capacity.

Kabuye Sugar Works SARL: BP 373; Kigali; tel. 575468; fax 572865; f. 1969; privatized 1997.

Office de la Valorisation Industrielle de la Banane du Rwanda (OVIBAR): BP 1002, Kigali; tel. 85857; f. 1978; mfrs of banana wine and juice; post-war activities resumed in Dec. 1994; 1995 production estimated at only 1% of pre-war capacity; activities suspended; Dir ALOYS MUTAGANDA.

Rwigass Cigarettes Co: BP 1286, Kigali; tel. 575535; fax 575516; production of cigarettes; Man. Dir R. ASSINAPOL.

Savonnerie de Kicukiro (SAKIRWA): BP 441, Kigali; tel. 572678; fax 575450; e-mail hram@rwandatel1.rwanda1.com; soap and washing powders; Chair. H. RAMJI.

Société Emballage—Rwanda: BP 1009, Kigali; tel. 575705; export of fruit and fruit products; production of soya- and cereal-based foods since 1997.

Société pour l'Hydraulique, l'Environnement et la Réhabilitation: rue de l'Akagera, Parcelle 3925, Nyarugenge, BP 1526, Kigali; tel. and fax 578630; fax 578851; e-mail rwanda@sher.be; internet www.sher.be; f. 1985; rural development; Chair. and Man. Dir PAUL GATIN; Rwandan Rep. MICHEL-HENRI BOURGE.

Société Rwandaise pour la Production et la Commercialisation du Thé (SORWATHE), SARL: Kigali; tel. 75461; f. 1978; tea.

TABARWANDA: BP 650, Kigali; tel. 85539; e-mail tbr@rwandatel1.rwanda1.com; produces cigarettes; Dir PIE MUGABO.

Tôlerie Industrielle du Rwanda (TOLIRWA): BP 521, Kigali; tel. 572129; produces sheet metal; Dir-Gen. JAFFER.

TRADE UNIONS

Centrale d'Education et de Coopération des Travailleurs pour le Développement/Alliance Coopérative au Rwanda (CECOTRAD/ACORWA): BP 295, Kigali; f. 1984; Pres. ELIE KATABARWA.

Centrale Syndicale des Travailleurs du Rwanda: BP 1645, Kigali; tel. 85658; fax 84012; e-mail cestrav@rwandatel1.rwanda1.com; Sec.-Gen. FRANÇOIS MURANGIRA.

Transport

RAILWAYS

There are no railways in Rwanda, although plans exist for the eventual construction of a line passing through Uganda, Rwanda and Burundi, to connect with the Kigoma–Dar es Salaam line in Tanzania. Rwanda has access by road to the Tanzanian railways system.

ROADS

In 2004 there were an estimated 14,008 km of roads, of which 2,662 km were paved. There are road links with Uganda, Tanzania, Burundi and the Democratic Republic of the Congo. Internal conflict during 1994 caused considerable damage to the road system and the destruction of several important bridges.

Office National des Transports en Commun (ONATRACOM): BP 609, Kigali; tel. 575564; Dir (vacant).

INLAND WATERWAYS

There are services on Lake Kivu between Cyangugu, Gisenyi and Kibuye, including two vessels operated by ONATRACOM.

CIVIL AVIATION

The Kanombe international airport at Kigali can process up to 500,000 passengers annually. There is a second international airport at Kamembe, near the border with the Democratic Republic of the Congo. There are airfields at Butare, Gabiro, Ruhengeri and Gisenyi, servicing internal flights.

Alliance Express Rwanda (ALEX): BP 1440, Kigali; tel. 82409; fax 82417; e-mail aev@aev.com.rw; f. 1998 to succeed fmr Air Rwanda as national carrier; 51% owned by Alliance Air (jtly owned by Govts of Uganda and South Africa and by South African Airways), 49% state-owned; domestic and regional passenger and cargo services; Chair. GERALD ZIRIMWABAGABO.

Rwandair Express: BP 3246, Kigali; tel. 577564; fax 577669; f. 1998; privately owned; operates two passenger aircraft; regional services; CEO PIERRE CLAVER KABERA (acting).

Tourism

Attractions for tourists include the wildlife of the national parks (notably mountain gorillas), Lake Kivu and fine mountain scenery. Since the end of the transitional period in late 2003, the Government has increased efforts to develop the tourism industry. In 1998 there were only an estimated 2,000 foreign visitors to Rwanda, but by 2001 the number of tourist arrivals had increased to 113,185. Total receipts from tourism were estimated at US $44m. in 2004.

Office Rwandais du Tourisme et des Parcs Nationaux (ORTPN): blvd de la Révolution 1, BP 905, Kigali; tel. 576514; fax 576515; e-mail webmaster@rwandatourism.com; internet www.rwandatourism.com; f. 1973; govt agency.

Defence

As assessed at November 2006, the total strength of the Rwandan armed forces was estimated at 33,000, comprising an army of 32,000 and an air force of 1,000. In addition, there were an estimated 2,000 local defence forces. Further restructuring of the army, which was expected to be reduced in size to number about 25,000, was planned.

Defence Expenditure: Estimated at 70,000m. Rwandan francs in 2006.

General Chief of Staff: Gen. JAMES KABAREEBE.

Education

Primary education, beginning at seven years of age and lasting for six years, is officially compulsory. Secondary education, which is not compulsory, begins at the age of 14 and lasts for a further six years, comprising two equal cycles of three years. In 2003, however, the Government announced plans to introduce a nine-year system of basic education, including three years of attendance at lower secondary schools. Schools are administered by the state and by Christian missions. In 2003/04 93.0% of children in the relevant age-group (males 91.5%, females 94.5%) were enrolled in primary schools, according to official estimates, while secondary enrolment was equivalent in 1999/2000 to only 12.1% of children in the appropriate age-group (males 12.4%, females 11.8%). Secondary enrolment was equivalent to 13.9% of children in that age-group in 2002. The Ministry of Education established 94 new secondary schools in 2003, and a further 58 in 2005. Rwanda has a university, with campuses at Butare and Ruhengeri, and several other institutions of higher education, but some students attend universities abroad, particularly in Belgium, France or Germany. In 2003 the number of students at the six public higher education institutions was 12,211, with a further 8,182 attending about seven private higher institutions. Estimated total expenditure by the central Government in 2003/04 represented 24.2% of total public expenditure.

Bibliography

Abdulai, N. (Ed.). *Genocide in Rwanda: Background and Current Situation*. London, Africa Research and Information Centre, 1994.

Adelman, H., and Suhrke, A. (Eds). *The Path of a Genocide: The Rwanda Crisis from Uganda to Zaire*. Piscataway, NJ, Transaction Publishers, 2000.

Bale, J. *Imagined Olympians: Body Culture and Colonial Representation in Rwanda*. Minneapolis, MN, University of Minnesota Press, 2002.

Barnett, M. N. *Eyewitness to a Genocide: The United Nations and Rwanda*. Ithaca, NY, Cornell University Press, 2002.

Berry, J. A. (Ed.). *Genocide in Rwanda: A Collective Memory*. Washington, DC, Howard University Press, 1999.

Braekman, C. *Rwanda: histoire d'un genocide*. Paris, Fayard, 1994.

Brauman, R. *Devant le mal. Rwanda, un génocide en direct*. Paris, Arléa, 1994.

Chrétien, J. P. *Rwanda, les Médias du génocide*. Paris, Editions Karthala, 1995.

Dallaire, R. *Shake Hands with the Devil: The Failure of Humanity in Rwanda*. Ontario, Random House of Canada Ltd, 2003.

Destexhe, A. *Rwanda and Genocide in the Twentieth Century*. London, Pluto Press, 1994.

Dorsey, L. *Historical Dictionary of Rwanda*. Lanham, MD, Scarecrow Press, 1999.

Dupaquier, J.-F. (Ed.). *La justice internationale face au drame rwandais*. Paris, Editions Karthala, 1996.

Gourevitch, P. *We Wish to Inform You That Tomorrow We Will Be Killed With Our Families: Stories from Rwanda*. New York, NY, Picador, 1999.

Grünfeld, F., and Huijboom, A. *The Failure to Prevent Genocide in Rwanda: The Role of Bystanders.* Boston, Martinus Nijhoff, 2007.

Guichaoua, A. (Ed.). *Les crises politiques au Burundi et au Rwanda (1993–1994)*. Paris, Editions Karthala, 1995.

Guillebaud, M. *Rwanda: The Land God Forgot?* Michigan, MI, Kregel Publications, 2002.

Harrell, P. E. *Rwanda's Gamble: Gacaca and a New Model of Transitional Justice*. Lincoln, NE, iUniverse, 2003.

Jones, B. D. *Peacemaking in Rwanda: The Dynamics of Failure (Project of the International Peace Academy)*. Boulder, CO, Lynne Rienner Publishers, 2001.

Kamukama, D. *Rwanda Conflict: Its Roots and Regional Implications*. Kampala, Fountain Publishers, 1993.

Khan, S. M., and Robinson, M. *The Shallow Graves of Rwanda*. London, I. B. Tauris & Co Ltd, 2001.

Kuperman, A. J. *The Limits of Humanitarian Intervention: Genocide in Rwanda*. Washington, DC, Brookings Institution, 2001.

Mamdani, M. *When Victims Become Killers: Colonialism, Nativism and the Genocide in Rwanda*. Princeton, NJ, Princeton University Press, 2001.

Waugh, C., M. *Paul Kagame and Rwanda: Power, Genocide and the Rwandan Patriotic Front*. Jefferson, NC, McFarland and Co, 2004.

Melvern, L. *A People Betrayed: the Role of the West in Rwanda's Genocide*. London, Zed Books, 2000.

Minear, L., and Guillot, P. *Soldiers to the Rescue: Humanitarian Lessons from Rwanda*. Paris, OECD, 1996.

Misser, F. *Vers un nouveau Rwanda?—Entretiens avec Paul Kagame*. Brussels, Editions Luc Pire, 1995.

Omaar, R. *Rwanda: Death, Despair and Defiance*. London, African Rights, 1994.

Pierce, J. R. *Speak Rwanda*. New York, NY, Picador USA, 2000.

Prunier, G. *The Rwanda Crisis 1959–1964: History of a Genocide*. London, Hurst, 1995.

Reyntjens, F. *Pouvoir et droit au Rwanda: droit public et évolution politique 1916–1973*. Tervuren, Musée royal de l'Afrique centrale, 1985.

L'Afrique des grands lacs en crise. Paris, Editions Karthala, 1994.

Rudakemwa, F. *Rwanda: à la recherche de la vérité historique pour une réconciliation nationale.* Paris, L'Harmattan, 2007.

Scherrer, C. P. *Genocide and Crisis in Central Africa: Conflict Roots, Mass Violence and Regional War*. Westport, CT, Praeger, 2001.

Sparrow, J. *Under the Volcanoes: Rwanda's Refugee Crisis*. Geneva, Federation of Red Cross and Red Crescent Societies, 1994.

Twagilimana, A. *The Debris of Hate: Ethnicity, Regionalism, and the 1994 Genocide*. Lanham, MD, University Press of America, 2003.

Uzabakiliho, F. *Flight for Life: A Journey from Rwanda*. New York, NY, Vantage Press, 2001.

Waller, D. *Rwanda: Which Way Now?* Oxford, Oxfam, 1993.

Willame, J. C. *Aux sources de l'hécatombe rwandaise*. Paris, L'Harmattan, 1995

SAINT HELENA

(WITH ASCENSION AND TRISTAN DA CUNHA)

Physical and Social Geography

Saint Helena, a rugged and mountainous island of volcanic origin, lies in the South Atlantic Ocean, latitude 16° S, longitude 5° 45′ W, 1,131 km south-east of Ascension and about 1,930 km from the south-west coast of Africa. The island is 16.9 km long and 10.5 km broad, covering an area of 122 sq km (47 sq miles). The highest elevation, Diana's Peak, rises to 823 m above sea-level. The only inland waters are small streams, few of them perennial, fed by springs in the central hills. These streams and rainwater are sufficient for domestic water supplies and a few small irrigation schemes.

The cool South Atlantic trade winds are continuous throughout the year. The climate is sub-tropical and mild: the temperature in Jamestown, on the sea-coast, is 21°C–29°C in summer and 18°C–24°C in winter. Inland it is some 5°C cooler. Annual rainfall varies from 200 mm to 760 mm in the centre of the island.

At the census of 8 March 1998 the total population was enumerated at 4,913. In December 2005 the population was estimated at 4,289, giving a density of 35.2 inhabitants per sq km.

Jamestown, the capital, is the only town and had a population of 850 at the 1998 census.

The language of the island is English and the majority of the population belong to the Anglican Communion.

Saint Helena has one of the world's most equable climates. Industrial pollution is absent from the atmosphere, and there are no endemic diseases of note. The island is of interest to naturalists for its rare flora and fauna; there are about 40 species of flora that are unique to Saint Helena.

Recent History

Revised by the editorial staff

The then uninhabited island of Saint Helena was discovered on 21 May 1502 by a Portuguese navigator, João da Nova, who named it in honour of St Helena, whose festival falls on that day. The British East India Co first established a settlement there in 1659, in order that the island might serve as a distant outpost from which to protect England's trade interests. The island was captured and briefly held by the Dutch in 1673. In that year a charter to occupy and govern Saint Helena was issued by King Charles II to the East India Co. In this charter the King confirmed the status of the island as a British outpost, and bestowed full rights of British citizenship on all those who settled on the island and on their descendants in perpetuity (see below). During 1815–21 the British Government temporarily assumed direct control of the island, owing to the exile there at Longwood House of Napoleon Bonaparte. In 1834 control over the island's affairs was transferred on a permanent basis from the East India Co to the British Government. However, Saint Helena was administered by the Foreign and Colonial Office (and classified as a colony), and not, as might have been expected, given its continuing use as a military outpost, by the War Office or the Admiralty. Its importance as a port of call on the trade route between Europe and India ceased with the opening of the Suez Canal in 1869.

In 1968 a South African concern, the South Atlantic Trading and Investment Co, acquired ownership of Solomon & Co (Saint Helena) Ltd, the local trading company. However, in view of the latter's dominant role in the island's economy, the British Government decided in 1974 to take full control of the enterprise. At the general election held in 1976, all but one of the 12 members elected to the Legislative Council strongly supported a policy of maintaining close economic links with the United Kingdom. This policy has been advocated by almost all members of the Legislative Council brought to office at subsequent elections (normally held every four years) up to and including that of August 2005.

In October 1981 the Governor announced the appointment of a commission to review the island's constitutional arrangements. The commission reported in 1983 that it was unable to find any proposal for constitutional change that would command the support of the majority of the islanders. In 1988, however, the Government obtained the introduction of a formal Constitution to replace the Order in Council and Royal Instructions under which Saint Helena was governed. This Constitution entered into force on 1 January 1989.

Underlying social discontent was expressed in two protest marches held in Jamestown during 1996, followed in April 1997 by an incident involving alleged arson attacks on police vehicles and a bus at Longwood. In the same month, the Governor (who exercises full executive and legislative authority in Saint Helena) refused to accept the nomination of a prominent critic of government policy to the post of Director of the Department of Social Welfare. Two members of the Executive Council (which acts in an advisory capacity) resigned in protest at the action of the Governor, who announced that elections to the Legislative Council would take place on 9 July. Following the elections, the Governor agreed to the nomination as Chairman of the Education Committee of the candidate he had previously refused to nominate to the Social Welfare Directorate.

Owing to the limited range of economic activity on the island, Saint Helena is dependent on development and budgetary aid from the United Kingdom. From 1981, when the United Kingdom adopted the British Nationality Act, which effectively removed the islanders' traditional right of residence in the United Kingdom, opportunities for overseas employment were limited to contract work, principally in Ascension and the Falkland Islands. In 1992 an informal 'commission on citizenship' was established by a number of islanders to examine Saint Helena's constitutional relationship with the United Kingdom, with special reference to the legal validity of the 1981 legislation as applied to Saint Helena. In April 1997 the commission obtained a legal opinion from a former acting Attorney-General of Saint Helena to the effect that the application of the Act to the population of Saint Helena was in contravention of the royal charter establishing British sovereignty in 1673. The commission indicated that it intended to pursue the matter further. In July 1997 private legislation was introduced in the British Parliament to extend full British nationality to 'persons having connections with' Saint Helena. In the following month the British Government indicated that it was considering arrangements under which islanders would be granted employment and residence rights in the United Kingdom. In February 1998, following a conference held in London, United Kingdom, of representatives of the British

Dependent Territories, it was announced that a review was to take place of the future constitutional status of these territories, and of means whereby their economies might be strengthened. It was subsequently agreed that the operation of the 1981 legislation in relation to Saint Helena would also be reviewed. As an immediate measure to ameliorate the isolation of Saint Helena, the British Government conceded permission for civilian air landing rights on Ascension Island, which, with the contemplated construction of a small airstrip on Saint Helena, could facilitate the future development of the island as a tourist destination. In March 1999 the British Government published draft legislation proposing that full British nationality, including the right of abode in the United Kingdom, was to be restored to the population of Saint Helena and its dependencies, under the reorganization of the British Dependent Territories as the United Kingdom Overseas Territories. However, this had still not been implemented in July 2000, when the citizens took their case to the UN Committee on Decolonization, seeking British passports, a new constitution and administration as a Crown dependency rather than as a colony. On 21 May 2002 Saint Helenians celebrated both the 500th anniversary of the island's discovery and the restoration of British citizenship under the British Overseas Territories Act, which reinstated those rights removed in 1981. In September 2002 an independent constitutional adviser visited Saint Helena and consulted extensively with the island's residents on the options for future constitutional development.

On 4 February 2002 a referendum was held in Saint Helena, Ascension Island, the Falkland Islands and on RMS *Saint Helena* on future access to Saint Helena; 71.6% of votes cast were in favour of the construction of an airport (the remainder of voters opted for a shipping alternative). Plans for the airport and associated commercial developments were cancelled in February 2003, on the grounds of unprofitability and environmental concerns; however, following protests by islanders, in April the Executive Council invited tenders for the construction of the airport. The project was expected to cost some £40m., of which the British Government was reported to have agreed to contribute some £26.3m., approximately equal to the cost of replacing the mail ship in 2010. The airport was scheduled to be fully functional by 2010. In July a public consultation procedure was undertaken on new draft tourism and investment policies, which were intended to provide a framework for private sector investment and tourism development, to maximize the opportunities that air access would bring to Saint Helena. However, in mid-2006 all three of the final contractors for the project declared that some of the commercial risks associated with the terms of the tender were unfeasible. Further negotiation was to ensue.

Meanwhile, a consultative poll on the draft for a new constitution, which, *inter alia*, proposed the creation of a ministerial form of government, took place on 25 May 2005. The draft document was rejected by 52.6% of voters. Concern was expressed at the low rate of voter participation, recorded at 43% of registered voters. Nevertheless, it was indicated that elements of the rejected constitution were expected to be adopted, including a change to the number of constituencies on Saint Helena. The British Government subsequently stated that it wished to identify any possible improvements to the existing Constitution in conjunction with the new Executive Council, which took office following the elections held on 31 August.

Economy

Revised by the editorial staff

From the 1980s increased benefits were made available to private farmers in a major effort to encourage greater local production, local utilization and farming efficiency. Grants, loans (of capital and labour) and free technical assistance have been offered and an increasing number of full-time smallholders have taken advantage of the scheme. Two major irrigation schemes using butyl-lined reservoirs have been completed. Following a notable rise in food production in the early 1980s, more land was rented or leased from the Government for this purpose. The Agricultural Development Authority farmed approximately one-half of the arable area and one-third of the grazing areas during 1975–96. Commonage grazing areas are now made available by the Government to private stock owners on a per head per month basis. Individuals hold land either in fee simple or by lease. Immigrants require a licence to hold land. Crown land may be leased on conditions approved by the Governor. At the 1998 census 10.2% of the employed labour force were engaged in agriculture and fishing. According to FAO, an estimated 66.6% of the economically active population were employed in the agricultural sector in mid-2005. Saint Helena was developing a reputation for niche organic products, such as coffee, and a project to develop honey production was also underway. It was also hoped that an integrated pest-management programme would lead to a greater range and output of agricultural production

A major reafforestation programme was begun during the mid-1970s, aimed at replacing flax and fostering land reclamation. A sawmill/timber treatment plant produces a proportion of the timber needed for construction and fencing requirements, but most timber continues to be imported. Timber sales amounted to 390 cu m in 1999. No mineral resources have been identified.

Fish of many kinds are plentiful in the waters around Saint Helena, and a fisheries corporation exists to exploit this resource. A freezing/storage unit is capable of storing 20 metric tons, allowing fish to be frozen for export as well as the local market. Fish exports comprise tuna—skipjack and dried salted skipjack—and in 2000 totalled 43.1 tons, with earnings amounting to £113,000. (Wild fish products from the island's inshore fishery recently became some of the first to receive organic certification from the British Soil Association.) A small quantity of coffee is the only other commodity exported.

In terms of offshore fishery, the Government has previously gained up to 20% of its revenue from the sale of licenses to international companies. International sales of the territory's postal stamps also comprise a significant proportion of local income.

Unemployment is a serious problem, and a large proportion of the labour force is forced to seek employment overseas, principally on Ascension and the Falkland Islands. In March 2001 551 Saint Helenians were working on Ascension, and in December 1999 371 were working on the Falkland Islands; approximately 1,700 members of the work-force were employed offshore at the end of 2005. However, a benefit of this arrangement was the volume of remittances entering the economy (see below). The rate of unemployment in Saint Helena was 12.7% in 2001/02. This has resulted in widespread reliance on welfare benefit payments and a concurrent decline in living standards for the majority of the population. Nearly 70% of employment on the island is provided by the Government (all key services and infrastructure, excluding telecommunications), although policies are actively being implemented to develop the private sector.

The main imports, by value, are foodstuffs, basic manufactures, machinery and transport equipment, chemicals and related products, mineral fuels, and beverages and tobacco. Total imports for 1994/95 were valued at £5,076,000; these were mainly supplied by the United Kingdom and South Africa. This figure was significantly greater than that of exports in the same year of some £200,000.

In 2006/07 Saint Helena was budgeted to receive £14,761m. in British aid (£3,056 for shipping purposes; £1,740 for development purposes; £3,016 for technical co-operation; and £6,949 as grant-in-aid). Local revenue was budgeted at £6.54m. in that year and total expenditure at £16.96m. Approximately one-third of the Government's annual recurrent budget and most capital investment is funded by the United Kingdom. Remittances from increasing offshore employment contribute some £2m. per year to the economy. The annual rate of inflation averaged 3.7% in 1990–2001. Consumer prices increased by an average of 3.5% in 2001.

The Saint Helena Growers' Co-operative Society is the only such association on the island. It is both a consumers' and a marketing organization, and provides consumer goods, such as seeds, implements and feeding stuffs, to its members, and markets their produce, mainly vegetables, locally, to visiting ships and to Ascension Island. The local market is limited and is soon over-supplied, and this, together with the decrease in the number of ships calling over recent years, has inhibited the growth of this enterprise.

The only port in Saint Helena is Jamestown, which is an open roadstead with a good anchorage for ships of any size.

There is no airport or airstrip as yet on Saint Helena and no railway, although in April 2003 the Executive Council invited tenders for the construction of an airport, which was expected to be completed by 2010. This development represented the potential to expand significantly both the private sector and the economy as a whole and plans included extensive infrastructural development to support the potential inflow of people and cargo. In 2006 new tourism and investment policies by expert consultants were commissioned, specifically to plan for the potential implications of the development, and put to public consultation. However, finding a contractor willing to undertake the commercial risks associated with the project was proving challenging. There are 118 km of all-weather roads, and a further 20 km of earth roads, which are used mainly by animal transport and are usable by motor vehicles only in dry weather. All roads have steep gradients and sharp curves.

In 1978, with the establishment of the Saint Helena Shipping Co, the Saint Helena Government assumed responsibility for the operation and maintenance of a charter vessel (known as the RMS *Saint Helena*, which entered operation in 1990), which carries cargo and passengers four times a year between Saint Helena and Cardiff, United Kingdom, via Vigo, Spain, and nine times a year between Saint Helena and Cape Town, South Africa (with calls at the Canary Islands); in addition, there are around 16 visits a year to Ascension Island, and one to Tristan da Cunha. The Saint Helena Shipping Co receives an annual subsidy from the British Government. There is a bulk fuel farm at Rupert's Valley, which is supplied at approximately three-month intervals with fuel from Europe.

Statistical Survey

Source (unless otherwise indicated): Development and Economic Planning Dept, Government of Saint Helena, Saint Helena Island, STHL 1ZZ; tel. 2777; fax 2830; e-mail depd@helanta.sh.

AREA AND POPULATION

Area: 122 sq km (47 sq miles).

Population: 5,644 at census of 22 February 1987; 5,157 (males 2,612, females 2,545) at census of 8 March 1998; 4,197 in December 2005.

Density (December 2005): 34.4 per sq km.

Principal Town (UN estimate, incl. suburbs): Jamestown (capital), population 1,787 in mid-2003 (Source: UN, *World Urbanization Prospects: The 2003 Revision*).

Births and Deaths (2005): Registered live births 34; Registered deaths 39.

Economically Active Population (1998 census): Agriculture, hunting and related activities 187; Fishing 20; Manufacturing 87; Electricity, gas and water 48; Construction 267; Wholesale and retail trade 344; Hotels and restaurants 24; Transport, storage and communications 181; Financial intermediation 17; Real estate, renting and business activities 7; Public administration and defence 293; Education 187; Health and social work 196; Other community services 87; Private household 74; Extra-territorial organizations 11; *Total employed* 2,037 (males 1,146; females 891); Unemployed 449 (males 290; females 159); *Total labour force* 2,486 (males 1,436, females 1,050). *2000:* Employed 2,637 (males 1,527, females 1,110); Registered unemployed 273 (Source: ILO). *Mid-2005* (estimates): Agriculture, etc. 2,000; Total labour force 3,000 (Source: FAO).

AGRICULTURE, ETC.

Livestock (2003 census): Cattle 996; Sheep 767; Pigs 751; Goats 1,190; Donkeys 134; Poultry 6,489.

Fishing (metric tons, live weight, including Ascension and Tristan da Cunha, 2005): Skipjack tuna 321; Yellowfin tuna 255; Tristan da Cunha rock lobster 373; Total catch (incl. others) 1,130. Figures include catches of rock lobster from Tristan da Cunha during the 12 months ending 30 April of the year stated. Source: FAO.

FINANCE

Currency and Exchange Rate: 100 pence (pennies) = 1 Saint Helena pound (£). *Sterling, Dollar and Euro Equivalents* (31 May 2007): £1 sterling = Saint Helena £1; US $1 = 50.57 pence; €1 = 68.04 pence; £10 = $19.77 = €14.70. *Average Exchange Rate* (£ per US dollar): 0.5462 in 2004; 0.5500 in 2005; 0.5435 in 2006. Note: The Saint Helena pound is at par with the pound sterling.

Budget (2006/07): *Revenue:* £21.30m. (United Kingdom assistance £14.76m., Local revenue £6.5m.); *Expenditure:* £16.96m.

Money Supply (£ '000, 2006/07): Currency in circulation 3,618 (excl. commemorative coins valued at 514).

Cost of Living (Consumer Price Index; base: 1990 = 100): 142.0 in 1999; 144.0 in 2000; 149.0 in 2001. Source: ILO.

EXTERNAL TRADE

Principal Commodities: *Imports* (1994/95, £ '000): Total 5,076 (Food and live animals 27.9%; Beverages and tobacco 8.5%; Mineral fuels, lubricants, etc. 8.5%; Chemicals and related materials 11.4%; Basic manufactures 12.7%; Machinery and transport equipment 11.7%; Miscellaneous manufactured articles 13.0%; Other commodities and transactions 3.3%); *Exports* (2000): fish £113,000; coffee n.a. Trade is mainly with the United Kingdom and South Africa. *2004/05* (trade with United Kingdom): Imports £6.4m.; Exports £0.8m.

TRANSPORT

Road Traffic (2004): 2,016 licensed vehicles.

Shipping: *Vessels Entered* (1999): 214. *Merchant Fleet* (31 December 2006): 2 vessels; Total displacement 2,322 grt (Source: Lloyd's Register-Fairplay, *World Fleet Statistics*).

COMMUNICATIONS MEDIA

Radio Receivers ('000 in use, 1997): 3. Source: UNESCO, *Statistical Yearbook*.

Television Subscribers (August 2006): 1,155.

Telephones (August 2006): 2,265.

EDUCATION

Primary (2006/07): 2 schools; 14 teachers; 115 pupils.

Amalgamated School (2006/07): 1 school; 15 teachers; 116 pupils.

Intermediate (2006/07): 2 schools; 17 teachers; 119 pupils.

Secondary (2006/07): 1 school; 42 teachers; 324 pupils.

Directory

The Constitution

The Saint Helena Constitution Order 1988, which entered into force on 1 January 1989, replaced the Order in Council and Royal Instructions of 1 January 1967. Executive and legislative authority is reserved to the British Crown, but is ordinarily exercised by others in accordance with provisions of the Constitution. The Constitution provides for the office of Governor and Commander-in-Chief of Saint Helena and its dependencies (Ascension Island and Tristan da Cunha). The Legislative Council for Saint Helena consists of the Speaker, three ex officio members (the Chief Secretary, the Financial Secretary and the Attorney-General) and 12 elected members; the Executive Council is presided over by the Governor and consists of the above ex officio members and five of the elected members of the Legislative Council. The elected members of the legislature choose from among themselves those who will also be members of the Executive Council. Although a member of both the Legislative Council and the Executive Council, the Attorney-General does not vote on either. Members of the legislature provide the Chairmen and a majority of the members of the various Council Committees. Executive and legislative functions for the dependencies are exercised by the Governor (although an advisory Island Council was inaugurated on Ascension in November 2002).

The Government

(August 2007)

Governor and Commander-in-Chief: MICHAEL CLANCY.

Chief Secretary: ETHEL YON (acting).

Financial Secretary: LINDA CLEMETT.

Chairmen of Council Committees:

Agriculture and Natural Resources: STEDSON GRAHAM FRANCIS.

Education: ERIC WILLIAM BENJAMIN.

Employment and Social Security: BRIAN WILLIAM ISAAC.

Public Health and Social Services: WILLIAM ERIC DRABBLE.

Public Works and Services: BERNICE ALICIA OLSSON.

Speaker of the Legislative Council: ERIC GEORGE.

GOVERNMENT OFFICES

Office of the Governor: The Castle, Jamestown, STHL 1ZZ; tel. 2555; fax 2598; e-mail ocs@helanta.sh; internet www.sainthelena.gov.sh.

Office of the Chief Secretary: The Castle, Jamestown, STHL 1ZZ; tel. 2555; fax 2598; e-mail ocs@helanta.sh.

Political Organizations

There are no political parties in Saint Helena. Elections to the Legislative Council, the latest of which took place in August 2005, are conducted on a non-partisan basis.

Judicial System

The legal system is derived from English common law and statutes. There are four Courts on Saint Helena: the Supreme Court, the Magistrate's Court, the Small Debts Court and the Juvenile Court. Provision exists for the Saint Helena Court of Appeal, which can sit in Jamestown or London.

Chief Justice: B. W. MARTIN (non-resident).

Attorney-General: KEN BADDON.

Sheriff: G. P. MUSK.

Magistrates: J. BEADON, D. BENNETT, D. CLARKE, R. COLEMAN, J. CORKER, L. CROWIE, J. FLAGG, P. FRANCIS, B. GEORGE, E. W. GEORGE, I. GEORGE, H. LEGG, V. MARCH, G. P. MUSK, R. PRIDHAM, G. SIM, S. STROUD, D. WADE, C. YON, P. YON, S. YOUDE.

Religion

The majority of the population belongs to the Anglican Communion.

CHRISTIANITY

The Anglican Communion

Anglicans are adherents of the Church of the Province of Southern Africa. The Metropolitan of the Province is the Archbishop of Cape Town, South Africa. St Helena forms a single diocese.

Bishop of Saint Helena: Rt Rev. JOHN SALT, Bishopsholme, POB 62, Saint Helena, STHL 1ZZ; tel. and fax 4471; e-mail bishop@helanta.sh; diocese f. 1859; has jurisdiction over the islands of Saint Helena and Ascension.

The Roman Catholic Church

The Church is represented in Saint Helena, Ascension and Tristan da Cunha by a Mission, established in August 1986. There were an estimated 87 adherents in the islands at 31 December 2000.

Superior: Rev. Fr MICHAEL MCPARTLAND (also Prefect Apostolic of the Falkland Islands); normally visits Tristan da Cunha once a year and Ascension Island two or three times a year; Vicar Delegate Rev. Fr JOSEPH WHELAN, Sacred Heart Church, Jamestown, STHL 1ZZ; tel. and fax 2535.

Other Christian Churches

The Salvation Army, Seventh-day Adventists, Baptists, New Apostolics and Jehovah's Witnesses are active on the island.

BAHÁ'Í FAITH

There is a small Bahá'í community on the island.

The Press

St Helena News Media Services: Saint Helena News Media Board, Broadway House, Jamestown, STHL 1ZZ; tel. 2612; fax 2802; e-mail sthelena.herald@helanta.sh; internet www.news.co.sh; f. 1986; govt-sponsored, independent; weekly; includes the *St Helena Herald* and St Helena Radio; Chief Exec. VERNON QUICKFALL; circ. 1,600.

Broadcasting and Communications

TELECOMMUNICATIONS

Cable & Wireless (St Helena) PLC: POB 2, Bishops Rooms, Jamestown, STHL 1ZZ; tel. 2155; fax 2206; e-mail webmaster@helanta.sh; internet www.cw.com/sthelena; f. 1899; provides national and international telecommunications.

BROADCASTING

Cable & Wireless PLC: The Moon, Jamestown, STHL 1ZZ; tel. 2200; f. 1995; provides a three channel television service 24 hours daily from five satellite channels.

Saint FM: Association Hall, Main St, Jamestown, STHL 1ZZ; tel. 2660; e-mail fm@helanta.sh; internet www.saint.fm; f. 2004; independent radio station; Station Man. MIKE OLSSON.

Radio St Helena: Saint Helena Information Office, Broadway House, Jamestown, STHL 1ZZ; tel. 4669; fax 4542; e-mail radio.sthelena@helanta.sh; internet www.sthelena.se/radiosth.htm; independent service; providing broadcasts for 24 hours per day; local programming and relays of British Broadcasting Corporation World Service programmes; Station Man. TONY LEO.

Finance

BANK

Bank of Saint Helena: Post Office Bldg, Main St, Jamestown STHL 1ZZ; tel. 2390; fax 2553; e-mail jamestown@sthelenabank.com; internet www.sainthelenabank.com; f. 2004; replaced the Government Savings Bank; total assets £30,182,375 (31 March 2006); 1 br. on Ascension; Chair. LYN THOMAS; Man. Dir JOHN TURNER.

INSURANCE

Solomon & Co PLC: Jamestown, STHL 1ZZ; tel. 2682; fax 2755; e-mail insurance@solomons.co.sh; internet www.solomons-sthelena.com; Solomon & Co operated an insurance agency on behalf of Royal SunAlliance Insurance Group during 1933–2002, until the latter co withdrew its interest from Saint Helena; negotiations for the foundation of a mutual insurance company on the island commenced in 2004; CEO Tony Green.

Trade and Industry

GOVERNMENT AGENCY

St Helena Development Agency: 2 Main St, POB 117, Jamestown, STHL 1ZZ; tel. 2920; fax 2166; e-mail enquiries@shda.co.sh; internet www.shda.helanta.sh; f. 1995; Man. Dir Dave Tyler.

CHAMBER OF COMMERCE

St Helena Chamber of Commerce: Jamestown, STHL 1ZZ; internet www.chamber.co.sh.

CO-OPERATIVE

St Helena Growers' Co-operative Society: Jamestown, STHL 1ZZ; tel. and fax 2511; vegetable marketing; also suppliers of agricultural tools, seeds and animal feeding products; 108 mems (1999); Chair. Stedson Francis; Sec. Peter W. Thorpe.

MAJOR COMPANIES

Argos Atlantic Cold Stores Ltd: POB 151, Jamestown; tel. 2333; fax 2334; f. 2000; processes, freezes and exports fish; owns five fishing vessels; head office in the Falkland Islands.

Island of St Helena Coffee Company Ltd: POB 119, Jamestown, STHL 1ZZ; tel. and fax 4944; e-mail info@st-helena-coffee.sh; internet www.st-helena-coffee.sh; f. 1994; organic arabica coffee, also sells chocolates online; Head David R. Henry.

St Helena Fisheries Corpn: Rupert's Valley, STHL 1ZZ; tel. 2430; fax 2552; e-mail shfc@helanta.sh; f. 1979; Gen. Man. Terry Richards.

St Helena Leisure Corpn Ltd (Shelco): Jamestown, STHL 1ZZ; e-mail joe.terry@shelco.sh; internet www.shelco.sh; Chair. Nigel Thompson.

Solomon & Co (St Helena) PLC: Main St, Jamestown, STHL 1ZZ; tel. 2380; fax 2423; e-mail generalenquiries@solomons.co.sh; internet www.solomons-sthelena.com; f. 1790; food production and retail, farming, construction, insurance, import and export, shipping and wharfage services.

W. A. Thorpe & Sons: Market St, POB 4, Jamestown, STHL 1ZZ; tel. 2781; fax 2318; e-mail office@thorpes.sh; internet www.thorpes.sh; f. 1860; imports groceries and hardware and maintains small cattle farm; 40 employees.

Transport

There are no railways in Saint Helena. In 2004 the Government conducted initial surveys for the construction of an airport, which was scheduled to be completed by 2008 and was to be situated on Prosperous Bay Plain.

ROADS

In 2002 there were 118 km of bitumen-sealed roads, and a further 20 km of earth roads, which can be used by motor vehicles only in dry weather. All roads have steep gradients and sharp bends.

SHIPPING

St Helena Line Ltd: Andrew Weir Shipping, Dexter House, 2 Royal Mint Court, London, EC3N 4XX, United Kingdom; tel. (20) 7265-0808; fax (20) 7481-4784; internet www.aws.co.uk; internet www.rms-st-helena.com; five-year govt contract renewed in August 2006; service subsidized by the British Govt by £1.5m. annually; operates two-monthly passenger/cargo services by the RMS *St Helena* to and from the United Kingdom and Cape Town, South Africa, calling at the Canary Islands, Ascension Island and Vigo, Spain, and once a year at Tristan da Cunha; also operates programme of shuttle services between Saint Helena and Ascension Island and the St Helena Liner Shipping Service; Chair. Garry Hopcroft.

Tourism

Although Saint Helena possesses flora and fauna of considerable interest to naturalists, as well as the house (now an important museum) in which the French Emperor Napoleon I spent his final years in exile, the remoteness of the island, which is a two-day sea voyage from Ascension Island, has inhibited the development of tourism. The construction of an airport on Saint Helena, which was scheduled to be fully operational by 2010, should greatly increase the island's accessibility to the limited number of visitors that can currently be accommodated. A total of 8,968 tourists visited Saint Helena in 1997. There are three hotels and a range of self-catering facilities.

St Helena Tourist Office: The Canister, Main St, Jamestown, STHL 1ZZ; tel. 2158; fax 2159; e-mail sthelena.tourism@helanta.sh; internet www.sthelenatourism.com; f. 1998; provides general information about the island; Dir Pamela Young.

Education

Education is compulsory and free for all children between the ages of five and 15 years, although power to exempt after the age of 14 can be exercised by the Education Committee. The standard of work at the secondary comprehensive school is orientated towards the requirements of the General Certificate of Secondary Education and the General Certificate of Education Advanced Level of the United Kingdom. During the second half of the 1980s the educational structure was reorganized from a two-tier to a three-tier comprehensive system, for which a new upper-school building was constructed.

There is a free public library in Jamestown, financed by the Government and managed by a committee, and a mobile library service in the country districts.

Ascension

The island of Ascension lies in the South Atlantic Ocean (7° 55′ S, 14° 20′ W), 1,131 km north-west of Saint Helena. It was discovered by a Portuguese expedition on Ascension Day 1501. The island was uninhabited until the arrival of Napoleon, the exiled French Emperor, on Saint Helena in 1815, when a small British naval garrison was placed there. Ascension remained under the supervision of the British Admiralty until 1922, when it was made a dependency of Saint Helena.

Ascension is a barren, rocky peak of purely volcanic origin, which was previously destitute of vegetation except above 450 m on Green Mountain (which rises to 875 m). The mountain supports a small farm producing vegetables and fruit. Since 1983 an alteration has taken place in the pattern of rainfall in Ascension. Total average annual rainfall has increased and the rain falls in heavy showers and is therefore less prone to evaporation. Grass, shrubs and flowers have grown in the valleys. Some topsoil has been produced by the decay of previous growth and root systems. The island is famous for green turtles, which land there from December to May to lay their eggs in the sand. It is also a breeding ground of the sooty tern, or 'wideawake', vast numbers of which settle on the island every 10 months to lay and hatch their eggs. All wildlife except rabbits and cats is protected by law. Shark, barracuda, tuna, bonito, marlin and other game fish are plentiful in the surrounding ocean. Following the decision by the British Government in February 1998 to open airfield facilities on Ascension to civilian flights, a modest eco-tourism sector is being developed.

The population in March 2001 was 982 (excluding British military personnel), of whom 760 were St Helenians. The majority of the remainder were expatriate civilian personnel of Merlin Communications International (MCI), which operates the British Broadcasting Corpn (BBC) Overseas World Service Atlantic relay station, Cable & Wireless PLC, which provides international communications services and operates the 'Ariane' satellite tracking station of the European Space Agency, and the US military base. Ascension does not raise its own finance; the costs of administering the island are borne collectively by the user organizations, supplemented by income from philatelic sales. Some revenue, which is remitted to the Saint Helena administration, is derived from fishing licences. On 31 March 2001 the joint venture between the BBC and Cable & Wireless, dating from 1984, to provide public services to the island was dissolved. The Ascension Island Government took over responsibility for health and education, the Ascension Island Works and Services Agency, a statutory body, was established to maintain transport and infrastructure, and any remaining services were taken over by the new Ascension Island Commercial Services Ltd (AICS) company. AICS was jointly owned by the Ascension Islands Government, the

BBC and Cable & Wireless and had the declared aim of privatizing the new enterprises by 2002. This development was regarded as highly significant in that it reorientated public-service provision to the demands of the resident population, rather than towards the needs of those organizations using the island.

Dissent developed among the resident population in June 2002, following the decision of the Foreign and Commonwealth Office to impose taxes for the first time on the island. The primary objection of the population was that this was 'taxation without representation', as the islanders do not possess the right to vote, to own property or even to live on the island. (Protests took the form of a petition and the threat of legal action under the European Convention on Human Rights.) The Governor responded with plans to introduce a democratically elected council that would have a purely advisory function and no decision-making powers. On 22–23 August a vote on the democratic options took place on the island, with 95% of the votes cast being in favour of an Island Council, rather than an Inter-Island Council plus Island Council structure; 50% of those eligible to vote did so. The Council was to be chaired by the Administrator, on behalf of the Governor, and was to comprise seven elected members, the Attorney-General, the Director of Finance and one or two appointed members. Elections for councillors took place in October, and the Island Council was inaugurated in the following month. A joint consultative council was also to be established, with representatives from both Ascension and Saint Helena, in order to develop policy relating to economic development and tourism common to both islands.

The British Government subsequently stated its intention to enact legislation granting the islanders right of abode and the right to own property. However, following a visit to the island by a delegation of British officials in November 2005, it was announced that the proposed reforms would not be carried out, on the basis that there was no indigenous population and that residents only lived and worked on the island for the duration of their employment contracts. The British Government cited its reluctance to change fundamentally the nature of the territory and also maintained that granting such rights would impose greater financial liabilities on British taxpayers, and would bring an unacceptable level of risk to the United Kingdom. In January 2006 the Island Council announced that it intended to seek clarification regarding the legality of the British Government's decision, observing that some residents had lived on the island for more than 40 years.

In May 2007 the Island Council was suspended and the Ascension Island Advisory Group was established to provide advice to the Administrator on certain policy issues. The suspension was expected to remain in place until May 2008, after elections would be held. It was anticipated that the Advisory Group would meet on a monthly basis, to be supplemented by informal meetings as necessary. Consultation papers were to be issued to encourage the people of Ascension to participate in the decision-making process.

In 1942 the US Government, by arrangement with the British Government, established an airbase, Wideawake, which it subsequently reoccupied and extended by agreement with the British Government in 1956, in connection with the extension of the long-range proving ground for guided missiles, centred in Florida. A further agreement in 1965 allowed the USA to develop tracking facilities on the island in support of the National Aeronautics and Space Administration's 'Apollo' space programme. This operation was terminated in 1990. In October 2003 the British Government concluded negotiations with the US authorities over the signing of an agreement to allow US air-charter access to the airfield.

Area: 88 sq km (34 sq miles).

Population: There are no indigenous inhabitants, but some 1,100 personnel and employees and their families are permanently resident (mostly nationals of Saint Helena, with some 200 UK nationals and 150 US nationals).

Budget: (2003/04, estimates, £ million, year ending 31 March): Revenue 4.3; Expenditure 4.0 (Recurrent expenditure 3.3, Capital expenditure 0.7).

Government: The Governor of Saint Helena, in his capacity as Governor of Ascension Island, is represented by an Administrator. Two advisory groups, one comprising senior managers of resident organizations, and one comprising their employees' representatives, assist the Administrator, who also has professional financial and technical advisers. In November 2002 an advisory Island Council, chaired by the Administrator and comprising seven elected members, the Attorney-General, the Director of Finance and two appointed members, was inaugurated.

Administrator: MICHAEL HILL, The Residency, Georgetown Ascension, ASCN 1ZZ; tel. 7000; fax 6152; e-mail aigenquiries@ascension .gov.ac; internet www.ascension-island.gov.ac.

Magistrate: (vacant).

Justices of the Peace: G. F. THOMAS, A. FOWLER, J. PETERS, C. PARKER-YON.

Religion: Ascension forms part of the Anglican diocese of Saint Helena, which normally provides a resident chaplain who is also available to minister to members of other denominations. There is a Roman Catholic chapel served by visiting priests, as well as a small mosque.

Transport: *Road vehicles* (1998): 830. *Shipping* (1998): ships entered and cleared 105. The St Helena Line Ltd (q.v.) serves the island with a two-monthly passenger/cargo service between Cardiff, in the United Kingdom, and Cape Town, in South Africa. A vessel under charter to the British Ministry of Defence visits the island monthly on its United Kingdom–Falkland Islands service. A US freighter from Cape Canaveral calls at three-month intervals. *Air services*: A twice-weekly Royal Air Force Tristar service between the United Kingdom and the Falkland Islands transits Ascension Island both southbound and northbound. There is a weekly US Air Force military service linking the Patrick Air Force Base in Florida with Ascension Island, via Antigua and Barbuda.

Tourism: Small-scale eco-tourism is encouraged, although accommodation on the island is limited and all visits require written permission from the Administrator. Access is available by twice-weekly flights operated from the United Kingdom by the Royal Air Force (see above), and by the RMS *St Helena* (see Saint Helena—Shipping).

Tristan da Cunha

Tristan da Cunha lies in the South Atlantic Ocean, 2,800 km west of Cape Town, South Africa and 2,300 km south-west of Saint Helena. Also in the group are Inaccessible Island, 37 km west of Tristan; the three Nightingale Islands, 37 km south; and Gough Island (Diego Alvarez), 425 km south. Tristan is volcanic in origin and nearly circular in shape, covering an area of 98 sq km (38 sq miles) and rising in a cone to 2,060 m above sea-level. The climate is typically oceanic and temperate. Rainfall averages 1,675 mm per year on the coast. The island provides breeding-grounds for albatrosses, rock-hopper penguins and seals, and a number of unique species, including the flightless land rail.

The British navy took possession of the island in 1816 during Napoleon's residence on Saint Helena, and a small garrison was stationed there. When the garrison was withdrawn, three men elected to remain and became the founders of the present settlement. Because of its position on a main sailing route the colony thrived until the 1880s, but with the replacement of sail by steam a period of decline set in. No regular shipping called and the islanders suffered at times from a shortage of food. Nevertheless, attempts to move the inhabitants to South Africa were unsuccessful. The islanders were engaged chiefly in fishing and agricultural pursuits.

The United Society for the Propagation of the Gospel has maintained an interest in the island since 1922, and in 1932 one of its missionary teachers was officially recognized as Honorary Commissioner and magistrate. In 1938 Tristan da Cunha and the neighbouring uninhabited islands of Nightingale, Inaccessible and Gough were made dependencies of Saint Helena, and in 1950 the office of Administrator was created. The Administrator is also the magistrate. The Island Council was established in 1952.

In 1942 a meteorological and wireless station was built on the island by a detachment of the South African Defence Force and was manned by the Royal Navy for the remainder of the Second World War. The coming of the navy reintroduced the islanders to the outside world, for it was a naval chaplain who recognized the possibilities of a crayfish industry on Tristan da Cunha. In 1948 a Cape Town-based fishing company was granted a concession to fish the Tristan da Cunha waters.

In June 2001 a hurricane in the main settlement of Edinburgh of the Seven Seas destroyed the hospital, community centre and numerous homes, and also killed many cattle; the satellite telephone link was lost and the island was without electricity for one week, although no serious injuries were sustained. The British Department for International Development granted a £75,000 emergency aid package in response to the disaster.

The island is remote, and regular communications are restricted to about six calls each year by vessels from Cape Town (usually crayfish trawlers), an annual visit from a British vessel, the RMS *St Helena*, from Cape Town and the annual call by a South African vessel with supplies for the island and the weather station on Gough Island. There is, however, a wireless station on the island which is in daily contact with Cape Town. A local broadcasting service was introduced in 1966 and a closed-circuit television system operated between 1983 and 1989, when it was replaced by a video lending-library. A satellite system, which provides direct dialling for telephone and fax facilities, was installed in 1992, and radio telex was installed at the island radio station in 1994. The cost of international communications was to diminish greatly from mid-2006, with the installation of a satellite internet and telephone exchange, part of the British Foreign and Commonwealth Office telecommunications network.

The island's major source of revenue derives from a royalty for the crayfishing concession, supplemented by income from the sale of postage stamps and other philatelic items, and handicrafts. The fishing industry and the administration employ all of the working population. Some 20 power boats operating from the island land their catches to a fish-freezing factory built by the Atlantic Islands Development Corpn, the fishing concession of which was transferred in January 1997 to a new holder, Premier Fishing (Pty) Ltd, of Cape Town. Premier also operates two large fishing vessels exporting the catch to the USA, France and Japan. Consultants were to assess the state of the island's harbour in late 2006, as its location makes it vulnerable to extreme weather conditions; however, raising the funding for its relocation to a safer position was likely to prove challenging. The island is largely self-sufficient.

Budget estimates for 2005/06 projected a deficit of £147,507. Development aid from the United Kingdom ceased in 1980, leaving the island financially self-sufficient. The United Kingdom, however, has continued to supply the cost of the salaries and passages of the Administrator, a doctor and visiting specialists (a dentist every two years and an optician every two years).

Area: Tristan da Cunha 98 sq km (38 sq miles); Inaccessible Island 10 sq km (4 sq miles); Nightingale Islands 2 sq km (3/4 sq mile); Gough Island 91 sq km (35 sq miles).

Population: (April 2005): 276 (including 10 expatriates) on Tristan; there is a small weather station on Gough Island, staffed, under agreement, by personnel employed by the South African Government.

Fishing: *Catch* (metric tons, year ending 30 April): Tristan da Cunha rock lobster 534 in 2003; 377 in 2004; 373 in 2005. Source: FAO.

Budget: (2005/06, estimates): Revenue £711,320; Expenditure £858,827 (with excess expenditure financed from capital reserves of £1.2m.).

Government: The Administrator, representing the Governor of Saint Helena, is assisted by an Island Council of eight elected members (of whom at least one must be a woman) and three appointed members, which has advisory powers in legislative and executive functions. The member receiving the largest number of votes at elections to the Council is appointed Chief Islander. The Council's advisory functions in executive matters are performed through 11 committees of the Council dealing with the separate branches of administration. Elections are held every three years. The last elections were held in March 2007.

Administrator: MICHAEL HENTLEY, The Administrator's Office, Edinburgh of the Seven Seas, Tristan da Cunha, TDCU 1ZZ; tel. (satellite) 874-1445434; fax (satellite) 874-1445435; e-mail admin@tristandc.com; internet www.tristandc.com/administator.php.

Legal System: The Administrator is also the Magistrate and Coroner.

Religion: Adherents of the Anglican church predominate on Tristan da Cunha, which is within the Church of the Province of Southern Africa, and is under the jurisdiction of the Archbishop of Cape Town, South Africa. There is also a small number of Roman Catholics.

Transport: The St Helena Line Ltd (q.v.), the MV *Hanseatic*, and MS *Explorer* and the SA *Agulhas* each visit the island once each year, and two lobster concession vessels each make three visits annually, remaining for between two and three months. Occasional cruise ships also visit the island. There is no airfield.

Tourism: Permission from the Administrator and the Island Council is required for visits to Tristan da Cunha. Facilities for tourism are limited, although some accommodation is available in island homes.

Bibliography

Ashmole, P., and Ashmole, M. *St Helena and Ascension Island: A Natural History.* Oswestry, Anthony Nelson, 2000.

Blackburn, J. *The Emperor's Last Island: A Journey to St Helena.* London, Secker & Warburg, 1992.

Blakeston, O. *Isle of Helena.* London, Sidgwick & Jackson, 1957.

Booy, D. M. *Rock of Exile: A Narrative of Tristan da Cunha.* London, Dent, 1957.

Castell, R. *St Helena: Island Fortress.* Old Amersham, Bucks, Byron Publicity Group, 1977.

Christopherson, E. (Ed.) *Results of the Norwegian Scientific Expedition to Tristan da Cunha, 1937–1938,* 16 parts. Oslo, Oslo University Press, 1940–62.

Cohen, R. (Ed.) *African Islands and Enclaves.* London, Sage Publications, 1983.

Cross, T. *St Helena: with chapters on Ascension and Tristan da Cunha.* Newton Abbot, David & Charles, 1981.

Day, A. (Ed.). *St Helena, Ascension and Tristan da Cunha* (World Bibliographical Series, Vol. 197). Santa Barbara, CA, ABC-Clio, 1997.

Eriksen, R. *St Helena Lifeline.* Norfolk, Mallett & Bell, 1999.

Gosse, P. *St Helena, 1502–1938.* London, Thomas Nelson, 1990 (reissue).

Hart-Davis, D. *Ascension: The Story of a South Atlantic Island.* London, Constable, 1972.

Mabbett, B. J. *St Helena: The Postal, Instructional and Censor Markings, 1815–2000.* Reading, West Africa Study Circle, 2002.

Mackay, M. M. *Angry Island: The Story of Tristan da Cunha (1506–1963).* London, Barker, 1963.

Munch, P. A. *Crisis in Utopia: The Ordeal of Tristan da Cunha.* New York, NY, Cromwell, 1971.

Royle, S. A. *A Geography of Islands: Small Island Insularity.* London, Routledge, 2001.

'Historic Communities: On a Desert Isle (Tristan da Cunha)' in *Communities, Journal of Co-operative Living,* No. 105, 1999.

Schreier, D., and Lavarello-Schreier, K. *Tristan da Cunha: History, People, Language.* London, Battlebridge Publishers, 2003.

The St Helena Research Group. *A Strategic Profile of St Helena, 2000 Edition* (Strategic Planning Series). Icon Group International Inc, 2000.

SÃO TOMÉ AND PRÍNCIPE

Physical and Social Geography

RENÉ PÉLISSIER

The archipelago forming the Democratic Republic of São Tomé and Príncipe is, after the Republic of Seychelles, the smallest independent state in Africa. Both the main islands are in the Gulf of Guinea on a south-west/north-east axis of extinct volcanoes. The boundaries take in the rocky islets of Caroço, Pedras and Tinhosas, off Príncipe, and, south of São Tomé, the Rôlas islet, which is bisected by the line of the Equator. The total area of the archipelago is 1,001 sq km (386.5 sq miles), of which São Tomé occupies an area of 859 sq km.

São Tomé is a former plantation island where the eastern slopes and coastal flatlands are covered by huge cocoa estates (*roças*) formerly controlled by Portuguese interests, alongside a large number of local smallholders. These plantations have been carved out of an extremely dense mountainous jungle which dominates this equatorial island. The highest point is the Pico de São Tomé (2,024 m), surrounded by a dozen lesser cones above 1,000 m in height. Craggy and densely forested terrain is intersected by numerous streams. The coast of Príncipe is extremely jagged and indented by many bays. The highest elevation is the Pico de Príncipe (948 m). Both islands have a warm and moist climate, with an average yearly temperature of 25°C. Annual rainfall varies from over 5,100 mm on the south-western mountain slopes to under 1,020 mm in the northern lowlands. The dry season, known locally as *gravana*, lasts from June to September.

The total population was 117,504 at the census of 4 August 1991, when São Tomé had 112,033 inhabitants and Príncipe 5,471. The population was 137,599 at the census of September 2001. In mid-2006, according to UN estimates, the population was 155,000, giving a density of 154.8 inhabitants per sq km. During 1995–2005, according to the World Bank, the population increased by an annual average of 2.1%. The capital city is São Tomé, with an estimated 53,570 inhabitants in 2003. It is the main export centre of the island. Inland villages on São Tomé are mere clusters of houses of native islanders. Príncipe has only one small town of about 1,000 people, Santo António.

The native-born islanders (*forros*) are the descendants of imported slaves and southern Europeans who settled in the 16th and 17th centuries. Intermarriage was common, but subsequent influxes of Angolan and Mozambican contract workers until about 1950 re-Africanized the *forros*. Descendants of slaves who escaped from the sugar plantations from the 16th century onwards, who formed a formidable maroon enclave in the south of São Tomé and became known as Angolares, are now mainly fishermen.

The widespread exodus of skilled Portuguese plantation administrators, civil servants and traders during the period just prior to independence in July 1975, together with the departure of most of the Angolan and Mozambican workers and the repatriation of more than 10,000 São Tomé exiles from Angola, caused considerable economic dislocation, the impact of which continues to be felt.

Recent History

GERHARD SEIBERT

São Tomé and Príncipe were colonized by Portugal in the 16th century. A nationalist group, the Comité de Libertação de São Tomé e Príncipe, was formed in 1960 and became the Movimento de Libertação de São Tomé e Príncipe (MLSTP) in 1972, under the leadership of Dr Manuel Pinto da Costa. Following the military coup in Portugal in April 1974, the Portuguese Government recognized the right of the islands to independence. In December Portugal appointed a transitional Government that included members of the MLSTP, which was recognized as the sole legitimate representative of the people. At elections for a Constituent Assembly held in July 1975, the MLSTP won all 16 seats. Independence as the Democratic Republic of São Tomé and Príncipe took effect on 12 July, with Pinto da Costa as President and Miguel Trovoada as Prime Minister. The Constitution promulgated in November effectively vested absolute power in the President and the political bureau of the MLSTP.

MLSTP GOVERNMENT

During 1976–82 serious ideological as well as personal divisions arose within the MLSTP, and in March 1978 Angolan soldiers were brought to the islands, following an alleged attempt to overthrow the Government. In 1979 Trovoada was dismissed as Prime Minister, arrested, accused of complicity in the census riots of the previous month and detained without trial until 1981, when he was permitted to leave the islands.

In its foreign relations, São Tomé and Príncipe avoided any formal commitment to the Eastern bloc, although close economic ties existed with the People's Republic of China and the German Democratic Republic. Gabon, the islands' nearest mainland neighbour, viewed these developments with disquiet, and relations consequently deteriorated. However, São Tomé and Príncipe extended the range of its international contacts by joining the IMF and the World Bank in 1977, acceding to the Lomé Convention in 1978 and participating in the foundation of the francophone Communauté économique des états de l'Afrique centrale (CEEAC) in 1983. The bulk of the country's trade continued to be transacted with Western Europe, and relations with Portugal remained generally cordial. In 1985, confronted by the threat of the complete collapse of the economy, Pinto da Costa began to abandon economic ties with the Eastern bloc in favour of capitalist strategies. The two main Western nations seeking to exert influence in the country were Portugal and France; however, trade with Portugal was much more substantial than with France, and negotiations concerning São Tomé's admission to the Franc Zone were eventually inconclusive.

Political Change

In October 1987 the Central Committee of the MLSTP announced major political and constitutional changes, including the election by universal suffrage of the Head of State, and of members of the legislative Assembleia Popular Nacional by secret ballot, as well as the admission of different political currents within the party. In January 1988 the post of Prime Minister was reintroduced, to which Celestino Rocha da Costa was appointed. Carlos Monteiro Dias da Graça, who had been pardoned in 1985 for an attempted *coup d'état* orchestrated from Gabon in 1978, was appointed Minister of Foreign Affairs. However, Miguel Trovoada, who had been invited to return from exile, remained in France, stating that the changes were insufficient. By 1987 three small overseas opposition groups were already in existence.

Increasingly concerned by the country's economic problems, and encouraged by a progressive faction within the party, the MLSTP embarked, in late 1989, on a transition to full multi-party democracy. In August 1990, in a national referendum, the electorate overwhelmingly approved the introduction of the new Constitution, proposed by the MLSTP Central Committee, which provided for a multi-party political system, and a maximum of two five-year terms of office for the President. At the MLSTP party congress, held in October 1990, da Graça succeeded Manuel Pinto da Costa as Secretary-General. In addition, the party's name was amended to the Movimiento de Libertação de São Tomé e Príncipe—Partido Social Democrata (MLSTP—PSD). Also in that year the Frente Democrata Cristã (FDC) was founded by members of a former opposition group based in Libreville, Gabon, and the Partido Democrático de São Tomé e Príncipe—Coligação Democrática de Oposição (PDSTP—CODO), a merger of two other opposition groups formerly in exile, was formed, under the leadership of Albertino Neto. However, the major challenge to the ruling party came from the Partido de Convergência Democrática—Grupo de Reflexão (PCD—GR), a coalition of former MLSTP dissidents, independents and young professionals, under the leadership of Leonel d'Alva.

At elections to the new Assembleia Nacional, held on 20 January 1991, the MLSTP—PSD secured only 30.5% of the total votes and 21 seats, while the PCD—GR obtained 54% of the votes and 33 seats; PDSTP—CODO took the one remaining seat. In February a transitional Government, headed by Daniel Daio, was installed, pending the forthcoming presidential election; President Pinto da Costa confirmed his decision not to run in the election. The MLSTP—PSD did not present an alternative candidate, and two of the three remaining candidates subsequently withdrew from the election. On 3 March Miguel Trovoada, the sole remaining contender, was elected President, receiving 82% of the votes cast. Trovoada took office the following month and officially inaugurated the PCD—GR Government, headed by Daio.

THE TROVOADA PRESIDENCY

In early 1992 a political crisis erupted when co-operation between the Government and the presidency began to break down after the PCD—GR attempted to introduce a constitutional amendment limiting presidential powers. Meanwhile, in June 1991 stringent austerity measures were imposed by the IMF and the World Bank as preconditions for economic assistance, which contributed to a sharp decline in the islanders' living standards. Following two mass demonstrations held in April 1992 to protest against the austerity programme, Trovoada dismissed the Daio Government, citing the 'institutional disloyalty' of the Prime Minister, who had publicly blamed the President for the country's economic plight and attendant political unrest. The PCD—GR, which initially condemned Trovoada's actions as an 'institutional coup', was invited to designate a new Prime Minister. In May Norberto Costa Alegre became Prime Minister and formed a new administration.

At local elections held in December 1992 the PCD—GR suffered a considerable reverse; however, the Government refused to accede to opposition demands that it resign, form a government of national unity or call new legislative elections. In April 1994 the Assembleia Nacional began discussion of a draft bill providing local autonomy for the island of Príncipe. Its proposals, approved later that year, included provision for the creation of a regional assembly and a five-member regional government. In March 1995 the first elections to a new seven-member Assembleia Regional (Regional Assembly) and five-member Regional Government were conducted on Príncipe, resulting in victory for the MLSTP—PSD, which won an absolute majority. The new Regional Government began functioning in April.

In early 1994 relations between the Government and the presidency again began to deteriorate. In April Trovoada publicly dissociated himself from government policy, and in July dismissed the Alegre administration citing 'institutional conflict'. On 4 July Trovoada appointed Evaristo do Espírito Santo de Carvalho (Minister of Defence and Security in the outgoing administration) as Prime Minister. The PCD—GR, which refused to participate in the new Government, subsequently expelled Carvalho from the party. An interim administration took office on 9 July. On the following day, in an attempt to resolve the political crisis, Trovoada dissolved the Assembleia Nacional and announced that a legislative election would be held on 2 October.

This election resulted in a decisive victory for the MLSTP—PSD, which secured 27 seats, one short of an absolute majority. The PCD—GR and the Acção Democrática Independente (ADI) each obtained 14 seats. The level of voter participation, which was as low as 52%, was believed to reflect public disillusionment at the failure of democracy to realize expectations of a transformation in the country's social and economic prospects. In late October 1994 da Graça was appointed Prime Minister and subsequently announced his intention to form a government of national unity with those parties represented in the legislature. However, both the ADI and the PCD—GR rejected the proposal. The Council of Ministers, which took office in late October, was thus composed almost entirely of members of the MLSTP—PSD.

On 15 August 1995, following a period of social unrest, a group of some 30 soldiers staged a *coup d'état* and detained Trovoada. The insurgents cited widespread corruption and political incompetence as justification for the coup. Following negotiations the military insurgents and the Government signed a 'memorandum of understanding', providing for the reinstatement of Trovoada and the restoration of constitutional order. In return, the Government gave an undertaking to restructure the armed forces, and the Assembleia Nacional granted a general amnesty to all those involved in the coup.

Consensus Government

At the end of December 1995 Armindo Vaz d'Almeida was appointed Prime Minister, at the head of a coalition Government of the MLSTP—PSD, the ADI, and the PDSTP—CODO.

At the presidential election of 30 June 1996 no candidate secured an absolute majority. Consequently, a second ballot, between the two leading candidates, was conducted on 21 July, at which Trovoada won 52.7% of the votes, defeating Pinto da Costa, who secured 47.3%. In mid-September the Vaz d'Almeida administration was dissolved, following its defeat in a confidence motion in the Assembleia Nacional. The motion had been proposed by Vaz d'Almeida's own party, the MLSTP—PSD, which accused the Government of inefficiency and corruption, and had received the support of the PCD—GR. In late October the MLSTP—PSD and the PCD—GR signed an accord providing for the establishment of a nine-member coalition government. In mid-November the President appointed Raúl Wagner da Conceição Bragança Neto, Assistant Secretary-General of the MLSTP—PSD, Prime Minister. The new coalition Government, which included five members of the MLSTP—PSD, three members of the PCD—GR and one independent, was inaugurated later that month.

The Premiership of Pósser da Costa

At an extraordinary congress of the MLSTP—PSD held in May 1998, the former President and party leader, Manuel Pinto da Costa, was elected unopposed as President of the party.

At a legislative election held on 8 November 1998 the MLSTP—PSD secured an absolute majority, with 31 seats, while the ADI won 16 seats and the PCD—GR obtained the remaining eight seats. The level of voter participation was 64.7%. In December 1998 Guilherme Pósser da Costa was appointed Prime Minister. However, the MLSTP—PSD accused Trovoada of interfering in areas outside his jurisdiction when, later that month, he vetoed Pósser da Costa's initial nominations for the Council of Ministers. A revised Council of Ministers was installed on 5 January 1999. At the instigation of the IMF, the number of ministries was limited to nine.

In January 2000 an estimated 3,500 civil servants and public-sector workers demanded an increase in the minimum wage from 40,000 to 600,000 dobras. The Government had earlier offered a minimum wage of 120,000 dobras, in accordance with IMF recommendations not to increase the total expenditure on salaries by more than 7%. The public-sector trade unions subsequently reduced their demands to 350,000 dobras. In April the unions accepted the Government's proposal to increase the minimum wage to 170,000 dobras, and a pledge to resume wage negotiations in August of that year.

PRESIDENTIAL AND LEGISLATIVE ELECTIONS

A presidential election took place on 29 July 2001. Among the five candidates hoping to succeed Trovoada were former President Manuel Pinto da Costa, the leader of the MLSTP—PSD, and Fradique de Menezes, a businessman standing for the ADI, who received the support of outgoing President Trovoada. In the event, de Menezes was elected to the presidency, winning 56.3% of the votes cast, while da Costa secured 38.7%. The rate of voter participation was 70.7%. De Menezes was inaugurated in early September. Later in that month, following disagreements with the MLSTP—PSD over the appointment of the former President's son, Patrice Trovoada (ADI), as foreign minister in a new Government, de Menezes appointed a Council of Ministers composed entirely of members of the parliamentary opposition, including the ADI's Evaristo de Carvalho as Prime Minister and Patrice Trovoada as foreign minister. However, in early February 2002 Trovoada resigned from that post, citing a lack of political confidence in President de Menezes, who had accused the Trovoada family of oligarchic attitudes.

In early November 2001 the MLSTP—PSD boycotted the Assembleia Nacional and urged President de Menezes to restore constitutional order, by returning the Government to the majority party or announcing early elections. In December Carlos Neves, hitherto leader of the ADI, and several of his followers left the party, following Trovoada's announcement of his candidacy for the party leadership. Later that month the dissident ADI members took leading positions in a new party created by supporters of de Menezes, the Movimento Democrático Força da Mudança (MDFM). Meanwhile, the President and representatives of political parties signed a pact advocating the formation of an all-party government after legislative elections, which were scheduled for 3 March 2002, in order to guarantee political stability. At the elections the MLSTP—PSD won 24 seats in the Assembleia Nacional and an alliance of the MDFM and the PCD (the suffix Grupo de Reflexão had been dropped the previous year) secured 23, while Uê Kédadji (UK—an alliance comprising the ADI and four smaller parties) obtained only eight seats. Following negotiations with the leader of the MLSTP—PSD, President de Menezes appointed Gabriel da Costa, a lawyer and hitherto ambassador to Portugal, as Prime Minister. In early April a Government of National Unity, which included members of the MLSTP—PSD, the MDFM-PCD and UK, as well as a number of independents, was installed.

In August 2002 the four deputies of the ADI left UK and formed a legislative group of independents. In mid-September a member of the Supreme Defence Council accused de Menezes of having illegally promoted the Minister of Defence and Internal Affairs, Victor Monteiro, to the highest rank of Lt-Col, since the minister had not met the necessary legal requirements. This affair provoked an open conflict between Monteiro and Prime Minister da Costa, who refused to continue working with the defence minister. Finally, on 27 September President de Menezes dismissed the da Costa Government, claiming that the conflict between Monteiro and the Prime Minister had created political instability. In October de Menezes appointed Maria das Neves de Souza (MLSTP—PSD), hitherto Minister of Trade, Industry and Tourism, as Prime Minister.

In late October 2002 the Assembleia Nacional initiated a revision of the Constitution in order to clarify ambiguous articles that had provoked conflicts between the President and the Government since 1991. The proposed amendments curbed the powers of the President and strengthened the position of government and the legislature. In response, President de Menezes fiercely condemned the proposed legislation and threatened to dissolve the legislature, if it could not reach consensus with him on the new Constitution. In early December the Assembleia Nacional unanimously approved the amendments to the Constitution, which were to come into effect after the end of the President's term in 2006. Following the refusal of the legislature to submit the amendments to a popular referendum, on 17 January 2003 de Menezes vetoed the new Constitution. On 22 January de Menezes dissolved the Assembleia Nacional and called early legislative elections for 13 April. However, Prime Minister das Neves and Alice de Carvalho, the President of the Supreme Court, successfully mediated in the conflict. On 24 January a memorandum of understanding was signed by the President and representatives of the parties in the Assembleia Nacional, according to which de Menezes revoked the dissolution of the legislature and promulgated the constitutional amendments, while the Assembleia Nacional agreed to submit the new Constitution to a popular referendum at the end of the President's mandate in 2006.

CIVIL UNREST AND MILITARY COUP

In mid-April 2003 a group of citizens published an open letter, signed by 80 people, which accused the Government and the President of having failed to improve living conditions and expressed concern over a lack of transparency in the country's oil negotiations. Furthermore, it accused the President of not having explained the remittance of US $100,000 by Chrome Oil Services to the Belgian bank account of his company, CGI, in February 2002 and of having conceded to his brother, João de Menezes, resident in Portugal, the exclusive rights for the exploitation of casinos and the airport in São Tomé. In response, President de Menezes held a controversial press conference, during which he accused a number of the signatories of the document of having committed acts of corruption themselves in the past. He declared that the payment of $100,000 from the Nigerian petroleum company was a donation to the MDFM-PCD campaign for the legislative elections.

On 16 July 2003, while President de Menezes was on a private visit to Nigeria, a group of military officers, led by Maj. Fernando Pereira ('Cobó'), together with the FDC, initiated a bloodless coup and detained a number of government ministers in the military barracks. Pereira and the leaders of the FDC, Sabino dos Santos and Alércio Costa established a Military Junta of National Salvation. The coup plotters claimed to have acted in response to continued corruption, widespread misery, and the widening gap between the few rich and the impoverished majority. The coup was quickly condemned by regional and world powers and organizations, which demanded the restitution of the constitutional order. On the fourth day of the rebellion the Military Junta commenced negotiations with international mediators from the Comunidade dos Países de Língua Portuguesa (CPLP), the CEEAC, the African Union (AU), Nigeria, the USA and South Africa. The mediators were co-ordinated by Rodolphe Adada, the foreign minister of the Republic of the Congo. On 22 July President de Menezes returned to São Tomé, accompanied by the Nigerian President, Olusegun Obasanjo, and on the same day the coup was ended when a memorandum of understanding was signed by de Menezes, Pereira and Adada. The agreement provided for a general amnesty for the coup leaders; the restoration of President de Menezes; respect by the President for the Constitution and the separation of powers; the formation of a new government; the approval of a law on the proper use of petroleum revenue by the Assembleia Nacional; the sound and transparent management of public funds by the Government; the improvement of the conditions of the armed forces; and the prohibition of foreign military intervention. A 13-member Commission, headed by a representative of the CEEAC, was created to monitor the implementation of the agreement. At the beginning of August Prime Minister das Neves resigned in preparation for the installation of a new Government. Das Neves was subsequently reappointed as Prime Minister, heading a government comprising representatives from the MLSTP—PSD, the MDFM and the ADI.

In mid-October 2003 the Assembleia Nacional entrusted a three-member parliamentary commission to present a draft for the petroleum revenue management law demanded by the IMF. In late October bidding for the first nine oil blocks in the Joint Development Zone (JDZ) was opened in São Tomé. In the following month, during a visit to São Tomé, an oil revenue management team from Columbia University in New York, USA, declared that it would assist the Assembleia Nacional with the drafting of petroleum legislation. In addition, on behalf of the World Bank, another team provided advice for the petroleum revenue law. Both expert teams submitted their draft proposals to the Assembleia Nacional in early 2004. The proposals include a petroleum fund for future generations.

In January 2004 the Audit Office (Tribunal de Contas), which had begun operations in early 2003 and was headed by Francisco Fortunato Pires, submitted its first report on government accounts to the Assembleia Nacional. The report criticized various irregularities in the management of public funds during 2003 and denounced the absence of record-keeping and of an inventory of state property. Fortunato Pires claimed that the massive waste of public monies during the 27 years before the existence of the Audit Office had totally bankrupted the state.

In March 2004 the unauthorized actions of two ministers of the President's party provoked a governmental crisis. It emerged that Tomé Vera Cruz, the Minister of Natural Resources and the Environment, had signed a controversial petroleum agreement with Energem Petroleum, while the Minister of Foreign Affairs, Mateus Rita, had tried to sign an air-transport agreement with the Angolan Government, both without the consent of Prime Minister das Neves. As a result of the affair, the MDFM resigned from the Government and the alliance UK joined the coalition.

In April 2004, at an extraordinary meeting, the MDFM re-elected Vera Cruz as party leader and renamed the party MDFM—Partido Liberal (PL). In mid-May President de Menezes appointed 11 advisors, whose portfolios corresponded to government ministries. The Head of State denied accusations that his extended staff represented a shadow executive and stated that it merely served to improve his capacity to examine government policies.

In mid-June 2004 de Menezes inaugurated the National Forum of Reconciliation that had been stipulated as part of the memorandum of understanding of 22 July 2003 to allow civil society and the political parties to debate the country's problems. The inaugural session of the Forum brought together 600 delegates of political parties and civil society to debate the country's problems and possible solutions for the future. Thereafter the Forum organized the 55 meetings to listen to the population's concerns and expectations. At the Forum's closing ceremony on July 12 a long list of recommendations and conclusions on a wide range of political and social-economic issues was presented.

DAS NEVES DISMISSED

In August 2004 an audit report of the accounts of the food aid agency, Gabinete de Gestão das Ajuda (GGA), embarrassed the country's political élite. The GGA was created in 1993 to administer the counterpart funds in dobras stemming from the local sale of foreign food aid. The report, covering the years 2001–04, revealed a series of irregularities, including the illegal concession of credits, the payment of fictitious services, and illicit financial transfers to the finance and economy ministries for extra-budgetary expenditure. In total, funds of US $1.9m. were diverted to local politicians and office holders. According to the document, Prime Minister das Neves had also taken various amounts from the GGA accounts. Although she denied the allegations, in mid-September 2004 das Neves and her coalition Government were dismissed by President de Menezes, who subsequently asked the MLSTP—PSD to form a new government. Days later a new Council of Ministers was installed by presidential decree, which, like the previous administration, was a coalition of the MLSTP—PSD, the ADI and two independents. Damião Vaz de Almeida, the former Minister of Labour, Employment and Security, was appointed Prime Minister. Six out of the 12 ministers had served in the previous Government.

After having twice declined the request of the public prosecutor, in early 2005 the Assembleia Nacional agreed to lift the parliamentary immunity of five deputies—namely former Prime Ministers Pósser da Costa and das Neves, and ex-ministers Arzemiro dos Prazeres (of the PCD), Basílio Diogo (MDFM), and Júlio Silva (ADI)—allowing them to be questioned about their alleged involvement in the GGA scandal. All five suspects denied any wrongdoing. In May the public prosecutor formally charged das Neves and dos Prazeres with embezzlement. The three other suspects were acquitted from any criminal responsibility and their cases were transferred to the Audit Office for investigation. In October 2006 the Government dissolved the corruption-ridden GGA. In April 2007 a judge dismissed the case against das Neves and dos Prazeres due to a lack of evidence. However, in June the public prosecutor filed an appeal against this decision at the Supreme Court.

Meanwhile, at the fourth party congress of the MLSTP—PSD in February 2005 Pósser da Costa was elected party President, replacing Manuel Pinto da Costa. Dionísio Dias, the current President of the Assembleia Nacional, was elected party Vice-President, while Homéro Salvaterra became Secretary-General. In March Pósser da Costa was sentenced by a local court to a suspended prison term for having attacked the Attorney-General, Adelino Pereira, in November 2004. Following the approval, in April 2005, of the budget for that year by the Assembleia Nacional, trade unions representing public-sector workers demanded an increase of the minimum salary from 300,000 dobras (US $30) to 1m. dobras ($100) per month. Citing budgetary constraints, the Government presented a proposal of only 428,000 dobras ($43), and on 30 May the unions commenced a five-day general strike. Following declarations by President de Menezes that the Government was responsible for the action, on the fourth day of the strike Prime Minister Vaz d'Almeida abruptly resigned, accusing de Menezes of a lack of institutional solidarity with the Government and of having ratified the petroleum block awards on 31 May to Nigerian companies of doubtful credibility (see Economy). The ruling MLSTP—PSD, having first asked for early elections, under pressure from donor countries to minimize instability in the country, acceded to the President's request that the party nominate a new prime minister.

On 9 June 2005 the Governor of the central bank (the Banco Central de São Tomé e Príncipe—BCSTP), Maria do Carmo Silveira, along with a new MLSTP—PSD Government, was sworn in as Prime Minister for the remaining nine-month term of the legislature. The ADI did not participate in the new Government, but promised to support it in the Assembleia Nacional. In late June, at the request of the Public Prosecutor, the Assembleia Nacional lifted the parliamentary immunity of Alcino Pinto, the parliamentary leader of the MLSTP—PSD. Pinto, the managing director of Air São Tomé e Príncipe, was charged with the alleged embezzlement of funds from the company's accounts. In early July the Government's legislative programme, which focused on sustainable development and improvement in the social sector, was approved by the Assembleia Nacional, and by early August a preliminary agreement on a 29% pay rise had been agreed between the Government and trade unions.

In mid-January 2006, following governmental pressure, the Minister of Foreign Affairs and Co-operation, Ovídio Manuel Barbossa Pequeno, who enjoyed close relations with de Menezes, resigned. It was alleged that Pequeno had spent an estimated US $500,000 of bilateral aid from Morocco, without the consent or knowledge of the Prime Minister on the purchase of cars and goods for the presidency and the foreign ministry. De Menezes had refused the Prime Minister's request that Pequeno be dismissed, and in early March it was announced that Pequeno had been appointed São Tomé e Príncipe's Permanent Representative to the UN.

In January 2006 about 50 disaffected members of the rapid-reaction police force, known as the 'Ninjas', seized the police headquarters and demanded higher salaries and the dismissal of the police commander, Armando Correia, who they accused of corruption and maltreatment. The dispute was resolved after a week of negotiations, with the mediation of the Portuguese ambassador to São Tomé e Príncipe, between a three-member government delegation and the police. The Government dismissed Correia, who was subsequently appointed as an advisor to the Minister of Defence.

THE 2006 ELECTIONS

In January 2006 the PCD and the MDFM formally renewed their electoral alliance for the legislative elections scheduled for 26 March. Prior to the elections President de Menezes ordered an audit of the computer system of the Comissão Eleitoral Nacional (CEN—National Electoral Commission) to impede possible electoral fraud. Nevertheless, the election campaign was marked by persistent reports of vote buying. In 13 localities some 9,600 out of the 89,850 registered voters were unable to vote owing to roadblocks erected by the local population in protest against poor access roads and the lack of other basic infrastructure. Elections in those localities were repeated on 2 April. In early April the Constitutional Court decided to recount all ballots to reconfirm the results announced by the CEN. The MDFM-PCD perceived this decision as a possible attempt by the MLSTP—PSD to defraud the electoral process, arguing that by law only contested ballots could be recounted. Shortly afterwards, at the behest of the Minister of Defence, Lt-Col Óscar Sousa, a confidant of President de Menezes, armed soldiers surrounded the court building where the recount was taking place, allegedly to protect the court against threats to public order. The outgoing MLSTP—PSD Government accused Sousa of having committed a military intervention without its consent and demanded his dismissal. On 28 April final election results were announced. The pro-de Menezes MDFM-PCD won 23 seats, the MLSTP—PSD and the ADI obtained 20 and 11 seats, respectively, while the newly established Novo Rumo took one seat.

In late April 2006 the MDFM-PCD formed a minority Government headed by Prime Minister Vera Cruz, the Secretary-General of the MDFM. In the government programme approved by the Assembleia Nacional in May, Vera Cruz promised to reach the conclusion point of debt forgiveness by the end of the year. The transformation of the country into a service centre was another government priority, with the aim of combating poverty, reforming the state apparatus, and promoting sustained development.

Also in late April 2006 President de Menezes announced that a presidential election would be held on 30 July, with local elections scheduled to take place on 9 July. In early June the Supreme Court refused to acknowledge 10 candidatures presented for the local elections since they had been submitted after the deadline of 25 May. The ADI and the MLSTP—PSD had not presented candidatures, and demanded that local elections be held after the presidential election. Following a protest by hundreds of demonstrators in Príncipe, led by the opposition União para a Mudança e Progresso do Príncipe (UMPP), against the court's decision, on 12 June the head of the island's Regional Government, Zeferino dos Prazeres (MLSTP—PSD), resigned. Subsequently the central Government appointed João Paulo Cassandra, the leader of revolt, as head of a provisional Regional Government pending the holding of the regional elections. In early July the elections were postponed until 27 August.

In late June 2006 the Government dismissed Silveira from her position as Governor of the BCSTP, and the bank's administrative board on the grounds that a proposed extension of the bank's premises had not been included in the bank's budget for 2006. The Government also dismissed the directors of several other state institutions. The MLSTP—PSD condemned the dismissals as politically motivated.

In mid-June 2006 President de Menezes announced that, as expected, he would stand as a candidate in the forthcoming presidential election. Days later Patrice Trovoada announced his candidacy. At the election which took place, as scheduled, on 30 July, de Menezes secured 60.58% of the votes cast, while Trovoada won 38.82% and a third candidate, Nilo de Oliveira Guimarães, received 0.59%. Some 64.9% of the 91,119 registered voters participated in the election. The election was praised by international monitors as having been 'free and fair'.

In the local elections of 27 August 2006, the first since December 1992, the MDFM-PCD secured control in five of São Tomé's six district councils, while the MLSTP—PSD obtained the majority in the Lembá district. In Príncipe, where regional elections had not been held since March 1995, the UMPP headed by José Cassandra gained an absolute majority.

Immediately after the local elections MLSTP—PSD leader Pósser da Costa resigned from his post due to the consecutive electoral defeats suffered by his party. At an extraordinary party congress in February 2007 Rafael Branco defeated António Quintas by 675 votes to 221 and became the party's new President. At the convention of the MDFM in May Prime Minister Vera Cruz was re-elected as the party's Secretary-General. At the same time the delegates elected President de Menezes as Chairman of the MDFM, despite the country's Constitution forbidding the Head of State to exercise other public functions. Having accepted the function, however, de Menezes opted not to assume the role publicly as long as he remained President.

FOREIGN RELATIONS

Following President Trovoada's unilateral decision in May 1997 to establish diplomatic relations with the Republic of China (Taiwan), the People's Republic of China (PRC) suspended diplomatic relations with São Tomé, ceased all development co-operation, and demanded the repayment of bilateral debts amounting to US $17m. In exchange for diplomatic recognition, Taiwan promised São Tomé $30m. in development aid over a three-year period. Trovoada declared that, in view of the economic condition of São Tomé, the Taiwanese aid could not be rejected. By contrast, the Government declared that the aid promised by Taiwan could not compensate for the loss of the long-standing co-operation enjoyed with the PRC. Consequently, the Government refused to accept $4.3m. in aid offered by Taiwan and prohibited its officials from receiving the four high-ranking diplomats appointed to represent Taiwan in São Tomé. In October, in order to avoid an open conflict with Trovoada, the Government withdrew its opposition to the diplomatic recognition of Taiwan and subsequently accepted the Taiwanese development aid. In January 1998 Taiwan's ambassador presented his credentials to Trovoada. In July 2002 the Taiwanese President, Chen Shui-bian, made a three-day visit to São Tomé. During the visit, President de Menezes declared his Government's support for Taipei's application for membership of the UN and other international organizations.

In late July 2002 Gen. Carlton Fulford, Deputy Commander-in-Chief of the US European Command (EUCOM), visited São Tomé for talks on security in the Gulf of Guinea. Fulford denied any intentions of the US Administration to establish a military base in the archipelago. US oil lobby groups, such as the African Oil Policy Initiative Group, had supported the creation of such a military presence. At the request of EUCOM, in March 2004 the US security company Military Professional Resources Incorporated (MPRI) dispatched a retired US colonel on a one-year mission to São Tomé to conduct an assessment of the local defence requirements. One of the objectives was to provide the country with the adequate naval equipment to patrol its Exclusive Economic Zone and the JDZ. At the invitation of the US military, in August President de Menezes and Defence Minister Óscar Sousa visited the EUCOM in Stuttgart, Germany. Later that month, General Charles Wald, Deputy Commander of EUCOM, paid a visit to São Tomé as part of a tour to West African oil producing countries to discuss co-operation in the petroleum and defence sectors. In February 2006 the USA donated a nine-crew patrol boat for São Tomé's coast guard. In June the US Navy selected São Tomé as regional centre of its Marine Domain Awareness, a surveillance radar programme for the identification and monitoring of shipping traffic to be shared among the neighbouring countries in the Gulf of Guinea region; installation of the system began in December. In Libreville in August 2006 the summit of the heads of state and government of the eight-country Gulf of Guinea Commission (GGC), which had been established in 1999, designated São Tomé as the GGC's Executive Secretary for a three-year period. Subsequently President de Menezes appointed Carlos Gomes, the former Chairman of the Joint Development Authority (JDA) in Abuja, as the Secretary of GGC, based in Luanda.

In March 2007 30 French soldiers based in Gabon held joint manoeuvres with 35 local military officers in São Tomé. The objective was to prepare the local armed forces for a peacekeeping unit in Central Africa financed by France. In the same month the guided-missile frigate USS *Kauffman* paid a four-day visit to São Tomé to strengthen the US maritime partnership with the archipelago. During the visit sailors of the frigate held joint exercises with São Tomé's coast guard. In May Vice-Admiral John Stufflebeem, Commander of the US Sixth Fleet based in the Mediterranean, promised US support to monitor the country's waters during a visit to São Tomé. In the same month the Nigerian Minister of Defence, Thomas I. Aguiyi-Ironsi, announced the establishment of a Gulf of Guinea Guard by Nigeria, Cameroon, Equatorial Guinea, São Tomé, Gabon, Angola, and the Democratic Republic of the Congo to protect their common maritime interests in the region.

In July 1996 São Tomé and Príncipe was among the five lusophone African countries which, together with Portugal and Brazil, formed the CPLP, a Portuguese-speaking commonwealth seeking to achieve collective benefits from co-operation in technical, cultural and social matters. In July 2004 São Tomé hosted the fifth Summit of the Heads of State and Government of the CPLP. At the end of the meeting Brazilian President Luís Inácio 'Lula' da Silva passed the CPLP's rotating presidency for the next two years to President de Menezes.

Economy

GERHARD SEIBERT

The economy of São Tomé and Príncipe, which until recently was based almost exclusively on the export of cocoa, has experienced a long period of decline since independence in 1975. The sudden loss of protected markets in Portugal and the mass exodus of skilled personnel were compounded by the negative effects of systematic nationalization and the relentless fall in the world price of cocoa after 1979. According to estimates by the World Bank, São Tomé's gross domestic product (GDP) increased, in real terms, by an annual average of 3.5% in 1998–2005. GDP growth in 2002 was 2.9%, 4.0% in 2003, 3.8% in 2004, 6.0% in 2005, and was estimated at 8.0% in 2006. According to the African Development Bank (ADB), in 2005 19.2% of GDP was derived from the primary sector, 17.4% from the secondary sector and 63.3% from the tertiary sector, the latter figure mainly reflecting the considerable size of the civil service.

President Pinto da Costa decided at independence to nationalize virtually all enterprises of any size. The Government also took a monopoly of foreign trade, and controlled prices and distribution through a network of 'people's shops'. São Tomé became a member of the IMF and the World Bank in 1977, and introduced a new currency unit, the dobra, to replace the Portuguese escudo at par. The dobra became increasingly overvalued, placing considerable strain on the balance of payments.

In 1985, confronted by the threat of economic collapse, the President initiated a process of economic liberalization. Following discussions during 1986 with the World Bank and the IMF, the Government widened the scope of its reforms with the introduction in 1987 of a three-year structural adjustment programme (SAP). This aimed to reduce the large trade and budget deficits, increase agricultural production, stimulate exports, and increase foreign earnings from tourism and fishing. Price controls were abolished on many goods, trade was liberalized, wages, taxes and duties were increased, and the dobra was devalued. The value of the dobra drifted downwards towards parallel rates, while further adjustments to controlled prices were made to bring these rates closer to market levels. Public-sector wages were raised periodically, but did not keep pace with the cost of living. In recognition of these reforms, a donors' meeting in Geneva, Switzerland, in 1989 pledged new loans and a rescheduling of debts, and in June the IMF approved a three-year SDR 2.8m. Structural Adjustment Facility (SAF). However, in 1990 the Government subordinated economic concerns to its own survival, causing the IMF to suspend payments, with the World Bank threatening to do the same. The budget deficit increased to US $4.5m., inflation reached 47%, and foreign-exchange reserves were severely depleted.

The currency was repeatedly devalued and by June 1993 the dobra was trading officially at approximately US $1 = 425 dobras, while 'black market' rates stood at about $1 = 600 dobras. By mid-1992 the IMF indicated that enough progress had been made for payments under the SAF to be resumed. This was a precondition to addressing the problem of the country's high level of external debt which, in 1993, stood at $254m., of which $225.8m. was long-term debt.

In 1994 the current account of the balance of payments, which had recorded a surplus equivalent to 1.3% of GDP in 1991–93, registered a deficit equivalent to 9.6% of GDP. Inflation increased from 20% in 1993 to 40% in 1994. By September 1994 none of the public finance targets set by the IMF had been met. Instead of a surplus of 1,040m. dobras, as scheduled by the IMF for the 1994 national budget, by September the deficit (excluding interest payments on debt) had already reached 442.4m. dobras. In order to reverse the negative trend, in December the Government increased fuel prices by some 30%. In addition the official and free-market exchange rates were unified. Successive devaluations of the currency implemented during 1994 totalled some 50%.

In 1995, following negotiations with a joint mission of the IMF and the World Bank, the Government announced a series of austerity measures aimed at facilitating the disbursement of a third tranche of credit under the SAF. With the implementation of successive increases in fuel prices in March and September 1995, the Government succeeded in facilitating the release of the structural adjustment credit of US $3.2m., which was disbursed in early 1996. Further increases in fuel prices were imposed in February and May 1996. In mid-1996 the Government announced a series of measures aimed at stemming the rapid depreciation of the currency and reducing the annual rate of inflation from 48% to about 25% by the end of the year. By October 1996 the current fiscal balance (excluding donations) had reached a deficit of 7,800m. dobras, compared with a targeted surplus for the year of 4,400m. dobras. The deficit resulted from low revenues, owing to tax evasion, the exemption of import duties on 73% of all imports, and excessive public spending. In February 1997 the World Bank issued an ultimatum to São Tomé, threatening the withdrawal of support if the country should fail to implement the necessary measures to qualify for the initiative for heavily indebted poor countries (HIPC).

In May 1997 the IMF advised the Government to take urgent measures to curb inflation and to stem the rapid devaluation of the currency. Expenditure on civil service salaries increased from 15.1% of total government spending in 1996 to 21.7% in 1997. In late 1997 the World Bank granted a loan of US $415,000 to strengthen the Government's preparation and execution of the budget. However, in April 1998 an IMF mission to São Tomé found that government expenditure had risen, owing to salary increases, while revenue had remained low. In addition, as the result of extra-budgetary spending, monetary financing of the budget was as high as 12,300m. dobras. As a result, the IMF announced that São Tomé would not qualify for debt cancellation under the HIPC.

As a consequence of vigorous adjustment measures imposed by the IMF, the country's economic and fiscal performance improved considerably in 1998. There was a surplus in the primary budget (excluding externally financed capital outlays) equivalent to 0.7% of GDP, compared with a deficit of 2.2% in 1997. The average annual inflation rate was reduced from 68.5% in 1997 to 42.3% in 1998, while the differential between the official rate of exchange of the dobra and the 'black market' rate was narrowed from 6.5% in 1996 to less than 1% in 1998.

Private investment increased to the equivalent of 18.4% of GDP in 1998, while gross national savings amounted to 21% of GDP in the same year. Owing to measures aimed at improving the tax administration, in 1998 government revenues increased to 54,500m. dobras (equivalent to 19.4% of GDP). Despite stricter budgetary controls, primary expenditure exceeded projections by 7,600m. dobras, mainly owing to government investments and an increase in public-sector wages. However, as a result of the primary budget surplus, the Government succeeded in settling all its domestic payment arrears in 1998 and in meeting its external debt-service requirements with regard to its multilateral creditors. Growth in money supply in 1998 was 16.3%, less than nominal GDP growth. The sale of petroleum concession rights and of shares in the fuel company ENCO contributed to a limited increase in net government bank credit. Following the reduction in inflation, the central bank reduced its reference interest rate from 55% to 29.5% in November 1998, and again to 24.5% in February 1999, and finally to 19% in May. The measure was expected to encourage investment and thus lead to greater economic growth.

In March 1999 the Government presented a memorandum of economic and financial policies outlining its objectives and economic policies for 1999–2002. The three-year programme included the development of a more prudent fiscal policy aimed at broadening the tax base, prioritizing expenditure on infrastructure and the social sector, the creation of a social programme to reduce poverty and improve educational and health services, the implementation of a tight monetary policy, and the introduction of accelerated structural reforms in an attempt to boost private-sector development and achieve sustainable economic growth.

In April 2000 the Government presented an interim Poverty Reduction Strategy Paper (PRSP) for 2000–02. According to the document, at least 40% of the local population lived below the poverty line, while some 33% were considered to live in extreme poverty, with an income sufficient to cover only one-half of minimum household food requirements. In late April the IMF granted São Tomé and Príncipe a three-year Poverty Reduction and Growth Facility (PRGF), worth some US $8.9m. The Government's three-year programme was to be monitored and evaluated on a yearly basis by the IMF; the successful implementation of the programme was a precondition for future debt reduction within the framework of the HIPC initiative. In May the 'Paris Club' group of donors agreed to reduce the interest on São Tomé and Príncipe's external debt by 95% until 2003, worth an estimated $26m.

Economic policy performance under the PRGF-supported programme in 2000 was negatively affected by a 1.5% deterioration in terms of trade, owing to lower cocoa prices and higher petroleum prices. However, as a result of growth in food crop production, tourism and construction, real GDP growth for 2000 was estimated at 3.0%. Consumer prices increased by an average of 12.2% in that year. The primary fiscal surplus increased to 2.1%, slightly less than expected because of higher government consumption of fuel and energy, as well as a higher wage bill caused by delays in the reduction of state bureaucracy. Influenced by higher petroleum prices and the nominal devaluation of the dobra, government revenue (excluding grants) increased by 19%, to 80,000m. dobras (21.7% of GDP), in 2000. The difference between the official and parallel exchange rate rose to 2.4%, significantly more than in the previous year.

In November 2000 the IMF declared São Tomé and Príncipe eligible for assistance under the enhanced HIPC initiative and in mid-December released a second disbursement of the PRGF worth US $1.2m. The IMF and the World Bank granted the country debt-service relief worth $200m. in nominal terms under the enhanced HIPC initiative. Nominal debt-relief savings for the following 20 years were estimated at $131m., or about $6.5m. per year. In April 2001 the ADB conceded São Tomé an 80% reduction in debt-service payments, equivalent to debt relief of $34.2m. The resources created by the reduction in debt-service payments were to be directed primarily to health, education, infrastructure, poverty reduction and improved governance. Some 70% of the assistance from the enhanced HIPC initiative was to be provided by multilateral creditors and 30% by bilateral donors. São Tomé was to receive full debt-relief assistance, if it took a series of agreed measures to achieve economic growth and poverty reduction, including at least one year's satisfactory implementation of the complete PRSP. Other conditions included the continued maintenance of a stable macroeconomic environment, improved public-expenditure management, transparency in the use of HIPC assistance and investment in the education and health sectors.

Following the Government's failure to observe structural performance criteria and other measures recommended by the IMF during the last quarter of 2000 and the first three quarters of 2001, the Fund suspended its PRGF-supported programme. The IMF had also criticized the lack of transparency in the negotiation of petroleum contracts in 2001. In order to secure a new PRGF medium-term programme, the Government was obliged to execute a six-month staff-monitored IMF programme (SMP), ending in June 2002. The debt rescheduling that 'Paris Club' donor countries had agreed in May 2000 became inoperative until the approval of a new PRGF arrangement.

Real GDP growth in 2001 achieved the targeted 4%. However, owing to higher petroleum prices, combined with a 5% devaluation of the dobra, the inflation rate was 9%. The overall fiscal deficit (on a commitment basis, including official grants) reached 15% of GDP, while the primary budget deficit (including HIPC-financed social spending) was 7% of GDP. The external current-account deficit (including official transfers) was reduced from 21% of GDP in 2000 to 11% of GDP in 2001. The difference between the official exchange rate and the parallel market rate was about 1% in 2001. There was a considerable increase in customs and consumption tax collection in that year, although overspending, amounting to almost 7% of GDP, resulted in a primary budget deficit of more than 3% of GDP, instead of a projected surplus of 2.7%.

For 2002 the Government's macroeconomic objectives agreed with the IMF included an inflation rate of 7%, an external current-account deficit (including official transfers) of less than 1%, and real GDP growth of 5%. In addition, the Government aimed to reduce the overall fiscal deficit (on a commitment basis, including official grants) to 5% of GDP and the primary budget deficit (including HIPC-financed social spending) to 3% of GDP. Government revenue was expected to increase by 15% (to 22.5% of GDP). However, government performance under the IMF SMP during the first half of 2002 was disappointing. Spending was higher than forecast, owing to wage demands, higher energy and utility costs, while expenditure related to the March 2002 elections more than offset higher revenue. Consequently, the primary fiscal deficit (including HIPC-financed social expenditure) increased to 3.2% of GDP in the first half of 2002, compared with a targeted deficit of 1.6% of GDP. The Government agreed to extend the SMP to December in order to re-establish a satisfactory track record of policy implementation. As part of the structural reforms, the Government had to apply mechanisms by which adjustments in the consumer prices of fuel, water and electricity reflected import and distribution costs; implement a privatization programme for the Empresa de Água e Electricidade (EMAE); adopt a revised investment code to strengthen incentives in the private sector; and submit to the Assembleia Nacional (National Assembly) a draft law on the management of petroleum resources and the establishment of a reserve fund. In July 2002 the legislature approved the annual budget for 2002, worth 458,757m. dobras (some US $50m.).

In January 2003 the Assembleia Nacional approved the annual budget for 2003, worth 522,000m. dobras (some US $55m.). Expenditure on education and health was to increase by 13% and 15%, respectively, and represented a combined 18% of the total budget. An IMF mission that visited São Tomé in July declared that the Government had fulfilled the required conditions for discussion of a new PRGF agreement and could benefit from a debt reduction of 83% (some $200m.), as part of the enhanced HIPC initiative, in the first quarter of 2004.

In November 2003 the Government submitted the annual budget for 2004, worth some US $65m., of which capital investment accounted for $42m. The budget included $13m. stemming from expected signature bonuses to be paid by petroleum companies in 2004. Health and education represented 17% and 18% of the budget, respectively, while the defence sector was also given priority. Salary expenditures and investment outlays were expected to increase by 23% and 32%, respectively. Government revenue was stipulated to increase by 30%, while GDP was forecast to grow by 5% and inflation was expected to be 9%. The Government committed itself to macroeconomic stability and poverty reduction, striving to qualify for debt forgiveness as part of the HIPC initiative. The IMF announced the preparation of a new three-year programme that would be conditional on the approval of an oil management law by the Assembleia Nacional. In mid-March 2004 the administrative board meeting of the IMF recognized that the Government had made progress in macroeconomic management during 2002–03. The Government observed five out of nine quantitative benchmarks and four out of six structural benchmarks. In 2003 real GDP growth was 4.5%, while the average inflation rate was 9.8%. The primary fiscal deficit (including HIPC-financed social outlays) was 12% of GDP. As a result of increased exports and modestly higher imports the external current account was estimated at 45% of GDP. The central bank estimated economic growth in 2004 of less than 4% and inflation, at 15%, was expected to exceed the targeted annual inflation rate of 13.3%.

In April 2005 the Assembleia Nacional approved the budget for 2005 worth 963,000m. dobras (US $90m.), of which 90,000m. dobras were expected to be provided from signature bonus payments. Current receipts accounted for 221,000m. dobras and capital receipts for 741,000m. Expenditure included debt service payments of 105,000m. dobras, public investments of 418,000m. dobras and debt payments to the Joint Development Zone (JDZ) and Angola of 189,000m. dobras. Compared with 2004, expenditure in health and education was reduced from 16.3% to 13.1% and from 16.4% to 13.4%, respectively. The budget included an increase in civil service salaries by 12%. Foreign assistance financed almost 90% of the budget. In August 2005 the IMF approved a new three-year PRGF worth $4.3m. The satisfactory implementation of the PRGF arrangement was a precondition for debt relief in the framework of the enhanced HIPC initiative.

In March 2006 the IMF concluded the first review of the PRGF arrangement. The IMF considered performance under the arrangement satisfactory and released an amount of US $600,000. In early March the Assembleia Nacional approved the 2006 national budget of $87m., of which 65% was capital investment, including debt service payments. Foreign donors provided $39m., while $15.6m. stemmed from the national oil account. The budget included the airport extension, infrastructural repairs, as well as indemnification payments for some 3,600 former public sector workers who received a total of 23,000m. dobras. In May the Minister of Planning and Finance, Maria dos Santos Lima da Costa Tebús Torres, declared that due to the lax financial policies of the former Government the country had failed to reach the HIPC conclusion point scheduled for June. Tebús Torres blamed the modalities of a $5m. credit received from Angola and the excessive use of central bank funds. In June an IMF mission declared that the country was close to reaching the conclusion point, provided that the action plan to contain expenditure presented by the new Government was implemented. In mid-June Tebús Torres negotiated the transformation of the $5m. Angolan commercial credit into a soft loan according to the criteria for HIPC. In early May President de Menezes and Tebús Torres visited Libya to ask for budgetary assistance. The Libyan Government agreed to provide financial aid and to send an expert team to assess technical needs in São Tomé. A visit was also made to Abuja, Nigeria, to request that President Obasanjo extend the deadline for the repayment of Nigerian loans worth $15m.

In March 2007 the Assembleia Nacional approved the annual budget 2007 of US $96m., of which 81% was externally financed. In the same month the IMF and the World Bank announced that the country had met the economic reform targets and was eligible for debt cancellation equivalent to $317m. under the enhanced HIPC initiative. The debt relief had been expected to be granted in 2006; however, due to delays in the implementation of the reform measurements the completion point was only reached in March 2007. In May the 'Paris Club' creditors agreed to write of bilateral debts of $24m. in nominal terms, thus reducing São Tomé's debt to 'Paris Club' creditors to $600,000.

AGRICULTURE

Agriculture (including forestry and fishing) contributed 19.2% of GDP in 2005 and employed 62.2% of the total labour force in 2003. At independence, São Tomé inherited a plantation economy, dominated by cocoa and partially protected from international price movements by a guaranteed home market. Most land was farmed by large Portuguese-owned enterprises. In 1975 the Government nationalized all landholdings of over 200 ha and grouped them into state enterprises, which covered over 80% of the cultivable land area. The nationalization of the estates led to the exodus of many of the skilled agricultural personnel. The state farms incurred substantial deficits and, within a decade, were brought to the point of financial collapse.

In 1985 the Government initiated a policy of partial privatization. Ownership of the estates was kept in the hands of the state, but foreign aid was sought to rehabilitate the plantations and foreign companies were invited to tender for management contracts of 15–20 years' duration. Privatization proceeded slowly under this system, and was confined to the prime land in the north-east of São Tomé island. By the early 1990s the strategy of estate management contracts was in crisis. Declining cocoa prices stifled the optimism of the late 1980s. In mid-1993, on the advice of the World Bank, the Government began the process of replacing management contracts with long leases.

An alternative strategy of breaking up the estates into smallholdings has been pursued since 1985. About 10,000 ha of land were distributed to small farmers during 1985–89. The Government viewed these areas as suitable only for domestic food production. At the instigation of the World Bank, which was providing finance of US $17.2m. for the process of land reform, the Government announced that some 20,000 ha of land would be transferred to smallholders between 1993 and 1998. Land distributed to smallholders since 1985 that had not been cultivated would be repossessed and redistributed by the State. Financing was subsequently forthcoming from international donors.

In December 2000 the Land Reform Programme, financed by the World Bank, ended. However, agrarian reform continued, as not all estate lands had been redistributed. In June 2001 smallholders complained about the lack of export opportunities for their products, since the output of tomatoes, bananas and other crops exceeded local demand, owing to the small market and the weak purchasing power of the population. Overproduction had resulted in lower prices, which did not cover the production costs of many small farmers. As a result, many had difficulty repaying the credits provided by the Government. In November the Government announced that a new support programme for some 11,000 smallholders, fishermen and market women was to commence in March 2002. The 12-year programme, which was expected to benefit some 58,000 people, was financed by the International Fund for Agricultural Development (IFAD) with US $13m. and was to replace the smallholder support project financed by France and the IFAD since 1995. According to figures provided by the IMF in 2004, only 43,522 ha were distributed in 1993–2003 to a total of 8,735 beneficiaries. The average size of the plots was 3.2 ha. In June 2003 the Government granted small farmers credits worth $500,000, of which $180,000 was to be administered by a local non-governmental organization, Micondó.

Since independence, cocoa has regularly accounted for well over 90% of exports by value. Cocoa covered 61% of the cultivated area on the 15 large estates in 1986. Production declined to around 4,000 metric tons per year in the 1980s, and export earnings from cocoa fell by 67% between 1979 and 1988. In 1985 the islands' cocoa trees were 30 years old on average, and some were much older. Black pod disease has spread because of a lack of phytosanitary treatment, and soil fertility has declined with the lack of fertilizer application. As cocoa prices fell still further in the early 1990s, production drifted down to a low point of 3,193 tons in 1991. According to FAO estimates, production in 2004 was 3,500 tons. Low yields were caused in part by an infestation of the insect *Heliothrips rubrocintus*, which affected 40% of the cocoa crop. The World Bank blamed the Government's poor provision of agricultural services for the spread of the infestation. In 2004 cocoa still accounted for 91.4% of exports, illustrating the failure of the Government's export diversification programme. However, in early 1999 the Government recognized that the cocoa and coffee rehabilitation programmes had failed and announced a shift in policy favouring smallholder agriculture and local food production. Nevertheless, some 60% of the arable land is still planted with cocoa. In the medium term cocoa will remain the main cash crop for both rural incomes and export production. In 2005 and 2006 cocoa exports of 2,413 tons and 2,434 tons represented incomes of US $2.4m. and $3.2m., respectively.

The islands' principal secondary crops are copra, coffee and palm oil and kernels. In 1986 coconut palms covered 23% of the cultivated area on the 15 state-owned estates, and copra was the country's only export of any significance apart from cocoa. By 1998 production of copra had fallen to 162 metric tons. By 2000, however, production had increased to 882 tons, although this fell to only 400 tons in 2003, according to FAO estimates. Oil palms accounted for 10% of the cultivated area on the estates in 1986 and coffee for 3%, but exports of these commodities ceased altogether in the latter half of the 1980s. Coffee output increased from 14 tons in 1992 to 36 tons in 1998, but declined to an estimated 20 tons by 2004. Exports of taro (also known as cocoyam, or matabala), plantain and citrus fruit to Gabon were also targeted for development. In October 1999 the Government adopted an agricultural policy charter, the Carta de Política e Desenvolvimento Rural, which, it hoped, would provide an integrated strategy for the entire sector. The charter emphasizes production, diversification, private-sector involvement, and the full participation of the rural population. Efforts were made to diversify into production of crops including ylang ylang, pepper, vanilla and other aromatic plants, fruits, vegetables, flowers and tubers. In June 2003 a private local company, Flora Speciosa, began exporting 15 varieties of tropical flowers to Europe.

Self-sufficiency in basic food crops has eluded the Government since independence, despite the high fertility of the islands' volcanic soils, the long growing season, the variety of micro-climates, and abundant rainfall. The apportionment of centrally fixed planning targets for food production among the nationalized estates proved unsuccessful, and by the mid-1980s the country was estimated to be importing 90% of its food requirements. By 1992 it was estimated that imports of food had fallen to around 45% of consumption. The only surviving large-scale food project is the oil palm plantation at Ribeira Peixe. Since the early 1980s, the European Community (EC, now the European Union—EU) has been providing funds to plant 610 ha of high-yielding oil palms and to establish a publicly owned palm oil factory on the 1,500-ha Ribeira Peixe estate in the south-east of São Tomé island. By 1992 the project was producing about 80,000 litres of oil a month and was able to meet the country's internal requirements. In April 2005, of the original 610 ha of palm trees only one-third were exploited, and there were only 93 workers left of the 300 formerly employed. Despite the capacity to produce 500 litres of palm oil per hour, the current production level was only 4,000 litres per week. Due to a lack of demand, the palm oil manufacturer EMOLVE had difficulties selling even this small quantity on the local market. The greatest obstacles to self-sufficiency in food are the virtual absence of a smallholder tradition, due to the plantation economy, and the impossibility of growing wheat for a population increasingly accustomed to eating bread and other wheat-based products. Average food consumption in the country is 300 metric tons per month, comprising mainly local food crops including plantain, bread-fruit, taro, cassava, sweet potatoes and vegetables. According to local statistics, annual plantain production increased from 10,250 tons in 1992 to 34,596 tons in 1998. Annual taro production increased from 5,000 tons in 1992 to 26,000 tons in 2003, according to FAO estimates.

The livestock sector has been seriously affected by the decline in veterinary services since independence and periodic outbreaks of swine fever. In 2003 swine fever reduced the number of pigs to some 2,500. Goats are widely reared, and are sometimes exported to Gabon. In 2000 there were 26,253 head of goat and sheep, and 63 tons of goat- and sheep-meat were produced; however, stocks in 2004 stood at only 2,800 sheep and 5,000 goats, with meat production of 25 tons. The islands are free of tsetse fly, but cattle have been badly affected by bovine tuberculosis. Beef production increased, however, from 12 tons in 1992 to an estimated 122 tons in 2004; the national herd numbered around 4,600 head in 2004. In late 1999 the ADB granted São Tomé US $3.8m. to finance the Projecto de Apoio ao Desenvolvimento Pecuário (Project for the Support of Livestock Development), which aimed to rehabilitate all infrastructures necessary for the sustainable development of livestock production. In May 2006 the African Development Fund approved a grant of $5.9m. for a five-year animal breeding development project that included 20,000 families.

Similar difficulties have beset the fishing sector, a priority area for economic diversification. In the early 1990s fishing was the second largest source of foreign exchange, due principally to revenue from fishing licences, and employed some 10% of the economically active population. A state-owned fishing company, Empesca, with two modern trawlers, was formed at independence. In June 1978 the Government established an Exclusive Economic Zone (EEZ) around the islands of 370 km (200 nautical miles), although the trawlers actually spent most of their time fishing in Angolan waters. In the late 1980s lack of maintenance on the trawlers led to a rapid decrease, and the industrial catch in 1988 was only one ton. In the long term the Government is basing its hopes for the fishing industry on the tuna resources of the area, and it is estimated that tuna catches could reach 17,000 tons a year without affecting stocks. In 2004 the total catch was estimated at 4,141 tons. In 2002 there were 4,687 fishermen and a total of 2,524 boats, of which 884 had an outboard motor. A fish-processing plant, the Sociedade Nacional de Comércio e Pesca (SNCP), financed with US $2m. of private capital, began operations in September 1995 in Ribeira Funda, some 20 km from the capital. Production was mainly destined for export.

In 1996 São Tomé renewed, for a further three-year period, its fishing agreement with the EU. In May 1999, and again in February 2002 and June 2005, the agreement was renewed. In March 2007 São Tomé signed a new four-year fishing agreement with the EU that became effective on 1 June. In return for an annual payment of €663,000 the agreement allowed 43 boats from Spain, France and Portugal to fish in the country's waters.

São Tomé and Príncipe's considerable forestry resources have been neglected, although it was estimated in 1984 that two-thirds of the country's energy consumption came from fuel wood and most housing is of wooden construction. Colonial legislation for the protection of forests was replaced by a new law in 1979, but it was not enforced and no barriers were placed on the uncontrolled cutting of trees. A commission was set up in 1988 to study the problems of forest preservation and reafforestation, and it began by drawing up a national forest inventory with foreign assistance. This revealed that 29% of the country was still covered in primary forest (*obó*), mainly in the inaccessible south-western quadrant of both islands. Some 245 sq km on São Tomé island and 45 sq km on Príncipe were identified as needing to be demarcated as 'ecological reserves', in areas where commercial agriculture is uneconomic. In addition, the inventory noted the existence of 30,000 ha of secondary forest, largely on abandoned plantation land and 32,000 ha of 'shade forest', covering commercial crops. The resources exploitable on a sustainable basis outside the 'ecological reserves' were estimated at between 70,000 cu m and 105,000 cu m of construction wood and between 43,000 cu m and 65,000 cu m of fuel wood per year. However, it was also estimated that the country needed 20,000 cu m of fuel wood for dry-processing cocoa, copra and other commercial crops, and a further 140,000 cu m for domestic purposes. In 1990 São Tomé was included in the Programme for Conservation and Rational Utilization of Forest Ecosystems in Central Africa (ECOFAC), an EC-funded Central African forest conservation project which was intended to lead to the demarcation and enforcement of forest reserves covering 32% of the total land area. The programme of land distribution to smallholders led to increasing deforestation, with the new occupants arbitrarily felling trees. Local observers fear serious ecological consequences. With the assistance of the UN Environment Programme, the Government formulated legislation, which was approved by the Assembleia Nacional in 1998, concerning management of the environment in order to address increasing problems of this kind. In 2000 the Government announced its intention formally to adopt a National Strategy for the Protection of the Environment and Sustainable Development. In January 2006 the European Commission granted São Tomé €930,000 as part of a new support programme for tropical rain forests called ECOFAC IV that amounted to a total of €38m. for seven countries. In August 2006 the two laws approved by the Assembleia Nacional in 2004 that created the Obô National Parks in São Tomé and on Príncipe, respectively, came into effect.

MANUFACTURING AND SERVICES

Industry, including construction and public utilities, employed 15.4% of the economically active population in 1998 and contributed an estimated 17.4% of GDP in 2004. The secondary sector comprises some 50 small and medium-sized enterprises and several hundred microenterprises. Industry is generally confined to production for the local market, but garments are exported to Angola. Many basic manufactured products are still imported, especially from Portugal. The Government aims to develop food-processing and the production of construction materials. All industrial companies were originally scheduled for privatization by the end of 1993. By early 1995 10 non-agricultural public enterprises had been privatized, liquidated or placed under foreign management. In mid-1997 the Government announced the sale of its minority shares in three enterprises: the brick manufacturer Cerámica de São Tomé, the clothing manufacturer Confecções Agua Grande Lda, and the construction materials supplier Cunha Gomes, SA (although by 2001 the latter had yet to be sold). In November 1998 the Government liquidated the pharmaceutical company Empresa Nacional de Medicamentos, and the slaughterhouse Empresa de Transformação de Carnes. Enterprises to remain under state control were the palm oil manufacturer, EMOLVE, the water and electricity utility, EMAE, the ports administration, the Empresa Nacional de Administração dos Portos (ENAPORT), the airport administration company, the Empresa Nacional de Aeroportos e Segurança Aérea (ENASA), the telecommunications company, the Companhia Santomese de Telecomunicaçoes (CST—49%) and the airline Air São Tomé e Príncipe (35%), all of which were to be transformed into limited-liability companies. In September 2000 the Government announced that the privatization of the state television and radio station had been postponed. As part of a new reform and privatization programme, the Government announced the adoption of a financial restructuring plan for EMAE, to be implemented by mid-2000. At the instigation of the IMF, the accounts of EMAE, ENAPORT and ENASA were to be submitted annually to external auditors.

The privately owned Banco Comercial do Equador (BCE), which in 2000 represented some 50% of bank credit conceded and about 40% of deposits in the country, was declared bankrupt in December 2002. In January 2003 the multinational air freight carrier Panalpina, which provided supplies to oil companies, ceased its weekly operations from Luxembourg to São Tomé and moved to Malabo, Equatorial Guinea. With the departure of Panalpina, São Tomé lost revenue of more than US $1m. per year. The expected petroleum wealth in the country attracted new investments in the banking sector. In December 2003 a branch office of the Cameroonian Afriland First Bank, with a capital stock of $1.8m., opened in São Tomé. The bankrupt BCE was recapitalized and reopened as Banco Equador in mid-March 2004, with a stock capital of $3m. Later in the same month President de Menezes inaugurated the National Investment Bank (NIB), owned by the private Portuguese airline Air Luxor (90%) and its subsidiaries in São Tomé and Cape Verde (5% each). The NIB announced plans to increase its capital of $2.5m. to $50m. within the next five years. In February 2005 Island Bank, SA, a subsidiary of the Nigerian Hallmark Bank, became the fifth commercial bank to open a branch office in São Tomé. In July the Cameroonian Commercial Bank Group, owned by Yves Michel Fotso, inaugurated the Commercial Bank—São Tomé e Príncipe with a stock capital of $3m. In July 2007 the private Togo-based Ecobank that operates in Central and West Africa opened a branch with an initial capital of $1.5m. in São Tomé.

ENERGY

There are no mineral resources on the islands, but offshore prospecting for hydrocarbons since the late 1980s has produced encouraging preliminary findings. In May 1997 the Government signed an accord with the Environmental Remedial Holding Corp (ERHC) and the South African Procura Financial Consultants (PFC) concerning the exploration and exploitation of petroleum, gas and mineral reserves in São Tomé's territory. The agreement, which was valid for 25 years, provided for an initial payment to the Government of US $5m. The ERHC and the PFC were then to finance the evaluation of the petroleum reserves, and a petroleum company was to be established with the Government, from which the State would receive 40% of the revenue. In November the Government submitted details of the country's 370-km EEZ, drafted by the ERHC, to the UN and the Gulf of Guinea Commission. In March 1998 São Tomé approved a law establishing the boundaries of the EEZ, which was presented to the UN Law of the Sea Commission in May. In July 1998 the Government and ERHC established a joint-venture petroleum company, Sociedade Nacional de Petróleos de São Tomé e Príncipe (STPETRO), with the Government holding 51% of the shares. In September STPETRO and the US company Mobil signed a technical assistance agreement to survey 22 deep-water blocks within an 18-month period. In January 1999 Schlumberger Geco/Prakla began a seismic survey of Mobil's concession area. In June 1999 President Trovoada and the President of Equatorial Guinea, Teodoro Obiang Nguema Mbasogo, signed a bilateral agreement on the delimitation of the two countries' maritime borders. In late April 2000 negotiations with Nigeria ended without an agreement on maritime boundaries between the two countries. The main obstacle had been Nigeria's refusal to agree to the Santomean proposal, which bases the boundary on equidistance from the continent. In March 1999 the Government assured the IMF of transparency in all future operations concerning petroleum exploration activities and promised to consult the international monetary institutions in all its negotiations with petroleum companies. Petroleum products were imported from Angola at concessionary rates after independence, but are now being supplied at commercial prices. At the request of the World Bank, in early 1998 the Government sold a 49% share of the state fuel company, ENCO, of which 40% was acquired by the Angolan petroleum company SONANGOL and 9% by local investors. In June 1999 the Government and Mobil signed an agreement on the partitioning of São Tomé's future petroleum production. Further negotiations on the matter took place in September 1999 and March 2000.

In October 1999 the Government rescinded the 1997 agreement with ERHC, on the grounds that the company had not met a number of commitments included in the contract. ERHC was subject to an investigation by the US Securities and Exchange Commission (SEC), due to missing accounting records. ERHC also failed to submit its latest annual report, arguing that it did not have the funds to pay the audit fees. ERHC subsequently declared its insolvency to the SEC and raised the possibility of commencing bankruptcy procedures. Despite the uncertainties over the future of ERHC, the Government resumed negotiations with the company in March. In May 2001, as part of an agreement brokered by the Nigerian Government, São Tomé settled the conflict with ERHC, which, in the mean time, had been taken over by the Nigerian company Chrome Energy Corporation. In exchange for the settlement of the dispute, the Government conceded ERHC far-reaching financial advantages, including working interests in licences, a share in signature bonuses and profit oil, and an overriding royalty in production.

In October 1999 the Government replaced the Comissão Nacional de Petróleo (National Petroleum Committee) with an inter-ministerial commission. Subsequently, there was a series of price increases. In October 2001 SONANGOL established a subsidiary in São Tomé.

In August 2000 Nigeria and São Tomé achieved an agreement on the joint exploration of petroleum in the oil-rich waters disputed by the two countries. According to the agreement, Nigeria was to receive 60% of the profits of the joint zone and São Tomé 40%. In February 2001 Presidents Obasanjo and Trovoada signed a treaty on the joint management of the waters lying between the two countries. The treaty demarcated the borders of a common development zone, which was to be managed by a joint commission and was to be jointly exploited. In March São Tomé allowed Nigeria exploitation rights in Block 246, which had been explored by Nigeria for several years and is situated in the JDZ, in exchange for compensation. In January 2002 a Joint Development Authority (JDA), based in Abuja, was created to direct the affairs of the JDZ. In the first half of 2002 it was agreed that São Tomé would receive 60,000 barrels per day (b/d) from Block 246. In July the Government received an advance payment of US $5m. on future signature bonuses from Nigeria. Petroleum exploration in the JDZ was not expected to commence before 2002, while petroleum production was not thought possible before 2006, with estimated production of 10,000 b/d. In February 2001 the Government and the Norwegian company Petroleum Geo-Services (PGS) signed an agreement on the execution of seismic studies outside Blocks 1–22, which had been conceded by ExxonMobil. The agreement gave PGS the option to acquire three blocks of its choice. PGS paid the Government a signature bonus of $2m. and started the seismic studies in the EEZ in late November. In late April 2002, after six months of studies, PGS confirmed the country's oil potential and stated that the identified blocks were commercially viable. In April 2001 São Tomé also reached an agreement with Gabon on the delimitation of the maritime borders between the two countries.

Following a critical assessment of São Tomé's oil agreements by US lawyers, conducted at the request of the IMF, in May 2002 President de Menezes demanded renegotiations of all oil contracts signed by previous Governments with Nigeria, ERHC/Chrome, ExxonMobil and PGS. In November the Nigerian Government suspended the licensing round for nine blocks in the JDZ scheduled for that month until São Tomé clarified the contentious issue of the agreement with third parties. In February 2003 Nigeria declared null and void the memorandum of understanding that promised São Tomé and Príncipe compensation for Block 246, 10% of which was located within the JDZ. In exchange, this part of Block 246 was returned to the JDZ. In the preceding months Nigeria had reduced the amount of petroleum it intended to supply from 60,000 b/d to 10,000 b/d. Nigeria had also failed to adhere to a number of other promises made in the memorandum, such as the concession of scholarships and the construction of a refinery. The three principal contracts with third parties were all renegotiated in early 2003. The new agreement with ExxonMobil, signed in January, gave the company pre-emptive rights to stakes of 40% in one and 25% each in two other blocks of its choice from any offered in the JDZ, while it was obliged to match signature bonuses and terms offered by other bidders. This was much more favourable to São Tomé than ExxonMobil's previous contract, which gave the company rights to five blocks of its choice for signature bonuses of only US $2m. each, in return for carrying out seismic and feasibility studies. The new agreement with PGS was concluded in early March, but no details were revealed. Finally, in mid-March ERHC/Chrome relinquished its rights to an overriding royalty interest, a share of signature bonuses and a share of profit in the JDZ. According to the new agreement, ERHC/Chrome increased its rights to participate in the JDZ from a total of 30% working interest in two blocks to a total of 125% working interest spread over six blocks, ranging from 15% to 30% each. In addition, the Nigerian company was not required to pay signature bonuses on four of the blocks. Analysts considered the new agreement excessively generous to ERHC/Chrome and out of line with international practice. In April the licensing round of the first nine of the 25 blocks in the JDZ was launched in Abuja. The licensing round was to be closed in mid-October in São Tomé. No initial offers of less than $30m. per block were to be accepted, and São Tomé expected at least $100m. as its share from signature bonuses, twice the value of the annual national budget.

In October 2003 Nigeria conceded a daily allocation of 30,000 b/d of crude to São Tomé and Príncipe at a guaranteed margin of US $0.13 per barrel until the end of 2004, for sale on the international market. The Government entrusted the Japanese-owned oil-trading company Arcadia with the sale of the crude. The country expected to earn $1.4m. annually through the agreement. Also in October at a ceremony in São Tomé 19 oil companies submitted 31 valid bids for seven of the nine oil blocks in the JDZ that had been put out for public tender in April. In mid-February 2004 the chairman of the JDA revealed that ExxonMobil would take the 40% stake in Block 1. However, the company hesitated to exercise its 25% preferential rights in two other blocks, thus delaying the entire process. Finally, in late March, ExxonMobil definitively declined to exercise the two options. Subsequently, in mid-April, ERHC/Chrome exercised four signature bonus-free options of 15%, 20%, 25% and 30%, respectively, in Blocks 6, 3, 4 and 2 and took another two stakes of 15% and 20% in Blocks 5 and 9, for which signature bonuses were payable. The four signature bonus-free options would cost São Tomé lost income of $75m. Later in April a meeting of the Nigeria-São Tomé Joint Ministerial Council (JMC) in Abuja was expected to announce the winners of the licensing round. However, the meeting only disclosed that the exploration rights for Block 1 were jointly awarded to ChevronTexaco (51%), ExxonMobil (40%) and Equity Energy Resources (9%). Surprisingly, the JMC decided to postpone the allocation of the remaining blocks to a later date. Later it was revealed that both the Nigerian and the São Tomé Governments wanted to avoid attributing the blocks to companies with uncertain financial and technical capacities. De Menezes announced the execution of new seismic studies by PGS before a new licensing round for the remaining eight blocks would be held. The sale of Block 1 entitled São Tomé to a signature bonus of $49m., much less than the $200m. expected from the auction at the time of the opening of the bids. ChevronTexaco promised to sign a product-sharing agreement with the JDA in August and start drilling in 2005. However, the eight-year Product Sharing Contract for Block 1 was only signed in February 2005. In late June in Abuja Presidents Obasanjo and de Menezes signed a nine-point agreement on transparency in payments, expenditure and other dealings in the transactions in the JDZ. The Abuja Joint Declaration adopted guide-lines for reporting promulgated by the United Kingdom's Extractive Industries Transparency Initiative.

In January 2004 the Canadian mining company DiamondWorks, which operates in 12 African countries, signed a memorandum of understanding (MoU) with the São Tomé Government for the creation of a joint venture for trading in refined petroleum products and in crude petroleum allocated to the country by other African petroleum producers. In mid-February DiamondWorks disclosed the signature of an expanded MoU by its subsidiary Energem Petroleum Corpn Ltd. This included the marketing of hydrocarbon products to be produced in São Tomé's EEZ and the establishment of a joint venture for the supply of fuel and petroleum products to enterprises operating in the EEZ. Under the agreement Energem would receive 70% of the profits stemming from the resale of crude from other African producers, while São Tomé would receive 30%. The agreement provoked a political crisis in São Tomé, since the Prime Minister, Maria das Neves, maintained that the agreement had been signed without her authorization. Consequently, on 4 March the Government declared the MoU null and void, although Energem maintained that the MoU was properly negotiated and was still operational.

In October 2004 the Government replaced the National Oil Commission with a 15-member Conselho Nacional de Petróleo (National Petroleum Council—CNP). Its members included the Head of State, the Prime Minister and various government ministers, although de Menezes resigned from the body in May 2005. At the same time, the Agência Nacional de Petróleo (ANP—National Petroleum Agency) was created as the regulatory body of the petroleum sector. The World Bank financed 50% of the ANP's US $1.3m. budget for 2005, and provided a capacity building training programme for its staff. In December 2004 President de Menezes signed legislation on petroleum revenue management. The legislation included provisions for control of oil receipts, transparency, conflict of interests, frequent auditing of accounts, and a permanent reserve fund. The law, which had been unanimously approved by the Assembleia Nacional in November, included the transparency principles of the Abuja Joint Declaration.

In December 2005 the company Equator Exploration, established by the Canadian national Wade Cherwayko in 2000, announced that it had acquired PGS's preferential rights in two blocks of its choice in São Tomé's EEZ through its subsidiary Aqua Exploration Ltd. In addition, Aqua Exploration had another option to participate to a maximum of 15% in any of the Government's participating options in the EEZ. Equator Exploration was also entitled to a share of licensing fees earned by PGS from the sale of seismic data of the EEZ and the JDZ.

In November 2004 the JDA organized a new licensing round for Blocks 2–6. Altogether, by the close of bidding on 15 December, 23 companies, mostly Nigerian, had presented 26 bids for the five blocks. The block awards of this second bidding round, expected in January 2005, were delayed by disagreements with Nigeria over signature bonuses. In April ExxonMobil declined to exercise its two 25% options, because it was refused the right to operate the desired blocks. At a meeting in late April in Abuja the JMC approved the awarding of the five blocks. However, the announcement was delayed by fierce accusations of irregularities by the Movimento de Libertação de São Tomé e Príncipe—Partido Social Democrata in São Tomé. In a report, the ANP accused the JDA of having carried out insufficient checks into bidders' backgrounds, and expressed fears that awards given to inexperienced Nigerian firms could discourage reputable petroleum companies. Patrice Trovoada, the leader of Acção Democrática Independente (ADI) and the presidential petroleum adviser, demanded a higher percentage for Equator Exploration. In response, President de Menezes dismissed Trovoada from his post, allegedly on the grounds that he had abused his function in order to conduct private business. De Menezes was also obliged to withdraw Mateus Meira Rita, the head of the presidential office, from the CNP and the JMC, since Rita's appointment to the two bodies violated the oil revenue management law. Pressured by Nigerian President Obasanjo, on 31 May, de Menezes approved the JMC's award recommendations unchanged. A consortium of ERHC and Devon Energy/Pioneer Natural Resources won a 65% stake of Block 2, while Block 4 was awarded to a consortium of ERHC and Noble Energy. Anadarko Petroleum Corpn, which had put in the highest bid for Block 4, received 51% of Block 3. An Iranian-Nigerian consortium was awarded the right to operate Block 5, while a Nigerian company became operator of Block 6. The five signature bonuses totalled US $283m. However, owing to ERHC's bonus-free options, São Tomé would only receive $57.2m.

In July 2005 Devon Energy withdrew from the consortium with ERHC owing to the low interest the company received as one of the three partners. In November the Geneva-based Addax Petroleum replaced Noble Energy in the ERHC/Noble consortium of Block 4. In February 2006 Pioneer Natural Resources withdrew from the operatorship of Block 2 and was replaced by the Chinese state company Sinopec and Addax. In the same month ERHC entered into a participation agreement with Addax Nigeria in Block 3. For the sale of interests to Addax and Sinopec ERHC received US $46m.

An investigation report into the second licensing round requested by the Assembleia Nacional in May 2005 and submitted by the Attorney-General, Adelino Pereira, to the local authorities in December revealed serious irregularities in the process of block awards, including vague selection criteria and the attribution of concessions to petroleum companies with doubtful technical and financial qualifications. Furthermore the document stated that ERHC's preferential rights would result in a loss of US $60m. in signature bonuses for São Tomé and suggested the company had made illegal payments to Santomean officials. The Attorney-General asked the US authorities to investigate the contracts awarded to ERHC. In response to the report, President de Menezes declared that it was impossible to cancel the block awards without Nigerian consent. The Nigerian Minister of Petroleum Resources, Edmund Dakoru, rejected the report's allegations as based on deficient information and a result of internal political wrangling in São Tomé. As a result of the report, in May 2006 a search warrant issued by a US court in Houston, Texas, was executed on ERHC for various records including correspondence with government officials in São Tomé and Nigeria. About 120 boxes of paper files and copies of computer hard drives were removed during the action. Due to the controversial report the signature of the production sharing contracts for the five blocks suffered considerable delays. Only in mid-March did the JDZ sign production sharing contracts with Addax and other consortium winners Conoil (20%), Gosonic Oil (5%), Hercules/Centurion (10%), and Overt (5%) of Block 4, with operator Anadarko and ERHC and other parties of Block 3 and with operator Sinopec, Addax and ERHC, A. and Hatman (Nigeria), Momo, and Equator Exploration in Block 2. The signature bonuses for these blocks were $90m., $40m., and $71m. respectively. Due to ERHC's bonus-free options São Tomé received only $28.6m. of the total amount. Owing to a lack of interest by bidders in April the JDA withdrew the Blocks 7, 8, and 9 from the licensing round.

In mid-January 2006 ChevronTexaco started drilling the first exploration well, Obó-1, located in some 1,700 m of water in Block 1. Drilling was completed in mid-March; however, it was not until late May that Chevron announced the discovery of oil and gas, although it stressed that it was premature to say if the deposits were commercially viable. Chevron announced that a second exploratory well out of a total of eight selected in the block would be drilled in late 2007. In mid-April 2006 Addax increased its interest in Block 4 to 38.3% by acquiring the 5% stake held by the Nigerian Overt Ventures for $10m. Later in that month Equator Exploration increased its share in Block 2 from 6% to 9% by acquiring, together with ONGC Videsh Ltd, a 7.5% interest held by A. and Hatman. In March 2007 the British Geological Service re-evaluated the seismic data on possible oil deposits in the country's EEZ produced by the Norwegian PGS in the early 2000s. Also in March 2007 Addax and Sinopec announced plans to drill five exploration wells in Blocks 2 and 4 in the period from 2008-2013. The costs of the drilling operation was estimated at US $74m. Later that month the Joint Ministerial Council increased the annual budget for the JDA in Abuja from $9m. in 2006 by 44% to $13m. in 2007.

Owing to increasing crude petroleum prices, in late April 2004 ENCO raised prices of petrol, diesel and kitchen kerosene from 7,000 dobras per litre to 8,500 dobras per litre, from 5,000 dobras per litre to 6,500 dobras per litre, and from 2,800 dobras per litre to 3,000 dobras per litre, respectively. ENCO announced that EMAE would be exempt from the higher prices to avoid an increase in electricity tariffs. In September 2003 ENCO had tried to increase fuel prices; however, at the time the Government refused authorization. The Government accepted ENCO's latest request since the company had already accumulated losses of 4,000m. dobras (US $350,000), which endangered its capacity to buy fuel from SONANGOL. In October 2004 the litre prices of petrol, diesel, and kitchen kerosene were increased to 10,500 dobras, 8,500 dobras, and 3,500 dobras, respectively.

In 2000 some 74% of electricity generation was derived from thermal sources, and 26% from hydroelectric sources. The capital city's recently rehabilitated generators still rely on fuel oil, and power cuts have become increasingly frequent as fuel prices have risen sharply. In 1996, with the installation of a new electricity generator with a capacity of 1,200 kWh, EMAE succeeded in reducing the energy deficit by 40%. A comprehensive energy plan was scheduled for the end of 1993, and the entire electricity and water distribution systems were to be replaced from 1994. Between 1993 and 1996 the Government invested US $13.5m. in EMAE. However, owing to poor financial and technical management, in 1996 the company still required government subsidies totalling $402,000, equivalent to almost 1% of GDP. In the budget for 1999 the Government planned to curb this expenditure to the equivalent of 0.6% of GDP. At the instigation of the IMF, EMAE was scheduled for privatization in 2001. However, in that year the company incurred a further deficit, of some $350,000, which the Government had to pay off. The Government promised the IMF that it would submit EMAE's accounts for the period 1995–98 to independent external auditors before the end of February 2002 and increase water and electricity tariffs by 16% in late March. Following continuous complaints by consumers, in July the Government created an emergency committee to solve EMAE's problems. Moreover, the Government returned the electricity rates and water rates, raised by 16% and 27% respectively in January, to their December 2001 levels, starting in July 2002. The Government announced plans for the privatization of EMAE in 2003.

The expansion of the electricity grid on Príncipe commenced in the second half of 2002, financed by the Portuguese Agency for Development Aid and including 13 km of power lines running from Picão in the north to Terreiro Velho in the south, with an extension to the airport through Santo Cristo. In January 2003 EMAE increased electricity tariffs by 5.6% to cover production costs. Despite higher tariffs, since December 2002 EMAE had been unable to pay for the fuel supplied by ENCO. When, in April 2004, the debts had reached some US $1m., ENCO stopped supplies, causing frequent energy cuts. EMAE claimed that it could not pay ENCO since the Government had not paid its energy bill. In turn, the Government created a commission to tackle EMAE's chronic problems. Das Neves announced the establishment of both a new thermal power plant outside the city and the construction of a hydroelectric dam at the Yô Grande river in the south of São Tomé by 2006 to increase the country's energy supply. In mid-2004 the Government and Synergie Investments (United Kingdom) signed a contract for the construction of a 25-gigawatt hydroelectric power plant on the Yô Grande and the repair of the small hydroelectric plant at the Contador river. In December the Government conceded Synergie Investments the concession for the exploration of the plant on the Contador river that produces some 20% of the country's electricity. However, in early 2005 11 EMAE technicians demanded the cancellation of the agreement arguing that it was prejudicial for the country. Furthermore, they maintained that the European Development Fund and the European Investment Bank had already conceded credits of €2m. and €1m., respectively, for the rehabilitation works of the Contador plant by the French company Cegelec. In response, the Government decided to review the contract with Synergie. In March EMAE announced plans to raise electricity tariffs by 25% owing to the increased price of diesel supplied by ENCO. In July 2005 petrol prices were increased from 10,500 dobras per litre to 12,500 dobras per litre, diesel went up from 9,000 dobras per litre to 11,000 dobras per litre, and kerosene was raised from 4,000 dobras per litre to 5,000 dobras per litre. In June 2006 the fuel prices were again raised to 16,000 dobras per litre, 14,000 dobras per litre, and 6,500 dobras per litre, respectively. At that time ENCO had accumulated debts of $3m. with the Angolan supplier SONANGOL. In November 2005 ENCO announced plans to increase the supply price for EMAE from 6,000 dobras per litre to 8,000 dobras per litre. At that time EMAE's debts with ENCO amounted to 26,800m. dobras. Consequently, ENCO ceased to concede credits to EMAE and did not pay tax debts of 14,000m. dobras to the treasury. In April 2006 EMAE announced it was to start a pilot project with a pre-paid electricity system for 3,000 of the company's 21,000 clients. In the same month, owing to higher fuel prices, EMAE increased the electricity tariffs by 33% for private customers, by 50% for embassies and international institutions, and by 60% for governmental departments. In May the new Government succeeded in convincing ENCO to pay part of the tax debts. In turn, the Government used this revenue to settle its own debts of 8,000m. dobras with EMAE. In November 2006 EMAE revealed that for several years some 40% of its monthly fuel supplies had been diverted. The criminal police was asked to investigate the fuel theft.

TRANSPORT, TOURISM AND COMMUNICATIONS

The asphalted road network of some 218 km suffered serious deterioration following independence, although a repair programme financed by foreign aid began in 1989, and by 1995 most roads outside the capital had been repaired with donor funds of almost US $10m. In 2000 the construction of the road from Monte Mário to Porto Alegre in the south of São Tomé, funded by the ADB with $7m., was completed and the repair of the road from Neves to Santa Catarina in the north, financed by Taiwan with $8m., was initiated. However, before 1997 the Government failed to provide for any expenditure on road maintenance, while the minimum annual expenditure necessary for routine road repairs was estimated at $300,000. Foreign donors are also upgrading three of the country's ports, although São Tomé city lacks a natural deep-water harbour and has been losing traffic to the better-endowed port of Neves, which handles petroleum imports and industrial fishing. Joint ventures were established in 1989 to replace the inefficient state enterprises for maritime communications and telecommunications. In February 2004 the US Trade and Development Agency (USTDA) announced grants of $450,000 and $350,000 to finance feasibility studies for the construction of a deep-sea port in São Tomé and the extension of the local international airport. The two grants, which were also motivated by strategic US interests, represented the first investments of USTDA in the archipelago.

In July 2006 the Assembleia Nacional approved a law on the creation of a free-trade zone at Agulhas Bay on Príncipe. The work for the extension of the runway of the airport in São Tomé from 2,100 m to 3,300 m, financed by Taiwan with US $2m., started in May 2007. In June Terminal Link S.A., a subsidiary of the French group CMA-CGM, and the Government signed a memorandum of understanding on the construction of a $400m. deep-water harbour at Fernão Dias in São Tomé.

In late 1993 a new airline, Air São Tomé e Príncipe, began operations. The company is managed by TAP-Air Portugal, which also holds a 40% share of the capital. The Government of São Tomé holds a 35% share, while the French companies Golfe International Air Service and Mistral Voyages hold 24% and 1%, respectively. Air São Tomé e Príncipe has been in debt since 1996, and the IMF and the World Bank urged the Government to privatize the company in 2001. In August 2002 the newly created Linhas Aéreas São-tomenses (LAS) inaugurated a regular charter flight from Lisbon. However, LAS was unable to continue flights. In March 2007 LAS became the representative of the Nigerian Aero Contractors when this company inaugurated a weekly flight to Lagos. In September of that year Air Luxor STP was established by the private Portuguese air carrier Air Luxor (49%) and three local shareholders (17% each). In mid-December Air Luxor STP began operating two weekly flights between Lisbon and São Tomé. In 2003 Air Luxor transported more passengers on the route than the total number of passengers previously transported by TAP Air Portugal. However, in late 2004 Air Luxor reduced the weekly flights from Lisbon to São Tomé to one. Air Luxor was sold to Longstock Financial Group in July 2006 ceased operating the flight to Lisbon due to bankruptcy in September 2006. In May 2006 Air São Tomé e Príncipe's only aeroplane, a 12-seat Twin Otter, crashed into the sea near the airport during an instruction flight killing the four people on board. In October 2006 Air São Tomé e Príncipe was dissolved and replaced by the newly created company STP Airways owned by the Government (35%) and private investors (65%). In February 2007 STP Airways inaugurated a twice-weekly direct flight to Luanda, Angola, operated by TAAG Angola Airlines.

In 1990 the telecommunications company CST was established as a joint venture between the State (49%) and the Portuguese Rádio Marconi (51%). In March 1997 an internet service was officially launched. In April 1999 Rádio Marconi threatened to withdraw from the CST if the Government did not revise legislation, approved in 1998, regarding free-trade zones which placed CST's monopoly in jeopardy by opening up the local telecommunications sector. In July 1999 CST completed the digitalization of the telecommunications system. Also in that month the Swedish internet provider Bahnhof AB purchased the country's principal domain, 'st', from the Government. The company hoped that the Government would attract foreign enterprises, through the provision of fiscal incentives, to use the internet services available at relatively low prices. The Government, with support from the World Bank, planned to open the local telecommunications market to other competitors in 2001. In April 2003 CST extended the mobile cellular telephone service to Santo António on Príncipe. At the instigation of the IMF, in February 2004 a law on the liberalization of the local telecommunications market was approved which, since 1989, had been a monopoly of the CST. Due to this monopoly São Tomé's international telephone rates were among the highest in the world. Under the new legislation the CST would maintain the exclusive right to operate the international telecommunications service and mobile phone service until the end of 2005, allowing the company to recoup investments in modernization made over the last 15 years. However, the implementation of this legislation was delayed and it was not until 2006 that the Government set up the Autoridade Geral de Regulação (AGER), the communication regulatory authority. In April 2004 the CST introduced the automatic roaming service for mobile telephone connections with the Portuguese TDM, a subsidiary of Portugal Telecom. The CST expected the number of subscribers of the mobile telephone service to equal those of the fixed telephone network within 12 months. By December 2004 the CST operated 7,050 telephone lines and had 7,745 mobile phone subscribers, representing telephone density rates of 4.9% and 5.4%, respectively. By May 2006 the CST reported the existence of almost 15,000 mobile telephone clients. In October CST reported that the mobile phone service represented 55% of the company's returns, while the fixed-phone network earned 30%.

The improvement in communications has been of great importance in sustaining efforts to develop tourism. The islands benefit from spectacular volcanic mountains and craters, beaches, unique bird life and flora, and have ample potential for game-fishing. However, the high rainfall during most of the year limits the duration of the tourist season, and the sea is usually dangerous to bathe in because of strong currents. In addition, the development of the industry has been hampered by high malaria incidence, expensive air fares and inadequate government policies. Nevertheless, the first modern tourist hotel, the Miramar, was completed in 1986 with a capacity of 50 beds, and it has attracted a modest current of tourists, mainly European expatriates and wealthy Gabonese. The Bombom Island luxury tourist complex on Príncipe island, which caters particularly for game-fishing, and the Santana tourist complex south of São Tomé city, also with emphasis on marine activities, were opened in late 1992. In late 1995 the Government leased the Miramar Hotel, for a period of 20 years, to a group of German investors, São Tomé Invest SA. The Portuguese company Rotas d'África inaugurated a 70 twin-bed bungalow complex on the Rolas Islet in June 2001. The US $800,000 complex, called Equator's Line, was to offer wind-surfing, submarine diving and big-game fishing. Although tourism has been identified as a growth sector for many years, failure to develop has confined its contribution to GDP to only 3%. The number of foreign visitor arrivals has increased steadily, from 5,584 in 1998 to 7,569 in 2001. In April 2001 the Government, UNDP and the World Tourism Organization signed an agreement on the joint elaboration of a tourism development strategy for the country. The strategic plan was presented in May 2002 and recommended that an additional capacity of 320 hotel rooms was necessary and an estimated 20,000 tourists were required to visit the country annually to make the investments profitable. In July the Government and local tour operators created a National Tourist Council to co-ordinate tourism promotion. The number of foreign visitors increased from 9,609 in 2003 to 10,705 in 2004, but then decreased to 10,516 in 2005 and 9,354 in 2006.

In March 2004 the Government announced plans to sell by public tender old plantation houses, in order to promote rural tourism and attempt to save from ruin the mostly dilapidated colonial architecture. Potential investors were obliged to maintain the original tropical architecture of the estate buildings. In early May the Government held a four-day round-table conference on tourism development to present a strategy for the development of the country's tourism to local and foreign investors. The priorities for tourism development identified by the local authorities included the improvement and diversification of the market, improving infrastructure, building capacity of local tourism agents, training of human resources, and the promotion of São Tomé's tourism potential. However, the event attracted very few potential investors from Europe's large tourist markets. At the end of the same month the Pestana Group, Portugal's largest hotel group, signed an agreement with the Government regarding the establishment of a five-star 100-room hotel with a casino and a discotheque in the country's capital. This investment, primarily destined for the oil business sector, was estimated at €25m. and was expected to employ some 600 local people. In September 2005 Pestana inaugurated the contruction works of its €30m. tourism project. In February of that year Pestana took over the management of the Rolas Islet Resort. In 2006 the Dutch company Consultant Designers of Separators (CDS), owned by Rombout Swanborn, purchased the Bom-Bom Island Resort in Príncipe and the Marlin Beach Hotel in São Tomé from International Hotel Development Corporation (IHDC), owned by the South African businessman Chris Hellinger. Swanborn planned to integrate the two hotels in his Gabon-based eco-tourism project Operation Loango.

Portugal, the USA and the Government launched a 10-year malaria eradication campaign, financed with US $16m., in 2001. In December 2005 the health authorities started a national anti-malaria campaign financed predominantly by Taiwan. By April 2006, due to the campaign, mortality by malaria had been reduced by more than 50% in the previous two years. The number of hospital admissions due to malaria decreased from 13,230 in 2004 to 5,560 in 2005. In March 2007 the health authorities announced that malaria cases had fallen from 67,156 in 2004 to 9,106 in 2006. Malaria mortality was reduced from 169 deaths from the disease in 2004 (19% of total mortality) to 26 in 2006 (3%).

FOREIGN TRADE AND PAYMENTS

Owing to the importance of cocoa and tourism, the islands' economic life is entirely dependent on external markets. Until 1980, the trade balance was usually positive because of the small value of imports. However, since then low world cocoa prices and low cocoa production, combined with the higher cost of food imports, have led to a continuing trade deficit. The deficit reached a record total of US $22.9m. in 2002. Shortages of essential supplies, especially fuel, have become more frequent. Portugal is the country's main supplier of goods, accounting for 60.0% of total imports in 2002, although there are considerable fluctuations from year to year. Since the mid-1980s São Tomé has sold its cocoa mainly to Germany and the Netherlands. In 2002 the Netherlands accounted for 58.8% of total exports.

In 1990 net foreign aid was equivalent to US $200 per head. UNDP, the World Bank, the EU, Portugal, France, Italy, Japan, the People's Republic of China and Arab countries have been especially prominent as donors. Since 1997 Taiwan, which provides $10m. in assistance annually, has replaced China as an important donor country. However, the institutional weakness of the country and the lack of co-ordination between donors has led to problems in the efficiency with which aid is utilized. The influx of aid has helped to deal with the deficit on the current account, but it has distorted prices. According to UN figures, in 1993 São Tomé received official development assistance of $378 per head, the highest level of any developing country. According to UNDP, in 1998 São Tomé received total official development assistance of $20.7m., a 54.5% decrease on the previous year. Technical co-operation represented 39.4% of the total, investment projects 53.4% and food aid 6.2%. Multilateral donors provided $8.2m. (58.9% less than in 1997), while bilateral donors allocated $12.5m. (a decrease of 51.1%). The principal donor countries were France (providing 24.4% of the total), Portugal (15.3%) and Taiwan (11.5%). Agriculture, forestry and fishing accounted for 21.5% of the total, while economic management, social development and development administration absorbed 17.2%, 14.8% and 13.8%, respectively. In 2002 outstanding debt totalled $264.8m., of which $5m. was short-term debt owed to Nigeria for an advance on oil contract signature bonuses. Multilateral and bilateral medium- and long-term debt amounted to $177.0m. and $82.8m., respectively. In addition to Nigeria, the most important bilateral creditors were Portugal ($27.9m.), the People's Republic of China ($16.6m.), Angola

($9.8m.), France ($6.6m.), Germany ($5.8m.), Italy ($5.5m.), Spain ($3.6m.) and Russia ($3.3m.). In June the ADB granted São Tomé and Príncipe a credit of $5.67m. to finance the development of human resources as part of poverty reduction measures. In July Taiwan signed a third three-year co-operation agreement with São Tomé and Príncipe, worth $35m. for the period 2003–06. Taiwan designated 60% of this funding for projects that would have considerable socio-economic impact, 20% for small projects, 10% for agriculture and 10% for small and medium-sized enterprises. In June 2004 Nigeria conceded São Tomé a third interest-free $5m. loan, bringing to $15m. the total owed by São Tomé to Nigeria. The amount would be deducted from future petroleum signature bonus payments. In October the World Bank granted a $5m. loan for strengthening the Government's economic, financial, and budgetary management capacities, particularly with regard to the oil revenue management law. Two months later Portugal and São Tomé signed a new co-operation agreement of €41m. for the period 2005–2007. In late 2004 the World Bank conceded an International Development Association (IDA) credit of $4.5m. and an IDA grant of $1.5m. for a five-year Social Sector Support Project focusing on basic health and education services. In March 2005 the EU granted a European Development Fund credit of $10.3m. for the improvement of the country's road network and road maintenance. In July the ADB announced a grant of $7.5m. for agriculture and good government. At a UNDP sponsored round-table donor conference in Brussels, Belgium, in early December the Government requested $130m. for poverty reduction and infrastructure projects; however, only $60m. was pledged. In February 2006 the World Food Programme announced a new five-year food aid programme worth $5.2m. Public investments declined by 33% from $28m. in 2004 to $19m. in 2005, of which 78% was financed by external donors. Taiwan contributed $7m., while the EU paid $3.4m. According to a World Bank report in May 2006, the country's total nominal debt represented 1,655% of the value of the export of goods and services or 666% of GDP, while debt service payments were equivalent to 44% of export of goods. In December 2006 the Government held a round-table donor conference for the infrastructure, education, and good governance sectors in São Tomé. The donors pledged $52m., considerably less than the $121m. requested by the Government. In March 2007 the EU promised European Development Fund financing of €13m. during the period 2008–13 for infrastructure improvement and road construction.

Statistical Survey

Source (unless otherwise stated): Instituto Nacional de Estatística, CP 256, São Tomé; tel. 221982.

AREA AND POPULATION

Area: 1,001 sq km (386.5 sq miles); São Tomé 859 sq km (331.7 sq miles), Príncipe 142 sq km (54.8 sq miles).

Population: 117,504 at census of 4 August 1991; 137,599 (males 68,236, females 69,363) at census of September 2001; 155,000 in 2006 (UN estimate at mid-year) (Source: UN, *World Population Prospects: The 2006 Revision*).

Density (mid-2006): 154.8 per sq km.

Population by District (census of 2001): Água-Grande 51,886, Mé-Zochi 35,105, Cantagolo 13,258, Caué 5,501, Lembá 10,696, Lobata 15,157, Pagué (Príncipe) 5,966; Total 137,599.

Principal Towns (population at census of 1991): São Tomé (capital) 42,300; Trindade 11,400; Santana 6,200; Santo Amaro 5,900; Neves 5,900. Source: Stefan Helders, *World Gazetteer* (internet www.world-gazetteer.com). *Mid-2005* (incl. suburbs): São Tomé (capital) 57,000 (Source: UN, *World Urbanization Prospects: The 2005 Revision*).

Births, Marriages and Deaths (2000): Registered live births 4,078 (birth rate 29.20 per 1,000); Registered marriages 210 (marriage rate 1.5 per 1,000); Registered deaths 1,030 (death rate 7.51 per 1,000). *2006:* Birth rate 32.5 per 1,000; Death rate 8.32 per 1,000 (Source: African Development Bank).

Expectation of Life (years at birth, WHO estimates): 59 (males 57; females 60) in 2004. (Source: WHO, *World Health Report*).

Economically Active Population (census of 2001): Agriculture and fishing 13,518; Industry, electricity, gas and water 2,893; Public works and civil construction 4,403; Trade, restaurants and hotels 8,787; Transport, storage and communications 792; Public administration 3,307; Health 776; Education 1,373; Other activities 7,088; *Total employed* 42,937. *Mid-2005* (estimates in '000): Agriculture, etc. 45; Total labour force 73 (Source: FAO).

HEALTH AND WELFARE

Key Indicators

Total Fertility Rate (children per woman, 2005): 3.8.

Under-5 Mortality Rate (per 1,000 live births, 2005): 118.

Physicians (per 1,000 head, 2004): 0.49.

Hospital Beds (per 1,000 head, 2003): 3.20.

Health Expenditure (2004): US $ per head (PPP): 141.4.

Health Expenditure (2004): % of GDP: 11.5.

Health Expenditure (2004): public (% of total): 86.2.

Access to Water (% of persons, 2004): 79.

Access to Sanitation (% of persons, 2004): 25.

Human Development Index (2004): ranking: 127.

Human Development Index (2004): value: 0.607.

For sources and definitions, see explanatory note on p. vi.

AGRICULTURE, ETC.

Principal Crops (metric tons, 2005, FAO estimates): Bananas 27,000; Maize 2,700; Cassava (Manioc) 6,890; Taro 28,000; Yams 1,547; Cocoa beans 3,534; Coconuts 26,277; Oil palm fruit 43,458; Coffee (green) 29; Cinnamon 30.

Livestock (head, 2005, FAO estimates): Cattle 4,600; Sheep 3,000; Goats 5,000; Pigs 2,500; Poultry 350,000.

Livestock Products (metric tons, 2005, FAO estimates): Cattle meat 122; Pig meat 75; Sheep meat 6; Goat meat 18; Chicken meat 667; Hen eggs 385; Cows' milk 144.

Forestry ('000 cubic metres, 1988): Roundwood removals 9; Sawnwood production 5. *1989–2005:* Annual output assumed to be unchanged since 1988.

Fishing (metric tons, live weight, estimates, 2005): Total catch 3,600 (Croakers and drums 110; Pandoras 160; Threadfins and tasselfishes 120; Wahoo 300; Little tunny 120; Atlantic sailfish 200; Flyingfishes 800; Jacks and crevalles 160; Sharks, rays and skates 170).

Source: FAO.

INDUSTRY

Production (metric tons, unless otherwise indicated): Bread and biscuits 3,768 (1995); Soap 261.1 (1995); Beer (litres) 529,400 (1995); Palm oil 2,000 (2005, FAO estimate); Electric energy (million kWh) 37.2 (2002). Sources: IMF, *Democratic Republic of São Tomé and Príncipe: Selected Issues and Statistical Appendix* (September 1998, February 2002, April 2004 and September 2006), and FAO.

FINANCE

Currency and Exchange Rates: 100 cêntimos = 1 dobra (Db). *Sterling, Dollar and Euro Equivalents* (29 December 2006): £1 sterling = 25,664.0 dobras; US $1 = 13,073.9 dobras; €1 = 17,218.3 dobras; 100,000 dobras = £3.90 = $7.65 = €5.81. *Average Exchange Rate* (dobras per US $): 9,902.3 in 2004; 10,558.0 in 2005; 12,445.4 in 2006.

Budget ('000 million dobras, 2005, estimates): *Revenue:* Taxation 184.0 (Direct 54.3, Indirect 129.7); Non-tax revenue 42.6; Grants 184.1; Oil signature bonuses 561.5; Total 972.2. *Expenditure:* Current expenditure 320.4 (Personnel costs 103.3, *of which* Wages and salaries 90.4, Goods and services 65.5, Interest on external debt 33.7. Interest on internal debt 1.9, Transfers 89.8, Other current expenditure 26.2); Capital expenditure 193.4; HIPC-related social expenditure 31.7; Total 545.5. Source: IMF, *Democratic Republic of São Tomé and Príncipe: Selected Issues and Statistical Appendix* (September 2006).

International Reserves (US $ million at 31 December 2006): IMF special drawing rights 0.07; Foreign exchange 34.12; Total 34.19. Source: IMF, *International Financial Statistics*.

Money Supply (million dobras at 31 December 2006): Currency outside banks 92,313; Demand deposits at commercial banks 341,746; Total money (incl. others) 435,181. Source: IMF, *International Financial Statistics*.

Cost of Living (Consumer Price Index; base: 1996 = 100): 437.2 in 2003; 503.8 in 2004; 590.5 in 2005. Source: IMF, *Democratic Republic of São Tomé and Príncipe: Selected Issues and Statistical Appendix* (September 2006).

Expenditure on the Gross Domestic Product (US $ million at current prices, 2006): Government final consumption expenditure 37.97; Private final consumption expenditure 57.24; Gross capital formation 65.91; *Total domestic expenditure* 160.42; Exports of goods and services 26.86; *Less* Imports of goods and services 104.14; *GDP in purchasers' values* 83.84. Source: African Development Bank.

Gross Domestic Product by Economic Activity ('000 million dobras at current prices, 2004, preliminary): Agriculture 83.7; Fishing 18.6; Manufacturing, electricity, gas and water 26.3; Construction 61.1; Trade and transport 175.0; Public administration 190.6; Financial institutions 69.4; Other services 4.4; *Total* 629.3. Source: IMF, *Democratic Republic of São Tomé and Príncipe: Selected Issues and Statistical Appendix* (September 2006).

Balance of Payments (US $ million, 2005, estimates): Exports of goods f.o.b. 3.8; Imports of goods f.o.b. −42.1; *Trade balance* −38.3; Net of service and income accounts −5.3; *Balance on goods, services and income* −43.6; Private transfers (net) 2.0; Official transfers (net) 18.4; *Current balance* −23.2; Project loans 3.9; Program loans 1.7; Oil signatures bonuses 49.2; Direct foreign investment 3.5; Other investment −0.6; Amortization −8.9; Short-term capital and errors and omissions 0.8; *Overall balance* 26.6. Source: IMF, *Democratic Republic of São Tomé and Príncipe: Selected Issues and Statistical Appendix* (September 2006).

EXTERNAL TRADE

Principal Commodities (US $ million, 2004): *Imports f.o.b.*: Foodstuffs 10.3; Beverages 5.0; Petroleum and petroleum products 6.2; Equipment 4.9; Transport equipment 4.4; Construction materials 2.9; Total (incl. others) 41.4. *Exports f.o.b.*: Cocoa 3.2; Coconuts 0.1; Total (incl. others) 3.5.

Principal Trading Partners (US $ million, 2004): *Imports c.i.f.*: Angola 6.6; Belgium 3.6; Gabon 0.6; Japan 2.5; Netherlands 0.4; Portugal 25.0; Total (incl. others) 41.3. *Exports f.o.b.*: Belgium 0.3; Gabon 0.1; Netherlands 1.8; Portugal 2.2; USA 0.2; Total (incl. others) 3.5. Source: Banco Central de São Tomé e Príncipe.

TRANSPORT

Road Traffic (registered vehicles, 1996, estimates): Passenger cars 4,000; Lorries and vans 1,540. Source: International Road Federation, *World Road Statistics*.

Shipping: *International Freight Traffic* (estimates, metric tons, 1992): Goods loaded 16,000; Goods unloaded 45,000. *Merchant Fleet* (registered at 31 December 2006): Number of vessels 34; Total displacement 32,659 grt (Source: Lloyd's Register-Fairplay, *World Fleet Statistics*).

Civil Aviation (traffic on scheduled services, 2003): Passengers carried ('000) 36; Passenger-km (million) 15; Total ton-km (million) 1. Source: UN, *Statistical Yearbook*.

TOURISM

Foreign Tourist Arrivals: 5,584 in 1998; 5,710 in 1999; 7,137 in 2000. Source: Tourism and Hotels Bureau.

Arrivals by Country of Residence (2005): Angola 552; Cape Verde 336; France 1,242; Gabon 286; Nigeria 473; Portugal 5,469; Spain 318; USA 154; Total (incl. others) 10,518. Source: World Tourism Organization.

Tourism Receipts (US $ million, excl. passenger transport): 10 in 2000; 10 in 2001; 10 in 2002. Source: World Tourism Organization.

COMMUNICATIONS MEDIA

Radio Receivers (1998): 45,000 in use. Source: UNESCO, *Statistical Yearbook*.

Television Receivers (1999): 33,000 in use. Source: UNESCO, *Statistical Yearbook*.

Newspapers and Periodicals (2000): Titles 14 (1997); Average circulation 18,500 copies.

Telephones ('000 main lines, 2003): 7.0 in use. Source: International Telecommunication Union.

Mobile Cellular Telephones ('000 subscribers, 2005): 12.0. Source: International Telecommunication Union.

Facsimile Machines (2000): 372 in use.

Internet Users (2004): 20,000. Source: International Telecommunication Union.

EDUCATION

Pre-primary (2001): 18 schools; 2,376 pupils.

Primary (2001): 73 schools; 623 teachers; 20,858 pupils.

General Secondary and Pre-university (2001): 11 schools; 630 teachers; 13,874 (including vocational education) pupils. There are also 2 vocational secondary schools.

Tertiary (2000/01): 1 polytechnic; 29 teachers; 117 pupils.

Source: mainly *Carta Escolar de São Tomé e Príncipe,* Ministério de Educação de Portugal.

Adult Literacy Rate (official estimate, 2001): 83.1%. Source: UN Development Programme, *Human Development Report*.

Directory

The Constitution

A new Constitution came into force on 4 March 2003, after the promulgation by the President of a draft approved by the Assembleia Nacional (National Assembly) in December 2002. A 'memorandum of understanding', which was signed in January 2003 by the President and the Assembleia Nacional, provided for the scheduling of a referendum on the system of governance in early 2006. However, the referendum did not take place. The following is a summary of the main provisions of the Constitution:

The Democratic Republic of São Tomé and Príncipe is a sovereign, independent, unitary and democratic state. Sovereignty resides in the people, who exercise it through universal, equal, direct and secret vote, according to the terms of the Constitution. There shall be complete separation between Church and State. There shall be freedom of thought, expression and information and a free and independent press, within the terms of the law.

Executive power is vested in the President of the Republic, who is elected for a period of five years by universal adult suffrage. The President's tenure of office is limited to two successive terms. He is the Supreme Commander of the Armed Forces and is accountable to the Assembleia Nacional. In the event of the President's death, permanent incapacity or resignation, his functions shall be assumed by the President of the Assembleia Nacional until a new President is elected.

The Council of State acts as an advisory body to the President and comprises the President of the Assembleia Nacional, the Prime Minister, the President of the Constitutional Tribunal, the Attorney-General, the President of the Regional Government of Príncipe, former Presidents of the Republic who have not been dismissed from their positions, three citizens of merit nominated by the President and three elected by the Assembleia Nacional. Its meetings are closed and do not serve a legislative function.

Legislative power is vested in the Assembleia Nacional, which comprises 55 members elected by universal adult suffrage. The Assembleia Nacional is elected for four years and meets in ordinary session twice a year. It may meet in extraordinary session on the proposal of the President, the Council of Ministers or of two-thirds of its members. The Assembleia Nacional elects its own President. In the period between ordinary sessions of the Assembleia Nacional its functions are assumed by a permanent commission elected from among its members.

The Government is the executive and administrative organ of State. The Prime Minister is the Head of Government and is appointed by the President. Other ministers are appointed by the President on the proposal of the Prime Minister. The Government is responsible to the President and the Assembleia Nacional.

Judicial power is exercised by the Supreme Court and all other competent tribunals and courts. The Supreme Court is the supreme judicial authority, and is accountable only to the Assembleia Nacional. Its members are appointed by the Assembleia Nacional. The right to a defence is guaranteed.

The Constitutional Tribunal, comprising five judges with a mandate of five years, is responsible for jurisdiction on matters of constitutionality. During periods prior to, or between, the installation of the Constitutional Tribunal, its function is assumed by the Supreme Court. The Constitution may be revised only by the Assembleia Nacional on the proposal of at least three-quarters of its members. Any amendment must be approved by a two-thirds' majority of the Assembleia Nacional. The President does not have right of veto over constitutional changes.

Note: In 1994 the Assembleia Nacional granted political and administrative autonomy to the island of Príncipe. Legislation was adopted establishing a seven-member Assembleia Regional and a five-member Regional Government; both are accountable to the Government of São Tomé and Príncipe.

The Government

HEAD OF STATE

President and Commander-in-Chief of the Armed Forces: FRADIQUE DE MENEZES (took office 3 September 2001; re-elected 30 July 2006).

COUNCIL OF MINISTERS

(August 2007)

The Government comprises members of the Movimento Democrático Força da Mudança, the Partido de Convergência Democrática and independents.

Prime Minister and Minister of Media and Regional Integration: TOMÉ SOARES VERA CRUZ.

Deputy Prime Minister and Minister of Planning and Finance: MARIA DOS SANTOS LIMA DA COSTA TEBÚS TORRES.

Minister of Foreign Affairs, Co-operation and Communities: CARLOS GUSTAVO DOS ANJOS.

Minister of Defence and Internal Order: Lt-Col ÓSCAR AGUÍAR SACRAMENTO E SOUSA.

Minister of Natural Resources and the Environment: MANUEL DE DEUS LIMA.

Minister of the Economy: CRISTINA MARIA FERNANDES DIAS.

Minister of Public Works and Infrastructure: DELFIM SANTIAGO DAS NEVES.

Minister of Education, Culture, Youth and Sport: MARIA DA FÁTIMA LEITE DE SOUSA ALMEIDA.

Minister of Health: ARLINDO VICENTE DE ASSUNÇÃO CARVALHO.

Minister of Justice and Parliamentary Affairs: JUSTINO TAVARES VEIGA.

Minister of Labour, Solidarity, Women and the Family: MARIA DO CRISTO HILÁRIO DE COSTA DE CARVALHO.

Minister of Public Administration, State Reform and Territorial Administration: ARMINDO VAZ RODRIGUES AGUIAR.

Provisional Government of the Autonomous Region of Príncipe

(August 2007)

President: JOÃO PAULO CASSANDRA.

Secretary for Social and Cultural Affairs: FELÍCIA FONSECA DE OLIVEIRA E SILVA.

Secretary for Economic and Financial Affairs: HÉLIO LAVRES.

Secretary for Infrastructure and the Environment: TIAGO ROSAMONTE.

Secretary for Political, Organizational and Institutional Affairs: CARLOS GOMES.

MINISTRIES

Office of the President: Palácio Presidêncial, São Tomé; internet www.presidencia.st.

Office of the Prime Minister: Rua do Município, CP 302, São Tomé; tel. 223913; fax 224679; e-mail gpm@cstome.net.

Ministry of Defence and Internal Order: Av. 12 de Julho, CP 427, São Tomé; tel. 222041; e-mail midefesa@cstome.net.

Ministry of the Economy: São Tomé.

Ministry of Education, Culture, Youth and Sport: Rua Misericórdia, CP 41, São Tomé; tel. 222861; fax 221466; e-mail mineducal@cstome.net.

Ministry of Foreign Affairs, Co-operation and Communities: Av. 12 de Julho, CP 111, São Tomé; tel. 221017; fax 222597; e-mail minecoop@cstome.net.

Ministry of Health: Av. Patrice Lumumba, CP 23, São Tomé; tel. 241200; fax 221306; e-mail msaude@cstome.net.

Ministry of Justice and Parliamentary Affairs: Av. 12 de Julho, CP 4, São Tomé; tel. 222318; fax 222256; e-mail emilioma@cstome.net.

Ministry of Labour, Solidarity, Women and the Family: Rua Município, Edif. Ministério do Trabalho, São Tomé; tel. 221466.

Ministry of Media and Regional Integration: São Tomé.

Ministry of Natural Resources and the Environment: CP 1093, São Tomé; tel. 225272; fax 226262; e-mail mirecurna@cstome.net.

Ministry of Planning and Finance: Largo Alfândega, CP 168, São Tomé; tel. 224173; fax 222683; e-mail mpfc@cstome.net.

Ministry of Public Administration, State Reform and Territorial Administration: Av. Kwame Nkrumah, CP 136, São Tomé; tel. 224750; fax 222824; e-mail mirna@cstome.net.

Ministry of Public Works and Infrastructure: São Tomé.

President and Legislature

PRESIDENT

Presidential Election, 30 July 2006

Candidate	Votes	% of votes
Fradique de Menezes	34,859	60.58
Patrice Emery Trovoada	22,339	38.82
Nilo de Oliveira Guimarães	340	0.59
Total	57,538	100.00

There were, in addition, 1,640 blank and other invalid votes.

ASSEMBLEIA NACIONAL

Assembleia Nacional: Palácio dos Congressos, CP 181, São Tomé; tel. 222986; fax 222835; e-mail romao.couto@parlamento.st; internet www.parlamento.st.

President: FRANCISCO DA SILVA.

General Election, 26 March and 2 April 2006

Party	% of valid votes	Seats
Movimento Democrático Força da Mudança-Partido de Convergência Democrática	36.79	23
Movimento de Libertação de São Tomé e Príncipe—Partido Social Democrata	29.47	20
Acção Democrática Independente (ADI)	20.00	11
Novo Rumo (NR)	4.71	1
Others	9.03	—
Total	100.00	55

Election Commission

Comissão Eleitoral Nacional (CEN): Av. Amílcar Cabral, São Tomé; tel. 227828; fax 224116; Pres. JOSÉ CARLOS BARREIRO.

Political Organizations

Acção Democrática Independente (ADI): Av. Marginal 12 de Julho, Edif. C. Cassandra, São Tomé; tel. 222201; f. 1992; Sec.-Gen. EVARISTO CARVALHO.

Frente Democrata Cristã—Partido Social da Unidade (FDC—PSU): São Tomé; f. 1990; Pres. ARLÉCIO COSTA; Vice-Pres. SABINO DOS SANTOS.

Geração Esperança (GE): São Tomé; f. 2005; Leader EDMILZA BRAGANÇA.

Movimento Democrático Força da Mudança (MDFM): São Tomé; f. 2001; formed alliance with PCD to contest legislative elections in 2006; Sec.-Gen. TOMÉ SOARES VERA CRUZ.

Movimento de Libertação de São Tomé e Príncipe—Partido Social Democrata (MLSTP—PSD): Estrada Riboque, Edif. Sede do MLSTP, São Tomé; tel. 222253; f. 1972 as MLSTP; adopted present name in 1990; sole legal party 1972–90; Pres. RAFAEL BRANCO; Sec.-Gen. JOSÉ VIEGAS.

Novo Rumo: São Tomé; f. 2006 by citizens disaffected by current political parties; Leader JOÃO GOMES.

Partido de Convergência Democrática (PCD): Av. Marginal 12 de Julho, CP 519, São Tomé; tel. and fax 223257; f. 1990 as Partido de Convergência—Grupo de Reflexão; formed alliance with MDFM to contest legislative elections in 2006; Pres. LEONEL MÁRIO D'ALVA; Sec.-Gen. MARCELINO COSTA.

Partido de Coligação Democrática (CÓDÓ): São Tomé; f. 1990 as Partido Democrático de São Tomé e Príncipe—Coligação Democrática da Oposição; renamed as above June 1998; Leader MANUEL NEVES E SILVA.

Partido Social e Liberal (PSL): São Tomé; f. 2005; promotes development and anti-corruption; Leader AGOSTINHO RITA.

Partido Popular do Progresso (PPP): São Tomé; f. 1998; Leader FRANCISCO SILVA.

Partido de Renovação Democrática (PRD): São Tomé; tel. 903109; e-mail prd100@hotmail.com; f. 2001; Pres. ARMINDO GRAÇA.

Partido Social Renovado (PSR): São Tomé; f. 2004; Leader HAMILTON VAZ.

Partido Trabalhista Santomense (PTS): CP 254, São Tomé; tel. 223338; fax 223255; e-mail pascoal@cstome.net; f. 1993 as Aliança Popular; Leader ANACLETO ROLIN.

União para a Democracia e Desenvolvimento (UDD): São Tomé; f. 2005; Leader MANUEL DIOGO.

União Nacional para Democracia e Progresso (UNDP): São Tomé; f. 1998; Leader PAIXÃO LIMA.

The União para a Mudança e Progresso do Príncipe (UMPP) operates on the island of Príncipe and there is also a local civic group, O Renascimento de Água Grande, in the district of Agua Grande, which includes the city of São Tomé.

Diplomatic Representation

EMBASSIES IN SÃO TOMÉ AND PRÍNCIPE

Angola: Av. Kwame Nkrumah 45, CP 133, São Tomé; tel. 222400; fax 221362; e-mail embrang@cstome.net; Ambassador PEDRO FERNANDO MAVUNZA.

Brazil: Av. Marginal de 12 de Julho 20, São Tomé; tel. 226060; fax 226895; e-mail brasembsaotome@cstome.net; Ambassador MANUEL INNOCENCIO DE LACERDA SANTOS, Jr.

China (Taiwan): Av. Marginal de 12 de Julho, CP 839, São Tomé; tel. 223529; fax 221376; e-mail rocstp@cstome.net; Ambassador YANG CHING-YUEN.

Equatorial Guinea: Rua Ex-Adriano Moreira, São Tomé; tel. 225427.

Gabon: Rua Damão, CP 394, São Tomé; tel. 224434; fax 223531; e-mail ambagabon@cstome.net; Ambassador BEKALÉ MICHEL.

Nigeria: Av. Kwame Nkrumah, CP 1000, São Tomé; tel. 225404; fax 225406; e-mail nigeria@cstome.net; Ambassador SUNDAY DOGONYARO OON.

Portugal: Av. Marginal de 12 de Julho, CP 173, São Tomé; tel. 221130; fax 221190; e-mail eporstp@cstome.net; Ambassador FERNANDO JOSÉ RODRIGUES RAMOS MACHADO.

Judicial System

Judicial power is exercised by the Supreme Court of Justice and the Courts of Primary Instance. The Supreme Court is the ultimate judicial authority. There is also a Constitutional Court, which rules on election matters.

Supremo Tribunal de Justiça: Av. Marginal de 12 de Julho, São Tomé; tel. and fax 222329; e-mail tsupremo@cstome.net; Pres. MARIA ALICE VERA CRUZ DE CARVALHO.

Religion

According to the 2001 census more than 80% of the population are Christians, almost all of whom are Roman Catholics.

CHRISTIANITY

The Roman Catholic Church

São Tomé and Príncipe comprises a single diocese, directly responsible to the Holy See. At 31 December 2004 an estimated 73.6% of the population were adherents. The bishop participates in the Episcopal Conference of Angola and São Tomé (based in Luanda, Angola).

Bishop of São Tomé and Príncipe: Rt Rev. MANUEL ANTÓNIO MENDES DOS SANTOS, Centro Diocesano, CP 104, São Tomé; tel. 223455; fax 227348; e-mail diocese@cstome.net.

Other Churches

Igreja Adventista do 7° Dia (Seventh-Day Adventist Church): Rua Barão de Água Izé, São Tomé; tel. 223349.

Igreja Evangélica: Rua 3 de Fevereiro, São Tomé; tel. 221350.

Igreja Evanélica Assembleia de Deus: Rua 3 de Fevereiro, São Tomé; tel. and fax 222442; e-mail iead@cstome.net.

Igreja Maná: Av. Amílcar Cabral, São Tomé; tel. and fax 224654; e-mail imana@cstome.net.

Igreja do Nazareno: Vila Dolores, São Tomé; tel. 223943; e-mail nszst@cstome.net.

Igreja Nova Apostólica: Fruta Fruta, São Tomé; tel. and fax 222406; e-mail inasaotome@cstome.net.

Igreja Universal do Reino de Deus: Travessa Imprensa, São Tomé; tel. 224047.

The Press

Correio da Semana: Av. Amílcar Cabral 382, São Tomé; tel. 225299; f. 2005; weekly; Publr RAFAEL BRANCO; Dir JUVENAL RODRIGUES; circ. 3,000.

Diário da República: Cooperativa de Artes Gráficas, Rua João Devs, CP 28, São Tomé; tel. 222661; internet dre.pt/stp; f. 1836; official gazette; Dir OSCAR FERREIRA.

Jornal Maravilha: São Tomé; tel. 911690; f. 2006; Dir NELSON SIGNO.

Jornal Tropical: Rua Padre Martinho Pinto da Rocha, São Tomé; tel. 923140; e-mail jornaltropical06@hotmail.com; internet www .jornaltropical.st; Dir OCTÁVIO SOARES.

O País: Av. Amílcar Cabral, CP 361, São Tomé; tel. 223833; fax 221989; e-mail iucai@cstome.net; f. 1998; Dir FRANCISCO PINTO DA SILVEIRA RITA.

O Parvo: CP 535, São Tomé; tel. 221031; f. 1994; weekly; Publr AMBRÓSIO QUARESMA; Editor ARMINDO CARDOSO.

Piá: Edif. Centro Cultural Português 1C, CP 600, São Tomé; tel. 226332; e-mail doriadesign@hotmail.com; f. 2002; monthly; Dir NILTON DÓRIA.

Téla Nón: Largo Água Grande, Edif. Complexo Técnico da CST, São Tomé; tel. 225099; e-mail diario_digital@cstome.net; internet www .cstome.net/diario; f. 2000; provides online daily news service; Chief Editor ABEL VEIGA.

Online newspapers include the Jornal de São Tomé e Príncipe (www.jornal.st) and Jornal Horizonte (www.cstome.net/jhorizonte).

PRESS ASSOCIATION

Associação Nacional de Imprensa (ANI): São Tomé; Pres. MANUEL BARRETO.

NEWS AGENCY

STP-Press: Av. Marginal de 12 de Julho, CP 112, São Tomé; tel. 223431; fax 221973; e-mail stp_press@cstome.net; internet www .cstome.net/stp-press; f. 1985; operated by the radio station in asscn with the Angolan news agency ANGOP; Dir MANUEL DÊNDE.

Lusa—Agência de Notícias de Portugal has a correspondent, Ricardo Neto, in São Tomé.

Broadcasting and Communications

TELECOMMUNICATIONS

Companhia Santomense de Telecomunicações, SARL (CST): Av. Marginal 12 de Julho, CP 141, São Tomé; tel. 222273; fax 222500; e-mail webmaster@cstome.net; internet www.cstome.net; f. 1989 by Govt of São Tomé (49%) and Grupo Portugal Telecom (Portugal, 51%) to facilitate increased telecommunications links and television reception via satellite; in March 1997 CST introduced internet services; Rádio Marconi's shares subsequently assumed by Portugal

Telecom SA; introduced mobile cellular telephone service in 2001; Pres. FELISBERTO AFONSO L. NETO; Sec. JORGE M. TAVARES MAGRO.

BROADCASTING

Portuguese technical and financial assistance in the establishment of a television service was announced in May 1989. Transmissions commenced in 1992, and the service currently broadcasts seven days a week. In 1995 Radio France Internationale and Rádio Televisão Portuguesa Internacional began relaying radio and television broadcasts, respectively, to the archipelago. In 1997 Voice of America, which had been broadcasting throughout Africa since 1993 from a relay station installed on São Tomé, began local transmissions on FM. In 2004 there were plans for Televisão Pública de Angola to begin transmitting by the end of the year. The liberalization of the sector was approved by the Government in early 2005 and Rádio Jubilar, Rádio Tropicana (operated by the Roman Catholic Church) and Rádio Viva FM subsequently began broadcasting. The French television channel, TV5, was due to begin broadcasting in 2007.

Radio

Rádio Nacional de São Tomé e Príncipe: Av. Marginal de 12 de Julho, CP 44, São Tomé; tel. 223293; fax 221973; e-mail rnstp@cstome.net; f. 1958; state-controlled; home service in Portuguese and Creole; Dir MÁXIMO CARLOS.

Rádio Jubilar: Rua Padre Martinho Pinto da Rocha, São Tomé; tel. 223455; f. 2005; operated by the Roman Catholic Church; Dir FERNANDO CORREIA.

Rádio Tropicana: Travessa João de Deus, CP 709, São Tomé; tel. 226856; f. 2005; Dir AGUINALDO SALVATERRA.

Television

Televisão Santomense (TVS): Bairro Quinta de Santo António, CP 393, São Tomé; tel. 221041; fax 221942; state-controlled; Dir MATEUS FERREIRA.

Finance

(cap. = capital; res = reserves; dep. = deposits; m. = million; br(s). = branch(es); amounts in dobras, unless otherwise indicated)

BANKING

Central Bank

Banco Central de São Tomé e Príncipe (BCSTP): Praça da Independência, CP 13, São Tomé; tel. 221300; fax 222777; e-mail bcstp@bcstp.st; internet www.bcstp.st; f. 1992 to succeed fmr Banco Nacional de São Tomé e Príncipe; bank of issue; cap. 100m., res 91,623m., dep. 125,154m.; Gov. ARLINDO AFONSO DE CARVALHO.

Commercial Banks

Afriland First Bank/STP: Praça da Independência, CP 202, São Tomé; tel. 226749; fax 226747; e-mail firstbank@afriland-firstbank.com; internet www.afrilandfirstbank.com; f. 2003; private bank; owned by Afriland First Bank, SA, Cameroon; cap. US $1.8m.; Gen. Man. AUGUSTIN DIAYO; Administrator-Delegate JOSEPH TINDJOU.

Banco Equador: Rua Moçambique 3, CP 361, São Tomé; tel. 226150; fax 226149; e-mail be@bancoequador.st; internet www.bancoequador.st; f. 1995 as Banco Comercial do Equador; restructured and name changed to above in 2003; owned by Monbaka (Angola) (40%) and Grupo António Mbakassi (40%); cap. US $3m.; Pres. DIONÍSIO MENDONÇA; Gen. Man. DOUGLAS PETERSEN; 1 br.

Banco Internacional de São Tomé e Príncipe (BISTP) (International Bank of São Tomé and Príncipe): Praça da Independência, CP 536, São Tomé; tel. 243100; fax 222427; e-mail bistp@cstome.net; f. 1993; 48% govt-owned, 30% owned by Banco Totta e Açores, SA (Portugal), 22% by Caixa Geral de Depósitos (Portugal); cap. US $3.0m., res $3.1m., dep. $22.2m. (2004); Pres. MANUEL FERNANDO MONTEIRO PINTO; 3 brs.

Commercial Bank—São Tomé e Príncipe: Av. Marginal 12 de Julho, CP 1109, São Tomé; tel. 227678; fax 227676; e-mail gi_sandjon@hotmail.com; f. 2005; subsidiary of Groupe Bancaire Commercial Bank (Cameroon); cap. US $3m. (2005); Chair. YVES MICHEL FOTSO; Gen. Man. JAQUES PAUL WOUENDJI.

Ecobank São Tomé: Edificio HB, Traversa de Pelorinho, CP 316, São Tomé; tel. 222141; fax 222672; e-mail ecobankstp@cstome.net; f. 2007; cap. US $1.5m.

Island Bank, SA: Rua de Guiné, CP 1044, São Tomé; tel. 222521; f. 2005; cap. US $1.8m. (2005); Pres. MARC WABARA; Dir CHRIS U. MMEJE.

The Ocean Offshore Bank, SA, was also active.

INVESTMENT BANK

National Investment Bank: Rua de Angola, São Tomé; tel. 908221; internet www.ni-bank.com; f. 2004; acquired by Superior Investments in 2005; cap. US $3.4m. (Dec. 2006); Chair. PAULO MIRPURI.

INSURANCE

Instituto de Segurança Social: Rua Soldado Paulo Ferreira, São Tomé; tel. 221382; e-mail inss@cstome.net; f. as Caixa de Previdência dos Funcionários Públicos, adopted present name 1994; insurance fund for civil servants; Pres. of Admin. Bd ALBINO GRAÇA DA FONSECA; Dir JUVENAL DO ESPÍRITO SANTO.

SAT INSURANCE: Av. 12 de Julho, CP 293, São Tomé; tel. 226161; fax 226160; e-mail satinsuran@cstome.net; f. 2001; general insurance; cap. US $0.6m.; Dir MICHEL SOBGUI.

Trade and Industry

GOVERNMENT AGENCIES

Agência Nacional do Petróleo de São Tomé e Príncipe (ANP—STP): Av. Nações Unidas, CP 1048, São Tomé; tel. 226940; fax 226937; e-mail anp_geral@cstome.net; internet www.anp-stp.gov.st; f. 2004; manages and implements govt policies relating to the petroleum sector; Exec. Dir LUÍS PRAZERES.

Nigeria-São Tomé and Príncipe Joint Development Authority (JDA): Plot 1101, Aminu Kano Cres., Wuse II, Abuja, Nigeria; Praça da UCCLA, São Tomé; tel. (234) 95241069; fax (234) 95241061; e-mail enquiries@nigeriasaotomejda.com; internet www.nigeriasaotomejda.com; f. 2002; manages development of petroleum and gas resources in Joint Development Zone; Chair. and Exec. Dir ADO YAKUBA WANKA.

DEVELOPMENT ORGANIZATION

Instituto para o Desenvolvimento Económico e Social (INDES): Travessa do Pelourinho, CP 408, São Tomé; tel. 222491; fax 221931; e-mail indes@cstome.net; f. 1989 as Fundo Social e de Infrastructuras; adopted present name 1994; channels foreign funds to local economy; Dir HOMERO JERÓNIMO SALVATERRA.

CHAMBER OF COMMERCE

Câmara do Comércio, Indústria, Agricultura e Serviços (CCIAS): Av. Marginal de 12 de Julho, CP 527, São Tomé; tel. 222723; fax 221409; e-mail ccias@cstome.net; Pres. ABÍLIO AFONSO HENRIQUES.

UTILITIES

Electricity and Water

Empresa de Água e Electricidade (EMAE): Av. Água Grande, CP 46, São Tomé; tel. 222096; fax 222488; e-mail emae@cstome.net; f. 1979; Synergie Investments (UK); state electricity and water co; privatized in 2004; Dir JÚLIO SILVA.

MAJOR COMPANIES

Empresa Industrial de Madeiras (EIM): Fruta Fruta, CP 137, Água Grande; tel. 222475; fax 222925; e-mail eim@cstome.net; mfrs of wood products.

Empresa Nacional de Combustíveis e Óleos (ENCO): Rua da Guiné, CP 50, São Tomé; tel. 222275; fax 222972; e-mail enco_1@cstome.net; Dir JOSÉ GOMES BARBOSA.

Flora Speciosa: Roça de São José; e-mail informacoes@floraspeciosa.com; internet www.floraspeciosa.com; f. 2003; production and international distribution of tropical flowers.

Sociedade de Construção Civil, SA (CONSTROMÉ): Av. 12 de Julho, CP 551, São Tomé; tel. 221775; e-mail constrome@cstome.net; construction.

TRADE UNIONS

Federação Nacional dos Pequenos Agricoltores (FENAPA): Rua Barão de Água Izé, São Tomé; tel. 224741; Pres. TEODORICO CAMPOS.

Organização Nacional de Trabalhadores de São Tomé e Príncipe (ONTSTP): Rua Cabo Verde, São Tomé; tel. 222431; e-mail ontstpdis@cstome.net; Sec.-Gen. JOÃO TAVARES.

Sindicato de Jornalistas de São Tomé e Príncipe (SJS): São Tomé; Pres. AMBRÓSIO QUARESMA.

Sindicato dos Trabalhadores do Estado (STE): São Tomé; Sec.-Gen. AURÉLIO SILVA.

União Geral dos Trabalhadores de São Tomé e Príncipe (UGSTP): Av. Kwame Nkrumah, São Tomé; tel. 222443; e-mail ugtdis@cstome.net; Sec.-Gen. COSTA CARLOS.

Transport

RAILWAYS

There are no railways in São Tomé and Príncipe.

ROADS

In 1999 there were an estimated 320 km of roads, of which 218 km were asphalted. In 2005 the European Union granted €930,000 towards upgrading the road network.

SHIPPING

The principal ports are at São Tomé city and at Neves on São Tomé island. At December 2005 São Tomé and Príncipe's registered merchant fleet comprised 37 vessels, totalling 46,657 grt.

Agência de Navegação e Turismo, Lda (AGENTUR): Rua Cabo Verde, São Tomé; tel. 224866; fax 221894.

Companhia Santomense de Navegação, SA (CSN): CP 49, São Tomé; tel. 222657; fax 221311; e-mail csn@setgrcop.com; internet www.navegor.pt; shipping and freight forwarding.

Empresa Nacional de Administração dos Portos (ENAPORT): Largo Alfândega, São Tomé; tel. 221841; fax 224949; e-mail enaport@cstome.net; Dir-Gen. DEODATO RODRIGUES.

Navetur-Equatour, Navegação e Turismo, Lda: Rua Viriato da Curz, CP 277, São Tomé; tel. 222122; fax 221748; e-mail navequatur@cstome.net; internet www.navetur-equatour.st; shipping and tourism.

Transportes e Serviços, Lda (TURIMAR): Rua Patrice Lumumba, CP 48, São Tomé; tel. 221869; fax 222162; e-mail turimar@cstome.net.

CIVIL AVIATION

The international airport is at São Tomé.

Empresa Nacional de Aeroportos e Segurança Aérea (ENASA): Aeroporto, CP 703, São Tomé; tel. 221878; fax 221154; e-mail enasa@cstome.net; Dir JORGE COELHO.

Linhas Aéreas São-tomenses (LAS): Rua Santo António do Príncipe, São Tomé; tel. 227282; fax 227281; e-mail hba.saotome@gmail.com; f. 2002; owned by Aerocontractors, Nigeria; Dir ANTÓNIO AGUIAR.

STP-Airways: Av. Marginal 12 de Julho, São Tomé; tel. 221160; fax 223449; e-mail stp-airways@cstome.net; f. 2006; 35% govt-owned; Dir FELISBERTO NETO.

Tourism

The islands benefit from spectacular mountain scenery, unspoilt beaches and unique species of flora and wildlife. Although still largely undeveloped, tourism is currently the sector of the islands' economy attracting the highest level of foreign investment. However, the high level of rainfall during most of the year limits the duration of the tourist season, and the expense of reaching the islands by air is also an inhibiting factor. There were 9,354 tourist arrivals in 2001, and receipts totalled some US $10m. in 2002.

Defence

In early 2005 the armed forces were estimated to number some 300. Military service, which is compulsory, lasts for 30 months. There is also a presidential guard numbering some 160. In 1992 a reorganization was initiated of the islands' armed forces and the police into two separate police forces, one for public order and another for criminal investigation. However, in December 1993, following increasing pressure from the military high command, parliament approved the new legal status of the armed forces, maintaining their role as military defenders of the nation. In late 1996 restructuring of the armed forces resumed, with technical assistance from Portugal. In late 2000 Portugal and São Tomé renewed the military agreement for the stationing of the 'Aviocar' and a crew of the Portuguese Air Force in the country. Since April 1988 the aeroplane has provided humanitarian emergency flights from Príncipe to São Tomé, as well as rescue operations for local fishermen along the coast. In 2004 a paramilitary unit, trained by the Angolan Government and comprising 200 men, was created. In mid-2006 army recruitment was broadened to include women.

Defence Expenditure: Budgeted at 1,100m. dobras (excl. capital expenditure) in 2000.

Commander-in-Chief of the Armed Forces: FRADIQUE DE MENEZES.

Chief of General Staff of the Armed Forces: Lt-Col IDALÉCIO PACHIRE.

Education

Primary education is officially compulsory for a period of four years between six and 14 years of age. Secondary education lasts for a further seven years, comprising a first cycle of four years and a second cycle of three years. In 2001 the country had 73 primary schools, with a total enrolment of 20,858 pupils. There were 13 secondary schools (including two devoted to vocational training) in that year, with a total enrolment of 13,874 pupils. There was one polytechnic institute (with an enrolment of 117 in 2000/01). The country's first university, Universidade Lusíada, was inaugurated in October 2006. In 2000 public investment in education (including culture and sport) amounted to US $1.3m., equivalent to 6.7% of total public investment. The budget for 2005 allocated 13.4% of total government expenditure to education.

Bibliography

Baptista, A. *Floripes Negra*. Coimbra, Cena Lusófona, 2001.

Caldeira, A. M. *Mulheres, Sexualidade e Casamento no Arquipelago de S. Tomé e Príncipe* (Seculos XV a XVII). Lisbon, Edições Cosmos, 1999.

Viagens de um piloto português do século XVI à costa de África e á São Tomé. Lisbon, Comissão Nacional para as Comemorações dos Descobrimentos Portugueses, 2000.

'A terra que seus pais povoaram e defenderam...' A questão do protonacionalismo em São Tomé e Príncipe nos séculos XVII e XVIII, in *Anais de História de Além-Mar,* Lisbon, Vol. II, 2001.

Chabal, P., Birmingham, D., Forrest, J., Newitt, M., Seibert, G., and Andrade, E. S. *History of Postcolonial Lusophone Africa*. Bloomington, IN, Indiana University Press, and London, Hurst, 2002.

Deus Lima, J. *História do Massacre de 1952 em S. Tomé e Príncipe: Em Busca de Nossa Verdadeira História*. São Tomé, 2002.

Economist Intelligence Unit. *Congo, São Tomé & Príncipe, Guinea-Bissau, Cape Verde, Country Report*. London, quarterly.

Congo, São Tomé & Príncipe, Guinea-Bissau, Cape Verde, Country Profile. London, annual.

Espírito Santo, C. *A Coroa do Mar*. Lisbon, Editorial Caminho, 1998.

Almas da Elite Santomense. Lisbon, Cooperação, 2000.

Aires de Menezes—O Leão. Lisbon, Cooperação, 2001.

Enciclopédia Fundamental de São Tomé e Príncipe. Lisbon, Cooperação, 2001.

A Guerra da Trindade. Lisbon, Cooperação, 2003.

Eyzaguirre, P. B. 'The Independence of São Tomé e Príncipe and Agrarian Reform', in *Journal of Modern African Studies,* April 1989.

'The Ecology of Swidden Agriculture and Agrarian History in São Tomé', in *Cahiers d'Etudes africaines*, Vol. XXVI, No. 101–102, 1986.

'Competing Systems of Land Tenure in an African Plantation Society', in Downs, R. E., and Reyna, S. P. (Eds), *Land and Society in Contemporary Africa*. Hanover, NH, University Press of New England, 1988.

Frynas, J. G., Wood, G., and Soares de Oliveira, R. M. S. 'Business and Politics in São Tomé and Príncipe: From Cocoa Monoculture to Petro-State', in *African Affairs*, No. 102, 2003.

Gallet, D. *São Tomé et Príncipe: Les îles du milieu du monde*. Paris, Editions Karthala, 2001.

Garfield, R. *A History of São Tomé Island 1470–1655: The Key to Guinea*. New York, Edwin Mellen Press, 1992.

Gaulme, F. 'São Tomé dix ans après la démocratisation, ou les apories d'un libéralisme systématique' in *Lusotopie. Enjeux contemporains dans les espaces lusophones,* 2000.

Gründ, F. *Tchiloli: Charlemagne à São Tomé sur l'île du milieu du monde*. Paris, Editions Magellan & Cie, 2006.

Guedes, A. M. *Litígios e Legitimação: Estado, Sociedade Civil e Direito em S. Tomé e Príncipe*. Coimbra, Almedina, 2002.

Henriques, I. C. *São Tomé e Príncipe: A Invenção de uma Sociedade*. Lisbon, Vega Editora, 2000.

Hipólito dos Santos, J. *O Desenvolvimento e a Mulher. Um outro mundo é possível*. Lisbon, SEIES, 2003.

Hodges, T., and Newitt, M. *São Tomé and Príncipe: From Plantation Colony to Microstate*. Boulder, CO, Westview Press, 1988.

Jones, P. J., Burlison, J. P., and Tye, A. *Conservação dos ecossistemas florestais da República Democrática de São Tomé e Príncipe*. Gland and Cambridge, UICN, 1991.

Liba, M. (Ed.). *Jewish Child Slaves in São Tomé*. Wellington, New Zealand Jewish Chronicle Publications, 2003.

Lloyed-Jones, S., and Costa Pinto, A. *The Last Empire. Thirty Years of Portuguese Decolonization*. Bristor and Portland, OR, Intellect Books, 2003.

Mata, I. *Emergência e Existência de uma Literatura. O Caso Santomense*. Linda-a-Velha (Portugal), ALAC–África, Literatura, Arte e Cultura, 1993.

Diálogo com as Ilhas. Sobre Cultura e Literatura de São Tomé e Príncipe. Lisbon, Edições Colibri, 1998.

Nascimento, A. 'Hegemonia das roças versus instituição municipal na ilha do Príncipe nos primeiros anos da República', in *O Município no Mundo Português*, Funchal, CEHA, 1998.

'S. Tomé e Príncipe no século XIX: um esboço de interpretação das mudanças sociais', in Alexandre, V. (Ed.), *O Império Africano. Séculos XIX e XX*, Lisbon, Edições Colibri e Instituto de História Contemporânea da Faculdade de Ciências Sociais e Humanas, Universidade Nova, 2000.

'O quotidiano dos europeus nas roças de S. Tomé: Primeiras décadas de Novecentos', in *Arquipélago. História*, 2nd Series, Vol. IV, No. 2, Ponta Delgado, Universidade dos Açores, 2000.

'Políticas coloniais, clivagens e representações sociais no associativismo são-tomense nas primeiras décadas de Novecentos', in *África e a instalação do sistema colonial (1885–1930). Actas da III Reunião Internacional de História de África*, Lisbon, 2000.

'Relações entre Angola e S. Tomé e Príncipe na época contemporânea', in *Construindo o pasado angolano: as fontes e a sua interpretação. Actas do II Seminário Internacional sobre a História de Angola*, Lisbon, Comissão Nacional para as Comemorações dos Descobrimentos Portugueses, 2000.

'Relações entre Brasil e S. Tomé e Príncipe: declínio e esquecimento', in *As ilhas e o Brasil*, Funchal, Centro de Estudos de História do Atlântico, 2000.

'Identidades e saberes na encruzilhada do nacionalismo são-tomense' in *Política Internacional,* No. 24, 2001.

Mutações sociais e políticas em S. Tomé e Príncipe nos séculos XIX-XX: uma síntese interpretativa. Lisbon, Agência Portuguesa de Apoio ao Desenvolvimento, 2001.

'São Tomé e Príncipe' in Marques, H. de (Ed.), *O império africano 1890–1930*, Lisbon, Estampa, 2001.

'A evolução da política colonial e padrões de recrutamento de caboverdianos para São Tomé e Príncipe', in *Portos, Escalas e Ilhéus no Relacionamento entre o Ocidente e o Oriente,* Lisbon, Universidade dos Açores e Comissão Nacional para as Comemorações dos Descobrimentos Portugueses, 2001.

'O papagaio e o falcão. A génese da automonia na ultra-periférica ilha do Príncipe', in *Autonomia e História das Ihas,* Funchal, Centro de Estudos de História do Atlântico, 2001.

Poderes e Quotidiano nas Roças de S. Tomé e Príncipe de finais de oitocentos a meados do novecentos. Lisbon, 2002.

Órfãos de Raça: Europeus Entre a Fortuna e a Desventura no S. Tomé e Príncipe Colonial. São Tomé, Instituto Camões—Centro Cultural Português, 2002.

O Sul da Diaspora: Cabo-Verdianos em Plantações de S. Tomé e Príncipe e Moçambique. Praia, Presidência da República da Cabo Verde, 2003.

Desterro e Contrato: Moçambicanos a caminho de S. Tomé e Príncipe (Anos 1940 a 1960). Maputo, Arquivo Histórico de Moçambique, 2003.

A Misericórdia na Voragem das Ilhas. Fragmentos da trajectória das Misericórdias de S. Tomé e do Príncipe. Lisbon, 2003.

Oliveira, J. E. *A Economia de São Tomé e Príncipe*. Lisbon, Instituto de Investigação Científica Tropical, 1993.

Pélissier, R. *Le Naufrage des Caravelles (1961–75)*. Orgeval, Editions Pélissier, 1979.

Explorar. Voyages en Angola et autres lieux incertains. Orgeval, Editions Pélissier, 1980.

Pereira, P. A. *Das Tchiloli von São Tomé: Die Wege des karolinischen Universums*. Frankfurt am Mein, Iko Verlkag, 2002.

Programa dos Nações Unidas para o Desenvolvimento (PNUD/UNDP). *Relatório do Desenvolvimento Humano São Tomé e Príncipe 1998*. São Tomé, 1999.

Ratelband, K. *Nederlanders in West-Afrika 1600–1650: Angola, Kongo en São Tomé*. Walburg Pers, Zutphen, 2000.

da Rosa, L. C. *Die lusographe Literatur der Inseln São Tomé und Príncipe: Versuch einer literaturgeschichtlichen Darstellung*. Frankfurt am Main, TFM/Domus Editoria Euroaea, 1994.

Santos, H. *Olhares Discretos*. São Tomé, Instituto Camões—Centro Cultural Português, 2002.

Seibert, G. 'A política num micro-estado: São Tomé e Príncipe, ou os conflitos pessoais e políticos na génese dos partidos políticos', in *Lusotopie, Enjeux contemporains dans les espaces lusophones*, Vol. 1995.

'São Tomé e Príncipe: Military Coup as a Lesson?', in *Lusotopie, Enjeux contemporains dans les espaces lusophones*, Vol. 1996.

'Le massacre de février à São Tomé: raison d'être du nationalisme santoméen', in *Lusotopie, Enjeux contemporains dans les espaces lusophones*, Vol. 1997.

'São Tomé e Príncipe: boatos, rádio Boca a Boca e panfletos anónimos na cultura política local', in *Revista Internacional de Estudos Africanos*, No. 18–22, Lisbon, 1995–1999.

'The February 1953 Massacre in São Tomé: Crack in the Salazarist Image of Multiracial Harmony and Impetus for Nationalist Demands for Independence', in *Portuguese Studies Review*, No. 10 (2), 2003.

'The Bloodless Coup of July 16 in São Tomé e Príncipe', in *Lusotopie. Enjeux contemporains dans les espaces lusophones*, Vol. 2003.

'São Tomé e Príncipe: The Difficult Transition from International Aid Recipient to Oil Producer', in *Resource Politics in Sub-Saharan Africa*. Hamburg, IAK, 2005

Comrades, Clients and Cousins: Colonialism and Democratization in São Tomé and Príncipe. (2nd edn) Leiden, Brill Academic Publishers, 2006.

Serafim, C. M. S. *As Ihas de São Tomé no século XVII*. Centro de História de Além-mar, Universidade Nova de Lisboa, 2000.

Shaw, C. S. *São Tomé and Príncipe*. Oxford, Clio Press (World Bibliographical Series, Vol. 172), 1994.

Silva, O. *São Tomé et Príncipe: Ecos da Terra do Ossobó*. Lisbon, Colibri, 2004

Tournadre, M. *São Tomé et Príncipe*. Aurillac, Editions Regads, 2000.

Valverde, P. *Máscara, Mato e Morte em São Tomé*. Oeiras, Celta Editora, 2000.

SENEGAL

Physical and Social Geography

R. J. HARRISON CHURCH

The Republic of Senegal, the most westerly state of mainland Africa, covers an area of 197,021 sq km (76,070 sq miles). The population was 9,956,202, according to provisional results of the census of December 2002, and had increased, according to official estimates, to 10,817,844 by mid-2005, giving a population density of 55.0 per sq km. According to the provisional results of the 2002 census, the capital, Dakar, the largest city in the country, had a population of 955,897, while Pikine, near Dakar, had a population of 768,826. Other large cities included Rufisque (284,263), Guediawaye (also near Dakar, 258,370), Thiès (237,849), Kaolack (172,305), Saint-Louis (154,555) and Mbour (153,503). In the early 2000s the authorities announced the intention of constructing a new capital city at Kébémer, north of Dakar. Senegal's southern border is with Guinea-Bissau, to the west, and with Guinea on the northern edge of the Primary sandstone outcrop of the Fouta Djallon. In the east the border is with Mali, in the only other area of bold relief in Senegal, where there are Pre-Cambrian rocks in the Bambouk mountains. The northern border with Mauritania lies along the Senegal river, navigable for small boats all the year to Podor and for two months to Kayes (Mali). The river has a wide flood plain, annually cultivated as the waters retreat. The delta soils are saline, but dams for power, irrigation and better navigation are being built or proposed. The commissioning in 1985 of the Djama dam has considerably improved navigability at the Senegal river delta. The Manantali scheme, completed in 1988, will eventually extend the all-year navigability of the river from 220 km to 924 km, as far as Kayes.

The Gambia forms a semi-enclave between part of southern Senegal and the sea, along the valley of the navigable Gambia river. This has meant that, since the colonial delimitation of the Gambia–Senegal borders in 1889, the river has played no positive role in Senegal's development and that the Casamance region, in the south, was isolated from the rest of Senegal until the opening of the Trans-Gambian Highway in 1958.

The Cap Vert (Cape Verde) peninsula, on which the capital, Dakar, stands, is of verdant appearance, resulting from exposure to south-westerly winds, and thus contrasts with the yellow dunes to the north. Basalt underlies much of Dakar, and its harbour was constructed in a sandy area east of (and sheltered by) the basaltic plateau. South of the peninsula, particularly in Casamance, the coast is a drowned one of shallow estuaries.

Apart from the high eastern and south-eastern borderlands most of the country has monotonous plains, which in an earlier period were drained by large rivers in the centre of the country. Relic valleys, now devoid of superficial water, occur in the Ferlo desert, and these built up the Sine Saloum delta north of The Gambia. In a later dry period north-east to south-west trending sand dunes were formed, giving Senegal's plains their undulating and ribbed surfaces. These plains of Cayor, Baol and Nioro du Rip are inhabited by Wolof and Serer cultivators of groundnuts and millet. The coast between Saint-Louis and Dakar has a broad belt of live dunes. Behind them, near Thiès, calcium phosphates are quarried (aluminium phosphates are also present) and phosphatic fertilizer is produced.

Although Senegal's mineral resources are otherwise relatively sparse, there are potentially valuable reserves of gold, in the south-east (production of which began in mid-1997), as well as deposits of high-grade iron ore, in considerable quantity, in the east. Reserves of natural gas are exploited offshore from Dakar, and there is petroleum off the Casamance coast.

Senegal's climate is widely varied, and the coast is remarkably cool for the latitude (Dakar 14° 38′ N). The Cap Vert peninsula is particularly breezy, because it projects into the path of northerly marine trade winds. Average temperatures are in the range 18°C–31°C, and the rainy season is little more than three months in length. Inland both temperatures and rainfall are higher, and the rainy season in comparable latitudes is somewhat longer. Casamance lies on the northern fringe of the monsoonal climate. Thus Ziguinchor (12° 35′ N) has four to five months' rainy season, with average annual rainfall of 1,626 mm, nearly three times that received by Dakar. The natural vegetation ranges from Sahel savannah north of about 15° N, through Sudan savannah in south-central Senegal, to Guinea savannah in Casamance, where the oil palm is common.

Recent History

PIERRE ENGLEBERT

Revised by KATHARINE MURISON

Following three centuries of French rule, Senegal became a self-governing member of the French Community in 1958. The Mali Federation with Soudan (now Mali) was formed in April 1959 and became independent in June 1960. However the Federation collapsed after only two months. The Republic of Senegal was proclaimed on 5 September, with Léopold Sédar Senghor, the founder of the Union progressiste sénégalaise (UPS), as its first President. After his Prime Minister, Mamadou Dia, was convicted of plotting a *coup d'état*, Senghor assumed the premiership himself in late 1962. A new Constitution, strengthening the powers of the President, was approved in a referendum in March 1963. Later in the year the UPS won a decisive victory in elections to the Assemblée nationale, and other parties were either outlawed or absorbed into the UPS, which by 1966 was the sole legal party.

In 1970 the office of the Prime Minister was revived and assigned to a young provincial administrator, Abdou Diouf. Elections in January 1973 returned both Senghor and the UPS with substantial majorities. In 1976 Senghor announced the creation of a three-party system, comprising the UPS (later renamed the Parti socialiste du Sénégal, PS), the Parti démocratique sénégalais (PDS) and a Marxist-Leninist party. At elections in February 1978 the PS won 83 of the 100 seats in the Assemblée nationale, while Senghor overwhelmingly defeated the PDS leader, Abdoulaye Wade, in the presidential election. In December a fourth political grouping, the right-wing Mouvement républicain sénégalais, was officially recognized.

DIOUF'S LEADERSHIP, 1981–2000

A period of economic decline and resultant austerity measures, in conjunction with intense pressure for political reform, led to Senghor's resignation in December 1980. Diouf assumed the presidency in January 1981 and undertook to reorganize the political system, by removing restrictions on political activity and allowing the official registration of previously unofficial parties.

In February 1983 Diouf led the PS to a clear victory in presidential and legislative elections. Diouf received 83.5% of the votes cast, and the PS candidates for the enlarged Assemblée nationale secured 111 of the 120 seats, with 79.9% of the votes.

Preliminary results of the February 1988 presidential and legislative elections indicated decisive victories for both Diouf and the PS. The PDS alleged widespread fraud, and Wade and Amath Dansokho, the leader of the Marxist-Leninist Parti de l'indépendance et du travail (PIT), were arrested, together with other opposition activists. The official results allocated 73.2% of the votes cast in the presidential election to Diouf and 25.8% to Wade. In the legislative elections the PS returned 103 deputies to the Assemblée nationale and the PDS 17. Trials began in April for incitement to violence and attacks on the internal security of the State. Dansokho and five others were acquitted, but in May Wade received a one-year suspended prison sentence, while three other PDS activists received prison terms of between six months and two years. However, all those who had been convicted of involvement in the post-election violence were included in a presidential amnesty later in the month.

In October 1989 the Assemblée nationale approved a series of electoral reforms. Changes to the electoral code were said to ensure a fair system of voter registration; a new system of partial proportional representation was to be introduced for legislative elections; and opposition parties were to be granted access to the state media. Many parties boycotted municipal and rural elections in November 1990 (at which the PS reportedly received the support of 70% of voters), claiming that Senegal's electoral code still permitted widespread malpractice.

Constitutional Concessions

In March 1991 the Assemblée nationale approved several constitutional amendments, notably the restoration of the post of Prime Minister. It was also agreed that opposition parties would, henceforth, be allowed to participate in government. Accordingly, in April Habib Thiam, a former premier, was restored to the post. His Government included four representatives of the PDS, among them Wade, as well as Dansokho. In September the Assemblée nationale adopted a series of amendments to the electoral code. Under the amended code, the presidential election would, henceforth, take place in two rounds, if necessary (to ensure that the President would be elected by at least one-quarter of registered voters and by an absolute majority of votes cast), every seven years, and an individual would be limited to a maximum of two terms of office. In October 1992 the PDS ministers resigned from the Government, stating that they had been excluded from the governmental process.

Eight candidates contested the presidential election of February 1993. Despite some irregularities, voting was reported to be well ordered in most areas, although there were serious incidents in the Casamance region (see below). According to official results, Diouf was re-elected, with 58.4% of the votes cast (51.6% of the electorate had voted), while Wade secured 32.0%.

Post-election Unrest

The PS won 84 seats at elections to the Assemblée nationale on 9 May 1993, while the PDS, with considerable support in urban areas, took 27 seats. Participation by voters was only 40.7%. Shortly after the announcement of the results the Vice-President of the Constitutional Council, Babacar Sèye, was assassinated. Although an organization styling itself the Armée du peuple claimed responsibility, Wade and three other PDS leaders were detained for three days in connection with the murder. Four people suspected of involvement in Sèye's murder were subsequently arrested: among those detained were Samuel Sarr, a close associate of Wade, and a PDS deputy, Mody Sy.

Wade and the PDS were excluded from Thiam's new Government, which was formed in June 1993. Dansokho, who had supported Diouf's presidential campaign, retained his position in the Council of Ministers, while other ministerial appointments included Abdoulaye Bathily, the leader of the Ligue démocratique—Mouvement pour le parti du travail (LD—MPT), and Serigne Diop, the leader of a PDS splinter group, the Parti démocratique sénégalais—Rénovation (PDS—R).

In October 1993 Wade was charged with complicity in the assassination of Sèye, and Wade's wife and a PDS deputy were charged with 'complicity in a breach of state security', although none was detained. In November Ousmane Ngom and Landing Savané, the leader of And Jëf—Parti africain pour la démocratie et le socialisme (AJ—PADS), were among those detained following a protest in Dakar to demand the cancellation of austerity measures introduced three months earlier. Ngom, Savané and more than 80 others were convicted of participating in an unauthorized demonstration and received six-month suspended prison sentences.

Diouf was regarded as a principal architect of the 50% devaluation, in January 1994, of the CFA franc, and the opposition accused the President of responsibility for resultant hardships. A demonstration in Dakar in February degenerated into serious rioting, as a result of which eight people were killed. Wade, Savané and more than 70 others were subsequently detained and charged with attacks on state security. Legal proceedings against them and 140 others implicated in the unrest were dismissed in July on the grounds of insufficient evidence. In May charges against Wade and his associates in connection with the murder of Sèye had also been dismissed. In October three of those accused of Sèye's murder were convicted and sentenced to between 18 and 20 years' imprisonment, with hard labour.

During the latter part of 1994 both the Government and opposition expressed their desire to restore a national consensus. In March 1995 Thiam named a new Council of Ministers, which included five PDS members, with Wade designated Minister of State at the Presidency. Djibo Kâ, a long-serving government member who recently, as Minister of the Interior, had been associated with the legal proceedings against Wade and other opposition leaders, left the Government. In September Dansokho and a minister-delegate, also a member of the PIT, were dismissed from the Council of Ministers, shortly after their party had issued a statement critical of the Government.

Elections and Political Sequels

In January 1996 Diouf announced that a Sénat was to be established as a second chamber of the legislature. At regional, rural and municipal elections in November, the PS won control of all regions, all principal towns and the majority of rural communities.

In August 1997 Diouf announced the creation of an electoral verification body, the Observatoire national des élections (ONEL), which was to operate under the aegis of the Ministry of the Interior; its nine members were to be appointed by the President, after consultations with various interested parties. Although the proposed new body fell short of the opposition's demands for a fully independent electoral commission, the Assemblée nationale overwhelmingly approved legislation providing for the creation of the ONEL.

In late 1997 serious divisions within the PS emerged, with the creation of a dissident grouping led by Kâ. In response to indications that the group was intending to present an independent list of candidates in the 1998 legislative elections, 11 of its leading members, including Kâ, were suspended from the PS for three months.

In February 1998 the PDS filed an appeal to the Constitutional Council to overturn legislation providing for an increase in the number of deputies in the Assemblée nationale from 120 to 140 members. Wade claimed that the proposed enlargement of the legislature would place an unnecessary added strain on the country's already limited resources. The Council annulled the proposed increase on procedural grounds. In March, however, the Assemblée nationale voted again to increase the number of deputies. Wade announced in late March that the PDS had withdrawn from the Government. Meanwhile, in early March Kâ and his associates had submitted a separate list of candidates for the elections, under the name Union pour le renouveau démocratique (URD), and at the end of the month they resigned from the PS. The URD formed an electoral alliance with two left-wing parties and the Alliance pour le progrès et la justice—Jëf-Jël (APJ—JJ).

The legislative elections, which took place on 24 May 1998, were reported to have proceeded in a generally peaceful atmosphere except in Casamance (see below). Following the elections, which were contested by a total of 18 parties and coalitions, the PDS and six other opposition parties accused the PS of instigating serious electoral fraud, but the Constitutional Council rejected their appeal for the annulment of the election results in the worst-affected areas. The PS retained 93 seats in the enlarged parliament, with 50.2% of the valid votes cast, while the number of PDS deputies was reduced to 23; Kâ's URD-APJ—JJ alliance secured 11 seats. Eight further groups won representation. The rate of participation by voters was only 39% of the registered electorate.

In June 1998 Ngom resigned from the PDS, following his demotion from the party's deputy chairmanship by Wade, and subsequently formed the Parti libéral sénégalais (PLS). The URD later announced that it was to form a parliamentary alliance with the LD—MPT, which held three seats and had announced that it would not participate in the new Government.

In July 1998 Thiam resigned as Prime Minister; he was replaced by Mamadou Lamine Loum, who had been recently appointed Minister of the Economy, Finance and Planning. Loum appointed a Council of Ministers that contained only one non-PS minister (Serigne Diop, Secretary-General of the PDS—R, as Keeper of the Seals, Minister of Justice).

In August 1998 the Assemblée nationale voted to revise the Constitution to remove the clause restricting the President to a maximum of two terms of office. The requirement that a President be elected by more than 25% of all registered voters was also removed. The opposition parties, which described the reforms as a constitutional *coup d'état*, boycotted the vote on the reforms, although declared that they would not boycott the presidential election.

On 24 January 1999 Senegal held elections to the newly created Sénat, in which 45 of the 60 senators were to be elected by members of the Assemblée nationale, together with local, municipal and regional councillors. Twelve senators were to be chosen by the President of the Republic, and three were to be elected by Senegalese resident abroad. Only the PS, the PLS and a coalition of the PIT and the AJ—PADS contested the elections. The main opposition parties had urged a boycott of the poll, describing the new chamber as unnecessary and costly, and accusing the Government of attempted electoral manipulation. The PS won all 45 seats contested, with 91.3% of the votes cast. The 12 senators nominated by Diouf included two opposition leaders, Marcel Bassène of the PLS and Majmout Diop of the Parti africain de l'indépendance.

In March 1999 a left-wing alliance of the AJ—PADS, the PIT, the PDS and the LD—MPT agreed to nominate Wade as their joint candidate in the presidential election scheduled for 2000. Wade had resigned his seat in the Assemblée nationale the previous July, in order to concentrate on the election. In June 1999 Moustapha Niasse, a former Minister of Foreign Affairs and Senegalese Abroad, also announced his intention of contesting the presidential election. Niasse, a founder member of the PS, additionally published a document criticizing the policies of Diouf and accusing the party of corruption; he subsequently formed his own party, the Alliance des forces de progrès (AFP).

THE WADE PRESIDENCY

Campaigning for the February 2000 presidential election began in earnest with Wade's return to Senegal at the end of October 1999 after a year of voluntary exile. Wade quickly succeeded in winning an endorsement from influential members of the Islamic Mouride brotherhood. Much of the campaigning centred on opposition accusations that the PS intended to manipulate the election, and there were persistent complaints about what were perceived to be false voter cards, which differed slightly in colour from the usual white cards.

In the presidential election, held on 27 February 2000, Diouf failed to win an overall majority, and Diouf and Wade therefore proceeded to a second round of voting. The three most successful candidates were Diouf with 41.3%, Wade with 31.0% and Niasse with 16.8%. Overall turn-out was estimated at 61.0%, and the ONEL described the poll as 'free and transparent'. In the following weeks Wade succeeded in gathering the support of Niasse and of the other opposition candidates, with the exception of Kâ, who lent his support to Diouf. At the second round of the election, held on 19 March, Wade gained a substantial victory, winning 58.5% of the vote. Turn-out was estimated at 60.1%. Both the victory for the 73-year-old political veteran and Diouf's dignified acceptance of defeat were acclaimed internationally as an example of a peaceful transition in Africa. Wade's Government was inaugurated in April, with Niasse as Prime Minister and Maj.-Gen. Mamadou Niang as Minister of the Interior.

Early in his tenure, Wade declared his priorities to be restoring peace in Casamance, applying the principle of transparency to the administration and guaranteeing the independence of the judiciary. He also promised to reform the agricultural sector, to attract foreign investment and to solve the country's youth unemployment problems. However, with the PS remaining the largest party in the Assemblée nationale and the Sénat, there remained the prospect of an institutional crisis. In May 2000 Wade promised to submit his preferred constitutional revisions to a referendum, with a view to calling new legislative elections in 2001.

The opening session of the Assemblée nationale in June 2000 was complicated by the defection from the URD of a number of deputies who had been alienated by Kâ's support for Diouf in the second round of the presidential election. In a move fiercely attacked in the press as undemocratic, the PS subsequently 'lent' the URD a number of deputies in order that the URD could continue to be registered as a group within the Assembly. In July the PS itself was affected by several important defections to Wade's PDS.

The new draft of the Constitution presented to a national referendum on 7 January 2001 included the following significant revisions: a reduction in the presidential term of office from seven to five years; a transfer of some powers from the President to the Prime Minister; the abolition of the Sénat; a reduction in the number of Assemblée nationale seats (from 140 to 120); the reintroduction of the requirement that a President be elected by more than 25% of all registered voters; and the introduction of a revised system of partial proportional representation (using a combination of national and regional lists of candidates). The major parties, including the PS, endorsed these amendments and, in the event, some 94.0% of those voting (65.8% of the registered electorate) supported the changes, which mostly took immediate effect, with the exception of those sections necessitating new legislative elections before their implementation.

In March 2001 Wade dismissed Niasse and other members of the AFP from the Government, effectively forcing the party into opposition ahead of the parliamentary elections. Mame Madior Boye, hitherto Minister of Justice and a non-partisan member of the Government, was appointed Prime Minister, becoming the first female premier of Senegal. In the general election of 29 April the PDS-led Sopi (Change) Coalition won a resounding victory, with 49.6% of the votes cast and a substantial majority of seats (89 of 120). The AFP and the PS won 11 and 10 seats, respectively. Electoral participation was measured at 67.5%. With his mandate now considerably strengthened, Wade was able to assemble a strong coalition behind him. Boye was reappointed as Prime Minister, leading a 24-member Government comprising 11 members of the PDS (who obtained most principal posts), nine representatives of civil society, and two members each of the AJ—PADS and the LD—MPT.

In August 2001 some 25 parties formed a pro-presidential electoral alliance, the Convergence des actions autour du Président en perspective du 21ième siècle (CAP-21). This kind of support was helpful in introducing organizational changes, especially the inauguration of a new Commission électorale nationale autonome (CENA). In delayed local and municipal elections, which were eventually held on 12 May 2002, CAP-21 won control of nine of the 11 regional governments, as well as a majority of municipal and communal seats.

Some 26 parties and alliances contested the elections, although turn-out was reportedly low. In October Diouf resigned from the chairmanship of the PS, in order to assume the elected position of Secretary-General of La Francophonie.

The sinking of a state-owned passenger ferry, the MV *Joola*, in September 2002, *en route* from Ziguinchor, the principal city of Casamance, to Dakar led to a national political crisis, even before the final death toll of the accident, subsequently enumerated at 1,863 people, became apparent. In early October the Minister of Capital Works and Transport, Youssouph Sakho, and the Minister of the Armed Forces, Yoba Sambou, resigned in response to the tragedy, as it became clear that the vessel had been severely overloaded; only 64 survivors were reported. Later in the month the head of the navy was dismissed, and Wade announced that the Government accepted responsibility for the disaster. In early November Wade dismissed Boye and her Government. Shortly afterwards an inquiry into the incident found that safety regulations had been widely violated on the *Joola*, and that the dispatch of rescue equipment and staff to the ship by the armed forces had been inexplicably delayed. Idrissa Seck, a close ally of Wade and previously a senior official in the PDS, was appointed as the new Prime Minister; several principal posts in the new Government remained unchanged.

During 2003 the consequences of the sinking of the *Joola* continued to be of political significance, and by mid-July relatives of the victims of the disaster had rejected three offers of compensation made by the Government as insufficient. However, at the end of July a further offer, amounting to a total of 20,000m. francs CFA, was accepted by relatives. In early August the Court of Cassation closed an investigation into the incident, stating that no further public action was feasible, as the commander of the ship, whom the court described as the sole person responsible for the overloading of the vessel, had perished in the disaster. However, the Chief of Staff of the Armed Forces and the Chief of Staff of the Air Force were subsequently dismissed as a result of disciplinary action related to the response to the sinking of the *Joola*.

In late 2003 opposition figures, including the Executive Secretary of the PS, Ousmane Tanor Dieng, identified several arson attacks that had occurred since 2000 against premises occupied by a trade union, a small opposition party and a publishing and broadcasting company as evidence of an apparent increase in politically motivated violence in Senegal during recent years. An attack on Talla Sylla, the President of the APJ—JJ, in Dakar in October 2003, by unknown individuals armed with a hammer, prompted a large demonstration against political violence. Members of the opposition described the assault on Sylla as an assassination attempt, and alleged that the attackers were associates of President Wade.

Political tensions intensified in early 2004 as several parties that had supported Wade's candidacy in the presidential election of 2000 and had ministerial representation in the Government, including the LD—MPT and AJ—PADS, declined to participate in celebrations organized to mark the fourth anniversary of Wade's accession to power. Moreover, while the President continued to announce his intention of forming a broadly based Government, most opposition parties, with the exception of the URD, reiterated their reluctance to participate in any such administration. In April Wade dismissed Seck's Government, appointing Macky Sall, hitherto Minister of State, Minister of the Interior and Local Communities, Government Spokesperson, as the new premier. Although the allocation of most strategic portfolios in the new Council of Ministers remained largely unchanged, Cheikh Sadibou Fall was accorded the post of Minister of the Interior, and two new ministers of state were appointed to the Government: Aminata Tall, as Minister of State, Minister of Local Communities and Decentralization, and the URD's Kâ, as Minister of State, Minister of the Maritime Economy.

Wade effected a minor government reshuffle in July 2004, notably replacing the hitherto Minister of Trade, Awa Guèye Kebé, with Ousmane Ngom, who had rejoined the PDS in 2003 and had subsequently been appointed as an adviser to the President on international relations. Ngom became Minister of the Interior in November, when Fall was dismissed as part of a further reorganization of the Government. In December the Assemblée nationale adopted legislation abolishing the death penalty.

In January 2005 the Assemblée nationale approved controversial legislation granting amnesty to perpetrators of election-related or politically motivated offences committed between 1983 and 2004, irrespective of whether they had been tried or not, and to all those involved in the murder of Babacar Sèye in May 1993 (see above). In February 2005 the Constitutional Council rejected an opposition appeal to declare the general amnesty unconstitutional, but ruled that the article specifically relating to Sèye's assassination did not conform with the Constitution. Wade subsequently promulgated the general amnesty law. (The three people convicted in October 1994 of Sèye's murder had been pardoned by Wade in February 2002.)

The two LD—MPT members of the Council of Ministers were dismissed and replaced with members of the PDS in March 2005, leaving AJ—PADS as the only party (other than the PDS) to retain ministerial representation from the alliance that supported Wade's presidential candidacy in 2000. The dismissals followed several months of discord between the PDS and the LD—MPT over the latter's criticism of Wade's presidency and its opposition to the amnesty legislation. In April 12 PDS deputies, who were reported to be close to former Prime Minister Seck, resigned from the majority parliamentary group, denouncing its management and a lack of consultation within the party, and formed their own group within the Assemblée nationale, the Forces de l'alternance (FAL). Amid ongoing tensions within the PDS, a further reorganization of the Government in May was interpreted as an attempt to strengthen support for the President, ahead of legislative elections due in 2006. New appointees included Awa Fall Diop, of AJ—PADS, as Minister of Relations with the Institutions, while the party's leader, Landing Savané, hitherto Minister of State, Minister of Industry and Crafts, became a Minister of State at the Presidency. Abdoulaye Diop remained Minister of the Economy and Finance, but was elevated to the position of Minister of State.

In May 2005 opposition leaders condemned the detention of Abdourahim Agne, the Secretary-General of a minor centre-left opposition party, the Parti de la réforme (PR), who was charged with threatening state security after he called for street demonstrations against the President. In mid-June Agne was provisionally released. Meanwhile, following a meeting between Wade and the 12 dissident PDS deputies, at which the President promised to address their grievances, the FAL was disbanded. Wade appointed members to a new CENA in early June. However, the opposition expressed concern at the composition of the commission, particularly the new Chairman, Moustapha Touré, whose wife was said to be an influential member of the PDS. In July the Assemblée nationale adopted legislation providing for the eventual creation of a new administrative and political capital some 150 km north-east of Dakar, near Kébémer.

Seck was questioned by police in mid-July 2005, after he was accused by President Wade of overspending on work to upgrade roads in Thiès, where he served as mayor. The former Prime Minister, whose house had been attacked in May, refuted any suggestion that he had misappropriated government funds intended for the project. Later that month Seck was formally charged with endangering national security; there was no immediate explanation of the charges, which Seck's defence lawyers claimed to be politically motivated. Widely regarded as a potential successor to Wade, Seck had made clear his presidential ambitions, although he had pledged not to stand against Wade if the President decided to seek a second term in the election due in 2007. In August 2005 the Assemblée nationale ruled that Seck and the Minister of Property, Housing and Construction, Salif Bâ, should be tried on embezzlement charges by the High Court of Justice, which is convened only to judge cases concerning offences allegedly committed by government members in the exercise of their duties. A few days later Bâ resigned from the Council of Ministers; he was replaced by Oumar Sarr in an ensuing minor reshuffle. Meanwhile, Seck and three other party officials close to the former Prime Minister were expelled from the PDS, having been accused of engaging in divisive activities. In October Seck was additionally charged with illegally sending correspondence from prison.

In December 2005 an ally of Seck, Yankhoba Diattara, who had created a new party, the Forces intégrées pour la démocratie et la liberté, in July, following his expulsion from the PDS, was sentenced to six months' imprisonment for inciting public disorder at an unauthorized demonstration in support of Seck in Thiès. He was released in March 2006, having been granted a presidential amnesty.

Despite strong resistance from opposition parties, in December 2005 the Assemblée nationale approved a proposal by Wade to extend deputies' mandates until February 2007, to allow legislative and presidential elections to be held concurrently. The President had initially announced the plan in August, stating that it would result in savings of some 7,000m. francs CFA, which would be used to rehouse people affected by recent flooding. However, opposition leaders claimed that the postponement was intended to give the PDS more time to resolve ongoing friction within the party.

Seck was released from prison in February 2006 after the High Court of Justice partially dismissed the charges of corruption and embezzlement against him owing to insufficient evidence; he had been cleared of endangering national security in the previous month. Bâ had been provisionally freed in January for health reasons. Minor government reshuffles took place in February and March. In April Seck declared his candidacy for the presidential election, and in September he formed a new political party, Rewmi (Nation). Meanwhile, several opposition parties, including the AFP, the LD—MPT, the PIT, the PR and the PS, announced the formation of the Coalition populaire pour l'alternative (CPA) to contest the legislative and presidential elections.

In April 2006 the arrest of the leaders of two opposition parties, the PIT's Dansokho and Jean-Paul Dias of the Bloc des centristes Gaïndé, provoked further political tension. Dias was accused of plotting against the authorities, following recent criticism of Wade's administration and a call for opposition politicians to ignore summonses from the criminal investigation division of the police, while Dansokho was charged with discrediting state institutions by disseminating false information, after alleging that the Government had illegally transferred state funds to foreign banks and that money looted from branches of the Banque centrale des états de l'Afrique de l'ouest in northern Côte d'Ivoire had been laundered in Senegal. Dias was released on bail in May, but rejected this measure, demanding a full exoneration. Dansokho received a two-month suspended sentence in June. Dias was arrested again in August and sentenced to one year's imprisonment, nine months of which were suspended, for spreading false information and issuing death threats against Wade and the Attorney-General; he was released on health grounds in September. Meanwhile, his son, Barthélémy Dias, leader of a movement allied to the PS, the Convergence socialiste, was also arrested in August, after he criticized Wade, and sentenced to six months' imprisonment; his sentence was reduced by two months in October, and he was pardoned by the President in the following month. Two former soldiers received five-year prison sentences in November, after they were convicted of involvement in a plot to overthrow President Wade in 2004.

In early November 2006 the Assemblée nationale narrowly adopted a constitutional amendment abolishing the requirement that a presidential candidate receiving a majority of votes in an election also secure the support of at least one-quarter of all registered voters to be elected at a first round of voting. Under the new system, winning more than 50% of the valid votes cast in the first round would be sufficient to ensure victory. A few days later the legislature also approved an increase in the number of deputies from 120 to 150. Opposition members criticized both changes. President Wade reshuffled the Council of Ministers in late November, appointing several new ministers from minor opposition parties. The CPA refused to participate in the new Government, although Abdourahim Agne, the Secretary-General of the PR, which had withdrawn from the opposition coalition in August, accepted the position of Minister of Micro-finance and Decentralized International Co-operation.

The elections to the Assemblée nationale were further postponed in January 2007, until 3 June, after the Council of State ruled that the distribution of legislative seats between constituencies had been inequitable. Opposition parties had complained that the President had allocated more seats to certain constituencies despite their populations being lower than those of others. In late January the Assemblée nationale approved the re-establishment of the Sénat; 65 of its 100 members were to be appointed by the President.

Political tensions heightened ahead of the presidential election, which was to be held, as scheduled, on 25 February 2007, despite the delay to the legislative polls. Three presidential candidates, Dieng of the PS, Niasse of the AFP and Bathily of the LD—MPT, were briefly detained in late January, along with several other opposition leaders, after police broke up an anti-Government demonstration that had earlier been banned owing to a lack of security. Several violent incidents were also reported during February, including clashes between supporters of Wade and Seck, in which several people were injured, and arson attacks on the houses of politicians. However, voting took place in largely peaceful conditions on the day of the election, which was contested by a total of 15 candidates and marked by a high turn-out of 70.6%. Wade won 55.9% of the valid votes cast, according to final results released by the Constitutional Council on 11 March, thus securing re-election without the need for a second round of voting. His closest rivals were Seck, with 14.9%, Dieng, with 13.6%, and Niasse, with 5.9%. The Council dismissed appeals by Dieng and Bathily, who had both rejected the results, alleging electoral irregularities. Meanwhile, two days after the election the AJ—PADS withdrew its five ministers from the Government, prompting a minor reshuffle. Wade was sworn in to serve a second term of office on 3 April.

Seventeen opposition parties, including the AFP, the LD—MPT, the PIT, the PS and Rewmi, grouped in an alliance styled the Front Siggil Sénégal (Restoring Dignity to Senegal), boycotted the legislative elections, after Wade refused to consider their demands for the revision of the voters' register and the replacement of the CENA with a new, independent electoral commission. The PDS-led Sopi Coalition consequently secured an overwhelming majority in the enlarged Assemblée nationale on 3 June 2007, winning 69.2% of the valid votes cast and 131 of the 150 seats (including all 90 seats determined by majority voting in constituencies). Twelve of the other 13 parties and coalitions that participated in the polls secured legislative representation, although none of them took more than three seats. The lack of effective opposition and the extremely low turn-out, of 34.7%, threatened to undermine the legitimacy of the new legislature. In mid-June the President appointed a new Prime Minister, Cheikh Hadjibou Soumaré, considered a technocrat and hitherto Minister-delegate at the Office of the Minister of State, Minister of the Economy and Finance, responsible for the Budget. The appointment of Soumaré, who was unaffiliated to any political party, was regarded as an attempt by Wade to ease tensions within the PDS over the question of who would succeed him at the end of his second, and final, term in office. Many of the other principal government posts remained unchanged.

SEPARATISM IN CASAMANCE

For many years there has been separatist sentiment among Diola communities in the southern region of Casamance, which is virtually isolated from the rest of Senegal by The Gambia. The emergence in the early 1980s of the Mouvement des forces démocratiques de la Casamance (MFDC) presented the Senegalese authorities with considerable security difficulties.

After demonstrations in the regional capital, Ziguinchor, in December 1982, several leaders of the MFDC were detained without trial. A more serious demonstration in December 1983 was suppressed by force, reportedly resulting in more than 100 deaths. Casamance was divided into two administrative regions, Ziguinchor and Kolda, in 1984. In January 1986 a leading Casamance independence campaigner was sentenced to life imprisonment, while other demonstrators received prison sentences ranging from two to 15 years. However, almost 100 detainees were provisionally released in April

1987, and a further 320 separatists reportedly benefited under the conditions of the May 1988 presidential amnesty.

The MFDC initiated an offensive in 1990 with a series of attacks in the Casamance region. Tensions escalated when military reinforcements were dispatched to the region, and in September 1990 a military Governor was appointed for Casamance. By April 1991 at least 100 people were said to have been killed as a result of violence in the region. In that month renewed action by separatists violated a truce that had apparently been negotiated by leaders of the MFDC and the new Thiam Government. In May Diouf announced the immediate release of more than 340 detainees who had been arrested in connection with the unrest in Casamance (including Fr Augustin Diamacouné Senghor, the Secretary-General and executive leader of the MFDC). This facilitated the conclusion, at talks in Guinea-Bissau, of a cease-fire agreement by representatives of the Senegalese Government and the MFDC. In June, as part of the demilitarization envisaged in the cease-fire accord, the military Governor was replaced by a civilian. An amnesty was ratified by the Assemblée nationale later in June, benefiting some 400 Casamançais (including separatists released in the previous month).

In January 1992 a peace commission, comprising government representatives and members of the MFDC, was established, with mediation by Guinea-Bissau. However, a resurgence of violence from July prompted the Government to redeploy armed forces in the region. This further exacerbated tensions and gave rise to MFDC protests that the 'remilitarization' of Casamance was in contravention of the cease-fire agreement. Evidence emerged of a split within the MFDC. The 'Front nord' and the MFDC Vice-President, Sidi Badji, appealed to the rebels to lay down their arms. The other faction, known as the 'Front sud', led by Diamacouné Senghor (himself now based in Guinea-Bissau), appeared determined to continue the armed struggle.

After an escalation of the conflict in late 1992 and early 1993, in which more than 500 people were killed, hundreds injured and tens of thousands forced to leave their homes, a new round of negotiations resulted in the signing of a cease-fire agreement, known as the Ziguinchor Accord, in July 1993. Guinea-Bissau was to act as a guarantor of the agreement, and the Government of France was to be asked to submit an historical arbitration regarding the Casamance issue. In December France issued its judgment that Casamance had not existed as an autonomous territory prior to the colonial period, and that independence for the region had been neither demanded nor considered at the time of decolonization.

From early 1995 renewed violence near the border with Guinea-Bissau indicated a re-emergence of divisions between the two factions of the MFDC. Rebels in the south were reportedly frustrated at the slow progress of the dialogue between the MFDC and the authorities, and accused the Senegalese armed forces of violating the provisions of the Ziguinchor Accord. Following the disappearance in April of four French tourists in southern Casamance, more than 1,000 élite troops were deployed in the region, and were assisted in their search by French reconnaissance aircraft. Although they failed to locate the missing tourists, in subsequent weeks the aim of the operation appeared increasingly to be to dislodge MFDC dissidents from the border region. Both factions of the MFDC denied any involvement in the apparent abduction of the tourists, who were never found. Diamacouné Senghor was placed under house arrest in Ziguinchor in late April, and the other members of the MFDC 'Political Bureau' were transported to Dakar and imprisoned. In June MFDC rebels announced an end to their cease-fire, again accusing the government forces of violating the 1993 Accord. Although Diamacouné Senghor appealed to the rebels not to break the truce, renewed violence in the south-west resulted in some 60 deaths.

In September 1995 the Government established a Commission nationale de paix (CNP). Members of the CNP travelled to Ziguinchor, where they reportedly sought a dialogue with Diamacouné Senghor and the MFDC's four other political leaders (all of whom remained under house arrest). Violence intensified, however. In December, following discussions with representatives of the Government and the CNP, Diamacouné Senghor made a televised appeal to the MFDC rebels to lay down their arms. He proposed that preliminary talks between his organization and the CNP take place in early 1996, to be followed by peace negotiations in a neutral country. The members of the MFDC 'Political Bureau' were released from house arrest in December 1995. Salif Sadio, the MFDC military leader, confirmed observance of a truce in January 1996, and preliminary discussions between the MFDC and the CNP took place in that month. After disagreements over the terms and location of further peace talks, there was a breakdown in negotiations in April. Diouf visited Ziguinchor in May (his first visit to Casamance since the 1993 election campaign), expressing his commitment to the pursuit of peace, while insisting that Casamance was an integral part of Senegal.

There was renewed optimism regarding the possible resumption of negotiations between a united MFDC and the authorities, following discussions in July 1996 between Diamacouné Senghor and Diouf's personal Chief of Staff in Ziguinchor. However, in March 1997 more than 40 rebels and two members of the armed forces were killed in clashes near the border with Guinea-Bissau. The MFDC denied that it had ended its cease-fire, stating that it would investigate these incidents. In that month four representatives of the MFDC had been permitted to travel to France, where they had spent three weeks meeting with representatives of the movement based in Europe.

While both the Senegalese authorities and the MFDC leadership appeared committed to reviving the peace process, the deaths of 25 soldiers in August 1997 near Ziguinchor prompted fears of a revival of the conflict. In September the armed forces launched a new offensive, in which rebel forces were reported to have sustained heavy losses. A further armed forces offensive in October, the largest such operation in Casamance since the 1995 cease-fire, involved as many as 3,000 soldiers and resulted in the deaths of 12 soldiers and 80 rebels in clashes near the border with Guinea-Bissau, according to Senegalese military sources. Sadio stated that the organization remained committed to the peace process, but maintained that its forces were justified in defending themselves against armed attack.

In January 1998 Diamacouné Senghor appealed to MFDC supporters to cease fighting and indicated that his organization would be prepared to abandon its demand for independence, on condition that the Government institute measures to ensure greater economic and social development in Casamance. Security operations in advance of the parliamentary elections resulted in the deaths of some 30 rebels in May, and six civilians were killed by separatists on the day before the election. Election results from 15 polling stations in Bignona were annulled by the Constitutional Council.

In February 1999 the Senegalese authorities released 123 rebels from prison, and in March serious fighting took place between security forces and rebels believed to have crossed into Casamance from Guinea-Bissau. In May the Government promised a large-scale investment programme for Casamance. However, from late May dissident elements within the MFDC, whom Diamacouné Senghor accused of seeking to sabotage the peace process, launched a series of mortar attacks near Ziguinchor.

In June 1999 talks between the various MFDC factions began in Banjul, the Gambian capital, although several leaders of military and exiled factions of the MFDC did not attend, claiming that Diamacouné Senghor was effectively a hostage of the Senegalese Government. At the meeting Léopold Sagna was confirmed as the head of the armed forces of the MFDC in place of Sadio, who was reportedly less prepared to compromise with government demands. The Senegalese authorities subsequently acceded to the MFDC conference's demand that Diamacouné Senghor be freed from house arrest, although his movements remained restricted.

In November 1999 Diamacouné Senghor agreed to recommence negotiations with the Senegalese Government, demanding, however, that the safety of MFDC negotiators be guaranteed, and that representatives of Casamançais civil society be included in the negotiations. At the meeting, held in Banjul in December, the Senegalese Government and the MFDC agreed to an immediate cease-fire and to create the conditions necessary to bring about lasting peace; the Governments of The Gambia and of Guinea-Bissau were to monitor the situation in the region; a further meeting between the two parties took place in January 2000.

Following his election as President in March 2000, Abdoulaye Wade announced that he would continue negotiations, but that his preference was to conduct direct dialogue with the MFDC. President Wade also declared that Diamacouné Senghor would henceforth be permitted full freedom of movement. In August Senegal and Guinea-Bissau announced that they would undertake joint military border patrols in order to restrict rebel activities in the region.

In November 2000 members of a peace commission, headed by the Minister of the Interior, Maj.-Gen. Mamadou Niang, and by Diamacouné Senghor, signed a joint statement that envisaged a series of official meetings between the Senegalese Government and the MFDC, the first of which would convene on 16 December. The Government simultaneously warned that legal action would be taken against any person actively promoting separatism. The discussions in mid-December were boycotted by representatives of the 'Front sud' of the MFDC, led by Ali Badji. However, a senior MFDC official present at the onset of negotiations, Alexandre Djiba (who had long been resident outside Senegal), subsequently reportedly met Ali Badji's representatives in Guinea-Bissau. The Senegalese Minister of the Armed Forces, Yoba Sambou, himself a native of Casamance, meanwhile stated that the Government preferred the rebels to unite into a single faction, so that more militant factions within the MFDC would not dispute the peace talks. As a result of renewed unrest, however, the MFDC postponed a proposed meeting in Banjul, to be held in January 2001, which had been intended to establish a common position between its various factions.

The overwhelming support in Casamance for the new Constitution, which was endorsed by 96% of voters in the region at the referendum in January 2001, prompted Wade to announce that Casamance had definitively voted to remain part of Senegal. In mid-January the Guinea-Bissau armed forces reportedly destroyed all the Casamance rebel bases in that country, in response to clashes between rival MFDC factions there. Continued unrest in the region south-west of Ziguinchor further delayed the signature of a cease-fire agreement, originally intended to take place at the meeting of mid-December, which had been rescheduled to occur in Dakar in early February.

In February 2001 Diamacouné Senghor announced that, in order to accelerate the peace process, several senior members of the MFDC, including Sidi Badji and Djiba, had been removed from their positions. However, Sidi Badji, who had served as the military affairs adviser to Diamacouné Senghor, rejected the legitimacy of his dismissal. Also in mid-February, in what was reportedly the most serious attack on civilian targets in Casamance for several years, separatist rebels killed some 13 civilians in an ambush. Both Sidi Badji and Diamacouné Senghor denied any knowledge of their supporters' involvement and condemned the attack. In early March Diamacouné Senghor accused Sadio of being implicated in the recent killings of civilians; in mid-March the Senegalese Government issued an international arrest warrant for Sadio, who had recently been removed from Guinea-Bissau, and announced that a reward of some US $200,000 would be paid for his capture.

In mid-March 2001 Niang and Diamacouné Senghor signed a cease-fire agreement at a meeting in Ziguinchor, which provided for the release of detainees, the return of refugees, the removal of landmines (which had been utilized in the region since 1998) and for economic aid to reintegrate rebels and to ameliorate the infrastructure of Casamance. Some 16 prisoners were released several days later. The Gambian Government issued a communiqué in mid-March, in which it promised to prevent armed rebel groups from operating on Gambian territory; it was suspected that the renewed violence had been co-ordinated by groups based in The Gambia. Later in March Niang and Diamacouné Senghor signed a further agreement, which provided for the disarmament of rebel groups and the confinement to barracks of military forces in Casamance. In April Wade and Sambou participated in negotiations with Diamacouné Senghor, at which other MFDC leaders, including Sidi Badji, were also present. In early May fighting was reported on the border with Guinea-Bissau between separatist forces and troops from Guinea-Bissau, reportedly in response to MFDC raids on villages in the region.

As a result of the renewed conflict, Diamacouné Senghor announced, in May 2001, that a proposed reconciliation forum, intended to unite the various factions of the MFDC, had been postponed indefinitely, and a number of members of the movement, including Djiba, were reportedly expelled. None the less, Diamacouné Senghor and Sidi Badji attended a meeting convened by the Gambian Government in Banjul in June, in an attempt to overcome the impasse. As tensions between factions within the MFDC intensified, with further clashes reported in June and July, Diamacouné Senghor was removed from the position of Secretary-General of the MFDC in August, at the much-delayed reconciliation forum, and appointed as honorary President. Jean-Marie François Biagui, who had previously been involved in the French-based section of the MFDC, became Secretary-General and de facto leader. Sidi Badji, who continued to question the tactics of Diamacouné Senghor, was appointed as the organization's head of military affairs. Biagui not only demonstrated considerable reluctance to play a leadership role, but was also apparently unable to prevent Sidi Badji, who was reputed to have support from the authorities in The Gambia, from becoming the dominant force in the movement.

Despite these personnel changes within the MFDC, President Wade met Diamacouné Senghor at the presidential palace in Dakar in September 2001; both leaders reiterated the importance of implementing the cease-fire agreement. In response to this meeting, it was reported that the new leadership of the MFDC had suspended all further negotiations with the Government. Following further attacks by rebels, Biagui resigned as Secretary-General in early November. Sidi Badji was announced as Biagui's successor, in an acting capacity, although Diamacouné Senghor rejected this appointment. In November MFDC rebels launched numerous attacks on civilians in Casamance. Violence in the province intensified in December, and several civilians were killed during attacks on villages. In an attempt to quell the rebellion, Diamacouné Senghor appointed an envoy, his nephew, Laurent Diamacouné, to seek negotiations with Sidi Badji, but with only limited success. In mid-December Diamacouné Senghor's position was further undermined, when an episcopal conference declared that his leadership of a movement that was using armed struggle to attain its ends was incompatible with his role as a Roman Catholic priest.

In mid-January 2002 Niang held talks with Diamacouné Senghor and Sidi Badji, although no date for the resumption of peace negotiations with the Government was forthcoming. In March further incidents of looting and robbery by MFDC militants were reported. In late March mediators from The Gambia and Guinea-Bissau met with MFDC representatives, with the intention of establishing a timetable for the resumption of peace talks. Following continued fighting, in which several civilians were killed, some 9,000 Casamançais were reported to have fled to The Gambia by the end of June.

In August 2002, following a joint declaration signed by Diamacouné Senghor and Sidi Badji urging the resumption of peace talks between the rebels and the Government, Wade appointed an official delegation, chaired by the Second Vice-President of the Assemblée nationale and President of Ziguinchor Regional Council, Abdoulaye Faye, and including among its membership Niang and Sambou, to undertake negotiations with the MFDC. Meanwhile, the holding of an intra-Casamance conference, in early September, appeared to indicate a decline in support for separatist aspirations, as the conference produced a declaration, signed by representatives of 10 ethnic groups resident in the region, in favour of a 'definitive peace in Casamance', and which referred to the region as 'belonging to the great and single territory of Senegal'. Moreover, the absence from the meeting of the MFDC faction loyal to Sidi Badji appeared to refute reports that the various wings of the MFDC had effectively reunited. In mid-September a further meeting between Faye and Niang, representing the Government, and Diamacouné Senghor and Sidi Badji, for the MFDC, was held in Ziguinchor. In late

September five civilians, including the brother of Sambou, were killed in an attack attributed to separatist rebels north of Ziguinchor. The internal disunity of the MFDC was emphasized in mid-October, when Biagui publicly demanded forgiveness from the people of Casamance and Senegal for the actions of the organization, and acknowledged that the MFDC was responsible for causing suffering to the populace; this statement was emphatically rejected by Sidi Badji. In spite of further discussions between the government commission and Diamacouné Senghor and Sidi Badji in January 2003, intermittent conflict and banditry continued to be reported in Casamance in early 2003, although by the end of April all members of the MFDC who had been imprisoned on charges other than murder had been released on bail.

In early May 2003 President Wade, meeting with a delegation of MFDC leaders, including Diamacouné Senghor, at the Republican Palace in Dakar, announced that several substantive measures towards the normalization of the political and economic situation in Casamance were to be implemented, notably major infrastructural projects and the rehabilitation of damaged villages. The Assemblée nationale was to consider an amnesty for all those implicated in crimes related to the conflict, following a convention of the MFDC, to be held, at an unspecified date, in Guinea-Bissau, prior to the conclusion of final peace talks between the MFDC and the Government. Wade also announced that the Government intended to accede to a further MFDC demand, by dismissing those implicated in the failed attempt to rescue the passengers of the stricken *Joola* ferry in September 2002 (see above), and arranging the provision of a replacement for the vessel, which had provided a key transport link between the Casamance region and Dakar. Mine-clearing operations, to involve both regular members of the army and former rebel fighters, were also to commence. (Sidi Badji had been a notable absentee from the delegation present at the meeting; his absence was attributed to ill health.) Meanwhile, Diamacouné Senghor reiterated on several occasions that the Casamance conflict had concluded.

In late May 2003 Diamacouné Senghor announced that the MFDC convention, comprising 460 participants from the various factions of the organization, was to be held in Guinea-Bissau in early June, although it was reported that factions opposed to the proposed peace agreement would refuse to attend the gathering. Following the death of Sidi Badji, from natural causes, in late May, the convention was postponed, initially to July. However, the Guinea-Bissau authorities announced that they would be unable to provide sufficient guarantees of security for participants, and the meeting was again postponed, until October, when the gathering was to be held in Ziguinchor. On this occasion, which was not attended by hardline factions of the MFDC loyal to Djiba, both Diamacouné Senghor and Biagui issued statements confirming that the conflict had ended, and announced that what was termed the emancipation of Casamance did not, as a matter of course, necessarily entail its independence from Senegal. Following the restoration of peace in Casamance, it was anticipated that some 15,000 displaced persons would return to their home villages in the Ziguinchor administrative region, while demining operations commenced in July. In March 2004 Diamacouné Senghor removed Biagui from the post of Secretary-General of the MFDC.

In April 2004, after many months of relative peace in Casamance, it was reported that three members of the armed forces had been killed and a further five injured while carrying out mine-clearing operations in Guidel, some 18 km south-east of Ziguinchor, in an attack attributed to the MFDC. The MFDC held a convention in Ziguinchor in May, at which it proposed the cantonment of its combatants while observing a unilateral one-month cease-fire, in return for the withdrawal of government troops deployed in Casamance since 1982. In July the Assemblée nationale adopted legislation providing for an amnesty for all MFDC combatants; however, MFDC leaders claimed that their members had done nothing from which they required amnesty and urged the Government to engage in negotiations with the organization. At a rally held later that month MFDC leaders reiterated their demand for the withdrawal of government troops from Casamance.

In September 2004 delegates at a general assembly of the MFDC dismissed Diamacouné Senghor as leader of the movement, designating him honorary President, as in mid-2001, and reappointed Biagui as Secretary-General and *de facto* leader. Biagui announced his intention to transform the MFDC into a political party, which would seek the establishment of a federal system of government, rather than full independence for Casamance. However, the MFDC remained divided. Its armed wing, known as Atika, rejected Biagui's proposals, insisting that independence remained the aim of the movement. Furthermore, a call by Diamacouné Senghor for an MFDC general assembly to be held at the end of November in an attempt at reconciliation was rejected by others in the political wing, while Abdoulaye Diédhiou, the head of Atika, claimed that he was the sole legitimate leader of the movement on the grounds that he had the support of its fighters. Nevertheless, the Government continued to regard Diamacouné Senghor as the MFDC's leader.

On 30 December 2004 a general peace accord was signed at a ceremony in Ziguinchor by the recently appointed Minister of the Interior, Ousmane Ngom, on behalf of the Government, and by Diamacouné Senghor, representing the MFDC. However, at least three factions of the MFDC—Atika, the 'Front nord' and more hardline elements of the diaspora based in France, led by Mamadou Nkrumah Sané—refused to sign or participate in the implementation of the agreement, which provided for a cease-fire, to be followed by negotiations on political and economic development. Under the terms of the accord, the MFDC committed itself to disarming its fighters, who would be granted amnesty by the Government and integrated into paramilitary units on a voluntary basis. President Wade, who attended the ceremony, pledged that 80,000m. francs CFA from the Government and donor agencies would finance reconstruction and development programmes in Casamance. Negotiations aimed at achieving a definitive resolution of the conflict in Casamance were opened by Prime Minister Sall on 1 February 2005 in the central town of Foundiougne, some 160 km south-east of Dakar, but were boycotted by Biagui and Diédhiou, who reportedly favoured further dialogue within the MFDC before engaging in talks with the Government. Both sides agreed to establish joint technical commissions to address reconstruction, economic and social development, and disarmament, demobilization and demining.

In June 2005 Diamacouné Senghor appointed Ansoumana Badji, formerly the MFDC's representative in Portugal, as Secretary-General of the movement; Badji stated that he aimed to persuade as many MFDC members as possible to join the peace process. Biagui rejected the legitimacy of Badji's appointment. In March 2006, however, Diamacouné Senghor dismissed Badji as Secretary-General of the MFDC, reappointing Biagui to that position. Meanwhile, in mid-2005 a number of attacks in Casamance were variously attributed to dissident members of the MFDC or to bandits. In an interview broadcast by the private radio station Sud FM in October, Salif Sadio, who had not participated in the recent peace negotiations, stated his intention to continue fighting for Casamance's independence. (The broadcast led to the temporary closure of Sud FM by the authorities.) Stalled talks between the MFDC and the Government were scheduled to resume in December, but were postponed at the request of the movement, which was attempting to reconcile its various factions. One year after the signing of the peace accord, the number of armed attacks in Casamance was reported to be increasing. In mid-March 2006 fierce fighting erupted in the border region with Guinea-Bissau between rival MFDC factions, with fighters led by Ismaïla Magne Dieme and César Badiate targeting territory held by Sadio and his supporters. The Guinea-Bissau armed forces subsequently intervened against Sadio's faction, which had established bases in northern Guinea-Bissau (see below), and by late April Sadio's forces had been expelled from Guinea-Bissau. Factional fighting continued in Casamance, however, and in mid-June it was reported that Sadio had seized control of several villages along the Gambian border from Dieme. The Senegalese armed forces mounted an offensive against Sadio's faction in mid-August, prompting an estimated 4,500 Senegalese to cross into The Gambia to escape the unrest, while several thousand others were thought to have been internally displaced within Casamance. The army took control of Sadio's main base in early October, although further clashes followed. Diamacouné Senghor died in January 2007 in a French military hospital; it remained to be seen what effect, if any, his death would have on the situation in Casamance. Later in January, following clashes between Senegalese government troops and rebels belonging to Badiate's faction near the border with Guinea-Bissau, more than 100 Senegalese were reported to have fled to northern Guinea-Bissau. Further fighting was reported between rival MFDC factions near the Gambian border in May.

REGIONAL AND INTERNATIONAL RELATIONS

From 1989 Senegal's traditional policy of peaceful coexistence with neighbouring countries was severely undermined by a series of regional disputes. Senegal's relations with both The Gambia and Guinea-Bissau were dominated by issues relating to the conflict in Casamance, which also led large numbers of displaced persons to seek refuge in neighbouring countries.

Senegal maintains good relations with France, which maintains a military presence in Senegal, and with the USA, which has provided training for Senegalese troops involved in peace-keeping missions. The French President, Jacques Chirac, paid a two-day state visit to Senegal in February 2005, his first since Wade's election to the presidency in 2000. In September 2006 the French Minister of State, Minister of the Interior and Land Management, Nicolas Sarkozy, and his Senegalese counterpart, Ousmane Ngom, signed an agreement in Dakar aimed at easing visa regulations for students and business people from both countries, while facilitating the repatriation of illegal immigrants; France also pledged to provide Senegal with €2.5m. in development aid. Following his election as French President in May 2007, Sarkozy returned to Senegal in July, when he offered to assist Senegal in organizing the trial of Hissène Habré (see below). Closer relations with the USA were also established from the late 1990s. In 1998 US President Bill Clinton visited Senegal and met President Diouf. In July 2003 Senegal and the USA signed an agreement, in accordance with which both countries undertook not to extradite the other's nationals to the proposed International Criminal Court; in that month President Wade met US President George W. Bush in Dakar.

In October 2005 Senegal severed diplomatic links with Taiwan, which had been maintained since 1996, in order to restore relations with the People's Republic of China. Senegal and China subsequently exchanged ambassadors, and ties were further strengthened during a six-day state visit by Wade to China in late June 2006, when several bilateral agreements were signed.

Following an influx of illegal immigrants into Spain's Canary Islands from Senegal (and other West African countries), in June 2006 the Spanish and Senegalese Governments agreed to co-operate on the establishment of a system of legal Senegalese emigration in an effort to discourage illegal migration. The agreement eased tensions that had arisen a few days earlier when the Senegalese Government had ordered a halt to the repatriation of its nationals from the Canaries after a first group of returning migrants claimed to have been mistreated. Later that month, at a meeting hosted by Senegal, officials from more than 50 African and European countries outlined a joint plan aimed at combating people-trafficking and promoting economic development to encourage would-be migrants to remain in Africa. The proposals were endorsed by a conference held in Morocco in July. In August Senegal and Spain agreed to conduct joint patrols of Senegal's coast in an attempt to curb illegal migration. The repatriation of Senegalese migrants from the Canaries resumed in the following month. During a visit to Dakar by the Spanish Prime Minister, José Luis Rodríguez Zapatero, in December, bilateral agreements were signed on increasing political and economic co-operation and on promoting legal migration. Zapatero also confirmed an earlier commitment to provide €20m. in funding for projects to create employment opportunities within Senegal.

Senegal is a significant contributor to peace-keeping activities world-wide. In early 2003 it was announced that Senegal was to contribute some 650 troops to the Economic Community of West African States (ECOWAS) military mission in Côte d'Ivoire (ECOMICI); Senegalese troops also participated in the UN Operation in Côte d'Ivoire (UNOCI) that assumed the responsibilities of ECOMICI from April 2004. Meanwhile, in August 2003 some 260 Senegalese troops were dispatched to serve in the ECOWAS Mission in Liberia (ECOMIL), which was replaced by the UN Mission in Liberia (UNMIL) in October. In August 2005 Senegal deployed 538 soldiers in the Darfur region of western Sudan as part of the enhanced African Union (AU) Mission in Sudan. However, in April 2007 the Senegalese Government threatened to withdraw its contingent from Sudan, following the death of five of its troops, citing the inadequate resources of the AU to ensure the security of its peace-keepers.

President Wade's assumption of power in 2000 was marked by a rise in Senegalese diplomatic influence in West Africa and across the continent. As one of a core group of recently elected democratic leaders, Wade campaigned for greater Western financial support for Africa. During 2001 his Government's Omega plan for African development was subsumed within the New Partnership for Africa's Development. At the AU summit held in Accra, Ghana, in July 2007, Wade emerged as a strong supporter of increased political integration within Africa, and most notably the formation of a single government for the continent, an initiative proposed by the Libyan leader, Col Muammar al-Qaddafi.

In July 2006 the AU decided that Hissène Habré, President of Chad during 1982–90, should be prosecuted in Senegal (where he had fled after being deposed in 1990) over alleged human rights abuses committed during his presidency. Earlier attempts to prosecute Habré in Senegal had failed, prompting his alleged victims to seek his extradition to stand trial in Belgium under its universal jurisdiction law. The Senegalese Government had referred Habré's case to the AU in November 2005, after a Senegalese court declared that it was not competent to rule on a Belgian extradition request. In November 2006 the Senegalese Government announced its intention to establish an inter-governmental commission to conduct preparations for Habré's trial.

Relations with Mauritania

In April 1989 the deaths of two Senegalese farmers, following a disagreement with Mauritanian livestock-breeders regarding grazing rights in the border region between the two countries, precipitated a crisis that was fuelled by long-standing ethnic and economic rivalries. Mauritanian nationals residing in Senegal were attacked and their businesses ransacked (the retail trade in Senegal had hitherto been dominated by an expatriate community of mainly light-skinned Mauritanians, estimated to number about 300,000), and Senegalese nationals in Mauritania suffered similar attacks. By early May it was believed that several hundred people, mostly Senegalese, had been killed. Operations to repatriate nationals of both countries were undertaken with international assistance, and Senegal granted asylum to Afro-Mauritanians who feared official persecution. None the less, diplomatic relations were severed in August. Renewed outbreaks of violence were reported in late 1989, while in early 1990 attempts at mediation were thwarted by military engagements in the border region. In March 1991 several deaths were reported to have resulted from a military engagement, on Senegalese territory, between members of the two countries' armed forces, following an incursion by Senegalese troops into Mauritania.

Diplomatic links, at ambassadorial level, were restored in April 1992, and the process of reopening the border began in May. None the less, the issues of border demarcation and the status of Mauritanian refugees in Senegal remained to be resolved. In December 1994, however, the Governments of Senegal and Mauritania agreed new co-operation measures, including efforts to facilitate the free movement of goods and people between the two countries. In January 1995, moreover, the Governments of Senegal, Mauritania and Mali undertook to co-operate in resolving joint border issues and in combating extremism, the smuggling of arms and drugs-trafficking. In October the Mauritanian authorities gave assurances that Mauritanian refugees in Senegal (estimated to number some

66,000) were free to return home. In January 1996, none the less, several hundred Mauritanian refugees took part in protests to denounce the Mauritanian authorities' arrangements for their return and to demand that their repatriation be organized under the auspices of the office of the UN High Commissioner for Refugees (UNHCR). However, the re-establishment of good relations with Mauritania remained a priority of the Senegalese Government. Thus, in May 1999 the two countries signed an agreement on the joint exploitation of fisheries, while in August Senegal, Mauritania and Mali agreed to establish a joint operational force in order to combat the ongoing insecurity in the border region.

In early June 2000 a new dispute broke out between Mauritania and Senegal, after the former accused the latter of threatening its interests by relaunching an irrigation programme in the fossil valleys area of the River Senegal. Claiming that the project would deprive its own lands of water, Mauritania instructed Senegalese nationals to leave the country within 15 days. Of the 345,000 Senegalese resident in Mauritania, some 25,000 returned home before the order was rescinded on 10 June. Wade immediately visited Nouakchott, the Mauritanian capital, and announced the cancellation of the irrigation project. However, following renewed negotiations, the visit of President Maawiya Ould Sid'Ahmed Taya of Mauritania to Dakar in April 2001, on the occasion of the 41st anniversary of the independence of Senegal, was widely regarded as indicating an improvement in relations between the countries. Presidents Taya and Wade again met in July 2003, when negotiations were conducted on a range of bilateral and international issues; Wade reiterated his support for Taya's administration, following an attempted *coup d'état* in Mauritania in the previous month. The extradition of one of the suspected coup plotters from Senegal to Mauritania was also interpreted as an indication of improved relations between the countries, as was the Mauritanian Government's decision to accord 270 temporary fishing licences to Senegalese fishermen in June 2004. In January 2006 Wade became the first foreign Head of State to visit Mauritania since the overthrow of Taya's regime in August 2005. Wade and Col Ely Ould Mohamed Vall, who had assumed the leadership of Mauritania, as President of a self-styled Military Council for Justice and Democracy, pledged to enhance co-operation in a number of areas, announcing that their Governments would henceforth hold regular joint committee meetings, and Wade expressed his support for the transitional process under way in Mauritania. Vall paid a reciprocal visit to Senegal in March 2006. In the following month the two countries signed an agreement regulating the seasonal migration of Mauritanian cattle into Senegal, an issue that had caused significant disputes in the past, notably in 1989. According to provisional UNHCR figures, 19,630 Mauritanian refugees remained in Senegal at the end of 2006. Following democratic elections and a return to civilian rule in Mauritania, in April 2007 the newly elected President, Sidi Mohammed Ould Cheikh Abdellahi, urged the refugees in Senegal to return to Mauritania, requesting assistance from UNHCR to facilitate their repatriation.

Relations with Guinea-Bissau

A dispute with Guinea-Bissau regarding the sovereignty of a maritime zone that is believed to contain reserves of petroleum, together with valuable fishing grounds, has caused tensions between the two countries. In July 1989 an international arbitration panel (to which the issue had been referred in 1985) judged the waters to be part of Senegalese territory. However, the Government of Guinea-Bissau refused to accept the judgment, and referred the matter to the International Court of Justice (ICJ) in The Hague, Netherlands. Moreover, the Government of Guinea-Bissau accused Senegal of repeated violations of both Guinea-Bissau's maritime borders and airspace during April 1990. Meetings between representatives of the two countries culminated, in May, in the signing of an accord whereby each country undertook to refrain from harbouring organizations hostile to the other and to maintain troops at a 'reasonable distance' from the border. In November 1991 the ICJ ruled that the existing delimitation of the maritime border remained valid, and Senegal and Guinea-Bissau signed a treaty recognizing this judgment in February 1993.

Although Guinea-Bissau (together with France) played an important role in the formulation of the 1991 cease-fire agreement between the Senegalese Government and the MFDC, relations were again strained in late 1992. In December an offensive by the Senegalese armed forces against MFDC strongholds close to the border with Guinea-Bissau resulted in the deaths of two nationals of that country. The Guinea-Bissau Government formally protested at Senegalese violations of its airspace. Although Senegal apologized for the incident, a further violation was reported in January 1993. None the less, Guinea-Bissau was again active in efforts to bring about a new cease-fire agreement between Senegal and the MFDC in mid-1993. In October of that year, moreover, the two countries signed a major 20-year agreement regarding the joint exploitation and management of fishing and petroleum resources in their maritime zones.

Renewed operations by the Senegalese military against MFDC rebels in southern Casamance, from early 1995, again affected relations with Guinea-Bissau. In April Guinea-Bissau temporarily deployed as many as 500 troops near the border with Senegal, as part of attempts to locate four missing French tourists. The October 1993 treaty on the joint exploration of maritime wealth was ratified in December 1995: fishing resources were to be shared equally between the two countries, while Senegal was to benefit from a majority share (85%) of petroleum deposits. A joint agency for the management of common resources was formally established during a visit to Guinea-Bissau by President Diouf in February 1996.

In January 1998 it was announced that the authorities in Guinea-Bissau had intercepted a consignment of armaments destined for MFDC rebels and that some 15 officers of the Guinea-Bissau armed forces had been arrested and suspended from duty, including their leader, Brig. (later Gen.) Ansumane Mané. In June, however, troops loyal to Mané rebelled, and civil war broke out in Guinea-Bissau. Senegalese troops intervened in support of the forces loyal to the Government, and were subsequently reinforced to number more than 2,500. Senegal's involvement became the subject of controversy, with Guinea-Bissau refugees accusing Senegalese troops of brutality against civilians. In July the Guinea-Bissau insurgents signed a cease-fire agreement with their Government, having apparently abandoned their previous pre-condition that foreign troops must leave the country before negotiations could take place. Under the terms of an agreement brokered by ECOWAS in November 1998, the final 800 Senegalese soldiers withdrew from Guinea-Bissau in March 1999. Following the overthrow of the President of Guinea-Bissau, João Bernardo Vieira, in a *coup d'état* in May, Senegal declared itself 'surprised and disappointed' by events.

Tensions between the two countries resurfaced in April 2000, when an armed group, reportedly composed of members of the MFDC operating from within Guinea-Bissau, attacked a Senegalese border post. In late April the common border was temporarily closed. In May Wade stated that he feared the prospect of an invasion by forces from Guinea-Bissau, calling on France to supply Senegal with military equipment in order to strengthen the country's position, and requesting that UN military observers be sent to the border area. The Government of Guinea-Bissau continued to deny supporting the MFDC rebels. In August the revision was announced of the agreement on the joint exploitation of petroleum resources; henceforth Guinea-Bissau was to receive 20% rather than 15% of the revenue generated. Relations between Senegal and Guinea-Bissau improved significantly following the killing of the dissident army commander Ansumane Mané during a failed coup attempt in Guinea-Bissau in November 2000, and Guinea-Bissau forces launched a new offensive against MFDC rebel bases in early 2001. Following a subsequent period of transitional rule in Guinea-Bissau, during the first half of 2005 President Wade assumed a mediatory role between rival candidates contesting a presidential election in that country in June and July of that year. Vieira was returned to the presidency of Guinea-Bissau in the elections.

In March 2006, following increasing instability along its border with Senegal, as rival factions of the MFDC clashed (see above), the Guinea-Bissau armed forces launched an offensive against bases established by Salif Sadio around the Guinea-Bissau town of São Domingos. Fighting between Guinea-Bissau troops and MFDC rebels continued until late April, leading to the displacement of several thousand Guinea-Bissau civilians, many of whom fled across the border to Ziguinchor. In January 2007 Guinea-Bissau deployed additional troops in its border area with Senegal, in response to reported clashes between Senegalese troops and forces belonging to César Badiate's MFDC faction.

Relations with The Gambia

In August 1981, following a *coup d'état* in The Gambia, President Diouf despatched Senegalese troops to restore the deposed Gambian President, Sir Dawda Jawara, to power. Senegalese forces were subsequently asked to remain, and Diouf and Jawara swiftly established a confederation of the two states, with co-ordinated policies in defence, foreign affairs and economic and financial matters. The agreement establishing the Senegambian Confederation came into effect in February 1982. Diouf was designated permanent President of a Joint Council of Ministers, and a Confederal Assembly was established. However, The Gambia resisted attempts by Senegal to proceed towards the full political and economic integration of the two countries.

In August 1989 the Diouf Government announced the withdrawal of 1,400 Senegalese troops from The Gambia, apparently in protest at a request by Jawara that his country be accorded more power within the Senegambian confederal agreement. Later in that month Diouf stated that, in view of The Gambia's reluctance to proceed towards full political and economic integration with Senegal, the functions of the Confederation should be suspended, and the two countries should endeavour to formulate more attainable co-operation accords. The Confederation was formally dissolved in September. In January 1991 the foreign ministers of the two countries signed a bilateral treaty of friendship and co-operation. However, Senegal's abrupt, unilateral decision to close the Senegalese–Gambian border in September 1993, apparently to reduce smuggling between the two countries, again strained relations. Negotiations subsequently took place between representatives of Senegal and The Gambia, in an attempt to minimize the adverse effects of the closure on The Gambia's regional trading links.

Following the *coup d'état* in The Gambia in July 1994, and the assumption of power by Yahya A. J. J. Jammeh, Jawara was initially granted asylum in Senegal. Despite the presence in Senegal of prominent opponents of the Gambian military regime, in January 1996 the two countries signed an agreement aimed at increasing bilateral trade and at minimizing cross-border smuggling. A further accord, concluded in April 1997, was to facilitate the trans-border movement of goods destined for re-export. In June the two countries agreed to take joint measures to combat insecurity, illegal immigration and trafficking in arms and illegal drugs. In early 1998 President Jammeh offered to act as a mediator between the Senegalese Government and the MFDC (see above) and subsequently hosted regular meetings between the Government and the MFDC.

None the less, intermittent disputes relating to transportation issues between the two countries have occurred, and in July 2002 the Gambian Secretary of State for Foreign Affairs, Blaise Baboucar Jagne, was prevented from entering Senegal by demonstrators protesting at the recent increase in fees for the transportation of foreign-registered vehicles on the ferry across the Gambia river, a principal trade route from the south of Senegal; the increase was revoked later in the month, following a meeting between Senegalese and Gambian officials. Tensions over transportation were renewed in August 2005 when The Gambia Ports Authority doubled the cost of using the ferry across the Gambia river. Many Senegalese lorry drivers refused to pay the increased fare, opting instead to take a long detour around The Gambia (aided by fuel subsidies granted by the Senegalese Government), while others blockaded the main border crossings between the two countries. Despite a 15% reduction in the ferry tariff in October, Senegalese trade union leaders insisted that the blockade would continue. Later that month, however, at talks mediated by President Olusegun Obasanjo of Nigeria, under the aegis of ECOWAS, Jammeh agreed to reverse the price increase that took effect in August pending further consultations, while Wade pledged to end the blockade of the border. Agreement was also reached on the construction of a bridge over the Gambia river. In December the Gambian and Senegalese Governments decided that the bridge project should be a regional initiative, to be undertaken by the Gambia River Basin Development Organization. Plans for the establishment of a permanent secretariat for bilateral co-operation were also announced.

Bilateral relations were again strained in March 2006, however, following allegations of Senegalese complicity in an abortive coup in The Gambia. One of those arrested in connection with the plot reportedly claimed to have been instructed by the alleged leader of the coup (who was believed to have fled to Senegal) to liaise with the Senegalese embassy in The Gambia. The Senegalese Government denied any involvement in the plot, which it condemned, and recalled its ambassador to The Gambia for consultations; a new ambassador was appointed in June.

Economy

RICHARD SYNGE

Based on an earlier article by EDITH HODGKINSON

Senegal retains some of the economic advantages derived from its leading position in pre-independence French West Africa. In 2005, according to the World Bank, Senegal's gross national income (GNI) was equivalent to US $700 per head, one of the highest levels in West Africa. Economic performance has been improving significantly in recent years. The economy responded positively to the 1994 devaluation of the CFA franc and the accompanying government reform programme, with real annual GDP growth rates averaging 4.1% per year in 1995–2006, according to the African Development Bank (ADB). In 2003 real GDP growth was recorded as 6.7%, and the revised estimates for 2004 and 2005 were 5.6% and 5.5%, respectively, although growth fell back to an estimated 3.3% in 2006. Inflation has remained low, at only 0.5% in 2004, 1.7% in 2005 and an estimated 1.9% in 2006. The major sources of foreign exchange—tourism, fishing and phosphates—initially responded particularly favourably to the change in relative prices and the liberalization of factor markets, although new constraints on performance in these sectors have arisen, and prospects for agro-industry and new mining ventures have begun to improve. Improvements in the country's electricity supply and transport infrastructure are regarded as central to the country's long-term economic prospects. Abdoulaye Wade, who was elected President in March 2000, indicated his intention to continue the process of economic reform and liberalization begun by his predecessor. The IMF has approved the Government's record of macro-economic performance and has extended the annual arrangements of its Poverty Reduction and Growth Facility (PRGF), although the Government has asked for this to be replaced by a Policy Support Instrument (PSI), which would continue close monitoring but without direct financial support. The Fund and other donors have also provided assistance under the initiative for heavily indebted poor countries (HIPC—see below).

The Wade Government declared its commitment to liberalizing markets, both by transforming the peasant economy into a private-sector-driven centre of agro-industry and services and by capitalizing on Senegal's relative proximity to Europe and the USA, in order to make the country a regional trading centre. The Government has also sought to attract private capital, in order to develop infrastructure, including a new international airport, road networks, ports, irrigation and an afforestation scheme to combat desert encroachment. There has, however, been considerable delay in achieving liberalization of the electricity sector (see below). During 2007 both the IMF and the World Bank were critical of poor fiscal management and new hindrances to private sector development.

Senegal's economy is vulnerable to competition in almost all areas of productive activity, and remains dependent on comparatively large inflows of foreign financial assistance. The agricultural base of the economy has been eroded by periodic droughts and the gradual desertification of large tracts of land. The agricultural sector's contribution to GDP declined from around 24% in 1970 to 17.0% in 2004. Following a substantial drift of population from rural to urban areas, approximately 44% of the country's total population is urban, of whom about one-half live in the overcrowded Dakar region. According to official statistics, poverty levels were reduced between 1994 and 2002, with those living below the poverty line falling from 68% to 57% of the total population. The Casamance region has the highest poverty levels, and Dakar has the lowest. Agriculture continues to be the predominant sector for employment, engaging some 72.8% of the total labour force in 2003.

Fishing, phosphate mining and tourism have developed to overtake groundnuts and groundnut products as the principal sources of foreign exchange. The importance of these sectors was further enhanced as a result of the devaluation of the CFA franc in January 1994, although many of Senegal's more import-dependent industrial activities have suffered payments difficulties. The phosphates industry, in particular, encountered severe financial difficulties and disruption of production in 2006. Since 1995 the Government has pursued a policy of gradually dismantling artificial protection barriers and promoting market-orientated incentives, in the face of considerable resistance from entrenched interest groups (particularly trade unions and organized élites). This was intensified in 2003 following the introduction of a programme supported by the World Bank that was designed to encourage new private investment and to reform a wide range of fiscal policies and incentives. In January 2004 there were important revisions to the 1987 Investment Code as well as to the tax regime, including a reduction in the corporate tax rate from 35% to 33% of profits.

Following the 1994 devaluation of the currency, Senegal received significant financial support from the IMF, the World Bank, France and other external donors. The Government undertook to accelerate its economic reforms, including the elimination of subsidies on some food commodities and the privatization of agricultural marketing, industrial units and some public utilities, such as the supply of drinking water. An ambitious privatization programme was adopted for the period 1994–97, with 22 major state-owned companies offered for sale and restructuring. A further round of privatization commenced in 2003.

AGRICULTURE AND FISHING

The principal food crops are millet, sorghum, rice and maize. Groundnuts are the leading cash crop, but the area under cultivation has declined in recent years, and output fluctuated somewhat. There has been a long-term shift from cash- to food-crop cultivation. In an attempt to stimulate marketing through official channels, groundnut purchasing was opened to private traders in 1985/86 and producer prices were increased sharply. After a decline in production in the early 1990s, groundnut production has fluctuated greatly, exceeding 1m. metric tons in both 1999 and 2000, falling sharply to 260,723 tons in 2002 before recovering to 440,709 tons in 2003 and to 602,621 tons in 2004, with a similar level of output estimated in 2005 and 2006. The Government has sought to link producer prices more closely to international price trends and, as part of structural adjustment efforts, has almost abandoned its policy of providing inputs (such as seed and fertilizer) to farmers of groundnuts and other agricultural products. The Government announced its intention of withdrawing public agencies from the collection and transportation of nuts and of introducing a factory-gate delivery system. However, the privatization of the groundnut-oil producer, the Société Nationale de Commercialisation des Oléagineux du Sénégal (SONACOS), was delayed by the failure of the private sector to purchase national output in 2002, at least partly as a result of a collapse in international groundnut prices, which caused financial losses to the company. After it received financial support from the European Union (EU), the sale of SONACOS to a private company was agreed in December 2004. However, despite liberalization, the Government has tended to overrule the body in charge of establishing the producer price each season, Comité National Interprofessionel de l'Arachide (CNIA), and has insisted that higher prices be paid to farmers. Meanwhile, heavy import taxes have been imposed on refined vegetable oils in order to try to protect SONACOS' falling share of the domestic market in edible oils. In February 2006, however, the World Bank stated that these taxes contravened an agreement between the Government and the Bretton Woods institutions, and modifications were made to the taxation regime; in 2007 IMF directors were still urging the authorities to eliminate the tax protecting the import operations of SONACOS.

The Government has attempted to reduce dependence on groundnuts by diversifying cash and food crops, in particular by expanding cotton, rice, sugar and market-garden produce. Production of unginned cotton rose rapidly, from only 460 metric tons in 1961 to 50,577 tons in 1991. Production averaged about 37,500 tons annually in 1992–97, but fell sharply to 11,628 tons in 1998, with a modest recovery thereafter, reaching 54,964 tons in 2003. Cotton production in the 2004/05 crop year was 39,668 tons, rising to 46,600 tons in 2005/06, according to preliminary figures. The state shareholding in the Société de Développement des Fibres Textiles (SODEFITEX) was reduced from 60.0% to 46.5% in November 2003, with a majority stake being acquired by the French company Dagris. Sugar is produced at the Richard Toll complex in the north, near Saint-Louis. Annual output of sugar cane, all of which is for domestic consumption, averaged around 820,000 tons in the early 2000s.

Output of rice has fluctuated widely. The annual average output of 169,686 metric tons recorded in 1990–96 fell far short of domestic demand (some 500,000 tons annually). Production in the 2004/05 crop year was 201,744 tons and that in 2005/06 of 251,027 tons. The shortfall is met by cheap imports of rice from the Far East; however, this seriously jeopardizes the viability of local produce, which in the past attracted a state subsidy. A number of small- and medium-scale projects, supported by foreign aid, have so far been largely unsuccessful in extending the area under irrigation for rice, although the Manantali project (see below) is expected to have a great impact on output levels and production costs in the future. Market gardening was begun in 1971, and, following initial difficulties, exports from this sector are viewed as having considerable potential, and exports were estimated to have increased four-fold between 2000 and 2006. Another agricultural initiative of recent years has been the experimental introduction of biofuels crops, including jatropha, castor oil and sunflowers, over large tracts of land near Kolda and Tambacounda, to test for the most efficient sources of production.

The traditional food sector has suffered reverses from recurring droughts, but the overall production level has risen. Production of millet and sorghum declined sharply, from 818,213 metric tons in 2003/04 to 450,244 tons in 2004/05, when it was badly affected by a locust invasion, but recovered to 752,540 tons in 2005/06. Maize production averaged 87,996 tons a year in 1993–2002, but increased dramatically to 400,907 tons in 2003 following the successful adoption by farmers of hybrid seeds, fertilizer, herbicides and insecticides, and a significant increase in the area harvested, from 108,114 ha in 2002 to 175,575 ha in the following year. Maize production in the 2004/05 crop year was 400,555 tons and in 2005/06 it was 399,958 tons.

In drought years at the end of the 20th century concessionary grain supplies amounted to more than 100,000 metric tons annually, while apparent consumption levels per head were declining. The attainment of food self-sufficiency remained a major priority. Of great relevance to this objective was the enormous increase in irrigated land that was due to result from the completion of the Manantali dam in Mali. The combined benefits of the anti-salt barrage at Diama and of the Manantali dam were expected to provide newly irrigated land totalling 240,000 ha in Senegal over a period of 25 years. (However, a World Bank report criticized the project's immediate impact on traditional farming methods, which rely on annual floods.) In the short term, it was hoped to stabilize rice imports at 340,000 tons per year, while promoting the increased cultivation and consumption of millet and sorghum.

Food crops are supplemented by output from fishing. This sector has potential and, including processing, regularly accounts for more than 20% of merchandise exports. The value of fish exports (including crustaceans and molluscs) in 2004 was US $14.3m. Annual catches averaged 443,333 metric tons in 2002–04. In 2005 the artisanal catch by local fishermen was 403,200 tons, compared to that of industrial fleets at 225,600 tons, making a total of 628,800 tons. Excessive artisanal fishing has been blamed for a perceived decline in fish stocks, which cause the industrial catch to fall most noticeably. The annual sustainable catch has been estimated at around 420,000 tons per year. Small-scale fishing by about 45,000 fishermen continues to predominate, although the political insecurity in the southern Casamance region (the main fishing area) has at times adversely affected the sector. Industrial fishing is practised both by national and foreign operators. It has been estimated that the fishing sector as a whole provides the livelihood for as many as 500,000 people, including those engaged in local canning factories. Fishing remains Senegal's leading source of foreign exchange, and constituted 24.5% of total exports in 2003.

After 1979 regular fishing agreements were concluded with the European Community (now the EU), for which Senegal received financial compensation of about €48m. in 1997–2001, and part of the catch made by EU vessels is landed for processing locally. Some 78 EU boats were licensed to fish in Senegal in 2000, but the agreement was not renewed in 2001, following government concern that industrial fishing activities by EU vessels were depleting stocks, and undermining the traditional fishing sector. A new agreement, however, was agreed between Senegal and the EU in June 2002, in accordance with which Senegal would receive €64m. in 2002–06; several conditions intended to protect fish stocks were included in the new agreement, including the institution of an annual two-month rest period. In May 1999 Senegal concluded an agreement with Mauritania on the long-term management of the two countries' fish resources. Senegal also faces increasing competition from Côte d'Ivoire, which has eroded Senegal's share of the French market.

Livestock is a significant sector of the traditional economy (although less important than in most other countries of this area), and is the base for the dairy and meat-processing industries. In 2005 the cattle herd stood at 3.1m. head, sheep at 4.9m., goats at 4.1m., pigs at 306,000 and horses at 509,000.

MINING

The mining sector's contribution to GDP was estimated at 1.3% of the total in 2004. However, including processed derivatives, the sector is the country's second largest source of merchandise export earnings. Mining in Senegal is dominated by the extraction of phosphates: reserves of calcium phosphates are estimated at 100m. metric tons, while there are reserves of 50m.–70m. tons of aluminium phosphates. Senegal accounts for about 1.5% of world output and 3% of world exports of phosphates. The Compagnie Sénégalaise des Phosphates de Taïba (CSPT) and the Société Sénégalaise des Phosphates de Thiès (SSPT, privatized in March 1998) have been the two companies extracting phosphates, which are then processed by Industries Chimiques du Sénégal (ICS). The merger of the activities of the CSPT and the ICS was announced in September 1996. The ICS complex sought to produce an annual output of phosphoric acid of 660,000 metric tons. Phosphate products in total generated around US $190m. in export revenue in 2003. Exports to countries of the EU have declined, partly because of the high cadmium content of Senegalese phosphates, although EU funding has been provided to finance a plant to remove the chemical. Expansion has been planned both at existing facilities and at new ones at Tobène, while a plant for the recovery of phosphates from tailings has been constructed at the ICS fertilizer complex, with World Bank support, to increase the life of the mine through the utilization of lower-quality deposits. There are also unexploited deposits at Semmé, estimated to contain 40m. tons of calcium phosphates.

As a result of rising costs of fuel and essential imports at the same time as market prices of its products have fallen, ICS suffered such severe financial difficulties in 2005 that it was declared bankrupt in 2006 and ceased production. The Government (with 46% of the shares) was under pressure to reach agreement with other shareholders, and particularly the Indian Farmers' Fertiliser Co-operative (IFFCO) and the Indian Government, which together were seeking to increase their joint equity stake from 26% to 51%. IFFCO and the Indian Government were continuing to pledge new loans and investments on condition that control was transferred to Indian management and debts were restructured.

At least 330m. metric tons of high-grade iron ore have been located at Falémé, in the east, but development would require new sources of electricity (the installation of the hydroelectric plant at the Manantali dam could provide such a source), a new, 740-km rail link to Dakar and new port facilities. Reflecting an increase in world demand for iron ore, in January 2006 Mittal Steel (of the Netherlands) signed a memorandum of understanding with the Government to explore the development and production of iron ore from Falémé. At the same time, Kumba Resources of South Africa claimed that it also held rights to the property, but Mittal declared that it understood that Kumba's earlier understandings with the Government had expired and indicated that it would proceed with their investigations into the potential of the deposits.

Gold deposits (estimated to amount to some 30 metric tons) have been discovered at Sabodala, in the south-east, and the Société Minière de Sabodala began production in 1997, but a dispute over legal titles interrupted production the following year; after a new agreement was reached with Mineral Deposits Ltd (of Australia) in 2004 (which thereby acquired a 70% state in the company), production was expected to resume. Other foreign companies, including South Africa's AngloGold Ashanti and Randgold, as well as Samax of the United Kingdom and several Canadian interests, have been awarded gold exploration permits in south-eastern Senegal. In 2002–2004 the US Geological Survey estimated the annual production of artisanal gold at 600 kg. Exploration for diamonds is also in progress. Commercially viable reserves of titanium were discovered in 1991: workable ores are estimated at some 10m. tons.

Deposits of petroleum, estimated at 52m.–58m. metric tons, have been located in the Dôme Flore field, off the Casamance coast, but the development of these reserves (which are overwhelmingly of heavy petroleum) was long regarded as economically unfeasible. Disagreement with Guinea-Bissau regarding sovereignty of waters in this region was a further obstacle to their development. In mid-1995, none the less, the two countries signed an agreement envisaging joint co-operation in prospecting for petroleum in adjoining territorial waters, and exploration rights were subsequently awarded to US interests, operating in partnership with the majority state-owned Société Nationale des Pétroles du Sénégal (PETROSEN). In 1997 PETROSEN announced the discovery of a natural gas deposit, with reserves estimated at 10,000m. cu m, in the Thiès region. The Government adopted a new petroleum code and a new mining code in 1997 and 1998, respectively, in an attempt to encourage the further exploitation of Senegal's mineral resources. The incentives include generous exploration rights if a deposit is located, while there is no requirement for government equity participation.

POWER

Senegal has in recent years undertaken significant public investment in boosting its sources of electricity. Most electric power comes from thermal stations, with the addition of 30 MW from the Manantali hydroelectric dam in 2003 bringing the country's total generating capacity to around 500 MW. The monopoly electricity company is Société Nationale d'Electricité (SENELEC), which has been scheduled for privatization since 1998. After negotiations with interested companies stalled in 2002, the Government agreed with the IMF that, initially at least, only power generation activities would be opened up to private participation, while SENELEC would retain its monopoly on transmission and distribution. Renewed efforts at privatization were initiated in 2004. In the meantime, significant advances have been made in rural electrification, using solar power. In November 2005 the Government renewed its commitment to privatize SENELEC without specifying a timetable. The company remained a significant burden on government finances, and the electricity regulation commission said the Government had to choose between increasing its financial assistance or increasing electricity tariffs. After the Government then agreed to a small increase in tariffs, but not to a sufficient level to cover SENELEC's increasing costs, there was a crisis in supply in March and April 2006, resulting in extensive power cuts in Dakar. The IMF reported in 2007 that government subsidies to SENELEC and the oil refinery were equivalent to 2% of GDP during the previous year, although they paid far below market prices for electricity and butane gas.

MANUFACTURING

Senegal has the most developed manufacturing sector in francophone West Africa after Côte d'Ivoire, with production accounting for some 15.2% of GDP in 2005. The main activity is light industry (most of which is located in or near Dakar), transforming basic local commodities and import substitution to satisfy domestic demand. The agro-industrial sector mainly comprises oil mills, sugar refineries, fish-canning factories, flour mills and drinks, dairy products and tobacco industries, which together account for 40% of total value added. Agro-industrial production has risen steadily since 1999, with food canning playing a major role, although the vegetable oil industry has been in decline. Extractive industries (mainly the processing of phosphates) constitute the second most important branch of industrial activity. The manufacturing of textiles, leather goods and chemicals are also important, while subsidiary activities include paper and packaging and the manufacture of wood products and building materials. Senegal's textiles industry is well equipped and is potentially the most important in francophone sub-Saharan Africa, but has performed badly hitherto. The immediate, short-term impact of devaluation in 1994 was, moreover, detrimental, as cotton was sold for higher prices abroad, leaving the domestic industry short of raw materials. The chemicals industry (soap, paints, insecticides, plastics, pharmaceuticals and a petroleum refinery) is aimed at import substitution, as are nearly all the metalworking, engineering and electrical plants (including three shipyards, and truck and bicycle assembly plants).

Senegal was for many years dependent on a single source of cement, a factory in Rufisque with a capacity of 1.5m. metric tons per year. A second cement plant at Kirène, near Thiès, commenced production in 2002, with initial annual output of 600,000 tons, expected to rise to 1.2m. tons. Cement has subsequently become an expanding export commodity. Senegal's oil refinery at M'Bao, near Dakar, produces 1.4m. tons of products a year, mainly for domestic consumption; the refinery's monopoly on importing and marketing of petroleum products was abolished in 1998.

After the devaluation of the CFA franc, new measures were undertaken in an attempt to stimulate private-sector participation in industry. Import licensing was abolished and the Government made further commitments to end the effective monopolies enjoyed by a few large companies, to reduce the rigidity of the statutory labour code and to privatize several state-owned companies and parastatals—including SONACOS, the main groundnut-oil producer. However, the Government's rejection in 1996 of several unacceptably low offers for state enterprises was endorsed by the World Bank. Performance in the manufacturing sector since the devaluation has been uneven, with some sectors (such as food processing and electronics) suffering a decline in output as protective barriers have been reduced. Loans for private-sector development and small and medium-sized enterprises were awarded by the International Development Association (IDA, the World Bank's concessionary lending agency) and the African Development Bank (ADB).

TRANSPORT INFRASTRUCTURE

Industrial development has been stimulated by, and has in turn boosted, the port at Dakar. Container-handling facilities were increased from 29,000 metric tons to more than 100,000 tons when a new terminal was inaugurated in 1988, and the extension of container facilities was completed in 1993. The port handles some 7m.–9m. tons of freight per year. Improvements to the fishing port at Dakar have also been carried out. There were proposals to construct a naval repair yard, to service bulk oil carriers, but plans were scaled down because of a downturn in the tanker market, and a smaller-scale dock, able to handle vessels up to 60,000 tons, entered service in 1981. Completion of the Manantali project will eventually extend the all-year navigability of the Senegal river, currently just 220 km, to 924 km, as far as Kayes in Mali.

Senegal possesses a good road network. In 2003 there were 13,576 km of classified roads, of which about 4,216 km were surfaced. A 163-km road between Dialakoto and Kédougou, the construction of which was financed by regional donor organizations, was inaugurated in March 1996. In 1999 new highways were completed in the east of Senegal, linking Tambacounda, Kidira and Bakel. Major investment in improving road transport facilities between Dakar and Bamako, Mali, has been indicated with the recent approval of loans from the African Development Fund and the Japan Bank for International Cooperation to contribute to a project costed at US $290m.

The rail infrastructure is also well developed, with 922 km of track, although only 70 km of this is two-way and the network would benefit from modernization. The two main lines run from Dakar to Kidira, from the west to the east and across the border with Mali to Bamako, and from Dakar, via Thiès, to Saint-Louis in the north, near the border with Mauritania. In late 1995 the Governments of Senegal and Mali agreed to establish, with a view to privatization, a joint company to operate the Dakar–Bamako line. In 2003 the two Governments granted a 25-year concession to a French/Canadian consortium, CANAC-Getmar, for which the company was to pay US $26.7m., in addition to making investments estimated at $60m.

There is an international airport at Dakar, which handles about 970,000 passengers and 26,000 metric tons of freight annually; in addition, there are three other major airports and about 15 smaller airfields. The construction of a new international airport at Ndiass, 50 km east of Dakar, commenced in 2003. A new company, with minority government ownership, has been created to oversee the project, and with a remit to finance the airport through a loan, which is to be reimbursed with receipts from an airport infrastructure development tax. In 2007 IMF directors urged the Government to ensure transparency in the implementation of the airport project. In accordance with the Government's overall strategy in the transport sector, Air Sénégal, the national carrier, was partially privatized in 1999, with Royal Air Maroc taking a 51% stake. The company was later renamed Air Sénégal International and Royal Air Maroc has contributed €20m. to its recovery programme.

COMMUNICATIONS

In mid-1997 the national telecommunications company, the Société Nationale des Télécommunications du Sénégal (SONATEL), was partially privatized, with France Câbles et Radio, a subsidiary of France Télécom, purchasing 33.3% of the company's capital. A further 10% of shares in the company were sold to SONATEL employees at a discounted rate, while a further 17% of the company's value was offered to institutions and the general public. Following the recapitalization of the company in 1999, France Câbles et Radio increased its share in SONATEL to 42.3%. In 1998 Millicom International Cellular, based in Luxembourg, was awarded a 20-year licence to construct Senegal's second mobile cellular telephone network; by mid-2003 the service, known as Sentel Sénégal GSM, had attracted 250,000 subscribers. Senegal's other mobile network, known as Alizé, is managed by SONATEL. According to the International Telecommunications Union, the total number of mobile phone subscribers in Senegal had increased to 1.8m. by the end of 2005, while it was estimated that the potential number of subscribers could increase to 3.8m. by 2009. The Government's investment promotion agency APIX has identified information technology as a key sector for promotion to investors, especially in the introduction of call centres.

TOURISM

Tourism has grown in importance since the early 1970s, and it now ranks as one of the country's major sources of foreign exchange. In 2003 gross earnings from tourism (excluding passenger transport) amounted to US $201m., and in 2005 visitor arrivals were recorded as 386,564. The Government hopes to increase visitor numbers to more than 1m. in future years and the APIX agency has commissioned feasibility studies for the construction of new resorts along the coast south of Dakar. Senegal has about 16,500 hotel beds of international tourist standard, and Dakar is of considerable importance as an international conference centre. The sector was estimated to provide direct employment for about 8,000 and indirect employment for about 16,000 people. The improving prospects for an enduring peace settlement in the Casamance region, where much tourist activity has been traditionally located, are expected to lead to further development of tourism in the future.

INVESTMENT AND FINANCE

Despite overall economic difficulties, the level of investment increased steadily in the 1960s, to reach 17% of GDP in 1971, although it had fallen back to about 13% by the early 1990s, as Senegal's economic structure became increasingly uncompetitive. Public investment has accounted for the majority of total gross investment (69% in 1990), with government borrowing—both internal and external—increasing, as budgetary revenue declined. Gross domestic savings have also tended to be low, but have risen since 1994. There has been an upward trend in private investment since 2000, both in industry and in services such as communications technology. Net private sector investment during 2002 and 2003 was estimated at over US $150m. per year. The World Bank reported that foreign direct investment in 2005 was $54m.

In its search for new sources of increased economic growth, the Government has commenced consultations with the private sector for five priority sectors: agriculture and agro-industry; fishing and the fishing industry; textiles; information technology and telecommunications; and tourism.

Considerable progress was made, under the austerity programmes of the early 1980s, in reducing the budget deficit. The increasing overvaluation of the currency had a negative impact on government revenues, however. Under the terms of its latest agreements with the IMF, the Government has agreed to prioritize social spending, while limiting overall expenditure. In 2003 the budgetary deficit (including grants and net lending) was 52,300m. francs CFA, equivalent to 1.4% of GDP. Fiscal performance in 2004 and 2005 was in line with programme targets. The overall fiscal deficit increased slightly to 3.5% of GDP in 2005, but was over-financed by concessional loans. However, the overall fiscal deficit (including grants) increased sharply, to 5.7% of GDP in 2006. Revenue performance remained strong, owing to higher revenues from corporate income tax and oil-related taxes, but total expenditure continued to increase, reflecting the growth of capital outlays and recurrent spending. The latter was due mainly to higher transfers to SENELEC and the oil refinery. The financial system has been burdened by a high share of non-performing loans and a concentration of credit. The IMF in 2006 urged the Government to address the financial problems of ICS (see Mining, above), in order to prevent eventual budgetary costs and reduce the exposure to risk of banks.

Since independence, Senegal has benefited from the consistent support of Western donors, which have been keen to assist the country's relatively stable, conservative Governments. Donors have always recognized that Senegal is poorly endowed with natural resources, and external aid and funding have been forthcoming. Relations with both the World Bank and the IMF have generally remained positive, although both institutions began markedly increasing their pressure on the Government in 2006 and 2007 for improved efficiency in public expenditure. They were also urging speedy implementation of the action plan for improving the business environment.

In March 1994 Senegal was the first Franc Zone member to reach agreement with the IMF on new funding (a stand-by credit of SDR 47.6m.), following the devaluation of the CFA franc, and a new Enhanced Structural Adjustment Facility (ESAF), of SDR 130.8m., was approved in August 1994. Principal among the donors of new loans were the World Bank, the ADB and France. In July 1995 the Consultative Group of donors, expressing broad satisfaction at the progress of adjustment measures hitherto, pledged US $1,500m. over a two-year period. Senegal was granted another three-year ESAF (later known as the PRGF), equivalent to about $144m., in April 1998. Subsequently, the major donors (including the World Bank, the EU and France) committed almost $2,000m. in aid pledges to support Senegal's 1998–2000 economic programme. Assistance has been directed in particular at the social sector, with schemes being developed for the more widespread provision of drinking water, improved nutrition and developing more feeder roads for rural communities. A further PRGF, equivalent to $33m., for the period 2003–06, was granted in April 2003.

FOREIGN TRADE AND PAYMENTS

Senegal's foreign trade and current-account balance have consistently been in deficit, with the size of the former varying in response to the groundnut crop. Since the mid-1970s, however, the fluctuations have tended to narrow, as exports have stabilized at higher levels, reflecting the expansion of exports of phosphates and fishery products. In nominal CFA franc terms, the value of both imports and exports increased substantially following the 50% devaluation of the currency in January 1994. In that year exports increased by 119% (in current prices) compared with 1993, to 439,100m. francs CFA, while the increase in expenditure on imports was limited to 84%, at 567,400m. francs CFA. The value of exports increased steadily in 1995–2000, reaching 654,900m. francs CFA (f.o.b.) in 2000. Imports increased by 9.4% per year in 1995–2000, and in 2000 were valued at 951,600m. francs CFA. The trade deficit widened to 470,000m. francs CFA in 2003 and 533,000m. francs CFA in 2004. There was a decline in some leading exports in 2005, although this was compensated for by a rise in exports of tomatoes and cement. Total exports in 2005 were US $1,600m., rising to $1,619m. in 2006, while imports were $2,924m. in 2005 and $3,028m. in 2006.

The chronic deficits on foreign trade and on imports and exports of services are to some degree offset on the current account of the balance of payments by inward cash transfers, consisting mainly of official development grants. There is also a strong inflow of receipts from tourism, remittances and private sources. According to official sources, the current account deficit was US $737m. in 2005, widening to $784m. in 2006.

Since the late 1970s the Government has had increasing recourse to external borrowing, and outstanding external long-term debt increased from US $1,114m. in 1980 to $3,504m. in 1998, before declining to $3,205m. in 2000, and then increasing to $4,051m. in 2003, before declining to $3,698m. in 2004. In that year the country's total debt stocks amounted to $3,938m., equivalent to 52.2% of GNI. Commercial bank debt is negligible following a World Bank initiated 'buy-back' of 'London Club' debt (at 16% of its face value) in December 1996. Substantial debt relief, including cancellations and reschedulings in accordance with the 'Trinidad terms', was approved by the 'Paris

Club' in March 1994, while France agreed to cancel one-half of Senegal's bilateral debt. Even more concessionary relief, involving some 87,000m. francs CFA of debt, was granted by official creditors in early 1995, in accordance with the new 'Naples terms', which allow the cancellation or rescheduling of as much as 67% of public debt.

In mid-2000 the IMF and the World Bank announced that Senegal was eligible for debt relief under the newly revised terms of the expanded HIPC initiative, since Senegal's external debt exceeded 150% of the value of exports and 250% of the value of fiscal revenue. The Bretton Woods institutions subsequently announced a debt-relief programme for Senegal, which, with the support of Senegal's other creditors, would be equivalent to some US $800m. The debt relief provided by the World Bank was equivalent to a 50% reduction in Senegal's obligations to that organization over the following nine years, while the relief provided by the IMF was equivalent to 20% of obligations to the IMF over the following seven years. As a result of the application of these measures, Senegal's annual debt-service obligations have been sharply reduced. According to the World Bank, the ratio of debt service to export revenue decreased from 20.7% in 1998 to 10.3% in 2003. Senegal reached 'completion point' under its HIPC arrangements in April 2004, becoming the 12th developing country in the world to do so. The total of debt relief was $850m. in nominal terms, or $488m. in net present value terms. Subsequently, various official creditors, including France, have announced official debt write-offs. In June 2005 Senegal was among 18 countries to be granted 100% debt relief on multilateral debt agreed by the Group of Eight leading industrialized nations (G-8), subject to the approval of the lenders. Senegal began receiving debt relief on its IMF and World Bank debts from the second half of 2006, and thereby benefited from a substantial reduction in debt service payments; the reduction in its annual debt service payments to the IMF was estimated to average 47% over the period 2005–09.

Statistical Survey

Source (unless otherwise stated): Agence nationale de la Statistique et de la Démographie, blvd de l'Est, Point E, BP 116, Dakar; tel. 824-03-01; fax 824-90-04; e-mail statsenegal@yahoo.fr; internet www.ansd.org.

Area and Population

AREA, POPULATION AND DENSITY

Area (sq km)	197,021*
Population (census results)†	
16 April 1976	5,085,388
27 May 1988	
Males	3,353,599
Females	3,543,209
Total	6,896,808
December 2002 (provisional result)	9,956,202
Population (official estimates at 31 December)	
2003	10,127,809
2004	10,564,303
2005	10,817,844
Density (per sq km) at 31 December 2005	55.0

* 76,070 sq miles.

† Figures for 1976 and 1988 refer to the *de jure* population. The de facto population at the 1976 census was 4,907,507, and at the 1988 census was 6,773,417.

POPULATION BY ETHNIC GROUP
(at 1988 census)

Ethnic group	Number	%
Wolof	2,890,402	42.67
Serere	1,009,921	14.91
Peul	978,366	14.44
Toucouleur	631,892	9.33
Diola	357,672	5.28
Mandingue	245,651	3.63
Rural-Rurale	113,184	1.67
Bambara	91,071	1.34
Maure	67,726	1.00
Manjaag	66,605	0.98
Others	320,927	4.74
Total	6,773,417	100.00

Source: UN, *Demographic Yearbook*.

REGIONS
(2002 census, provisional results)

	Area (sq km)	Population	Density (per sq km)
Dakar	547	2,267,356	4,145.1
Diourbel	4,903	1,049,954	214.1
Fatick	7,910	613,000	77.5
Kaolack	15,449	1,066,375	69.0
Kolda	21,112	836,230	39.6
Louga	25,254	677,533	26.8
Matam	29,041	423,041	14.6
Saint-Louis	19,241	688,767	35.8
Tambacounda	59,542	605,695	10.2
Thiès	6,670	1,290,265	193.4
Ziguinchor	7,352	437,986	59.6
Total	197,021	9,956,202	50.5

PRINCIPAL TOWNS
(2002 census, provisional results)

Dakar (capital)	955,897	Mbour	153,503
Pikine	768,826	Diourbel	95,984
Rufisque	284,263	Louga	73,662
Guediawaye	258,370	Tambacounda	67,543
Thiès	237,849	Kolda	53,921
Kaolack	172,305	Mbacké	51,124
Saint-Louis	154,555		

Note: Data given pertains to communes, except for Dakar, Pikine, Rufisque and Guediawaye, where the population figure given is that of the département.

Mid-2005 ('000, incl. suburbs, UN estimate): Dakar 2,159 (Source: UN, *World Urbanization Prospects: The 2005 Revision*).

BIRTHS AND DEATHS
(annual averages, UN estimates)

	1990–95	1995–2000	2000–05
Birth rate (per 1,000)	41.5	39.0	37.6
Death rate (per 1,000)	11.8	10.6	9.8

Source: UN, *World Population Prospects: The 2006 Revision*.

Expectation of life (years at birth, WHO estimates): 55 (males 54; females 57) in 2004 (Source: WHO, *World Health Report*).

ECONOMICALLY ACTIVE POPULATION
('000 persons, 1990, ILO estimates)

	Males	Females	Total
Agriculture, hunting, forestry and fishing	1,319	1,190	2,508
Industry	195	51	246
Manufacturing	177	50	227
Services	370	145	516
Total	1,884	1,386	3,269

Source: ILO.

Unemployed (general survey, February–March 1999): 157,063 (males 99,892, females 57,171).

Mid-2005 (estimates in '000): Agriculture, etc. 3,746; Total labour force 5,189 (Source: FAO).

Health and Welfare

KEY INDICATORS

Total fertility rate (children per woman, 2005)	4.8
Under-5 mortality rate (per 1,000 live births, 2005)	136
HIV/AIDS (% of persons aged 15–49, 2005)	0.9
Physicians (per 1,000 head, 2004)	0.06
Hospital beds (per 1,000 head, 1998)	0.40
Health expenditure (2004): US $ per head (PPP)	72.1
Health expenditure (2004): % of GDP	5.9
Health expenditure (2004): public (% of total)	40.3
Access to water (% of persons, 2004)	76
Access to sanitation (% of persons, 2004)	57
Human Development Index (2004): ranking	156
Human Development Index (2004): value	0.460

For sources and definitions, see explanatory note on p. vi.

Agriculture

PRINCIPAL CROPS
('000 metric tons)

	2003	2004	2005
Rice (paddy)	231.8	201.7	279.1
Maize	400.9	400.6	400.0
Millet	628.4	323.8	608.6
Sorghum	189.8	126.5	144.0
Cassava (Manioc)	181.7	401.4	281.5
Sugar cane	829.6	828.5	828.5*
Pulses*	35.0	12.3	93.2
Cashew nuts*	4.5	4.5	4.5
Groundnuts (in shell)	440.7	602.6	703.4
Oil palm fruit*	70	70	70
Cottonseed	30.0†	17.0*	16.0*
Tomatoes	52.1	81.5	114.1
Dry onions*	46.8	40.0	45.0
Watermelons	398.5	275.8	241.4
Oranges	32.9	24.4	35.5
Guavas, mangoes and mangosteens*	85.4	65.8	61.6
Cotton (lint)	22.0†	21.7†	22.0*

* FAO estimate(s).
† Unofficial figure.

Source: FAO.

LIVESTOCK
('000 head, year ending September)

	2003	2004	2005
Cattle	3,018	3,039	3,070
Sheep	4,614	4,739	4,872
Goats	3,969	4,025	4,105
Pigs	303	300	306
Horses	500	504	509
Asses, mules or hinnies	400	412	416
Camels	4	4	4
Poultry	25,649	26,245	26,959

Source: FAO.

LIVESTOCK PRODUCTS
('000 metric tons)

	2003	2004	2005
Cattle meat	43.3	43.1	45.8
Sheep meat	14.8	15.2	16.0
Goat meat	9.5*	9.9	10.2
Pig meat	9.9	9.3	9.9
Horse meat*	6.9	6.9	7.0
Chicken meat	25.1*	26.0	26.5
Other meat*	6.5	6.6	6.6
Cows' milk	92.3	95.9	95.9
Sheep's milk	8.4	8.5	8.6
Goats' milk	9.7	9.8	10.0
Hen eggs*	23	24	27

* FAO estimate(s).

Source: FAO.

Forestry

ROUNDWOOD REMOVALS
('000 cubic metres, excl. bark, FAO estimates)

	2003	2004	2005
Sawlogs, veneer logs and logs for sleepers*	40	40	40
Other industrial wood†	754	754	754
Fuel wood	5,210	5,243	5,276
Total	6,004	6,037	6,070

* Annual output assumed to be unchanged since 1986 (FAO estimates).
† Annual output assumed to be unchanged since 1999 (FAO estimates).

Source: FAO.

SAWNWOOD PRODUCTION
('000 cubic metres, incl. railway sleepers)

	1989	1990	1991
Total (all broadleaved)	15	22	23

1992–2005: Annual production as in 1991 (FAO estimates).

Source: FAO.

Fishing

('000 metric tons, live weight)

	2003	2004	2005
Capture*	478.5	445.3	405.1
Freshwater fishes*	38.4	38.4	38.4
Sea catfishes	8.6	18.8	18.8
Round sardinella	107.6	137.6	114.0
Madeiran sardinella	149.0	115.3	118.4
Bonga shad	23.6	21.8	19.2
Octopuses	10.9	5.0	1.8
Aquaculture	0.1	0.2	0.2
Total catch*	478.6	445.5	405.3

* FAO estimates.

Source: FAO.

Mining

('000 metric tons, unless otherwise stated)

	2003	2004*	2005*
Cement, hydraulic	1,694	1,700	1,700
Gold (kg)†	600	600	600
Calcium phosphates	1,761	1,576	1,451
Aluminium phosphates	4	4	4
Fuller's earth (attapulgite)	195	200	200
Salt (unrefined)	235	240	240

* Estimates.

† Government estimate of unreported production of artisanal gold.

Source: US Geological Survey.

Industry

PETROLEUM PRODUCTS

('000 metric tons)

	2002	2003	2004
Jet fuels	72	126	132
Motor gasoline (petrol)	140	151	148
Kerosene	23	26	19
Gas-diesel (distillate fuel) oils	375	463	471
Residual fuel oils	255	316	327
Lubricating oils	5	5	5
Liquefied petroleum gas	9	12	10

Source: UN, *Industrial Commodity Statistics Yearbook*.

SELECTED OTHER PRODUCTS

('000 metric tons, unless otherwise indicated)

	2001	2002	2003
Raw sugar	95.0*	95.0†	95.0†
Sugar cubes	27.2	19.8	23.2
Tobacco products (tons)	2,132	2,245	2,218
Groundnut oil—crude	125.3	98.1	39.2
Vegetable oil—refined	70.6	78.5	75.7
Canned tuna	12.1	10.7	6.9
Footwear (million pairs)	0.6	n.a.	n.a.
Cotton yarn (tons)	411	n.a.	n.a.
Soap	38.6	34.8	33.4
Paints and varnishes	4.6	4.3	4.6
Cement	1,539.0	1,653.2	1,693.9
Metal cans (million)	113.2	185.2	182.2
Electricity (million kWh)	1,651.2	1,557.3	1,855.5

* Unofficial figure.

† FAO estimate.

Source: mainly IMF, *Senegal: Selected Issues and Statistical Appendix* (May 2005).

Nitrogenous fertilizers (nitrogen content, '000 metric tons, unofficial figures): 38.8 in 1998; 24.5 in 1999; 19.4 in 2000 (Source: FAO).

Phosphate fertilizers (phosphoric acid content, '000 metric tons, unofficial figures): 67.5 in 1998; 45.0 in 1999; 32.4 in 2000 (Source: FAO).

Source: IMF, *Senegal: Statistical Appendix* (June 2003).

Cement ('000 metric tons): 1.0 annually in 2001–03 (Source: US Geological Survey).

Finance

CURRENCY AND EXCHANGE RATES

Monetary Units

100 centimes = 1 franc de la Communauté financière africaine (CFA).

Sterling, Dollar and Euro Equivalents (31 May 2007)

£1 sterling = 964.116 francs CFA;
US $1 = 487.592 francs CFA;
€1 = 655.957 francs CFA;
10,000 francs CFA = £10.37 = $20.51 = €15.24.

Average Exchange Rate (francs CFA per US $)

2004 528.29
2005 527.47
2006 522.89

Note: An exchange rate of 1 French franc = 50 francs CFA, established in 1948, remained in force until January 1994, when the CFA franc was devalued by 50%, with the exchange rate adjusted to 1 French franc = 100 francs CFA. This relationship to French currency remained in effect with the introduction of the euro on 1 January 1999. From that date, accordingly, a fixed exchange rate of €1 = 655.957 francs CFA has been in operation.

BUDGET

('000 million francs CFA)

Revenue*	2001	2002	2003
Tax revenue	576.8	629.2	677.0
Taxes on income and property	130.6	145.9	159.3
Individual	58.8	74.7	80.8
Corporate	48.9	54.2	55.9
Taxes on goods and services (excl. petroleum)	254.8	258.3	308.9
Value-added tax on domestic goods	90.5	114.6	128.7
Value-added tax on imported goods	112.7	86.4	119.8
Taxes on imports (excl. petroleum)	107.3	107.7	107.9
Taxes on petroleum products	84.1	115.4	100.9
Value-added tax	38.6	64.4	37.3
Excises	44.7	44.8	56.4
Non-tax revenue	25.9	35.4	43.1
Total	602.7	664.6	720.1

* Excluding grants received ('000 million francs CFA): 61.7 in 2001; 62.1 in 2002; 77.7 in 2003.

Expenditure*	2001	2002	2003
Current expenditure	516.6	478.2	529.5
Wages and salaries	177.3	199.4	203.7
Other operational expenses	309.0	239.0	281.2
Interest payments on public debt	30.3	39.8	44.6
External	23.7	35.4	40.0
Capital expenditure	232.3	275.9	338.5
Treasury special accounts and correspondents (net)	3.8	–18.2	–11.1
Total	752.7	735.9	856.9

* Excluding net lending ('000 million francs CFA): –4.6 in 2001; –5.6 in 2002; –6.8 in 2003.

Source: IMF, *Senegal: Selected Issues and Statistical Appendix* (May 2005).

2004 ('000 million francs CFA): Revenue 776.8 (Tax revenue 738.5, Non-tax revenue 38.3), Expenditure 953.2 (Current expenditure 553.8, Capital expenditure 413.3, Net treasury special accounts and correspondents –25.0, Structural reform costs 11.3). Figures exclude grants received: 88.0 and net lending: 12.3.

INTERNATIONAL RESERVES

(excluding gold, US $ million at 31 December)

	2004	2005	2006
IMF special drawing rights	7.3	1.4	0.0
Reserve position in IMF	2.4	2.2	2.4
Foreign exchange	1,376.7	1,187.4	1,331.8
Total	1,386.4	1,191.0	1,334.2

Source: IMF, *International Financial Statistics*.

MONEY SUPPLY

('000 million francs CFA at 31 December)

	2004	2005	2006
Currency outside banks	342.3	378.6	451.9
Demand deposits at deposit money banks	532.5	576.0	633.8
Checking deposits at post office	12.8	7.6	12.5
Total money (incl. others)	887.9	962.7	1,098.7

Source: IMF, *International Financial Statistics*.

COST OF LIVING

(Consumer Price Index, Dakar, annual averages; base: 1996 = 100)

	2003	2004	2005
Food and non-alcoholic beverages	113.1	114.0	118.4
Alcoholic beverages, tobacco, stimulants, etc.	116.6	117.5	118.6
Clothing	92.5	89.9	87.1
Housing, water, electricity and gas	116.4	117.1	117.4
All items (incl. others)	109.9	110.5	112.4

NATIONAL ACCOUNTS

('000 million francs CFA at current prices)

Expenditure on the Gross Domestic Product

	2004	2005*	2006†
Final consumption expenditure	3,862.4	4,106.2	4,332.7
Households; Non-profit institutions serving households	3,280.1	3,479.5	3,665.9
General government	582.3	626.7	666.8
Gross capital formation	884.6	995.2	1,085.1
Gross fixed capital formation	961.9	1,038.4	1,123.8
Changes in inventories; Acquisitions, less disposals, of inventories	–77.3	–43.2	–38.7
Total domestic expenditure	4,747.0	5,101.4	5,417.8
Exports of goods and services	1,121.7	1,185.4	1,261.0
Less Imports of goods and services	1,670.2	1,790.5	1,962.5
Statistical discrepancy	—	64.9	182.8
GDP in purchasers' values	4,198.5	4,561.2	4,899.1
GDP in constant 1999 prices	3,874.0	4,109.1	4,316.0

* Estimates.

† Provisional.

Gross Domestic Product by Economic Activity

	2004	2005*	2006†
Agriculture, hunting, forestry and fishing	589.5	668.3	714.9
Mining and quarrying	48.3	45.2	48.2
Manufacturing	606.4	631.6	648.7
Electricity, gas and water	92.1	106.3	114.3
Construction	179.8	207.3	240.1
Trade	674.6	715.9	756.4
Transport, storage and communications	363.7	409.6	457.6
Education and training	142.3	156.1	166.5
Health and social services	58.0	61.2	64.7
Government services	291.0	322.2	349.7
Other services	627.9	664.2	714.8
Sub-total	3,673.6	3,987.9	4,275.9
Import taxes and duties	524.9	573.4	623.1
GDP in purchasers' values	4,198.5	4,561.2	4,899.1

* Estimates.

† Provisional.

BALANCE OF PAYMENTS

(US $ million)

	2002	2003	2004
Exports of goods f.o.b.	1,066.5	1,257.0	1,509.4
Imports of goods f.o.b.	–1,603.9	–2,065.5	–2,495.8
Trade balance	–537.4	–808.5	–986.4
Exports of services	456.2	569.0	670.1
Imports of services	–474.3	–591.3	–698.1
Balance on goods and services	–555.5	–830.8	–1,014.4
Other income received	65.1	86.4	95.2
Other income paid	–195.1	–222.6	–225.9
Balance on goods, services and income	–685.5	–967.0	–1,145.1
Current transfers received	414.4	595.6	715.1
Current transfers paid	–45.8	–65.2	–83.1
Current balance	–316.8	–436.6	–513.1
Capital account (net)	126.8	150.4	750.0

—continued	2002	2003	2004
Direct investment abroad	–34.0	–2.7	–13.1
Direct investment from abroad	78.1	52.5	77.0
Portfolio investment assets	–25.0	–56.3	–47.5
Portfolio investment liabilities	–13.1	10.6	0.8
Financial derivatives assets	–1.9	1.6	0.7
Financial derivatives liabilities	–0.4	0.7	–0.8
Other investment assets	11.9	58.0	6.0
Other investment liabilities	–103.8	–61.9	–76.9
Net errors and omissions	30.8	10.8	15.9
Overall balance	–247.3	–272.8	199.1

Source: IMF, *International Financial Statistics*.

External Trade

PRINCIPAL COMMODITIES
(distribution by SITC, US $ million)

Imports c.i.f.	2002	2003	2004
Food and live animals	449.2	563.5	661.3
Cereals and cereal preparations	257.4	297.9	349.3
Rice	184.4	217.2	243.2
Rice, broken	183.9	216.0	236.6
Crude materials (inedible) except fuels	41.6	87.5	110.0
Mineral fuels, lubricants, etc.	729.7	444.7	522.1
Petroleum, petroleum products, etc.	688.4	399.4	460.7
Crude petroleum oils, etc.	417.4	276.3	333.0
Petroleum products, refined	266.3	117.8	115.8
Animal and vegetable oils, fats and waxes	40.2	86.7	98.4
Fixed vegetable oils and fats	32.6	74.2	82.3
Chemicals and related products	191.9	255.2	325.8
Medicinal and pharmaceutical products	64.6	79.7	99.9
Medicaments (incl. veterinary)	59.3	71.2	90.5
Basic manufactures	224.8	304.2	403.5
Iron and steel	49.5	75.1	137.6
Machinery and transport equipment	248.1	486.8	530.2
General industrial machinery, equipment and parts	34.7	89.7	98.9
Road vehicles and parts (excl. tyres, engines and electrical parts)	108.6	160.9	146.9
Passenger motor vehicles (excl. buses)	61.0	83.1	70.6
Miscellaneous manufactured articles	65.1	105.8	152.2
Total (incl. others)	2,031.0	2,391.5	2,848.8

Exports f.o.b.	2002	2003	2004
Food and live animals	50.5	343.1	417.8
Fish, crustaceans and molluscs, and preparations thereof	0.4	282.0	314.3
Fish, fresh, chilled or frozen	0.2	104.1	166.9
Fish, fresh or chilled, excl. fillets	—	14.5	82.1
Fish, frozen, excl. fillets and minced fish	—	62.3	76.8
Crustaceans and molluscs, fresh, chilled, frozen, salted, etc	—	142.0	118.9
Crustaceans, frozen	—	41.2	43.8
Shrimps and prawns, frozen	—	38.7	42.7
Molluscs and aquatic invertebrates, fresh, frozen, dried, etc.	—	100.8	74.3
Cuttlefish, octopus and squid, frozen, dried, salted or in brine	—	97.0	70.2
Beverages and tobacco	11.2	46.7	14.7
Tobacco and tobacco manufactures	10.4	36.8	13.5
Tobacco, manufactured (whether or not containing tobacco substitutes)	10.1	36.4	11.4
Crude materials (inedible) except fuels	63.5	77.1	86.5
Crude fertilizers and crude minerals	36.0	31.3	37.8
Mineral fuels, lubricants, etc.	157.5	231.5	256.3
Petroleum, petroleum products, etc.	156.8	230.7	255.4
Crude petroleum and oils obtained from bituminous materials	21.2	43.5	37.7
Refined petroleum products	133.7	184.4	215.3
Animal and vegetable oils, fats and waxes	53.5	37.4	27.3
Fixed vegetable oils and fats	53.4	36.9	26.8
Crude fixed vegetable oils and fats	53.0	36.5	26.0
Chemicals and related products	267.7	260.6	337.4
Inorganic chemicals	171.2	139.9	180.4
Phosphorus pentoxide and phosphoric acids	170.3	138.0	179.4
Oils and perfume materials; toilet and cleansing preparations	28.9	39.0	47.9
Manufactured fertilizers	37.5	49.7	69.0
Nitrogen-phosphorus-potassium fertilizer	35.1	48.0	62.6
Basic manufactures	40.8	55.4	87.6
Machinery and transport equipment	24.2	48.2	50.9
Miscellaneous manufactured articles	26.0	51.0	40.5
Total (incl. others)	694.7	1,151.2	1,319.2

Source: UN, *International Trade Statistics Yearbook*.

PRINCIPAL TRADING PARTNERS
(US $ million)

Imports c.i.f.	2002	2003	2004
Argentina	37.0	26.1	25.5
Belgium	55.5	67.1	81.8
Brazil	34.7	70.9	108.1
China, People's Republic	41.9	64.2	97.1
Côte d'Ivoire	75.0	86.1	100.4
France (incl. Monaco)	427.0	588.9	691.1
Germany	50.0	82.4	78.3
India	39.3	52.6	40.6
Ireland	28.0	28.7	45.7
Italy	85.2	86.0	89.9
Japan	36.6	57.8	68.9
Netherlands	76.8	71.3	73.8
Nigeria	385.4	280.7	334.3
Russia	22.9	42.4	30.1
Saudi Arabia	26.8	14.3	6.2
South Africa	20.4	24.1	40.4
Spain	67.4	103.5	117.5
Thailand	151.0	173.9	177.2
Ukraine	—	16.2	65.5
United Kingdom	31.3	49.2	52.4
USA	35.0	86.0	88.7
Viet Nam	20.5	21.9	53.9
Total (incl. others)	2,031.0	2,391.5	2,848.8

Exports f.o.b.	2002	2003	2004
Benin	21.8	32.7	24.3
Burkina Faso	6.3	29.5	23.0
China, People's Republic	0.6	15.3	6.4
Côte d'Ivoire	28.1	61.4	40.2
France (incl. Monaco)	53.5	137.5	125.1
The Gambia	33.8	42.8	65.9
Greece	—	16.6	27.5
Guinea	17.7	59.9	38.7
Guinea-Bissau	21.2	—	46.2
India	196.0	147.2	183.1
Italy	22.5	95.6	92.6
Mali	86.1	114.9	180.6
Mauritania	30.9	33.3	32.0
Netherlands	14.4	9.8	11.3
Spain	2.2	56.3	88.0
Togo	8.5	14.9	18.7
Total (incl. others)	694.7	1,151.2	1,319.9

Source: UN, *International Trade Statistics Yearbook*.

Transport

RAILWAYS
(traffic)

	2002	2003	2004
Passenger-km (million)	105	129	122
Net ton-km (million)	345	375	358

Passengers ('000): 4,789 in 1999.

Freight carried ('000 metric tons): 2,017 in 1999.

ROAD TRAFFIC
(motor vehicles in use)

	1997	1998	1999
Passenger cars	76,971	85,805	98,260
Buses and coaches	9,236	9,974	10,477
Lorries and vans	21,693	23,851	25,276
Road tractors	2,110	2,278	2,458
Motorcycles and mopeds	3,624	4,155	4,515

Source: IRF, *World Road Statistics*.

SHIPPING

Merchant Fleet
(vessels registered at 31 December)

	2004	2005	2006
Number of vessels	178	181	183
Total displacement ('000 grt)	40.8	41.6	42.5

Source: Lloyd's Register-Fairplay, *World Fleet Statistics*.

International Sea-borne Freight Traffic
('000 metric tons)

	2003	2004	2005
Goods loaded	3,028	2,875	2,911
Goods unloaded	7,521	7,144	8,026

Source: Port Autonome de Dakar.

CIVIL AVIATION
(traffic on scheduled services)*

	2001	2002	2003
Kilometres flown (million)	4	7	6
Passengers carried ('000)	176	231	130
Passenger-km (million)	319	572	388
Total ton-km (million)	116	20	35

* Including an apportionment of the traffic of Air Afrique.

Source: UN, *Statistical Yearbook*.

Tourism

FOREIGN TOURIST ARRIVALS BY NATIONALITY*

	2003	2004	2005
African states	85,664	89,660	87,565
Belgium, Luxembourg and the Netherlands	17,025	16,160	21,712
East Asian and Pacific states	2,273	3,705	3,837
France	181,470	172,878	191,580
Germany	7,985	8,374	9,615
Italy	9,279	9,413	11,493
Spain	12,680	13,415	15,353
United Kingdom	3,063	4,092	4,380
USA	8,518	10,422	11,080
Total (incl. others)	353,539	363,490	386,564

* Figures refer to arrivals at hotels and similar establishments.

Receipts from tourism (US $ million, excl. passenger transport): 201 in 2003; n.a. in 2004; n.a. in 2005.

Source: World Tourism Organization.

Communications Media

	2003	2004	2005
Telephones ('000 main lines in use)	228.8	244.9	266.6
Mobile cellular telephones ('000 subscribers)	782.4	1,121.3	1,730.1
Personal computers ('000 in use)	220	242	n.a.
Internet users ('000)	225	482	n.a.

Television receivers ('000 in use): 380 in 2000.

Radio receivers ('000 in use): 1,240 in 1997.

Daily newspapers: 1 (average circulation 45,000 copies) in 1996; 4 in 1997; 5 in 1998.

Non-daily newspapers: 6 (average circulation 37,000 copies) in 1995.

Sources: mainly International Telecommunication Union; UNESCO, *Statistical Yearbook*, UNESCO Institute for Statistics.

Education

(2003/04, unless otherwise indicated)

			Students ('000)		
	Institutions*	Teachers	Males	Females	Total
Pre-primary	460	1,983	26.3	28.5	54.8
Primary	5,670	32,005	715.4	667.4	1,382.7
Secondary	591	13,654	210.2	149.8	360.0
Tertiary	n.a.	n.a.	n.a.	n.a.	52.3

* 2002/03 (Source: Ministry of Education, Dakar).

Source: UNESCO Institute for Statistics.

Adult literacy rate (UNESCO estimates): 39.3% (males 51.1%; females 29.2%) in 2003 (Source: UN Development Programme, *Human Development Report*).

Directory

The Constitution

The Constitution of the Republic of Senegal was promulgated following its approval by popular referendum on 7 January 2001, and entered into force thereafter, with the exception of those sections relating to the Assemblée nationale and the relations between the executive and legislative powers (articles 59–87), which took effect following legislative elections on 29 April 2001. The main provisions are summarized below:

PREAMBLE

The people of Senegal, recognizing their common destiny, and aware of the need to consolidate the fundaments of the Nation and the State, and supporting the ideals of African unity and human rights, proclaim the principle of national territorial integrity and a national unity respecting the diverse cultures of the Nation, reject all forms of injustice, inequality and discrimination, and proclaim the will of Senegal to be a modern democratic State.

THE STATE AND SOVEREIGNTY

Articles 1–6: Senegal is a secular, democratic Republic, in which all people are equal before the law, without distinction of origin, race, sex or religion. The official language of the Republic is French; the national languages are Diola, Malinké, Pular, Sérère, Soninké, Wolof and any other national language that may be so defined. The principle of the Republic is 'government of the people, by the people and for the people'. National sovereignty belongs to the people who exercise it, through their representatives or in referenda. Suffrage may be direct or indirect, and is always universal, equal and secret. Political parties and coalitions of political parties are obliged to observe the Constitution and the principles of national sovereignty and democracy, and are forbidden from identifying with one race, one ethnic group, one sex, one religion, one sect, one language or one region. All acts of racial, ethnic or religious discrimination, including regionalist propaganda liable to undermine the security or territorial integrity of the State are punishable by law. The institutions of the Republic are: the President of the Republic; the Assemblée nationale; the Government and the Constitutional Council; the Council of State; the Final Court of Appeal (Cour de Cassation); the Revenue Court (Cour de Comptes); and Courts and Tribunals.

PUBLIC LIBERTIES AND THE HUMAN PERSON; ECONOMIC AND SOCIAL RIGHTS AND COLLECTIVE RIGHTS

Articles 7–25: The inviolable and inalienable rights of man are recognized as the base of all human communities, of peace and justice in the world, and are protected by the State. All humans are equal before the law. The Republic protects, within the rule of law, the right to free opinion, free expression, a free press, freedom of association and of movement, cultural, religious and philosophical freedoms, the right to organize trade unions and businesses, the right to education and literacy, the right to own property, to work, to health, to a clean environment, and to diverse sources of information. No prior authorization is required for the formation of an organ of the press. Men and women are guaranteed equal rights to possess property.

Marriage and the family constitute the natural and moral base of the human community, and are protected by the State. The State is obliged to protect the physical and moral health of the family, in particular of the elderly and the handicapped, and guarantees to alleviate the conditions of life of women, particularly in rural areas. Forced marriages are forbidden as a violation of individual liberty. The State protects youth from exploitation, from drugs, and from delinquency.

All children in the Republic have the right to receive schooling, from public schools, or from institutions of religious or non-religious communities. All national educational institutions, public or private, are obliged to participate in the growth of literacy in one of the national languages. Private schools may be opened with the authorization of, and under the control of, the State.

Freedom of conscience is guaranteed. Religious communities and institutions are separate from the State.

All discrimination against workers on grounds of origins, sex, political opinions or beliefs are forbidden. All workers have the right to join or form trade or professional associations. The right to strike is recognized, under legal conditions, as long as the freedom to work is not impeded, and the enterprise is not placed in peril. The State guarantees sanitary and human conditions in places of work.

THE PRESIDENT OF THE REPUBLIC

Articles 26–52: The President of the Republic is elected, for a term of five years, by universal direct suffrage. The mandate may be renewed once. Candidates for the presidency must be of solely Senegalese nationality, enjoy full civil and political rights, be aged 35 years or more on the day of elections, and must be able to write, read and speak the official language fluently. All candidates must be presented by a political party or a legally constituted coalition of political parties, or be accompanied by a petition signed by at least 10,000 electors, including at least 500 electors in each of six administrative regions. Candidates may not campaign predominately on ethnic or regional grounds. Each political party or coalition of political parties may present only one candidate. If no candidate receives an absolute majority of votes cast in the first round, representing the support of at least one-quarter of the electorate, a second round of elections is held between the two highest-placed candidates in the first round. In the case of incapacity, death or resignation, the President's position is assumed by the President of the Assemblée nationale, and in the case of his or her incapacity, by one of the Vice-Presidents of the Assemblée nationale, in all cases subject to the same terms of eligibility that apply to the President. The President presides over the Council of Ministers, the Higher Council of National Defence, and the National Security Council, and is the Supreme Chief of the Armed Forces. The President appoints a Prime Minister, and appoints ministers on the recommendation of the Prime Minister.

THE GOVERNMENT

Articles 53–57: The head of the Government is the Prime Minister. In the event of the resignation or removal from office of a Prime Minister, the entire Government is obliged to resign.

THE OPPOSITION

Article 58: The Constitution guarantees the right to oppose to political parties that are opposed to Government policy, and recognizes the existence of a parliamentary opposition.

THE ASSEMBLÉE NATIONALE

Article 59–66: Deputies of the Assemblée nationale are elected by universal direct suffrage, for a five-year mandate, subject only to the dissolution of the Assemblée nationale. Any serving deputy who resigns from his or her party shall have his or her mandate removed. Deputies enjoy immunity from criminal proceedings, except with the authorization of the bureau of the Assemblée nationale. The Assemblée nationale votes on the budget. Deputies vote as individuals and must not be obligated to vote in a certain way. Except in exceptional and limited circumstances, sessions of the Assemblée nationale are public.

RELATIONS BETWEEN THE EXECUTIVE AND LEGISLATIVE POWERS

Articles 67–87: The Assemblée nationale is the sole holder of legislative power, votes on the budget and authorizes a declaration of war. The President of the Republic may, having received the opinion of the Prime Minister and the President of the Assemblée nationale, pronounce by decree the dissolution of the Assemblée nationale, except during the first two years of any Assemblée.

INTERNATIONAL TREATIES

Articles: 88–91: The President of the Republic negotiates international engagements, and ratifies or approves them with the authorization of the Assemblée nationale. The Republic of Senegal may conclude agreements with any African State that would comprise a partial or total abandonment of national sovereignty in order to achieve African unity.

JUDICIAL POWER

Articles 92–98: The judiciary is independent of the legislature and the executive power. The judiciary consists of the Constitutional Council, the Council of State, the Court of Final Appeal, the Revenue Court and Courts and Tribunals. The Constitutional Council comprises five members, including a President, a Vice-President and three judges. Each member serves for a mandate of six years (which may not be renewed) with partial renewals occurring every two years. The President of the Republic appoints members of the Constitutional Council, whose decisions are irreversible.

THE HIGH COURT OF JUSTICE

Articles 99–101: A High Court of Justice, presided over by a magistrate and comprising members elected by the Assemblée nationale, is instituted. The President of the Republic can only be brought to trial for acts accomplished in the exercise of his duties in the case of high treason. The High Court of Justice tries the Prime Minister and other members of the Government for crimes committed in the exercise of their duties.

LOCAL GOVERNMENT

Article 102: Local government bodies operate independently, by means of elective assemblies, in accordance with the law.

ON REVISION

Article 103: Only the President of the Republic or the deputies of the Assemblée nationale, of whom a three-quarters' majority must be in favour, may propose amending the Constitution. Amendments may be approved by referendum or, at the initiative of the President of the Republic, solely by approval by the Assemblée nationale, in which case a three-fifths' majority must be in favour.

The Government

HEAD OF STATE

President: ABDOULAYE WADE (took office 1 April 2000, re-elected 25 February 2007).

COUNCIL OF MINISTERS

(August 2007)

Prime Minister: CHEIKH HADJIBOU SOUMARÉ.

Minister of State, Minister of Foreign Affairs: CHEIKH TIDIANE GADIO.

Minister of State, Minister of the Economy and Finance: ABDOULAYE DIOP.

Minister of State, Keeper of the Seals, Minister of Justice: CHEIKH TIDIANE SY.

Minister of State, Minister of the Interior: OUSMANE NGOM.

Minister of State, Minister of the Maritime Economy: DJIBO LEÏTY KÂ.

Minister of State, Minister of Infrastructure, Urban Hydraulics and Sanitation: HABIB SY.

Minister of State, Minister of the Environment and Conservation: SOULEYMANE NDÉNÉ NDIAYE.

Minister of the Armed Forces: BÉCAYE DIOP.

Minister of Town Planning, Housing and Construction: OUMAR SARR.

Minister of Decentralization and Local Communities: OUSMANE MASSECK NDIAYE.

Minister of Education: Prof. MOUSTAPHA SOURANG.

Minister of Micro-finance and Decentralized Co-operation: ABDOURAHIM AGNE.

Minister of the Family and Female Entrepreneurship: AWA NDIAYE.

Minister of Crafts, Mining and Industry: MADICKÉ NIANG.

Minister of Telecommunications, Posts and Information and Communication Technologies: SOPHIE GLADIMA SIBY.

Minister of Scientific Research: YAYE KENE GASSAMA DIA.

Minister of Health and Preventive Medicine: ISSA MBAYE SAMB.

Minister of Rural Hydraulics, the National Hydrographic Network, Retention Basins and Man-made Lakes: ADAMA SALL.

Minister of Culture and Protected National Heritage: MAME BIRAME DIOUF.

Minister of Rural Development and Agriculture: HAMATH SALL.

Minister of Livestock-rearing: OUMOU KHAÏRY GUÈYE SECK.

Minister of Land and Air Transport: FARBA SENGHOR.

Minister of Information and Relations with the Institutions, Spokesperson for the Government: BACAR DIA.

Minister of Sports: El Hadj DAOUDA FAYE.

Minister of the Quality of Life and Public Hygiene: MAÏMOUNA SOURANG NDIR.

Minister of National Solidarity: FATOU BINTOU TAYA NDIAYE.

Minister of Youth and Employment: MAMADOU LAMINE KEÏTA.

Minister of Energy: SAMUEL AMÈTE SARR.

Minister of the Civil Service, Labour and Professional Organizations: INNOCENCE NTAP.

Minister of Competitiveness and Good Governance: FATOU DANIELLE DIAGNE.

Minister of Trade: AMADOU HABIBOU NDIAYE.

Minister of Technical and Professional Training: MOUSSA SAKHO.

Minister of Senegalese Nationals Abroad: AMINATA LÔ.

Minister of Tourism: FATOU GASSAMA.

Minister of National Languages and Francophone Affairs: MAMADOU MAKALOU.

Minister-delegate at the Office of the Minister of State, Minister of the Economy and Finance, responsible for the Budget: IBRAHIMA SARR.

Minister-delegate at the Ministry of Rural Development and Agriculture, responsible for Rural Development: FATOU GAYE SAR.

MINISTRIES

Office of the President: ave Léopold Sédar Senghor, BP 168, Dakar; tel. 823-10-88; internet www.gouv.sn/institutions/president.html.

Office of the Prime Minister: Bldg Administratif, ave Léopold Sédar Senghor, BP 4029, Dakar; tel. 849-70-00; fax 822-55-78; internet www.gouv.sn.

Ministry of the Armed Forces: Bldg Administratif, ave Léopold Sédar Senghor, BP 4041, Dakar; tel. 823-56-13; fax 823-63-38; internet www.forcesarmees.gouv.sn.

Ministry of Biofuels and Renewable Energy Resources: Dakar.

Ministry of the Built Environment, Housing and Construction: blvd Dial Diop, pl. de l'ONU, BP 15363, Dakar; tel. 869-15-45; fax 864-59-32; internet www.habitat.gouv.sn.

Ministry of the Civil Service, Labour, Employment and Professional Organizations: Bldg Administratif, BP 4007, Dakar; tel. 823-52-19; fax 842-73-03; e-mail mineladiallo@yahoo.fr; internet www.fonctionpublique.gouv.sn.

Ministry of Competitiveness and Good Governance: Dakar.

Ministry of Crafts and Tourism: rue Calmette, BP 4049, Dakar; tel. 821-11-26; fax 822-94-13; internet www.tourisme.gouv.sn.

Ministry of Culture and Protected National Heritage: Bldg Administratif, ave Léopold Sédar Senghor, BP 4001, Dakar; tel. 822-95-49; fax 822-16-38; internet www.culture.gouv.sn.

Ministry of Decentralization and Local Communities: Bldg Administratif, ave Léopold Sédor Senghor, Dakar; tel. 849-75-12; fax 849-67-63.

Ministry of the Economy and Finance: ave Carde, Bâtiment CEPOD, Dakar; tel. 823-34-27; fax 821-83-12; e-mail i_diouf@minfinances.sn; internet www.finances.gouv.sn.

Ministry of Education: rue Alpha Hachamiyou Tall, BP 4025, Dakar; tel. 849-54-54; fax 821-12-28; internet www.education.gouv.sn.

Ministry of Energy: Dakar.

Ministry of the Environment and Conservation: Bldg Administratif, BP 4055, Dakar; tel. 889-02-34; fax 822-21-80; e-mail mepn@environnement.gouv.sn; internet www.environnement.gouv.sn.

Ministry of Foreign Affairs: pl. de l'Indépendance, BP 4044, Dakar; tel. 889-13-00; e-mail cheikhgadio@senegal.diplomatie.sn; internet www.diplomatie.gouv.sn.

Ministry of Health and Preventive Medicine: Fann Résidence, rue Aimé Césaire, BP 4024, Dakar; tel. 869-42-68; fax 869-42-69; e-mail mspmwebsante@sentoo.sn; internet www.sante.gouv.sn.

Ministry of Information and Relations with the Institutions: 58 blvd de la République, BP 4027, Dakar; tel. 823-10-65; fax 821-45-04; internet www.information.gouv.sn.

Ministry of Infrastructure, Capital Works and Land Transport: Ex-Camp Lat Dior, Corriche, Dakar; tel. 849-07-59; fax 823-82-79; internet www.equipement.gouv.sn.

Ministry of the Interior: pl. Washington, BP 4002, Dakar; tel. 823-41-51; fax 821-05-42; e-mail mint@primature.sn; internet www.interieur.gouv.sn.

Ministry of International Co-operation and Decentralized Co-operation: Dakar; tel. 842-58-47; fax 860-16-05; e-mail mcdpr@primature.sn; internet www.mcdpr.gouv.sn.

Ministry of Justice: Bldg Administratif, ave Léopold Sédar Senghor, BP 4030, Dakar; tel. 849-70-00; fax 823-27-27; e-mail justice@justice.gouv.sn; internet www.justice.gouv.sn.

Ministry of Land and Air Transport: Dakar.

Ministry of Livestock-rearing: VDN, BP 45677, Dakar-Fann; tel. 864-50-91; fax 864-50-90.

Ministry of the Maritime Economy and Maritime Transport: Bldg Administratif, BP 4050, Dakar; tel. 823-34-26; fax 823-87-20; e-mail abdoumbodj@yahoo.fr; internet www.ecomaritime.gouv.sn.

Ministry of Micro-finance and Decentralized International Co-operation: Bldg Administratif, 6e étage, ave Léopold Sédar Senghor, BP 36008, Dakar; tel. 849-72-71; fax 842-02-92; e-mail mpme@pme.gouv.sn; internet www.pme.gouv.sn.

Ministry of Mining and Industry: 4e étage, Bldg Administratif, BP 4029, Dakar; tel. 849-70-00; fax 823-44-70.

Ministry of National Languages and Francophone Affairs: Dakar.

Ministry of National Solidarity: Dakar.

Ministry of NEPAD, African Economic Integration and the Politics of Good Governance: 94 rue Félix Faure, Dakar; tel. 889-11-60; fax 842-42-65; e-mail dgnepad@sentoo.sn; internet www.nepad.gouv.sn.

Ministry of Planning, Sustainable Development and International Co-operation: 8 rue du Dr Guillet, BP 4010, Dakar; tel. 823-29-93; fax 823-14-37; e-mail xadijabousso@hotmail.com; internet www.plan.gouv.sn.

Ministry of Preventive Care, Public Hygiene and Decontamination: 2 rue Béranger Ferraud, angle ave Assane Ndoye, Dakar; tel. 889-17-04; fax 842-84-25; e-mail mphpa@sentoo.sn; internet www.prevention.gouv.sn.

Ministry of the Quality of Life and Leisure: Dakar.

Ministry of Relations with the Institutions: Bldg Administratif, ave Léopold Sédar Senghor, BP 49, Dakar; tel. 821-80-60; fax 821-88-50; e-mail mmbodj@sentoo.sn; internet www.mri.gouv.sn.

Ministry of Rural Development and Agriculture: Bldg Administratif, BP 4005; Dakar; tel. 823-39-74; fax 821-32-68; e-mail agric@agric.gouv.sn; internet www.agriculture.gouv.sn.

Ministry of Rural Hydraulics, the National Hydrographic Network, Retention Basins and Man-made Lakes: Dakar.

Ministry of Scientific Research: Bldg Administratif, ave Léopold Sédar Senghor, BP 36005, Dakar; tel. 849-75-52; fax 822-45-63; internet www.recherche.gouv.sn.

Ministry of Senegalese Nationals Abroad: Dakar; tel. 864-50-87; fax 864-50-89.

Ministry of Sports: rue Carnot 58, BP 4019, Dakar; tel. 822-46-21; fax 822-48-31; internet www.sports.gouv.sn.

Ministry of Technical and Professional Training: Dakar.

Ministry of Telecommunications, Posts and Information and Communication Technologies: 2 rue Béranger Ferraud, angle ave Assane Ndoye, Dakar; tel. 887-17-15; fax 842-87-24; internet www.telecom.gouv.sn.

Ministry of Town Planning and Territorial Administration: Ex-Camp Lat Dior, Dakar; tel. 842-08-13; fax 842-08-12; e-mail muat@sentoo.sn; internet www.muat.gouv.sn.

Ministry of Trade: Bldg Administratif, ave Léopold Sédar Senghor, BP 4029, Dakar; tel. 849-70-00; fax 821-91-32; internet www.commerce.gouv.sn.

Ministry of Women, the Family, Social Development and Female Entrepreneurship: Bldg Administratif, Dakar; tel. 849-70-63; fax 822-94-90; internet www.famille.gouv.sn.

Ministry of Youth and Employment: Bldg Administratif, Dakar; tel. 849-59-00; fax 822-97-64; e-mail contact@jeunesse.gouv.sn; internet www.jeunesse.gouv.sn.

President and Legislature

PRESIDENT

Presidential Election, 25 February 2007

Candidate	Votes	% of valid votes
Abdoulaye Wade	1,914,403	55.90
Idrissa Seck	510,922	14.92
Ousmane Tanor Dieng	464,287	13.56
Moustapha Niasse	203,129	5.93
Robert Sagna	88,446	2.58
Abdoulaye Bathily	75,797	2.21
Landing Savané	70,780	2.07
Others	97,162	2.84
Total	3,424,926	100.00

LEGISLATURE

Assemblée nationale

pl. Soweto, BP 86, Dakar; tel. 823-10-99; fax 823-67-08; e-mail assnat@assemblee-nationale.sn; internet www.assemblee-nationale.sn.

President: PAPE DIOP.

General Election, 3 June 2007

Party	Votes	% of votes	Seats
Sopi Coalition*	1,190,609	69.21	131
Takku Defaraat Sénégal Coalition	86,621	5.04	3
And Defar Sénégal Coalition	84,998	4.94	3
Waar Wi Coalition	74,919	4.35	3
Rassemblement pour le peuple (RP)	73,083	4.25	2
Front pour le socialisme et la démocratie—Benno Jubël (FSD—BJ)	37,427	2.18	1
Alliance Jëf-Jël	33,297	1.94	1
Convergence pour le renouveau et la citoyenneté (CRC)	30,658	1.78	1
Parti socialiste authentique (PSA)	26,320	1.53	1
Union nationale patriotique (UNP)	22,271	1.29	1
Mouvement de la réforme pour le développement social (MRDS)	20,041	1.16	1
Rassemblement des écologistes du Sénégal (RES)	17,267	1.00	1
Parti social-démocrate—Jant Bi (PSD—JB)	15,968	0.93	1
Rassemblement patriotique sénégalais—Jammi Rewmi (RPS—JR)	6,847	0.40	—
Total	1,720,326	100.00	150

* A coalition of some 40 parties and movements, led by the PDS.

Election Commission

Commission électorale nationale autonome (CENA): Dakar; f. 2005; Pres. MAMADOU MOUSTAPHA TOURÉ.

Political Organizations

In early 2006 there were more than 70 political parties registered in Senegal, of which the following were among the most important:

Alliance des forces de progrès (AFP): rue 1, angle rue A, point E, BP 5825, Dakar; tel. 825-40-21; fax 864-07-07; e-mail admin@afp-senegal.org; internet www.afp-senegal.org; f. 1999; mem. of opposition Cadre permanent de concertation (f. 2001); Sec.-Gen. MOUSTAPHA NIASSE.

Alliance Jëf-Jël: BP 7838, Dakar; tel. 652-22-32; fax 630-44-51; e-mail tallasylla@hotmail.com; internet tallasylla-president.com; f. 1997; mem. of opposition Cadre permanent de concertation (f. 2001); Pres. TALLA SYLLA.

And Defar Sénégal Coalition: Kolda; Leader LANDING SAVANÉ.

And Jëf—Parti africain pour la démocratie et le socialisme (AJ—PADS): Villa 1, Zone B, BP 12136, Dakar; tel. 825-76-67; fax 823-58-60; e-mail webmaster@ajpads.org; internet x.ajpads.org; f. 1992; Sec.-Gen. LANDING SAVANÉ.

Bloc des centristes Gaïndé (BCG): Villa no 734, Sicap Baobabs, Dakar; tel. 825-37-64; e-mail issa_dias@sentoo.sn; f. 1996; Pres. and First Sec. JEAN-PAUL DIAS.

Convergence pour le renouveau et la citoyenneté (CRC): Leader ALIOU DIA.

Front pour le socialisme et la démocratie—Benno Jubël (FSD—BJ): contested 2001 election as mem. of Sopi Coalition; Leader ABDOULAYE DIÈYE.

Ligue démocratique—Mouvement pour le parti du travail (LD—MPT): ave Bourguiba, Dieuppeul 2, Villa 2566, BP 10172, Dakar Liberté; tel. 825-67-06; fax 827-43-00; regd 1981; social-democrat; Sec.-Gen. ABDOULAYE BATHILY.

Mouvement pour la démocratie et le socialisme—Naxx Jarinu (MDS—NJ): Unité 20, Parcelles Assainies, Villa no 528, Dakar; tel. 869-50-49; f. 2000; Leader OUMAR KHASSIMOU DAI.

Mouvement de la réforme pour le développement social (MRDS): HLM 4, Villa 858, Dakar; tel. 644-31-70; f. 2000; Pres. IBRAHIMA DIENG; Sec.-Gen. Imam BABACAR NIANG.

Mouvement pour le socialisme et l'unité (MSU): HLM 1, Villa 86, Dakar; tel. 825-85-44; f. 1981 as Mouvement démocratique populaire; mem. of opposition Cadre permanent de concertation (f. 2001); National Co-ordinator-Gen. MOUHAMADOU BAMBA N'DIAYE.

Mouvement républicain sénégalais (MRS): Résidence du Cap-Vert, 10e étage, 5 pl. de l'Indépendance, BP 4193, Dakar; tel. 822-03-19; fax 822-07-00; e-mail agaz@omnet.sn; Sec.-Gen. DEMBA BA.

Parti africain de l'indépendance (PAI): Maison du Peuple, Guediewaye, BP 820, Dakar; tel. 837-01-36; f. 1957; reorg. 1976; Marxist; Sec.-Gen. MAJMOUT DIOP.

Parti démocratique sénégalais (PDS): blvd Dial Diop, Immeuble Serigne Mourtada Mbacké, Dakar; tel. 823-50-27; fax 823-17-02; e-mail cedobe@aol.com; internet www.sopionline.com; f. 1974; liberal democratic; Sec.-Gen. Me ABDOULAYE WADE.

Parti de l'indépendance et du travail (PIT): route front de terre, BP 10470, Dakar; tel. 827-29-07; fax 820-90-00; e-mail pit@telecomplus.sn; regd 1981; Marxist-Leninist; mem. of opposition Cadre permanent de concertation (f. 2001); Sec.-Gen. AMATH DANSOKHO.

Parti libéral sénégalais (PLS): 13 ave Malick Sy, BP 28277, Dakar; tel. and fax 823-15-60; f. 1998 by breakaway faction of PDS; Leader Me OUSMANE NGOM.

Parti populaire sénégalais (PPS): Quartier Escale, BP 212, Diourbel; tel. 971-11-71; regd 1981; populist; mem. of opposition Cadre permanent de concertation (f. 2001); Sec.-Gen. Dr OUMAR WANE.

Parti pour le progrès et la citoyenneté (PPC): Quartier Merina, Rufique; tel. 836-18-68; absorbed Rassemblement pour le progrès, la justice et le socialisme in 2000; Sec.-Gen. Me MBAYE JACQUES DIOP.

Parti pour la renaissance africaine—Sénégal (PARENA): Sicap Dieuppeul, Villa no 2685/B, Dakar; tel. 636-87-88; fax 823-57-21; e-mail mariamwane@yahoo.fr; f. 2000; Sec.-Gen. MARIAM MAMADOU WANE LY.

Parti de la renaissance et de la citoyenneté: Liberté 6, Villa 7909, Dakar; tel. 827-85-68; f. 2000; supports Pres. Wade; Sec.-Gen. SAMBA DIOULDÉ THIAM.

Parti social-démocrate—Jant Bi (PSD—JB): Leader MAMOUR CISSE.

Parti socialiste authentique (PSA): Leader SOUTY TOURÉ.

Parti socialiste du Sénégal (PS): Maison du Parti Socialiste Léopold Sédar Senghor, Colobane, BP 12010, Dakar; tel. and fax 824-77-44; e-mail partisocialiste@sentoo.sn; internet www.partisocialiste.sn; f. 1958 as Union progressiste sénégalaise; reorg. 1978; democratic socialist; mem. of opposition Cadre permanent de concertation (f. 2001); First Sec. OUSMANE TANOR DIENG.

Rassemblement des écologistes du Sénégal—Les verts (RES): rue 67, angle rue 52, Gueule Tapée, BP 25226, Dakar-Fann; tel. and fax 842-34-42; e-mail lesverts@arc.sn; f. 1999; Sec.-Gen. OUSMANE SOW HUCHARD.

Rassemblement national démocratique (RND): Sacré-Coeur III, Villa no 972, Dakar; tel. 827-50-72; e-mail wourydiouf@hotmail.com; f. 1976; legalized 1981; mem. of opposition Cadre permanent de concertation (f. 2001); Sec.-Gen. MADIOR DIOUF.

Rassemblement patriotique sénégalais—Jammi Rewmi (RPS—JR): Leader ELY MADIODO FALL FALL.

Rassemblement des travailleurs africains—Sénégal (RTA—S): Villa 999, HLM Grand Yoff, BP 13725, Dakar; tel. 827-15-79; e-mail sambmomar@hotmail.com; f. 1997; Co-ordinator El Hadj MOMAR SAMBE.

Takku Defaraat Sénégal Coalition: VDN à côté de la Poste; tel. 860-50-19; fax 860-50-20; internet www.robertsagna.com; f. 2000; Leader ROBERT SAGNA.

Union nationale patriotique (UNP): Leader NDÈYE FATOU TOURÉ.

Union pour le renouveau démocratique (URD): Bopp Villa 234, rue 7, Dakar; tel. 820-55-98; fax 820-73-17; f. 1998 by breakaway faction of PS; mem. of opposition Cadre permanent de concertation (f. 2001); Sec.-Gen. DJIBO LEÏTY KÂ.

Waar Wi Coalition: Leader MOUDOU DIAGNE FADA.

In August 2001 some 25 pro-Government parties, which were formerly members of the Sopi (Change) Coalition that contested the legislative elections in April 2001, formed an electoral alliance, the **Convergence des actions autour du Président en perspective du 21ième siècle (CAP-21)**, to contest municipal and local elections in May 2002. In May 2001 several opposition parties (numbering eight in February 2004 and led by the AFP) formed an opposition consultative framework, the **Cadre permanent de concertation (CPC)**, which was also to operate as an electoral alliance in the municipal and local elections.

The **Mouvement des forces démocratiques de la Casamance (MFDC)** was founded in 1947; it had paramilitary and political wings and formerly sought the independence of the Casamance region of southern Senegal. The MFDC is not officially recognized as a political party (the Constitution of 2001 forbids the formation of parties on a geographic basis) and waged a campaign of guerrilla warfare in the region from the early 1980s. Representatives of the MFDC have participated in extensive negotiations with the Senegalese Government on the restoration of peace and the granting of greater autonomy to Casamance, and in December 2004 a cease-fire agreement was signed between the two sides, pending further peace negotiations. The Honorary President of the MFDC, Fr AUGUSTIN DIAMACOUNÉ SENGHOR, died in January 2007; the post of Secretary-General was disputed between JEAN-MARIE FRANÇOIS BIAGUI and ANSOUMANA BADJI.

Diplomatic Representation

EMBASSIES IN SENEGAL

Algeria: 5 rue Mermoz, Plateau, Dakar; tel. 849-57-00; fax 849-57-01; e-mail ambalgdak@orange.sn; Ambassador Dr ABDELHAMID CHEBCHOUB.

Austria: 18 rue Emile Zola, BP 3247, Dakar; tel. 849-40-00; fax 849-43-70; e-mail dakar-ob@bmaa.gv.at; Ambassador GERHARD DOUJAK.

Belgium: ave des Jambaars, BP 524, Dakar; tel. 821-25-24; fax 821-63-45; e-mail ambelda@sentoo.sn; internet www.diplomatie.be/dakar; Ambassador LUC WILLEMARCK.

Brazil: Immeuble Fondation Fahd, 4e étage, blvd Djily Mbaye, angle rue Macodou Ndiaye, BP 136, Dakar; tel. 823-14-92; fax 823-71-81; e-mail embdakar@sentoo.sn; Ambassador KÁTIA GODINHO GILABERTE DO NASCIMENTO BORGES.

Burkina Faso: Sicap Sacré Coeur III, Extension VDN No. 10628B, BP 11601, Dakar; tel. 864-58-24; fax 864-58-23; e-mail ambabf@sentoo.sn; Ambassador SALAMATA SAWADOGO.

Cameroon: 157–9 rue Joseph Gomis, BP 4165, Dakar; tel. 849-02-92; fax 823-33-96; Ambassador EMMANUEL MBONJO-EJANGUE.

Canada: rue Galliéni, angle Brière de l'Isle, BP 3373, Dakar; tel. 889-47-00; fax 889-47-20; e-mail dakar@international.gc.ca; internet www.dakar.gc.ca; Ambassador LOUISE R. MARCHAND.

Cape Verde: 3 blvd El-Hadji Djilly M'Baye, BP 11269, Dakar; tel. 822-42-85; fax 821-06-97; e-mail acvc.sen@metissacana.sn; Ambassador RAÚL JORGE VERA CRUZ BARBOSA.

China, People's Republic: rue 18 prolongée, BP 342, Dakar-Fann; tel. 864-77-75; fax 864-77-80; Ambassador LU SHAYE.

Congo, Democratic Republic: Fenêtre Mermoz, Dakar; tel. 825-12-80; Chargé d'affaires a.i. FATAKI NICOLAS LUNGUELE MUSAMBYA.

Congo, Republic: Statut Mermoz, BP 5242, Dakar; tel. 634-50-22; fax 825-78-56; Ambassador VALENTIN OLLESSONGO.

Côte d'Ivoire: ave Birago Diop, BP 359, Dakar; tel. 869-02-70; fax 825-21-15; e-mail cmrci@ambaci-dakar.org; internet www.ambaci-dakar.org; Ambassador FATIMATA TANOE TOURÉ.

Cuba: 43 rue Aimé Césaire, BP 4510, Dakar-Fann; tel. 869-02-40; fax 864-10-63; e-mail embacubasen@sentoo.sn; Ambassador LLUSIF SADIN TASSE.

Egypt: 22 ave Brière de l'Isle, Plateau, BP 474, Dakar; tel. 889-24-74; fax 821-89-93; e-mail ambegydk@telecomplus.sn; Ambassador SANAA ISMAIL ATTA ALLAH.

Ethiopia: 18 blvd de la République, BP 379, Dakar; tel. 821-98-96; fax 821-98-95; e-mail ethembas@sentoo.sn; Ambassador ATO HASSEN ABDULKADIK.

France: 1 rue El Hadj Amadou Assane Ndoye, BP 4035, Dakar; tel. 839-51-00; fax 839-51-81; e-mail webmestre.dakar-amba@diplomatie.gouv.fr; internet www.ambafrance-sn.org; Ambassador JEAN-CHRISTOPHE RUFIN.

Gabon: ave Cheikh Anta Diop, cnr Fann-Résidence, BP 436, Dakar; tel. 865-22-34; fax 864-31-45; Ambassador VINCENT BOULE.

The Gambia: 11 rue de Thiong, BP 3248, Dakar; tel. 821-44-16; fax 821-62-79; Ambassador GIBRIL SEMAN JOOF.

Germany: 20 ave Pasteur, angle rue Mermoz, BP 2100, Dakar; tel. 889-48-84; fax 822-52-99; e-mail reg1@daka.auswaertiges-amt.de; internet www.dakar.diplo.de; Ambassador DORETTA LOSCHELDER.

Ghana: Lot 27, Parcelle B, Almadies, BP 25370, Dakar; tel. 869-19-90; fax 820-19-50; Ambassador FREDERICK DANIEL LARYEA.

Guinea: rue 7, angle B&D, point E, BP 7123, Dakar; tel. 824-86-06; fax 825-59-46; Ambassador HADJA KOUMBA DIAKITÉ.

Guinea-Bissau: rue 6, angle B, point E, BP 2319, Dakar; tel. 823-00-59; fax 825-29-46; Ambassador LANSANA TOURÉ.

Holy See: rue Aimé Césaire, angle Corniche-Ouest, Fann Résidence, BP 5076, Dakar; tel. 824-26-74; fax 824-19-31; e-mail vatemb@orange.sn; Apostolic Nuncio Most Rev. GIUSEPPE PINTO (Titular Archbishop of Anglona).

India: 5 rue Carde, BP 398, Dakar; tel. 822-58-75; fax 822-35-85; e-mail indiacom@sentoo.sn; internet www.ambassadeinde.sn; Ambassador PARBATI SEN VYAS.

Indonesia: ave Cheikh Anta Diop, BP 5859, Dakar; tel. 825-73-16; fax 825-58-96; e-mail kbri@sentoo.sn; internet www.indonesia-senegal.org; Ambassador AHZAM BAHDARI RAZIF.

Iran: rue AX8, point E, BP 735, Dakar; tel. 825-25-28; fax 824-23-14; e-mail ambiiran@telecomplus.sn; Ambassador MOHAMMAD HOSEINI.

Israel: Immeuble SDIH, 3 pl. de l'Indépendance, BP 2096, Dakar; tel. 823-79-65; fax 823-64-90; e-mail info@dakar.mfa.gov.il; internet dakar.mfa.gov.il; Ambassador DANIEL PINHASI.

Italy: rue Alpha Achamiyou Tall, BP 348, Dakar; tel. 822-05-78; fax 821-75-80; e-mail ambasciata.dakar@esteri.it; internet sedi.esteri.it/dakar; Ambassador AGOSTINO MATHIS.

Japan: blvd Martin Luther King, Corniche-Ouest, BP 3140, Dakar; tel. 849-55-00; fax 849-55-55; Ambassador AKIRA NAKAJIMA.

Korea, Republic: 4e étage, Immeuble Fayçal, 3 rue Parchappe, BP 3338, Dakar; tel. 822-58-22; fax 821-66-00; e-mail senegal@mofat.go.kr; internet www.mofat.go.kr/senegal; Ambassador JAE CHOL HAHN.

Kuwait: blvd Martin Luther King, Dakar; tel. 824-17-23; fax 825-08-99; Ambassador MUHAMMAD AZ-ZUWAIKH.

Lebanon: 56 ave Jean XXIII, BP 234, Dakar; tel. 822-02-55; fax 823-58-99; e-mail ambaliban@sentoo.sn; Ambassador MICHEL HADDAD.

Libya: route de Ouakam, Dakar; tel. 824-57-10; fax 824-57-22; Ambassador AL HADY SALEM HAMMAD.

Madagascar: Immeuble rue 2, angle Ellipse, Point E, BP 25395, Dakar; tel. 825-26-66; fax 864-40-86; e-mail ambadak@yahoo.fr; internet www.ambamad.sn; Ambassador LILA HANITRA RATSIFANDRIHAMANANA.

Malaysia: 7 Extension VDN, Fann Mermoz, BP 15057, Dakar; tel. 825-89-35; fax 825-47-19; e-mail mwdakar@sentoo.sn; Chargé d'affaires a.i. SHARWANA BIN IDRISS.

Mali: Fann Résidence, Corniche-Ouest, rue 23, BP 478, Dakar; tel. 824-62-52; fax 825-94-71; e-mail ambamali@sentoo.sn; Ambassador N'TJI LAÏCO TRAORÉ.

Mauritania: 37 blvd Charles de Gaulle, Dakar; tel. 823-53-44; fax 823-53-11; Ambassador MOHAMED EL-MOCTAR OULD MOHAMED YAHYA.

Morocco: 73 ave Cheikh Anta Diop, BP 490, Dakar; tel. 824-69-27; fax 825-70-21; e-mail ambmadk@sentoo.sn; Ambassador MOHA OUALI TAGMA.

Netherlands: 37 rue Jaques Bugnicourt, BP 3262, Dakar; tel. 849-03-60; fax 821-70-84; e-mail dak@minbuza.nl; internet www.nlambassadedakar.org; Ambassador Dr J. W. G. JANSING.

Nigeria: 8 ave Cheikh Anta Diop, BP 3129, Dakar; tel. 869-86-00; tel. 869-86-00; fax 825-81-36; e-mail info@nigeriandakar.sn; Ambassador AZUKA CECILIA UZOKA-EMEJULU.

Pakistan: Stèle Mermoz, Villa no 7602, BP 2635, Dakar; tel. 824-61-35; fax 824-61-36; e-mail parepdakar@sentoo.sn; Ambassador ABDUL MALIK ABDULLAH.

Poland: Villa 'Les Ailes', Fann Résidence, angle Corniche-Ouest, BP 343, Dakar; tel. 824-23-54; fax 824-95-26; e-mail ambassade.pl@sentoo.sn; internet www.ambassade-pologne.sn; Ambassador ANDRZEJ MICHAL LUPINA.

Portugal: 5 ave Carde, BP 281, Dakar; tel. 864-03-17; fax 864-03-22; e-mail ambportdakar@sentoo.sn; Ambassador ANTÓNIO AUGUSTO MONTENEGRO VIEIRA CARDOSO.

Qatar: 25 blvd Martin Luther King, BP 5150, Dakar; tel. 820-95-59; fax 869-10-12; Ambassador ALI ABDUL LATIF AHMED AL-MASALAMANI.

Romania: rue A prolongée, point E, BP 3171, Dakar; tel. 825-20-68; fax 824-91-90; e-mail romania@sentoo.sn; Ambassador SIMONA CORLAN-IOAN.

Russia: ave Jean Jaurès, angle rue Carnot, BP 3180, Dakar; tel. 822-48-21; fax 821-13-72; e-mail ambrus@sentoo.sn; Ambassador ALEKSANDR A. ROMANOV.

Saudi Arabia: route Corniche-Ouest, face Olympique Club, BP 3109, Dakar; tel. 864-01-41; fax 864-01-30; e-mail snemb@mofa.gov.sa; Chargé d'affaires a.i. FAHD NASSER AL BIHAIRAN.

South Africa: Memoz SUD, Lotissement Ecole de Police, BP 21010, Dakar-Ponty; tel. 865-19-59; fax 864-23-59; e-mail ambafsud@sentoo.sn; internet www.saesenegal.info; Ambassador T. C. MAJOLA-EMBALO.

Spain: 18–20 ave Nelson Mandela, BP 2091, Dakar; tel. 821-11-78; fax 821-68-45; e-mail ambespsn@mail.mae.es; Ambassador FERNANDO MORÁN CALVO-SOTELO.

Sudan: 31 route de la Pyrotechnie, Mermoz, BP 15033, Dakar-Fann; tel. 824-98-53; fax 824-98-52; e-mail sudembse@sentoo.sn; Ambassador MAHMOUD HASSAN EL-AMIN.

Sweden: 18 rue Emile Zola, BP 6087, Dakar; tel. 849-03-33; fax 849-03-40; e-mail ambassaden.dakar@foreign.ministry.se; internet www.swedenabroad.com/dakar; Ambassador AGNETA BOHMAN.

Switzerland: rue René N'Diaye, angle rue Seydou, BP 1772, Dakar; tel. 823-05-90; fax 822-36-57; e-mail dak.vertretung@eda.admin.ch; internet www.eda.admin.ch/dakar; Ambassador LIVIO HÜRZELER.

Syria: rue 1, point E, angle blvd de l'Est, BP 498, Dakar; tel. 824-62-77; fax 825-17-55; Ambassador HAMZEH DAWALIBI.

Thailand: 10 rue Léon Gontran Damas, BP 3721, Dakar-Fann; tel. 869-32-90; fax 824-84-58; e-mail thaidkr@sentoo.sn; internet www.mfa.go.th/web/2366.php; Ambassador ITTI DITBANJONG.

Tunisia: rue Alpha Hachamiyou Tall, BP 3127, Dakar; tel. 823-47-47; fax 823-72-04; Ambassador JALEL LAKHDAR.

Turkey: ave des Ambassadeurs, Fann Résidence, BP 6060, Etoile, Dakar; tel. 869-25-42; fax 825-69-77; e-mail trambdkr@sentoo.sn; Ambassador YALÇIN KAYA ERENSOY.

United Kingdom: 20 rue du Dr Guillet, BP 6025, Dakar; tel. 823-73-92; fax 823-27-66; e-mail britemb@sentoo.sn; internet www.britishembassy.gov.uk/senegal; Ambassador CHRIS TROTT.

USA: ave Jean XXIII, angle rue Kleber, BP 49, Dakar; tel. 823-42-96; fax 823-51-63; e-mail usadakar@state.gov; internet dakar.usembassy.gov; Ambassador JANICE L. JACOBS.

Judicial System

In 1992 the Supreme Court was replaced by three judicial bodies. The Constitutional Council verifies that legislation and international agreements are in accordance with the Constitution. It decides disputes between the Executive and the Legislature, and determines the relative jurisdictions of the Council of State and the Court of Cassation. The Council of State judges complaints brought against the Executive. It also resolves electoral disputes. The Court of Cassation is the highest court of appeal, and regulates the activities of subordinate courts and tribunals. The Revenue Court supervises the public accounts.

Constitutional Council: BP 45732, Dakar; tel. 822-52-52; fax 822-81-87; e-mail magou_51@hotmail.com; internet www.gouv.sn/institutions/conseil_const.html; 5 mems; Pres. MIREILLE NDIAYE.

Council of State: rue Béranger Ferraut, Dakar; tel. 822-47-86; internet www.gouv.sn/institutions/conseil_etat.html; Pres. ABDOU AZIZ BA.

Court of Cassation: blvd Martin Luther King, BP 15184, Dakar-Fann; tel. 889-10-10; fax 821-18-90; e-mail pasakho@yahoo.fr; internet www.gouv.sn/institutions/cour_cassation.html; First Pres. PAPA OUMAR SAKHO; Procurator-Gen. ABDOULAYE CRAYE; Sec.-Gen. MAMADOU BADIO CAMARA.

Revenue Court (Cour des Comptes): 15 ave Franklin Roosevelt, BP 9097, Peytavin, Dakar; tel. 849-40-01; fax 849-43-62; e-mail askonte@courdescomptes.sn; internet www.courdescomptes.sn; Pres. ABDOU BAME GUEYE; Sec.-Gen. El Hadji MALICK KONTE; Pres. of Chambers ABBA GOUDIABY, MOUSTAPHA GUEYE, MAMADOU HADY SARR; Chief Administrator ABDOURAHMANE DIOUKNANE.

High Court of Justice: Dakar; competent to try the Prime Minister and other members of the Government for crimes committed in the exercise of their duties; The President of the Republic may only be brought to trial in the case of high treason; mems elected by the Assemblée nationale.

Religion

At the time of the 1988 census almost 94% of the population were Muslims, while some 4% professed Christianity (the dominant faith being Roman Catholicism); a small number, mostly in the south, followed traditional beliefs.

ISLAM

There are four main Islamic brotherhoods active in Senegal: the Tidjanes, the Mourides, the Layennes and the Qadiriyas.

Association pour la coopération islamique (ACIS): Dakar; f. 1988; Pres. Dr THIERNAO KÂ.

Grande Mosquée de Dakar: Dakar; tel. 822-56-48; Grand Imam El Hadj BAYE DAME DIÈNE.

CHRISTIANITY

The Roman Catholic Church

Senegal comprises one archdiocese and six dioceses. At 31 December 2004 there were an estimated 544,292 adherents of the Roman Catholic Church, representing about 5.3% of the total population.

Bishops' Conference

Conférence des Evêques du Sénégal, de la Mauritanie, du Cap-Vert et de Guinée-Bissau, BP 941, Dakar; tel. 836-33-09; fax 836-16-17; e-mail archevchedkr@sentoo.sn.

f. 1973; Pres. Most Rev. JEAN-NOËL DIOUF (Bishop of Tambacounda).

Archbishop of Dakar: Most Rev. THÉODORE-ADRIEN SARR, Archevêché, ave Jean XXIII, BP 1908, Dakar; tel. 823-69-18; fax 823-48-75; e-mail archevechedkr@sentoo.sn.

The Anglican Communion

The Anglican diocese of The Gambia, part of the Church of the Province of West Africa, includes Senegal and Cape Verde. The Bishop is resident in Banjul, The Gambia.

Protestant Church

Eglise Protestante du Sénégal: 65 rue Wagane Diouf, BP 22390, Dakar; tel. 821-55-64; fax 821-71-32; f. 1862; Pastor ETITI YOMO DJERIWO.

BAHÁ'Í FAITH

National Spiritual Assembly: Point E, rue des Ecrivains, 2è impasse à droite après la Direction de la statistique, BP 1662, Dakar; tel. 824-23-59; e-mail bahai@sentoo.sn; internet www.sn.bahai.org; regd 1975; Sec. ABOUBAKRINE BA.

The Press

DAILY NEWSPAPERS

L'Actuel: route du Front de Terre, angle ave Bourguiba, Immeuble Dramé, BP 11874, Dakar; tel. 864-26-01; fax 864-26-02; e-mail lactuel@sentoo.sn.

Dakar Soir: Dakar; tel. and fax 832-10-93; e-mail dakar-soir@telecomplus.sn; f. 2000.

Dekeu Bi: Quartier Casier, Thiès; tel. 557-29-15.

L'Evénement du Soir: Fann Résidence, rue A, angle rue 4, point E, BP 16060, Dakar; tel. 864-34-30; fax 864-36-00; evenings.

Frasques Quotidiennes: 51 rue du Docteur Thèze, BP 879, Dakar; tel. 842-42-26; fax 842-42-77; e-mail frasques@arc.sm.

L'Info 7: Sicap rue 10, BP 11357, Dakar; tel. and fax 864-26-58; e-mail comsept@sentoo.sn; f. 1999.

Le Matin: route de l'Aéroport Léopold Sédar Senghor, BP 6472, Dakar; tel. 825-73-59; fax 825-73-58; e-mail lematin@metissacana.sn; daily; independent; Dir MAME LESS CAMARA; Editor-in-Chief ALIOUNE FALL.

La Pointe: Dakar; tel. 820-50-35; fax 820-50-43.

Le Populaire: 114 ave Peytavin, Immeuble Serigne Massamba Mbacké, Dakar; tel. 822-79-77; fax 822-79-27; e-mail populaire@sentoo.sn; f. 2000; Editor-in-Chief MAMADOU THIERNO TALLA.

Scoop: route du Service Géographique, BP 92, Dakar; tel. 859-59-59; fax 859-60-50.

Le Soleil: Société sénégalaise de presse et de publications, route du Service géographique, Hann, BP 92, Dakar; tel. 859-59-40; fax 859-60-50; e-mail lesoleil@lesoleil.sn; internet www.lesoleil.sn; f. 1970; Dir-Gen. and Dir of Publication MAMADOU SEYE; Editors-in-Chief HABIB DEMBA FALL, IBRAHIMA MBODJ; circ. 25,000 (2005).

Sud Quotidien: Immeuble Fahd, BP 4130, Dakar; tel. 821-33-38; fax 822-52-90; e-mail info@sudonline.sn; internet www.sudonline.sn; independent; Dir ABDOULAYE NDIAGA SYLLA; circ. 30,000.

Tract: 13 rue de Thann, BP 3683, Dakar; tel. and fax 823-47-25; e-mail tract.sn@laposte.net; f. 2000.

Le Volcan: Dakar; tel. 820-50-35; fax 820-50-43.

Wal Fadjri/L'Aurore (The Dawn): Sicap Sacré-Coeur no 8542, BP 576, Dakar; tel. 824-23-43; fax 824-23-46; e-mail walf@walf.sn; internet www.walf.sn; f. 1984; Exec. Dir MBAYE SIDY MBAYE; circ. 15,000.

PERIODICALS

Afrique Médicale: 10 rue Abdou Karim Bourgi, BP 1826, Dakar; tel. 823-48-80; fax 822-56-30; f. 1960; 11 a year; review of tropical medicine; Editor P. CORREA; circ. 7,000.

Afrique Nouvelle: 9 rue Paul Holle, BP 283, Dakar; tel. 822-51-22; f. 1947; weekly; development issues; Roman Catholic; Dir RENÉ ODOUN; circ. 15,000.

Afrique Tribune: Dakar; tel. and fax 821-15-92; monthly.

Amina: BP 2120, Dakar; e-mail amina@calva.net; monthly; women's magazine.

Le Cafard Libéré: 10 rue Tolbiac, angle Autoroute, Soumédioune, BP 7292, Dakar; tel. 822-84-43; fax 822-08-91; e-mail caflibere@sentoo.sn; f. 1987; weekly; satirical; Editor PAPE SAMBA KANE; circ. 12,000.

Construire l'Afrique: Dakar; tel. 823-07-90; fax 824-19-61; f. 1985; six a year; African business; Dir and Chief Editor CHEIKH OUSMANE DIALLO.

Le Courrier du Sud: BP 190, Ziguinchor; tel. 991-11-66; weekly.

Démocratie: Liberté V, 5375 M, 71 rue du rond-point Liberté V et VI; tel. 824-86-69; fax 825-18-79.

Eco Hebdo: 22 x 19 rue Médina, BP 11451, Dakar; tel. and fax 837-14-14; weekly.

L'Equipe Sénégal: Dakar; tel. 824-00-13; e-mail lequipesenegal@yahoo.fr; weekly; sports.

Ethiopiques: BP 2035, Dakar; tel. and fax 821-53-55; f. 1974; literary and philosophical review; publ. by Fondation Léopold Sédar Senghor.

Le Journal de l'Economie: 15 rue Jules Ferry, BP 2851, Dakar; tel. 823-87-33; fax 823-60-07; weekly.

Journal Officiel de la République du Sénégal: Rufisque; f. 1856; weekly; govt journal.

Momsareew: BP 820, Dakar; f. 1958; monthly; publ. by PAI; Editor-in-Chief MALAMINE BADJI; circ. 2,000.

Nord Ouest: Immeuble Lonase, BP 459, Louga; tel. 680-79-43; e-mail lenordouest@yahoo.fr; regional monthly; Dir of Publication PAPE MOMAR CISSÉ.

Nouvel Horizon: Dakar; tel. and fax 822-74-14; weekly.

Nuit et Jour: Dakar; tel. 832-15-70; weekly.

Le Politicien: Dakar; tel. and fax 827-63-96; f. 1977; weekly; satirical.

Promotion: BP 1676, Dakar; tel. 825-69-69; fax 825-69-50; e-mail giepromo@telecomplus.sn; f. 1972; fortnightly; Dir BOUBACAR DIOP; circ. 5,000.

République: BP 21740, Dakar; tel. 822-73-73; fax 822-50-39; e-mail republike@yahoo.fr; f. 1994.

Sénégal d'Aujourd'hui: Dakar; monthly; publ. by Ministry of Culture; circ. 5,000.

Sopi (Change): 5 blvd Dial Diop, Dakar; tel. 824-49-50; fax 824-47-00; f. 1988; weekly; publ. by PDS; Dir of Publishing JOSEPH NDONG; Editor CHEIKH KOUREYSSI BA.

Le Témoin: Gibraltar II, Villa no 310, Dakar; tel. 822-32-69; fax 821-78-38; f. 1990; weekly; Editor-in-Chief MAMADOU OUMAR NDIAYE; circ. 5,000.

Unir Cinéma: 1 rue Neuville, BP 160, Saint Louis; tel. 861-10-27; fax 861-24-08; f. 1973; quarterly African cinema review; Editor PIERRE SAGNA.

Vive La République: Sicap Amitié III, Villa no 4057, Dakar; tel. 864-06-31; weekly.

Xareli (Struggle): BP 12136, Dakar; tel. 822-54-63; fortnightly; publ. by AJ—PADS; circ. 7,000.

NEWS AGENCIES

Agence Panafricaine d'Information—PANA-Presse SA: ave Bourjuiba, BP 4056, Dakar; tel. 824-13-95; fax 824-13-90; e-mail panapress@panapress.com; internet www.panapress.com; f. 1979 as Pan-African News Agency (under the auspices of the Organization of African Unity), restructured as 75% privately owned co in 1997; Co-ordinator-Gen. BABACAR FALL.

Agence de Presse Sénégalaise: 58 blvd de la République, BP 117, Dakar; tel. 823-16-67; fax 822-07-67; e-mail aps@aps.sn; internet www.aps.sn; f. 1959; govt-controlled; Dir AMADOU DIENG.

Foreign Bureaux

Agence France-Presse (AFP): Immeuble Maginot, 7e étage, BP 363, Dakar; tel. 823-21-92; fax 822-16-07.

Xinhua (New China) News Agency (People's Republic of China): Villa 1, 2 route de la Pyrotechnie, Stèle Mermoz, BP 426, Dakar; tel. 823-05-38.

ANSA (Italy), ITAR—TASS (Russia) and UPI (USA) are also represented in Dakar.

PRESS ORGANIZATION

Syndicat des Professionnels de l'Information et de la Communication du Sénégal (SYNPICS): BP 21722, Dakar; tel. 842-42-56; fax 842-02-69; e-mail synpics@yahoo.fr; Sec.-Gen. DIATA CISSÉ.

Publishers

Africa Editions: BP 1826, Dakar; tel. 823-48-80; fax 822-56-30; f. 1958; general, reference; Man. Dir JOËL DECUPPER.

Agence de Distribution de Presse: km 2.5, blvd du Centenaire de la Commune de Dakar, BP 374, Dakar; tel. 832-02-78; fax 832-49-15; e-mail adpresse@telecomplus.sn; f. 1943; general, reference; Man. Dir PHILIPPE SCHORP.

Centre Africain d'Animation et d'Echanges Culturels Editions Khoudia: BP 5332, Dakar-Fann; tel. 821-10-23; fax 821-51-09; f. 1989; fiction, education, anthropology; Dir AISSATOU DIA.

Editions Clairafrique: 2 rue El Hadji Mbaye Guèye, BP 2005, Dakar; tel. 822-21-69; fax 821-84-09; f. 1951; politics, law, sociology, anthropology, literature, economics, development, religion, school books.

Editions des Ecoles Nouvelles Africaines: ave Cheikh Anta Diop, angle rue Pyrotechnie, Stèle Mermoz, BP 581, Dakar; tel. 864-05-44; fax 864-13-52; e-mail eenas@sentoo.sn; youth and adult education, in French.

Editions Juridiques Africaines (EDJA): 18 rue Raffenel, BP 22420, Dakar-Ponty; tel. 821-66-89; fax 823-27-53; e-mail edja.ed@sentoo.sn; f. 1986; law; Dir SALIMATA NGOM DIOP.

Editions des Trois Fleuves: blvd de l'Est, angle Cheikh Anta Diop, BP 123, Dakar; tel. 825-79-23; fax 825-59-37; f. 1972; general non-fiction; luxury edns; Dir GÉRARD RAZIMOWSKY; Gen. Man. BERTRAND DE BOISTEL.

Enda—Tiers Monde Editions (Environmental Development Action in the Third World): 54 rue Carnot, BP 3370, Dakar; tel. 822-98-90; fax 823-51-57; e-mail editions@enda.sn; internet www.enda.sn; f. 1972; third-world environment and development; Dir GIDEON PRISLER OMOLU; Exec. Sec. JACQUES BUGNICOURT.

Grande imprimerie africaine (GIA): 9 rue Amadou Assane Ndoye, Dakar; tel. 822-14-08; fax 822-39-27; f. 1917; law, administration; Man. Dir CHEIKH ALIMA TOURÉ.

Institut fondamental d'Afrique noire (IFAN)—Cheikh Anta Diop: BP 206, Campus universitaire, Dakar; tel. 825-98-90; fax 824-49-18; e-mail bifan@telecomplus.sn; internet www.afrique-ouest.auf.org; f. 1936; scientific and humanistic studies of Black Africa, for specialist and general public.

Nouvelles éditions africaines du Sénégal (NEAS): 10 rue Amadou Assane Ndoye, BP 260, Dakar; tel. 822-15-80; fax 822-36-04; e-mail neas@telecomplus.sn; f. 1972; literary fiction, schoolbooks; Dir-Gen. SAYDOU SOW.

Per Ankh: BP 2, Popenguine; history.

Société africaine d'édition: 16 bis rue de Thiong, BP 1877, Dakar; tel. 821-79-77; f. 1961; African politics and economics; Man. Dir PIERRE BIARNES.

Société d'édition 'Afrique Nouvelle': 9 rue Paul Holle, BP 283, Dakar; tel. 822-38-25; f. 1947; information, statistics and analyses of African affairs; Man. Dir ATHANASE NDONG.

Société nationale de Presse, d'édition et de publicité (SONAPRESS): Dakar; f. 1972; Pres. OBEYE DIOP.

Sud-Communication: BP 4100, Dakar; operated by a journalists' co-operative; periodicals.

Xamal, SA: BP 380, Saint-Louis; tel. 961-17-22; fax 961-15-19; e-mail xamal@sentoo.sn; general literature, social sciences, in national languages and in French; Dir ABOUBAKAR DIOP.

GOVERNMENT PUBLISHING HOUSE

Société sénégalaise de presse et de publications—Imprimerie nationale (SSPP): route du Service géographique, BP 92, Dakar; tel. 832-46-92; fax 832-03-81; f. 1970; 62% govt-owned; Dir SALIOU DIAGNE.

Broadcasting and Communications

TELECOMMUNICATIONS

Regulatory Authority

Agence de Régulation des Télécommunications et des Postes (ARTP): route de Ngor Angle Dioulikayes, BP 14130, Dakar-Peytavin; tel. 869-03-69; fax 869-03-70; e-mail contact@artp.sn; internet www.artp.sn; f. 2001; Ppres. Prof. ABDOULAYE SAKHO; Dir-Gen. DANIEL G. GOUMALO SECK.

Service Providers

Excaf Telecom: Domaine Industriel SODIDA, rue 14 Prolongée, BP 1656, Dakar; tel. 824-24-24; fax 824-21-91; internet www.excaf.com.

Sentel Sénégal GSM: ave Nelson Mandela, angle ave Moussé Diop. BP 146, Dakar; tel. 675-42-02; fax 823-18-73; internet www.sentel.sn; mobile cellular telephone operator in Dakar, most western regions, and in selected localities nation-wide; 75% owned by Millicom International Cellular (Luxembourg), 25% by Senegalese private investors; Gen. Man. YOUVAL ROSH; 250,000 subscribers (2003).

Société Nationale des Télécommunications du Sénégal (SONATEL): 46 blvd de la République, BP 69, Dakar; tel. 839-11-18; fax 823-60-37; e-mail webmaster@sonatel.sn; internet www.sonatel.sn; f. 1985; 42.3% owned by France Câbles et Radio (France Télécom, France), 27.67% owned by Govt; Pres. MICHEL HIRSCH; Man. Dir CHEIKH TIDIANE MBAYE; 1,673 employees (2003).

Alizé: 46 blvd de la République, BP 2352, Dakar; tel. 839-17-00; fax 839-17-54; e-mail webmaster@alize.sn; internet www.alize.sn; f. 1996 as Sonatel Mobiles.

Télécom Plus SARL: 20 rue Amadou Assane Ndoye, BP 21100, Dakar; tel. 839-97-00; fax 823-46-32; telecommunications products and services.

BROADCASTING

Regulatory Authority

Haut Conseil de l'Audiovisuel: Immeuble Fahd, Dakar; tel. and fax 823-47-84; f. 1991; Pres. AMINATA CISSÉ NIANG.

Radio

Société nationale de la Radiodiffusion-Télévision Sénégalaise (RTS): Triangle sud, angle ave Malick Sy, BP 1765, Dakar; tel. 849-12-12; fax 822-34-90; e-mail rts@rts.sn; internet www.rts.sn; f. 1992; state broadcasting co; broadcasts two national and eight regional stations; Dir-Gen. DAOUDA NDIAYE.

Radio Sénégal Internationale: Triangle sud, angle ave El Hadj Malick Sy, BP 1765, Dakar; tel. 849-12-12; fax 822-34-90; f. 2001; broadcasts news and information programmes in French, English, Arabic, Portuguese, Spanish, Italian, Soninké, Pulaar and Wolof from 14 transmitters across Senegal and on cable; Dir CHÉRIF THIAM.

RST1: Triangle sud, angle ave El Hadj Malick Sy, BP 1765, Dakar; tel. 849-12-12; fax 822-34-90; f. 1992; broadcasts in French, Arabic and six vernacular languages from 16 transmitters across Senegal; Dir MANSOUR SOW.

JDP FM (Jeunesse, Développement, Paix): BP 17040, Dakar; tel. 827-20-97; fax 824-07-41; e-mail sarrabdou@sentoo.sn.

Radio Nostalgie Dakar: BP 21021, Dakar; tel. 821-21-21; fax 822-22-22; e-mail nostafric@globeaccess.net; f. 1995; music; broadcasts in French and Wolof; Gen. Man. SAUL SAVÎOTE.

Oxy-Jeunes: Fojes BP 18303, Pikine, Dakar; tel. 834-49-19; fax 827-32-15; e-mail cheikh_seck@eudoramail.com; f. 1999; youth and community radio station supported by the World Asscn of Community Radio Stations and the Catholic Organization for Development and Peace.

Radio PENC-MI: BP 51, Khombole; tel. 957-91-03; fax 824-58-98; e-mail rdoucoure@oxfam.org.uk.

Radio Rurale FM Awagna de Bignona: BP 72, Bignona; tel. 994-10-21; fax 994-19-09; e-mail mksonko2000@yahoo.fr.

Sud FM: Immeuble Fahd, 5e étage, BP 4130, Dakar; tel. 822-53-93; fax 822-52-90; e-mail info@sudonline.sn; f. 1994; operated by Sud-Communication; regional stations in Saint-Louis, Kaolack, Louga, Thiès, Ziguinchor and Diourbel; Man. Dir CHERIF EL-WAHIB SEYE.

Wal Fadjri FM: Sicap Sacré-Coeur no 8542, BP 576, Dakar; tel. 824-23-43; fax 824-23-46; f. 1997; Islamic broadcaster; Exec. Dir MBAYE SIDY MBAYE.

Broadcasts by the Gabonese-based Africa No. 1, the British Broadcasting Corporation and Radio France Internationale are received in Dakar.

Television

Radiodiffusion-Télévision Sénégalaise (RTS): see Radio; Dir of Television DAOUDA NDIAYE.

Canal Horizons Sénégal: 31 ave Albert Sarrault, BP 1390, Dakar; tel. 823-25-25; fax 823-30-30; e-mail canalh@sonatel.sn; internet www.canalhorizons.com; f. 1990; private encrypted channel; 18.8% owned by RTS and Société Nationale des Télécommunications du

Sénégal, 15% by Canal Horizons (France); Man. Dir JACQUES BARBIER DE CROZES.

Réseau MMDS-EXCAF Télécom: rue 14 prolongée, HLM 1, Domaine Industriel SODIDA, BP 1656, Dakar; tel. 824-24-24; fax 824-21-91; broadcasts selection of African, US, European and Saudi Arabian channels.

The French television stations, France-2, TV5 and Arte France, are also broadcast to Senegal.

Finance

(cap. = capital; res = reserves; dep. = deposits; m. = million; br(s). = branch(es); amounts in francs CFA)

BANKING

Central Bank

Banque centrale des états de l'Afrique de l'ouest (BCEAO): National HQ: blvd du Général de Gaulle, angle Triangle Sud, BP 3159, Dakar; tel. 823-53-84; fax 823-57-57; e-mail akangni@bceao.int; internet www.bceao.int; f. 1962; bank of issue for mem. states of the Union économique et monétaire ouest africaine (UEMOA, comprising Benin, Burkina Faso, Côte d'Ivoire, Guinea-Bissau, Mali, Niger, Senegal and Togo); cap. 134,120m., res 949,521m., dep. 1,226,294m. (Dec. 2004); Gov. DAMO JUSTIN BARO (acting); Dir in Senegal SEYNI NDIAYE; brs at Kaolack and Ziguinchor.

Commercial Banks

Attijariwafa Bank Sénégal: 5 rue Victor Hugo, angle ave Léopold Sédar Senghor, Dakar; f. 2004; 100% owned by Attijariwafa Bank Maroc (Morocco); Pres. and Dir-Gen. SAÏD RAKI.

Bank of Africa—Sénégal: Résidence Excellence, 4 ave Léopold Sédar Senghor, BP 1992, Dakar; tel. 849-62-40; fax 842-16-67; e-mail boadg@sentoo.sn; internet www.bkofafrica.net/senegal.htm; f. 2001; 59.32% owned by African Financial Holding, 15.00% by Bank of Africa—Benin; cap. and res 1,661.2m., total assets 20,588.0m. (Dec. 2003); Pres. MAMADOU AMADOU AW; Dir-Gen. BERNARD PUECHALDOU; 1 br.

Banque Internationale pour le Commerce et l'Industrie du Sénégal (BICIS): 2 ave Léopold Sédar Senghor, BP 392, Dakar; tel. 839-03-90; fax 823-37-07; e-mail bicis@bicis.sn; internet www.bicis.sn; f. 1962; 54.09% owned by Groupe BNP Paribas (France); cap. and res 15,638m., total assets 227,702m. (Dec. 2003); Pres. LANDING SANÉ; Dir-Gen. AMADOU KANE; 17 brs.

Citibank Dakar: Immeuble SDIH, 4e étage, 2 pl. de l'Indépendance, BP 3391, Dakar; tel. 849-11-11; fax 823-88-17; e-mail thioro.ba@citicorp.com; f. 1975; wholly owned subsidiary of Citibank NA (USA); cap. 1,626m., total assets 84,864m. (Dec. 2001); Pres. JOHN REED; Dir-Gen. MICHAEL GROSSMAN; 1 br.

Compagnie Bancaire de l'Afrique Occidentale (CBAO): 1 pl. de l'Indépendance, BP 129, Dakar; tel. 839-96-96; fax 823-20-05; e-mail cbao@cboa.sn; f. 1853; 76% owned by Groupe Mimran; cap. 9,000m., res 13,509m., dep. 307,312m. (Dec. 2005); Pres. JEAN CLAUDE MIMRAN; Dir-Gen. PATRICK MESTRALLET; 24 brs.

Compagnie Ouest Africaine de Crédit Bail (LOCAFRIQUE): Immeuble Coumaba Castel, 11 rue Galandou Diouf, BP 292, Dakar; tel. 822-06-47; fax 822-08-94; e-mail locafrique@are.sn; f. 1977; cap. 579m., total assets 1,241m. (Dec. 2003); Dir-Gen. IBRAHIMA SOUR.

Crédit Lyonnais Sénégal (CLS): blvd El Hadji Djily Mbaye, angle rue Huart, BP 56, Dakar; tel. 849-00-00; fax 823-84-30; e-mail cl_senegal@creditlyonnais.fr; internet www.creditlyonnais.sn; f. 1989; 95% owned by Calyon Global Banking (France); 5% state-owned; cap. 2,000m., res 8,018m., dep. 100,817m. (Dec. 2004); Pres. and Chair. BAUDOUIN MERLET; Dir-Gen. JEAN PAUL VERU; 1 br.

Crédit National du Sénégal (CNS): 7 ave Léopold Sédar Senghor, BP 319, Dakar; tel. 823-34-86; fax 823-72-92; f. 1990 by merger; 87% state-owned; cap. 1,900m., total assets 2,032m. (Dec. 1996); Pres. ABDOU NDIAYE.

Ecobank Sénégal: 8 ave Léopold Sédar Senghor, BP 9095, Dakar; tel. 849-20-00; fax 823-47-07; e-mail ecobank.sn@ecobank.com; internet www.ecobank.com; 41.45% owned by Ecobank Transnational Inc (Togo, operating under the auspices of the Economic Community of West African States), 17.0% by Ecobank Bénin, 12.43% by Ecobank Côte d'Ivoire, 4.56% by Ecobank Niger, 4.56% by Ecobank Togo; cap. and res 3,181m., total assets 48,591m. (Dec. 2003); Pres. MAHENTA BIRIMA FALL; Dir-Gen. EVELYNE TALL.

Société Générale de Banques au Sénégal (SGBS): 19 ave Léopold Sédar Senghor, BP 323, Dakar; tel. 839-55-00; fax 823-90-36; e-mail sgbs@sentoo.sn; internet www.sgbs.sn; f. 1962; 57.72% owned by Société Générale (France), 35.23% owned by private Senegalese investors; cap. 4,528m., res 22,026m., dep. 325,030m. (Dec. 2004); Pres. PAPA-DEMBA DIALLO; Dir-Gen. SANDY GILLIOT; 30 brs and sub-brs.

Development Banks

Banque de l'Habitat du Sénégal (BHS): 69 blvd du Général de Gaulle, BP 229, Dakar; tel. 839-33-33; fax 823-80-43; e-mail bdld10@calva.com; internet www.bhs.sn; f. 1979; cap. and res 19,661.0m., total assets 132,554.6m. (Dec. 2003); Pres. AHMED YÉRO DIALLO; Dir-Gen. SOULEYMANE LY; 2 brs.

Banque Sénégalo-Tunisienne (BST): Immeuble Kebe, 97 ave André Peytavin, BP 4111, Dakar; tel. 849-60-60; fax 823-82-38; e-mail bst@bst.sn; internet www.banquesenegalotunisienne.com; f. 1986; 56.6% owned by Compagnie Africaine pour l'Investissement; cap. 4,200m., res 2,206m., dep. 81,587m. (Dec. 2004); Pres. and Chair. MAMADOU TOURÉ; Dir-Gen. ABDOUL MBAYE; 7 brs.

Caisse Nationale de Crédit Agricole du Sénégal (CNCAS): pl. de l'Indépendance, Immeuble ex-Air Afrique, 31–33 rue El Hadji Asmadou Assane Ndoye, angle ave Colbert, Dakar; tel. 839-36-36; fax 821-26-06; e-mail cncas@cncas.sn; internet www.cncas.sn; f. 1984; 23.8% state-owned; cap. 2,300m., res 3,952m., dep. 59,196m. (Dec. 2003); Pres. ABDOULAYE DIACK; Dir-Gen. ARFANG BOUBACAR DAFFE; 13 brs.

Société Financière d'Equipement (SFE): 2e étage, Immeuble Sokhna Anta, rue Dr Thèze, BP 252, Dakar; tel. 823-66-26; fax 823-43-37; e-mail sfe@telecomplus.sn; 59% owned by Compagnie Bancaire de l'Afrique Occidentale; cap. and res 388m., total assets 6,653m. (Dec. 1999); Pres. ARISTIDE ORSET ALCANTARA; Dir-Gen. MOHAMED A. WILSON.

Islamic Bank

Banque Islamique du Sénégal (BIS): Immeuble Abdallah Fayçal, rue Huart, angle rue Amadou Ndoye, BP 3381, 18524 Dakar; tel. 849-62-62; fax 822-49-48; e-mail contact@bis-bank.com; internet www.bis-bank.com; f. 1983; 44.5% owned by Dar al-Maal al-Islami (Switzerland), 33.3% by Islamic Development Bank (Saudi Arabia), 22.2% state-owned; cap. 2,706m., res 4,120m., dep. 38,845m. (Dec. 2006); Pres. of Bd of Administration BADER EDDINE NOUIOUA; Dir-Gen. AZHAR S. KHAN; 4 brs.

Banking Association

Association Professionnelle des Banques et des Etablissements Financiers du Sénégal (APBEF): 5 pl. de l'Indépendance, BP 6403, Dakar; tel. 823-60-93; fax 823-85-96; e-mail apbef@sentoo.sn; Pres. EVELYNE TALL (Dir-Gen. of Ecobank Sénégal).

STOCK EXCHANGE

Bourse Régionale des Valeurs Mobilières (BRVM): BP 22500, Dakar; tel. 821-15-18; fax 821-15-06; e-mail osane@brvm.org; internet www.brvm.org; f. 1998; national branch of BRVM (regional stock exchange based in Abidjan, Côte d'Ivoire, serving the member states of UEMOA); Man. OUSMANE SANE.

INSURANCE

AGF Sénégal Assurances: rue de Thann, angle ave Abdoulaye Fadiga, Dakar; tel. 849-44-00; fax 823-10-78; Dir-Gen. BERNARD GIRARDIN.

Les Assurances Conseils Dakarois A. Gueye et cie: 20 rue Mohamed V, BP 2345, Dakar; tel. 822-69-97; fax 822-86-80.

Assurances Générales Sénégalaises (AGS): 43 ave Albert Sarraut, BP 225, Dakar; tel. 839-36-00; fax 823-37-01; e-mail ags@metissacana.sn; f. 1977; cap. 2,990m.; Dir-Gen. IBRAHIM GUEYE.

AXA Assurances Sénégal: 5 pl. de l'Indépendance, BP 182, Dakar; tel. 849-10-10; fax 823-46-72; e-mail info@axa.sn; f. 1977; fmrly Csar Assurances; 51.5% owned by AXA (France); cap. 1,058m. (Mar. 2004); Pres. MOUSTAPHA CISSÉ; Dir-Gen. ALIOUNE NDOUR DIOUF.

V. Capillon Assurances: BP 425, Dakar; tel. 821-13-77; fax 822-24-35; f. 1951; cap. 10m.; Pres. and Man. Dir GILLES DE MONTALEMBERT.

Compagnie d'Assurances-Vie et de Capitalisation (La Nationale d'Assurances-Vie): 7 blvd de la République, BP 3853, Dakar; tel. 822-11-81; fax 821-28-20; f. 1982; cap. 80m.; Pres. MOUSSA DIOUF; Man. Dir BASSIROU DIOP.

Compagnie Sénégalaise d'Assurances et de Réassurances (CSAR): 5 pl. de l'Indépendance, BP 182, Dakar; tel. 823-27-76; fax 823-46-72; f. 1972; cap. 945m.; 49.8% state-owned; Pres. MOUSTAPHA CISSÉ; Man. Dir MAMADOU ABBAS BA.

Gras Savoye Sénégal: 15 blvd de la République, BP 9, Dakar; tel. 823-01-00; fax 821-54-62; e-mail olivier.destriau@grassavoye.sn; affiliated to Gras Savoye (France); Man. OLIVIER DESTRIAU.

Intercontinental Life Insurance Co (ILICO): BP 1359, Dakar; tel. 821-75-20; fax 822-04-49; f. 1993; life insurance; fmrly American Life Insurance Co; Pres. and Dir-Gen. MAGATTE DIOP.

Mutuelles Sénégalaises d'Assurance et de Transport (MSAT): Dakar; tel. 822-29-38; fax 823-42-47; f. 1981; all branches; Dir MOR ATJ.

La Nationale d'Assurances: 5 ave Albert Sarrault, BP 3328, Dakar; tel. 822-10-27; fax 821-28-20; f. 1976; fire, marine, travel and accident insurance; privately owned; Pres. AMSATA DIOUF; also La Nationale d'Assurances—Vie; life insurance.

La Sécurité Sénégalaise (ASS): BP 2623, Dakar; tel. 849-05-99; e-mail ass.dk@sentoo.sn; f. 1984; cap. 500m. (2002); Pres. MOUSSA SOW; Man. Dir MBACKE SENE.

Société Africaine d'Assurances: Dakar; tel. 823-64-75; fax 823-44-72; f. 1945; cap. 9m.; Dir CLAUDE GERMAIN.

Société Nationale d'Assurances Mutuelles (SONAM): 6 ave Léopold Sédar Senghor, BP 210, Dakar; tel. 823-10-03; fax 820-70-25; f. 1973; cap. 1,464m.; Pres. ABDOULAYE FOFANA; Man. Dir DIOULDÉ NIANE.

Société Nouvelle d'Assurances du Sénégal (SNAS): rue de Thann, BP 2610, Dakar; tel. 823-41-76; fax 823-10-78; e-mail snas@telecomplus.sn; Dir-Gen. FRANÇOIS BURGUIERRE.

Société Sénégalaise de Courtage et d'Assurances (SOSECODA): 16 ave Léopold Sédar Senghor, BP 9, Dakar; tel. 823-54-81; fax 821-54-62; f. 1963; cap. 10m.; 55% owned by SONAM; Man. Dir A. AZIZ NDAW.

Société Sénégalaise de Réassurances SA (SENRE): 6 ave Léopold Sédar Senghor, angle Carnot, BP 386, Dakar; tel. 822-80-89; fax 821-56-52; cap. 600m.

Insurance Association

Syndicat Professionel des Agents Généraux d'Assurances du Sénégal: 43 ave Albert Sarraut, BP 1766, Dakar; Pres. URBAIN ALEXANDRE DIAGNE; Sec. JEAN-PIERRE CAIRO.

Trade and Industry

GOVERNMENT AGENCIES

Agence de Développement et d'Encadrement des Petites et Moyennes Entreprises (ADEPME): BP 333, Dakar-Fann; tel. 860-13-63; e-mail adepme@sentoo.sn; f. 2001; assists in the formation and operation of small and medium-sized enterprises; Dir MARIE THÉRÈSE DIEDHIOU.

Agence nationale pour la promotion des investissements et des grands travaux (APIX): 52–54 rue Mohamed V, BP 430, 18524 Dakar; tel. 849-05-55; fax 823-94-89; e-mail contact@apix.sn; internet www.investinsenegal.com; f. 2000; promotes investment and major projects; Dir-Gen. AMINATA NIANE.

Agence Sénégalaise de Promotion des Exportations (ASEPEX): Dakar; f. 2005; promotes exports; Dir-Gen. MAIMOUNA SAVANÉ.

Société de Développement Agricole et Industriel (SODAGRI): BP 222, Dakar; tel. 821-04-26; fax 822-54-06; cap. 120m. francs CFA; agricultural and industrial projects; Pres. and Dir-Gen. AMADOU TIDIANE WANE.

Société de Gestion des Abattoirs du Sénégal (SOGAS): BP 14, Dakar; tel. 854-07-40; fax 834-23-65; e-mail sogas@sentoo.sn; f. 1962; cap. 619.2m. francs CFA; 28% state-owned; livestock farming; Dir-Gen. SOW SADIO.

Société Nationale d'Aménagement et d'Exploitation des Terres du Delta du Fleuve Sénégal et des Vallées du Fleuve Sénégal et de la Falémé (SAED): 200 ave Insa Coulibaly-Sor, BP 74, Saint-Louis; tel. 961-15-33; fax 961-14-63; e-mail saed@refer.sn; internet www.saed.sn; f. 1965; cap. 2,500m. francs CFA; 100% state-owned; controls the agricultural development of more than 40,000 ha around the Senegal river delta; Dir-Gen. MAMOUDOU DEME.

Société Nationale d'Etudes et de Promotion Industrielle (SONEPI): Dakar; tel. 825-21-30; fax 824-654-65; f. 1969; cap. 150m. francs CFA; 28% state-owned; promotion of small and medium-sized enterprises; Chair. and Man. Dir HADY MAMADOU LY.

Société Nouvelle des Etudes de Développement en Afrique (SONED—AFRIQUE): 22 rue Moussé Diop, BP 2084, Dakar; tel. 823-94-57; fax 823-42-31; e-mail sonedaf@telecomplus.sn; f. 1974; cap. 150m. francs CFA; Pres. ABDOU WAHAH TALLA; Man. Dir El Hadj AMADOU WONE.

DEVELOPMENT ORGANIZATIONS

Agence Française de Développement (AFD): 15 ave Mandela, BP 475, Dakar; tel. 849-19-99; fax 823-40-10; e-mail afddakar@groupe-afd.org; Country Dir JEAN-MARC GRAVELLINI.

Association Française des Volontaires du Progrès (AFVP): BP 1010, route de la VDN, Sacré coeur 3, Villa no 9364, Dakar; tel. 827-40-75; fax 827-40-74; e-mail afvp@telecomplus.sn; internet www.afvp.org; f. 1972; Regional Delegate for Senegal, Cape Verde, Guinea, Guinea-Bissau, Mali and Mauritania JEAN-LOUP CAPDEVILLE; Nat. Delegate KARIM DOUMBIA.

Centre International du Commerce Extérieur du Sénégal: route de l'Aéroport, BP 8166, Dakar-Yoff, Dakar; tel. 827-54-66; fax 827-52-75; e-mail cices@metissacana.sn; Sec.-Gen. AMADOU SY.

Service de Coopération et d'Action Culturelle: BP 2014, Dakar; tel. 839-53-05; administers bilateral aid from France; fmrly Mission Française de Coopération et d'Action Culturelle; Dir XAVIN ROZE.

CHAMBERS OF COMMERCE

Union Nationale des Chambres de Commerce, d'Industrie et d'Agriculture du Sénégal: 1 pl. de l'Indépendance, BP 118, Dakar; tel. 823-71-69; fax 823-93-63; f. 1888; restructured 2002; Pres. MAMADOU LAMINE NIANG.

Chambre de Commerce, d'Industrie et d'Agriculture de Dakar: 1 pl. de l'Indépendance, BP 118, Dakar; tel. 823-71-89; fax 823-93-63; e-mail cciad@sentoo.sn; internet www.cciad.sn; f. 1888; Pres. MAMADOU LAMINE NIANG; Sec.-Gen. ALY MBOUP (acting).

Chambre de Commerce, d'Industrie et d'Agriculture de Diourbel: BP 7, Diourbel; tel. 971-12-03; fax 971-38-49; e-mail ccdiour@cyg.sn; f. 1969; Pres. MOUSTAPHA CISSÉ LO; Sec.-Gen. MAMADOU NDIAYE.

Chambre de Commerce de Fatick: BP 66, Fatick; tel. and fax 949-14-25; e-mail ccfatick@cosec.sn; Pres. BABOUCAR BOP; Sec.-Gen. SEYDOU NOUROU LY.

Chambre de Commerce et d'Industrie de Kaolack: BP 203, Kaolack; tel. 941-20-52; fax 941-22-91; e-mail cciak@netcourrier.com; internet www.cciak.fr.st; Pres. IDRISSA GUÈYE; Sec.-Gen. SALIMATA S. DIAKHATE.

Chambre de Commerce d'Industrie et d'Agriculture de Kolda: BP 23, Quartier Escale, Kolda; tel. 996-12-30; fax 996-10-68; Pres. AMADOU MOUNIROU DIALLO; Sec.-Gen. YAYA CAMARA.

Chambre de Commerce, d'Industrie et d'Agriculture de Louga: BP 26, Louga; tel. 967-11-14; fax 967-08-25; e-mail ccial@sentoo.sn; Pres. CHEIKH MACKÉ FAYE; Sec.-Gen. DOUDOU NIANG.

Chambre de Commerce, d'Industrie et d'Agriculture de Matam: BP 95, Matam; tel. and fax 966-65-91; Pres. MAMADOU NDIADE; Sec.-Gen. MOUSSA NDIAYE.

Chambre de Commerce, d'Industrie et d'Agriculture de Saint-Louis: 10 rue Blanchot, BP 19, Saint-Louis; tel. 961-10-88; fax 961-29-80; f. 1879; Pres. El Hadj ABIBOU DIEYE; Sec.-Gen. MOUSSA NDIAYE.

Chambre de Commerce, d'Industrie et d'Agriculture de Tambacounda: BP 127, Tambacounda; tel. 981-10-14; fax 981-29-95; e-mail cham.comm.tamba@sentoo.sn; Pres. DJIBY CISSÉ; Sec.-Gen. TENGUELLA BA.

Chambre de Commerce, d'Industrie et d'Agriculture de Thiès: 96 ave Lamine Guèye, BP 3020, Thiès; tel. 951-10-02; fax 952-13-97; e-mail ccthies@cosec.sn; f. 1883; 38 mems; Pres. ATTOU NDIAYE; Sec.-Gen. ABDOULKHADRE CAMARA.

Chambre de Commerce, d'Industrie et d'Artisanat de Ziguinchor: rue du Gen. de Gaulle, BP 26, Ziguinchor; tel. 991-13-10; fax 991-52-38; f. 1908; Pres. MAMADOU DIALLO; Sec.-Gen. ALASSANE NDIAYE.

EMPLOYERS' ASSOCIATIONS

Chambre des Métiers de Dakar: route de la Corniche-Ouest, Soumbedioune, Dakar; tel. 821-79-08; Sec.-Gen. MBAYE GAYE.

Confédération Nationale des Employeurs du Sénégal: Dakar; tel. 821-76-62; fax 822-96-58; e-mail cnes@sentoo.sn; Pres. MANSOUR CAMA.

Conseil National du Patronat du Sénégal (CNP): 70 rue Jean Mermoz, BP 3537, Dakar; tel. 821-58-03; fax 822-28-42; e-mail cnp@sentoo.sn; Pres. YOUSSOUPHA WADE; Sec.-Gen. MABOUSSO THIAM.

Groupement Professionnel de l'Industrie du Pétrole du Sénégal (GPP): rue 6, km 4.5, blvd du Centenaire de la Commune de Dakar, BP 479, Dakar; tel. and fax 832-52-12; e-mail noeljp@sentoo.sn; Sec.-Gen. JEAN-PIERRE NOËL.

Organisation des Commerçants, Agriculteurs, Artisans et Industriels: Dakar; tel. 823-67-94.

Rassemblement des Opérateurs Economiques du Sénégal (ROES): Dakar; tel. 825-57-17; fax 825-57-13.

Syndicat des Commerçants Importateurs, Prestataires de Services et Exportateurs de la République du Sénégal (SCIMPEX): 2 rue Parent, angle ave Abdoulaye Fadiga, BP 806, Dakar; tel. and fax 821-36-62; e-mail scimpex@sentoo.sn; f. 1943; Pres. PAPE ALSASSANE DIENG.

Syndicat Patronal de l'Ouest Africain des Petites et Moyennes Entreprises et des Petites et Moyennes Industries: BP 3255, 41 blvd Djily M'Baye, Dakar; tel. 821-35-10; fax 823-37-32;

e-mail moctarniang@yahoo.fr; f. 1937; Pres. BABACAR SEYE; Sec.-Gen. MOCTAR NIANG.

Syndicat Professionnel des Entrepreneurs de Bâtiments et de Travaux Publics du Sénégal: ave Abdoulaye Fadiga, BP 593, Dakar; tel. 823-43-73; f. 1930; 130 mems; Pres. CHRISTIAN VIRMAUD.

Syndicat Professionnel des Industries du Sénégal (SPIDS): BP 593, Dakar; tel. 823-43-24; fax 822-08-84; e-mail spids@syfed .refer.sn; f. 1944; 110 mems; Pres. CHRISTIAN BASSE.

Union des Entreprises du Domaine Industriel de Dakar: BP 10288, Dakar-Liberté; tel. 825-07-86; fax 825-08-70; e-mail snisa@ sentoo.sn; Pres. ARISTIDE TINO ADEDIRAN.

Union Nationale des Chambres de Métiers: Domaine Industriel SODIDA, ave Bourguiba, BP 30040, Dakar; tel. 825-05-88; fax 824-54-32; f. 1981; Pres. El Hadj SEYNI SECK; Sec.-Gen. BABOUCAR DIOUF.

Union Nationale des Commerçants et Industriels du Sénégal (UNACOIS): BP 11542, 3 rue Valmy, Dakar; tel. 826-15-19.

UTILITIES

Electricity

Société Nationale d'Electricité (SENELEC): 28 rue Vincent, BP 93, Dakar; tel. 839-30-00; fax 823-82-46; e-mail senelec@senelec.sn; internet www.senelec.sn; f. 1983; 100% state-owned; Dir-Gen. SAMUEL SARR.

Gas

Société Sénégalaise des Gaz: Dakar; tel. 832-82-12; fax 823-59-74.

Water

Société Nationale des Eaux du Sénégal (SONES): route de Front de Terre, BP 400, Dakar; tel. 839-78-00; fax 832-20-38; e-mail sones@sones.sn; internet www.sones.sn; f. 1995; water works and supply; state-owned; Pres. ABDOUL ALY KANE; Dir-Gen. AMADOU NDIAYE.

Sénégalaise des Eaux (SDE): BP 224, Dakar; tel. 839-37-37; fax 839-37-05; e-mail bdtt@sde.sn; f. 1996; subsidiary of Groupe Saur International (France); water distribution services; Pres. ABDOULAYE BOUNA FALL; Dir-Gen. BERNARD DEBENEST.

MAJOR COMPANIES

The following are some of the largest companies in terms of either capital investment or employment.

AfricaMer: Nouveau Quai de Pêche-Môle 10, BP 8214, Dakar; tel. 821-68-93; fax 821-44-26; e-mail africamer@cyg.sn; fishing and export of frozen fish and seafood; sales US $17.0m. (2001); Dir-Gen. GIORGIO GABRIELLI; 2,700 employees (2002).

Compagnie Commerciale Industrielle du Sénégal (CCIS): route du Front de Terre, angle Service géographique, BP 137, Dakar; tel. 832-33-44; fax 832-68-22; f. 1972; cap. 1,969.6m. francs CFA; mfrs of PVC piping and plastic for shoes; Man. Dir NAYEF DERWICHE.

Compagnie Sucrière Sénégalaise (CSS): ave Félix Eboué, BP 2031, Dakar; tel. 832-28-86; fax 832-91-92; e-mail css@sentoo.sn; f. 1970; cap. 13,586m. francs CFA; sales 48,955.8m. francs CFA (2001); growing of sugar cane and refining of cane sugar; Dir-Gen. ROBERT CHAVANE; 5,222 employees (April 2002).

Crown Sénégal: route du Service Géographique, Hann, BP 3850, Dakar; tel. 849-32-32; fax 832-37-25; f. 1959; cap. 900m. francs CFA; 77% owned by Crown Holding (France); fmrly CarnaudMetalbox Sénégal; mfrs of metal packaging; Chair. LAURENT DONDIN; Man. Dir MICHEL BOREAU.

Les Grands Moulins de Dakar (GMD): ave Félix Eboué, BP 2068, Dakar; tel. 839-97-97; fax 832-89-47; e-mail gmd@gmd.sn; f. 1946; cap. 1,180m. francs CFA; sales US $96.8m. (2004); production of wheat flour and animal food; Chair. JEAN-CLAUDE MIMRAN; Dir PHILIPPE STEFFAN; 300 employees (2004).

Industries Chimiques du Sénégal (ICS): BP 3835, Dakar; tel. 879-10-00; fax 834-08-14; e-mail icssg@ics.sn; internet www.ics.sn; f. 1975; cap. 130,000m. francs CFA; 46.4% state-owned, 19.1% owned by Indian Farmers' Fertiliser Co-operative (India), 7.0% owned by Govt of India; mining of high-grade calcium phosphates at Taïba, production of sulphuric and phosphoric acid at two factories at Darou, fertilizer factory at M'Bao; Chair. and Man. Dir PIERRE KAMA; 2,000 employees (2001).

Lesieur Afrique (Dakar): pl. Amílcar Cabral, BP 236, Dakar; tel. 823-10-66; f. 1942; cap. 1,796m. francs CFA; subsidiary of Lesieur Afrique (Morocco); groundnut-shelling plant (annual capacity: 350,000 metric tons) and vegetable oil refining plant (capacity: 30,000 tons) at Dakar; Man. Dir MAMBAYE DIAW.

Manufacture de Tabacs de l'Ouest Africain (MTOA): km 2.5, blvd du Centenaire de la Commune de Dakar, BP 76, Dakar; tel. 849-25-00; fax 849-25-55; e-mail mtoa@telecomplus.sn; f. 1951; mfrs of tobacco products; cap. 3,129.6m. francs CFA; sales US $42.8m. (2000); Pres. PIERRE IMBERT; Dir-Gen. HENRI LUQUET; 300 employees.

Mobil Oil Sénégal: blvd du Centenaire de la Commune de Dakar, BP 227, Dakar; tel. 859-30-00; fax 859-31-00; subsidiary of Exxon-Mobil (USA); marketing and sale of petroleum and petroleum products; sales US $105.8m. (2001); Pres. MOULAYE ALI HAIDARA; Dir-Gen. RICHARD WILLEMS; 80 employees (2002).

Les Moulins Sentenac (MS): 50 ave Lamine Guèye, BP 451, Dakar; tel. 839-90-00; fax 823-80-69; e-mail sentenac@sentoo.sn; f. 1943; cap. 1,056m. francs CFA (April 2004); milling, production of wheat and millet flour and other food products and of livestock feed; Chair. of Bd DONALD BARON; 137 employees (2004).

Nestlé Senegal-Codripal: km 14, route de Rufisque, BP 796, Dakar; tel. 839-83-00; fax 834-17-02; e-mail nestle-senegal .senegal@nestle.com; f. 1960; cap. 1,620m. francs CFA; mfrs of sweetened and unsweetened condensed milk and culinary products; wholly owned by Nestlé (Switzerland); sales US $34.2m. (2001); Man. Dir JEAN-MARIE MAUDUIT.

La Rochette Dakar (LRD): km 13.7, blvd du Centenaire de la Commune de Dakar, BP 891, Dakar; tel. 839-82-82; fax 834-28-26; e-mail contact@rochette.sn; internet www.rochette.sn; f. 1946; cap. 500m. francs CFA; mfrs of paper and cardboard packaging; Chair. and Man. Dir ADEL SALHAB; 166 employees (2002).

Senbus Industries: près du Chemin de fer, Dakar; tel. 952-00-39; 93% owned by SIE—Société d'intervention financière, 7% state-owned; f. 2003; assembly of passenger coaches and buses; Pres. and Dir-Gen. OUSMANE JOSEPH DIOP.

Sénégal Pêche: Môle 10, Pont de Pêche, BP 317, Dakar; tel. 822-30-35; owned by China International Fisheries Corpn.

Shell Sénégal: route des Hydrocarbures, BP 144, Dakar; tel. 849-37-37; fax 823-87-30; internet www.shell.com/home/ Framework?siteId=sn-en; f. 1961; marketing and distribution of petroleum and gas; Pres. and Dir-Gen. MICHEL GOURY; 193 employees (2002).

Société Africaine de Raffinage (SAR): BP 203, Dakar; tel. 834-84-39; fax 821-10-10; f. 1963; 54% owned by Total (France), 30% by Royal Dutch Shell (Netherlands); cap. 1,000m. francs CFA; petroleum refinery at M'Bao; sales US $346.2m. (2001); Pres. ABDOU SIBY; 220 employees (2002).

Société des Brasseries de l'Ouest Africain (SOBOA): route des Brasseries, BP 290, Dakar; tel. 832-01-90; fax 832-54-69; f. 1928; cap. 820m. francs CFA; mfrs of beer and soft drinks; Man. Dir PIERRE TRAVERSA.

Société de Conserves Alimentaires du Sénégal (SOCAS): 50 ave Lamine Guèye, BP 451, Dakar; tel. 839-90-00; fax 823-80-69; e-mail socas@sentoo.sn; f. 1963; cap. 726m. francs CFA (April 2004); mfrs of tomato concentrate, vegetable canning, export of fresh vegetables; Chair. of Bd DONALD BARON; 315 employees (2003).

Société de Développement et des Fibres Textiles (SODEFITEX): km 4.5, blvd du Centenaire de la Commune de Dakar, BP 3216, Dakar; tel. 889-79-50; fax 832-06-75; e-mail dg@sodefitex.sn; internet www.sodefitex.sn; f. 1974; 51.0% owned by Dagris (France), 46.5% state-owned; responsible for planning and development of cotton industry and rural sustainable development; cap. 3,000m. francs CFA; Pres. YOUSSOU DAOU; Dir-Gen. AHMED BACHIR DIOP.

Société Industrielle Moderne des Plastiques Africains (SIMPA): 50 ave du Président Lamine Guèye, BP 451, Dakar; tel. 823-43-25; fax 821-80-69; f. 1958; cap. 551m. francs CFA; mfrs of injection-moulded and extruded plastic articles; Chair. and Man. Dir RAYMOND GAVEAU.

Société Industrielle de Papeterie au Sénégal (SIPS): km 11, route de Rufisque, BP 1818, Dakar; tel. 834-09-29; fax 834-23-03; f. 1972; cap. 750m. francs CFA; mfrs of paper goods; Chair. OMAR ABDEL KANDER GHANDOUR; Man. Dir ALI SALIM HOBALLAH.

Société Minière de Sabodala (SMS): 7 rue Mermoz, BP 268, Dakar; tel. 821-95-60; fax 823-38-64; 70% owned by Mineral Deposits Ltd (Australia), 30% owned by private Senegalese interests; exploration and exploitation of gold mines in Sabodala region.

Société Nationale des Pétroles du Sénégal (PETROSEN): route du Service Géographique, Hann, POB 2076, Dakar; tel. 839-92-98; fax 832-18-99; e-mail petrosen@petrosen.sn; internet www .petrosen.sn; f. 1981; 90% state-owned; exploration and exploitation of hydrocarbons; Gen. Man. SERIGNE MBOUP.

Société Nouvelle des Salins du Sine Saloum (SNSS): BP 200, Diohrane, Kaolack; tel. 941-19-04; fax 941-16-29; e-mail salins@ sentoo.sn; f. 1965; 51% owned by Salins (Compagnie des Salins du Midi—France), 49% state-owned; production and marketing of sea-salt; cap. 723m. francs CFA; Dir LUC LEROY.

Société de Produits Industriels et Agricoles (SPIA): 56 ave Faidherbe, BP 3806, Dakar; tel. 821-43-78; fax 821-66-37; f. 1980; cap. 640m. francs CFA; mfrs of plant-based medicines at Louga; Chair. DJILLY MBAYE; Dir-Gen. CHEIKH DEMBA KAMARA.

Société Sénégalaise d'Engrais et de Produits Chimiques (SSEPC): Dakar; tel. 834-02-79; f. 1958; cap. 727m. francs CFA; mfrs of fertilizers, insecticides and livestock feed; Chair. Bernard Portal; Man. Dir Paul Sasportes.

Société Sénégalaise des Phosphates de Thiès (SSPT): 39 ave Jean XXIII, BP 241, Dakar; tel. 823-32-83; fax 823-83-84; e-mail miller@telecomplus.sn; f. 1948; cap. 1,000m. francs CFA; owned by TOLSA SA (Spain); production of phosphates and attapulgite, mfrs of phosphate fertilizers; Chair. Míren Larrea; Man. Eduardo Miller Mendez.

Société Textile de Kaolack (SOTEXKA): Dakar; tel. 821-89-99; fax 821-23-01; f. 1977; cap 8,628m. francs CFA; 63% state-owned; transfer pending to private ownership; textile and garment-assembling complex; Man. Dir Abdourahmane Touré.

SUNEOR: 32–36 rue du Dr Calmette, BP 639, Dakar; tel. 849-17-00; fax 821-99-70; e-mail siege@sonacos.sn; internet www.suneor.sn; f. 1975 as Société Nationale de Commercialisation des Oléagineux du Sénégal (SONACOS); cap. 22,626.6m. francs CFA; majority share owned by Advens (France); comprises five factories, processing and export of edible oils, cattle feed, bleach and vinegar; Pres. Abbas Jaber; Dir-Gen. Franck Bavard; 339 permanent and 201 seasonal employees (2007).

Total Sénégal: Km 3, blvd du Centenaire de la Commune de Dakar, BP 355, Dakar; tel. 839-54-54; distribution of petroleum.

Société des Produits Pétroliers (SPP): Zone des Hydrocarbures, Terre Plein Nord-Est, Port de Commerce, BP 97, Dakar; tel. 849-32-00; Total Sénégal is sole shareholder; import, storage and distribution of petroleum products, mfrs of lubricating oil.

TRADE UNIONS

Confédération Nationale des Travailleurs du Sénégal (CNTS): 7 ave du Président Laminé Gueye, BP 937, Dakar; tel. 821-04-91; fax 821-77-71; e-mail cnts@sentoo.sn; f. 1969; affiliated to PS; Sec.-Gen. Mody Guiro.

Confédération Nationale des Travailleurs du Sénégal—Forces de Changement (CNTS—FC): Dakar; f. 2002; following split from CNTS; Sec.-Gen Cheikh Diop; 31 affiliated asscns.

Confédération des Syndicats Autonomes (CSA): BP 10224, Dakar; tel. 835-09-51; fax 893-52-99; e-mail csasenegal@yahoo.com; organization of independent trade unions; Sec.-Gen. Mamadou Diouf.

Union Démocratique des Travailleurs du Sénégal (UDTS): BP 7124, Médina, Dakar; tel. 835-38-97; fax 854-10-70; 18 affiliated unions; Sec.-Gen. Alioune Sow.

Union Nationale des Syndicats Autonomes du Sénégal (UNSAS): BP 10841, HLM, Dakar; fax 824-80-13; Sec.-Gen. Mademba Sock.

Transport

RAILWAYS

There are 922 km of main line including 70 km of double track. One line runs from Dakar north to Saint-Louis (262 km), and the main line runs to Bamako (Mali). All the locomotives are diesel-driven.

Société Nationale des Chemins de Fer du Sénégal (SNCS): BP 175A, Thiès; tel. 951-10-13; fax 951-13-93; e-mail siamoncs@telecomplus.sn; f. 1905; state-owned; operates passenger and freight services on Dakar–Thiès and Djourbel–Kaoulack lines, following transfer of principal Dakar–Bamako (Mali) line to private management in 2003; suburban trains operate on Dakar–Thiès route as 'Le Petit Train Bleu', pending their proposed transfer to private management by 2006; Pres. Drame Alia Diene; Man. Dir Diouf Mbaye.

ROADS

In 2003 there were 13,576 km of roads, of which 4,216 km were main roads. Some 3,972 km of the network were paved. A 162.5 km road between Dialakoto and Kédougou, the construction of which (at a cost of some 23,000m. francs CFA) was largely financed by regional donor organizations, was inaugurated in March 1996. The road is to form part of an eventual transcontinental highway linking Cairo (Egypt) with the Atlantic coast, via N'Djamena (Chad), Bamako (Mali) and Dakar. In 1999 new highways were completed in the east of Senegal, linking Tambacounda, Kidira and Bakel.

Comité Executif des Transports Urbains de Dakar (CETUD): Résidence Fann, route du Front de Terre, Dakar; tel. 832-47-42; fax 832-47-44; e-mail cetud@telecomplus.sn; f. 1997; regulates the provision of urban transport in Dakar; Pres. Ousmane Thiam.

Dakar-Bus: Dakar; f. 1999; operates public transport services within the city of Dakar; owned by RATP (France), Transdev (France), Eurafric-Equipment (Senegal), Mboup Travel (Senegal) and Senegal Tours (Senegal).

INLAND WATERWAYS

Senegal has three navigable rivers: the Senegal, navigable for three months of the year as far as Kayes (Mali), for six months as far as Kaédi (Mauritania) and all year as far as Rosso and Podor, and the Saloun and the Casamance. Senegal is a member of the Organisation de mise en valeur du fleuve Gambie and of the Organisation pour la mise en valeur du fleuve Sénégal, both based in Dakar. These organizations aim to develop navigational facilities, irrigation and hydroelectric power in the basins of the Gambia and Senegal rivers, respectively.

SHIPPING

The port of Dakar is the second largest in West Africa, after Abidjan (Côte d'Ivoire), and the largest deep sea port in the region, serving Senegal, Mauritania, The Gambia and Mali. It handled more than 7m. metric tons of international freight in 1999. The port's facilities include 40 berths, 10 km of quays, and also 53,000 sq m of warehousing and 65,000 sq m of open stocking areas. There is also a container terminal with facilities for vessels with a draught of up to 11 m. In March 2005 the Governments of Mauritania, Morocco and Senegal agreed that a shipping line linking the three countries and to transport merchandise was to commence operations, following the completion of a tendering process.

Compagnie Sénégalaise de Navigation Maritime (COSENAM): Dakar; tel. 821-57-66; fax 821-08-95; f. 1979; 26.1% state-owned, 65.9% owned by private Senegalese interests, 8.0% by private French, German and Belgian interests; river and ocean freight transport; Pres. Abdourahim Agne; Man. Dir Simon Boissy.

Conseil Sénégalais des Chargeurs (COSEC): BP 1423, Dakar; tel. 849-07-07; fax 823-11-44; e-mail cosec@cyg.sn; Dir-Gen. Amadou Kane Diallo.

Dakarnave: Dakar; tel. 823-82-16; fax 823-83-99; e-mail commercial@dakarnave.sn; internet www.dakarnave.com; responsible for Senegalese shipyards; owned by Chantier Navals de Dakar, SA (Dakarnave), a subsidiary of Lisnave International, Portugal; Dir-Gen. José António Ferreira Mendes.

Maersk Sénégal: route de Rufisque, BP 3836, Dakar; tel. 859-11-11; fax 832-13-31; e-mail senmkt@maersk.com; internet www.maersksealand.com/senegal; f. 1986.

SDV Sénégal: 47 ave Albert Sarrault, BP 233, Dakar; tel. 839-00-00; fax 839-00-69; e-mail sdvdir@sentoo.sn; f. 1936; 51.6% owned by Groupe Bolloré (France); shipping agents, warehousing; Pres. André Guillabert; Dir-Gen. Bernard Fraud.

Société pour le Développement de l'Infrastructure de Chantiers Maritimes du Port de Dakar (Dakar-Marine): Dakar; tel. 823-36-88; fax 823-83-99; f. 1981; privately controlled; operates facilities for the repair and maintenance of supertankers and other large vessels; Man. Yoro Kante.

Société Maritime de l'Atlantique (SOMAT): c/o Port Autonome de Dakar, BP 3195, Dakar; f. 2005; 51% owned by Compagnie Marocaine de Navigation, COMANAV (Morocco), 24.5% by Conseil Sénégalais des Chargeurs, COSEC, 24.5% by Société Nationale de Port Autonome de Dakar, PAD; operates foot passenger and freight ferry service between Dakar and Ziguinchor (Casamance).

Société Nationale de Port Autonome de Dakar (PAD): 21 blvd de la Libération, BP 3195, Dakar; tel. 823-45-45; fax 823-36-06; e-mail pad@sonatel.senet.net; internet www.portdakar.sn; f. 1865; state-owned port authority; Pres. and Dir-Gen. Bara Sady.

SOCOPAO-Sénégal: BP 233, Dakar; tel. 823-10-01; fax 823-56-14; f. 1926; warehousing, shipping agents, sea and air freight transport; Man. Dir Gilles Cuche.

TransSene: 1 blvd de l'Arsenal, face à la gare ferroviaire, Dakar; tel. 821-81-81; e-mail transsen@telecomplus.sn; internet www.transsene.sn.

Yenco Shipping: Fondation Fahd, blvd Djily Mbaye, Dakar; tel. 821-27-26; fax 822-07-81; e-mail yencoshi@sentoo.sn; f. 1988; Dir of Finance M. Dianka; Dir of Shipping M. Diokhane.

CIVIL AVIATION

The international airport is Dakar-Léopold Sédar Senghor. There are other major airports at Saint-Louis, Ziguinchor and Tambacounda, in addition to about 15 smaller airfields. Facilities at Ziguinchor and Cap-Skirring were upgraded during the mid-1990s, with the aim of improving direct access to the Casamance region. In 1998 the Islamic Development Bank agreed to fund a new international airport at Tobor, Casamance. In 2000 work began to extend the runway at Saint-Louis in order to accommodate larger aircraft. The construction of a new international airport, at Ndiass, commenced in 2003.

Agence nationale de l'aviation civile du Sénégal (ANACS): BP 8184, Dakar; fax 820-04-03; civil aviation authority; Dir-Gen. MATHIACO BESSANE.

Aeroservices: Dakar; f. 1996; charter flights; Sec.-Gen. El Hadj OMAR BA.

African West Air: Dakar; tel. 822-45-38; fax 822-46-10; f. 1993; services to western Europe and Brazil; Man. Dir J. P. PIEDADE.

Air Sénégal International (ASI): 45 ave Albert Serraut, Dakar; tel. 842-41-00; e-mail siege@airsenegalinternational.sn; internet www.air-senegal-international.com; f. 2000; 51% owned by Royal Air Maroc, 43% state-owned; domestic, regional and international services; Dir-Gen. MOHAMED FATTAHI.

Tourism

Senegal's attractions for tourists include six national parks (one of which, Djoudj, is listed by UNESCO as a World Heritage Site) and its fine beaches. The island of Gorée, near Dakar, is of considerable historic interest as a former centre for the slave-trade. In 1993 the number of foreign tourist arrivals declined dramatically, largely as a result of the suspension of tourist activity in the Casamance region in that year. The sector recovered strongly from 1995 onwards, and in 2005 visitor arrivals of 386,564 were recorded; receipts from tourism in 2003 were US $201m.

Ministry of Tourism and Air Transport: rue Calmette, BP 4049, Dakar; tel. 821-11-26; fax 822-94-13; internet www.tourisme.gouv .sn.

Defence

As assessed at November 2006, Senegal's active armed forces comprised a land army of 11,900, a navy of 950, and an air force of 770. There was also a 5,000-strong paramilitary gendarmerie. Military service is by selective conscription and lasts for two years. France and the USA provide technical and material aid, and in November 2006 there were 840 French troops stationed in Senegal.

Defence Expenditure: Estimated at 70,000m. francs CFA in 2006.

Chief of Staff of the Armed Forces: Gen. ABDOULAYE FALL.

Education

Primary education, which usually begins at seven years of age, lasts for six years and is officially compulsory. In 2003/04 primary enrolment included 66% of children in the relevant age-group (males 68%; females 64%), according to UNESCO estimates. The 1995–2008 Educational and Training Plan places special emphasis on increasing levels of female enrolment, and is intended to raise overall levels of pupil enrolment by 5% annually. Secondary education usually begins at the age of 13, and comprises a first cycle of four years (also referred to as 'middle school') and a further cycle of three years. According to UNESCO estimates, in 2003/04 secondary enrolment was equivalent to only 15% of children in the relevant age-group (males 18%; females 13%). There are two universities in Senegal, the Université Cheikh Anta Diop in Dakar and the Université Gaston Berger in Saint-Louis. Since 1981 the reading and writing of national languages has been actively promoted, and is expressly encouraged in the 2001 Constitution. Current government expenditure on education in 2000 was some 100,400m. francs CFA (representing 24.4% of total current expenditure). Some 40% of the Senegalese budget for 2005 was designated for the educational sector.

Bibliography

Adedeji, A., Senghor, C., and Diouf, A. *Towards a Dynamic African Economy.* Ilford, Frank Cass Publishers, 1989.

Barry, B. *Le royaume du Waalo: le Sénégal avant la conquête.* Paris, Editions Karthala, 1985.

Bellitto, M. *Une histoire du Sénégal et de ses entreprises publiques.* Paris, L'Harmattan, 2002.

Biondi, J.-P. *Senghor, ou, la tentation de l'universel: l'aventure coloniale de la France.* Paris, Denoël, 1993.

Boone, C. *Merchant Capital and the Roots of State Power in Senegal.* Cambridge, Cambridge University Press, 1992.

Camara, A. *La philosophie politique de Léopold Sédar Senghor.* Paris, L'Harmattan, 2002.

Clark, A. F., and Phillips, L. C. *Historical Dictionary of Senegal.* 2nd Edn. Metuchen, NJ, Scarecrow Press, 1994.

Coulibaly, A. L. *Le Sénégal à l'épreuve de la démocratie: Enquête sur 50 ans de lutte et de complots au sein de l'élite socialiste.* Paris, L'Harmattan, 1999.

Wade, un opposant au pouvoir: L'alternance piégée. Dakar, Editions Sentinelles, 2003.

Coulon, C. *Le Marabout et Le Prince: Islam et Pouvoir en Sénégal.* Paris, A. Pedone, 1981.

Cruise O'Brien, D. B. *The Mourides of Senegal: The Political and Economic Organization of an Islamic Brotherhood.* Oxford, Clarendon, 1971.

Cruise O'Brien, D. B., Diop, M. C., and Diouf, M. *La construction de l'Etat au Sénégal.* Paris, Editions Karthala, 2002.

Cruise O'Brien, D. B., Dunn, J., and Rathbone, R. (Eds). *Contemporary West African States.* Cambridge, Cambridge University Press, 1989.

Dahou, T. *Entre parenté et politique: Développement et clientélisme dans le Delta du Sénégal.* Paris, Editions Karthala, 2005.

Diagne, A. *Abdou Diouf, le maître du jeu.* Dakar, Agence Less Com, 1996.

Diagne, A. and Daffé, G. (Eds). *Le Sénégal en quête d'une croissance durable.* Paris, Editions Karthala, 2002.

Diallo, M. L. *Le Sénégal, un lion économique?* Paris, Editions Karthala, 2004.

Diop, A.-B. *La société Wolof.* Paris, Editions Karthala, 1983 (reissue).

Diop, M—C. (Ed.). *Senegal: Essays in Statecraft.* Dakar, CODESRIA, 1993.

La société sénégalaise entre le local et le global. Paris, Editions Karthala, 2002.

Le Sénégal contemporain. Paris, Editions Karthala, 2003.

Diouf, M. *Sénégal, les ethnies et la nation.* Paris, UN Research Institute for Social Development, Forum du Tiers-Monde and L'Harmattan, 1994.

L'Endettement puis l'ajustement: L'Afrique des institutions Bretton-Woods. Paris, L'Harmattan, 2002.

Eades, J., and Dilley, R. *Senegal.* Santa Barbara, CA, ABC Clio, 1993.

Fauvelle, F. X. *L'Afrique de Cheikh Anta Diop: histoire et idéologie.* Paris, Editions Karthala, 1996.

Gellar, S. *Senegal: An African Nation between Islam and the West.* 2nd Edn. Boulder, CO, Westview Press, 1995.

Getz, T. R. *Slavery and reform in West Africa: toward emancipation in nineteenth-century Senegal and the Gold Coast.* Athens, OH, Ohio University Press, 2004.

Harrison Church, R. J. *West Africa.* 8th Edn. London, Longman, 1979.

Harvey, C., and Robinson, M. *The Design of Economic Reforms in the Context of Economic Liberalization: The Experience of Mozambique, Senegal and Uganda.* Brighton, Institute of Development Studies, 1995.

Hesseling, G. *Histoire politique du Sénégal.* Paris, Editions Karthala, 1983.

Hymans, J. L. *Léopold Sédar Senghor.* Edinburgh University Press, 1972.

Johnson, G. W. *Naissance du Sénégal contemporain.* Paris, Editions Karthala, 1991.

Jus, C. *Soudan français–Mauritanie, une géopolitique coloniale (1880–1963): tracer une ligne dans le désert.* Paris, L'Harmattan, 2003.

Linares, O. *Power, Prayer and Production: The Jola of Casamance.* Cambridge, Cambridge University Press, 1993.

Loum, N. *Médias et l'état au Sénégal: L'impossible autonomie.* Paris, L'Harmattan, 2003.

Magassouba, M. *L'Islam au Sénégal: Demain les Mollahs?* Paris, Editions Karthala, 1985.

Makédonsky, E. *Le Sénégal: La Sénégambie.* 2 vols, Paris, L'Harmattan, 1987.

Milcent, E., and Sordet, M. *Léopold Sédar Senghor et la naissance de l'Afrique moderne.* Paris, Editions Seghers, 1969.

Robinson, D. *Sociétés musulmanes et pouvoir colonial français au Sénégal et en Mauritanie 1880–1920.* Paris, Editions Karthala, 2004.

Roche, C. *Histoire de la Casamance: conquête et résistance, 1850–1920.* Paris, Editions Karthala, 1985.

Le Sénégal à la conquête de son indépendance: 1939–1960: chronique de la vie politique et syndicale, de l'Empire français à l'indépendance. Paris, Editions Karthala, 2001.

Saint-Martin, Y.-J. *Le Sénégal sous le second empire.* Paris, Editions Editions Karthala, 1989.

Schaffer, F. C. *Democracy in Translation: Understanding Politics in an Unfamiliar Culture.* Ithaca, NY, Cornell University Press, 2000.

Seck, A. *Sénégal émergence d'une démocratie moderne, 1945-2005: Un itinéraire politique.* Paris, Editions Karthala, 2005.

Senghor, L. S. *Liberté I, Négritude et Humanisme; Liberté II, Nation et voie africaine du socialisme.* Editions du Seuil, 1964 and 1971.

Snipe, T. *Arts and Politics in Senegal, 1960–1996.* Lawrenceville, NJ, Africa World Press Inc, 1997.

Sweeney, P. (Ed.). *The Gambia and Senegal.* London, APA, 1996.

Vandermotten, C. *Géopolitique de la vallée du Sénégal: les flots de la discorde.* Paris, L'Harmattan, 2004.

Vaillant, J. G. *Vie de Léopold Sédar Senghor: Noir, Français et Africain.* Paris, Editions Karthala, 2006.

Villalon, L. *Islamic Society and State Power in Senegal: Disciples and Citizens in Fatick.* Cambridge, Cambridge University Press, 1995.

Wade, A. *Un destin pour l'Afrique.* Paris, Editions Karthala, 1992.

Wane, A. M. *Le Sénégal entre deux naufrages?: Le Joola et l'Alternance.* Paris, L'Harmattan, 2003.

Wolf, Franziska *Senegal: Entwicklungsland im Globalisierungswettlauf.* Frankfurt am Main, Peter Lang, 2004.

Yansané, A. Y. *Decolonization in West African states, with French Colonial Legacy: Comparison and Contrast: Development in Guinea, the Ivory Coast, and Senegal, 1945–1980.* Cambridge, MA, Schenkman Publishing Co, 1984.

Zarour, C. *La Coopération arabo-sénégalaise.* Paris, L'Harmattan, 2000.

SEYCHELLES

Physical and Social Geography

The Republic of Seychelles comprises a scattered archipelago of granitic and coralline islands, lying about 1,600 km east of continental Africa and ranging over some 1m. sq km of the western Indian Ocean. The exact number of islands is unknown, but has been estimated at 115, of which 41 are granitic and the remainder coralline. The group also includes numerous rocks and small cays. At independence in June 1976, the Aldabra Islands, the Farquhar group and Desroches (combined area 28.5 sq km, or 11 sq miles), part of the British Indian Ocean Territory since 1965, were reunited with Seychelles, thus restoring the land area to 308 sq km (119 sq miles). Including the Aldabra lagoon, the country's area is 455.3 sq km (175.8 sq miles).

The islands take their name from the Vicomte Moreau de Séchelles, Controller-General of Finance in the reign of Louis XV of France. The largest of the group is Mahé, which has an area of about 148 sq km (57 sq miles) and is approximately 27 km long from north to south. Mahé lies 1,800 km due east of Mombasa, 3,300 km south-west of Bombay, and 1,100 km north of Madagascar. Victoria, the capital of Seychelles and the only port of the archipelago, is on Mahé. It is the only town in Seychelles of any size and had a population of 24,324 (including suburbs) at the census of August 1987; Mahé itself had an estimated population of 72,100 at mid-2004 (with Praslin accounting for 7,200 people and La Digue and the outer islands some 3,200 people). The islanders have a variety of ethnic origins—African, European, Indian and Chinese. In 1981 Creole (Seselwa), the language spoken by virtually all Seychellois, replaced English and French as the official language. The total population was enumerated at 75,876 at the August 1997 census, and at 84,600 at mid-2006, giving a density of 185.8 persons per sq km.

The granitic islands, which are all of great scenic beauty, rise fairly steeply from the sea and Mahé has a long central ridge, which at its highest point, Morne Seychellois, reaches 912 m. Praslin, the second largest island in the group, is 43 km from Mahé and the other granitic islands are within a radius of 56 km. The coral islands are reefs in different stages of formation, rising only marginally above sea-level.

For islands so close to the Equator, the climate is surprisingly equable. Maximum shade temperature at sea-level averages 29°C, but during the coolest months the temperature may fall to 24°C. There are two seasons, hot from December to May, and cooler from June to November while the south-east trade winds are blowing. Rainfall varies over the group; the greater part falls in the hot months during the north-west trade winds and the climate then tends to be humid and somewhat enervating. The mean annual rainfall in Victoria is 2,360 mm and the mean average temperature nearly 27°C. All the granitic islands lie outside the cyclone belt.

Recent History

Revised by KATHARINE MURISON

The archipelago now forming the Republic of Seychelles was occupied by French settlers in 1770. Following its capture in 1811 by British naval forces, Seychelles was formally ceded by France to Britain in 1814. The islands were administered as a dependency of Mauritius until 1903, when Seychelles became a separate Crown Colony.

During the 1960s political activity was focused on the socialist-orientated Seychelles People's United Party (SPUP), led by France Albert René, and the centre-right Seychelles Democratic Party (SDP), led by James (later Sir James) Mancham, who became the islands' Chief Minister in 1970. The SPUP sought full independence for the islands, while the SDP favoured a form of economic integration with the United Kingdom. This option was not acceptable to the British Government, and in 1974 the SDP adopted a pro-independence policy. The two parties formed a coalition Government in 1975, and the independent Republic of Seychelles, with Mancham as President and René as Prime Minister, was proclaimed on 29 June 1976.

SINGLE-PARTY GOVERNMENT

In June 1977 supporters of the SPUP staged an armed coup while Mancham was absent in the United Kingdom, and installed René as President. René claimed that Mancham had intended to postpone the 1979 elections (a charge that Mancham denied), but there was little doubt that the ex-President's extravagant lifestyle and capitalist philosophy had displeased many of the islanders. The SDP had intended to develop Seychelles as a financial and trading centre and placed great emphasis on the tourism industry. The SPUP considered the development of agriculture and fishing to be as important as tourism to the economy, and planned to ensure a more equitable distribution of wealth.

A new Constitution was promulgated in 1979. The SPUP, now redesignated the Seychelles People's Progressive Front (SPPF), was declared the sole legal party, and legislative and presidential elections were held to legitimize the new political order. The Government's socialist programme, however, led to discontent, particularly among the islands' small middle class. Two plots to overthrow René were suppressed in 1978, and a third and more serious attempt, involving South African mercenaries, was thwarted in 1981. In 1982 the Government put down both an army mutiny and a further coup plot. In 1983 another attempt to depose René was quelled. This sustained anti-Government activism was blamed by the Government on pro-Mancham exile groups, although Mancham denied any involvement in the conspiracies. Dissent within the SPPF itself was evident, however, in the enforced resignations of two government ministers: Dr Maxime Ferrari, the Minister of Planning and External Relations, left the islands in 1984, and two years later the Minister of Youth and Defence, Col Ogilvy Berlouis, was removed from office after the discovery of another alleged conspiracy against the Government.

During the mid-1980s there was a series of violent attacks upon, and disappearances of, exiled opponents of the SPPF. Notable among these was the murder in London in 1985 of Gérard Hoarau, a former government official and leader of the Mouvement pour la Résistance. In 1987 an elaborate plan to overthrow the Seychelles Government was discovered by police in the United Kingdom.

Until the early 1990s, exiled opposition to René remained split among a number of small groups based principally in London. In July 1991 five of these parties, including the Rassemblement du Peuple Seychellois pour la Démocratie (subsequently renamed the Seychelles Christian Democrat Party, SCDP), founded by Dr Maxime Ferrari, established a coalition, the United Democratic Movement (UDM), under

Ferrari's leadership, while ex-President Mancham rallied his supporters in a 'Crusade for Democracy'.

During 1991 the René Government came under increasing pressure from France and the United Kingdom, the islands' principal aid donors, to return Seychelles to a democratic political system. Internally, open opposition to the SPPF was voiced by the newly formed Parti Seselwa (PS), led by a Protestant clergyman, Wavel Ramkalawan. In August Maxime Ferrari returned from exile to organize support for the UDM, and in November René invited all political dissidents to return to the islands.

RESUMPTION OF MULTI-PARTY POLITICS

In December 1991 the SPPF conceded its political monopoly, and agreed that, from January 1992, political groups numbering at least 100 members could be granted official registration, and that multi-party elections would take place in July for a Constituent Assembly, whose proposals for constitutional reform would be submitted to a national referendum, with a view to holding multi-party parliamentary elections in December. In April Mancham returned from exile to lead the New Democratic Party (NDP).

Elections for a 20-seat commission to draft a new constitution took place in July 1992. The SPPF won 58.4% of the votes, while the NDP received 33.7%. The PS, which took 4.4% of the votes, was the only other political party to obtain representation on the commission. The commission, which comprised 11 representatives from the SPPF, eight from the NDP (now renamed the Democratic Party, DP) and one from the PS, completed its deliberations in October. In September, however, the DP withdrew its delegation, on the grounds that the SPPF had allegedly refused to permit a full debate of reform proposals. Following publication of the draft Constitution, the DP focused its opposition on proposed voting arrangements for a new National Assembly, whose members were to be elected on a basis of one-half by direct vote and one-half by proportional representation. The latter formula was to reflect the percentage of votes obtained by the successful candidate in presidential elections, and was intended to ensure that the President's party would secure a legislative majority. Other sections of the proposed Constitution, relating to social issues, were strongly opposed by the Roman Catholic Church, to which more than 90% of the islanders belong.

The draft Constitution, which required the approval of at least 60% of voters, was endorsed by only 53.7% at a referendum held in November 1992. A second constitutional commission began work in January 1993. In May the second commission unanimously agreed on a new draft Constitution, in which a compromise plan was reached on the electoral formula for a new National Assembly. With the joint endorsement of René and Mancham, the draft Constitution was approved by 73.9% of voters at a national referendum in June. Opponents of the new constitutional arrangements comprised the PS, the Seychelles National Movement (SNM) and the National Alliance Party (NAP). At the presidential and legislative elections that followed in July, René received 59.5% of the vote, against 36.7% for Mancham and 3.8% for Philippe Boullé, who was representing an alliance of the PS, the SCDP, the SNM and the NAP. In the legislative elections, the SPPF secured 28 of the 33 seats, while the DP took four and the PS one. Immediately following the elections, René, whose decisive victory was widely attributed to his promise of increased expenditure on social programmes, carried out an extensive reshuffle of the Council of Ministers.

Socio-Economic Transition

Following the 1993 elections, the Government began to promote a gradual transition from socialism to free-market policies, aimed at maximizing the country's potential as an 'offshore' financial and business centre. State-owned port facilities were transferred to private ownership in 1994, when plans were also announced for the creation of a duty-free international trade zone to provide transhipment facilities. Arrangements also proceeded during 1995 for the privatization of government activities in tourism, agriculture and tuna-processing.

In early 1995 tensions developed within the DP, whose only directly elected deputy, Christopher Gill, sought to remove Mancham from the party leadership on the grounds that the former President was insufficiently vigorous in opposing the policies of the René Government. Gill was suspended from the DP in June, and subsequently formed a breakaway 'New Democratic Party'. The official registration of active political organizations, affording them corporate status, led to the formal amalgamation of the PS, the SNM, the SCDP and the NAP as a single party, the United Opposition (UO), under the leadership of Ramkalawan.

In the furtherance of its efforts to promote Seychelles as an international 'offshore' financial centre, the Government introduced, in November 1995, an Economic Development Act (EDA), under whose provisions investors of a minimum US $10m. would receive immunity in Seychelles from extradition or seizure of assets. It was feared in international financial circles, however, that the operation of the EDA would make Seychelles a refuge for the proceeds of drugs-trafficking and other crimes. Protest was led by the United Kingdom, France and the USA, and in February 1996 the EDA was described as a 'serious threat to world financial systems' by the Paris-based Financial Action Task Force on Money Laundering (which was established in 1989 on the recommendation of the 'Group of Seven' leading industrial countries). The Government, while refusing to rescind the EDA, established an Economic Development Board under the chairmanship of René, to vet potential EDA investors. In April the Government introduced legislation aimed at preventing the use of the EDA for 'laundering' illicit funds. The EDA was repealed in 2000. Meanwhile, it was disclosed in April 1997 that 243 foreign nationals had obtained Seychelles passports, in return for individual payments of $25,000, under an Economic Citizenship Programme (ECP) introduced in the previous year to attract foreign investors to the republic. It was claimed, however, by opposition groups that many of the grantees had never visited the islands, and that the names of some of these absentee citizens had been added to electoral lists. In early 1998 the Minister of Foreign Affairs stated that the ECP in its existing form was 'finished', but that consideration was being given to a new citizenship scheme to be linked to investment in the Seychelles economy.

In July 1996 the SPPF introduced a series of constitutional amendments, creating the post of Vice-President, to which James Michel, the Minister of Finance, Communications and Defence and a long-standing political associate of René, was appointed in August. The constitutional changes also provided for revisions in constituency boundaries, which were generally interpreted as favouring SPPF candidates in future legislative elections. Measures were also implemented whereby the number of directly elected members of the National Assembly was to be increased from 22 to 25, and the number of seats allocated on a proportional basis reduced from 11 to a maximum of 10.

Elections

In January 1998 René announced that presidential and legislative elections would be held in March, and that he was to seek the second of a maximum of three consecutive five-year terms as President permitted under the 1993 Constitution. The outcome of the elections provided the SPPF with a decisive victory. René obtained 66.7% of the presidential ballot, while his party secured 30 of the 34 seats in the enlarged National Assembly. Ramkalawan, with 19.5% of the presidential vote, substantially exceeded support for Mancham, who received 13.8%. In the National Assembly the UO increased its representation from one seat to three seats, with the DP losing three of the four seats previously held. Mancham, who lost his seat, announced his temporary withdrawal from active politics. In July 1998 the party changed its name to the Seychelles National Party (SNP).

In July 2001 René announced that the presidential election was to be held two years before it was due, in order to reassure investors of the political stability of the country, which was suffering from a lack of foreign earnings and a decline in tourism. At the election, which was held on 31 August–2 September, René was re-elected as President, with 54.2% of the valid votes cast, defeating the SNP's Ramkalawan, who secured 45.0%. Ramkalawan subsequently appealed to the Constitutional Court to nullify the election results, alleging malpractice by the SPPF. Philippe Boullé, the first independent candidate in the country's history (who had contested the presidential election in July 1993 for an opposition alliance), secured only 0.9% of the votes.

Legislative elections, which were due in 2003, were also held early, on 4–6 December 2002. The SPPF retained its majority in the National Assembly, but with the loss of seven seats, securing 23 of the 34 seats; the SNP, with 11 seats, won significantly more than in the previous election. In early 2003, for the first time, President René officially acknowledged Vice-President Michel as his successor, also announcing that he was to relinquish certain presidential duties to Michel.

On 14 April 2004 René officially resigned from the presidency; Michel was inaugurated as President of the Republic on the same day and Joseph Belmont subsequently succeeded him as Vice-President. Michel was regarded as a leader who would be prepared to implement certain much-needed reforms within the country and the economy. (René retained the position of President of the SPPF, however, to which he was re-elected in May 2005.)

In February 2005 President Michel reduced the number of government ministries from nine to seven. The Minister of Foreign Affairs, Jérémie Bonnelame, was appointed Permanent Representative to the United Nations and the USA and replaced by Patrick Pillay, hitherto Minister of Health. In a further political development in that month, Mancham resigned from the chairmanship of the DP and was succeeded on an interim basis by Nichol Gabriel, who also assumed the post of Secretary-General of the party. In March 2006 Paul Chow was elected leader of the DP; Gabriel remained Secretary-General.

A presidential election was held on 28–30 July 2006, and monitored by more than 20 regional and international observers (compared with 12 in 2001). Michel won a narrow victory, securing his first elected term in office, with 53.7% of the votes cast. Ramkalawan, who was supported by the DP, as well as his own SNP, received 45.7% of the vote, while Boullé, standing again as an independent, took only 0.6%. A turn-out of 88.7% of the electorate was recorded. Economic concerns had dominated the electoral campaign. Ramkalawan, who had called for the devaluation of the national currency, the rupee, accepted defeat, but claimed that the SPPF candidate had won owing to the large amounts of finance the party had devoted to its campaign. President Michel was sworn in to serve a five-year term on 1 August. A new Government, which included three new ministers, was inaugurated on 9 August.

Ramkalawan and several other SNP members were injured outside the National Assembly building in October 2007, when the security forces attempted to disperse protesters demonstrating against a ban on political and religious groups from establishing private radio and television stations. The SNP condemned police use of tear gas and rubber bullets during the disturbance, but the police commissioner maintained that his officers had been forced to take such measures after SNP leaders had refused requests to ask their supporters to leave. Ramkalawan and two other SNP leaders were charged with organizing an unlawful assembly, although the charges were later suspended. Michel ordered an official inquiry into the incident, which opened in March 2007.

In March 2007, in response to a five-month boycott of the legislature by the SNP, Michel dissolved the National Assembly. Early elections were held on 10–12 May, at which a turn-out of 85.9% was recorded. With 56.2% of the votes cast, the SPPF secured 23 of the 34 seats, the same number it had held in the previous legislature, while an alliance of the SNP and the DP took the remaining 11 seats. Michel restructured the Government in early July, reducing the number of ministries from 10 to eight.

EXTERNAL RELATIONS

Seychelles, a member of the Commonwealth, the African Development Bank, the Common Market for Eastern and Southern Africa (COMESA), the African Union (formerly the Organization of African Unity) and, until recently, the Southern African Development Community (SADC), has traditionally pursued a policy of non-alignment in international affairs. In July 2003 the country announced its withdrawal from SADC and the Indian Ocean Rim Association for Regional Co-operation with effect from July 2004, as part of a five-year comprehensive macroeconomic plan. However, in mid-2007 Seychelles' readmission into SADC was under consideration. President Michel was seeking to rejoin the Community in an effort to increase trade and encourage foreign investment.

In 1983 Seychelles, Madagascar and Mauritius agreed to form an Indian Ocean Commission (IOC) with the aim of increasing regional co-operation. The first such agreement under the IOC was signed by the three countries in January 1984. Comoros joined the IOC in 1985. In early 1986 Seychelles withdrew its objections to the admission to membership of France (as the representative of Réunion), despite its reluctance to recognize permanent French sovereignty over Réunion, and disagreements over the demarcation of regional tuna-fishing rights. Relations with France improved in 1987, despite Seychelles' opposition to the accession of France to the presidency of the IOC. France signed three new economic assistance agreements with Seychelles during that year, and the French Minister of Co-operation visited the islands and opened an electricity generator that had been provided by the French Government. The French Minister of Co-operation visited Seychelles in February 2001, thus improving relations, which had once again cooled over accumulated debt owed by Seychelles to the Agence Française de Développement and the consequent cessation of funding from that body.

In 1988 Seychelles established diplomatic relations with the Comoros and with Mauritius. In 1989 diplomatic relations were established with Morocco, Madagascar and Côte d'Ivoire, and in 1990 with Kenya. During 1992 formal relations were established with Israel and South Africa, and in 1998 Seychelles proposed to establish a diplomatic mission in Malaysia to expand its relations in Asia and Oceania. Libya opened a diplomatic mission in Seychelles in January 2000. In July 2003 the Government announced that it intended to close its high commissions in Malaysia, South Africa and the United Kingdom for economic reasons.

During the 1980s President René actively pursued initiatives for the creation of an Indian Ocean 'peace zone' and the demilitarization of the British Indian Ocean Territory, which includes the atoll of Diego Garcia. Until 1983 Seychelles allowed limited use of its naval facilities to warships of all nations, but only on condition that an assurance was issued that they were not carrying nuclear weapons. Neither the British nor the US Governments would agree to this condition, and their refusal to do so caused their respective naval fleets to be effectively banned from using Seychelles port facilities. It is thought that this embargo lost Seychelles a considerable amount of foreign exchange, and that this may have been one reason for the lifting of the guarantee requirement in September 1983. Seychelles continues, theoretically, to refuse entry to ships carrying nuclear weapons.

Relations with Japan were restored in 2001, with the granting of a SR 31m. subsidy towards fishery development; this was rumoured to be in connection with the reversal of Seychelles' policy on whaling. James Michel continued to foster strong relations with India, paying a state visit to the country in July 2005, following which India pledged a US $10m. aid package to assist the Government's economic reform programme and agreed to reschedule the debt owed by Seychelles. Similarly, Michel had visited Mauritius in March of that year, establishing various trade and co-operation agreements with the Mauritius Government, and a more wide-ranging agreement on co-operation was signed at the end of the seventh session of the Seychelles-Mauritius Commission on Bilateral Co-operation in December. In February and December 2006 Michel paid official visits to Qatar and the United Arab Emirates, respectively, where discussions focused on increasing investment in Seychelles. The Government also sought to encourage further investment from the People's Republic of China, hoping to capitalize on that country's greatly expanded Africa programme. Relations with China were strengthened during a state visit to that country by Michel in November 2006, when he held talks with the Chinese President, Hu Jintao, and Premier, Wen Jiabao, and attended the summit of the Forum on China-Africa Co-operation. President Hu paid a reciprocal visit to Seychelles during a tour of eight African countries in February 2007; five agreements on bilateral co-operation were signed during the visit. Meanwhile, in January of that year Seychelles and South Africa signed a General Co-operation Agreement aimed at enhancing bilateral ties.

Economy

DONALD L. SPARKS

Seychelles is a prosperous country in the African context and is classified by the World Bank as an upper-middle-income economy, one of only six states in the region thus designated. In 2005, according to the World Bank, Seychelles' gross national income (GNI) was US $8,180 per head (this compares to a regional average of US $746). In addition, its life expectancy, which was 72.2 years at birth in 2006, is (along with that of Mauritius) the region's highest (compared to a sub-Saharan African average of 47 years), and 97% of its population has access to safe water and sanitation (compared to a regional average of about 50%). The services sector (tourism, transport and communications) has dominated the economy in recent years and traditionally accounts for about 70% of GDP. The nation's gross domestic product (GDP) increased, in real terms, at an average annual rate of 4.4% during 1995–2002, somewhat higher than the regional average of 3.2%. However, the economy slowed over subsequent years; GDP declined by 5.9% in 2003 and by 2.9% in 2004, according to the IMF. Seychelles experienced its worst natural disaster when the Indian Ocean tsunami struck on 26 December 2004. The direct loss to the economy, according to the Government, was $30m., equal to about 4% of GDP. Fortunately, owing to its distance from the epicentre and adequate forewarning, only two lives were lost. GDP grew slowly in 2005, at 1.2%. The economy recovered faster than many expected in 2006, with an estimated GDP growth of 4.5%, according to the IMF. This growth was attributed mainly to expansion in the tourism and construction sectors and higher government spending. Tourist arrivals of 140,627 were the highest on record and foreign direct investment increased from $82m. in 2005 to $120m. in 2006. In the same year unemployment was recorded at 2.7%. Soon after independence, successive governments favoured a socialist agenda with price controls and state ownership of business. In April of 2004 Albert René resigned and James Michel took over as President; Michel formerly served as Minister of Finance and was welcomed as representing a reformist economic policy agenda (see below).

TOURISM

The economy is heavily dependent on tourism, which in 2004 provided more than 10% of total GDP. In 2005 tourism earned 43% of total foreign revenue in the country. However, it has been estimated that more than 60% of gross earnings from tourism leaves the country as payment for imported food and other goods, and by way of remittances to tour operators.

The tourism industry began in 1971 with the opening of Mahé international airport. In that year there were only 3,175 visitors; by 1981 the number had risen to 60,425. Tourist arrivals remained fairly constant during the mid- and late 1990s and increased to 130,046 by 2000. Despite the aftermath of the terrorist attacks in the USA on 11 September 2001, the industry was only slightly damaged: 129,762 tourists visited Seychelles in that year, and a record 132,246 in 2002. Tourism was already reduced when the tsunami (see above) struck in late 2004. The number of arrivals had declined to 122,038 in 2003 and was down to 120,765 in 2004. The number of visitors increased in 2005 to 128,654 and by 9% in 2006, to a record 140,627. In 2006 Europeans remained the largest source of tourists, with 80%, of whom French visitors comprised 20%, Italians 16%, Germans 14% and British 12% Unfortunately, the western Indian Ocean region was affected by the mosquito-borne virus 'chikungunya' in 2006. While not fatal, it is serious and there is no effective treatment. By early 2006 there had been 2,000 cases in Seychelles. The Government responded with a massive anti-mosquito spraying programme and the reported cases began to decline. It should be noted that the nation is malaria free.

Seychelles has developed an extensive network of international air links, although it pared back significantly in 2004. Kenya Airways flies three times each week to Nairobi. British Airways halted its twice-weekly London–Seychelles flights, owing to the decline in visitor business, and its difficulty in repatriating its profits in hard currency. Air France, Air Mauritius and Alitalia maintain joint flight agreements with Air Seychelles, operating services to Paris (France), Mauritius, Milan and Rome (Italy). However, Air Seychelles (the national state-owned airline) cancelled its service to Dubai (United Arab Emirates), Frankfurt (Germany), the Maldives, Mumbai (India) and Zurich (Switzerland) during 2004. This service reduction was accompanied by the redundancy of 100 of its 700 employees. In addition, competition from Emirates and Qatar airlines (three weekly flights for each started in 2004) would erode Air Seychelles' market share, which was previously about 80%. Charter flights, which had been discouraged previously, were also now welcome. The country hoped to become a centre for aircraft registration. In 2004 the Government announced a US $3m. renovation of the arrivals and departures lounges at the Seychelles International Airport, which would allow two aircraft to be serviced at the same time. The project, funded by the Arab Bank for Economic Development in Africa, was expected to be completed in 2006.

From the mid-1980s the Government rehabilitated and improved existing tourist facilities, and developed new attractions, including a craft village, a national aquarium and historical sites. The occupancy rate of hotels in 2004 was 46%. The Government estimated the islands' maximum tourist capacity, without detriment to the environment, at 200,000 visitors annually. It was hoped to attract an increasing proportion of visitors interested in the ecological aspects of the archipelago, and to this end attention was focused in the late 1990s on the tourism potential of the outlying islands. A conglomerate based in Dubai purchased land near Victoria with a view to constructing a marina village, to include yachting facilities, a golf course, a conference centre and a 320-room hotel. The Banyan Tree Group (a Singapore-based chain) opened a five-star resort in South Mahé in late 2002, and the Mauritius-based company Beachcomber purchased Reef Hotel. In 2006 the Hilton group acquired the £28m. Northolme resort on Mahé, adding further to the high-end range of hotel brands available, which included the Shangri-La group, Le Meridien, the Four Seasons and Lemuria. Seychelles signed the World Tourism Organization's Global Code of Ethics for Tourism, and, despite concerns that large-scale projects were inconsistent with Seychelles' ethos of sustainable tourism, the Ministry of Finance affirmed that it would welcome as many as 15 further hotel developments. From 1993 the Government divested itself of most of its parastatal holdings in the tourism sector, and foreign investment was actively sought. A series of new taxes on the tourism industry, introduced by the Government, includes a hotel licence fee, which is levied according to the number of beds per hotel. In late 2001 the Government retracted the exemption of five-star luxury hotels from the 7% tax on goods and services previously offered. Seychelles was instrumental in establishing the Indian Ocean Tourism Organization.

AGRICULTURE, FISHERIES AND MINERALS

As the area of cultivable land is limited to about 6,000 ha of Seychelles' total land area and the soil is often poor, it is unlikely that the republic will ever become self-sufficient in agriculture. (In 2006 FAO declared that less than 3,000 ha were available for agricultural production, compared to 12,000 ha in the 1980s.) The islands are heavily dependent on imported food, which, together with drink and tobacco, generally has accounted for up to 25% of the total import bill, although this proportion was slowly reduced. The Government is seeking to stimulate greater self-sufficiency in vegetables, fruit, meat and milk. There are a number of large farms and about 650 small farms and numerous smallholdings, about one-half of them run by 'part-time' farmers. The transfer of government-owned agricultural land to smallholder farmers was proceeding in the early 2000s. In addition, the African Development Bank (ADB) provided substantial financial assistance to an integrated agricultural development project to develop roads and irrigation facilities. Agriculture, forestry and fishing were estimated to have contributed 2.6% of total GDP in 2003 and 2004. Seychelles' food production per head increased at an average annual rate of 2.2% in 1990–2001 (compared to a 0.2% decline for sub-Saharan Africa). The main agricultural exports have traditionally been coconuts (especially for copra), frozen fish and cinnamon (exported as bark). However, in 1987, the first year of its production, canned tuna became the most significant export commodity. Minor export crops include patchouli, vanilla, tea and limes. Cup copra is processed locally into oil, and the by-product made into animal feed. The value of cinnamon bark exports increased by an average of 55.5% per year between 1990 and 1994, and stood at SR 0.5m. in 2004. Bark production totalled 204 metric tons in 2004. Tea is grown for domestic consumption, and there is a small surplus for export. Output amounted to 183 tons in 2004. The Government is encouraging the production of bananas, mangoes and avocados. Seychelles is self-sufficient in eggs and poultry, and there has been a large increase in the number of pigs, although animal feed has to be imported. The islands possess a fruit and vegetable canning plant and an integrated poultry unit.

Seychelles' fish consumption per head is one of the highest in the world and, at 57.5 kg per person in 2000, the highest in sub-Saharan Africa. The small artisnal fish catch fell by 3% in 2006, to 4,237 metric tons. However, in 2007 Japan granted the Seychelles Fisheries Association US $400,000 to develop small-scale artisanal fishing and processing. In 2005 the fisheries sector earned $290m., a 16% increase over the previous year. A modern fishing industry, operated by the Fishing Development Co (FIDECO), is concentrating on industrial tuna fishing through joint-venture operations, including the Société Thonière de Seychelles (of which 49% is owned by French interests), which has two freezer ships, and a tuna canning plant at Victoria that began operation in 1987 as a joint venture between the Governments of Seychelles and France. In 1995 the US multinational foods group H. J. Heinz acquired a 60% interest in the tuna-canning factory. The Government retained a 40% holding in the company, which was reorganized as the Indian Ocean Tuna Co (IOT) and has established Seychelles as the largest centre for tuna processing in the Indian Ocean, and one of the largest in the world. In 2005 canned tuna production stood at 41,162 tons. The tuna catch rose by 8.3% in 2006, to 388,000 tons.

In 2006 Heinz sold its European seafood division, which includes the 60% share in the IOT cannery, for US $505m. About 99% of tuna produced at the factory is exported to Europe through the port at Victoria, which has become the principal centre in the Indian Ocean for tuna transhipment. Although Victoria is still responsible for shipping nearly 90% of the region's tuna, it was likely to lose business to neighbouring states (especially Mauritius and Madagascar) because of the poor service being offered to the foreign fishing fleets. Of the 150 licences issued for long-line fishing in 2005, only 18% of licences called at Port Victoria. These services earn Seychelles about SR 235m. annually. However, in 2006 a development plan was launched whereby the fisheries sector was allocated 40 ha of land for industrial development at St Anne resort, which would include the expansion of existing quays and the creation of new ones on reclaimed land; the Government was to provide $60m. and it was hoped that the further $140m. necessary could be raised from investors. The scheme was considered likely to double fisheries income and create some 2,000 jobs.

In 1978 Seychelles declared an exclusive economic zone (EEZ), extending 370 km (200 nautical miles) from the coast, to curtail the activities of large foreign fleets, which until then had been freely catching almost 24,000 metric tons per year of deep-sea tuna. Agreements were thereafter concluded with several foreign governments. A new agreement, covering the period 2005–11 was signed by the European Parliament and the EU Council of Ministers in early 2006. That agreement will guarantee Seychelles US $5.13m. annually for the tuna catch up to 55,000 tons, and an additional $93 per ton for catches in excess of that amount. The agreement commits 35% for developing sustainable fisheries. In addition, any EU fishing vessel will have to employ two Seychellois workers (or pay a penalty of $40 per day). The fisheries development plan announced in 2006 (see above) included scope to increase landings by vessels operating in the EEZ from 30% to 80%, through value-added activities such as cold storage, processing, canning and re-export.

Additional revenue is derived from supplying vessels at Victoria and through leasing the expanded port facilities to foreign vessels, including cruise ships. The Fisheries Reserves Regulation launched in 2001 regulates the fishing industry in 16 specific areas in an effort to reduce illegal fishing. In late 2001 the Seychelles Fishing Authority required fishermen in outlying islands, who had formerly been exempt, to be licensed from January 2002. It also announced its intention to take stronger action against unlicensed lobster fishermen. Much of the lobster catch is sold to hotels and restaurants, where guests pay in hard currency, modestly adding to the country's foreign-exchange earnings. Seychelles' first tuna-seiner, with a capacity of 250 metric tons, began operations in late 1991. Assistance in expanding the fishing industry sector has been forthcoming from the ADB, France, Japan and the United Kingdom. In 1991 Seychelles joined Madagascar and Mauritius to form a tuna-fishing association. According to the Indian Ocean Tuna Commission (IOTC), the regional tuna catch substantially exceeds sustainable limits and there were fears of stock depletion. In early 2004 the EU began funding a US $17m. tuna-tagging programme in conjunction with the IOTC. The programme was to tag about 100,000 fish over a 30-month period to determine their migration, and was to be useful in the fight against illegal fishing. In 2004 the aquaculture production of giant tiger prawn had reached 1,175 tons. In 1999 a Chinese company was licensed to catch 100 tons annually of grouper, destined for the Asian gourmet food market. There is also future potential for Seychelles to exploit its rich stock of marine algae, for use in the manufacture of fertilizers, adhesives, beverages and medicines. The prawn farm on Coetivy Island has not been as successful as many had hoped. Production there reached 642 tons in 1998, but declined in the early 1990s, before recovering to over 1,000 tons in 2003 and 2004. Due to the Asian tsunami of December 2004, however, production fell to 772 tons.

The islands' sole mineral export is guano. In mid-2007 the Government was investigating the possibility of processing local coral into lime for a cement factory. India has collaborated in surveys for polymetallic nodules in the EEZ. Several petroleum companies have conducted exploration operations in Seychelles waters over the years, although thus far without success, and there have not been any significant operations for the past decade. In early 2005, however, the Seychelles National Oil Company signed an agreement with the US firm Petroquest to begin explorations for a nine-year period over an area covering 30,000 sq km. With higher petroleum prices and new exploration technologies Seychelles has become a more attractive possibility for findings.

INFRASTRUCTURE, ENERGY AND MANUFACTURING

The network of roads is generally good and an improvement programme is proceeding. It should be noted that the 2004 tsunami caused damage to the main road from the capital to the international airport where parts were washed away, and two bridges were destroyed. In 2004 there were 498 km of roads, of which 478 km were paved. Most surfaced roads are on Mahé and Praslin. The international airport on Mahé has been expanded, its runway has been strengthened to bear Boeing 747s, and a new domestic terminal has been built. There are airstrips on several outlying islands.

Seychelles' major infrastucture project, the Mahé east coast development plan, includes the modernization and expansion of Victoria port and the construction of a new road linking Victoria to the airport. Another major project is the five-year, US $450m., Eden Island. When completed this resort will have 450 luxury villas (with prices of over $1.2m.), a hotel complex and a marina. The project is located on reclaimed land near Victoria, and will require a $2.6m. causeway to link it from the mainland. The commercial port can accommodate vessels of up to 214 m in length, but there is only one berth. Additional berthing capacity is planned, with some facilities for containerization, and possibly a repair dock. In early 1999 the Government announced plans for a major land reclamation project on Mahé, costing an estimated $100m. and encompassing a new harbour and anchorage for cruise ships. In early 2003 some 300 stevedores went on strike at Victoria's fishing port, calling for a wage increase from SR 2 per metric ton unloaded to SR 4 per ton. The Spanish fishing firm affected refused to meet the demands, and claimed that many customers had become reluctant to use Seychelles as a port, at a cost of $1,200m. per month in lost revenues.

Commercial energy in Seychelles comes from imported petroleum, of which over one-half is used in the transportation and construction sectors, and the remaining converted into electricity. The Seychelles Petroleum Corporation, a parsatatal, is in charge of oil imports, with Malaysia's Petronas being the major supplier. The Seychelles Electricity Corpn was established in 1980 as a parastatal organization which was to finance its own recurrent costs. The extension of electricity supply to the islands of Mahé, Praslin and La Digue has been completed. Power supplies are generated entirely from petroleum. Generally mineral fuels account for 10.0% of the value of total imports. Seychelles imports about 6,000 barrels of oil per day, however, the vast majority of fuel imports are re-exported, mainly as bunker sales to visiting ships and aircraft. Seychelles generated a record US $65.3m. in petroleum re-exports in 2003. Studies have been conducted on the use of windmills, solar and wave power for electricity generation.

The recurring problem of water shortages should be eased eventually by the completion of the Baie Lazare water supply scheme, in the south of Mahé, with the capacity to supply 18,000 people in the Victoria area. In 2002 a US $29m. government-constructed desalination plant opened with the aim of relieving the situation. Seychelles is also considering building a dam at Grand Anse, which, if approved, would be due for completion in 2010. The second largest private company (after the tuna cannery), Seychelles Breweries Ltd (Seybrew—a soft-drink and beer producer), was forced to suspend bottling production owing to water shortages in late 2001 (and the tuna-processing cannery had water shortages in 2002). A lack of bottles has also been a problem for Seybrew, although it was able to import 750,000 bottles from Kenya in 2002. In that year the company was able to increase its production by 20% over its previous best month's output. In addition, the company has suffered from a lack of foreign exchange for vital imported inputs. Sales in 2003 decreased by 22% and the company was facing competition from imported beer (perhaps illegally shipped in by the Seychelles Marketing Board). In 2003 the company was compelled to make some 30–40 of its 180 workers redundant, and reduce its two daily shifts to one. Since then it has been bought by Diageo, a British conglomerate. In 2006 the Government retained its tax on imported beer (SR 35 per litre), but reduced the tax on locally brewed beers to SR 19.45, which was expected to provide a boost for Seybrew.

Manufacturing's contribution to GDP has increased in recent years, and accounted for 15.8% in 2006. Several small industries have been established, including brewing, plastic goods, salt, coconut oil, cinnamon essence distilling, soft drinks, detergents, cigarettes, soap, boat building, furniture, printing and steel products, together with animal feed, meat and fish processing, dairy products, paints, television assembly, and handicrafts for the tourist industry. A series of incentives was introduced in 2000 to aid small businesses; these included the creation of an Export Development and Promotion Facility and an Export Marketing Fund, as well as a Small Business Finance Fund. Also, as part of a new trade tax concession, export businesses were to be able to claim a full refund of trade tax. The tuna-canning factory (see above) remains pre-eminent in the industrial sector. Foreign direct investment increased from US $46m. in 1995 to $59m. in 2001, but decreased to $37m. in 2004, before increasing slightly, to $40m., in 2005. In 2006 Seychelles lost its appeal to the International Centre for Settlement of Investment Disputes, and has caused some uncertainty over the perception of its credit-worthiness. The country has a well-developed telecommunications infrastructure, and is thus well positioned to attract additional investment, however. Indeed, the nation ranks the highest in sub-Saharan Africa in the number of mobile phone users (704 per 1,000, against a regional average of 113). Only South Africa can claim near similar figures, with 654 users per 1,000 people. Seychelles was also one of the leaders of the region in personal computer usage; in 2004 personal computer use was 247 per 1,000 people, against the regional average of 26. In 2003 a South African firm and a Namibian firm agreed to establish a short-message telecommunications service in Seychelles.

TRADE, FINANCE AND DEBT

Seychelles traditionally sustains a substantial visible trade deficit. However, this deficit is partly offset by earnings from tourism and by capital inflows in the form of aid and private investment. The current account has generally been in deficit. The deficit was US $51m. in 2000, reaching $123m. in 2001 and $131m. in 2002, but improved dramatically in 2003 to only $16m. The deficit continued in 2004 and 2005, however, at $60m. and $195m., respectively. The current-account deficit was estimated at $157 for 2005. Seychelles' total external debt was $614.8m. at the end of 2004. In that year the cost of debt-servicing was equivalent to 8% of the value of exports of goods and services. In 2007 Seychelles issued a global bond raising $200m., much of which was used to pay off external debt. The Government was able to pay the Bank of Tokyo Mitsubishi $65m., the African Development Bank $47m., the World Bank $2.7m., and the European Investment Bank $3.4m. The Government has not yet started talk with bilateral creditors via the 'Paris Club'. Reserves of foreign exchange, which declined steadily during the late 1980s and first half of the 1990s, amounted to $20.6m. in 1996, recovering to $37.1m. in 2001, and increased to $69.8m. in 2002, before declining to $34.6m. in 2004, then rising again to $56.2m. in 2005.

In 2005 Seychelles' exports were estimated at US $355m., and imports at $620m., resulting in a trade deficit of $265m. That year its main suppliers of imports were Saudi Arabia (23% of the total), Spain (14%), France (8%), and Singapore (7%). Seychelles' principal export markets were the United Kingdom (45% of the total), France (23%), Spain (12%) and Japan (10%). In that year Seychelles' most significant exports were canned tuna ($176m.), petroleum re-exports ($134m.) and frozen and fresh fish ($125m.). Its principal imports that year were manufactured goods ($175m.), fuel ($135M.), fuel ($135m.), food and live animals ($125m.), and chemicals ($37.).

In 1993 Seychelles joined the Preferential Trade Area for Eastern and Southern Africa (PTA, which in 1994 became the Common Market for Eastern and Southern Africa—COMESA) and benefits from the clearing house function, which facilitates the use of member countries' currencies for regional transactions. This has reduced the pressure on foreign exchange resources, particularly from trade with Mauritius, another COMESA member. Trade between Seychelles and other members of the Indian Ocean Commission (IOC) accounts for only 2%–3% of the country's total official trade, owing principally to Seychelles' high import duties. Seychelles is a member of the ADB, as well as of the IOC. In 2004 it remained at odds with the African Union (AU) over unpaid dues (its voting rights remained suspended as of mid-2007), and also in that year Seychelles withdrew from membership of both SADC and the Indian Ocean Rim Association for Regional Co-operation (IOR—ARC), claiming that the benefits were not commensurate with the costs. However, in 2006 Seychelles applied to rejoin SADC, if a financial agreement could be reached on arrears owing to that body. Application has been made for membership of the World Trade Organization (WTO).

Government spending increased dramatically following independence in 1976, as the new administration expanded its provision of social services and raised its levels of defence spending. British grant support ended in 1979. The budget deficit rose to nearly 10% of GDP in 1989. In 1999 Seychelles recorded a budgetary deficit of SR 348m., equivalent to 11.0% of GDP. The deficit increased to SR 480m. in 2002 (equivalent to 14% of GDP), compared with a target of SR 248m. The Government succeeded in achieving a surplus in 2004 of SR 179m., equal to 4.7% of GDP, significantly less than earlier projections. President Michel presented the 2006 budget in late 2005, and it was similar to the previous two, in that it sought a surplus, this time of SR 178m., or 5% of GDP. Total spending was budgeted at SR 1,751m., with revenues expected of SR 1,929m. The 2006 budget also specified an increase in senior citizens' social security payments of SR 100 a month; an arrangement where every new baby is given a SR 1,000 bank account at birth; salary increases for civil servants (at a cost of SR 252m. annually); and an increase in public housing. The 2007 budget anticipated revenues of SR 2,420m. (an increase of 26% over the previous year) and spending of SR 1,900m. (25% higher than 2005). The expected surplus was SR 327m., equivalent to 7% of GDP.

Due to its relatively high GDP per head, Seychelles has never been particularly favoured for international aid. None the less, Seychelles does receive development assistance from a wide variety of sources, including the World Bank, the EU (particularly France, amounting to US $5.2m. in 2004), and other Western European countries, the ADB, the Banque Arabe pour le Développement Economique en Afrique, the USA, India, Canada, Arab countries and the People's Republic of China. Total official development assistance declined from $24m. in 1998 to $14m. in 2001, and averaged $11.8m. during 2000–04. Aid as a percentage of GDP decreased from 4.0% in 1998 to 1.1% in 2002. In spite of its decline from $308 in 1998 to $101 in 2003, aid per head remains at one of the highest levels in the world (with aid of $34 per head the average for sub-Saharan Africa). In 2006 the Belgian Government agreed to a 15-year rescheduling of $10m. of debt owed to it by Seychelles, following what it regarded as positive local economic reforms. The country also signed the first double tax-avoidance treaty of any EU-member state with Seychelles. Many other European creditors insisted on negotiating debt rescheduling via the 'Paris Club' of donors, however, which would entail implementation of IMF-recommended reforms.

In 1996 legislation came into effect under which it became compulsory to remit all foreign currency earnings to local banks. In 1997 the existing foreign exchange allocation system was abandoned and commercial banks assumed control of the allocation of foreign currency. Recipients of foreign exchange may claim up to 20% of their earnings in foreign exchange, but the amount allocated is decided on a discretionary basis by the commercial bank concerned. The Seychelles Marketing Board (SMB) requires hotels to charge in foreign exchange, and some local retailers demand partial payment in US dollars for imported foods.

The Seychelles rupee, previously tied to sterling, was linked to the IMF special drawing right (SDR) in 1979. In March 1981 the mid-point exchange rate was set at SDR 1 = 7.2345 SR. This remained in effect until February 1997, when the fixed link with the SDR was ended. Since then the currency has been pegged to a trade and tourism weighted basket, comprising the US dollar (11%), the pound sterling (30%), and the euro (59%). The exchange rate was US $1 = SR 5.45 at June 2006, virtually unchanged from 2003–05, although it declined to US $ 1=SR 6.18 in June 2007. Because of government price controls on fuel and certain food items, inflation has remained low: annual increases were 3.3% in 2003, 3.8% in 2004, 0.9% in 2005 and 0.4% in 2006. In 2006 the Government established a National Statistical Bureau to help data collection and analysis. Foreign direct investment (FDI) increased to US $120m. in 2006, compared with $82m. in 2005 and $37m. in 2004.

ECONOMIC PROSPECTS

Since the early 1990s the Government has encouraged foreign investment, both public and private, particularly in tourism, farming, fisheries and small-scale manufacturing. There is, however, an official preference for joint ventures where foreign investors are concerned. Until 2005 the Seychelles Marketing Board retained a monopoly on importing and exporting a wide range of products. However, the Government will retain a strategic reserve in many food items. Taxed profits can be repatriated freely. Certain aspects of the Economic Development Act (EDA), introduced in 1995 to assist in establishing Seychelles as a centre for international 'offshore' financial services, attracted intense criticism, on the grounds that they could provide a shelter for illegally obtained funds (see Recent History). The EDA was repealed in 2000. However, in 1996 Seychelles launched a controversial scheme called the Economic Citizenship Programme, whereby foreign nationals could buy, for US $25,000, Seychelles citizenship and passports. In 2006 the Government had not reached an agreement with the IMF, which continued to advocate a devaluation of the rupee and more broad-based economic liberalization. Such an agreement is important, as it would allow the Seychelles to enter into debt rescheduling negotiations with the 'Paris Club' group of creditors.

Seychelles' desire to become an international business centre has gained limited momentum. Measures to promote the development of an international business centre for financial services, trading and transhipment commenced in 1995 with the formation of the Seychelles International Business Authority as the regulatory authority. Legislation introduced in early 1997 provided tax incentives for the establishment of service-provider businesses. The Seychelles International Business Association licensed 13,500 international business companies (although many of these are inactive). The offshore sector accounted for US $5.8m. in foreign exchange earnings in 2003. In 2004 Seychelles established the Seychelles Investment Bureau (SIB), which has approved investments amounting to some $51m. According to the Government, 58 projects (mostly in the tourism sector) worth SR 1,400m. have been attracted under the SIB, of which 94% were from foreign investors. In addition, Barclays Bank opened the nation's first offshore bank in early 2005. In late 2005 the National Assembly approved a new investment code that was developed with the assistance of UNIDO and the World Bank. The code aimed to: guarantee against expropriation; allow foreign investors to repatriate their rupee earnings; and, establish a dispute settlement authority. Many local economic activities, such as taxis, tour operators, small-scale agriculture and fishing, internet providers and other small businesses will be reserved for local investors only.

In 1993 the Government created the National Economic Consultative Committee, with a membership including business leaders as well as members of the political opposition. In 1994, with the implementation of the Investment Promotion Act, the Government offered a range of incentives to stimulate increased private-sector investment in tourism, agriculture, manufacturing and services. None the less, the Government remains heavily involved in the economy and social sectors, through parastatals and inclusive services. In 2006 the Government finally re-launched its privatization programme with the sale of the state-owned insurance firm State Assurance Corporation of Seychelles, which has since been renamed the Seychelles Assurance Company Limited. The Government also planned to divest the Seychelles Savings Bank and parts of the Seychelles Marketing Board, eliminating its monopoly on imports of many basic goods. During the past two years President Michel has outlined a number of initiatives including liberalizing the trade and investment regimes, greater independence for the central bank, and more business-friendly rules to enable more private sector growth while still providing essential state services. The IMF, in its latest consultation with the Government in 2007, generally reacted favourably to these initiatives, but also highlighted the need for further and deeper reforms, especially in price controls.

Seychelles has the potential to become a regional player in e-commerce, given its high literacy rate, well-developed telecommunications infrastructure and the ability of most citizens to speak three languages (English, French and Creole). Should recent political and policy changes translate into genuine economic reform, the country may well be within reach of further increases in income per head and an extended period of sustained economic growth and development.

Statistical Survey

Source (unless otherwise stated): Statistics and Database Administration Section, Management and Information Systems Division, POB 206, Victoria; e-mail misdstat@seychelles.net; internet www.nsb.gov.sc.

AREA AND POPULATION

Area: 455.3 sq km (175.8 sq miles), incl. Aldabra lagoon (145 sq km).

Population: 74,331 at census of 26 August 1994; 75,876 (males 37,589, females 38,287) at census of 29 August 1997. *Mid-2006* (official estimate): 84,600 (males 42,875, females 41,725).

Density (mid-2006): 185.8 per sq km.

Principal Town: Victoria (capital), estimated population 60,000 (incl. suburbs) in 1994. *Mid-2003* (incl. suburbs, UN estimate): Victoria 20,050. (Source: UN, *World Urbanization Prospects: The 2003 Revision*).

Births, Marriages and Deaths (registrations, 2006): Live births 1,467 (birth rate 17.3 per 1,000); Marriages (of residents) 385 (marriage rate 4.6 per 1,000); Deaths 664 (death rate 7.8 per 1,000).

Expectation of Life (years at birth, official estimates): 72.2 (males 68.9; females 75.7) in 2006.

Employment (2006, averages): Agriculture, forestry and fishing 1,189; Manufacturing 4,465; Electricity and water 1,089; Quarrying and construction 3,717; Trade, restaurants and hotels 7,978; Transport, storage and communications 3,366; Other services 17,758; *Total* 39,561. (Figures exclude self-employed persons, unpaid family workers and employees in private domestic services; total may not be equal to the sum of components, owing to rounding).

HEALTH AND WELFARE

Key Indicators

Total Fertility Rate (children per woman, 2005): 2.1.

Under-5 Mortality Rate (per 1,000 live births, 2005): 13.

Physicians (per 1,000 head, 2004): 1.51.

Hospital Beds (per 1,000 head, 2004): 5.04.

Health Expenditure (2004): US $ per head (PPP): 634.2.

Health Expenditure (2004): % of GDP: 6.1.

Health Expenditure (2004): public (% of total): 75.3.

Access to Water (% of persons, 2004): 88.

Human Development Index (2004): ranking: 47.

Human Development Index (2004): value: 0.842.

For sources and definitions, see explanatory note on p. vi.

AGRICULTURE, ETC.

Principal Crops (metric tons, 2005, FAO estimates): Coconuts 3,200; Vegetables 1,940; Bananas 1,970; Other fruit 505; Tea (green leaf) 213; Cinnamon 200.

Livestock ('000 head, 2005, FAO estimates): Cattle 1; Pigs 19; Goats 5.

Livestock Products ('000 metric tons, 2005, FAO estimates): Pig meat 1; Chicken meat 1; Hen eggs 2.

Fishing ('000 metric tons, live weight, 2005): Capture 106.6 (Skipjack tuna 46.0; Yellowfin tuna 43.8; Bigeye tuna 10.4); Aquaculture 0.8 (Giant tiger prawn 0.8); *Total catch* 107.3.

Source: FAO.

INDUSTRY

Industrial Production (2006): Canned tuna 40,222 metric tons; Beer 6,737,000 litres; Soft drinks 9,225,000 litres; Cigarettes 19 million; Electric energy 252 million kWh.

FINANCE

Currency and Exchange Rates: 100 cents = 1 Seychelles rupee (SR). *Sterling, Dollar and Euro Equivalents* (31 May 2007): £1 sterling = 12.123 rupees; US $1 = 6.131 rupees; €1 = 8.248 rupees; 100 Seychelles rupees = £8.25 = $16.31 = €12.12. *Average Exchange Rate* (Seychelles rupees per US $): 5.5000 in 2004; 5.5000 in 2005; 5.5197 in 2006. Note: In November 1979 the value of the Seychelles rupee was linked to the IMF's special drawing right (SDR). In March 1981 the mid-point exchange rate was set at SDR 1 = 7.2345 rupees. This remained in effect until February 1997, when the fixed link with the SDR was ended.

Budget (SR million, 2006): *Revenue:* Taxation 1,245.6 (Taxes on income, etc. 297.0, Domestic taxes on goods and services 723.1, Import duties 225.5); Other current revenue 1,157.6; Total 2,403.2, excl. grants received (73.0). *Expenditure:* General government services 371.5; Community and social services 377.6; Education 189.2; Health 179.3; Economic services 47.7; Agriculture, environment and fishing 67.5; Transport and communications 62.8; Other purposes 199.7; Interest payments 405.9; Capital 403.8; Total 2,305.0, excl. lending minus repayments (–3.2). Note: Figures represent the consolidated accounts of the central Government, covering the operations of the Recurrent and Capital Budgets and of the Social Security Fund.

International Reserves (US $ million at 30 December 2006): IMF special drawing rights 0.0; Foreign exchange 112.92; Total 112.92. Source: IMF, *International Financial Statistics*.

Money Supply (SR million at 30 December 2006): Currency outside banks 392.8; Demand deposits at commercial banks 1,951.8; Total money (incl. others) 2,344.6. Source: IMF, *International Financial Statistics*.

Cost of Living (Consumer Price Index; base: 2001 = 100): All items 107.5 in 2004; 108.5 in 2005; 108.1 in 2006.

Expenditure on the Gross Domestic Product (US $ million at current prices, 2006): Government final consumption expenditure 172.68; Private final consumption expenditure 304.95; Gross fixed capital formation 152.39; *Total domestic expenditure* 630.02; Exports of goods and services 848.57; *Less* Imports of goods and services 732.23; *GDP in purchasers' values* 746.36. Source: African Development Bank.

Gross Domestic Product by Economic Activity (SR million at current prices, 2006): Agriculture, forestry and fishing 107.4; Manufacturing 673.8; Electricity and water 107.0; Construction 540.7; Trade, restaurants and hotels 929.6, Transport, storage and communications 801.2; Finance, insurance, real estate and business services 566.9; Government services 562.0; *Sub-total* 4,288.6; Import duties 204.8; *Less* Imputed bank service charge 240.8; *GDP in purchasers' values* 4,252.6.

Balance of Payments (US $ million, 2006): Exports of goods f.o.b. 422.82; Imports of goods f.o.b. –710.05; *Trade balance* –287.23; Exports of services 430.60; Imports of services –311.63; *Balance on goods and services* –168.26; Other income received 10.27; Other income paid –53.95; *Balance on goods, services and income* –211.95; Current transfers received 46.56; Current transfers paid –10.10; *Current balance* –175.49; Capital account (net) 13.24; Direct investment abroad –8.01; Direct investment from abroad 145.82; Portfolio investment assets –0.05; Portfolio investment liabilities 198.21; Other investment assets –8.48; Other investment liabilities –74.03; Net errors and omissions 2.04; *Overall balance* 93.25. Source: IMF, *International Financial Statistics*.

EXTERNAL TRADE

Principal Commodities (distribution by SITC, US $ million, 2004): *Imports c.i.f.:* Food and live animals 121.0 (Frozen fish, excl. fillets 73.8); Mineral fuels and lubricants 130.5 (Petroleum and petroleum products 129.2); Animal and vegetable oils, fats and waxes 12.4 (Olive oil 6.2); Chemicals and related products 24.8; Basic manufactures 80.5 (Paper and paperboard 15.1; Iron and steel 11.1; Other metal manufactures 30.6); Machinery and transport equipment 74.3 (General industrial machinery 15.7; Telecommunications equipment 11.3; Road vehicles 14.8); Miscellaneous manufactured articles 41.7; Total (incl. others) 496.6. *Exports f.o.b.:* Food and live animals 182.9 (Tuna, whole or pieces 169.3); Petroleum oils (not crude) 87.1; Chemicals and related products 15.4 (Medicaments 15.2); Total (incl. others) 290.8 (Source: UN, *International Trade Statistics Yearbook*). *2006* (SR million, provisional): Total imports c.i.f. 4,180.5; Total exports f.o.b. 2,100.3 (Canned tuna 1,030.4; Fish (fresh/frozen) 14.4; Frozen prawns 23.7; Fish meal 25.1; Medicaments, etc. 80.3. Note: Exports comprise domestic exports SR 1,185.7m. and re-exports SR 914.7m.

Principal Trading Partners (US $ million, 2004): *Imports c.i.f.:* France (incl. Monaco) 49.0; India 12.9; Italy 37.8; Japan 5.2; Malaysia 6.2; Mauritius 20.1; Netherlands 7.3; Saudi Arabia 128.9; Singapore 35.7; South Africa 44.8; Spain 45.4; United Arab Emirates 10.7; United Kingdom 30.9; USA 8.3; Total (incl. others) 496.6. *Exports f.o.b.:* France (incl. Monaco) 58.3; Germany 16.3; Italy 22.0; Saudi Arabia 86.4; United Kingdom 92.6; Total (incl. others) 290.8 (Source: UN, *International Trade Statistics Yearbook*). *2006* (SR million): Total imports c.i.f. 4,180.5; Total domestic exports f.o.b. 1,185.7 (United Kingdom 498.3; France 313.1; Italy 214.1; Germany 45.4); Re-exports 914.7.

TRANSPORT

Road Traffic (registered motor vehicles, 2006): Private 6,766; Commercial 2,581; Taxis 304; Self-drive 1,125; Motor cycles 21; Omnibuses 215; *Total* 11,012.

Shipping: *Merchant Fleet* (registered at 31 December 2006): Vessels 47; Total displacement 115,616 grt (Source: Lloyd's Register-Fairplay, *World Fleet Statistics*); *International Sea-borne Freight Traffic* (2006): Freight ('000 metric tons): Imports 534; Exports 4,604; Transhipment (of fish) 74.

Civil Aviation (traffic on scheduled services, 2002): Kilometres flown 12 million; Passengers carried 518,000; Passenger-km 1,397 million; Total ton-km 153 million (Source: UN, *Statistical Yearbook*). *2006:* Aircraft movements 3,194; Passengers embarked 186,000; Passengers disembarked 189,000; Freight embarked 1,503 metric tons; Freight disembarked 5,380 metric tons.

TOURISM

Foreign Tourist Arrivals ('000): 120.8 in 2004; 128.7 in 2005; 140.6 in 2006.

Arrivals by Country of Residence (2005): CIS 4,248; France 27,592; Germany 17,011; Italy 18,377; South Africa 5,395; Switzerland 4,473; United Kingdom 16,497. Source: World Tourism Organization.

Tourism Receipts (SR million, central bank estimates): 818 in 2004; 824 in 2005; 885 in 2006.

COMMUNICATIONS MEDIA

Radio Receivers (1997): 42,000 in use. Source: UNESCO, *Statistical Yearbook*.

Television Receivers (2000): 16,500 in use. Source: International Telecommunication Union.

Telephones (2006): 22,039 main lines in use.

Facsimile Machines (2002): 590 in use.

Mobile Cellular Telephones (2006): 72,019 subscribers.

Personal Computers (2004): 15,000 in use. Source: International Telecommunication Union.

Internet Users (2006): 3,872 accounts.

Book Production (1980): 33 titles (2 books, 31 pamphlets).

Daily Newspapers (2006): 1.

Non-daily Newspapers (2006): 3.

EDUCATION

Pre-primary (2007): 32 schools; 191 teachers; 2,825 pupils.

Primary (2007): 25 schools; 687 teachers; 8,802 pupils.

Secondary (2007): 13 schools; 588 teachers; 7,816 pupils.

Post-secondary (2007): 9 schools; 209 teachers; 1,906 pupils.

Vocational (2004): 7 institutions; 82 teachers; 1,099 pupils.

Adult Literacy Rate (official estimate): 96% (males 96%; females 96%) in 2007.

Directory

The Constitution

The independence Constitution of 1976 was suspended after the coup in June 1977 but reintroduced in July with substantial modifications. A successor Constitution, which entered into force in March 1979, was superseded by a new Constitution, approved by national referendum on 18 June 1993.

The President is elected by popular vote simultaneously with elections for the National Assembly. The President fulfils the functions of Head of State and Commander-in-Chief of the armed forces and may hold office for a maximum period of three consecutive five-year terms. The Assembly, elected for a term of five years, consists of 34 seats, of which 25 are filled by direct election and nine are allocated on a proportional basis. Constitutional amendments, introduced in July 1996, provided for an Assembly of 25 directly elected seats and a maximum of 10 proportionally allocated seats. There is provision for an appointed Vice-President. The Council of Ministers is appointed by the President and acts in an advisory capacity to him. The President also appoints the holders of certain public offices and the judiciary.

The Government

HEAD OF STATE

President: JAMES MICHEL (took office 14 April 2004, elected 28–30 July 2006).

Vice-President: JOSEPH BELMONT.

COUNCIL OF MINISTERS
(August 2007)

President, with additional responsibility for Defence, the Police, Information and Public Relations, Legal Affairs and Risk and Disaster Management: JAMES MICHEL.

Vice-President, Minister of Tourism, and Minister of Public Administration and Internal Affairs: JOSEPH BELMONT.

Minister of Finance: DANNY FAURE.

Minister of Foreign Affairs: PATRICK PILLAY.

Minister of National Development: JACQUELIN DUGASSE.

Minister of the Environment, Natural Resources and Transport: JOEL MORGAN.

Minister of Community Development, Youth, Sports and Culture: VINCENT MERITON.

Minister of Education: BERNARD SHAMLAYE.

Minister of Employment and Human Resources Development: MACSUZY MONDON.

Minister of Social Development and Health: MARIE-PIERRE LLOYD.

MINISTRIES

Office of the President: State House, POB 55, Victoria; tel. 224155; fax 224985; e-mail jmichel@statehouse.gov.sc.

Office of the Vice-President: State House, POB 1303, Victoria; tel. 225509; fax 225152; e-mail jbelmont@statehouse.gov.sc.

Ministry of Community Development, Youth, Sports and Culture: Oceangate House, POB 731, Victoria; tel. 225477; fax 225254; e-mail frevet@seychelles.net.

Ministry of Education: POB 48, Mont Fleuri; tel. 283283; fax 224859; e-mail pamedu@seychelles.net; internet www.education.gov.sc.

Ministry of Employment and Human Resources Development: Independence House, POB 1097, Victoria; tel. 676250; fax 610795; e-mail department@employment.gov.sc; internet www.employment.gov.sc.

Ministry of the Environment, Natural Resources and Transport: Independence House, POB 166, Victoria; tel. 611120; fax 225438; e-mail minister@env.gov.sc; internet www.env.gov.sc.

Ministry of Finance: Liberty House, POB 113, Victoria; tel. 382004; fax 225265; e-mail psf@finance.gov.sc.

Ministry of Foreign Affairs: Maison Queau de Quincy, POB 656, Mont Fleuri; tel. 283500; fax 225398; e-mail dazemia@mfa.gov.sc; internet seychelles.diplomacy.edu.

Ministry of National Development: International Conference Centre, POB 648, Victoria; tel. 611200; fax 225374; e-mail mmep@seychelles.sc.

Ministry of Social Development and Health: POB 52, Mont Fleuri; tel. 388000; fax 226042; e-mail minister@moh.gov.sc.

President and Legislature

PRESIDENT

Election, 28–30 July 2006

Candidate	Votes	% of votes
James Michel (SPPF)	30,119	53.73
Wavel Ramkalawan (SNP)	25,626	45.71
Philippe Boullé (Independent)	314	0.56
Total	56,059	100.00

NATIONAL ASSEMBLY

Speaker: PATRICK HERMINIE.

Election, 10–12 May 2007

Party	Votes	% of votes	Seats*
Seychelles People's Progressive Front (SPPF)	30,571	56.2	23
Seychelles National Party (SNP)-Democratic Party (DP)	23,869	43.8	11
Total	54,440	100.0	34

* Of the Assembly's 34 seats, 25 were filled by direct election and nine by allocation on a proportional basis.

Election Commission

Electoral Commission: POB 741, Victoria; Suite 203, Aarti Bldg, Mont Fleuri; tel. 225847; fax 225474; e-mail hendrick@seychelles.net; Electoral Commissioner HENDRICK PAUL GAPPY.

Political Organizations

Democratic Party (DP): POB 169, Mont Fleuri; tel. 224916; fax 224302; internet www.dpseychelles.com; f. 1992; successor to the Seychelles Democratic Party (governing party 1970–77); Leader PAUL CHOW; Sec.-Gen. NICHOL GABRIEL.

Mouvement Seychellois pour la Démocratie: Mont Fleuri; tel. 224322; fax 224460; f. 1992; Leader JACQUES HODOUL.

Seychelles National Party (SNP): Arpent Vert, Mont Fleuri, POB 81, Victoria; tel. 224124; fax 225151; e-mail snpseychelles@gmail.com; internet www.snpseychelles.sc; f. 1995 as the United Opposition, comprising the fmr mem. parties of a coalition formed to contest the 1993 elections; adopted present name in 1998; Leader Rev. WAVEL RAMKALAWAN; Sec. ROGER MANCIENNE.

Seychelles People's Progressive Front (SPPF): POB 1242, Victoria; tel. 324622; fax 225070; e-mail people@sppf.sc; internet www.sppf.sc; fmrly the Seychelles People's United Party (f. 1964), which assumed power in 1977; renamed in 1978; sole legal party 1978–91; Pres. FRANCE ALBERT RENÉ; Sec.-Gen. JAMES MICHEL.

Diplomatic Representation

EMBASSIES AND HIGH COMMISSIONS IN SEYCHELLES

China, People's Republic: POB 680, St Louis; tel. 266588; fax 266866; e-mail china@seychelles.net; internet sc.china-embassy.org/eng/; Ambassador GENG WENBING.

Cuba: Belle Eau, POB 730, Victoria; tel. 224094; fax 224376; e-mail cubasey@seychelles.net; Ambassador DOMINGO ANGEL GARCÍA RODRÍGUEZ.

France: La Ciotat Bldg, Mont Fleuri, POB 478, Victoria; tel. 382500; fax 382510; e-mail ambafrance@intelvision.net; internet www.ambafrance-sc.org; Ambassador MICHEL TRÉTOUT.

India: Le Chantier, POB 488, Francis Rachel St, Victoria; tel. 610301; fax 610308; e-mail hicomind@seychelles.net; internet www.seychelles.net/hicomind; High Commissioner MALAY MISHRA.

Russia: Le Niol, POB 632, St Louis, Mahé; tel. 266590; fax 266653; e-mail rfembsey@seychelles.net; Ambassador ALEXANDER VLADIMIROV.

United Kingdom: 3rd Floor, Oliaji Trade Centre, POB 161, Victoria; tel. 283666; fax 283657; e-mail bhcvictoria@fco.gov.uk; internet www.bhcvictoria.sc; High Commissioner PHILIPPA THOMPSON (acting).

Judicial System

The legal system is derived from English Common Law and the French Code Napoléon. There are three Courts, the Court of Appeal, the Supreme Court and the Magistrates' Courts. The Court of Appeal hears appeals from the Supreme Court in both civil and criminal cases. The Supreme Court is also a Court of Appeal from the Magistrates' Courts as well as having jurisdiction at first instance. The Constitutional Court, a division of the Supreme Court, determines matters of a constitutional nature, and considers cases bearing on civil liberties. There is also an industrial court and a rent tribunal.

Supreme Court: POB 157, Victoria; tel. 224071; fax 224197; Chief Justice VIVEKANAND ALLEEAR.

President of the Court of Appeal: STEPHEN BWANA (acting).

Justices of Appeal: ANNEL SILUNGWE, A. PILLAY, G. P. S. DE SILVA, K. P. MATADEEN.

Puisne Judges: RANJAN PERERA, D. KARUNAKARAN, N. JUDDOO.

Attorney-General: ANTHONY F. FERNANDO.

Religion

The majority of the inhabitants are Christians, of whom more than 90% are Roman Catholics and about 8% Anglicans. Hinduism, Islam, and the Bahá'í Faith are also practised, however.

CHRISTIANITY

The Anglican Communion

The Church of the Province of the Indian Ocean comprises six dioceses: four in Madagascar, one in Mauritius and one in Seychelles. The Archbishop of the Province is the Bishop of Antananarivo, Madagascar.

Bishop of Seychelles: Rt Rev. SANTOSH MARRAY, POB 44, Victoria; tel. 224242; fax 224296; e-mail angdio@seychelles.net.

The Roman Catholic Church

Seychelles comprises a single diocese, directly responsible to the Holy See. At 31 December 2004 there were an estimated 70,090 adherents in the country, representing 85% of the total population.

Bishop of Port Victoria: Rt Rev. DENIS WIEHE, Bishop's House-Evêché, Olivier Maradan St, POB 43, Victoria; tel. 322152; fax 324045; e-mail rcchurch@seychelles.net.

Other Christian Churches

Pentecostal Assemblies of Seychelles: Victoria; tel. 224598; e-mail paos@seychelles.net; Pastor HERMITTE FREMINOT.

The Press

L'Echo des Iles: POB 12, Victoria; tel. 322262; fax 321464; monthly; French, Creole and English; Roman Catholic; Editor Fr EDWIN MATHIOT; circ. 2,800.

Le Nouveau Seychelles Weekly: Victoria; supports the Democratic Party.

The People: Maison du Peuple, Revolution Ave, Victoria; tel. 224455; owned by the SPPF; monthly; Creole, French and English; circ. 1,000.

Seychelles Nation: Information Technology and Communication Division, POB 800, Victoria; tel. 225775; fax 321006; e-mail seynat@seychelles.net; internet www.seychelles-online.com.sc; f. 1976; govt-owned; Mon.–Sat.; English, French and Creole; the country's only daily newspaper; Dir DENIS ROSE; circ. 3,500.

Seychelles Review: POB 29, Mahé, Victoria; tel. 241717; fax 241545; e-mail surmer@seychelles.net; monthly; business, politics, real estate and tourism; Editor ROLAND HOARAU.

Seychellois: POB 32, Victoria; f. 1928; publ. by Seychelles Farmers Assen; quarterly; circ. 1,800.

Vizyon: Arpent Vert, Mont Fleuri, Victoria; tel. 224507; fax 224987; e-mail regar@seychelles.net; internet www.regar.sc; f. 2007; political fortnightly magazine of the opposition SNP; successor to weekly Regar; Creole, English and French; Editor ROGER MANCIENNE.

NEWS AGENCY

Seychelles Agence de Presse (SAP): Victoria Rd, POB 321, Victoria; tel. 224161; fax 226006.

Broadcasting and Communications

TELECOMMUNICATIONS

Cable and Wireless (Seychelles) Ltd: Mercury House, Francis Rachel St, POB 4, Victoria; tel. 284000; fax 322777; e-mail cws@seychelles.net; internet www.cwseychelles.com; f. 1990; Chief Exec. CHARLES HAMMOND.

Atlas (Seychelles) Ltd: POB 903, Victoria; tel. 304060; fax 324565; e-mail atlas@seychelles.net; internet www.seychelles.net; f. 1996 by a consortium of Space95, VCS and MBM; acquired by Cable and Wireless (Seychelles) Ltd in 2006; internet service provider; Gen. Man. ANTHONY DELORIE.

Telecom Seychelles Ltd (AirTel): POB 1358, Providence; tel. 345505; fax 345499; e-mail custcare@airtel.sc; internet www.airtel.sc; f. 1998; 80% owned by private investors, 10% by Govt of Seychelles; provides fixed-line, mobile and satellite telephone and internet services; Chief Exec. RAJAN SWAROOP.

BROADCASTING

Radio

Seychelles Broadcasting Corpn (SBC): Hermitage, POB 321, Victoria; tel. 224161; fax 225641; e-mail sbcradtv@seychelles.sc; internet www.sbc.sc; f. 1983; reorg. as independent corpn in 1992; programmes in Creole, English and French; Man. Dir IBRAHIM AFIF.

SBC Radio: Union Vale, POB 321, Victoria; tel. 289600; fax 289720; e-mail sbcradtv@seychelles.sc; internet www.sbc.sc; f. 1941; programmes in Creole, English and French; Man. Dir IBRAHIM AFIF.

Television

Seychelles Broadcasting Corpn (SBC): see Radio.

SBC TV: Hermitage, POB 321, Mahé; tel. 224161; fax 225641; e-mail sbcradtv@seychelles.sc; f. 1983; programmes in Creole, English and French; Head of TV Production JUDE LOUANGE.

Finance

(cap. = capital; res = reserves; dep. = deposits; m. = million; brs = branches; amounts in Seychelles rupees)

BANKING

Central Bank

Central Bank of Seychelles (CBS): Independence Ave, POB 701, Victoria; tel. 225200; fax 224958; e-mail cbs@seychelles.sc; internet www.cbs.sc; f. 1983; bank of issue; cap. 1.0m., res 82.6m., dep. 830.6m. (Dec. 2005); Gov. FRANCIS CHANG-LENG; Gen. Man. (vacant).

National Banks

Development Bank of Seychelles: Independence Ave, POB 217, Victoria; tel. 224471; fax 224274; e-mail devbank@dbs.sc; internet www.dbs.sc; f. 1978; 55.5% state-owned; cap. 39.2m., res 43.7m., dep. 11.5m. (Dec. 2000); Chair. ANTONIO LUCAS; Man. Dir R. TOUSSAINT.

Seychelles International Mercantile Banking Corporation Ltd (Nouvobanq) (SIMBC): Victoria House, State House Ave, POB 241, Victoria; tel. 293000; fax 224670; e-mail nvb@nouvobanq.sc; f. 1991; 78% state-owned, 22% by Standard Chartered Bank (UK); cap. 50.0m., res 50.0m., dep. 1,664.9m. (Dec. 2004); Chair. VISWANATHAN SHANKAR; Pres. AHMED SAEED; 2 brs.

Seychelles Savings Bank Ltd (SSB): Kingsgate House, POB 531, Victoria; tel. 294000; fax 224713; e-mail ssb@savingsbank.sc; f. 1902; state-owned; term deposits, savings and current accounts; cap. and res 7.8m. (Dec. 1992), dep. 356.4m. (1999); Chair. JOSEPH NOURRICE; 4 brs.

Foreign Banks

Bank of Baroda (India): Trinity House, Albert St, POB 124, Victoria; tel. 323038; fax 324057; e-mail ce.seychelles@bankofbaroda.com; f. 1978; Man. M. S. PHOGAT.

Barclays Bank (Seychelles) Ltd (United Kingdom): Independence Ave, POB 167, Victoria; tel. 383838; fax 224678; e-mail barclays.seychelles@barclays.com; f. 1959; Seychelles Dir M. P. LANDON; 3 brs and 4 agencies.

Habib Bank Ltd (Pakistan): Frances Rachel St, POB 702, Victoria; tel. 224371; fax 225614; e-mail habibsez@seychelles.net; f. 1976; Vice-Pres. and Chief Man. SOHAIL ANWAR.

Mauritius Commercial Bank (Seychelles) Ltd (MCB Seychelles): POB 122, Manglier St, Victoria; tel. 284555; fax 322676; e-mail contact@mcbseychelles.com; internet www.mcbseychelles.com; f. 1978 as Banque Française Commerciale (BFCOI); changed name in 2003; cap. 14.0m., res 14.0m., dep. 958.4m. (Dec. 2003); Man. Dir JOCELYN AH-YU; 5 brs.

INSURANCE

H. Savy Insurance Co Ltd (HSI): Maison de la Rosière, 2nd Floor, POB 887; Victoria; tel. 322272; fax 321666; e-mail insurance@mail.seychelles.net; f. 1995; all classes; majority-owned by Corvina Investments; Gen. Dir JEAN WEELING-LEE.

Seychelles Assurance Company Ltd (SACL): Pirate's Arms Bldg, POB 636, Victoria; tel. 225000; fax 224495; e-mail sacos@sacos.sc; internet www.sacos.sc; f. 1980; state-owned; scheduled for privatization (excluding the Life Insurance Fund); all classes of insurance; subsidiaries include SUN Investments (Seychelles) Ltd, property-development company; fmrly State Assurance Corporation of Seychelles—SACOS; current name adopted 2006; Exec. Chair. ANTONIO A. LUCAS.

Trade and Industry

GOVERNMENT AGENCIES

Seychelles Fishing Authority (SFA): POB 449, Fishing Port, Victoria; tel. 670300; fax 224508; e-mail management@sfa.sc; internet www.sfa.sc; f. 1984; assessment and management of fisheries resources; Man. Dir RONDOLPH PAYET; Chair. FINLAY RACOMBO.

Seychelles Marketing Board (SMB): Latanier Rd, POB 634, Victoria; tel. 285000; fax 224735; e-mail mail@smb.sc; internet www.smb.sc; f. 1984; manufacturing and marketing of products, retailing, trade; CEO PATRICK VEL.

DEVELOPMENT ORGANIZATIONS

Indian Ocean Tuna Commission (IOTC) (Commission de Thons de l'Océan Indien): POB 1011, Victoria; tel. 225494; fax 224364; e-mail secretariat@iotc.org; internet www.iotc.org; f. 1997; an intergovernmental organization mandated to manage tuna and tuna-like species in the Indian Ocean and adjacent seas; to promote co-operation among its members with a view to ensuring, through appropriate management, the conservation and optimum utilisation of stocks and encouraging sustainable development of fisheries based on such stocks; Exec. Sec. ALEJANDRO ANGANUZZI.

Seychelles Agricultural Development Co Ltd (SADECO): POB 172, Victoria; tel. 375888; f. 1980; Gen. Man. LESLIE PRÉA (acting).

Seychelles Industrial Development Corporation (SIDEC): POB 537, Victoria; tel. 323151; fax 324121; e-mail sidec@sidec.sc; internet www.sidec.sc; f. 1988; promotes industrial development and manages leased industrial sites; CEO MAXWELL JULIE.

Seychelles International Business Authority (SIBA): POB 991, Victoria; Bois de Rose Ave, Roche Caiman; tel. 380800; fax 380888; e-mail siba@seychelles.net; internet www.siba.net; f. 1995 to supervise registration of companies, transhipment and 'offshore' financial services in an international free-trade zone covering an area of 23 ha near Mahé International Airport; Chief Exec. and Man. Dir AHMED AFIF.

Seychelles Investment Bureau (SIB): POB 1167, Caravelle House, 2nd floor, Manglier St, Victoria; tel. 295500; fax 225125; e-mail sib@seychelles.sc; internet www.sib.sc; f. 2004; Chief Exec. JOSEPH NOURRICE.

CHAMBER OF COMMERCE

Seychelles Chamber of Commerce and Industry: Ebrahim Bldg, 2nd Floor, POB 1399, Victoria; tel. 323812; fax 321422; e-mail scci@seychelles.net; Chair. BERNARD POOL; Sec.-Gen. NICHOLE TIRANT-GHÉRARDI.

EMPLOYERS' ORGANIZATION

Federation of Employers' Associations of Seychelles (FEAS): POB 214, Victoria; tel. 324969; fax 324996; Chair. BASIL SOUNDY.

UTILITIES

Electricity

Public Utilities Corporation (Electricity Division): Electricity House, POB 174, Roche Caiman; tel. 678000; fax 321020; e-mail pmorin@puc.sc; Man. Dir PHILIPPE MORIN.

Water

Public Utilities Corporation (Water and Sewerage Division): Unity House, POB 34, Victoria; tel. 322444; fax 325612; e-mail pucwater@seychelles.net; Man. Dir STEPHEN ROUSSEAU.

MAJOR COMPANIES

Abhaye Valabhji (PTY) Ltd: POB 175, Victoria; tel. 373881; fax 373848; e-mail abeval@seychelles.net; f. 1964; furniture, household appliances, marine engines and motor vehicles; Chair. ABHAYE VALABHJI; Man. Dir ANIL VALABHJI.

Allied Builders (Seychelles) Ltd: POB 215, Les Mamelles, Victoria; tel. 344600; fax 344560; e-mail allied@seychelles.net; f. 1980; building and civil engineering construction; Chair K. K. PATEL; 400 employees.

Aluminium and Steel Works (Pty) Ltd: POB 121, Victoria; tel. 344545; fax 344012; Man. Dir CHARLES LOIZEAU.

Amalgamated Tobacco Co (Seychelles) Ltd: Anse des Genêts, POB 679, Victoria; tel. 373118; fax 373322; e-mail atc@seychelles.net; mfrs of cigarettes; Man. Dir R. LATIMER; Gen. Man. J. HIPWAYE.

Corvina Investment Co Ltd: POB 738, Maison la Rosière, Victoria; tel. 321655; e-mail corvina@seychelles.net; f. 1998; holds investments in 30 Seychelles companies and one in Mauritius; holds interests in shipping, tourism, trading, manufacturing, and financial and management services; Chair. GUY ADAM; Man. Dir ABOO AUMEERUDDY.

Indian Ocean Tuna Co: POB 676, Victoria; tel. 282500; fax 224628; e-mail iotmdpa@seychelles.net; fmrly Conserveries de l'Océan Indien; reorg. 1995; Lehman Brothers Inc. (USA) acquired 60% in 2006 and Seychelles Govt owns 40%; tuna-processing; largest private-sector employer in Seychelles, with c. 2,000 employees; Dir DAVID BENTLEY.

Oceana Fisheries Co Ltd: POB 71, Victoria; tel. 224754; fax 224661; exports fish; Dir JOE TIRANT.

Seychelles Breweries (SeyBrew) Ltd: O'Brien House, POB 273, Victoria; tel. 344555; fax 344573; e-mail seybrew@seychelles.net; sole producer of beer and soft drinks; Chair. DAVID HAMPSHIRE.

Seychelles National Oil Co Ltd (SNOC): Maison du Peuple, POB 230, Victoria; tel. 225182; fax 225177; e-mail snoc@seychelles.net; internet www.snoc.sc; f. 1984; merged with Seychelles Petroleum Co (SEPEC) in June 2003, retaining its own name; petroleum exploration in the exclusive economic zone; Chair. GUY ADAM; Man. Dir PATRICK R. JOSEPH.

Seychelles Petroleum Co Ltd (SEPEC): New Port Rd, POB 222, Victoria; tel. 224240; fax 224556; e-mail elizabethb@seychelles-petroleum.com; internet www.seychelles-petroleum.com; f. 1985; merged with Seychelles National Oil Co in June 2003, only to retain its name for international transactions; distributing fuel and lubricants; state-owned; Exec. Chair. GUY ADAM.

Seychelles Timber Co (SEYTIM): Grande Anse, Mahé; tel. 278343; logging, timber sales, joinery and furniture; operates sawmill at Grande Anse.

United Concrete Products (Seychelles) Ltd (UCPS): POB 382, Victoria; tel. 373100; fax 373142; manufactures concrete products; Exec. Dir J. ALBERT; Gen. Man. S. PAYET.

Victoria Computer Services (Pty) Ltd: POB 724, Victoria; tel. 323790; fax 324056; e-mail vcs@seychelles.net; f. 1991; computers and accessories, internet service provider, computer training, telecommunications; Chair. K. MASON; Man. Dir MARC HOUAREAU.

TRADE UNION

Seychelles Federation of Workers' Unions (SFWU): Maison du Peuple, Latanier Rd, POB 154, Victoria; tel. 224455; fax 225351; e-mail sfwu@seychelles.net; f. 1978 to amalgamate all existing trade unions; affiliated to the Seychelles People's Progressive Front; 25,200 mems; Pres. OLIVIER CHARLES; Gen. Sec. ANTOINE ROBINSON.

Transport

RAILWAYS

There are no railways in Seychelles.

ROADS

In 2004 there were 498 km of roads, of which 478 km were surfaced. Most surfaced roads are on Mahé and Praslin.

SHIPPING

Privately owned ferry services connect Victoria, on Mahé, with the islands of Praslin and La Digue. At 31 December 2005 Seychelles' merchant fleet numbered 40 vessels, totalling 104,238 grt.

Port and Marine Services Division, Ministry of Tourism and Transport: POB 47, Mahé Quay, Victoria; tel. 224701; fax 224004; e-mail marineservices@seychellesports.sc; Dir-Gen. (Port of Victoria) Capt. W. ERNESTA.

Aquarius Shipping Agency Ltd: POB 865, Victoria; tel. 225050; fax 225043; e-mail aqua@seychelles.net; Gen. Man. ANTHONY SAVY.

Hunt, Deltel and Co Ltd: Victoria House, POB 14, Victoria; tel. 380300; fax 225367; e-mail hundel@seychelles.net; internet www.hundel.sc; f. 1937; Man. Dir E. HOUAREAU.

Mahé Shipping Co Ltd: Maritime House, POB 336, Victoria; tel. 380500; fax 380538; e-mail maheship@seychelles.net; shipping agents; Chair. Capt. G. C. C. ADAM.

Harry Savy & Co Ltd: POB 20, Victoria; tel. 322120; fax 321421; e-mail hsavyco@seychelles.net; shipping agents; Man. Dir GUY SAVY.

Seychelles Shipping Line Ltd: POB 977, Providence, Victoria; tel. 373737; fax 373647; e-mail ssl@gondwana.sc; f. 1994; operates freight services between Seychelles and Durban, South Africa; Chair. SELWYN GENDRON; Man. Dir HASSAN OMAR.

CIVIL AVIATION

Seychelles International Airport is located at Pointe Larue, 10 km from Victoria. A new international passenger terminal and aircraft parking apron were to be constructed by 2007 on land reclaimed in 1990; the existing terminal (which underwent SR 3m. in renovations in 2002) was to be converted into a cargo terminal. The airport also serves as a refuelling point for aircraft traversing the Indian Ocean. There are airstrips on several outlying islands.

Seychelles Civil Aviation Authority (SCAA): POB 181, Victoria; tel. 384000; fax 384009; e-mail dcaadmin@seychelles.net; formerly Directorate of Civil Aviation; offers ground and cargo handling and refuelling services, as well as holding responsibility for the Flight Information Region of 2.6m. sq km of Indian Ocean airspace; Chair. GERARD LAFORTUNE; Chief Exec. CONRAD BENOÎTON.

Air Seychelles: The Creole Spirit Bldg, Quincy St, POB 386, Victoria; tel. 224305; fax 225933; e-mail airseymd@seychelles.net; internet www.airseychelles.net; f. 1979; operates scheduled internal flights from Mahé to Praslin; also charter services to Bird, Desroches and Denis Islands and to outlying islands of the Amirantes group; international services to Europe, Far East, East and South Africa; Chief Exec. Capt. DAVID SAVY.

Emirates Airlines: 5th June Ave and Manglier St, Victoria; tel. 292700; f. 2005; Dir ABDULRAHMAN AL BALOOSHI.

Tourism

Seychelles enjoys an equable climate, and is renowned for its fine beaches and attractive scenery. There are more than 500 varieties of flora and many rare species of birds. Most tourist activity is concentrated on the islands of Mahé, Praslin and La Digue, although the potential for ecological tourism of the outlying islands received increased attention in the late 1990s. It is government policy that the development of tourism should not blight the environment, and strict laws govern the location and construction of hotels. In 1998 the Government indicated that up to 200,000 visitors (although not more than 4,000 at any one time) could be accommodated annually without detriment to environmental quality. However, several new luxury resorts were constructed in the early 2000s, and the yachting sector was also under development. Receipts from tourism totalled an estimated SR 885m. in 2006. In that year there were 140,600 tourist arrivals; most visitors (approximately 65.2%% in 2005) are from Europe; in 2004 there were an average of 5,030 hotel beds available.

Compagnie Seychelloise de Promotion Hotelière Ltd: POB 683, Victoria; tel. 224694; fax 225291; e-mail cosproh@seychelles.net; promotes govt-owned hotels.

Seychelles Tourism Board (STB): POB 1262, Victoria, Mahe; tel. 671300; fax 620620; e-mail info@seychelles.com; internet www.seychelles.travel; f. 1998 as Seychelles Tourism Marketing Authority; merged with Seychelles Tourism Office in 2005; Chair. MAURICE LOUSTEAU-LALANNE.

Defence

As assessed at November 2006, the army numbered 400 men, including a coastguard of 200. Paramilitary forces comprised a 250-strong national guard. Seychelles was to contribute servicemen to the East African Stand-by Brigade, a part of the African Union stand-by peace-keeping force.

Defence Expenditure: Budgeted at SR 70m. in 2006.

Commander-in-Chief of Seychelles Armed Forces: Col LÉOPOLD PAYET.

Education

Education is free and compulsory for children between six and 16 years of age. A programme of educational reform, based on the British comprehensive schools system, was introduced in 1980. The language of instruction in primary schools is English. The duration of primary education is six years, while that of general secondary education is five years (of which the first four years are compulsory), beginning at 12 years of age. Pre-primary and special education facilities are also available. There were 1,837 students in post-secondary (non-tertiary) education in 2005. A number of students study abroad, principally in the United Kingdom. Government expenditure on education in 2004 was SR 165.8m., or about 11.2% of total expenditure.

Bibliography

Barclays Bank International. *Seychelles: Economic Survey*. London, William Lea, 1972.

Benedict, B. *People of the Seychelles*. London, HMSO, 1966.

Benedict, M., and Benedict, B. *Men, Women and Money in Seychelles*. Berkeley, CA, University of California Press, 1982.

Bennett, G., and Bennett, P.R. *Seychelles* (World Bibliographical Series). Santa Barbara, CA, ABC-Clio, 1993.

Bradley, J. T. *History of Seychelles*. Victoria, Clarion Press, 1940.

Central Bank of Seychelles. *Quarterly Review*. Victoria, Central Bank of Seychelles.

Cohen, R. (Ed.) *African Islands and Enclaves*. London, Sage Publications, 1983.

Doyle, S., Ewing, D., Kelly, R. C., and Youngblood, D. *Seychelles Country Review 2000*. Houston, TX, CountryWatch.com, 1999.

Franda, M. *Quiet Turbulence in the Seychelles: Tourism and Development*. Hanover, NH, American Field Staff Reports, Asia Series No. 10, 1979.

The Seychelles. Boulder, CO, Westview Press, 1981.

Gabby, R., and Ghosh, R. N. *Seychelles Marketing Board: Economic Development in a Small Island Economy*. Singapore, Academic Press International, 1992.

International Monetary Fund. *Seychelles—Recent Economic Developments*. Washington, DC, IMF, 1996.

Lee, C. *Seychelles: Political Castaways*. London, Hamish Hamilton, 1976.

Leymarie, P. *Océan indien, nouveau coeur du monde*. Paris, Editions Karthala, 1983.

Lionnet, G. *The Seychelles*. Newton Abbot, David and Charles, 1972.

Mancham, Sir J. R. *Paradise Raped: Life, Love and Power in the Seychelles*. London, Methuen, 1983.

Island Splendour. London, Methuen, 1984.

Maubouche, R., and Hadjitarkhani, N. *Seychelles Economic Memorandum*. Washington, DC, World Bank, 1980.

Scarr, D. *Seychelles since 1770: History of a Slave and Post-Slavery Society*. New Jersey, NJ, Africa World Press, Inc, 2000.

Skerrett, J., and Skerrett, A. *Seychelles*. London, APA, 1994.

Thomas, A. *Forgotten Eden*. London, Longman, 1968.

Toussaint, A. *History of the Indian Ocean*. London, Routledge and Kegan Paul, 1966.

USA International Business Publications. *Seychelles Country Study Guide* (World Country Study Guide). 2000.

Webb, A. W. T. *Story of Seychelles*. Seychelles, 1964.

World Bank. *Seychelles' Economic Memorandum*. Washington, DC, World Bank, 1980.

SIERRA LEONE

Physical and Social Geography

PETER K. MITCHELL

The Republic of Sierra Leone, which covers an area of 71,740 sq km (27,699 sq miles), rises from the beaches of the south-west to the broad plateaux of the Atlantic/Niger watershed at the north-eastern frontier. Despite the general horizontal aspect of the landscapes, developed over millennia upon largely Pre-Cambrian structures, there are a number of abrupt ascents to older uplifted erosion surfaces—most impressively along sections of a major escarpment, 130 km inland, separating a western lowland zone (c. 120 m above sea-level) from the country's more elevated interior half (c. 500 m). Incised valleys, interspersed by minor waterfalls, carry drainage south-westwards; only locally or along a coastal sedimentary strip do rivers flow through open terrain.

A geologically recent submergence of major floodplains, particularly north of Cape St Ann, has brought tide-water into contact with the rocky margins of the ancient shield, impeding up-river navigation. Water-borne trade has found compensation in sheltered deep-water anchorages, notably off Freetown, the principal port and capital, where a line of coastal summits rising to almost 900 m above sea-level facilitates an easy landfall.

Intrusive gabbros form the peninsular range; elsewhere, isolated blocks or hill groups consist of rock-bare granites or the metamorphic roots of long-vanished mountain chains, which provide mineral deposits: iron, chromite, gold, rutile and bauxite. Reserves of kimberlite in the southern high plateaux are approaching exhaustion. The pipes and dikes of kimberlite may provide the basis for future deep mining.

Differences in seasonal and regional incidence of humidity and rainfall are important. Prolonged rains (May to October, with heaviest rains from July to September) are bracketed by showery weather with many squally thunderstorms, such spells beginning earlier in the south-east. Consequently, the growing season is longest here (although total rainfall—over 5,000 mm locally—is greater along the coast) and the 'natural' vegetation is tropical evergreen forest; the cultivation of cash crops such as cocoa, coffee, kola and oil-palm is successful in this area, and the more productive timber areas, although limited, are concentrated here. The savannah-woodlands of the north-east have less rain (1,900 mm–2,500 mm), a shorter period for plant growth and a dry season made harsh by harmattan winds, with cattle-rearing, groundnuts and tobacco as potential commercial resources. Semi-deciduous forest occupies most intervening areas, but long peasant occupation has created a mosaic of short-term cropland, fallow regrowth plots and occasional tracts of secondary forest.

Permanent rice-lands have been created from mangrove swamp in the north-west, and much encouragement is being given to the improvement of the many small tracts of inland valley swamp throughout the east. Such innovation contrasts with a widespread bush-fallowing technique, giving low yields of rain-fed staples, normally rice, but cassava (especially on degraded sandy soils) and millet in the north. Sierra Leone's agricultural sector is able to provide most of the country's food requirements.

Sierra Leone's third national census, which was held in December 1985, enumerated 3,515,812 inhabitants, representing a population density of 49 inhabitants per sq km. However, there was believed to have been underenumeration, and the census total was subsequently adjusted to 3.7m. At mid-2006, according to UN estimates, Sierra Leone had 5,743,000 inhabitants and a population density of 80.1 inhabitants per sq km.

Traditional *mores* still dominate, in spite of the Westernizing influences of employment in mining, of education and of growing urbanization. A large proportion of the population follows animist beliefs, although there are significant Islamic and Christian communities. Extended family, exogamous kin-groups and the paramount chieftaincies form a social nexus closely mirrored by a hierarchy of hamlet, village and rural centre: 29,000 non-urban settlements including isolated impermanent homesteads. The towns, however, are expanding. Greater Freetown had almost 470,000 inhabitants at the 1985 census, while Koindu, the centre of the Kono diamond fields, had about 82,000 inhabitants; in 1985 there were, in total, 10 towns with more than 10,000 people. By mid-2005 the population of Freetown was estimated by the UN to have increased to 799,000. Diamond mining has attracted settlers to many villages in the mining areas. In the first quarter of 2003, according to the office of the UN High Commissioner for Refugees, about 8,250 Sierra Leonean refugees were repatriated from Guinea (with some 52,380 remaining in Guinea).

The official language of the country is English, while Krio (Creole), Mende, Limba and Temne are also widely spoken.

Recent History

RICHARD SYNGE

Based on an earlier article by CHRISTOPHER CLAPHAM

In 1896 a British protectorate was proclaimed over the hinterland of the coastal colony of Sierra Leone, which had been under British administration since 1787. In 1951, following the introduction of a Constitution, elections were won by the Sierra Leone People's Party (SLPP), led by Dr (later Sir) Milton Margai, who became Chief Minister in 1953 and Prime Minister in 1958. On 27 April 1961 Sierra Leone became an independent state within the Commonwealth. The SLPP retained power in elections in 1962. Sir Milton died in 1964 and was succeeded as Prime Minister by his half-brother, Dr (later Sir) Albert Margai. The main opposition party, the All-People's Congress (APC), led by Dr Siaka Stevens, gained a parliamentary majority at general elections in 1967, but was prevented from taking power by a military coup. Following an army mutiny in April 1968, a civilian Government was restored, with Stevens as Prime Minister. A period of political instability followed, culminating in an attempted military coup in March 1971, which was suppressed with the aid of troops from neighbouring Guinea. In April a republican Constitution was introduced, with Stevens as executive President. The SLPP offered no candidates in the 1973 general elections, and Stevens, as sole candidate, was elected to a further presidential term.

In 1978 the APC was constitutionally established as the sole legal party, upon which a number of prominent supporters of the SLPP joined the APC and received ministerial posts. The Government encountered increasing opposition in 1981, following a scandal involving government officials and several cabinet ministers in the misappropriation of public funds. Amid serious outbreaks of violence, general elections took place in May 1982 and a new Government was formed.

In April 1985 Stevens announced that he was to leave office upon the expiry of his existing mandate later that year. At a conference of the APC in August, Maj.-Gen. Joseph Saidu Momoh, a cabinet minister and the Commander of the Armed Forces, was nominated as sole candidate for the presidency and for the leadership of the party. In October Momoh received 99% of votes cast in a presidential election, and was inaugurated as President on 28 November. Although retaining his military affiliation, Momoh installed a civilian Cabinet, which included several members of the previous administration. Elections to the House of Representatives took place in May 1986.

In 1987 Momoh initiated measures to combat financial corruption in the public sector. In July the Minister of Agriculture, Natural Resources and Forestry resigned after allegations of accountancy irregularities in the distribution of domestic sugar supplies, and was later ordered by Momoh to make financial restitution. In November, following a series of strikes by workers in the public sector, which resulted from the Government's inability to pay their salaries, Momoh declared a state of emergency in the economy, announced measures to prevent hoarding of currency and essential goods, and intensified the campaign against smuggling. Under the new measures, corruption was redefined as a criminal offence, and people accused of any crime could be tried *in absentia*. Severe penalties were introduced for the publication of 'defamatory' articles in newspapers, and government censorship was imposed.

By early 1990 there was widespread popular support for the restoration of a multi-party system; this was initially rejected by Momoh, although he emphasized that he would continue to encourage broadly based participation in the one-party state. In mid-August, however, Momoh conceded the necessity of electoral reforms, and announced an extensive review of the Constitution. The Central Committee of the APC approved a number of proposed amendments to the Constitution, and in November Momoh appointed a 30-member National Constitutional Review Commission, which, in March 1991, submitted a draft Constitution, providing for the restoration of a plural political system. The maximum duration of the President's tenure of office was to be two five-year terms. The President was to appoint the Cabinet, which was to include one Vice-President, rather than two. Legislative power was to be vested in a bicameral legislature, elected by universal adult suffrage for a term of five years. The Government subsequently accepted the majority of the Commission's recommendations. It presented the draft Constitution to the House of Representatives and announced that the parliamentary term, which was due to end in June, was to be extended for a further year, owing to the disruption caused by the conflict between government forces and Liberian rebels in the south of the country. The general elections, which were scheduled for May, were also to be postponed for a year to allow time for the transition to a plural political system. However, political activity by parties other than the APC remained illegal until the new Constitution took effect. At a national referendum, which was conducted during 23–30 August, the new Constitution was approved by 60% of voters, with 75% of the electorate participating.

REBEL ACTIVITY AND MILITARY RULE

In March 1991 repeated border incursions by Liberian rebels, reported to be members of the National Patriotic Front of Liberia (NPFL), resulted in the deaths of several Sierra Leoneans. The Sierra Leone Government, which had already committed 500 of its troops to the peace-keeping operation in Liberia authorized by the Economic Community of West African States (ECOWAS) Monitoring Group (ECOMOG), subsequently deployed another 2,150 troops on the Liberian border and, in early April, attacked rebel bases in Liberian territory. The Government alleged that the rebel offensive had been instigated by the NPFL leader, Charles Taylor, in an attempt to force Sierra Leone's withdrawal from ECOMOG. The newly created Revolutionary United Front (RUF), which was apparently led by a former Sierra Leone army photographer, Cpl Foday Sankoh, began to support the NPFL in its attacks against Sierra Leone army positions. In mid-1991 Sierra Leonean troops, by now assisted by military units from Nigeria and Guinea, initiated a counter-offensive against the RUF rebels, and succeeded in recapturing several towns in the east and south of the country. Government forces were also joined by some 1,200 former members of the Liberian armed forces, who had fled to Sierra Leone in September 1990, while a number of other countries, including the United Kingdom and the USA, provided logistical support to Sierra Leone.

In late September 1991 six newly created political associations established an alliance, known as the United Front of Political Movements (UNIFOM), and demanded that the Government give way to an interim administration. Shortly afterwards the first Vice-President, Abubakar Kamara, and the second Vice-President, Salia Jusu-Sheriff, resigned from both the APC and the Government. In December Momoh and leaders of the registered political parties agreed to co-operate in the establishment of a multi-party system.

On 29 April 1992 members of the armed forces, who had arrived in Freetown to protest against the deprivations being endured by troops engaged in suppressing the rebellion in the border region, seized a radio station in the capital and occupied the presidential offices. Their leader, Capt. Valentine Strasser, subsequently declared that the Momoh Government had been replaced by a five-member military junta. Momoh sought assistance from the Guinean Government, which dispatched troops to Freetown, and more than 100 people were killed in the ensuing fighting. Momoh fled to Guinea, and Strasser announced the formation of a National Provisional Ruling Council (NPRC), while making pledges about the introduction of a multi-party system and an end to the conflict in the country, and assuring ECOWAS of the continued participation of Sierra Leone in ECOMOG. The NPRC suspended the Constitution, dissolved the House of Representatives, imposed a state of emergency and curfew, and temporarily closed the country's air, sea and land borders.

On 1 May 1992 the NPRC (which comprised 18 military officers and four civilians) was formally convened under Strasser's chairmanship. All political activity was suspended, and it was subsequently reported that some 55 people, including members of the former Cabinet, had been arrested. On 6 May Strasser was sworn in as Head of State. Later that month the new Government established a commission of inquiry to investigate the activities of members of the former regime. In August Strasser announced the establishment of an advisory council, which, among its other functions, was to review the provisions of the 1991 Constitution. In early September 1992 Capt. Solomon Musa, the Deputy Chairman of the NPRC, became the acting Head of State during Strasser's absence in the United Kingdom to obtain medical treatment for injuries sustained in his earlier operations against the rebels. In December Musa was appointed Chief Secretary of State and the Government announced that it had foiled a coup attempt by a group known as the Anti-Corruption Revolutionary Movement (which included former members of the army and security forces). Among those reported to have been killed by security forces was the alleged instigator of the plot, Sgt Lamin Bangura. Shortly afterwards nine of those accused of involvement in the conspiracy were tried by a military tribunal, and, together with 17 prisoners who had been convicted in November on charges of treason, were summarily executed. In January 1993 the United Kingdom announced the suspension of economic aid to Sierra Leone, in protest at the executions. Later that month, in an apparent attempt to allay further accusations of human rights violations, the military regime released several former members of the Momoh Government, who had been detained since May 1992.

In April 1993 Strasser announced that a programme providing for a return to civilian Government by 1996 had been adopted. He also stated that measures were being taken to reduce the powers of the security services. In a government reorganization in July, Musa was replaced as Deputy Chairman of the NPRC and Chief Secretary of State by Capt. Julius Maada Bio, ostensibly on the grounds that false allegations against him had proved detrimental to the stability of the administration. Musa (who was widely blamed for the repressive measures undertaken by the Government) took refuge in the Nigerian High Commission in Freetown, amid widespread speculation regarding his dismissal, and subsequently sought refuge in the United Kingdom. Also in July a number of political prisoners were released.

By April 1993 it was reported that only Kailahun District in the extreme east of Sierra Leone, near the border with Liberia, and Pujehun District in the south of the country, still remained under the control of rebel forces. Government forces later also made advances in Kailahun District, regaining control of the significant diamond-mining town of Koidu, 250 km east of Freetown, in November. In January 1994 the Government claimed that it had regained control of further rebel bases in Pujehun District and the town of Kenema near the border with Liberia, but the RUF managed to regroup and there was a subsequent intensification of the fighting in the south and east of Sierra Leone. In April it was reported that the RUF, which had been joined by disaffected members of the armed forces, had initiated attacks in the north of the country.

In November 1993 Strasser announced a two-year transitional programme, which provided for the installation of a civilian government by January 1996. In December 1993, in accordance with the transitional programme, a five-member Interim National Electoral Commission (INEC), under the chairmanship of Dr James Jonah (the assistant Secretary-General of the UN, in charge of political affairs), was established to organize the registration of voters and the demarcation of constituency boundaries, in preparation for the forthcoming local government elections. In the same month the National Advisory Council submitted several constitutional proposals (which included a number of similar provisions to the 1991 Constitution), stipulating that only Sierra Leonean nationals of more than 40 years of age were to qualify to contest a presidential election (thereby precluding Strasser and the majority of members of the NPRC, on the grounds of age). In April 1994 several senior members of the armed forces were dismissed, following criticism of the Government's failure to end the RUF rebellion. By this time there were widespread rumours of collusion between military officers and the rebels, who proved able to make extraordinary advances, taking over the mining installations of Sierra Leone Ore and Metal Co (SIEROMCO) and Sierra Rutile in January 1995, and seizing numerous foreign hostages.

After frequent changes of government personnel in 1994, in March 1995 Musa was apparently ordered to retire from the armed forces, after Strasser rejected his proposal for the installation of a transitional civilian government. Lt-Col Akim Gibril became Chief Secretary of State, replacing Maada Bio, who was appointed Chief of the Defence Staff. In late April, on the third anniversary of the NPRC coup, Strasser announced that the ban on political activity would be lifted and that a National Consultative Conference was to be convened to discuss the transitional process. He indicated that elections would take place by the end of the year, with the installation of a civilian government in January 1996, in accordance with the provisions of the transitional programme. The ban on political parties was formally rescinded on 21 June. The RUF, which was making large advances, refused to participate in the political process.

Continued atrocities perpetrated against civilians were increasingly attributed to 'sobels', disaffected members of the armed forces who engaged in acts of looting, banditry and indiscriminate killing. By early 1995 some 900,000 civilians had been displaced as a result of the increase in the civil conflict, of whom about 185,000 had fled to Guinea, 90,000 to Liberia and some 500,000 had settled around the capital. Despite the successful counter-offensives by government forces, the RUF made some advances towards Freetown and initiated attacks against towns in the vicinity (including Songo, which was situated only 35 km east of Freetown), apparently prior to besieging the capital. The Governments of Guinea and Nigeria dispatched additional troops to Sierra Leone, while it was reported that mercenaries recruited from South Africa were assisting the authorities with military training and logistics. The RUF indicated that humanitarian organizations would be prevented from operating in territory that the movement controlled, and there were increasing reports of massacres and other violations of human rights perpetrated by the rebels against the civilian population. In November the RUF regained control of Kailahun, and a further 10 towns in Moyamba District. In December an Organization of African Unity (OAU, now the African Union) mission conducted negotiations with RUF representatives in Abidjan, Côte d'Ivoire.

FALL OF STRASSER AND ELECTION OF KABBAH

In December 1995 it was announced that the presidential and legislative elections were to take place concurrently in February 1996. In January, however, Strasser was deposed by military officers, led by Bio, in a bloodless coup. Bio, who assumed the office of Head of State, announced that the coup had been instigated in response to efforts by Strasser to remain in power. (It was reported that Strasser had indicated that he intended to amend restrictions on the age of prospective candidates to enable himself to contest the elections.) A reconstituted Supreme Council of State and Council of Secretaries were formed, and, following a meeting of the new military leadership, and representatives of the political parties and the INEC, it was announced that the elections would proceed as scheduled. Following the refusal of Bio to accede to the RUF's request for a postponement of the elections pending a peace agreement, the rebels abandoned a cease-fire in early February and subsequently launched a series of attacks in various parts of the country, killing large numbers of civilians, in an apparent attempt to undermine the electoral process.

On 26 February 1996 presidential and legislative elections, which were contested by 13 political parties and were monitored by international observers, took place as scheduled. The reconstituted SLPP secured 36% of votes cast in the legislative elections, while its presidential candidate, Ahmed Tejan Kabbah, also received most support, with 36% of votes. Seven of the political parties, including the National Unity Party (which had supported Bio), demanded that the results be annulled, owing to the disruption of the elections in several regions caused by rebel violence. Since none of the candidates had achieved the requisite majority of 55% of the votes, a second round of the presidential election, which took place on 15 March, was contested by Kabbah and the candidate of the United National People's Party (UNPP), John Karefa-Smart (who had obtained 23% of votes cast in the first round): Kabbah was elected President by 60% of the votes. Later in March seats in the new 80-member Parliament were allocated on a basis of proportional representation, with the SLPP securing 27, the UNPP 17, the People's Democratic Party 12 and the reconstituted APC only five; the 12 provincial districts were represented in the legislature by Paramount Chiefs. Kabbah was inaugurated on 29 March, when the military Government officially relinquished power to the new civilian administration. In July the Parliament adopted legislation that formally reinstated the Constitution of 1991.

Following discussions between President Kabbah and the rebel leader, Foday Sankoh, in April 1996, both the Government and the RUF made a commitment to a cessation of hostilities, and announced the establishment of three joint committees, which would consider issues regarding the demobilization of rebel forces. Sankoh refused, however, to recognize the legitimacy of the new Government, and demanded that a transitional administration be installed, pending further elections. At further discussions between the Government and the rebel leadership in July, Sankoh demanded that members of the RUF be allocated ministerial posts as a precondition to the cessation of hostilities.

In September 1996 Kabbah ordered the compulsory retirement of some 20 officers, including Strasser and Bio, from the armed forces. Shortly afterwards it was reported that a plot against the Government had been discovered by senior military officers. Later that month the Government announced that a team of specialists from Nigeria was to assist the armed forces in the investigation of the planned coup attempt. About 17 members of the armed forces were arrested, of whom nine were subsequently charged with involvement in the conspiracy. Following reports of a further plot to overthrow the

Government in January 1997, Kabbah announced that the Nigerian investigative mission had concluded that former members of the NPRC administration had instigated the coup conspiracy of the previous September.

MILITARY AND RUF IN ALLIANCE

On 25 May 1997 dissident members of the armed forces, led by Maj. Johnny Paul Koroma, seized power, deposing Kabbah, who fled to Guinea. Koroma claimed that the coup, which prompted international condemnation, was in response to the Government's failure to implement a peace agreement with the RUF, reached in November 1996. The Nigerian Government demanded that the junta relinquish power, and increased its military strength in Freetown. The new authorities imposed a curfew in Freetown, following widespread violent looting by armed factions; most foreign nationals were evacuated. In early June Nigerian forces initiated a naval bombardment of Freetown in an effort to force the new military leaders to resign. However, forces loyal to the coup leaders, assisted by RUF members, succeeded in repelling Nigerian attacks; it was reported that about 62 people were killed in the fighting. Some 300 Nigerian troops were taken hostage, but were subsequently released. Koroma announced the establishment of a 20-member Armed Forces Revolutionary Council (AFRC), with himself as Chairman and Sankoh as Vice-Chairman (*in absentia*, since he was being detained in Abuja by the Nigerian authorities). The AFRC (which was not internationally recognized as the legitimate Government) included a further three members of the RUF and several civilians. All political activity, the existing Constitution and government bodies were suspended, although Koroma pledged that democratic rule would be restored, following new elections. Nigeria reiterated that it intended to reinstate the ousted Government with the support of ECOWAS, and a further two Nigerian warships were dispatched to the region; further clashes between Nigerian troops and supporters of the new military leaders occurred at the international airport at Lungi.

In mid-June 1997 the AFRC announced that it had suppressed a coup attempt, following the arrest of 15 people, including several senior military officers. In the same month it was reported that troops supporting the junta had repulsed an attack by Kamajors, who remained loyal to Kabbah, at the town of Zimmi, 250 km south-east of Freetown. On 17 June Koroma was formally installed as the self-proclaimed Head of State. However, despite appeals from Koroma, civilians continued to observe a campaign of civil disobedience, which had been organized by the labour congress in protest at the coup. In the same month members of the disbanded legislature, who had met in defiance of the ban on political activity, proposed a peace agreement, under which a government of national unity representing all political parties and the RUF would be established, and ECOMOG and UN forces would be deployed throughout the country.

By July 1997 the new military Government had become completely isolated by the international community. The Commonwealth ministerial action group (which had been established to respond to unlawful activities by member states) suspended Sierra Leone from meetings of the Commonwealth, pending the restoration of constitutional order and the reinstatement of a democratically elected government. The UN Security Council also condemned the coup, and expressed support for ECOWAS efforts to resolve the situation. The effective imposition of an ECOWAS embargo against Sierra Leone, enforced through the naval blockade and occupation of Lungi airport by Nigerian troops, resulted in increasing shortages of food, crude petroleum and other essential commodities. Meanwhile, a four-nation committee, comprising representatives of Nigeria, Côte d'Ivoire, Guinea and Ghana, which had been established by ECOWAS to monitor a return to constitutional rule, urged the Government to relinquish power during a series of negotiations with an AFRC delegation. In an apparent effort to consolidate power, Koroma formed a Cabinet, known as the Council of Secretaries, comprising representatives of the RUF and the army, together with a number of civilians. In late July, following further reports of clashes between Kamajors and government forces in the south of the country, AFRC representatives and the ECOWAS committee, meeting in Abidjan, Côte d'Ivoire, agreed to an immediate cease-fire; negotiations were to continue, with the aim of restoring constitutional order. However, Nigeria subsequently accused the AFRC of violating the cease-fire, while further clashes between the Kamajors and the AFRC forces were reported at Zimmi. Renewed skirmishes between Nigerian and AFRC troops also occurred at Lungi airport following an attempt by forces loyal to the junta to locate a clandestine radio station, which had been allegedly established by supporters of Kabbah. At the end of August the ECOWAS members agreed to impose a total embargo on all supplies of petroleum products, armaments and military equipment to the military junta, and they sought the endorsement of the UN in strengthening these sanctions. The UN Security Council subsequently approved the adoption of sanctions against Sierra Leone. The ECOMOG military presence at Lungi airport was increased, and a base was established at Jui, on the principal road linking Freetown to the rest of the country. ECOMOG enforced the economic blockade on Freetown by launching aerial bombardments against merchant ships in the port. During September there was an escalation of hostilities between the AFRC's forces and ECOMOG, resulting in numerous deaths; thousands of Freetown residents subsequently fled from the capital.

Amid increasing ECOMOG military pressure and mounting popular resistance, the military junta apparently acceded to ECOWAS demands that the AFRC relinquish power by 22 April 1998, as part of an agreement that also provided for the imposition of a cease-fire, and the disarmament and demobilization of combatant forces. However, subsequent major disagreements over the terms of the accord prompted further confrontations between the AFRC and ECOMOG. Despite Koroma's demands that ECOMOG begin to withdraw its forces as a precondition for his adherence to the agreement, ECOMOG's Nigerian forces were strengthened. There was no progress on the disarmament programme, which had been scheduled to begin in December.

KABBAH'S RESTORATION TO POWER,

International efforts to restore Kabbah to power intensified during January 1998, when the United Kingdom appointed a former ambassador to Angola, John Flynn, to co-operate with the UN and ECOWAS officials to this end. According to subsequent reports in the British media, Kabbah contracted a British military consultancy, Sandline International, to undertake the supply of armaments, and to provide military support and training, both to Sierra Leonean forces loyal to the ousted Government and to ECOMOG. Following armed clashes near the ECOMOG base at Jui at the end of January, the ECOMOG Force Commander, Col Maxwell Khobe, ordered a final offensive against the capital in early February. The presidential mansion was captured after several days of fighting and full control of Freetown was achieved by mid-February; it was estimated that about 100 people had been killed during the operation. Following the seizure of the capital, ECOMOG ended the military embargo and opened Lungi airport to commercial traffic. A special task force was established to supervise government activities and to expedite the delivery of humanitarian aid. International donors pledged to provide emergency food and medical supplies, and mine-clearance expertise. The Kamajor forces (now operating under the name of Civil Defence Forces) initially seized Bo and Koidu in mid-February; however, intensive fighting for control of the area ensued, while violence and looting continued in many parts of the country. Some AFRC officers were quickly captured by ECOMOG, while others fled to the northern region; Koroma was reported to have taken refuge in a village in the south-east of the country. Many refugees, including RUF activists, fled into Liberia. Nigerian troops undertook most of the operations to suppress continuing rebel activity, ousting the RUF from Kenema and forcing AFRC troops to surrender in Makeni. ECOMOG only finally gained control of Bo in late February, but fighting continued in the surrounding countryside for some weeks thereafter. On 10 March Kabbah returned to Freetown and was formally inaugurated. Although international donors pledged substantial support, the stability of his Government was initially dependent on the continued presence of the ECOMOG forces, then numbering 7,000 (principally Nigerians, but also including Ghanaians and Guineans). In mid-April Kabbah appointed Khobe as Chief of National Security. During April the reinstated Government charged a total of 59 people, including the former President, Joseph Momoh, with treason and collaboration with the AFRC.

In May 1998 government and ECOMOG troops continued to launch attacks against rebel forces, which remained in control of Kailahun District and part of Kono District. In late July the UN Security Council established a 70-member United Nations Observer Mission in Sierra Leone (UNOMSIL); the force, which had an initial mandate to remain in the country for a six-month period, was to monitor the security situation, and the disarmament of former combatants based in secure regions of the country. In August 16 people were convicted and sentenced to death for their involvement in the May 1997 coup. After appeals for clemency, their sentences were reviewed, but in October 24 former members of the armed forces were executed, after having been convicted of collaborating with the ousted junta. At the end of October Sankoh, who had in July been returned from detention in Nigeria, was convicted and sentenced to death for treason and murder, owing to his support for the May 1997 coup; he immediately launched an appeal. In November a further 15 civilians were sentenced to death for treason, and ex-President Momoh received a 10-year prison sentence.

The death sentence imposed on Sankoh prompted an upsurge in attacks by RUF forces, in alliance with former AFRC members, after October 1998. There were increased reports of atrocities being perpetrated against civilians as the rebels began the systematic recruitment and abduction of minors, both to act as combatants and to transport ammunition and goods. Fighting spread rapidly in the eastern diamond district of Kono and in northern areas of the country. ECOMOG launched further air attacks in November. The RUF issued a general threat of retaliation if Sankoh was harmed. Despite a rapid reinforcement of the ECOMOG contingent to 15,000 troops, and the deployment of Kamajors, the rebels seized Koidu in the east and the northern town of Makeni, before advancing into Lunsar and Waterloo, closer to Freetown. Fighting subsequently erupted throughout the capital in early January 1999; the rebels attacked civilians and forced them to flee towards the city centre, thus securing cover for a rapid advance. Over a period of three weeks an estimated 5,000 people were killed in Freetown, including thousands of civilians, at least 800 ECOMOG troops and hundreds of RUF rebels, while many thousands of city residents were assaulted or mutilated. A subsequent investigation by a human rights organization concluded that these widespread abuses were authorized at a high level within the RUF's command structure. The investigation also identified violations of human rights committed by ECOMOG forces, especially with regard to their policy of summary execution of captured rebels.

As the rebels withdrew from the city they set alight buildings and caused widespread destruction. ECOMOG was eventually able to restore a semblance of order to Freetown, but in view of an implied threat of a complete withdrawal by the Nigerian forces, owing to the heavy losses they had suffered, there was a renewed international initiative for negotiations with the RUF. With mediation by the UN, the OAU, the Commonwealth, the United Kingdom and the USA, the discussions began in Lomé, Togo, following a UN-supervised release of Sankoh in April 1999. In May the Sierra Leonean Government and the RUF signed a cease-fire agreement, although violations were subsequently reported. Continuing negotiations on the proposed participation of the RUF in a transitional administration followed. In early July the Government and the RUF reached a power-sharing agreement, after the Government acceded to rebel demands that Sankoh be appointed Vice-President, with responsibility for the mineral resources industry, and the RUF be allocated a further eight cabinet posts. The accord provided for the release of civilians who had been abducted by the rebels, and the disarmament and reintegration into the armed forces of former combatants; the RUF was to be reconstituted as a political organization. However, the UN High Commissioner for Refugees and human rights organizations objected to a general amnesty for perpetrators of human rights violations granted under the provisions of the peace agreement.

In Freetown the uncertainties surrounding the RUF's commitment to complying with the agreement were reflected in the prolonged delay in the return from Liberia of both Foday Sankoh and Johnny Paul Koroma, whose mutual alliance was by now under severe strain. Eventually arriving in the capital in early October 1999, Sankoh issued a prepared apology for atrocities committed during the war, but under questioning from journalists, he continued to deny most accusations that had been levelled against the RUF. Negotiations ensued on the composition of the Government, in which the former AFRC junta had expected to be allocated senior posts. Sankoh was eventually ceded powers equivalent to those of a Vice-President, as well as the chairmanship of a new commission for strategic resources, national reconstruction and development, while four RUF members were allocated government positions, with the AFRC effectively excluded from participation in the new administration. During November the RUF clashed with AFRC supporters in the north of the country; Sankoh's RUF forces took control of the towns of Makeni and Lunsar, previously held by the AFRC.

UN AND BRITISH MILITARY DEPLOYMENT

The political climate was already highly uncertain by the time the UN Security Council eventually approved the UN Mission to Sierra Leone (UNAMSIL) on 22 October 1999, and tension increased as the UN peace-keeping force, at first mainly comprising troops from Commonwealth countries, began to arrive and be deployed in the country during November. UNAMSIL was to consist of 6,000 troops, who were to join the remaining 5,000-strong Nigerian ECOMOG contingent. In accordance with the Lomé agreement, the RUF was registered as a political party during November, but Sankoh showed little inclination to moderate the aggressive culture of the movement or to oblige it to adhere to the disarmament timetable, which was considerably behind schedule. In January 2000 the UN Secretary-General, Kofi Annan, asked the Security Council to increase the size of UNAMSIL to 11,000 troops, to allow for the complete replacement of ECOMOG.

RUF hostility to the proposed disarmament of its fighters was increased by the UN's decision not to pay for surrendered armaments. Sankoh's associates also reacted with antagonism to the prospect of being charged with crimes committed during the earlier war. These developments contributed to the increasing strain on the cease-fire between the Government and rebels, just as the UNAMSIL force was beginning to be deployed around the country. The disarmament process, which had been scheduled to end in December 1999, did not proceed as planned, with most RUF combatants refusing to relinquish their weapons and some being rearmed through supply lines from Liberia, especially after the joint border between the two countries was opened in November. Only 2,500 of an estimated 45,000 former combatants surrendered any armaments. The rate of disarmament accelerated only in those areas that were controlled by the AFRC; by early 2000 some 12,000 combatants had complied. In January there were confrontations between ECOMOG and RUF forces, and these were followed in February by the RUF's refusal to allow Indian and Ghanaian UNAMSIL forces to be deployed in the east of the country.

Nigeria agreed in January 2000 to suspend the progressive withdrawal of its ECOMOG troops from Sierra Leone, on the understanding that many of them would be transferred to UNAMSIL control at the end of April. While the RUF became increasingly aggressive, it was also undergoing division between Sankoh's loyalists and those of Sam Bockarie and other leaders operating from bases in Liberia. The RUF's refusal to disarm was, in April, condemned by the other militias, in particular the AFRC and the Kamajors, who pledged to force the rebel movement's followers to surrender their weapons. The formal ending of the ECOMOG mission on 30 April was accompanied by a severe loss of control by UNAMSIL. The deployment of newly arrived Jordanian troops was almost cancelled as a result of unconfirmed rumours of an RUF advance on Freetown. At the same time the leadership of the Sierra Leone army was also thrown into confusion by the unexpected death, in April, of its Nigerian Chief of Staff, Brig.-Gen. Khobe.

By the end of April 2000 it was estimated that about 20,000 armed RUF rebels were still able to operate freely in the country. The UN force at this stage amounted to only 8,500 troops, many of them on unarmed monitoring duties. At the beginning of May the RUF clashed with the UN forces at a number of locations, and after a few days some 500 UN troops were reported missing, presumed kidnapped. This development prompted the British Government to start preparations for a rescue mission, on behalf of both the UN and the Sierra Leone armed forces. On 8 May the United Kingdom dispatched a force of 800 paratroopers, with strong air force and naval support. After first securing the airport, the British forces were deployed throughout Freetown and surrounding areas, pre-empting an RUF offensive against Waterloo, near the capital, on 11 and 12 May. British helicopters transported Jordanian peace-keepers to defensive positions, while army experts assisted the UN in preparing new military tactics. A renewed RUF attempt to advance on Freetown was successfully repelled, while Sankoh, after a brief disappearance, was arrested and detained on behalf of the Government on 17 May.

In mid-May 2000 British forces declared Freetown to be secure, and it was reported that the RUF had commenced the release of some of its hostages, after Liberian mediation. For their part, ECOWAS leaders urged the UN to expand its peace-keeping mandate to allow the use of force, whereupon Nigeria campaigned to be allowed to retain the military leadership of the peace-keeping exercise in Sierra Leone, but also demanded international assistance to be able to undertake the task. After further deliberations, ECOWAS defence chiefs agreed to resume sending troops to the country, but under a changed command structure that would reflect the military role played by Nigeria and would expand the mandate from peace-keeping to peace enforcement. In mid-May the UN Security Council approved a further increase in the size of UNAMSIL, to 13,000, by immediately deploying 3,000 West African and 800 Bangladeshi troops. The RUF released most of the UN hostages.

In mid-June 2000 many of the British forces were withdrawn, although some 250 British troops subsequently remained in the country. In early July the UN Security Council adopted a resolution, proposed by the United Kingdom, for an international embargo on the purchase of diamonds mined from RUF-controlled regions. Later that month some 233 peace-keeping personnel (mainly Indian) held hostage by the RUF at Kailahun were rescued in a military operation, staged by UNAMSIL, with the endorsement of the UN Security Council. Meanwhile, increasing divisions in the pro-Government forces were reported. In late August one of the most notorious of the militia groups supporting the former AFRC junta, the West Side Boys (WSB), abducted 11 British military personnel and one member of the Sierra Leone army. The WSB subsequently issued a number of demands, including the release from detention of their leader, as a precondition to freeing the hostages. Five of the British personnel were released a few days later, but additional British troops were dispatched to Sierra Leone following the failure of negotiating officials to secure an agreement over the remaining hostages. In early September about 150 British troops attacked the WSB base, and succeeded in freeing the remaining hostages; one British serviceman and 25 WSB members were killed during the rescue mission. Later that month the Indian Government announced that the Indian contingent, numbering 3,073, was gradually to be withdrawn from UNAMSIL. The overall British military presence was again reinforced by an increase in the number of ground troops to about 600, and it was also disclosed that about 5,000 British troops were being held in reserve for possible rapid deployment if necessary. These military arrangements constituted the background to the signing of a new cease-fire agreement between the Government and RUF in Abuja, Nigeria, on 11 November; under its terms, the RUF was committed to return the weapons and ammunition that it had previously seized, as well as to commence a comprehensive programme of disarmament, demobilization and reintegration of troops. On the following day a British helicopter carrier and other naval vessels arrived offshore at Freetown, and, in a demonstration of military strength, 300 Royal Marines were landed by helicopter near the capital. With Sankoh under arrest, the leadership of the RUF had been assumed by the movement's military commander, 'Gen.' Issa Sesay, although his authority was reportedly challenged by a commander based in Makeni, known as 'Strongman' Mingo, who was believed to be largely responsible for the creation of close links with dissidents from neighbouring Guinea. With RUF support, these Guinean rebels established a series of bases along the border, most of them inside Sierra Leone itself. Thus, a new conflict situation, involving the armed forces of Guinea, developed rapidly in the second half of 2000.

ADVANCES IN PACIFICATION, DISARMAMENT AND ELECTIONS

In early 2001 the RUF continued to exert its control over rather more than one-half of the country, especially the north and east, including, for a short period, the entire border region with Guinea. The rebel movement continued to demand the release of Sankoh and the control of the eight ministerial posts that it had been promised under the Lomé peace agreement. However, Kabbah appointed leading members of other opposition parties to the government posts, and in February requested that Parliament defer elections, scheduled to take place later that month, by a period of six months. In response to this extension, there were indications that the RUF might be preparing to contest the elections. The movement appointed a new leader, Omrie Golley, who represented those in favour of reviving the peace process. In May there was a substantial advance, when the demobilization and disarmament process was resumed, with the formal surrender to UNAMSIL of 10,000 armaments in Freetown. At the same time hundreds of the RUF's child soldiers were transferred to the authority of UNAMSIL and humanitarian agencies. In the following weeks RUF combatants began to disarm much more rapidly than ever before and also relinquished control of the regions bordering Guinea. Disarmament commenced in July in the diamond-producing region at Kono, and UNAMSIL was soon able to deploy forces throughout nearly all Sierra Leone. A Pakistani battalion was deployed in Kono from the beginning of August, while Bangladeshi forces were stationed in Kabala and Koinadugu. The overall troop strength of UNAMSIL was reinforced to its authorized total of 17,500, including 260 military observers and 60 civilian police.

The Kabbah Government agreed in August 2001 to postpone elections for a further period, in order to allow for the prior completion of the disarmament process. Meetings of a specially convened National Consultative Forum succeeded in bringing together all sides of political opinion and in achieving compromises in some of the more difficult political issues before a resumption of more normal political processes. More than 20 political associations were represented at an important meeting of the Forum in November, where new electoral measures were discussed. It was agreed that elections would be organized on a constituency basis, rather than by proportional representation.

By the end of 2001 a total of 36,000 combatants had been disarmed, both from the RUF and the Civil Defence Forces (CDF—constituted from the Kamajors). The transfer of armaments had also commenced in the RUF strongholds of Kailahun and Tongo Field. In January 2002, as the disarmament process was being finally concluded, Golley declared the war to be ended. The now officially dissolved RUF established the Revolutionary United Front Party (RUFP), with the aim of contesting the forthcoming elections with other political associations, including the ruling SLPP, the revived APC and the newly formed Peace and Liberation Party (PLP) of Johnny Paul Koroma.

The election campaign commenced in April 2002, with Kabbah again nominated as the SLPP presidential candidate, Ernest Koroma representing the APC and Pallo Bangura standing for the RUFP. The elections, which took place on 14 May, were conducted almost entirely peacefully. Kabbah was overwhelmingly re-elected as President, with 70.1% of the vote, and the SLPP won 83 seats, thereby securing a comfortable majority of the 112 elective seats in Parliament. The APC won 27 seats and the PLP two, while the RUFP failed to secure any representation in the legislature. The UN declared that the elections had proceeded successfully, but also indicated that it did not envisage an early withdrawal of its peace-keeping forces. On 20 May Kabbah was officially inaugurated for a second term in office. Solomon Berewa (hitherto Minister of Justice) became Vice-President, and a reorganized Cabinet was installed. In July a seven-member Truth and Reconciliation Commission (TRC) was established.

With a measure of peace returning to the country during 2002 and 2003, allowing a gradual reduction in the UN military presence, the Government attempted to establish the conditions for economic recovery, and to restore health and education facilities. The national disarmament process was eventually concluded in February 2004, following the demobilization of 72,490 combatants, of whom 6,845 were child soldiers. The majority of the former combatants had been given short-term allowances and some education or vocational training to assist their return to civilian life, with the total cost of the programme estimated at US $36.5m. The UNAMSIL force was reduced to 3,200 troops during 2005. Prior to the termination of its mandate at the end of that year, the UN Security Council unanimously approved the establishment of a successor operation, the UN Integrated Office for Sierra Leone (UNIOSIL) from January 2006, with an initial mandate of 12 months. UNIOSIL's primary responsibilities would be: to help the Government reinforce human rights; to ensure the holding of free and fair elections in 2007; to co-ordinate efforts against arms- and human-trafficking; and to assist in providing security for the UN-sponsored Special Court (see below).

The TRC conducted its hearings during 2003, receiving statements from about 9,000 individuals and organizations relating to the abuses committed during the 10 years of civil conflict. Its provisional final report, published in October 2004, concluded that the origins of conflict lay in the 'bad governance, endemic corruption and the denial of basic human rights' of earlier years. The Commission blamed the leaderships of the RUF, AFRC and CDF alike for their authorization, instigation or tolerance of human rights abuses, but discovered that the RUF leaders were the worst offenders in this respect. It also noted that both Libya and Liberia had played a key role in supporting the RUF rebellion, and it proposed that Libya should pay compensation. The TRC made several 'imperative' recommendations, including the abolition of the death penalty, judicial reforms and the renewal of efforts to end corruption in the mining industry and in government administration. Its report stated that corruption remained 'rampant' and that no culture of tolerance or inclusion in political discourse had yet emerged. At the end of June 2005 the Government published its proposals for implementing the TRC's recommendations. In several cases, the Government pointed to actions it had already taken, such as the establishment of a human rights commission. However, nearly all human rights and civil society organizations were critical of the Government's proposals, some condemning them as 'vague' and 'non-committal'. The Government's human rights record had already been questioned following the conviction and imprisonment for libel of the Editor of the privately owned *For di People* newspaper, Paul Kamara. Kamara's successor, Harry Yanssaneh, was badly assaulted, allegedly by government supporters, at the newspaper's offices in May 2005 and later died of his injuries.

The SLPP Government suffered a reverse during local government elections in May 2005, when, in what was widely regarded as a vote of protest against the continuing poor state of the economy and the Government's failure to address corruption, the opposition APC won majorities in the municipal councils of both Freetown and Makeni. Subsequently, the Chairman of the Electoral Commission, Eugene Davis, complained of 'political interference' and resigned. When the SLPP held its delegates' conference in September, Vice-President Solomon Berewa was elected party leader and therefore the party's presidential candidate in the 2007 election. One of his leading rivals for the position, Charles Margai, the son of the Sierra Leone's first Prime Minister, Sir Albert Margai, left the party shortly afterwards and established his own association, the People's Movement for Democratic Change (PMDC), potentially weakening support for the SLPP in the south and east of the country. Margai's challenge took on an additional dimension when in February 2006 he adopted, in his professional capacity as a lawyer, the case of three RUF supporters who had been arrested in late January and accused of conspiring to overthrow the Government.

Kabbah hoped to stage a referendum on his preferred constitutional changes (including establishing an upper chamber in Parliament) to coincide with the 2007 elections. However, a combination of organizational and political factors appeared to rule out any referendum, while the elections themselves were postponed from late July until 11 August to allow time for political campaigning and for the opening of new polling booths to reduce the difficulties of voting during the rainy season. The APC, led by Ernest Koroma, and the new PMDC, led by Charles Margai, appeared equally confident of taking votes away from the SLPP by attacking both its record in office and its apparent failure to reduce corruption during its years in power. According to provisional results, the APC secured 59 of the 112 seats, while the SLPP took 43 and the PMDC 10.

INDICTMENTS AND REGIONAL CHANGES

The UN and the Government reached agreement in 2002 on the establishment of a Special Court to apply both local and international law to cases of crimes against humanity, in co-operation with the TRC. In March the Special Court issued the first indictments against seven former leaders of the combatant groups, notably Foday Sankoh, Sam Bockarie, Johnny Paul Koroma and Hinga Norman. However, Sankoh died in custody shortly after the indictments and Bockarie was reported to have been killed in Liberia in May 2003, while the whereabouts of Koroma were unknown. In June Taylor was officially indicted for crimes against humanity, resulting from his involvement in the Sierra Leone conflict, and an international warrant was issued for his arrest, but he accepted an offer of asylum in Nigeria shortly afterwards. In January 2004 the Special Court judges decided to try the nine indictees already in custody in three separate groups, according to the organizations with which they were identified. The CDF group comprised Hinga Norman, Moinina Fofana and Allieu Kondewa, the RUF group Issa Hassan Sesay, Morris Kallon and Augustine Gbao, and the AFRC group Alex Tamba Brima, Brima Bazzy Kamara and Santigie Borbor Kanu. Norman's trial did not get fully under way until January 2006; when he gave testimony to answer the charges against him, he argued that he could not be held responsible for the acts of the CDF, since he was only the organization's civilian co-ordinator, and that many people, including President Kabbah and senior foreign diplomats, had been in active support of the Kamajor combatants, who were closely allied to the CDF. The verdict in Norman's case had not been delivered when he died in February 2007 after being flown to Senegal for surgery.

Taylor was finally surrendered to the Special Court in March 2006, after the Liberian Government formally requested that the Nigerian authorities extradite him (see chapter on Liberia). In late April the Court petitioned the International Criminal Court in The Hague, Netherlands, to make its facilities available for Taylor's trial, because of security concerns in Freetown. The United Kingdom agreed to allow Taylor to serve his term in a British prison if he were convicted, and Taylor was transferred to the facilities of the International Criminal Court in The Hague in June; his trial eventually commenced in the first half of 2007.

Economy

LINDA VAN BUREN

Sierra Leone's post-war economic recovery continued in 2006 and 2007, according to a February 2007 IMF assessment. Despite fiscal and monetary 'slippages' in late 2005, the Government of Ahmed Tejan Kabbah 'took corrective measures' and was able to report lower import costs (despite high international oil prices), higher export revenue, a narrowing current-account deficit, single-digit inflation, and higher gross international reserves, all adding up to 'substantial progress' in Sierra Leone's post-conflict transition. The Fund had described the country's economic performance as 'mixed' in 2005, after 'broadly satisfactory' in 2002 and 2003.

Agricultural output grew significantly after the 1991–2001 civil war ended, and the improved security situation allowed farmers to return to their land and resume cultivation of crops. Sierra Leone's economy was poorly developed even prior to the civil conflict of the 1990s. Much of the country's infrastructure was destroyed during the conflict, and gross domestic product (GDP) declined at an average annual rate of 2.2% in 1990–1999. In 1997 alone, GDP contracted by 17.6%. However, positive growth returned in 2000 at 3.8%, and positive real GDP growth continued, reaching 9.5% in 2003, 7.4% in 2004, 7.3% in 2005 and an estimated 7.4% in 2006. Slightly more modest targets were set for the future, at 6.5% for 2007 and 6.1% for 2008. Inflation is one of the areas in which the Kabbah Government produced a 'slippage'; after achieving a commendable 2.1% in 2001 and 3.3% in 2002, it subsequently allowed inflation to rise into double digits, when it reached 14.2% in 2004 and 12.1% in 2005. However, the rate declined to 9.5% in 2006, and the IMF forecast it to decline further, to 8.4% in 2007. These lower rates were achieved by reining in monetary growth; the broad money supply was allowed to grow by 26.2% in 2003, by 18.9% in 2004 and by 32.8% in 2005 but was held to just 3.9% in 2006.

The lack of progress in infrastructural development, both before and after the war, has rendered large areas of the country untouched by monetization or by the valorization of formal trade. A majority of the population survive by subsistence agriculture and by informal trading activities, which, however, suffered much disruption during the civil conflict. Poor implementation of economic policies meant that modernization projects often failed, even before the civil conflict, which destroyed much of the remaining infrastructure and caused severe disruption to the traditional economy, as well as to the few mining operations that provided earnings of foreign exchange. Mining of both bauxite and rutile (titanium dioxide) ceased (see below). At about the same time as the world began to draw a distinction between conflict diamonds and other diamonds, civil conflict erupted in Sierra Leone.

The economy became export-orientated early in the colonial period, when emphasis was placed on the production of primary commodities for overseas industrial markets, which were also the principal suppliers of the country's import requirements. Favourable terms of trade in the 1950s, in conjunction with an expansion in the diamond industry, resulted in a rapid increase in income, allowing imports and government expenditure to rise sharply. Increasing state expenditure during the Stevens Government, together with slow export and revenue growth in the early 1960s, led to a financial crisis, which was exacerbated in the mid-1960s by an overly ambitious programme of investment in plantations and oil-palm mills by the Sierra Leone Produce Marketing Board (SLPMB), the sole exporter of the country's crops.

By the 1980s Sierra Leone suffered high inflation, an acute shortage of foreign exchange and heavy external debt, while the country's natural mineral resources remained underutilized. Official revenue from exports (particularly diamonds) was adversely affected by smuggling, which was encouraged by government policies on price controls and the exchange rate. In 1986 the Momoh Government of 1985–92 implemented an economic reform programme, based on IMF recommendations, which included the introduction of a 'floating' exchange rate, the elimination of government subsidies on rice and petroleum, the liberalization of trade, and increases in producer prices, with the aim of encouraging self-sufficiency in rice and other foods. In 1988, however, the IMF withdrew its support for the programme, declaring Sierra Leone ineligible for assistance until arrears in repayments were received. This pattern of payment arrears and unsustainable levels of debt continued to plague Sierra Leone for the next 17 years. Internal unrest throughout the 1990s impeded government efforts to achieve economic stability, although the Strasser regime that assumed power in April 1992 agreed to implement the final stage of the IMF-endorsed economic programme and to continue the implementation of structural reforms, including the reduction of civil-service employees and privatization measures. An extensive privatization programme, involving 19 enterprises (including the Sierra Leone Petroleum Refining Co), was initiated in 1994; it was announced that a certain percentage of shares would be reserved for Sierra Leone citizens, while the State would also place shares on the international market. The civil conflict, which had affected mainly the southern and eastern regions of the country, escalated in early 1995, forcing the closure of the bauxite and rutile mining operations, which formed the principal sources of official export earnings. Major long-term foreign investors withdrew from the country. With the disruption of nearly all export activity, Sierra Leone became increasingly dependent on the small amounts of foreign assistance that were available from the International Development Association (IDA) and the European Union (EU), as well as on emergency humanitarian aid.

During the nine-month period from May 1997 to February 1998, more than 2m. Sierra Leoneans were internally and externally displaced, economic and social infrastructure was virtually destroyed, and the financial system was severely disrupted. The World Food Programme (WFP) provided relief food supplies to 200,000 Sierra Leonean civilians affected by the conflict in May 2000 alone. With the cessation of hostilities, and with the benefit of favourable weather, many of these displaced people returned to their homes, and stability improved markedly, although renewed fighting in neighbouring Liberia in 2003 caused substantial numbers of refugees from that country to flee into south-eastern Sierra Leone. Even before this influx of refugees, WFP estimated that 135,000 rural Sierra Leonean families required emergency food aid in 2003. Generally, efforts to persuade Sierra Leonean refugees to return to Sierra Leone were much more successful than efforts to persuade Liberian refugees in Sierra Leone to return to Liberia have been. In 2006 and 2007 WFP activity in Sierra Leone was focused on Liberian refugees, who numbered about 63,000 in June 2007. A two-year WFP programme to benefit Liberian refugees in Sierra Leone was to have ended in December 2006 but was extended until June 2007. WFP was attempting to reduce the inflow of food and other refugee aid and to channel it to a much smaller number of particularly vulnerable refugees. The aim was two-fold: to make it more attractive for Liberian refugees to leave Sierra Leone and to lessen the impact that food aid had on the market forces operating in nearby Sierra Leonean villages. Not all the refugees are in camps; some have attempted to blend into nearby communities. As for Sierra Leone itself, the majority of Sierra Leoneans were able to return to their country in 2003 and to return to their fields, and good harvests were collected in 2004/05, 2005/06 and 2006/07. Nevertheless, large sections of the country still had no access to the electricity grid in 2007, and even Freetown was still experiencing daily extensive power cuts, to the detriment of industry, as well as general economic and social activity. Some regional towns have also been without water or electricity for long periods of time.

AGRICULTURE AND FISHING

Sierra Leone's economy is predominantly agricultural; some 70% of the labour force were engaged in the agricultural sector in 2007, primarily in subsistence farming, and agriculture contributes more than 30% of official GDP. Some 70 different crops have been cultivated in the country, but only a few (mainly coffee, cocoa, palm kernels and piassava, a fibre crop) have been exported, and these were produced by fewer than 10% of the country's farmers. Prior to the civil conflict of the 1990s, about three-quarters of farmers were engaged in the cultivation of the staple food crop, rice, but production met only about 75% of domestic demand, and the shortfalls were offset by imports (adding some US $68m. to the cost of imports in 2002 alone). After the end of the civil war, the harvest of paddy rice recovered from only 199,134 tons in 2000 to an estimated 265,000 tons in 2005. In contrast, Sierra Leone's domestic requirement for rice was estimated at about 550,000 tons per year. The Income Tax Act of 2000 contained measures to stimulate agricultural production, but rice was originally exempted, further deterring local cultivation. In 2002 the amount of surface area planted with rice increased by 47%, to about 78% of the pre-war level, largely owing to the distribution of 5,772 tons of seed rice to 144,000 families and to the 2002 budget's extension of the provisions of the Income Tax Act to rice-growing. Both incorporated and unincorporated businesses cultivating rice were to be exempt from the payment of income tax for a period of 10 years from the date of the commencement of the activity. By October 2006 the Kabbah Government reported that distribution of seed rice to farmers had increased from 62,000 bushels in 2002 to 100,000 bushels in 2006 and claimed that 'all farmers are now considered self-sufficient in seed rice'.

During the time of the fierce civil conflict, the effects on agricultural production were devastating, with production of all major food and cash crops suffering. The sorghum crop, estimated at 24,000 metric tons in 1994, had fallen dramatically to 8,100 tons in 2000. With the return of peace, this crop proved the resilience for which it is known: output had recovered to 27,000 tons by 2006. Even worse affected by the conflict was the millet crop, which declined from 26,000 tons in 1994 to a mere 3,636 tons in 2000, according to FAO estimates; however, millet's recovery was also sustained, with 10,529 tons harvested in 2002 and with the 2003, 2004, 2005 and 2006 crops all exceeding 10,000 tons. Cassava production declined from 289,200 tons in 1998 to 239,597 tons in 1999, but recovered to an estimated 390,000 tons in 2005. As for cash crops, production of groundnuts in shells declined from 35,400 tons in 1998 to 29,010 tons in 1999 and to only 14,704 tons in 2000; by 2005 output had risen only to 16,000 tons. Production of coffee, mainly robusta, decreased dramatically, by 41%, from an estimated 26,000 tons in 1998 to 15,350 tons in 1999; after the end of the civil war, output has fluctuated, from a low of 960 tons in 2004 to a high of 3,420 tons in 2005. The 2006 crop was estimated at 1,500 tons (the coffee year runs from 1 October to 30 September). Exports of green coffee beans rose from 1,695 tons in the year to 31 May 2006 to 2,716 tons in the year to 31 May 2007. Output of cocoa beans fell from 13,000 tons in 1998 to 10,920 tons in 1999, a decline of 16%; scarcely any recovery had been achieved by 2005.

The fishing sector, particularly marine fisheries, was seriously affected by the civil conflict. The total catch, which had amounted to 59,437 metric tons in 1999, was 41,909 tons in 2006. Overfishing by foreign vessels within Sierra Leone's coastal waters (including the continental shelf of some 25,000 sq km) is believed to have depleted the available stocks of sardinellas and other common species. It was estimated that illegal fishing deprived the Government of some US $30m. per year in revenue in the mid-1990s. In the mid-2000s Sierra Leone's fishermen continued to campaign to gain a viable share of the country's coastal waters.

MINING

Mining, which began in Sierra Leone in the 1930s, was, prior to the civil conflict, the second most important commodity-producing sector and the main source of foreign exchange. During the civil conflict, with severe disruption to the agricultural sector as well as to most mining operations, the matter of which side had access to Sierra Leone's diamonds became an issue of military importance. In 2000 increasing international acknowledgement of this factor emerged. A June World Bank report, entitled *Economic Causes of Civil Conflict and Their Implications for Policy*, studied 47 civil wars in various areas of the world between 1960 and 1999. This study concluded that the primary cause motivating rebel groups to attempt to seize power was not that of political, ethnic or religious differences, but the desire to gain control of lucrative economic resources (in Sierra Leone, diamond reserves). The diamonds sold on the open market by rebel groups became known as 'conflict diamonds'. On 5 July 2000 the UN Security Council imposed an international embargo on the sale of rough diamonds from Sierra Leone. The UN directly stated that the reason for doing so was to halt the flow of funds to the rebels of the Revolutionary United Front (RUF), who were then in control of most of the country's alluvial diamond-mining areas. Under the embargo, which was initially imposed for a period of 18 months and was renewed in 2002 for a further 18 months, it was declared illegal to buy any diamonds from Sierra Leone unless they were accompanied by a certificate of origin from the Government. However, the embargo did not specifically name Liberia as a conduit for the illicit sale of Sierra Leone diamonds, primarily owing to the fact that the then Liberian President, Charles Taylor, was at the time involved in sensitive negotiations to release UN peace-keeping personnel held by the RUF in Kailahun. The UN embargo was finally ended in June 2003, following the Kabbah Government's introduction of a certification system. The US Congress adopted the Clean Diamond Trade Act in April 2003. The Kimberley Process Certification Scheme also sought to document the origin of diamonds, from the mine to the point of sale. The Kabbah Government also reduced the export tariff from 15% to 3%, in an acknowledgement that the tariff had been providing a significant economic incentive to encourage illicit trade. In 2002 it was estimated that as much as 40% of the diamonds produced in Sierra Leone were smuggled out of the country. The combined effects in export tariff reductions and the Certification Scheme helped boost official diamond export revenue from just US $1.5m. in 1999 to more than $126.6m. in 2004.

Historically, alluvial diamond mining was carried out by numerous small prospectors, while larger-scale mining operations were conducted by the Sierra Leone Selection Trust (SLST), in which the government-controlled National Diamond Mining Co (NDMC, also known as DIMINCO) held a majority share. This enterprise, however, was adversely affected by management, financial and technical problems, and by 1992 its production made only a negligible contribution to foreign-exchange receipts. By 1995 the NDMC had ceased operations. The marketing of Sierra Leone diamonds was subsequently conducted by the Government Gold and Diamond Office (GGDO). This was superseded by the Gold and Diamond Department (GDD), and it is the GDD that is responsible for implementing the Kimberley Process Certification Scheme in Sierra Leone. Legal exports of diamonds declined from 2m. carats in 1970 to 31,929 carats in 1996. Following the 1997 coup, fighting continued in the region of the diamond-mining areas, followed by large-scale looting and destruction of equipment. Mining companies carried out emergency evacuations of their foreign staff, and production ceased. After the return to civilian government in March 1998, some mining companies expressed their intention to resume production. However, the new civilian Government under President Kabbah announced in April 1998 that all foreign nationals would be banned from gold-mining areas, while in May it was proclaimed that all diamond mining in the country was to cease until a new mining policy could be promulgated. After the end of the civil war, securing and returning the Koidu diamond mine to production was a priority. To this end, Energem of Canada (40%), Magma Diamond Resources Ltd (35%) and BSG Resources Ltd (25%) formed Koidu Holdings Ltd. In May 2007 Energem sold its 40% stake in Koidu Holdings to BSG Resources for US $18.25m. The Koidu mine has estimated reserves of 2.4m. carats and the capacity to produce some 250,000 carats per year. An important discovery in late 2003, not only of diamonds but also of gold, centred on a site near Kamakwie. Mining had taken place in the 1930s in the vicinity, but new finds of diamonds (some as large as 56 carats) caused more than 10,000 artisanal miners to rush to the area by mid-2004.

In response to uncertainties in the organization of both the production and the marketing of Sierra Leone's diamonds, operators had increasingly turned to the 'black' market, even prior to the civil conflict of the late 1990s. In early 1994, in an effort to reduce illicit trade, the Strasser Government offered informants rewards of up to 40% of the value of anything recovered. This offer resulted in the recovery in June of that year of a particularly large (172-carat) diamond, which obtained US $2.8m. for the Government from its sale by public auction. In April 2000 illicit exports of diamonds were estimated to cost the country $250m. per year.

Sierra Leone's second most important mineral export was formerly iron ore, but operations were suspended in 1985. The Sierra Leone Ore and Metal Co (SIEROMCO), a subsidiary of Alusuisse of Switzerland, began mining bauxite at Mokanji in 1964. Exports reached an average of 1.7m. metric tons per year in 1984–88, but thereafter the volume declined, amounting to only 735,000 tons in 1994. Shortly afterwards, RUF forces seized the mine in January 1995, obliging SIEROMCO to suspend all operations. Government forces regained control in the following month, but the company did not resume production. Looters subsequently inflicted damage estimated at US $30m., and in September 1996 the company announced its withdrawal from the country, owing to the cost that the resumption of operations would involve.

Sierra Leone has the world's largest deposit of rutile, an essential ingredient of paint pigment. Prior to the disruption resulting from the civil conflict, Sierra Leone was, after Australia, the world's second largest producer of rutile, and the reserves at the Sierra Rutile-owned mine are reported to be the largest and highest-grade natural rutile resource in the world. Australia's Consolidated Rutile bought a 50% interest in Sierra Rutile in 1994 and undertook, in partnership with the Nord Resources Corpn of the USA, to continue expansion of the mining activity and to increase production to 190,000 metric tons per year by 1996, with investment amounting to US $72m. In 1993 rutile provided 57% of Sierra Leone's official mineral export earnings, which totalled $108m. In the year to June 1994 rutile production was 144,000 tons, but in January 1995 all production was suspended when RUF forces overran the mining operation. After the rebels were driven out in February, the company took renewed steps to secure the property but was unable to resume production. In September 1996 Sierra Rutile indicated that the IMF and the World Bank had pledged $18m. towards the reopening of the mine, which was projected to cost a total of $80m. However, the coup in May 1997 disrupted those plans, and Nord Resources applied for $15.7m. in compensation under insurance provisions of the US Government's Overseas Private Investment Corpn (OPIC). After an initial payment of $1m., the remaining $14.2m. was paid in May 1998. Nord Resources used the compensation to restructure Sierra Rutile's $34.2m. debt to various development banks (one-half of which was guaranteed by Nord Resources, as a 50% partner in Sierra Rutile). Nord Resources sold its holding in Sierra Rutile to MIL (Investments) in 1999. According to official figures, the country exported rutile valued at $1.15m. in June 1999, but no rutile was exported for the remainder of 1999, nor in the next two years. With the return of peace, the Kabbah Government announced that resuming production at Sierra Rutile was a priority. The EU extended a grant of $25m. towards the $114m. needed to rehabilitate the company. The USA became closely involved in the plans, and in March 2003 OPIC announced that it was to provide a $25m. investment guarantee to a US firm for Sierra Rutile's project to restart and expand its mineral-sands operation.Phase I, when completed, was expected to result in annual average production of 110,000 tons of rutile and 20,000 tons of ilmenite. Exports of rutile resumed in the first half of 2006 and amounted to an estimated 100,000 metric tons in that year, earning $3.6m. It was forecast in late 2006 that over the medium term, the operation has the capacity to produce 220,000 tons of rutile per year. About 1,000 workers are employed in mining rutile.

Exports of bauxite resumed in March 2006, and by August of that year, 400,000 metric tons of the ore had been exported. In the nine months to 31 December 2006, exports amounted to an estimated 1m. tons, earning US $2.9m. The bauxite operation employed 300 workers in 2007.

No significant investment has been made in the gold industry, although some corporate interest had been shown in this activity prior to the civil conflict. Gold mining was principally carried out by petty diggers, and most of the production in the 1990s was believed to have been smuggled out of the country. Foreign nationals were banned from gold-mining areas in April 1998. Official figures indicated that Sierra Leone exported no gold from 1999 onwards.

MANUFACTURING, TRADE AND TRANSPORT

With the introduction in 1960 of the Development Ordinance, Sierra Leone adopted a policy of industrial development using an import-substitution strategy. Under the Ordinance, the Government extended generous tax incentives, which included duty-free importation of equipment and raw materials and tax 'holidays', and established an industrial estate at Wellington, near Freetown, with basic services and an employment exchange. At first the prospects for this sector were good, as the country began to produce alcoholic and non-alcoholic beverages, cigarettes and several other goods that had been principal imports. By the late 1970s, however, the manufacturing sector had suffered as a result of the extensive shortages of foreign exchange, unreliable electricity and water supplies, poor telecommunications and rising costs of imported raw materials. By the late 1990s the sector comprised mainly palm-oil production and other agro-based industries, textiles and furniture-making. The sector was severely affected by the 1997 coup, which forced most manufacturers to shut down; widespread looting and destruction of factories occurred during the nine-month period in government of the junta. The damage was so extensive that many companies were unlikely ever to reopen after peace was restored. However, one that did resume operations was Sierra Leone Breweries (SLB), in April 1998. The company reconstructed its brewery, which had been destroyed during the conflict. After producing no beer at all during 1999, Sierra Leone resumed production in June 2000. In June 2001 it launched a new product, a 'cold filtered beer', amid acclaim at its Wellington industrial estate premises, which was aimed in part at encouraging other industrial concerns to resume production. SLB commissioned a new €6m. bottling plant in 2004. Foreign shareholders in SLB include Heineken, Guinness and Paterson Zochonis. Production of beer and stout increased from 305,970 cartons in 2000 to 770,430 cartons in 2001; by 2004 output had increased to 809,000 cartons. Among the industrial activities that resumed after mid-1999 were the manufacture of plastic footwear, paint, confectionery, soap, cement and soft drinks. Output of acetylene and oxygen also resumed. Industry (including mining, manufacturing, construction and power) accounted for 37.1% of GDP in 2006, while the manufacturing sector contributed 6.3%.

High priority was accorded to road construction in the 1970s, especially after the closure in 1971 of the 292-km narrow-gauge government railway. The country had 11,300 km of classified roads in 2002, including 2,138 km of main roads and 1,950 km of secondary roads; however, only about 904 km of the network was paved, and most of the network was in a poor state of repair, even before the renewed fighting of 1997 and 1998. In June 2005 the EU extended funds of US $11.4m. to rehabilitate 650 km of feeder roads in four agricultural districts of Sierra Leone. Improvements to the road system were an essential prerequisite for the resumption of viable agricultural activity in most parts of the country. In March 2001 a bridge was opened linking Port Loko to the northerly Kambia district, some 65 km north of Freetown. Inland waterways and coastal shipping are important features of internal transport. There are almost 800 km of established routes for launches, which include the coastal routes from Freetown northward to the areas served by the Great and Little Scarcies rivers and southward to the important seaport of Bonthe.

The services and facilities of the international airport at Lungi, north of Freetown, were improved, with financial assistance from the UNDP, but the civil conflict subsequently disrupted services. Services have remained, for financial, security and other reasons, subject to periods of disruption. In mid-2007 a weekly service, operated by the British-based carrier Astraeus, was inaugurated between Lungi and London Gatwick. Lungi is linked to Abidjan, Accra, Banjul, Conakry, Dakar, Lagos and Monrovia by three regional carriers: GR-Avia of Guinea, Slok Air International of The Gambia and Bellview Airlines of Nigeria.

EXTERNAL TRADE AND PAYMENTS

Sierra Leone is heavily dependent on foreign trade. Exports amounted to US $136.1m. in 2006, of which 73%, or $99.4m., was contributed by mineral products, with diamonds contributing $77m. Rutile exports contributed $3.6m., and bauxite exports added $2.9m. While exports exhibited strong growth in 2006, boosted mainly by peace-time mining export resumption, they still were dwarfed by the level of imports, at $238.3m. Export revenue covered just 57% of import costs in 2006, and the visible trade deficit was $102.2m. The current account of the balance of payments, which is continually in deficit, carried a shortfall of $177.3m. excluding official transfers in 2005, followed by an estimated deficit excluding transfers of $151.6m. in 2006. These deficits were equivalent to 7.7% of GDP in 2005 and to an estimated 5.4% of GDP in 2006. The 2006 current-account deficit, if transfers were excluded, was equivalent to 10.3% of GDP, with 10.5% of GDP forecast for 2007. These proportions are significantly higher than the IMF would like. Growth in mineral exports will provide an opportunity to reduce the current-account balance, but only if concerted effort is made to curb import growth. The overall balance of payments, which carried a small deficit in 2005, is estimated to have moved back into surplus in 2006, equivalent to 9% of GDP. Gross international reserves grew to $168.3m. in 2005 and to an estimated $169m. in 2006, enough to cover over three months' worth of imports of goods and services.

In October 2001 the 'Paris Club' of official creditors restructured Sierra Leone's external debt under the 'Naples terms' and cancelled $72m. of the total. At the end of 2004 external debt totalled $1,612m., of which $1,400m. was long-term public debt. In March 2002 the IMF and the World Bank, under the enhanced initiative for heavily indebted poor countries, rescheduled $950m. of Sierra Leone's external debt. As a result of its protracted foreign-exchange crisis (see below), Sierra Leone had a poor record of servicing its foreign debt and had little access to loans at concessionary rates until 2001. Total public debt, including arrears, was equivalent to 69% of GDP in 1980/81 and to no less than 285% of GDP in 2000. In December 2006 Sierra Leone was granted debt relief under the provisions of the IMF and World Bank enhanced initiative for heavily indebted poor countries. The decision reduced Sierra Leone's total external bilateral debt from an estimated $1,197.6m. at 31 December 2005 to $483m. at 31 December 2006. The IMF and the World Bank have urged private-sector creditors to follow suit.

PUBLIC FINANCE

The 2007 budget, presented in October 2006, requested total expenditure of Le 1,220,000m. and forecast total revenue at Le 674,900m., excluding grants and anticipated (and subsequently confirmed) debt relief. This meant revenue from internal sources was expected to cover just 55.3% of total spending. The deficit, excluding grants, of Le 355,900m., was equivalent to 8.3% of GDP, well outside the IMF's preferred parameters. Total projected revenue was 21.8% higher than in 2005; however, total expenditure was less positive, and possibly unsustainable, at 35.6% higher than in 2005. Also of concern to the IMF was the extent of the Sierra Leone Government's borrowing from domestic bank sources. These concerns also featured prominently in the IMF's performance review of May 2005. In the May 2006 assessment, the focus of concern had shifted to monetary policy. Sierra Leone had indeed slowed its rate of domestic borrowing, but it had increased the broad money supply by 32.8% in 2005. This had a direct and detrimental effect on inflation. After allowing broad money-supply growth of 32.8% in 2005, the Kabbah Government clamped down in 2006, allowing broad money supply to grow only by 3.9%. Correspondingly, inflation was reduced to 9.5% in that year and was forecast to fall further in 2007, to 8.4%.

Weekly foreign-exchange auctions were introduced by the Kabbah Government in February 2000. The Government reported that the difference between the official and parallel market exchange rates had narrowed from 24% in December 1999 to 6% in October 2000. According to the 2000 budget speech, this was a reflection of the increased external assistance and the improved management of the foreign-exchange market, following the introduction of the weekly foreign-exchange auctions. The IMF acknowledged that the difference in rates had narrowed from 31% in December 1999 to 6% in November 2000. Meanwhile, on the parallel market, the leone strengthened, from an annual average of Le 2,443 = US $1 in 1999 to an annual average of Le 2,315 = $1 in 2000. In December 2001 the budget speech for 2002 stated that the foreign-exchange auctions had 'emerged as the reference rate for the pricing of all foreign-exchange transactions'. The exchange rate of the leone strengthened to Le 1,930 = $1 in July 2002, but thereafter weakened year-on-year, to yearly averages of Le 2,099 = $1 in 2002, Le 2,348 = $1 in 2003, Le 2,735 = $1 in 2004 and Le 2,894 = $1 in 2005. By 30 June 2007 the rate stood at Le 2,954.37 = $1.

ECONOMIC PROSPECTS

The protracted civil conflict throughout the 1990s resulted in the cumulative and severe deterioration of the economy. Agricultural activity, both in food and cash crops, was sharply reduced, leaving the mining sector to generate essential foreign exchange, until production in that sector was also severely disrupted. International condemnation of the May 1997 coup resulted in the imposition of an ECOWAS blockade. Even the distribution of emergency food aid to civilians was disrupted by the activities of armed groups and by lack of co-operation from the military junta, which in July 1997 ordered the International Red Cross to cease all operations in Sierra Leone. After the Kabbah Government was restored in March 1998, the fragile Lomé peace accord of July 1999 was followed by a resumption of rebel activity. From this low point, the Kabbah Government was confronted with the formidable challenge of reconstructing the devastated Sierra Leonean economy and, indeed, with raising the living standard of the population above the poverty level, a task that, even before the 10-year civil war, no Government had ever achieved. Sierra Leone has one of the lowest per-head gross national incomes in the world, at just US $220, and an estimated two-thirds of the population live below the poverty line. The World Bank in July 2004 extended a $35m. IDA credit for the struggling National Power Authority (NPA), to contribute to alleviating the daily lengthy power cuts, curbing the high levels of energy loss (estimated at as much as 40%) and improving the low level of revenue collection. The 50-MW Bumbuna hydroelectric power station was 85% complete when the civil war forced the abandonment of construction work in May 1997; legislation was enacted in 2006 to recommence construction of the Bumbuna facility, with completion scheduled for 2009. The power cuts were not only inconvenient for Freetown residents but also expensive for manufacturing companies. A return to regular supplies of electricity in the capital would have a positive real effect on the economy, as well as improve the morale of the citizens who have suffered so much hardship for so many years. In the countryside, good harvests in 2004/05, in 2005/06 and again in 2006/07 have raised morale, but much more is needed. The Kabbah presidency ends in 2007, and elections in August–September will bring a new leader to power, who will take office facing a long list of economic challenges.

Statistical Survey

Source (unless otherwise stated): Central Statistics Office, PMB 595, Tower Hill, Freetown; tel. (22) 223287; fax (22) 223897; internet www.sierra-leone.org/cso.html and www.statistics-sierra-leone.org.

Area and Population

AREA, POPULATION AND DENSITY

Area (sq km)	71,740*
Population (census results)†	
14 December 1985	3,515,812
4 December 2004‡	
Males	2,412,860
Females	2,550,438
Total	4,963,298
Population (UN estimates at mid-year)§	
2004	5,390,000
2005	5,586,000
2006	5,743,000
Density (per sq km) at mid-2006	80.1

* 27,699 sq miles.

† Excluding adjustment for underenumeration, estimated to have been 9% in 1985.

‡ Provisional.

§ Source: UN, *World Population Prospects: The 2006 Revision*.

PRINCIPAL TOWNS
(population at 1985 census)

Freetown (capital)	384,499	Kenema	52,473
Koindu	82,474	Makeni	49,474
Bo	59,768		

Mid-2005 (incl. suburbs, UN estimate): Freetown 799,000 (Source: UN, *World Urbanization Prospects: The 2005 Revision*).

BIRTHS AND DEATHS
(annual averages, UN estimates)

	1990–95	1995–2000	2000–05
Birth rate (per 1,000)	47.5	47.1	46.9
Death rate (per 1,000)	26.3	24.5	23.5

Source: UN, *World Population Prospects: The 2006 Revision*.

Expectation of life (years at birth, WHO estimates): 39 (males 37; females 40) in 2004 (Source: WHO, *World Health Report*).

ECONOMICALLY ACTIVE POPULATION
(% of labour force)

	1994/95	1995/96	1996/97
Agriculture, etc.	61.08	60.96	60.83
Industry	16.99	17.04	17.10
Services	21.93	22.00	22.07

Mid-2005 (estimates in '000): Agriculture, etc. 1,249; Total labour force 2,103 (Source: FAO).

Health and Welfare

KEY INDICATORS

Total fertility rate (children per woman, 2005)	6.5
Under-5 mortality rate (per 1,000 live births, 2005)	282
HIV/AIDS (% of persons aged 15–49, 2005)	1.6
Physicians (per 1,000 head, 2004)	0.03
Hospital beds (per 1,000 head, 2006)	0.40
Health expenditure (2004): US $ per head (PPP)	34.1
Health expenditure (2004): % of GDP	3.3
Health expenditure (2004): public (% of total)	59.0
Access to water (% of persons, 2004)	57
Access to sanitation (% of persons, 2004)	39
Human Development Index (2004): ranking	176
Human Development Index (2004): value	0.335

For sources and definitions, see explanatory note on p. vi.

Agriculture

PRINCIPAL CROPS
('000 metric tons)

	2003	2004	2005
Rice (paddy)	445.6	542.0	738.0
Maize	16.1	32.1	39.1
Millet*	10	15	20
Sorghum†	21.0	15.9	14.1
Sweet potatoes†	25.5	25.5	26.0
Cassava (Manioc)	377.2	390.0†	390.0†
Sugar cane†	69	70	70
Groundnuts (in shell)	70.5	91.1	104.7
Oil palm fruit†	195.0	174.9	166.1
Tomatoes†	15.0	15.1	15.1
Plantains†	33.0	30.8	30.5
Citrus fruit†	85.0	82.4	82.3
Coffee (green)†	18.0	16.4	15.5
Cocoa beans†	12.0	9.7	8.7

* Unofficial figures.

† FAO estimate(s).

Source: FAO.

LIVESTOCK
('000 head, year ending September)

	2003	2004	2005
Cattle	170.0	200.0	250.0
Pigs*	52	52	52
Sheep	200	300	375
Goats	258	350	438
Chickens*	7,500	7,500	7,500
Ducks*	70	70	70

* FAO estimates.

Source: FAO.

LIVESTOCK PRODUCTS
('000 metric tons, FAO estimates)

	2003	2004	2005
Chicken meat	11.3	10.8	10.8
Pig meat	2.3	2.3	2.4
Game meat	2.5	2.5	2.5
Cows' milk	21.3	21.3	21.3
Hen eggs	8.3	8.3	8.3

Source: FAO.

Forestry

ROUNDWOOD REMOVALS
('000 cubic metres, excl. bark, FAO estimates)

	2003	2004	2005
Sawlogs, veneer logs and logs for sleepers*	3.6	3.6	3.6
Other industrial wood†	120.0	120.0	120.0
Fuel wood	5,386.7	5,403.1	5,422.8
Total	5,510.3	5,526.7	5,546.4

* Annual output assumed to be unchanged since 1993.
† Annual output assumed to be unchanged since 1980.

Source: FAO.

SAWNWOOD PRODUCTION
('000 cubic metres, incl. railway sleepers)

	1991	1992	1993
Total (all broadleaved)	9.0	9.0*	5.3

* FAO estimate.

1994–2005: Annual production as in 1993 (FAO estimates).

Source: FAO.

Fishing

('000 metric tons, live weight of capture)

	2003	2004	2005
West African ilisha	1.5	3.1	3.5
Tonguefishes	1.2	1.0	1.1
Bobo croaker	5.8	7.3	7.9
Sardinellas	15.4	18.2	22.1
Bonga shad	28.5	51.0	52.7
Tuna-like fishes	0.8	2.5	2.0
Marine molluscs	3.1	1.3	1.9
Total catch (incl. others)	96.9	134.4	146.0

Source: FAO.

Mining

(metric tons, unless otherwise indicated)

	2003	2004	2005
Gypsum	4,000	—	—
Diamonds ('000 carats)	507	693	669
Salt	1,005	827	—

Source: US Geological Survey.

Industry

PETROLEUM PRODUCTS
('000 metric tons, estimates)

	2002	2003	2004
Jet fuels	20	20	21
Motor spirit (petrol)	31	31	32
Kerosene	10	10	10
Distillate fuel oils	74	74	n.a.
Residual fuel oils	55	55	55

Source: UN, *Industrial Commodity Statistics Yearbook*.

SELECTED OTHER PRODUCTS
('000 metric tons, unless otherwise indicated)

	2005	2006
Beer and stout ('000 cartons)	669	582
Malt drink ('000 cartons)	160	160
Soft drinks ('000 crates)	1,908	2,089
Confectionery ('000 lbs)	2,074	2,330
Soap (metric tons)	417	467
Paint ('000 gallons)	136	143
Cement	172	234
Flour	19	14

Source: Bank of Sierra Leone, *Annual Report*.

Finance

CURRENCY AND EXCHANGE RATES

Monetary Units

100 cents = 1 leone (Le).

Sterling, Dollar and Euro Equivalents (31 May 2007)

£1 sterling = 5,900.680 leones;
US $1 = 2,984.210 leones;
€1 = 4,014.656 leones;
10,000 leones = £1.69 = $3.35 = €2.49.

Average Exchange Rate (leones per US $)

2004 2,701.30
2005 2,889.59
2006 2,961.91

BUDGET
(Le million)

Revenue*	2003	2004	2005
Taxes on income and profit	73,046	93,963	110,153
Taxes on goods and services	63,742	85,257	103,501
Taxes on international trade	114,166	166,137	172,283
Other taxes	2,535	3,7173	4,288
Non-tax revenue	4,168	7,893	25,756
Total	287,657	356,966	415,982

Expenditure	2003	2004	2005
Recurrent expenditure	485,368	555,046	620,728
Wages and salaries	152,003	178,751	229,440
Goods and services	222,088	191,172	202,468
Emergency defence	40,774	35,244	33,976
Subsidies and transfers	27,506	55,559	63,233
Education	19,000	21,187	20,549
Local government	417	—	15,508
Pensions/Others	8,088	34,372	27,176
Interest	83,771	129,564	125,588
Development Expenditure and net lending	112,631	133,046	207,575
Total	597,999	688,092	828,304

* Excluding grants received (Le million): 179,344 in 2003; 259,376 in 2004; 351,870 in 2005.

Source: IMF, *Sierra Leone: Statistical Appendix* (January 2007).

INTERNATIONAL RESERVES
(US $ million at 31 December)

	2004	2005	2006
IMF special drawing rights	51.0	32.8	29.2
Foreign exchange	74.1	137.7	154.7
Total	125.1	170.5	183.9

Source: IMF, *International Financial Statistics*.

MONEY SUPPLY
(Le million at 31 December)

	2004	2005	2006
Currency outside banks	204,733	231,274	275,405
Demand deposits at commercial banks	127,416	176,649	195,870
Total money (incl. others)	344,524	424,173	489,298

Source: IMF, *International Financial Statistics*.

COST OF LIVING
(Consumer Price Index for Freetown; base: 2000 = 100)

	2001	2002	2003
Food	105.2	104.4	112.2
All items (incl. others)	102.2	98.8	106.3

All items: 121.3 in 2004; 135.9 in 2005; 148.9 in 2006.

Source: IMF, *International Financial Statistics*.

NATIONAL ACCOUNTS
()

National Income and Product
(Le million at current prices, year ending 30 June)

	1992/93	1993/94	1994/95*
Compensation of employees	86,503.1	107,650.3	138,658.6
Operating surplus	313,873.8	352,605.6	467,380.1
Domestic factor incomes	400,376.9	460,255.8	606,038.7
Consumption of fixed capital	30,097.2	35,104.2	41,907.3
Gross domestic product (GDP) at factor cost	430,474.1	495,360.0	647,946.1
Indirect taxes, *less* subsidies	36,713.4	48,351.0	62,443.2
GDP in purchasers' values	467,187.5	543,711.0	710,389.3
Factor income received from abroad *Less* Factor income paid abroad	−66,914.8	−70,237.5	−84,216.0
Gross national product (GNP)	400,272.7	473,473.5	626,173.3
Less Consumption of fixed capital	30,097.2	35,104.2	41,907.3
National income in market prices	370,175.5	438,369.3	584,265.9
Other current transfers received from abroad *Less* Other current transfers paid abroad	11,483.0	12,438.6	15,067.8
National disposable income	381,658.5	450,807.9	599,333.7

* Provisional figures.

Expenditure on the Gross Domestic Product
(US $ million at current prices)

	2004	2005	2006
Government final consumption expenditure	145.25	163.36	182.96
Private final consumption expenditure	980.03	1,065.97	1,286.40
Gross capital formation	113.11	208.40	222.60
Total domestic expenditure	1,238.39	1,437.73	1,691.96
Exports of goods and services	239.02	291.08	399.38
Less Imports of goods and services	405.98	515.88	634.59
GDP in purchasers' values	1,071.43	1,212.94	1,456.74
GDP at constant 2000 prices	1,085.64	1,164.32	1,250.28

Source: African Development Bank.

Gross Domestic Product by Economic Activity
(Le million at current prices, year ending 30 June)

	1992/93	1993/94	1994/95*
Agriculture, hunting, forestry and fishing	162,194.6	188,884.1	275,327.5
Mining and quarrying	98,615.8	96,748.8	119,229.2
Manufacturing	39,567.0	47,816.7	61,475.3
Electricity, gas and water	469.8	757.3	2,816.8
Construction	4,655.4	12,544.4	15,788.2
Trade, restaurants and hotels	69,139.9	77,251.0	98,270.1
Transport, storage and communications	37,056.5	50,047.1	61,267.5
Finance, insurance, real estate and business services	15,947.0	17,988.0	14,732.2
Government services	14,500.0	17,884.0	19,844.9
Other community, social and personal services	8,998.3	9,769.0	12,308.9
Sub-total	451,144.3	519,690.4	681,060.6
Import duties	18,994.0	27,410.0	32,942.0
Less Imputed bank service charge	2,950.8	3,389.8	3,612.3
GDP in purchasers' values	467,187.5	543,711.0	710,389.3

* Provisional figures.

BALANCE OF PAYMENTS
(US $ million)

	2003	2004	2005
Exports of goods f.o.b.	110.8	154.1	185.1
Imports of goods f.o.b.	−310.7	−274.3	−361.7
Trade balance	−199.9	−120.2	−176.6
Exports of services	66.1	61.4	78.0
Imports of services	−93.8	−92.3	−90.6
Balance on goods and services	−227.6	−151.2	−189.2
Other income received	1.7	4.1	5.4
Other income paid	−16.7	−71.1	−56.3
Balance on goods, services and income	−242.6	−218.2	−240.1
Current transfers received	148.5	80.3	73.5
Current transfers paid	−5.0	−2.8	−2.0
Current balance	−99.1	−140.8	−168.6
Capital account (net)	16.0	18.4	36.8
Direct investment abroad	—	—	7.5
Direct investment from abroad	8.6	61.2	58.6
Other investment assets	0.5	10.1	−1.9
Other investment liabilities	24.4	5.0	−26.1
Net errors and omissions	−50.3	−53.5	−35.9
Overall balance	−99.9	−99.7	−129.6

Source: IMF, *International Financial Statistics*.

External Trade

PRINCIPAL COMMODITIES
(US $'000)

Imports c.i.f.	2005	2006
Food and live animals	53,115.2	56,139.8
Beverages and tobacco	9,920.2	9,295.3
Crude materials (inedible) except fuels	8,754.2	21,702.6
Mineral fuels, lubricants, etc.	115,596.9	147,080.4
Animal and vegetable oils and fats	1,306.7	3,327.1
Chemicals	22,746.8	23,999.9
Basic manufactures	40,674.4	48,601.3
Machinery and transport equipment	71,824.1	69,110.9
Miscellaneous manufactured articles	17,125.1	15,571.3
Total	341,063.6	394,828.6

Exports f.o.b.	2005	2006
Coffee	873.8	1,093.4
Cocoa beans	5,236.8	11,570.7
Diamonds	142,202.1	125,041.2
Total (incl. others)	159,010.6	231,037.1

Source: Bank of Sierra Leone.

PRINCIPAL TRADING PARTNERS

Imports c.i.f. (US $ million)	2002
Canada	23.0
China, People's Repub.	11.8
Côte d'Ivoire	129.1
Germany	9.1
India	13.2
Japan	14.9
Netherlands	19.4
United Kingdom	11.9
USA	17.4
Total (incl. others)	352.0

Source: UN, *International Trade Statistics Yearbook*.

Exports (Le million)	1992	1993	1994
Belgium	25,770	54	11,412
Germany	1,060	2,486	1,328
Guinea	1,315	817	1,331
Netherlands	5,307	1,201	2,815
Switzerland	7,546	486	215
United Kingdom	5,567	5,988	11,767
USA	13,832	17,564	30,431
Total (incl. others)	75,034	67,077	67,930

Source: Central Statistics Office, Freetown.

Transport

ROAD TRAFFIC
(motor vehicles in use at 31 December)

	2000	2001	2002
Passenger cars	2,045	2,263	11,353
Buses and coaches	2,597	3,516	4,050
Goods vehicles	2,309	2,898	3,565
Motorcycles	1,398	1,532	1,657

Source: IRF, *World Road Statistics*.

SHIPPING

Merchant Fleet
(registered at 31 December)

	2004	2005	2006
Number of vessels	46	69	194
Displacement (gross registered tons)	26,999	77,244	293,872

Source: Lloyd's Register-Fairplay, *World Fleet Statistics*.

International Sea-borne Freight Traffic
(estimates, '000 metric tons)

	1991	1992	1993
Goods loaded	1,930	2,190	2,310
Goods unloaded	562	579	589

Source: UN Economic Commission for Africa, *African Statistical Yearbook*.

CIVIL AVIATION
(traffic on scheduled services)

	2000	2001	2002
Kilometres flown (million)	1	1	1
Passengers carried ('000)	19	14	14
Passenger-km (million)	93	73	74
Total ton-km (million)	18	13	13

2003: Figures assumed to be unchanged from 2002.

Source: UN, *Statistical Yearbook*.

Tourism

	2003	2004	2005
Tourist arrivals	38,107	43,560	40,023
Tourism receipts (US $ million, excl. passenger transport)	60	58	n.a.

Source: World Tourism Organization.

Communications Media

	2000	2001	2002
Television receivers ('000 in use)	64	65	n.a.
Telephones ('000 main lines in use)	19.0	22.7	24.0
Mobile cellular telephones ('000 subscribers)	11.9	26.9	67.0
Internet users ('000)	5	7	8

2003 ('000): Mobile cellular telephones (subscribers) 113.2; Internet users 9.

2004–05 ('000): Mobile cellular telephones (subscribers) 113.2 (estimates); Internet users 10.

Radio receivers ('000 in use): 1,120 in 1997.

Facsimile machines (number in use, year beginning 1 April): 2,500 in 1998.

Daily newspapers: 1 (average circulation 20,000) in 1996.

Sources: UNESCO, *Statistical Yearbook*; UN, *Statistical Yearbook*; and International Telecommunication Union.

Education

(2001/02)

	Schools	Teachers	Number of pupils		
			Males	Females	Total
Primary	2,704	14,932	323,924	230,384	554,308
Secondary	246	5,264	66,745	41,031	107,776
University*	n.a.	n.a.	1,163	300	1,463

* Full time undergraduate students in 1995.

2003/04: *Primary:* Teachers 17,327; Pupils 1,158,399 (males 670,079, females 488,320). *Secondary:* Pupils 94,366 (males 46,449, females 47,917) (Source: UNESCO Institute for Statistics).

Adult literacy rate (UNESCO estimates): 35.6% (males 46.9%; females 24.4%) in 2004 (Source: UN Development Programme, *Human Development Report*).

Directory

The Constitution

Following the transfer of power to a democratically elected civilian administration on 29 March 1996, the Constitution of 1991 (which had been suspended since April 1992) was reinstated. The Constitution provided for the establishment of a multi-party system, and vested executive power in the President, who was to be elected by the majority of votes cast nationally and by at least 25% of the votes cast in each of the four provinces. The maximum duration of the President's tenure of office was limited to two five-year terms. The President was to appoint the Cabinet, subject to approval by the Parliament. The Parliament was elected for a five-year term and comprised 124 members, 112 of whom were elected by a system of proportional representation, in 14 constituencies, while 12 Paramount Chiefs also represented the provincial districts in the legislature. Members of the Parliament were not permitted concurrently to hold office in the Cabinet.

The Government

HEAD OF STATE

President and Commander-in-Chief of the Armed Forces: Alhaji AHMED TEJAN KABBAH (took office 29 March 1996; reinstated 10 March 1998; re-elected 14 May 2002).

Vice-President: SOLOMON BEREWA.

CABINET

(August 2007)

Minister of Foreign Affairs and International Co-operation: MOMODU KOROMA.

Minister of Finance: JOHN OPONJO BENJAMIN.

Minister of Development and Economic Planning: MOHAMED B. DARAMY.

Minister of Trade and Industry: Dr KADI SESAY.

Minister of Transport and Communications: (vacant).

Minister of Marine Resources: Dr CHERNOR JALLOH.

Minister of Health and Sanitation: ABBATOR THOMAS.

Minister of Education, Science and Technology: Dr ALPHA T. WURIE.

Minister of Mineral Resources: Alhaji MOHAMED SWARRAY DEEN.

Minister of Local Government and Community Development: SIDIKIE BRIMA.

Minister of Tourism and Culture: OKERE ADAMS.

Minister of Country Planning, Forestry and the Environment: Dr ALFRED BOBSON SESAY.

Minister of Information and Broadcasting: Prof. SEPTIMUS KAIKAI.

Minister of Works, Housing and Technical Maintenance: Dr CAISER J. BOIMA.

Minister of Labour and Industrial Relations, and Social Security: ALPHA O. TIMBO.

Minister of Social Welfare, Gender and Children's Affairs: SHIRLEY GBUJAMA.

Minister of Justice and Attorney-General: FRANCIS M. CAREW.

Minister of Internal Affairs: PASCAL EGBENDA.

Minister of Youth and Sports: Dr DENNIS BRIGHT.

Minister of Energy and Power: LLOYD DURING.

Minister of Agriculture and Food Security: Dr SAMA S. MONDEH.

Minister of Political and Parliamentary Affairs: EYA MBAYO.

Minister of State of Presidential Affairs: Dr SHEKU SESAY.

Minister of the Northern Region: ALEX ALIE KARGBO.

Minister of the Southern Region: Dr S. U. M. JAH.

Minister of the Eastern Region: SAHR RANDOLPH FILLIE-FABOE.

MINISTRIES

Office of the President: Freetown; tel. (22) 232101; fax (22) 231404; e-mail info@statehouse-sl.org; internet www.statehouse-sl.org/president.html.

Ministry of Agriculture and Food Security: Youyi Bldg, 3rd Floor, Brookfields, Freetown; tel. (22) 222242; fax (22) 241613.

Ministry of Country Planning, Forestry and the Environment: Youyi Bldg, 4th Floor, Brookfields, Freetown; tel. (22) 242013.

Ministry of Defence: State Ave, Freetown; tel. (22) 227369; fax (22) 229380.

Ministry of Development and Economic Planning: Youyi Bldg, 6th Floor, Brookfields, Freetown; tel. (22) 225236; fax (22) 241599.

Ministry of Education, Science and Technology: New England, Freetown; tel. (22) 240881; fax (22) 240137.

Ministry of Energy and Power: Electricity House, Siaka Stevens St, Freetown; tel. (22) 226566; fax (22) 228199.

Ministry of Finance: Secretariat Bldg, George St, Freetown; tel. (22) 225612; fax (2) 228472.

Ministry of Foreign Affairs and International Co-operation: Gloucester St, Freetown; tel. (22) 223260; fax (22) 225615; e-mail mfaicsl@yahoo.com.

Ministry of Health and Sanitation: Youyi Bldg, 6th Floor, Brookfields, Freetown; tel. (22) 240427; fax (22) 241613.

Ministry of Information and Broadcasting: Youyi Bldg, 8th Floor, Brookfields, Freetown; tel. (22) 240339; fax (22) 241757.

Ministry of Internal Affairs: Liverpool St, Freetown; tel. (22) 226979; fax (22) 227727.

Ministry of Justice: Guma Bldg, Lamina Sankoh St, Freetown; tel. (22) 227444; fax (22) 229366.

Ministry of Labour and Industrial Relations, and Social Security: New England, Freetown; tel. (22) 241947.

Ministry of Local Government and Community Development: New England, Freetown; tel. (22) 226589; fax (22) 222409.

Ministry of Marine Resources: Marine House, 11 Old Railway Line, Brookfields, Freetown; tel. (22) 242117.

Ministry of Mineral Resources: Youyi Bldg, 5th Floor, Brookfields, Freetown; tel. (22) 240142; fax (22) 241757.

Ministry of Political and Parliamentary Affairs: State House, State Ave, Freetown; tel. (22) 228698; fax (22) 222781.

Ministry of Presidential Affairs: State House, State Ave, Freetown; tel. (22) 229728; fax (22) 229799.

Ministry of Social Welfare, Gender and Children's Affairs: New England, Freetown; tel. (22) 241256; fax (22) 242076.

Ministry of Trade and Industry: Ministerial Bldg, George St, Freetown; tel. (22) 225211.

Ministry of Transport and Communications: Ministerial Bldg, George St, Freetown; tel. (22) 221245; fax (22) 227337.

Ministry of Tourism and Culture: Ministerial Bldg, George St, Freetown; tel. (22) 222588.

Ministry of Works, Housing and Technical Maintenance: New England, Freetown; tel. (22) 240937; fax (22) 240018.

Ministry of Youth and Sports: New England, Freetown; tel. (22) 240881; fax (22) 240137.

President and Legislature

PRESIDENT

Presidential Election, 14 May 2002

Candidate	% of votes
Ahmed Tejan Kabbah (SLPP)	70.06
Ernest Bai Koroma (APC)	22.35
Johnny Paul Koroma (PLP)	3.00
Pallo Bangura (RUFP)	1.73
Dr John Karefa-Smart (APC)	1.04
Dr Raymond Kamara (GAP)	0.59
Zainab Hawa Bangura (MOP)	0.55
Bamidele Thompson (CUPP)	0.47
Andrew Turay (YPP)	0.20
Total	100.00

PARLIAMENT

Speaker: Justice E. K. COWAN.

General Election, 11 August 2007, provisional results

Party	Seats
All-People's Congress (APC)	59
Sierra Leone People's Party (SLPP)	43
People's Movement for Democratic Change (PMDC)	10
Total	112*

* A further 12 seats were allocated to Paramount Chiefs, who represented the 12 provincial districts.

Election Commission

National Electoral Commission (NEC): Wellington Industrial Esate, Freetown; internet www.necsierraleone.org; f. 2000; Chair. CHRISTIANA AYOKA MARY THORPE.

Political Organizations

A ban on political activity was rescinded in June 1995. Numerous political parties were officially granted registration, prior to elections in May 2002.

All-People's Congress (APC): 137H Fourah Bay Rd, Freetown; e-mail info@new-apc.org; internet apcparty.org; f. 1960; sole authorized political party 1978–91; merged with the Democratic People's Party in 1992; reconstituted in 1995; Leader ERNEST BAI KOROMA.

Citizens United for Peace and Progress (CUPP): e-mail info@cupp.org; internet www.cupp.org; f. 2002; Chair. ABUBAKARR YANSSANEH.

Grand Alliance Party (GAP): Freetown; f. 2002; Pres. Dr RAYMOND KAMARA.

Movement for Progress (MOP): Freetown; f. 2002; Pres. ZAINAB HAWA BANGURA.

National Alliance Democratic Party (NADP): Leader MOHAMED YAHYA SILLAH.

National Democratic Alliance (NDA): Leader AMADU M. B. JALLOH.

National Unity Movement (NUM): Leader DESMOND LUKE.

National Unity Party (NUP): e-mail johnben@nupsl.org; internet www.nupsl.org; Leader JOHN OPONJO BENJAMIN (acting).

Peace and Liberation Party (PLP): Freetown; f. 2002; Leader JOHNNY PAUL KOROMA.

People's Democratic Party (PDP): Freetown; supported Sierra Leone People's Party in May 2002 elections; Leader OSMAN KAMARA.

People's Movement for Democratic Change (PMDC): Freetown; f. April 2006 by fmr mems of Sierra Leone People's Party; Leader CHARLES MARGAI; Sec.-Gen. ANSU LANSANA.

People's National Convention (PNC): Leader EDWARD JOHN KARGBO.

People's Progressive Party (PPP): Leader ABASS CHERNOR BUNDU.

Sierra Leone People's Party (SLPP): 29 Rawdon St, Freetown; tel. and fax (22) 228222; e-mail sq-slpp@hotmail.com; internet www.slpp.ws; Nat. Chair. Alhaji U. N. S. JAH; Leader SOLOMAN BEREWA.

Social Democratic Party (SDP): Leader ANDREW VICTOR LUNGAY.

United National People's Party (UNPP): Leader Dr JOHN KAREFA-SMART.

Young People's Party (YPP): 19 Lewis St, Freetown; tel. (22) 232907; e-mail info@yppsl.org; internet www.yppsl.org; f. 2002; Leader SYLVIA BLYDEN; Sec.-Gen. ABDUL RAHMAN YILLA.

Diplomatic Representation

EMBASSIES AND HIGH COMMISSIONS IN SIERRA LEONE

China, People's Republic: 29 Wilberforce Loop, POB 778, Freetown; tel. and fax (22) 231797; e-mail chinaemb_sl@mfa.gov.cn; internet sl.china-embassy.org; Ambassador CHENG WENJU.

Egypt: 174C Wilkinson Rd, POB 652, Freetown; tel. (22) 231245; fax (22) 234297; Ambassador MAHMOUD YEHIA M. EZZAT.

The Gambia: 6 Wilberforce St, Freetown; tel. (22) 225191; fax (22) 226846; High Commissioner DEMBO BADJIE.

Ghana: 13 Walpole St, Freetown; tel. (22) 223461; fax (22) 227043; High Commissioner KABRAL BLAY-AMIHERE.

Guinea: 6 Wilkinson Rd, Freetown; tel. (22) 232584; fax (22) 232496; Ambassador MOHAMED LAMIN SOMPARE.

Lebanon: 22A Spur Rd, Wilberforce, Freetown; tel. (22) 222513; fax (22) 234665; Ambassador GHASSAN ABDEL SATER.

Liberia: 10 Motor Rd, Brookfields, POB 276, Freetown; tel. (22) 230991; Chargé d'affaires a.i. SAMUEL PETERS.

Libya: 1A and 1B P. Z. Compound, Wilberforce, Freetown; tel. (22) 235231; fax (22) 234514; Chargé d'affaires a.i. ALI TELLISI.

Nigeria: 37 Siaka Stevens St, Freetown; tel. (22) 224224; fax (22) 2242474; High Commissioner ADAMU A. ABBAS.

United Kingdom: 6 Spur Rd, Wilberforce, Freetown; tel. (22) 232565; fax (22) 232070; e-mail bhc@sierratel.sl; internet www.britishhighcommission.gov.uk/sierraleone; High Commissioner SARAH MACINTOSH.

USA: Leicester, Freetown; tel. (22) 515000; fax (22) 515355; e-mail TaylorJB2@state.gov; internet freetown.usembassy.gov; Ambassador JUNE CARTER PERRY.

Judicial System

The Supreme Court

The ultimate court of appeal in both civil and criminal cases. In addition to its appellate jurisdiction, the Court has supervisory jurisdiction over all other courts and over any adjudicating authority in Sierra Leone, and also original jurisdiction in constitutional issues.

Chief Justice: DESMOND LUKE.

Supreme Court Justices: C. A. HARDING, AGNES AWUNOR-RENNER.

The Court of Appeal

The Court of Appeal has jurisdiction to hear and determine appeals from decisions of the High Court in both criminal and civil matters, and also from certain statutory tribunals. Appeals against its decisions may be made to the Supreme Court.

Justices of Appeal: S. C. E. WARNE, C. S. DAVIES, S. T. NAVO, M. S. TURAY, E. C. THOMPSON-DAVIS, M. O. TAJU-DEEN, M. O. ADOPHY, GEORGE GELAGA KING, Dr A. B. Y. TIMBO, VIRGINIA A. WRIGHT.

High Court

The High Court has unlimited original jurisdiction in all criminal and civil matters. It also has appellate jurisdiction against decisions of Magistrates' Courts.

Judges: FRANCIS C. GBOW, EBUN THOMAS, D. E. M. WILLIAMS, LAURA MARCUS-JONES, L. B. O. NYLANDER, A. M. B. TARAWALLIE, O. H. ALGHALLI, W. A. O. JOHNSON, N. D. ALHADI, R. J. BANKOLE THOMPSON, M. E. T. THOMPSON, C. J. W. ATERE-ROBERTS (acting).

Magistrates' Courts: In criminal cases the jurisdiction of the Magistrates' Courts is limited to summary cases and to preliminary investigations to determine whether a person charged with an offence should be committed for trial.

Local Courts have jurisdiction, according to native law and custom, in matters that are outside the jurisdiction of other courts.

Religion

A large proportion of the population holds animist beliefs, although there are significant numbers of Islamic and Christian adherents.

ISLAM

In 1990 Islamic adherents represented an estimated 30% of the total population.

Ahmadiyya Muslim Mission: 15 Bath St, Brookfields, POB 353, Freetown; Emir and Chief Missionary KHALIL A. MOBASHIR.

Kankaylay (Sierra Leone Muslim Men and Women's Association): 15 Blackhall Rd, Kissy, POB 1168, Freetown; tel. (22) 250931; e-mail kankaylay@yahoo.com; f. 1972; 500,000 mems; Pres. Alhaji IBRAHIM ALPHA TURAY; Lady Pres. Haja MARIAM TURAY.

Sierra Leone Muslim Congress: POB 875, Freetown; Pres. Alhaji MUHAMMAD SANUSI MUSTAPHA.

CHRISTIANITY

Council of Churches in Sierra Leone: 4A King Harman Rd, Brookfields, POB 404, Freetown; tel. (22) 240568; fax (22) 241109;

e-mail ccsl@sierratel.sl; f. 1924; 17 mem. churches; Pres. Rev. MOSES B. KHANU; Gen. Sec. ALIMAMY P. KOROMA.

The Anglican Communion

Anglicans in Sierra Leone are adherents of the Church of the Province of West Africa, comprising 12 dioceses, of which two are in Sierra Leone. The Archbishop of the Province is the Bishop of Koforidua, Ghana.

Bishop of Bo: Rt Rev. SAMUEL SAO GBONDA, MacRobert St, POB 21, Bo, Southern Province.

Bishop of Freetown: Rt Rev. JULIUS O. PRINCE LYNCH, Bishopscourt, Fourah Bay Rd, POB 537, Freetown.

Baptist Churches

Sierra Leone Baptist Convention: POB 64, Lunsar; Pres. Rev. JOSEPH S. MANS; Sec. Rev. N. T. DIXON.

The Nigerian Baptist Convention is also active.

Methodist Churches

Methodist Church Sierra Leone: Wesley House, George St, POB 64, Freetown; tel. (22) 222216; autonomous since 1967; Pres. of Conf. Rev. GERSHON F. H. ANDERSON; Sec. Rev. CHRISTIAN V. A. PEACOCK; 26,421 mems.

United Methodist Church: Freetown; Presiding Bishop T. S. BANGURA; 36,857 mems.

Other active Methodist bodies include the African Methodist Episcopal Church, the Wesleyan Church of Sierra Leone, the Countess of Huntingdon's Connexion and the West African Methodist Church.

The Roman Catholic Church

Sierra Leone comprises one archdiocese and two dioceses. At 31 December 2004 there were an estimated 195,552 adherents in the country, representing about 3.3% of the total population.

Inter-territorial Catholic Bishops' Conference of The Gambia and Sierra Leone

Santanno House, POB 893, Freetown; tel. (22) 228240; fax (22) 228252.

f. 1971; Pres. Rt Rev. GEORGE BIGUZZI (Bishop of Makeni).

Archbishop of Freetown and Bo: Most Rev. JOSEPH HENRY GANDA, Santanno House, POB 893, Freetown; tel. (22) 224590; fax (22) 224075; e-mail archbis@hotmail.com.

Other Christian Churches

The following are represented: the Christ Apostolic Church, the Church of the Lord (Aladura), the Evangelical Church, the Missionary Church of Africa, the Sierra Leone Church and the United Brethren in Christ.

AFRICAN RELIGIONS

There is a diverse range of beliefs, rites and practices, varying between ethnic and kinship groups.

The Press

DAILIES

Daily Mail: 29–31 Rawdon St, POB 53, Freetown; tel. (22) 223191; f. 1931; state-owned; Editor AIAH MARTIN MONDEH; circ. 10,000.

For di People: Freetown; independent; Editor PAUL KAMARA.

PERIODICALS

African Crescent: 15 Bath St, POB 353, Brookfields, Freetown; Editor MAULANA-KHALIL A. MOBASHIR.

The Catalyst: Christian Literature Crusade Bookshop, 92 Circular Rd, POB 1465, Freetown; tel. (22) 224382; Editor ELIAS BANGURA.

Concord Times: 139 Pademba Rd, Freetown; 3 a week; Editor DOROTHY GORDON.

Leonean Sun: 49 Main Rd, Wellington, Freetown; tel. (22) 223363; f. 1974; monthly; Editor ROWLAND MARTYN.

Liberty Voice: 139 Pademba Rd, Freetown; tel. (22) 242100; Editor A. MAHDIEU SAVAGE.

New Breed: Freetown; weekly; independent; Man. Editor (vacant).

New Citizen: 5 Hanna Benka-Coker St, Freetown; tel. (22) 241795; Editor I. BEN KARGBO.

The New Globe: 49 Bathurst St, Freetown; tel. (22) 228245; weekly; Man. Editor SAM TUMOE; circ. 4,000.

The New Shaft: 60 Old Railway Line, Brookfields, Freetown; tel. (22) 241093; 2 a week; independent; Editor FRANKLIN BUNTING-DAVIES; circ. 10,000.

The Pool Newspaper: 1 Short St, 5th Floor, Freetown; tel. and fax (22) 220102; e-mail pool@justice.com; internet www.poolnewspaper.tripod.com; f. 1992; 3 a week; independent; Man. Dir CHERNOR OJUKU SESAY; circ. 3,000.

Progress: 1 Short St, Freetown; tel. (22) 223588; weekly; independent; Editor FODE KANDEH; circ. 7,000.

Sierra Leone Chamber of Commerce Journal: Sierra Leone Chamber of Commerce, Industry and Agriculture, Guma Bldg, 5th Floor, Lamina Sankoh St, POB 502, Freetown; tel. (22) 226305; fax (22) 228005; monthly.

Unity Now: 82 Pademba Rd, Freetown; tel. (22) 227466; Editor FRANK KPOSOWA.

The Vision: 60 Old Railway Line, Brookfields; tel. (22) 241273; Editor SIAKA MASSAQUOI.

Weekend Spark: 7 Lamina Sankoh St, Freetown; tel. (22) 223397; f. 1983; weekly; independent; Editor ROWLAND MARTYN; circ. 20,000.

Weekly Democrat: Freetown; Editor JON FORAY.

NEWS AGENCY

Sierra Leone News Agency (SLENA): 15 Wallace Johnson St, PMB 445, Freetown; tel. (22) 224921; fax (22) 224439; f. 1980; Man. Dir ABDUL KARIM JALLOH (acting).

Publishers

Njala University Publishing Centre: Njala University College, PMB, Freetown; science and technology, university textbooks.

Sierra Leone University Press: Fourah Bay College, POB 87, Freetown; tel. (22) 22491; fax (22) 224439; f. 1965; biography, history, Africana, religion, social science, university textbooks; Chair. Prof. ERNEST H. WRIGHT.

United Christian Council Literature Bureau: Bunumbu Press, POB 28, Bo; tel. (32) 462; books in Mende, Temne, Susu; Man. Dir ROBERT SAM-KPAKRA.

Broadcasting and Communications

TELECOMMUNICATIONS

Sierra Leone Telecommunications Co (SIERRATEL): 7 Wallace Johnson St, POB 80, Freetown; tel. (22) 222804; fax (22) 224439.

BROADCASTING

Sierra Leone Broadcasting Service: New England, Freetown; tel. (22) 240403; f. 1934; state-controlled; programmes mainly in English and the four main Sierra Leonean vernaculars, Mende, Limba, Temne and Krio; weekly broadcast in French; television service established 1963; Dir-Gen. JEANA BANDATOMO.

Finance

(cap. = capital; res = reserves; dep. = deposits; m. = million; br(s). = branch(es); amounts in leones)

BANKING

Central Bank

Bank of Sierra Leone: Siaka Stevens St, POB 30, Freetown; tel. (22) 226501; fax (22) 224764; e-mail info@bankofsierraleone-centralbank.org; internet www.bankofsierraleone-centralbank.org; f. 1964; cap. 24,001.5m., res –177,362.3m., dep. 717,290.7m. (Dec. 2005); Gov. JAMES D. ROGERS; Dep. Gov. MOHAMED S. FOFANA; 1 br.

Other Banks

Guaranty Trust Bank: Sparta Bldg, 12 Wilberforce St, Freetown; tel. (22) 228493; fax (22) 228318; e-mail gtbsl@sierratel.sl; f. Feb. 2002 through the acquisition of 90% of shareholding of First Merchant Bank of Sierra Leone by Guaranty Trust Bank of Nigeria; cap. 2,261.0m., total assets 17,769.0m. (Dec. 2003); Chair. TAYO ADERINOKUN.

National Development Bank Ltd: Leone House, 6th Floor, 21–23 Siaka Stevens St, Freetown; tel. (22) 226792; fax (22) 224468; e-mail ndbrisk@sierratel.sl; f. 1968; 99% state-owned; provides medium- and long-term finance and tech. assistance to devt-orientated enterprises; cap. 1,604.3m., total assets 2,200m. (Dec. 2003); Chair. MURRAY E. S. LAMIN; Man. Dir MOHAMED M. TURAY; 3 brs.

Rokel Commercial Bank of Sierra Leone Ltd: 25–27 Siaka Stevens St, POB 12, Freetown; tel. (22) 222501; fax (22) 222563; e-mail rokelsl@sierratel.sl; internet www.rokelsl.com; f. 1971; cap. 1,119.7m., res 1,776.7m., dep. 141,581.1m. (Dec. 2005); 51% govt-owned; Chair. YAYAH TOBIAS SESAY; Man. Dir HENRY AKIN MACAULEY; 10 brs.

Sierra Leone Commercial Bank Ltd: 29–31 Siaka Stevens St, Freetown; tel. (22) 225264; fax (22) 225292; e-mail slcb@sierratel.sl; internet www.slcb.biz; f. 1973; state-owned; cap. 1,000.0m., res 19,090.2m., dep. 148,960.7m. (Dec. 2005); Chair. VICTOR F. JAMINA; Man. Dir Alhaji ABDULAI KAKAY; 8 brs.

Standard Chartered Bank Sierra Leone Ltd: 9 and 11 Lightfoot-Boston St, POB 1155, Freetown; tel. (22) 225022; fax (22) 225760; e-mail scbsl@sierratel.sl; f. 1971; cap. and res 13,073.0m., total assets 102,179.9m. (Dec. 2003); Chair. LLOYD A. DURING; Man. Dir LAMIN KEMBA MANJANG; 14 brs.

Union Trust Bank Ltd: Howe St, PMB 1237, Freetown; tel. (22) 226954; fax (22) 226214; e-mail utb@sierratel.sl; fmrly Meridien BIAO Bank Sierra Leone Ltd; adopted present name in 1995; cap. and res 8,221.1m., total assets 29,025.0m. (Dec. 2003); Chair. S. B. NICOL-COLE; Man. Dir JOHN D. OKRAFO-SMART.

INSURANCE

Aureol Insurance Co Ltd: Kissy House, 54 Siaka Stevens St, POB 647, Freetown; tel. (22) 223435; fax (22) 229336; f. 1987; Man. Dir S. G. BENJAMIN.

National Insurance Co Ltd: 18–20 Walpole St, PMB 84, Freetown; tel. (22) 222535; fax (22) 226097; e-mail nic@sierratel.sl; f. 1972; state-owned; Chair. P. J. KUYEMBEH; CEO ARTHUR NATHANIEL YASKEY.

New India Assurance Co Ltd: 18 Wilberforce St, POB 340, Freetown; tel. (22) 226453; fax (22) 222494; Man. Dir A. CHOPRA.

Reliance Insurance Trust Corpn Ltd: 24 Siaka Stevens St, Freetown; tel. (22) 225115; fax (22) 228051; e-mail oonomake@yahoo.com; f. 1985; Chair. MOHAMED B. COLE; Man. Dir ALICE M. ONOMAKE.

Sierra Leone Insurance Co Ltd: 31 Lightfoot Boston St, POB 836, Freetown; tel. (22) 224920; fax (22) 222115; Man. Dir IDRISSE YILLE.

Trade and Industry

GOVERNMENT AGENCY

Government Gold and Diamond Office (GGDO): c/o Bank of Sierra Leone, Siaka Stevens St, Freetown; tel. (22) 222600; fax (22) 229064; f. 1985; govt regulatory agency for diamonds and gold; combats illicit trade; Chair. Alhaji M. S. DEEN.

CHAMBER OF COMMERCE

Sierra Leone Chamber of Commerce, Industry and Agriculture: Guma Bldg, 5th Floor, Lamina Sankoh St, POB 502, Freetown; tel. (22) 226305; fax (22) 228005; e-mail cocsl@sierratel.sl; internet www.cocsl.com; f. 1961; 215 mems; Pres. Alhaji MOHAMED MUSA KING.

TRADE AND INDUSTRIAL ASSOCIATIONS

Sierra Leone Export Development and Investment Corpn (SLEDIC): 18–20 Walpole St, PMB 6, Freetown; tel. (22) 227604; fax (22) 229097; e-mail sledic@sierratel.sl; f. 1993; Man. Dir CHRIS JASABE.

Small-Medium Scale Businesses Association (Sierra Leone): O.A.U. Dr., Tower Hill, PMB 575, Freetown; tel. (22) 222617; fax (22) 224439; Dir ABU CONTEH.

EMPLOYERS' ORGANIZATIONS

Sierra Leone Employers' Federation: POB 562, Freetown; Chair. AMADU B. NDOEKA; Exec. Officer L. E. JOHNSON.

Sierra Leone Chamber of Mines: POB 456, Freetown; tel. (22) 226082; f. 1965; mems comprise the principal mining concerns; Pres. D. J. S. FRASER; Exec. Officer N. H. T. BOSTON.

UTILITIES

Electricity

National Power Authority: Electricity House, Siaka Stevens St, Freetown; tel. (30) 700000; fax (22) 227584; e-mail Sierra_Leone@iaeste.org; supplies all electricity in Sierra Leone.

Water

Guma Valley Water Co: Guma Bldg, 13/14 Lamina Sankoh St, POB 700, Freetown; tel. (22) 25887; e-mail gumasl@yahoo.co.uk; f. 1961; responsible for all existing water supplies in Freetown and surrounding villages, including the Guma dam and associated works.

MAJOR COMPANIES

Aureol Tobacco Co Ltd: Wellington Industrial Estate, POB 109, Freetown; tel. (22) 223435; fax (22) 263138; f. 1959; cigarette mfrs; Chair. Prof. K. KOSO-THOMAS; Man. Dir A. D. A. M'CORMACK; 75 employees.

Bata Shoe Co Sierra Leone Ltd: Wallace Johnson St, POB 111, Freetown; footwear mfrs and distributors. Assoc. co:

Plastic Manufacturing Sierra Leone Ltd: Wilkinson Rd, POB 96, Freetown; footwear mfrs.

Chanrai Sierra Leone Ltd: Wellington Industrial Estate, POB 57, Freetown; tel. (22) 263292; fax (22) 263305; f. 1893; importers of motor spares, air-conditioners, refrigerators, building materials, textiles and provisions; mfrs of soaps and polyethylene bags; Dir R. K. LAKHANPAL; 115 employees.

Dalcon International: Spiritus House, 8 Howe St, Freetown; tel. (22) 228325; fax (22) 228223; e-mail dalcon_c@yahoo.com; f. 1991; export trade in cocoa and coffee; Chair. IBRAHIM K. TURAY.

The Diamond Corpn (West Africa) Ltd: 25–27 Siaka Stevens St, POB 421, Freetown; purchase and export of diamonds; Dir S. L. MATTURI.

KPMG Peat Marwick: Ludgate House, Wallace-Johnson St, Freetown; tel. (22) 222061; fax (22) 228149; e-mail kpmg@sierratel.sl; f. 1960; accounting and consultancy services; Dir DAVID CAREW.

Rokel Leaf Tobacco Development Co Ltd: POB 29, Makeni; f. 1974; production of leaf tobacco; Chair. J. T. SHORT.

Sierra Leone Breweries Ltd: POB 721, Freetown; tel. (22) 263384; fax (22) 263118; e-mail slbl@sierratel.sl; f. 1961; brewing and marketing of Guinness stout and Star lager; Man. Dir V. L. THOMAS.

Sierra Leone National Petroleum Co: NP House, Cotton Tree, POB 277, Freetown; tel. (22) 225040; fax (22) 226892; e-mail enpee@sierratel.sl; petroleum products; Chair. MICHAEL A. CARROL; CEO MOHAMED BABAIUDE COLE.

Sierra Leone Ore and Metal Co (SIEROMCO): POB 725, Freetown; tel. (22) 226777; fax (22) 227276; mining of bauxite; operations suspended since 1995; Chair. K. WOLFENSBERGER; Man. Dir JAMES WESTWOOD.

Sierra Rutile Ltd: PMB, Freetown; tel. and fax (22) 228144; f. 1971; jtly owned by US and Australian interests; mining of rutile and ilmenite (titanium-bearing ores); Dir JOHN B. SISAY; 1,600 employees.

TRADE UNIONS

Artisans', Ministry of Works Employees' and General Workers' Union: 4 Pultney St, Freetown; f. 1946; 14,500 mems; Pres. IBRAHIM LANGLEY; Gen. Sec. TEJAN A. KASSIM.

Sierra Leone Labour Congress: 35 Wallace Johnson St, POB 1333, Freetown; tel. (22) 226869; f. 1966; 51,000 mems in 19 affiliated unions; Pres. H. M. BARRIE; Sec.-Gen. KANDEH YILLA.

Principal affiliated unions:

Clerical, Mercantile and General Workers' Union: 35 Wallace Johnson St, Freetown; f. 1945; 3,600 mems; Pres. M. D. BENJAMIN; Gen. Sec. M. B. WILLIAMS.

Sierra Leone Association of Journalists: Freetown; Pres. SIAKA MASSAQUOI.

Sierra Leone Dockworkers' Union: 165 Fourah Bay Rd, Freetown; f. 1962; 2,650 mems; Pres. D. F. KANU; Gen. Sec. A. C. CONTEH.

Sierra Leone Motor Drivers' Union: 10 Charlotte St, Freetown; f. 1960; 1,900 mems; Pres. A. W. HASSAN; Gen. Sec. ALPHA KAMARA.

Sierra Leone Teachers' Union: Regaland House, Lowcost Step—Kissy, POB 477, Freetown; f. 1951; 18,500 mems; Pres. FESTUS E. MINAH; Sec.-Gen. A. O. TIMBO.

Sierra Leone Transport, Agricultural and General Workers' Union: 4 Pultney St, Freetown; f. 1946; 1,600 mems; Pres. S. O. SAWYERR-MANLEY; Gen. Sec. S. D. KARGBO.

United Mineworkers' Union: 35 Wallace Johnson St, Freetown; f. 1944; 6,500 mems; Pres. H. M. BARRIE; Gen. Sec. S. D. GBENDA.

Also affiliated to the Sierra Leone Labour Congress: **General Construction Workers' Union, Municipal and Local Government Employees' Union, Sierra Leone National Seamen's Union.**

Transport

RAILWAYS

There are no passenger railways in Sierra Leone.

Marampa Mineral Railway: Delco House, POB 735, Freetown; tel. (22) 222556; 84 km of track linking iron ore mines at Marampa (inactive since 1985) with Pepel port; Gen. Man. SYL KHANU.

ROADS

In 2002 there were an estimated 11,300 km of classified roads, including 2,138 km of main roads and 1,950 km of secondary roads; about 904 km of the total network was paved.

Sierra Leone Road Transport Corpn: Blackhall Rd, POB 1008, Freetown; tel. (22) 250442; fax (22) 250000; f. 1965; state-owned; operates transport services throughout the country; Gen. Man. DANIEL R. W. FAUX.

INLAND WATERWAYS

Established routes for launches, which include the coastal routes from Freetown northward to the Great and Little Scarcies rivers and southward to Bonthe, total almost 800 km. Although some of the upper reaches of the rivers are navigable only between July and September, there is a considerable volume of river traffic.

SHIPPING

Freetown, the principal port, has full facilities for ocean-going vessels.

Sierra Leone National Shipping Co Ltd: 45 Cline St, POB 935, Freetown; tel. (22) 229883; fax (22) 229513; e-mail nsc@sierratel.sl; f. 1972; state-owned; shipping, clearing and forwarding agency; representatives for foreign lines; Chair. Alhaji B. M. KOROMA; Man. Dir SYLVESTER B. FOMBA.

Sierra Leone Ports Authority: Queen Elizabeth II Quay, PMB 386, Cline Town, Freetown; tel. (22) 226480; fax (22) 226443; f. 1965; parastatal body, supervised by the Ministry of Transport and Communications; operates the port of Freetown; Gen. Man. Capt. P. E. M. KEMOKAI.

Sierra Leone Shipping Agencies Ltd: Deep Water Quay, Clinetown, POB 74, Freetown; tel. (22) 223453; fax (22) 220021; e-mail slsa@sl.dti.bollore.com; f. 1949; Man. Dir MICHEL MEYNARD.

Silver Star Shipping Agency Ltd: PMB 1023, Freetown; tel. (22) 221035; fax (22) 226653; e-mail silver2_star@hotmail.com; Dir Capt. H. A. BLOOMER.

CIVIL AVIATION

There is an international airport at Lungi.

Directorate of Civil Aviation: Ministry of Transport and Communications, Ministerial Bldg, George St, Freetown; tel. (22) 221245; Dir T. T. A. VANDY.

Sierra National Airlines: Leone House, 25 Pultney St, POB 285, Freetown; tel. (22) 222075; fax (22) 222026; internet www.flysna.com; f. 1982; state-owned; operates domestic and regional services, and a weekly flight to Paris, France; operations resumed, following civil conflict, in Nov. 2000; Chair. TAMBA MATTURI; Man. Dir ADAM CORMACK.

Tourism

The main attractions for tourists are the coastline, the mountains and the game reserves. Civil conflict throughout most of the 1990s effectively suspended tourist activity. By 2005, however, according to the World Tourism Organization, tourist arrivals had increased to 40,023, compared with 10,615 in 1999. Receipts from tourism totalled an estimated US $58m. in 2004.

National Tourist Board of Sierra Leone: Cape Sierra Hotel, Room 100, Aberdeen, POB 1435, Freetown; tel. (22) 236620; fax (22) 236621; e-mail info@welcometosierraleone.org; internet www.visitsierraleone.org; f. 1990; Gen. Man. CECIL J. WILLIAMS.

Defence

As assessed at March 2006, the armed forces of the Republic of Sierra Leone numbered about 12,000–13,000, with a navy of 200. In October 1999 the UN Security Council adopted a resolution establishing the UN Mission in Sierra Leone (UNAMSIL), which was to supervise the implementation of a peace agreement between the Government and rebel forces, signed in July of that year. Following the completion of disarmament in January 2002, a new army, restructured with British military assistance, was established. In September 2004 UNAMSIL transferred primary responsibility for security to the armed forces but retained its own rapid intervention capacity. Some 100 British troops remained in the country to support peace-keeping operations and to continue reorganization of the Sierra Leone armed forces. The mandate of UNAMSIL (which had been reduced from nearly its maximum authorized strength of 17,500 to about 3,400) ended at the end of 2005. Following a UN Security Council resolution in August, the United Nations Integrated Office in Sierra Leone (UNIOSIL) was established in the capital, Freetown, on 1 January 2006, for an initial period of one year. UNIOSIL, which had a mandate to support state institutions and strengthen security in the country, numbered 274 local and international staff, and 24 UN volunteers in September.

Defence Expenditure: Estimated at Le 75,000m. in 2005.

Commander-in-Chief of the Armed Forces: Pres. Alhaji AHMED TEJAN KABBAH.

Chief of Staff of the Armed Forces: Maj.-Gen. SAM MBOMA.

Education

Primary education begins at five years of age and lasts for seven years. Secondary education, beginning at the age of 12, also lasts for a further seven years, comprising a first cycle of five years and a second cycle of two years. In 1987 tuition fees for government-funded primary and secondary schools were abolished. In 2000/01 primary enrolment was equivalent to 92.8% of children in the relevant age-group (males 106.0%; females 79.8%), while about 26.5% of children of the relevant age-group were enrolled at secondary secondary schools (males 29.0%; females 24.0%). In 2003/04 85% of the total school-age population was enrolled at primary and secondary schools. There is one university, which comprises six colleges. A total of 8,795 students were enrolled in tertiary education in 2000/01. At the end of 2001 school enrolment continued to be affected by the large displacement of civilians and the destruction of school facilities. Budgetary expenditure on education by the central Government in 2001 was estimated at Le 30,700m., increasing to a projected Le 36,400m. in 2002.

Bibliography

Allie, Joe. *A New History of Sierra Leone.* London, Macmillan, 1990.

Ashby, P. *Against All Odds: Escape from Sierra Leone.* London, St Martin's Press, 2004.

Bergner, D. *In the Land of Magic Soldiers: a Story of White and Black in West Africa.* New York, NY, Farrar Straus & Giroux, 2003.

Bundu, A., and Karefa-Smart, J. *Democracy by Force? A Study of International Military Intervention in the Conflict in Sierra Leone from 1991–2000.* Parkland, FL, Universal Publishers, 2001.

Campbell, G. *Blood Diamonds: Tracing the Deadly Path of the World's Most Precious Stones.* Boulder, CO, Westview Press, 2003.

Conteh-Morgan, E., and Dixon-Fyle, M. *Sierra Leone at the End of the Twentieth Century: History, Politics and Society.* Berne, Peter Lang, 1999.

Cox, T. S. *Civil-Military Relations in Sierra Leone: A Case Study of African Soldiers in Politics.* Bridgewater, NJ, Replica Books, 2001.

Cruise O'Brien, D. B., Dunn, J., and Rathbone, R. (Eds). *Contemporary West African States.* Cambridge, Cambridge University Press, 1989.

Daramy, S. B. *Constitutional Developments in the Post-Colonial State of Sierra-Leone 1961–1984.* Lewiston, NY, Edwin Mallen, 1993.

Fashole Luke, D. *Labour and Parastatal Politics in Sierra Leone: A Study in African Working-class Ambivalence.* Lanham, MD, University Press of America, 1984.

Ferme, M. C. *The Underneath of Things: Violence, History, and the Everyday in Sierra Leone.* Berkeley, CA, University of California Press, 2001.

Francis, D. J. *The Politics of Economic Regionalism: Sierra Leone in ECOWAS (The International Political Economy of New Regionalisms).* Burlington, VT, Ashgate Publishing Co, 2002.

Fyle, C. M. *The History of Sierra Leone: A Concise Introduction.* London, 1981.

(Ed.) *The State and Provision of Social Services in Sierra Leone Since Independence.* Dakar, CODESRIA, 1993.

Greenhalgh, P. *West African Diamonds: An Economic History 1919–83.* Manchester, Manchester University Press, 1985.

Hayward, M. F. *Elections in Independent Africa.* Boulder, CO, Westview Press, 1987.

Hinton, S. S. *University Student Protests and Political Change in Sierra Leone (Studies in African Education, 4).* Lewiston, NY, Edwin Mellen Press, 2002.

Hirsch, J. L. *Sierra Leone: Diamonds and the Struggle for Democracy (International Peace Academy Occasional Paper Series).* Boulder, CO, Lynne Rienner Publishers, 2001.

Kamarah, U. I. *Sustainable Rural Development: Semantics or Substance? The Study of Rural Projects in North Western Sierra Leone (1985–1995).* Lanham, MD, University Press of America, 2001.

Karamoh, K. *A Mother's Saga: An Account of the Rebel War in Sierra Leone.* New South Wales, Universal Publishers, 2003.

Kargbo, M. *British Foreign Policy And the Conflict in Sierra Leone, 1991-2001.* Oxford, Peter Lang, 2006.

Keen, D. *Conflict and Collusion in Sierra Leone.* New York, Palgrave Macmillan, 2005.

Koroma, A. K. *Sierra Leone: Agony of a Nation.* Freetown, Afro Media, 1996.

Land, J. *Blood Diamonds.* New York, Tor Books, 2002.

Luke, D. F., and Riley, S. P. *Economic Decline and the New Reform Agenda in Africa: The Case of Sierra Leone.* Manchester, Manchester University Press, 1991.

Makannah, T. J. (Ed.). *Handbook of the Population of Sierra Leone.* Freetown, Toma Enterprises, 1996.

Megill, E. L. *Sierra Leone Remembered.*Bloomington, IN, Authorhouse, 2004.

Osagie, I. F., and L. F. *The Amistead Revolt: Memory, Slavery and the Politics of Identity in the United States and Sierra Leone.* Athens, GA, University of Georgia Press, 2003.

Paracka, D. J. *The Athens of West Africa: a History of International Education at Fourah Bay College, Sierra Leone (African Studies).* London, Routledge, 2003.

Reno, W. *Corruption and State Politics in Sierra Leone.*Cambridge, Cambridge University Press, 1995.

Richards, P. *Fighting for the Rain Forest: War, Youth and Resources in Sierra Leone.* Oxford, James Currey, 1996.

Rimmer, D. *The Economies of West Africa.* London, Weidenfeld and Nicolson, 1984.

Shaw, R. *Memories of the Slave Trade: Ritual and the Historical Imagination in Sierra Leone.* Chicago, IL, University of Chicago Press, 2002.

Stevens, S. *What Life Has Taught Me.* London, Kensal Press, 1984.

Thomas, A. C. *The Population of Sierra Leone: An Analysis of Population Data.* Freetown, Fourah Bay College, 1983.

Thompson, B. *The Constitutional History and Law of Sierra Leone, 1961–1995.* Lanham, MD, University Press of America, 1997.

Turay, E. D. A., and Abraham, A. *The Sierra Leone Army: A Century of History.* London, Macmillan, 1988.

United Nations Institute for Disarmament Research. Weeks, J. *Development Strategy and the Economy of Sierra Leone.* New York, St Martin's Press, 1992.

Bound to Cooperate: Conflict, Peace and People in Sierra Leone. New York, NY, United Nations Publications, 2001.

Voeten, T. *How de Body? One Man's Terrifying Journey Through an African War.* New York, NY, Thomas Dunne Books, 2002.

Wyse, A. *The Krio of Sierra Leone: An Interpretive History.* London, Hurst, 1989.

H. C. Bankole-Bright and Politics in Colonial Sierra Leone, 1919–1958. Cambridge, Cambridge University Press, 2003.

Zack-Williams, A. *Tributors, Supporters and Merchant Capital: Mining and Underdevelopment in Sierra Leone.* Aldershot, Avebury, 1995.

SOMALIA

Physical and Social Geography

I. M. LEWIS

The Somali Democratic Republic covers an area of 637,657 sq km (246,201 sq miles). It has a long coastline on the Indian Ocean and the Gulf of Aden, forming the 'Horn of Africa'. To the north, Somalia faces the Arabian peninsula, with which it has had centuries of commercial and cultural contact. To the north-west, it is bounded by the Republic of Djibouti, while its western and southern neighbours are Ethiopia and Kenya. The country takes its name from its population, the Somali, a Muslim Cushitic-speaking people who stretch into these neighbouring states.

Most of the terrain consists of dry savannah plains, with a high mountain escarpment in the north, facing the coast. The climate is hot and dry, with an average annual temperature of 27°C, although temperate at higher altitudes and along the coast during June–September, with annual rainfall rarely exceeding 500 mm in the most favourable regions. Only two permanent rivers—the Juba and Shebelle—water this arid land. Both rise in the Ethiopian highlands, but only the Juba regularly flows into the sea. The territory between these two rivers is agriculturally the richest part of Somalia, and constitutes a zone of mixed cultivation and pastoralism. Sorghum, millet and maize are grown here, while along the rivers, on irrigated plantations, bananas (the mainstay of Somalia's exports) and citrus fruits are produced. This potentially prosperous zone contains remnants of Bantu groups—partly of ex-slave origin—and is also the home of the Digil and Rahanwin, who speak a distinctive dialect and are the least nomadic element in the population. Of the other Somali clans—the Dir, Isaaq, Hawiye and Darod, primarily pastoral nomads who occupy the rest of the country—the Hawiye along the Shebelle valley are the most extensively engaged in cultivation. A small subsidiary area of cultivation (involving Dir and Isaaq) also occurs in the north-west highlands.

In this predominantly pastoral country, permanent settlements are small and widely scattered, except in the agricultural regions, and for the most part are tiny trading centres built around wells. There are few large towns. Mogadishu, the capital, which dates from at least the 10th century as an Islamic trading post, had an estimated population of 1,219,000 in 2000. The other main centres are Kismayu (population 70,000 in 1981) and Berbera (65,000 in 1981), the main southern and northern ports, respectively. The northern town of Hargeysa (population 70,000 in 1981) was declared the capital of the secessionist 'Republic of Somaliland' in 1991.

According to the census of 1975, the population of Somalia was 3,253,024 (excluding adjustment for underenumeration). The 1986 census recorded a total of 7,114,431. According to UN estimates, the mid-year population in 2006 was 8,445,000, giving a density of 13.2 inhabitants per sq km. Important demographic changes took place from the later decades of the 20th century, beginning with the serious drought that affected the north of the country in 1974–75 and led to the resettlement of large numbers of people in the south. During 1980–88 successive influxes of refugees from Ethiopia created a serious refugee problem before repatriations began in 1990. Of greatest consequence, however, has been the dislocation of Somalia's population during the civil unrest that has raged since the late 1980s. In early 1993 it was estimated that three-quarters of the population had been internally displaced by civil conflict; by late 2006 there were an estimated 400,000 internally displaced Somalis. More than 460,000 refugees from Somalia were resident outside the country at the end of 2006, including an estimated 173,702 in Kenya, 91,587 in Yemen, 72,546 in the USA, 34,138 in the United Kingdom and 16,576 in Ethiopia.

Recent History

WALTER S. CLARKE

Of those who live in the largely desertic lowlands of the Horn of Africa, the Somalis maintain a notable independence of spirit and resilience in the face of multiple natural and man-made adversities. Many of them will soon have lived for 17 years without a central governmental authority. Somali history, culture and external events may have been influential in preventing Somalia from forging national political unity. These same factors are also relevant to understanding how Somalis cope with chronic state and societal failure.

COLONIALISM IN THE HORN OF AFRICA

The peopling of the Horn of Africa provides a fascinating story in which Somalis have played a number of critical roles. Their historical tradition centres on their lives as nomads with intimate knowledge of water sources and trade routes to and from the Abyssinian highlands and the Arab and Persian coastal settlements. Like nomads everywhere Somalis are rugged individualists who defend to the best of their abilities their rights to move their families and flocks safely subject to predictable patterns of nature. Islam appeared early in the Horn of Africa, and Somalis adopted Sunni Islam, strongly influenced by the spiritual beliefs of *Sufism*.

Mogadishu became a significant Indian Ocean *entrepôt*. The famous Muslim traveller, Ibn Batuta, reported that the Sultan of Mogadishu was native to the region and that he spoke both Arabic and the local language with equal fluency. Over the centuries, the ebb and flow of Somali clan groups around the Horn of Africa has been affected by external forces, including the depredations by Portuguese marauders during the 16th and early 17th centuries. They looted and burned various coastal cities including Berbera, Zeila, Mogadishu, Merca and Brava. After the defeat of the Portuguese at Fort Jesus in Mombasa harbour in 1728 by Swahili and Omani forces, the Banaadir coast came under Omani suzerainty. Although there were a number of Somali sheikhs and sultans along the coast and rivers whose influence rose and fell with time, there was never an undisputed Somali ruler who could claim dominion over the majority of Somalis.

Not all Somalis share the nomadic tradition. In the relatively fertile valleys between the Juba and Shebelle rivers, significant numbers of African Bantu farmers and grazers work the fickle fields of central and southern Somalia. In years of drought, they starve; in good rain years, they prosper, but they are obliged to defend their communities from the depredations of mounted bandits. They usually ally themselves with nomadic groups, and are obliged to surrender a portion of their crops in return for protection.

The world of the Somalis and the Horn of Africa was the subject of renewed interest to European powers after the

United Kingdom established its foothold in Aden, Yemen, in 1839. Aden originally proved useful as an anti-piracy base and observation point in the Middle East, but it became a strategic point after the opening of the Suez canal in 1869. In 1886 the United Kingdom gained control over the northern coast of the Horn of Africa by offering protection to various chiefs. The area became known as British Somaliland and was vital for safe-guarding trade routes to the East and as a reliable source of provisions for the military garrison and growing commercial activities in Aden. In Somaliland the British encountered serious resistance from a religious scholar, Sayyid Mohammed Abdullah Hassan, who inspired Dulbahante militancy and active rebellion between 1899 and 1920. The long military campaign against the 'Mad Mullah', as he was called by the British colonial forces, involved the first use of aircraft in an African war. Abdullah Hassan was never caught before he died of natural causes in 1920.

The French Consul in Aden negotiated a treaty of protection with the local chief in 1859, providing for anchorage in the Gulf of Tadjoura near the town of Obock. In 1862 a representative of the Sultan of Tadjoura made an official visit to Paris to sign a treaty ceding Obock and a portion of the northern coast of the Gulf of Tadjoura to France. The French established their first presence at Obock in 1884, when they needed a coaling station after the United Kingdom expressed its displeasure with French activities in what was soon to become Indo-China by closing facilities in Aden to French naval vessels. These first treaties were made with leaders of the Afar ethnic group, which extends far into Ethiopia and present-day Eritrea. After the French established the colonial capital in present-day Djibouti town in 1894, work soon began on building a railway linking it to Addis Ababa, Ethiopia, and there came a substantial influx of Somalis to French Somaliland, which became the northern-most extension of the Somali sphere.

After only concluding its own unification in 1870, Italy was late in establishing colonies in Africa. In 1885 the Italian state looked to East Africa and negotiated agreements with the Sultan of Zanzibar, giving it certain commercial advantages in the region. Additional treaties were concluded with the sultans of Obbia and Caluula in 1889, placing them under Italian protection. In succeeding years Italy agreed the remaining frontiers for its colonies in negotiations with the Governments of Ethiopia and the United Kingdom.

North-west Kenya has a large population of Somalis and, historically, this population and the British colonial authorities had many disagreements during the colonial period. Kismayu and the lower coast of Somalia were administered by British East African authorities until 1926, when it was handed over to Italian Somaliland.

Although the colonial period for the British, French and Italian Somalilands was not as long as for many other African states that joined the revolution of African independence that began with freedom in Ghana in 1957, the Somalis in the three colonial dependencies none the less experienced very different colonial styles and traditions which left their marks on Somali politics after independence.

INDEPENDENCE AND PAN-SOMALISM

On 26 June 1960 British Somaliland became the first Somali dependency to be accorded independence. The Italian UN Trust Territory of Somalia received its independence on 1 July and, as the result of earlier agreements with Somaliland leaders, joined with the former British Somaliland that same day to form the Somali Republic. The Italians had held the Trust Territory's first election in March 1959, in which the Somali Youth League (SYL) took 83 of the 90 seats in the Legislative Assembly. The former British Somaliland had experienced largely decentralized governance; the former Italian trusteeship had seen more direct rule with policies aimed at diminishing the roles of clan chiefs and religious leaders. The two new partners decided that the Presidency would be held by a figure from the former Italian side; the premiership would be the responsibility of a Somali from the former British territory. A coalition was built between the SYL and the two leading northern parties after independence. The early years of the new Somali Republic were not easy. The original coalition developed many cleavages and the SYL split into competing factions.

National elections were held in 1967 in which Dr Abd ar-Rashid Ali Shermarke was elected President and Mohamed Ibrahim Egal, a highly respected politician from Somaliland, was named Prime Minister. The National Assembly became highly fractured as clan-based factions formed; confidence in the Government was waning. Following indecisive legislative elections in 1969, Shermarke was assassinated.

SIAD BARRE AND SOCIALIST REALISM

After the death of Shermarke it appeared that a replacement closely allied to Egal might become President. Justifying its action as an effort to prevent chaos, the military assumed control of the Government and a Supreme Revolutionary Council (SRC) was formed. The country was renamed the Somali Democratic Republic. The President of the SRC, a former national police chief, Maj.-Gen. Mohammed Siad Barre, became Head of State.

Siad Barre perceived himself as a revolutionary and sought a close relationship with the Soviet Union. The Soviet Union embraced its new client and provided military training and equipment for the Somali Army. A single national party, the Somali Revolutionary Socialist Party, was invested with the role of fostering 'socialist realism'. Drought, mismanagement and corruption caused Siad Barre's plans for a wide-scale transformation of Somali society to falter. To inspire the dispirited Somali people, Siad Barre promoted one of Somalia's most persistent dreams, the notion of uniting all Somali peoples under the same flag. Pan-Somalism implied the liberation of Somalis in Kenya, Ethiopia and Djibouti to join the Somali Democratic Republic.

The ill-health of the aged Emperor Haile Selassie and rising opposition to his arbitrary rule encouraged Siad Barre to imagine that it was the right time to bring the Somali populations of the Ethiopian Ogaden under his protection. In 1976 he restructured the Western Somali Liberation Front (WSLF) to prepare it for insurgency operations in the Ogaden. As Siad Barre prepared for war—efforts that did not escape the attention of Soviet military advisers attached to his army—the Soviet Union attempted to mediate between Siad Barre and Lt-Col Mengistu Haile Mariam, one of the leaders in the movement to oust the Ethiopian Emperor. The Soviet efforts were summarily rejected by Siad Barre, and the Soviets removed their military advisers (many of whom went directly to Ethiopia) and ended their military supply relationship with Somalia. Sensing an opportunity, the USA reactivated an earlier military agreement and provided some support to the Somalis. The WSLF initiated guerrilla actions in the Ogaden in May 1977. The first attacks of the WSLF were to blow up three bridges on the rail line connecting Djibouti to Dire Dawa in the Ogaden and to Addis Ababa. Somali regular forces entered the Ogaden in support of the WSLF in July and advanced quickly to the foothills of the Ethiopian plateau in the vicinity of Harar. The Soviet Union used its vast logistical resources to bring in Cuban military forces (from Angola) and supplies, and more advisers, stopping the Somali advance in January 1978. Exhausted, demoralized and ill-supplied, Somali forces returned to Somalia and in March the Ethiopians claimed total victory over the invaders.

DETERIORATION OF THE SOMALI STATE

The abject defeat of Somali forces in the Ogaden ignited opposition to Siad Barre throughout the country. The peoples of the former British Somaliland were deeply resentful of the costly human and financial losses brought about by the war. Opposition groups formed, including the Somali Salvation Democratic Front (SSDF), a Mijertein-based group, and the Somali National Movement (SNM), rooted in the Isaaq sub-clan, developed with Ethiopian support, in Somaliland. The SSDF captured two border towns in 1981 but did not have much success afterward. Siad Barre made peace with Mengistu in 1988 by restoring diplomatic relations, and the SNM was ordered to vacate its Ogaden bases. The SNM subsequently captured Burao and occupied a part of Hargeysa, the regional capital. Siad Barre ordered his former son-in-law, Gen. Mohamed Siad 'Morgan' to make an example of the northern dissidents. Using South African mercenary pilots and heavy artillery to bombard the city, Morgan's forces systematically killed and raped the Somali population of the city and then mined the ruins. An estimated 40,000 Somalis were killed by their own Government in this operation and some 400,000 refugees fled to Ethiopia.

As Siad Barre's rule became more onerous, his range of advisers grew smaller and the corruption of his family became more apparent. He made several attempts to make his Government more palatable to the people. In 1979 he introduced a new Constitution with an elected National Assembly, all chosen from within a single party. This experiment was abandoned in 1984, and all powers were returned to the presidency. In 1987 Siad Barre reluctantly permitted the creation of a Prime Minister position, to be held by Gen. Mohamed Ali Samater, a former Vice-President and Minister of Defence. In August 1989, with his regime under pressure from nearly all clans except his own Marehan, Siad Barre announced that opposition parties would be permitted. This experiment had a brief existence and in January 1990 the President dismissed the Government, bitterly criticizing Samater.

While the President desperately searched for a formula to assuage the forces gathering to overthrow his inept rule, the opposition was growing in strength. Siad Barre's military experienced a few minor victories over the SNM in the north, but more significantly, the Hawiye, Somalia's largest clan group, was preparing for major operations. Hawiye forces initiated large-scale attacks on government installations and military facilities in and around Mogadishu in November 1990. Gen. Mohamed Farah Aidid, who had been imprisoned early in the Siad Barre presidency and subsequently released and appointed Ambassador to India, gathered troops while marching south from Galkayo. He advanced steadily on Siad Barre's positions in Mogadishu. Unable to stand up to Aidid's United Somali Force (USF) and Hawiye forces and abandoned by all but his family, Siad Barre left Mogadishu on 26 January 1991, fleeing south with his family and the remnants of his army. The former President made an abortive attempt to recapture Mogadishu in mid-1991 but was pushed back over the Kenyan border. Having failed to obtain political asylum in Kenya, Siad Barre moved on to Nigeria where he died in January 1995.

The people of Somalia gained little from the fall of Siad Barre. The administration of the country had largely evaporated and the exultant victors of the battles of Mogadishu and elsewhere had little governmental experience. The business community in Mogadishu feared Aidid; many of them joined in establishing the 'manifesto group' within the United Somali Congress (USC). In January 1991 this group selected Ali Mahdi Mohamed, a well-respected Hawiye Abgal businessman and former government minister, as the new leader of Somalia. Aidid could not accept this action and in February his followers in the USC elected Omar Arteh Ghalib, an Isaaq, as head of Somalia.

Bitter fighting broke out between sub-clan militia groups as Ali Mahdi's Hawiye Abgal fighters confronted Aidid's Hawiye Habr Gidr forces. The city was soon separated by a rubble-filled 'green line' demarcating the largely north–south sub-clan ethnic boundaries of shattered Mogadishu. In the 1991–92 civil war that consumed most of Mogadishu it was estimated that some 35,000 civilians were killed and many more thousands displaced. In southern Somalia fighting broke out between sub-clan groups vying for control of the strategic city of Kismayu.

In March 1992 the UN Security Council supported an effort to achieve a cease-fire in Somalia and in April it authorized a very limited observation operation under the title UN Operation in Somalia (UNOSOM). The Secretary-General sent his personal representative, Muhammad Sahnoun, a well-respected Algerian diplomat, to Mogadishu in May to work with the faction leaders to achieve a cease-fire. Aidid by that time was the master of southern Mogadishu with control of the airport. He was firmly opposed to any international mandates to intervene in Somali affairs and restricted UN peace-keepers' access to the airport.

Aidid sent troops to Kismayu where they sided with the Somali Patriotic Movement (SPM) faction, led by Omar Jess. In May 1992 the combined Aidid-Jess force prevailed over a mixed force of local clans and a USC faction group affiliated with Ali Mahdi. In October Marehan militia head Gen. Morgan and Somali National Force (SNF) commander Gen. Ahmed Warsame regained control of Kismayu.

Continued battles in Mogadishu and in the south, combined with the policies of Aidid and other warlords to prevent the distribution of food and medicine to the region known as the 'triangle of death', bordered by Merca, south of Mogadishu, Baidoa and Kismayu, led to hundreds of thousands of deaths between mid-1991 and late 1992. Persons displaced by Aidid's takeover of southern Mogadishu were mostly government officials and businessmen associated with the Siad Barre regime. For Aidid, who had used the seized properties as rewards to his commanders, there was no question of permitting the displaced Marehan to return to Mogadishu to regain their properties, and starvation kept them in place.

FIRST INTERNATIONAL INTERVENTION

In August 1992 US President George Bush authorized a humanitarian operation to fly food from Mombasa, Kenya, to airports in Somalia. In an arrangement with the US Government, a US-led UN peace-keeping operation was authorized to enter Somalia to relieve the starvation situation and restore order. The first US troops of the Unified Task Force (UNITAF) landed at Mogadishu in early December as part of 'Operation Restore Hope'. More than 20 nations contributed troops to UNITAF and by 28 December, one month ahead of schedule, UNITAF controlled Mogadishu and had completed the various national deployments to the famine zone. The warehouses in Mogadishu and routes to the interior were reopened and food flows were quickly restored. Aidid was displeased with these developments but the incoming forces attempted to establish working relationships with him and most of the other warlords.

UNITAF facilitated two reconciliation conferences (in January and March 1993, both in Addis Ababa) during its five-month deployment in Somalia. There was little time to prepare the Somali political terrain for these hurried meetings, a problem that was exacerbated when Aidid obtained virtual veto power over the attendance lists. UNITAF imposed the issuance of invitations to the conferences to a large contingent of Somali women and civil society. These convocations were very expensive and neither conference produced anything of significance other than the benefit of temporary cease-fires.

UNITAF handed over the operation to a UN-led peace-keeping force headed by Gen. Çevik Bir of Turkey on 4 May 2003. Although 30 countries contributed to UNOSOM II, the UN force was about one-half of the size of UNITAF at its peak (approximately 30,000 at the end of January). Aidid was upset at the open-ended international operation and in June, having been advised of a UN inspection of a weapons site at the former national radio station under his control, he launched an ambush of the Pakistani military unit that was to undertake the inspection. There was also a simultaneous ambush of a lightly-armed Pakistani food distribution detail. In these confrontations the Pakistanis lost 24 men and dozens more were wounded. The following day the UN Security Council held an emergency session in New York, USA, to condemn the attack and to call for punishment of the perpetrators. There was little doubt regarding responsibility for this unprovoked attack and UNOSOM II launched a number of unsuccessful operations to find Aidid. In a US-led helicopter operation on 4 October to capture Aidid's followers meeting at the Olympic Hotel in Mogadishu, two helicopters were shot down and 18 US military personnel were killed. Lacking heavily armoured vehicles, the US response force took several hours to bring relief to the survivors of the helicopter crashes and to recover the dead. Under heavy pressure from the US Congress, President Bill Clinton decided to withdraw US forces from Somalia and the US element of the operation ended in March 1994. UNOSOM II concluded its operations in February 1995 when its remaining troops were removed under the protection of a combined US-Italian task force.

RETURN TO ANARCHY

With the departure of the international force, the Somali clans and sub-clans recommenced their internal rivalries. Aidid's Somali National Alliance (SNA) began to dissipate as Aidid attempted to make leadership changes. In a meeting convened in mid-June 1995 Aidid convoked 15 affiliated faction heads to a 'reconciliation' conference in which he was elected President. To placate the usual stresses that were generated when a leadership change occurred, Aidid named five Vice-Presidents. The results of this meeting were immediately rejected by Ali Mahdi and Aidid's former ally, Osman Hassan Ali 'Ato'.

Sporadic gunfights between members of the two groups followed during May and August 1996. On 1 August, while participating in a battle with rival forces in Mogadishu's suburbs, Aidid was reportedly shot through the liver. He died the following day. His son, Hussein Mohamed Aidid, who had been raised in California and was a US Marine Corps reservist, was elected leader of the SNA and factional fighting continued.

The SNA was not invited to a reconciliation conference held in Sodere, Ethiopia, in December 1996. A total of 26 Somali factions accepted invitations from the Intergovernmental Authority on Development (IGAD) and the Ethiopian Government to attend the conference, which created a National Salvation Council (NSC) of 41 members representing all Somali clan groups. Hussein Aidid condemned the NSC, claiming that he was the legitimate President of Somalia.

NATIONAL RECONCILIATION

From the time of the collapse of the Siad Barre regime in 1991 until March 1998, 12 national conferences were convened, sponsored variously by the UN, the US, Ethiopia and Egypt. In March 1998 IGAD proposed another reconciliation meeting and Ismael Omar Gelleh, the President of Djibouti, saw this as an opportunity to make an impact on the region. Believing that the power of the warlords needed to be diluted if there was to be any chance of success, he invited 1,500 Somalis from all branches of society to attend a national reconciliation conference in the town of Arta, west of Djibouti town. Representatives from the self-declared regions of 'Somaliland' and 'Puntland' (see below) refused to attend. Gelleh's plan was to have the delegates elect a new national legislature that would be established in Mogadishu. The legislature would then elect a President who would appoint a Prime Minister. The Arta discussions opened on 2 May 2000. It took several weeks for the delegations to agree on an electoral formula: each of the four major clan families (Darod, Dir, Rahanwin and Hawiye) would be allotted 24 seats in a Transitional National Assembly (TNA) and an equal number would be made available to the smaller clan groups. An additional 25 seats would be reserved for women, with each of the five previous groups empowered to select five women to hold a seat in the TNA. To overcome the impasse in the negotiations after long discussions of the manner of allocation of legislative seats between clans and sub-clans, the delegations requested that President Gelleh intervene. He was asked to apportion an additional 20 seats, thereby raising the number of legislators to 245. This last-minute effort to assuage the ambitions of representatives of smaller clan and sub-clan groups was successful.

The TNA met for the first time on 13 August 2000 with 166 delegates present. In a subsequent session Abdallah Deerow Isa, formerly director of the political wing of the Rahanwin Resistance Army (RRA), was elected Speaker. On 26 August Abdulkasim Salad Hasan, a Hawaye who had held several ministerial positions in the Siad Barre regime, was elected interim President of Somalia by the TNA with 145 of 245 votes. His principal opponent was Abdullah Ahmed Adow, a former Ambassador to the US, who received 92 votes. Attending the ceremonies were the Heads of Government of Eritrea, Ethiopia, Sudan, Yemen and Djibouti. Representatives of the UN, the European Union (EU), the Arab League, the Organization of African Unity (OAU, later the African Union—AU), France, Italy, Kuwait and Libya were also present. President Abdulkasim flew to Mogadishu on 30 August, where he was reportedly met by a welcoming crowd of 100,000 Somalis. After wide-ranging consultations with clan leaders, on 8 October the new President appointed Ali Khalif Galaydh, a Dulbuhante from Burao in 'Somaliland', as Prime Minister. Later that month Galaydh announced the composition of a 32-member Transitional National Government (TNG).

Despite early euphoria over the formation of the new Government, the TNG very quickly became unpopular. Many of its members were recognizable as former members of the Siad Barre regime; its actions were interpreted by many Somalis as those of just another armed faction. After a group of 100 legislators flew into Mogadishu in early October 2000 to mark a positive step towards creation of a central government, they came under heavy gunfire as their bus approached their hotel. One gunman was killed but none of the new representatives was hurt. A Mogadishu newspaper lamented that the senior leadership of the TNG constituted the 'very faction leaders who plunged the country into anarchy for the past 10 years'. Hussein Aidid quickly declared himself opposed to the TNG and the Transitional National Charter (TNC) and objected specifically to the requirement in the TNC that the President must be at least 40 years of age; at the time, he was 38.

In late February 2001 Hussein Aidid and several other disgruntled faction leaders met in Addis Ababa and formed the Somali Reconciliation and Restoration Council (SRRC). Other SRRC leaders included Abdulhi Sheikh Ismail (Southern Somali National Movement), Hassan Mohamed Nur (RRA), Aden Abdulahi Nur (Somali Patriotic Movement), and Hilowle Iman Omer (United Somali Congress-Mogadishu North faction). To demonstrate its opposition to the TNG, the SRRC, under the leadership of Aidid, called on all Somali political parties, clan and religious leaders, civil society and the business community to join in an all-inclusive conference in order to establish a legitimate representative government of national unity.

The security situation in Somalia continued to deteriorate at an alarming rate, with various international aid workers kidnapped (although they were usually released within a few days) and gun fights in various cities and towns along the border. The SRRC held a general meeting in Baidoa in mid-April 2001. The delegations roundly criticized the Arta Group for its inability to restore stability and delegates asked the Governments of Egypt and Saudi Arabia to end their support of the Arta Group, which they accused of attempting to reignite the civil war. Also at the meeting Aidid accused Yemen, Saudi Arabia, Libya and Sudan of providing arms to the TNG, charges which were promptly denied.

The main task confronting the TNG in mid-2001 was to begin building something resembling an administration. In early June the Government introduced the collection of taxes in Mogadishu. Senior members of the SRRC protested, claiming that the taxes were illegal. The TNG also took measures to boost the value of the Somali shilling. Members of the TNG and legislators fanned out across the country to prepare for the establishment of regional administrations and President Abdulkasim announced that he was willing to meet dissident faction leaders on their terms. Many local businessmen were very reluctant to turn in their weapons, uncertain about the ability of the Government to provide security. Newly recruited police officers began to take up the administration of law at the local level. At the end of June the police began to demolish illegal structures such as sheds and shops that had been built on public thoroughfares in the years without government. The TNG arranged a public ceremony on 1 July marking the anniversary of the country's independence, the first such ceremony in a decade. A few days later the President and a substantial delegation departed for Lusaka, Zambia to attend an OAU summit, the first Somali delegation at the OAU since the Siad Barre Government dissolved in January 1991.

By mid-2001 reports were coming in from the countryside of fierce fighting as various sub-clans attempted to extend their areas of control. Heavy fighting broke out in Mogadishu on 12 July 2001 between militia groups affiliated with Hussein Aidid, Osman 'Ato' and militias loyal to the TNG. It later became apparent that much of the fighting was between Habr Gedir sub-clans. National reconciliation was not working at most levels, and on 25 July the highly respected Chairman of the TNG Reconciliation Committee, Abdirazzaq Haji Husayn, resigned. He accused Prime Minister Galaydh of failing to support the committee's work since its inception on 6 May. By the end of September it was clear that the TNG had failed in its effort to create a central administration for the country and was unable to maintain cohesion within the new institutions. The Prime Minister admitted that there were important differences between him and President Abdulkasim and with the TNA.

In mid-September 2001 the EU advised its non-governmental agencies to withdraw their staff temporarily from Somalia. On 24 September the UN evacuated all international staff from Somalia after its war risk insurance was withdrawn because of anticipated claims arising from the 11 September al-Qa'ida attacks on New York and Washington, DC. Only 45 international staff were affected, including those in 'Somaliland'. The TNG announced that it had no ties with terrorism, and on 2 October, it set up an anti-terrorism task force.

Somalia's TNA began debating a motion of 'no confidence' in the TNG in mid-October 2001. The major issue concerned the inability or unwillingness of the Prime Minister and his Government to promote national reconciliation. The motion also noted that in one year, the TNG had failed to constitute a single regional administration. The Prime Minister was also accused of corruption in handing out 1,600 mobile cellular telephones to friends and political colleagues which resulted in a cost to the treasury of US $700,000. After one week of debate in the Assembly, the Government lost the vote of 'no confidence' by 141 votes to 29. The Government would remain in place until President Abdulkasim nominated a new Prime Minister. According to the TNC, the President had 30 days to present a new name to the Assembly.

After the fall of the Somali Government, Kenyan President Daniel arap Moi invited the Somali President and representatives of the opposition SRRC to Nairobi, Kenya, to discuss the future course of the reconciliation process. Moi lectured his guests on the need to lay down their guns and dedicate themselves to achieving reconciliation. On 5 November 2001 the four-day talks ended and the two Somali delegations pronounced them a success. To show his satisfaction with the talks, President Moi announced that the Kenya–Somali border would be reopened immediately. No date was given for further discussions between the Somali groups, but the final statement of the meeting outlined the agenda for the next meeting, which was to cover the implementation of all previous resolutions adopted by the OAU, the UN Security Council and IGAD. The agenda would also include clan-based power-sharing, the denouncement of violence as a means of settling political differences and co-operation with the international community on eradicating terrorism. The agenda also provided for all Somali state laws to be reviewed in accordance with the requirements of the reconciliation process. A Kenyan official from the Ministry of Foreign Affairs told a UN news representative that the agenda agreed upon in Nairobi provided the basis for further reconciliation to deepen the Arta process.

On 12 November 2001 President Abdulkasim announced his nomination for post of Prime Minister. Hassan Abshir Farah, a former military officer and hitherto Minister of Minerals and Water Resources, was a member of the Ise Mahmud sub-clan of the Mijertein, and a native of Garowe, the capital of the so-called Republic of 'Puntland' in Somalia's north-east. The Prime Minister-designate stated that national reconciliation would be his first priority and he pledged to open dialogue with regions that had administrations (referring to 'Somaliland' and 'Puntland') and declared that he would not hesitate to ask for assistance from IGAD and Somalia's immediate neighbours, Ethiopia, Djibouti and Kenya. He promised to reactivate TNG Reconciliation Committee, which had been set up in May but had been inactive since the resignation of its Chairman in July.

The new Prime Minister delayed naming a new Cabinet for several weeks. Farah hoped to advance the reconciliation process by sending a message to TNG opponents in which he stated that anyone willing to join the Government would be accommodated. Farah indicated that he would announce the new Cabinet at the opening of the reconciliation conference in Nairobi in mid-December 2001. The SRRC and the RRA both signalled that they would not attend the conference. After several days of delay reconciliation talks opened in Nairobi on 21 December. The SRRC was represented by its Secretary-General, Mawlid Ma'ane, and other faction leaders present included Hussein Aidid, representing his SNA, Umar Finish, a deputy of Muse Sudi Yalahow, leader of the United Somalia Congress—Somali Salvation Alliance, and Osman 'Ato', leader of another SRRC faction. After four days of discussions the participants announced that a peace agreement would be signed on 24 December in Nakuru, Kenya. In a joint statement the sides agreed to the establishment of an 'all-inclusive Government' to ensure an equitable distribution of power. The participants also agreed to the enlargement of the TNA and the Cabinet, and to the establishment of a permanent secretariat in Nairobi to oversee the implementation of the Somali peace process and to secure funding for it. Prime Minister Farah signed for the TNG and all the faction leaders present also signed the agreement except for Hussein Aidid who, at the last minute, declined to sign, stating in an interview with Agence France Presse that his party rejected the deal completely.

The following day fighting broke out in the Medina area of Mogadishu as Yalahow's militia attacked supporters of his former deputy, Umar Finish. Both Yalahow and Finish belonged to the same Da'ud sub-clan of the Abgal clan. Prime Minister Farah failed in his gamble to use the formation of a new Cabinet as a means of encouraging broader representation. He named a new Cabinet of 31 members in mid-February 2002 without persuading any dissidents, including those who signed the December 2001 declaration, into participation. The new Government included Dr Saynab Aways Husayn with the portfolio of women's development and family affairs, the first woman to hold a cabinet position in Somalia's history.

On 10–11 January 2002 IGAD held a summit in Khartoum, Sudan, which focused on Somalia's inability to effect national reconciliation. In the concluding act of the summit it was stated that a reconciliation conference should be convened in Nairobi within two months. The date of the proposed conference quickly changed to April. The IGAD conference agreed to set up a technical committee, again composed of representatives of the three states bordering Somalia, to prepare for the conference. Opponents of the TNG held a three-day conference in the Ethiopian town of Dire Dawa in late February to plot their strategy for the impending conference in Kenya. They declared that they would attend the IGAD-sponsored April reconciliation meeting in Nairobi.

In mid-March 2002 President Abdulkasim embarked on a tour of Somali regions, his first since being elected President in 2000. He flew directly to Dhusa Mareb, the capital of Galgudud, about 400 km north-east of Mogadishu. He was met by the Governor, other senior officials and a large crowd of supporters at the airport. Later he met with community leaders and discussed ways of establishing a functioning regional administration and emphasized the importance of local initiatives. On 14 March the President left for the Abud Waq district, about 50 km west of Dhusa Mareb.

Hoping to buoy the efforts of the regional organizations and to bring the Somali representatives together for discussions, the UN Secretary-General announced the formation of a Contact Group on Somalia (CGS) in late March 2002. The group of about 30 members would be composed of representatives of all members of the Security Council, the co-chairs of IGAD, the Partners Forum (Italy and Norway) and representatives of other organizations in which Somalia has membership; countries that had undertaken peace initiatives with Somalia and the European Union, which has also been actively engaged in the search for resolution to the Somali problem, were also represented. The CGS would have offices in New York and Nairobi. In a presidential statement from the UN Security Council on 28 March, endorsing the action by the Secretary-General, it was stated that the initiative was taken to promote the completion of the Arta peace process. The CGS held its first meeting in Nairobi on 25 July.

On 1 April the RRA, which controlled the Bay and Bakool regions, declared that it was establishing an autonomous region based in Baidoa, which would be known as the State of South-western Somalia (SSWS). The RRA central committee reportedly elected Col Hasan Muhammad Nur Shatigadud as President by acclamation. Shatigadud was already known to

Somalis as a former member of the feared National Security Service (NSS) of former dictator Siad Barre. He had been instrumental in establishing the RRA in 1995 to resist the intimidation of Muhammad Farah Aidid whose forces invaded the Bay area that year. Observers believed that the RRA took the action of establishing an autonomous state in order to raise its status at the forthcoming Nairobi talks from that of a faction to that of a functioning administration. To dispel suggestions that the declaration would undermine the SRRC, which had its main base of support in the area of the new autonomous zone, Baidoa Governor Muhammad Ali Adan Qalinle announced that the Government of the SSWS would go to Nairobi as a new state but under the SRRC umbrella. Despite these assurances, other members of the SRRC, including several high-level officials, soon condemned the decision to create the new autonomous region, claiming that it was an attempt to sabotage the Nairobi conference.

The technical committee named to prepare for the Nairobi conference met in Nairobi on 3–5 April 2002 to establish the terms of reference for the conference. These included the Declaration on Cessation of Hostilities, recognition of steps taken so far in national reconciliation, the criteria for attendance, the number of attendees and ways of monitoring the results of the conference. Sources close to the organizing group said that they expected the number of attendees to be between 100–150, including representatives of the TNG, the SRRC, signatories of the Nakuru accords and all other Somali parties 'without conditions'. These arrangements needed to be ratified by the IGAD principals before implementation.

Activity related to the Nairobi conference continued quietly as the technical committee travelled throughout Somalia, including 'Somaliland' and 'Puntland', attempting to brief all prospective attendees. 'Somaliland' officials announced after the visit of the technical team that it would not participate in the proposed conference either as delegates or observers. In mid-May 2002 President Moi appointed Elijah Mwangale, a former cabinet minister, as his special envoy to Somalia. He would be responsible for arranging a summit conference on Somalia to be held in Nairobi in mid-July. This seemingly positive development was immediately followed by the collapse of talks with the technical committee. The Djibouti participant claimed that the failure of the technical discussions was due to the inability of the members of the technical committee to present a united front. He explained that this meant that there was no clear understanding of the objectives of the proposed meeting. According to the Djibouti diplomat, the Ethiopian delegation wanted to start the discussions of Somali reconciliation with a clean slate. Djibouti believed that recent achievements should not be discarded.

With Mwangale's help, the full technical committee visited Kismayu in the south and Jowhar and Beled Weyne in central Somalia in late July 2002. The technical committee had yet to produce its report for the IGAD executive, and it appeared unlikely that the delayed national reconciliation conference would be held in September. Recent outbreaks of fighting in Mogadishu, Jowhar, Baidoa and 'Puntland' made it unlikely that the clans would be prepared to negotiate constructively.

Mogadishu continued to be the focal point of fighting between the TNG and opposition forces. During May 2002 there were many attacks by one force against another, including a full-scale attack by a militia belonging to Muhammad Dhere on the north Mogadishu home of Dahir Shaykh Dayah, the TNG Minister of Internal Affairs. His bodyguards were overwhelmed and his home was looted and destroyed. The TNG forces were gaining in strength, as well as in confidence, and observers feared that these localized attacks would expand into larger, more generalized, conflicts. In late May there was a significant gun battle in north Mogadishu between TNG forces and the militia of faction leader Yalahow, leaving 60 killed and over 100 wounded. Militia units of faction leaders Osman 'Ato' and Hussein Aidid were believed to have joined the fight on the side of Yalahow after the hostilities began. Many of the dead were civilians caught in cross-fire. This battle was reportedly the bloodiest confrontation in Mogadishu in years. The fighting in the city led to significant displacement as families attempted to flee the conflict. The office of the UN High Commission for Refugees (UNHCR) continued to warn of catastrophe if the fighting in Mogadishu and elsewhere continued.

Preparations for the national reconciliation conference continued. IGAD officials were intent on ensuring that the next attempt at engineering some form of power-sharing acceptable to the truculent warlords and militia leaders would be successful. The Nairobi reconciliation conference was originally to take place in April 2002. As the intensive preparations led to more and more delays, the starting date for the conference was put back to July and then to September. The fragility of the organizational dynamics of the process was illustrated when aides of the self-styled SSWS returned from Nairobi in early June with a special invitation to its leader from the Kenyan Government. This invitation for special discussions with the Kenyan organizers was expected to ensure that Shatigadud would attend the conference. However, at the time, he was very reluctant to leave Baidoa for fear of being replaced during his absence. In fact, Baidoa experienced continuous conflict for several weeks until 1 August, when Shatigadud announced that he had driven out the dissident forces of his former deputies, Shaykh Adan Madobe and Muhammad Ibrahim Habsade, and that he was in full control. When forces loyal to Madobe and Habsade set up camp a few miles from Baidoa, elders attempted to mediate, but they were unsuccessful and the situation in the area remained tense.

At a press conference in Mogadishu on 7 August 2002 President Abdulkasim expressed his deep disappointment at the lack of international support for the rehabilitation of Somalia. He complained of the continuing supply of arms to dissident forces. The frustrated President hoped that the forthcoming reconciliation conference would complete the Arta process and not just be another unsuccessful meeting. He implored all factions to attend the conference, and he pledged that his Government would abide by any decisions made at the conference.

THE 14TH SOMALI NATIONAL RECONCILIATION CONFERENCE

In mid-August 2002 it was announced that the IGAD-sponsored Somali national reconciliation conference would convene at Eldoret, Kenya, on 16 September. The Kenyan Minister of Foreign Affairs, Marsden Madoka, told the press that the conference was expected to last two weeks, but that depending upon its achievements it could last longer.

Complaints and reservations soon began to emerge from the usual dissident sources. Concerns were raised over the preparations for the conference: the technical team was accused of failing to inform faction leaders of the expected outcomes of the conference and 'Puntland' officials believed the conference was being rushed.

A ministerial-level meeting of IGAD was scheduled for Nairobi prior to the main conference at which the ministers responsible for foreign affairs of Djibouti, Ethiopia and Kenya would review the Somali peace process. The IGAD meeting of ministers responsible for foreign affairs was held in Nairobi in the first week of September and it was agreed that the Somali national reconciliation conference would convene on 15 October. Registration would open on 12 October for the 300 delegates then expected to attend.

The town of Baidoa changed hands on 3 October 2002 after contingents of the RRA, under the command of Shatigadud's former deputies Madobe and Habsade, entered the town. Although Shatigadud and his troops left the town with little resistance, the new leaders of Baidoa were unable to control the looting that followed. Madobe and Habsade later explained that the looting was carefully targeted and that they were in control. They soon took over Buur Hakaba, the second most important town in the area.

On 8 October 2002 IGAD sent invitations for the oft-postponed reconciliation conference to all political entities. Invitations to civil society were to be distributed the following day. However, there was a complication when the new authorities in Baidoa stated that they would not attend unless all of the RRA invitations were reserved for them. The IGAD technical committee explained that the RRA had been allocated 28 seats with one-half earmarked for Shatigadud, while the Madobe-Habsade group would receive the other half.

President Moi of Kenya opened the Somali national reconciliation conference in Eldoret on 15 October 2002 by welcoming the many delegations and expressing hope that this would be the last such conference. The UN Secretary-General's representative promised the gathered Somali leaders that if they could produce a peaceful environment, the UN would provide increased development assistance and humanitarian aid. Somali delegations in Eldoret included the TNG, representatives of 'Puntland', the SRRC, the Juba Valley Alliance (JVA) and various Mogadishu warlords including Hussein Aidid and Yalahow. Other representatives included some from civil society, women's groups and the Somali diaspora. The rules of procedure were adopted on the second day, although IGAD technical committee chairman Mwangale observed that not all groups were present. Mwangale also noted that the number of registrations on the second day of the conference totalled 450, a significant increase from the 300 invited. In a press conference on the third day of the conference Mwangale stated that the number of delegations was well beyond expectations, but he was encouraged by the numbers and believed that the conference could reach discussion of constitutional and governing structures within a month rather than the three months originally planned.

Mwangale explained the process through which this goal could be reached: in the first two weeks of the conference a committee would define the six or seven key issues. Committees to examine each issue would have 12–16 members. This would mean the number of delegates in the second stage of the conference could be reduced to between 75 and 100. He noted that 450 delegates were far too many; every head of delegation had arrived with more members than they had been allocated. It would be necessary to reason with the delegation heads to bring the number of delegates to a more manageable number. When the conference reconvened on 21 October 2002 there were reportedly over 500 delegates registered. By 23 October it was reported that considerable tension had developed between the representatives of civil society and the political leaders. The political leaders decided to hold closed meetings and civil society representatives complained that the organizers had permitted the political leaders to hijack the conference. They objected to giving the factions veto power over all decisions and stated that if the factions controlled who could participate and who could not, the conference was doomed to failure.

The conference entered its second phase on 4 November 2002. Six committees would be formed to study and draft requisite documents outlining the steps to achieve their agenda item. These included: federalism and provisional federal charter; demobilization and disarmament; land and property rights; economic institution building and resource mobilization; conflict resolution and reconciliation; and regional and international relations. Each committee would include 15 members but unfortunately, no formula had been agreed on how members of the committees would be selected. When this plan was tabled the conference immediately reached a deadlock. The technical committee and its chairman, Mwangale, began a round of individual meetings with members of the leaders' committee. At the time of the impasse over committee membership on 8 November there were more than 700 delegates registered at the conference. It was imperative to reduce the size of the delegations. Delegation leaders were not able to reduce the number of delegates, and they left it to the IGAD technical committee which reduced the number of delegates from 700 to 362. Many delegations protested at the choices that were made. Muhammad Qanyare Afrah, one of the most important faction leaders from Mogadishu, was joined by seven other faction heads in sending a letter protesting over the methodology used for the technical committee's selection. They noted that the SRRC had been allocated delegates not only as a group but also as individuals. This, they claimed, resulted in duplications, which favoured their rivals.

Representation issues continued to plague the conference. Searching for different criteria for representation, the organizers proposed a clan-based formula. On 20 November 2002 the following was suggested: each of the four major Somali clans (Hawiye, Darod, Dir and Rahanwin) would be allocated 84 seats each, with 22 seats held for discretionary seating, giving a total of 358. At that time the number of delegates present in Eldoret had risen to over 800 as each faction strove to improve its numbers before the seating matter was finally resolved. Prime Minister Farah told a news conference that although he had turned away from clan-based traditions two years previously, he was prepared to accept distribution of seats on the basis of clan membership in a new transitional Government if this was negotiated at the conference. The SRRC was also uncomfortable with the formula but it was willing to study the proposal. Hoping to proceed with the second phase of the reconciliation conference, IGAD organizers proffered a plan to reduce the number of delegates to 400. They also increased the pressure on delegates, demanding that they cease their wrangling and produce concrete results. On 26 November the organizers became more optimistic when three major clans and minority groups delivered their lists of participants in the technical committees. Each of the technical committees was to receive 30 members selected from the clan lists, with an additional 18 seats from minorities. Despite fears that it would be difficult to implement this system (many delegates assumed that if they were not on a technical committee they would not have a role in the next Government) the committee lists were accepted and the second phase of the conference could begin.

The vital second phase of the Somali reconciliation conference was initiated on 2 December 2002. As an indication of growing positivity, in a side negotiation parallel with the conference, the TNG and five Mogadishu-based factions signed a cease-fire agreement. This news was received with some scepticism in Mogadishu, where the population had seen many agreements that did not produce results.

In further negotiations with participants the delegations finally agreed to limit the number of participants in phase two to a maximum of 400. Part of the problem of representation in the conference was simple logistics; although Eldoret was an international tourist centre, the largest hotel had only 300 rooms, while costs had exceeded the initial budget. IGAD agreed to cover the costs of sending excess delegates back to Somalia providing that they registered before a fixed date. When the peace talks resumed on 6 January 2003, there were still many dozens of Somalis present in Eldoret whose names had been struck from conference rolls. The response of the hosts was direct and Kenyan police went to each hotel ordering Somalis not on the approved delegate list to leave. There were some complaints but the actions of the Kenyan authorities were supported by delegation chiefs who told their compatriots to obey the instructions.

By mid-January 2003 Mwangale was again encouraging action by the delegations with the second phase to be completed by the end of the month. Power-sharing was to be the subject of phase three and it was generally considered to present the greatest challenges to the conference. There was growing anxiety in the international community about the slow progress in Eldoret. The security situation in Somalia was worsening despite all delegations agreeing to suspend all aggressive activities when the talks opened. Fighting had again broken out in Baidoa as the contending factions of the RRA manoeuvred to gain military advantage. There were armed confrontations and attacks in Las Anod in the north-east and in the Bari, Bay, Bakoi, Gedo and lower Shebelle regions. In Mogadishu, in December 2002, there was an attack on a school bus that killed at least six schoolchildren. In addition, there was a gradual erosion within the delegations in Eldoret. Qanyare Afrah had been the first to leave, when he returned home in late November claiming frustration at the slow progress of the conference. The leader of the JVA, Col Barre Hiiraale, returned to Kismayu after the departure of Qanyare Afrah. Prominent Mogadishu faction leader Yalahow decided to return to his section of the Somali capital in mid-January. Conference organizers feared that rising tensions in Somalia and delegation heads departing from Eldoret would affect the discussions and lessen the credibility of any potential outcome of the conference.

On 18 January 2003 the Government of Kenya announced that a retired diplomat, Bethwel Kiplagat, would replace Mwangale. This was not unexpected as Mwangale had been the focus of many complaints from Somalis in the conference for his 'dictatorial' manner. Kiplagat was introduced to the conference on 22 January and promised more consultation and transparency with the delegations.

In early February 2003 the talks broke down when the available delegates in Eldoret could not constitute a quorum. Many of the organizers and foreign representatives were also absent from Eldoret. Kenyan authorities decided to move the conference from Eldoret to Nairobi. An EU-financed professional administrative and financial management team was contracted to put the conference on a more solid path.

The conference was moved to Nairobi on 17 February 2003. In recognition of the continuing dispute over seats in the conference, Kiplagat announced the creation of an arbitration committee to resolve seating issues, comprising representatives of Somalia's clans. Each clan group was to select three people such as elders and other leaders to employ traditional Somali mediation techniques to resolve the problems. Kiplagat claimed that he had been involved in mediation issues every day from morning to night, and that henceforth all such problems would be referred to the Somali arbitration committee.

In late April 2003 the Somali business community recognized the fact that the reconciliation conference could come up with recommendations that would affect their interests and requested to take part in the Nairobi proceedings. The business community stated that it supported an all-inclusive Government which it was prepared to support morally, materially and physically. Muhammad Jirde Husayn, an executive member of the Dubai-based Somali Business Council, led a 27-member team to Nairobi to demonstrate their support for a successful conference.

The technical committees continued to meet and on 15 May 2003 their results were revealed. There was no agreement on the size of the future interim Parliament although most delegates expected that all 361 of them would be included. In June several of the factional groups, including the SRRC, proposed a 450-member interim Assembly, but this was considered excessive and uneconomical by observers from prospective donor states.

On 5 July 2003 delegates to the peace talks in Nairobi signed what was hailed as an historic agreement to set up a transitional federal government. However, this was immediately followed by a series of denunciations from leaders such as TNG President Abdulkasim. His differences with Prime Minister Farah were already manifest in the conference and he soon left. Mogadishu faction leader Yalahow, who had earlier walked out of the conference, based his rejection largely on the fact that he had not been party to the process. Conference organizers imported dozens of traditional Somali elders to take part in the talks, hoping they would be useful in the selection of future parliamentarians and would lend greater credibility to the process. On 25 August the first reading of the draft national charter was concluded. It was generally well-received, but Article 19, dealing with existing administrations, was proving problematic. The delegate from 'Puntland' was particularly unhappy with the use of the term 'regional administrations', preferred by most delegates. 'Puntland' considered itself a state rather than a region.

After receiving many messages from the peace talks imploring them to return to Nairobi, the main dissenters met in Mogadishu in early September. TNG President Abdulkasim, Hiiraale of the JVA, Mogadishu leaders Yalahow and Osman 'Ato' and RRA leader Habsade attempted to salvage the conference, requesting that international constitutional experts be engaged to resolve many of the problems in the draft charter. Abdulkasim and Hiiraale, and representatives of Yalahow and Habsade subsequently returned to Nairobi.

On 15 September 2003 the delegates at the reconciliation conference adopted a Transitional Federal Charter which would lead to the establishment of a TNA with a mandate of four years. Its membership would be selected by traditional elders and politicians invited to the talks. President Abdulkasim and Yalahow's representative continued their opposition to the new charter. Their protestations were rejected by the collected delegates. The organizers announced that the conference had entered its third and last phase on 16 September.

In a press conference on 26 October 2003 Abdulkasim blamed the IGAD technical committee for what he termed 'the total breakdown' of the Nairobi conference. He claimed that the Kenyan organizers gave Ethiopia too strong a role in the running of the conference. As a result of the machinations of the organizers, he observed, the official delegates of the TNG became a minority group in the face of a dozen factions created and supported by Ethiopia.

In an effort to focus the deliberations in Nairobi, the organizers announced an enlargement of the number of international sponsors and their intention to hold a retreat in Mombasa with the leaders of the conference. Kiplagat announced that the list would consist of the 24 leaders who signed the Declaration on Cessation of Hostilities and Abdulkasim. The retreat would be opened by the IGAD President, the President of Uganda, Yoweri Kaguta Museveni. President Mwai Kibaki of Kenya and President Joaquim Chissano of Mozambique were also expected to attend. The Mombasa meeting was originally scheduled for 9 December 2003, but it was repeatedly postponed. President Museveni proposed holding a meeting of Somali leaders in Kampala prior to the Mombasa meeting. When Museveni arrived in Nairobi on 8 January 2004, he met with Somali delegation heads. Rather than continuing to Mombasa, Museveni remained in Nairobi and held the retreat there. Progress was made on a number of contentious issues: the Parliament would comprise 275 members, with 12% of seats allocated to women; they would be selected for a period of five years by the political leaders who were party to the original Declaration on Cessation of Hostilities, and politicians were officially invited to take part in the technical committees, in consultation with traditional leaders. Each of the four major clans would select 61 members and 31 positions would be allocated to the minority clans. Once formed, the Parliament would choose a President who would nominate a Prime Minister to lead a Government. The amended TNC was signed on 29 January by the TNG and the assembled political faction chiefs. One of the signatories was Asha Haji Ilmi, a civil society leader and the first Somali woman to sign a peace agreement.

The amended agreement was to enter into effect after its adoption by the plenary session in Nairobi and the TNA in Mogadishu. Agreement to the new charter was soon achieved in Nairobi and on 8 February 2004, after only three days of debate, the TNA gave its approval. At the vote 155 members of the 245-member TNA were present; of those, 136 members voted in favour, one voted against, and 18 members abstained. The positive vote of the TNA was echoed by 60 elders representing all Hawiye sub-clans. After the TNA vote, President Abdulkasim signed a decree making the charter legal and binding on his Government.

The third phase of the peace talks could not be initiated until the formal launching of the TNC by IGAD ministers in Nairobi. Many objections were lodged against Article 30 of the charter, which dealt with the appointment of Assembly members. Some believed Article 30 was unclear on how the selection would be made and who would select them. While Article 30 was being discussed in various locations in Somalia, plans moved forward in Kenya to launch the TNC. The new parliamentarians would be sworn in and would elect a new speaker and his or her deputies. They would oversee the election of the President of the Republic. The new Government would be inaugurated in Nairobi.

Dozens of militia men and bystanders were killed in various confrontations in mid-2004. Two members of Somalia's new Assembly were killed in separate incidents. Disgruntled politicians showed their anger and frustration. Some humanitarian workers were kidnapped and eventually released by their captors. Negotiations within and between clan groups continued apace in both Somalia and Kenya. The organizers abandoned their orderly plans and decided that new Assembly members would be sworn in as the completed lists were received from the clans. On 29 August a second group of legislators was sworn in, bringing the number of legislators to give the oath of office to 258. On 1 September, following standard practice throughout the parliamentary world, the Assembly selected an interim Speaker on the basis of age, in this case Hersi Bulhan Farah, aged 83. Parliamentarians were relieved when Hussein Aidid, who had hitherto shunned all of the ceremonies pertaining to the TNA, indicated an interest in joining the Assembly; he was promptly selected and sworn in.

On 16 September 2004 11 candidates presented themselves for election as Speaker of the TNA. A businessman Shariff Hassan Sheikh Adan won with 161 of the 267 votes cast. His closest opponent, Adan Muhammad Nur, received 105 votes and protested at alleged electoral irregularities.

Election of a new President of Somalia began on 10 October 2004 in Nairobi. After the first round, the three leading candidates were Abdullahi Yussuf Ahmed, former military ruler of the self-declared breakaway region of 'Puntland', Abdullahi Addou, former finance minister, and Mogadishu warlord Qanyare Afrah. Yussuf secured victory in the second round. In 1998 he had led the north-eastern Somali provinces in the formation of 'Puntland' and his record there did not demonstrate a strong commitment to democracy (see below). The new President took his oath of office in Nairobi on 14 October. The inauguration ceremony attendees included President Olusegun Obasanjo of Nigeria in his role as President of the AU, and the Presidents of Kenya, Rwanda, Burundi, Djibouti and Yemen. Sudan was represented by Vice-President Ali Osman Muhammad Taha and Ethiopia by Minister of Foreign Affairs Seyoum Mesfin. On 4 November President Yussuf appointed Ali Mohammed Ghedi as transitional Prime Minister.

The main issue now confronting Somalia's Transitional Federal Government (TFG), after two years of negotiations in Djibouti and Kenya, was how and where to establish its base. One of Ghedi's first statements after being appointed was to call upon the AU and the UN for peace-keepers. The press believed that the Government intended to relocate to Mogadishu in January 2005. President Yussuf and Prime Minister Ghedi toured Somalia in February and March to determine the location of the TNA. They went to Jowhar, Beled Weyne, Garowe, Bossaso, Galkayo and Baidoa, but notably did not visit Mogadishu. Meanwhile, the Somali Government remained in Kenya. Observers noted that a 'government in exile' could quickly be seen as irrelevant and that a cabinet should be named promptly.

On 1 December 2004 Prime Minister Ghedi announced a Cabinet that would consist of 31 ministers, 31 deputy ministers and five ministers of state. The Cabinet appeared to be inclusive with all clan groups appropriately represented, but regional analysts observed that it was too large for Somalia's requirements and that the Government could not afford to maintain so many ministers. The Cabinet was later rejected by the TNA. In mid-January 2005 a new Cabinet which included many former warlords was announced. Hussein Aidid was made Deputy Prime Minister and Minister of Interior and Security. Qanyare Afrah became Minister of National Security. Other familiar names on the cabinet list included Yalahow, Osman 'Ato', Shatigadud and Nur. Abdullahi Shaykh Isma'il was appointed Minister of Foreign Affairs.

In January 2005 IGAD promised to provide peace-keepers for Somalia, but in early February the issue of moving the Somali Government to Mogadishu had still not been resolved. Nevertheless, some Somali deputies began to relocate. On 3 February 30 deputies arrived in Mogadishu. Three days later an additional 50 deputies joined their colleagues in the country's capital. Contrary to the fears of many Assembly members, the arrival of the officials was warmly welcomed with thousands of cheering citizens lining the streets. Some Government members, however, were fired upon while touring the city. As the notion of peace-keeping troops being deployed to Mogadishu began to emerge, demonstrations were held opposing the possible presence of foreign troops.

Most of the Somali Government stayed in Nairobi during May 2005. President Yussuf in particular remained reluctant to return to Mogadishu. Prime Minister Ghedi believed that he could be safer in nearby Jowhar (90 km north of Mogadishu), while Yussuf decided to install the presidency temporarily in Baidoa, a town held by warlord Habsade, who opposed the idea. Severe fighting broke out in Baidoa in late May between supporters and opponents of the relocation of the presidency to that town. The Speaker, Sheikh Adan, was keen to return to Mogadishu, but was hesitant to call a meeting of the Assembly until the security of the city was assured. The Assembly met in May to approve the deployment of peace-keepers to Mogadishu. In early June local warlords agreed to remove illegal barriers and roadblocks in Mogadishu.

On 7 June 2005 the Government of Kenya broke the deadlock over the movement of the Government to Somalia by ordering the Cabinet ministers to leave Kenya by 14 June. By 21 June the TNA announced that it was able to convene in Jowhar. President Yussuf also established offices in Jowhar. Speaker Sheikh Adan had been in Mogadishu for several weeks and this separation created an impasse within the TFG. With most of the Government in Jowhar and the remainder in Mogadishu, the TFG quickly became seen as irrelevant. The situation of a dispersed administration worsened as security conditions in Jowhar became more uncertain.

The President and the parliamentarians moved to Baidoa in February 2006. Although it was initially denied by TFG officials, it was reported that Ethiopian forces had entered Somalia to provide protection for the new administration in Baidoa.

THE RISE OF THE ISLAMIC COURTS

Although many foreign policy experts appeared surprised when the Union of Islamic Courts (UIC) emerged in 2006, and assumed that it was a move engineered by al-Qa'ida, the religious authorities had been a factor in Somali lives for some years. According to a Chatham House study, the Islamic Courts owed their origin to the early 1990s when Abgal politicians in north Mogadishu saw the need for an institution to restore law and order to the chaotic city. They turned to local Hawiye clerics who co-operated by founding a *Shari'a* court. The Chatham study emphasized that the origin of the UIC was more due to the communal need for security than out of an Islamist imperative.

There did not appear to be a direct line of association between the Islamic Union Party (al-Ittihad al-Islam—AIAI) and the Islamic Courts. AIAI was a fundamentalist sect that was based in Luuq, north of Baidoa near the border with Ethiopia. Quiet for years during the Siad Barre regime, AIAI became more militant in the early 1990s and fought with Aidid in 1991 and with Yussuf in 1992. After AIAI shifted its base to the Gedo region, Ethiopia feared that it represented a threat to its territory and in 1996 launched an attack that eliminated the organization's military capacity. Remnants of AIAI took refuge in south Mogadishu where they joined the growing Islamic Courts movement.

In June 2001 the TFG announced that it would 'nationalize' the Islamic Courts. This was announced by President Abdulkasim as he presided over the incorporation of some judges from the Islamic Courts into the normal judiciary. Soon after the 11 September attacks in New York and Washington, DC, the US Government froze AIAI assets in the USA. The alleged affiliation of AIAI with al-Qa'ida came as a surprise to most regional observers. AIAI was widely credited with having established some Islamic Courts in Mogadishu in recent years, but it was believed to have handed those courts over to the Government in June 2002.

The Islamic judges were assigned to the High Court as Islamic *qadis* responsible for adjudicating family affairs. The Islamic Court in Mogadishu, also known as the Shirkole Islamic Court, had been set up in south Mogadishu in the mid-1990s along clan lines in order to combat the dramatic increase in crime that followed the collapse of the Siad Barre regime. Each Shirkole court maintained its own militia to deal with criminals and to provide protection. The Islamic Court militia were set to be absorbed by official security services. In spite of efforts to nationalize all of the Islamic Courts, some of them continued to operate in some parts of Mogadishu, especially in the northern sectors.

In November 2005 there was a violent confrontation between Islamists and the warlords in Mogadishu after the militants attempted to close down video stores and improvised motion picture theatres. The warlords, who were paid a percentage of the takings by the store owners, simply wanted to protect their incomes.

The rapid takeover of Mogadishu and most of Somalia south of Galkayo by the UIC in 2006 alarmed many foreign powers and dramatically altered the course of Somali politics. The rising strength of the Islamic Courts contributed to the decision of the USA to facilitate the foundation of the Alliance for the Restoration of Peace and Counter-Terrorism (ARPCT) in March. The warlord collaborators in this venture did not have any great successes, but the event served as a rallying cry for the subsequent explosive offensive launched by the Islamic Courts in March and April. By mid-April the Islamic Courts had invested in many strategic points of Mogadishu. A brief truce between the UIC fighters and the warlords in mid-May was quickly broken. The UIC militias were relentless in their fighting against the so-called anti-terrorist forces. Resistance collapsed in early June, and the UIC was declared victorious on 6 June. Early evidence of the success of the UIC was the reopening of the city of Mogadishu to both its inhabitants and the outside world. Journalists flocked to the city, while residents marvelled at the disappearance of road blocks. There were 11 Islamic Court groups within the UIC, and they represented a number of different Islamic tendencies. Some of these communicated to the US Government their interest in establishing relations.

In late June 2006, at a meeting in Khartoum sponsored by the Arab League, the Islamists and the TFG signed a series of accords, in which they agreed to recognize each other and to work towards peace. On 27 June a UIC delegation met with representatives of the US Embassy in Khartoum. The Islamists laid out a list of complaints (the restrictions imposed on charities and financial organizations and US backing of warlords) and recent favourable actions (the creation of the CGS and positive comments about the Arab League-sponsored meeting with the TFG). The US Embassy delegation indicated that the US Government was considering sending an observer team to Khartoum to oversee a second round of negotiations with the UIC.

The following months in Mogadishu and central Somalia revealed several tendencies of the UIC (now renamed the Supreme Somali Islamic Courts Council—SSICC). The hardliners appeared to be in control in Mogadishu, where dancing, singing and mixed entertainment was firmly suppressed, and women were required to wear veils. As essentially an instrument created by the Hawiye clans, the Islamic Courts were working in familiar territory when they drove the warlords out of Mogadishu. The public perception of the courts shifted when they were able to take over Kismayu in late September 2006. In Kismayu, the UIC was treading on uncertain ground and risked uniting previous adversaries in common opposition to the courts.

While maintaining a low profile, the Ethiopian military continued to monitor the TFG in Baidoa. It was also becoming clear that Eritrea was furnishing arms to the SSICC as the overextended SSICC forces gradually grew in strength. The downfall of the Islamists came even quicker than their victory over the warlords. On 12 December 2006 the leaders of the military wing of the courts voiced an ultimatum to the Ethiopian Government, allowing it one week to withdraw from Somalia or be forced out. On 20 December there was an exchange of fire between Ethiopian and SSICC forces near Baidoa. Ethiopian forces pressed south and east, first capturing the town of Bandiiradley, about 60 km south of Galkayo, and then sweeping through towns and villages before marching unopposed into Mogadishu on 28 December. Under Ethiopian protection the TFG moved into the capital. By 13 January 2007 the Ethiopian army had driven the remnants of the SSICC forces into the southern tip of Somalia at Ras Kamboni where the Islamists were attacked by US air and sea forces with undetermined success.

A FURTHER RECONCILIATION CONFERENCE

The defeat of the Islamists in January 2007 created more questions than it did answers, most notably about their location since relatively few had escaped to the forests at Ras Kamboni. Some of the leaders were able to flee to Yemen and some further afield, while the foot soldiers simply blended back into the population. However, the Islamist groups remained active, raising the issue of why the security situation in Mogadishu continues to fester. In July 2007 conflict erupted in the Bakhara market, the lifeblood of the city's economy. Yet, in the long term, there seems little to be gained from such episodes. The port of Kismayu also remains a critical part of the southern Somali economy, but following the takeover of the port by Marehan forces in April 2007, the TFG-appointed local administrator was expelled. The TFG lost all authority in Kismayu. In the lower Shebelle region, TFG forces continue to come under fire from militia groups claiming allegiance to a previous administration. The location of Sheikh Hassan Dahir Aweys, the radical Chairman of the SSICC, remains unknown, prompting concerns over how to respond should he re-emerge on the local political scene. The Chinese National Offshore Oil Corporation signed a contract with President Yussuf in May 2006 to explore for oil in the Mudug. The Mudug is currently the focus for competition between the Darod Mijertein and the Hawiye Habr Gedir. The oil contract adds a significant dimension to prospective developments.

These were some of the issues to be discussed by the latest reconciliation conference. It opened, after the inevitable delays, in Mogadishu on 15 July 2007, although the opening ceremony was boycotted by the Hawiye elders and the Islamists. The talks lasted six weeks, but opinion was divided over the success of the negotiations. Some 1,000 delegates attended the conference, which appeared to run peacefully. However, Hawiye elders maintained that the conference was not inclusive and that little progress had been made in ending violence in Somalia with hundreds reported to have been killed in fighting since the talks began.

'THE REPUBLIC OF SOMALILAND'

With collapse of the Siad Barre regime in January 1991, there seemed little doubt that the only course for the people of the former British Somaliland would be to terminate their association with the Republic of Somalia. The Great Conference of the Northern Peoples convened in May 1991, entrusted the SNM with the task of forming a Government and drafting a constitution for the Republic of Somaliland. 'Somaliland' celebrates 19 May 1991 as the date of its second independence. Without international recognition it first proved difficult to attract aid, and this in turn meant the Government had no means to settle the claims of ex-guerrilla fighters, nor could it afford to demobilize them. Only assistance from NGOs enabled the Government to begin the work of repairing the war-damaged infrastructure of the region, and some progress was made in the removal of mines (it has been estimated that there were about 2m. such devices to be cleared).

Since 1991 the single fundamental issue of 'Somaliland's' foreign policy has been the quest for international recognition, a goal that continues to elude the Government. 'Somaliland's' relations with its neighbours have vacillated between confrontation and co-operation. As President, Dahir Riyale Kahin has struggled to resolve the recognition dilemma and to normalize regional relations. The representatives of 'Somaliland' show great imagination in their quest, and usually receive and invitation for many international meetings and festivities. The only meetings that the Government of 'Somaliland' resolutely refuses to attend are those that involve Somali national reconciliation or integration.

The AU remained bound by the principle of respect of borders existing at the time of independence. 'Somaliland' rejects this interpretation because it first gained independence on 26 June 1960, four days before it voluntarily joined the Somali Republic, when that territory was granted independence. 'Somaliland's' first President was Abidirahman Mohamed Ali 'Tur. The Somalilanders turned to their traditional elders to select a new 'national' leader to succeed 'Tur. After protracted discussions at Borama, the elders selected Mohamed Ibrahim Egal, an elder statesman who had served as the first Prime Minister of the Republic of Somalia in 1960 and served in several governments in Somalia before the central administration dissolved in 1991. Egal was successful in negotiating with the 'Somaliland' clans, was able to disarm factions and set the candidate state on a solid path. After Egal's death in 2002 he was succeeded by his Kahin.

Without the approval of the AU, western Governments were unlikely to recognize 'Somaliland' as a state. In December 2005 President Kahin submitted an application for 'Somaliland' membership of the AU, but it was not accepted. On 23 May 2006 the International Crisis Group (ICG) published a report entitled Somaliland: Time for African Union Leadership, in which it recommended that the AU appoint a special envoy to report on the dispute between 'Somaliland' and Somalia; to survey the factual and legal issues involved, and offer options for resolution; to organize a consultative process with appropriate scholars and experts, and pending final resolution, to grant 'Somaliland' interim observer status to enable it to participate in the AU consultative process.

Relations with Djibouti have historically been strained because of former President Egal's refusal to participate in the Djibouti-sponsored Somali national reconciliation process. Looking back to the pre-colonial period, 'Somaliland' would like to re-establish Berbera as an alternate port for Ethiopia. There have also been a number of political disagreements and minor border disputes between 'Somaliland' and its neighbours. Relations with 'Puntland' suffer because of disputed ownership of the regions of Sanaag and Sool, which were part of British Somaliland but whose inhabitants, the Harti, are more closely related to clans in 'Puntland'. Since the late 1990s the dispute over Sanaag and Sool has caused numerous low-level armed confrontations. In late October 2004 fighting erupted at the village of Adi-Addeye, north of Sool's capital, Las Anod, which resulted in the deaths of 109 people. 'Somaliland' protested to the AU, IGAD, the UN Security Council and various foreign Governments, and accused TFG President Yussuf (the former leader of 'Puntland') of engineering the violence to justify his request for international peace-keepers in Somalia.

The most recent dispute between 'Somaliland' and 'Puntland' took place on 14 April 2007 when troops of the two sides fought over the ownership of a strip of desert. This event took place almost immediately after the 'Puntland' military commander in Sool defected to 'Somaliland'. There were few casualties from the battles in Sool, and both sides claimed victory. The following day 'Somaliland' Minister of Defence, Adan Mire Walkaf, was dismissed for disobeying a direct order and cutting off communications with President Kahin.

According to results published by the 'Somaliland' Election Commission, at the presidential election held on 14 April 2003, Kahin defeated his nearest rival, Ahmad Muhammad Silanyo, by just 80 votes. Kahin received 205,595 votes (42.08%), while Silanyo obtained 205,515 votes (42.07%). A third candidate, Faysal Ali Warabe, received 77,433 (15.5%), of the total 498,639 votes cast around the country. An estimated 800,000 of 'Somaliland's' population were eligible to vote. Silanyo immediately contested the result of the election and announced his intention to appeal against the outcome. However, the following month the 'Somaliland' constitutional court confirmed the legitimacy of Kahin's victory; Kahin was sworn in as President on 16 May. On 28 September 2005 elections were held to select the 82 members of the country's lower parliamentary chamber. The first session of the newly elected body met on 1 December. The meeting was marred by student protests at a recent police killing of one of their comrades and a police confrontation with the opposition.

In 2005 Yussuf accused Djibouti of supplying arms to 'Somaliland' and encouraging attacks on 'Puntland'. Djibouti dismissed the charges as unfounded but urged 'Puntland' to withdraw its forces from Las Anod. Tensions between 'Somaliland' and 'Puntland' remained high, with no indication that the dispute over Sool and Sanaag would be swiftly resolved. Signs of improving relations between the two regions were demonstrated in December 2005 when authorities in both areas exchanged detainees taken a year earlier during the height of the dispute over the Sool border.

President Kahin opposed the election of Yussuf as President of Somalia, largely because Yussuf claimed to be President of the entire country, including 'Somaliland'. Kahin stated that he would oppose discussions about the reunification of the two states and would forcibly oppose any attempt by Yussuf to lay claim to 'Somaliland' or to dispute the territory's secession. Two days later the AU encouraged the two parties to resolve their differences through negotiation. On a visit to 'Somaliland' in October a junior member of the British Government told the 'Somaliland' Parliament that the United Kingdom would oppose a forced reintegration between 'Somaliland' and the south and also urged the parliamentarians to support the southern peace process and to begin bilateral negotiations with Yussuf's administration.

In March 2005 the Berbera Port Authority and the Ethiopian Maritime and Transit Service Enterprises concluded an agreement to increase Ethiopian transit trade through Berbera. Officials also explored ways to improve trade between Somalia and 'Somaliland'. Also in March the trial of 10 men accused of murdering four foreign aid workers in October 2003 began in Hargeysa, 'Somaliland'; authorities claimed that the perpetrators were terrorists but failed to present any evidence to substantiate the charge. In June 2005 the UN rehabilitated the Berbera and Dhoqoshey police stations in 'Somaliland' and offered training courses for the Internal Control Unit, the Special Protection Unit and the Criminal Investigations Department. Additionally, the UN supported the territory's Law Review Commission and the University of Hargeysa Legal Clinic.

'PUNTLAND' REGIONAL ADMINISTRATION

In May 1998 delegates from three north-eastern regions of Somalia met in Garowe to establish a single administration for the area as an autonomous state within Somalia. They named the region 'Puntland' or Land of Frankincense, one of its main exports, and designated Garowe as its capital. In July the delegates elected Yussuf, a former leader of the SSDF and later President of Somalia, as their President, and Muhammad Abdi Hashi as Vice-President. In August Yussuf established a 69-member parliament and a nine-member cabinet. In February 2001 a group of 78 elders, intellectuals and other prominent members of society issued a statement that accused the 'Puntland' government of committing human rights violations, concluding secret marine agreements, secretly joining the pro-Ethiopian and southern-controlled SRRC Council, printing counterfeit money and sabotaging peace in the region. Yussuf rejected these accusations and pledged to reform 'Puntland' politics extensively. In late June the 'Puntland' house of representatives approved a three-year extension to the region's administration, the mandate of which had been about to expire. The high court of 'Puntland' unsuccessfully sought to overturn this decision by issuing a decree that placed all government institutions under its control. However, in early July 'Puntland' authorities announced that Yussuf had been sworn in for a second term. The Chief Justice of 'Puntland', Yussuf Haji Nur, subsequently proclaimed himself President of the territory; senior clan elders confirmed Haji Nur as acting President until 31 August. However, Abdullahi Yussuf rejected this decision, and heavy fighting ensued between followers of Yussuf and Haji Nur. In late August 1998 a general congress, attended by representatives of all major 'Puntland' clans, opened in Garowe, the region's capital, to elect a new President and Vice-President, as well as members of a new 'Puntland' assembly. In mid-November Jama Ali Jama and Ahmad Mahmud Gunle were sworn in as President and Vice-President, respectively. Ali Jama, a former military officer, had links to the TNG, which alarmed Ethiopia, as it remained determined to remove the TNG. Abdullahi Yussuf, however, refused to recognize the election, and just days later violent clashes were reported to have taken place in Garowe between troops loyal to Yussuf and those supporting Ali Jama. The SRRC favoured Yussuf, and in December Ethiopian troops intervened in 'Puntland' in support of his campaign against Ali Jama.

In January 2002 Ethiopian troops again intervened in 'Puntland', claiming that Ali Jama was harbouring AIAI militants, a charge he denied. Offers by Ethiopia to mediate in the dispute between Yussuf and Ali Jama were rejected by both men. In April Yussuf declared a state of emergency and suspended the 'Puntland' constitution. He claimed that the action was necessary to resolve the confusions created by the TNG and its supporters. In early May Yussuf recaptured Bossaso, with military support from Ethiopia, after a three-day campaign that had been launched from Garowe. Fighting continued throughout late 2002 and early 2003, as forces loyal to Yussuf battled against Ali Jama's troops. In mid-May 2003 Yussuf sought to stabilize 'Puntland' by concluding a power-sharing agreement with opposition forces. Under the agreement, the opposition was to provide three ministers, two deputy ministers, two governors, two mayors and the commander of either the police force or the army. The opposition militia was to be integrated into 'Puntland' security forces.

In mid-February 2004 the house of representatives approved an extension of the mandate of the region's administration by 39 votes to six, with four abstentions and 17 members absent. Yussuf had opposed the extension as he wished to hold elections, but Vice-President Muhammad Abdi Hashi and his allies favoured the action because of drought, lack of financial resources and growing tensions with 'Somaliland' over Sool and Sanaag. Others were concerned, however, that if the ongoing Kenyan-sponsored Somali peace conference were successfully to precipitate the creation of a new Somali national Government, a dangerous power vacuum would be created if elections were not held.

When Yussuf was elected President of Somalia in October 2004, he was succeeded in 'Puntland' by Muhammad Abdi Hashi who served until January 2005, when he was defeated in his bid for re-election to parliament. On 8 January 2005 65 representatives of the regions of 'Puntland' elected Gen. Mohamud Muse Hersi 'Adde' to a three-year term as the territory's new President, defeating Hashi by 35 votes to 30. The new President pledged to reduce tensions with 'Somaliland' over the disputed Sool and Sanaag regions, a move welcomed by 'Somaliland'. Commentators believed that Muse's election reflected the growing desire for a federalist government. In June the UN announced that it had completed construction of 'Puntland's' Armo Police Academy with the capacity for 300 cadets.

Economy

WALTER S. CLARKE

INTRODUCTION

According to a report from the British Department for International Development, the population of Somalia is between 6m. and 9m. (with an estimated annual growth rate of 4.2%), comprising mainly pastoral nomads. The gross national income (GNI) per head was put at US $130, and 43% of the population earn less than $1 per day. The primary school enrolment rate is falling and only some 17%, with only one-third of those enrolled being girls. The average life expectancy is 47 years, and 225 children out of 1,000 die before the age of five years. The World Health Organization (WHO) estimated maternal mortality as one per 100 live births. The average prevalence of the human inmmunodeficiency virus (HIV) among the population is estimated at 0.9%. Access to improved water sources is estimated to be 29%.

In November 2004 the World Bank's private sector office published a report entitled 'Anarchy and Invention: How does Somalia's Private Sector Cope without Government?' (*Public Policy Journal*, Note No. 280). The authors praised the innovative nature of Somalia's private sector. They noted that competition was strong in markets where transactions are simple, such as in retail sales and construction. The rule has limited relevance in more complex environments, such as telecommunications and electricity production. The public sector is only sorely missed when critical issues such as roads, currency, laws, education and international monetary transfers are concerned. Somalia is the prototypical failed state, but the Somali people have generally worked out creative methods of replacing services usually provided by government. They have replaced domestic government in such matters as airline safety, currency stability and contractual law with a reliance on outside institutions ('importing governance'). The Somali clan system creates a natural trust network that fosters the enforcement of contracts and the safe transmission of funds. The result, according to the authors, is that while Somalia is one of the poorest countries in the world it possesses infrastructure that, in some cases, is of higher capacity than other, wealthier countries in Africa.

The natural resilience of Somalis was sorely tested after the 2004 observations were made. The people endured an interminable period of political negotiation, in which clan leaders closeted themselves in one foreign country or another while the home front struggled for survival. When the Union of Islamic Courts (UIC) overthrew the chaotic warlords in Mogadishu in mid-2006, it introduced a period of relative peace in central and southern Somalia that had not been seen for years. The harsh version of Islam which the UIC espoused soon proved wearisome for most of the population, but it seemed worth the price of peace for most. However, as it worked out, the Islamists preached their tough form of Islam and imposed restrictions on the lives of many, but they could not govern. When the Transitional Federal Government (TFG) and supporting Ethiopian soldiers marched into Mogadishu in December 2006, most Islamists simply melted back into their clans. Some of the UIC leadership fled the country, but the day after their disappearance, the qat sellers were back plying their trade in the streets of Mogadishu.

The entry of the TFG and their Ethiopian allies into Mogadishu signalled the return of the 'bad old days', with roadblocks, arbitrary theft and seizure of property, and fighting between armed groups, including now the Ethiopian occupiers and, later, some UN-authorized Ugandan peace-keepers (under what became the African Union Mission in Somalia—AMISOM). The new Government instituted a night-time curfew (19.00–07.00) in Mogadishu, which severely limited the movement of people going to or looking for work and in the unending search for food for their families. In the months succeeding the arrival of the TFG in Mogadishu, thousands of people fled the capital. Most of these internally displaced persons (IDPs) moved west and south towards those regions where most crops are grown in Somalia. The February 2007 monthly UN report on the humanitarian situation in Somalia noted that the situation was dire and that, in a worst case scenario, the number of people in need of critical assistance would increase from 1.7m. to 1.8m, excluding the 400,000 IDPs country-wide. The same monthly analysis reported that polio, which had disappeared from Somalia in October 2002, had returned; 194 cases of wild polio had been confirmed in the previous seven months. Other diseases were also on the increase.

AGRICULTURE AND FISHING

In July 2007 the assessment following the Gu rains ('long' wet season of March–May, as opposed to the Deyr or 'short' rains of October–December) indicated that the fertile middle and lower Shebelle regions in central Somalia were in a state of humanitarian emergency. The regions of Gedo, Hakol and Bay experienced almost total crop failure in the first half of 2007. Civil insecurity and the inability to access markets after the closure of the port of Mogadishu (because of piracy) and of the Bakhara market in Mogadishu (a source of illegal arms sales) added to the growing desperation of Somalis. The July 2007 survey noted that at that time there were about 238 check-points in south-central Somalia; taxes were imposed on humanitarian commodities and considerable delays caused. Humanitarian workers were subject to harassment and attack and, in 'Puntland', it was necessary to withdraw some aid workers.

The World Bank noted in a 2006 study that 'livestock is at the root of Somali literature and cultural identity'. Animal husbandry remains the dominant component of Somalia's agriculture and economy, providing a livelihood for more than one-half of the population and about 80% of export earnings. The most important livestock are sheep, goats, cattle and camels. The lack of veterinary services and, therefore, the lack of sanitary certificates remained a significant problem. During the 1990s periodic import bans were imposed on Somali animals by Saudi Arabia, Yemen and various states of the Persian (Arabian) Gulf, but with the assistance of donors and government-funded programmes, most were not long-lasting. In the mid-2000s the Government of 'Somaliland' contracted the Djibouti Government to provide sanitary certificates for cattle exports from 'Somaliland'.

In April 2003 representatives from the Somali Transitional National Government (TNG), 'Somaliland' and 'Puntland' had met in Dubai, UAE, with officials from several Middle Eastern countries. They hoped to end export bans to Saudi Arabia and other Middle Eastern countries by agreeing to establish a Somali Livestock Board to regulate the industry by improving disease surveillance, inspection and certification. Implementation of the activities of such a body remained theoretical in mid-2007. The droughts in East Africa, meanwhile, had caused the deaths of a significant number of larger animals, especially camels.

Crops are mainly grown in the west and south. Traditionally, the most important crops are maize, sorghum, cassava, bananas (which accounted for around one-10th of exports before the civil war) and sesame seed, and to a lesser extent sugar cane, citrus fruits and pulses. The most productive plantations, in the lower Shebelle region, have been controlled by competing Habr Gedir clansmen, who channelled the revenues into their war efforts. Bananas and other fruits, now chiefly for local consumption, are grown on plantations in that area. Sugar cane is a significant crop with a small surplus available for export. In 2005 an estimated 200,000 metric tons of sugar cane were produced. The area between the Juba and Shebelle rivers, of which at present only some 700,000 ha of an estimated potential of 8.2m. ha are under cultivation, also traditionally provides the subsistence maize and sorghum crops of the southern Somalis. The full utilization of this fertile belt, envisaged in development plans, could eventually satisfy the grain needs of the domestic market and provide a subsidiary export crop—experiments in rice cultivation, assisted by the People's Republic of China, might eventually enable Somalia to dispense with costly imports of this grain. Sorghum production waxes and wanes on the basis of rainfall, and the low-value nature of the crop makes it unattractive to looters. In 2005 sorghum production was some 150,000 tons. Cereal production in 2001/02 totalled 267,000 metric tons, some 17% less than in the previous year. Maize production was 170,000 tons in 2003, 202,000 tons in 2004 and, falling back slightly, 190,000 tons in 2005. All crops had suffered from the three-year drought that ended in the spring of 2006 with the Gu rains; the food security situation in many parts of the country remained precarious.

From 1991 Somalia increased exports of acacia charcoal to Kenya and the Gulf states. Areas of charcoal production include the region south of Kismayu, parts of Bay and the middle Shebelle region, and several areas in 'Somaliland' and 'Puntland'. This expanding charcoal trade created a serious environmental problem. The World Bank believed that certain areas in southern Somalia might no longer be suitable for traditionally vital pastoral use. In the absence of effective government, no effort was made to end the increasingly destructive, but highly lucrative, charcoal trade.

The World Bank noted that an historical peak of fish production was attained in 1989, with an estimated 21,000 metric tons of large and small pelagic fish species, including sharks, and 4,700 tons of crustaceans (mostly lobster, but some shrimp). The World Bank estimated that the long, coastal Somali exclusive economic zone could produce an annual sustainable catch of 300,000 tons of fish and 10,000 tons of crustaceans. FAO assumed the 2002–05 annual catches to be similar to the 27,500 tons landed in 2001, but a far greater quantity of fish is caught in Somali waters.

The absence of a national coast guard leads to illegal fishing by foreign ships, with hundreds of foreign vessels conducting illegal fishing operations along Somalia's coastline. The ships, mainly from India, Italy, Japan, the Republic of Korea, Pakistan, Spain and Yemen, operate without concern for the future of the fish resources. Somali fishermen, with the help of motor boats donated by local non-governmental organizations (NGOs), often attack the ships, fining the captains and holding the crews for ransom. In the past some Somali warlords undercut the fishermen by selling fishing rights to foreign companies, using the revenues to purchase weapons and ammunition. A May 2007 report on livelihoods and food security from the UN Office for the Co-ordination of Humanitarian Affairs (OCHA) estimated that Somalia lost about US $100m. annually to illegal fishing.

MINERALS AND INDUSTRIAL PRODUCTS

Somalia's mineral resources include salt, limestone, gypsum, gold, silver, nickel, copper, zinc, lead, manganese, uranium and iron ore. Iron ore reserves estimated at 170m. metric tons have been located in the Bur region and deposits of uranium ore exist to the west of Mogadishu. Somalia contains the world's largest gypsum deposits, near Berbera, and in 2004 an estimated 2,000 tons were mined. The mining sector contributed only 0.3% of GDP in 1988.

In May 2006 the China National Offshore Oil Company (CNOOC) signed an agreement with the TFG according to which Somalia would received US $50m. in bonuses for any wells that would yield 200,000 barrels per day for 75 consecutive days. According to the *Financial Times* of London (United Kingdom), CNOOC and a smaller partner also from the People's Republic of China, China International Oil and Gas (CIOG) would have the right to 49% of the profits from any petroleum found, with 51% going to the TFG. Plans to start petroleum exploration off Somalia's Indian Ocean coast had been announced by Mobil Corpn and Pecten, the US subsidiary of Shell, in 1990, but were postponed as the civil war intensified later in that year. The interim Somali legislature in July 2007 enacted an affirmation of the prospecting rights acquired by oil companies under previous governments.

According to the *Indian Ocean Newsletter* (published in Paris, France, by Indigo Publications), in October 2005 an Australian company, Range Resources Ltd, was accorded exclusive prospecting rights for petroleum and minerals in the whole of 'Puntland', an area of some 212,000 sq km. Under the agreement, Range could contract with third parties and, in April 2006, the Korea National Oil Corpn (KNOC) took 75% of Range's concession in the Noogal valley against a payment of US $10m. and a promise to invest $25m. in exploration over the following two years.

Such other industrial activities as still exist in Somalia since the civil war are small in scale and mostly based on agriculture, meat and fish processing, textiles and leather goods. Even in 1988, however, the sector had only accounted for some 5.0% of GDP. In 2002 industry was estimated to employ some 12% of the labour force.

THE ROLE OF THE SOMALI DIASPORA

There are no reliable figures for the numbers of Somalis living in Somalia or overseas. It is believed that at least 1.1m. Somalis reside outside the country, with large populations in the United Kingdom, Canada and the USA, but with the most significant populations in Saudi Arabia, the UAE and Yemen. At a December 2005 conference in Washington, DC (USA), sponsored by the World Bank and the UN Development Programme (UNDP), it was estimated that 1m. expatriate Somalis remitted between US $825m. and $1,000m. to Somalia during 2004. More than 50% of remittances were believed destined to consumption, but a significant portion went into investment.

In November 2001 the USA closed the al-Barakat money-transfer company, which operated in 40 countries, and seized its assets, worth some US $43m., owing to its suspected links to terrorist organizations. At the time al-Barakat was Somalia's biggest employer, with radio and telecommunications interests in addition to its remittance business. After several years of investigation by international banking authorities, a single employee in Scandinavia was found to have suspicious ties and, after his dismissal in 2005, al-Barakat was permitted to reopen.

THE 'DOLLARIZATION' OF THE ECONOMY

By 2000 the paper currency of Somalia had been in use for at least 10 years and the money packages (old shillings were usually packed into 5,000-shilling bricks) had become very shabby. The result was a proliferation of counterfeit or regional Somali currencies. During May–June at least four consignments of Indonesian-produced currency, worth some US $9.5m., were delivered to 'Puntland'. In August more than $2.5m. worth of 'new' currency arrived in Mogadishu and, in late October, currency printed in Canada, worth almost $3m., arrived in the Somali capital; the TNG used the money to pay its newly established militia. At about the same time, however, the TNG publicly condemned the import of illegal currency. In November a further $2m. arrived in 'Puntland' from Indonesia and Malaysia, the fourth consignment of new banknotes to arrive that month. This process continued into the 2000s in various guises and, as well as deterring potential international investors, the proliferation of counterfeit and regional currencies caused sharp rises in the shilling prices of essential commodities throughout Somalia. In 1990–2001 the average annual rate of inflation was 20.6%. Consumer prices only increased by 11.5% in 2001, but by 2004 the annual inflation rate had increased to some 15%.

FOREIGN AID AND DEVELOPMENT

During 1960–69 Somalia received a substantial amount of foreign aid, chiefly from Italy, the USA and the USSR, without producing any proportionate return. During 1963–70 the Government launched a series of plans to improve the country's resources. Although the plans proved too ambitious, much was accomplished during those years, notably in road-building, the construction of ports at Berbera (with aid from the USSR) and Kismayu (with US aid) and the building of schools and a large hospital at Mogadishu, financed by the European Community (EC, now the European Union—EU). Few projects for livestock management and agricultural development had successfully progressed beyond the planning stage by 1969.

Until 1977 the major source of aid was the USSR; aid was also provided by the People's Republic of China, the European Development Fund, the Federal Republic of Germany (West Germany), IDA and UN specialized agencies. Since 1974 Arab states have also been important contributors, especially Libya, the UAE and Saudi Arabia, which reportedly supplied considerable military aid in the war with Ethiopia over the Ogaden. In 1987 bilateral discussions were reported to have taken place with the Arab funds to reschedule Somalia's external debt. Following the 1980 agreement permitting US forces to use Somalia's military bases, the USA became a major donor. Its support was particularly important for Somalia's transport systems, which were among Africa's poorest.

In 1985 work finished on a US-sponsored US $37.5m. project to double the number of berths at Berbera port and to deepen its harbour, which handled a large volume of cattle exports. Soon afterwards, a $42m. development of Kismayu port began, designed to equip it to handle livestock in addition to bananas. The USA also provided finance for the expansion of the main runway at Mogadishu airport. US assistance was suspended in 1988 after publicity alleging government abuses of human rights and because of the protracted civil war. A more traditional benefactor was Italy, which in 1985 offered more than $200m. in special assistance from its emergency aid fund for Africa, mostly for the construction of a road linking Garowe to Bossaso, providing access to the isolated north-east. In 1989 Italy financed the reconstruction and expansion of Mogadishu airport.

The traditional wired telephone system was one of the first casualties of Somalia's civil war. The advent of wireless communications permitted Somali entrepreneurs to establish one of the most efficient and inexpensive telecommunications systems in Africa: international calls were the cheapest in Africa; new subscribers could be connected within three days; internet use was less than $10 per month; and there were no taxes. Connectivity between systems was being developed by 2007, and it might soon not be necessary to call a neighbour through a European connection. Telecommunications companies included Amana, Netexchange, GteleAtlantic, Olympic Telecommunications, NationLink Telecommunications Co and Hormud Telecom Somalia, which had used the equipment and premises of the al-Barakat money-transfer firm (closed in late 2001 for some years—see above).

In January 2004 the UN, in co-operation with the World Bank, UNDP and several other UN agencies, released a new socio-economic survey for Somalia, the first since the collapse of the Siad Barre regime in 1991. Reliable data were expected to assist donors to divert funds to those sectors in most need of development. (In the mid-2000s Somalia received some US $100m. in assistance each year.) Some key findings in the report were that 43% of Somalis lived on income of $1 per day or less and that 'Somaliland' and 'Puntland' had better income levels than the rest of the country because the degree of conflict in those territories was lower than in the south. In July a new Coca-Cola beverage factory opened in Mogadishu. Somali businessmen had invested $8.3m. in the factory, which employed 150 people; some 70 others were employed with distributors for the company. The factory was capable of producing 36,000 bottles per hour. A subsequent World Bank report was published in early 2006: 'Somalia: From Resilience towards Recovery and Development. A Country Economic Memorandum for Somalia'. This very useful survey examines many issues of the Somali failed state and supplements the statistics provided in the earlier report.

FOREIGN TRADE

There are no reliable recent trade statistics, meaningful figures being impossible to produce since the civil war. Despite a considerable narrowing of the trade deficit in 1988, to US $157.6m., Somalia's foreign trade deficit (almost entirely financed by foreign aid) was estimated at $278.6m. in 1989, with the deficit on the current account of the balance of payments increasing from $98.5m. in 1988 to $156.7m. in 1989. In 2003 Somalia's main export destinations were reckoned to include the UAE ($37m.), Yemen ($22m.), Oman ($10m.), Nigeria ($4m.), Bahrain ($3m.) and India ($3m.). The main suppliers of imports included Kenya ($58m.), Djibouti ($26m.), Brazil ($25m.), India ($12m.), Thailand ($16m.) and the United Kingdom ($6m.).

ECONOMIC ACTIVITIES IN A FAILED STATE

The collapse of Siad Barre's regime ushered in a period of chronic instability that continues to impede the country's economic rehabilitation. Throughout the early 1990s millions of Somalis were displaced and in danger, or at risk, of starvation. By the later 1990s Somalia remained dependent on international aid, especially during times of environmental disasters such as drought or flooding. However, the continuation of factional fighting during 1998–2000 led many NGOs and other humanitarian agencies to re-evaluate their presence in Somalia. In September 1998 the International Committee of the Red Cross (ICRC) announced that it would no longer send expatriate staff to Somalia and would reduce its activities. By the mid-2000s most international humanitarian agencies with operations in Somalia based their operations in Nairobi, Kenya.

Despite such problems, there have been some economic improvements. The re-establishment of security in some regions stimulated a revival of livestock and fruit exports. The north-eastern town of Bossaso (the largest town and the commercial capital of 'Puntland') became a major point of entry for goods into Somalia, and the fishing and livestock sectors expanded throughout the relatively stable north-east, thanks largely to Bossaso's tax-free environment. By late 1997 there were 14 aviation companies, with 62 aircraft, operating out of Bossaso, compared to one aviation firm with three aircraft prior to the war. Improvement works planned for the airport from the mid-2000s proved politically controversial (see below). In March 2001 Air Somalia (a new airline formed to replace Somali Airlines, which ceased operations in 1990) commenced flights from Mogadishu to destinations throughout the country. The US global 'war on terror', however, was also to have an impact on Somalia's transportation sector. In mid-June 2004 the Kenya Airports Authority (KAA) imposed a ban on flights to Somalia after the US Administration raised concerns that suspected terrorists were using Nairobi's Wilson Airport to enter and exit Kenya.

In March 2001 the Central Bank of Somalia reopened and a new Governor, Mahmoud Mohamed Ulusow, was appointed; in mid-2007 the Governor was Bashir Isse Ali. The bank had been closed shortly after the collapse of the Siad Barre regime in 1991. However, money flows in the country were still dependent on private companies and were severely compromised by the USA's closure of the al-Barakat company towards the end of 2001 (see above). In January 2002 the Dahabshil remittance company received a new licence in the USA, after stricter regulations had been imposed on money-transfer companies. In April Dahabshil announced that it operated in 50 countries and was the largest private-sector business in Somalia and 'Somaliland'. At about the same time a group of Somali businessmen opened the Universal Bank of Somalia (UBS), with headquarters in Brussels, Belgium, and Dubai, UAE. The major foreign investors were from Belgium, Ireland, the Netherlands and Norway. The bank planned to commence operations with an operating capital of US $10m. and to maintain relations with 62 correspondence banks in 72 countries. However, in January 2002 the Central Bank of Somalia announced that the UBS had failed to follow the proper procedures in establishing a private bank. In early 2003 UNDP continued its efforts to devise a transparent system that ensured the flow of remittances, which contributed $750m. to the country's economy prior to the closure of al-Barakat. The UAE also agreed to support efforts to create a more transparent remittance system, while Norway lifted a ban on remittance companies.

In December 2003 a group of Somali remittance companies and financial regulators from Europe and the USA established the Somali Financial Services Association (SFSA) in London, United Kingdom. This organization, which was supported by UNDP, represented 14 money-transfer companies and aimed to provide both advocacy and technical support to the industry, while also serving as a conduit between members and authorities in foreign countries on issues such as legislation. According to the SFSA Secretary-General, Muhammed Jirdeh Hussein, such companies remitted about US $750m. annually from Somalis in the diaspora and were the largest employers in Somalia. Many remittance transactions related to investments, commerce and social development projects.

In 2004 the World Food Programme (WFP) was in the second year of a Protracted Relief and Recovery Operation (PRRO) in Somalia, covering January 2003–December 2005 and providing assistance to some 2.8m. people. The PRRO was to support tuberculosis and HIV/AIDS patients and to fund hospitals, mother-and-child health care, orphanages, school feeding and emergency relief programmes. There were also provisions for drought and flood relief. In July 2004 WFP appealed for more than US $14m. to help drought-affected people and to fund other humanitarian operations for the remainder of that year. The three-year PRRO estimated some 64,000 metric tons of food aid would be required, at a cost of $51m. Four years of poor rainfall had severely reduced the size of herds in the northern and central regions, especially southern Togdher, Sool, Sanaag, southern Bari, Nugaal, northern Mudug, southern Mudug, Galgadud and some lower Juba districts; livestock deaths were up to 80% of herds in some places. Ongoing instability throughout much of the country impeded relief deliveries and economic recovery. Nevertheless, by early 2004 WFP had distributed more than 3,000 tons of relief aid to some 145,000 people in northern and eastern Somalia. In mid-April the UN reported that 123,000 Somalis faced a food-security crisis, 95,000 of whom were in a critical condition. To address this problem, UN agencies and NGOs in Somalia requested 4,110m. tons in emergency food and development aid for about 750,000 Somalis. In June 2005 Prime Minister Ali Mohammed Ghedi opened a recently renovated canal in Jowhar that would enable about 50,000 people to irrigate their fields with water from the Shebelle river and would protect them from perennial floods. The WFP, under a food-for-work project, provided 600 tons of food for those who helped repair the canal.

'SOMALILAND'

The relative stability of the self-proclaimed 'Republic of Somaliland', following its secession in 1991, contributed to improvements in the economy of that territory. More than one-half of the 3.5m. population of 'Somaliland' were nomadic pastoralists. As in Somalia proper, a substantial portion of regional income was derived from remittances. Population growth, drought and general poverty ensured that the agricultural sector was unable to sustain real development. The lack of international recognition effectively closed access to international financial institutions such as the World Bank and the IMF.

The pursuit of international aid for projects in 'Somaliland' remained a priority of the Government. In January 1997 the Intergovernmental Authority on Development (IGAD) announced a project (estimated to cost US $18m.) to improve communications between Berbera and several other East African ports. Meanwhile, the EU agreed to fund the reconstruction of several roads, and an Italian relief agency, Cooperazione Internazionale, was to rehabilitate Berbera's water system. In September 1998 an Islamic Development Bank (IDB) delegation arrived in Hargeysa to consider developing the veterinary, education and water sectors in 'Somaliland'. In December a British company, Digital Exchange Products, announced that it had been appointed by Somaliland Telecommunications Corpn to reinstall a telecommunications system (destroyed during the civil war) and to design and maintain a website for the 'Somaliland' Government. In October 1998 the UN Conference on Trade and Development (UNCTAD) embarked on a programme to rehabilitate the port of Berbera and to train Somalis to become port managers, mechanics, cargo-handlers and clerks. The programme also included the port of Bossaso, in 'Puntland'. In May 1999 the EU granted 'Somaliland' $1m. to finance water projects and to train staff in water management and maintenance of water installations. In February 1998 President Mohamed Ibrahim Egal protested to WHO about Saudi Arabia's decision to suspend livestock imports from 'Somaliland' for fear that the animals suffered from the Rift Valley fever that had broken out in Kenya. The ban devastated the economy, which depends on livestock sales for foreign-exchange earnings amounting to some $100m. annually. The export of goats reportedly declined from 1m. head in March 1997 to 481,000 in March 1998, while sheep exports fell from 1.2m. head in April 1997 to about 514,000 in April 1998.

In November 1998 Saudi Arabia and the UAE lifted the livestock ban. A few months later FAO reported that the territory's livestock was healthy and free of disease, notably of Rift Valley fever. In late 2000 'Somaliland' and Iran concluded a series of agreements about the export of livestock, hides and skins. In September 2000 Saudi Arabia and the Gulf states imposed a livestock import embargo. 'Somaliland' initially suffered millions of dollars in lost livestock sales. However, by early 2003 the Government had developed some alternative markets, although sales did not match the levels achieved in the late 1990s. In April 2003 the different parts of Somalia sought to address this recurring problem by beginning discussions to create a joint Somali Livestock Board to regulate the livestock industry and to open a modern slaughter house in Burao. By late 2003 all the Gulf states, but not Saudi Arabia, had lifted the livestock ban. Despite these positive developments, 'Somaliland' and 'Puntland' continued to experience significant losses of sales, exports taxes and port revenues. As a result, in 2003 sheep and goat exports totalled only 1.5m. head, cattle 71,228 and camels 4,259.

In late 1999 the EU had begun using the port of Berbera for food aid bound for Ethiopia. According to the EU, the shipment of 16,670 metric tons of food aid constituted a pilot project to assess the suitability of 'Somaliland' as a transhipment point. The use of Berbera was necessary owing to congestion at the port of Djibouti, the main supply route into Ethiopia.

In January 2000 President Egal approved a plan for Total Red Sea, the local subsidiary of the French oil company, to assume management responsibility for the port of Berbera's petroleum-storage facilities. On 18 April 2001 a 'Somaliland' newspaper announced that a British company, Rovagold, had received permission to commence prospecting for offshore petroleum. Rovagold, which had signed agreements in 1999 with two Chinese companies, Continental Petroleum Engineering Co and China Petrochemical Corpn, planned to start exploration activities off the coast of Berbera. In mid-October 2002 'Somaliland' signed an agreement with the Seminal Copenhagen Group to begin petroleum exploration in late 2002.

Compared to the war-torn south, the economy of 'Somaliland' has experienced relative stability. On 26 March 2000 Egal announced that the 2000 budget would balance at US $26m. This was an increase over the previous year and attributed to increased revenue collection in Berbera, which remains the Government's main source of income. In November 2000 'Somaliland' and Ethiopia concluded a trade and communications agreement. The terms of the accord included a plan to increase Ethiopian use of the port of Berbera by improving the road to the Ethiopian border. The Ethiopian authorities also agreed to build a microwave communication link between Burao, Hargeysa and Berbera. In August 2001 the Great Wall Chinese Oil Co announced that it planned to sink seven deep onshore wells at several locations in 'Somaliland', including Sahil Sail, Sanaag Sail, Tahil, Gabiley and Borama. The project was reportedly funded by a number of companies from the People's Republic of China, Bahrain and the UAE. At about the same time experts from the UAE carried out mineral exploration on the outskirts of Berbera and other parts of 'Somaliland'. In 2003 'Somaliland' reported that tax revenue from the port of Berbera totalled $13.2m. in 2002, contributing some 81% of the Government's total revenue of $16.2m. The diaspora also contributed some $150m. to 'Somaliland' in 2002. In September 2003 US-based Tecore Wireless Systems announced that it would install a wireless Global System for Mobile Communications which would link 'Somaliland' and Somalia.

The economic rehabilitation of 'Somaliland' remains stymied because there is no formal operational banking structure. The Bank of Somaliland, which has little capital, sought to work with public and private sectors, but had yet to attract enough savings clients. To resolve this problem, the Bank of Somaliland continued to encourage the Somali diaspora, which sends as much as US $250m. to 'Somaliland' annually, to use its services instead of those of the remittance companies. However, this initiative failed, as the latter could transfer money to 'Somaliland' within hours, whereas the Bank of Somaliland required seven working days to process such transfers. The Bank of Somaliland hoped to establish relations with the Commercial Bank of Ethiopia, the Bank of Djibouti and Germany's Commerzbank to secure links to the international financial world.

'PUNTLAND'

The regional administration of 'Puntland' was established in mid-1998, incorporating the areas of Bari and Nugaal, and parts of Mudug, Sanaag and Sool regions. The main economic activity of Puntland is cattle rearing, while frankincense is one of the region's principal exports. In mid-2000 two US companies won a contract to provide US $1m. worth of telecommunications equipment to the North East Telecom Corpn.

In December 1998 drought crippled the economic viability of 'Puntland'. Officials appealed to the UN and to foreign governments and relief agencies for food and medical supplies for the populations of Mudug and Nugaal regions, both of which were suffering from severe drought. To make matters worse, some 200,000 people displaced from southern Somalia sought refuge in 'Puntland'. Some 900,000 were facing starvation and famine, out of an estimated 2.4m. people in 'Puntland'. In April 1999 'Puntland' declared a state of emergency. At about the same time WFP announced the arrival at Bossaso port of a shipment of 335 metric tons of food aid for 'Puntland'. The food, donated by the EU, was part of a 1,400-ton consignment to feed some 100,000 famine victims. Oxfam also warned that the situation had become acute in Nugaal and Mudug because of water shortages. Oxfam, in co-operation with other humanitarian agencies, planned to transport 1,500 tanker-loads of water to key grazing areas over a six-week period. Meanwhile, the UN Children's Fund (UNICEF) launched a $1.3m. appeal for drought-stricken areas in northern Somalia. In March 2002 there were reports that a Chinese petroleum exploration company had been active along stretches of the 'Puntland' coastline. In December 2005 the Governments of the USA and Saudi Arabia reportedly registered their opposition to the award of a contract for airport work in Bossaso to the Saudi Binladin Group (a company owned by the family of the notorious terrorist, Osama bin Laden, denounced by most of his family). The project was to be financed by the UAE Emirate of Sharjah, which selected the Binladin company for the multimillion dollar project.

Statistical Survey

Sources (unless otherwise stated): Economic Research and Statistics Dept, Central Bank of Somalia, Mogadishu, and Central Statistical Dept, State Planning Commission, POB 1742, Mogadishu; tel. (1) 80385.

Area and Population

AREA, POPULATION AND DENSITY

Area (sq km)	637,657*
Population (census results)†	
7 February 1975	3,253,024
February 1986 (provisional)	
Males	3,741,664
Females	3,372,767
Total	7,114,431
Population (UN estimates at mid-year)‡	
2004	7,954,000
2005	8,196,000
2006	8,445,000
Density (per sq km) at mid-2006	13.2

* 246,201 sq miles.

† Excluding adjustment for underenumeration.

‡ Source: UN, *World Population Prospects: The 2006 Revision*.

PRINCIPAL TOWNS
(estimated population in 1981)

Mogadishu (capital)	500,000	Berbera	65,000
Hargeysa	70,000	Merca	60,000
Kismayu	70,000		

Mid-2005 ('000, including suburbs, UN estimate): Mogadishu 1,320 (Source: UN, *World Urbanization Prospects: The 2005 Revision*).

BIRTHS AND DEATHS
(annual averages, UN estimates)

	1990–95	1995–2000	2000–05
Birth rate (per 1,000)	45.7	47.7	45.8
Death rate (per 1,000)	23.5	20.3	18.5

Source: UN, *World Population Prospects: The 2006 Revision*.

Expectation of life (years at birth, WHO estimates): 44 (males 43; females 45) in 2004 (Source: WHO, *World Health Report*).

ECONOMICALLY ACTIVE POPULATION
(estimates, '000 persons, 1991)

	Males	Females	Total
Agriculture, etc.	1,157	1,118	2,275
Industry	290	46	336
Services	466	138	604
Total labour force	1,913	1,302	3,215

Source: UN Economic Commission for Africa, *African Statistical Yearbook*.

2002 (percentage distribution): Agriculture 66.9; Industry 12.0; Services 21.1 (Source: The World Bank and United Nations Development Programme, *Socio-Economic Survey 2002 Somalia*).

Mid-2005 (estimates in '000): Agriculture, etc. 2,572; Total labour force 3,737 (Source: FAO).

Health and Welfare

KEY INDICATORS

Total fertility rate (children per woman, 2005)	6.2
Under-5 mortality rate (per 1,000 live births, 2005)	225
HIV/AIDS (% of persons aged 15–49, 2005)	0.9
Physicians (per 1,000 head, 1997)	0.04
Hospital beds (per 1,000 head, 1997)	0.42
Health expenditure (2001): US $ per head (PPP)	18
Health expenditure (2001): % of GDP	2.6
Health expenditure (2001): public (% of total)	44.6
Access to water (% of persons, 2004)	29
Access to sanitation (% of persons, 2004)	26

For sources and definitions, see explanatory note on p. vi.

Agriculture

PRINCIPAL CROPS
('000 metric tons)

	2003	2004	2005
Rice (paddy)	12*	18*	4†
Maize	170*	202*	190†
Sorghum	121*	145*	150†
Sweet potatoes†	7	7	7
Cassava (Manioc)†	80	85	85
Sugar cane†	200	200	200
Groundnuts (in shell)	4*	9*	4
Sesame seed†	30	30	30
Vegetables†	53	53	55
Watermelons	6*	8*	6†
Grapefruit and pomelos†	6	6	6
Bananas†	38	38	38
Oranges†	9	9	9
Lemons and limes†	8	8	8
Dates†	12	12	12

* Unofficial figure.
† FAO estimate(s).

Source: FAO.

LIVESTOCK
('000 head, year ending September, FAO estimates)

	2003	2004	2005
Cattle	5,350	5,350	5,350
Sheep	14,350	14,500	13,100
Goats	12,800	12,800	12,700
Pigs	4	4	4
Asses and mules	41	41	41
Camels	7,200	7,000	7,000
Chickens	3	3	3

Source: FAO.

LIVESTOCK PRODUCTS
('000 metric tons, FAO estimates)

	2000	2001	2002
Cows' milk	530	557	557
Goats' milk	390	392	392
Sheep's milk	430	445	445
Cattle meat	59	63	62
Sheep meat	35	43	43
Goat meat	37	32	38
Hen eggs	3	3	3

2003–05: Figures assumed to be unchanged from 2002 (FAO estimates).

Source: FAO.

Forestry

ROUNDWOOD REMOVALS
('000 cubic metres, excl. bark, FAO estimates)

	2003	2004	2005
Sawlogs, veneer logs and logs for sleepers*	28	28	28
Other industrial wood	82	82	82
Fuel wood	10,141	10,466	10,803
Total	10,251	10,576	10,913

* Annual output assumed to be unchanged since 1975.

Source: FAO.

SAWNWOOD PRODUCTION
('000 cubic metres, incl. railway sleepers)

	1973	1974	1975
Total (all broadleaved)	15*	10	14

* FAO estimate.

1976–2005: Annual production as in 1975 (FAO estimates).

Source: FAO.

Fishing

('000 metric tons, live weight, FAO estimates)

	1999	2000	2001
Marine fishes	23.5	19.8	26.3
Total catch (incl. others)	24.8	20.8	27.5

2002–05: Figures assumed to be unchanged from 2001 (FAO estimates).

Source: FAO.

Mining

('000 metric tons, estimates)

	2002	2003	2004
Salt	1	1	1
Gypsum	2	2	2

Source: US Geological Survey.

Industry

SELECTED PRODUCTS
('000 metric tons, unless otherwise indicated)

	1986	1987	1988
Sugar*	30.0	43.3	41.2
Canned meat (million tins)	1.0	—	—
Canned fish	0.1	—	—
Pasta and flour	15.6	4.3	—
Textiles (million yards)	5.5	3.0	6.3
Boxes and bags	15.0	12.0	5.0
Cigarettes and matches	0.3	0.2	0.1
Petroleum products	128	44	30
Electric energy (million kWh)†	253	255‡	257‡

Sugar (unofficial estimates, '000 metric tons)*: 21 in 1996; 18 in 1997; 19 in 1998.

Electric energy (million kWh)†: 282 in 2002; 284 in 2003; 286 in 2004.

* Data from FAO.

† Source: UN, *Industrial Commodity Statistics Yearbook*.

‡ Provisional figure.

Finance

CURRENCY AND EXCHANGE RATES

Monetary Units
100 cents = 1 Somali shilling (So. sh.).

Sterling, Dollar and Euro Equivalents (30 April 2007)
£1 sterling = 28,734 Somali shillings;
US $1 = 14.406 Somali shillings;
€1 = 19,599 Somali shillings;
100,000 Somali shillings = £3.48 = $6.94 = €5.10.

Average Exchange Rate (Somali shillings per US $)
1987 105.18
1988 170.45
1989 490.68

Note: A separate currency, the 'Somaliland shilling', was introduced in the 'Republic of Somaliland' in January 1995. The exchange rate was reported to be US $1 = 2,750 'Somaliland shillings' in March 2000.

CURRENT BUDGET
(million Somali shillings)

Revenue	1986	1987	1988
Total tax revenue	8,516.4	8,622.4	12,528.1
Taxes on income and profits	1,014.8	889.7	1,431.0
Income tax	380.5	538.8	914.8
Profit tax	634.3	350.9	516.2
Taxes on production, consumption and domestic transactions	1,410.4	1,274.2	2,336.4
Taxes on international transactions	6,091.2	6,458.5	8,760.6
Import duties	4,633.2	4,835.2	6,712.1
Total non-tax revenue	6,375.2	8,220.4	7,623.4
Fees and service charges	274.1	576.1	828.8
Income from government property	633.4	656.4	2,418.9
Other revenue	5,467.2	6,987.9	4,375.7
Total	14,891.6	16,842.8	20,151.5

Expenditure	1986	1987	1988
Total general services	11,997.7	19,636.7	24,213.6
Defence	2,615.9	3,145.0	8,093.9
Interior and police	605.0	560.7	715.4
Finance and central services	7,588.3	14,017.8	12,515.6
Foreign affairs	633.0	1,413.9	2,153.1
Justice and religious affairs	248.5	290.2	447.0
Presidency and general administration	93.0	148.0	217.4
Planning	189.0	24.9	24.3
National Assembly	25.0	36.2	46.9
Total economic services	1,927.6	554.1	600.3
Transportation	122.2	95.2	94.5
Posts and telecommunications	94.3	76.7	75.6
Public works	153.9	57.5	69.8
Agriculture	547.2	59.4	55.3
Livestock and forestry	459.0	89.5	109.9
Mineral and water resources	318.8	85.2	93.1
Industry and commerce	131.0	45.1	43.9
Fisheries	101.2	45.5	58.2
Total social services	1,050.5	900.1	930.8
Education	501.6	403.0	478.1
Health	213.8	203.5	255.2
Information	111.5	135.0	145.8
Labour, sports and tourism	139.6	49.3	51.7
Other	84.0	109.3	—
Total	14,975.8	21,091.0	25,744.7

1989 (estimates): Budget to balance at 32,429.0m. Somali shillings.

1990 (estimates): Budget to balance at 86,012.0m. Somali shillings.

1991 (estimates): Budget to balance at 268,283.2m. Somali shillings.

CENTRAL BANK RESERVES
(US $ million at 31 December)

	1987	1988	1989
Gold*	8.3	7.0	6.9
Foreign exchange	7.3	15.3	15.4
Total	15.6	22.3	22.3

* Valued at market-related prices.

Source: IMF, *International Financial Statistics*.

MONEY SUPPLY
(million Somali shillings at 31 December)

	1987	1988	1989
Currency outside banks	12,327	21,033	70,789
Private-sector deposits at central bank	1,771	1,555	5,067
Demand deposits at commercial banks	15,948	22,848	63,971
Total money	30,046	45,436	139,827

Source: IMF, *International Financial Statistics*.

COST OF LIVING
(Consumer Price Index; base: 2000 = 100)

	2001	2002	2003
All items	111.5	133.8	133.8

2004–06: Consumer prices assumed to be unchanged from 2003.

Source: African Development Bank.

NATIONAL ACCOUNTS

Expenditure on the Gross Domestic Product*
(estimates, million Somali shillings at current prices)

	1988	1989	1990
Government final consumption expenditure	33,220	58,530	104,760
Private final consumption expenditure	240,950	481,680	894,790
Increase in stocks	14,770	n.a.	n.a.
Gross fixed capital formation	44,780	134,150	240,030
Total domestic expenditure	333,720	674,360	1,239,580
Exports of goods and services	7,630	8,890	8,660
Less Imports of goods and services	49,430	57,660	58,460
GDP in purchasers' values	291,920	625,580	1,189,780

* Figures are rounded to the nearest 10m. Somali shillings.

Source: UN Economic Commission for Africa, *African Statistical Yearbook*.

Gross Domestic Product by Economic Activity
(million Somali shillings at constant 1985 prices)

	1986	1987	1988
Agriculture, hunting, forestry and fishing	54,868	59,378	61,613
Mining and quarrying	291	291	291
Manufacturing	4,596	4,821	4,580
Electricity, gas and water	77	62	57
Construction	3,289	3,486	2,963
Trade, restaurants and hotels	8,587	9,929	8,599
Transport, storage and communications	6,020	6,153	5,873
Finance, insurance, real estate and business services	3,743	4,095	3,890
Government services	1,631	1,530	1,404
Other community, social and personal services	2,698	2,779	2,863
Sub-total	85,800	92,524	92,133
Less Imputed bank service charges	737	748	748
GDP at factor cost	85,064	91,776	91,385
Indirect taxes, *less* subsidies	5,301	4,250	3,262
GDP in purchasers' values	90,365	96,026	94,647

GDP at factor cost (estimates, million Somali shillings at current prices): 249,380 in 1988; 500,130 in 1989; 923,970 in 1990 (Source: UN Economic Commission for Africa, *African Statistical Yearbook*).

BALANCE OF PAYMENTS
(US $ million)

	1987	1988	1989
Exports of goods f.o.b.	94.0	58.4	67.7
Imports of goods f.o.b.	–358.5	–216.0	–346.3
Trade balance	–264.5	–157.6	–278.6
Imports of services	–127.7	–104.0	–122.0
Balance on goods and services	–392.2	–261.6	–400.6
Other income paid	–52.0	–60.6	–84.4
Balance on goods, services and income	–444.2	–322.2	–485.0
Current transfers received	343.3	223.7	331.2
Current transfers paid	–13.1	—	–2.9
Current balance	–114.0	–98.5	–156.7
Investment liabilities	–22.8	–105.5	–32.6
Net errors and omissions	39.0	22.4	–0.8
Overall balance	–97.9	–181.7	–190.0

Source: IMF, *International Financial Statistics*.

External Trade

PRINCIPAL COMMODITIES
(million Somali shillings)

Imports*	1986	1987	1988
Foodstuffs	1,783.3	3,703.6	1,216.1
Beverages and tobacco	298.1	183.6	6.2
Manufacturing raw materials	230.0	626.9	661.4
Fertilizers	1.8	238.0	2,411.4
Petroleum	2,051.0	3,604.2	3,815.9
Construction materials	981.4	2,001.9	307.8
Machinery and parts	1,098.3	1,203.6	957.1
Transport equipment	1,133.8	1,027.6	195.2
Total (incl. others)	8,443.4	13,913.7	11,545.5

* Figures cover only imports made against payments of foreign currencies. The total value of imports in 1986 was 20,474 million Somali shillings.

Exports	1986	1987	1988
Livestock	4,420.3	7,300.0	3,806.5
Bananas	1,207.2	2,468.8	3,992.3
Hides and skins	294.0	705.2	492.0
Total (incl. others)	6,372.5	10,899.9	9,914.1

1992 (estimates, US $ million): Imports 150; Exports 80.

PRINCIPAL TRADING PARTNERS
('000 Somali shillings)

Imports	1980	1981	1982
China, People's Repub.	46,959	40,962	89,772
Ethiopia	43,743	146,853	155,775
Germany, Fed. Repub.	104,117	430,548	214,873
Hong Kong	5,351	13,862	3,972
India	41,467	19,638	4,801
Iraq	2,812	67,746	402
Italy	756,800	662,839	1,221,146
Japan	28,900	54,789	48,371
Kenya	86,515	105,627	198,064
Saudi Arabia	120,208	160,583	82,879
Singapore	18,569	15,592	73,652
Thailand	19,296	40,527	106,474
United Kingdom	172,613	935,900	238,371
USA	201,662	141,823	154,082
Total (incl. others)	2,190,627	3,221,715	3,548,805

Exports	1980	1981	1982
Djibouti	6,640	3,209	2,458
Germany, Fed. Repub.	11,376	1,956	20,086
Italy	107,661	58,975	77,870
Kenya	2,425	6,929	4,211
Saudi Arabia	583,768	803,631	1,852,936
United Kingdom	1,233	—	3,169
USA	1,301	—	6,970
Yemen, People's Dem. Repub.	3,182	—	—
Total (incl. others)	844,012	960,050	2,142,585

Source: the former Ministry of Planning, Mogadishu.

1986: *Imports* (estimates, million Somali shillings) USA 1,816; Japan 836; China, People's Repub. 553; United Kingdom 773; France 341; Germany, Fed. Repub. 1,481; Total (incl. others) 8,443; *Exports* (estimates, million Somali shillings) USA 5; China, People's Repub. 4; United Kingdom 31; France 27; Germany, Fed. Repub. 11; Total (incl. others) 6,373 (Source: UN Economic Commission for Africa, *African Statistical Yearbook*).

Transport

ROAD TRAFFIC
(estimates, '000 motor vehicles in use)

	1994	1995	1996
Passenger cars	2.8	2.0	1.0
Commercial vehicles	7.4	7.3	6.4

Source: International Road Federation, *World Road Statistics*.

SHIPPING

Merchant Fleet
(registered at 31 December)

	2004	2005	2006
Number of vessels	18	18	19
Total displacement ('000 grt)	7.3	2.8	10.3

Source: Lloyd's Register-Fairplay, *World Fleet Statistics*.

International Sea-borne Freight Traffic
('000 metric tons)

	1989	1990	1991
Goods loaded	325	324	n.a.
Goods unloaded	1,252*	1,118	1,007*

* Estimate.

Source: UN Economic Commission for Africa, *African Statistical Yearbook*.

CIVIL AVIATION
(traffic on scheduled services)

	1989	1990	1991
Kilometres flown (million)	3	3	1
Passengers carried ('000)	89	88	46
Passenger-km (million)	248	255	131
Freight ton-km (million)	8	9	5

Source: UN, *Statistical Yearbook*.

Tourism

	1996	1997	1998
Tourist arrivals ('000)	10	10	10

Source: World Bank.

Communications Media

	1995	1996	1997
Radio receivers ('000 in use)	400	450	470
Television receivers ('000 in use)	124	129	135
Telephones ('000 main lines in use)*	15	15	15
Daily newspapers	1	2	n.a.

* Estimates.

2003: Mobile cellular telephones (subscribers) 200,000; Telephones (main lines in use, estimate) 100,000.

2004: Mobile cellular telephones (subscribers) 500,000; Telephones (main lines in use, estimate) 100,000; Internet users 86,000.

2005: Mobile cellular telephones (subscribers) 500,000; Telephones (main lines in use, estimate) 100,000; Internet users 90,000.

Sources: UNESCO, *Statistical Yearbook*; International Telecommunication Union.

Education

(1985)

	Institutions	Teachers	Pupils
Pre-primary	16	133	1,558
Primary	1,224	10,338	196,496
Secondary:			
general	n.a.	2,149	39,753
teacher training	n.a.	30*	613*
vocational	n.a.	637	5,933
Higher	n.a.	817†	15,672†

* Figure refers to 1984.
† Figure refers to 1986.

Source: UNESCO, *Statistical Yearbook*.

1990 (UN estimates): 377,000 primary-level pupils; 44,000 secondary-level pupils; 10,400 higher-level pupils.

1991: University teachers 549; University students 4,640.

Adult literacy rate (UNESCO estimates): 24.0% in 2002 (Source: UN Development Programme, *Human Development Report*).

Directory

The Constitution

The Constitution promulgated in 1979 and amended in 1990 was revoked following the overthrow of President Siad Barre in January 1991. In July 2000 delegates at the Somali national reconciliation conference in Arta, Djibouti, overwhelmingly approved a national Charter, which was to serve as Somalia's constitution for an interim period of three years. The Charter, which is divided into six main parts, guarantees Somali citizens the freedoms of expression, association and human rights, and distinctly separates the executive, the legislature and the judiciary, as well as guaranteeing the independence of the latter.

The Government

HEAD OF STATE

President: Col ABDULLAHI YUSSUF AHMED (took office 14 October 2004).

CABINET
(August 2007)

Prime Minister: ALI MOHAMMED GHEDI.

Deputy Prime Minister and Minister of Culture and Higher Education: SALIM ALIOW IBROW.

Minister of Public Works and Housing: HUSSEIN MOHAMED AIDID.

Minister of Finance: HASAN MOHAMED NUR.

Minister of Information: MADOBE NUNOW MUHAMMAD.

Minister of Justice: HASAN DIMBIL WARSAME.

Minister of Religious Affairs and Endowment: SHEIKH HASSAN ISMA'IL BILE.

Minister of Foreign Affairs: HUSAYN ELABE FAHIYE.

Minister of Defence: BARE ADAN SHIRE.

Minister of National Security: ABDULLAHI SHEIKH ISMA'IL GARUN.

Minister of Agriculture: ABDULKADIR NUR ARALE.

Minister of Fishery and Marine Resources: HASSAN ABSHIR FARAH.

Ministry of Livestock Husbandry, Forestry and Wildlife: ALI AHMAD JAMA JANGALI.

Minister of Trade: ABDULLAHI AHMAD AFRAH.

Minister of Health: QAMAR ADAN ALI.

Minister of Minerals and Water Resources: MUHAMMAD NUURANI BAKAR.

Minister of Aviation and Land Transport: MOHAMED IBRAHIM HABSADE.

Minister of Ports and Sea Transport: ALI ISMA'IL ABDI GIIR.

Minister of Posts and Telecommunications: ABDI MUHAMMAD TARAH.

Minister of Energy and Fuel: ABDULLAHI YUSUF MUHAMMAD.

Minister of Internal Affairs: MOHAMED MAHMUD GULEED.

Minister of Industry: MOHAMED ABDULLAHI MOHAMED KAAMIL.

Minister of Reconstruction and Resettlement: ADBIRAHMAN JAMA ABDALLA.

Minister of Education: ISMA'IL MUHAMMAD HURRE 'BUBA'.

Minister for the Environment: MUHAMMAD MAHMUD HAYD.

Minister of Tourism and Wildlife: ALI MUHAMMAD MAHMUD.

Minister of Labour Development: SALAH ALI FARAH.

Minister of Sports and Youth Affairs: MOWLID MA'ANE MAHMUD.

Minister of Reconciliation and Somali Communities Abroad: MUHAMMAD ABDI HAYIR.

Minister of National Planning: ALI ABDULAHI OSOBLE.

Minister of Constitutional and Federal Affairs: ABDULLAHI SHEIKH ISMA'IL.

Minister of Women's Development and Family Affairs: AMINA MUHAMMAD MURSAL.

MINISTRIES

Until mid-2005 the Somali Government was based in Nairobi, Kenya, for security reasons. The President, the Prime Minister and several ministers relocated to Jowhar, Somalia, in June; however, a significant number of ministers returned to Mogadishu in defiance of the President. The Transitional Parliament (TP) held its first meeting in Baidoa, some 250 km north-west of Mogadishu, in February 2006 and the town was subsequently declared the seat of government. In mid-March 2007 the TP voted to move the Cabinet to Mogadishu, and in early April the first five ministries were relocated; the remaining ministries were expected to be re-opened in the capital during 2007.

Legislature

TRANSITIONAL PARLIAMENT

Speaker: SHAYKH ADAN MADOBE.

In August 2000, following the successful completion of the Somali national reconciliation conference, which commenced in Arta, Djibouti, in May, a Transitional National Assembly (TNA), comprising 245 members, was established. Despite the expiry of its mandate in August 2003, the TNA remained in place, pending the election of a new legislative body. In late January 2004, following protracted negotiations in Kenya, an agreement was signed that provided for the establishment of a new 275-member transitional national parliament, to comprise 61 representatives from each of the four major clans and 31 from an alliance of smaller clans. Members were sworn in to the Transitional Parliament in late August.

Political Organizations

Alliance Party: Hargeysa; f. 2001; Chair. SULAYMAN MAHMUD ADAN.

Islamic Party (Hizb al-Islam): radical Islamist party; Chair. Sheikh AHMAD QASIM.

Islamic Union Party (al-Ittihad al-Islam): aims to unite ethnic Somalis from Somalia, Ethiopia, Kenya and Djibouti in an Islamic state.

Juba Valley Alliance (JVA): f. 1999; alliance of militia and businessmen from the Habr Gedir and Marehan clans; Pres. BARE ADAN SHIRE.

National Democratic League: Beled Weyne; f. 2003; Chair. Dr ABDIRAHMAN ABDULLE ALI; Sec.-Gen. ABDIKARIM HUSAYN IDOW.

Northern Somali Alliance (NSA): f. 1997 as alliance between the United Somali Front and the United Somali Party.

United Somali Front (USF): f. 1989; represents Issas in the north-west of the country; Chair. ABD AR-RAHMAN DUALEH ALI; Sec.-Gen. MOHAMED OSMAN ALI.

United Somali Party (USP): opposes the SNM's declaration of the independent 'Republic of Somaliland'; Leader MOHAMED ABDI HASHI.

Peace and Development Party: Mogadishu; f. 2002; Chair. ABDULLAHI HASAN AFRAH.

Rahanwin Resistance Army (RRA): guerrilla force active around Baidoa; Chair. MOHAMED HASAN NUR.

Somali Democratic Alliance (SDA): f. 1989; represents the Gadabursi ethnic grouping in the north-west; opposes the Isaaq-dominated SNM and its declaration of an independent 'Republic of Somaliland'; Leader MOHAMED FARAH ABDULLAH.

Somali Democratic Movement (SDM): represents the Rahanwin clan; movement split in early 1992, with this faction in alliance with Ali Mahdi Mohamed; Leader ABDULKADIR MOHAMED ADAN.

Somali Eastern and Central Front (SECF): f. 1991; opposes the SNM's declaration of the independent 'Republic of Somaliland'; Chair. HIRSI ISMAIL MOHAMED.

Somali National Alliance (SNA): f. 1992 as alliance between the Southern Somali National Movement (which withdrew in 1993) and the factions of the United Somali Congress, Somali Democratic Movement and Somali Patriotic Movement given below; Chair. HUSSEIN MOHAMED AIDID.

Somali Democratic Movement (SDM): represents the Rahanwin clan; Chair. ADAM UTHMAN ABDI; Sec.-Gen. Dr YASIN MA'ALIM ABDULLAHI.

Somali Patriotic Movement (SPM): f. 1989; represents Ogadenis (of the southern Darod clan); Chair. GEDI UGAS MADHAR.

United Somali Congress (USC): f. 1989; overthrew Siad Barre in 1991; party split in mid-1991, and again in mid-1995; Chair. OSMAN HASSAN ALI 'ATO'.

Somali National Front (SNF): f. 1991; guerrilla force active in southern Somalia, promoting Darod clan interests and seeking restoration of SRSP Govt; a rival faction (led by OMAR HAJI MASALEH) is active in southern Somalia; Leader Gen. MOHAMED SIAD HERSI 'MORGAN'.

Somali National Salvation Council: f. 2003; Chair. MUSE SUDI YALAHOW.

Somali Patriotic Movement (SPM): f. 1989 in southern Somalia; represents Ogadenis (of the Darod clan) in southern Somalia; this faction of the SPM has allied with the SNF in opposing the SNA; Chair. Gen. ADEN ABDULLAHI NOOR ('Gabio').

Somali Peace Loving Party: Mogadishu; f. 2002; Dr KHALID UMAR ALI.

Somali People's Democratic Union (SPDU): f. 1997; breakaway group from the SSDF; Chair. Gen. MOHAMED JIBRIL MUSEH.

Somali Reconciliation and Restoration Council (SRRC): f. 2001 by faction leaders opposed to the establishment of the Hasan administration; aims to establish a rival national govt; Co-Chair. HUSSEIN MOHAMED AIDID, HILOWLE IMAN UMAR, ADEN ABDULLAHI NOOR, HASAN MOHAMED NUR, ABDULLAHI SHAYKH ISMA'IL; Sec.-Gen. MOWLID MA'ANEH MOHAMED.

Somali Revolutionary Socialist Party (SRSP): f. 1976 as the sole legal party; overthrown in Jan. 1991; conducts guerrilla operations in Gedo region, near border with Kenya; Sec.-Gen. (vacant); Asst Sec.-Gen. AHMED SULEIMAN ABDULLAH.

Somali Salvation Democratic Front (SSDF): f. 1981 as the Democratic Front for the Salvation of Somalia (DFSS), as a coalition of the Somali Salvation Front, the Somali Workers' Party and the Democratic Front for the Liberation of Somalia; operates in cen. Somalia, although a smaller group has opposed the SNA around Kismayu in alliance with the SNF; Chair. MOHAMED ABSHIR MONSA.

Somali Solidarity Party: Mogadishu; f. 1999; Chair. ABD AR-RAHMAN MUSA MOHAMED; Sec.-Gen. SA'ID ISA MOHAMED.

Southern Somali National Movement (SSNM): based on coast in southern Somalia; Chair. ABDI WARSEMEH ISAR.

Supreme Somali Islamic Courts Council: formerly the Union of Islamic Courts; seeks to create a Somali state under the guiding principles of *Shari'a* (Islamic) law; Chair. Sheikh HASSAN DAHIR AWEYS.

United Somali Congress (USC): f. 1989 in cen. Somalia; overthrew Siad Barre in Jan. 1991; party split in 1991, with this faction dominated by the Abgal sub-clan of the Hawiye clan, Somalia's largest ethnic group; Leader ABDULLAHI MA'ALIN; Sec.-Gen. MUSA NUR AMIN.

United Somali Congress—Somali National Alliance (USC—SNA): f. 1995 by dissident mems of the SNA's USC faction; represents the Habr Gedir sub-clan of the Hawiye; Leader OSMAN HASSAN ALI 'ATO'.

United Somali Congress—Somali Salvation Alliance (USC—SSA): Leader MUSE SUDI YALAHOW.

Unity for the Somali Republic Party (USRP): f. 1999; the first independent party to be established in Somalia since 1969; Leader ABDI NUR DARMAN.

In November 1993 interim President Ali Mahdi Mohamed was reported to have assumed the leadership of the **Somali Salvation Alliance (SSA)**, a coalition of 12 factions opposed to Gen. Aidid, including the Somali African Muki Organization (SAMO), the Somali National Union (SNU), the USF, the SDA, the SDM, the SPM, the USC (pro-Mahdi faction), the SSDF, the Somali National Democratic Union (SNDU), the SNF and the SSNM. In May 1994 the SNU announced its intention to leave the alliance and join the SNA.

Diplomatic Representation

EMBASSIES IN SOMALIA

Note: Following the overthrow of Siad Barre in January 1991, all foreign embassies in Somalia were closed and all diplomatic personnel left the country. Some embassies were reopened, including those of France, Sudan and the USA, following the arrival of the US-led Unified Task Force (UNITAF) in December 1992; however, nearly all foreign diplomats left Somalia in anticipation of the withdrawal of the UN peace-keeping force, UNOSOM, in early 1995.

Algeria: POB 2850, Mogadishu; tel. (1) 81696.

Cuba: Mogadishu.

Djibouti: Mogadishu.

Iran: Via al-Mukarah, POB 1166, Mogadishu; tel. (1) 80881.

Korea, Democratic People's Republic: Via Km 5, Mogadishu; Ambassador KIM RYONG SU.

Kuwait: First Medina Rd, Km 5, POB 1348, Mogadishu.

Libya: Via Medina, POB 125, Mogadishu; Ambassador MOHAMED ZUBEYD.

Pakistan: Via Afgoi, Km 5, POB 339, Mogadishu; tel. (1) 80856.

Sudan: Via al-Mukarah, POB 552, Mogadishu; Chargé d'affaires a.i. ALI HASSAN ALI.

Turkey: Via Km 6, POB 2833, Mogadishu; tel. (1) 81975.

United Arab Emirates: Via Afgoi, Km 5, Mogadishu; tel. (1) 23178.

United Kingdom: Waddada Xasan Geedd Abtoow 7/8, POB 1036, Mogadishu; tel. (1) 20288.

Yemen: K4, Mogadishu; Ambassador AHMED HAMID ALI UMAR.

Judicial System

Constitutional arrangements in operation until 1991 provided for the Judiciary to be independent of the executive and legislative powers. Laws and acts having the force of law were required to conform to the provisions of the Constitution and to the general principles of Islam.

Attorney-General: ABDULLAH DAHIR BARRE.

Supreme Court: Mogadishu; the court of final instance in civil, criminal, administrative and auditing matters; Chair. Sheikh AHMAD HASAN.

Military Supreme Court: Mogadishu; f. 1970; tried mems of the armed forces.

National Security Court: Mogadishu; heard cases of treason.

Courts of Appeal: Mogadishu; sat at Mogadishu and Hargeysa, with two sections, General and Assize.

Regional Courts: There were eight Regional Courts, with two sections, General and Assize.

District Courts: There were 84 District Courts, with Civil and Criminal Divisions. The Civil Division had jurisdiction over all controversies where the cause of action had arisen under *Shari'a* (Islamic) Law or Customary Law and any other Civil controversies where the matter in dispute did not involve more than 3,000 shillings. The Criminal Division had jurisdiction with respect to offences punishable with imprisonment not exceeding three years, or fines not exceeding 3,000 shillings, or both.

Qadis: District Courts of civil jurisdiction under Islamic Law.

In September 1993, in accordance with Resolution 865 of the UN Security Council, a judiciary re-establishment council, composed of Somalis, was created in Mogadishu to rehabilitate the judicial and penal systems.

Judiciary Re-establishment Council (JRC): Mogadishu; Chair. Dr ABD AL-RAHMAN HAJI GA'AL.

Following the withdrawal of the UN peace-keeping force, UNOSOM, in early 1995, most regions outside Mogadishu reverted to clan-based fiefdoms where Islamic (*Shari'a*) law (comprising an Islamic Supreme Council and local Islamic high courts) prevailed. In October 1996 Ali Mahdi Mohamed endorsed a new Islamic judicial system under which appeals could be lodged on all sentences passed by Islamic courts, and no sentence imposed by the courts could be implemented prior to an appeal court ruling. In August 1998 the Governor of the Banaadir administration announced the application of *Shari'a* law in Mogadishu and its environs thenceforth.

Religion

ISLAM

Islam is the state religion. Most Somalis are Sunni Muslims.

Imam: Gen. MOHAMED ABSHIR.

CHRISTIANITY

The Roman Catholic Church

Somalia comprises a single diocese, directly responsible to the Holy See. At 31 December 2004 there were an estimated 100 adherents.

Bishop of Mogadishu: (vacant), POB 273, Ahmed bin Idris, Mogadishu; tel. (1) 20184.

The Anglican Communion

Within the Episcopal Church in Jerusalem and the Middle East, the Bishop in Egypt has jurisdiction over Somalia.

The Press

The Country: POB 1178, Mogadishu; tel. (1) 21206; f. 1991; daily.

Dalka: POB 388, Mogadishu; tel. (1) 500533; e-mail dalka@somalinternet.com; internet www.dalka-online.com; f. 1967; current affairs; weekly.

Heegan (Vigilance): POB 1178, Mogadishu; tel. (1) 21206; f. 1978; weekly; English; Editor MOHAMOUD M. AFRAH.

Horseed: POB 1178, Mogadishu; tel. (1) 21206; e-mail horseednet@gmail.com; internet www.horseednet.com; weekly; in Somali and English.

Huuriya (Liberty): Hargeysa; daily.

Jamhuuriya (The Republic): Hargeysa; e-mail webmaster@jamhuuriya.info; internet www.jamhuuriya.info; independent; daily; Editor-in-Chief HASSAN SAÏD FAISAL ALI; circ. 2,500.

Al Mujeehid: Hargeysa; weekly.

New Era: POB 1178, Mogadishu; tel. (1) 21206; quarterly; in English, Somali and Arabic.

Qaran Press (Maalinle Madaxbannaan): Mogadishu; tel. (1) 215305; e-mail qaranpress@hotmail.com; internet www.qaranpress.com; financial information; daily; in Somali; Editor ABDULAHI AHMED ALI; circ. 2,000.

Riyaaq (Happiness): Bossaso.

Sahan (Pioneer): Bossaso; Editor MUHAMMAD DEEQ.

Somalia in Figures: Ministry of National Planning, POB 1742, Mogadishu; tel. (1) 80384; govt statistical publ; 3 a year; in English.

Somalia Times: POB 555, Mogadishu BN 03040; e-mail info@somalpost.com; internet www.somaliatimes.com; Somali; weekly; circ. 50,000.

NEWS AGENCIES

Horn of Africa News Agency: Mogadishu; e-mail info@hananews.org; internet www.hananews.org; f. 1990.

Somali National News Agency (SONNA): POB 1748, Mogadishu; tel. (1) 24058; Dir MUHAMMAD HASAN KAHIN.

Foreign Bureaux

Agence France-Presse (AFP) (France): POB 1178, Mogadishu; Rep. MOHAMED ROBLE NOOR.

Agenzia Nazionale Stampa Associata (ANSA) (Italy): POB 1399, Mogadishu; tel. (1) 20626; Rep. ABDULKADIR MOHAMOUD WALAYO.

Publishers

Government Printer: POB 1743, Mogadishu.

Somalia d'Oggi: Piazzale della Garesa, POB 315, Mogadishu; law, economics and reference.

Broadcasting and Communications

TELECOMMUNICATIONS

Ministry of Information: POB 1748, Mogadishu; tel. (1) 999621; Dir-Gen. A. ALI ASKAR.

Somali Telecom (Olympic Telecommunications): Mogadishu.

Somaliland Telecommunications Corpn: Hargeysa; Dir MOHAMED ARWO.

BROADCASTING

Radio

Holy Koran Radio: Mogadishu; f. 1996; religious broadcasts in Somali.

Radio Awdal: Boorama, 'Somaliland'; operated by the Gadabursi clan.

Radio Banaadir: Tahlil Warsame Bldg, 4 Maka al-Mukarama Rd, Mogadishu; tel. (5) 944176; e-mail rbb@radiobanadir.com; internet www.radiobanadir.com; f. 2000; serves Mogadishu and its environs.

Radio Free Somalia: f. 1993; operates from Galacaio in north-eastern Somalia; relays humanitarian and educational programmes.

Radio Gaalkayco: operates from 'Puntland'.

Radio Hargeysa, the Voice of the 'Republic of Somaliland': POB 14, Hargeysa; tel. 155; e-mail radiohargeysa@yahoo.com; internet www.radiosomaliland.com/radiohargeisa.html; serves the northern region ('Somaliland'); broadcasts in Somali, and relays Somali and Amharic transmission from Radio Mogadishu; Dir of Radio IDRIS EGAL NUR.

Radio HornAfrique: Mogadishu; f. 1999; commercial independent station broadcasting music and programmes on social issues; Dir AHMAD ABDI SALAN HAJI ADAN.

Radio Mogadishu, Voice of the Masses of the Somali Republic: southern Mogadishu; f. 1993 by supporters of Gen. Aidid after the facilities of the fmr state-controlled radio station, Radio Mogadishu (of which Gen. Aidid's faction took control in 1991), were destroyed by UNOSOM; broadcasts in Somali, Amharic, Arabic, English and Swahili; Chair. FARAH HASAN AYOBOQORE.

Radio Mogadishu, Voice of Somali Pacification: Mogadishu; f. 1995 by supporters of Osman Hassan Ali 'Ato'; broadcasts in Somali, English and Arabic; Dir-Gen. MUHAMMAD DIRIYEH ILMI.

Radio Mogadishu, Voice of the Somali Republic: northern Mogadishu; f. 1992 by supporters of Ali Mahdi Mohamed; Chair. FARAH HASSAN AYOBOQORE.

Radio Somaliland: e-mail radio@radiosomaliland.com; internet www.radiosomaliland.com.

Voice of Peace: POB 1631, Addis Ababa, Ethiopia; f. 1993; aims to promote peace and reconstruction in Somalia; receives support from UNICEF and the AU.

Some radio receivers are used for public address purposes in small towns and villages.

Note: In January 2007 the Transitional National Government was granted emergency powers to proscribe four media companies in an attempt to restore order in Mogadishu. HornAfrique Media and Shabelle Media were believed to have ceased operations although others condemned the ban and refused to close.

Television

A television service, financed by Kuwait and the United Arab Emirates, was inaugurated in 1983. Programmes in Somali and Arabic are broadcast for three hours daily, extended to four hours on Fridays and public holidays. Reception is limited to a 30-km radius of Mogadishu.

Somali Television Network (STN): Mogadishu; f. 1999; broadcasts 22 channels in Somali, English, French, Hindi, Gujarati, Bengali, Punjabi, Italian and Arabic; Man. Dir ABURAHMAN ROBLEY ULAYEREH.

Television HornAfrique: Mogadishu; f. 1999; broadcasts 6 channels in Somali and Arabic; CEO ALI IMAN SHARMARKEH.

Finance

(cap. = capital; res = reserves; m. = million; brs = branches; amounts in Somali shillings unless otherwise stated)

BANKING

Central Bank

Central Bank of Somalia (Bankiga Dhexe ee Soomaaliya): Corso Somalia 55, POB 11, Mogadishu; tel. (1) 657733; f. 1960; bank of issue; cap. and res 132.5m. (Sept. 1985); Gov. BASHIR ISSE ALI; Gen. Man MOHAMED MOHAMED NUR.

A central bank (with 10 branches) is also in operation in Hargeysa (in the self-proclaimed 'Republic of Somaliland').

Commercial Banks

Commercial Bank of Somalia: Via Primo Luglio, POB 203, Mogadishu; tel. (1) 22861; f. 1990 to succeed the Commercial and Savings Bank of Somalia; state-owned; cap. 1,000m. (May 1990); 33 brs.

Universal Bank of Somalia: Mogadishu; f. 2002; cap. US $10m.; Gen. Man. MAHAD ADAN BARKHADLE (acting).

Private Bank

Somali-Malaysian Commercial Bank: Mogadishu; f. 1997; cap. US $4m.

Development Bank

Somali Development Bank: Via Primo Luglio, POB 1079, Mogadishu; tel. (1) 21800; f. 1968; state-owned; cap. and res 2,612.7m. (Dec. 1988); Pres. MOHAMED MOHAMED NUR; 4 brs.

INSURANCE

Cassa per le Assicurazioni Sociali della Somalia: POB 123, Mogadishu; f. 1950; workers' compensation; Dir-Gen. HASSAN MOHAMED JAMA; 9 brs.

State Insurance Co of Somalia: POB 992, Mogadishu; f. 1974; Gen. Man. ABDULLAHI GA'AL; brs throughout Somalia.

Trade and Industry

DEVELOPMENT ORGANIZATIONS

Agricultural Development Corpn: POB 930, Mogadishu; f. 1971 by merger of fmr agricultural and machinery agencies and grain marketing board; supplies farmers with equipment and materials and purchases growers' cereal and oil seed crops; Dir-Gen. MOHAMED FARAH ANSHUR.

Livestock Development Agency: POB 1759, Mogadishu; Dir-Gen. HASSAN WELI SCEK HUSSEN; brs throughout Somalia.

Somali Co-operative Movement: Mogadishu; Chair. HASSAN HAWADLE MADAR.

Somali Oil Refinery: POB 1241, Mogadishu; Chair. NUR AHMED DARAWISH.

Water Development Agency: POB 525, Mogadishu; Dir-Gen. KHALIF HAJI FARAH.

CHAMBER OF COMMERCE

Chamber of Commerce, Industry and Agriculture: Via Asha, POB 27, Mogadishu; tel. (1) 3209; Chair. MOHAMED IBRAHIM HAJI EGAL.

TRADE ASSOCIATION

National Agency of Foreign Trade: POB 602, Mogadishu; major foreign trade agency; state-owned; brs in Berbera and over 150 centres throughout Somalia; Dir-Gen. JAMA AW MUSE.

UTILITIES

Water Development Agency: POB 525, Mogadishu; Dir-Gen. KHALIF HAJI FARAH.

INDUSTRIAL COMPANY

Industrie Chimique Somale: POB 479, Mogadishu; soap and detergent mfrs; Man. Dir HIREI GASSEM.

TRADE UNIONS

General Federation of Somali Trade Unions: POB 1179, Mogadishu; Chair. MOHAMED FARAH ISSA GASHAN.

National Union of Somali Journalists (NUSOJ): Tree Biano Bldg, Via al-Mukarah Km4, Mogadishu; fax (1) 859944; e-mail nusoj@nusoj.org; internet www.nusoj.org; f. 2002 as Somali Journalists' Network (SOJON) ; name changed as above in 2005; Sec.-Gen. OMAR FARUK OSMAN; 6 brs across Somalia.

Transport

RAILWAYS

There are no railways in Somalia.

ROADS

In 1999 there were an estimated 22,100 km of roads, of which some 11.8% were paved.

SHIPPING

Merca, Berbera, Mogadishu and Kismayu are the chief ports. An EU-sponsored development project for the port of Berbera (in 'Somaliland') was announced in February 1996. It was reported that the port of Mogadishu, which had been largely closed since 1995, was reopened to commercial traffic in August 2006. In 2005 the International Maritime Bureau warned ship operators to avoid the coast of Somalia following an increase in piracy.

Somali Ports Authority: POB 935, Mogadishu; tel. (1) 30081; Port Dir MOHAMED JUMA FURAH.

Juba Enterprises Beder & Sons Ltd: POB 549, Mogadishu; privately owned.

National Shipping Line: POB 588, Mogadishu; tel. (1) 23021; state-owned; Gen. Man. Dr ABDULLAHI MOHAMED SALAD.

Puntland Shipping Service: Bossaso.

Shosman Commercial Co Ltd: North-Eastern Pasaso; privately owned.

Somali Shipping Corpn: POB 2775, Mogadishu; state-owned.

CIVIL AVIATION

Mogadishu has an international airport. There are airports at Hargeysa and Baidoa and six other airfields. It was reported that a daily service had been inaugurated in April 1994 between Hargeysa (in the self-declared 'Republic of Somaliland') and Nairobi, Kenya. Mogadishu international airport (closed since 1995) was officially reopened in mid-1998, but continuing civil unrest hampered services. In August 2006 the airport reopened to commercial flights.

Air Somalia: Mogadishu; f. 2001; operates internal passenger services and international services to destinations in Africa and the Middle East; Chair. ALI FARAH ABDULLEH.

Jubba Airways: POB 6200, 30th St, Mogadishu; tel. (1) 217000; fax (1) 227711; e-mail jubbaair@emirates.net.ae; internet www.jubba-airways.com; f. 1998; operates domestic flights and flights to destinations in Djibouti, Saudi Arabia, the United Arab Emirates and Yemen.

Defence

Of total armed forces of 64,500 in June 1990, the army numbered 60,000, the navy 2,000 and the air force 2,500. In addition, there were 29,500 members of paramilitary forces, including 20,000 members of the People's Militia. Following the overthrow of the Siad Barre regime in January 1991, there were no national armed forces. Somalia was divided into areas controlled by different armed groups, which were based on clan, or sub-clan, membership. In March 1994 the UN announced that 8,000 former Somali police officers had been rehabilitated throughout the country, receiving vehicles and uniforms from the UN. Following the UN withdrawal from Somalia in early 1995, these police officers ceased receiving payment and their future and their hitherto neutral stance appeared uncertain. In December 1998 a 3,000-strong police force was established for the Banaadir region (Mogadishu and its environs). An additional 3,000 members (comprising former militiamen and police officers) were recruited to the force in early 1999; however, the force was disbanded within months. Following his election to the presidency in August 2000, Abdulkasim Salad Hasan announced his intention some to recruit former militiamen into a new national force: by December some 5,000 Somalis had begun training under the supervision of Mogadishu's Islamic courts. However, efforts to establish a new national armed force have made little progress since the Government's return to Somalia from exile in 2005. In August 2004 the total armed forces of the self-proclaimed 'Republic of Somaliland' were estimated to number 7,000.

Chief of General Staff: Col ABDI AHMAD GULED.

Air Force Commander: NUR ILMI ADAWE.

Navy Commander: Col MUSE SA'ID MOHAMED.

Army Commander: Gen. ABDULAHI ALI OMAR.

Commander of Rapid Reaction Forces: Gen. ABDI'AZIZ ALI BARRE.

Education

All private schools were nationalized in 1972, and education is now provided free of charge. Primary education, lasting for eight years, is officially compulsory for children aged six to 14 years. In 2002 enrolment at primary schools was equivalent to only 16.9% of the school-age population (boys 20.8%; girls 12.7%). Secondary education, beginning at the age of 14, lasts for four years but is not compulsory. In 1985 enrolment of children at secondary schools included 3% (boys 4%; girls 2%) of those in the relevant age-group. Current expenditure on education in the 1988 budget was 478.1m. Somali shillings (equivalent to 1.9% of total current spending). Following the overthrow of Siad Barre's Government in January 1991 and the ensuing internal disorder, Somalia's education system collapsed. In January 1993 a primary school was opened in the building of Somalia's only university, the Somali National University in Mogadishu (which had been closed in early 1991). The only other schools operating in the country were a number under the control of fundamentalist Islamic groups and some that had been reopened in the 'Republic of Somaliland' in mid-1991.

Bibliography

Ahmed, A. J. (Ed.). *The Invention of Somalia*. Lawrenceville, KS, Red Sea Press, 1995.

Beachey, R. *The Warrior Mullah: The Horn Aflame 1892–1920*. London, Bellew Publishing, 1990.

Besteman, C., and Cassanelli, L. V. (Eds). *The Struggle for Land in Southern Somalia: The War Behind the War*. Boulder, CO, and Oxford, Westview Press, 1996.

Bongartz, M. *The Civil War in Somalia: Its Genesis and Dynamics*. Uppsala, Scandinavian Institute for African Studies, 1991.

Burnett, John S. *Where Soldiers Fear to Tread: At Work in the Fields of Anarchy*. London, William Heinemann, 2005.

Cassanelli, L. V. *The Shaping of Somali Society: Reconstructing the History of a Pastoral People, 1600–1900*. Philadelphia, PA, Pennsylvania University Press, 1982.

Clarke, W., and Herbst, J. (Eds). *Learning from Somalia: The Lessons of Armed Humanitarian Intervention*. Boulder, CO, Westview Press, 1997.

Contini, P. *The Somali Republic: An Experiment in Legal Integration*. 1969.

DeLong, K., and Tuckey, S. *Mogadishu: Heroism and Tragedy*. Westport, CT, and London, Praeger, 1994.

de Waal, R., and de Waal, A. *Somalia: Crimes and Blunders*. London, James Currey Publishers, 1995.

Drysdale, J. *Whatever Happened to Somalia?* London, Haan Associates, 1994.

Dualeh, H. A. *From Barre to Aidid: The Story of Somalia and the Agony of a Nation*. Nairobi, Stellagraphics, 1994.

Farah, A. O., Muchie, M., and Gundel, J. *Somalia: Diaspora and State Reconstitution in the Horn of Africa*. London, Adonis & Abbey Publishers, 2007.

Fitzgerald, N. J. *Somalia: History, Issues and Bibliography*. Hauppauge, NY, Nova Science Publishers, 2002.

Ghalib, J. M. *The Cost of Dictatorship. The Somali Experience*. New York, NY, and Oxford, Lilian Barber Press, 1995.

Hashim, A. B. *The Fallen State: Dissonance, Dictatorship and Death in Somalia*. Lanham, MD, University Press of America, 1997.

Hess, R. L. *Italian Colonialism in Somalia*. 1966.

Hirsch, J. L., and Oakley, R. B. *Somalia and 'Operation Restore Hope': Reflections on Peacemaking and Peacekeeping*. Washington, DC, United States Institute of Peace Press, 1995.

Issa-Salwe, A. M., and Cissa-Salwe, C. *The Collapse of the Somali State*. London, Haan Associates, 1994.

Kusow, A. (Ed.). *Putting the Cart before the Horse: Contested Nationalism and the Crisis of the Nation-state in Somalia*. Lawrenceville, NJ, Red Sea Press, 2005.

Laitin, D. D., and Saïd, S. S. *Somalia: Nation in Search of a State*. Boulder, CO, Westview Press, 1987.

Lewis, I. M. *A Modern History of Somalia: Nation and State in the Horn of Africa*. Boulder, CO, Westview Press, 1988.

Blood and Bone: The Call of Kinship in Somali Society. Trenton, NJ, Red Sea Press, 1994.

Saints and Somalis: Popular Islam in a Clan-Based Society. Lawrenceville, NJ, Red Sea Press, 1998.

Little, P. D. *Somalia: Economy without State (African Issues)*. London, James Currey Publishers, 2003.

Lyons, T., and Samatar, A. I. *Somalia: State Collapse, Multilateral Intervention and Strategies for Political Reconstruction*. Washington, DC, Brookings Institution, 1995.

Makinda, S. M. *Seeking Peace from Chaos: Humanitarian Intervention in Somalia*. Boulder, CO, Lynne Rienner Publishers, 1993.

Mburu, N. *Bandits on the Border: The Last Frontier in the Search for Somali Unity*. Lawrenceville, NJ, Red Sea Press, 2005.

Morin, D. *Littérature et politique en Somalie*. Talenco Cedex, Université Montesquieu—Bordeaux IV, 1997.

Mubarak, J. A. *From Bad Policy to Chaos in Somalia: How an Economy Fell Apart.* Westport, CT, and London, Praeger, 1996.

An Economic Policy Agenda for Post-Civil War Somalia: How to Build a New Economy, Sustain Growth and Reduce Poverty. Lewiston, NY, The Edwin Mellen Press, 2006

Mukhtar, M. H. *Historical Dictionary of Somalia: New Edition.* Metuchen, NJ, Scarecrow Press, 2003.

Nenova, T., and Harford, T. Anarchy and Invention: How does Somalia's Private Sector Cope without Government? *Public Policy Journal*, Note No. 280. Washington, DC, World Bank, Nov. 2004.

Omar, M. O. *Somalia: A Nation Driven to Despair.* New Delhi, Somali Publications, 1996.

Osman, A. A., and Souare, I. K. *Somalia at the Crossroads: Challenges and Perspectives in Reconstituting a Failed State.* London, Adonis & Abbey Publishers, 2007.

Pankhurst, E. S. *Ex-Italian Somaliland.* New York, NY, Philosophical Library, 1951.

Sahnoun, M. *Somalia: The Missed Opportunities.* Washington, DC, United States Institute of Peace Press, 1994.

Salih, M. A. M., and Wohlgemuth, L. (Eds). *Crisis Management and the Politics of Reconciliation in Somalia*. Uppsala, Scandinavian Institute for African Studies, 1994.

Samatar, A. I. (Ed.). *The Somali Challenge: From Catastrophe to Renewal?* Boulder, CO, Lynne Rienner, 1994.

Samatar, S. S. *Somalia: A Nation in Turmoil.* London, Minority Rights Group, 1991.

Simons, A. *Networks of Dissolution: Somalia Undone*. Boulder, CO and Oxford, Westview Press, 1995.

Stevenson, J. *Losing Mogadishu: Testing US Policy in Somalia.* Annapolis, MD, Naval Institute Press, 1995.

United Nations, Dept of Public Information. *The United Nations and Somalia 1992–1996*. New York, NY, United Nations, 1996.

Wam, P. E. *Conflict in Somalia: Drivers and Dynamics.* Herndon, VA, World Bank Publications, 2005.

World Bank. *Somalia: From Resilience Towards Recovery and Development. A Country Economic Memorandum for Somalia*. Report No. 34356. Washington, DC, World Bank, 2006.

SOUTH AFRICA

Physical and Social Geography

A. MacGREGOR HUTCHESON

The Republic of South Africa occupies the southern extremity of the African continent and, except for a relatively small area in the northern Transvaal, lies poleward of the Tropic of Capricorn, extending as far as latitude 34° 51′ S. The republic covers a total area of 1,219,080 sq km (470,689 sq miles) and has common borders with Namibia to the north-west, with Botswana to the north, and with Zimbabwe, Mozambique and Swaziland to the north-east. Lesotho is entirely surrounded by South African territory, lying within the eastern part of the republic.

PHYSICAL FEATURES

Most of South Africa consists of a vast plateau with upwarped rims, bounded by an escarpment. Framing the plateau is a narrow coastal belt. The surface of the plateau varies in altitude from 600 m to 2,000 m above sea-level, but is mostly above 900 m. It is highest in the east and south-east and dips fairly gently towards the Kalahari Basin in the north-west. The relief is generally monotonous, consisting of undulating to flat landscapes over wide areas. Variation is provided occasionally by low ridges and *inselberge* (or *kopjes*) made up of rock more resistant to erosion. There are three major sub-regions:

(i) the Highveld between 1,200 m and 1,800 m, forming a triangular area which occupies the southern Transvaal and most of the Free State;

(ii) a swell over 1,500 m high, aligned WNW–ESE, part of which is known as the Witwatersrand, rising gently from the plateau surface to the north of the Highveld and forming a major drainage divide; and

(iii) the Middleveld, generally between 600 m and 1,200 m, comprising the remaining part of the plateau.

The plateau's edges, upwarped during the Tertiary Period, are almost everywhere above 1,500 m. Maximum elevations of over 3,400 m occur in the south-east in Lesotho. From the crests the surface descends coastwards by means of the Great Escarpment which gives the appearance of a mountain range when viewed from below, and which is known by distinctive names in its different sections. An erosional feature, dissected by seaward-flowing rivers, the nature of the Escarpment varies according to the type of rock which forms it. Along its eastern length it is known as the Drakensberg; in the section north of the Olifants river fairly soft granite gives rise to gentle slopes, but south of that river resistant quartzites are responsible for a more striking appearance. Further south again, along the KwaZulu/Natal–Lesotho border, basalts cause the Drakensberg to be at its most striking, rising up a sheer 1,800 m or more in places. Turning westwards the Great Escarpment is known successively as the Stormberg, Bamboes, Suurberg, Sneeuberg, Nieuwveld and Komsberg, where gentle slopes affording access to the interior alternate with a more wall-like appearance. The Great Escarpment then turns sharply northwards through the Roggeveld mountains, following which it is usually in the form of a simple step until the Kamiesberg are reached; owing to aridity and fewer rivers the dissection of this western part of the Escarpment is much less advanced than in the eastern (Drakensberg) section.

The Lowland margin which surrounds the South African plateau may be divided into four zones:

(i) the undulating to flat Transvaal Lowveld, between 150 m and 600 m above sea-level, separated from the Mozambique coastal plain by the Lebombo mountains in the east, and including part of the Limpopo valley in the north;

(ii) the south-eastern coastal belt, a very broken region descending to the coast in a series of steps, into which the rivers have cut deep valleys. In northern KwaZulu/Natal the Republic possesses its only true coastal plain, some 65 km at its widest;

(iii) the Cape ranges, consisting of the remnants of mountains folded during the Carboniferous era, and flanking the plateau on the south and south-west. On the south the folds trend E–W and on the south-west they trend N–S, the two trends crossing in the south-western corner of the Cape to produce a rugged knot of mountains and the ranges' highest elevations (over 2,000 m). Otherwise the Cape ranges are comparatively simple in structure, consisting of parallel anticlinal ridges and synclinal valleys. Narrow lowlands separate the mountains from the coast. Between the ridges and partially enclosed by them, e.g. the Little Karoo, is a series of steps rising to the foot of the Great Escarpment. The Great Karoo, the last of these steps, separates the escarpment from the Cape ranges; and

(iv) the western coastal belt is also characterized by a series of steps, but the slope from the foot of the Great Escarpment to the coast is more gentle and more uniform than in the south-eastern zone.

The greater part of the plateau is drained by the Orange river system. Rising in the Drakensberg within a short distance of the Escarpment, as do its two main perennial tributaries, the Vaal and the Caledon, the Orange flows westward for 1,900 km before entering the Atlantic Ocean. However, the western part of its basin is so dry that it is not unknown for the Orange to fail to reach its mouth during the dry season. The large-scale Orange River Project, a comprehensive scheme for water supply, irrigation and hydroelectric generation, aids water conservation in this western area and is making possible its development. The only other major system is that of the Limpopo, which rises on the northern slopes of the Witwatersrand and drains most of the Limpopo Province to the Indian Ocean. Apart from some interior drainage to a number of small basins in the north and north-west, the rest of the Republic's drainage is peripheral. Relatively short streams rise in the Great Escarpment, although some rise on the plateau itself, having cut through the escarpment, and drain directly to the coast. With the exception of riparian strips along perennial rivers, most of the country relies for water supplies on underground sources supplemented by dams. None of the Republic's rivers is navigable.

CLIMATE AND NATURAL VEGETATION

Except for a small part of Limpopo Province the climate of South Africa is subtropical, although there are important regional variations within this general classification. Altitude and relief forms have an important influence on temperature and on both the amount and distribution of rainfall, and there is a strong correlation between the major physical and the major climatic regions. The altitude of the plateau modifies temperatures and because there is a general rise in elevation towards the Equator there is a corresponding decrease in temperature, resulting in a remarkable uniformity of temperature throughout the Republic from south to north (mean annual temperatures: Cape Town, 16.7°C; and Pretoria, 17.2°C). The greatest contrasts in temperature are, in fact, between the east coast, warmed by the Mozambique Current, and the west coast, cooled by the Benguela Current (respectively, mean monthly temperatures: Durban, January 24.4°C, July 17.8°C; and Port Nolloth, January 15.6°C, July 12.2°C). Daily and annual ranges in temperature increase with distance from the coast, being much greater on the plateau (mean annual temperature range: Cape Town, 8°C; Pretoria, 11°C).

The areas of highest annual rainfall largely coincide with the outstanding relief features, over 650 mm being received only in the eastern third of South Africa and relatively small areas in the southern Cape. Parts of the Drakensberg and the seaward slopes of the Cape ranges experience over 1,500 mm. West of the Drakensberg and to the north of the Cape ranges there is a marked rain-shadow, and annual rainfall decreases progressively westwards (Durban 1,140 mm, Bloemfontein 530 mm, Kimberley 400 mm, Upington 180 mm, Port Nolloth 50 mm). Virtually all the western half of the country, apart from the southern Cape, receives less than 250 mm and the western coastal belt's northern section forms a continuation of the Namib Desert. Most of the rain falls during the summer months (November to April) when evaporation losses are greatest, brought by tropical marine air masses moving in from the Indian Ocean on the east. However, the south-western Cape has a winter maximum of rainfall with dry summers. Only the narrow southern coastal belt between Cape Agulhas and East London has rainfall distributed uniformly throughout the year. Snow may fall occasionally over the higher parts of the plateau and the Cape ranges during winter, but frost occurs on an average for 120 days each year over most of the interior plateau, and for shorter periods in the coastal lowlands, except in KwaZulu/Natal, where it is rare.

Variations in climate and particularly in annual rainfall are reflected in changes of vegetation, sometimes strikingly, as between the south-western Cape's Mediterranean shrub type, designed to withstand summer drought and of which the protea—the national plant—is characteristic, and the drought-resistant low Karoo bush immediately north of the Cape ranges and covering much of the semi-arid western half of the country. The only true areas of forest are found along the wetter south and east coasts—the temperate evergreen forests of the Knysna district and the largely evergreen subtropical bush, including palms and wild bananas, of Eastern Cape and KwaZulu/Natal, respectively. Grassland covers the rest of the Republic, merging into thornveld in the north-western Cape and into bushveld in Limpopo Province.

MINERAL RESOURCES

South Africa's mineral resources, outstanding in their variety, quality and quantity, overshadow all the country's other natural resources. They are mainly found in the ancient Pre-Cambrian foundation and associated intrusions and occur in a wide curving zone which stretches from Limpopo Province through the Free State and Northern Cape to the west coast. To the south of this mineralized zone, one of the richest in the world, the Pre-Cambrian rocks are covered by Karoo sedimentaries which generally do not contain minerals, with the exception of extensive deposits of bituminous coal, the country's only indigenous mineral fuel. These deposits occur mainly in the eastern Transvaal Highveld, the northern Free State and northern KwaZulu/Natal, mostly in thick, easily worked seams fairly near to the surface. Coal is of particular importance to South Africa because of relatively low production elsewhere in the continent south of the Equator, and South Africa's current dependence on imported petroleum.

The most important mineral regions are the Witwatersrand and the northern Free State, producing gold, silver and uranium; the diamond areas centred on Kimberley, Pretoria, Jagersfontein and Koffiefontein; and the Transvaal bushveld complex containing multiple occurrences of a large number of minerals, including asbestos, chrome, copper, iron, magnesium, nickel, platinum, tin, uranium and vanadium. In the Northern Cape important deposits of manganese, iron ore and asbestos occur in the Postmasburg, Sishen and Kuruman areas, while in the north-western Cape reserves of lead, zinc, silver and copper are being exploited. This list of occurrences and minerals is by no means exhaustive, and prospecting for new mineral resources is continuing. In 1988 exploitable petroleum deposits were discovered near Hondeklip Bay, off the western Cape coast, and a substantial reserve of natural gas and petroleum was discovered south-west of Mossel Bay, off the south coast of the Cape.

ETHNIC GROUPS AND POPULATION

Five major ethnic groups make up South Africa's multiracial society. The 'Khoisan' peoples—Bushmen, Hottentots and Bergdamara—are survivors of the country's earliest inhabitants. The negroid Bantu-speaking peoples fall into a number of tribal groupings. The major groups are formed by the Nguni, comprising Zulu, Swazi, Ndebele, Pondo, Tembu and Xhosa on the one hand, and by the Sotho and Tswana on the other. The European or 'white' peoples, who once dominated the political and social organization of the Republic and continue to exercise considerable economic influence, are descended from the original 17th-century Dutch settlers in the Cape, refugee French Huguenots, British settlers from 1820 onwards, Germans and more recent immigrants from Europe and ex-colonial African territories. The remainder of the population comprises Coloureds (people of mixed race) and Asians, largely of Indian origin. At the October 2001 census the total population was 44,819,770, while the ethnic composition of the total population was: Africans (blacks) 79.0%; Europeans (whites) 9.6%; Coloureds 8.9%; and Asians 2.5%. The official languages are Afrikaans, English, isiNdebele, Sesotho sa Leboa, Sesotho, siSwati, Xitsonga, Setswana, Tshivenda, isiXhosa and isiZulu.

The overall density of the population was 36.8 inhabitants per sq km at the census of October 2001, but its distribution is extremely uneven. It is generally related to agricultural resources, more than two-thirds living in the wetter eastern third of the Republic and in the southern Cape. The heaviest concentrations are found in the Witwatersrand mining area—at mid-2005 some 3,254,000 people were estimated to be living in the Johannesburg Metropolitan Area—and in and around the major ports of Cape Town (3,083,000 at mid-2005) and Durban (2,631,000 at mid-2005). The fourth largest city is Pretoria (the greater Metropolitan Area had an estimated population of 1,271,000 at mid-2005). Cape Town is the legislative capital of the country, Pretoria the administrative capital and Bloemfontein the judicial capital. Europeans have a widespread geographical distribution, but more than 80% reside in towns. Relatively few Africans are resident in Western Cape and, while an increasing number are moving to the large black townships on the periphery of the major urban centres, more than 60% continue to reside in those rural areas that comprised the former tribal reserves. These extend in a great horseshoe along the south-eastern coast and up to Limpopo Province and then south-westwards to the north-eastern Cape. The Coloured population is mainly resident in the Cape, and the Asian population is concentrated largely in KwaZulu/Natal and the Witwatersrand. The total population was estimated at 47,850,064 at mid-2007, giving a population density of 39.3 per sq km.

Recent History

CHRISTOPHER SAUNDERS

Based on an earlier article by J. D. OMER-COOPER

HISTORICAL BACKGROUND

Hunter-gatherers lived in many parts of South Africa for hundreds of thousands of years, leaving behind evidence of their activities in rock art. About 2,000 years ago descendants of the San (Bushman) people who had acquired sheep arrived from the north. These pastoralists, the Khoikhoi (Hottentot), were the first indigenous people to interact with European seafarers along the coast from the late 15th century. From about 1,500 years ago Bantu-speaking farmers moved into the northern parts of South Africa. Growing their own crops, they rapidly increased in numbers and began to develop small kingdoms, some of which enjoyed brief periods of relative wealth. Trading routes began to link the coastal areas with the interior. Over time these farmers spread southwards into what is now the Transkei and the Free State. In the early 19th century a process of political centralization led to the emergence, in what is today KwaZulu/Natal, of the relatively large Zulu state. The Zulu and other black African peoples fought to resist white encroachment in the 19th century.

The Dutch East India Company established a settlement at the Cape in 1652. About 150 years later the British took over a sizeable white-ruled colony from the Dutch. Friction between the British authorities at the Cape and the Dutch (Afrikaner or Boer) frontier farmers led many of the latter, after the abolition of slavery in 1834, to embark upon a northward trek to establish an independent polity. Britain subsequently annexed the trekker Republic of Natalia (now part of the province of KwaZulu/Natal), but permitted the creation of two independent Boer republics, the Orange Free State (OFS), between the Orange and Vaal rivers, and the South African Republic or Transvaal. When a large diamond deposit was discovered at what became known as Kimberley in 1871, the British quickly intervened and brought the contested diamond-rich territory under British rule. The rapid development of gold-mining in the Transvaal after 1886, together with the emergence of the South African Republic as the most powerful state in the region, were perceived by British interests as a threat to their paramountcy; the consequent exertion of pressure on the Transvaal and the OFS provoked the Anglo-Boer (or South African) war of 1899–1902. During the war the Boer republics passed under British control, and on 31 May 1910 the Union of South Africa, comprising the two conquered Boer republics and the two British colonies of the Cape and Natal, was formally declared a dominion under the British crown.

The Constitution of the new Union gave the franchise to white males only, except in the Cape, where the existing voting rights were protected. The two Afrikaner parties in the ex-republics amalgamated with the Cape's South Africa Party to form the national South Africa Party (SAP). Led by two Boer generals, Louis Botha and Jan Smuts, the SAP formed the first Government of the new Union. In 1912 another general, J. B. M. Hertzog, broke away to found the National Party (NP), devoted to the exclusive interests of Afrikaners. In the same year members of the African élite, under the leadership of Pixley Seme, established the South African Native National Congress, soon renamed the African National Congress (ANC). The Congress protested in vain against the 1913 Land Act, which denied Africans the right to buy land outside the Native Reserves or to lease white-owned land. As a consequence of an economic crisis, Hertzog's NP, in power from 1924, entered a coalition with the SAP under Smuts, and the two parties subsequently merged to form the United Party. A small group of Afrikaner nationalists, under Daniel Malan, rejected the coalition and merger, and formed a 'purified' NP, the party that eventually introduced apartheid when it came to power in 1948.

APARTHEID

Afrikaner farmers, who feared the loss of their low-wage African labour to the towns, and Afrikaner workers in the towns, who feared black competition, supported the intensification of racial segregation, which the NP called 'apartheid'. In the 1948 general election the NP secured a narrow parliamentary majority. Malan formed a Government and began putting apartheid into practice. In 1954 he was replaced by the hardline J. G. Strydom, who died in 1958 and was succeeded by Hendrik Verwoerd, apartheid's chief architect and leading ideologue. Verwoerd believed that each race should be kept apart so that each could develop along its own lines. Each racial group was to have its own territorial area within which to develop its unique cultural personality. Of the areas envisaged for the African peoples, the overwhelming majority, however, were the poverty-stricken Native Reserves, comprising only 13% of the national territory.

The period 1948–59 saw the introduction of a series of interrelated laws and measures aimed at restructuring South African society to conform to apartheid doctrine. The Population Registration Act provided for the classification of the entire population on the basis of race. Inter-racial marriages were forbidden and the Immorality Act, banning sexual relations between whites and blacks, was extended to include relations between whites and Coloureds. The Group Areas Act of 1950 provided for the designation of particular residential areas for specific races. Existing provisions for the reservation of categories of employment for particular races were strengthened. Race segregation in public places, trains and buses, post-offices, hospitals and even ambulances was introduced wherever it had not been previously practised. Under the terms of the Separate Amenities Act, amenities provided for different races did not have to be of equal standard. The Extension of University Education Act removed the right of non-white students to attend the previously open universities of Cape Town and the Witwatersrand. To strengthen its hand against radical opposition the Government introduced the Suppression of Communism Act, which forced the Communist Party of South Africa to disband, only to regroup underground as the South African Communist Party (SACP).

The repressive policies of the NP prompted the ANC to embark on a programme of mass civil disobedience, for which the ANC Youth League had been pressing. After the Defiance Campaign of 1952, a Congress Alliance was formed, which drew together the ANC and other Congresses, including the South African Indian Congress. At the Congress of the People held in June 1955, a Freedom Charter was adopted, setting out a vision of a new South Africa. Some within the ANC did not approve of the Congress Alliance's assertion that South Africa belonged to all who lived in it, regardless of colour, and in 1958 the Africanists in the ANC, led by Robert Sobukwe, broke away and, in April 1959, formed the Pan-Africanist Congress (PAC).

In March 1960 police in the township of Sharpeville, south of Johannesburg, opened fire on a crowd of unarmed black Africans who were surrounding the police station in response to a PAC demonstration, killing 69 people. The Sharpeville massacre aroused international indignation to an unprecedented degree: South Africa sustained a net outflow of foreign investment capital, and appeals for military, economic and sporting boycotts began to be given serious attention. In 1961, following a referendum among white voters in October 1960, South Africa became a republic, and left the Commonwealth.

In response to demonstrations within South Africa in protest at the Sharpeville massacre, the Government banned both the ANC and the PAC. In 1961 some within the ANC, together with white members of the SACP, formed a military organization, Umkhonto we Sizwe (MK—'Spear of the Nation'). Under the leadership of Nelson Mandela, it aimed to force the Government to negotiate by attacking white-owned property, while avoiding harm to people. Mandela was arrested in 1962 and then, along with others, sentenced to life imprisonment on charges of sabotage in 1964.

Verwoerd argued that the Native Reserves constituted the historic 'homelands' (Bantustans) of different African nations. The 'homelands' were to be led to self-government under constitutions giving scope to the elective principle, but with the balance of power in the hands of government-appointed chiefs. Transkei was accorded 'self-government' under such a system in 1963. Ciskei, Bophuthatswana, Lebowa, Venda, Gazankulu, Qwaqwa and KwaZulu followed in the early 1970s. The replacement of explicit racism by separate nationality as a rationale for the denial of civil rights to blacks gave new urgency to reducing the settled African population in white areas. Stricter controls were imposed to prevent Africans acquiring permanent residence in urban areas. Wherever possible, jobs performed by settled blacks were given to migrant labourers. A massive campaign was launched to rid the white areas of 'surplus Bantu' and force them into the overcrowded 'homelands'. In the 1960s more than 1.5m. people were forcibly resettled. These measures, more drastic than those of the first phase of apartheid, required more ruthless repression to enforce them. Under John Vorster, the Minister of Justice, the powers of the security police were massively extended. Vorster succeeded Verwoerd as Prime Minister in 1966 when Verwoerd was assassinated.

South Africa took control of South West Africa (later to become Namibia) in 1915 and after the First World War ruled the territory as a mandate under the League of Nations. After the Second World War South Africa's application to annex the territory was rejected by the new United Nations and in 1960 Ethiopia and Liberia brought a case before the International Court of Justice (ICJ) in which they claimed that South Africa was violating the mandate and should therefore withdraw from South West Africa. South Africa fought the case, but at the same time began to introduce the Bantustan system in the territory. After the ICJ dismissed the case in 1966, the UN General Assembly resolved to revoke South Africa's mandate and place the territory under direct UN administration. This was subsequently confirmed by the Security Council, but South Africa refused to co-operate. From 1966 South Africa fought a low-intensity war in northern Namibia against guerrillas of the South West Africa Peoples's Organization (see the chapter on Namibia).

INTERNAL PRESSURES FOR CHANGE

In the 1970s the South African Government endeavoured to confer formal independence on the 'Bantustans'. Transkei accepted this status in 1976, Bophuthatswana in 1977, Venda in 1979 and Ciskei in 1981. All remained dependent on South African financial support and their 'independence' was not internationally recognized. The imposition of 'independence' was resisted by KwaNdebele and, still more determinedly, by KwaZulu under the leadership of Chief Mangosuthu Buthelezi, who used the political immunity conferred by his position to attack the apartheid system. He attempted to transform Inkatha, the Zulu cultural movement that he had founded, into a national political force.

In June 1976 the agglomeration of segregated African townships to the south-west of Johannesburg known as Soweto (South-West Townships) erupted, after police opened fire on school children protesting against being forced to use Afrikaans as the medium of instruction for some of their school subjects. Resistance spread not only to other black townships around the Rand and Pretoria but to Natal and the Cape, where Coloured and Indian youths joined in. Repeatedly and violently repressed, the uprisings were not brought under control until the end of the year. Thousands of young people were arrested but many others escaped across the borders to join the liberation movements. The ANC proved far more successful than the PAC in attracting this cadre of prospective freedom fighters, thus consolidating its political hold over the loyalties of the majority. The Black Consciousness Movement leader Steve Biko was arrested by the police and died in police custody in September 1977. At the subsequent inquest into his death, details were revealed of how the police had tortured him. The national and international outcry led the Government to ban the black consciousness organizations in October and the UN to impose a mandatory arms embargo on South Africa in November.

P. W. Botha, who had been Minister of Defence and who took over from Vorster as Prime Minister in 1978, altered the balance of influence within the state security network in favour of the armed forces, as opposed to the police. The State Security Council, which brought together politicians and key officials in the security forces, became the main decision-making organ, with the roles of the NP and Parliament (where the Progressive Federal Party—PFP now led the opposition) increasingly reduced. In the face of the increasing pressure on the apartheid regime, Botha introduced some reforms. Racial job restrictions were gradually abolished and trade-union rights extended to black Africans. Africans with urban rights of residence were allowed to move from one town to another. Restrictions on multiracial sports were reduced and the laws against interracial marriage and extra-marital sexual relations were repealed. The ineffective Senate was replaced by a President's Council, which proposed the establishment of a tricameral Parliament, comprising separate houses for whites, Coloureds and Indians. Though white domination was not threatened by this, any sharing of power with non-whites was rejected by the hardliners in the NP, who broke away and formed the Conservative Party (CP). Botha, however, proceeded to implement his constitutional plan. In November 1983 white voters approved the creation of a tricameral legislature in a referendum. Elections for the Coloured House of Representatives and the Indian House of Delegates followed in August 1984, and in September P. W. Botha became the country's first executive President.

The introduction of the new Constitution was the catalyst for a rebellion in the black townships which exceeded the scale of the 1976 Soweto upheaval. It was supported by strikes, notably in the economically crucial mining industry, while resistance to apartheid, and to the new Constitution, had been galvanized by the coming together of hundreds of local civic and other groups in the United Democratic Front. The Congress of South African Trade Unions (COSATU), a federation of black trade unions that were politically aligned with the ANC, was formed in December 1985, and demanded the abolition of pass restrictions, the withdrawal of foreign investment and the release of Mandela. The township rebellion escalated in March 1985, when the police opened fire on an unarmed African procession in Uitenhage, killing 20 and wounding many more. In July the Government declared a state of emergency in 36 magisterial districts, but the violence continued to increase. Black policemen, community councillors and suspected informers were killed in growing numbers. Demands intensified for the Government to introduce major reforms, but in August Botha, in a much publicized speech, rejected outside interference in dealing with the country's problems. With US banks refusing to roll over short term loans, the currency plummeted and the leaders of big business met with the ANC in exile in Zambia. As internal resistance escalated, in June 1986 the Government extended the state of emergency to cover the whole country. This provoked further international condemnation of South Africa. European banks suspended new lending and the European Community (EC, now the European Union—EU) and the USA introduced limited sanctions.

Among Afrikaner intellectuals, professionals and businessmen and within the NP itself, opinion was already growing that apartheid would have to be abandoned and an accommodation reached with an effective African leadership. While liberal Afrikaner opinion was moving towards this view, a proliferation of movements on the extreme right expressed the growing desperation of the poorer sections of the white community at the erosion of their privileged position. A paramilitary organization, the Afrikaanse Weerstandsbeweging, founded in 1977 and led by Eugene Terre'Blanche, actively recruited among the security forces.

A general election to the white House of Assembly in 1987 saw the NP emerge with a secure majority but a considerably reduced vote. The CP obtained more seats than the PFP and became the official opposition. In 1989 the PFP was reconstituted as the Democratic Party (DP). In January that year,

Botha suffered a stroke and decided to relinquish the NP leadership, while remaining State President. The NP members of Parliament then elected F. W. de Klerk as the new NP leader. Botha met with Mandela—still serving out a life sentence—in July, thus effectively recognizing the ANC leader's position as the potential alternative Head of Government, and relinquished the presidency, with some unwillingness, in mid-August. Prior to the September parliamentary elections, de Klerk, still only the acting Head of State, gave little indication of any radical intentions. At the election, the opposition parties made considerable gains, but the NP retained a clear majority, and de Klerk was confirmed as State President.

During 1989 international and internal pressures on the Government increased. The greater part of the NP and the Afrikaner intellectual élite was convinced that apartheid was unsustainable and that the ANC must be accepted as a negotiating partner. The ANC, meanwhile, lost its military facilities in Angola as part of the deal that brought Namibia its independence in March 1990, and had to move its camps even further away from South Africa. In the USA President George Bush initiated a more active approach towards democratic change in South Africa. During 1989 informal meetings were held in the United Kingdom between representatives of the ANC, the NP, a number of African states, and the USA and the USSR. In September US officials indicated that if no move to release Mandela had taken place within six months President Bush would assent to an extension of sanctions.

THE NEGOTIATED SETTLEMENT

Addressing the three Houses of Parliament on 2 February 1990, President de Klerk made the dramatic announcement that Nelson Mandela would be released and that the ban had been lifted on the ANC, the PAC, the SACP and 33 other organizations. It was the Government's intention to open negotiations with black leaders, with a view to devising a new constitution based on universal franchise. Equality of all citizens, regardless of race, was to be guaranteed by an independent judiciary, and protection for individual rights entrenched. On 11 February 1990 Mandela was released after 27 years in prison. ANC refugees soon began to return from exile. However, the ANC faced major problems in bringing the spontaneous loyalties of the great majority of the black population within a disciplined organizational framework, and urged the continuation of sanctions until the abandonment of apartheid had become demonstrably irreversible.

The ANC and the Government met in May 1990 to discuss conditions for the opening of full constitutional negotiations, and again in August, when the ANC agreed to the formal suspension of its guerrilla activities. The ANC favoured the election by universal franchise of a constituent assembly to draw up the new constitutional order, while the Government instead favoured a multi-party conference giving each party an equal voice. In January 1991 the Government agreed to a proposal by the ANC that a multi-party conference should determine the procedures for drawing up a new constitution.

On 1 February 1991 de Klerk again took the initiative in an address to Parliament by announcing that all the remaining legislation enshrining apartheid, including the Group Areas Act and the Population Registration Act, was to be repealed. By the end of June this legal revolution was complete. The NP even changed its own constitution to open membership to all races, and began to attract significant numbers of Indians and Coloureds, as well as smaller numbers of black members. The EC and the USA abandoned most sanctions, and contacts between South Africa and black African states expanded. In early July, at its national congress, the ANC elected a new National Executive. Mandela became President, and the leader of the National Union of Mineworkers, Cyril Ramaphosa, Secretary-General.

The main obstacle impeding constitutional negotiations was the continuing violence between Inkatha and ANC supporters and the suspicion that elements of the state security forces were involved. In early April 1991 the ANC threatened to withdraw from negotiations if the Government failed to take effective action to stop the violence, and demanded the dismissal of the Minister of Defence, Magnus Malan, and the Minister of Law and Order, Adriaan Vlok. In July it was admitted that secret payments had been made from government funds to Inkatha during 1989–90, and Malan and Vlok were demoted to minor cabinet posts. Suspicions of official complicity in the violence were not fully dispelled, however, and the ANC insisted on the formation of an interim government in which it would be represented during the transition to a democratic order.

A multi-party conference, called the Convention for a Democratic South Africa (CODESA), met to begin drafting a new constitution in December 1991. The commencement of constitutional discussions intensified the hostility of the extreme right and, after losing a parliamentary by-election to the CP, de Klerk called a referendum of white voters for 17 March 1992. Despite demonstrations and campaigning by the far right, the Government achieved a more than two-thirds' majority in support of continuing negotiations towards a democratic constitution. The CODESA talks were resumed, but the Government insisted on provisions that appeared to give it a veto. The talks came to an impasse, after which the ANC called for a campaign of non-violent mass action by its supporters to put pressure on the Government. Then, on 17 June, a number of residents of the settlement of Boipatong, including women and children, were massacred, apparently by Inkatha supporters who had allegedly been brought to the scene by police trucks. The ANC broke off negotiations with the Government, and demanded effective action to stop the violence, including the disbandment of groups involved in covert operations.

In early September 1992 the armed forces of the nominally independent 'homeland' of Ciskei fired on a procession of ANC supporters, killing 28 people and wounding about 200 others. The ANC blamed the South African Government for complicity in the massacre, but realized that there would be further bloodshed unless negotiations were resumed. Informal contacts between Ramaphosa and the Government's chief negotiator, Roelf Meyer, paved the way for a meeting between Mandela and de Klerk which approved a 'record of understanding', allowing for the resumption of full bilateral negotiations. In November the ANC announced its acceptance of a proposal that a government of national unity should be formed for five years after the first democratic elections. The legislature elected then would also act as a constitutional assembly to draw up a new Constitution.

With substantial agreement between the two main negotiating partners achieved, the multi-party negotiating forum was reconvened in April 1993. Buthelezi, who protested vigorously at the bilateral agreements between the Government and the ANC, initiated meetings between representatives of Inkatha, a number of movements based in the 'homelands' and the CP, who formed the Concerned South Africans Group to act as a pressure group at the negotiating forum in favour of extreme regional autonomy. In early April, however, on the eve of the talks, CP leader Chris Hani was assassinated by a white right-wing extremist; the aim was to disrupt the negotiations, but instead the negotiators came under greater pressure than before to reach consensus on the way forward. By mid-year it had been decided that the elections would be held in April 1994, and that a set of constitutional principles would have to be observed in the final constitution. The interim Constitution was finalized in November, and embodied major compromises by both the main negotiating partners. Its regional proposals provided for some measure of federalism, but not enough to persuade Buthelezi to accept them. There were now to be nine provinces: Western Cape, Eastern Cape, Northern Cape, Orange Free State (renamed Free State in June 1995), North-West, Natal (soon redesignated KwaZulu/Natal), Eastern Transvaal (subsequently renamed Mpumalanga), Northern Transvaal (renamed Northern Province in June 1995 and Limpopo in February 2002) and Pretoria, Witwatersrand and Vereeniging (PWV—subsequently renamed Gauteng). The former 'homelands', including those purported to be 'independent', were to disappear as distinct entities and be absorbed into one or more of the new provinces. Each of the new provinces was to be provided with an elected assembly, to be chosen by proportional representation, and a regional government with extensive local authority and autonomy.

The central Parliament was to comprise a House of Assembly of 400 members, all elected by proportional representation but on a basis of one-half from national and one-half from regional lists. There was to be an upper house or Senate of 90 members chosen by the regional assemblies. The executive would be headed by an executive President, to be chosen by Parliament, and under the terms of the agreement on a government of national unity, any party obtaining 20% of the national vote would be entitled to one of two vice-presidential positions. In the event that only one party achieved this total, the second position would go to any grouping with the second largest support. Any party receiving 5% or more of the vote would be entitled to a position in the national Cabinet. The national and regional assemblies and governments were to function within the limitations of a justiciable interim bill of rights. The interim Parliament was to function as the national legislature for a maximum period of five years and was also to act as a Constitutional Assembly charged with the responsibility for drafting the definitive Constitution for the country within two years. The adoption of the new Constitution was to require a two-thirds' majority in the Constitutional Assembly.

Buthelezi was persuaded to register the Inkatha Freedom Party (IFP) for the election, but he then reverted to demands for postponement and threats of a boycott. By early April 1994, however, he was under great pressure from those of his supporters who wished to participate in the elections. He finally agreed that the IFP would contest the elections in return for the enhancement of the status of the Zulu monarchy by the transfer of extensive state lands to a trust in the name of the Zulu monarch, King Goodwill Zwelithini. Since the IFP had missed the deadline for the registration of candidates and was not on the ballot papers which had already been printed, additional strips were required to be attached to ballot papers during the voting procedure.

The general election, involving 19 political parties, commenced on 26 April 1994, as scheduled, and continued for three days. The logistical difficulties of organizing an election on this scale for the first time, compounded by the complex voting procedures (which were further exacerbated by the need to affix the Inkatha strips to ballot papers), resulted in much frustration and long delays. Although there were abundant opportunities for errors and electoral fraud, the overall outcome was clear beyond doubt. The ANC gained an overwhelming majority at national level, although short of the two-thirds' majority which would have enabled it to rewrite the Constitution unilaterally. It also gained control of seven of the nine provinces. The NP was the only other grouping to secure more than 20% of the votes and it won control of the Western Cape Province. Inkatha won 10% of the votes cast, and was credited with a 51% victory in KwaZulu/Natal. The PAC, with its radical Africanist approach, and the white-led DP each received less than 2% of the votes.

THE MANDELA GOVERNMENT

On 9 May 1994 the National Assembly elected Mandela as President, and on the following day he was inaugurated as Head of State at a ceremony attended by a large number of international dignitaries. In accordance with the interim Constitution (which had taken effect on 27 April), an interim Cabinet of National Unity was formed, in which the ANC, the NP and the IFP were represented in proportion to the number of seats that they had won in the general election. Thabo Mbeki of the ANC and de Klerk (NP) became Deputy Presidents, while Buthelezi was allocated the portfolio of home affairs. Ramaphosa remained outside the Cabinet, but was selected to preside over the Constitutional Assembly, which comprised the National Assembly and the Senate. Following the installation of a democratic Government, South Africa was admitted into the Organization of African Unity (OAU—subsequently the African Union—AU), the Commonwealth and the Southern African Development Community (SADC), and resumed its seat in the General Assembly of the UN. The arms embargo that the UN had imposed in 1977 was finally removed. South Africa's standing in the Commonwealth was acknowledged with a royal visit from Queen Elizabeth II in March 1995.

The Government of National Unity focused on the maintenance of stability and the promotion of economic growth, with initial emphasis laid on a Reconstruction and Development Programme (RDP), which included an undertaking to construct 1m. homes in a period of five years, and to extend basic educational and health facilities to all. The Government planned to finance the RDP through savings on security-related expenses and increased revenue resulting from economic growth, and Japan and other countries provided sizeable contributions, but implementation proved much more difficult than the Government had anticipated. In early 1996 it was announced that the separate ministry for the RDP was to be abolished and that a new macroeconomic policy called the Growth, Employment and Redistribution programme (GEAR), in which growth came first and redistribution last, had been adopted. This signalled that the Government aimed to lure foreign investment to stimulate economic growth. Although the Government's schemes to provide electricity and clean water to those without these services were initially among its most successful, unemployment remained very high in the townships and many communities continued to refuse to pay for services and rents, despite the government campaign to persuade them to do so.

Aware of a possible threat from right-wing extremists, Mandela continued efforts to appear reconciliatory towards whites. A Volkstaat Council was established to debate the issue of self-determination for right-wing Afrikaners. Various plans were proposed, but none of these was practicable, and Mandela insisted that he would not consider a new structure based on racial criteria. Many Afrikaners opposed the downgrading of Afrikaans from one of two official languages to one of 11, which was reflected, for example, in the great reduction in the use of Afrikaans in television broadcasting. Afrikaners, English-speaking whites and Coloureds resented 'affirmative action' (discrimination in favour of black Africans) in job appointments. However, there was no significant protest by whites against the new system, and the threat of armed resistance by the extreme right-wing receded after the election in April 1994.

A number of communities began to use vigilante methods in response to the police force's apparent inability to combat an increase in violent crime, which also prompted demands for the restoration of the death penalty, outlawed by the Constitutional Court in June 1995. The process of transforming the police into a force that was regarded by the public as legitimate and credible was hindered by evidence which emerged about the measures that had, during the period of apartheid, been used against opponents of that system. A number of members of the former police force were placed on trial, most notably Col Eugene de Kock, the former head of a clandestine police base near Pretoria from which political assassinations had been carried out. After proceedings lasting 18 months, de Kock was convicted in 1996 on 89 charges of murder and other crimes, and sentenced to over 200 years in jail. In another trial, which came to an end in that year, Gen. Magnus Malan, the former Minister of Defence, and prominent officials in the former armed forces were acquitted of complicity in a massacre, perpetrated in KwaZulu in 1987 by commandos who had been trained in Namibia. As a result of such trials, and the proceedings of the Truth and Reconciliation Commission (TRC, see below), much was revealed of the illicit activities that had been employed during apartheid and the transitional period.

On 8 May 1996 Parliament approved the final version of the new Constitution and the document was subsequently referred to the Constitutional Court for confirmation that it accorded with the constitutional principles that had been established in negotiations prior to the 1994 elections. In September the Court returned some sections for reconsideration. The Court subsequently ratified the Constitution, which was signed by President Mandela at Sharpeville on 10 December 1996, and it entered into force on 4 February 1997. The new Constitution provided for the establishment of a 'commission for the promotion and protection of the rights of cultural, religious and linguistic communities', while a National Council of Provinces replaced the Senate as the upper house of Parliament, increasing the influence of the provinces on central government policy.

Following the approval of the draft of the new Constitution, the NP announced that it was to leave the Cabinet of National

Unity from the end of June 1996, to form a parliamentary opposition. Although Buthelezi continued to assert his differences with the ANC, the IFP remained in the Government. Efforts by Mandela to persuade the PAC to join the Government were unsuccessful. After the NP ministers left the Cabinet, their portfolios were allocated to ANC members and de Klerk became the official leader of the opposition. The NP, though reinvented as a non-racial party, continued to receive almost all its support from the white and Coloured communities. Roelf Meyer, who had played a significant role in the negotiations of 1992–93 and (as Secretary-General of the party) was the designated successor to de Klerk, became increasingly concerned with the NP's inability to attract black African voters. Following his suggestion that the NP disband and re-form as part of a realigned opposition, he was obliged to resign from the party. In September 1997 he formed a new political party, the United Democratic Movement (UDM), with Bantu Holomisa, the former ruler of Transkei. By mid-1998 Holomisa had become leader of the party, with Meyer his deputy and a former ANC activist from Natal, Sifiso Nkabinde, as Secretary-General. The UDM began to attract significant support, most notably in the former 'homeland' of Transkei. Meanwhile, in August 1997 de Klerk unexpectedly resigned as leader of the NP, on the grounds that this was in the interests of the party, and the party's Secretary-General, Marthinus van Schalkwyk, took over as leader.

At the ANC congress in December 1997 Mandela resigned from the presidency of the party and was succeeded by Thabo Mbeki, who was elected unopposed. Jacob Zuma (hitherto the party Chairman) was elected Deputy President at the congress. Although Mandela remained active as Head of State, Mbeki was already effectively in control of government administration.

Following Mandela's assumption of office, it became evident that the new Government intended to maintain cordial relations with regimes that were regarded with disapproval by the USA and other Western countries, but which had provided substantial support to the ANC during the apartheid era, most notably those of Iran, Cuba and Libya. Nevertheless, South Africa's links with the USA strengthened following the transition to democratic rule. South Africa was the location for a number of important international meetings, including those of the Non-aligned Movement and the Commonwealth Heads of Government. Mandela's personal stature, in addition to the success of the country's transition to democracy, enhanced South Africa's prestige internationally.

After a prolonged debate, the EU in March 1996 agreed on a framework for negotiations with South Africa on the proposed establishment of a joint free-trade area. It was another three years before the EU and South Africa reached agreement on a comprehensive free-trade agreement in the final months of the Mandela administration, although details of the accord were not finalized until well into the Mbeki presidency (see below), delaying its implementation. In November 1996 Mandela announced that South Africa would transfer diplomatic recognition from Taiwan (Republic of China) to the People's Republic of China, with effect from the end of 1997. Taiwan immediately severed diplomatic relations, announced the suspension of most of its aid projects in South Africa and banned South African Airways from flying to Taipei, the Taiwanese capital. The South African decision was influenced by the return of Hong Kong to Chinese rule in 1997 and its wish to secure a permanent seat on an enlarged UN Security Council.

After becoming Chairman of SADC in September 1996, Mandela pursued a more active foreign policy, frequently intervening personally in an effort to resolve regional problems. In early 1997 he was involved in intensive diplomatic activity aimed at ending the civil war in Zaire (now the Democratic Republic of the Congo—DRC), meeting both the then Zairean rebel leader, Laurent Kabila, and the Zairean President, Mobutu Seso Seko. Mandela also sought to mediate in the dispute over Indonesia's annexation of East Timor in 1976 and in the continuing civil war in southern Sudan.

THE TRUTH AND RECONCILIATION COMMISSION (TRC)

In 1995, following protracted disputes regarding its method of operating, Parliament approved the establishment of the TRC, and in December of that year 17 members were appointed to the Commission by Mandela. Desmond Tutu (whose term of office as Anglican Archbishop of Cape Town ended in 1996) became Chairman. The Commission began by conducting public hearings throughout the country, at which former victims of human-rights violations gave evidence. The TRC's amnesty committee considered applications by perpetrators of such abuses, and from August 1996 began to grant amnesty to those who had given a full account of their actions. After the mandate of the Commission was extended from December 1993 to 10 May 1994 (as requested by both the Freedom Front and the PAC), more applications for amnesty were received.

From August 1996 the TRC heard representations from political parties. Although de Klerk formally apologized for the policy of apartheid, he denied that he or other members of the previous Government had ordered or condoned illegal activities. The ANC admitted responsibility for some violations of human rights committed by its members in the 1980s, and asserted that these were justified in the context of the struggle against apartheid. Buthelezi refused to co-operate with the TRC, claiming that he had already apologized for acts of violence perpetrated by IFP supporters. In May 1997 the NP suspended participation in the Commission and threatened legal action against Tutu, after he accused de Klerk of responsibility for human-rights violations. Although the legal action was abandoned, and relations improved when van Schalkwyk replaced de Klerk as the leader of the NP, many in the NP remained deeply suspicious of the TRC, which they regarded as biased towards the ANC. P. W. Botha, having refused to testify, was brought before a court, which in August 1998, following considerable delays, sentenced him to a fine of R10,000, or 12 months' imprisonment, for being in contempt of the TRC. However, Botha subsequently won an appeal against the conviction, on the technical grounds that the TRC's subpoena was invalid since the Commission's mandate had temporarily expired.

One of the most serious perceived failings of the TRC was its inability to investigate thoroughly the numerous human-rights violations which South Africans had committed in neighbouring countries. It was unable to demand testimony relating to such acts because it could not guarantee defendants' indemnity from prosecution in those countries. In 1998 horrifying revelations emerged concerning the apartheid regime's clandestine project to produce a chemical and biological weapons capability; it was claimed that pharmaceutical substances had been developed with specific properties to incapacitate blacks. Further details were revealed when Wouter Basson, head of the secret chemical and biological warfare programme, was brought to trial in Pretoria. More than 150 witnesses were called, one of whom revealed that hundreds of captured Namibian guerrillas had been thrown from planes, some of them still alive, into the sea off the Namibian coast. Eventually, the judge found Basson not guilty because of insufficient evidence.

Tutu submitted the initial five-volume TRC report to Mandela in October 1998, after de Klerk had won a legal challenge preventing the release of a section in the report concerning his role in human-rights violations. The ANC failed in an attempt to delay publication of the report, on the grounds that it 'criminalized' its role in the struggle against apartheid. The amnesty process continued, and many of the decisions provoked considerable controversy. A number of members of the Azanian People's Liberation Army were granted amnesty for the indiscriminate killing of whites, but the members of the security forces who murdered Biko in 1977 were refused amnesty, on the grounds that the killing was not politically motivated. The amnesty applications of the two right-wing extremists who killed Hani in 1993 (see above) were also rejected, as they were judged not to have made full disclosure. Tutu, Mandela and others rejected any suggestion that a general amnesty might be granted to perpetrators of abuses. It was not until May 2001 that the work of the amnesty committee finally came to an end. That left the TRC with a last task of compiling a further report, and the final two volumes were handed to the Government in March 2003. While the TRC's reparations committee had recommended that R3,000m. be granted to compensate victims, the Government made only about R65m. available, which equated to a one-off payment of about R30,000 to the 22,000 victims identified by the TRC. In his speech to Parliament on the TRC in April 2003, President Mbeki rejected the idea of a wealth tax to pay for reparations, as suggested by the TRC, and voiced strong disapproval of the cases being brought against multinational companies for their alleged complicity in apartheid, on the grounds that such cases would threaten future foreign investment. For many, the Government's response to the recommendations of the TRC was inadequate, and it remained unclear whether any of those who had not applied for amnesty, or had not been granted amnesty, would be prosecuted successfully.

THE 1999 GENERAL ELECTION AND MBEKI'S FIRST TERM

In the later years of the Mandela presidency Mbeki increasingly assumed responsibility for government administration, and accumulated power in the Office of the First Deputy President. One of his major achievements was to contribute to the restoration of relative peace in KwaZulu/Natal, and to improve relations between the ANC and Inkatha. Although he lacked Mandela's personal charisma, he proved to be a competent campaigner for the ANC in the 1999 general election campaign. The ANC urged voters to award it a decisive mandate to continue with the process of change and transformation. The NP, reconstituted as the New National Party (NNP), lost Coloured support to the ANC and white support to the DP under the leadership of Tony Leon. On 2 June 1999 almost 17m. voters participated in the elections, which were judged to be substantially 'free and fair' by domestic and international observers. The ANC obtained 266 seats, narrowly failing to secure a two-thirds' majority in the National Assembly. Support for the opposition fragmented, with the NNP winning only 28 seats. The DP was the main beneficiary of this, increasing its representation in the National Assembly from seven to 38 seats (thus becoming the official opposition). The IFP, which won 34 seats in the National Assembly, entered into a coalition with the ANC, and Buthelezi remained Minister of Home Affairs. Jacob Zuma, long a close associate of Mbeki, became Deputy President. As a result of the coalition, the ANC achieved much more than a two-thirds' majority in the legislature.

On 16 June 1999 Thabo Mbeki was formally inaugurated as President. His Cabinet was larger than Mandela's, despite a prior commitment to a more rationalized government structure. There were a number of unexpected appointments, but the two principal economic ministers, Trevor Manuel, the Minister of Finance, and Alec Erwin, the Minister of Trade and Industry, were retained in their posts, signalling that Mbeki had no wish to alter the macroeconomic strategies on which the Mandela Government had embarked. Mbeki also pledged that the privatization of parastatal companies would proceed with more urgency. However, there was a gradual shift of emphasis away from privatization and towards private investment in state-owned enterprises.

In July 1999 public-sector workers took strike action in large numbers in support of a demand for a 10% increase in wages. The Government offered them a rise of 6%, which was just less than the annual rate of inflation. COSATU, which supported the strike, had helped the ANC to reach its large majority in the general election the previous month, but there was now much speculation that a dissolution of the alliance between the ANC Government and its allies, COSATU and the SACP, was inevitable, especially if President Mbeki attempted to renege on the Government's concessions to the trade unions, to provide for greater flexibility in the labour market. In mid-2000 the Minister of Labour proposed amendments aimed at rendering the Government's labour regime more attractive to foreign investors: COSATU vehemently opposed such changes. Although there was talk of privatizing major parastatals, such as ESKOM (electricity), and Spoornet and Transnet (transport), progress was extremely slow.

One of Mbeki's main aims in foreign policy was to secure a peaceful settlement in the DRC. He assisted in the arrangement of a cease-fire there in June 1999, and subsequently endeavoured to persuade the rebels to observe it. South Africa agreed to contribute a small number of troops to the UN peace-keeping force in the DRC. In the Angolan conflict, the South African Government had for some time made efforts to prevent supplies reaching the UNITA insurgency movement from its territory, but found this difficult to enforce. Mbeki sought to continue, and strengthen, links with states such as Cuba, Libya and Iraq, while at the same time travelling to Western countries to win support for his Millennium African Recovery Plan, a programme for good governance and economic reform for the continent, subsequently incorporated into the New Partnership for Africa's Development (NEPAD). Meanwhile, Mandela took a leading role in trying to bring about peace in war-torn Burundi, and in October 2001 South African soldiers were sent to that country as part of a peace-keeping mission to enforce national security and support the formation of a new multi-ethnic transitional government. In 2004 they were brought under the authority of the AU, and some South African troops were also deployed in the DRC. It was expected that South Africa would in time commit troops to a proposed AU standby-force.

Mbeki endeavoured to promote the case for economic justice on behalf of poorer countries to the developed world, and at many international forums emphasized the importance of debt relief and the elimination of global poverty. In June 2002 he presented NEPAD to the meeting of the Group of Eight leading industrialized countries (G-8) in Canada, in an attempt to attract increased foreign aid to the continent. The G-8 countries promised to provide an extra US $6,000m. a year, a figure that many African observers considered insufficient. In July Mbeki presided over a conference in Durban, at which the OAU was relaunched as the AU, of which he became the first Chairman. In August South Africa hosted the UN World Summit on Sustainable Development in Johannesburg, which was convened to confront poverty in developing countries, promote sustainable development and build upon measures for the protection of the environment that had been discussed at the Earth Summit in Rio de Janeiro, Brazil, in 1992. By July 2003 Mbeki had handed over the chairmanship of both the Non-aligned Movement and the AU, but his Government continued to devote much effort to trying to bring peace to the DRC and Burundi, and the AU also asked him to mediate in the crisis in Côte d'Ivoire. In that he was not successful, and he took advantage of South Africa's election as a non-permanent member of the UN Security Council to withdraw from his role there. From 2004 it was a major concern of the Government to secure a permanent seat on an enlarged UN Security Council. To that end, numerous countries were visited and lobbied. However, when South Africa took up its non-permanent seat in January 2007, it came under much criticism for arguing that the Council was over-reaching itself and for voting not to take a stand against human rights abuses in countries such as Myanmar and Zimbabwe.

When the invasion of white-owned farms in neighbouring Zimbabwe began, Mbeki was urged to condemn what was happening in that country. Not only did he fail to criticize the Zimbabwean President, Robert Mugabe, but he delayed announcing clearly that the seizure of land by violent means would not be tolerated in South Africa. Identifying land inequalities as a major issue to be addressed, he stated his preference of implementing 'quiet diplomacy' with Mugabe, to influence him to hold a free and fair election and to deal with the land issue peacefully. In May 2000 Mbeki attempted in vain to raise funds internationally to pay for land transfers in Zimbabwe. After Mugabe's controversial re-election as President in March 2002, Mbeki agreed reluctantly to comply with the wishes of President Olesegun Obasanjo of Nigeria and Prime Minister John Howard of Australia and recommend the suspension of Zimbabwe from the Commonwealth, but still refused to criticize Mugabe's increasingly authoritarian rule and the extreme measures taken against both white farmers and supporters of the Zimbabwean opposition Movement for

Democratic Change (MDC). In June 2003 Mbeki stated publicly that the Zimbabwean crisis would be resolved by June 2004; when that date arrived he had to admit that his policy of quiet diplomacy, which aimed to bring the MDC into a unity government, had not been successful, but he repeated that there was no alternative. Not only were no sanctions of any kind imposed on Zimbabwe, but Mbeki ignored those who argued that his failure to condemn Mugabe's rule was threatening to undermine his entire NEPAD strategy. When the Mugabe regime destroyed homes and made hundreds of thousands homeless in 2005, Mbeki again offered no public criticism. In 2007 he stated that South Africa would have to live with the millions of refugees from Zimbabwe who poured across the border, but in March that year he was deputed by SADC to mediate in the crisis. In mid-2007 it remained unclear whether his intervention would bring about the resolution of the crisis.

As the Zimbabwean crisis developed, some foreign investors began to fear that land invasions might occur in South Africa—as happened on a small scale in mid-2001—and that the Government might not stand firm on the rule of law. The programme for land restitution in South Africa proceeded slowly, mainly owing to a cumbersome bureaucratic process. By mid-2007 all but 5,100 claims remained to be settled, but they were the most difficult ones, and it appeared that the deadline of completing the process by 2008 would not be met. Of the 73,000 claims that had been settled, most had been resolved by monetary compensation rather than the return of land. Meanwhile, the Communal Land Rights Act of 2004 aimed to clarify the tenure rights of 15m. people in the former 'homelands'. An estimated 86% of all rural land remained in the hands of approximately 60,000 white commercial farmers, and attacks on white farmers continued at a high level, with well over 1,000 killed since 1994.

It was on the subject of HIV/AIDS that Mbeki was most severely criticized by the national and international media, because of statements he made in support of dissident scientists who questioned whether AIDS was caused by HIV, and for promoting the idea that an indigenous cure might be found for the disease. While there was widespread support for his view that AIDS must be considered in the context of poverty in Africa, his often ambiguous statements served to divert attention from the question of how best to tackle the pandemic. By the end of 2001 an estimated 4.7m. South Africans were infected with HIV, about one-fifth of the population aged between 15 and 49 years. While the Ministry of Health claimed in mid-2002 that the rate of infection was slowing, others believed it was gaining momentum. Although the lobby group Treatment Action Campaign (TAC) won a court case in late 2001 in which the Government was ordered to provide antiretroviral drugs for pregnant women, the Mbeki Government argued that a system of monitoring would be required, which South Africa could not afford, and that the drugs themselves were too expensive. However, the Ministry of Health did campaign for multinational pharmaceuticals companies to lower the prices of anti-AIDS drugs or to allow generic alternatives to be used, and in April 2001 the companies withdrew from a court case they had brought against the Government. In February 2002 Buthelezi, as Minister of Home Affairs, ordered the distribution of antiretrovirals in Kwazulu/Natal, in contravention of government policy. In March the High Court upheld the ruling that ordered state provision of antiretroviral drugs; the Government sought leave to appeal the ruling, but it was overturned by the Constitutional Court in July. In October the Government finally announced that it would investigate ways of providing antiretrovirals through the public health system. Peter Mokaba, the former President of the ANC Youth League, died of what was widely believed to be AIDS in June, but he and many other victims would not admit to suffering from the disease. In August one of the largest employers in South Africa, Anglo American PLC, agreed to distribute antiretroviral drugs to its employees free of charge. The measure was intended to provide for employees without medical insurance, and to save the company the cost of replacing infected workers. Very reluctantly, the Government agreed in 2003 to accept that it should make antiretrovirals freely available, but the roll-out proceeded slowly, amid much confusion regarding the Government's commitment and plans, and the TAC continued to accuse the Government of stalling the process and to demand that the Minister of Health be dismissed. It was not until 2006 that the Government committed itself to a new AIDS policy which the TAC could support. Although Mbeki retained the Minister of Health, the TAC found that it could work with the new Deputy President, and it now apparently accepted that the Government had abandoned its previous tardy approach to the pandemic.

Although the rate of overall crime remained at a high level, with some particularly violent crimes having an apparent racial aspect to them, certain categories of crime declined in the early years of the new century, in part because of the establishment of a new élite anti-crime unit, known as the Scorpions. The Department of Safety and Security claimed that the number of murders had fallen by one-third between 1994 and 2002, but refused to disclose detailed statistics. The underfunded police were often unable to detain offenders, there were numerous escapes from jails, and those detained were often released back into society because of the inadequacy of the justice system. State agents did, however, successfully infiltrate a right-wing extremist group, members of which were put on trial for plotting to overthrow the state. The so-called Boeremag trial that followed was still continuing in mid-2007, its proceedings having been delayed in part by the escape from court of two of the leading figures on trial, who were then able to evade the police for one year before being recaptured. White emigration increased as a result of rising crime and the impact of events in Zimbabwe, and as a consequence of legislation that required all companies and organizations to set targets for making their work-force more representative of the demographics of the country. Many young white males saw no prospect of employment. Mbeki and some members of his Government continued to argue that privileged whites were not doing enough to address the inequalities in society. As a small, well-connected, black élite benefited massively from the Government's Black Economic Empowerment programme (see Economy), Mbeki defended the rapid emergence of a black bourgeoisie as a means to greater social stability, and accused those whom he called 'fishers of corrupt men' of adhering to racist stereotypes of Africans as inherently corrupt.

The alliance formed by the DP and the NNP in the Western Cape in June 1999 led in mid-2000 to the establishment of the Democratic Alliance (DA), which linked the two parties nationally, under the leadership of Tony Leon, with the NNP leader Marthinus van Schalkwyk as his deputy. Although the DP claimed that it held firm to its liberal principles, there were few black Africans in the new Alliance and the ANC was able to present the DA as an anti-African front. When municipal elections were held in late 2000 to replace the more than 800 existing local government structures with 284 new municipalities, the main urban centres became 'uni-cities', each under one authority. Cape Town's was controlled initially by the DA. In KwaZulu/Natal the loose alliance between the ANC and IFP brought relative stability, although the chiefs (*inkosi*), who were now paid by the Government, feared that the new local government system would reduce their powers, and sought unsuccessfully to challenge the demarcation of the new structures. In late 2001 a series of crises in the Western Cape, involving alleged corruption by the mayor of Cape Town, provided an opportunity for the NNP faction of the DA, led by van Schalkwyk, to suspend its participation in the alliance and enter into a partnership with the ANC instead. These two parties then entered into a power-sharing agreement in the Western Cape, and van Schalkwyk became Premier of the Western Cape. The NNP was weakened, however, by legislation passed in June 2002 enabling elected members of Parliament and of local government bodies to change parties without the need to seek re-election. The result was disastrous for the UDM, which had opposed the floor-crossing legislation; it lost most of its members of Parliament to other parties. The DA gained members from the NNP, and the ANC was able to take power in the Western Cape at local level. Although many expected the ANC also to gain a majority in the KwaZulu/Natal legislature, the IFP managed to remain in power until the 2004 elections.

Perhaps the single most important decision of the Mbeki Government was to allocate some R30,000m. to purchase arms from the United Kingdom, Germany and Sweden, despite much criticism that the weapons were not necessary. The purchase was justified in part by the promised 'offsets', which were supposed to bring foreign capital into the country and create jobs. However, there was much scepticism about whether the offsets would materialize and, as the value of the rand fell, the cost of the arms escalated, so that by mid-2002 it was estimated at R60,000m. The arms deal was to remain a running sore for the Government, as critics alleged that there had been massive corruption in the arms-procurement process. For a time it seemed that the Government wanted to hinder investigations into the matter, as it refused to allow the Special Investigation Unit, set up by Mandela and headed by Judge Willem Heath, to probe the matter. Eventually in 2001, public hearings were held in Pretoria, under the auspices of the Auditor-General, the National Director of Public Prosecutions and the Public Protector. The report these bodies issued in November of that year failed to find evidence of serious wrongdoing, but opposition parties accused the ANC of manipulating and suppressing certain parts of the report, and criticized the Government for forcing the resignation of Heath during the investigation. The ANC's chief whip, Tony Yengeni, was subsequently forced to resign, following allegations that he had received favours from one of the contractors in the arms deal while Chairman of the Parliamentary Defence Committee. He was sentenced to four years' imprisonment in March 2003 for defrauding the Government. The Scorpions then began to investigate allegations that Jacob Zuma, the Deputy President, had solicited a bribe from a French manufacturer bidding for an arms contract that was part of the multi-million rand arms deal. The National Director of Public Prosecutions, Bulelani Ngcuka, in August 2003 said that there was a *prima facie* case of corruption, but insufficient evidence to convict Zuma, and thus he would not be prosecuted. Infuriated by this, Zuma lodged a complaint against Ngcuka with the Public Protector in October 2003, and a number of Zuma's associates claimed that Ngcuka had worked for the apartheid Government. A judicial commission appointed by President Mbeki could, however, find no evidence to substantiate the claims.

THE 2004 ELECTIONS AND BEYOND

In 2004 South Africa celebrated 10 years of democracy, and a relatively peaceful transition from an apartheid order, and the threat of civil war, to an apparently stable democratic order. The celebration coincided with the holding of the third democratic elections, which took place on 14 April 2004. Of the 20m. registered voters (an estimated 7m. eligible persons had not registered), 5m. did not vote. Official results, announced on 17 April, confirmed the overwhelming victory of the ANC, which won 279 of the National Assembly's 400 seats, with 69.7% of the valid votes cast. The DA took 50 seats, with 12.4% of votes cast, and the IFP 28, with 7.0%. For the first time the ANC won control of all nine provincial governments, although it failed to win outright majorities in Kwazulu/Natal and Western Cape. On 23 April members of the National Assembly voted unanimously to re-elect Mbeki to the presidency, and he was sworn in to serve a second term on 27 April. He reshuffled the Cabinet, retaining Zuma as Deputy President and Manto Tshabalala-Msimang as Minister of Health, despite her record on HIV/AIDS. The leader of the NNP, Marthinus van Schalkwyk, was appointed Minister of Environment and Tourism, and the Cabinet's leading intellectual, Kader Asmal, who had been a forceful Minister of National Education, was removed, as was Buthelezi.

In the aftermath of the election, the NNP, which won only 1.7% of the vote, decided to disband: Van Schalkwyk joined the ANC, but most NP support was transferred to the DA. The loss of KwaZulu/Natal precipitated a major crisis in the IFP, which continued to be headed by the marginalized Buthelezi. In the Western Cape the ANC, which had taken power before the election after entering into an alliance with the NNP, remained in control, but with an ANC Premier, Ebrahim Rasool. However, ANC control of the province was soon again jeopardized by internecine feuding between a Coloured-led faction under Rasool and a black African faction led by Mcebisi Skwatsha. At the party's provincial congress in mid-2005, Rasool failed in his attempt to be re-elected as provincial Chairman, but he remained Premier of the province and tried to promote it as a 'home for all'. Holomisa's UDM, which had lost support to the ANC and other parties, especially during the window period for floor-crossing, emerged from the 2004 election with nine seats and one deputy minister. Patricia de Lille, formerly a prominent member of the PAC, had broken away from that party to form the Independent Democrats (ID), which won seven seats, most of them in the Western Cape. The ID was to proclaim itself a social democratic party, and stated that in the 2009 elections it would take on the ANC on the issue of growing inequalities in the country.

After the local government elections held in March 2006, no clear winner emerged in Cape Town; however, the DA and a coalition of small parties defeated the ANC, allied with the ID, by one vote. A former DA member of parliament, Helen Zille, was elected mayor. She dismissed the ANC-appointed city manager and began a more efficient and open administration of the city. In January 2007 she was able to forge a multi-party coalition with the ID to strengthen her position as mayor. One of the most pressing issues she faced was the cost and location of the stadium to be constructed for the 2010 Association Football World Cup, which the ANC had announced would be in a wealthy suburb and not near the poorer parts of the city. In May 2007 Leon stepped down as DA leader, and Zille was elected in his place, combining the post with that of mayor. Sandra Botha was subsequently elected as parliamentary leader of the DA.

Meanwhile, in May 2005 the Public Protector issued a report criticizing the National Director of Prosecutions for improperly prejudicing the Deputy President, whom many saw as the natural successor to Mbeki. The crisis over the allegations of corruption involving Zuma came to a head during the lengthy trial of his long-term acquaintance and financial adviser, the Durban businessman Schabir Shaik. In June Shaik was found guilty of corruption and fraud and sentenced to 15 years' imprisonment by the Durban High Court. The Court found that there had been a 'generally corrupt relationship' between Shaik and Zuma, and that a series of payments made by Shaik on behalf of Zuma were intended to influence Zuma to benefit Shaik's business. Although Zuma did not give evidence, the trial revealed that Zuma had been party to a bid to solicit a bribe from the French defence company Thales, one of the contractors in the controversial arms deal (see above).

Mbeki came under increasing pressure to dismiss Zuma and after a period of deliberation, the President called a joint sitting of both houses of Parliament, and announced that Zuma would be 'released' from his duties as Deputy President of the country. Mbeki appointed Phumzile Mlambo-Ngcuka, hitherto the Minister of Energy and Mineral Affairs, and the wife of the former National Director of Prosecutions, to replace Zuma. The new National Director of Prosecutions subsequently issued a summons against Zuma on two charges of corruption, but when the trial began the judge threw the case out, leaving the door open for Zuma to be prosecuted at a later date when the National Prosecuting Authority (NPA) had assembled more evidence. Further cases followed in which the NPA sought legal permission to use documents seized from Zuma and a key diary held in Mauritius that allegedly showed that he had accepted a bribe. In November 2005 Zuma was accused of raping a HIV-positive family friend at his home. In March 2006 he pleaded not guilty to the offence and claimed that unprotected sexual intercourse between the two had been consensual. Zuma, a former head of the South African National AIDS Council, shocked observers by arguing that he believed there was little danger of contracting HIV from unprotected sex, and that by taking a shower after intercourse with the woman he had reduced the risk of transmission. Doctors and health activists feared that his testimony would undermine prevention campaigns against the HIV virus.

In mid-May 2006 Zuma was acquitted of the rape charge. His supporters claimed that the trial was part of a political conspiracy to prevent him from succeeding Mbeki as President in 2009. Mbeki's successor as President of the ANC was to be chosen at a party congress to be held in late 2007 and Mbeki had expressed his preference for a female successor. Nevertheless, Zuma remained Deputy President of the ANC, and enjoyed wide support among Zulu-speakers and those to the left of the tripartite alliance of the ANC Youth League, the SACP and COSATU. The SACP subsequently accused the ANC of 'reformism' and of abandoning its revolutionary character in favour of deracializing and 'managing' capitalism, while COSATU claimed that under Mbeki the country was drifting towards a dictatorship. When it was suggested that Mbeki might seek to remain as the party's President after 2007, the ANC Youth League was quick to reject the idea, although it was taken up by the Eastern Cape ANC. Others criticized Mbeki's remote and autocratic leadership style and his reluctance to remove failing cabinet ministers. His supporters pointed to the successful way the economy was being managed, to his role on the world stage and to his mid-2006 veto of a number of bills put before Parliament by the Government that would, many observers believed, have interfered with the independence of the judiciary.

The succession issue became almost all-consuming in 2007, with COSATU professing neutrality but giving strong indications that it was in the anti-Mbeki camp, and Mosima Gabriel (Tokyo) Sexwale, a former guerrilla who had become premier of Gauteng Province and subsequently a successful businessman, emerging as a possible candidate. A bitter strike by public servants, who initially demanded a 12% wage increase but eventually settled for 7.5%, helped fuel tensions in the run up to the ANC policy conference held in June—the prelude to the party's national conference, to be held in Polokwane in December, which would decide who was to be the party's, and probably the country's, President in succession to Mbeki. (Mbeki had pledged that he would not seek to have the Constitution revised to allow him a third term in that position).

There was a series of scandals during Mbeki's second term. In the so-called 'oilgate' scandal, it was alleged that Imvume Management, a company that had obtained crude oil from Iraq during the era of Saddam Hussain, had been a front for the ANC, to which it had allegedly paid a large sum before the 2004 elections. Mbeki appointed a commission of inquiry, which began work in May 2006; however, before it could reveal how much the Government knew of payments on transactions under the oil-for-food programme, its work was halted for procedural reasons. Meanwhile, in June 2005 five members of Parliament were obliged to resign their seats after being convicted of using travel vouchers for fraudulent purposes; up to 200 other deputies were implicated in the controversy and the 'travelgate' scandal weakened the reputation of Parliament, which was increasingly marginalized in the political system. By mid-2006 investigations into the 44,000 government employees receiving social welfare grants revealed that 21,588 were found to have made fraudulent claims.

In 2005 Barclays Bank, of the United Kingdom, returned to South Africa by purchasing a 60% share of the ABSA banking group and stated that it hoped to extend its new network across the continent from its new base in South Africa. Many South African firms were now operating in other African countries, and the state-owned oil prospector was involved in the search for petroleum in Equatorial Guinea and elsewhere. South African Breweries, having successfully taken over a major US brewery, assumed control of one of the largest breweries in South America, and Old Mutual acquired a leading insurance company in Sweden. However, greater foreign direct investment in South Africa was hampered by the Government's affirmative action policy, which critics maintained was creating a new system of racial classification and setting unrealistic targets for black economic empowerment. Rejecting calls for more state intervention to tackle poverty, the Government instead announced an Accelerated Shared Growth Initiative (Asgi-SA), which aimed to stimulate job creation through investment and increase economic growth to 6%, while halving poverty and unemployment by 2014. The new Deputy President promoted the initiative on visits to potential donor countries, with little apparent success.

Despite the legacies of apartheid, the ravages of HIV/AIDS, the economic catastrophe in neighbouring Zimbabwe, and the Government's failure to tackle poverty effectively, the Johannesburg Stock Exchange rose to record highs. In 2006 South Africa was reviewed in terms of the AU's African Peer Review Mechanism. In July the team preparing the review was given South Africa's self-assessment of its system of governance, which apparently accepted that poverty, unemployment and underdevelopment remained huge challenges, and took note of concerns over poor monitoring of services and limited skills. When the report on South Africa was completed, it was not released as expected early in 2007, apparently because the Government was unhappy with its emphasis on corruption. While the inequalities between the races had lessened since 1994, inequalities between different income groups had widened, and South Africa remained one of the most unequal societies in the world. The income of black Africans, who constituted almost 80% of the population, contributed just 40% of the country's total. Social spending had increased greatly, to over R50,000m. per year, and by 2007 12m. people, representing 27% of the population, were receiving welfare. A public works programme, begun in 2004, failed to cause a visible reduction in unemployment, which was higher than ever, although the Government maintained that much informal employment was disguised. An estimated 20m. people, about 45% of the population, lived in poverty. The lack of service delivery in black townships, where many continued to live in squatter camps, provoked a number of demonstrations, in particular in the Free State and the Western Cape. In the latter, the demonstrations were in some cases linked to tensions between Coloured and black residents, with the former alleging that the latter were being given preference in the allocation of new housing. Despite the construction of over 2m. houses since 1994, the housing backlog was still growing. More than 600 people were dying from HIV/AIDS every day, and South Africa had more HIV-positive citizens than any other country in the world. It remained to be seen whether a country with problems of such magnitude would survive as a vibrant democracy.

Economy

LINDA VAN BUREN

'South Africa has been enjoying its longest economic expansion on record,' proclaimed the IMF in November 2006, 'thanks in large measure to sound macroeconomic management.' The Minister of Finance, Trevor Manuel, had described the financial year ending on 31 March 2006 as 'the year of plenty' in his February 2006 budget speech. Basing his February 2007 budget speech on the theme 'Human life has equal worth', he introduced the framework for a broad-based social-security system embracing all South Africans. Real gross domestic product (GDP) growth amounted to 4.9% in 2006 and was forecast at 4.8% in 2007. A June 2007 government review of development indicators revealed a number of positive figures. For example, real per-head GDP growth, which had been negligible or even sometimes negative during the 1990s, increased substantially in the mid-2000s, reaching 3.4% in 2004, 3.7% in 2005 and 3.6% in 2006. Government debt as a percentage of GDP stood at 43.5% in 1994, the year that the apartheid Government left power, but had declined to 31.3% by 2007 and was forecast to decline further, to 24.3% by 2010. In addition, 90% of the population had access to the water-supply infrastructure in 2006; the Government's target was for 100% of South Africans to have access to potable water by 2008. Of South Africa's 12.98m. households, 9.56m., or 73.7%, had access to electricity. The Government's Free Basic Electricity

Programme also made available a basic monthly allocation of 50 kWh for free. The number of severely malnourished children under the age of five years declined from 88,971 in 2001 to 30,082 in 2005. By contrast, the incidence of HIV prevalence rose from 8.5% of the total population in 2001 to 11.1% in 2007. The adult literacy rate was 74.2% in 2005, compared with 69.6% in 1995. In general, the South African economy continued to exhibit a fundamental strength, stability and resilience in the post-apartheid era. President Thabo Mbeki was among five key middle-income countries' heads of state invited to attend the Group of Eight leading industrialized nations (G-8) summit at Gleneagles, in Scotland, United Kingdom, in July 2005. Known as the 'G-8+5' summit, the gathering also included representatives from Brazil, the People's Republic of China, India and Mexico.

The rand recovered from its substantial depreciation during the second half of 2001; and, even when the economy was threatened by weak international prices for one of its key commodities—gold—and by the negative regional publicity emanating from neighbouring Zimbabwe, the outflow of investment resources that some had predicted simply did not occur. Investment grew by 6.3% in 2002 and by 11.7% in just the first nine months of 2006, especially in construction, finance, transport, communications and manufacturing. Some 280,000 new jobs per year were created between 2000 and 2004, but this rate rose to about 500,000 per year by 2006, Manuel stated. The unemployment rate still stood at 26.4% in 2006, compared to about 26.7% in 2005. The fact that the unemployment rate remained static from year to year even though 500,000 jobs were being created annually was an indication of how fast new school-leavers were entering the job market. A reduction in the rate of unemployment could be one of the best ways of countering the country's high crime rate, which was a major topic of discussion from 1999 onwards. The 2002 budget allocated R5,200m. towards the fight against crime for 2002–05, including the recruitment of 16,000 additional police officers, the strengthening of the judicial system to cope with more criminal trials and the expansion of the prison system to accommodate a burgeoning prisoner population. The Government allocated R33,000m. to the police in 2006/07, and this figure was forecast to rise to R44,000m. in 2009/10. A further R1,500m. was earmarked for the justice department over the three-year period 2007–09 to improve court capacity, reduce case backlogs and modernise the administration of justice. Both the Government and the private sector have introduced job-creation schemes and initiatives such as Black Economic Empowerment (BEE—see below), as well as various training and skills programmes. At the end of any training course, however, a worker would still need to find employment, and his chances would be limited if growth remained moderate. The Growth and Development Summit of 2003 set a target of reducing South Africa's unemployment rate by one-half by 2014.

NATURAL RESOURCES

South Africa's diverse climate permits the cultivation of a wide range of crops, even though only 13% of the land surface is suitable for arable farming, owing largely to inadequate or erratic rainfall, and only 11% of the total land area, or 132,000 sq km, is under major crops. Topographic difficulty is the main factor limiting the extent of irrigation, although ambitious irrigation schemes—such as the one originally dubbed the 'Orange River Project' in 1928 but now extending well beyond the river system of the Orange—are expected eventually to increase the total irrigated area by about 300,000 ha, or 37.5%. Despite improvements in farming methods and conservation techniques in the 1980s and the 1990s, South Africa remains a relatively poor crop-raising country. This situation also imposes limits on animal husbandry, for which South Africa is better suited, although even here, the carrying capacity of the land is fairly low by international standards. Nevertheless, owing to a high degree of specialization, experience and advanced methods, along with considerable capital investment, certain branches of farming, such as the fruit and wool sectors, continue to make a substantial contribution to the economy and to exports in particular. The 2004 budget gave priority to the provision of comprehensive agricultural support to developing farmers, and the 2005 budget followed up with a new credit scheme for small-scale farmers. The 2006 budget proposed a 16% increase in expenditure for the agricultural sector. Nevertheless, the 2007 budget described agricultural performance as 'poor'.

It is in mineral deposits, though, that South Africa's greatest wealth lies. The discovery, first of diamonds and then, more importantly, of gold, during the latter part of the 19th century, formed the basis of the country's modern economic development. A huge complex of heavy and light industry, based initially on the gold-mining sector, grew up in the interior, although South Africa's share in the volume of world gold production (excluding the former USSR) declined from 70% in 1980 to 20% in 2000, owing to a fall in the average grade of ore mined and to increases in output in other parts of the world. Nevertheless, at the start of the 21st century, South Africa remained the largest gold producer in the world, supplying one-fifth of the world total. South Africa has five of the 12 largest gold mines and seven of the 20 largest gold-mining companies in the world; among them is AngloGold Ashanti (formerly Anglo American Corpn), the world's second largest. The country also has abundant deposits of many other important minerals. South Africa has the world's largest proven reserves not only of gold but also of platinum-group metals, manganese, vanadium, vermiculite, chrome and alumino-silicates. The production of minerals other than gold accounted for 50% of the total value of mining output in 2004; more than 50 different minerals are commercially exploited. There are huge reserves of coal—28,600m. metric tons, the seventh largest in the world—with a pit-head price that is probably the lowest in the world. The country's iron-ore reserves rank ninth in the world. In 2004 South Africa possessed about three-quarters of the world's reserves of manganese ore, more than two-thirds of the world's chromium, more than one-half of world reserves of platinum-group metals in general and more than one-quarter of its zirconium-group minerals, plus a significant proportion of the world's titanium minerals and fluorspar. In addition, South Africa is a major producer of copper, lead, zinc, antimony and uranium.

South Africa's long coastline has few natural harbours, but close to its shores are some of the richest fishing areas in the world. The catch includes Southern African anchovy, Cape hakes, Southern African pilchard, Cape horse mackerel and Whitehead's round herring. Demand for Cape hakes in southern European markets grew significantly in 2006, after European hake stocks became depleted and the European Union (EU), in December 2005, implemented strict quotas on the fishing of this species in European waters. The total marine fish catch was 576,551 metric tons in 2005, ranking South Africa 23rd in the world and 2nd in Africa (after Morocco).

POPULATION

The chief characteristic of South Africa's population, and the one that dominates its society, is the great racial, linguistic and cultural heterogeneity of its people, with Africans, Asians, Europeans and mixed-race citizens making up the population.

South Africa's total population as recorded in national censuses was 44,819,770 in October 2001, up from 40,583,573 in October 1996 and representing an average annual population growth of 2.1%. People are no longer officially classified according to race, as they were during apartheid, but, in order to gain some idea of the figures involved, in the 2001 census South Africans were invited to classify themselves. The result was that 79% of those enumerated described themselves as African (black), 10% as white, 9% as Coloured (of mixed race) and 2% as Asian. Official mid-2007 estimates put the population at 47.9m., of whom 38.1m. (79.6%) were African, 4.4m. (9.1%) were white, 4.2m. (8.9%) were Coloured and 1.2m. (2.5%) were Asian.

The occupational distribution of the economically active population in 2005 was as follows: of the estimated 12,110,500 persons aged 15–65 years who were in employment, about 2,360,000 worked in community, social and personal services (19.5%), 1,707,500 in manufacturing (14.1%), 2,555,500 in wholesale and retail trade (21.1%), 1,235,500 in private households (10.2%), 1,126,500 in financial, insurance, real estate and business services (9.3%), 654,000 in construction (5.4%), 520,500 in mining and quarrying (4.3%), and 581,500 in transport, storage and communications (4.8%). The most drastic structural change in the economy has been an apparently sharp decline in the proportion of the population engaged in agriculture, hunting, forestry and fishing; from 28% at the 1970 census, the number employed in the sector had fallen to 1,247,500 in 2005, 10.3% of the economically active population.

NATIONAL INCOME

Real GDP increased by an annual average of 5.9% between 1960 and 1970, an increase rivalling that of Japan. At the same time, GDP per head increased by 2.9% per year. This rate fell sharply in the 1970s, however, with real GDP growing at an average of only 3.9% (and by about 1% per head) per year in the period 1970–80. Real GDP growth slowed to an average of only 1.0% per year in 1980–90; with the population increasing at an average annual rate of 2.6% in that decade, income per head was in decline. Despite an improvement in the racial distribution of personal income in recent years, income remains very unevenly distributed in South Africa. It was estimated in 1988 that the 13% of South Africans who were white received about 54% of total personal income, while the 76% of the population classified as Africans received only 36% of the wealth. In 1988 the differential in earnings per employee between whites and Africans in the manufacturing sector was 3.5:1, increasing to 5:1 in mining and quarrying. The income-tax threshold is set at a level that requires only 4m. South Africans to be registered as income-tax payers; however, other, more regressive taxes, such as value-added tax, take in a much wider tax base.

The contribution to national income of the three main productive sectors—manufacturing, mining and agriculture—changed markedly over the years. Manufacturing steadily increased its relative position, overtaking mining as the leading sector in the 1940s. By the first quarter of 2006 manufacturing contributed 16.4% of GDP at factor cost, mining and quarrying 6.3% and agriculture only 2.6%. The services sector contributed 60.8%, the highest such proportion in Africa. In the first quarter of 2006 agriculture, forestry and fishing output declined by 6.9%, and mining and quarrying production fell by 2.9%. However, manufacturing output grew by 4.3%, construction by 13.7% and services also showed positive growth. Manufacturing grew by more than 4% per year in 2004, 2005 and 2006.

INVESTMENT AND SAVING

Since the discovery of diamonds and gold in the 19th century, foreign investment has played a vital role in developing these industries and the economy in general. From 1984 until the accession of the administration of Nelson Mandela (1994–99), foreign investment was strongly in a negative direction. Thereafter, the flow was reversed and, a decade later, the net flow was still inward. In 2005 foreign direct investment was strongest in the information-technology and electronics sector, followed by the metals and automotive sector, the tourism sector, the clothing and textiles sector and the chemicals sector. The tourism sector showed particularly strong growth in 2006, with 8,508,806 tourist arrivals in that year, 14.5% more than in 2005. Gross fixed capital formation grew by at least 8% per year in 2003–05, and the forecast for 2006–08 was for growth of between 9% and 10% annually. Gross fixed capital formation rose from 17.3% of GDP in 2005 to 19.2% of GDP in 2006. South Africa's gross external debt stood at US $56,263m. at 31 March 2007, up from $53,091m. one year earlier and from $45,857m. at 31 March 2005. At the time of the transition to majority rule, South Africa had a record of foreign borrowing that was especially low for a country of South Africa's level of development, and many predicted that this situation would change after South Africa, following its political transition, gained access to institutions such as the World Bank and was more favourably treated by the international financial community. These fears initially proved unfounded, although the level of foreign debt climbed steadily after 2000. The first World Bank loan to post-apartheid South Africa—and indeed the first lending from the Bank to the country in over 30 years—was a 1997 arrangement for $46m. of funding for industrial competitiveness and job creation, repayable over 15 years.

MANUFACTURING INDUSTRY

Unlike its counterparts in the rest of Africa, South Africa's manufacturing industry is the largest of the productive sectors of the national economy, measured in terms of contribution to GDP (16.4% in the first quarter of 2006). At September 2004 the sector employed 1.7m. workers, or 14.1% of the employed labour force.

Industrial GDP declined by an annual average of 1.1% in 1980–90, but increased at an annual average rate of 1.8% in 1995–2004. Manufacturing output rose by an annual average above 4% in 2004–06 and by 7.1% year on year in February 2007. Industry is heavily concentrated in four industrial areas: Gauteng, Western Cape, Durban-Pinetown and Port Elizabeth-Uitenhage. More than 50% of the country's industry is now located in Gauteng alone, and the tendency has been for this concentration to increase at the expense of the ports and the rural areas.

Metal Products and Engineering

This comprises the largest sector of industry (including basic metals, metal products, machinery and transport equipment), employing about 500,000 workers in 2005. The steel industry is the most important branch of this sector, with production of crude steel valued at some R14,000m. per year. Following its transfer from state to private-sector ownership in 1989, the Iron and Steel Corpn of South Africa (Iscor) dominated the industry. In 1997 it operated 10 ore mines and four steel mills, with a fifth, at a projected cost of US $1,550m., entering production in 1998 at Saldanha Bay. The company was renamed Ispat-Iscor in July 2004, after merging with LNM Group of India, the world's second largest steel-maker, and became Mittal Steel South Africa Limited in March 2005. The company, which produces 7.3m. metric tons of liquid steel per year, is the largest steel producer in Africa. It commissioned a R204m. pulverized coal injection plant for its N5 blast furnace in June 2005. In 2000 Duferco of Switzerland entered into a joint venture with South Africa's Industrial Development Corpn (IDC) to build a R1,500m. steel-rolling and galvanizing plant, also at Saldanha Bay; Duferco Steel Processing (Pty) South Africa produced 600,000 tons of steel and employed 320 people in 2005. With favourable costs of location, raw materials and labour, and an efficient scale of production, South African steel is among the cheapest in the world.

Three manganese plants were upgraded in 1997, at Sasolburg, Meyerton and Witbank, and Gencor rehabilitated its Impala platinum refinery. The aluminium enterprise ALUSAF—45% owned by Gencor and 20% by the IDC—commissioned its Hillside aluminium smelter in April 1997, five months earlier than scheduled. The total cost of the project was finally estimated at R6,000m.; it had already achieved full production in June 1996, and its output reached 636,000 metric tons in its first year, about three-quarters of which was exported. ALUSAF's production cost, at US $750 per ton, was one of the lowest in the world. In July 2002 Péchiney of France and South African interests entered into a joint venture to build and operate an aluminium smelter in the government-promoted Coega industrial development zone in the Eastern Cape. Following the takeover of Péchiney by Alcan Inc. of Canada in July 2003, the final decision on the smelter was put on hold; as of June 2007, construction of the R19,000m. facility was to begin in 2008, with first metal production expected in 2010. At full production, the smelter would produce 660,000 tons of aluminium per year.

The motor industry is another important branch of the engineering sector, employing some 33,000 people in 2004 and contributing 5.7% of the GDP. The vast majority of new cars contain at least 66% local content by weight, thereby qualifying for special tariff rates as 'locally manufactured' models. In common with this industry in other developing countries, vehicle manufacturing faces the problem of rising costs with increasing local content, because of the lack of those economies of scale that are enjoyed in the major producing countries. With its potential market size of over 44m. people,

South Africa would offer better opportunities to achieve economies of scale if incomes were more evenly distributed and a larger proportion of the population could afford to buy basic luxuries such as motor vehicles. In March 2004 Volkswagen announced that a new R750m. production line was to be installed at its South African plant at Uitenhage in the Eastern Cape. In July 2004 the company finalized an export programme to markets in the Far East and Australasia worth R2,500m. over the five years through 2008.

Food, Beverages and Tobacco

Industries processing local farm produce were among the first to develop in South Africa and contribute significantly to exports. Food, beverages and tobacco accounted for about 20% of the value of manufacturing output in 2000. The end of the apartheid era created suitable conditions for South African Breweries (SAB) to become, in a short space of time, the second largest brewing company in the world. SAB embarked on a period of rapid expansion, taking over existing breweries elsewhere in Africa before expanding into Asia, with a major investment in India, and also into the USA, with the acquisition of a 64% stake in the US brewing giant Miller from Philip Morris for US $5,600m. in May 2002; the conglomerate that resulted was renamed SABMiller, headquartered in the United Kingdom. In a major example of new inward foreign investment after South Africa's transition to majority rule, the US company Coca-Cola in 1995 joined South African Bottling Co in a $400m. venture, which was aimed not only at the South African market but also at those of other African countries. The country's wine industry was established in the 17th century by Protestant immigrants from France. The industry established very high standards, but suffered as a result of sanctions during the apartheid era. In the post-apartheid era the industry experienced a rapid growth in exports, and its reputation for quality continues.

Clothing and Textiles

The clothing industry, which was well established before the Second World War, by the 2000s supplied 90% of local demand and employed more than 100,000 workers. The textile industry (other than clothing) was essentially a post-war development; it met 60% of the country's textile needs. Textiles, wearing apparel and footwear contributed about 8% of the value of manufacturing output in 2004. The local textile industry was adversely affected in the 1990s by mass illegal imports of textile products, and some 20,000 jobs in the sector were lost. The textile industry benefited from the provisions of the African Growth and Opportunity Act (AGOA), enabling US $127m.-worth of South African textile products to enter the USA duty free in 2003. With the elimination of curbs on US imports of textile products from major producers such as China and India in January 2005, South Africa's share of the US market came under threat, as did those of other African textile exporters. The South African textile industry faced the challenge of lowering its costs in order to complete with low-cost Asian competitors.

Chemicals

South Africa's chemical industry employed about 124,000 workers in 1999. The industry had an early beginning, with the manufacture of explosives for the gold mines; the Modderfontein factory, near Johannesburg, is now one of the world's largest privately owned explosives factories. Production of fertilizers is also a significant branch of this industry. However, the most important development in the late 20th century was the establishment by the state-owned South African Coal, Oil and Gas Corpn (SASOL) of its first oil-from-coal plant (SASOL 1), which began production in the northern part of the then Orange Free State in 1955. Based on cheap, low-grade coal with a high ash content, this establishment was, until the commissioning of SASOL 2 and SASOL 3, the largest plant of its kind in the world. Besides producing a small but significant percentage of South Africa's petrol requirements, the development of synthetic fuel production led to the establishment of a huge petrochemicals complex capable of manufacturing about 110 products, some of which, like coal-tar products, were only by-products of a coal-using process. Owing to the absence of local supplies of natural mineral oil, attempts at a petroleum embargo and the huge rise in world petroleum prices in 1973, it was decided in 1974 to build SASOL 2 with 10 times the capacity of SASOL 1. SASOL was privatized in 1979. Production at SASOL 2, which had a capital cost of R2,400m., reached full capacity in 1982. Following the change of regime in Iran in 1979 and the consequent loss by South Africa of its main source of supply of crude petroleum, it was decided to build SASOL 3 at a capital cost of R3,200m. This plant began operation in 1983 and reached full production in 1985. The three plants in full production provided about 40% of South Africa's fuel requirements.

In the post-apartheid and post-sanctions era, the Government reconstituted its relationship with the hydrocarbons sector. A government report on energy in June 1998 proposed a sweeping liberalization, with the government subsidies to SASOL and Mossgas (the state-owned gas-to-fuel producer) to be removed completely. Government controls over the import and export of crude petroleum were to end, with the result that SASOL would be free to market its output directly to the public by establishing its own retail network and also would be allowed to export its product. At the same time, other enterprises would be allowed to import crude petroleum and sell it in competition on the South African market. In 1997 SASOL commissioned a new acetic acid plant at Secunda, near Johannesburg; the R167m. plant had the capacity to produce 16,000 metric tons per year of acetic acid and 7,000 tons per year of propionic acid. Also at Secunda, a R1,000m. plant came on stream in February 2003, producing 120,000 tons per year of alcohol. SASOL announced in 2000 that it was to build four new chemicals plants in Sasolburg at a cost of R1,430m.; they were to produce 'world-scale' crude acrylic acid, normal-butyl acrylate, ethyl acrylate and glacial (high-purity) acrylic acid. Output was forecast at 80,000 tons per year of crude acrylic acid. The acrylate facility was commissioned in March 2004, at a time of growing international demand. In addition, another plant in Sasolburg producing 150,000 tons of normal butanol per year was commissioned in February 2003. In December 2005 SASOL announced that it would build a second methyl isobutylketone (MIBK—a solvent for resins used in surface coatings) plant at Sasolburg, due for completion in 2008 with a capacity of 30,000 tons per year. SASOL also received support from the World Bank's Multilateral Investment Guarantee Agency for its US $1,200m. Mozambique–South Africa natural-gas project, Sasol Petroleum Temane (SPT). The first Mozambican gas flowed into the SPT gas-processing plant in Temane in November 2003.

AGRICULTURE

Agriculture's role as a source of income in the South African economy is a declining one, despite major successes in some sub-sectors. Maize is the staple food of the African population and the most important single item in South African farming; this New World crop was introduced into South Africa during the colonial period. From a record output of 13.6m. metric tons in 1981, production fell to only 3.4m. tons during the 1983 drought, resulting in maize imports. Poor rainfall in maize-growing areas reduced the 2007 crop to an estimated 7m. metric tons (continuing a decline from a 2005 peak of 12m. tons); this output was less than the country's annual maize demand of about 8m. tons, necessitating maize imports. The short supply of this staple food crop in local marketplaces had already driven the retail price of maize up by 28% in the year to 31 December 2006. Sorghum production fell from 473,000 tons in 2000 to 206,000 tons in 2001, causing hardship for many of the most vulnerable South Africans in rural areas. This drought-resistant grain thereafter exhibited a significant recovery, dramatically in 2004, at 449,100 tons, although it fell back to 354,400 tons the following year. In 2006 the South African Government rejected an application from a US company to grow genetically modified (GM) sorghum in the country. Wool, although prone to wide fluctuations in price, is one of South Africa's most important agricultural exports (along with maize, fruit and cane sugar). The country grows a wide range of cash crops, fruits and vegetables both for domestic consumption and for the export market. The low overall productivity of farming, relative to other sectors, was also reflected in the fact that, although engaging 10% of the employed labour force at February 2006, the sector contributed only 2.5% of GDP in 2006, owing principally to poor crop yields obtained by large numbers of inefficient African subsistence farmers in the former 'homelands'. However, even commercial farms, which were relatively efficient, obtained comparatively low yields by international standards. In maize farming, for example, yields per hectare were only 23% of those in the USA in 2001; according to FAO, South Africa's average maize yield in 2000 (a year not affected by drought) was 2,736 kg per ha, compared with 8,700 kg per ha in Egypt and 8,603 kg per ha in the USA. The GDP of the agricultural sector declined by 6.9% in the first quarter of 2006.

MINING

Despite having given way to manufacturing as the leading sector, mining is still of great importance in external trade. The sector contributed 6.3% of GDP in the first quarter of 2006. The low international price for gold in the late 1990s resulted in major structural changes in the sector (see below).

South Africa is the world's leading gold producer. Since 1945 new gold mines in the Free State, Far West Rand, Klerksdorp and Evander areas not only replaced output from the worked-out mines on the old Rand, but also greatly increased total production. In the absence of new discoveries, however, gold output was expected to continue the decline that began in the early 1970s, after a record 1,000 metric tons was mined in 1970. This was largely a result of a policy by the industry of lowering the grade of ore mined as the price rose. (Unless there is a compensating increase in tonnage milled when the average grade of ore mined is lowered, output falls.) In 1996 South Africa's production of gold fell below 500 tons for the first time since 1956. In December 1997 a government report announced a major liberalization of the gold-marketing sector. Whereas previously all gold producers were required to hand over any newly mined gold to the South African Reserve Bank within 30 days, under the new policy producers were to be allowed to market their output directly to foreign buyers. By late July 1999 the international gold price had declined to $252.90 per troy oz. In comparison, the average cost of producing gold for many companies had been $347 per oz in 1997 and $305 per oz in 1998. Of the 48 gold-mining companies in South Africa in 1994, only 11 were still operating in 2004, most having been merged into one of four major companies: AngloGold Ashanti, Gold Fields, Harmony Gold or Durban Roodeport Deep. It was not until 2003 that the global gold price climbed above the average cost of production. By July 2004 the gold price had recovered to $392 per oz, and by July 2007 it had risen to $657 per oz. The sector's role as an employer fluctuated along similar lines; the gold-mining companies in total employed 338,658 people in 1997, but by 2001 the figure had fallen to 201,698. The continuing strength of the rand in 2003 led to further mine closures by Harmony Gold and Durban Roodeport Deep; at that time, analysts reported that only 40% of mines in the country were operating at a profit, and companies were looking abroad for cheaper resources. Between 1994 and 2004 some 120,000 jobs were lost in the Free State Province goldfields. In 2003 Anglo American and Khula Enterprise Finance established a R40m. mining fund, in support of BEE, which would help establish small and medium-sized businesses to supply the Anglo American (now AngloGold Ashanti) group with non-core goods and services.

The output of other minerals rapidly gained in importance after 1945. Gold accounted for about 80% of South Africa's mineral production in 1946, but for only 50% by 1993 and 27% by 2006. A great expansion took place in the output of uranium, platinum, palladium, nickel, copper, coal, antimony, diamonds, vanadium, asbestos, iron ore, fluorspar, chromium, manganese and limestone, to name only the most important. When it was reported that the Impala platinum refinery had been affected by strike action in 1997, the international price of platinum increased from US $445 to $460 per troy oz. By July 2007 the global platinum price had reached $1,312 per oz. South Africa's platinum-group mines employed more than 99,571 workers in 2001. Exports of platinum-group metals earned R25,133.8m. in 2005.

Silver production, for which South Africa ranks only 18th overall globally, has been a sector in decline; South Africa's output in 2001, at 109.4m. metric tons of ore, was only about one-half of the output level in the 1980s. Copper-ore production declined from 144,263 tons in 1999 to 137,092 tons in 2000. The conversion of the copper mine at Phalaborwa from open-pit to underground, undertaken by Palabora Mining Co at a projected cost of R1,500m., was completed in 2002. Anglo American, while selling off its non-core sectors in 1999 and 2000, announced in May 2000 a new R700m. expansion at its Black Mountain mine at Aggeneys in the Northern Province. The mine, which Anglo had purchased from Gold Fields of South Africa and Phelps Dodge in 1998, produces zinc, lead and copper. The new expansion involved the sinking of a new vertical shaft to a depth of 1,750 m, which was expected to extend the life of the mine until 2013. However, work on Anglo's proposed zinc project at Gamsberg, in the Northern Cape, was postponed, pending an improvement in the global zinc market; the scheme would have created 1,000 permanent jobs. Lead output fell from 75,280 tons in 2000 to 50,771 tons in 2002. The South African Department of Energy and Mines, in its forecasts to 2006, reported that cobalt production offered the best growth prospects, at 9% annually, while prospects for copper were the least optimistic, with a predicted contraction of 3.4% annually, on average.

Diamonds were traditionally the country's second most important export commodity after gold, but by the 1980s they had been overtaken by coal, and by 2001 South Africa ranked only fifth in the world in terms of rough-diamond production. South African diamond production had been conducted for some time at five mine locations. After discoveries in 1980, a sixth mine, Venetia, was opened in 1992; it soon became the country's top producer. Trivalence Mining Corpn's 2,082-ha kimberlite concession at Palmietgat, about 70 miles (113 km) north of Pretoria, entered production in April 2000. The open-pit operation consisted of six kimberlite pipes and produced 6,602 carats in its first three months of operation. In April 2002 De Beers sold its Kamfersdam operation to Nare Diamond Company (NDC) of Australia. NDC brought Kamfersdam into production in April 2006, producing 420,000 metric tons of gravel per month for the remainder of the year; output rose to 1m. tons per month in 2007. The diamonds produced are to be sold to De Beers, which would in turn sell them on to South African diamond cutters. South African diamond production totalled 15.8m. carats in 2005. Diamond exports earned the country R12,231.1m. in 2005, an increase of 27% compared with the previous year.

The coal-mining industry, which stagnated for many years owing to low prices and slow growth, acquired renewed vigour after the petroleum crisis in 1973. Exports grew rapidly, helped by the opening of the new rail link and coal terminal at Richards Bay in northern KwaZulu/Natal. In 2006 South Africa ranked fifth in terms of international coal reserves, fifth in terms of production and fourth in terms of exports. Exports of coal and lignite earned R20,771.2m. in 2005, 31.% more than in 2004. In 2000 Anglo Coal initiated a study into the redevelopment of the Kriel South coal reserves in Mpumalanga, and in July 2003 it was announced that the project would go ahead. With investments of US $96m. by Anglo Coal and $40m. by SASOL, Kriel South was expected to produce between 9m. and 10m. tons per year, all to be used for SASOL's synthetic-fuels plant at Secunda. In July 2004 Anglo Coal and Ingwe Collieries, a subsidiary of BHP Billiton, signed a memorandum of understanding into joining and expanding their resources in the Western Complex, effectively creating a 'mega-mine'.

South Africa is the continent's leading producer of iron ore; exports to Japan in particular became important in the late 1980s, as did, in recent years, exports to China. A railway line from the high-grade deposits of the Sishen area, in the Northern Cape, carries iron ore to Saldanha Bay. In 2004 Kumba Resources was producing 30m. metric tons of iron ore annually; plans to expand production by up to 20m. tons were constrained by a lack of capacity on the railway line, and Kumba entered a pricing agreement in March 2005 with the railway operator, Transnet, with regard to upgrading the line, in preparation for an increase in iron-ore exports through the

Sishen–Saldanha corridor from 23.5m. tons per year to 35m. tons. South Africa has proven petroleum reserves of just 29.4m. tons, but daily production levels are on the decline. SASOL produces 155,000 barrels per day (b/d) at its oil-from-coal plant (see above), but domestic consumption in 2002 ran at an estimated 469,000 b/d. Imports of petroleum and gas cost South Africa R41,216m. in 2005 and comprised 60% of the total import bill. In February 1985 the Southern Oil Exploration Corpn (Soekor), a government-owned company that had been involved since 1965 in an intensive search for petroleum deposits, announced that a discovery off shore at Mossel Bay, off the south coast of Cape Province, had yielded a daily output of 2,600 barrels of light crude and about 28,300 cu m of natural gas. While the petroleum potential of this field was thought to be limited, the natural-gas reserves were estimated to be substantial, at about 30,000m. cu m. In 1987 the Government decided to proceed with the establishment of a plant to convert this natural gas into liquid fuel, at a cost of R5,500m. This plant was designed to supply 10% of South Africa's liquid-fuel requirements when it came into operation in 1992. Soekor announced in May 1997 that Petrol SA Ltd and Phillips Petroleum of the USA were to explore an area of the Indian Ocean off South Africa's east coast. Other participants in the venture, for which Phillips was the operator, with a 40% share, were Pan Canadian Petroleum (Africa) Ltd of Canada (20%), Energy Africa Bredasdorp (Pty) Ltd of South Africa (20%) and SASOL (20%). Phillips was to spend US $8m. in gathering seismic data and was to drill at least one exploratory well over the four-year period of the lease (which could be extended for up to two subsequent periods of three years each). In 2002 Soekor merged with Mossgas and elements of the Strategic Fuel Fund to form the Petroleum Oil and Gas Corpn of South Africa (PetroSA). In 2003 the Government passed the Minerals and Petroleum Resources Development Act, providing a structured framework for oil and gas exploration. Petroleum exploration continues, with particular interest in waters off the west coast of South Africa. In November 2000 the liquid-fuels industry became the first to sign a BEE charter, which specified that 25% of the industry should be transferred to black ownership by 2010; at 2004 this figure stood at 17%. In 2006 total BEE transactions reached R56,000m.

TRANSPORT AND COMMUNICATIONS

South Africa's transport system is entirely dependent on its rail and road network, with air transport playing a small but increasing role. The number of people employed in the transport, storage and communications sectors increased from 483,652 in 1996 to some 578,000 in February 2007. In 1999–2000 the Government was proceeding with plans to construct the country's first new railway line in 15 years, and the transport sector was forecast to grow at a faster rate than the economy as a whole. In 1990 the transport parastatal, Transnet Ltd, was created to remove the transport system from direct governmental control. At the time, Transnet was the largest commercial employer in South Africa, with a work-force of 168,419, although by 2002 this figure had fallen to 77,000. Transnet originally encompassed Spoornet for the rail network, Portnet for the port authorities, South African Airways (SAA) for aviation, Autonet for the road network, Petronet for petroleum pipelines and PX for the delivery of parcels. Since then, restructuring has left Transnet with 12 divisions, including Metrorail, Propnet, Transtel and Transwerk. Spoornet oversees a rail network covering 31,400 route-km in 2000 (about one-third of all the railway track length in sub-Saharan Africa). Some 87% of the rail network is electrified, and the system was computerized in 1980. Spoornet came under pressure to reduce costs in the 1990s and began to curtail its work-force. In 1999 it announced that it was to dismiss more than one-half of its remaining employees, with the further loss of 27,000 jobs. In 2004 the Government ruled out the privatization of Transnet but was investigating the potential for public-private partnerships in the sector. The selling of concessions to use private rolling-stock on the Transnet rail network was proposed in September 2004. Control of the passenger rail network would also pass to the Ministry of Transport.

Portnet's seven commercial ports—Durban, Richards Bay, East London, Port Elizabeth, Mossel Bay, Cape Town and Saldanha Bay—handled 162m. metric tons of cargo in 2002. The entrance channel to the port of Durban is being widened from 110 m to 220 m, and its depth is to be a minimum of 16 m; completion is expected by the end of 2009. In January 2005 Transnet announced a R2,075m. investment to improve its container-port facilities. Safmarine and Unicorn, the two largest shipping companies, are both in the private sector. In 1999 Portnet was divided into two entities, the port authority and the port operators, and two ancillary divisions were sold. A ports bill went before the National Assembly in 2004, proposing to allow private-sector involvement in the provision of port services and facilities. South African Port Operations (SAPO), a division of Transnet, operated 13 ports in six locations in 2006.

In 1993 the country's nine major airports were placed under the management of the Airports Co Ltd, which was 100% owned by the Government but was, nevertheless, operating the airports on a commercial basis. The national carrier is South African Airways (SAA), one of the world's oldest airlines, founded in 1934. Its fleet comprises 55 jet aircraft, including six Boeing 747s. but the airline sector was deregulated in 1990, and SAA is now exposed to competition from private-sector carriers, both on domestic and on international routes. More than 20 private-sector airlines provided about 70 routes to 546 towns in South Africa in 2007. Following the end of apartheid, SAA expanded services to the rest of Africa, forming partnerships with several national carriers and serving 20 destinations on the African continent. In 1999 SAA was reconstituted as South African Airways (Pty) Ltd. Swissair purchased a 20% share in the carrier in the same year, at a cost of R1,400m., in the second largest privatization exercise at that time. However, following massive losses at Swissair in 2001, the South African Government was forced to buy back the shares, albeit at a reduced price. The Government later had to underwrite a R7,000m. debt incurred by SAA, the result of a foreign-exchange hedging loss in 2003–04. In March 2007 SAA announced that, following 'several years of continued losses', it was embarking on a 'deep and fundamental restructuring', to be managed by Seabury Airline Planning Group of the USA.

Freight Dynamics, formerly Autonet, oversees an extensive road network, with more than 500,000 km of classified roads. While this figure includes some motorways, less than 25% of all roads were paved in 2005. In 2002 there were 4,135,037 registered light passenger motor vehicles, 326,798 load vehicles, 159,266 motorcycles and 296,518 special vehicles. Private long-distance road haulage was for many years restricted by government legislation designed to protect the railways. The illegal haulage of freight by road is an ongoing problem. Freight Dynamics was offered for privatization in July 2006, along with Viamax, which manages a fleet of 7,000 road vehicles.

The telecommunications network is fairly extensively developed, with an estimated 4.7m. telephone lines in use in 2005 (down from 4.9m. in the previous year). The use of mobile cellular telephones increased dramatically from the late 1990s; between 1998 and 2005 the number of subscribers increased from 3.3m. to 34.0m. In 2004 there were also 77.5 internet hosts per 10,000 inhabitants; the number of users rose from 3.6m. in total in that year to 5.1m. in 2005. In 1997 Telkom, the then state telecommunications company, and Telecom Malaysia revealed plans for the construction of a US $360m. Indian Ocean undersea cable, which would link Cape Town to Penang, Malaysia, via Port Louis, Mauritius. Telkom was offered for privatization in 1997, in the hope that the sale of part of its equity would generate revenue amounting to about R5,000m. In March 1997 the sale to the Malaysian consortium Thintana of a 30% stake in Telkom for R5,600m. was completed, in South Africa's largest privatization exercise. The South African Government's share in June 2004 was 38.3%. In 2006 Telkom faced competition both from Sentech and from the Second Network Operator (SNO).

POWER AND WATER

Electricity

The Government-owned Electricity Supply Commission (ESKOM) produces 95% of South Africa's electricity and claims to be one of the lowest-cost generators of electricity in the world. In addition to generating, transmitting and distributing electricity in South Africa, ESKOM wholly owns ESKOM Enterprises, which supplies electricity elsewhere in Africa, as far away as Uganda, Nigeria and Mali. ESKOM's highly diversified network of 20 power stations in South Africa was capable of producing 38,000 MW in 2007, most of it from coal-fired generators. In fact, ESKOM is the world's largest single buyer of coal, burning more than 100m. metric tons of coal in 2005. Also in 2005 ESKOM was engaged in discussions with Alcan of Canada over the proposed aluminium smelter at Coega (see above); aluminium smelting requires vast amounts of electricity. The abundance of domestic resources means that coal is likely to remain the country's main power source until the 2020s, by which time the coal-fired stations will be due for decommissioning. However, concerns that the country is too dependent on coal, as well as increasing environmental issues, have prompted the Government to investigate alternative energy supplies. The remaining 11% of ESKOM's output currently comes from its mix of nuclear, pumped-storage, hydroelectric and petroleum-fired gas-turbine power stations. In 1976 ESKOM commissioned the building of the 1,800-MW Koeberg nuclear power station at Duynefontein, between Cape Town and Saldanha Bay, by a French consortium. It has remained the only nuclear reactor in Africa. However, in mid-2004 the Government gave its support to a 10-year project to develop a new reactor in co-operation with France, the United Kingdom and the USA. Some peak-load power is provided by the hydroelectric stations of the Orange River Project; ESKOM also entered into a new agreement in 1998 to buy 900 MW of power from the Cahora Bassa dam in Mozambique, an amount which increased to 2,000 MW by 2007. ESKOM also planned to return three renovated generating plants to service, adding 3,600 MW to the national grid by 2009. In addition, open-cycle gas-turbine technology was to be introduced by the end of 2007 at the Atlantis and Mossel Bay stations. Plans to privatize ESKOM were put on hold in mid-2004; however, the Government announced that it would issue tenders for new power stations with a view to producing electricity by 2008. ESKOM estimated that R100,000m. would have to be invested in power generation and transmission over the five-year period to 2010 to ensure adequate electricity supplies.

Water

Water supply is increasingly becoming a problem for the future location of industry. The Vaal river, which is the main source of water supply for the large concentration of manufacturing industry and mining in Gauteng and the northern Free State, is nearing the limit of its capacity. Even with planned increases in supply to the Vaal from the Tugela basin in KwaZulu/Natal, it is unlikely that this river will meet future requirements for much longer. It is likely, therefore, that KwaZulu/Natal, with its much greater water supply, will have a higher rate of growth of industry than Gauteng in the future. In March 1988 South Africa and Lesotho signed the final protocols for the Lesotho Highlands Water Project (LHWP); the arrangements were reconfirmed in the mid-1990s after South Africa's change of leadership. At a projected cost of US $3,770m., the LHWP proposed the diversion of water from Lesotho's rivers for export to South Africa. The prospective throughput of water was projected at 77 cu m per second by the time the scheme is completed in 2017, although at the end of the $2,500m. Phase 1A in 1998, the rate was about 18 cu m per second. The first water deliveries flowed in 1997, and South Africa made the first annual royalty payment, of R110m. At completion, the scheme would provide South Africa with 2,428m. cu m of water annually. About 75% of the cost of Phase 1A was raised in southern Africa (including some 57% from banks), with diversified external sources providing the balance, including $110m. from the World Bank in 1989. The commercial segment of the debt was to be met from royalty payments on water purchases by South Africa. Phase 1B, with a total projected cost of $1,100m., was also to be funded largely from South African capital and money markets and from the water users ($825m. in all, also equivalent to 75%). Phase 1B received the necessary backing to proceed; however, some observers doubted that the remaining five proposed dams would ever be built. With the completion of Phase 1B, the whole of Phase 1 was officially inaugurated with a ceremony at Mohale on 16 March 2004, attended by King Letsie III of Lesotho and President Thabo Mbeki of South Africa. In 1997 the Rand Water Board planned to construct a second reservoir, at a cost of R100m., which was located at KlipriViersberg, south of Johannesburg, and was to serve Johannesburg and Gauteng. In 1999 the Government had identified 1,020 water-supply projects, at various stages of planning or execution, which were aimed at supplying 25 litres of drinkable water per person per day to every community. The water sector was also chosen to provide jobs in some of the country's poorest communities. In February 2006 90% of all households in South Africa were within 200 m of a piped-water source.

FOREIGN TRADE

South Africa is highly dependent on international trade. The value of merchandise imports rose to R349,381.76m. in 2005, while the value of visible exports increased to R331,314.77m. in that year. The visible trade deficit nearly doubled to R18,067m. A trend that has emerged in the structure of South Africa's imports since the ending of economic sanctions in the first half of the 1990s is an increase in the import of products manufactured by unskilled workers. Products of this nature accounted for 23.5% of all imports in 1993, but by 1998 their share had risen to 48.2%. The country remains heavily dependent, therefore, on manufacturing, mining (of gold in particular) and agriculture to pay for imports. In 2005 manufactures accounted for 42% of total exports. In that year the major purchaser of South Africa's exports was Japan (which accounted for 10% of the total), followed by the USA, the United Kingdom, Germany and the Netherlands. In the same year South Africa's principal supplier was Germany (which accounted for 14% of the total), followed by China, Japan, the USA, France, the United Kingdom, Saudi Arabia, Iran and Italy.

On 29 August 1994 South Africa became a member of the Southern African Development Community (SADC). After four years of negotiations, South Africa and the EU finally signed a Free Trade Agreement in March 1999. The development was not well received by the Common Market for Eastern and Southern Africa (COMESA), however, which threatened to challenge the agreement if it were found to be to the detriment of COMESA members (who included most of the other members of SADC). The USA also complained that the accord would render its exports to South Africa less competitive.

Despite massive outflows of foreign capital in 1985–93, the balance-of-payments position and reserves remained fairly steady. With the widespread abandonment of international sanctions on trade and investment from 1991, a more favourable climate for South Africa's balance of payments was achieved. The year-end figures for 1994 confirmed that the flow of capital could indeed be reversed: South Africa achieved a net inflow of short-term capital of R1,430m. as well as a net inflow of long-term capital of R3,780m., totalling a net capital inflow of R5,210m. The current account of the balance of payments has recorded deficits in most years since 1995. These deficits were small enough not to place undue negative pressure on the overall balance of payments. The current-account deficit for 2005 was equivalent to 3.7% of GDP. The current-account deficit was equivalent to 4.9% of GDP in 2006. (Prior to 1998, trade data refer to the Southern African Customs Union, which includes Botswana, Lesotho, Namibia, South Africa and Swaziland.)

FINANCE

The South African currency is the rand, issued by the South African Reserve Bank. The 'commercial' rand's link with the US dollar was freed and allowed to float in 1979, and non-residents were allowed to buy 'security' rands at a discount for direct investment purposes. In 1983 the 'security' rand was abolished and merged with the commercial rand for non-residents. Owing to the outbreak of political disturbances in 1984, the rand depreciated sharply against the dollar and all other major currencies. Coupled with the unwillingness of foreign banks to reschedule short-term loans, a moratorium on debt repayments was imposed by the apartheid Government in September 1985, together with the reintroduction of the two-tier system of exchange control on foreign investors. In March 1987, however, an agreement was reached with foreign creditor banks, allowing a three-year rescheduling of US $13,000m. of outstanding debt. In August 1994 the commercial rand stood at R3.57 = US $1, and the financial rand at R5.56 = $1, while the discount on the financial rand was 20.59%, reflecting the continued outflow of foreign capital. By March 1995, however, the outflow had been reversed (see above), and the Government announced the abolition of the financial rand and the termination of the dual exchange-rate system. The exchange rate weakened to R7.02 = $1 in May 2000 and to R8.07 = $1 by June 2000 and by late December had reached R13.44 = $1. Thereafter, the currency recovered; by 7 July 2006 the exchange rate stood at R7.22 = $1. In the year to 7 July 2007, it had appreciated to R7.01 = $1. Public finance is conducted along orthodox lines, although there has been a steady trend for public spending to grow as a proportion of GDP, despite repeated attempts to prevent further increases in real terms. In 1991/92 expenditure was 29.7% of GDP, compared with 25.5% in 1977/78. From 1994 economies in outlays on defence expenditure have been more than offset by large increases in social expenditure on housing, health and education for the African population, which, together with the weak performance of the economy, led to stagnating revenues and spiralling deficits. The first post-election budget, presented in June 1994, essentially followed the conservative tradition of previous budgets. The planned 6.5% increase in expenditure to R135,100m. was below the prevailing rate of inflation, so that the fiscal deficit was forecast to shrink substantially to some 6.6% of GDP. The 2007/08 national budget forecast a budgetary surplus equivalent to 0.6% of GDP and advocated an increase in total expenditure from an out-turn of R470,600m. in 2006/07 to R534,000m.

The post-apartheid Government committed itself to a programme of privatization of public enterprises. Emphasis was placed on deregulation, liberalization and the removal of subsidies, even in such principal sectors as gold mining and oil-from-coal production. Although this policy was in agreement with IMF and World Bank principles, it also contributed to greater unemployment and to popular discontent.

ECONOMIC OUTLOOK

Between 1989 and 1993, real GDP fell by 4%, signalling South Africa's longest recession of the 20th century. International recession, as well as severe drought and the volatility of the political climate, were all contributory factors. The most serious manifestation of the recession was the decline in investment, which was equivalent to only 15% of GDP in 1992 and had been well below earlier levels (24% on average during 1982–85) since the late 1980s. This low level of investment undermined the economy's future ability to generate growth and absorb job-seekers. Following the establishment of the African National Congress (ANC) administration, a major reversal of the flow of investment took place. In 1994 South Africa achieved a record net inflow of foreign investment of R821m., while in 1995 this figure increased almost five-fold, to R3,900m. Disinvestment, in contrast, was less than R50m. per year in 1994 and 1995. Direct foreign investment by country at January 2005 was led by the USA (636 companies), followed by Germany (467), the United Kingdom (271), Belgium (150), the Netherlands (136) and France (135).

During 1990–2001 job losses amounted to 300,000 in mining, 100,000 in public utilities, 100,000 in transport and 60,000 in manufacturing. In 2000–04, an estimated 280,000 new jobs were created each year, giving a total of 1.4m. The rate increased to 500,000 jobs per year thereafter. Despite this, unemployment was officially estimated at 26.7% in 2005 and at 26.4% in 2006. Most of the unemployed were blacks, especially those who lived in rural areas. Moreover, the outlook was not good: the rate of creation of new jobs was falling far short of the rate of increase in the number of job seekers or, at best, was barely keeping pace. The BEE initiative, which sought to create jobs for black South Africans, was introduced in 2003, whereby major companies such as Telkom gave preference to black-run suppliers for their purchases. A quota system was also in force to achieve 'employment equity', which required that 80% of a company's work-force be black, 54% be female and 5% have disabilities.

The first years of the Mbeki administration posed even more challenges than any of the previous five years. The Government's measures to redistribute wealth more evenly must do so in a way that is effective, without deterring potential private-sector investors, whose funds are badly needed. Progress on this front was debated. A change in the way figures were calculated, not only for employment but also for other economic indicators, was criticized. In the matter of employment, the revised figures showed that unemployment was reduced during 2003—but employment also declined in 2003. The seeming contradiction reflected a somewhat worrying trend: people who had formerly been actively seeking jobs in the formal sector, without success, simply gave up, removing themselves both from the employment figures and from the unemployment figures. Nowhere in any of these figures was there a solution to the problem that people in this category still faced. Even more importantly, South Africa's economic planners must find a way to increase the country's wealth. Through all means possible, the Mbeki administration would have to create sustainable jobs in large numbers. New investment, both by local companies and by foreign enterprises, would be an essential element of any strategy to achieve that end. Even with apartheid laws no longer in place, a bitter legacy of that system remained in the extreme polarization of incomes. In some respects, the South African economy can boast of spectacular global successes, in terms of diamond and gold mining, minerals and brewing. Yet far more needed to be done to create business opportunities inside South Africa. With a market of nearly 47m. potential consumers, sales of products such as motor vehicles and household goods could be much larger, if every South African household had the means to buy them, a situation that was unrealizable in the 2000s. Even a modest achievement towards lifting more households above the poverty level would provide an impetus not only to badly needed investment, but also to the job creation that such investment could bring. To address these issues, the Government in 2007 announced a proposed mandatory earnings-related social-security scheme that would provide improved unemployment insurance, disability benefits and death benefits 'targeted at the income needs of dependants' and a standard retirement savings arrangement. The scheme was to be financed by a social-security tax that would be administered by the South African Reserve Bank and would be held in individual accounts in the name of every contributor. The target date for implementation of the scheme was 2010.

Statistical Survey

Source (unless otherwise indicated): Statistics South Africa, Private Bag X44, Pretoria 0001; tel. (12) 3108911; fax (12) 3108500; e-mail info@statssa.pwv.gov.za; internet www.statssa.gov.za.

Area and Population

AREA, POPULATION AND DENSITY*

Area (sq km)	1,219,090†
Population (census results)	
9 October 1996	40,583,573
9 October 2001	
Males	21,434,033
Females	23,385,737
Total	44,819,770
Population (official estimates at mid-year)	
2005	46,892,424
2006	47,391,029
2007	47,850,064
Density (per sq km) at mid-2007	39.3

* Excluding data for Walvis Bay (area 1,124 sq km or 434 sq miles, population 22,999 in 1991), sovereignty over which was transferred from South Africa to Namibia on 1 March 1994.

† 470,693 sq miles.

ETHNIC GROUPS

(at census of October 2001)*

	Number	% of total
Africans (Blacks)	35,416,164	79.02
Europeans (Whites)	4,293,638	9.58
Coloureds	3,994,507	8.91
Asians	1,115,461	2.49
Total	44,819,770	100.00

* Figures exclude the effect of additional deaths caused by HIV/AIDS.

PROVINCES

(official estimates at mid-2007)

	Area (sq km)	Population	Density (per sq km)	Capital
KwaZulu/Natal	92,100	10,014,500	108.7	Pietermaritzburg
Gauteng*	17,010	9,688,100	569.6	Johannesburg
Eastern Cape	169,580	6,906,200	40.7	Bisho
Limpopo†	123,910	5,402,900	43.6	Pietersburg
Western Cape	129,370	4,839,800	37.4	Cape Town
North-West	116,320	3,394,200	291.8	Mmabatho
Mpumalanga‡	79,490	3,536,300	44.5	Nelspruit
Free State§	129,480	2,965,600	22.9	Bloemfontein
Northern Cape	361,830	1,102,200	3.0	Kimberley
Total	1,219,090	47,849,800	39.33	

* Formerly Pretoria-Witwatersrand-Vereeniging.

† Known as Northern Province (formerly Northern Transvaal) until February 2002.

‡ Formerly Eastern Transvaal.

§ Formerly the Orange Free State.

Note: Figures for population are rounded estimates based on the cohort-component compilation method.

PRINCIPAL TOWNS

(metropolitan areas, population at 2001 census)

Johannesburg	3,225,812	Springs	80,776
Durban	3,090,122	Vanderbiljpark	80,201
Cape Town*	2,893,247	Vereeniging	73,288
Pretoria*	1,985,983	Uitenhage	71,668
Port Elizabeth	1,005,779	Rustenburg	67,201
Soweto	858,649	Kimberley	62,526
Tembisa	348,687	Brakpan	62,115
Pietermaritzburg	223,518	Witbank	61,092
Botshabelo	175,820	Somerset West	60,609
Mdantsane	175,783	Klerksdorp	59,511
Boksburg	158,650	Midrand	44,566
East London	135,560	Newcastle	44,119
Bloemfontein*	111,698	Welkom	34,158
Benoni	94,341	Potchefstroom	26,725
Alberton	89,394	Carletonville	18,362
Krugersdorp	86,618	Westonaria	8,440

* Pretoria is the administrative capital, Cape Town the legislative capital and Bloemfontein the judicial capital.

Mid-2005 ('000, incl. suburbs, UN estimates): Johannesburg 3,254; Cape Town 3,083; East Rand (Ekurhuleni) 2,817; Durban 2,631; Pretoria 1,271; Vereeniging 1,027; Port Elizabeth 999 (Source: UN, *World Urbanization Prospects: The 2005 Revision*).

BIRTHS AND DEATHS

(annual averages, UN estimates)

	1990–95	1995–2000	2000–05
Birth rate (per 1,000)	27.7	25.3	24.1
Death rate (per 1,000)	8.2	9.2	13.5

Source: UN, *World Population Prospects: The 2006 Revision*.

Registered live births ('000): 1,433 in 2001; 1,518 in 2002; 1,677 in 2003.

Registered deaths: 413,969 in 2000; 451,936 in 2001; 499,268 in 2002.

Registered marriages: 134,581 in 2001; 177,002 in 2002; 178,689 in 2003.

Expectation of life (years at birth, UN estimates): 47.0 (males 45.7; females 48.2) in 2004 (Source: UN Development Programme, *Human Development Report*).

IMMIGRATION AND EMIGRATION

	2001	2002	2003
Immigrants:			
Africa	1,419	2,472	4,961
Europe	1,714	1,847	2,567
Asia	1,289	1,738	2,328
Americas	213	244	354
Oceania	51	65	99
Total (incl. others and unspecified)	4,832	6,545	10,578
Emigrants:			
Africa	1,584	1,461	2,611
Europe	5,316	4,637	6,827
Asia	226	218	445
Americas	1,713	1,473	2,090
Oceania	2,912	2,523	3,248
Total (incl. others and unspecified)	12,260	10,890	16,165

Immigrants (2004): Africa 5,235; Europe 2,638; Asia 2,225; Americas 343; Oceania 2,638; Total (incl. others) 10,714.

ECONOMICALLY ACTIVE POPULATION
(household survey, '000 persons aged 15 to 65 years, September 2001)*

	Males	Females	Total
Agriculture, hunting, forestry and fishing	727	324	1,051
Mining and quarrying	470	17	487
Manufacturing	1,004	602	1,605
Electricity, gas and water	80	15	95
Construction	534	60	594
Trade, restaurants and hotels	1,186	1,212	2,397
Transport, storage and communications	448	94	543
Financing, insurance, real estate and business services	547	428	975
Community, social and personal services	878	1,110	1,988
Private households	150	905	1,055
Total employed (incl. others)	6,049	4,783	10,833
Unemployed†	2,139	2,386	4,525
Total labour force	8,188	7,169	15,358

* Figures have been assessed independently, so that totals are not always the sum of the component parts.

† Based on the official definition. According to the expanded definition, the number of unemployed (in '000) was 7,698 (males 3,280, females 4,418).

September 2005 ('000): Agriculture, hunting, forestry and fishing 925; Mining and quarrying 411; Manufacturing 1,706; Electricity, gas and water 100; Construction 935; Wholesale and retail 3,024; Transport, storage and communications 616; Financing, insurance, real estate and business services 1,296; Community, social and personal services 2,192; Total employed (incl. others) 12,301; Unemployed 4,487; Total labour force 16,788.

September 2006 ('000): Agriculture, hunting, forestry and fishing 1,088; Mining and quarrying 398; Manufacturing 1,737; Electricity, gas and water 119; Construction 1,024; Wholesale and retail 3,055; Transport, storage and communications 611; Financing, insurance, real estate and business services 1,309; Community, social and personal services 2,319; Total employed (incl. others) 12,800; Unemployed 4,391; Total labour force 17,191.

Health and Welfare

KEY INDICATORS

Total fertility rate (children per woman, 2005)	2.7
Under-5 mortality rate (per 1,000 live births, 2005)	68
HIV/AIDS (% of persons aged 15–49, 2005)	18.8
Physicians (per 1,000 head, 2004)	0.77
Health expenditure (2004): US $ per head (PPP)	748.0
Health expenditure (2004): % of GDP	8.6
Health expenditure (2004): public (% of total)	40.4
Access to water (% of persons, 2004)	88
Access to sanitation (% of persons, 2004)	65
Human Development Index (2004): ranking	121
Human Development Index (2004): value	0.653

For sources and definitions, see explanatory note on p. vi.

Agriculture

PRINCIPAL CROPS
('000 metric tons)

	2003	2004	2005
Wheat	1,546.8	1,687.0	2,034.3
Barley	240	185	248.6
Maize	9,705	9,965	11,996
Oats	32.9	36.9	36.9*
Sorghum	264.3	449.1	354.4
Potatoes	1,496.0	1,786.0	1,878.0
Sweet potatoes	50.1	54.8	64.5
Sugar cane	20,418.9	19,094.8	21,725.1
Dry beans	68.3	85.1	71.7
Soybeans	136.5	220.0	227.1
Groundnuts (in shell)	66.9	128.0	85.0
Sunflower seed	682.2	677.4	691.0
Cottonseed	41.1	71.7	52.2
Cabbages	171.4	174.0	175*
Tomatoes	413.6	436.5	493.7
Pumpkins, squash and gourds	357.1	367.8	378.8
Onions (dry)	360.4	403.3	426.1
Carrots	124.2	132.9	135.3
Green corn (maize)*	322	320	320
Watermelons	61.2	64.9	70.1
Other vegetables (incl. melons)*	899.0	918.9	982.7
Bananas	209.7	279.8	321.7
Oranges	1,330.2	1,139.9	992.7
Tangerines, mandarins, clementines and satsumas	112.2	112.6	112.6
Lemons and limes	197.6	215.0	234.4
Grapefruit and pomelos	256.2	233.3	212.3
Apples	701.7	769.3	778.6
Pears	309.6	342.8	342.9
Apricots	50.1	97.8	82.0
Peaches and nectarines	249.3	178.2	184.8
Plums	57.5	70.2	75.8
Grapes	1,663.5	1,761.9	1,682.8
Mangoes	81.8	77.2	91.1
Avocados	63.3	56.2	59.5
Pineapples	163.8	162.4	172.2
Other fruit (excl. melons)*	161.8	214.0	204.3
Tobacco (leaves)	37.4	25.2	23.7

* FAO estimate(s).

Source: FAO.

LIVESTOCK
('000 head, year ending September)

	2003	2004	2005
Cattle	13,538	13,512	13,764
Pigs	1,662	1,651	1,648
Sheep	25,820	25,360*	25,317
Goats	6,358	6,372	6,407
Horses*	270	270	270
Asses, mules or hinnies*	164	164	164
Chickens	144,000*	145,000*	121,000
Ducks*	360	360	360
Geese*	128	130	130
Turkeys*	410	500	500

* FAO estimate(s).

Source: FAO.

LIVESTOCK PRODUCTS
('000 metric tons)

	2003	2004	2005
Cattle meat	610	632	672
Sheep meat	120	120	120
Goat meat*	36	36.4	36.5
Pig meat	134	145	140*
Chicken meat*	960.6	966.4	980.1
Cows' milk	2,642	2,552	2,552
Hen eggs	340	328	339
Wool: greasy	44.2	44.2*	44.2*

* FAO estimate(s).

Source: FAO.

Forestry

(including Namibia)

ROUNDWOOD REMOVALS
('000 cubic metres, excl. bark)

	2003	2004	2005
Sawlogs, veneer logs and logs for sleepers	5,235.9*	5,237.1†	5,079.2†
Pulpwood	14,833.3*	14,833.3†	14,833.3†
Other industrial wood	1,090.2	1,260.9	1,158.6
Fuel wood†	12,000	12,000	12,000
Total	33,159.4*	33,331.3†	33,071.1†

* Unofficial figure.
† FAO estimate(s).

Source: FAO.

SAWNWOOD PRODUCTION
('000 cubic metres, incl. railway sleepers)

	2003*	2004	2005
Coniferous (softwood)	2,076.6	2,689.0	2,579.5
Broadleaved (hardwood)	94.7	134.8	80.8
Total	2,171.3	2,823.8	2,660.3

* Unofficial figures.

Source: FAO.

Fishing

('000 metric tons, live weight)

	2003	2004	2005
Capture*	822.9	881.9	817.6
Cape hakes (Stokvisse)	139.2	153.3	144.0
Southern African pilchard	290.0	373.8	246.8
Whitehead's round herring	42.5	47.2	28.9
Southern African anchovy	258.9	190.1	282.7
Cape horse mackerel	28.3	34.1	35.1
Aquaculture	4.9	3.2	3.1
Total catch*†	827.8	885.1	820.7

* FAO estimate(s).
† Excluding aquatic plants ('000 metric tons, FAO): 20.2 in 2003; 25.6 in 2004; 9.6 in 2005.

Note: Figures exclude aquatic animals, recorded by number rather than weight. The number of Nile crocodiles captured was: 31,321 in 2003; 35,760 in 2004; 16,384 in 2005. The number of toothed whales caught was 70 in 2003; 77 in 2004; 77 in 2005.

Source: FAO.

Mining

('000 metric tons, unless otherwise indicated)

	2003	2004	2005*
Hard coal	239,311	243,372	245,007
Crude petroleum ('000 barrels)	4,068	6,769	7,277
Natural gas†	2,230	2,011	2,000
Iron ore‡	24,200	24,800	24,900
Copper ore (metric tons)‡	120,800	102,574	103,856
Nickel ore (metric tons)‡	40,842†	39,851	42,392
Lead concentrates (metric tons)‡	39,941	37,485	42,159
Zinc ore (metric tons)‡	41,400	32,001	32,112
Manganese ore and concentrates (metallurgical and chemical)§	3,501	4,282	4,611
Chromium ore§	7,406	7,677	7,494
Vanadium ore (metric tons)‡	27,172	23,302	22,604
Zirconium concentrates (metric tons)†	300,000	400,000	410,000
Antimony concentrates (metric tons)‡	5,291	4,967	8,600†
Cobalt ore (metric tons)†‡	400	460	400
Silver (kg)	79,817	70,913	87,874
Uranium oxide (metric tons)	894	887	795
Gold (kg)	373,300	337,223	294,671
Platinum-group metals (kg)	266,150	276,401	302,981
Kaolin	86.4	81.9	59.4
Magnesite—crude	86.1	65.9	66.0†
Phosphate rock§	2,643	2,735	2,577
Fluorspar	235.0	265.0	245.0†
Salt	441.3	332.7	399.1
Diamonds ('000 carats)	12,684	14,295	15,776
Gypsum—crude	394.1	452.3	547.6
Asbestos	6.2	—	—
Mica (metric tons)	1,003	901	924
Talc (metric tons)	6,719	8,141	8,469
Pyrophyllite (metric tons)	14,350	28,987	60,267

* Preliminary figures.
† Estimate(s).
‡ Figures refer to metal content of ores and concentrates.
§ Gross weight.

Source: US Geological Survey.

Industry

SELECTED PRODUCTS
('000 metric tons, unless otherwise indicated)

	2001	2002	2003
Wheat flour	1,926	2,070	2,073
Sugar—refined	1,096	1,141	1,653
Cotton yarn—incl. mixed	74.5	78.8	69.7
Woven cotton fabrics (million sq metres)	216	215	198
Footwear ('000 pairs)	17,552	19,699	17,317
Mechanical wood pulp	550	550	276
Chemical wood pulp	2,648	2,648	2,667
Newsprint paper	656	656	972
Other printing and writing paper	1,066	1,066	1,128
Other paper and paperboard	1,406	1,406	1,436
Rubber tyres ('000)	10,923	12,038	12,804
Nitrogenous fertilizers	467	657	656
Phosphate fertilizers	309	369	538
Motor spirit (petrol)	7,948	8,567	n.a.
Kerosene	691	691	n.a.
Jet fuel	1,690	1,924	n.a.
Distillate fuel oils	7,150	7,992	n.a.
Lubricating oils	402	391	n.a.
Petroleum bitumen—asphalt	231	266	n.a.
Cement*	9,165	9,624	10,163
Pig-iron*	5,820	5,823	6,234
Crude steel*	9,100	9,100	9,481
Refined copper—unwrought*	132.1	101.0	111.0
Colour television receivers ('000)	260	271	359
Passenger motor cars—assembled ('000)	294	300	306
Lorries—assembled ('000)	126	129	125
Electric energy (million kWh)	219,839	228,781	n.a.

* Source: US Geological Survey.

Source: UN, *Industrial Commodity Statistics Yearbook*.

Electric energy (consumption, million kWh): 213,461 in 2003; 221,934 in 2004; 223,257 in 2005.

Finance

CURRENCY AND EXCHANGE RATES

Monetary Units
100 cents = 1 rand (R).

Sterling, Dollar and Euro Equivalents (31 May 2007)
£1 sterling = 14.21 rand;
US $1 = 7.19 rand;
€1 = 9.67 rand;
100 rand = £7.04 = $13.92 = €10.35.

Average Exchange Rate (rand per US $)

2004	6.4597
2005	6.3593
2006	6.7716

BUDGET

(million rand, year ending 31 March)

Revenue	2005/06	2006/07*	2007/08*
Tax revenue (gross)	417,334.0	489,662.0	556,562.0
Taxes on incomes and profits	230,803.6	247,300.0	312,150.0
Individuals	125,645.3	139,000.0	155,335.0
Companies (including secondary tax)	98,438.4	130,471.0	154,515.0
Retirement funds	4,783.1	2,750.0	—
Other	1,936.7	2,079.0	2,300.0
Taxes on payroll and workforce	4,872.0	5,850.0	6,500.0
Taxes on property	11,137.5	10,345.0	10,995.0
Domestic taxes on goods and services	151,361.9	174,667.0	199,210.0
Value-added tax	114,351.6	134,562.0	155,068.0
Excise duties	14,546.5	16,100.0	17,792.4
Levies on fuel	20,506.7	21,750.0	23,937.7
Air departure tax	458.2	500.0	520.0
Other	341.7	455.0	477.0
Stamp duties and fees	792.8	600.0	222
State Miscellaneous Revenue	—	—	—
Taxes on international trade and transactions	18,201.9	23,900.0	27,485.0
Other current revenue	7,642.3	9,532.5	9,185.2
Capital revenue	916.5	1,813.1	1,907.4
Sub-total	425,892.8	501,007.6	567,654.6
Less SACU payments†	14,144.9	25,172.0	23,053.0
Total	411,747.9	475,835.6	544,601.6

Expenditure	2005/06‡	2006/07*	2007/08*
Central government administration	25,054.1	35,372.6	40,798.7
The Presidency	190.1	238.9	254.7
Parliament	673.8	782.1	835.7
Foreign affairs	2,687.7	3,042.1	3,856.4
Home affairs	3,172.1	2,800.4	3,314.6
Provincial and local government	15,976.1	25,392.3	28,844.2
Public works	2,354.3	3,116.8	3,693.1
Financial and administrative services	17,013.2	18,807.6	21,718.1
Government communication and information system	253.6	294.6	375.8
National treasury	13,100.7	16,752.9	19,708.2
Public services and administration	197.0	442.4	357.3
Public service commission	91.1	97.0	105.4
SA management development institute	55.4	58.9	71.1
Statistics South Africa	643.9	1,161.8	1,100.3
Social services	80,295.4	91,919.1	102,686.2
Arts and culture	1,121.0	1,330.1	1,608.0
Education	12,436.8	14,299.2	16,000.9
Health	9,937.1	11,454.0	12,655.1
Labour	1,295.9	1,493.5	2,032.9
Social development	55,067.8	62,382.4	67,232.1
Sport and Recreation South Africa	436.8	959.9	3,157.2
Justice and protection services	67,710.5	72,800.1	79,940.8
Correctional services	9,631.2	9,831.5	10,742.3
Defence	23,510.5	23,902.9	25,922.3
Independent complaints directorate	54.5	65.9	80.9

Expenditure—*continued*	2005/06‡	2006/07*	2007/08*
Justice and constitutional development	5,153.5	6,478.6	7,277.8
Safety and security	29,360.8	32,521.2	35,917.5
Economic services and infrastructure	34,345.8	47,286.8	54,034.0
Agriculture	1,906.8	2,367.6	2,281.2
Communications	1,034.4	1,322.3	1,423.5
Environmental affairs and tourism	1,775.7	2,061.8	2,590.8
Housing	5,248.8	7,333.7	8,877.6
Land affairs	2,876.9	3,730.2	5,678.5
Minerals and energy	2,191.6	2,635.1	2,966.1
Public enterprises	2,671.5	2,869.9	1,064.0
Science and technology	2,041.3	2,617.1	3,142.5
Trade and industry	3,056.4	3,942.0	4,845.6
Transport	10,409.9	13,746.8	15,857.9
Water affairs and forestry	3,804.0	4,660.3	5,306.3
Unallocated funds / Projected underspending	—	–2,100.0	—
Contingency reserve	—	—	3,000.0
Sub-total	224,419.1	264,086.5	302,177.7
State debt costs	50,912.0	52,588.1	52,916.0
Provincial equitable share	135,291.6	150,752.9	171,271.4
Skills levy and seats	4,883.3	5,500.0	6,000.0
Members' remuneration	211.7	229.2	242.4
Judges' salaries	1,040.1	1,071.1	1,263.5
President and deputy-president salary	2.0	2.2	2.2
Total	416,759.9	474,229.9	533,873.3

* Estimates.

† Payments to Botswana, Lesotho, Namibia and Swaziland, in accordance with Southern African Customs Union agreements.

‡ Preliminary outcome.

Source: National Treasury, Pretoria.

INTERNATIONAL RESERVES

(US $ million at 31 December)

	2004	2005	2006
Gold (national valuation)	1,578	2,051	2,530
IMF special drawing rights	346	319	355
Reserve position in IMF	1	1	1
Foreign exchange	12,794	18,260	22,720
Total	14,719	20,630	25,606

Source: IMF, *International Financial Statistics*.

MONEY SUPPLY

(million rand at 31 December)

	2004	2005	2006
Currency outside banks	39,080	43,419	49,951
Demand deposits at deposit money banks	204,947	248,103	287,612
Total (incl. others)	244,027	291,522	337,563

Source: IMF, *International Financial Statistics*.

COST OF LIVING

(Consumer Price Index; base: 2000 = 100)

	2004	2005	2006
Food	134.9	137.9	147.8
Housing	111.2	n.a.	n.a.
Electricity, gas and other fuels	129.0	n.a.	n.a.
All items (incl. others)	123.8	128.0	134.0

Source: ILO.

NATIONAL ACCOUNTS

(million rand at current prices, preliminary)

National Income and Product

	2004	2005	2006
Compensation of employees	627,411	679,206	740,435
Net operating surplus	426,122	469,015	544,233
Consumption of fixed capital	172,966	189,892	214,803
Gross domestic product (GDP) at factor cost	1,226,499	1,338,113	1,499,471
Taxes on production	177,820	210,219	238,921
Less Subsidies	6,162	9,079	11,704
GDP at market prices	1,398,157	1,539,253	1,726,688
Primary incomes received from abroad	20,973	29,550	40,234
Less Primary incomes paid abroad	48,823	60,975	75,990
Gross national income at market prices	1,370,307	1,507,828	1,690,932
Current transfers received from abroad	1,621	1,536	1,792
Less Current transfers paid abroad	12,947	14,311	18,978
Gross national disposable income at market prices	1,358,981	1,495,053	1,673,746

Expenditure on the Gross Domestic Product

	2004	2005	2006
Government final consumption expenditure	273,708	301,338	336,073
Private final consumption expenditure	870,806	963,291	1,080,074
Increase in stocks	20,989	18,484	30,027
Gross fixed capital formation	226,808	262,432	320,642
Residual item	11,301	7,892	18,012
Total domestic expenditure	1,403,612	1,553,437	1,784,828
Exports of goods and services	372,722	423,022	515,355
Less Imports of goods and services	378,177	437,206	573,495
GDP at market prices	1,398,157	1,539,253	1,726,688
GDP at constant 2000 prices	1,062,187	1,118,155	1,189,015

Gross Domestic Product by Economic Activity

	2004	2005	2006
Agriculture, forestry and fishing	39,432	37,625	41,632
Mining and quarrying	89,290	100,515	120,222
Manufacturing	237,100	254,993	278,793
Electricity, gas and water	29,645	31,574	33,579
Construction (contractors)	29,838	33,161	39,274
Wholesale and retail trade, catering and accommodation	175,738	191,549	213,233
Transport, storage and communication	122,240	131,955	145,044
Finance, insurance, real estate and business services	260,151	293,481	336,950
Government services	193,420	209,614	226,360
Other community, social and personal services	76,998	84,055	94,327
Gross value added at basic prices	1,253,852	1,368,522	1,529,413
Taxes, less subsidies, on products	144,305	170,731	197,275
GDP at market prices	1,398,157	1,539,253	1,726,688

Source: South African Reserve Bank.

BALANCE OF PAYMENTS

(US $ million)

	2004	2005	2006
Exports of goods f.o.b.	48,237	55,280	63,767
Imports of goods f.o.b.	-48,518	-56,484	-69,941
Trade balance	-281	-1,204	-6,175
Exports of services	9,682	11,157	12,022
Imports of services	-10,328	-12,155	-14,291
Balance on goods and services	-928	-2,201	-8,444
Other income received	3,259	4,640	5,944
Other income paid	-7,576	-9,569	-11,238
Balance on goods, services and income	-5,246	-7,130	-13,737
Current transfers received	257	240	261
Current transfers paid	-2,015	-2,251	-2,800
Current balance	-7,003	-9,142	-16,276
Capital account (net)	52	30	30
Direct investment abroad	-1,305	-909	-6,496
Direct investment from abroad	701	6,133	-11
Portfolio investment assets	-950	-911	-2,021
Portfolio investment liabilities	7,357	5,698	21,814
Other investment assets	-216	-3,503	-7,301
Other investment liabilities	2,065	4,896	8,545
Net errors and omissions	5,623	3,474	5,427
Overall balance	6,324	5,766	3,711

Source: IMF, *International Financial Statistics*.

External Trade

PRINCIPAL COMMODITIES

(distribution by SITC, US $ million)

Imports c.i.f.	2002	2003	2004
Food and live animals	925.1	1,185.6	1,626.8
Crude materials (inedible) except fuels	843.2	1,098.9	1,497.0
Mineral fuels, lubricants, etc.	3,269.2	4,105.3	6,885.8
Petroleum, petroleum products, etc.	3,134.7	3,934.5	6,647.6
Crude petroleum oils, etc.	2,796.4	3,597.9	5,937.6
Chemicals and related products	3,181.3	3,813.9	4,771.8
Basic manufactures	3,191.8	4,172.1	5,320.9
Non-metallic mineral manufactures	825.9	1,082.6	1,276.4
Machinery and transport equipment	9,839.8	13,595.0	18,905.6
Power generating machinery and equipment	581.6	809.3	1,040.6
Machinery specialized for particular industries	1,335.9	1,712.8	2,196.3
General industrial machinery, equipment and parts	1,444.9	1,986.1	2,266.4
Office machines and automatic data-processing equipment	1,080.4	1,616.0	2,329.7
Telecommunications and sound equipment	1,613.5	1,722.7	2,614.7
Other electrical machinery, apparatus, etc.	1,184.9	1,542.6	1,883.7
Road vehicles	1,662.5	2,441.5	3,818.7
Passenger motor vehicles (excl. buses)	959.7	1,455.2	2,568.0
Other transport equipment	737.7	1,486.6	2,391.6
Miscellaneous manufactured articles	2,307.3	2,887.9	3,989.2
Total (incl. others)	26,212.1	34,543.1	47,794.3

Exports f.o.b.	2002	2003	2004
Food and live animals	1,898.9	2,381.5	2,670.4
Vegetables and fruit	846.4	1,238.0	1,548.2
Beverages and tobacco	482.1	670.1	786.6
Crude materials (inedible) except fuels	2,435.4	2,744.6	3,094.4
Metalliferous ores and metal scrap	1,305.5	1,348.8	1,650.3
Mineral fuels, lubricants, etc.	2,853.2	3,105.8	3,658.9
Coal, lignite and peat	1,839.0	1,804.8	2,432.6
Petroleum, petroleum products, etc.	1,009.6	1,296.9	1,217.4
Chemicals and related products	2,154.3	2,395.9	3,152.9
Basic manufactures	6,714.9	12,045.0	16,897.6
Non-metallic mineral manufactures	1,750.1	2,010.3	2,326.5
Pearl, precious and semi-precious stones, unworked or worked	1,550.9	1,764.0	2,008.2
Diamonds (non-industrial), not mounted or set	1,543.8	1,754.6	1,998.5
Iron and steel	2,411.4	3,877.4	5,642.0
Pig-iron, etc.	1,109.8	1,722.4	2,776.5
Non-ferrous metals	1,099.1	4,423.5	6,927.8
Silver, platinum and other platinum group metals	20.3	3,206.7	4,641.2
Platinum group metals, unwrought, unworked or semi-manufactured	0.1	3,196.1	4,631.2
Aluminium	887.8	956.5	1,386.4
Aluminium and aluminium alloys, unwrought	704.2	679.0	1,017.9
Machinery and transport equipment	5,260.4	6,544.2	7,927.4
General industrial machinery, equipment and parts	1,294.8	1,650.7	1,955.7
Road vehicles	2,396.7	3,114.5	3,540.6
Passenger motor vehicles (excl. buses)	1,614.5	2,099.3	2,451.9
Miscellaneous manufactured articles	1,193.5	1,487.0	1,664.7
Total (incl. others)	23,064.4	31,635.9	40,206.1

Source: UN, *International Trade Statistics Yearbook*.

PRINCIPAL TRADING PARTNERS
(US $ million)*

Imports f.o.b.	2002	2003	2004
Australia	741.1	797.8	1,128.4
Austria	279.0	364.2	429.6
Belgium-Luxembourg	371.2	506.0	599.2
Brazil	467.2	715.1	1,000.8
China, People's Repub.	1,358.9	2,218.8	3,589.2
France (incl. Monaco)	1,075.7	2,063.7	2,901.7
Germany	4,076.2	5,128.4	6,778.1
India	280.5	417.7	708.9
Iran	920.8	1,251.6	2,376.2
Ireland	290.4	376.5	634.0
Italy	943.8	1,128.9	1,444.8
Japan	1,818.6	2,433.9	3,270.0
Korea, Repub.	427.7	558.3	1,013.5
Malaysia	345.8	402.6	593.3
Netherlands	478.4	579.8	707.8
Nigeria	344.0	405.1	810.7
Saudi Arabia	1,299.5	1,966.3	2,665.6
Spain	337.3	511.8	673.1
Sweden	316.7	448.8	641.3
Switzerland-Liechtenstein	453.9	466.4	483.6
Thailand	283.0	426.3	666.0
United Kingdom	2,372.0	3,000.7	3,269.7
USA	3,084.0	3,425.6	4,128.8
Total (incl. others)	26,212.0	34,543.1	47,794.3

Exports f.o.b.	2002	2003	2004
Angola	322.6	447.3	481.2
Australia	486.6	745.3	1,025.4
Belgium-Luxembourg	865.6	985.3	1,124.7
China, People's Repub.	450.3	889.1	1,054.2
France (incl. Monaco)	664.4	743.0	892.5
Germany	1,883.6	2,439.7	3,231.9
Hong Kong	316.1	423.2	527.3
India	351.5	380.3	566.3
Israel	521.2	508.1	634.7
Italy	743.0	931.1	1,188.9
Japan	1,490.2	3,147.7	4,104.5
Korea, Repub.	478.1	580.1	697.5
Mauritius	255.0	271.3	269.3
Mozambique	600.8	745.5	786.4
Netherlands	1,188.8	1,508.7	1,838.0
Nigeria	258.8	334.1	443.9
Spain	641.6	830.8	1,109.2
Switzerland-Liechtenstein	240.5	762.8	1,125.1
United Kingdom	2,519.1	3,197.4	4,209.4
USA	2,439.2	3,844.2	4,682.8
Zimbabwe	692.3	858.6	927.7
Total (incl. others)	23,064.4	31,635.8	40,206.1

* Imports by country of origin; exports by country of destination.

Source: UN, *International Trade Statistics Yearbook*.

Transport

RAILWAYS
(traffic, year ending 31 March)*

	1997/98	1998/99	1999/2000
Passenger-km (million)	1,775	1,794	3,930
Net ton-km (million)	103,866	102,777	106,786

* Including Namibia.

Source: UN, *Statistical Yearbook*.

ROAD TRAFFIC
(registered motor vehicles)

	2002
Heavy load vehicles	326,798
Heavy passenger motor vehicles	164,369
Light load vehicles	1,875,234
Light passenger motor vehicles	4,135,037
Motorcycles	159,266
Special vehicles	296,518
Other vehicles	17,955
Total (incl. others)	6,975,177

SHIPPING

Merchant Fleet
(vessels registered at 31 December)

	2004	2005	2006
Number of vessels	246	243	242
Displacement ('000 grt)	170.0	180.6	173.1

Source: Lloyd's Register-Fairplay, *World Fleet Statistics*.

International Sea-borne Freight Traffic

	2003	2004	2005
Goods loaded (metric tons)	128,477,183	124,370,762	127,408,557
Goods unloaded (metric tons)	42,845,843	43,820,161	43,847,748
Containers loaded (TEU)	1,194,400	1,290,883	1,484,009
Containers unloaded (TEU)	1,220,167	1,341,888	1,530,227

Source: National Ports Authority of South Africa.

CIVIL AVIATION
(traffic on scheduled services)

	2001	2002	2003
Kilometres flown (million)	167	170	188
Passengers carried ('000)	7,948	8,167	9,160
Passenger-km (million)	22,061	22,914	24,666
Total ton-km (million)	2,746	2,853	3,125

Source: UN, *Statistical Yearbook*.

Tourism

FOREIGN VISITOR ARRIVALS*

Country of origin	2003	2004	2005
Botswana	797,315	806,820	798,455
France	130,365	111,636	103,674
Germany	261,194	249,564	253,471
Lesotho	1,291,242	1,479,802	1,668,826
Mozambique	474,790	405,579	648,526
Namibia	216,978	226,525	220,045
Netherlands	122,565	122,271	117,855
Swaziland	809,049	852,636	911,990
United Kingdom	463,021	463,176	476,627
USA	192,561	213,322	238,934
Zambia	115,650	122,512	128,390
Zimbabwe	568,626	558,093	783,100
Total (incl. others and unspecified)	6,640,095	6,815,202	7,517,258

* Figures include same-day visitors (excursionists), but exclude arrivals of South African nationals resident abroad. Border crossings by contract workers are also excluded.

Tourism receipts (US $ million, incl. passenger transport): 6,147 in 2003; 6,729 in 2004; n.a. in 2005.

Source: World Tourism Organization.

Communications Media

	2003	2004	2005
Telephones ('000 main lines in use)	4,821.0	4,850.0	4,729.0
Mobile cellular telephones ('000 subscribers)	16,860.0	20,839.0	33,960.0
Internet users ('000)	3,325.0	3,566.0	5,100.0
Personal computers in use ('000)	3,513	3,740	3,966

2001: Radio receivers ('000 in use): 11,696; Television receivers ('000 in use): 7,708; Daily newspapers (average circulation, '000): 1,233.4, (titles) 21.

Facsimile machines (number in use): 150,000 in 1997.

Book production: 5,418 titles in 1995.

Sources: partly UNESCO, *Statistical Yearbook*; UN, *Statistical Yearbook*; International Telecommunication Union.

Education

(2004)*

	Institutions	Teachers	Students
Primary	16,286	177,861	6,320,479
Secondary	5,887	114,755	3,717,780
Combined	3,911	53,305	1,755,083
Intermediate and middle	795	11,416	383,049
ABET centres†	2,339	15,954	272,725
ELSEN centres‡	408	7,392	86,388
Further education and training§	50	6,477	394,027
ECD‖	4,146	7,363	189,254
Higher education§	29	15,375	744,488

* Figures for public and independent institutions, unless otherwise indicated.

† Adult basic education and training.

‡ Education for learners with special needs.

§ Figures refer to public institutions only.

‖ Early childhood development.

Source: Department of Education.

Adult literacy rate (UNESCO estimates): 82.4% (males 84.1%; females 80.9%) in 1995–99 (Source: UN Development Programme, *Human Development Report*).

Directory

The Constitution

The Constitution was adopted by the Constitutional Assembly (comprising the National Assembly and the Senate) on 8 May 1996, and entered into force on 4 February 1997. Its main provisions are summarized below:

FOUNDING PROVISIONS

The Republic of South Africa is one sovereign democratic state founded on the following values: human dignity, the achievement of equality and advancement of human rights and freedoms; non-racialism and non-sexism; supremacy of the Constitution and the rule of law; universal adult suffrage, a national common voters' roll, regular elections, and a multi-party system of democratic government, to ensure accountability, responsiveness and openness. There is common South African citizenship, all citizens being equally entitled to the rights, privileges and benefits, and equally subject to the duties and responsibilities of citizenship.

BILL OF RIGHTS

Everyone is equal before the law and has the right to equal protection and benefit of the law. The state may not unfairly discriminate directly or indirectly against anyone on one or more grounds, including race, gender, sex, pregnancy, marital status, ethnic or social origin, colour, sexual orientation, age, disability, religion, conscience, belief, culture, language and birth. The rights that are enshrined include: protection against detention without trial, torture or any inhuman form of treatment or punishment; the right to privacy; freedom of conscience; freedom of expression; freedom of assembly; political freedom; freedom of movement and residence; the right to join or form a trade union or employers' organization; the right to a healthy and sustainable environment; the right to property, except in the case of the Government's programme of land reform and redistribution, and taking into account the claims of people who were dispossessed of property after 19 June 1913; the right to adequate housing; the right to health care, food and water and social security assistance, if needed; the rights of children; the right to education in the official language of one's choice, where this is reasonably practicable; the right to use the language and to participate in the cultural life of one's choice, but not in a manner inconsistent with any provision of this Bill of Rights; access to state information; access to the courts; the rights of people who have been arrested or detained; and the right to a fair trial.

CO-OPERATIVE GOVERNMENT

Government is constituted as national, provincial and local spheres of government, which are distinctive, interdependent and interrelated. All spheres of government and all organs of state within each sphere must preserve the peace, national unity and indivisibility of the Republic; secure the well-being of the people of the Republic; implement effective, transparent, accountable and coherent government for the Republic as a whole; respect the constitutional status, institutions, powers and functions of government in the other spheres; not assume any power or function except those conferred on them in terms of the Constitution.

PARLIAMENT

Legislative power is vested in a bicameral Parliament, comprising a National Assembly and a National Council of Provinces. The National Assembly has between 350 and 400 members and is elected, in general, by proportional representation. National and provincial legislatures are elected separately, under a 'double-ballot' electoral system. Each provincial legislature appoints six permanent delegates and nominates four special delegates to the 90-member National Council of Provinces, which is headed by a Chairperson, who is elected by the Council and has a five-year term of office. Parliamentary decisions are generally reached by a simple majority, although constitutional amendments require a majority of two-thirds.

THE NATIONAL EXECUTIVE

The Head of State is the President, who is elected by the National Assembly from among its members, and exercises executive power in consultation with the other members of the Cabinet. No person may hold office as President for more than two terms. Any party that holds a minimum of 80 seats in the National Assembly (equivalent to 20% of the national vote) is entitled to nominate an Executive Deputy President. If no party, or only one party, secures 80 or more seats, the party holding the largest number of seats and the party holding the second largest number of seats in the National Assembly are each entitled to designate one Executive Deputy President from among the members of the Assembly. The President may be removed by a motion of no-confidence or by impeachment. The Cabinet comprises a maximum of 27 ministers. Each party with a minimum of 20 seats in the National Assembly (equivalent to 5% of the national vote) is entitled to a proportional number of ministerial portfolios. The President allocates cabinet portfolios in consultation with party leaders, who are entitled to request the replacement of ministers. Cabinet decisions are reached by consensus.

JUDICIAL AUTHORITY

The judicial authority of the Republic is vested in the courts, which comprise the Constitutional Court; the Supreme Court of Appeal; the High Courts; the Magistrates' Courts; and any other court established or recognized by an Act of Parliament. (See Judicial System.)

PROVINCIAL GOVERNMENT

There are nine provinces: Eastern Cape, Free State (formerly Orange Free State), Gauteng (formerly Pretoria-Witwatersrand-Vereeniging), KwaZulu/Natal, Limpopo (formerly Northern Transvaal, subsequently Northern Province), Mpumalanga (formerly Eastern Transvaal), Northern Cape, North-West and Western Cape. Each province is entitled to determine its legislative and executive structure. Each province has a legislature, comprising between 30 and 80 members (depending on the size of the local electorate), who are elected by proportional representation. Each legislature is entitled to draft a constitution for the province, subject to the principles governing the national Constitution, and elects a Premier, who heads a Cabinet. Parties that hold a minimum of 10% of seats in the legislature are entitled to a proportional number of portfolios in the Cabinet. Provincial legislatures are allowed primary responsibility for a number of areas of government, and joint powers with central government in the principal administrative areas.

LOCAL GOVERNMENT

The local sphere of government consists of municipalities, with executive and legislative authority vested in the Municipal Council. The objectives of local government are to provide democratic and accountable government for local communities; to ensure the provision of services to communities; to promote social and economic development, and a safe and healthy environment; and to encourage the involvement of communities and community organizations in the matters of local government. The National Assembly is to determine the different categories of municipality that may be established, and appropriate fiscal powers and functions for each category. Provincial Governments have the task of establishing municipalities, and of providing for the monitoring and support of local government in each province.

STATE INSTITUTIONS SUPPORTING CONSTITUTIONAL DEMOCRACY

The following state institutions are designed to strengthen constitutional democracy: the Public Protector (whose task is to investigate any conduct in state affairs, or in the public administration in any sphere of government, that is alleged or suspected to be improper); the Human Rights Commission; the Commission for the Protection and Promotion of the Rights of Cultural, Religious and Linguistic Communities; the Commission for Gender Equality; the Auditor-General; and the Electoral Commission.

TRADITIONAL LEADERS

The institution, status and role of traditional leadership, according to customary law, are recognized, subject to the Constitution. A traditional authority that observes a system of customary law may function subject to any applicable legislation and customs. National and provincial legislation may provide for the establishment of local or provincial houses of traditional leaders; the National Assembly may establish a national council of traditional leaders.

The Government

HEAD OF STATE

President: THABO MBEKI (inaugurated 16 June 1999; re-elected by vote of the National Assembly 23 April 2004).

Deputy President: PHUMZILE MLAMBO-NGCUKA (ANC).

THE CABINET

(August 2007)

The African National Congress of South Africa (ANC), the Azanian People's Organization (AZAPO) and the South African Communist Party (SACP) are represented in the Cabinet.

Minister of Agriculture and Land Affairs: LULAMA XINGWANA (ANC).

Minister of Arts and Culture: Dr Z. PALLO JORDAN (ANC).

Minister of Communications: IVY MATSEPE-CASABURRI (ANC).

Minister of Correctional Services: NGCONDE BALFOUR (ANC).

Minister of Defence: MOSIUOA LEKOTA (ANC).

Minister of Education: G. NALEDI PANDOR (ANC).

Minister of Environmental Affairs and Tourism: MARTHINUS VAN SCHALKWYK (ANC).

Minister of Finance: TREVOR A. MANUEL (ANC).

Minister of Foreign Affairs: NKOSAZANA C. DLAMINI-ZUMA (ANC).

Minister of Health: MANTOMBAZANA (MANTO) TSHABALALA-MSIMANG (ANC).

Minister of Home Affairs: NOSIVIWE MAPISA-NQAKULA (ANC).

Minister of Housing: LINDIWE NONCEBA SISULU (ANC).

Minister of Intelligence: RONNIE KASRILS (ANC).

Minister of Justice and Constitutional Development: BRIGITTE S. MABANDLA (ANC).

Minister of Labour: MEMBATHISI M. S. MDLADLANA (ANC).

Minister of Minerals and Energy: BUYELWA P. SONJICA (ANC).

Minister of Provincial and Local Government: F. SYDNEY MUFAMADI (ANC).

Minister of Public Enterprises: ALEC ERWIN (ANC).

Minister of Public Service and Administration: GERALDINE J. FRASER-MOLEKETI (ANC).

Minister of Public Works: ANGELA THOKO DIDIZA (ANC).

Minister of Safety and Security: CHARLES NQAKULA (SACP).

Minister of Science and Technology: MOSIBUDI MANGENA (AZAPO).

Minister of Social Development: ZOLA S. T. SKWEYIYA (ANC).

Minister of Sport and Recreation: Rev. MAKHENKESI STOFILE (ANC).

Minister of Trade and Industry: MANDISI B. M. MPAHLWA (ANC).

Minister of Transport: JEFFREY T. RADEBE (ANC).

Minister of Water Affairs and Forestry: LINDIWE HENDRICKS (ANC).

Minister in the Presidency: Dr ESSOP G. PAHAD (ANC).

MINISTRIES

The Presidency: Union Bldgs, West Wing, Government Ave, Pretoria 0001; Private Bag X1000, Pretoria 0001; tel. (12) 3005200; fax (12) 3238246; e-mail president@po.gov.za; internet www.gov.za/president/index.html.

Ministry of Agriculture and Land Affairs: Agriculture Bldg, 20 Beatrix St, Arcadia, Pretoria 0002; Private Bag X250, Pretoria 0001; tel. (12) 3197298; fax (12) 3218558; e-mail nanaz@nda.agric.za; internet www.nda.agric.za.

Ministry of Arts and Culture: 481 Church St, 10th Floor, cnr Church and Beatrix Sts, Kingsley Centre, Arcadia, Pretoria; Private Bag X899, Pretoria 0001; tel. (12) 32440968; fax (12) 3242687; e-mail sandile.memela@dac.gov.za; internet www.dac.gov.za.

Ministry of Communications: Nkululeko House, iParioli Office Park, 399 Duncan St, cnr Park St, Hatfield, Pretoria 0083; Private

Bag X860, Pretoria 0001; tel. (12) 4278000; fax (12) 4278026; e-mail elna@doc.gov.za; internet www.doc.gov.za.

Ministry of Correctional Services: Poyntons Bldg, West Block, cnr Church and Schubart Sts, Pretoria 0002; Private Bag X853, Pretoria 0001; tel. (12) 3072000; fax (12) 3286149; e-mail communications@dcs.gov.za; internet www.dcs.gov.za.

Ministry of Defence: Armscor Bldg, Block 5, Nossob St, Erasmusrand 0181; Private Bag X161, Pretoria 0001; tel. (12) 3556321; fax (12) 3556398; e-mail info@mil.za; internet www.mil.za.

Ministry of Education: Sol Plaatje House, 123 Schoeman St, Pretoria 0002; Private Bag X895, Pretoria 0001; tel. (12) 3125911; fax (12) 3256260; e-mail webmaster@doe.gov.za; internet www.education.gov.za.

Ministry of Environmental Affairs and Tourism: Fedsure Forum Bldg, North Tower, cnr Van der Walt and Pretorius Sts, Pretoria; Private Bag X447, Pretoria 0001; tel. (12) 3103911; fax (12) 3222682; internet www.environment.gov.za.

Ministry of Foreign Affairs: Union Bldgs, East Wing, 1 Government Ave, Arcadia, Pretoria 0002; Private Bag X152, Pretoria 0001; tel. (12) 3511000; fax (12) 3510253; e-mail minister@foreign.gov.za; internet www.dfa.gov.za.

Ministry of Health: DTI Bldg, Rm 1105, Prinsloo St, Pretoria 0001; Private Bag X828, Pretoria 0001; tel. (12) 3120000; fax (12) 3264395; e-mail masint@health.gov.za; internet www.health.gov.za.

Ministry of Home Affairs: 270 Maggs St, Watloo; Private Bag X114, Pretoria 0001; tel. (12) 3148911; fax (12) 3216491; internet www.home-affairs.gov.za.

Ministry of Housing: Govan Mbeki House, 240 Walker St, Sunnyside, Pretoria 0002; Private Bag X644, Pretoria 0001; tel. (12) 4211311; fax (12) 3418510; internet www.housing.gov.za.

Ministry of Intelligence: Bogare Bldg, 2 Atterbury Rd, Menlyn, Pretoria 0063; POB 37, Menlyn 0063; tel. (12) 3670700; fax (12) 3670749.

Ministry of Justice and Constitutional Development: Momentum Centre, 329 Pretorius St, cnr Pretorius and Prinsloo Sts, Pretoria 0001; Private Bag X276, Pretoria 0001; tel. (12) 3151332; fax (12) 3151749; e-mail znqayi@justice.gov.za; internet www.doj.gov.za.

Ministry of Labour: Laboria House, Schoeman St, Pretoria 0002; Private Bag X117, Pretoria 0001; tel. (12) 3094000; fax (12) 3094030; e-mail page.boikanyo@labour.gov.za; internet www.labour.gov.za.

Ministry of Minerals and Energy: Mineralia Centre, 391 Andries St, Pretoria 0002; Private Bag X59, Pretoria 0001; tel. (12) 3179000; fax (12) 3204327; internet www.dme.gov.za.

Ministry of Provincial and Local Government: 87 Hamilton St, Arcadia, Pretoria 0001; Private Bag X804, Pretoria 0001; tel. (12) 3340600; fax (12) 3340603; e-mail enquiry@dplg.gov.za; internet www.dplg.gov.za.

Ministry of Public Enterprises: Infotech Bldg, Suite 401, 1090 Arcadia St, Hatfield, Pretoria 0083; Private Bag X15, Hatfield 0028; tel. (12) 4311000; fax (86) 5012624; e-mail info@dpe.gov.za; internet www.dpe.gov.za.

Ministry of Public Service and Administration: Batho Pele House, 22nd Floor, Vermeulen and van der Walts Sts, Pretoria 0002; Private Bag X916, Pretoria 0001; tel. (12) 3147911; fax (12) 3232386; internet www.dpsa.gov.za.

Ministry of Public Works: Central Government Bldg, cnr Bosman and Vermeulen Sts, Pretoria 0002; Private Bag X65, Pretoria 0001; tel. (12) 3372000; fax (12) 3252856; internet www.publicworks.gov.za.

Ministry of Safety and Security: Van Erkom Bldg, 8th Floor, Van Erkom Arcade, 217 Pretorius St, Pretoria 0002; Private Bag X922, Pretoria 0001; tel. (12) 3392500; fax (12) 3392536; e-mail stratfordm@saps.org.za; internet www.gov.za/sss.

Ministry of Science and Technology: Oranje Nassau Bldg, 7th Floor, 188 Schoeman St, Pretoria 0001; Private Bag X727, Pretoria 0001; tel. (12) 3174302; fax (12) 3242687; e-mail nelvis.qekema@dst.gov.za; internet www.dst.gov.za.

Ministry of Social Development: HSRC Bldg, North Wing, 134 Pretorius St, Pretoria 0002; Private Bag X901, Pretoria 0001; tel. (12) 3127654; fax (12) 3127943; internet www.welfare.gov.za.

Ministry of Sport and Recreation: Oranje Nassau Bldg, 3rd Floor, 188 Schoeman St, Pretoria; Private Bag X896, Pretoria 0001; tel. (12) 3343220; fax (12) 3264026; e-mail greg@srsa.gov.za; internet www.srsa.gov.za.

Ministry of Trade and Industry: 77 Meintjies St, Sunnyside, Pretoria 0002; Private Bag X84, Pretoria 0001; tel. (12) 2549405; fax (12) 2549406; e-mail contactus@thedti.gov.za; internet www.thedti.gov.za.

Ministry of Transport: 159 Forum Bldg, 159 Struben St, Pretoria 0002; Private Bag X193, Pretoria 0001; tel. (12) 3093000; fax (12) 3285926; e-mail khozac@dot.gov.za; internet www.transport.gov.za.

Ministry of Water Affairs and Forestry: Sedibeng Bldg, 10th Floor, 185 Schoeman St, Pretoria 0002; Private Bag X313, Pretoria 0001; tel. (12) 3368733; fax (12) 3284254; internet www-dwaf.pwv.gov.za.

National Treasury: 40 Church Sq., Pretoria 0002; Private Bag X115, Pretoria 0001; tel. (12) 3155111; fax (12) 3155234; e-mail thoraya.pandy@treasury.gov.za; internet www.treasury.gov.za.

Legislature

PARLIAMENT

National Council of Provinces

Chairman: MOSIUOA LEKOTA.

The National Council of Provinces (NCOP), which replaced the Senate under the new Constitution, was inaugurated on 6 February 1997. The NCOP comprises 90 members, with six permanent delegates and four special delegates from each of the nine provinces.

National Assembly

Speaker: BALEKA MBETE.

General Election, 14 April 2004

Party	Votes	% of votes	Seats
African National Congress	10,878,251	69.68	279
Democratic Alliance	1,931,201	12.37	50
Inkatha Freedom Party	1,088,664	6.97	28
United Democratic Movement	355,717	2.28	9
Independent Democrats	269,765	1.73	7
New National Party	257,824	1.65	7
African Christian Democratic Party	250,272	1.60	6
Freedom Front Plus	139,465	0.89	4
United Christian Democratic Party	117,792	0.75	3
Pan-Africanist Congress of Azania	113,512	0.73	3
Minority Front	55,267	0.35	2
Azanian People's Organisation	41,776	0.27	2
Others	113,161	0.72	—
Total	15,612,667	100.00	400

Provincial Governments

(August 2007)

EASTERN CAPE

Premier: NOSIMO BALINDLELA (ANC).

Speaker of the Legislature: NOXOLO KIVIET (ANC).

FREE STATE

Premier: BEATRICE MARSHOFF (ANC).

Speaker of the Legislature: MXOLISI DUKWANA (ANC).

GAUTENG

Premier: MBHAZIMA SHILOWA (ANC).

Speaker of the Legislature: RICHARD MDAKANE (ANC).

KWAZULU/NATAL

Premier: SIBUSISO NDEBELE (ANC).

Speaker of the Legislature: WILLIES MCHUNU (ANC).

LIMPOPO

Premier: SELLO MOLOTO (ANC).

Speaker of the Legislature: DR TSHENUWANI FARISANI (ANC).

MPUMALANGA

Premier: SAMPSON PHATHAGE (THABANG) MAKWETLA (ANC).

Speaker of the Legislature: YVONE (PINKY) PHOSA (ANC).

NORTHERN CAPE

Premier: DIPUO PETERS (ANC).

Speaker of the Legislature: CONNIE SEOPOSENGWE (ANC).

NORTH-WEST

Premier: EDNA MOLEWA (ANC).

Speaker of the Legislature: THANDI MODISE (ANC).

WESTERN CAPE

Premier: EBRAHIM RASOOL (ANC).

Speaker of the Legislature: SHAUN BYNEVELDT (ANC).

Election Commission

Independent Electoral Commission: Election House, 260 Walker St, Sunnyside, Pretoria; tel. (12) 4285700; fax (12) 4285784; e-mail iec@elections.org.za; internet www.elections.org.za; f. 1996; Chair. Dr BRIGALIA BAM.

Political Organizations

A total of 21 parties contested the elections to the National Assembly in April 2004, while 37 parties presented candidates in the concurrent provincial elections.

African Christian Democratic Party (ACDP): Stats Building, 1st Floor, 2 Fore St, POB 1677, Alberton; tel. (11) 8693941; fax (11) 8693942; e-mail office@acdp.org.za; internet www.acdp.org.za; f. 1993; Leader Rev. KENNETH MESHOE.

African National Congress of South Africa (ANC): 54 Sauer St, Johannesburg 2001; POB 61884, Marshalltown 2107; tel. (11) 3761000; fax (11) 3761134; e-mail nmtyelwa@anc.org.za; internet www.anc.org.za; f. 1912; in alliance with the South African Communist Party (SACP) and the Congress of South African Trade Unions (COSATU); governing party since April 1994; Pres. THABO MBEKI; Deputy Pres. JACOB ZUMA; Sec.-Gen. KGALEMA MOTLANTHE.

Afrikaner Eenheidsbeweging (AEB) (Unity Movement): Pretoria; right-wing movement; Leader CASPERUS AUCAMP.

Afrikaner Weerstandsbeweging (AWB) (Afrikaner Resistance Movement): POB 274, Ventersdorp 2710, Johannesburg; tel. and fax (18) 2642516; e-mail awb@awb.co.za; internet www.awb.co.za; f. 1973; Afrikaner (Boer) nationalist group seeking self-determination for the Afrikaner people in South Africa; Leader EUGENE TERRE' BLANCHE.

Azanian People's Organization (AZAPO): 100 President St, 7th Floor, Balmoral House, Johannesburg 2001; POB 4230, Johannesburg 2000; tel. (11) 3363551; e-mail azapo@sn.apc.org; internet www.azapo.org.za; f. 1978; to seek the establishment of a unitary, democratic, socialist republic; excludes white mems; Pres. MOSIBLIDI MANGENA; Nat. Chair. ZITHULELE N. A. CINDI.

Blanke Bevrydingsbeweging (BBB) (White Protection Movement): f. 1987; extreme right-wing activist group; Leader Prof. JOHAN SCHABORT.

Boerestaat Party (Boer State Party): POB 3456, Randburg 2125; tel. and fax (11) 7081988; f. 1988; seeks the reinstatement of the Boer Republics in a consolidated Boerestaat; Leader COEN VERMAAK.

Cape Democrats: f. 1988; white support; liberal.

Democratic Alliance (DA): POB 15, Cape Town 8000; e-mail info@da.org.za; internet www.da.org.za; f. 2000 by opposition parties, incl. the Democratic Party, the Federal Alliance and the New National Party (NNP), to contest that year's municipal elections; NNP withdrew in late 2001; Leader HELEN ZILLE; Chair. JOE SEREMANE.

Democratic Reform Party (DRP): f. 1988; Coloured support; Leader CARTER EBRAHIM.

Democratic Workers' Party (DWP): Cape Town; f. 1984 by breakaway faction of the People's Congress Party; mainly Coloured support; Leader DENNIS DE LA CRUZ.

Freedom Front Plus (Vryheidsfront Plus—FF Plus/VF Plus): 203 Soutpansberg Ave, Rietondale, Pretoria; POB 74693, Lynnwood Ridge 0040; tel. (12) 3291220; fax (12) 3291229; e-mail info@vf.co.za; internet www.vf.co.za; f. 1994 as Freedom Front; name changed after incorporating the Conservative Party and Afrikaner Eenheidsbeweging in Sept. 2003; right-wing electoral alliance, incl. mems of the CPSA; Leader Dr PIETER W. A. MULDER; Sec.-Gen. Col (retd) PIET UYS.

Freedom Party: Coloured support; Leader ARTHUR BOOYSEN.

Herstigte Nasionale Party (HNP): 199 Neethling St, Eloffsdal, POB 1888, Pretoria 0001; tel. (12) 3358523; fax (12) 3358518; e-mail info@hnp.org.za; internet www.hnp.org.za; f. 1969 by fmr mems of the National Party; advocates 'Christian Nationalism'; Leader WILLEM MARAIS; Gen. Sec. LOUIS J. VAN DER SCHYFF.

Independent Democrats (ID): Rm 28, Marks Bldg, Parliament Plein St, POB 751, Cape Town 8000; tel. (21) 4038696; fax (21) 4032350; e-mail id@id.org.za; internet www.id.org.za; f. 2003; Leader PATRICIA DE LILLE.

Inkatha Freedom Party (IFP): Albany House North, 4th Floor, Albany Grove, POB 4432, Durban 4000; tel. (31) 3651300; fax (31) 3010252; internet www.ifp.org.za; f. as Inkatha Movement, liberation movement with mainly Zulu support; reorg. in 1990 as a multiracial political party; Leader Chief MANGOSUTHU GATSHA BUTHELEZI; Nat. Chair. L. P. H. M. MTSHALI; Sec.-Gen. M. ZAKHELE KHUMALO.

Justice and Freedom Alliance (JAFA): ME Store Bldg, 4th Floor, 155 Smit St, Johannesburg; Private Bag X49, Johannesburg; tel. (11) 3397129; fax (11) 3396982; f. 1997; CEO BARRY NILSSON; Sec.-Gen. A. DLOMO.

Minority Front: Law Society Bldg, Suite 17, Chancery Lane, Pietermaritzburg; tel. (33) 3557667; internet www.mf.org.za; f. 1993; Indian support; formed political alliance with the ANC in June 1999; Leader AMICHAND RAJBANSI.

New Freedom Party of Southern Africa: 15 Eendrag St, Bellville 7530; Coloured support.

New Solidarity: POB 48687, Qualbert 4078; tel. (11) 3055692; fax (11) 3011077; f. 1989; Indian support; Leader Dr J. N. REDDY.

Pan-Africanist Congress of Azania (PAC): Umoya House, 5th Floor, 2–6 cnr Rissik and New South Sts, Ghandi Sq., Johannesburg; POB 6010, Johannesburg 2000; tel. (11) 3372193; fax (11) 3376400; internet www.paca.org.za; f. 1959; Pres. Dr MOTSOKO PHEKO; Sec.-Gen. THAMI PLAATJIE.

Progressive Independent Party (PIP): Indian support; Leader FAIZ KHAN.

South African Communist Party (SACP): Cosatu House, 3rd Floor, 1 Leyds St, Braamfontein; POB 1027, Johannesburg 2000; tel. (11) 3393633; fax (11) 3396880; e-mail info@sacp.org.za; internet www.sacp.org.za; f. 1921; reorg. 1953; supports the ANC; Chair. GWEDE MANTASHE; Gen. Sec. BLADE NZIMANDE.

Transvaal Indian Congress: f. 1902; reactivated 1983; Pres. Dr ESSOP JASSAT.

United Christian Democratic Party (UCDP): POB 3010, Mmabatho; tel. (18) 3815691; fax (18) 3817346; e-mail ucdpheadoff@ucdp.org.za; internet www.ucdp.org.za; f. 1972 as the Bophuthatswana Nat. Party; name changed to Bophuthatswana Dem. Party in 1974; present name adopted in 1991; multiracial; Leader KGOSI L. M. MANGOPE; Sec.-Gen. M. N. MATLADI; Nat. Chair. I. SIPHO MFUNDISI.

United Democratic Movement: Tomkor Bldg, 2nd Floor, cnr Vermeulen and Du Toit Sts, Pretoria; POB 26290, Arcadia 0007; tel. (12) 3210010; fax (12) 3210014; e-mail research@udm.org.za; internet www.udm.org.za; f. 1997; multiracial support; demands effective measures for enforcement of law and order; Pres. BANTU HOLOMISA.

United Democratic Reform Party: POB 14048, Reigerpark 1466; f. 1987 by merger; mainly Coloured and Indian support; Leader JAKOBUS (JAC) ALBERT RABIE; Nat. Chair. NASH PARMANAND.

Workers' Organization for Socialist Action (WOSA): c/o University of Cape Town, Private Bag, Rondebosch 7701; e-mail nalexand@humanities.uct.ac.za; f. 1990; Trotskyist; Chair. Dr NEVILLE ALEXANDER; Gen. Sec. C. BRECHER.

Diplomatic Representation

EMBASSIES AND HIGH COMMISSIONS IN SOUTH AFRICA

Algeria: 950 Arcadia St, Hatfield, Pretoria 0083; POB 57480, Arcadia 0007; tel. (12) 3425074; fax (12) 3426479; Ambassador MOURAD BENCHEIKH.

Angola: 1030 Schoeman St, Hatfield, Pretoria 0083; POB 8685, Pretoria 0001; tel. (12) 3420049; fax (12) 3427039; Ambassador MIGUEL GASPAR FERNANDES NETO.

Argentina: 200 Standard Plaza, 440 Hilda St, Hatfield, Pretoria 0083; POB 11125, Pretoria 0028; tel. (12) 4303524; fax (12) 4303521; e-mail argembas@global.co.za; Ambassador CARLOS SERSALE DI CERISANO.

Australia: 292 Orient St, Pretoria; Private Bag X150, Pretoria 0001; tel. (12) 4236000; fax (12) 3428442; e-mail pretoria.info@dfat.gov.au; internet www.australia.co.za; High Commissioner PHILIP GREEN.

Austria: Momentum Office Park, 1109 Duncan St, Brooklyn, Pretoria 0181; POB 95572, Waterkloof 0145; tel. (12) 4529155; fax (12) 4601151; e-mail pretoria-ob@bmeia.gv.at; internet www.bmeia.gv.at/pretoria; Ambassador Dr HELMUT FREUDENSCHUSS.

Bangladesh: 410 Farenden St, Sunnyside, Pretoria 0002; tel. (12) 3432105; fax (12) 3435222; e-mail bangladeshpta@iburst.co.za; High Commissioner NASIMA HAIDER.

Belarus: 327 Hill St, Arcadia, Pretoria 0083; POB 4107, Pretoria 0001; tel. (12) 4307664; fax (12) 3426280; e-mail sa@belembassy.org; Ambassador Dr Anatoly Akhramchuk.

Belgium: 625 Leyds St, Muckleneuk, Pretoria 0002; tel. (12) 4403201; fax (12) 4403216; e-mail pretoria@diplobel.org; internet www.diplomatie.be/pretoria; Ambassador Jan Mutton.

Benin: 900 Park St, cnr Orient and Park Sts, Arcadia, Pretoria 0083; POB 26484, Arcadia 0007; tel. (12) 3426978; fax (12) 3421823; e-mail embbenin@yebo.co.za; Chargé d'affaires a.i. Pamphile C. Goutondji.

Bosnia and Herzegovina: 25 Stella St, Brooklyn, Pretoria 0181; POB 11464, Hatfield 0028; tel. (12) 3465547; fax (12) 3462295; e-mail bih@mweb.co.za; Ambassador Dragan Pjević.

Botswana: 24 Amos St, Colbyn, Pretoria 0083; POB 57035, Arcadia 0007; tel. (12) 4309640; fax (12) 3421845; High Commissioner Motlhware Kgori James Masisi.

Brazil: Hillcrest Office Park, Woodpecker Pl., 1st Floor, 177 Dyer Rd, Hillcrest, Pretoria 0083; POB 3269, Pretoria 0001; tel. (12) 3665200; fax (12) 3665299; e-mail pretoria@brazilianembassy.org.za; internet www.brazilianembassy.org.za; Ambassador Lucio Amorim.

Bulgaria: 1071 Church St, Hatfield, Pretoria 0083; POB 29296, Arcadia 0007; tel. (12) 3423720; fax (12) 3423721; e-mail embulgsa@iafrica.com; internet www.bulgarianembassy.co.za; Ambassador V. C. Neykov.

Burundi: 20 Glyn St, Colbyn, Pretoria 0083; POB 12914, Hatfield 0028; tel. (12) 3424881; fax (12) 3424885; Ambassador Patrice Rwimo.

Cameroon: 924 Pretorius St, Arcadia 0083; POB 13790, Hatfield 0028; tel. (12) 3624731; fax (12) 3624732; e-mail hicocam@cameroon.co.za; High Commissioner Njoteh Albert Fobatong (acting).

Canada: 1103 Arcadia St, cnr Hilda St, Hatfield, Pretoria 0083; Private Bag X13, Hatfield 0028; tel. (12) 4223000; fax (12) 4223052; e-mail pret@international.gc.ca; internet www.dfait-maeci.gc.ca/southafrica/menu-en.asp; High Commissioner Ruth Archibald.

Chile: Brooklyn Gardens, cnr Veale St and Middle St, Block B, 1st Floor, New Muckleneuk, Pretoria; POB 2449, Brooklyn Sq. 0075; tel. (12) 4608090; fax (12) 4608093; e-mail chile@iafrica.com; internet www.embchile.co.za; Ambassador Claudio E. Herrera Alamos.

China, People's Republic: 965 Church St, Arcadia, Pretoria 0083; POB 95764, Waterkloof 0145; tel. (12) 3424194; fax (12) 3424154; e-mail reception@chinese-embassy.org.za; internet www.chinese-embassy.org.za; Ambassador Zhong Jianhua.

Colombia: 1105 Park St, 3rd Floor, Hatfield, Pretoria 0083; POB 12791, Hatfield 0028; tel. (12) 3420211; fax (12) 3420216; e-mail info@embassyofcolombia.co.za; Ambassador Carlos Moreño de Caro.

Congo, Democratic Republic: 791 Schoeman St, Arcadia, Pretoria 0083; POB 28795, Sunnyside 0132; tel. (12) 3441478; fax (12) 3441510; e-mail rdcongo@lantic.net; Ambassador Bene M'Poko.

Congo, Republic: 960 Arcadia St, Arcadia, Pretoria 0083; POB 40427, Arcadia 0007; tel. (12) 3425508; fax (12) 3425510; Ambassador Roger Issombo.

Côte d'Ivoire: 795 Government Ave, Arcadia, Pretoria 0083; POB 13510, Hatfield 0028; tel. (12) 3426913; fax (12) 3426713; Ambassador Boubakar Kone.

Croatia: 1160 Church St, Colbyn, Pretoria 0083; POB 11335, Hatfield 0028; tel. (12) 3421206; fax (12) 3421819; Ambassador Ivan Picukarić.

Cuba: 45 Mackenzie St, Brooklyn, Pretoria 0181; POB 11605, Hatfield 0028; tel. (12) 3462215; fax (12) 3462216; e-mail sudafri@iafrica.com; Ambassador Esther Armenteros Cárdenas.

Cyprus: cnr Church St and Hill St, Arcadia, Pretoria 0083; POB 14554, Hatfield 0028; tel. (12) 3425258; fax (12) 3425596; e-mail cyprusjb@mweb.co.za; High Commissioner Costa Leontiou.

Czech Republic: 936 Pretorius St, Arcadia, Pretoria 0083; POB 13671, Hatfield 0028; tel. (12) 4312380; fax (12) 4302033; e-mail pretoria@embassymzv.cz; Ambassador Jaroslav Siro.

Denmark: iParioli Office Park, Block B2, Ground Floor, 1166 Park St, Hatfield, Pretoria; POB 11439, Hatfield 0028; tel. (12) 4309340; fax (12) 3427620; e-mail pryamb@um.dk; internet www.ambpretoria.um.dk; Ambassador Dan E. Frederiksen.

Egypt: 270 Bourke St, Muckleneuk, Pretoria 0002; POB 30025, Sunnyside 0132; tel. (12) 3431590; fax (12) 3431082; e-mail egyptemb@global.co.za; Ambassador Mona Omar Muhammad Attia.

Equatorial Guinea: 48 Florence St, Colbyn, Pretoria; POB 12720, Hatfield 0028; tel. (12) 3429945; fax (12) 3427250; Ambassador Juan Antonio Bibang Nchuchuma.

Eritrea: 1281 Cobham Rd, Queenswood, Pretoria 0186; POB 11371, Queenswood 0121; tel. (12) 3331302; fax (12) 3332330; e-mail eremb@lantic.net; Ambassador Tesfamicael Gerahtu Ogbaghiorghis.

Ethiopia: 47 Charles St, Bailey's Muckleneuk, Brooklyn 0181; POB 11469, Hatfield 0028; tel. (12) 3463542; fax (12) 3463867; e-mail ethiopia@sentechsa.com; Ambassador Melese Marimo Marasso.

Finland: 628 Leyds St, Muckleneuk, Pretoria 0002; POB 443, Pretoria 0001; tel. (12) 3430275; fax (12) 3433095; e-mail sanomat.pre@formin.fi; internet www.finland.org.za; Ambassador Heikki Tuunanen.

France: 250 Melk St, cnr Melk and Middle Sts, New Muckleneuk, Pretoria 0181; tel. (12) 4251600; fax (12) 4251689; e-mail france@ambafrance-rsa.org; internet www.ambafrance-rsa.org; Ambassador Denis Pietton.

Gabon: 921 Schoeman St, Arcadia, Pretoria 0083; POB 9222, Pretoria 0001; tel. (12) 3424376; fax (12) 3424375; e-mail embagarsap@telkomsa.net; Ambassador Marcel-Jules Odongui-Bonnard.

Germany: 180 Blackwood St, Arcadia, Pretoria 0083; POB 2023, Pretoria 0001; tel. (12) 4278900; fax (12) 3433606; e-mail GermanEmbassyPretoria@gonet.co.za; internet www.pretoria.diplo.de; Ambassador Dieter Walter Haller.

Ghana: 1038 Arcadia St, Hatfield, Pretoria 0083; POB 12537, Hatfield 0028; tel. (12) 3425847; fax (12) 3425863; High Commissioner J. B. Heymann.

Greece: 1003 Church St, Arcadia, Pretoria 0083; tel. (12) 3427136; fax (12) 4304313; e-mail embgrsaf@global.co.za; Ambassador Aristidis Sandis.

Guinea: 336 Orient St, Arcadia, Pretoria 0083; POB 13523, Hatfield 0028; tel. (12) 3420893; fax (12) 3427348; e-mail embaguinea@iafrica.com; Ambassador Alexandre Cécé Loua.

Haiti: 808 George St, Arcadia, Pretoria 0007; POB 14362, Hatfield 0028; tel. (12) 4307560; fax (12) 3427042; Ambassador Yolette Azor-Charles.

Holy See: 800 Pretorius St, Arcadia, Pretoria 0083; POB 26017, Arcadia 0007; tel. (12) 3443815; fax (12) 3443595; e-mail nunziosa@iafrica.com; Apostolic Nuncio Most Rev. James Patrick Green.

Hungary: 959 Arcadia St, Hatfield, Pretoria 0083; POB 13843, Hatfield 0028; tel. (12) 4303020; fax (12) 4303029; e-mail huembprt@mweb.co.za; Ambassador András Dallos.

Iceland: iParioli Office Park, Phase II, Block A2, 1166 Park St, Pretoria; POB 14325 Hatfield 0028; tel. (12) 3425885; fax (12) 3420883; e-mail emb.pretoria@mfa.is; internet www.iceland.org/za; Ambassador Dr Sigridur Duna Kristmundsdottir.

India: 852 Schoeman St, Arcadia, Pretoria 0083; POB 40216, Arcadia 0007; tel. (12) 3425392; fax (12) 3425310; e-mail polinf@hicomind.co.za; High Commissioner R. K. Bhatia.

Indonesia: 949 Schoeman St, Arcadia, Pretoria 0083; POB 13155, Hatfield 0028; tel. (12) 3423350; fax (12) 3423369; e-mail fpanggabean@indonesia-pretoria.org.za; internet www.indonesia-pretoria.org.za; Ambassador Sugeng Rahardjo.

Iran: 1002 Schoeman St, Hatfield, Pretoria 0083; POB 12546, Hatfield 0083; tel. (12) 3425880; fax (12) 3421878; internet www.iranembassy.org.za; Ambassador Mohammad Ali Ghanezadeh.

Iraq: 803 Duncan St, Brooklyn 0181, Pretoria; POB 11089, Hatfield 0028; tel. (12) 3622048; fax (12) 3622027; Ambassador Qasim Abdlbaqi Shakir.

Ireland: Southern Life Plaza, 1st Floor, 1059 Schoeman St, cnr Festival and Schoeman Sts, Arcadia, Pretoria 0083; POB 4174, Arcadia 0001; tel. (12) 3425062; fax (12) 3424752; e-mail pretoria@dfa.ie; internet www.embassyireland.org.za; Ambassador Colin Wrafter.

Israel: 428 King's Hwy, Elizabeth Grove St, Lynnwood, Pretoria; POB 3726, Pretoria 0001; tel. (12) 3480470; fax (12) 3488594; e-mail operator@pretoria.mfa.gov.il; internet pretoria.mfa.gov.il; Ambassador Ilan Baruch.

Italy: 796 George Ave, Arcadia, Pretoria 0083; tel. (12) 4230000; fax (12) 4305547; e-mail segreteria.pretoria@esteri.it; internet www.ambpretoria.esteri.it; Ambassador Alessandro Cevese.

Japan: 259 Baines St, cnr Frans Oerder St, Groenkloof, Pretoria 0181; Private Bag X999, Pretoria 0001; tel. (12) 4521500; fax (12) 4603800; e-mail info@embjapan.org.za; internet www.japan.org.za; Ambassador Akihiko Furuya.

Jordan: 252 Olivier St, Brooklyn, Pretoria 0075; POB 14730, Hatfield 0028; tel. (12) 346861517; fax (12) 3468611; e-mail embjordpta@telkomsa.net; Ambassador Dr Mazen Izzedine Tal.

Kenya: 302 Brooks St, Menlo Park, Pretoria 0081; POB 35954, Menlo Park 0012; tel. (12) 3622249; fax (12) 3622252; e-mail info@kenya.org.za; High Commissioner Tabitha J. Seii.

Korea, Democratic People's Republic: 958 Waterpoort St, Faerie Glen, Pretoria; POB 1238, Garsfontein 0042; tel. (12) 9918661; fax (12) 9918662; e-mail dprkembassy@lantic.net; Ambassador An Hui Jong.

Korea, Republic: Greenpark Estates, Bldg 3, 27 George Storrar Dr., Groenkloof, Pretoria 0081; POB 939, Groenkloof 0027; tel. (12) 4602508; fax (12) 4601158; Ambassador KIM KYUN-SEOP.

Kuwait: 890 Arcadia St, Arcadia, Pretoria 0083; Private Bag X920, Pretoria 0001; tel. (12) 3420877; fax (12) 3420876; e-mail safarku@global.co.za; Ambassador SALEM AL-ZAMANAN.

Lebanon: 290 Lawley St, Waterkloof, Pretoria 0081; POB 941, Groenkloof 0027; tel. (12) 3467020; fax (12) 3467022; Ambassador MICHEL KATRA.

Lesotho: 391 Anderson St, Menlo Park, Pretoria 0081; POB 55817, Arcadia 0007; tel. (12) 4607648; fax (12) 4607469; High Commissioner MOSUOE CHARLES MOTEANE.

Liberia: Infotech Bldg, Suite 105/113, 1090 Arcadia St, Hatfield, Pretoria 0083; POB 25917, Monument Park 0105; tel. (12) 3460880; fax (12) 3468006; Chargé d'affaires B. S. COLLINS.

Libya: 900 Church St, Arcadia, Pretoria 0083; POB 40388, Arcadia 0007; tel. (12) 3423902; fax (12) 3423904; Ambassador Dr ABDULLAH ABDUSSALAM AL-ZUBEDI.

Madagascar: 90B Tait St, Colbyn, Pretoria; POB 11722, Queenswood 0121; tel. (12) 3420983; fax (12) 3420995; e-mail consul@infodoor.co.za; Ambassador (vacant).

Malawi: 770 Government Ave, Arcadia, Pretoria 0083; POB 11172, Hatfield 0028; tel. and fax (12) 3421759; High Commissioner MICHAEL KAMPHAMBE-NKHOMA.

Malaysia: 1007 Schoeman St, Arcadia, Pretoria 0083; POB 11673, Hatfield 0028; tel. (12) 3425990; fax (12) 4307773; High Commissioner YAHAYA BIN ABDUL JABAR.

Mali: 876 Pretorius St, Arcadia 0083; POB 12978, Hatfield, Pretoria 0028; tel. (12) 3427464; fax (12) 3420670; Ambassador SINALY COULIBALY.

Mauritius: 1163 Pretorius St, Hatfield, Pretoria 0083; tel. (12) 3421283; fax (12) 3421286; e-mail mhcpta@mweb.co.za; High Commissioner MOHAMED ISMAEL DOSSA.

Mexico: 1 Hatfield Sq., 3rd Floor, 1101 Burnett St, Hatfield, Pretoria 0083; POB 9077, Pretoria 0001; tel. (12) 3622822; fax (12) 3621380; e-mail embamexza@mweb.co.za; Ambassador (vacant).

Morocco: 799 Schoeman St, cnr Farenden St, Arcadia, Pretoria 0083; POB 12382, Hatfield 0028; tel. (12) 3430230; fax (12) 3430613; e-mail sifmapre@mwebbiz.co.za; Chargé d'affaires HABIB DEFOUAD.

Mozambique: 529 Edmund St, Arcadia, Pretoria 0083; POB 40750, Arcadia 0007; tel. (12) 4010300; fax (12) 3266388; High Commissioner FERNANDO ANDRADE FAZENDA.

Myanmar: 201 Leyds St, Arcadia, Pretoria 0083; POB 12121, Queenswood 0121; tel. (12) 3415207; fax (12) 3413867; e-mail euompta@global.co.za; Ambassador U OHN THWIN.

Namibia: 197 Blackwood St, Arcadia, Pretoria 0083; POB 29806, Sunnyside 0132; tel. (12) 4819100; fax (12) 3445998; e-mail secretary@namibia.org.za; High Commissioner PHILEMON KAMBALA.

Netherlands: 825 Arcadia St, Arcadia, Pretoria 0083; POB 117, Pretoria 0001; tel. (12) 3443910; fax (12) 3439950; internet www.dutchembassy.co.za; Ambassador FRANS A. ENGERING.

New Zealand: Block C, Hatfield Gardens, 1110 Arcadia St, Hatfield, Pretoria 0083; Private Bag X17, Hatfield 0028; tel. (12) 3428656; fax (12) 3428640; e-mail enquiries@nzhc.co.za; internet www.nzhc.co.za; High Commissioner MALCOLM MCGOUN.

Nigeria: 971 Schoeman St, Arcadia, Pretoria 0083; POB 27332, Sunnyside 0132; tel. (12) 3420805; fax (12) 3421668; High Commissioner Dr OLUGBENGA AYODEJI ASHIRU.

Norway: iParioli Bldg, A2, 1166 Park St, Hatfield, Pretoria 0083; POB 11612, Hatfield 0028; tel. (12) 3426100; fax (12) 3426099; e-mail emb.pretoria@mfa.no; internet www.norway.org.za; Ambassador OVE THORSHEIM.

Oman: 42 Nicholson St, Muckleneuk, Pretoria 0081; POB 2650, Brooklyn 0075; tel. (12) 3460808; fax (12) 3461660; e-mail sult-oman@telkom.net; Chargé d'affaires a.i. FAKHRI MOHAMMED SAID AL-SAID.

Pakistan: 312 Brooks St, Menlo Park, Pretoria 0181; POB 11803, Hatfield 0028; tel. (12) 3624072; fax (12) 3623967; e-mail pareppretoria@worldonline.co.za; High Commissioner ASHRAF QURESHI.

Paraguay: 189 Strelitzia Rd, Waterkloof Heights, Pretoria 0181; POB 95774, Waterkloof 0145; tel. (12) 3471047; fax (12) 3470403; Chargé d'affaires a.i. ARNALDO R. SALAZAR.

Peru: Infotech Bldg, Suite 202, 1090 Arcadia St, Hatfield, Pretoria 0083; POB 907, Groenkloof 0027; tel. (12) 3422390; fax (12) 3424944; Ambassador FÉLIX CÉSAR CALDERÓN.

Philippines: 54 Nicholson St, Muckleneuk, 0181 Pretoria; POB 2562, Brooklyn Sq. 0075; tel. (12) 3460451; fax (12) 3460454; e-mail pretoriape@mweb.co.za; internet mzone.mweb.co.za/residents/pretoriape/; Ambassador VIRGILIO A. REYES, Jr.

Poland: 14 Amos St, Colbyn, Pretoria 0083; POB 12277, Queenswood 0121; tel. (12) 4302621; fax (12) 4302608; e-mail amb.pol@pixie.co.za; Ambassador ROMUALD SZUNIEWICZ.

Portugal: 599 Leyds St, Muckleneuk, Pretoria 0002; POB 27102, Sunnyside 0132; tel. (12) 3412340; fax (12) 3413975; e-mail portemb@global.co.za; Ambassador PAULO COUTO BARBOSA.

Qatar: 355 Charles St, Waterkloof, Pretoria 0181; Private Bag X13, Brooklyn Sq. 0075; tel. (12) 4521700; fax (12) 3466732; e-mail qatar-emb@lantic.net; Ambassador ZAYED RASHED AL-NAEMI.

Romania: 117 Charles St, Brooklyn, Pretoria 0181; POB 11295, Hatfield 0028; tel. (12) 4606940; fax (12) 4606947; e-mail romembsa@global.co.za; Ambassador VALER GABRIEL PAUL POTRA.

Russia: 316 Brooks St, Menlo Park, Pretoria 0081; POB 6743, Pretoria 0001; tel. (12) 3621337; fax (12) 3620116; e-mail ruspospr@mweb.co.za; internet www.russianembassy.org.za; Ambassador ANATOLY A. MAKAROV.

Rwanda: 983 Schoeman St, Arcadia, Pretoria; POB 55224, Arcadia 0007; tel. (12) 3426536; fax (12) 3427106; e-mail ambapretoria@minaffet.gov.rw; Ambassador JAMES KIMONYO.

Saudi Arabia: 711 Duncan St, cnr Lunnon St, Hatfield, Pretoria 0083; POB 13930, Hatfield 0028; tel. (12) 3624230; fax (12) 3624239; Ambassador Dr ABDULLAH KHOUJ.

Senegal: Charles Manor, 57 Charles St, Baileys Muckleneuk, Pretoria 0181; POB 2948, Brooklyn Sq. 0075; tel. (12) 4605263; fax (12) 3465550; e-mail ambassenepta@telkomsa.za; Ambassador MAÏMOUNA DIOP SY.

Serbia: 163 Marais St, Brooklyn, Pretoria; POB 13026, Hatfield 0028; tel. (12) 4605626; fax (12) 4606003; e-mail info@scgembassy.org.za; internet www.scgembassy.org.za; Ambassador JOVAN MARIĆ.

Singapore: 980 Schoeman St, Arcadia, Pretoria 0083; POB 11809, Hatfield 0028; tel. (12) 4306035; fax (12) 3424425; e-mail sporehc@mweb.co.za; High Commissioner MOHIDEEN P. H. RUBIN.

Slovakia: 930 Arcadia St, Pretoria 0083; POB 12736, Hatfield 0028; tel. (12) 3422051; fax (12) 3423688; e-mail slovakemb@telkomsa.net; internet www.mfa.sk/zu; Ambassador PAVOL IVAN.

Spain: 337 Brooklyn Rd, Menlo Park, Pretoria 0181; POB 1633, Pretoria 0001; tel. (12) 4600123; fax (12) 4602207; e-mail emb.pretoria@mae.es; Ambassador RAMÓN GIL-CASARAES SATRÚSTEGUI.

Sri Lanka: 410 Alexander St, Brooklyn, Pretoria 0181; tel. (12) 4607690; fax (12) 4607702; e-mail srilanka@global.co.za; internet www.srilanka.co.za; High Commissioner A. RAJAKARUNA.

Sudan: 1203 Pretorius St, Hatfield, Pretoria 0083; POB 25513, Monument Park 0105; tel. (12) 3424538; fax (12) 3424539; internet www.sudani.co.za; Ambassador KUOL ALOR.

Swaziland: 715 Government Ave, Arcadia, Pretoria 0007; POB 14294, Hatfield 0028; tel. (12) 3441910; fax (12) 3430455; High Commissioner PHILLIP NHLANHLA MUNTU MSWANE.

Sweden: iParioli Bldg, 1166 Park St, Hatfield, Pretoria 0028; POB 13477, Hatfield 0028; tel. (12) 4266400; fax (12) 4266464; e-mail sweden@iafrica.com; internet www.swedenabroad.com/Sydafrika; Ambassador ANDERS MÖLLANDER.

Switzerland: 225 Veale St, Parc Nouveau, New Muckleneuk, Pretoria 0181; POB 2508, Brooklyn Sq. 0075; tel. (12) 4520660; fax (12) 3466605; e-mail vertretung@pre.rep.admin.ch; internet www.swissembassy.co.za; Ambassador VIKTOR CHRISTEN.

Syria: 963 Schoeman St, Arcadia, Pretoria 0083; POB 12830, Hatfield 0028; tel. (12) 3424701; fax (12) 3424702; e-mail syriaemb@telkomsa.net; Chargé d'affaires a.i. Dr M. KHODUR.

Tanzania: 822 George Ave, Arcadia, Pretoria 0007; POB 56572, Arcadia 0007; tel. (12) 3424393; fax (12) 4304383; e-mail thc@tanzania.org.za; internet www.tanzania.org.za; High Commissioner EMMANUEL A. MWAMBULUKUTU.

Thailand: 428 cnr Hill and Pretorius Sts, Arcadia, Pretoria 0028; POB 12080, Hatfield 0083; tel. (12) 3424600; fax (12) 3424805; e-mail info@thaiembassy.co.za; internet www.thaiembassy.co.za; Ambassador DOMEDEJ BUNNAG.

Tunisia: 850 Church St, Arcadia, Pretoria 0083; POB 56535, Arcadia 0007; tel. (12) 3426282; fax (12) 3426284; Ambassador ALI GOUTALI.

Turkey: 1067 Church St, Hatfield, Pretoria 0083; POB 56014, Arcadia 0007; tel. (12) 3426055; fax (12) 3426052; e-mail pretbe@global.co.za; internet www.turkishembassy.co.za; Ambassador FERHAT ATAMAN.

Uganda: 882 Church St, Pretoria 0083; POB 12442, Hatfield 0083; tel. (12) 3426031; fax (12) 3426206; e-mail ugacomer@mweb.co.za; High Commissioner KWERONDA RUHEMBA.

Ukraine: 398 Marais St, Brooklyn, Pretoria 0181; POB 36463, Menlo Park 0102; tel. (12) 4601943; fax (12) 4601944; e-mail emb_za@mfa.gov.ua; Ambassador MYKHAYLO V. SKURATOVSKYI.

United Arab Emirates: 992 Arcadia St, Arcadia, Pretoria 0083; POB 57090, Arcadia 0007; tel. (12) 3427736; fax (12) 3427738; e-mail uae@mweb.co.za; Ambassador ISMAEL OBAID YUSUF AL-ALI.

United Kingdom: 255 Hill St, Arcadia, Pretoria 0002; tel. (12) 4217500; fax (12) 4217555; e-mail media.pretoria@fco.gov.uk; internet www.britain.org.za; High Commissioner PAUL BOATENG.

USA: 877 Pretorius St, Arcadia, Pretoria 0083; POB 9536, Pretoria 0001; tel. (12) 4314000; fax (12) 3422299; e-mail embassypretoria@state.gov; internet southafrica.usembassy.gov; Ambassador ERIC M. BOST.

Uruguay: 301 MIB House, 3rd Floor, Hatfield Sq., 1119 Burnett St, Hatfield, Pretoria 0083; POB 3247, Pretoria 0001; tel. (12) 3626521; fax (12) 3626523; Ambassador GUILLERMO JOSÉ POMI BARIOLA.

Venezuela: Hatfield Gables South Bldg, 1st Floor, Suite 4, 474 Hilda St, Pretoria 0083; POB 11821, Hatfield 0028; tel. (12) 3626593; fax (12) 3626591; e-mail embasudaf@icon.co.za; Ambassador ANTONIO MONTILLA-SALDIVIA.

Viet Nam: 87 Brooks St, Brooklyn, Pretoria 0181; POB 13692, Hatfield 0028; tel. (12) 3628119; fax (12) 3628115; e-mail embassy@vietnam.co.za; Ambassador Dr TRAN DUY THI.

Yemen: 329 Main St, Waterkloof 0181; POB 13343, Hatfield 0028; tel. (12) 4250760; fax (12) 4250762; e-mail info@yemenembassy.org.za; internet www.yemenembassy.org.za; Chargé d'affaires a.i. MOHAMED JAMIL MUHARRAM.

Zambia: 570 Ziervogel St, Arcadia, Pretoria 0083; POB 12234, Hatfield 0028; tel. (12) 3261854; fax (12) 3262140; High Commissioner LESLIE SAINOT MBULA.

Zimbabwe: Zimbabwe House, 798 Merton St, Arcadia, Pretoria 0083; POB 55140, Arcadia 0007; tel. (12) 3425125; fax (12) 3425126; Ambassador SIMON KHAYA MOYO.

Judicial System

The common law of the Republic of South Africa is the Roman-Dutch law, the uncodified law of Holland as it was at the time of the secession of the Cape of Good Hope in 1806. The law of England is not recognized as authoritative, although the principles of English law have been introduced in relation to civil and criminal procedure, evidence and mercantile matters.

The Constitutional Court, situated in Johannesburg, consists of a Chief Justice, a Deputy Chief Justice and nine other justices. Its task is to ensure that the executive, legislative and judicial organs of government adhere to the provisions of the Constitution. It has the power to reverse legislation that has been adopted by Parliament. The Supreme Court of Appeal, situated in Bloemfontein, comprises a President, a Deputy President and a number of judges of appeal, and is the highest court in all but constitutional matters. There are also High Courts and Magistrates' Courts. A National Director of Public Prosecutions is the head of the prosecuting authority and is appointed by the President of the Republic. A Judicial Service Commission makes recommendations regarding the appointment of judges and advises central and provincial government on all matters relating to the judiciary.

THE SUPREME COURT OF APPEAL

President: CRAIG HOWIE.

THE CONSTITUTIONAL COURT

Chief Justice: PIUS N. LANGA.

Religion

Some 80% of the population profess the Christian faith. Other religions that are represented are Hinduism, Islam, Judaism and traditional African religions.

CHRISTIANITY

At mid-2000 there were an estimated 12.4m. Protestants and 18.7m. adherents of other forms of Christianity.

South African Council of Churches: POB 62098, Marshalltown 2107; tel. (11) 2417817; fax (11) 8384818; e-mail tmm@sacc.org.za; internet www.sacc.org.za; f. 1968; 26 mem. churches; Pres. Prof. RUSSEL BOTMAN; Gen. Sec. EDDIE MAKUE.

The Anglican Communion

Most Anglicans in South Africa are adherents of the Church of the Province of Southern Africa, comprising 26 dioceses (including Angola, Lesotho, Namibia, St Helena, Swaziland and two dioceses in Mozambique). The Church had an estimated 4.5m. communicant members at mid-2006.

Archbishop of Cape Town and Metropolitan of the Province of Southern Africa: Most Rev. NJONGONKULU WINSTON HUGH NDUNGANE, 20 Bishopscourt Dr., Bishopscourt, Claremont, Cape Town 7700; tel. (21) 7612531; fax (21) 7614193; e-mail archbish@bishopscourt-cpsa.org.za; internet www.cpsa.org.za.

The Dutch Reformed Church (Nederduitse Gereformeerde Kerk–NGK)

In 2005/06, including confirmed and baptized members, the Dutch Reformed Churches in South Africa consisted of: the Dutch Reformed Church, with 1,155,001 (mainly white) members; the Uniting Reformed Church, with 1,039,606 (mainly Coloured and black) members; the Reformed Church in Africa, with 1,708 Indian members; and the Dutch Reformed Church in Africa, with an estimated 150,000 (mainly black) members. All congregations were desegregated in 1986.

General Synod: POB 13528, Hatfield, Pretoria 0028; tel. (12) 3420092; fax (12) 3420380; e-mail algemenesinode@ngkerk.org.za; internet www.ngkerk.org.za; Moderator Prof. PIET STRAUSS; Gen. Sec. Dr KOBUS GERBER.

The Lutheran Churches

Lutheran Communion in Southern Africa (LUCSA): POB 7170, Bonaero Park 1622; tel. (11) 9731873; fax (11) 3951615; e-mail info@lucsa.org; f. 1991; co-ordinating org. for the Lutheran churches in southern Africa, incl. Angola, Botswana, Malawi, Mozambique, Namibia, South Africa, Swaziland, Zambia and Zimbabwe; 1,618,720 mems (1999); Pres. Bishop C. K. MOENGA; Exec. Dir Bishop Dr A. MOYO.

Evangelical Lutheran Church in Southern Africa (ELCSA): POB 7231, 1622 Bonaero Park; tel. (11) 9731853; fax (11) 3951888; e-mail elcsaadmin@mweb.co.za; f. 1975 by merger of four non-white churches; Pres. Bishop LOUIS SIBIYA; 624,567 mems.

Evangelical Lutheran Church in Southern Africa (Cape Church): POB 3466, 7602 Matieland; tel. (21) 8869747; fax (21) 8869748; e-mail rohwernj@adept.co.za; Pres. Bishop NILS ROHWER; 4,108 mems.

Evangelical Lutheran Church in Southern Africa (N-T): Church Council, 24 Geldenhuys Rd, Bonaero Park, Johannesburg; POB 7095, Bonaero Park 1622; tel. (11) 9731851; fax (11) 3951862; e-mail elksant@elksant.co.za; internet www.elcsant.org.za; f. 1981; Pres. Bishop DIETER R. LILJE; 9,800 mems (2006).

Moravian Church in Southern Africa: POB 24111, Lansdowne 7779; tel. (21) 7614030; fax (21) 7614046; e-mail mcsa@iafrica.com; f. 1737; Pres. ANGELENE H. SWART; 100,000 mems (2002).

The Roman Catholic Church

South Africa comprises four archdioceses, 21 dioceses and one Apostolic Vicariate. At 31 December 2004 there were an estimated 3,139,115 adherents in the country, representing about 6.5% of the total population.

Southern African Catholic Bishops' Conference (SACBC)
Khanya House, 399 Paul Kruger St, Pretoria 0002; POB 941, Pretoria 0001; tel. (12) 3236458; fax (12) 3266218; internet www.sacbc.org.za.

f. 1947mems representing South Africa, Botswana and Swaziland; Pres. Cardinal WILFRID NAPIER (Archbishop of Durban; until Jan. 2007); Pres. Archbishop BUTI TLHAGALE (Bishop of Johannesburg; from Jan. 2007); Sec.-Gen. Fr RICHARD MENATSI.

Archbishop of Bloemfontein: JABULANI ADATUS NXUMALO, Archbishop's House, 7A Whites Rd, Bloemfontein 9301; POB 362, Bloemfontein 9300; tel. (51) 4481658; fax (51) 4472420; e-mail bfnarch@mweb.co.za.

Archbishop of Cape Town: Most Rev. LAWRENCE HENRY, Cathedral Place, 12 Bouquet St, Cape Town 8001; POB 2910, Cape Town 8000; tel. (21) 4622417; fax (21) 4619330; e-mail archbishop@catholic-ct.co.za; internet www.catholic-ct.co.za.

Archbishop of Durban: Cardinal WILFRID NAPIER, Archbishop's House, 154 Gordon Rd, Durban 4001; POB 47489, Greyville 4023; tel. (31) 3031417; fax (31) 3121848; e-mail chancery@catholic-dbn.org.za.

Archbishop of Pretoria: Most Rev. GEORGE FRANCIS DANIEL, Jolivet House, 140 Visagie St, Pretoria 0002; POB 8149, Pretoria 0001; tel. (12) 3265311; fax (12) 3253994; e-mail ptadiocese@absamail.co.za.

Other Christian Churches

In addition to the following Churches, there are a large number of Pentecostalist groups, and more than 4,000 independent African Churches.

African Gospel Church: POB 32312, 4060 Mobeni; tel. (31) 9074377; Moderator Rev. F. D. Mkhize; Gen. Sec. O. Mtolo; 100,000 mems.

Afrikaanse Protestantse Kerk (Afrikaans Protestant Church): POB 11488, Hatfield 0028; tel. (12) 3621390; fax (12) 3622023; f. 1987 by fmr mems of the Dutch Reformed Church (Nederduitse Gereformeerde Kerk) in protest at the desegregation of church congregations; c. 46,400 mems.

Apostolic Faith Mission of South Africa: POB 890197, 2106 Lyndhurst; tel. (11) 7868550; fax (11) 8871182; e-mail afmgens@mweb.co.za; f. 1908; Gen. Sec. Pastor M. G. Mahlabo; 136,000 mems.

Assemblies of God: POB 51065, Musgrave 4062; tel. (31) 231341; fax (31) 231342; f. 1915; Chair. Rev. Isaac Hleta; Gen. Sec. Rev. C. P. Watt; 300,000 mems.

Baptist Union of Southern Africa: Private Bag X45, Wilropark 1731; tel. (11) 7685980; fax (11) 7685983; f. 1877; Pres. Rev. Stephen Mann; Gen. Sec. Rev. Angelo Scheepers; 51,769 mems (2004).

Black Dutch Reformed Church: POB 137, Bergvlei 2012; Leader Rev. Sam Buti; c. 1m. mems.

Church of England in South Africa: POB 2180 Clareinch 7740; tel. (21) 6717070; fax (21) 6712553; e-mail cameronb@cesa.org.za; internet www.cesa.org.za; Bishop Rt Rev. F. Retief (presiding), Bishop Rt Rev. M. Morrison, Bishop Rt Rev. Dr W. Cole-Edwardes, Bishop Rt Rev. D. Inglesby; 207 churches.

Evangelical Presbyterian Church in South Africa: POB 31961, Braamfontein 2017; tel. (11) 3391044; Gen. Sec. Rev. J. S. Ngobe; Treas. Rev. H. D. Masangu; 60,000 mems.

The Methodist Church of Southern Africa: Methodist Connexional Office, POB 50216, Musgrave 4062; tel. (31) 2024214; fax (31) 2017674; internet www.users.club.co.za/mco; f. 1883; Pres. Bishop I. M. Abrahams; Sec. Rev. Ross A. J. Oliver; 696,353 mems.

Nederduitsch Hervormde Kerk van Afrika: POB 2368, Pretoria 0001; tel. (12) 3228885; fax (12) 3227907; internet www.nhk.co.za; e-mail fanie@nhk.co.za; Gen. Sec. Dr S. P. Pretorius; 193,561 mems.

Nederduitse Gereformeerde Kerk in Afrika: Portland Pl., 37 Jorissen St, 2017 Johannesburg; tel. (11) 4031027; 6 synods (incl. 1 in Swaziland); Moderator Rev. S. P. E. Buti; Gen. Sec. W. Raath; 350,370 mems.

Presbyterian Church of Africa: POB 54840, Umlazi 4031; tel. (31) 9072366; f. 1898; 8 presbyteries (incl. 1 in Malawi and 1 in Zimbabwe); Chief Clerk Rev. S. A. Khumalo; 1,231,000 mems.

Reformed Church in South Africa (Die Gereformeerde Kerke): POB 20002, Noordbrug 2522, Potchefstroom; tel. (148) 2973986; fax (148) 2931042; f. 1859; Prin. Officer Dr C. J. Smit; 158,973 mems.

Seventh-day Adventist Church: POB 468, Bloemfontein 9300; tel. (51) 4478271; fax (41) 4488059; e-mail sau.president@adventist.org.za; internet www.adventist.org.za; Pres. Pastor F. Louw; Sec. Pastor T. Kunene; 150,000 mems.

United Congregational Church of Southern Africa: POB 96014, Brixton; tel. and fax (21) 6839665; e-mail dave@uccsa.co.za; internet www.uccsa.org.za; f. 1799; Pres. Rev. Ian Booth; Gen. Sec. Rev. Des van der Water; 400,000 mems in 350 churches.

Uniting Presbyterian Church in Southern Africa: POB 96188, Brixton 2019; tel. (11) 3392471; fax (11) 3396938; e-mail gensec@presbyterian.org.za; internet www.upcsa.org.za; f. 1999; Moderator Rt Rev W. D. Pool; Gen. Sec. Rev. V. S. Vellem; Clerk of the Assembly T. W. Coulter; 130,000 mems.

Zion Christian Church: Zion City, Moria; f. 1910; South Africa's largest black religious group; Leader Bishop Barnabas Lekganyane; c. 4m. mems.

ISLAM

In 2003 there were some 455 Mosques and 408 Muslim colleges in South Africa.

United Ulama Council of South Africa (UUCSA): POB 4118, Cape Town 8000; tel. (21) 6965150; fax (21) 6968502; f. 1994; Pres. Sheikh Ebrahim Gabriels; Sec.-Gen. Moulana Yusuf Patel.

JUDAISM

According to the South African Jewish Board of Deputies, in 2006 there were about 80,000 Jews in South Africa, and about 200 organized Jewish communities.

African Jewish Congress: POB 51663, Raedene 2124; tel. (82) 4402621; fax (86) 6146724; e-mail moshe@beyachad.co.za; internet www.africanjewishcongress.com; f. 1994; co-ordinating body representing Jewish communities in sub-Saharan Africa; Pres. Mervyn Smith; Spiritual Leader Rabbi Moshe Silberhaft.

South African Jewish Board of Deputies: POB 87557, Houghton 2041; tel. (11) 6452523; fax (11) 6452559; e-mail sajbod@iafrica.com; internet www.jewish.org.za; f. 1903; the representative institution of South African Jewry; Pres. Russell Gaddin; Chair. Michael Bagraim; Nat. Dir Wendy Kahn.

BAHÁ'Í FAITH

National Spiritual Assembly: 209 Bellairs Dr., North Riding 2169, POB 932, Banbury Cross 2164; tel. (11) 4620100; fax (11) 4620129; e-mail nsa.sec@bahai.org.za; internet www.bahai.org.za; f. 1956; Sec. Shohreh Rawhani; 11,000 mems resident in 320 localities.

The Press

Government Communication and Information System (GCIS): Midtown Bldg, cnr Vermeulen and Prinsloo Sts, Pretoria; Private Bag X745, Pretoria 0001; tel. (12) 3142911; fax (12) 3252030; e-mail govcom@gcis.gov.za; internet www.gcis.gov.za; govt agency; CEO Themba Maseko.

South African Press Ombudsman: POB 47221, Parklands 2121, Johannesburg; tel. (11) 7884837; fax (11) 7884990; e-mail pressombudsman@ombudsman.org.za; internet www.ombudsman.org.za; Ombudsman Joe Thloloe.

DAILIES

Eastern Cape

Die Burger (Oos-Kaap): 52 Cawood St, POB 525, Port Elizabeth 6001; tel. (41) 5036111; fax (41) 5036138; f. 1937; morning; Afrikaans; Editor Leon van der Vyver; circ. 23,849.

Daily Dispatch: 35 Caxton St, POB 131, East London 5200; tel. (43) 7022000; fax (43) 7022968; e-mail phyliciao@dispatch.co.za; internet www.dispatch.co.za; f. 1872; publ. by Dispatch Media (Pty) Ltd; afternoon; also publ. *Weekend Dispatch* (Sat.); English; Editor Phylicia Oppelt; circ. 33,338 (Mon.–Fri.), 27,927 (Sat.).

The Herald: Newspaper House, 19 Baakens St; POB 1117, Port Elizabeth 6000; tel. (41) 5047911; fax (41) 5853947; f. 1845; fmrly *Eastern Province Herald*; publ. by Johnnic Publishing Ltd; morning; English; Editor Ric Wilson; circ. 29,719 (Mon.–Fri.), 25,000 (Sat.).

Free State

Die Volksblad: 79 Voortrekker St, POB 267, Bloemfontein 9300; tel. (51) 4047600; fax (51) 4306949; e-mail nuus@volksblad.com; internet www.naspers.com; f. 1904; publ. by Media 24; morning; Afrikaans; Editor Jonathan Crowther; circ. 29,018 (Mon.–Fri.), 23,000 (Sat.).

Gauteng

Beeld: Media Park, Kingsway 69, Auckland Park, Johannesburg; POB 333, Auckland Park 2006; tel. (11) 7139000; fax (11) 7139960; e-mail ggrobler@beeld.com; f. 1974; publ. by Media 24; morning; weekly: *Kampus-Beeld*, student news and information, and *JIP* youth supplement; Afrikaans; Editor Peet Kruger; Gen. Man. Lucille van Niekerk; circ. 105,618 (Mon.–Fri.), 88,402 (Sat.).

Business Day: POB 1745, Saxonwold 2132; tel. (11) 2803000; fax (11) 2805505; internet www.bday.co.za; f. 1985; publ. by BDFM Publrs (Pty) Ltd; afternoon; English; financial; incl. *Wanted* arts and leisure magazine; Editor Jim Jones; circ. 40,451 (Mon.–Fri.).

The Citizen: POB 43069, Industria 2042; tel. (11) 2486000; fax (11) 2486213; e-mail news@citizen.co.za; f. 1976; publ. by Caxton Publrs & Printers Ltd; morning; English; Editor M. A. Johnson; circ. 76,183 (Mon.–Fri.), 57,935 (Sat.).

The Pretoria News: 216 Vermeulen St, Pretoria 0002; POB 439, Pretoria 0001; tel. (12) 3002000; fax (12) 3257300; f. 1898; publ. by Independent Newspapers Gauteng Ltd; afternoon; English; Editor Philani Mgwaba; circ. 28,690 (Mon.–Fri.), 17,406 (Sat.).

Sowetan: 61 Commando Rd, Industria West, Johannesburg 2000; POB 6663, Johannesburg 2000; tel. (11) 4714000; fax (11) 4748834; e-mail editor@sowetan.co.za; internet www.sowetan.co.za; f. 1981; publ. by New Africa Publs (NAP) Ltd; morning; English; Editor Z. Aggrey Klaaste; circ. 4,122,825 (Mon.–Fri.).

The Star: 47 Sauer St, POB 1014, Johannesburg 2000; tel. (11) 6339111; fax (11) 8343918; e-mail starnews@star.co.za; internet www.star.co.za; f. 1887; publ. by Independent Newspapers Gauteng Ltd; morning; English; also publ. *The Saturday Star*; Editor Moegsien Williams; circ. 166,461 (Mon.–Fri.), 137, 385 (Sat.).

KwaZulu/Natal

The Daily News: 18 Osborne St, Greyville 4001; POB 47549, Greyville 4023; tel. (31) 3082107; fax (31) 3082185; internet www.iol.co.za; f. 1878; Mon.–Fri., afternoon; English; Editor D. Pather; circ. 50,000.

The Mercury: 18 Osborne St, Greyville 4001; POB 47397, Greyville 4023; tel. (31) 3082472; fax (31) 3082662; e-mail mercnews@inl.co.za;

internet themercury.co.za; f. 1852; publ. by Independent Newspapers KZN; morning; English; Editor DAVID CANNING; circ. 39,343 (Mon.–Fri.).

Witness: 45 Willowton Rd, POB 362, Pietermaritzburg 3200; tel. (33) 3551111; fax (33) 3551122; e-mail johnc@witness.co.za; internet www.witness.co.za; f. 1846; publ. by Natal Witness Printing and Publishing Co Ltd; morning; English; also publ. *Weekend Witness*; Editor J. CONYNGHAM; circ. 23,700 (Mon.–Fri.), 29,000 (Sat.).

Northern Cape

Diamond Fields Advertiser: POB 610, cnr Bean and Villiers Sts, Kimberley 8300; tel. (53) 8326261; fax (53) 8328902; e-mail pbe@independent.co.za; internet www.iol.co.za; publ. by Independent Newspapers Gauteng Ltd; morning; English; Editor KEVIN RITCHIE; circ. 8,948 (Mon.–Fri.).

North-West

Rustenburg Herald: 13 Coetzer St, POB 2043, Rustenburg 0300; tel. (14) 5928329; fax (14) 5921869; e-mail mailbag@rustenburgherald.co.za; f. 1924; English and Afrikaans; Man. Editor C. THERON; circ. 20,368.

Western Cape

Die Burger: 40 Heerengracht, POB 692, Cape Town 8000; tel. (21) 4062222; fax (21) 4062913; f. 1915; publ. by Media 24; morning; Afrikaans; Editor E. DOMMISSE; circ. 104,102 (Mon.–Fri.), 117,092 (Sat.).

Cape Argus: 122 St George's St, POB 56, Cape Town 8000; tel. (21) 4884911; fax (21) 4884075; f. 1857; publ. by Independent Newspapers Cape Ltd; afternoon; English; also publ. *Weekend Argus*; Editor MOEGSIEN WILLIAMS; circ. 73,230 (Mon.–Fri.), 103,953 (Sat. and Sun.).

Cape Times: Newspaper House, 122 St George's Mall, Cape Town 8001; POB 56, Cape Town 8000; tel. (21) 4884911; fax (21) 4884744; e-mail tyrone.august@inl.co.za; internet www.capetimes.co.za; f. 1876; publ. by Independent Newspapers Cape Ltd; morning; English; Editor TYRONE AUGUST; circ. 49,526 (Mon.–Fri.).

WEEKLIES AND FORTNIGHTLIES

Eastern Cape

Weekend Post: Private Bag X6071, Port Elizabeth 6000; tel. (41) 5047251; fax (41) 5854966; e-mail weekend@johnnicec.co.za; internet www.weekendpost.co.za; publ. by Johnnic Publishing Co Ltd; English; Editor CHARMAIN NAIDOO; circ. 33,372 (Sat.).

Free State

Vista: POB 1027, Welkom 9460; tel. (57) 3571304; fax (57) 3532427; e-mail avaneck@volksblad.com; internet www.media24.com/eng/newspapers/vista.html; f. 1971; weekly; English and Afrikaans; Editor MARTI WILLN; circ. 38,000 (2005).

Gauteng

Benoni City Times en Oosrandse Nuus: 28 Woburn Ave, POB 494, Benoni 1500; tel. (11) 8451680; fax (11) 4224796; English and Afrikaans; Editor HILARY GREEN; circ. 32,000.

City Press: POB 3413, Johannesburg 2000; tel. (11) 7139002; fax (11) 7139977; e-mail news@citypress.co.za; f. 1983; publ. by RCP Media Bpk; weekly; English; Editor-in-Chief KHULU SIBIYA; circ. 173,922 (Sun.).

Financial Mail: Johncom Bldg, 4 Biermann Ave, Rosebank 2196; POB 1744, Saxenwold 2132; tel. (11) 2803016; fax (11) 2805800; e-mail fmmail@fm.co.za; internet www.financialmail.co.za; weekly; English; Editor BARNEY MTHOMBOTHI; circ. 33,000.

The Herald Times: POB 31015, Braamfontein 2017; tel. (11) 8876500; weekly; Jewish interest; Man. Dir R. SHAPIRO; circ. 5,000.

Mail and Guardian: POB 91667, Auckland Park 2006; tel. (11) 7277000; fax (11) 7277110; publ. by M&GMedia (Pty) Ltd; weekly; English; CEO GOVIN REDDY; Editor PHILIP VAN NIEKERK; circ. 40,162 (Fri.).

Engineering News/Mining Weekly: POB 75316, Garden View 2047; tel. (11) 6229350; fax (11) 6229350; e-mail newsdesk@engineeringnews.co.za; internet www.miningweekly.co.za; f. 1979; publ. by Creamer Media; weekly; circ. 10,000.

Die Noord-Transvaler: POB 220, Ladanna, Pietersburg 0704; tel. (152) 931831; fax (152) 932586; weekly; Afrikaans; Editor A. BUYS; circ. 12,000.

Noordwes Gazette: POB 515, Potchefstroom 2520; tel. (18) 2930750; e-mail potchherald@media24.com; weekly; English and Afrikaans; Editor H. STANDER; circ. 35,000.

Northern Review: 16 Grobler St, POB 45, Pietersburg 0700; tel. (152) 2959167; fax (152) 2915148; weekly; English and Afrikaans; Editor R. S. DE JAGER; circ. 10,300.

Potchefstroom and Ventersdorp Herald: POB 515, Potchefstroom 2520; tel. (18) 2930750; fax (18) 2930759; e-mail potchherald@media24.com; f. 1908; Friday; English and Afrikaans; Editor H. STANDER; Man. Dir RASSIE VAN ZYL; circ. 8,000.

Rapport: POB 333, Auckland Park 2006; tel. (11) 7139002; fax (11) 7139977; e-mail rapport@rapport.co.za; internet www.naspers.co.za/rapport; publ. by RCP Media; weekly; Afrikaans; Sr Gen. Man. and Publr SAREL DU PLESSIS; Editor IZAK DE VILLIERS; circ. 322,731 (Sun.).

South African Jewish Report: Suite 175, Postnet X10039, Randburg 2125; tel. (11) 8860162l; fax (11) 8864202; e-mail geoffs@icon.co.za; weekly; publ. by SA Jewish Report (Pty) Ltd; Editor GEOFF SIFRIN.

Springs and Brakpan Advertiser: POB 138, Springs 1560; tel. (11) 8121600; fax (11) 8121908; f. 1916; English and Afrikaans; Editor CATHY GROSVENOR; circ. 13,000.

Sunday Times: POB 1742, Saxonwold 2132; tel. (11) 2805101; fax (11) 2805111; e-mail makhanyam@sundaytimes.co.za; internet www.sundaytimes.co.za; publ. by Johnnic Publishing Co Lt; weekly; English; Editor MONDLI MAKHANYA; circ. 505,402 (Sun.).

Vaalweekblad: 27 Ekspa Bldg, D. F. Malan St, POB 351, Vanderbijlpark 1900; tel. (16) 817010; fax (16) 810604; weekly; Afrikaans and English; Editor W. J. BUYS; circ. 16,000.

Die Vrye Afrikaan: PO Box 675, Durbanville 7551; tel. (12) 3268646; e-mail redakteur@vryeafrikaan.co.za; f. 2004; weekly; Afrikaans; Editor JOHANN ROUSSOUW; circ. 13,000.

KwaZulu/Natal

Farmers' Weekly: POB 32083, Mobeni 4060; tel. (31) 422041; fax (31) 426068; f. 1911; weekly; agriculture and horticulture; Editor CORRIE VENTER; circ. 17,000.

Ilanga: 19 Timeball Blvd, The Point, Durban 4001; POB 2159 Durban 4000; tel. (31) 3374000; fax (31) 3379785; e-mail peterc@ilanganews.co.za; f. 1903; publ. by Mandla Matla Publishing Co (Pty) Ltd; 2 a week; also publ *Ilanga Lange Sonto* (Sun. circ. 70,000); Zulu; Editor S. NGOBESE; circ. 107,000; circ. 100,000 (Mon. and Thurs.).

Kwana in the City: POB 35559, Northway 4065; tel. (31) 5641230; fax (31) 5649807; e-mail vrydag@eastcoast.co.za; internet www.kwana.co.za; f. 1995; publ. by Kwana Group; English; free community newspaper with focus on consumer and human rights issues; also publ. *Kwana on Track* (f. 2004, English and Zulu, circ. 50,000) aimed at rail commuters; Publr SHELLEY SEID; Editor Dr HILDA GROBLER; circ. 20,000.

Independent On Saturday: 18 Osborne St, Greyville 4001; POB 47397, Greyville 4023; tel. (31) 3082900; fax (31) 3082185; e-mail satmail@inl.co.za; internet www.nn.independent.co.za; f. 1878; publ. by Independent Newspapers KZN; English; Editor CLYDE BAWDEN; circ. 56,216.

Ladysmith Gazette: POB 10019, Ladysmith 3370; tel. (36) 6376801; fax (36) 6372283; f. 1902; weekly; English, Afrikaans and Zulu; Editor DIANA PROCTER; circ. 7,000.

Post: 18 Osborne St, Greyville, Durban 4000; POB 47397, Greyville 4023; tel. (31) 3082400; fax (31) 3082427; e-mail post@inl.co.za; internet www.iol.co.za; f. 1955 as *Golden City Post*; publ. by Independent Newspapers KZN; weekly; English; focus on the Indian community; Editor BRIJLALL RAMGUTHEE; circ. 45,500 (Wed.).

Sunday Tribune: 18 Osborne St, POB 47549, Greyville 4023; tel. (31) 3082911; fax (31) 3082662; e-mail tribnews@nn.independent.co.za; internet www.iol.co.za; f. 1937; publ. by Independent Newspapers KZN; weekly; English; Editor ALAN DUNN; circ. 109,774 (Sun.).

Umafrika: 35A Intersite Ave, Umgeni Business Park, Durban; tel. (31) 2684500; fax (31) 2684545; e-mail editor@umafrika.co.za; f. 1911; Friday; Zulu and English; Editor CYRIL MADLALA; circ. 32,000.

Northern Cape

Die Gemsbok: POB 60, Upington 8800; tel. 27017; fax 24055; English and Afrikaans; Editor D. JONES; circ. 8,000.

Western Cape

Drum: Naspers Bldg, 7th Floor, 5 Protea Place, Sandown 2096; POB 653284, Benmore 2010; tel. (11) 3220888; fax (11) 3220891; e-mail pmdluli@media24.com; f. 1951; English and Zulu; Editor ESMARE WEIDEMAN; Publr JOHN RELIHAN; circ. 79,895 (2006).

Eikestadnuus: 44 Alexander St, POB 28, Stellenbosch 7600; tel. (2231) 72840; fax (2231) 99538; weekly; English and Afrikaans; Editor R. GERBER; circ. 7,000.

Fair Lady: POB 785266, Cape Town 2146; tel. (11) 3220858; fax (11) 8836611; e-mail flmag@fairlady.com; internet www.fairlady.com; fortnightly; English; Editor SUZY BROKENSHA; circ. 103,642.

Huisgenoot: 40 Heerengracht, POB 1802, Cape Town 8000; tel. (21) 4062279; fax (21) 4063316; e-mail eweidema@media24.com; internet www.huisgenoot.com; f. 1916; weekly; Afrikaans; Editor ESMARÉ WEIDEMAN; circ. 355,487.

Move! Magazine: Media City, 10th Floor, 1 Heerengracht St, Foreshore, Cape Town 8001; tel. (21) 4461232; fax (21) 4461206; e-mail move@media24.com; f. 2005; weekly; English; Editor SBU MPUNGOSE.

The Southern Cross: POB 2372, Cape Town 8000; tel. (21) 4655007; fax (21) 4653850; e-mail scross@global.co.za; internet www.thesoutherncross.co.za; f. 1920; publ. by Catholic Newspapers and Publishing Co Ltd; weekly; English; Roman Catholic interest; Editor GÜNTHER SIMMERMACHER; circ. 11,000 (Wed.).

tvplus: Media City, 10th Floor, 1 Heerengracht St, Cape Town 8001; POB 7197, Roggebaai 8012; tel. (21) 4461222; fax (21) 4461206; e-mail tvplus@media24.com; internet www.tvplus.co.za; f. 2000; weekly; English and Afrikaans; Editor WICUS PRETORIUS.

Tyger-Burger: 40 Heerengracht, POB 2271, Cape Town 8000; tel. (21) 4062121; fax (21) 4062913; weekly; Afrikaans and English; Editor ABIE VON ZYL.

Weekend Argus: 122 St George's Mall, POB 56, Cape Town 8000; tel. (21) 4884911; fax (21) 4884762; internet www.iol.co.za; f. 1857; Sat. and Sun.; English; Editor CHRIS WHITFIELD; circ. 108,294.

You Magazine: Naspers Bldg, 7th Floor, 40 Heerengracht St, Cape Town 8001; POB 7167, Roggebaai 8012; tel. (21) 4062166; fax (21) 4062937; e-mail you@you.co.za; internet www.you.co.za; f. 1987; weekly; English; Editor ESMARÉ WEIDEMAN; circ. 222,845 (2004).

MONTHLIES

Free State

Wamba: POB 1097, Bloemfontein; publ. in seven vernacular languages; educational; Editor C. P. SENYATSI.

Gauteng

Nursing News: POB 1280, Pretoria 0001; tel. (12) 3432315; fax (12) 3440750; f. 1978; English and Afrikaans; magazine of the Dem. Nursing Org; circ. 76,000.

KwaZulu/Natal

Bona: POB 32083, Mobeni 4060; tel. (31) 422041; fax (31) 426068; f. 1956; English, Sotho, Xhosa and Zulu; Editor DAIZER MQHABA; circ. 256,631.

Living and Loving: POB 218, Parklands, Johannesburg 2121; tel. (11) 8890621; fax (11) 8890668; e-mail livingandloving@caxton.co.za; internet www.livingandloving.co.za; publ. by Caxton Magazines; English; lifestyle magazine; Editor CARLIEN WESSELS; circ. 55,000.

Rooi Rose: POB 412982, Craighall 2024; tel. (11) 8890665; fax (11) 8890975; e-mail rooirose@caxton.co.za; internet www.rooirose.co.za; Afrikaans; women's interest; Editor MARTIE PANSEGROUW; circ. 122,296.

World Airnews: POB 35082, Northway 4065; tel. (31) 5641319; fax (31) 5637115; e-mail tom@airnews.co.za; internet www.airnews.co.za; f. 1973; aviation news; Editor TOM CHALMERS; circ. 12,428 (2007).

Your Family: POB 32083, Mobeni 4060; tel. (31) 422041; fax (31) 426068; f. 1973; English; cooking, crafts, DIY; Editor ANGELA WALLER-PATON; circ. 164,115.

Western Cape

Boxing World: 5A Dover St, Randburg, Gauteng; tel. (11) 8868558; e-mail info@boxingworld.co.za; f. 1976; Editor PETER LEOPENG; circ. 10,000.

Car: Ramsay, Son & Parker (Pty) Ltd, Digital Publishing, 3 Howard Dr., Pinelands, Cape Town; POB 180, Howard Place 7450; tel. (21) 5303100; fax (21) 5322698; e-mail car@rsp.co.za; internet www.cartoday.com; English; Editor J. WRIGHT; circ. 105,934 (2004).

Femina: 21 St. John's St, POB 3647, Cape Town 8000; tel. (21) 4646248; fax (21) 4612501; e-mail robynne@assocmags.co.za; Editor ROBYNNE KAHN; circ. 68,591.

Reader's Digest (South African Edition): 5 Protea Pl., Protea Park, Sandown, Johannesburg 2146; POB 785266, Sandton 2146; tel. (11) 3220700; fax (11) 8839495; e-mail magazine.sa@readersdigest.com; internet www.readersdigest.co.za; f. 1948; English; Editor ANTHONY JOHNSON; circ. 62,399.

Sarie: POB 785266, Sandton 2146; tel. and fax (21) 4062366; e-mail mvanbre@sarie.com; internet www.natmags.com; monthly; Afrikaans; women's interest; Editor MICHELLE VAN BREDA; circ. 137,970 (2004).

South African Medical Journal: MASA House, Central House, Private Bag X1, Pinelands 7430; tel. (21) 5306520; fax (21) 5314126; f. 1884; publ. by the South African Medical Assn; Editor DANIEL J. NCAYIYANA; circ. 20,000.

Die Unie: POB 196, Cape Town 8000; tel. (21) 4616340; fax (21) 4619238; e-mail saoukaap@jaywalk.com; f. 1905; educational; publ. by the South African Teachers' Union; Editor H. M. NEL; circ. 7,200.

Die Voorligter: Private Bag, Tyger Valley 7536; tel. (21) 9177000; fax (21) 9141333; e-mail lig@cnw-inter.net; internet www.christene.co.za; f. 1937; journal of the Dutch Reformed Church of South Africa; Editor Dr F. M. GAUM; circ. 50,000.

Wineland Magazine: VinPro, POB 1411, Suider-Paarl 7624; tel. (21) 8634524; fax (21) 8634851; e-mail cas@wineland.co.za; internet www.wineland.co.za; f. 1931; publ. by VinPro wine producers' org.; viticulture and the wine and spirit industry; incorporates *Wynboer* technical guide for wine producers; Editor CASSIE DU PLESSIS; circ. 10,000.

The Wisden Cricketer: POB 16368, Vlaeberg 8018; tel. (21) 4083813; e-mail aevlambi@touchline.co.za; internet www.wisdencricketer.co.za; f. 2005; Publr NIC WIDES; Editor ROB HOUWING.

Woman's Value: POB 1802, Cape Town 8000; tel. (21) 4062629; fax (21) 4062929; e-mail wvdited@womansvalue.com; internet www.women24.com/women24/womanswalue/wv_template; English; Editor and Publr TERENA LE ROUX; circ. 134,749.

PERIODICALS

Eastern Cape

African Journal of AIDS Research (AJAR): Centre for AIDS Development, Research and Evaluation, Institute of Social and Economic Research, Rhodes University, POB 94, Grahamstown 6140; tel. (46) 6038553; fax (46) 6038770; e-mail ajar@ru.ac.za; internet www.cadre.org.za; f. 2002; quarterly; Man. Editor KEVIN KELLY.

Gauteng

Africa Insight: Africa Institute of South Africa, POB 630, Pretoria 0001; tel. (12) 3286970; fax (12) 3238153; internet www.ai.org.za; f. 1970; quarterly; journal of the Africa Institute of South Africa; Editor ELIZABETH LE ROUX; circ. 1,200.

African Journal of Political Science: 195 Beckett St, Arcadia, Pretoria; POB 13995, The Tramshed 0126; tel. (12) 3430409; fax (12) 3443622; e-mail program@aaps.org.za; 2 a year; articles in English and French; Editor ADEKUNLE AMUWO.

Africanus: Unisa Press, POB 392, UNISA, 0003 Pretoria; tel. (12) 4292953; fax (12) 4293449; e-mail delpoa@unisa.ac.za; 2 a year; journal of the Centre for Development Studies, Unisa; African and Third World developmental issues; Editor LINDA CORNWELL.

Codicillus: Unisa Press, POB 392, UNISA, 0003 Pretoria; tel. (12) 4292953; fax (12) 4293449; e-mail delpoa@unisa.ac.za; 2 a year; journal of the School of Law at the Univ. of South Africa; South African and international law; Editor Prof. H. C. ROODT.

The Motorist: Highbury Monarch Pty, 8th Floor, Metlife Centre, 7 Coen Steytler Ave, Foreshore, 8001 Cape Town; tel. (21) 4160141; fax (21) 4187312; e-mail themotorist@monarchc.co.za; f. 1966; journal of the Automobile Assn of SA; Editor FIONA ZERBST; circ. 131,584 (2000).

The ScienceScope: POB 395, Pretoria 0001; tel. (12) 8414625; fax (12) 8413789; e-mail edaconceicao@csir.co.za; internet www.csir.co.za; f. 1991 as *Technobrief*; quarterly; publ. by the South African Council for Scientific and Industrial Research; Editor EUNICE DA CONCEIÇÃO; circ. 6,000.

South African Journal of Chemistry: POB 806, Ruimsig 1732; tel. (16) 9604715; fax (11) 5222034; e-mail wolfgang.meyer@sasol.com; internet search.sabinet.co.za/sajchem/; f. 1921; digital; Editor WOLFGANG H. MEYER.

South African Journal of Economics: 4.45 EBW Bldg, University of Pretoria, Pretoria 0002; POB 73354, Lynnwood Ridge 0040; tel. (12) 4203525; fax (12) 3625266; e-mail saje@up.ac.za; internet www.essa.org.za; f. 1933; quarterly; English and Afrikaans; journal of the Economic Soc. of South Africa; publ. by Blackwells; Man. Editor P. A. BLACK.

Kwa/Zulu Natal

African Journal on Conflict Resolution: ACCORD, Private Bag X018, Umhlanga Rocks 4320; tel. (31) 5023908; fax (31) 5024160; e-mail info@accord.org.za; internet www.accord.org.za/ajcr/intro.htm; f. 1999; annually; conflict transformation in Africa; Chair. Prof. JAKES GERWEL; Man. Editor RICHARD KAMIDZA; Editor JANNIE MALAN.

Indilinga: African Journal of Indigenous Knowledge Systems (IAJIKS): POB 13789, Cascades, Pietermaritzburg 3202; tel. (31) 9077000; fax (31) 9073011; e-mail nmkabela@hotmail.com; internet www.indilinga.org.za; f. 2002; 1–2 a year; issues relating to the transmission of local or traditional knowledge; Editor-in-Chief QUEENETH MKABELA.

North-West

Historia: c/o Dept of Historical and Heritage Studies, Faculty of Humanities, Humanities Bldg (Main Campus), University of Pretoria, Pretoria 0002; tel. (12) 4202323; fax (12) 4202656; e-mail moutofa@unisa.ac.za; f. 1956; 2 a year; journal of the Historical Asscn of South Africa; South African and African history; Co-ordinating Editor ALEX MOULTON.

Western Cape

African Finance Journal: African Finance Association, ACIA, University of Stellenbosch Business School, POB 610, Bellville 7535; tel. (21) 9184347; fax (21) 9184262; e-mail afa@acia.sun.ac.za; f. 1999; 2 a year; finance, accounting and economics; Exec. Editor NICHOLAS BIEKPE.

Economic Prospects: Bureau for Economic Research, Economics and Management Sciences Bldg, 7th Floor, Bosman St, Stellenbosch 7600; Private Bag 5050, Stellenbosch 7599; tel. (21) 8872810; fax (21) 8839225; e-mail hhman@sun.ac.za; quarterly; forecast of the South African economy for the coming 18–24 months; Man. Editor P. LAUBSCHER.

Ecquid Novi: c/o South African Journal for Journalism Research, POB 106, Stellenbosch 7599; tel. (21) 8082625; fax (21) 8083488; e-mail novi@sun.ac.za; internet www.sun.ac.za/ecquidnovi; f. 1980; 2 a year; focus on role of the media in southern Africa and Africa; Editor ARNOLD S. DE BEER.

Journal for the Study of Religion: Dept of Religious Studies, Room 5.40, Leslie Social Science Bldg, Upper Campus, University of Cape Town, Private Bag, Rondebosch 7701; tel. (21) 6503452; fax (21) 6897575; e-mail abdulkader.tayob@uct.ac.za; 2 a year; Editor Prof. DAVID CHIDESTER; Man. Editor RAFFAELLE DELLE DONNE.

South African Journal of Wildlife Research: POB 217, Bloubergstrand 7436; tel. (21) 5541297; e-mail elma@mweb.co.za; internet www.sawma.co.za; f. 1970; journal of the Southern African Wildlife Management Asscn; 2 a year; Editor Dr MICHAEL SOMERS.

South African Law Journal: Faculty of Law, University of Cape Town, Private Bag Rondebosch 7700; POB 24299, Lansdowne 7779; tel. (21) 7633600; fax (21) 7970121; e-mail salj@law.uct.ac.za; f. 1884; Editor C. H. LEWIS; circ. 1,000.

NEWS AGENCIES

East Cape News (ECN) Pty Ltd: POB 897, Grahamstown 6140; tel. (46) 6361050; e-mail editor@ecn.co.za; internet www.ecn.co.za; f. 1997; fmrly East Cape News Agencies; Dir MIKE LOEWE.

South African Press Association (SAPA): Cotswold House, Greenacres Office Park, cnr Victory and Rustenburg Rds, Victory Park; POB 7766, Johannesburg 2000; tel. (11) 7821600; fax (11) 7821587; e-mail comms@sapa.org.za; internet www.sapa.org.za; f. 1938; Man. WIM J. H. VAN GILS; Editor MARK A. VAN DER VELDEN; 40 mems.

Foreign Bureaux

Agence France-Presse (AFP): 37 Keyes Ave, Rosebank, Johannesburg; POB 952, Parklands, Johannesburg 2000; tel. (11) 5309900; fax (11) 8809987; e-mail stephane.barbier@afp.com; Bureau Chief STÉPHANE BARBIER.

Agencia EFE (Spain): 321 Main Rd, Bryanston, Johannesburg-Postnet Suite 189, Private Bag X51, Bryanston 2021; tel. (11) 4631618; fax (11) 4635674; e-mail sudafrica@efe.com; Bureau Chief AGUSTÍN DE GRACIA.

Agenzia Nazionale Stampa Associata (ANSA) (Italy): POB 2762, Saxonwold 2132; tel. and fax (21) 7888001.

Associated Press (AP) (USA): Mentone Centre, 5th Floor, 1 Park Rd; POB 880, Auckland Park 2006; tel. (11) 6287700; fax (11) 6287710; e-mail tleonard@ap.org; Bureau Chief TERRY LEONARD.

Central News Agency (Taiwan): Kine Centre, 1st Floor, 141 Commissioner St, Johannesburg 2001; POB 78328, Sandton 2146; tel. and fax (11) 8840658; e-mail jenkins5168@telkomsa.net; Chief CHENG-CHING LIU.

Deutsche Presse-Agentur (dpa) (Germany): 1 Park Rd, Richmond 2092, Johannesburg; tel. (11) 4823077; fax (11) 4822381; e-mail dpa@jhb.stormnet.co.za; Chief RALF E. KRÜGER.

ITAR—TASS (Information Telegraphic Agency of Russia—Telegraphic Agency of the Sovereign Countries): 1261 Park St, Atfield, Pretoria; tel. (12) 436677; fax (12) 3425017; Bureau Chief YURII K. PICHUGIN.

IPS—Inter Press Service (Italy): Suite 283, Dunkeld West Centre, cnr Bompas and Jan Smuts Aves, Dunkeld 2196, Johannesburg; POB 1062, Auckland Park 2006; tel. (11) 3252675; fax (11) 3252891; internet www.ipsnews.net/africa; Regional Dir (Africa) FARAI SAMHUNGU.

Kyodo News (Japan): Sandton Office Towers, 6th Floor, cnr Rivonia Rd and 5th St; POB 787522 Sandton 2146; tel. (11) 8834995; fax (11) 8834996; e-mail sakamoto.yasuyuki@kyodonews.jp; Bureau Chief YASUYUKI SAKAMOTO.

News Agency of Nigeria (Nigeria): Southern Africa Bureau, 7 Margaret Rose St, Sandringham 2192, Johannesburg; tel. and fax (11) 6405945; e-mail waletimi@yahoo.com; f. 1978; Bureau Chief WALE OJETIMI.

Reuters Ltd (UK): 138 West St, Sandton, Johannesburg; POB 2662, Johannesburg 2000; e-mail john.chiahemen@reuters.com; Chief Correspondent JOHN CHIAHEMEN.

United Press International (UPI) (USA): Nedbank Centre, 2nd Floor, POB 32661, Braamfontein 2017; tel. (11) 4033910; fax (11) 4033914; Bureau Chief PATRICK COLLINS.

Xinhua News Agency (China, People's Repub): POB 2482, Parklands 2121; tel. (11) 7281719; fax (11) 7285819; e-mail mingchen_china@hotmail.com; Bureau Chief MING CHEN.

PRESS ASSOCIATIONS

Foreign Correspondents' Association of South Africa: POB 1136, Auckland Park, 2006; tel. and fax (11) 4860490; e-mail fca@onwe.co.za; internet www.fcasa.co.za; represents 175 int. journalists; Chair. JOHN CHIAHEMEN; Sec. MARTINA SCHWIKOWSKI.

Newspaper Association of South Africa: Nedbank Gardens, 5th Floor, 33 Bath Ave, Rosebank 2196, Johannesburg; POB 47180, Parklands 2121; tel. (11) 7213200; fax (11) 7213254; e-mail na@printmedia.org.za; internet www.printmedia.org.za; f. 1882; represents 42 national daily and weekly newspapers, and 178 community newspapers; Pres. TREVOR NCUBE.

Print Media SA: North Wing, Nedbank Gardens, 5th Floor, 33 Bath Ave, Rosebank 2196, Johannesburg; POB 47180, Parklands 2121; tel. (11) 7213200; fax (11) 7213254; e-mail printmediasa@printmedia.org.za; internet www.printmedia.org.za; f. 1995 following the restructuring of the Newspaper Press Union of Southern Africa; represents all aspects of the print media (newspapers and magazines); 680 mems; Pres. TREVOR NCUBE.

Publishers

Acorn Books: POB 4845, Randburg 2125; tel. (11) 8805768; fax (11) 8805768; e-mail acorbook@iafrica.com; f. 1985; Africana, general, natural history; Propr and Publr ELEANOR-MARY CADELL.

Jonathan Ball Publishers: 10–14 Watkins St, Denver Ext. 4, Johannesburg 2094; POB 33977, Jeppestown 2043; tel. (11) 6222900; fax (11) 6227610; e-mail orders@jonathanball.co.za; acquired by Via Afrika (Naspers Group) in 1992; fiction, reference, bibles, textbooks, general; imprints incl. AD Donker (literature), Delta (general fiction and non-fiction) and Sunbird; Man. Dir JONATHAN BALL.

BLAC Publishing House: POB 17, Athlone, Cape Town; f. 1974; general fiction, poetry; Man. Dir JAMES MATTHEWS.

Bible Society of South Africa: POB 5500, Tyger Valley 7536; tel. (21) 9108777; fax (21) 9108799; e-mail turleym@biblesociety.co.za; internet www.biblesociety.co.za; f. 1820; bibles and religious material in 11 official languages; CEO Rev. G. S. KRITZINGER.

Brenthurst Press (Pty) Ltd: POB 87184, Houghton 2041; tel. (11) 6466024; fax (11) 4861651; e-mail orders@brenthurst.co.za; internet www.brenthurst.org.za; f. 1974; Southern African history; Dir MARCELLE GRAHAM.

Clever Books: POB 13186, Hatfield 0028; tel. (12) 3423263; fax (12) 432376; e-mail elizabeth@cleverbooks.co.za; f. 1981; subsidiary of MacMillan Publrs; Man. Dir STEVEN CILLIERS.

Christelike Uitgewersmaatskappy (CUM): POB 1599, Vereeniging 1930; tel. (16) 4407000; fax (16) 4211748; e-mail orders@cabooks.co.za; internet www.cum.co.za; religious fiction and non-fiction.

Fisichem Publishers: Private Bag X3, Matieland 7602; tel. (21) 8870900; fax (21) 8839635; e-mail fisichem@iafrica.com; science study guides; Man. RETHA JORDAAN.

Flesch Publications: 11 Peninsula Rd, Zeekoevlei, Cape Town 7941; POB 31353, Grassy Park 7888; tel. (21) 7054317; fax (21) 7060766; e-mail sflesch@iafrica.com; f. 1954; biography, cookery, aviation; CEO STEPHEN FLESCH.

Fortress Books: POB 2475, Knysna 6570; tel. (44) 3826805; fax (44) 3826848; e-mail fortress@iafrica.com; internet www.uys.com/fortress; f. 1973; military history, biographies, financial; Man. Dir I. UYS.

Heinemann Publishers (Pty) Ltd: Heinemann House, Grayston Office Park, Bldg 3, 128 Peter Rd, Atholl Ext. 12, Sandton 2196; POB 781940, Sandown, Sandton 2146; tel. (11) 3228600; fax (11) 3228715; e-mail customerliaison@heinemann.co.za; internet www.heinemann.co.za; educational; incl. imprints Lexicon, Isando and Centaur; Man. Dir ORENNA KRUT.

Home Economics Publishers (Huishoudkunde Uitgewers): POB 7091, Stellenbosch 7599; tel. and fax (21) 8864722; e-mail mcv1@sun.ac.za; Man. M. C. VOSLOO.

Juta and Co Ltd: POB 14373, Kenwyn 7790, Cape Town; tel. (11) (21) 7633600; fax (21) 7627424; e-mail books@juta.co.za; internet www.juta.co.za; f. 1853; academic, educational, law, electronic; imprints incl. Double Storey (general contemporary), and University of Cape Town Press (scholarly and academic); CEO R. J. WILSON.

LAPA Publishers (Lees Afrikaans Praat Afrikaans): 380 Bosman St, POB 123, Pretoria 0001; tel. (12) 4010700; fax (12) 3244460; f. 1996 as the publishing arm of the Afrikaans Language and Culture Asscn; present name adopted in 2000; Afrikaans; general fiction and non-fiction; CEO WIM DE WET.

Learning Matters Africa: 341 West St, Durban 4001; POB 466, Durban 4000; tel. (31) 3053791; fax (31) 3077356; e-mail padams@adamsbooks.co.za; educational; CEO BRYAN PHILLIPS.

Lemur Books (Pty) Ltd (The Galago Publishing (1999) (Pty) Ltd): POB 1645, Alberton 1450; tel. (11) 9072029; fax (11) 8690890; e-mail lemur@mweb.co.za; internet www.galago.co.za; f. 1980; military, political, history, hunting, general; Man. Dir F. STIFF.

LexisNexis Butterworths SA: 215 North Ridge Rd, Morningside, Durban 4001; POB 792, Durban 4000; tel. (31) 2683111; fax (31) 2683108; e-mail customercare@lexisnexis.co.za; internet www.lexisnexis.co.za; f. 1948 as Butterworths; adopted LexisNexis name in 2001; jtly owned by Reed Elsevier, USA, and Kagiso Media; law, tax, accountancy; Chair. W. ROGER JARDINE; CEO WILLIAM J. LAST.

Lux Verbi-BM: POB 1822, Cape Town 8000; tel. (21) 8648237; fax (21) 8648292; e-mail epi@luxverbi-bm.co.za; internet www.luxverbi-bm.com; f. 1818 as the Dutch Reformed Church Publishing Co; merged with Bible Media in 1999; subsidiary of the Naspers Group; imprints incl. Hugenote, NG Kerk Uitgewers, Protea, and Waterkant; Christian media; CEO H. S. SPIES; Editor-in-Chief D. FOURIE.

Maskew Miller Longman (Pty) Ltd: cnr Forest Dr. and Logan Way, Pinelands 7405; POB 396, Cape Town 8000; tel. (21) 5326000; fax (21) 5310716; e-mail tembela@mml.co.za; internet www.mml.co.za; f. 1893 as Miller Maskew; merged with Longman in 1983; jtly owned by Pearson Education and Caxton Publrs and Printers Ltd; imprints incl. Kagiso Publishing (f. 1994; fmrly De Jager-HAUM) and Phumelela Books; educational and general; CEO JAPIE PIENAAR.

Methodist Publishing House: POB 13128, Woodstock, Cape Town 7915; tel. (21) 4483640; fax (21) 4483716; e-mail george@methbooks.co.za; f. 1894; religion and theology; Gen. Man. GEORGE VINE (acting).

NB Publishers: Naspers Bldg, 12th Floor, 40 Heerengracht, Roggebai 8012; POB 5050, Cape Town 8000; tel. (21) 4063033; fax (21) 4063812; e-mail nb@nb.co.za; internet www.nb.co.za; English, Afrikaans, Xhosa and Zulu; Human & Rousseau (f. 1959; general, children's and youth literature, cookery and self-help), Kwela (f. 1994; fiction), Pharos (dictionaries), Tafelberg (f. 1950; fiction and non-fiction, politics, children's and youth literature) and Best Books (educational texts); Head of Publishing C. T. BREYTENBACH.

Nasou—Via Afrika: 40 Heerengracht, Cape Town 8001; POB 5197, Cape Town 8000; tel. (21) 4063005; fax (21) 4063086; e-mail mdewitt@nasou.com; internet www.nasou-viaafrika.com; f. 1963; subsidiary of Via Afrika (Naspers Group); educational; imprints incl. Acacia, Action Publrs, Afritech, Afro, Atlas, Era, Juta, KZN Books, Gariep, Idem, Phoenix Education, Shortland and Y-Press Grade R-3; CEO LOUISE NAUDÉ.

Oxford University Press: POB 12119, N1 City, Cape Town 7463; tel. (21) 5962300; fax (21) 5961234; e-mail oxford.za@oup.com; internet www.oxford.co.za; f. 1914; Man. Dir LIEZE KOTZE.

Protea Book House: 1067 Burnett St, Hatfield, Pretoria; POB 35110, Menlo Park, 0102 Pretoria; tel. (12) 3623444; fax (12) 3625688; e-mail protea@intekom.co.za; internet www.proteaboekhuis.co.za; f. 1997; art and photography, Afrikaans fiction, South African history, spiritual, academic and general; Dir NICOL STASSEN.

Random House (Pty) Ltd South Africa: POB 2002, Houghton 2041; tel. (11) 4843538; fax (11) 4846180; e-mail mail@randomhouse.co.za; f. 1966; general fiction; Man. Dir S. E. JOHNSON.

Shuter & Shooter Publishers (Pty) Ltd: 21C Cascades Cres., KwaZulu-Natal 3201; POB 13016, Cascades, Pietermaritzburg 3202; tel. (33) 3476100; fax (33) 3476130; internet www.shuters.com; f. 1921; educational, general and African languages; Man. Dir DAVE F. RYDER.

Struik New Holland Publishing (South Africa) (Pty) Ltd: 80 Mckenzie St, Gardens, Cape Town 8001; POB 1144, Cape Town 8000; tel. (21) 4624360; fax (21) 4619378; e-mail inquiry@booksite.co.za; general fiction and non-fiction, religious, women's issues, maps; imprints incl. Books of Africa, New Holland, Oshun, Struik, Two Dogs and Zebra; CEO BRIAN D. WOOTON.

University of KwaZulu-Natal Press (UKZN Press): Private Bag X01, Scottsville 3209; tel. (33) 2605226; fax (33) 2605801; e-mail books@ukzn.ac.za; internet www.ukznpress.co.za; academic and scholarly; Publr GLENN COWLEY; Editor SALLY HINES.

Van Schaik Publishers: POB 12681, Hatfield 0028; tel. (12) 3422765; fax (12) 4303563; e-mail vanschaik@vanschaiknet.com; internet www.vanschaiknet.com; f. 1915; acquired by Nasionale Pers, latterly (Via Afrika-Naspers Group) in 1986; English and Afrikaans; academic and scholarly; CEO. LEANNE MARTINI.

Wits University Press: PO Wits, Johannesburg 2050; tel. (11) 4845910; fax (11) 4845971; e-mail Veronica.Klipp@wits.ac.za; internet witspress.wits.ac.za; f. 1922; general trade, non-fiction and scholarly; Publr VERONICA KLIPP.

PUBLISHERS' ASSOCIATION

Publishers' Association of South Africa: Suite 305, 2nd Floor, The Foundry, Prestwich St, Green Point, Cape Town 8005; tel. (21) 4252721; fax (21) 4213270; e-mail dudley@publishsa.co.za; internet www.publishsa.co.za; f. 1992; Exec. Dir. DUDLEY H. SCHROEDER.

Broadcasting and Communications

REGULATORY AUTHORITY

Independent Communications Authority of South Africa (ICASA): Pinmill Farm, Blocks A, B, C and D, 164 Katherine St, Sandton 2146; Private Bag X10002, Marlboro 2063; tel. (11) 3218200; fax (11) 4441919; e-mail info@icasa.org.za; internet www.icasa.org.za; f. 2000 as successor to the Independent Broadcasting Authority (f. 1993) and South African Telecommunications Regulatory Authority (f. 1996); regulates telecommunications and broadcasting; Chair. PARIS MASHILE.

TELECOMMUNICATIONS

Cell C (Pty) Ltd: 150 Rivonia Rd, Sandown 2196; Private Bag X36, Benmore 2010, Johannesburg; e-mail custserv@cellc.co.za; internet www.cellc.co.za; f. 2000; subsidiary of 3C Telecommunications (60% owned by Oger Telecom South Africa, 40% by CellSAf); mobile cellular telecommunications provider; Chair. TALAAT LAHAM; CEO JEFFREY HEDBERG.

Mobile Telephone Networks (Pty) Ltd (MTN): PMB 9955, Sandton 2146; tel. (11) 3016000; fax (11) 3016111; internet www.mtn.co.za; f. 1994; mobile cellular telecommunications provider; operations in 21 countries in Africa and the Middle East; 11m. subscribers in South Africa (2006); Chair. MATAMELA CYRIL RAMAPHOSA; Group Pres. and CEO PHUTHUMA NHLEKO.

Telkom SA Ltd: Telkom Towers North, 152 Proes St, Pretoria 0002; POB 925, Pretoria 0001; tel. (12) 3111007; fax (12) 3114031; e-mail letlapll@telkom.co.za; internet www.telkom.co.za; f. 1991; 38% govt-owned; ICT solutions service provider; Chair. SHIRLEY LUE ARNOLD; Exec. Dir PAPI MOLOTSANE.

Virgin Mobile South Africa (Pty) Ltd (VMSA): Citicorp Bldg, 2nd Floor, 145 West St, Sandton, Johannesburg; POB 78331, Sandton 2146; tel. (11) 3244000; fax (11) 3244113; e-mail paia@virginmobile.co.za; internet www.virginmobile.co.za; f. 2006; jt venture btwn Cell C and Virgin Mobile Telecoms Ltd, United Kingdom; mobile cellular telecommunications provider; CEO SAJEED SACRANIE.

Vodacom Group (Pty) Ltd: Vodacom Corporate Park, 082 Vodacom Blvd, Vodavalley, Midrand 1685; tel. (11) 6535000; e-mail corporate.affairs@vodacom.co.za; internet www.vodacom.co.za; f. 1993; 50% owned by Telkom SA Ltd, 50% by Vodafone Group PLC, United Kingdom; subsidiaries in the DRC (f. 2002), Lesotho (f. 1996), Mozambique (f. 2003) and Tanzania (f. 1999); Chair. OYAMA MABANDLA.

BROADCASTING

Radio

South African Broadcasting Corpn (SABC)—Radio: Private Bag X1, Auckland Park 2006; tel. (11) 7143407; fax (11) 7142635; e-mail info@sabc.co.za; internet www.sabc.co.za; f. 1936; comprises 15 public radio stations and three commercial radio stations broadcasting in 11 languages; Chair. Prof. PAULUS ZULU; CEO CHARLOTTE MAMPANE.

Domestic Services

Radio South Africa; Afrikaans Stereo; Radio 5; Radio 2000; Highveld Stereo; Good Hope Stereo; Radio Kontrei; RPN Stereo; Jacaranda Stereo; Radio Algoa (regional services); Radio Lotus (Indian service in English); Radio Metro (African service in English); Radio Lebowa; Radio Ndebele; Radio Sesotho; Setswana Stereo; Radio Swazi; Radio Tsonga; Radio Xhosa; Radio Zulu.

External Service

Channel Africa Network: POB 91313, Auckland Park 2006; tel. (11) 7142255; fax (11) 7142072; e-mail ntentenit@sabc.co.za; internet www.channelafrica.org; f. 1966; external service of SABC; broadcasts 217 hours per week in English, French, Portuguese, Kiswahili, Chinyanja and Silozi; Exec. Editor THAMI NTENTENI.

Television

South African Broadcasting Corpn (SABC)—Television: Private Bag X41, Auckland Park 2006; tel. (11) 7149111; fax (11) 7145055; e-mail info@sabc.co.za; internet www.sabc.co.za; transmissions began in 1976; broadcasts television services in 11 languages over three channels; Channel One (TV1) broadcasts in English and Afrikaans; Channel Two (CCV-TV) broadcasts in English, Northern and Southern Sotho, Tswana, Xhosa and Zulu; Channel Three (NNTV) broadcasts documentaries, educational programmes and sport; Chair. Prof. PAULUS ZULU; CEO MOLEFE MOKGATLE.

Finance

(cap. = capital; auth. = authorized; res = reserves; dep. = deposits; m. = million; brs = branches; amounts in rand)

BANKING

In 2006 there were 30 commercial banks and 1,354 microfinance institutions operating in South Africa. The five largest banks—Standard Bank, Nedbank, ABSA, FirstRand, and Investec—controlled some 86% of total banking assets.

Central Bank

South African Reserve Bank: 370 Church St, POB 427, Pretoria 0002; tel. (12) 3133911; fax (12) 3133197; internet www.resbank.co.za; f. 1921; cap. 2.0m., res 3,429.1m., dep. 71,821.9m. (March 2002); Gov. TITO T. MBOWENI; Sen. Dep. Gov. X. P. GUMA; 7 brs.

Commercial Banks

ABSA Bank Ltd: ABSA Towers East, 3rd Floor, 170 Main St, Johannesburg 2001; tel. (11) 3504000; fax (11) 3503768; e-mail absa@absa.co.za; internet www.absa.co.za; total assets 306,848m. (Mar. 2004); Chair. Dr DANIE CRONJÉ; CEO STEVE F. BOOYSEN; 726 brs.

African Bank Investments Ltd: 59 16th Rd, Private Bag X170, Midrand 1685; tel. (11) 2569000; fax (11) 2569217; internet www.abil.co.za; f. 1975; cap. 1,876.4m., res 186.7m., dep. 706.2m. (Sept. 2002); CEO LEONIDAS KIRKINIS; 268 brs.

Albaraka Bank Ltd: 134 Commercial Rd, 1st Floor, Durban 4001; POB 4395, Durban 4000; tel. (31) 3662800; fax (31) 3052631; internet www.albaraka.co.za; f. 1989; operates according to Islamic principles; cap. 41.0m., res 13.5m., dep. 551.7m. (Dec. 2002); Chair. A. A. SABBAHI; Deputy CEO M. G. MCLEAN.

AMB Holdings Ltd: 18 Fricker Rd, Illovo, Sandton 2196; POB 786833, Sandton 2146; tel. (11) 2152000; fax (11) 268886; e-mail asprague@amb.co.za; internet www.amb.co.za; Exec. Dir ZENZO LUSENGO; CEO ANDREW SPRAGUE.

Brait South Africa Ltd: 9 Fricker Rd, Illovo Blvd, Illovo, Sandton 2196; Private Bag X1, Northlands 2116; tel. (11) 5071000; fax (11) 5071001; internet www.brait.com; f. 1998; subsidiary of Brait SA, Luxembourg; total assets 802.3m. (Mar. 2004); CEO JOHN COULTER.

FirstRand Bank Ltd: 4 Merchant Place, 4th Floor, cnr Fredman Dr. and Rivonia Rd, Sandton 2196; POB 786273, Sandton 2146; tel. (11) 2821808; fax (11) 2828065; e-mail information@firstrand.co.za; internet www.firstrand.co.za; f. 1971 as First National Bank of Southern Africa; merged with Rand Bank in 1998; total assets 323,500m. (June 2004); Chair. GERRIT T. FERREIRA; CEO LAURITZ L. DIPPENAAR; 650 brs.

GBS Mutual Bank: 18–20 Hill St, Grahamstown 6139; POB 114, Grahamstown 6140; tel. (46) 6227109; fax (46) 6228855; e-mail gbs@gbsbank.co.za; internet www.gbsbank.co.za; f. 1877; total assets 301.1m. (Dec. 2003); Chair. C. K. M. STONE; Man. Dir T. C. S. TAGG; 1 br.

HBZ Bank Ltd: 135 Jan Hofmeyr Rd, Westville, Durban 3631; POB 1536, Wandsbeck 3631; tel. (31) 2674400; fax (31) 2671193; e-mail sazone@hbzbank.co.za; internet www.habibbank.com; f. 1995; subsidiary of Habib Bank Ltd; total assets 650.4m. (Dec. 2003); Chair. MUHAMMAD HABIB; CEO ZAFAR ALAM KHAN; 4 brs.

Imperial Bank Ltd: 140 Boeing Rd, East Elma Park, Edenvale, Gauteng 1610; POB 3567, Edenvale 1610; tel. (11) 8792000; fax (11) 8792234; e-mail phassim@imperialbank.co.za; internet www.imperialbank.co.za; f. 1996; 51.1% owned by Nedbank, 49.9% Imperial Holdings; total assets 12,955.0m. (Dec. 2003); Chair. W. G. LYNCH; CEO R. VAN WYK.

Meeg Bank Ltd: Meeg Bank Bldg, 60 Sutherland St, Umtata; POB 332, Umtata 5100; tel. (47) 5026200; fax (47) 5311098; internet www.meegbank.co.za; f. 1977; fmrly Bank of Transkei; name changed Oct. 1998; total assets 782.4m. (March 2003); Chair. Prof. WISEMAN LUMKILE NKUHLU; Man. Dir. EMIL G. KALTENBRÜNN; 5 brs.

Mercantile Bank Ltd: Mercantile Lisbon House, 142 West St, Sandown 2196; POB 782699, Sandton 2146; tel. (11) 3020300; fax (11) 3020729; internet www.mercantile.co.za; f. 1965; subsidiary of Mercantile Lisbon Bank Holdings; total assets 2,224.8m. (Dec. 2003); Chair. Dr JOAQUIM A. S. DE ANDRADE CAMPOS; CEO D. J. BROWN; 14 brs.

Nedbank Ltd: 135 Rivonia Rd, Sandown 2196, Johannesburg 2001; POB 1144, Johannesburg 2000; tel. (11) 2940999; fax (11) 2950999; e-mail nedbankgroupir@nedbank.co.za; internet www.nedbankgroup.co.za; f. 1988; name changed from Nedcor Bank Ltd Nov. 2002; subsidiary of Nedbank Group Ltd; cap. 14,400m., res 6,300m., dep. 271,200m. (June 2006); Chair. REUEL J. KHOZA; CEO TOM BOARDMAN; 459 brs.

Rennies Bank Ltd: Rennie House, 11th Floor, 19 Ameshoff St, Braamfontein 2001, Johannesburg; POB 185, Johannesburg 2000; tel. (11) 4073000; fax (11) 4073322; e-mail agent2@bank.rennies.co.za; internet www.renniesbank.co.za; f. 1850; subsidiary of Bidvest Group Ltd; foreign exchange, trade finance and related activities; total assets 313,772m. (June 2003); Chair. J. J. PAMENSKY; CEO DAVID WALKER; over 60 brs.

South African Bank of Athens Ltd: Bank of Athens Bldg, 116 Marshall St, Johannesburg 2001; POB 7781, Johannesburg 2000; tel. (11) 6344300; fax (11) 8381001; e-mail karenc@bankofathens.co.za; internet www.bankofathens.co.za; f. 1947; 99.46% owned by National Bank of Greece; cap. 94.5m., dep. 531.7m. (Dec. 2004); Chair. TAKIS ARAPOGLOU; CEO HECTOR ZARCA; 10 brs.

Standard Bank Ltd: Standard Bank Centre, 5 Simmonds St, Johannesburg 2000; POB 7725, Johannesburg 2000; tel. (11) 6369111; fax (11) 6364207; e-mail information@standardbank.co.za; internet www.standardbank.co.za; f. 1862; cap. 5,703.0m., res 9,472.0m., dep. 204,812.0m. (Dec. 2003); Chair. DEREK E. COOPER; CEO JACKO H. MAREE; 997 brs.

Teba Bank Ltd: Sanhill Park, 1 Eglin Rd, Sunninghill; Private Bag X101, Sunninghill 2157; tel. (11) 5185000; fax (11) 2031554; e-mail corpcomm@tebabank.com; internet www.tebabank.co.za; f. 2000; fmrly Teba Savings Fund; specializes in micro-finance and providing financial services to mining communities; total assets 2,200.0m. (Feb. 2006); Man. Dir ZIENZI MUSAMIRAPAMWE; 23 brs, 70 mine outlets and 29 agencies.

Merchant Bank

Marriott Merchant Bank Ltd: Kingsmead Office Park, Durban 4001; POB 3211, Durban 4000; tel. (31) 3661007; fax (31) 3661250; e-mail mmb@marriott.co.za; internet www.marriott.co.za; f. 1994; CEO D. A. POLKINGHORNE.

Investment Banks

Cadiz Investment Bank Ltd: Fernwood House, 1st Floor, The Oval, 1 Oakdale Rd, Newlands 7700; POB 44547, Claremont 7735; tel. 6578300; fax 6578301; e-mail reception@cadiz.co.za; internet www.cadiz.co.za; f. 1993; 15% owned by Investec, 11% Makana Financial Services; total assets 298.1m. (Dec. 2003); Chair. COLIN HALL; CEO RAM BARKAI.

Investec Bank Ltd: 100 Grayston Dr., Sandown, Sandton 2196; POB 785700, Sandton 2146; tel. (11) 2867000; fax (11) 2867777; e-mail investorrelations@investec.com; internet www.investec.com; f. 1974; cap. 12.6m., res 7.7m., dep. 70.0m. (Sept. 2006); CEO S. KOSEFF; 6 brs.

Sasfin Bank Ltd: Sasfin Pl., 13–15 Scott St, Waverley 2090; POB 95104, Grant Park 2051; tel. (11) 8097500; fax (11) 8872489; e-mail info@sasfin.com; internet www.sasfin.com; f. 1951; subsidiary of Sasfin Holdings Ltd; total assets 2,460m. (2006); Chair. MARTIN GLATT; CEO ROLAND SASSOON.

Development Bank

Development Bank of Southern Africa (DBSA): 1258 Lever Rd, Headway Hill; POB 1234, Halfway House, Midrand 1685; tel. (11) 3133911; fax (11) 3133086; e-mail info@dbsa.org; internet www.dbsa.org; total assets 23,684.5m. (March 2004); f. 1983; Chair. JAYASEELAN NAIDOO; CEO MANDLA S. V. GANTSHO.

Bankers' Association

Banking Council of South Africa: 17 Harrison St, 10th Floor, POB 61674, Marshalltown 2107; tel. (11) 3703500; fax (11) 8365509; e-mail banking@banking.org.za; internet www.banking.org.za; f. 1993; 15,000 mems; Chair. E. R. Bosman; CEO Robert S. K. Tucker.

STOCK EXCHANGE

JSE Ltd: 2 Gwen Lane, Sandown, Sandton; Private Bag X991174, Sandton 2146; tel. (11) 5207000; fax (11) 5208584; internet www.jse .co.za; f. 1887 as Johannesburg Stock Exchange; present name adopted in 2005; in late 1995 legislation was enacted providing for the deregulation of the Stock Exchange; automated trading commenced in June 1996; demutualized in July 2005 and became a listed co in June 2006; CEO R. M. Loubser.

INSURANCE

In 2003 South Africa was served by 96 short-term and 69 long-term insurers, and six reinsurance firms.

Allianz Insurance Ltd: 40 Ashford Rd, Parkwood, Johannesburg 2001; POB 62228, Marshalltown 2107; tel. (11) 4421111; fax (11) 4421125; Chair. D. du Preez; Man. Dir Ian Bain.

Clientèle Life Assurance Co: Clientèle House, Morning View Office Park, cnr Rivonia and Alon Rds, Morningside, Johannesburg; POB 1316, Rivonia 2128; tel. (11) 3203333; e-mail services@ clientelelife.com; internet www.clientelelife.com; f. 1997; subsidiary of Hollard Insurance Group; Chair. G. Q. Routledge; Man. Dir G. J. Soll.

Credit Guarantee Insurance Corpn of Africa Ltd: 31 Dover St, POB 125, Randburg 2125; tel. (11) 8897000; fax (11) 8861027; e-mail info@cgic.co.za; internet www.creditguarantee.co.za; f. 1956; Chair. Bruce Campbell; Man. Dir Mike Truter.

Discovery: Discovery Bldg, 155 West St cnr Alice Lane, Sandton 2146; POB 786722, Sandton 2146; tel. (11) 5292888; fax (11) 5293590; e-mail worldinfo@discovery.co.za; internet www.discoveryworld.co .za; f. 1992; 64% owned by FirstRand; health and life assurance; Chair. Lauritz L. Dippenaar; CEO Adrian Gore.

Liberty Life: Liberty Life Centre, 1 Ameshoff St, Braamfontein, Johannesburg 2017; POB 10499, Johannesburg 2000; tel. (11) 4083911; fax (11) 4082109; e-mail info@liberty.co.za; internet www .liberty.co.za; f. 1958; Chair. D. E. Cooper; CEO Bruce Hemphill.

Metropolitan Life Ltd: Parc du Cap Complex, Mispel Rd, Cape Town; POB 2212, Bellville 7535; tel. (21) 9405911; fax (21) 9405730; e-mail info@metropolitan.co.za; internet www.metropolitan.co.za; Chair. D. E. Moseneke; Man. Dir P. R. Doyle.

Momentum Life Assurers Ltd: 268 West Ave, Centurion, Gauteng 0157; POB 7400, Centurion 0046; tel. (12) 6718911; fax (12) 6636288; e-mail corporate@momentum.co.za; internet www.momentum.co .za; f. 1967; Chair. Laurie Dippenaar; Man. Dir Hillie P. Meyer.

Mutual & Federal Insurance Co Ltd: Mutual Federal Centre, 75 President St, POB 1120, Johannesburg 2000; tel. (11) 3749111; fax (11) 3742652; internet www.mf.co.za; f. 1970; Chair. K. T. M. Saggers; Man. Dir B. Campbell.

Old Mutual (South African Mutual Life Assurance Society): Mutualpark, Jan Smuts Dr., POB 66, Cape Town 8001; tel. (21) 5099111; fax (21) 5094444; e-mail contact@oldmutual.com; internet www.oldmutual.com; f. 1845; Chair. Michael J. Levett; CEO James Sutcliffe.

Santam Ltd: Santam Head Office, 1 Sportica Cres., Bellville 7530; POB 3881, Tyger Valley 7536; tel. (21) 9157000; fax (21) 9140700; internet www.santam.co.za; f. 1918; Chair. M. H. Daling; Man. Dir Steffen Gibert.

South African Eagle Insurance Co Ltd: SA Eagle House, The Braes, 193 Bryanston Dr., Bryanston 2021; POB 61489, Marshalltown 2107; tel. (11) 5404000; fax (11) 5404444; internet www.saeagle .co.za; Chair. M. C. South; CEO N. V. Beyers.

South African National Life Assurance Co Ltd (SANLAM): 2 Strand Rd, Bellville; POB 1, Sanlamhof 7532; tel. (21) 9165000; fax (21) 9479440; e-mail life@sanlam.co.za; internet www.sanlam.co.za; f. 1918; Chair. Dr J. van Zyl.

Association

South African Insurance Association (SAIA): JCC House, 3rd Floor, 27 Owl St, Milpark; POB 30619, Braamfontein 2017; tel. (11) 7265381; fax (11) 7265351; e-mail info@saia.co.za; e-mail info@saia .co.za; internet www.saia.co.za; f. 1973; represents short-term insurers; Chair. Adam Samie; CEO Barry Scott.

Trade and Industry

DEVELOPMENT ORGANIZATIONS

Business Partners Ltd: 5 Wellington Rd, Parktown, Johannesburg 2193; POB 7780, Johannesburg 2000; tel. (11) 4808700; fax (11) 6422791; e-mail enquiries@businesspartners.co.za; internet www .businesspartners.co.za; f. 1981 as Small Business Devt Corpn; invests in, and provides services to, small and medium enterprises; Chair. Johann Rupert; Man. Dir Jo' Schwenke.

Industrial Development Corpn of South Africa Ltd (IDC): 19 Fredman Dr., Sandown 2196; POB 784055, Sandton 2146; tel. (11) 2693000; fax (11) 2693116; e-mail callcentre@idc.co.za; internet www.idc.co.za; f. 1940; promotes entrepreneurship and competitiveness; total assets 36,593m.; Chair. Dr Wendy Y. N. Luhabe; CEO G. M. Qhena.

The Independent Development Trust: Glenwood Office Park, cnr Oberon and Sprite Sts, Faerie Glen, Pretoria; POB 73000, Lynnwood Ridge 0040; tel. (12) 8452000; fax (12) 3480939; f. 1990; advances the national. devt programme working with govt and communities in fields incl. poverty relief, infrastructure, empowerment, employment and capacity building; CEO Thembi Nwedamustwu.

National Productivity Institute: Private Bag 235, Midrand 1685; tel. (11) 8485300; fax (11) 8485555; e-mail info@npi.co.za; internet www.npi.co.za; f. 1968; Exec. Dir Dr Yvonne Dladla.

CHAMBER OF COMMERCE

South African Chamber of Business (SACOB): 24 Sturdee Ave, Rosebank, Johannesburg; POB 213, Saxonwold 2132; tel. (11) 4463800; fax (11) 4463847; internet www.sacob.co.za; f. 1990 by merger of Asscn of Chambers of Commerce and Industry and South African Federated Chamber of Industries; Pres. D. Penfold; CEO James Lennox.

CHAMBERS OF INDUSTRIES

Bloemfontein Chamber of Commerce and Industry: Stabilitas Bldg, Maitland St, Bloemfontein 9301; POB 87, Bloemfontein 9301; tel. (51) 4473368; fax (51) 4475064; e-mail bcci@intekom.co.za; internet www.bcci.co.za; c. 550 mems (2006).

Cape Town Regional Chamber of Commerce and Industry: Cape Chamber House, 19 Louis Gradner St, Foreshore, Cape Town 8001; tel. (21) 4024300; fax (21) 4024302; e-mail info@capechamber .co.za; internet www.capechamber.co.za; f. 1804; Pres. Janine Myburgh; 4,632 mems.

Chamber of Commerce and Industry–Johannesburg: JCC House, 6th Floor, Empire Rd, Milpark; Private Bag 34, Auckland Park 2006; tel. (11) 7265300; fax (11) 4822000; e-mail info@jcci.co.za; internet www.jcci.co.za; f. 1890; CEO Keith Brebnor; 3,800 mems.

Durban Chamber of Commerce and Industry: POB 1506, Durban 4000; tel. (31) 3351000; fax (31) 3321288; e-mail chamber@durbanchamber.co.za; internet www.durbanchamber.co .za; CEO Prof. Bonke Dumisa; 3,500 mems.

Gauteng North Chamber of Commerce and Industry (GNCCI): Tshwane Events Centre, Soutter St, Pretoria; POB 2164, Pretoria 0001; tel. (12) 3271487; fax (12) 3271490; internet www.gncci.co.za; f. 1929; fmrly Pretoria Business and Agricultural Centre; merged with Pretoria Sakekamer in 2004; Chair. Bert Badenhorst; CEO Wim du Plessis; over 900 mems.

Pietermaritzburg Chamber of Business (PCB): POB 11734, Dorpspruit, Pietermaritzburg 3206; tel. (33) 3452747; fax (33) 3944151; e-mail pcb@pcb.org.za; internet www.pcb.org.za; f. 2002 as successor to the Pietermaritzburg Chamber of Commerce and Industries (f. 1910); CEO Andrew Layman; 880 mems.

Port Elizabeth Regional Chamber of Commerce and Industry (PERCCI): 200 Norvic Dr., Greenacres, Port Elizabeth 6045; KPMG House, POB 63866, Greenacres 6057; tel. (41) 3731122; fax (41) 3731142; e-mail info@pechamber.org.za; internet www.percci.co.za; f. 1995; CEO Odwa Mtati; 814 mems.

Wesvaal Chamber of Business (WESCOB): POB 7167, Flamwood 2572; tel. (18) 4842952; fax (86) 6936365; e-mail chamber@gds .co.za; f. 1898; Pres. Johan Smit; c. 320 mems.

INDUSTRIAL AND TRADE ORGANIZATIONS

Association of Cementitious Material Producers: POB 10181, Centurion 0046; tel. (12) 6635146; fax (12) 6636036; e-mail naudek .acmp@mweb.co.za; f. 2002; Chair. Orrie Fenn.

Cape Wools: POB 2191, Port Elizabeth 6056; tel. (41) 544301; fax (41) 546760; e-mail onav@capewools.co.za; internet www.capewools .co.za; f. 1946 as the South African Wool Board; 12 mems: nine appointed by wool-growers and three by the Minister of Agriculture and Land Affairs; Chair. H. F. Prinsloo; Gen. Man. André Strydom.

Chamber of Mines of South Africa: Chamber of Mines Bldg, 5 Hollard St, POB 61809, Marshalltown 2107; tel. (11) 4987100; fax (11) 0865024757; e-mail webmaster@bullion.org.za; internet www.bullion.org.za; f. 1889; Pres. LAZARUS ZIM.

Clothing Trade Council (CloTrade): 35 Siemers Rd, 6th Floor, Doornfontein; POB 2303, Johannesburg 2000; tel. (11) 4020664; fax (11) 4020667; f. 2002; successor to the Clothing Fed. of South Africa; Pres. JACK KIPLING.

Grain Milling Federation: POB 7262, Centurion 0046; tel. (12) 6631660; fax (12) 6633109; e-mail info@grainmilling.org.za; internet www.grainmilling.org.za; f. 1944; Exec. Dir JANNIE DE VILLIERS.

Industrial Rubber Manufacturers' Association of South Africa: POB 91267, Auckland Park 2006; tel. (11) 4822524; fax (11) 7261344; f. 1978; Chair. Dr D. DUNCAN.

Master Builders South Africa (MBSA): POB 1619, Halfway House, Midrand 1685; tel. (11) 2059000; fax (11) 3151644; e-mail info@mbsa.org.za; f. 1904; fmrly known as Building Industries Fed. South Africa; 4,000 mems.

Master Diamond Cutters' Association of South Africa: S.A. Diamond Centre, Suite 310, 240 Commissioner St, Johannesburg 2001; tel. (11) 3341930; fax (11) 3341933; e-mail diam@pixie.co.za; f. 1928; 76 mems.

National Association of Automobile Manufacturers of South Africa: Nedbank Plaza, 1st Floor, cnr Church and Beatrix Sts, Pretoria 0002; POB 40611, Arcadia 0007; tel. (12) 3232980; fax (12) 3263232; e-mail naamsa@iafrica.com; f. 1935; Dir N. M. W. VERMEULEN; 18 full mems and 10 associate mems.

National Chamber of Milling, Inc: POB 7262, Centurion 0046; tel. (12) 6631660; fax (12) 6633109; e-mail info@grainmilling.org.za; internet www.grainmilling.org.za; f. 1936; Exec. Dir JANNIE DE VILLIERS.

National Textile Manufacturers' Association: POB 1506, Durban 4000; tel. (31) 3013692; fax (31) 3045255; f. 1947; Sec. PETER MCGREGOR; 9 mems.

Plastics Federation of South Africa: 18 Gazelle Rd, Corporate Park South, Old Pretoria Rd, Midrand; Private Bag X68, Halfway House, Midrand 1685; tel. (11) 3144021; fax (11) 3143764; internet www.plasticsinfo.co.za; f. 1979; Exec. Dir DAVID HUGHES; 10 mems.

Printing Industries Federation of South Africa (PIFSA): Printech Ave, Laser Park, POB 1084, Honeydew 2040; tel. (11) 6993000; fax (11) 6993010; e-mail pifsa@pifsa.org; internet www.pifsa.org; f. 1916; CEO C. W. J. SYKES; c. 900 mems (representing 65% of printers in South Africa).

Retail Motor Industry Organization (RMI): POB 2940, Randburg 2125; tel. (11) 8866300; fax (11) 7894525; e-mail rmi@rmi.org.za; internet www.rmi.org.za; f. 1908; affiliates throughout southern Africa; CEO JEFF OSBORNE; 7,800 mems.

South African Dairy Foundation: POB 72300, Lynnwood Ridge, Pretoria 0040; tel. (2712) 3485345; fax (2712) 3486284; f. 1980; Sec. S. L. VAN COLLER; 59 mems.

South African Federation of Civil Engineering Contractors (SAFCEC): POB 644, Bedfordview 2008; tel. (11) 4551700; fax (11) 4501715; e-mail admin@safcec.org.za; internet www.safcec.org.za; f. 1939; Dir H. P. LANGENHOVEN; 300 mems.

South African Fruit and Vegetable Canners' Association (Pty) Ltd (SAFVCA): Hoofstraat 258 Main St, POB 6175, Paarl 7620; tel. (21) 8711308; fax (21) 8725930; e-mail jill@safvca.co.za; f. 1953; Gen. Man. JILL ATWOOD-PALM; 9 mems.

South African Inshore Fishing Industry Association (Pty) Ltd: POB 2066, Cape Town 8000; tel. (21) 251500; f. 1953; Chair. W. A. LEWIS; Man. S. J. MALHERBE; 4 mems.

South African Oil Expressers' Association: Cereal Centre, 6th Floor, 11 Leyds St, Braamfontein 2017; tel. (11) 7251280; f. 1937; Sec. Dr R. DU TOIT; 14 mems.

South African Paint Manufacturers' Association: POB 751605, Gardenview, Johannesburg 2047; tel. (11) 4552503; fax (11) 4552502; e-mail sapma@sapma.org.za; internet www.sapma.org.za; Chair. DERYCK SPENCE; 80 mems.

South African Petroleum Industry Association (SAPIA): ABSA Centre, 14th Floor, Adderley St, Cape Town 8001; POB 7082, Roggebai 8012; tel. (21) 4198054; fax (21) 4198058; internet www.sapia.co.za; e-mail colinmcclelland@sapia.co.za; f. 1994; represents South Africa's six principal petroleum cos; Chair. RASHID YUSOF; Dir COLIN MCCLELLAND.

South African Sugar Association (SASA): 170 Flanders Dr., POB 700, Mount Edgecombe 4300; tel. (31) 5087000; fax (31) 5087199; internet www.sugar.org.za; Exec. Dir M. K. TRIKAM.

Includes:

South African Sugar Millers' Association Ltd (SASMAL): POB 1000, Mt Edgecombe 4300; tel. (31) 5087300; fax (31) 5087310; e-mail sasmal@sasa.org.za; represents interests of sugar millers and refiners within the operations of SASA; Exec. Dir D. W. HARDY; 6 mem. cos.

Sugar Manufacturing and Refining Employers' Association (SMREA): POB 1000, Mount Edgecombe 4300; tel. (31) 5087300; fax (31) 5087310; e-mail sasmal@sasa.org.za; f. 1947; regulates relations between mems and their employees; participates in the Bargaining Council for the sugar manufacturing and refining industry; Chair. C. H. KYLE; 6 mem. cos.

South African Wool Textile Council: POB 2201, North End, Port Elizabeth 6056; tel. (41) 4845252; fax (41) 4845629; Sec. BEATTY-ANNE STARKEY.

Steel and Engineering Industries Federation of South Africa (SEIFSA): POB 1338, Johannesburg 2000; tel. (11) 2989400; fax (11) 2989500; e-mail info@seifsa.co.za; internet www.seifsa.co.za; f. 1943; Exec. Dir. BRIAN ANGUS; 38 affiliated trade asscns representing 2,350 mems.

VinPro (SA): POB 1411, Suider-Paarl 7624; tel. (21) 8073322; fax (21) 8632079; e-mail info@vinpro.co.za; internet www.vinpro.co.za; f. 1979; represents wine producers; Chair. ABRIE BOTHA; Exec. Dir JOS LE ROUX.

UTILITIES

Electricity

Electricity Supply Commission (ESKOM): POB 1091, Johannesburg 2000; tel. (11) 8008111; fax (11) 8004390; internet www.eskom.co.za; f. 1923; state-controlled; CEO A. J. MORGAN.

Gas

SASOL Gas: POB 4211, Randburg 2125; tel. (11) 8897600; fax (11) 8897955; internet www.sasol.com/gas; f. 1964; Man. Dir HANS NAUDÉ.

Water

Umgeni Water: 310 Burger St, Pietermaritzburg 3201; tel. (331) 3411111; fax (331) 3411167; internet www.umgeni.co.za/contact.html.

Water Research Commission: Private Bag X03, Gezina 0031; tel. (12) 3300340; fax (12) 3312565; e-mail orders@wrc.org.za; internet www.wrc.org.za; Chair. Prof. H. C. KASAN; CEO Dr SNOWY KHOZA.

MAJOR COMPANIES

The following are among the leading companies in South Africa.

AECI Ltd: Private Bag X21, Gallo Manor 2052; tel. (11) 8068700; fax (11) 8068701; e-mail groupcomms@aeci.co.za; internet www.aeci.co.za; f. 1924; cap. and res R2,264m., sales R6,745m. (Dec. 2001); mfrs of explosives, industrial and agricultural chemicals and fibres; Chair A. E. PEDDER; CEO L. C. VAN VUGHT; 8,200 employees.

Barloworld Ltd: 180 Katherine St, POB 782248, Sandton 2146; tel. (11) 4451000; fax (11) 4443643; e-mail barlowpr@barloworld.com; internet www.barloworld.com; f. 1902; total assets 27,842m. (Sept. 2004); conducts industrial brand management in 31 countries; represents principals incl. Caterpillar (machines and engines), Hyster (lift trucks), Freightliner (trucks) and other motor vehicle mfrs; subsidiary producers incl. PPC Surebuild (cement), Plascon, Taubmans, Bristol and White Knight (coatings), Melles Griot (photonics) and Bibby Sterilin (laboratory equipment); Avis licensee for southern Africa; Chair. WARREN A. M. CLEWLOW; CEO A. J. 'TONY' PHILLIPS; c. 12,500 employees (South Africa).

Frame Textile Group: POB 81, New Germany 3620; tel. (31) 7104444; fax (31) 7056329; e-mail framexec@iafrica.com; internet www.frame.co.za; f. 1928; fmrly Consolidated Frame Textiles Ltd; mfrs of fabrics for clothing and textile industries; Group Man. Dir WALTER SIMEONI; 3,900 employees.

Grinaker-LTA: Block A, Jurgens St, Jet Park, Boksburg 1459; POB 1517, Kempton Park 1620; tel. (11) 5786000; fax (11) 5786161; e-mail dduplessis@grinaker-lta.co.za; internet www.grinaker-lta.com; f. 2000 by merger of LTA Ltd (f. 1965) and Grinaker Holdings (f. 1964); 75% owned by Aveng Ltd, 25% owned by Qakazana Investment Holdings (Pty) Ltd (Tiso Group); total assets R4,886.4m., sales R8,561.7m. (Dec. 2005); holding co; multidisciplinary construction and engineering group specializing in infrastructure, energy and mining; Exec. Chair. CARL GRIM; Sec. JOHN BAXTER; 17,828 employees.

Holcim (South Africa) (Pty): POB 6367, Weltevredenpark 1715; tel. (11) 6705500; fax (11) 6705793; internet www.alpha.co.za; f. 1934; fmrly Alpha (Pty) Ltd; present name adopted in 2004; subsidiary of Holcim Ltd Switzerland; cap. and res R1,122.8m., sales R1,967.2m. (Dec. 1997); major producer of cement, stone aggregates, lime, industrial minerals and ready-mixed concrete, with extensive interests in manufacture of paper sacks and fertilizers; Chair. BASIL E. HERSOV; 4,583 employees.

ICS Holdings Ltd: Harrowdene Office Park, Bldg 4, Western Service Rd, Woodmead, POB 783854, Sandton 2146; tel. (11) 8045780; fax (11) 8044173; f. 1902; cap. R10.7m.; processes and distributes red meat, poultry and meat products, milk and milk products, ice cream, fish; Chair. R. A. WILLIAMS; Man. Dir R. V. SMITHER; 14,400 employees.

Illovo Sugar Ltd: Illovo Sugar Park, 1 Montgomery Dr., Mount Edgecombe; POB 194, Durban 4000; tel. (31) 5084300; fax (31) 5084525; e-mail gdknox@illovo.co.za; internet www.illovosugar.com; f. 1891; sales R5,468.80m. (March 2006); Africa's largest sugar producer (annual output of some 1.9m. metric tons of raw and refined sugar in Southern Africa); downstream producer of syrup, furfural and its derivatives, ethyl alcohol and lactulose; agricultural, manufacturing and other interests in six southern African countries; Man. Dir D. G. MACLEOD; 12,886 permanent employees.

Irvin and Johnson Ltd: 70 Prestwhich St, Cape Town 8001; POB 1628, Cape Town 8000; tel. (21) 4029200; fax (21) 4029282; internet www.ij.co.za; f. 1910; sales R2,836.0m. (2000); trawler operators; processors, distributors and exporters of frozen fish; Man. Dir R. C. GORDON; 6,099 employees.

Malesela Taihan Electric Cable (Pty) Ltd: Steel Rd, Peacehaven, Vereeniging, 1930 Gauteng; tel. (16) 4508200; fax (16) 4508202; e-mail info@m-tec.co.za; internet www.m-tec.co.za; f. 1911 as Union Steel Corpn of South Africa; cap. R20m. (June 2000); mfr of copper and aluminium conductor and associated products; Chair. M. K. MADUNGANDABA; CEO C. H. KIM; 354 employees.

Nampak Ltd: 114 Dennis Rd, Athol Gardens, POB 784324, Sandton 2146; tel. (11) 7196300; fax (11) 4445761; e-mail mcleishsa@nampak.co.za; internet www.nampak.co.za; f. 1968; total assets 12,435.6m. (2006); mfrs of packaging in various forms based on paper, paper board, metal, glass and plastics; there are subsidiaries in the service area and fields allied to packaging; CEO JOHN BORTOLAN; Man. Dir Africa NEIL CUMMING; 15,345 employees.

Petroleum, Oil and Gas Corporation of South Africa (Pty) Ltd (PetroSA): Portswood Sq., Foyer 2, Dock Rd, V&A Waterfront, Cape Town 8001; Private Bag X1, Waterfront 8002; tel. (21) 4173000; fax (21) 4173144; e-mail petrosa@petrosa.co.za; internet www.petrosa.co.za; f. 2002 by merger of Mossgas, Soekor and parts of the Strategic Fuel Fund Asscn; undertakes exploration and production of oil and natural gas off the coast of South Africa; Pres. and CEO SIPHO MKHIZE.

Pretoria Portland Cement Co Ltd: PPC Bldg, 180 Katherine St, Barlow Park ext., Sandton; POB 787416, Sandton 2146; tel. (11) 3869000; fax (11) 3869001; e-mail contactus@ppc.co.za; internet www.ppc.co.za; f. 1892; cap. R614.9m., sales R2,071.2m. (Sept. 2001); mfrs and distributors of cement, lime and limestone products, paper sacks and other containers; also mines and markets gypsum; CEO JOHN E. GOMERSALL; 3,004 employees.

Protea Holdings Cape (Pty) Ltd: POB 3839, Cape Town 8000; tel. (21) 512357; f. 1963; Man. Dir A. WOLFAARDT; 100 employees.

SAPPI Ltd: POB 31560, Braamfontein 2017; tel. (11) 4078111; fax (11) 3391846; internet www.sappi.com; f. 1936 as South African Pulp and Paper Industries Ltd; sales US $4,184m. (Sept. 2001); eight pulp and paper mfg and processing subsidiaries; Exec. Chair. EUGENE VAN AS; 18,235 employees.

SASOL Ltd: POB 5486, Johannesburg 2000; tel. (11) 4413111; fax (11) 7885092; e-mail sasolltd@sasol.com; internet www.sasol.com; f. 1950; sales R61,578.0m. (June 2002); group of cos operating the world's largest complex of oil-from-coal petrochemical installations; produces. 120 products; Chair. PAUL DU P. KRUGER; CEO PIETER COX; 31,000 employees.

South African Breweries Ltd: 65 Park Lane, Sandown; POB 782178, Sandton 2146; tel. (11) 8818111; fax (11) 3391830; internet www.sabreweries.com; f. 1895; owned by SABMiller PLC; cap. and res US $1,703m., sales US $6,184m. (March 1999); largest non-mining industrial group in sub-Saharan Africa; brewing and marketing of beer; mfrs, wholesalers and retailers of furniture, footwear, domestic appliances, plate glass, textiles, natural fruit juices and soft drinks; discount department, food and fashion chain stores; also owns and operates hotels; Man. Dir TONY VAN KRALINGEN; 8,600 employees.

Stewarts and Lloyds Trading (Pty) Ltd: POB 1137, Johannesburg 2000; tel. (11) 4933000; fax (11) 4931440; internet www.stewartsandlloyds.co.za; f. 1903; acquired by Stockwell in 2001; cap. R12m.; suppliers of metal products and services to the engineering, mining, water, chemical and petro-chemical, automotive, construction and agricultural industries; Export Man. P. KEMP.

L. Suzman Ltd: 2 Elray St, Raedene POB 2188, Johannesburg 2192; tel. (11) 4851020; fax (11) 6401325; f. 1889; cap. R2.1m.; wholesale distribution of tobacco products and other consumer products; operates 26 brs in South Africa; Chair. P. R. S. THOMAS; Man. Dir C. J. VAN DER WALT; 1,000 employees.

Tongaat-Hulett Group Ltd: Amanzimnyama Hill Rd, Tongaat, KwaZulu/Natal, 4400; POB 3, Tongaat 4400; tel. (32) 4394019; fax (32) 9453333; e-mail info@tongaat.co.za; internet www.tongaat.co.za; f. 1892; total assets R9,056m. (Jan. 2007); incorporating Hulett Aluminium, African Products (starch and glucose mfrs), Tongaat-Hulett Sugar, and Moreland (property devt); 38% owned by Anglo South Africa Capital (Pty) Ltd; agri-processing business incl. integrated components of land management, property development and agriculture; Chair. CEDRIC SAVAGE; CEO PETER STAUDE; 30,000 employees (2006).

Mining Companies

Anglo American Corpn of South Africa Ltd: 44 Main St, Johannesburg; POB 61587, Marshalltown 2107; tel. (11) 6389111; fax (11) 6382455; f. 1917; wholly owned subsidiary of Anglo American PLC; group sales US $19,245m. (1999); mining and natural resource group; a world leader in gold, platinum group metals and diamonds, with significant interests in coal, base and ferrous metals, industrial minerals, forestry and financial services; Non-Exec. Chair. JULIAN OGILVIE THOMPSON; CEO TONY TRAHAR.

AngloGold Ltd: 76 Jeppe St, Newtown, Johannesburg 2001; POB 62117, Marshalltown 2107; tel. (11) 6376000; e-mail cjlandman@anglogoldashanti.com; internet www.anglogold.co.za; cap. and res R21,680m. (Dec. 1998); world's largest gold producer; Chair. RUSSELL EDEY; CEO ROBERT M. GODSELL; 93,000 employees.

Anglovaal Mining Ltd: POB 1885, Saxonwold 2132; tel. (11) 2830000; fax (11) 2830007; internet www.avmin.co.za; f. 1933; cap. and res R3,125m., sales R2,489m. (June 1999); mining, financial and industrial group with divisions operating in precious metal and base mineral mining and beneficiation, fishing, food and rubber production, packaging, construction, engineering, electronics, information technology, textiles; Chair. KENNEDY MAXWELL; CEO RICK MENELL; 70,000 employees.

De Beers Consolidated Mines Ltd: 36 Stockdale St, POB 616, Kimberley 8300; tel. (53) 8394111; fax (53) 8394210; internet www.edata.co.za; cap. and res R23,349m., sales R15,957m. (Dec. 1998); group of diamond mining cos and allied interests; reorg. 1990, when foreign interests were transferred to De Beers Centenary AG, Switzerland; Chair. NICHOLAS F. OPPENHEIMER; Man. Dir GARY RALFE; 14,000 employees.

Gencor Ltd: Postnet Suite 222, Private Bag X30500, Houghton 2041; tel. (11) 6476200; fax (11) 4841654; f. 1895; fmrly General Mining Union Corpn; cap. and res R3,674m., sales R2,261m. (June 1998); diversified group with investments in several cos, incl. GENMIN, which administers mines producing coal, platinum, ferro-alloys, and ENGEN, which has interests in petroleum refining and retail petrol sales; Chair. A. S. DU PLESSIS.

Gold Fields of South Africa Ltd: Postnet Suite 252, Private Bag X30500, Houghton 2041; tel. (11) 6442460; fax (11) 4840639; internet www.goldfields.co.za; cap. and res R1,342m., sales R200m. (June 1999); incl. five gold-producing cos, platinum, coal and base metals; Chair. J. P. RUPERT; Man. Dir IAN COCKERILL.

JCI Gold Ltd: Consolidated Bldg, cnr Fox and Harrison Sts, Johannesburg 2001, POB 590, Johannesburg 2000; tel. (11) 3739111; fax (11) 4921070; f. 1889; cap. and res R1,555.5m., sales R100.4m. (March 1999); mining house with major investments in gold, ferrochrome, coal and base metals; Chair. Prof. W. L. NKUHLU; CEO J. BROWNRIGG.

Palabora Mining Co Ltd: Copper Rd, POB 65, Phalaborwa 1390; tel. (15) 7802911; fax (15) 7810448; cap. R28.9m., sales R1,985.0m. (Dec. 2001); 49% owned by Rio Tinto, 30% owned by Anglo American; mining of copper, with by-products of magnetite, zirconia metals, uranium oxide, anode slimes, nickel sulphate, sulphuric acid and vermiculite; produces c. 80,000 metric tons of refined copper per year; Chair. RUFUS MARUMA; Man. Dir KEITH MARSHALL; c. 2,000 employees.

Randgold and Exploration Co Ltd: POB 82291, Southdale 2135; tel. (11) 8370706; fax (11) 8372396; e-mail haddond@randgold.co.za; internet www.randgold.co.za; f. 1992; to acquire gold-mining interests of Rand Mines Ltd; cap. and res R310.8m., sales R309.2m. (March 1999); mineral exploration and devt; Chair. ROGER KEBBLE.

TRADE UNIONS

According to COSATU, some 40% of workers were unionized at March 2005. Under amendments to the Labour Relations Act (LRA), 1995, introduced in 2002, the Government sought to eliminate illegitimate trade unions and employers' organizations. The provisions of the LRA also stipulated that organizations that failed to provide annual audited financial accounts would be deregistered.

Trade Union Federations

Confederation of South African Workers' Unions: Constancia Bldg, 7th Floor, Room 701, 291 Andries St, Pretoria; POB 877, Pretoria 0001; tel. (12) 322 4961; fax (12) 322 4964; e-mail consawu@mweb.co.za; internet www.consawu.co.za; f. 2003; affiliated to World Confed. of Labour and Dem. Org. of African Workers' Trade Unions; Pres. JOEL MFINGWANA; Gen. Sec. KHULILE NKUSHUBANA.

Affiliates with 20,000 or more mems include:

National Union of Public Service and Allied Workers (NUPSAW): Mercedes Benz Bldg, 2nd Floor, 11 Schoemen St, Pretoria; POB 11459, Tramshed 0126; tel. (12) 3282236; fax (012) 3286410; e-mail nupsaw@mweb.co.za; internet www.nupsaw.co.za; f. 1998; Pres. EZRA MFINWANA; Gen. Sec. SUCCESS MATAITSANE; c. 42,000 (2005).

Other organizations affiliated to CONSAWU include: the Asscn of Metal, Iron and General Workers' Union; the Asscn Trade Union of South African Workers; the Brick and General Workers' Union; Building, Wood and Allied Workers' Union of South Africa; the Building Workers' Union; the Food and Gen. Workers' Union; the Commercial Workers' Union of South Africa; the Food, Cleaning and Security Workers' Union; the Fed. Council of Retail and Allied Workers'; the Hotel and Allied Restaurant Workers' Union; the Movement for Social Justice; the Nat. Certified Fishing and Allied Workers' Union; the Nat. Construction, Building and Allied Workers' Union; the Nat. Union of Tertiary Education of South Africa; the Professional Educators' Union; the Professional Employees' Trade Union of South Africa; the Progressive Gen. Employees Asscn of South Africa; the Progressive Trade Union of South Africa; Solidarity; the South African Building and Allied Workers' Org.; the South African Domestic and Gen. Workers' Union; the South African Food, Retail and Agricultural Workers' Union; the Transport Action, Retail and Gen. Workers' Union; the Trawler and Line Fishermen's Union; the Westcoast Workers' Union; and the Workers' Labour Council–South Africa.

Congress of South African Trade Unions (COSATU): COSATU House, 4th Floor, 1–5 Leyds St, Braamfontein; POB 1019, Johannesburg 2000; tel. (11) 3394911; fax (11) 3396940; internet www.cosatu.org.za; f. 1985; 21 trade union affiliates representing c. 1.8m. paid-up mems; Pres. WILLIE MADISHA; Gen. Sec. ZWELINZIMA VAVI.

Affiliates with 20,000 or more mems include:

Chemical, Energy, Paper, Printing, Wood and Allied Workers' Union (CEPPWAWU): Umoya House, 3rd Floor, 2–6 New St, South Ghandi Sq., Johannesburg 2001; POB 3219, Johannesburg 2000; tel. (11) 8332870; fax (11) 8332883; e-mail secretariat@ceppwawu.org.za; f. 1999 by merger of the Chemical Workers' Industrial Union and Paper, Printing, Wood and the Allied Workers' Union; represents workers in the petrochemical, consumer chemical, rubber, plastics, glass and ceramics, printing, pulp and paper, furniture and woodworking industries; Pres. PASCO DYANI; Gen. Sec. WELILE NOLINGO; Nat. Treas. MARY NXUMALO; 61,768 mems (2006).

Communication Workers' Union (CWU): 29 Rissik St, 3rd Floor, Johannesburg 2001; POB 10248, Johannesburg 2000; tel. (11) 8388188; fax (11) 8388727; e-mail membership@cwu.org.za; internet www.cwu.org.za; f. 1996 by merger of the Post Office Employees Asscn, the Post and Telecommunication Workers Asscn and the South African Post Telecommunication Employees Asscn; Pres. JOE CHAUKE; Gen. Sec. MACVICAR B. DYASOPU; 44,000 mems (2006).

Democratic Nursing Organisation of South Africa (DENOSA): 605 Church St, Pretoria 0001; POB 1280, Pretoria 0001; tel. (12) 3432315; fax (12) 3440750; internet www.denosa.org.za; f. 1996; Pres. EPHRAIM P. MAFALO; Gen.-Sec. THEMBEKA T. GWAGWA; 64,165 mems (2006).

Food and Allied Workers' Union (FAWU): Vuyisile Mini Centre, cnr NY1 and NY110, Guguletu, Cape Town; POB 1234, Woodstock 7915; tel. (21) 6379040; fax (21) 6379190; e-mail admin@fawu.org.za; affiliated to the Int. Union of Food, Agricultural, Hotel, Restaurant, Catering, Tobacco and Allied Workers' Asscns; Pres. (vacant); Gen. Sec. KATISHI MASEMOLA; 111,029 mems (2006).

National Education, Health and Allied Workers' Union (NEHAWU): 56 Marshall St, Marshalltown, Johannesburg; POB 10812, Johannesburg 2000; tel. (11) 8332902; fax (11) 8343416; e-mail bongi@nehawu.org.za; internet www.nehawu.org.za; f. 1987; affiliated to the Public Services International; Pres. NOLUTHANDO MAYENDE-SIBIYA; Gen. Sec. FIKILE MAJOLA; 192,739 mems (2006).

National Union of Metalworkers of South Africa (NUMSA): NUMSA Bldg, 153 Bree St, cnr Becker St, Newtown, Johannesburg 2001; POB 260483, Excom 2023; tel. (11) 6891700; fax (11) 8336408; internet www.numsa.org.za; affiliated to the Int. Metalworkers' Fed.; represents workers in the engineering, motor, tyre, rubber and automobile assembly industries; Pres. MTHUTHUZELI TOM; Gen. Sec. SILUMKO NONDWANGU; 216,808 mems (2006).

National Union of Mineworkers (NUM): 7 Rissik St, cnr Frederick St, Johannesburg 2000; POB 2424, Johannesburg 2000; tel. (11) 3772000; fax (11) 8360367; e-mail zmakue@num.org.za; internet www.num.org.za; f. 1982; represents workers in the mining, energy, construction, building material manufacturing, civil engineering and building industries; Pres. SENZENI ZOKWANA; Gen. Sec. FRANS BALENI; 262,042 mems (2006).

Police and Prisons Civil Rights Union (POPCRU): POPCRU House, 97–99 Simmonds St, Braamfontein; POB 8657, Johannesburg 2000; tel. (11) 4030406; fax (11) 4039377; Pres. ZIZAMELE CEBEKHULU; Gen. Sec. ABBEY WITBOOI; 95,864 mems (2006).

SASBO: The Finance Union: SASBO House, Fourmall Office Park West, 1 Percy St, Fourways; Private Bag X84, Bryanston 2021; tel. (11) 4670192; fax (11) 4670188; e-mail michelek@sasbo.org.za; internet www.sasbo.org.za; f. 1916 as the South African Soc. of Bank Officials; Gen. Sec. SHAUN OELSCHIG; 63,470 mems (2007).

Southern African Clothing and Textile Workers' Union (SACTWU): Industria House, 350 Victoria Rd, Salt River, Cape Town; POB 1194, Woodstock 7915; tel. (21) 4474570; fax (21) 4474593; e-mail aldenea@sactwu.org.za; affiliated to the Int. Textile, Garment and Leather Workers' Fed.; Pres. JOHN ZIKHALI; Gen. Sec. EBRAHIM PATEL; 110,216 mems (2006).

South African Commercial, Catering and Allied Workers Union (SACCAWU): SACCAWU House, 11 Leyds St, Braamfontein; POB 10730, Johannesburg 2000; tel. (11) 4038333; fax (11) 4030309; e-mail secretariatadmin@saccawu.org.za; f. 1975; affiliated to the Union Network International; represents workers in the service industry, commercial, catering, tourism, hospitality and finance sectors; Pres. AMOS MOTHAPO; Gen. Sec. BONES SKULU; 107,553 mems (2006).

South African Democratic Teachers' Union (SADTU): Matthew Goniwe House, cnr Goud and Marshall Sts, Johannesburg 2000; POB 6401, Johannesburg 2000; tel. (11) 3344830; fax (11) 3344836; e-mail tntshangase@sadtu.org.za; internet www.sadtu.org.za; f. 1990; affiliated to Education Int.; Pres. WILLIAM MADISHA; Gen. Sec. THULAS NXESI; 224,387 mems (2006).

South African Municipal Workers Union (SAMWU): Trade Union House, 8 Beverly St, Athlone, Cape Town; Private Bag X9, Athlone 7760; tel. (21) 6971151; fax (21) 6969175; e-mail soraya.solomon@samwu.org.za; internet www.samwu.org.za; f. 1987; affiliated to the Public Services International; Pres. PETRUS MASHISHI; Gen. Sec. MTHANDEKI NHLAPO; 118,973 (2006).

South African Transport and Allied Workers' Union (SATAWU): Marble Towers, 6th Floor, cnr Jeppe and Von Wielligh Sts, Johannesburg 2000; POB 9451, Johannesburg 2001; tel. (11) 3336127; fax (11) 3338918; e-mail cecilia@satawu.org.za; internet www.satawu.org.za; f. 2000; affiliated to the Int. Transport Workers' Fed.; Pres. EZROM MABYANA; Gen. Sec. RANDALL HOWARD; 134,000 mems (2006).

Other organizations affiliated to COSATU include: the Musicians' Union of South Africa; the Performing Arts Workers' Equity; the Public and Allied Workers' Union of South Africa; the South African Democratic Nurses' Union; the South African Football Players' Union; the South African Medical Association; and the South African State and Allied Workers' Union.

Federation of Unions of South Africa (FEDUSA): Fedusa House, 10 Kingfisher St, Horizon Park, Roodepoort 1725; POB 7779, Westgate 1734; tel. (11) 2791800; fax (11) 2791821; e-mail fedusa@fedusa.org.za; internet www.fedusa.org.za; f. 1997 by merger of the Fed. of South African Labour Unions and Fed. of Civil Servants; 22 mem. unions representing 550,000 workers; politically non-aligned; affiliated to the Int. Trade Union Confed.; proposed 'super fed.' with the Nat. Council of Trade Unions and Confed. of South African Workers' Unions delayed in 2006; Pres. MARY MALETE; Gen. Sec. DENNIS GEORGE.

Affiliated unions with 10,000 or more mems include:

Health and Other Services Personnel Trade Union of South Africa (HOSPERSA): POB 12266 Queenswood, Pretoria 0121; tel. (12) 3652021; fax (12) 3652043; internet www.hospersa.co.za; affiliated to the Public Services International; represents workers in the public and private health, welfare and services sectors, and the public safety and security and education sectors; Pres. GAVIN MOULTRIE; Gen. Sec. JOHAN STEYN; 62,272 mems (2005).

National Security and Unqualified Workers' Union (NASAWU): United Bldg, 10th Floor, 58 Field St, Durban; POB 63015, Bishopsgate, Durban 4008; tel. (31) 3059320; fax (31) 3059621; Gen. Sec. HAROLD MDINEKA; 13,000 mems (2006).

National Union of Leather and Allied Workers (NULAW): Mercury House, 6th Floor, Rm 67, 320 Smith St, Durban; POB 839,

Durban 4000; tel. (31) 3076420; fax (31) 3043077; e-mail nulaw.mar@mweb.co.za; affiliated to the Int. Textile, Garment and Leather Workers' Fed.; Gen. Sec. MARTIN PAULSEN; 13,180 mems (2005).

Professional Transport Workers' Union (PTWU): Sable Centre, 3rd Floor, 41 De Korte St, Braamfontein, Johannesburg; POB 31415, Braamfontein 2017; tel. (11) 3394249; fax (11) 6820444; e-mail ptwu@wol.co.za; represents workers in the road freight, private security and cleaning sectors; Gen. Sec. PAUL WA MALEMA; c. 10,000 mems (2002).

South African Typographical Union (SATU): SATU House, 166 Visagie St, Pretoria 0001; POB 1993, Pretoria 0001; tel. (12) 3236097; fax (12) 3231284; e-mail martind@satu.co.za; f. 1982; represents workers in the printing, newspaper and packaging industries; Gen. Sec. MARTIN DEYSEL; 17,796 mems (2001).

Suid-Afrikaanse Onderwysersunie (SAOU) (South African Teachers' Union): SAOU Bldg, 278 Serene St, Garsfontein, Pretoria; POB 90120, Garsfontein 0042; tel. (12) 3489641; fax (12) 3482478; e-mail liezla@saou.co.za; internet www.saou.co.za; Pres. JOHANNES S. ROUX; CEO EDWARD H. DAVIES; 24,247 (2006).

United Association of South Africa (UASA): UASA Office Park, 42 Goldman St, Florida 1709; POB 565, Florida 1710; tel. (11) 4723600; fax (11) 6744057; e-mail jplbez@uasa.org.za; internet www.uasa.org.za; f. 1998 by merger of the Administrative, Technical and Electronic Asscn of South Africa and Officials' Asscn of South Africa; fed. of 31 unions incl. the fmr Nat. Employees' Trade Union; represents workers in the mining, motor, transport, manufacturing and engineering industries; CEO J. P. L. 'KOOS' BEZUIDENHOUT; c. 100,000 mems (2006).

Other organizations affiliated to FEDUSA include: the Airline Pilots' Association of South Africa; the Care, Catering and Retail Allied Workers Union of South Africa; the Construction and Engineering Industrial Workers Union; the Insurance and Banking Staff Association; the Internal Staff Association; the Jewellers and Goldsmiths Union; the Millennium Workers Union; the Mouth Peace Workers Union; the National Democratic Change and Allied Workers Union; the National Teachers Union; the National Union of Hotel, Restaurant, Catering, Commercial, Health and Allied Workers; the South African Communications Union; the South African Parastatal and Tertiary Institutions Union; the United National Public Servants Association of South Africa and Allied Workers Union; and the United Transport and Allied Trade Union.

National Council of Trade Unions (NACTU): Metropolitan Life Centre, 4th Floor, 108 Fox St, Johannesburg; POB 10928, Johannesburg 2000; tel. (11) 8331040; fax (11) 8331032; e-mail info@nactu.org.za; internet www.nactu.org.za; f. 1986 by merger of the Council of Unions of South Africa and Azanian Confed. of Trade Unions; fed. of 22 African trade unions; aligned to the Pan-Africanist Congress of Azania party; Pres. JOSEPH MAQHEKENI; Gen. Sec. MAHLOMOLA SKHOSANA; 327,000 mems (2004).

Affiliates with 10,000 or more mems include:

Building, Construction and Allied Workers' Union (BCAWU): Glencairn Bldg, 8th Floor, 73 Market St, Johannesburg; POB 96, Johannesburg 2000; tel. (11) 3339180; fax (11) 3339944; e-mail bcawu@netactive.co.za; f. 1974; affiliated to the Building and Wood Workers International; Gen. Sec. NARIUS MOLOTO; c. 25,000 mems (2003).

Media Workers' Association of South Africa (MWASA): North State Bldg, 5th Floor, cnr Market and Kruis Sts, Johannesburg; POB 11136, Johannesburg 2000; tel. (11) 3336306; fax (11) 3338616; f. 1978 as the Writers Asscn of South Africa, successor to the Union of Black Journalists; present name adopted in 1986; affiliated to the Int. Fed. of Journalists and Union Network Int.; applied to become a political party in 2005; Pres. TUWANI GUMANI; Sec.-Gen. THEMBA HLATSHWAYO; c. 27,000 mems (1998).

Metal and Electrical Workers' Union of South Africa (MEWUSA): Elephant House, 5th Floor, 107 Market St, Johannesburg; POB 3669, Johannesburg 2000; tel. (11) 3369369; fax (11) 3369120; e-mail mewusa@lantic.net; f. 1989; affiliated to the Int. Metalworkers' Fed.; Gen. Sec. NKRUMAH RAYMOND KGAGUDI; c. 10,000 paid-up mems (2005).

National Union of Food, Beverages, Wine, Spirit and Allied Workers (NUFBWSAW): 8 Stannic Bldg, 4th Floor, New St, South Ghandi Sq., Johannesburg; POB 5718, Johannesburg 2000; tel. (11) 8331140; fax (11) 8331503; Pres. ARMSTRONG NTOYAKHE; Nat. Organizer ANTHONY HENDRICKS; c. 10,000 mems (2005).

South African Chemical Workers' Union (SACWU): 29 Klerk St, btwn Harrison and Dirk Sts, 11th Floor, Johannesburg; POB 236, Johannesburg 2000; tel. (11) 8386581; fax (11) 8386622; e-mail samela@sacwu.co.za; Pres. JOSEPH MAQHEKENI; c. 40,000 mems (2003).

Other organizations affiliated to NACTU include: the Banking, Insurance and Finance Workers' Union; the Hospitality Industry and Allied Workers' Union; the Hotel, Liquor, Catering, Commercial and Allied Workers' Union of South Africa; the Municipality, Education, State, Health And Allied Workers' Union; the National Clothing and Textile Workers' Union of South Africa; the National Services and Allied Workers' Union; the National Union of Farm Workers; the National Union of Furniture and Allied Workers; the Parliamentary Staff Union; Transport and Allied Workers Union; and the Transport and Omnibus Workers' Union.

Non-affiliated Union

Public Servants' Association of South Africa (PSA): PSA Head Office Bldg, 563 Belvedere St, Arcadia, Pretoria; POB 40404, Arcadia 0007; tel. (12) 3036500; fax (12) 3036652; e-mail ask@psa.co.za; internet www.psa.co.za; withdrew affiliation from FEDUSA in 2006; Chair. PAUL SELLO; Pres. KOOT MYBURGH; Gen. Man. DANNY ADONIS; 185,500 mems (2006).

Transport

Most of South Africa's railway network and the harbours and airways are administered by the state-owned Transnet Ltd. There are no navigable rivers. Private bus services are regulated to complement the railways.

Transnet Ltd: 8 Hillside Rd, Parktown, Johannesburg; POB 72501, Parkview 2122; tel. (11) 4887055; fax (11) 4887511; internet www.transnet.co.za; Chair. BONGANI AUG KHUMALO; CEO MARIA RAMOS.

RAILWAYS

With the exception of commuter services, the South African railways system is operated by Spoornet Ltd (the rail division of Transnet). The network comprised 31,400 track-km in 1996, of which 16,946 km was electrified. Extensive rail links connect Spoornet with the rail networks of neighbouring countries.

Spoornet: Paul Kruger Bldg, 30 Wolmarans St, Private Bag X47, Johannesburg 2001; tel. (11) 7735090; fax (11) 7733033; internet www.spoornet.co.za; CEO SIYABONGA GAMA.

ROADS

In 2001 there were an estimated 36,131 km of classified roads, including 239 km of motorways. In 2004 there were 7,200 km of main roads.

South African National Roads Agency Ltd (SANRAL): Ditsela Pl., 1204 Park St, cnr Duncan St, Hatfield, Pretoria; POB 415, Pretoria 0001; tel. (12) 4266000; fax (12) 3622116; e-mail info@nra.co.za; internet www.nra.co.za; f. 1998; responsible for design, construction, management and maintenance of 13,933 km of the national road network (2005); Chair. LOT NDLOVU; CEO NAZIR ALLI.

SHIPPING

The principal harbours are at Richards Bay, Durban, Saldanha, Cape Town, Port Elizabeth, East London and Mossel Bay. Construction of an eighth port, at Ngqura (Coega), was ongoing in early 2006. The deep-water port at Richards Bay has been extended and its facilities upgraded. Both Richards Bay and Saldanha Bay are major bulk-handling ports, while Saldanha Bay also has an important fishing fleet. More than 30 shipping lines serve South African ports.

National Ports Authority (NPA): POB 32696, Braamfontein 2017; tel. (11) 2424022; fax (11) 2424027; internet www.npa.co.za; f. 2000; fmrly part of Portnet; subsidiary of Transnet; controls and manages the country's seven major seaports; CEO KHOMOTSO PHIHLELA (acting).

South African Maritime Safety Authority: Block E, Hatfield Gardens, 333 Grosvenor St, Hatfield, Pretoria; SAMSA, POB 13186, Hatfield 0028; tel. (12) 3423049; fax (12) 3423160; e-mail samsa@iafrica.com; advises the Govt on matters connected with sea transport to, from or between South Africa's ports, incl. safety at sea, and prevention of pollution by petroleum; CEO Capt. B. R. WATT.

South African Port Operations (SAPO): Marine Parade, POB 10124, Durban 4056; tel. (31) 3088333; fax (31) 3088352; e-mail webmaster@saportops.co.za; internet www.saponet.co.za; f. 2000; fmrly part of Portnet; subsidiary of Transnet; operates 13 container, bulk, breakbulk and car terminals at six of the country's major ports; CEO TAU MORWE.

CIVIL AVIATION

Civil aviation is controlled by the Minister of Transport. The Chief Directorate: Civil Aviation Authority at the Department of Transport is responsible for licensing and control of domestic and international air services.

Airports Company South Africa (ACSA): 24 Johnson Rd, Riverwoods, Bedfordview 2008; POB 75480, Gardenview 2047; tel. (11) 9216991; internet www.airports.co.za; f. 1993; owns and operates

South Africa's nine principal airports, of which three (at Johannesburg, Cape Town and Durban) are classified as international airports; Chair. TOMMY OLIPHANT; Man. Dir MONHLA HLAHLA.

Civil Aviation Authority (CAA): Ikhaya Lokundiza, Bldg 16, Treur Close, Waterfall Park, Bekker St, Midrand; Private Bag X73, Halfway House 1685; tel. (11) 5451000; fax (12) 5451465; e-mail mail@caa.co.za; internet www.caa.co.za; Chair. ZAKES MYEZA (acting).

Air Cape (Pty) Ltd: POB D. F. Malan Airport, Cape Town 7525; tel. (21) 9340344; fax (21) 9348379; scheduled internal passenger services and charters, engineering services and aerial surveys; Chair. Dr P. VAN ASWEGEN; Gen. Man. G. A. NORTJE.

Airlink Airline: POB 7529, Bonaero Park 1622; tel. (11) 3953579; fax (11) 3951319; internet www.saairlink.co.za; f. 1992; internal and external scheduled services and charters in Southern Africa; Man. Dirs RODGER FOSTER, BARRIE WEBB.

COMAIR Ltd: POB 7015, Bonaero Park 1622; tel. (11) 9210111; fax (11) 9733913; e-mail cr@comair.co.za; internet www.comair.co.za; f. 1946; scheduled domestic, regional and international services; Chair. D. NOVICK; Jt CEOs ERIK VENTER, GIDON NOVICK.

Safair (Pty) Ltd: POB 938, Kempton Park 1620; tel. 9280000; fax 3953060; e-mail marketing@safair.co.za; internet www.safair.co.za; f. 1965; subsidiary of Imperial Holdings Ltd; aircraft leasing, engineering and maintenance services; Chair. R. J. BOËTTGER; CEO C. KOK.

South African Airways (SAA): Airways Park, Jones Rd, Private Bag X13, Johannesburg 1627; tel. (11) 9781111; fax (11) 9781106; internet www.flysaa.com; f. 1934; state-owned; internal passenger services linking all the principal towns; international services to Africa, Europe, North and South America and Asia; Chair. JAKES GERWEL; CEO KHAYA NGQULA.

Tourism

Tourism is an important part of South Africa's economy. The chief attractions for visitors are the climate, scenery and wildlife reserves. In 2005 some 7.5m. tourists visited South Africa. In 2004 receipts from tourism receipts amounted to US $6,729m.

South African Tourism: Bojanala House, 90 Protea Rd, Chislehurston, Johannesburg 2196; Private Bag X10012, Sandton 2146; tel. (11) 8953000; fax (11) 8953001; e-mail info@southafrica.net; internet www.southafrica.net; f. 1947; 11 overseas brs; CEO MOEKETSI MOSOLA.

Defence

As assessed at November 2006, the South African National Defence Force (SANDF) totalled about 62,334: army 41,350, navy 5,801, air force 9,183 and a medical corps numbering 6,000. The SANDF comprised members of the former South African armed forces, together with personnel from the former military wings of the ANC and the Pan-Africanist Congress, and the former 'homelands' militias. In 2006 some 2,157 South African troops were stationed abroad, attached to UN missions throughout Africa; of these, 39 were serving in an advisory capacity and 67 were observers.

Defence Expenditure: Budgeted at R24,600m. in 2007.

Chief of the South African National Defence Force: Lt-Gen. GODFREY NHLANHLA NGWENYA.

Chief of the South African Air Force: Lt-Gen. CARLO GAGIANO.

Chief of the South African Army: Maj.-Gen. SOLLY ZACHARIA SHOKE.

Chief of the South African Navy: Vice-Adm. JOHANNES REFILOE MUDIMU.

Education

School attendance is compulsory for children of all population groups between the ages of seven and 16 years. From 1991 state schools were permitted to admit pupils of all races, and in 1995 the right to free state education for all was introduced. According to UNESCO estimates, in 2002/03 enrolment at primary schools included 89% of pupils in the relevant age-group (males 88%; females 89%), while in 1999/2000 secondary enrolment included 62% of pupils in the relevant age-group (males 58%; females 65%). During the 1980s universities, which were formerly racially segregated, began to admit students of all races. In 1999 there were 21 universities and 15 'technikons' (tertiary education institutions offering technological and commercial vocational training); in 2002 it was announced that the number of universities was to be reduced to 11, the number of technikons reduced to six, and that four comprehensive institutions and two national higher education institutes would be created. Revised budget estimates for 2005/06 indicated the allocation of R12,397.1m. (3.0% of total expenditure) to education.

Bibliography

Abedian, I., and Standish, P. (Eds). *Economic Growth in South Africa: Selected Policy Issues.* Cape Town, Oxford University Press, 1992.

Abel, R. L. *Politics by Other Means: Law in the Struggle Against Apartheid, 1980–1994.* London, Routledge, 1995.

Adam, H., *et al. Comrades in Business: Post-Liberation Politics in South Africa.* Cape Town, Tafelberg, 1997.

African National Congress. *The Reconstruction and Development Programme.* Johannesburg, Umanyano Publications, 1994.

Alden, C. and Le Pere, G. *South Africa's Post-apartheid Foreign Policy: From Reconciliation to Revival?* Oxford, Oxford University Press for the International Institute for Strategic Studies, 2003.

Asmal, K., Asmal, L., and Robert, R. S. *Reconciliation Through Truth: A Reckoning of Apartheid's Criminal Governance.* Cape Town, David Philip, 1996.

Barker, F. S. *The South African Labour Market.* Pretoria, Van Schaik, 2003.

Barnard, N., and Du Toit, J. *Understanding the South African Macro-Economy.* Pretoria, Van Schaik, 1992.

Beinart, W. *Twentieth-Century South Africa.* Cape Town, Oxford University Press, 1994.

Bloomberg, C. *Christian Nationalism and the Rise of the Afrikaner Broederbond in South Africa, 1918–1948.* Bloomington, IN, Indiana University Press, 1989.

Callinicos, L. *People's History of South Africa.* Johannesburg, Ravan Press. 3 vols. 1981–93.

Cameron, T., and Spies, S. B. (Eds). *Illustrated History of South Africa.* 3rd Edn. Gauteng, Halfway House, Southern Book Publishers, 1996.

Central Statistical Services, *South African Statistics.* Pretoria, Government Printer, biennial.

Christopher, A. J. *South Africa.* London, Longman, 1982.

Clark, N. L., and Worger, H. *South Africa: The Rise and Fall of Apartheid.* Harlow, Longman, 2004.

Cloete, J. J. N. *Accountable Government and Administration for the Republic of South Africa.* Pretoria, Van Schaik, 1996.

Cole, K. (Ed.). *Sustainable Development for a Democratic South Africa.* London, Earthscan, 1994.

Davies, R., O'Meara, D., and Dlamini, S. *The Struggle for South Africa: A Reference Guide to Movements, Organizations and Institutions.* 2 vols. London, Zed Books, 1984.

De Beer, J., and Lourens, L. *Local Government: The Road to Democracy.* Midrand, Educum Publishers, 1995.

De Kock, L., Bethlehem, L., and Laden, S. (Eds). *South Africa in the Global Imaginary.* Pretoria, University of South Africa Press, 2004.

De Ville, J., and Steytler, N. (Eds). *Voting in 1999: Choosing an Electoral System.* Durban, Butterworth Publishers, 1996.

Du Pre, R. H. *Separate but Unequal: The 'Coloured' People of South Africa: A Political History.* Johannesburg, Jonathan Ball, 1994.

Du Toit, P. *State Building and Democracy in Southern Africa: Botswana, Zimbabwe and South Africa.* Washington, DC, US Institute of Peace Press, 1995.

Falkena, H. B. *Fundamentals of the South African Financial System.* Gauteng, Halfway House, Southern Book Publishers, 1993.

(Ed.). *South African Financial Institutions.* Gauteng, Halfway House, Southern Book Publishers, 1992.

Faure, M., and Lane, J. E. (Eds). *South Africa: Designing New Political Institutions.* London, Sage Publications, 1996.

Gastrow, S. *Who's Who in South African Politics.* 5th Edn. Johannesburg, Ravan Press, 1995.

Giliomee, H. *The Afrikaners: Biography of a People.* London, C. Hurst & Co, 2003

Hain, P. *Sing the Beloved Country: The Struggle for the New South Africa.* London, Pluto Press, 1996.

Hall, M. *The Changing Past: Farmers, Kings and Traders in Southern Africa, 1800–1860.* Cape Town, David Philip, 1987.

Hammond-Tooke, D. *The Roots of Black South Africa: An Introduction to the Traditional Culture of the Black People of South Africa.* Johannesburg, Jonathan Ball, 1993.

Hentz, J. J. *South Africa and the Logic of Regional Co-operation.* Bloomington, IN, Indiana University Press, 2005.

Heyns, S. *Parliamentary Pocketbook.* Cape Town, Institute for Democracy in South Africa, 1996.

Hodge, T. *South African Politics since 1994.* Cape Town, David Philip, 1999.

Jacobs, D. F. *Suggestions for Alternative Budget Balances for South Africa.* Washington, DC, IMF, 2002.

James, W., *et al.* (Eds). *Now That We Are Free: Coloured Communities in a Democratic South Africa.* Rondebosch, Institute For a Democratic South Africa, 1996.

Johnson, R. W. *South Africa: The first Man, the Last Nation.* London, Weidenfeld & Nicolson, 2004.

Johnson, R. W., and Schlemmer, L. (Eds). *Launching Democracy in South Africa: The First Open Election, April 1994.* New Haven, CT, Yale University Press, 1996.

Joyce, P. *Concise Dictionary of South African Biography.* Cape Town, Francolin, 1999.

Keegan, T. *Colonial South Africa and the Origins of Racial Order.* Cape Town, David Philip, 1996.

Konczacki, Z. A., and Konczacki, J. M. (Eds). *An Economic and Social History of South Africa.* London, Frank Cass, 1980.

Konczacki, Z. A., Parpart, J. L., and Shaw, T. M. (Eds). *Studies in the Economic History of Southern Africa.* Vol. II. London, Frank Cass, 1991.

Laband, J. P. C. *Rope of Sand: The Rise and Fall of the Zulu Kingdom in the Nineteenth Century.* Johannesburg, Jonathan Ball, 1995.

Le May, G. H. L. *The Afrikaners: An Historical Interpretation.* Oxford, Blackwell Publishers, 1995.

Lipton, M. *Capitalism and Apartheid: South Africa 1910–1984.* Aldershot, Maurice Temple Smith/Gower, 1985.

Lodge, T. *Politics in South Africa: From Mandela to Mbeki.* Cape Town, David Philip; and Oxford, James Currey, 2003.

Marais, H. *South Africa: Limits to Change—The Political Economy of Transformation.* London, Zed Books, 1998.

Marks, S., and Trapido, S. *The Politics of Race, Class and Nationalism in Twentieth Century South Africa.* London and New York, Longman, 1987.

Marsh, R. *With Criminal Intent: The Changing Face of Crime in South Africa.* Kenilworth, Ampersand Press, 1999.

Mayekiso, M. *Township Politics: Civic Struggles For a New South Africa.* New York, Monthly Review Press, 1996.

Maylam, P. *History of the African People of South Africa.* Cape Town, David Philip, 1986.

Meli, F. *South Africa Belongs To Us: A History of the ANC.* London, James Currey; Cape Town, David Philip; and Bloomington, IN, Indiana University Press, 1989.

Musiker, N., and Musiker, R. *Historical Dictionary of Greater Johannesburg.* Lanham, MD, Scarecrow Press, 1999.

Nattrass, N., and Ardington, E. (Eds). *Political Economy of South Africa.* Cape Town, Oxford University Press, 1990.

Nicholson, J. (Ed.). *User's Guide to the South African Economy.* Durban, Y Press, 1994.

Nuttall, T., *et al. From Apartheid to Democracy: South Africa 1948–1994.* Pietermaritzburg, Shuter & Shooter, 1998.

Oden, B., *et al. The South African Tripod: Studies on Economics, Politics and Conflict.* Uppsala, Nordiska Afrikainstitutet, 1994.

O'Meara, D. *Forty Lost Years: The Apartheid State and the Politics of the National Party.* Johannesburg, Ravan Press, 1996.

Omer-Cooper, J. D. *History of Southern Africa.* 2nd Edn. Cape Town, David Philip, 1994.

Pakenham, T. *The Boer War.* London, Weidenfeld & Nicolson, 1979; Johannesburg, Jonathan Ball, 1992 (reprint).

Pampallis, J. *Foundations of the New South Africa.* London, Zed Books; and Cape Town, Maskew Miller Longman, 1991.

Piper, L. (Ed.) *et al. South Africa's 2004 Election: the Quest for Democratic Consolidation.* Johannesburg, EISA, 2005.

Pollock, N. C., and Agnew, S. *An Historical Geography of South Africa.* London, Longman, 1963.

Preston-Whyte, E., and Rogerson, C. (Eds). *South Africa's Informal Economy.* Cape Town, Oxford University Press, 1991.

Purkitt, H. E. *South Africa's Weapons of Mass Destruction.* Bloomington, IN, Chesham/Indiana University Press, Combined Academic, 2005.

Ramphela, M. *The Affirmative Action Book: Towards an Equity Government.* Rondebosch, Institute for a Democratic South Africa, 1995.

Reader's Digest. *Illustrated History of South Africa.* 3rd Edn. Cape Town, 1994.

Reynolds, A. (Ed.). *Election '94 South Africa: The Campaigns, Results and Future Prospects.* Cape Town, David Philip, 1994.

Rogerson, C., and McCarthy, J. (Eds). *Geography in a Changing South Africa: Progress and Prospects.* Cape Town, Oxford University Press, 1992.

Roux, A. *Everyone's Guide to the South African Economy.* 4th Edn. Wynberg, Sandton, Zebra Books, 1996.

Saunders, C., and Southey, N. *Dictionary of South African History.* Cape Town, David Philip, 1998.

Schrire, R. (Ed.). *Wealth or Poverty: Critical Choices for South Africa.* Cape Town, Oxford University Press, 1992.

Seegers, A. *The Military in the Making of Modern South Africa.* London, I. B. Taurus, 1997.

Simon, D. (Ed.). *South Africa in Southern Africa: Reconfiguring the Region.* Athens, OH, Ohio University Press, 1998.

Simons, H. J., and Simons, R. E. *Class and Colour in South Africa, 1850–1950.* Harmondsworth Penguin Books, 1969.

Smollan, R. *Black Advancement in the South African Economy.* Johannesburg, Macmillan Boleswa, 1993.

South African Institute of Race Relations. *South African Survey.* Johannesburg, annual.

Sparks, A. *Tomorrow is Another Country: The Inside Story of South Africa's Road to Change.* New York, NY, Hill & Wang, 1995.

Terreblanche, S. *A History of Inequality in South Africa 1652–2002.* Scottsville, University of Natal Press, 2003

Thompson, L. *The Unification of South Africa 1902–1910.* Oxford, Clarendon Press, 1960.

History of South Africa. New Haven, CT, Yale University Press, 1990.

United Nations. *United Nations and Apartheid 1984–1994.* New York, NY; and Geneva, United Nations Publications, 1995.

Vosloo, W. B. (Ed.). *Entrepreneurship and Economic Growth.* Pretoria, Human Sciences Research Council, 1994.

Wentzel, J. *The Liberal Slideaway.* Johannesburg, South African Institute of Race Relations, 1995.

White, L. *South Africa-Mercosur: Long Process, Little Progress.* Braamfontein, South African Institute of International Affairs, 2002.

Wilson, M., and Thompson, L. (Eds). *The Oxford History of South Africa.* Oxford, Clarendon Press, 1969–71.

Wilson, R. *The Politics of Truth and Reconciliation in South Africa: Legitimizing the Post-Apartheid State.* Cambridge, Cambridge University Press, 2001.

History of South Africa to 1870. (Revised Edn of Vol. 1 of *The Oxford History of South Africa.*) Cape Town, David Philip, 1982.

Woods, D. *Rainbow Nation Revisited: South Africa's Decade of Democracy.* London, André Deutsch, 2000.

World Economic Forum. *South Africa at 10: Perspectives by Political, Business and Civil Leaders.* Cape Town, Human & Rousseau, 2004.

SUDAN

Physical and Social Geography

J. A. ALLAN

THE NILE

The River Nile and its tributaries form the basis of much of the economic activity of Sudan, and of most of the future activity that is now envisaged. The river traverses diverse landscapes, from the relatively humid tropical forest in the south to the arid deserts in the north. The Republic of Sudan has a total area of 2,505,813 sq km (967,500 sq miles), and the Nile waters that enter Sudan just south of Juba either evaporate or flow 3,000 km until they reach Lake Nubia on the Egyptian border. Even those which flow down the Blue Nile travel 2,000 km. The distances are vast, and the remoteness of places on the Nile system, not to speak of those in the deserts, savannah and swamps of the rest of the country, explains much of the character of Sudan's land use. The other important factor is climate, which influences vegetation and, more significantly, affects the seasonal flow of the Nile tributaries.

The Blue Nile is the main tributary, both in the volume of water which it carries (four-sevenths of the total average flow of the system) as well as in the area of irrigated land, of which it supports over 40% of the present area and 70% of potential irrigable land. The Blue Nile and other east-bank tributaries are sustained by monsoon rains over the Ethiopian highlands, which cause the river to flood at the end of July, reach a peak in August and remain high through September and the first half of October. The Atbara, another seasonal east-bank tributary, provides a further one-seventh of the flow in the system, and the remaining two-sevenths come from the White Nile. The sustained flow of the White Nile arises first because its main source is Lake Victoria, which regulates the flow, and secondly because the swamps of the Sudd and Machar act as a reservoir, absorbing the irregular stream flow from the south while discharging a regular flow, much reduced by evaporation, in the north.

The River Nile is an international river system, and Sudan depends on river flows from seven other states. Sudan does not yet use all of the 18,500m. cu m of annual flow agreed with Egypt in 1959 as its share of the total average flow at Aswan of 84,000m. (Egypt receives 55,500m. cu m, while 10,000m. cu m are assumed to evaporate annually from Lake Nasser/Nubia.) In anticipation of future additional demand by upstream states such as Ethiopia, and in view of Egypt's rising demand for water, Sudan and Egypt jointly embarked in 1978 on the construction of the Jonglei Canal project, which will eventually conserve some 4,000m. cu m of the 33,000m. cu m of water lost annually through evaporation in the Sudd swamp. The Machar swamps will also yield water at a rate as yet undetermined, but likely to be about 4,000m. cu m per year (3,240m. cu m at Aswan).

PHYSICAL FEATURES AND CLIMATE

Sudan is generally a flat, featureless plain reflecting the proximity to the surface of the ancient Basement rocks of the African continent. The Basement is overlain by the Nubian Sandstone formation in the centre and north-west of the country, and by the Umm Ruwaba formation in the south. These formations hold groundwater bodies of agricultural significance. No point in the country is very high above sea-level. Elevations rise to 3,187 m on Mt Kinyeti, near the Uganda border, and to 3,071 m on Jabel Marrah, an extinct volcano, in west central Sudan near the frontier with Chad. Some idea of the level character of the landscape is provided by the small amount of the fall in the Blue Nile, which starts its 2,000-km flow through Sudan at 500 m above sea-level at the Ethiopian border and formerly flowed past Wadi Halfa (now flooded) at an elevation of 156 m. It now flows into Lake Nubia at 180 m above sea-level. The White Nile, as it emerges from Uganda, falls some 600 m between the border and Khartoum, a distance of 1,700 km, but falls only 17 m in the last 700 km from entering the southern clay plains.

Average temperatures and rainfall change steadily from month to month, except where the effect of the Ethiopian highlands disturbs the east–west trend in the climatic belts in the south-east. The north of Sudan is a desert, with negligible rainfall and high average daily temperatures (summer 35°C, winter 20°C). Low temperatures occur only in winter. Rainfall increases steadily south of Khartoum (200 mm per year), reaching over 1,000 mm per year at the southern border. Rainfall varies from year to year, especially in the north, and is seasonal. In the south it falls in the period April–October; the rainy season is progressively shorter towards the north, where it lasts only from July until August. Potential evaporation approaches 3,000 mm per year in the north and is always over 1,400 mm per year, even in the humid south.

VEGETATION AND SOILS

The soil resources of Sudan are rich in agricultural potential. Their exploitation, however, depends on the availability of the limiting factor, water, and only a small proportion of the clay plains of central and east Sudan are currently farmed intensively. Clay soils also occur in the south, being deposits of the White Nile and Sobat streams. Recent alluvium provides a basis for productive agriculture in the narrow Nile valley north of Khartoum. Elsewhere, in the west and north the soils are sandy, with little agricultural potential, except in the dry valleys, which generally contain some soil moisture.

Vegetation is closely related to the climatic zones. From the desert in the north vegetation gradually improves through semi-arid shrub to low woodland savannah characterized by acacia and short grasses. Progressively higher rainfall towards the south promotes trees and shrubs as well as herbs, while the more reliably watered rangeland of the Bahr al-Arab provides an important seasonal resource for the graziers from the poor pastures of Darfur and Kordofan. The flooded areas of the Sudd and Machar and environs support swamp vegetation and grassland. On the uplands of the southern border, rainfall is sufficient to support tropical rainforest.

During 1984–85 and again in the early 1990s large areas of Sudan were affected by drought, and it was estimated that thousands of people faced starvation, particularly in the western provinces of Darfur and Kordofan.

POPULATION

The population of Sudan was enumerated at 24,940,683 at the census held in April 1993, compared with 20,594,197 in February 1983 and 14,113,590 in April 1973. The population increased at an estimated average annual rate of 2.1% in 1995–2005. According to UN estimates, the population was 37,707,000 at mid-2006, giving an estimated population density of 15.0 per sq km. At the 1983 census about 71% of the population resided in rural areas, 18% in urban and semi-urban areas and the remaining 11% were nomadic. The population is concentrated in Khartoum province and the Central Region, where population densities were, respectively, 55 and 28 per sq km in 1973, compared with 3.6–6.8 per sq km elsewhere. Agricultural development in the two most populous regions created employment opportunities and this led to the doubling of these populations during 1956–1973, compared with rises of between zero and 50% elsewhere. There are local concentrations of population in the Nuba mountains and higher densities than average in better-farmed parts of the Southern and Darfur regions.

The ethnic origin of the people of Sudan is mixed, and the country is still subject to significant immigration by groups from Nigeria and Chad, such as the Fulani. In the south the Nuer, the Dinka and the Shilluki are the most important of the Nilotic peoples. Arab culture and language predominate in the north, which includes the most populous provinces and the capital, Khartoum. The South is predominantly Christian and this cultural difference, added to the ethnic separateness and its extreme remoteness, has been expressed in economic backwardness and a tendency to political distinctness, which have been the main cause of persistent unrest in Southern Sudan.

Khartoum had an estimated population of 947,483 at the 1993 census. It is the main administrative, commercial and industrial centre of the country. The neighbouring city of Omdurman had 1,271,403 inhabitants in 1993, thus creating, with Khartoum, a conurbation of some 2.2m. inhabitants. In 2000 the UN estimated the population of this conurbation to total about 2.7m. As communications are very poor and since Khartoum is at least 1,000 km away from 80% of the country, the influence that the capital exerts on the rest of the country is small. The relatively advanced character and general success of much of the irrigated farming on the east-central clay plains has led to a predominance of investment there, and to the misguided impression that the success of the east-central plains could be transferred to other parts of the country where the resources are unfortunately much less favourable. Much of Sudan is so dry for part of each year that the only possible way to use the land and vegetation resources is by grazing, and tribes such as the Bagara traverse the plains and plateaux of Darfur and Kordofan in response to the availability of fodder.

Recent History

THOMAS OFCANSKY

Revised by PETER WOODWARD

The British-led military reconquest of the Sudan, formerly an Egyptian territory from the invasion of 1820 until the Mahdist revolt of 1881–85, was completed during 1896–98. A British-dominated Anglo-Egyptian administration governed the territory until the revolt of 1924, after which a system of 'Indirect Rule' through tribal chiefs was introduced, and Egyptian involvement effectively ceased. Nationalist movements, which began to mobilize in the mid-1930s, exerted pressure for increased Sudanese participation in government in preparation for full independence. In 1953 elections were held, resulting in a victory for the National Unionist Party (NUP), the leader of which, Ismail al-Azhari, became the first Sudanese Prime Minister in January 1954. On 19 December 1955 Sudan declared itself to be an independent republic. The United Kingdom and Egypt were left with no choice but to recognize this independence, which formally took effect on 1 January 1956.

Soon after independence, Azhari's Government was replaced by an unstable coalition of the Mahdist-supported Umma Party (UP) and the People's Democratic Party (PDP), the political organ of a rival religious fraternity, the Khatmiyya, with Abdallah Khalil, the UP Secretary-General, as Prime Minister. A military coup in November 1958 by Gen. Ibrahim Abboud won the support of civilian politicians with assurances by the junta that it aimed merely to restore stability and would relinquish power when this was achieved. The Abboud regime had some success in the economic sphere, but the extent of military involvement in government and allegations of corruption created growing discontent. The Government also pursued a military solution to the rebel uprising in the predominantly Christian south, where its operations against the *Anya Nya* rebels forced thousands of southerners to flee to neighbouring countries. In 1964 Abboud transferred power to a transitional Government, which was formed with representatives from all parties, including, for the first time, the Sudanese Communist Party (SCP) and the Muslim Brotherhood. Following elections held in June 1965, a coalition Government was formed by the UP and the NUP, with the UP's Muhammad Ahmad Mahgoub as Prime Minister and Azhari as permanent President of the committee that acted as collective Head of State.

The new Government faced serious rebel activity in the south and large numbers of southerners were killed by government troops. The Government itself became increasingly right-wing, and in late 1965 the SCP was banned. A split meanwhile developed within the UP, with the more moderate members rallying around the party President, Sadiq al-Mahdi, in opposition to the Prime Minister. Mahgoub resigned in July 1966 and al-Mahdi was elected Prime Minister at the head of another UP-NUP coalition, which collapsed in May 1967. Mahgoub again became Prime Minister. However, domestic problems were neglected by the new Government, which severed diplomatic relations with the USA and the United Kingdom following the Arab–Israeli war in June and developed closer relations with the Eastern bloc. Faced by worsening violence in the south and growing divisions within the coalition, the Government was overthrown in a bloodless coup, led by Col Gaafar Muhammad Nimeri, in May 1969.

THE NIMERI REGIME, 1969–85

Nimeri's first two years in power were characterized by the adoption of socialist policies and the forging of an alliance between the new military leadership and the SCP. The foundations for a one-party state were laid with the formation of the Sudanese Socialist Union (SSU), and the country was renamed the Democratic Republic of the Sudan. Internal opposition was ruthlessly suppressed. The Government declared its commitment to regional administrative autonomy for the south and created a Ministry for Southern Affairs. It developed closer relations with the Eastern bloc and followed a policy of militant support for the Palestinian cause. However, the announcement in November 1970 that Nimeri, President Anwar Sadat of Egypt and Libyan leader Col Muammar al-Qaddafi had decided to unite their three countries as a single federal state proved unacceptable to the communists, who staged a military coup, led by Maj. Hashim al-Ata, which resulted in the temporary overthrow of Nimeri in July 1971. With popular support, Nimeri was restored to power within three days.

The attempted coup was followed by a cooling of relations with the Eastern bloc and led to a surge in the personal popularity of Nimeri, who won the first presidential election in Sudanese history in October 1971. The SSU became the sole legal political party. The Addis Ababa Agreement, signed in March 1972 between the Government and the *Anya Nya* rebels, appeared to establish the basis for a settlement by introducing regional autonomy for the three southern provinces. A Regional People's Assembly was established in the regional capital of southern Sudan, Juba with representatives in the National People's Assembly and a Higher Executive Council (HEC) of its own.

Following the break in relations with the Eastern bloc, Sudan sought to improve its relations with Egypt and in 1974 signed a 10-year agreement providing for political and economic integration and close co-operation in foreign policy, security and development. The Sudanese Government was troubled by Sadat's decision to make peace with Israel, a move opposed by most of the Arab world, but Nimeri eventually expressed his support for the move. The assassination of Sadat in October 1981, and growing fears of Libyan attempts to destabilize the Nimeri regime, increased the desire of Egypt and Sudan for close co-operation. Along with Egypt, Sudan had been developing closer ties to the USA, which increased its provision of aid to both countries, especially in the area of security.

Prolonged discussions about decentralization led to the adoption in January 1980 of a plan whereby Sudan was to be divided into five regions (Northern, Eastern, Central, Kordofan and Darfur) in addition to Khartoum and the south, which would continue to enjoy a special status and administrative structure. However, relations between the Government and the south were again deteriorating. A decision to subdivide the south into three sub-regions to avoid the domination of one ethnic group (the Dinka), eventually implemented in May 1983, was opposed by many southerners, who feared it would weaken their collective position *vis-à-vis* the north. Southern resentment was further aroused by the decision that petroleum from the newly discovered oilfields astride the traditional boundaries of the two regions would not be refined locally but exported via a pipeline to Port Sudan, and by fears that the Jonglei Canal project (see Economy) would benefit northerners and Egypt, but have an adverse effect on the southern population.

A major factor in the deepening crisis was the adoption by the Nimeri regime, after September 1983, of certain aspects of Islamic *Shari'a* law, followed by the introduction, after April 1984, of martial law. Despite the general popularity, in principle, of Islamization among the northern Muslim majority, and official assurances that non-Muslims would not be adversely affected, many southern Sudanese were now alienated to the point of armed insurrection. Commonly known as *Anya Nya II*, the revitalized rebel groups were organized into political and military wings, the Sudan People's Liberation Movement (SPLM) and Sudan People's Liberation Army (SPLA), respectively. During 1983–84 the rebels engaged government forces in a series of battles, especially in Upper Nile and Bahr al-Ghazal.

Meanwhile, Nimeri's commitment to Islamization continued to attract some support among the mainly Muslim population of the north. However, opposition also increased with Sadiq al-Mahdi, *inter alia*, viewing Nimeri's Islamization policies as a gross distortion of Islamic principles. Relations between Nimeri and a faction of the Muslim Brotherhood led by Hassan at-Turabi deteriorated, both because the Brotherhood was ignored in the formulation of Islamization policies and because it was potentially a formidable contender for political power, although formally allied to the regime since 1977. By February 1985 disillusionment with the regime and its policies, both internal and external, was rapidly crystallizing. At this late juncture, Nimeri moved to deal with the Muslim Brotherhood by putting its leaders on trial for sedition and, by so doing, alienated his last vestiges of popular support. Nimeri reacted to this situation by adopting a conciliatory stance. The state of emergency was lifted, and the operation of the special courts was suspended, while an offer was made to revoke the redivision of the south if a majority of southerners desired it.

MILITARY COUP

Public discontent with Nimeri's regime reached its culmination in March 1985, exacerbated by substantial increases in the price of food and fuel, and Khartoum was immobilized by a general strike. On 6 April, while Nimeri was visiting the USA, he was deposed in a bloodless military coup, led by Lt-Gen. Abd ar-Rahman Swar ad-Dahab, the Minister of Defence and Commander-in-Chief of the armed forces. A state of emergency was declared, and a Transitional Military Council (TMC) was appointed. A 15-member Council of Ministers, including three non-Muslim southerners, was subsequently announced. Dr Gizuli Dafallah, a trade unionist who had been a prominent organizer of the general strike, was appointed Prime Minister. The Council of Ministers was to be responsible to the TMC during a 12-month transitional period prior to the holding of free elections, scheduled for April 1986. Hundreds of Nimeri's officials were arrested, and the SSU was dissolved.

In response to the coup, the SPLM initially declared a ceasefire, but presented the new regime with a series of demands concerning the Southern Region. Ad-Dahab offered various concessions to the south, including the cancellation of the redivision and the reinstatement of the southern HEC in Juba, with Maj.-Gen. James Loro, a member of the TMC, as its interim president. The SPLM rejected these terms and resumed hostilities. In an attempt to reach agreement with the SPLM, a conference was held in March 1986 in Addis Ababa, Ethiopia, between the SPLM and the National Alliance for Salvation (NAS), a semi-official alliance of trade unionists and politicians who supported the Government. The SPLM insisted that the retention of the *Shari'a* remained a major obstacle to national unity; the NAS agreed to abolish *Shari'a* law and, in response to another of the rebels' demands, to end military links with Libya and Egypt; however, these measures were not implemented by the TMC before the April 1986 election.

Despite these difficulties, ad-Dahab promised a return to civilian rule after a 12-month interim period. A transitional Constitution was signed in October 1985; under its provisions, numerous political groupings began to emerge in preparation for the forthcoming general election. In December the name of the country was changed to 'the Republic of Sudan', thus restoring the official designation to its pre-1969 form.

The TMC's foreign policy during its 12-month rule reversed Nimeri's strongly pro-Western stance. While advocating a policy of non-alignment, the TMC sought to improve relations with Ethiopia, Libya and the USSR, to the concern of Sudan's former allies, Egypt and the USA. A military co-operation agreement was signed with Libya in July 1985, and diplomatic relations were quickly restored between Sudan, Libya and Ethiopia. Relations also improved with Iran, which had been one of the main adversaries of Nimeri's Government. In November links with Egypt were reaffirmed. Relations with the USA, already viewed with suspicion (owing to the US Government's former support for Nimeri), were further strained after an attack on Libya by US aircraft in April 1986.

CIVILIAN COALITIONS AND REGIONAL UNREST

More than 40 political parties participated in the general election held in April 1986. As expected, no single party won an outright majority of seats in the National Assembly, but Sadiq al-Mahdi's UP won the largest number (99), followed by the Democratic Unionist Party (DUP), formed in 1968 by a merger of the PDP and the NUP and now led by Osman al-Mirghani (with 63 seats), and the National Islamic Front (NIF) of at-Turabi (with 51 seats). The Council of Ministers comprised a coalition of the UP and the DUP, with, in addition, four portfolios allocated to southern parties. Sadiq al-Mahdi became Prime Minister and Minister of Defence. He urged the southern rebels to negotiate a peaceful settlement, and promised that *Shari'a* law would be abolished and the state of emergency lifted. In foreign policy, al-Mahdi undertook to maintain the non-aligned policy of the TMC, which was dissolved in preparation for the return to civilian rule. Swar ad-Dahab relinquished the posts of Head of State (being replaced by a six-member Supreme Council, installed in May) and of military Commander-in-Chief.

In an attempt to make the new Government acceptable to the southerners, a special portfolio, the Ministry of Peace and Unity, had been created for a member of the NAS, and Col John Garang, leader of the SPLM, had been offered a post in the Council of Ministers. However, the SPLM refused either to recognize or take part in the new Government. Tensions in the south continued to worsen; in early 1986 the SPLM launched a new offensive, and captured the town of Rumbek. In July al-Mahdi and Garang held direct talks for the first time, in Addis Ababa; however, further negotiations, held in August, between the NAS and the SPLM ended abruptly when the SPLM shot down a Sudan Airways aircraft, killing 60 civilians on board. The SPLM launched a new offensive, with the aim of recapturing the four strategic southern towns of Juba, Wau, Malakal and Bentiu. By May the military situation in the south had become so unstable that it appeared possible that the Government might consent to the outright secession of three southern provinces.

In mid-1997 al-Mahdi stated that the coalition parties had agreed on mutually acceptable guide-lines for the conduct of government policy, with special reference to the abrogation of religiously based legislation unacceptable to the south. It was stated that laws based on a 'Sudanese legal heritage' would replace those unacceptable to non-Muslims, who would be exempted from Islamic punishments and the system of *zakat* (alms) taxation. Such a compromise, however, was rejected by the SPLM, which continued to demand the total abrogation of *Shari'a* law as a precondition to peace negotiations, while the fundamentalist NIF restated its demand that the Islamic code be applied to the country as a whole. In late July the Government imposed a 12-month state of emergency, aimed at resolving the country's worsening economic crisis.

In January 1988 representatives of the Government and 17 political parties signed a 'transitional charter', which aimed to define Sudan's political structure pending a proposed constitutional conference. The 'transitional charter' stressed Sudan's commitment to multi-party democracy; stipulated that the Government of the south would be in accordance with the 1972 system of autonomous regional government; and requested that the Government replace *Shari'a* law with an alternative legal system before the constitutional conference was convened.

In April 1988 al-Mahdi requested that the Supreme Council dissolve his coalition Government, following a vote by the National Assembly in favour of the formation of a new 'government of national unity'. Following his re-election as Prime Minister by the National Assembly later that month, al-Mahdi declared that, while the precise nature of the relationship between the state and religion should be established at the proposed constitutional conference, the Muslim majority had the right to choose laws that governed Muslims in so far as they did not infringe upon the rights of non-Muslims.

The formation of a new 27-member 'Government of National Unity', comprising members of the UP, the DUP, the NIF and a number of southern Sudanese political parties, was completed in May 1988. Al-Mahdi announced that the new Government would deal with the critical economic and security problems facing the country. Few observers, however, expected the new administration to be able to resolve the problem of the war in the south, especially since the fundamentalist NIF had joined the coalition on condition that a 'replacement' *Shari'a* code be introduced within 60 days of its formation.

In November 1988 representatives of the SPLM met senior members of the DUP and reached agreement on proposals to end the civil war. In December, however, a state of emergency was again declared amid reports that a military coup had been attempted (see below). The DUP withdrew its six ministers from the coalition Government, following a request by al-Mahdi that the National Assembly convene a national constitutional conference, without the agreement between the SPLM and the DUP being incorporated into his proposal.

In February 1989 at-Turabi was appointed Deputy Prime Minister. This appointment, while strengthening the position of the NIF in the Government, reduced the likelihood of an early solution to the war in the south. In March al-Mahdi agreed to form a new, broadly based Government which would begin negotiations with the SPLM. Thirty political parties and 17 trade unions had previously signed an agreement endorsing the peace agreement drawn up by the DUP and the SPLM in November 1988. However, the NIF refused to endorse the agreement (which called for the suspension of Islamic laws as a prelude to the negotiation of a peace settlement to the civil war), and was excluded from the new Government formed in March 1989. Peace negotiations between a government delegation and the SPLM commenced in Ethiopia in April.

AL-BASHIR SEIZES POWER

On 30 June 1989 a bloodless *coup d'état*, led by Brig. (later Lt-Gen.) Omar Hassan Ahmad al-Bashir, removed al-Mahdi's Government and formed a 15-member Revolutionary Command Council for National Salvation (RCC), which declared its primary aim to be the resolution of the southern conflict. Al-Bashir rapidly dismantled the civilian ruling apparatus: the Constitution, National Assembly and all political parties and trade unions were abolished, and a state of emergency was declared. Civilian newspapers were closed. About 30 members of the former Government were detained, including al-Mahdi, although three of the ex-ministers were included in the new 21-member Cabinet announced in early July. Its composition included 16 civilians, of whom four were southerners, as well as several members who were understood to be sympathetic towards Islamic fundamentalism. Internationally, the RCC regime received immediate diplomatic recognition from Chad, Egypt, Libya, the People's Democratic Republic of Yemen and Saudi Arabia, and the new Government was generally welcomed as a potentially stabilizing influence in the region.

In February 1991 al-Bashir signed a decree introducing a new penal code, based, like its predecessor, on *Shari'a* law. The code, which was to take effect from 22 March, was not to apply, for the present, in the three southern regions of Equatoria, Upper Nile and Bahr al-Ghazal. This exemption, however, appeared to cover only five of the code's 186 articles, and it was stated that the code would be applicable to non-Muslim Sudanese residents in the north, notably the estimated 2m. refugees who had fled to the Khartoum area from the civil war in the south.

In April 1991 al-Bashir announced the immediate release of all the country's political prisoners. Human rights organizations subsequently claimed, however, that at least 60 of the Government's opponents remained in detention. Al-Mahdi was among those released. In late June al-Bashir announced that a political system based on Libyan-style 'people's congresses' was to be introduced.

In May 1991, with rebel forces remaining in control of most of southern Sudan, Col Garang marked the eighth anniversary of the start of the civil war by inviting the Government to take part in peace negotiations. The Government responded by stating that it was willing at any time to discuss terms for a settlement, but it reiterated its view that the administrative reforms introduced in February already represented a considerable degree of compromise. The overthrow, on 21 May, of the Ethiopian Government led by Mengistu Haile Mariam had implications for the SPLA, which had in the past enjoyed Ethiopian support; armed clashes within Ethiopia between SPLA forces and those of the new Ethiopian regime were reported in late May. On 29 May the Sudanese Government declared its recognition of, and support for, the new Ethiopian Government.

International efforts to achieve a peace settlement within Sudan gained renewed momentum in mid-1991. In mid-June the Government announced that it would consider proposals made by the US Government, providing for the partial withdrawal of government forces from southern Sudan, the withdrawal of the SPLA forces from government-held areas and the declaration of Juba, the southern capital, as an 'open' city. On 14 June the SPLA endorsed the Government's suggestion that the Nigerian Head of State, Ibrahim Babangida, should act as a mediator. At the beginning of July, following further initiatives by the USA, Garang was reported to have agreed to begin unconditional peace negotiations with the Government. However, in August, as part of a cabinet reshuffle, which was carried out during the absence abroad of al-Bashir, a prominent Islamic fundamentalist, at-Tayeb Ibrahim Muhammad Khair, was appointed Governor of the southern province of Darfur. This appointment was viewed as unlikely to improve the prospects of a definitive peace settlement in the immediate future.

An alleged coup attempt in late August 1991 resulted in the arrest of 10 army officers and a number of civilians and was officially ascribed to unspecified 'foreign powers'. Subsequent official statements alleged that those implicated included members of the National Democratic Alliance (NDA, a grouping formed in 1989 by the SPLA and some of the other former political parties, including the UP and the DUP) and the previously unknown organization, Ana al-Sudan ('I am Sudan'). The NDA claimed at the end of September that some 70 people had been arrested and that Sadiq al-Mahdi had been among those interrogated. The subsequent trial by a military court of 15 people accused of involvement in the coup attempt resulted in death sentences for 10 army officers, commuted in December to life imprisonment.

Reports of a split within the SPLA, circulated from Khartoum at the end of August 1991, were immediately denied by Garang. Three SPLA field commanders—Riek Mashar Teny-

Dhurgon, Lam Akol and Kerubino Kuanyin Bol—claimed to have taken over the leadership of the SPLA and accused Garang of dictatorial behaviour. The dissidents were reported to favour a policy of secession for the south, whereas the aim of Garang and his supporters, based at Kapoeta, remained a united, secular state. The split was also along ethnic lines, with the Dinka supporting Garang and the Nuer the breakaway faction. The SPLA's divisions led to a postponement of the first round of peace talks due to be held under the auspices of the Organization of African Unity (OAU, now the African Union—AU) in Abuja, Nigeria, at the end of October. Fierce fighting between the two SPLA factions was reported in November and resulted in the massacre of several thousand civilians in the southern towns of Bor and Kongor before a cease-fire was negotiated in mid-December. At the end of November the Government announced a one-month amnesty for rebels who wished to surrender.

Proposals for constitutional reform were announced by al-Bashir on 1 January 1992. A 300-member transitional National Assembly was to be appointed, with full legislative functions and the power to veto decisions of the RCC. The Assembly, which convened for the first time on 24 February, included—as well as all members of the RCC (excluding al-Bashir), state governors and representatives of the army and police—former members of the banned UP and DUP, and former aides to ex-President Nimeri, reflecting the Government's desire to broaden its support in the wake of the introduction of an unpopular programme of economic austerity measures. A further alleged coup attempt was reported to have been foiled in mid-April.

PEACE TALKS FAIL

Contacts between the Government and the various rebel factions took place in Uganda and Kenya during February 1993, with a view to resuming the peace process following unsuccessful attempts to do so in 1992. In mid-March Col Garang announced a unilateral cease-fire; the Government subsequently responded with its own announcement of a cease-fire. Garang also urged the establishment of safety zones to allow the delivery of food supplies to starving people. However, at the end of March fighting was reported at Kongor between Garang's forces and the 'Forces of Unity' faction of the SPLA, led by William Nyuon.

Peace talks between the Government and the faction of the SPLA led by Col Garang resumed in Abuja in April 1993. The talks adjourned on 18 May, having made little progress on the main issues dividing the parties. Although the Government claimed the talks would resume in June, the SPLA said they had been a failure and that the cease-fire was at an end. Meanwhile, in Nairobi, talks were also taking place between a government delegation and SPLA—United, an alliance formed in early April between the Nasir faction, the 'Forces of Unity' and a faction led by Kerubino Kuanyin Bol. The Nairobi talks, after a break in early May, resumed during 7–26 May and ended with agreement on the concept of a unified federal state and on the rights of state governments to introduce laws supplementary to federal legislation—allowing the implementation of *Shari'a* law in the north, but not in the south. No agreement was reached, however, on the length of the period of transition before the holding of a referendum on future divisions of power.

In October 1993 al-Bashir announced political reforms in preparation for presidential and legislative elections to be held in 1994 and 1995, respectively. The RCC had been dissolved three days previously, after it had appointed al-Bashir as President and as head of a new civilian Government. Cabinet ministers were requested to remain in office until elections took place. Al-Bashir appointed a new Minister of Defence—a portfolio that he had formerly held himself—and a new Vice-President. Western observers regarded the dissolution of the RCC as reinforcing the position of the NIF within the Government during the transition to civilian rule. In early February 1994, by constitutional decree, Sudan was redivided into 26 states instead of the previous nine. The executive and legislative powers of each state government were to be expanded, and southern states were expected to be exempted from *Shari'a* law.

CONFLICT CONTINUES

At the beginning of 1994 the civil war in southern Sudan remained in stalemate. As in previous years, the Government's 1993–94 southern offensive involved the deployment of army and Popular Defence Force (PDF) units from sizeable garrisons in Juba and Wau, largely along main roads, to locations along the borders with Zaire (now the Democratic Republic of the Congo—DRC) and Uganda. In late October al-Bashir announced the start of a dual offensive to sever the SPLA's supply lines from Uganda and Zaire before the next government offensive. The President also announced that his goal was to liberate southern Sudan from the SPLA and, at the same time, to pursue efforts to negotiate with the rebels. The offensive did not proceed as planned, however, and army and PDF units suffered several defeats in the area of Mangall and Terakeka, north of Juba. By mid-December the fighting was taking place primarily around the government-held town of Kapoeta. The Government acknowledged that its forces had suffered another military defeat east of Torit, on the supply route to Kapoeta. According to Col Garang, the SPLA had killed more than 1,000 government troops. By January 1995 there were reports that rebel forces had surrounded Kapoeta, and had captured part of the town. In March, in spite of these losses, government forces managed to capture Nasir, a stronghold of the South Sudan Independence Movement (SSIM) near the Ethiopian border; later that month, however, the SSIM captured intact an armoured military convoy of government forces at the town of Lafon. This development was significant in that the Sudanese Government had previously provided support to the SSIM. With the SSIM now in conflict with the Government, a reconciliation between the SSIM commander, Dr Riek Mashar Teny-Dhurgon, and Col Garang became more likely. Indeed, on 27 April the two commanders signed the Lafon Declaration, which provided for a cease-fire and a cessation of hostilities between their forces, reunification, reintegration of military forces, and a general amnesty. In early February the Cabinet was reshuffled, the pattern of changes suggesting a reinforcement of the Islamic character of the Government.

An unexpected development in the southern conflict occurred in late March 1995, when former US President Jimmy Carter persuaded the Sudanese Government to declare a unilateral two-month cease-fire and to offer the rebel groups an amnesty if they surrendered their weapons. Three days later the SPLA also declared a two-month cease-fire and requested the deployment of international observers to monitor the truce. Finally, in early April, the SSIM issued a cease-fire declaration. In May the Sudanese Government extended its cease-fire for two months. However, it soon became apparent that the army was continuing to conduct military operations. Four days prior to the extension of the government cease-fire, the SSIM claimed that government forces had launched a new offensive in Latjor state, which brought the number of government violations of the Carter-mediated cease-fire to 21.

In mid-June 1995 a conference took place in Asmara, Eritrea, of groups and parties opposed to the Government. The conference, hosted by the Eritrean People's Front for Democracy and Justice (PFDJ) and organized by the Asmara-based NDA, was attended, among others, by representatives of the DUP, the UP, the SCP and the SPLA. At its conclusion the conference issued a communiqué in which opposition leaders pledged (once the al-Bashir regime had been ousted) to support the right of self-determination for all Sudanese peoples, based on the results of future referendums; and to establish a decentralized government for a four-year interim period. The communiqué also envisaged the future separation of religion and politics and the abolition of *Shari'a* law. The creation of a Government-in-exile was announced and the conference was also reported to have achieved a rapprochement between the SPLA and the other opposition groups: the NDA announced details of a forthcoming military campaign to be undertaken by its military wing in alliance with, among others, Col Garang's faction of the SPLA.

In August 1995 a cabinet reshuffle was announced. The DUP claimed that ministers who were dismissed had been involved in planning the attempted assassination of President Mubarak of Egypt in June (see below). Later in August President al-Bashir announced that legislative and presidential elections which had been scheduled to take place in 1994 and 1995, respectively, would now be held in 1996. Political prisoners who were released in a government amnesty on 24–25 August 1995 included Sadiq al-Mahdi, who had been placed under arrest in May for having alleged that state funds were being misused.

In November 1995, having begun a new offensive in late October, Col Garang's SPLA forces were reported to be advancing on the southern town of Juba. The retreat of government forces which this provoked appeared to be regarded as more serious than other, similar retreats in the past: the Government declared a mass mobilization, urging all sectors of the population to defend the country. On 11 November the Government claimed that its forces had inflicted a major defeat on the SPLA and on Ugandan and Eritrean forces allied with it. The Governments of Uganda and Eritrea denied the involvement of their forces in the fighting. By late 1996 the SPLA claimed to have taken control of all of Western Equatoria and all of the rural regions of Eastern Equatoria.

POST-ELECTION DOMESTIC ISSUES

The first legislative and presidential elections to be held in Sudan since 1989 took place during 6–17 March 1996. Some 5.5m. of Sudan's 10m. eligible voters were reported to have participated in the election of 275 deputies to a new, 400-seat National Assembly. The remaining 125 deputies had been appointed at a national conference in January. In the presidential election al-Bashir obtained 75.7% of the total votes cast, and formally commenced a five-year term of office on 1 April. On the same day at-Turabi was unanimously elected President of the National Assembly. Representatives of opposition groups and parties alleged that electoral malpractice had been widespread and that many voters had been intimidated into participating.

A peace agreement concluded by the Government and the SSIM in February 1996—initially in order to facilitate the provision of emergency food aid to areas of need in southern Sudan—appeared, in April, to culminate in a substantial breakthrough in the southern conflict. On 10 April the Government, the SSIM and the SPLA—United signed an agreement—described as a 'political charter for peace'—under which they pledged to preserve Sudan's national unity and to take joint action to develop those areas of the country which had been affected by the civil war. The charter also provided for the holding of a referendum as a 'means of realizing the aspirations of southern citizens' and affirmed that *Shari'a* law would be the basis of future legislation. Other opposition groups, however, rejected the charter. On 17 April Sudan's First Vice-President was reported to have invited Garang to sign the charter on behalf of the faction of the SPLA under his control, and there was speculation that this was part of an attempt to form a new government of national unity. However, the new Cabinet, announced on 21 April, retained the military, Islamic cast of its predecessor.

In April 1997 a further peace agreement was concluded between the Government and six of the southern factions. In this agreement self-determination was promised for the southern states, as was, after a four-year transitional period, a referendum on independence. The SPLA refused to sign, claiming that the pact was devised in such a way as to divide and weaken the southern opposition. Although the SPLA and the NDA carried out some successful military offensives during 1997 and 1998, neither grouping came close to scoring a decisive military victory over the Sudan People's Armed Forces (SPAF).

In early August 1997, in accordance with the terms of the peace treaty, the Southern States Co-ordination Council (SSCC) was established; Dr Riek Mashar Teny-Dhurgon, leader of the SSIM, was appointed its Chairman. Dr Lam Akol, leader of the SPLA—United, signed a peace agreement with the Government in September and returned to Khartoum in the following month. (The SPLA—United was the third largest of the southern insurgent groups, and controlled northern Upper Nile state.) In early 1998 Riek Mashar announced that the six southern rebel factions that had made peace with the Government had agreed to unify their troops with his Southern Sudan Defence Force (SSDF). Unification of the former factions' troops left two armed organizations, the SPAF and the SSDF, operating in the south, which was expected to facilitate the war against the SPLA. Discontent among southern politicians became evident in February when many of them threatened to rejoin rebel ranks unless they received positions in the proposed state governments; four were already expected to have done so, including Maj.-Gen. Kerubino Kuanyin Bol, one of the founders of the SPLA.

CONSTITUTIONAL AMENDMENTS

In October 1997 a 277-member constitutional committee was formed to draft a new Constitution. This document was approved by the National Assembly in April 1998 and then submitted to al-Bashir. A referendum on the new Constitution was held during 1–20 May; results, announced in late June, showed that 96.7% of voters were in favour of the Constitution, which came into force on 1 July 1998. Under its terms, executive power was vested in the Council of Ministers, which was appointed by the President but responsible to the National Assembly. Legislative power was vested in the National Assembly. The Constitution also contained guarantees of freedoms of thought and religion, and the right to political association, provided that such associations complied with the law. Fighting continued in the south in November, and in that month a state of emergency was declared in Darfur region and in Northern Kordofan.

New legislation approved in November 1998 provided for the establishment of an independent election commission, to prepare guidelines for elections and referendums, and of a Constitutional Court, and for the legalization of political associations. In January 1999 the age of eligibility to vote was reduced to 17 years. Registration of political parties began in that month; all parties were required to have 100 founding members, none of whom was to have a criminal record. The first registration documents were issued in early February; however, the northern parties affiliated to the NDA were not included.

In early 1999 it was announced that elections would be held in mid-1999 for the state legislative assemblies. However, critics claimed that this schedule would not give the new parties time to prepare themselves for elections. In April voting was postponed in the south until November, as adverse weather conditions would impede the movement of citizens, and thus their ability to register and to vote. Elections in the northern and central states were to be completed in early June. On 9 May al-Bashir granted an amnesty to ex-President Nimeri. Two days later a licence was granted to Nimeri's followers to form a political party called the Alliance of the People's Working Forces. On 22 May Nimeri returned to Khartoum from exile in Egypt. During that month the opposition claimed a series of victories in the south and on 31 May Col Garang of the SPLA, Sadiq al-Mahdi of the UP and Mubarak al-Mahdi of the NDA held closed meetings in Kampala, Uganda, to discuss several issues regarding their armed campaign against the Government.

President al-Bashir gradually sought to steer Sudan away from its hard-line, isolationist domestic and foreign policies. He sought, *inter alia*, reconciliation with northern opposition groups in the NDA, which had relocated to Eritrea. In November 1999 al-Bashir and UP leader al-Mahdi met for talks in Djibouti; al-Mahdi had previously met with at-Turabi in Geneva, Switzerland. The Djibouti meeting ended with a joint declaration that envisaged a federal system of government and the holding of a referendum within four years to allow southerners to choose between the division of the country or unity with decentralized powers. The Government later announced it would accept the result of such a referendum. The agreement was welcomed by many parties; however, the NDA responded by stating that it would escalate the war in the south rather than end it. SPLA leader John Garang later condemned and disavowed the Djibouti agreement.

AL-BASHIR ASSUMES GREATER CONTROL

By 2000 it was apparent that al-Bashir remained in firm control of the Government. In December 1999 he had declared a three-month state of emergency and suspended the National Assembly, and in January 2000 he announced the formation of a new Government and appointed new governors in 25 of the 26 states. In early February al-Bashir stated that the dissolution of the National Assembly was irrevocable and relocated several senior army officers in order to prevent a possible coup. The state of emergency was extended from three to 12 months in March, and in April it was reported that presidential elections were planned for October. Observers interpreted the announcement as yet another step to curb at-Turabi's power. Most opposition parties, including the UP, indicated that they would boycott any elections prior to the convening of a national conference to discuss the problems in Sudan. In March the UP had announced its decision to suspend its membership of the NDA. Relations between these two groups had deteriorated after December 1999 when al-Mahdi initiated independent talks with al-Bashir following the dissolution of the National Assembly. On 6 May al-Bashir took a further step against at-Turabi by suspending him as Secretary-General of the ruling National Congress (NC). Throughout 1999 at-Turabi had become increasingly vociferous in his criticism of the Government, expressing the desire for a more open political system. Despite his removal, at-Turabi still enjoyed considerable support within the NC, the Muslim Brotherhood, the SPAF, the People's Defence Force and various other Islamic militias. In late June at-Turabi responded to his dismissal by creating a new political party, the Popular National Congress (PNC).

Presidential and legislative elections were held concurrently over a 10-day period in mid-December 2000, although they were boycotted by the main opposition parties. As expected, al-Bashir was re-elected President, securing 86.5% of the votes cast, according to results released by the General Elections Commission (GEC), thus comfortably defeating his nearest rival, former President Nimeri, who obtained 9.6% of the vote. Voting did not take place in three southern states, and opposition leaders dismissed the official turn-out figures. The NC secured 355 seats in the new 360-member National Assembly; the remaining five seats were taken by small opposition parties. A nine-member OAU team of observers praised the manner in which the elections had been conducted, although it also noted that 'logistical challenges' had affected voting in some areas. Monitors from the OAU, the Arab League and the Non-aligned Movement endorsed the election. On 3 January 2001 al-Bashir extended the state of emergency for a further year.

On 21 February 2001 at-Turabi was arrested at his home in Khartoum after it was announced that the PNC and the SPLM had, two days earlier, signed a memorandum of understanding in Geneva, which called for the Sudanese people to participate in 'peaceful popular resistance' against the al-Bashir regime. Over the following days some 30 associates of at-Turabi were also taken into police custody, and in early March at-Turabi and three members of the PNC's leadership council were reported to have been charged with criminal conspiracy, undermining the constitutional order, waging war on the state and calling for violent opposition to public authority. The day after at-Turabi's arrest al-Bashir implemented a major reorganization of the Cabinet and replaced many of the country's state governors. Several new ministries were created, and, although the new 32-member Cabinet was dominated by NC members, al-Bashir incorporated four members of two minor opposition parties into the Government. Two members of the UDSF retained their positions in the Cabinet; however, the UP, despite earlier indications to the contrary, refused to participate in the new administration and officially stated that it would not accept ministerial posts before the holding of free and fair elections in the south of the country and the resolution of the armed conflict in that region.

In May 2001 the Government announced the suspension of air strikes against southern rebel groups, but stated that it reserved the right to protect individuals and lines of supply and to counter any rebel offensives. The cessation proved short-lived, as heavy fighting swiftly broke out, and in early June an SPLA offensive resulted in the capture of the strategically important town of Raga in the Bahr al-Ghazal province. Just days later the Government officially revoked the suspension of air strikes, although it stated that it would attempt to avoid the bombing of densely populated areas. In mid-December the state of emergency, first imposed in 1999, was extended for a further 12 months. There was little public opposition to the move.

The situation in the south remained as unclear as that in the north of the country. In January 2002 Riek Mashar, the military commander of the Sudan People's Defence Force, announced that the group had merged with the SPLA and that both would conduct joint military operations against the SPAF. Despite this significant development, neither the southern rebels nor government troops seemingly possessed the capabilities to score a decisive military victory. In April al-Bashir consolidated his hold on power after the consultative council of the National Congress approved resolutions that increased his constitutional powers and strengthened his position against the provincial and national parliaments. Notably, al-Bashir was granted the right to appoint provincial governors, and the two-term limit on the presidential mandate was abolished. Additionally, these changes further isolated at-Turabi by impeding his ability to cultivate parliamentary support and to mount an effective presidential campaign. The amendments were condemned by several opposition parties.

In mid-January 2002 talks sponsored jointly by the USA and Switzerland commenced in Bürgenstock, Switzerland. Following six days of intensive discussions, the Sudanese Government and the SPLM agreed to observe a six-month cease-fire, to be supervised by a joint military commission in the central Nuba region in order to facilitate the delivery of vital aid supplies to the area. However, in February the USA announced that it had suspended discussions with the Sudanese Government after two separate incidents earlier that month in which Sudanese air force planes had bombed civilians collecting food supplies in the Bahr al-Ghazal province. In the second incident at least 24 civilians were killed when a UN World Food Programme (WFP) relief centre came under fire. Although the Government insisted that the earlier incident, which resulted in the deaths of two children, was accidental, the US Department of State insisted that discussions would not recommence until it had received a full explanation for the attacks from the Sudanese Government. Talks resumed, however, following the issuing of an apology for the attacks by the Sudanese Minister of External Relations, and in mid-March a US-brokered agreement was concluded between the SPLM and the Sudanese Government, which aimed to guarantee the protection of civilians from military attacks; the agreement was to be monitored by two teams of international observers.

In May 2002 the Minister of Finance, Adb ar-Rahim Muhammad Hamdi, reportedly resigned owing to ill health. There was, however, speculation that he had been dismissed by al-Bashir following the implementation of several unpopular economic measures. Hamdi was subsequently replaced by Muhammad al-Hasan az-Zubayr. In June three members of the NC, including the Minister of Transport, Dr Lam Akol, resigned from the party in protest at the increasing dominance of al-Bashir. Akol went on to establish a new political party, the Justice Party, in early September and was dismissed from his ministerial post by al-Bashir later that month. Meanwhile, al-Bashir reorganized the Council of Ministers in August, to bring into government eight members of the UP breakaway faction that opposed Sadiq al-Mahdi. Having been placed under a detention order the previous year, in September at-Turabi was removed from house arrest and transferred to prison. In late December Parliament approved al-Bashir's request to extend the state of emergency for another year. He justified the action by stating that there were 'exceptional security threats' in Sudan; however, some observers maintained that the state of emergency had been prolonged to reinforce al-Bashir's political position by allowing him to continue to rule by decree, nullify existing laws, and detain prisoners without trial. Also in late

December al-Bashir appointed three new ministers of state and three new federal ministers. In part, the reshuffle further co-opted the opposition by including an additional three members of the DUP.

At the PNC's national convention, which took place in mid-October 2003, the party leadership urged the Government to conclude a comprehensive peace agreement with the SPLM and called upon all political forces to join the PNC to foster national unity and democracy. Later that month the authorities released at-Turabi and lifted the ban on the PNC and its publications. At-Turabi's freedom proved to be short-lived, however. In late March 2004 the Sudanese Government announced that it had uncovered a coup plot and had arrested 10 army officers, 10 police officers and seven PNC members, including at-Turabi; all PNC activities were also suspended. Further arrests followed and the authorities accused at-Turabi of encouraging Darfurian rebels (see below), particularly the Sudan Justice and Equality Movement (SJEM), to take up arms against the Government.

REGIONAL PEACE INITIATIVES

Throughout much of the 1990s the Intergovernmental Authority on Drought and Development (IGADD, now the Intergovernmental Authority on Development—IGAD) sought to broker a settlement between the Sudanese Government and the SPLM. By 2000 the IGAD peace process had made little progress despite donor efforts to 'invigorate' the talks by establishing a Nairobi-based IGAD secretariat headed by senior Kenyan diplomat Daniel Mboya. Funding and organizational problems, coupled with the intransigence of the warring parties, prevented the secretariat from making any meaningful accomplishments. A further round of discussions was due to be held in mid-May 2000; however, early that month the SPLM announced that it had suspended its participation in the peace negotiations in protest at the Government's alleged continued bombing of civilian targets. It reaffirmed its commitment to the unification of the IGAD process and the joint Egyptian-Libyan initiative (see below), but did not indicate on what conditions it would resume talks. In June the SPLM announced it would rejoin the peace talks and in that month President al-Bashir declared a general amnesty for all opponents of the Government; however, it was rejected by a number of opposition groups, including the SPLA. Later in June al-Bashir proposed a national forum of all political forces and national leaders, which was to attempt to negotiate an end to the country's civil war.

In August 1999 Egypt and Libya proposed a five-point peace initiative which envisaged a cease-fire and a national reconciliation conference, which would welcome all parties, including the NDA, which had been excluded from the IGAD process. In January 2000 the Libyan and Egyptian Ministers of Foreign Affairs visited Sudan and held talks with President al-Bashir, during which they discussed recent developments in Sudan; at the end of the meeting they stressed that the joint Egyptian-Libyan peace initiative would continue. In May SPLM leader Col Garang informed the Egyptian Minister of Foreign Affairs that he favoured combining the Egyptian-Libyan peace initiative with the IGAD process. However, by mid-2001 Egypt and Libya had still not been successful in their attempts to persuade IGAD to join their initiative, largely owing to opposition by Kenya and the USA. In June al-Bashir and Garang attended another IGAD meeting in Nairobi—significantly, this was the first time the two men had attended the same peace talks since 1997. However, they did not meet in person, and, although the two sides agreed to redouble their efforts to end the conflict, no agreement regarding a cease-fire was reached.

In mid-June 2002 a new round of IGAD-sponsored peace talks between the Government and the SPLM opened in Machakos, Kenya. Despite the ongoing discussions, fighting between the two sides continued, and there were numerous reports of heavy civilian casualties following bombing raids on southern towns by government forces. Nevertheless, following five weeks of protracted talks, a major breakthrough in the conflict was achieved on 20 July, when delegations from the SPLM and the Government signed an accord, known as the Machakos Protocol, which provided for the holding of a referendum, after a transitional period of six years, on self-determination for the south. The Protocol also stated that Sudan's Constitution would be rewritten to ensure that *Shari'a* law would not be applied to non-Muslim southerners. The Machakos Protocol was not a definitive peace agreement, but rather a framework for future negotiations, and the Government stated that the accord would only be implemented following the cessation of hostilities between the two sides. Government and SPLM delegations reconvened in Machakos in mid-August for talks. Despite reports of further fighting, on 17 October the Government and the SPLM agreed to a cease-fire covering the whole of Sudan. In November the second round of talks in Machakos ended with the signing of a memorandum of understanding that proposed a structure for an interim government. The document's main provisions included an agreement for the creation of a directly elected bicameral parliament and a government of national unity, in which the south would have proportional representation. Southerners would also receive a share of senior and mid-level civil service positions.

In September 2003 the Sudanese Government and the SPLM signed an accord in Naivasha, Kenya, which provided for the withdrawal from southern Sudan of 100,000 government troops within two and a half years, in addition to the withdrawal of rebel forces from eastern Sudan within a year. An integrated 'third force', comprising some 40,000 troops, was also to be established and deployed in areas disputed by both sides. During a six-year interim period, government and rebel troops were to be treated equally as the Sudan Armed Forces (SAF). It was also agreed that, in the case of the south rejecting self-determination at a referendum following the six-year interim period, a new Sudanese national army would be established. In early December 2003 SPLM delegates visited Khartoum for the first time since the escalation of the north–south conflict in 1983, prior to convening for further talks with the Government in Naivasha. Later that month the Government and the SPLM agreed 'in principle' to divide petroleum revenues between the north and the south, and it was reported that they had also reached preliminary agreement on the distribution of tax revenues and the role of the new central bank. Nevertheless, no final agreement was concluded by the end of the month, and talks recommenced in early January 2004. On 7 January the two sides signed an accord on wealth- and revenue-sharing, which also provided for the establishment of two separate banking systems for the north and the south, as well as a new national currency on the signing of a final peace settlement. In mid-April the UN announced it had been forced to suspend aid operations in southern Sudan, owing to renewed violence, and that some 50,000 people had fled their homes in the region during the previous month.

In late May 2004 the Sudanese Government and the SPLM signed three protocols that covered power-sharing arrangements—Garang would assume the post of First Vice-President in a proposed 'government of national unity' and would also be appointed President of southern Sudan—and the administration of the three disputed provinces. Other provisions approved the allocation of 50% of Sudan's net revenue (not including petroleum revenues) to the proposed southern Government and both parties agreed that 3% of oil revenues would be given to the province that produced the petroleum with the remainder being divided equally between the Sudanese Government and the SPLM.

On 9 January 2005 the Government and the SPLM signed a Comprehensive Peace Agreement (CPA) in Nairobi, thus opening a new chapter in the country's history and officially ending the civil war in the south that had lasted for more than two decades, during which at least 2m. people had been killed and more than 4m. displaced. The accord included eight protocols, including agreements that political power and Sudan's national wealth would be shared between the national Government and the south; that the SPAF and the SPLA would remain separate forces within the national army, in addition to contributing equally to new Joint Integrated Units that would be deployed on both sides of the north–south border, and that all militias would be disbanded within a year; that oil revenues would be shared equally between the north and the south; that the SPLA and other southern groups would hold 30% of government positions in the north, while holding 70% in the south; that the contested regions of the Blue Nile and the Nuba mountains would be governed by an administration in which 55% of the seats would be taken by government officials and 45% by the SPLM, while the petroleum-rich region of Abeyi would be granted special status under the presidency; that the application of *Shari'a* law would be limited to the north; and that Garang, would become Sudan's First Vice-President and would act as President of Southern Sudan and head of the SPLA forces during the six-year period of autonomy, after which a referendum on secession would be held.

THE COMPREHENSIVE PEACE AGREEMENT

The Interim National Constitution was promulgated on 9 July 2005, in accordance with the terms stipulated in the CPA. On 1 August, however, Garang was killed in a helicopter accident while en route to Rumbek, in southern Sudan, from Uganda. The announcement of Garang's death was followed by several days of rioting in Khartoum, during which more than 130 people were killed. Garang was replaced as leader of the SPLA/SPLM by Commdr Salva Kiir Mayardit, hitherto deputy leader of the organization. Salva Kiir was later appointed First Vice-President in the national Government and assumed the presidency of the new Government of Southern Sudan (GOSS). In September 2005 a Government of National Unity was established, which was dominated by the NC and the SPLM but eventually included some representatives of the NDA; however, the new Government was boycotted by the UP and the PNC. By the end of the year the new National Assembly was also functioning. The process of nominating national commissions to implement the CPA in a number of policy areas also commenced. By mid-2007 four had been established: those for the Constitutional Court, the national judiciary, the north–south border and the national Constitution; however, those responsible for elections, human rights and the civil service were yet to be created. Nevertheless, doubts persisted regarding the future stability of the Government of National Unity, with particular concern over the potentially acrimonious national elections scheduled to be held by and amid general accusations that the NC sought to delay implementation of the CPA.

In addition to the GOSS, a new Transitional Southern Sudan Legislative Assembly was established and regional administrations were also created. In December 2005 a new Constitution for the south was promulgated. Security remained a difficult issue. In addition to the forces of the SPLA a number of other rebel groups were known to be active in the south, including the SSDF, which was comprised predominantly from the Nuer people of Upper Nile region. The Ugandan Lord's Resistance Army (LRA) has also carried out attacks in the south. It has been suggested that both groups have enjoyed the support of the NC in an attempt to undermine the power base of the SPLA/SPLM. However, since the signing of the CPA, Salva Kiir has reached agreement with the main SSDF leader, Paulino Matip, while the new Vice-President of the GOSS, Riek Mashar, has met with LRA leader Joseph Kony in an attempt to facilitate peace talks between the LRA and the Ugandan Government. There are also concerns about the SPLA/SPLM's capacity to transform itself from an armed force into a solely political entity and the repatriation of refugees and internally displaced persons (IDPs) currently in northern Sudan and neighbouring Uganda. In December 2005 the office of the United Nations High Commissioner for Refugees (UNHCR) announced that it would begin to repatriate some 500,000 refugees from neighbouring countries; earlier in that month 90,000 refugees had returned to southern Sudan from northern Kenya under UNHCR auspices. In addition, many southerners who were displaced to the north of the country have begun to return to their homes in the south, though the rate of return remains comparatively slow and facilities to receive those who do go back are very limited.

The border between northern Sudan and the south remains unresolved. In accordance with the CPA, a commission, headed by the former US Ambassador to Sudan, Donald Petterson, decided that Abyei region belonged to southern Sudan, a decision rejected by the Missiriya Arabs, despite the fact that all parties had promised to honour the 'binding and final' agreement. In addition, the NC continued to reject the commission's findings stating that the experts had exceeded their terms of reference, thus causing tension between the NC and the SPLM. The two other disputed areas of Blue Nile and the Nuba Mountains were less problematic but still presented challenges. Observers feared that tension over the border issue could increase in the period leading up to the referendum on southern self-determination scheduled to take place in 2011, particularly with regard to Sudan's newly discovered petroleum reserves, much of which lie in the disputed border areas. In early 2006 there was a series of disagreements between the national Government and the GOSS over the distribution of petroleum revenues and the right to grant licences for exploration and extraction in the south (see Economy essay). Representatives of the NC and the SPLM met in May to discuss progress in implementing the CPA, but a number of divisive issues remained unresolved in mid-2007.

THE WAR IN DARFUR

In February 2003 two rebel groups, the Sudanese Liberation Movement (SLM), which reportedly comprised as many as 2,500 armed troops, and the SJEM, a force estimated to number several hundred men, organized a rebellion against the Government in an attempt to end political oppression and economic neglect in the Darfur region of western Sudan. The SLM and the SJEM also feared that the peace process with the south would lead to a new national government that would focus on southern Sudan's political and economic development at the expense of Darfur. The Sudanese Government responded to this aggression by employing pro-Government ethnic Arab militias—the *Janjaweed*—to suppress the revolt. Militia operations forced hundreds of thousands of people from towns, villages and other populated areas and rebel counter-attacks increased the number of displaced persons. International observers reported that the Government's brutal tactics against Darfur's Fur, Masaalit and Zaghawa ethnic groups included targeted killings, mass rapes, the burning of villages and food stocks and the contamination of water supplies. By 2006 estimates indicated that up to 200,000 had died directly or indirectly as a result of the conflict. Another 250,000 had sought refuge in neighbouring Chad, with a further 2m. displaced in Darfur. In total the UN was providing food for some 2.7m. people, while humanitarian organizations active in the region accused the Government of obstructing their efforts to reach the estimated 800,000 people who required support.

International pressure on the Sudanese Government to take measures to halt the atrocities in Darfur continued in 2004. The USA and the UN stated that they had evidence that the Sudanese Government was providing support to the *Janjaweed* and that the militia forces had carried out summary executions of civilians. On 8 April Chadian-brokered talks resulted in the declaration of a 45-day cease-fire, to be monitored by the AU. However, the agreement swiftly collapsed and clashes between rebel fighters and the *Janjaweed* continued. In July Sudan and the UN signed a joint communiqué that committed the former to disarming the *Janjaweed*, improving humanitarian access to Darfur, providing security for the internally displaced and ending impunity for perpetrators of human rights abuses. The UN promised to deliver aid to those in need and to support initiatives for a peace settlement. In mid-July AU-sponsored peace talks between the Sudanese Government and the rebels opened in Addis Ababa. The talks swiftly collapsed after the Government rejected the conditions for further negotiations stipulated by the SLA and the SJEM, which included the disarmament of the *Janjaweed* and the removal of those *Janjaweed* fighters absorbed by the police and army; the observation of the April cease-fire agreement; the prosecution of the perpetrators of crimes and an inquiry into allegations of genocide; unimpeded humanitarian access for aid agencies; the release of prisoners of war; and a 'neutral' venue for future talks. In late July the US House of Representatives approved a resolution declaring the human rights abuses in Darfur a 'genocide' and on 30 July the UN Security Council adopted Resolution 1556 that called on the Sudanese Government to end the conflict in Darfur, to facilitate the delivery of humanitarian aid, and to grant AU peace monitors access to the region. Should the Sudanese Government fail to achieve these goals within 30 days, the UN would take 'further measures' against the country. The Government announced that it 'reluctantly' accepted the UN resolution, although the AU subsequently delayed its decision on plans to deploy a peace-keeping mission to Darfur and there were continuing reports of attacks being carried out by the *Janjaweed*. In September the Security Council approved Resolution 1564, which stated that the Council would consider imposing sanctions on Sudan's petroleum industry should the Government fail to act to disarm the *Janjaweed* and to protect civilians from further attacks. Later that month talks were held between the SLA, the SJEM and the Government in Abuja, Nigeria, which ended without agreement. The talks resumed the following month and in November all sides pledged to cease hostilities and the Government agreed to establish a 'no-fly zone' over the region. Nevertheless, during late 2004 AU officials and humanitarian agencies continued to report attacks by forces on both sides of the conflict and several aid agencies temporarily withdrew their staff from the region.

In March 2005 the UN Security Council adopted Resolution 1593, referring the situation in Darfur to the Prosecutor of the International Criminal Court—(ICC, based in The Hague, Netherlands). The resolution urged all parties to co-operate fully with the ICC, which was to undertake preparatory studies prior to making a decision on whether to launch a full investigation into alleged crimes against humanity committed in Darfur. Al-Bashir subsequently vowed not to send any Sudanese national to The Hague for trial and mass demonstrations were held in the capital against the ICC. The President's declaration was put to the test in January 2007 when the ICC issued indictments against two men, Ahmed Haroun, a Minister of State, and Ali Kushayb, a *Janjaweed* leader, only for al-Bashir to repeat the refusal to co-operate. Meanwhile, the AU announced in April 2005 that it was to increase its African Mission in Sudan (AMIS) to an authorized strength of 7,731 troops and in June further talks between the Government and rebels commenced in Abuja, in which a declaration of principles was signed. In the following month the SLA and SJEM agreed to normalize relations following discussions in Tripoli, Libya. A further round of talks in Abuja commenced in mid-September, despite the absence of an SLM faction. Violence continued to escalate, however, and in early October four AU peace-keepers were killed in southern Darfur, prompting the UN to withdraw all non-essential staff from the region. Peace talks resumed in Abuja in November, but these ended without any real progress. In January 2006 one Senegalese peace-keeper was killed in an attack on a battalion of 30 AU peace-keeping troops in western Darfur. The Sudanese Government blamed the attack on rebels supported by the Chadian Government. At a meeting in March the AU agreed to extend the mandate of AMIS to 31 September, while announcing its intention to transfer control of the mission to the UN following the mandate's expiry. The UN Security Council approved Resolution 1672 in late April, imposing sanctions upon four individuals suspected of committing crimes against humanity in Darfur.

Efforts to reach a negotiated peace settlement continued in late April 2006 under AU auspices in Abuja. AU mediators submitted a peace proposal on 30 April and, finally, following days of deliberations the Government and one of the SLM factions, led by Minni Minawi, agreed to accept the proposal, although the other main SLM leader, Abd al-Wahid Muhammad Nur, and the SJEM leader, Khalil Ibrahim, refused to sign the agreement, known as the Darfur Peace Agreement (DPA). Rebel negotiators had insisted on the creation of a national Vice-President's position, but eventually agreed to accept the role of Senior Assistant to the President on Darfur (to be included in the presidency). The Senior Assistant would also chair a new Transitional Darfur Regional Authority (TDRA). They had also sought recognition of Darfur as a region rather than as three separate states in the current federal structure. The DPA provided for a referendum in 2008 to decide upon this issue. Nevertheless, concerns were raised, not least by rebel groups which had refused to sign the DPA, regarding the proposal that the Government enforce the disarmament of its *Janjaweed* proxy. Throughout 2006 the UN continued its preparations to send a peace-keeping force to Darfur, despite increasing opposition from the Sudanese Government. In late May the UN Secretary-General's Special Adviser, Lakhdar Brahimi, held discussions with al-Bashir aimed at persuading the President to allow a UN force to enter the region. A UN team was subsequently given permission to enter Darfur in order to undertake preliminary analysis for the proposed deployment of UN peace-keepers. However, in late June al-Bashir gave a speech in which he insisted that no such force would be allowed to enter the country.

It was becoming increasingly clear that AMIS was undermanned, under-equipped and under-funded, and on 31 August 2006 the UN Security Council approved Resolution 1706, calling for the UN Mission in Sudan currently deployed in the south of the country to be increased by up to 17,300 military personnel, and for its mandate to be extended to encompass the responsibilities of AMIS in Darfur. The resolution envisaged a force of 'a strong African character', which was to be deployed before 31 December. Earlier in August the UN Under Secretary-General for Humanitarian Affairs, Jan Egeland, had warned of an impending 'catastrophe of an unprecedented scale' in Darfur, should UN efforts to intervene in the crisis fail. The UN, the AU, Amnesty International and humanitarian agencies all continued to express concern at continuing violence in the region, and alleged that the forces of Minni Minawi (now Senior Assistant to the President on Darfur) had joined government troops and *Janjaweed* fighters in attacks against the SJEM and other rebel groups. According to these reports, the killing and rape of civilians and the systematic burning of villages also continued. By late 2006, despite international pressure, the Government refused to grant permission for the United Nations Mission in Sudan to deploy troops in Darfur and, in the wake of the failure of the DPA, the situation in Darfur appeared critical. Relations between the Government and the UN continued to deteriorate and in October the UN Special Representative for Sudan, Jan Pronk, was expelled from the country following comments he made on his website regarding defeats of government forces by rebels.

With the situation continuing to deteriorate in Darfur in 2007, and the rebels fragmenting into as many as 19 armed factions, there were further efforts to secure agreement from the Government to strengthen the AMIS force. Eventually, in January a tentative agreement was made for 3,000 UN troops to give support to AMIS; however, this was still well short of the 17,300 military personnel plus 3,000 civilians that the UN wanted to deploy. At the same time Salva Kiir, President of the GOSS, endeavoured to mediate with the rebel groups.

REBELLION IN THE EAST

As the situation in Darfur deteriorated, so fears grew that rebellion might spread to eastern Sudan. Resentment towards the national Government had increased among the mostly rural population, especially the Rashaida and the Beja communities, which had been severely affected by decades of drought and famine. The success of the SPLA in forcing the Sudanese Government to negotiate, as well as the revolt in Darfur, led some young Beja to launch an armed struggle, helped by the presence of NDA and SPLA forces in eastern Sudan, which had opened up a second front against the Government in the late 1990s.

The Beja Congress, which emerged in the 1960s, was joined in the late 1990s by the Rashaida Free Lions group. The two groups had similar objectives and in 2005 joined forces to form the Eastern Front. The Front's forces were far smaller than those of the SPLA or rebel groups in Darfur, but were active in a region of strategic importance to the national Government. Sudan's sole outlet to the sea was Port Sudan on the Red Sea coast, which was connected to central Sudan by road and rail links, and more recently by an oil pipeline, which was inaugurated in 1999. The Eastern Front perpetrated numerous attacks on roads in the region and on the pipeline, threatening to destabilize Sudan's growing economy, largely based on the export of petroleum through the pipeline.

After several military offensives in the region by Government forces had failed to prevent the Eastern Front from staging attacks on the region's economic and transport infrastructure, the Government finally agreed to hold talks with the Eastern Front. In June 2006 representatives from both sides met in Asmara for talks presided over by the Eritrean authorities and on 19 June the Government and the Eastern Front signed a declaration of principles and agreed a cessation of hostilities. Talks resumed in mid-July and in October the Eastern Sudan Peace Agreement (ESPA) was signed. Under it the Eastern Front was given some representation in the Council of Ministers, as well as promises of economic support. In contrast with the situation in Darfur it appeared that by mid-2007 the EPSA was holding.

FOREIGN RELATIONS

Since al-Bashir seized power in 1989 Sudan's foreign policy has passed through several phases. Initially, the new regime sought to preserve relations with the West, but as the Government became increasingly determined to spread radical Islamic fundamentalism throughout eastern Africa and the Middle East, the regime experienced periods of increased tension with its neighbours. Sudan provided refuge to a number of radical Islamist groups, including the al-Qa'ida (Base) organization of Osama bin Laden, who was based in Khartoum during 1991–96. This aggressive policy of support of 'Islamization' contributed to the deterioration of relations with neighbouring countries, including Uganda, Eritrea, Ethiopia, Kenya, Egypt and Libya; however, the People's Republic of China, South Africa and Russia all continued to pursue the burgeoning economic opportunities in Sudan. The Government's policies also fostered new links with Middle Eastern countries including Iraq, which supplied arms to the Government and received reciprocal support for its invasion of Kuwait in 1990, and Iran. Meanwhile, the USA condemned the Sudanese Government in the strongest terms for its alleged role in the organization of international terrorism and sought to isolate the country, especially after Sudan was implicated in the attempted assassination of President Mubarak of Egypt in 1995. By the late 1990s, however, al-Bashir was determined to improve relations with the West, especially the USA.

In the early 2000s, under the new Administration of President George W. Bush, US-Sudanese relations showed modest signs of improvement. Following the suicide attacks on New York and Washington, DC, in September 2001 the Sudanese Government pledged to support the global 'war on terrorism' by providing intelligence about bin Laden and al-Qa'ida, which the USA held responsible for the attacks. US officials welcomed this development, but refused to remove unilateral sanctions, which were extended for a further year in November, and Sudan continued to be listed by the US Department of State as a sponsor of terrorism. Furthermore, two Sudanese banks (Ash-Shamal Islamic Bank and Tadamon Islamic Bank) were among numerous institutions under US investigation as possible sources of financial support for bin Laden. The Bush Administration tacitly supported the UN's decision in September to lift sanctions against Sudan. Nevertheless, Sudan condemned the US-led military campaign in Afghanistan.

In November 2001 John Danforth, a former US senator and Bush's special envoy to Sudan, proposed four confidence-building measures to the Sudanese Government to help end the country's 18-year civil war. These measures included improved humanitarian access in conflict areas; the creation of zones and periods of tranquillity, in which immunization efforts and other humanitarian activities could proceed in peace; an end to bombing and other military attacks on civilian targets; and an end to the abduction of civilians. In late April 2002 Danforth released a report that endorsed an internal political settlement based on a 'one state, two systems' strategy. Despite IGAD's lack of success in advancing the Sudanese peace process, the US Administration continued to rely on that organization to initiate a lasting solution to the civil war. On 21 October Bush signed the Sudan Peace Act, which provided for punitive financial and diplomatic steps against the Sudanese authorities and for the suspension of aid to areas not under the Government's control, if the USA believed that the Sudanese Government was acting in bad faith at the peace talks. The Act also authorized US $100m. of appropriations in each of the fiscal years 2003, 2004 and 2005 for assistance to areas outside government control to prepare the population for peace and democratic governance, including support for civil administration, communications infrastructure, education, health and agriculture. Additionally, the Act condemned human rights violations by all sides involved in the conflict. Finally, the Act required Bush to certify within six months of enactment, and each six months thereafter, that the Sudanese Government and the SPLM were negotiating in good faith and that negotiations should continue. If Bush certified that the Sudanese Government had not engaged in negotiations in good faith or had unreasonably interfered with humanitarian efforts, the USA could seek a UN Security Council resolution for an arms embargo on Sudan; oppose loans, credits and guarantees by international financial institutions; take steps to deny Sudan access to oil revenues to ensure that the funds were not used for military purposes; and downgrade or suspend diplomatic relations. If the USA determined that the SPLM was not negotiating in good faith, none of the above provisions would apply to the Government of Sudan. In mid-2003 President Bush certified that Sudan and the SPLM were 'negotiating in good faith and that negotiations should continue'. Some observers maintained that US reluctance to impose sanctions reflected its unwillingness to jeopardize Sudanese co-operation over international terrorism. Meanwhile, in its annual *Trends in Global Terrorism* report, the US Administration listed Sudan as a 'state sponsor of terrorism' owing to its links with some hard-line anti-Israeli groups. However, the report also noted that the USA was satisfied with Sudan's anti-terrorism co-operation. Many observers believed the Act was biased in that it contained no provisions for penalizing the SPLM for obstructing the search for peace. In October US Secretary of State Colin Powell secured assurances from the Sudanese Government and the SPLM that a comprehensive settlement would be reached by the end of the year. Nevertheless, later in October US sanctions on Sudan (see below) were extended for a further 12 months, as the USA maintained that the Sudanese Government's policies continued to threaten US national security.

Relations between the two countries became increasingly tense owing to the ongoing crisis in the Darfur region (see above). Nevertheless, on 18 May 2004 the USA removed Sudan from a blacklist of countries deemed not to be co-operating with US anti-terrorism efforts. However, Sudan, which allows terrorist organizations such as Hamas and the Palestinian Islamic Jihad to maintain offices in Khartoum, remained on the State Department's list of 'state sponsors of terrorism', inclusion on which also bans arms sales. In late 2004 and early 2005 US-Sudanese relations focused on the implementation of the CPA and attempts to end the fighting in Darfur. In late July the US Secretary of State, Condoleezza Rice, visited Khartoum to express concern over the Darfur crisis to President al-Bashir. She also visited the Abu Shouk refugee camp near el-Fasher, where more than 50,000 people were being supported by the international community. In August 2006 the USA and the United Kingdom co-sponsored a draft resolution to the UN Security Council, urging the deployment of a UN peace-keeping force (see above). In late August the Assistant Secretary of State for African Affairs, Jendayi Frazer, visited Khartoum for talks with senior Government officials and urged the Sudanese Government to accept the deployment of UN troops in Darfur. However, Frazer departed without having reached an agreement. With frustration growing in the USA over Darfur, in May 2007 President Bush announced new sanctions against Sudan designed to increase the pressure to reach agreement with the UN, although critics feared that the move might only make the Sudanese Government more intransigent.

Sudan's relations with China took a new turn in 2007. Seen since the beginning of the oil development in the 1990s China has been a close commercial partner of Sudan, and an opponent in the Security Council of sanctions over Darfur. However, during 2007 China became more public in its efforts to encourage the Sudanese Government towards peace in the troubled region. At the start of that year the Chinese President, Hu Jintao, visited Sudan during the course of an African tour, and in May China appointed Liu Giujin as special envoy to Sudan. As a further sign of its concern China also announced that month that it would send 300 military engineers to assist in Darfur.

Relations between Sudan and Uganda continued to experience periods of tension, largely owing to Uganda's support for the SPLA and Sudan's links to Ugandan rebel groups, such as the Lord's Resistance Army (LRA). In December 1999 Sudan and Uganda concluded an agreement under the terms of which both countries pledged to disarm terrorists, respect one another's borders, exchange prisoners of war, free abductees taken by the insurgent LRA, stop rebel activity on each side of their common border, and offer amnesties to those who renounced the use of force. In January 2000 Sudan released 58 people who had been abducted by the LRA, while Uganda freed 72 Sudanese prisoners of war. Despite this exchange and several follow-on meetings between Sudanese and Ugandan officials, relations between the countries remained difficult. At its centre was the unwillingness of Uganda to talk with the LRA while unable to defeat it, and the Sudanese Government's continuing connections with it as a counter to the SPLM. In May 2006 the SPLM held talks with representatives of the LRA in an effort to facilitate discussions between the LRA and the Ugandan Government. In late June the GOSS invited the Ugandan Government to a meeting with the LRA in Juba. Talks began in mid-July without eventual success and the situation remained unresolved.

Sudan's relations with Eritrea have also been marred by repeated cross-border incidents involving clashes with the Sudanese-supported Eritrean Islamic Jihad (EIJ), which reportedly aims to overthrow the Eritrean Government. Eritrea's support for the NDA also contributed to the tense state of relations between the two countries. The unwillingness of both Governments to compromise undermined several diplomatic efforts to resolve their differences.

In November 1998 Eritrea and Sudan explored the possibility of improving relations and following negotiations, mediated by Qatar, they signed the Doha Agreement in May 1999, which provided for a restoration of diplomatic relations, the formation of joint committees to resolve any differences and a cessation of hostile propaganda between the two countries. However, by mid-1999 Sudan and Eritrea had yet to re-establish diplomatic relations and in June Sudan accused Eritrea of breaking the agreement following talks which Eritrea held with the Sudanese opposition. In January 2000 Sudan and Eritrea finally restored diplomatic relations and agreed to reopen the land route between the two countries and to adopt procedures for issuing travel permits to those wanting to cross the common border. In the same month the Eritrean Government ordered the NDA to evacuate the Sudanese embassy in Asmara, which it had been using as a headquarters. In February President al-Bashir and President Issaias Afewerki of Eritrea met in Khartoum and declared that they would not allow opposition groups located in their respective countries to launch cross-border raids. In October Afewerki visited Khartoum where he held talks with al-Bashir, during which both sides expressed their desire for a fresh beginning to their bilateral relations and agreed to take measures to resolve differences between the two countries in a peaceful manner. Later that month Eritrea sponsored talks between the Sudanese Government and the Asmara-based NDA, although attempts to persuade NDA Chairman al-Mirghani to return to Sudan proved unsuccessful.

In April 2002 the Sudanese First Vice-President, Ali Osman Muhammad Taha, expressed the hope that his country could improve relations with Eritrea. However, the fact that Eritrea continued to provide shelter and support to the NDA suggested that it remained unlikely that there would be reconciliation between the two countries in the near future. In October Sudan closed its border with Eritrea following an NDA attack on the town of Hamashkoreb in Kassala state. Eritrea rejected Sudan's accusation that it had been involved in the operation. Nevertheless, Sudan maintained diplomatic relations with Eritrea and allowed the repatriation of tens of thousands of Eritrean refugees from camps in Sudan to continue. Sudan expelled 10 Eritrean government officials who had been working with the office of the UN High Commissioner for Refugees in the refugee camps. Shortly after the NDA attack, Eritrea accused Sudan of fabricating charges of a Khartoum-NDA link as a pretext to obstructing peace negotiations with the SPLA. Sudan retorted by announcing that it continued to support the memorandum of understanding with the SPLA, but that the document did not cover military operations or 'Eritrean aggression' in north-east Sudan. In October Sudanese-Eritrean relations were further strained after the Sudanese Government accused Eritrea of participating in the NDA offensive in north-eastern Sudan and of providing support to the SLM/SJEM campaign in Darfur. Following these developments, the border was closed and Sudan rejected offers of mediation by the AU. Sudan has retaliated by providing aid to the opposition Eritrean National Alliance (ENA), which maintains offices in Khartoum. In November Sudan, Ethiopia and Yemen agreed to enhance their common security in the region. Eritrea, which had denounced an earlier meeting between these three countries as an attempt to form an 'axis of belligerence', did not participate in the talks. In early 2003 tension between Sudan and Eritrea intensified, as each accused the other of mounting terrorist attacks on the other's territory. In April the NDA met in Asmara to discuss Sudan's peace process. Sudan criticized the meeting claiming it violated the 'spirit' of the IGAD-sponsored peace talks.

During 2003–04 Eritrea repeatedly denied that it had been providing aid to the SLM/SJEM rebels in Darfur (see above), as the region was 'too far away'. Nevertheless, Eritrea hosted a number of SLM representatives who, in January 2004, joined the Asmara-based Beja Congress, which was a member of the NDA. The two groups promised to 'continue their struggle together' until they had eliminated 'marginalization, poverty, ignorance and backwardness'. At about the same time Eritrea complained that the Sudanese Government had arrested some of its nationals without charge or trial and had closed several community centres used by Eritreans. In March an estimated 1,700 Eritrean refugees in eastern Sudan returned to Eritrea. The repatriation allowed the Sudanese authorities to close 10 of 18 camps in eastern Sudan. However, some 200,000 Eritrean refugees remained in eastern Sudan. Only some 35,000 of them had signed up for voluntary repatriation in 2004 while more than 29,000 families had applied to remain in Sudan as refugees. Eritrean-Sudanese relations improved in 2006. In June the new Eritrean ambassador presented credentials to al-Bashir in Khartoum, and later in that month the Eritrean Government, having previously supported rebel groups active in the east of Sudan, offered to host talks between the Sudanese Government and the Eastern Front. Following the success of these talks, relations between the two Governments have moved closer to normalization.

Until late 1995 Sudan enjoyed relatively harmonious links with Ethiopia. In September, however, Ethiopia accused Sudan of harbouring three terrorists implicated in the attempted assassination of President Mubarak of Egypt in Addis Ababa in June and announced that it would close some Sudanese diplomatic facilities in the country and all non-governmental organizations (NGOs) connected with Sudan. Over the next few years, relations remained tense. However, in November 1999 and January 2000 Sudan and Ethiopia conducted talks that resulted in the reopening of their common border. Additionally, the two countries agreed to improve road links, reactivate a joint ministerial committee, and install telephone lines between their respective capitals, while Ethiopia indicated that it would no longer demand the repatriation of those suspected of launching the failed assassination attempt against Mubarak. Bilateral co-operation commissions met regularly to discuss security and economic issues, and in December 2000 Sudan and Ethiopia announced an ambitious long-term rail project. It was proposed that a 2,200-km railway link would be constructed between Port Sudan and Moyale on the Kenyan–Ethiopian border, at a cost of some US $1,400m. In December 2001 Sudan and Ethiopia agreed to demarcate their border and assess the issues of security, refugees and water management. The two countries also agreed to accelerate the construction of the Metemma–Gonder–Gallabat road.

In April 2002 Taha visited Ethiopia; at the end of his four-day visit he announced that a 'new era' in relations with Ethiopia had begun, and that the two countries had concluded a preferential trade agreement, as well as accords on the economy, commerce, infrastructure and telecommunications. In

May Sudan and Ethiopia signed four co-operation agreements in areas of agriculture, livestock, culture, and tourism. Sudan's Minister of External Relations, Mustafa Osman Ismail, also expressed hope that relations between the two countries would be an example for other African nations to follow, and praised the efforts made by the border demarcation committee between the two countries. In January 2003 Sudan delivered its first oil shipment to Ethiopia under an agreement that had been concluded in mid-2002. Eventually, Sudan planned to supply up to 10,000 metric tons of benzene, butane and kerosene per month. It was estimated that each shipment would save the Government around US $30 per ton on its current supplies. Also in January Ethiopia and Sudan announced the opening of a 184-km, $18.2m. road that linked the two countries between Gedarif and Metemma. In late March Ethiopian Prime Minister Meles expressed his desire to expand trade between the two countries and to seek funding from sources such as the African Development Bank, the European Union, the Organization of the Petroleum Exporting Countries Fund, the Arab Bank for Economic Development in Africa and the Chinese Government for additional road projects. In June Sudan and Ethiopia signed an agreement ending a seven-year border dispute. Under the accord, Ethiopia returned small pockets of land to the al-Qadaref region. In late March 2004 the African Development Fund (ADF) announced that it had awarded $2.59m. to Ethiopia and Sudan to study the irrigation and drainage of the eastern Nile. According to ADF officials, the study would enhance food security, reduce rural poverty, preserve the environment through sustainable natural resource management and encourage an integrated approach to irrigation and drainage development in the eastern Nile sub-basin. In July the Paris-based *Indian Ocean Newsletter* reported that Ethiopia and a German company, Thormaehlen Schweisstechnik, had signed an agreement with the SPLM and Kenyan and Ugandan authorities to build a rail link between Juba and Nakuru via Lokichokio. Additional rail lines could be constructed in the future to link southern Sudan with the Uganda towns of Arua and Gulu; however, given the estimated construction costs (€3,000m.), it seemed unlikely that this railway would be constructed by the end of the decade.

The Kenyan Government has sought to maintain good relations with all of the opposing forces in Sudan. However, its support of the SPLA frequently has alienated the Sudanese Government. Over the years, there have been numerous accusations that the Government of Kenya and certain Kenyan-based NGOs have provided weapons and other military supplies to the SPLA. Moreover, Garang and other senior rebel leaders maintained a strong presence in Nairobi. The UN-administered Operation Lifeline Sudan (OLS), which is headquartered in Nairobi, has transported food relief supplies into southern Sudan. Kenya also has played a major role in peace negotiations between the Sudanese Government and the rebels. During 2002–03 Kenya supported the IGAD-sponsored Sudanese peace talks by providing Gen. Lazaro Sumbeiywo of Kenya as chief negotiator. In July 2002 he concluded the Machakos Protocol that committed the Sudanese Government and the SPLM to a referendum on unity or secession for southern Sudan after a six-year transition period. The subsequent negotiations on the various protocols took place in Naivasha, and the signing of the CPA in Nairobi on 9 January 2005 underscored Kenya's importance as East Africa's diplomatic hub. The Moi Foundation, established by former Kenyan President Daniel arap Moi in 2003, also contributed to the southern Sudanese reconciliation process by sponsoring a conference between Garang and other southern leaders in late April 2005. Following the signing of the CPA commercial relations between Kenya and southern Sudan have expanded rapidly.

Sudanese-Egyptian relations historically have vacillated between confrontation and co-operation. However, they reached a new low on 26 June 1995, following an unsuccessful assassination attempt against President Mubarak in Addis Ababa. The Egyptian Government immediately accused Sudan of involvement in the attack, and relations quickly deteriorated. After a number of conciliatory measures, relations between the two countries had improved markedly by late 1999, when al-Bashir visited Egypt and the two countries agreed to normalize diplomatic relations. In April 2000 al-Bashir visited the Egyptian capital, Cairo, and met with President Mubarak at an Africa-Europe summit. Later that month Egypt appointed a new ambassador to Sudan, for the first time since the assassination attempt on Mubarak in 1995. The two countries also agreed to take steps to establish an Egyptian-Sudanese joint committee. Sudan and Egypt subsequently reached an agreement about Sudan's US $70m. debt to Egypt. Afterwards, Egypt abandoned the 10% levy on exports from Sudan. In September 2000 the Sudanese and Egyptian Ministers of Foreign Affairs held the first session of the Egyptian-Sudanese Commission for 10 years during which the two countries expressed their commitment to further bilateral economic development. The new IGAD Sudan peace initiative, backed by the USA, alarmed Egypt which feared that an independent southern Sudan would jeopardize the 1959 Nile water-sharing agreement, which gives Egypt the right to more than 80% of water flows. To protect its interests, Egypt in co-operation with Libya, had fostered its own peace plan, which offered no prospect of southern independence, but under pressure, notably from the US, the plan was dropped. In early May 2003 Mubarak and al-Bashir held talks in Khartoum, emphasizing their commitment to good relations. Shortly afterwards Garang met with Mubarak in Cairo, and the Secretary-General of the Arab League and former Egyptian Minister of Foreign Affairs, Amr Moussa, led a delegation to southern Sudan to 'build understanding and confidence' with the SPLA leadership. In late May Egypt hosted talks between the SPLA and northern opposition groups not included in the Machakos talks. During a meeting, held in mid-July, of the joint Sudanese-Egyptian higher committee in Khartoum, Taha claimed that relations between the two countries would achieve 'unprecedented progress', partially as a result of the implementation of 19 bilateral co-operation pacts. By 2006 Egypt, together with other Arab states, notably Saudi Arabia, had accepted the CPA and pledged to work with the GOSS to maintain the unity of Sudan.

Sudan and Libya have traditionally had mixed relations. Having been in dispute during most of the Nimeri era, relations were much closer when al-Mahdi became Prime Minister. In March 1990 the two Governments signed a 'declaration of integration' which provided for the merging of the two countries, but the increasingly Islamic fundamentalist character of the Sudanese regime after 1989 contributed to a cooling of relations. However, the Libyan leader, Col Muammar al-Qaddafi maintained links with the SPLM and was reported on various occasions to have attempted to mediate between the al-Bashir regime and more hostile neighbouring governments, notably Uganda in 1996. Qaddafi was also involved in attempts to mediate in the Darfur conflict, hosting a meeting between the SLA and SJEM in mid-2005 (see above). Thousands of Darfurians have sought refuge in Libya, and Libya has also provided a route for the safe passage of humanitarian aid convoys. In mid-2006 Qaddafi facilitated a resumption in relations between Sudan and Chad, following a dispute in late 2005 (see below). He continued to remain involved in 2007, hosting further talks involving Sudan and Egypt.

The ongoing crisis in Darfur has also affected Sudan's relations with Chad. Darfur and Chad have long-standing links and both President Hissène Habré and the current President, Idriss Deby Itno, launched coups with Sudanese assistance from bases in Darfur. Deby's seizure of power was supported by both Libya and Sudan, but relations with the latter have deteriorated sharply since late 2005 as the Chadian Government expressed fears that the conflict in Darfur could spread across the border. In December Chad declared 'a state of beligerence' with Sudan and, in response, Sudan has supported opposition movements operating both within Chad and in Darfur that seek to overthrow Deby. In April 2006 Deby severed relations with Sudan, accusing the Sudanese Government of supporting an attempted coup. However, relations improved in July when the two Governments agreed to withdraw support for rebel groups on both sides of the border. In August, following mediation by Libya, Deby and al-Bashir announced that full diplomatic relations would be restored later in 2006, although in practice relations remained difficult despite meetings in 2007 between the two Presidents.

FOOD AID AND REFUGEE PROBLEMS

The population of Sudan has suffered from both natural disasters and the civil war in recent years. In March 1994 the SPLA and the SPLA—United concluded an agreement under which they undertook to deliver food aid to all those in need of it, regardless of their locations. Despite this pledge, both factions continued to obstruct the famine relief process. In April, for example, the Government, the SPLA and the SPLA—United concluded an agreement under the auspices of the then IGADD, which provided for the safe shipment of food to southern Sudanese war zones. According to the Sudanese Government, the agreement collapsed when Col Garang refused to sign the final document. As a result, relief activities came to a halt throughout many parts of southern Sudan. Nevertheless, the Government succeeded in delivering some relief food to areas under its control. By mid-1994 the UN estimated that about 1.3m. Sudanese required emergency food aid. The situation in southern Sudan subsequently improved, however, and in January 1995, the UN resident co-ordinator in Sudan announced that better security in some areas had allowed people to acquire food on their own rather than rely on humanitarian aid.

In January 1996 a meeting of donor nations in Geneva approved the establishment of the UN Inter-Agency Consolidated Appeal for Sudan in order to assist in the co-ordination of relief activities. In the same month an FAO/WFP assessment team, working in conjunction with the OLS, estimated that at least 2.1m. Sudanese would require food aid during 1996. However, the Sudanese Minister of Agriculture claimed that international food aid was unnecessary as the country produced enough food to feed the population, and rejected the UN's assessment. In February, nevertheless, the UN requested its members to provide US $107.6m. in aid for southern Sudan, in particular the war-afflicted provinces of Bahr al-Ghazal, Jonglei and Upper Nile.

In mid-1998 FAO estimated that more than 1.2m. Sudanese were in need of food and non-food aid. However, international relief efforts were hampered by the war. In February the Government suspended OLS air operations in Bahr al-Ghazal and Lakes regions on security grounds. Limited air operations resumed later that month and were extended on 31 March. In April many aid agencies warned of widespread famine in the south if immediate action was not taken, but by mid-year the OLS had succeeded in gaining only 7% of the US $109.3m. that it had requested for its emergency operations in Bahr al-Ghazal. In August the OLS announced that Sudan was facing its worst humanitarian aid crisis in 10 years, with up to 2.6m. people at risk throughout the country. In response to the crisis, the OLS launched its most comprehensive humanitarian operation since its formation and urged other humanitarian organizations to join the relief effort. In mid-1999 the Government and the SPLA held a meeting of the Technical Committee on Humanitarian Assistance in Oslo, Norway. Both sides renewed their commitment to a humanitarian cease-fire in Bahr el-Ghazal and to security protocols for the railway and roads used by OLS. The Government and the SPLA also agreed to take steps to protect OLS personnel and property.

In early July 2004 WFP commenced the airlifting of enriched food from Addis Ababa to Darfur, where an estimated 1.2m. people required food aid every month until October. Initially, two WFP-chartered Ilyushin cargo planes made 44 trips to Nyala in south Darfur and el-Fasher in northern Darfur. Their cargoes included 2,000 metric tons of enriched flour, enough to feed some 300,000 people for one month. The airlifts ensured that at least some relief would arrive in Darfur during the rainy season which caused severe problems for transporters and trucks loaded with WFP food. In many areas the fighting and displacements had drastically reduced harvests and government, militia and rebel forces had looted livestock and food stocks. Cereal stocks in the markets were low and costs had increased more than 30% compared with the previous year's prices. Insecurity had nearly cut off all food commodity flows from usual surplus-to-deficit areas while fuel prices were rising due to insecurity and low supplies. Reportedly, there were no longer functioning markets in remote pastoral areas. The crisis severely disrupted 2004/05 agriculture activities, as the majority of the displaced and local residents in conflict-affected areas would be unable to plant and harvest crops in 2004. WFP expected the number of people in need of food assistance to rise to 2m. by the end of 2004, since most people missed the planting season. The destruction of seeds and farm implements meant that Darfur's humanitarian crisis would continue into 2005, even had many displaced people returned home. In addition, the movement of returning IDPs and refugees had already commenced in southern Sudan ahead of a complete peace agreement. Even if only 25% of IDPs moved, this would still represent some 1m. people. It was expected that most would cover large distances on foot, with little water and food, and WFP intended to be prepared with high-energy biscuits for situations where urgent nutrition was required.

By early 2005 there were an estimated 5.3m.–6.2m. IDPs in Sudan and some 600,000 Sudanese refugees or asylum seekers in other countries. There were more than 225,900 refugees from other countries in Sudan, including some 191,000 from Eritrea, 15,000 from Ethiopia, 7,900 from Uganda and 5,000 from Chad. Refugees were required by the Sudanese authorities to live in camps, but individuals were allowed to leave for medical care, education or employment. However, only about 90,000 refugees lived in camps, while some 65,000 resided in urban areas. By early 2005 the fighting in Darfur had claimed 70,000–140,000 lives, while disease and malnutrition had claimed a further 130,000–260,000 lives. Moreover, some 30% of Darfur's population had been internally displaced. Humanitarian relief and some protection against violence was provided by 11 UN agencies, at least 77 NGOs and more than 9,000 aid workers. About one-half of those affected by the conflict had access to clean water, but only 62% received food aid or had access to medical care. Moreover, by February of that year donors had supplied only 55% of the food aid required in Darfur and 8% of that required by all other areas. Throughout 2005–07 conditions for the delivery of relief supplies continued to deteriorate. Attacks against international NGOs increased in frequency and a number of Sudanese NGO personnel were killed in mid-2006, leading to the withdrawal from the country of some NGOs. In addition to worsening conditions, money for relief was increasingly in short supply. The humanitarian situation also contributed to worsening relations between Jan Egeland and the Sudanese Government. On the ground, the number of IDPs requiring assistance continued to grow and there were fears that the camps were becoming semi-permanent with large areas of the countryside being deserted by civilians fleeing the escalating violence.

HUMAN RIGHTS ISSUES

According to the US Department of State's 2003 human rights report, Sudan's human rights record remained 'extremely poor', despite improvements in some areas. Citizens lacked the ability to change their government peacefully. Security forces and pro-Government militias undertook extra-judicial killings and arbitrarily beat, harassed, arrested, tortured or detained incommunicado opponents or suspected opponents of the al-Bashir regime. Security forces and pro-Government militias also assaulted refugees and raped women abducted during raids. The Civilian Protection Monitoring Team (CPMT), created by an agreement between the Sudanese Government and the SPLA following the 2002 Machakos Protocol, and the Joint Military Commission operating in the Nuba mountains, had some success in monitoring and curbing serious abuses during 2003. However, in Darfur government forces and pro-Government militias committed serious human rights abuses in response to rebel attacks against government troops. As many as 3,000 unarmed civilians were killed, more than 600,000 civilians were internally displaced, and an estimated 100,000 refugees had fled to neighbouring Chad by the end of 2003. In July 2004 the UN reported that some 50,000 Sudanese had died and that more than 1m. had fled their homes. Other areas of concern included harsh and at times life-threatening prison conditions and prolonged detention, the absence of due process in civilian or military courts, and the infringement of citizens' privacy rights. Neither the Sudanese Government nor the SPLA respected the conventions of war in the southern insurgency, and neither side took many prisoners—as they regularly executed those who surrendered. Both also failed to co-operate fully with the International Committee of the Red Cross regarding access to or treatment of prisoners of war. Government co-operation with UN-sponsored relief operations in southern Sudan improved significantly as relief flights started operating in early 2004. However, government forces restricted the flow of humanitarian aid to Darfur. Restrictions on press freedom under the National Security Emergency decree increased as the authorities suspended many publications and newspapers during 2003. Security forces frequently arrested editors and journalists who criticized or disagreed with government policy. There were also restrictions on freedom of speech, assembly, association, religion and movement. In 2004 reports by Amnesty International, Human Rights Watch and other human rights organizations agreed that there had been no improvement in any of these areas. In March 2005 the UN resolved to refer allegations of human rights abuses in Darfur to the ICC. Later in that year a sealed list of some 50 names of those suspected of involvement in such crimes was sent to the ICC for investigation and inquiries extended into 2006; two indictments were handed down in 2007 (see above). However, the Sudanese Government continued to refuse to co-operate with ICC investigators, not least owing to speculation that the list contained the names of senior government officials.

Economy

THOMAS OFCANSKY

Revised by PETER WOODWARD

Sudan is primarily an agricultural and pastoral country, with about 65% of the economically active population engaged in the agricultural sector—the majority in essentially subsistence production. Industry is largely based around agriculture and the increasingly important petroleum sector, and accounted for an estimated 27.8% of gross domestic product (GDP) in 2006 (compared with 2% in the early 1960s). A major expansion of rain-fed production, which provides most staple foods and some export crops, in the 1970s helped to generate vigorous economic growth. By the early 1980s, however, the progressively deteriorating rainfall in the west and east of Sudan began to reduce production, and the contribution of agriculture to GDP declined sharply. Nevertheless, agriculture remains a major component of GDP, accounting for an estimated 38.7% of GDP in 2005. Since 1999 Sudan has been a net exporter of petroleum, and this has sharply boosted economic growth. Production was expected to rise, and in 2005–06 there were also significant rises in international oil prices. By 2006 the oil sector accounted for over 25% of GDP. In May 2006 Sudan was invited to become a full member of the Organization of Petroleum Exporting Countries (OPEC), of which it has previously held observer status. Commercial banking activity grew at an unprecedented level in 2005, following the emergence of several new agents on the world market (particularly in the Gulf states). Overall, the service sector (mainly financial services, commerce and hospitality) constituted 33.6% of Sudan's GDP in that year.

During 1995–2005, it was estimated, GDP per head increased, in real terms, at an average annual rate of 4.1%, while the population increased at an average annual rate of 2.1%. According to World Bank estimates, Sudan's GDP increased by an annual average of 0.4% in 1980–90 and by an average of 6.3% per year in 1998–2005. According to the IMF, real GDP increased by 6.4% in 2002, by 5.6% in 2003 by 5.2% in 2004. and by 8% in 2005. GDP was estimated to have increased by 13% in 2006 and was forecast to grow further in 2007.

Until the early 1970s Sudan's trade deficit was minimal despite a steady growth of imports, thanks to high domestic production and good world prices for cotton (the crop which had dominated Sudan's exports since the late 1920s). Since the early 1990s, however, Sudan has experienced a sharp increase in the value of its exports, mainly as a result of the commencement of the exportation of petroleum. The value of Sudanese exports amounted to US $2,542.2m. in 2003, $3,777.8m. in 2004 and $4,824.3m. in 2005. In 2005 Sudan recorded an estimated trade deficit of US $1,121.7m.,a result attributed to the rising level of imports required to sustain economic growth. The deficit on the current account of the balance of payments was equal to $614.5m. in that year. The gradual elimination of subsidies on many basic commodities and the devaluation of the Sudanese pound in 1991 and 1992 led to a sharp increase in inflation: during 1992–2000 the average annual rate of inflation was 64.8%. Consumer prices were estimated to have risen by 6.3% in 2003 and by 8.3% in 2004. According to the IMF, the average annual rate of inflation in 2005 was 8.5% and 7% in 2006.

Attempts to resolve Sudan's economic crisis (largely the result of overspending on a grandiose development programme, heavy government borrowing and inefficiency and corruption in the public sector earlier in the 1970s) began in 1978 and for the next five years consisted of repeated debt reschedulings and donor aid, underpinned by the IMF, World Bank-sponsored austerity measures and structural adjustment programmes aimed at restoring some balance to the external account by stimulating the production of export crops. After 1981 the new policies, especially towards the irrigated sector, began to have an effect. However, the Islamization of economic policies and the legal code in 1983, in an attempt to suppress growing popular opposition to the Government of Col Gaafar Muhammad Nimeri, and the fall in living standards associated with the austerity programmes, brought this improvement to an abrupt end. This dislocation of the domestic economy alienated foreign donors and creditors, leading to the suspension of several important rehabilitation schemes and the collapse of the vital support programme of debt relief and economic aid. By exacerbating civil unrest in the south, Islamization also created security uncertainties, which led to the suspension of activity, in 1984, on two projects that had been viewed as vital to Sudan's long-term recovery: the Jonglei Canal scheme and the exploitation of petroleum reserves.

The situation remained little changed for the first two years following the overthrow of Nimeri in April 1985, with drought compounding the problems of political instability and continuing civil conflict in the south. Various programmes aimed at attracting multilateral and bilateral loans were initiated by the al-Mahdi Government, but all eventually lapsed (see below). Following the June 1989 coup, the military regime of Lt-Gen. al-Bashir introduced strict measures in its attempt to ameliorate the economic situation, and government economic policies have since attempted—with little success—to achieve food self-sufficiency, stricter control of the budget and a reduction of the government deficit through the privatization of state enterprises. A decade after Nimeri's ousting, the economy remained stifled by high inflation, a huge external debt (US $17,603m. at the end of 1995), an acute shortage of 'hard' currencies and declining foreign aid. In mid-1997 it appeared that Sudan had resolved its dispute with the IMF over the management of its debt to the Fund. In November, however, economic sanctions were imposed by the USA for Sudan's alleged involvement in terrorist activities. By the end of 2005 Sudan's external debt totalled some $27,700m., according to preliminary estimates by the IMF, $24,400m. of which was in arrears. However, strong economic growth facilitated a decline in the ratio of external debt to GDP—equivalent to 156.7% in 2001—to 100% in 2005.

AGRICULTURE

Approximately one-third of Sudan's total area of about 2.5m. sq km is considered to be suitable for some form of agriculture. Of this, about 84m. ha is potential arable land and the remainder pastoral. Only about 15%, however, of the available arable area is cropped, reflecting the critical role of water availability in the development of the sector. The vast majority of settled cultivation has, until recently, been limited to the permanent water-courses of the Blue and White Niles and their tributaries in north-central Sudan. It is these areas which, within the framework of Sudan's 2m. ha of irrigation schemes, have been the focus of modern, commercial agriculture—producing the major export crop, cotton, as well as vital import substitutes such as sugar and wheat.

In contrast, some 60% of Sudan's area is occupied by the 11% of the population (estimated at 37.7m. in 2006) who are fully or partly nomadic—combining cultivation of subsistence crops and some cash crops with seasonal migration, with their herds, along well-defined routes, determined by the location of sources of drinking water during the wet and dry seasons.

The rainlands account for virtually all output of the staple grains—sorghum, millet and wheat—as well as of meat, milk and some vegetable products, and output in normal rainfall years has usually been enough for self-sufficiency. Livestock have also been an important export, as have other rain-fed products such as sesame seed. Sudan exports sorghum to Eritrea, Japan, Saudi Arabia and several European countries. In 2005 sorghum production was an estimated 4.3m. metric tons.

Chronic drought has had a severe impact on Sudan's agricultural output. In January 1985 Sudan was included on the UN list of 10 most severely drought-affected countries. In 1986 inadequate rains and the disruptions caused by the civil war created major food shortages. The civil war caused relief efforts to be constantly interrupted during 1987 and 1988, and the problem of distribution, both of local surpluses and food aid, has remained acute. In September 1988 it was stated that the levels of malnutrition and the percentage of those dying from starvation among the thousands of refugees from the civil war in the south were the worst hitherto recorded world-wide. In March 1989 the Government endorsed a UN-sponsored proposal to call a one-month cease-fire to the war in the south in order to facilitate the supply of 170,000 metric tons of food and medical supplies to victims of the conflict. 'Operation Lifeline Sudan' (OLS) was launched in April and its first phase ended in October 1989. After a four-month delay, the second phase of OLS got under way in early April 1990 after the Government and the insurgent Sudan People's Liberation Army (SPLA) ended their opposition to relief flights. The 1990 programme of 'OLS' aimed to transport 100,000 tons of relief supplies by air, road, river and rail. The World Food Programme maintained airlifts of food under 'OLS' from Uganda to the south in 1990 and 1991. However, by the turn of the century improved growing conditions, owing to stronger rainfall patterns, gave rise to some optimistic assessments. In 2006 FAO reported a sharp rise in cereal production, to 5.5m. metric tons.

Historically, drought and disease have had a significant impact on livestock exports. Nevertheless, by 1999 overseas sales of cattle, sheep, goats and camels were estimated by FAO to have contributed about 14.7% of the total value of exports. In September 2000 there was an outbreak of Rift Valley fever in Saudi Arabia. The Saudi Government blamed the problem on livestock imported from East Africa, and Saudi Arabia and several other Gulf states subsequently banned livestock imports from the region. This action had a devastating impact on Sudan's livestock sector. The growing population of unexported animals reduced local meat and livestock prices. In May 2002 Sudan sought to resolve this problem by imposing new hygiene regulations on producers and offering free livestock vaccinations. Most Gulf states subsequently lifted the ban, but by mid-2002 sales remained below their 2000 levels. Official figures indicated that livestock exports comprised 3.2% of the total value of exports in 2000 and just 0.1% in 2001 (partly owing to the increasing contribution of petroleum exports). This increased to 7.9% in 2002, however.

Almost 12% of Sudan's area is classified as forest land, but a minimal amount is under commercial plantations, largely fuel-wood developments in the central region. Exploitation of the natural forest is also predominantly limited to fuel wood, other than gum arabic, which is by far the most important forest product. Until the 1970s Sudan was the world's largest single producer of edible gum, accounting for some 92% of production, but this was reduced to about 80% with the advent of new producers and artificial substitutes and with it the importance of gum in exports. The value of exports of gum arabic amounted to US $32m. in 2002 and $21m. in 2003, since when the crisis in Darfur had a damaging impact on production of the crop.

Of the 2m. ha of land under irrigation, about 50% is in the Gezira scheme, which is located between the Blue and White Niles. First developed by the British in the 1920s, the Gezira became the world's largest farming enterprise under one management—the parastatal Sudan Gezira Board. The remaining irrigated land is also predominantly under publicly administered schemes: the small-scale farmer pump schemes on the Blue, White and main Niles; the New Halfa scheme developed in the 1960s on the Gash river to resettle people displaced by the Aswan high dam flooding; and the Rahad scheme, on the Blue Nile, inaugurated in 1977. Although these schemes account for over 60% of Africa's total irrigated area, they represent less than 50% of Sudan's estimated potential. In 1994 Sudan embarked on a programme of privatization of irrigation schemes.

Expansion into new areas has been limited by capital costs, and by the terms of agreements with Egypt governing the use of the Nile waters. By the late 1970s Sudan was close to drawing its full quota of 20,500m. cu m per year and began, in joint venture with Egypt, construction of the Jonglei Canal in southern Sudan. This scheme aimed at conserving, by the construction of a 360-km canal, some 4,000m. cu m of the 33,000m. cu m of water lost annually through evaporation in the Sudd swamp. The additional yield was to have been divided equally between the two countries, enabling Sudan to develop an additional 12,600 ha of land on the west bank of the Nile and reclaim up to 1.5m. ha of potential agricultural land. Work began in 1978 but had to be suspended in 1984, with 250 km completed, following attacks on construction workers by the SPLA. The persistence of civil conflict in the south effectively delayed any substantial progress towards completing this scheme, and although a peace agreement was signed in 2005 its future remained uncertain.

The major irrigated crop is cotton. The main types of cotton grown in Sudan are medium-staple Akala variety; long-staple Barakat; and long-medium staple Shambat B. A small amount of rain-fed short-staple cotton is also grown. The share of cotton in Sudan's total exports declined from 65% in 1979 to less than 45% in 1980, partly as a result of government policies that emphasized the development of wheat and other new crops, and the expansion of the mechanized rain-fed sector. A reversal of official policy in mid-1979, under IMF pressure to improve export crop production, brought the start of a large-scale rehabilitation programme for the irrigated sector, which was focused on the Gezira scheme. Gezira currently provides more than one-half of Sudan's cotton output, which totalled 520,000 bales in 1996/97 (compared with around 1.3m. bales in 1970/71). In that year the total area under cotton was 290,000 ha, compared with 324,000 ha in the early 1980s. In 1997 overseas sales of cotton represented 17.8% of the total value of Sudan's exports; however, by 2003 this figure had declined to just 3.2%. In 2001/02 Sudan produced 60,000 metric tons of cotton. Projections for the 2002/03 growing season suggested that cotton production would rise to 76,000 tons and in 2003/04 it was predicted that production would reach 120,000 tons.

The development of sugar production began in the 1960s to reduce the cost of Sudan's single most expensive import commodity after petroleum. The largest of the parastatal sugar enterprises, the Kenana Scheme, was officially opened in 1981, and played a major role in eliminating Sudan's sugar import costs in 1986. In early 1999 plans were announced for the construction of a US $500m. sugar production facility in the White Nile region. The majority of the finance was expected to be provided by the Chinese Government. Moreover, Sudan and the People's Republic of China agreed to build a sixth sugar plant, which would further increase production. In May 2002

Sudan inaugurated a new facility at the state-owned Sudan Sugar Co in New Halfa, which would increase production to 600 metric tons per day. There were also reports that several Gulf-based investors were considering investing in the Sudanese sugar industry. In 2004 Sudan produced 750,000 tons of sugar and in May 2005 the Council of Ministers approved a $71m. loan agreement with the Arab Fund for Economic and Social Development to fund the White Nile sugar project, intended to build water pumps and irrigation works. The project was expected to produce 340,000 tons of sugar and 40,000 tons of other cash crops annually. In 2005 Sudan exported 5.5m. metric tons of sugar.

Wheat, Sudan's other major irrigated crop, is also an import substitute, although attempts to increase irrigated domestic production have had very limited success owing to the unsuitability of the climate south of the Egyptian border area. This causes yields to be very low. In July 2005 the Government launched the US $75m. Sondos Agricultural Project, which was to be implemented by Sudan's Eastern Jebel-Awlia firm and the China Engineering Company and would cover 40,500 ha of land across the three states of Khartoum, White Nile and Gezira. The project was intended to expand production of grains, vegetables and livestock, increase job opportunities in agriculture and promote social development services, in an attempt to enable the country to feed itself.

INDUSTRY

The ginning of cotton encouraged the beginning of industry in Sudan in the early 20th century. With the expansion of cotton production, the number of ginning factories has increased, with the Gezira Board alone operating the world's largest single ginning complex. The country is not yet self-sufficient in basic cotton cloth, however, owing to a disparity between spinning and weaving capacity. Cotton seeds are partly decorticated, while exports of cotton-seed oil and oil-cake are increasing. Groundnuts are also partly processed, with oil and cake dominating exports of groundnut products. Minerals (including copper, iron, mica, chromite and, most recently, gold), which are exported in the crudest form, previously constituted less than 1% of exports. However, in 1999 gold accounted for 7.1% of the total value of exports, and this industry was being increasingly developed: in 2000 gold accounted for 3.0% of the total value of exports, but by 2002 this figure had increased to 4.5%.

With the exception of enterprises producing cement, soap, soft drinks and vegetable oils, large-scale manufacturing of import substitutes started in Sudan only after 1960. State involvement expanded dramatically after the 1971 nationalizations. A shift in emphasis towards a more mixed economy followed the overthrow of Nimeri in 1985, but the trend towards privatization gained new momentum in 1988 as part of the medium-term economic recovery programme approved by the IMF and the World Bank. Plans were announced to privatize two agricultural schemes, as well as the four state-owned commercial banks and some new industrial concerns. At the same time, plans were announced to rehabilitate existing public-sector concerns, and in March 1989 the Government initiated a programme for the rehabilitation and modernization of the cotton-spinning sector.

Average annual industrial growth declined from 3.1% in 1965–80 to 2.5% during 1980–90. In 1995–2002 industrial GDP increased at an average annual rate of 8.0%, increasing by an estimated 7.5% in 2002. The amount of idle capacity in the textile and food industries has been of particular concern, as Sudan has imported many goods that it could produce itself. At the time of the military coup of June 1989 it was estimated that many factories were operating at only 5% of capacity.

In July 1999 Sudan announced that work was progressing on the Red Sea Free Trade Zone between Port Sudan and the port of Suwakin, which will be accessible by a road linking the coast with Khartoum. The project, which eventually will cover a 600 sq km area, began with a 26 sq km zone, which encompasses warehouse, industrial and commercial areas. Investors are from a variety of countries, including Qatar, Saudi Arabia and the United Arab Emirates (UAE). In January 2000 a co-operation agreement was signed between the Red Sea Free Trade Zone and the Free Trade Zone of Jebel Ali, UAE. Under its terms, the UAE pledged to help Sudan to establish free zone areas at all of Sudan's border areas, linking trade between East Asia and Africa via Sudan, to increase marketing and shipping activities, and exchange manpower and technical information. A similar agreement was also signed with Saudi Arabia's Jeddah Free Trade Zone. In February the Sudan authorities officially opened the Red Sea Free Trade Zone. In October President al-Bashir opened the US $450m. Jiad industrial town, some 50 km south of Khartoum. The town included factories for manufacturing cables, cars, electricity wires, steel, trucks and pipeline products. There were also housing, health and education facilities. However, in February 2002 reports indicated that just seven of the factories in the Red Sea Free Trade Zone were still functioning, and since then the Zone has collapsed.

MINERALS

From 1973 a number of international companies showed an interest in exploring for petroleum and Chevron prepared for production when the resumption of civil war in the south in 1983 halted the project. It was not until the mid-1990s that Sudan began to take steps to commence production.

In August 1995 Arakis Energy, a Canadian company, announced that it had concluded a US $750m. arrangement with a Saudi Arabian financier to fund the construction of a pipeline project from southern Sudan's petroleum fields to Port Sudan, but this collapsed one month later and Arakis was subsequently reported to be seeking financing for the project from French and Asian sources. It appeared likely, however, that any effective development of the scheme would have to await the settlement of the conflict in southern Sudan. In January 1997 China was granted the right to exploit Sudan's largest oilfield with proven oil reserves of 220m. metric tons. In March it was awarded a contract to build a refinery in Jaili just north of Khartoum with a capacity of 50,000 barrels per day (b/d).

Sudan has pursued other opportunities to develop its petroleum industry. In June 1995 Sudan and the China established a joint venture to explore for petroleum. Sudan was to provide 30% of the finance for the company, while China agreed to provide the remaining 70% and to train Sudanese technicians. China subsequently agreed to accord Sudan a grant of US $15m. for the exploitation of its petroleum reserves. In October 1995 the Qatar General Petroleum Corpn agreed to participate in a joint venture with Sudan's Concorp to exploit petroleum reserves in central Sudan, while the French bank Paribas was reported to be involved in discussions with the Sudanese Ministry of Finance and the Bank of Sudan regarding a $25m. rehabilitation scheme for the oil refinery at Port Sudan. In March 1997 an agreement was signed with four international companies—from Malaysia, Canada, China and Sudan—allowing for shared petroleum production and the construction of a $1,000m. pipeline which will transport petroleum to Port Sudan.

In the late 1990s the development of the petroleum industry became a national priority. In 1997 Arakis began production in the Heglig field. In May 1998 the China National Petroleum Co (CNPC) and the Sudanese Ministry of Energy and Mining started work on the Port Sudan refinery. In 1998 it became clear that Arakis lacked the capital to continue its operations. At the end of the year, however, Talisman Energy, a Canadian firm, finalized its take-over of Arakis. Talisman subsequently agreed a partnership with CNPC and Sudapet to develop the Heglig and Unity oilfields and to construct the pipeline from the southern oilfields to Port Sudan. On 31 May 1999 the 1,610-km oil pipeline was inaugurated. The line, which has a capacity of 150,000 b/d, links Southern Kordofan's Heglig petroleum field with a loading terminal at Port Sudan, via a petroleum refinery being built at al-Jeili, 30 km north of Khartoum. The pipeline was largely financed by Chinese, Malaysian, Argentine, Canadian and British companies. To protect the pipeline and other petroleum facilities from attack by the SPLA and other rebel groups, the Sudanese authorities deployed troops to strategically important areas throughout the oil-producing region. In late August 1999 Sudan began exporting crude petroleum from this facility, which has a storage capacity of 2m. barrels. Petroleum production reached about 397,000 b/d by the end of 2006. According to the BP *Statistical Review of World Energy*, proven reserves of petroleum were equivalent to 6,400m. barrels in 2006.

Foreign interest in Sudan's burgeoning oil industry remains high, despite the claims of many humanitarian and special interest groups that the development of the country's petroleum sector sustains the conflict in southern Sudan. Western companies, such as Talisman Energy, which in 2002 sold its 25% stake in the Greater Nile Petroleum Operating Co (GNPOC) to India's ONGC Videsh and Slavneft of Russia, which withdrew in August 2002 in part owing to 'substantial domestic risks' in Sudan, remained sensitive to such tactics. However, the CNPC, which belongs to the GNPOC, announced plans to build a second pipeline from Block 6 to Port Sudan. Shortly afterwards, CNPC discovered new oil reserves in Block 7. In October 2002 the US Administration adopted legislation (the Sudan Peace Act) that allowed the USA to enforce further sanctions on Sudan, including the suspension of multilateral loans, in an attempt to force the Government to negotiate an end to the civil war in the south of the country. However, legislators withdrew the provision that would have prevented firms that invested in Sudan's oil sector from having access to US capital markets. During 2002 Sudan conducted talks with several foreign firms that had expressed interest in helping to develop the country's oilfields. Discussions with Petrel Resources (Ireland) focused on the exploration of an offshore block and areas in western, central, and northern Sudan. Sonatrach of Algeria, was interested in developing Block 15, while Rompetrol, a Romanian firm, was considering Block 8. Several Arab, European, Indian, Indonesian, Japanese, Korean, Malaysian and Russian companies also were examining the possibility of initiating operations in Sudan.

In September 2003 the Austrian government-controlled OMV petroleum company sold its US $115m. interest in the Sudanese petroleum industry to ONGC Videsh. OMV cited 'strategic and economic' reasons for its decision to withdraw from Sudan, although it donated €6.5m. to support various health and sanitation programmes in the country. OMV was the third Western company (after Talisman and Lundin) to leave Sudan as a result of reports about human rights abuses. In November the US-based human rights organization, Human Rights Watch, accused international petroleum companies in Sudan of complicity in displacing hundreds of thousands of civilians from oil concession areas. According to the report, petroleum company executives had 'turned a blind eye' to attacks on civilians and civilian targets, including the aerial bombings of hospitals, churches, relief operations and schools. These claims were rejected and the petroleum companies maintained that they assisted the region by providing development opportunities for local Sudanese while also promoting human rights. In 2003 domestic petroleum consumption was about 70,000 b/d, which left approximately 200,000 b/d for export. Oil revenues have risen substantially with the rising price on world markets. In December 2004 the French oil company, Total, renewed its oil agreement with Sudan that had lapsed in 1985. However, in February 2005 a British company, White Nile Petroleum, signed a contract with a company founded by the Sudan People's Liberation Movement to manage southern oil interests, Nile Petroleum, that re-awarded the Total concession to White Nile. Total disputed this award and the matter was in 2006 the subject of a legal dispute. Also in February 2005 the Sudanese Government announced that ONGC Videsh would build a new $1,200m. oil refinery at Port Sudan that would reportedly have the capacity to produce 100,000 b/d. Port Sudan's existing refinery was more than 40 years old and only had a 25,000 b/d capacity. In the same year Sudan announced the first offshore exploration concession, which was expected to yield significant reserves of natural gas. In 2006 Kenya also raised the possibility of a new pipeline from southern Sudan to Lamu, on the Kenyan coast. In April of that year work was completed on a new 740-km pipeline to the export terminal at al-Khair, near Port Sudan. In July CNPC announced that it had completed work to upgrade the production capacity of the al-Jeili refinery from 50,000 b/d to some 100,000 b/d.

Sudan's other known mineral resources include marble, mica, chromite and gypsum. Gold deposits in the Red Sea hills have been known since pharaonic times, and there are uranium reserves on the western borders with Chad and the Central African Republic. Until recently, only the chromite deposits in the Ingessana Hills near the Ethiopian border were exploited on a substantial scale by the state-owned Sudan Mining Co, which produces 10,000–15,000 metric tons per year for export. The known reserves exceed 1m. tons of high-quality chromite. In November 1988 it was reported that Northern Quarries and Mines (United Kingdom) was planning to develop an iron ore and gypsum mine in the Fodikwan area. It is now estimated that there are four or five deposits in the Fodikwan area, with reserves of more than 500m. tons of ore. Sudan has benefited from a resurgence of interest among foreign companies in reworking gold deposits in the Red Sea hills, which, using new processing technology, have a high recoverable gold content. Gold production at the Hassai mine, which is carried out by a joint Sudanese-French venture, reached an estimated 1.6 tons in 1993. British and Irish mining interests have also become involved in developing the country's gold-mining sector. In late 1996 the Ariab mining company announced that it had mined 3 tons of gold to the year ending August 1996. In 1998 it mined 5 tons of gold and estimated that there were reserves of a further 25 tons. In 2004 some 5 tons of gold were mined. Sudan's offshore sea-bed is known to be rich in precious minerals, as well as copper, zinc and iron, and plans are under consideration for these to be exploited jointly with Saudi Arabia.

FOREIGN TRADE AND BALANCE OF PAYMENTS

Previously, more than 90% of Sudan's export earnings were from primary agricultural products. However, in recent years petroleum has become the dominant export, replacing cotton, whose share of earnings declined from 65% in the late 1970s to just 3.2% in 2003. Meanwhile, the share of export earnings from petroleum and its products increased from 35.4% in 1999 to 81.0% in 2003. The total value of imports in 2005 was US $5,946.0.2m., while the value of exports totalled $4,824.3m.

In 2005 Sudan's main sources of imports included China (20.5%), Saudi Arabia (9.3%), the UAE (5.8%) and Japan (5.0%). China was Sudan's most important export market, receiving 71.0% of the country's exports in 2005. Japan (12.0%) and Saudi Arabia (2.8%) were also significant recipients of Sudanese exports. Total external debt increased from US $16,900m. in 2003 to an estimated $17,400m. in 2005.

Sudan has had a deficit on the current account of its balance of payments since independence in 1956, but the deficits were relatively insignificant until the mid-1970s, when government policies resulted in escalating deficits on the balance of trade and rising debt-service requirements. By 1995, despite a number of IMF agreements, austerity programmes and currency devaluations during the 1980s, the current-account deficit stood at US $499.9m. By 2002 the deficit had reached $1,008.1m.; however, it was reduced slightly, to $955.4m., in 2003, and again, to $870.9m., in 2004. In 2005 the deficit increased to some $3,013.1m. In November 2000 Sudan was one of nine founding members of the Common Market for Eastern and Southern Africa's Free Trade Area (FTA), the others being Djibouti, Egypt, Kenya, Madagascar, Malawi, Mauritius, Zambia and Zimbabwe. The countries were committed to removing all tariff and non-tariff barriers to internal trade and to establishing a common customs union by 2004. The FTA also planned to authorize free movement of labour between countries and right of residence in member countries by 2014 and to establish a common currency by 2025.

FOREIGN AID

Throughout the post-independence period Sudan's economic well-being depended on ever increasing amounts of foreign aid. During the Cold War the USA became Sudan's largest single donor; other important bilateral donors included Egypt, Libya, the United Kingdom, Kuwait, China and Saudi Arabia. The principal multilateral donors included the World Bank, the European Community (now the European Union, EU) and the IMF. The end of the Cold War coincided with the rise of the al-

Bashir regime, and Sudan's economic performance for much of the period that followed was increasingly poor, resulting in international sanctions and isolation, and difficulties with the World Bank and IMF.

In August 1999 the IMF lifted its nine-year sanction against Sudan following the latter's efforts to reduce its arrears and implement economic reforms. Sudan repaid some US $58m. in 1998 and about $25m. during the first eight months of 1999. In May 2000, in accordance with an IMF-approved structural adjustment programme, Sudan introduced a value-added tax, which represented 10% of the value of transactions involving goods and services in the country, and exempted capital goods from import duties. The Sudanese Government also planned to expand its privatization programme in the agro-industrial, communications and transport sectors. The performance of the privatized Sudan Telecom Co (SUDATEL) suggests that the IMF strategy may be paying some dividends. In April 2000 SUDATEL reported that its 1999 earnings totalled $55m. According to its five-year plan, SUDATEL planned to invest $620m. and increase the number of its subscribers to 1.5m. In August 2000 the IMF announced that Sudan had repaid $64m. in total thus far and had commenced a programme of economic reforms. As a result, Sudan regained full membership and voting rights in the IMF. According to the World Bank, Sudan was among 36 countries with an unsustainable debt burden and thus a candidate for the international community's initiative for heavily indebted poor countries (HIPC). In October the Government announced that it would sell its remaining SUDATEL shares. The Sudanese authorities planned to use the proceeds to improve the country's transport sector.

In March 2000 Sudan signed two concessionary loan agreements worth US $114m. with the Arab Fund for Economic and Social Development (AFESD). Sudan planned to use the loans to finance highways out of Khartoum and to upgrade an existing dam that stores Nile flood waters for irrigation. At about the same time, the Government arranged a $16m. loan from the Islamic Development Bank (IDB) to fund several water and research projects. Furthermore, the OPEC Fund for International Development provided $10m. for upgrades to Sudan's power sector. In April Sudan announced that it had rejoined the AFESD after coming to an agreement about the issue of its arrears, which amounted to $214m. In September Sudan appealed for greater investment from Arab countries during the Arab Agricultural Day celebration of the Arab Organization for Agricultural Development in Khartoum. In April 2001 the IDB announced that it had granted Sudan a loan of $6.5m to fund a project to assist those displaced by the civil war in Southern Kordofan State. The project included digging 10 deep drinking-water wells and constructing five water barriers and 10 water reservoirs. The loan was also for the construction of 10 health centres and 20 primary schools.

During 2001–02 Sudan remained committed to maintaining good relations with the IMF. In July 2001 Sudan announced that it intended to accelerate its privatization programme by identifying 175 projects to be developed by domestic and foreign investors. In November the Sudanese authorities reduced the subsidy on domestic fuel supplies. As a result, the price of petrol increased by 25% and benzene by 40%. Both these actions conformed with the IMF-approved economic reform programme. In May 2002 the Minister of Finance, Adb ar-Rahim Muhammad Hamdi, was replaced by Muhammad al-Hasan az-Zubayr, who stressed his commitment to maintaining good relations with the IMF by facilitating economic reforms and liberalization. However, some observers believed that he lacked the experience and expertise to ensure that the IMF remained satisfied with Sudan's economic policies. Moreover, Sudan's 2002 budget projected a deficit equivalent to 2.4% of GDP, thus exceeding the limits set by the IMF. In November the IMF released a report that praised the progress Sudan had made since its reform programme began in 1997, but criticized 'slippages' in several areas, including military spending and government subsidies on goods such as food, over the previous 18 months. The IMF sought to encourage Sudan's commitment to the reform programme by lowering its payments to the Fund to US $2m. per month. In return, Sudan pledged to reduce its projected deficit from 2.4% of GDP in the 2002 budget to 1% of GDP, and to reduce military spending by 13%.

In January 2002 the EU announced that it had decided to resume aid to Sudan, which could total as much as US $155m. in 2002–07. In May Sudan was instrumental in the establishment of the Malaysian-based Islamic Financial Services Board. Meanwhile, in late 2001 Sudan became a founding member of the Bahrain-based Islamic Money Market. The Government believed that its participation in these two organizations could significantly increase the amount of foreign aid it received. In July 2002 the OPEC Fund for International Development announced that it would provide $40m. for various irrigation projects, 80% of the funding for the construction of a $3m. bridge over the Nile in Atbara and $5m. for the cost of new telephone exchanges. In August the IDB signed an agreement with the Kuwait Fund for Arab Development, whereby the latter would provide $200m. to Sudan for several development projects, including $100m. for the refurbishment of the Roseires Dam. The Abu Dhabi Fund for Economic and Social Development, the AFESD, Qatar and a number of other Arab and Islamic development funds pledged some $1,000m. towards the construction of a hydroelectric plant at Merowe. In April 2003 the World Bank announced that Sudan was one of Africa's economic successes, largely because of an average annual real growth rate of 6.2% over the past decade. This made Sudan the fifth fastest growing economy in Africa. At May 2004 the World Bank had approved, through the International Development Association, 52 credits for Sudan, totalling approximately $1,520m. However, the World Bank's lending programme in Sudan remained inactive.

According to the IMF's 2005 staff report, Sudan's commitment to the Staff Monitored Programme was 'commendable', largely because of its improving growth rate and an ambitious economic reform agenda. The IMF also announced that Sudan's policy performance and its payment on arrears was, for the third consecutive year, in line with the IMF's Rights Accumulation Programme, which rewarded countries with favourable consideration for future IMF loans. In mid-June 2005 the director of the IMF office in Cairo, Egypt, arrived in Khartoum to reopen the IMF office in Sudan.

PUBLIC FINANCE, PLANNING AND DEVELOPMENT

The Sudanese Government, like governments in many other less developed countries, historically has depended heavily on indirect taxes, especially import duties, for its main source of revenue. Since the late 1970s, however, the share of indirect taxes in total revenue has declined in parallel with the economy, reflecting the cut-backs in imports that have been imposed in continuing attempts to reduce the balance-of-payments deficit.

In mid-December 1999 the Government passed its 2000 budget by decree. The budget, which was in line with the IMF's economic restructuring plan, emphasized economic stability and liberalization and envisaged a reduction in the rate of inflation, the acceleration of the privatization programme, an easing of trade restrictions, and a growth rate of 6.5%. It was projected that revenue would total 298,000m. Sudanese dinars and that expenditure would amount to 335,000m. Sudanese dinars, an increase of 34% compared with the previous year. The commencement of exports of crude petroleum led the Minister of Finance to predict a 68% rise in the value of exports from 1999, and in 2000 total export earnings actually increased by 132%. In January 2000 the Sudanese authorities announced subsidy cuts on several basic goods. This action resulted in a 20% increase in petrol and diesel prices and a 30% increase in the price of beef, chicken and other foodstuffs. To allay complaints about the subsidy cuts by trade unions, the al-Bashir regime pledged to implement a 15% pay rise for public-sector workers. In April 2001 Sudan announced a series of tax reforms to encourage local and foreign direct investment. The reforms removed most provincial taxes on agricultural outputs. The Government planned to use petroleum revenues to compensate provincial governments for the loss of tax revenues. The reforms also lowered import tariffs on agricultural inputs and machinery. According to IMF projections, budget revenue in 2005 was 1,472,900m.

dinars and expenditure was 1,593,900m. dinars, resulting in a projected fiscal deficit of 121,000m. dinars, equivalent to 1.8% of GDP.

POWER, TRANSPORT AND COMMUNICATIONS

Sudan's electricity sector has been beset by poor infrastructure, frequent outages, and a small customer base. In 2004 Sudan had 728 MW of electric generation capacity, which included roughly equal amounts of thermal (mainly oil) and hydropower capacity. Sudan's main generating facility is the 280-MW Roseires Dam located about 315 miles south-east of Khartoum. In 2002 Sudan's total electricity generation was 2,400m. kWh. Electricity was transmitted via two interconnected electrical grids; however, these grids cover only a small portion of the country. Regions not covered by the grid rely on small-scale, diesel-fired generators. In total, only an estimated 30% of the country's population has access to electricity. The Sudanese Government has announced it will spend US $3,000m. to increase that number to 90% in coming years. In the 1990s the electricity sector deteriorated as a result of a lack of funding. By 2000 a Rehabilitation and Performance Improvement Programme to upgrade the electricity infrastructure and to improve the adequacy and reliability of the electricity supply had been launched. This programme was supported by a $10m. loan from the OPEC Fund for International Development and $15m.-worth of funding from Saudi Arabia, Qatar, and other Arab investors. One of the largest projects was the proposed Merowe and Kajbar hydroelectric facilities in northern Sudan. The 1,250-MW Merowe facility was to be located 250 miles north of Khartoum at the River Nile's Fourth Cataract. In October 2002 two consortia (China International Water and Electric and China National Water Resources and Hydropower Engineering Corpn; and a joint venture of Consolidated Contractors International Co of Greece and Salini Costruttori of Italy) agreed to build three sections of the civil works portion of the dam, at an estimated cost of $1,900m. In December 2003 the French company Alstom agreed to a $300m. contract to construct the dam, while China's Harbin Power signed an agreement to build seven substations and around 1,000 miles of transmission lines. Egypt has thus far voiced no major objections to the project's planned diversion of River Nile flows. Construction is scheduled for completion in July 2008. The Kajbar Dam, located at the Nile's Second Cataract, is currently under construction, and will have a capacity of 300 MW. China was to finance 75% of the project (costing a total of some $200m.), with Sudan providing the remaining 25%. Environmental groups have expressed concern about the Kajbar Dam, citing potential damage to the Nile river's ecosystem and to the culture of the displaced Nubian residents of the area. In April 2002 Sudan and Ethiopia agreed to link their power grids. In September Ethiopian television reported that the two nations had agreed to take necessary steps to implement previously proposed development projects through joint use of Nile waters, though the report did not give details about what was expected from each nation.

Although Sudan still depends heavily on railways for transport, the road network has played an increasingly important role since 1980. More than 48,000 km of tracks are classed as 'motorable'; there were more than 3,160 km of main roads and 739 km of secondary roads in 1985. In 2004, according to UN statistics, there were 3,599 km of paved roads and 2,611 km of gravelled roads in Sudan. The completion in 1980 of a 1,190-km highway between Khartoum and Port Sudan encouraged a rapid increase in the number of road haulage firms, and, as a result, road transport now accounts for over 60% of internal haulage traffic. By 1997 work had been completed on a 270-km road linking Jaili with Atbara, as part of a project to provide an alternative route from Khartoum to the coast, and work on a 510-km road from Omdurman to Dongola began in mid-1992. In the same year Iran agreed to assist in the construction of the road from Kosti to Malakal and Juba. In January 1997 al-Bashir inaugurated the second phase of the Challenge Highway which is expected to link eastern and northern Sudan. He also laid the foundation stone for the third phase of the Atbara–Haiya road. In early 1999 Sudan announced plans to rehabilitate the 126-km road linking Khartoum and Wad Medani. The project was estimated to cost $11m. A company based in the UAE was to finance 62% of the project, in return for a 20-year monopoly on all services on the road. In February 2004 the Arab Fund for Economic and Social Development granted a loan of $31.5m. to finance the construction of the Gedaref–Doka–Galabat road linking the east of Sudan with Ethiopia. In late May 2005 the SPLA leader, John Garang, announced that a project would be started to develop the roads in southern Sudan once the interim period of autonomy in the south had commenced. The project would include the construction of 12 asphalt roads joining the southern towns and linking the south to Uganda, Kenya and the Democratic Republic of the Congo.

In 2002 the total length of railway operated by the Sudan Railways Corpn (SRC) was 5,978 km. The main line runs from Wadi Halfa, on the Egyptian border, to el-Obeid, via Khartoum. Lines from Atbara and Sinnar connect with Port Sudan. There are lines from Sinnar to Damazin on the Blue Nile (227 km) and from Aradeiba to Nyala in the south-western province of Darfur (689 km), with a 445-km branch line from Babanousa to Wau in Bahr al-Ghazal province. The Sudan Gezira Board also operated 1,400 km of railway in 1994, serving the country's cotton plantations. Shortages of spare parts and the impact of import controls on the rehabilitation requirements of track and rolling stock have considerably impeded the country's railway system. The rehabilitation of both lines and rolling stock was announced in September 1997, in order to facilitate the transportation of petroleum. In May 1999 the SRC announced plans to privatize its passenger and cargo services by the end of 2001. Under this proposal, the SRC would retain the responsibility for the management of the rails, the stations and signalling equipment. In April 2001 the IDB announced that it had granted Sudan a loan worth US $10.7m. in order to purchase 180 railway cargo wagons to enhance the railway's transport capabilities. The SRC planned to link el-Obeid with the refinery and to build another line at Sharif field (production area). There also would be a line in the southern White Nile area to link the second refinery with the petroleum pipeline. The SRC claimed that these projects are 'ready for operation'.

Although Sudan has about 4,068 km of navigable river, with some 1,723 km open throughout the year, river transport has, until recently, been minimal. The most frequently used waterway is the 1,435-km section of the White Nile route between Karima and Dongola.

Following the reopening of the Suez Canal in 1975, work began on modernizing and enlarging the facilities at Sudan's principal port, Port Sudan. Work on the project, financed by the World Bank and the United Kingdom, started in 1978. It would increase cargo-handling capacity to 13m. metric tons per year, and container, 'roll on, roll off' and new deep-water berths were being added. The first phase was completed in 1982, and a revised second phase began in 1983. The port at Suakin has the capacity to handle about 1.5m. tons of cargo annually.

Sudan Airways, the national carrier, is under the control of the Ministry of Transport, Roads and Bridges. At mid-2005 the company had 500 employees and an air fleet that included five Fokker 50 aircraft, two Beech King Air B200s, a Beech King Air C90, and two leased Boeing 737-200s, which are used for flights to Egypt, Kenya, the Persian (Arabian) Gulf and some domestic destinations. The Government was seeking to buy two Airbus 300-600R aircraft but, because of US economic sanctions, Airbus had yet to agree to the sale. The Sudan Airways route network includes 15 domestic destinations, 11 in Saudi Arabia and the Persian Gulf, six in the Middle East, seven in east and southern Africa, five in Europe and three in West Africa. The company's training centre offers technical, engineering, commercial, financial, computer and management courses. It was announced in 2004 that the Government would begin privatization of the company, with 30% of the shares in the new firm being held by the Government, 21% by Sudan's private sector and 49% by foreign investors. Sudan Airways had a US $65m. debt in early 2005; however, in early February Airbus cancelled the $45m. owed to it by the airline. In return, it was agreed that Airbus would win the majority of Sudan Airways' contracts for new aircraft. Over the past few years, air passenger traffic in Sudan has grown at an average annual rate of 49%; however, safety remained an issue and since 2000 there have been at least 26 air accidents. There are 47 charter companies in Sudan (31 for air transport, 11 for air spraying, and five for servicing the country's oilfields). In June 2005 the Government announced that the initial stages of construction work for a new $530m. international airport 40 km south-west of the capital had been completed. In June 2006 Sudan's Civil Aviation Authority opened the bidding process for the contract to construct core facilities at the airport, including two passenger terminals; the project was expected to be completed by 2010. Also in June 2005, Sudan Airways announced that it had concluded an $82m. contract for the purchase of six Antonov planes from Ukraine, and the construction of a maintenance centre at Khartoum International Airport at a cost of $8.8m. At the end of that month the Civil Aviation Authority allocated $452m. to finance the development and upgrade of 17 airports in the capital cities of the Sudanese states.

By 2004 there were more than 1m. main, fixed telephone lines in use in Sudan. A mobile cellular telephone network for Khartoum State was inaugurated in February 1997. By 2004 there were about 1m. SUDATEL mobile cellular telephone subscribers in 17 cities. The programme was expected to cost some US $620m. In July 2002 SUDATEL awarded the German electrical engineering and electronics company Siemens a contract worth $21.9m. to undertake expansion work on Sudan's fixed-line telephone network. Work on the expansion was scheduled to commence by the end of the year. In 2002 Sudan commissioned SR Telecom, a Canadian company, to install a multi-point system for low-density applications. SR Telecom also announced that 85 rural and urban areas would soon be connected to a single grid. In December 2004 Kanartel, a consortium led by Emirates Telecommunications Corpn (Etisalat), announced that it would begin to improve Sudan's second nation-wide fixed-line service by providing 500,000 fixed lines during its first year of operation.

Statistical Survey

Source (unless otherwise stated): Department of Statistics, Ministry of Finance and National Economy, POB 735, Khartoum; tel. (183) 777563; fax (183) 775630; e-mail info@mof-sudan.net; internet www.mof-sudan.net.

Area and Population

AREA, POPULATION AND DENSITY

Area (sq km)	2,505,813*
Population (census results)†	
1 February 1983	20,594,197
15 April 1993‡	
Males	12,518,638
Females	12,422,045
Total	24,940,683
Population (UN estimates at mid-year)§	
2004	36,145,000
2005	36,900,000
2006	37,707,000
Density (per sq km) at mid-2006	15.0

* 967,500 sq miles.

† Excluding adjustments for underenumeration, estimated to have been 6.7% in 1993.

‡ Provisional result.

§ Source: UN, *World Population Prospects: The 2006 Revision*.

PROVINCES
(1983 census, provisional)*

	Area (sq miles)	Population	Density (per sq mile)
Northern	134,736	433,391	3.2
Nile	49,205	649,633	13.2
Kassala	44,109	1,512,335	34.3
Red Sea	84,977	695,874	8.2
Blue Nile	24,009	1,056,313	44.0
Gezira	13,546	2,023,094	149.3
White Nile	16,161	933,136	57.7
Northern Kordofan	85,744	1,805,769	21.1
Southern Kordofan	61,188	1,287,525	21.0
Northern Darfur	133,754	1,327,947	9.9
Southern Darfur	62,801	1,765,752	28.1
Khartoum	10,883	1,802,299	165.6
Eastern Equatoria	46,073	1,047,125	22.7
Western Equatoria	30,422	359,056	11.8
Bahr al-Ghazal	52,000	1,492,597	28.7
Al-Buhayrat	25,625	772,913	30.2
Sobat	45,266	802,354	17.7
Jonglei	47,003	797,251	17.0
Total	967,500	20,564,364	21.3

* In 1991 a federal system of government was inaugurated, whereby Sudan was divided into nine states, which were sub-divided into 66 provinces and 281 local government areas. A constitutional decree, issued in February 1994, redivided the country into 26 states.

PRINCIPAL TOWNS
(population at 1993 census)

Omdurman	1,271,403	Nyala	227,183
Khartoum (capital)	947,483	El-Gezira	211,362
Khartoum North	700,887	Gedaref	191,164
Port Sudan	308,195	Kosti	173,599
Kassala	234,622	El-Fasher	141,884
El-Obeid	229,425	Juba	114,980

Source: UN, *Demographic Yearbook*.

Mid-2005 ('000, including suburbs, UN estimate): Khartoum 4,518 (Source: UN, *World Urbanization Prospects: The 2005 Revision*).

BIRTHS AND DEATHS
(annual averages, UN estimates)

	1990–95	1995–2000	2000–05
Birth rate (per 1,000)	40.0	37.9	34.4
Death rate (per 1,000)	13.1	11.9	11.2

Source: UN, *World Population Prospects: The 2006 Revision*.

Expectation of life (years at birth, WHO estimates): 58 (males 56; females 60) in 2004 (Source: WHO, *World Health Report*).

ECONOMICALLY ACTIVE POPULATION*
(persons aged 10 years and over, 1983 census, provisional)

	Males	Females	Total
Agriculture, hunting, forestry and fishing	2,638,294	1,390,411	4,028,705
Mining and quarrying	5,861	673	6,534
Manufacturing	205,247	61,446	266,693
Electricity, gas and water	42,110	1,618	43,728
Construction	130,977	8,305	139,282
Trade, restaurants and hotels	268,382	25,720	294,102
Transport, storage and communications	209,776	5,698	215,474
Financing, insurance, real estate and business services	17,414	3,160	20,574
Community, social and personal services	451,193	99,216	550,409
Activities not adequately defined	142,691	42,030	184,721
Unemployed persons not previously employed	387,615	205,144	592,759
Total	4,499,560	1,843,421	6,342,981

* Excluding nomads, homeless persons and members of institutional households.

Mid-2005 (estimates in '000): Agriculture, etc. 8,220; Total 14,558 (Source: FAO).

Health and Welfare

KEY INDICATORS

Total fertility rate (children per woman, 2005)	4.2
Under-5 mortality rate (per 1,000 live births, 2005)	90
HIV/AIDS (% of persons aged 15–49, 2005)	1.6
Physicians (per 1,000 head, 2004)	0.22
Hospital beds (per 1,000 head, 2004)	0.70
Health expenditure (2004): US $ per head (PPP)	54.0
Health expenditure (2004): % of GDP	4.1
Health expenditure (2004): public (% of total)	35.4
Access to water (% of persons, 2004)	70
Access to sanitation (% of persons, 2004)	34
Human Development Index (2004): ranking	141
Human Development Index (2004): value	0.516

For sources and definitions, see explanatory note on p. vi.

Agriculture

PRINCIPAL CROPS
('000 metric tons)

	2003	2004	2005
Wheat	332	435*	415*
Rice (paddy)	16	36	20
Maize	53*	46†	60†
Millet*	784	281	745
Sorghum (Durra)*	5,188	2,704	4,275
Potatoes	309	336	385
Cassava (Manioc)†	10	11	11
Yams†	137	142	145
Sugar cane†	—	6,984	7,186
Dry beans	11	14	15
Dry broad beans	171	173	112
Other pulses†	72	72	72
Groundnuts (in shell)	790*	790	520
Sunflower seed	18	7	12
Sesame seed	325*	399	277
Melonseed†	46	46	46
Cottonseed	162	155	202
Tomatoes	547	556	484
Pumpkins, squash and gourds†	68	71	72
Aubergines (Eggplants)†	230	255	272
Dry onions†	59	59	59
Garlic†	18	18	19
Melons†	28	29	30
Watermelons†	145	152	157
Dates	328	336	328
Oranges†	18	19	19
Lemons and limes†	63	64	66
Grapefruits and pomelos†	68	70	71
Guavas, mangoes and mangosteens†	195	213	225
Bananas†	74	76	78

* Unofficial figure(s).
† FAO estimate(s).

Source: FAO.

LIVESTOCK
('000 head, year ending September)

	2003	2004	2005
Horses*	26	26	26
Asses and mules*	751	751	751
Cattle	39,760	39,760	40,468
Camels	3,503	3,724	3,908
Sheep	48,440	48,910	49,797
Goats	42,030	42,179	42,526
Poultry*	37,000	37,000	37,000

* Estimates.

Source: FAO.

LIVESTOCK PRODUCTS
('000 metric tons)

	2003	2004	2005
Sheep meat*	144	n.a.	n.a.
Goat meat	138	139	186
Chicken meat*	30	29	29
Other meat*	714	717	769
Cows' milk	5,494	5,384	5,480
Sheep's milk	464	475	487
Goats' milk	1,384	1,500	1,519
Hen eggs*	47	47	47
Wool: greasy*	46	46	46

* Estimates.

Source: FAO.

Forestry

ROUNDWOOD REMOVALS
('000 cubic metres, FAO estimates)

	2003	2004	2005
Sawlogs, veneer logs and logs for sleepers	123	123	123
Other industrial wood	2,050	2,050	2,050
Fuel wood	17,272	17,482	17,698
Total	19,445	19,655	19,871

Source: FAO.

Gum arabic ('000 metric tons, year ending 30 June): 24 in 1993/94; 27 in 1994/95; 25 in 1995/96 (Source: IMF, *Sudan—Recent Economic Developments*, March 1997).

Fishing

('000 metric tons, live weight, FAO estimates)

	2003	2004	2005
Capture	59.0	57.0	62.0
Nile tilapia	20.0	20.0	21.5
Other freshwater fishes	34.0	34.0	35.0
Marine fishes	4.9	4.9	5.4
Aquaculture	1.6	1.6	1.6
Total catch	60.6	58.6	63.6

Source: FAO.

Mining

('000 metric tons, unless otherwise stated)

	2003	2004	2005*
Crude petroleum ('000 barrels)	103,400	118,000	120,000
Salt (unrefined)	61.1	62.0	62.0
Chromite	37.0	26.0	26.0
Gold ore (kilograms)†	5,106	5,000	4,728

* Estimated figures.
† Figures refer to the metal content of ores.

Source: US Geological Survey.

Industry

PETROLEUM PRODUCTS
('000 metric tons)

	2002	2003	2004
Motor spirit (petrol)	985	1,111	1,228
Naphtha	26	26	28
Jet fuels	169	170	192
Kerosene	34	36	41
Gas-diesel (distillate fuel) oils	1,123	1,273	1,400
Residual fuel oils	290	328	361

Source: UN, *Industrial Commodity Statistics Yearbook*.

SELECTED OTHER PRODUCTS

	2002	2003	2004
Wheat flour ('000 metric tons)	840	890	870
Raw sugar ('000 metric tons)	732	686	n.a.
Cement ('000 metric tons)	190*	272	280

* Estimate.

2002: Refined sugar ('000 metric tons) 674; Vegetable oils ('000 metric tons) 63.

Source: UN, *Industrial Commodity Statistics Yearbook*.

Finance

CURRENCY AND EXCHANGE RATES

Monetary Units
100 piastres = 1 Sudanese dinar.

Sterling, Dollar and Euro Equivalents (31 May 2007)
£1 sterling = 396.71 dinars;
US $1 = 200.63 dinars;
€1 = 269.91 dinars;
1,000 Sudanese dinars = £2.53 = $4.98 = €3.70.

Average Exchange Rate (Sudanese dinars per US $)
2004 257.91
2005 243.61
2006 217.15

Note: On 1 March 1999 the Sudanese pound (£S) was replaced by the Sudanese dinar, equivalent to £S10. The pound was withdrawn from circulation on 31 July 1999. A new Sudanese pound, equivalent to 100 dinars (and 1,000 old pounds) was introduced on 10 January 2007. The new currency was to circulate along with previous currencies (the old pound had continued to circulate in some regions) for a transitional period, but was to become the sole legal tender on 1 July 2007.

CENTRAL GOVERNMENT BUDGET
('000 million Sudanese dinars)

Revenue	2003	2004	2005*
Tax revenue	270.0	420.5	472.1
Direct taxes	52.3	74.7	92.2
Indirect taxes	217.7	345.8	379.9
Non-tax revenue	471.9	684.0	1,000.8
Departmental fees	10.7	14.1	15.3
National revenues	461.2	669.9	985.5
Non-petroleum revenues	38.7	90.6	84.5
Petroleum revenues	422.6	579.3	901.0
Total	741.9	1,104.5	1,472.9

Expenditure	2003	2004	2005*
Current expenditure	563.8	762.5	1,382.7
Wages, salaries and pensions	191.1	273.8	301.1
Other current spending	321.3	404.6	651.0
Debt service paid	73.0	81.1	86.2
Goods and services	54.5	71.0	72.4
General reserve	104.0	144.3	123.3
Other obligations	89.8	108.1	369.1
Transfers to states	51.4	84.2	430.7
Capital expenditure	135.2	277.2	227.6
Locally financed	112.8	227.5	178.1
Foreign financed	22.4	49.7	49.5
Statistical discrepancy	9.3	–20.2	–16.4
Total	708.4	1,019.5	1,593.9

* Preliminary figures.

Source: IMF, *Sudan: 2006 Article IV Consultation and Staff-Monitored Program—Staff Report; Staff Statement; Public Information Notice on the Executive Board Discussion; and Statement by the Executive Director for Sudan* (May 2006).

INTERNATIONAL RESERVES
(US $ million at 31 December)

	2004	2005	2006
IMF special drawing rights	—	0.1	—
Foreign exchange	1,338.0	1,868.5	1,659.9
Total	1,338.0	1,868.6	1,659.9

Source: IMF, *International Financial Statistics*.

MONEY SUPPLY
('000 million Sudanese dinars at 31 December)

	2004	2005	2006
Currency outside banks	304.90	376.13	535.53
Demand deposits at deposit money banks	279.46	393.72	481.39
Total money (incl. others)	604.37	813.01	1,052.41

Source: IMF, *International Financial Statistics*.

COST OF LIVING
(Consumer Price Index; base: 1992 = 100)

	1998	1999	2000
Food, beverages and tobacco	3,930.8	4,670.3	4,883.3
Clothing and footwear	3,615.7	4,010.5	3,985.6
Housing	3,826.8	5,257.2	6,192.9
Household operations	3,677.7	3,899.3	3,706.4
Health care	5,277.9	6,313.5	6,984.7
Transport and communications	7,107.7	8,661.7	9,082.8
Entertainment	2,261.2	3,046.0	4,149.7
Education	5,947.8	7,057.0	8,048.7
All items (incl. others)	4,299.8	5,077.0	5,451.9

Source: Bank of Sudan.

All items (Consumer Price Index; base: 2000 = 100): 134.0 in 2004; 145.5 in 2005; 155.9 in 2006 (Source: IMF, *International Financial Statistics*).

NATIONAL ACCOUNTS

(estimates, '000 million Sudanese dinars at current prices)

Expenditure on the Gross Domestic Product

	1997	1998	1999
Government final consumption expenditure	91.3	88.5	118.3
Private final consumption expenditure	1,465.9	1,882.2	2,172.6
Gross fixed capital formation	210.7	259.1	318.7
Total domestic expenditure	1,767.9	2,229.8	2,609.6
Exports of goods and services	98.4	122.4	205.7
Less Imports of goods and services	255.4	393.9	383.8
GDP in purchasers' values	1,676.9	2,062.1	2,536.3
GDP at constant 1981/82 prices*	1,201.9	1,262.1	1,338.2

* Million Sudanese dinars.

Source: IMF, *Sudan—Statistical Appendix* (July 2000).

Gross Domestic Product by Economic Activity

	1997	1998	1999
Agriculture and forestry	745.7	841.6	1,040.3
Mining and quarrying	4.2	5.5	20.9
Manufacturing and handicrafts	100.7	177.4	217.3
Electricity and water	14.3	16.1	19.0
Construction	73.1	132.5	156.8
Trade, restaurants and hotels	260.5	405.9	492.0
Transport and communications	150.5	116.3	142.3
Other services	266.0	290.8	354.1
GDP at factor cost	1,615.1	1,986.0	2,442.7
Indirect taxes, *less* subsidies	61.9	76.1	93.6
GDP in purchasers' values	1,677.0	2,062.1	2,536.3

Source: IMF, *Sudan—Statistical Appendix* (July 2000).

BALANCE OF PAYMENTS

(US $ million)

	2004	2005	2006
Exports of goods f.o.b.	3,777.8	4,824.3	5,656.6
Imports of goods f.o.b.	–3,586.2	–5,946.0	–7,104.7
Trade balance	191.6	–1,121.7	–1,448.1
Exports of services	44.1	113.9	205.6
Imports of services	–1,064.5	–1,844.4	–2,789.5
Balance on goods and services	–828.8	–2,852.2	–4,032.0
Other income received	21.8	44.1	89.3
Other income paid	–1,134.5	–1,405.9	–2,103.3
Balance on goods, services and income	–1,941.5	–4,214.0	–6,046.0
Current transfers received	1,580.2	1,680.5	1,877.1
Current transfers paid	–509.6	–479.6	–940.7
Current balance	–870.9	–3,013.1	–5,109.6
Direct investment from abroad	1,511.1	2,304.6	3,534.1
Portfolio investment assets	19.9	50.6	–0.1
Portfolio investment liabilities	—	—	–35.3
Other investment assets	598.8	1,134.7	208.2
Investment liabilities	–702.0	–605.3	1,031.7
Net errors and omissions	225.5	743.0	–219.9
Overall balance	782.4	614.5	–590.6

Source: IMF, *International Financial Statistics*.

External Trade

PRINCIPAL COMMODITIES

(US $ million)

Imports c.i.f.	2001	2002	2003
Food and live animals	328.3	411.6	402.7
Cereals and cereal preparations	187.3	242.8	214.3
Unmilled durum wheat	133.4	203.3	186.2
Mineral fuels, lubricants, etc.	43.1	120.1	88.9
Refined petroleum products	39.5	117.5	85.1
Chemicals and related products	221.6	261.5	302.6
Medicinal and pharmaceutical products	57.9	73.2	85.1
Basic manufactures	382.6	495.0	641.7
Textiles and textile products (excl. clothing)	77.7	90.1	123.0
Cement	50.6	91.8	103.7
Iron and steel	83.8	113.0	185.1
Machinery and transport equipment	772.1	945.0	1,112.4
Power generating machinery and equipment	90.3	122.3	107.7
Machinery specialized for particular industries	123.5	166.9	197.7
Miscellaneous industrial machinery	94.2	112.8	125.7
Telecommunication and recording equipment	72.8	73.2	125.1
Road vehicles	267.5	285.0	353.3
Passenger vehicles (excl. buses)	76.4	91.1	102.1
Lorries and special purpose vehicles	88.5	96.9	112.9
Miscellaneous manufactured articles	136.3	172.3	242.2
Total (incl. others)	1,958.0	2,492.8	2,898.1

Exports f.o.b.	2001	2002	2003
Food and live animals	57.7	193.8	168.6
Live animals	1.5	124.6	97.7
Sheep and goats	—	122.2	85.3
Sheep	—	121.0	83.5
Crude materials (inedible) except fuels	194.5	172.9	248.5
Oil seeds and oleaginous fruit	121.9	82.4	89.8
Sesame seeds	97.8	68.8	74.3
Cotton	47.3	55.2	106.4
Mineral fuels, lubricants, etc.	1,480.0	1,118.0	1,969.5
Petroleum and petroleum products	1,458.1	1,100.0	1,938.3
Crude petroleum and bituminous oils	—	128.8	—
Refined petroleum products	1,458.1	971.2	1,938.3
Other commodities and transactions	48.6	73.4	55.5
Non-monetary gold, unwrought	48.6	72.7	55.5
Total (incl. others)	1,812.1	1,616.6	2,480.6

Source: UN, *International Trade Statistics Yearbook*.

PRINCIPAL TRADING PARTNERS
(US $ million)

Imports c.i.f.	2003	2004	2005
Brazil	6.3	23.9	54.3
China, People's Repub.	229.1	529.6	1,383.0
France (incl. Monaco)	50.9	72.8	220.7
Germany	142.6	185.1	81.2
India	115.9	197.1	317.8
Italy	52.4	118.5	257.6
Japan	85.0	165.1	341.8
Jordan	33.2	35.1	45.3
Korea, Repub.	51.1	89.3	149.8
Netherlands	40.5	60.1	93.4
Russia	17.1	19.0	57.5
Saudi Arabia	723.9	471.5	627.5
Sweden	27.2	46.6	82.0
United Arab Emirates	180.0	239.2	394.8
United Kingdom	125.6	151.3	221.9
USA	11.1	34.0	129.7
Total (incl. others)	2,882.0	4,075.2	6,756.8

Exports f.o.b.	2003	2004	2005
Bangladesh	17.3	14.4	19.7
China, People's Repub.	1,761.9	2,527.0	3,427.1
France	12.0	23.8	26.1
Germany	18.7	34.3	27.3
Italy	11.3	14.3	19.1
Japan	167.7	402.2	577.5
Korea, Repub.	18.3	23.5	7.9
Saudi Arabia	114.8	164.2	136.4
Syria	12.1	15.8	12.7
United Arab Emirates	83.0	90.2	90.0
United Kingdom	66.4	56.1	21.8
USA	2.7	2.9	12.4
Yemen	3.7	3.5	10.8
Total (incl. others)	2,542.2	3,777.8	4,824.3

Source: Bank of Sudan.

Transport

RAILWAY TRAFFIC*

	1991	1992	1993
Freight ton-km (million)	2,030	2,120	2,240
Passenger-km (million)	1,020	1,130	1,183

* Estimates.

Source: UN Economic Commission for Africa, *African Statistical Yearbook*.

2000 (passengers carried): 258,000 (Source: Sudan Railways).

ROAD TRAFFIC
(motor vehicles in use)

	2000	2001	2002
Passenger cars	46,000	46,400	47,300
Commercial vehicles	60,500	61,800	62,500

Source: UN, *Statistical Yearbook*.

SHIPPING

Merchant Fleet
(registered at 31 December)

	2004	2005	2006
Number of vessels	17	17	19
Displacement (grt)	15,650	15,650	25,904

Source: Lloyd's Register-Fairplay, *World Fleet Statistics*.

International Sea-borne Freight Traffic
(estimates, '000 metric tons)

	1991	1992	1993
Goods loaded	1,290	1,387	1,543
Goods unloaded	3,800	4,200	4,300

Source: UN Economic Commission for Africa, *African Statistical Yearbook*.

CIVIL AVIATION
(traffic on scheduled services)

	2001	2002	2003
Kilometres flown (million)	6	6	7
Passengers carried ('000)	415	409	420
Passenger-km (million)	761	767	786
Total ton-km (million)	98	98	103

Source: UN, *Statistical Yearbook*.

Tourism

	2002	2003	2004
Tourist arrivals	52,000	52,291	60,577
Tourism receipts (US $ million, excl. passenger transport)	108	118	n.a.

Source: World Tourism Organization.

Communications Media

	2003	2004	2005
Telephones ('000 main lines in use)	936.8	1,028.9	670.0
Mobile cellular telephones ('000 subscribers)	527.2	1,049	1,828
Personal computers ('000 in use)	348	606	3,250
Internet users ('000)	937	1,140	2,800

Source: International Telecommunication Union.

1996: Daily newspapers 5 (average circulation 737,000 copies) (Source: UNESCO, *Statistical Yearbook*).

1997: Radio receivers ('000 in use) 7,550 (Source: UNESCO, *Statistical Yearbook*).

1998: Non-daily newspapers 11 (average circulation 5,644,000); Periodicals 54 (average circulation 68,000 copies) (Source: UN, *Statistical Yearbook*).

2000: Television receivers ('000 in use) 8,500 (Source: International Telecommunication Union).

Education

(2004)

	Institutions*	Teachers	Students
Pre-primary	5,984	13,616	445,763
Primary	11,982	105,142†	3,208,186
Secondary	3,512	52,673	1,292,619
Universities, etc.	n.a.	4,486‡	200,538‡

* Figures refer to 1998.
† Estimates for 2003.
‡ Estimates for 2000.

Source: UNESCO Institute for Statistics.

1999/2000: Primary: 11,923 schools. Secondary: 1,694 schools (Source: Ministry of Education).

Adult literacy rate (UNESCO estimates): 60.9% (males 71.1%; females 51.8%) in 2004 (Source: UN Development Programme, *Human Development Report*).

Directory

The Constitution

Following the coup of 6 April 1985, the Constitution of April 1973 was abrogated. A transitional Constitution, which entered into force in October 1985, was suspended following the military coup of 30 June 1989. In April 1998 a new Constitution was approved by the National Assembly, and presented to President al-Bashir. At a referendum held in June, the new Constitution was endorsed by 96.7% of voters. This Constitution, which entered into force on 1 July 1998, vests executive power in the Council of Ministers, which is appointed by the President but responsible to the National Assembly. Legislative power is vested in the National Assembly. The Constitution guarantees freedom of thought and religion, and the right to political association, provided that such activity complies with the law.

On 9 July 2005 the National Assembly approved an interim Constitution, as part of the Comprehensive Peace Agreement signed in January between the Sudanese Government and the Sudan People's Liberation Movement (SPLM). The Interim National Constitution provided for the establishment of a Government of National Unity (GONU), representation in which was to be divided between northerners and southerners, with the former holding 70% and the latter 30% of the posts. In the GONU, the National Congress shall be represented by 52% (49% northerners and 3% southerners); the SPLM shall be represented by 28% (21% southerners and 7% northerners); other northern political forces shall be represented by 14%; and other southern political forces shall be represented by 6%.

The Interim National Constitution also stipulated that, pending legislative elections, which were to be held by no later than the end of the fourth year of the interim period, the National Assembly shall be composed of 450 members who shall be appointed by the President of the Republic in consultation with the First Vice-President, according to the 70%:30% north-south ratio.

Provision was also made in the Interim National Constitution for the election of the President of the Government of Southern Sudan and for the establishment of a transitional Southern Sudan Assembly. The President of Government of Southern Sudan shall be elected directly by the people of Southern Sudan for a five-year mandate, renewable only once. The transitional Southern Sudan Assembly shall be an inclusive, constituent legislature composed of 170 appointed members with 70% representing the SPLM, 15% representing the National Congress, and 15% representing the other southern Sudanese political forces.

The Government

HEAD OF STATE

President: Lt-Gen. Omar Hassan Ahmad al-Bashir (took power as Chairman of the Revolutionary Command Council for National Salvation (RCC) on 30 June 1989; appointed President by the RCC on 16 October 1993; elected President in March 1996; re-elected in December 2000).

First Vice-President: Commdr Salva Kiir Mayardit.

Second Vice-President: Ali Osman Muhammad Taha.

COUNCIL OF MINISTERS
(August 2007)

Prime Minister: Lt-Gen. Omar Hassan Ahmad al-Bashir (National Congress).

Minister of Foreign Affairs: Dr Lam Akol (SPLM).

Minister of the Interior: Prof. Zubeir Beshir Taha (National Congress).

Minister of the Presidency: Maj. Gen. Bakri Hassan Saleh (National Congress).

Minister of Cabinet Affairs: Deng Alor Kol (SPLM).

Minister of Defence: Maj.-Gen. Eng. Abd ar-Rahim Muhammad Hussein (National Congress).

Minister of Justice: Muhammad Ali al-Mardi (National Congress).

Minister of Information and Communication: Zahawi Ibrahim Malek (UP).

Minister of Federal Government: Abd al-Basit Saleh Sabdarat (National Congress).

Minister of Finance and National Economy: Az-Zobeir Ahmed Hassan (National Congress).

Minister of Foreign Trade: George Boreng Niyami (SPLM).

Minister of International Co-operation: At-Tijani Saleh Fedail (National Congress).

Minister of Industry: Jalal Yusuf Muhammad ad-Duqayr (DUP).

Minister of Investment: Malek Agar Ayar (SPLM).

Minister of Agriculture and Forestry: Muhammad al-Amin Issa Alaghbash (National Congress).

Minister of Animal Resources: Galwak Deng (National Congress).

Minister of Irrigation and Water Resources: Eng. Kamal Ali Muhammad (National Congress).

Minister of Energy and Mining: Dr Awad Ahmad al-Jaz (National Congress).

Minister of Transport, Roads and Bridges: Kuwal Maniang Ajok (SPLM).

Minister of Culture, Youth and Sport: Muhammad Yussuf Abdallah (National Congress).

Minister of Tourism and Wildlife: Josef Malwal (UDSF).

Minister of Higher Education and Scientific Research: Peter Niyot Kok (SPLM).

Minister of Education: Paul Mithanq (SPLM).

Minister of Labour, Public Services and Development of Human Resources: Maj.-Gen. (retd) Alison Manani Magaya (National Congress).

Minister of Health: Dr Tabita Sokaya (SPLM).

Minister of Humanitarian Affairs: Kosti Manyebi (SPLM).

Minister of Religious Affairs and Waqf: Azhari at-Tigani Awad as-Sid (National Congress).

Minister of Welfare and Social Development: Samia Ahmad Muhammad.

Minister of the Environment and Urban Development Construction: Ahmed Babkir Nahar (National Congress).

Minister of Parliamentary Affairs: Joseph Okello (USAP).

In addition, there is one presidential adviser and 33 Ministers of State. The President also has 12 special advisers who are considered part of the Government.

GOVERNMENT OF SOUTHERN SUDAN
(August 2007)

President: Commdr Salva Kiir Mayardit.

Vice-President and Minister for Housing, Lands and Public Service: Dr Riek Machar.

Minister for Presidential Affairs: Dr Justin Yaac Arop.

Minister for Police and Security: Daniel Awet.

Minister of Finance and Economic Planning: Artha Akwin Chuol.

Minister of Regional Co-operation: Dr Barnaba Marial Benjamin.

Minister for Legal Affairs and Constitutional Development: Michael Makuei.

Minister for Education, Science and Technology: Dr Michael Mila Hussein.

Minister for Health: Dr Theophilus Ochan.

Minister for Industry and Mining: Maj.-Gen. (Retd) Albino Akol.

Minister for Trade and Supplies: Anthony Lino Makana.

Minister for Information, Broadcasting and Television: Dr Samson Kwaje.

Minister for Communication and Postal Services: Geer Chan.

Minister for Transport and Roads: Rebecca Nyan Deng de Mabior.

Minister for Environment and Protection of Wildlife: Lt-Gen. James Loro.

Minister for Agriculture and Forestry: Dr Martin Alia.

Minister for Public Services and Human Resource Development: David Deng Athorbi.

Minister for Animal Resources and Fisheries: Dr Festo Kumba.

Minister for Culture, Youth and Sports: Dr John Luk.

Minister for Diversity and Social and Religious Affairs: Mary Kiden.

Minister for Water and Irrigation: Joseph Dwer.

In addition, there are seven presidential advisers.

MINISTRIES

Ministry of Agriculture and Forestry: POB 285, al-Gamaa Ave, Khartoum; tel. (183) 780951; e-mail moafcc@sudanmail.net.

Ministry of Animal Resources: Khartoum.

Ministry of Cabinet Affairs: Khartoum.

Ministry of Culture, Youth and Sport: Khartoum.

Ministry of Defence: POB 371, Khartoum; tel. (183) 774910.

Ministry of Education: Khartoum; tel. (183) 772808; e-mail moe-sd@moe-sd.com; internet www.moe-sd.com.

Ministry of Energy and Mining: POB 2087, Khartoum; tel. (183) 775595; fax (183) 775428.

Ministry of the Environment and Urban Development Construction: POB 300, Khartoum; tel. (183) 462604.

Ministry of Federal Government: Khartoum.

Ministry of Finance and National Economy: POB 735, Khartoum; tel. (183) 777563; fax (183) 775630; e-mail info@mof-sudan.net; internet mof-sudan.com.

Ministry of Foreign Affairs: POB 873, Khartoum; tel. (183) 773101; fax (183) 772941; e-mail ministry@mfa.gov.sd; internet www.sudanmfa.com.

Ministry of Foreign Trade: Khartoum; tel. (183) 772793; fax (183) 773950.

Ministry of Health: POB 303, Khartoum; tel. (183) 773000; e-mail inhsd@sudanet.net; internet www.fmoh.gov.sd.

Ministry of Higher Education and Scientific Research: POB 2081, Khartoum; tel. (183) 779312; e-mail mhesr@sudanmail.net.

Ministry of Humanitarian Affairs: POB 1976, Khartoum; tel. (183) 780675; e-mail human@mha.gov.sd; internet www.mha.gov.sd.

Ministry of Industry: POB 2184, Khartoum; tel. (183) 777830.

Ministry of Information and Communication: Khartoum.

Ministry of the Interior: POB 2793, Khartoum; tel. (183) 776554.

Ministry of International Co-operation: POB 2092, Khartoum; tel. (183) 772169; fax (183) 780115; e-mail info@micsudan.com; internet www.micsudan.com.

Ministry of Investment: POB 6286, Khartoum; tel. (183) 787194; fax (183) 787199; e-mail investment@sudanmail.net; internet www.sudaninvest.gov.sd.

Ministry of Irrigation and Water Resources: POB 878, Khartoum; tel. (183) 783221; fax (183) 773388; e-mail oehamad@hotmail.com.

Ministry of Justice: POB 302, an-Nil Ave, Khartoum; tel. (183) 774842; fax (183) 771479.

Ministry of Labour, Public Services and Development of Human Resources: Khartoum.

Ministry of Parliamentary Affairs: Khartoum.

Ministry of Religious Affairs and Waqf: Khartoum.

Ministry of Tourism and Wildlife: POB 2424, Khartoum; tel. (183) 471329; fax (183) 471437; e-mail admin@sudan-tourism.com.

Ministry of Transport, Roads and Bridges: POB 300, Khartoum; tel. (183) 781629; fax (183) 780507.

Ministry of Welfare and Social Development: Khartoum.

STATE GOVERNORS

(August 2007)

Al-Buhayrat: Lt-Gen. DANIEL WET AKOT.

Bahr al-Jabal: Maj.-Gen. CLEMENT WANI KONGA.

Blue Nile: ABDALLAH UTHMAN AL-HAJ.

Eastern Equatoria: ALOYSIO AMOR.

Gadarif: ABD AR-RAHMAN AHMED AL-KHADR.

Gezira: Lt-Gen. (retd) ABD AR-RAHMAN SIR AL-KHATIM.

Jonglei: PHILLIP THON LEEK.

Kassala: Lt-Gen. FARUQ HASAN MUHAMMAD NUR.

Khartoum: Dr ABD-AL-HALIM ISMAIL AL-MUTA'AFI.

Northern: Maj.-Gen. (retd) AL-HADI BUSHRA HASSAN.

Northern Bahr al-Ghazal: MARYANG AKOI AGO.

Northern Darfur: OSMAN MUHAMMAD YUSUF KIBIR.

Northern Kordofan: GHULAM AD-DIN UTHMAN.

Red Sea: Maj.-Gen. (retd) HATIM AL-WASIL ASH-SHAYKH AS-SAMMANI.

River Nile: Dr BDELLA MASAR.

Sennar: AHMED ABBAS.

Southern Darfur: ADAM HAMID MUSA.

Southern Kordofan: SOMI ZAYDAN ATTIYAH.

Upper Nile: Dr DAK DOK BISHOK.

Wahdah: Brig. TABAN DENG GAI.

Warab: ANTHONY BOL MADUT.

Western Bahr al-Ghazal: MARK NABIBOSH OBONG.

Western Darfur: Staff Maj.-Gen. (retd) SULAYMAN ABDALLAH ADAM.

Western Equatoria: Commdr SAMUEL ABU JOHN KABASHI.

Western Kordofan: Maj.-Gen. AT-TAYIB ABD AR-RAHMAN MUKHTAR.

White Nile: MAJDHUB YUSUF BABIKIR.

President

PRESIDENT

Election, 13–22 December 2000

Candidate	% of total votes cast
Omar Hassan Ahmad al-Bashir (National Congress)	86.5
Gaafar Muhammad Nimeri (Alliance of the People's Working Forces)	9.6
Malik Hussain	1.6
as-Samawi'it Husayn Osman Mansur (Independent Democrats)	1.0
Mahmoud Ahmad Juna	1.0

Legislature

MAJLIS WATANI

(National Assembly)

Speaker: AHMAD IBRAHIM AT-TAHIR.

Deputy Speakers: ANGELO BEDA, ABDALLAH AL-HARDELLO.

Election, 13–22 December 2000

	Seats
National Congress	355
Others	5
Total	360*

* Of the 360 members, 270 are directly elected in single seat constituencies, 35 members represent women, 26 represent university graduates and 29 represent trade unions.

According to the interim Constitution approved by the National Assembly in July 2005, the National Assembly shall be composed of 450 members who shall be appointed by the President of the Republic in consultation with the First Vice-President. Legislative elections were to be held by no later than the end of the fourth year of the interim period.

Election Commission

General Election Commission (GEC): PO 14416, Omdurman; tel. (15) 558537; fax (15) 560950; e-mail info@sudan-parliament.org; comprises of a chairman and two mems appointed for the election period only; mems appointed by the President, subject to the approval of the National Assembly; responsible for the election of the President, provincial magistrates, and national, provincial and local assembly mems; Chairman ABD AL-MUN'IM AL-ZAYN AL-NAHHAS.

Political Organizations

National Congress: Khartoum; successor to National Islamic Front; Pres. Lt-Gen. OMAR HASSAN AHMAD AL-BASHIR; Sec.-Gen. Prof. IBRAHIM AHMAD UMAR.

The right to political association, subject to compliance with the law, was guaranteed in the Constitution approved by referendum in June 1998. (All political organizations had been banned following the military coup of 30 June 1989.) The registration of parties began in January 1999. The following parties are among the most active:

Alliance of the People's Working Forces: Khartoum; Head GAAFAR MUHAMMAD NIMERI; Acting Sec.-Gen. KAMAL AD-DIN MUHAMMAD ABDULLAH.

Democratic Unionist Party (DUP): Khartoum; Leader OSMAN AL-MIRGHANI; participates in National Democratic Alliance (see below).

Free Sudanese National Party (FSNP): Khartoum; Chair. Fr PHILIP ABBAS GHABBUSH.

Independent Democrats: Khartoum; Leader AS-SAMAWI'IT HUSAYN OSMAN MANSUR.

Islamic-Christian Solidarity: Khartoum; Founder HATIM ABDULLAH AZ-ZAKI HUSAYN.

Islamic Revival Movement: Khartoum; Founder SIDDIQ AL-HAJ AS-SIDDIQ.

Islamic Socialist Party: Khartoum; Leader SALAH AL-MUSBAH.

Islamic Ummah Party: Khartoum; Chair. WALI AD-DIN AL-HADI AL-MAHDI.

Justice Party: Khartoum; f. 2002 by fmr members of the National Congress.

Moderate Trend Party: Khartoum; Leader MAHMUD JIHA.

Muslim Brotherhood: Khartoum; Islamic fundamentalist; Leader Dr HABIR NUR AD-DIN.

National Democratic Party: Khartoum; f. 2002 following merger of the Union of Nationalistic Forces, the Communist Party and the National Solidarity Party.

Nile Valley Conference: Khartoum; Founder Lt-Gen. (retd) UMAR ZARUQ.

Popular Masses' Alliance: Khartoum; Founder FAYSAL MUHMAD HUSAYN.

Popular National Congress (PNC): Khartoum; f. 2000; Founder HASSAN AT-TURABI.

Socialist Popular Party: Khartoum; Founder SAYYID KHALIFAH IDRIS HABBANI.

Sudan Green Party: Khartoum; Founder Prof. ZAKARAIA BASHIR IMAM.

Sudan People's Liberation Movement (SPLM): e-mail webmaster@splmtoday.com; internet www.splmtoday.com; Leader Commdr SALVA KIIR MAYARDIT; Sec.-Gen. PAGAN AMUM.

Sudanese Central Movement: Khartoum; Founder Dr MUHAMMAD ABU AL-QASIM HAJ HAMAD.

Sudanese Initiative Party: Khartoum; Leader J'AFAR KARAR.

Sudanese National Party (SNP): Khartoum; Leader HASAN AL-MAHI; participates in the National Democratic Alliance (see below).

Umma Party (UP): e-mail hq@umma.org; internet www.umma.org; Mahdist party based on the Koran and Islamic traditions; Chair. Dr UMAR NUR AD-DA'IM; Leader SADIQ AL-MAHDI; withdrew from the National Democratic Alliance (see below) in March 2000.

Union of Sudan African Parties (USAP): f. 1987; Chair. JOSEPH OKELLO; Sec.-Gen. Prof. AJANG BIOR.

United Democratic Salvation Front (UDSF): Khartoum; political wing of the Sudan People's Defence Force; Chair. Dr RIEK MASHAR TENY-DHURGON.

A number of opposition movements are grouped together in the Asmara-based **National Democratic Alliance (NDA)** (Chair. OSMAN AL-MIRGHANI; Sec.-Gen. JOSEPH OKELU). These include the **Beja Congress** (Sec.-Gen. Amna Dirar), the **Legitimate Command (LC)**, the **Sudan Alliance Forces (SAF)** (f. 1994; Commdr-in-Chief Brig. ABD EL-AZIZ KHALID OSMAN), the **Sudan Federal Democratic Alliance (SFDA)** (f. 1994; advocates a decentralized, federal structure for Sudan; Chair. AHMAD DREIGE).

In 2003 two rebel groups, the **Sudan Liberation Movement (SLM)** (Leader MINNI ARKUA MINAWI) and the **Sudan Justice and Equality Movement (SJEM)**, began an armed rebellion in the Darfur region of western Sudan.

At a meeting convened in Asmara in 2006 the **National Redemption Front (NRF)** was formed by the leader of the SJEM, Dr KHALIL IBRAHIM MOHAMED, his counterpart, AHMAD DREIGE of the SFDA, and KHAMIS ABDALLA ABAKAR, the former Deputy Chairman of Abd al-Wahid Muhammad an-Nur's faction of the SLM, and leader of the **Group of 19 (G-19)**. The G-19 emerged as the principal faction of the NRF, originally formed as a group of commanders who defected from an-Nur's faction during the Abuja negotiations. In December 2006 a group of Arab rebels, opposed to the Sudanese army and the *Janjaweed*, formed an alliance called the **Popular Forces Troops (PFT)**.

Diplomatic Representation

EMBASSIES IN SUDAN

Afghanistan: Madinatol Riyadh, Shareol Moshtal Sq. 10, House No. 81, Khartoum; tel. (183) 221852; fax (183) 222059; e-mail afembsudan@hotmail.com; Chargé d'affaires a.i. KHALILURRAHMAN HANANI.

Algeria: Blvd El-Mechtel Eriad, POB 80, Khartoum; tel. (183) 234773; fax (183) 224190; Ambassador SALIH BEN KOBBI.

Bulgaria: St 31, House No. 9, Block 10, al-Amarat, POB 1690, 11111 Khartoum; tel. (183) 560106; fax (183) 560107; e-mail bgembsdn@yahoo.co.uk; Chargé d'affaires SVILEN BOZHANOV.

Chad: St 57, al-Amarat, Khartoum; tel. (183) 471612; Ambassador MOUSSA MAHAMAT SEID MEDELA.

China, People's Republic: POB 1425, Khartoum; tel. (183) 272730; fax (183) 271138; e-mail ssddssgg@yahoo.com.cn; Ambassador LI CHENGWEN.

Congo, Democratic Republic: St 13, Block 12 CE, New Extension, 23, POB 4195, Khartoum; tel. (183) 471125; Chargé d'affaires a.i. BAWAN MUZURI.

Egypt: University St, POB 1126, Khartoum; tel. (183) 777646; fax (183) 778741; e-mail sphinx-egysud@yahoo.com; Ambassador MOHAMED ABDEL MONEIM EL SHAZLY.

Eritrea: St 39, House No. 26, POB 1618, Khartoum 2; tel. (183) 483834; fax (183) 483835; e-mail erena@sudanet.net; Ambassador Gen. ISSA AHMED ISSA.

Ethiopia: Plot No. 4, Block 384BC, POB 844, Khartoum; tel. (183) 471379; fax (183) 471141; e-mail eekrt@hotmail.com; Ambassador Dr KADAFO MOHAMMED HANFARE.

France: al-Amarat, St 13, Plot No. 11, Block 12, POB 377, 11111 Khartoum; tel. (183) 471082; fax (183) 465928; e-mail cad.khartoum@diplomatie.gouv.fr; internet www.ambafrance-sd.org; Ambassador CHRISTINE ROBICHON.

Germany: 53 Baladia St, Block No. 8D, Plot 2, POB 970, Khartoum; tel. (183) 777990; fax (183) 777622; e-mail reg1@khar.auswaertiges-amt.de; internet www.khartum.diplo.de; Ambassador Dr STEPHAN KELLER.

Greece: Sharia al-Gamhouria, Block 5, No. 30, POB 1182, Khartoum; tel. (183) 765900; fax (183) 765901; e-mail grembkrt@mfa.gr; Ambassador GEORGIOS VEIS.

Holy See: Kafouri Belgravia, POB 623, Khartoum (Apostolic Nunciature); tel. (183) 330037; fax (183) 330692; e-mail kanuap@yahoo.it; Apostolic Nuncio Most Rev. LEO BOCCARDI (Titular Archbishop of Bitettum).

India: 61 Africa Rd, POB 707, Khartoum II; tel. (183) 574001; fax (183) 574050; e-mail ambassador@indembsdn.com; internet www.indembsdn.com; Ambassador DEEPAK VOHRA.

Indonesia: St 60, 84, Block 12, ar-Riyadh, POB 13374, Khartoum; tel. (183) 225106; fax (183) 225528; e-mail kbri_khartoum@sudanmail.com; Ambassador SYAMSUDIN YAHYA.

Iran: Sq. 15, House No. 4, Mogran, POB 10229, Khartoum; tel. (183) 781490; fax (183) 778668; e-mail iranemb_khartoum@mfa.gov.ir; Ambassador REZA AMERI.

Iraq: Sharia ash-Shareef al-Hindi, POB 1969, Khartoum; tel. (183) 271867; fax (183) 271855; e-mail krtemb@iraqmofamail.net; Ambassador SAMIR KHAIREE ALNEEMA.

Italy: St 39, POB 793, Khartoum; tel. (183) 471615; fax (183) 471217; e-mail ambasciata.khartoum@esteri.it; internet www.ambkhartoum.esteri.it; Ambassador LORENZO ANGELONI.

Japan: St 43, House No. 67, POB 1649, Khartoum; tel. (183) 471601; fax (183) 471600; Ambassador YUICHI ISHII.

Jordan: St 33, House No. 13, POB 1379, Khartoum; tel. (183) 483125; fax (183) 471038; e-mail joremb@sudanmail.net; Ambassador MUNTHER QUBAAH.

Kenya: St 3, POB 8242, Khartoum; tel. (183) 265163; fax (183) 281233; Ambassador Col (Retd) ELIJAH MALEKYA MATIBO.

Korea, Republic: House No. 2, St 1, New Extension, POB 2414, Khartoum; tel. (183) 451136; fax (183) 452822; e-mail ssudan@mofat.go.kr; Ambassador DONG EOK KIM.

Kuwait: Africa Ave, near the Tennis Club, POB 1457, Khartoum; tel. (183) 781525; Ambassador MUNTHIR BADR SALMAN.

Lebanon: Khartoum; Ambassador AHMAD SHAMMATT.

Libya: 50 Africa Rd, POB 2091, Khartoum; Secretary of People's Bureau GUMMA AL-FAZANI.

Malaysia: St 3, Block 2, al-Amarat, POB 11668, Khartoum; tel. (183) 482763; fax (183) 482762; e-mail mwktoum@kln.gov.my; Ambassador HAJI ZAINAL HAMZAH.

Morocco: St 19, 32, New Extension, POB 2042, Khartoum; tel. (183) 473068; fax (183) 471053; e-mail sifmasoud@sudan.mail.net; Ambassador MUHAMMAD MAA EL-AININE.

Netherlands: St 47, House No. 76, POB 391, Khartoum; tel. (183) 471200; fax (183) 471204; e-mail nlgovkha@mail.com; internet www.mfa.nl/kha; Ambassador J. H. M. WOLFS.

Nigeria: St 17, Sharia al-Mek Nimr, POB 1538, Khartoum; tel. (183) 779120; Ambassador IBRAHIM KARLI.

Norway: St 49, House No. 63, POB 13096, Khartoum; tel. (183) 578336; fax (183) 577180; e-mail emb.khartoum@mfa.no; internet www.norway-sudan.org; Ambassador FRIDTJOV THORKILDSEN.

Oman: St 1, New Extension, POB 2839, Khartoum; tel. (183) 471606; fax (183) 471017; Ambassador SALIM BIN FANKHAR AL-SHANFARI.

Pakistan: Dr Mehmood Sharif St, House No. 13, Block 35, POB 1178, Khartoum; tel. (183) 265599; fax (183) 273777; e-mail parepkhartoum@yahoo.com; Ambassador KHALID HUSSAIN YOUSFANI.

Qatar: ELmanshia Block 92H, POB 223, Khartoum; tel. (183) 261113; fax (183) 261116; e-mail qatarembkht@yahoo.com; Ambassador ALI HASSAN ABDULLAH AL-HAMADI.

Romania: Kassala Rd, Plot No. 172–173, Kafouri Area, POB 1494, Khartoum North; tel. (185) 338114; fax (185) 341497; e-mail ambro_khartoum@hotmail.com; Ambassador Dr EMIL GHITULESCU.

Russia: A10 St, B1, New Extension, POB 1161, Khartoum; tel. (183) 471042; fax (183) 471239; e-mail rfsudan@hotmail.com; Ambassador VALERII Y. SUKHIN.

Saudi Arabia: St 11, New Extension, Khartoum; tel. (183) 741938; Ambassador SAYED MOHAMMED SIBRI SULIMAN.

Somalia: St 23–25, New Extension, POB 1857, Khartoum; tel. (183) 744800; Ambassador Sheikh MUHAMMAD AHMED.

South Africa: St 11, House No. 16, Block B9, al-Amarat, POB 12137, Khartoum; tel. (183) 585301; fax (183) 585082; e-mail khartoum@foreign.gov.za; Ambassador REDDY MAMPANE.

Switzerland: St 15, House No. 7, Amarat, POB 1707, Khartoum; tel. (183) 471010; fax (183) 471115; e-mail vertretung@kha.rep.admin.ch; Ambassador ANDREJ MOTYL.

Syria: St 3, New Extension, POB 1139, Khartoum; tel. (183) 471152; fax (183) 471066; Ambassador MOHAMMED AL-MAHAMEED.

Tunisia: St 15, 35, al-Amarat, Khartoum; tel. (183) 487947; fax (183) 487950; e-mail at_khartoum@yahoo.fr; Ambassador ABDESSALEM BOUAÏCHA.

Turkey: St 29, 31, New Extension, POB 771, Khartoum; tel. (183) 794215; fax (183) 794218; e-mail trembkh@sudanmail.net; Ambassador Dr ALI ENGIN OBA.

Uganda: POB 2676, Khartoum; tel. (183) 158571; fax (183) 797868; e-mail ugembkht@hotmail.com; Ambassador MULL KATENDE.

United Arab Emirates: St 3, New Extension, POB 1225, Khartoum; tel. (183) 744476; Ambassador ISA ABDULLAH AL-BASHAR.

United Kingdom: St 10, off Baladia St, POB 801, Khartoum; tel. (183) 777105; fax (183) 776457; e-mail Media.Khartoum@fco.gov.uk; internet www.britishembassy.gov.uk/sudan; Ambassador IAN CLIFF.

USA: Ali Abd al-Latif St, POB 699, Khartoum; tel. (183) 774701; internet khartoum.usembassy.gov; Chargé d'affaires ALBERTO M. FERNANDEZ.

Yemen: St 11, New Extension, POB 1010, Khartoum; tel. (183) 743918; Ambassador ABDOULJALIL AZZOUZ.

Judicial System

Until September 1983 the judicial system was divided into two sections, civil and Islamic, the latter dealing only with personal and family matters. In September 1983 President Nimeri replaced all existing laws with Islamic (*Shari'a*) law. Following the coup in April 1985, the *Shari'a* courts were abolished, and it was announced that the previous system of criminal courts was to be revived. In June 1986 the Prime Minister, Sadiq al-Mahdi, reaffirmed that the *Shari'a* law was to be abolished. It was announced in June 1987 that a new legal code, based on a 'Sudanese legal heritage', was to be introduced. In July 1989 the military Government established special courts to investigate violations of emergency laws concerning corruption. It was announced in June 1991 that these courts were to be incorporated in the general court administration. Islamic law was reintroduced in March 1991, but was not applied in the southern states of Equatoria, Bahr al-Ghazal and Upper Nile.

Chief Justice: GALAL ED-DIN MUHAMMAD OSMAN.

Religion

The majority of the northern Sudanese population are Muslims, while in the south the population are principally Christians or animists.

ISLAM

Islam is the state religion. Sudanese Islam has a strong Sufi element, and is estimated to have more than 15m. adherents.

CHRISTIANITY

Sudan Council of Churches: Inter-Church House, St 35, New Extension, POB 469, Khartoum; tel. (183) 742859; f. 1967; 12 mem. churches; Chair. Most Rev. PAOLINO LUKUDU LORO (Roman Catholic Archbishop of Juba); Gen. Sec. Rev. CLEMENT H. JANDA.

Roman Catholic Church

Latin Rite

Sudan comprises two archdioceses and seven dioceses. At 31 December 2004 there were an estimated 4,020,548 adherents, representing about 9.1% of the total population.

Sudan Catholic Bishops' Conference

General Secretariat, POB 6011, Khartoum; tel. (183) 724365; fax (183) 724866.

f. 1971; Pres. Most Rev. PAOLINO LUKUDU LORO (Archbishop of Juba); Sec.-Gen. JOHN DINGI MARTIN.

Archbishop of Juba: Most Rev. PAOLINO LUKUDU LORO, Catholic Church, POB 32, Juba, Equatoria State; tel. 20303; fax 20755.

Archbishop of Khartoum: Cardinal GABRIEL ZUBEIR WAKO, Catholic Church, POB 49, Khartoum; tel. (183) 782174; fax (183) 783518; e-mail ayoung@yahoo.com.

Maronite Rite

Maronite Church in Sudan: POB 244, Khartoum; Rev. Fr YOUSEPH NEAMA.

Melkite Rite

Patriarchal Vicariate of Egypt and Sudan: Greek Melkite Catholic Patriarchate, 16 Sharia Daher, 11271 Cairo, Egypt; tel. (2) 5905790; fax (2) 5935398; e-mail grecmelkitecath_egy@hotmail.com; General Patriarchal Vicar in Egypt and Sudan Mgr (JOSEPH) JULES ZEREY (Titular Archbishop of Damietta); Patriarchal Vicar in Sudan Mgr Exarkhos GEORGE BANNA; POB 766, Khartoum; tel. (183) 777910.

Syrian Rite

Syrian Church in Sudan: Under the jurisdiction of the Patriarch of Antioch; Protosyncellus Rt Rev. JOSEPH-CLÉMENT HANNOUCHE (Bishop of Cairo).

Orthodox Churches

Coptic Orthodox Church

Metropolitan of Khartoum, Southern Sudan and Uganda: Rt Rev. ANBA DANIAL, POB 4, Khartoum; tel. (183) 770646; fax (183) 785646; e-mail metaous@email-sudan.net.

Bishop of Atbara, Omdurman and Northern Sudan: Rt Rev. ANBA SARABAMON, POB 628, Omdurman; tel. (183) 550423; fax (183) 556973.

Greek Orthodox Church

Metropolitan of Nubia: POB 47, Khartoum; tel. (183) 772973; Archbishop DIONYSSIOS HADZIVASSILIOU.

The Ethiopian Orthodox Church is also active.

The Anglican Communion

Anglicans are adherents of the (Episcopal) Church of the Province of the Sudan. The Province, with 24 dioceses and about 1m. adherents, was established in 1976.

Archbishop in Sudan: Most Rev. JOSEPH BIRINGI HASSAN MARONA, POB 110, Juba; tel. (183) 20065.

Other Christian Churches

Evangelical Church: POB 57, Khartoum; c. 1,500 mems; administers schools, literature centre and training centre; Chair. Rev. RADI ELIAS.

Presbyterian Church: POB 40, Malakal; autonomous since 1956; 67,000 mems (1985); Gen. Sec. Rev. THOMAS MALUIT.

The Africa Inland Church, the Sudan Interior Church and the Sudanese Church of Christ are also active.

The Press

DAILIES

Press censorship was imposed following the 1989 coup.

Abbar al-Youm: Khartoum; tel. (183) 779396; daily; Editor AHMED AL-BALAL AT-TAYEB.

Al-Anbaa: Khartoum; tel. (183) 466523; f. 1998; Editor-in-Chief NAJIB ADAM QAMAR AD-DIN.

Al-Wan: Khartoum; tel. (183) 775036; e-mail alwaan@cybergates.net; daily; independent; pro-Govt; Editor HOUSSEN KHOGALI.

An-Nasr: Khartoum; tel. (183) 772494; Editor Col YOUNIS MAHMOUD.

Ar-Rai al-Akhar: Khartoum; tel. (183) 777934; daily; Editor MOHI AD-DIN TITTAWI.

Ar-Rai al-Amm: Khartoum; tel. (183) 778182; fax (183) 772176; e-mail info@rayaam.net; internet www.rayaam.net; daily; Editor SALAH MUHAMMAD IBRAHIM.

Khartoum Monitor: St 61, New Extension, Khartoum; e-mail Khartoummonitor@hotmail.com; Chair. and Editor ALFRED TABAN; Man. Editor WILLIAM EZEKIEL.

Sudan Mirror: POB 59163, 00200 Nairobi, Kenya; tel. and fax (20) 3876439; fax (20) 3876439; e-mail info@sdt.co.ke; internet www.sudanmirror.com; f. 2003; Dir DAN EIFFE.

Sudan Standard: Ministry of Information and Communication, Khartoum; daily; English.

PERIODICALS

Al-Guwwat al-Musallaha (The Armed Forces): Khartoum; f. 1969; publs a weekly newspaper and monthly magazine for the armed forces; Editor-in-Chief Maj. MAHMOUD GALANDER; circ. 7,500.

New Horizon: POB 2651, Khartoum; tel. (183) 777913; f. 1976; publ. by the Sudan House for Printing and Publishing; weekly; English; political and economic affairs, development, home and international news; Editor AS-SIR HASSAN FADL; circ. 7,000.

Sudanow: POB 2651, Khartoum; tel. (183) 777913; f. 1976; publ. by the Sudan House for Printing and Publishing; monthly; English; political and economic affairs, arts, social affairs and diversions; Editor-in-Chief AHMED KAMAL ED-DIN; circ. 10,000.

NEWS AGENCIES

Sudan News Agency (SUNA): Sharia al-Gamhouria, POB 1506, Khartoum; tel. (183) 775770; e-mail suna@sudanet.net; internet www.sudanet.net/suna.htm; Dir-Gen. ALI ABD AR-RAHMAN AN-NUMAYRI.

Sudanese Press Agency: Khartoum; f. 1985; owned by journalists.

Foreign Bureaux

Middle East News Agency (MENA) (Egypt): Dalala Bldg, POB 740, Khartoum.

Xinhua (New China) News Agency (People's Republic of China): No. 100, 12 The Sq., Riad Town, POB 2229, Khartoum; tel. (183) 224174; Correspondent SUN XIAOKE.

The Agence Arabe Syrienne d'Information—SANA (Syria) also has a bureau in Khartoum.

Publishers

Ahmad Abd ar-Rahman at-Tikeine: POB 299, Port Sudan.

Al-Ayyam Press Co Ltd: Aboulela Bldg, POB 363, United Nations Sq., Khartoum; f. 1953; general fiction and non-fiction, arts, poetry, reference, newspapers, magazines; Man. Dir BESHIR MUHAMMAD SAID.

As-Sahafa Publishing and Printing House: POB 1228, Khartoum; f. 1961; newspapers, pamphlets, fiction and govt publs.

As-Salam Co Ltd: POB 944, Khartoum.

Claudios S. Fellas: POB 641, Khartoum.

Khartoum University Press: POB 321, Khartoum; tel. (183) 776653; f. 1964; academic, general and educational in Arabic and English; Man. Dir ALI EL-MAK.

GOVERNMENT PUBLISHING HOUSE

El-Asma Printing Press: POB 38, Khartoum.

Broadcasting and Communications

TELECOMMUNICATIONS

A mobile cellular telephone network for Khartoum State was inaugurated in 1997.

Ministry of Information and Communication: Khartoum; regulatory body; Sec.-Gen. Eng. AWAD E. WIDAA.

Posts and Telegraphs Public Corpn: Khartoum; tel. (183) 770000; fax (183) 772888; e-mail sudanpost@maktoob.com; regulatory body; Dir-Gen. AHMAD AT-TIJANI ALALLIM.

Sudan Telecom Co (SUDATEL): Sudatel Tower, POB 11155, Khartoum; tel. (183) 797400; fax (183) 782322; e-mail info@sudatel.net; internet www.sudatel.net; f. 1993; service provider for Sudan; Chair. Dr AHMAD MAGZOUB; Gen. Man. EMAD ALDIN HUSSAIN AHMAD.

BROADCASTING

Radio

Sudan Radio: POB 572, Omdurman; tel. (187) 559315; fax (187) 560566; e-mail info@sudanradio.info; internet www.sudanradio.info; f. 1940; state-controlled service broadcasting daily in Arabic, English, French and Swahili; Dir-Gen. MUTASIM FADUL USUD.

Voice of Sudan: e-mail sudanvoice@umma.org; active since 1995; run by the National Democratic Alliance; Arabic and English.

Television

An earth satellite station operated on 36 channels at Umm Haraz has much improved Sudan's telecommunications links. A nation-wide satellite network is being established with 14 earth stations in the provinces. There are regional stations at Gezira (Central Region) and Atbara (Northern Region).

Sudan Television: POB 1094, Omdurman; tel. (15) 550022; internet www.sudantv.net; f. 1962; state-controlled; 60 hours of programmes per week; Head of Directorate HADID AS-SIRA.

Finance

(cap. = capital; res = reserves; dep. = deposits; m. = million; brs = branches; amounts in Sudanese dinars, unless otherwise indicated)

BANKING

All domestic banks are controlled by the Bank of Sudan. Foreign banks were permitted to resume operations in 1976. In December 1985 the Government banned the establishment of any further banks. It was announced in December 1990 that Sudan's banking system was to be reorganized to accord with Islamic principles. In 2000 there were a total of 25 banks in Sudan. In May 2000 the Bank of Sudan issued new policy guide-lines under which Sudan's banks were to merge into six banking groups to improve their financial strength and international competitiveness; however, the mergers had not been implemented by early 2007.

Central Bank

Bank of Sudan: Gamaa Ave, POB 313, Khartoum; tel. (187) 056000; fax (183) 780273; e-mail sudanbank@sudanmail.net; internet www.bankofsudan.org; f. 1960; bank of issue; cap. 1,200.0m., res 7,474.9m., dep. 772,433.7m. (Dec. 2004); Gov. Dr SABIR MUHAMMAD HASSAN; 9 brs.

Commercial Banks

Al-Baraka Bank: Al-Baraka Tower, Zubeir Pasha St, POB 3583, Khartoum; tel. (183) 783927; fax (183) 778948; e-mail baraka2000@sudanmail.net; internet www.albarakasudan.com; f. 1984; 87.8% owned by Al-Baraka Banking Group (Bahrain); investment and export promotion; cap. 1,365.5m., res 3,748.7m., dep. 23,286.0m. (Dec. 2004); Chair. OSMAN AHMED SULIMAN; Gen. Man. ABDALLAH KHAIRY HAMID; 24 brs.

Ash-Shamal Islamic Bank: Ash-Shamal Islamic Tower, as-Sayid Abd ar-Rahman St, POB 10036, 11111 Khartoum; tel. (183) 779078; fax (183) 772661; e-mail info@alshamalbank.com; internet www.alshamalbank.com; f. 1990; total assets 18,258.0m. (Dec. 2003); Pres. GAFAAR OSMAN FAGIR; Gen. Man. ABDELMONEIM HASSAN SAYED (acting); 17 brs.

Bank of Khartoum Group: Intersection Gamhouria St and El-Gaser St, POB 1008, Khartoum; tel. (183) 772800; fax (183) 781120; e-mail admin@bankofkhartoum.net; internet www.bankofkhartoum.net; f. 1913; 55% owned by Dubai Islamic Bank PLC; absorbed National Export/Import Bank and Unity Bank in 1993; cap. 11,800m., res 450.1m., dep. 48,600m. (Dec. 2003); Chair. OSMAN ALHADI IBRAHIM; Gen. Man. MUHAMMAD SALAH ELDIN; 118 brs.

Blue Nile Mashreg Bank: Parliament St, POB 984, Khartoum; tel. (183) 784690; fax (183) 782562; e-mail info@bluemashreg.com; internet www.bluemashreg.com; cap. 1,531.8m., res 277.7m., dep. 13,076.4m. (Dec. 2004); Chair. MUHAMMAD ISMAIL MUHAMMAD; Gen. Man. ABDEL KHALIG ALSAMANI ABDEL RAZIG.

Farmers Commercial Bank: POB 11984, Al-Qasr Ave, Khartoum; tel. (183) 774960; fax (183) 773687; f. 1960 as Sudan Commercial Bank; name changed as above in 1999 following merger with Farmers Bank for Investment and Rural Development; cap. 3,001.0m., res 1,162.0m., dep. 19,466.9m. (Dec. 2004); Chair. ET-TAYB ELOBEID BADR; Gen. Man. SULIMAN HASHIM MUHAMMAD; 28 brs.

National Bank of Sudan: Kronfli Bldg, Zubeir Pasha St, POB 1183, Khartoum; tel. (183) 778153; fax (183) 779545; f. 1982; 70% owned by Bank Audi SAL, Lebanon; cap. 593.0m., res 313.6m., dep. 8,384.0m. (Dec. 2001); Chair. HASSAN IBRAHIM MALIK; Gen. Man. MUHAMMAD KHEIR ISMAIL; 13 brs in Sudan, 2 abroad.

Omdurman National Bank: Al-Qaser Ave, POB 11522, Khartoum; tel. (183) 770400; fax (183) 777219; e-mail omb@sudanmail.net; internet www.omd-bank.com; f. 1993; cap. 6,096.3m., res 8,362.2m., dep. 342,391.2m. (Dec. 2005); Gen. Man. ABDEL RAHMAN HASSAN ABDEL RAHMAN; 19 brs; 890 employees.

Sudanese French Bank: Plot No. 6, Block A, Al-Qasr Ave, POB 2775, Khartoum; tel. (183) 771730; fax (183) 771740; e-mail sfbankb@sudanet.net; f. 1978 as Sudanese Investment Bank; name changed as above in 1993; cap. 5,067.3m., res 1,671.1m., dep. 48,598.9m. (Dec. 2006); Chair. Dr EZZELDEIN EBRAHIM; Gen. Man. MASSAD MOHAMMED AHMED; 11 brs.

Tadamon Islamic Bank: Baladia St, POB 3154, Khartoum; tel. (183) 771505; fax (183) 773840; e-mail info@tadamonbank-sd.com; internet www.tadamonbank-sd.com; f. 1981; cap. 6,775.5m., res 1,363.9m., dep. 66,768.0m. (Dec. 2006); Chair. Dr HASSAN OSMAN SAKOTA; Gen. Man. ABDALLAH NOGD ALLAH AHMAIDI; 18 brs.

Foreign Banks

Byblos Bank Africa Ltd: 21 Al-Amarat St, POB 8121, Khartoum; tel. (183) 566444; fax (183) 566454; internet www.byblosbank.com.lb; f. 2003; cap. 6,375m., res 207m., dep. 13,408m.; Chair. Dr FRANÇOIS S. BASSIL; Gen. Man. NADIM GHANTOUS.

Faisal Islamic Bank (Sudan) (Saudi Arabia): Faiha Bldg, Ali al-Latif St, POB 2415, Khartoum; tel. (183) 777920; fax (183) 780193; e-mail fibsudan@fibsudan.com; internet www.fibsudan.com; f. 1977; cap. 3,000.0m., res 834.4m., dep. 24,677.2m. (Dec. 2004); Chair. Prince MUHAMMAD AL-FAISAL AS-SAUD; Gen. Man. ALI OMAR IBRAHIM FARAH; 28 brs.

Habib Bank (Pakistan): Al-Qasr St, POB 8246, Khartoum; tel. (183) 782820; fax (183) 781497; e-mail hblsudan@sudanmail.net.sd; internet www.habibbankltd.com; f. 1982; cap. and res 13.8m. Sudanese pounds, total assets 27.3m. (Dec. 1987); Gen. Man. BAZ MUHAMMAD KHAN.

National Bank of Abu Dhabi (United Arab Emirates): Taka Bldg, Atbara St, POB 2465, Khartoum; tel. (183) 787203; fax (183) 774892; e-mail nbadkh@sudanmail.net; internet www.nbad.com; f. 1976; cap. and res 16.9m. Sudanese pounds, total assets 12.5m. (Dec. 1987); Man. GAAFER OSMAN MUHAMMAD.

Saudi Sudanese Bank: Baladia St, POB 1773, Khartoum; tel. (183) 776700; fax (183) 781836; e-mail saudi-sud@saudisb.com; internet www.saudisb.com; f. 1986; Saudi Arabian shareholders have a 57.3% interest, Sudanese shareholders 42.7%; cap. 422.6m., res 2,630.5m., dep. 26,072.2m. (Dec. 2004); Chair. ABDEL GALIL EL-WASIA; Gen. Man. MUDATHIR ALI AL-BASHIR (acting); 13 brs.

Development Banks

Agricultural Bank of Sudan: Ghoumhoria Ave, POB 1263, Khartoum; tel. (183) 777432; fax (183) 778296; e-mail agribank@yahoo.com; f. 1957; cap. 5,200.0m., res 3,609.4m., dep. 18,864.9m. (Dec. 2003); provides finance for agricultural projects; Pres. AS-SAYID GAFFAR MUHAMMAD AL-HASSAN; Gen. Man. AS-SAYID AL-KINDI MUHAMMAD OSMAN; 40 brs.

Islamic Co-operative Development Bank (ICDB): Et-Tanmha Tower, Kolyat Eltib St, POB 62, Khartoum; tel. (183) 780223; fax (183) 777715; f. 1983; cap. and res 3,821.0m., total assets 28,250.4m. (Dec. 2003); Chair. EL-HAJ ATTA EL-MANAN IDRIS; 6 brs.

El-Nilein Industrial Development Bank: United Nations Sq., POB 1722, Khartoum; tel. (183) 771117; fax (183) 771984; e-mail info@nidbg.com; internet www.nidbg.com; f. 1993 by merger of El-Nilein Bank and Industrial Bank of Sudan; partially privatized in 2006; 40% govt-owned, 60% owned by Dubai-based Amlak Finance; provides tech. and financial assistance for private-sector industrial projects and acquires shares in industrial enterprises; cap. 3,096.9m., res 779.6m., dep. 33,713.8m. (Dec. 2003); Chair. Dr SABIR MUHAMMAD EL-HASSAN; Man. Dir WAGIE ALLA EL NAW; 43 brs.

NIMA Development and Investment Bank: Hashim Hago Bldg, As-Suk al-Arabi, POB 665, Khartoum; tel. (183) 779496; fax (183) 781854; f. 1982 as National Devt Bank; name changed as above 1998; 90%-owned by NIMA Groupe, 10% private shareholders; finances or co-finances economic and social devt projects; cap. 4,000m. Sudanese pounds, res 106m. (Dec. 1998); Dir-Gen. SALIM EL-SAFI HUGIR; 6 brs.

Sudanese Estates Bank: Baladia St, POB 309, Khartoum; tel. (183) 777917; fax (183) 779465; f. 1967; mortgage bank financing private-sector urban housing devt; cap. and res 1,700m. Sudanese pounds, total assets 9,500m. (Dec. 1994); Chair. Eng. MUHAMMAD ALI EL-AMIN; 6 brs.

STOCK EXCHANGE

Sudanese Stock Exchange: Al-Baraka Tower, 5th Floor, POB 10835, Khartoum; tel. (183) 776235; fax (183) 776134; f. 1995; Chair. HAMZA MUHAMMAD JENAWI; 27 mems.

INSURANCE

African Insurance Co (Sudan) Ltd: New Abu Ella Bldg, Parliament Ave, Khartoum; tel. (183) 173402; fax (183) 177988; f. 1977; fire, accident, marine and motor; Gen. Man. AN-NOMAN AS-SANUSI.

Blue Nile Insurance Co (Sudan) Ltd: Al-Qasr Ave, POB 2215, Khartoum; tel. (183) 170580; fax (183) 172405; Gen. Man. MUHAMMAD AL-AMIN MIRGHANI.

Foja International Insurance Co Ltd: POB 879, Khartoum; tel. (183) 784470; fax (183) 783248; fire, accident, marine, motor and animal; Gen. Man. MAMOON IBRAHIM ABD ALLA.

General Insurance Co (Sudan) Ltd: El-Mek Nimr St, POB 1555, Khartoum; tel. (183) 780616; fax (183) 772122; f. 1961; Gen. Man. ELSAMAWL ELSAYED HAFIZ.

Islamic Insurance Co Ltd: Al-Faiha Commercial Bldg, Ali Abdullatif St, POB 2776, Khartoum; tel. (183) 772656; e-mail islamicins@sudanmail.net; f. 1979; all classes; CEO Dr OTHMAN ABDUL WAHAB.

Khartoum Insurance Co Ltd: Al-Taminat Bldg, Al-Jamhouriya St, POB 737, Khartoum; tel. (183) 778647; f. 1953; Chair. MUDAWI M. AHMAD; Gen. Dir YOUSIF KHAIRY.

Juba Insurance Co Ltd: Al-Baladiya St, Sayen Osnam Al-Amin Bldg, 2nd Floor, POB 10043, Khartoum; tel. (183) 783245; fax (183) 781617; Gen. Man. ABDUL AAL ELDAWI ABDUL AAL.

Middle East Insurance Co Ltd: Al-Qasr St, Kuronfuli Bldg, 1st Floor, POB 3070, Khartoum; tel. (183) 772202; fax (183) 779266; f. 1981; fire, marine, motor and general liability; Chair. AHMAD I. MALIK; Gen. Dir ALI MUHAMMAD AHMED EL-FADL.

Sudanese Insurance and Reinsurance Co Ltd: Al-Gamhouria St, Nasr Sq., Middle Station Makati Bldg, 3rd Floor, POB 2332, Khartoum; tel. (183) 770812; f. 1967; CEO HASSAN ES-SAYED MUHAMMAD ALI.

United Insurance Co (Sudan) Ltd: Makkawi Bldg, Al-Gamhouria St, POB 318, Khartoum; tel. (183) 776630; fax (183) 770783; e-mail abdin@unitedinsurance.ws; internet www.unitedinsurance.ws; f. 1968; Chair. HASHIM EL-BERIER; Dir-Gen. MUHAMMAD ABDEEN BABIKER.

Trade and Industry

GOVERNMENT AGENCIES

Agricultural Research Corpn: POB 126, Wadi Medani; tel. (5118) 42226; fax (5118) 43213; e-mail arcsudan@sudanet.net; f. 1967; Dir-Gen. Prof. SALIH HUSSEIN SALIH.

Animal Production Public Corpn: POB 624, Khartoum; tel. (183) 778555; Gen. Man. Dr FOUAD RAMADAN HAMID.

General Petroleum Corpn: POB 2649, Khartoum; tel. (183) 777554; fax (183) 773663; e-mail secretarygeneral@spc.sd; f. 1976; Chair. Dr AWAD AHMED AL JAZZ; Sec.-Gen. Dr AOMER MOHAMED KHEIR.

Gum Arabic Co Ltd: POB 857, Khartoum; tel. (183) 461061; fax (183) 471336; e-mail info@gum-arab.com; internet www.gum-arab.com; f. 1969; Chair. ABD EL-HAMID MUSA KASHA; Gen. Man. HASSAN SAAD AHMED.

Industrial Production Corpn: POB 1034, Khartoum; tel. (183) 771278; f. 1976; Dir-Gen. OSMAN TAMMAM.

Cement and Building Materials Sector Co-ordination Office: POB 2241, Khartoum; tel. (183) 774269; Dir T. M. KHOGALI.

Food Industries Corpn: POB 2341, Khartoum; tel. (183) 775463; Dir MUHAMMAD AL-GHALI SULIMAN.

Leather Industries Corpn: POB 1639, Khartoum; tel. (183) 778187; f. 1986; Man. Dir IBRAHIM SALIH ALI.

Oil Corpn: POB 64, Khartoum North; tel. (183) 332044; Gen. Man. BUKHARI MAHMOUD BUKHARI.

Spinning and Weaving General Co Ltd: POB 765, Khartoum; tel. (183) 774306; f. 1975; Dir MUHAMMAD SALIH MUHAMMAD ABDALLAH.

Sudan Tea Co Ltd: POB 1219, Khartoum; tel. (183) 781261.

Sudanese Mining Corpn: POB 1034, Khartoum; tel. (183) 770840; f. 1975; Dir IBRAHIM MUDAWI BABIKER.

Sugar and Distilling Industry Corpn: POB 511, Khartoum; tel. (183) 778417; Man. MIRGHANI AHMAD BABIKER.

Mechanized Farming Corpn: POB 2482, Khartoum; Man. Dir AWAD AL-KARIM AL-YASS.

National Cotton and Trade Co Ltd: POB 1552, Khartoum; tel. (183) 80040; f. 1970; Chair. ABD EL-ATI A. MEKKI; Man. Dir ABD AR-RAHMAN A. MONIEM; Gen. Man. ZUBAIR MUHAMMAD AL-BASHIR.

Port Sudan Cotton Trade Co Ltd: POB 590, Port Sudan; POB 590, Khartoum; Gen. Man. SAÏD MUHAMMAD ADAM.

Public Agricultural Production Corpn: POB 538, Khartoum; Chair. and Man. Dir ABDALLAH BAYOUMO; Sec. SAAD AD-DIN MUHAMMAD ALI.

Public Corpn for Building and Construction: POB 2110, Khartoum; tel. (183) 774544; Dir NAIM AD-DIN.

Public Corpn for Irrigation and Excavation: POB 619, Khartoum; tel. (183) 780167; Gen. Sec. Osman an-Nur.

Public Corpn for Oil Products and Pipelines: POB 1704, Khartoum; tel. (183) 778290; Gen. Man. Abd ar-Rahman Suliman.

Rahad Corpn: POB 2523, Khartoum; tel. (183) 775175; financed by the World Bank, Kuwait and the USA; Man. Dir Hassan Saad Abdalla.

State Trading Corpn: POB 211, Khartoum; tel. (183) 778555; Chair. E. R. M. Tom.

Automobile Corpn: POB 221, Khartoum; tel. (183) 778555; importer of vehicles and spare parts; Gen. Man. Dafalla Ahmad Siddiq.

Captrade Engineering and Automobile Services Co Ltd: POB 97, Khartoum; tel. (183) 789265; fax (183) 775544; e-mail cap1@sudanmail.net; f. 1925; importers and distributors of engineering and automobile equipment; Gen. Man. Essam Mohd el-Hassan Kambal.

Gezira Trade and Services Co: POB 215, Khartoum; tel. (183) 772687; fax (183) 779060; e-mail gtco@sudanmail.net; f. 1980; importer of agricultural machinery, spare parts, electrical and office equipment, foodstuffs, clothes and footwear; exporter of oilseeds, grains, hides and skins and livestock; provides shipping insurance and warehousing services; agents for Lloyds and P and I Club; Chair. Nasr ed-Din M. Omer.

Khartoum Commercial and Shipping Co: POB 221, Khartoum; tel. (183) 778555; f. 1982; import, export and shipping services, insurance and manufacturing; Gen. Man. Idris M. Salih.

Silos and Storage Corpn: POB 1183, Khartoum; stores and handles agricultural products; Gen. Man. Ahmad at-Taieb Harhoof.

Sudan Cotton Co Ltd: POB 1672, Khartoum; tel. (183) 771567; fax (183) 770703; e-mail sccl@sudanmail.net.sd; internet www.sudancottonco.com; f. 1970; exports and markets cotton; Chair. Abbas Abd al-Bagi Hammad; Dir-Gen. Dr Abdin Muhammad Ali.

Sudan Gezira Board: POB 884, HQ Barakat Wadi Medani, Gezira Province; tel. 2412; Sales Office, POB 884, Khartoum; tel. (183) 740145; responsible for Sudan's main cotton-producing area; the Gezira scheme is a partnership between the Govt, the tenants and the board. The Govt provides the land and is responsible for irrigation. Tenants pay a land and water charge and receive the work proceeds. The Board provides agricultural services at cost, technical supervision and execution of govt agricultural policies relating to the scheme. Tenants pay a percentage of their proceeds to the Social Development Fund. The total potential cultivable area of the Gezira scheme is c. 850,000 ha and the total area under systematic irrigation is c. 730,000 ha. In addition to cotton, groundnuts, sorghum, wheat, rice, pulses and vegetables are grown for the benefit of tenant farmers; Man. Dir Prof. Fathi Muhammad Khalifa.

Sudan Oilseeds Co Ltd: Parliament Ave, POB 167, Khartoum; tel. (183) 780120; f. 1974; 58% state-owned; exporter of oilseeds (groundnuts, sesame seeds and castor beans); importer of foodstuffs and other goods; Chair. Sadiq Karar at-Tayeb; Gen. Man. Kamal Abd al-Halim.

DEVELOPMENT CORPORATIONS

Sudan Development Corpn (SDC): 21 al-Amarat, POB 710, Khartoum; tel. (183) 472151; fax (183) 472148; e-mail sdc@sudanmail.net; f. 1974 to promote and co-finance devt projects with special emphasis on projects in the agricultural, agri-business, and industrial sectors; cap. p.u. US $200m.; Man. Dir Abdel Wahab Ahmed Hamza.

Sudan Rural Development Co Ltd (SRDC): POB 2190, Khartoum; tel. (183) 773855; fax (183) 773235; e-mail srdfc@hotmail.com; f. 1980; SDC has 27% shareholding; cap. p.u. US $20m.; Gen. Man. El-Awad Abdalla H. Hijazi (designate).

Sudan Rural Development Finance Co (SRDFC): POB 2190, Khartoum; tel. (183) 773855; fax (183) 773235; f. 1980; Gen. Man. Omran Muhammad Ali.

CHAMBER OF COMMERCE

Union of Sudanese Chambers of Commerce: POB 81, Khartoum; tel. (183) 772346; fax (183) 780748; e-mail chamber@sudanchamber.org; internet www.sudanchamber.org; f. 1908; Pres. Eltayeb Ahmed Osman; Sec.-Gen. Ibrahim Muhammad Osman.

INDUSTRIAL ASSOCIATION

Sudanese Industries Association: Africa St, POB 2565, Khartoum; tel. (183) 773151; f. 1974; Chair. Fath ar-Rahman al-Bashir; Exec. Dir A. Izz al-Arab Yousuf.

UTILITIES

Public Electricity and Water Corpn: POB 1380, Khartoum; tel. (183) 81021; Dir Dr Yasin al-Haj Abdin.

CO-OPERATIVE SOCIETIES

There are about 600 co-operative societies, of which 570 are officially registered.

Central Co-operative Union: POB 2492, Khartoum; tel. (183) 780624; largest co-operative union operating in 15 provinces.

MAJOR COMPANIES

The following are among the larger companies, either in terms of capital investment or employment.

Aboulela Cotton Ginning Co Ltd: POB 121, Khartoum; tel. (183) 770020; cotton mills.

Bata (Sudan) Ltd: POB 88, Khartoum; tel. (183) 732240; f. 1950; cap. £S1.7m.; mfrs and distributors of footwear; Man. Dir A. A. Ali; 1,070 employees.

Blue Nile Brewery: POB 1408, Khartoum; f. 1954; cap. £S734,150; brewing, bottling and distribution of beer; Man. Dirs Ibrahim Elyas, Hussein Muhammad Kemal, Omer az-Zein Sagayroun; 336 employees.

Central Desert Mining Co Ltd: POB 20, Port Sudan; f. 1946; cap. £S150,000; prospecting for and mining of gold, manganese and iron ore; Dirs Abd al-Hadi Ahmad Bashir, Abou-Bakr Said Bashir; 274 employees.

Cotton Textile Mills Ltd: POB 203, Khartoum; tel. (183) 731414; f. 1976; yarns and fabrics; Man. Abdel Marouf ZeinElabdeen.

Gabaco (Sudan) Ltd: POB 1155, Khartoum; tel. (183) 780253; f. 1959; cap. £S15.8m.; distribution of petroleum products; Pres. E. Campoli; Gen. Man. G. Baronio; 187 employees.

Kenana Sugar Co Ltd: POB 2632, Khartoum; tel. (183) 224703; fax (183) 220563; e-mail info@kenana.com; internet www.kenana.com; f. 1971; financed by Sudanese Govt and other Arab nations; 15,500 employees; Man. Dir Osman Abdullah el-Nazir.

Shell Co of Sudan Ltd: Shell House, Aboullela Bldg, Parliament Ave, POB 320, Khartoum; tel. (187) 014150; fax (183) 781632; internet www.shell.com/home/content/sd-en; marketing of petroleum products; Chair. Muhammad el-Shafie.

TRADE UNIONS

All trade union activity was banned following the 1989 coup. The following organizations were active prior to that date.

Federations

Sudan Workers Trade Unions Federation (SWTUF): POB 2258, Khartoum; tel. (183) 777463; includes 42 trade unions representing c. 1.75m. public-service and private-sector workers; affiliated to the Int. Confed. of Arab Trade Unions and the Org. of African Trade Union Unity; Pres. Muhammad Osman Gama; Gen. Sec. Yousuf Abu Shama Hamed.

Sudanese Federation of Employees and Professionals Trade Unions: POB 2398, Khartoum; tel. (183) 773818; f. 1975; includes 54 trade unions representing 250,000 mems; Pres. Ibrahim Awadallah; Sec.-Gen. Kamal ad-Din Muhammad Abdallah.

Transport

RAILWAYS

The total length of railway in operation in 2002 was 5,978 route-km. The main line runs from Wadi Halfa, on the Egyptian border, to al-Obeid, via Khartoum. Lines from Atbara and Sinnar connect with Port Sudan. There are lines from Sinnar to Damazin on the Blue Nile (227 km) and from Aradeiba to Nyala in the south-western province of Darfur (689 km), with a 445-km branch line from Babanousa to Wau in Bahr al-Ghazal province. In 2001 plans were announced for the construction of a rail link between Port Sudan and Moyale, Ethiopia.

Sudan Railways Corpn (SRC): POB 65, Atbara; tel. 2000; f. 1875; Gen. Man. Omar Muhammad Nur.

ROADS

Roads in northern Sudan, other than town roads, are only cleared tracks and often impassable immediately after rain. Motor traffic on roads in the former Upper Nile province is limited to the drier months of January–May. There are several good gravelled roads in Equatoria and Bahr al-Ghazal provinces which are passable all the year, but in these districts some of the minor roads become impassable after rain.

Over 48,000 km of tracks are classed as 'motorable'; there were 3,160 km of main roads and 739 km of secondary roads in 1985. A 1,190-km tarmac road linking the capital with Port Sudan was completed during 1980. In 1996, according to World Bank estimates, some 36.3% of Sudan's roads were paved. By 1997 a 270-km road linking Jaili with Atbara had been completed, as part of a scheme to provide an alternative route from Khartoum to the coast. A 484-km highway linking Khartoum, Haiya and Port Sudan was scheduled for completion in 2006.

National Transport Corpn: POB 723, Khartoum; Gen. Man. MOHI AD-DIN HASSAN MUHAMMAD NUR.

Public Corpn for Roads and Bridges: POB 756, Khartoum; tel. (183) 770794; f. 1976; Chair. ABD AR-RAHMAN HABOUD; Dir-Gen. ABDOU MUHAMMAD ABDOU.

INLAND WATERWAYS

The total length of navigable waterways served by passenger and freight services is 4,068 km, of which approximately 1,723 km is open all year. From the Egyptian border to Wadi Halfa and Khartoum navigation is limited by cataracts to short stretches, but the White Nile from Khartoum to Juba is almost always navigable.

River Transport Corpn (RTC): POB 284, Khartoum North; operates 2,500 route-km of steamers on the Nile; Chair. ALI AMIR TAHA.

River Navigation Corpn: Khartoum; f. 1970; jtly owned by Govts of Egypt and Sudan; operates services between Aswan and Wadi Halfa.

SHIPPING

Port Sudan, on the Red Sea, 784 km from Khartoum, and Suakin are the only commercial seaports.

Axis Trading Co Ltd: POB 1574, Khartoum; tel. (183) 775875; f. 1967; Chair. HASSAN A. M. SULIMAN.

Red Sea Shipping Corpn: POB 116, Khartoum; tel. (183) 777688; fax (183) 774220; e-mail redseaco@sudan.net; Gen. Man. OSMAN AMIN.

Sea Ports Corpn: Port Sudan; f. 1906; Gen. Man. MUHAMMAD TAHIR AILA.

Sudan Shipping Line Ltd: POB 426, Port Sudan; tel. 2655; POB 1731, Khartoum; tel. (183) 780017; f. 1960; 10 vessels totalling 54,277 dwt operating between the Red Sea and western Mediterranean, northern Europe and United Kingdom; Chair. ISMAIL BAKHEIT; Gen. Man. SALAH AD-DIN OMER AL-AZIZ.

United African Shipping Co: POB 339, Khartoum; tel. (183) 780967; Gen. Man. MUHAMMAD TAHA AL-GINDI.

CIVIL AVIATION

In June 2005 the Government announced that preliminary construction work had been completed for a new international airport at a site 40 km south-west of Khartoum. Work to build runways and two passenger terminals was scheduled to begin in 2007. The airport was expected to open in 2010.

Civil Aviation Authority: Sharia Sayed Abd ar-Rahman, Khartoum; tel. (183) 772264; Dir-Gen. ABOU BAKR GAAFAR AHMAD.

Air West Express: POB 10217, Khartoum; tel. (183) 452503; fax (183) 451703; f. 1992; passenger and freight services to destinations in Africa; Chair. SAIF M. S. OMER.

Azza Transport: POB 11586, Mak Nimir St, Khartoum; tel. (183) 783761; fax (183) 770408; e-mail sawasawa@sudanet.net; f. 1993; charter and dedicated freight to Africa and the Middle East; Man. Dir Dr GIBRIL I. MOHAMED.

Sudan Airways Co Ltd: POB 253, Sudan Airways Complex, Obeid Khatim St 19, Khartoum; tel. (183) 243708; fax (183) 243722; internet www.sudanair.com; f. 1947; internal flights and international services to Africa, the Middle East and Europe; Man. Dir AHMED ISMAEL ZUMRAWI.

Sudanese Aeronautical Services (SASCO): POB 8260, al-Amarat, Khartoum; tel. (183) 7463362; fax (183) 4433362; fmrly Sasco Air Charter; chartered services; Chair. M. M. NUR.

Trans Arabian Air Transport (TAAT): POB 1461, Africa St, Khartoum; tel. (183) 451568; fax (183) 451544; e-mail ftaats@sudanmail.net; f. 1983; dedicated freight; services to Africa, Europe and Middle East; Man. Dir Capt. EL-FATI ABDIN.

United Arabian Airlines: POB 3687, Office No. 3, Elekhwa Bldg, Atbara St, Khartoum; tel. (183) 773025; fax (183) 784402; e-mail krthq@uaa.com; internet www.uaa.com; f. 1995; charter and dedicated freight services to Africa and the Middle East; Man. Dir M. KORDOFANI.

Tourism

Public Corpn of Tourism and Hotels: POB 7104, Khartoum; tel. (183) 781764; f. 1977; Dir-Gen. Maj.-Gen. EL-KHATIM MUHAMMAD FADL.

Defence

As assessed at November 2006, the armed forces comprised: army an estimated 104,800; navy an estimated 1,800; air force 3,000. A paramilitary Popular Defence Force included 17,500 active members and 85,000 reserves. Military service is compulsory for males aged 18–30 years and lasts for two years.

Defence Expenditure: Budgeted at US $535m. for 2006.

Commander-in-Chief of the People's Armed Forces: Pres. Lt-Gen. OMAR HASSAN AHMAD AL-BASHIR.

Education

The Government provides free primary education from the ages of six to 13 years. Secondary education begins at 14 years of age and lasts for up to three years. In 2000/01 enrolment at primary schools included 49% of children in the relevant age-group (boys 54%; girls 45%), according to UNESCO estimates, while in 1998/99 enrolment at secondary schools was equivalent to 30% of children in the relevant age-group (boys 31%; girls 29%). About 15% of current government expenditure in 1985 was for primary and secondary education. Pupils from secondary schools are accepted at the University of Khartoum, subject to their reaching the necessary standards. (The University of Khartoum was closed in January 1997 to allow students to join the armed forces.) The Khartoum branch of Egypt's Cairo University was appropriated and renamed Nilayn University by the Sudanese Government in 1993. In August 2006 construction work began on a new branch of the University of Cairo in Khartoum. There were also plans to open a branch of Egypt's University of Alexandria in Juba. There are three universities at Omdurman: Omdurman Islamic University; Omdurman Ahlia University; and Ahfad University for Women. New universities were opened at Juba and Wadi Medani (University of Gezira) in 1977. There is also a University of Science and Technology in Khartoum.

Bibliography

Abdel-Rahim, M. *Imperialism and Nationalism in the Sudan: A Study in Constitutional and Political Developments 1899–1956*. Oxford, Oxford University Press, 1969.

Abdel-Rahim, M., *et al. Sudan since Independence*. London, Gower, 1986.

Adar, K. G. *The Sudan Peace Process*. Pretoria, Africa Institute of South Africa, 2005.

Africa Watch. *War in South Sudan: The Civilian Toll*. New York, NY, Africa Watch, 1993.

African Rights. *Facing Genocide: The Nuba of Sudan*. London, African Rights, 1995.

Alier, A. *Southern Sudan: Too Many Agreements Dishonoured*. Exeter, Ithaca Press, 1990.

Amnesty International. *The Ravages of War: Political Killings and Humanitarian Disaster*. New York, Amnesty International, 1993.

An-Náim, A. A., and Kok, P. N. *Fundamentalism and Militarism: A Report on the Root Causes of Human Rights Violations in the Sudan*. New York, NY, The Fund for Peace, 1991.

Arkell, A. J. *History of Sudan from Earliest Times to 1821*. 2nd Edn. London, Athlone Press, 1961.

Asher, M. *Khartoum: The Ultimate Imperial Adventure*. London, Viking, 2005.

Barbour, K. M. *The Republic of the Sudan: A Regional Geography*. London, University of London Press, 1961.

Beasley, I., and Starkey, J. (Eds). *Before the Winds Change: Peoples, Places and Education in the Sudan*. Oxford, Oxford University Press, 1991.

Beshir, M. O. *The Southern Sudan: Background to Conflict*. London, C. Hurst, and New York, Praeger, 1968.

Revolution and Nationalism in the Sudan. New York, NY, Barnes and Noble, 1974.

(Ed.). *Sudan: Aid and External Relations, Selected Essays*. University of Khartoum, Graduate College Publications No. 9, 1984.

Brown, R. P. C. *Public Debt and Private Wealth: Debt, Capital Flight and the IMF in Sudan*. Basingstoke, Macmillan (in association with the Institute of Social Studies), 1992.

Burr, J. M., and Collins, R. O. *Requiem for the Sudan: War, Drought and Disaster Relief on the Nile*. Boulder, CO, Westview Press, 1995.

Butler, V., Carney, T., and Freeman, M. *Sudan: The Land and the People*. London, Thames & Hudson, 2005.

Collins, R. O. *Shadows in the Grass: Britain in the Southern Sudan 1918–1956*. New Haven, CT, Yale University Press, 1983.

Craig, G. M. (Ed.). *Agriculture of the Sudan*. Oxford, Oxford University Press, 1991.

Daly, M. W. *Imperial Sudan*. New York, NY, Cambridge University Press, 1991.

Daly, M. W., and Sikainga, A. A. *Civil War in the Sudan*. London, British Academic Press, 1993.

Deng, F. M. *War of Visions: Conflict of Identities in the Sudan*. Washington, DC, Brookings Institution, 1995.

Deng, F. M., and Khalil, M. *Sudan's Civil War: The Peace Process Before and Since Machakos*. Pretoria, Africa Institute of South Africa, 2005.

Doornbos, M., Cliffe, L., Ahmed, A. G. M., and Markakis, J. (Eds). *Beyond Conflict in the Horn: The Prospects of Peace and Development in Ethiopia, Somalia, Eritrea and Sudan*. Lawrenceville, KS, Red Sea Press, 1992.

El-Affendi, A. *Turabi's Revolution: Islam and Power in Sudan*. London, Grey Seal Books, 1991.

Eprile, C. L. *War and Peace in the Sudan 1955–1972*. Newton Abbot, David and Charles, 1974.

Flint, J., and de Waal, A. *Darfur: A Short History of a Long War*. London, Zed Books, 2005.

Fluehr-Lobban, C., Fluehr-Lobban, R.A., and Voll, J. *Historical Dictionary of the Sudan*. 2nd Edn. Metuchen, NJ, Scarecrow Press, 1992.

Fukui, K., and Markakis, J. (Eds). *Ethnicity and Conflict in the Horn of Africa*. London, James Currey, 1994.

Gabriel, W. *Islam, Sectarianism and Politics in Sudan since Mahdiyya*. London, C. Hurst, 2003

Garang, J. *The Call for Democracy in Sudan* (Ed. Khalid, M.). 2nd Edn. London, Kegan Paul International, 1992.

Gurdon, C. (Ed.). *The Horn of Africa*. London, University College London Press, 1994.

Hill, R., and Hogg, P. A. *Black Corps d'Elite*. East Lansing, MI, Michigan State University Press, 1995.

Hodgkin, R. A. *Sudan Geography*. London, 1951.

Holt, P. M., and Daly, M. W. *The History of the Sudan from the Coming of Islam to the Present Day*. 4th Edn. London and New York, NY, Longman, 1988.

Hurst, H. E., and Philips, P. *The Nile Basin*. 7 vols. London, 1932–38.

Iyob, R., and Khadiagala, G. M. *Sudan: The Elusive Quest for Peace*. Boulder, CO, Lynne Rienner Publishers, 2006.

Johnson, D. H. *The Root Causes of Sudan's Civil Wars*. London, James Currey, 1995.

Karrar, A. S. *The Sufi Brotherhoods in the Sudan*. London, C. Hurst, 1992.

Katsuyoshi, F., and Markakis, J. *Ethnicity and Conflict in the Horn of Africa*. London, James Currey, 1994.

Keen, D. *The Benefits of Famine: A Political Economy of Famine and Relief in Southwestern Sudan, 1983–1989*. Princeton, NJ, Princeton University Press, 1994.

Khalid, M. *War and Peace in Sudan: A Tale of Two Countries*. London, Kegan Paul International, 2003.

Khalifa, M. E. *Reflections on the Sudanese Political System*. Khartoum, Sudan House, 1995.

Kibreab, G. *People on the Edge: Displacement, Land Use and the Environment in the Gedaref Region, Sudan*. London, James Currey, 1996.

Mackie, I. *Trek into Nuba*. Edinburgh, Pentland Press, 1994.

Metz, H. C. (Ed.). *Sudan: A Country Study*. Washington, DC, US Government Printing Office, 1991.

Minority Rights Group. *Sudan: Conflict and Minorities*. London, Minority Rights Group, 1995.

Niblock, T. *Class and Power in Sudan: The Dynamics of Sudanese Politics 1898–1985*. Albany, NY, State University Press of New York, 1987.

Nyaba, P. A. *The Politics of Liberation in South Sudan: An Insider's View*. Kampala, Fountain Publishers, 1997.

O'Ballance, E. *The Secret War in the Sudan 1955–1972*. London, Faber and Faber, 1977.

Oduho, J., and Deng, W. *The Problem of the Southern Sudan*. Oxford, Oxford University Press, 1963.

Petterson, D. *Inside Sudan: Political Islam, Conflict, and Catastrophe*. Philadelphia, PA, Westview, 1999.

Prendergast, J. *Sudanese Rebels at a Crossroads: Opportunities for Building Peace in a Shattered Land*. Washington, DC, Center of Concern, 1994.

Prunier, G. *From Peace to War: The Southern Sudan (1972–1984)*. Hull, University of Hull, 1986.

Darfur: The Ambiguous Genocide. London, Hurst, 2005.

Ramcharan, R. *Money, Meat and Inflation: Using Price Data to Understand an Export Shock in Sudan*. Washington, DC, IMF, 2002.

Reilly, H. *Seeking Sanctuary: Journeys to Sudan*. Bridgnorth, Eye Books, 2005

Rolandsen, O. H. *Guerrilla Government: Political Changes in the Southern Sudan during the 1990s*. Uppsala, Nordic Africa Institute, 2005.

Rone, J., *et al.* (Eds). *Civilian Devastation: Abuses by the Parties in the War in Southern Sudan*. New York, NY, Human Rights Watch, 1994.

Ruay, D. D. A. *The Politics of Two Sudans: The South and the North, 1921–1969*. Uppsala, Nordic Africa Institute, 1994.

Santi, P., and Hill, R. (Eds). *The Europeans in the Sudan 1834–1878*. Oxford, Oxford University Press, 1980.

Sidahmed, A. S. *Politics and Islam in Contemporary Sudan*. Richmond, Curzon Press, 1996.

Sidahmed, A.S., and Sidahmed, A. *Sudan*. Abingdon, Routledge, 2004.

Sikainga, A. A. *Slaves into Workers: Emancipation and Labor in Colonial Sudan*. Austin, TX, University of Texas Press, 1996.

Simone, T. A. M. *In Whose Image?* Chicago, IL, University of Chicago Press, 1994.

Sylvester, A. *Sudan under Nimeri*. London, Bodley Head, 1977.

Thomas, G. F. *Sudan: Struggle for Survival, 1984–1993*. London, Darf, 1993.

Voll, J. O. (Ed.). *Sudan: State and Society in Crisis*. Bloomington, IN, Indiana State University Press, 1991.

Woodward, P. *Sudan 1898–1989: The Unstable State*. Boulder, CO, Lynne Rienner Publishers, 1990.

SWAZILAND

Physical and Social Geography

A. MacGREGOR HUTCHESON

The Kingdom of Swaziland is one of the smallest political entities of continental Africa. Covering an area of only 17,363 sq km (6,704 sq miles), it straddles the broken and dissected edge of the South African plateau, surrounded by South Africa on the north, west and south, and separated from the Indian Ocean on the east by the Mozambique coastal plain.

PHYSICAL FEATURES

From the Highveld on the west, averaging 1,050 to 1,200 m in altitude, there is a step-like descent eastwards through the Middleveld (450 to 600 m) to the Lowveld (150 to 300 m). To the east of the Lowveld the Lebombo Range, an undulating plateau at 450–825 m, presents an impressive westward-facing scarp and forms the fourth of Swaziland's north–south aligned regions. Drainage is by four main systems flowing eastwards across these regions: the Komati and Umbeluzi rivers in the north, the Great Usutu river in the centre, and the Ngwavuma river in the south. The eastward descent is accompanied by a rise in temperature and by a decrease in mean annual rainfall from a range of 1,150–1,900 mm in the Highveld to one of 500–750 mm in the Lowveld, but increasing again to about 850 mm in the Lebombo range. The higher parts, receiving 1,000 mm, support temperate grassland, while dry woodland savannah is characteristic of the lower areas.

RESOURCES AND POPULATION

Swaziland's potential for economic development in terms of its natural resources is out of proportion to its size. The country's perennial rivers represent a high hydroelectric potential and their exploitation for irrigation in the drier Middleveld and Lowveld has greatly increased and diversified agricultural production. Sugar, however, is the dominant industry and has traditionally been the principal export commodity. Other major crops include cotton (in terms of the number of producers, this is the most important cash crop), maize, tobacco, rice, vegetables, citrus fruits and pineapples. The well-watered Highveld is particularly suitable for afforestation and over 120,000 ha (more than 100 plantations) have been planted with conifers and eucalyptus since the 1940s, creating the largest man-made forests in Africa. In 1998 there were some 98,000 ha of planted forest in the country.

Swaziland is also rich in mineral wealth. Once a major exporter of iron ore, this industry ceased with the exhaustion of high-grade ores, although considerable quantities of lower-grade ore remain. World demand for Swaziland's exports of chrysolite asbestos has declined in recent years as the result of health problems associated with this mineral. Coal holds the country's most important mineral potential, with reserves estimated at 1,000m. metric tons. Coal is currently mined at Maloma, mostly for export, and further reserves have been identified at Lobuka. Other minerals of note are cassiterite (a tin-bearing ore), kaolin, talc, pyrophyllite and silica.

Nearly one-half of the population live in the Middleveld, which contains some of the best soils in the country. This is Swaziland's most densely peopled region, with an average of 50 inhabitants per sq km, rising to more than 200 per sq km in some rural and in more developed areas. The total population of Swaziland (excluding absentee workers) was enumerated at 929,718 at the census of 1997, giving an overall density of 53.5 inhabitants per sq km. Preliminary results of this census indicated that nearly 50% of the population was under 15 years of age. According to UN estimates, the population at mid-2006 was 1,134,000, giving a population density of 65.3 per sq km.

A complex system of land ownership, with Swazi and European holdings intricately interwoven throughout the country, is partly responsible for considerable variations in the distribution and density of the population. Only about 40% of the country was under Swazi control at the time of independence in 1968, but this proportion steadily increased in subsequent years, as non-Swazi land and mineral concessions were acquired through negotiation and purchase. The Swazi Nation, to which most of the African population belongs, has now regained all mineral concessions.

Recent History

HUGH MACMILLAN

Based on an earlier article by RICHARD LEVIN

Swaziland, which began to emerge as a nation in the early 19th century, became a British protectorate following the Anglo-Boer War in 1903, and in 1907 became one of the High Commission Territories. A preoccupation of King Sobhuza II during his 61-year reign, which began in 1921, was the recovery of lands granted to settlers and speculators—and lost to neighbouring countries—in the late 19th century.

Moves towards the restoration of independence in the early 1960s were accompanied by a growth in political activity. The Ngwane National Liberatory Congress (NNLC), an African nationalist party formed in 1962 and led by Dr Ambrose Zwane, advocated independence on the basis of universal adult suffrage and a constitutional monarchy. Royalist interests formed the rival Imbokodvo National Movement, which won all seats in the new House of Assembly in the pre-independence elections in April 1967. The independence Constitution vested legislative authority in a bicameral parliament, with a proportion of its membership nominated by the King. Formal independence followed on 6 September 1968.

The post-independence rule of Sobhuza was characterized by stability and a significant expansion of the economy as investment flowed in, much of it from South Africa. Growing reliance on South African capital, along with Swaziland's membership of the Southern African Customs Union, restricted the country's economic and political choices. During this period the royal authorities acquired a significant material base in the economy through their control of Tibiyo Taka Ngwane and Tisuka Taka Ngwane, royal corporations that managed the investment of mineral royalties. Politically, the King extended his influence through his indirect control of the country's Tinkhundla (singular: Inkhundla), local authorities each grouping a small number of chieftaincies. In 1973, in accordance with a resolution of the House of Assembly, Sobhuza decreed a suspension of the Constitution and a formal ban on party political activity. Parliament effectively voted itself out of existence. By the time of Sobhuza's diamond jubilee in 1981, the authority of the Swazi monarchy was absolute. Sobhuza's death in August 1982 precipitated a prolonged and complex power struggle both within the royal family and among contending factions of the Liqoqo, a traditional advisory body. By early 1985, however, supporters of the Regent, Queen Ntombi Latfwala, mother of the 14-year-old heir apparent, Prince Makhosetive, had emerged as the group most likely to ensure an orderly succession and to overcome fractious and corrupt elements within the Liqoqo, the powers of which were substantially curtailed in 1985.

ACCESSION OF MSWATI III

Prince Makhosetive was installed as King Mswati III in April 1986. The young King, or his advisers, moved quickly to assert his authority. The Liqoqo was disbanded in May and the Cabinet reshuffled. In October Sotsha Dlamini, a former assistant commissioner of police, was appointed as Prime Minister. Despite the factionalism and personal intrigue within the royal family, both the King and the new Prime Minister indicated a determination to eliminate corruption from the administration. In September 1987 the legislature was dissolved in preparation for elections to be held in November, one year ahead of schedule. In November the electoral college duly appointed 40 members of the House of Assembly (none of whom had previously been members). Of the 10 additional members nominated by the King, eight were former deputies. The new House of Assembly and King Mswati each appointed 10 members of the Senate. A new Cabinet, appointed in late November, included Sotsha Dlamini, as Prime Minister, and three members of the previous Cabinet. The low turn-out at the polls for the election of the electoral college was widely interpreted as an indication of dissatisfaction with the Tinkhundla system. In October 1988 a majority of the members of the upper house supported a motion demanding a comprehensive review of the legislative structure. Sotsha Dlamini and the King both opposed the motion, claiming that political stability was best served by the maintenance of the Tinkhundla. Some 40 chiefs advocated the introduction of direct legislative elections in 1989.

RE-EMERGENCE OF PUDEMO

In July 1989 the King dismissed Sotsha Dlamini for 'disobedience' and replaced him as Prime Minister with Obed Dlamini, a founder member and former Secretary-General of the Swaziland Federation of Trade Unions (SFTU). This appointment was viewed as an attempt to allay labour unrest, which had led to strikes in the banking and transport systems. Until late 1989 open criticism of Mswati's maintenance of autocratic rule had been restricted to sporadic appearances of anti-Liqoqo pamphlets linked to the People's United Democratic Movement (PUDEMO), an organization that had been formed in 1983 during the regency. PUDEMO returned to prominence in 1990 with the distribution of new pamphlets that advocated a constitutional monarchy. PUDEMO criticized the King for his alleged excesses, condemned corruption and called for democratic reform.

By mid-1991 there appeared to be widespread public support for PUDEMO and in the second half of the year the organization began to establish civic structures in order to advance its objectives through legal organizations. The most prominent of these were the Swaziland Youth Congress (SWAYOCO) and the Human Rights Association of Swaziland. The King finally agreed to review the Tinkhundla and established a commission, under the chairmanship of Prince Masitsela, which became known as the Vusela ('Greeting') committee, to test opinion on political reforms.

In the second half of 1991 PUDEMO rejected the Vusela process and set out five demands, including the suspension of the state of emergency and the establishment of a constituent assembly to draw up a new constitution. In February 1992, the King announced the establishment of a second committee (Vusela 2) and included a member of PUDEMO among the commissioners.

PRESSURE FOR REFORM

In October 1992 the King approved a number of proposals, which had been submitted by Vusela 2. The House of Assembly (which was to be called the National Assembly) was to be expanded to 65 deputies and the Senate to 30 members. In addition, detention without trial was to cease, and a new constitution, confirming the monarchy, the fundamental rights of the individual and the independence of the judiciary, was to be drafted. Opposition groups protested at the committee's failure to recommend the immediate restoration of a multi-party political system.

PUDEMO announced its opposition to the reforms, and demanded that the Government organize a national convention to determine the country's constitutional future. King Mswati subsequently dissolved parliament and announced that he was to rule by decree, with the assistance of the Cabinet, pending the adoption of the new constitution and the holding of parliamentary elections.

The first round of elections to the expanded National Assembly took place on 25 September 1993. At the end of September the King repealed the legislation providing for detention without trial and also dissolved the Cabinet. The second round of parliamentary elections, which took place on 11 October, was contested by the three candidates in each Inkhundla who had obtained the highest number of votes in the first poll. In early November the former Minister of Works and Construction, Prince Jameson Mbilini Dlamini, was appointed Prime Minister, and a new Cabinet was formed.

In early 1995 there were outbreaks of arson and incendiary attacks on the properties of government officials, and on the parliament and high court buildings. The focus of opposition shifted from illegal political organizations to the trade union movement. On 13–14 March the SFTU brought the economy to a standstill with a general strike, staged in protest at the Government's failure to respond to demands that had been put forward in January of the previous year. In November 1995 a conference of political organizations (including PUDEMO and SWAYOCO) and the SFTU urged Mswati to leave the country for a temporary period of exile, pending the establishment of a multi-party democracy.

In January 1996 PUDEMO announced a campaign of civil disobedience, and later that month the SFTU initiated an indefinite general strike and there were clashes with the police. The SFTU subsequently suspended its industrial action to allow negotiations with the Government to proceed. In July King Mswati appointed a Constitutional Review Commission (CRC), comprising chiefs, political activists and unionists, to draft proposals for a new constitution. At the same time, Dr Barnabas Sibusiso Dlamini, an Executive Director of the IMF and a former Minister of Finance, was appointed Prime Minister.

The draft of the new Constitution was finally presented to the King in April 2001 and published in August of that year. It recommended the extension of the King's powers, the strengthening of traditional structures such as the Tinkhundla and the continuation of the ban on political parties. In December the King announced the appointment of a 15-member team—the Constitution Drafting Committee (CDC). Opposition groups considered this as yet another delaying tactic and accused the Government of manipulating the Commission's report. In February 2002 it was announced that the CDC would be chaired by the King's brother, Prince David Dlamini.

Continued Labour Unrest and Public Discontent

Meanwhile, the Industrial Relations Bill, which had been presented to parliament in 1998, was finally approved by the King in May 2000, as a result of pressure from the USA and the International Labour Organization (ILO). Swaziland was threatened with sanctions by the USA, however, when it became clear that the last-minute changes were unacceptable to both that country and the ILO, and changes to the legislation were agreed after talks with the ILO in mid-November. The enactment of new amendments was expedited and they received royal assent in time to meet the US deadline of 30 November. These changes were made against a background of continuous industrial action and popular protest, beginning in September 2000, with strike action against the labour legislation, and intensifying in October, with protests against the eviction from their land by the armed forces of 200 followers of two local chiefs in eastern Swaziland. This was the climax of a protracted dispute between Chief Mliba Fakudze of Macetjeni and Chief Mfutse Dlamini of KaMkhweli, on the one hand, and Prince Maguga Dlamini, an elder half-brother of King Mswati, on the other. The evictions were carried out under the terms of the Swaziland Administration Order of 1998, which gave the King the power to dismiss chiefs and purported to remove such issues from the jurisdiction of the courts.

In mid-October 2000 police dispersed a demonstration organized by the Swaziland National Association of Teachers in Mbabane in protest against the evictions, and the Government announced a ban on all trade union meetings in the country and the closure of the University of Swaziland. The Prime Minister also threatened to reintroduce detention without trial. In response to these measures, the trade unions called a meeting of their members at Nelspruit, South Africa, in early November. The resulting 'Nelspruit Declaration' called for the establishment of an interim government outside Swaziland, for strike action in mid-November and for a three-day closure of the Swazi borders at the end of the month. At the time of the strike Mario Masuku, the President of PUDEMO, was detained, but was released a few days later after court action, while the SFTU leader, Jan Sithole, was placed under police surveillance with his movements restricted. The border blockade at the end of the month received the support of the Congress of South African Trade Unions (COSATU) and was partially successful.

PRESS RELATIONS

Apart from the trade unions, the press continued to be a major focus of opposition and to bear the brunt of government pressure in 1999–2001. The editor of the Sunday edition of *The Times of Swaziland*, Bheki Makhubu, was detained in early October 1999 and charged with defamation under a colonial ordinance, following a series of articles that were critical of King Mswati's choice of Senteni Masango as one of two new royal fiancées.

In March 2000 the Government suddenly closed its own newspaper, the *Swaziland Observer*, which had been founded in 1981 as an alternative to the long-established *Times of Swaziland*. It had recently increased its circulation under an editor who had adopted a more independent stance and had published articles about government corruption and scandals. The Government denied that it was responsible for the closure of the newspaper, and in March 2001, on the anniversary of its closure, it resumed publication, apparently without explanation.

The press was one of the main targets of a royal decree issued in June 2001, which allowed the Minister of Broadcasting and Information, acting on behalf of the King, to ban newspapers without reason and to deny them the right of appeal to the courts. Other measures in the decree prevented any person or body, including the courts, from challenging the King, and allowed him to appoint and dismiss judges personally and to prevent the courts from considering matters that related to royal prerogatives. The SFTU threatened industrial action and there was a wave of protest from opposition leaders and foreign governments. The Government revoked the decree in July, in response to international diplomatic pressure and the threat of economic sanctions from the USA; a new decree was issued shortly afterwards, which retained certain sections of the original decree, including a provision allowing the detention of Swazi citizens without the option of bail for some offences.

INTERNAL SECURITY BILL

In June 2002 the King introduced the Internal Security Bill, intended to suppress political dissent. Popularly known as the 'makhundu', or fighting club, this provided for the imposition of a fine of up to E2,000 (some US $200) or a sentence of up to two years' imprisonment for anyone found guilty of wearing or carrying a banner or flag of any political formation and for the imprisonment for up to one year, without the option of a fine, of any person who incited others to participate in mass strikes or boycotts. People undertaking guerrilla training outside the country in order to commit acts of insurgency in Swaziland could be sentenced to up to 20 years' imprisonment. The Bill provoked harsh criticism from leaders of PUDEMO and the SFTU, as well as foreign governments, which considered it inconsistent with the proposed new Constitution and bill of rights.

JUDICIAL CRISIS

The monarchy was embroiled in controversy in October 2002 when Lindiwe Dlamini sought a High Court injunction against two royal courtiers, claiming that they had abducted her 18-year-old daughter, Zena Mahlangu, from her school near Mbabane on the instructions of King Mswati. The courtiers admitted taking Mahlangu, who the King had chosen to be his wife, but claimed that she was not taken against her will and that the King had been courting her by telephone. The Chief Justice, Stanley Sapire, issued a court order instructing whoever was holding the girl to release her. Security guards at the royal palace where she was alleged to be held refused to accept the court order, and lawyers acting for her mother subsequently sought an order holding them in contempt of court, which was denied by Sapire. Mahlangu eventually announced that she was not being held against her will, and that she was happy to marry the King. The case was then suspended indefinitely. Sapire stated that he had been threatened by the Attorney-General and the heads of the army police and prisons service, but King Mswati denied any knowledge of this alleged intimidation. Sapire resigned in April 2003 amid rumours that he was to be demoted and replaced by another South African judge, Jacobus Annandale. The President of the Swaziland Law Association, Paul Shilubane, described Sapire's demotion as a case of 'constructive dismissal'. The formal marriage of King Mswati to Zena Mahlangu, as his 11th wife, was announced in June 2004.

It was announced at the end of November 2002 that the six South African judges of the Swaziland Court of Appeal, led by Leon Steyn, had resigned in protest at the refusal of the Government to uphold two rulings: one, that the King had no power to overrule the National Assembly and rule by decree; and another, that held the Chief of Police in contempt for obstructing a court order. Prime Minister Sibusiso Dlamini reportedly stated that the Government would not be bound by the rulings of the Court of Appeal and the Attorney-General declared that the judges were under 'external influence'. The judges of the High Court subsequently announced that they would refuse to sit or set dates for hearings; a strike by members of the legal profession followed. In April 2003 the International Bar Association issued a report in which it stated that the ongoing judicial crisis was due to a 'blurring of the lines' between the executive, legislature and judiciary. A report by the IMF in May 2004 referred to an economic crisis, a widening deficit and to the detrimental effects of the legal crisis on investor confidence.

In mid-September 2004 the Government announced the resolution of the judicial crisis and called upon the Court of Appeal to reconstitute itself. This followed intervention by the Commonwealth Secretariat which brokered an agreement allowing for the restoration of the rule of law. Under the terms of this deal the Government withdrew statements that had been made in November 2002 by the Attorney-General impugning the integrity of the Court and suggesting that it was under external influence. It also undertook to correct its failure to implement various court orders and to release prisoners awaiting trial, who had been held in detention since 2002 in defiance of bail orders. In mid-November 2004 it was reported that the judges of the Court had returned to work in the belief that their orders had been implemented. After discovering that this was not the case, they announced that they could not resume their duties. It later became apparent that the Government had released 29 prisoners awaiting trial, but was still reluctant to implement other outstanding orders, including those relating to the evicted people of KwaMkheli and Macetjeni. In April 2005 the Government declared the 'rule of law crisis' to be over, and reports indicated that some evicted people were returning to their homes. In late 2006, however, it was reported that some of the evictees remained in internal exile or in South Africa. By that time the Court of Appeal had been reconstituted with new personnel. Early in 2007 a new Chief Justice, Francis Banda, a Malawian, was appointed, and there were complaints that his appointment on a fixed-term contract undermined the independence of the judiciary.

CONSTITUTIONAL CRISIS

In addition to the legal crisis, the ongoing constitutional crisis created further controversy. In April 2003 police fired teargas at demonstrators who were commemorating the 30th anniversary of the suspension of the Constitution in 1973. On 31 May King Mswati announced the dissolution of the National Assembly and promised to hold elections in October. At the same time Prince David, the King's brother and Chairman of the CDC, announced that the new draft Constitution had been completed. He made it clear, however, that the forthcoming elections would be held under the Tinkhundla system, which was enshrined in the draft Constitution as 'the unifying symbol in the kingdom'. The new Constitution was not formally presented to the King until November—after the general election. In what appeared to be a further delaying tactic, it was announced that it would not be published until it had been translated into the national language, siSwati.

In May 2004 a newly formed pressure group, the National Constituent Assembly (NCA), which brought together churches and civic associations, announced a legal challenge to what it claimed was the King's intention of promulgating the new Constitution by decree. In June the NCA petitioned the High Court, demanding that the CDC should be required to hold public hearings and receive submissions from interested parties. The High Court agreed that it would hear the petition in August, though no date was fixed. Although it had been promised that the final draft of the Constitution would be presented to the National Assembly early in 2004, it was not, in fact, presented to the Assembly until June 2005.

GENERAL ELECTION, SEPTEMBER–OCTOBER 2003

The general election was held in two stages. In the primary elections held on 20 September 2003, 1,500 candidates contested the 55 constituencies; of this number, 333 were chosen to go through as candidates in the second round. Only 20 sitting deputies were selected to go through to the second round and only 30 of the second-round candidates were women. Some 228,000 people were registered to vote out of a potential electorate of 400,000. A number of foreign groups observed the election, including the Commonwealth Observer Group (COG). In its final report the COG entirely rejected the credibility of the electoral process in a country where, it said, the parliament had no power and political parties were banned. It was also highly critical of the draft Constitution for its lack of provision for the transfer of power from the King to the legislature. The COG recommended that the draft Constitution be amended accordingly, that there should be an independent electoral commission and that political parties should be legalized. Although none of the 'underground' political parties contested the election, the leader of the NNLC, former Prime Minister Obed Dlamini, was elected to the new National Assembly. He was reported to have stood for election as an individual and not as a representative of the party.

King Mswati had dissolved the cabinet before the second round of the 2003 election and removed the long-serving Prime Minister Sibusiso Dlamini from office. After the election the King appointed a new Government. Eight of its members were drawn from the 10 nominated members of the National Assembly. He also appointed a new Prime Minister, Absolom Themba ('AT') Dlamini, who had served for 10 years as Managing Director of Tibiyo Taka Ngwane, the national development agency. Albert Shabangu was appointed as Deputy Prime Minister.

ROYAL EXTRAVAGANCE

In January 2004 the UN's World Food Programme reported that it was feeding 250,000 people in Swaziland—about one-quarter of the population—and in February the King spoke of a humanitarian disaster in the country as a result of famine and HIV/AIDS. The country's nurses went on strike in February and March, demanding the payment of overtime arrears, which dated back to 2001. Against this backdrop, it was reported in January 2004 that the Government was planning to spend US $14m. on the construction of a palace for each of the King's 11 wives. There were also press reports in April of lavish expenditure on the King's public birthday celebrations in Mbabane. In March the opening of the new sitting of parliament had been postponed when the Speaker of the House of Assembly, Marwick Khumalo, was forced to resign; no official explanation was given, but Khumalo had opposed the King's plans to buy an executive jet aeroplane. He was replaced by the Deputy Speaker, Trusty Gina. The King reopened the legislature later that month with the announcement that some $18m. would be channelled into humanitarian programmes.

During 2004–05 there were continued reports of royal extravagance. These focused on the purchase by the King for US $500,000 of a DaimlerChrysler Maybach limousine, said to be one of the most expensive cars in the world and the only one to have been sold to southern Africa. It was also reported that luxury vehicles were being bought for each of the King's wives at a total cost of E5m. and that the building of palaces for the King's wives and the widows of his father, King Sobhuza, was continuing. In April 2005 there was further criticism of the expenditure of $1m. on the King's birthday celebrations, which were held in the Manzini Stadium with a crowd of 20,000 people. Linked to reports of royal extravagance had been reports in February that the King had taken two new fiancées. Protests regarding the King's birthday celebrations again occurred in 2007 and it was reported earlier that year that he had married his 13th wife, Phindile Nkambule, that he had taken another fiancée, and that he had, by that time, fathered 30 children.

INTRODUCTION OF THE NEW CONSTITUTION AND ABORTIVE PROTESTS

In early January 2005 the trade union leadership called for a two-day national strike at the end of the month in protest against royal extravagance and the terms of the new Constitution. At the same time PUDEMO promised more direct political action. There appeared, however, to have been a disappointing response to these appeals and it was reported that only a small number of the country's workers participated in the strike and public meetings.

The constitutional legislation was presented for approval to a joint sitting of the Senate and the National Assembly in June 2005. The Constitution concentrated executive power in the King and preserved the Tinkhundla as the basis of the parliamentary system. The King would have the power to appoint the Prime Minister and the Cabinet, the principal secretaries and the judges. He could also dissolve the legislature. Political parties were not banned, but neither was there any provision for their recognition: indeed, they were not mentioned at all. The bill of rights guaranteed freedoms of speech and assembly, but gave the King the right to abrogate these in the public interest. In introducing the Constitution Bill, Prince David had asked the legislature to pass the Bill without amendments. The Bill was approved by the legislature in mid-June, but the King then demanded that there should be a further joint sitting to reconsider a clause recognizing Christianity as the official religion of Swaziland and another relating to taxation of the royal family. Having met with the King's approval, an amended version of the Constitution was finally signed on 26 July; *inter alia*, it confirmed the King as absolute monarch, but included a clause that would allow for his removal and replacement by the Queen Mother under certain conditions (it was not clear, however, when, or how, this might occur). The King was immune from prosecution by the courts and members of the royal family were exempt from paying tax. It was announced that the new Constitution would come into effect within six months and that there would then be parliamentary elections.

On 10 February 2006 King Mswati announced to a gathering of 5,000 people at the Ludzidzini royal residence that the new Constitution had entered into force. There was continuing uncertainty, however, as to the position of political parties under the new dispensation. In April King Mswati stated that there was no ban on political parties, but he was also quoted as saying that parties were a minority interest in Swaziland and that the country could not afford them. There was evidence that the opposition was divided on how to respond to the new Constitution. The leader of the NNLC, Obed Dlamini, suggested that his party would try to register in order to test the legal position. The leader of PUDEMO, Mario Masuku, indicated that his party rejected the Constitution outright because of the lack of consultation with the opposition on its formulation, the veto over legislation that it appeared to give to the King and the fact that it had been introduced by royal edict, rather than by legislative vote; furthermore, the party refused to participate in any elections organized under the terms of the 'royal Constitution'. PUDEMO was critical of the Commonwealth Secretary-General, Don MacKinnon, who visited Swaziland in February and greeted the new Constitution as 'not perfect' but 'a step forward'.

The attention of the political parties had been distracted by the arrest between December 2005 and January 2006 of 16 political activists who were charged with treason for alleged involvement in a spate of petrol bomb attacks against government offices and police houses. Those charged included Ignatius Dlamini, the Secretary-General of PUDEMO, and Wandile Dludlu, a student leader at the University of Swaziland. In granting bail of E3,000 to each of the accused in March, the Chief Justice, Jacobus Annandale, stated that the prosecution had brought no evidence to link the accused to the bombings and instructed the Government to investigate allegations made by the accused of torture and beatings. In February one of the accused, Mduduzi Dlamini, had pleaded guilty to treason and to involvement in the bombing of the Sandleni constituency centre in August 2005. He was sentenced to two years' imprisonment, one of which was suspended, with the option of a E10,000 fine. Opposition spokesmen claimed that his plea had been extracted through torture and that the light sentence implied that the Government intended to use him as a state witness.

PUDEMO held its first conference for five years in Mlumati, South Africa in June–July 2006. The conference's concluding declaration spoke of the oppression of women and the corruption of the royal élite in Swaziland. It also protested at what it said was the continued concentration of legislative, executive and judicial power in the monarchy. A legal challenge to the Constitution, demanding the publication of evidence of popular support, was mounted by the NCA in September, but had yet to reach a conclusion by mid-2007. A general election was scheduled to take place in 2008; however, the legal status of political parties remained obscure.

In July 2006 COSATU published a report which pointed to serious divisions within the SFTU; three unions, including the important Swaziland National Association of Civil Service had been suspended from it. The report also pointed to continuing tension between the leaders of the SFTU and PUDEMO, as well as between the SFTU and the rival Swaziland Federation of Labour. These divisions weakened the SFTU and the political opposition at a time when formal employment and trade union membership was in significant decline.

A march on the Prime Minister's office by university students protesting at the suspension of scholarships was broken up by riot police in September 2006 and a number of people were injured or arrested. In early December police dispersed a gathering of PUDEMO and SWAYOCO members in Manzini before they could begin a planned protest march.

THE HIV/AIDS CRISIS

Perhaps the greatest single problem confronting Swaziland is the HIV/AIDS pandemic. The rejection by Parliament during the latter half of 1999 of proposed public health legislation, which included measures relating to HIV/AIDS, was regarded by some as symbolizing the failure of the country to come to terms with the pandemic. The UN estimated that 33.4% of Swaziland's adult population (aged between 15 and 49 years) was living with HIV/AIDS in 2005. In October 2000 it was reported that the infection rate among children aged between five and 14 years was 14%. The Swaziland National Aids Programme reported in March 2001 that the rate of HIV infection detected in women attending ante-natal clinics in the country was 34.2%, compared with 3.6% in 1992. Representatives of AIDS organizations in the country protested at a government decision to transfer the HIV/AIDS budget of E13m., which had been criticized as inadequate, from education to the purchase of antiretroviral drugs. In August 2002 the Government announced that antiretrovirals would be made available to pregnant women in order to prevent the transmission of HIV to their children, and that universal provision would be made when sufficient medical and financial resources became available. In June 2003 the King announced the establishment of the Royal Initiative to Combat Aids.

In June 2005 Faith Dlamini, the Co-ordinator for AIDS Prevention, stated that the situation was so acute that it threatened the very existence of the Swazi people. It was estimated that one child in every 15 had been orphaned as a result of HIV/AIDS and that the proportion would reach one child in eight within five years. Spokespersons for concerned non-governmental organizations believed that the cancellation of World Aids Day in Swaziland in December 2005, on the grounds that it coincided with the beginning of the Ncwala festival, reflected a continuing lack of seriousness about the situation. The South African Treatment Action Committee in a statement in April 2006 linked Swaziland's high HIV/AIDS statistics to the lack of democracy in the country. There was also criticism of the announcement by King Mswati in August 2005 of the end of the *umcwasho*—a period of compulsory abstinence from sexual relations by, or with, girls younger than 18. In November 2006 there was an unprecedented boycott of parliament by deputies protesting against an announcement by the Minister of Health and Social Welfare, Njabulo Mabuza, that the Government was unable to pay grants to the elderly, many of whom were responsible for the care of HIV/AIDS orphans. It was estimated that there were by then 80,000 HIV/AIDS orphans in the country. In June 2007 a crisis in food security that threatened 400,000 people was linked not only to a serious drought, but also to the loss of family labour through HIV/AIDS.

EXTERNAL RELATIONS

After achieving independence in 1968 Swaziland joined a number of international organizations, including the Commonwealth, the UN and the Organization of African Unity (now the African Union). It later also became a member of the Southern African Development Community. During the Cold War Swaziland adopted a conservative position with regard to international relations and maintained close links with the United Kingdom and the USA. It also maintained diplomatic relations with Israel and Taiwan and received substantial development assistance from those countries. With the end of the Cold War, Swaziland came under increasing pressure from the USA to move towards the establishment of a multi-party democracy. The relocation, from Swaziland to Botswana, of the regional office of the United States Agency for International Development and the withdrawal of the US Peace Corps from the kingdom were announced in 1996. These moves were widely seen as signifying US disapproval of the slow pace of political reform in Swaziland. The US Government continued to apply pressure for democratization and the reform of industrial legislation. In February 2002 Denmark suspended development aid to Swaziland in protest at its human rights record. During 2004–05 there were frequent adverse comments in the British and South African press regarding Swaziland's human rights record and its failure to implement democratic reform. These comments focused on royal extravagance and the King's frequent marriages, which were associated in the media with the HIV/AIDS crisis and food shortages. Swaziland was linked with Zimbabwe as a southern African country with a similar, or even less satisfactory, record of governance and disregard for the rule of law.

In what was seen as a major blow to Swaziland's international status, the British Government announced in December 2004 that it was to close its High Commission in Mbabane at the end of 2006. It would appoint an honorary consul and would otherwise conduct its relations with Swaziland from the High Commission in Pretoria, South Africa. This would mark the end of more than a century of direct British representation in the country. Although this was presented as an economizing measure, and Lesotho was to suffer a similar demotion, it was widely regarded as a rebuke to Swaziland's poor record of governance. In February 2006 the new British High Commissioner to South Africa, Paul Boateng, who was also accredited to Swaziland, presented his credentials to King Mswati. His remarks on the need for the recognition of political parties were widely reported and earned a rebuke from King Mswati in April. In May it was reported that the European Union was suspending direct aid to the Swazi Government, citing problems of governance and inadequate fiscal controls.

As a small and land-locked country, Swaziland's most important bilateral relationships have been with its two neighbours, South Africa and Mozambique. From the mid-1950s until shortly before Swaziland's independence in 1968, South Africa regarded the country as the potential nucleus of a Swazi 'Bantustan' ('homeland'). Conversely, King Sobhuza II harboured the ambition of reclaiming from South Africa areas in the eastern Transvaal and northern Natal that were separated from the Swazi kingdom in the 19th century. The achievement of independence by Mozambique in 1975 created a situation in which the exiled African National Congress (ANC) of South Africa was able to use Swaziland as a corridor for the movement of recruits from South Africa and for the infiltration of guerrilla fighters. This posed a threat to South Africa's security and provided the basis for negotiations between the Governments of Swaziland and South Africa about a possible 'land deal.' South Africa offered to transfer to Swaziland the KaNgwane 'Bantustan' in the Transvaal and the Ingwavuma district in northern Natal (the acquisition of the latter area would have afforded Swaziland direct access to the sea) in exchange for the imposition of more stringent restrictions on the activities of the ANC. The first step in these negotiations was the conclusion in February 1982 of a secret security agreement between the two countries. King Sobhuza's death in August removed the only obstacle to an all-out offensive on the ANC, and by the end of that year the first of a series of round-ups and 'deportations' of alleged ANC members had occurred. However, as a result of legal obstacles and strong opposition in South Africa, the proposals for the land transfer were finally abandoned in 1984.

In 1984, within days of the signing of the Nkomati Accord between South Africa and Mozambique, the Swazi Government revealed the existence of its security agreement with South Africa. The systematic suppression of ANC activities intensified, and open collaboration between the two countries led to gun battles in Manzini as speculation increased that this policy was being orchestrated by a South African trade mission that was established in Mbabane earlier that year. In January 1985 the Swazi Prime Minister defended his Government's close relationship with South Africa and implied that the attacks against the ANC would continue. The ANC responded by creating a sophisticated underground network in Swaziland. The conflict escalated in 1986 and armed raids by South African security personnel resulted in a number of ANC deaths in border areas and in Manzini. Increased public outrage at these activities led the Swazi Prime Minister publicly to accuse South Africa of responsibility and to condemn a raid in August as an 'illegal act of aggression', the first open attack on South African policies by a Swaziland Government. None the less, South African security forces continued to carry out operations within Swaziland, in which ANC activists were abducted or murdered. The era of political reform within South Africa that followed the release of Nelson Mandela in February 1990 brought a general improvement in relations between the two countries, and in late 1993 formal diplomatic relations were established.

It emerged in February 2001 that King Mswati had still not abandoned his determination to reincorporate parts of the Mpumalanga and KwaZulu/Natal provinces into Swaziland. He declared this intention in a letter to South African President Thabo Mbeki, which he handed to the Deputy President, Jacob Zuma, during a visit by the latter to the kingdom in that month. In June 2003 Prince Khuzulwandle, Chairman of the Swaziland Border Adjustment Committee, criticized Mbeki for refusing to discuss realignments to the border. In November 2006 the Swazi Government announced that it would be taking the border dispute to the International Court of Justice (ICJ) at The Hague, Netherlands. A meeting between President Mbeki and King Mswati to discuss the dispute, which had apparently been proposed by Mbeki in 2005, had still not taken place by mid-2007.

During 1996–97 prominent South African organizations, including the ANC and COSATU, expressed support for the SFTU's demands for political reform, prompting the Swazi Government to protest at interference in its domestic affairs. In October 1997 the South African Broadcasting Corporation's coverage of strike action organized by the SFTU was condemned as inaccurate and biased by the Swazi Government; its broadcasts in Swaziland were subsequently suspended. In April 2006 COSATU organized blockades within South Africa at several of the border crossings into Swaziland, including Oshoek and Golela. At the Matsamo border post the South African police opened fire with rubber bullets and injured a number of people. Among those arrested was Joel Nkosi, First Deputy President of COSATU. (Nkosi and the others were eventually acquitted.) In an indication of tension between COSATU and the SFTU, SFTU leader Jan Sithole had earlier advised Swazi trade unionists not to participate in these blockades. This tension was reported to be related an ongoing investigation by COSATU, on behalf of the International Confederation of Free Trade Unions, into alleged irregularities in the affairs of the SFTU.

During the prolonged period of civil unrest within Mozambique, considerable numbers of Mozambicans crossed into Swaziland in search of food and employment, an influx that was linked by Swazi police to an increase in armed crime, and resulted in several mass arrests in urban areas. A sizeable 'unofficial' population of Mozambicans gathered in urban areas; these Mozambicans, many of whom were highly skilled workers, were perceived as a threat to the jobs of Swazi urban residents. The presence of Mozambican refugees in rural areas also caused tension, owing to a shortage of land to accommodate them. In June 1990 the Governments of Swaziland and Mozambique signed an extradition agreement providing for the repatriation of alleged criminals and illegal immigrants, which was designed to reduce the incidence of smuggling between the two countries. In 1992, however, tension at the border with Mozambique increased, following reports of raids against Swazi farms by members of the Mozambican armed forces. Following the ratification of a Mozambican peace accord in October 1992, an agreement, which was signed by the Governments of Swaziland and Mozambique and the UN High Commissioner for Refugees in August 1993, provided for the repatriation of some 24,000 Mozambican nationals resident in Swaziland. In early 1994 discussions took place between Swazi and Mozambican officials to seek mutually satisfactory arrangements for the joint patrol of the border, and in 1995 it was announced that the Mhlumeni border post, closed since the 1970s, would reopen as the second official transit point between the two countries.

In recent years an area of conflict, and co-operation, between Swaziland, South Africa and Mozambique has been the use of the water resources of the Komati river. The apparently excessive use of the river for hydroelectric projects and irrigation schemes in South Africa and Swaziland has severely reduced the flow of water into Mozambique and led that country to take a claim for compensation to the ICJ. In 1995 the Swedish Government provided funds, through the Swedish International Development Agency, for the establishment of the Inkomati Shared River Basin Initiative (ISRBI). This resulted in the presentation by the three countries to the Second World Water Security Forum at The Hague in March 2000 of a proposed scheme for fair and equal access to the water of the river. Mozambique's representative on the ISRBI stated that this plan might encourage the country to withdraw its claim for compensation. Mozambique did not, however, become a signatory to the related Nkomati River Basin Accord until 2002. In the following year the Maguga Dam, the water from which was shared by South Africa and Swaziland on a 60:40

basis, was opened. Mozambique subsequently protested at the reduced flow of the river across its border. In 1998 the Lubombo Spatial Development Initiative (see Economy) was established by the three countries to encourage investment in communications and tourism in the Lubombo, Pongola, St Lucia Bay, Nkosi Bay and Ponto do Ouro areas. The first phase of the initiative involved expenditure of more than E600m. on improvements to transport infrastructure.

Economy

DONALD L. SPARKS

Based on an earlier article by GRAHAM MATTHEWS

Swaziland is the second smallest state in mainland Africa. In 2005, according to the World Bank, the kingdom's gross national income (GNI) was US $2,280 per head, about three times the regional average of US $746, placing it in the world's 'lower middle income' group of countries. From 1985–94 Swaziland recorded impressive average annual growth of its gross domestic product (GDP) of 7.3%, the region's highest after Botswana. During 1995–2005 GDP per head increased, in real terms, by an average of 0.4% per year. Overall GDP increased, in real terms, at an average annual rate of 2.4% in 1998–2005, below the regional average; growth in 2002 was 3.4%, declining in 2003 to 2.2%, 2.1% in 2004, 1.8% in 2005 and an estimated 1.2% in 2006. That slower growth was due to the continued appreciation of the currency (affecting exports), drought, problems associated with the HIV/AIDS pandemic (with an infection rate of 33% of those between the ages 15–49, Swaziland has one of the world's highest HIV/AIDS prevalence rates) and competition from Asian textile producers. Bad weather conditions have had a significant negative impact on farming, affecting at least 25% of the population. Since independence there has been significant diversification of the economy away from early dependence upon agriculture and mining. Industry and services contributed the largest shares of GDP in 2005, with 48.0% and 40.4%, respectively; agriculture and forestry contributed 11.6%. Despite its relative diversification and wealth, Swaziland has not escaped the extremes of income distribution familiar elsewhere in Africa. More than two-thirds of the resident population comprises families earning generally poor incomes from smallholder cash cropping or subsistence agriculture on Swazi Nation Land (SNL). Moreover, the condition of the rural poor has been largely unimproved by periods of rapid growth since independence.

Swaziland's development has been dominated in many ways by South Africa, the principal regional power. South African capital and imports, the Southern African Customs Union (SACU), the South African labour market and the Common Monetary Area (CMA) have shaped the economy and restricted the scope for an independent economic policy. However, a consistent determination to maintain an investment climate attractive to foreign business and a policy of accepting the dominance of its powerful neighbour have brought Swaziland a rate of post-independence capital formation not achieved in most African states. In the late 1980s the kingdom benefited as foreign and South African companies relocated to Swaziland, often to escape anti-apartheid sanctions. In the early 1990s, however, Swaziland experienced the negative repercussions of political uncertainty and economic recession in South Africa. Also, since the mid-1990s, many firms that might have chosen to locate, or relocate, in Swaziland have opted for South Africa, given the political uncertainty and lack of skilled manpower in Swaziland. Swaziland traditionally supplied the South African mines with labour, and those miners' remittances back to Swaziland provided a substantial income base. However, during the past few years the number of Swazi miners has fallen, along with their remittances. This has been partially balanced by an increasing number of Swazi professionals moving to South Africa and the United Kingdom.

AGRICULTURE AND FORESTRY

Although the agricultural sector accounts for a declining share of GDP (11.6% in 2005 compared with 14.3% in 2004), it remains the backbone of the economy, employing about one-third of the labour force. Agro-industry continues to contribute the majority of manufacturing value added; it provides a significant amount of formal employment. Over one-half of the total land area is SNL, where traditional subsistence farming is conducted on land held by the monarchy, access to which is managed by the Swazi aristocracy and local chiefs. However, more than one-half of all SNL is designated as Rural Development Areas, and cash cropping of rain-watered crops, particularly maize and cotton, contributes significantly to total agricultural production when climatic conditions are favourable. The remainder of the land, the Title Deed Land (TDL), comprises individual tenure farms, owned by commercial companies, wealthy Swazis and white settlers. The principal agricultural commodities are sugar (of which Swaziland is continental Africa's second largest exporter), maize, citrus fruits, pineapples (for canning) and cotton. Livestock-rearing is an important sub-sector of the economy, particularly on SNL, where cattle serve as a store of value, a unit of account, and are used for various cultural purposes (for example, bride price).

Swaziland has been under a long-lasting drought, and the hardest hit areas have been in the southern and eastern areas of Shiselweni and Lubombo. About 200,000 people are surviving on food aid due to severe crop failures. The National Disaster Task Team announced in 2007 that the country is likely to face a food shortage as bad as that experienced in 1992. In addition, as South Africa is also experiencing bad weather, it will be unlikely to export sufficient maize to Swaziland. In 2006–07 the price of maize rose about 90%, from E1,250 to E2,300 per metric ton.

Sugar is the dominant agricultural export, earning US $184m. in 2004. The 2004 season was adversely affected by the worst drought in a century, with sugar cane growers at a particular disadvantage since they could not irrigate to normal levels. Output declined from 628,191 metric tons in the 2003 season to 539,000 tons in 2004. In addition, world price declines have decreased profits, especially for smallholders. The world price at mid-2007 was actually lower than Swazi production costs (including transportation costs and a stronger rand). Brazilian sugar has also become competitive in the SACU market, causing both South Africa and Swaziland to cut their prices by 7% in late 2003. Output in 2006 was 623,357 tons, down from 652,735 tons in 2005.

Since 1987 increased quantities of sugar have been sold and refined locally, with the establishment of Coca-Cola's soft drink concentrate plant, Cadbury's confectionery factory and a new sugar refinery. Soft drink concentrates became Swaziland's major export in 1996, with sales of US $170m. more than doubling, to $384m., in 1998, before declining in 1999, to $276m. Conco is Swaziland's largest privately owned foreign-exchange earner. There are three sugar mills in the country, in which the Swazi Nation has substantial shareholdings. The sugar industry was adversely affected by the industrial action that disrupted economic activity across the country in 1996 and 1997. In terms of production, 12,000 tons of white sugar, worth E24m., were lost.

Recent cereal harvests have failed to meet domestic requirements. The 2000 maize crop was badly affected by adverse weather conditions and production was 91,000 metric tons in that year, compared with 112,500 tons in 1999. Production in 2001 was 74,400 tons and 76,200 tons in 2002; according to unofficial estimates, the 2003 crop was 69,300 tons. Maize growers were faced with declining prices and higher costs to the extent that by 2004 the cost of production (E1,100–E1,500 per ton) was greater than the offered price (of E1,000 per ton). It was estimated that some 70% of the maize crop was destroyed by drought in February 2005.

Supported by the role of cattle as a store of wealth in customary society, the national herd represents a significant environmental problem in terms of the overgrazing of SNL. Frozen and canned meat is exported to the European Union (EU) under quota. South African cattle from Mpumalanga province brought foot-and-mouth disease into Swaziland in late 2000. Swaziland instituted strict quarantine operations and closed, for several months, the abattoir in Matasapha. Mozambique quickly banned Swazi beef imports and the effects were also experienced on the EU market. Several thousand head of cattle in the northern part of Swaziland were scheduled for slaughter, and an intensive vaccination programme was carried out. The disease was eradicated from the country in 2001.

Swaziland achieved production of citrus fruit (mainly oranges and grapefruit) in the range of 66,000–72,000 metric tons annually through the early 1990s. Sales of citrus and canned fruit fell drastically in 1998, to US $30m., compared with $133m. in 1996. In 2001 exports of canned fruit earned only $10m.

Smallholders on SNL grow most of the kingdom's cotton. The diversification of certain sugar estates into raising an irrigated crop and the rapid expansion of the area planted to cotton by SNL farmers combined to raise output from 9,127 metric tons of seed cotton in 1983 to a record 39,900 tons in 1991. The number of cotton producers fell from more than 10,000 in the early 1990s to less than 4,000 by 1999. Cotton prices fell by 16% during 1999, and by mid-2001 land cultivated for cotton production had declined to around 17,000 ha, down from 35,000 ha in 1998/99. Due to a drop in cotton prices from E4 per kg in 2003 to E2.10 per kg in 2005, the Government launched a E1m.-subsidy programme for cotton farmers. However, there were delays in getting the funds to many farmers, who had to postpone their planting. This programme was expected to last for the next six years.

In 1998 Swaziland had some 98,000 ha of planted forest, representing 6% of the country's total land area. Of the total, more than one-half was devoted to supplying the kingdom's main forestry industry, the Usutu pulp mill, which produces unbleached wood pulp. The mill is Swaziland's third largest source of export earnings and the Usutu Pulp Co currently produces around 250,000 metric tons annually. In 2002 the company had 1,539 employees, but was considering making 900 workers redundant. In 2004 the People's Republic of China became Swaziland's primary destination for wood pulp exports, surpassing South Africa, Japan, the USA and Europe for the first time. Wood pulp exports increased to 176,775 tons in 2004, from 156,340 tons the previous year. These exports were valued at E410.5m. Of the remaining area planted to timber, 27,331 ha was for sawlogs in 1991; a further 12,331 ha (mostly gum) was planted for mine timber. The kingdom has three saw mills supplying a small but diversified timber products industry, and pine shelving of Swazi manufacture is sold in the British market, in 'kit' form.

In 2006, as a result of new production from the Kpmati basin irrigation scheme, the sugar-cane crop was expected to increase. However, cotton and citrus production has fallen. Owing to low maize output, food security remains unstable in rural areas.

MINING AND MANUFACTURING

Mining and quarrying have represented a declining proportion of GDP overall since independence, although the kingdom is relatively rich in mineral resources. From 10% in the 1960s, the sector's contribution to GDP fell to 0.6% in 2004. The asbestos mine remained the major contributor to this sector, accounting for E46.5m. in 1996. The poor performance was due to reduced output at the Maloma colliery and to the phasing-out of the diamond mine, which closed at the end of 1996. In addition to the exported minerals, quarry stone is produced to meet the needs of the local construction industry. Asbestos was the first mineral product to be exploited in the country on a large scale. The Havelock mine was developed in the 1930s, and it was not until 1962 that it was overtaken by the sugar industry as the territory's leading export earner. Since then, however, the identification of health problems associated with asbestos and the depletion of reserves have resulted in the decline of this sub-sector. A steady 30,000–40,000 metric tons were exported annually for decades, but production declined to 22,804 tons in 1988. Output fluctuated thereafter, reaching 22,912 tons in 1999, before falling in 2000, to 12,690 tons. Asbestos mining ceased in 2001.

Coal holds the country's most important mineral potential, with reserves estimated at 1,000m. metric tons. Coal production was estimated to have reached a record 550,000 tons in 2004.

Dwyka Diamonds Ltd, an Australian mining company with South African operations, conducted an initial geological exploration of the 425 sq km Swazigold area where there is potential for high-grade gold deposits.

Except for processing agricultural and forestry products, the majority of Swaziland's manufacturing is based at the Matsapha industrial estate, south of the capital. Prior to the new investment in the sector in the latter part of the 1980s, four-fifths of manufaturing's value added derived from agroindustries of various kinds, ranging from sugar, timber and woodpulp mills to fruit, cotton-and meatprocessing plants. Manufacturing contributed 37.2% of GDP in 2005.

Despite these developments within the kingdom, arguably the single most important factor in the improved fortunes of the manufacturing sector in the late 1980s was renewed unrest in South Africa and the imposition of international sanctions against that country in the aftermath of its suppression under a state of emergency. It was against this background that Coca-Cola relocated its regional concentrate plant to Swaziland in 1987. This single decision added some 5% to real value added in manufacturing by 1988.

Since the late 1980s there has been encouraging diversification of the manufacturing sector, and Swaziland now ranks among some of the most industrialized of African economies. The pace of investment slowed in the 1990s, however, as a combined result of drought, regional recession, labour unrest and a drift back to post-apartheid South Africa of earlier relocations. Several smaller factories producing knitwear, footwear, gloves, refrigerators, office equipment, beverages, confectionery, pine furniture, safety glass and bricks were established during the investment boom, creating many new jobs.

Refrigerators have become an important source of export earnings for Swaziland, with sales of US $69m. in 1999. The Fridge Master factory was to increase production in 1999 to supply US-based General Electric with its new line of products for African markets; a further 200 workers were to be employed, increasing the work-force to 1,500. However, by 1999 the company had become embroiled in a dispute with the authorities, which questioned the high number of deaths among its staff. Denying the accusation that these were caused by toxic chemicals used in the manufacturing process, the company attributed the deaths to HIV/AIDS. Owing to the controversy, Fridge Master threatened to locate its planned new stove factory in Botswana. In February 2001 the Government placed Fridge Master under provisional liquidation.

Formal employment grew strongly over the five years to 1990, when the total informal employment reached an estimated 92,000. Employment has since stagnated. According to the central bank, total employment (including both the formal and informal sectors) grew by only 0.7% in 2000, from 110,776 workers in 1999 to 111,578 in 2000. According to FAO, Swaziland's labour force increased from 281,000 in 1990 to 372,000 at mid-2003. The problem of unemployment is serious and growing, especially among young people: 54% of the jobless are under 25 years of age and a further 29% are aged between 25 and 34.

Swaziland's textile industry has seen significant changes during the past decade. Swaziland was granted provisions by the USA's African Growth and Opportunity Act (AGOA) in July 2001, which was expected to benefit the local textile industry; under the terms of the Act, Swaziland enjoyed unrestricted access to the US market for the export of textiles and clothes, without having to pay tariffs. Indeed, the garment industry has grown rapidly. However, the current AGOA expires in 2007, and after that time Swaziland must use its own fabric (or fabric from other sub-Saharan African states or from the USA) in production rather than that sourced elsewhere (mostly Asia). Of all SACU countries, Swaziland ranks third, after South Africa and Lesotho, in textile exports to the USA. In 2003, for example, Swaziland exported textiles to the USA worth US $134m. out of a total $2,228.5m. (South Africa sold $1,668.7m. of the total). However, Swaziland is a relatively high-cost producer. The average wage in the textile industry is about $200 per month, compared with about $40 per month in southern and eastern Asia, the major competitors. In addition, the WTO's agreement on textiles and clothing also expired at the end of 2004, and import quotas from other major producers (principally the People's Republic of China and Bangladesh) will be reduced. The industry has been under intense pressure and in decline for at least three years. Two textile firms (GMS Textiles and First Garments) left Swaziland in 2003. In 2004 and 2005 14 textile factories closed, and the Swaziland Textile Exporter's Association estimated that the industry had lost some 15,000 of the 30,000 people employed in the industry. Two major unions signed new contracts, which included wage freezes for the first half of 2005. Natex, one of Swaziland's largest employers and its leading textile producer, which was threatened with closure because of low demand in South Africa and competition from Asia, was bought by Tatex Investment Swaziland of Taiwan in 2002, which invested E180m. in the company.

South Africa's decision to recognize the People's Republic of China greatly benefited Swaziland. Taiwan suspended new investment in South Africa, and reduced its trade and commercial ties with that country. Much Taiwanese investment, originally intended for South Africa, was expected to be relocated to Swaziland, and the kingdom consolidated its economic ties with Taiwan, with the Prime Minister paying a visit there in 1997 to discuss new investment projects. These included Taiwanese nylon-casting operation, at a cost of a E12m., and a jumper manufacturer, Gold Investment, which was planning to employ an additional 300 workers to cater for a planned increase in its exports to the USA.

Net foreign direct investment (FDI) has been erratic in recent years. In 1998 Swaziland attracted a record sum of US $130m. in FDI, which fell to $43m. by 2003, before declining further to $16.1m. in 2005.

POWER, TRANSPORT AND COMMUNICATIONS

The country has a comparatively well developed and maintained physical infrastructure, but the Swaziland Electricity Board (SEB) still imports from South Africa most of the power it supplies, and the proportion has risen steadily during the recent period of historically low rainfall. In 2000 Swaziland's electricity grid was connected to the 400-kv 'Motraco' line delivering power from South Africa's Camden plant to the new Mozal aluminium smelter in Maputo, Mozambique. The SEB was also investigating the possibility of drawing power from the Cahora Bassa hydroelectric plant in central Mozambique. Such a project would probably take several years and a massive capital outlay would have to be realized, especially if it was to involve constructing a direct power line through Mozambican territory. A Taiwanese-funded project is expected to add 700 km of line to the country's electricity network, supplying power to an additional 50,000 people.

The kingdom's first railway line was built during 1962–64 to connect the Ngwenya iron-ore mine in the far west of the country, via the then railhead across the eastern border at Goma, to the port of Maputo (then Lourenço Marques) and so to its Japanese customers. Long disused west of the Matsapha industrial estate, the line was finally taken up in 1995. A southern link via Lavumisa and connecting to the South African port of Richards Bay was completed in 1978, while a northern link, crossing the border near Mananga and running to the South African town of Komatipoort, was opened in 1986. These lines established a direct link between the eastern Transvaal and the Natal ports, integrating the Swazi lines into the South African network. In 1995 the northern link carried 3.3m. metric tons of transit traffic, which represented 78% of all tonnages hauled by the Swaziland Railway Board. Swaziland is studying the feasibility of linking its rail network to Mpumalanga province in South Africa. This route could compete with existing lines between South Africa and Mozambique, and add alternatives to Durban. The Italian Government has announced financial support to help rehabilitate Swaziland's east–west line. By mid-1999 Swaziland Railways had invested E15.8m. in purchasing materials for the rehabilitation of the east–west line to Maputo, in addition to E12.2m. already spent on upgrading the southern link to Lavumisa. In mid-2004 it was announced that the company would be privatized. In 1993 Swaziland established an inland container depot, which saw rapid growth (ranging from 10%–20% annually). The inland port receives imports and moves exports that are transported by rail from Durban, South Africa.

The kingdom's road network is comparatively well developed. In 2002 there were an estimated 3,594 km of roads. About 28.2% of the road network was paved in 1994. The ratio of roads to inhabitants in Swaziland is twice the regional average. Road projects have dominated the capital expenditure programmes of recent development plans and in 1991 work began on the rebuilding of the kingdom's main road artery connecting the capital, Mbabane, to Manzini, via Matsapha. The highway was completed in 1999, behind schedule and well over budget. By the end of 1999 a large-scale infrastructure investment programme was in place. It included resurfacing and upgrading the main road from Manzini to Lomahasha on the Mozambican border. A new E21m. bridge and approach roads over the Komati river have already been completed. Several other roads are also being upgraded, including Siteki to Mhlumeni in the east of the country, Nhlangano to Lavumisa in the south and Luvengo to Sicunusa in the west. In February 2001 the Japanese Bank for International Co-operation signed a loan agreement for E300m. for the construction of two main roads in the north of the country. The Ministry of Works and Transport has recently suggested introducing toll roads (as in South Africa) and establishing a Roads Authority.

Most of Swaziland can now be reached telephonically by dialling directly; a satellite link was inaugurated in 1983, allowing the kingdom's subscribers to bypass South Africa when contacting Europe and North America. At the end of 2005 Swaziland had an estimated 35,000 main telephone lines in use. The Swaziland Posts and Telecommunications Corpn (SPTC) introduced new telephone codes in late 1998 to include area codes as a prefix for the existing numbers, bringing Swaziland into line with most international telephone exchange systems. The level of internet use, with 36,000 subscribers in 2004, is considered high by African standards. The fastest growing service was the mobile operator MTN Swaziland, an SPTC joint venture. MTN began six new transmission facilities at a cost of E32m. in 1999 and increased its coverage from 40% to 65% of the country. At the end of 2002 the number of mobile cellular telephone subscribers exceeded the number of fixed-line telephones. Indeed, Swaziland had an average of 88 mobile phones per 1,000 people in 2003, and by 2005 fixed-line and mobile phone coverage reached 207 per 1,000 people.

In the planned reform of the state-owned sector, the SPTC was to be broken up into separate postal and telecommunications companies in preparation for their future privatization. In 2001 the Development Bank of Southern Africa awarded the SPTC a loan of E43m. to upgrade the telecommunications sector, including installing 1,500 lines in rural areas and 5,000 lines in urban areas. In 2005 the SPTC was declared insolvent with debts to UT Star Communications of the USA amounting to E59m. A US company, Spirit Telecoms, subsequently proposed a joint venture arrangement. An estimated 95% of the population have access to two radio stations operated by the Swaziland Broadcasting and Information Service. One television channel is run by the Swaziland Television Broadcasting Corpn.

TOURISM

Swaziland is blessed with an abundance of natural beauty and fairly well developed tourism infrastructure (by regional standards). Tourism in Swaziland was largely depressed during the early 1980s, owing primarily to the economic recession in South Africa (whence the majority of the tourists come), together with strong competition from new hotel complexes in the South African 'homelands'. There were significant improvements after 1985, when the total number of arrivals was stimulated by growth in the number of business visitors as well as by renewed tourist interest.

Facilities in the central Ezulwini valley (the heart of the Swazi tourism industry) are dominated by the South African Sun International chain. Visitor arrivals rose to 287,796 in 1990, but thereafter stagnated. In 1994 an improvement in the industry's fortunes was reflected in a 24% increase in tourist arrivals at hotels compared with the previous year (reaching 335,933). In 1997 arrivals increased further, to 322,000, and receipts from tourism rose to US $40m. Tourism declined in the late 1990s and early 2000s. However, in 2004 the number of tourists increased to 352,040 (from 218,813 the previous year); receipts amounted to $109m. in 2004.

A E503m. luxury resort, the Royal Jozini Big Six, completed the required environmental impact assessment in 2005. In 2007 the South African resort developer, the Elan Group, became a partner in the project. When completed, the resort aims to attract eco-tourists.

TRADE AND BALANCE OF PAYMENTS

The national currency is the lilangeni (plural: emalangeni—E), introduced in 1974. The terms of the Trilateral Monetary Agreement, signed with South Africa and Lesotho to form the Common Monetary Area (CMA) in 1986, allowed the Swazi authorities the option of determining the lilangeni's exchange rate independently. Under the amended Multilateral Monetary Agreement (signed in early 1992 to formalize Namibia's de fact membership), this freedom is maintained, but the currency has remained pegged at par to the South African rand. By June 2006 the exchange rate was US $1 = E6.6, unchanged since the year before, although depreciating to US $1 = E7.08 in June 2007.

As a member of the CMA, Swaziland was affected by South Africa's decision in 1997 to relax further its controls on the availability of foreign exchange. The limits on capital investment by companies in the Southern African Development Community (SADC) region have also been relaxed, and thus Swaziland will have to become more competitive, if it is to attract further capital and investment from South Africa. In 1999 South Africa launched a 14% value-added tax (VAT) on exports and imports to and from the other members of SACU. Swaziland was concerned about the delays that trucks will experience at the border, although South African customs officials have guaranteed that the delay will be minimal. Despite the disagreement between the SACU members over the introduction of VAT, there was progress in late 1998 on the renegotiation of the SACU agreement. Receipts from SACU represent about one-half of total government recurrent revenue, but the current government budget suggests that those revenues will decline from 54.2% of the budget funding to 46.5% in 2005/06 (see below). The recent signing of the South African-EU free-trade agreement is likely to have a negative impact on Swaziland's revenue from SACU. However, in 2001 an agreement between SACU and the EU was concluded in principle; under the scheme, Swaziland was to receive some E1,900m. in revenue annually, compared with E1,700m. under the previous arrangements. In February 2003 the five members of SACU met the US special trade representative to discuss the creation of a possible bilateral free-trade area. South Africa was to take the lead in such negotiations, but was required to take into account the concerns of the other members, including Swaziland.

The Customs Union was renegotiated in 2002 and the new agreement guarantees a duty rate of 17% between Botswana, Lesotho, Namibia and Swaziland, reducing the yearly fluctuations of the past. In addition, each SACU member will now receive customs revenues based on its relative share of SACU GDP, of which Swaziland has 0.9%. Swaziland's share of the total for 2005/06, at E2,800m., is only slightly up from the E2,700m. the previous year. Although these are not major changes, the new agreement is more democratic as each member has more say in the arrangement. SACU is also negotiating for a free-trade arrangement with the European Free Trade Association. None the less, receipts from the Customs Union played an even more important role in the past two years. By 2005 those revenues comprised 62% of the budget, up from 54% in 2004. Customs revenues expanded by 57% in 2006, with the Government projecting that such receipts would comprise 71% of total revenue by 2008.

In 2004 the country's merchandise exports amounted to US $1,877.9m., with merchandise imports of $1,909.9m., resulting in a visible trade deficit of $32m., down from $42.7m. the year before. In 2003 Swaziland's principal exports were soft drink concentrates ($762m.), cottonseed ($220m.), sugar ($118m.) and wood pulp ($178m.). Principal imports in that year included machinery and transport equipment ($452m.), manufactured goods ($363m.), food and live animal products ($203m.) and chemicals ($190m.). The major destinations for Swaziland's exports in 2000 were South Africa, accounting for 59.7% of the total, followed by the EU (8.8%), the USA (8.2%) and Mozambique (6.2%). South Africa was also the principal source of imports (95.6%); other suppliers included the EU, Japan and Singapore (each with less than 1.0% of the total). In 2006 the Ministry of Foreign Affairs developed a national export strategy for 2006–09, focusing on seven sectors. The strategy aimed to diversify exports, strengthen existing markets and foster stronger public-private partnerships. The plan detailed several priority areas: agriculture (specifically, forestry, sugar and citrus), manufacturing (handicrafts and food and beverages), tourism and information technology.

The current account has remained in surplus in recent years: reaching US $57.7m. in 2002, $36.3m. in 2003 and $39.8m. in 2004. Swaziland is a member of SACU, SADC and the Common Market for Eastern and Southern Africa (COMESA), but has not elected to join COMESA's free-trade area, in common with other CMA members. The Swaziland Stock Exchange, with a capitalization of $146m. in 2002, increased the minimum amount of capital requirements for listed companies from E1m. to E5m. in 2003. This requirement is similar to those of other SADC members and was implemented to harmonize regional stock-exchange regulations.

PUBLIC FINANCE, DEBT AND FOREIGN AID

Swaziland's public finances are characterized by a heavy dependence upon receipts from South Africa from the SACU revenue pool. Over and above the revenue raised in customs and excise duty on the kingdom's own trade and excisable production, these include cash compensation for the distorting effects of high import tariffs, which protect South African producers' dominance of the Swazi market.

In late 1995 a programme for the reform of public enterprises was introduced, and in 1996 an extensive reform of the tax system was initiated, as part of the Government's continuing austerity programme. In June 1999 the corporate tax rate was reduced from 37.5% to 30.0%, the same as South Africa's. Earlier in that year an additional petrol tax of 7 cents per litre was proposed. The Government also announced that it wanted to diversify its revenue base, especially given probable cuts in SACU customs receipts over the long term.

The government budgets of the early 1980s were introduced against a background of chronic public finance problems, successive (often large) deficits and growing domestic and external debt. However, the economy's buoyancy in the late 1980s and early 1990s turned the deficits into persistent surpluses. The pattern was repeated over the next five years. The finance ministry's routine revisions of the budget projections in July and December–January of each fiscal year showed higher than expected revenue, tight control of recurrent outgoings and underspending of the capital budget.

The 2007/08 budget was introduced in February 2007. The main components of that budget were similar to the previous year's, including: civil service reform; an anti-corruption bill; a tourism levy; an increase in health and primary education and health spending, especially on HIV/AIDS. Total grants and revenues were projected at around E9,000m. with expenditures at around E8,500m. resulting in a government budget surplus of E552m., equivalent to 2.6% of GDP. The increase in SACU customs receipts was the principal reason for the surplus. In 2006 Swaziland had an external debt of E3,200m., equal to about 18% of the country's GDP. Swaziland's debt service to export ratio stood at a modest 1.9% in 2005. Net official development assistance fell from US $29m. in 1999 to $13m. in 2000, but increased to $25m. in 2002 and $46m. by 2005. In 1990–2002 the average annual rate of inflation was 9.5%; consumer prices increased by 7.3% in 2003, by a lower rate of 3.4% in 2004, by 5.3% in 2005 and by 5.7% in 2006. All CMA members keep their interest rates roughly aligned, and the prime lending rate of commercial banks in South Africa and Swaziland was 12.5% in June 2007. Swaziland's official reserves stood at E3,200m. in 2006 (an increase of 69% over 2005), and equalled about 3 months' worth of imports.

ECONOMIC PROSPECTS

Swaziland faces serious challenges in the near term. It is now ranked as the country with the world's highest percentage of its population infected with HIV/AIDS, while FDI is virtually stagnant. Some 60% of the population live below the official poverty line. Labour productivity is low, unemployment is estimated at 40%, labour relations are particularly strained and there is general political instability (portions of the new Constitution that took effect in early 2006 were being contested in 2007). Despite this, there are some areas of growth. For example, in 1998 the Lubombo Spatial Development Initiative (SDI—see Recent History) was launched. The SDI is a joint E600m. project by the Governments of South Africa, Swaziland and Mozambique to attract investment to eastern Swaziland, southern Mozambique and parts of the South African provinces of Mpumalanga and KwaZulu/Natal. Potential projects for Swaziland include tourism and agricultural developments, and road improvements from the southern border with KwaZulu/Natal. Many hoped that the King's Millennium Projects, including US $26m. budgeted in 2005 for the airport in the east of the country (the location of which is controversial due to its lack of proximity to any population centre), and a new conference centre, would stimulate the construction industry in particular and the economy in general. None the less, the IMF and others in the international community expressed concern about these projects, as well as the King's recent spending excesses (see Recent History). This lavish lifestyle is causing a backlash domestically. Civil servants have threatened mass protests against such spending, and have been critical of the proposed airport as part of the Millennium Project. The leading political organization, the People's United Democratic Movement, has called for the international community to isolate and ostracize the King. In early 2006 the IMF finalized its Article IV consultation which called for privatizations, a reduction in the size of the civil service and a government restructuring. In May 2004 a proposed Electricity Act foresaw the development of independent power producers and it was expected that the Government's forthcoming National Development Plan would outline details for restructuring at SPTC, RSNAC and the Central Transport Administration. The Fund was also concerned about expanding and diversifying the Government's revenue base and keeping government expenditure under firmer control. Additional criticism of the Government's attempts to limit the judiciary's independence in 2002–03 came from the EU and the USA. The latter threatened to withdraw Swaziland's eligibility for AGOA and to reduce official aid; exclusion from AGOA and the preferential duty treatment it brings would severely damage Swaziland's textile industry (see above). It should be noted that many in Swaziland have been critical of the AGOA, claiming that most of the benefits have gone to foreign rather than local firms, as foreign firms are typically larger, better equipped and can more easily meet the needs of overseas buyers.

Swaziland's economy has undergone many changes during the past decade. The most important has been in its relationship with its neighbour, South Africa, with which Swaziland's economic future is in many ways linked. None the less, there are a number of areas where Swaziland will have to make changes independently of that relationship. Most importantly, Swaziland will have to find ways of accommodating strong desire for political reform in order to establish the domestic and international confidence needed for economic growth and poverty reduction.

Statistical Survey

Source (unless otherwise stated): Central Statistical Office, POB 456, Mbabane; internet www.gov.sz/home.asp?pid=75.

Area and Population

AREA, POPULATION AND DENSITY

Area (sq km)	17,363*
Population (census results)†	
25 August 1986	681,059
11–12 May 1997	929,718
Population (UN estimates at mid-year)‡	
2004	1,114,000
2005	1,125,000
2006	1,134,000
Density (per sq km) at mid-2006	65.3

* 6,704 sq miles.

† Excluding absentee workers.

‡ Source: UN, *World Population Prospects: The 2006 Revision*.

ETHNIC GROUPS

(census of August 1986)

Swazi	661,646
Other Africans	14,468
European	1,825
Asiatic	228
Other non-Africans	412
Mixed	2,403
Unknown	77
Total	681,059

REGIONS

(population at census of May 1997; provisional figures, excluding absentee workers)

	Area (sq km)	Population	Density (per sq km)
Hhohho	3,569	247,539	69.4
Manzini	5,945	276,636	46.5
Shiselweni	4,070	198,084	48.7
Lebombo	3,779	190,617	50.4
Total	17,363	912,876	52.6

PRINCIPAL TOWNS
(population at census of May 1997)

Mbabane (capital)	57,992	Manzini	25,571

Mid-2005 (incl. suburbs, UN estimate): Mbabane 73,000 (Source: UN, *World Urbanization Prospects: The 2005 Revision*).

BIRTHS AND DEATHS
(annual averages, UN estimates)

	1990–1995	1995–2000	2000–05
Birth rate (per 1,000)	38.7	33.3	30.4
Death rate (per 1,000)	9.7	11.2	17.2

Source: UN, *World Population Prospects: The 2006 Revision*.

Expectation of life (years at birth, WHO estimates): 37 (males 36; females 39) in 2004 (Source: WHO, *World Health Report*).

EMPLOYMENT
(labour force sample survey, '000 persons in paid employment, June 1996)

	Males	Females	Total
Agriculture, hunting, forestry and fishing	18.34	4.10	22.44
Mining and quarrying	1.10	0.04	1.14
Manufacturing	12.53	3.64	16.17
Electricity, gas and water	1.05	0.14	1.19
Construction	4.81	0.19	5.00
Trade, restaurants and hotels	6.79	5.10	11.89
Transport, storage and communications	2.44	0.27	2.70
Financing, insurance, real estate and business services	4.17	2.00	6.17
Community, social and personal services	12.31	10.86	23.17
Total employed	63.54	26.32	89.86

Source: ILO.

Mid-2005 (estimates in '000): Agriculture, etc. 115; Total labour force 370 (Source: FAO).

Health and Welfare

KEY INDICATORS

Total fertility rate (children per woman, 2005)	3.7
Under-5 mortality rate (per 1,000 live births, 2005)	160
HIV/AIDS (% of persons aged 15–49, 2005)	33.4
Physicians (per 1,000 head, 2004)	0.16
Health expenditure (2004): US $ per head (PPP)	367.2
Health expenditure (2004): % of GDP	6.3
Health expenditure (2004): public (% of total)	63.8
Access to water (% of persons, 2004)	62
Access to sanitation (% of persons, 2004)	48
Human Development Index (2004): ranking	146
Human Development Index (2004): value	0.500

For sources and definitions, see explanatory note on p. vi.

Agriculture

PRINCIPAL CROPS
('000 metric tons)

	2003	2004	2005
Maize	69.3	68.1	74.5
Potatoes*	6	6	6
Sweet potatoes*	2.3	2.5	2.6
Sugar cane*	4,500	4,500	5,200
Groundnuts (in shell)*	4.1	4.6	4.8
Cottonseed*	4.0	3.4	2.8
Cotton (lint)*	2	2	2
Tomatoes*	3.4	3.3	3.2
Oranges*	36	36	36
Grapefruit and pomelo*	37	35	34
Pineapples*	32	16	9

* FAO estimates.

Source: FAO.

LIVESTOCK
('000 head, year ending September)

	2003	2004	2005
Horses*	1.4	1.4	1.4
Asses, mules or hinnies*	14.9	14.9	14.9
Cattle*	520	580	580
Pigs*	30	30	30
Sheep*	35	27	27
Goats	273.6†	274.0*	274*
Chickens*	3,200	3,200	3,200

* FAO estimate(s).
† Unofficial figure.

Source: FAO.

LIVESTOCK PRODUCTS
('000 metric tons)

	2001	2002	2003
Cattle meat	8.0	12.5	12.5*
Goat meat*	2.9	2.4	1.9
Pig meat*	1.1	1.1	1.1
Chicken meat*	6.0	5.0	5.0
Cows' milk*	37.5	37.5	37.5

* FAO estimate(s).

2004–05: Figures assumed to be unchanged from 2003 (FAO estimates).

Source: FAO.

Forestry

ROUNDWOOD REMOVALS
('000 cubic metres, excl. bark, FAO estimates)

	1996	1997	1998
Sawlogs, veneer logs and logs for sleepers	260	260	260
Pulpwood	604	604	—
Other industrial wood	70	70	70
Fuel wood	560	560	560
Total	1,494	1,494	890

1999–2005: Production as in 1998 (FAO estimates).

Source: FAO.

SAWNWOOD PRODUCTION
('000 cubic metres, incl. railway sleepers, FAO estimates)

	1995	1996	1997
Total (all coniferous)	90	100	102

1998–2005: Production as in 1997.

Source: FAO.

Fishing

(metric tons, live weight)

	1999	2000*	2001*
Capture	70*	70	70
Aquaculture	61	69	72
Common carp	18	20	20
Mozambique tilapia	20	25	25
Redbreast tilapia	12	13	15
North African catfish	5	6	6
Red claw crayfish	6	5	6
Total catch	131*	139	142

* FAO estimate(s).

2002–05 (metric tons, live weight, FAO estimate): Capture 70.

Source: FAO.

Mining

(metric tons, unless otherwise indicated)

	2003	2004	2005
Coal	448,664	488,314	221,701
Ferrovanadium	1,011	1,150	345
Quarrystone ('000 cu m)	324	230	567

Source: US Geological Survey.

Industry

SELECTED PRODUCTS
('000 metric tons, unless otherwise indicated)

	2001	2002	2003
Raw sugar	334	406	616
Wood pulp	191	191	191
Electrical energy (million kWh)*	475	475	475

* Estimates.

Source: UN, *Industrial Commodity Statistics Yearbook*.

Electrical energy (million kWh, excl. self-generated power of some industrial units): 203.7 in 2002; 123.0 in 2003; 103.5 in 2004.

Sources: Swaziland Electricity Board and IMF, *Kingdom of Swaziland: Statistical Appendix* (March 2006).

Finance

CURRENCY AND EXCHANGE RATES

Monetary Units
100 cents = 1 lilangeni (plural: emalangeni).

Sterling, Dollar and Euro Equivalents (31 May 2007)
£1 sterling = 14.2069 emalangeni;
US $1 = 7.185 emalangeni;
€1 = 9.6660 emalangeni;
100 emalangeni= £7.04 = $13.92 = €10.35.

Average Exchange Rate (emalangeni per US $)
2004 6.460
2005 6.359
2006 6.772

Note: The lilangeni is at par with the South African rand.

BUDGET
(million emalangeni, year ending 31 March)

Revenue*	2002/03	2003/04	2004/05
Tax revenue	3,107.4	3,660.5	4,627.8
Taxes on net income and profits	827.5	1,105.4	1,164.0
Companies	259.6	322.4	324.0
Individuals	494.1	698.7	742.0
Non-resident dividends and interest	73.8	84.3	98.0
Taxes on property	6.0	9.0	12.0
Taxes on goods, services, and international trade	2,269.2	2,540.8	3,445.8
Receipts from Southern African Customs Union	1,618.6	1,878.1	2,772.8
Levies on sugar exports	21.8	12.1	22.0
Hotel and gaming taxes	3.7	4.4	5.0
Sales tax	528.6	547.7	549.0
Licenses and other taxes	96.6	98.5	97.0
Other taxes	4.7	5.3	6.0
Other current revenue	157.1	104.9	98.0
Property income	108.6	52.0	46.0
Fees, fines, and non-industrial sales	48.5	52.9	52.0
Total	3,264.5	3,765.4	4,725.8

Expenditure†	2002/03	2003/04	2004/05
Current expenditure	3,045.0	3,437.2	4,294.9
Wages and salaries	1,417.1	1,668.9	1,964.0
Other purchases of goods and services	905.6	1,003.0	1,421.0
Interest payments	167.3	173.8	168.0
Domestic	0.0	37.0	49.0
Foreign	163.7	136.8	119.0
Subsidies and other current transfers	555.0	591.5	742.0
Capital expenditure	935.5	817.8	1,259.0
Education	48.0	13.0	27.9
Agriculture	31.0	48.0	104.5
Transport and communications	427.0	125.0	347.6
Other	407.5	571.8	696.4
Total	3,980.5	4,255.0	5,553.9

* Excluding grants received (million emalangeni): 163.0 in 2002/03; 137.7 in 2003/04; 116.0 in 2004/05.

† Excluding net lending (million emalangeni): 37.7 in 2002/03; 59.0 in 2003/04; 3.0 in 2004/05.

Source: IMF, *Kingdom of Swaziland: Statistical Appendix* (March 2006).

INTERNATIONAL RESERVES
(excl. gold, US $ million at 31 December)

	2004	2005	2006
IMF special drawing rights	3.84	3.55	3.74
Reserve position in IMF	10.19	9.38	9.87
Foreign exchange	309.53	230.97	358.91
Total	323.56	243.90	372.52

Source: IMF, *International Financial Statistics*.

MONEY SUPPLY
(million emalangeni at 31 December)

	2004	2005	2006
Currency outside banks	235.85	242.08	255.98
Demand deposits at deposit money banks	843.08	1,046.03	1,106.01
Total	1,078.93	1,288.11	1,361.99

COST OF LIVING
(Consumer Price Index; base: 2000 = 100)

	2003	2004	2005
Food	145.7	155.7	169.2
Fuel	114.0	119.2	123.9
Clothing	114.4	115.2	116.9
Housing	105.7	117.5	119.6
All items (incl. others)	129.0	133.5	139.9

Source: ILO.

NATIONAL ACCOUNTS

Expenditure on the Gross Domestic Product
(US $ million at current prices)

	2004	2005	2006
Government final consumption expenditure	529.84	751.75	731.96
Private final consumption expenditure	1,463.75	1,496.66	1,508.52
Gross capital formation	438.35	485.09	454.08
Total domestic expenditure	2,431.94	2,733.50	2,694.56
Exports of goods and services	2,356.63	2,435.76	2,478.45
Less Imports of goods and services	2,440.89	2,619.02	2,640.06
GDP in purchasers' values	2,347.68	2,550.23	2,532.95
GDP in constant 2000 prices	1,050.44	1,070.70	1,089.97

Source: African Development Bank.

Gross Domestic Product by Economic Activity
(million emalangeni at current prices)

	2002	2003	2004*
Agriculture and forestry	1,075.0	1,050.5	1,063.6
Mining	47.3	50.4	57.0
Manufacturing	2,983.3	3,269.7	3,403.0
Electricity and water	127.5	130.6	134.0
Construction	504.2	539.0	797.3
Wholesale and retail trade	642.5	715.7	797.3
Hotels and restaurants	143.2	146.8	147.8
Transport and communications	434.8	481.7	479.7
Banking, finance and insurance	285.1	314.2	382.4
Real estate	86.3	89.4	93.2
Government services	1,496.1	1,687.3	1,856.0
Other services	85.0	86.7	89.2
Owner-occupied dwellings	158.0	161.0	165.7
Sub total	8,068.3	8,723.0	9,466.2
Less Imputed bank service charge	192.6	212.3	240.9
GDP at factor cost	7,875.7	8,510.7	9,225.3
Indirect taxes *Less* Subsidies	4,684.3	5,911.7	7,037.0
GDP at purchasers' values	12,560.0	14,422.4	16,262.3

* Estimates.

Source: IMF, *Kingdom of Swaziland: Statistical Appendix* (March 2006).

BALANCE OF PAYMENTS
(US $ million)

	2003	2004	2005
Exports of goods f.o.b.	1,625.6	1,738.4	1,827.7
Imports of goods f.o.b.	–1,508.1	–1,598.6	–1,754.6
Trade balance	117.5	139.8	73.0
Exports of services	255.4	463.9	282.5
Imports of services	–299.5	–632.1	–457.6
Balance on goods and services	73.4	–28.4	–102.1
Other income received	143.5	144.0	132.4
Other income paid	–147.1	–124.7	–112.8
Balance on goods, services and income	69.8	–9.1	–82.5
Current transfers received	333.3	367.1	396.3
Current transfers paid	–287.0	–242.6	–268.0
Current balance	116.2	115.5	45.9
Capital account (net)	—	–2.1	1.1
Direct investment abroad	–10.5	1.5	25.0
Direct investment from abroad	–60.9	70.6	–16.2
Portfolio investment assets	–0.3	–10.7	3.7
Portfolio investment liabilities	–0.1	–0.3	0.3
Other investment assets	64.4	–167.3	40.7
Other investment liabilities	–20.0	–45.6	26.6
Net errors and omissions	–133.0	19.9	–129.5
Overall balance	–44.1	–18.5	–2.4

Source: IMF, *International Financial Statistics*.

External Trade

PRINCIPAL COMMODITIES
(distribution by SITC, US $ million)

Imports c.i.f.	2000	2001	2002
Food and live animals	164.9	129.4	131.9
Beverages and tobacco	27.3	19.7	18.1
Crude materials (inedible) except fuels	34.2	31.9	27.2
Mineral fuels and lubricants	138.5	95.7	19.9
Petroleum and petroleum products	121.3	84.9	3.9
Chemicals and related products	115.0	101.8	95.1
Manufactures classified chiefly by materials	179.7	145.1	182.6
Machinery and transport equipment	299.0	192.7	201.1
Specialized machinery	34.4	33.0	35.7
General industrial machinery	89.2	29.2	29.2
Electric machinery, apparatus appliances and parts	44.6	21.0	20.6
Road vehicles	96.6	79.2	73.6
Miscellaneous manufactures	114.4	99.9	98.8
Total (incl. others)	1,098.6	832.0	797.8

Exports f.o.b.	2000	2001	2002
Food and live animals	283.9	257.5	125.6
Sugar, sugar preparations and honey	120.1	96.5	74.6
Crude materials (inedible) except fuels	102.7	87.4	79.9
Wood pulp	60.5	60.7	56.3
Chemicals and related products	178.6	143.9	465.5
Manufactures classified chiefly by materials	44.9	28.3	31.9
Textile yarn, fabrics and related products	21.4	12.7	16.2
Machinery and transport equipment	86.4	31.2	35.3
General industrial machinery	26.8	6.5	9.3
Electric machinery, apparatus appliances and parts	30.2	3.1	4.9
Miscellaneous manufactures	174.1	114.1	211.8
Clothing and accessories	124.0	79.5	173.5
Total (incl. others)	890.8	677.8	974.1

Source: UN, *International Trade Statistics Yearbook*.

PRINCIPAL TRADING PARTNERS
(US $ million)

Imports c.i.f.	2000	2001	2002
China, People's Repub.	4.2	3.9	12.9
Hong Kong	11.9	8.2	19.6
Japan	8.1	7.5	8.1
South Africa	1,023.4	786.5	675.3
Total (incl. others)	1,098.6	832.0	797.8

Exports f.o.b.	2000	2001	2002
Angola	5.8	10.0	7.5
Mozambique	55.5	31.4	52.2
South Africa	531.5	528.6	657.5
Tanzania	27.1	9.4	13.3
United Kingdom	33.0	7.2	12.3
USA	78.8	26.8	78.3
Zimbabwe	33.4	7.3	28.2
Total (incl. others)	890.8	677.8	974.1

Source: UN, *International Trade Statistics Yearbook*.

Transport

RAILWAYS
(traffic)

	2002	2003	2004
Net total ton-km (million)	728	726	710

Source: UN, *Statistical Yearbook*.

ROAD TRAFFIC
(motor vehicles in use at 31 December 2003)

Passenger cars	44,113
Buses and coaches	6,424
Lorries and vans	42,576
Motorcycles and mopeds	3,184

Source: International Road Federation, *World Road Statistics*.

CIVIL AVIATION
(traffic on scheduled services)

	1998	1999	2000
Kilometres flown (million)	1	1	2
Passengers carried ('000)	41	12	90
Passenger-km (million)	43	13	68
Total ton-km (million)	4	1	6

Source: UN, *Statistical Yearbook*.

Tourism

TOURIST ARRIVALS
(at hotels)

Country of residence	2003	2004	2005
Australia	701	1,725	1,527
Mozambique	11,642	17,619	15,597
Portugal	8,666	828	733
South Africa	85,899	112,027	99,176
United Kingdom	13,702	17,776	15,737
Total (incl. others)	218,813	352,040	311,656

Tourism receipts (US $ million, incl. passenger transport): 113 in 2003; 109 in 2004; n.a. in 2005.

Source: World Tourism Organization.

Communications Media

	2003	2004	2005
Telephones ('000 main lines in use)	46.2	46.2*	35.0
Mobile cellular telephones ('000 subscribers)	85.0	113.0	200.0
Personal computers ('000 in use)	30	36	n.a.
Internet users ('000)	27.0	36.0	n.a.

* Estimate.

Source: International Telecommunication Union.

Radio receivers (year ending 31 March 1998): 155,000 in use (Source: UN, *Statistical Yearbook*).

Television receivers (2002): 32,000 in use (Source: International Telecommunication Union).

Daily newspapers (1996): 3 (estimated circulation 24,000) (Source: UN, *Statistical Yearbook*).

Education

(2002/03, unless otherwise indicated)

	Institutions	Teachers	Students
Primary	541*	6,680	208,444
Secondary	182*	3,684	62,401
University†	1‡	328§	6,594

* Figure for 2001/02.

† Figures exclude vocational, technical and teacher-training colleges. In 2000, there were 1,822 students enrolled at these institutions, which numbered 10 in 2003.

‡ Figure for 2000.

§ Figure for 2003/04.

Source: UNESCO Institute for Statistics.

Adult literacy rate (UNESCO estimates): 79.6% (males 80.9%; females 78.3%) in 2004 (Source: UN Development Programme, *Human Development Report*).

Directory

The Constitution

The Constitution of 13 October 1978 vests supreme executive and legislative power in the hereditary King (Ngwenyama—the Lion). Succession is governed by traditional law and custom. In the event of the death of the King, the powers of Head of State are transferred to the constitutional dual monarch, the Queen Mother (Indlovukazi—Great She Elephant), who is authorized to act as Regent until the designated successor attains the age of 21. The Constitution provides for a bicameral legislature, comprising a House of Assembly and a Senate. The functions of the Swaziland National Council (Libandla) are confined to debating government proposals and advising the King. Executive power is exercised through the Cabinet (later redesignated the Council of Ministers), which is appointed by the King. The Libandla, which comprises members of the royal family, and is headed by the King and Queen Mother, advises on matters regulated by traditional law and custom. The Constitution affirms the fundamental rights of the individual.

Following amendments to the electoral system, which were approved by the King in October 1992, the House of Assembly (which was redesignated as the National Assembly) was expanded to 65 deputies (of whom 55 are directly elected from candidates nominated by traditional local councils, known as Tinkhundla, and 10 appointed by the King) and the Senate to 30 members (of whom 20 are appointed by the King and 10 elected by the National Assembly). Elections to the National Assembly are conducted by secret ballot, in two rounds of voting; the second round of the elections is contested by the three candidates from each of the Tinkhundla who secure the highest number of votes in the first poll. In July 1996 the King appointed a commission to prepare proposals for a draft constitution, which would subsequently be submitted for approval by the Swazi people. The commission submitted its report in August 2001, and in February 2002 a committee began drafting a new constitution, based on the commission's recommendations. In May 2003 the completion of the draft document was announced.

The draft Constitution was approved by a joint sitting of the National Assembly and the Senate in mid-June 2005, but was initially rejected by King Mswati. The King approved and signed an amended version on 26 July. The new Constitution came into effect on 7 February 2006. Executive power remained concentrated in the King, who appoints the Prime Minister and the Council of Ministers and who has the power to dissolve the bicameral legislature. Further details of the new Constitution were not immediately made available.

The Government

HEAD OF STATE

King: HM King MSWATI III (succeeded to the throne 25 April 1986).

COUNCIL OF MINISTERS
(August 2007)

Prime Minister: ABSALOM THEMBA DLAMINI.

Deputy Prime Minister: CONSTANCE SIMELANE.

Minister of Justice and Constitutional Affairs: Prince DAVID.

Minister of Finance: MAJOZI SITHOLE.

Minister of Home Affairs: Prince GABHENI.

Minister of Foreign Affairs and Trade: MOSES MATHENDELE DLAMINI.

Minister of Education: THEMBA MSIBI.

Minister of Regional Development and Youth Affairs: Chief SIPHO SHONGWE.

Minister of Agriculture and Co-operatives: MTITI FAKUDZE.

Minister of Enterprise and Employment: LUTFO DLAMINI.

Minister of Economic Planning and Development: Rev. ABSALOM DLAMINI.

Minister of Health and Social Welfare: NJABULO MABUZA.

Minister of Public Service and Information: CHARLES S'GAYOYO MAGONGO.

Minister of Public Works and Transport: ELIJAH SHONGWE.

Minister of Natural Resources and Energy: DUMSILE SUKATI.

Minister of Tourism, the Environment and Communication: THANDI SHONGWE.

Minister of Housing and Urban Development: MABILI DLAMINI.

MINISTRIES

Office of the Prime Minister: POB 433, Swazi Plaza, Mbabane; tel. 4042251; fax 4043943; internet www.gov.sz.

Office of the Deputy Prime Minister: POB 433, Swazi Plaza, Mbabane; tel. 4042723; fax 4044085.

Ministry of Agriculture and Co-operatives: POB 162, Mbabane; tel. 4042731; fax 4044700.

Ministry of Economic Planning and Development: POB 602, Mbabane; tel. 4043765; fax 4042157.

Ministry of Education: POB 39, Mbabane; tel. 4042491; fax 4043880.

Ministry of Enterprise and Employment: POB 451, Mbabane; tel. 4043201; fax 4044711; e-mail sglabour@realnet.co.sz.

Ministry of Finance: POB 443, Mbabane; tel. 4048148; fax 4043187; e-mail minfin@realnet.co.sz.

Ministry of Foreign Affairs and Trade: POB 518, Mbabane; tel. 4042661; fax 4042669.

Ministry of Health and Social Welfare: POB 5, Mbabane; tel. 4042431; fax 4042092.

Ministry of Home Affairs: POB 432, Mbabane; tel. 4042941; fax 4044303.

Ministry of Housing and Urban Development: POB 1832, Mbabane; tel. 4041739; fax 4045290.

Ministry of Justice and Constitutional Affairs: POB 924, Mbabane; tel. 4046010; fax 4043533; e-mail ps@justice.gov.sz.

Ministry of Natural Resources and Energy: POB 57, Mbabane; tel. 4046244; fax 4042436; e-mail nergyswa@realnet.co.sz.

Ministry of Public Service and Information: POB 338, Mbabane; tel. 4042761; fax 4042774.

Ministry of Public Works and Transport: POB 58, Mbabane; tel. 4042321; fax 4042364.

Ministry of Regional Development and Youth Affairs: Phutfumani Bldg, Warner St, Mbabane; POB 125, Mbabane H100.

Ministry of Tourism, the Environment and Communication: POB 2652, Mbabane; tel. 4046556; fax 4045415; internet www.mintour.gov.sz.

Legislature

SENATE

There are 30 senators, of whom 20 are appointed by the King and 10 elected by the National Assembly.

President: MUNTU MSAWANE.

NATIONAL ASSEMBLY

There are 65 deputies, of whom 55 are directly elected from candidates nominated by the Tinkhundla and 10 appointed by the King. The latest elections to the National Assembly took place on 18 October 2003.

Speaker: PRINCE GUDUZA.

Election Commission

National Elections Office: POB 4842, Mbabane; tel. 4162813; fax 4161970; Chief Electoral Officer ROBERT TWALA.

Political Organizations

Party political activity was banned by royal proclamation in April 1973, and formally prohibited under the 1978 Constitution. Since 1991, following indications that the Constitution was to be revised, a number of political associations have re-emerged. Following the introduction of the new Constitution in February 2006, the legal status of party political activity remained unclear.

Imbokodvo National Movement (INM): f. 1964 by King Sobhuza II; traditionalist movement, which also advocates policies of devt and the elimination of illiteracy; Leader (vacant).

Ngwane National Liberatory Congress (NNLC): Ilanga Centre, Martin St, Manzini; tel. 5053935; f. 1962 by fmr mems of the SPP; advocates democratic freedoms and universal suffrage, and seeks abolition of the Tinkhundla electoral system; Pres. OBED DLAMINI; Sec.-Gen. DUMISA DLAMINI.

People's United Democratic Movement (PUDEMO): POB 4588, Manzini; tel. and fax 5054181; internet www.members.nbci.com/pudemo; f. 1983; seeks constitutional limitation of the powers of the monarchy; affiliated orgs include the Human Rights Asscn of Swaziland and the Swaziland Youth Congress (SWAYOCO—Pres. ALEX LANGWENYA; Sec.-Gen. KENNETH KUNENE); Pres. MARIO BONGANI MASUKU; Sec. SIKHUMBUZO PHAKATHI.

Swaziland National Front (SWANAFRO): Mbabane; Pres. ELMOND SHONGWE; Sec.-Gen. GLENROSE DLAMINI.

Swaziland Progressive Party (SPP): POB 6, Mbabane; tel. 2022648; f. 1929; Pres. J. J. NQUKU.

Swaziland United Front (SUF): POB 14, Kwaluseni; f. 1962 by fmr mems of the SPP; Leader MATSAPA SHONGWE.

Diplomatic Representation

EMBASSIES IN SWAZILAND

China (Taiwan): Makhosikhosi St, Mbabane; tel. 4044739; fax 4046688; e-mail rocembassy@africaonline.co.sz; Ambassador LEONARD CHAO.

Mozambique: Princess Dr., POB 1212, Mbabane; tel. 4043700; fax 4048402; Ambassador AMOUR ZACARIAS KAPELA.

South Africa: The New Mall, 2nd Floor, Plasmall St, POB 2597, Mbabane; tel. 4044651; fax 4044335; e-mail sahc@africaonline.co.sz; High Commissioner Dr MZOLISI MABUDE.

USA: 2350 Mbabane Pl., Mbabane; tel. 4046441; fax 4045959; internet mbabane.usembassy.gov; Ambassador LEWIS W. LUCKE.

Judicial System

Swaziland's legal system operates on a dual basis, comprising both traditional Swazi National Courts as well as Constitutional Courts. The latter are based on Roman-Dutch law and comprise a High Court (which is a Superior Court of Record) with subordinate courts in all the administrative districts. The Court of Appeal sits at Mbabane. The Constitutional Courts are headed by a Chief Justice, subordinate to whom are judges and magistrates. There is also an Industrial Court.

There are 17 Swazi National Courts, including two Courts of Appeal and a Higher Court of Appeal, which have limited jurisdiction in civil and criminal cases. Their jurisdiction excludes non-Swazi nationals. The Constitutional Courts have the final ruling in the event of any conflict between the two legal systems.

Chief Justice: RICHARD BANDA.

Judge President of the Court of Appeal: RAY LEON.

Religion

About 60% of the adult Swazi population profess Christianity. Under the new Constitution, which came into effect on 7 February 2006, Christianity ceased to be recognized as the country's official religion. At mid-2005 there was a growing Muslim population, reported to number some 10,000 adherents. Most of the remainder of the population hold traditional beliefs.

CHRISTIANITY

At mid-2000 there were an estimated 153,000 Protestants and 466,000 adherents professing other forms of Christianity.

Council of Swaziland Churches: Mandlenkosi Ecumenical House, 142 Esser St, Manzini; POB 1095, Manzini; tel. 5053697; fax 5055841; e-mail c.o.c@africaonline.co.sz; f. 1976; Chair. Bishop NCAMISO LOUIS NDLOVU; Gen. Sec. KHANGEZILE I. DLAMINI; 10 mem. churches incl. Roman Catholic, Anglican, Kukhany'okusha Zion Church and Lutheran.

League of African Churches: POB 230, Lobamba; asscn of 48 independent churches; Chair. SAMSON HLATJWAKO.

Swaziland Conference of Churches: 175 Ngwane St, POB 1157, Manzini; tel. 5055259; fax 5054430; f. 1929; Pres. Rev. NICHOLAS NYAWO; Gen. Sec. JOHANNES V. MAZIBUKO.

The Anglican Communion

Swaziland comprises a single diocese within the Church of the Province of Southern Africa. The Metropolitan of the Province is the Archbishop of Cape Town, South Africa. The Church had some 40,000 members at mid-2000.

Bishop of Swaziland: Rt Rev. MESHACK BOY MABUZA, Bishop's House, Muir St, POB 118 Mbabane; tel. 4043624; fax 4046759; e-mail anglicanchurch@africaonline.co.sz.

The Roman Catholic Church

The Roman Catholic Church was established in Swaziland in 1913. For ecclesiastical purposes, Swaziland comprises the single diocese of Manzini, suffragan to the archdiocese of Pretoria, South Africa. At 31 December 2004 there were an estimated 55,000 adherents in Swaziland (some 5.1% of the total population). The Bishop participates in the Southern African Catholic Bishops' Conference (based in Pretoria, South Africa).

Bishop of Manzini: Rt Rev. LOUIS NCAMISO NDLOVU, Bishop's House, Sandlane St, POB 19, Manzini; tel. 5056900; fax 5056762; e-mail bishop@africaonline.co.sz.

Other Christian Churches

Church of the Nazarene: POB 1460, Manzini; tel. 5054732; f. 1910; 7,649 adherents (1994).

The Evangelical Lutheran Church in Southern Africa: POB 117, Mbabane; tel. 4046453; f. 1902; Bishop M. D. BIYELA; 2,800 adherents in Swaziland (1994).

Mennonite Central Committee: POB 329, Mbabane; tel. 4042805; fax 4044732; f. 1971; Co-ordinator HLOB'SILE NXUMALO.

The Methodist Church in Southern Africa: POB 218, Mbabane; tel. 4042658; f. 1880; 2,578 adherents (1992).

United Christian Church of Africa: POB 1345, Nhlangano; tel. 2022648; f. 1944; Pres. Rev. WELLINGTON B. MKHALIPHI; Founder and Gen. Sec. Dr J. J. NQUKU.

The National Baptist Church, the Christian Apostolic Holy Spirit Church in Zion and the Religious Society of Friends (Quakers) are also active.

BAHÁ'Í FAITH

National Spiritual Assembly: POB 298, Mbabane; tel. 5052689; f. 1960; mems resident in 153 localities.

ISLAM

Ezulwini Islamic Institute: Al Islam Dawah Movement of Swaziland, POB 133, Ezulwini; c. 3,000 adherents (1994).

The Press

PRINCIPAL NEWSPAPERS

The Guardian of Swaziland: POB 4747, Mbabane; tel. 404838; f. 2001; daily newspaper; publ. suspended May 2001, resumed Sept. 2001; Editor THULANI MTHETHWA.

The Swazi News: Sheffield Rd, POB 156, Mbabane; tel. 4042520; fax 4042438; e-mail swazinews@times.co.sz; internet www.times.co.sz; f. 1983; weekly; English; owned by *The Times of Swaziland*; Editor THULANI THWALA; circ. 24,000.

Swazi Observer: Observer House, 3 West St, POB A385, Swazi Plaza, Mbabane; tel. 4049600; fax 4045503; e-mail info@observer.org.sz; internet www.observer.org.sz; f. 1981; owned by Tibiyo Taka Ngwane; Mon.–Sat.; *Weekend Observer* (Sun.); publ. suspended Feb. 2000, resumed March 2001; CEO S. MYZO MAGAGULA; Editor-in-Chief MUSA NDLANGAMANDLA.

Swaziland Today: POB 395, Mbabane; tel. 4041432; fax 4043493; weekly; govt newsletter.

The Times of Swaziland: Sheffield Rd, POB 156, Mbabane; tel. 4042211; fax 4042438; e-mail editor@times.co.sz; internet www.times.co.sz; f. 1897; Mon.–Fri., Sun.; also monthly edn; English; other publs incl. *What's Happening* (tourist interest); Editor MARTIN DLAMINI; circ. 18,000.

PRINCIPAL PERIODICALS

Farming in Swaziland: POB 592, Mbabane; tel. and fax 4041839; e-mail cft@realnet.co.sz; quarterly; Editor CHRISTINA FORSYTH-THOMPSON; circ. 3,000.

The Nation: Mbabane House, 3rd Floor, Warner St, POB 4547, Mbabane; tel. and fax 4046611; e-mail thenation@realnet.co.sz; f. 1997; monthly; independent news magazine; publ. suspended briefly May 2001; Editor BHEKI MAKHUBU.

Swaziview: Mbabane; tel. 4042716; monthly magazine; general interest; circ. 3,500.

UNISWA Journal of Agriculture: Faculty of Agriculture, University of Swaziland, Luyengo Campus, PO Luyengo M205; tel. and fax 5283021; e-mail mwendera@agric.uniswa.sz; annually; Editor-in-Chief Prof. EMMANUEL J. MWENDERA.

UNISWA Research Journal of Agriculture, Science and Technology: Private Bag 4, Kwaluseni; tel. 5184011; fax 5185276; e-mail research@uniswa.sz; internet www.uniswa.sz; 2 a year; publ. of the

Faculties of Agriculture, Health Sciences and Science of the Univ. of Swaziland; Chair. Prof. E. M. Ossom.

Publishers

Apollo Services (Pty) Ltd: POB 35, Mbabane; tel. 4042711.

GBS Printing and Publishing (Pty) Ltd: POB 1384, Mbabane; tel. 5052779.

Jubilee Printers: POB 1619, Matsaka; tel. 5184557; fax 5184558.

Longman Swaziland (Pty) Ltd: POB 2207, Manzini; tel. 5053891.

Macmillan Boleswa Publishers (Pty) Ltd: POB 1235, Manzini; tel. 5184533; fax 5185247; e-mail macmillan@africaonline.co.sz; f. 1978; textbooks and general; CEO Dusanka Stojakovic.

Swaziland Printing & Publishing Co Ltd: POB 28, Mbabane; tel. 4042716; fax 4042710.

Whydah Media Publishers Ltd: Mbabane; tel. 4042716; f. 1978.

Broadcasting and Communications

TELECOMMUNICATIONS

MTN Swaziland: Smuts St, POB 5050, H100 Mbabane; tel. 4060000; fax 4046217; e-mail yellohelp@mtn.co.sz; internet www.mtn.co.sz; f. 1998; jt venture btwn MTN Group, South Africa, and Swaziland Posts and Telecommunications Corpn; operates mobile cellular telephone network; 213,000 subscribers (2005); CEO Themba Khumalo.

Swaziland Posts and Telecommunications Corpn (SPTC): Phutfumani Bldg, Warner St, POB 125, H100 Mbabane; tel. 4052000; fax 4052020; e-mail info@sptc.co.sz; internet www.sptc.co.sz; f. 1983; Chair. Sabelo Masuku; Man. Dir Elijah N. Dlamini.

BROADCASTING

Radio

Swaziland Broadcasting and Information Service: POB 338, Mbabane; tel. 4042763; fax 4046953; e-mail sbisnews@africaonline.co.sz; f. 1966; broadcasts in English and siSwati; Dir Stan Motsa.

Swaziland Commercial Radio (Pty) Ltd: POB 1586, Alberton 1450, South Africa; tel. (11) 4344333; fax (11) 4344777; privately owned commercial service; broadcasts to southern Africa in English and Portuguese; music and religious programmes; Man. Dir A. de Andrade.

Trans World Radio: POB 64, Manzini; tel. 5052781; fax 5055333; f. 1974; religious broadcasts from five transmitters in 30 languages to southern, central and eastern Africa and to the Far East; Pres. David Tucker.

Television

Swaziland Television Authority (Swazi TV): POB A146, Swazi Plaza, Mbabane; tel. 4043036; fax 4042093; e-mail swazitv.eng@africaonline.co.sz; f. 1978; state-owned; broadcasts seven hours daily in English; colour transmissions; CEO Vukani Maziya.

Finance

(cap. = capital; res = reserves; dep. = deposits; m. = million; brs = branches; amounts in emalangeni)

BANKING

Central Bank

Central Bank of Swaziland: POB 546, Mahlokohla St, Mbabane; tel. 4082000; fax 4042636; e-mail info@centralbank.org.sz; internet www.centralbank.org.sz; f. 1974; bank of issue; cap. 21.8m., res 31.4m., dep. 303.7m. (March 2006); Gov. Martin G. Dlamini; Dep. Gov. S. G. Mdluli.

Commercial Banks

First National Bank of Swaziland Ltd: Sales House Bldg, 2nd Floor, POB 261, Mbabane; tel. 4045401; fax 4044735; e-mail hnsibande@fnb.co.za; f. 1988; fmrly Meridien Bank Swaziland Ltd; cap. and res 61.5m., dep. 484.5m. (June 2002); Chair. Dr D. M. J. von Wissel; Man. Dir I. J. M. Leyenaar; 7 brs and 1 agency.

Nedbank (Swaziland) Ltd: Nebank House, Dr Sishayi and Sozisa Rds, Swazi Plaza, POB 68, Mbabane; tel. 4081000; fax 4044060; e-mail info@nedbank.co.sz; internet www.nedbank.co.sz; f. 1974; fmrly Standard Chartered Bank Swaziland Ltd; 23.1% state-owned; cap. 11.9m., res 84.3m., dep. 711.3m. (Dec. 2005); Chair. Zacheus M. Nkosi; Man. Dir Ambrose Dlamini; 6 brs and 1 agency.

Development Banks

Standard Bank Swaziland Ltd: Standard House, 1st Floor, Swazi Plaza, POB A294, Mbabane; tel. 4046930; fax 4045899; internet www.standardbank.co.sz; f. 1988; fmrly Stanbic Bank Swaziland, present name adopted 1997; merged with Barclays Bank of Swaziland in Jan. 1998; 10% state-owned; cap. 14.6m. res 89.3m., dep. 1,454.3m. (Dec. 2005); Chair. R. J. Rossouw (acting); Man. Dir Mervyn Lubbe; 10 brs, 1 agency.

Swaziland Development and Savings Bank (SwaziBank—Libhange LeSive): Engungwini Bldg, Gwamile St, POB 336, Mbabane; tel. 4042551; fax 4042550; internet www.swazibank.sz; f. 1965; state-owned; taken over by central bank in 1995; under independent management since 2000; cap. and res 143.0m., total assets 557.9m. (Mar. 2002); Chair Nokukhanya Gamedze; Man. Dir Stanley M. N. Matsebula; 8 brs.

Financial Institution

Swaziland National Provident Fund: POB 1857, Manzini; tel. 5082000; fax 5082001; internet www.snpf.co.sz; f. 1974; provides benefits for employed persons on retirement from regular employment or in the event of becoming incapacitated; employers are required by law to pay a contribution for every eligible staff member; total assets 290m. (June 1996); CEO Prince Lonkhokhela Dlamini.

STOCK EXCHANGE

Swaziland Stock Exchange: Capital Markets Development Unit, Infumbe Bldg, 1st Floor, Warner St, POB 546, Mbabane; tel. 4082164; fax 4049493; e-mail info@ssx.org.sz; internet www.ssx.org.sz; f. 1990 as Swaziland Stock Market (SSM); state-owned; Chair. Martin G. Dlamini.

INSURANCE

Between 1974 and 1999 the state-controlled Swaziland Royal Insurance Corpn (SRIC) operated as the country's sole authorized insurance company, although cover in a number of areas not served by SRIC was available from several specialized insurers. In 1999 it was proposed that legislation would be enacted to end SRIC's monopoly and provide for the company's transfer to private-sector ownership. The legislation was passed as the Insurance Act in 2005.

Insurance Company

Swaziland Royal Insurance Corpn (SRIC): SRIC House, Somhlolo Rd, Gilfillan St, POB 917, H100 Mbabane; tel. 4043231; fax 4046415; e-mail zrmagagula@sric.sz; internet www.sric.sz; 41% state-owned; 59% owned by Munich-Reinsurance Co of Africa Ltd, Mutual and Fed. Insurance Co of South Africa Ltd, Swiss Re Southern Africa Ltd, S.A. Eagle Insurance Co Ltd, Old Mutual, and Mutual and Federal; sole auth. insurance co 1974–99; Chair. Dr E. T. Gina; Gen. Man. Zombodze R. Magagula.

Insurance Association

Insurance Brokers' Association of Swaziland (IBAS): POB 1072, Mbabane H100; tel. 4043394; fax 4045035; f. 1983; Chair. Keith P. Dukes; 4 mems.

Trade and Industry

GOVERNMENT AGENCY

Small Enterprise Development Co (SEDCO): POB A186, Swazi Plaza, Mbabane; tel. 4042811; fax 4040723; e-mail business@sedco.co.sz; internet www.sedco.ws; f. 1970; devt agency; supplies workshop space, training and expertise for 165 local entrepreneurs at eight sites throughout the country; CEO Dorington Matiwane.

Swaziland Investment Promotion Authority (SIPA): Mbandzeni House, 7th Floor, Church St, POB 4194, Mbabane; tel. 4040472; fax 4043374; e-mail info@sipa.org.sz; internet www.sipa.org.sz; f. 1998; Gen. Man. John W. Creamer (acting).

DEVELOPMENT ORGANIZATIONS

National Industrial Development Corpn of Swaziland (NIDCS): POB 866, Mbabane; tel. 4043391; fax 4045619; f. 1971; state-owned; administered by Swaziland Industrial Devt Co; Admin. Dir P. K. Thamm.

Swaziland Coalition of Concerned Civic Organisations (SCCCO): Smithco Industrial Centre, Mswati III Ave, 11th St, Matsapha; POB 4173, Mbabane; tel. and fax 5187688; e-mail webmaster@swazicoalition.org.sz; internet www.swazicoalition.org

.sz; f. 2003; promotes constitutional democracy, poverty alleviation, fiscal discipline, economic stability, competitive regional and international trade, social justice, and the rule of law; Sec.-Gen. MUSA HLOPE; 9 mems:

Coordinating Assembly of Non-Governmental Organisations (CANGO): POB A67, Swazi Plaza, Mbabane; tel. 4044721; fax 4045532; e-mail director@cango.org.sz; internet www.cango.org.sz; f. 1983; Exec. Dir EMMANUEL NDLANGAMANDLA; over 70 mem. orgs.

Federation of Swaziland Employers and Chamber of Commerce (FSECC): POB 72, Mbabane; tel. 4040768; fax 4090051; e-mail fsecc@business-swaziland.com; internet www.business-swaziland.com; f. 2003 by merger of Fed. of Swaziland Employers (f. 1964) and Swaziland Chamber of Commerce (f. 1916); CEO ZODWA MABUZA; c. 500 mems (2005).

Association of the Swazi Business Community.

Federation of the Swazi Business Community.

Swaziland Association of Teachers.

Swaziland Federation of Labour.

Swaziland Federation of Trade Unions.

Swaziland Law Society.

Women and Law Southern Africa.

Swaziland Industrial Development Co (SIDC): Dhlan'Ubeka House, 5th Floor, cnr Tin and Walker Sts, POB 866, Mbabane; tel. 4044010; fax 4045619; e-mail info@sidc.co.sz; internet www.sidc.co.sz; f. 1986; 34.9% state-owned; finances private-sector projects and promotes local and foreign investment; cap. E24.1m., total assets E178.4m. (June 1999); Chair. TIM ZWANE; Man. Dir TAMBO GINA.

Swaki (Pty) Ltd: Liqhaga Bldg, 4th Floor, Nkoseluhlaza St, POB 1839, Manzini; tel. 5052693; fax 5052001; e-mail info@swaki.co.sz; jtly owned by SIDC and Kirsh Holdings; comprises a number of cos involved in manufacturing, services and the production and distribution of food.

Tibiyo Taka Ngwane (Bowels of the Swazi Nation): POB 181, Kwaluseni; tel. 5184306; fax 5184399; e-mail info@tibiyo.com; internet www.tibiyo.com; f. 1968; national devt agency, with investment interests in all sectors of the economy; participates in domestic and foreign jt investment ventures; total assets: E604m. (1999); Chair. Prince MANGALISO; Man. Dir NDUMISO MAMBA.

Swaziland Solidarity Network (SSN): c/o COSATU House, 3rd Floor, 1–5 Leyds St, Braamfontein, South Africa; POB 1027, Johannesburg 2000; tel. (11) 3393621; fax (11) 3394244; e-mail ssnnetwork@gmail.org.za; internet www.swazisolidarity.org; f. 1997; umbrella org. promoting democracy; incorporates mems from Swaziland and abroad incl. PUDEMO, SWAYOCO, and the Swaziland Democratic Alliance (f. 1999); also incl., from South Africa, the ANC, SACP and COSATU.

CHAMBERS OF COMMERCE

Sibakho Chamber of Commerce: POB 2016, Manzini; tel. 5057347.

Swaziland Chamber of Commerce and Industry: see Fed. of Swaziland Employers and Chamber of Commerce.

INDUSTRIAL AND TRADE ASSOCIATIONS

National Agricultural Marketing Board: POB 4261, Manzini; tel. 5055314; fax 5054072; internet www.swazibusiness.com/namboard; Chair. Prince MABANDLA; CEO OBED HLONGWANE.

National Maize Corpn: POB 158, Manzini; tel. 5187432; fax 5184461; f. 1985.

Swaziland Citrus Board: Sokhamila Bldg, cnr Dzeliwe and Mdada Sts, POB 343, Mbabane H100; tel. 4044266; fax 4043548; e-mail citrus@realnet.co.sz; f. 1969; Chair. H. C. NODDEBOE.

Swaziland Commercial Board: POB 509, Mbabane; tel. 4042930; Man. Dir J. M. D. FAKUDZE.

Swaziland Cotton Board: POB 230, Manzini; tel. 5052775; Gen. Man. TOM JELE.

Swaziland Dairy Board: Liqhaga Bldg, 3rd Floor, POB 2975, Manzini; tel. 5058262; fax 5058260; e-mail ceo-swazidairy@africaonline.co.sz; Gen. Man. N. T. GUMEDE.

Swaziland Sugar Association: 4th Floor, cnr Dzeliwe and Msakato Sts, POB 445, Mbabane; tel. 4042646; fax 4045005; e-mail info@ssa.co.sz; internet www.ssa.co.sz; CEO Dr MICHAEL MATSEBULA.

EMPLOYERS' ORGANIZATIONS

Building Contractors' Association of Swaziland: POB 518, Mbabane; tel. 4040071; fax 4044258.

Swaziland Association of Architects, Engineers and Surveyors: Swazi Plaza, POB A387, Mbabane; tel. 4042309.

Swaziland Institute of Personnel and Training Managers: c/o UNISWA, Private Bag, Kwaluseni; tel. 5184011; fax 5185276.

UTILITIES

Electricity

Swaziland Electricity Board: Mhlambanyatsi Rd, Eluvatsini House, POB 258, Mbabane; tel. 4042521; fax 4042335; internet www.seb.co.sz; statutory body; f. 1963; Man. Dir (vacant).

Water

Swaziland Water Services Corpn: Dhlan'Ubeka House, 6th and 7th Floor, POB 20, Mbabane; tel. 4043161; fax 4045585; internet www.swsc.co.sz; state authority; Chair. ESAU N. ZWANE; CEO PETER N. BHEMBE.

MAJOR COMPANIES

Cadbury Swaziland (Pty) Ltd: POB 679, Matsapha M202; tel. 5186168; fax 5186173; f. 1989; mfrs of confectionery; Gen. Man. GREG STOCK.

Mantenga Craft Centre: POB 364, Eveni; tel. 4161136; fax 4161040; internet www.mantengacrafts.com; f. 1975; handcrafts; incorporates 11 shops; Man. Dir DARREN RARAW.

Natex Swaziland Ltd: Matsapha Industrial Sites, POB 359, Manzini; tel. 5186133; fax 5186029; f. 1987; textiles; Man. Dir A. N. KUMAR; 410 employees.

Neopac Swaziland Ltd: Matsapha Industrial Sites, POB 618, Manzini M200; tel. 5186204; fax 5184277; f. 1968; mfrs of corrugated containers for agriculture and industry; Man. Dir WILLIE HORSBURGH.

Ngwane Mills (Pty) Ltd: Matsapha Industrial Sites, POB 1169, Manzini; tel. 5185011; fax 5185112; f. 1992; subsidiary of Namib Management Services, South Africa; wheat and maize millers; exports wheat flour to South Africa; Man. Dir DAWIE FOURIE.

Palfridge Ltd: POB 424, Matsapha; tel. 5184104; fax 5184126; e-mail info@palfridge.com; internet www.palfridge.com; f. 2001; mfrs of domestic, commercial, medical and camping refrigerators and freezers; Chair. COLIN FOSTER; CEO PETER MCCULLOUGH; 500 employees.

Royal Swaziland Sugar Corpn (RSSC): Simunye Sugar Estate, POB 1, Simunye L301; tel. 3134000; fax 3838171; e-mail info@rssc.co.sz; internet www.rssc.co.sz; f. 1977; 53% owned by Tibiyo Taka Ngwane, 25.9% owned by TSB Sugar Int., 6.5% owned by the Govt of Nigeria; mfrs of sugar, and potable alcohol (80% for export); estates at Mhlume and Simunye; incorporates Royal Swazi Distillers (RSD); Chair. MAMBA NDUMISO; Man. Dir JOHN DU PLESSIS; c. 3,200 employees.

Sappi Kraft (Pty) Ltd (Sappi Usutu): Bhunya, Private Bag, Mbabane H100; tel. 4026010; fax 4026032; internet www.sappi.com; f. 1961; fmrly Usutu Pulp Co Ltd; subsidiary of Sappi, South Africa; mfrs of unbleached kraft pulp; Pres. I. FORBES; Mill Man. SHANE PERROW; 1,539 employees (2002); c. 70,000 ha of timber plantations.

Spintex Swaziland (Pty) Ltd: Mswati III Ave, POB 6, Matsapha; tel. 5186166; fax 5186038; e-mail spintex@africaonline.co.sz; internet www.spintex.co.sz; f. 1991; mfrs of cotton and poly-cotton combed yarns, sewing thread, core yarns, lycra core yarns and open-end yarns; CEO ALEX MNGOMEZULU; 400 employees.

Swazi Paper Mills Ltd: POB 873, Mbabane; tel. 4086024; fax 4086091; f. 1987; Swaziland's largest privately-owned concern; produces paper and paper products; Man. Dir P. SHARMA.

Swazispa Holdings Ltd: POB 331, Mbabane; tel. 4165000; fax 4161606; e-mail swazisun@sunint.co.za; f. 1962; 50.6% owned by All Saints (Pty) Ltd, 39.7% owned by Tibiyo Taka Ngwane; leisure, casino and hospitality operator with interests in property devt and finance; Chair. DAVID D. DLAMINI; Area Gen. Man. A. C. STEYN; 368 employees.

Swazi Timber Products Ltd: POB 2313, Manzini M200; tel. and fax 5186291; fax 5187952; f. 1987; Man. Dir M. RAMKOLOWAN.

Swaziland Brewers Ltd: POB 100, Matsapha; tel. 5186033; fax 5186309; f. 1976; 40% owned by Tibiyo Taka Ngwane; annual production of 250,000 hl of beer; Group Man. Dir M. B. MANYATSHE; 181 employees.

Swaziland Meat Industries Ltd: POB 446, Manzini; tel. 5184165; fax 5190069; e-mail simunyemeats@smi.co.sz; f. 1965; operates an abattoir and deboning plant at Matsapha to process beef for local and export markets; Gen. Man. J. C. WILLIAMS.

Swaziland Safety Glass: Matsapha Industrial Estate, POB 3058, Manzini; tel. 5085366; fax 5085361; f. 1990; mfrs of glass for transport industry; Man. Dir BRIAN BROOKS.

Top-Pine Furniture (Pty) Ltd: POB 4, Piggs Peak H108; tel. 4371344; fax 4371457; e-mail tpfswazi@mweb.co.za; mfrs of pine furniture; Chair. JOHN MORE; Man. Dir. RONNIE BORRAGEIRO; 180 employees.

Ubombo Sugar Ltd: POB 23, Big Bend L311; tel. 3638000; fax 3636330; f. 1958; 60% owned by Illovo Sugar Group, (South Africa), 40% owned by Tibiyo Taka Ngwane; produces raw and refined sugar; Man. Dir EDDIE WILLIAMS.

YKK Zippers (Swaziland) (Pty) Ltd: POB 1425, Mbabane; tel. 5186026; fax 5186132; e-mail s.magagula@ykkafrica.com; f. 1977; mfrs of zip fasteners; Man. Dir T. SHIMIZU.

CO-OPERATIVE ASSOCIATIONS

Swaziland Central Co-operatives Union: POB 551, Manzini; tel. 5052787; fax 5052964.

There are more than 123 co-operative associations, of which the most important is:

Swaziland Co-operative Rice Co Ltd: handles rice grown in Mbabane and Manzini areas.

TRADE UNIONS

At mid-2005 there were 55 organizations recognized by the Department of Labour. Only non-managerial workers may belong to a union.

Trade Union Federations

Swaziland Amalgamated Trade Unions (SATU): POB 7138, Manzini; tel. 5059544; fax 5052684; f. 2003 by merger of five industrial unions; affiliated to the Int. Metalworkers' Fed.; Sec.-Gen. FRANK NKULULEKO MNCINA; 3,500 mems (2005).

Swaziland Federation of Labour (SFL): Swazi Plaza, POB 1173, Mbabane; tel. 4045216; fax 4044261; e-mail sufiaw@realnet.co.sz; affiliated to the Int. Trade Union Confed.; Sec.-Gen. VINCENT V. NCONGWANE; 4,000 mems (2002).

Swaziland Federation of Trade Unions (SFTU): POB 1158, Manzini; tel. and fax 5056575; internet www.cosatu.org.za/sftu; f. 1973; affiliated to the Int. Trade Union Confed.; prin. trade union org. since mid-1980s; represents workers in the agricultural, private and public sectors; Pres. RICHARD NXUMALO; Sec.-Gen. JAN SITHOLE; 83,000 mems.

21 affiliated mem. unions incl.:

Swaziland Agriculture and Plantation Workers' Union (SAPWU): POB 2010, Manzini; tel. 4526010; fax 4526106.

Swaziland Communications Workers' Union (SCWU): c/o Swaziland Post and Telecommunications Corpn, POB 125, Mbabane; fax 4042093; fmrly Swaziland Post and Telecommunications Workers' Union; present name adopted in 2006; Pres. KENNEDY DLAMINI; Sec.-Gen. MANDLA MDLULI.

Swaziland Manufacturing and Allied Workers' Union (SMAWU): Agora Shopping Complex, King Mswati III Ave, Matsapha, POB 2379, Manzini; tel. 5186503; fax 5187028; e-mail smawu@realnet.co.sz; affiliated to the Int. Textile, Garment and Leather Workers' Fed.; Gen. Sec. SIPHO PETERSON MAMBA; 7,000 mems (2004).

Swaziland National Association of Civil Service (SNACS): POB 2811, Manzini M200; tel. 557882; fax 557887; e-mail snacs@swazi.net; f. c. 1980; affiliated to the Public Services Int.; Pres. CHARLES KHUMALO; Gen. Sec. ABSOLOM DLAMINI; 3,855 mems (2002).

Swaziland Nurses Association (Swaziland National Association of Nurses): POB 6191, Manzini; tel. and fax 5058070; f. 1965; affiliated to the Public Services Int.; Pres. PATRICK MASITSELA MHLANGA; Gen. Sec. JULIA JABULILE ZIYANÉ.

Swaziland Transport and Allied Workers' Union (STAWU): POB 3362, Manzini; affiliated to the Int. Transport Workers' Fed.

Other unions affiliated to the SFTU include the Building and Construction Workers' Union of Swaziland; the Swaziland Commercial and Allied Workers' Union; the Swaziland Conservation Workers' Union; the Swaziland Electricity Supply, Maintenance and Allied Workers' Union; the Swaziland Hotel, Catering and Allied Workers' Union; the Swaziland Manufacturing and Allied Workers' Union; the Swaziland Media and Publications Workers' Union; the Swaziland Mining, Quarrying and Allied Workers' Union; the Swaziland Motor Engineering Allied Workers' Union; the Swaziland Union of High Learning Institutions; the Workers' Union of Swaziland Security Guards; the Workers' Union of Town Councils; and the Swaziland Water and Co-operation Workers' Union.

Swaziland National Association for Teachers (SNAT): POB 1575, M200 Manzini; tel. 5052603; fax 5060386; e-mail snatcentre@africaonline.co.sz; affiliated to Education Int.; Pres. SIMON BRIAN MAKHANYA; Sec.-Gen. DOMINIC NXUMALO; 6,000 mems.

Swaziland Union of Financial Institutions and Allied Workers (SUFIAW): 100 Johnson St, Mbabane; tel. 4044261; fax 4045216; e-mail sufiaw@realnet.co.sz; Pres. VINCENT V. NCONGWANE.

Other registered unions include the Association of Lecturers and Academic Personnel of the University of Swaziland; the University of Swaziland Workers' Union; and the Workers' Union of Swaziland Security Guards.

Staff Associations

Three staff associations exist for employees whose status lies between that of worker and that of management: the Nyoni Yami Irrigation Scheme Staff Association, the Swazican Staff Association and the Swaziland Electricity Board Staff Association.

Transport

Buses are the principal means of transport for many Swazis. Bus services are provided by private operators who are required to obtain annual permits for each route from the Road Transportation Board, which also regulates fares.

RAILWAYS

The rail network, which totalled 297 km in 1998–99, provides a major transport link for imports and exports. Railway lines connect with the dry port at Matsapha, the South African ports of Richards Bay and Durban in the south, the South African town of Komatipoort in the north and the Mozambican port of Maputo in the east. Goods traffic is mainly in wood pulp, sugar, molasses, coal, citrus fruit and canned fruit. In June 1998 the Trans Lebombo rail service was launched to carry passengers from Durban to Maputo via Swaziland. The service was terminated in May 2000, owing to insufficient demand. In August 2004 the Government announced plans to privatize Swaziland Railways.

Swaziland Railways: Swaziland Railway Bldg, cnr Johnston and Walker Sts, POB 475, Mbabane; tel. 4047211; fax 4047210; f. 1962; Chair. B. A. G. FITZPATRICK; CEO GIDEON J. MAHLALELA.

ROADS

In 2002 there were an estimated 3,594 km of roads, including 1,465 km of main roads and 2,129 km of secondary roads. About 28.2% of the road network was paved in 1994. The rehabilitation of about 700 km of main and 600 km of district gravel-surfaced roads began in 1985, financed by World Bank and US loans totalling some E18m. In 1991 work commenced on the reconstruction of Swaziland's main road artery, connecting Mbabane to Manzini, via Matsapha, and in 2001 the Government announced the construction of two main roads in the north of the country, financed by Japanese loans.

Roads Department: Ministry of Public Works and Transport, POB 58, Mbabane; tel. 4042321; fax 4042364; e-mail tshabalala@gov.sz; Chief Roads Engineer T. M. TSHABALALA.

SHIPPING

Royal Swazi National Shipping Corpn Ltd: POB 1915, Manzini; tel. 5053788; fax 5053820; f. 1980 to succeed Royal Swaziland Maritime Co; 76% owned by Tibiyo Taka Ngwane; owns no ships, acting only as a freight agent; Gen. Man. M. S. DLAMINI.

CIVIL AVIATION

Swaziland's only airport is at Matsapha, near Manzini, about 40 km from Mbabane. In mid-1997 the Government initiated a three-year programme to upgrade the airport. In early 2003 construction began of an international airport at Sikhupe, in eastern Swaziland. In March 2006 Swaziland Airlink was one of 92 airlines banned from landing at European Union airports owing to safety concerns.

Swaziland Airlink: POB 939, Matsapha Airport, Manzini; tel. 5186155; fax 5186148; f. 1999; fmrly Royal Swazi Nat. Airways Corpn; jt venture between SA Airlink, South Africa, (40%) and the Govt of Swaziland; scheduled passenger services from Manzini to Johannesburg, South Africa; Chair. LINDIWE KHUMALO-MATSE.

Tourism

Swaziland's attractions for tourists include game reserves (at Malolotja, Hawane, Mlawula and Mantenga) and magnificent mountain scenery. In 2005 tourist arrivals fell to 311,656 from 352,040 in 2004; receipts fell from US $113m. in 2003 to $109m. in 2004.

Hotel and Tourism Association of Swaziland: Oribi Court, 1st Floor, Gwamile St, 462, Mbabane; tel. 4042218; fax 4044516; e-mail aliand@realnet.co.sz; internet www.visitswazi.com/tourismassoc; f. 1979.

Swaziland National Trust Commission (SNTC): POB 100, Lobamba; tel. 4161516; fax 4161875; e-mail director@sntc.org.sz (parks and wildlife); e-mail curator@sntc.org.sz (museums and monuments); internet www.sntc.org.sz; f. 1972; parastatal org. responsible for conservation of nature and cultural heritage (national parks, museums and monuments); CEO S. MAMBA.

Swaziland Tourism Authority: POB A1030, Swazi Plaza, Mbabane; tel. 4049693; fax 4049683; e-mail secretary@tourismauthority.org.sz; internet www.welcometoswaziland.com; CEO ERIC SIPHO MASEKO.

Defence

The Umbutfo Swaziland defence force, created in 1973, totalled 2,657 regular troops in November 1983. There is also a paramilitary police force. Compulsory military service of two years was introduced in 1983.

Defence Expenditure: Budgeted at E168m. for 2001/02.

Deputy Commander of the Umbutfo Swaziland Defence Force: Brig. JEFFREY SHABALALA.

Education

Education is not compulsory in Swaziland. Primary education begins at six years of age and lasts for seven years. Secondary education begins at 13 years of age and lasts for up to five years, comprising a first cycle of three years and a second of two years. According to UNESCO estimates, in 2002/03 77% of children in the relevant age-group (males 76%; females 77%) were enrolled at primary schools, while in that year secondary enrolment included 29% of children in the appropriate age-group (males 26%; females 32%). In 2003/04 4,198 students were enrolled at the University of Swaziland, which has campuses at Luyengo and Kwaluseni. There are also a number of other institutions of higher education: in 2000, there were 1,822 students enrolled at 10 vocational, technical and teacher-training colleges. According to the IMF, of total expenditure by the central Government in 2001/02, E607m. (18.4%) was for education.

Bibliography

Bischoff, P.-H. *Swaziland's International Relations and Foreign Policy: A Study of a Small African State in International Relations*. Berne, P. Lang, 1990.

Booth, A. R. *Historical Dictionary of Swaziland*. Metuchen, NJ, Scarecrow Press, 1975.

Swaziland: Tradition and Change in a Southern African Kingdom. Boulder, CO, Westview Press, 1983; London, Gower Publishers, 1984.

Booth, M. Z. *Culture and Education: The Social Consequences of Western Schooling in Contemporary Swaziland*. Lanham, MD, University Press of America, 2004.

Daniel, J., and Stephen, M. F. (Eds). *Historical Perspectives on the Political Economy of Swaziland*. Kwaluseni, University of Swaziland, 1986.

Davies, R. H., *et al.* (Eds). *The Kingdom of Swaziland: A Profile*. London, Zed Press, 1985.

Forster, S., and Nsibande, B. S. (Eds). *Swaziland: Contemporary Social and Economic Issues*. Aldershot, Ashgate Publishing Ltd, 2000.

Funnell, D. C. *Under the Shadow of Apartheid: Agrarian Transformation in Swaziland*. Aldershot, Avebury, 1991.

Gillis, D. H. *The Kingdom of Swaziland*. Westport, CT, Greenwood Publishing Group, 1999.

Gosnell, P. J. *Big Bend: A History of the Swaziland Bushveld*. Durban, Peter J. Gosnell, 2001.

Konczacki, Z. A., *et al.* (Eds). *Studies in the Economic History of Southern Africa*. Vol. II. London, Cass, 1991.

Leliveld, A. *Social Security in Developing Countries: Operation and Dynamics of Social Security Mechanisms in Rural Swaziland*. Amsterdam, Thesis Publishers, 1994.

Matsebula, J. S. *A History of Swaziland*. 2nd Edn. Cape Town, Maskew Miller, Longmans, 1988.

Okpalmba, Chuks, *et al.* (Eds). *Human Rights in Swaziland: The Legal Response*. Kwaluseni, University of Swaziland, 1997.

Oluikpe, B. O. *Swazi*. New York, NY, Rosen Publishing Co, 1997.

Organization for Social Science Research in Eastern and Southern Africa (OSSREA). *Democracy, Transformation, Conflict and Public Policy in Swaziland*. Kwaluseni, OSSREA Swaziland Chapter, 2003.

Issues in the Economy and Politics of Swaziland since 1968. Kwaluseni, OSSREA Swaziland Chapter, 2003.

Rose, L. L. *The Politics of Harmony: Land Dispute Strategies in Swaziland*. Cambridge, Cambridge University Press, 1992.

Schwager, D. *Swaziland*. Mbabane, Websters, 1984.

Simelane, H. S. *Colonialism and Economic Change in Swaziland 1940–1960*. Manzini, Jan Publishing Centre, 2003.

Simelane, N. C. (Ed.). *Social Transformation: The Swaziland Case*. Dakar, CODESRIA, 1995.

TANZANIA

Physical and Social Geography

L. BERRY

PHYSICAL FEATURES AND CLIMATE

The 945,087 sq km (364,900 sq miles) of the United Republic of Tanzania (incorporating mainland Tanganyika and a number of offshore islands, including Zanzibar, Pemba, Latham and Mafia) have a wide variety of land forms, climates and peoples. The country includes the highest and lowest points in Africa—the summit of Mt Kilimanjaro (5,892 m above sea-level) and the floor of Lake Tanganyika (358 m below sea-level). The main upland areas occur in a northern belt—the Usambara, Pare, Kilimanjaro and Meru mountains; a central and southern belt—the Southern highlands, the Ugurus and the Ulugurus; and a north–south trending belt, which runs southwards from the Ngorongoro Crater. The highest peaks are volcanic, although block faulting has been responsible for the uplift of the plateau areas. Other fault movements have resulted in the depressed areas of the rift valleys; Lakes Tanganyika, Malawi, Rukwa, Manyara and Eyasi occupy part of the floor of these depressions. Much of the rest of the interior comprises gently sloping plains and plateaux, broken by low hill ranges and scattered isolated hills. The coast includes areas with wide sandy beaches and with developed coral reefs, but these are broken by extensive growth of mangroves, particularly near the mouths of the larger rivers.

With the exception of the high mountain areas, temperatures in Tanzania are not a major limiting factor for crop growth, although the range of altitude produces a corresponding range of temperature regimes from tropical to temperate. Rainfall is variable, both from place to place and time to time, and is generally lower than might be expected for the latitude. About one-fifth of Tanzania can expect with 90% probability more than 750 mm of rainfall annually, and only about 3% normally receives more than 1,250 mm. The central third of the country is semi-arid (less than 500 mm), with evaporation exceeding rainfall in nine months of the year. For much of Tanzania most rain falls in one rainy season, December–May, though two peaks of rainfall in October–November and April–May are found in some areas. Apart from the problem of the long dry season over most parts of the country, there is also a marked fluctuation in annual rainfall from one year to the next, and this may be reflected in the crop production and livestock figures.

The surplus water from the wetter areas drains into the few large perennial rivers. The largest of these, the Rufiji, drains the Southern highlands and much of southern Tanzania. With an average discharge of 1,133 cu m per second, it is one of the largest rivers in Africa, and has major potential for irrigation and hydroelectric power development. The Ruvu, Wami and Pangani also drain to the Indian Ocean. The Pangani has already been developed for hydroelectric power, which supplies Arusha, Moshi, Tanga, Morogoro and Dar es Salaam. Apart from the Ruvuma, which forms the southern frontier, most other drainage is to the interior basins, or to the Lakes Tanganyika, Victoria and Malawi.

The most fertile soils in Tanzania are the reddish-brown soils derived from the volcanic rocks, although elsewhere *mbuga* and other alluvial soils have good potential. The interior plateaux are covered with tropical loams of moderate fertility. The natural vegetation of the country has been considerably modified by human occupation. In the south and west-central areas there are large tracts of woodland covering about 30% of the country, while on the uplands are small but important areas of tropical rain forest. Clearly marked altitudinal variations in vegetation occur around the upland areas and some distinctive mountain flora is found. Tanzania has set aside about one-third of its land for national parks and game and forest reserves.

POPULATION AND RESOURCES

According to the census of 25 August 2002, Tanzania had a population of 34,569,232. In August 2002 some 593,623 people resided in the autonomous Zanzibar region (the islands of Pemba and Zanzibar). According to UN estimates, Tanzania had a population of 39,459,000 in mid-2006, and a population density of 41.8 people per sq km. Most of the country's inhabitants are of African origin, although people of Indian and Pakistani ancestry comprise a significant component of the urban population. Tanzania is one of the least urbanized countries of Africa. According to official estimates, the population of the principal towns at mid-1988 was: Dar es Salaam (1,360,850), Mwanza (223,013), Dodoma (203,833), Tanga (187,455), Zanzibar town (157,634) and Mbeya (152,844). There are more than 120 ethnic groups in Tanzania, of which the largest are the Sukuma and the Nyamwezi. None, however, exceeds 10% of the total population.

Traditionally, the main features of the pattern of population distribution have been, firstly, sharp variations in density, with a number of densely populated areas separated from each other by zones of sparse population; secondly, the comparatively low density of population in most of the interior of the country; and, thirdly, the preponderance in rural areas of scattered individual homesteads. Since the late 1960s, however, the majority of the rural population have been settled in nucleated villages. The highest population densities, reaching over 250 per sq km, occur on the fertile lower slopes of Mt Kilimanjaro and on the shores of Lake Malawi. Most other upland areas have relatively high densities, as does the area south of Lake Victoria known as Sukumaland.

Agriculture, which employs about four-fifths of the economically active population, is geared in large part towards subsistence farming. The main cash crops are coffee, cotton, cashew nuts, cloves (Zanzibar's principal export, cultivated mainly on the island of Pemba), tobacco, tea, sisal, pyrethrum, coconuts, sugar, cardamom and groundnuts. Exports of cut flowers commenced in the mid-1990s. Tanzania's mineral resources include diamonds, other gemstones, gold, salt, phosphates, coal, gypsum, kaolin, tin, limestone and graphite, all of which are exploited. There are also reserves of nickel, silver, copper, cobalt, lead, soda ash, iron ore, tungsten, pyrochlore, magnesite, niobium, titanium, vanadium, uranium and natural gas.

Dar es Salaam is the main port, the dominant industrial centre, and the focus of government and commercial activity. Dar es Salaam has been growing at a substantial rate and attempts are being made to decentralize industrial development to other centres. Arusha has also been growing rapidly in recent years, partly because of its importance to tourism.

Considerable variation in the pattern of development occurs within Tanzania. In some areas agriculture is becoming much more orientated towards cash crops. In such a large country distance to market is an important factor, and in successive development plans major attempts have been made to improve the main and subsidiary communication networks. The Tan-Zam road and Tazara railway are an important addition, leaving only the far west and the south-east without good surface links to the rest of the country.

Recent History

GRAHAM MATTHEWS

Revised by MICHAEL JENNINGS

European interest in the area that now forms the United Republic of Tanzania was attracted in the 17th century by the mercantile opportunities of the Omani-controlled caravan trade from Zanzibar into the eastern Congo and Buganda. British trading interests on the island and its then extensive coastal possessions expanded rapidly after 1841. Zanzibar declared its independence from Oman in 1856, and its mainland areas were acquired by the United Kingdom and Germany in 1886–90, when a British protectorate was established over the islands of Zanzibar and Pemba.

Mainland Tanganyika was declared a German protectorate in 1885. In 1920, following the defeat of Germany in the First World War, Tanganyika was placed under a League of Nations mandate, with the United Kingdom as the administering power, and in 1946 became a UN trust territory, still under British administration. The politicization of indigenous Africans began in 1929, with the formation of the Tanganyika African Association, which evolved in 1954 into the Tanganyika African National Union (TANU), under the leadership of Julius Nyerere.

THE NYERERE PERIOD, 1959–85

TANU won decisive victories in general elections held in Tanganyika in 1959 and 1960, when Nyerere became Chief Minister. Nyerere duly became Prime Minister when internal self-government was granted in May 1961. Full independence followed on 9 December. In January 1962 Nyerere resigned as Prime Minister; he was succeeded by Rashidi Kawawa. In December Tanganyika became a republic, with Nyerere returning to power as the country's first President, having been elected in the previous month. Kawawa became Vice-President.

Zanzibar (together with the neighbouring island of Pemba and several smaller islets), became an independent sultanate in December 1963. The Sultan was overthrown in an armed uprising in January 1964, following which a republic was declared and the Afro-Shirazi Party (ASP) took power. In April an Act of Union between Tanganyika and Zanzibar was signed. The leader of the ASP, Abeid Karume, became the United Republic's First Vice-President, as well as being Chairman of the ruling Supreme Revolutionary Council of Zanzibar. The Union was named Tanzania in October.

A new Constitution, introduced in July 1965, provided for a one-party state (although, until 1977, TANU and the ASP remained the respective official parties of mainland Tanzania and Zanzibar, and co-operated in affairs of state). Nyerere was re-elected as President in September 1965, and subsequently in the 1970, 1975 and 1980 elections. Early in 1967 TANU adopted a programme of socialism and self-reliance, known as the Arusha Declaration. National development was to be based upon that of the rural sector via community (*ujamaa*) villages. Commercial banks and many industries were immediately nationalized. The National Assembly voted in June 1975 to incorporate the fundamental principles of socialism and self-reliance into the Constitution. The programme ran into difficulties in the 1970s, facing increased resistance from those being forced into *ujamaa* villages.

In Zanzibar, Karume was assassinated in April 1972. His successor, Aboud Jumbe, reorganized the islands' Government in that month by extending the powers of the ASP. Despite its incorporation into Tanzania, Zanzibar retained a separate administration, which ruthlessly suppressed all opposition.

In 1972 Kawawa was reappointed to the revived post of Prime Minister. In February 1977 TANU and the ASP merged to form the Chama Cha Mapinduzi (CCM—Revolutionary Party), of which Nyerere was elected Chairman and Jumbe Vice-Chairman. A government reshuffle followed, in which Kawawa was replaced as premier by Edward Sokoine. In April the National Assembly adopted a permanent Constitution for Tanzania, providing for the election of 10 Zanzibari representatives to the National Assembly. In October 1979 the Supreme Revolutionary Council of Zanzibar adopted a separate Constitution, governing Zanzibar's internal administration, with provisions for a popularly elected President and a legislative House of Representatives elected by delegates of the CCM.

In early 1984 demands were made for greater autonomy for Zanzibar, sparking a political crisis. Jumbe and three of his ministers resigned in January, and in April Ali Hassan Mwinyi was elected President of Zanzibar (thus also becoming Vice-President of Tanzania). A new, more liberal, Constitution for the islands was introduced in January 1985, providing for the House of Representatives to be directly elected by universal suffrage and for the introduction of a Commonwealth legal system.

In October 1985 Mwinyi was elected as President of Tanzania with 96% of the valid votes cast. Idris Abdul Wakil (formerly Speaker of the Zanzibar House of Representatives) was elected President of Zanzibar to replace Mwinyi. After taking office in November, Mwinyi appointed Joseph Warioba, previously Minister of Justice, as Prime Minister and First Vice-President.

THE MWINYI PRESIDENCY, 1985–95

The change of President coincided with a worsening economic crisis (see below). The new administration was forced to accept a range of policy proposals from the IMF, including greater encouragement to the private sector, and policies on budgeting, agricultural reform and currency valuation to persuade continued aid flows from key donors.

In February 1990 the CCM initiated a campaign against corruption among government officials and in the following month Mwinyi dismissed seven ministers who had allegedly opposed plans for economic reform and presided over corrupt or irresponsible ministries. In August, following the resignation of Nyerere, Mwinyi was appointed Chairman of the CCM. In October concurrent parliamentary and presidential elections were held in Zanzibar. The sole presidential candidate, Dr Salmin Amour, was elected as Wakil's successor with 97.7% of the votes cast. At the end of October national parliamentary and presidential elections took place. Mwinyi, the sole candidate in the presidential election, was re-elected, receiving 95.5% of the votes cast. Warioba was replaced as Prime Minister by John Malecela.

In May 1992 the Constitution was amended to implement a plural political system. The amendment stipulated that all new political organizations should command support in both Zanzibar and mainland Tanzania, and should be free of tribal, religious and racial bias.

In early 1993 the Zanzibar Government attempted to join the Organization of the Islamic Conference (OIC). The National Assembly ruled that Zanzibar's membership of the OIC was unconstitutional, and it withdrew in August. Relations between the islands and mainland worsened. In November foreign donors suspended aid disbursements following allegations of official connivance in widespread tax evasion. Malecela, Kolimba and Kighoma Ali Malima, the Minister of Finance, were dismissed and Cleopa Msuya reappointed to the premiership.

In July 1995 the CCM convened a special national conference to select a candidate to contest the forthcoming presidential election. Under Nyerere's influence the shortlist was restricted to three candidates: Msuya, Lt-Col Jakaya Kikwete, the Minister of Finance, and Benjamin Mkapa, the Minister of Science, Technology and Higher Education. Mkapa was nominated following Nyerere's intervention.

Opposition and Division

By the mid-1990s more than a dozen opposition movements were officially recognized. Nevertheless, the first multi-party by-election in April 1993 was boycotted by all but one of the newly registered parties, and the CCM won by default. In February 1994 the CCM won the third by-election of the multi-party era. However, in a significant judgment delivered in August, the High Court upheld the petition of the opposition Chama Cha Demokrasia na Maendeleo (Chadema) that the seat had been won by unfair means. The CCM's authority was further challenged in early 1995, when Augustine Mrema joined the opposition National Convention for Construction and Reform (NCCR—Mageuzi). In June, following allegations of personal financial irregularities, the Minister of Industry and Trade, Malima, was forced to resign from the Government. Malima defected to the opposition National Reconstruction Alliance (NRA), briefly leading the party until his death in August.

THE 'THIRD PHASE' GOVERNMENT

In October 1995 multi-party legislative and presidential elections were held for the first time both in Zanzibar (see below) and throughout the Tanzanian Union. The CCM won 186 of the 232 elective seats in the National Assembly, while the Civic United Front (CUF), a party favouring Zanzibari autonomy (see below), secured 24 seats; NCCR—Mageuzi won 16, and both Chadema and the United Democratic Party (UDP) took three seats. Mkapa was elected national President, winning 61.8% of the votes cast. Omar Ali Juma (hitherto the Chief Minister of Zanzibar) was appointed Vice-President. Mkapa appointed Frederick Sumaye (formerly Minister of Agriculture) as Prime Minister. The opposition refused to participate in the new administration (known as the 'third phase' Government) in protest at alleged electoral fraud by the CCM.

In January 1996 Mkapa appointed a special presidential commission, under the chairmanship of the former premier, Warioba, to investigate corruption in high public office. At a special congress of the CCM, held in June, Mkapa was elected party Chairman. In September the Minister of Finance, Simon Mbilinyi, resigned after a parliamentary select committee investigating bribery allegations recommended that he be made accountable for having illegally granted tax exemptions. In December the Warioba commission issued a report asserting that corruption was widespread in the public sector.

In early August 1998 a powerful bomb exploded outside the US embassy in Dar es Salaam (concurrently with a similar attack at the US mission in Nairobi, Kenya); 11 people were killed in Dar es Salaam and some 86 were injured. The attacks were believed to have been co-ordinated by international Islamist terrorists led by a Saudi-born dissident, Osama bin Laden. Two suspects were charged with murder by the Tanzanian authorities in mid-September in connection with the Dar es Salaam attack. In February 2001 the trial of four men accused of involvement in the bombings began in New York, USA. All four were convicted at the end of May and sentenced to life imprisonment.

In late April 1999 Mrema and his faction of NCCR—Mageuzi defected to the Tanzania Labour Party (TLP). Mrema initially assumed the chairmanship of the TLP; in mid-May, however, he was banned by the High Court from holding any official post in the party.

THE OCTOBER 2000 ELECTIONS

In June 1999 six opposition parties without representation in the National Assembly formed the Outside Parliament Political Parties Organization, under the chairmanship of Emmanuel Makaidi, leader of the National League for Democracy (NLD). Other parties represented in the coalition included the NRA, the Tanzania Democratic Alliance Party (TADEA), the Popular National Party (PONA), the Union for Multi-Party Democracy of Tanzania (UMD) and the United People's Democratic Party (UPDP).

In October 1999 the report of the committee charged with assessing public opinion on constitutional reform suggested that some 96.3% of Zanzibaris and 85.0% of mainland Tanzanians favoured a 'two-tier' government for the United Republic; the committee itself recommended the establishment of a 'three-tier' system. In so doing it was adjudged by Mkapa to have exceeded its mandate. In February 2000 the National Assembly approved draft legislation to amend the Constitution in accordance with the citizens' recommendations as reported by the committee. Opposition deputies declared that they would legally challenge the proposed legislation if necessary to prevent its enactment.

The National Election Commission (NEC) announced various measures in an attempt to guarantee free and fair elections, reflecting opposition concerns over voting procedures: polling booths were to be introduced, replacing voting in the open; ballot boxes were to be transparent; and NEC division offices were not to be used as polling stations, nor division officers appointed as returning officers, owing to many NEC staff having their own political interests. In July 2000 the media agreed new guide-lines, which urged journalists to report objectively during the elections; it was reported that media coverage of the elections was to be monitored by a Tanzanian non-governmental organization (NGO), the Legal and Human Rights Centre. However, in the same month the publicly funded media were accused of broadcasting pro-Government propaganda by a human rights group, ARTICLE 19.

In late July 2000 seven parties (the CCM, NCCR—Mageuzi, TADEA, the UMD, PONA, the Tanzania People's Party—TPP—and the UPDP) agreed on a code of conduct during a joint meeting with the NEC. The code barred politicians from using prayer meetings or places of worship to carry out political campaigns, and banned religious leaders from using their positions to campaign for political parties or candidates during prayer sessions. Two parties rejected the code of conduct completely. The CUF complained that voter registration centres were located in centres belonging to the CCM and in military bases. There were reported incidents, in the north-western region of the mainland, of police dispersing rallies organized by the CUF and Chadema, on the grounds that the official campaigning period had not begun. The CUF and Chadema protested, however, that the rallies were part of their campaign to mobilize people to register as voters.

At the presidential election, held on 29 October 2000, Mkapa was re-elected, securing 71.7% of votes cast; Ibrahim Lipumba, the Chairman of the CUF, secured 16.3%, Mrema 7.8% and John Cheyo, the Chairman of the UDP, 4.2%. The participation rate was 84%. At the parliamentary elections, held concurrently, the CCM secured 244 seats in the National Assembly. The CUF took 15 seats; Chadema, the TLP and the UDP won four, three and two seats, respectively. The polls were declared by international observers to have been freely and fairly conducted, in marked contrast to the controversial events in Zanzibar (see below). In November Mkapa appointed a new national Cabinet, reappointing Sumaye as Prime Minister (official confirmation of the national election results had been delayed until after some Zanzibari constituencies had conducted new polls).

DOMESTIC ISSUES PRIOR TO THE 2005 ELECTIONS

In the run-up to the 2005 elections political attention within the CCM turned to the issue of the successor to Mkapa, who was coming to the end of his two-term limit. The internal campaign to nominate a candidate became increasingly bitter, and exposed serious divisions within the party. Mkapa and former Vice-President Kawawa both indicated their support for the Minister of Foreign Affairs and International Co-operation, Jakaya Kikwete, who in the event defeated his nearest rival Dr Salim Ahmed Salim by 1,072 to 476 votes to be chosen as the CCM's candidate. Meanwhile, the opposition remained fragmented across 17 political parties, and made little headway in presenting a serious challenge to the dominance of the CCM (with the exception of Zanzibar, where the CUF maintained a strong presence).

In early August 2005 12 of the 18 registered political parties signed a code of conduct for the election campaigning period. The agreement guaranteed equal media space and fair coverage for all candidates and parties, and advised religious leaders not to participate or influence campaigns, and politicians not to use places of worship as venues for rallies or other political events. The Government agreed to ensure that the security services did not use excessive force in the maintenance of order, and not to interfere with rallies and meetings sanctioned by the NEC. Candidates also agreed to campaign in Kiswahili, not in local languages or in English. The NCCR accused the NEC of being too weak to effectively regulate and control the CCM, but nevertheless signed up to the agreement, leaving the Forum for the Restoration of Democracy as the only registered party refusing to adhere to it. The official presidential and parliamentary election campaign began on 21 August. In September violence connected to campaigning increased in intensity on the mainland, and at the end of the month it was announced that security was being increased across the country in response.

THE KIKWETE ADMINISTRATION

On 25 October 2005, five days before the elections were to be held, Jumbe Rajab Jumbe, Chadema's vice-presidential candidate, died. As a result the mainland elections were initially postponed until 18 December, although they were subsequently rescheduled to take place on 14 December. The elections proceeded on 14 December and were generally peaceful and well attended. Kikwete was elected as Tanzania's fourth president, taking 80.28% of the votes cast, a larger margin of victory than expected by many analysts. The CCM won an overwhelming majority in the legislative elections, securing 206 of the 232 elective seats in the National Assembly, an increase of six seats compared with 2000. The CUF won 19 seats, Chadema took five seats and the TLP and UDF each won one seat. Around 11.9m. people voted, equating to voter turnout of 72.4%. Following the allocation of seats reserved for women, presidential nominees and members of the Zanzibari House of Representatives, the CCM received a total of 266 seats, the CUF 28, Chadema 11 and the TLP and UDP one each. In January 2006 Kikwete announced his Cabinet, having designated Edward Lowassa, hitherto the Minister of Water and Livestock Development, as Prime Minister in late December. The number of women at cabinet level was significantly increased, accounting for seven of the 19 ministers, and 10 of the 30 deputy ministers. Most notably, Zakia Meghji was promoted to Minister for Finance, and Dr Asha-Rose Migiro to the Ministry of Foreign Affairs and International Co-operation. In early 2007 Migiro was appointed to the post of Deputy UN Secretary-General, the first African to hold the position, and a minor reorganization of the Cabinet was carried out.

Meanwhile, in May 2006 the Government began the politically sensitive task of forcibly evicting around 1,000 pastoralists living in the Ihefu Basin, in Mbeya region. Riot police were deployed to assist the process, and police held more than 1,000 head of cattle. The Government was concerned about land degradation and conservation in the area, a major source of water for the Great Ruaha river and the several hydroelectric dams downstream. However, pastoralist groups complained that no provision had been made for their resettlement.

In June 2006, in an effort to assert his authority over the divided CCM, Kikwete assumed the presidency of the party, and appointed key allies to senior positions within the organization. However, divisions over his succession remained. In October the Cabinet was reshuffled, in part to give a visible indication of the Government's continued determination to quicken the pace of modernization, but largely in response to the growing crisis in the energy sector. Dr Ibrahim Msabaha was moved from the energy and minerals portfolio to the Ministry of East African Co-operation, following a sustained period of controversy over continued poor supplies in energy and power that threatened the collapse of the energy sector. He was replaced by Mustapha Kalamagi. The move, designed to restore confidence in Kikwete's administration, nevertheless failed to end the energy crisis, and in January 2007 areas within Dar es Salaam were still without power for up to 18 hours each day. Plans to privatize the state-owned energy company, the Tanzania Electric Supply Company Ltd, were revealed in 2007, and the 2007/08 budget, announced in June 2007, withdrew Ts. 10,000m. of state subsidies to the energy sector.

Kikwete's Government appeared to be impressing foreign donors during 2006 and 2007. The World Bank's 'Doing Business 2007: How to Reform' report stated that Tanzania was among the 10 best global reformers in 2005–06, giving warm support to Kikwete's efforts to encourage foreign direct investment (FDI). The annual report of the UN Conference on Trade and Development for 2006 named the country as the 12th most effective in Africa in securing FDI.

Further concerns over Tanzania's infrastructure, and Dar es Salaam's in particular, arose in light of a cholera epidemic that affected the city in late 2006, transmitted through the city's poor water supplies. In November Lowassa presented the city's authorities with an ultimatum: to curb the spread of cholera within two weeks or face dismissal. The epidemic peaked in mid-December with an average of 17 deaths each day since the beginning of the month. City health officials began a programme of purifying water wells with chlorine, banned the cultivation of vegetables within Dar es Salaam (claiming farmers often used toxic water), and made regular inspections of restaurants, hotels and bars.

In January 2007 Rift Valley fever, which had broken out in Kenya in late 2006, had spread to Tanzania. The Government immediately instituted measures to prevent the spread of the disease. The movement of cattle between Kenya and Tanzania was banned, and restrictions were placed on the internal movement of livestock. A cattle vaccination campaign was begun and 500,000 doses were purchased from South Africa. By May 109 people had died of the disease (almost double the fatality rate of the epidemic in Kenya), and 684 people had been infected.

In February 2007 opposition parties issued a joint statement threatening to boycott the 2010 elections unless constitutional reforms were made. In the same month the controversy over possible corruption in relation to the purchase of an air traffic radar system from the British company BAE Systems in 2001 continued. The Government announced that it would seek compensation from the United Kingdom if an inquiry into the purchase of the British system showed evidence of corruption and overcharging. Kikwete also announced that any officials found guilty of accepting bribes would be prosecuted.

TENSIONS IN ZANZIBAR

In early 1988 political tensions began to increase in Zanzibar, reflecting rivalries between the inhabitants of the main island and those of the smaller island of Pemba, between Zanzibar's African and Arab populations and between supporters and opponents of the Union.

In January 1988, following allegations of a coup plot, President Wakil suspended the Supreme Revolutionary Council and assumed control of the armed forces. The Chief Minister, Seif Sharif Hamad, was dismissed, together with five other ministers. All were subsequently expelled from the CCM, and in May 1989 Hamad was arrested for allegedly being in possession of secret government documents and for attending an 'illegal meeting' in Pemba. Omar Ali Juma, a senior government official, was appointed as the new Chief Minister.

The continuation of the Union was increasingly questioned by dissident groups such as the Movement for Democratic Alternative (MDA) and a smaller, religiously based group on Pemba, the Bismillah Party, which had emerged before the adoption of multi-party politics in 1992. Opposition in Zanzibar coalesced around the Kamati ya Mageuzi Huru (Kamahuru), led by Shaaban Mloo, which merged with the mainland-based Chama cha Wananchi to form the CUF in 1992.

The CCM secured 26 of the 50 elective seats in the October 1995 elections to the House of Representatives. The CUF, campaigning for increased Zanzibari autonomy, took 24 seats, including every constituency on Pemba. The ZEC credited Satmin Amour (who had succeeded Wakil in October 1990) with a narrow victory with 50.2% of the votes cast. Hamad, representing the CUF, secured 49.8%. Rejecting Nyerere's advice to form a government of national unity with the opposition, Amour appointed a new Supreme Revolutionary Council, with Dr Mohamed Gharib Bilali as Chief Minister.

The CUF refused to accept the election result and demanded the contest be restaged. The newly elected CUF delegates refused to take up their seats in the legislature.

During 1996 external donors began to suspend aid disbursements to Zanzibar, in view of the continuing political impasse between the islands' administration and the CUF; the Government repeatedly claimed that Zanzibar was being destabilized by an 'external plot'. The Zanzibari CCM, meanwhile, came under considerable pressure from senior mainland CCM officials to reach an agreement with the CUF, while that party's leadership eventually resigned itself to accepting Amour's tenure of the presidency until the end of his term in 2000. A mutual accord was finally concluded in early June 1999. CUF deputies took up the 24 seats that they had boycotted, in return for promises of constitutional, judicial and electoral reform intended to ensure free and fair elections. In May 2000 the CCM reneged on the agreement, stating that any reforms would not be implemented until after the October elections.

In the run up to the October 2000 elections, the CUF complained that its politicians and supporters were being intimidated by state security services. In April 18 CUF members, awaiting trial since detention in 1997 and 1998, were refused bail. Although they were named in July 2000 as CUF candidates, they were still in detention in August and therefore ineligible to stand. In May Hamad was charged with assault and violent robbery, and the CUF was charged with 114 criminal acts including alleged terrorism. Frequent clashes between CCM and CUF supporters occurred during the voter-registration procedure and in mid-August armed troops were deployed on Zanzibar, ostensibly to ensure security during the elections. The CUF reported that security services had detained over 120 of its agents and candidates, and that over 7,000 CUF supporters had been barred from registering to vote.

Presidential and legislative elections were held on Zanzibar and Pemba on 29 October 2000, amid widespread accusations of electoral fraud. Voting in 16 of the 50 constituencies was annulled (all areas of strong CUF support) and new elections arranged. The ZEC rejected calls from opposition parties and Commonwealth observers for a complete rerun of the elections, and following a week of violent clashes between police and opposition supporters, the annulled polls were held on 5 November. The CCM claimed it had won 34 seats in the House of Representatives, securing 67% of the vote. The CUF refused to recognize the results and demanded a complete rerun of the election. Popular unrest and violence continued, with a wave of bomb attacks across the islands. On 27–28 January 2001 clashes between police and demonstrators left at least 40 people dead (including six members of the security forces) and 100 people injured. Over 400 people were arrested and imprisoned, and the police used tear gas and live ammunition to disperse crowds, while troops were deployed in Pemba to restore order. Police reportedly refused to allow local hospitals to treat the wounded, and many fled to Kenya to seek treatment and escape detention. By February 636 Zanzibari refugees had claimed asylum in Kenya. Two prominent CUF politicians were arrested in that month, charged with murdering a policeman in the January demonstrations. Amnesty International condemned the charges as politically motivated.

Efforts to mediate a peaceful solution continued throughout 2001. Upon his election as President, Amani Abeid Karume of the CCM withdrew the treason charges against the 18 CUF members. A series of secret negotiations concluded with the signing of a *muafaka* (peace accord) between the CUF and the CCM in October. All charges related to the January disturbances were withdrawn, and a joint presidential monitoring commission was appointed by Karume. The accord recommended amendments to the Zanzibari constitution, approved by the House of Representatives in April 2002, bringing opposition representatives onto the electoral commission, and removing residential qualifications for voter registration deemed unfair by the CUF. A right to appeal High Court decisions was also established. Nevertheless, tensions on the islands remained high, and a wave of political and religious militancy swept across Zanzibar in 2003 and 2004. In February 2004 supporters of the Association for the Revival and Propagation of the Islamic Faith (Uamsho) clashed with police forces. In March the organization led demonstrations calling for the establishment of the *Shari'a* (Islamic law) on Zanzibar, and attacked religious and secular leaders who did not support their demands. Police attempts to end the demonstrations led to two days of violence; 32 were arrested and eight people injured. The Mufti condemned Uamsho and called upon Muslims to boycott the organization.

In 2004 the *muafaka* agreement appeared to break down following claims by the CUF that the Government was delaying reform of the electoral commission and establishing a permanent voter's register. The Government denied the allegations, and claimed that it had implemented most of the agreement. In an effort to appease more radical elements, the Government approved a new flag for Zanzibar.

THE 2005 ELECTIONS ON ZANZIBAR AND THEIR AFTERMATH

The violent attacks continued into 2005 in the run-up to the October elections. Arson attacks were committed against CCM and CUF offices, as well as government buildings and churches, and a CCM official was murdered in April. The CUF accused the Government of preventing over 30,000 CUF supporters from registering to vote, and of supporting a local militia, known locally as the *Janjaweed*, in its attacks on CUF supporters. In mid-April Hamad was banned from standing in the elections, as he had not resided on Zanzibar for three consecutive years. The move provoked strong protests, and the ruling was overturned on appeal. In July the East Africa Law Society reported that there was evidence of corruption in the registration process on Zanzibar. At the end of August several international donors issued a statement calling for free and fair elections on Zanzibar. President Mkapa responded by demanding that international donors refrain from interfering in the electoral process, and the Zanzibar Electoral Commission announced tha it would no longer accept donor support for the running of the elections. During September at least 100 people were injured in clashes between CCM and CUF supporters. The CUF continued to allege malpractice over the voter lists, claiming that 100,000 names on the lists were false; however, the ZEC stated that it had discovered only 700 instances where names had been entered more than once. Nevertheless, one week before the polling day the ZEC struck off 2,000 'bogus' names. In October police opened fire on a CUF demonstration, wounding 18 and arresting dozens of CUF supporters. Prior to the elections, 30,000 members of the security forces were deployed across Zanzibar in an effort to ensure control. The deployment was condemned by the CUF as being politically motivated and designed to intimidate CUF supporters.

The elections on Zanzibar took place on 30 October 2005 in comparative calm, and international observers noted the poll on Zanzibar was generally free and fair. Karume was re-elected as president of Zanzibar, winning 53.18% of the votes cast; Hamad won 46.06%. The CCM won 31 seats, and the CUF 19 seats. The results in one constituency were annulled by the electoral commission and reheld on 14 December. For several days following the election there were violent clashes between the police and CUF supporters in Stone Town. The CUF claimed that the poll had been subject to serious electoral fraud, that at least 47,000 people had been prevented from voting and that the ZEC had failed to make the voter lists transparent. Hamad claimed that he had actually won the poll with 50.63% of the vote. Despite the claims, Karume was sworn in to office.

A law requiring citizens of Zanzibar to hold national identity cards in order to receive salaries and public services came into effect on 1 April 2006. The CUF claimed it was a political strategy to identify and target opposition supporters.

In April 2007 Zanzibari journalists criticized a draft bill that would limit freedom to report on the Island's House of Representatives. The proposed new law, which would impose reporting restrictions on closed sessions, and would prohibit the press from publishing details of proposed laws and discussions without permission from the Speaker or a House Committee, was condemned as undermining press freedom in Zanzibar.

SECURITY CONCERNS

The US-led 'war on terror' continued to impact on Tanzania, with repeated security warnings issued by the USA and United Kingdom in particular. In June 2003 President Mkapa stated that the suspensions of flights and security warnings against travelling to East Africa were harming the economy. Security warnings continued throughout 2003 and the first half of 2004, with the USA in particular advising against travel to the region, and specifically to Zanzibar. The USA claimed in January that it had, together with Tanzanian security forces, foiled a plot by individuals associated with the radical al-Haramain Islamic Foundation to attack tourist hotels in late 2003. In mid-March 2004 warnings were issued of potential attacks against ports, airports and tourist targets in the region, as well as other Western commercial interests. The USA continued to insist that Tanzania, in common with other East African countries, draft new security bills and implement heightened security measures designed to counter the risk from radical Islamist groups in the region. In March 2007 a Tanzanian national, Ahmed Khalfan Ghailani, who had been transported to the US military base at Guantanamo Bay, Cuba, by US authorities, admitted to delivering explosives used in the 1998 bombing of the US embassy in Dar es Salaam (see above), although he claimed he had not known of the plans to attack the embassy building.

FOREIGN RELATIONS

Tanzania's relations with neighbouring Uganda deteriorated in the early 1970s. Border fighting was reported in October 1978 and, in the following month, Uganda announced the annexation of Tanzania's bordering Kagera region. Ugandan troops withdrew after pressure from the Organization of African Unity (OAU, subsequently restyled as the African Union—AU), but border fighting continued. In January 1979 a full-scale invasion force entered Uganda from Tanzania. The force, comprising approximately 20,000 members of the Tanzanian People's Defence Forces and 1,200 members of the Uganda National Liberation Front (UNLF), rapidly gained control of southern Uganda. The Ugandan army capitulated and an interim UNLF Government was proclaimed in April. In July 1999 Uganda reportedly agreed to pay compensation for costs incurred during the operation to defeat former President Idi Amin Dada.

Tanzania's relations with Burundi also began to deteriorate in the early 1970s. A failed coup attempt in 1972 caused thousands of refugees to enter Tanzania, and Tanzanian border villages were raided by Burundian troops. In October 1993 another failed coup attempt in Burundi sent a wave of refugees into Tanzania's Kigoma and Kagera regions. In March 1995 further influxes of both Rwandan and Burundian refugees led to the controversial closure by Tanzania of its border with Burundi. In early 1996 former President Nyerere mediated in peace talks between the warring parties in Burundi. This initiative failed, however, and in July the democratically elected Hutu Government was overthrown in a Tutsi-led military coup under Maj. Pierre Buyoya (President of Burundi 1987–93). Tanzania subsequently imposed economic sanctions against the new Burundi regime, in co-operation with other countries of the region. Renewed peace talks between the Burundian Government and opposition parties, again with Nyerere as mediator, were convened in Arusha during 1998 and 1999. Following the death of Nyerere in October, the former President of South Africa, Nelson Mandela, became the chief mediator in the Arusha peace negotiations. Efforts to promote voluntary repatriation of Burundian refugees in Tanzania began in May 2001. By March 2002 30,000 refugees had registered for voluntary repatriation. Peace negotiations between the Burundian transitional Government and rebel groups took place in Dar es Salaam in 2002 and 2003. In August 2004 a power-sharing agreement was signed at a meeting in Tanzania, with most former-rebel groups joining the Government. In May 2006 peace talks in Dar es Salaam brought the last remaining rebel group into the power-sharing agreement.

At the end of November 2006 Kikwete announced that Tanzania would press for voluntary repatriation of Burundian refugees under the auspices of the UN High Commissioner for Refugees (UNHCR). However, with more than 200,000 refugees still residing in camps in western Tanzania, he called for UN and Burundian officials to help speed up the repatriation process. By January 2007 numbers had dropped significantly, with 287,000 refugees voluntarily returning home. Camps in western Kibondo and Muyovosi districts were closed down by UNHCR. In mid-2007 an agreement was reached under which 8,500 Burundians who had fled to Tanzania in 1972 would be resettled in the USA. The first group left at the end of May with the remainder expected to follow by the end of the year.

In April 1994 a massive and sudden influx of Rwandans into Tanzania followed the genocide perpetrated in that country. The International Criminal Tribunal for Rwanda, authorized by the UN to try Rwandan nationals accused of direct participation in the genocide, was inaugurated in June 1995 in Arusha. In December 1996 some of the Rwandan refugees remaining in Tanzania returned to their homeland, following the threat of forcible repatriation by the Tanzanian Government. In June 1997 it was agreed to repatriate some 100,000 refugees to the Democratic Republic of the Congo (DRC—formerly Zaire). At the end of December UNHCR estimated that some 74,300 refugees from the DRC remained in Tanzania. In May 2003 Tanzania hosted peace negotiations between DRC President, Joseph Kabila, and representatives of opposition militias, at which a cease-fire agreement was signed. In September 2005 Tanzania and the DRC agreed to a programme of repatriation of Congolese refugees living in camps in western Tanzania. In October 282 refugees returned to the DRC as part of an initial campaign to repatriate over 150,000 refugees.

In early September 2003 the last group of 900 Rwandan Hutu refugees left Tanzania after their claims for asylum were finally rejected. The refugees complained that they were given no time to take their possessions with them, and UNHCR declared itself to be disappointed with the Tanzanian Government in pursuing the forced repatriation operation.

In November 2006 the Tanzanian Government announced that it would begin repatriating foreign pastoralist families who had settled in Kagera region in western Tanzania having fled conflicts in Burundi, Rwanda and Uganda. However, progress was slow, and by the middle of the month, just 50 people had been returned, out of an estimated 100,000 immigrants. Officials faced difficulties in identifying immigrants and Tanzanian citizens. Efforts to speed up the repatriation led to tens of thousands of Rwandans being deported by March 2007, many of whom had been living in the country since the 1960s. The Rwandan Government condemned the expulsions.

In January 2007 there were in Tanzania 154,412 refugees from Burundi; 127,967 from the DRC; 2,086 from Somalia; and 2,600 from other African countries. However, the Tanzanian Government estimated that 300,000–500,000 refugees from Burundi and the DRC were long-term settlers in villages in north-western Tanzania.

In January 2005 the United Kingdom signed a debt relief agreement with the Tanzanian Government. The United Kingdom agreed to pay 10% of Tanzania's repayments to the World Bank and IMF, amounting to US $6.4m. each year. In July all of Tanzania's debts to the World Bank, the IMF and the African Development Bank were declared eligible for immediate cancellation under the terms of an agreement brokered at the Group of Eight leading industrialized nations (G-8) summit held at Gleneagles, Scotland. Tanzania's 2007/08 budget, issued in June 2007, received substantial support from the World Bank and other donors. The Bank committed $190m. towards supporting the budget, and the United Kingdom's Department for International Development provided $239m. Total general budget support from external donors reached around $600m. In March 2007 plans were finalized for the AU's African Court of Human and People's Rights to be established in Arusha.

In November 1993 the Presidents of Tanzania, Uganda and Kenya signed a protocol on renewed co-operation among their countries. In March 1996 the three leaders formally inaugurated the Secretariat of the Permanent Tripartite Commission for East African Co-operation, which aimed to revive the East African Community (EAC) that had collapsed in its original form in 1977. A treaty for the re-establishment of the EAC provided for the creation of a free trade area (with the eventual introduction of a single currency), for the development of infrastructure, tourism and agriculture within the Community, and for the establishment of a regional legislative assembly and regional court. In September Tanzania left the Common Market for Eastern and Southern Africa. The EAC Treaty was signed by the Presidents of Tanzania, Kenya and Uganda in Arusha in November 1999 and it came into force in July 2000. The new East African Council of Ministers held its first meeting in Tanzania in January 2001. In March 2004 the three EAC members signed a protocol establishing the East African Customs Union (EACU). The EACU took effect in January 2005.

In December 2006 Rwanda and Burundi were accepted as members of the EAC, expanding the bloc to include around 90m. people. In March 2007 the East African Court of Justice in Arusha rejected Kenya's nominees for the East African Legislative Assembly (EALA), after a case was filed by Kenyan opposition activists. The Court demanded that the EAC members harmonize election procedures to the EALA, and the ruling further delayed the establishment of the Assembly, already delayed since November 2006. The EAC presented a US $28.3m. budget in June 2007, focusing on establishing a common market and on consolidating the customs union.

As Zimbabwe's political crisis deepened (see the chapter on Zimbabwe), Tanzania hosted a summit for heads of state from South African Development Community countries in late March 2007. Initial statements called on South Africa in particular to mediate in the crisis, but the meeting ended without significant pressure being placed on Zimbabwean President Robert Mugabe to resolve the situation.

Economy

LINDA VAN BUREN

Following independence in 1961, Tanzania, under the leadership of its first President, Julius Nyerere, embarked on a socialist path that placed more emphasis on the alleviation of illiteracy, poverty and disease than on the productive sectors. The landmark Arusha Declaration of 1967 envisaged the elimination of these ills by means of a programme of socialism and self-reliance. At the time a large proportion of the population was either nomadic or dispersed in widely scattered homesteads. By 1974, however, the majority of the rural population had been settled into planned and permanent villages (*ujamaa vijijini*). The main objective of 'villagization' was originally to raise output through collectivization and larger-scale farming methods; however, from an agronomic viewpoint, the results were largely unsuccessful, with ineffective management and shortages of materials contributing to low levels of crop production. The emphasis was gradually moved from the agricultural to the social benefits, with the *ujamaa* villages envisaged as centres for social and infrastructural services. The Nyerere Government also pursued a policy of nationalizing important economic sectors, particularly major industries and distribution and marketing. However, more than a decade of severe economic decline brought the country to a condition of economic collapse by 1985, when President Nyerere voluntarily left office. In order to obtain continuing aid from international donors, the Government under the second President, Ali Hassan Mwinyi, adopted a more pragmatic approach to economic planning. By the late 1990s efforts by the Government of the third President, Benjamin Mkapa, to restructure Tanzania's state-owned concerns were under way on a large scale, with privatization for many of them as the stated intention. The humanitarian aims of the Arusha Declaration had not been fully achieved, and indeed by the 1990s Tanzania performed significantly less well than its northerly neighbour Kenya, even in comparisons based on national education and health statistics.

The fourth President of Tanzania, Jakaya Mrisho Kikwete, was swift to proclaim his economic priorities. The former finance minister unequivocally embraced 'sound, consistent and predictable macroeconomic policies with low inflation' and vowed to practise good governance, to adhere to the rule of law, to promote private-sector development and to expand foreign direct investment (FDI). The first budget of his administration, presented to the National Assembly in June 2006, called for total expenditure of Ts. 4,850,588m., 50% of which was to be met by domestic revenue. Official development assistance (ODA) was to cover the remaining 50%. The previous year, in presenting the 10th and final budget of the Mkapa administration, the then Minister for Finance, Basil Mramba, used the occasion to compare the economic situation in 2005 with that of 1996. He reported significant progress in stabilizing the long-troubled economy. Average annual inflation, which had been 21% in 1996, was contained at 4.1% in the year to 31 March 2005, although rising global petroleum prices and drought subsequently increased the rate to 6.9% by 30 April 2006 and to 6.7% in the year to 31 December 2006. Inflation climbed to 7.2% in the year to 31 March 2007 and, although it fell to an annual 6.1% in April 2007, the target of 4.0% by 30 June 2007 was not met. The budget for the fiscal year ending on 30 June 2008 set a new inflation target of 4.5% by the end of the 2007/08 financial year. Real economic growth, in terms of gross domestic product (GDP), amounted to 6.2% in 2006 and to 6.8% in 2005, compared with 4.2% in 1996; the 2006 figure exceeded the target of 5.9%. However, with a population growth rate of almost 3% per year, Tanzania's GDP needed to grow at a rate of at least 10% per year if the country was to meet its goal of becoming a middle-income country by 2025. By 31 March 2007 foreign-exchange reserves were sufficient to cover 5.3 months' worth of imports, down from 6.4 months' worth at 31 December 2005.

According to the Bank of Tanzania, the central bank, in 2002 Tanzania achieved a surplus on the current account of the balance of payments for the first time in many years, of US $$83.6m.; this returned to a deficit thereafter, of $87.5m. in 2003, but escalating to a provisional $1,458.7m. by 2006 (the overall balance, however, remained in surplus for the three years of 2002–04). With abundant rainfall at the right time of year in 2007, Tanzania was predicted to harvest an abundant crop of maize, the staple food, in the 2007/08 season. In contrast, drought in 2005 had caused food to be in short supply and had placed upward pressure on retail food prices and therefore on inflation. The Government waived import taxes on food imports to calm inflationary tendencies. The UN World Food Programme (WFP) estimated in August 2005 that 600,000 Tanzanians were 'food insecure'. Distributions from the Government's Strategic Grain Reserve began in October 2005. By January 2006 the situation had deteriorated, and WFP found that 3.7m. Tanzanians were in need of 99,600 metric tons of food aid in the period to May 2006, when the harvest in the unimodal (one crop season) parts of the country would begin. Ironically, just two years earlier, the retail price of maize had been the lowest in East Africa, and the supply of maize in most Tanzanian markets, including Dar es Salaam, had been relatively abundant, placing downward pressure on retail prices and encouraging exports of Tanzanian maize into neighbouring states, especially into Kenya. This boom-and-bust pattern is exacerbated by time delays in the delivery of food aid, which often arrives after the next crop is in the ground.

AGRICULTURE

The agricultural sector is the mainstay of Tanzania's economy, providing a livelihood for some 80% of the economically active population and contributing 47% of GDP in 2006. Subsistence farming accounted for about 40% of total agricultural output. No more than about 8% of the country's land area is cultivated, and only about 3% of the cultivated land is irrigated, yet the growing of field crops heavily dominates the agricultural sector as a whole. The northern and south-western areas of the country are the most fertile, receiving the highest rainfall in most years. The main food crop is maize, which is the staple food in most parts of the country. The staple in the west is green bananas. Other food crops include cassava, paddy rice, sorghum, plantains, sweet potatoes, potatoes, beans and millet. In 1999, following intensive efforts to revitalize the cashew-nut sector, this tree crop overtook coffee as Tanzania's main agricultural export, earning US $98.94m., compared to $76.62m. for green coffee beans. The main reason for the change in ranking was a 52% increase in the dollar price for cashew nuts in 1999, compared with the previous year, while at the same time the price for coffee fell by 17%; the export volume for both crops in fact declined. In 2006/07 cashew nuts accounted for 5.0% of total exports, while coffee accounted for 3.5%. Other important export crops in 2006/07 were tea, clove stems (from Zanzibar), tobacco, cotton and sisal. The 2006/07 budget speech lamented that nearly all of Tanzania's foreign exchange came from ODA and announced that boosting Tanzania's foreign-exchange earnings from exports was to be a priority. Cashew nuts and coffee were initially to lead this drive, but the Government was also hoping to identify and develop new sources of export earnings.

During the 1980s successive increases in producer prices for all the major crops were diluted by the weakness of the shilling, but new foreign-exchange support from international aid donors led to better availability of imported agricultural inputs and contributed to improved harvests. In 1991 legislation was adopted to end the state monopoly over agricultural marketing, permitting private traders to market crops alongside co-operatives; in 2003 five private-sector companies were engaged in the purchasing of food crops. Implementation of the legislation was particularly slow regarding the marketing of cotton.

Production of cashew nuts fell from an annual 145,000 metric tons in 1973–74 to only 7,400 tons in 1990, partly because of low producer prices, long delays in payments to growers, disease, poor husbandry and lack of imported inputs, but also partly because growers were moved away from their trees to *ujamaa* villages. Efforts to revitalize the sector included the creation of the Cashewnut Industry Development Fund (CIDEF). Among other measures, in 1998 CIDEF arranged a US $100m. overdraft facility from EXIM Bank to overcome the cash-flow problem that often made it impossible to make timely payments to producers for their crop. Output of cashew nuts rose steadily during the 1990s, and by 2003 had almost reached 100,000 tons, according to FAO, but declined thereafter (72,000 tons in 2005). The total annual processing capacity in the country is nominally just over 100,000 tons, but 10 of the 11 processing factories were built mostly in the mid-1970s (ironically, just as the growers were being moved away) and are badly in need of updating. In May 2007 a new cashew-nut-processing factory was commissioned 60 km west of Dar es Salaam. It inauguration was overshadowed by a lack of electric power, even though Tanzania Electricity Supply Co (TANESCO) power lines were visible from the factory.

Coffee is grown mainly by some 400,000 smallholders. The main growing area is in the Kilimanjaro region in the north, where the arabica variety is grown. The centre for the growing of robusta is west of Lake Victoria. Tanzania's coffee crop in 2005/06 was 63.7% arabica and 36.3% robusta, in volume terms; on global markets, arabica fetched almost double the price of robusta. Coffee accounted for 49% of export earnings in 1986, but this share had fallen to just 3.5% 10 years later. A record crop of 67,300 metric tons was produced in 1980/81, but thereafter output fluctuated. According to the International Coffee Organization, of which Tanzania is a member, production reached 49,440 metric tons in the coffee year ending in June 2002, fell back to 36,720 tons in 2002/03, but was more stable in the following three years, reaching an official estimate of 45,000 tons in 2005/06. In the ensuing exporting year, which ended in July 2007, some 44,186 tons of green coffee beans were exported.

Cotton is grown mainly by smallholders. Cotton's fortunes have followed the same pattern as in other African countries. From 2001 onwards, the USA's African Growth and Opportunity Act (AGOA) spurred growth by allowing qualifying African textile producers preferential access to the US market; these textile producers in turn gave a major boost to demand for raw cotton. This situation was reinforced by the Mulitfibre Agreement (MFA), which placed quotas on Chinese and Indian textiles in a bid to give a boost to African producers. The number of textile producers soon mushroomed in Tanzania and other African countries as a result. In Tanzania, the area planted with cotton jumped from 213,300 ha in 2000 to 419,960 ha in 2001. However, the MFA expired in January 2005, ending restrictions on Chinese and Indian products, with the result that large quantities of Chinese textiles entered the US market at a low price, creating difficult trading conditions for African producers such as Tanzania. Even before the MFA expired, allowing major cotton producers including the People's Republic of China and India direct access to the US market, Tanzania's cotton sector was struggling, buoyed up only by favourable quotas. Without those quotas, the sector was in danger of collapse. African textile producers requested that the US Government amend AGOA to increase its effectiveness. As a result, the USA in November 2005 entered into the US-Chinese Memorandum of Understanding (MoU), which placed restrictions on 34 categories of textile and clothing imports into the USA from China from 1 January 2006 to 31 December 2008. Nevertheless, the production of seed cotton in Tanzania, which had jumped from a low 139,829 metric tons in 2003/04 to 341,789 tons in 2004/05 and 376,591 in 2005/06, fell back to only 130,585 tons because of severe drought in the cotton year ending in July 2007 (Tanzania Cotton Board figures). Despite flooding delaying planting in June 2007, it was hoped that the cotton harvest of 2007/08 would regain a level of some 300,000 tons. The 2006 collapse in production was evident in the figures for exports of cotton lint in July–October, which were only 19% of the volume and value levels in the same period the year before; in 2005/06 as a whole exports of lint had totalled 97.1m. tons (up 28% on the previous year), earning US $116.1m. (up 27%). In 2003 Tanzania set up Export Processing Zones (EPZs) to encourage local textile manufacturers to take advantage of AGOA. However, it was reported in May 2004 that one year after the EPZs had been launched, only three companies had been licensed to produce for the US market. In other words, Tanzania's notorious 'red tape' and slowness in processing applications had meant that it was less able to take advantage of AGOA provisions than some other countries.

Tea was first planted in Tanzania by German settlers in 1904. Production recovered after private-sector investment in the late 1980s and 1990s. The output of made tea rose from 8,492 metric tons in 1970 to 30,700 tons in 2005. The Tea Board of Tanzania, established in 1997, is responsible for regulating the tea industry. The country had 18 tea-processing factories in 2007. The estates were rehabilitated throughout the 1990s and some now produce organic teas, which command high prices. The revived East African Community (EAC) liberalized the tea sector in the three member states (Tanzania, Kenya and Uganda), and the 2004 Tanzania budget exempted black tea and packaged tea from value-added tax (VAT) so as to enable Tanzanian tea to compete in the three-nation market. Overseas, innovative marketing and participation with fair-trade marketing organizations have placed Tanzanian tea in a number of superior international coffee and tea outlets, under branding such as Kibena tea. Tanzania Tea Packers Ltd (Tatepa) garnered a 70% share of the local market for tea and launched four brands of herbal tea, which also found markets in neighbouring Kenya.

Tobacco production increased significantly from the early 1990s and peaked at 51,102 metric tons of unmanufactured leaf in 1997. Output fell back to 24,270 tons in 2001, but then grew steadily thereafter, reaching some 52,000 tons in 2006.

Production of sisal was just over 250,000 metric tons in 1964, but output fell drastically when more than one-half of the estates were nationalized in 1976. World prices for sisal recovered in the late 1980s from the very low levels of the 1970s, as the product began to compete successfully with synthetic substitutes, particularly in some specialized uses.

Production rose from 20,600 tons in 2000 to 27,800 tons in 2006. Renewed world demand in 2000 had encouraged investment in sisal, and several foreign groups bought estates or started joint ventures with the Tanzania Sisal Development Board (TSDB), which the Mkapa Government had transferred to private-sector control in April 1998. In November 2004 construction began on a pilot plant to produce bio-gas, electricity and fertilizers from sisal waste at Kwarguru Estate in Tanga region (see below).

Cloves, cultivated mainly on Pemba, are the main export of Zanzibar, providing about 80% of the islands' foreign-exchange earnings. Zanzibar, once the world's largest clove producer, ranked only third in 2000, behind Indonesia and Madagascar. When Indonesia, the world's largest consumer, became self-sufficient in cloves in 1983, Zanzibar had to compete for much smaller markets in India, Thailand, Singapore and the Netherlands. Compared with up to 20,000 metric tons per year in the mid-1960s, output had fallen to only 1,575 tons in 1995. Insufficient profit incentives were blamed for the sector's poor performance in the 1990s. Together with low producer prices, the industry suffered the effects of smuggling, tree diseases and, in 1997, fires (the result of prolonged drought), which destroyed thousands of clove trees. Production fluctuated in the late 1990s, but by 2000 a sustained recovery was under way, with output rising steadily to 12,271 tons in 2005. The recovery was helped by the increase in the producer price for cloves, which, according to the IMF, was Ts. 1,688 per kg in the 2000/01 season and Ts. 5,024 per kg in the 2001/02 season (compared to just Ts. 216 in the 1995/96 season). A clove distillery at Chake Chake produces clove-bud oil and clove-stem oil for export. The distillery also produces other exotic oils, primarily for the lucrative aromatherapy industry; among them are cinnamon, vetiver, eucalyptus and lemon-grass oils. Oil of vetiver is also used in perfumery and commands a very high price. A project begun in 2002 seeks to add clove-leaf oil and eugenol to the distillery's output. Alternative export crops now being encouraged and which are increasingly widely grown on the islands of Zanzibar and Pemba, include tobacco, rubber, cardamom, nutmeg, vanilla and peppermint. In the 1990s seaweed became an important export crop for Zanzibar. Output rose fairly steadily, reaching a peak of 4,991 tons in 2000.

Other cash crops include sugar cane, copra, groundnuts (peanuts), oil-palm fruits, sunflower seeds, sesame seeds (simsim), cocoa beans, soya beans and pyrethrum. Tanzania's output of raw centrifugal cane sugar doubled from 134,600 metric tons in 2001 to 269,200 tons in 2006, according to FAO estimates. Local demand is about 415,000 tons per year. Despite this deficit, Tanzania exports 10,000 tons per year to European Union (EU) countries. The smuggling of cheaper foreign sugar into Tanzania was widespread in the late 1990s. By May 2000 the Mkapa Government had banned the import of sugar into all but the three largest ports in a bid to stem the practice. Output of simsim amounted to 48,000 tons in 2006, according to FAO figures, but output of processed sesame oil declined from 11,969.6 tons in 2001 to just 4,055.2 tons in 2006, owing to shortages of electricity supply at processing factories. Fresh fruit, vegetables and flowers are potentially important export crops, and small quantities are air-freighted to European markets. This non-traditional trade was stimulated by the encouragement of private enterprise, but it was still severely constrained by many factors, including the very limited chilled storage facilities at Dar es Salaam international airport. Honey and beeswax produced by Tabora Beekeepers' Co-operative were being exported in small quantities, after a gap of some years; Zanzibar exported clove honey. Grapes are cultivated in central Tanzania, with output totalling some 13,283 tons in 2006; some local wine is produced in the area around Dodoma. The 2004/05 budget sought to increase the production of grapes by exempting from excise duty wine and brandy made from locally grown grapes.

Tanzania is one of Africa's largest cattle producers, with an estimated national herd of 17.2m. in 2006. Epidemics of lung disease and rinderpest threatened stocks in the mid-1990s, but production gradually recovered in the last part of the decade, continuing after 2000. An outbreak of Rift Valley fever in December 2006 afflicted 46,680 cattle, of which 5,610 died; this disease is also infectious to humans and, according to the Ministry of Agriculture, Livestock and Co-operatives, 'several' people died. The country's resources of commercial species of timber, including camphor wood, podo and African mahogany, are exploited. Total roundwood removals amounted to 24m. cu m in 2005, of which 77,420 cu m were exported, earning US $6.9m. Fishing, on both a commercial and subsistence basis, contributed 7% of GDP in 2005. The total fish catch is about 350,000 metric tons per year. Of the total catch in 2005, 87% was freshwater fish, including Nile perch, dagaas and tilapias; other species caught included sardinellas, Indian mackerel and tuna from the Indian Ocean. The African Fishing Co, the country's first deep-sea fishing company, was licensed in 1997, with authorization to run six vessels for deep-sea trawling. The Deep Sea Fishing Act, promulgated in May 1998, imposed tighter controls on the monitoring of Tanzania's fish stocks. In May 1998 two new deep-sea fishing vessels entered service, increasing the Tanzanian fleet to four, out of a total of 14 vessels licensed to fish the country's coastal waters in the 1998 fishing season. Tanzania also produces modest amounts of prawns, molluscs and sea urchins. Having exempted agricultural inputs and fishing equipment from VAT, the Government gave a boost to local producers of fishing equipment in the 2004/05 budget by exempting their raw-material inputs from VAT as well.

During 2005, as in 2000 and in the early 1990s, severe food shortages were experienced in some areas. WFP estimated in January 2006 that 3.7m. Tanzanians, mainly in the central and north-eastern parts of the country, were at risk from drought following poor rainfall. The smuggling of Tanzanian grain into Kenya in pursuit of higher prices exacerbated the situation, but the biggest problem was the inability of the authorities to transport maize within Tanzania from areas of surfeit to areas of deficit. In addition, an estimated 30%–40% of all crops are lost through post-harvest pest infestation and other damage.

INDUSTRY AND POWER

According to estimates by the World Bank, the average annual growth rate of industrial GDP was 3.4% in 1980–90 and 4.4% in 1990–2003. Many factories closed down or suspended operations for long periods during the 1980s. Industries suffered from rising costs of fuel and other imports and from a severe lack of foreign exchange to pay for raw materials, machinery, equipment and spares, as well as from frequent interruptions to water and electricity supplies. In 2005 and 2006 the lack of a reliable source of electricity to factories was a key hindrance to the manufacturing sector. In June 2007 the IMF commented on the importance of a 'reliable and ample energy supply' for economic growth and on how critical was 'rapid progress towards the commercial viability of the energy parastatal, TANESCO'. The IMF urged government vigour in support of the TANESCO financial recovery programme, emphasizing the 'forthcoming application for an electricity tariff increase', which was intended to enable the 'full recovery of operating costs'.

A few signs of improvement appeared from 1986, mainly as more foreign exchange became available through the IMF and various aid donors. By mid-1990 most factories were operating at 20%–40% of capacity and a few had reached 70%. Industrial output increased by an annual average of 9.7% during 1990–94. The sector's growth rate slowed to just 0.4% in 1995, and interruptions to the supply of power in the late 1990s also hindered manufacturing output. Manufacturing contributed 9.9% of GDP in 2003; industry as a whole contributed 16.7% of GDP in 2004, down from 21.2% in 2003.

The industrial sector is based on the processing of local commodities (with agro-industrial companies manufacturing sugar, sisal twine and cigarettes) and on import substitution. However, the Government is seeking to encourage the production of manufactured goods for export, in order to lessen dependence on agricultural commodities. Some industrial goods—textiles, clothing, footwear, tyres, batteries, transformers, switch gear, electric cookers, bottles, cement and paper—are exported to neighbouring countries. Principal manufactures in 2007 were beer, wheat flour, rope, sugar, vegetable oils, animal feeds, batteries, iron sheets, rolled steel, paint, textiles and carpets. Other industrial activities include petroleum refining, fertilizer production, metalworking, vehicle assembly, fruit canning, engineering (spares for industrial machinery and for vehicles), railway-wagon assembly and the manufacture of pulp and paper, paperboard, cement, soft drinks, gunny bags, glassware, ceramics, hoes, pharmaceutical products, oxygen, carbon dioxide, bricks and tiles, light bulbs, electrical goods, wood products, machine tools, footwear and disposable hypodermic syringes. Kagera Sugar Co Ltd, which had ceased production in 1998 after producing just 960 metric tons in that year, reopened in 2004 after rehabilitation and privatization. Kagera was forecast to produce 110,000 tons of sugar per year by the time it reached full capacity in 2010.

According to IMF figures, revenue from exports of manufactured goods peaked in 1996, at US $122.8m., and then began a steady decline until, in 1999, exports of Tanzanian manufactured goods earned only $30.1m., the lowest level for eight years. By 2001, however, this had improved somewhat, to $56.2m., and in 2003/04 revenue from manufactured goods amounted to an estimated $95.5m. High production costs, unreliable electricity supply and reliance on imported content, however, remained a barrier to international competitiveness.

There are three cement plants, at Mbeya, at Wazo Hill near Dar es Salaam and at Tanga. After several years of severe cement shortage, rehabilitation of the plants, mainly with Danish and Swedish assistance, allowed production to increase. Combined capacity in 2000 was about 1m. metric tons per year. In 2001 these plants were operating near this capacity, and produced 900,000 tons of cement. Total cement production was estimated at 1.2m. tons in 2003. Finnish Valmet tractors are assembled at Trama-Valmet, and Swedish Scania trucks are assembled at the Tanzania Automobile Manufacturing Co Ltd (TAMCO) in Kibaha. TAMCO, owned 90% by the Tanzanian Government and 10% by Scania AB of Sweden, is scheduled for privatization.

Southern Paper Mills' US $260m. pulp and paper mill at Mgololo (in Mufindi district, on the Tanzania–Zambia Railway Authority—Tazara railway line) commenced production in 1985. It was envisaged that the nearby Sao Hill forest would eventually supply the mill's timber needs, but, meanwhile, the plant used imported chemical pulp. The eventual target output was 75,000 metric tons per year, in seven grades of paper, although additional investment was required to attain that level of production. Meanwhile, in 1999 the mill's capacity was 60,000 tons per year. It was estimated in 1999 that the operation would initially require $29m. in capital investment, followed by two further instalments of $10m. for the rehabilitation and modernization of the paper machines, the bleaching plant and the finishing sections, and in order to expand the rated capacity to the targeted 75,000 tons per year. In 2004 RAI group of companies, based in Eldoret, Kenya, purchased Southern Paper Mills at a cost of $1m. plus a commitment to invest $25m. in rehabilitating the mill and returning it to full production.

The World Bank's International Development Association (IDA) extended a loan of US $44m. towards a $104m. petroleum distribution improvement project, which is regarded as a key component of overall infrastructure improvement plans. A pipeline to transport natural gas from the gas fields at Songo Songo Island in the Indian Ocean to Dar es Salaam was completed in May 2004, and the first gas reached the capital city in July 2004.

From the 1990s the Government expressed its intention to privatize, restructure or dissolve 410 state-owned companies. It established the Presidential Parastatal Sector Reform Commission (PPSRC) in 1992 to oversee the privatization exercise. Between April 1993 and June 1999 191 parastatals were privatized or disposed of, and by 2003 the number had grown to 266. The majority were small companies engaged in agro-industrial activities, but mining entities attracted the largest sums of investment money. The two principal obstacles in negotiations with potential investors were the assumption of the often very large debts of these parastatals, and the burden of severance compensation costs for any workers to be dismissed by the new investors as part of a cost-cutting exercise. In December 1999 IDA approved two loans in support of Tanzania's private-sector development. The first was of US $41.2m. towards the $103.4m., 12-year, three-phase Public Service Reform Programme, aimed at improving sustainable performance by concentrating on core capacity while contracting out non-core activities. The second was a $45.9m. credit to the $76.81m. Privatization and Private Sector Development Project. Among the companies already privatized are the Dar es Salaam Water Supply Authority, the Kagera Sugar Co and Southern Paper Mills. Earmarked for privatization but not yet privatized by mid-2007 were the Tanzania Telecommunications Co Ltd (TTCL), the Tanzania Railways Corpn (TRC) and the Tanzania Ports Authority (TPA).

Only about 11% of Tanzania's population have access to the electricity grid. Tanzania's total electricity generating capacity was 641 MW in 2006, including 80 MW from diesel-powered generating stations, although less than one-half of this capacity was operational. Lack of reliable electricity supply is often identified as the biggest hindrance to manufacturing growth in Tanzania. In 1999 TANESCO projected that the country's electricity requirements would rise to 2,312 MW by 2025 and indicated that 1,440 MW of new electricity-generating capacity would be required to meet this demand. Of the total generating capacity in 2006, 87% was supplied by hydroelectric facilities. The largest is the Kidatu hydroelectric complex on the Great Ruaha river, with a capacity of 204 MW following its expansion in the late 1980s. An eight-year investment programme for the power sector was initiated in 1991 and included the US $410m. development of the 180-MW Kihansi power station, the expansion of the 68-MW Pangani Falls power station and the $107m. construction of a 220-kilovolt transmission line from Singida to Arusha. The Mtera hypropower station has a capacity of 80 MW. In the mid-1990s the production of electricity was opened to private-sector investment, but in mid-2001 less than 5% of output was generated by such operations. In 1997 Independent Power Tanzania Ltd (IPTL), a joint venture between Malaysian and Tanzanian investors, began the construction of a large-scale, 100-MW, $163m. thermoelectric power generation plant at Sala Sala, 18 km north of Dar es Salaam. Work was carried out by Dutch and Finnish contractors. Electricity was to be produced by 10 diesel-fuelled generators, each with a capacity of 10 MW. All 10 were commissioned in 1998. In 2004 a feasibility study was conducted into the viability of converting IPTL's electricity generation from diesel to natural gas. Although IPTL was by far the largest private-sector investment in Tanzania's power sector, it was not the first. The Tanganyika Wattle Co in Njombe and the Kiwira coal-powered station in Mbeya had already begun contributing 2.5 MW and 3.96 MW, respectively. In November 2004 construction began on a pilot plant to produce bio-gas, electricity and fertilizers from sisal waste at Kwarguru Estate in Tanga region. Projected to produce 40 MW of electricity, it was expected to make Tanga region self-sufficient in electricity. Meanwhile, the privatization of TANESCO, which remained heavily indebted, stalled in 2006.

MINERALS

Tanzania's mining sector provided an estimated 2.3% of GDP in 2006. Mineral exports earned US $614.1m. in 2006, compared with earnings of $27m. in 1990. New policies introduced in the late 1990s regarding mineral exploitation encouraged prospectors to sell more of their gemstone finds into the formal economic system. As a result, official diamond receipts more than doubled in volume, and gold receipts increased 10-fold in 1999 and three-fold in 2000. Gold became the leading export earner, accounting for 49.7% of exports in 2003/04. Exports of gold alone rose from $7.6m. in the year to 30 April 1999 to $254m. in 2001, after key mines became operational. In 2003/04 this figure had increased to $581.6m. Output of diamonds rose from 97,800 carats in 1998 to 304,000 carats by 2004, before falling back to 220,000 carats in the following year. Gold, diamonds, salt, various gemstones, phosphates, coal, gypsum, kaolin, limestone, graphite and tin are exploited. Deposits of lead, iron ore, silver, tungsten, pyrochlore, magnesite, nickel, copper, cobalt, soda ash, uranium, niobium, titanium and vanadium have also been identified.

Gold production virtually ceased in the 1970s, but renewed interest in the 1990s led to a major revitalization in the sector. Gold output increased dramatically in the late 1990s, from 427 kg in 1998, to 4,767 kg in the following year. In 2003 output was recorded at 48,018 kg and by 2005 52,236 kg. Ashanti Goldfields of Ghana and AngloGold (now merged, as AngloGold Ashanti) brought their joint-venture gold project at Geita into production in June 2000, three months ahead of schedule. Output at Geita, 80 km south-west of Mwanza, was projected at 500,000 troy oz (15,550 kg) per year, at a cost of US $180 per oz. Diamond drilling of the Geita Hill down-dip extension mineralization continued in July 2005, and step-out drilling continued to the north-east at Geita Hill, tracing gold mineralization along the strike and down-dip to define areas for infill drilling. Additional drilling information from Nyankanga West and Geita Hill defined an additional 800,000 oz to the mineral resource in 2004. At 31 December 2005 Geita had 22.1m. metric tons of proven ore reserves containing 75.1 tons of gold, plus another 40.4m. tons of probable ore reserves containing 189.2 tons of gold. The $48m. Golden Pride gold mine at Lusu, near Nzega, in central Tanzania, began exporting in 1999. Golden Pride, which is 100% owned by Resolute Mining Ltd of Australia, produced 149,866 oz in 2005 at a cost of $269 per oz; this mine was expected to reach the end of its life in 2008 or 2009. Canada's Toronto-based Barrick Gold Corpn, which through acquisitions had become the world's largest gold-mining company, owned three gold operations in Tanzania: Bulyanhulu, North Mara and Tulawaka. The $211m. underground gold mine at Bulyanhulu in Kahama district had proven reserves of 3.8m. oz in 1999, but by 31 December 2005 the potential had grown to 10.7m. of proven and probable gold reserves. The mine produced 311,000 oz of gold at a cash cost of $358 per oz in 2005, well exceeding initial forecasts of 180,000 oz of gold annually for 15 years, starting in 2001. Output at Bulyanhulu in 2006 was 330,000 oz of gold at a cost of $339 per oz. The North Mara operation, comprising three open-pit gold mines, lies 100 km east of Lake Victoria and just 20 km south of the Kenyan border. It produced 372,000 oz of gold in 2006, up from 250,000 oz in 2005, at a 2006 cost of $279 per oz. Proven and probable reserves stood at 3.3m. oz of gold as of 31 December 2006. The Tulawaka open-pit gold mine, a joint venture 70% owned by Barrick and 30% by Northern Mining Explorations Ltd, entered production in the first quarter of 2005 and produced 124,000 oz at a cash cost of $253 per oz. Located 120 km west of the Bulyanhulu mine, it produced 140,000 oz at a cash cost of $228 per oz. Proven and probable reserves at Tulawaka were in excess of 470,000 oz of gold as of 31 December 2006. In addition, Barrick in 2007 proceeded with the construction, at a cost of $400m., of the Buzwagi open-pit gold mine, lying 80 kilometres south of the Bulyanhulu gold mine. Buzwagi had proven and probable reserves of 2.64m. oz of gold and 118m. lb (53.5m. kg) of copper 'within the gold reserves'. Buzwagi was expected to produce 240,000–250,000 oz of gold per year during the projected 10-year life of the mine. Pre-stripping and mining activities were due to begin in 2008. Another Canadian company, Tan Range Exploration Corpn of Vancouver, announced in December 2005 that its drilling programme had 'significantly expanded' the resource potential of its Luhala concession, in the Lake Victoria greenstone belt. Tan Range is also drilling, in partnership with Northern Mining, near the Tulawaka mine.

Tanzania has extensive reserves of precious and semiprecious stones, and new discoveries are continuing to be made, generating a high level of foreign interest, especially in the southern half of the country. The Longido ruby mine, established in 1949 after spectacular discoveries, is the largest in the world, although growth in production has been slow since the mine reopened in 1994, following a temporary halt in operations. The Umba River Valley yields rubies and sapphires, with particular interest in the gem market centring on a fiery reddish-orange sapphire to rival the famous and increasingly scarce paparadzha sapphire of Sri Lanka. Sapphires have been discovered at Songea, and alluvial deposits at Tunduru have yielded sapphires, tourmalines, alexandrites, chrysoberyls and spinels; nine prospecting licences have been granted. Both Songea and Tunduru have been overrun by illegal prospectors. Deposits of tanzanite, a blue semiprecious stone that was first discovered in the Merelani Hills near Arusha in 1967 and is found nowhere else in the world, have been exploited by unlicensed miners. The Government was attempting to curtail this activity and at the same time was reviving the Tanzania Gemstone Industry enterprise, which buys and processes gemstones. Demand for tanzanite rose significantly in the USA from 2005, following aggressive television marketing. The 2003/04 budget banned the export of uncut tanzanites in a bid to add more value to the semiprecious stones within Tanzania before export.

Lake Natron, the most caustic body of water in the world, is a bright orange red lake in the Rift Valley with large deposits of soda ash for the production of caustic soda. Used in the production of fibreglass and fibre-optics, natural soda ash has advantages over synthetic soda ash. In March 2007 the Tanzanian Government announced plans for a US $600m. project to exploit Lake Natron's soda-ash potential. Salt is produced at coastal salt pans and is a potential export. The feasibility of extracting salt from Lake Eyasi, 200 km west of Arusha, was being investigated. Salt output declined to 35,900 metric tons in 1999, but had recovered to 59,000 tons in 2003 and 57,000 tons in 2004, before increasing dramatically to 135,000 in 2005. Barrick and Falconbridge Ltd formed a 50:50 joint venture to develop the 26.4m. tons of nickel deposits in Kabanga, north-western Tanzania. Xstrata of Switzerland, which acquired Falconbridge in 2006, committed a further $95m. to the project in February 2007, at which time Barrick described Kabanga as 'among the world's most attractive undeveloped nickel sulphide deposits'. In 1992 Canada's Sutton Resources, later acquired by Barrick, commenced exploration of 26,400 sq km of the Kagera basin, searching for nickel, cobalt, copper, lead, zinc and platinum. In that year a scheme to exploit deposits of nickel, copper and cobalt, which had already been located in the region, was launched, at a projected cost of $750m. The Chinese-built Songwe-Kiwira coal mine in the south-west, which came into production in 1988, had an annual capacity of 100,000 tons, but the coal's high ash content rendered it unsuitable for use by the intended major customers, Southern Paper Mills and Mbeya Cement Co. The mine produced electricity for the national grid. In September 1996 a $2m. rehabilitation of the Kiwira coal mine was announced, which was to increase its annual production capacity to 150,000 tons. Kiwira produced 78,980 tons of coal in 2002, well below its potential. In April 2007 the Tanzanian Government announced plans to establish a $600m. open-cast colliery, Mchuchuma, producing 1.5m. tons of coal per year. The coal from Mchuchuma would then be used to fuel the production of sponge iron 2 km away, in order to supply the country's steel producers, enabling them to source their raw material domestically and reducing their dependence on imports. Coal is mined on a smaller scale at Ilima in the Mbeya region. Iron ore is mined at Chunya. Tin is mined on a small scale near the Congolese border.

Prospecting for petroleum and natural gas has been continuing for many years. In the 1970s there were reports of the discovery of petroleum in the Songo Songo island area, offshore from Kilwa, south of Dar es Salaam; the presence of an estimated 42,890m. cu m of natural gas in the area was later confirmed. In 1998 Songas Ltd announced plans to develop the Songo Songo reserves. The US $375m. project is funded by a $200m. IDA credit, a $50m. equity investment by TransCanada and Ocelot of Canada and a $37m. European Investment Bank (EIB) loan, as well as by several smaller equity investments. In October 2001 IDA approved a $183m. interest-free credit for the Songo Songo gas scheme. Songas built two gas-processing units on Songo Songo island, as well as a 25-km underwater pipeline to deliver the gas from the island to Somanga, on the mainland, and a 207-km underground pipeline to deliver the gas from Somanga northwards to Dar es Salaam, where it supplies the 122-MW Ubungo power plant (whose four turbines were to be converted to run on gas) and the cement plant at Wazo Hill. The scheme entailed several infrastructural developments on Songo Songo island, including the construction of an airstrip. The pipelines were completed in May 2004 and the first gas from Songo Songo arrived in Dar es Salaam in July 2004. Songo Songo had a projected lifetime of 20 years. There is a much larger offshore gas field at

Kimbiji, 40 km south-east of Dar es Salaam, where recoverable reserves were estimated at 130,000m. cu m. Results of petroleum exploration so far have been disappointing, but a number of international companies from Australia, Canada, India, Italy, the Netherlands, Norway, Switzerland, the United Kingdom and the USA have been active, in both on- and offshore areas (in some cases grouped in consortia). The Tanganyika Oil Co Ltd drilled an exploratory well in 1999 to test the East Lika prospect at the Mandawa Jurassic Salt Basin. Petroleum and petroleum products accounted for 18.6% of imports in 2003, but this proportion increased in 2005 and 2006.

TOURISM

During the privatization era Tanzania's tourism sector aroused more investor interest than any other sector except mining. Tourism revenue contributed 17% of GDP and 25% of exports of goods and services in 2006. The sector was growing by some 10% annually in the 2000s. According to the Tanzanian Association of Tourism Operators (TATO), out of the 281 licensed tour operators in 2007, 247 were Tanzanian and only 34 were foreign. However, the 34 foreign operators were responsible for between 70% and 80% of the tourist arrivals in the country. An estimated 700,000 tourists arrived in Tanzania in 2006, earning the country US $862m. in that year. The forecast was for 1m. annual tourist arrivals by 2010. During the period when the old EAC was active, the tourism sector in Tanzania was an adjunct of the Kenyan tourist industry. Most travellers merely visited Tanzania's tourist attractions on one-day excursions, pre-paid in Kenya. The dissolution of the EAC and the closure of the Kenya–Tanzania border in 1977 led to a fall in visitor arrivals; only 60,218 tourists visited Tanzania in 1983, compared with 178,000 in 1974. Hotels, lodges and access roads were allowed to deteriorate badly. From 1986 onwards, however, the tourism sector began to recover, with the growing recognition of Tanzania's promising potential as a tourist destination (based on the country's unspoiled beaches and superb game parks, covering one-quarter of its area, as well as its long-term political stability). By 1996 tourist arrivals had reached a record 326,000, according to government figures. Gross receipts from tourism were estimated at US $392.4m. in 1997, when the sector overtook coffee to become Tanzania's primary source of foreign exchange (it was subsequently overtaken by gold exports). Devaluation of the shilling benefited tourism, because Tanzania was previously an extremely expensive destination. The sector is co-ordinated by the state-owned Tanzania Tourist Board. Investment was forthcoming from several local and foreign private companies. Most new investment was in the so-called 'northern circuit', linking the Serengeti National Park, the Ngorongoro Crater and Mount Kilimanjaro. Hotel capacity in this area, including Arusha, was about 13,400 beds. The Government intended to encourage the development of tourism in the 'southern circuit', which included the Selous National Park. Other destinations include the soda-rich Lake Natron, where flamingos gather in large numbers, and Lake Eyasi. Tourism arrivals declined after the terrorist attacks in New York, USA, in September 2001, but 2003 saw a recovery. The 2004/05 budget reduced the business visa fee from $200 to $50, bringing it into line with the tourism fee, in order to stop arriving business travellers from masquerading as tourists. A 'visa sticker' system was also introduced, to replace the rubber-stamping of visas, a system that had been subject to abuse; the new system was expected to generate some Ts. 19,823m. in additional revenue for the Government. Zanzibar, which had an estimated 87,000 visitors in the year to June 2000, expanded and upgraded its tourist facilities, in particular through an agreement signed with the Aga Khan Fund for Economic Development to build two new hotels (one of which was opened in March 1997), develop a tourism centre and repair historic buildings in the old capital. The Serena Group, part of the Aga Khan Development Network, established five new international tourist-class hotels and lodges and one luxury tented camp in Tanzania between 1996 and 2001. Zanzibar's Ras Nungwi peninsula, at the northern end of the island, offers beach-front hotel holidays with water sports and tours to the surrounding area. The number of hotel beds in Zanzibar reportedly increased from 3,000 in 1986 to 5,352 in 2000. In 2007 the Tanzania Tourist Board was promoting deep-sea diving and snorkelling off the country's Indian Ocean coast.

TRANSPORT AND COMMUNICATIONS

The concentration of Tanzania's population on the periphery of the country, leaving the central part relatively sparsely populated, poses considerable problems in transport and communications.

Tanzania has two distinct railway systems. They are Tazara and the TRC, both of which were scheduled to be privatized. The Tazara rail line was designed to provide an alternative sea outlet to landlocked Zambia, and has eased the problem of transportation to the rich Kilombero valley as well as the Iringa and Mbeya regions. The Chinese-built 1,860-km Tazara line initially experienced financial and technical problems, together with lack of equipment and spare parts. Following the political changes that took place in South Africa during the early 1990s, Zambia started to make greater use of the much more reliable southern transport routes, creating new problems for the Tazara line. Tazara was built with a capacity of 5m. metric tons per year, but in 2000 less than 500,000 tons was carried. Tazara had 76 active locomotives and 1,800 active 40-ft wagons in 2000. In mid-2007 the Governments of Tanzania and Zambia had held discussions about the future of Tazara and had mapped out a privatization model, but Tazara had not yet been added to the PPSRC's privatization list. The other railway, the TRC, was still state-owned but was earmarked for privatization. It operates Tanzania's central railway system, which has two main lines and four branches. One line runs from the Indian Ocean port city of Dar es Salaam to Tabora, where it splits into two branches. One branch links Tabora to Kigoma, on Lake Tanganyika, thereby serving the landlocked neighbouring countries of Burundi and Rwanda and the eastern part of the Democratic Republic of the Congo (DRC—formerly Zaire); the other branch links Tabora to Mwanza, on Lake Victoria, where a ferry connects the service to landlocked Uganda. The other TRC main line runs from Ruvu to Korogwe, where it splits into two branches. One branch links Korogwe to the Indian Ocean port of Tanga and the other links Korogwe to Moshi, then connecting with the Kenya Railways system. Canada provided finance and technical assistance for TRC's development programme. IDA agreed in 1991 to lend US $76m. for five years for TRC's $279m. rehabilitation project. The network comprises 2,101 km of main-line track and 405 km of branch-line track. In 2000 the fleet included 71 active locomotives, 2,237 active 40-ft freight wagons and about 100 passenger coaches. The 2006/07 budget removed VAT from locomotives and rolling stock to help reduce the cost of these imports for the railway companies. TRC also formerly operated marine services and ferry services across Lake Victoria, from Mwanza to Ugandan lake ports, and across Lake Tanganyika to the DRC. In addition, TRC formerly operated services across the north of Lake Malawi to Malawi, but these do not connect to its rail system. Those ferry services were separated as part of the unbundling of TRC and were then operated by the Marine Services Company. TRC's hotels were leased out and its catering services contracted out, in preparation for privatization.

Air Tanzania Corpn (ATC), which was founded in 1977, operates domestic and regional services. The airline has on several occasions had to suspend international flights because of financial problems. In 1992 the Government proposed the partial privatization of ATC. In 2004 South African Airways (SAA) and Air Tanzania announced the creation of a new carrier, Air Tanzania Ltd (ATL), of which 49% was owned by SAA and 51% was still owned by the Tanzanian Government. In 2006 ATL's domestic routes linked Dar es Salaam to Kilimanjaro, Mwanza, Mtwara and Zanzibar, while its international regional routes included Entebbe in Uganda, Johannesburg in South Africa and Hahaya in the Comoros. Zanzibar's airport runway has been extended, with aid from Oman, to enable long-haul aircraft to land. In 1998 a British-led consortium won a 25-year contract to handle all airport services at Kilimanjaro International Airport. Precisionair, a joint venture between Kenya Airways (49%) and a private-sector Tanzanian businessman (51%), is based in Dar es Salaam. It operates domestic services to 11 Tanzanian cities, including Zanzibar; regional services to the Kenyan cities of Nairobi and Mombasa, to Entebbe in Uganda, to the Malawian cities of Lilongwe and Blantyre (in partnership with Air Malawi) and to Pemba in Mozambique; and longer-haul services to Dubai.

The TPA, formerly the Tanzania Harbours Authority, was unbundled and was to be partially privatized. TPA's US $220m. improvement programme for Dar es Salaam port, including the development of container-handling facilities, received funding from the World Bank, Finland, Denmark, Italy, the Netherlands, Norway, the United Kingdom and the EIB. The container terminal came into service in 1989, and an inland container depot was developed at Ubungo, 15 km from Dar es Salaam. The container portion of TPA was privatized in 2000, when ownership passed to a consortium including two companies from the Philippines.

The road network in Tanzania is in a state of poor repair, despite significant investment in the sector. In 1999 only about 14% of Tanzania's 88,200 km of roads were said to be in 'good' condition.

An international telephone service giving direct-dialling facilities was inaugurated in 1991. A satellite earth station at Mwenge, built in 1979, was replaced by a new installation supplied by an Italian company, giving access to Atlantic as well as Indian Ocean satellites. Plans to privatize the TTCL were announced in 1996, and in February 2001 a 35% share was sold to a consortium of Mobile Systems International of the Netherlands and Detecon of Germany. The Tanzanian Government subsequently reduced its stake from 65% to 36%. The land telephone network is extremely limited, but the number of main telephone lines per 1,000 inhabitants rose from 3.7 in 1998 to 4.2 in 2003. As access to mobile cellular networks increased, the demand for land lines slackened, with the 149,100 in use in 2004 dropping off slightly to 148,400 in 2005; the number of mobile network subscribers steadily rose, from 0.9m. in 2003 to 1.6m. in 2004 and 1.9m. in 2005. The first cellular network in the capital had been inaugurated in 1994. In 2003 Tanzania had 5.7 personal computers per 1,000 inhabitants.

EXTERNAL TRADE

The leading visible export is gold, followed by cashew nuts, coffee beans and raw cotton. Gold contributed about 70% of visible export revenue in 2006. Other exports include fish and prawns, cloves, beans, gemstones, timber and aromatic oils. Industrial exports include textiles, hides, wattle-bark extract and spray-dried instant coffee. Non-traditional exports developed in the 1990s included fresh fruit, vegetables and cut flowers. Visible exports free on board (f.o.b.) grew steadily in the mid-2000s, reaching US $1,830m. in 2006 (up 15% on 2004). At the same time imports f.o.b. proliferated to $4,081m. in 2006 (up 50% on 2004). The resulting visible trade deficit ballooned from $1,134m. in 2004 to $1,700m. in 2005 and $2,251m. in 2006.

An encouraging feature of Tanzania's trade performance has been the success of small private exporters, demonstrating how quickly many of them responded to trade-liberalization measures. Improved relations between Tanzania and its neighbours Kenya and Uganda during the late 1990s led to the re-establishment of the EAC through treaties signed in 2001 and 2004. In March 2004 President Mkapa, President Mwai Kibaki of Kenya and President Yoweri Museveni of Uganda signed a protocol on the creation of a customs union, eliminating most duties on goods within the EAC. The protocol came into force on 1 January 2005. However, surveys conducted in 2007 found that Tanzanians were significantly less enthusiastic about the EAC than Kenyans and Ugandans.

BALANCE OF PAYMENTS, INTERNATIONAL AID AND PUBLIC FINANCE

Tanzania's visible trade account, current account and overall balance of payments were all chronically in deficit throughout the 1990s and, even with growing tourism receipts, the goods and services account showed a series of deficits. All three balances were in deficit every year from 1999 as well, with the exception of the overall balance in 2003 and 2006. The deficit on goods and services increased by 124% between 2004 and 2006, reaching US $1,907.2m. in the latter year; the income balance made little difference, but once the failure of transfers to keep up with the widening gap had been taken into consideration, the deficit on the current account had increased by 276% to $1,442.7m. This trend worried the IMF. Gross official foreign reserves stood at $2,048m. at 31 December 2006 and were sufficient at 31 March 2007 to cover 5.3 months' worth of imports of goods and non-factor services. Tanzania's total external debt stood at $9,219.3m. at 31 December 2004, equivalent to 77.5% of GDP. Tanzania's level of debt-servicing in 1999 yielded a debt-service ratio equivalent to 33.6% of exports of goods and non-factor services. In addition, the Tanzanian Government owed Ts. 919,000m. (about $1,350m.) in domestic debt at the end of March 1999. During that month it paid Ts. 5,900m. in service on this debt, making a negligible impact on the outstanding arrears, which stood at Ts. 107,500m. Under a debt conversion programme inaugurated by the Bank of Tanzania in 1990, foreign private creditors were permitted to convert their claims into equity or into cash to invest in certain sectors, on a basis that reduced the local costs involved in starting a business in Tanzania. In April 2000 the World Bank and the IMF agreed a $1,200m. package of debt-relief assistance for Tanzania; the sums were to be dispersed over a 20-year period and were to cover 69.1% of Tanzania's debt-service obligations to IDA. In November 2001 the World Bank and the IMF granted Tanzania $3,000m. in debt relief under their enhanced initiative for heavily indebted poor countries (HIPC). This facility, according to the Bretton Woods institutions, reduced the present net value of Tanzania's total external debt by 54%. Debt-service obligations were reduced from $193m. in fiscal 1999/2000 (year ending 30 June) to an average of $116m. per year in the period 2000/01–2010/11. They amounted to about $130.27m. in 2004/05. The Mkapa Government rigorously began seeking debt relief from the time it came into office and, by mid-June 2004, the Minister of Finance was able to proclaim that 'all Paris Club creditors except Brazil have offered debt relief through partial cancellation (90%) or full cancellation'. The result of these cancellations was that the World Bank estimated the 'present value' of Tanzania's debt in 2002 at $1,800m. and changed Tanzania's classification to the category of a 'less indebted' country. Nevertheless, Tanzania was listed among the 18 HIPCs that were eligible for immediate debt cancellation under the terms of the agreement reached by the Group of Eight leading industrialized nations (G-8) in July 2005 at Gleneagles, in Scotland, United Kingdom. The IMF subsequently confirmed that Tanzania was among 19 countries eligible for '100% debt relief' in 2006. Tanzania's public external debt-service paid plunged from $124m. in 2004 to $32m. in 2006, and its debt-service ratio as a percentage of exports of goods and non-factor services declined to just 1% in 2006.

Tanzania's relations with the World Bank and the IMF, which had been strained for many years, much improved under the Mkapa Government, particularly by 2002, and remained cordial into 2007. In November 1994 foreign donors had suspended aid disbursements in protest at alleged high-level government connivance in widespread tax evasion, during the Mwinyi era. In response, the Mkapa Government, within months of entering office, established a new regulatory body, the Tanzania Revenue Authority (TRA), which became operational in July 1996. In February 1997 the TRA enforced a harmonization of import tariffs throughout the country, following donor concerns that the lower rate of duty in Zanzibar encouraged smuggling to the mainland. IMF credit was restored in November 1996, following the implementation of measures to improve revenue collection, to reduce expenditure and to contain inflation. The Fund in July 2003 approved a new three-year US $27m. Poverty Reduction and Growth Facility (PRGF) arrangement, followed by further disbursements, including a $4.2m. tranche in February 2007. These disbursements signalled the Fund's confidence in Tanzania's National Strategy for Growth and Reduction of Poverty, better known in Tanzania by its Swahili name, Mkukuta. The Income Tax Act

2004 had the stated aim of strengthening government revenue while at the same time providing tax incentives to activities that would enable growth and alleviate poverty.

Measures to deregulate the banking sector were introduced during the 1990s. When the Mkapa Government came to power in November 1995 there were just two banks in Tanzania. By March 1996 the Bank of Tanzania (in its new role as 'regulator and supervisor' of the banking sector) had licensed eight private commercial banks and four non-bank financial institutions. By June 2005 26 banks were operating in Tanzania. From April 1991 a number of bureaux de change opened throughout the country, and in 1996 the Government announced plans to remove all remaining controls on currency convertibility.

The 2006/07 budget projected total revenue at Ts. 2,460,995m. and called for total expenditure of Ts. 4,850,588m. The revenue target—even if achieved, which it was—covered scarcely 50% of the proposed expenditure. VAT remained unchanged, at 20%, despite the business sector's complaint that it made the expense of doing business in Tanzania higher than in neighbouring Kenya, where VAT was levied at 17%. The out-turn showed total domestic revenue at Ts. 2,600,000m. in the 2006/07 financial year. The 2007/08 budget projected total domestic revenue at Ts. 3,502,000m. and total expenditure at Ts. 6,067,000m.; domestic revenue was expected to cover less than 58% of total expenditure. The budget forecast foreign grants and loans to cover the gap at Ts. 2,549,000m. Of total expenditure, 63.7%, or Ts. 3,866,000m., was recurrent, and 36.3%, or Ts. 2,201,000m., was for development.

CONCLUSION

Evidence that Tanzania's earlier period of significant economic decline had been arrested became apparent by the late 1980s. The Mwinyi Government persevered with the policies formulated in the economic reform programmes approved by the IMF and other donors, albeit less rapidly than the donors wished. The Mkapa Government accelerated the pace of recovery, although it still remained slower than some donors wished. The Kikwete Government made it clear from the outset that it intended to continue in the same vein, working in close co-operation with the IMF, the World Bank and bilateral development partners to make Mkukuta succeed in improving the lives of Tanzanians. An inflation rate of 6.9% in 2005 gave no cause for alarm, as the reasons were clear and unavoidable—drought and high prices for imported petroleum products—and donors and investors continued to show confidence in Tanzania's economic management. Nevertheless, the infrastructure of Tanzania remained weakened by decades of neglect, hindering economic growth, especially in the agricultural sector, in which more than 80% of the Tanzanian people earned their livelihoods. The 2006/07 budget speech placed improved export performance prominently in the frame as the preferred engine of growth. How this was to be achieved was not disclosed in detail; however, it was apparent that the attraction of foreign investors, particularly in the mining sector, to Tanzania was of increasing importance to the country's prospects. Tanzania's mineral reserves were indeed attracting foreign investment, but much more would be needed to make significant inroads into the country's widespread poverty. The inability to provide a reliable electricity supply even to the 11% of the population with access to the national grid was a huge shackle on the country's manufacturers. The country has a widespread reputation for excessive bureaucracy, 'red tape' that often deters investment in non-mining sectors of the economy. Then too, corruption was a problem. Even so, Tanzania continued to win the favour of the IMF. In June 2007 the IMF observed that the Tanzanian authorities seemed to be committed to improving governance and transparency, trying to strengthen the Prevention of Corruption Bureau and to address allegations of improprieties about the management of the Government's external payment arrears account at the Bank of Tanzania; the Fund commented that the 'forthcoming special audit of this account should be conducted in a timely manner and in line with best international standards.'

Statistical Survey

Source (unless otherwise stated): Economic and Research Policy Dept, Bank of Tanzania, POB 2939, Dar es Salaam; tel. (22) 2110946; fax (22) 2113325; e-mail info@hq.bot-tz.org; internet www.bot-tz.org.

Area and Population

AREA, POPULATION AND DENSITY

Area (sq km)	945,087*
Population (census results)	
28 August 1988	23,126,310
25 August 2002	
Males	16,910,321
Females	17,658,911
Total	34,569,232
Population (UN estimates at mid-year)†	
2004	37,508,000
2005	38,478,000
2006	39,459,000
Density (per sq km) at mid-2006	41.8

* 364,900 sq miles. Of this total, Tanzania mainland is 942,626 sq km (363,950 sq miles), and Zanzibar 2,461 sq km (950 sq miles).

† Source: UN, *World Population Prospects: The 2006 Revision*.

ETHNIC GROUPS

(private households, census of 26 August 1967)

African	11,481,595	Others	839
Asian	75,015	Not stated	159,042
Arabs	29,775	**Total**	11,763,150
European	16,884		

REGIONS

(at census of 25 August 2002)

Arusha	1,292,973	Mwanza	2,942,148
Dar es Salaam	2,497,940	Pwani	889,154
Dodoma	1,698,996	North Pemba†	186,013
Iringa	1,495,333	North Unguja†	136,953
Kagera	2,033,888	Rukwa	1,141,743
Kigoma	1,679,109	Ruvuma	1,117,166
Kilimanjaro	1,381,149	Shinyanga	2,805,580
Lindi	791,306	Singida	1,090,758
Manyara*	603,691	South Pemba†	176,153
Mara	1,368,602	South Unguja†	94,504
Mbeya	2,070,046	Urban West†	391,002
Morogoro	1,759,809	Tabora	1,717,908
Mtwara	1,128,523	Tanga	1,642,015

* Before the 2002 census Manyara was included in the region of Arusha.

† Part of the autonomous territory of Zanzibar.

PRINCIPAL TOWNS
(estimated population at mid-1988)

Dar es Salaam	1,360,850	Mbeya	152,844
Mwanza	223,013	Arusha	134,708
Dodoma	203,833	Morogoro	117,760
Tanga	187,455	Shinyanga	100,724
Zanzibar	157,634		

Source: UN, *Demographic Yearbook*.

Mid-2005 ('000, incl. suburbs, UN estimate): Dar es Salaam 2,676 (Source: UN, *World Urbanization Prospects: The 2005 Revision*).

BIRTHS AND DEATHS
(annual averages, UN estimates)

	1990–1995	1995–2000	2000–05
Birth rate (per 1,000)	42.4	41.5	42.1
Death rate (per 1,000)	14.8	15.4	14.6

Source: UN, *World Population Prospects: The 2006 Revision*.

Expectation of life (years at birth, WHO estimates): 48 (males 47; females 49) in 2004 (Source: WHO, *World Health Report*).

ECONOMICALLY ACTIVE POPULATION
(Mainland Tanganyika only, persons aged 10 years and over, at March 2001)

	Males	Females	Total
Agriculture, forestry, hunting and fishing	6,698.6	7,191.2	13,890.1
Mining and quarrying	15.5	13.8	29.2
Manufacturing	161.7	83.8	245.4
Electricity, gas and water supply	13.5	1.2	14.7
Construction	147.5	4.2	151.7
Wholesale and retail trade and restaurants and hotels	565.5	697.5	1,263.0
Transport, storage and communications	103.9	7.6	111.6
Financing, insurance, real estate and business services	22.2	4.3	26.5
Community, social and personal services	622.8	559.9	1,182.7
Total employed	8,351.3	8,563.5	16,914.8
Unemployed	388.4	524.4	912.8
Total labour force	8,739.7	9,087.9	17,827.6

Source: ILO.

Mid-2005 (estimates in '000): Agriculture, etc. 15,802; Total labour force 20,224 (Source: FAO).

Health and Welfare

KEY INDICATORS

Total fertility rate (children per woman, 2005)	4.8
Under-5 mortality rate (per 1,000 live births, 2005)	122
HIV/AIDS (% of persons aged 15–49, 2005)	6.5
Physicians (per 1,000 head, 2004)	0.02
Hospital beds (per 1,000 head, 1992)	0.89
Health expenditure (2004): US $ per head (PPP)	28.5
Health expenditure (2004): % of GDP	4.0
Health expenditure (2004): public (% of total)	43.6
Access to water (% of persons, 2004)	62
Access to sanitation (% of persons, 2004)	47
Human Development Index (2004): ranking	162
Human Development Index (2004): value	0.430

For sources and definitions, see explanatory note on p. vi.

Agriculture

PRINCIPAL CROPS
('000 metric tons)

	2003	2004	2005
Wheat	75.0	74.0	115.0
Rice (paddy)	713.0	586.0	957.0
Maize	2,322.0	3,232.0	3,288.0
Millet	139.0	215.0	155.0*
Sorghum	488.0	820.1	890.0*
Potatoes	196.0	260.0†	260.0†
Sweet potatoes†	970.0	970.0	970.0
Cassava (Manioc)	5,284	6,152	7,000†
Sugar cane	2,000.0†	2,000.0†	n.a.
Dry beans	333.3	280.0†	290.0†
Cashew nuts	95.0	79.0	72.0
Groundnuts (in shell)*	52.0	54.0	54.0
Coconuts†	370.0	370.0	370.0
Oil palm fruit†	65.0	65.0	65.0
Seed cotton*	155.0	330.0	330.0
Tomatoes	129.6	145.0†	145.0†
Onions (dry)	36.1	55.0†	55.0†
Bananas	141.2	147.8	150.0†
Plantains	564.8	591.2	600.0†
Mangoes	336.0	195.0†	200.0†
Pineapples†	77.5	77.5	77.5
Coffee (green)	61.6	32.5	54.0
Tea (made)	27.6	30.1	30.7
Cloves (whole and stems)†	12.5	12.5	12.5
Tobacco (leaves)	28.0	34.0	47.0
Cotton (lint)*	50.0	118.0	100.0

* Unofficial figure(s).
† FAO estimate(s).

Source: FAO.

LIVESTOCK
('000 head, year ending September)

	2003	2004	2005
Asses, mules or hinnies*	182.0	182.0	182.0
Cattle	17,704.0	17,472.1	17,719.1
Pigs	455.0	455.0	455.0
Sheep	3,521.2	3,521.0	3,521.0
Goats	12,556.2	12,550.0*	12,550.0*
Chickens*	30,000	30,000	30,000

* FAO estimate(s).

Source: FAO.

LIVESTOCK PRODUCTS
('000 metric tons, FAO estimates)

	2003	2004	2005
Cattle meat	246.3	246.3	246.3
Sheep meat	10.3	10.3	10.3
Goat meat	30.6	30.6	30.6
Pig meat	13.0	13.0	13.0
Chicken meat	47.0	47.0	47.0
Cows' milk	840.0	840.0	840.0
Goats' milk	104.0	104.0	104.0
Hen eggs	35.1	35.1	35.1
Honey	27.0	27.0	27.0

Source: FAO.

Forestry

ROUNDWOOD REMOVALS
('000 cubic metres, excluding bark, FAO estimates)

	2003	2004	2005
Sawlogs, veneer logs and logs for sleepers	317	317	317
Pulpwood	153	153	153
Other industrial wood	1,844	1,844	1,844
Fuel wood	21,310	21,505	21,712
Total	23,624	23,819	24,026

Source: FAO.

SAWNWOOD PRODUCTION
('000 cubic metres, including railway sleepers, FAO estimates)

	1992	1993	1994
Coniferous (softwood)	26	21	13
Broadleaved (hardwood)	22	18	11
Total	48	39	24

1995–2005: Production assumed to be unchanged from 1994 (FAO estimates).

Source: FAO.

Fishing

('000 metric tons, live weight)

	2003	2004	2005*
Capture	351.1	347.8	348.1
Tilapias	50.0	51.7	51.7
Nile perch	98.5	98.5	98.5
Other freshwater fishes	98.8	97.0	97.0
Dagaas	43.5	40.0	40.0
Sardinellas	14.2	15.0	15.0
Aquaculture*	0.0	0.0	0.0
Total catch	351.1	347.8	348.1

* FAO estimates.

Note: Figures exclude aquatic plants ('000 metric tons): 9.5 (capture 2.5, aquaculture 7.0) in 2003; 6.2 (capture 0.2, aquaculture 6.0) in 2004; 6.2 (capture 0.2, aquaculture 6.0) in 2005. Also excluded are aquatic mammals, recorded by number rather than by weight. The number of Risso's dolphins caught was: 1 in 2003; 1 in 2004; nil in 2005. The number of Indo-Pacific hump-backed dolphins caught was: 4 in 2003; 1 in 2004; nil in 2005. The number of Bottlenose dolphins caught was: 16 in 2003; 6 in 2004; nil in 2005. The number of Spinner dolphins caught was: 10 in 2003; 3 in 2004; nil in 2005. The number of other spotted dolphins caught was: 2 in 2003; 1 in 2004; nil in 2005. The number of Nile crocodiles caught was: 1,469 in 2003; 1,560 in 2004; 1,467 in 2005.

Source: FAO.

Mining

('000 metric tons, unless otherwise indicated)

	2003	2004	2005
Coal (bituminous)	55	65	75
Diamonds ('000 carats)*	237	304	220
Gold (refined, kilograms)	48,018	48,178	52,236
Salt	59	57	135
Gypsum and anhydrite	33	59	63
Limestone, crushed	1,206	1,391	2,780
Pozzolanic materials	106	153	163
Sand	2,036	2,400†	2,800†

* Estimated at 85% gem-quality and 15% industrial-quality stones. Excluding smuggled artisanal production.

† Estimate.

Source: US Geological Survey.

Industry

SELECTED PRODUCTS
('000 metric tons, unless otherwise indicated)

	2001	2002	2003*
Sugar	184.0	189.6	212.9
Cigarettes (million)	3.5	3.8	3.9
Beer (million litres)	175.7	175.9	194.1
Non-alcoholic beverages (million litres)	198.7	208.7	208.4
Textiles (million sq metres)	84.3	106.3	125.8
Cement	900.0	1,026.0	1,186.0
Rolled steel	16.1	25.4	39.6
Iron sheets	25.9	35.1	33.6
Aluminium	0.1	0.1	0.2
Sisal ropes	4.5	5.9	6.9
Paints (million litres)	9.0	13.6	16.8

* Provisional.

Source: IMF, *Tanzania—Selected Issues and Statistical Appendix* (September 2004).

Cement ('000 metric tons): 1,281 in 2004; 1,375 in 2005 (Source: US Geological Survey).

Finance

CURRENCY AND EXCHANGE RATES

Monetary Units
100 cents = 1 Tanzanian shilling.

Sterling, Dollar and Euro Equivalents (31 May 2007)
£1 sterling = 2,488.37 Tanzanian shillings;
US $1 = 1,258.47 Tanzanian shillings;
€1 = 1,693.02 Tanzanian shillings;
10,000 Tanzanian shillings = £4.02 = $7.95 = €5.91.

Average Exchange Rate (Tanzanian shillings per US $)
2004 1,089.33
2005 1,128.93
2006 1,251.90

BUDGET
('000 million shillings, year ending 30 June)*

Revenue†	2001/02	2002/03	2003/04‡
Tax revenue	938.5	1,105.7	1,325.1
Import duties	88.9	106.4	130.1
Value-added tax	352.3	424.3	494.8
Excises	177.6	187.3	216.6
Income tax	228.4	276.1	360.4
Other taxes	91.3	111.7	123.2
Non-tax revenue	104.5	111.8	122.3
Ministries and regions	68.0	78.0	85.4
Total	1,042.9	1,217.5	1,447.3

Expenditure	2001/02	2002/03	2003/04‡
Recurrent expenditure	1,171.4	1,488.6	1,887.1
Wages	342.0	397.8	464.1
Interest	121.1	99.8	121.7
Goods, services and transfers	708.3	991.1	1,301.4
Clearance of domestic payment arrears	59.1	—	—
Development expenditure and net lending	291.3	500.9	644.4
Local	50.2	95.7	136.1
Foreign	241.1	405.2	508.3
Total	1,521.9	1,989.5	2,531.5

* Figures refer to the Tanzania Government, excluding the revenue and expenditure of the separate Zanzibar Government.
† Excluding grants received.
‡ Provisional.

Source: IMF, *Tanzania—Selected Issues and Statistical Appendix* (September 2004).

2004/05: ('000 million shillings): Total revenue (including grants) 2,736.0; Total expenditure (including lending minus repayments) 3,275.6.

2005/06 ('000 million shillings): Total revenue (including grants) 3,078.0; Total expenditure (including lending minus repayments) 3,914.9 (Source: IMF, *International Financial Statistics*).

INTERNATIONAL RESERVES
(excl. gold, US $ million at 31 December)

	2004	2005	2006
IMF special drawing rights	0.1	0.7	0.1
Reserve position in IMF	15.5	14.3	14.3
Foreign exchange	2,280.1	2,033.8	2,033.8
Total	2,295.7	2,048.8	2,048.2

Source: IMF, *International Financial Statistics*.

MONEY SUPPLY
('000 million shillings at 31 December)

	2004	2005	2006
Currency outside banks	664.16	843.16	989.23
Demand deposits at commercial banks	651.45	915.65	961.10
Total money	1,315.61	1,758.81	1,950.33

Source: IMF, *International Financial Statistics*.

COST OF LIVING
(Consumer Price Index)

Tanganyika
(base: 2000 = 100)

	2003	2004	2005
Food (incl. beverages)	112.0	118.6	125.6
Fuel, light and water	107.7	112.9	107.6
Clothing (incl. footwear)	106.6	109.0	113.2
Rent	111.2	113.8	122.4
All items (incl. others)	109.8	114.5	119.4

Source: ILO.

Zanzibar
(base: 2001 = 100)

	2002	2003
Food (incl. beverages)	106.9	116.7
Fuel, light and water	100.0	106.0
Clothing (incl. footwear)	106.7	128.3
Rent	104.9	118.0
All items (incl. others)	105.2	114.7

2004: Food (incl. beverages) 128.6; All items (incl. others) 124.0.

2005: Food (incl. beverages) 143.7; All items (incl. others) 136.1.

Source: ILO.

NATIONAL ACCOUNTS
(Tanzania mainland, current prices)

National Income and Product
(million shillings, provisional)

	1992	1993	1994
Compensation of employees	88,230	119,119	148,194
Operating surplus	906,923	1,132,774	1,462,193
Domestic factor incomes	995,153	1,251,894	1,610,387
Consumption of fixed capital	35,802	36,697	49,542
Gross domestic product (GDP) at factor cost	1,030,955	1,288,591	1,659,929
Indirect taxes	109,442	183,389	260,039
Less Subsidies	9,801	67,611	97,398
GDP in purchasers' values	1,130,596	1,404,369	1,822,570
Factor income received from abroad	2,563	7,934	8,648
Less Factor income paid abroad	72,969	67,842	78,173
Gross national product (GNP)	1,060,190	1,344,460	1,753,045
Less Consumption of fixed capital	35,802	36,697	49,542
National income in market prices	1,024,387	1,307,763	1,703,504
Other current transfers from abroad (net)	282,813	291,673	308,518
National disposable income	1,307,200	1,599,436	2,084,022

Expenditure on the Gross Domestic Product
('000 million shillings)

	2003	2004	2005
Government final consumption expenditure	712.7	855.3	1,037.7
Private final consumption expenditure	8,549.1	9,980.2	11,407.3
Increase in stocks	19.7	28.3	31.1
Gross fixed capital formation	2,239.3	2,570.7	3,118.3
Total domestic expenditure	11,520.8	13,434.5	15,594.4
Exports of goods and services	1,887.7	2,847.6	3,259.7
Less Imports of goods and services	2,811.2	3,646.4	4,319.2
Sub-total	10,597.3	12,635.7	14,534.9
Statistical discrepancy	80.5	–270.1	–325.7
GDP in purchasers' values	10,677.8	12,365.6	14,209.2
GDP at constant 1992 prices	1,962.4	2,094.5	2,237.1

Source: IMF, *International Financial Statistics*.

Gross Domestic Product by Economic Activity
('000 million shillings)

	2001	2002	2003*
Agriculture, forestry, fishing and hunting	1,919.7	2,205.2	2,508.9
Mining and quarrying	120.5	153.0	191.2
Manufacturing	564.7	638.7	711.0
Electricity and water	124.8	145.8	157.0
Construction	335.9	389.7	454.2
Trade, restaurants and hotels	926.9	1,038.1	1,153.3
Transport and communications	361.6	404.9	454.0
Public administration	723.1	810.3	869.3
Financial and business services	421.5	494.8	564.3
Other services	73.9	82.7	86.9

—continued	2001	2002	2003*
Sub-total	5,572.4	6,363.1	7,150.0
Less Imputed bank service charge	157.8	168.8	182.3
Total monetary GDP	5,414.6	6,194.3	6,967.7
Non-monetary GDP	2,210.0	2,505.6	2,843.8
Agriculture, forestry, fishing and hunting	1,486.4	1,679.4	1,909.0
Construction	69.2	80.3	92.0
Owner-occupied dwellings	654.3	745.9	842.9
Total GDP at factor cost	7,624.6	8,699.9	9,811.6
Net taxes	650.0	745.6	880.9
Total GDP at market prices	8,274.6	9,445.5	10,692.4

* Provisional figures.

Source: IMF, *Tanzania—Selected Issues and Statistical Appendix* (September 2004).

BALANCE OF PAYMENTS
(US $ million)

	2004	2005	2006
Exports of goods f.o.b.	1,473.1	1,675.8	1,723.0
Imports of goods f.o.b.	–2,482.8	–2,997.6	–3,864.1
Trade balance	–1,009.8	–1,321.8	–2,141.1
Exports of services	1,133.6	1,269.2	1,483.2
Imports of services	–974.7	–1,207.3	–1,249.4
Balance on goods and services	–850.9	–1,260.0	–1,907.2
Other income received	81.8	80.9	80.2
Other income paid	–200.9	–198.0	–165.2
Balance on goods, services and income	–970.0	–1,377.0	–1,992.1
Current transfers received	651.7	563.0	615.6
Current transfers paid	–65.0	–66.5	–65.6
Current balance	–383.3	–880.6	–1,442.7
Capital account (net)	459.9	633.2	5,292.9
Direct investment from abroad	330.6	447.6	474.5
Other investment assets	–11.0	–61.5	–175.0
Portfolio investment liabilities	2.4	2.5	2.6
Other investment liabilities	–46.4	276.6	–4,589.3
Net errors and omissions	–148.4	–671.7	873.8
Overall balance	203.9	–253.8	437.4

Source: IMF, *International Financial Statistics*.

External Trade

PRINCIPAL COMMODITIES
(US $ million)

Imports c.i.f.	2002	2003	2004
Food and live animals	156.0	188.9	277.1
Cereals and cereal preparations	94.9	133.9	202.8
Wheat and meslin, unmilled	58.4	76.8	119.2
Mineral fuels, lubricants, etc.	197.6	405.8	417.4
Petroleum, petroleum products, etc.	195.5	401.7	409.4
Petroleum products, refined	188.6	394.4	400.7
Motor spirit, incl. aviation spirit	61.7	394.2	—
Gas oils	99.4	—	—
Animal and vegetable oils, fats and waxes	67.4	85.9	85.1
Fixed vegetable oils and fats	63.2	78.1	77.0
Palm oil	57.0	73.9	74.3
Chemicals and related products	219.4	265.8	354.7
Medicinal and pharmaceutical products	38.0	54.1	56.3
Artificial resins and plastic materials, cellulose esters, etc.	54.8	65.4	—
Basic manufactures	270.7	341.2	382.4
Iron and steel	57.1	81.5	98.7

Imports c.i.f.*—continued*	2002	2003	2004
Other metal manufactures	55.3	83.1	76.4
Machinery and transport equipment	601.7	698.6	775.4
Power generating machinery and equipment	25.3	45.6	43.9
Rotating electric plant, and parts thereof	14.0	20.4	23.8
Electric motors (incl. ac/dc motors), other than direct current	1.2	1.3	3.1
Machinery specialized for particular industries	138.0	141.4	166.9
General industrial machinery, equipment and parts	68.5	85.4	108.2
Telecommunications, sound recording and reproducing equipment	49.4	60.8	59.7
Telecommunication equipment, parts and accessories	42.2	52.9	50.3
Other electrical machinery, apparatus and appliances, and parts	56.1	53.9	82.3
Road vehicles	198.1	213.4	223.5
Passenger motor vehicles, excl. buses	63.6	71.9	78.2
Lorries and special purpose motor vehicles	73.4	68.1	78.2
Vehicles for the transportation of goods or materials	67.8	64.4	72.6
Miscellaneous manufactured articles	117.9	139.2	172.7
Total (incl. others)	1,691.2	2,189.5	2,531.2

Exports f.o.b.	2002	2003	2004
Food and live animals	315.1	384.9	399.0
Fish, crustaceans, molluscs and preparations thereof	116.7	134.5	125.6
Fish, fresh, chilled or frozen	103.6	116.4	110.1
Fish fillets, fresh or chilled	43.3	69.9	75.7
Fish fillets, frozen	59.3	44.1	30.6
Cereals and cereal preparations	35.2	63.0	61.3
Vegetables and fruit	70.0	76.9	95.6
Fruit and nuts, fresh, dried	49.0	46.3	70.4
Cashew nuts, fresh or dried	47.2	43.5	68.7
Coffee, tea, cocoa, spices, and manufactures thereof	77.7	93.4	98.0
Coffee and coffee substitutes	36.0	49.9	50.1
Coffee, not roasted; coffee husks and skins	35.0	49.1	49.4
Beverages and tobacco	57.4	54.4	70.1
Tobacco and tobacco manufactures	56.2	51.6	66.1
Tobacco, wholly or partly stripped	25.8	33.5	55.4
Crude materials, inedible, except fuels	160.0	179.6	256.9
Textile fibres (not wool tops) and their wastes (not in yarn)	38.1	56.4	83.5
Raw cotton, excl. linters, not carded or combed	25.9	40.8	50.3
Metalliferous ores and metal scrap	75.8	64.4	107.3
Ores and concentrates of precious metals	75.2	61.0	105.5
Basic manufactures	72.1	89.0	121.3
Non-metallic mineral manufactures	53.7	53.4	58.5
Pearl, precious and semi-precious stones, unworked or worked	42.2	43.1	49.1
Diamonds cut or otherwise worked, but not mounted or set	21.2	24.3	23.4
Gold, non-monetary, unwrought or semi-manufactured	268.5	438.1	524.6
Total (incl. others)	901.4	1,218.4	1,465.8

Source: UN, *International Trade Statistics Yearbook*.

PRINCIPAL TRADING PARTNERS
(US $ million)

Imports c.i.f.	2002	2003	2004
Australia	73.2	54.7	75.2
Bahrain	79.8	116.1	171.7
Belgium	23.4	33.4	35.3
Canada	17.8	31.3	39.8
China, People's Repub.	79.8	116.1	171.7
Denmark	15.8	20.4	21.8
France	39.4	40.8	40.6
Germany	60.6	68.8	75.4
India	107.9	167.4	216.4
Indonesia	62.7	75.9	86.6
Italy	45.4	39.7	40.6
Japan	140.2	169.7	180.9
Kenya	96.2	116.2	130.3
Korea, Repub.	18.5	28.0	27.0
Malaysia	12.7	17.6	19.4
Netherlands	27.6	32.1	42.8
Saudi Arabia	47.8	51.3	55.5
South Africa	190.7	306.3	331.0
Sweden	22.2	38.5	23.7
Switzerland	23.0	22.9	18.8
Thailand	36.3	20.6	29.7
United Arab Emirates	98.0	146.5	184.9
United Kingdom	95.9	108.2	110.4
USA	92.1	69.5	78.2
Total (incl. others)	1,691.2	2,189.5	2,531.2

Exports f.o.b.	2002	2003	2004
Belgium	21.5	35.6	26.9
Congo, Democratic Repub.	16.0	36.5	41.6
France	156.2	79.5	12.3
Germany	27.9	30.9	34.3
Hong Kong	11.3	9.9	12.4
India	64.9	74.4	104.2
Ireland	14.2	0.0	0.1
Italy	24.7	23.4	28.3
Japan	97.3	88.7	65.0
Kenya	35.7	83.4	90.0
Malawi	18.0	13.1	22.8
Netherlands	54.5	67.8	60.5
Saudi Arabia	17.0	8.5	12.7
Singapore	4.0	13.3	15.6
South Africa	16.7	39.1	120.3
Switzerland	5.7	12.6	30.1
Uganda	5.5	48.1	55.6
United Arab Emirates	14.6	16.6	18.7
United Kingdom	159.2	386.9	473.2
USA	13.7	11.4	15.2
Zambia	17.6	24.9	16.3
Total (incl. others)	901.4	1,218.4	1,465.8

Source: UN, *International Trade Statistics Yearbook*.

Transport

RAILWAYS

	2003	2004	2005
Passengers ('000)	666	464	514
Freight ('000 metric tons)	1,443	1,002	1,169

Source: National Bureau of Statistics, *Tanzania in Figures 2005*.

ROAD TRAFFIC
(estimates, '000 motor vehicles in use)

	1994	1995	1996
Passenger cars	28.0	26.0	23.8
Buses and coaches	78.0	81.0	86.0
Lorries and vans	27.2	27.7	29.7
Road tractors	6.7	6.7	6.6

Source: IRF, *World Road Statistics*.

SHIPPING

Merchant fleet
(registered at 31 December)

	2004	2005	2006
Number of vessels	51	50	52
Displacement ('000 grt)	38.9	36.8	37.5

Source: Lloyd's Register-Fairplay, *World Fleet Statistics*.

International sea-borne traffic

	2003	2004	2005
Vessels docked	2,350	2,898	3,895
Cargo ('000 metric tons)	5,346	4,179	4,307
Passengers ('000)	648	525	1,072

Source: National Bureau of Statistics, *Tanzania in Figures 2005*.

CIVIL AVIATION
(traffic on scheduled services)

	2001	2002	2003
Kilometres flown (million)	4	3	4
Passengers carried ('000)	175	134	150
Passenger-km (million)	181	136	151
Total ton-km (million)	21	14	16

Source: UN, *Statistical Yearbook*.

Tourism

FOREIGN VISITOR ARRIVALS
(by country of origin)

	2003	2004	2005
Burundi	11,907	3,157	5,767
Canada	10,354	10,613	10,922
Congo, Democratic Repub.	6,850	8,030	9,479
France	22,103	21,849	23,547
Germany	19,222	19,222	18,170
India	22,215	14,804	17,598
Italy	24,675	44,045	49,829
Kenya	119,406	124,967	112,766
Malawi	14,267	16,868	19,999
Netherlands	15,272	14,594	15,805
Rwanda	12,061	6,089	17,037
South Africa	35,071	25,849	28,922
Spain	9,565	11,168	11,709
Uganda	34,664	24,253	25,373
United Kingdom	43,656	59,547	52,442
USA	36,419	40,248	47,621
Zambia	10,670	25,405	29,120
Total (incl. others)	576,198	582,807	612,754

Tourism receipts (US $ million, incl. passenger transport): 468 in 2003; 610 in 2004; n.a. in 2005.

Source: World Tourism Organization.

Communications Media

	2003	2004	2005
Telephones ('000 main lines in use)	149.1	149.1	148.4
Mobile cellular telephones ('000 subscribers)	891.2	1,640.0	1,942.0
Personal computers ('000 in use)	200	278	278
Internet users ('000)	250	333	333

Source: International Telecommunication Union.

Television receivers ('000 in use, 2000): 700.

Radio receivers ('000 in use, estimate, 1997): 8,800 (Source: UNESCO, *Statistical Yearbook*).

Daily newspapers (1996): 3; average circulation ('000 copies, estimate) 120 (Source: UNESCO, *Statistical Yearbook*).

Education

(2005)

	Institutions	Teachers	Students
Primary (state)	14,053	132,409	1,853,000
Primary (private)	204	2,604	16,154
Secondary (state)	1,202	13,448	199,602
Secondary (private)	543	10,457	90,753
Higher (state)*	64	n.a.	15,384
Higher (private)†	31	n.a.	1,388

* Comprising 34 teacher training colleges, 4 technical colleges, 5 full universities, 3 constituent universities and 18 other higher institutions.
† Comprising 18 teacher training colleges and 13 universities.

Source: National Bureau for Statistics, *Tanzania in Figures 2005*.

Adult literacy rate (UNESCO estimates): 69.4% (males 77.5%; females 62.2%) in 2004 (Source: UN Development Programme, *Human Development Report*).

Directory

The Constitution

The United Republic of Tanzania was established on 26 April 1964, when Tanganyika and Zanzibar, hitherto separate independent countries, merged. An interim Constitution of 1965 was replaced, on 25 April 1977, by a permanent Constitution for the United Republic. In October 1979 the Revolutionary Council of Zanzibar adopted a separate Constitution, governing Zanzibar's internal administration, with provisions for a popularly elected President and a legislative House of Representatives elected by delegates of the then ruling party. A new Constitution for Zanzibar, which came into force in January 1985, provided for direct elections to the Zanzibar House of Representatives. The provisions below relate to the 1977 Constitution of the United Republic, as subsequently amended.

GOVERNMENT

Legislative power is exercised by the Parliament of the United Republic, which is vested by the Constitution with complete sovereign power, and of which the present National Assembly is the legislative house. The Assembly also enacts all legislation concerning the mainland. Internal matters in Zanzibar are the exclusive jurisdiction of the Zanzibar executive, the Supreme Revolutionary Council of Zanzibar, and the Zanzibar legislature, the House of Representatives.

National Assembly

The National Assembly comprises both directly elected members (chosen by universal adult suffrage) and nominated members (including five members elected from the Zanzibar House of Representatives). The number of directly elected members exceeds the number of nominated members. The Electoral Commission may review and, if necessary, increase the number of electoral constituencies before every general election. The National Assembly has a term of five years.

President

The President is the Head of State, Head of the Government and Commander-in-Chief of the Armed Forces. The President has no power to legislate without recourse to Parliament. The assent of the President is required before any bill passed by the National Assembly becomes law. Should the President withhold his assent and the bill be repassed by the National Assembly by a two-thirds' majority, the President is required by law to give his assent within 21 days unless, before that time, he has dissolved the National Assembly, in which case he must stand for re-election.

The President appoints a Vice-President to assist him in carrying out his functions. The President presides over the Cabinet, which comprises a Prime Minister and other ministers who are appointed from among the members of the National Assembly.

JUDICIARY

The independence of the judges is secured by provisions which prevent their removal, except on account of misbehaviour or incapacity when they may be dismissed at the discretion of the President. The Constitution also makes provision for a Permanent Commission of Enquiry, which has wide powers to investigate any abuses of authority.

CONSTITUTIONAL AMENDMENTS

The Constitution can be amended by an act of the Parliament of the United Republic, when the proposed amendment is supported by the votes of not fewer than two-thirds of all the members of the Assembly.

The Government

HEAD OF STATE

President: Lt-Col (Retd) JAKAYA MRISHO KIKWETE (took office 21 December 2005).

Vice-President: Dr ALI MOHAMMED SHEIN.

CABINET
(August 2007)

President and Commander-in-Chief of the Armed Forces: Lt-Col (Retd) JAKAYA MRISHO KIKWETE.

Prime Minister: EDWARD LOWASSA.

Minister of Foreign Affairs and International Co-operation: BERNARD KAMILLIUS MEMBE.

Minister of East African Co-operation: Dr IBRAHIM SAID MSABAHA.

Minister of Finance: ZAKIA MEGHJI.

Minister of Planning, Economy and Empowerment: Dr JUMA NGASONGWA.

Minister of Industry, Trade and Marketing: BASIL MRAMBA.

Minister of Agriculture, Food Security and Co-operatives: STEPHEN WASSIRA.

Minister of Natural Resources and Tourism: Prof. JUMANNE ABDALLAH MAGHEMBE.

Minister of Water: Dr SHUKURU JUMANNE KAWAMBWA.

Minister of Energy and Minerals: NAZIR MUSTAFA KARAMAGI.

Minister of Infrastructure Development: ANDREW JOHN CHENGE.

Minister of Health and Social Welfare: Prof. DAVID HOMELI MWAKYUSA.

Minister of Education and Vocational Training: MARGARETH SIMWANZA SITTA.

Minister of Science, Technology and Higher Education: Prof. PETER MAHMOUD MSOLLA.

Minister of Labour, Employment and Youth Development: Capt. JOHN ZEFENIA CHILIGATI.

Minister of Land and Human Settlements: JOHN POMBE MAGUFULI.

Minister of Information, Culture and Sports: MUHAMMED SEIF KHATIB.

Minister of Defence and National Service: Prof. JUMA ATHUMAN KAPUYA.

Minister of Public Safety and Security: BAKARI HARITH MWAPACHU.

Minister of Home Affairs: JOSEPH JAMES MUNGAI.

Minister of Justice and Constitutional Affairs: Dr MARY MICHAEL NAGU.

Minister of Community Development: SOFIA MATTAYO SIMBA.

Minister of Livestock Development: ANTHONY MWANDU DIALLO.

Ministers of State in the President's Office: HAWA ABDULRAHMAN GHASIA (Public Service Management), PHILIP SANKA MARMO (Good Governance), KINGUNGE NGOMBALE MWIRU (Politics and Social Relations).

Ministers of State in the Vice-President's Office: Dr HUSSEIN MWINYI (Union Affairs), Prof. MARK MWANDOSYA (Environment).

Ministers of State in the Prime Minister's Office: MIZENGO PETER PINDA (Regional Administration and Local Governments), Dr BATILDA SALHA BURIAN (Parliamentary Affairs).

MINISTRIES

Office of the President: State House, POB 9120, Dar es Salaam; tel. (22) 2116679; fax (22) 2113425.

Office of the Vice-President: POB 5380, Dar es Salaam; tel. (22) 2113857; fax (22) 2113856; e-mail makamu@twiga.com.

Office of the Prime Minister: POB 980, Dodoma; tel. (26) 233201.

Ministry of Agriculture, Food Security and Co-operatives: POB 9192, Dar es Salaam; tel. (22) 2862480; fax (22) 2862077; e-mail psk@kilimo.go.tz.

Ministry of Community Development: POB 3448, Dar es Salaam; tel. (22) 2115074; fax (22) 2132647.

Ministry of Defence and National Service: POB 9544, Dar es Salaam; tel. (22) 2117153; fax (22) 2116719.

Ministry of East African Co-operation: Dar es Salaam.

Ministry of Education and Vocational Training: POB 9121, Dar es Salaam; tel. (22) 2110146; fax (22) 2113271; e-mail ps-moec@twiga.com.

Ministry of Energy and Minerals: POB 2000, Dar es Salaam; tel. (22) 2112791; fax (22) 2121606; e-mail madini@africaonline.co.tz.

Ministry of Finance: POB 9111, Dar es Salaam; tel. (22) 2111174; fax (22) 2138573.

Ministry of Foreign Affairs and International Co-operation: POB 9000, Dar es Salaam; tel. (22) 2111906; fax (22) 2116600.

Ministry of Health and Social Welfare: POB 9083, Dar es Salaam; tel. (22) 2120261; fax (22) 2139951; e-mail moh@cats-net.com.

Ministry of Home Affairs: POB 9223, Dar es Salaam; tel. (22) 2112034; fax (22) 2139675.

Ministry of Industry, Trade and Marketing: POB 9503, Dar es Salaam; tel. (22) 2181397; fax (22) 2182481.

Ministry of Information, Culture and Sports: Dar es Salaam.

Ministry of Infrastructure Development: Dar es Salaam.

Ministry of Justice and Constitutional Affairs: POB 9050, Dar es Salaam; tel. (22) 2117099.

Ministry of Labour, Employment and Youth Development: POB 1422, Dar es Salaam; tel. (22) 2120419; fax (22) 2113082.

Ministry of Lands and Human Settlements: POB 9132, Dar es Salaam; tel. (22) 2121241; fax (22) 2113224; e-mail ps-ardhi@africaonline.co.tz.

Ministry of Livestock Development: Dar es Salaam.

Ministry of Natural Resources and Tourism: POB 9372, Dar es Salaam; tel. (22) 2111061; fax (22) 2110600; e-mail nature.tourism@mnrt.org; internet www.mnrt.org.

Ministry of Planning, Economy and Empowerment: Dar es Salaam.

Ministry of Public Safety and Security: Dar es Salaam.

Ministry of Science, Technology and Higher Education: POB 2645, Dar es Salaam; tel. (22) 2666376; fax (22) 2666097; e-mail msthe@msthe.go.tz.

Ministry of Water: POB 9153, Dar es Salaam; tel. (22) 2117153; fax (22) 37138; e-mail dppmaj@raha.com.

SUPREME REVOLUTIONARY COUNCIL OF ZANZIBAR
(August 2007)

President and Chairman and Minister of Finance and Economic Planning: AMANI ABEID KARUME.

Chief Minister: SHAMSI VUAI NAHODHA.

Deputy Chief Minister and Minister of Information, Culture and Sport: ALI JUMA SHAMHUNA.

Minister of Communication and Transport: ADAM MWAKANJUKI.

Minister of Education and Vocational Training: HAROUN ALI SULEIMAN.

Minister of Employment, Youth, Women and Children: ASHA ABDALLAH JUMA.

Minister of Agriculture, Livestock and Co-operatives: BURHANI SAADAT HAJI.

Minister of Water, Works, Energy and Land: MANSOUR YUSSUF HIMID.

Minister of Tourism, Trade and Investment: SAMIA SULUHU HASSAN.

Ministers of State in the President's Office: MWINYIAHJI MAKAME MWADINI (Finance and Economic Affairs), SULEIMAN OTHMAN NYANGA (Regional Administration, Local Government and Special Forces), RAMADHAN ABDALLAH SHAABAN (Constitutional Affairs and Good Governance).

Minister of State in the Chief Minister's Office: SALUM JUMA OTHMAN.

MINISTRIES

Office of the President: POB 776, Zanzibar; tel. (24) 2230814; fax (24) 2233722.

Office of the Chief Minister: POB 239, Zanzibar; tel. (24) 2311126; fax (24) 233788.

Ministry of Agriculture, Livestock and Co-operatives: Zanzibar; tel. (24) 232662.

Ministry of Communication and Transport: POB 266, Zanzibar; tel. (24) 2232841.

Ministry of Education and Vocational Training: POB 394, Zanzibar; tel. (24) 232827.

Ministry of Employment, Youth, Women and Children: POB 884, Zanzibar; tel. (24) 30808.

Ministry of Finance and Economic Planning: POB 1154, Zanzibar; tel. (24) 231169.

Ministry of Information, Culture and Sport: POB 236, Zanzibar; tel. (24) 232640.

Ministry of Tourism, Trade and Investment: POB 772, Zanzibar; tel. (24) 232321.

Ministry of Water, Works, Energy and Land: Zanzibar.

President and Legislature

PRESIDENT

Election, 14 December 2005

Candidate	Votes	% of votes
Lt-Col (Retd) Jakaya Mrisho Kikwete (CCM)	9,123,952	80.28
Prof. Ibrahim Haruna Lipumba (CUF)	1,327,125	11.68
Freeman Mbowe (Chadema)	668,756	5.88
Augustine Lyatonga Mrema (TLP)	84,901	0.75
Sengondo Mvungi (NCCR—Mageuzi)	55,819	0.49
Others	104,924	0.92
Total	11,365,477	100.00

NATIONAL ASSEMBLY

Speaker: SAMUEL SITTA.

Election, 14 December 2005

Party	Seats*
Chama Cha Mapinduzi (CCM)	266
Civic United Front (CUF)	28
Chama Cha Demokrasia na Maendeleo (Chadema)	11
Tanzania Labour Party (TLP)	1
United Democratic Party (UDP)	1
Total	307

* In addition to the 232 elective seats, 75 seats are reserved for women (included in the figures above). Furthermore, 10 seats are reserved for presidential nominees and five for members of the Zanzibar House of Representatives; the Attorney-General is also an ex officio member of the National Assembly.

ZANZIBAR PRESIDENT

Election, 30 October 2005

Candidate	Votes	% of votes
Amani Abeid Karume	239,832	53.18
Seif Sharif Hamad	207,733	46.06
Haji Mussa Kitole	2,110	0.47
Others	1,293	0.29
Total	450,968	100.00

ZANZIBAR HOUSE OF REPRESENTATIVES

Speaker: (vacant).

Election, 30 October 2005

Party	Seats*
Chama Cha Mapinduzi (CCM)	31
Civic United Front (CUF)	18
Total	49

* In addition to the 50 elective seats, five seats are reserved for regional commissioners, 10 for presidential nominees, 15 for women (on a party basis in proportion to the number of elective seats gained) and one for the Attorney-General. Results in one constituency were invalidated; a fresh ballot was held on 14 December 2005 for which results were yet to be released.

Election Commission

National Election Commission of Tanzania (NEC): Posta House, POB 10923, Ghana/Ohio St, 6th and 7th Floor, Dar es Salaam; tel. (22) 2114963; fax (22) 2116740; e-mail info@nec.go.tz; internet www.nec.go.tz; f. 1993; Chair. Lewis M. Makame; Dir of Elections R. R. Kiravu.

Political Organizations

Bismillah Party: Pemba; seeks a referendum on the terms of the 1964 union of Zanzibar with mainland Tanzania.

Chama Cha Amani na Demokrasia Tanzania (CHADETA): House No. 41, Sadan St Ilala, POB 15809, Dar es Salaam; tel. (744) 889453; granted temporary registration in 2003.

Chama Cha Demokrasia na Maendeleo (Chadema—Party for Democracy and Progress): House No. 170 Ufipa St, POB 31191, Dar es Salaam; tel. (22) 2182544; supports democracy and social development; Chair. Edwin I. M. Mtei; Sec.-Gen. Bob Nyanga Makani.

Chama Cha Haki na Usitawi (Chausta—Party for Justice and Development): Drive Inn Oysterbay, POB 5450, Dar es Salaam; tel. (741) 247266; f. 1998; officially regd 2001; Chair. James Mapalala.

Chama Cha Mapinduzi (CCM) (Revolutionary Party of Tanzania): Kuu St, POB 50, Dodoma; tel. 2180575; e-mail katibumkuu@ccmtz.org; internet www.ccmtz.org; f. 1977 by merger of the mainland-based Tanganyika African National Union (TANU) with the Afro-Shirazi Party, which operated on Zanzibar and Pemba; sole legal party 1977–92; socialist orientation; Chair. Jakaya Mrisho Kikwete; Vice-Chair. John S. Malecela, Amani A. Karume; Sec.-Gen. Philip Mangula.

Civic United Front (CUF): Mtendeni St at Malindi, POB 3637, Zanzibar; tel. (24) 2237446; fax (24) 2237445; e-mail headquarters@cuftz.org; internet www.cuftz.org; f. 1992 by merger of Zanzibar opposition party Kamahuru and the mainland-based Chama Cha Wananchi; commands substantial support in Zanzibar and Pemba, for which it demands increased autonomy; Chair. Prof. Ibrahim Haruna Lipumba; Sec.-Gen. Seif Sharif Hamad.

Democratic Party (DP): Ilala Mchikichini, POB 63102, Dar es Salaam; tel. (741) 430516; e-mail dp_watanganyika@yahoo.com; f. 2002; Chair. Rev. Christopher Mtikila.

Demokrasia Makini (MAKINI): Kibo Ubungo, POB 75636, Dar es Salaam; tel. (744) 295670; officially regd 2001.

Forum for Restoration of Democracy (FORD): House No. 6, Rufiji St, Kariakoo, POB 15587, Dar es Salaam; tel. (741) 292271; f. 2002.

Movement for Democratic Alternative (MDA): Zanzibar; seeks to review the terms of the 1964 union of Zanzibar with mainland Tanzania; supports democratic institutions and opposes detention without trial and press censorship.

National Convention for Construction and Reform (NCCR—Mageuzi): Plot No. 2 Kilosa St, Ilala, POB 72444, Dar es Salaam; tel. (744) 318812; f. 1992; Chair. Dr Kassim Magutu; Sec.-Gen. Mabere Marando.

National League for Democracy (NLD): Plot No. 7310 Sinza, POB 352, Dar es Salaam; f. 1993; Chair. Emmanuel J. E. Makaidi; Sec.-Gen. Michael E. A. Mhina.

National Reconstruction Alliance (NRA): Bububu St, Tandika Kilimahewa, POB 45197, Dar es Salaam; tel. (744) 496724; f. 1993; Chair. Ulotu Abubakar Ulotu; Sec.-Gen. Salim R. Matinga.

Popular National Party (PONA): Plot 104, Songea St, Ilala, POB 21561, Dar es Salaam; Chair. Wilfrem R. Mwakitwange; Sec.-Gen. Nicolaus Mchaina.

Tanzania Democratic Alliance Party (TADEA): Buguruni Malapa, POB 482, Dar es Salaam; tel. (22) 2865244; f. 1993; Pres. John D. Lifa-Chipaka; Sec.-Gen. Charles Dotto Lubala.

Progressive Party of Tanzania (PPT-Maendeleo): Wibu St, Kinondoni, POB 31932, Dar es Salaam; tel. (744) 300302; f. 2003; Leader Peter Mziray; Sec.-Gen. Ahmed Hamad.

Tanzania Labour Party (TLP): Argentina Manzese, POB 7273, Dar es Salaam; tel. (22) 2443237; f. 1993; Chair. Leo Lwekamwa.

Tanzania People's Party (TPP): Mbezi Juu, Kawe, POB 60847, Dar es Salaam; removed from register of political parties 2002; Chair. Alec H. Che-Mponda; Sec.-Gen. Gravel Limo.

United Democratic Party (UDP): Mbezi Juu, SLP 5918, Dar es Salaam; tel. (748) 613723; f. 1994; Leader John Momose Cheyo.

United People's Democratic Party (UPDP): Mtaa wa Shariff Muss, POB 3121, Zanzibar; tel. (744) 753075; f. 1993; Chair. Khalfani Ali Abdullah; Sec.-Gen. Ahmed M. Rashid.

Union for Multi-Party Democracy (UMD): House No. 84, Plot No. 630, Block No. 5, Kagera St. Magomeni, POB 2985, Dar es Salaam; tel. (744) 478153; f. 1993; Chair. Abdallah Fundikira.

Diplomatic Representation

EMBASSIES AND HIGH COMMISSIONS IN TANZANIA

Algeria: 34 Ali Hassan Mwinyi Rd, POB 2963, Dar es Salaam; tel. (22) 2117619; fax (22) 2117620; e-mail algemb@twiga.com; Ambassador Abdelmoun'aam Ahriz.

Angola: Plot 78, Lugalo Rd, POB 20793, Dar es Salaam; tel. (22) 2117674; fax (22) 2132349; e-mail sinangocom@zamnet.zm; Ambassador (vacant).

Belgium: Ocean Rd, POB 9210, Dar es Salaam; tel. (22) 2112688; fax (22) 2117621; e-mail daressalaam@diplobel.be; internet www.diplomatie.be/dar-es-salaam; Ambassador Peter Maddens.

Burundi: Plot 1007, Lugalo Rd, POB 2752, Upanga, Dar es Salaam; tel. (22) 238608; e-mail burundemb@raha.com; Ambassador Leandre Amuri Bangengwanubusa.

Canada: 38 Mirambo St, Garden Ave, POB 1022, Dar es Salaam; tel. (22) 2163300; fax (22) 2116897; e-mail dslam@international.gc.ca; internet www.dfait-maeci.gc.ca/tanzania; High Commissioner Janet Siddal.

Congo, Democratic Republic: 438 Malik Rd, POB 97, Upanga, Dar es Salaam; tel. (22) 2150282; fax (22) 2153341; e-mail drcemba@intafrica.com; Chargé d'affaires a.i. Nsingi Zi Lubaki.

Cuba: Plot 313, Lugalo Rd, POB 9282, Upanga, Dar es Salaam; tel. (22) 2115928; fax (22) 2115927; e-mail embacuba.tz@raha.com; Ambassador Felipe Ruiz O'Farrill.

Denmark: Ghana Ave, POB 9171, Dar es Salaam; tel. (22) 2113887; fax (22) 2116433; e-mail daramb@um.dk; internet www.ambdaressalaam.um.dk; Ambassador Bjarne Henneberg Sørensen.

Egypt: 24 Garden Ave, POB 1668, Dar es Salaam; tel. (22) 2117622; fax (22) 2112543; e-mail egypt.emb.tz@Cats-net.com; Ambassador Sabry Magdy Sabry.

Finland: Mirambo St and Garden Ave, POB 2455, Dar es Salaam; tel. (22) 2196565; fax (22) 2196573; e-mail sanomat.dar@formin.fi; internet www.finland.or.tz; Ambassador Juhani Toivonen.

France: Ali Hassan Mwinyi Rd, POB 2349, Dar es Salaam; tel. (22) 2198800; fax (22) 2198815; e-mail ambfrance@africaonline.co.tz; internet www.ambafrance-tz.org; Ambassador Jacques Champagne de Labriolle.

Germany: Umoja House, Mirambo St/Garden Ave, 2nd Floor, POB 9541, Dar es Salaam; tel. (22) 2117409; fax (22) 2112944; e-mail german.embassy@bol.co.tz; internet www.daressalam.diplo.de; Ambassador Wolfgang Ringe.

Holy See: Oyster Bay, Plot 146, Haile Selassie Rd, POB 480, Dar es Salaam (Apostolic Nunciature); tel. (22) 2666422; fax (22) 2668059; e-mail nunzio@cats-net.com; Apostolic Nuncio Most Rev. JOSEPH CHENNOTH (Titular Archbishop of Milevum).

Indonesia: 299 Ali Hassan Mwinyi Rd, POB 572, Dar es Salaam; tel. (22) 2119119; fax (22) 2115849; e-mail kbridsm@raha.com; Ambassador TRIJONO MARJONO.

Ireland: 353 Toure Dr., POB 9612, Oyster Bay, Dar es Salaam; tel. (22) 2602355; fax (22) 2602362; e-mail daressalaamembassy@dfa.ie; Ambassador JOHN MCCULLAGH.

Italy: Plot 316, Lugalo Rd, POB 2106, Dar es Salaam; tel. (22) 2115935; fax (22) 2115938; e-mail segr.dar@esteri.it; internet www.ambdaressalaam.esteri.it; Ambassador FRANCESCO CATANIA.

Japan: 1018 Ali Hassan Mwinyi Rd, POB 2577, Dar es Salaam; tel. (22) 2115827; fax (22) 2115830; internet www.tz.emb-japan.go.jp; Ambassador MAKOTO ITO.

Kenya: Plot 127 Mafinga St, Kinondoni, POB 5231, Dar es Salaam; tel. (22) 2668285; fax (22) 2668213; e-mail info@kenyahighcom.tz.org; internet www.kenyahighcomtz.org; High Commissioner BOAZ KIDIGA MBAYA.

Korea, Democratic People's Republic: Plot 5, Ursino Estate, Kawawa Rd, Msasani, POB 2690, Dar es Salaam; tel. (22) 2775395; fax (22) 2700838; Ambassador SOON CHUN LEE.

Korea, Republic: Plot 8/1, Tumbawe Rd, Oyster Bay, POB 154, Dar es Salaam; tel. (22) 2600496; fax (22) 2600559; e-mail rok@intafrica.com; Ambassador AHN HYO-SEUNG.

Libya: 386 Mtitu St, POB 9413, Dar es Salaam; tel. (22) 2150188; fax (22) 2150068; Secretary of People's Bureau Dr AHMED IBRAHIM EL-ASHHAB.

Malawi: Plot 38, Ali Hassan Mwinyi Rd, POB 7616, Dar es Salaam; tel. (22) 2666284; fax (22) 2668161; e-mail mhc@africaonline.co.tz; High Commissioner (vacant).

Mozambique: 25 Garden Ave, POB 9370, Dar es Salaam; tel. and fax (22) 2116502; High Commissioner ZACARIAS KUPELA.

Netherlands: Umoja House, 4th Floor, Garden Ave, POB 9534, Dar es Salaam; tel. (22) 2110000; fax (22) 2110044; e-mail nlgovdar@intafrica.com; internet www.netherlands-embassy.go.tz; Ambassador KAREL VAN KESTEREN.

Nigeria: 83 Haile Selassie Rd, POB 9214, Oyster Bay, Dar es Salaam; tel. (22) 2666000; fax (22) 2668947; e-mail nhc-dsm@raha.com; High Commissioner AHMED M. USMAN.

Norway: 160 Mirambo St, POB 2646, Dar es Salaam; tel. (22) 2113366; fax (22) 2116564; e-mail emb.daressalaam@mfa.no; internet www.norway.go.tz; Ambassador JON LOMØY.

Poland: 63 Alykhan Rd, Upanga, POB 2188, Dar es Salaam; tel. (22) 2115271; fax (22) 2115812; e-mail polamb@wingrouptz.com; Chargé d'affaires a.i. EUGENIUSZ RZEWUSKI.

Russia: Plot No. 73, Ali Hassan Mwinyi Rd, POB 1905, Dar es Salaam; tel. (22) 2666005; fax (22) 2666818; e-mail embruss@bol.co.tz; Ambassador LEONARD ALEKSEEVIC.

Rwanda: Plot 32, Ali Hassan Mwinyi Rd, POB 2918, Dar es Salaam; tel. (22) 2115889; fax (22) 2115888; e-mail ambadsm@minaffet.gov.rw; Ambassador ZEPHYR MUTANGUHA.

South Africa: Plot 1338/1339, Mwaya Rd, Msaski, POB 10723, Dar es Salaam; tel. (22) 2601800; fax (22) 2600684; e-mail highcomm@sahc-tz.com; High Commissioner S. G. MFENYANA.

Spain: 99B Kinondoni Rd, POB 842, Dar es Salaam; tel. (22) 2666936; fax (22) 2666938; e-mail embesptz@mail.mae.es; Ambassador GERMÁN ZURITA SÁENZ DE NAVARRETE.

Sudan: 'Albaraka', 64 Ali Hassan Mwinyi Rd, POB 2266, Dar es Salaam; tel. (22) 2117641; fax (22) 2115811; e-mail sudan.emb.dar@raha.com; Ambassador ELMUGHIRA ALI OMAR.

Sweden: Mirambo St and Garden Ave, POB 9274, Dar es Salaam; tel. (22) 2111235; fax (22) 2113420; e-mail ambassaden.dar-es-salaam@sida.se; internet www.swedenabroad.se/daressalaam; Ambassador STAFFAN HERRSTROM.

Switzerland: 79 Kinondoni Rd/Mafinga St, POB 2454, Dar es Salaam; tel. (22) 2666008; fax (22) 2666736; e-mail dar.vertretung@eda.admin.ch; Ambassador EMMANUEL JENNI.

Syria: 246 Alykhan Rd, Upanga, POB 2442, Dar es Salaam; tel. (22) 2117656; fax (22) 2115860; Chargé d'affaires a.i. M. B. IMADI.

Uganda: Extelcom Bldg, 7th Floor, Samora Ave, POB 6237, Dar es Salaam; tel. (22) 2667391; fax (22) 2667224; e-mail ugadar@intafrica.com; High Commissioner IBRAHIM MUKIIBI.

United Kingdom: Umoja House, Garden Ave, POB 9200, Dar es Salaam; tel. (22) 2110101; fax (22) 2110102; e-mail bhc.dar@fco.gov.uk; internet www.britishhighcommission.gov.uk/tanzania; High Commissioner PHILIP PARHAM.

USA: 686 Old Bagamoyo Rd, Msasani, POB 9123, Dar es Salaam; tel. (22) 2668001; fax (22) 2668238; e-mail embassyd@state.gov; internet tanzania.usembassy.gov; Ambassador MARK GREEN.

Yemen: 353 United Nations Rd, POB 349, Dar es Salaam; tel. (22) 2117650; fax (22) 2115924; Chargé d'affaires a.i. MOHAMED ABDULLA ALMAS.

Zambia: 5–6 Ohio St/Sokoine Dr. Junction, POB 2525, Dar es Salaam; tel. and fax (22) 2112977; e-mail zhcd@raha.com; High Commissioner JOHN KASHONKA CHITAFU.

Zimbabwe: 2097 East Upanga, off Ali Hassan Mwinyi Rd, POB 20762, Dar es Salaam; tel. (22) 2116789; fax (22) 2112913; e-mail zimdares@cats-net.com; Ambassador J. M. SHAVA.

Judicial System

Permanent Commission of Enquiry: POB 2643, Dar es Salaam; tel. (22) 2113690; fax (22) 2111533; Chair. and Official Ombudsman Prof. JOSEPH F. MBWILIZA; Sec. A. P. GUVETTE.

Court of Appeal

Consists of the Chief Justice and four Judges of Appeal.

Chief Justice of Tanzania: BARNABAS SAMATTA.

Chief Justice of Zanzibar: HAMID MAHMOUD HAMID.

High Court: headquarters at Dar es Salaam, but regular sessions held in all Regions; consists of a Jaji Kiongozi and 29 Judges.

District Courts: situated in each district and presided over by either a Resident Magistrate or District Magistrate; limited jurisdiction, with a right of appeal to the High Court.

Primary Courts: established in every district and presided over by Primary Court Magistrates; limited jurisdiction, with a right of appeal to the District Courts and then to the High Court..

Attorney-General: ANDREW CHENGE.

Director of Public Prosecutions: KULWA MASSABA.

People's Courts were established in Zanzibar in 1970. Magistrates are elected by the people and have two assistants each. Under the Zanzibar Constitution, which came into force in January 1985, defence lawyers and the right of appeal, abolished in 1970, were reintroduced.

Religion

Religious surveys were eliminated from all government census reports after 1967. However, religious leaders and sociologists generally believe that the country's population is 30%–40% Christian and 30%–40% Muslim, with the remainder consisting of practitioners of other faiths, traditional indigenous religions and atheists. Foreign missionaries operate in the country, including Roman Catholics, Lutherans, Baptists, Seventh-day Adventists, Mormons, Anglicans and Muslims.

ISLAM

The Muslim population is most heavily concentrated on the Zanzibar archipelago and in the coastal areas of the mainland. There are also large Muslim minorities in inland urban areas. Some 99% of the population of Zanzibar is estimated to be Muslim. Between 80% and 90% of the country's Muslim population is Sunni; the remainder consists of several Shi'a groups, mostly of Asian descent. A large proportion of the Asian community is Isma'ili.

Ismalia Provincial Church: POB 460, Dar es Salaam.

National Muslim Council of Tanzania: POB 21422, Dar es Salaam; tel. (22) 234934; f. 1969; supervises Islamic affairs on the mainland only; Chair. Sheikh HEMED BIN JUMA BIN HEMED; Exec. Sec. Alhaj MUHAMMAD MTULIA.

Supreme Muslim Council: Zanzibar; f. 1991; supervises Islamic affairs in Zanzibar; Mufti Sheikh HARITH BIN KALEF.

Wakf and Trust Commission: POB 4092, Zanzibar; f. 1980; Islamic affairs; Exec. Sec. YUSUF ABDULRAHMAN MUHAMMAD.

CHRISTIANITY

The Christian population is composed of Roman Catholics, Protestants, Pentecostals, Seventh-day Adventists, members of the Church of Jesus Christ of Latter-day Saints (Mormons) and Jehovah's Witnesses.

Jumuiya ya Kikristo Tanzania (Christian Council of Tanzania): Church House, POB 1454, Dodoma; tel. (26) 2324445; fax (26) 2324352; f. 1934; Chair. Rt Rev. DONALD LEO MTETEMELA (Bishop of the Anglican Church); Gen. Sec. Rev. Dr LEONARD AMOS MTAITA.

The Anglican Communion

Anglicans are adherents of the Church of the Province of Tanzania, comprising 16 dioceses.

Archbishop of the Province of Tanzania and Bishop of Ruaha: Most Rev. DONALD LEO MTETEMELA, POB 1028, Iringa; fax (26) 2702479; e-mail ruaha@maf.or.tz.

Provincial Secretary: Dr R. MWITA AKIRI (acting), POB 899, Dodoma; tel. (26) 2321437; fax (26) 2324265; e-mail cpt@maf.org.

Greek Orthodox

Archbishop of East Africa: NICADEMUS OF IRINOUPOULIS (resident in Nairobi, Kenya); jurisdiction covers Kenya, Uganda and Tanzania.

Lutheran

Evangelical Lutheran Church in Tanzania: POB 3033, Arusha; tel. (57) 8855; fax (57) 8858; 1.5m. mems; Presiding Bishop Rt Rev. Dr SAMSON MUSHEMBA (acting); Exec. Sec. AMANI MWENEGOHA.

The Roman Catholic Church

Tanzania comprises five archdioceses and 25 dioceses. There were an estimated 10,476,621 adherents at 31 December 2004, equivalent to about 27.0% of the total population.

Tanzania Episcopal Conference

Catholic Secretariat, Mandela Rd, POB 2133, Dar es Salaam; tel. (22) 2851075; fax (22) 2851133; e-mail tec@cats-net.com; internet www.rc.net/tanzania/tec.

f. 1980; Pres. Mgr SEVERINE NIWEMUGIZI (Bishop of Rulenge).

Archbishop of Arusha: Most Rev. JOSAPHAT LOUIS LEBULU, Archbishop's House, POB 3044, Arusha; tel. (27) 2544361; fax (27) 2548004; e-mail archbishoplebulu@habari.co.tz.

Archbishop of Dar es Salaam: Cardinal POLYCARP PENGO, Archbishop's House, POB 167, Dar es Salaam; tel. (22) 2113223; fax (22) 2125751; e-mail nyumba@cats-net.com.

Archbishop of Mwanza: Most Rev. ANTHONY MAYALA, Archbishop's House, POB 1421, Mwanza; tel. and fax (68) 501029; e-mail mwanza-archdiocese@cats-net.com.

Archbishop of Songea: Most Rev. NORBERT WENDELIN MTEGA, Archbishop's House, POB 152, Songea; tel. (65) 602004; fax (65) 602593; e-mail songea-archdiocese@cats-net.com.

Archbishop of Tabora: Most Rev. MARIO EPIFANIO ABDALLAH MGULUNDE, Archbishop's House, Private Bag, PO Tabora; tel. (62) 2329; fax (62) 4536; e-mail archbishops-office@yahoo.co.uk.

Other Christian Churches

Baptist Mission of Tanzania: POB 9414, Dar es Salaam; tel. (22) 2170130; fax (22) 2170127; f. 1956; Admin. FRANK PEVEY.

Christian Missions in Many Lands (Tanzania): German Branch, POB 34, Tunduru, Ruvuma Region; f. 1957; Gen. Sec. THOMAS MÜHLING.

Moravian Church in Tanzania: POB 377, Mbeya; 113,656 mems; Gen. Sec. Rev. O. M. T. MPAYO.

Pentecostal Church: POB 34, Kahama.

Presbyterian Church: POB 2510, Dar es Salaam; tel. (22) 229075.

BAHÁ'Í FAITH

National Spiritual Assembly: POB 585, Dar es Salaam; tel. and fax (22) 2152766; e-mail bahaitz@africaonline.tz; mems resident in 2,301 localities.

OTHER RELIGIONS

Many people follow traditional beliefs. There are also some Hindu communities.

The Press

NEWSPAPERS

Daily

The African: Sinza Rd, POB 4793, Dar es Salaam; e-mail dimba@africaonline.co.tz; Editor-in-Chief JOHN KULEKANA.

Alasiri: POB 31042, Dar es Salaam; Swahili; Editor LUCAS MNUBI.

Daily News: POB 9033, Dar es Salaam; tel. (22) 2110165; fax (22) 2112881; f. 1972; govt-owned; Man. Editor SETHI KAMUHANDA; circ. 50,000.

The Democrat: Dar es Salaam; independent; Editor IDRISS LUGULU; circ. 15,000.

The Guardian: POB 31042, Dar es Salaam; tel. (22) 275250; fax (22) 273583; e-mail guardian@ipp.co.tz; internet www.ippmedia.com; f. 1994; English and Swahili; Man. Dir KIONDO MSHANA; Man. Editor PASCAL SHIJA.

Kipanga: POB 199, Zanzibar; Swahili; publ. by Information and Broadcasting Services.

Majira: POB 71439, Dar es Salaam; tel. (22) 238901; fax (22) 231104; independent; Swahili; Editor THEOPHIL MAKUNGA; circ. 15,000.

Nipashe: POB 31042, Dar es Salaam; Swahili; Editor HAMISI MZEE.

Uhuru: POB 9221, Dar es Salaam; tel. (22) 2182224; fax (22) 2185065; e-mail uhuru@intafrica.com; f. 1961; official publ. of CCM; Swahili; Man. Editor SAIDI NGUBA; circ. 100,000.

Weekly

Business Times: POB 71439, Dar es Salaam; tel. (22) 238901; fax (22) 231104; e-mail majira@bcsmedia.com; internet www.bcstimes.com; independent; English; Editor ALLI MWAMBOLA; circ. 15,000.

The Express: POB 20588, Dar es Salaam; tel. (22) 2180058; fax (22) 2182665; e-mail express@raha.com; internet www.theexpress.com; independent; English; Editor FAYAZ BHOJANI; circ. 20,000.

The Family Mirror: Faru/Nyamwezi St, Karikoo Area, POB 6804, Dar es Salaam; tel. (22) 181331; Editor ZEPHANIAH MUSENDO.

Gazette of the United Republic: POB 9142, Dar es Salaam; tel. (22) 231817; official announcements; Editor H. HAJI; circ. 6,000.

Government Gazette: POB 261, Zanzibar; f. 1964; official announcements.

Kasheshe: POB 31042, Dar es Salaam; Swahili; Editor VENANCE MLAY.

Leta Raha: POB 31042, Dar es Salaam; Swahili; Editor EDMOND MSANGI.

Mfanyakazi (The Worker): POB 15359, Dar es Salaam; tel. (22) 226111; Swahili; trade union publ.; Editor NDUGU MTAWA; circ. 100,000.

Mzalendo: POB 9221, Dar es Salaam; tel. (22) 2182224; fax (22) 2185065; e-mail uhuru@intafrica.com; f. 1972; publ. by CCM; Swahili; Man. Editor SAIDI NGABA; circ. 115,000.

Nipashe Jumapili: POB 31042, Dar es Salaam; Swahili.

Sunday News: POB 9033, Dar es Salaam; tel. (22) 2116072; fax (22) 2112881; f. 1954; govt-owned; Man. Editor SETHI KAMUCHANDA; circ. 50,000.

Sunday Observer: POB 31042, Dar es Salaam; e-mail guardian@ipp.co.tz; Man. Dir VUMI URASA; Man. Editor PETER MSUNGU.

Taifa Letu: POB 31042, Dar es Salaam; Swahili.

PERIODICALS

The African Review: POB 35042, Dar es Salaam; tel. (22) 2410130; e-mail mubakar@udsm.ac.tz; 2 a year; journal of African politics, development and international affairs; publ. by the Dept of Political Science, Univ. of Dar es Salaam; Chief Editor Dr MOHAMMED BAKARI; circ. 1,000.

Eastern African Law Review: POB 35093, Dar es Salaam; tel. (22) 243254; f. 1967; 2 a year; Chief Editor N. N. N. NDITI; circ. 1,000.

Elimu Haina Mwisho: POB 1986, Mwanza; monthly; circ. 45,000.

Habari za Washirika: POB 2567, Dar es Salaam; tel. (22) 223346; monthly; publ. by Co-operative Union of Tanzania; Editor H. V. N. CHIBULUNJE; circ. 40,000.

Jenga: POB 2669, Dar es Salaam; tel. (22) 2112893; fax (22) 2113618; journal of the National Development Corpn; circ. 2,000.

Kiongozi (The Leader): POB 9400, Dar es Salaam; tel. (22) 229505; f. 1950; fortnightly; Swahili; Roman Catholic; Editor ROBERT MFUGALE; circ. 33,500.

Kweupe: POB 222, Zanzibar; weekly; Swahili; publ. by Information and Broadcasting Services.

Mlezi (The Educator): POB 41, Peramiho; tel. 30; f. 1970; every 2 months; Editor Fr DOMINIC WEIS; circ. 8,000.

Mwenge (Firebrand): POB 1, Peramiho; tel. 30; f. 1937; monthly; Editor JOHN P. MBONDE; circ. 10,000.

Nchi Yetu (Our Country): POB 9142, Dar es Salaam; tel. (22) 2110200; f. 1964; govt publ.; monthly; Swahili; circ. 50,000.

Nuru: POB 1893, Zanzibar; f. 1992; bi-monthly; official publ. of Zanzibar Govt; circ. 8,000.

Safina: POB 21422, Dar es Salaam; tel. (22) 234934; publ. by National Muslim Council of Tanzania; Editor YASSIN SADIK; circ. 10,000.

Sikiliza: POB 635, Morogoro; tel. and fax (23) 2604374; quarterly; Seventh-day Adventist; Editor MIKA D. MUSA; circ. 100,000.

Taamuli: POB 899, Dar es Salaam; tel. (22) 243500; 2 a year; journal of political science; publ. by the Dept of Political Science, Univ. of Dar es Salaam; circ. 1,000.

Tantravel: POB 2485, Dar es Salaam; tel. (22) 2111244; fax (22) 2116420; e-mail safari@ud.co.tz; internet www.tanzaniatouristboard.com; quarterly; publ. by Tanzania Tourist Board; Editor STEVE FISHER.

Tanzania Education Journal: POB 9121, Dar es Salaam; tel. (22) 227211; f. 1984; 3 a year; publ. by Institute of Education, Ministry of Education; circ. 8,000.

Tanzania Trade Currents: POB 5402, Dar es Salaam; tel. (22) 2851706; fax (22) 851700; e-mail betis@intafrica.com; bi-monthly; publ. by Board of External Trade; circ. 2,000.

Uhuru na Amani: POB 3033, Arusha; tel. (57) 8855; fax (57) 8858; quarterly; Swahili; publ. by Evangelical Lutheran Church in Tanzania; Editor ELIZABETH LOBULU; circ. 15,000.

Ukulima wa Kisasa (Modern Farming): Farmers' Education and Publicity Unit, POB 2308, Dar es Salaam; tel. (22) 2116496; fax (22) 2122923; e-mail fepu@twiga.com; f. 1955; bi-monthly; Swahili; publ. by Ministry of Food and Agriculture; Editor H. MLAKI; circ. 15,000.

Ushirika Wetu: POB 2567, Dar es Salaam; tel. (22) 2184081; e-mail ushirika@covision2000.com; monthly; publ. by Tanzania Federation of Co-operatives; Editor SIMON J. KERARYO; circ. 40,000.

Wela: POB 180, Dodoma; Swahili.

NEWS AGENCIES

Press Services Tanzania (PST) Ltd: POB 31042, Dar es Salaam; tel. and fax (22) 2119195.

Foreign Bureaux

Inter Press Service (IPS) (Italy): 304 Nkomo Rd, POB 4755, Dar es Salaam; tel. (22) 229311; Chief Correspondent PAUL CHINTOWA.

Newslink Africa (UK): POB 5165, Dar es Salaam; Correspondent NIZAR FAZAL.

RIA—Novosti (Russian Information Agency—News): POB 2271, Dar es Salaam; tel. (22) 223897; Dir ANATOLII TKACHENKO.

Xinhua (New China) News Agency: 72 Upanga Rd, POB 2682, Dar es Salaam; tel. (22) 223967; Correspondent HUAI CHENGBO.

Reuters (UK) is also represented in Tanzania.

Publishers

Central Tanganyika Press: POB 1129, Dodoma; tel. (26) 23000; fax (26) 2324565; e-mail ctzpress@maf.or.tz; f. 1954; religious; Man. PETER MAKASSI MANGATI.

DUP (1996) Ltd: POB 7028, Dar es Salaam; tel. and fax (22) 2410137; e-mail director@dup.udsm.ac.tz; f. 1979; educational, academic and cultural texts in Swahili and English; Dir Dr N. G. MWITTA.

Eastern Africa Publications Ltd: POB 1002 Arusha; tel. (57) 3176; f. 1979; general and school textbooks; Gen. Man. ABDULLAH SAIWAAD.

Inland Publishers: POB 125, Mwanza; tel. (68) 40064; general non-fiction, religion, in Kiswahili and English; Dir Rev. S. M. MAGESA.

Oxford University Press: Maktaba Rd, POB 5299, Dar es Salaam; tel. (22) 229209; f. 1969; literature, literary criticism, essays, poetry; Man. SALIM SHAABAN SALIM.

Tanzania Publishing House: 47 Samora Machel Ave, POB 2138, Dar es Salaam; tel. (22) 2137402; e-mail tphhouse@yahoo.com; f. 1966; educational and general books in Swahili and English; Gen. Man. PRIMUS ISIDOR KARUGENDO.

GOVERNMENT PUBLISHING HOUSE

Government Printer: Office of the Prime Minister, POB 9124, Dar es Salaam; tel. (22) 2860900; fax (22) 2866955; e-mail gptz@pmo.go.tz; Dir KASSIAN C. CHIBOGOYO.

Broadcasting and Communications

TELECOMMUNICATIONS

Tanzania Communications Regulatory Authority (TCRA): POB 474, Dar es Salaam; tel. (22) 2118947; fax (22) 2116664; e-mail dg@tcra.go.tz; internet www.tcra.go.tz; f. 1993; licenses postal and telecommunications service operators; manages radio spectrum; acts as ombudsman.

MIC Tanzania Ltd: POB 2929, Dar es Salaam; tel. (22) 2126510; fax (741) 123014; e-mail mobitel@mobitel.co.tz; internet www.mobitel.co.tz; operates mobile cellular telecommunications services through Mobitel network.

Tanzania Telecommunications Co Ltd (TTCL): POB 9070, Dar es Salaam; tel. (22) 2110055; fax (22) 2113232; e-mail ttcl@ttcl.co.tz; 35% sold to consortium of Detecon (Germany) and Mobile Systems International (Netherlands) in Feb. 2001; Man. Dir ASMATH N. MPATWA.

Tritel Tanzania Ltd: POB 1853, Dar es Salaam; tel. (22) 2862191; fax (22) 2862710; e-mail info@tritel.co.tz; internet www.tritel.co.tz; mobile cellular telephone operator.

Vodacom (Tanzania) Ltd: POB 2369, Dar es Salaam; tel. (744) 702220; fax (744) 704014; e-mail care@vodacom.co.tz; internet www.vodacom.co.tz; mobile cellular telephone operator.

Zanzibar Telecom (Zantel): Zanzibar; f. 1999; mobile cellular telephone operator for Zanzibar; CEO MOHAMMED AHMED SALIM.

CelTel Ltd also provides telecommunications services.

BROADCASTING

Radio

Radio FM Zenj 96.8: Zanzibar; f. 2005; owned by Zanzibar Media Corpn; broadcasts to 60% of Zanzibar, to be extended to all of Zanzibar and mainland coast from southern Tanzania to Kenya; Gen. Man. AUSTIN MAKANI.

Radio Kwizera: N'Gara; tel. (28) 2223679; fax (28) 2223795; e-mail rkngara@jrstz.co.tz; f. 1995; station's objective is to educate, entertain and inform refugee and local communities, with the aim of bringing about peace and reconciliation; Dir DAMAS S. J. MISSANGA.

Radio One: POB 4374, Dar es Salaam; tel. (22) 275914; e-mail ipptech@ipp.co.tz; internet www.ippmedia.com.

Radio Tanzania Dar es Salaam (RTD): POB 9191, Dar es Salaam; tel. (22) 2860760; fax (22) 2865577; f. 1951; state-owned; domestic services in Swahili; external services in English; Dir ABDUL NGARAWA.

Radio Tanzania Zanzibar: state-owned.

Radio Tumaini (Hope): 1 Bridge St, POB 167, Dar es Salaam; tel. (22) 2117307; fax (22) 2112594; e-mail tumaini@africaonline.co.tz; broadcasts in Swahili within Dar es Salaam; operated by the Roman Catholic Church; broadcasts on religious, social and economic issues; Dir Fr JEAN-FRANÇOIS GALTIER.

Sauti Ya Tanzania Zanzibar (The Voice of Tanzania Zanzibar): POB 1178, Zanzibar; f. 1951; state-owned; broadcasts in Swahili on three wavelengths; Dir SULEIMAN JUMA.

Television

Dar Television (DTV): POB 21122, Dar es Salaam; tel. (22) 2116341; fax (22) 2113112; e-mail franco.dtv@raha.com; Man. Dir FRANCO TRAMONTANO.

Independent Television (ITV): Dar es Salaam.

Television Zanzibar: POB 314, Zanzibar; f. 1973; Dir JAMA SIMBA.

Finance

(cap. = capital; res = reserves; dep. = deposits; m. = million; brs = branches; amounts in Tanzanian shillings, unless otherwise indicated)

BANKING

Central Bank

Bank of Tanzania (Benki Kuu Ya Tanzania): 10 Mirambo St, POB 2939, Dar es Salaam; tel. (22) 2110946; fax (22) 2113325; e-mail info@hq.bot-tz.org; internet www.bot-tz.org; f. 1966; bank of issue; cap. 10,000m., res 343,825m., dep. 948,562m. (June 2005); Gov. and Chair. Dr DAUDI T. S. BALLALI; 4 brs.

Principal Banks

African Banking Corpn (Tanzania) Ltd: Barclays House, 1st Floor, Ohio St, POB 31, Dar es Salaam; tel. (22) 2119303; fax (22) 2112402; e-mail abct@africanbankingcorp.com; internet www.africanbankingcorp.com; wholly owned by African Banking Corpn Holdings Ltd; cap. 5,404m. (Dec. 2003); Chair. Dr JONAS KIPOKOLA.

Akiba Commercial Bank Ltd: TDFL Bldg, Ali Hassan Mwinyi Rd, POB 669, Dar es Salaam; tel. (22) 2118340; fax (22) 2114173; e-mail akiba@cats-net.com; cap. 2,793m., res 115m., dep. 21,951m. (Dec. 2004); Chair. D. M. MOSHA; Man. Dir J. LYALE.

Azania Bancorp Ltd: POB 9271, Dar es Salaam; tel. (22) 2117997; fax (22) 2118010; e-mail info@azaniabank.co.tz; internet www.azaniabank.co.tz; 55% owned by National Social Security Fund, 31% owned by Parastatal Pension Fund, 9% owned by East African

Development Bank, 5% owned by individuals; cap. 6,168m. (Dec. 2003); Chair. N. NSEMWA; CEO CHARLES SINGILI.

Barclays Bank (Tanzania) Ltd: Barclays House, Ohio St, POB 5137, Dar es Salaam; tel. (22) 2129381; fax (22) 2129757; e-mail karl .stumke@barclays.com; 99.9% owned by Barclays PLC (United Kingdom), 0.1% owned by Ebbgate Holdings Ltd; cap. 18,750m. (Dec. 2003); Chair. J. K. CHANDE; Man. Dir KARL STUMKE.

Capital Finance Ltd: TDFL Bldg, 5th Floor, 1008 Ohio St/Upanga Rd, POB 9032, Dar es Salaam; tel. (22) 2135152; fax (22) 2135150; e-mail mail@cfl.co.tz; wholly owned by Tanzania Development Finance Co Ltd; cap. 4,000m. (Dec. 2003); Chair. H. K. SENKORO; CEO J. H. MCGUFFOG.

CF Union Bank Ltd: Jivan Hirji Bldg, Indira Gandhi/Mosque St, POB 1509, Dar es Salaam; tel. (22) 2110212; fax (22) 2118750; e-mail cfunionbank@raha.com; f. 2002 by merger of Furaha Finance Ltd and Crown Finance & Leasing Ltd; cap. 4m. (Dec. 2006); Chair. MUNIR ASGARALI BHARWANI; CEO SUBRAMANIAN GOPALAN.

Citibank Tanzania Ltd: Ali Hassan Mwinyi Rd, POB 71625, Dar es Salaam; tel. (22) 2117575; fax (22) 2113910; 99.98% owned by Citibank Overseas Investment Corpn; Chair. EMEKA EMUWA.

CRDB Bank: Azikiwe St, POB 268, Dar es Salaam; tel. (22) 2117442; fax (22) 2116714; e-mail crdb@crdb.com; internet www.crdb.com; f. as Co-operative and Rural Development Bank in 1947, transferred to private ownership and current name adopted 1996; 30% owned by DANIDA Investment; provides commercial banking services and loans for rural development; cap. 12,367m., res 13,730m., dep. 662,811m. (Dec. 2005); Chair JERRY SOLOMON; Man. Dir Dr CHARLES S. KIMEI; 34 brs.

Dar es Salaam Community Bank Ltd (DCB): Arnautoglu Bldg, Bibi Titi Mohamed St, POB 19798, Dar es Salaam; tel. (22) 2180253; fax (22) 2180239; e-mail dcb@africaonline.co.tz; f. 2001; cap. 1,796m. (Dec. 2003); Chair. PAUL MILVANGE RUPIA; Man. Dir EDMUND PANCRAS MKWAWA.

Diamond Trust Bank Tanzania Ltd: POB 115, cnr of Mosque St and Jamaat St, Dar es Salaam; tel. (22) 2114888; fax (22) 2114210; f. 1946 as Diamond Jubilee Investment Trust; converted to bank and adopted current name in 1996; 33.4% owned by Diamond Trust Bank Kenya Ltd, 31.2% owned by Aga Khan Fund for Economic Development SA (Switzerland); cap. 1,108m., res 222m., dep. 49,069m. (Dec. 2005); Chair. MAHMOOD MANJI; CEO SANJEEV KUMAR.

Eurafrican Bank (Tanzania) Ltd: NDC Development House, cnr Kivukoni Front and Ohio St, POB 3054, Dar es Salaam; tel. (22) 2111229; fax (22) 2113740; e-mail eab@eurafricanbank-tz.com; f. 1994; 78.8% owned by Belgolaise/Fortis Bank Group; other shareholders: FMO-Netherlands Development Co (9.83%), Tanzania Development Finance (9.41%), others (1.96%); cap. 6,478m. (Dec. 2002); Chair. FULGENCE M. KAZAURA; Man. Dir JUMA KISAAME.

EXIM Bank (Tanzania) Ltd: NIC Investment House, Samora Ave, POB 1431, Dar es Salaam; tel. (22) 2113091; fax (22) 2119737; e-mail enquiry@eximbank-tz.com; internet www.eximbank-tz.com; cap. 12,900m., res 31m., dep. 179,159m. (Dec. 2005); Chair. YOGESH MANEK; Man. Dir S. M. J. MWAMBENJA.

FBME Bank Ltd: POB 8298, Samora Ave, Dar es Salaam; tel. (22) 2126000; fax (22) 2126006; e-mail headoffice@fbme.com; internet www.fbme.com; f. 1982 in Cyprus as Federal Bank of the Middle East Ltd, subsidiary of Federal Bank of Lebanon SAL (Lebanon); changed country of incorporation to Cayman Islands in 1986, and to Tanzania in 2003; present name adopted 2005; cap. US $43m., res US $2m., dep. US $676m. (Dec. 2005); Chair. AYOUB-FARID M. SAAB, FADI M. SAAB; Gen. Man. (Tanzania) JAN VAN JAAREN.

Habib African Bank Ltd: India St, POB 70086, Dar es Salaam; tel. (22) 2111107; fax (22) 2111014; cap. 1,300m. (Dec. 2003); Chair. HABIB MOHAMMED D. HABIB; Man. Dir MANZAR A. KAZMI.

International Bank of Malaysia (Tanzania) Ltd: Upanga/Kisutu St, POB 9363, Dar es Salaam; tel. (22) 2110518; fax (22) 2110196; e-mail ibm@afsat.com; Chair. JOSEPHINE PREMLA SIVARETNAM; CEO M. RAHMAT.

Kenya Commercial Bank (Tanzania) Ltd: National Audit House, Samora/Ohio St, POB 804, Dar es Salaam; tel. (22) 2115386; fax (22) 2115391; e-mail kbctanzania@kcb.co.tz; internet www.kcb.ke; cap. 6,000m. (Dec. 2003); Chair. S. MUDHUME; Man. Dir BAZRA TABULO.

Kilimanjaro Co-operative Bank Ltd: Mawenzi Rd, POB 1760, Moshi; tel. (27) 54470; fax (27) 53570; Chair. A. P. KAVISHE; Gen. Man. J. KULAYA.

Mufindi Community Bank: POB 147, Mafinga; tel. and fax (26) 2772165; e-mail mucoba@africaonline.co.tz; cap. 100m. (Dec. 2003); Chair. J. J. MUNGAI; Gen. Man. DANY MPOGOLE.

Mwanga Community Bank: Mwanga Township, POB 333, Mwanga, Kilimanjaro; tel. and fax (27) 2754235; Man. Dir CHRIS HALIBUT.

National Microfinance Bank Ltd (NMB): Samora Ave, POB 9213, Dar es Salaam; tel. (22) 2124048; fax (22) 2110077; e-mail ceo@nmbtz.com; internet www.nmbtz.com; f. 1997 following disbandment of The National Bank of Commerce; Chair. M. NGATUNGA; CEO JOHN R. GILES.

NBC Ltd (National Bank of Commerce Ltd): NBC House, Sokoine Drive, POB 1863, Dar es Salaam; tel. (22) 2112082; fax (22) 2112887; e-mail nbcltd@nbctz.com; internet www.nbctz.com; f. 1997 following disbandment of National Bank of Commerce; 55% owned by ABSA Group Ltd (South Africa), 30% by Govt and 15% by International Finance Corpn; cap. 12,000m., res 26,349m., dep. 546,831m. (Dec. 2005); Chair. CHARLES M. NYIRABU; Man. Dir CHRISTO DE VRIES; 33 brs.

People's Bank of Zanzibar Ltd (PBZ): POB 1173, Stone Town, Zanzibar; tel. (24) 2231119; fax (24) 2231121; e-mail pbzltd@zanlik .com; f. 1966; controlled by Zanzibar Govt; cap. 16m. (June 1991); Chair. ABDUL RAHMAN M. JUMBE; Man. Dirs J. M. AMOUR, N. S. NASSOR; 3 brs.

Savings & Finance Ltd: Mission St/Samora Ave, POB 20268, Dar es Salaam; tel. (22) 2118625; fax (22) 2116733; Man. Dir SURANJAN GHOSH.

Stanbic Bank Tanzania Ltd: Sukari House, cnr Ohio St and Sokoine Drive, POB 72647, Dar es Salaam; tel. (22) 2112195; fax (22) 2113742; e-mail tanzaniainfo@stanbic.com; internet www .stanbic.co.tz; f. 1993; wholly owned by Standard Africa Holdings PLC; cap. 2,000m., res 871m., dep. 230,804m. (Dec. 2005); Chair ARNOLD B. S. KILEWO; Man. Dir BASHIR AWALEO; 4 brs.

Standard Chartered Bank Tanzania Ltd: International House, 1st Floor, cnr Shaaban Robert St and Garden Ave, POB 9011, Dar es Salaam; tel. (22) 2122160; fax (22) 2113770; f. 1992; wholly owned by Standard Chartered Holdings (Africa) BV, Netherlands; cap. 1,000m., res 20,613m., dep. 351,182m. (Dec. 2004); Man. Dir H. SHAH.

Tanzania Development Finance Co Ltd (TDFL): TDFL Bldg, Plot 1008, cnr Upanga Rd and Ohio St, POB 2478, Dar es Salaam; tel. (22) 2116417; fax (22) 2116418; e-mail mail@tdfl.co.tz; f. 1962; owned by Govt (32%), govt agencies of the Netherlands and Germany (5% and 26% respectively), the Commonwealth Development Corpn (26%) and the European Investment Bank (11%); cap. 3,303m. (Dec. 2001); Chair. H. K. SENKORO; CEO J. MCGUFFOG.

Tanzania Investment Bank (TIB): cnr Zanaki St and Samora Machel Ave, POB 9373, Dar es Salaam; tel. (22) 2111708; fax (22) 2113438; e-mail tib-tz@intafrica.com; internet www.tib.co.tz; f. 1970; provides finance, tech. assistance and consultancy, fund administration and loan guarantee for economic devt; 99% govt-owned; cap. 7,641m., res 838m., dep. 32,515m. (Dec. 2003); Man. Dir WILLIAM A. MLAKI.

Tanzania Postal Bank (TPB): Extelecoms Annex Bldg, Samora Ave, POB 9300, Dar es Salaam; tel. (22) 2112358; fax (22) 2114815; e-mail md@postalbank.co.tz; internet www.postalbank.co.tz; f. 1991; state-owned; cap. 1,041m. (Dec. 2003); Chair. PAUL JUSTIN MKANGA; Man. Dir and CEO ALPHONSE R. KIHWELE; 4 brs and 113 agencies.

Ulc (Tanzania) Ltd: POB 31, Dar es Salaam; tel. (22) 2118888; fax (22) 2118953; e-mail dtbank@intafrica.com; cap. 2,204m. (Dec. 1999); Chair. Dr JONAS KIPOKOLA; CEO JAMES MACHARIA.

United Bank of Africa Ltd: PPF House, Ground/Mezzanine Floors, Samora Ave/Morogoro Rd, POB 9640, Dar es Salaam; tel. (22) 2130113; fax (22) 2130116; e-mail uba@cats-net.com; cap. 2,532m. (Dec. 2002); Chair. N. N. KITOMARI; Man. Dir I. J. MITCHELL.

STOCK EXCHANGE

Dar es Salaam Stock Exchange: Twigga Bldg, 4th Floor, Samora Ave, POB 70081, Dar es Salaam; tel. (22) 2133659; fax (22) 2122421; e-mail des@cats-net.com; internet www.darstockexchange.com; f. 1998; Chair. GABINUS MAGANGA; Chief Exec. Dr HAMISI S. KIBOLA.

INSURANCE

Jubilee Insurance Co of Tanzania Ltd (JICT): Dar es Salaam; 40% owned by Jubilee Insurance Kenya, 24% by local investors, 15% by the IFC, 15% by the Aga Khan Fund for Economic Devt, 6% by others; cap. US $2m.

National Insurance Corporation of Tanzania Ltd (NIC): POB 9264, Dar es Salaam; tel. (22) 2113823; fax (22) 2113403; f. 1963; state-owned; all classes of insurance; Chair. Prof. J. L. KANYWANYI; Man. Dir OCTAVIAN W. TEMU; 30 brs.

Trade and Industry

GOVERNMENT AGENCIES

Board of External Trade (BET): POB 5402, Dar es Salaam; tel. (22) 2851706; fax (22) 2851700; e-mail betis@intafrica.com; f. 1978; trade and export information and promotion, market research, marketing advisory and consultancy services; Dir-Gen. MBARUK K. MWANDORO.

Board of Internal Trade (BIT): POB 883, Dar es Salaam; tel. (22) 228301; f. 1967 as State Trading Corpn; reorg. 1973; state-owned; supervises seven national and 21 regional trading cos; distribution of general merchandise, agricultural and industrial machinery, pharmaceuticals, foodstuffs and textiles; shipping and other transport services; Dir-Gen. J. E. MAKOYE.

Parastatal Sector Reform Commission (PSRC): Sukari House, POB 9252, Dar es Salaam; tel. (22) 2115482; fax (22) 2113065; e-mail masalla@raha.com.

Tanzania Investment Centre (TIC): POB 938, Dar es Salaam; tel. (22) 2116328; fax (22) 2118253; e-mail information@tic.co.tz; internet www.tic.co.tz; f. 1997; promotes and facilitates investment in Tanzania; Exec. Dir SAMUEL SITTA.

CHAMBERS OF COMMERCE

Dar es Salaam Chamber of Commerce: Kelvin House, Samora Machel Ave, POB 41, Dar es Salaam; tel. (744) 270438; fax (22) 2112754; e-mail dcc1919@yahoo.com; f. 1919; Exec. Dir Y. P. MSEKWA.

Tanzania Chamber of Commerce, Industry and Agriculture: POB 9713, Dar es Salaam; tel. and fax (22) 2119437; e-mail tccia .info@cats-net.com; internet www.tccia.co.tz; f. 1988; Pres. E. MUSIBA.

Zanzibar Chamber of Commerce: POB 1407, Zanzibar; tel. (24) 2233083; fax (24) 2233349.

DEVELOPMENT CORPORATIONS

Capital Development Authority: POB 1, Dodoma; tel. (26) 2324053; f. 1973 to develop the new capital city of Dodoma; govt-controlled; Dir-Gen. EVARIST BABISI KEWBA.

Economic Development Commission: POB 9242, Dar es Salaam; tel. (22) 2112681; f. 1962 to plan national economic development; state-controlled.

National Development Corporation: Kivukoni Front, Ohio St, POB 2669, Dar es Salaam; tel. (22) 2112893; fax (22) 2113618; e-mail epztz@ndctz.com; internet www.ndctz.com; f. 1965; state-owned; cap. Ts. 30.0m.; promotes progress and expansion in production and investment.

Small Industries Development Organization (SIDO): POB 2476, Dar es Salaam; tel. (22) 2151946; fax (22) 2152070; e-mail sido-dg@africaonline.co.tz; internet www.sido.go.tz; f. 1973; promotes and assists development of small-scale enterprises in public, co-operative and private sectors, aims to increase the involvement of women in small businesses; Chair. JAPHET S. MLAGALA; Dir-Gen. MIKE LAISOR.

Sugar Development Corporation: Dar es Salaam; tel. (22) 2112969; fax (22) 230598; Gen. Man. GEORGE G. MBATI.

Tanzania Petroleum Development Corporation (TPDC): POB 2774, Dar es Salaam; tel. (22) 2181407; fax (22) 2180047; f. 1969; state-owned; oversees petroleum exploration and undertakes autonomous exploration, imports crude petroleum and distributes refined products; Man. Dir YONA S. M. KILLAGANE.

There is also a development corporation for textiles.

INDUSTRIAL AND TRADE ASSOCIATIONS

Cashewnut Board of Tanzania: POB 533, Mtwara; tel. (59) 333445; fax (59) 333536; govt-owned; regulates the marketing, processing and export of cashews; Chair. GALUS ABEID; Gen. Man. Dr ALI F. MANDALI.

Confederation of Tanzania Industries (CTI): POB 71783, Dar es Salaam; tel. (22) 2123802; fax (22) 2115414; e-mail cti@cti.co.tz; f. 1991; Chair. REGINALD Mengi ; Exec. Dir CHRISTINE KILINDU.

National Coconut Development Programme: POB 6226, Dar es Salaam; tel. (22) 2700552; fax (22) 275549; e-mail arim@arim .africaonline.co.tz; f. 1979 to revive coconut industry; processing and marketing via research and devt in disease and pest control, agronomy and farming systems, breeding and post-harvest technology; based at Mikocheni Agricultural Research Inst.; Dir Dr ALOIS K. KULLAYA.

Tanganyika Coffee Growers' Association Ltd: POB 102, Moshi.

Tanzania Association of Floriculture (TAFA): POB 11123, Arusha; tel. (57) 4432; fax (57) 4214; e-mail aru.cut@kabari.co.tz; Sec. MATTHIAS OLE KISSAMBU.

Tanzania Coffee Board (TCB): POB 732, Moshi; tel. (55) 52324; fax (55) 53033; e-mail coffee@eoltz.com; internet www.newafrica .com; Man. Dir LESLIE OMARI.

Tanzania Cotton Board: Pamba House, Garden Ave, POB 9161, Dar es Salaam; tel. (22) 2122565; fax (22) 2112894; e-mail tclb@ tancotton.co.tz; internet www.tancotton.co.tz; f. 1984; regulates, develops and promotes the Tanzanian cotton industry; Dir Gen. Dr J. C. B. KABISSA.

Tanzania Exporters' Association: Plot No. 139, Sembeti Rd, POB 1175, Dar es Salaam; tel. (22) 2781035; fax (22) 2112752; e-mail smutabuz@hotmail.com.

Tanzania Pyrethrum Board: POB 149, Iringa; f. 1960; Chair. Brig. LUHANGA; CEO P. B. G. HANGAYA.

Tanzania Sisal Authority: POB 277, Tanga; tel. (53) 44401; fax (53) 42759; Chair. W. H. SHELLUKINDO; Man. Dir S. SHAMTE.

Tanzania Tobacco Board: POB 227, Mazimbu Rd, Morogoro; tel. (23) 2603364; fax (23) 2604401; Chair. V. KAWAWA; CEO FRANK S. URIO.

Tanzania Wood Industry Corporation: POB 9160, Dar es Salaam; Gen. Man. E. M. MNZAVA.

Tea Association of Tanzania: POB 2177, Dar es Salaam; tel. (22) 2122033; e-mail trit@twiga.com; f. 1989; Chair. Dr NORMAN C. KELLY; Exec. Dir DAVID E. A. MGWASSA.

Tea Board of Tanzania: POB 2663, Dar es Salaam; tel. and fax (22) 2114400; Chair. A. MDEE; Exec. Dir H. S. MIJINGA.

Zanzibar State Trading Corporation: POB 26, Zanzibar; govt-controlled since 1964; sole exporter of cloves, clove stem oil, chillies, copra, copra cake, lime oil and lime juice; Gen. Man. ABDULRAHMAN RASHID.

UTILITIES

Electricity

Tanzania Electric Supply Co Ltd (TANESCO): POB 9024, Dar es Salaam; tel. (22) 2112891; fax (22) 2113836; e-mail mdtan@ intafrica.com; internet www.tanesco.com; state-owned; placed under private management in May 2002; privatization pending; Chair. FULGENCE M. KAZAURA; Man. Dir RUDY HUYSEN.

Gas

Enertan Corpn Ltd: POB 3746, Dar es Salaam.

Songas Ltd: POB 6342, Dar es Salaam; tel. (22) 2117313; fax (22) 2113614; internet www.songas.com; f. 1998; Gen. Man. JIM MCCARDLE.

Water

Dar es Salaam Water and Sanitation Authority: POB 1573, Dar es Salaam; e-mail dawasapiu@raha.com; privatization pending.

National Urban Water Authority: POB 5340, Dar es Salaam; tel. (22) 2667505.

MAJOR COMPANIES

The following are some of the largest companies in terms either of capital investment or employment.

Aluminium Africa Ltd (ALAF): Pugu Rd, POB 2070, Dar es Salaam; tel. (22) 2863306; fax (22) 2864690; e-mail galco@cats-net .com; mfrs of aluminium circles, corrugated and plain sheets, galvanized corrugated iron sheets, furniture tubes, steel billets, galvanized pipes, cold rolled steel sheets and coils; sales US $32.0m. (2000); Chair. M. P. CHANDARIA; CEO S. N. SALGAR; 550 employees.

Brooke Bond Liebig Tanzania Ltd: POB 4955, Dar es Salaam; tel. (22) 2863400; fax (22) 2865293; e-mail norman.kelly@unilever.com; wholly owned by Unilever PLC; production and sale of tea; sales US $16.0m. (2000); Man. Dir NORMAN KELLY; 6,500 employees.

Friendship Textiles Mill Ltd: POB 20842, Dar es Salaam; tel. (22) 2189841; fax (22) 2183689; f. 1966; wholly owned by National Textile Corpn; dyed and printed fabric mfrs; 5,400 employees.

IPP Ltd: POB 163, Dar es Salaam; tel. (22) 2119349; fax (22) 2119360; e-mail ipp@raha.com; internet www.ippmedia.com; f. 1978; holding co; Exec. Chair. REGINALD A. MENGI; 2,000 employees.

Katani Ltd: POB 123, Tanga; tel. (27) 2644401; fax (27) 2642409; e-mail katani@twiga.com; f. 1997; mfrs of steel products; sales US $5.0m. (2000); Exec. Chair. A. MPUNGWE; 2,500 employees.

KJ Motors Ltd: POB 9440, Dar es Salaam; tel. (22) 2863588; fax (22) 2863036; f. 1959; mfrs of light and heavy commercial vehicles, construction equipment and motor cycles; sales Ts. 8,000.0m. (1999); Man. Dir NOORALLY K. J. DHANANI; 400 employees.

Mwanza Textiles Ltd: POB 1344, Mwanza; tel. (068) 40466; f. 1966; spinners, weavers, dyers and printers of cotton; 3,901 employees.

National Chemical Industries: POB 9643, Dar es Salaam; tel. (22) 2135287; fax (22) 2155287; manufacture of industrial chemicals; Man. Dir M. DARESOI; 2,000 employees.

National Milling Corporation (NMC): 74/1 Mandela/Nyerere Rd, POB 9502, Dar es Salaam; tel. (22) 2860260; fax (22) 2863817; f. 1968; stores and distributes basic foodstuffs, owns grain milling establishments and imports cereals as required; Chair. T. SIWALE; Gen. Man. VINCENT M. SEMESI; 1,300 employees.

Sunflag (Tanzania) Ltd: POB 3123, Arusha; tel. (27) 3739; fax (27) 8210; f. 1967; mfrs of textiles and clothing; Chair. SATYA DEV BHARDWAJ; 3,500 employees.

Tanga Cement Co Ltd: POB 5053, Tanga; tel. (27) 44500; fax (27) 46180; wholly owned by Tanzania Saruji Corpn; mfrs of Portland cement; Gen. Man. P. FRAZER; 650 employees.

Tanpack Tissues Ltd: POB 21359, Dar es Salaam; tel. (22) 2773901; fax (22) 2700890; e-mail tanpack@cats-net.com; internet www.chandaria.com; f. 1996; wholly owned by Chandaria Industries Ltd; mfrs of paper and tissue; sales Ts. 2,500m. (2004); Man. Dir MAHESH M. CHANDARIA; Gen. Man. RAJESH SHA; 140 employees.

Tanzania Breweries Ltd: Ururo St, POB 9013, Dar es Salaam; tel. (22) 2182780; fax (22) 2181458; e-mail info@tbl.co.tz; f. 1960; subsidiary of South African Breweries International; manufacture, bottling and distribution of malt beer; sales Ts. 135,059.05m. (2002); Chair. PAUL L. BOMANI; CEO J. Q. O'DONOVAN; 1,266 employees.

Tanzania Cigarette Co Ltd: POB 40114, Dar es Salaam; tel. (22) 2860150; fax (22) 2865730; e-mail tcc@cats-net.com; f. 1965; 75% owned by JT International; manufacture and marketing of cigarettes; sales Ts. 77,597.0m. (1999); Chair. and CEO NATWAR GOTECHA; 700 employees.

Tanzania Daesung Cable Co Ltd: POB 508, Dar es Salaam; tel. and fax (22) 2862907; f. 1978; owned by Nexans (Repub. of Korea); production of cables; sales Ts. 3,498.0m. (2000); Chair. S. B. YANG; 76 employees.

Tanzania Distillers Ltd: POB 9412, Dar es Salaam; tel. (22) 2860510; fax (22) 5865202; distillers; sales Ts. 9.525.0m. (2000); CEO N. T. JENKINSON; 78 employees.

Tanzania Portland Cement Co Ltd: POB 1950, Dar es Salaam; tel. (22) 2630130; fax (22) 2630139; e-mail arne.tvedt@tpcc.raha.com; f. 1959; jt venture; mfrs of ordinary Portland cement; capacity: 520,000 metric tons per year; sales US $30.0m. (1999); Chair. FINN ARNOLDSEN; Man. Dir ARNE TVEDT; 390 employees.

TOL Ltd: POB 911, Dar es Salaam; tel. (22) 2860047; fax (22) 2864041; e-mail ccsm@tol.co.tz; f. 1950; 11.4% owned by Govt; manufacture and distribution of industrial and chemical gases; sales Ts. 2,919.8m. (2003); Chair. E. MASSAWE; 107 employees.

Toyota Tanzania Ltd: POB 9060, Dar es Salaam; tel. (22) 2118990; fax (22) 2112987; e-mail sales@toyota.co.tz; f. 1825; wholly owned by Karimjee Jivanjee Ltd; distribution of Toyota motor vehicles; sales US $34.6m. (2000); Chair. HATIM KARIMJEE; 300 employees.

CO-OPERATIVES

There are some 1,670 primary marketing societies under the aegis of about 20 regional co-operative unions. The Co-operative Union of Tanzania is the national organization to which all unions belong.

Tanzania Federation of Co-operatives Ltd: POB 2567, Dar es Salaam; tel. (22) 2184082; fax (22) 2184081; e-mail ushirika@ushirika.co.tz; internet www.ushirika.coop; f. 1962; Exec. Sec. GERALD P. MALIMA; 700,000 mems.

Department of Co-operative Societies: POB 1287, Zanzibar; f. 1952; promotes formation and development of co-operative societies in Zanzibar.

Principal Societies

Bukoba Co-operative Union Ltd: POB 5, Bukoba; 74 affiliated societies; 75,000 mems.

Kilimanjaro Native Co-operative Union (1984) Ltd: POB 3032, Moshi; tel. (27) 2752785; fax (27) 2754204; e-mail kncu@kilinet.co.tz; f. 1984; 88 regd co-operative societies.

Nyanza Co-operative Union Ltd: POB 9, Mwanza.

TRADE UNIONS

Union of Tanzania Workers (Juwata): POB 15359, Dar es Salaam; tel. (22) 226111; f. 1978; Sec.-Gen. JOSEPH C. RWEGASIRA; Dep. Secs-Gen. C. MANYANDA (mainland Tanzania), I. M. ISSA (Zanzibar).

Agricultural Workers: Sec. G. P. NYINDO.

Central and Local Government and Medical Workers: Sec. R. UTUKULU.

Commerce and Construction: Sec. P. O. OLUM.

Communications and Transport Workers: Sec. M. E. KALUWA.

Domestic, Hotels and General Workers: Sec. E. KAZOKA.

Industrial and Mines Workers: Sec. J. V. MWAMBUMA.

Railway Workers: Sec. C. SAMMANG' OMBE.

Teachers: Sec. W. MWENURA.

Principal Unaffiliated Unions

Organization of Tanzanian Trade Unions (OTTU): Dar es Salaam; Sec.-Gen. BRUNO MPANGAL.

Workers' Department of Chama Cha Mapinduzi: POB 389, Vikokotoni, Zanzibar; f. 1965.

Transport

RAILWAYS

Tanzania Railways Corporation (TRC): POB 468, Dar es Salaam; tel. and fax (22) 2110599; e-mail ccm_shamte@trctz.com; internet www.trctz.com; f. 1977 after dissolution of East African Railways; privatization pending; operates 2,600 km of lines within Tanzania; Chair. J. K. CHANDE; Dir-Gen. LINFORD MBOMA.

Tanzania-Zambia Railway Authority (Tazara): POB 2834, Dar es Salaam; tel. (22) 2862191; fax (22) 2862474; e-mail acistz@twiga.com; internet www.tazara.co.tz; jtly owned and administered by the Tanzanian and Zambian Govts; operates a 1,860-km railway link between Dar es Salaam and New Kapiri Mposhi, Zambia, of which 969 km are within Tanzania; Chair. SALIM MSOMA; Man. Dir K. MKANDAWIRE; Regional Man. (Tanzania) A. F. S. NALITOLELA.

ROADS

In 2004 Tanzania had an estimated 85,000 km of classified roads, of which some 5,169 km were paved. A 1,930-km main road links Zambia and Tanzania, and there is a road link with Rwanda. A 10-year Integrated Roads Programme, funded by international donors and co-ordinated by the World Bank, commenced in 1991. Its aim was to upgrade 70% of Tanzania's trunk roads and to construct 2,828 km of roads and 205 bridges, at an estimated cost of US $650m.

The island of Zanzibar has 619 km of roads, of which 442 km are bituminized, and Pemba has 363 km, of which 130 km are bituminized.

INLAND WATERWAYS

Steamers connect with Kenya, Uganda, the Democratic Republic of the Congo, Burundi, Zambia and Malawi. A joint shipping company was formed with Burundi in 1976 to operate services on Lake Tanganyika. A rail ferry service operates on Lake Victoria between Mwanza and Port Bell.

SHIPPING

Tanzania's major harbours are at Dar es Salaam (eight deep-water berths for general cargo, three berths for container ships, eight anchorages, lighter wharf, one oil jetty for small oil tankers up to 36,000 gross tons, offshore mooring for oil supertankers up to 100,000 tons, one 30,000-ton automated grain terminal) and Mtwara (two deep-water berths). There are also ports at Tanga (seven anchorages and lighterage quay), Bagamoyo, Zanzibar and Pemba. A programme to extend and deepen the harbour entrance at Dar es Salaam commenced in 1997.

Tanzania Ports Authority (TPA): POB 9184, Dar es Salaam; tel. (22) 2116258; fax (22) 232066; e-mail dp@tanzaniaports.com; internet www.tanzaniaports.com; f. 2005 to replace the Tanzania Harbours Authority, in preparation for privatization; Dir-Gen. EPHRAIM MGAWE.

Chinese-Tanzanian Joint Shipping Co: POB 696, Dar es Salaam; tel. (22) 2113389; fax (22) 2113388; f. 1967; services to People's Republic of China, South East Asia, Eastern and Southern Africa, Red Sea and Mediterranean ports.

National Shipping Agencies Co Ltd (NASACO): POB 9082, Dar es Salaam; f. 1973; state-owned shipping co; Man. Dir D. R. M. LWIMBO.

Tanzania Central Freight Bureau (TCFB): POB 3093, Dar es Salaam; tel. (22) 2114174; fax (22) 2116697; e-mail tcfb@cats-net.com.

Tanzania Coastal Shipping Line Ltd: POB 9461, Dar es Salaam; tel. (22) 237034; fax (22) 2116436; regular services to Tanzanian coastal ports; occasional special services to Zanzibar and Pemba; also tramp charter services to Kenya, Mozambique, the Persian (Arabian) Gulf, Indian Ocean islands and the Middle East; Gen. Man. RICHARD D. NZOWA.

CIVIL AVIATION

There are 53 airports and landing strips. The major international airport is at Dar es Salaam, 13 km from the city centre, and there are also international airports at Kilimanjaro, Mwanza and Zanzibar. The management of Kilimanjaro International Airport was privatized in 1998. In 2005 it was reported that privatization was to be extended to the management of airports at Dar es Salaam, Mtware and Mwanza.

Tanzania Civil Aviation Authority (TCAA): IPS Bldg, cnr Samora Machel Ave and Azikiwe St, POB 2819, Dar es Salaam; tel. (22) 2115079; fax (22) 2118905; e-mail tcaa@tcaa.go.tz; internet www.tcaa.go.tz; f. 2003; replaced Directorate of Civil Aviation

(f. 1977); ensures aviation safety and security, provides air navigation services; Dir-Gen. MARGARET T. MUNYAGI.

Air Tanzania: ATC House, Ohio St/Garden Ave, POB 543, Dar es Salaam; tel. (22) 2197200; fax (22) 2125221; e-mail bookings@airtanzania.com; internet www.airtanzania.com; f. 1977; operates an 18-point domestic network and international services to Africa, the Middle East and Europe; Chair. MUSTAFA NYANG'ANYI; CEO DAVID MATTAKA.

Air Zanzibar: POB 1784, Zanzibar; f. 1990; operates scheduled and charter services between Zanzibar and destinations in Tanzania, Kenya and Uganda.

New ACS Ltd: Peugeot House, 36 Upanga Rd, POB 21236, Dar es Salaam; fax (22) 237017; operates domestic and regional services; Dir MOHSIN RAHEMTULLAH.

Precisionair: New Safari Hotel Bldg, Boma Rd, POB 1636, Arusha; tel. (27) 2502818; fax (27) 2508204; e-mail jgwaseko@precisionairtz.com; internet www.precisionairtz.com; f. 1993; operates scheduled and charter domestic and regional services.

Tanzanair: Royal Palm Hotel, POB 364, Dar es Salaam; tel. (22) 2843131; fax (22) 2844600; e-mail info@tanzanair.com; internet www.tanzanair.com; f. 1969; operates domestic and regional charter services, offers full engineering and maintenance services for general aviation aircraft.

Tourism

Mount Kilimanjaro is a major tourist attraction. Tanzania has set aside about one-quarter of its land area for 12 national parks, 17 game reserves, 50 controlled game areas and a conservation area. Other attractions for tourists include beaches and coral reefs along the Indian Ocean coast, and the island of Zanzibar (which received 86,495 tourists in 1997 and is expanding and upgrading its tourism facilities). Visitor arrivals totalled 612,754 in 2005, and in 2004 revenue from tourism was US $610m. (excluding revenue from passenger transport).

Tanzania Tourist Board: IPS Bldg, 3rd Floor, POB 2485, Dar es Salaam; tel. (22) 2111244; fax (22) 2116420; e-mail safari@ud.co.tz; internet www.tanzaniatouristboard.com; state-owned; supervises the development and promotion of tourism; Man. Dir GEOFREY E. TENGENEZA.

Tanzania Wildlife Co: POB 1144, Arusha; tel. (57) 8830; fax (57) 8239; e-mail info@tanzaniaquest.com; internet www.tanzaniaquest.com; f. 1974; organizes hunting, photographic, horseback and adventure safaris; also exports and deals in live animals, birds and game-skin products; Man. Dir LEON LAMPRECHT.

Zanzibar Tourist Corporation: POB 216, Zanzibar; tel. (24) 2238630; fax (24) 2233417; e-mail ztc@zanzinet.com; internet www.zanzibartouristcorporation.com; f. 1985; operates tours and hotel services; Gen. Man. SABAAH SALEH ALI.

Defence

As assessed at November 2006, the total armed forces numbered 27,000, of whom an estimated 23,000 were in the army, 1,000 in the navy and 3,000 in the air force. Paramilitary forces comprise a 1,400-strong Police Field Force and an 80,000-strong reservist Citizens' Militia.

Defence Expenditure: Budget estimated at Ts. 183,000m. in 2004.

Commander-in-Chief of the Armed Forces: President JAKAYA MRISHO KIKWETE.

Head of the People's Defence Forces: Maj.-Gen. DAVIS MWAMUNYANGE.

Education

In 2004/05 enrolment at pre-primary level was 23% (23% of both boys and girls). Education at primary level is officially compulsory and is provided free of charge. In secondary schools a government-stipulated fee is paid: from January 1995 this was 8,000 shillings per year for day pupils at state-owned schools and 50,000–60,000 shillings per year for day pupils at private schools. Villages and districts are encouraged to construct their own schools with government assistance. Almost all primary schools are government-owned. Primary education begins at seven years of age and lasts for seven years. In 2004/05 enrolment at primary level was 82% (83% of boys; 81% of girls). Secondary education, beginning at the age of 14, lasts for a further six years, comprising a first cycle of four years and a second of two years. Secondary enrolment in 1999/2000 included only 6% of children in the appropriate age-group (males 6%; females 5%), according to UNESCO estimates. In November 2001 it was announced that approximately 7m. children were to be enrolled in primary schools, under the Government's five-year plan to reintroduce universal primary education by 2005. Enrolment at tertiary level was included just 1% of those in the relevant age-group in 2004/05 (males 2%; females 1%). There is a university at Dar es Salaam. Tanzania also has an agricultural university at Morogoro, and a number of vocational training centres and technical colleges. Education was allocated 23% of total recurrent budgetary expenditure by the central Government in 1994.

Bibliography

Admassu Kebede, J. *The Changing Face of Rural Policy in Tanzania*. London, Minerva Press, 2000.

Angelsen, A., and Fjeldstad, O.-H. *Land Reforms and Land Degradation in Tanzania: Alternative Economic Approaches*. Bergen, CMI, 1995.

Bagachwa, M. S. D. *Financial Integration and Development in Sub-Saharan Africa: A Study of Informal Finance in Tanzania*. London, Overseas Development Institute, 1995.

(Ed.). *Poverty Alleviation in Tanzania: Recent Research Issues*. Dar es Salaam University Press, 1994.

Bagachwa, M. S. D., and Mbelle, A. V. Y. (Eds). *Economic Policy under a Multiparty System in Tanzania*. Dar es Salaam University Press, 1993.

Bryceson, D. F. *Liberalizing Tanzania's Food Trade: Public and Private Faces of Urban Marketing Policy 1939–1988*. Geneva, UN Research Institute for Social Development; Tanzania, Mkuki Na Nyota, 1993.

Buchert, L. *Education in the Development of Tanzania, 1919–1990*. London, James Currey Publishers, 1994.

Campbell, H., and Stein, H. *Tanzania and the IMF: The Dynamics of Liberalization*. Boulder, CO, Westview Press, 1990.

Creighton, C., and Omazi, C. K. (Eds). *Gender, Family and Household in Tanzania*. Brookfield, VT, Ashgate Publishing, 1995.

Drysdale, H. *Dancing with the Dead: A Journey through Zanzibar and Madagascar*. London, Hamish Hamilton, 1991.

Elgstrom, O. *Foreign Aid Negotiations: The Swedish-Tanzanian Aid Dialogue*. Aldershot, Avebury, 1992.

Fair, L. *Pastimes and Politics*. London, James Currey Publishers, 2001.

Feierman, S. *Peasant Intellectuals: Anthropology and History in Tanzania*. Madison, University of Wisconsin Press, 1990.

Forster, P. G., and Maghimbi, S. (Eds). *The Tanzanian Peasantry: Economy in Crisis*. Aldershot, Avebury, 1992.

The Tanzanian Peasantry: Further Strides. Brookfield, VT, Ashgate Publishing, 1995.

Agrarian Economy, State and Society in Contemporary Tanzania. Brookfield, VT, Ashgate Publishing, 1999.

Gibbon, P. (Ed.). *Liberalized Development in Tanzania: Studies on Accumulation Processes and Local Institutions*. Uppsala, Nordiska Afrikainstitutet, 1995.

Giblin, J. L. *A History of the Excluded: Making Family a Refuge from State in Twentieth Century Tanzania (Eastern African Studies)*. Oxford, James Currey Publishers, 2003.

Giblin, J. L., *et al.* (Eds). *In Search of a Nation: Histories of Authority and Dissidence in Tanzania (Eastern African Studies)*. Oxford, James Currey Publishers, 2003.

Hansen, A., and Sommers, M. *Fear in Bongoland*. Oxford, Berghahn Books, 2001.

Havenik, K. J. *Tanzania: The Limits to Development From Above*. Uppsala, SIAS, 1993.

Hyden, G., and Mukandala, R. (Eds). *Agencies in Foreign Aid*. London and Basingstoke, Palgrave, 2000.

International Monetary Fund. *Tanzania—Statistical Appendix*. Washington, DC, IMF, 1998.

Kaijage, F., and Tibaijuka, A. *Poverty and Social Exclusion in Tanzania.* Geneva, International Labour Organisation, 1996.

Kikula, I. S. *Policy Implications on Environment: The Case of Villagization in Tanzania.* Uppsala, Nordiska Afrikainstitutet, 1998.

Kimambo, I. N. *Penetration and Protest in Tanzania: The Impact of the World Economy on the Pare, 1860–1960.* London, James Currey Publishers, 1991.

Lange, S. *From Nation-Building to Popular Culture: The Modernization of Performance in Tanzania.* Bergen, CMI, 1995.

Lapperre, P., and Szirmai, A. (Eds). *The Industrial Experience of Tanzania.* London and Basingstoke, Palgrave, 2001.

Legum, C., and Mmari, G. (Eds). *Mwalimu: The Influence of Nyerere.* London, James Currey Publishers, 1995.

Lovejoy, P. E. *Slavery and the Muslim Diaspora: African Slaves in Dar Es-Salaam.* Princeton, NJ, Markus Wiener Publishers, 2003.

Luvanga, N. and Shitundu, J. *The Role of Tourism in Poverty Alleviation in Tanzania.* Dar es Salaam, Mkuki na Nyota Publishers, 2005.

Maddox, G., Giblin, J. L., and Kimambo, I. N. (Eds). *Custodians of the Land: Environment and Hunger in Tanzanian History.* London, James Currey Publishers, 1995; Athens, OH, Ohio University Press, 1996.

Martin, D. *Serengetu Tanzania: Land, People, History.* Harare, APG, 1997.

Mbelle, A., and Mjema, G. D. (Eds). *The Nyerere Legacy and Economic Policy Making in Tanzania.* (2nd Edn) Dar es Salaam University Press, 2004.

Mbogoni, L. E. Y. *The Cross Versus the Crescent: Religion and Politics in Tanzania from the 1880s to the 1990s.* Dar es Salaam, Mkuki na Nyota Publishers, 2005.

McHenry, D. E., Jr. *Limited Choices: The Political Struggle for Socialism in Tanzania.* Boulder, CO, Lynne Rienner Publishers, 1994.

Mmuya, M. (Ed.). *Functional Dimensions of the Democratization Process: Tanzania and Kenya.* Dar es Salaam University Press, 1994.

Mmuya, M., and Chaligha, A. *Political Parties and Democracy in Tanzania.* Dar es Salaam University Press, 1994.

Mukandala, R., and Othman, H. *Liberalization and Politics: The 1990 Election in Tanzania.* Dar es Salaam University Press, 1994.

Mwakikagile, G. *Nyerere and Africa: End of an Era.* Atlanta, GA, Protea Publishing, 2002.

Nyerere, J. K. *Freedom and Socialism: A Selection from Writings and Speeches, 1965–67.* Dar es Salaam and London, Oxford University Press, 1968; contains the Arusha Declaration and subsequent policy statements.

Ofcansky, T. P., and Yeager, R. *Historical Dictionary of Tanzania.* Lanham, MD, Scarecrow Press, 1997.

Okema, M. *Political Culture in Tanzania.* Lewiston, Edwin Mellen, 1996.

Othman, H. I. B., and Okema, M. *Tanzania: Democracy in Transition.* Dar es Salaam University Press, 1990.

Rosch, P. G. *Der Prozess der Strukturanpassung in Tanzania.* Hamburg, Institut für Afrika-Kunde, 1995.

Sheriff, A. *Slaves, Spices and Ivory in Zanzibar: Integration of an East African Commercial Empire into the World Economy, 1770–1873.* London, James Currey Publishers, 1987.

Shivji, I. G. *Law, State and the Working Class in Tanzania.* London, James Currey Publishers, 1986.

Tanzania: the Legal Foundations of the Union. Dar es Salaam University Press, 1999.

Tripp, A. M. *Changing the Rules.* Berkeley, University of California Press, 1997.

Wange, S. M., *et al.* (Eds). *Traditional Economic Policy and Policy Options in Tanzania.* Dar es Salaam, Mkuki na Nyota Publishers, 1998.

Weiss, B. *Sacred Trees, Bitter Harvests: Globalizing Coffee in Colonial Northwest Tanzania.* Westport, CT, Greenwood Press, 2003.

World Bank. *Tanzania: the Challenge of Reforms: Growth, Incomes and Welfare.* Washington, DC, World Bank, 1996.

Tanzania at the Turn of the Century: Background Papers and Statistics (World Bank Country Study). Washington, DC, World Bank, 2002.

TOGO

Physical and Social Geography

R. J. HARRISON CHURCH

The Togolese Republic, a small state of West Africa (bordered to the west by Ghana, to the east by Benin and to the north by Burkina Faso), covers an area of 56,600 sq km (21,853 sq miles), and comprises the eastern two-thirds of the former German protectorate of Togoland. From a coastline of 56 km on the Gulf of Guinea, Togo extends inland for about 540 km. According to UN estimates, at mid-2006 the population numbered 6,410,000, giving a density of 113.3 persons per sq km (higher than average for West Africa). Northern Togo is more ethnically diverse than the south, where the Ewe predominate. The most numerous ethnic group in 1995 was the Kabré, who represented an estimated 23.7% of the population, when the Ewe accounted for 21.9%. The official languages are French, Ewe and Kabiyé. According to official estimates, the population of the capital, Lomé, located on the coast, amounted to 839,000 in 2003.

The coast, lagoons, blocked estuaries and Terre de Barre regions are identical to those of Benin, but calcium phosphate, the only commercially exploited mineral resource, is quarried north-east of Lake Togo. Pre-Cambrian rocks with rather siliceous soils occur northward, in the Mono tableland and in the Togo-Atacora mountains. The latter are, however, still well wooded and planted with coffee and cocoa. To the north is the Oti plateau, with infertile Primary sandstones, in which water is rare and deep down. On the northern border are granite areas, remote but densely inhabited, as in neighbouring Ghana and Burkina Faso. Togo's climate is similar to that of Benin, except that Togo's coastal area is even drier: Lomé, the capital, had an average annual rainfall of 734 mm in 1999–2000, around one-half of the rainfall recorded in northern regions. Thus Togo, although smaller in area than Benin, is physically, as well as economically, more varied than its eastern neighbour.

Recent History

PIERRE ENGLEBERT

Revised by KATHARINE MURISON

Togoland, of which the Togolese Republic was formerly a part, became a German protectorate in 1894. The territory was occupied by Anglo-French forces in 1914, and was designated a League of Nations mandate in 1919. France was awarded the larger eastern section, while the United Kingdom administered the west. This partition divided the homeland of the Ewe people of the southern part of the territory, and became a continuing source of internal friction. Ewe demands for reunification were intensified during the UN trusteeship system that took effect after the Second World War. In May 1956 a UN-supervised plebiscite in British Togoland produced, despite Ewe opposition, majority support for a merger with the neighbouring territory of the Gold Coast, then a British colony. The region was transferred to the independent state of Ghana in the following year. In October 1956, in a further plebiscite, French Togoland voted to become an autonomous republic within the French Community.

Political life in French Togoland was dominated by the Comité de l'unité togolaise (usually known as the Unité togolaise), led by Sylvanus Olympio, and the Parti togolais du progrès, led by Nicolas Grunitzky. Following independence on 27 April 1960, Olympio, a campaigner for Ewe reunification, became President.

In January 1963 Olympio was overthrown and killed in a military coup led by Sgt (later Gen.) Etienne (Gnassingbé) Eyadéma, a Kabiye from the north of the country, who invited Grunitzky to return from exile as head of state. Subsequent efforts by Grunitzky to achieve constitutional multi-party government proved unsuccessful, and in January 1967 Eyadéma, by then army Chief of Staff, assumed power. Political activity remained effectively suspended until the creation in 1969 of the Rassemblement du peuple togolais (RPT), which served as a vehicle for integrating the army into political life. Plots to overthrow Eyadéma were suppressed in 1970 and again in 1977, when the exiled sons of ex-President Olympio were accused of organizing a mercenary invasion. The introduction of a new Constitution in 1980 made little impact on Eyadéma's authoritarian style of government. In 1985 the Constitution was amended to allow candidates for election to the Assemblée nationale to be adopted without prior approval by the RPT, which, however, remained the only legal political party.

POLITICAL REPRESSION

A series of bomb attacks in Lomé in August 1985 led to the arrest of at least 15 people. When one of the detainees died shortly following his arrest, exiled supporters of Olympio claimed that the Government had used the pretext of the bomb attacks to unleash a 'wave of repression', and in 1986 a visiting delegation of French jurists concluded that torture was being used against political prisoners. Many of those who had been arrested following the bombings were released under a presidential amnesty in January 1986.

In September 1986 some 19 people were detained following an apparent attempted coup, in which some 13 people were killed. In December Eyadéma was re-elected as President, reportedly winning almost 100% of votes cast. At trials in the same month 13 people were sentenced to death, and 14 to life imprisonment, for complicity in the events in September. Gilchrist Olympio, son of the former President, was one of three people sentenced to death *in absentia*. In the aftermath of the alleged coup attempt Eyadéma combined measures to increase his personal security with reforms aimed at apparent political democratization. In October 1987 a national human rights commission, the Commission nationale des droits de l'homme (CNDH), was established, while most of the death sentences imposed in the previous December were commuted.

At elections to the Assemblée nationale in March 1990, 230 candidates, all of whom declared their allegiance to the RPT, contested the Assemblée's 77 seats.

THE COLLAPSE OF LEGITIMACY

In October 1990 a commission was established to draft a new constitution, to be submitted to a national referendum in December 1991. The constitutional commission presented its draft document, which provided for the establishment of a multi-party political system, in late 1990.

In early 1991 several opposition movements formed a co-ordinating organization, the Front des associations pour le renouveau (FAR), to campaign for the immediate introduction of a multi-party political system. Eyadéma subsequently consented to an amnesty for all political dissidents, and agreed to the legalization of political parties and to the organization of a national forum.

The approval of legislation regarding the general amnesty and the legalization of political parties was overshadowed by the discovery, in April 1991, of about 26 bodies in a lagoon in Lomé. Opposition allegations that the bodies were those of demonstrators who had been beaten to death by the security forces were denied by the Government, which ordered the CNDH to investigate the deaths. (In July the CNDH concluded that the security forces had been responsible for the deaths of at least 20 of those whose bodies had been discovered.) Fearing an inter-ethnic conflict between the Kabiye and Ewe ethnic groups, Eyadéma appealed for national unity, and announced that a new constitution would be introduced within one year, and that multi-party legislative elections would be organized.

The FAR was disbanded in April 1991, to allow for the establishment of independent political parties. Yawovi Agboyibo, hitherto leader of the FAR, formed the Comité d'action pour le renouveau (CAR), while numerous other movements obtained official status, and in May 10 parties (including the CAR) formed a coalition, the Front de l'opposition démocratique (FOD), which was later renamed the Coalition de l'opposition démocratique (COD).

Negotiations between the Government and the opposition, in preparation for the national forum, took place amid conditions of social and labour unrest. In June 1991 it was announced that the Government and the FOD had reached agreement regarding the mandate of what was to be known henceforth as the national conference.

The national conference was opened on 8 July 1991, attended by some 1,000 delegates (representing, among others, the organs of state and the country's newly legalized political organizations, together with workers', students' and religious leaders). A resolution by the conference, in mid-July, to declare itself sovereign, to suspend the Constitution and to dissolve the Assemblée nationale prompted the Government to boycott the proceedings for one week. Upon their return to the conference, government representatives refused to endorse these resolutions. In late July the conference resolved to sequester the assets of the RPT and its former trade union affiliate, and to create an authority to control the finances of state and parastatal organizations, with the aim of preventing the transfer of state funds abroad.

On 26 August 1991 Eyadéma, deprived by the national conference of most of his powers, abruptly suspended the conference. Opposition delegates responded by proclaiming a provisional Government under the leadership of Joseph Kokou Koffigoh, a prominent lawyer and the head of the independent Ligue togolaise des droits de l'homme (LTDH). The conference also voted to dissolve the RPT and to form an interim legislature, the Haut conseil de la république (HCR). Fearing renewed unrest, Eyadéma hastily signed a decree confirming Koffigoh as transitional Prime Minister.

Koffigoh's Council of Ministers, appointed in September 1991, was composed mainly of technocrats who had not previously held political office. The Prime Minister assumed personal responsibility for defence, and it was envisaged that Eyadéma would remain only nominally head of the military. However, the events of subsequent months were to demonstrate that the Kabiye-dominated armed forces looked to Eyadéma for their command. In October a group of soldiers seized control of the offices of the state broadcasting service in Lomé, demanding the resignations of Koffigoh and his Government, but returned to barracks on Eyadéma's orders. Five people were killed during the incident. One week later, presidential guards attempted unsuccessfully to abduct Koffigoh, although Eyadéma again ordered a return to barracks. Seven deaths were reported, as demonstrations by civilian supporters of Koffigoh degenerated into looting and violence.

CONSTITUTIONAL TRANSITION

The brief political calm ended in late November 1991, when the HCR responded to attempts to convene a congress of the RPT by reaffirming the ban on the former ruling party. Clashes between supporters of Eyadéma and Koffigoh resulted in further casualties. The military retook the broadcasting headquarters and surrounded government offices, demanding that the transitional authorities be disbanded. The troops returned to barracks on 30 November, and conciliation talks began. Two days later, however, the military reoccupied strategic positions in the capital, and on the following day captured the Prime Minister. Following negotiations between Eyadéma and Koffigoh, in late December the formation was announced of a 'Government of National Unity', which included many members of the outgoing Council of Ministers, although two key portfolios were allocated to close associates of Eyadéma. The HCR also restored legal status to the RPT.

In July 1992 the Government was reorganized and proposals for a new electoral schedule were announced, beginning with a constitutional referendum in August. The political climate deteriorated shortly after the reshuffle, when a prominent opposition leader, Tavio Ayao Amorin, was killed. In response, a new opposition coalition, the Collectif de l'opposition démocratique (COD-2), comprising some 25 political organizations and trade unions, organized a widely observed general strike in Lomé.

An attempt to resolve the political crisis was made in July 1992, when representatives of Eyadéma and of the country's eight leading political parties began a series of meetings. In August the HCR restored a number of powers to the President, empowering Eyadéma to preside over the Council of Ministers and to represent Togo abroad, and obliging the Prime Minister to make government appointments in consultation with the Head of State. Moreover, the draft Constitution was amended to permit members of the armed forces seeking election to the new democratic organs of state to retain their commissions.

The transitional Government was dissolved on 1 September 1992, and a new electoral schedule was announced. In mid-September a new transitional Government was formed: Koffigoh remained as Prime Minister, but the most influential posts were allocated to members of the RPT. On 27 September the new Constitution was approved in a referendum by 98.1% of the votes cast (the rate of participation by voters was about 66%). At the end of the month, however, a further rescheduling of the elections was announced. In October members of the armed forces stormed a meeting of the HCR, holding some of its members hostage. In November Koffigoh dismissed two ministers (both supporters of the RPT) for their conduct during the attack on the HCR, but his decision was overruled by Eyadéma. In the same month a general strike was organized by the COD-2, to support their demands for elections, the neutrality of the armed forces, the formation of a non-military 'peace force', and the bringing to justice of those responsible for the attacks on the HCR. The strike was widely observed, except in the north of Togo (where support for Eyadéma was strongest), and continued for nine months, causing considerable economic disruption.

In January 1993 Eyadéma dissolved the Government, but reappointed Koffigoh as Prime Minister. The President stated that he would appoint a new government of national unity, whose principal task would be the expedited organization of elections. His action provoked protests by the opposition parties, which claimed that, according to the Constitution, the HCR should appoint a prime minister since the transition period had now expired. Later in January, representatives of the French and German Governments visited Togo to offer mediation in the political crisis. During their visit at least 20 people were killed when police opened fire on anti-Government protesters. Thousands of Togolese subsequently fled from Lomé, many taking refuge in Benin and Ghana. In February discussions in France, attended by representatives of Eyadéma, the RPT, Koffigoh, the HCR and the COD-2, failed when the presidential delegation left after one day. The formation of a new 'Crisis Government' was announced shortly afterwards; supporters of Eyadéma retained the principal posts. Declaring that they now regarded Koffigoh as an obstacle to democratization, in March COD-2 member parties nominated a 'parallel' Prime Minister, Jean-Lucien Savi de Tové.

On 25 March 1993 more than 20 people were killed during an armed attack on the military camp in Lomé where Eyadéma had his residence, after which about 110 members of the armed forces fled the country. The Government declared that the attack had been instigated by Gilchrist Olympio, with assistance from the Ghanaian authorities.

In July 1993 the Government and the COD-2 agreed on 25 August as the date for the presidential poll. Agreement was also reached on the issue of security during the election campaign (the Togolese armed forces would be confined to barracks, under the supervision of a multinational military team) and the establishment and functions of an independent national electoral commission. International observers were to be invited to monitor the elections. Edem Kodjo, the leader of the Union togolaise pour la démocratie (UTD), was chosen as the presidential candidate of the COD-2. Four other opposition candidates, including Agboyibo and Gilchrist Olympio, were selected to contest the election. However, the Supreme Court disallowed Olympio's candidature, on a legal technicality.

As the election campaign gained momentum during August 1993, opposition demands, supported by the national electoral commission, that the election be postponed intensified, and Kodjo (widely regarded as Eyadéma's strongest challenger) and Agboyibo effectively withdrew from the election. The COD-2 and Olympio's Union des forces de changement (UFC) appealed to their supporters to boycott the poll, and US and German observers withdrew from Togo, alleging irregularities in electoral preparations. As voting began, on 25 August, the Government announced that a coup attempt, plotted by Togolese dissidents in Ghana, had been detected on the eve of polling. Shortly after the poll, it was revealed that at least 15 opposition supporters, arrested in connection with attacks on polling stations in Lomé, had died while in detention. According to official results, Eyadéma was re-elected President by 96.5% of voters. Only about 36% of the electorate voted. Eyadéma was sworn in as President of the Fourth Republic on 24 September.

THE FOURTH REPUBLIC

In January 1994 an armed attack on Eyadéma's official residence was reported. As in March 1993, the Government alleged that the attack had been organized by Gilchrist Olympio, with Ghanaian support: this was denied both by Olympio and by the Ghanaian Government. A total of 67 people were officially reported to have died in the violence. It was claimed by the international human rights organization Amnesty International that the armed forces had carried out at least 48 summary executions.

In the elections to the Assemblée nationale, which took place on 6 and 20 February 1994, after several postponements, 347 candidates contested 81 seats. Despite the murder of a newly elected CAR candidate after the first round, and some incidents of violence at polling stations during the second round, international observers expressed themselves satisfied with the conduct of the elections. The final result revealed a narrow victory for the opposition, with the CAR winning 36 seats and the UTD seven; the RPT obtained 35 seats and two smaller pro-Eyadéma parties won three. During March Eyadéma consulted the main opposition parties on the formation of a new Government. In March the CAR and the UTD reached agreement on the terms of their alliance and jointly proposed the candidacy of Agboyibo for Prime Minister. In March and April the Supreme Court declared the results of the legislative elections invalid in three constituencies (in which the CAR had won two seats and the UTD one) and ordered by-elections. The CAR and the UTD refused to attend the new Assemblée nationale in protest. In April Eyadéma nominated Kodjo as Prime Minister. Kodjo accepted the appointment, despite assertions by the CAR that to do so was a violation of the agreement between the party and the UDT, which stipulated that their candidate for the premiership should be a CAR member. The CAR subsequently announced that it would not participate in an administration formed by Kodjo. Kodjo took office on 25 April. It was not until late May that he announced the formation of his Government, which comprised eight members of the RPT and other pro-Eyadéma parties, three members of the UTD, and eight independents. On 25 November the by-elections, due to be held on 27 November, were postponed.

Political and Constitutional Manoeuvres

In December 1994 the Assemblée nationale declared a general amnesty covering all persons who had been charged with political offences committed before 15 December 1994.

In early 1995 the Government and the major opposition parties reached agreement on equal representation on national, district and local electoral commissions. In November Kodjo implemented a major reorganization of the Council of Ministers. The CAR, which was not represented in the new Government, expressed concern at the level of representation given to supporters of Eyadéma; of the 13 new members, 11 were considered to be close allies of the President.

In April 1996 a CAR deputy resigned from the party, thus reducing its representation in the Assemblée nationale to 33 seats. In May the CAR announced its withdrawal from the by-elections, after the Government rejected its demand that they be organized according to the terms of the accord of July 1993, in the presence of an international monitoring committee. In that month a UTD deputy was dismissed from the party, thus reducing its representation in the Assemblée nationale to five seats.

At the by-elections, conducted in August 1996 in the presence of 22 international observers, the RPT won control of the three constituencies being contested. Consequently, the RPT and its political allies were able to command a legislative majority, thus forcing the resignation of the Kodjo administration. On 20 August Eyadéma appointed Kwassi Klutse, hitherto Minister of Planning and Territorial Development, as Prime Minister. Both the CAR and the UTD refused to participate in a proposed government of national unity, and consequently the new Council of Ministers, appointed in late August, comprised almost exclusively supporters of Eyadéma.

In October 1996 a further CAR deputy left the party, transferring his allegiance to the RPT. In November the Union pour la justice et la démocratie, which held two seats in the legislature, announced that it was to merge with the RPT, thus giving the RPT 41 seats and an overall majority. In December legislation on the creation of a Constitutional Court was approved by the Assemblée nationale, in the absence of the CAR and the UTD, which boycotted the vote.

Electoral Controversies

In March 1998 the Government announced that the presidential election would take place on 7 June. In April the RPT nominated Eyadéma as its presidential candidate. In the same month Gilchrist Olympio returned from exile in Ghana and announced his candidacy for the UFC. Following a postponement, the presidential election eventually took place on 21 June. On the following day, as early voting figures indicated that Eyadéma might lose the election, the vote count was suspended. On 23 June five of the nine members of the electoral commission, including the Chairman, resigned, reportedly as a result of intimidation. The vote count was not resumed, and on 24 June the Minister of the Interior and Security declared Eyadéma to have won the election with 52.1% of the vote. European Union (EU) observers expressed serious concern at the suspension of the vote count and called on the Togolese authorities to complete the process. Monitors reported that Olympio had received a greater share of the vote than Eyadéma in much of Lomé, and, according to observers, all indications were of a victory for Olympio. Supporters of the UFC staged demonstrations in protest at the announced results, prompting the Government to impose a ban on all organized protests.

In August 1998 armed attacks on an army post and a police station near the border with Ghana were blamed by the authorities on supporters of Gilchrist Olympio. Olympio, however, speaking from Ghana, accused the Government of exploiting the disturbances to attack the opposition, noting that during the disturbances the residence of two UFC leaders and the party headquarters had been ransacked.

In September 1998 Klutse announced his new Council of Ministers. Despite Eyadéma's stated desire for a government of national unity, no opposition figures were willing to be included, and few new appointments were made. In November the Government survived a vote of 'no confidence' tabled by the CAR and the UTD.

In January 1999 the Government announced that the first round of legislative elections would take place on 7 March. In February the opposition parties called for discussions with the Government prior to the elections, on the grounds that the issue of the disputed presidential election should be settled before legislative elections were held. The Government agreed to postpone the elections until later in March, but rejected the opposition's suggestion that the Constitution be amended in order to allow the extension of the incumbent Assemblée nationale's mandate. The main opposition parties therefore boycotted the elections.

The elections to the Assemblée nationale took place on 21 March 1999, and were contested by the RPT, by 12 independent candidates, and by two small parties loyal to Eyadéma. The Constitutional Court ruled that the RPT had won 77 seats, and that independent candidates had taken two seats, while fresh elections were scheduled in two constituencies. Turn-out was officially estimated at 66%, although the opposition estimated that it was little more than 10%. In April Klutse tendered his Government's resignation, and in May Eugène Koffi Adogboli, a former UN official, was appointed Prime Minister. In June Adogboli appointed a new Council of Ministers dominated by supporters of Eyadéma.

Discussions took place in Lomé in July 1999 between the Government, the opposition and four international facilitators, representing France, Germany, the EU and La Francophonie. Gilchrist Olympio demanded that his party, the UFC, should meet government representatives separately, to resolve the issue of the disputed presidential election. However, this proposal was rejected by both the Government and the opposition, and Olympio therefore withdrew from discussions and returned to Ghana, although the UFC continued to be represented in the talks. Eyadéma's announcement, reportedly advocated by President Jacques Chirac of France, that he would not stand for re-election, and that new legislative elections would be held in 2000, was widely credited with breaking the deadlock in negotiations, and, after the opposition had agreed to accept Eyadéma's victory in the presidential election, an accord was signed on 29 July by all the parties involved in negotiations. The accord made provision for the establishment of an independent electoral body, which was to create a definitive electoral register.

In August 1999 the first meeting was held of the 24-member Comité paritaire de suivi (CPS) responsible for the implementation of the accord, composed equally of representatives of the opposition and supporters of Eyadéma, and also including a group of intermediaries from the EU. Harry Octavianus Olympio, the cousin of Gilchrist Olympio and the Minister for the Promotion of Democracy and the Rule of Law, was appointed to head the CPS. Agreement on the mechanism for announcing election results was reached in September, and in December agreement was reached on a revised electoral code, providing for the establishment of an independent electoral commission. In April 2000 Eyadéma obliged the Assemblée nationale (which had initially refused to adopt the revised document) to accept the new electoral code.

In May 2000 Harry Octavianus Olympio announced that he had survived an attempted assassination. However, in June Olympio was dismissed from the Government, after evidence was discovered indicating that he had himself engineered the supposed attempt.

In August 2000 Adogboli was overwhelmingly defeated in a vote of 'no confidence' in his premiership, and therefore presented his resignation and that of his Government to Eyadéma. In late August Eyadéma appointed Agbéyomé Kodjo, hitherto the President of the Assemblée nationale, as Prime Minister. In January 2001 the Commission électorale nationale indépendante (CENI) announced that the legislative elections would be held in October 2001. The CENI also announced that, instead of compiling new voters' lists, the electoral registers from the 1998 presidential election would be used in the forthcoming polls.

In June 2001 Harry Octavianus Olympio was sentenced to 18 months' imprisonment, having been convicted of the illegal possession and manufacture of explosives. In August Agboyibo, the leader of the CAR, was jailed for six months and fined 100,000 francs CFA, having been found guilty on charges of libelling the Prime Minister. Agboyibo had alleged that Kodjo was involved in the organization of an armed militia group when he was director of the port at Lomé in 1998. In October 2001 Eyadéma pardoned Harry Octavianus Olympio. In November Eyadéma implied that he would be prepared to offer a pardon to Agboyibo, should he request one. However, Agboyibo instead launched an appeal against his conviction. Although the appeals court found in favour of Agboyibo in January 2002, he was immediately rearrested on charges of conspiring to commit violence during the 1998 presidential election campaign.

Meanwhile, in August 2001 the Prime Minister announced that, owing to technical and financial difficulties, the legislative elections would be further postponed until 2002. In February 2002 the Assemblée nationale approved amendments to electoral legislation and to the remit of the CENI; henceforth all candidates for legislative elections were required to have been continuously resident in Togo for six months prior to elections, with presidential candidates to have been resident for a continuous 12 months. The CENI was also to be reduced in size from 20 to 10 members. The UFC opposed the amendments, which effectively prevented its leader, Gilchrist Olympio, who remained resident in Ghana, from seeking election. In response to the amendments, the EU announced the suspension of financial assistance intended to fund the elections. Five opposition parties accused the Government of breaking the conditions of the accord signed in July 1999, and in March 2002 they rejected an invitation by Kodjo to nominate representatives to the CENI. The Government consequently announced that no date for the legislative elections could be announced until a complete electoral commission had been formed.

Agboyibo was released from prison in March 2002. Eyadéma stated that the release, which he had ordered, was intended to facilitate national reconciliation. The President also ordered that the charges of conspiring to commit violence against Agboyibo be lifted. Following Agboyibo's release, 10 opposition parties that had not been party to the accord signed in 1999, and were therefore excluded from the CPS, announced the formation of a Coordination des partis de l'opposition constructive, headed by Harry Octavianus Olympio. In mid-May a committee of seven judges (the Comité de sept magistrats—C-7), charged with monitoring the electoral process, was appointed, in accordance with a provision of the revised electoral code that permitted the appointment of such a committee in the event that the CENI could not be formed by consensus. The CAR, the Convergence patriotique panafricaine (CPP—formed in 1999 by a merger of the UTD and three other parties) and other opposition parties condemned this decision, and announced their intention to boycott any elections organized by the C-7. At the end of May the EU announced that it would not renew funding for the three facilitators it supported, in view of the continued lack of progress towards democracy in Togo.

At the end of June 2002 Eyadéma dismissed Kodjo as Prime Minister, following a dispute between factions within the RPT. Eyadéma appointed Koffi Sama, hitherto Minister of National Education and Research, as Prime Minister, and a new Government, which included several principal members of the former administration, was appointed in early July. Kodjo subsequently issued a statement criticizing the 'monarchic, despotic' regime of Eyadéma, and—in contrast to his former stated position—called for measures to ensure that Eyadéma would be unable to amend the Constitution to stand for a further term of office; it was subsequently reported that the former premier had received death threats from a relation of the President. Moreover, the state prosecutor filed a suit against Kodjo on charges of disseminating false information and demeaning the honour of the President, in response to statements issued by Kodjo alleging corruption and human rights abuses by representatives of the Government; Kodjo subsequently left the country, taking up residence in France.

In August Kodjo was expelled from the RPT, and in September an international warrant was issued for his arrest, on charges of fraud. However, in October Kodjo's bank accounts in France were 'unfrozen', after a judicial inquiry failed to establish that the accounts had been used fraudulently.

Meanwhile, in August 2002 four parties, including the CAR, announced the formation of an opposition alliance, the Front uni de l'opposition (Le Front), headed by Agboyibo. In late August concern about the freedom of the press in Togo arose, following the approval by the Council of Ministers of a draft text of modifications to the press code; notably, journalists convicted of insulting the President could be sentenced to five years' imprisonment under the new proposed legislation. In September the authorities announced that the legislative elections were to be held on 27 October.

In October 2002 Eyadéma dissolved the Assemblée nationale, although deputies were to retain their responsibilities and powers until the holding of the forthcoming legislative elections. These measures, which were approved by the outgoing Assemblée nationale, provoked controversy, as the Constitution required 30 days to elapse between the dissolution of the legislature and the holding of elections. In late October nine opposition parties that had declined to participate in the elections announced the formation of a new alliance, the Coalition des forces démocrates (CFD), chaired, on an interim basis, by Edem Kodjo of the CPP; other members of the grouping included the CAR and the UFC, in addition to a faction of 'renovators' within the RPT (which subsequently became the Pacte socialiste pour le renouveau—PSR). Meanwhile, a group of 'constructive' opposition parties (including Harry Octavianus Olympio's Rassemblement pour le soutien de la démocratie et du développement—RSDD), which were prepared to participate in the electoral process and form alliances with the RPT, formed the Coordination des partis politiques de l'opposition constructive (CPOC). The elections proceeded as scheduled, without the participation of the principal opposition parties, on 27 October. The 81 seats of the Assemblée nationale were contested by 15 parties and eight independent candidates, although the RPT was the sole party to contest every seat. The RPT won 72 seats (of which 46 had been secured unopposed) and the RSDD three, while three other parties won a total of five seats, and one independent candidate was elected. The C-7, which now comprised six judges (following the resignation of one member of the committee on the day before the elections), estimated electoral turn-out at 67.4%, although the CFD claimed that no more than 10% of the electorate had voted.

Eyadéma reappointed Sama as Prime Minister in November 2002; a new Government, comprising 21 ministers, was formed in December. All ministers were members of the RPT, with the exception of Harry Octavianus Olympio, who was appointed Minister responsible for Relations with Parliament.

In December 2002 the Assemblée nationale approved several constitutional amendments regarding the eligibility of presidential candidates. The restriction that had limited the President to serving two terms of office was removed, and the age of eligibility was reduced from 45 to 35 years. (It was widely believed that these measures were intended to permit Eyadéma to serve a further term of office, and also to permit the possible candidacy of Eyadéma's son, Faure Gnassingbé.) Candidates were henceforth to be required to hold solely Togolese citizenship, although those holding dual or multiple nationalities were to be permitted to renounce them, prior to seeking election. Although these measures were adopted unanimously, they were vociferously denounced by the extra-parliamentary opposition. In February 2003 the UFC withdrew from the CFD, after other parties within the grouping agreed to appoint representatives to the CENI prior to the holding of a presidential election later in the year. In March Gilchrist Olympio announced that he intended to contest the presidential election, although his candidacy was rejected in May, as he did not meet residency requirements. Emmanuel Bob Akitani, the First Vice-President of the UFC, was subsequently announced as his party's candidate.

Eyadéma was returned to office in the presidential election, which was held on 1 June 2003, receiving 57.8% of the votes cast. His nearest rivals were Bob Akitani, with 33.7% of the votes, and Agboyibo, with 5.1%. Several of the six defeated candidates, including Bob Akitani, Edem Kodjo and Maurice Dahuku Pere, representing the PSR, declared that the election had been conducted fraudulently, although observers from the Economic Community of West African States (ECOWAS), the African Union (AU—formerly the Organization for African Unity—OAU) and the Conseil de l'Entente stated that only minor irregularities had been witnessed. Eyadéma was inaugurated for a further term of office on 20 June. Sama was reappointed as premier on 1 July, apparently with instructions from Eyadéma to form a government of national unity. However, most opposition parties reportedly declined to participate, and the new Government included only two representatives of the 'constructive' opposition, including Harry Octavianus Olympio, who was reappointed as Minister responsible for Relations with Parliament. Faure Gnassingbé received his first ministerial posting, as Minister of Equipment, Mines, Posts and Telecommunications. Olympio resigned in August, expressing dissatisfaction at the post to which he had been appointed. Later in August the RSDD was reportedly expelled from the CPOC. In September the Assemblée nationale elected new members of the CENI, prompting speculation that local elections would be held soon; the UFC and the CAR refused to propose representatives to serve on the commission. In December, however, the local elections were postponed indefinitely.

Democratic Reforms

Discussions between the Government and the EU on the conditions for a resumption of economic co-operation commenced in April 2004 in Brussels, Belgium; the government delegation pledged to implement 22 measures, such as revising the press code, introducing more transparent conditions for fair elections and guaranteeing political parties the freedom to conduct their activities without fear of harassment. Under pressure from the EU to strengthen democracy, President Eyadéma officially opened talks between the Government and opposition parties in late May, despite a boycott of the ceremony by the CAR, the UFC and the Convention démocratique des peuples africains—Branche Togolaise (CDPA—BT), which criticized the lack of preparations prior to the discussions; the UFC also deplored the exclusion of its President, Gilchrist Olympio, who, it claimed, had been denied entry into Togo. An EU mission charged with assessing Togo's progress in implementing democratic reforms held meetings with the Government, political leaders, human rights organizations and religious leaders over four days at the beginning of June. Later that month Sama commenced a series of separate consultations with leaders of several opposition parties, including the UFC, and representatives of civil society organizations as part of the national dialogue opened in late May by Eyadéma. However, following the meetings, the CAR, the UFC and the CDPA—BT criticized Sama's approach to conducting the national dialogue, and the three parties refused to participate in a multi-party commission established in July to consider the revision of the electoral code and the funding of political parties, urging that a more structured framework for the dialogue be formulated. In early August it was reported that Gilchrist Olympio had been provided with a Togolese passport. Some 500 prisoners were released in mid-August, having been granted a presidential pardon. Later that month the Assemblée nationale adopted amendments to the press code, notably abolishing prison sentences for offences such as defamation and repealing the powers of the Ministry of the Interior, Security and Decentralization to order the closure or seizure of newspapers. A few days later the Government, the main opposition parties (including the CAR, the UFC and the CDPA—BT) and a number of civil society associations agreed on a framework for a new round of national dialogue.

In November 2004 the EU announced a partial resumption of economic co-operation with Togo, expressing satisfaction at the opening of dialogue with opposition parties, the reform of the press code and the release of prisoners. A full restoration of development aid was made conditional on the organization of transparent legislative elections. The inter-Togolese national dialogue resumed in December, although the CAR, the UFC and the CDPA—BT were again critical of procedural aspects of the discussions. Later that month Eyadéma announced that legislative elections would be held during the first quarter of 2005. In January 2005 the Assemblée nationale approved several amendments to the electoral code, notably strengthening the powers of the CENI and increasing its membership to 13, to include two representatives of civil society.

Presidential Succession

On 5 February 2005 Prime Minister Sama announced that President Eyadéma had died while being transported to France for medical treatment. Two hours later the Chief of General Staff of the armed forces, Gen. Zakari Nandja, declared that the Constitution had been suspended and named Faure Gnassingbé as his father's successor. Gnassingbé's appointment as President was in clear contravention of the Constitution, which provided for the assumption of the functions of head of state by the President of the Assemblée nationale for up to 60 days pending an election. However, the military had closed Togo's airports, seaports and land borders immediately after Eyadéma's death, thus preventing the legislative chairman, Ouattara Fambaré Natchaba, from returning to the country from a visit to Europe. Nandja justified Gnassingbé's appointment as being necessary to avoid a power vacuum. The AU denounced the military's installation of Gnassingbé as Head of State as a *coup d'état*, while the UN, ECOWAS and La Francophonie urged the Togolese authorities to respect the terms of the Constitution. On the following day, amid continuing international condemnation, the Assemblée nationale attempted to legitimize Gnassingbé's assumption of power. Deputies abolished the constitutional provision requiring an election to take place within 60 days of the death of an incumbent President, instead authorizing the new head of state to serve the remainder of his predecessor's term, and amended the electoral code to allow ministers to reassume their mandates as deputies on resigning from the Government (thus rendering them eligible for election to the presidency of the legislature). The Assemblée then voted to remove Natchaba from his post as President of the legislature, electing Gnassingbé in his place.

Gnassingbé was formally sworn in as President of the Republic on 7 February 2005 in a ceremony that was boycotted by diplomats from the UN, the EU, France, Nigeria and the USA. After the Government announced a ban on demonstrations for the duration of a two-month period of mourning for Eyadéma, a coalition of six so-called 'radical' opposition parties, including the CAR, the CDPA—BT and the UFC, instead called a two-day strike in protest at what they also termed a coup, but it was only partially observed. Two days after Gnassingbé's inauguration La Francophonie suspended Togo's membership of the organization, while the Heads of State of nine ECOWAS countries, meeting at an extraordinary summit in Niamey, Niger, agreed that the intervention of the military constituted a coup and condemned the subsequent 'manipulation' of the Constitution by the legislature, threatening to impose sanctions against the new regime if constitutional order was not restored. Protests subsequently broke out in Lomé against Gnassingbé's seizure of power and the closure by the authorities of several private radio and television stations on the grounds of alleged non-payment of taxes and incitement to rebellion. A week after Eyadéma's death at least three people were killed in the Lomé district of Bè, a traditional opposition stronghold, as the security services suppressed a demonstration organized by the opposition and attended by several thousand people; it was reported that police had used tear gas and, in some instances, live ammunition to disperse the protesters. Two days later a second call to strike by the opposition was largely unheeded except in Bè, where a further death was reported.

ECOWAS continued to exert pressure on Gnassingbé's administration to apply the Constitution as it stood before Eyadéma's death. Prime Minister Sama held talks with President Mamadou Tandja, the President of Niger and Chairman of ECOWAS, in Niamey on 13 February 2005, and two days later an ECOWAS delegation travelled to Lomé for negotiations with Gnassingbé. Gnassingbé then visited the Nigerian capital, Abuja, for a meeting with Nigeria's President, Olusegun Obasanjo, who reiterated ECOWAS's position. On 18 February, in a televised speech, Gnassingbé pledged to hold an election within 60 days, but stated his intention to remain in power in the mean time. The Assemblée nationale subsequently reversed the constitutional changes adopted following Eyadéma's death. The day after Gnassingbé's declaration ECOWAS suspended Togo's membership of the Community, imposed an arms embargo on the country, banned its government ministers from travelling in the region and ordered the recall of ambassadors of member states from Lomé. Meanwhile, at least 10,000 people participated in a protest march organized by the opposition in Bè, while several thousand others attended a rally in support of Gnassingbé outside the presidential palace; the Government had lifted the ban on public demonstrations on the previous day.

On 25 February 2005, following consultations with the leaders of Gabon and Libya and the imposition of sanctions against Togo by the AU, Gnassingbé bowed to international pressure and announced his resignation from the presidency of the Assemblée nationale, and therefore from the presidency of the Republic. He was to be replaced, in an interim capacity, by the Vice-President of the legislature, Abass Bonfoh. Earlier that day Gnassingbé had been acclaimed President of the RPT, at a special congress of the party, and endorsed as the party's candidate for the forthcoming presidential election. Gnassingbé's decision to stand down was widely welcomed by the international community, and ECOWAS rescinded its sanctions against Togo and pledged to assist with election preparations. However, opposition parties continued to insist that Natchaba should be appointed interim President, and largely peaceful demonstrations were held in support of this demand, although violent disturbances were again reported in Bè; five corpses believed to be those of protesters were later discovered.

In March 2005 the CENI announced that the presidential election would take place on 24 April. The six-party 'radical' opposition coalition subsequently united behind Bob Akitani, of the UFC, as its sole candidate, while Harry Octavianus Olympio, of the RSDD, and Nicolas Lawson, the leader of the Parti du renouveau et de la rédemption, were to represent the 'constructive' opposition. As in 2003, Gilchrist Olympio, who returned to Togo in mid-March, was barred from standing owing to his failure to meet the residency requirements.

Tensions mounted in April 2005, as the date of the election approached. Isolated violent incidents were reported across the country at the beginning of the month, with people claiming to have been prevented from registering to vote. The opposition alliance, accusing the authorities of irregularities, urged the Government and the CENI to postpone the election. The official opening of election campaigning on 8 April was overshadowed by the death of a demonstrator in confrontations between opposition supporters and the security forces. At least seven people were reportedly killed, and around 150 injured, in violent clashes in Lomé between opposition and government supporters on 16 April. On the following day an estimated 30,000 people attended a rally at which Gnassingbé pledged to introduce free primary education and to secure the full restoration of EU development aid, if elected. President Tandja convened a meeting of all four presidential candidates in Niamey on 20 April, amid growing regional concern regarding the recent violence, but Bob Akitani refused to attend, insisting that it was too late for talks and that the election should be delayed. Two days later the Minister of the Interior, Security and Decentralization, Maj. François Akila Esso Boko, was dismissed after he, too, called for a postponement, citing a risk that the election could lead to civil war whatever its outcome. Bonfoh announced that the election would proceed as planned. Lawson withdrew his candidacy on the following day in protest at alleged irregularities in the electoral process (although his name remained on the ballot).

Voting in the presidential election took place in relatively peaceful conditions in most areas on 24 April 2005, although some violent incidents were reported, and at least three people were believed to have died in clashes between supporters of rival candidates. In an attempt to avert further violence, the day after the election Obasanjo, in his capacity as Chairman of the AU, summoned Gnassingbé and Gilchrist Olympio to Abuja for emergency talks, at which it was agreed that a government of national unity would be formed after the election if either Gnassingbé or Bob Akitani was elected as President. However, the announcement by the CENI, on 26 April, that preliminary results indicated a clear victory for Gnassingbé provoked widespread rioting, particularly in Lomé and Aného, east of the capital. The security forces quelled the unrest after two days. The six-party opposition coalition later stated that 106 people had been killed in the violence, although the Government estimated the death toll at 22, while thousands of others fled the country for neighbouring Benin and Ghana. Meanwhile, Bob Akitani refused to concede defeat, declaring that he had won the election. However, ECOWAS observers, while acknowledging that there had been some irregularities, stated that these had not been such as to invalidate the result. The EU had declined to send official monitors owing to concerns regarding the speed with which the election had been organized; however, a confidential EU report on the election that later surfaced apparently revealed that Western diplomats had observed incidents of fraud and intimidation of voters by the security forces. It was alleged that the names of some 900,000 non-existent voters had appeared on the electoral register. Gnassingbé and the international community appealed for reconciliation, while ECOWAS dispatched a delegation to Lomé in an attempt to negotiate a political solution to the crisis, but there was little evidence of any progress.

On 3 May 2005 the Constitutional Court declared the official results of the election, proclaiming Gnassingbé President, with 60.2% of the votes cast, and rejecting an opposition appeal for the polls to be annulled in nearly one-half of Togo's districts. Bob Akitani, Gnassingbé's closest rival, was attributed 38.3% of the votes. A turn-out of 63.6% of the electorate was recorded. Gnassingbé was inaugurated on the following day, amid increased security. By this time the office of the UN High Commissioner for Refugees (UNHCR) had registered 22,600 refugees in Benin and Ghana, mostly from southern areas of Togo. In mid-May the LTDH claimed that 790 people had been killed and 4,345 injured between 28 March (when the authorities began updating the electoral register) and 5 May, much higher figures than previous estimates. However, another human rights group, aligned to the Government, reported 58 deaths during this period. Gnassingbé later appointed a national commission of inquiry into the violence, headed by former Prime Minister Koffigoh. Meanwhile, the European Parliament adopted a resolution criticizing the conduct of the election and condemning the 'brutal repression' perpetrated by the police against people disputing its regularity. Nevertheless, the election result was generally accepted by the international community.

On 19 May 2005 Obasanjo chaired a reconciliation summit in Abuja, under the aegis of ECOWAS and the AU, which was attended by Gnassingbé, Gilchrist Olympio and other opposition leaders, as well as the Heads of State of Benin, Burkina Faso, Gabon, Ghana and Niger. (Bob Akitani was unable to participate owing to ill health.) The talks ended without agreement, however, as the 'radical' opposition alliance continued to reject the legitimacy of Gnassingbé's victory and demanded a full and independent investigation of alleged election irregularities as a precondition for engaging in substantive negotiations on a power-sharing arrangement. None the less, Gnassingbé subsequently held meetings with a number of opposition leaders to discuss the formation of a government of national unity. A split emerged in the six-party coalition, as most members decided to join the talks, while the UFC remained steadfast in its refusal to participate. In late May the AU removed sanctions against Togo, declaring that it considered conditions in Togo to be constitutional. Meanwhile, refugees continued to flee Togo, amid reports that opposition supporters were being arrested or kidnapped by the security forces, and by late May 34,416 had been registered by UNHCR (19,272 in Benin and 15,144 in Ghana). It was estimated that a further 10,000 people had been internally displaced within Togo. In June Gnassingbé created a High Commission for Refugees and Humanitarian Action.

On 8 June 2005 Gnassingbé designated Edem Kodjo, the leader of the moderate opposition CPP, as Prime Minister, replacing Sama. Gnassingbé's talks with five of the 'radical' opposition parties, which had hoped that one of their representatives would be appointed to the premiership, had earlier broken down when the President rejected a series of proposals presented by the parties, including demands for a rerun of the presidential election and increased powers for the Prime Minister. The formation of a 30-member Council of Ministers was announced later that month. The new Government was dominated by the RPT, although some members of the opposition and civil society received posts. Notably, Tchessa Abi of the PSR (part of the 'radical' opposition) was appointed as Keeper of the Seals, Minister of Justice; the other five members of the six-party coalition refused to participate and later condemned Abi's acceptance of a ministerial position, deciding to expel the PSR from the coalition. Zarifou Ayéva, the leader of the moderate opposition Parti pour la démocratie et le renouveau (PDR), became Minister of State, Minister of Foreign Affairs and African Integration, while an elder brother of the President, Kpatcha Gnassingbé, joined the Government as Minister-delegate at the Presidency of the Republic, responsible for Defence and Veterans. In September the UFC expelled Gabrial Sassouvi Dosseh-Anyroh from the party for accepting the position of Minister of Culture, Tourism and Leisure.

Reconciliation Efforts

Efforts to promote national reconciliation and to encourage the return of refugees dominated the new Government's agenda. The return of the refugees was discussed by Gnassingbé and Gilchrist Olympio at a meeting in Rome, Italy, in July 2005, at which the two men also condemned violence and agreed that political prisoners arrested during the electoral process should be released. Earlier that month the Government had announced that some 170 prisoners were to be released, including 48 opposition supporters who had been detained following the electoral violence. By early August the number of refugees in Benin exceeded 24,500, although no new arrivals had been registered in Ghana since the end of May and the number of internally displaced people was estimated to have declined from 10,000 to less than 4,000. In September the Government announced the establishment of a commission charged with re-examining Togo's history and making recommendations regarding the proposed rehabilitation of former Togolese leaders and other notable figures, including Sylvanus Olympio, the country's first President. Later that month Gnassingbé stated that he intended to organize legislative elections as quickly as possible, in conditions acceptable to all concerned. The EU had recently agreed to finance an electoral census.

In late September 2005 the office of the UN High Commissioner for Human Rights (UNHCHR) released a report stating that 400–500 people had been killed in Togo between 5 February and 5 May and that responsibility for the political violence and human rights violations that occurred during this period lay principally with the security forces, although opposition leaders were also criticized for failing to control militant supporters. The Togolese Government disputed UNHCHR's findings, and in November the national commission of inquiry into the violence reported that 154 people had died.

Representatives of Gnassingbé and Olympio held further talks in Rome in November 2005. Some 460 prisoners were released from detention in Lomé in that month; many of those freed were opposition supporters who had been involved in the post-election unrest. In December opposition supporters staged a protest march in Lomé, demanding the arrest and trial of those responsible for the deaths that followed the election.

The UFC criticized official celebrations held on 13 January 2006 to mark Liberation Day (the anniversary of the 1967 coup in which Eyadéma assumed power), claiming that they contradicted the new administration's promise of reconciliation. Nevertheless, on the same day a mass was also organized by the authorities in honour of Sylvanus Olympio, who was assassinated on 13 January 1963. Moreover, acting on a proposal made by the commission on Togo's history, for the first time in some 40 years the Government held festivities to celebrate Independence Day on 27 April. (However, the UFC refused to participate in the official celebrations, organizing its own event, which Gilchrist Olympio briefly returned from exile to attend.) Meanwhile, in a further gesture of reconciliation, four streets in Lomé were renamed after Sylvanus Olympio.

In March 2006, in an attempt to encourage the return of refugees, the Government abandoned judicial proceedings against alleged perpetrators of acts of violence related to the 2005 election, with the exception of those accused of 'bloody crimes'. Despite repeated government calls for their return, 19,870 Togolese refugees remained in Benin and 14,100 in Ghana in April, according to UNHCR.

The inter-Togolese national dialogue, which had broken down following the death of Eyadéma, finally resumed in Lomé in April 2006, with the participation of six political parties (the CAR, the CDPA—BT, the CPP, the PDR, the RPT and the UFC), as well as two civil society organizations and the Government; issues to be addressed included the revision of the electoral framework, institutional reform, the restructuring of the security forces and the situation of the refugees. The EU welcomed the renewed dialogue as an important stage in the implementation of the 22 measures agreed in April 2004 for the resumption of full economic co-operation. In July participants in the dialogue designated the President of Burkina Faso, Blaise Compaoré, to act as a facilitator in future negotiations. Meanwhile, following a meeting in Brussels to consider Togo's progress in strengthening democracy, the EU decided to disburse €15m. (some 10,000m. francs CFA) to the Government in support of further reform.

Following talks, held in the Burkinabè capital, Ouagadougou, under the mediation of Compaoré, on 20 August 2006 the nine participants in the national dialogue formally signed a comprehensive political accord at a ceremony in Lomé. The agreement provided, *inter alia*, for the formation of a government of national unity, the organization of legislative elections by October 2007, the re-establishment of the CENI, the revision of the electoral register, the creation of a commission of inquiry into past political violence and the establishment of a committee charged with accelerating the return of refugees from Benin and Ghana (now estimated to number a total of 16,500). In early September 2006, during a European tour that included visits to Brussels and Paris, France, Gnassingbé was successful in securing financial support for the transitional process.

In mid-September 2006 Agboyibo, who had chaired the board of the national dialogue, was designated Prime Minister. The transitional Council of Ministers, which included members of six political parties, as well as several representatives of civil society, was formed a few days later. The UFC, which had initially been allocated four portfolios, refused to participate in the new administration, rejecting Agboyibo's appointment and complaining that the RPT had secured the most significant portfolios, although the party's Second Vice-President, Amah Gnassingbé, accepted the post of Minister of State on an 'individual basis'. Former Prime Minister Edem Kodjo was appointed Minister of State at the Presidency later that month. In mid-October the Assemblée nationale named the 19 members of the new CENI, which comprised five members from the presidential coalition, 10 from opposition parties (including the UFC), two from civil society organizations and two from the Government. Shortly afterwards the CENI proposed that the legislative elections be held on 24 June 2007.

From November 2006 monthly meetings of the nine signatory parties to the August accord were held to monitor the progress of its implementation. These talks were brokered by Compaoré and also attended by representatives of the EU and ECOWAS. The Assemblée nationale adopted amendments to the electoral code in February 2007, notably returning full responsibility for organizing, as well as supervising, elections to the CENI. In May the legislative elections were delayed until 5 August, and in July they were postponed indefinitely owing to ongoing difficulties in finalizing preparations. Voter registration was scheduled to be completed on 17 August.

HUMAN RIGHTS ISSUES

In early May 1999 Amnesty International published a report detailing numerous abuses of human rights allegedly committed by the security forces in Togo, claiming that hundreds of political opponents of Eyadéma had been killed following the 1998 presidential election. The Government reacted with indignation to the report, and threatened to institute legal proceedings against the organization. In early May four human rights activists, all members of the opposition CDPA—BT, were detained by the authorities, accused of providing Amnesty with false information. The four men were released on bail in June. In the same month Amnesty accused the Togolese security forces of the detention and torture of one of their members, Amen Ayodole, although the authorities claimed that Ayodole had been detained on suspicion of drugs-smuggling.

In July 1999 a human rights organization in Benin reported that, following the 1998 presidential election in Togo, corpses had been discovered on the beaches of Benin. The Government of Benin, however, stated that it had received no such intelligence, and called for witnesses to come forward with evidence. In late July Eyadéma agreed to the establishment of an international commission of inquiry into the allegations, and he urged the UN and the OAU to assist in the creation of a suitable independent body. A commission of inquiry was subsequently established in June 2000. In January 2001 Amnesty International issued demands that the report by the UN-OAU joint commission of inquiry be made public. In February the Minister of the Interior, Security and Decentralization, Gen. Sizing Walla, accused Amnesty International of having received US $500,000m. from Gilchrist Olympio prior to the publication of its 1999 report. Walla claimed that the Government was in possession of letters, reportedly written by Olympio, to the Secretary-General of Amnesty International, Pierre Sané, which confirmed these allegations, although the UFC rejected these claims. Later in February the report of the joint UN-OAU commission was published, concluding that 'systematic violations of human rights' had occurred in Togo in 1998, and that allegations of extra-judicial executions, particularly of opposition party activists, could not be refuted. Although the commission had been unable to establish the quantity of corpses found in the sea or on beaches following the election, or to confirm reports that bodies had been dropped into the sea by aircraft, it stated that individuals linked to the security forces appeared to be responsible for such killings, and recommended that the authorities punish those responsible, and that a special rapporteur be appointed to monitor human rights in Togo. However, both the Government and the President of the Assemblée nationale, Ouattara Fambaré Natchaba, dismissed the report's conclusions, emphasizing that the commission had been unable to substantiate some of its findings. In March 2001 Prime Minister Agbéyomé Kodjo appeared before UNHCHR to deny the findings of the report.

During its discussions with the EU in April 2004 (see above), the Government pledged to release all political prisoners and guarantee the absence in Togo of extra-judicial executions, torture and other inhumane and degrading acts. In May the Government stated that it had been unable to identify any political prisoners, but was to consult with non-governmental organizations in this regard; the UFC claimed that 11 of its members were in detention, including nine who had been convicted earlier that month of public order offences and illegal possession of weapons. The International Federation of Human Rights Leagues (FIDH), which had visited Togo in February, released a report severely criticizing the Government's human rights record in June; the Government rejected the allegations contained in the report. Seven UFC militants were among some 494 prisoners released in August, having been pardoned by the President, although the authorities denied that they had been political detainees.

Following the presidential election in April 2005, human rights groups expressed serious concerns about human rights in Togo, claiming that the thousands of people leaving the country for Benin and Ghana were fleeing severe harassment from the security forces. In May the FIDH denounced a 'serious and systematic' abuse of human rights in Togo, urging the UN and the AU to conduct an international inquiry into the alleged violations. In mid-June UNHCHR commenced an investigation into allegations of killings, abductions and political persecution. In an attempt to address concerns, a new Ministry of Human Rights, Democracy and Reconciliation was created later that month from the restructuring of the former Ministry of the Promotion of Democracy and the Rule of Law. In mid-July the LTDH claimed that it was still receiving complaints of political persecution from opponents of the Government, despite government assurances that it was safe for those who had fled the country to return. The Government dismissed allegations of human rights abuses. Meanwhile, the Government announced plans to release some 170 prisoners, including political detainees; a further 460 prisoners were freed in November. Later in July Amnesty International issued a report denouncing human rights violations allegedly perpetrated by the Togolese security forces and pro-Government militias before and after the presidential election. The Togolese Government condemned the organization's investigation, which was based on testimony from refugees in camps in Benin. UNHCHR's report on pre- and post-election violence and alleged human rights violations, which was published in September (see above), stated that torture and inhumane treatment had been widely used by the security forces during the unrest. In April 2006 Amnesty International released a report criticizing the Government for failing to prosecute those responsible for crimes committed during the 2005 election period and claiming that a culture of impunity had existed in Togo for more than 30 years. In response, the Minister of Justice defended the Government's actions since taking office, stating that people suspected of lesser acts of violence had been freed in the interests of national reconciliation and that the issue of impunity would be addressed by the national dialogue that had resumed that month. Following the signature of a memorandum of understanding with the Togolese Government in July 2006, UNHCHR opened an office in Lomé. Amnesty International issued a further report in January 2007, again urging the Togolese authorities to prosecute those suspected of perpetrating violent crimes in 2005. More than 100 Togolese were reported to have filed cases related to the election violence with the judiciary. The Government insisted that progress was being made in this regard, making reference to the commitment made in the political accord of August 2006 to create a commission to investigate past political violence.

FOREIGN RELATIONS

The issue of Ewe reunification has at times led to difficult relations with Ghana. In the late 1950s President Kwamé Nkrumah of Ghana assisted Togo in its campaign for independence, but with the intention of integrating Togo into Ghana. When this objective failed, Nkrumah subjected Togo to constant harassment, through trade embargoes and border closures. Relations improved after the assassination of Sylvanus Olympio, and Nkrumah was the first to recognize the new Government. However, relations between the two countries deteriorated as Togo's political crisis of the early 1990s intensified, and the presence of Togolese opposition leaders in Ghana prompted renewed suspicion in Lomé that the Ghanaian authorities were supporting elements that might seek to destabilize the Eyadéma regime.

By late 1994 relations with Ghana had improved considerably. In November full diplomatic relations, suspended since 1982, were formally resumed, and in December Togo's border with Ghana, which had been closed since January 1994, was reopened. In July 1995, following talks between Eyadéma and President Jerry Rawlings of Ghana, agreement was reached providing for the reactivation of the Ghana-Togo Joint Commission for Economic, Social and Technical Co-operation and the Ghana-Togo Border Demarcation Commission. In August Togo signed an accord with UNHCR, providing for the introduction of a programme of voluntary repatriation for Togolese exiles from Ghana and Benin. By December 1996 some 40,500 Togolese exiles, of an estimated total of 48,000, had reportedly been repatriated from Ghana. The newly elected President of Ghana, John Kufuor, visited Togo to mark the celebrations for Liberation Day on 13 January 2001; this visit, while said by Kufuor to reflect his desire to promote good relations with neighbouring countries, provoked controversy internationally, within Ghana and among the Togolese opposition. The Togolese authorities emphasized that the annual holiday commemorated the bloodless coup of 13 January 1967, and not the military uprising that occurred on the same day under Eyadéma's leadership in 1963. Thousands of Togolese sought refuge in Benin and Ghana from late April 2005, fleeing the violence that followed the presidential election (see above). By the end of 2005 UNHCR had registered 26,632 Togolese refugees in Benin and 14,136 in Ghana. Many refugees subsequently returned to Togo, following the restoration of stability, and by the end of 2006 9,444 remained in Benin and 8,517 in Ghana. Repatriation efforts continued in 2007.

Relations with France have improved in recent years, following the resumption of civil co-operation with Togo in June 1994. Relations were further strengthened with the election in 1995 of Jacques Chirac as French President. In 1998 the French authorities criticized the lack of opposition participation in the legislative elections, and in June 1999 the French Government hosted talks in Paris between the Government and opposition groups, which led to an agreement to hold further talks in Lomé in July. In July, while on an official visit to West Africa, Chirac visited Lomé and met the participants in the reconciliation talks. Gilchrist Olympio, however, refused to meet Chirac, accusing him of favouring Eyadéma. Prior to his visit to Togo, Chirac received an open letter from Amnesty International, asking him to exert pressure on Eyadéma to improve Togo's record on human rights, which Amnesty had recently criticized in a published report. Chirac, however, condemned Amnesty's report as a 'manipulation', and vigorously denied accusations of French complicity in Togolese abuses. Following Eyadéma's re-election in June 2003, it was reported that France favoured a relaxation of EU sanctions against Togo, on the grounds that the international observers of the polls had not reported any flagrant irregularities, and Chirac subsequently attempted to persuade his European counterparts to resume co-operation with Togo. Chirac urged the Togolese authorities to respect the Constitution following Faure Gnassingbé's installation as President in February 2005, and welcomed Gnassingbé's subsequent decision to stand down. Chirac congratulated Gnassingbé on his victory in the presidential election held in April. During a visit by Gnassingbé to Paris in September 2006, Chirac announced the provision of €5m. to assist the political transition in Togo. A further €3m. was granted by France in July 2007 for the organization of forthcoming legislative elections. Additional aid was disbursed by the EU for this purpose.

From mid-1998, in his capacity as Chairman of the Authority of Heads of State and Government of ECOWAS, Eyadéma mediated in the conflict in Guinea-Bissau. A contingent of Togolese troops was sent to Guinea-Bissau as part of the ECOWAS cease-fire monitoring group, and a peace conference was held in Lomé in February 1999. In June, after the failure of the peace agreement, the Togolese contingent withdrew from Guinea-Bissau. Eyadéma also mediated in the conflicts in Sierra Leone in 1999, and in Côte d'Ivoire from late 2002. Togo contributed troops to the ECOWAS military mission that was deployed in Côte d'Ivoire from January 2003 and to the UN Operation in Côte d'Ivoire (UNOCI) that succeeded it in April 2004. In September 2003 a contingent of 150 Togolese troops was dispatched to serve in the ECOWAS Mission in Liberia (ECOMIL), which was replaced by the UN Mission in Liberia (UNMIL) in October. In March 2004 the former President of the Central African Republic, Ange-Félix Patassé, who had been deposed in March 2003, was granted asylum in Togo.

Gnassingbé's assumption of power following the death of his father, Eyadéma, in February 2005 (see above) was condemned by West African countries and the wider international community. Relations with Nigeria were particularly strained that month when the Togolese authorities refused to allow an aeroplane carrying an advance delegation of President Olusegun Obasanjo's aides to land in Lomé ahead of planned talks between an ECOWAS mission and Gnassingbé. However, Obasanjo subsequently assumed a significant role in regional efforts to persuade Gnassingbé to stand down, and later mediated between Gnassingbé and Togolese opposition leaders. Gnassingbé's resignation as Head of State at the end of February, to allow an election to take place, was widely welcomed, and his victory in the poll in April was generally accepted by the international community, despite some concerns over electoral irregularities. At a summit meeting held in

Abuja in February 2007, Obasanjo, Gnassingbé and the President of Benin, Boni Yayi, announced the formation of a Co-Prosperity Alliance Zone, aimed at accelerating the integration of their national economies and promoting peace, stability and development in West Africa. Later that month the electricity networks of Benin and Nigeria were officially connected, enabling energy to be supplied from Nigeria to Togo (via Benin) at a lower cost.

Economy

CHARLOTTE VAILLANT

Based on an earlier article by EDITH HODGKINSON

At independence in 1960, Togo's economy, compared with those of most of its neighbours, was relatively advanced. Over the last 25 years, however, the economy has declined to such an extent that Togo is now classified as a 'least developed country'. This in part reflected strained relationships with donors, concomitant with poor economic management. In 2005, according to estimates by the World Bank, Togo's gross national income (GNI) per head was US $350, the third lowest in the Union économique et monétaire de l'Afrique de l'Ouest, after Guinea-Bissau and Niger.

In the years following independence, rates of population growth and urbanization continued at a high level, and population density is markedly higher than the average for countries of the West Africa region. In 2003 some 35.2% of the population were estimated to live in urban areas. According to World Bank estimates, annual population growth in 1995–2005 averaged 3.1% In most years there is seasonal migration, of around 100,000 Togolese annually, to neighbouring Ghana and Benin.

Severe economic problems which beset the country during the 1980s (see below) reduced growth in gross domestic product (GDP) to an average of 0.5% per year in 1981–90. GDP was estimated to have decreased each year in 1981–83 because of drought, the slump in phosphate production, the recession in neighbouring economies, and measures of economic adjustment in response to these adverse trends. There was an upturn in 1988–89, when average annual growth of 4.0% was recorded, reflecting increases in both production of and international prices for phosphates and an easing in the financing constraint following the rescheduling of the public debt (see below). GDP declined by 1.0% in 1990, as a result of lower world prices for Togo's export commodities. Despite a three-year programme of economic reform that was adopted in 1989 (with support from IMF funds), GDP continued to contract, by an annual average of 9.7% in 1991–93, as political unrest disrupted agricultural distribution and phosphate production. Foreign aid and investment flows also declined dramatically in response to the political unrest, severely weakening the country's fiscal and external payments position. In January 1994 the CFA franc underwent a 50% devaluation, and in mid-year the Government adopted a comprehensive adjustment strategy. The resultant increase in economic activity led to real GDP growth of 13.9% in that year, although this represented little more than economic recovery from the downturn of 1992–93. Further GDP growth, averaging 6.6%, was recorded in 1995–96, owing largely to improved performances in the mining and manufacturing sectors and a recovery in the cash-crop sector.

The Government's economic programme for 1997–99, supported by programmes from the IMF and World Bank, aimed to achieve sustained and diversified economic growth and a viable external position, although not all of the targets of the programme were fulfilled. According to the IMF, real GDP growth was 4.3% in 1997. Real GDP declined by 2.3% in 1998 before increasing by 2.4% in 1999. It declined again by 1.6% in 2000, but the economy recovered in 2001 and 2002 owing to increased agricultural and phosphate productions and real GDP growth rose by 2.9% and 4.1%, respectively. Real GDP contracted by 1.3% in 2003, but rebounded to 3.7% in 2004, despite a fall in phosphate output, largely owing to good agricultural performance and increased port activity. It is worth noting that these GDP figures have recently been revised, with crop years now being categorized in the calendar year they begin. According to the IMF, real GDP growth was positive but subdued in 2006, at an estimated 1.8%. Consumer prices remained constant in 1999 and increased by 1.9% in 2000, although more substantial increases, of 3.9% and 3.1%, were recorded in 2001 and 2002, respectively. Consumer prices declined by 0.9% in 2003, and remained broadly constant in 2004. According to preliminary figures, they increased by 6.8% in 2005, reflecting higher prices for food and petroleum products. Average inflation declined in 2006, to 2.2%.

At mid-2007 the country's long-term economic prospects remained dependent on progress made towards the restoration of relations with international donors and the resumption of external assistance, notably from the European Union (EU).

AGRICULTURE

Agriculture (including livestock, forestry and fishing) was by far the dominant economic activity in 2006, accounting for 37.8% of GDP, while accounting for an estimated 56.7% of the economically active population in mid-2005, according to FAO. During 1995–2005, according to the World Bank, agricultural GDP increased at an average annual rate of 3.2%; agricultural GDP increased by 3.7% in 2005. In non-drought years Togo is self-sufficient in basic foodstuffs. Food supplies are supplemented by fishing, but Togo's narrow coastline constrains activity, which is mainly artisanal. None the less, modern vessels are used, although the total catch—29,500 tons in 2004—is insufficient to satisfy domestic demand. The livestock sector contributes to—but does not satisfy—the local meat and dairy market. Livestock numbers in 2004, according to FAO estimates, were 1.9m. sheep, 1.5m. goats, 320,000 pigs and 280,000 cattle.

Production in the cash-crop sector has, on the whole, recovered since the decline recorded in the mid-1970s. The most important contribution has come from cotton, which is now the country's principal export crop. After falling to negligible levels in the second half of the 1970s, output of seed cotton rose strongly, reaching 99,600 metric tons in 1990, reflecting increases in the area under cultivation. Output in subsequent years increased, reaching 180,000 tons in 1998 and averaged 173,200 tons in 2001–04. However, delays by the cotton parastatal in paying farmers resulted in a marked switch to other crops, and consequently cotton output declined sharply to 65,400 tons in 2005 and 45,300 tons in 2006.

Coffee output fluctuated widely in the 1980s, increasing significantly in the second half of the decade, as a result of an improvement in climatic conditions, the impact of replanting programmes and higher producer prices. Annual output in the second half of the 1990s fluctuated in the range 10,000–22,000 metric tons. Annual output has since remained below 10,000 tons, amounting to 9,300 tons in 2005. Groundnut production has also fluctuated markedly, with annual output in the 1990s ranging from the 21,843 tons recorded in 1991 to record production of 55,420 tons in 1996. Annual output in 2001–05 stabilized at an annual average of 36,821 tons. Output of cocoa beans declined from a peak of 29,000 tons in 1971 until the early 2000s, largely owing to the ageing of cocoa bushes, which consequently produce lower yields. Output fell further from 10,200 tons in 2000 to 3,700 tons in 2003 and has since remained roughly at 4,000 tons per year.

The Government's agricultural development programme has received substantial foreign support, including grants from the European Development Fund (EDF) and France's Fonds d'Aide et de Coopération (FAC), for the development of coffee, cocoa and cotton production in the south, the most developed area. Credits have also come from the concessionary lending body of the World Bank, the International Development Association (IDA), for rural development projects, intended to increase the area under cultivation and to introduce cotton, maize, sorghum and groundnut crops. It is also planned to develop irrigated agriculture—rice, sugar cane, fruits and vegetables. The Anié sugar complex, in central Togo, was inaugurated in 1987. The complex has the capacity to refine 60,000 metric tons of sugar cane annually. Other projects intend to increase self-sufficiency in animal protein by encouraging the rearing of cattle, pigs and poultry.

MINING AND POWER

Traditionally the main stimulus to Togo's exports—and overall economic growth—has come from phosphate mining. Phosphates were discovered in Togo in 1952, and exports began in 1961. Togo's phosphate deposits are the richest in the world, with a mineral content of 81%. Reserves of first-grade ore are estimated at 260m. metric tons, while there are more than 1,000m. tons of carbon phosphates, which, although of a lower quality, have the advantage of a significantly lower cadmium content (see below). In the early 1990s the country ranked fifth among the world's producers of calcium phosphates, and they accounted for almost one-half of Togo's domestic export receipts (excluding re-exports) in 1991. However, with the relatively rapid growth of cotton and non-traditional exports since 1994, the contribution of phosphate to Togo's export revenue has declined. Phosphates accounted for 27.4% of domestic export earnings (excluding re-exports) in 1998, and subsequently declined further; they contributed to only 12.6% of Togo's export revenue in 2001 and 7.5% in 2003. In 2004 they accounted for an estimated 6.9% of export earnings. National output of phosphates declined steadily in the late 1990s, from 2,250m. tons in 1998 to 1,067m. tons in 2001, as increasing concern was expressed at the high cadmium content of Togolese phosphates. Revenue from exports of phosphates totalled 40,100m. francs CFA in 1999, compared with the 55,800m. francs CFA achieved in 1998. After lengthy negotiations with creditors, the Government agreed to open the heavily indebted Office Togolais des Phosphates (OTP) to private ownership, and in 1997 a 38% share in the company's capital was offered for sale. At the end of 2001 the OTP was dissolved and replaced by a new management company, International Fertilizers Group-Togo (IFG-TG). The new company rehabilitated the production equipment associated with phosphate mining, resulting in an increase in output, to 1,271m. tons in 2002 and to 1,471m. tons in 2003. Exports of phosphates subsequently rose from 1,328m. tons in 2002 to 1,356m. tons in 2003. However, the new management contract was broken in 2003 following a dispute with the Government, which resulted in a significant decline in phosphate production in 2004 and 2005, to 1,115m. tons and 1,021m. tons, respectively. Production in 2006 remained largely unchanged.

Togo also possesses extensive limestone reserves (some 200m. metric tons), utilization of which began in 1981 at a large-scale cement plant run by Ciments de l'Afrique de l'Ouest (CIMAO), with an output of 600,000 tons of clinker (one-half of capacity). Although CIMAO went into liquidation in 1989, the construction industry revived in the following two years, with continued work on the Nangbeto dam (see below) and on offices of the regional central bank and the Economic Community of West African States. Cement production has therefore continued under the Société des Ciments du Togo (CIMTOGO), a parastatal organization operated in co-operation with Norwegian interests, with an annual capacity of 780,000 tons. Some 2.4m. tons of limestone were extracted in 2003, according to the US Geological Survey. Production of cement and clinker rose from 987,000 tons in 2002 to 2.3m. tons in 2003, before easing off to 1.7m. tons in 2004, 1.5m. tons in 2005 and 1.5m. tons in 2006. Exploitation of reserves of marble at Gnaoulou and Pagola (estimated at 20m. tons) began in 1970 by the Société Togolaise de Marbrerie (later restructured, with Norwegian participation, as the Nouvelle Société Togolaise de Marbrerie et de Matériaux—Nouvelle SOTOMA). In 1999 it was reported that deposits of petroleum and gas had been discovered in Togolese territorial waters by Petroleum Geo-Service of Norway. In October 2002 the Togolese Government, the Hunt Oil Co of the USA and Petronas Carigali of Malaysia signed a joint-venture oil-production agreement, providing for the first offshore drilling in Togolese territorial waters. However, following unsuccessful exploration tests, Hunt Oil withdrew from the project in mid-2005. A two-year exploration deal was signed with Oranto Petroleum of Nigeria in January 2007. Mining and quarrying accounted for 2.7% of GDP in 2006.

Electricity shortages have long impaired Togo's economy. Despite progress being made in building its domestic capacity, the country is still dependent on unreliable supply from the Akosombo hydroelectric installation in Ghana and, to a lesser extent, Côte d'Ivoire's gas-fired station in Azito. The economy was particularly affected by the shortages of electricity in 1998 and 2003, owing to receding water levels in Lake Volta, Ghana, which feeds the Akasombo hydroelectric dam. Domestic electricity was, in the past, generated mainly at a thermal plant in Lomé and a small hydroelectric installation at Kpalimé. Beginning in 1988, however, supplies were enhanced by the 65-MW hydroelectric plant at Nangbeto, on the Mono river, constructed in co-operation with Benin. The plant has a maximum capacity of 150m. kWh, and also provides irrigation for 43,000 ha of land. In 2001 domestic electricity generation was 85m. kWh. In early 2004 the Togolese and Beninois authorities announced that the Adjarala hydroelectric installation, also on the Mono river, was to be modernized, and its production capacity increased markedly; however this has not been implemented as a result of disagreement between the governments of Benin and Togo over the project's funding.

In August 1999 six companies including Chevron, Royal Dutch Shell, and the Société Togolaise de Gaz concluded arrangements to construct a US $400m. pipeline, which will supply natural gas from Nigeria to Togo, Benin and Ghana. A government agreement on the pipeline was reached in February 2000. After continuous delays, construction works began in the last quarter of 2005. The pipeline is now expected to come on stream by the end of 2007. The electricity grid of Togo and Benin was in the mean time connected to that of Nigeria in early 2007. In 2005, according to the Union Monétaire et Économique de l'Afrique de l'Ouest, domestic production in Togo totalled 50,600 MWh, while imports amounted to 478,000 MWh. An estimated 18% of the population had access to electricity, falling to 5% in rural areas.

In 2000 the management of the CEET, which was subsequently renamed Togo Electricité, was ceded to a consortium consisting of Hydro-Québec of Canada and Elyo of France under a 20-year contract. The Government was, however, to retain control of the company. But the relationship with the consortium deteriorated in 2005 over a contractual dispute and, in February 2006, the Government eventually cancelled the 20-year contract.

INDUSTRY

The manufacturing sector is small and relatively undeveloped, accounting for 7.5% of GDP in 2006. Continued electricity shortages, a weak financial sector and low economic growth hamper its development and performance. Manufacturing was, in the past, centred on the processing of agricultural commodities (palm oil extraction, coffee roasting, cassava flour milling, and cotton ginning) and import substitution of consumer goods—textiles, footwear, beverages, confectionery, salt and tyres. An integrated textile mill, which cost 10,000m. francs CFA and has a capacity of 24,000 metric tons per year, began operations at Kara in 1981, and the expansion of domestic cotton production led to the establishment of two further plants, at Notse and Atakpamé. A cotton-ginning plant was inaugurated at Talo in January 1991, with a total capacity of 50,000 tons of seed cotton per year. By 1999 Togo had a total cotton-ginning capacity of 150,000 tons, of which 110,000 tons was located in state-owned factories. At early 1999 some 230,000 Togolese were reported to depend on the cotton sector for their livelihoods. New palm oil mills have been installed to complement the development of plantations. On the whole, however, the industrialization programme of the late 1970s proved to be an expensive failure, and large-scale projects have not featured in subsequent plans.

In order to improve economic efficiency and reduce the fiscal burden of financing unproductive investments, the Government has gradually withdrawn from its dominant role in the productive sectors. It has sold (either wholly or partially) or leased a number of state enterprises to the private sector as well as liquidating the most unprofitable ventures. By the end of 1990 the assets of 30 companies had been transferred to private ownership, and 18 others were intended for privatization. Following the resumption of the economic reform programme in 1994, there were renewed efforts to further the privatization process; the Government has continued to reduce its holdings in a number of hotels, in cement production and in agri-processing. Only little progress was made by the government in the privatization of state-owned banks, but private management contracts were awarded for several companies with the aim of improving their financial position prior to divestiture. Meanwhile, it was expected that manufacturing aimed at export markets would be stimulated by the establishment of a free-trade zone at Lomé, which was inaugurated in 1990. By the end of 1991 a total of 15 companies had invested some 56,000m. francs CFA in the zone; most of these, however, suspended operations during 1992–93, owing to the political upheaval. In 1994 the Government resumed the promotion of its free-trade zone project, and by mid-1996 some 30 companies were operating in the zone. A second free-trade zone was subsequently opened, and provision was made for free-zone terms to apply to certain businesses operating outside the regions. Instability in Côte d'Ivoire caused some businesses to relocate their activity in neighbouring countries, which benefited Togo's free trade zone in 2003 and 2004.

TRANSPORT AND TOURISM

Communications are made difficult by the country's long, narrow shape. However, the road network (7,520 km in 1996, of which 2,376 km were paved) was substantially updated during the 1980s, with aid from the EDF, IDA and FAC. The railways, with 355 km of track, are generally in need of modernization, and two lines, to Palimé and Aného, have been closed to passenger traffic. The national railway company, the Société Nationale des Chemins de Fer du Togo, was transferred to private ownership in January 2002. The new owners, West African Cement (Wacem), were expected further to develop the railway's freight capacity, which had become increasingly significant in the late 1990s, as the number of passengers declined. The port of Lomé handled about 2m. metric tons of freight per year in the late 1980s and early 1990s, following an increase in its capacity at the beginning of the 1980s, which afforded new facilities for handling minerals and for fishing. In 1986 work began in Lomé on the first bulk grain transhipment facility in West Africa. The level of freight handled declined to 1.1m. tons in 1993, as the political crisis in Togo resulted in the diversion of a large proportion of transit trade to Benin. The level of freight later recovered substantially, to reach 2.0m. tons in 1996 and 2.8m. tons in 1999. In 1995 the BOAD approved a loan of 5,000m. francs CFA to help finance the rehabilitation of the infrastructure at Lomé port. The port was transferred to private-sector management in January 2002 and further investments were planned. As a result of the civil conflict that commenced in Côte d'Ivoire in September 2002 the port has been a beneficiary of entrepôt trade displaced from that country; although the political instability in Togo in mid-2005 that followed the death of President Gnassingbé Eyadéma, had the effect of diverting some of this trade to other neighbouring countries, this trend was reversed after the holding of presidential elections. Overall, since the port has been under private management, container traffic has increased markedly, from 60,000 TEU (twenty-foot equivalent unit) in 2001 to 212,000 TEU in 2005. There are international airports at Tokoin, near Lomé, and at Niamtougou, in the north of the country, as well as several smaller airfields.

Tourism, formerly a major source of foreign exchange, suffered from the political crises of the 1990s. Visitor numbers, which reached a record 143,000 in 1982, declined to a low of 22,244 in 1993. In 2003 there were 60,952 international arrivals, the highest figure recorded since 1999, and arrivals further increased, to 82,686, in 2004, before declining marginally to 80,763 in 2005. Receipts from tourism (including passenger transport) increased from US $11m. in 2000 to $26m. in 2003 but were likely to have suffered from political instability in 2005. The privatization of most state-owned hotels was initiated in early 1997. In addition to recreational tourism, efforts have been made to promote Togo as an international conference centre, for which the country is reasonably well equipped.

PUBLIC FINANCE

In the past Togo's official investment targets have been attained or even exceeded, but in the late 1970s and early 1980s development spending had to be reduced as part of the Government's austerity programme. Reflecting the influence of the IMF, the 1985–90 Development Plan involved relatively modest targets: an average rise in real GNI of 1.9% per year, and an emphasis on the maintenance and rehabilitation of existing investment projects, particularly in areas such as infrastructure and rural development. By the late 1980s, however, funding at the anticipated level had not been procured, rendering the investment target unattainable.

One of the major objectives of the Development Plans was the strengthening of the Government's revenue position. Togo was able to finance a rising capital programme in the 1970s because of the strong expansion in budget revenue, largely owing to higher receipts from phosphate mining and indirect taxation. However, the worsening in the payments situation after 1978 (and a downturn in phosphate production from 1980) necessitated recourse to IMF capital support, which required, in turn, a reduction in the growth of spending to an average of 5% per year in 1979–81. Fiscal austerity continued in 1982–84, with increases in taxation, a continuation of constraints on development spending, and a 'freeze' on public-sector salaries. These trends were scheduled to continue throughout the 1985–90 Plan period. However, with the ending of the public-sector salary 'freeze' in 1987, and as a result of lower commodity prices and higher producer prices, the budget deficit almost doubled in 1987, to the equivalent of 6.8% of GDP. However, the proportion was reduced in 1988, to 3.3%, as a result of higher receipts from taxation, strict controls on current expenditure, and a sharp decline in capital spending. The deficit was little changed in 1989 and 1990, and the primary budget (excluding interest payments) was estimated to have been almost in balance in 1991. However, with the onset of political unrest and suspension of financial support by major external creditors, total budget receipts declined considerably, by 47.4% in 1993. The situation in 1993 was exacerbated by the nine-month general strike (beginning in November 1992), which directly affected both generation and collection of revenue, with the larger than expected budgetary shortfall requiring recourse to foreign reserves. By March 1995 the majority of major external creditors had resumed financial co-operation. In July the Government introduced value-added tax on commercial operations, replacing the general business tax, primarily in order to simplify fiscal management. However, reductions in domestic and external debt arrears, undertaken following pressure from creditors, resulted in an overall budget deficit of 35,000m. francs CFA in 1995 (equivalent to some 6.3% of GDP). Togo's overall budget deficit for 2000 was 43,200m. francs CFA (equivalent to 4.7% of GDP). The deficit narrowed to 19,600m. francs CFA (2.1% of GDP) in 2001 and to 15,900m. francs CFA (1.6% of GDP) in 2002. In 2003 Togo's budget balance moved to a surplus, at 24,400 francs CFA (2.5% of GDP) owing to increased revenue, which accounted for 17% of GDP, compared with 12.3% in 2002. In April 2004 the IMF expressed concern at Togo's continued accumulation of domestic and external payments arrears and urged the authorities to further improve revenue collection. However, a stagnation in revenue and increased expenditure resulted in the budget surplus decreasing to 9,800m. francs CFA in 2004 (0.9% of

GDP). This trend was exacerbated in 2005, when Togo recorded a budget deficit of 27,000m. francs CFA (2.4% of GDP). The fiscal situation improved after the Government agreed a staff monitored programme with the IMF in late 2006. The IMF notably commended the Government for recovering tax arrears, curtailing off-budget operations and paying back some domestic arrears. External arrears continued to accumulate, however (see below). The 2006 budget saw the deficit increase to 32,300m. francs CFA, equivalent to 2.8% of GDP.

FOREIGN TRADE AND PAYMENTS

Togo's chronic deficit on foreign trade worsened after the mid-1970s, as export earnings declined as a proportion of import spending. A record trade deficit, of US $173.8m., was achieved in 1979, although the deficit then narrowed substantially (and in 1984 even recorded a modest surplus) as earnings from both phosphates and cocoa improved, while imports were restricted. In 1986, with the renewed decline in international prices for Togo's export commodities, the trade deficit widened again, to $56.2m. It remained close to this level for the rest of the 1980s. The situation worsened considerably in 1992 and 1993, as political disorder resulted in a decrease in exports exceeding the concurrent contraction in imports, producing a deficit of $127.7m. and $111.3m. respectively, according to the IMF. However, these figures do not take into account smuggling, the importance of which would have increased substantially during the political unrest. According to IMF figures, the deficit declined to $37.1m. in 1994. In 2002 Togo recorded a visible trade deficit of $151.4m., when a current-account deficit of $139.9m. was recorded. In 2003 the trade deficit was $156.8m., and the deficit on the current account of the balance of payments was $161.9m.

Falling exports coupled with rising oil and food imports caused the trade deficit to widen to 133,300m. francs CFA (equivalent to $251.8m.) in 2004 and to an estimated 182,800 francs CFA in 2005 and 224,000 francs CFA in 2006. Private transfers continued in part to compensate for the trade deficit, although the current account deficit rose from 30,200m. francs CFA (3% of GDP) in 2004 to 58,900m. francs CFA (5.3% of GDP) in 2005, and to 70,100m. francs CFA (6.0% of GDP) in 2006.

In 2002 the principal source of imports was France (20.4%); other major suppliers were Côte d'Ivoire, Canada, Belgium and Germany. However, in 2003 the People's Republic of China became Togo's principal supplier of imports, accounting for 27.7% of total imports in 2005. India was second (11.6%) and France was the third largest supplier (10.5%). The principal markets for exports are regional neighbouring countries: in 2005 Burkina Faso took 15.9% of Togo's total exports; other significant purchasers were Ghana, Benin and Mali. The principal exports in 2004 were cotton and phosphates. The principal imports in 2004 were capital goods, petroleum products and foodstuffs.

Since the services side of the current payments account shows a structural deficit, it is usually left to grants and loans to cover the shortfall. Togo's receipts of Official Development Assistance (ODA) from bilateral and multilateral creditors have tended to be lower, and on slightly less concessionary terms, than those of other countries in francophone West Africa. In 1991–95 the country received an annual average of US $168m. of ODA. In 1991, in order to exert pressure on the Eyadéma administration to expedite democratic reform, France, Germany and the USA (the three leading sources of bilateral aid) suspended development aid, while military assistance from the USA and France was suspended in 1992. By 1996 ODA flows had increased to $166m., which, according to the World Bank, constituted about 12% of GDP and 85% of gross domestic investment. Net ODA to Togo had declined to $70m. by 2000, however, and declined further in 2001, to $44m., before increasing slightly, to $51m., in 2002. Net ODA totalled $47m. in 2003 and increased to $61m. in 2004. France typically contributes more than one-half of the country's ODA.

From 1993 the EU confined the aid it grants to Togo to 'vital projects' in disease control, sanitation and education. The bulk of the seventh EDF grant—some 31,000m. francs CFA—remained suspended, although individual EU member states, notably France, resumed development aid. Meanwhile, Togo successfully sought aid from other sources, including the Islamic Development Bank, of which Togo became a member in November 1998, the African Development Bank and the African Development Fund. In late 2004 the EU announced a partial resumption of aid to Togo, but the failure to implement democratic or human-rights reforms inhibited a resumption of full assistance. In 2005 the EU defined the launch of a successful inter-party dialogue and the holding of free and fair legislative elections preconditions to the full resumption of relations and assistance. In November 2006, after the electoral commission named 24 June 2007 as the provisional date of the legislative election, the EU confirmed that Togo was eligible for funding of €40m. (US $52m.) under the Ninth European Development Fund.

The steep rise in foreign borrowing in the late 1970s, stimulated by the commodity price increases which took place in preceding years, brought Togo's external debt to US $1,122m. at the end of 1980 (102.4% of total GNI in that year), of which $970m. was long-term public debt. In 1982 Togo's reclassification by its official creditors as a 'least developed country' resulted in the cancellation of one-sixth of its outstanding bilateral debt. In 1984 and 1985, however, the increase in the exchange value of the US dollar, in which much of Togo's foreign debt is denominated, kept the debt-service ratio at a high level (an estimated 27.3% of foreign earnings in 1985), despite a continued growth in the value of exports. This necessitated the conclusion of further rescheduling agreements, within the context of the long-term austerity programme negotiated with the IMF. Togo clearly could not service its debt at such rates, and further agreements were reached in 1988, under the terms of which the 'Paris Club' of Western official creditors agreed to reschedule all debts due to the end of that year over 16 years, with eight years' grace and with lower interest spreads. More rescheduling of official debt liabilities over a 12-month period followed, in 1989, 1990 and 1992, when relief was accorded on payments due on one-half of Togo's total external debt. These agreements helped to reduce the debt-service ratio, in relation to the value of exports of goods and services, from 15.6% in 1989 to 6.1% in 1992. However, political uncertainty obstructed further rescheduling agreements, while external debt, which stood at $1,281m. at the end of 1990, remained substantial in relation to the size of the economy, being equivalent to 80.1% of GNI in that year. Moreover, the devaluation of the franc CFA in January 1994 effectively doubled the external debt in local currency terms, and Togo, while it benefited from the French Government's cancellation of debt following the devaluation, was unable initially to draw on the special grants and concessionary loans promised by France, the IMF and the World Bank. In September 1994 France resumed financial co-operation with Togo with the release of 26,000m. francs CFA towards economic restructuring and rural development. That month the IMF approved a series of credits, totalling $95m., in support of Togo's 1994–97 economic programme. In February 1995 the 'Paris Club' rescheduled some $237m. of Togo's debt-service obligations. In May France agreed to the cancellation of 17,000m. francs CFA of Togolese debt and to the rescheduling of a further 19,000m. francs CFA. Despite limited external lending (as a result of the breakdown in relations with donors), with no new rescheduling deals taking place, Togo's total external debt remains high. Around 29% of total external debt at the end of 2005 consisted of arrears. According to the World Bank, Togo's stock of external debt amounted to US $1,470m. at the end of 2005, with 61.4% of its long-term debt obligations being owed to multilateral lenders. The country could qualify for debt relief under the initiative for heavily indebted poor countries and the Multilateral Debt Relief Initiative, if the Government is successful in negotiating a three-year facility with the IMF and resuming relationships with bilateral donors.

Statistical Survey

Source (except where otherwise indicated): Direction de la Statistique, BP 118, Lomé; tel. 221-62-24; fax 221-27-75; e-mail dgscn_tg@yahoo.fr; internet www.stat-togo.org.

Area and Population

AREA, POPULATION AND DENSITY

Area (sq km)	56,600*
Population (census results)	
1 March–30 April 1970	1,997,109
22 November 1981	2,703,250
Population (UN estimates at mid-year)†	
2004	6,071,000
2005	6,239,000
2006	6,410,000
Density (per sq km) at mid-2006	113.3

* 21,853 sq miles.

† Source: UN, *World Population Prospects: The 2006 Revision*.

Ethnic Groups (percentage of total, 1995): Kabré 23.7; Ewe 21.9; Kabiyé 12.9; Watchi 10.1; Guin 6.0; Tem 6.0; Mobamba 4.9; Gourmantché 3.9; Lamba 3.2; Ncam 2.4; Fon 1.2; Adja 0.9; Others 2.9 (Source: La Francophonie).

ADMINISTRATIVE DIVISIONS
(2003, official estimates)

Region	Area (sq km)	Population ('000)	Density (per sq km)	Principal city
Centrale	13,317	478	35.9	Sokodé
Kara	11,738	647	55.1	Kara
Maritime	6,100	2,113	346.4	Lomé
Plateaux	16,975	1,142	67.3	Atakpamé
Savanes	8,470	590	69.7	Dapaoug
Total	56,600	4,970	87.8	

PRINCIPAL TOWNS
(2003, official estimates)

Lomé (capital)	839,000	Atakpamé	68,000
Golfe Urbain	355,000	Kpalimé	68,000
Sokodé	101,000	Dapaong	49,000
Kara	95,000	Tsevie	44,300

BIRTHS AND DEATHS
(annual averages, UN estimates)

	1990–95	1995–2000	2000–05
Birth rate (per 1,000)	43.1	41.3	39.6
Death rate (per 1,000)	11.2	10.7	10.8

Source: UN, *World Population Prospects: The 2006 Revision*.

Expectation of life (years at birth, WHO estimates): 54 (males 52; females 56) in 2004 (Source: WHO, *World Health Report*).

ECONOMICALLY ACTIVE POPULATION
(census of 22 November 1981)

	Males	Females	Total
Agriculture, hunting, forestry and fishing	324,870	254,491	579,361
Mining and quarrying	2,781	91	2,872
Manufacturing	29,307	25,065	54,372
Electricity, gas and water	2,107	96	2,203
Construction	20,847	301	21,148
Trade, restaurants and hotels	17,427	87,415	104,842
Transport, storage and communications	20,337	529	20,866
Financing, insurance, real estate and business services	1,650	413	2,063
Community, social and personal services	50,750	12,859	63,609
Activities not adequately defined	14,607	6,346	20,953
Total employed	484,683	387,606	872,289
Unemployed	21,666	7,588	29,254
Total labour force	506,349	395,194	901,543

Mid-2005 (estimates in '000): Agriculture, etc. 1,485; Total labour force 2,621 (Source: FAO).

Health and Welfare

KEY INDICATORS

Total fertility rate (children per woman, 2005)	5.1
Under-5 mortality rate (per 1,000 live births, 2005)	139
HIV/AIDS (% of persons aged 15–49, 2005)	3.2
Physicians (per 1,000 head, 2004)	0.04
Hospital beds (per 1,000 head, 2005)	0.90
Health expenditure (2004): US $ per head (PPP)	62.6
Health expenditure (2004): % of GDP	5.5
Health expenditure (2004): public (% of total)	20.7
Access to water (% of persons, 2004)	52
Access to sanitation (% of persons, 2004)	35
Human Development Index (2004): ranking	147
Human Development Index (2004): value	0,495

For sources and definitions, see explanatory note on p. vi.

Agriculture

PRINCIPAL CROPS
('000 metric tons)

	2003	2004	2005
Rice (paddy)	62.0	68.5	72.9
Maize	538.0	523.7	509.5
Millet	47.1	35.0	42.2
Sorghum	163.3	169.8	206.0
Cassava (Manioc)	778.9	679.1	678.2
Taro (Coco Yam)	19.6	17.8	12.9
Yams	615.0	636.3	585.4
Dry beans	43.6	49.4	67.4
Groundnuts (in shell)	38.2	34.9	33.4
Coconuts*	14.5	14.5	14.5
Oil palm fruit*	115	115	115
Cottonseed†	90	87	86
Bananas*	18	17	17
Oranges*	12.1	12.1	12.1
Cotton (lint)†	71	71	69
Coffee (green)†	13.5	13.5	8.4
Cocoa beans†	7.9	21.7	59.0

* FAO estimates.
† Unofficial figures.

Source: FAO.

LIVESTOCK
('000 head, year ending September, FAO estimates)

	2003	2004	2005
Cattle	279	279	280
Sheep	1,800	1,850	1,850
Pigs	310	320	320
Goats	1,470	1,480	1,480
Horses	2	2	2
Asses, mules or hinnies	3	3	3
Poultry	8,500	9,000	9,000

Source: FAO.

LIVESTOCK PRODUCTS
('000 metric tons, FAO estimates)

	2003	2004	2005
Cattle meat	5.7	5.7	5.7
Sheep meat	3.9	4.1	4.1
Goat meat	3.7	3.7	3.7
Pig meat	4.8	4.2	4.0
Chicken meat	10.4	10.9	11.2
Game meat	4.5	4.5	4.5
Cows' milk	9.2	9.2	9.3
Hen eggs	6.3	6.4	6.4

Source: FAO.

Forestry

ROUNDWOOD REMOVALS
('000 cubic metres, excluding bark)

	2003	2004	2005
Sawlogs, veneer logs and logs for sleepers	43	44	86
Other industrial wood	191	210	80
Fuel wood	5,653*	4,424	5,762
Total	5,887	4,678	5,928

* FAO estimate.

Source: FAO.

Fishing

('000 metric tons, live weight)

	2003	2004	2005
Capture	27.5	28.0	27.7
Tilapias	3.5	3.5	3.5
Other freshwater fishes	1.5	1.5	1.5
West African ilisha	0.5	2.2	1.2
Bigeye grunt	0.4	1.5	0.8
Round sardinella	4.0	4.7	9.4
European anchovy	11.5	6.9	6.5
Atlantic bonito	1.7	1.4	1.2
Marlins, sailfishes	0.9	0.1	0.0
Jack and horse mackerels	0.6	0.9	0.5
Jacks, crevalles	0.7	1.2	1.0
Other mackerels	1.9	2.0	n.a.
Aquaculture	1.2	1.5*	1.5
Total catch	28.7	29.5	29.3

* FAO estimate.

Source: FAO.

Mining

('000 metric tons)

	2003	2004	2005
Limestone*	2,400	2,400	2,400
Phosphate rock (gross weight)	1,471	1,115	1,021
Phosphate content	530*	418	368*

* Estimate(s).

Source: US Geological Survey.

Industry

SELECTED PRODUCTS
('000 metric tons, unless otherwise indicated)

	2002	2003	2004
Palm oil	7.0	7.0	7.0
Cement	800	800	800
Electric energy (million kWh)	234	291	262

Sources: FAO; US Geological Survey; UN, *Industrial Commodity Statistics Yearbook*.

Finance

CURRENCY AND EXCHANGE RATES

Monetary Units
100 centimes = 1 franc de la Communauté financière africaine (CFA).

Sterling, Dollar and Euro Equivalents (31 May 2007)
£1 sterling = 964.116 francs CFA;
US $1 = 487.592 francs CFA;
€1 = 655.957 francs CFA;
10,000 francs CFA = £10.37 = $20.51 = €15.24.

Average Exchange Rate (francs CFA per US $)
2004 528.29
2005 527.47
2006 522.89

Note: An exchange rate of 1 French franc = 50 francs CFA, established in 1948, remained in force until January 1994, when the CFA franc was devalued by 50%, with the exchange rate adjusted to 1 French franc = 100 francs CFA. This relationship to French currency remained in effect with the introduction of the euro on 1 January 1999. From that date, accordingly, a fixed exchange rate of €1 = 655.957 francs CFA has been in operation.

BUDGET

('000 million francs CFA)

Revenue*	2004	2005	2006
Tax revenue	161.0	162.1	179.1
Direct tax revenue	50.0	43.5	46.9
Indirect tax revenue	110.0	118.5	132.3
Taxes on international trade	68.9	81.0	92.3
Other current revenue	10.7	12.8	16.8
Total	171.7	174.9	195.9

Expenditure†	2004	2005	2006
Current expenditure	153.9	184.1	202.5
Salaries and wages	51.7	49.2	59.3
Other operational expenses	20.8	35.9	9.6
Interest payments on public debt	4.9	0.7	0.5
External	13.0	10.9	10.0
Capital expenditure	15.8	30.9	41.6
Externally financed	12.8	17.3	18.2
Total†	169.8	215.0	244.2

* Excluding grants received ('000 million francs CFA): 7.9 in 2004; 13.1 in 2005; 16.0 in 2006.

† Including lending minus repayments.

Source: IMF, *Togo: Statistical Appendix* (June 2007).

INTERNATIONAL RESERVES

(excluding gold, US $ million at 31 December)

	2004	2005	2006
IMF special drawing rights	—	—	0.1
Reserve position in IMF	0.5	0.5	0.5
Foreign exchange	359.2	194.1	373.9
Total	359.7	194.6	374.5

Source: IMF, *International Financial Statistics*.

MONEY SUPPLY

('000 million francs CFA at 31 December)

	2004	2005	2006
Currency outside banks	73.3	63.3	100.4
Demand deposits at deposit money banks	116.9	121.5	145.3
Total money (incl. others)	192.9	186.7	248.4

Source: IMF, *International Financial Statistics*.

COST OF LIVING

(Consumer Price Index for Lomé; base: 1996 = 100)

	2004	2005	2006
Food, beverages and tobacco	101.9	113.0	111.7
Clothing	114.9	116.0	115.3
Housing, water, electricity and gas	109.1	112.4	120.5
All items (incl. others)	115.3	123.1	125.8

Source: IMF, *Togo: Statistical Appendix* (June 2007).

NATIONAL ACCOUNTS

('000 million francs CFA at current prices)

Expenditure on the Gross Domestic Product

	2004	2005	2006
Final consumption expenditure	1,063.4	1,168.7	1,234.7
Households; Non-profit institutions serving households	958.8	1,028.5	1,094.0
General government	104.6	140.2	140.7
Gross capital formation	113.5	131.8	151.2
Gross fixed capital formation	125.1	126.6	151.2
Changes in inventories; Acquisitions, less disposals, of valuables	−11.6	5.2	0.0
Total domestic expenditure	1,176.9	1,300.5	1,385.9
Exports of goods and services	421.1	448.4	468.9
Less Imports of goods and services	574.7	636.2	696.0
GDP at market prices	1,023.3	1,112.7	1,158.8
GDP at constant 2000 prices	966.5	978.5	998.1

Gross Domestic Product by Economic Activity

	2004	2005	2006
Agriculture, hunting, forestry and fishing	370.8	436.7	432.4
Mining and quarrying	29.9	33.0	31.0
Manufacturing	83.9	95.3	83.6
Electricity, gas and water	35.7	36.1	36.0
Construction	26.0	27.3	36.5
Trade, restaurants and hotels	126.8	124.2	156.4
Transport, storage and communications	57.9	56.8	69.1
Banking and insurance	21.6	23.1	24.6
Non-market services	103.4	99.1	98.7
Other services	77.1	80.6	89.2
Sub-total	933.1	1,012.3	1,057.4
Import duties and taxes	90.2	100.3	101.4
GDP in purchasers' values	1,023.3	1,112.7	1,158.8

Source: IMF, *Togo: Statistical Appendix* (June 2007).

BALANCE OF PAYMENTS

('000 million francs CFA at current prices)

	2004	2005	2006
Exports of goods f.o.b.	317.5	314.2	319.8
Imports of goods f.o.b.	−450.8	−497.0	−543.8
Trade balance	−133.3	−182.8	−224.0
Exports of services	103.6	134.2	149.1
Imports of services	−123.9	−139.2	−152.1
Balance on goods and services	−153.6	−187.8	−227.0
Other income (net)	−17.7	−9.4	−13.2
Balance on goods, services and income	−171.3	−197.2	−240.2
Current transfers (net)	141.1	138.3	170.2
Current balance	−30.2	−58.9	−70.1
Direct investment abroad (net)	38.0	24.2	39.8
Portfolio investment assets (net)	15.7	12.7	33.7
Other investment assets net)	−21.9	−29.3	27.7
Overall balance	1.6	−51.3	31.1

Source: IMF, *Togo: Statistical Appendix* (June 2007).

External Trade

PRINCIPAL COMMODITIES
(US $ million)

Imports c.i.f.	2002	2003	2004
Food and live animals	65.4	65.2	53.1
Fish, crustaceans and molluscs and preparations thereof	6.9	7.6	4.9
Fish, fresh, chilled or frozen	6.0	6.7	4.0
Fish, frozen, excl. fillets	5.8	6.6	3.9
Cereals and cereal preparations	38.3	35.5	26.7
Wheat and meslin, unmilled	29.2	25.6	16.7
Mineral fuels, lubricants, etc.	61.0	106.9	125.9
Petroleum products, refined	60.3	106.3	124.9
Animal and vegetable oils, fats and waxes	12.6	13.6	14.3
Chemicals and related products	42.6	59.1	52.9
Medicinal and pharmaceutical products	15.4	20.8	23.6
Basic manufactures	99.5	135.4	141.8
Textile yarn, fabrics, made-up articles and related products	14.4	18.7	27.5
Cotton fabrics, woven*	9.4	8.9	11.3
Other woven fabrics, 85% plus of cotton, bleached, etc., finished	8.2	7.7	10.1
Non-metallic mineral manufactures	33.8	43.2	45.6
Lime, cement and fabricated construction materials	30.3	36.4	40.5
Cement	29.0	34.4	38.8
Iron and steel	31.0	44.1	44.6
Iron and steel bars, rods, shapes and sections	15.6	27.6	24.9
Iron and steel bars, rods, shapes and sections, of other than high carbon or alloy steel	14.9	26.7	23.3
Machinery and transport equipment	79.8	126.8	75.9
Telecommunications, sound recording and reproducing equipment	9.2	7.7	6.7
Telecommunication equipment, parts and accessories	8.6	5.8	3.4
Road vehicles	33.1	36.0	35.1
Passenger motor vehicles (excl. buses)	11.0	13.2	11.6
Miscellaneous manufactured articles	22.5	29.0	38.5
Total (incl. others)	405.3	568.4	548.1

Exports f.o.b.	2002	2003	2004
Food and live animals	41.7	45.3	73.6
Cereals and cereal preparations	11.6	10.6	8.9
Coffee, tea, cocoa, spices, and manufactures thereof	10.5	12.9	27.7
Coffee, not roasted; coffee husks and skins	2.9	1.1	2.7
Crude materials, inedible, except fuels	86.6	114.2	111.2
Textile fibres and their waste†	40.0	70.2	59.6
Cotton	39.9	69.5	58.8
Raw cotton, excl. linters, not carded or combed	26.4	53.4	48.4
Cotton, carded or combed	13.4	16.0	10.3
Crude fertilizers and crude minerals	41.7	37.9	47.6
Crude fertilizers and crude minerals (unground)	41.4	35.0	47.5
Basic manufactures	93.1	166.0	148.8
Non-metallic mineral manufactures	66.8	124.2	97.8
Cement	66.3	73.2	66.4
Iron and steel	18.5	28.1	40.7
Iron and steel bars, rods, shapes and sections	8.4	12.6	27.3
Machinery and transport equipment	5.9	111.8	5.0
Total (incl. others)	250.6	494.6	384.4

* Excluding narrow or special fabrics.
† Excluding wool tops and wastes in yarn.

Source: UN, *International Trade Statistics Yearbook*.

PRINCIPAL TRADING PARTNERS
(US $ million)

Imports c.i.f.	2002	2003	2004
Belgium	20.5	21.9	26.5
Canada	23.6	9.9	7.3
China, People's Repub.	11.7	23.4	45.7
Côte d'Ivoire	25.5	33.0	33.2
France (incl. Monaco)	82.4	118.7	106.8
Germany	20.4	25.7	18.0
Ghana	8.1	13.5	9.6
Hong Kong	7.3	10.1	14.0
India	4.8	8.2	9.6
Indonesia	7.8	10.5	11.3
Italy	14.6	25.1	20.5
Japan	7.8	8.2	8.9
Mauritania	4.5	4.2	3.2
Netherlands	13.0	68.3	18.4
Russia	6.1	4.6	6.0
Senegal	5.5	8.1	4.8
South Africa	8.1	23.6	7.9
Spain	10.7	17.2	15.7
Ukraine	12.9	17.2	12.2
United Kingdom	6.8	5.2	11.2
USA	18.6	6.5	13.3
Total (incl. others)	405.3	568.4	548.1

Exports f.o.b.	2002	2003	2004
Australia	9.2	4.5	6.4
Belgium	1.2	1.5	10.4
Benin	33.1	46.2	46.8
Brazil	0.6	3.3	4.2
Burkina Faso	32.6	72.3	50.2
France (incl. Monaco)	2.3	5.1	15.3
Ghana	53.8	68.0	45.6
India	5.0	10.4	15.4
Indonesia	2.9	8.2	7.9
Italy	4.5	4.5	3.3
Malaysia	5.0	5.4	2.4

Exports f.o.b.—*continued*	2002	2003	2004
Morocco	2.7	4.1	2.9
Netherlands	4.9	99.6	15.2
New Zealand	8.5	5.5	7.4
Niger	11.6	19.2	12.9
Nigeria	5.0	6.1	7.2
Poland	5.9	0.8	1.3
South Africa	5.9	3.8	5.2
Thailand	4.3	2.7	3.6
USA	0.9	10.4	1.5
Total (incl. others)	250.6	494.6	384.4

Source: UN, *International Trade Statistics Yearbook*.

Transport

RAILWAYS
(traffic)

	1997	1998	1999
Passengers carried ('000)	152.0	35.0	4.4
Freight carried ('000 metric tons)	250	759	1,090
Passenger-km (million)	12.7	3.4	0.4
Freight ton-km (million)	28.8	70.6	92.4

Source: Société Nationale des Chemins de Fer du Togo, Lomé.

ROAD TRAFFIC
(motor vehicles registered at 31 December)

	1994	1995	1996*
Passenger cars	67,936	74,662	79,200
Buses and coaches	529	547	580
Goods vehicles	31,457	32,514	33,660
Tractors (road)	1,466	1,544	1,620
Motorcycles and scooters	39,019	52,902	59,000

* Estimates.

Source: IRF, *World Road Statistics*.

SHIPPING

Merchant Fleet
(registered at 31 December)

	2004	2005	2006
Number of vessels	26	27	26
Total displacement ('000 grt)	19.5	20.6	18.5

Source: Lloyd's Register-Fairplay, *World Fleet Statistics*.

International Sea-borne Freight Traffic
('000 metric tons)

Port Lomé	1997	1998	1999
Goods loaded	432.4	794.6	1,021.4
Goods unloaded	1,913.9	1,912.9	1,812.4

Source: Port Autonome de Lomé.

CIVIL AVIATION
(traffic on scheduled services)*

	1999	2000	2001
Kilometres flown (million)	3	3	1
Passengers carried ('000)	84	77	46
Passenger-km (million)	235	216	130
Total ton-km (million)	36	32	19

* Including an apportionment of the traffic of Air Afrique.

Source: UN, *Statistical Yearbook*.

Tourism

FOREIGN TOURIST ARRIVALS*

	2003	2004	2005
Belgium, Luxembourg and the Netherlands	509	1,024	3,517
Benin	5,111	7,434	5,909
Burkina Faso, Mali and Niger	5,953	8,132	8,069
Côte d'Ivoire	4,134	5,860	5,916
France	14,154	17,674	16,511
Germany	830	879	1,092
Ghana	1,585	2,161	1,880
Italy	570	960	674
Nigeria	3,152	3,572	3,356
United Kingdom	655	879	619
USA	1,384	2,097	2,141
Total (incl. others)	60,592	82,686	80,763

* Arrivals at hotels and similar establishments, by country of residence.

Receipts from tourism (US $ million, incl. passenger transport): 26 in 2003; n.a. in 2004; n.a. in 2005.

Source: World Tourism Organization.

Communications Media

	2003	2004	2005
Telephones ('000 main lines in use)	61.1	65.9	58.6
Mobile cellular telephones ('000 subscribers)	243.6	332.6	443.6
Personal computers ('000 in use)	160	171	185
Internet users ('000)	210	221	300

Television receivers ('000 in use): 150 in 2000.

Radio receivers ('000 in use): 940 in 1997.

Facsimile machines ('000 in use): 17 in 1997.

Daily newspapers: 1 (average circulation 10,000 copies) in 1999; 1 (average circulation 10,000 copies) in 2000.

Book production (number of titles): 5 in 1998.

Sources: International Telecommunication Union; UNESCO, *Statistical Yearbook*, UNESCO Institute for Statistics; UN, *Statistical Yearbook*.

Education

(2003/04, unless otherwise indicated)

	Institutions*	Teachers	Students		
			Males	Females	Total
Pre-primary	319	707	6,580	6,465	13,045
Primary	4,701	22,210	535,541	449,305	984,846
Secondary	n.a.	11,029	250,693	124,692	375,385
Tertiary	n.a.	388*	15,336†	3,119†	18,455†

* 1999/2000.

† 2000/01.

Source: UNESCO Institute for Statistics.

Adult literacy rate (UNESCO estimates): 53.0% (males 68.5%; females 38.3%) in 2003 (Source: UN Development Programme, *Human Development Report*).

Directory

The Constitution

The Constitution that was approved in a national referendum on 27 September 1992, and subsequently amended, defines the rights, freedoms and obligations of Togolese citizens, and defines the separation of powers among the executive, legislative and judicial organs of state.

Executive power is vested in the President of the Republic, who is elected, by direct universal adult suffrage, with a five-year mandate. The legislature, the Assemblée nationale, is similarly elected for a period of five years, its 81 members being directly elected by universal suffrage. The President of the Republic appoints a Prime Minister who is able to command a majority in the legislature, and the Prime Minister, in consultation with the President, appoints other government ministers. A Constitutional Court is designated as the highest court of jurisdiction in constitutional matters.

Constitutional amendments, approved by the Assemblée nationale in late December 2002, removed the previous restriction limiting the President to serving two terms of office; reduced the minimum age for presidential candidates from 45 to 35 years; and required presidential candidates holding dual or multiple citizenships to renounce their non-Togolese nationality or nationalities.

An amendment authorizing an interim President to serve the remainder of a deceased predecessor's term was approved by the Assemblée nationale in February 2005; later that month, however, the amendment was reversed.

The Government

HEAD OF STATE

President: FAURE GNASSINGBÉ (inaugurated 4 May 2005).

COUNCIL OF MINISTERS
(August 2007)

Prime Minister: YAWOVI MADJI AGBOYIBO.

Minister of State: AMAH GNASSINGBÉ.

Minister of State, Minister of Foreign Affairs and African Integration: ZARIFOU AYÉVA.

Minister of State, Minister of Health: CHARLES KONDI AGBA.

Minister of State, Minister of Mines and Energy: LÉOPOLD MESSAN GNININVI.

Minister of Trade, Industry and Crafts: JEAN-LUCIEN SAVI DE TOVÉ.

Minister of Primary and Secondary Education: KOMI SÉLOM KLASSOU.

Minister of Finance, the Budget and Privatization: ADJI AYASSOR.

Minister of the Environment and Forest Resources: ISSIFOU OKOULOU-KANTCHATI.

Minister of Defence and Veterans: KPATCHA GNASSINGBÉ.

Minister of Communication and Civil Training: Me GAHOUN EGBOR.

Minister of Land Management and Decentralization: YENDJA YENTCHABRÉ.

Minister of Agriculture, Stockbreeding and Fisheries: YVES MADO NAGOU.

Minister of Security: Col ATCHA TITIKPINA.

Minister of Labour, Employment and the Civil Service: KATARI FOLI-BAZI.

Minister of Relations with the Institutions of the Republic: Me TCHESSA ABI.

Minister of Territorial Administration: SÉLÉAGODJI AHUMEY-ZUNU.

Minister of Co-operation and the New Partnership for Africa's Development (NEPAD): GILBERT BAWARA.

Minister of Higher Education and Research: MESSAN ADIMADO ADUAYOM.

Minister of the Economy and Development: DANIEL KLOUTSÈ.

Minister of Human Rights and Democracy: CÉLESTINE AKOUAVI AÏDAM.

Minister of Culture, Tourism and Leisure: GABRIEL SASSOUVI DOSSEH-ANYRON.

Minister of Technical Education and Professional Training: ANTOINE AGBÉWANOU EDOH.

Minister of Towns and Town Planning: COMLAN MALLY.

Minister of Water and Water Resources: YAO FLORENT MAGANAWÉ.

Minister of Small and Medium-sized Enterprises and the Promotion of the Free Zone: BERNARD WALLA.

Keeper of the Seals, Minister of Justice: SELA POLO.

Minister of Social Affairs and the Promotion of Women: MAÏNOUNATOU IBRAHIMA.

Minister-delegate at the Presidency, responsible for Capital Works, Transport, Post, Telecommunications and Technological Innovations: KOKOUVI DOGBÉ.

Minister-delegate at the Presidency, responsible for National Reconciliation and ad hoc Institutions: Me MASSAN LORETTA ACOUETEY.

Minister-delegate to the Minister of Territorial Administration, responsible for Local Communities: OURO BOSSI TCHACONDOH.

Minister-delegate to the Minister of Small- and Medium-sized Enterprises and the Promotion of the Free Zone, responsible for the Informal Sector: LYDIA ADANLÉTÉ.

Minister-delegate to the Minister of Social Affairs and Promotion of Women, responsible for the Protection of Children and Elderly Persons: AGNÉLÉ CHRISTINE MENSAH.

Secretary-of-State at the Ministry of Youth and Sports, responsible for the Promotion of Young Persons, and acting Minister of Youth and Sports: GILBERT KODJO ATSU.

MINISTRIES

Office of the President: Palais Présidentiel, ave de la Marina, Lomé; tel. 221-27-01; fax 221-18-97; e-mail presidence@republicoftogo.com; internet www.republicoftogo.com.

Office of the Prime Minister: Palais de la Primature, BP 1161, Lomé; tel. 221-15-64; fax 221-37-53; internet www.gouvernement.tg.

Ministry of Agriculture, Stockbreeding and Fisheries: ave de Sarakawa, BP 341, Lomé; tel. 221-04-82; fax 221-87-92.

Ministry of Capital Works, Transport, Post, Telecommunication and Technological Innovations: ave de Sarakawa, BP 389, Lomé; tel. 223-14-00; fax 221-68-12; e-mail eco@republicoftogo.com.

Ministry of Communication and Civic Training: BP 40, Lomé; tel. 221-29-30; fax 221-43-80; e-mail info@republicoftogo.com.

Ministry of Co-operation and the New Partnership for Africa's Development (NEPAD): Lomé.

Ministry of Culture, Tourism and Leisure: 47 ave des Nations Unies, BP 3146, Lomé; tel. and fax 222-41-97.

Ministry of Defence and Veterans: Lomé; tel. 221-28-12; fax 221-88-41.

Ministry of the Economy and Development: Lomé.

Ministry of the Environment and Forest Resources: Lomé; tel. 221-56-58; fax 221-03-33.

Ministry of Finance, the Budget and Privatization: CASEF, ave Sarakawa, BP 387, Lomé; tel. 221-00-37; fax 221-25-48; e-mail eco@republicoftogo.com.

Ministry of Foreign Affairs and African Integration: place du Monument aux Morts, BP 900, Lomé; tel. 221-36-01; fax 221-39-74; e-mail diplo@republicoftogo.com.

Ministry of Health: rue Branly, BP 386, Lomé; tel. 221-35-24; fax 222-20-73.

Ministry of Higher Education and Research: rue Colonel de Roux, BP 12175, Lomé; tel. 222-09-83; fax 222-07-83.

Ministry of Human Rights and Democracy: Lomé.

Ministry of Justice: ave de la Marina, rue Colonel de Roux, Lomé; tel. 221-26-53; fax 222-29-06.

Ministry of Labour, Employment and the Civil Service: angle ave de la Marina et rue Kpalimé, BP 372, Lomé; tel. 221-41-83; fax 222-56-85.

Ministry of Land Management and Decentralization: Lomé.

Ministry of Mines and Energy: Lomé.

Ministry of Primary and Secondary Education: Lomé.

Ministry of Relations with the Institutions of the Republic: Lomé.

Ministry of Security: rue Albert Sarraut, Lomé; tel. 222-57-12; fax 222-61-50; e-mail info@republicoftogo.com.

Ministry of Small and Medium-sized Enterprises and the Promotion of the Free Zone: Lomé.

Ministry of Social Affairs and the Promotion of Women: Lomé.

Ministry of Technical Education and Professional Training: BP 398, Lomé; tel. 221-20-97; fax 221-89-34.

Ministry of Territorial Administration: Lomé.

Ministry of Towns and Town Planning: Lomé.

Ministry of Trade, Industry and Crafts: 1 ave de Sarakawa, face au Monument aux Morts, BP 383, Lomé; tel. 221-20-25; fax 221-05-72; e-mail eco@republicoftogo.com.

Ministry of Water and Water Resources: Lomé.

Ministry of Youth and Sports: BP 40, Lomé; tel. 221-22-47; fax 222-42-28.

President and Legislature

PRESIDENT

Presidential Election, 24 April 2005

Candidate	Votes	% of votes
Faure Gnassingbé (RPT)	1,323,622	60.16
Emmanuel Bob Akitani (UFC)	841,642	38.25
Nicolas Lawson (PRR)	22,979	1.04
Harry Octavianus Olympio (RSDD)	12,033	0.55
Total	2,200,276	100.00

LEGISLATURE

Assemblée nationale

Palais des Congrès, BP 327, Lomé; tel. 222-57-91; fax 222-11-68; e-mail assemblee.nationale@syfed.tg.refer.org.

President: El Hadj ABASS BONFOH.

General Election, 27 October 2002

Party	Seats
Rassemblement du peuple togolais (RPT)	72
Rassemblement pour le soutien de la démocratie et du développement (RSDD)	3
Union pour la démocratie et le progrès social (UDPS)	2
Juvento—Mouvement de la jeunesse togolaise	2
Mouvement des croyants pour l'égalité et la paix (MOCEP)	1
Independents	1
Total	81

Election Commission

Commission électorale nationale indépendante (CENI): rue des Ekis, Lomé; tel. 222-39-61; Pres. KISSEM TCHANGAI-WALLA.

Political Organizations

In late 2005 there were around 70 registered political parties. Of those active in early 2006, the following were among the most influential:

Alliance démocratique pour la Patrie (ADP): Lomé; f. 2006; opposed to regime of Pres. Faure Gnassingbé; Leaders AGBEYOME KODJO, MAURICE DAHUKU PERE.

Alliance togolaise pour la démocratie (ATD): Lomé; Leader ADANI IFÉ ATAKPAMEVI.

Coalition des forces démocrates (CFD): Lomé; f. Oct. 2002 by nine parties that boycotted legislative elections held in that month; opposed the administration of fmr Pres. Eyadéma; the UFC left the coalition in Feb. 2003; Chair. EDEM KODJO (acting).

In mid-2003 constituent parties and groupings included:

Convergence patriotique panafricaine (CPP): BP 12703, Lomé; tel. 221-58-43; f. 1999 by merger of the Parti d'action pour la démocratie (PAD), the Parti des démocrates pour l'unité (PDU), the Union pour la démocratie et la solidarité (UDS) and the Union togolaise pour la démocratie (UTD); did not participate in legislative elections in 2002; Pres. EDEM KODJO; First Vice-Pres. JEAN-LUCIEN SAVI DE TOVÉ.

Front uni de l'opposition (Le Front): Lomé; f. 2002; Co-ordinator Me YAWOVI AGBOYIBO.

Alliance des démocrates pour le développement intégral (ADDI): Lomé; tel. 221-47-90; Leader Dr NAGBANDJA KAMPATIBE.

Comité d'action pour le renouveau (CAR): 58 ave du 24 janvier, BP06, Lomé; tel. 222-05-66; fax 221-62-54; e-mail yagboyibo@bibway.com; moderately conservative; Leader Me YAWOVI AGBOYIBO; Sec.-Gen. DODJI APEVON; 251,349 mems (Dec. 1999).

Convention démocratique des peuples africains—Branche togolaise (CDPA—BT): 2 rue des Cheminots, BP 13963, Lomé; tel. 221-71-75; fax 226-46-55; e-mail cdpa-bt@cdpa-bt.org; internet www.cdpa-bt.org; f. 1991; socialist; Gen.-Sec. LÉOPOLD GNININVI; First Sec. Prof. EMMANUEL Y. GU-KONU.

Union pour la démocratie et la solidarité—Togo (UDS—Togo): 276 blvd Circulaire, BP 8580, Lomé; tel. 222-55-64; fax 221-81-95; e-mail uds-togo@wanadoo.fr; Leader ANTOINE FOLLY.

Pacte socialiste pour le renouveau (PSR): Lomé; f. 2003 by fmr 'renovationist' mems of RPT; Leader TCHESSA ABI.

Coordination des partis politiques de l'opposition constructive (CPOC): Lomé; f. 2002; alliance of 'constructive opposition' parties that favoured working with the regime of fmr Pres. Eyadéma.In mid-2003 members included:

Juvento—Mouvement de la jeunesse togolaise: Lomé; f. 2001; nationalist youth movement; Leaders MONSILIA DJATO, ABALO FIRMIN.

Mouvement des croyants pour l'égalité et la paix (MOCEP): Lomé; Leader COMLANGAN MAWUTOÈ D'ALMEIDA.

Union pour la démocratie et le progrès social (UDPS): Lomé; Sec.-Gen. SEKODONA SEGO.

Coordination nationale des forces nouvelles (CFN): Lomé; f. 1993; centrist; Pres. Me JOSEPH KOKOU KOFFIGOH.

Parti démocratique togolais (PDT): Lomé; Leader M'BA KABASSÉMA.

Parti du renouveau et de la rédemption (PRR): Lomé; Pres. NICOLAS LAWSON.

Parti des travailleurs (PT): 49 ave de Calais, BP 13974, Nyékonakpoé, Lomé; tel. 913-65-54; socialist; Co-ordinating Sec. CLAUDE AMEGANVI.

Rassemblement du peuple togolais (RPT): pl. de l'Indépendance, BP 1208, Lomé; tel. 226-93-83; e-mail rpttogo@yahoo.fr; f. 1969; sole legal party 1969–91; Pres. FAURE GNASSINGBÉ; Sec.-Gen. SOLITOKI ESSO.

Rassemblement pour le soutien de la démocratie et du développement (RSDD): Lomé; tel. 222-38-80; expelled from the CPOC (q.v.) in August 2003; Leader HARRY OCTAVIANUS OLYMPIO.

Union des forces de changement (UFC): 59 rue Koudadzé, Lom-Nava, BP 62168 Lomé; tel. and fax 221-33-32; e-mail contact@ufctogo.com; internet www.ufctogo.com; f. 1992; social-democratic; First Vice-Pres. Emmanuel Bob Akitani contested presidential election in June 2003 under the designation Parti des forces de changement—Union des forces de changement; Pres. GILCHRIST OLYMPIO; First Vice-Pres. EMMANUEL BOB AKITANI; Sec.-Gen. JEAN-PIERRE FABRE.

Union des libéraux indépendants (ULI): f. 1993 to succeed Union des démocrates pour le renouveau; Leader KWAMI MENSAN JACQUES AMOUZOU.

Diplomatic Representation

EMBASSIES IN TOGO

China, People's Republic: 1381 rue de l'Entente, BP 2690, Lomé; tel. 222-38-56; fax 221-40-75; e-mail chinaemb_tg@mfa.gov.cn; Ambassador YANG MIN.

Congo, Democratic Republic: Lomé; tel. 221-51-55; Ambassador LOKOKA IKUKELE BOMOLO.

Egypt: 1163 rue de l'OCAM, BP 8, Lomé; tel. 221-24-43; fax 221-10-22; Ambassador ADEL MOSTAFA AHMED EL-SALASY.

France: rue de la Marina, BP 7485, Lomé; tel. 223-46-40; fax 223-46-56; e-mail Eric.BOSC@diplomatie.fr; internet www.ambafrance-tg.org; Ambassador ALAIN HOLLEVILLE.

Gabon: Lomé; tel. 222-18-93; fax 222-18-92; Ambassador (vacant).

Germany: blvd de la République, BP 1175, Lomé; tel. 221-23-70; fax 222-18-88; e-mail amballtogo@cafe.tg; Ambassador HELMUT KOLB.

Ghana: 8 rue Paulin Eklou, Tokoin-Ouest, BP 92, Lomé; tel. 221-31-94; fax 221-77-36; e-mail ghmfa01@cafe.tg; Ambassador KWABENA MENSA-BONSU.

Guinea: Lomé; tel. 221-74-98; fax 221-81-16.

Korea, Democratic People's Republic: Lomé; Ambassador KIM PYONG GI.

Libya: blvd du 13 janvier, BP 4872, Lomé; tel. 221-40-63; Chargé d'affaires a.i. AHMED M. ABDULKAFI.

Nigeria: 311 blvd du 13 janvier, BP 1189, Lomé; tel. and fax 221-59-76; Ambassador BABA GANA ZANNA.

USA: rue Kouenou, angle rue 15 Beniglato, BP 852, Lomé; tel. 221-29-94; fax 221-79-52; e-mail RobertsonJJ2@state.gov; internet togo.usembassy.gov; Ambassador DAVID BERNARD DUNN.

Judicial System

Justice is administered by the Constitutional Court, the Supreme Court, two Appeal Courts and the Tribunaux de première instance, which hear civil, commercial and criminal cases. There is a labour tribunal and a tribunal for children's rights. In addition, there are two exceptional courts, the Cour de sûreté de l'Etat, which judges crimes against internal and external state security, and the Tribunal spécial chargé de la répression des détournements de deniers publics, which deals with cases of misuse of public funds.

Constitutional Court: 32 ave Augustino de Souza, Lomé; tel. 221-72-98; fax 221-07-40; f. 1997; seven mems; Pres. ATSU KOFFI AMEGA.

Supreme Court: BP 906, Lomé; tel. 221-22-58; f. 1961; consists of three chambers (judicial, administrative and auditing); Chair. FESSOU LAWSON; Attorney-General KOUAMI AMADOS-DJOKO.

State Attorney: ATARA NDAKENA.

Religion

It is estimated that about 50% of the population follow traditional animist beliefs, some 35% are Christians and 15% are Muslims.

CHRISTIANITY

The Roman Catholic Church

Togo comprises one archdiocese and six dioceses. At 31 December 2004 there were an estimated 1,397,193 adherents in the country, representing about 23.2% of the total population.

Bishops' Conference

Conférence Episcopale du Togo, 561 rue Aniko Palako, BP 348, Lomé; tel. 221-22-72; fax 222-48-08.

Statutes approved 1979; Pres. Most Rev. PHILIPPE FANOKO KOSSI KPODZRO (Archbishop of Lomé).

Archbishop of Lomé: Most Rev. PHILIPPE FANOKO KOSSI KPODZRO, Archevêché, 561 rue Aniko Palako, BP 348, Lomé; tel. 221-22-72; fax 222-48-08; e-mail archlome@lome.ocicnet.net.

Protestant Churches

There are about 250 mission centres, with a personnel of some 250, affiliated to European and US societies and administered by a Conseil Synodal, presided over by a moderator.

Directorate of Protestant Churches: 1 rue Maréchal Foch, BP 378, Lomé; Moderator Pastor AWUME (acting).

Eglise Evangélique Presbytérienne du Togo: 1 rue Tokmake, BP 2, Lomé; tel. 221-46-69; fax 222-23-63; Moderator Rev. Dr KODJO BESSA.

Fédération des Evangéliques du Togo: Lomé; Co-ordinator HAPPY AZIADEKEY.

BAHÁ'Í FAITH

Assemblée spirituelle nationale: BP 1659, Lomé; tel. 221-21-99; e-mail asnbaha@yahoo.fr; Sec. ALLADOUM NGOMNA; 19,002 adherents (2006).

The Press

DAILY

Togo-Presse: BP 891, Lomé; tel. 221-53-95; fax 222-37-66; f. 1961; official govt publ; French, Kabiye and Ewe; political, economic and cultural; circ. 8,000.

PERIODICALS

L'Aurore: Lomé; tel. 222-65-41; fax 222-65-89; e-mail aurore37@caramail.com; weekly; independent; Editor-in-Chief ANKOU SALVADOR; circ. 2,500.

Carrefour: 596 rue Ablogame, BP 6125, Lomé; tel. 944-45-43; e-mail carrefour1@caramail.com; f. 1991; pro-opposition; weekly; Dir HOLONOU HOUKPATI; circ. 3,000 (2000).

Cité Magazine: 50 ave Pas de Souza, BP 6275, Lomé; tel. and fax 222-67-40; e-mail citemag@cafe.tg; internet www.cafe.tg/citemag; monthly; Editor-in-Chief GAËTAN K. GNATCHIKO.

Le Citoyen: Lomé; tel. 221-73-44; independent.

La Colombe: Lomé; f. 2001; weekly.

Le Combat du Peuple: 62 rue Blagogee, BP 4682, Lomé; tel. 904-53-83; fax 222-65-89; e-mail combat@webmails.com; f. 1994; pro-opposition weekly; Editor LUCIEN DJOSSOU MESSAN; circ. 3,500 (2000).

Le Courrier du Golfe: rue de l'OCAM, angle rue Sotomarcy, BP 660, Lomé; tel. 221-67-92.

Crocodile: 299 rue Kuévidjin, no 27 Bé-Château, BP 60087, Lomé; tel. 221-38-21; fax 226-13-70; e-mail crocodile@caramail.com; f. 1993; pro-opposition; weekly; Dir VIGNO KOFFI HOUNKANLY; Editor FRANCIS-PEDRO AMAZUN; circ. 3,500 (2000).

Le Débat: BP 8737, Lomé; tel. 222-42-84; f. 1991; 2 a month; Dir PROSPER ETEH.

La Dépêche: BP 20039, Lomé; tel. and fax 221-09-32; e-mail ladepeche@hotmail.com; f. 1993; 2 a week; Editor ESSO-WE APPOLINAIRE MÈWÈNAMÈSSÈ; circ. 3,000.

L'Etoile du matin: S/C Maison du journalisme, Casier no 50, Lomé; e-mail wielfridsewa18@hotmail.com; f. 2000; weekly; Dir WIELFRID SÉWA TCHOUKOULI.

Etudes Togolaises: Institut National de la Recherche Scientifique, BP 2240, Lomé; tel. 221-57-39; f. 1965; quarterly; scientific review, mainly anthropology.

L'Eveil du Peuple: Lomé; weekly; re-established in 2002, having ceased publication in 1999.

L'Evénement: 44–50 rue Douka, Kotokoucondji, BP 1800, Lomé; tel. 222-65-89; f. 1999; independent; weekly; Dir MENSAH KOUDJODJI; circ. 3,000 (2000).

L'Exilé: Maison du journalisme, Casier no 28, Lomé; e-mail jexil@hotmail.com; f. 2000; weekly; independent; Editor HIPPOLYTE AGBOH.

Game su/Tev Fema: 125 ave de la Nouvelle Marché, BP 1247, Lomé; tel. 221-28-44; f. 1997; monthly; Ewe and Kabiye; govt publ. for the newly literate; circ. 3,000.

Hébdo-forum: 60 rue Tamakloe, BP 3681, Lomé; weekly.

Journal Officiel de la République du Togo (JORT): BP 891, Lomé; tel. 221-37-18; fax 222-14-89; government acts, laws, decrees and decisions.

Kpakpa Désenchanté: BP 8917, Lomé; tel. 221-37-39; weekly; independent; satirical.

Kyrielle: BP 81213, Lomé; e-mail noel@journaliste.org; f. 1999; monthly; culture, sport; Dir CREDO TETTEH; circ. 3,000 (2000).

Libre Togovi: BP 81190, Lomé; tel. 904-43-36; e-mail libretogovi@mail.com; 2 a week; pro-democracy, opposed to Govt of fmr Pres. Eyadéma; distributed by the Comité presse et communication de la concertation nationale de la société civile.

La Matinée: Tokoin Nkafu, rue Kpoguédé, BP 30368, Lomé; tel. 226-69-02; f. 1999; monthly; Dir KASSÉRÉ PIERRE SABI.

Le Miroir du Peuple: 48 rue Defale, BP 81231, Lomé; tel. 946-60-24; e-mail nouveau90@hotmail.com; f. 1998; fmrly Le Nouveau Combat; weekly; independent; Dir ELIAS EDOH HOUNKANLY; circ. 1,000 (2000).

Motion d'Information: Lomé; f. 1997; weekly; pro-opposition.

Nouvel Echo: BP 3681, Lomé; tel. 947-72-40; f. 1997; pro-opposition; weekly; Dir ALPHONSE NEVAME KLU; Editor JULIEN AYIH.

Nouvel Eclat: Lomé; tel. 945-55-42; e-mail nouvel.eclat@caramail.com; f. 2000; weekly; Dir CHARLES PASSOU; circ. 2,500 (2000).

Nouvel Horizon: Maison du journalisme, Casier no 38, BP 81213, Lomé; tel. 222-09-55; f. 2000; weekly; Dir DONNAS A. AMOZOUGAN; circ. 3,000 (2000).

La Nouvelle République: Lomé; tel. 945-55-43; e-mail nouvelle.republique@caramail.com; f. 1999; Dir WIELFRID SÉWA TCHOUKOULI; circ. 2,500 (2000).

La Parole: Lomé; tel. 221-55-90.

Politicos: Lomé; tel. 945-32-66; fax 226-13-70; e-mail politicos@hotmail.com; f. 1993; weekly; Editor ELVIS A. KAO; circ. 1,500 (2000).

Le Regard: BP 81213, Lomé; tel. 222-65-89; fax 226-13-70; e-mail leregard@webmails.com; f. 1996; weekly; pro-opposition; supports promotion of human rights; Editor ABASS MIKAÏLA SAIBOU ; circ. 3,000 (2000).

Le Reporter des Temps Nouveaux: Maison du journalisme, Casier no 22, BP 1800, Lomé; tel. 945-40-45; fax 226-18-22; e-mail le_reporter@hotmail.com; f. 1998; weekly; independent; political criticism and analysis; Man. Editor ROMAIN ATTISO KOUDJODJI; circ. 3,000 (2000).

Le Scorpion—Akéklé: S/C Maison du journalisme, BP 81213, Lomé; tel. 944-43-80; fax 226-13-70; e-mail lescorpion@webmails

.com; f. 1998; opposition weekly; Dir DIDIER AGBLETO; circ. 3,500 (2000).

Le Secteur Privé: angle ave de la Présidence, BP 360, Lomé; tel. 221-70-65; fax 221-47-30; monthly; publ. by Chambre de Commerce et d'Industrie du Togo.

Le Soleil: Lomé; tel. 944-41-97; e-mail joel12@dromadaire.com; f. 1999; weekly; Dir ARISTO GABA; circ. 2,000 (2000).

Témoin de la Nation: Maison du journalisme, Casier no 48, BP 434, Lomé; tel. 221-24-92; f. 2000; weekly; Dir ELIAS EBOH.

Tingo Tingo: 44–50 rue Douka, Kotokoucondji, BP 80419, Lomé; tel. 222-17-53; e-mail jtingo-tingo@yahoo.fr; f. 1996; weekly; independent; Editor AUGUSTIN ASIONBO; circ. 3,500 (2000).

Togo-Images: BP 4869, Lomé; tel. 221-56-80; f. 1962; monthly series of wall posters depicting recent political, economic and cultural events in Togo; publ. by govt information service; Dir AKOBI BEDOU; circ. 5,000.

Togo-Presse: BP 891, Lomé; tel. 221-53-95; fax 22-37-66; f. 1962; publ. by Govt in French, Ewe and Kabre; political, economic and cultural affairs; Dir WIYAO DADJA POUWI; circ. 5,000 (2000).

La Tribune du Peuple: Lomé; weekly; pro-opposition; Dir KODJO AFATSAO SILIADIN.

PRESS ASSOCIATION

Union des Journalistes Indépendants du Togo: BP 81213, Lomé; tel. 226-13-00; fax 226-13-70; e-mail maison-du-journalisme@ids.tg; also operates Maison de Presse; Sec.-Gen. GABRIEL AYITÉ BAGLO.

NEWS AGENCY

Agence Togolaise de Presse (ATOP): 35 rue des Medias, BP 891, Lomé; tel. 221-53-95; fax 222-37-66; f. 1975; Dir-Gen. SEEDEM ABASSA.

Publishers

Centre Togolais de Communication Evangélique—Editions Haho (CTCE—Editions Haho): 1 rue de Commerce, BP 378, Lomé; tel. 221-45-82; fax 221-29-67; e-mail ctcte@cafe.tg; f. 1983; general literature, popular science, poetry, school textbooks, Christian interest; Dir KODJO MAWULI ETSÉ.

Editions Akpagnon: BP 3531, Lomé; tel. and fax 222-02-44; e-mail yedogbe@yahoo.fr; f. 1978; general literature and non-fiction; Man. Dir YVES-EMMANUEL DOGBÉ.

Editions de la Rose Bleue: BP 12452, Lomé; tel. 222-93-39; fax 222-96-69; e-mail dorkenoo_ephrem@yahoo.fr; general literature, poetry; Dir EPHREM SETH DORKENOO.

Les Nouvelles Editions Africaines du Togo (NEA-TOGO): 239 blvd du 13 janvier, BP 4862, Lomé; tel. and fax 222-10-19; e-mail neatogo@yahoo.fr; general fiction, non-fiction and textbooks; Dir-Gen. KOKOU A. KALIPE; Editorial Dir TCHOTCHO CHRISTIANE EKUE.

Les Presses de l'Université du Lomé: BP 1515, Lomé; tel. 225-48-44; fax 225-87-84.

Société Nationale des Editions du Togo (EDITOGO): BP 891, Lomé; tel. 221-61-06; f. 1961; govt-owned; general and educational; Pres. BIOSSEY KOKOU TOZOUN; Man. Dir WIYAO DADJA POUWI.

Broadcasting and Communications

TELECOMMUNICATIONS

Télécel Togo: Cité Maman N'Danida, route de Kpalimé, BP 14511, Lomé; tel. 225-82-50; fax 225-82-51; e-mail telecel@telecel.tg; internet www.telecel.tg; operates mobile cellular telecommunications network in Lomé and six other towns.

Togo Télécom: ave N. Grunitzky, BP 333, Lomé; tel. 221-44-01; fax 221-03-73; e-mail contact@togotel.net.tg; internet www.togotel.net.tg; Dir-Gen. KOSSIVI PAUL AYIKOE.

Togo Cellulaire—Togocel: Lomé; tel. 004-05-06; e-mail togocel@togocel.tg; internet www.togocel.tg; f. 2001; provides mobile cellular communications services to more than 70% of the territory of Togo.

BROADCASTING

Radio

Legislation providing for the liberalization of radio broadcasting was ratified in November 1990. However, no definitive licences for radio stations had been issued by mid-2002, when 11 private stations were, nevertheless, in operation.

Radiodiffusion du Togo (Internationale)—Radio Lomé: BP 434, Lomé; tel. 221-24-93; fax 221-24-92; e-mail radiolome@yahoo.fr; f. 1953; state-controlled; radio programmes in French, English and vernacular languages; Dir AMÉVI DABLA.

Radiodiffusion du Togo (Nationale): BP 21, Kara; tel. 660-60-60; f. 1974 as Radiodiffusion Kara (Togo); state-controlled; radio programmes in French and vernacular languages; Dir M'BA KPENOUGOU.

Radio Avenir: BP 20183, 76 blvd de la Kara, Doumassessé, Lomé; tel. 221-20-88; fax 221-03-01; f. 1998; broadcasts in French, English, Ewe and Kotokoli; Dir KPÉLE-KOFFI AHOOMEY-ZUNU.

Radio Carré Jeunes: BP 2550, Adidogomé, Lomé; tel. 225-77-44; e-mail carrejeunes@yahoo.fr; f. 1999; community radio stn; popular education, cultural information; broadcasts in French, Ewe, Kabyè and other local languages; Dir FOLY ALODÉ GLIDJITO AMAGLI.

Radio de l'Evangile-Jésus Vous Aime (JVA): Klikamé, Bretelle Atikoumé, BP 2313, Lomé; tel. 225-44-95; fax 225-92-81; e-mail radio.jva@fatad.org; f. 1995; owned by the West Africa Advanced School of Theology (Assemblies of God); Christian; education and development; broadcasts on FM frequencies in Lomé and Agou in French, English and 12 local languages; Dir Pastor DOUTI LALLEBILI FLINDJA.

Radio Galaxy: BP 20822, 253 rue 48, Doumassessé, Lomé; tel. and fax 221-63-18; e-mail radiogalaxy@yahoo.fr; f. 1996; broadcasts in French, English, Ewe and Kabyè; Dir PAUL S. TCHASSOUA.

Radio Kanal FM: Immeuble Decor, blvd du 13 janvier, BP 61554, Lomé; tel. 221-33-74; fax 220-19-68; e-mail kanalfm@cafe.tg; f. 1997; broadcasts in French and Mina; independent; Dir MODESTE MESSAVUSSUA-KUE.

Radio Maria Togo: BP 30162, 155 de la rue 158, Hédzranawoé, Lomé; tel. 226-11-31; fax 226-35-00; e-mail rmariatg@ids.tg; f. 1997; Roman Catholic; broadcasts in French, English and six local languages; Dir R. P. GUSTAVE SANVEE.

Radio Metropolys: 157 rue Missahoé, Tokoin Hôpital, derrière Pharmacie Ave Marie, Lomé; tel. 222-86-81; e-mail metropolys.lome@voila.fr; internet site.voila.fr/metropolys; f. 2000; secular and apolitical broadcasts in French only; Dir NOËLIE ASSOGBAVI.

Radio Nana FM: BP 6035, Immeuble du Grand Marché du Lomé, Lomé; tel. 221-02-63; e-mail petdog2@yahoo.fr; f. 1999; broadcasts in French and Mina; community stn; political, economic and cultural information; Dir PETER DOGBE.

Radio Nostalgie: 14 ave de la Victoire, Quartier Tokoin-Hôpital, BP 13836, Lomé; tel. 222-25-41; fax 221-07-82; e-mail nostalgietogo@yahoo.fr; internet www.nostalgie.tg; f. 1995; broadcasts in French, Ewe and Mina; Pres. and Dir-Gen. FLAVIEN JOHNSON.

Radio Tropik FM: BP 2276, Quartier Wuiti, Lomé; tel. 226-11-11; e-mail tropikfm@nomade.fr; f. 1995; broadcasts in French, Kabyè and Tem; Dir BLAISE YAO AMEDODJI.

Radio Zion: BP 13853, Adidogomé, Lomé; tel. 225-64-99; f. 1999; religious; broadcasts in French, Ewe and Kabyè; Dir LUC ADJAHO.

Television

Télévision Togolaise: BP 3286, Lomé; tel. 221-53-57; fax 221-57-86; e-mail televisiontogolaise@yahoo.fr; internet www.tvt.tg; f. 1973; state-controlled; three stations; programmes in French and vernacular languages; Dir KUESSAN YOVODEVI.

Broadcasting Association

Organisation Togolaise des Radios et Télévisions Indépendantes (ORTI): Lomé; tel. 221-33-74; e-mail kawokou@syfed.tg.refer.org; Pres. RAYMOND AWOKOU KOUKOU.

Finance

(cap. = capital; res = reserves; dep. = deposits; m. = million; br(s). = branch(es); amounts in francs CFA, unless otherwise indicated)

BANKING

Central Bank

Banque centrale des états de l'Afrique de l'ouest (BCEAO): rue Branly, BP 120, Lomé; tel. 221-25-12; fax 221-76-02; e-mail ocourrier@lome.bceao.int; internet www.bceao.int; HQ in Dakar, Senegal; f. 1962; bank of issue for the mem. states of the Union économique et monétaire ouest-africaine (UEMOA, comprising Benin, Burkina Faso, Côte d'Ivoire, Guinea-Bissau, Mali, Niger, Senegal and Togo); cap. and res 859,313m., total assets 5,671,675m. (Dec. 2002); Gov. DAMO JUSTIN BARO (acting); Dir in Togo AYÉWANOU AGETOHO GBEASOR; br. at Kara.

Commercial Banks

Banque Internationale pour l'Afrique au Togo (BIA—Togo): 13 rue de Commerce, BP 346, Lomé; tel. 221-32-86; fax 221-10-19; e-mail bia-togo@cafe.tg; f. 1965; fmrly Meridien BIAO—Togo; 57.5% owned by Banque Belgolaise (Belgium); cap. and res 567m., total assets 51,793m. (Dec. 2003); Pres. KOMLA ALIPUI; Dir-Gen. JEAN-PAUL LE CALM; 7 brs.

Banque Togolaise pour le Commerce et l'Industrie (BTCI): 169 blvd du 13 janvier, BP 363, Lomé; tel. 223-55-00; fax 221-32-65; e-mail btci@btci.tg; f. 1974; 48.5% by Groupe BNP Paribas (France) 24.8% owned by Société Financière pour les Pays d'Outre-mer; cap. 1,700m. (Dec. 2006); Pres. BARRY MOUSSA BARQUÉ; Dir-Gen. YAO PATRICE KANEKATOUA; 9 brs.

Ecobank Togo (Ecobank-T): 20 ave Sylvanus Olympio, BP 3302, Lomé; tel. 221-72-14; fax 221-42-37; e-mail ecobanktg@ecobank.com; internet www.ecobank.com; f. 1988; 80.7% owned by Ecobank Transnational Inc (operating under the auspices of the Economic Community of West African States), 14.0% by Togolese private investors; cap. and res 6,031.7m., total assets 80,556.0m. (Dec. 2004); Dir-Gen. ROGER DAHA CHINAMON; 2 brs.

Ecobank Transnational Inc: 2 ave Sylvanus Olympio, BP 3261, Lomé; tel. 221-03-03; fax 221-51-19; e-mail info@ecobank.com; internet www.ecobank.com; f. 1985; holding co for banking cos in Benin, Burkina Faso, Cameroon, Côte d'Ivoire, Ghana, Guinea, Liberia, Mali, Niger, Nigeria, Senegal and Togo, Ecobank Development Corpn and EIC Bourse; cap. and res US $105.5m., total assets $1,523.1m. (Dec. 2003); Pres. and Dir-Gen. PHILIP C. ASIODU.

Financial Bank Togo: 11 ave du 24 janvier, Lomé; tel. 271-32-71; fax 271-48-51; e-mail jean-yves.le-paulmier@financial-bank.com; f. 2004; cap. 1,500m. (2004); Pres. MENSAVI LULU MENSAH.

Société Interafricaine de Banque (SIAB): 14 rue de Commerce, BP 4874, Lomé; tel. 221-28-30; fax 221-58-29; e-mail siab@bibway.com; f. 1975; fmrly Banque Arabe Libyenne-Togolaise du Commerce Extérieur; 86% owned by Libyan Arab Foreign Bank, 14% state-owned; cap. and res 181m., total assets 6,999m. (Dec. 2003); Pres. ESSOWÈDÉOU AGBA; Dir-Gen. KHALIFA ACHOUR ETTLUAA.

Union Togolaise de Banque (UTB): blvd du 13 janvier, Nyékonakpoé, BP 359, Lomé; tel. 221-64-11; fax 221-22-06; e-mail utbsg@cafe.tg; f. 1964; 100% state-owned; transfer to majority private ownership proposed; cap. and res −12.3m., total assets 49.0m. (Dec. 2003); Pres. ESSOWÉDÉOU AGBA; Dir-Gen. YAOVI ATTIGBÉ ITOU; 11 brs.

Development Banks

Banque Ouest-Africaine de Développement (BOAD): 68 ave de la Libération, BP 1172, Lomé; tel. 221-42-44; fax 221-72-69; e-mail boadsiege@boad.org; internet www.boad.org; f. 1973; promotes West African economic development and integration; cap. 682,100m., total assets 849,993m. (Dec. 2004); Interim Pres. ISSA COULIBALY.

Banque Togolaise de Développement (BTD): ave des Nîmes, angle ave N. Grunitzky, BP 65, Lomé; tel. 221-36-41; fax 221-44-56; e-mail togo_devbank@bibway.com; f. 1966; 43% state-owned, 20% owned by BCEAO, 13% by BOAD; transfer to majority private ownership pending; cap. and res 10,111m., total assets 33,418m. (Dec. 2003); Pres. ESSO KANDJA; Dir-Gen. ZAKARI DAROU-SALIM; 8 brs.

Société Nationale d'Investissement et Fonds Annexes (SNI & FA): 11 ave du 24 janvier, BP 2682, Lomé; tel. 221-62-21; fax 221-62-25; e-mail sni@ids.tg; f. 1971; 23% state-owned; cap. 2,600m., total assets 13,219m. (Dec. 2001); Pres. PALOUKI MASSINA; Dir-Gen. RICHARD K. ATTIPOE.

Savings Bank

Caisse d'Epargne du Togo (CET): 23 ave de la Nouvelle Marché, Lomé; tel. 221-20-60; fax 221-85-83; e-mail cet@ids.tg; internet www.cet.tg; state-owned; privatization proposed; cap. and res −3,617m., total assets 18,961m. (Dec. 2003); Pres. GNANDI SEMONDJI.

Credit Institution

Société Togolaise de Crédit Automobile (STOCA): 3 rue du Mono, BP 899, Lomé; tel. 221-37-59; fax 221-08-28; e-mail stoca@ids.tg; f. 1962; 93.3% owned by SAFCA; cap. and res −112m., total assets 1,677m. (Dec. 2003); Pres. DIACK DIAWAR; Dir-Gen. DÉLALI AGBALE.

Bankers' Association

Association Professionnelle des Banques et Etablissements Financiers du Togo: Lomé; tel. 221-24-84; fax 221-85-83.

STOCK EXCHANGE

Bourse Régionale des Valeurs Mobilières (BRVM): BP 3263, Lomé; tel. 221-23-05; fax 221-23-41; e-mail natcholi@brvm.org; internet www.brvm.org; f. 1998; national branch of BRVM (regional stock exchange based in Abidjan, Côte d'Ivoire, serving the member states of UEMOA); Man. in Togo NATHALIE BITHO ATCHOLI.

INSURANCE

Colina Togo: 10 rue du Commerce, BP 1349, Lomé; tel. 221-79-91; fax 221-73-58; e-mail c-togo@colina-sa.com; internet www.colina-sa.com; affiliated to Colina SA (Côte d'Ivoire); Dir-Gen. MARCUS LABAN.

Compagnie Commune de Réassurance des Etats Membres de la CICA (CICA—RE): ave du 24 janvier, BP 12410, Lomé; tel. 221-62-69; fax 221-49-64; e-mail cicare@cafe.tg; f. 1981; reinsurance co operating in 12 west and central African states; cap. 1,500m.; Chair. LÉON-PAUL N'GOULAKIA; Gen. Man. DIGBEU KIPRE.

Groupement Togolais d'Assurances (GTA): route d'Atakpamé, BP 3298, Lomé; tel. 225-60-75; fax 225-26-78; f. 1974; 62.9% state-owned; all classes of insurance and reinsurance; Pres. Minister of the Economy, Finance and Privatization; Man. Dir KOSSI NAMBEA.

Sicar Gras Savoye Togo: 140 blvd du 13 janvier, BP 2932, Lomé; tel. 221-35-38; fax 221-82-11; e-mail sicargs@sicargs.tg; internet www.grassavoye.com; affiliated to Gras Savoye (France); Dir GUY BIHANNIC.

UAT: Immeuble BICI, 169 blvd du 13 janvier, BP 495, Lomé; tel. 221-10-34; fax 221-87-24.

Trade and Industry

ECONOMIC AND SOCIAL COUNCIL

Conseil Economique et Social: Lomé; tel. 221-53-01; f. 1967; advisory body of 25 mems, comprising five trade unionists, five reps of industry and commerce, five reps of agriculture, five economists and sociologists, and five technologists; Pres. KOFFI GBODZIDI DJONDO.

GOVERNMENT AGENCIES

Direction Générale des Mines et de la Géologie: BP 356, Lomé; tel. 221-30-01; fax 221-31-93; organization and administration of mining in Togo; Dir-Gen. ANKOUME P. AREGBA.

EPZ Promotion Board: BP 3250, Lomé; tel. 221-13-74; fax 221-52-31; promotes the Export Processing Zone at Lomé internationally.

Société d'Administration des Zones Franches (SAZOF): BP 2748, Lomé; tel. 221-07-44; fax 221-43-05; administers and promotes free zones; Dir Gen. YAZAZ EGBARÉ.

Société Nationale de Commerce (SONACOM): 29 blvd Circulaire, BP 3009, Lomé; tel. 221-31-18; f. 1972; cap. 2,000m. francs CFA; importer of staple foods; Dir-Gen. JEAN LADOUX.

DEVELOPMENT ORGANIZATIONS

Agricultural development is under the supervision of five regional development authorities, the Sociétés régionales d'aménagement et de développement.

Agence Française de Développement (AFD): 437 ave de Sarakawa, BP 33, Lomé; tel. 221-04-98; fax 221-79-32; e-mail afdlome@groupe-afd.org; internet www.afd.fr; Country Dir GENEVIÈVE JAVALOYES.

Association Française des Volontaires du Progrès (AFVP): BP 1511, Lomé; tel. 221-09-45; fax 221-85-04; e-mail afvp@togo-imet.com; internet www.afvp.org; f. 1965; Nat. Del. MARC LESCAUDRON.

Association Villages Entreprises: BP 23, Kpalimé; tel. and fax 441-00-62; e-mail averafp@hotmail.com; Dir KOMI AFELETE JULIEN NYUIADZI.

Office de Développement et d'Exploitation des Forêts (ODEF): 59 QAD rue de la Kozah, BP 334, Lomé; tel. 221-79-86; fax 221-34-91; f. 1971; develops and manages forest resources; Man. Dir BADÉKÉNÉ K. KOMMONGOU.

Recherche, Appui et Formation aux Initiatives d'Autodéveloppement (RAFIA): BP 43, Dapaong; tel. 770-80-89; fax 770-82-37; f. 1992; Dir NOIGUE TAMBILA LENNE.

Service de Coopération et d'Action Culturelle: BP 91, Lomé; tel. 221-21-26; fax 221-21-28; e-mail scac-lome@tg.refer.org; administers bilateral aid from the French Ministry of Foreign Affairs; Dir HENRI-LUC THIBAULT.

Société d'Appui a la Filière Café-Cacao-Coton (SAFICC): Lomé; f. 1992; development of coffee, cocoa and cotton production.

CHAMBER OF COMMERCE

Chambre de Commerce et d'Industrie du Togo (CCIT): ave de la Présidence, angle ave Georges Pompidou, BP 360, Lomé; tel. 221-70-65; fax 221-47-30; e-mail ccit@ccit.tg; internet www.ccit.tg; f. 1921; Pres. ALEXIS LAMSEH LOOKY; Sec.-Gen. DJAHLIN BROOHM (acting); br. at Kara.

EMPLOYERS' ORGANIZATIONS

Conseil National du Patronat: 55 ave N. Grunitzky, BP 12429, Lomé; tel. and fax 221-08-30; f. 1989; Pres. A. J. KOUDOYOR.

Groupement Interprofessionnel des Entreprises du Togo (GITO): BP 345, Lomé; Pres. CLARENCE OLYMPIO.

Syndicat des Commerçants Importateurs et Exportateurs du Togo (SCIMPEXTO): BP 1166, Lomé; tel. 222-59-86; Pres. C. SITTERLIN.

Syndicat des Entrepreneurs de Travaux Publics, Bâtiments et Mines du Togo: BP 12429, Lomé; tel. 221-19-06; fax 221-08-30; Pres. JOSÈPHE NAKU.

UTILITIES

Electricity

Communauté Electrique du Bénin: ave de la Kozah, BP 1368, Lomé; tel. 221-61-32; fax 221-37-64; e-mail dg@cebnet.org; f. 1968 as a jt venture between Togo and Benin to exploit the energy resources in the two countries; Chairs KOFFI DJERI, Z. MARIUS HOUNKPATIN; Man. CYR M'PO KOUAGOU.

Togo Electricité: 426 ave du Golfe, BP 42, Lomé; tel. 221-27-43; fax 221-64-98; e-mail m.ducommun@ids.tg; internet www.togoelectricite.com; f. 2000; to replace Compagnie Energie Electrique du Togo; production, transportation and distribution of electricity; Man. Dir MARC DUCOMMUN-RICOUX.

Gas

Société Togolaise de Gaz SA (Togogaz): BP 1082, Lomé; tel. 221-44-31; fax 221-55-30; 71% privatization pending; Dir-Gen. JOËL POMPA.

Water

Société Togolaise des Eaux (STE): 53 ave de la Libération, BP 1301, Lomé; tel. 221-34-81; fax 221-46-13; f. 2003 to replace Régie Nationale des Eaux du Togo; production and distribution of drinking water.

MAJOR COMPANIES

The following are among the country's largest companies in terms of either capital investment or employment:

Amina Togo SA: 32 blvd de la Paix, BP 10230, Lomé; tel. 226-84-04; fax 226-92-72; production of synthetic hair; operates in the Export Processing Zone; South Korean-owned; Man. LEE DAE.

Atlantic Produce: Plantes ornamentales, route de Kegue, BP 3170, Lomé; tel. 226-31-64; fax 226-28-49; exporter of tropical houseplants; Danish-owned; operates in the Export Processing Zone; Man. M. TINGGARRARD.

Boncomm International Togo: Immeuble TABA, BP 13124, Lomé; tel. 227-88-77; fax 227-08-33; Indian-owned clothing manufacturer; exports to Europe and the USA; operates in the Export Processing Zone; Man. M. SIRINIVAS.

Brasserie BB Lomé: 47 rue du Grand Marché, BP 896, Lomé; tel. 221-50-62; fax 221-38-59; f. 1964 as Brasserie du Bénin; cap. 2,500m. francs CFA; 25% owned by Castel, France; mfrs of beer and soft drinks at Lomé and Kara; Chair. and Man. Dir JOACHIM HAASE; Dirs ELMAR VAN BOEMMEL, OSCAR BOSSHARD; 530 employees (2001).

CEREKEM Exotic Togo: BP 2082, Lomé; f. 1987; cap. 400m. francs CFA; agro-industrial complex at Adétikopé for cultivation and processing of aromatic plants; Chair. and Man. Dir OLE RASMUSSEN; 400 employees.

Cotonfil: Cacavéli, BP 1481, Lomé; tel. 225-14-45; fax 222-38-44; cotton producer; jt Spanish and Togolese ownership; Man. M. MORA.

Crustafric: BP 2051, Lomé; tel. 227-82-52; fax 227-48-86; processor and exporter of seafood; operates in the Export Processing Zone; Italian-owned; Man. M. INGLEESE.

Industrie Togolaise des Plastiques (ITP): PK 12+, Zone Industrielle du Port de Lomé, BP 9157, Lomé; tel. 227-49-83; fax 227-15-58; e-mail itp@itp.tg; internet www.itp.tg; f. 1980; 51.7% owned by Groupement Togolaise d'Investissement et de Participation, 15% by WAVIN (Netherlands), 15% by Pumpenboese PB (Germany), 15% by IFU—Danish Fund for Investment in Developing Countries; mfr and marketing of moulded articles, etc.; cap. 1,100m. francs CFA; Pres. MESSANVI CREPPY; 88 employees (2001).

International Fertilizers Group-Togo (IFG-TG): BP 379, Lomé; tel. 221-39-01; fax 221-71-52; e-mail ifgtogo@ifgtogo.com; internet www.ifgtogo.com/bienvenue.htm; f. 2002 to replace the Office Togolais des Phosphates (f. 1974); cap. 15,000m. francs CFA; production and marketing of phosphates; Dir-Gen. STEPHANE CUNY; 2,500 employees (2002).

Nouvelle Industrie des Oléagineux du Togo (NIOTO): Zone Industrielle du Port, BP 3086, Lomé; tel. 227-23-79; fax 227-68-33; e-mail nioto@nioto-togo.com; internet www.nioto-togo.com; f. 1976; cap. 1,000m. francs CFA; affiliate of Groupe Dagris (France); production and marketing of edible plant oils; sales 10,436m. francs CFA (2005); Man. Dir GEORGES ORSONI; 171 permanent employees (Dec. 2005).

Nouvelle Société Togolaise de Marbrerie et de Matériaux (Nouvelle SOTOMA): Lomé; tel. 221-29-22; fax 221-71-32; cap. 500m. francs CFA; exploitation of marble at Gnaoulou and Pagola; transfer to private sector pending; Man. Dir K. PEKEMSI.

Sagefi: route de l'Aéroport, BP 4566, Lomé; tel. 221-55-43; fax 221-64-24; f. 1976; mfrs of electronic equipment; Chair. K. HOFFER.

Société Agricole Togolaise-Arabe-Libyenne (SATAL): 329 blvd du 13 janvier, BP 3554, Lomé; tel. 221-69-18; fax 222-50-75; f. 1977; cap. 1,400m. francs CFA; 50% state-owned, 50% owned by Govt of Libya; production, processing and marketing of agricultural goods; Pres. JARALAH MOHAMED; Man. Dir FATROUCH MOHAMED; 22 employees (2001).

Société des Ciments du Togo (CIMTOGO): Zone Industrielle Portuaire PK 12, BP 1687, Lomé; tel. 227-08-59; fax 227-71-32; f. 1969; cap. 750m. francs CFA; owned by Heidelberg Cement Group (Norway); production and marketing of cement and clinker; Man. Dir DAG MOEN.

Sociéte Générale des Moulins du Togo (SGMT): Zone Industrielle Portuaire, BP 9098, Lomé; tel. 227-43-77; fax 227-74-64; e-mail sgmtsa@yahoo.fr; f. 1971; cap. 300m. francs CFA; flour milling at Lomé; Chair. KOUDJOLOU DOGO; Man. Dir VASKEN BAKALIAN.

Société Industrielle de Coton (SICOT): BP 12465, Lomé; tel. 227-00-69; fax 227-75-35; ginning and marketing of cotton; Dir-Gen. ENSELME GOUTHON.

Société Nationale pour le Développement de la Palmeraie et des Huileries (SONAPH): Lomé; tel. 221-22-32; f. 1968; cap. 1,320m. francs CFA; state-owned; cultivation of palms and production of palm oil and palmettoes; Chair. Dr FOLI AMAIZO BUBUTO; Man. Dir ANANI ERNEST GASSOU.

Société Togolaise des Boissons (STB): Zone Industrielle Portuaire, BP 2239, Lomé; tel. 227-21-97; f. 1970; cap. 264m. francs CFA; manufacture, bottling and sale of soft drinks; owned by Castel, France; Chair. PIERRE CASTEL; Dir-Gen. E. VAN BÖMMEL; 90 employees (2001).

Société Togolaise du Coton (SOTOCO): BP 219, Atakpamé; tel. 440-01-53; fax 440-00-33; f. 1974 to promote and develop cotton cultivation; absorbed cotton production and marketing activities of fmr Office des Produits Agricoles du Togo in 2001; transfer to private ownership proposed; Dir-Gen. KAMBIA ESSOBEHEYI.

Société Togolaise et Danoise de Savons (SOTODAS): Lomé; tel. 221-52-03; fax 221-52-04; f. 1987; cap. 205m. francs CFA; 40% owned by Domo Kemi (Denmark), 20% by private Togolese interests; mfrs of detergents and cleansers; Man. Dir S. RAZVI.

Société Togolaise de Sidérurgie (STS): Lomé; tel. 221-10-16; cap. 700m. francs CFA; steel production; Chair. JOHN MOORE; Man. Dir STANLEY CLEVELAND.

Société Togolaise de Stockage de Lomé (STSL): BP 3283, Lomé; tel. 221-50-64; fax 227-52-11; f. 1976; cap. 4,000m. francs CFA; exploitation and commercialization of hydrocarbons; Dir-Gen. M. BLAZJENVICZ.

Togo et Shell: rue du Lac, BP 797, Lomé; tel. 221-17-51; fax 221-74-15; marketing and sale of petroleum and petroleum products; owned by Royal Dutch Shell.

Togotex International: Lomé; tel. 221-33-25; fax 221-60-49; f. 1990; cap. 2,250m. francs CFA; owned by Cha Chi Ming (Hong Kong); operates textile mills; Pres. CHA CHI MING; Man. Dir VICTOR CHA.

Total Togo: 69 blvd de la Paix, BP 312, Lomé; tel. 226-26-00; distribution of petroleum.

TRADE UNIONS

Collectif des Syndicats Indépendants (CSI): Lomé; f. 1992 as co-ordinating org. for three trade union confederations.

Confédération Nationale des Travailleurs du Togo (CNTT): Bourse du Travail, BP 163, 160 blvd du 13 janvier, Lomé; tel. 222-02-55; fax 221-48-33; f. 1973; Sec.-Gen. DOUEVI TCHIVIAKOU.

Confédération Syndicale des Travailleurs du Togo (CSTT): 14 rue Van Lare, BP 3058, Lomé; tel. 222-11-17; fax 222-44-41; e-mail cstt-tg@cstt-togo.org; f. 1949, dissolved 1972, re-established 1991; comprises 36 unions and 7 professional federations (Agro-Alimentation, Education, General Employees, Industry, Public Services, Transport, Woodwork and Construction); Sec.-Gen. BELIKI ADRIEN AKOUETE; 50,000 mems.

Union Nationale des Syndicats Indépendants du Togo (UNSIT): Tokoin-Wuiti, BP 30082, Lomé; tel. 221-32-88; fax 221-95-66; e-mail unsit@netcom.tg; f. 1991; Sec.-Gen. NORBERT GBIKPI-BENISSAN; 17 affiliated unions.

Transport

RAILWAYS

Société Nationale des Chemins de Fer du Togo (SNCT): BP 340, Lomé; tel. 221-43-01; fax 221-22-19; f. 1900; owned by West African Cement (Wacem) since Jan. 2002; total length 355 km, incl. lines running inland from Lomé to Atakpamé and Blitta (280 km); a coastal line, running through Lomé and Aného, which links with the Benin railway system, was closed to passenger traffic in 1987 (a service from Lomé to Palimé—119 km—has also been suspended); passengers carried (1999): 4,400 (compared with 628,200 in 1990); freight handled (1999): 1.9m. metric tons; Gen. Man. ROY GEMMELL.

ROADS

In 1996 there were an estimated 7,520 km of roads, of which 2,376 km were paved. The rehabilitation of the 675-km axis road that links the port of Lomé with Burkina Faso, and thus provides an important transport corridor for land-locked West African countries, was considered essential to Togo's economic competitiveness; in 1997 the World Bank provided a credit of US $50m. for the rehabilitation of a severely deteriorated 105-km section of the road between Atakpamé and Blitta. In 1998 Kuwait awarded Togo a loan of 6,000m. francs CFA francs to improve the Notse-Atakpamé highway. Other principal roads run from Lomé to the borders of Ghana, Nigeria and Benin.

Africa Route International (ARI—La Gazelle): Lomé; tel. 225-27-32; f. 1991 to succeed Société Nationale de Transports Routiers; Pres. and Man. Dir BAWA S. MANKOUBI.

SHIPPING

The major port, at Lomé, generally handles a substantial volume of transit trade for the land-locked countries of Mali, Niger and Burkina Faso, although political unrest in Togo, in the early 1990s, resulted in the diversion of much of this trade to neighbouring Benin. In 1995 the Banque ouest-africaine de développement approved a loan of 5,000m. francs CFA to help finance the rehabilitation of the infrastructure at Lomé port. The project aimed to re-establish Lomé as one of the principal transit ports on the west coast of Africa, and further upgrading of the port's facilities, including the computerization of port operations and the construction of a new container terminal, was implemented in the late 1990s, with private-sector funding. By 1999 freight traffic had recovered to 2.8m. metric tons, compared with only 1.1m. tons in 1993. There is another port at Kpémé for the export of phosphates.

Port Autonome de Lomé: BP 1225, Lomé; tel. 227-47-42; fax 227-26-27; e-mail togoport@togoport.tg; internet www.togoport.tg; f. 1968; transferred to private management in Jan. 2002; Pres. ASSIBA AMOUSSOU-GUENOU; Man. Dir Intendant Mil. AWA BELEYI; 1,600 employees (2003).

Conseil National des Chargeurs Togolais (CNCT): BP 2991, Lomé; tel. 223-71-00; fax 227-08-37; e-mail cnct@cnct.tg; internet www.cnct.tg; f. 1980; restructured 2001; Dir-Gen. MAGUÉNANI KOMOU.

Ecomarine International (Togo): Immeuble Ecomarine, Zone Portuaire, BP 6014, Lomé; tel. 227-48-04; fax 227-48-06; e-mail kegbeto@ecomarineint.com; f. 2001 to develop container-handling facility at Lomé Port; operates maritime transport between Togo, Senegal and Angola; Chief Exec. KOFI I. J. EGBETO.

Société Ouest-Africaine d'Entreprises Maritimes Togo (SOAEM—Togo): Zone Industrielle Portuaire, BP 3285, Lomé; tel. 221-07-20; fax 221-34-17; f. 1959; forwarding agents, warehousing, sea and road freight transport; Pres. JEAN FABRY; Man. Dir JOHN M. AQUEREBURU.

Société Togolaise de Navigation Maritime (SOTONAM): pl. des Quatre Etoiles, rond-point du Port, BP 4086, Lomé; tel. 221-51-73; fax 227-69-38; state-owned; privatization pending; Man. PAKOUM KPEMA.

SOCOPAO—Togo: 18 rue du Commerce, BP 821, Lomé; tel. 221-55-88; fax 221-73-17; f. 1959; freight transport, shipping agents; Pres. GUY MIRABAUD; Man. Dir HENRI CHAULIER.

SORINCO—Marine: 110 rue de l'OCAM, BP 2806, Lomé; tel. 221-56-94; freight transport, forwarding agents, warehousing, etc.; Man. AHMED EDGAR COLLINGWOOD WILLIAMS.

Togolaise d'Armements et d'Agence de Lignes SA (TAAL): 21 blvd du Mono, BP 9089, Lomé; tel. 222-02-43; fax 221-06-09; f. 1992; shipping agents, haulage management, crewing agency, forwarding agents; Pres. and Man. Dir LAURENT GBATI TAKASSI-KIKPA.

CIVIL AVIATION

There are international airports at Tokoin, near Lomé (Gnassingbé Eyadéma International Airport), and at Niamtougou. In addition, there are smaller airfields at Sokodé, Sansanné-Mango, Dapaong and Atakpamé.

Air Togo—Compagnie Aérienne Togolaise: Aéroport International de Lomé-Tokoin, BP 20393, Lomé; tel. 226-22-11; fax 226-22-30; e-mail airtogo@airtogo.net; internet www.airtogo.net; f. 1963; cap. 5m. francs CFA; scheduled internal services; Man. Dir AMADOU ISAAC ADE.

Peace Air Togo (PAT): Lomé; tel. and fax 222-71-40; internal services and services to Burkina Faso, Côte d'Ivoire and Ghana; Man. Dir PELSSEY NORMAN.

Société aéroportuaire de Lomé-Tokoin (SALT): Aéroport International de Lomé-Tokoin, BP 10112, Lomé; tel. 223-60-60; fax 226-88-95; e-mail salt@cafe.tg; Dir-Gen. Dr AKRIMA KOGOE.

Transtel Togo: Lomé; f. 2001; flights between Togo and France and Belgium; Gen. Man. M. MOROU.

Tourism

Togo's tourist industry declined precipitously in the wake of the political instability of the early 1990s; occupancy rates in the capital's hotels dropped from 33% in 1990 to 10% in 1993. The tourist industry did, however, recover in the late 1990s. Some 80,763 foreign tourist arrivals were reported in 2005. In 2003 receipts from tourism totalled US $26m.

Office National Togolais du Tourisme (ONTT): BP 1289, Lomé; tel. 221-43-13; fax 221-89-27; internet www.togo.tourisme.com; f. 1963; Dir FOLEY DAHLEN (acting).

Defence

As assessed at November 2006, Togo's armed forces officially numbered about 8,550 (army 8,100, air force 250, naval force 200). Paramilitary forces comprised a 750-strong gendarmerie. Military service is by selective conscription and lasts for two years. Togo receives assistance with training and equipment from France.

Defence Expenditure: Estimated at 18,000m. francs CFA in 2005.

Chief of General Staff: Gen. ZAKARI NAMDZA.

Education

Primary education, which begins at six years of age and lasts for six years, is (in theory) compulsory. Secondary education, beginning at the age of 12, lasts for a further seven years, comprising a first cycle of four years and a second of three years. According to UNESCO estimates, in 2003/04 enrolment at primary schools included 79% of children in the relevant age-group (85% of boys; 72% of girls), while in 1999/2000 secondary enrolment was equivalent to 22% of the relevant age group (boys 30%; girls 14%). Proficiency in the two national languages, Ewe and Kabiye, is compulsory. Mission schools are important, educating almost one-half of all pupils. In 1998 15,028 students were enrolled in institutions providing higher education. The Université du Lomé (formerly the University du Bénin) had about 14,000 students in the early 2000s, and scholarships to French universities are available. A second university opened in Kara, in the north of Togo, in early 2004.

Bibliography

Agboyibo, Y. *Combat pour un Togo démocratique: une méthode politique*. Paris, Editions Karthala, 1999.

Ameagbleame, S. *Histoire, littérature et société au Togo*. Frankfurt, IKO Verlag, 1997.

Amenumey, D. *The Ewe Unification Movement: A Political History*. Accra, Ghana University Press, 1989.

Atisso, F. S. *La problématique de l'alternance politique au Togo*. Paris, L'Harmattan, 2001.

Cornevin, R. *Le Togo: des origines à nos jours*. Paris, Académie des sciences d'outre-mer, 1987.

Decalo, S. *Togo*. Paris, ABC-Clio, 1995.

Historical Dictionary of Togo. 3rd Edn. Metuchen, NJ, Scarecrow Press, 1996.

Degli, J. Y. *Togo: La Tragédie Africaine*. Ivry-sur-Seine, Editions Nouvelles du Sud, 1996.

Delval, R. *Les musulmans au Togo*. Paris, Académie des sciences d'outre-mer, 1984.

Dossouvi Logo, H. *Lutter pour ses droits au Togo*. Paris, L'Harmattan, 2004.

Feuillet, C. *Le Togo 'en général': La Longue Marche de Gnassingbé Eyadéma*. Paris, Afrique Biblio Club, 1976.

François, Y. *Le Togo*. Paris, Editions Karthala, 1993.

Harrison Church, R. J. *West Africa*. 8th Edn. London, Longman, 1979.

Houngnikpo, M. C. *Determinants of Democratization in Africa: A Comparative Study of Benin and Togo*. Lanham, MD, University Press of America, 2001.

Nugent, P. *Smugglers, Secessionists and Loyal Citizens on the Ghana–Togo Frontier: the Lie of the Borderlands since 1914*. Oxford, James Currey, 2002.

Schuerkens, U. *Du Togo allemand aux Togo et Ghana indépendants: Changement social sous régime colonial*. Paris, L'Harmattan, 2001.

Stoecker, H. (Ed.). *German Imperialism in Africa*. London, Hurst Humanities, 1987.

Tété-Adjalogo, T. G. *De la colonisation allemande au Deutsche-Togo Bund*. Paris, L'Harmattan, 1998.

Démocratisation à la togolaise. Paris, L'Harmattan, 1998.

Histoire du Togo: La palpitante quête de l'Ablodé (1940–1960). Créteil, NM7, 2000.

Toulabor, C. *Le Togo sous Eyadéma*. Paris, Editions Karthala, 1986.

Verdier, R. *Le pays kabiyé Togo*. Paris, Editions Karthala, 1983.

Yagla, O. W. *L'édification de la nation togolaise: naissance d'une conscience nationale dans un pays africain*. Paris, L'Harmattan, 1978.

Les indigènes du Togo à l'assaut du pouvoir colonial, 1920–1958: l'histoire politique d'un peuple africain. Lomé, Nouvelles Editions Africaines du Togo, 1992.

UGANDA

Physical and Social Geography

B. W. LANGLANDS

PHYSICAL FEATURES AND CLIMATE

The Republic of Uganda is located on the eastern African plateau, at least 800 km inland from the Indian Ocean, and has a total area of 241,551 sq km (93,263 sq miles), including 44,228 sq km of inland water. There are several large freshwater lakes, of which Lakes Victoria, Edward and Albert are shared with neighbouring states. These lakes and most of the rivers form part of the basin of the upper (White) Nile, which has its origin in Uganda. At the point where the upper Nile leaves Lake Victoria, it is harnessed for hydroelectricity by the Owen Falls dam.

Of the land area (excluding open water), 84% forms a plateau at 900 m–1,500 m above sea-level, with a gentle downwarp to the centre to form Lake Kyoga. The western arm of the east African rift system accounts for the 9% of the land area at less than 900 m; this includes the lowlands flanking the rift lakes (Edward and Albert) and the course of the Albert Nile at little more than 620 m. Some 5% of the land area lies at an altitude of 1,500 m–2,100 m, including (in the eastern and western extremities) the shoulders of rift valley structures, and also the foothills of the mountains referred to below; this altitude accommodates some of the most heavily populated regions, as it is free of malaria. Mountains of over 2,100 m occupy the remaining 2% of the land area and these lands are above the limit of cultivation. The highest point is Mt Stanley, 5,109 m, in the Ruwenzori group on the border with the Democratic Republic of the Congo (formerly Zaire), but larger areas of highland are included in the Uganda portion of the volcanic mass of Mt Elgon, near the Kenyan border.

Geologically, the great proportion of the country is made up of Pre-Cambrian material, largely of gneisses and schists into which granites have been intruded. In the west, distinct series of metamorphosed rocks occur, mainly of phyllites and shales, in which mineralized zones contain small quantities of copper, tin, tungsten and beryllium. Deposits of cobalt and nickel have also been identified, and also potentially substantial reserves of gold-bearing ores. Small quantities of gold, tungsten and tin concentrates are currently mined. In the east of the country there are extensive reserves of magnetite, apatite and crystalline limestone. The apatite provides the basis for a superphosphate industry and the limestone for a cement industry.

NATURAL RESOURCES

The economy of Uganda depends upon agriculture and this, in turn, is affected by climate. The country's location, between 1° 30′ S and 4° N, gives little variation in temperature throughout the year, affording an equatorial climate modified by altitude. Rainfall is greatest bordering Lake Victoria and on the mountains, where small areas have over 2,000 mm per year. The high ground of the west, the rest of the Lake Victoria zone, and the eastern and north-central interior all have more than 1,250 mm annually. Only the north-east (Karamoja) and parts of the south (east Ankole) have less than 750 mm. However, total amounts of rain are less significant agriculturally than the length of the dry season. For much of the centre and west there is no more than one month with less than 50 mm and this zone is characterized by permanent cropping of bananas for food, and coffee and tea for cash crops. To the south the dry season increases to three months (June–August); in the north it increases to four months (December–March) and in the north-east the dry season begins in October. Where the dry season is marked, as in the north and east, finger millet provides the staple food and cotton the main cash crop. In the driest parts pastoralism predominates, together with some sorghum cultivation.

Western Uganda, where there is a greater range of different physical conditions, and generally where population densities are below average, shows a diversity of land use, with tropical rainforest, two game parks, ranch lands, fishing, mining and the cultivation of coffee and tea. The north and east is more monotonous, savannah-covered plain with annually sown fields of grain and cotton. Most of the country's coffee comes from the Lake Victoria zone (*Coffea robusta*) and Mt Elgon (*Coffea arabica*). The economy relies heavily upon smallholding peasant production of basic cash crops.

POPULATION

The latest census, conducted in November 2002, enumerated a population of 24,748,977, giving a density of about 102.6 inhabitants per sq km. According to official estimates, the population had risen to 28,247,300 by mid-2007. The population is predominantly rural; in 2001 only about 13.7% of the populace resided in urban centres. In 2002 the population of Kampala, the capital, was estimated at 1,208,544. The annual birth rate was 47.3 per 1,000 of the population in 2000–05. Average life expectancy at birth in 2004 was 49 years, according to WHO estimates. Demographic patterns in the late 1990s and beyond were expected to be significantly affected by the high rate of incidence of AIDS, which, by the early 1990s, had reportedly reached epidemic proportions in parts of Uganda. According to estimates by the World Bank almost 10% of the adult population were infected with HIV in 1997. By 2005, however, following mass education and prevention campaigns, the percentage of adults living with HIV/AIDS had been reduced to 6.7%.

In 1959 about two-thirds of the population, mainly in the centre and south, were Bantu-speaking, about one-sixth Nilotic-speaking and a further one-sixth Nilo-Hamitic (Paranilotic). In 1969 there were 74,000 people of Indian and Pakistani origin, engaged mainly in commerce, and 9,500 Europeans, mostly in professional services. Since the 1972 expulsions of non-citizen Asians (who comprised the majority of the resident Asian population), both of these totals have fallen substantially.

Recent History

ALAN RAKE

Revised by MICHAEL JENNINGS

British colonial activity in Uganda, which commenced after 1860, was consolidated in 1891 by a treaty with the Kabaka (king) of Buganda, the dominant kingdom. In 1894 Buganda was declared a protectorate, and the same status was subsequently conferred on the kingdoms of Bunyoro, Toro, Ankole and Bugosa. For the next 50 years debate over the position of Buganda within a future self-governing state inhibited the creation of a united nationalist movement. In 1954 the Democratic Party (DP) was formed, favouring a unitary independent state of Uganda and opposing the ambitions of the Baganda people, who did not wish Buganda's influence to be diminished after independence. The Uganda National Congress (UNC), meanwhile, advocated greater African control of the economy in a federal independent state. In 1958 seven African members of the protectorate's Legislative Council, including two members of the UNC, joined another faction, led by Dr Milton Obote, to form the Uganda People's Congress (UPC). By 1960 the UPC, the DP (led by Benedicto Kiwanuka) and the Lukiiko (legislature) of Buganda were the principal political forces in Uganda.

In 1961, at the first country-wide election to the Legislative Council, the DP won a majority of the seats. Kiwanuka was appointed Chief Minister, but he proved to be unacceptable to the ruling élite of Buganda. The Kabaka Yekka (KY, or King Alone), a political party representing the interests of the Bugandan Lukiiko, was formed to ally with the UPC against the DP. Uganda was granted self-government in 1962, with Kiwanuka as Prime Minister. At pre-independence elections to a National Assembly, held in April, the UPC won a majority of seats. The UPC-KY coalition formed a Government, led by Obote. The new Constitution provided for a federation of four regions—Buganda, Ankole, Bunyoro and Toro—each with considerable autonomy. In October Uganda became independent, within the Commonwealth, and a year later, on 9 October 1963, the country became a republic, with Mutesa II, the Kabaka of Buganda, as non-executive President.

OBOTE AND THE UPC

During the first years of independence the UPC-KY alliance was placed under increasing strain. By the end of 1964 sufficient KY and DP members of the National Assembly had defected to the UPC for the alliance to be no longer necessary. The UPC had also gained control of all district councils and kingdom legislatures, except in Buganda. The UPC itself, however, was split between conservative, centrist and radical elements of the party. In February 1966 the National Assembly approved a motion demanding an investigation into gold-smuggling, in which Obote, the Minister of Defence, and the second-in-command of the army, Col Idi Amin Dada, were alleged to be involved. Later in that month Obote led a pre-emptive coup against his opponents within the UPC. Five government ministers were arrested, the Constitution suspended, the President deposed and all executive powers transferred to Obote. In April an interim Constitution was introduced, withdrawing regional autonomy and introducing an executive presidency. Obote became head of state. In May, when the Lukiiko demanded the restoration of Buganda's autonomy, government troops, commanded by Amin, seized the palace of the Kabaka (who escaped abroad) and a state of emergency was imposed in Buganda. A new Constitution was adopted in September 1967, establishing a unitary republic and abolishing traditional rulers and legislatures. National elections were postponed until 1971.

During the late 1960s the Obote regime came to rely increasingly on detention and armed repression by the paramilitary and intelligence services. Estrangement began to develop, however, between Obote and the army. In December 1969 Obote was wounded in an assassination attempt in Kampala; Amin (still commander of the army) immediately fled to a military base in his home area.

THE AMIN REGIME

Amin seized power in January 1971, while Obote was out of the country. In February Amin declared himself head of state, promising a return to civilian rule within five years. Amin consolidated his military position by massacring troops and police (particularly those of the Langi and Acholi tribes) who had supported the Obote regime. Soon after taking power Amin suspended political activity and most civil rights. The National Assembly was dissolved, and Amin ruled by decree. The jurisdiction of military tribunals was extended to cover the entire population, and several agencies were established to enforce state security. In August 1972 Amin announced the expulsion of all non-citizen Asians (who comprised the majority of the resident Asian population). The order was subsequently extended to include all Asians, and although this was later rescinded, under internal and external pressure, all but 4,000 Ugandan Asians left the country. Most went to the United Kingdom, which severed diplomatic relations and imposed a trade embargo against Uganda. In December all British companies in Uganda were nationalized without compensation.

Former Chief of Staff, David Oyite-Ojok and Yoweri Museveni, a senior officer, led an attempt to oust Amin by invading from Tanzania in September 1972. In retaliation, Amin's air force bombed Tanzanian towns. The Amin regime was supplied with military aid by Libya and the USSR, and by the end of 1972 virtually all Western aid had ceased. No coherent economic development policy existed, and the country's infrastructure deteriorated.

In October 1978 Amin sought to divert the attention of the armed forces from internal divisions (which had led to another abortive coup in August) by invading Tanzania, claiming the rightful possession of the Kagera salient. The attempt was unsuccessful. President Julius Nyerere of Tanzania encouraged political exiles to form a united political front to remove Amin. In January 1979 the Tanzanian armed forces invaded Uganda, assisted by the Uganda National Liberation Army (UNLA) under the command of Oyite-Ojok and Museveni. They met little resistance and captured Kampala in April. Amin fled the country, eventually taking refuge in Saudi Arabia, where he remained until his death in August 2003.

TRANSITIONAL GOVERNMENT

A provisional government, the National Executive Council (NEC), was established in April 1979 from the ranks of the Uganda National Liberation Front (UNLF, a coalition of 18 previously exiled groups), with Dr Yusuf Lule, a former vice-chancellor of Makerere University, as President. When Lule attempted to reshuffle the NEC in June, opposition from within the UNLF forced his resignation. Lule was succeeded by Godfrey Binaisa (a former Attorney-General), who was, in turn, overthrown by the Military Commission of the UNLF in May 1980. The Military Commission was chaired by Paulo Muwanga (an associate of Obote), supported by Oyite-Ojok and with Museveni as Vice-Chairman.

OBOTE AND OKELLO

The elections held in December 1980 were contested by four parties: the UPC, under Obote; the DP, led by Paul Ssemogerere; the Uganda Patriotic Movement (UPM), a regrouping of the radical faction of the UPC, led by Museveni; and the Conservative Party (CP), a successor to the KY. The UPC gained a majority of seats, and Obote was proclaimed President for the second time in mid-December.

Dissatisfaction with the conduct and outcome of the elections caused several factions to initiate guerrilla operations. The three main guerrilla movements were the Uganda National Rescue Front (UNRF), comprising supporters of Amin who were active in the West Nile area, the Uganda Freedom Movement (UFM), led by Balaki Kirya and Andrew Kayiira, and the National Resistance Army (NRA), led by Museveni, with the former President, Lule, now in exile, as chairman of its political wing, the National Resistance Movement (NRM). (Following Lule's death in 1985 Museveni became sole leader of the NRM and NRA.)

In March 1983, during a UNLA campaign to combat the NRA, attacks on refugee camps resulted in the deaths of hundreds of civilians, and more than 100,000 people were displaced. The offensive against the NRA was renewed in late 1984, with civilians again suffering the main impact of attacks. In mid-1985 the human rights organization Amnesty International alleged widespread torture and murder of civilians by the security forces.

In July 1985 Obote (a Langi) was overthrown in an Acholi military coup, led by Brig. (later Lt-Gen.) Basilio Okello. (The deposed President was subsequently granted political asylum by Zambia.) A Military Council, headed by Lt-Gen. (later Gen.) Tito Okello, the Commander-in-Chief of the army, was established to govern the country, pending elections to be held a year later. In subsequent months opposition groups, with the exception of the NRA/NRM, accepted positions on the Military Council. An amnesty was declared for exiles who had supported Amin. By late September the NRA controlled much of southern Uganda. Its control of the region's cash crops placed an economic stranglehold on the Kampala Government. A peace accord signed in December 1985 soon broke down, and Museveni returned to south-west Uganda to push for a final offensive.

THE MUSEVENI PRESIDENCY

NRA troops took control of Kampala in January 1986. Museveni was sworn in as President of the country and formed a National Resistance Council (NRC), with both civilian and military members drawn from across the political spectrum. Samson Kisekka was appointed Prime Minister. Elections were postponed for at least three years and the activities of political parties were officially suspended in March. The defeat of Okello's remaining UNLA troops was officially completed by the end of March.

Museveni announced a policy of national reconciliation. He established a commission to investigate breaches of human rights during the regimes of Amin, Obote and Okello. Following an investigation of the activities of the police force, more than 2,500 of its members were dismissed in July 1986. During 1986 the Museveni Government developed a system of resistance committees at local and district level; these were to be partly responsible for the maintenance of security and the elimination of corruption.

In March 1986 an armed movement seeking the overthrow of Museveni, the Uganda People's Democratic Movement (UPDM), was formed, with Obote's former premier, Eric Otema Allimadi, as leader. This, together with raids by remnants of the UNLA, chronic problems with armed cattle-rustlers in the north-east and the lack of any basic infrastructure of law and order, prevented President Museveni from consolidating his control over Uganda. Museveni refused to restore Uganda's traditional monarchies until stability had returned to the country.

In October 1986 26 people, including Paulo Muwanga, Obote's former Vice-President, and Kayiira, were arrested for treason. Although charges against some of these were later withdrawn, the murder of Kayiira in March 1987 caused the UFM to withdraw its support for the Government. The trial of seven of the 26 who had been arrested began in August 1987, and in the following March three were sentenced to death, while the remaining four were acquitted.

The largest uprising in the period immediately following Museveni's accession to power was led by a charismatic cult leader, Alice Lakwena, whose religious sect attracted both peasant farmers from the Acholi tribe and former soldiers of the UNLA. The rebel Holy Spirit Movement, as it became known, was crushed in late 1987 and Lakwena fled to Kenya. However, remaining members of the movement subsequently regrouped themselves as the Lord's Resistance Army (LRA), under the leadership of Joseph Kony, Lakwena's nephew.

In June 1987 an amnesty was declared for insurgents (except those accused of murder or rape), which was subsequently repeatedly extended; by April 1988 Ugandan officials reported that almost 30,000 rebels had surrendered. Peace talks with the armed wing of the UPDM led to agreement in June under the leadership of Lt-Col John Angelo Okello. However, a faction of the UPDA regrouped, under the leadership of Odong Latek, and continued to oppose the Government. In mid-1989 the NRC launched a major offensive against guerrilla forces.

A major cabinet reshuffle in February 1988 increased the number of ministers originating from the north-east of Uganda, where opposition to the Government was most prevalent. An abortive mutiny by members of the NRA in April resulted in the detention of some 700 army officers and soldiers. In May the NRC approved legislation validating the NRC as the country's official legislature.

Post-election Reforms

In February 1989 the first national election since 1980 was held. The NRC, which had previously comprised only members nominated by the President, was expanded from 98 to 278 members, to include 210 elected representatives. While a total of 20 ministerial posts were reserved for nominated members of the NRC, 50 were allocated to elected members. Following the election, Museveni appointed a constitutional commission to gauge public opinion on Uganda's political future and to draft a new constitution. In October 1989 (despite opposition from the DP) the NRC approved draft legislation to extend the Government's term of office by five years from January 1990.

In May 1991 President Museveni formally invited all *émigré* Ugandan Asians, who had been expelled during the Amin regime, to return. A report by Amnesty International, which was released in early December, accused the NRA of torturing and summarily executing prisoners during anti-insurgency operations.

In December 1992 the constitutional commission recommended continuing the non-party democracy system against the opposition of the UPC and the DP. In April the NRC passed legislation authorizing the establishment of a Constituent Assembly.

In July 1993 legislation was approved which provided for the restoration of each of Uganda's traditional monarchies; these were, however, to be limited to ceremonial and cultural functions. At the end of that month Prince Ronald Mutebi, the claimant to the throne of Buganda, was enthroned as the Kabaka of Buganda, and in early August the realm's Lukiiko was re-established. A new Omukama of Toro, Patrick Olimi Kaboyo, was installed in July, and a new Omugabe of Ankole, John Barigye, in November. In June 1994 Museveni agreed to the coronation of Solomon Gafabusa Iguru as Omukama of Bunyoro. Kaboyo died in August 1995 and was succeeded as Omukama of Toro in September 1996 by his infant son, Oyo Nyimba Iguru. The kingdom of Busoga was restored in February 1996, with Henry Wako Muloki installed as the Kyabazinga.

In October 1993 Lt-Col James Oponyo, the commander of the UPA in the Teso area in north-eastern Uganda, surrendered to government forces. In January 1994 two other rebel groups, the Ugandan Democratic Alliance (UDA) and the Uganda Federal Army (UFA), also agreed to suspend their guerrilla operations. However, in early 1994 Peter Otai, a former leader of the UPA, formed a new rebel group, known as the Uganda People's Freedom Movement (UPFM). In March renewed clashes occurred in northern Uganda between the forces of Kony's LRA and the Government, following the collapse of short-lived negotiations between the two sides which had commenced in January.

The return of *émigré* Asians to reclaim the property which was expropriated by the Amin regime continued in 1994, although the process provoked jealousies and racial antagonism, with indigenous businessmen claiming that they had not been sufficiently compensated. Despite sporadic acts of violence, the Government adhered to its compensation policy and extended from October 1993 to April 1994 the deadline for Asians to return and reclaim their expropriated assets.

Political and Constitutional Changes

Elections to the newly created 288-member Constituent Assembly took place in March 1994. Museveni and the NRM won overwhelming support. Although candidates were officially required to stand on a non-party basis, tacit official tolerance of party campaigning was reflected in the leaders of three parties—the DP, the CP and the UPC—being given access to national radio and television during the weeks prior to the election. The ruling alliance won an estimated 150 of the 214 seats, most of which were in Buganda, the Western region and parts of the east, while the opposition (supporters of the UPC and DP) secured most seats in the north and the north-east. The Constituent Assembly, which also comprised nominated representatives of the armed forces, political parties, trade unions and various special interest groups, was empowered to debate, amend and finally to enact the draft constitution. Amendments to the draft required a two-thirds' majority of the Assembly; changes that received majority support but less than two-thirds were to be submitted to referendum. The new Constitution, under the terms of which a national referendum on the future introduction of a multi-party political system was to be staged in 2000, was eventually promulgated in October 1995.

In November 1994 Museveni reshuffled the Cabinet, replacing Adyebo as Prime Minister with Kintu Musoke, hitherto Minister of State for Security, and appointing Dr Speciosa Wandira Kazibwe, the Minister of Women's Affairs and Community Development, as Vice-President. Brig. Moses Ali rejoined the Cabinet.

In June 1995 the Constituent Assembly rejected the immediate restoration of multi-party democracy. Consequently, candidates at the legislative and presidential elections would be required to seek election without official reference to their respective political affiliations. The Constituent Assembly's decision was strongly opposed by the UPC and other unofficial opposition parties.

The presidential and legislative election dates were postponed several times in 1996. The main challenger to Museveni was Ssemogerere, the leader of the DP. Museveni campaigned with the full backing of the army, police and security forces. The presidential election was held on 9 May; Museveni won convincingly, securing 74.2% of the votes cast (Ssemogerere took 23.7%). The election was declared free and fair by international observers and Museveni immediately declared that he would not restore multi-party democracy for at least five years. Elections to the Parliament (as the NRC had been restyled under the 1995 Constitution), which now consisted of 276 seats, comprising 214 elected and 62 nominated representatives, took place in June. In the same month elections were held for new local councils (to replace the resistance committees).

The referendum on Uganda's non-party system took place on 29 June 2000. Opposition parties boycotted the poll. Electoral monitors from the Organization of African Unity (OAU, now the African Union—AU) declared that the referendum had been conducted fairly and peacefully. The existing system was supported by 90.7% of voters, although the participation rate was only around 45%. The Referendum Act was passed in Parliament, but declared null and void by the Supreme Court in August. The Court decided that the law had been passed with less than the 93 deputies present required to form a quorum. However, the Parliament reversed this decision at the end of the month, by enacting a validation of the referendum and all other laws passed since October 1996.

MUSEVENI RE-ELECTED

The 2001 presidential election was contested by a number of candidates, the most serious challenge to Museveni being his former physician, Dr Kizza Besigye. Besigye commanded significant support within the UPDF in particular, and his criticism of Uganda's continued involvement in the Democratic Republic of Congo (DRC) also won much popular support. The campaign was accompanied by violence, and opposition groups complained that state security services targeted their members and supporters for intimidation. The presidential election was held on 12 March, and Museveni was re-elected President with 69% of the votes cast. Besigye won 28%, and Aggrey Awori and Mohamed Kibirige Mayanja both won 1%. There were reports of electoral malpractice and intimidation during the poll, but international observers concluded the election was generally free and fair. A number of bombings in the country took place in the immediate aftermath, one in Kampala coming just after the results were announced. Although no group claimed responsibility, the Government accused Besigye of being linked to the attacks and barred him from leaving the country. Museveni purged the UPDF of Besigye supporters and was sworn in as President in May. Besigye fled to the USA in August. Legislative elections took place on 26 June 2001. The NRM secured more than 70% of seats (the total number of seats having been increased to 292—214 elected and 78 nominated). A new Cabinet was appointed in July, including 10 ministers who had failed to retain their seats in the elections.

In late 2003 and early 2004 the Government faced international criticism for its management of the media. In early September it accused the only independent newspaper of treason and of supporting the LRA after it called for a negotiated settlement to the conflict. In November, the Attorney-General announced that news media could not publish financial details of political leaders, widely interpreted as an attempt to prevent investigations into the activities of ministers and political leaders. In March 2004 Human Rights Watch published a report accusing the Government of using torture and violence to suppress political opposition; the Government denied the accusations. In October the Uganda Human Rights Commission similarly noted the use of torture by state security services. It noted progress in closing the network of safe-houses used by security services to illegally detain and interrogate political opponents, but suggested that such practices were still widespread. Reports from human rights groups in 2005 reported similar practices, and suggested that the Government routinely accused opposition politicians of supporting rebel groups and treason. In particular, the Forum for Democratic Change (FDC), an opposition group established in December 2004 and led by Besigye, was accused of being linked to the People's Redemption Army, an accusation widely discredited by international observers.

In February 2004 the seven main opposition parties—the DP, the UPC, the CP, the Justice Forum, the National Democratic Forum, the Free Movement and the Reform Agenda—established a coalition known as the Group of Seven (G7). Talks between the G7 and the Government over the transition to multi-party democracy repeatedly broke down. In April the G7 accused the Government of creating around 50 new opposition parties to undermine their members. Throughout 2004 and 2005 opposition politicians regularly accused the Government of banning rallies and undermining their campaigns. In November 2004 the Constitutional Court overturned legislation preventing parties other than the NRM-O (as the NRM had been renamed in 2003) from contesting elections, and allowing candidates who lived abroad to lead political parties. Nevertheless, the Government continued to harass opposition politicians. In April 2005 two FDC deputies were accused of murdering a local official three years earlier. In response to what it claimed was a politically motivated trial, the FDC called on donors to suspend aid in protest at government efforts to undermine political opposition. Donors, already concerned at the lack of progress towards multi-party democracy, responded by putting pressure on the Government. In February the Dutch Minister of Development Co-operation, on a visit to Uganda, called on Museveni not to stand for a third term. In March the British Government called for an easing of restrictions on opposition parties.

The Succession Question

In 2003 there began a series of machinations designed to allow Museveni to run for a then unconstitutional third term in office, despite his formal protestations that he had no intention of doing so. In late May a number of ministers who had opposed plans to revoke the presidential two-term limit were dismissed from the Cabinet. Pro-government civil society organizations and politicians were mobilized to build up popular support for the move. In September the Cabinet presented proposals for amending the Constitution to the Constitutional Review Commission. In April 2004 Museveni formally retired from the UPDF, having been promoted to the rank of General, in order to comply with legislation barring serving members of the armed forces from active membership of a political party, and thereby removing one obstacle to his running for political office in 2006. In June 2005 Parliament passed legislation officially restoring multi-party democracy and lifting the presidential time limit. On 28 July 92.5% of voters at a national referendum ratified the changes (albeit with a relatively low turn-out of 47%). The Government's actions in opening the opportunity for Museveni to stand in the presidential election were criticized by opposition parties, which alleged that the Government had bribed deputies to support the 2005 legislative changes. Museveni was also accused of attempting to undermine the independence of the judiciary when he declared unacceptable a June 2004 decision by the Constitutional Court that the referendum confirming support for the non-party system in 2000 was invalid (the Supreme Court overturned the ruling in September 2004).

The 2006 Elections

In November 2005 Museveni made the long-expected announcement that he would stand in the presidential elections for a third term. On 14 November, three weeks after his return from self-imposed exile, Besigye was arrested and imprisoned on charges of rape and treason. The arrests led to two days of rioting in Kampala, with one opposition supporter shot dead by police. A few days later heavily armed soldiers surrounded the court in which Besigye and 14 co-defendants were attending a bail hearing. Although they were granted bail, Besigye and his co-defendants returned to jail over concerns for their safety should they be released. The UPDF later stated that the soldiers had been present to re-arrest the accused. The action was widely condemned both within Uganda and internationally, and the head of the High Court denounced the UPDF for attacking the rule of law. In December the Electoral Commission announced that Besigye could file his election nomination papers from prison, overruling a call from the Attorney-General that Besigye be denied the opportunity to stand in the election.

International donors became increasingly concerned over the transition to democracy in Uganda, especially following the arrest of Besigye, and allegations of intimidation and violence against opposition supporters and politicians. In November 2005 the outgoing US ambassador voiced concern over the levels of political violence in Uganda, and the Secretary-General of the Commonwealth Secretariat met with Museveni to discuss the Government's apparent willingness to use force and intimidation against political opposition. The British Government announced in December that it would reduce its aid to the country by £15m. (US $26m.), owing to concerns over the level of democracy in the country. The payment of an additional £4m. was also delayed until the British Government could assess the conduct of the forthcoming elections. The Swedish Government announced that it had similarly diverted £4.6m. away from the Government to aid agencies in the north.

In January 2006 two FDC deputies were acquitted of murder. The judge criticized the prosecution case, and the acquitted deputies claimed that the charges were politically motivated. In mid-February two FDC supporters were killed and six injured after security officials fired into a crowd in Kampala that had gathered to celebrate the adjournment of Besigye's treason trial until after the election. The Government claimed the crowd had attacked a state security agent's car.

Presidential and parliamentary elections took place on 23 February 2006. Museveni was re-elected President after securing 59.3% of the votes cast; Besigye, who had been released on bail by the High Court, won 37.4%. Voter turn-out of some 68% was recorded. In the parliamentary elections the NRM-O was reported to have won 202 seats. Its nearest rival, the FDC, was reported to have won 40 seats. The remaining seats were split between the DP (10 seats), the UPC (nine seats), the CP (one seat), the Justice Forum (one seat), and 28 independents. It was reported that 80 deputies lost their seats in the elections, including 17 ministers. The President's wife, Janet Museveni, was elected to Parliament; overall, women made up 19% of deputies. International observers did not challenge the overall result of the election, although they noted some irregularities—such as Besigye's arrest and the media bias towards Museveni—as well as broader problems with the electoral process. Furthermore, the head of the EU observer team called for the reintroduction of laws limiting the President to two terms of office.

On 7 March 2006 Besigye filed a petition challenging the election results and alleging significant irregularities in its conduct. In April the Supreme Court ruled by four votes to three that there was no evidence that the election had been significantly fraudulent or beset by major irregularities. It did, however, find that names had been struck off the electoral list, evidence of irregularities in the counting of votes, the use of bribery, intimidation and violence, and some examples of multiple voting and ballot-stuffing. Despite this, the Court concluded that the failures had not seriously affected the overall result, and confirmed Museveni's victory. Museveni was sworn in as President in May 2006.

Museveni's Third Term

Between October and December 2006 150 people were killed and around 1,000 internally displaced in Karamoja region following clashes between armed pastoralists and government security forces. In March 2007 the British non-governmental organization Save the Children alleged that an army operation in the region had killed 66 children. The army denied the allegations.

Although Besigye was aquitted of rape in March 2006, his trial for treason continued. After a ruling in January that he and the 22 co-defendants could not be tried before a court martial, the trial was moved to the High Court. However, the judge charged with hearing the case withdrew in February, and the trial was rescheduled to April. The second judge also withdrew soon after. The trial eventually resumed in June 2007, when Besigye appeared with 10 co-defendants.

In January 2007 police prevented the DP from organizing a rally in Kampala to mark the 20th anniversary of the assassination of Kayiira, the former rebel and leader of the UFM (see above). The DP accused members of the armed forces of his murder, and announced that it intended to make public their names. Throughout 2006 and 2007 opposition politicians continued to allege government and security forces intimidation, and restrictions were placed on opposition rallies and demonstrations. Questions were also asked over the Government's perceived lack of willingness to ensure the independence of the judiciary. In March 2007, in a repetition of events from November 2005, police and prison guards stormed the High Court to re-arrest nine individuals linked to Besigye (who had been granted bail on charges of treason). The judiciary reacted by holding a three-day strike in protest at what it called government interference in the legal system, and opposition supporters marched in Kampala in support of the action. Museveni wrote to Chief Justice Benjamin Odoki apologizing for the confrontation and providing assurances that the Government would ensure that such action was not repeated.

Concerns over growing anti-Asian feelings in Uganda were heightened following riots in mid-April 2007 in which one Asian Ugandan was stoned to death and a Hindu temple was attacked, as were shops and individuals. The riots followed protests organized against the Ugandan-Asian-owned Sugar Corporation of Uganda, which had been given substantial forest areas by the Government for cultivating sugar. Police were required to protect over 100 individuals from being attacked by the protesters in Kampala, and two opposition members of Parliament, Beatrice Atim and Hussein Kyanjo, who had organized the protests, were arrested, along with 26 others, on charges of inciting anti-Indian violence. In response to the arrests opposition supporters demonstrated in Kampala; the police used water cannons, tear gas and live ammunition against the protesters.

In May 2007 former Minister of Health Maj.-Gen. Jim Muhwezi was charged with embezzlement and abuse of office over a US $4.3m. child vaccination fund. Three other officials were also arrested and charged over the affair. All denied the charges.

Internal Security Concerns

From the mid-1990s three main rebel groups in northern and western Uganda challenged the Museveni administration. Firstly, in the north, the LRA (backed by Sudan) was becoming increasingly disruptive. 'Operation Clean', launched in mid-1996, met with initial success. However, the LRA soon resumed its attacks. During 1993–98 the LRA killed as many as 10,000 people, while a further 220,000 sought refuge in protected camps; economic activity in the region was devastated. During the late 1990s the authorities introduced a programme to provide a number of protected villages for northerners. However, the Government strongly resisted pressure to resume negotiations with the LRA, prompting some speculation that Museveni (a southerner) might be prepared to profit from the disablement of opposition strongholds in the northern region. In the west, meanwhile, the UPDF was challenging the serious threat posed by both the West Nile Bank Front (WNBF), led by a former Minister of Foreign Affairs, Col Juma Oris, until his death in action in February 1997, and the Allied Democratic Front (ADF), mainly comprising Ugandan Islamist fundamentalists and former soldiers of the defeated UNLA, assisted by exiled Rwandan Hutu militiamen and by former soldiers from Zaire (which, in May 1997, became the DRC).

WNBF activities subsided in mid-1997 following the killing of several hundred of its members by Sudanese rebels on good terms with the Ugandan Government. However, the ADF mounted a persistent terror campaign from mid-1997 against western Ugandan targets. In October the ADF carried out a series of attacks in the Ruwenzori mountains (where its bases were) and in Kilembe district, prompting the Ugandan and DRC armies to launch a joint military operation against the rebels. Libya and Iran were accused of supporting the ADF with military equipment and financial aid.

The inability of the UPDF to eliminate the guerrilla threat in the north and west of the country, and allegations of corruption concerning some senior UPDF officers, increasingly concerned Museveni. In December 1997 the security services established a special task force to investigate allegations that a number of officers had been offered money to carry out an assassination attempt against the President. This led to a major purge of the UPDF in January 1998, when several high-ranking officers were dismissed. Maj.-Gen. Salim Saleh—Museveni's half-brother—was promoted to Minister of State for Defence, while the UPDF commander Maj.-Gen. Mugisha Muntu was replaced by Maj.-Gen. Jeje Abubaker Odongo. Museveni also redressed the perceived ethnic imbalance in the UPDF by appointing more non-westerners to important posts. During April a combination of WNBF guerrillas, former Zairean soldiers and Sudanese government troops were reported to be operating just across the Uganda–DRC border. In June the ADF attacked the Kichwambwa Technical Institute, in the foothills of the Ruwenzori, killing an estimated 80 students and reportedly abducting more than 100 others. Reports subsequently emerged that UPDF troops guarding the college had abandoned their posts and fled during the incident, prompting many citizens in the region to lose confidence in the ability of the state to protect them, and consequently seriously diminishing Museveni's local popularity. Following the Kichwambwa atrocity the President came under mounting pressure to master the national security crisis, if needs be by abandoning his policy of refusing to negotiate with the guerrillas. His immediate response was to promise disciplinary action against the incompetent soldiers and compensation for the victims of the attack, and to appoint his trusted UPDF Chief of Staff, Brig. James Kazini, as regional commander for the Ruwenzori area. By early 1999 the ADF had reportedly displaced about 70,000 western Ugandans.

The LRA intensified its campaign in the first half of 1999. In May Museveni issued an amnesty to the rebels and promised Kony, the LRA leader, a cabinet post should he be democratically elected to government. A series of bomb attacks between 1997 and the first half of 1999 on civilian targets in Kampala were believed to be the work of the ADF. By mid-1999 it was estimated that 55 people had been killed and at least 183 injured by the attacks. By July more than 120 alleged dissidents had reportedly been arrested and interrogated in connection with the atrocities, prompting a number of protests from human rights organizations. Some 13 of those arrested were charged with terrorism and treason in June. In December 1999 Parliament passed a bill granting a general amnesty to all rebels who had been fighting to overthrow the Museveni Government and who were prepared to renounce rebellion.

An agreement signed in Kenya in December 1999 by the Presidents of Uganda and Sudan (see below) included provisions for the disarmament and disbandment of terrorist groups and the cessation of support for rebel groups. At further meetings in Kampala in September 2000 Uganda and Sudan agreed to disarm the LRA and to relocate it at least 1,000 km deeper within Sudanese territory. Improved relations and co-operation between Uganda and Sudan (see below) resulted in a number of successful UPDF offensives against LRA bases in Sudan in 2002, when Sudan allowed Ugandan troops to operate within its territory.

Following the UPDF attacks on LRA bases in Sudan during 2002, LRA forces began to return to northern Uganda. In May 2003 large numbers of LRA fighters crossed from Sudan into Uganda, reportedly heading for the northern town of Kitgum. Soon afterwards the conflict escalated, as the LRA carried out renewed attacks and abductions in northern Uganda. Both Kony and Museveni appeared to have abandoned efforts to find a peaceful solution. A brigade of 3,000 UPDF troops was deployed to defend the region, and the Government began to use newly acquired helicopter gunships to attack the rebels.

Following the terrorist attacks of 11 September 2001 in the USA, the LRA was placed on the US register of terrorist groups. In 2003 and 2004 the scale of violence in northern Uganda appeared to increase. In one 10-day period in November 2003 around 150 civilians were killed by the LRA. Two LRA attacks in February 2004 on camps near Lira left over 130 civilians dead. In May nearly 100 people were killed in two rebel attacks on Lokodi village and a displaced persons camp. A report issued by the World Refugee Survey in June 2004 estimated Uganda had 1.4m. internally displaced persons, mostly as a result of the conflict in the north. A report issued by the UN suggested at least 10,000 children had been abducted since October 2002, the majority forced to fight with the LRA. The Government's response was to step up its military operations against the LRA, criticizing international donors that sought to limit military expenditure to 2% of the overall budget. Donors refused to sanction the 2004/05 budget in May 2004, calling for negotiation rather than continued military effort to stop the violence. In March 2004 the Government renewed a protocol with the Sudanese Government allowing Ugandan forces to cross into Sudan in pursuit of LRA fighters. That month, major operations were launched against LRA bases in southern Sudan, killing more than 50 rebel soldiers. In April Museveni offered to order a cease-fire if the LRA leadership agreed to peace talks. Observers suggested that the offer was intended to placate international criticism and not a genuine commitment to a negotiated settlement. With no response from the LRA, the Government renewed its military operation. In June the Government announced that 781 rebel soldiers had been killed and over 1,500 hostages freed over the past six months. An operation in July nearly succeeded in trapping Kony, and captured four of his wives and some of his children.

By the end of 2004 LRA attacks appeared to be declining in number, and increasing numbers of LRA fighters were taking advantage of the government amnesty. The LRA spokesman, Brig. Sam Kolo, announced the rebels were seeking peace talks, and the Government offered a seven-day cease-fire in response. The cease-fire was repeatedly extended until the end of December, when the LRA refused to sign a permanent agreement; the following month Museveni ordered military action to be resumed. In February 2005 a new cease-fire came into effect as unofficial negotiations continued. Two senior LRA leaders, Col. Onon Kamdulu and Sam Kolo, took advantage of the amnesty and fled the LRA. This cease-fire proved short-lived and ended without agreement at the end of the month, leading to renewed LRA attacks throughout 2005. In July 2004 the International Criminal Court (ICC) at the

Hague, Netherlands, opened an investigation into war crimes committed by the LRA since July 2002. Some Ugandan officials expressed concern that the proposed trial might hamper efforts to negotiate a settlement. Nevertheless, in October 2005, the ICC issued arrest warrants for Joseph Kony and four other LRA commanders (deputy leader Vincent Otti, Raska Lukwiya, Okot Odhiambo and Dominic Ongwen).

In September 2005 a large force of LRA fighters moved from their bases in southern Sudan to the DRC. Led by Vincent Otti, the group set up base in Garamba National Park. In September UN officials met with a delegation of the LRA in north-eastern DRC. A senior member of the Congolese armed forces was also present at the meeting, and urged the rebels to disarm. In late 2005 the LRA renewed attacks on civilians and began to target aid agencies in particular. (The LRA also expanded its field of operation into the DRC, where eight UN peace-keepers were killed in an ambush in January 2006.) Despite an increase in attacks, the deputy commander of the LRA called for peace talks in late November. The Minister of Internal Affairs, Dr Ruhakana Rugunda, announced that the Government would be willing to meet with the LRA to discuss a peace settlement, although it was not clear whether the Government was truly committed to peace talks. In February 2006 a report issued by a consortium of 50 Ugandan and international non-governmental organizations suggested that 146 people were dying as a direct result of conflict-related violence each week in the camps in Gulu, Kitgum and Pader. In April the UN Secretary-General for Humanitarian Affairs and Emergency Relief, Jan Egeland, described the situation in northern Uganda as the worst instance of terrorism in the world.

In May 2006 there were signs that progress towards a negotiated peace settlement between the LRA and the Government was gaining ground. Through a series of carefully orchestrated public appearances, Kony seemed to signal his willingness to meet with the Government. That month Kony accepted the Government of Southern Sudan's offer to mediate in negotiations between the LRA and the Ugandan Government. In June Kony, in an interview with the British media, announced his willingness to meet government officials for peace talks, but denied allegations of atrocities including kidnapping children and forcing them to become soldiers, and the use of violence against civilians. He alleged that the UPDF was responsible for such actions, seeking to discredit the LRA. In July Museveni confirmed that he would be prepared to offer Kony an amnesty should peace talks proceed successfully, despite the ICC reiterating in June that the international arrest warrant for Kony was still valid. Talks were scheduled to take place in Juba, Sudan, in mid-July, but debates over the constitution of the LRA delegation delayed their start. At the same time, the Ugandan Minister in Charge of Security travelled to the ICC to gain support for the offer of an amnesty to senior LRA members if they attended peace negotiations.

In mid-August 2006 government soldiers killed Raska Lukwiya, a senior LRA commander and one of those named in the ICC arrest warrants, casting doubts over the opportunities for success of talks between the two sides. However, despite tensions engendered by the military operation, later that month the Government and the LRA signed a truce. Under the terms of the agreement the LRA agreed to move its fighters to camps in southern Sudan, and in return the Government would cease military operations against the rebels. The Government announced it was enacting a three-year plan to resettle internally displaced persons in the north, costing an estimated US $336m. By January 2007 some 230,000 people had returned to their villages as security in the north continued to improve. However, an estimated 1.2m. people remained in the camps.

Throughout August 2006 LRA fighters left their base in the DRC for camps in southern Sudan. Kony and Otti arrived in Ri Kwangba camp in September. However, the LRA claimed that the Ugandan army had surrounded the rally points, and halted plans to relocate their soldiers. The Government denied the charges, and following renewed talks the cease-fire was extended by two months. In October senior army commanders announced they would resume operations against any LRA members still based in Uganda. Despite signing a renewed truce to revive negotiations, the following month the LRA suspended its participation in the talks, accusing the Government of killing three rebels as they headed to the assembly areas. In December the Government agreed to withdraw troops in an effort to restore confidence in the talks. Museveni held face to face talks with LRA deputy leader Vincent Otti, the first time he had had direct contact with the leaders of the rebel group. The President agreed to keep government troops east of the Nimule–Juba road, if the LRA kept its fighters north of the Juba–Torit road. The cease-fire was extended again.

In an effort to end the impasse, former Mozambican President Joaquim Chissano was appointed as UN special envoy to mediate between the Government and the LRA in December 2006. However, at the start of 2007 peace talks stalled once more as the LRA leaders demanded that the negotiations be moved from southern Sudan to Kenya. They demanded that Southern Sudan's Vice-President, Riek Machar, be replaced as chief mediator after Southern Sudan's President, Salva Kiir Mayardit, reportedly announced that LRA rebels were no longer welcome in the country. The Kenyan Government refused the LRA's request, but the Ugandan Government announced that it would consider changing the location, possibly to South Africa. In mid-April 2007 the LRA and the Ugandan Government signed a new truce. Under its terms the LRA committed to moving its soldiers to the border area adjoining the DRC within six weeks, while the Government guaranteed their security. Both sides agreed to restart talks in Juba, Southern Sudan. The tortured pace of talks continued into mid-2007.

REGIONAL RELATIONS

During 1987 Uganda's relations with neighbouring Kenya deteriorated, with the Museveni Government accusing Kenya of sheltering Ugandan rebels. In March the Kenyan authorities expelled hundreds of Ugandans. In December clashes occurred between Kenyan and Ugandan security forces and the border was temporarily closed. Discussions between the heads of state of the two countries led to an improvement in relations, and in August 1990 President Daniel arap Moi of Kenya visited Museveni, indicating a renewed *détente* between Uganda and Kenya. Relations worsened again during early 1995 when Uganda granted refugee status to an alleged Kenyan guerrilla leader. Relations between Uganda and Kenya remained strained until January 1996, when, following the intervention of the newly elected President Benjamin Mkapa of Tanzania, Museveni and Moi were publicly reconciled. In March 1996 Museveni, Moi and Mkapa formally inaugurated the secretariat of the permanent tripartite commission for East African co-operation. A treaty for the re-establishment of the defunct East African Community (EAC), providing for the creation of a free trade area and for the establishment of a regional legislative assembly and regional court, was signed in November 1999. In January 2005 the East African Customs Union came into effect.

In December 2006 Rwanda and Burundi were accepted as members of the EAC, expanding the block to include around 90m. people. In March 2007 the East African Court of Justice in Arusha rejected Kenya's nominees for the East African Legislative Assembly (EALA), after a case was filed by Kenyan opposition activists. The Court demanded that the three EAC members harmonize election procedures to the EALA, and the ruling further delayed the establishment of the Assembly, already deferred from November 2006. The EAC presented a US $28.3m. budget in June 2007, focusing on establishing a common market and consolidating the customs union. In February 2004 Uganda joined four other East African countries in forming the Eastern African Standby Brigade (EASB), which was to form part of the AU's African Standby Force (ASF). The ASF was intended to form the heart of Africa's response to conflict on the continent, and the EASB was one of five regional brigades to be established. In March 2007 Uganda sent 1,700 troops to Somalia as part of an AU peace-keeping force.

During 1988 tension arose along Uganda's border with Zaire, owing to a number of attacks by Zairean troops on NRA units; further border clashes occurred in 1992. In November 1996 Ugandan rebels were reportedly operating from within Zaire with the support of Zairean troops. In late 1996 and early 1997 the Ugandan authorities repeatedly denied allegations that Ugandan forces were occupying territory in eastern Zaire; however, it was widely reported that Uganda was supplying armaments and tactical support, if not troops, to Kabila's Alliance des forces démocratiques pour la libération du Congo-Zaïre, which overthrew the Government of President Mobutu Sese Seko in May 1997. The Museveni administration, however, subsequently withdrew its support from the Kabila regime in the renamed DRC, as Kabila made no attempt to sever the ongoing supply of arms to Ugandan rebels operating from the DRC–Uganda border region. When, in August 1998, anti-Kabila elements launched a rebellion from the eastern part of the DRC, Uganda intervened, at first covertly, on the side of the rebels. Uganda eventually admitted that it had deployed troops in the DRC in co-operation with the Rwandan Government, asserting that they were protecting Ugandan and Rwandan interests by creating a 'security zone'. In November the two Governments formed a joint military command. By 1999 the Ugandan Government was seeking to extricate itself from the conflict, and held unilateral talks with Kabila. However, an agreement reached in April was superseded by a comprehensive cease-fire agreement concluded in Lusaka, Zambia, in early July, signed by the heads of state of all the countries involved in the conflict (Kabila, Museveni and the Rwandan President, as well as the Presidents of Angola, Namibia and Zimbabwe, who had entered the conflict in support of the DRC Government). Under the Lusaka accord a joint military commission was to be formed to supervise the cease-fire and all foreign troops were to withdraw from the DRC and be replaced by a UN peace-keeping force. Disagreements subsequently emerged over the schedule for the evacuation of the foreign forces, and Uganda continued to station about 16,000 troops in the DRC. Meanwhile, tensions had arisen between Uganda and Rwanda when, in May, the DRC rebel group, the Rassemblement congolais démocratique, which they had been jointly supporting, split into two factions, with the Ugandan and Rwandan Governments suspending their co-operation to back rival rebel leaders. In mid-August fighting erupted between Ugandan and Rwandan troops in Kisangani, in the DRC. A cease-fire agreement was signed after three days. In September Museveni transferred leading UPDF commanders from Kisangani to Uganda, in an attempt to reduce tension between Ugandan and Rwandan troops. In May 2000 the DRC Government signed an agreement in which it consented to the deployment of 500 UN military observers and 5,000 support troops, the Mission des nations unies en République démocratique du Congo, to monitor the frequently violated cease-fire that had been inaugurated by the Lusaka accord. Nevertheless, further fighting occurred in June.

In mid-March 2001 the groups involved in the conflict commenced the military disengagement of their forces. However, in April the UN reported that Burundi, Rwanda and Uganda were illegally exploiting the DRC's mineral reserves. Museveni announced that Uganda would withdraw its remaining troops from the DRC and pull out of the UN-sponsored Lusaka accord. In late 2001 Rwandan troops occupied positions in the eastern DRC that had been vacated by the UPDF in June of that year, prompting fears that clashes would again erupt between Rwandan and Ugandan forces. In October it was reported that a new rebel group, known as the People's Redemption Army, had been formed in the Rwanda-controlled part of the DRC by dissident UPDF officers who had defected earlier in the year. However, negotiations between Museveni and Maj.-Gen. Paul Kagame, the President of Rwanda, saw relations stabilize once more. Despite the redeployment of Ugandan troops in the north-east of the DRC in January 2002, to prevent escalating fighting between the rebel factions from reaching the border with Uganda, negotiations between Uganda and Rwanda continued, with British mediation, and in April 2002 the two countries signed a peace agreement in Kigali. In mid-August the DRC and Uganda reached an accord in the Angolan capital, Luanda, providing for the normalization of relations between the two countries, and the full withdrawal of Ugandan troops in the DRC. Most Ugandan troops were reported to have withdrawn from the DRC by early May.

The establishment of camps in the DRC by LRA rebels in mid-2005 led to increasing strains in the relationship between the two Governments. Uganda threatened to send troops over the border to pursue the rebels, and the DRC rejected requests for joint operations against the LRA. In late April 2006 the DRC accused the UPDF of illegally crossing into its territory as part of an operation against the LRA. The Ugandan Government denied that its troops had entered the country illegally. In December thousands fled into Uganda following renewed fighting in the DRC between government soldiers and those loyal to rebel leader Laurent Nkunda. Later that month leaders from the Great Lakes countries signed a security and development agreement in Kenya. It included measures to demobilize rebel groups, act against arms-smuggling and provide more co-ordinated assistance to refugees. Security plans were reinforced in April 2007 when army chiefs from Burundi, the DRC, Rwanda and Uganda agreed joint military action against rebel groups destabilizing the region.

During the late 1980s and early 1990s Sudanese troops reportedly made repeated incursions into Ugandan territory in pursuit of Sudanese rebels, and Sudanese aircraft were alleged to have dropped bombs in northern Uganda on several occasions. In 1992 and 1993 some 130,000 Sudanese refugees fled into Uganda. Relations between the two countries deteriorated seriously in 1994, when each Government accused the other of harbouring and supporting their respective outlawed guerrilla groups; in April 1995 Uganda severed diplomatic relations with Sudan. In September 1996 Sudan and Uganda resumed diplomatic relations, and in the following month a preliminary accord was signed in the Iranian capital, Tehran. In April 1997, despite continuing discussions under the auspices of Iran and Libya, the Sudanese authorities claimed that their forces had killed several hundred Ugandan soldiers who had been assisting Sudanese rebels from within Sudan. In December 1999 Presidents Museveni and Omar al-Bashir met in Nairobi and signed a peace agreement, brokered by the former US President Jimmy Carter. Each country agreed to stop hosting guerrilla groups directed against each other. The two Presidents also agreed to resume full diplomatic relations. In January 2000 the Ugandan Government released the last group of 72 Sudanese prisoners of war. The Sudanese Government announced that it was reopening its embassy in Kampala, which had been closed since 1995.

In August 2001 the Ugandan embassy reopened in the Sudanese capital, Khartoum, and a chargé d'affaires was appointed; relations were upgraded to ambassadorial level in April 2002. In August 2001 al-Bashir announced that his Government would no longer provide support for the LRA, and in December bank accounts used by the LRA in London, United Kingdom, were frozen. In March 2002 it was announced that Sudan was to allow the UPDF to deploy forces within its borders in order to pursue operations against the LRA, and later that month the Ugandan Government announced that its troops had captured all four main bases in Sudan belonging to the LRA.

In August 2003 the Ugandan Government accused the Sudanese Government of supplying arms to the LRA, alleging that Kony had returned to southern Sudan to re-supply the LRA. The Sudanese Government denied the allegations, and declared that it was adhering to the military protocol between the two countries under which Sudan agreed to stop supporting the LRA and to allow the Ugandan army to cross the border in pursuit of LRA fighters. In March 2004 the southern rebel Southern People's Liberation Movement (SPLM) announced it had launched attacks on the LRA, claiming that the Sudanese Government was backing the Ugandan rebels. The campaign was launched following reports of LRA attacks on SPLM positions south of Juba. With the conclusion of a peace settlement between the SPLM and the Sudanese Government in Khartoum, some of the 160,000 refugees from the conflict began to head home. In October 2005 the UPDF was granted permission by the Sudanese Government to pursue LRA rebels beyond the 62-mile limit accepted in previous negotiations. In January the International Crisis Group accused the Sudanese military of continuing to support the LRA.

In October 2006 the UN's High Commissioner for Refugees (UNHCR) temporarily suspended its repatriation programme for southern Sudanese based in Uganda, following attacks in southern Sudan that killed at least 40 people. It resumed operations by the end of the month after assurances from the Southern Sudan Government that it was taking action to prevent violent attacks. The LRA were initially blamed, although Sudanese armed groups were later suspected. However, in January 2007 the LRA launched two attacks in southern Sudan, killing 13 people.

During the late 1980s an estimated 250,000 Rwandan refugees were sheltering in Uganda. Relations with Rwanda deteriorated in October 1990, following the infiltration of northern Rwanda by an invasion force of some 4,000 Rwandan rebels who had been based in Uganda. Their leader, Maj.-Gen. Fred Rwigyema (who was killed by the Rwandan armed forces), was a deputy commander of the NRA and a former Ugandan deputy defence minister. In November President Museveni dismissed all non-Ugandan members of the NRA. The victory in Rwanda of the Front patriotique rwandais (FPR) in mid-1994 brought about a significant change in bilateral relations; Maj.-Gen. Paul Kagame, Rwandan Vice-President and Minister of National Defence, had previously served in the Ugandan NRA, as had other members of the FPR administration. In August 1995 Museveni made an official visit to Rwanda, and both countries made commitments to enhance economic and social co-operation. In August 1998 Uganda and Rwanda jointly deployed troops in the DRC, although tensions subsequently emerged between the two forces (see above). However, this tension eased when both armies withdrew from Kisangani during May 2000, and in July Museveni and Kagame (now President of Rwanda) met to discuss relations between their respective countries. In early May 2003 Rwanda mobilized troops along its border with Uganda, claiming that rebel Interahamwe militia were planning to attack from the Kabale District in Uganda (although the Ugandan Government was not directly accused of supporting it).

At the end of 2004, according to UNHCR, there were a total of 248,557 refugees in Uganda, including 214,673 from Sudan and 18,902 from Rwanda.

Economy

LINDA VAN BUREN

'Uganda's macroeconomic performance over the past 15 years has been exceptional,' proclaimed the IMF in January 2007, adding that per-head gross domestic product (GDP) growth had exceeded the average for sub-Saharan Africa, while inflation had remained reasonably stable. Furthermore, Uganda's stock of international reserves had been replenished and the rate of poverty had vastly improved. According to IMF data, Uganda's economy grew by an annual average of 6.0% in 1995–2005 and by a further 5.4% in 2006. The Fund noted, however, that GDP per head had failed to rise at a concomitant level over the last few years. The Government's Poverty Eradication Action Plan (PEAP), launched in May 2005, received the backing of the IMF's Policy Support Instrument (PSI) programme. Corruption, the Fund added, has also 'cut into government revenues and has led to wasteful spending'. In 2005 Uganda asked the IMF to waive the non-observance of two performance criteria: the accumulation of domestic arrears under the commitment control system; and new lending by the Uganda Development Bank (UDB). The Fund did indeed in January 2006 agree to waive these criteria. Uganda's economy is no longer reliant on just one export commodity, coffee, which traditionally contributed up to 95% of export revenue. Spearheaded by the Government's Strategic Export Programme (SEP), export diversification has been achieved. By 2002 coffee accounted for only 13.5% of total export earnings. In 2004/05 the largest share of public spending was allocated to paying wages and salaries; the Government, with a payroll of 600,000 people, was still the nation's largest employer. However, 2005/06 saw a major 'payroll cleaning exercise', in which phantom workers were detected and removed from the payroll. Some 4,000 teachers' records and about 2,500 records on the general government payrolls had been deleted by June 2006. The 2006/07 budget statement proclaimed that all government accounting officers would be held accountable for any discrepancies, would be surcharged and would have their non-wage provisions reduced by the amounts of any discrepancies.

AGRICULTURE

Agriculture is the most important sector in this land-locked country. In 2006 it accounted for 30.3% of GDP and provided a livelihood for over three-quarters of Uganda's people. According to data collated during the 2002 census, 68% of Ugandan households engaged in the practice of subsistence agriculture. The 2007/08 budget, presented in June 2007, committed funding to support the Bonna Bagaggawale ('Prosperity for All') scheme, which aimed to bring more Ugandan households into the monetary economy. This scheme placed emphasis on 'correct enterprise selection', and was mostly designed for farmers of five acres or less. Households presiding over these small plots of land would be encouraged to abandon the production of low-value crops such as maize or tobacco, and instead engage in zero-grazing dairy cattle, fruit growing, fish farming or the raising of chickens or pigs. More lucrative crops were also suggested, such as pharmaceutical herbs or mulberry for silk farming. The development of the whole economy is heavily influenced by the agricultural sector's performance, yet the Government remains keen to diversify activities and President Museveni signalled Uganda's long-term growth strategy in June 2007 when he declared that 'enhanced agricultural production must be accompanied with rapid industrialization'. After severe dependence on coffee for decades, the early 2000s saw a revival in the production of other crops, for example cotton and tobacco, which had been important before Idi Amin Dada came to power in 1971, but which had been virtually dormant for some 30 years. Also performing well was a non-traditional subsector, horticulture, and by 2005 fish exports were also becoming significant. Soils are generally fertile, and apart from some parts of the north-east and the north-west, the country has a climate favourable to both field crops and livestock production. Smallholder mixed farming predominates, with estate production confined mainly to tea and sugar cane. Under Museveni's presidency, efforts have been made to rehabilitate the sector, although continuing security problems in northern and western regions have slowed the pace of recovery.

Coffee

Coffee is grown by some 2.5m. small-scale farmers. Production fell steadily throughout the 1970s, from a record 3.75m. 60-kg bags in 1973 to only 1.62m. bags in 1981. Once the recovery of the 1990s was under way, 2001's 3.16m. bags became the high-water mark. Total production in 2006 was 2.35m. bags. Most of the crop is Robusta; less than 15% is Arabica, which commands a significantly higher price than robusta. The Coffee Marketing Board (CMB), which was the sole purchaser and exporter of coffee during the 1980s, had persistent problems with crop finance, which adversely affected deliveries from farmers. The sector exhibited many of the problems that beset commodity-marketing arrangements in a number of African countries: a state-run commodity marketing board held a statutory monopoly over the purchase of the crop; prices were fixed by the Government; and farmers often had to wait for long periods of time for their payments, owing to cash-flow crises at the commodity board. However, unlike many slow privatization programmes in Africa, the coffee sector in Uganda underwent a thorough and fundamental transformation during the 1990s.

In 1990 the CMB's monopoly of coffee marketing was abolished. Five coffee co-operatives joined forces to form Union Export Services (UNEX), and by mid-1992 UNEX was handling 20% of coffee sales. By the mid-1990s Uganda had 12 coffee-marketing co-operatives and 167 licensed coffee exporters. However, in a climate of fierce local competition and flagging international demand mergers and takeovers became commonplace. By 1996/97 the number of licensed exporters had fallen by more than one-half, to 76, and, of these, 10 were reportedly accounting for 75% of total coffee exports. Of the 46 Ugandan licensed coffee exporters in 1997/98, only 37 renewed their permits in 1998/99, and, reportedly, only 26 actually exported any coffee. The largest firm accounted for 17.8% of total exports in the latter year, while a further five companies provided more than 50% of the total. The Government undertook to unbundle the CMB's assets into smaller, more attractive units, in order to accelerate its privatization. However, investor interest in the former monopoly's facilities was lukewarm, and non-Ugandan-backed companies preferred to finance new factory plants. The Uganda Coffee Development Authority (UCDA) was established in 1991, with responsibility for policy-making, as well as for research and development, for promotion, for the co-ordination of marketing and for quality control. Prior to 1991, growers competed with each other to sell their crop to a single buyer and earned less than 20% of the value that their coffee fetched on the world market. In contrast, the top five coffee buyers accounted for about 60% of the market in 2007.

The Uganda Investment Authority in the 1990s and the early 2000s sought investors in coffee nurseries and enterprises for roasting, packaging, processing, blending and the utilization of coffee by-products. Private-sector coffee nurseries introduced seedlings with higher yields; the first major crop of these seedlings began to mature in 1995, with more maturing every year thereafter. During 2001/02 the Government distributed 16.5m. coffee seedlings to 85,000 households and established five new coffee nurseries in a bid to sustain production, so that when the volatile price began to rise again, Uganda would be ready to exploit the situation. In 2005, after a long period of low prices, coffee prices began to rise again, and Uganda did benefit in part, but many growers had abandoned coffee growing in favour of more lucrative crops, and a lower volume of coffee was available for export, so that the country was unable to take full advantage of the price rise. An estimated 1.5m. Ugandan coffee trees per year were destroyed because of coffee wilt disease during the late 1990s, but most of the country's 330m. coffee trees were not affected, and a larger contributing factor to lower coffee output was the abandonment of coffee growing in favour of other crops. The UCDA is responsible for replanting coffee trees and for conducting research into areas such as cloning techniques, in an attempt to introduce trees that are resistant to diseases. Under the SEP, between September 2001 and June 2003, 46m. coffee seedlings were distributed to 200,000 households, and 16 coffee-processing machines were imported, with a capacity to wet-process 20,000 metric tons of arabica coffee per year. Uganda's coffee exports declined from 2.55m. bags in 2004/05 to 2.14m. bags in 2005/06, but then recovered to 2.48m. bags in 2006/07.

The United Kingdom has traditionally been Uganda's largest customer for coffee, taking about one-third of the total. The USA, Japan and Germany are also important markets. Most of Uganda's coffee is transported to the Kenyan port of Mombasa by road and rail, although the Museveni Government would prefer to effect a transfer to rail freight for all Ugandan trade, in order to reduce costs. The Government introduced an organic-coffee certification scheme in 2002, and by June 2003 16,000 coffee growers had been granted certificates.

Cotton

The cotton sector, regulated since its founding in 1994 by the Cotton Development Organization (CDO), has experienced mixed fortunes. Cotton output reached a peak of 266,422 bales (each of 217.7 kg) in 1997, after having declined from a peak of 467,000 bales in 1970 to a low of 10,000 bales in 1987. The causes of the decline were the very low official prices paid to producers and the physical deterioration of the ginneries during Amin's rule, as well as security problems in the main cotton-growing areas in the north and east of the country. Exports ceased altogether during the 1970s, resuming in 1982. In 1986 the Museveni Government initiated the Emergency Cotton Production Programme. The US $15m. programme was funded by the World Bank, the United Kingdom and other donors. The derelict state of the ginneries frequently resulted in stockpiles awaiting ginning, even when harvests were low. Ginneries were privatized during 1995–97, and the ensuing competition, together with the distribution of free high-quality seed by the Government in 1996 and the liberalization of seed distribution in 1997, contributed to increased yields. The country has 29 ginneries, of which 27 are double-roller gins. Ginning capacity doubled between 1993 and 2001. A high proportion of Uganda's output is long-staple cotton, which commands a price premium sometimes as high as 20%. The cotton sector is a particular focus of the Government's bid to increase the amount of value added to agricultural products before export (see below). Cotton exports earned US $30m. in 2006/07, more than 90% of which was exported as raw lint. In the local vegetable oil industry, cottonseed oil faces stiff competition from imported palm oil. A growth area within the cotton sector is organic cotton, the production of which rose from 3,500 bales in 2005/06 to 13,000 bales in 2006/07.

Horticulture

Horticulture became significant in Uganda in the late 1990s. The export of fresh cut flowers was singled out in the 2005/06 budget as a potential growth sector. Uganda's revenue from the export of horticultural produce rose from US $2.3m. in 1995 to $10.9m. in 2001. Horticultural produce ranges from beans and peas to tomatoes, onions, pimientos, ginger, simsim (sesame seeds) and vanilla pods. Vanilla performed well enough to be singled out in the 2002/03 budget speech for its success. About 6,000 Ugandans work in the horticultural sector, about 80% of them women. According to FAO, Uganda produced about 556,000 metric tons of fresh vegetables in 2006. In an effort to add more value locally before export, some vegetables are exported frozen. Limiting factors are high air freight charges and inadequate storage facilities at Entebbe to keep horticultural produce fresh while it awaits air freight space to Europe. In 2000 the Ugandan Flower Exporters' Association and the Horticultural Exporters' Association set up Fresh Handling Services Limited to organize the logistics of exporting these perishable commodities to distant markets, especially the Netherlands. Ugandan horticultural exporters pay air freight costs of $2.40 per kg, whereas Kenyan and Ethiopian exporters pay $1.70 per kg and $1.50 per kg, respectively. A cold storage facility at the old Entebbe Airport, built in 1997 with funding from US AID, was in the final stages of privatization in July 2007. After negotiating for three years, the Civil Aviation Authority (CAA) announced that it would hand over the facility in September 2007 to Fresh Handling Services, which had previously been renting the facility from the CAA. Uganda's flower growers specialize in small roses and, to a lesser extent, chrysanthemums. A new 13 ha joint venture announced in July 2007 between Madhvani of Uganda and Flower Direct of the Netherlands is to specialize in chrysanthemums. Roses are grown on 142 ha, and chrysanthemums are grown on 32 ha. Uganda exports some 7,500 metric tons of flowers per year, earning export revenue of $30m. The number of flower-growing companies grew from three in 1993 to 18 in 2007. Of the 18, seven were owned by Ugandans, three were owned jointly by Ugandan and foreign investors, and eight were owned by foreign investors, including three Dutch firms.

Tea

The tea sector experienced a sustained recovery in the 1990s. Prior to the regime of Idi Amin and his nationalization of tea plantations in 1972, Uganda had been second only to Kenya among African tea producers. However, production declined each year thereafter until 1980, by which time Uganda's tea exports were negligible. In 1980 the United Kingdom-based company Mitchell Cotts, former owner of three groups of tea estates until these were nationalized by Amin, was invited back to establish a joint venture with the Government to own and operate the estates. The Toro and Mityana Tea Co (Tamteco) was formed in 1980, with 51% of the shares owned by the Government, and work began on a US $8.8m. programme to rehabilitate the overgrown plantations and near-derelict factories. Tamteco, with 2,300 ha under cultivation, was fully privatized in 1995. In addition to its cultivation of tea, Tamteco has branched out into growing lemon grass and rosemary for use in herbal teas and infusions. Other tea producers include Rwenzori Highlands Tea Co, which comprised six tea estates covering over 3,000 ha in western Uganda, along the border with the Democratic Republic of Congo (DRC). Smallholders, numbering about 1m. and cultivating some 9,500 ha, market their output through the Uganda Tea Growers' Asscn. The Uganda Tea Authority organizes research into growing methods and oversees the sector. Tea estates still face some of the problems that have hindered the sector for decades, such as a shortage of pickers and transport difficulties. The sector has, however, benefited from the success of Uganda's economic reform programme, with higher real wages attracting harvest labour. Uganda harvested 6,740 metric tons of made tea in 1990, which earned the country $3.57m.; by 2006 output had risen by more than five-fold, to 37,734 tons. In 2001/02 the Government distributed 2m. tea seedlings to 1,000 households in a bid to bring more Ugandan farmers into the cash-crop economy. In 2002/03 300,000 'improved clones' were imported for multiplication, and 5m. tea seedlings were distributed to 1,300 households. Also during that year, 150 tea nurseries were established, with the capacity to nurture 9m. tea seedlings, and more than 100 nursery operators were trained.

Other Crops

Tobacco output was frequently adversely affected by unfavourable weather conditions and recurrent fighting during the 1980s and the 1990s in the West Nile region, where it is grown. Tobacco's performance improved in the late 1990s, despite declining global demand. Production of tobacco leaves rose from 11,333 metric tons in 1998 to 36,000 tons in 2005. By 2005/06 Ugandan tobacco growers were experiencing the same market forces as the world's other growers: continued weakening of demand in the major importing countries which meant that buyers could drive a hard bargain when negotiating with growers (see especially Malawi's experience). The 2007/08 budget stated that Ugandan tobacco farmers were to be encouraged to grow other crops.

Production of raw sugar had fallen to only 2,400 metric tons by 1984, compared with a peak of 152,000 tons in 1968. Local demand is estimated at some 235,000 tons per year. Lack of transport and problems with the maintenance of mechanical equipment contributed to this drastic fall in output, but the major cause was the expulsion of the Asian families who ran much of the sugar industry, on three large estates. The Madhvani and Mehta families returned in 1980 to begin the rehabilitation of the estates and factories, in joint-venture companies with the Government. A US $58m. project to rehabilitate the state-owned Kinyara Sugar Works (which was in the process of being privatized in 2007) began in 1992, partly financed by Kuwait, the Arab Bank for Economic Development in Africa and the Saudi Fund for Development. Once rehabilitated, Kinyara's capacity was rated at 37,000 tons of sugar per year. This rose to 64,000 tons in 2004, and Kinyara has the capacity to produce 93,000 tons per year. In 1985 a branch of the Madhvani family signed an agreement with the Government to establish a new company, Kakira Sugar Works. Upon completion of the rehabilitation work, Kakira had an annual capacity of 120,000 tons of cane sugar; it produced an estimated 70,000 tons in 1997. In 2004 the Madhvani Group announced an investment of $2m. to improve outgrower conditions and to attract some 4,000–5,000 additional outgrowers by mid-2006. The 2002/03 budget raised the excise duty on imported sugar from 10% to 20%, which was welcomed by local sugar producers but perhaps not by the IMF and the World Bank. The 2005/06 budget levied an excise duty not only on imported sugar but also on domestically produced sugar. A 100% excise duty on sugar imported from countries not in the East African Community (i.e. countries other than Kenya and Tanzania) was due to expire in March 2008. Controversially, this duty applied to sugar from other member-states of COMESA. In 2007 Ugandan sugar producers were lobbying for the 100% excise duty to be extended beyond 2008. Uganda harvested 1.6m. tons of sugar cane in 2005.

Cocoa production declined significantly during the Amin regime and then slowly recovered during the late 1980s and the 1990s. Production rose steadily in the second half of the 1990s and beyond, rising to an estimated 5,000 metric tons of cocoa beans in 2006. During 2001/02 the Government distributed 1.1m. cocoa seedlings to 2,933 households, in a move designed both to alleviate poverty and to stimulate export revenue. The groundnut sector also experienced steady growth from the 1990s onwards; output of groundnuts in shells was 158,000 tons in 2006. Uganda's staple food crop is matoke, a form of plantain. Output of matoke is over 9m. tons per year. Also contributing towards national food requirements in 2005 were 5.47m. tons of cassava, 2.63m. tons of sweet potatoes, 700,000 tons of finger millet, 420,000 tons of sorghum, 573,000 tons of potatoes (the fifth significant increase in a row) and 711,300 tons of various pulses (mainly dry beans, pigeon peas and dry cowpeas). Both pulses and potatoes are seen as growth sectors among food crops. There are three rice-growing projects in the country. The International Finance Corpn (IFC), an affiliate of the World Bank, provided a US $2.4m. loan to Tilda Uganda Ltd for the development of an integrated rice-growing and -processing facility at Kibimba, in eastern Uganda. The rice mill, with a capacity of 5 tons per hour, processes rice grown locally by smallholders in addition to that cultivated on the main farm. Uganda produced 153,000 tons of rice in 2006. Maize cultivation is expanding, both for subsistence and as a cash crop, although transport problems and the poor state of rural roads hamper the evacuation of crops; the 2006 harvest was 1.17m. tons. Production of soya beans grew steadily throughout the 1990s, increasing from 53,000 tons in 1992 to a record 187,000 tons in 2003, before falling back to an estimated 158,000 per year in 2004–05. In 2005 Uganda also harvested about 623,913 tons of sweet bananas, 173,000 tons of sunflower seeds, 161,000 tons of sesame seeds, 14,698 tons of tomatoes, 15,000 tons of wheat, and 3,231 tons of chick peas. Small amounts of vanilla, pepper, ginger and allspice were also produced. The Government's National Agricultural Advisory Service (NAADS) was extended to eight new districts in 2005/06, bringing the total to 37 districts.

Livestock, Fishing and Forestry

Beef and dairy cattle are kept by smallholders and on large commercial ranches. The country has good-quality pasture, but the prevalence of several endemic diseases and cattle-rustling (the armed theft of cattle) are persistent problems. The total number of cattle was estimated at 6.97m. in 2006. The dairy sector underwent a revitalization in the early 2000s, funded by several UN agencies, the African Development Bank (ADB), the European Development Fund (EDF) and Denmark. The project aimed at improving the processing, collection and transport of dairy produce to urban markets. Dairy cattle account for about one-third of the national cattle herd. Goats, sheep, pigs, bees and poultry are also important. In the mid-1990s the Government invited foreign companies to invest in cattle, sheep and goat ranching; in chicken, peking duck and ostrich farming; in beekeeping; in hide, skin and leather processing; in cattle-horn processing; in preserved-meat processing and in crocodile farming and processing. Potential was particularly identified in beekeeping; Uganda had more than 75,000 beehives in 2006, and honey exports could be increased with better marketing overseas.

Uganda has an abundance of lakes and rivers, and fishing is an important rural industry in this land-locked country, with considerable scope for further development, particularly in inshore fish farming, eels and freshwater prawns. The total catch rose from 220,948 metric tons in 1998 to an estimated 415,000 tons in 2006, of which some 40,000 tons was produced by fish farming. Important types included tilapia and other cichlid species. In 1989 an Italian company began to develop an integrated fisheries centre at Masese to smoke and dry tilapia and Nile perch. Concerns were raised in 1996 that the country's fish stocks were being depleted, and the licensing of processing factories was suspended (20 were licensed at the time, although not all were operational). Fish exports contributed over 15% of total export revenue and earned about US $100m.

in 2006. In 2002 the ADB extended a loan of $23m. to Uganda to revitalize the fisheries industry. About two-thirds of the total was designated for the construction of 30 modern refrigeration factories. Nevertheless, Ugandan fisheries authorities complained that while neighbouring Kenya owns only 6% of Lake Victoria compared with the 43% owned by Uganda, Kenya has 16 fish-processing plants on its shore of the lake and earns $200m. a year from the export of Lake Victoria fish.

Forests and woodland cover some 7.5m. ha of the country. Total roundwood removals amounted to 40.0m. cu m in 2005, of which 36.8m. cu m ended up as wood fuel; only about 4,000 metric tons were exported.

INDUSTRY

The manufacturing sector had been recording strong growth during the mid-1990s and early 2000s. During 1995–2005 manufacturing GDP increased by an average of 9.4% per year. The 1998/99 fiscal year realised a particularly good performance from this sector, which reportedly grew by 13.7%. However, manufacturing declined sharply in 2005/06, falling by 1.6%, as compared to growth of 11.1% recorded in 2004/05. The Uganda Manufacturing Association (UMA) attributed the decline in manufacturing output to the country's faltering electricity supply. The sector's main industries involve the processing of the country's agricultural produce, including coffee, cotton, tea, sugar, tobacco, edible oils and dairy products, and grain milling and brewing. There has also been some activity in the areas of vehicle assembly and the manufacture of textiles, steel, metal products, hoes, wheelbarrows, mattresses, cement, soap, shoes, animal feeds, fertilizers, paints, cigarettes and matches. The output of all these industries fell drastically during the 1970s. Much plant and machinery was in a poor state of repair, and shortages of fuel, spare parts and technical and managerial skills also hampered the sector. Another problem was the poor purchasing power of the currency, which encouraged the labour force to avoid wage labour in favour of activities rewarded with food or other consumables. The industrial sector as a whole contributed 20.4% of GDP in 2004/05 and grew by 10.8% in that year, although the growth rate fell to 4.5% in 2005/06. The Government has sought to encourage private-sector investment in a myriad of manufacturing activities, ranging from packaging materials to fish sausages. President Museveni, on his return from a visit to the USA in 2005, urged Uganda Breweries to market its *waragi*, well-known throughout East Africa, to the USA as 'banana gin'.

The textile industry suffered a severe lack of skilled personnel and spare parts in the 1990s, but considerable amounts of aid from the ADB, the EU and Arab funds are helping to establish new ginneries, spinning and weaving mills and are enabling the industry to repair existing plants and equipment. There are four fully integrated textile mills, with a total rated capacity of 66m. linear m of cloth per year. Yarn is also produced. Uganda's largest textile factory, Nyanza Textiles Industries (NYTIL) at Jinja, reopened in 1996 under private management, after several years of dormancy. In June 1999 a review of NYTIL's performance alleged that some 3.7m. sq m of textiles were being smuggled into Uganda every month. The 2002/03 budget increased the excise duty on *mivumba* (imported second-hand clothing) by 5%. The US African Growth and Opportunity Act (AGOA) of 2000 gave a significant boost to trade with Uganda, in both directions. Spurred largely by textile products made in Uganda from Ugandan long-staple cotton, Uganda's exports to the USA more than doubled in a single year, from US $15.3m. in 2002 to $34.9m. in 2003. However, the 2004/05 removal of quotas limiting the export of textile goods into the US market from large, cost-effective producers such as the People's Republic of China and India had a detrimental effect on most African textile exporters, including those in Uganda. The subsequent extension of AGOA to 2015 offered new opportunities to African exporters.

The country's first vehicle-assembly plant, operated by GM Co, was a joint venture between the local Spear Motors and Peter Bauer of Germany. Capacity is 490 commercial vehicles and 360 trailers per year, with about 40% available for export. In 1989 the Madhvani Group began to bring nine of its 10 industrial companies back into production; at that time, only its textile firm, Mulco, was still operating. By 1997 the group was producing tea, beer, cooking oil, sugar, confectionery, steel bars, fencing, cables, matches, bottle tops, glassware, cut flowers, twine and cardboard boxes, and in 1998 it ventured into the assembly of televisions. In addition, in 2001, the company was involved in vehicle distribution and servicing, flour milling, software development, air-charter services, tourism and the distribution of television programming. It was also manufacturing 12,000 metric tons of soap per year and producing rhizobium, an agrochemical used to increase yields of leguminous crops. In 1995 the Government awarded KW Uganda Ltd a licence to import beer from South Africa, thereby opening the Ugandan beer market to foreign competition. In 1997 Nile Breweries announced a joint venture with South African Breweries (SAB, which later became SABMiller), to produce South African brands of beer in Uganda. SAB took a 41% stake in Nile Breweries, which was increased to a majority share in 2001. The company launched a beer called Eagle, which was made from locally grown sorghum yet resembled imported beers in appearance. A local firm, Century Bottling Co, obtained the franchise to produce Coca-Cola in the Ntinda industrial area, outside Kampala. Lake Victoria Bottling Co Ltd produces Pepsi-Cola. A tannery has been opened at Jinja, and it is hoped that Uganda will become self-sufficient in leather goods.

There are two cement plants, at Tororo (near the Kenyan border) and at Hima (about 500 km to the west), with rated annual capacities of 150,000 metric tons and 300,000 tons respectively, although in 1995 their combined output was only 84,000 tons. Total domestic requirements are 650,000 tons per year. In 1995 the Kenya-based Rawal group bought the Hima plant for US $20.5m., while the Kenyan company Corrugated Sheets Limited purchased the Tororo complex for $5.7m. Total cement production amounted to 367,500 tons in 2000. Renovation work has been carried out by a Turkish company at Tororo and by a German company at Hima. Tororo was fully rehabilitated by 2003, with a production capacity of 1,000 tons per day.

During 1992–95 the Uganda Investment Authority identified 1,600 new investment projects in agro-processing, tourism, mining, banking and communications. It is seeking investors in radio, television and video assembly and in the manufacture of office equipment, household durables and electrical goods. Other areas in which investment was invited in 2001 were meat processing, tea processing and packaging, fruit-juice processing, cashew-nut, honey and vanilla processing, floriculture, packaging generally, fish farming, tanning, rice milling, tourism, storage, electronics and the production of edible oils, soap, scrap steel, pharmaceuticals and metal products.

MINERALS

Copper, apatite, tungsten, beryl, columbo-tantalite, gold, bismuth, phosphate, limestone and tin are among the minerals Uganda produced, albeit mostly on a small scale, before Amin came to power. Prior to the Amin period, a stockpile of copper pyrites accumulated at the Kilembe mines in western Uganda. The Kasese Cobalt Co, a joint venture between the state-owned Kilembe Mines Ltd and the then Banff Resources of Canada (later MFC Bancorp Ltd of Canada and now KHD Humboldt Wedag International Limited), which had a 64% interest, aims to extract cobalt from these tailings in a scheme with an estimated cost of US $125m.; the venture came into operation in 2000, and its target annual production is 1,000 metric tons of cobalt. Prior to the Amin period, Uganda exploited substantial deposits of apatite (used in superphosphate fertilizers) at Tororo. Investors were being sought in the early 2000s to exploit the silica sands at four locations along the Ugandan shore of Lake Victoria, as well as on two islands in the lake; these deposits are said to be suitable for making container glass. In 1996, following the removal of a 5% royalty on the metal, gold was Uganda's second largest export; an unquantified proportion, however, had allegedly been smuggled into the country from the DRC. Gold mining has begun in Mubende district, and gold tailings in Busia are being processed. Vermiculite is produced in Wakiso district. During 2002/03 an evaluation study of Uganda's columbo-tantalite resources was completed, which identified seven sites in Ntungamo district for further evaluation. A study, financed by the World Bank, was made by US and French consultants on a phosphate fertilizer project using phosphate deposits in the Sukulu hills, estimated at 220m.–225m. tons. The study recommended construction of a plant to make single superphosphates, with an initial capacity of 80,000 tons per year. The total cost of the project was to be about $102m. High-grade iron-ore deposits at Kigezi have not yet been exploited. A group of 20 Ugandan investors formed a consortium, Muko Iron Ore Development Co (MIDECO), in July 2000 to exploit haematite iron ore in Kabale district, in the south-west, with a view to supplying domestic iron and steel operations. Geological surveys have been carried out in the Lake Albert and Rift Valley areas. The concession to mine tungsten at a remote site in the Nyamuliro Wolfram Hills near Kabale was awarded to the Ugandan company Krone Uganda Limited, but operations could not commence until a road and a bridge had been built through the swamp that separates the mine from Kabale.

Petroleum exploration has proceeded slowly. In 1990 Uganda and Zaire (now the DRC) signed an agreement for the joint exploration and exploitation of petroleum reserves beneath Lakes Albert and Edward. Geological surveys in Lake Albert were completed in 1994, followed by those in the Lake Edward basin. In 1995 the Ugandan Government awarded a US-affiliated firm, the Uganda General Works and Engineering Co, a licence to exploit reserves in the Lake Albert area. A further exploration licence was awarded in January 1997 to Heritage Oil of Canada, which in 2001 formed an equal partnership with Energy Africa. Three exploratory wells have been drilled to the south of Lake Albert. Turaco-1, spudded in September 2002, and Turaco-2, dug in October 2003, both showed the presence of hydrocarbons; Turaco-3 was drilled in September 2004. Exploration wells were dug in 2005 at two locations in western Uganda, Mputa and Waraga, and the Government stated that petroleum had been found at both sites; the commercial viability of extraction was being studied in mid-2006. In July 2007 the Kenya Pipeline Company (KPC) announced plans to begin construction of the long-awaited US $80m., 320-km long, 8-mm diameter oil pipeline. The pipeline was to connect Eldoret in Kenya to Kampala in Uganda, and construction had been scheduled to begin in 2004. The pipeline is to deliver 220,000 litres of petroleum per hour. The pipeline will link up with existing pipeline from Kenya's oil refineries at Mombasa to Nairobi to Eldoret.

POWER

Power shortages are the major factor hindering Uganda's economic growth and development. In 2007 a poll was conducted to gauge the performance of Uganda's manufacturing sector. Of the 150 companies surveyed, 18 reported that the frequent power shortages were forcing them to contemplate permanent closure. The shortages were exacerbated by drought in 2006 which reduced the supply of water to the country's hydroelectric facilities. This reduction in supply, coupled with growing demand, left Uganda's national grid with a shortfall of almost 200 MW at peak periods in 2006. In June 2007 load-shedding amounted to some 30 hours per week.

Electricity is generated at the Nalubaale (formerly Owen Falls) hydroelectric station at Jinja, which has an installed capacity of 180 MW, of which about 18% is exported. Power, sometimes as much as 30 MW, has been exported, under contract, to Kenya under an arrangement that began in 1955, prior to the independence of both countries. By the mid-1990s domestic demand for electricity was considerably in excess of supply; after exports of power, barely one-half of Uganda's domestic requirement was being met. The monopoly held by the Uganda Electricity Board (UEB) over electricity supply was removed from September 1996, opening the sector to competition. Companies in all fields were encouraged to establish 'build, own and operate' (BOO) schemes to provide electricity to meet their own demands, while selling power to others as a means of recouping some of their investment. A typical example is Tilda's Kibimba rice project in eastern Uganda; the facility includes its own electricity-generating plant. A new US $500m., 250-MW dam at Bujagali Falls, near Jinja, was proposed by the Madhvani Group and AES of the USA; despite objections from environmentalists, promoters of the project won the approval of the Cabinet, of Parliament and of the people living at the proposed site. In 2001 the World Bank placed the project into a 120-day-long 'open comment' period, during which all interested parties were invited to put their cases for or against proceeding with the construction of the dam. The project would involve the construction of a dam 30 m in height on the Victoria Nile, 100 km of transmission lines and two sub-stations. In mid-2002 the project became embroiled in a bribery scandal, in which it was alleged that a European contractor had bribed a Ugandan official. AES alerted the World Bank, which suspended deliberations on the funding of the project pending the outcome of the resulting court case. In April 2007, the World Bank approved the project and pledged some $360m. worth of loans and guarantees. Completion was forecast for 2011, and the cost was reassessed in 2007 at $799m.

Work began in early 2002 on a third, 40-MW unit at the Kiira power plant, and the 2002/03 budget stated that financing had been secured for the fourth and fifth units at Kiira, also of 40 MW each. Together they were to add 120 MW to the national grid, increasing its total level to 400 MW. In late 2002 the Electricity Supply Commission of South Africa (ESKOM) was awarded a contract to manage the Kiira and Nalubaale hydropower facilities at Owen Falls. The 240 MW Kiyara Power Station near Jinja, built at a cost of US $230m., came on stream in 2000 and produces power both for Uganda and for export to Kenya. An Electricity Regulatory Authority became operational in 2002. The 2006/07 budget proposed two solutions: the 'immediate' procurement of 100 MW in additional thermal power capacity; and the establishment of an Energy Fund to finance the development of the Bujagali and Karuma hydropower projects in partnership with the private sector.

TOURISM

During the 1960s and until 1972, tourism was, after coffee and cotton, the third most important source of foreign exchange. In 1971 85,000 visitors went to Uganda, and receipts were US $27m. Tourism ceased during Amin's rule, with wildlife parks and hotels totally neglected. Under the post-Amin Government of Milton Obote, the sector began to be slowly rehabilitated. The number of visitors of all categories rose from 8,622 in 1982 to an estimated 189,000 in 1995 and to more than 500,000 in 2004/05. Revenue from the tourism sector rose from some $90m. in 1995 to $185m. in 2002. In that year there were 29 tour operators in Uganda. The country has eight national parks, and approval was given in 2000 for the creation of a new park in the Kibale forest. The kidnapping and killing by Rwandan Hutu rebels of foreign visitors to Bwindi National Park in March 1999 (see Recent History) precipitated a large increase in tourist cancellations. The 2005/06 budget allocated $2,000m. for tourism development, and the 2006/07 budget gave priority to infrastructural development and security for tourists.

The state-owned Uganda Hotels Corpn and all hotels in Uganda have been privatized. In 1988 a consortium of Italian companies, led by Viginter, agreed to construct four four-star hotels, in Masaka, Fort Portal, Jinja and Mbale. The Sheraton Kampala, with 237 'newly renovated' rooms, and the Nile Hotel International Kampala provide high-rise accommodation in the capital, while the 89-room Hotel Equatoria and the 109-room Grand Imperial Hotel are both run by Imperial Hotels. In 2004 Imperial Hotels also opened a new 181-room, six-storey Imperial Resort Beach Hotel at Entebbe, on a 27-acre site on the shores of Lake Victoria. In 2003 more than one-half of all tourists to Uganda arrived by road from neighbouring states, especially from Kenya. The Uganda Tourist Board promotes the country as an up-scale long-haul destination, specializing in niche holidays such as ecotourism, adventure holidays, sport fishing and bird-watching. In 2007 plans were unveiled to develop the dilapidated Entebbe airport facility into a tourist attraction. An aviation museum was to be constructed, to commemorate the notorious Entebbe raid. (In 1976 an Air

France A300 Airbus flight from Tel Aviv and Athens en route to Paris was hijacked by Palestinian rebels. The jet was later diverted to Libya, where non-Israeli and non-Jewish passengers were released, before being flown on to Entebbe, where Israeli forces mounted a rescue operation to free the hostages.)

TRANSPORT AND COMMUNICATIONS

In 2006 the road network comprised 10,800 km of national (trunk) roads, 27,500 km of district roads, 4,300 km of urban roads and some 30,000 km of community roads. The Government's Road Sector Development Programme in 2005/06 completed the upgrading the Kagamba–Rukungiri and Gayaza–Kalagi trunk roads. As of June 2006 work was in progress on the upgrading or rehabilitation of 554 km of trunk roads, including the Fort Portal–Hima, Hima–Kasese and Kasese–Kilembe roads and the Kampala northern bypass.

India, France and Germany supplied locomotives and rolling stock that were urgently needed by the Uganda Railways Corpn (URC), established following the dissolution of East African Railways. The United Kingdom, France, Italy, Germany and the EU have all assisted with a programme to rehabilitate the railway system, which also forms part of the 'northern corridor'. The URC operates a wagon-ferry service on Lake Victoria between Jinja and the Tanzanian lake port of Mwanza. In theory, this provides an alternative route to the sea, via the Tanzanian ports of Tanga and Dar es Salaam. However, in practice, poor road conditions in Tanzania have limited the practicality of this alternative route, and most Ugandan freight traffic still goes via Kenya to and from the port of Mombasa. The URC carries about 1m. metric tons of freight per year, according to official estimates. The company opted to pursue a strategy of 'privatization from within', selling non-core activities such as locomotive maintenance. Following the withdrawal of government subsidies, the URC suspended operations on unprofitable lines, retaining just two routes: Kampala–Kasese and Kampala–Jinja–Tororo; the 333-km Kampala–Kasese line was subsequently also closed, leaving only the route from Kampala east to the Kenyan border in operation. In 1999 the East African Railways Development Corpn offered to invest US $12.6m. in these two routes, announcing plans to reopen the Kasese line and to carry out repairs and update equipment. In June 2004 the URC was actively recruiting financing for the $24m. cost of re-opening the Kampala–Kasese line. After negotiations, in 2004 the Governments of Uganda and Kenya agreed to merge their two railways and offer them for commerialization as a single unit. In April 2006 the Governments of Uganda and Kenya signed a 25-year concession agreement with Rift Valley Railways (RVR), whereby RVR undertook to make new investment of not less than $18m. towards the rehabilitation of existing infrastructure. The core infrastructure and existing assets are to remain under the ownership of the relevant government. RVR took over full operation of the active rail system in both countries in July 2006.

Uganda Airlines Corpn (UAC), established by the Government in 1976, was liquidated in 2001. Alliance Air was founded in 1994 as a joint venture between UAC, Air Tanzania Corpn and South African Airways and the Tanzanian and Ugandan Governments, in order to compete with major international airlines. However, heavy debts grounded the carrier in October 2000 and led to a change of ownership. Uganda sold its 30% share to Dairo Air Cargo Services, and Tanzania sold its 30% to Infra Investment Ltd, a consortium of Tanzanian private-sector interests. The remaining share, held by South Africa's Transnet, was to be sold to Dairo Air Services and Infra Investment in exchange for the purchasers' agreement to take over Transnet's debts in respect of Alliance Air. However, plans to relaunch SA Alliance Air in 2002 failed, and the airline collapsed. Two new airlines, AfricaOne and East African Airlines (EAA), commenced operating passenger services within Africa and to the Middle East in 2002. However, AfricaOne was forced to suspend flights after only eight months and was wound up in 2003. Meanwhile, EAA pressed the Ugandan Government to grant it 'national carrier' status, as the only Ugandan-based international airline still operating. This was granted, and EAA was also awarded one of the five weekly Entebbe–Nairobi routes, all five previously operated by Kenya Airways. In July 2005 the Ugandan Government granted EAA a one-year waiver on the payment of landing and parking fees at Entebbe, but even so, debts to creditors, suppliers and operational partners mounted. In May 2006 EAA was sold to Africa Direct Uganda Ltd and to a Ugandan businessman. The new owners planned to maintain full services on the existing routes, to Nairobi, Johannesburg, Harare and Dubai, and to agree a financial restructuring with the airline's creditors. However, as of mid-2007, it was reported that the airline was not operating.

In 1993 Uganda had only one telephone line per 1,000 inhabitants; by 2001, the ratio had improved to 2.8 lines per 1,000, although this had declined somewhat to 2.4 lines per 1,000 by 2003. In 2003 Uganda had 61,000 fixed telephone lines and about 776,200 cellular subscribers—a ratio typical of many African countries. Mobile telephone services were provided in Kampala from 1995 by CelTel Ltd (which had approximately 3,000 customers in 1996), and Kenya's Wilken Group received a licence in 1994 to establish a V-Sat (a small-aperture satellite terminal) to provide voice, data and facsimile links in remote areas of the country. South African, Swedish, Ugandan and Rwandan interests, grouped together in a consortium known as MTN Uganda Ltd, entered a successful US $5.8m. bid for a licence to become the country's second national operator. The consortium committed itself to investing $60m. and providing 89,000 new telephone lines in the first five years, beginning in August 1998. The licence covered a full range of services, including fixed lines, international links, cellular services and broadband. MTN, in co-operation with Ericsson of Sweden, underwent a $52m. network upgrade in 2006, due for completion by the end of 2007. The 2003/04 Ugandan budget raised the level of excise duty on mobile-phone air time to 7%, the 2004/05 budget raised the level to 10% and the 2005/06 budget raised it to 12%. In 2001 Uganda had 3.1 personal computers per 1,000 people, six times as many as in 1995; by 2003 this had risen to 4.0 personal computers per 1,000 people. Under a Rural Communication Development Programme, a scheme was launched in 2003 to provide every district of Uganda with an internet-access point, to extend the telephone network to 154 sub-counties and to ensure that each sub-county had at least one public-access telephone.

EXTERNAL TRADE

Traditionally, Uganda's four leading export commodities were coffee, tea, cotton and copper. However, copper exports dwindled from US $20.6m. in 1970 to nil by 1979, with the halting of production at Kilembe. Coffee alone for many years provided about 95% of total export earnings. In the 1990s the profile of Uganda's exports began to change. The value of coffee exports declined sharply in 1993, contributing only about 53% of total export revenue, and by 2002 they contributed only 13.5%. This sharp fall in coffee's share of exports had two main causes: lower world coffee prices and, at the same time, a marked increase in exports of other commodities. Export revenue in dollar terms free-on-board (f.o.b.) exceeded $1,000m. for the first time in 2004/05, up 10% from the previous year. The United Kingdom, previously the main market for Uganda's exports, was overtaken in 2000 by Switzerland and Kenya, and also by the Netherlands in 2001. The USA moved rapidly up the list of Uganda's export clients thanks in large measure to AGOA (see above), and imports from the USA also experienced rapid growth in 2003. Leading the visible exports in 2003/04 were non-coffee exports, which grew by about 30% to $521m.; notable performers among these were maize, cotton, tea, flowers and fish. Imports on a cost, insurance and freight (c.i.f.) basis grew more slowly than exports in 2002/03, 2003/04 and 2004/05.

THE EAST AFRICAN COMMUNITY

Uganda was a partner, with Kenya and Tanzania, in the EAC, which came into existence in December 1967. The EAC disintegrated, however, as a result of continual disagreements among the partners over financial and political issues. In November 1983 agreement was finally reached, after nearly six years of negotiations, on the division of the EAC's assets and liabilities. The final accounts of the EAC, produced by the World Bank, were approved by the three heads of state in July 1986. The surviving EAC institution, the East African Development Bank (based in Kampala), was given a new charter in August 1980 and gradually expanded its lending programme. In January 1996 the presidents of Uganda, Kenya and Tanzania undertook to co-operate over an initiative to relaunch the EAC. The permanent tripartite commission for East African co-operation was formally inaugurated in March 1996. A treaty for the re-establishment of the EAC, providing for the creation of a free trade area (with the eventual introduction of a single currency) and for the development of infrastructure, tourism and agriculture within the community, was ratified in June 2000. Uganda, Kenya and Tanzania have held discussions towards eventual full currency convertibility. On 2 March 2004 Uganda, Kenya and Tanzania signed a Protocol for the establishment of a customs union between the three countries. Under the agreement, goods entering the EAC are to be subject to common rules; a common legal, institutional and administrative structure; and a Common External Tariff (CET). The EAC CET came into effect on 1 January 2005.

PUBLIC FINANCE

The currency, the Uganda shilling, has a troubled past and for years it was virtually worthless; remedial measures included replacing the old shilling with a new shilling and several demonetizations of banknotes. In the 12 months leading up to 1 July 2007, the shilling 'appreciated' from Us. 1,790.00 per US $1 to Us. 1,650.00 per $1. However, there was no substantial increase in the purchasing power of the shilling, thus much of the currency appreciation could be attributed to the weakening of the US dollar.

Underlying inflation (excluding food) was assessed at 6.1% (7.8% including food) in 2006/07, up from 5.2% in 2005/06 and 4.7% in 2004/05. Poor harvests led to a shortage of foodstuffs in the marketplace in 2005 and to a food-price rise averaging 23%.

Under the 1996/97 budget, the former sales tax (at 15%) was replaced by a value-added tax (VAT), at an initial rate of 17%. The 2005/06 budget raised the VAT rate from 17% to 18%; the 2006/07 and 2007/08 budgets left the rate unchanged. The Government was also to pay VAT on its purchases, thereby providing a means for businesses to claim refunds where applicable. Although the new tax was proclaimed a success and company registration was high, traders protested that they felt unable to pass on the increased cost to their customers. The 2004/05 budget speech lamented the poor performance of tax administration, particularly concerning VAT. The level of taxation in Uganda was reported to be the highest in Africa. The 2006/07 budget envisaged total expenditure of Us. 4,255,000m., an 18% rise over the previous year, which itself was a 20% rise over 2004/05. Total domestic revenue was projected to cover 59% of total expenditure, up from 54% in 2004/05. The remainder of expenditure was to be covered by support from donor partners. Part of the remainder, however, has been financed from borrowing, both from overseas and on the domestic market, so much so that in 2006/07 interest payments were forecast to account for Us. 408,000m., leaving Us. 3,847,000m. for spending on economic and social development. The resulting forecast budgetary deficit for 2006/07 was equivalent to 9.2% of GDP, well outside the World Bank/IMF preferred ceiling of 5%.

BALANCE OF PAYMENTS

The current account of the balance of payments is traditionally and regularly in deficit, both before and after official transfers. According to the IMF, Uganda's current account deficit was equal to US $130.8m. in 2006, despite a substantial increase in transfer payments, which rose to $2,075.1m. In that year, imports increased by 26% and amounted to $2,249.1m., while exports rose by 16.2% to $1,003.9m. End-of-year foreign reserves amounted to $1,577m. at 31 December 2006, up from $1,408m. a year earlier. However, the forward import cover provided by these reserves was the same for both years, at 5.3 months' worth.

The IMF assessed the present value of Uganda's total external debt at the end of 2005 at 168.6% of GDP. The 2004/05 budget speech admitted that Uganda's external-debt burden was 'quickly becoming unsustainable'. In December 2003 the IMF granted Uganda's request for waivers on the non-performance of three criteria, allowing a small disbursement of US $3m. under the three-year September 2002 Poverty-Reduction and Growth Facility (PRGF). The criteria in question were that Uganda accumulated more new domestic arrears than had been agreed; Uganda did not complete by the agreed deadline its plan to clear the existing outstanding stock of domestic arrears; and Uganda had not privatized the Uganda Development Bank (UDB) by the agreed deadline. As a result, 15 months into the 36-month PRGF term, Uganda had been allowed to draw only $5m. of the $19m. total. The Fund approved a new three-year Policy Support Instrument for Uganda in December 2006.

Uganda benefited from the Multilateral Debt Relief Initiative (MDRI) that followed the G-8 summit at Gleneagles, Scotland in July 2005. Whereas before the initiative Uganda's debt-service obligations alone were equivalent to 8.0% of GDP in 2002/03, after the initiative, in 2006 the total external debt stock was equivalent to 7.7% of GDP.

ECONOMIC DEVELOPMENT

In early 1995 the Government established a privatization unit, later known as the Privatization and Utility Sector Reform Project (PUSRP), and transferred to the Ministry of Finance and Economic Planning responsibility for those parastatals that were to be divested. Some 13 former state-owned enterprises had already been privatized in 1994/95, realizing combined gross proceeds of Us. 57,720m. Net proceeds were, however, expected to be at a much lower level, because the Government was required to settle the large debts that some of the organizations had accumulated. In June 2006 the Government proclaimed that 128 entities had been divested in one way or another. On the basis of per-head GDP (only US $280 in 2006), Uganda was among the 15 poorest countries in the world. The recovery experienced after 2000 enabled GDP to grow at a faster rate than the population was increasing, with the result that in 2004/05 GDP per capita grew by 11%. The Museveni administration's implementation of effective economic recovery plans, supported by the IMF and the World Bank, has been greeted with approval by Uganda's donors and business partners. By mid-1990 the short-term prospects for recovery seemed to be reasonably favourable; there had been a considerable influx of aid, and inflation was greatly reduced. In 1997 the Kampala Stock Exchange was launched, under the supervision of a Capital Markets Authority. The Government has made efforts to encourage investment from abroad, in order to reduce Uganda's significant dependence on aid. Foreign direct investment amounted to $261m. in 2005/06, or 2.8% of GDP. Economic growth has been consistent since the early 1990s; GDP grew by 6.5% in 2006/07, for example, despite high global oil prices and major power cuts. Nevertheless, obstacles to economic recovery include the cost of combating rebel insurrections (and the loss in tourism receipts because of insecurity and the perception of insecurity), as well as a dilapidated infrastructure, poor power supply and an increasing domestic debt burden. These and many other problems will have to be overcome before the country can begin to benefit from its unquestionable advantages: a generally favourable climate, fertile soils and an abundance of natural resources. However, Uganda has another potential resource, for which it was well known in the days before Idi Amin: a relatively well-educated and skilled labour force.

Long periods of devastation and insecurity led many Ugandans to fear sending their children to school, so that the education sector, as other sectors, fell into decay. A major initiative to redress this situation was launched in 1997, in the form of the introduction of free primary education for up to four children in every Ugandan family. In the first year after fees were abolished enrolment nearly doubled, from 2.7m. pupils in 1996 to 5.2m. in 1997, and it has grown every year since then. Schools began operating two shifts daily, and a system of community-based school management was introduced, whereby parents and teachers determined each school's budgetary priorities. This is a major undertaking that aims to prepare the nation for a potentially favourable economic future; however, its success owes much to the patience of Uganda's teachers, many of whom have kept their posts in their classrooms despite having accumulated salary arrears going back more than eight years. The Government allocated funding in the 2004/05 budget to the building of houses for teachers and eventually acknowledged that these teachers' salary arrears needed to be paid. In June 2001 it paid Us. 9,000m. in back pay owed to teachers since 1993. However, if Uganda is to maintain its reputation for a good education system, the Government still has much to do to improve its record for teacher payments. The 2006/07 budget raised monthly salaries for primary school teachers from Us. 125,000 to Us. 150,000—but even after the rise, teachers earned only about US $83 per month. Price stability, steady GDP growth and significant export diversification have been achieved, but export revenue still needs to grow substantially if it is to cover the burgeoning import bill, let alone become an engine for growth capable of lifting the income levels and living standards of the people. With the revival of the EAC, Uganda's future should include closer co-operation with Kenya and Tanzania, and the joint concessioning of the Ugandan and Kenyan railways is a step in that direction. If good intentions can be translated into action, a market of over 100m. people could open up new opportunities for all three member states, which would be particularly significant for Uganda, the land-locked one of the three. Considerable structural adjustment remains necessary in Uganda if substantial foreign investment is to be realized. The continued development of infrastructure—particularly the consolidation of the electricity supply—is vital if Uganda is to improve its investment profile.

Statistical Survey

Sources (unless otherwise stated): Uganda Bureau of Statistics, POB 13, Entebbe; tel. (41) 320165; fax (41) 320147; e-mail ubos@infocom.co.ug; internet www.ubos.org; Statistics Department, Ministry of Finance, Planning and Economic Development, POB 8147, Kampala.

Area and Population

AREA, POPULATION AND DENSITY

Area (sq km)	
Land	197,323
Inland water and swamp	44,228
Total	241,551*
Population (census results)	
12 January 1991	16,671,705
12 September 2002	
Males	11,929,803
Females	12,512,281
Total	24,442,084
Population (official estimates at mid-year)	
2005	26,494,600
2006	27,356,900
2007	28,247,300
Density (per sq km) at mid-2007	116.9

* 93,263 sq miles.

PRINCIPAL ETHNIC GROUPS
(at census of 12 September 2002)*

Acholi	1,145,357	Basoga	2,062,920
Baganda	4,126,370	Iteso	1,568,763
Bagisu	1,117,661	Langi	1,485,437
Bakiga	1,679,519	Lugbara	1,022,240
Banyakole	2,330,212		

* Ethnic groups numbering more than 1m. persons, excluding population enumerated in hotels.

DISTRICTS
(population, official estimates at mid-2004)

Central	7,015,300	Northern	5,812,700
Kalangala	41,400	Adjumani	225,100
Kampala	1,290,500	Apac	716,800
Kayunga	306,800	Arua	915,500
Kiboga	249,200	Gulu	491,000
Luwero	496,100	Kitgum	307,500
Masaka	777,300	Kotido	705,400
Mpigi	424,300	Lira	805,200
Mubende	742,400	Moroto	185,500
Mukono	845,800	Moyo	229,800
Nakasongola	129,200	Nakapiripirit	170,500
Rakai	485,700	Nebbi	453,500
Sembabule	190,700	Pader	315,300
Wakiso	1,035,800	Yumbe	291,500
Eastern	6,712,400	Western	6,761,500
Bugiri	464,800	Bundibugyoi	232,900
Busia	239,500	Busheny	746,400
Iganga	757,300	Hoima	380,000
Jinja	436,100	Kabale	479,400
Kaberamaido	130,600	Kabarole	368,300
Kamuli	753,200	Kamwenge	312,300
Kapchorwa	208,600	Kanungu	212,300
Katakwi	343,800	Kasese	568,600
Kumi	417,500	Kibaale	454,100
Mayuge	346,800	Kisoro	224,300
Mbale	760,800	Kyenjojo	405,700
Pallisa	552,000	Masindi	512,900
Sironko	305,700	Mbarara	1,142,500
Soroti	406,800	Ntungamo	400,000
Tororo	589,300	Rukungiri	322,000

PRINCIPAL TOWNS
(population according to provisional results of census of 12 September 2002)*

Kampala (capital)	1,208,544	Entebbe	57,518
Gulu	113,144	Kasese	53,446
Lira	89,971	Njeru	52,514
Jinja	86,520	Mukono	47,305
Mbale	70,437	Arua	45,883
Mbarara	69,208	Kabale	45,757
Masaka	61,300	Kitgum	42,929

* According to administrative divisions of 2002.

Mid-2005 ('000, incl. suburbs, UN estimate): Kampala 1,319 (Source: UN, *World Urbanization Prospects: The 2005 Revision*).

BIRTHS AND DEATHS
(annual averages, UN estimates)

	1990–95	1995–2000	2000–05
Birth rate (per 1,000)	49.6	48.2	47.3
Death rate (per 1,000)	16.0	17.7	15.5

Source: UN, *World Population Prospects: The 2006 Revision*.

Expectation of life (years at birth, WHO estimates): 49 (males 48; females 51) in 2004 (Source: WHO, *World Health Report*).

EMPLOYMENT
(persons aged 10 years and over, census of 12 September 2002)*

	Males	Females	Total
Agriculture, hunting and forestry	2,545,962	2,649,779	5,195,741
Fishing	102,043	16,743	118,786
Mining and quarrying	13,613	6,127	19,740
Manufacturing	108,653	45,594	154,247
Electricity, gas and water supply	12,860	1,509	14,369
Construction	105,769	2,939	108,708
Wholesale and retail trade, repair of motor vehicles, motorcycles and personal and household goods	191,191	143,145	334,336
Hotels and restaurants	23,741	64,099	87,840
Transport, storage and communications	119,437	5,798	125,235
Financial intermediation; Real estate, renting and business activities	14,539	7,562	22,101
Public administration and defence, compulsory social security	146,319	27,278	173,597
Education	124,167	85,015	209,182
Health and social work	54,327	53,108	107,435
Other community, social and personal service activities	22,736	26,734	49,470
Private households with employed persons	14,019	19,115	33,134
Not classifiable by economic activity	120,219	76,167	196,386
Total employed	3,719,595	3,230,712	6,950,307

* Excluding population enumerated at hotels.

Health and Welfare

KEY INDICATORS

Total fertility rate (children per woman, 2005)	7.1
Under-5 mortality rate (per 1,000 live births, 2005)	136
HIV/AIDS (% of persons aged 15–49, 2005)	6.7
Physicians (per 1,000 head, 2004)	0.08
Hospital beds (per 1,000 head, 2004)	0.70
Health expenditure (2004): US $ per head (PPP)	135.3
Health expenditure (2004): % of GDP	7.6
Health expenditure (2004): public (% of total)	32.7
Access to water (% of persons, 2004)	60
Access to sanitation (% of persons, 2004)	43
Human Development Index (2004): ranking	145
Human Development Index (2004): value	0.502

For sources and definitions, see explanatory note on p. vi.

Agriculture

PRINCIPAL CROPS
('000 metric tons)

	2003	2004	2005
Rice (paddy)	132	121	153
Maize	1,300	1,080	1,170
Millet	640	659	672
Sorghum	421	399	449
Potatoes	557	573	585
Sweet potatoes	2,610	2,650	2,478
Cassava (Manioc)	5,450	5,500	5,576
Sugar cane*	1,995	2,203	2,150
Dry beans	525	455	478
Cow peas, dry	67	69	71
Pigeon peas	84	84	85
Soybeans	187	158	158

—continued	2003	2004	2005
Groundnuts (in shell)	130	155	159
Sesame seed	113*	125	161
Seed cotton†	78	110	160
Onions, dry†	147	147	147
Bananas†	615	615	624
Plantains	9,700	9,686	9,045
Coffee (green)	151	170	158
Tea (made)	37	36	38
Tobacco (leaves)	34	33	31
Cotton (lint)*	20	30	44

* Unofficial figure(s).
† FAO estimates.

Source: FAO.

LIVESTOCK
('000 head, year ending September)

	2003	2004*	2005
Asses, mules or hinnies*	18	18	18
Cattle	6,519	6,567	6,770
Sheep	1,175	1,552	1,600
Goats	7,092	7,566	7,800
Pigs	1,778	1,940	2,000
Chickens	35,903	31,622	25,174

* FAO estimates.

Source: FAO.

LIVESTOCK PRODUCTS
('000 metric tons, FAO estimates)

	2003	2004	2005
Cattle meat	110	106	106
Sheep meat	8	8	6
Goat meat	29	29	29
Pig meat	60	60	60
Chicken meat	38	38	44
Cows' milk	700	700	700
Poultry eggs	20	20	20

Source: FAO.

Forestry

ROUNDWOOD REMOVALS
('000 cubic metres, excl. bark, FAO estimates)

	2003	2004	2005
Sawlogs, veneer logs and logs for sleepers	1,055	1,055	1,055
Other industrial wood	2,120	2,120	2,120
Fuel wood	35,683	36,235	36,797
Total	38,858	39,410	39,972

Source: FAO.

SAWNWOOD PRODUCTION
('000 cubic metres, incl. railway sleepers)

	1997	1998	1999
Coniferous (softwood)	57	61	67
Broadleaved (hardwood)	172	184	197
Total	229	245	264

2000–05: Production assumed to be unchanged from 1999 (FAO estimates).

Source: FAO.

Fishing

('000 metric tons, live weight)

	2003	2004	2005
Capture	241.8	372.4	417.1
Cyprinids	8.3	22.9	25.7
Tilapias	97.3	138.8	155.6
African lungfishes	4.6	12.9	14.5
Characins	9.5	20.0	22.4
Nile perch	112.8	156.3	175.2
Aquaculture	5.5	5.5	10.8
Total catch	247.3	377.9	427.9

Source: FAO.

Mining

('000 metric tons, unless otherwise indicated)

	2003	2004	2005
Cement (hydraulic)	507.1	559.0	630.0*
Tantalum and niobium (columbium) concentrates (kilograms)	16,240	376	273
Cobalt (metric tons)	0	436	638
Gold (kilograms)	40	1,447	46
Limestone	226.4	228.8	540.8
Salt (unrefined)*	5	5	5

* Estimate(s).

Source: US Geological Survey.

Industry

SELECTED PRODUCTS
('000 metric tons, unless otherwise indicated)

	2003	2004	2005
Soft drinks (million litres)	78.5	111.5	163.5
Sugar	139.5	189.5	182.9
Soap	101.3	93.4	127.6
Cement	507.1	559.0	692.7
Paint (million litres)	1.9	2.2	8.2
Edible oil and fat	56.0	58.1	43.3
Animal feed	20.9	19.6	17.3
Footwear (million pairs)	3.4	3.6	46.3
Wheat flour	42.2	25.7	20.3
Processed milk (million litres)	14.9	19.6	18.5
Cotton and rayon fabrics (million sq metres	11.1	10.1	13.6
Clay bricks, tiles, etc.	33.3	15.4	36.2
Corrugated iron sheets	39.2	48.8	61.6

Source: Bank of Uganda.

Finance

CURRENCY AND EXCHANGE RATES

Monetary Units
100 cents = 1 new Uganda shilling.

Sterling, Dollar and Euro Equivalents (31 May 2007)
£1 sterling = 3,347.7 new Uganda shillings;
US $1 = 1,693.1 new Uganda shillings;
€1 = 2,277.7 new Uganda shillings;
10,000 new Uganda shillings = £2.99 = $5.91 = €4.39.

Average Exchange Rate (new Uganda shillings per US $)
2004 1,810.3
2005 1,780.7
2006 1,831.5

Note: Between December 1985 and May 1987 the official exchange rate was fixed at US $1 = 1,400 shillings. In May 1987 a new shilling, equivalent to 100 of the former units, was introduced. At the same time, the currency was devalued by 76.7%, with the exchange rate set at $1 = 60 new shillings. Further adjustments were implemented in subsequent years. Foreign exchange controls were mostly abolished in 1993.

BUDGET
(million new shillings, year ending 30 June)

Revenue	2003/04	2004/05	2005/06
Revenue*	1,669,200	1,948,000	2,267,000
Grants	1,188,000	1,198,000	1,136,000
Total	2,857,200	3,146,000	3,403,000

Expenditure	2003/04	2004/05	2005/06
Recurrent expenditure	1,868,000	1,977,900	2,234,000
Wages and salaries	683,000	774,000	867,000
Interest payments	264,000	229,000	250,000
Development expenditure	1,094,000	1,187,100	1,262,000
External expenditure	439,000	487,100	519,000
Domestic expenditure	635,000	700,000	743,000
Net lending and investment	80,700	47,400	26,000
Total	3,042,700	3,212,400	3,522,000

* Tax revenue excludes tax refunds and government payments.

INTERNATIONAL RESERVES
(US $ million at 31 December)

	2004	2005	2006
IMF special drawing rights	0.7	1.1	0.1
Foreign exchange	1,307.4	1,343.1	1,801.8
Total	1,308.1	1,344.2	1,801.9

Source: IMF, *International Financial Statistics*.

MONEY SUPPLY
('000 million new shillings at 31 December)

	2004	2005	2006
Currency outside banks	588.61	710.22	885.87
Demand deposits at commercial banks	752.63	894.22	1,020.61
Total money	1,341.24	1,604.45	1,906.49

Source: IMF, *International Financial Statistics*.

COST OF LIVING
(Consumer Price Index for all urban households; base: 2000 = 100)

	2004	2005	2006
Food	111.4	126.1	139.1
Clothing	100.5	102.3	n.a.
Rent, fuel and light	121.0	130.1	n.a.
All items (incl. others)	114.5	124.1	133.3

Source: ILO.

NATIONAL ACCOUNTS

(million new shillings at current prices)

Expenditure on the Gross Domestic Product

	2004	2005	2006
Government final consumption expenditure	2,055,645	2,356,983	2,676,574
Private final consumption expenditure	10,790,811	12,344,208	14,860,021
Increase in stocks	15,338	51,390	58,277
Gross fixed capital formation	3,227,081	3,696,936	4,510,215
Total domestic expenditure	16,088,875	18,449,517	22,105,087
Exports of goods and services	1,884,120	2,350,966	2,327,573
Less Imports of goods and services	3,862,172	4,601,102	5,952,580
Statistical discrepancy	–29,267	68,939	128,350
GDP in purchasers' values	14,081,557	16,268,320	18,608,430
GDP at constant 1997/98 prices	11,004,238	11,606,298	12,393,135

Gross Domestic Product by Economic Activity

	2004	2005	2006
Agriculture, hunting, forestry and fishing	2,305,118	2,665,779	2,946,685
Mining and quarrying	106,317	112,402	149,460
Manufacturing	1,201,543	1,350,166	1,468,481
Electricity, gas and water	165,425	180,045	171,027
Construction	1,283,379	1,496,825	1,795,422
Wholesale and retail trade	1,418,825	1,648,988	1,925,792
Hotels and restaurants	400,588	464,567	528,547
Transport, storage and communications	1,010,031	1,287,910	1,656,035
General government services	570,512	638,701	695,900
Education	870,960	1,003,333	1,162,376
Health	333,096	406,644	497,513
Other services	957,803	1,065,422	1,154,623
Total monetary GDP	10,623,596	12,320,782	14,151,862
Non-monetary GDP			
Agriculture	1,700,122	1,993,882	2,202,455
Construction	66,731	74,771	82,853
Owner-occupied dwellings	482,526	508,359	538,738
Total GDP at factor cost	12,872,975	14,897,795	16,975,908
Taxes on production and imports (net)	1,208,581	1,370,525	1,632,522
GDP at market prices	14,081,557	16,268,320	18,608,430

BALANCE OF PAYMENTS

(US $ million)

	2004	2005	2006
Exports of goods f.o.b.	708.9	864.2	1,003.9
Imports of goods f.o.b.	–1,467.1	–1,784.4	–2,249.1
Trade balance	–758.2	–920.2	–1,245.2
Exports of services	358.3	507.7	463.5
Imports of services	–665.8	–800.3	–972.1
Balance on goods and services	–1,065.8	–1,212.7	–1,753.8
Other income received	35.7	49.8	71.9
Other income paid	–205.6	–208.8	–183.8
Balance on goods, services and income	–1,235.7	–1,371.1	–1,865.8
Current transfers received	1,229.5	1,414.3	2,075.1
Current transfers paid	–208.9	–319.4	–340.0
Current balance	–215.2	–276.8	–130.8
Direct investment from abroad	222.2	257.1	286.9
Portfolio investment assets	—	—	—
Portfolio investment liabilities	6.2	–13.4	21.7
Other investment assets	0.2	–7.1	–17.0
Other investment liabilities	113.1	106.9	130.8
Net errors and omissions	–4.0	15.1	31.1
Overall balance	122.5	81.7	322.6

Source: IMF, *International Financial Statistics*.

External Trade

PRINCIPAL COMMODITIES

(distribution by SITC, US $ '000)

Imports c.i.f.	2003	2004	2005
Food and live animals	144,836	189,910	212,121
Cereals and cereal preparations	106,698	134,431	141,194
Crude materials (inedible) except fuels	47,703	49,504	54,197
Mineral fuels, lubricants, etc.	188,770	219,745	348,474
Petroleum, petroleum products and related materials	187,255	217,762	343,159
Animal and vegetable oils, fats and waxes	64,523	72,070	73,707
Chemicals and related products	180,354	224,882	268,415
Medicinal and pharmaceutical products	74,920	80,137	85,721
Plastics in primary forms	28,332	43,886	62,606
Basic manufactures	270,623	322,438	362,764
Non-metallic mineral manufactures	51,862	57,269	68,576
Iron and steel	77,755	96,020	118,823
Machinery and transport equipment	344,098	473,729	537,299
Telecommunications and sound recording/reproducing apparatus	48,936	82,764	100,410
Electrical machinery, apparatus, etc.	52,178	61,971	56,843
Road vehicles (incl. air-cushion vehicles) and parts (excl. tyres, engines and electrical parts)	115,096	144,695	192,198
Miscellaneous manufactured articles	130,046	155,222	186,404
Total (incl. others)	1,375,106	1,726,238	2,054,137

Exports f.o.b.	2003	2004	2005
Food and live animals	272,838	318,434	419,261
Fish, crustaceans, molluscs and preparations thereof	84,649	100,028	139,864
Cereals and cereal preparations	17,592	26,360	31,040
Coffee, tea, cocoa, spices and manufactures	157,646	174,832	223,691
Beverages and tobacco	45,764	43,698	39,509
Tobacco and tobacco manufactures	43,212	40,805	32,281
Crude materials (inedible) except fuels	61,726	94,649	106,478
Textile fibres (not wool tops) and their wastes (not in yarn)	22,180	49,329	39,267
Crude animal and vegetable materials n.e.s.	29,845	35,234	39,823
Mineral fuels, lubricants and related materials	41,664	40,219	37,839
Petroleum, petroleum products and related materials	27,884	28,145	32,979
Basic manufactures	19,394	31,068	52,193
Iron and steel	11,035	18,123	29,699
Machinery and transport equipment	19,208	25,713	42,582
Miscellaneous manufactured articles	18,515	27,143	13,343
Gold, non-monetary (excl. gold ores and concentrates)	33,726	61,200	73,074
Total (incl. others)	534,106	665,090	812,857

PRINCIPAL TRADING PARTNERS
(US $ '000)

Imports c.i.f.	2003	2004	2005
Argentina	2,191	17,806	24,507
Belgium	23,087	35,321	31,073
Canada	8,283	19,115	27,150
China, People's Repub.	70,248	103,090	109,217
France	15,596	35,525	35,317
Germany	39,151	36,346	49,256
Hong Kong	16,805	13,377	16,511
India	102,160	121,773	131,813
Italy	23,320	20,433	49,222
Japan	90,361	121,984	146,552
Kenya	357,327	399,198	520,686
Malaysia	42,062	67,430	47,214
Netherlands	25,015	37,165	43,875
Saudi Arabia	12,270	14,893	22,776
Sweden	8,811	30,343	22,643
South Africa	98,984	140,899	143,676
United Arab Emirates	80,416	84,881	136,702
United Kingdom	86,411	84,422	99,405
USA	78,129	103,390	78,143
Total (incl. others)	1,375,106	1,726,238	2,054,137

Exports f.o.b.	2003	2004	2005
Australia	9,214	3,417	3,967
Belgium	12,899	26,685	33,147
Burundi	10,076	18,113	20,801
Congo, Democratic Repub.	12,891	28,913	60,404
France	5,116	22,702	39,581
Germany	12,024	17,677	33,768
Hong Kong	12,300	15,845	12,936
Japan	10,006	5,975	5,220
Kenya	78,432	76,903	72,437
Netherlands	48,955	57,860	85,413
Rwanda	20,803	24,683	36,088
Saudi Arabia	12,527	1,625	14
Singapore	13,859	22,799	28,945
South Africa	29,632	9,250	9,796
Spain	14,526	13,914	17,988
Sudan	13,765	22,676	50,487
Switzerland	72,993	108,779	74,857
Tanzania	5,832	12,155	15,445
United Arab Emirates	345	33,458	84,389
United Kingdom	33,883	29,438	26,831
USA	12,693	15,714	15,892
Total (incl. others)	534,106	665,090	812,857

Transport

RAILWAYS
(traffic)

	1994	1995	1996
Passenger-km (million)	35	30	28
Freight ton-km (million)	208	236	187

Freight traffic ('000 ton-km): 212,616 in 2003; 229,439 in 2004; 185,559 in 2005.

ROAD TRAFFIC
(vehicles in use)

	2003	2004	2005
Passenger cars	56,837	59,786	65,472
Buses and coaches	20,572	23,443	28,436
Lorries and vans	64,650	70,215	71,887
Motorcycles	80,088	89,212	108,207

CIVIL AVIATION
(traffic on scheduled services)

	2001	2002	2003
Kilometres flown (million)	2	2	2
Passengers carried ('000)	41	41	40
Passenger-km (million)	235	237	237
Total ton-km (million)	42	42	44

Source: UN, *Statistical Yearbook*.

Tourism

FOREIGN TOURIST ARRIVALS

Country of residence	2003	2004	2005
India	6,639	9,366	10,691
Kenya	114,499	220,062	138,346
Rwanda	50,143	65,298	80,522
Tanzania	30,534	67,885	50,723
United Kingdom	17,181	22,402	28,227
USA	13,179	18,898	21,968
Total (incl. others)	305,719	512,379	467,728

Tourism receipts (US $ million, incl. passenger transport): 202 in 2002; 219 in 2003; 306 in 2004 (Source: World Tourism Organization).

Communications Media

	2003	2004	2005
Telephones ('000 main lines in use)	65.8	82.5	100.8
Mobile cellular telephones ('000 subscribers)	893.0	1,165.0	1,525.1
Personal computers ('000 in use)	103	120	250
Internet users ('000)	125	200	500

Source: partly International Telecommunication Union.

Television receivers ('000 in use, 2000): 610.

Radio receivers ('000 in use, 1997): 2,600.

Facsimile machines (number in use, year ending 30 June 1996): 3,000 (estimate).

Book production (titles, excl. pamphlets and govt publications, 1996): 288.

Daily newspapers (1996): titles 2; average circulation ('000 copies) 40.

Sources: mainly UNESCO, *Statistical Yearbook*; UN, *Statistical Yearbook*.

Education

(2004)

	Institutions	Teachers	Students
Primary	n.a.	147,291	7,377,292
Secondary	n.a.	29,061	697,507
Teacher training colleges	10	n.a.	16,170
Technical schools and institutes	25	n.a.	7,999
Universities	18	n.a.	58,823

Adult literacy rate (UNESCO estimates): 66.8% (males 76.8%; females 57.7%) in 2004 (Source: UN Development Programme, *Human Development Report*).

Directory

The Constitution

Following the military coup in July 1985, the 1967 Constitution was suspended, and all legislative and executive powers were vested in a Military Council, whose Chairman was Head of State. In January 1986 a further military coup established an executive Presidency, assisted by a Cabinet of Ministers and a legislative National Resistance Council (NRC). In September 1995 a Constituent Assembly (comprising 214 elected and 74 nominated members) enacted a draft Constitution. The new Constitution was promulgated on 8 October 1995. Under its terms, a national referendum on the introduction of a multi-party political system was to take place in 2000. The referendum produced an overwhelming vote in favour of retaining the existing 'no-party' system; however, the referendum was annulled by the Constitutional Court in 2004. A direct presidential election took place in May 1996, followed in June of that year by legislative elections to the Parliament. This body, comprising 214 elected members and 62 nominated members, replaced the NRC. At the general election of June 2001 the number of nominated members was increased to 78. Legislation outlining the transition to multi-party politics was passed by the Parliament on 28 June 2005 and approved by 92.5% of voters in a national referendum held on 28 July 2005. The legislation also removed the two-term limit on the presidency.

The Government

HEAD OF STATE

President: Gen. (retd) YOWERI KAGUTA MUSEVENI (took office 29 January 1986; elected 9 May 1996, re-elected 12 March 2001 and 23 February 2006).

Vice-President: Prof. GILBERT BALIBASEKA BUKENYA.

THE CABINET
(August 2007)

Prime Minister: Prof. APOLLO NSIBAMBI.

First Deputy Prime Minister and Minister in Charge of East African Affairs: ERIYA KATEGAYA.

Second Deputy Prime Minister and Minister of Public Service: HENRY MUGANWA KAJURA.

Third Deputy Prime Minister and Minister of Information and National Guidance: KIRUNDA KIVEJINJA.

Minister for Security: AMAMA MBABAZI.

Minister in Charge of the Presidency: BEATRICE WABUDEYA.

Minister in the Office of the Prime Minister: ADOLF MWESIGE.

Minister of Agriculture, Animal Industry and Fisheries: HILLARY ONEK.

Minister of Defence: Dr CRISPUS KIYONGA.

Minister of Relief and Disaster Preparedness: TARSIS KABWEGYERE.

Minister of Education and Sports: NAMIREMBE BITAMAZIRE.

Minister of Energy and Minerals: DAUDI MIGEREKO.

Minister of Internal Affairs: Dr RUHAKANA RUGUNDA.

Minister of Finance: Dr EZRA SURUMA.

Minister of Works: JOHN NASASIRA.

Minister of Justice and Constitutional Affairs and Attorney-General: GERALD KIDDU MAKUBUYA.

Minister of Gender, Labour and Social Services: SYDA BUMBA.

Minister of Trade and Industry: JANAT MUKWAYA.

Minister of Water and Environment: MARIA MUTAGAMBA.

Minister of Lands, Housing and Urban Development: OMARA ATUBO.

Minister of Health: Dr STEVEN MALLINGA.

Minister of Foreign Affairs: SAM KUTESA.

Minister of Information Communication Technology: HAMU MULIIRA.

Minister of Local Government: Maj.-Gen. KAHINDA OTAFIIRE.

Minister without Portfolio: DOROTHY HYUHA.

In addition to the Cabinet Ministers, there are 44 Ministers of State. The Chief Whip is also a member of the Cabinet.

MINISTRIES

Office of the President: Parliament Bldg, POB 7168, Kampala; tel. (41) 2258441; fax (41) 2256143; e-mail info@gouexecutive.net; internet www.gouexecutive.net.

Office of the Prime Minister: POB 341, Kampala; tel. (41) 2259518; fax (41) 2242341.

Ministry of Agriculture, Animal Industry and Fisheries: POB 102, Entebbe; tel. (41) 2320987; fax (41) 2321255; e-mail psmaaif@infocom.co.ug; internet www.agriculture.go.ug.

Ministry of Defence: Bombo, POB 7069, Kampala; tel. (41) 2270331; fax (41) 2245911.

Ministry of Education and Sports: Embassy House and Development Bldg, Plot 9/11, Parliament Ave, POB 7063, Kampala; tel. (41) 2234451; fax (41) 2230437; e-mail pro@education.go.ug; internet www.education.go.ug.

Ministry of Energy and Minerals: Amber House, Kampala Rd, Kampala; tel. (41) 2311111; e-mail psmemd@energy.go.ug; internet www.energyandminerals.go.ug.

Ministry of Finance: Appollo Kaggwa Rd, Plot 2/4, POB 8147, Kampala; tel. (41) 2234700; fax (41) 2230163; e-mail webmaster@finance.go.ug; internet www.finance.go.ug.

Ministry of Foreign Affairs: Embassy House, POB 7048, Kampala; tel. (41) 2345661; fax (41) 2258722; e-mail info@mofa.go.ug; internet www.mofa.go.ug.

Ministry of Gender, Labour and Social Affairs: Udyam House, Jinja Rd, POB 7168, Kampala; tel. (41) 2258334.

Ministry of Health: Plot 6, Lourdel Rd, Wandegeya, POB 7272, Kampala; tel. (41) 2340884; fax (41) 2340887; e-mail info@health.go.ug; internet www.health.go.ug.

Ministry of Information Communication Technology: Kampala.

Ministry of Information and National Guidance: Kampala.

Ministry of Internal Affairs: Jinja Rd, POB 7191, Kampala; tel. (41) 2231103; fax (41) 2231188; e-mail psmia@infocom.co.ug.

Ministry of Justice and Constitutional Affairs: Parliament Bldg, POB 7183, Kampala; tel. (41) 2230538; fax (41) 2254829; e-mail mojca@africaonline.co.ug; internet www.justice.go.ug.

Ministry of Lands, Housing and Urban Development: Kampala.

Ministry of Local Government: Uganda House, 8/10 Kampala Rd, POB 7037, Kampala; tel. (41) 2341224; fax (41) 2258127; e-mail info@molg.go.ug; internet www.molg.go.ug.

Ministry of Security: Kampala.

Ministry of Disaster Preparedness, Relief and Refugees: POB 341, Kampala; tel. (41) 4236967; e-mail psopms@infocom.co.ug.

Ministry of Trade and Industry: 6/8 Parliament Ave, POB 7103, Kampala; tel. (41) 2232971; fax (41) 2242188; e-mail ps@mintrade.org.

Ministry of Water and Environment: POB 7096, Kampala; tel. (41) 2342931; e-mail mwle@mwle.go.ug; internet www.mwle.go.ug.

Ministry of Works: POB 10, Entebbe; tel. (42) 2320101; fax (42) 2320135; e-mail mowhc@utlonline.co.ug; internet www.miniworks.go.ug.

President and Legislature

PRESIDENT

Election, 23 February 2006

Candidate	Votes	% of votes
Gen. (Retd) Yoweri Kaguta Museveni (NRM-O)	4,078,677	59.28
Kizza Besigye (FDC)	2,570,572	37.36
John Ssebaana Kizito (DP)	109,055	1.59
Abed Bwanika (Ind.)	65,344	0.95
Miria Obote Kalule (UPC)	56,584	0.82
Total	6,880,232	100.00

PARLIAMENT

Speaker: EDWARD SSEKANDI.

Deputy Speaker: REBECCA KADAGA.

The National Resistance Movement, which took office in January 1986, established a National Resistance Council (NRC), initially comprising 80 nominated members, to act as a legislative body. National elections were held on 11–28 February 1989, at which 210 members of an expanded NRC were elected by members of district-level Resistance Committees (themselves elected by local-level Resistance Committees, who were directly elected by universal adult suffrage). The remaining 68 seats in the NRC were reserved for candidates nominated by the President (to include 34 women and representatives of youth organizations and trades unions). Political parties were not allowed to participate in the election campaign. In October 1989 the NRC approved legislation extending the Government's term of office by five years from January 1990, when its mandate was to expire. The Constituent Assembly (see Constitution) extended further the NRM's term of office in November 1994. Under the terms of the Constitution that was promulgated in October 1995, the NRC was restyled as the Ugandan Parliament. Legislative elections to the Parliament took place in June 1996 (again officially on a 'no-party' basis). The total membership of the Parliament was reduced from 278 to 276, comprising 214 elected and 62 nominated representatives. A national referendum on the future introduction of a multi-party political system was staged in June 2000, at which 90.7% of participants voted in favour of retaining the 'no-party' political system—the referendum was nullified in mid-2004 (see Recent History). Legislation was adopted by the Parliament in June 2005, and ratified by a national referendum on 28 July of that year, restoring multi-party politics and lifting the two-term limit on the presidency. Multi-party legislative elections were held on 23 February 2006, following which the number of seats in Parliament stood at 319, comprising 215 directly elected representatives, 69 nominated female representatives, 10 nominated representatives from the UPDF, five nominated representatives for young people, five nominated representatives for people with disabilities, five nominated representatives for workers and 10 ex officio members.

Election Commission

Electoral Commission: 53–56 Jinja Rd, POB 22678, Kampala; tel. (41) 2337500; fax (41) 4341907; e-mail info@ec.or.ug; internet www.ec.or.ug; independent; Chair. Dr BADRU M. KIGGUNDU.

Political Organizations

Political parties were ordered to suspend active operations, although not formally banned, in March 1986. At a referendum on the future restoration of a plural political system, which took place on 29 June 2000, the retention of the existing 'no-party' system was overwhelmingly endorsed by voters. However, the result was nullified by the Constitutional Court in mid-2004. Following a successful challenge to the Political Parties and Organisations Act 2002, political parties were permitted to resume their activities nationally from March 2003. Discussions on a proposed transition to multi-party politics commenced in 2004. By April of that year some 60 new political parties had emerged, but only 13 had sought registration. In mid-2005 legislation was passed allowing for a return to full multi-party democracy; the legislation was approved by 92.5% of voters in a national referendum held on 28 July 2005. By mid-2006 33 parties had been officially registered.

Bazzukulu ba Buganda (Grandchildren of Buganda): Bagandan separatist movement.

Buganda Youth Movement: f. 1994; seeks autonomy for Buganda; Leader STANLEY KATO.

Conservative Party (CP): f. 1979; Leader JEHOASH MAYANJA-NKANGI.

Democratic Party (DP): City House, Plot 2/3 William St, POB 7098, Kampala; tel. and fax (41) 2252536; e-mail info@dpuganda.org; internet www.dpuganda.org; f. 1954; main support in southern Uganda; seeks a multi-party political system; Pres. JOHN SSEBAANA KIZITO; Vice-Pres. ZACHARY OLUM.

Federal Democratic Movement (FEDEMO): Kampala.

Forum for Democratic Change (FDC): f. 2004 by a merger of the Reform Agenda, the Parliamentary Advocacy Forum and the National Democratic Forum; Leader REAGAN OKUMU.

Forum for Multi-Party Democracy: Kampala; Gen. Sec. JESSE MASHATTE.

Justice Forum: Leader MUHAMMAD KIBIRIGE MAYANJA.

Movement for New Democracy in Uganda: based in Zambia; f. 1994 to campaign for multi-party political system; Leader DAN OKELLO-OGWANG.

National Resistance Movement Organisation (NRM-O): f. as National Resistance Movement to oppose the UPC Govt 1980–85; also opposed the mil. Govt in power from July 1985 to Jan. 1986; its fmr mil. wing, the National Resistance Army (NRA), led by Lt-Gen. (later Gen. retd) Yoweri Kaguta Museveni, took power in Jan. 1986; name changed as above on registration in 2003; Chair. Dr SAMSON KISEKKA.

Nationalist Liberal Party: Kampala; f. 1984 by a breakaway faction of the DP; Leader TIBERIO OKENY.

Uganda Democratic Alliance (UDA): Leader APOLO KIRONDE.

Uganda Democratic Freedom Front: Leader Maj. HERBERT ITONGA.

Uganda Freedom Movement (UFM): Kampala; mainly Baganda support; withdrew from NRM coalition Govt in April 1987; Sec.-Gen. (vacant).

Uganda Independence Revolutionary Movement: f. 1989; Chair. Maj. OKELLO KOLO.

Uganda Islamic Revolutionary Party (UIRP): Kampala; f. 1993; Chair. IDRIS MUWONGE.

Uganda National Unity Movement: Chair. Alhaji SULEIMAN SSALONGO.

Uganda Patriotic Movement (UPM): Kampala; f. 1980; Sec.-Gen. JABERI SSALI.

Uganda People's Congress (UPC): POB 1951, Kampala; internet www.members.home.net/upc; f. 1960; socialist-based philosophy; mainly northern support; ruling party 1962–71 and 1980–85, sole legal political party 1969–71; Nat. Leader Dr JAMES RWANYARARE.

Ugandan People's Democratic Movement (UPDM): seeks democratic reforms; support mainly from north and east of the country; includes mems of fmr govt armed forces; signed a peace accord with the Govt in 1990; Chair. ERIC OTEMA ALLIMADI; Sec.-Gen. EMMANUEL OTENG.

Uganda Progressive Union (UPU): Kampala; Chair. ALFRED BANYA.

In August 2006 12 parties merged to form an opposition group styled The People's Platform (TPP). Those parties included the **Forum for Integrity in Leadership (FIL)**, the **Movement for Democratic Change (MDC)** and the **National Peasant Party (NPP)**. The Chairman of the FIL, EMMANUEL TUMUSIIME, assumed the chairmanship of TPP

The following organizations are in armed conflict with the Government:

Alliance of Democratic Forces (ADF): active since 1996 in south-eastern Uganda; combines Ugandan Islamic fundamentalist rebels, exiled Rwandan Hutus and guerrillas from the Democratic Republic of the Congo; Pres. Sheikh JAMIL MUKULU.

Lord's Resistance Army (LRA): f. 1987; claims to be conducting a Christian fundamentalist 'holy war' against the Govt; forces est. to number up to 1,500, operating mainly from bases in Sudan; Leader JOSEPH KONY; a breakaway faction (LRA—Democratic) is led by RONALD OTIM KOMAKECH.

Uganda National Rescue Front Part Two (UNRF II): based in Juba, Sudan; Leader ALI BAMUZE.

Uganda People's Freedom Movement (UPFM): based in Tororo and Kenya; f. 1994 by mems of the fmr Uganda People's Army; Leader PETER OTAI.

West Nile Bank Front (WNBF): operates in northern Uganda.

Diplomatic Representation

EMBASSIES AND HIGH COMMISSIONS IN UGANDA

Algeria: 14 Acacia Ave, Kololo, POB 4025, Kampala; tel. (41) 2232918; fax (41) 2341015; e-mail ambalgka@imul.com; Ambassador ABDELKADER AZIRIA.

Belgium: Rwenzori House, 3rd Floor, Plot 1, Lumumba Ave, POB 7043, Kampala; tel. (41) 2345559; fax (41) 2347212; e-mail kampala@diplobel.org; internet www.diplomatie.be/kampala; Ambassador JAN DE BRUYNE.

China, People's Republic: 37 Malcolm X Ave, Kololo, POB 4106, Kampala; tel. (41) 2259881; fax (41) 2235087; e-mail chinaemb_ug@mfa.gov.cn; internet ug.china-embassy.org; Ambassador FAN GUIJIN.

Congo, Democratic Republic: 20 Philip Rd, Kololo, POB 4972, Kampala; tel. (41) 2250099; fax (41) 2340140; Chargé d'affaires a.i. BISELELE WA MUTSHIPAYI.

Cuba: KAR Dr., 16 Lower Kololo Terrace, POB 9226, Kampala; tel. (41) 2233742; fax (41) 2233320; e-mail ecuba@africaonline.co.ug; Ambassador RICARDO ANTONIO DANZA SIGAS.

Denmark: Plot 3, Lumumba Ave, POB 11243, Kampala; tel. (31) 2263211; fax (31) 2264624; e-mail kmtamb@um.dk; internet www.ambkampala.um.dk; Ambassador STIG BARLYNG.

Egypt: 33 Kololo Hill Dr., POB 4280, Kampala; tel. (41) 2254525; fax (41) 2232103; e-mail egyembug@utlonline.co.ug; Ambassador REDA ABDEL RAHMAN BEBARS.

Ethiopia: 3L Kitante Close, off Kira Rd, POB 7745, Kampala; tel. (41) 2348340; fax (41) 2341885; e-mail ethiokam@starcom.co.ug; Ambassador Ato TERFA MENEGESHA.

France: 16 Lumumba Ave, Nakasero, POB 7212, Kampala; tel. (41) 2342120; fax (41) 2341252; e-mail ambafrance.kampala@diplomatie.gouv.fr; internet www.ambafrance-ug.org; Ambassador BERNARD GARANCHER.

Germany: 15 Philip Rd, Kololo, POB 7016, Kampala; tel. (41) 2501111; fax (41) 2501115; e-mail info@kampala.diplo.de; internet www.kampala.diplo.de; Ambassador REINHARD BUCHHOLZ.

Holy See: Chwa II Rd, Mbuya Hill, POB 7177, Kampala (Apostolic Nunciature); tel. (41) 2505619; fax (41) 2221774; e-mail nuntius@utlonline.co.ug; Apostolic Nuncio (vacant).

India: 11 Kyaddondo Rd, Nakasero, POB 7040, Kampala; tel. (41) 2257368; fax (41) 2254943; e-mail hoc@hicomindkampala.org; High Commissioner SIBARATA TRIPATHI.

Iran: 9 Bandali Rise, Bugolobi, POB 24529, Kampala; tel. (41) 2221689; fax (41) 2223590; e-mail iranemb@infocom.co.ug; Ambassador ABOUTALEBI MORTEZA.

Ireland: 25 Yusuf Lule Rd, Nakasero, POB 7791, Kampala; tel. (41) 2340400; fax (41) 2344353; e-mail kampalaembassy@dfa.ie; Chargé d'affaires a.i. AINE HEARNS.

Italy: 11 Lourdel Rd, Nakasero, POB 4646, Kampala; tel. (41) 4250442; fax (41) 4250448; e-mail segreteria.kampala@esteri.it; internet www.ambkampala.esteri.it; Ambassador UMBERTO PLAJA.

Japan: Plot 8, Kyaddondo Rd, Nakasero, POB 23553, Kampala; tel. (41) 2349542; fax (41) 2349547; e-mail jembassy@jembassy.co.ug; Ambassador RYUUZI KIKUCHI.

Kenya: 41 Nakasero Rd, POB 5220, Kampala; tel. (41) 2258235; fax (41) 2258239; e-mail kenyahicom@africaonline.co.ug; High Commissioner JAPHETH R. GETUGI.

Korea, Democratic People's Republic: 10 Prince Charles Dr., Kololo, POB 5885, Kampala; tel. (41) 2546033; fax (41) 2250224; Ambassador PAK HYON JAE.

Libya: 26 Kololo Hill Dr., POB 6079, Kampala; tel. (41) 2344924; fax (41) 2344969; Sec. of People's Bureau ABDALLA ABDULMAULA BUJELDAIN.

Netherlands: Rwenzori Courts, 4th Floor, Plot 2, Nakasero Rd, POB 7728, Kampala; tel. (41) 2346000; fax (41) 2231861; e-mail kam@minbuza.nl; internet www.netherlandsembassyuganda.org; Ambassador JEROEN VERHEUL.

Nigeria: 33 Nakasero Rd, POB 4338, Kampala; tel. (41) 2233691; fax (41) 2232543; e-mail nighicom-sgu@africaonline.co.ug; High Commissioner CHUKUDI DIXON ORIKE.

Norway: 8A John Babiiha Ave, Kololo, POB 22770, Kampala; tel. (41) 2343621; fax (41) 2343936; e-mail emb.kampala@mfa.no; internet www.norway.go.ug; Ambassador BJØRG SCHONHOWD LEITE.

Russia: 28 Malcolm X Ave, Kololo, POB 7022, Kampala; tel. (41) 2233676; fax (41) 2345798; e-mail russemb@imul.com; Ambassador VALERY I. UTKIN.

Rwanda: 2 Nakaima Rd, POB 2468, Kampala; tel. (41) 2344045; fax (41) 2258547; e-mail ambakampala@minaffet.gov.rw; Ambassador IGNACE KAMALI KAREGESA.

Saudi Arabia: 3 Okurut Close, Kololo, POB 22558, Kampala; tel. (41) 2340614; fax (41) 2254017; e-mail reskala@infocom.co.ug; Chargé d'affaires MAJED ABDULRAHMAN M. MARTHA AL-OTAIBI.

South Africa: 2B Nakasero Hill Lane, POB 22667, Kampala; tel. (41) 2343543; fax (41) 2348216; e-mail sahc@utlonline.co.ug; High Commissioner THANDUYISE HENRY CHILIZA.

Sweden: 24 Lumumba Ave, Nakasero, POB 22669, Kampala; tel. (41) 2340970; fax (41) 2340979; e-mail ambassaden.kampala@foreign.ministry.se; internet www.swedenabroad.com/kampala; Ambassador ANDERS JOHNSON.

Tanzania: 6 Kagera Rd, Nakasero, POB 5750, Kampala; tel. (41) 2256272; fax (41) 2343973; e-mail tzrepkla@imul.com; High Commissioner RAJAB H. GAMAHA.

United Kingdom: Plot 4, Windsor Loop Rd, POB 7070, Kampala; tel. (31) 2312000; fax (41) 2257304; e-mail bhcinfo@starcom.co.ug; internet www.britishhighcommission.gov.uk/uganda; High Commissioner FRANCOIS GORDON.

USA: Plot 1577, Ggaba Rd, POB 7007, Kampala; tel. (41) 2259791; fax (41) 2259794; e-mail KampalaWebContact@state.gov; internet kampala.usembassy.gov; Ambassador STEVEN A. BROWNING.

Judicial System

Courts of Judicature: POB 7085, Kampala; tel. (41) 2233420; e-mail hclib@imul.com; internet www.judiciature.go.ug.

The Supreme Court

Kabaka Anjagala Rd, Mengo.

Hears appeals from the Court of Appeal. Also acts as a Constitutional Court.

Chief Justice: BENJAMIN ODOKI.

Deputy Chief Justice: L. E. M. MUKASA-KIKONYOGO.

The Court of Appeal: 5 Parliament Ave, Kampala; hears appeals from the High Court; the Court of Appeal consists of the Deputy Chief Justice and no fewer than seven Justices of Appeal, the number thereof being prescribed by Parliament.

The High Court

POB 7085, Kampala; tel. (41) 2233422.

Has full criminal and civil jurisdiction and also serves as a Constitutional Court. The High Court consists of the Principal Judge and 27 Puisne Judges.

Principal Judge: JAMES OGOOLA.

Magistrates' Courts: These are established under the Magistrates' Courts Act of 1970 and exercise limited jurisdiction in criminal and civil matters. The country is divided into magisterial areas, presided over by a Chief Magistrate. Under the Chief Magistrate there are two categories of Magistrates. The Magistrates preside alone over their courts. Appeals from the first category of Magistrates' Court lie directly to the High Court, while appeals from the second categories of Magistrates' Court lie to the Chief Magistrate's Court, and from there to the High Court. There are 27 Chief Magistrates' Courts, 52 Magistrates' Grade I Courts and 428 Magistrates' Grade II Courts.

Religion

Christianity is the majority religion—its adherents constitute approximately 75% of the population. Muslims account for approximately 15% of the population. A variety of other religions, including traditional indigenous religions, several branches of Hinduism, the Bahá'í Faith and Judaism, are practised freely and, combined, make up approximately 10% of the population. There are few atheists in the country. In many areas, particularly in rural settings, some religions tend to be syncretistic: deeply held traditional indigenous beliefs are blended into or observed alongside the rites of recognized religions, particularly in areas that are predominantly Christian. Missionary groups of several denominations are present and active in the country, including the Pentecostal Church, the Baptist Church, the Episcopal Church/Church of Uganda, the Church of Christ and the Mormons.

CHRISTIANITY

The Roman Catholic and Anglican Churches claim approximately the same number of followers, accounting for approximately 90% of the country's professed Christians. The Seventh-day Adventist Church, the Church of Jesus Christ of Latter-day Saints (Mormons), the Orthodox Church, Jehovah's Witnesses, the Baptist Church, the Unification Church and the Pentecostal Church, among others, are also active.

The Anglican Communion

Anglicans are adherents of the Church of the Province of Uganda, comprising 29 dioceses. In 2002 there were about 8m. adherents.

Archbishop of Uganda and Bishop of Kampala: Most Rev. LIVINGSTONE MPALANYI-NKOYOYO, POB 14123, Kampala; tel. (41) 2270218; fax (41) 2251925; e-mail couab@uol.co.ug.

Greek Orthodox Church

Archbishop of East Africa: NICADEMUS OF IRINOUPOULIS (resident in Nairobi, Kenya); jurisdiction covers Kenya, Tanzania and Uganda.

The Roman Catholic Church

Uganda comprises four archdioceses and 15 dioceses. At 31 December 2004 there were an estimated 11,628,291 adherents (equivalent to some 42.7% of the total population).

Uganda Episcopal Conference

Uganda Catholic Secretariat, POB 2886, Kampala; tel. (41) 2510398; fax (41) 2510545.

f. 1974; Pres. Most Rev. PAUL BAKYENGA (Archbishop of Mbarara).

Archbishop of Gulu: Most Rev. JOHN BAPTISTE ODAMA, Archbishop's House, POB 200, Gulu; tel. (471) 232026; fax (471) 223593; e-mail metrog@africaonline.co.ug.

Archbishop of Kampala: Cardinal EMMANUEL WAMALA, Archbishop's House, POB 14125, Mengo, Kampala; tel. (41) 2270183; fax (41) 2345441; e-mail rubaga@africaonline.co.ug.

Archbishop of Mbarara: Most Rev. PAUL BAKYENGA, POB 184, Mbarara; tel. (485) 220052; fax (485) 221249; e-mail mbarch@utlonline.co.ug.

Archbishop of Tororo: Most Rev. JAMES ODONGO, Archbishop's House, POB 933, Mbale; tel. (45) 22233269; fax (45) 22233754; e-mail tororoad@africaonline.co.ug.

ISLAM

Muslims are mainly Sunni, although there are Shi'a followers of the Aga Khan among the Asian community.

The Uganda Muslim Supreme Council: POB 1146, Kampala; tel. (41) 2344499; fax (41) 2256500; e-mail umsc@utlonline.co.ug; Mufti of Uganda Sheikh SHABAN MUBAJJE; Chief Kadi and Pres. of Council HUSAYN RAJAB KAKOOZA.

BAHÁ'Í FAITH

National Spiritual Assembly: POB 2662, Kampala; tel. (31) 2262681; e-mail ugangabahai@gmail.com; mems resident in 2,721 localities.

JUDAISM

There is a small Jewish community, the Abayudaya, in central Uganda, with 600 members and six synagogues.

The Press

DAILY AND OTHER NEWSPAPERS

The Citizen: Kampala; official publ. of the Democratic Party; English; Editor JOHN KYEYUNE.

The Economy: POB 6787, Kampala; weekly; English; Editor ROLAND KAKOOZA.

Financial Times: Plot 17/19, Station Rd, POB 31399, Kampala; tel. (41) 2245798; bi-weekly; English; Editor G. A. ONEGI OBEL.

Focus: POB 268, Kampala; tel. (41) 2235086; fax (41) 2242796; f. 1983; publ. by Islamic Information Service and Material Centre; 4 a week; English; Editor HAJJI KATENDE; circ. 12,000.

Guide: POB 5350, Kampala; tel. (41) 2233486; fax (41) 2268045; f. 1989; weekly; English; Editor-in-Chief A. A. KALIISA; circ. 30,000.

The Monitor: POB 12141, Kampala; tel. (41) 2232367; fax (41) 2232369; e-mail info@monitor.co.ug; internet www.monitor.co.ug; f. 1992; daily; English; Man. Dir CONRAD NKUTU; Exec. Editor Dr PETER MWESIGE; circ. 22,000 (Mon.–Sat.), 24,000 (Sun.).

Mulengera: POB 6787, Kampala; weekly; Luganda; Editor ROLAND KAKOOZA.

Munnansi News Bulletin: POB 7098, Kampala; f. 1980; weekly; English; owned by the Democratic Party; Editor ANTHONY SGEKWEYAMA.

Munno: POB 4027, Kampala; f. 1911; daily; Luganda; publ. by the Roman Catholic Church; Editor ANTHONY SSEKWEYAMA; circ. 7,000.

New Vision: POB 9815, Kampala; tel. (41) 2235846; fax (41) 2235221; e-mail wpike@newvision.co.ug; internet www.newvision.co.ug; f. 1986; official govt newspaper; daily; English; Editor WILLIAM PIKE; circ. 34,000 (Mon.–Sat.), 42,000 (Sun.).

Bukedde: daily; Luganda; Editor MAURICE SSEKWAUNGU; circ. 16,000.

Etop: weekly; vernacular; Editor KENNETH OLUKA; circ. 5,000.

Ormuri: tel. (485) 221265; e-mail visionmb@infocom.co.ug; weekly; vernacular; Editor JOSSY MUHANGI; circ. 11,000.

Rupiny: weekly; vernacular; Editor CHRIS BANYA; circ. 5,000.

Ngabo: POB 9362, Kampala; tel. (41) 2242637; f. 1979; daily; Luganda; Editor MAURICE SEKAWUNGU; circ. 7,000.

The Star: POB 9362, Kampala; tel. (41) 2242637; f. 1980; revived 1984; daily; English; Editor SAMUEL KATWERE; circ. 5,000.

Taifa Uganda Empya: POB 1986, Kampala; tel. (41) 2254652; f. 1953; daily; Luganda; Editor A. SEMBOGA; circ. 24,000.

Weekly Topic: POB 1725, Kampala; tel. (41) 2233834; weekly; English; Editor JOHN WASSWA; circ. 13,000.

PERIODICALS

Eastern Africa Journal of Rural Development: Dept of Agricultural Economics and Agribusiness, Makerere University, POB 7062, Kampala; tel. (77) 2616540; fax (41) 2530858; e-mail bkiiza@infocom.co.ug; annual; Editor BARNABAS KIIZA; circ. 800.

The Exposure: POB 3179, Kampala; tel. (41) 2267203; fax (41) 2259549; monthly; politics.

Leadership: POB 2522, Kampala; tel. (41) 222407; fax (41) 2221576; f. 1956; 11 a year; English; Roman Catholic; circ. 7,400; Editor Fr CARLOS RODRÍGUEZ.

Mkombozi: c/o Ministry of Defence, Republic House, POB 3798, Kampala; tel. (41) 2270331; f. 1982; military affairs; Editor A. OPOLOTT.

Musizi: POB 4027, Mengo, Kampala; f. 1955; monthly; Luganda; Roman Catholic; Editor F. GITTA; circ. 30,000.

Pearl of Africa: POB 7142, Kampala; monthly; govt publ.

Uganda Confidential: POB 5576, Kampala; tel. (41) 2250273; fax (41) 2255288; e-mail ucl@swiftuganda.com; internet www.swiftuganda.com/~confidential; f. 1990; monthly; Editor TEDDY SSEZI-CHEEYE.

NEWS AGENCIES

Uganda News Agency (UNA): POB 7142, Kampala; tel. (41) 2232734; fax (41) 2342259; Dir CRISPUS MUNDUA (acting).

Foreign Bureaux

Inter Press Service (IPS) (Italy): Plot 4, 3rd St, Industrial Area, POB 16514, Wandegeya, Kampala; tel. (41) 2235846; fax (41) 2235211; Correspondent DAVID MUSOKE.

Newslink Africa (United Kingdom): POB 6032, Kampala.

RIA—Novosti (Russian Information Agency—News): POB 4412, Kampala; tel. (41) 2232383; Correspondent Dr OLEG TETERIN.

Xinhua (New China) News Agency (People's Republic of China): Plot 27, Prince Charles Dr., Kampala; tel. (41) 2347109; fax (41) 2254951; Chief Correspondent WANG SHANGZHI.

Publishers

Centenary Publishing House Ltd: POB 6246, Kampala; tel. (41) 2241599; fax (41) 2250427; f. 1977; religious (Anglican); Man. Dir Rev. SAM KAKIZA.

Fountain Publishers Ltd: POB 488, Kampala; tel. (41) 2259163; fax (41) 2251160; e-mail fountain@starcom.co.ug; internet www.fountainpublishers.co.ug; f. 1989; general, school textbooks, children's books, academic, scholarly; Man. Dir JAMES TUMUSIIME.

Longman Uganda Ltd: POB 3409, Kampala; tel. (41) 2242940; f. 1965; Man. Dir M. K. L. MUTYABA.

Uganda Printing and Publishing Corporation: POB 33, Entebbe; tel. (41) 2220639; fax (41) 2220530; f. 1993; Man. Dir P. A. BAKER.

Broadcasting and Communications

TELECOMMUNICATIONS

CelTel Ltd: POB 6771, Kampala; tel. (41) 2230110; fax (41) 2230106; e-mail customercare@ug.celtel.com; internet www.ug.celtel.com; Man. Dir YESSE OENGA.

MTN Uganda Ltd: POB 24624, Kampala; tel. (31) 2212053; fax (31) 2212333; internet www.mtn.co.ug; f. 1998.

Uganda Communications Commission: Communications House, 12th Floor, 1 Colville St, POB 7376, Kampala; tel. (41) 2348830; fax (41) 2348832; e-mail ucc@ucc.co.ug; internet www.ucc.co.ug; f. 1998; regulatory body; Chair. Dr A. M. S. KATAHOIRE; Exec. Dir PATRICK MASAMBU.

Uganda Telecom Ltd (UTL): Rwenzori Courts, Plot 2/4A, Nakasero Rd, POB 7171, Kampala; tel. (41) 2333200; fax (41) 2345907; e-mail Customercare.info@utl.co.ug; internet www.utl.co.ug; f. 1998; state-owned; privatization pending; Man. Dir ABDULBASET ELAZZABI.

BROADCASTING

Regulatory Body

Uganda Broadcasting Council (UBC): Broadcasting Council Secretariat, Worker's House, Northern wing, 6th Floor, Plot 1 Pilkington Rd, POB 27553, Kampala; tel. (41) 2251452; fax (41) 2250612; e-mail info@broadcastug.com; internet www.broadcastug.com; f. 1998; statutory body enacted by the Electronic Media Act of 2000; main functions include licensing and regulating radio and television stations, video and cinema operators and libraries for hiring out video recordings or cinema films; consists of 12 mems appointed by the Minister of Information Communication Technology; Chair. GODFREY MUTABAAZI; Dir-Gen. EDGAR TABAARO.

Radio

91.3 Capital FM: POB 7638, Kampala; tel. (41) 2235092; fax (41) 2344556; e-mail capital@imul.com; f. 1993; independent music station broadcasting from Kampala, Mbarara and Mbale; Chief Officers WILLIAM PIKE, PATRICK QUARCOO.

Central Broadcasting Service (CBS): POB 12760, Kampala; tel. (41) 2272993; fax (41) 2340031; e-mail cbs@imul.com; f. 1996; independent station broadcasting in local languages and English to most of Uganda.

Radio One: POB 4589, Kampala; tel. (41) 2348211; fax (41) 2348311.

Radio Uganda: POB 7142, Kampala; tel. (41) 2257256; fax (41) 2256888; f. 1954; state-controlled; broadcasts in 24 languages, including English, Swahili and Ugandan vernacular languages; Commr for Broadcasting JACK TURYAMWIJUKA.

Sanyu Radio: Katto Plaza, Nkrumah Rd, Kampala; f. 1993; independent station broadcasting to Kampala and its environs.

Voice of Toro: POB 2203, Kampala.

Television

Sanyu Television: Naguru; f. 1994; independent station broadcasting to Kampala and its environs.

Uganda Television (UTV): POB 7142, Kampala; tel. (41) 2254461; f. 1962; state-controlled commercial service; programmes mainly in English, also in Swahili and Luganda; transmits over a radius of 320 km from Kampala; five relay stations are in operation, others are under construction; Controller of Programmes FAUSTIN MISANVU.

Finance

(cap. = capital; res = reserves; dep. = deposits; m. = million; brs = branches; amounts in new Uganda shillings, unless otherwise indicated)

BANKING

Central Bank

Bank of Uganda: 37–43 Kampala Rd, POB 7120, Kampala; tel. (41) 2258441; fax (41) 2255983; e-mail info@bou.or.ug; internet www.bou.or.ug; f. 1966; bank of issue; cap. 20,000m., res 291,993m., dep. 2,659,751m. (June 2005); Gov. EMMANUEL TUMUSIIME-MUTEBILE; Dep. Gov. DAVID G. OPIOKELLO (acting).

State Bank

Uganda Development Bank Ltd (UDBL): 15A Clemen Hill Rd, POB 7210, Kampala; tel. (414) 230446; fax (414) 258571; e-mail info@udbl.co.ug; f. 1972; state-owned; reorg. 2001; privatization pending; cap. 11m. (Dec. 1993); CEO ANTHONY K. APPIAH.

Commercial Banks

Bank of Africa—Uganda Ltd: Plot 45 Jinja Rd, POB 2750, Kampala; tel. (41) 2236535; fax (41) 2230439; e-mail boa@boa-uganda.com; internet www.boa-uganda.com; f. 1986 as Allied Bank International (Uganda); name changed as above in 2005; 46% owned by Bank of Africa—Kenya, 22% by FMO, 22% by Aureos Capital, 10% by Central Holdings Ltd; cap. 4,001m., res 5,361m., dep. 60,553m. (Dec. 2006); Chair. JOHN CARRUTHERS; Man. Dir KWAME AHADZI; 5 brs.

Cairo International Bank: 30 Kampala Rd, POB 7052, Kampala; tel. (41) 2235666; fax (41) 2230130; e-mail cib@spacenetuganda.com; 44.4% owned by Banque du Caire, 36.1% owned by Kato Aromatics SAE, 6.5% each owned Bank of Egypt, Bank Misr and Bank of Alexandria; cap. 7,135m. (Dec. 2003); Chair. Dr IBRAHIM KAMEL; Man. Dir NABIL GHANEM.

Crane Bank Ltd: Crane Chambers, 38 Kampala Rd, POB 22572, Kampala; tel. (41) 2231337; fax (41) 2231578; e-mail cranebank@cranebanklimited.com; internet www.cranebanklimited.com; 17% by M/S Meera Investments Ltd, remainder owned by private investors; cap. 5,000m., dep. 107,435m. (Dec. 2003); Chair. SAMSON MUWANGUZI; Man. Dir A. R. KALAN (acting).

DFCU Bank Ltd: Impala House, 13 Kimathi Ave, POB 70, Kampala; tel. (41) 2231784; fax (41) 2231687; e-mail dfcubank@dfcugroup.com; internet www.dfcugroup.com; f. 1984 as Gold Trust Bank Ltd; current name adopted 2000; cap. 5,200m., res 5,097m., dep. 172,645m. (Dec. 2004); Chair. Dr WILLIAM KALEMA; Man. Dir COLIN MCCORMACK.

Diamond Trust Bank (Uganda) Ltd: Diamond Trust Bldg, Plot 17–19, Kampala Rd, POB 7155, Kampala; tel. (41) 2259331; fax (41) 2342286; e-mail info@dtbuganda.co.ug; 40% owned by The Diamond Jubilee Investment Trust, 33.3% owned by Aga Khan Fund for Economic Development, 26.7% owned by Diamond Trust Bank Kenya Ltd; cap. 4,000m., dep. 31,757m. (Dec. 2005); Chair. MAHMOOD MANJI; CEO MANMATH K. DALAI.

Mercantile Credit Bank Ltd: Plot 10, Old Port Bell Rd, POB 620, Kampala; tel. and fax (41) 2235967; e-mail mcb@afsat.com; cap. 1,000m. (Dec. 2003); Chair. PALLE MOELLER; Man. NELSON LUGOLOBI.

National Bank of Commerce (Uganda) Ltd: Cargen House, Plot 13A, Parliament Ave, POB 23232, Kampala; tel. (41) 2347699; fax (41) 2347701; e-mail nbc@swiftuganda.com; cap. 4,631m. (Dec. 2003); Chair. AMOS NZEYI; Man. Dir G. BANGERA.

Nile Bank Ltd: Spear House, Plot 22, Jinja Rd, POB 2834, Kampala; tel. (41) 2346904; fax (41) 2257779; e-mail info@nilebank.co.ug; internet www.nilebank.co.ug; f. 1988; 15.88% owned by East African Development Bank, remainder owned by private investors; cap. 4,000m., res 889m., dep. 111,053m. (Dec. 2005); Chair. J. B. BYAMUGISHA; Man. Dir RICHARD P. BYARUGABA; 8 brs.

Orient Bank Ltd: Orient Plaza, Plot 6/6A, Kampala Rd, POB 3072, Kampala; tel. (41) 2236012; fax (41) 2236066; e-mail mail@orient-bank.com; internet www.orient-bank.com; f. 1993; cap. 5,000m., res 3,377m., dep. 91,020m. (Dec. 2005); Chair. KETAN MORJARIA; Man. Dir SAMWIRI H. K. NJUKI; 6 brs.

Post Bank Uganda Ltd: Plot 11/13, Nkrumah Rd, POB 7189, Kampala; tel. (41) 2258551; fax (41) 2347107; e-mail postbank@imul.com; wholly state-owned; cap. 2,000m. (Dec. 2003); Chair. STEPHEN MWANJE.

Development Banks

Capital Finance Corpn Ltd: 4 Pilkington Rd, POB 21091, Kampala; tel. (41) 2345200; fax (41) 2258310; e-mail cfc@starcom.co.ug; 70% owned by City Credit Bank Ltd; Chair. KEMAL LALANI; Man. Dir and CEO GHULAM HAIDER DAUDANI.

Centenary Rural Development Bank: 7 Entebbe Rd, POB 1892, Kampala; tel. (41) 2251276; fax (41) 2251273; e-mail crdb@imul.com; cap. 4,110m. (Dec. 2003); Chair. Dr JOHN DDUMBA SSENTAMU; CEO HUNG LIHN.

Development Finance Co of Uganda Ltd: Rwenzori House, 1 Lumumba Ave, POB 2767, Kampala; tel. (41) 2231215; fax (41) 2259435; e-mail dfcu@dfcugroup.com; internet www.dfcugroup.com; owned by Commonwealth Devt Corpn (60%), Uganda Devt Corpn (18.5%) and International Finance Corpn (21.5%); cap. 3,978m. (Dec. 2003); Chair. WILLIAM S. KALEMA; Man. Dir C. MCCORMACK.

East African Development Bank (EADB): East African Development Bank Bldg, 4 Nile Ave, POB 7128, Kampala; tel. (41) 2230021; fax (41) 2259763; e-mail admin@eadb.com; internet www.eadb.com; f. 1967; Govts of Kenya, Uganda and Tanzania 25.46% each; remaining 23.62% shared between FMO (Netherlands); Deutsche Investitions- und Entwicklungs-GmbH (Germany); SBIC—Africa Holdings; Commercial Bank of Africa (Kenya); Nordea AB (Sweden); Standard Chartered Bank (United Kingdom); Barclays Bank PLC (United Kingdom); provides financial and tech. assistance to promote industrial development within Uganda, Kenya and Tanzania; regional offices in Nairobi and Dar es Salaam; cap. US $69m., res US $8m. (Dec. 2005); Chair. GRAY S. MGONJA.

Housing Finance Co Uganda Ltd: Investment House, 25 Kampala Rd, POB 1539, Kampala; tel. (41) 2341227; fax (41) 2341429; e-mail hfcultd@infocom.co.ug; 50% owned by Govt, 50% owned by National Social Security Fund; cap. 1,000m. (Dec. 2003); Chair. ALOYSIUS SEMANDA; CEO J. OKWIR.

Foreign Banks

Bank of Baroda (Uganda) Ltd (India): 18 Kampala Rd, POB 7197, Kampala; tel. (41) 2233680; fax (41) 2230781; e-mail bobho@spacenetuganda.com; internet www.bankofbaroda.com; f. 1969; wholly owned by Bank of Baroda (India); cap. 4,000m., res 5,647m., dep. 126,995m. (Dec. 2004); Chair. M. B. SAMANT; Man. Dir K. K. SHUKLA; 6 brs.

Barclays Bank of Uganda Ltd (United Kingdom): POB 7101, Barclay House, Plot 4, Harrington Rd, Kampala; tel. (31) 218300; fax (31) 218393; e-mail uganda.barclays@barclays.com; internet www.barclays.com/uganda.htm; f. 1969; wholly owned by Barclays Bank PLC (United Kingdom); cap. 4,000m., res 15,236m., dep. 328,553m. (Dec. 2005); Chair. GEORGE EGADU; Man. Dir NICK MBUVI; 4 brs.

Citibank (Uganda) Ltd (USA): Plot 4, Centre Court, Ternan Ave, Nakasero, POB 7505, Kampala; tel. (41) 2340951; fax (41) 2340624; internet www.citibank.com/eastafrica/uganda.htm; 99.9% owned by Citicorp Overseas Investment Corpn, 0.1% owned by Foremost Investment; cap. 21,285m. (Dec. 2003); Chair. Prof. J. M. L. SSEBUWUUFU; Man. Dir NADEEM LODHI.

Stanbic Bank Uganda Ltd (United Kingdom): Crested Towers, Short Tower, 17 Hannington Rd, POB 7131, Kampala; tel. (41) 2231152; fax (41) 2231116; e-mail ugandainfo@stanbic.com; internet www.stanbic.co.ug; f. 1906 as National Bank of India

Uganda; adopted present name 1993; wholly owned by Stanbic Africa Holdings Ltd (United Kingdom); merged with Uganda Commercial Bank Ltd 2002; cap. 5,119m., res 50,703m., dep. 828,150m. (Dec. 2005); Chair. Dr MARTIN ALIKER; Man. Dir KITILI MBATHI; 2 brs.

Standard Chartered Bank Uganda Ltd (United Kingdom): 5 Speke Rd, POB 7111, Kampala; tel. (41) 42258211; fax (41) 4231473; e-mail sbc.uganda@ug.standardchartered.com; internet www .standardchartered.com/ug; f. 1912; wholly owned by Standard Chartered Bank PLC; cap. 4,000m., res 15,553m., dep. 544,863m. (Dec. 2005); Chair. JAMES MULWANA; CEO LAMIN MANJANG; 5 brs.

Tropical Africa Bank Ltd (Libya): Plot 27, Kampala Rd, POB 9485-7292, Kampala; tel. (41) 2341408; fax (41) 2232296; e-mail tabu10@calva.com; f. 1972; 50% govt-owned, 50% owned by Libyan Arab Foreign Bank; cap. 7,000m. (Dec. 2003); Chair. C. M. KASSAMI; Gen. Man. and CEO MOHAMED A. WAHRA.

STOCK EXCHANGE

Uganda Securities Exchange: Workers' House, 2nd Floor, Northern Wing, 1 Pilkington Rd, POB 23552, Kampala; tel. (41) 2343297; fax (41) 2343841; e-mail info@use.or.ug; internet www.use.or.ug; f. 1997; Chair. GEOFFREY A. ONEGI-OBEL; Chief Exec. SIMON RUTEGA.

INSURANCE

East Africa General Insurance Co Ltd: Plot 14, Kampala Rd, POB 1392, Kampala; tel. (31) 22262221; fax (41) 2343234; e-mail vkrishna@eagen.co.ug; internet www.eagen.co.ug; f. 1949; public shareholding co; fire, life, motor, marine and accident; CEO VYASA KRISHNA.

National Insurance Corporation: Plot 3, Pilkington Rd, POB 7134, Kampala; tel. (41) 2258001; fax (41) 2259925; f. 1964; general and life; Man. Dir S. SEBUUFU.

Pan World Insurance Co Ltd: POB 7658, Kampala; tel. (41) 2341618; fax (41) 2341593; e-mail pwico@imul.com; Gen. Man. GORDON SENTIBA.

Uganda American Insurance Co Ltd: POB 7077, Kampala; tel. and fax (41) 2533781; f. 1970; Man. Dir STAN MENSAH.

Uganda Co-operative Insurance Ltd: Plot 10, Bombo Rd, POB 6176, Kampala; tel. (41) 2241836; fax (41) 2258231; f. 1982; general; Chair. EPHRAIM KAKURU; Gen. Man. (vacant).

Trade and Industry

GOVERNMENT AGENCIES

Capital Markets Authority: East African Development Bank Bldg, 4 Nile Ave, POB 24565, Kampala; tel. (41) 2342788; fax (41) 2342803; e-mail cma@starcom.co.ug; f. 1996 to develop, promote and regulate capital markets sector; Chair. TWAHA KIGONGO KAAWAASE.

Enterprise Development Unit (EPD): Kampala; oversees privatization programme; Exec. Dir LEONARD MUGANWA.

Export and Import Licensing Division: POB 7000, Kampala; tel. (41) 2258795; f. 1987; advises importers and exporters and issues import and export licences; Prin. Commercial Officer JOHN MUHWEZI.

Uganda Advisory Board of Trade: POB 6877, Kampala; tel. (41) 2233311; f. 1974; issues trade licences and service for exporters.

Uganda Export Promotion Board: POB 5045, Kampala; tel. (41) 2230233; fax (41) 2259779; e-mail uepc@starcom.co.ug; internet www.ugandaexportsonline.com; f. 1983; provides market intelligence, organizes training, trade exhbns, etc.; Exec. Dir FLORENCE KATE.

Uganda Investment Authority: Investment Centre, Plot 28, Kampala Rd, POB 7418, Kampala; tel. (41) 2251561; fax (41) 2342903; e-mail info@ugandainvest.com; internet www .ugandainvest.com; f. 1991; promotes foreign and local investment, assists investors, provides business information, issues investment licences; Exec. Dir Dr MAGGIE KIGOZI.

DEVELOPMENT ORGANIZATIONS

Agriculture and Livestock Development Fund: f. 1976; provides loans to farmers.

National Housing and Construction Corpn: Crested Towers, POB 659, Kampala; tel. (41) 2257461; fax (41) 2258708; e-mail nhcc@imul.com; internet www.nhcc.ug.com; f. 1964; govt agent for building works; also develops residential housing; Chair. Dr COLIN SENTONGO; Gen. Man. M. S. KASEKENDE.

Uganda Industrial Development Corpn Ltd (ULDC): 9–11 Parliament Ave, POB 7042, Kampala; f. 1952; Chair. SAM RUTEGA.

CHAMBER OF COMMERCE

Uganda National Chamber of Commerce and Industry: Plot 2, 1st Floor, Parliament Ave, Jumbo Plaza, POB 3809, Kampala; tel. (41) 503024; fax (41) 230231; e-mail info@ugandachamber.com; internet www.chamberuganda.com; Chair. BONEY KATATUMBA.

INDUSTRIAL AND TRADE ASSOCIATIONS

CMB Ltd (Coffee Marketing Board): POB 7154, Kampala; tel. (41) 2254051; fax (41) 2230790; state-owned; privatization pending; purchases and exports coffee; Chair. Dr DDUMBA SSENTAMU; Man. Dir SAM KIGGUNDU.

Cotton Development Organization: POB 7018, Kampala; tel. (41) 2232968; fax (41) 2232975; Man. Dir JOLLY SABUNE.

Produce Marketing Board: POB 3705, Kampala; tel. (41) 2236238; Gen. Man. ESTHER KAMPAMPARA.

Uganda Coffee Development Authority (UCDA): Coffee House, Plot 35, Jinja Rd, POB 7267, Kampala; tel. (41) 2256940; fax (41) 2256994; e-mail ucdajc@ugandacoffee.org; internet www .ugandacoffee.org; f. 1991; enforces quality control and promotes coffee exports, maintains statistical data, advises Govt on local and world prices and trains processors and quality controllers; Man. Dir HENRY NGABIRANO.

Uganda Importers', Exporters' and Traders' Association: Kampala.

Uganda Manufacturers' Association (UMA): POB 6966, Kampala; tel. (41) 2221034; fax (41) 2220285; e-mail uma@starcom.co.ug; internet www.uganda.co.ug/uma.htm; promotes mfrs' interests; Chair. JAMES KALIBBALA.

Uganda Tea Authority: POB 4161, Kampala; tel. (41) 2231003; state-owned; controls and co-ordinates activities of the tea industry; Gen. Man. MIRIA MARGARITA MUGABI.

EMPLOYERS' ORGANIZATION

Federation of Uganda Employers: POB 3820, Kampala; tel. (41) 2220201; fax (41) 2221257; e-mail fue@infocom.co.ug; internet www .employers.co.ug; Chair. ALOYSIUS K. SSEMMANDA; Exec. Dir ROSEMARY N. SSENABULYA.

UTILITIES

Electricity

Uganda Electricity Board (UEB): POB 7059, Kampala; tel. (41) 2254071; fax (41) 2235119; e-mail okumu@infocom.co.ug; f. 1948; privatization pending; Chair. J. E. N. KAGULE-MAGAMBO; 36 brs.

Water

National Water & Sewerage Corpn: Plot 39, Jinja Rd, POB 7053, Kampala; tel. (41) 2256596; fax (41) 2346532; e-mail nwscmd@infocom.co.ug; internet www.nwsc.co.ug; f. 1972; privatization pending; Man. Dir WILLIAM TSIMWA MUHAIRWE; 12 brs.

MAJOR COMPANIES

The following are some of the largest companies in terms either of capital investment or employment.

African Textile Mills Ltd: POB 242, Mbale; tel. (45) 2234373; fax (45) 2234549; f. 1968; cap. Us. 12,000m.; textile mfrs; operates one mill; Man. Dir J. V. PATEL; 260 employees.

Blenders Uganda Ltd: POB 3515, Kampala; tel. (41) 2259152; fax (41) 2232510; tea- and coffee-blending, packaging and distribution; Gen. Man. DIPAK BANERJEE.

British American Tobacco (BAT) Uganda: Plot 69/71 Jinja Rd, POB 7100, Kampala; tel. (31) 2200100; fax (41) 2256425; f. 1928; 90% owned by BAT (United Kingdom); tobacco mfrs and exporters; Man. Dir PHILIP PAYNE; 650 employees.

International Distillers Uganda Ltd: POB 3221, Kampala; tel. (41) 2221111; fax (41) 2221903; f. 1964; cap. US $15m.; production of potable spirits; Man. Dir IVOR H. KINSTON; 70 employees.

Kilembe Mines Ltd: POB 1, Kilembe; tel. and fax (41) 2234909; f. 1950; mining of cobalt and copper, generation hydroelectric power, production of lime, foundry production; 90% govt-owned; Gen. Man. AMOS GEORGE BASAZA; 576 employees.

Kinyara Sugar Works Ltd: POB 7474, Kampala; tel. (41) 2236382; fax (41) 2236383; f. 1990; sugar production; sales Us. 35.7m. (1999); Gen. Man. J. G. POLLOCK; 3,700 employees.

Lonrho Motors Uganda Ltd: Plot 45, Jinja Rd, POB 353, Kampala; tel. (41) 2231395; fax (41) 2254388; e-mail toyota@toyotauganda .com; distributors of motor vehicles and parts.

Madhvani Group: POB 6361, Kampala; tel. (41) 2259390; fax (41) 2259399; e-mail madhvani@madhvani.org; internet www.madhvani .org; f. 1905; involved in the beer, cardboard, cooking oils, crown corks, fencing, glass containers, soap, steel, sugar and tea industries;

maintains interests in Kenya, Rwanda, Tanzania and Zambia as well as India, Jordan, Lebanon, Saudi Arabia and the UAE; sales Us. 1,500m. (1998); Chair. Dr J. LUYUMBYA; 13,000 employees.

Kakira Sugar Works (1985) Ltd: POB 121, Jinja; tel. and fax (43) 2121475; e-mail kakira@kakira.com; internet www.kakira.com; f. 1985; jtly owned by Madhvani Group (70%) and Uganda Govt; mfrs of some 70,000 metric tons of sugar annually; joint Man. Dirs MAYUR MADHVANI, MANUBHAI MADHVANI; 7,000 employees.

Mulco Textiles Ltd: POB 54, Jinja; tel. (43) 2120511; fax (43) 2130174; e-mail madhvani@madhvani.org; f. 1963; mfrs of cotton textiles.

Nile Breweries Ltd: Yusuf Lule Rd, POB 762, Jinja; tel. (43) 2130060; fax (43) 2120759; e-mail cruhui@nilebrew.com; internet www.nilebeer.com; f. 1951; 40% owned by South African Breweries Ltd; mfrs some 400,000 crates per month; CEO HENRY RUOD; 700 employees.

Mukwano Industries (Uganda) Ltd: 30 Mukwano Rd, POB 2671, Kampala; tel. (41) 2235701; fax (41) 2235704; e-mail marketing@mukwano.com; internet www.mukwano.com; f. 1984; refining of crude palm and sunflower oils, tea production, mfrs of vegetable cooking oils, soaps, detergents, cardboard boxes and plastics; sales Us. 200m. (1998); subsidiaries: A. K. Oils & Fats Ltd; Mukwano Personal Care Products Ltd; A. K. Plastics (U) Ltd; Mukwano Sweets & Confectionaries; A. K. Transporters Ltd; Chair. AMIRALI KARMALI; Exec. Dir ALYKHAN KARMALI; 7,000 employees.

Roko Construction Ltd: POB 172, Kampala; tel. (41) 2567305; fax (41) 2567784; e-mail roko@roko.co.ug; f. 1969; civil engineering and construction; sales US $16m. (2004); Chair. R. KOEHLER; Snr Dir M. ROHRER; 1,650 employees.

Southern Range Nyanza Ltd: POB 408, Jinja; tel. (43) 2120205; fax (43) 2120241; f. 1949; as Nyanza Textile Industries Ltd (NYTIL); owned by Picfare Ltd; went into receivership in May 2000; in 2001 Government agreed rescue package; textile mfrs; Man. Dir Mr ONEG-OBEL.

Toro and Mityana Tea Co Ltd: POB 6641, Kampala; tel. (41) 2259885; fax (41) 2243121; e-mail prinsloo@africaonline.co.ug; f. 1980; wholly owned subsidiary of Mitchell Cotts Uganda Ltd (UK) and Probert Investments Inc.; production, processing and export of tea; Man. Dir J. PRINSLOO; 2,500 employees.

Tororo Industrial Chemicals and Fertilisers Ltd: POB 254, Tororo; f. 1962; mfrs of single super-phosphate fertilizer, sulphuric acid and insecticide.

Uganda Breweries Ltd: POB 7130, Kampala; tel. (41) 2220224; fax (41) 2220059; produces Bell, Pilsner, Tusker and Guinness beers for the domestic market; Man. Dir PATRICK CARDWELL; 700 employees.

Uganda Grain Milling Co Ltd: POB 895, Jinja; tel. (43) 2120171; fax (43) 2120060; f. 1957; 51% owned by Greenland Investments; production of flour, animal feeds and bread; Exec. Chair. Dr S. KIGUNDU; 600 employees.

CO-OPERATIVES

In 2000 there were 6,313 co-operative societies, grouped in 34 unions. There is at least one co-operative union in each administrative district.

Uganda Co-operative Alliance: Kampala; co-ordinating body for co-operative unions, of which the following are among the most important:

Bugisu Co-operative Union Ltd: Palisa Rd, Private Bag, Mbale; tel. (45) 2233027; f. 1954; processors and exporters of Bugisu arabica coffee; 226 mem. socs; Gen. Man. WOMUTU.

East Mengo Growers' Co-operative Union Ltd: POB 7092, Kampala; tel. (41) 2270383; fax (41) 2243502; f. 1968; processors and exporters of coffee and cotton; 280 mem. socs; Chair. FRANCIS MUKAMA; Man. JOSEPH SSEMOGERERE.

Kakumiro Growers' Co-operative Union: POB 511, Kakumiro; processing of coffee and cotton; Sec. and Man. TIBIHWA-RUKEERA.

Kimeeme Livestock Co-operative Society: Mwanga II Rd, POB 6670, Kampala; f. 1984; farming and marketing of livestock; Chair. SAMUSI LUKIMA.

Lango Co-operative Union: POB 59, Lira; f. 1956; ginning and exporting of conventional and organic cotton produce; Gen. Man. PATRICK ORYANG.

Masaka Co-operative Union Ltd: POB 284, Masaka; tel. (481) 220260; f. 1951; coffee, dairy farming, food processing, carpentry; 245 primary co-operative socs; Chair. J. M. KASOZI; Gen. Man. EDWARD C. SSERUUMA.

Nyakatonzi Growers Co-operative Union: Fort Portal Rd, POB 32, Kasese; tel. (483) 244370; fax (483) 244135; f. 1957; processors and exporters of coffee and cotton; Gen. Man. ADAM BWAMBALE.

South Bukedi Co-operative Union: 6 Busia Rd, POB 101, Tororo; tel. (45) 2244327; f. 1952; ginning and export of cotton lint; Gen. Man. MICHAEL O. OGUNDY.

South-west Nile Co-operative Union: POB 33, Pakwach, Nebbi; f. 1958; ginning and export of cotton; Gen. Man. PHILIP UPAKRWOTH.

Uganda Co-operative Savings and Credit Society: 62 Parliament Ave, POB 9452, Kampala; tel. (41) 2257410; f. 1973; Chair. PATRICK KAYONGO.

Uganda Co-operative Transport Union: 41 Bombo Rd, POB 5486, Kampala; tel. and fax (41) 256506; e-mail uctultd@infocom.co.ug; f. 1971; general transport, imports of motor vehicles, vehicle repair and maintenance; Gen. Man. NUWAGIRA NABOTH MWEJUNE.

Wamala Growers' Co-operative Union Ltd: POB 99, Mityana; tel. (46) 2222036; f. 1968; coffee and cotton growers, real estate agents, cattle ranchers, printers, mfrs of edible oils, bricks, tiles and clay products; 250 mem. socs; Gen. Man. HERBERT KIZITO.

West Mengo Growers' Co-operative Union Ltd: POB 7039, Kampala; tel. (41) 2567511; f. 1948; cotton growing and buying, coffee buying and processing, maize milling; 250 mem. socs; Chair. H. E. KATABALWA MIIRO.

West Nile Tobacco Co-operative Union: Wandi, POB 71, Arua; f. 1965; growing, curing and marketing of tobacco; Gen. Man. ANDAMAH BABWA.

TRADE UNION

National Organization of Trade Unions (NOTU): POB 2150, Kampala; tel. (41) 2256295; f. 1973; Chair. E. KATURAMU; Sec.-Gen. MATHIAS MUKASA.

Transport

RAILWAYS

In 1992 there were 1,241 km of 1,000-mm-gauge track in operation. A programme to rehabilitate the railway network is under way.

Uganda Railways Corporation (URC): Nasser Rd, POB 7150, Kampala; tel. (41) 2254961; fax (41) 2344405; f. 1977 following the dissolution of East African Railways; management of operations assumed by Rift Valley Railways consortium in Nov. 2006; Man. Dir D. C. MURUNGI.

ROADS

Uganda's road network consists of approximately 10,000 km of national or trunk roads (of which some 2,200 km are bituminized, the rest being gravel), 25,000 km of district or feeder roads, 2,800 km of urban roads (comprising roads in Kampala City, the 13 municipal councils and the 50 town councils in the country) and 30,000 km of community roads. There are also private roads, some of which are open to the general travelling public. Road transport remains the dominant mode of transport in terms of scale of infrastructure and the volume of freight and passenger movement. The National (Trunk) Road Network carries 80% of Uganda's passenger and freight traffic and includes international routes linking Uganda to neighbouring countries and to the sea (via Kenya and Tanzania), and internal roads linking areas of high population and large administrative and commercial centres. It provides the only form of access to most rural communities. The Government is implementing a programme of continuous upgrading of key gravel roads to bitumen standard.

INLAND WATERWAYS

A rail wagon ferry service connecting Jinja with the Tanzanian port of Tanga, via Mwanza, was inaugurated in 1983, thus reducing Uganda's dependence on the Kenyan port of Mombasa. In 1986 the Uganda and Kenya Railways Corporations began the joint operation of Lake Victoria Marine Services, to ferry goods between the two countries via Lake Victoria.

CIVIL AVIATION

The international airport is at Entebbe, on Lake Victoria, some 40 km from Kampala. There are also several small airfields.

Civil Aviation Authority (CAA): POB 5536, Kampala; Passenger Terminal Bldg, 2nd floor, Entebbe International Airport; tel. (41) 320516; fax (41) 320571; e-mail info@caa.co.ug; internet www.caa.co.ug; Man. Dir AMBROSE AKANDONDA.

Principal Airlines

Dairo Air Cargo Services: 24 Jinja Rd, POB 5480, Kampala; tel. (41) 2257731.

Eagle Air Ltd: Entebbe International Airport, POB 7392, Kampala; tel. (41) 2344292; fax (41) 2344501; e-mail eagle@swiftuganda.com;

internet www.eagleuganda.com; f. 1994; domestic services, charter flights to neighbouring countries; Man. Dir Capt. ANTHONY RUBOMBORA.

East African Airlines (EEC): Airways House, 6 Colville St, POB 5740, Kampala; tel. (41) 2232990; fax (41) 2257279; f. 2002; services to Africa and the Middle East; CEO BENEDICT MUTYABA.

Inter Air: Nile Ave, POB 22658, Kampala; tel. (41) 2255508.

Tourism

Uganda's principal attractions for tourists are the forests, lakes, mountains and wildlife and an equable climate. A programme to revive the tourist industry by building or improving hotels and creating new national parks began in the late 1980s. There were 467,728 tourist arrivals in 2005 (compared with 12,786 in 1983). Revenue from the sector in 2004 was estimated at US $306m., including revenue from the transport of passengers.

Uganda Tourist Board: Impala House, 13/15 Kimatti Ave, POB 7211, Kampala; tel. (41) 2342196; fax (41) 2342188; e-mail utb@visituganda.com; internet www.visituganda.com; Chair. PETER KAMYA; Gen. Man. IGNATIUS NAKISHERO.

Defence

As assessed at November 2006, the Uganda People's Defence Forces (UPDF, formerly the National Resistance Army) was estimated to number 40,000–45,000 men, including paramilitary forces (a border defence unit of about 600 men, a police air wing of about 800 men, about 400 marines and local defence units totalling about 3,000 men). The Lord's Resistance Army (LRA) was thought to have over 1,500 members, with about 600 in Uganda and the remainder in Sudan. The Allied Democratic Front (also known as the Uganda Allied Democratic Army) was believed to comprise some 200 men. The West Nile Bank Front was thought to number 1,000, but had not launched any attacks in the previous 12 months and was therefore considered dormant.

Defence Expenditure: Budgeted at Us. 347,000m. in 2006.

Chief of Defence Forces: Gen. ARONDA NYAKARIMA.

Education

Education is not compulsory. Most schools are supported by the Government, although a small proportion are sponsored by missions. Traditionally all schools have charged fees. In 1997, however, the Government introduced an initiative known as Universal Primary Education (UPE), whereby free primary education was to be phased in for up to four children per family. In January 2007 the Government initiated free secondary school education in 700 public schools as part of a phased programme to introduce universal free education. Primary education begins at six years of age and lasts for seven years. Secondary education, beginning at the age of 13, lasts for a further six years, comprising a first cycle of four years and a second of two years. In 2002/03, according to UNESCO, enrolment at pre-primary level was 3% (for both boys and girls). In that year, 141% of children in the appropriate age-group (males 142%; females 139%) were enrolled at primary schools. According to UNESCO estimates, enrolment at secondary schools was 16% (males 17%; females 16%), while just 3% of those in the relevant age group (males 4%; females 2%) were enrolled in tertiary education. In addition to Makerere University in Kampala there is a university of science and technology at Mbarara, and a small Islamic university is located at Mbale. In 2004 58,823 students were enrolled in Ugandan universities. Education expenditure in the financial year ending 30 June 1997 accounted for 24.9% of government current expenditure.

Bibliography

Ahluwalia, D. P. S. *Plantations and the Politics of Sugar in Uganda.* Kampala, Fountain Publishers, 1995.

Armstrong, J. *Uganda's AIDS Crisis: Its Implications for Development.* Washington, DC, World Bank, 1995.

Barter, J. *Idi Amin (Heroes & Villains).* San Diego, CA, Lucent Books, 2005.

Bigsten, A., and Kayizzi-Mugerwa, S. *Is Uganda an Emerging Economy?* Uppsala, Nordiska Afrikainstitutet, 2001.

Hansen, H. B., and Twaddle, M. (Eds). *Uganda Now.* London, James Currey, 1988.

Changing Uganda: The Dilemmas of Structural Management Adjustment and Revolutionary Change. London, James Currey, 1991.

Developing Uganda. Oxford, James Currey, 1998.

Ingham, K. *Obote.* London, Routledge, 1994.

International Monetary Fund (IMF). *Adjustment for Growth.* Washington, DC, IMF, 1996.

Jørgensen, J. J. *Uganda: A Modern History.* London, Croom Helm, 1981.

Karugire, S. R. *A Political History of Uganda.* London, Heinemann, 1980.

Roots of instability in Uganda. Kampala, Fountain Publrs, 1996.

Kasozi, A. B. K. *Social Origins of Violence in Uganda, 1964–1985.* London, University College London Press, 1995.

Langseth, P., and Katotobo, J. (Eds). *Uganda: Landmarks in Rebuilding a Nation.* Kampala, Fountain Publrs, 1993.

Lubanga, F., and Villadsen, S.(Eds). *Democratic Decentralisation in Uganda.* Kampala, Fountain Publrs, 1997.

Mamdani, M. *Imperialism and Fascism in Uganda.* London, Heinemann Educational, 1983.

Measures, R., and Walker, T. *Amin's Uganda.* Whitstable, Oyster Press, 2002.

Mukholi, D. *A Complete Guide to Uganda's Fourth Constitution: History, Politics and the Law.* Kampala, Fountain Publrs, 1995.

Museveni, Y. K. *Sowing the Mustard Seed: The Struggle for Freedom and Democracy in Uganda.* London, Macmillan, 1997.

Mutibwa, P. *Uganda since Independence: A Story of Unfulfilled Hopes.* London, Hurst, 1992.

Nzita, R., and Mbaga-Niwampa. *Peoples and Cultures of Uganda.* 2nd edn. Kampala, Fountain Publrs, 1995.

Oghojafor, K. *Uganda (Countries of the World).* Milwaukee, WI, Gareth Stevens Publishing, 2004.

Okoth, G. P., and Muranga, M. (Eds). *Uganda: A Century of Existence.* Kampala, Fountain Publrs, 1995.

Okuku, J. *Ethnicity, State Power and the Democratisation Process in Uganda (Discussion Paper).* Uppsala, Nordiska Afrikainstitutet, 2002.

Pirouet, M. L. *Historical Dictionary of Uganda.* Metuchen, NJ, Scarecrow Press, 1995.

Reid, R. J. *Political Power in Pre-Colonial Buganda.* Athens, OH, Ohio University Press, 2003.

Rotberg, R. I. (Ed.). *Uganda (Africa: Continent in the Balance).* Broomall, PA, Mason Crest Publishers, 2005.

Roth, M., Cochrane, J., and Kisamba-Mugerwa, W. *Tenure Security, Credit Use and Farm Investment in the Rujumbura Pilot Land Registration Scheme, Rukungiri District, Uganda.* Madison, WI, University of Wisconsin Press, 1993.

Rubongoya, J. B. *Regime Hegemony in Museveni's Uganda: Pax Musevenica.* Basingstoke, Palgrave Macmillan, 2007.

Ruzindana, A., *et al.* (Eds). *Fighting Corruption in Uganda.* Kampala, Fountain Publrs, 1998.

Soghayroun, I. E.-Z. *The Sudanese Muslim Factor in Uganda.* Khartoum, Khartoum University Press, 1981.

Ssekamnsa, I. C. *History and Development of Education in Uganda.* Kampala, Fountain Publrs, 1997.

Tripp, A. M. *Women and Politics in Uganda.* Madison, WI, University of Wisconsin Press, 2000.

Whyte, S. R. *Questioning Misfortune.* Cambridge, Cambridge University Press, 1998.

World Bank. *Uganda: Growing out of Poverty.* Washington, DC, World Bank, 1993.

The Challenge of Growth and Poverty Reduction. Washington, DC, World Bank, 1996.

Uganda. Washington, DC, World Bank, 2000.

ZAMBIA

Physical and Social Geography

GEOFFREY J. WILLIAMS

PHYSICAL FEATURES

The Republic of Zambia is a land-locked state occupying elevated plateau country in south-central Africa. Zambia has an area of 752,614 sq km (290,586 sq miles). The country is irregularly shaped, and shares a boundary with eight other countries.

The topography of Zambia is dominated by the even skylines of uplifted planation surfaces. Highest elevations are reached on the Nyika plateau on the Malawi border (2,164 m). Elevations decline westward, where the country extends into the fringe of the vast Kalahari basin. The plateau surfaces are interrupted by localized downwarps (occupied by lakes and swamp areas, such as in the Bangweulu and Lukanga basins) and by the rifted troughs of the mid-Zambezi and Luangwa.

Katangan rocks of upper-Pre-Cambrian age yield the copper ores exploited on the Copperbelt. Younger Karoo sedimentaries floor the rift troughs of the Luangwa and the mid-Zambezi rivers, while a basalt flow of this age has been incised by the Zambezi below the Victoria Falls to form spectacular gorges. Coal-bearing rocks in the Zambezi trough are of this same system. Over the western third of the country there are extensive and deep wind-deposited sands.

The continental divide separating Atlantic from Indian Ocean drainage forms the frontier with the Democratic Republic of the Congo (DRC), then traverses north-east Zambia to the Tanzanian border. Some 77% of the country is drained to the Indian Ocean by the Zambezi and its two main tributaries, the Kafue and Luangwa, with the remainder being drained principally by the Chambeshi and Luapula via the River Congo to the Atlantic. Rapids occur along most river courses so that the rivers are of little use for transportation. The country's larger lakes, including the man-made Lakes Kariba and Itezhitezhi, offer possibilities of water use as yet relatively little developed.

Zambia's climatic year can be divided into three seasons: a cool dry season (April–August), a hot dry season (August–November) and a warm wet season (November–April). Temperatures are generally moderate. Mean maximum temperatures exceed 35°C only in southern low-lying areas in October, most of the country being in the range 30°–35°C. July, the coldest month, has mean minima of 5°–10°C over most of the country, but shows considerable variability. Rainfall is highest on the high plateau of the Northern Province and on the intercontinental divide west of the Copperbelt (exceeding 1,200 mm per year). In the south-west and the mid-Zambezi valley, annual mean rainfall is less than 750 mm.

The eastern two-thirds of the country has generally poor soils. Soils on the Kalahari Sands of the west are exceptionally infertile, while seasonal waterlogging of soils in basin and riverine flats makes them difficult to use. Savannah vegetation dominates, with miombo woodland extensive over the plateau, and mopane woodland in the low-lying areas. Small areas of dry evergreen forest occur in the north, while treeless grasslands characterize the flats of the river basins.

RESOURCES AND POPULATION

Zambia's main resource is its land, which, in general, is underutilized. Although soils are generally poor, altitudinal modifications of the climate make possible the cultivation of a wide range of crops. Cattle numbers are greatest in the southern and central areas, their range being limited by large tsetse-infested areas in the Kafue basin and the Luangwa valley. In the Western Province their numbers are less, but their importance to the local economy is even greater. Subsistence farming characterizes most of the country, with commercial farming focusing along the 'line of rail'. Commercial forestry is important on the Copperbelt, where there are extensive softwood plantations, and in the south-west, where hardwoods are exploited. The main fisheries are located on the lakes and rivers of the Northern Province, with the Kafue Flats, Lukanga and Lake Kariba also contributing significantly. Game parks cover 7.9% of the country.

For many years, the mining of copper has been the mainstay of Zambia's economy, although its contribution has fallen sharply since the mid-1980s, reflecting price fluctuations on international commodity markets. By the mid-1990s the country remained Africa's largest producer, although only the 11th largest in terms of copper output world-wide. It has been estimated that, at current production rates, Zambia's economically recoverable reserves will be virtually exhausted by 2010. Cobalt, a by-product of copper mining, has recently gained in significance, and Zambia has been steadily expanding its cobalt production in an attempt to offset falls in copper output. Since the collapse of cobalt output in Zaire (now the DRC) in 1992, Zambia has been the world's leading cobalt-producing country. Lead and zinc are mined at Kabwe, although the reserves of the Broken Hill Mine are nearing exhaustion. Coal, of which Zambia has the continent's largest deposits outside South Africa, is mined in the Zambezi valley, although this industry is in need of re-equipment and modernization. Manganese, silver and gold are produced in small quantities. Deposits of uranium have been located, and prospects exist for the exploitation of iron ore. No petroleum deposits have yet been located. However, Zambia is rich in hydropower, developed and potential.

At the census of October 2000 Zambia's population was 9,885,591, equivalent to 13.1 inhabitants per sq km. This level of population density is low, by African standards, for a state which contains no truly arid area. However, this average figure is misleading, for Zambia is one of the most urbanized countries in mainland sub-Saharan Africa, with 46.9% of its population in 2000 classified as urban by the African Development Bank. Some 78% of the urban population was, in fact, located in the 10 largest urban areas, all situated on the 'line of rail', extending south from the Copperbelt, through Lusaka, to the Victoria Falls, forming the major focus of Zambia's economic activity. Lusaka is the largest single urban centre, but the Copperbelt towns together constitute the largest concentration of urban population (47.1% of the total). By mid-2006, according to UN estimates, Zambia's total population had increased to 11,696,000. While the increasing rate of population growth for the country as a whole (2.0% per year in 1995–2005) is a problem, the sustained influx to urban areas is even more acute as this growth has not been matched by employment and formal housing provision.

There are no fewer than 73 different ethnic groups among Zambia's indigenous population. Major groups are: the Bemba of the north-east, who are also dominant on the Copperbelt; the Nyanja of the Eastern Province, also numerous in Lusaka; the Tonga of the Southern Province; and the Lozi of the west. Over 80 languages have been identified, of which seven are recognized as 'official' vernaculars. English is the language of government.

Recent History

GREGORY MTHEMBU-SALTER

Based on an earlier article by ANDREW D. ROBERTS

Zambia's colonial history began in the 1890s, when British colonial troops forced land-ceding treaties on African leaders north of the Zambezi river, extending territory they had earlier annexed south of the river. The first territory captured became known as Southern Rhodesia (now Zimbabwe) and the second as Northern Rhodesia (now Zambia). By the mid-1930s, following earlier discoveries of vast copper deposits, the large-scale exploitation of the northern region of Northern Rhodesia, soon known as the Copperbelt, was firmly established. The colonial authorities granted Northern Rhodesia's best agricultural land to white farmers, removing Africans to 'native reserves' on inferior land, thus retarding the development of African farming—a legacy with which Zambia lives to this day. A major focus of the administration was to create a mining labour pool, both for the copper mines and the gold mines of the South African Witwatersrand. Little effort was made to establish a manufacturing sector. Instead, Northern Rhodesia was intended as a primary market for manufactured goods from Southern Rhodesia, where there was appreciable investment during the colonial era in the industrial sector.

Mining helped foster an industrial class-consciousness among Northern Rhodesians, which was both hindered and radicalized by the prohibition of African trade unions by the colonial authorities. Miners, and later other African workers, instead formed 'welfare societies', which by 1951 had emerged as a cohesive, anti-colonial political force, the Northern Rhodesia African National Congress. The Congress unsuccessfully opposed federation with Southern Rhodesia, and in 1953 the colony became part of the Central African Federation (CAF) with Southern Rhodesia and Nyasaland (now Malawi). In 1958 leadership of the Congress passed to Kenneth Kaunda, whose demands for the dissolution of the CAF and the independence of Northern Rhodesia, under the name of Zambia, led to his imprisonment and the banning of the Congress in 1959. On his release, a few months later, Kaunda became leader of the newly formed United National Independence Party (UNIP). In 1962, following a sustained civil disobedience campaign, led by UNIP, the British Government introduced a Constitution for Northern Rhodesia, which would create an African majority in the legislature. UNIP agreed to participate in the ensuing elections, and formed a coalition Government with the remaining supporters of Congress. The CAF was formally dissolved in December 1963 and Northern Rhodesia became independent as the Republic of Zambia on 24 October 1964, with Kaunda as President.

Kaunda advocated self-reliant black African nationalism, but this was structurally undermined by the fact that the Zambian economy was dependent on the industrial complex of white-ruled southern Africa. UNIP sought to lessen this reliance by investing in import-substitution industries and developing routes to seaports that did not pass through Southern Rhodesia and South Africa. Southern Rhodesia's unilateral declaration of independence in November 1965, and the subsequent imposition of international sanctions, further stimulated these efforts, particularly in relation to fuel, hydroelectric power and rail communications, although only very limited success was achieved.

UNIP was returned to power at general elections in 1968, but popular support for the party was in decline. Sensing an opportunity, in 1971 Simon Kapwepwe, a former Vice-President of Zambia who had a strong following among the country's numerous Bemba population, left UNIP and formed the United People's Party (UPP), intending to challenge UNIP at the polls. The UPP, however, was suppressed, and in December 1972 Zambia was declared a one-party state. Legislative elections took place in December 1973, and Kaunda was re-elected for a further term of office.

In January 1973 the Government of Rhodesia (formerly Southern Rhodesia) closed the border along the Zambezi to all Zambian exports except copper, damaging the economy. The Zambian Government's subsequent decision to divert copper exports using routes to Tanzania and Angola resulted in further economic deterioration, which was compounded, following the outbreak of civil war in Angola in late 1975, by the closure of the Benguela railway. During 1974–76, moreover, world copper prices fell and export revenues plummeted. By the end of the year there was widespread domestic discontent at high food prices, import restrictions and increasing unemployment. His apparent belief that external forces were exploiting this unrest prompted Kaunda to declare a state of emergency in January 1976.

In 1978 Kapwepwe rejoined UNIP after being courted by Kaunda who wanted a recognized Bemba leader at a time of acute internal instability. In October 1978 rail links with Rhodesia were restored, and an agreement was reached on the shipping of exports via South Africa. From 1977, however, Zambia had openly harboured members of the Zimbabwe African People's Union (ZAPU) wing of the Patriotic Front, and in 1978 and 1979 Rhodesian forces attacked ZAPU bases in Zambia and carried out air raids on Lusaka. Zambia suffered further disruption from Rhodesian bombing until the implementation, in December 1979, of an agreement providing for the internationally recognized independence of Rhodesia, as Zimbabwe, which came into effect in April 1980.

ECONOMIC PROBLEMS AND POLITICAL UNREST

Political dissent increased towards the end of 1980, as economic conditions worsened further. In October several prominent businessmen, government officials and UNIP members allegedly staged a coup attempt. Kaunda claimed South African involvement, but many of those subsequently arrested for their involvement in the alleged coup were ethnic Bemba. In January 1981 the suspension from UNIP of 17 officials of the Mineworkers' Union of Zambia (MUZ) and the Zambia Congress of Trade Unions (ZCTU) prompted a widely observed strike, and riots.

Despite the introduction of unpopular austerity measures, as the sole candidate, Kaunda won the presidential election in October 1983, receiving 93% of the votes cast. In March 1985, following strikes by public-sector employees demanding higher wages, Kaunda assumed emergency powers to ban strikes in essential services. Austerity measures inspired by the IMF were imposed in that year, leading to an increase in retail prices, provoking angry demonstrations in Lusaka in October. There were further strikes in early 1987, and in April of that year the Government was forced to rescind a 70% increase in the price of fuel, following protests in Lusaka. In May Kaunda announced that an economic austerity programme advocated by the IMF was to be replaced by a government-devised strategy involving greater state controls, and a new Minister of Finance was appointed.

Meanwhile, the Government became increasingly preoccupied with internal security. In early 1987 Kaunda alleged that the South African Government, with the assistance of local businessmen and members of the armed forces, was conspiring to destabilize his administration, which was followed by arrests and prosecutions of a number of people for alleged coup plotting and spying offences.

In late October 1988 presidential and legislative elections took place. Kaunda, again the only candidate, received 95.5% of all votes cast in the presidential election. There followed continued unrest among workers and students, and the Government threatened to ban trade unions involved in strike action. Increases in the prices of essential goods in mid-1989 raised political tensions still further, and led to renewed rioting in the Copperbelt region in July. In June 1990 an announcement that the price of maize meal was to increase by more than 100% resulted in severe rioting in Lusaka, in which at least 30 people were reported to have been killed. On 30 June a junior army officer, Lt Mwamba Luchembe, announced on the state radio that Kaunda had been overthrown by the armed forces. Luchembe was immediately arrested, although he was subsequently pardoned and released.

Earlier, in April 1990, and despite the rapidly deteriorating political climate, the UNIP general conference rejected proposals for the introduction of a multi-party political system in Zambia. Showing a surer grasp of the public mood, however, in May Kaunda announced that a referendum on the introduction of multi-party politics would be conducted in October of that year, and that proponents of such a system were allowed to campaign and hold public meetings. In early July the Movement for Multi-party Democracy (MMD), an informal alliance of political opponents of the Government, was formed, under the leadership of a former Minister of Finance, Arthur Wina, and the Chairman of the ZCTU, Frederick Chiluba. In addition, the ZCTU demanded an end to the existing state of emergency, the creation of an independent body to monitor the referendum and equal access to the media for both those supporting and opposing the introduction of a multi-party system. Kaunda's initial response was hostile, announcing in July that the referendum would be postponed until August 1991. By September, however, Kaunda had changed his mind, and he proposed abandoning the referendum and instead pressing ahead with organizing multi-party elections. UNIP quickly endorsed the new proposals and elections were scheduled for October 1991.

CONSTITUTIONAL TRANSITION

In December 1990 Kaunda formally adopted constitutional amendments, approved by the National Assembly earlier that month, which allowed a multi-party system. Shortly afterwards, the MMD was granted official recognition as a political organization; the establishment of a further 11 opposition movements followed in subsequent months. In early 1991 several prominent members of UNIP resigned from the party and declared their support for the MMD, while the ZCTU officially transferred its allegiance to the MMD. In February Kaunda announced that he would permit other members of UNIP to contest the presidential election, despite previous statements to the contrary.

The constitutional commission presented its recommendations in June 1991, but they were immediately rejected by the MMD, which threatened to boycott the elections if the National Assembly accepted the proposals. The MMD objected in particular to amendments permitting the appointment of non-elected ministers from outside the National Assembly, and the vesting of supreme authority in the President rather than in the National Assembly. The Government meanwhile rejected MMD demands that foreign observers monitor the elections. In July, following intense negotiations, Kaunda conceded to opposition demands that ministers be appointed only from members of the National Assembly and that the proposed establishment of a constitutional court be abandoned; presidential powers to impose martial law were also to be rescinded. On 2 August the National Assembly formally adopted the new draft Constitution, which included these amendments. Later in August Kaunda agreed to permit foreign observers to monitor the forthcoming elections, to counter opposition allegations that UNIP would perpetrate electoral fraud. In a further attempt to increase the distance between party and state, Kaunda announced that leaders of the armed forces would henceforth be obliged to retire from membership of UNIP's Central Committee.

In September 1991 the National Assembly was dissolved in preparation for the presidential and legislative elections, which were scheduled for 31 October. On the same day Kaunda formally announced the disassociation of UNIP from the state and banned public-sector workers from engaging in party-political activity. While welcoming these developments, international observers expressed concern none the less at UNIP bias in the state-owned media, at open support for the party from parastatal organizations and that the state of emergency remained in force.

THE CHILUBA PRESIDENCY

Despite these concerns, international observers reported that the elections, which took place on 31 October 1991, were free and fair. In the presidential election Chiluba, who received 75.8% of votes cast, soundly defeated Kaunda, who obtained 24.2% of the vote. In the legislative elections, which were contested by 330 candidates representing six political parties, the MMD again triumphed, securing 125 seats in the National Assembly, while UNIP won just 25 seats; only four members of the previous Government were returned to the National Assembly. On 2 November Chiluba was inaugurated as President; he appointed Levy Mwanawasa, a lawyer, as Vice-President and Leader of the National Assembly, and formed a new 22-member Cabinet. In addition, a minister was appointed to each of the country's nine provinces, which were previously administered by governors. Two days later the Government allowed the state of emergency to lapse. During his first month in office Chiluba began a major restructuring of the civil service and parastatal organizations, replacing Kaunda's appointees with people loyal to himself.

Internal 'Conspiracies' and Official Investigations

In December 1991, following a road accident in which Mwanawasa was severely injured, the Minister without Portfolio, Brig.-Gen. Godfrey Miyanda, was accused of plotting his death. In March 1992, however, following an investigation by British detectives into the circumstances of the accident, Miyanda was exonerated.

In early March 1993 Chiluba declared a state of emergency, following the apparent discovery of documents emanating from UNIP detailing an alleged conspiracy (referred to as the 'Zero Option') to destabilize the Government by inciting unrest and civil disobedience. Prominent members of UNIP, including Kaunda's three sons, were subsequently arrested. Shortly afterwards, the National Assembly approved the state of emergency, which was to remain in force for a further three months. Owing to pressure from Western governments, however, Chiluba reduced the maximum period of detention without trial from 28 to seven days. Responding to growing domestic and international concern about corruption, Chiluba reshuffled his Cabinet in April 1993, but although several ministers were dismissed, those most strongly suspected of corruption—including foreign affairs minister Vernon Mwaanga—kept their jobs. Later that month the state of emergency was lifted.

Political Realignments

In July 1993 UNIP called for civil disobedience in protest at the economic austerity measures, but was largely ignored by the general population. The persistence of divisions within the MMD was laid bare in August when 15 prominent members left the party. The rebels accused the Government of protecting corrupt cabinet ministers and failing to respond to numerous reports linking senior party officials with the illegal drugs trade. Their opposition to Chiluba's Government was consolidated later in the month by the formation of a new political group, the National Party (NP).

Following continued allegations of his links to illegal drug trafficking, Mwaanga resigned in January 1994, while denying any misconduct. In early July 1994 Mwanawasa resigned as Vice-President, citing long-standing differences with Chiluba, and was replaced by Miyanda. In the same month former-President Kaunda, despite having earlier resigned as leader of UNIP and stating that he was to retire from politics, unexpectedly announced that he was considering contesting the presidential election scheduled to be held in 1996. In June 1995, at an extraordinary congress of UNIP, Kaunda was elected party President by a large majority. Proposed constitutional reforms from the MMD, however, threatened to deny Kaunda the opportunity, through the inclusion of a clause banning any President from a third term of office and barring candidates from seeking election as President if their parents were not both of Zambian origin. Kaunda's parents were both born in Malawi.

In early September 1995 the Munyama Commission on Human Rights alleged that torture and other abuses of human rights had been carried out in cells beneath the presidential residence during Kaunda's reign. A month later the Minister of Legal Affairs announced that Kaunda had not officially relinquished Malawian citizenship until 1970 (and had therefore governed illegally for six years) and that he had not obtained Zambian citizenship through the correct procedures. There followed widespread reports that Kaunda would be deported, but later that month the Government relented and ordered the security forces to suspend investigations into his citizenship.

Electoral Controversies

The Government was determined, however, to press on with its proposed constitutional changes despite the resignation of two ministers over the issue during early 1996, ignoring demands from opposition parties that it negotiate with them on the matter. In May UNIP deputies withdrew from a parliamentary debate on the proposed Constitution, which was subsequently approved by a large majority in the National Assembly. On 28 May, despite continuing criticism, the new Constitution, which, as anticipated, contained clauses intended to prevent Kaunda from standing as a presidential candidate, was officially adopted by Chiluba. Donors reduced aid in protest, while Kaunda announced that he would contest the presidency despite the ban. In the same month eight senior UNIP officials, including the party Vice-President, were arrested and charged in connection with a series of bomb attacks against official buildings, which were officially attributed to a clandestine anti-Government organization called 'Black Mamba'.

In August 1996 Chiluba and Kaunda met for discussions in Lusaka, following which the Government made minor concessions regarding the conduct of forthcoming elections, while rejecting UNIP's central demand that the elections be conducted according to the 1991 Constitution. UNIP threatened again to boycott the elections and to organize a campaign of civil disobedience, and soon after a further six political parties also decided on an electoral boycott. Further undermining the credibility of the polls, there was widespread criticism of the voter-registration process, in which fewer than one-half of the estimated 4.6m. eligible voters were listed.

The 1996 Elections

Elections took place on 18 November 1996, with the boycott by the main opposition parties ensuring that Chiluba and the MMD were returned to power by a large majority. In the presidential election Chiluba defeated the four other candidates, with 72.5% of the valid votes cast. His nearest rival (with only 12.5%) was Dean Mung'omba, who had challenged Chiluba for the MMD leadership in 1995, but had subsequently founded the Zambia Democratic Congress (ZADECO). The MMD secured 131 of the 150 seats in the National Assembly. Of the eight other parties that finally contested the legislative elections, only the NP (five seats), ZADECO (two seats) and Agenda for Zambia (two seats) won parliamentary representation, with independent candidates taking the remaining 10 seats. The rate of participation was low. Despite the verdict of the Electoral Commission of Zambia (ECZ) that the elections had been conducted fairly, allegations of fraud were made by opposition parties and local monitoring groups, which criticized voter registration procedures and accused the MMD of buying votes.

Chiluba was inaugurated for a second presidential term on 21 November 1996. Amid demands for his resignation and fresh elections, Chiluba dissolved the Cabinet and put the military on alert at the end of the month. In early December a new Government was appointed: there were no changes to the main portfolios, except for the appointment of Lawrence Shimba (a professor of law at the University of Zambia) as Minister of Foreign Affairs. Four opposition parties filed petitions with the Supreme Court challenging Chiluba's citizenship (and therefore his eligibility as President) and accusing the ECZ of conspiring with the MMD to commit electoral fraud; the petitions were dismissed in early 1997.

In early February 1997 a human rights report prepared for the US Department of State condemned police brutality and prison conditions in Zambia, but claimed that there had been no evidence of significant electoral fraud in the 1996 elections. In the same month an African human rights group released a report that called for further investigation into the deaths of five opposition politicians during 1995–96. In March 1997 the Government established a permanent commission to investigate human rights violations, but opposition parties refused to participate.

Internal Tensions

Voter cards were burnt at a series of opposition rallies in mid-1997, and in late July security forces dispersed demonstrators at a protest march against the MMD after government vehicles were stoned. In mid-August the Government accused the opposition of inciting unrest after market-traders rioted when their stalls were destroyed by fire; 56 people were arrested in the disturbances. Later that month Kaunda and Roger Chongwe, the leader of the Liberal Progressive Front, were shot and wounded when the security forces opened fire on an opposition gathering, following the cancellation of a rally in Kabwe, north of Lusaka. Kaunda's subsequent allegation that the shooting was an assassination attempt organized by the Government was strongly denied by Chiluba. The Government announced in November 1997 that all public-sector wages would be frozen in 1998 to allow for the financing of major civil service redundancies, as part of its public-sector reform programme. In March 1998 the ZCTU organized a general strike in protest, but the action collapsed after the Government threatened the strikers with dismissal. In June 1999 Zambia's industrial relations court ruled that the 1998 wage freeze had been illegal, but the Government ignored the ruling, prompting further strike action from public-sector workers.

In the early morning of 28 October 1997 rebel officers, led by Capt. Stephen Lungu, briefly captured the national television and radio station from where they proclaimed the formation of a military regime. The attempted coup was suppressed within a few hours by regular military units; 15 people, including Lungu, were arrested during the operation and one man was killed. Chiluba declared a state of emergency on 29 October, providing for the detention for 28 days without trial of people suspected of involvement in the attempted coup. Several non-governmental organizations, including the Law Association of Zambia (LAZ), described the state of emergency as an abuse of human rights. Mung'omba was among 84 people arrested in the immediate aftermath of the coup attempt, and in November the High Court ordered that he undergo a medical examination to investigate injuries allegedly sustained during interrogation by the police.

Chiluba carried out an extensive cabinet reshuffle in early December 1997, which saw the demotion of ministers who were widely perceived to be potential rivals to Chiluba within the MMD. Lt-Gen. Christon Tembo, hitherto the Minister of Mines and Mineral Development, replaced Miyanda as Vice-President.

On 25 December 1997 Kaunda was arrested under emergency powers and imprisoned, shortly after his return to Zambia from more than two months abroad. Numerous regional and international governments expressed serious concern at the detention of Kaunda, who refused food until the end of the month when Julius Nyerere, the former President of Tanzania, visited him. On the following day Kaunda was placed under house arrest at his home in Lusaka. He was arraigned in court in January 1998 and in mid-February he was formally notified that he was to stand trial for 'misprision of treason', on the grounds that he had failed to report in advance to the authorities details allegedly known to him of the attempted coup of October 1997. Meanwhile, in late January the National Assembly voted to extend the state of emergency for a further three months; Chiluba eventually revoked the state of emergency in mid-March, following pressure from external donors. Three days later, Chiluba dismissed another powerful cabinet figure, Minister of Finance and Economic Development, Ronald Penza. Kaunda was released from detention in early June, after charges against him were withdrawn, apparently owing to lack of evidence. His subsequent resignation as UNIP President in July created a split within the party over the nomination of a replacement. The MMD was also divided over an eventual successor to Chiluba, despite a ban within the party on presidential campaigning, amid suggestions that Chiluba might seek a third term of office in 2001, contrary to the Constitution.

In November 1998 Penza was murdered at his home in Lusaka. Shortly afterwards the police shot dead five of six suspects whom they had earlier apprehended, prompting widespread allegations of a cover-up. In mid-December Mung'omba and Princess Nakatindi Wina, a former minister and the MMD's National Chairperson for Women, were released from prison, as no witnesses had provided evidence against them since their detention on charges of treason following the failed coup attempt of October 1997.

In late March 1999 the High Court delivered its judgment in a case concerning Kaunda's citizenship, declaring him to be stateless. Kaunda appealed to the Supreme Court, and at around the same time survived a reported assassination attempt, when a group of armed men opened fire on his car. In November Chiluba demoted Mwila to the Ministry of Energy and Water Development, after increasingly transparent hints from Mwila that he intended to contest the presidency in 2001. Kaunda's son, Maj. Wezi Kaunda, whom he had been grooming to succeed him as UNIP President, was shot dead in early November outside his Lusaka home. Kaunda later alleged the murder had been politically motivated, while police sources stated that Wezi Kaunda had been the victim of an attempted car hijack.

In January 2000 Chiluba announced the creation of provincial District Administrators (DAs), who were to be appointed by, and answer directly to, the President. Opposition parties accused the DAs of being detested Kaunda-era governors in disguise and reminded the MMD that it had campaigned for their abolition in 1990. Kenneth Kaunda resigned once again as President of UNIP in late March, and an extraordinary party congress elected Francis Nkhoma as its new leader in mid-May. Nkhoma had been Governor of the central bank during Kaunda's presidency, but had joined the MMD after its election victory, prior to rejoining UNIP in 1998. Another of Kaunda's sons, Tilyenji, was appointed as UNIP's new Secretary-General. Nkhoma was suspended as President by senior UNIP officials in November, although he contested the legality of the suspension, and in January 2001 the UNIP Central Committee returned to the Kaunda dynasty, adopting Tilyenji Kaunda as its President.

Mwila publicly declared his intention to bid for the presidency in May 2000, and was later expelled from the MMD. At least 10 other prominent MMD members were also expelled from the ruling party for supporting Mwila. Mwila's expulsion again raised the issue of Chiluba's intentions regarding the forthcoming presidential election, scheduled to be held in or before November 2001. A constitutional amendment introduced by the Government in 1996 prohibited Chiluba from contesting another election, having already served two terms. However, towards the end of 2000 many MMD cadres began calling for a further constitutional amendment to allow Chiluba to stand again. The newly appointed DAs were among the most vocal in their support for a third term for Chiluba, making it increasingly clear that the President, who declined to speak publicly on the subject, none the less backed the pro-third term campaign.

Debate over whether the Constitution should be amended to allow Chiluba to stand for a third term intensified during 2001. Prominent civil society organizations, including trade unions, churches, the LAZ and many smaller bodies were against the proposal and in late February adopted the 'Oasis Declaration', which vigorously opposed the proposed third term. The declaration was quickly endorsed by opposition parties. Conventions of the provincial branches of the MMD discussed the third-term bid during early 2001, often in an atmosphere of heavy-handed intimidation. Seven provinces endorsed changing the Constitution, while two—Lusaka and Southern—did not. In late March the MMD National Executive Committee (NEC) scheduled a special convention of the party for late April to decide the issue. As the date approached, opposition to the third term within the MMD grew markedly, and in mid-April 50 MMD deputies, including 21 ministers, signed a petition opposing the bid. The MMD convention at the end of the month was highly controversial; party members opposed to a third term were physically prevented from attending, while pro-third term delegates were presented with a range of gifts before proceeding to nominate Chiluba as the party's presidential candidate.

On 2 May 2001 Chiluba dismissed all those in his Cabinet who had signed the petition against his re-election bid, including Vice-President Tembo, and the MMD expelled them from the party. Those removed from the MMD contested the legality of their expulsion in the courts, but also established their own political party, the Forum for Democracy and Development (FDD). On 3 May 65 deputies signed a motion to impeach Chiluba for alleged violations of the Constitution. However, the Speaker of the National Assembly, Amusaa Mwanamwambwa, controversially prevented a parliamentary debate on the motion. After this, the National Assembly did not sit for five months. Mwanamwambwa's move secured Chiluba some time, but in early May Chiluba bowed to the pressure, and publicly stated that he would not seek a third term in office.

Public-sector workers went on strike in late May 2001, angry at the spending of state resources on the third-term bid, and demanding a substantial pay increase. Fearful that the industrial action might damage the forthcoming summit of the Organization of African Unity (OAU, now the African Union—AU) in Lusaka in early July, the Government eventually reached an agreement with public-sector unions only days before the summit began.

THE MWANAWASA PRESIDENCY

In July 2001 Chiluba selected Levy Mwanawasa as the MMD's presidential candidate, angering serving MMD cabinet ministers and other influential party members, since Mwanawasa had not been active in politics since the mid-1990s. Despite the tensions, the MMD officially endorsed Mwanawasa's candidature in August. The FDD held its first national convention in mid-October, electing Tembo as the party President. Tembo and other opposition party leaders then held talks to try to agree on just one candidate from among them to oppose Mwanawasa, but the presidential ambitions of each party leader proved too strong, and the talks failed. In November Chiluba set the election date for late December, and campaigning began in earnest. International observers monitoring poll preparations later noted the substantial deployment of state resources to assist the MMD's campaign, and found that DAs worked openly for the party in most areas.

The elections took place peacefully on 27 December 2001; turn-out was 67% of registered voters. According to the ECZ, Mwanawasa narrowly won the presidential election—with 29.15% of the votes cast, defeating his closest rival, Mazoka of the UPND, who won 27.20% of the votes—by fewer than 34,000 votes. Mazoka immediately alleged the poll was rigged and that he was the true winner. The complaint was formalized in mid-January 2002, when Mazoka and other opposition party leaders petitioned the Supreme Court that the poll was neither free nor fair, and that the official result should be set aside. In the National Assembly elections, the MMD won 69 seats and opposition parties 80, of which the UPND took 49; one independent was elected. The Constitution allowed Mwanawasa to appoint eight new members to the Assembly, who were then brought into the Government, but—in a first for Zambian politics—he still lacked a majority in the Assembly. In early February the European Union (EU) election monitoring team stated the election results were unsafe and alleged a wide range of malpractice, including state media bias and the deliberate failure to supply ballot boxes in marginal constituencies.

Mwanawasa was sworn in as President on 2 January 2002 and a new Government was announced a few days later. Emmanuel Kasonde was appointed as Minister of Finance and Economic Development, and seven ministers from Chiluba's Cabinet were retained, including Enoch Kavindele as Vice-President and Kalumba, who was moved from the Ministry of Finance and Economic Development to the Ministry of Foreign Affairs. Later in January Mwanawasa effected major changes in the armed forces and intelligence services high command and the senior levels of the civil service, removing Chiluba appointees and replacing them with his own.

A rift between Mwanawasa and Chiluba, who had remained MMD President, became evident soon after Mwanawasa assumed office. Following a ruling by the courts that Chiluba would not be entitled to his benefits package as a former Head of State if he continued in active politics, Chiluba relinquished the MMD presidency in late March. Meanwhile, Mwanawasa continued with his civil service reforms, replacing the heads of the Treasury, the Bank of Zambia, the revenue authority and the privatization agency. In March 2002 EU parliamentarians visited Lusaka to discuss the EU's relations with the new Government. The EU later opted to support the new administration, despite its concerns about the election, and in June made substantial new aid pledges.

Following growing demands that he take action against corruption, Mwanawasa called a special sitting of the National Assembly in mid-July, and implicated Chiluba in several major corruption scandals. Mwanawasa also announced the formation of a new anti-corruption task force. In response to a request from Mwanawasa, the Assembly subsequently lifted Chiluba's immunity from prosecution. Chiluba stalled charges being laid against him for several months by applying to the courts for a ruling on the validity of the Assembly's decision, but in February 2003 Chiluba was arrested and charged with over 200 counts of corruption and embezzlement after the Supreme Court ruled in favour of the National Assembly.

Several people closely associated with Chiluba were arrested in August 2002, including Richard Sakala, previously in charge of the former President's public relations. In that month the former head of intelligence services, Xavier Chungu, was arrested for vehicle theft—a non-bailable offence in Zambia—and detained.

Mwanawasa and Kasonde's differences over economic policy were made public in December 2002 after correspondence between them was leaked to the media, apparently by the President's office: Kasonde defended privatization while Mwanawasa opposed it. Later that month the National Assembly approved a motion calling on the Government to halt the privatization process. Meanwhile, the IMF warned the Government that Zambia's continued access to its Poverty Reduction and Growth Facility (PRGF) was dependent on the ongoing privatization process, particularly the divestitures of the Zambia Electricity Supply Corpn and the Zambia National Commercial Bank (ZNCB).

As part of a government reshuffle, Mwanawasa appointed several opposition party members to his Cabinet in early February 2003, including Dipak Patel of the FDD, who became Minister of Commerce, Trade and Industry. Mwanawasa presented the reshuffle as a bid to unite Zambians, but opposition party leaders complained that the appointments had been made without consultation and that Mwanawasa had, in fact, intended to weaken the opposition.

After announcing in early 2003 that the Constitution required review, Mwanawasa charged a newly appointed commission with this task in mid-April. Prominent civil society organizations, however, refused to join the commission, demanding instead the establishment of a constituent assembly with sovereign powers. Undeterred, however, the commission held its first public hearings in August.

Inclusive Politics or Swallowing?

UNIP announced a formal alliance with the MMD in May 2003, angering many UNIP supporters, although party President Tilyenji Kaunda defended the agreement. At the end of the month Mwanawasa reshuffled his Cabinet again, dismissing Kasonde and Kavindele, whom he later accused of corruption. Kavindele was replaced by Nevers Mumba, an evangelical pastor who had previously led an opposition party, the National Citizens' Coalition.

In mid-August 2003, despite several influential MMD members voting against him, Mwanawasa survived an attempt by opposition members of the National Assembly to impeach him over the manner of Mumba's appointment and the President's alleged corruption. Mwanawasa removed the offenders from the MMD NEC soon after. Subsequent victories in 12 parliamentary by-elections by the end of the year gave the MMD its first majority in the National Assembly since Mwanawasa became President. Several of the by-elections had been necessitated by the defection of the UPND incumbents to the MMD. In each case, much to the displeasure of UPND President Anderson Mazoka, the defector was the MMD candidate at the by-election.

A national one-day strike was held in mid-February 2004 by the ZCTU and the Federation of Free Trade Unions of Zambia—the two main trade union umbrella bodies—to protest at a public-sector wage freeze announced in the 2004 budget. The wage freeze was the Government's response to the IMF and other donors' insistence that public sector spending be tightly contained as a condition for their continued balance-of-payments assistance. The strike was well-attended and, following threats of further industrial action by trade unions, the Government promised in March that it would consider demands for a 15% pay increase. However, following donor indications that they would not accept such an increase, in April the Government jettisoned the proposal. At the end of the month, the IMF favourably reviewed the Government's fiscal performance during the first quarter of the year, and a new PRGF was agreed in mid-June. The previous PRGF had lapsed in March 2003 and was not renewed because of IMF concerns about alleged government overspending.

In a controversial move, in early 2004 Mwanawasa dismissed the Director of Public Prosecutions (DPP), Mukelabai Mukelabai, for allegedly not conducting himself properly during the Chiluba corruption trial. Mukelabai protested that his removal was illegal, and his petition was subsequently upheld by a legal tribunal, which called for his reinstatement. Ignoring the ruling, Mwanawasa appointed Mukelabai's deputy, Caroline Sokoni, who dropped some of the charges against Chiluba and prepared new ones, to which Chiluba again pleaded not guilty. Meanwhile, Mwanawasa dismissed Vice-President Mumba in October, replacing him with Lupando Mwape, a former transport minister.

The Supreme Court ruled in February 2005 that Mwanawasa's election as President in 2001 was valid, prompting a strong protest from Mazoka, who linked the ruling to pay awards that the Government had recently awarded the judiciary.

CONSTITUTIONAL DEBATES

With presidential and legislative elections due in 2006, during late 2004 and early 2005 opposition parties and civil society bodies intensified their demands for prior constitutional reform, insisting that changes be made before the elections, preferably by a constituent assembly. Mwanawasa, however, insisted that constitutional change would only be possible in 2008 and rejected calls for a constituent assembly. In February 2005 the Government rejected proposals for electoral reform from a technical committee constituted for the purpose in 2004 by Mwanawasa. One of the proposals made by the committee was that in the event of a dispute about the probity of a presidential election, no candidate should be sworn in to the presidency until the matter was resolved in the Supreme Court.

Mwanawasa's imposition of a wage freeze in the public sector during 2004 infuriated trade unions and reduced domestic political support for the President, but the decision garnered its reward in April 2005 when the IMF and World Bank announced that Zambia had reached the completion point under the enhanced initiative for heavily indebted poor countries, qualifying the country for debt relief valued at US $3,900m. This was despite the Government's failure to dispose of the ZNCB, which had been a core condition imposed by the Bretton Woods institutions. Shortly after the IMF's announcement, the Government signalled that the ending of the public-sector wage freeze by offering teachers a 25% pay increase for 2005.

In late June 2005 the Chairman of the Constitutional Review Commission (CRC), Willa Mung'omba, presented the first draft of the CRC's recommendations. Mung'omba recommended a new constitution be adopted through a constituent assembly rather than the National Assembly, and also argued that candidates must win at least 51% of the popular vote to become President, rather than the simple majority required at present. The National Assembly subsequently debated an opposition motion endorsing the CRC's 51% proposition, but the MMD opposed it, and the motion was defeated. Two weeks later the

MMD held its national convention in Kabwe, where Enoch Kavindele challenged Mwanawasa unsuccessfully for the post of party President. Around the same time as the convention, striking miners at Konkola Copper Mines (KCM—see Economy), the country's largest copper producer, responsible for 70% of national output, rioted after rejecting a 30% wage increase offer; the workers were demanding a 100% salary increase. An explosive device was also set off on KCM property. Later that month, alleging that the strike and the bomb were the result of political conspiracy, Mwanawasa ordered the arrest of Michael Sata, leader of the Patriotic Front (PF) opposition party, accusing him of involvement. Sata was later arraigned in court on charges including sedition and espionage. The Minister of Mines and Mineral Development, Kaunda Lembalemba, was removed from the Government the following month.

In November 2005 opposition parties and civil society activists grouped under the umbrella of the Oasis Forum (named after the 2001 Oasis Declaration opposing Chiluba's third-term bid) held a public demonstration in Lusaka to call for the adoption of a new constitution before the 2006 elections. The Forum also reiterated calls for the constitution to be adopted by a constituent assembly rather than the National Assembly. A secret ballot of MMD deputies in early 2006 on the constitutional issue indicated an overwhelming majority of them supported the constitution's adoption by a constituent assembly. In February 2006, to the approval of the Oasis Forum, Mwanawasa reversed his long-standing opposition to the reform, promising that the new constitution would be introduced this way. Mwanawasa insisted, however, that the change must first be approved by a national referendum, and—contrary to the wishes of the Oasis Forum—could not be introduced before the 2006 elections.

MWANAWASA SECURES A SECOND TERM

In March 2006 the three main opposition parties—the UPND, the FDD and UNIP—announced that they would endorse a single presidential candidate to challenge the MMD candidate, under a new grouping styled the United Democratic Alliance (UDA). Zambian opposition parties had tried and failed to achieve similar agreements in past elections, helping to ensure continued victories for the ruling party. Mwanawasa was rushed to London, United Kingdom, for medical treatment on 30 March, after suffering a stroke, raising concerns about whether he would be well enough to stand in the forthcoming elections; however, he soon returned to Zambia, insisting that he was in good health. In May UPND leader Anderson Mazoka died, following a long illness. His death immediately sparked a succession battle within the party, and created uncertainty about who would lead the UDA, since it had previously been assumed this would be Mazoka, as the leader of the largest party within the alliance. A new electoral law was passed in May that notably failed to incorporate many of the earlier demands made of it by opposition parties and the Oasis Forum. Most significantly, the new law made no change to the way in which the President should be elected, retaining the previous requirement of a simple majority rather than the 51% demanded by reformists. In June the UPND selected Hakainde Hichilema (a former managing director of accountancy and financial services provider Grant Thornton Ltd in Zambia) as its new leader. On 26 July Mwanawasa dissolved the National Assembly and announced that the elections would be held on 28 September. There followed intense and at times acrimonious discussions within the UDA regarding the identity of its presidential candidate, and on 2 August its member parties finally settled on Hichilema. The FDD President, Edith Nawakwi, was selected as the UDA vice-presidential candidate, while the UNIP President, Tilyenji Kaunda, became the UDA National Chairman. Mwanawasa announced his own candidacy for the presidency on 12 August.

Sata concentrated his electoral campaign in Lusaka and the Copperbelt where, to the delight of many voters, he villified foreign, and particularly Chinese, investors in the mining industry, promising to increase Zambian control in mines and improve conditions for mineworkers if elected. Mwanawasa's campaign, by contrast, made little impact in these urban areas but was more successful in rural areas where, for many voters, the President was the only politician they knew. Sata's candidacy was supported by Chiluba, while Kaunda publicly backed Hichilema. Voting took place as scheduled on 28 September with a high turn-out, later announced at over 70% by the Electoral Commission of Zambia. Mwanawasa gained 42.98% of the presidential poll, a significant improvement on his 2001 showing, and enough to secure him a comfortable victory. Sata was his nearest opponent with 29.37%, and while he protested he was the victim of electoral fraud Sata did not take his case to court, presumably fearing that even if fraud were proved, it would not be found sufficient to reverse the final result. Hichilema secured 25.32%, demonstrating that a united opposition would have easily defeated Mwanawasa. In the parliamentary elections that were held concurrently, the MMD secured 73 seats, again a sharp increase compared with its 2001 performance, to which were added eight nominated seats, bringing its total to 81. Sata's PF gained 43, the UDA won 26 seats and smaller parties and independents secured the remaining seven elected seats, leaving the MMD with a slender overall majority of just five seats.

Most electoral observers judged the polls to have been free and fair, although the EU observer group stated that there had been insufficient regulation of campaign spending which had benefited Mwanawasa and the MMD. The observer group also found that administrative problems, including the lack of proper verification of the voters' register prior to the vote, had created the suspicion of vote rigging. This was the view of many PF supporters, and there were riots in Lusaka and parts of the Copperbelt for two days after the results were declared, which only ended after Sata appealed for calm. Mwanawasa was sworn in as President on 4 October 2006.

The President's new Cabinet was similar to his previous administration; Ng'andu Peter Magande was reappointed as Minister of Finance and National Planning, Kalombo Mwansa retained his position as Minister of Mines and Mineral Development, while Ronnie Shikapwasha was moved from the foreign affairs to the home affairs portfolio. One significant change, however, was the replacement of Lupando Mwape (who lost his seat at the election) at the vice-presidency with veteran politician Rupiah Banda. Banda had not held public office since he was Minister of Foreign Affairs under Kaunda in the mid-1970s, but helped deliver a substantial vote for the MMD in the Eastern Province during the 2006 election.

Considerable tensions persisted between the MMD and the PF, and personally between Mwanawasa and Sata, during the remainder of 2006. In a development that was widely held to be politically motivated, Sata was arrested in early December for alleged false declaration of assets. The case was, however, dismissed later in the month after the High Court determined that the state had failed to prove its case beyond reasonable doubt. Meanwhile, Sata ordered PF local councillors not to co-operate with the national Government, but in April 2007 softened this stance, permitting co-operation on the condition that the chanting of anti-Sata slogans was forbidden at government functions.

In May 2007 a court in London found Chiluba guilty of conspiring to defraud Zambia of US $46m. via a London account of the ZNCB, and ordered the former President and his co-conspirators to repay 85% of the money. The case was held in London following a decision by Zambia's Attorney-General in 2006 to launch a civil prosecution case against Chiluba in the United Kingdom, as the Zambian criminal trial against him had stalled. Chiluba, who had refused to testify in the case, denounced the verdict as a conspiracy between Mwanawasa and the British Prime Minister, Anthony Blair, and said he would not recognize it. However, the Minister of Information and Broadcasting Services, Mike Mulongoti, announced that the Government would soon domesticate the judgment by filing it in the Lusaka High Court. If the ruling is enforced, Chiluba is widely expected to be bankrupted.

Zambian courts overturned the results of three parliamentary elections in June 2007, on the grounds that the victors, all representing the MMD, had bribed voters. Two of the candidates involved appealed against the verdicts, while the third stood for re-election in his constituency and won. In mid-July a petition to have Magande's election declared invalid was rejected by the High Court.

REGIONAL RELATIONS

Relations between Zambia and newly independent Zimbabwe were initially tense, owing to Kaunda's long-standing support for Robert Mugabe's political rival, Joshua Nkomo. However, the two countries' shared experience as 'front-line' states opposed to apartheid South Africa did much to improve relations. The Chiluba Government also enjoyed good relations with Mugabe's Government, but accused it of economic protectionism and 'dumping'. Chiluba often stood in rhetorical solidarity with the Zimbabwean Government, calling on other African leaders to support Mugabe during his 'persecution' by foreign forces. Mwanawasa initially adopted the same policy but became increasingly agitated with developments in Zimbabwe, and in 2006 he publicly compared Zimbabwe to the sinking ship 'Titanic'. Prior to Mwanawasa's appointment as Chairman of the Southern African Development Community (SADC) in August 2007, the Zambian President attempted to heal the rift between himself and Mugabe, dispatching Vice-President Banda to Harare for talks with the Zimbabwean leader.

Kaunda assumed a leading role in peace initiatives in southern Africa and supported both the South West Africa People's Organisation of Namibia (SWAPO), allowing it to operate from Zambian territory, and the African National Congress of South Africa (ANC), which, until its return to South Africa in mid-1990, maintained its headquarters in Lusaka. In September 1985 Kaunda was appointed Chairman of the 'front-line' states, and in July 1987 he was elected to the chairmanship of the OAU. Owing to Kaunda's support for SWAPO and the ANC, Zambia was frequently subjected to military reprisals by South Africa. South African political reforms from 1990 onwards, however, eased relations, and in mid-1993 the South African President, F. W. de Klerk, made an official visit to Zambia (the first by a South African Head of State). Relations between the MMD Government and the ANC, which has ruled South Africa since 1994, were cordial, but not warm, during Chiluba's presidency, and were negatively affected by Chiluba's treatment of Kaunda; the situation improved after Mwanawasa took office, particularly following his decision to affect the political rehabilitation of Kaunda. The South African Government endorsed Mwanawasa's controversial first election victory and, in return, Mwanawasa supported Mbeki's proposal for the New Partnership for Africa's Development.

The Namibian and Zambian authorities have co-operated since SWAPO came to power to suppress Lozi nationalism. In 1999 Lozi nationalists from the Caprivi strip in Namibia fled to Zambia seeking asylum, but were detained in Lusaka and subsequently returned to Namibia by the Zambian Government. Lozi nationalists clashed with Namibian troops in Caprivi that year, and the Zambia-based Lozi nationalist Imasiku Mutangelwa, the leader of the Barotse Patriotic Front (BPF—a militant group based in Zambia), was arrested by the Zambian authorities for allegedly declaring his support for their actions. Mutangelwa had initially sought refuge in the South African High Commission in Lusaka, but the South Africans handed him over to the Zambian police.

Zambia's support for the Governments of Angola and Mozambique during the Kaunda era resulted in retaliatory attacks by União Nacional para a Independência Total de Angola (UNITA) rebels and by Mozambican guerrillas of the Resistência Nacional Moçambicana (Renamo). Renamo attacks ceased after a peace agreement was reached between Renamo and the Government of Mozambique in October 1992. Zambia subsequently contributed 950 troops for a UN peacekeeping force that was deployed in Mozambique. It was frequently alleged by the Angolan Government during the Chiluba presidency that senior members of the Zambian Government were supporting UNITA. Chiluba denied the charges, which were never proved, but it was none the less widely suspected that covert Zambian assistance for UNITA was taking place, even though in early 1996 Zambia contributed some 1,000 troops to the UN Angola Verification Mission. In early 1999 tensions between the two countries peaked when the Angolan Government accused Chiluba's administration of complicity in a mysterious bomb blast that severely damaged the Angolan embassy in Lusaka. The two Governments later signed an agreement aimed at resolving their differences, but the Angolan Government was angered that Chiluba refused to allow its troops to pursue UNITA forces onto Zambian territory, and in December 1999 Angolan military aircraft bombed border areas of Zambia's North-Western Province. The UNITA leader, Jonas Savimbi, was killed in early 2002, and a peace agreement was reached between the Angolan Government and UNITA in April. Following the agreement, peace largely returned to the border region and the refugees began to go home in substantial numbers. However, by early 2007 an estimated 64,000 Angolans were still living in Zambian refugee camps, together with at least another 25,000 Angolans elsewhere in Zambia, according to the office of the UN High Commissioner for Refugees (UNHCR).

The Zambian Government became involved in regional efforts to find a political solution to the conflict in the DRC, after a rebellion was mounted against its Government in August 1998, and Chiluba was appointed to co-ordinate SADC and OAU peace initiatives on the crisis. A summit held in Lusaka in June–July 1999 resulted in a cease-fire document that provided a timetable for the withdrawal of foreign forces from the DRC and for political reform in the country, which was hailed at the time as a major diplomatic achievement by Chiluba. The diplomatic initiative to end the war was subsequently taken by South Africa; Mwanawasa played only a minimal role in later diplomacy. Mwanawasa's relations with Congolese President Joseph Kabila, while cordial, show little evidence of warmth, and Mwanawasa remained careful not to offend the DRC Government. When former Vice-President Mumba appeared to insult Kabila in 2004, Mwanawasa dismissed him. Meanwhile, Zambia continues to host tens of thousands of Congolese refugees who fled the DRC during the conflict, most of whom live in camps assisted by UNHCR. With the ending of general hostilities in the DRC, many of the refugees returned home, but continued conflict in eastern DRC led to new arrivals, and the Congolese refugee population in the country was estimated by UNHCR at 61,000 in mid-2007. UNHCR then launched a voluntary repatriation programme among this population and expressed the hope that 20,000 would return home.

Economy

LINDA VAN BUREN

In 2006, after some 30 years, Zambia finally reduced the rate of inflation to below 10%. The recorded rate of 8.2% was a significant improvement over the 2005 rate of 15.9%. Real growth of gross domestic product (GDP) was estimated at 5.5% in 2006, which was below the 6% target but exceeded growth in 2005, which stood at 5.2%. The deficit on the current account of the balance of payments was also brought under control. It was 11.8% of GDP in 2005—well above the IMF's usual maximum preference of 5%—but declined to just 2.3% of GDP in 2006. Gross international reserves were enough to cover over 1.5 months' worth of imports at 31 December 2005 and two months' worth one year later. Relations between the Government of President Levy Mwanawasa and the IMF remained good in 2007; the Fund approved Zambia's request for waivers for the non-observance of several performance criteria in 2006 and 2007, on grounds that Zambia had subsequently taken corrective action. Growth in 2006 was attributed to mining, construction and transport, but other sectors, such as agriculture, tourism and manufacturing, also performed well.

Positive economic indicators in 2006 and 2007 followed decades of over-dependence on copper. During the 1960s and the early 1970s the Zambian economy expanded rapidly, owing to high price levels for that commodity. Despite considerable investment in physical and social infrastructure, however, the Government of President Kenneth Kaunda failed to develop other sectors of the economy, and a fall in the level of copper prices in the mid-1970s led to severe economic setbacks for Zambia. Development was subsequently constrained by a shortage of foreign exchange with which to import essential inputs, and by a lack of skilled manpower, a poor transport network and high debt-service obligations. Economic mismanagement during the Kaunda period brought about a further deterioration in domestic conditions, with severe food shortages and a dramatic increase in inflation rates and unemployment. Hopes were high in the early 1990s that an economic recovery would follow the establishment of a new Government in 1991 by President Frederick Chiluba and the resumption of an IMF-approved austerity programme. Signs of improvement, however, were slow to appear, and when Chiluba left office 10 years later, Zambians were still beset by food shortages, worrying inflation rates and high unemployment. The Mwanawasa Government, elected in December 2001, inherited an economy suffering from crop failure, food shortages, weak global prices for copper and cobalt (Zambia's principal exports), and the impending withdrawal of a major copper investor. Copper remains the mainstay of Zambia's formal economy, but agriculture provides a livelihood for most of the population.

Although the 21st century has so far been a period of sustained positive economic growth for Zambia, a higher level of growth—7% or more—is required if poverty is to be reduced. Erratic rains turned the country from a net maize exporter in 2004 to a net maize importer in 2005, while favourable weather led to a strong maize harvest of 1.4m. metric tons in 2005/06. The national annual requirement is about 1.6m. tons. Continued strong global demand maintained high copper prices in 2005, 2006 and the first half of 2007. After an initial period of cordial relations, during which the IMF proclaimed, in November 2002, that the Zambian authorities under President Mwanawasa were 'to be commended for their continued commitment to sound macroeconomic policies and structural reforms', Zambia briefly fell out of favour with the Fund. In June 2003 the IMF withheld a US $100m. disbursement under the Poverty Reduction and Growth Facility (PRGF), pending Zambia's resolution of its budget deficit; the shortfall was equivalent to 3% of GDP, whereas the forecast had been a deficit of just 1.6%. In June 2004 the IMF eventually approved a larger PRGF arrangement for $320.4m. over a three-year period, and by January 2007 over $300m. had been disbursed. The three-year PRGF arrangement was extended until 30 September 2007.

AGRICULTURE

Zambia's topography, with its varied elevation, enables a variety of crops to be grown, although only about 7% of the surface area is under cultivation, while some 40% serves as permanent pasture and 43% is under forest. The Government estimates that, of the country's 60m. ha of arable land, only about 15% is currently being exploited. In the Mwanawasa Government's first budget, announced in March 2002, the then Minister of Finance and Economic Development, Emmanuel Kasonde, observed that Zambian agriculture was too heavily dependent on rainfall, especially given the country's under-used water and arable land resources. He therefore proposed to direct government funding towards the construction of irrigation dams, to encourage private-sector investment in irrigation, to contract large-scale commercial farmers to grow maize under irrigation and to develop 'appropriate technologies' for small-scale farmers. He also announced his intention to establish a Crop Marketing Authority (CMA) as a buyer of last resort for selected crops in outlying areas, while pledging to supply farmers with 80,000 metric tons of fertilizer in the 2002/03 season, for which small-scale farmers would benefit from a K50,000m. price subsidy. The Food Reserve Agency (FRA) was to be gradually abolished, as it had, Kasonde claimed, failed to execute its statutory functions of buyer of last resort and keeper of strategic food reserves. Kasonde noted that he was prepared to cover only K30,000m. of the FRA's total outstanding debt of K112,000m. relating to the 2001/02 season, and that the FRA would have to recover the rest of the debt before its closure. The CMA was given responsibility for maintaining the national strategic food reserve. In July 2003, however, the FRA was still functioning and was embroiled in a dispute with the North-Western Province Co-operative Union over the FRA's insistence that farmers in the province sell their maize to two designated private-sector transport companies for K30,000 per 50-kg bag, as stipulated by the Government. Maize is the staple food crop of Zambia, consumed in the form of *nshima*, a porridge-like dish. With the poor crop of 2005 in mind, Zambians in mid-2006 again debated the nation's food-reserve policy. On the one hand, a sufficient proportion of the crop needed to be retained as a strategic grain reserve, to feed the nation in years of crop failure. On the other hand, the country has only limited capacity for storing grain, as the cost of maintaining an excessive proportion of maize is prohibitive. Besides maize, Zambia also produces cassava, wheat, millet, vegetables, sugar cane, groundnuts, sweet potatoes, melons, fruits, cotton, sorghum, barley, pulses, soya beans, tobacco, sunflower seeds and paddy rice. In 2006 the agricultural sector (including forestry and fishing) grew by 2.4%.

A number of lakes and rivers, particularly Lake Kariba on the southern border and those in the Northern Province, offer considerable potential for fishing; the annual total catch is about 70,000 metric tons. The 2007/08 budget allocated K25,700m. for fisheries development.

Zambia has 323,000 sq km of forested land, 265,000 sq km of which is open to exploitation. Commercial forestry is important on the Copperbelt, where there are numerous softwood tree plantations, and in the hardwood areas of the south-west, which are rich in African teak. Total roundwood removals amount to about 8m. cu m per year, but over 7m. cu m is consumed locally in the form of wood fuel. The 2005 budget introduced a 25% export duty on unprocessed timber, in a bid to encourage the adding of more value locally.

Zambia has several hundred large commercial farms, situated mostly near the railway lines, which account for about 45% of the country's agricultural output. The number of smallholders who cultivate cash crops is increasing and stood at about 800,000 in 2007. Most subsistence farmers use traditional methods, without adequate inputs or infrastructural support, although some improvement took place from 2003 onwards through such schemes as fertilizer support, food-security packs, outgrower programmes and improved access to agricultural credit. Agriculture accounted for an estimated 25% of GDP in 2006 and employed 85% of the economically active population in that year. Maize determines the fortunes of the agricultural sector, and the country consumes about 1.6m. metric tons of maize annually. Zambia's maize farmers consistently achieve a substantially higher yield than their counterparts south of the border; in 2000, before political events in Zimbabwe caused severe disruption to the farming sector, that country's average maize yield was 1,488 kg per ha, whereas Zambia's was 1,502 kg per ha, even in a relatively poor growing season. By 2004 the gap had widened dramatically; Zambia's yield was 1,548 kg per ha, whereas Zimbabwe's had declined to 714 kg per ha. Zimbabwe produced nearly three times as much maize in 2000 as Zambia; yet by 2005, even though Zimbabwe grew maize on nearly three times as much land area, and even though Zambia's maize crop was 29% smaller than the previous year's harvest, Zambia still produced the greater amount of maize, at 866,190 tons. In Zambia the area under maize declined from a high of 671,000 ha in 2003 to 465,830 ha in 2005.

Financial losses, principally resulting from overproduction, posed an ongoing problem, and experts advocated a comprehensive strategic maize policy that would assure adequate stocks to meet domestic requirements in times of drought, as well as sufficient storage for that purpose, while avoiding costly maintenance of excessive stocks. The Mwanawasa Government's reaction to the drought of 2001/02 was efficient enough that when good rains returned, the country had plenty of seed to plant and was able to harvest a much larger crop in the following season. The Government also took swift action to halt exports in March 2005, after the previous month's poor rains. Efforts to deliver seed and fertilizers to grain farmers in time for the planting of the 2005/06 crop were hampered in some parts of the country by excessive rains that washed out roads and bridges.

The ratios for other crops followed a similar pattern. Zimbabwe produced 250,000 metric tons of wheat to Zambia's 75,000 tons in 2001; but by 2005 Zambia harvested 136,830 tons to Zimbabwe's estimated 95,000 tons. In Zambia, wheat is grown almost exclusively on large commercial farms, usually under irrigation. The country's flour mills require some 140,000 tons per year to keep the nation supplied with bread; even in very productive seasons wheat has to be imported, although in 2004 and 2005 Zambia was nearly self-sufficient.

Zambia has about 300,000 cash-crop smallholders, the majority of whom produce cotton and tobacco. Smallholders grow most of the nation's cotton crop. Textile factories in the country required some 12,000 metric tons of cotton lint per year under the US African Growth and Opportunities Act (AGOA), and in most years the domestic cotton crop is large enough to meet all of the demand and to allow for cotton exports. In 1997 the Zambia Agricultural High Value Crops Asscn was formed, with the aim of encouraging Zambian smallholders to grow high-value cash crops, such as cotton, castor-bean, sesame and paprika. The 2005 budget promised continued government support for the cotton, tobacco, beekeeping, paprika, cashew-nut and coffee sectors.

In 2003 the harvest of sugar cane peaked at 2.3m. metric tons, but output declined subsequently, to 2.2m. tons in 2005. Zambia Sugar PLC produced 1.4m. tons of cane and 271,000 tons of sugar in 2006, the year in which Illovo Sugar of South Africa acquired an 89.1% stake in Zambia Sugar for US $20m. A two-year R1,400m. expansion began in April 2007. The coffee sector produces arabica. Exports of green coffee declined from 137,333 60-kg bags in 2003/04 (based on a coffee year of July to June) to just 55,470 bags in 2006/07, according to International Coffee Organization (ICO) figures. The ICO also assessed Zambia's coffee production at 100,000 bags in 2006, down from 117,000 bags in 2004.

The horticultural sector experienced strong growth in the 1990s, with the export of fruits, vegetables and flowers to Europe. The sector's interests are overseen by the Zambia Export Growers' Asscn (ZEGA), which, among other things, lobbies for affordable airfreight charges. In November 2000 ZEGA complained that Zambian horticultural exporters had to pay US $2.00 per kg to send their flowers to Europe on charter airfreight flights, whereas their competitors in Kenya paid only $1.50 per kg. Zambia has more than 30 flower farms, covering 135 ha, growing more than 50 varieties of roses and some 20 kinds of summer flowers for export.

About 70% of livestock is owned by traditional farmers. The national cattle herd numbered about 2.6m. head in 2005. A small amount of beef is generally exported, and in 2003 Zambia was a net exporter of beef. Foot-and-mouth disease constitutes a problem in some areas of the country. The 2005 budget pledged measures to control animal diseases in areas with high potential for livestock production. The Central Veterinary Research Institute in Chilanga produces livestock vaccines for the local market and for export. Zambeef Products PLC, the largest meat company in Zambia, has an annual turnover of some K200,000m. and employs over 1,400 workers throughout the country. All of its shares are quoted on the Lusaka Stock Exchange. Zambeef slaughters 60,000 head of cattle annually, produces 8m. litres of milk, processes 3.5m. chickens, produces over 20m. eggs, tans 60,000 hides for export (earning US $1.2m. in foreign exchange), distributes meat in the Zambian marketplace through 85 outlets and even makes shoes. It also grows maize, wheat, lucerne and soya beans on 4,000 ha of land, of which 2,500 ha are under irrigation. In late 2006 Zambeef set up a subsidiary in Nigeria, forming the joint venture Master Meats with Shoprite of South Africa.

Although rural development was accorded a high priority during the Kaunda period, most of the schemes and programmes yielded disappointing results. Nearly 18% of total development expenditure in 1980 was for agriculture. However, poor organization, lack of skills, inadequate marketing and transport infrastructure, the high incidence of HIV/AIDS and migration to urban areas all impeded growth. The sector was additionally constrained by low producer prices, late and unreliable payments to farmers for their crops, inefficient marketing and inadequate supply of inputs. Twenty years after liberalization was introduced in 1986, however, farmers continued to face most of these impediments. The Mwanawasa Government's first budget acknowledged that input availability had been poor in 2001 and pledged K100,000m. to supply 80,000 metric tons of fertilizer during the 2002/03 growing season. Although agricultural liberalization has produced mixed results, some subsectors, such as horticulture, have benefited significantly, and results from 2003 onwards show that the more traditional subsectors have also begun to benefit.

MINING

Mining output rose by 11.8% in 2006, and copper output increased by 7%, from 459,324 metric tons in 2005 to 492,016 tons in 2006. The mining sector as a whole contributed 18.8% of GDP in 1990 but just 3.2% in 2004. The sector employed nearly 50,000 people in 2007. Copper accounted for about 93% of all Zambia's foreign-exchange earnings in 1991, but the proportion fell to 54% in 2000, although it amounted, with cobalt (found in association with copper), to 64% in 2005. Other minerals exploited include zinc, lead, gold, silver, selenium, marble, emeralds, amethysts, aquamarines, tourmalines and garnets. The mining industry in Zambia was established during the colonial period, with the opening in 1906 of the Broken Hill lead and zinc mine at Kabwe. Copper mining was begun in the 1920s by Zambian Anglo American (later Nchanga Consolidated Copper Mines) and Roan Selection Trust (later Roan Consolidated Mines), which, in 1982, united to form Zambia Consolidated Copper Mines (ZCCM), in which the Government took a 60.3% share. Growth continued after independence in 1964, and by 1969 Zambia had become a leading producer of unrefined copper, with a record output of 747,500 tons, accounting for 12% of global production. After the mid-1970s, however, copper output and revenues declined significantly; production dropped from 700,000 tons in 1976 to 249,000 tons in 2000.

Following Zambia's change of government in 1991, the Chiluba administration announced a number of remedial measures, including the transfer of ZCCM to private-sector ownership. A range of reforms within ZCCM was carried out, and higher production targets for copper were set. Potential bidders' plans for the expansion of productive capacity and a wide-ranging programme of exploration and modernization were an important part of the evaluation of bids. In 1996 the Government announced that ZCCM was to be privatized as four separate entities, and the process was to be completed by late 1998. After continually reviewing the complicated privatization of this huge conglomerate, it was eventually decided that nine 'packages' of ZCCM assets would be offered, and by February 1997 15 companies had entered 26 bids for them.

Konkola is potentially the richest of Zambia's copper mines, possessing reserves of 44.3m. metric tons, with a copper content of 3.9%, while reserves at Nchanga have a copper content of 3.8% and those at Mufulira have a content of 3.2%; Nkana is the largest mine, with 95.5m. tons of reserves, but with a copper content of only 2.3%. Konkola Copper Mines PLC, 51% of which is owned by Vedanta of the United Kingdom and 28.4% by Anglo's Zambia Copper Investments Limited of Bermuda, was already the largest mining company in Zambia when in May 2007 it announced plans to mine even deeper. The US $400m. Konkola Deep Mining Project (KDMP), the largest-ever single mining investment in Zambia, is to take the mine down to a depth of 1,490 m. KDMP is to extend the life of the mine to 2035 and is to increase its throughput from 2m. tons of copper ore to 6m. tons. In February 2003 First Quantum of Canada announced the favourable results of a feasibility study of the Kansanshi copper and gold deposits near Solwezi, in North-Western Province. During the first phase of the project, expected to last 16 years, the operation would produce 1.6m. tons of copper, with a by-product of 25,000 oz of gold annually. The US company Cyprus Amax Minerals purchased the rights to develop the Kansanshi mine for $28m. Subsequently, Cyprus Amax was acquired by Phelps Dodge of the USA, which in 2001 sold its 80% Kansanshi shareholding to First Quantum. The total cost of the project was estimated at between $200m. and $300m., and the mine entered production in December 2004, with the creation of 1,300 new jobs. Also in the North-Western Province, the 1,355-sq km open-pit Lumwana copper mine was expected to produce 140,000 tons of copper per year and was to enter full production in January 2008, followed by a productive lifespan of 37 years. An estimated 500,000 tons of copper concentrates per year was forecast for its first five years.

An 85% stake in the Chambeshi copper mine, known as ZCCM (D) or 'D Co', was purchased by China Non-Ferrous Metal Industry in 1998. ZCCM (B), or 'B Co', comprising the Luanshya and Baluba facilities, was sold to the Binani group of India for US $35m. in 1997. The mine was subsequently acquired by Roan Antelope Mining Company of Zambia (Ramcoz), which later went into receivership. In 2005 the Government selected J & W Investments of Switzerland, an affiliate of International Mineral Resources AG of Switzerland (but with operations in Kazakhstan), to take over the Luanshya and Baluba assets for $7.5m. The Chibuluma mine assets were sold to a Canadian-South African consortium led by South Africa's Metorex for $17m. The new owners pledged to invest $34m. in the facility, the production capacity of which was described as 480,000 metric tons of ore per year. In 2006 Metorex opened a new mine at Chibuluma South, the first new underground mine to open on the Copperbelt in 30 years.

The Mwanawasa Government is actively seeking private-sector investment in the mining sector. Incentives to potential mining investors include a 10% reduction in the corporate tax rate for mining investors and also relief from several other types of tax, such as the withholding tax on dividends, royalties and management fees. The tax on mineral royalties was reduced from 2% to 0.6%. The mining corporation tax declined from 35% to 25% for all companies, whereas previously only KCM and Mopani Copper Mines had enjoyed the lower rate. Meanwhile, the global copper price began a sustained rise, reached US $1.64 per lb in July 2005 and $3.56 per lb in July 2006, owing in large measure to increased demand from the People's Republic of China, which in 2002 had overtaken the USA as the world's largest importer of copper. The price in July 2007 was $3.48 per lb.

Zambian output of cobalt increased from 2,934 metric tons in 1995 to 11,900 tons in 1998, but had declined to 4,600 tons by 2000. Cobalt production declined from 5,537 tons in 2005 to 4,658 tons in 2006. The global price for cobalt was even weaker than that for copper during 2001, when the cobalt price decreased by 31%. Low world prices were cited as the reason for Orion's decision to close its cobalt plant in Kabwe in 2001. Zambia mines gemstones such as emeralds, aquamarines, amethysts and some diamonds. Two gem companies identified for privatization in 1999 were Kariba Minerals Ltd and Kariba Amethyst Marketing Ltd, an equal joint venture between the Zambian Government and Lonmin, and Zambia Emeralds Industries, which extracts, polishes and markets emeralds, aquamarines, amethysts, garnets and tourmalines. Zambia boasts the world's second largest deposits of emeralds, after Colombia, and Zambian emeralds accounted for a significant and growing share of the coloured-gem market by the mid-1990s and held a dominant position near the top end of the market by 1997. Zambian emeralds are valued almost as highly as those from Colombia. Most gemstones are mined on a small scale, but the sector is thought to offer significant potential for growth. Smuggling of gemstones is a major problem; the Government estimated that some 70% of Zambia's emeralds were exported illegally in 1999, costing the treasury US $600m. per year in lost revenue.

Marble deposits in Lusaka province and elsewhere in Zambia range from pure white to pale pink, deep salmon pink and dark green, and some varieties are hard-wearing enough for use in flooring. Zambian granite tends to be dark and suitable for kitchen counters in homes, but a rare blue granite has been found near Solwezi. Metorex of South Africa acquired a Kabwe processing plant from Sable Zinc in February 2005; renovation work was taking place in mid-2007, and the plant was to be commissioned by September 2007. Chilanga Cement, 84.5% of which is owned by Lafarge of France, has plants in Lusaka and Ndola. Petroleum exploration took place in the 1980s, but no significant discoveries have emerged.

INDUSTRY

Manufacturing's share of GDP has changed little over the years; it contributed 9.1% of GDP in 1990 and 10.4% in 2005. Growth in the manufacturing sector was for many years very moderate, rarely achieving a whole percentage point; but in 2004 manufacturing grew by 4.7%, primarily owing to the Mwanawasa Government's decision to reduce the import duty on imported raw materials. Growth in the manufacturing sector slowed to 2.9% in 2005, but recovered to 3.3% in 2006. The slowdown was attributed almost entirely to the reduced prospects of the textiles subsector.

After the traumatic unbundling and privatization of ZCCM (see above), the mining sector was not the only area of business to feel the effects; the new owners of former ZCCM companies found lower-cost suppliers elsewhere in the region and stopped buying from higher-priced Zambian suppliers. Zambia's manufacturing sector has experienced a variety of problems, not least a chronic shortage of foreign exchange with which to import raw materials and inputs. The sector was also constrained, especially during the Kaunda years, by state intervention in many manufacturing activities, investment in inappropriate schemes and a corresponding lack of funds to invest in more suitable undertakings. The state-owned Industrial Development Corpn of Zambia (INDECO) acquired 26 companies in 1968 and continued to acquire majority shareholdings in a number of other enterprises thereafter. By 1991 INDECO accounted for 75% of Zambia's manufacturing activity. During the Kaunda era, the Government, usually through INDECO, formed a number of joint ventures with foreign enterprises, to establish a chemical-fertilizer plant, a petroleum refinery, an explosives plant, a glass-bottle factory, a battery factory, a brickworks, a textile factory, a copper-wire factory, two vehicle-assembly operations and an iron-and-steel project. However, a number of these ventures subsequently ended in failure. Activities that exhibited positive growth in 2006 included food processing, beverages, tobacco, chemicals, rubber, plastics, fabricated metal products, base metal products, paper and paper products.

Nitrogen Chemicals of Zambia (NCZ) opened a K32m. sulphuric-acid plant in 1983, while its fertilizer operation at Kafue, with an estimated cost of K300m., was the country's largest non-mining enterprise. The Chiluba Government earmarked the conglomerate for privatization, and the Mwanawasa Government opted in March 2002 to allocate K20,000m. in state funding to revive NCZ. NCZ was 'available for immediate sale' in mid-2007. In March 2005 MB International of Zambia purchased Kafue Textiles in a deal that included the paying of some debts and the writing off of others.

Zambia Breweries was divided in 1994, when its Copperbelt holdings became Northern Breweries. Lonmin bought a 70% share of Northern Breweries for US $9m., while the management bought 10%. South African Breweries (SAB—later SABMiller, with headquarters in the United Kingdom) invested in the remaining part of Zambia Breweries. In 1998 Zambia Breweries purchased Lonmin's 70% holding, announcing a 'rights' issue on the LuSE to finance the transaction; the move left both halves of the old Zambia Breweries in the possession of its parent company, SABMiller, which also acquired National Breweries.

In 1983 the Kaunda Government introduced an arrangement whereby companies that exported non-traditional items were allowed to retain 50% of foreign exchange from those exports for use in paying for imported inputs, thereby compensating for lack of foreign currency. After only one year, exports of non-metal products exhibited a fivefold increase. In 1987, however, companies lost this concession, after the Kaunda Government adopted the former system of strict import licensing, an artificially revalued exchange rate and other similar measures. The Investment Act of 1991 partially restored the facility, allowing companies holding investment licences to retain 70% of gross foreign-exchange earnings for three years, 60% for the following two years and 50% for the remaining period of the investment licence's validity. The Chiluba Government subsequently revised the Investment Act to allow the full retention of foreign-exchange earnings by investors. Among the incentives offered to boost interest in the LuSE were a 30% corporate tax rate for listed companies, as well as the absence of restrictions on foreign ownership and of exchange controls.

Meanwhile, the Zambia Privatisation Agency (ZPA) was conducting the privatization programme; by 2001, 262 companies had been transferred to private-sector ownership or had completed the negotiation stage. However, the fact that no further privatizations had been completed by mid-2006 indicated a loss of momentum in the programme. To that end, the Zambia Development Agency (ZDA) was created in 2006 and succeeded the ZPA in January 2007 as the country's privatization vehicle. ZDA was tasked with investigating the high cost of doing business in Zambia and with simplifying licensing procedures. In mid-2007 the number of enterprises that had been privatized remained at 262.

ENERGY

Zambia became self-sufficient in hydroelectric power in 1974 and began exporting power to Zimbabwe (then Rhodesia) and the Democratic Republic of the Congo (DRC, then Zaire). The Zambia Electricity Supply Corpn (Zesco), still earmarked for privatization as of mid-2007, oversees the country's power generation and distribution. Zambia had 1,670 MW of electric-power capacity in 2007, the year in which national demand rose to meet national supply. Load-shedding led to frequent power cuts at peak demand times in 2007, while exports continued at off-peak times. Major hydroelectric facilities are at Kafue Gorge, Kariba North and Victoria Falls. Zesco has long-term plans to add 120 MW at Itezhi-Tezhi, 360 MW through an extension at Kariba North and 750 MW at Kafue Gorge Lower.

Rural electrification is a stated priority, and some extension of the national grid has been achieved, but many areas of rural Zambia still do not have access to mains power supply. Charcoal and fuel wood remain the main sources of energy supply for cooking and heating purposes for most people in both urban and rural areas.

Coal production commenced in 1965 but was subsequently affected by shortages of equipment and spare parts. The remaining colliery, at Maamba, operated substantially below capacity in 1987. Following a rehabilitation programme, however, the mine met its production target of 560,000 metric tons in 1987/88 and began exporting coal to the DRC (then Zaire), Malawi and Tanzania. By 1994, however, annual output of hard coal had declined to an estimated 380,000 tons. Thereafter output declined further, and in 1997 a 70% share in Maamba Collieries Ltd was designated for privatization. In 2007 the Government chose ZCCM Investment Holdings to take over this percentage of equity. The Maamba Katuya consortium, comprising French, South African and Zambian interests, had been designated the preferred bidder.

TRANSPORT

At independence in 1964 Zambia had only one tarred road and one railway line. The railway line extended from the Copperbelt, in the north, through Lusaka and Livingstone to Zimbabwe (then Southern Rhodesia), and connected with the Rhodesian rail network, providing access to South African ports. In 1965 the unilateral declaration of independence by Rhodesia prompted sanctions against that country, which severely disrupted the flow of Zambia's traffic on its only transport link to the outside world.

The Zambian Government invested substantial sums in improving infrastructure, with the construction of the TanZam oil pipeline from the Tanzanian port of Dar es Salaam, which was completed in 1968. The TanZam pipeline (now Tazama) was in July 2007 still on the list for 'future' privatization. Under the first phase of the Road Sector Investment Programme (1997–2002) some 59% of the country's road network was paved. Both the Great North Road to Tanzania and parts of the Great East Road to Malawi and beyond to the Mozambican ports of Nacala and Beira were rehabilitated under the programme. The Tanzania-Zambia Railway Authority (Tazara) railway line leading to Dar es Salaam was built and financed by China with an interest-free loan during the early 1970s. The complete route was opened to regular service in October 1975, ahead of the original schedule, and proved to be essential, after the closure of the Lobito railway to Angola in August 1975. However, limited port facilities at Dar es Salaam and unavailability of rolling stock resulted in severe delays, and Tazara incurred losses for the Zambian Government in its first eight years of operation. In October 1978 Zambia resumed its use of the Rhodesian rail route to South Africa. Tazara finally moved into profit in mid-1983, although it did not consistently achieve profits until 1988. An option study into private-sector participation in Tazara had been completed by March 2005. Although the intention of privatizing Tazara has been proclaimed both by Tanzania and by Zambia, in July 2007 Tazara was still on Zambia's list for 'future' privatization. Zambia Railways underwent restructuring in 1999–2001, with assistance from Sweden and the World Bank, ultimately with a view to privatization. In February 2003 a consortium of mainly South African business interests, known as New Limpopo Bridge Projects Investments, and Spoornet won a 20-year concession to run Zambia Railways in exchange for an annual payment to the Zambian Government, amounting to US $253m., plus 5% of annual turnover. The World Bank's International Development Association had approved $27m. in credit in November 2000 to help prepare the company for this change of ownership. Zambia's only port, Mpulungu, is on Lake Tanganyika. The ZPA concessioned Mpulungu harbour, port operations and assets to Mpulungu Harbour Management Ltd for 25 years. In 2005 the High Court blocked the Government's attempt to recover possession of the port.

The BotZam Highway links Kazungula with Nata, in Botswana. A new German-financed €8.2m. road bridge across the Zambezi river at Katima Mulilo opened in 2004, facilitating cross-border passage and potentially enabling Zambia to use Namibia's Walvis Bay port for cargo transportation. The 2007/08 budget allocated K787,000m. to road construction, rehabilitation and maintenance.

The national airline, Zambia Airways, went into liquidation in 1995. Some 3,000 creditors in 50 countries presented claims against the company's assets. By January 1996 most of the assets had been sold, including overseas operations in 13 countries. Two local airlines, Roan Air and Eastern Air, subsequently took many of the routes previously flown by Zambia Airways. Roan Air was awarded the right to operate the long-haul routes to London, Frankfurt and Amsterdam, in addition to 19 regional routes; the company subsequently adopted the name Zambian Airways. Eastern Air, now Zambia Skyways, operates long-haul routes to Dubai and London, as well as several regional routes. The National Airports Corpn Ltd (NACL) operates Lusaka International Airport, in addition to the Ndola, Livingstone and Mfuwe airports; as of mid-2007, NACL was still government-owned.

TOURISM

The Mwanawasa Government has identified tourism as a growth sector and the number of tourist arrivals increased from 650,000 in 2005 to 670,000 in 2006, while tourism receipts rose from US $164.8m. in 2005 to $176.7m. in 2006. Growth of this sector was 12.1% in 2000 and was some 24.1% in 2001, owing to a large extent to the events in neighbouring Zimbabwe. The two countries boast one of the great tourist attractions of the world in Victoria Falls, on the Zambezi river on their shared border. Until the recent crisis in Zimbabwe, that country attracted a far larger share of the tourists visiting the Falls and had the more highly developed tourism infrastructure. On the Zambian side of the river, the town of Livingstone is the focus of renewed tourism development. The number of flights into Livingstone International Airport rose sharply in 2000 and 2001, and the Mwanawasa Government has granted hotel accommodation in the Livingstone District Area a zero rating for value-added tax. All these factors contributed to 12.1% growth in tourism in 2005, up from 6.4% in 2004. Tourist arrivals at Livingstone Airport increased to 56,527 in 2004, 39% more than in 2003. Tourist interest in Zambia has expanded beyond Victoria Falls; the country's game parks received 9% more tourists in 2004 than in 2003, and tourist arrivals at Mfuwe Airport increased by 17% compared with 2003. The 2005 budget speech acknowledged that the potential of the tourism sector was not being fully exploited because of 'relatively poor' infrastructure, especially in the majority of the national parks, and 'high administrative burdens'. The Tourism Development Credit Facility, launched in 2004, facilitated private-sector interest in rapidly building tourism infrastructure such as lodges, guesthouses and camping sites, so that Zambia could capitalize on the boom opportunities.

FOREIGN TRADE AND PAYMENTS

Zambia generally maintained a visible trade surplus from independence until 1991. The principal export commodity is copper, although its share of total exports declined from the early 1990s onwards. The value of total merchandise exports in dollar terms rose by 77%, from US $2,200m. in 2005 to $3,900m. in 2006. Increased revenues from exports can be attributed to higher copper prices. There was growth of 29% in non-traditional exports (known as NTEs) such as copper wire, electricity cables, scrap metal, gemstones, fresh vegetables and fresh flowers. This very successful export performance was accompanied by greater import restraint. The value of total merchandise imports rose by just 23%, from $2,200m. in 2005 to $2,700m. in 2006. As a result, the trade deficit of $121m. in 2005 became a surplus of $1,200m. in 2006. The principal suppliers of Zambia's imports in 2005 were South Africa, with 25.6% (down from 50.3% in 2004), the United Kingdom (17.0%), Switzerland (16.0%), Tanzania (7.4%), the DRC (7%) and Zimbabwe (5.8%—down from 13.2% in 2004). Zambia's main export clients in 2005 were South Africa, with 46.2% (up from 13.2% in 2004), the United Kingdom (14.2%), the United Arab Emirates (7.1%) and Zimbabwe (6.0%). Another important client for Zambia's NTEs is the Common Market for Eastern and Southern Africa (COMESA), which in 2006 imported from Zambia such items as chemicals, cement, maize, fresh meat and eggs, refined petroleum and sugar. One item among the principal non-mineral exports that declined sharply in importance from the 1990s onwards was tobacco.

The current account of the balance of payments also registered a notable improvement. From a deficit of US $32.7m. in 2005, or 11.8% of GDP, the current-account shortfall fell to 2.3% of GDP in 2006. This compared favourably with the shortfalls of $584m. in 2000 and $743m. in 2001.

GOVERNMENT FINANCE

The 2003/04 budgetary deficit of K3,254,500m. became a divisive issue between the Government and the IMF and led to the Fund's refusal to release balance-of-payments support in the first half of 2003. The 2004/05 budget, announced in early February 2004, called for total expenditure of K8,328,600m., an amount equivalent to 33% of GDP. Domestic revenue was to cover only 63.5% of the total, with the remainder to be financed by domestic borrowing of K504,450m., an amount equivalent to 2% of GDP. This budget was prepared in close consultation with the World Bank and the IMF, with the Fund subsequently, four months later, releasing funding under the PRGF. However, Zambia was expected to make significant improvements to its revenue-collection measures in order to source a much higher proportion of budgetary funding locally—without borrowing—in future.

The 2005/06 budget showed that while the Government had continued to borrow domestically, raising the domestic debt stock from K5,186,170m. at December 2003 to K5,498,800m. at December 2004, its rate of borrowing had slowed significantly, from an increase of 31% in 2003 to an increase of 6% in 2004. The Government had committed itself to a domestic borrowing target equivalent to not more than 2.2% of GDP, and this target was achieved. The 2005/06 budget called for revenue and expenditure of K9,779,020m. However, a breakdown of the revenue showed that only K5,722,250m. was to be raised domestically in tax and other non-borrowing revenue, with the remainder to come from donors and a sum limited to K500,000m. to come from domestic borrowing. The 2006/07 budget called for total expenditure of K10,236,600m., equivalent to 26.9% of GDP. The 2007/08 budget, presented in February 2007, set a number of targets: real GDP growth of not less than 7%; inflation of not more than 5%; government domestic borrowing of not more than 1.2% of GDP; and gross international reserves sufficient to cover not less than 2.5 months' worth of imports. It called for total expenditure of K12,042,400m., equivalent to 26.6% of projected GDP of K45,282,000m. Of this total spending figure, 72% was to be financed from domestic resources.

Zambia remains one of the poorest countries in the world, with the ninth-lowest life expectancy, at 40 years. In December 2000 Zambia received assistance under the IMF and the World Bank's enhanced initiative for heavily indebted poor countries (HIPCs). Although the publicized amount was US $3,800m., the 'present value' of this debt relief was, by the IMF's own assessment, $2,500m. Even with this assistance, Zambia agreed to pay an average of $260m. per year in 2000–05 and some $130m. per year in 2006–15.

In 2006, owing to debt relief from the IMF, the World Bank and the African Development Bank, Zambia was able to shed its status as a 'highly indebted poor country'. Zambia's total external debt had stood at US $7,300m. at 31 December 2001. Various debt-reduction initiatives succeeded in reducing that figure to $4,500m. at 31 December 2005. After the 2005 Group of Eight (G-8) summit in Gleneagles, Scotland, called for complete debt cancellation for the world's poorest countries, the IMF, through its Multilateral Debt Relief Initiative (MDRI), in January 2006 announced that Zambia was eligible for 100% debt relief on all debt incurred by Zambia to the IMF prior to 1 January 2005 that was still outstanding. This MDRI reduced Zambia's total external debt from $4,500m. at the beginning of 2006 to $635m. at 31 December 2006. Correspondingly, Zambia's debt-service costs declined from $373.2m. in 2004 to a projected $33.9m. in 2007.

The annual rate of inflation in 1991 had been assessed by the IMF as 92.6% but was unofficially estimated by banking and business sources at 400%. The Chiluba Government's aim to reduce the official rate of inflation by one-half by the end of 1992 was not realized, and inflation remained above 100% until 1994, when it finally began to decrease. The Chiluba Government managed to reduce year-end inflation from 30.1% in December 2000 to 18.7% in December 2001, according to the Mwanawasa Government's first budget speech, which set a target of 13% by December 2002. This target, too, was not met; annual inflation in 2002 was 26.7%, although inflation excluding the cost of food in this drought-stricken year was 17.2%. The generous harvest helped drive down food prices in the marketplace in 2003, enabling the Government to rein in inflation from 26.7% at the end of 2002 to 17.2% at the end of 2003. The 2004 target had been 15%, but this was not met; 2004 inflation was 17.5%. The 2005 target was set at 15%, a clear indication that a single-digit level was not yet within the economic planners' sights; in the out-turn, inflation was 15.9% in 2005. The improved 8.2% inflation achieved in 2006 owed more to the strong maize harvest than to any restraint in money-supply growth, which the Government admitted was still 'rapid' in 2006.

As part of its reform programme, the Chiluba Government liberalized its exchange-rate policy. The first bureaux de change, which opened in October 1992, were permitted to set their own rates for the buying and selling of foreign currency; Zambian residents were initially limited to purchases of US $2,000 per transaction. The exercise proved extremely successful, and the kwacha fared far better during its initial period as a free-market currency than any other African currency had in similar circumstances. In December 2001, when Chiluba was defeated in the presidential election by Mwanawasa, the kwacha lost 24.6% of its value overnight. Currency stability was achieved in the next 12 months, however, and by 1 August 2004 the exchange rate stood at K4,755 = $1. This stability continued, and on 1 August 2005 the exchange rate had appreciated to K4,635 = $1. Much of the appreciation was accounted for by US dollar weakness rather than a kwacha strengthening, but the kwacha kept its stability despite double-digit inflation. In 2005 and 2006 the kwacha appreciated significantly, strengthening from K4,635 = $1 in July 2005 to K3,780 = $1 in July 2006, an appreciation of 22% in a single 12-month period. The currency depreciated moderately in the next 12 months and stood at K3,861 = $1 in July 2007.

Decades after copper became Zambia's main source of foreign exchange, the economy is still heavily dependent on the commodity. Some significant success has been achieved in encouraging alternative exports, mostly of agricultural commodities, and strenuous efforts are being made to persuade Zambian farmers to cultivate high-value crops such as paprika, cauliflower and roses. Trade figures indicate that these NTEs have increased their share of export earnings; however, these activities are still young and fragile. They face formidable competition in their intended markets. The world copper price, long known for its volatility, entered a trough in 1998, just as the disposal of ZCCM's assets was prompting potential buyers to make careful assessments of the sector's future potential; on the other hand, in the year to July 2006, the price more than doubled. Shortages of the country's staple food, maize, vastly increases its price in the nation's marketplaces, whereas in years of abundant harvests, the price plummets. In addition, pressure from the IMF and the World Bank to collect huge sums of unpaid taxes from companies such as the power authority and the distributor of petroleum products has led to rises in electricity tariffs and fuel prices, placing further strong upward pressure on the inflation rate. Adverse publicity south of the border in Zimbabwe, as well as the perceived threat of global terrorism, have had a negative effect on tourism to the region as a whole, although Zambia's share of this smaller industry has already increased. The problems in Zimbabwe, then, may not be entirely negative for Zambia; the LuSE has been promoting itself as a haven for 'offshore investment across the Zambezi'. In comparison with the tense situation prevailing in Zimbabwe in 2000–07, Zambia may have seemed a safer option.

The Mwanawasa Government has demonstrated its flexibility where negotiations with the IMF, the World Bank and the 'Paris Club' creditors are concerned, since its poverty-reduction measures cannot succeed without their financing. Domestically, bumper maize harvests were reaped in 2003, 2004 and 2006, lifting morale throughout the country. This upturn gave the Government an opportunity to boost the agricultural sector with measures to help make farmers less vulnerable to the vagaries of the weather. Indications are that government efforts to improve irrigation and to provide much-needed agricultural inputs in a timely manner did make a contribution towards returns to good harvests. However, funding for these measures will depend on overseas donors, and they will want to see tougher and more effective domestic revenue measures in place.

Statistical Survey

Source (unless otherwise indicated): Central Statistical Office, POB 31908, Lusaka; tel. (1) 211231; internet www.zamstats.gov.zm.

Area and Population

AREA, POPULATION AND DENSITY

Area (sq km)	752,612*
Population (census results)	
20 August 1990	7,383,097
25 October 2000	
Males	4,946,298
Females	4,939,293
Total	9,885,591
Population (UN estimates at mid-year)†	
2004	11,270,000
2005	11,478,000
2006	11,696,000
Density (per sq km) at mid-2006	15.5

* 290,585 sq miles.

† Source: UN, *World Population Prospects: The 2006 Revision*.

PROVINCES

(2000 census)

	Area	Population	Density
Central	94,394	1,012,257	10.7
Copperbelt	31,328	1,581,221	50.5
Eastern	69,106	1,306,173	18.9
Luapula	50,567	775,353	15.3
Lusaka	21,896	1,391,329	63.5
Northern	147,826	1,258,696	8.5
North-Western	125,826	583,350	4.6
Southern	85,283	1,212,124	14.2
Western	126,386	765,088	6.1
Total	752,612	9,885,591	13.1

PRINCIPAL TOWNS

(population at 2000 census)

Lusaka (capital)	1,084,703	Lundazi	236,833
Kitwe	376,124	Petauke	235,879
Ndola	374,757	Choma	204,898
Chipata	367,539	Solwezi	203,797
Chibombo	241,612	Mazabuka	203,219

Mid-2005 ('000, incl. suburbs, UN estimate): Lusaka 1,260 (Source: UN, *World Urbanization Prospects: The 2005 Revision*).

BIRTHS AND DEATHS
(annual averages, UN estimates)

	1990–95	1995–2000	2000–05
Birth rate (per 1,000)	43.9	43.8	41.9
Death rate (per 1,000)	17.5	21.3	21.7

Source: UN, *World Population Prospects: The 2006 Revision*.

Expectation of life (years at birth, WHO estimates): 40 (males 40; females 40) in 2004 (Source: WHO, *World Health Report*).

ECONOMICALLY ACTIVE POPULATION
(living conditions survey, '000 persons aged 12 years and over)

	1996
Agriculture, hunting, forestry and fishing	2,261
Mining and quarrying	60
Manufacturing	171
Electricity, gas and water	14
Construction	36
Wholesale and retail trade; restaurants and hotels	406
Transport, storage and communication	58
Financial, insurance, real estate and business services	48
Community, social and personal services	312
Total employed	3,368
Unemployed*	614
Total labour force	3,982

* Figure obtained as a residual.

Source: ILO Sub-Regional Office for Southern Africa.

Mid-2005 (estimates in '000): Agriculture, etc. 3,293; Total labour force 4,968 (Source: FAO).

Health and Welfare

KEY INDICATORS

Total fertility rate (children per woman, 2005)	5.4
Under-5 mortality rate (per 1,000 live births, 2005)	182
HIV/AIDS (% of persons aged 15–49, 2005)	17.0
Physicians (per 1,000 head, 2004)	0.12
Hospital beds (per 1,000 head, 2004)	0.20
Health expenditure (2004): US $ per head (PPP)	62.8
Health expenditure (2004): % of GDP	6.3
Health expenditure (2004): public (% of total)	54.7
Access to water (% of persons, 2004)	58
Access to sanitation (% of persons, 2004)	55
Human Development Index (2004): ranking	165
Human Development Index (2004): value	0.407

For sources and definitions, see explanatory note on p. vi.

Agriculture

PRINCIPAL CROPS
('000 metric tons)

	2003	2004	2005
Wheat	135*	85*	137
Rice (paddy)	12†	12	13
Maize	1,040.0	1,214.0	866.2
Millet	35*	39.8	29.6
Sorghum	20*	24.5	18.7
Potatoes	11†	11†	14
Sweet potatoes	53*	53†	67
Cassava (Manioc)	957	957	900
Sugar cane	1,800*	1,800†	n.a.
Pulses†	17	17	17
Soybeans (Soya beans)*	12	14	12
Groundnuts (in shell)*	40	40	40
Sunflower seed*	8	9	8
Cottonseed*	109	125	125
Dry onions†	27	27	27
Tomatoes†	25	25	25
Cotton (lint)†	70	75	76
Tobacco (leaves)†	4.8	4.8	4.8

* Unofficial figure(s).
† FAO estimate(s).

Source: FAO.

LIVESTOCK
('000 head, year ending September)

	1999	2000	2001*
Cattle	2,905	2,621	2,600
Sheep	120†	140†	150
Goats	1,069†	1,249†	1,270
Pigs	324†	309	340
Chickens*	28,000	29,000	30,000

* FAO estimates.
† Unofficial figure.

2002–05: Figures assumed to be unchanged from 2001 (FAO estimates).

Source: FAO.

LIVESTOCK PRODUCTS
('000 metric tons, FAO estimates)

	1999	2000	2001
Cattle meat	46.5	40.8	40.8
Pig meat	10.6	10.1	11.0
Chicken meat	33.5	35.0	36.5
Other meat	37.4	38.6	38.8
Cows' milk	61.5	64.2	64.2
Hen eggs	44.8	46.4	48.0
Cattle hides	6.3	5.4	5.4

2002–05: Hen eggs 46.4 in 2003, all other figures assumed to be unchanged from 2001 (FAO estimates).

Source: FAO.

Forestry

ROUNDWOOD REMOVALS
('000 cubic metres, FAO estimates)

	1997	1998	1999
Sawlogs, veneer logs and logs for sleepers	319	319	319
Other industrial wood	492	504	515
Fuel wood	7,219	7,219	7,219
Total	8,030	8,042	8,053

2000–05: Production as in 1999 (FAO estimates).

Source: FAO.

SAWNWOOD PRODUCTION
('000 cubic metres, incl. railway sleepers, FAO estimates)

	1995	1996	1997
Coniferous (softwood)	300	230	145
Broadleaved (hardwood)	20	15	12
Total	320	245	157

1998–2005: Annual production as in 1997 (FAO estimates).

Source: FAO.

Fishing

('000 metric tons, live weight)

	2003	2004	2005*
Capture	65.0*	65.0*	65.0
Dagaas	8.5*	8.5*	8.5
Other freshwater fishes	56.5*	56.5*	56.5
Aquaculture	4.5	5.1	5.1
Three-spotted tilapia	2.3	2.0	2.0
Total catch*	69.5	70.1	70.1

* FAO estimate(s).

Note: Figures exclude aquatic animals, recorded by number rather than weight. The number of Nile crocodiles caught was: 28,019 in 2003; 26,353 in 2004; 23,133 in 2005.

Source: FAO.

Mining

	2003	2004*	2005*
Coal ('000 metric tons)	71.8	240.0	240.0
Copper ore ('000 metric tons)†	348.0	426.9	447.0
Cobalt ore (metric tons)†	11,300	10,000	9,300
Amethysts ('000 kilograms)	1,000	1,100	1,100

* Estimated production.

† Figures refer to the metal content of ore.

Source: US Geological Survey.

Copper production ('000 metric tons): 465 in 2005.

Industry

SELECTED PRODUCTS
('000 metric tons, unless otherwise indicated)

	2003	2004*	2005*
Cement	350	390	435
Copper (unwrought): smelter	268	280	270
Copper (unwrought): refined	350	410	399
Cobalt (refined, metric tons)	6,620	5,791	5,422

* Estimates.

Raw sugar ('000 metric tons): 189 in 2000; 279 in 2001; 232 in 2002.

Electric energy (million kWh): 7,625 in 2000; 7,998 in 2001; 8,910 in 2002.

Sources: FAO; US Geological Survey; UN, *Industrial Commodity Statistics Yearbook*.

Finance

CURRENCY AND EXCHANGE RATES

Monetary Units

100 ngwee = 1 Zambian kwacha (K).

Sterling, Dollar and Euro Equivalents (31 May 2007)

£1 sterling = 7,875.9 kwacha;
US $1 = 3,983.2 kwacha;
€1 = 5,358.5 kwacha;
10,000 Zambian kwacha = £1.27 = $2.51 = €1.87.

Average Exchange Rate (Zambian kwacha per US $)

2004 4,778.88
2005 4,463.50
2006 3,603.07

CENTRAL GOVERNMENT BUDGET
(K '000 million)

Revenue	2003	2004	2005*
Tax revenue	3,548	4,546	5,513
Income tax	1,622	2,032	2,455
Excise taxes	482	607	768
Value-added tax (VAT)	1,034	1,362	1,633
Domestic VAT	393	453	623
VAT on imports	642	909	1,010
Customs duty	409	544	656
Non-tax revenue	132	194	130
Total†	3,680	4,740	5,643

Expenditure	2003	2004	2005*
Current expenditure	4,002	4,654	6,082
Wages and salaries	1,728	2,012	2,455
Public service retrenchment	10	20	44
Other current expenditures	1,465	1,711	2,709
Domestic interest (paid)	563	746	731
External interest (paid)	229	152	133
Contingency	6	13	10
Capital expenditure	2,335	2,265	2,267
Total	6,337	6,919	8,350

* Preliminary figures.

† Excluding grants received (K '000 million): 1,424 in 2003; 1,433 in 2004; 1,825 in 2005 (preliminary figure).

Source: IMF, *Zambia: Fourth Review of the Three-Year Arrangement Under the Poverty Reduction and Growth Facility, Request for Modification of Performance Criteria, and Financing Assurances Review—Staff Report; and Press Release on the Executive Board Consideration* (July 2006).

INTERNATIONAL RESERVES
(US $ million at 31 December)

	2004	2005	2006
IMF special drawing rights	24.8	15.7	13.3
Foreign exchange	312.2	544.0	706.4
Total	337.1	559.8	719.7

Source: IMF, *International Financial Statistics*.

MONEY SUPPLY
(K '000 million at 31 December)

	2004	2005	2006
Currency outside banks	727.0	752.5	1,066.4
Demand deposits at commercial banks	1,104.8	1,338.3	2,264.8
Total money (incl. others)	1,841.0	2,099.7	3,340.1

Source: IMF, *International Financial Statistics*.

COST OF LIVING
(Consumer Price Index; low-income group; base: 2000 = 100)

	2001	2002	2003
Food (incl. alcohol and tobacco)	118.9	151.1	184.5
Clothing and footwear	120.5	139.4	168.8
Fuel and rent	121.4	145.1	176.5
All items (incl. others)	121.4	148.4	180.1

Food (incl. alcohol and tobacco): 214.7 in 2004; 254.5 in 2005.

All items: 212.5 in 2004; 251.4 in 2005.

Source: ILO.

NATIONAL ACCOUNTS

Expenditure on the Gross Domestic Product
(US $ million at current prices)

	2004	2005	2006
Final consumption expenditure	4,695.00	5,805.43	8,193.24
Households	3,676.67	4,809.90	6,753.33
General government	1,018.33	995.53	1,439.91
Gross fixed capital formation	1,617.30	1,669.82	2,576.73
Total domestic expenditure	6,312.40	7,475.25	10,769.97
Exports of goods and services	1,525.61	2,465.15	3,304.85
Less Imports of goods and services	2,397.84	2,670.38	3,130.27
GDP in purchasers' values	5,440.07	7,270.02	10,944.55

Source: African Development Bank.

Gross Domestic Product by Economic Activity
(K '000 million at current prices)

	2002	2003	2004
Agriculture, forestry and fishing	3,247.4	4,244.6	5,568.2
Mining and quarrying	575.1	564.8	809.7
Manufacturing	1,693.6	2,241.0	2,802.9
Electricity, gas and water	488.3	595.1	694.7
Construction	1,067.7	1,590.0	2,443.3
Wholesale and retail trade, restaurants and hotels	3,004.1	3,873.8	4,827.3
Transport and communications	1,055.9	1,058.2	1,220.5
Finance and insurance	1,493.1	1,847.7	2,282.7
Real estate and business services	1,041.2	1,341.2	1,658.4
Restaurants and hotels	406.8	527.7	659.3
Community, social and personal services*	1,414.4	1,757.0	2,041.6
Sub-total	15,487.6	19,641.1	25,008.6
Import duties	1,630.8	1,899.9	2,219.1
Less imputed bank service charge	858.1	1,061.8	1,311.8
GDP in purchasers' values	16,260.4	20,479.2	25,915.9

* Includes public administration, defence, sanitary services, education, health, recreation, and personal services.

Source: IMF, *Zambia: Selected Issues and Statistical Appendix* (March 2006).

BALANCE OF PAYMENTS
(US $ million)

	2003	2004	2005*
Exports of goods f.o.b.	1,061	1,779	2,161
Imports of goods f.o.b.	–1,393	–1,727	–2,161
Goods procured by airlines	29	31	32
Trade balance	–302	82	32
Services (net)	–238	–215	–237
Balance on goods and services	–540	–133	–205
Income (net)	–143	–424	–466
Interest payments	–126	–121	–110
Balance on goods, services and income	–683	–557	–671
Current transfers (net)	–3	–25	–24
Current account	–686	–581	–696
Capital and financial accounts (net)	457	180	1,120
Net errors and omissions	46	58	–354
Overall balance	–275	–343	70

* Preliminary figures.

Source: IMF, *Zambia: Fourth Review of the Three-Year Arrangement Under the Poverty Reduction and Growth Facility, Request for Modification of Performance Criteria, and Financing Assurances Review—Staff Report; and Press Release on the Executive Board Consideration* (July 2006).

External Trade

PRINCIPAL COMMODITIES
(US $ million)

Imports f.o.b.	2002	2003	2004
Food and live animals	148.5	160.8	89.8
Cereals and cereal preparations	100.2	98.1	38.3
Crude materials (inedible) except fuels	36.2	59.0	64.5
Mineral fuels, lubricants, etc.	88.0	129.3	226.3
Petroleum and petroleum products	79.3	101.2	191.9
Chemicals and related products	191.7	291.7	330.4
Fertilizers (manufactured)	50.3	67.7	81.3
Basic manufactures	156.8	250.0	295.7
Iron and steel	37.3	62.4	89.2
Manufactures of metals	27.7	46.4	65.3
Machinery and transport equipment	390.0	505.0	637.5
Machinery specialized for particular industries	83.3	135.1	177.0
General industrial machinery, equipment and parts	66.0	81.2	112.3
Telecommunications and sound equipment	28.9	49.0	39.8
Other electrical machinery, apparatus, etc.	55.5	70.5	80.1
Road vehicles and parts	109.9	107.8	154.3
Passenger motor vehicles (excl. buses)	32.6	27.3	35.0
Goods vehicles (lorries and trucks)	43.4	35.5	64.7
Miscellaneous manufactured articles	209.0	142.3	331.8
Printed matter	141.3	67.4	238.5
Total (incl. others)	1,252.7	1,573.6	2,017.1

Exports f.o.b.	2002	2003	2004
Food and live animals	67.8	75.3	138.9
Sugar and honey	35.1	33.7	31.6
Crude materials (inedible) except fuels	49.9	91.4	228.3
Metal ores and scrap	16.0	31.2	36.3
Basic manufactures	684.9	742.9	932.4
Textile yarn, fabrics and related products	24.8	24.1	23.3
Cotton yarn	22.9	22.1	22.3
Non-metallic mineral manufactures	29.6	86.4	33.2
Non-ferrous metals	569.5	573.7	634.0
Refined copper, unwrought	464.3	394.4	462.0
Base metals and cements	83.0	84.6	—
Manufactures of metals	55.2	52.1	234.6
Machinery and transport equipment	45.5	8.1	16.3
Miscellaneous manufactured articles	8.5	10.9	21.5
Total (incl. others)	929.5	980.7	1,461.5

Source: UN, *International Trade Statistics Yearbook*.

PRINCIPAL TRADING PARTNERS
(US $ million)

Imports f.o.b.	2002	2003	2004
China, People's Repub.	34.5	43.2	43.8
Finland	7.8	27.0	21.2
France	25.5	30.2	57.5
Germany	15.1	24.0	21.3
India	45.4	35.5	78.6
Japan	40.6	23.4	27.6
Kenya	11.7	24.1	32.5
South Africa	641.6	766.5	932.7
Tanzania	14.9	23.7	27.1
United Kingdom	153.5	92.4	286.5
USA	18.3	32.5	33.8
Zimbabwe	97.8	202.7	120.5
Total (incl. others)	1,252.7	1,573.6	2,017.1

Exports f.o.b.	2002	2003	2004
Belgium	17.3	27.9	35.1
China, People's Repub.	2.7	16.6	29.3
Congo, Democratic Repub.	39.7	41.6	101.8
Finland	5.8	12.2	5.8
Hong Kong	4.7	24.7	2.6
India	17.0	34.4	14.4
Japan	7.2	16.2	7.0
Malawi	19.4	24.5	42.9
Netherlands	11.3	27.4	43.1
South Africa	213.9	211.4	374.5
Switzerland-Liechtenstein	57.1	76.8	234.2
Tanzania	71.1	122.7	107.6
United Kingdom	393.6	254.1	249.1
USA	5.3	6.9	17.7
Zimbabwe	14.0	18.9	85.3
Total (incl. others)	929.5	980.7	1,461.5

Source: UN, *International Trade Statistics Yearbook*.

Transport

ROAD TRAFFIC
(estimates, '000 motor vehicles in use at 31 December)

	1994	1995	1996
Passenger cars	123	142	157
Lorries and vans	68	74	81

Source: IRF, *World Road Statistics*.

CIVIL AVIATION
(traffic on scheduled services)

	2001	2002	2003
Kilometres flown (million)	2	2	2
Passengers carried ('000)	49	47	45
Passenger-km (million)	16	16	14
Total ton-km (million)	1	1	1

Source: UN, *Statistical Yearbook*.

Tourism

VISITOR ARRIVALS BY NATIONALITY
(provisional figures)

	2003	2004	2005
Australia	5,597	7,490	16,336
South Africa	62,604	110,710	110,272
Tanzania	30,776	33,502	65,881
United Kingdom	31,072	37,520	44,369
USA	15,879	20,547	23,895
Zimbabwe	138,288	123,573	148,436
Total (incl. others)	412,675	515,000	668,862

Tourism receipts (US $ million, incl. passenger transport): 149 in 2003; 161 in 2004; n.a. in 2005.

Source: World Tourism Organization.

Communications Media

	2003	2004	2005
Telephones ('000 main lines in use)	88.4	91.7	91.7
Mobile cellular telephones ('000 subscribers)	241.0	464.4	735.0
Personal computers ('000 in use)	95	113	113
Internet users ('000)	110.0	231.0	231.0

Radio receivers ('000 in use): 1,436 in 1999.

Television receivers ('000 in use): 540 in 2001.

Facsimile machines (number in use): 1,005 (estimate) in year ending 31 March 1999.

Daily newspapers (1996): 3; average circulation: 114,000 copies.

Sources: UNESCO, *Statistical Yearbook*; UN, *Statistical Yearbook*; International Telecommunication Union.

Education

(2003/04 unless otherwise indicated)

	Institutions	Teachers	Students
Primary	4,221*	61,251†	2,251,357
Secondary	n.a.	33,964†	363,163
Tertiary	n.a.	n.a.	24,553‡

* 1998 figure.
† 2002/03 estimate.
‡ 1999/2000 estimate.

Source: UNESCO Institute for Statistics.

Adult literacy rate (UNESCO estimates): 68.0% (males 76.3%; females 59.8%) in 1995–99 (Source: UN Development Programme, *Human Development Report*).

Directory

The Constitution

The Constitution for the Republic of Zambia, which was formally adopted on 28 May 1996 (amending the Constitution of 1991), provides for a multi-party form of government. The Head of State is the President of the Republic, who is elected by popular vote at the same time as elections to the National Assembly. The President's tenure of office is limited to two five-year terms. Foreign nationals and those with foreign parentage are prohibited from contesting the presidency. The legislature comprises a National Assembly of 158 members: 150 are elected by universal adult suffrage, while the remaining eight are nominated by the President. The President appoints a Vice-President and a Cabinet from members of the National Assembly.

The Constitution also provides for a House of Chiefs numbering 27: four from each of the Northern, Western, Southern and Eastern Provinces, three each from the North-Western, Luapula and Central Provinces and two from the Copperbelt Province. It may submit resolutions to be debated by the Assembly and consider those matters referred to it by the President.

The Supreme Court of Zambia is the final Court of Appeal. The Chief Justice and other judges are appointed by the President. Subsidiary to the Supreme Court is the High Court, which has unlimited jurisdiction to hear and determine any civil or criminal proceedings under any Zambian law.

The Government

HEAD OF STATE

President: LEVY PATRICK MWANAWASA (took office 2 January 2002; re-elected 28 September 2006).

THE CABINET
(August 2007)

President: LEVY PATRICK MWANAWASA.

Vice-President: RUPIAH BANDA.

Minister of Home Affairs: RONNIE SHIKAPWASHA.

Minister of Foreign Affairs: KABINGA PANDE.

Minister of Defence: GEORGE MPOMBO.

Minister of Finance and National Planning: NG'ANDU PETER MAGANDE.

Minister of Commerce, Trade and Industry: FELIX MUTATI.

Minister of Justice: GEORGE KUNDA.

Minister of Agriculture, Food and Fisheries: BEN KAPITA.

Minister of Communications and Transport: SARAH SAYIFWANDA.

Minister of Energy and Water Development: KENNETH KONGA.

Minister of Tourism, the Environment and Natural Resources: MICHAEL KAINGU.

Minister of Education: GEOFFREY LUNGWANGWA.

Minister of Science, Technology and Vocational Training: PETER DAKA.

Minister of Health: Brig.-Gen. Dr BRIAN CHITUWO.

Minister of Local Government and Housing: SYLVIA MASEBO.

Minister of Works and Supply: KAPEMBWA SIMBAO.

Minister of Community Development and Social Services: CATHERINE NAMUGALA.

Minister of Sport, Youth and Child Development: GABRIEL NAMULAMBE.

Minister of Lands: BRADFORD MACHILA.

Minister of Labour and Social Security: RONALD MUYKUMA.

Minister of Mines and Mineral Development: KALOMBO MWANSA.

Minister of Information and Broadcasting Services: MIKE MULONGOTI.

Minister of Gender and Development: PATRICIA MULASIKAWANDA.

There are, in addition, 23 Deputy Ministers.

MINISTRIES

Office of the President: POB 30208, Lusaka; tel. (1) 218282; internet www.statehouse.gov.zm.

Ministry of Agriculture, Food and Fisheries: Mulungushi House, Independence Ave, Nationalist Rd, POB RW50291, Lusaka; tel. (1) 213551.

Ministry of Commerce, Trade and Industry: Kwacha Annex, Cairo Rd, POB 31968, Lusaka; tel. (1) 213767.

Ministry of Communications and Transport: Fairley Rd, POB 50065, Lusaka; tel. (1) 251444; fax (1) 253260.

Ministry of Community Development and Social Welfare: Fidelity House, POB 31958, Lusaka; tel. (1) 228321; fax (1) 225327.

Ministry of Defence: POB 31931, Lusaka; tel. (1) 252366.

Ministry of Education: 15102 Ridgeway, POB RW50093, Lusaka; tel. (1) 227636; fax (1) 222396.

Ministry of Energy and Water Development: Mulungushi House, Independence Ave, Nationalist Rd, POB 36079, Lusaka; tel. and fax (1) 252589.

Ministry of Finance and National Planning: Finance Bldg, POB 50062, Lusaka; tel. (1) 253512; fax (1) 251078.

Ministry of Foreign Affairs: POB RW50069, Lusaka; tel. (1) 213822; fax (1) 222440.

Ministry of Gender and Development: Lusaka.

Ministry of Health: Woodgate House, 1st–2nd Floors, Cairo Rd, POB 30205, Lusaka; tel. (1) 227745; fax (1) 228385.

Ministry of Home Affairs: POB 32862, Lusaka; tel. (1) 213505.

Ministry of Information and Broadcasting Services: Independence Ave, POB 32245, Lusaka; tel. (1) 228202; fax (1) 253457.

Ministry of Justice: Fairley Rd, POB 50106, 15101, Ridgeway, Lusaka; tel. (1) 228522.

Ministry of Labour and Social Security: Lechwe House, Freedom Way, POB 32186, Lusaka; tel. (1) 212020.

Ministry of Lands: POB 50694, Lusaka; tel. (1) 252288; fax (1) 250120.

Ministry of Local Government and Housing: Church Rd, POB 34204, Lusaka; tel. (1) 253077; fax (1) 252680.

Ministry of Mines and Mineral Development: Chilufya Mulenga Rd, POB 31969, 10101 Lusaka; tel. (1) 251402; fax (1) 252095.

Ministry of Science, Technology and Vocational Training: POB 50464, Lusaka; tel. (1) 229673; fax (1) 252951.

Ministry of Sport, Youth and Child Development: Memaco House, POB 50195, Lusaka; tel. (1) 227158; fax (1) 223996.

Ministry of Tourism, the Environment and Natural Resources: Electra House, Cairo Rd, POB 30575, Lusaka; tel. (1) 227645; fax (1) 222189.

Ministry of Works and Supply: POB 50003, Lusaka; tel. (1) 253088; fax (1) 253404.

President and Legislature

PRESIDENT

Presidential Election, 28 September 2006

Candidate	Votes	% of votes
Levy Patrick Mwanawasa (MMD)	1,177,846	42.98
Michael C. Sata (PF)	804,748	29.37
Hakainde Hichilema (UDA)	693,772	25.32
Brig.-Gen. Godfrey K. Miyanda (HP)	42,891	1.57
Winright K. Ngondo (APC)	20,921	0.76
Total	2,740,178	100.00

NATIONAL ASSEMBLY

Speaker: AMUSAA KATUNDA MWANAMWAMBWA.

General Election, 28 September 2006*

Party	Seats
Movement for Multi-party Democracy (MMD)	75
Patriotic Front (PF)	43
United Democratic Alliance (UDA)†	26
Independents	3
United Liberal Party (ULP)	2
National Democratic Focus (NDF)	1
Total	150

* Includes the results of voting in two constituencies where the elections were postponed until 26 October 2006, owing to the deaths of candidates.

† Coalition of the Forum for Democracy and Development (FDD), the United National Independence Party (UNIP) and the United Party for National Development (UPND).

House of Chiefs

The House of Chiefs is an advisory body which may submit resolutions for debate by the National Assembly. There are 27 Chiefs, four each from the Northern, Western, Southern and Eastern Provinces, three each from the North-Western, Luapula and Central Provinces, and two from the Copperbelt Province.

Election Commission

Electoral Commission of Zambia (ECZ): Ndeke Annex, Haile Selassie Ave, POB 50274, Longacres, Lusaka; tel. (1) 253155; fax (1) 253884; e-mail elections@electcom.org.zm; internet www.elections.org.zm; f. 1996; independent; Chair. IRENE MAMBILIMA; Dir DAN KALALE.

Political Organizations

Democratic Party (DP): Plot C4, President Ave (North), POB 71628, Ndola; f. 1991; Pres. EMMANUEL MWAMBA.

Heritage Party (HP): POB 51055, Lusaka; f. 2001 by expelled mems of the MMD; Pres. Brig.-Gen. GODFREY K. MIYANDA.

Liberal Progressive Front (LPF): POB 31190, Lusaka; f. 1993; Pres. Dr RODGER CHONGWE.

Movement for Multi-party Democracy (MMD): POB 30708, Lusaka; f. 1990; governing party since Nov. 1991; Nat. Chair. BONIFACE KAWIMBE; Nat. Sec. VERNON MWAANGA.

National Democratic Front: Lusaka; f. 2006 to contest the presidential election; Acting Chair. NEVERS MUMBA (RP).

Comprising:

All Peoples' Congress Party (APC): Lusaka; f. 2005 by fmr mems of the FDD; Pres. WINRIGHT K. NGONDO.

Party for Unity, Democracy and Development (PUDD): Lusaka; f. 2004 by fmr mems of the MMD; Pres. CHITALU SAMPA.

Reform Party: Lusaka; f. 2005 by fmr mems of the MMD; Pres. NEVERS MUMBA; Nat. Chair. EVA SANDERSON; Sec.-Gen. CLEMENT MICHELO.

Zambia Democratic Conference (ZADECO): Lusaka; f. 1998 as the Zambia Democratic Congress Popular Front by fmr mems of the Zambia Democratic Congress; disbanded in 1999; reformed after 2001 election by fmr mems of the ZAP; Pres. Rev. Dr DAN PULE.

Zambia Republican Party (ZRP): Lusaka; f. 2001 by merger of the Republican Party (f. 2000) and the Zambia Alliance for Progress (f. 1999); Gen. Sec. SILVIA MASEBO; Nat. Chair. BEN KAPITA.

National Leadership for Development (NLD): POB 34161, Lusaka; f. 2000; Pres. Dr YOBERT K. SHAMAPANDE.

Patriotic Front (PF): f. 2001 by expelled mems of the MMD; Pres. MICHAEL C. SATA; Sec.-Gen. GUY SCOTT.

United Democratic Alliance (UDA): Kenneth Kaunda House, Cairo Rd, Lusaka; f. 2006 to contest that year's elections; Nat. Chair. TILYENJI KAUNDA (FDD).

Comprising:

Forum for Democracy and Development (FDD): POB 35868, Lusaka; f. 2001 by expelled mems of the MMD; Pres. EDITH NAWAKWI; Chair. SIMON ZUKAS.

United National Independence Party (UNIP): POB 30302, Lusaka; tel. (1) 221197; fax (1) 221327; f. 1959; sole legal party 1972–90; Pres. TILYENJI KAUNDA; Nat. Chair. KEN KAIRA.

United Party for National Development (UPND): POB 33199, Lusaka; internet www.upnd.org; f. 1998; incl. fmr mems of the Progressive People's Party and Zambia Dem. Party; Pres. HAKAINDE HICHILEMA.

Unity Party for Democrats (UPD): POB RW28, Ridgeway, Lusaka; f. 1997; Pres. MATHEW PIKITI.

Zambia Alliance for Progress (ZAP): Lusaka; f. 1999; re-registered as ZAP in 2001 after splitting from Zambia Republican Party; Pres. (vacant).

Diplomatic Representation

EMBASSIES AND HIGH COMMISSIONS IN ZAMBIA

Angola: Plot 108, Great East Rd, Northmead, POB 31595, 10101 Lusaka; tel. (1) 34764; fax (1) 221210; e-mail sinangocom@zamnet.zm; Ambassador (vacant).

Botswana: 5201 Pandit Nehru Rd, Diplomatic Triangle, POB 31910, 10101 Lusaka; tel. (1) 250555; fax (1) 250804; High Commissioner LAPOLOGANG CAESAR LEKOA.

Brazil: 74 Anglo American Bldg, Independence Ave, POB 33300; tel. (1) 250400; fax (1) 251652; e-mail brasemblusaca@iconnect.zm; Chargé d'affaires a.i. PAULO M. G. DE SOUSA.

Canada: Plot 5199, United Nations Ave, POB 31313, 10101 Lusaka; tel. (1) 250833; fax (1) 254176; e-mail lsaka@international.gc.ca; High Commissioner JOHN DEYELL.

China, People's Republic: Plot 7430, United Nations Ave, Longacres, POB 31975, 10101 Lusaka; tel. (1) 251169; fax (1) 251157; Ambassador LI QIANGMIN.

Congo, Democratic Republic: Plot 1124, Parirenyatwa Rd, POB 31287, 10101 Lusaka; tel. and fax (1) 235679; Ambassador JOHNSON WA BINANA.

Cuba: 5574 Mogoye Rd, Kalundu, POB 33132, 10101 Lusaka; tel. (1) 291308; fax (1) 291586; e-mail sikulem@zamnet.zm; Ambassador NARCISO MARTÍN MORA DÍAZ.

Denmark: 4 Manenekela Rd, POB 50299, Lusaka; tel. (1) 254277; fax (1) 254618; e-mail lunamb@um.dk; internet www.amblusaka.um.dk/en; Ambassador ORLA BAKDAL.

Egypt: Plot 5206, United Nations Ave, Longacres, POB 32428, Lusaka 10101; tel. (1) 250229; fax (1) 254149; Ambassador MOHAMED TAMER SAAD ELDIN MANSOUR.

Finland: Haile Selassie Ave, opposite Ndeke House, Longacres, POB 50819, 15101 Lusaka; tel. (1) 251988; fax (1) 253783; e-mail sanomat.lus@formin.fi; internet www.finland.org.zm; Ambassador SINIKKA ANTILA.

France: Anglo American Bldg, 4th Floor, 74 Independence Ave, POB 30062, 10101 Lusaka; tel. (1) 251322; fax (1) 254475; e-mail france@ambafrance-zm.org; internet www.ambafrance-zm.org; Ambassador FRANCIS SAUDUBRAY.

Germany: Plot 5209, United Nations Ave, POB 50120, 15101 Ridgeway, Lusaka; tel. (1) 250644; fax (1) 254014; e-mail info@lusaka.diplo.de; internet www.lusaka.diplo.de; Ambassador Dr IRENE HINRICHSEN.

Holy See: 283 Los Angeles Blvd, POB 31445, 10101 Lusaka; tel. (1) 251033; fax (1) 250601; e-mail nuntius@coppernet.zm; Apostolic Nuncio Most Rev. NICOLA GIRASOLI (Titular Archbishop of Egnazia Appula).

India: 1 Pandit Nehru Rd, POB 32111, 10101 Lusaka; tel. (1) 253159; fax (1) 254118; High Commissioner YOGESH K. GUPTA.

Ireland: 6663 Katima Mulilo Rd, Olympia Park, POB 34923, 10101 Lusaka; tel. (1) 290650; fax (1) 290482; Ambassador BILL NOLAN.

Italy: Plot 5211, Embassy Park, Diplomatic Triangle, POB 50497, Lusaka; tel. (1) 250781; fax (1) 254929; e-mail ambasciata.lusaka@esteri.it; internet www.amblusaka.esteri.it; Ambassador Dr GIOVANNI CERUTI.

Japan: Plot 5218, Haile Selassie Ave, POB 34190, 10101 Lusaka; tel. (1) 251555; fax (1) 254425; e-mail jez@zamtel.zm; internet www.zm.emb-japan.go.jp; Ambassador MASAAKI MIYASHITA.

Kenya: 5207 United Nations Ave, POB 50298, 10101 Lusaka; tel. (1) 250722; fax (1) 253829; e-mail kenhigh@zamnet.zm; High Commissioner ESTHER MSHAI TOLLE.

Libya: 251 Ngwee Rd, off United Nations Ave, Longacres, POB 35319, 10101 Lusaka; tel. (1) 253055; fax (1) 251239; Ambassador KHALIFA OMER SWIEXI.

Malawi: 31 Bishops Rd, Kabulonga, POB 50425, Lusaka; tel. (1) 213750; fax (1) 265764; e-mail mhcomm@zamtel.zm; High Commissioner Dr CHRISSIE MUGHOGHO.

Mozambique: Kacha Rd, Plot 9592, POB 34877, 10101 Lusaka; tel. (1) 220333; fax (1) 220345; High Commissioner SHAHARUDDIN MOHAMMED SOM.

Namibia: 30B Mutende Rd, Woodlands, POB 30577, 10101 Lusaka; tel. (1) 260407; fax (1) 263858; High Commissioner FRIEDA NANGULA ITHETE.

Netherlands: 5208 United Nations Ave, POB 31905, 10101 Lusaka; tel. (1) 253819; fax (1) 253733; e-mail lus@minbuza.nl; internet www.netherlandsembassy.org.zm; Ambassador EDUARD J. M. MIDDELDORP.

Nigeria: 5208 Haile Selassie Ave, Longacres, POB 32598, 10101 Lusaka; tel. (1) 253177; fax (1) 253560; High Commissioner Chief IBIRONKE O. VAUGHAN-ADEFOPE.

Norway: cnr Birdcage Walk and Haile Selassie Ave, Longacres, POB 34570, 10101 Lusaka; tel. (1) 252188; fax (1) 253915; e-mail emb.lusaka@mfa.no; internet www.norway.org.zm; Ambassador TERJE VIGTEL.

Russia: Plot 6407, Diplomatic Triangle, POB 32355, 10101 Lusaka; tel. (1) 252120; fax (1) 253582; internet www.russianembassy.biz/zambia-lusaka.htm; Ambassador ANVAR AZIMOV.

Saudi Arabia: 27BC Leopards Hill Rd, Kabulonga, POB 34411, 10101 Lusaka; tel. (1) 266861; fax (1) 266863; e-mail saudiemb@uudial.zm; Ambassador TALAT SALEM RADWAN.

Serbia: Plot 5216, Diplomatic Triangle, POB 33379, 10101 Lusaka; tel. (1) 250235; fax (1) 253889; e-mail ambscg@zamnet.zm; Chargé d'affaires a.i. MIRKO MANOJLOVIC.

Somalia: G3/377A Kabulonga Rd, POB 34051, Lusaka; tel. (1) 262119; Ambassador Dr OMAN UMAL.

South Africa: D26, Cheetah Rd, Kabulonga, Private Bag W369, Lusaka; tel. (1) 260999; fax (1) 263001; e-mail sahc@zamnet.zm; High Commissioner MASALA MZIWANDILA.

Sudan: 31 Ng'umbo Rd, Longacres, POB RW179X, 15200 Lusaka; tel. (1) 215570; fax (1) 40653; Ambassador ABDALLAH KHIDIR BASHIR.

Sweden: Haile Selassie Ave, POB 50264, 10101 Lusaka; tel. (1) 251711; fax (1) 254049; e-mail ambassaden.lusaka@foreign.ministry.se; internet www.swedenabroad.com/lusaka; Ambassador LARS RONNÅS.

Tanzania: Ujamaa House, Plot 5200, United Nations Ave, POB 31219, 10101 Lusaka; tel. (1) 253222; fax (1) 254861; e-mail tzreplsk@zamnet.zm; High Commissioner GEORGE MWANJABALA.

United Kingdom: Plot 5201, Independence Ave, POB 50050, 15101 Ridgeway, Lusaka; tel. (1) 251133; fax (1) 253798; High Commissioner ALISTAIR HARRISON.

USA: cnr Independence and United Nations Aves, POB 31617, Lusaka; tel. (1) 250955; fax (1) 252225; internet zambia.usembassy.gov; Ambassador CARMEN M. MARTINEZ.

Zimbabwe: 11058, Haile Selassie Ave, Longacres, POB 33491, 10101 Lusaka; tel. (1) 254012; fax (1) 227474; Ambassador KOSHO DUBE.

Judicial System

The judicial system of Zambia comprises a Supreme Court, composed of a Chief Justice, a Deputy Chief Justice and five Justices; a High Court comprising the Chief Justice and 30 Judges; Senior Resident and Resident Magistrates' Courts, which sit at various centres; and Local Courts, which deal principally with customary law, but which also have limited criminal jurisdiction.

Supreme Court of Zambia

Independence Ave, POB 50067, Ridgeway, Lusaka; tel. (1) 251330; fax (1) 251743.

Chief Justice: ERNEST L. SAKALA.

Deputy Chief Justice: DAVID M. LEWANIKA.

Supreme Court Judges: LOMBE CHIBESAKUNDA, DENNIS CHIRWA, PETER CHITENGI, IREEN MAMBILIMA, SANDSON SILOMBA.

Religion

CHRISTIANITY

Council of Churches in Zambia: Church House, Cairo Rd, POB 30315, Lusaka; tel. (1) 229551; fax (1) 224308; e-mail info@ccz.org.zm; f. 1945; Chair. Rt Rev. THUMA HAMUKANG'ANDU (Brethren in Christ Church); Gen. Sec. JAPHET NDHLOVU; 22 mem. churches and 18 affiliate mem. orgs.

The Anglican Communion

Anglicans are adherents of the Church of the Province of Central Africa, covering Botswana, Malawi, Zambia and Zimbabwe. The Church comprises 15 dioceses, including five in Zambia. The Archbishop of the Province is the Bishop of Upper Shire in Malawi. There are an estimated 80,000 adherents in Zambia.

Bishop of Central Zambia: Rt Rev. DEREK G. KAMUKWAMBA, POB 70172, Ndola; tel. (2) 612431; fax (2) 615954; e-mail adcznla@zamnet.zm.

Bishop of Eastern Zambia: Rt Rev. WILLIAM MUCHOMBO, POB 510154, Chipata; tel. and fax (6) 221294; e-mail dioeastzm@zamnet.zm.

Bishop of Luapula: Rt Rev. ROBERT MUMBI, POB 710210, Mansa, Luapula.

Bishop of Lusaka: Rt Rev. DAVID NJOVU, Bishop's Lodge, POB 30183, Lusaka; tel. (1) 264515; fax (1) 262379; e-mail angdiolu@zamnet.zm.

Bishop of Northern Zambia: Rt Rev. ALBERT CHAMA, POB 20798, Kitwe; tel. (2) 223264; fax (2) 224778; e-mail dionorth@zamnet.zm.

Protestant Churches

At mid-2000 there were an estimated 2.7m. Protestants.

African Methodist Episcopal Church: POB 31478, Lusaka; tel. (1) 264013; Presiding Elder Rev. L. SICHANGWA; 440 congregations, 880,000 mems.

Baptist Church: Lubu Rd, POB 30636, Lusaka; tel. (1) 253620.

Baptist Mission of Zambia: Baptist Bldg, 3062 Great East Rd, POB 50599, 15101 Ridgeway, Lusaka; tel. (1) 222492; fax (1) 227520; e-mail bmzambia@zamnet.zm; internet bmoz.org.

Brethren in Christ Church: POB 630115, Choma; tel. (3) 20228; fax (3) 20127; e-mail biccz@zamtel.zm; internet www.bic.org; f. 1906; Bishop Rev. E. SHAMAPANI; 165 congregations, 17,623 mems.

Reformed Church in Zambia: POB 38255, Lusaka; tel. (1) 295369; f. 1899; African successor to the Dutch Reformed Church mission; 147 congregations, 400,000 mems.

Seventh-day Adventist Church: Plot 9221, cnr Burma Rd and Independence Ave, POB 31309, Lusaka; tel. (1) 255197; fax (1) 255191; e-mail zbupre@zamnet.zm; f. 1905; Pres. Dr CORNELIUS MULENGA MATANDIKO; Sec. HARRINGTON SIMUI AKOMBWA; 534,126 mems.

United Church of Zambia: Synod Headquarters, Nationalist Rd at Burma Rd, POB 50122, Lusaka; tel. (1) 250641; fax (1) 252198; e-mail uczsynod@zamnet.zm; f. 1965; Synod Bishop Rev. MUTALE MULUMBWA (Interim Synod Bishop); Gen. Sec. Rev. Prof. TEDDY KALONGO; c. 3m. mems.

Other denominations active in Zambia include the Assemblies of God, the Church of Christ, the Church of the Nazarene, the Evangelical Fellowship of Zambia, the Kimbanguist Church, the Presbyterian Church of Southern Africa, the Religious Society of Friends (Quakers) and the United Pentecostal Church. At mid-2000 there were an estimated 2m. adherents professing other forms of Christianity.

The Roman Catholic Church

Zambia comprises two archdioceses and eight dioceses. At 31 December 2004 there were an estimated 3.5m. adherents in the country, equivalent to 28.4% of the total population.

Bishops' Conference

Zambia Episcopal Conference, Catholic Secretariat, Unity House, cnr Freedom Way and Katunjila Rd, POB 31965, Lusaka; tel. (1) 212070; fax (1) 220996.

f. 1984; Pres. Rt Rev. TELESPHORE GEORGE MPUNDU (Bishop of Mpika).

Archbishop of Kasama: Most Rev. JAMES SPAITA, Archbishop's House, POB 410143, Kasama; tel. (4) 221248; fax (4) 222202; e-mail archkasa@zamtel.zm.

Archbishop of Lusaka: Most Rev. MEDARDO JOSEPH MAZOMBWE, 41 Wamulwa Rd, POB 32754, 10101 Lusaka; tel. (1) 239257; fax (1) 237008.

ISLAM

There are about 10,000 members of the Muslim Association in Zambia.

BAHÁ'Í FAITH

National Spiritual Assembly: Sekou Touré Rd, Plot 4371, Private Bag RW227X, Ridgeway 15102, Lusaka; tel. and fax (1) 254505; e-mail nsa@zamnet.zm; f. 1952; Sec.-Gen. MARGARET K. LENGWE; mems resident in 1,456 localities.

The Press

DAILIES

The Post: 36 Bwinjimfumu Rd, Rhodespark, Private Bag E352, Lusaka; tel. (97) 788200; fax (1) 229271; internet www.postzambia.com; f. 1991; privately owned; Editor-in-Chief FRED M'MEMBE; circ. 29,000.

The Times of Zambia: Kabelenga Ave, POB 70069, Ndola; tel. (2) 621305; fax (2) 617096; internet www.times.co.zm; f. 1943; govt-owned; English; Deputy Editor-in-Chief DAVEY SAKALA; circ. 25,000.

Zambia Daily Mail: Zambia Publishing Company, POB 31421, Lusaka; tel. (1) 225131; fax (1) 225881; internet www.daily-mail.co.zm; f. 1968; govt-owned; English; Man. Editor EMMANUEL NYIRENDA; circ. 40,000.

PERIODICALS

African Social Research: Institute of Economic and Social Research, University of Zambia, POB 32379, Lusaka; tel. (1) 294131; fax (1) 253952; f. 1944; 2 a year; Editor MUBANGA E. KASHOKI; circ. 1,000.

The Challenge: Mission Press, Chifubu Rd, POB 71581, Ndola; tel. (2) 680456; fax (2) 680484; e-mail miha@missionpress.org; internet www.missionpress.org; f. 1999; quarterly; English; social, educational and religious; Roman Catholic; edited by Franciscan friars; circ. 9,000.

Chipembele Magazine: POB 30255, Lusaka; tel. (1) 254226; 6 a year; publ. by Wildlife Conservation Soc. of Zambia; circ. 20,000.

Chronicle: Lusaka; bi-weekly; independent.

Farming in Zambia: POB 50197, Lusaka; tel. (1) 213551; f. 1965; quarterly; publ. by Ministry of Agriculture, Food and Fisheries; Editor L. P. CHIRWA; circ. 3,000.

Imbila: POB RW20, Lusaka; tel. (1) 217254; f. 1953; monthly; publ. by Zambia Information Services; Bemba; Editor D. MUKAKA; circ. 20,000.

Intanda: POB RW20, Lusaka; tel. (1) 219675; f. 1958; monthly; publ. by Zambia Information Services; Tonga; Editor J. SIKAULU; circ. 6,000.

Journal of Adult Education: University of Zambia, POB 50516, Lusaka; tel. (1) 216767; f. 1982; Exec. Editor FRANCIS KASOMA.

Journal of Science and Technology: School of Natural Sciences, Dept of Biological Sciences, University of Zambia, POB 32379, Lusaka 10101; tel. (1) 293008; fax (1) 253952; e-mail press@admin.unza.zm; f. 1996; science and technology journal of the Univ. of Zambia; 2 a year; Editor-in-Chief Prof. J. N. ZULU (acting).

Konkola: Zambia Consolidated Copper Mines Ltd, PR Dept, POB 71505, Ndola; tel. (2) 640142; f. 1973 as *Mining Mirror*; monthly; English; Editor G. MUKUWA; circ. 30,000.

Leisure Magazine: Farmers House, Cairo Rd, POB 8138, Woodlands, Lusaka; monthly; general interest.

Liseli: POB RW20, Lusaka; tel. (1) 219675; monthly; publ. by Zambia Information Services; Lozi; Editor F. AMNSAA; circ. 8,000.

The Lowdown: Lusaka; internet www.lowdown.co.zm; f. 1995; monthly; English; Editor HEATHER CHALCRAFT.

Lukanga News: POB 919, Kabwe; tel. (5) 217254; publ. by Zambia Information Services; Lenje; Editor J. H. N. NKOMANGA; circ. 5,500.

National Mirror: Multimedia Zambia, 15701 Woodlands, POB 320199, Lusaka; tel. (1) 263864; fax (1) 263050; f. 1972; fortnightly; news, current affairs and foreign affairs; publ. by Multimedia Zambia; Editor SIMON MWANZA; circ. 40,000.

Ngoma: POB RW20, Lusaka; tel. (1) 219675; monthly; Lunda, Kaonde and Luvale; publ. by Zambia Information Services; Editor B. A. LUHILA; circ. 3,000.

Outlook: TBM Publicity Enterprises Ltd, POB 40, Kitwe; f. 1971; monthly; general interest.

Speak Out!: POB 70244, Ndola; tel. (2) 612241; fax (2) 620630; e-mail speakout@zamnet.zm; f. 1984; 6 a year; Christian; aimed at youth readership; Man. Editor CONSTANTIA TREPPE; circ. 25,000.

The Sportsman: POB 31762, Lusaka; tel. (1) 214250; f. 1980; monthly; Man. Editor SAM SIKAZWE; circ. 18,000.

Sunday Express: Lusaka; f. 1991; weekly; Man. Editor JOHN MUKELA.

Sunday Times of Zambia: Kabelenga Ave, POB 70069, Ndola; tel. (2) 614469; fax (2) 617096; e-mail times@zamtel.zm; internet www.times.co.zm/sunday; f. 1965; owned by UNIP; English; Man. Editor ARTHUR SIMUCHOBA; circ. 78,000.

Tsopano: POB RW20, Lusaka; tel. (1) 217254; f. 1958; monthly; publ. by Zambia Information Services; Nyanja; Editor S. S. BANDA; circ. 9,000.

Voters' Voice: Lusaka; monthly; independent.

Workers' Voice: POB 20652, Kitwe; tel. (2) 211999; f. 1972; fortnightly; publ. by Zambia Congress of Trade Unions.

Youth: POB 30302, Lusaka; tel. (1) 211411; f. 1974; quarterly; publ. by UNIP Youth League; Editor-in-Chief N. ANAMELA; circ. 20,000.

Zambia Government Gazette: POB 30136, Lusaka; tel. (1) 228724; fax (1) 224486; f. 1911; weekly; English; official notices.

NEWS AGENCY

Zambia News Agency (ZANA): Mass Media Complex, 2nd Floor, Alick Nkhata Rd, POB 30007, Lusaka; tel. (1) 219673; fax (1) 251631; internet www.zana.gov.zm; f. 1969; Dir LEWIS MWANANGOMBE; Editor-in-Chief VILLIE LOMBANYA; headquarters in Lusaka and nine regional offices.

Foreign Bureaux

Agence France-Presse: Plot 3814, Martin Mwamba Rd, POB 32295, Lusaka; tel. (9) 7767887; Bureau Chief DICKSON JERE.

ITAR—TASS (Information Telegraphic Agency of Russia—Telegraphic Agency of the Sovereign Countries): POB 33394, Lusaka; tel. (1) 254201; Correspondent ANDREY K. POLYAKOV.

Panapress (PANA) (Senegal): Impala House, Cha Cha Cha Rd, POB 37065, Lusaka; tel. (1) 220772; fax (1) 221897; e-mail mildred.mulenga@panapress.com; internet www.panapress.com; Dir MILDRED MULENGA.

Reuters (United Kingdom): Woodgate House, 3rd Floor, Cairo Rd, Lusaka; tel. 96843609; tel. and fax (1) 235698; e-mail shapi@reuters.com.zm; Correspondent SHAPI K. SHACINDA.

RIA—Novosti (Russia Information Agency—News): Lusaka; tel. (1) 252849; Rep. VIKTOR LAPTUKHIN.

Xinhua (New China) News Agency (People's Republic of China): United Nations Ave, POB 31859, Lusaka; tel. (1) 252227; fax (1) 251708; e-mail xinhuana@zamnet.zm; Chief Correspondent CHAI SHIKUAN.

PRESS ASSOCIATION

Press Association of Zambia (PAZA): c/o The Times of Zambia, Kabelenga Ave, POB 70069, Ndola; tel. (2) 621305; fax (2) 617096; f. 1983; Pres. ANDREW SAKALA; Chair. ROBINSON MAKAYI.

Publishers

Africa: Literature Centre, POB 21319, Kitwe; tel. (2) 210765; fax (2) 210716; general, educational, religious; Dir JACKSON MBEWE.

African Social Research: Institute of Economic and Social Research, University of Zambia, POB 32379, Lusaka; tel. (1) 294131; fax (1) 253952; social research in Africa; Editor MUBANGA E. KASHOKI.

Bookworld Ltd: Lottie House, Cairo Rd, POB 31838, Lusaka; tel. (1) 225282; fax (1) 226710; e-mail bookwld@zamtel.zm.

Daystar Publications Ltd: POB 32211, Lusaka; f. 1966; religious; Man. Dir S. E. M. PHEKO.

Directory Publishers of Zambia Ltd: Mabalenga Rd, POB 30963, Lusaka; tel. (1) 237915; fax (1) 237912; f. 1958; trade directories; Gen. Man. W. D. WRATTEN.

Multimedia Zambia: Woodlands, POB 320199, Lusaka; tel. and fax (1) 261193; f. 1971; religious and educational books, audio-visual materials; Exec. Dir EDDY MUPESO.

University of Zambia Press (UNZA Press): POB 32379, 10101 Lusaka; tel. (1) 290740; fax (1) 290409; e-mail press@admin.unza.zm; f. 1938; academic books, papers and journals.

Zambia Educational Publishing House: Chishango Rd, POB 32708, 10101 Lusaka; tel. (1) 222324; fax (1) 225073; f. 1967; educational and general; Man. Dir BENIKO E. MULOTA.

Zambia Printing Co Ltd: POB 34798, 10101 Lusaka; tel. (1) 227673; fax (1) 225026; Gen. Man. BERNARD LUBUMBASHI.

GOVERNMENT PUBLISHING HOUSES

Government Printer: POB 30136, Lusaka; tel. (1) 228724; fax (1) 224486; official documents and statistical bulletins.

Zambia Information Services: POB 50020, Lusaka; tel. (1) 219673; state-controlled; Dir BENSON SIANGA.

PUBLISHERS' ASSOCIATION

Booksellers' and Publishers' Association of Zambia: POB 31838, Lusaka; tel. (1) 222647; fax (1) 225195; Chair. RAY MUNAMWIMBU; Sec. BASIL MBEWE.

Broadcasting and Communications

TELECOMMUNICATIONS

Celtel Zambia: POB 320001, Nyerere Rd, Woodlands, Lusaka; tel. (1) 250707; e-mail customerservice@zm.celtel.com; internet www.zm.celtel.com; f. 1997 as ZamCell Ltd; acquired by Celtel Int. BV, Netherlands, in 1998; mobile cellular telephone operator; Chair. GEORGE SOKOTA; Man. Dir DAVID VENN; c. 500,000 subscribers.

MTN (Zambia) Ltd: POB 35464, Lusaka; tel. (1) 750072; fax (1) 750750; internet www.mtnzambia.co.zm; f. 1997 as Telecel (Zambia) Ltd; acquired by MTN Group, South Africa, in 2005; 152,000 subscribers (2006); mobile cellular telecommunications provider; CEO MIKE BLACKBURN.

Zambia Telecommunications Co Ltd (ZAMTEL): Provident House, POB 71660, Ndola; tel. (2) 611111; fax (2) 611399; internet www.zamtel.zm; transfer to private sector abandoned in 2005; commercialization pending; operates Cell-Z cellular network (f. 1995); Chair. BASIL SICHALI; Man. Dir SIMON TEMBO.

BROADCASTING

Zambia National Broadcasting Corpn: Mass Media Complex, Alick Nkhata Rd, POB 50015, Lusaka; tel. (1) 252005; fax (1) 254013;

internet www.znbc.co.zm; f. 1961; state-owned; two national radio stations (Radio 1 and Radio 2) and one line-of-rail station (Radio 4); television broadcasts along the line of rail, from Livingstone to Chililabombwe; services in English and seven Zambian languages; Dir-Gen. EDDY MUPESO.

Radio

Breeze FM: POB 511178, Chipata; tel. (6) 221175; e-mail breezefm@zamtel.zm; internet www.breezefm.com; f. 2003; Nyanja and English; community radio; broadcasts to the Eastern Province; Managing Dir MIKE DAKA.

Educational Broadcasting Services: Headquarters: POB 50231, Lusaka; tel. (1) 251724; radio broadcasts from Lusaka; audio-visual aids service from POB 50295, Lusaka; Controller MICHAEL MULOMBE.

Radio Maria Zambia: POB 510307, Chipata; tel. and fax (6) 221154; e-mail info.zam@radiomaria.org; internet www.radiomaria.org; f. 1999; part of The World Family of Radio Maria, Italy; Roman Catholic religious programming; broadcasts to Eastern Province; Dir MWANZA GABRIEL KWAKU.

Radio Phoenix: Private Bag E702, Lusaka; tel. (1) 223581; fax (1) 226839; e-mail rphoenix@zamnet.zm; commercial radio station; Chair. ERROL T. HICKEY.

Yatsani Radio: Leopards Hill Rd, Bauleni Catholic Church, POB 320147, Lusaka; tel. (1) 261082; fax (1) 265842; internet yatsani.com; f. 1999; owned by the Archdiocese of Lusaka; Roman Catholic religious community; broadcasts to Lusaka; Dir Most Rev. MEDARDO JOSEPH MAZOMBWE (Archbishop of Lusaka).

Television

Educational Broadcasting Services: POB 21106, Kitwe; television for schools; Controller MICHAEL MULOMBE.

Finance

(cap. = capital; auth. = authorized; res = reserves; dep. = deposits; m. = million; br(s). = branch(es); amounts in kwacha)

BANKING

From 30 June 1996 all banks operating in Zambia were required to have capital of not less than K2,000m. in order to receive a banking licence or to continue to function.

Central Bank

Bank of Zambia: Bank Sq., Cairo Rd, POB 30080, 10101 Lusaka; tel. (1) 228888; fax (1) 221722; internet www.boz.zm; f. 1964; bank of issue; cap. 10m., res 31,675m., dep. 2,459,106m. (Dec. 2002); Gov. and Chair. Dr CALEB FUNDANGA; br. in Ndola.

Commercial Banks

Finance Bank Zambia Ltd: 2101 Chanik House, Cairo Rd, POB 37102, 10101 Lusaka; tel. (1) 229733; fax (1) 227290; e-mail fbz@financebank.co.zm; internet www.financebank.co.zm; f. 1987; cap. and res 92,636m., dep. 390,086m. (Dec. 2002); Chair. Dr R. L. MAHTANI; Man. Dir DICK KING; 32 brs and 9 agencies.

National Savings and Credit Bank of Zambia: Plot 248B, Cairo Rd, POB 30067, Lusaka; tel. (1) 227534; fax (1) 223296; e-mail natsave@zamnet.zm; internet www.webnet.co.zm/nscb.htm; f. 1972; total assets 6,598m. (Dec. 1998); Man. Dir REGINALD MFULA.

New Capital Bank PLC: Anchor House, Mezzanine Floor, Sapele Rd, POB 36452, Lusaka; tel. (1) 229508; fax (1) 224055; f. 1992; cap. and res 4,510m., total assets 18,538m. (Dec. 2001); Chair. WILA D. MUNG'OMBA; CEO and Gen. Man. GODFREY P. MSISKA.

Union Bank Zambia Ltd: Zimco House, Cairo Rd, POB 34940, Lusaka; tel. (1) 229392; fax (1) 221866; cap. and res 3,775m., total assets 35,506m. (Dec. 1998); Chair. J. R. NAYEE; Man. Dir L. CHONGO.

Zambia National Commercial Bank PLC (ZNCB): POB 33611, Lusaka; tel. (1) 228979; fax (1) 223106; e-mail support@zanaco.co.zm; internet www.zanaco.co.zm; f. 1969; partial privatization agreed in 2005: 25% to remain govt-owned; 25.8% to be sold to Zambian citizens through the Zambian Privatisation Trust Fund; cap. and res 63,370m., total assets 584,667m. (Dec. 2000); Chair. MBIKUSITA W. LEWANIKA; Man. Dir LIKOLO NDALAMEI; 43 brs.

Foreign Banks

Bank of China (Zambia) Ltd (China): Amandra House, Ben Bella Rd, POB 34550, Lusaka; tel. (1) 238711; fax (1) 235350; e-mail boc@zamnet.zm; cap. and res 5,731m., total assets 73,237m. (Dec. 2001); Chair. PING YUE; Gen. Man. HONG XINSHENG.

Barclays Bank of Zambia PLC (United Kingdom): Kafue House, Cairo Rd, POB 31936, Lusaka; tel. (1) 228858; fax (1) 222519; e-mail barclays.zambia@barclays.com; internet www.africa.barclays.com; f. 1971; cap. and res 114,618m., total assets 809,515m. (Dec. 2001); Chair. A. BRUCE MUNYAMA; Man. Dir MARGARET MWANAKATWE; 5 brs.

Citibank Zambia Ltd (USA): Citibank House, Cha Cha Cha Rd, POB 30037, Southend, Lusaka; tel. (1) 229025; fax (1) 226264; f. 1979; cap. 521.2m., dep. 237,176m. (Dec. 2001); Man. Dir SURINIVASAN SRIDHAR; 1 br.

Indo-Zambia Bank (IZB): Plot 6907, Cairo Rd, POB 35411, Lusaka; tel. (1) 224653; fax (1) 225090; e-mail izb@zamnet.zm; internet www.izb.co.zm; f. 1984; cap. and res 34,312m., dep. 200,770m. (March 2002); Chair. ORLENE Y. MOYO; Man. Dir CYRIL PATRO; 7 brs.

Stanbic Bank Zambia Ltd: Woodgate House, 6th Floor, Nairobi Place, Cairo Rd, POB 31955, Lusaka; tel. (1) 229071; fax (1) 221152; internet www.stanbic.co.zm; f. 1971; wholly owned by Standard Bank Investment Corpn; cap. and res 55,064m., total assets 425,746m. (Dec. 2001); Chair. D. A. R. PHIRI; Man. Dir A. H. S. MACLEOD; 7 brs.

Standard Chartered Bank Zambia Ltd (United Kingdom): Standard House, Cairo Rd, POB 32238, Lusaka; tel. (1) 229242; fax (1) 222092; f. 1971; cap. 2,048m., res 75,575m., dep. 450,784m. (Dec. 2001); Chair. A. K. MAZOKA; Man. Dir J. A. H. JANES; 14 brs.

Development Banks

Development Bank of Zambia: Development House, Katondo St, POB 33955, Lusaka; tel. (1) 228576; fax (1) 222426; internet www.dbz.co.zm; f. 1973; 99% state-owned; provides medium- and long-term loans and administers special funds placed at its disposal; cap. and res 7,580.0m., total assets 145,976.6m. (March 1998); Chair. J. M. MTONGA; Man. Dir DIPAK MALIK; 2 brs.

Lima Bank: Kulima House, Cha Cha Cha Rd, POB 32607, Lusaka; tel. (1) 213111; fax (1) 228077; cap. 57m. (March 1986); Chair. N. MUKUTU; Man. Dir K. V. KASAPATU.

Zambia Agricultural Development Bank: Society House, Cairo Rd, POB 30847, Lusaka; tel. (1) 219251; f. 1982; loan finance for devt of agriculture and fishing; auth. cap. 75m.; Chair. K. MAKASA; Man. Dir AMON CHIBIYA.

Zambia Export and Import Bank Ltd: Society House, Cairo Rd, POB 33046, Lusaka; tel. (1) 229486; fax (1) 222313; f. 1987; cap. 50m. (March 1992), dep. 50.9m. (March 1990); Man. Dir LIKANDO NAWA.

STOCK EXCHANGE

Lusaka Stock Exchange (LuSE): Farmers House, 3rd Floor, Cairo Rd, POB 34523, Lusaka; tel. (1) 228537; fax (1) 225969; e-mail info@luse.co.zm; internet www.luse.co.zm; f. 1994; Chair. JOHN JANES; Gen. Man. JOSEPH CHIKOLWA.

INSURANCE

African Life Assurance Zambia: Mukuba Pension House, 4th Floor, Dedan Kimathi Rd, POB 31991; tel. (1) 225452; fax (1) 225435; e-mail customercare@african-life.com.zm; f. 2002; life insuarnce; CEO STEVE WILLIAMS.

Cavmont Capital Insurance Corpn Ltd: Farmers House, 3rd Floor, POB 38474, Lusaka; tel. (1) 228929; e-mail info@cavmont.com.zm; f. 2003; subsidiary of Cavmont Capital Holdings Ltd; Man. Dir MOSES MALUNGA.

Goldman Insurance Ltd: Zambia National Savings and Credit Bank Bldg, 2nd Floor, Cairo Rd, Private Bag W395, Lusaka; tel. (1) 235234; fax (1) 227262; f. 1992; Chair. BWALYA CHITI.

Madison Insurance Co Ltd: Plot 255, Kaleya Rd, Roma, POB 37013, Lusaka; tel. (1) 295311; fax (1) 295320; internet www.madisonzambia.com; f. 1992; general and micro-insurance; Chair. DAVID A. R. PHIRI; Man. Dir LAWRENCE S. SIKUTWA.

NICO Insurance Zambia Ltd (NIZA): 1131 Parirenyatwa Rd, Fairview, POB 32825, Lusaka; tel. (1) 222862; fax (1) 222863; e-mail nicozam@zamnet.zm; internet www.nicomw.com/zambia; f. 1997; subsidiary of NICO Group, Malawi; general insurance; Chair. JOHN MWANAKATWE; Gen. Man. TITUS KALENGA.

Professional Insurance Corpn Zambia Ltd (PICZ): Professional Insurance House, Heroes Pl., POB 34264, Lusaka; tel. (1) 227509; fax (1) 222151; e-mail ho@picz.co.zm; internet www.picz.co.zm; f. 1992; Exec. Dir GEORGE SILUTONGWE; Man. Dir ASHOK CHAWLA.

Zambia State Insurance Corpn Ltd: Premium House, Independence Ave, POB 30894, Lusaka; tel. (1) 229343; fax (1) 222263; e-mail zsic@zsic.co.zm; internet www.zsic.co.zm; f. 1968; sole authorized insurance provider in Zambia 1971–92; transfer to private sector pending; Chair. ALBERT WOOD; Man. Dir IRENE MUYENGA.

ZIGI Insurance Co Ltd: Mukuba Pension House, 5th Floor, POB37782, Lusaka; tel. (1) 226835; fax (1) 231564; e-mail zigi@zamnet.zm; f. 1998; Chair. and CEO SAVIOUR H. KONIE.

Trade and Industry

In 2006 the National Assembly was considering the Zambia Development Agency Bill, which proposed merging into one body the Export Board of Zambia, the Export Processing Zones Authority, the Small Enterprises Development Board, the Zambia Investment Centre and the Zambia Privatisation Agency.

GOVERNMENT AGENCIES

Export Board of Zambia (EBZ): Woodgate House, 5th Floor, Cairo Rd, Heroes Pl., POB 30064, Lusaka; tel. (1) 228106; fax (1) 222509; e-mail ebz@ebz.co.zm; internet www.ebz.co.zm; f. 1985; develops and promotes non-traditional exports.

Export Processing Zones Authority (EPZA): Plot No. 18939, cnr Great East and Katima Mulilo Rds, POB 337110, Lusaka; tel. (1) 212403; fax (1) 212406; e-mail zepza@uudial.zm; f. 2002; Chair. LOVEMORE CHIHOTA.

Small Enterprises Development Board (SEDB): SEDB House, Cairo Rd (South End), POB 35373, Lusaka; tel. and fax (1) 222176; f. 1981 as the Small Industries Devt Org.; to promote devt of small and village industries.

Zambia Investment Centre: Los Angeles Blvd, POB 34580, 10101 Lusaka; tel. (1) 255240; fax (1) 252150; e-mail invest@zamnet.zm; internet www.zic.org.zm; f. 1991; Dir-Gen. JACOB LUSHINGA.

Zambia Privatisation Agency: Privatisation House, Nasser Rd, POB 30819, Lusaka; tel. (1) 223859; fax (1) 225270; e-mail zpa@zpa.org.zm; internet www.zpa.org.zm; f. 1992; responsible for the divestment of various state-owned enterprises; 262 cos privatized by mid-2006, 22 privatizations pending; Chair. LUKE MBEWE; CEO ANDREW CHIPWENDE.

DEVELOPMENT ORGANIZATIONS

Industrial Development Corpn of Zambia Ltd (INDECO): Indeco House, Buteko Place, POB 31935, Lusaka; tel. (1) 228026; fax (1) 228868; f. 1960; auth. cap. K300m.; taken over by the Nat. Housing Authority in May 2005; Chair. R. L. BWALYA; Man. Dir S. K. TAMELÉ.

Mpongwe Development Company: Block 4450, Mpongwe, POB 90599, Luanshya; tel. (2) 510584; fax (2) 511713; promotes the production of crops for domestic and regional markets; CEO HENK MARMELSTEIN.

CHAMBERS OF COMMERCE

Zambia Association of Chambers of Commerce and Industry: Great East Rd, Showgrounds, POB 30844, Lusaka; tel. (1) 252483; fax (1) 253020; e-mail secretariat@zacci.co.zm; internet www.zacci.org.zm; f. 1938; Chair. WAMULUME KALABO; 10 district chambers.

Member chambers and associations include:

Chamber of Mines of Zambia: POB 22100, Kitwe; tel. (2) 214122; f. 1941 as Northern Rhodesia Chamber of Mines; replaced by the Copper Industry Service Bureau 1965–2000; represents mining employers; 19 mems.

Zambia Association of Manufacturers: POB 30036, Lusaka; tel. (1) 242780; fax (1) 222912; e-mail babbar@zamnet.zm; f. 1985; Chair. D. BABBAR; 180 mems.

Chamber of Small and Medium Business Associations.

INDUSTRIAL AND TRADE ASSOCIATIONS

Tobacco Board of Zambia (TBZ): POB 31963, Lusaka; tel. (1) 288995; fax (1) 287118; e-mail tbz@zamnet.zm; promotes, monitors and controls tobacco production; Sec. JONATHAN M. CHIZUNI.

Zambia Farm Employers' Association (ZFEA): Farmers' Village, Lusaka Agricultural and Commercial Showgrounds, POB 30395, Lusaka; tel. (1) 252649; fax (1) 252648; e-mail znfu@zamnet.zm; Chair. R. DENLY; 350 mems.

Other associations include: the Bankers Asscn of Zambia; the Cotton Asscn of Zambia; the Environmental Conservation Asscn of Zambia; the Insurance Brokers Asscn of Zambia; the Kapenta Fishermen Asscn; the National Aquaculture Asscn of Zambia; the National Council for Construction; the Poultry Asscn of Zambia; Tobacco Asscn of Zambia; the Wildlife Producers Asscn of Zambia; the Young Farmers Clubs of Zambia; the Zambia Asscn of Clearing and Forwarding; the Zambia Asscn of Manufacturers; the Zambia Coffee Growers Asscn; the Zambia Export Growers Asscn; and the Zambian Women in Agriculture.

UTILITIES

Electricity

Zambia Electricity Supply Corpn (Zesco): Stand 6949, Great East Rd, POB 33304, Lusaka; tel. (1) 226084; fax (1) 222753; internet www.zesco.co.zm; e-mail mchisela@zesco.co.zm; f. 1970; privatization under way in 2006; Man. Dir RHODNIE P. SISALA.

MAJOR COMPANIES

The following are among the largest companies in terms either of capital investment or employment. The Government traditionally has a controlling interest in major strategic industries, but it instituted a privatization programme in 1992.

BP Zambia PLC: Mukuba Pension House, Dedani Kamathi Rd, POB 31999, Lusaka; tel. (1) 228684; fax (1) 223645; f. 1963; privatized in 1996; 75% owned by BP Africa; retail and distribution of petroleum products; Man. Dir D. MOROKA; c. 380 employees.

British American Tobacco (Zambia) PLC: POB 30622; tel. (1) 248082; fax (1) 241602; e-mail keith_gretton@bat.com; revenue K67,231m. (2005).

Chilanga Cement PLC: Kafue Rd, POB 32639, Lusaka; tel. (1) 279029; fax (1) 278134; e-mail chilanga.cement@lafarge.com; f. 1949; privatized in 1994; subsidiary of Lafarge Cement; cement plants at Chilanga and Ndola; manufacture and marketing of cement; Chair. M. HANTUBA; 445 employees.

Kafue Textiles (Z) Ltd (KTZ): POB 360131, Kafue; tel. (1) 311501; fax (1) 311514; f. 1969; subsidiary of MB Int. Ltd; privatized March 2005; mfrs of drills, denims, twills and poplins; dress prints and African prints; industrial and household textiles; Chair. S. C. KOPULANDE; Gen. Man. and CEO J. P. BONDAZ; c. 400 employees.

Konkola Copper Mines PLC (KCM): Stand M/1408, Fern Ave, Private Bag KCM (C) 2000, Chingola; tel. (2) 350000; e-mail samuel.equamo@kcm.co.zm; internet www.kcm.co.zm; f. 2000; 51% owned by Vedanta Resources, India; 28.4% by Zambia Copper Investments Ltd; and 20.6% by ZCCM Investment Holdings PLC; acquired ZCCM mining operations in 2000; mines at Chingola (Nchanga), Chililabombwe (Konkola) and Nampundwe; smelter and refinery at Kitwe; produces around one-half of national copper output; Chair. N. AGARWAL; CEO K. K. KAURA; 10,500 permanent employees and 2,600 contract employees.

ZCCM—Investment Holdings PLC (ZCCM-IH): Mukuba Pension House, 1st Floor, Plot 5309, Dedan Kimathi Rd, POB 30048, Lusaka 10101; tel. (1) 221023; fax (1) 221957; e-mail corporate@zccm-ih.com.zm; f. 1982 pursuant to privatization of Consolidated Copper Mines and Roan Consolidated Mines Ltd; 87.6% govt owned; Chair. ALFRED J. LUNGU.

Metal Fabricators of Zambia Ltd (ZAMEFA): Cha Cha Cha Rd, POB 90295, Luanshya; tel. (2) 510453; fax (2) 512637; e-mail jzulu@zamefa.co.zm; f. 1967; privatized in 1996; 82% owned by Phelps Dodge Int. Corpn, USA; 18% by Zambia Privatisation Trust Fund; mfrs of copper rods, and copper and aluminium wire and cables; CEO J. REVUELTA; c. 800 employees.

Minestone (Zambia) Ltd: POB 31870, Lusaka; tel. (1) 228748; fax (1) 222301; f. 1954; cap. K1.9m.; building, civil and mechanical contractors; Gen. Man. MARK CHISANGA (acting); 3,900 employees.

Mopani Copper Mines PLC (MCM): Central Ave, Kitwe; tel. (2) 247000; f. 1932; privatized in 2000; 73% owned by Glencore Int. AG, Switzerland; 16.9% by First Quantum Minerals Ltd, Canada; 10% by ZCCM-IH; copper mine, smelter and refinery at Mufuklira; copper mine and cobalt plant at Nkana; annual production: 160,000 tons of copper ore, 2,000 tons of cobalt (2004); CEO TIM HENDERSON; 9,600 permanent employees and 6,400 contractors.

National Milling Co Ltd (NMC): POB 31980, Lusaka; tel. (1) 248045; fax (1) 242022; e-mail seaboard@seaboardcorp.com; privatized in 1996; acquired by Seaboard Corpn, USA, in 1998; mfrs of maize flour and stockfeeds; Man. Dir COTAN; five maize mills.

Nitrogen Chemicals of Zambia Ltd (NCZ): POB 360226, Kafue; tel. (1) 312279; fax (1) 321706; f. 1967; privatization pending; production of ammonium nitrate for fertilizer and explosives, nitric acid, ammonium sulphate, sulphuric acid, methanol, compound fertilizers and liquid carbon dioxide; revenue K27,004m. (2004); Chair. LUKE MBEWE; CEO MAYBIN M. MWINGA; 676 employees.

Parmalat Zambia: POB 34930, Lusaka; tel. (1) 286855; fax (1) 289388; f. 1964 as Dairy Produce Board of Zambia; bought by Bonnita, South Africa, in 1996; acquired by Parmalat Int., Italy, in 1998; producers of milk and mfrs of dairy products and fruit juices; Man. Dir PIET THERON.

Shoprite Zambia: Cairo Rd, (old NHS Bldg), POB 37226, Lusaka; tel. (1) 221706; fax (1) 235437; f. 1995; wholly owned subsidiary of Shoprite Group, South Africa; supermarket retail and distribution; revenue K276,000,000m. (2002); 1,698 employees (2003).

Zambeef Products PLC: Plot 1164, House No. 1, Nkanchibaya Rd off Addis Ababa Dr., Rhodes Park, Private Bag 17, Woodlands, Lusaka; tel. (1) 252476; fax (1) 252496; e-mail info@zambeef.co.zm; internet www.zambeef.com; interests in arable and livestock farming and processing, feedlotting, and retail; group comprises Zamleather Ltd and Zambeef Retailing Ltd subsidiaries; revenue

US $43m. (2005); Chair. JACOB MWANZA, FRANCIS GROGAN; Jt Man. Dirs CARL IRWIN, FRANCIS GROGAN; 1,531 employees.

Zambezi Sawmills (2005) Ltd: Livingstone; tel. and fax (3) 322853; f. 1911; nationalized in 1968 as Zambezi Sawmills (1968) Ltd; privatized in 1991; production ceased in 1996; went into liquidation in 2001; revived in 2005; Exec. Chair. SIKOTA WINA.

Zambia Sugar PLC: POB 670240, Mazabuka; tel. (3) 230666; fax (3) 230116; e-mail administrator@zamsugar.zm; privatized 1995; 89.7% of Illovo Sugar Ltd, South Africa; accounts for 45% of domestic market; exports 10% of production to the EU; revenue K486,083m. (2005); Chair. G. J. CLARK; Man. Dir J. M. MOULT.

Zambia Breweries PLC: POB 31293, Mungwi Rd, Lusaka; f. 1951; opened in Lusaka 1966; privatized 1994; subsidiary of SABMiller Africa BV, Netherlands; revenue K107,512m. (2006); brewing, bottling and distribution of beers and soft drinks; Chair. V. CHITALU; Man. Dir W. TIEDT; 1,300 employees.

CO-OPERATIVES

Zambia Co-operative Federation Ltd: Co-operative House, Cha Cha Cha Rd, POB 33579, Lusaka; tel. (1) 220157; fax (1) 222516; agricultural marketing; supply of agricultural chemicals and implements; cargo haulage; insurance; agricultural credit; auditing and accounting; property and co-operative devt; Chair. B. TETAMASHIMBA; Man. Dir G. Z. SIBALE.

TRADE UNIONS

Zambia Congress of Trade Unions (ZCTU): Solidarity House, Oxford Rd, POB 20652, Kitwe; tel. (2) 211999; fax (2) 228284; e-mail zctu@microlink.zm; f. 1965; Pres. LEONARD HIKAUMBA; Sec.-Gen. SYLVESTER TEMBO; c. 400,000 mems.

Affiliated Unions

Airways and Allied Workers' Union of Zambia: Lusaka International Airport, 2nd Floor, Terminal Bldg, POB 30175, 10101 Lusaka; affiliated to the Int. Transport Workers' Fed.; Pres. F. MULENGA; Gen. Sec. B. CHINYANTA.

Civil Servants' Union of Zambia (CSAWUZ): Plot 5045A, Mumbwa Rd, POB 50160, Lusaka; tel. and fax (1) 287106; e-mail csuz@zamnet.zm; f. 1975; Chair. L. C. HIKAUMBA; Gen. Sec. DARISON CHAALA; 35,000 mems.

Guards Union of Zambia (GUZ): POB 21882, Kitwe; tel. (2) 216189; e-mail uni-africa@union-network.org; f. 1972; affiliated to the Union Network Int.; Chair. D. N. S. SILUNGWE; Gen. Sec. MICHAEL S. SIMFUKWE; 13,500 mems.

Hotel Catering Workers' Union of Zambia: POB 35693, Lusaka; affiliated to the Int. Union of Food, Agricultural, Hotel, Restaurant, Catering, Tobacco and Allied Workers' Asscns; Chair. IAN MKANDAWIRE; Gen. Sec. STOIC KAPUTU; 9,000 mems.

Mineworkers' Union of Zambia (MUZ): POB 20448, Kitwe; tel. (2) 214022; affiliated to the Int. Fed. of Chemical, Energy, Mine and Gen. Workers' Unions; Pres. ANDREW MWANZA; Sec.-Gen. OSWELL MUNYENYEMBE; 50,000 mems.

National Union of Building, Engineering and General Workers (NUBEGW): City Sq., Millers Bldg, Plot No. 1094, POB 21515, Kitwe; tel. (2) 224468; fax (2) 661119; e-mail nubegw@zamtel.zm; affiliated to the Building and Wood Workers Int. and the Int. Metalworkers' Fed.; Chair. LUCIANO MUTALE (acting); Gen. Sec. P. N. NZIMA; 18,000 mems.

National Union of Commercial and Industrial Workers (NUCIW): 17 Obote Ave, POB 21735, Kitwe; tel. (2) 228607; fax (2) 225211; e-mail nuciw@zamtel.zm; f. 1982; affiliated to the Int. Fed. of Chemical, Energy, Mine and Gen. Workers' Unions, the Int. Textile, Garment and Leather Workers' Fed., the Int. Union of Food, Agricultural, Hotel, Restaurant, Catering, Tobacco and Allied Workers' Asscns and the Union Network Int.; Chair. I. M. KASUMBU; Gen. Sec. JOHN M. BWALYA; 16,000 mems.

National Union of Communication Workers: POB 70751, Ndola; tel. (2) 611345; fax (2) 614679; e-mail nucw@zamtel.zm; affiliated to the Union Network Int.; Pres. PATRICK KAONGA; Gen. Sec. CHELLA WELLINGTON; 5,000 mems.

National Union of Plantation and Agricultural Workers: POB 80529, Kabwe; tel. (5) 224548; affiliated to the Int. Union of Food, Agricultural, Hotel, Restaurant, Catering, Tobacco and Allied Workers' Asscns; Pres. MUDENDA RISHER; Gen. Sec. MAILONI KABULAYI; 15,155 mems.

National Union of Public Services' Workers (NUPSW): POB 32523, Lusaka; tel. (1) 227451; fax (1) 287105; e-mail znslib@zamtel.zm; affiliated to the Public Services Int.; Gen. Sec. DAVIS J. CHINGONI.

National Union of Transport and Allied Workers (NUTAW): Chachacha House, Rm 4, 1st Floor, POB 30068, Cario Rd, Lusaka; tel. (1) 214756; e-mail sapphiri2005@yahoo.com; Pres. PATRICK C. CHANDA; Gen. Sec. SAM A. P. PHIRI.

Railway Workers' Union of Zambia: POB 80302, Kabwe; tel. (5) 224006; affiliated to the Int. Transport Workers' Fed.; Chair. H. K. NDAMANA; Gen. Sec. BENSON L. NGULA; 10,228 mems.

University of Zambia and Allied Workers' Union: POB 32379, Lusaka; tel. (1) 213221; f. 1968; Chair. BERIATE SUNKUTU; Gen. Sec. SAINI PHIRI.

Zambia Electricity Workers' Union: POB 70859, Ndola; f. 1972; Chair. COSMAS MPAMPI; Gen. Sec. ADAM KALUBA; 3,000 mems.

Zambia National Farmers' Union: ZNFU Head Office, Tiyende Pamodzi Rd, opposite Polo Grounds, Farmers' Village, Zambia Agricultural and Commercial Showgrounds, POB 30395, Lusaka; tel. (1) 252649; fax (1) 252648; e-mail znfu@zamnet.zm; internet www.znfu.org.zm; Exec. Dir SONGOWAYO ZYAMBO.

Zambia National Union of Teachers: POB 31914, Lusaka; tel. (1) 214623; fax (1) 214624; e-mail znut@microlink.zm; affiliated to Education Int.; Chair. RICHARD M. LIYWALII; Gen. Sec. ROY MWABA; 2,120 mems.

Zambia Graphical and Allied Workers' Union (ZATAWU): c/o UNI-Africa, POB 71760, Ndola; tel. (2) 612889; fax (2) 613054; e-mail zatawu@yahoo.com; affiliated to the Union Network Int.; Gen. Sec. DAVID S. MWABA.

Zambia Union of Journalists: POB 70956, Ndola; tel. (2) 613290; fax (2) 614229; Gen. Sec. OFFERING KAJIMALWENDO.

Zambia Union of Local Government Officers: f. 1997; Pres. ISAAC MWANZA.

Zambia Union of Skilled Mineworkers: f. 1998; Chair. ALEX MOLOI.

Zambia United Local Authorities Workers' Union (ZULAWU): Mugala House, POB 70575, Ndola; tel. (2) 615022; affiliated to the Public Services Int.; Chair. ABRAHAM M. MUTAKILA; Gen. Sec. AMON DAKA (acting).

Principal Non-Affiliated Union

Zambian African Mining Union: Kitwe; f. 1967; 40,000 mems.

Transport

RAILWAYS

Total length of railways in Zambia was 2,162 km (including 891 km of the Tanzania–Zambia railway) in 2000. There are two major railway networks: the Zambia Railways network, which traverses the country from the Copperbelt in northern Zambia and links with the National Railways of Zimbabwe to provide access to South African ports, and the Tanzania–Zambia Railway (Tazara) network, linking New Kapiri-Mposhi in Zambia with Dar es Salaam in Tanzania. The Tazara railway line increased its capacity from 1976, in order to reduce the dependence of southern African countries on trade routes through South Africa. A 10-year rehabilitation programme, assisted by the USA and EC (now EU) countries, began in 1985. In April 1987 the Governments of Zambia, Angola and Zaire (now the Democratic Republic of the Congo) declared their intention to reopen the Benguela railway, linking Zambian copper mines with the Angolan port of Lobito, following its closure to international traffic in 1975 as a result of the guerrilla insurgency in Angola. In 1997 a programme of repairs was begun, and plans were announced in June 2002 to rebuild the Benguela railway. It was announced in 2003 that a line would be built linking the Zambian port of Mpulungu to the Tazara network. In April 2005 Northwest Railways undertook to develop a new line between Chingola, in the Copperbelt Province, and Lumwana, in the North-Western Province. It was anticipated that the line could eventually be linked to the Benguela railway.

Tanzania–Zambia Railway Authority (Tazara): POB T01, Mpika; Head Office: POB 2834, Dar es Salaam, Tanzania; tel. (4) 370684; fax (4) 370228; f. 1975; operates passenger and freight services linking New Kapiri-Mposhi, north of Lusaka, with Dar es Salaam in Tanzania, a distance of 1,860 km, of which 891 km is in Zambia; jtly owned and administered by the Govts of Tanzania and Zambia; Chair. SALIM H. MSOMA; Man. Dir CLEMENT MWIYA.

Zambia Railways Ltd: cnr Buntungwa St and Ghana Ave, POB 80935, Kabwe; tel. (5) 222201; fax (5) 224411; f. 1967; management assumed in 1998 by consortium of Hifab Int. AB, Sweden, and DE Consult, Germany; concession of assets and operations to consortium of New Limpopo Bridge Project Investments Ltd and Spoornet, South Africa, agreed in early 2003; Chair. B. NONDE; Man. Dir GÖRAN MALMBERG.

ROADS

In 2001 there was a total road network of 91,440 km, including 4,222 km of main roads and 8,948 km of secondary roads. The main arterial roads run from Beitbridge (Zimbabwe) to Tunduma (the Great North Road), through the copper-mining area to Chingola and

Chililabombwe (hitherto the Zaire Border Road), from Livingstone to the junction of the Kafue river and the Great North Road, and from Lusaka to the Malawi border (the Great East Road). In 1984 the 300-km BotZam highway linking Kazungula with Nata, in Botswana, was formally opened. A 1,930-km main road (the TanZam highway) links Zambia and Tanzania. In 1998 the Government initiated a 10-year Road Sector Investment Programme with funding from the World Bank, and in its second phase the European Union.

Road Development Agency: POB 50003, Lusaka; tel. (1) 253088; fax (1) 253404; e-mail rda_hq@roads.gov.zm; internet www.roads.gov.zm; fmrly Dept of Roads; Dir of Roads W. Ng'ambi.

CIVIL AVIATION

In 1984 there were 127 airports, aerodromes and air strips. An international airport, 22.5 km from Lusaka, was opened in 1967.

National Airports Corpn Ltd (NACL): Lusaka International Airport, POB 30175, Lusaka; tel. (1) 271281; fax (1) 224777; e-mail naclmd@zamnet.zm; f. 1973; air cargo services; Man. Dir Chileshe M. Kapwepwe.

Zambia Skyways (Eastern Air): Plot 6, Addis Ababa Rd, POB 32661, Lusaka; tel. (1) 250987; fax (1) 250767; e-mail zskyways@yahoo.com; internet www.zambiatourism.com/zambiaskyways/index.htm; f. 1995; operates scheduled passenger services to domestic destinations and South Africa; Man. Dir Yoosuf Zumla.

Zambian Airways: Lusaka International Airport, POB 310277, Lusaka; tel. (1) 271230; fax (1) 271054; e-mail roanhq@zamnet.zm; internet www.zambiaairways.co.zm; f. 1988 as Roan Air; present name adopted in 1999; operates domestic and regional routes; CEO Donald MacDonald.

Tourism

Zambia's main tourist attractions, in addition to the Victoria Falls, are its wildlife, unspoilt scenery and diverse cultural heritage; there are 19 national parks and 36 game management areas. In 2005 668,862 tourists visited Zambia, up from 515,000 in the previous year; tourism receipts increased from US $149m. in 2003 to $161m. in 2004.

Tourism Council of Zambia: Holiday Inn Cottage, Church Rd, Lusaka; tel. (1) 252859; fax (1) 255337; e-mail tcz@zamnet.zm; internet www.zambiatourism.com/travel/localnews/tcz.htm; Chair. Bruce Chapman.

Zambia National Tourist Board: Century House, Lusaka Sq., POB 30017, Lusaka; tel. (1) 229087; fax (1) 225174; e-mail zntb@zambiatourism.org.zm; internet www.zambiatourism.com; Chair. Errol Hickey; Man. Dir Chanda Charity Lumpa.

Defence

As assessed at November 2006, Zambia's armed forces officially numbered about 15,100 (army 13,500, airforce 1,600). Paramilitary forces numbered 1,400. Military service is voluntary. There is also a national defence force, responsible to the Government. In 2005 some 456 Zambian troops were stationed abroad, attached to UN missions in Africa and Europe; of these 103 were serving as observers.

Defence Expenditure: Estimated at K884,000m. for 2006.

Commander of the Army: Lt-Gen. Isaac Soda Arizona Chisuzi.

Commander of the Air Force: Lt-Gen. Christopher Singogo.

Education

Between 1964 and 1979 enrolment in schools increased by more than 260%. Primary education, which is compulsory, begins at seven years of age and lasts for seven years. Secondary education, beginning at the age of 14, lasts for a further five years, comprising a first cycle of two years and a second of three years. According to UNESCO estimates, in 2003/04 80% of children (80% of boys; 80% of girls) in the relevant age-group attended primary schools, while enrolment at secondary schools included 24% of children (27% of boys; 21% of girls) in the relevant age-group. There are two universities: the University of Zambia at Lusaka, and the Copperbelt University at Kitwe (which is to be transferred to Ndola). There are 14 teacher training colleges. In 2005 expenditure on education was K1,062.0m. The 2006 budgetary allocation for 2006 was K1,647.0m., some 26.9% of the overall budget. The Government recruited an additional 8,000 teachers in 2005 and planned to recruit a further 4,500 in 2006.

Bibliography

Akashambatwa, M. *Milk in a Basket: The Political-Economic Malaise in Zambia*. Lusaka, Zambia Research Foundation, 1990.

Andersson, P., Bigsten, A., and Persson, H. *Foreign Aid, Debt and Growth in Zambia*. Uppsala, Nordiska Africainstitutet, 2001.

Bonnick, G. G. *Zambia Country Assistance Review: Turning an Economy Around*. Washington, DC, World Bank, 1997.

Carmody, B. P. *The Evolution of Education in Zambia*. Lusaka, Bookworld Publrs, 2004.

Chan, S. *Zambia and the Decline of Kaunda 1984–1998*. Lewiston, NY, Edward Mellen Press, 2000.

Crehan, K. *The Fractured Community: Landscapes of Power and Gender in Rural Zambia*. Berkeley, CA, University of California Press, 1997.

Ferguson, J. *Expectations of Modernity*. Berkeley, CA, University of California Press, 1999.

Grotpeter, J. J., Siegel, B. V., and Pletcher, J. R. *Historical Dictionary of Zambia*. Lanham, MD, Scarecrow Press, 1998.

Hamalengwa, M. *Class Struggle in Zambia, 1884–1989, and the Fall of Kenneth Kaunda, 1990–1991*. Lanham, MD, University Press of America, 1992.

Hill, C. B., and McPherson, M. F. *Promoting and Sustaining Economic Reform in Zambia*. Cambridge, MA, Harvard University Press, 2003.

Ihonvbere, J. O. *Economic Crisis, Civil Society and Democratization: The Case of Zambia*. Trenton, NJ, Africa World Press, 1996.

Larmer, M. *Mineworkers in Zambia: Labour and Political Change in Post-colonial Africa*. London, Tauris Academic Studies, 2006.

Macmillan, H., and Shapiro, F. *Zion in Africa—The Jews of Zambia*. London and New York, NY, I. B. Tauris, 1999.

Makungu, K. *The State of the Media in Zambia: From the Colonial Era to December 2003*. Lusaka, Media Institute of Southern Africa, Zambian Chapter, 2004.

Mutale, E. *The Management of Urban Development in Zambia*. Aldershot, Ashgate, 2004.

Meebelo, H. S. *Reaction to Colonialism: A Prelude to the Politics of Independence in Northern Zambia, 1839–1939*. International Academic Publrs, 2001.

Moore, H., and Vaughan, M. *Cutting Down Trees: Gender, Nutrition and Agricultural Change in Northern Province, Zambia, 1890–1990*. Zambia, University of Zambia Press, 1994.

Moore, R. C. *The Political Reality of Freedom of the Press in Zambia*. Lanham, MD, University Press of America, 1992.

Mwanakatwe, J. M. *End of Kaunda Era*. Lusaka, Multimedia, 1994.

Mwanza, A. M. (Ed.). *The Structural Adjustment Programme in Zambia: Lessons from Experience*. Harare, SAPES Books, 1992.

Rakner, L. *Trade Unions in Processes of Democratisation: A Study of Party Labour Relations in Zambia*. Bergen, Michelsen Institute, 1992.

Saasa, O., and Carlsson, J. *The Aid Relationship in Zambia: A Conflict Scenario*. Uppsala, Nordiska Afrikainstitutet, 1996.

Saasa, O., Wilson, F., and Chingambo, L. *The Zambian Economy in Post-Apartheid Southern Africa: A Critical Analysis of Policy Options*. Lusaka, IAS Consultancy Services, 1992.

Sichone, O., and Chikulo, B. *Democracy in Zambia*. Aldershot, Avebury, 1997.

Van Binsbergen, W. *Tears of Rain: Ethnicity and History in Central Western Zambia*. London, Kegan Paul International, 1992.

Wood, A. P. (Ed.). *Dynamics of Agricultural Policy and Reform in Zambia*. Ames, IO, Iowa State University Press, 1990.

ZIMBABWE

Physical and Social Geography

GEORGE KAY

The Republic of Zimbabwe, covering an area of 390,757 sq km (150,872 sq miles), is land-locked and is bounded on the north and north-west by Zambia, on the south-west by Botswana, by Mozambique on the east and on the south by South Africa. The census of August 1997 enumerated 11,789,274 persons. By mid-2006 the population had increased to 13,228,000, according to UN estimates, giving an average density of 33.9 inhabitants per sq km.

Zimbabwe lies astride the high plateaux between the Zambezi and Limpopo rivers. It consists of four relief regions. The Highveld, comprising land more than 1,200 m above sea-level, extends across the country from south-west to north-east; it is most extensive in the north-east. The Middleveld, land of 900 m–1,200 m above sea-level, flanks the Highveld; it is most extensive in the north-west. The Lowveld, land below 900 m, occupies the Zambezi basin in the north and the more extensive Limpopo and Sabi-Lundi basins in the south and south-east. These three regions consist predominantly of gently undulating plateaux, except for the narrow belt of rugged, escarpment hills associated with faults along the Zambezi trough. Also, the surfaces are broken locally where particularly resistant rocks provide upstanding features. For example, the Great Dyke, a remarkable intrusive feature over 480 km in length and up to 10 km wide, gives rise to prominent ranges of hills. The fourth physical region, the eastern highlands, is distinctive because of its mountainous character. Inyangani rises to 2,594 m and many hills exceed 1,800 m.

Temperatures vary by altitude. Mean monthly temperatures range from 22°C in October and 13°C in July on the Highveld to 30°C and 20°C in the low-lying Zambezi valley. Winters are noted for a wide diurnal range; night frosts can occur on the high plateaux and can occasionally be very destructive.

Rainfall is largely restricted to the period November–March and, except on the eastern highlands, is extremely variable; in many regions it is too low for commercial crop production. Mean annual rainfall ranges from 1,400 mm on the eastern highlands, to 800 mm on the north-eastern Highveld and to less than 400 mm in the Limpopo valley. The development of water resources for economic uses is a continually pressing need which, to date, has been met by a major dam-building programme. Underground water resources are limited. Large-scale irrigation works in the south-eastern Lowveld have overcome climatic limitations, and the area around Chiredzi, once suitable only for ranching, is now a major developing region.

Soils vary considerably. Granite occurs over more than one-half of the country and mostly gives rise to infertile sandy soils; these are, however, amenable to improvement. Kalahari sands are also extensive and provide poor soils. Soil-forming processes are limited in the Lowveld and, except on basalt, soils there are generally immature. Rich, red clays and loams occur on the limited outcrops of Basement Schists, which are also among the most highly mineralized areas of Zimbabwe.

Climatic factors are the chief determinants of agricultural potential and six broad categories of land have been defined largely on bio-climatic conditions: Region I (1.6% of the country) with good, reliable rainfall; suitable for specialized and diversified farming, including tree crops; Region II (18.7%) with moderately high rainfall; suitable for intensive commercial crop production with subsidiary livestock farming; Region III (17.4%) with mediocre rainfall conditions; suitable for semi-extensive commercial livestock farming with supplementary production of drought-resistant crops; Region IV (33%) with low and unreliable rainfall; suitable for semi-extensive livestock production; Region V (26.2%) semi-arid country; suitable only for extensive ranching; and Region VI (3.1%—probably underestimated) which, because of steep slopes, skeletal soils, swamps, etc., is unsuitable for any agricultural use. The seizure of white-owned commercial farms from 2000 adversely affected agricultural production (see Economy).

Zimbabwe possesses a wide variety of workable mineral deposits, which include gold, platinum, asbestos, copper, chrome, nickel, palladium, cobalt, tin, iron ore, limestone, iron pyrites, phosphates and coal. Most mineralization occurs on the Highveld and adjacent parts of the Middleveld.

The population of Zimbabwe is diverse. At mid-1980 it was estimated to include some 223,000 persons of European descent and some 37,000 Asians and Coloureds, all of them a legacy of the colonial era. The indigenous inhabitants, who accounted for over 98% of the population at mid-1987, broadly comprise two ethnic or linguistic groups, the Ndebele and the Shona. The Shona, with whom political power now rests, outnumber the Ndebele by 4:1. There are, in addition, several minor ethnic groups, such as the Tonga, Sena, Hlengwe, Venda and Sotho. The official languages are English, ChiShona and SiNdebele.

In recent years urban growth has proceeded rapidly. The urban poor, operating within the highly competitive 'informal economy', are now a large and increasing part of the urban social structure. During 1982–92 the population of Harare, the capital, grew from 656,000 to 1,189,103, while that of Bulawayo increased from 413,800 to 621,742. In 2003 the population of Harare (including suburbs) was estimated at 1,469,149.

Most rural African households still reside on communal lands, where they have traditionally depended upon subsistence production, augmented by small irregular sales of surplus produce, by casual employment and by remittances from migrant labourers. However, the cohesion of this rural society is being eroded by the selective effects of migration.

The socio-economic difficulties of rural African society are compounded by ecological problems. While some extensive areas (notably in remote northern parts of the country) remain sparsely populated, the greater part of the communal lands suffers from overpopulation and overstocking. Deforestation, soil erosion and a deterioration of wildlife and water resources are widespread, and in some areas they have reached critical dimensions. Desertification is a real danger in the semi-arid regions of the country.

Recent History

RICHARD BROWN

Revised by CHRISTOPHER SAUNDERS

The boundaries of modern Zimbabwe were demarcated after Cecil Rhodes, mine magnate and then Prime Minister of the British Cape Colony, sent whites to settle north of the Limpopo river in 1890. The mineral deposits found there proved much more limited than Rhodes had hoped, but within a decade large areas of agricultural land had been seized from the Shona and Ndebele people and occupied by white farmers, mainly from Britain and South Africa. In 1923 the small white population of Southern Rhodesia, as the territory was then known, was accorded self-government. In 1953 Southern Rhodesia was united by the British Government with Northern Rhodesia and Nyasaland (now Zambia and Malawi, respectively) in a Central African Federation, which was opposed by Africans in all three territories. The British Government eventually recognized the strength of African hostility in Northern Rhodesia and Nyasaland, and conceded independence to those territories, breaking up the federation in 1963. Whites in Southern Rhodesia viewed these developments as the outcome of British appeasement, and in 1962 voted into office the newly formed Rhodesian Front (RF), dedicated to upholding white supremacy and demanding full independence from the United Kingdom and the retention of the existing minority-rule Constitution. When the United Kingdom refused independence on this basis, the RF appointed the intransigent Ian Smith as Prime Minister. In November 1965 Smith carried out the long-threatened unilateral declaration of independence (UDI), renaming the territory 'Rhodesia'.

Repressive measures preceding UDI had seriously weakened the black African nationalist opposition, which in 1963 had split into the Zimbabwe African People's Union (ZAPU), led by Joshua Nkomo, and the breakaway Zimbabwe African National Union (ZANU), led by Rev. Ndabaningi Sithole and subsequently Robert Mugabe. These nationalists embarked upon a 'people's war' to overthrow the Smith regime. ZAPU, based mainly in Zambia, received training and armaments from the USSR. ZANU developed strong links with the Frente de Libertação de Moçambique (Frelimo) movement fighting the Portuguese in Mozambique, and with the People's Republic of China. It concentrated on infiltration and rural mobilization in the Chishona-speaking areas in the north-east, and later in the eastern and central areas of the country. From 1976 a combined struggle was waged in the name of the Patriotic Front (PF), an uneasy alliance formed by ZAPU and ZANU, and backed by the 'front-line' states, i.e. those African countries most involved in the Rhodesian conflict. Within the country, mounting economic difficulties, resulting in large part from the imposition of economic sanctions by the international community (with the effective exception of South Africa), together with declining white morale and guerrilla advances in the rural areas, led the Smith regime in 1979 to fashion what was termed an 'internal settlement'. This took the form of a black surrogate regime under the leadership of Bishop Abel Muzorewa. Within less than a year all the parties to the conflict agreed to participate in the Lancaster House constitutional conference, in London, United Kingdom, under the chairmanship of the British Secretary of State for Foreign and Commonwealth Affairs, which was to lead to the emergence of the independent state of Zimbabwe on 18 April 1980.

THE INDEPENDENCE SETTLEMENT

The Lancaster House conference lasted for 14 weeks, an agreement being signed on 21 December 1979. Administrative continuity was stressed in the adoption of the prime ministerial system in preference to an executive presidency, and in the disproportionate political influence reserved to the white minority (20 of the 100 seats in the House of Assembly). However, the compensation clause attached to land reform was strongly opposed by the PF, and was accepted only after vague assurances had been given about a future multinational fund to assist in the urgent problems of land redistribution. At elections in February 1980 Mugabe's ZANU—PF won 57 of the 80 'common roll' (black African) seats in the House, receiving 63% of the votes. Nkomo's PF won 20 seats and Muzorewa's United African National Council (UANC) three seats. Between them the two parties that had conducted the armed struggle received 87% of the votes in a turn-out estimated at 94% (in an earlier and separate election, the RF won all 20 seats reserved for whites). Rev. Canaan Banana, a prominent figure in the nationalist struggle, became Zimbabwe's first President, with ceremonial duties only.

In the immediate period following his massive victory, Mugabe adopted a markedly conciliatory stance. To restore stability, he quickly stressed the need for reconciliation; disavowed rapid change towards his stated socialist goals; emphasized non-alignment in foreign affairs; and included two whites in his Cabinet. Nevertheless, the new Government was faced with formidable problems arising from the ravages of war and the expectations aroused in the struggle against settler rule. For most Zimbabweans the struggles of recent decades had been about recovering the land, and the later stages of the guerrilla war to some extent resembled a peasant uprising. The importance of the established commercial farming sector made the problem of meeting peasant needs daunting. The pace of official resettlement, slowed by drought, manpower shortages, restrictive provisions in the Lancaster House agreement and perhaps by lack of will, was not sufficient to head off uncontrolled resettlement or to prevent the land issue from fuelling discontent.

Zimbabwe established diplomatic relations with other countries in Africa, with Western countries, with the People's Republic of China and its allies and, more hesitantly, with the USSR and its allies. A conference on Reconstruction and Development (Zimcord), held in March 1981, succeeded in substantially meeting its targets for aid. Zimbabwe also began to play a prominent part in the Southern African Development Co-ordination Conference (SADCC, now the Southern African Development Community—SADC). Mugabe made it clear that political and diplomatic support would be given to the movements fighting to liberate neighbouring South Africa.

POLITICS AND SECURITY

There remained serious internal and external threats posed by disaffected supporters of the former regime, by unresolved tensions within the governing coalition, and by South Africa. In December 1981 the ZANU—PF headquarters were destroyed in a bomb attack. Subsequently, vital transport routes and petroleum facilities in Mozambique were sabotaged, the homes of government ministers attacked, and a substantial part of the air force destroyed as part of a campaign by South Africa to destabilize Zimbabwe.

Meanwhile, there was increasing discussion of the need for a one-party state. Mugabe believed that such a development should come about through persuasion, but other members of his party urged the need for speed and attacked the restrictive clauses of the Lancaster House Constitution. Nkomo, who later made it known that he did not consider the election results to be valid and who had rejected Mugabe's offer of the presidency following the independence elections, refused to accept that a ZAPU merger with ZANU—PF was the best solution to the sharp regional polarization between the two coalition parties. In January 1981 Nkomo was demoted from his home affairs portfolio to a lesser cabinet office, and one year later he and some of his colleagues were dismissed altogether. Mugabe threatened to bring Nkomo to trial on charges of plotting a coup, but also stressed again his policy of reconciliation. The ZAPU ministers who had remained were promoted, and Mugabe also added two ex-RF deputies to his Government. Still under the leadership of Ian Smith, the RF, restyled the Republican Front in 1981, adopted a negative attitude to the new Government. In 1985 it reconstituted itself as the Conservative Alliance of Zimbabwe (CAZ).

The Government's authority was increasingly challenged by acute land problems in Mabeteland, allied to the effects of a devastating drought, which heightened the tense political situation there. During 1982 dissidents from the Zimbabwe People's Revolutionary Army (ZAPU's former guerrilla army), and former colleagues who had deserted from the new national army, perpetrated numerous indiscriminate acts of violence. Their exact link with Nkomo and his party was not fully established, but the Government held ZAPU largely to blame for the worsening situation.

In the first general election since independence, held at the end of June 1985 for the 20 'guaranteed' white seats and in early July for the 80 'common roll' seats, Ian Smith's CAZ won 15 of the 20 reserved seats. ZANU—PF increased its representation in the House of Assembly by six seats to 64, although it failed to gain any of the Matabeleland seats held by Joshua Nkomo's ZAPU. Outside Matabeleland, ZAPU lost all five of the seats that it held in the previous legislature. ZANU—Sithole secured one seat, but Muzorewa's UANC failed to gain any representation. Following the election, several CAZ representatives in the House of Assembly either joined the ruling party or became independents.

ZANU—PF CONSOLIDATES

Following the elections, the drive towards a de facto one-party state was resumed, with reprisals against supporters of minority parties. The Government's vigorous campaign against ZAPU led to a critical report by the human rights organization Amnesty International, but that did not prevent the resumption of unity talks between ZAPU and ZANU—PF. In April 1987, however, Mugabe abruptly abandoned the unity negotiations on the grounds that they had been deadlocked for too long. A resurgence of violence in Matabeleland and further measures against ZAPU's political activities followed the cancellation of the unity talks. Nkomo, however, continued to deny any involvement with the dissidents, and in July ZAPU indicated its continuing wish for negotiations with the ruling party by voting in favour of renewing the state of emergency.

A particularly brutal massacre in Matabeleland in November 1987 and the worsening security situation on the eastern border (see below) precipitated a unity agreement between ZAPU and ZANU—PF, healing the split of almost 25 years in the nationalist ranks. The agreement to merge the two parties, under the name of ZANU—PF, was signed by Mugabe and Nkomo in December and was ratified by both parties in April 1988. According to the agreement, the new party was to be committed to the establishment of a one-party state with a Marxist-Leninist doctrine. The party was to be led by Mugabe, with Nkomo as one of two Vice-Presidents. Nkomo was offered a senior position in a new Cabinet, while two other ZAPU officials were given government posts. An amnesty, proclaimed in April 1988, led to a rapid improvement in political and security conditions in Matabeleland.

Meanwhile, constitutional changes moved Zimbabwe closer to becoming a one-party state. The reservation for whites of 20 seats in the House of Assembly and 10 seats in the Senate was finally abolished in September 1987. In the following month the 80 remaining members of the Assembly elected 20 candidates who were all nominated by ZANU—PF, including 11 whites, to fill the vacant seats. Candidates nominated by ZANU—PF, including four whites, were then elected to the vacancies in the Senate by the new House of Assembly. In October Parliament adopted another major constitutional reform, whereby the ceremonial presidency was replaced by an executive presidency incorporating the post of Prime Minister. Robert Mugabe was nominated as sole candidate for the office, and on 31 December he was inaugurated as Zimbabwe's first executive President. His new enlarged Cabinet included Joshua Nkomo as one of three senior ministers in the President's office who were to oversee policy and review ministerial performance. In November 1989 the House of Assembly voted to abolish the Senate. The single chamber was then expanded from 100 to 150 seats, with effect from the next general election. In addition to 120 elected members, the change provided for eight provincial governors, 10 chiefs and 12 presidential nominees to be members of the Assembly.

DISCONTENT AND 'CORRUPTION'

As unemployment and prices rose in 1988, open public and parliamentary criticism of corrupt government officials mounted. An anti-Government demonstration by students in September resulted in many arrests. In October a former Secretary-General of ZANU—PF, Edgar Tekere, was expelled from the party for his persistent denunciation of its leadership and policies, including the plans to introduce a one-party state. He had previously disavowed any intention of forming a new party, but he now founded the Zimbabwe Unity Movement (ZUM).

The Government was embarrassed during 1989 by a series of conflicts with the judiciary and by strikes in the public service sector, but it was criticism by students that provoked the most serious political disturbances. In July a clash occurred between students and security police during a rally of ZUM supporters at the University of Zimbabwe. Following further serious clashes, the University was closed from October 1990 to April 1991. When the Zimbabwe Congress of Trade Unions (ZCTU) issued a statement supporting the students, its Secretary-General, Morgan Tsvangirai, was arrested and detained for six weeks. Although the state of emergency was discontinued, owing to the reduction of tension in South Africa, the Government retained wide powers of arrest and detention.

Political debate intensified during the ZANU—PF congress in December 1989. The congress was convened to complete the merger process with ZAPU, begun two years earlier (see above), but there was controversy concerning a proposed constitutional amendment to create a second vice-presidency, specifically for Joshua Nkomo, the former ZAPU leader. (Nkomo was officially appointed Vice-President, in addition to the existing Vice-President, Simon Muzenda, in August 1990.) Although Mugabe re-committed the new ZANU—PF to Marxism-Leninism and the one-party state, opposition to a one-party state was expressed within and outside the congress. Indeed, in August 1990 the ZANU—PF politburo voted to reject plans for the creation of a one-party state in Zimbabwe.

For the general election of March 1990, ZANU—PF chose to campaign against the ZUM, its only serious opponent among the four opposition parties, on the general issue of national unity rather than on that of the one-party state. The election was marred by political violence, but the result of the poll appeared to be a fair reflection of the Government's popularity. ZANU—PF secured 117 of the 120 elective seats. The ZUM obtained two seats and ZANU—Ndonga (formerly ZANU—Sithole) retained one. However, electoral participation had declined sharply in comparison with the two previous general elections. Overall, the distribution of votes in the election indicated that the ZUM had achieved something approaching national status as an opposition party. At the concurrent election for the presidency, Tekere received 413,840 votes, while Mugabe secured 2.03m. votes.

Mugabe's new Cabinet included three whites, but its overall composition, to the annoyance of former ZAPU members, was little altered. Nevertheless, few doubted that, under the surface, the final year of the decade since independence had witnessed a substantial political shift. With more than 50% of the population below the age of 25 years, and with severe unemployment and other domestic problems, appeals by ZANU—PF to the heroism of the pre-independence struggle were no longer as relevant or powerful as previously.

IDEOLOGICAL AND OTHER REASSESSMENTS

After the adoption in 1991 of an Economic Structural Adjustment Programme (ESAP), 'Marxism-Leninism' was increasingly replaced in official discourse by references to 'pragmatic socialism' and 'indigenous capitalism'. Vigorous debate followed the expiry of the remaining restrictions of the Lancaster House agreement on 18 April 1990. Constitutional amendments that restored corporal and capital punishment and denied recourse to the courts in cases of compulsory purchase of land by the Government were enacted in April 1991, despite fierce criticism from the judiciary and from human rights campaigners.

Despite the Government's evident unpopularity, the disorganized and divided state of the opposition continued to protect the Government from serious challenge. A split in the ZUM led to the formation in September 1991 of the ineffective Democratic Party. In July 1992 ZANU—Ndonga, the UANC, ZUM and the CAZ formed an informal alliance, the United Front (UF), with the aim of defeating the Government at the general election due in 1995, but divisions soon emerged within the new grouping.

The ZCTU found itself unable to capitalize on the widespread industrial unrest that took place in 1994. The organization was weakened by the resignation of its Secretary-General, Morgan Tsvangirai, and by the loss of members as a result of the economic recession. When the ZCTU rejected the suggestion that it form its own party, a group of non-union figures opposed to the ESAP announced the formation of a Movement for Democracy in June 1994.

Meanwhile, amid the rising urban discontent fuelled by corruption scandals, falling real wages and the social consequences of the ESAP, the Government was increasingly preoccupied by the land issue, which it continued to regard as the key to retaining its grip on power. The Land Acquisition Act (LAA), drafted following the expiry of the Lancaster House provisions, passed its final legislative phase on 19 March 1992. The new legislation, which provided for the compulsory acquisition of land by the state, brought the Government into conflict with the powerful white-dominated Commercial Farmers' Union (CFU) and with Western aid donors. Both groups were angered by the decision in April 1993 to designate 70 commercial white-owned farms for purchase. Many of them were productive holdings, which, it had been understood, were to be exempt from compulsory purchase. The Government eventually allowed appeals in a sufficient number of cases to suggest that an uneasy compromise had been reached. For its part, the CFU announced in September that it would assist in the Government's resettlement programme, and its members were represented on the commission set up in November to make proposals for land tenure reforms. However, in March 1994 the Government found itself once again under intense pressure when it was revealed that the first of the farms acquired under the LAA had been allocated to government minister Witness Mangwende, who had been Minister of Agriculture when the act was passed. The scandal escalated when the press revealed that most of the first 98 farms acquired by compulsory purchase had been leased to prominent party figures and civil servants and were not being used for peasant resettlement. The President responded by ordering the cancellation of all relevant leases. In November the High Court ruled against three white farmers who had attempted to prove that the confiscation of their land was unconstitutional; the farmers subsequently lost an appeal to the Supreme Court against the verdict. Government plans to resettle 100,000 smallholders over five years were impeded by a lack of available resources. Indeed, the funds made available for resettlement were more than halved in the 1995/96 budget. In mid-1996 Mugabe requested financial assistance from the United Kingdom for the implementation of the land redistribution programme.

In spite of the popular discontent that had characterized its last term of office, the Government won a fourth decisive general election victory on 8–9 April 1995. Of the six opposition parties that contested the election, only the regionally based ZANU—Ndonga won any seats in the House of Assembly (two). ZANU—PF received more than 82% of the votes cast and secured 118 of the 120 elective seats (55 of them uncontested), as well as control of the 30 nominated and reserved seats. Most independent observers agreed that the elections had been largely 'free and fair', but they criticized aspects of the registration procedures, the ruling party's domination of the media and the Political Parties (Finance) Act of 1992, under which only organizations with at least 15 assembly members (that is, effectively only ZANU—PF) were entitled to state support. In August 1995 the High Court nullified the election result in the bitterly contested Harare South constituency, when it was established that more votes had been cast than there were registered electors. This lent credence to opposition claims of widespread electoral malpractices by the Mugabe administration (despite the favourable pronouncement of the majority of independent observers), and calls were made for both the annulment of all the results and the convening of an all-party constitutional conference to debate means of improving the implementation of democratic principles in the *de facto* one-party state. Nevertheless, Mugabe was returned to office at a presidential election on 16–17 March 1996, winning 93% of the votes cast. There was, however, a turn-out of only 32% of the eligible electorate.

ECONOMIC CRISIS AND LAND REFORM

During 1997 and 1998 the Mugabe administration increasingly came under attack for corruption, arrogance and maladministration. In 1997 allegations arose that official contracts were being unfairly tendered and that ministerial funds were being used to finance the construction of homes for civil servants, government ministers and Mugabe's wife. Mugabe himself publicly acknowledged in July 1999 that corruption existed within his administration.

The Government announced in August 1997 that the war veterans (an increasingly powerful lobby) were to be awarded a number of substantial benefits, which had not been included in the budget. It was reported that Tsvangirai had been severely assaulted in his office by unknown assailants at that time, who were subsequently reported to be war veterans. The weak Zimbabwe dollar and soaring food prices, compounded by an excessively high level of unemployment, aggravated the nation-wide mood of discontent. In January 1998 unprecedented food riots erupted in most of the country's urban areas in protest at successive rises in the price of the staple maize meal. In response Mugabe agreed to withdraw the most recent price increase. However, the army was deployed to suppress the disturbances and was authorized to open fire on protesters; nine people were reportedly killed and some 800 rioters were arrested. The ZCTU organized a further two-day strike in March, to protest against the continuing rise in living costs; soon afterwards the organization's Bulawayo office was destroyed in an arson attack. Meanwhile, in early 1998, despite the ongoing economic crisis, Mugabe presented legislation to Parliament that provided for a number of luxury retirement benefits for himself, his family, the two Vice-Presidents and their families. Further consumer price increases were followed by renewed rioting. A series of one-day strikes over pay were called by unions and action took place until banned by Mugabe. In February 1999, however, the ban was ruled to be illegal. In that month growing unrest followed an address to the nation by Mugabe in which he attacked the judiciary, the independent media and 'British agents'. He also accused white Zimbabweans of 'fomenting unrest'.

In October 1997, in an attempt to revive his declining popularity, Mugabe announced that the hitherto slow pace of the national land resettlement programme would be accelerated. He declared that the constitutional right of white commercial farmers to receive full and fair compensation for confiscated land would not be honoured and challenged the United Kingdom, in its role as former colonial power, to take responsibility for assisting them. A list of 1,471 properties to be reallocated forthwith was published in November. In January 1998, however, the IMF required an assurance from the Mugabe administration that it would respect the Constitution during the land resettlement procedure as a condition for the release of financial assistance. Such an assurance was given in early March, and the IMF allocated a substantial loan in June.

There was broad support for the land resettlement programme, providing that members of the ruling élite did not become beneficiaries, and that the success of the thriving commercial farming sector was not prejudiced. However, when Mugabe announced the second phase of the programme, to resettle 150,000 families on 1m. ha of land each year for the next seven years, and appealed to Western donors for funds, the potential donors dismissed the scheme as too ambitious and costly. Under pressure, the Government agreed to reduce its plans, but in November 1998 841 white-owned farms were ordered to be confiscated, with compensation deferred.

Renewed pressure exerted by the IMF brought an assurance from Mugabe that his administration would not break agreements for a gradual programme of land reform, but at the end of March 1999 the President contravened this undertaking, announcing a plan to acquire a further 529 white-owned farms. He accused the USA and the United Kingdom of 'destabilizing' Zimbabwe through their alleged control over the IMF, and threatened to sever Zimbabwe's relations with the IMF and the World Bank.

REJECTION OF THE NEW CONSTITUTION

In October 1998 the Government embarked on discussions with a National Constitutional Assembly (NCA) of opposition interests on proposed changes to the country's Constitution. The Mugabe administration confirmed its commitment to an open process that would not allow government domination, and expressed its intention that a new constitution would be in operation prior to the elections due to take place by 2000. However, the NCA suspended negotiations in November after about 50 protesters urging greater constitutional democratization were prevented from marching by riot police. In March 1999 Mugabe unilaterally appointed a 395-member commission of inquiry, dominated by ZANU—PF, to make recommendations on a new constitution. They were given seven months for the task. The NCA refused to participate in the commission, and announced its intention to hold a rival 'people's convention'.

An international constitutional conference was held in November 1999, but several experts suspected that a draft had already been created, and that they had been invited to make presentations primarily to give the process credibility. In late November a document bearing no relation to that prepared by the constitutional commission was declared to have been 'adopted by acclamation', despite vigorous protests. A drafting committee overseen by ZANU—PF had deleted crucial clauses proposed by the commission, particularly relating to the reduction of the President's powers.

In January 2000 Mugabe announced that a constitutional referendum would take place on 12–13 February. The opposition believed that the high level of confusion before the polls over such issues as eligibility to vote and the location of polling stations was orchestrated by ZANU—PF to maximize its chances of victory. The Registrar-General announced that the electoral roll was to be used, which was known to be outdated, 25% of those listed having died and another 30% having changed constituencies. Despite fears that a lack of supervision of the ballot had led to widespread irregularities by ZANU—PF, 55% of the 26% of the electorate who participated in the polls voted to reject the proposed new constitutional document. The level of participation was highest in urban areas, where support for the Movement for Democratic Change (MDC—formed in September 1999 under the leadership of Morgan Tsvangirai) was strong, while voters in the Government's rural strongholds were apathetic, despite promises that the new constitution would grant them redistributed white land. In a televised address a few days later, Mugabe accepted the result.

In mid-May 2000 Mugabe announced that a parliamentary election was to be held on 24–25 June. The MDC obtained a postponement at the High Court of the deadline for nominations until 3 June, as ZANU—PF had been given exclusive access to the details of electoral constituency boundaries. The MDC feared that more constituencies might have been created in rural areas where support for the ruling party was strong. The main issues dominating the election were land reform and the economy. International aid to Zimbabwe had been suspended in October 1999, while the budget deficit was growing ever larger and huge arrears to overseas suppliers for fuel, partly owing to a shortage of foreign currency reserves, led to the suspension of petroleum supplies in December. In the following month rationing caused unrest and long queues at petrol stations. In February 2000 the Minister of Transport and Energy, Enos Chikowore, assumed responsibility for the fuel crisis and resigned. In April white farmers urged a substantial devaluation of the currency and threatened not to take their tobacco crop to auction until this happened. The banks agreed that devaluation was needed to avoid mass default. The Government, however, fearing that devaluing the currency might adversely affect its chances of retaining power, refused to act. (Following the election, the Government devalued the Zimbabwe dollar in early August.) Meanwhile, in March the Minister of Agriculture, Kumbirai Kangai, appeared in court on charges of manipulating tenders for grain imports. He was the first minister to face corruption charges since Mugabe had come to power.

FARM OCCUPATIONS AND THE JUNE 2000 ELECTION

In late February 2000 a state-sponsored campaign of illegal occupations of white-owned farms began, perpetrated by so-called 'war veterans', many of whom were too young to have taken part in the war of independence. The security forces refused to act against the occupiers, declaring that this 'political issue' lay outside their jurisdiction. The police failed to take steps to evict the protesters following a ruling by the High Court in mid-March in favour of the white farmers (which was ignored by the 'veterans'). Although Mugabe repeatedly denied that his administration was behind the occupations, he made no secret of his support for them. The invasions became increasingly violent, and two farmers were killed in April. A few days earlier, Mugabe had threatened war against farmers who refused to give up their land voluntarily, and following the violence he declared that they were 'enemies of the state', in what he now termed the third 'Chimurenga' (a Shona word for struggle).

The international community condemned this state-sponsored violence, which was directed in large part against supporters of the MDC. When a 500-strong mob violently attacked a peace march in Harare in April 2000, no action was taken against the perpetrators of the attack. A constitutional amendment approved in April, shortly before the dissolution of the House of Assembly to prepare for the election, stated that white farmers dispossessed of their land would have to apply to the 'former colonial power', the United Kingdom, for compensation (see below). Following worsening unrest, the MDC threatened to boycott the election, but in May Mugabe called for an end to the violence. He met with the self-styled 'war veterans' and white farmers and announced the creation of a land commission to redistribute farmland. Shortly afterwards, however, he signed a law allowing the seizure of 841 white-owned farms without compensation. Political violence continued, and in early June a list was published of 804 farms that were to be confiscated. Farmers were granted approximately one month to contest the list. By August farmers had contested the acquisition of 593 of the 804 properties listed, and a further 2,237 farms had been identified by the land commission for confiscation. Meanwhile, the settlement of black families had commenced on 211 farms acquired without objection.

In the period prior to the election, 34 people were killed, and there were reports of widespread intimidation and use of torture by ZANU—PF against members of the opposition. The authorities refused to permit the accreditation of some 200 foreign monitors, and most international observers concluded that the election had not been free and fair. ZANU—PF won 62 of the 120 contested seats in the House of Assembly. The MDC, which won 57 seats, subsequently challenged the results in 37 constituencies, on the grounds of either voter intimidation or electoral irregularities. The Supreme Court nullified thousands of postal votes cast in the elections by troops serving in the DRC, ruling that the ballot papers had been issued invalidly.

THE CRISIS DEEPENS

Following the June 2000 parliamentary election, the political and economic crisis deepened. Mugabe, now 77, declared that he would seek a fifth term in the 2002 presidential ballot. The MDC was increasingly targeted by ZANU—PF youths and thugs. As lawlessness spread throughout the country, there were numerous reports of assaults on individuals by soldiers and police-officers. Some opposition leaders were arrested, and

Tsvangirai was the target of more than one assassination attempt.

In late August 2000 the security forces took action for the first time against the self-styled 'war veterans' occupying white-owned farms. Several hundred squatters were evicted, and dwellings erected by 'veterans' on council-owned land were demolished. However, following angry demonstrations by the 'war veterans' and their followers, the Government apologized and offered compensation for the damage to their properties, provoking condemnation from the MDC. In September the CFU announced its intention to challenge the Government's right to seize land without paying compensation, after the Government apparently refused to negotiate with the farmers. By then, however, the Government had taken steps to weaken the judiciary; a number of judges were threatened until they took early retirement. In January 2001, two days after the Minister of State for Information and Publicity, Jonathan Moyo, had threatened to close down the *Daily News*, the only independent daily newspaper in Zimbabwe, the paper's printing presses were bombed.

Meanwhile, increasing numbers of white-owned farms were listed for appropriation, until by mid-2001 the CFU, which had offered 1m. ha for resettlement, stated that 95% of all commercial farms, totalling 8.3m. ha, were destined for take-over. As a direct consequence of the continuing land invasions, there was a sharp decline in agricultural production, and relatively little new maize or tobacco was planted. As lawlessness spread, poaching of animals and killing of protected wildlife intensified. By mid-2001 the Government claimed to have little foreign currency, and there was a severe fuel crisis. The manufacturing sector, long in decline, was especially adversely affected; some 400 manufacturers were forced to close their businesses within one year. An estimated 60% of the workforce was unemployed, and an estimated 80% of the population was living below the poverty line.

In mid-2001 the Government began to admit that there would be severe food shortages; at least 500,000 metric tons of imported maize would be needed. Despite shortages of foreign currency, new equipment was imported from Israel for the police, to help them deal with internal disorder. The Government also found almost Z.$1,000m. in unbudgeted funds to give further increases to the so-called war veterans. After the death in June 2001 of their leader, Chenjerai 'Hitler' Hunzvi, notorious for his inflammatory rhetoric, relations between the 'veterans' and the ZANU—PF leadership became even closer. When the Supreme Court ruled that the fast-track land reform programme could only continue if the Government presented a clear plan of action, Mugabe chose to interpret this as an invitation to continue to pursue the policy of seizing commercial farmland, much of which was taken over by members of the ruling élite.

In February 2001 Tsvangirai was charged with having threatened to use violence to remove Mugabe from office if he did not retire peacefully. In a by-election in the predominantly rural constituency of Bindura, north of Harare, in July 2001 there was considerable violence, and a motorcade carrying Tsvangirai was fired upon. It now seemed that ZANU—PF would sanction any means, including the use of violence, to ensure that Mugabe would win the forthcoming presidential election. The fast-track land reform programme was a way of moving thousands of registered and potential voters from the urban to the rural areas, in the hope that, having been given land, they would support ZANU—PF.

THE 2002 PRESIDENTIAL ELECTION

Violence increased in the period preceding the presidential election in March 2002, the principal target of which was the MDC, and its supporters were reported to have been systematically harassed and ill-treated by members of ZANU—PF and war veterans. In February Tsvangirai and two other senior members of the MDC were arrested and charged with treason for allegedly plotting to assassinate Mugabe. Land owned by white commercial farmers (12 of whom had been killed by mid-2002) continued to be seized. However, many of the previously landless people who occupied the land of commercial farmers had no expertise in farming, and production declined dramatically. At least 70,000 farm-workers lost their jobs as a consequence of the land reform programme. Torture and intimidation of opposition supporters was reported to be widespread, with the police and army, and members of the youth brigades, known as the 'green bombers', apparently behaving with impunity.

When the presidential election took place, on 9–10 March 2002, with Mugabe and Tsvangirai the two principal candidates, the voting period was extended by one day by the High Court, in response to a request from the MDC, which claimed that the number of polling stations in urban areas, where support for the MDC was strong, had been reduced by some 45%, while those in rural areas had been increased. The MDC alleged that many stations closed early, before numerous voters had been able to cast their ballots, and that a number of its agents had been abducted from polling stations and detained by the police. According to official results, Mugabe won 56.2% of the votes, and Tsvangirai 42.0%. To the astonishment of other observer missions, the South African mission declared that the election was 'legitimate', if not free and fair. Most other observer groups, including that of the Commonwealth, found that conditions had not allowed for a free expression of the will of the electorate. The Presidents of South Africa, Nigeria and Malawi attempted to broker talks between ZANU—PF and the MDC, but ZANU—PF withdrew after the MDC challenged the election result in the courts.

After the election, another 2,900 white farmers were given a deadline by which to vacate their farms under the LAA. About one-half left their properties, but the rest remained and awaited the outcome of legal challenges to the legislation. Many of these were then arrested. In mid-September 2002 the House of Assembly adopted an amendment to the LAA, which provided for the eviction of farmers within seven days of being served notice, rather than the 90-day deadline hitherto in force. Although Mugabe announced in early 2003 that his fast-track land redistribution programme was at an end, and instituted an audit of what had been achieved, seizures of white-owned land continued to take place.

Much of the first half of 2003 was dominated by the treason trial of Tsvangirai and his two co-defendants. Following a new wave of demonstrations in June, many MDC supporters, including Tsvangirai himself, were arrested. He was charged with a new count of treason, for seeking to overthrow the Mugabe regime. While the MDC continued to express its willingness to enter into discussions with ZANU—PF, Mugabe insisted that it must first recognize that his re-election as President was legitimate, and withdraw its legal challenge to the 2002 election. The MDC refused and won a number of victories in court as results in the legislative elections in individual constituencies were overturned. In mid-2003 it was finally announced that its case on the legality of the presidential election would be heard in November. Various church leaders, including the Anglican Archbishop of Cape Town, attempted to mediate between the two parties, and for a time informal talks took place between Patrick Chinamasa, the Minister of Justice, for ZANU—PF, and Welshman Ncube, Secretary-General of the MDC, but no significant progress was made. Mugabe insisted that the MDC sever its alleged ties with the West before talks could continue. Tsvangirai continued to be encumbered by his trial on treason charges; in July 2004 the High Court postponed indefinitely judgment on his trial.

As the crisis intensified, Zimbabwe's position on the UN Human Development Index plummeted. Life expectancy, which had been 61 years in 1991, fell to 36 years in 2004, and an estimated 6,000 people were dying each week from AIDS-related diseases. Around one-third of the adult population aged between 15 and 49 years was living with HIV/AIDS, and the rate of infection continued to rise because of the lack of measures to address the pandemic. Meanwhile, the country's economy contracted at a dramatic rate. Inflation soared to over 600%, and an estimated 75% of the population was unemployed. Many industries were forced to close, and agricultural production continued to decline. Shortages of foreign currency, fuel, power, basic commodities and food became commonplace. Although the Government blamed drought and even economic sabotage by the opposition, its land redistribution policies were largely responsible for the massive decline of 67% in cereal production since 1999. Stocks of maize held by some commercial farmers were seized, and all maize producers had to sell their grain to the state-owned Grain Marketing Board; maize meal, cooking oil, salt and sugar became increasingly scarce. As the food crisis worsened, the UN World Food Programme (WFP) imported vast quantities of food. The Government continued to harass journalists whom it considered to have misrepresented the situation in the country. The Access to Information and Privacy Act required all journalists working in the country to seek approval from the state. By mid-2002 more than 10 journalists had been detained, and the few foreign journalists who remained were soon expelled from the country.

Mugabe often claimed that the country's white population was financing the MDC. In mid-2003 he announced plans to extend his land policy to the seizure of white-owned mines and industries, and to introduce legislation to force companies to offer one-fifth of their shares to local black investors. Although whites, who had constituted 5% of the total population in 1980, now made up only 0.5% of the population, they owned more than one-half of the companies listed on the Zimbabwe Stock Exchange. Meanwhile, an estimated 500,000 skilled Zimbabweans had left the country, mostly to settle in the United Kingdom, Botswana and South Africa, often illegally in the case of the latter. The health sector was particularly badly affected by the emigration of professionals, but other public services also suffered.

One of the severest blows to democracy in Zimbabwe occurred when in September 2003 the *Daily News*, which claimed 1m. readers, was forced to close down after the Media and Information Commission (MIC) refused to grant it a licence to publish. The paper briefly published again the following month, but the Supreme Court upheld the closure, and the paper went out of business. This was followed by the banning of the weekly *Tribune* newspaper, on the grounds that it had changed ownership without authorization from the MIC.

As he turned 80 in February 2004, Mugabe announced that he would not retire until his term of office ended in 2008, but infighting among the senior echelons of ZANU—PF suggested that a struggle to succeed him was under way. Corruption charges levelled at some senior party officials were thought to be politically motivated. In early 2004 the reputation of Jonathan Moyo, the influential Minister of Information and Publicity, declined after he clashed openly with the country's Vice-President, Joseph Msika; John Nkomo, the Ndebele ZANU—PF Chairman, emerged as a possible successor to Mugabe in place of Mnangagwa, who was thought to be Mugabe's own preferred successor.

In December 2003 the IMF began procedures to suspend Zimbabwe for failing to repay its debt, which by that month stood at US $273m. A new Governor of the Reserve Bank of Zimbabwe, Gideon Gono, took steps to prevent expulsion. Interest rates were raised, slowing inflation, and the fixed exchange rate system was replaced by currency auctions in an attempt to eliminate the black market. However, the country's gross domestic product (GDP), which had declined by some 30% since 1999, continued to contract. The new Minister of Finance and Economic Development, appointed in February 2004, was soon arrested on foreign currency charges, after the South African media disclosed that he owned three valuable properties in Cape Town. The IMF postponed Zimbabwe's suspension until the end of 2004, after payments totalling US $9m. were made to the Fund; at mid-July 2004 the arrears had risen to US $295m.

By mid-2004 MDC structures had been virtually destroyed in large parts of the country and the party had few resources with which to challenge ZANU—PF in the parliamentary election due in March 2005. The MDC's representation in the 150-seat House of Assembly had been reduced to 52 members as a result of a series of by-elections marred by violence and allegations of vote rigging.

Under pressure from the other countries in the region (see below), ZANU—PF suddenly announced in July 2004 the reform of the electoral process in Zimbabwe; however, the suggested changes, such as introducing transparent ballot boxes, did not meet MDC demands. The MDC pointed to vast intimidation and widespread abuses of human rights perpetrated in the name of ZANU—PF. Those responsible for such acts were not brought to justice, and the judicial system was instead used to harass the opposition. Foreign journalists were unable to operate, and only three small and relatively expensive weekly newspapers expressed independent views. Police approval was required for any gathering of more than three people, MDC supporters were often targets of physical attack, and activists were routinely arrested and detained. While foreign funding of political parties was outlawed, ZANU—PF used state funds for party political purposes. The so-called Independent Electoral Commission, led by an army officer and mostly staffed by military personnel, was not autonomous. The MDC was unable to inspect the voters' roll, but claimed that 2m. of the 6m. names on it were of 'ghost' voters. Large parts of the country were virtually 'no-go' areas for the MDC and civil society, and polling stations there would be controlled by ZANU—PF faithful and security force personnel. Unsurprisingly, some in the MDC thought that the party should boycott the 2005 election. One of Mugabe's main critics, the outspoken Roman Catholic Archbishop of Bulawayo, Pius Ncube, believed that political repression and economic collapse had gone so far that the country faced the prospect of full-scale violent civil conflict.

In late 2004 internecine conflict within ZANU—PF came to a head over the appointment of a new Vice-President, to fill the vacancy created by the death of Simon Muzenda. It was widely expected that the new appointee would succeed Mugabe. A group within ZANU—PF led by Mnangagwa, whom many had seen as the heir apparent, and Jonathan Moyo met to try to prevent the elevation of Joyce Mujuru, who had been in the Cabinet since independence and was Mugabe's choice for the post. Moyo was removed from the party's politburo and then from the Cabinet. After Mujuru was appointed Vice-President, it was clearer than ever that most of the key figures in ZANU—PF were from the Zezuru clan among the Shona, to which Mugabe belonged.

THE 2005 LEGISLATIVE ELECTIONS AND BEYOND

In the period prior to the parliamentary elections, which were held on 31 March 2005, many urged the MDC not to participate. Up to one-third of the population of the country was now living abroad and the Supreme Court had ruled in mid-March that those resident outside Zimbabwe would not be eligible to vote. However, after lengthy deliberation, the MDC decided to participate in the ballot. The Government excluded foreign observers considered unsympathetic to its cause, and delayed accrediting other observers until one month before the poll. In that period overt political violence rescinded and the elections were held in relative calm. SADC and South African observers reported a credible process that 'reflected the will of the Zimbabwean people', but the USA and the European Union (EU), along with Amnesty International and several others, condemned the elections as 'phoney'. Many potential voters had been turned away from the polls, and there were gross discrepancies between official figures for the numbers of voters and the results announced.

According to official results, the MDC won 41 of the 120 contested seats (securing 39.5% of the total votes cast), 16 fewer than in 2000. It alleged gross electoral fraud, and filed petitions at the Electoral Court challenging the results in 13 constituencies. Nevertheless, MDC members took up their seats in the House of Assembly, and the party welcomed the election of the relatively conciliatory John Nkomo as the new legislative Speaker. Jonathan Moyo won a seat as an independent, the only independent to do so. ZANU—PF won 78 of the contested seats (with 59.6% of the vote). Under the Constitution the President could allocate 12 seats in the House of Assembly to candidates of his choosing and appoint the eight provincial governors; a further 10 seats were reserved for tribal chiefs, also loyal to Mugabe. Thus, the party controlled 108 seats and the two-thirds' majority necessary to pass constitutional reforms. When Parliament convened in June 2005, the Government introduced legislation providing for the reintroduction of a second chamber. Meanwhile, it was announced that white farmers who had lost their farms during the resettlement programme would be compensated for the value of assets and improvements but not for the land itself, which the Government maintained was the responsibility of the United Kingdom. It was estimated that the white population in Zimbabwe had fallen from 200,000 in 2000 to around 25,000 at March 2005; of these, some 500 were farmers.

In mid-April 2005 Mugabe announced his new Government, which he described as a 'development Cabinet': the former Zimbabwean ambassador to the United Kingdom, Simbarashe Mumbengegwi, was appointed Minister of Foreign Affairs replacing Stanislaus Mudenge, who moved to head the Ministry of Higher and Tertiary Education; Tichaona Jokonya, formerly Zimbabwe's Permanent Representative to the UN, assumed the hitherto vacant post of Minister of State for Information and Publicity; Didymus Mutasa was appointed Minister of State for National Security; Herbert Murerwa was confirmed as Minister of Finance; and the two newly created posts of Minister of Economic Development and Minister of Rural Housing and Social Amenities were awarded to Rugare Gumbo and Emmerson Mnangagwa, respectively. Sixteen ministers retained their portfolios, including Patrick Chinamasa as Minister of Justice, Legal and Parliamentary Affairs.

After the election the economic situation deteriorated further: fuel was again in very short supply, and a devaluation of the currency in May 2005 did little to improve matters. Mugabe had claimed that there would be no need for food aid, but WFP, which was feeding over 1m. Zimbabweans, estimated that up to one-third of the population needed assistance. Also in May the police suddenly began what they termed 'Operation Restore Order' and 'Operation Murambatsvina' ('Sweep Away the Rubbish'). What were said to be illegal structures, informal shops and markets were bulldozed. The largest market in the country, Mbare in Harare, was entirely demolished, as were many houses. The destruction was carried out in a ruthless fashion, leaving hundreds of thousands of people homeless. Some were placed in temporary accommodation, others were driven into the countryside. Mugabe claimed that the operation had long been planned and was designed to clean up the cities and end illegal activity, but critics countered that no provision had been made for those left homeless, and many suspected that the destruction was, at least in part, an act of vengeance against those who had voted for the MDC in the March election.

The regime seemed taken aback by the international outcry against the destruction and evictions, although once again other African leaders failed to respond, and the African Union (AU) maintained that the destruction was merely an internal matter for Zimbabwe. The UN Secretary-General dispatched an envoy, Anna Tibaijuka, to Zimbabwe to report on the situation, and before the meeting of the Group of Eight leading industrialized nations (G-8) at Gleneagles, United Kingdom, in early July 2005, Tsvangirai met South African President Thabo Mbeki in Pretoria and implored him to use his influence in the ever-deepening crisis in Zimbabwe, arguing that under 'quiet diplomacy' the economic and humanitarian situation had deteriorated further. The South African Deputy President, Phumzile Mlambo-Ngcuka, subsequently visited Harare, with the Mugabe regime under increasing pressure from the IMF, which, after a number of warnings, threatened to expel Zimbabwe if it did not repay the large arrears it owed. Mlambo-Ngcuka was reported to have informed Mugabe that the demolition of 'illegal' structures must cease. The destruction was then suspended, after the High Court had dismissed a case brought against the Government for defying an earlier court order stopping evictions until alternative accommodation was provided. Tibaijuka's report, released in mid-July, harshly criticized those responsible for the evictions, but the Zimbabwean Government rejected the report, claiming it was biased and ill-informed. Although the Government suggested it would build new homes for those made homeless by 'Operation Murambatsvina', no action was taken and evictions continued.

The MDC proved unable to capitalize on the ongoing crisis. Its call for a national boycott at the time of the opening of Parliament in June 2005 was not widely observed. Mugabe continued to accuse the MDC of being in league with foreign enemies of the country, and to claim that the country's economic problems were a result of sabotage by Western governments opposed to the seizure of white land. Human rights groups charged that the police were implicated in numerous cases of arbitrary actions, assaults and various forms of ill-treatment. Freedom of expression and assembly remained severely curtailed. Numerous journalists, including two working for Botswana television, were arrested for failing to seek accreditation from the MIC. Attempts to restart the *Daily News* came to nothing and the staff of *Voice of the People*, an independent radio station, was severely harassed.

In late 2005 the MDC split over the question of participating in the election of members of the new Senate. In that election, held on 26 November, turn-out was very low and ZANU—PF won 43 of the 50 directly elected seats. Most members of the MDC, led by Tsvangirai, rejected the idea of participating, but a small faction led by Gibson Sibanda, the party Vice-President, and Welshman Ncube, the Secretary-General, insisted on doing so. Arthur Mutambara, a scientist who returned from exile, took over leadership of the breakaway group, but Tsvangirai was able to reassert his leadership over the main body of MDC supporters. He called for a Truth and Justice Commission to investigate political and human rights abuses and corruption and expressed the fear that mounting frustration would lead to violence. Mugabe warned the MDC leader that mass protests would be met with force.

In March 2006 Peter Hitschmann, a former Rhodesian soldier, was arrested, along with several MDC activists, after an arms cache was found at his home. The state claimed that he and others planned to assassinate Mugabe and begin an insurgency. That same month Roy Bennett, a former MDC deputy suspected of involvement in the alleged assassination plot, who had previously served eight months of a one-year prison sentence after being convicted by a parliamentary committee of assaulting Patrick Chinamasa in May 2004, fled the country and sought asylum in South Africa. Charges against the detained MDC officials were dropped, but Hitschmann was tried and in 2007 sentenced to three years' imprisonment for illegal possession of weapons.

The economic crisis worsened in 2006, with inflation reaching over 1,200%. Somehow Zimbabwe found the means to make further payments to the IMF, to avoid expulsion, but it still owed the organization a considerable sum and in March the IMF refused to provide new financial support. Well-connected individuals prospered as the economy declined: houses in the northern suburbs of Harare were sold for Z.$50,000m. (US $500,000), while the average monthly salary was Z.$20m. (US $200), and the monthly cost of a basic food basket for a family of six was Z.$60m. (US $600). Because there was so little available foreign exchange, there were shortages of almost all imported items, including fuel, electricity, medicines, schoolbooks, agricultural inputs and spare parts. Most productive activity declined, and hundreds of thousands fled, most of them to South Africa. From November of that year, in what was called 'Operation Chikorokoza' Chapera ('No to Illegal Mining'), people who were desperately looking for gold and other minerals were rounded up and sometimes beaten. In certain rural areas there were reports of mass starvation.

Central bank Governor Gono was among those who now acknowledged that the problems the country faced were in part caused by widespread corruption. Politicians and army generals with no experience of farming had received large-scale commercial farms and had often sold what they found on the farms for massive financial gains. Since the land redistribution exercise began in 2000, commercial agricultural production had fallen by 60%–70%. The commercial herd had fallen from 1.2m. cattle to just 150,000, and milk production had been halved. The Government deployed soldiers to monitor the operations of newly resettled small-scale farmers, to ensure that they use the land effectively, but with little success.

In 2006 the power struggle within the ruling party intensified. Vice-President Mujuru appeared to be the leading candidate to succeed Mugabe, but many believed that Emmerson Mnangagwa remained a strong contender. Meanwhile, Mugabe refused Msika's request to step down from his position as Vice-President for reasons of ill health, fearing further infighting over Msika's successor. When Mugabe suggested changing the Constitution to delay the March 2008 presidential poll until 2010, when a parliamentary election was scheduled, it was at first unclear whether this was to allow him to remain in office for a further two years, or to give his successor two years in office before they would have to face a presidential election. Regardless, Mugabe's proposition was rejected in March 2007 by ZANU—PF's central committee, which resolved instead that the general election would be brought forward, so that the two ballots would take place concurrently in 2008. The House of Assembly was to be increased in size from 150 to 210 members, with the new constituencies located mainly in the rural areas from which ZANU—PF drew its main support. Mugabe then made it clear that he intended to run in the 2008 presidential election, and ZANU—PF announced that he would be its sole candidate. Mugabe also received the support of traditional chiefs, who praised him for resisting what they called Western attempts to recolonize the country. As registration of voters for the 2008 elections began, there were numerous complaints of irregularities, and a litany of reports of abduction and intimidation of members of the opposition, as well as torture and arbitrary killings. As a campaign of intimidation against the opposition continued, the outspoken Archbishop of Bulawayo, Pius Ncube, continued to urge people to rise up to overthrow Mugabe.

On 11 March 2007 Tsvangarai and other leading MDC figures were savagely beaten by the police when trying to hold what they called a prayer rally organized by the Save Zimbabwe Campaign; one MDC activist was killed in the incident. Justifying the attack, Mugabe claimed that the MDC was responsible for a spate of petrol bombings earlier in the month aimed at bringing about regime change. In April Edward Chikomba, a photographer believed responsible for supplying graphic images of police brutality during the 11 March incident to the international media, was kidnapped and killed; the security forces were widely held responsible. In the following months, the Zimbabwe dollar continued to fall in value until it became virtually worthless. In late June businesses were ordered to cut their prices by 50%, and company executives and shopkeepers who failed to do so were arrested. Supermarkets and shops soon emptied, and manufacturing, which had already declined by over 50% in the previous decade, collapsed further. There was speculation that this latest step in the long process of economic collapse would at last precipitate the political change that many had been anticipating for years.

EXTERNAL RELATIONS

Regional instability and the issue of apartheid in South Africa dominated Zimbabwe's foreign relations in the first decade of independence. High priority was given to co-operation with Zimbabwe's partners in SADCC (now SADC—see above) and the Preferential Trade Area for Eastern and Southern African States (later superseded by the Common Market for Eastern and Southern Africa). Mugabe's strong support for mandatory sanctions against South Africa brought him into conflict with the United Kingdom and the USA, but enhanced Zimbabwe's standing in the Non-aligned Movement.

The activities of the South African-backed insurgent guerrilla group, the Resistência Nacional Moçambicana (Renamo) in Mozambique posed a threat to Zimbabwe's alternative access to the sea via the Beira corridor during the 1980s and early 1990s, and as a result Zimbabwe provided military assistance to the Mozambique Government. Following the death of President Machel of Mozambique in an air crash in October 1986, Mugabe reiterated his support for the Mozambique leadership. Renamo consequently declared war on the Zimbabwe Government, and cross-border incursions and civilian deaths became a regular occurrence. Mugabe played a leading role in mediating the cease-fire between the Mozambique Government and Renamo. In late 1992–early 1993, under the terms of a cease-fire, Zimbabwean troops, who had been stationed in Mozambique since 1982, were withdrawn. By 1992 it was estimated that 250,000 Mozambican refugees were sheltering in Zimbabwe. Plans for the repatriation of some 145,000 Mozambican refugees were announced in March 1993; this scheme, under the auspices of the office of the UN High Commissioner for Refugees, was completed during the mid-1990s.

The support given by Zimbabwe to the Mozambique Government, and the leading role taken by Mugabe in advocating the imposition of economic sanctions against South Africa, resulted in direct retaliatory action against Zimbabwe by the South African Government during the 1980s. In 1987 South African security forces launched two raids on alleged bases of the African National Congress of South Africa (ANC) in Harare. In June 1988 an attempt by a South African commando unit to release five alleged South African agents who were awaiting trial in Zimbabwe was thwarted by Zimbabwean security forces; three of the detainees were found guilty in June 1989 of taking part in bomb attacks on ANC targets. The detainees were eventually released in July 1990. Diplomatic relations with South Africa were resumed following the holding of democratic elections in that country in April 1994, and in March 1997 a mutual defence co-operation agreement was concluded. In February 2000 South Africa denied reports that it had offered a substantial loan to Zimbabwe to help the country to resolve its financial crisis. However, South African President Thabo Mbeki offered to negotiate on Zimbabwe's behalf with the IMF and the World Bank for emergency aid to prevent the collapse of the economy. Following an SADC summit in Harare in August 1998, the Zimbabwe Government dispatched troops and arms to the DRC to support the regime of President Laurent-Désiré Kabila against advancing rebel forces. There were repeated attempts to negotiate a peaceful solution to the conflict, but by May 1999 it was reported that Zimbabwe had spent at least Z.$500m. on its military intervention. Despite conservative official figures for losses and casualties, the action was domestically unpopular and placed Zimbabwe's financial and military resources under considerable strain. A cease-fire agreement was signed at Lusaka, Zambia, on 10 July, and troop withdrawals were supposed to follow within the next few months. However, within a few days both the rebels and the allies of the DRC were accused of violating the accord, and the Zimbabwean troops remained in the DRC in support of Kabila, enabling the Mugabe Government to benefit economically from exploiting the DRC's natural resources, especially diamonds. Following the assassination of Kabila in January 2001 and the succession of his son, Joseph, to the DRC presidency, efforts to agree a solution to the conflict were accelerated, and all countries involved in the conflict agreed to withdraw their forces by May, pending the deployment of a UN force. Nevertheless, in April 2002 an estimated 6,000–7,000 Zimbabwean troops remained in the DRC, from an initial deployment of 11,000. In October Zimbabwean troops completed their withdrawal from the DRC, following a number of positive developments in the peace process in that country.

Land reform issues dominated relations with the United Kingdom. During talks in April 2000 the British Government offered aid towards resettlement, but insisted that illegal farm seizures and political violence cease, free and fair elections be held and that only the black rural poor be allocated redistributed land. Harare rejected these terms. Meanwhile, relations deteriorated sharply between the two countries when customs officials at Harare airport ordered the opening of British diplomatic baggage. The British Government denounced this as a grave breach of the Vienna convention on diplomatic protocol and briefly recalled its High Commissioner to London for consultations. Zimbabwe countered by condemning the United Kingdom for smuggling goods into the country.

As the crisis in Zimbabwe deepened, African leaders, at meetings of the Organization of African Unity (now the AU) and elsewhere, failed to criticize Mugabe's lawless and authoritarian rule. Mugabe had to surrender the chairmanship of the SADC organ on politics, defence and security in 2001, but otherwise remained effectively untouched. The man with the most leverage, Thabo Mbeki, failed in his statements to distinguish between the principle of land redistribution and the violent means used in Zimbabwe to seize land. Nor did he criticize the harassment of the opposition; instead, Mbeki claimed that there was no alternative to 'quiet diplomacy'.

Meanwhile, Zimbabwe forged a new alliance with Libya, which provided credit to enable Zimbabwe to buy petroleum, and soon 70% of the country's supply was coming from Libya. In July 2001 Col Muammar al-Qaddafi visited Zimbabwe, declared that all whites should leave, and offered further supplies of fuel in exchange for Zimbabwean products. He also promised a large donation to ZANU—PF funds for the forthcoming presidential election, although, ironically, Zimbabwean law had recently been changed to prohibit foreign funding for political parties. Mugabe obtained support from the Chinese Government, which offered Zimbabwe an interest-free loan. By mid-2001 the Commonwealth had failed to take any effective action against Mugabe's increasingly lawless rule, but the US Congress moved to impose a range of sanctions on Zimbabwe; the Zimbabwe Democracy and Economic Recovery Act 2001 provided for sanctions to be lifted when the rule of law was restored and if the presidential election was adjudged free and fair. In September, under pressure from the Commonwealth and SADC, the Zimbabwe Government agreed at Abuja, Nigeria, to conduct future land redistribution lawfully (with funding from the United Kingdom), but it soon became apparent that this agreement would not be respected. The international community subsequently sought to secure the right to monitor the presidential election, threatening sanctions if observers were prevented from entering the country.

Relations between the United Kingdom and Zimbabwe had deteriorated further in February 2001, when an official at the British embassy was accused of obstructing the investigation into the activities of a British journalist, who was subsequently expelled from the country. Before the 2002 presidential election, the EU withdrew its observer mission after the chief of the mission was prevented from continuing his work, and then imposed so-called 'smart' sanctions, preventing Mugabe and his associates from travelling to EU countries and 'freezing' their assets. After the election, the Presidents of South Africa and Nigeria and the Prime Minister of Australia, who had been nominated by the Commonwealth to consider the conduct of the election and to formulate the organization's response, decided to suspend Zimbabwe from meetings of the Commonwealth for one year. After six months, the two African leaders were prepared to lift the suspension, but the Commonwealth did not accept this. The suspension was extended for a further nine months in March 2003, pending consideration by the next summit of the Commonwealth Heads of Government, scheduled to be held in December. Other countries did not follow the example of the USA and the EU in imposing selective sanctions. Speaking at the UN World Summit on Sustainable Development in Johannesburg, South Africa, in August–September 2002, Mugabe renewed his attack on the British Government, accusing it of neo-colonialism in its attitude to land distribution in Zimbabwe.

Mbeki, much criticized for doing little to resolve the Zimbabwe crisis, attempted to pressurize ZANU—PF to create the conditions for a parliamentary election in early 2005 that would be accepted as legitimate by the international community. He also sought to persuade SADC to agree to norms for free and fair elections in the region as a whole. However, the ZANU—PF politburo approved only minor electoral changes, which the MDC immediately criticized as inadequate. As the Zimbabwe crisis worsened in 2005–06, the AU, SADC and Mbeki all continued to avoid taking effective action. In 2005 the AU appointed former Mozambican President Joaquim Chissano to help address Zimbabwe's problems, and in 2006 SADC appointed former Tanzanian head of state Benjamin Mkapa to mediate between the Zimbabwean and British Governments, but neither was able to achieve anything significant. When, in March 2007, MDC leaders were beaten by police (see above), the South African Government merely issued a mild statement, despite widespread international condemnation of the incident. The USA and the EU tightened sanctions against Zimbabwe's ruling élite, and Zambian President Levy Mwanawasa broke ranks with others in SADC and admitted that quiet diplomacy had failed and that Zimbabwe was like 'a sinking Titanic' that was harming its neighbours. An emergency SADC summit was held in Dar es Salaam, Tanzania, later in March, at which Mbeki was appointed SADC mediator on Zimbabwe, but the summit also called for sanctions against the country to be lifted. Furthermore, the AU continued to insist that Mugabe be invited to a planned meeting of European and African leaders to be held in Lisbon, Portugal, in December. In mid-2007 Mbeki tried to bring together ZANU—PF and MDC representatives to negotiate a set of proposals on how the 2008 election should be conducted. However, Mbeki and SADC had condoned gross irregularities in previous elections in Zimbabwe, few thought the prospects were good for any kind of solution through such mediation. Meanwhile, the exodus of Zimbabweans continued, with South Africa absorbing most of the refugees, thought by 2007 to number perhaps as many as 4m.—almost one-quarter of the country's population.

International attention was for a time diverted from developments inside Zimbabwe by the saga of a group of alleged mercenaries who were arrested in Harare in March 2004 when they arrived by air from South Africa. Also arrested at Harare airport were the alleged leader of the group, former British army officer Simon Mann, and two former members of the South African security forces. The 70 men were then held in jail in Zimbabwe while investigations into their alleged mission to Equatorial Guinea were carried out. They were finally brought to trial in Harare in July 2004, and charged with, *inter alia*, attempting to buy weapons in Zimbabwe. Mann was jailed for four years and the others for lesser periods. By mid-2005 most had been released, but Mann remained in jail in mid-2007 while Zimbabwe and Equatorial Guinea discussed the latter's request for his extradition to stand trial there.

Economy

LINDA VAN BUREN

In 2007 the economy of Zimbabwe lay in ruins, with widespread hunger in the country that used to be known as the 'breadbasket of Southern Africa', with hyperinflation, with a worthless currency and with business activity at a virtual standstill. The UN World Food Programme (WFP) warned in August 2007 that 4.1m. Zimbabweans, both urban and rural, faced 'severe food shortages' prior to the next harvest, due in April 2008, unless they received WFP assistance. The WFP attributed the crisis to bad weather, a shortage of key inputs such as fertilizers and tractors, the crumbling irrigation system and the disincentive effect of the price controls put in place by the Government of Robert Mugabe. The accumulated effect of these shortcomings contributed to the poor maize harvest in 2006/07, which at 799,000 metric tons, fell far short of Zimbabwe's annual consumption requirements of 2.3m. tons and represented a 44% decline on output in the 2005/06 marketing year. In mid-2005 more than 1m. Zimbabweans, already struggling to survive without the support of a workable economic infrastructure, saw their homes bulldozed and their livelihoods destroyed when at least 200,000 homes were razed to the ground by the Mugabe's Government. Mugabe had alienated all traditional donors and lenders, inflation was running in four figures and real gross domestic product (GDP) contracted by 7.2% in 2005, having already contracted by one-third in 1999–2003. GDP contracted by a further 2.5%, in 2006, according to government estimates. In 2007 the Government forbade the Central Statistical Office from publishing inflation figures; none the less, an unreleased Government assessment reported that year-on-year inflation stood at 4,530% in 31 May 2007. This rate far exceeded hyper-inflation experienced elsewhere in the world, yet independent financial resources placed inflation at a far higher rate, with some estimating levels as high as 13,000%. An IMF source quoted in a local Zimbabwe business newspaper warned that by the end of 2007, inflation could reach six figures, at 100,000%.

International food-aid organizations were forced to withdraw their teams from Zimbabwe in May 2004 after the Government suddenly cancelled their food-supply assessment mission. Wide discrepancies existed between the Zimbabwe Government's estimate of the 2005 and 2006 maize harvests and assessments by external sources. The Government claimed that the 2004/05 crop amounted to 1m. metric tons, whereas the WFP estimated the crop at not more than 500,000 tons. In either case the figure was well below Zimbabwe's annual maize requirement. The Zimbabwe Government claimed that the 2005/06 maize crop totalled 1.7m. metric tons, but FAO reported that, even with the improved rains, the 2006 crop had increased only to between 1m. and 1.2m. tons. For its part, the US Department of Agriculture in February 2006 estimated Zimbabwe's maize harvest at 900,000 tons. FAO predicted in July 2006 that Zimbabwe would need to import 300,000 tons of maize in 2006/07. WFP had terminated its operations in Zimbabwe in April 2004, but in August 2005 WFP stated that it was standing by with food aid and was awaiting a formal request from the Zimbabwe Government for food assistance. Otherwise, filling the 1m. ton food gap would necessitate maize imports, and Zimbabwe, devoid of balance-of-payments support, was unlikely to possess the necessary funds to pay for imported maize. WFP resumed its vulnerable group feeding programme in time for the worst of the 2005 food crisis, and when it terminated it at the end of April 2006, it was because of increased availability of food in the country after the better harvest. The programme, which involved 11 non-governmental organizations (NGOs), had provided 3.6m. Zimbabweans with a monthly food ration saving many Zimbabweans from starvation. Other WFP activities in Zimbabwe continued in 2006 and 2007, supporting some 1m. Zimbabweans through such programmes as school feedings, support for orphans and assistance for the chronically ill. While President Mugabe proclaimed a 'food surplus' and an 'economic revival' in 2003, the UN warned of a huge food shortage. Economic performance indicators from 2004 showed that Mugabe's 'revival' had yet to occur, and that the predicted food shortage had ensued, peaking in 2005, when WFP reported that many Zimbabweans had resorted to hunting and searching for wild food to eat.

Zimbabwe has been in continuous arrears with the IMF since February 2001. In December 2003 the IMF took the unprecedented step of initiating compulsory withdrawal procedures against Zimbabwe. As negotiations continued, in February 2005 the Fund granted Zimbabwe six months to put in place measures to address the crisis situation. An IMF mission visited Zimbabwe in July 2005 and described talks as 'cordial'. Zimbabwe repaid some of its arrears to the Fund in early 2006, but in March 2006 the IMF declared that Zimbabwe remained ineligible for new lending because it still had outstanding arrears of US $119m. A subsequent IMF mission in December 2006 noted that Zimbabwe continued to endure 'deteriorating economic conditions' and that little progress had been made since its previous visit in March of that year.

In the five years between 31 July 2001 and 31 July 2006, the Zimbabwe dollar lost 99.94% of its official value. In a surprise three-hour speech on national television on 31 July 2006, the Governor of the Reserve Bank of Zimbabwe (RBZ), Gideon Gono, blamed Zimbabwe's monetary woes on 'three zeroes' and then announced that three zeroes would be removed from the currency to rectify this situation. At the same time, he announced a 60% devaluation of the currency, which altered the exchange rate from Z.$100,828 = US $1 to Z.$250,000 = US $1. The removal of the three zeroes left the official daily interbank exchange rate at Z.$250 = US $1. Gono also announced that old banknotes and bearer cheques (issued during the 2003 cash crisis and still in use in 2006) would be demonetized on 21 August 2006, leaving anyone holding these old instruments three weeks to present them at banks for conversion to the new banknotes. Various measures were included to trap those hoarding large sums of cash, defined as Z.$5m. in old money. In a country where a loaf of bread cost Z.$1m. (at that time equivalent to US $9.92), anyone who had sufficient cash to buy five loaves of bread was over the limit and exposed to punitive measures. Their cash would not be readily converted to the new currency but instead would be converted into two-year Anti-Money Laundering Zero Coupon Bonds (known as AMOLAZEBO) pending investigation. The day after the announcement the authorities seized Z.$100,000,000m. at borders as parties who had exported Zimbabwean dollars tried to reimport them ahead of the 21 August deadline. This devaluation had immediate negative effects: the Zimbabwean people were bewildered and even more mistrusting of the Zimbabwean dollar, and the black-market rate for the currency plunged further. On the 'black' market, the exchange rate fell from Z.$100,828 = US $1 on 31 July to Z.$650,000 = US $1 on 2 August. One year later nearly all sectors of the economy had ceased to use the Zimbabwe dollar and the 'three zeroes' had reappeared. In August 2007 the 'black' market exchange rate was estimated at Z.$400,000 = US $1, which, had it not been for the 2006 removal of three digits, would have been Z.$4,000,000 = US $1.

Foreign-exchange reserves have been negligible throughout the current crisis, and at 31 December 2005 they stood at US $24.8m., enough to cover only six days' worth of imports of goods and services. The 2006/07 budget made no attempt to quantify gross international reserves. Export volume was still declining, by 7.3% in 2005, although this decline was slower than the rate of decline in 2003, when export volume plummeted by 19.3%. Balance-of-payments support had never been more necessary than in June 2003, when the IMF suspended Zimbabwe's voting rights, and it was still much needed four years later: both the current account and the overall balance of payments had been in deficit, before and after official transfers, since the beginning of the existing crisis. Although a drought was the immediate cause, the difference from past droughts, when the agricultural system was organized well enough for commercial farmers—both large- and small-scale—to produce enough in good years to create sufficient reserves, was that many commercial farms had been confiscated by the Mugabe Government since 2000, severely affecting crop yields. With the virtual collapse of the agricultural infrastructure, thousands of farm labourers no longer had employment or food.

As annual statistics for 2000 emerged, every economic indicator reflected the worsening situation, and figures for each subsequent year demonstrated further serious deterioration. Financial institutions made their own assessments, which differed radically from the official version of key indicators issued by the Government. In the first two decades following independence in 1980, even though the same political leadership was in power, little was done to redistribute wealth, and until the late 1990s only modest progress was achieved in establishing a mechanism for an orderly reallocation of resources. Suddenly, in the election year of 2000, the Mugabe Government decided to act. The land-redistribution arrangements that had been agreed at negotiating tables over the preceding three years were discarded, inducing fear. In February 2000 squatters, styling themselves 'war veterans' (the war ended in 1980, and many of these squatters were clearly too young to have been fighting 20 years earlier), invaded white farms. Observed by the world's media, some invaded peacefully and, although not welcomed, were received peacefully; in numerous other cases violent confrontations took place, and lives were lost. The result was that in an economy already in decline, virtually all remaining business optimism and confidence, whether foreign or domestic, vanished. In 2001 Zimbabweans suffered shortages of electricity, fuel and food, in this relatively resource-rich country. Morale descended to unprecedented depths across the entire racial and economic spectrum in the aftermath of the controversial presidential election in March 2002 (see Recent History), leaving the Mugabe Government even more isolated than before, at a time when Zimbabwean citizens needed help more than ever. The heavy price of this political isolation was to take a ruinously costly economic toll in subsequent years.

Population growth was 1.9% per year during 1990–2003, according to the World Bank. However, in 1995–2004 population growth slowed to 1.0% per year, owing largely to the impact of HIV/AIDS and an increase in emigration. Zimbabwe had the second highest rate of HIV infection in Africa in 2005, and it has been estimated that by 2015 the labour force will be one-sixth smaller than it would have been in the absence of the

HIV/AIDS pandemic. Some demographic experts predicted that Zimbabwe could soon reach zero population growth as a result of the AIDS pandemic alone; the simultaneous increase in emigration would only compound the trend. In 2007 Zimbabwe had the third-lowest life expectancy in the world, at 37 years.

LAND POLICIES AND FOOD INSECURITY

Before independence, the country's land was divided into five grades. The most productive cropland was classified as Grade I, the least productive as Grade V. Whites were allocated 78% of all Grade I and II land. Grade IV and V land, deemed fit only for the grazing of livestock, accounted for 75% of the land allocated to smallholders in the pre-independence era, in what were known as the 'communal areas'. At 1 January 2000 some 11m. black Zimbabweans were still crowded on unproductive communal lands, and 4,500 principally white commercial farmers still owned 11m. ha of prime land.

After independence, the Mugabe Government reiterated its pre-election pledge to 'resettle' landless Zimbabweans on commercial farmland acquired from willing sellers among the white commercial farmers. By 1990 about 52,000 families had been resettled on 2.7m. ha, but this figure constituted only about 32% of the target set in the 1982–85 Transitional National Development Plan, which envisaged the resettlement of 162,000 families by 1985. Moreover, after a whole decade, fewer than 1% of those hoping for resettlement had been resettled. This took place in an orderly manner, albeit at much too slow a pace in the view of the many who had waited for so long. Under the 1980 Constitution, the Government was permitted, until 1990, to acquire land compulsorily for purposes of resettlement if it was 'under-utilized'. After 1990, expectations were directed towards an acceleration in land-reform measures. In March 1992 the House of Assembly unanimously approved the Land Acquisition Act, which permitted the compulsory acquisition of land by the state, facilitating the purchase of 5.5m. ha of the 11m. ha of land then still held by white farmers. The declared intention was to use the purchased land to resettle small-scale farmers from the communal areas. After much debate, the Act stopped short of detailing the white farmers' guarantee of fair compensation. This matter thus remained unresolved until President Mugabe, in August 2000, proclaimed that there was to be no compensation unless the United Kingdom wished to compensate these 'British' white farmers (most of whom held Zimbabwean nationality).

In 1996 it was announced that the acquisition of land by foreign investors would be permissible only in areas of low rainfall, and only in cases (subject to government approval) where a project would upgrade an economically marginal area, would either bring significant industrialization to a primary agricultural region, create major employment opportunities, or introduce a new form of export processing. Later, foreigners and companies were barred from owning land, following the announcement in June 1997 that the National Land Acquisition Committee had concluded its programme of identifying land for reallocation. Nevertheless, by August 1997 only 3.4m. ha of land had been acquired in the 17 years since independence, and only about 70,000 families had been resettled—a figure that still constituted scarcely 1% of those hoping for resettlement. Also in August 1997 plans were announced to acquire 1,072 farms, covering 3.2m. ha, to resettle some 100,000 landless peasants; a further 700 farms, covering 1.3m. ha, were to be used for indigenous commercial farming. The Government published its full list of 1,471 commercial farms designated for compulsory acquisition in November 1997. Controversially, Mugabe proclaimed that farmers would be compensated for the improvements they had made to their farms but not for the land itself. In January 1998, however, the IMF stipulated as a condition for the release of further financial assistance that the Mugabe administration must make assurances that it would offer full and fair compensation for land seized under the land-resettlement programme. The Mugabe Government did indeed make just such a pledge in March 1998, and it was subsequently announced that 112 farms would be acquired before the commencement of the 1998/99 growing season in November 1998. The Commercial Farmer's Union (CFU) speculated that, consequently, commercial-farm revenue would fall from Z.$14,000m. to Z.$8,000m. annually, that exports from the sector would decline from Z.$10,000m. to Z.$6,600m. per year, and that job losses would be substantial. At the time, many viewed these predictions as overly pessimistic; however, the next few years proved that, if anything, the predictions were optimistic.

A three-day international donors' conference on land reform took place in September 1998 in Harare, at which 24 countries and seven international organizations were represented. The Zimbabwean Government, which sought Z.$40,000m. from donors to support its land-acquisition programme, presented its case, as did the CFU and other interested parties. Although the donors acknowledged in principle the need for land reform in Zimbabwe, and some pledged financial support, they were unwilling to provide the full funding requirement for the scheme as proposed at that time. However, a 24-month Inception Phase was approved, to begin immediately. In November the Mugabe Government announced compulsory acquisition orders for a further 841 farms covering 2.24m. ha. In May 1999 the Cabinet approved an Inception Phase Framework Plan (IPFP), which the CFU agreed was practicable and would allow for proper land reform, leaving intact the 'basis of the economy'. The IPFP called for the resettlement of 77,700 families on 1m. ha by 2001. Of this land, 223,112 ha was to come from 120 farms that were voluntarily offered for sale in 1998, with the balance representing uncontested acquisitions under the Government's scaled-down list of 800 farms for compulsory purchase and what were described as 'novel approaches' for 'better utilization of farmland'. In May 1999 the World Bank pledged US $5m. towards the Inception Phase. Hard work at the negotiating table was, however, to be overtaken by events about to unfold in the countryside.

In February 2000 'war veterans' began occupying white-owned farms. By April nearly 1,000 farms had been occupied, four people had been killed, six had been abducted, hundreds of black employees working on white farms had been beaten, and several homes were burned down. It was alleged that only some 15% of the squatters were in fact 'war veterans', while the other 85% were unemployed youths who were paid Z.$50 per day by Mugabe's ruling party. Meanwhile, Zimbabwe's annual tobacco auction opened in April 2000 with fewer than 7,000 bales for sale—less than one-third of the 25,000 bales usually offered on the first day—because land occupations had disrupted the growing, harvesting, drying and curing of this labour-intensive crop. By mid-May 2000 tourist arrivals had declined to fewer than one-half of the usual levels. In the same month the World Bank halted all funding to Zimbabwe after the Mugabe Government failed to repay a government-guaranteed loan to the electricity parastatal and exceeded the 60-day grace period (see below). The World Bank placed Zimbabwe, indefinitely, on non-payment status on 3 October 2000. Following the general elections held in June 2000, the Mugabe Government, still in power but with a significantly reduced majority, resumed talks with donors. A series of contradictory policy statements then ensued. In July 2000 the new Minister of Industry and International Trade, Nkosana Moyo, reportedly acknowledged the need to work with the IMF, given the country's lack of resources. A few days later, however, Mugabe apparently stated that donors' funds were not required, and that land would not be given up to satisfy donors. On 1 August 2000 the Government devalued the Zimbabwe dollar by 24%, from Z.$38 = US $1 to Z.$50 = US $1, in an attempt to prevent 'a massive uncontrolled devaluation'; even before the devaluation the rate of inflation had been more than 50%. The following day a one-day general strike called by the trade unions was held peacefully. On 3 August, during a one-day visit by President Thabo Mbeki of South Africa, Mugabe promised that the exercise of removing squatters from occupied farms would be completed 'within the month'. None the less, on the following day Mugabe proclaimed that the squatters were not to be removed at all but instead would be allowed to stay on the farms until they were properly 'resettled'. In this climate of almost daily contradictory statements, investor confidence, already at an extremely low ebb, vanished altogether.

As 2000 drew to a close, and as annual statistics began to be compiled, they quantified a severe downward spiral. The Confederation of Zimbabwe Industries (CZI) revealed that more than 400 companies had closed in 2000, with the loss of some 10,000 jobs. Gold, tobacco, maize, wheat and horticultural production was significantly lower. Visible exports declined in terms of both volume and value, and tourism revenue dissipated overnight. The budgetary deficit, which had been forecast at 3.8% of GDP, expanded to 23% of GDP. Inflation continued to increase. Three-digit inflation, while not unknown in some other African countries, had been unprecedented in Zimbabwe, and it went on to become four-digit inflation. Hyperinflation created a major and lasting change in the daily lives of the Zimbabwean people, of all races and of all economic levels. Fuel shortages and electricity cuts plagued the nation, and the food supply would not stretch from one harvest to the next. The IMF made a last-ditch attempt in September 2001 to persuade the Mugabe Government to honour the 1998 Inception Phase agreement. Its mission failed, and later that month the Fund declared Zimbabwe ineligible to use general IMF resources and removed it from the list of countries eligible to borrow resources under the Poverty Reduction and Growth Facility (PRGF—see below). The US Senate had already approved the Zimbabwe Democracy and Economic Recovery Act of 2001 in July, which encompassed not only trade restrictions but also a ban on travel to the USA by President Mugabe, his immediate family, cabinet members and officials of the ruling party. Donors in 2001 expressed a willingness to ease their stance on compassionate grounds and send emergency food aid to avert a true famine, but only on the condition that the sole distributor of such food aid would be the UN Development Programme. The Mugabe Government rejected this condition.

Excessive rain in late 2001 raised hopes for a better harvest, but severe drought was experienced in January–April 2002 (the main harvest is in April–May). Total cereal production for the 2001/02 season was estimated to be 57% less than the previous year's already poor yield. Output of maize, the staple food, was 67% lower than in 2000/01 and 77% less than in 1999/2000. A major source of contention for donors was that the Government insisted that all cereal imports be processed through the Grain Marketing Board (GMB), which not only held a monopoly over grain imports but also fixed retail grain prices and restricted grain movements within the country. The GMB reported in May 2002 that it needed to distribute 5,000 metric tons of maize per day in order to provide for all those in need, but it was able to distribute only amounts varying from 400 tons to 2,000 tons per day. The GMB registered a loss of Z.$24,800m. in 2002. WFP began distributing emergency food aid in Zimbabwe in July 2002; by February 2003 it had distributed 204,000 tons to 4m. people in 49 out of the country's 57 districts, and by March the Programme had supplied 5m. people. This situation was followed by two successive maize harvests of less than one-half of the national annual requirement; even though the Mugabe Government suspended WFP attempts to assess the food-aid requirement in May 2004, enough information was known for severe food shortages to be forecast by both WFP and FAO. In August 2002 the European Union (EU) allocated food aid worth about US $35m. to the Zimbabwean Government. Although President Mugabe publicly stated in May 2004 that Zimbabwe would not import food in 2004, it was reported the following month that the South African Grain Information Service, by monitoring ships' manifests, had recorded consignments totalling nearly 200,000 tons from Argentina and the USA bound for Zimbabwe. With another poor harvest in 2006/07, food shortages worsened in 2007 (see above).

NATIONAL INCOME

The much-publicized land invasions of 2000 exacerbated an already troubled economic situation in Zimbabwe. In contrast, high levels of economic growth had been recorded in the first two fiscal years following independence. GDP grew, in real terms, by 11% in 1980 and by 13% in 1981. A major factor in these growth levels was the withdrawal, in 1980, of economic sanctions, which had crippled the economy during the 15 years of unilaterally declared independence; increased trade with the outside world rapidly stimulated economic activity. These growth levels demonstrated a temporary overinflation of the economy, to an extent that was illustrated graphically in the following fiscal years; GDP stagnated in 1982 and contracted by 3.5% in 1983, coinciding with serious drought, which lasted three years. None the less, GDP grew by an annual average rate of 3.6% during 1980–90, the first decade of independence, and by 0.1% annually in 1990–2002. In 1999, however, Zimbabwe entered a period of severe economic contraction, from which it has not recovered. GDP decreased in real terms by 4.1% in 1999, by 6.8% in 2000, by 8.4% in 2001, by 4.4% in 2002, by 10.4% in 2003, by 4.2% in 2004, by 7.2% in 2005 and by 2.5% in 2006, according to official estimates. Overall, the economy is estimated to be less that 63% of its size in 1999. The IMF estimated that GDP per head had declined by a cumulative 23% between 1997 and 2001. The population was enumerated at 11.8m. at the census of August 1997 and was estimated at about 13.2m. in mid-2007.

Although Zimbabwe has historically had one of sub-Saharan Africa's most successful agricultural sectors, agriculture would normally rank third, behind services and industry, in terms of contribution to GDP. Services accounted for about 60% of GDP in 2004, followed by industry at some 18% (including manufacturing at 11%) and agriculture at an estimated 22%, according to RBZ figures. Growth prospects for all these sectors were dismal from 2002. The occupation of white farms by squatters severely reduced the harvest of maize, wheat, tobacco and other crops; low investor confidence, a tightening of exchange controls and hyperinflation hindered manufacturing; depressed world gold prices lowered the value of mining output; and a decrease in tourists adversely affected the services sector, as well as placing downward pressure on invisible export receipts. Before the crisis of 2000, tourism had contributed 6% of GDP and had been a growth sector, increasing by 20%–40% per year. Tourist arrivals declined by 11% in 2000, and hotel-room occupancy rates were less than 20% at the height of the tourist season, although arrivals did increase by 11% in 2001. The Zimbabwe Tourism Authority offered free 'educationals' (also known as 'fam'—or familiarization—trips) to international tour operators in a bid to coax them back to the country. An estimated 100 tour operators in Zimbabwe closed in the year after the crisis began, and tour operators catering for visitors to Victoria Falls began transferring their bases across the Zambezi river to Livingstone, Zambia.

The most notable trend in domestic expenditure in the 1980s was the decline in the private sector's share, from 63% in 1980 to 44% in 1989. The downward trend was reversed in 1990, when the private sector accounted for 53% of total spending; the sector's share grew to 61% in 1991 and to 71% in 1992, reflecting almost immediately the Economic Structural Adjustment Programme (ESAP) that had been introduced in 1991, which envisaged continued growth of private consumption. The private sector's share in domestic expenditure had increased to 78% in 1996. Although these figures are somewhat dated, they are more indicative of the economic capabilities of Zimbabwe than the dismal figures of the 21st century.

By 1995 relations between the Zimbabwean Government and the Bretton Woods institutions had deteriorated significantly, and the IMF suspended assistance worth US $100m. in that year, pending a reduction in Zimbabwe's budgetary deficit. Multilateral credit and bilateral balance-of-payments support remained suspended until June 1998, when the IMF resumed lending with a US $175m., 13-month stand-by credit in support of Zimbabwe's 1998 economic reform programme, of which US $52m. was disbursed immediately, with the remainder to be released subsequently, 'subject to Zimbabwe's meeting performance targets'. The last IMF credit approved was in August 1999 (see above). Zimbabwe fell behind in repayments to the IMF for the first time in February 2001 and has remained in continuous arrears since that time. In September 2001 the Fund formally declared Zimbabwe ineligible for general and PRGF borrowing. By mid-2002 Zimbabwe's arrears to the IMF had grown to US $132m., of which US $58m. was made payable to the PRGF Trust. Although Zimbabwe made a US $3m. payment to the Fund in the first half of 2002, its arrears continued to mount. In June 2002 the IMF proclaimed a 'declaration of non-compliance' and suspended technical assistance to Zimbabwe. By August 2003 Zimbabwe's arrears to all creditors had increased to US $1,500m., equivalent to 29% of total debt. In December 2003 the IMF initiated compulsory withdrawal procedures against Zimbabwe, citing the Government's lack of active co-operation and a failure to address the country's economic problems with comprehensive and consistent policies (see Recent History).

AGRICULTURE

Zimbabwe has had, and could have again, a diversified and well-developed agricultural sector, in terms of food production, cash crops and livestock. Of the total land area, 8.3% is arable. The principal rainy season is from November to March, and the harvest is in April and May. In 2001 about two-thirds of the total labour force and about one-quarter of the formal-sector labour force were engaged in agricultural activity, although the farm confiscations made many Zimbabweans redundant and in many cases homeless and hungry. WFP estimated in May 2002 that retrenched farm workers and their dependants numbered about 825,000. Agriculture (including forestry) contributed an estimated 22% of GDP in 2004, compared with 12.4% in 1990. Although the agricultural sector in Zimbabwe has been no more immune to fluctuations of price and unfavourable weather than in any other country, in the first 19 years of independence it proved to be resilient. After the squatter occupations of February 2000, however, depressing economic indicators revealed the scale of the damage this exercise had inflicted on Zimbabwe's agricultural sector. Agricultural lenders reported that few farmers were arranging new loans and that some had stopped servicing their existing loans, while manufacturing companies dependent on the supply of locally produced agricultural commodities registered a fall in capacity utilization of up to 60%. Several resorted to laying off production staff, and some closed down altogether. At first, the plight of manufacturers was in the form of knock-on effects from the invasion of commercial farms; but by mid-2004 several manufacturing companies had suffered invasions of their own premises. Freight hauliers reported a sharp decline in demand at a time when fuel was increasingly scarce and costs were rising; by mid-2001 at least five freight-forwarding companies had closed down. By August 2003 an estimated 500,000 Zimbabweans had become 'displaced persons' as a result of the land confiscations, nearly all of them black former employees on white farms and their families, and more than 240,000 farm workers had lost their jobs. By the end of 2006 unemployment was officially assessed at 70%.

The staple food crop is maize, and other cereal crops grown include wheat, millet, sorghum and barley. Despite the fact that the country's best farmland was still concentrated overwhelmingly in the commercial sector, the share of agricultural output contributed by small-scale farmers in the communal areas rose from 9% in 1983 to 50% in 1990 and to 60% in 1999, before the onslaught of the 'troubles' on the occupied commercial farms. The area planted with maize in the communal and resettled areas increased by 14% in 2001/02, although drought and other factors lowered yields per ha, and the size of the harvest declined. The area planted with maize on commercial farms declined from 74,000 ha in 2000/01 to 61,000 ha in 2001/02, representing a fall of 62% from the 1999/2000 level. The total area planted with maize declined from 1.64m. ha in 1997 to a low of 1.22m. ha in 2001, reflecting the increasing difficulty of growing maize in the deteriorating economic conditions prevailing in Zimbabwe. After 2001 the area under maize increased somewhat, reflecting the need to return to maize-growing at subsistence level, in a market of scarce supplies. FAO figures revealed that the maize yield declined from 1,199 kg per ha in 2001 to just 378 kg per ha in 2002. Zambia's maize farmers consistently achieve a substantially higher yield than their counterparts south of the border: in 2000, before political events caused severe disruption to the farming sector, Zimbabwe's average maize yield was 1,488 kg per ha, whereas Zambia's was 1,502 kg per ha, even in a relatively poor growing season. By 2004 the gap had widened dramatically: Zambia's yield was 1,548 kg per ha, whereas Zimbabwe's had plunged to 714 kg per ha. Adverse weather conditions—drought followed by excessive rains—accounted for only part of the problem from 2002; lack of agricultural inputs, marketing difficulties and poor producer prices, in real terms, all took their toll.

In 2002 the Government raised the producer price for maize from Z.$15,000 to Z.$28,000 per metric ton; meanwhile, the GMB fixed the retail price at Z.$9,600. At this rate, a government subsidy was to cover nearly two-thirds of the price of every ton of maize sold in Zimbabwe. Despite this measure, the CFU called for a producer price of Z.$60,000 per ton to cover the cost of production, which it assessed at Z.$43,000 (US $781) per ton. In a climate of hyperinflation, producer price rises such as these have little effect.

In June 1999 the National Bakers' Association warned the Government that if its proposal to limit the retail price of bread to Z.$8.72 per standard white loaf went ahead, its members would suspend production. In 2002 it was reported that the baking industry was losing Z.$33,000 per day. In July 2001 the GMB, which had once been the only legal marketer of grain in the country (until stripped of its monopoly during the reform years), once again found itself the sole buyer of maize and wheat, when President Mugabe declared these two crops to be 'controlled'. Farmers reacted angrily to this move, threatening the emergence of a parallel market in these two essential grains. The Government fixed the producer price of maize at Z.$7,500 per metric ton; a ton of maize had previously been selling on the open market for Z.$9,329. Within weeks of this move, it was estimated that maize was selling on the 'black' market for four to five times the controlled price. Subsequently, according to WFP, the black-market price of maize rose by a further 167% between August 2002 and August 2003. The Government also granted the GMB a monopoly over the movement of grain within the country. Although food shortages in Zimbabwe were nationwide by mid-2002, some areas suffered more than others, as the GMB failed to move available grain there, and the private sector was forbidden to move it. One of the main reasons for the failure to move food was a lack of availability of fuel, owing to the shortage of foreign exchange with which to import it. In August 2001, in the face of dwindling stocks, the Southern African Development Community had agreed to allow Zimbabwe to import at least 100,000 tons of maize from South Africa; this amount was, however, far less than the minimum 600,000 tons urgently needed to feed the population. The announcement of the decision to import grain ran counter to Mugabe's denials that Zimbabwe was facing food shortages and was seen as an attempt to prevent food riots. Zimbabwe consumes about 400,000 tons of wheat per year and must import wheat even in years of good harvests. Local wheat production declined from 320,000 tons in 1999 to 250,000 tons in 2001, to 150,000 tons in 2002, but recovered, according to FAO, to 213,000 tons in 2003. In 2006, a good crop was approaching harvest time, and the only legal buyer of farmers' maize was the GMB. Despite this, most farmers were selling their maize on the 'black' market. The GMB offered a set fixed subsidized price, whereas the black market was paying far less; but the GMB's form of payment was to issue, a month or two after it took possession of the grain, a cheque that then took even more time to clear; the black marketeers offered cash on the spot.

During the 1990s National Breweries Ltd produced 8,000–10,000 metric tons of malt per year for export. Zimbabwe's barley output fluctuates according to weather conditions, ranging from 30,000 tons in 1989 to 4,500 tons in 1992. FAO figures indicate that barley production amounted to an estimated 30,000 tons in 2003 and to 25,000 tons in 2004. In 2005, according to FAO, Zimbabwe produced an estimated 40,000 tons of millet (compared with 14,648 tons in 2002 and 115,000 tons in 1997), about 80,000 tons of sorghum (compared with 110,300 tons in 2001) and an estimated 150,000 tons of groundnuts in shells (compared with 190,890 tons in 2000). Millet and sorghum began to fill an increasing proportion of the rural Zimbabwean diet, as maize stocks ran out; however, not even these crops could feed the nation.

The horticultural sector performed well in the late 1990s, displaying a diversity unequalled in many other African countries. Both for domestic consumption and for export, Zimbabwean fruit growers produced apples, pears, peaches, nectarines, apricots, plums, mangoes, papayas, melons, strawberries, raspberries, currants, grapes, oranges, lemons, limes, tangerines and grapefruits. Other horticultural crops included green peas, green beans, broad beans, cucumbers, artichokes, asparagus, mushrooms, chillies, cabbages, lettuces, carrots, cauliflower, onions, leeks, garlic, chestnuts and vanilla. Horticultural produce was regularly freighted to Europe. The sector exhibited phenomenal growth, averaging some 20% per year throughout the 1990s, and became the second largest visible foreign-exchange earner after tobacco, contributing 4.5% of GDP in 1999. Horticultural production (not including flowers) reached 13,597 metric tons in 1999, but output in 2000, as with other sectors, suffered, reaching only 10,217 tons, 56% of the forecast. Earnings from floriculture reached US $88.4m. in 1999, but output declined by 2.3% in 2000, falling 23% short of forecasts.

Zimbabwe's principal cash crops are tobacco, cotton and sugar. During the 1980s tobacco cultivation employed about 12% of the labour force and contributed about two-thirds of agricultural export revenue. In the 1990s declining demand in export markets placed downward pressure on prices. Zimbabwe's golden-yellow 'lemon leaf' variety is highly prized by blenders. Tobacco auctions each year normally begin in April and last for 25 weeks. Exports of Zimbabwean tobacco in 1996 earned Z.$6,800m., with the EU and the Far East the most important destinations. During the 1990s smallholders became increasingly involved in the cultivation of burley tobacco. The flue-cured sector is far larger, with commercial farmers accounting for most of the output. In 1996 the Government imposed an effective 10% tax on tobacco sales. Farmers and merchants bitterly opposed the tax and urged its abolition, claiming that it would damage the sector. A record tobacco crop of 260m. kg was harvested in 1998. In June 1999 the Government agreed to halve the levy. In early 2001, in the face of extremely bleak prospects for two of its most important agricultural export commodities, the Government introduced an allowance for tobacco and cotton farmers to retain 20% of foreign-exchange earnings, to permit them to pay for essential imported inputs. The disbursement of funds under this scheme reportedly commenced in July 2001, after a delay of several months. According to WFP, however, both tobacco and cotton experienced significant reductions in both production and export in 2001/02. Between 1990 and 2004 the number of commercial tobacco growers dropped from 1,299 to 700. Tobacco remained a valuable source of foreign currency (valued at US $321m.) in 2003. Prior to the troubles of 2000, Zimbabwe had enjoyed a favourable yield, and the area planted under tobacco had set a record in 1997, at 99,293 ha. Yield per ha plummeted from 2,387 kg per ha in 2001/02 to 1,783 kg per ha in 2002/03, the surface area planted with tobacco fell by more than one-half, from 55,547 ha to 23,240 ha, and production of tobacco leaves weakened from 195.9m. kg in 2001 to about 80m. kg per year in 2004. In April 2006 the RBZ introduced a Delivery and Early Delivery Bonus, whereby growers who delivered their tobacco to the auction floor by 31 July would receive a 30% bonus and those who delivered their leaf by 31 August would receive 15%. This bonus was in addition to a 65% subsidy known as the Tobacco Performance, Research and Development Facility. The two programmes together constitute a 95% subsidization of tobacco prices.

In the cotton sector, small-scale communal producers account for just over one-half of total production. In contrast to most crops, the cotton sector performed well in 1999/2000, with a harvest of 327,000 metric tons of seed cotton, an increase of 22% from the previous year, which yielded 199,470 tons of cottonseed and 127,530 tons of cotton lint. By 2002 the harvest of seed cotton had declined to 200,417 tons. The US company Monsanto had expressed an interest in investing Z.$150m. in a controversial venture to grow genetically engineered cottonseed in Zimbabwe, conditional on its being allowed to retain a controlling 51% share, but permission was not granted, and the plan was abandoned in 1999. Conditions in Zimbabwe were such that the country's textile industry was not in a position to take advantage of the US African Growth and Opportunity Act (AGOA) benefits enjoyed by textile producers in many of the neighbouring countries.

The harvest of sugar cane amounted to 3.3m. metric tons in 2005, according to FAO, compared with 4.5m. tons in 2003. An irrigation scheme has been proposed to make this very thirsty crop less vulnerable to drought in future, although the current financial crisis has placed most major investment schemes of all types on hold. In 1999 Hippo Valley Estates strongly criticized government intervention in sugar prices, pointing out that the domestic price of sugar in Zimbabwe was less than one-half that in neighbouring countries. This anomaly has provided a significant incentive for the legal and illegal export of Zimbabwean sugar and, according to Hippo Valley Estates, costs the Government Z.$110m. per year in lost tax revenue, together with a further Z.$313m. in price subsidies. In April 2004 the Zimbabwe Government, having enacted amendments to the land-appropriation legislation, sought to confiscate 49 properties comprising 24,838 ha of the total of 60,165 ha that comprise Hippo Valley Estates.

Coffee export revenue for Zimbabwe's mild arabicas reached Z.$75m. in the 1986/87 marketing year. The arabica crop doubled in 1988/89 to 12,500 metric tons, following favourable weather conditions; however, the value of exports was only Z.$54m., because of depressed world prices. Output declined to 9,100 tons in 2000 and to 7,500 tons in 2001; however, production recovered to 10,000 tons in 2003. The official estimate of the 2005 crop was 7,000 tons. According to the International Coffee Organization, Zimbabwe produced 58,000 60-kg bags of coffee in 2005, down from 96,000 bags in 2004, and exports amounted to 50,755 bags in 2005/06, down from 80,878 bags in 2004/05.

Zimbabwe is one of only a few sub-Saharan African countries allowed to export beef to EU member states; exports began in 1985, although Zimbabwe was unable to meet its quota of 8,100 metric tons in the first two years. In 1998 Zimbabwe's EU quota was 9,100 tons, but the country was still able to fill only 84% of it, at 7,653 tons. Zimbabwe also enjoys a 5,000 ton-per-year quota of beef exports to South Africa. The national herd was estimated at 5.4m. head of cattle, 2.97m. goats, 610,000 sheep, 62,000 pigs and 27,500 horses in 2004. Good rains in April 2002 unexpectedly improved grazing and water availability. However, according to WFP, the national herd of commercial beef cattle declined from 500,000 in 1999 to 282,000 in May 2002, owing to destocking. From 2005 both the commercial and communal livestock sectors suffered from a lack of grain, which is used to make animal feed, and prices fell. As feed became scarcer, distress sales increased, causing prices to decline further.

In forestry, Zimbabwe's total roundwood removals amount to some 9.1m. cu m annually, about 90% of which goes towards fuelwood. Exports of sawnwood declined from 112,000 cu m in 2000 to 25,400 cu m in 2001, in volume terms, and from US $24.9m. in 2000 to US $6.1m. in 2001, in value terms. Along with the white-owned farms targeted, the Government listed 55 forest plantations for compulsory acquisition under its land-resettlement programme, placing more than 20,000 timber workers' jobs at risk. Wildfires in 2005 claimed 12% of Zimbabwe's forests and destroyed US $992m. worth of timber.

Zimbabwe's total fish catch was estimated at 16,000 metric tons by 2004. Freshwater species account for about one-third of the total. The predominant fish caught are dagaas (various species of shad), which migrate between saltwater and freshwater; dagaas accounted for 67% of the total catch in 2003.

The capacity of authorities to accurately capture agricultural performance continued to decline and by 2007 official assessments were published infrequently and widely regarded as implausible by independent observers. Indeed, while WFP was signalling a severe crop failure in 2006/07 and warning that millions of Zimbabweans faced hunger and starvation, the 2006/07 budget proclaimed that 'the outlook for agriculture for the 2006/07 season is promising'.

MINING AND MANUFACTURING

The mining sector experienced negative growth in 2005, contracting by 5.7%. The 2006 budget blamed 'deteriorating international mineral prices' and 'rampant smuggling of gold, diamonds and other precious minerals'. Gold accounted for 44% of all mineral production, and during 2005 the global gold price rose from US $444 to US $513 per troy oz, so it would appear that the rampant gold smuggling was the main culprit in gold's lacklustre performance in Zimbabwe. The Government proposed to combat this smuggling not with financial disincentives but instead with tougher policing measures. The index of mineral production declined dramatically in 2000, and little improvement occurred subsequently. In fact, Zimbabwe's official gold output declined by more than 50% in 1999–2003.

In the late 1990s Zimbabwe produced more than 40 different minerals. Gold, platinum, nickel, asbestos, coal, copper, chromite, iron ore, tin, silver, emeralds, graphite, lithium, granite, cobalt, tungsten, quartz, silica sands, kyanite, vermiculite, corundum, magnesite, kaolin and mica are the main mineral products. About 25% of Zimbabwe's gold production is derived from the tailings of earlier gold-mining activities. In November 1993 Cluff Resources of the United Kingdom (later acquired by Ashanti Goldfields of Ghana, now AngloGold Ashanti) reached an agreement with the Eastern and Southern African Trade and Development Bank for a 52,000-oz gold loan to finance underground development of the Freda Rebecca gold mine, which had become Zimbabwe's largest gold mine by the end of 1994. The loan was repayable over five years and gave the borrower the choice of repaying in gold or US dollars. In 2004 AngloGold Ashanti sold the Freda Rebecca gold mine to Mwana Africa Holdings and subsequently sold six smaller gold mines in Zimbabwe, thereby disposing of all of its assets in Zimbabwe.

Production at one of the country's largest mines, Rio Tinto's Renco mine in Masvingo, fell by 15%, from 12,796 troy oz in the third quarter of 1998, to 10,919 oz in the second quarter of 1999. Rio Tinto closed its unprofitable Brompton gold mine near Kadoma in 1998. Falcon Gold closed its Dalny gold mine in the same year and its Venice mine in 2000. Delta Gold bought three mines from Falcon Gold and proceeded with the development of the 10.5-ton Eureka mine near Guruve, capable of processing 75,000 oz of gold annually. Following a series of acquisitions, the Eureka gold mine became an asset of Placer Dome in 2005, when that company sold it to a Zimbabwean consortium comprising Mmakau Mining (Pty) Ltd and Shaft Sinkers (Pty) Ltd. The global mining community is staying away from Zimbabwe despite known very attractive mineral resources. Meanwhile, the RBZ resumed its gold-price support scheme amid weak gold prices in 2001 and 2002, paying Zimbabwean gold producers US $343.00 per oz, effectively amounting to a 36% subsidy. This subsidization of maize, gold and other commodities not only contradicts IMF and World Bank principles but also places a heavy strain on scarce government resources.

The world nickel price increased dramatically at the end of the 20th century, doubling to US $8,370 per metric ton in 1999. Nickel traditionally ranks second in Zimbabwe's mineral export revenue; output was 12,872 tons in 1998 but declined to 8,160 tons in 2000, although production recovered to an estimated 8,556 tons in 2005. In a market in which almost all trends were downward, Bindura Nickel's share price rose from Z.$1.05 at 1 January 1999, to Z.$14.00 at 31 December 1999, and to Z.$21.00 at 1 March 2000. Production of asbestos, which accounted for 10.6% of total mining output in 2005, grew by 8.5% in 2005. Output of coal, which accounted for 12.6% of total mineral production in 2005, grew by 21.8% in that year. Rio Tinto Zimbabwe (which became RioZim Ltd in 2004—see below) announced in 1990 that it was to develop the Sengwa coalfield in western Zimbabwe, which has a projected annual output of 100,000 tons of low-sulphur coal; the project was to be the second largest investment in Zimbabwe since independence. However, in 2005 RioZim was looking, without success, for investment partners to bring in the US $2,000m. needed to progress with the Sengwa scheme. Reserves at Lubimbi coalfield are estimated to exceed 20,000m. tons. Zimbabwe's total coal reserves are estimated at 28,000m. tons. Shangani Energy Exploration was granted a licence in May 1998 to mine coal-bed methane gas in Bulawayo mining district. RioZim Ltd in 2004 announced the discovery of new nickel reserves at its Chimakasa concession.

Platinum holds significant revenue potential, and substantial reserves, first discovered in 1914, are located in the Great Dyke mineral belt in central Zimbabwe. The first platinum mine opened at Wedza in 1926. In 1993 BHP of Australia made an investment equivalent to US $211m., said to be the largest single private-sector investment in Zimbabwe since independence, to enable the Hartley project to go ahead. The mine, which has a projected life span of 70 years, has been forecast to produce annually, at full capacity, 150,000 oz of platinum metal, as well as 110,000 oz of palladium, 23,000 oz of gold, 11,500 oz of rhodium, 3,200 tons of nickel, 23,000 tons of copper, and 2,000 tons of cobalt. In 1994 the Zimbabwean Government agreed to the venture, and construction work commenced. An underground mine came into operation in 1996, creating 3,573 mining jobs, but the project ran into technical problems, which caused the date for entry into full production to be postponed. In the late 1990s a mill, a concentrator, a smelter, a converter and a base-metal refinery were built, and in 1997 the project produced its first shipment of platinum concentrate. Modifications to the smelter costing Z.$72m. had to be made in order to deal with the geological conditions encountered. In 1998 Delta Gold sold its 33% share in the Hartley concession to Zimbabwe Platinum Mines Ltd (Zimplats). In June 1999 BHP announced the closure of the mine, owing to geological problems and unstable ground conditions that rendered the mine unsafe, and claiming that it had earned only US $40m. from the mine after investing US $585m. BHP sold its 67% share for a token sum to Zimplats in late 1999. The Government hastened to claim that the Hartley closure was temporary and that production would resume once the mine could be made safe underground. At full production of 180,000 metric tons of platinum-bearing ore per month, Hartley would account for about 10% of total world output of the precious metal and would establish Zimbabwe as Africa's second most significant producer of platinum, after South Africa. Production was about 71,000 tons per month in mid-1998. Operating costs at Zimplats rose from US $9.9m. in the first quarter of 2003 to US $15.3m. in the second quarter. Areas adjacent to Hartley are also being explored for possible exploitation. In 1995 Delta Gold announced plans to develop a further platinum and gold project at Ngezi, 57 km south of the Hartley complex. While reserves of platinum at Hartley are assessed at 14m. oz, those at Ngezi are evaluated at 24m. oz. Anglo Zimbabwe has announced plans to develop a platinum mine at Unki, near Shurugwe, at a cost of US $90m., in a joint venture with the Zimbabwean Government. Unki was expected to produce 1.02m. tons of ore per year at a richness of 5.4 g per ton of platinum-grade metals and gold. The scheme was expected to generate Z.$4,000m. per year in export revenue and create 1,400 jobs. In 1996 the Zimbabwe Mining and Smelting Co was reported to be developing a smaller platinum mine in Midlands Province.

The parastatal Zimbabwe Mining Development Corpn is developing the copper deposits at the Copper Queen and King mines, and it is planned to manufacture copper cable locally as an import-substitution venture, aimed at saving Z.$6.6m. in foreign exchange annually. There is also import-substitution potential in the manufacture of ferrochrome derivatives, chemicals and pesticides. Another parastatal organization, the Minerals Marketing Corpn of Zimbabwe, markets all the country's minerals, except gold, abroad. Established in 1982, its operations were consistently profitable for the following 15 years. Major private-sector mining companies, such as Anglo American, Rio Tinto-Zinc and Lonmin, have also been active in Zimbabwe. In 1989 a gold refinery, with a capacity of 50 metric tons per year, was opened in Harare. Built at a cost of Z.$4m., the refinery is owned by the RBZ and is operated by Fidelity Printers and Refiners. It was expected to lessen Zimbabwe's dependence on South Africa, which had previously possessed the only gold refineries in Africa. Gemstones hold considerable growth potential. In 1991 the British company Reunion Mining began prospecting for diamonds over a 43,597 sq km area near Beitbridge. In the following month Auridiam Consolidated of Australia obtained a permit to develop the River Ranch diamond concession at a cost of US $10m.–$12m. The company completed its exploration activities in 1992, confirming that diamonds had been found at the concession and announcing plans to build a small-scale production plant. A 500,000 ton-per-year processing plant at River Ranch was commissioned in January 1994. The River Ranch mine had been expected to reach full production of 1.5m. tons of ore annually in 1996 and to produce 500,000 carats per year during its projected 10-year life span. However, low world diamond prices resulted in the company losing Z.$40m. for every ton of ore processed, and in February 1998 the mine closed down with the loss of 400 jobs. It went into voluntary liquidation in May of that year; immediately 12 potential purchasers (both local and foreign) reportedly came forward, but the number subsequently dwindled to only two.

Interest in mining diamonds in Zimbabwe remained keen, and in 1998 a number of licences were granted to companies to prospect for them. In March 2001 Rio Zimbabwe, Trans Hex Zimbabwe Ltd and Somabula Explorations Ltd set up a joint venture to prospect for diamonds in kimberlite pipes in three concessions in southern Zimbabwe. Although Zimbabwe's mineral resources are attractive to overseas investors, the current political and economic crisis has caused investor interest to fall to a very low level. In May 2004 Rio Tinto Ltd restructured its relationship with Rio Tinto Zimbabwe in an arrangement whereby the parent company traded its holding in Rio Tinto Zimbabwe in exchange for a 22% share in the US $10m. Murowa diamond mine, which had been a 50:50 joint venture between the parent and the Zimbabwe affiliate. Rio Tinto Zimbabwe became RioZim Ltd, an entirely Zimbabwean entity, and Rio Tinto ceased to be an ordinary shareholder in RioZim. Rio Tinto denied that the move was a reaction to the 'unrest' in Zimbabwe, although the announcement followed the April 2004 revocation by the Zimbabwe Government of 13 exclusive mining concessions by three companies, one of which was Rio Tinto. Meanwhile, development of the Murowa mine, with reserves of 18.7m. tons of ore evaluated at 0.9 carats per ton, continued; the mine entered production in the last quarter of 2004. Production amounted to 30,222 tons of treated ore in 2004 and 29,380 tons in the first quarter of 2005. Rio Tinto sold its 59% share of Murowa to RioZim in 2005. Further investment was being sought in July 2005 to boost production beyond the current capacity of an annualized 200,000 tons of treated ore. The mineral sector has the potential to recover rapidly if the political climate improves, although the pace of recovery will depend on the global prices prevailing at the time.

Zimbabwe produces a wide variety of manufactured products, both for the local market and for export. Growth of manufactured exports on a regional basis was hindered by lack of foreign exchange in neighbouring countries in the 1990s and by reductions of up to 55% in the amount of foreign exchange allocated to manufacturers for the import of essential raw materials, even before the foreign-exchange crisis from 2000 onwards. The weak Zimbabwe dollar was a fillip to those companies with low import costs manufacturing for export, but it placed further pressure on those with high import costs manufacturing for the local market. Companies with low import costs make wide use of local raw materials, not least Zimbabwe's own agricultural output; however, the drought rendered most of those materials scarce, so that such companies also were operating well below capacity in 2002 and beyond. The manufacturing sector accounted for 11% of GDP in 2004, a decline from 19% in 1996 and from the 30% annually achieved in 1992–93. Manufacturing output contracted by 3% in 2005 and by 7% in 2006.

Manufacturing in the country's Export Processing Zones (EPZs) flourished in the late 1990s. As of August 1998, 28 companies had been established, creating 6,242 jobs and generating Z.$2,000m. in export revenue; a further 72 projects had been approved, with the potential to create 12,000 jobs. In July 2001 the Ministry of Finance and Economic Development called for the Export Processing Zone Authority and the Zimbabwe Investment Centre to be merged, in order to save Z.$1.76m. in administrative costs. In November 2003 it was announced that EPZ companies were to lose their exemption from Zimbabwean exchange controls, in a bid to eradicate foreign-currency 'leakages' in the sector. The manufacturing sector came under severe pressure during the economic crisis of 1999 and the subsequent troubles. It was reported that 85 companies in 12 sectors had gone into liquidation during 1999 and that 400 had closed in 2000. These companies had been engaged in trade, farming, manufacturing, tourism and construction. Of the 1999 figure, 43 companies went into voluntary liquidation, while the other 42 were forcibly liquidated by creditors. Whereas 6,357 companies had defaulted on debt repayments in the whole of 1999, no fewer than 2,820 had been issued with default judgements in the first four months of 2000. A severe shortage of fuel in the country from 2005 hindered the movement of manufactured goods, mining equipment and the entire transport sector in general, increasing the cost of conducting business in Zimbabwe significantly. Last but certainly not least, hyperinflation placed an unsustainable burden on a number of manufacturers.

INTERNATIONAL TRADE AND BANKING

With terms of trade deteriorating and with the deficit on the current account of the balance of payments widening, Zimbabwe was reportedly entering into barter arrangements to pay for imports with tobacco and minerals. Visible exports, which had amounted to US $2,496m. in 1996, totalled just US $1,398m. in 2002, falling to an estimated US $1,225m. in 2003. Imports totalled US $1,923m. in 2002, falling to US $1,627m. in 2003. The revised visible trade balance for 2001, originally stated to register a surplus of US $270m., was actually in deficit, at US $217m. The shortfall for 2002 widened to US $525m., but the fall in imports in 2003 led to a narrowing of the deficit in 2003, to an estimated US $402m. The overall balance of payments carried a deficit of US $273m. in 2001, rising to US $639m. in 2002 and falling to about US $574m. in 2003. The 2006/07 budget stopped short of quantifying 2006 exports and imports, but did reveal that total exports declined by 6% and that total imports declined by 1.6% in that year. The Government also placed the current account deficit on the balance of payments at US $543.3m. in 2006 and admitted that, overall, the balance of payments was 'under severe pressure'. Generally, in normal circumstances, tobacco, horticultural produce and gold are Zimbabwe's principal exports, but together they contribute less than 50%; other export earners in normal years are cotton lint, textile products, footwear, ferro-alloys, food and live animals, crude inedible non-food materials, chrome, nickel, asbestos, copper, raw sugar, iron and steel bars, ingots and billets, electric cables and radios. This list illustrates an unusually high level of export diversity for an African country. Exports of ivory (officially to Japan only) recommenced on a limited scale in 1999, following a vote at a conference of the Convention on International Trade in Endangered Species (CITES), and Zimbabwe had already arranged to sell 20 metric tons of ivory to Japan of its estimated ivory stock of 38 tons. An auction of 80 tons of processed elephant hides in June 1998 earned Z.$17m. in export revenue. In April 2000, however, CITES decided to suspend again all trade in ivory. The main imports in 2005 and 2006 were fuel, food and electricity.

Zimbabwe's principal trading partners vary significantly from year to year. In 2003 the principal source of imports (52.6%) was South Africa; in 2002 that country was also the principal destination for exports (18.5%). Other major trading partners in those years were the United Kingdom, Germany, Japan, Switzerland, Italy and the USA. A survey in South Africa found that by mid-2000 46% of South African manufacturers had reported a decline in exports to Zimbabwe.

Zimbabwe's membership of the Common Market for Eastern and Southern Africa (COMESA), formerly the Preferential Trade Area for Eastern and Southern Africa, has, in theory, provided access to new directions in regional trade. In practice, however, Zimbabwean exporters have been somewhat disappointed. In the 1990s Zimbabwe produced many items that the other member states needed to import, but the potential trade partners lacked the foreign exchange to pay for them. The historic change of government in South Africa made it politically acceptable for countries and companies in the region to source their imports from there, often with better value for money, and Zimbabwe's share of the market dwindled. South Africa was able to take an even larger share of Zimbabwe's domestic market following the increase in trade liberalization in the late 1990s. Zimbabwe ratified the COMESA treaty in 1999.

Zimbabwe's external debt rose sharply during the 1980s, climbing from US $696m. at the end of 1980, just after independence and Mugabe's accession to power, to US $3,906m. at the end of 1995. Total external debt at 31 December 2001 stood at US $3,784m., equivalent to 46.4% of GDP. By July 2006, according to the RBZ, it stood at US $4,000m., a sum that had remained static for several years because Zimbabwe had not had access to lending. The 2006/07 budget assessed Zimbabwe's total external debt at US $4,100m. while total external payment arrears were placed at US $2,200m. as of 31 October 2006. In July 1999 the Mugabe Government assured the IMF that the exchange rate would be determined by market forces, with the central bank intervening only to smooth out fluctuations and achieve its international reserve objectives. Thereafter, however, the RBZ's role in Government finance was very different. Debt-servicing costs were equivalent to 29% of the value of exports of goods and services in 2000, up from 22% in 1999; the IMF assessed the debt-service ratio at 31.0% at the end of 2002. Significantly, total domestic debt had increased to Z.$108,212m. by 31 May 2000, a rise of 164% in just 17 months. The Government had financed its budgetary deficits through two principal means: short-term Treasury bills and an RBZ overdraft window. The 2006 budget speech, delivered 1 December 2005, stated that a full 93% of public domestic debt was short-term and admitted that this structure of debt was 'expensive and not sustainable'. Using the RBZ overdraft window was, the budget statement confessed, 'highly inflationary'; for this reason, the 2006 budget left the statutory limit on that overdraft unchanged at Z.$1,600,000m.

As the post-2000 crisis deepened and government funds dwindled, the Government resorted to huge increases in the money supply in order to pay its own obligations. This action was the largest single contributing factor to the hyperinflation that ensued. It was reported that the printing of money was accelerated in the first half of 2000 in order to meet the pay increases of civil servants in the months preceding the June election. This sudden, literal increase in the money supply placed great upward pressure on an already excessive inflation rate. This practice continued, and the broad money supply grew by 165% in 2002 and by 207% in the year to 31 March 2003, even according to official assessments. It was announced in 2001 that the RBZ was to issue a new Z.$500 banknote and a new Z.$5 coin; less than one year later the RBZ was forced to launch a new Z.$1,000 banknote. However, the Government was still allowed to buy foreign exchange at a more favourable rate. By mid-2001 it was clear that not even officially authorized currency dealers were transacting at the official rate, except for the regulated 40% of all export receipts (increased from 25% previously) that were required by law to go to the National Oil Co of Zimbabwe (NOCZIM) for fuel imports and to the Zimbabwe Electricity Supply Authority (ZESA) for power. Airlines were quoting fares at the black-market rate, much to the disapproval of the Government. This situation led to the sudden demonetization announced by the RBZ Governor in July 2006 (see above).

ENERGY

A critical fuel shortage permeated the Zimbabwean economy in late 1999, and it worsened significantly in 2000 and 2001. The Government raised pump prices in June 1999 by 27% for petrol and by 32% for diesel fuel and then imposed a 74% fuel-price increase in June 2001. In order to find the foreign currency to pay for fuel imports, the Government decreed that 25% of all export proceeds must by law be surrendered by exporters to NOCZIM and ZESA to pay for fuel and electricity imports; this sum was in 2001 raised to 40%, providing a severe disincentive for exporting from Zimbabwe. In July 2001 press reports in Harare claimed to have discovered that high-ranking government officials were abusing 'direct' fuel-import licences and were stockpiling fuel for their own self-enrichment in storage tanks in Gweru and Chivhu. Libya and Zimbabwe announced a bilateral arrangement in 2001, whereby Libya would provide US $360m. worth of petroleum in exchange for Zimbabwean exports; this amount was equivalent to about nine months' worth of Zimbabwe's petroleum imports. Petroleum products enter the landlocked country through a 300-km pipeline running between Mutare and the Mozambique port of Beira. Zimbabwe consumes some 800,000 metric tons of petroleum products (including diesel fuel) annually.

Zimbabwe shares with Zambia the huge Kariba dam, on the Zambezi river. For many years Kariba's only hydroelectric power plant was on the Zambian side, and Zimbabwe imported some Z.$20m. worth of energy annually from its northern neighbour. In 1987, however, Zimbabwe added 920 MW of new thermal capacity to its own national grid, eliminating the need for these imports. The Hwange thermal power station, constructed at a cost of Z.$230m., accounted for 920 MW of total national generating capacity of 1,900 MW in 1989. However, the Hwange facility's performance has been disappointing, owing to design faults and a shortage of spare parts. Work to refurbish Units 1–4 of the facility during the first half of the 1990s was funded by the World Bank. The shared Central African Power Corpn was replaced in 1986 by ZESA, which had the stated aim of maximizing the operational efficiency of existing installed capacity, while furthering a longer-term development programme directed towards a forecast demand of 2,800 MW by 2004. In 1991, after many delays, the Government agreed to the construction of a Z.$500m. hydroelectric extension facility at Kariba South and of a joint Zambia-Zimbabwe Batoka Gorge hydroelectric facility costing Z.$1,000m., which was to add 1,600 MW by 2003; however, the Zambian Government withdrew from the project, leaving the Zimbabwean authorities to seek private finance for the scheme. A Z.$154m. plan to rehabilitate three thermal power plants was also approved. Work on an interconnector linking Mozambique's Cahora Bassa facility to Matimba and Bindura in Zimbabwe began in 1994 and added 500 MW to Zimbabwe's national grid. Peak demand in mid-2004 was 2,100 MW. By March 2004 ZESA had accrued external debts of over US $200m.; the company was dissolved in October and was unbundled into smaller companies. The Zimbabwe Electricity Regulatory Commission took over the regulation of the sector on a temporary basis. Plans to build a new 1,400-MW power station at Gokwe were abandoned in 2003. In August RioZim was attempting to revive interest in a coal-fired project at Sengwa where the company had estimated coal reserves of 2,200m. metric tons. Funding for the rehabilitation of the Hwange power station was one of the few details known to have emerged from the July 2005 visit to China by Mugabe and other senior government members.

Also in August 2003 it was reported that ZESA owed Wankie Colliery Co Ltd (WCC—latterly renamed Hwange Colliery Co Ltd) some Z.$9,000m, one month after WCC had failed to open a new mine because of a shortage of funds. In 2003 WCC production was running at less than 40%; the new mine would have trebled monthly coal production to 150,000 metric tons and could have gone some way towards addressing the problems of undersupply that were affecting other sectors of the economy reliant on coal, such as, in particular, tobacco producers. It was a government-guaranteed loan to ZESA that triggered the World Bank's suspension of lending to Zimbabwe in May 2000. A crucial repayment due in March was not made on time, nor was it made during the subsequent 60-day grace period. Although the repayment was eventually made, the World Bank's arrears procedures required other debt arrears to be paid before lending could resume.

In May 2007 it was announced that the daily electricity supply to households was to be rationed to four hours in order to divert supplies to farms for irrigation. Frequent power cuts, owing to declining capacity in ageing power plants, were additionally affecting the mining and manufacturing sectors at this time.

LABOUR, WAGES AND INFLATION

Inflation has, with the exception of 1988, affected lower-income urban families more than it has higher-income urban families in every year since independence in 1980. By the time high inflation became hyperinflation, everyone was affected at a fundamental level. Virtually all transactions were being conducted at black-market rates of exchange by mid-2001.

Since independence, the Government has continually stated its determination to narrow the wide gap in incomes between rich and poor Zimbabweans. The Minimum Wage Act of 1980 established minimum wages on a sliding scale depending on type of employment. Industrial action took place on a number of occasions in the 1990s, and one-day general strikes in 2000 and 2001, both of them peaceful, achieved a high level of participation. In July 2001 civil servants demanded a 20% cost-of-living salary increase; the public-sector wage bill was equivalent to 17% of GDP in 2000, but the Government warned that it would have to be maintained within 12% in 2001. However, percentages like these have little meaning in an economy in a state of collapse. Prior to 1999 there was a tendency to blame the IMF for job losses, pay cuts and price 'liberalization', which always seemed to mean price increases; but, by the third quarter of 1999, the Mugabe Government was managing Zimbabwe's economy without interference (or lending) from the IMF. However, the job losses and high prices grew steadily worse; an estimated 50,000 jobs were lost in the private sector between January and June 2000, and by 2005 unemployment was officially estimated at 70%. Mugabe, despite the absence of any balance-of-payments support from donors and lenders, reinstated price controls, but later removed them for all but a few key commodities. The Government's strategy embraced fixed prices, subsidization and a state monopoly on the import and transportation of food and other commodities, in direct opposition to the dictates of the IMF and the World Bank. Lenders and donors largely refrained from providing money under these circumstances, and potential foreign investors stayed away. Declining export revenue further narrowed the Government's options for obtaining foreign exchange. Proceeds from privatization had also fallen, as investor confidence disappeared. The Privatisation Agency of Zimbabwe raised only one-quarter of the revenue it expected to raise. The privatization programme was suspended in 2003; however, in mid-2005 the Government was considering proposals to restructure parastatals including Air Zimbabwe, Zimbabwe Power Co, National Railways of Zimbabwe, Zisco, and the Forestry Co of Zimbabwe; plans for public-private partnerships through concessioning or investment were being explored. Mugabe retained power in the presidential election of March 2002, and the threat of full economic sanctions remained a possibility. Domestically, police were guarding maize distribution points, as it became increasingly clear that the Government's supply of foreign exchange was insufficient to import nearly as much grain as the country required. Meanwhile, the people of Zimbabwe were resorting to what the WFP termed 'coping mechanisms' of gold-panning, prostitution, foraging in the wild for food and the sale of household assets.

PROSPECTS FOR 2006 AND BEYOND

In May 2005 the Mugabe Government launched Operation Murambatsvina (which translates as 'Sweep Away the Rubbish'), destroying some 200,000 homes in shanty towns, leaving at least 700,000 people homeless and resulting in virtually unanimous international condemnation. These former shanty-town residents constituted a 'grey' market that contributed no less than 60% of total economic activity in Zimbabwe. The result of the razing of these communities was that they moved from the 'grey' economy into the 'black' economy; where previously they had sold their services in the streets, selling everything from vegetables to rubber sandals and purveying various services, now they sold vegetables and offered services, but they did it in secret. In May 2007 President Mugabe signed legislation to establish a new Incomes and Pricing Commission, which was to have sole authority to set rates for price-controlled items including basic foodstuffs, school fees and public transport. Critics of the policy considered that such controls would force suppliers out of business and further divert goods to the parallel market. No positive benefit to any Zimbabwean, not even to the Government, has resulted from Operation Murambatsvina. On 31 July 2006 the sudden demonetization did figuratively to the entire nation what the previous year's bulldozers had done literally to the 'grey' market. Life savings hung in the balance for Zimbabwe's sizeable middle class. It was increasingly clear that a viable solution to Zimbabwe's desperate situation would not take place while Mugabe remained in office. But after his departure, be it sooner or later, the people of Zimbabwe would again have an opportunity to exhibit their collective resilience, as they have done before. The underlying potential for a marked, and remarkable, economic recovery remains.

Statistical Survey

Source (unless otherwise stated): Central Statistical Office, Ministry of Finance and Economic Development, Blocks B, E and G, Composite Bldg, cnr Samora Machel Ave and Fourth St, Private Bag 7705, Causeway, Harare; tel. (4) 706681; fax (4) 728529; internet www.mofed.gov.zw.

Area and Population

AREA, POPULATION AND DENSITY

Area (sq km)	390,757*
Population (census results)	
18 August 1992	10,412,548
18 August 1997	
Males	5,647,090
Females	6,142,184
Total	11,789,274
Population (UN estimates at mid-year)†	
2004	13,025,000
2005	13,120,000
2006	13,228,000
Density (per sq km) at mid-2006	33.9

* 150,872 sq miles.

† Source: UN, *World Population Prospects: The 2006 Revision*.

PRINCIPAL TOWNS
(population at census of August 1992)

Harare (capital)	1,189,103	Masvingo	51,743
Bulawayo	621,742	Chinhoyi (Sinoia)	43,054
Chitungwiza	274,912	Hwange (Wankie)	42,581
Mutare (Umtali)	131,367	Marondera (Marandellas)	39,384
Gweru (Gwelo)	128,037	Zvishavane (Shabani)	32,984
Kwekwe (Que Que)	75,425	Redcliff	29,959
Kadoma (Gatooma)	67,750		

Mid-2005 ('000, incl. suburbs, UN estimate): Harare 1,515 (Source: UN, *World Urbanization Prospects: The 2005 Revision*).

BIRTHS AND DEATHS
(annual averages, UN estimates)

	1990–95	1995–2000	2000–05
Birth rate (per 1,000)	35.5	31.9	28.9
Death rate (per 1,000)	8.7	15.3	20.5

Source: UN, *World Population Prospects: The 2006 Revision*.

Expectation of life (years at birth, WHO estimates): 36 (males 37; females 34) in 2004 (Source: WHO, *World Health Report*).

ECONOMICALLY ACTIVE POPULATION
(sample survey, persons aged 15 years and over, 1999)

	Males	Females	Total
Agriculture, hunting, forestry and fishing	1,215,661	1,584,839	2,800,500
Mining and quarrying	46,946	3,367	50,313
Manufacturing	283,090	94,667	377,757
Electricity, gas and water	10,158	n.a.	10,158
Construction	98,908	6,659	105,567
Trade, restaurants and hotels	154,198	178,341	332,539
Transport, storage and communications	93,289	8,288	101,577
Financing, insurance, real estate and business services	100,425	20,749	121,174
Community, social and personal services	320,020	258,505	578,525
Activities not adequately defined	63,052	124,286	187,338
Total employed	2,385,747	2,279,701	4,665,448
Unemployed	187,142	110,669	297,811
Total labour force	2,572,889	2,390,370	4,963,259

2004 ('000 employees, annual average): Agriculture, hunting, forestry and fishing 154; Mining and quarrying 50; Manufacturing 136; Electricity, gas and water 11; Construction 25; Trade, restaurants and hotels 114; Transport, storage and communications 38; Financing, insurance, real estate and business services 38; Public administration 68; Education 151; Health 26; Domestic 102; Other services 88; *Total employed* 999 (Source: IMF, *Zimbabwe: Selected Issues and Statistical Appendix*—October 2005).

Mid-2005 (estimates in '000): Agriculture, etc. 3,688; Total labour force 6,180 (Source: FAO).

Health and Welfare

KEY INDICATORS

Total fertility rate (children per woman, 2005)	3.4
Under-5 mortality rate (per 1,000 live births, 2005)	86
HIV/AIDS (% of persons aged 15–49, 2005)	20.1
Physicians (per 1,000 head, 2004)	0.16
Hospital beds (per 1,000 head, 1990)	0.51
Health expenditure (2004): US $ per head (PPP)	138.6
Health expenditure (2004): % of GDP	7.5
Health expenditure (2004): public (% of total)	46.1
Access to water (% of persons, 2004)	81
Access to sanitation (% of persons, 2004)	53
Human Development Index (2004): ranking	151
Human Development Index (2004): value	0.491

For sources and definitions, see explanatory note on p. vi.

Agriculture

PRINCIPAL CROPS
('000 metric tons)

	2003	2004	2005
Wheat	213	140*	140*
Barley	30*	25*	29†
Maize	929.6	550.0*	900.0*
Millet*	44.8	40.0	40.0
Sorghum*	39.6	80.0	80.0
Potatoes†	35	35	35
Cassava (Manioc)†	190	198	207
Dry beans†	52	52	52
Sugar cane*	4,533	4,121	3,290
Soybeans (Soya beans)*	93	84	100
Groundnuts (in shell)	147*	152†	160†
Sunflower seed*	11	10	13
Oranges†	93	96	99
Bananas†	85	86	87
Coffee (green)	10	6*	4*
Tea (made)†	22	22	22
Tobacco (leaves)	102.7	62.3*	65.0†
Cotton (lint)*	85	100	75

* Unofficial figure(s).
† FAO estimate(s).

Source: FAO.

LIVESTOCK
('000 head, year ending September)

	2001	2002	2003
Horses*	27.0	27.0	27.5
Asses, mules or hinnies*	108	110	112
Cattle	5,752	5,600*	5,400*
Sheep	600	600*	610*
Pigs	604	605*	620*
Goats	2,968	2,950*	2,970*
Chickens	20,000	22,000*	22,000*

* FAO estimate(s).

2004–05: Figures assumed to be unchanged from 2003 (FAO estimates).

Source: FAO.

LIVESTOCK PRODUCTS
('000 metric tons, FAO estimates)

	2001	2002	2003
Cattle meat	101.3	99.0	96.8
Goat meat	12.8	12.7	12.8
Pig meat	27.0	27.0	27.5
Chicken meat	38.1	35.2	36.6
Other meat	28.9	29.4	31.4
Cows' milk	310	280	248
Poultry eggs	22	22	22

2004–05: Figures assumed to be unchanged from 2003 (FAO estimates).

Source: FAO.

Forestry

ROUNDWOOD REMOVALS
('000 cubic metres, excl. bark)

	2000	2001	2002*
Sawlogs, veneer logs and logs for sleepers	773	786	786
Pulpwood	93	94	94
Other industrial wood*	112.4	112.4	112.4
Fuel wood*	8,115	8,115	8,115
Total*	9,094.4	9,108.4	9,108.4

* FAO estimates.

2003–05: Figures assumed to be unchanged from 2002 (FAO estimates).

Source: FAO.

SAWNWOOD PRODUCTION
('000 cubic metres, incl. railway sleepers)

	1999	2000	2001
Coniferous (softwood)	395	343	354
Broadleaved (hardwood)	43	43*	43*
Total	438	386	397

* FAO estimate.

2002–05: Figures assumed to be unchanged from 2001 (FAO estimates).

Source: FAO.

Fishing

('000 metric tons, live weight, FAO estimates)

	2003	2004	2005
Capture	13.0	13.0	13.0
Tilapias	0.8	0.8	0.8
Other freshwater fishes	1.8	1.8	1.8
Dagaas	10.4	10.4	10.4
Aquaculture	2.6	3.0	2.5
Total catch	15.6	16.0	15.5

Note: Figures exclude aquatic animals, recorded by number rather than weight. The number of Nile crocodiles caught was: 73,707 in 2003; 60,185 in 2004; 76,970 in 2005 (all FAO estimates).

Source: FAO.

Mining

('000 metric tons, unless otherwise indicated)

	2003	2004	2005*
Asbestos	147	104	122
Chromium ore	637.1	668.4	614.7
Coal	2,872	2,476	2,891
Cobalt ore (metric tons)†	79	59	281
Copper ore‡	2.8	2.4	2.6
Gold (kilograms)	12,564	21,330	14,024
Iron ore	367	283	377
Limestone	922	41	84
Magnesite (metric tons)	1,333	749	893
Nickel ore (metric tons)	9,516	9,776	8,556
Phosphate rock	95.5	83.4	45.7
Silver (kilograms)	747	3,216	187

* Preliminary figures.

† Figures include metal content of compounds and salts and may include cobalt recovered from nickel-copper matte.

‡ Figures refer to the metal content of ores and concentrates.

Source: US Geological Survey.

Industry

SELECTED PRODUCTS
('000 metric tons, unless otherwise indicated)

	2003	2004	2005*
Coke (metallurgical)	228	180	200
Cement†	400	400	400
Pig-iron	182	145	125
Ferro-chromium	245.3	193.1	218.1
Crude steel	152	150	119
Refined copper—unwrought (metric tons)	7,200	7,000†	7,000
Refined nickel—unwrought (metric tons)	12,657	12,200†	12,000†

* Preliminary figures.

† Estimate(s).

Source: US Geological Survey.

Raw sugar ('000 metric tons): 585 in 2000; 639 in 2001 (Source: UN, *Industrial Commodity Statistics Yearbook*).

Electric energy (million kWh): 8,587 in 2002; 8,799 in 2003; 9,719 in 2004.

Finance

CURRENCY AND EXCHANGE RATES

Monetary Units
100 cents = 1 Zimbabwe dollar (Z.$).

Sterling, US Dollar and Euro Equivalents (31 August 2006)
£1 sterling = Z.$476.8999;
US $1 = Z.$250.0000;
€1 = Z.$321.2748;
Z.$1,000 = £2.10 = US $4.00 = €3.11.

Average Exchange Rate (Z.$ per US dollar)
2003 697.4240
2004 5,068.6600
2005 22,363.6000

BUDGET
(Z.$ '000 million, year ending 30 June)

Revenue	2002	2003	2004
Taxation	284.6	1,325.8	7,763.0
Taxes on income and profits	158.3	734.7	4,076.9
Personal income	116.4	588.8	3,184.8
Companies	30.0	80.6	604.9
Domestic dividends and interest	4.5	22.2	206.3
Other income taxes	7.5	43.2	80.9
Customs duties	27.2	92.9	930.0
Excise duties	18.8	94.6	278.8
Sales tax / Value-added tax	76.2	382.3	2,377.0
Miscellaneous taxes	4.0	21.3	100.4
Revenue from investments and properties	1.2	1.8	3.0
Fees paid for departmental facilities and services	1.1	2.5	16.4
Other revenue	17.3	44.7	289.3
Total	304.2	1,374.8	8,071.7

Expenditure*	2002	2003	2004
Recurrent	320.7	1,233.2	8,410.7
Goods and services	216.0	924.3	5,016.3
Salaries, wages and allowances	123.9	528.0	3,657.6
Subsistence and transport	6.4	34.1	181.9
Incidental expenses	20.8	43.7	860.6
Maintenance of capital works	3.9	18.3	269.8
Other recurrent expenditure	61.1	300.3	46.7
Interest payments	49.5	69.2	1,302.1
Foreign	9.2	3.3	568.0
Domestic	40.3	65.9	734.0
Transfers and subsidies	55.2	239.7	2,092.4
Pensions	22.6	77.2	772.1
Capital	25.2	107.7	1,220.2
Total	345.9	1,340.9	9,630.9

* Excluding loans (Z.$ '000 million): 5.4 in 2002; 53.7 in 2003; 139.8 in 2004.

Source: IMF, *Zimbabwe: Selected Issues and Statistical Appendix* (October 2005).

INTERNATIONAL RESERVES
(US $ million at 31 December)

	2000	2001	2002
Gold*	45.4	27.5	22.7
IMF special drawing rights	0.2	—	—
Reserve position in IMF	0.4	0.4	0.4
Foreign exchange	192.5	64.3	82.9
Total	238.5	92.2	106.0

* Valued at a market-related price which is determined each month.

2003–06 (US $ million at 31 December): Reserve position in IMF 0.5.

Source: IMF, *International Financial Statistics*.

MONEY SUPPLY
(Z.$ '000 million at 31 December)

	2003	2004	2005
Currency outside banks	441.71	1,655.89	9,875.8
Demand deposits at deposit money banks	1,636.45	5,148.17	34,048.0
Total money (incl. others)	2,086.70	6,856.61	44,746.2

Source: IMF, *International Financial Statistics*.

COST OF LIVING
(Consumer Price Index; base: 2000 = 100)

	2003	2004	2005
Food	2,238.4	8,792.0	42,868.1
All items (incl. others)	2,255.8	8,625.7	34,688.3

Source: ILO.

NATIONAL ACCOUNTS

Expenditure on the Gross National Product
(US $ million at current prices, estimates)

	2004	2005	2006
Government final consumption expenditure	153.99	142.52	248.64
Private final consumption expenditure	4,730.58	3,442.12	6,545.78
Gross capital formation	240.73	150.47	243.57
Total domestic expenditure	5,125.30	3,735.11	7,037.99
Exports of goods and services	2,006.24	1,443.83	1,838.76
Less Imports of goods and services	2,419.48	1,806.43	1,843.03
GDP in purchasers' values	4,712.06	3,372.50	7,033.72

Source: African Development Bank.

Gross Domestic Product by Economic Activity
(Z.$ million, at factor cost)

	1997	1998	1999
Agriculture, hunting, forestry and fishing	17,042	27,135	35,812
Mining and quarrying	1,400	2,400	3,380
Manufacturing	16,208	20,708	30,538
Electricity and water	2,849	3,139	5,171
Construction	2,544	3,640	5,132
Trade, restaurants and hotels	17,163	22,652	36,261
Transport, storage and communications	5,192	6,712	11,373
Finance, insurance and real estate	9,797	15,679	26,917
Government services	13,640	16,916	22,913
Other services	5,320	6,806	8,273
Sub-total	91,155	125,762	185,770
Less Imputed bank service charges	1,149	1,242	1,357
Total	90,006	124,540	184,413

BALANCE OF PAYMENTS
(US $ million)

	2002	2003	2004*
Exports of goods f.o.b.	1,802	1,670	1,680
Imports of goods f.o.b.	–1,821	–1,778	–1,989
Trade balance	–18	–108	–310
Exports of services	217	185	317
Imports of services	–398	–401	–424
Balance on goods and services	–199	–324	–417
Investment income (net)	–242	–191	–208
Balance on goods, services and income	–441	–515	–625
Private transfers (net)	228	169	204
Current balance	–213	–346	–421
Official transfers (net)	38	38	24
Direct investment (net)	23	4	9
Portfolio investment (net)	–2	4	2
Long-term capital (net)	–281	–228	–221
Short-term capital (net)	–94	–27	17
Net errors and omissions	74	79	344
Overall balance	–456	–476	–247

* Estimates.

Source: IMF, *Zimbabwe: Selected Issues and Statistical Appendix* (October 2005).

External Trade

PRINCIPAL COMMODITIES
(US $ million)

Imports f.o.b.	2002	2003	2004*
Food	337	206	161
Tobacco and beverages	39	36	44
Crude materials	87	79	96
Fuel and electricity	352	456	462
Petroleum products	149	110	342
Oils and fats	27	25	30
Chemicals	361	328	401
Machinery and transport equipment	375	341	417
Other manufactured goods	241	220	269
Total (incl. others)	1,821	1,778	1,989

Exports†	2002	2003	2004*
Agricultural exports	646.6	516.0	384.2
Tobacco	434.7	321.3	226.7
Sugar	64.2	54.8	53.9
Cold Storage Co beef	2.3	0.2	—
Coffee	5.4	5.9	4.1
Horticulture	126.6	118.7	84.1
Mineral exports	297.8	390.8	604.2
Gold‡	159.5	152.3	262.8
Asbestos	39.3	42.4	19.4
Nickel	31.8	68.5	95.7
Platinum	14.5	77.4	174.4
Copper	8.9	4.6	2.6
Manufacturing exports	287.3	691.2	620.9
Ferrous alloys	106.8	119.8	185.1
Cotton lint	53.2	67.2	122.1
Iron and steel	22.3	39.9	22.9
Textiles and clothing	17.7	28.2	13.8
Machinery and equipment	5.2	12.8	1.9
Chemicals	3.5	5.1	9.6
Total (incl. others)§	1,397.9	1,670.3	1,679.7

* Estimates.

† Value of exports based on official exchange rates.

‡ Based on unit value of US dollar per ounce.

§ Excluding unidentified exports and internal freight.

Source: IMF, *Zimbabwe: Selected Issues and Statistical Appendix* (October 2005).

PRINCIPAL TRADING PARTNERS
(US $ million)

Imports f.o.b.	2001	2002	2004
Botswana	33.6	47.2	88.9
Congo, Democratic Repub.	96.1	2.9	7.1
France (incl. Monaco)	27.7	31.9	20.4
Germany	47.7	134.3	37.5
Japan	29.5	72.4	24.0
Kuwait	6.9	54.1	44.3
Mozambique	89.9	46.7	49.7
South Africa	802.6	1,297.8	1,159.8
United Kingdom	54.3	120.7	83.2
USA	48.4	87.0	41.4
Total (incl. others)	1,714.9	2,466.7	2,203.8

Exports f.o.b.	2001	2002	2004
Botswana	12.8	68.0	48.3
China, People's Repub.	104.8	13.3	110.5
Germany	155.8	109.6	77.2
Japan	117.1	122.3	55.5
Malawi	10.6	120.1	47.6
Mozambique	3.7	69.0	19.5
Netherlands	25.8	89.8	27.0
South Africa	122.3	431.4	565.2
Spain	32.5	70.5	29.2
Switzerland (incl. Liechtenstein)	12.5	303.7	133.7
United Arab Emirates	3.4	8.9	12.0
United Kingdom	130.3	140.4	131.3
USA	61.5	104.7	41.0
Zambia	11.6	215.5	71.6
Total (incl. others)	1,206.8	2,327.4	1,926.1

* Figures for 2003 unavailable.

Source: UN, *International Trade Statistics Yearbook*.

Transport

RAIL TRAFFIC
(National Railways of Zimbabwe, including operations in Botswana)

	1998	1999	2000
Total number of passengers ('000)	1,787	1,896	1,614
Revenue-earning metric tons hauled ('000)	12,421	12,028	9,422
Gross metric ton-km (million)	9,248	8,962	6,953
Net metric ton-km (million)	4,549	4,375	3,326

ROAD TRAFFIC
('000 motor vehicles in use, estimates)

	1998	1999	2000
Passenger cars	540	555	573
Commercial vehicles	37	38	39

2002: Passenger cars 570,866; Lorries and vans 84,456; Motorcycles 45.

CIVIL AVIATION
(traffic on scheduled services)

	2001	2002	2003
Kilometres flown (million)	15	8	6
Passengers carried ('000)	308	251	201
Passenger-km (million)	723	674	437
Total ton-km (million)	224	87	58

Source: UN, *Statistical Yearbook*.

Tourism

VISITOR ARRIVALS BY NATIONALITY

	2003	2004	2005
Australia and New Zealand	40,141	28,540	13,369
Botswana	242,750	135,860	189,751
Canada and USA	54,572	60,093	39,779
Mozambique	313,954	299,122	183,792
South Africa	882,726	653,352	626,677
United Kingdom	58,354	42,260	42,525
Zambia	295,103	220,060	194,311
Total (incl. others)	2,256,205	1,854,488	1,558,501

Tourism receipts (US $ million, incl. passenger transport): 61 in 2003; 194 in 2004; n.a. in 2005.

Source: World Tourism Organization.

Communications Media

	2003	2004	2005
Telephones ('000 main lines in use)	305.9	317.0	328.0
Mobile cellular telephones ('000 subscribers)	363.7	423.6	699.0
Personal computers ('000 in use)	620	1,000	1,200
Internet users ('000)	800	820	1,000

Radio receivers ('000 in use): 4,488 in 1999.

Television receivers ('000 in use): 410 in 2000.

Facsimile machines: 4,100 in use in year ending 30 June 1995.

Daily newspapers (1996): 2; average circulation: 209,000 copies.

Sources: UNESCO, *Statistical Yearbook*; UN, *Statistical Yearbook*; International Telecommunication Union.

Education

(2002/03, unless otherwise indicated)

	Institutions*	Teachers	Students
Pre-primary	n.a.	19,588	448,124
Primary	4,699	61,521	2,361,588
Secondary	1,539	33,964	758,229
Tertiary	n.a.	n.a.	21,631†

* 1998 figures.
† Estimate.

Source: UNESCO Institute for Statistics.

Adult literacy rate (UNESCO estimates): 90.0% (males 93.8%; females 86.3%) in 2002 (Source: UN Development Programme, *Human Development Report*).

Directory

The Constitution

The Constitution of the Republic of Zimbabwe took effect at independence on 18 April 1980. Amendments to the Constitution must have the approval of two-thirds of the members of the House of Assembly (see below). The provisions of the 1980 Constitution (with subsequent amendments) are summarized below:

THE REPUBLIC

Zimbabwe is a sovereign republic and the Constitution is the supreme law.

DECLARATION OF RIGHTS

The declaration of rights guarantees the fundamental rights and freedoms of the individual, regardless of race, tribe, place of origin, political opinions, colour, creed or sex.

THE PRESIDENT

Executive power is vested in the President, who acts on the advice of the Cabinet. The President is Head of State and Commander-in-Chief of the Defence Forces. The President appoints two Vice-Presidents and other Ministers and Deputy Ministers, to be members of the Cabinet. The President holds office for six years and is eligible for re-election. Each candidate for the Presidency shall be nominated by not fewer than 10 members of the House of Assembly; if only one candidate is nominated, that candidate shall be declared to be elected without the necessity of a ballot. Otherwise, a ballot shall be held within an electoral college consisting of the members of the House of Assembly.

PARLIAMENT

Legislative power is vested in a bicameral Parliament, consisting of a House of Assembly and a Senate. The House of Assembly comprises 150 members, of whom 120 are directly elected by universal adult suffrage, 12 are nominated by the President, 10 are traditional Chiefs and eight are Provincial Governors. The life of the House of Assembly is ordinarily to be five years. The Senate comprises 66 members, of whom 50 are directly elected by universal adult suffrage, six are nominated by the President and 10 are traditional Chiefs. The life of the Senate is ordinarily to be five years.

OTHER PROVISIONS

An Ombudsman shall be appointed by the President, acting on the advice of the Judicial Service Commission, to investigate complaints against actions taken by employees of the Government or of a local authority.

Chiefs shall be appointed by the President, and shall form a Council of Chiefs from their number in accordance with customary principles of succession.

Other provisions relate to the Judicature, Defence and Police Forces, public service and finance.

The Government

HEAD OF STATE

President: ROBERT GABRIEL MUGABE (took office 31 December 1987; re-elected March 1990, 16–17 March 1996 and 9–11 March 2002).

THE CABINET

(August 2007)

Vice-President: JOSEPH MSIKA.

Vice-President: JOYCE MUJURU.

Minister of Special Affairs in the President's Office, responsible for Lands, Land Reform and Resettlement: FLORA BHUKA.

Minister of Defence: SYDNEY SEKERAMAYI.

Minister of Home Affairs: KEMBO MOHADI.

Minister of Justice, Legal and Parliamentary Affairs: PATRICK ANTHONY CHINAMASA.

Minister of Public Service, Labour and Social Welfare: NICHOLAS GOCHE.

Minister of Local Government, Public Works and National Housing: Dr IGNATIUS MORGAN CHIMINYA CHOMBO.

Minister of Agriculture and Rural Resettlement: RUGARE GUMBO.

Minister of Rural Housing and Social Amenities: EMMERSON MNANGAGWA.

Minister of Industry and International Trade: OBERT MPOFU.

Minister of Energy and Power Development: MICHAEL NYAMBUYA.

Minister of Mines and Mining Development: AMOS MIDZI.

Minister of the Environment and Tourism: FRANCIS NHEMA.

Minister of Foreign Affairs: SIMBARASHE MUMBENGEGWI.

Minister of Finance: SAMUEL MUMBENGEGWI.

Minister of Economic Development: SYLVESTER NGUNI.

Minister of Higher and Tertiary Education: I. STANISLAUS GORERAZVO MUDENGE.

Minister of Education, Sports and Culture: AENEAS CHIGWEDERE.

Minister of Health and Child Welfare: DAVID PARIRENYATWA.

Minister for Information and Publicity: Dr SKHANYISO NDLOVU.

Minister of Science and Technology: OLIVIA MUCHENA.

Minister of Transport and Communications: CHRIS MUSHOHWE.

Minister of Women Affairs, Gender and Community Development: OPPAH MUCHINGURI.

Minister of Small and Medium Enterprises Development: SITHEMBISO NYONI.

Minister of Youth Development, Gender and Employment Creation: Brig. (retd) AMBROSE MUTINHIRI.

Minister of Water Resources and Infrastructural Development: MUNACHO MUTEZO.

Minister of State for National Security: DIDYMUS MUTASA.

Minister of State for Policy Implementation: WEBSTER SHAMU.

Minister of State for Indigenization and Empowerment: MUNYARADZI PAUL MANGWANA.

Minister of State for State Enterprises, Anti-Monopolies and Anti-Corruption: SAMUEL UNDENGE.

Minister without Portfolio: ELLIOT MANYIKA.

MINISTRIES

Office of the President: Munhumutapa Bldg, Samora Machel Ave, Private Bag 7700, Causeway, Harare; tel. (4) 707091.

Office of the Vice-Presidents: Munhumutapa Bldg, Samora Machel Ave, Private Bag 7700, Causeway, Harare; tel. (4) 707091.

Ministry of Agriculture and Rural Resettlement: Ngungunyana Bldg, Private Bag 7701, Causeway, Harare; tel. (4) 792223; fax (4) 734646.

Ministry of Defence: Defence House, Union Ave and Third St, Private Bag 7713, Causeway, Harare; tel. (4) 700155; fax (4) 727501.

Ministry of Economic Development: Harare; internet www.mofed.gov.zw.

Ministry of Education, Sports and Culture: Ambassador House, Union Ave, POB CY121, Causeway, Harare; tel. (4) 734051; fax (4) 707599.

Ministry of Energy and Power Development: Karigamombe Centre, Private Bag 7753, Causeway, Harare; tel. (4) 751720; fax (4) 734075.

Ministry of the Environment and Tourism: Kaguvi Bldg, 12th Floor, cnr 4th St and Central Ave, Private Bag 7753, Causeway, Harare; tel. (4) 701681; fax (4) 252673; e-mail metlib@zarnet.ac.zw; internet www.met.gov.zw.

Ministry of Finance: Blocks B, E and G, Composite Bldg, cnr Samora Machel Ave and Fourth St, Private Bag 7705, Causeway, Harare; tel. (4) 738603; fax (4) 792750; internet www.mofed.gov.zw.

Ministry of Foreign Affairs: Munhumutapa Bldg, Samora Machel Ave, POB 4240, Causeway, Harare; tel. (4) 727005; fax (4) 705161.

Ministry of Health and Child Welfare: Kaguvi Bldg, Fourth St, POB CY198, Causeway, Harare; tel. (4) 730011; fax (4) 729154.

Ministry of Higher Education and Technology: Government Composite Bldg, cnr Fourth St and Samora Machel Ave, Union Ave, POB UA275, Harare; tel. (4) 796441; fax (4) 728730; e-mail thesecretary@mhet.ac.zw; internet www.mhet.ac.zw.

Ministry of Home Affairs: Mukwati Bldg, Fourth St, Private Bag 7703, Causeway, Harare; tel. (4) 703299; fax (4) 707231.

Ministry of Indigenization and Empowerment: Harare.

Ministry of Industry and International Trade: Mukwati Bldg, Fourth St, Private Bag 7708, Causeway, Harare; tel. (4) 702731; fax (4) 729311.

Ministry of Information and Publicity: Linquenda House, Baker Ave, POB CY825, Causeway, Harare; tel. (4) 703894; fax (4) 707213.

Ministry of Justice, Legal and Parliamentary Affairs: Corner House, cnr Samora Machel Ave and Leopold Takawira St, Private Bag 7751, Causeway, Harare; tel. (4) 774620; fax (4) 772999.

Ministry of Local Government, Public Works and National Housing: Mukwati Bldg, Fourth St, Private Bag 7755, Causeway, Harare; tel. (4) 7282019; fax (4) 708493.

Ministry of Mines and Mining Development: Harare.

Ministry of National Security: Chaminuka Bldg, POB 2278, Harare; tel. (4) 700501; fax (4) 732660.

Ministry of Policy Implementation: Harare.

Ministry of Public Service, Labour and Social Welfare: Compensation House, cnr Central Ave and Fourth St, Private Bag 7707, Causeway, Harare; tel. (4) 790871.

Ministry of Transport and Communications: Kaguvi Bldg, POB CY595, Causeway, Harare; tel. (4) 700991; fax (4) 708225.

Ministry of Water Resources, Infrastructural Development, and Small and Medium Enterprises: Makombe Complex, Private Bag 7701, Causeway, Harare; tel. (4) 706081.

Ministry of Youth Development, Gender and Employment Creation: ZANU—PF Bldg, Private Bag 7762, Causeway, Harare; tel. (4) 734691; fax (4) 732709.

PROVINCIAL GOVERNORS
(August 2007)

Bulawayo: CAIN MATHEMA.

Harare: DAVID KARIMANZIRA.

Manicaland: TINAYE CHIGUDU.

Mashonaland Central: EPHRAIM MASAWI.

Mashonaland East: RAY KAUKONDE.

Mashonaland West: NELSON SAMKANGE.

Masvingo: WILLARD CHIWEWE.

Matabeleland North: THOKOZILE MATHUTHU.

Matabeleland South: ANGELINA MASUKU.

Midlands: CEPHAS MSIPA.

President and Legislature

PRESIDENT

Election, 9–11 March 2002

Candidate	Votes	% of votes
Robert Gabriel Mugabe	1,685,212	56.2
Morgan Tsvangirai	1,258,401	42.0
Wilson Kumbala	31,368	1.0
Shakespeare Maya	11,906	0.4
Paul Siwela	11,871	0.4
Total	2,998,758	100.0

HOUSE OF ASSEMBLY

Speaker: JOHN NKOMO.

Election, 31 March 2005

	Votes	% of votes	Seats*
ZANU—PF	1,569,867	59.59	78
MDC	1,041,292	39.52	41
Independents	16,223	0.62	1
ZANU—Ndonga	6,608	0.25	—
Others	655	0.02	—
Total	2,634,645	100.00	120

* In addition to the 120 directly elective seats, 12 seats are held by nominees of the President, 10 by traditional Chiefs and eight by Provincial Governors.

SENATE

Speaker: EDNA MADZONGWE.

Election, 26 November 2005

	Votes	% of votes	Seats*
ZANU—PF	449,860	73.71	43
MDC	123,628	20.26	7
Others	36,807	6.03	—
Total	610,295	100.00	50

* In addition to the 50 directly elective seats, 6 seats are held by nominees of the President, and 10 by traditional Chiefs.

Election Commissions

Electoral Delimitation Commission (EDC): Harare; appointed by and responsible to the President; establishes constituency boundaries; Chair. GEORGE CHIWESHE.

Zimbabwe Electoral Commission (ZEC): Harare; f. 2005; the President appoints six commrs and also the Chair. in consultation with the Judicial Service Commission; superseded and replaced the Electoral Supervisory Commission (abolished Aug. 2005); responsible for voter registration and conducting elections; Chair. GEORGE CHIWESHE.

Political Organizations

Committee for a Democratic Society (CODESO): f. 1993; Karanga-supported grouping, based in Matabeleland; Leader SOUL NDLOVU.

Conservative Alliance of Zimbabwe (CAZ): POB 242, Harare; f. 1962; known as the Rhodesian Front until 1981, and subsequently as the Republican Front; supported by sections of the white community; Pres. GERALD SMITH; Chair. MIKE MORONEY.

Democratic Party: f. 1991 by a breakaway faction from ZUM; Nat. Chair. GILES MUTSEKWA; Pres. DAVIDSON GOMO.

Forum Party of Zimbabwe (FPZ): POB 74, Bulawayo; f. 1993; conservative; Pres. WASHINGTON SANSOLE.

Front for Popular Democracy: f. 1994; Chair. Prof. AUSTIN CHAKAWODZA.

General Conference of Patriots: Harare; f. 1998; opposes the Govt; aims to organize and direct dissent; Leader OBEY MUDZINGWA.

Independent Zimbabwe Group: f. 1983 by a breakaway faction from the fmr Republican Front; Leader BILL IRVINE.

Movement for Democratic Change (MDC): Harvest House, 6th Floor, cnr Angwa St and Nelson Mandela Ave, Harare; internet www.mdczimbabwe.org; f. 1999; allied to Zimbabwe Congress of Trade Unions; opposes the Mugabe Govt; a 'pro-Senate' splinter faction emerged in Dec. 2005 led by Prof. ARTHUR MUTAMBARA and WELSHMAN NCUBE; Pres. MORGAN TSVANGIRAI; Sec.-Gen. TENDAI BITI.

National Democratic Union: f. 1979; conservative grouping with minority Zezuru support; Leader HENRY CHIHOTA.

National Progressive Alliance: f. 1991; Chair. CANCIWELL NZIRAMASANGA.

United National Federal Party (UNFP): Harare; f. 1978; conservative; seeks a federation of Mashonaland and Matabeleland; Leader Chief KAYISA NDIWENI.

United Parties (UP): f. 1994; Leader Bishop ABEL MUZOREWA.

Zimbabwe Active People's Unity Party: Bulawayo; f. 1989; Leader NEWMAN MATUTU NDELA.

Zimbabwe African National Union—Ndonga (ZANU—Ndonga): POB UA525, Union Ave, Harare; tel. and fax (4) 481180; f. 1977; breakaway faction from ZANU, also includes fmr mems of United African Nat. Council; supports free market economy; Pres. (vacant); Sec.-Gen. EDWIN C. NGUWA.

Zimbabwe African National Union—Patriotic Front (ZANU—PF): cnr Rotten Row and Samora Machel Ave, POB 4530, Harare; tel. (4) 753329; fax (4) 774146; internet www.zanupfpub.co.zw; f. 1989 by merger of PF—ZAPU and ZANU—PF; Pres. ROBERT GABRIEL MUGABE; Vice-Pres SIMON VENGAYI MUZENDA, JOSEPH W. MSIKA; Nat. Chair. JOHN LANDAU NKOMO.

Zimbabwe Congress Party: Harare; f. 1994; Pres. KENNETH MANO.

Zimbabwe Democratic Party: Harare; f. 1979; traditionalist; Leader JAMES CHIKEREMA.

Zimbabwe Federal Party (ZFPO): Stand 214, Nketa 6, P.O. Nkulumane, Bulawayo; f. 1994; aims to create national federation of five provinces; Leader RICHARD NCUBE.

Zimbabwe Integrated Programme: f. 1999; seeks economic reforms; Pres. Prof. HENEDI DZINOCHIKIWEYI.

Zimbabwe National Front: f. 1979; Leader PETER MANDAZA.

Zimbabwe Peoples' Democratic Party: f. 1989; Chair. ISABEL PASALK.

Zimbabwe Union of Democrats: Harare; f. 1998; aims to create an effective opposition in the national parliament; Pres. MARGARET DONGO.

Zimbabwe Unity Movement (ZUM): f. 1989 by a breakaway faction from ZANU—PF; merged with United African National Council in 1994; Leader EDGAR TEKERE.

Diplomatic Representation

EMBASSIES IN ZIMBABWE

Angola: 26 Speke Ave, POB 3590, Harare; tel. (4) 770075; fax (4) 770077; Ambassador JOAQUIM DE LEMOS.

Australia: 1 Green Close, Borrowdale, Harare, POB 4541, Harare; tel. (4) 852471; fax (4) 870566; e-mail zimbabwe.embassy@dfat.gov.au; internet www.dfat.gov.au/missions/countries/zw.html; Ambassador JON SHEPPARD.

Austria: 13 Duthie Rd, Alexandra Park, POB 4120, Harare; tel. (4) 702921; fax (4) 705877; e-mail harare-ob@bmeia.gv.at; Ambassador Dr GERHARD ZIEGLER.

Bangladesh: 9 Birchenough Rd, POB 3040, Harare; tel. (4) 727004; Ambassador NASIMA HAIDER.

Botswana: 22 Phillips Ave, Belgravia, POB 563, Harare; tel. (4) 729551; fax (4) 721360; Ambassador PELOKGALE SELOMA.

Brazil: Old Mutual Centre, 9th Floor, Jason Moyo Ave, POB 2530, Harare; tel. (4) 790740; fax (4) 790754; e-mail brasemb@ecoweb.co.zw; Chargé d'affaires a.i. FRANCISCO CARLOS SOARES LUZ.

Bulgaria: 15 Maasdorp Ave, Alexandra Park, POB 1809, Harare; tel. (4) 730509; fax (4) 732504; e-mail bgembhre@ecoweb.co.zw; Ambassador CHRISTO TEPAVITCHAROV.

Canada: 45 Baines Ave, POB 1430, Harare; tel. (4) 252181; fax (4) 252186; e-mail hrare@dfait-maeci.gc.ca; internet www.harare.gc.ca; Ambassador ROXANNE DUBÉ.

China, People's Republic: 30 Baines Ave, POB 4749, Harare; tel. and fax (4) 794155; e-mail chinaemb_zw@mfa.gov.cn; internet www.chinaembassy.org.zw; Ambassador NANSHENG YUAN.

Congo, Democratic Republic: 5 Pevensey Rd, Highlands, POB 2446, Harare; tel. (4) 481172; fax (4) 796421; Ambassador Dr KIKAYA BIN KARUB (acting).

Cuba: 5 Phillips Ave, Belgravia, POB 4139, Harare; tel. (4) 720256; Ambassador BUENAVENTURA REYES ACOSTA.

Czech Republic: 4 Sandringham Dr., Alexandra Park, GPO 4474, Harare; tel. (4) 700636; fax (4) 720930; e-mail harare@embassy.mzv.cz; internet www.mzv.cz/harare; Ambassador VÁCLAV JÍLEK.

Egypt: 7 Aberdeen Rd, Avondale, POB A433, Harare; tel. (4) 303445; fax (4) 303115; Ambassador MUHAMMAD FARED MONEIB.

Ethiopia: 14 Lanark Rd, Belgravia, POB 2745, Harare; tel. (4) 701514; fax (4) 701516; e-mail embassy@ecoweb.co.zw; Ambassador DINA MUFTI.

France: Bank Chambers, 11th Floor, 74–76 Samora Machel Ave, POB 1378, Harare; tel. (4) 703216; fax (4) 730078; internet www.ambafrance-zw.org; Ambassador GABRIEL JUGNET.

Germany: 30 Ceres Rd, Avondale, Harare; tel. (4) 308655; fax (4) 303455; e-mail botschaft_harare@gmx.de; Ambassador KARIN BLUMBERGER-SAUERTEIG.

Ghana: 11 Downie Ave, Belgravia, POB 4445, Harare; tel. (4) 700982; fax (4) 701014; e-mail ghcom25@africaonline.co.zw; Ambassador JOHN K. GBENAH.

Greece: 8 Deary Ave, Belgravia, POB 4809, Harare; tel. (4) 793208; fax (4) 703662; e-mail grembha@zol.co.zw; Ambassador DIMITRI M. ALEXANDRAKIS.

Holy See: 5 St Kilda Rd, Mount Pleasant, POB MP191, Harare (Apostolic Nunciature); tel. (4) 744547; fax (4) 744412; e-mail nunzim@zol.co.zw; Apostolic Nuncio Most Rev. EDWARD JOSEPH ADAMS (Titular Archbishop of Scala).

Hungary: 20 Lanark Rd, Belgravia, POB 3594, Harare; tel. (4) 733528; fax (4) 730512; Ambassador TAMÁS GÁSPÁR GÁL.

India: 12 Natal Rd, Belgravia, POB 4620, Harare; tel. (4) 795955; fax (4) 722324; e-mail hci@samara.co.zw; Ambassador AJIT KUMAR.

Indonesia: 3 Duthie Ave, Belgravia, POB Cy 69 Causeway, Harare; tel. (4) 251799; fax (4) 796587; e-mail indohar@ecoweb.co.zw; internet www.indonesia-harare.org; Ambassador HUPUDIO SUPARDI.

Iran: 8 Allan Wilson Ave, Avondale, POB A293, Harare; tel. (4) 726942; Ambassador RASOUL MOMENI.

Italy: 7 Bartholomew Close, Greendale North, POB 1062, Harare; tel. (4) 498190; fax (4) 498199; e-mail segreteria.ambzimbabwe@esteri.it; internet www.ambitalia.co.zw; Ambassador MARIO BOLOGNA.

Japan: Social Security Centre, 4th Floor, Julius Nyerere Way, cnr Sam Nujoma St, POB 2710, Harare; tel. (4) 250025; fax (4) 250111; internet www.zw.emb-japan.go.jp; Ambassador TAKEO YOSHIKAWA.

Kenya: 95 Park Lane, POB 4069, Harare; tel. (4) 704820; fax (4) 723042; e-mail kenhicom@africaonline.co.zw; Ambassador Prof. JOHN ABDUBA.

Korea, Democratic People's Republic: 102 Josiah Chinamano Ave, Greenwood, POB 4754, Harare; tel. (4) 724052; Ambassador RI MYONG CHOL.

Kuwait: 1 Bath Rd, Avondale, POB A485, Harare; Ambassador SAUD FAISAL AL-DAWESS.

Libya: 124 Harare St, POB 4310, Harare; tel. (4) 728381; Ambassador MAHMOUD YOUSEF AZZABI.

Malawi: 9–11 Duthie Rd, Alexandra Park, POB 321, Harare; tel. (4) 798584; fax (4) 799006; e-mail malahigh@africaonline.co.zw; Ambassador Dr BENSON M. TEMBO.

Malaysia: 40 Downie Ave, Avondale, POB 5570, Harare; tel. (4) 334413; fax (4) 334415; e-mail malharare@kln.gov.my; Ambassador CHEAH CHOONG KIT.

Mozambique: 152 Herbert Chitepo Ave, cnr Leopold Takawira St, POB 4608, Harare; tel. (4) 790837; fax (4) 732898; Ambassador VINCENTE MEBUNIA VEKOSO.

Netherlands: 2 Arden Rd, Highlands, POB HG601, Harare; tel. (4) 776701; fax (4) 776700; e-mail nlgovhar@mweb.co.zw; Ambassador JOSEPH WETERINGS.

Nigeria: 36 Samora Machel Ave, POB 4742, Harare; tel. (4) 253900; Ambassador ANTHONY U. OSULA.

Norway: 5 Lanark Rd, Belgravia, POB A510, Avondale, Harare; tel. (4) 252426; fax (4) 252430; e-mail emb.harare@mfa.no; internet www.norway.org.zw; Ambassador PER GULLIK STAVNUM.

Pakistan: 314 Pipendale Rd, Barrowadalf, Harare; tel. (4) 720293; fax (4) 722446; e-mail pakhar@icon.zw; Ambassador RIFFAT IQBAL.

Poland: 16 Cork Rd, Belgravia, POB 3932, Harare; tel. (4) 253442; fax (4) 253710; Ambassador JAN WIELINSKI.

Portugal: 12 Harvey Brown Ave, Milton Park, Harare; tel. (4) 253023; fax (4) 253637; e-mail embport@harare.dgaccp.pt; Ambassador João Carlos Versteeg.

Romania: 105 Fourth St, POB 4797, Harare; tel. (4) 700853; fax (4) 725493; Chargé d'affaires a.i. Luminita Florescu.

Russia: 70 Fife Ave, POB 4250, Harare; tel. (4) 701957; fax (4) 700534; e-mail russemb@africaonline.co.zw; internet www.zimbabwe.mid.ru; Ambassador Sergei Kryukov.

South Africa: 7 Elcombe Rd, Belgravia, POB A1654, Harare; tel. (4) 753147; fax (4) 749657; e-mail admin@saembassy.co.zw; Ambassador Mlungisi Makalima.

Spain: 16 Phillips Ave, Belgravia, POB 3300, Harare; tel. (4) 250740; fax (4) 795261; e-mail emb.harare@mae.es; Ambassador Santiago Martínez-Caro de la Concha-Castañeda.

Sudan: 4 Pascoe Ave, Harare; tel. (4) 700111; fax (4) 703450; e-mail sudan@africaonline.co.zw; internet www.sudaniharare.org.zw; Ambassador Hassan Ahmed Fageeri.

Sweden: 32 Aberdeen Rd, Avondale, POB 4110, Harare; tel. (4) 302636; fax (4) 302236; e-mail ambassaden.harare@foreign.ministry.se; internet www.swedenabroad.com; Ambassador Sten Rylander.

Switzerland: 9 Lanark Rd, POB 3440, Harare; tel. (4) 703997; fax (4) 794925; e-mail har.vertretung@eda.admin.ch; Ambassador Marcel Stutz.

Tanzania: Ujamaa House, 23 Baines Ave, POB 4841, Harare; tel. (4) 792714; fax (4) 792747; e-mail tanrep@icon.co.zw; Ambassador Adadi Rajabu.

Tunisia: Harare; tel. (4) 791570; fax (4) 727224; Ambassador Hamid Zaouche.

United Kingdom: Corner House, cnr Samora Machel Ave and Leopold Takawira St, POB 4490, Harare; tel. (4) 772990; fax (4) 774617; e-mail consular.harare@fco.gov.uk; internet www.britishembassy.gov.uk/zimbabwe; Ambassador Dr Andrew Pocock.

USA: 172 Herbert Chitepo Ave, POB 3340, Harare; tel. (4) 758803; fax (4) 796488; e-mail hararepas@state.gov; internet harare.usembassy.gov; Ambassador Christopher W. Dell.

Zambia: Zambia House, cnr Union and Julius Nyerere Aves, POB 4698, Harare; tel. (4) 773777; fax (4) 773782; Ambassador Prof. E. C. Mumba.

Judicial System

The legal system is Roman-Dutch, based on the system which was in force in the Cape of Good Hope on 10 June 1891, as modified by subsequent legislation.

The Supreme Court has original jurisdiction in matters in which an infringement of Chapter III of the Constitution defining fundamental rights is alleged. In all other matters it has appellate jurisdiction only. It consists of the Chief Justice and eight Judges of Appeal. A normal bench consists of any five of these.

The High Court consists of the Chief Justice, the Judge President, and 11 other judges. Below the High Court are Regional Courts and Magistrates' Courts with both civil and criminal jurisdiction presided over by full-time professional magistrates.

The Customary Law and Local Courts Act, adopted in 1990, abolished the village and community courts and replaced them with customary law and local courts, presided over by chiefs and headmen; in the case of chiefs, jurisdiction to try customary law cases is limited to those where the monetary values concerned do not exceed Z.$1,000 and in the case of a headman's court Z.$500. Appeals from the Chiefs' Courts are heard in Magistrates' Courts and, ultimately, the Supreme Court. All magistrates now have jurisdiction to try cases determinable by customary law.

Chief Justice: Godfrey Chidyausiku.

Judges of Appeal: W. Sandura, Anele Matika, Tadius Karwi, Susan Mavangira, Lavender Makoni.

Judge President: Paddington Garwe.

Attorney-General: Sobuza Gula-Ndebele.

Religion

AFRICAN RELIGIONS

Many Africans follow traditional beliefs.

CHRISTIANITY

About 55% of the population are Christians.

Zimbabwe Council of Churches: 128 Mbuya Nehanda St, POB 3566, Harare; tel. (4) 772043; fax (4) 773650; e-mail zcc@africaonline.co.zw; f. 1964; Pres. Rt Rev. Dr Wilson Sitshebo; Gen. Sec. Densen Mafiyani; 24 mem. churches, nine assoc. mems.

The Anglican Communion

Anglicans are adherents of the Church of the Province of Central Africa, covering Botswana, Malawi, Zambia and Zimbabwe. The Church comprises 15 dioceses, including five in Zimbabwe. The current Archbishop of the Province is the Bishop of Upper Shire, Malawi. The Church had an estimated 320,000 members at mid-2000.

Bishop of Central Zimbabwe: Rt Rev. Ishmael Mukuwanda, POB 25, Gweru; tel. (54) 21030; fax (54) 21097.

Bishop of Harare: Rt Rev. Dr Nolbert Kunonga, Bishopsmount Close, POB UA7, Harare; tel. (4) 702253; fax (4) 700419; e-mail angbishophre@mango.zw.

Bishop of Manicaland: (vacant), 115 Herbert Chitepo St, Mutare; tel. (20) 64194; fax (20) 63076; e-mail diomani@syscom.co.zw; internet www.anglicandioceseofmanicaland.co.zw.

Bishop of Masvingo: Rt Rev. Godfrey Toanezvi, POB 1421, Masvingo; tel. (39) 362536; e-mail anglicandiomsv@comone.co.zw.

Bishop of Matabeleland: Rt Rev. Wilson Sitshebo, POB 2422, Bulawayo; tel. (9) 61370; fax (9) 68353; e-mail angdiomat@telconet.co.zw.

The Roman Catholic Church

For ecclesiastical purposes, Zimbabwe comprises two archdioceses and six dioceses. At 31 December 2004 there were some 1.3m. adherents, equivalent to an estimated 8.8% of the total population.

Zimbabwe Catholic Bishops' Conference (ZCBC)

ZCBC Secretariat, Africa Synod House, 29–31 Selous Ave, POB CY738 Causeway, Harare; tel. (4) 705368; fax (4) 704001; internet www.zcbc.co.zw.

f. 1969; Pres. Most Rev. Robert C. Ndlovu (Archbishop of Harare).

Archbishop of Bulawayo: (vacant), cnr Lobengula St and 9th Ave, POB 837, Bulawayo; tel. (9) 63590; fax (9) 60359; e-mail archdbyo@mweb.co.zw.

Archbishop of Harare: Most Rev. Robert C. Ndlovu, Archbishop's House, 66 Fifth St, POB CY330, Causeway, Harare; tel. (4) 727386; fax (4) 721598; e-mail hrearch@zol.co.zw.

Other Christian Churches

At mid-2000 there were an estimated 4.8m. adherents professing other forms of Christianity.

Dutch Reformed Church in Zimbabwe (Nederduitse Gereformeerde Kerk): 35 Samora Machel Ave, POB 503, Harare; tel. (4) 774738; fax (4) 774739; e-mail pvanvuuren@mango.zw; f. 1895; 10 congregations in Zimbabwe and two in Zambia; Chair. Rev. Piet F. J. van Vuuren; Sec. Rev. J. Haasbroek; 1,400 mems.

Evangelical Lutheran Church: POB 2175, Bulawayo; tel. (9) 254991; e-mail elczhead@mweb.co.zw; f. 1903; Sec. Rt Rev. L. M. Dube; 57,000 mems.

Greek Orthodox Church: POB 2832, Harare; tel. and fax (4) 744991; e-mail zimbabwe@greekorthodox-alexandria.org; internet www.greekorthodox-zimbabwe.org; Archbishop George.

Methodist Church in Zimbabwe: POB CY71, Causeway, Harare; tel. (4) 250523; fax (4) 723709; f. 1891; Presiding Bishop Rev. Margaret M. James; Sec. of Conference Rev. Simon U. Madhiba; 112,529 mems.

United Congregational Church of Southern Africa: 40 Jason Moyo St, POB 2451, Bulawayo; tel. (9) 63686; internet www.uccsa.org.za/zimbabwe-synod; Chair. Rev. B. Mathema (acting); Sec. Rev. Majaha Nthliziyo.

United Methodist Church: POB 3408, Harare; tel. (4) 704127; f. 1890; Bishop of Zimbabwe Abel Tendekayi Muzorewa; 45,000 mems.

Among other denominations active in Zimbabwe are the African Methodist Church, the African Methodist Episcopal Church, the African Reformed Church, the Christian Marching Church, the Church of Christ in Zimbabwe, the Independent African Church, the Presbyterian Church (and the City Presbyterian Church), the United Church of Christ, the Zimbabwe Assemblies of God and the Ziwezano Church.

JUDAISM

The Jewish community numbered 897 members at 31 December 1997; by 2006 that number had fallen to around 300.

Zimbabwe Jewish Board of Deputies: POB 1954, Harare; tel. (4) 702507; fax (4) 702506; Pres. P. Sternberg; Sec. E. Alhadeff.

BAHÁ'Í FAITH

National Spiritual Assembly: POB GD380, Greendale, Harare; tel. (4) 495945; fax (4) 744611; internet www.bahai.co.zw; Nat. Sec. Derek Sithole; f. 1970; mems resident in 57 clusters.

The Press

DAILIES

The Chronicle: 9th Ave and George Silundika St, POB 585, Bulawayo; tel. (9) 888871; fax (9) 888884; e-mail editor@chronicle.co.zw; internet www.chronicle.co.zw; f. 1894; publ. by the Govt-controlled co Zimpapers; circulates throughout south-west Zimbabwe; English; English; Editor MAKUWERERE BWITITI; circ. 25,000 (2004).

Daily Mirror (Zim Mirror): Charter House, 70 Samora Machel Ave, Harare; tel. (4) 725251; fax (4) 729607; internet www.zimmirror.co.zw; f. 2002; publ. by Zimbabwe Mirror Newspapers Group; also publ. *Sunday Mirror* (f. 1997 as *The Zimbabwe Mirror Weekly*, circ. c. 15,000); English; CEO and Editor-in-Chief IBBO MANDAZA.

The Daily News: 18 Sam Nujoma St and cnr Speke Ave, Harare; tel. (4) 753027; fax (4) 753024; publ. by Associated Newspapers of Zimbabwe; English; publ. suspended Sept. 2003; Editor NQOBILE NYATHI; CEO SAM SIPEPA NKOMO; Chair. STRIVE MASIYIWA; circ. c. 80,000 (2003).

The Herald: POB 396, Harare; tel. (4) 795771; fax (4) 700305; internet www.herald.co.zw; f. 1891; publ. by the Govt-controlled co Zimpapers; English; Editor PIKIRAYI DEKETEKE; circ. c. 60,000 (2006).

WEEKLIES

Financial Gazette: Coal House, 5th Floor, cnr Nelson Mandela Ave and Leopold Takawira St, Harare; tel. (4) 781571; fax (4) 781578; e-mail schamunorwa@fingaz.co.zw; internet www.fingaz.co.zw; f. 1969; publ. by ZimInd Publrs (Pvt) Ltd; affiliated to the ZANU—PF party; Editor-in-Chief SUNSLEEY CHAMUNORWA; Gen. Man. JACOB CHISESE; circ. c. 40,000 (2004).

Indonsakusa/Ilanga: c/o CNG, POB 6520, Harare; tel. (4) 796855; fax (4) 703873; publ. by Community Newspaper Group (Mass Media Trust); distributed in north and south Matabeleland, respectively; circ c. 10,000.

Kwayedza: POB 396, Harare; tel. (4) 795771; fax (4) 791311; internet www.kwayedza.co.zw; publ. by the Govt-controlled co Zimpapers; f. 1985; ChiShona; Editor GERVASE M. CHITEWE; circ. c. 15,000 (2003).

Manica Post: POB 960, Mutare; tel. (20) 61212; fax (20) 61149; f. 1893; publ. by the Govt-controlled co Zimpapers; English; Editor PAUL MAMBO; circ. 15,000 (2004).

Mashonaland Guardian/Telegraph: c/o CNG, POB 6520, Harare; tel. (4) 796855; fax (4) 703873; publ. by Community Newspaper Group (Mass Media Trust); distributed in Mashonaland; circ. c. 10,000.

Masvingo Mirror: POB 1214, Masvingo; tel. (39) 64372; fax (39) 64484; independent; Editor NORNA EDWARDS.

Masvingo Star: 2–3 New Market Centre, R. Tangwena Ave, POB 138, Masvingo; tel. and fax (39) 63978; e-mail thestar@africaonline.co.zw; publ. by Community Newspaper Group (Mass Media Trust); English; distributed in Masvingo province; Editor TAPERA CHIKUWIRA; circ. c. 10,000.

Midlands Observer: POB 533, Kwekwe; tel. (55) 22248; fax (55) 23985; e-mail nelson_mashiri@yahoo.com; f. 1953; weekly; English; Editor R. JARIJARI; circ. 20,000.

North Midlands Gazette: POB 222, Kadoma; tel. and fax (68) 3731; f. 1912; Editor C. B. KIDIA.

The Standard: 1st Block, 3rd Floor, Ernst and Young Bldg, 1 Kwame Nkrumah Ave, POB 661730, Kopje, Harare; tel. 1750401; fax 1773854; internet www.thestandard.co.zw; f. 1997; publ. by ZimInd Publrs (Pvt) Ltd; Sun.; Exec. Chair and CEO TREVOR NCUBE; circ. 42,000 (2004).

Sunday Mail: POB 396, Harare; tel. (4) 795771; fax (4) 700305; internet www.sundaymail.co.zw; f. 1935; publ. by the Govt-controlled co Zimpapers; English; Chair. THOMAS SITHOLE; Editor WILLIAM CHIKOTO; circ. 110,000 (2004).

Sunday News: POB 585, Bulawayo; tel. (9) 540071; fax (9) 540084; f. 1930; publ. by the Govt-controlled co Zimpapers; English; Editor BREZHNEV MALABA; circ. 30,000 (2004).

The Times: c/o CNG, POB 6520, Harare; tel. (4) 796855; fax (4) 703873; f. 1897; fmrly *The Gweru Times*; publ. by Community Newspaper Group (Mass Media Trust); distributed in Mashonaland; English; circ. c. 5,000.

uMthunywa (The Messenger): 9th Ave and George Silundika, POB 585 Bulawayo; tel. (09) 880888; fax (09) 888884; e-mail advertising@chronicle.co.zw; internet www.umthunywa.co.zw; f. 2004; SiNdebele; publ. by the Govt-controlled co Zimpapers; Editor BHEKITHEMBA J. NCUBE.

The Vanguard: Zimbabwe National Students' Union, 21 Wembley Cres., Eastlea, Harare; tel. (4) 788135; e-mail zinasu@gmail.com; internet www.zinasu.org/vanguards/latest.html; publ. by the Zimbabwe Nat. Students' Union.

The Zimbabwean: POB 248, Hythe, SO45 4WX, United Kingdom; e-mail feedback@thezimbabwean.co.uk; internet www.thezimbabwean.co.uk; f. 2005; independent; publ. in the United Kingdom and South Africa; focus on news in Zimbabwe and life in exile; Publr and Editor WILF MBANGA.

Zimbabwe Independent: Zimind Publishers (Pvt) Ltd, Suites 23/24, 1 Union Ave, POB BE1165, Belvedere, Harare; e-mail trevorn@mg.co.za; internet www.theindependent.co.zw; f. 1996; publ. by ZimInd Publrs (Pvt) Ltd; English; Publr TREVOR NCUBE; Editor DUMISANI MULEYA; circ. 30,500 (2005).

Zimbabwean Government Gazette: POB 8062, Causeway, Harare; official notices; Editor L. TAKAWIRA.

PERIODICALS

The Agenda: Information Department, 348 Herbert Chitepo Ave, Harare; tel. (4) 736338; fax (4)721146; e-mail info@nca.org.zw; internet www.nca.org.zw; f. 1997; publ. by the Nat. Constitutional Assembly; quarterly; civil rights issues.

Central African Journal of Medicine (CAJM): University of Zimbabwe Publications, POB A195, Avondale, Harare; tel. (4) 791630; fax (4) 791995; e-mail cajm@medsch.uz.ac.zw; internet www.ajol.info; f. 1955; monthly; Editor-in-Chief Prof. G. I. MUGUTI.

Chamber of Mines Journal: Stewart House, North Wing, 4 Central Ave, POB 712, Harare; tel. (4) 702841; fax (4) 707983; e-mail chamines@utande.co.zw; publ. by Thomson Publs; monthly.

Chaminuka News: POB 650, Marondera; f. 1988; publ. by Community Newspaper Group (Mass Media Trust); fortnightly; English and ChiShona; distributed in Manicaland and Mashonaland North provinces; Editor M. MUGABE; circ. c. 10,000.

Indonsakusa: Hwange; f. 1988; monthly; English and SiNdebele; Editor D. NTABENI; circ. 10,000.

The Insider: Insider Publications, POB FM 415, Famona, Bulawayo; tel. (11) 789-739; e-mail charlesrukuni@insiderzim.com; e-mail charlesrukuni@yahoo.com; internet www.insiderzim.com; f. 1990; monthly; digital newsletter; news and current affairs; Editor and Publr CHARLES RUKUNI.

JASSA: Journal of Applied Science in Southern Africa: University of Zimbabwe Publications, POB MP203, Mount Pleasant, Harare; tel. (4) 303211; fax (4) 333407; e-mail uzpub@admin.uz.ac.zw; internet www.uz.ac.zw/publications; applied science journal of the Univ. of Zimbabwe; 2 a year; Editor-in-Chief Prof. C. F. B. NHACHI.

Journal of Social Development in Africa: School of Social Work, Private Bag 66022, Kopje, Harare; 2 a year; Editor CAROLE PEARCE.

Mahogany: POB UA589, Harare; tel. (4) 752063; fax (4) 752062; f. 1980; 6 a year; English; women's interest; Editor TENDAI DONDO; circ. 240,000.

Masiye Pambili (Let Us Go Forward): POB 591, Bulawayo; tel. (9) 75011; fax (9) 69701; f. 1964; 2 a year; English; Editor M. N. NDLOVU; circ. 21,000.

Moto (Fire): POB 890, Gweru; tel. (54) 24886; fax (54) 28194; e-mail moto@telco.co.zw; f. 1959; monthly; publ. by the Govt-controlled co Zimpapers; banned in 1974; relaunched in 1980 as a weekly newspaper, then in magazine format in 1982; Roman Catholic; Editor SYDNEY SHOKO; circ. 22,000.

Mukai-Vukani Jesuit Journal for Zimbabwe: Jesuit Communications, 1 Churchill Ave, Alexandra Park, POB ST194, Southerton, Harare; tel. (4) 744571; fax (4) 744284; e-mail owermter@zol.co.zw; internet www.jescom.co.zw; 4–6 a year; Catholic; Editor Fr OSKAR WERMTER; circ. 2,000.

Nehanda Guardian: Bindura; f. 1988; weekly; English and ChiShona; Editor K. MWANAKA; circ. 10,000.

New Farmer: Herald House, cnr George Sikundika and Sam Nujoma Sts, POB 55, Harare; tel. (4) 708296; fax (4) 702400; e-mail advertising@chronicle.co.zw; internet www.newfarmer.co.zw; f. 2002; publ. by the Govt-controlled co Zimpapers; weekly; English; Editor GEORGE CHISOKO.

The Outpost: POB HG106, Highlands; tel. (4) 724571; fax (4) 703631; e-mail theoutpostmag@yahoo.com; f. 1911; publ. of the Zimbabwe Republic Police; monthly; English; Editor NKOSANA DLAMINI; circ. c. 25,000 (2005).

Railroader: National Railways of Zimbabwe, cnr Fife St and 10th Ave, POB 596, Bulawayo; tel. (9) 363716; fax (9) 363502; f. 1952; publ. by Nat. Railways of Zimbabwe; monthly; Editor M. GUMEDE; circ. 10,000.

Southern African Political and Economic Monthly (SAPEM): Southern Africa Political Economy Series Trust, 2-6 Deary Ave, Belgravia, POB MP111, Mt Pleasant, Harare; tel. (4) 252962; fax (4) 252964; f. 1987; monthly; publ. by the SAPES Trust; incorporating

Southern African Economist; Editor-in-Chief KHABELE MATLOSA; circ. 16,000.

Trends: 9th Ave and George Silundika St, POB 585 Bulawayo; tel. (09) 880888; fax (09) 888884; e-mail advertising@chronicle.co.zw; internet www.zimtrends.co.zw; f. 2003; publ. by the Govt-controlled co Zimpapers; monthly; English; leisure and entertainment; Editor EDWIN DUBE.

The Worker: ZCTU, Chester House, 9th Floor, Speke Ave and Third St, POB 3549, Harare; tel. (4) 794742; fax (4) 728484; e-mail info@zctu.co.zw; publ. by the Zimbabwe Congress of Trade Unions; News Editor BRIGHT CHIBVURI.

Zambezia: University of Zimbabwe Publications, POB MP203, Mount Pleasant, Harare; tel. (4) 303211; fax (4) 333407; e-mail uzpub@admin.uz.ac.zw; internet www.uz.ac.zw/publications; publ. by the Univ. of Zimbabwe; 2 a year; humanities and general interest; Editor Dr ZIFIKILE MGUNI-GAMBAHAYA.

Zimbabwe Agricultural Journal: Dept of Research and Specialist Services, 5th St, Extension, POB CY594, Causeway, Harare; tel. (4) 704531; fax (4) 728317; f. 1903; 6 a year; Editor R. J. FENNER; circ. 2,000.

Zimbabwean Travel: Herald House, cnr George Sikundika and Sam Nujoma Sts, POB 55, Harare; tel. (4) 708296; fax (4) 702400; e-mail advertising@chronicle.co.zw; internet www.zimtravel.com; f. 2003; publ. by the Govt-controlled co Zimpapers; monthly; English; Editor NOMSA NKALA.

Zimbabwe National Army Magazine: Ministry of Defence, Defence House, cnr Kwame Nkuruma and 3rd Sts, Harare; tel. (4) 700316; f. 1982; 4 a year; Dir of Communications Col LIVINGSTONE CHINEKA; circ. 5,000.

The Zimbabwe Farmer: POB 1683, Harare; tel. (4) 736836; fax (4) 749803; monthly; fmrly *Tobacco News*; present name adopted in 2003; publ. by Thomson Publs; Editor D. MILLER; circ. 2,000.

Zimbabwe Journal of Educational Research: HRRC, Faculty of Education, University of Zimbabwe, POB MP167, Mount Pleasant, Harare; e-mail hrrc@education.uz.ac.zw; internet www.uz.ac.zw/education/zjer; 3 a year; Editor-in-Chief Prof. F. ZINDI.

Zimbabwe Veterinary Journal: Zimbabwe Veterinary Asscn, POB CY168, Causeway, Harare; e-mail rjestewart@yahoo.com; f. 1970; journal of the Zimbabwe Veterinary Asscn; 2 a year; Editor-in-Chief S. MUKARATIRWA; Publ. Man. Dr R. STEWART.

NEWS AGENCIES

NewZiana (Pvt) Ltd: Mass Media House, 19 Selous Ave, POB CY511, Causeway, Harare; tel. (4) 251754; fax (4) 794336; e-mail mukrati@ziana.co.zw; internet www.newziana.co.zw; f. 1981 as Zimbabwe Inter-Africa News Agency; present name adopted in 2003; owned by the Govt-controlled co Multimedia Investment Trust (fmrly Zimbabwe Mass Media Trust); operates 10 community newspapers; CEO MUNYARADZI MATANYAIRE.

Foreign Bureaux

Agence France-Presse (AFP): Robinson House, Union Ave, POB 1166, Harare; tel. (4) 758017; fax (4) 753291; Rep. FRANÇOIS-BERNARD CASTÉRAN.

ANGOP (Angola): Mass Media House, 3rd Floor, 19 Selous Ave, POB 6354, Harare; tel. (4) 736849.

Agenzia Nazionale Stampa Associata (ANSA) (Italy): 2 Boundary Rd, Highlands, Harare; tel. (4) 723881; Rep. IAN MILLS.

Associated Press (AP) (USA): POB 785, Harare; tel. (4) 706622; fax (4) 703994; Rep. JOHN EDLIN.

Deutsche Presse-Agentur (dpa) (Germany): Harare; tel. (4) 755259; fax (4) 755240; Correspondent JAN RAATH.

ITAR—TASS (Information Telegraphic Agency of Russia—Telegraphic Agency of the Sovereign Countries): Mass Media House, 19 Selous Ave, POB 4012, Harare; tel. (4) 790521; Correspondent YURII PITCHUGIN.

Inter Press Service (IPS) (Italy): 127 Union Ave, POB 6050, Harare; tel. (4) 790104; fax (4) 728415; Rep. KENNETH BLACKMAN.

News Agency of Nigeria (NAN): Harare; tel. (4) 703041.

Pan-African News Agency (PANA) (Senegal): 19 Selous Ave, POB 8364, Harare; tel. (4) 730971; Bureau Chief PETER MWAURA.

Prensa Latina (Cuba): Mass Media House, 3rd Floor, 19 Selous Ave, Harare; tel. (4) 731993; Correspondent HUGO RIUS.

Press Trust of India (PTI): Mass Media House, 3rd Floor, 19 Selous Ave, Harare; tel. (4) 795006; Rep. N. V. R. SWAMI.

Reuters (United Kingdom): Harare; Correspondent MACDONALD DZIRUTWE.

RIA—Novosti (Russian Information Agency—News): 503 Robinson House, cnr Union Ave and Angwa St, POB 3908, Harare; tel. (4) 707232; fax (4) 707233; Correspondent A. TIMONOVICH.

United Press International (UPI) (USA): Harare; tel. (4) 25265; Rep. IAN MILLS.

Xinhua (New China) News Agency (People's Republic of China): 4 Earls Rd, Alexander Park, POB 4746, Harare; tel. and fax (4) 731467; Chief Correspondent LU JIANXIN.

Publishers

Academic Books (Pvt) Ltd: POB 567, Harare; tel. (4) 755408; fax (4) 781913; educational; Editorial Dir IRENE STAUNTON.

Amalgamated Publications (Pvt) Ltd: POB 1683, Harare; tel. (4) 736835; fax (4) 749803; f. 1949; trade journals.

Anvil Press: POB 4209, Harare; tel. (4) 751202; fax (4) 739681; f. 1988; general; Man. Dir PAUL BRICKHILL.

The Argosy Press: POB 2677, Harare; tel. (4) 755084; magazine publrs; Gen. Man. A. W. HARVEY.

Baobab Books (Pvt) Ltd: POB 567, Harare; tel. (4) 665187; fax (4) 665155; general, literature, children's.

The Bulletin: POB 1595, Bulawayo; tel. (9) 78831; fax (9) 78835; fmrly Directory Publrs Ltd; educational; CEO BRUCE BEALE.

College Press Publishers (Pvt) Ltd: 15 Douglas Rd, POB 3041, Workington, Harare; tel. (4) 754145; fax (4) 754256; f. 1968; educational and general; Man. Dir B. B. MUGABE.

Graham Publishing Co (Pvt) Ltd: POB 2931, Harare; tel. (4) 752437; fax (4) 752439; f. 1967; general; Dir GORDON M. GRAHAM.

Harare Publishing House: Chiremba Rd, Hatfield, Harare; tel. (4) 570342; f. 1982; Dir Dr T. M. SAMKANGE.

HarperCollins Publishers Zimbabwe (Pvt) Ltd: Union Ave, POB UA201, Harare; tel. (4) 721413; fax (4) 732436; Man. S. D. MCMILLAN.

Longman Zimbabwe (Pvt) Ltd: POB ST125, Southerton, Harare; tel. (4) 62711; fax (4) 62716; f. 1964; general and educational; Man. Dir N. L. DLODLO.

Mambo Press: Senga Rd, POB 779, Gweru; tel. (54) 24017; fax (54) 21991; f. 1958; religious, educational and fiction in English and African languages.

Modus Publications (Pvt) Ltd: Modus House, 27–29 Charter Rd, POB 66070, Kopje, Harare; tel. (4) 738722; Man. Dir ELIAS RUSIKE.

Munn Publishing (Pvt) Ltd: POB UA460, Union Ave, Harare; tel. (4) 481048; fax (4) 7481081; Man. Dir I. D. MUNN.

Standard Publications (Pvt) Ltd: POB 3745, Harare; Dir G. F. BOOT.

Southern African Printing and Publishing House (SAPPHO): 109 Coventry Rd, Workington, POB MP1005, Mount Pleasant, Harare; tel. (4) 621681; fax (4) 666061; internet www.zimmirror.co.zw; Editor-in-Chief Dr IBBO MANDAZA.

University of Zimbabwe Publications: University of Zimbabwe, POB MP203, Mount Pleasant, Harare; tel. (4) 303211; fax (4) 333407; e-mail uzpub@admin.uz.ac.zw; internet www.uz.ac.zw/publications; f. 1969; Dir MUNANI SAM MTETWA.

Zimbabwe Newspapers (1980) Ltd (Zimpapers): POB 55, Harare; tel. (4) 704088; fax (4) 702400; e-mail theherald@zimpapers.co.zw; internet www.herald.co.zw; f. 1981; 51% state-owned; publ. the newspapers *The Herald, The Sunday Mail, The Manica Post, The Chronicle, The Sunday News, Kwayedza, Umthunywa* and *The Southern Times* (based in Namibia); and magazines incl. *The Zimbabwean Travel, Trends Magazine* and *New Farmer Magazine*; Chair. HERBERT NKALA; Group CEO JUSTIN MUTASA.

ZPH Publishers (Pvt) Ltd: 183 Arcturus Rd, Kamfinsa, GD510, Greendale, Harare; tel. (4) 497548; fax (4) 497554; f. 1982 as Zimbabwe Publishing House Ltd; Chair. BLAZIO G. TAFIREYI.

Broadcasting and Communications

TELECOMMUNICATIONS

Econet Wireless Zimbabwe: Econet Park, No.2 Old Mutare Rd, Msasa, POB BE1298, Belvedere, Harare; tel. (91) 793500; fax (4) 486120; e-mail info@econet.co.zw; internet www.econet.co.zw; f. 1998; mobile cellular telecommunications operator; Chair. TAWANDA NYAMBIRAI; CEO DOUGLAS MBOWENI.

Net.One Ltd: POB CY579, Causeway, Harare; tel. (4) 707138; e-mail marketing@netone.co.zw; internet www.netone.co.zw; f. 1998; state-owned; mobile cellular telecommunications operator; Chair. CALLISTUS NDLOVU; CEO REWARD KANGAI.

Posts and Telecommunications Corpn (PTC): POB CY331, Causeway, Harare; tel. (4) 728811; fax (4) 731980; Chair. Dr M. MHLOYI; CEO BRIAN MUTANDIRO.

Telecel Zimbabwe: 148 Seke Rd, Graniteside, POB CY232, Causeway, Harare; tel. (4) 748321; fax (4) 748328; e-mail info@telecelzim.co.zw; internet www.telecel.co.zw; f. 1998; 60% owned by Telecel Int. and 40% owned by Empowerment Corpn; mobile cellular telecommunications operator; Chair. JAMES MAKAMBA; Man. Dir JOHN SWAIM.

TelOne: Runhare House, 107 Union Ave, POBCY331, Causeway, Harare; tel. (4) 798111; e-mail webmaster@telone.co.zw; internet www.telone.co.zw; state-owned; sole fixed-line telecommunications operator.

BROADCASTING

There are four govt-controlled radio stations (National FM, Power FM, Radio Zimbabwe and Spot FM) and one television station. Radio Voice of the People was established as an alternative to state broadcasting. An independent radio station, SW Radio Africa, broadcasts to Zimbabwe from London, United Kingdom. Since 2003 Voice of America has broadcast a weekday news and entertainment programme (Studio 7) from the USA in ChiShona, English and SiNdebele.

Radio

Voice of the People (VOP): POB 5750, Harare; tel. (4) 707123; e-mail voxpopzim@yahoo.co.uk; internet www.vopradio.co.zw; f. 2000 by fmr ZBC staff; broadcasts one hour per day; relayed by Radio Netherlands transmitters in Madagascar; news and information in ChiShona, SiNdebele and English; Chair. DAVID MASUNDA; Exec. Dir JOHN MASUKU.

Zimbabwe Broadcasting Corpn: Broadcasting Center, Pockets Hill, POB HG444, Highlands, Harare; tel. (4) 498610; fax (4) 498613; e-mail zbc@zbc.co.zw; internet www.zbc.co.zw; f. 1957; programmes in English, ChiShona, SiNdebele and 14 minority languages, incl. Chichewa, Venda and Xhosa; broadcasts a general service (mainly in English), vernacular languages service, light entertainment, and educational programmes; Editor-in-Chief CHRISTINA TARUVINGA.

Television

Zimbabwe Broadcasting Corpn: (see Radio).

The main broadcasting centre is in Harare, with a second studio in Bulawayo; broadcasts on two commercial channels (one of which, Joy TV, serves the Harare area only) for about 95 hours per week.

Finance

(cap. = capital; res = reserves; dep. = deposits; m. = million; br(s). = branch(es); amounts in Zimbabwe dollars)

BANKING

Central Bank

Reserve Bank of Zimbabwe: 80 Samora Machel Ave, POB 1283, Harare; tel. (4) 703000; fax (4) 706450; e-mail lchitapi@rbz.co.zw; internet www.rbz.co.zw; f. 1964; bank of issue; cap. 2m., res 6m., dep. 11,734,195m. (Dec. 2004); Gov. Dr GIDEON GONO.

Commercial Banks

Barclays Bank of Zimbabwe Ltd: Barclays House, cnr First St and Jason Moyo Ave, POB 1279, Harare; tel. (4) 758281; fax (4) 752913; e-mail barclays.zimbabwe@barclays.com; internet www.barclays.co.zw; f. 1912; commercial and merchant banking; cap. 1,000m., res 19,000m., dep. 1,779,000m. (Dec. 2004); Chair. Dr ROBBIE MATONGO MUPAWOSE; CEO CHARITY JINYA; 44 brs.

Jewel Bank: Union House, 60 Union Ave, POB 3313, Harare; tel. (4) 758081; fax (4) 758085; e-mail cbzinfo@africaonline.co.zw; state-owned; cap. and res 2,551m., total assets 36,057m. (Dec. 2001); f. 1980; fmrly Commercial Bank of Zimbabwe; present name adopted 2004; Chair. RICHARD V. WILDE; 9 brs.

Kingdom Bank Ltd: 6th Floor, Karigamombe Centre, 53 Samora Machel Ave, Harare; tel. (4) 749400; fax (4) 755201; e-mail kmb@kingdom.co.zw; internet www.kingdom.co.zw; f. 2000; cap. 102m., res 14,655m., dep. 522,437m.; Man. Dir MARK WOOD.

Stanbic Bank Zimbabwe Ltd: Stanbic Centre, 1st Floor, 59 Samora Machel Ave, POB 300, Harare; tel. (4) 759480; fax (4) 751324; e-mail zimbabweinfo@stanbic.com; internet www.stanbic.co.zw; f. 1990; cap. 1,000m., res 1,761,842m., dep. 7,386,055m. (Dec. 2005); Chair. S. MOYO; Man. Dir PINDIE NYANDORO; 16 brs.

Standard Chartered Bank Zimbabwe Ltd: John Boyne House, cnr Inez Terrace and Speke Ave, POB 373, Harare; tel. (4) 252623; fax (4) 758076; internet www.standardchartered.com/zw; f. 1983; cap. and res 3,422.7m., total assets 558,124m. (2003); Chair. H.P. MKUSHI; CEO WASHINGTON MATSAIRA; 28 brs.

Trade and Investment Bank Ltd: Cabs Centre, 10th Floor, 74 Jason Moyo Ave, POB CY1064, Causeway, Harare; tel. (4) 703791; fax (4) 705491; f. 1997; cap. and res 32m., total assets 421m. (Dec. 1997); Chair. Dr BERNARD THOMAS CHIDZERO; CEO Dr KOMBO JAMES MOYANA.

Zimbabwe Banking Corpn Ltd (Zimbank): Zimbank House, Speke Ave and First St, POB 3198, Harare; tel. (4) 757471; fax (4) 757497; e-mail finhold@finhold.co.zw; internet www.finhold.co.zw; f. 1951; state-owned; cap. 102m., res 178,293m., dep. 821,214m. (Sept. 2004); Chair. RICHARD CHEMIST HOVE; Group CEO ELISHA N. MUSHAYAKARARA; 35 brs.

Development Banks

African Export-Import Bank (Afreximbank): Eastgate Bldg, 3rd Floor, Gold Bridge (North Wing), Second St, POB 1600 Causeway, Harare; tel. (4) 729751; fax (4) 729756; internet www.afreximbank.com.

Infrastructure Development Bank of Zimbabwe (IDBZ): 99 Rotten Row, Harare; tel. (4) 774226; fax (4) 774225; e-mail enquiries@zdb.co.zw; internet www.zdb.co.zw; f. 2005.

Zimbabwe Development Bank (ZDB): ZDB House, 99 Rotten Row, POB 1720, Harare; tel. (4) 774226; fax (4) 774225; internet www.zdb.co.zw; f. 1985; 33.3% state-owned; cap. and res 355m., total assets 2,317m. (Dec. 2001); Chair. Dr T. MASAYA; Man. Dir CORNELIUS MARADZA; 3 brs.

Merchant Banks

African Banking Corpn of Zimbabwe Ltd (ABC): ABC House, 1 Endeavour Cres., Mount Pleasant Business Park, Mount Pleasant, POB 2786, Harare; tel. (4) 369260; fax (4) 369939; e-mail abcmail@africanbankingcorp.com; internet www.africanbankingcorp.com; f. 1956 as Rhodesian Acceptances Ltd; name changed to First Merchant Bank of Zimbabwe Ltd in 1990; merged with Heritage Investment Bank in 1997; present name adopted in 2002; subsidiary of ABC Holdings Ltd, Botswana; cap. and res 36.8m., total assets 475.6m. (Dec. 2001); Chair. O. M. CHIDAWU; Man. Dir F. M. DZANYA; 1 br.

MBCA Bank Ltd: Old Mutual Centre, 14th Floor, cnr Third St and Jason Moyo Ave, POB 3200, Harare; tel. (4) 701636; fax (4) 708005; e-mail mbca@mbca.co.zw; internet www.mbca.co.zw; f. 1956; cap. 500.1m., res 10,946.7m., dep. 3,366,941.3m. (Dec. 2004); Chair. E. D. CHIURA; Man. Dir D. DENYA.

NMB Bank Ltd: Unity Court, 4th Floor, cnr Union Ave and First St, POB 2564, Harare; tel. (4) 759651; fax (4) 759648; e-mail enquiries@nmbz.co.zw; internet www.nmbz.com; f. 1993; fmrly Nat. Merchant Bank of Zimbabwe; cap. 32m., res 391,485m., dep. 2,610,982m. (Dec. 2005); Chair. Dr GIBSON MANYOWA MANDISHONA; CEO Dr DAVID T. HATENDI; 10 brs.

Standard Chartered Merchant Bank Zimbabwe Ltd: Standard Chartered Bank Bldg, cnr Second St and Nelson Mandela Ave, POB 60, Harare; tel. (4) 708585; fax (4) 725667; f. 1971; cap. and res 78m., dep. 83m. (Dec. 1998); Chair. BARRY HAMILTON; Man. Dir EBBY ESSOKA.

Discount Houses

African Banking Corpn Securities Ltd: 69 Samora Machel Ave, POB 3321, Harare; tel. (4) 752756; fax (4) 790641; cap. and res 68m. (Dec. 1999); fmrly Bard Discount House Ltd; Chair. N. KUDENGA; Man. Dir D. DUBE.

The Discount Co of Zimbabwe (DCZ): 70 Park Lane, POB 3424, Harare; tel. (4) 705414; fax (4) 731670; cap. and res 8.9m., total assets 377.4m. (Feb. 1995); Chair. S. J. CHIHAMBAKWE.

Intermarket Discount House: Unity Court, 5th Floor, Union Ave, POB 3290, Harare.

National Discount House Ltd: MIPF House, 5th Floor, Central Ave, Harare; tel. (4) 700771; fax (4) 792927; internet www.ndh.co.zw; cap. and res 168.4m., total assets 2,365.2m. (Dec. 2000); Chair. EDWIN MANIKAI; Man. Dir LAWRENCE TAMAYI.

Banking Organizations

Bankers' Association of Zimbabwe (BAZ): Kuwana House, 4th Floor, Union Ave and First St, POB UA550, Harare; tel. (4) 728646; Pres. ELISHA MUSHAYAKARA; Dir FRANK READ.

Institute of Bankers of Zimbabwe: Union Ave, POB UA521, Harare; tel. (4) 752474; fax (4) 750281; e-mail info@iobz.co.zw; internet www.iobz.co.zw; f. 1973; Chair. S. BIYAM; Pres. M. L. WOOD; Dir I. E. H. HELBY; 7,000 mems.

STOCK EXCHANGE

Zimbabwe Stock Exchange: Chiyedza House, 5th Floor, cnr First St and Kwame Nkrumah Ave, POB UA234, Harare; tel. (4) 736861;

fax (4) 791045; e-mail zse@econet.co.zw; internet www.zse.co.zw; f. 1946; Chair. G. MHLANGA; CEO EMMANUEL MUNYUKWI.

INSURANCE

Export Credit Guarantee Corpn of Zimbabwe (Pvt): 6 Earles Rd, Alexandra Park, POB CY2995, Causeway, Harare; tel. and fax (4) 744644; e-mail ecgc@telco.co.zw; internet www.ecgc.co.zw; f. 1999 as national export credit insurance agency; also provides export finance guarantee facilities; 100% owned by Reserve Bank of Zimbabwe; Chair. J. A. L. CARTER; Man. Dir RAPHAEL. G. NYADZAYO.

Credit Insurance Zimbabwe (Credsure): Credsure House, 69 Sam Nujoma St, POB CY1584, Causeway, Harare; tel. (4) 706101; fax (4) 706105; e-mail headoffice@credsure.co.zw; export credit insurance; Man. Dir BRIAN HILLEN-MOORE.

Fidelity Life Assurance of Zimbabwe (Pvt) Ltd: 66 Julius Nyerere Way, POB 435, Harare; tel. (4) 750927; fax (4) 751723; f. 1977; 52% owned by Zimre Holdings Ltd; pensions and life assurance; Chair. J. P. MKUSHI; Man. Dir SIMON B. CHAPAREKA.

Intermarket Life Assurance Ltd: Intermarket Life Towers, 77 Jason Moyo Ave, POB 969, Harare; tel. (4) 708801; fax (4) 703186; e-mail info@interlife.co.zw; internet www.intermarket.co.zw; f. 1964; life insurance; Man. Dir AMBROSE G. CHINEMBIRI.

NICOZ Diamond: Shell House, Samora Machel and Leopold Takawira Ave, POB 1256, Harare; tel. (4) 704911; fax (4) 704134; internet www.nicozdiamond.co.zw; f. 2003 by merger of National Insurance Co of Zimbabwe and Diamond Insurance of Zimbabwe; Chair. PHINEAS S. CHINGONO; Man. Dir GRACE MURADZIKWA.

Old Mutual PLC: Old Mutual Central Africa CABS Bldg, Northend Close, Northridge Park, Highlands, Harare; POB 1346, Harare; tel. (4) 851484-88; fax (4) 485480; e-mail info@oldmutual.co.zw; internet www.oldmutual.co.zw; f. 1845; life and general insurance, asset management, and banking services; Chair. M. J. LEVETT; CEO J. H. SUTCLIFFE.

Zimnat Lion Insurance Co Ltd: Zimnat House, cnr Nelson Mandela Ave and Third St, POB CY1155, Causeway, Harare; tel. (4) 701177; fax (4) 735060; f. 1998 by merger of Zimnat Insurance Co Ltd and Lion of Zimbabwe Insurance; merged with AIG Zimbabwe in 2005; short-term insurance; Chair. S. MUTASA; Man. Dir CARLSON CHISWO.

Trade and Industry

GOVERNMENT AGENCIES

Export Processing Zones Authority (EPZA): POB 661484, Kopje, Harare; tel. (4) 780147; fax (4) 773843; e-mail info@epz.co.zw; internet www.epz.co.zw; f. 1996; administers and regulates export processing zones established since 1994; Chair. LOVEMORE CHIHOTA; Chief Exec. WALTER CHIDHAKWA.

Industrial Development Corpn of Zimbabwe (IDC): 93 Park Lane, POB CY1431, Causeway, Harare; tel. (4) 706971; fax (4) 250385; e-mail administrator@idc.co.zw; internet www.idc.co.zw; f. 1963; state investment agency; Gen. Man. MIKE NDUDZO.

Privatisation Agency of Zimbabwe (PAZ): Club Chambers, 9th Floor, cnr Nelson Mandela Ave and Third St, Private Bag 7728, Causeway, Harare; tel. (4) 251620; fax (4) 253723; internet www.paz.co.zw; f. 1999; CEO ANDREW N. BVUMBE.

Zimbabwe Investment Centre (ZIC): Investment House, 109 Rotten Row, POB 5950, Harare; tel. (4) 757931; fax (4) 757937; e-mail info@zic.co.zw; internet www.zic.co.zw; f. 1993; promotes domestic and foreign investment; CEO RICHARD MBAIWA (acting).

ZimTrade: 904 Premium Close, Mount Pleasant Business Park, POB 2738, Harare; tel. (4) 369330; fax (4) 369244; internet www.zimtrade.co.zw; f. 1991; national export promotion org.; Chair. FLORENCE SIGUDU MATAMBO; CEO ELIZABETH NERWANDE.

DEVELOPMENT ORGANIZATIONS

Alternative Business Association (ABA): Stand No. 15295, cnr First St and Eighth Cres., Sunningdale, Harare; tel. (4) 589625; fax (4) 799600; f. 1999 to address urban and rural poverty; programme areas include, agriculture, micro-mining, cross-border trade, microenterprise devt and micro-finance; Dir ISRAEL MABHOU.

Indigenous Business Development Centre (IBDC): Pocket Bldg, 1st Floor, Jason Moyo Ave, POB 3331, Causeway, Harare; tel. (4) 748345; f. 1990; Pres. BEN MUCHECHE; Sec.-Gen. Enoch KAMUSHINDA.

Indigenous Business Women's Organisation (IBWO): 73B Central Ave, POB 3710, Harare; tel. (4) 702076; fax (4) 614012; Pres. JANE MUTASA.

Zidco Holdings: 88 Robert Mugabe Rd, POB 1275, Harare; tel. (4) 253682; fax (4) 704391; f. 1981; fmrly Zimbabwe Devt Corpn; privatized in 2001; CEO (vacant).

Zimbabwe Human Rights NGO Forum: Blue Bridge, 8th Floor, Eastgate, POB 9077, Harare; tel. (4) 250511; fax (4) 250494; e-mail admin@hrforum.co.zw; internet www.hrforumzim.com; f. 1998; provides legal and 'psycho-social' assistance to the victims of organized violence; comprises 16 mem. orgs.

Zimbabwe Women's Bureau: 43 Hillside Rd, POB CR 120, Cranborne, Harare; tel. (4) 747809; fax (4) 707905; e-mail zwbtc@africaonline.co.zw; f. 1978; promotes entrepreneurial and rural community devt; Dir BERTHA MSORA.

CHAMBERS OF COMMERCE

Manicaland Chamber of Industries: 91 Third St, POB 92, Mutare; tel. (20) 61718; f. 1945; Pres. KUMBIRAI KATSANDE; 60 mems.

Mashonaland Chamber of Industries: POB 3794, Harare; tel. (4) 772763; fax (4) 750953; f. 1922; Pres. CHESTER MHENDE; 729 mems.

Matabeleland Chamber of Industries: 104 Parirenyatwa St, POB 2317, Bulawayo; tel. (9) 60642; fax (9) 60814; f. 1931; Pres. FELIX TSHUMA; 75 mems (2003).

Midlands Chamber of Industries: POB 213, Gweru; tel. (54) 2812; Pres. Dr BILL MOORE; 50 mems.

Zimbabwe National Chamber of Commerce (ZNCC): ZNCC Business House, 42 Harare St, POB 1934, Harare; tel. (4) 749335; fax (4) 750375; internet www.zncc.co.zw; f. 1983; represents small and medium businesses; Pres. LUXON ZEMBE; CEO CAIN MPOFU (acting); 2,500 mems; 8 brs.

INDUSTRIAL AND TRADE ASSOCIATIONS

Chamber of Mines of Zimbabwe: Stewart House, North Wing, 4 Central Ave, POB 712, Harare; tel. (4) 702841; fax (4) 707983; internet www.chamines.co.zw; f. 1939 by merger of the Rhodesian Chamber of Mines (Bulawayo) and Salisbury Chamber of Mines; Pres. Dr JACK MUREHWA; Chief Exec. and Sec. DAVID E. H. MURANGARI.

Confederation of Zimbabwe Industries (CZI): 31 Josiah Chinamano Ave, POB 3794, Harare; tel. (4) 772763; fax (4) 750953; internet www.czi.org.zw; f. 1957; Pres. PATTISON SITHOLE; CEO CALLISTO JOKONYA.

Specialized affiliate trade associations include:

CropLife Zimbabwe: POB AY78, Amby, Harare; tel. (4) 620191; fax (4) 660590; e-mail maxm@ecomed.co.zw; fmrly Agricultural Chemical Industry Asscn; Chair. MAX MAKUVISE.

Furniture Manufacturers' Association: c/o CZI, 31 Josiah Chinamano Ave, POB 3794, Harare; Pres. MATT SNYMAN.

Zimbabwe Association of Packaging: 17 Conventry Rd, Workington, Harare; tel. (4) 753800; fax (4) 882020.

Construction Industry Federation of Zimbabwe: Conquenar House, 256 Samora Machel Ave East, POB 1502, Harare; tel. (4) 746661; fax (4) 746937; Pres. GILBERT MATIKA; CEO MARTIN CHINGAIRA; c. 460 mems.

Grain Marketing Board (GMB): Dura Bldg, 179–187 Samora Machel Ave, POB CY77, Harare; tel. (4) 701870; fax (4) 251294; e-mail seedco@seedcogroup.com; f. 1931; responsible for maintaining national grain reserves and ensuring food security; CEO SAMUEL MUVUTI (acting).

Indigenous Petroleum Group of Zimbabwe (IPGZ): Harare; f. 2004 following split from Petroleum Marketers' Asscn of Zimbabwe; Chair. HUBERT NYAMBUYA; represents 68 importers.

Minerals Marketing Corpn of Zimbabwe (MMCZ): 90 Mutare Rd, Msasa, POB 2628, Harare; tel. (4) 487200; fax (4) 487161; internet www.mmcz.co.zw; f. 1982; sole authority for marketing of mineral production (except gold); Chair. MERCY MKUSHI (acting); Gen. Man. and CEO ONESIMO MAZAI MOYO.

Petroleum Marketers' Association of Zimbabwe (PMAZ): 142 Samora Machel Ave, Harare; tel. (4) 797556; represents private importers of petroleum-based products; Chair. GORDON MUSARIRA.

Timber Council of Zimbabwe: Conquenar House, 256 Samora Machel Ave, POB 3645, Harare; tel. (4) 746645; fax (4) 746013; Exec. Dir MARTIN DAVIDSON.

Tobacco Growers' Trust (TGT): POB AY331, Harare; tel. (4) 781167; fax (4) 781722; f. 2001; manages 20% of tobacco industry foreign exchange earnings on behalf of Reserve Bank of Zimbabwe; affiliated orgs include Zimbabwe Tobacco Asscn and Zimbabwe Farmers' Union; Chair. WILFANOS MASHINGAIDZE; Gen. Man. ALBERT JAURE.

Tobacco Industry and Marketing Board: POB 10214, Harare; tel. (4) 613310; fax (4) 613264; e-mail timb@timb.co.zw; internet www.timb.co.zw; f. 1936; Chair. NJODZI MACHIRORI; CEO STANLEY MUTEPFA.

Tobacco Trade Association: c/o 4–12 Paisley Rd, POB ST180, Southerton, Harare; tel. (4) 773858; fax (4) 773859; e-mail tta@zol.co.zw; f. 1948; represents manufacturers and merchants.

Zimbabwe National Traditional Healers' Association (ZINATHA): Red Cross House, 2nd Floor, Rm 202, 98 Cameron St, POB 1116, Harare; tel. and fax (11) 606771; f. 1980; certifies and oversees traditional healers and practitioners of herbal medicine through the Traditional Medical Practitioners Council; promotes indigenous methods of prevention and treatment of HIV/AIDS; Pres. Prof. GORDON CHAVUNDUKA; 55,000 mems (2004).

Zimbabwe Tobacco Association (ZTA): 108 Prince Edward St, POB 1781, Harare; tel. (4) 796931; fax (4) 791855; e-mail fctobacco@zta.co.zw; internet www.zta.co.zw; f. 1928; represents growers; Pres. ANDREW FERREIRA; CEO RODNEY AMBROSE; c. 5,500 mems.

EMPLOYERS' ASSOCIATIONS

Commercial Farmers' Union (CFU): Agriculture House, cnr Adylinn Rd and Marlborough Dr., Marlborough; POB WGT390, Westgate, Harare; tel. (4) 309800; fax (4) 309849; e-mail aisd3@cfu.co.zw; internet www.cfu.co.zw; f. 1942; Pres. DOUGLAS TAYLOR-FREEME; Dir HENDRIK W. OLIVIER; 1,200 mems.

Cattle Producers' Association (CPA): Agriculture House, cnr Adylinn Rd and Marlborough Dr., Marlborough; POB WGT390, Westgate, Harare; tel. and fax (4) 309837; e-mail cpa@cfu.co.zw; Chair. MARYNA ERASMUS.

Coffee Growers' Association: Agriculture House, cnr Adylinn Rd and Marlborough Dr., Marlborough; POB WGT390, Westgate, Harare; tel. and fax (4) 750238; e-mail pres@cfu.co.zw; f. 1961; Chair. T. GIFFORD; Dir H. OLIVIER.

Commercial Cotton Growers' Association: Agriculture House, cnr Adylinn Rd and Marlborough Dr., Marlborough; POB WGT390, Westgate, Harare; tel. (4) 309800; fax (4) 309849; f. 1951; Chair. NEVILLE BROWN.

Crops Association: Agriculture House, cnr Adylinn Rd and Marlborough Dr., Marlborough; POB WGT390, Westgate, Harare; tel. (4) 309843; fax (4) 309850; e-mail copa@cfu.co.zw; comprises the Commercial Oilseeds Producers' Asscn (COPA), the Zimbabwe Cereal Producers' Asscn (ZCPA) and the Zimbabwe Grain Producers' Asscn (ZGPA); Chair. DENNIS LAPHAM; Man. (Crops) GEORGE HUTCHISON; represents c. 800 producers.

National Association of Dairy Farmers: Agriculture House, cnr Adylinn Rd and Marlborough Dr., Marlborough; POB WGT390, Westgate, Harare; tel. (4) 309800; fax (4) 309837; e-mail nadf@cfu.co.zw; f. 1953; CEO ROB J. VAN VUUREN; 174 mems.

Ostrich Producers' Association of Zimbabwe (TOPAZ): Agriculture House, cnr Adylinn Rd and Marlborough Dr., Marlborough; POB WGT390, Westgate, Harare; tel. (4) 309800; fax (4) 309862; Chair. CEDRIC WILDE; Exec. Dir CLARE DAVIES.

Zimbabwe Association of Tobacco Growers (ZATG): Agriculture House, cnr Adylinn Rd and Marlborough Dr., Marlborough; POB WGT390, Westgate, Harare; f. 2001; Pres. JULIUS NGORIMA; CEO CANAAN RUSHIZHA; 1,500 mems.

Zimbabwe Poultry Association (Commercial Poultry Producers' Association): Agriculture House, cnr Adylinn Rd and Marlborough Dr., Marlborough; POB WGT390, Westgate, Harare; tel. (4) 309800; fax (4) 309849; Chair. PETER DRUMMOND; represents c. 200 producers.

Employers' Confederation of Zimbabwe (EMCOZ): Stewart House, 4 Central Ave, 2nd Floor, POB 158, Harare; tel. (4) 739647; fax (4) 739630; e-mail emcoz@emcoz.co.zw; Pres. MIKE C. BIMHA; Exec. Dir JOHN W. MUFUKARE.

Horticultural Promotion Council (HPC): 12 Maasdorp Ave, Alexandra Park; POB WGT290, Westgate, Harare; tel. (4) 745492; fax (4) 745480; Chief Exec. BASILIO SANDAMU; represents c. 1,000 producers.

Export Flower Growers' Association of Zimbabwe (EFGAZ): 12 Maasdorp Ave, Alexandra Park; POB WGT290, Westgate, Harare; tel. (4) 725130; fax (4) 795303; Dir MARY DUNPHY; c. 300 mems.

National Employment Council for the Construction Industry of Zimbabwe: St Barbara House, Nelson Mandela Ave and Leopold Takawira St, POB 2995, Harare; tel. (4) 773966; fax (4) 773967; CEO STANLEY R. MAKONI; represents over 19,000 mem. cos (2002).

National Employment Council for the Engineering and Iron and Steel Industry: Adven House, 5th Floor, cnr Inez Terrace and Speke Ave, POB 1922, Harare; tel. (4) 775144; fax (4) 775918; f. 1943; Gen. Sec. E. E. SHARPE.

Zimbabwe Association of Consulting Engineers (ZACE): 16 Murandy Sq. East, POB HG836, Highlands, Harare; tel. (4) 746010; fax (4) 746010; e-mail zace@mango.zw.

Zimbabwe Building Contractors' Association: Caspi House, Block C, 4 Harare St, Harare; tel. (4) 780411; represents small-scale building contractors; CEO CONCORDIA MUKODZI.

Zimbabwe Commercial Farmers' Union (ZCFU): 53 Third St, Mutare; tel. (20) 67163; fmrly Indigenous Commercial Farmers' Union; Pres. DAVISON MUGABE; Dir. JOHN MAUTSA; represents c. 11,000 black farmers (2003).

Zimbabwe Farmers' Union (ZFU): POB 3755, Harare; tel. (4) 704763; fax (4) 700829; Pres. SILAS HUNGWE; Exec. Dir KWENDA DZAVIRA; represents c. 200,000 small-scale black farmers (2002).

UTILITIES

Electricity

Rural Electrification Agency (REA): Megawatt House, 6th Floor, 44 Samora Machel Ave Harare, POB 311, Harare; tel. (4) 770666; fax (4) 101661; e-mail emidzi@zesa.co.zw; f. 2002; manages the Rural Electrification Fund to expand and accelerate the electrification of rural areas; Chair. Dr SYDNEY GATA; CEO EMMANUEL MIDZI.

Zimbabwe Electricity Regulatory Commission (ZERC): Harare; f. 2004 to oversee the unbundling from ZESA of the Zimbabwe Power Co, the Zimbabwe Electricity Transmission Co and the Zimbabwe Electricity Distribution Co; Dir-Gen. MAVIS CHIDZONGA.

Zimbabwe Electricity Supply Authority (ZESA): 25 Samora Machel Ave, POB 377, Harare; tel. (4) 774508; fax (4) 774542; operates one hydroelectric and four thermal power stations; Chair. and CEO Dr SIDNEY GATA; dependable generation capacity of 1,700 MW.

Oil

National Oil Company of Zimbabwe (Pvt) Ltd (NOCZIM): NOCZIM House, 100 Leopold Takawira St, POB CY223, Causeway, Harare; tel. (4) 748543; fax (4) 748525; responsible for importing liquid fuels; Chair. CHARLES CHIPATO; Man. Dir ZVINECHIMWE CHURA.

Water

Zimbabwe National Water Authority (ZINWA): POB CY1215, Causeway, Harare; tel. and fax (4) 793139; e-mail mtetwa@utande.co.zw; f. 2001; fmrly Dept of Water, privatized in 2001; construction of dams, water supply, resources planning and protection; Chief Exec. ALBERT MUYAMBO.

MAJOR COMPANIES

African Distillers Ltd (AFDIS): POB WGT900, Westgate, Harare; tel. (4) 308351; fax (4) 308083; e-mail headoffice@afdis.co.zw; f. 1944; mfrs and importers of wines and spirits; Chair. J. S. MUTIZWA.

Almin Metal Industries: POB ST394, Southerton, Harare; tel. (4) 620110-121; fax (4) 620123; internet www.almin.co.zw; f. 1969; semi-fabricators in non-ferrous metals; Man. Dir A. P. PYLE; 188 employees.

Bindura Nickel Corpn Ltd: 70 Samora Machel AvePOB 1108, Harare; tel. (4) 704461; fax (4) 725509; f. 1966; 52.9% owned by Anglo American Corpn; sales Z.$1,500m. (Dec. 1998); mining, smelting and refining of nickel; Chair. G. G. GOMWE; CEO Dr L. R. CHIMIMBA; 2,800 employees.

Circle Cement Ltd: Manresa Works, Arcturus Rd, POB GD160, Greendale, Harare; tel. (4) 491028; fax (4) 491044; e-mail janice.johnny@lafarge.com; f. 1954; cap. and res Z.$449.6m., sales Z.$456.5m. (Nov. 1998); acquired by Lafarge, France, in 2001; mfrs and distributors of cement and allied products; Chair. M. A. MASUNDA; Man. Dir I. BINGWA; 305 employees.

Cotton Co of Zimbabwe Ltd (COTTCO): 1 Lytton Rd, Workington, POB 2697, Harare; tel. (4) 771981; fax (4) 753854; e-mail cottco@cottco.co.zw; internet www.thecottoncompany.com; f. 1994; provides services to cotton growers at every stage of the production and sales process; Chair. PATISON SITHOLE.

Dairibord Zimbabwe Ltd (DZL): 1225 Rekayi Tangwena Ave, POB 2512, Harare; tel. (4) 793761; fax (4) 795220; e-mail SamudzimuB@dairibord.co.zw; internet www.dairibord.com/dairibordzimbabwe; f. 1994; milk processors and mfrs of dairy products, and beverages; privatized in 1997; incorporates Lyons, NFB Logistics, and Dairibord Malawi; Man. Dir BENSON P. SAMUDZIMU; 1,530 employees at seven factories.

Delta Corpn Ltd: Sable House, Northridge Close, Northridge Park; POB BW294, Borrowdale, Harare; tel. (4) 883865; fax (4) 883864; e-mail h.gaitskell@delta.co.zw; internet www.delta.co.zw; f. 1898; brewers and mfrs of soft drinks and agro-industrial products; Chair. Dr R. M. MUWAPOSE; CEO J. S. MUTIZWA; 7,115 employees (2005).

Falcon Gold Zimbabwe Ltd (Falgold): Forestry Commission House, 1st Floor, Life St, POB 4096, Bulawayo; tel. (9) 76826; fax (9) 64028; e-mail citygroup@dial.pipex.com; f. 1991; subsidiary of Halogen Investments Holdings S.A., Luxembourg; gold mining and exploration; Group Chair. D. C. MARSHALL; Man. Dir ANDREW BEATTIE.

Hippo Valley Estates Ltd: POB 1108, Harare; tel. (4) 336802; e-mail amasunda@hippo.co.zw; f. 1956; cap. Z.$192.8m., sales Z.$3,663.4m. (Dec. 2005); production and milling of sugar from cane and other farming operations; Chair. G. G. GOMWE; CEO S. D. MTSAMBIWA; 4,890 employees (2005).

Hwange Colliery Co Ltd (Wankie Colliery Co Ltd): Coal House, 17 Nelson Mandela Ave, cnr Leopold Takawira St; POB 2870, Harare; tel. (4) 781985; fax (4) 781988; e-mail hccanalyst@zol.co.zw; internet www.hwangecolliery.co.zw; f. 1925; 40% state-owned; coal mining and production of coke and by-products; Chair. TENDAI SAVANHU; Man. Dir GODFREY DZINOMWA; 3,200 employees.

OK Zimbabwe Ltd: Ramon Rd, Graniteside, POB 3081, Harare; tel. (4) 757311; fax (4) 757028; f. 1940; retailers of groceries, clothing, houseware and furniture; Chair. M. E. KAHARI; CEO V. W. ZIREVA.

Rio Tinto Zimbabwe Ltd (RioZim): 1 Kenworth Rd, Highlands; POB CY1243, Causeway, Harare; tel. (4) 746141; fax (4) 746228; f. 1956; nickel and copper refining; gold mining; also diamonds and coal prospecting; Chair. M. ERIC KAHARI; CEO JOHN L. NIXON; 1,900 employees.

Zimbabwe Alloys and Smelting Co Ltd (Zimasco): Pegasus House, 6th Floor, Samora Machel Ave, POB 3110, Harare; tel. (4) 739622; fax (4) 707758; f. 1923; chromite mines at Shurugwi and Mutorashanga, smelter at Kwekwe; CEO SYDWELL JENA; 3,500 employees.

Ziscosteel: Private Bag 2, Redcliff; tel. (55) 62401; fax (55) 68666; 89% state-owned; fmrly Zimbabwe Iron and Steel Co Ltd; annual capacity of 1m. tons of liquid steel; Man. Dir GABRIEL MASANGA; 3,200 employees.

TRADE UNIONS

Zimbabwe Congress of Trade Unions (ZCTU): Chester House, 9th Floor, Speke Ave and Third St, POB 3549, Harare; tel. (4) 794742; fax (4) 728484; e-mail info@zctu.co.zw; internet www.zctu.co.zw; f. 1981 by merger of the African Trade Union Congress, the Nat. African Trade Union Congress, the Trade Union Congress of Zimbabwe, the United Trade Unions of Zimbabwe, the Zimbabwe Fed. of Labour and the Zimbabwe Trade Union Congress; affiliated to the Int. Trade Union Confed., the Org. of African Trade Union Unity and the Southern African Trade Union Co-ordination Council; co-ordinating org. for trade unions; Pres. LOVEMORE MATOMBO; Sec.-Gen. WELLINGTON CHIBEBE; c. 163,000 mems (2002).

In 2005 there were 35 affiliated unions. Affiliates with over 3,000 mems include:

Associated Mineworkers' of Zimbabwe (AMWZ): St. Andrew's House, 4th Floor, Leopold Takawira St and Samora Machel Ave, POB 384, Harare; tel. (4) 700287; fax (4) 706543; e-mail amwz@mweb.co.zw; affiliated to the Int. Fed. of Chemical, Energy, Mine and Gen. Workers' Unions; Nat. Pres. TINAGO EDMUND RUZIVE; 10,000 mems (2002).

Commercial Workers' Union of Zimbabwe (CWUZ): CWUZ House, 15 Sixth Ave, Parktown; POB 3922 Harare; tel. (4) 664701; e-mail cwuz@africaonline.co.zw; Pres. TAITUS MAGAYA; Gen. Sec. LOVEMORE MUSHONGA (acting); 22,000 mems (2003).

Communication and Allied Services Workers Union of Zimbabwe (CASWUZ): Morgan House, 4th Floor, G. Silundika Ave, POB 739, Harare; tel. (4) 794763; e-mail caswuz@africaonline.co.zw; fmrly the Zimbabwe Post and Telecommunication Workers' Union; present name adopted 2002; Gen. Sec. REWARD S. MUSIWOKUWAYA; 5,700 mems (2002).

Federation of Food and Allied Workers' Union of Zimbabwe (FFAWUZ): c/o ZCTU, Chester House, 9th Floor, Speke Ave and Third St, POB 3549, Harare; tel. (4) 74150; f. 1962; affiliated to the Int. Union of Food, Agricultural, Hotel, Restaurant, Catering, Tobacco and Allied Workers' Asscns; Gen. Sec. LEONARD KUZONDISHAYA; 3,000 mems (2002).

General Agricultural and Plantation Workers' Union (GAPWUZ): POB 1952, Harare; tel. (4) 734141; fax (4) 797918; e-mail alb@cfu.co.zw; affiliated to the Building and Wood Workers Int. and the Int. Union of Food, Agricultural, Hotel, Restaurant, Catering, Tobacco and Allied Workers' Asscns; Gen. Sec. GERTRUDE HAMBIRA; 5,000 mems (2002).

National Engineering Workers' Union (NEWU): St Barbara House, cnr Nelson Mandela Ave and Leopold Takawira St, Harare; tel. (4) 759597; fax (4) 759598; e-mail information@newu.org.zw; affiliated to the Int. Metalworkers' Fed.; Pres. ISAAC MATONGO; Gen. Sec. JAPHET MOYO; 9,000 mems (2002).

National Union of Clothing Industry Workers' Union (NUCI): Union House, 139A Lobengula St with 13th Ave, POB RY28, Raylton, Bulawayo; tel. (9) 64432; fax (9) 71089; affiliated to the Int. Textile, Garment and Leather Workers' Fed.; Gen. Sec. FRED MPOFU; 4,500 mems (2002).

Progressive Teachers' Union of Zimbabwe (PTUZ): 14 McLaren Rd, Milton Park, Harare; POB CR620, Cranborne, Harare; tel. (4) 757746; fax (4) 741937; e-mail ptuz@mweb.co.zw; f. 1997; Pres. TAKAVAFIREI ZHOU; Sec.-Gen. RAYMOND MAJONGWE; 12,000 mems (2002).

Public Service Association: PSA House, 9 Livingstone Ave, POB 179, Harare; tel. (4) 726506; fax (4) 704971; e-mail psahq@mweb.co.zw; f. 1919; affiliated to the Public Services Int.; Pres. CECILIA ALEXANDER; Gen. Sec. MAXWELL KAITANO; 20,689 mems (2003).

Mem. orgs incl. the Administrative and Exec. Officers Asscn, the Govt Officers Asscn, the Govt Workers Asscn, Professional and Technical Officers Asscn and:

Civil Service Employees' Association (CSEA): PSA House, 3rd floor, 9 Livingstone Ave, POB CY 202, Causeway, Harare; tel. (4) 701123; fax (4) 707208; e-mail civilsea@africaonline.co.zw; f. 1966; represents public-sector employees; Pres. MASIMBA KADZIMU; Gen. Sec. GEORGE NASHO WILSON; 5,000 mems (2006).

Zimbabwe Amalgamated Railwaymen's Union (ZARU): Unity House, 13th Ave, Herbert Chitepo St, POB 556, Bulawayo 10; tel. (9) 60948; affiliated to the Int. Transport Workers' Fed.; Gen. Sec. GIDEON P. SHOKO; 7,000 mems (2002).

Zimbabwe Banks and Allied Workers' Union (ZIBAWU): 1 Meredith Dr., Eastlea, POB 966, Harare; tel. (4) 703744; e-mail bankunion@zol.co.zw; Pres. GEORGE KAWENDA; Gen. Sec. COLLEN GWIYO; 4,560 mems (2002).

Zimbabwe Catering and Hotel Workers' Union (ZCHWU): Nialis Bldg, 1st Floor, Manyika, POB 3913, Harare; tel. (4) 753338; affiliated to the Int. Union of Food, Agricultural, Hotel, Restaurant, Catering, Tobacco and Allied Workers' Asscns; 8,500 mems (2002).

Zimbabwe Chemical, Plastics and Allied Workers' Union (ZCPAWU): St Andrew's House, 2nd Floor, Leopold Takawira St and Samora Machel Ave, POB 4810, Harare; tel. (4) 796533; Gen. Sec. F. P. GOMBEDZA; 3,723 mems (2002).

Zimbabwe Construction and Allied Trades Workers' Union (ZCAWU): St Barbara House, Office 306, Nelson Mandela Ave with Leopold Takawira St, POB 1291, Harare; tel. (4) 750159; fax (4) 773967; affiliated to the Building and Wood Workers Int.; Gen. Sec. CHARLES GUMBO; 3,000 mems (2002).

Zimbabwe Electricity and Energy Workers' Union (ZEEWU): Crossroads House, 43 Julius Nyere Way, POB 5537, Harare; tel. and fax (4) 724430; e-mail zeewu@comone.co.zw; affiliated to the Int. Fed. of Chemical, Energy, Mine and Gen. Workers' Unions and the Building and Wood Workers Int.; Gen. Sec. IAN MUNJOMA; 3,075 mems (2002).

Zimbabwe Furniture, Timber and Allied Trades Union (ZFTATU): St Andrew's House, 4th Floor, Samora Machel Ave, POB 4793, Harare; tel. (4) 728056; fax (4) 737686; e-mail inviolata@lantic.net; affiliated to the affiliated to the Building and Wood Workers Int.; Gen. Sec. L. CHISHAKWE; 3,500 mems (2002).

Zimbabwe Graphical Workers' Union (ZGWU): 6 Harare St, POB 494, Harare; tel. (4) 775627; fax (4) 775727; represents employees in the printing and packaging industries; Gen. Sec. MADZIVO CHIMHUKA; 5,000 mems (2005).

Zimbabwe Leather Shoe and Allied Workers' Union (ZLSAWU): POB 4450, Harare; tel. (4) 727925; fax (4) 727926; e-mail zlsawu@telco.co.zw; affiliated to the Int. Textile, Garment and Leather Workers' Fed.; Gen. Sec. ISIDORE MANHANDO ZINDOGA; 6,745 mems (2002).

Zimbabwe Textile Workers' Union (ZTWU): 50 Jason Moyo Ave, Pockets Bldg, 2nd Floor, South Wing, Hillside, POB 10245, Harare; tel. (4) 770226; fax (4) 758233; e-mail ztwu@mweb.co.zw; affiliated to the Int. Textile, Garment and Leather Workers' Fed.; Gen. Sec. SILAS KUVEYA; 11,636 mems (2004).

Zimbabwe Tobacco Industry Workers' Union (ZTIWU): St Andrew's House, 2nd Floor, Samora Machel Ave, POB 2757, Harare; tel. (4) 702339; Gen. Sec. ESTEVAO CUMBULANE; 3,000 mems (2002).

Zimbabwe Urban Councils Workers' Union (ZUCWU): POB CY 1859, Causeway, Harare; tel. (4) 729412; f. 1990; represents workers in engineering, housing and community services, health and emergency services, and clerical and treasury services; affiliated to the Public Services Int.; Pres. SIMON TAYALI; Gen. Sec. MOSES TSHIMKENI-MAHLANGU; 10,200 mems (2003).

Other ZCTU affiliates include the Automotive and Allied Workers' Union, the Cement and Lime Workers' Union, the Employment Council Workers' Union, the National Airways Workers' Union, the Railway Artisans' Union, the Railway Association of Enginemen, Transport and General Workers' Union, the Zimbabwe Domestic and Allied Workers' Union, the Zimbabwe Education, Scientific and Social Welfare Workers' Union, the Zimbabwe Ferro-alloys Workers' Union, the Zimbabwe Pulp and Paper Workers' Union, the Zimbabwe

Sugar Milling Workers' Union, the Zimbabwe Soft Drinks Manufacturing Workers' Union, and the Zimbabwe Radio, Television, Electronics Manufacturing Union.

Zimbabwe Federation of Trade Unions: Makombe Complex, Causeway, Harare; f. 1996 as alternative to ZCTU; 23 affiliated unions (2006); Gen. Sec. ADAMS VERENGA.

Affiliated unions include:

Zimbabwe Teachers' Union (ZITU): POB GV1, Glen View, Harare; tel. (4) 692454; fax (4) 708929; f. 2002; Gen. Sec. SIMPLISIO K. MATUMBA.

Other reported ZFTU affiliates include the Clothing Industry Workers' Union, the Zimbabwe Mining, Quarrying, Iron and Steel Workers' Union and the Zimbabwe National Drivers' Union.

Non-affiliated Unions

Zimbabwe National Students'Union (ZINASU): 21 Wembley Cres., Eastlea, Harare; tel. (4) 788135; e-mail zinasu@gmail.com; internet www.zinasu.org; represents students in more than 43 tertiary institutions; Sec.-Gen. BELOVED CHIWESHE; Nat. Co-ordinator WASHINGTON KATEMA; c. 260,000 mems (2006).

Zimbabwe Nurses' Association (ZINA): 47 Livingstone Ave, POB 2610, Harare; tel. and fax (4) 700479; e-mail zimnurse@mweb.co.zw; f. 1980; affiliated to the Public Services Int.; Gen. Sec. VANZAI MAJADA; 4,500 mems (2003).

Zimbabwe Teachers' Association (ZIMTA): POB 1440, Harare, Zimbabwe; tel. (4) 728438; fax (4) 791042; e-mail zimta@telco.co.zw; affiliated to Education Int.; Pres. TENDAI CHIKOWORE; Sec.-Gen. RICHARD GUNDANI (acting); 55,000 mems (2004).

Transport

RAILWAYS

In 1998 the rail network totalled 2,592 km, of which 313 km was electrified. Trunk lines run from Bulawayo south to the border with Botswana, connecting with the Botswana railways system, which, in turn, connects with the South African railways system; north-west to the Victoria Falls, where there is a connection with Zambia Railways; and north-east to Harare and Mutare connecting with the Mozambique Railways' line from Beira. From a point near Gweru, a line runs to the south-east, making a connection with the Mozambique Railways' Limpopo line and with the Mozambican port of Maputo. A connection runs from Rutenga to the South African Railways system at Beitbridge. A 320-km line from Beitbridge to Bulawayo was opened in 1999.

National Railways of Zimbabwe (NRZ): cnr Fife St and 10th Ave, POB 596, Bulawayo; tel. (9) 363716; fax (9) 363502; f. 1899; reorg. 1967; privatization under way; Chair. Brig. DOUGLAS NYIKAYARAMBA; Gen. Man. Air Commodore MIKE TICHAFA KARAKADZAI.

ROADS

In 2002 the road system in Zimbabwe totalled an estimated 97,267 km; some 18,481 km of the total network was paved. In December 2005 tollgates were introduced at the borders to raise funds to maintain the road network.

CIVIL AVIATION

AirZim operates an effective monopoly over air travel and transport within Zimbabwe. International and domestic air services connect most of the larger towns.

Civil Aviation Authority of Zimbabwe (CAAZ): Harare Int. Airport Terminal, Level 3, Private Bag CY7716, Causeway, Harare; tel. (4) 585009; fax (4) 585112; e-mail ais@caaz.co.zw; internet www.caaz.co.zw; f. 1999; operates eight airports incl. Harare Int. Airport and Joshua Mqabuko Nkomo Int. Airport (fmrly Bulawayo Airport); CEO DAVID CHAWOTA.

Air Zimbabwe (Pvt) Ltd (AirZim): POB AP1, Harare Airport, Harare; tel. (4) 575111; fax (4) 575068; internet www.airzimbabwe.com; f. 1967; scheduled domestic and international passenger and cargo services to Africa, Australia and Europe; plans were announced in Apr. 2006 to separate operations, creating the new cos Air Zimbabwe Technical, Air Zimbabwe Cargo, Nat. Handling Services and Galileo Zimbabwe, in addition to Air Zimbabwe; Chair. MIKE BIMHA; CEO Dr PETER CHIKUMBA.

Tourism

The principal tourist attractions are the Victoria Falls, the Kariba Dam and the Hwange Game Reserve and National Park. Zimbabwe Ruins, near Fort Victoria, and World's View, in the Matapos Hills, are also of interest. There is climbing and trout-fishing in the Eastern Districts, around Umtali. In 2005 1,558,501 tourists visited Zimbabwe, down from 1,854,488 in 2004 and 2,256,205 in 2003; however, revenue from tourism rose sharply in 2004, to US $194m., from US $61m. in the previous year.

Zimbabwe Tourism Authority (ZTA): POB CY286, Causeway, Harare; tel. (4) 758748; fax (4) 758826; e-mail info@ztazim.co.zw; internet www.zimbabwetourism.co.zw; f. 1984; promotes tourism domestically and from abroad; Chair. EMMANUEL FUNDIRA.

Associations licensed by the ZTA include:

Zimbabwe Association of Tour and Safari Operators (ZATSO): 18 Walter Hill Ave, Eastlea, Harare; tel. (4) 702402; fax (4) 707306; e-mail enquiries@soaz.net; CEO PAUL MATAMISA (acting).

Defence

As assessed at November 2006, total armed forces numbered about 29,000: 25,000 in the army and 4,000 in the air force. In 2000 the strength of the air force was reduced. Reductions in the army were made following the withdrawal of Zimbabwean troops from the Democratic Republic of the Congo in late 2002; there were further reductions the following year. Paramilitary forces comprise a police force of 19,500 and a police support unit of 2,300.

Defence Expenditure: Budgeted at Z.$14,900,000m. for 2006.

Commander-in-Chief of the Armed Forces: Pres. ROBERT GABRIEL MUGABE.

Head of the Armed Forces: Lt-Gen. CONSTANTINE CHIWENGA.

Commander of the Zimbabwe National Army: Lt-Gen. PHILLIP V. SIBANDA.

Education

Primary education, which begins at six years of age and lasts for seven years, is free and has been compulsory since 1987. Secondary education begins at the age of 13 and lasts for six years. According to UNESCO estimates, in 2002/03 enrolment at primary schools included 82% of children in the relevant age-group (males 81%; females 82%), while the comparable ratio for secondary enrolment was 34% of children (males 35%; females 33%). In 1998 some 11,451 students were attending universities, while 36,830 students were enrolled at other institutions of higher education. There are two state-run universities, the University of Zimbabwe, which is located in Harare, and the University of Science and Technology, at Bulawayo. There are also two private universities, Africa University in Mutare and Solusi University in Figtree. Education was allocated Z.$6,800,000m. by the central Government in the budget for 2005, 24.7% of total expenditure for that year.

Bibliography

Baynham, S. *Zimbabwe in Transition.* Stockholm, Almqvist and Wiksell International; Pretoria, Africa Institute of South Africa, 1992.

Bhebe, N., and Ranger, T. (Eds). *Society in Zimbabwe's Liberation War.* Portsmouth, NH, Heinemann, 1993.

Soldiers in Zimbabwe's Liberation War. Portsmouth, NH, Heinemann, 1993.

Blair, D. *Degrees in Violence: Robert Mugabe and the Struggle for Power in Zimbabwe.* London, Continuum International Publishing Group, 2002.

Bond, P. and Manyanya, M. *Zimbabwe's Plunge: Exhausted Nationalism, Neoliberalism and the Struggle for Social Justice.* Scottsville, University of Natal Press; London, Merlin; Harare, Weaver Press, 2002.

Bourdillon, M. F. C. *Where are the Ancestors? Changing Culture in Zimbabwe.* Harare, University of Zimbabwe Publications, 1993.

Bowyer-Bower, T. A. S., and Stoneman, C. (Eds). *Land Reform in Zimbabwe: Constraints and Prospects.* Aldershot, Ashgate Publishing Ltd, 2000.

Chikuhwa, J. W. *Zimbabwe at the Crossroads.* Bloomington, IN; Milton Keynes, Authorhouse, 2006.

Chung, F., and Ngara, E. *Socialism, Education and Development.* Harare, Zimbabwe Publishing House, 1995.

Dashwood, H. S. *Zimbabwe: the Political Economy of Transformation.* Toronto, University of Toronto Press, 2000.

De Waal, V. *The Politics of Reconciliation: Zimbabwe's First Decade.* London, Hurst, 1990; Harare, Longman Zimbabwe, 1992.

Engel, U. *Foreign Policy of Zimbabwe.* Hamburg, Institute of African Affairs, 1994.

Gibbon, P. (Ed.). *Structural Adjustment and the Working Poor in Zimbabwe: Studies on Labour, Women, Informal Sector Workers and Health.* Uppsala, Nordiska Afrikainstitutet, 1995.

Goebel, A. *Gender and Land Reform: The Zimbabwe Experience.* Montréal, McGill-Queen's University Press, 2005.

Gore, C. *The Case for Sustainable Development in Zimbabwe: Conceptual Problems, Conflicts and Contradictions.* Harare, Zero, 1992.

Grier, B. C. *Invisible Hands: Child Labor and the State in Colonial Zimbabwe.* Portsmouth, NH, Heinemann, 2006.

Harrold-Barry, D. (Ed.). *Zimbabwe: The Past is the Future: Rethinking Land, State, and Nation in the Context of Crisis.* Harare, Weaver Press, 2004.

Herbst, J. *State Politics in Zimbabwe.* Berkeley, CA, University of California Press; Harare, University of Zimbabwe Publications, 1990.

Hill, G. *What Happens After Mugabe?* Cape Town, Zebra Press, 2005.

Killick, T., *et al. European Aid and the Reduction of Poverty in Zimbabwe.* London, Overseas Development Institute, 1998.

Kriger, N. *Guerrilla Veterans in Post-war Zimbabwe: Symbolic and Violent Politics, 1980–1987.* Cambridge, Cambridge University Press, 2003.

Lindenthal, R. *Co-operative Development and Economic Structural Adjustment in Zimbabwe.* Geneva, International Labour Organization, 1994.

Mararike, C. G. *Grassroots Leadership: The Process of Rural Development in Zimbabwe.* Harare, University of Zimbabwe Publications, 1995.

Mbiba, B. *Urban Agriculture in Zimbabwe: Implications for Urban Management and Poverty.* Aldershot, Avebury; Brookfield, VT, Ashgate Publishing, 1995.

Meredith, M. *Our Votes, Our Guns: Robert Mugabe and the Tragedy of Zimbabwe.* New York, NY, Public Affairs, 2002.

Mlambo, A. S., and Pangeti, E. S. *The Political Economy of the Sugar Industry in Zimbabwe, 1920–1990.* Harare, Zimbabwe Publishing House, 1996.

Moore, D. S. *Suffering for Territory: Race, Place, and Power in Zimbabwe.* Durham, NC, Duke University Press, 2005.

Moyo, J. N. *Voting for Democracy: A Study of Electoral Politics in Zimbabwe.* Harare, University of Zimbabwe Publications, 1992.

Moyo, S. *Economic Nationalism and Land Reform in Zimbabwe.* Harare, Southern African Printing and Publishing House, 1994.

The Land Question in Zimbabwe. Harare, Southern African Printing and Publishing House, 1995.

Mudenge, S. I. G. *A Political History of Munhumutapa, c.1400–1902.* Portsmouth, NH, Heinemann, 1989.

Mungazi, D. A. *Colonial Policy and Conflict in Zimbabwe: A Study of Cultures in Collision, 1890–1979.* New York, NY, Crane Russak, 1992.

Munkonoweshuro, E. G. *Zimbabwe: Ten Years of Destabilisation: A Balance Sheet.* Stockholm, Bethany Books, 1992.

Mutizwa-Mangiza, N. D., and Helmsing, A. H. J. *Rural Development and Planning in Zimbabwe.* Aldershot, Avebury, 1991.

Ndhlovu, T. *Zimbabwe: A Decade of Development.* London, Zed Books, 1992.

Nklwane, S. M. (Ed.). *Zimbabwe's International Borders: A Study in National and Regional Development in Southern Africa.* Harare, University of Zimbabwe Publications, 1997.

Nyathi, P. *Zimbabwe's Cultural Heritage.* Bulawayo, 'amaBooks, 2005.

Palmer, R., and Birch, I. *Zimbabwe: A Land Divided.* Oxford, Oxfam, 1992.

Phimister, I. *Wangi Kolia: Coal, Capital and Labour in Colonial Zimbabwe, 1894–1994.* Harare, Baobab Books, 1994.

Pikirayi, I. *The Zimbabwe Culture: Origins and Decline of Southern Zambezian States.* Walnut Creek, CA, AltaMira Press, 2002.

Raftopoulos, B. and Savage, T. (Eds). *Zimbabwe: Injustice and Political Reconciliation.* Cape Town, Institute for Justice and Reconciliation, 2004.

Rasmussen, R. K., and Rubert, S. C. *Historical Dictionary of Zimbabwe.* 2nd Edn. Metuchen, NJ, Scarecrow Press, 1991.

Schmidt, E. *Peasants, Traders and Wives: Shona Women in the History of Zimbabwe, 1870–1939.* London, James Currey; Portsmouth, NH, Heinemann, 1992.

Shadur, M. A. *Labour Relations in a Developing Country: A Case Study on Zimbabwe.* Aldershot, Avebury, 1994.

Sibanda, E. M. *The Zimbabwe African People's Union, 1961–87: A Political History of Insurgency in Southern Rhodesia.* Trenton, NJ, Africa World Press, 2005.

Simon, D., Gaitskell, D. and Schumaker, L. (Eds). *Zimbabwe's Crisis.* Abingdon, Routledge, 2006.

Sithole, M. *Democracy and the One-party State in Africa: The Case of Zimbabwe.* Harare, SAPES Books, 1992.

Staunton, I. (Ed.). *Mothers of the Revolution: War Experiences of Thirty Zimbabwean Women.* Harare, Baobab Books, 1991.

Stiff, P. *Cry Zimbabwe: Independence—Twenty Years On.* Johannesburg, Galago Publishing Co, 2002.

Sylvester, C. *Zimbabwe: The Terrain of Contradictory Development.* Boulder, CO, Westview Press, 1991.

Tamarkin, M. *The Making of Zimbabwe.* London, Frank Cass, 1990.

Weiss, R. *Zimbabwe and the New Elite.* London, British Academic Press, 1994.

Whyte, B. *Yesterday, Today and Tomorrow: A 100 Year History of Zimbabwe, 1890–1990.* Harare, David Burke, 1990.

Zvobgo, R. J. *Colonialism and Education in Zimbabwe.* Harare, SAPES Books, 1994.

PART THREE

Regional Information

REGIONAL ORGANIZATIONS

THE UNITED NATIONS

Address: United Nations, New York, NY 10017, USA.

Telephone: (212) 963-1234; **fax:** (212) 963-4879; **internet:** www.un.org.

The United Nations (UN) was founded on 24 October 1945. The organization, which has 192 member states, aims to maintain international peace and security and to develop international co-operation in addressing economic, social, cultural and humanitarian problems. The principal organs of the UN are the General Assembly, the Security Council, the Economic and Social Council, the International Court of Justice and the Secretariat. The General Assembly, which meets for three months each year, comprises representatives of all UN member states. The Security Council investigates disputes between member countries, and may recommend ways and means of peaceful settlement: it comprises five permanent members (the People's Republic of China, France, Russia, the United Kingdom and the USA) and 10 other members elected by the General Assembly for a two-year period. The Economic and Social Council comprises representatives of 54 member states, elected by the General Assembly for a three-year period: it promotes co-operation on economic, social, cultural and humanitarian matters, acting as a central policy-making body and co-ordinating the activities of the UN's specialized agencies. The International Court of Justice comprises 15 judges of different nationalities, elected for nine-year terms by the General Assembly and the Security Council: it adjudicates in legal disputes between UN member states.

In March 2005 the Secretary-General announced a series of proposals for extensive reforms of the UN.

Secretary-General: BAN KI-MOON (Republic of Korea) (2007–11).

MEMBER STATES IN AFRICA SOUTH OF THE SAHARA

(with assessments for percentage contributions to UN budget for 2007–09, and year of admission)

Angola	0.003	1976
Benin	0.001	1960
Botswana	0.014	1966
Burkina Faso	0.002	1960
Burundi	0.001	1962
Cameroon	0.009	1960
Cape Verde	0.001	1975
Central African Republic	0.001	1960
Chad	0.001	1960
Comoros	0.001	1975
Congo, Democratic Republic	0.003	1960
Congo, Republic	0.001	1960
Côte d'Ivoire	0.009	1960
Djibouti	0.001	1977
Equatorial Guinea	0.002	1968
Eritrea	0.001	1993
Ethiopia	0.003	1945
Gabon	0.008	1960
The Gambia	0.001	1965
Ghana	0.004	1957
Guinea	0.001	1958
Guinea-Bissau	0.001	1974
Kenya	0.010	1963
Lesotho	0.001	1966
Liberia	0.001	1945
Madagascar	0.002	1960
Malawi	0.001	1964
Mali	0.001	1960
Mauritania	0.001	1961
Mauritius	0.011	1968
Mozambique	0.001	1975
Namibia	0.006	1990
Niger	0.001	1960
Nigeria	0.048	1960
Rwanda	0.001	1962
São Tomé and Príncipe	0.001	1975
Senegal	0.004	1960
Seychelles	0.002	1976
Sierra Leone	0.001	1961
Somalia	0.001	1960
South Africa	0.290	1945
Sudan	0.010	1956
Swaziland	0.002	1968
Tanzania	0.006	1961
Togo	0.001	1960
Uganda	0.003	1962
Zambia	0.001	1964
Zimbabwe	0.008	1980

Diplomatic Representation

PERMANENT MISSIONS TO THE UNITED NATIONS

(September 2007)

Angola: 125 East 73rd St, New York, NY 10021; tel. (212) 861-5656; fax (212) 861-9295; e-mail ang-un@angolamissionun.org; internet www.angolamissionun.org; Permanent Representative ISMAEL ABRAÃO GASPAR MARTINS.

Benin: 4 East 73rd St, New York, NY 10021; tel. (212) 249-6014; fax (212) 988-3714; e-mail benin@un.int; internet www.un.int/benin; Permanent Representative JEAN-MARIE EHOUZOU.

Botswana: 103 East 37th St, New York, NY 10016; tel. (212) 889-2277; fax (212) 725-5061; e-mail botswana@un.int; Permanent Representative SAMUEL OTSILE OUTLULE.

Burkina Faso: 115 East 73rd St, New York, NY 10021; tel. (212) 288-7515; fax (212) 772-3562; e-mail burkinafaso@un.int; Permanent Representative MICHEL KAFANDO.

Burundi: 336 East 45th St, 12th Floor, New York, NY 10017; tel. (212) 499-0001; fax (212) 499-0006; e-mail burundi@un.int; Permanent Representative JOSEPH NTAKIRUTIMANA.

Cameroon: 22 East 73rd St, New York, NY 10021; tel. (212) 794-2296; fax (212) 249-0533; e-mail info@cameroonmission.org; internet www.cameroonmission.org; Permanent Representative MARTIN BELINGA EBOUTOU.

Cape Verde: 27 East 69th St, New York, NY 10021; tel. (212) 472-0333; fax (212) 794-1398; e-mail capeverde@un.int; Permanent Representative ANTONIO PEDRO MONTEIRO LIMA.

Central African Republic: 386 Park Ave South, Rm 1114, New York, NY 10016; tel. (212) 679-8089; fax (212) 545-8326; e-mail caf@un.int; Permanent Representative FERNAND POUKRE-KONO.

Chad: 211 East 43rd St, Suite 1703, New York, NY 10017; tel. (212) 986-0980; fax (212) 986-0152; e-mail chad@un.int; Permanent Representative MAHAMAT ALI ADOUM.

Comoros: 420 East 50th St, New York, NY 10022; tel. (212) 972-8010; fax (212) 983-4712; e-mail comoros@un.int; internet www.un.int/comoros; Chargé d'affaires a.i. MAHMOUD MOHAMED ABOUD.

Congo, Democratic Republic: 866 United Nations Plaza, Suite 511, New York, NY 10017; tel. (212) 319-8061; fax (212) 319-8232; e-mail drcongo@un.int; internet www.un.int/drcongo; Permanent Representative CHRISTIAN ILEKA ATOKI.

Congo, Republic: 14 East 65th St, New York, NY 10021; tel. (212) 744-7840; fax (212) 744-7975; e-mail congo@un.int; Permanent Representative BASILE IKOUEBE.

Côte d'Ivoire: 46 East 74th St, New York, NY 10021; tel. (212) 717-5555; fax (212) 717-4492; e-mail ivorycoast@un.int; internet www.un.int/cotedivoire; Chargé d'affaires ILAHIRI ALCIDE DJEDJE.

Djibouti: 866 United Nations Plaza, Suite 4011, New York, NY 10017; tel. (212) 753-3163; fax (212) 223-1276; e-mail djibouti@nyct.net; Permanent Representative ROBLE OLHAYE.

Equatorial Guinea: 57 Magnolia Ave, Mount Vernon, NY 10553; tel. (914) 667-8999; fax (914) 667-8778; e-mail eqguinea@un.int; Permanent Representative LINO SIMA EKUA AVOMO.

Eritrea: 800 Second Ave, 18th Floor, New York, NY 10017; tel. (212) 687-3390; fax (212) 687-3138; e-mail eritrea@un.int; internet www.un.int/eritrea; Permanent Representative ARAYA DESTA.

Ethiopia: 866 Second Ave, 3rd Floor, New York, NY 10017; tel. (212) 421-1830; fax (212) 754-0360; e-mail ethiopia@un.int; internet www.un.int/ethiopia; Permanent Representative DAWIT YOHANNES.

Gabon: 18 East 41st St, 9th Floor, New York, NY 10017; tel. (212) 686-9720; fax (212) 689-5769; e-mail gabon@un.int; Permanent Representative DENIS DANGUE RÉWAKA.

The Gambia: 800 Second Ave, Suite 400F, New York, NY 10017; tel. (212) 949-6640; fax (212) 808-4975; e-mail gambia@un.int; Permanent Representative TAMSIR JALLOW.

Ghana: 19 East 47th St, New York, NY 10017; tel. (212) 832-1300; fax (212) 751-6743; e-mail ghanaperm@aol.com; Permanent Representative LESLIE KOJO CHRISTIAN.

Guinea: 140 East 39th St, New York, NY 10016; tel. (212) 687-8115; fax (212) 687-8248; e-mail guinea@un.int; Permanent Representative MAMADY TRAORÉ.

Guinea-Bissau: 211 East 43rd St, Rm 704, New York, NY 10017; tel. (212) 338-9394; fax (212) 293-0264; e-mail guinea-bissau@un.int; Chargé d'affaires a.i. ALFREDO LOPES CABRAL.

Kenya: 866 United Nations Plaza, Rm 486, New York, NY 10017; tel. (212) 421-4740; fax (212) 486-1985; e-mail kenya@un.int; internet www.un.int/kenya/; Permanent Representative ZACHARY DOMINIC MUBURI-MUITA.

Lesotho: 204 East 39th St, New York, NY 10016; tel. (212) 661-1690; fax (212) 682-4388; e-mail lesotho@un.int; internet www.un.int/lesotho; Permanent Representative LEBOHANG FINE MAEMA.

Liberia: 820 Second Ave, 13th Floor, New York, NY 10017; tel. (212) 687-1033; fax (212) 687-1035; e-mail liberia@un.int; Permanent Representative NATHANIEL BARNES.

Madagascar: 820 Second Ave, Suite 800, New York, NY 10017; tel. (212) 986-9491; fax (212) 986-6271; e-mail repermad@ren.com; internet www.un.int/madagascar; Permanent Representative ZINA ANDRIANARIVELO-RAZAFY.

Malawi: 600 Third Ave, 21st Floor, New York, NY 10016; tel. (212) 949-0180; fax (212) 599-5021; e-mail malawiun@aol.com; Permanent Representative STEVE DICK TENNYSON MATENJE.

Mali: 111 East 69th St, New York, NY 10021; tel. (212) 737-4150; fax (212) 472-3778; e-mail malionu@aol.com; Permanent Representative CHEICK SIDI DIARRA.

Mauritania: 211 East 43rd St, Suite 2000, New York, NY 10017; tel. (212) 986-7963; fax (212) 986-8419; e-mail mauritania@un.int; Permanent Representative MOHAMED OULD TOLBA.

Mauritius: 211 East 43rd St, 15th Floor, New York, NY 10017; tel. (212) 949-0190; fax (212) 697-3829; e-mail mauritius@un.int; Permanent Representative SOMDUTH SOBORUN.

Mozambique: 420 East 50th St, New York, NY 10022; tel. (212) 644-5965; fax (212) 644-5972; e-mail mozambique@un.int; internet www.un.int/mozambique; Permanent Representative FILIPE CHIDUMO.

Namibia: 135 East 36th St, New York, NY 10016; tel. (212) 685-2003; fax (212) 685-1561; e-mail namibia@un.int; internet www.un.int/namibia; Permanent Representative Dr KAIRE MUNIONGANDA MBUENDE.

Niger: 417 East 50th St, New York, NY 10022; tel. (212) 421-3260; fax (212) 753-6931; e-mail nigerun@aol.com; internet www.un.int/niger; Permanent Representative ABOUBACAR IBRAHIM ABANI.

Nigeria: 828 Second Ave, New York, NY 10017; tel. (212) 953-9130; fax (212) 697-1970; e-mail nigeria@un.int; Permanent Representative AMINU BASHIR WALI.

Rwanda: 124 East 39th St, New York, NY 10016; tel. (212) 679-9010; fax (212) 679-9133; e-mail rwanda@un.int; Permanent Representative JOSEPH NSENGIMANA.

São Tomé and Príncipe: 400 Park Ave, 7th Floor, New York, NY 10022; tel. (212) 317-0533; fax (212) 317-0580; e-mail stp@un.int; Chargé d'affaires a.i. OVIDIO MANUEL BARBOSA PEQUENO.

Senegal: 238 East 68th St, New York, NY 10021; tel. (212) 517-9030; fax (212) 517-3032; e-mail senegal@un.int; internet www.un.int/senegal; Permanent Representative PAUL BADJI.

Seychelles: 800 Second Ave, Rm 400C, New York, NY 10017; tel. (212) 972-1785; fax (212) 972-1786; e-mail seychelles@un.int; Permanent Representative RONALD JEAN JUMEAU.

Sierra Leone: 245 East 49th St, New York, NY 10017; tel. (212) 688-1656; fax (212) 688-4924; e-mail sierraleone@un.int; Permanent Representative JOE ROBERT PEMAGBI.

Somalia: 425 East 61st St, Suite 702, New York, NY 10021; tel. (212) 688-9410; fax (212) 759-0651; e-mail somalianet@hotmail.com; internet www.iaed.org/somalia; Permanent Representative ELMI AHMED DUALE.

South Africa: 333 East 38th St, 9th Floor, New York, NY 10016; tel. (212) 213-5583; fax (212) 692-2498; e-mail soafun@worldnet.att.net; internet www.southafrica-newyork.net/pmun; Permanent Representative DUMISANI SHADRACK KUMALO.

Sudan: 655 Third Ave, Suite 500-510, New York, NY 10017; tel. (212) 573-6033; fax (212) 573-6160; e-mail sudan@un.int; Permanent Representative ABDALMAHMOOD ABDALHALEEM MOHAMAD.

Swaziland: 408 East 50th St, New York, NY 10022; tel. (212) 371-8910; fax (212) 754-2755; e-mail swaziland@un.int; Permanent Representative PHESHEYA MBONGENI DLAMINI.

Tanzania: 201 East 42nd St, 17th Floor, New York, NY 10017; tel. (212) 972-9160; fax (212) 682-5232; e-mail tzrepny@aol.com; Permanent Representative AUGUSTINE PHILIP MAHIGA.

Togo: 112 East 40th St, New York, NY 10016; tel. (212) 490-3455; fax (212) 983-6684; e-mail togo@un.int; e-mail onu@republicoftogo.com; Permanent Representative ROLAND YAO KPOTSRA.

Uganda: 336 East 45th St, New York, NY 10017; tel. (212) 949-0110; fax (212) 687-4517; e-mail ugandaamb@aol.com; internet www.un.int/uganda; Permanent Representative FRANCIS BUTAGIRA.

Zambia: 237 East 52nd St, New York, NY 10022; tel. (212) 888-5770; fax (212) 888-5213; e-mail zambia@un.int; internet www.un.int/zambia; Permanent Representative LAZAROUS KAPAMBWE.

Zimbabwe: 128 East 56th St, New York, NY 10022; tel. (212) 980-9511; fax (212) 308-6705; e-mail zimbabwe@un.int; Permanent Representative T. J. B. BONIFACE GUWA CHIDYAUSIKU.

OBSERVERS

African Union: 346 East 50th St, New York, NY 10022; tel. (212) 319-5490; fax (212) 319-7135; Permanent Representative AMADOU KÉBÉ.

Asian-African Legal Consultative Organization: 404 East 66th St, Apt 12C, New York, NY 10021; tel. (212) 734-7608; e-mail aalco@un.int; Permanent Representative K. BHAGWAT-SINGH (India).

Commonwealth Secretariat: 800 Second Ave, 4th Floor, New York, NY 10017; tel. (212) 599-6190; fax (212) 808-4975; e-mail comsec@thecommonwealth.org.

La Francophonie: 801 Second Ave, Suite 605, New York, NY 10017; tel. (212) 867-6771; fax (212) 867-3840; e-mail francophonie@un.int; Permanent Representative RIDHA BOUABID.

International Committee of the Red Cross: 801 Second Ave, 18th Floor, New York, NY 10017; tel. (212) 599-6021; fax (212) 599-6009; e-mail log.nyc@icrc.org; Head of Delegation DOMINIQUE BUFF.

IUCN—The World Conservation Union: 406 West 66th St, New York, NY 10023; tel. and fax (212) 734-7608.

Organization of the Islamic Conference: 130 East 40th St, 5th Floor, New York, NY 10016; tel. (212) 883-0140; fax (212) 883-0143; e-mail oic@un.int; internet www.oicun.org; Permanent Representative MOKHTAR LAMANI.

The African, Caribbean and Pacific Group of States, the African Development Bank, the African Union, the Economic Community of West African States and the Southern African Development Community are among several intergovernmental organizations that have a standing invitation to participate as observers but do not maintain permanent offices at the UN.

United Nations Information Centres/Services

Burkina Faso: BP 135, 14 ave de la Grande Chancellerie, Secteur no 4, Ouagadougou; tel. 50-30-60-76; fax 50-31-13-22; e-mail cinu.oui@fasonet.bf; internet www.ouagadougou.unic.org; also covers Chad, Mali and Niger.

Burundi: BP 2160, ave de la Révolution 117, Bujumbura; tel. (2) 225018; fax (2) 241798; e-mail unicbuj@undp.com; internet bujumbura.unic.org.

Cameroon: PB 836, Immeuble Tchinda, rue 2044, Yaoundé; tel. 221-23-67; fax 221-23-68; e-mail unic.cm@undp.org; internet yaounde.unic.org; also covers the Central African Republic and Gabon.

Congo, Democratic Republic: PB 7248, blvd du 30 juin, Kinshasa; tel. 884-5537; fax 884-3675; e-mail unic.kinshasa@undp.org.

Congo, Republic: POB 13210, ave Foch, Case ORTF 15, Brazzaville; tel. 661-20-68; fax 81-27-44; e-mail prosper.mihindou@undp.org; internet brazzavile.unic.org.

Eritrea: Andinet St, Zone 4 Admin. 07, Airport Rd, Asmara; tel. (1) 151166; fax (1) 151081; e-mail mohammed.salih@undp.org; internet asmara.unic.org.

Ethiopia: POB 3001, Africa Hall, Addis Ababa; tel. (11) 5515826; fax (11) 5510365; e-mail ecainfo@un.org.

Ghana: POB 2339, Gamel Abdul Nassar/Liberia Rds, Accra; tel. (21) 665511; fax (21) 665578; e-mail info@unic-ghana.org; internet accra.unic.org; also covers Sierra Leone.

Kenya: POB 30552, United Nations Office, Gigiri, Nairobi; tel. (20) 7623292; fax (20) 7624349; e-mail nairobi.unic@unon.org; internet www.unicnairobi.org; also covers Seychelles and Uganda.

Lesotho: POB 301, Maseru 100; tel. (22) 312496; fax (22) 310042; e-mail unic.maseru@undp.org; internet maseru.unic.org.

Liberia: Dubar Bldg, Virginia, Monrovia; tel. 2260195; fax 205407; e-mail registry.1r@undp.org.

Madagascar: PB 1348, 22 rue Rainitovo, Antasahavola, Antananarivo; tel. (20) 2224115; fax (20) 2237506; e-mail unic.ant@dts.mg; internet www.antananarivo.unic.org.

Namibia: Private Bag 13351, Paratus Bldg, 372 Independence Ave, Windhoek; tel. (61) 233034; fax (61) 233036; e-mail unic@un.na; internet windhoek.unic.org.

Nigeria: POB 1068, Alfred Rewane Rd, Ikoyi, Lagos; tel. (1) 269-4886; fax (1) 269-1934; e-mail uniclag@unicnig.org; internet www.unicnig.org.

Senegal: BP 154, rues de Thann et Dajorne, Dakar; tel. 889-11-89; fax 822-14-06; e-mail unicdakar@cinu-dakar.org; internet dakar.unic.org; also covers Cape Verde, Côte d'Ivoire, The Gambia, Guinea, Guinea-Bissau and Mauritania.

South Africa: Metro Park Bldg, 351 Schoemann St, POB 12677, Pretoria 0126; tel. (12) 354-8506; fax (12) 354-8501; e-mail unic@un.org.za; internet pretoria.unic.org.

Sudan: POB 1992, UN Compound, Gamma'a Ave, Khartoum; tel. (11) 773121; fax (11) 773772; e-mail registry.sd@undp.org; also covers Somalia.

Tanzania: Msimbazi Creek Housing Estate Ltd, King's Way, Mafinga St, Plot 134/140, Kinondoni, Dar es Salaam; tel. (22) 2199297; fax (22) 2668749; e-mail maravanyika@un.org; internet daressalaam.unic.org.

Togo: BP 911, 107 blvd du 13 janvier, Lomé; tel. and fax 221-23-06; e-mail cinutogo@cafe.tg; also covers Benin.

Zambia: POB 32905, Lusaka 10101; tel. (1) 228478; fax (1) 222958; e-mail unic@zamtel.zm; internet lusaka.unic.org; also covers Botswana, Malawi and Swaziland.

Zimbabwe: POB 4408, Sanders House, 2nd Floor, First St/Jason Moyo Ave, Harare; tel. (4) 777060; fax (4) 750476; e-mail unic@mweb.co.zw.

Economic Commission for Africa—ECA

Address: Menelik II Ave, POB 3001, Addis Ababa, Ethiopia.

Telephone: (11) 5517200; **fax:** (11) 5514416; **e-mail:** ecainfo@uneca.org; **internet:** www.uneca.org.

The UN Economic Commission for Africa (ECA) was founded in 1958 by a resolution of the UN Economic and Social Council (ECOSOC) to initiate and take part in measures for facilitating Africa's economic development.

MEMBERS

Algeria
Angola
Benin
Botswana
Burkina Faso
Burundi
Cameroon
Cape Verde
Central African Republic
Chad
Comoros
Congo, Democratic Republic
Congo, Republic
Côte d'Ivoire
Djibouti
Egypt
Equatorial Guinea
Eritrea
Ethiopia
Gabon
The Gambia
Ghana
Guinea
Guinea-Bissau
Kenya
Lesotho
Liberia
Libya
Madagascar
Malawi
Mali
Mauritania
Mauritius
Morocco
Mozambique
Namibia
Niger
Nigeria
Rwanda
São Tomé and Príncipe
Senegal
Seychelles
Sierra Leone
Somalia
South Africa
Sudan
Swaziland
Tanzania
Togo
Tunisia
Uganda
Zambia
Zimbabwe

Organization

(September 2007)

COMMISSION

The Commission may only act with the agreement of the government of the country concerned. It is also empowered to make recommendations on any matter within its competence directly to the government of the member or associate member concerned, to governments admitted in a consultative capacity, and to the UN Specialized Agencies. The Commission is required to submit for prior consideration by ECOSOC any of its proposals for actions that would be likely to have important effects on the international economy.

CONFERENCE OF MINISTERS

The Conference, which meets every two years, is attended by ministers responsible for economic or financial affairs, planning and development of governments of member states, and is the main deliberative body of the Commission.

The Commission's responsibility to promote concerted action for the economic and social development of Africa is vested primarily in the Conference, which considers matters of general policy and the priorities to be assigned to the Commission's programmes, considers inter-African and international economic policy, and makes recommendations to member states in connection with such matters.

OTHER POLICY-MAKING BODIES

A Conference of Ministers of Finance and a Conference of Ministers Responsible for Economic and Social Development and Planning meet in alternate years to formulate policy recommendations. Each is served by a committee of experts. Five intergovernmental committees of experts attached to the Sub-regional Offices (see below) meet annually and report to the Commission through a Technical Preparatory Committee of the Whole, which was established in 1979 to deal with matters submitted for the consideration of the Conference.

Seven other committees meet regularly to consider issues relating to the following policy areas: women and development; development information; sustainable development; human development and civil society; industry and private sector development; natural resources and science and technology; and regional co-operation and integration.

SECRETARIAT

The Secretariat provides the services necessary for the meeting of the Conference of Ministers and the meetings of the Commission's subsidiary bodies, carries out the resolutions and implements the programmes adopted there. It comprises an Office of the Executive Secretary and the following divisions: Trade, Finance and Economic Development; Food Security and Sustainable Development; Governance and Public Administration; Information and Science and Technology for Development; the African Centre for Gender and Social Development; and NEPAD and Regional Integration.

Executive Secretary: ABDOULIE JANNEH (Gambia).

SUB-REGIONAL OFFICES

The Sub-regional Offices (SROs) aim to enable member states to play a more effective role in the process of African integration and to facilitate the integration efforts of the other UN agencies active in the sub-regions. In addition, the SROs act as the operational arms of ECA at national and sub-regional levels with a view to: ensuring harmony between the objectives of sub-regional and regional programmes and those defined by the Commission; providing advisory services; facilitating sub-regional economic co-operation, integration and development; collecting and disseminating information; stimulating policy dialogue; and promoting gender issues. Under the radical restructuring of the ECA, completed in 2006, the SROs were given an enhanced role in shaping the Commission's agenda and programme implementation, and were also designated as privileged partners of the regional economic communities. (There are 14 African regional economic communities; the following five of these are regarded as the five pillars of the envisaged African Economic Community: the Common Market for Eastern and Southern Africa—COMESA, the Communauté économique des états de l'Afrique centrale—CEEAC, the Economic Community of West African States—ECOWAS, the Southern African Development Community—SADC, and the Union of the Arab Maghreb.)

Central Africa: POB 14935, Yaoundé, Cameroon; tel. 23-14-61; fax 23-31-85; e-mail sroca@uneca.org; Officer-in-Charge HACHIM KOUMARÉ.

East Africa: POB 4654, Kigali, Rwanda; tel. 586549; fax 586546; e-mail mdiouf@uneca.org; Dir MBAYE DIOUF.

North Africa: 22 rue Jabal Al Ayachi, POB 827, Méchouar-Rabat, Morocco; tel. (3) 767-45-95; fax (3) 767-52-82; e-mail srdc-na@uneca.org; internet www.uneca-na.org; Dir KARIMA BOUNEMRA BEN SOLTANE.

Southern Africa: POB 30647, Lusaka, Zambia; tel. (1) 228503; fax (1) 236949; e-mail srdsa.uneca@un.org; internet www.uneca.org/eca-sa; Officer-in-Charge JENNIFER KARGBO.

West Africa: POB 744, Niamey, Niger; tel. 72-29-61; fax 72-28-94; e-mail srdcwest@eca.ne; Dir HALIDOU OUEDRAOGO.

Activities

The Commission's activities are designed to encourage sustainable socio-economic development in Africa and to increase economic co-operation among African countries and between Africa and other parts of the world. The Secretariat has been guided in its efforts by major regional strategies including the Abuja Treaty establishing the African Economic Community signed under the aegis of the Organization of African Unity (OAU, now African Union—AU) in 1991, the UN System-wide Special Initiative on Africa (launched in 1996, see below), and the UN New Agenda for the Development of Africa, which covered the period 1991–2000. In 2006 the Executive Secretary of the ECA appointed a Task Force to assist with redirecting the strategic orientation of the commission, with a view to better supporting efforts to advance development in Africa, and also to address means of strengthening the ECA's presence at sub-regional level and to examine the Commission's partnership with other regional stakeholders. A radical restructuring of the ECA's divisions was implemented in that year, with more emphasis to be placed on knowledge generation and networking; advocacy; and advisory services and technical co-operation. The main focus of ECA's work programme for 2006–07 was on enhancing member states' capacity to formulate and implement appropriate policies and programmes to facilitate accelerated and sustained rates of economic growth with the aim of achieving poverty reduction, consistent with internationally agreed development goals such as the UN's Millennium Development Goals (MDGs) and priorities agreed by the New Partnership for Africa's Development (NEPAD), launched in October 2001. Other ECA priorities were to expand and upgrade the statistical capacities of member countries; to address HIV/AIDS issues; to foster sustainable development by improving management of the nexus of food security, population, human settlements, natural resources and the environment; to improve good governance practices; to further strengthen the African information society; to promote intraregional and international trade and transport and communications integration; to promote the advancement of women; to support sub-regional activities for development; and to enhance development planning and administration.

INFORMATION, SCIENCE AND TECHNOLOGY FOR DEVELOPMENT

The Information and Science and Technology for Development Division has responsibility for co-ordinating the implementation of the Harnessing Information Technology for Africa project (in the context of the UN System-wide Special Initiative on Africa) and for implementing the African Information Society Initiative (AISI), a framework for creating an information and communications infrastructure; for overseeing quality enhancement and dissemination of statistical databases; for improving access to information by means of enhanced library and documentation services and output; and for strengthening geo-information systems for sustainable development. In addition, ECA encourages member governments to liberalize the telecommunications sector and stimulate imports of computers in order to enable the expansion of information technology throughout Africa. ECA manages the Information Technology Centre for Africa (see below). The Commission administers the Partnership for Information and Communication Technologies in Africa (PICTA), which was established in 1999 as an informal grouping of donors and agencies concerning with developing an information society in Africa. ECA provided institutional and logistical support to an African Ministerial Committee which was established in April 2004 to consider proposals of the first phase of the World Summit on Information Society (WSIS), convened in December 2003. ECA co-ordinated preparations for the African Regional Preparatory Conference (held in Accra, Ghana, in February 2005) for the second phase of the WSIS, which was convened in Tunis, Tunisia, in November of the same year.

ECA assists its member states in population data collection and data processing; analysis of demographic data obtained from censuses or surveys; training demographers at the Regional Institute for Population Studies (RIPS) in Accra, Ghana, and at the Institut de formation et de recherche démographiques (IFORD) in Yaoundé, Cameroon; formulation of population policies and integrating population variables in development planning, through advisory missions and through the organization of national seminars on population and development; and dissemination of demographic information.

In 1999 ECA's Committee on Development Information established the African Virtual Library and Information Network (AVLIN) as a hub for the exchange of data among African researchers and policy-makers. In August 2000 ECA launched the Africa Knowledge Networks Forum (AKNF). The Forum, to be convened on an annual basis under ECA auspices, was to facilitate co-operation in information-sharing and research between professional research and development networks, and also between these and policy-makers, educators, civil society organizations and the private sector. It was to provide technical support to the ADF process (see below). In May 2003 the Committee on Development Information, convened to address the theme 'Information for Governance', urged governments to make consistent use of information systems in decision-making and in the decentralization of services and resources. During that month ECA launched the e-Policy Resource Network for Africa, under the Global e-Policy Resource Network initiative aimed at expanding the use and benefits of information and communication technologies.

In August 2007 ECA and the World Health Organization (WHO) commissioned, within the framework of the AISI, a joint regional needs assessment and study in respect of WHO's Africa Health Infoway (AHI) programme, which supports the collection of sub-national health data and statistics for analysis, dissemination and use to support decision-making in the health sector, and aims to strengthen the capacity of African countries in using information in decision-making.

GOVERNANCE AND PUBLIC ADMINISTRATION

ECA aims to assist governments, public corporations, universities and the private sector in improving their financial management; strengthening policy-making and analytical capacities; adopting measures to redress skill shortages; enhancing human resources development and utilization; and promoting social development through programmes focusing on youth, people with disabilities and the elderly. The Secretariat organizes training workshops, seminars and conferences at national, sub-regional and regional levels for ministers, public administrators and senior policy-makers, as well as for private and non-governmental organizations.

In October 1999 the first African Development Forum (ADF) was held in Addis Ababa, Ethiopia. The ADF process was initiated by ECA to formulate an agenda for effective, sustainable development in African countries through dialogue and partnership between governments, academics, the private sector, donor agencies, etc. It was intended that the process would focus towards an annual meeting concerned with a specific development issue. The first Forum was convened on the theme 'The Challenge to Africa of Globalization and the Information Age'. It reviewed the AISI (see above) and formulated country action plans and work programmes. The four issues addressed were: strengthening Africa's information infrastructure; Africa and the information economy; information and communication technologies for improved governance; and democratizing access to the information society. The second ADF, convened in October 2000 on the theme 'AIDS: the Greatest Leadership Challenge', addressed the impact on Africa of the HIV/AIDS epidemic and issued a Consensus and Plan of Action. The third ADF, held in March 2002, addressed the theme 'Defining Priorities for Regional Integration'. ADF IV took place in October 2004 with the theme of 'Governance for a Progressing Africa'. ADF V, convened in November 2006, adopted a Consensus Document, which included proposals for launching an African Youth Volunteer Corps to encourage skills development and to address manpower shortages, and an African Youth Exchange Programme to promote the idea of citizenship and a common identity.

In 1997 ECA hosted the first of a series of meetings on good governance, in the context of the UN System-wide Special Initiative on Africa. The second African Governance Forum (AGF II) was held in Accra, Ghana, in June 1998. The Forum focused on accountability and transparency, which participants agreed were essential elements in promoting development in Africa and should involve commitment from both governments and civil organizations. AGF III was convened in June 1999 in Bamako, Mali, to consider issues relating to conflict prevention, management and governance. The fourth AGF, which took place in Kampala, Uganda, in September 2000, focused on parliamentary processes and their role in consolidating good governance on the continent. AGF V, addressing the role of local government in reducing poverty in Africa, was held in Maputo, Mozambique, in May 2002. In 2003 28 countries participated in a study to assess and monitor progress towards good governance in Africa. A synopsis of the ensuing report, the *Africa Governance Report*, was presented at ADF IV in October 2004; a second *Africa Governance Report* was issued in May 2006. The sixth AGF was held in Kigali, Rwanda, in April of that year, and focused on NEPAD's implementation of the African Peer Review Mechanism, whereby participating member Governments mutually monitor policy and practice.

AFRICAN CENTRE FOR GENDER AND SOCIAL DEVELOPMENT

ECA aims to improve the socio-economic prospects of women through the promotion of equal access to resources and opportunities, and equal participation decision-making. An African Centre for Gender and Development was established in 1975 to service all national, sub-regional and regional bodies involved in development issues relating to gender and the advancement of women. The Centre manages the African Women's Development Fund, which was established in June 2000. The preliminary results of a new African Gender and Development Index were presented in January 2005.

A Commission on HIV/AIDS and Governance in Africa, with its secretariat based at ECA headquarters, was launched in September 2003. The Commission, an initiative of the UN Secretary-General, was mandated to assess the impact of the HIV/AIDS pandemic on national structures and African economic development and to incorporate its findings in a Final Report; this was issued in October 2005.

FOOD SECURITY AND SUSTAINABLE DEVELOPMENT

ECA aims to strengthen the capacity of member countries to design institutional structures and implement policies and programmes, in areas such as food production, population, environment and human settlements, to achieve sustainable development. It also actively promotes the use of science and technology in achieving sustainable development. In 1995 ECA published its first comprehensive report and statistical survey of human development issues in African countries. The *Human Development in Africa Report*, which was to be published every two years, aimed to demonstrate levels of development attained, particularly in the education and child health sectors, to identify areas of concern and to encourage further action by policy-makers and development experts. A *Bulletin on Sustainable Development* aims to monitor, review and disseminate information regarding development research and activities, in particular in respect of implementation of recommendations ensuring from the World Summit on Sustainable Development, held in August–September 2002 in Johannesburg, South Africa.

ECA is actively involved in the promotion of food security in African countries through raising awareness of the relationship between population, food security, the environment and sustainable development; encouraging the advancement of science and technology in member states; and providing policy analysis support and technical advisory services. The strengthening of national population policies was an important element of ECA's objective of ensuring food security in African countries.

TRADE, FINANCE AND ECONOMIC DEVELOPMENT DIVISION

The Trade, Finance and Economic Development Division (TFED), established in 2006, is concerned with issues relating to macroeconomic analysis, and also deals with international trade, international trade negotiations development, finance and financial sector policies, debt, aid, investment, and industrial policies. The Division comprises: the Industry and Sectoral Policies Section, the Financing Development Section, the Trade and International Negotiations Section, the Macroeconomic Analysis Section, and the African Trade Policy Center (ATPC). Every year the Commission publishes the *Survey of Economic and Social Conditions in Africa* and the *Economic Report on Africa*. The ECA's African Centre for Statistics promotes the compilation, analysis, and dissemination of statistics, with the aim of enabling national policymakers to make informed choices. The Advisory Board on Statistics in Africa, which was inaugurated in 2004 and comprises 15 experts from national statistical offices, sub-regional bodies and training institutes, advises ECA on statistical developments in Africa and guides its statistical activities.

The Financing Development Section is responsible for researching and analyzing challenges in the area of development finance relating to the attainment of sustained growth and poverty reduction. The Section provides support to member states, regional and national institutions, academics, and private-sector and civil society interests, and also engages in policy advocacy work. Principal focus areas are: foreign aid, debt, private capital flows, and savings and remittances. The Section produces publications and provides training, seminars and workshops.

The Industry and Sectoral Policies Section assists African countries to formulate and implement effective industrial policies, strategies and programmes aimed at enhancing their competitiveness in the global production system. The Section undertakes policy research and outreach activities and aims to improve the access of local policy researchers to analytical tools and information.

The Macroeconomic Analysis Section assists member states to improve their capacity to formulate, implement and monitor sound macroeconomic policies and better institutional frameworks, with a view to achieving sustainable development. The Section also focuses on policy advocacy and collaboration with development organizations and institutions. The section produces publications and provides training, conferences and workshops. It undertakes macroeconomic research and policy analysis in the following areas: macroeconomic modelling and planning, growth strategies, fiscal and monetary policies and debt management. The Section also preparares background documents for the annual Conference of African Ministers of Finance, Planning, and Economic Development.

The Trade and International Negotiations Section conducts research and outreach activities aimed at ensuring best practice in trade policy development and undertakes research and dissemination activities on bilateral and international trade negotiations (such as the ongoing multilateral trade negotiations under the World Trade Organization) with a view to helping African countries to benefit from globalization through trade.

The African Trade Policy Centre (ATPC), established in May 2003, aims to strengthen the human, institutional and policy capacities of African governments to formulate and implement sound trade policies and participate more effectively in international trade negotiations. The Centre takes both a national and regional perspective, and provides a rapid response to technical needs arising from on-going trade negotiations.

ECA provides guidance to the policy-making organs of the UN and the AU on the formulation of policies supporting the achievement of Africa's development objectives. It contributes to the work of the General Assembly and other specialized agencies by providing an African perspective in the preparation of development strategies. In March 1996 the UN announced its System-wide Special Initiative on Africa to mobilize resources and to implement a series of political and economic development objectives over a 10-year period. ECA's Executive Secretary is the Co-Chairperson, with the Administrator of the UNDP, of the Steering Committee for the Initiative.

In November 2000 an informal 'Big Table' meeting convened between ministers of finance from African countries and OECD ministers of development co-operation focused on transforming Africa's relationship with its development partners; a second Big Table meeting in October 2001 addressed means of establishing a new African co-operation framework. The third Big Table meeting, held in January 2003, considered the role played by the IMF in low-income countries. A special session was convened in October 2003, and in October 2004 the fourth Big Table meeting was held to discuss stimulating private investment in Africa.

In April 2003 ECA and the African Development Bank synchronized their annual legislative meetings in an effort to find a common position on addressing the principal challenges confronting the continent. They concluded that development was constrained by national debt, a persistent decline in exports, and weak economic growth rates. They also urged a thorough review of development strategies to determine whether poor outcomes were the result of bad policy, poor implementation or external factors. ECA's Executive Secretary proposed the establishment of a mechanism to monitor both the use of donor funds and the honouring of donor commitments; he also emphasized the need to focus on domestic resource mobilization and good economic management. ECA and OECD proposed that a joint review should be conducted every two years with a view to advancing policy coherence and mutual accountability between African countries and their external partners.

NEPAD AND REGIONAL INTEGRATION DIVISION

The NEPAD and Regional Integration Division, established in 2006, focuses on regional integration, infrastructure, natural resources development and support for NEPAD.

ECA supports the implementation of the AU's regional integration agenda, through research; policy analysis; strengthening capacity and the provision of technical assistance to the regional economic communities; and working on transboundary initiatives and activities across a variety of sectors. In June 2002 ECA issued its first *Annual Report on Regional Integration*. A report entitled *Assessing Regional Integration in Africa* was published in July 2004.

ECA was designated as the main body responsible for identifying and preparing programmes on economic and corporate governance under NEPAD. The Commission supports NEPAD's African Peer Review Mechanism process. In July 2006 ECA and NEPAD adopted a framework document aimed at providing a more structured basis for guiding future collaboration between the two organizations. It was envisaged that the framework document would be elaborated into a formal Memorandum of Understanding.

ECA was appointed lead agency for the second United Nations Transport and Communications Decade in Africa (UNTACDA II), covering the period 1991–2000. The principal aim of UNTACDA II was the establishment of an efficient, integrated transport and communications system in Africa. ECA and the World Bank jointly co-ordinate the sub-Saharan Africa Transport Programme (SSATP), established in 1987, which aims to facilitate policy development and related capacity-building in the continent's transport sector. A meeting of all participants in the programme is held annually. In September 2004 the SSATP conference, hosted by ECA, recognized the importance of the transport sector in achieving the MDGs and proposed a ministerial review to ensure the integration of transport issues in MDG strategies. The regional Road Management Initiative (RMI) under the SSATP seeks to encourage a partnership between the public and private sectors to manage and maintain road infrastructure more efficiently and thus to improve country-wide communications and transportation activities. An Urban Mobility component of the SSATP aims to improve sub-Saharan African urban transport services, while a Trade and Transport component aims to enhance the international competitiveness of regional economies through the establishment of more cost-effective services for shippers. The Railway Restructuring element focuses on the provision of financially sustainable railway enterprises. In December 2003 the first Central African Forum on Transport Infrastructure and Regional Integration, organized by TRID, was convened in Yaoundé, Cameroon. In November 2005 a meeting of sub-Saharan African ministers of transport, convened in Bamako, Mali, on the fringes of the SSATP Annual General Meeting, adopted a resolution aimed at developing Africa's transport infrastructure, focusing on the importance of incorporating transport issues into poverty reduction strategies, ensuring sustainable financing for Africa's road programmes, and prioritizing road safety issues. The African Road Safety Conference, convened in Accra, Ghana, in February 2007 by African ministers responsible for transport and health, reaffirmed road safety as a key development priority and pledged to set and achieve measurable national targets for road safety and the prevention of traffic injuries in all member states.

The Fourth Regional Conference on the Development and Utilization of Mineral Resources in Africa, held in March 1991, adopted an action plan that included the formulation of national mineral exploitation policies; and the promotion of the gemstone industry, small-scale mining and the iron and steel industry. ECA supports the Southern African Mineral Resources Development Centre in Dar-es-Salaam, Tanzania, and the Central African Mineral Development Centre in Brazzaville, Republic of the Congo, which provide advisory and laboratory services to their respective member states.

ECA's Energy Programme provides assistance to member states in the development of indigenous energy resources and the formulation of energy policies to extricate member states from continued energy crises. In May 2004 ECA was appointed as the secretariat of a new UN-Energy/Africa initiative which aimed to facilitate the exchange of information, good practices and knowledge-sharing among UN organizations and with private sector companies, non-governmental organizations, power utilities and other research and academic institutions.

ECA assists member states in the assessment and use of water resources and the development of river and lake basins common to more than one country. ECA encourages co-operation between countries with regard to water issues and collaborates with other UN agencies and regional organizations to promote technical and economic co-operation in this area. In 1992, on the initiative of ECA, the Interagency Group for Water in Africa (IGWA) was established to co-ordinate and harmonize the water-related activities of the UN and other organizations on the continent. ECA has been particularly active in efforts to promote the integrated development of the water resources of the Zambezi river basin and of Lake Victoria. In December 2003 ECA hosted the Pan-African Implementation and Partnership Conference on Water (PANAFCON).

ASSOCIATED BODY

Information Technology Centre for Africa (ITCA): POB 3001, Addis Ababa, Ethiopia; tel. (11) 5514534; fax (11) 5510512; e-mail mfaye@uneca.org; internet www.uneca.org/itca; aims to strengthen the continent's communications infrastructure and promote the use of information and communications technologies in planning and policy-making; stages exhibitions and provides training facilities.

Finance

For the two-year period 2006–07 ECA's proposed regular budget, an appropriation from the UN budget, was estimated at US $107.4m.

Publications

Africa in Figures.
African Governance Report.
African Statistical Yearbook.
African Trade Bulletin (2 a year).
African Women's Report (annually).
Africa's Population and Development Bulletin.
Annual Report on Regional Integration.
Assessing Regional Integration in Africa.
ECA Development Policy Review.
ECA Environment Newsletter (3 a year).
ECANews (monthly).
Economic Report on Africa (annually).
Focus on African Industry (2 a year).
GenderNet (annually).
Human Development in Africa Report (every 2 years).
Human Rights Education.
Report of the Executive Secretary (every 2 years).
Survey of Economic and Social Conditions in Africa (annually).
TRIDNews (monthly).
Country reports, policy and discussion papers, reports of conferences and meetings, training series, working paper series.

United Nations Children's Fund—UNICEF

Address: 3 United Nations Plaza, New York, NY 10017, USA.

Telephone: (212) 326-7000; **fax:** (212) 887-7465; **e-mail:** info@unicef.org; **internet:** www.unicef.org.

UNICEF was established in 1946 by the UN General Assembly as the UN International Children's Emergency Fund, to meet the emergency needs of children in post-war Europe. In 1950 its mandate was expanded to respond to the needs of children in developing countries. In 1953 the General Assembly decided that UNICEF should become a permanent branch of the UN system, with an emphasis on programmes giving long-term benefits to children everywhere, particularly those in developing countries. In 1965 UNICEF was awarded the Nobel Peace Prize.

Organization

(September 2007)

EXECUTIVE BOARD

The Executive Board, as the governing body of UNICEF, comprises 36 member governments from all regions, elected in rotation for a three-year term by ECOSOC. The Board establishes policy, reviews programmes and approves expenditure. It reports to the General Assembly through ECOSOC.

SECRETARIAT

The Executive Director of UNICEF is appointed by the UN Secretary-General in consultation with the Executive Board. The administration of UNICEF and the appointment and direction of staff are the responsibility of the Executive Director, under policy directives laid down by the Executive Board, and under a broad authority delegated to the Executive Director by the Secretary-General. In January 2007 there were more than 8,000 UNICEF staff positions, of which about 85% were in field offices.

Executive Director: ANN M. VENEMAN (USA).

UNICEF OFFICES

Regional Office for Eastern and Southern Africa: POB 44145, Nairobi, Kenya 00100; tel. (20) 621234; fax (20) 622678; e-mail unicefesaro@unicef.org.

Regional Office for West and Central Africa: POB 29720, Dakar-Yoff, Senegal; tel. 869-58-58; fax 820-89-65; e-mail wcaro@unicef.org.

UNICEF Innocenti Research Centre: Piazza SS. Annunziata 12, 50122 Florence, Italy; tel. (055) 20330; fax (055) 2033220; e-mail florence@unicef.org; internet www.unicef-irc.org; f. 1988.

UNICEF Supply Division: UNICEF Plads, Freeport 2100, Copenhagen, Denmark; tel. 35-27-35-27; fax 35-26-94-21; e-mail supply@unicef.org; internet www.unicef.org/supply.

NATIONAL COMMITTEES

UNICEF is supported by 37 National Committees, mostly in industrialized countries, whose volunteer members, numbering more than 100,000, raise money through various activities, including the sale of greetings cards. The Committees also undertake advocacy and awareness campaigns on a number of issues and provide an important link with the general public.

Activities

UNICEF is dedicated to the well-being of children, adolescents and women and works for the realization and protection of their rights within the frameworks of the Convention on the Rights of the Child, which was adopted by the UN General Assembly in 1989 and by 2007 was almost universally ratified, and of the Convention on the Elimination of All Forms of Discrimination Against Women, adopted by the UN General Assembly in 1979. Promoting the full implementation of the Conventions, UNICEF aims to ensure that children world-wide are given the best possible start in life and attain a good level of basic education, and that adolescents are given every opportunity to develop their capabilities and participate successfully in society. The Fund also continues to provide relief and rehabilitation assistance in emergencies. Through its extensive field network in some 156 developing countries and territories, UNICEF undertakes, in co-ordination with governments, local communities and other aid organizations, programmes in health, nutrition, education, water and sanitation, the environment, gender issues and development, and other fields of importance to children. Emphasis is placed on low-cost, community-based programmes. UNICEF programmes are increasingly focused on supporting children and women during critical periods of their life, when intervention can make a lasting difference. UNICEF is actively involved in global-level partnerships for child protection, including the Inter-Agency Co-ordination Panel on Juvenile Justice; the Inter-Agency Working Group on Unaccompanied and Separated Children; the Donors' Working Group on Female Genital Mutilation/Cutting; the Better Care Network; the Study on Violence Against Children; the Inter-Agency Standing Committee (IASC) Task Force on Protection from Sexual Exploitation and Abuse in Humanitarian Crises; and the IASC Task Force on Mental Health and Psychological Support in Emergency Settings.

The five principal themes of UNICEF's medium-term strategic plan for the period 2006–09 are: young child survival and development; basic education and gender equality, including the Fund's continued leadership of the UN Girls' Education Initiative (UNGEI); HIV/AIDS and children, including participation in the Joint UN Programme on HIV/AIDS (UNAIDS—see below); child protection from violence, exploitation and abuse; and policy advocacy and partnerships for children's rights. These priorities are guided by the relevant UN Millennium Development Goals (MDGs) adopted by world leaders in 2000, and by the 'A World Fit for Children' declaration and plan of action endorsed by the UN General Assembly Special Session on Children in 2002 (see below).

UNICEF served as the substantive secretariat for, and played a leading role in helping governments and other partners prepare for, the UN General Assembly Special Session on Children, which was held in May 2002 to assess the outcome of the World Summit for Children convened in 1990 (which had made commitments to reducing mortality rates for infants and children; reducing the maternal mortality rate; reducing severe malnutrition amongst children under five; ensuring universal access to safe drinking water and to sanitary means of excreta disposal; and ensuring universal access to basic education) and to determine a set of actions and objectives for the next 10 years. At the Session the General Assembly adopted a declaration entitled 'A World Fit for Children', reaffirming its commitment to the agenda of the 1990 summit, and outlining a plan of action that resolved to achieve as yet unmet World Summit goals by 2010 and to work towards the attainment by 2015 of 21 new goals and targets supporting the MDGs in the areas of education, health and the protection of children. The latter included: a reduction of mortality rates for infants and children under five by two-thirds; a reduction of maternal mortality rates by three-quarters; a reduction by one-third in the rate for severe malnutrition among children under the age of five; and enrolment in primary education by 90% of children. The UN General Assembly was to review the progress towards 'A World Fit for Children' in 2007. UNICEF's annual publication *The State of the World's Children* includes social and economic data relevant to the well-being of children.

In 2000 UNICEF launched a new initiative, the Global Movement for Children—comprising governments, private- and public-sector bodies, and individuals—which aimed to rally world-wide support to improve the lives of all children and adolescents. In April 2001 a 'Say Yes for Children' campaign was adopted by the Global Movement, identifying 10 critical actions required to further its objectives. These were: eliminating all forms of discrimination and exclusion; putting children first; ensuring a caring environment for every child; fighting HIV/AIDS; eradicating violence against and abuse and exploitation of children; listening to children's views; universal education; protecting children from war; safeguarding the earth for children; and combating poverty. In 2003 UNICEF, WHO, the World Bank and other partners established a new Child Survival Partnership, which was to act as a forum for the promotion of co-ordinated action in support of efforts to reduce the level of child mortality in 42 targeted developing countries.

UNICEF, in co-operation with other UN agencies, promotes universal access to and completion of basic and good quality education. The Fund, with UNESCO, UNDP, UNFPA and the World Bank, co-sponsored the World Conference on Education for All, held in Thailand in March 1990, and undertook efforts to achieve the objectives formulated by the conference, which included the elimination of disparities in education between boys and girls. UNICEF participated in and fully supports the objectives and framework for action adopted by the World Education Forum in Dakar, Senegal, in April 2000. The Fund supports education projects in sub-Saharan Africa, South Asia and countries in the Middle East, North Africa, and Latin America and the Caribbean, and leads and acts as the secretariat of the United Nations Girls' Education Initiative (UNGEI), which aims to increase the enrolment of girls in primary schools in more than 100 countries. In 2002 more than 115m. school-age children world-wide, of whom more than 53% were girls, remained deprived of basic education. Some 28% of the Fund's programme assistance was allocated to girls' education in 2005. In that year approximately 500,000 girls in Afghanistan were enrolled in schools for the first time. Major 'back-to-school' campaigns and enrolment drives were launched in countries struck by the December 2004 Indian Ocean tsunamis; within three months of the disaster 90% of affected children had returned to school. UNICEF's annual publication *The State of the World's Children* includes social and economic data relevant to the well-being of children. It was reported in this publication in 2007 that one of the most powerful constraints to realizing children's rights and achieving the MDGs was discrimination against women.

UNICEF works to improve safe water supply, sanitation and hygiene, and thereby reduce the risk of diarrhoea and other water-borne diseases. In partnership with other organizations the Fund supports initiatives to make schools in more than 90 developing countries safer through school-based water, sanitation and hygiene programmes. UNICEF places great emphasis on increasing the testing and protection of drinking water at its source as well as in the home. In 2006 UNICEF and partners established the Global Task Force on Water and Sanitation with the aim of providing all children with access to safe water, and accelerating progress towards MDG targets on safe drinking water and basic sanitation.

UNICEF aims to break the cycle of poverty by advocating for the provision of increased development aid to developing countries, and aims to help poor countries obtain debt relief and to ensure access to basic social services. UNICEF is the leading agency in promoting the 20/20 initiative, which was endorsed at the World Summit for Social Development, held in Copenhagen, Denmark, in March 1995. The initiative encourages the governments of developing and donor countries to allocate at least 20% of their domestic budgets and official development aid respectively, to healthcare, primary education and low-cost safe water and sanitation. During the G-8 summit held in Gleneagles, United Kingdom, in July 2005, UNICEF convened a parallel summit, known as the C-8 Children's Forum, in nearby Dunblane to encourage children to participate in the global dialogue on alleviating poverty.

UNICEF estimates that the births of some 50m. children annually are not officially registered, and promotes universal registration in order to prevent the abuse of children without proof of age and nationality, for example through trafficking, forced labour, early marriage and military recruitment. It estimates that some 218m. children were involved in exploitative labour (excluding domestic work) in 2004, and approximately 126m. children aged five–17 were believed to be engaged in hazardous work. It is estimated that, annually, around 1.2m. children world-wide are trafficked. The Fund, which vigorously opposes the exploitation of children as a violation of their basic human rights, works with ILO and other partners to promote an end to exploitative and hazardous child labour, and supports special projects to provide education, counselling and care in developing countries. UNICEF co-sponsored and actively participated in the Second Congress Against Commercial Sexual Exploitation of Children held in Yokohama, Japan, in December 2001. Some 10% of the Fund's direct programme assistance was allocated to the improved protection of children in 2005.

In 2005 UNICEF allocated 38% of its programme assistance to early childhood development and 19% to its Immunization Plus activities (focusing on the promotion of improved child-care practices, the strengthening of local health systems, and the delivery of other life-saving services—such as the provision of vitamin A supplements and insecticide-treated mosquito nets to help prevent malaria—during immunization campaigns). The Fund estimates that around 11m. children under five years of age die each year, mainly in developing countries, and the majority from largely preventable causes. UNICEF has worked with WHO and other partners to increase global immunization coverage against the following six diseases: measles, poliomyelitis, tuberculosis, diphtheria, whooping cough and tetanus. In 2003 UNICEF, WHO, the World Bank and other partners established a new Child Survival Partnership, which acts as a forum for the promotion of co-ordinated action in support of efforts to save the children's lives in 42 targeted developing countries. In September 2005 UNICEF, WHO and other partners launched the Partnership for Maternal, Newborn and Child Health, formed to accelerate progress towards MDGs four and five, which aim to reduce child and maternal mortality respectively. In 2000 UNICEF, WHO, the World Bank and a number of public- and private-sector partners launched the Global Alliance for Vaccines and Immunization (GAVI), which aimed to protect children of all nationalities and socio-economic groups against vaccine-preventable diseases. GAVI's strategy included improving access to sustainable immunization services, expanding the use of existing vaccines, accelerating the development and introduction of new vaccines and technologies and promoting immunization coverage as a focus of international development efforts.

The results of integrated approaches to child health, such as the Accelerated Child Survival and Development (ACSD) strategy and community-based Integrated Management of Childhood Illnesses (IMCI) programme, have demonstrated new potential to reduce child mortality. The ACSD strategy, implemented by UNICEF since 2002, is an intensive combination of life-saving interventions including the promotion of antenatal care, vaccination and breast-feeding, volunteer health-worker follow-up of newborns and the distribution of insecticide-treated mosquito nets. Focused in 97 high-mortality districts in 11 mainly West African countries, ACSD has reached around 16m. people, including 2.8m. children under the age of five. In May 2005 it was reported that UNICEF planned to expand the project to help more children across Africa.

At the UN General Assembly Special Session on Children, in 2002, goals were set to reduce measles deaths by 50%. Expanded efforts by UNICEF, WHO and other partners led to a reduction in world-wide measles deaths by around 60% between 1999 and 2005.

UNICEF-assisted programmes for the control of diarrhoeal diseases promote the low-cost manufacture and distribution of prepackaged salts or home-made solutions. The use of 'oral rehydration therapy' has risen significantly in recent years, and is believed to prevent more than 1m. child deaths annually. During 1990–2000 diarrhoea-related deaths were reduced by one-half. UNICEF also promotes the need to improve sanitation and access to safe water supplies in developing nations in order to reduce the risk of diarrhoea and other water-borne diseases (see 20/20 initiative, above). To control acute respiratory infections, another leading cause of death in children under five in developing countries, UNICEF works with WHO in training health workers to diagnose and treat the associated diseases. Around 1m. children die from malaria every year, mainly in sub-Saharan Africa. In October 1998 UNICEF, together with WHO, UNDP and the World Bank, inaugurated a new global campaign, Roll Back Malaria, to fight the disease. UNICEF is actively engaged in developing innovative and effective ways to distribute highly-subsidized insecticide-treated mosquito nets at local level, thereby increasing the proportion of children and pregnant women who use them.

According to UNICEF estimates, around 25% of children under five years of age are underweight, while each year malnutrition contributes to about one-half of the child deaths in that age group and leaves millions of others with physical and mental disabilities. More than 2,000m. people world-wide (mainly women and children in developing countries) are estimated to be deficient in one or more essential vitamins and minerals, such as vitamin A, iodine and iron. UNICEF supports national efforts to reduce malnutrition, for example, fortifying staple foods with micronutrients, widening women's access to education, improving the nutritional status of pregnant women, improving household food security and basic health services, providing food supplies in emergencies, and promoting sound childcare and feeding practices. Since 1991 more than 19,000 hospitals in about 130 countries have been designated 'baby-friendly', having implemented a set of UNICEF and WHO recommendations entitled '10 steps to successful breast-feeding'. In 1996 UNICEF expressed its concern at the impact of international economic embargoes on child health, citing as an example the extensive levels of child malnutrition recorded in Iraq. UNICEF remains actively concerned at the levels of child malnutrition and accompanying diseases in Iraq and in the Democratic People's Republic of Korea, which has also suffered severe food shortages.

UNICEF estimates that more than 500,000 women die every year during pregnancy or childbirth, largely because of inadequate maternal healthcare. For every maternal death, approximately 30 further women suffer permanent injuries or chronic disabilities as a result of complications during pregnancy or childbirth. With its partners in the Safe Motherhood Initiative—UNFPA, WHO, the World Bank, the International Planned Parenthood Federation, the Population Council, and Family Care International—UNICEF promotes measures to reduce maternal mortality and morbidity, including improving access to quality reproductive health services, educating communities about safe motherhood and the rights of women, training midwives, and expanding access to family planning services. Under the Global Partnership for Maternal, Newborn and Child Health, UNICEF works with WHO, UNFPA and other partners in countries with high maternal mortality to improve maternal health and prevent maternal deaths. UNICEF and partners work with governments and policy-makers to ensure that emergency obstetric care is a priority in national health plans. In 2005 UNICEF activities in this area included support for obstetric facilities and training in, and advocacy of, women's health issues such as avoiding child marriage, eliminating female genital mutilation/cutting (FGM/C), and preventing malaria and promoting the uptake of tetanus toxoid vaccinations and iron and folic acid supplements among pregnant women.

UNICEF is concerned at the danger posed by HIV/AIDS to the realization of children's rights and in 2005 allocated 8% of its programme expenditure to this area. At the end of 2006 it was estimated that 2.3m. children under the age of 15 were living with HIV/AIDS world-wide. During that year some 530,000 children under the age of 15 were estimated to have been newly infected with the HIV virus, while 380,000 died as a result of AIDS and AIDS-related illnesses. It was estimated that more than one-half of all new HIV infections in 2006 occurred in young people, aged below 25. It is believed that more than 15m. children world-wide have lost one or both parents to AIDS since the start of the pandemic. UNICEF's priorities in this area include prevention of infection among young people (through, for example, support for education programmes and dissemination of information through the media), reduction in mother-to-child transmission, care and protection of orphans and other vulnerable children, and care and support for children, young people and parents living with HIV/AIDS. UNICEF works closely in this field with governments and co-operates with other UN agencies in the Joint UN Programme on HIV/AIDS (UNAIDS), which became operational on 1 January 1996. In July 2002 UNICEF, UNAIDS and WHO jointly produced a study entitled *Young People and HIV/AIDS: Opportunity in Crisis*, examining young people's sexual behaviour patterns and knowledge of HIV/AIDS. UNICEF advocates Life Skills-Based Education as a means of empowering young people to cope with challenging situations and encouraging them to adopt healthy patterns of behaviour. In July 2004 UNICEF and other partners produced a *Framework for the Protection, Care and Support of Orphans and Vulnerable Children Living in a World with HIV and AIDS*. In October 2005 UNICEF launched Unite for Children, Unite Against AIDS, a campaign that was to provide a platform for child-focused advocacy aimed at reversing the spread of HIV/AIDS amongst children, adolescents and young people; and to provide a child-focused framework for national programmes based on the following four pillars: the prevention of mother-to-child HIV transmission, improved provision of paediatric treatment, prevention of infection among adolescents and young people, and protection and support of children affected by HIV/AIDS. In January 2007 UNICEF issued *Children and AIDS: A stocktaking report* detailing the progress and challenges of the previous year.

At December 2005 it was estimated that around 2m. children under 15 were living with HIV/AIDS in sub-Saharan Africa (including 240,000 both in Nigeria and South Africa), while some 12m. children aged 0–17 in the region were reported to have been orphaned by AIDS-related illnesses. It was estimated that, of young people in sub-Saharan Africa aged between 15–24, some 4.3% of females and 1.5% of males were infected with HIV/AIDS. In July 2004 a Task Force on Women, Girls and AIDS in Southern Africa, convened by the UN Secretary-General in the previous year, issued a report of its findings.

UNICEF provides emergency relief assistance to children and young people affected by conflict, natural disasters and food crises. In situations of violence and social disintegration the Fund provides support in the areas of education, health, mine-awareness and psychosocial assistance, and helps to demobilize and rehabilitate child soldiers. In recent years several such operations have been undertaken, including in Afghanistan, Burundi, Democratic Republic of the Congo, Iraq, Liberia, the Palestinian territories, Sierra Leone, Somalia and Sudan. In 2005 UNICEF provided emergency assistance to children in more than 50 countries. In 1999 UNICEF adopted a Peace and Security Agenda to help guide international efforts in this field. Emergency education assistance includes the provision of 'Edukits' in refugee camps and the reconstruction of school buildings. In the area of health the Fund co-operates with WHO to arrange 'days of tranquility' in order to facilitate the immunization of children in conflict zones. Psychosocial assistance activities include special programmes to support traumatized children and help unaccompanied children to be reunited with parents or extended families.

By December 2005 UNICEF had received US $660m. in donor funding in support of its relief and recovery response to the devastating December 2004 Indian Ocean tsunamis. In 2005 the Fund assisted an estimated 1.5m. children and young people who had been displaced from their homes by the tsunamis. UNICEF's relief and recovery efforts included the provision of emergency immunization to prevent an increase in the prevalence of fatal childhood diseases; the provision of basic medicines; supply of safe water and provision of basic sanitation; provision of fortified supplementary food to young children and to pregnant and lactating women; care for traumatized children; identification and protection of the large numbers of orphans and children who had been separated from their families; and the provision of education kits for children whose schooling had been disrupted by the natural disaster and the rehabilitation of schools.

By the end of 2005, in response to severe food insecurity in Niger, UNICEF, jointly with the World Food Programme and other partners, had opened more than 860 feeding centres which provided medical and nutritional therapy to some 325,000 moderately and acutely malnourished children. Other activities undertaken by the Fund in Niger in that year included the formulation and dissemination of a uniform protocol for treating malnutrition, restocking cereal banks, the provision of nutritional supplies and medicines to health facilities, and the supply of water and sanitation kits to malnourished families. This assistance continued in 2006.

In 2005 UNICEF provided primary health care to some 2m. people in Darfur, Sudan, and worked with partners to supply camps with safe water and basic sanitation to the region. Many children were immunized against measles and polio, interrupting wild polio virus transmission after a major outbreak in 2004.

In 2005 UNICEF country offices prepared contingency plans for a possible future avian influenza pandemic among humans, with a particular focus on children, as part of the inter-agency response to the threat.

An estimated 250,000 children are involved in armed conflicts as soldiers, porters and forced labourers. UNICEF encourages ratification of the Optional Protocol to the Convention on the Rights of the Child on the involvement of children in armed conflict, which was adopted by the General Assembly in May 2000 and entered into force in February 2002, and bans the compulsory recruitment of combatants below the age of 18. The Fund also urges states to make unequivocal statements endorsing 18 as the minimum age of voluntary recruitment to the armed forces. It is estimated that land-mines kill and maim between 8,000 and 10,000 children every year. The Convention on the Prohibition of the Use, Stockpiling, Production and Transfer of Anti-Personnel Mines and on their Destruction was adopted in December 1997 and entered into force in March 1999. By November 2006 the Convention had been ratified by 152 countries. UNICEF is committed to campaigning for its universal ratification and full implementation, and also supports mine-awareness campaigns.

Finance

UNICEF is funded by voluntary contributions from governments and non-governmental and private-sector sources. UNICEF's income is divided into contributions for 'regular resources' (used for country programmes of co-operation approved by the Executive Board, programme support, and management and administration costs) and contributions for 'other resources' (for special purposes, including expanding the outreach of country programmes of co-operation and ensuring capacity to deliver critical assistance to women and children, for example during humanitarian crises). Total income in 2005 amounted to US $2,762m., of which 53% was from governments and intergovernmental organizations, and 38% from private-sector sources.

In 2005 some 45% of the Fund's total expenditure was allocated to activities in Africa South of the Sahara, and 22% to activities in South Asia.

Publications

Progress for Children (in English, French and Spanish).

The State of the World's Children (annually, in Arabic, English, French, Russian and Spanish and about 30 other national languages).

UNICEF Annual Report (in English, French and Spanish).

UNICEF at a Glance (in English, French and Spanish).

Young People in Changing Societies (annually).

Reports and studies; series on children and women; nutrition; education; children's rights; children in wars and disasters; working children; water, sanitation and the environment; analyses of the situation of children and women in individual developing countries.

United Nations Development Programme—UNDP

Address: One United Nations Plaza, New York, NY 10017, USA.

Telephone: (212) 906-5295; **fax:** (212) 906-5364; **e-mail:** hq@undp.org; **internet:** www.undp.org.

The Programme was established in 1965 by the UN General Assembly. Its central mission is to help countries to eradicate poverty and achieve a sustainable level of human development, an approach to economic growth that encompasses individual well-being and choice, equitable distribution of the benefits of development, and conservation of the environment. UNDP advocates for a more inclusive global economy. UNDP is the focus of UN efforts to achieve the Millennium Development Goals.

Organization

(September 2007)

UNDP is responsible to the UN General Assembly, to which it reports through ECOSOC.

EXECUTIVE BOARD

The Executive Board is responsible for providing intergovernmental support to, and supervision of, the activities of UNDP and the UN Population Fund (UNFPA). It comprises 36 members: eight from Africa, seven from Asia and the Pacific, four from eastern Europe, five from Latin America and the Caribbean and 12 from western Europe and other countries. Members serve a three-year term.

SECRETARIAT

Offices and divisions at the Secretariat include: an Operations Support Group; Offices of the United Nations Development Group, the Human Development Report, Development Studies, Audit and Performance Review, Evaluation, and Communications; and Bureaux for Crisis Prevention and Recovery, Resources and Strategic Partnerships, Development Policy, and Management. Five regional bureaux, all headed by an assistant administrator, cover: Africa; Asia and the Pacific; the Arab states; Latin America and the Caribbean; and Europe and the Commonwealth of Independent States.

Administrator: Kemal Derviş (Turkey).

Associate Administrator: Ad Melkert (Netherlands).

Assistant Administrator and Director, Regional Bureau for Africa: Gilbert Fossoun Houngbo (Togo).

COUNTRY OFFICES

In almost every country receiving UNDP assistance there is an office, headed by the UNDP Resident Representative, who usually also serves as UN Resident Co-ordinator, responsible for the co-ordination of all UN technical assistance and operational development activities, advising the Government on formulating the country programme, ensuring that field activities are undertaken, and acting as the leader of the UN team of experts working in the country. The offices function as the primary presence of the UN in most developing countries.

OFFICES OF UNDP REPRESENTATIVES IN AFRICA SOUTH OF THE SAHARA

Angola: Rua Major Kanhangulo 197, CP 910, Luanda; tel. (2) 331181; fax (2) 335609; e-mail registry.ao@undp.org; internet mirror.undp.org/angola; Resident Rep. (vacant).

Benin: Lot 3, Zone Residentielle, BP 506, Cotonou; tel. 21-31-30-45; fax 21-31-57-86; e-mail fo.ben@undp.org; internet www.undp.org.bj; Resident Rep. EDITH GASANA.

Botswana: UN Place, Khama Crescent, POB 54, Gaborone; tel. 3952121; fax 356093; e-mail undp.bw@undp.org; internet www.unbotswana.org.bw; Resident Co-ordinator KRISTAN SCHOULTZ.

Burkina Faso: Immeuble des Nations Unies, rue Maurice Bishop, 01 BP 575, Ouagadougou 01; tel. 50-30-67-65; fax 50-31-04-70; e-mail registry.bf@undp.org; internet www.pnud.bf; Resident Co-ordinator GEORG CHARPENTIER.

Burundi: Chausée du Peuple Murundi, BP 1490, Bujumbura; tel. (2) 301100; fax (2) 301190; e-mail registy.bi@undp.org; internet www.bi.undp.org; Resident Co-ordinator IBRAHIMA FALL.

Cameroon: Immeuble Foul'assi, Nouvelle Route Bastos, Rue 1775, BP 836, Yaoundé; tel. 220-0800; fax 220-0796; e-mail registry.cm@undp.org; internet www.cm.undp.org; Resident Rep. SOPHIE DE CAEN.

Cape Verde: Maison des Nations Unies, Avda OUA, Achada de Santo António, CP 62, Praia; tel. 260-96-12; fax 62-13-52; e-mail anita.pinto@cv.jo.un.org; internet www.cv.jo.org.

Central African Republic: ave Boganda, Bangui; tel. 61-19-77; fax 61-17-32; e-mail registry.cf@undp.org; internet www.cf.undp.org; Resident Rep. TOBY LANZER.

Chad: ave Colonel D'Ornano, BP 906, N'Djamena; tel. 51-41-00; fax 51-63-30; e-mail registry.td@undp.org; internet www.td.undp.org; Resident Co-ordinator KINGSLEY AMANING.

Comoros: Hamramba, BP 648, Moroni; tel. 73-15-58; fax 73-15-77; e-mail fo.coi@undp.org.

Congo, Democratic Republic: Immeuble Royal, blvd du 30 juin, BP 7248, Commune de la Gombe, Kinshasa; tel. (810) 555-3300; fax (810) 555-3305; internet www.undp.org.cd.

Congo, Republic: ave du Maréchal Foch, BP 465, Brazzaville; tel. 81-57-63; fax 81-16-79; e-mail registry.cg@undp.org; internet mirror.undp.org/cong.

Côte d'Ivoire: angle rue Gourgas et ave Marchand, Abidjan-Plateau, 01 BP 1747, Abidjan 01; tel. 20-21-29-95; fax 20-21-13-67; e-mail fo.civa@undp.org; internet www.ci.undp.org.

Djibouti: blvd Maréchal Joffre, Plâteau du Serpent, BP 2001, Djibouti; tel. 354354; fax 350587; e-mail pnud@intnet.dj; internet www.undp.org.dj.

Equatorial Guinea: Esquina Calle de Kenia con Calle Rey Boncoro, CP 399, Malabo; tel. (9) 2275; fax (9) 2153; e-mail registry.gq@undp.org; internet www.gq.undp.org.

Eritrea: UN Offices, HDAY St, POB 5366, Asmara; tel. (1) 151468; fax (1) 151081; e-mail registry.er@undp.org; internet www.er.undp.org; Resident Rep. Mr MACLEOD NYIRONGO.

Ethiopia: Africa Hall, Old ECA Bldg, 7th Floor, Menelik II Ave, POB 5580, Addis Ababa; tel. (11) 551-5177; fax (11) 551-4599; e-mail registry.et@undp.org; internet www.et.undp.org.

Gabon: BP 2183, Libreville; tel. 73-88-87; fax 73-88-91; e-mail registry.ga@undp.org; internet www.ga.undp.org; Resident Rep. FATOUMATA BINTOU DJIBO.

The Gambia: 5 ave Kofi Annan, Cape Point, POB 553, Banjul; tel. 4494760; fax 4494758; e-mail registry.gm@undp.org; internet www.gm.undp.org; Resident Rep. Dr. FADZAI GWARADZIMBA.

Ghana: Ring Rd Dual Carriage, nr Police HQ, POB 1423, Accra; tel. (21) 777890; fax (21) 773899; e-mail fo.gha@undp.org.

Guinea: Maison Commune, Rue MA 002, Coléah Corniche Sud, Commune de Matam, BP 222, Conakry; tel. 46-88-98; fax 13- 68-64; e-mail registry.gn@undp.org; internet www.gn.undp.org.

Guinea-Bissau: Rua Rui Djassi, 72 A/B, POB 1011, Bissau; tel. 201368; fax 201753; e-mail registry.gw@undp.org; internet www.gw.undp.org.

Kenya: Kenyatta International Conference Center, Harambee Ave, POB 30218, Nairobi; tel. (20) 621234; fax (20) 624489; e-mail registry.ke@undp.org; internet www.ke.undp.org; Resident Rep. ELIZABETH LWANGA.

Lesotho: cnr Hilton and Nightingale Rds, POB 301, Maseru 100; tel. 313790; fax 310042; e-mail fo.lso@undp.org; internet www.undp.org.ls; Resident Rep. HODAN A. HAJI-MOHAMUD.

Liberia: Sekou Toure Ave, Mamba Point, POB 0274, Monrovia 10; tel. 226195; fax 226210; e-mail fo.lbr@undp.org; internet www.lr.undp.org; Resident Rep. JORDAN RYAN.

Madagascar: rue Rainitovo, Antsahavola, BP 1348, Antananarivo 10147; tel. (20) 2236650; fax (20) 2336794; e-mail registry.mg@unep.org; internet www.snu.mg/pnud; Resident Rep. BOUVI SANHOUIDI.

Malawi: Plot No 7, Area 40, POB 30135, Lilongwe 3; tel. 773500; fax 774637; e-mail information.mw@undp.org; internet www.undp.org.mw; Resident Rep. MICHAEL KEATING.

Mali: Immeuble Me Hamaciré N'Douré, Badalabougou-Est, BP 120, Bamako; tel. 222-20-52; fax 222-62-98; e-mail fo.ml@undp.org; internet www.undp.org/fomli.

Mauritania: 203, rue 42–133, Lot K, Lots No. 159–161, BP 620, Nouakchott; tel. (2) 525-24-09; fax (2) 525-26-16; e-mail registry.mr@undp.org; internet www.pnud.mr.

Mauritius: Anglo-Mauritius House, 6th Floor, Intendance St, POB 253, Port Louis; tel. 212-3726; fax 208-4871; e-mail registry.mu@undp.org; internet un.intnet.mu; Resident Rep. CLAUDIO CALDARONE.

Mozambique: Avda Kenneth Kaunda, 921/931, POB 4595, Maputo; tel. (21) 481400; fax (21) 491691; e-mail undpmz@undp.org; internet www.undp.org.mz.

Namibia: Sanlam Centre, 154 Independence St, Private Bag 13329, Windhoek 9000; tel. (61) 2046111; fax (61) 2046203; e-mail fo.nam@undp.org; Resident Rep. SIMON R. NHONGO.

Niger: Maison des Nations Unies,, BP 11207, Niamey; tel. 73-21-04; fax 72-36-30; e-mail registry.ne@undp.org; internet www.pnud.ne; Resident Rep. MICHELE FALAVIGNA.

Nigeria: United Nations House, Plot 617/618, Diplomatic Zone, Central Area District, PMB 2851, Garki; tel. (9) 461-8600; fax (9) 461-8546; e-mail registry.ng@undp.org; internet www.undp.org.ng; Resident Rep. ALBÉRIC KACOU.

Rwanda: , BP 445, Kigali; tel. 590400; fax 576263; e-mail registry.rw@undp.org; internet www.unrwanda.org/undp; Resident Rep. MOUSTAPHA SOUMARE.

São Tomé and Príncipe: Avda das Naçoes Unidas, CP 109, São Tomé; tel. 221123; fax 222198; e-mail registry.st@undp.org; internet www.uns.st/undp.

Senegal: Immeuble Faycal, 19 rue Parchappe, BP 154, Dakar; tel. 839-90-50; fax 823-55-00; e-mail registry.sn@undp.org; internet www.undp.org.sn.

Seychelles: covered by office in Mauritius.

Sierra Leone: United Nations House, 76 Wilkinson Rd, POB 1011, Freetown; tel. (22) 231311; fax (22) 233075; e-mail registry.sl@undp.org; internet www.sl.undp.org.

Somalia: covered by office in Kenya.

South Africa: Metropark Bldg, 9th and 10th Floors, 351 Schoeman St, POB 6541, Pretoria 0001; tel. (12) 338-5063; fax (12) 320-4353; e-mail fo.zaf@undp.org; internet www.undp.org.za.

Sudan: House No 7, Block 5, R.F.E., Gama'a Ave, POB 913, 11111 Khartoum; tel. 1 83 783 820; fax 1 83 783 764; e-mail registry.sd@undp.org; internet www.sd.undp.org; Resident Rep. MANUEL ARANDA DA SILVA.

Swaziland: Lilunga House, 5th Floor, Somhlolo St, PO Box 261, Mbabane; tel. 4042301; fax 4045341; e-mail registry.sz@undp.org; internet www.undp.org.sz; Resident Rep. CHINWE DIKE.

Tanzania: Matasalamat Mansions, 2nd Floor, Zanaki St, POB 9182, Dar es Salaam; tel. (22) 26680000; fax (22) 2668749; e-mail registry.tz@undp.org; internet www.tz.undp.org.

Togo: 40 ave des Nations Unies, le étage, BP 911, Lomé; tel. 221-20-22; fax 221-16-41; e-mail registry.tg@undp.org; internet www.tg.unpd.org.

Uganda: UN House, 15 Clement Hill Rd, POB 7184, Kampala; tel. (41) 233440; fax (41) 344801; e-mail undp@imul.com; internet www.imul.com/undp.

Zambia: Plot No. 11867, Alick Nkhata Ave, Longacres, POB 31966, Lusaka; tel. (1) 250800; fax (1) 253805; e-mail registry.zm@undp.org; internet www.undp.org.zm.

Zimbabwe: Takura House, 9th Floor, 67–69 Union Ave, POB 4775, Harare; tel. (4) 792681; fax (4) 725973; e-mail registry.zw@undp.org; internet www.undp.org.zw.

Activities

UNDP provides advisory and support services to governments and UN teams with the aim of advancing sustainable human development and building national development capabilities. Assistance is mostly non-monetary, comprising the provision of experts' services, consultancies, equipment and training for local workers. Developing countries themselves contribute significantly to the total project costs in terms of personnel, facilities, equipment and supplies. UNDP also supports programme countries in attracting aid and utilizing it efficiently. A network of nine Sub-regional Resource Facilities (SURFs) has been established to strengthen and co-ordinate UNDP's role as a global knowledge provider and channel for sharing knowledge and experience.

During the late 1990s UNDP undertook an extensive internal process of reform, 'UNDP 2001', which placed increased emphasis on its activities in the field and on performance and accountability. In

2001 UNDP established a series of Thematic Trust Funds to enable increased support of priority programme activities. In accordance with the more results-oriented approach developed under the 'UNDP 2001' process UNDP introduced a new Multi-Year Funding Framework (MYFF), which outlined the country-driven goals around which funding was to be mobilized, integrating programme objectives, resources, budget and outcomes. The MYFF was to provide the basis for the Administrator's Business Plans for the same duration and enables policy coherence in the implementation of programmes at country, regional and global levels. A Results-Oriented Annual Report (ROAR) was produced for the first time in 2000 from data compiled by country offices and regional programmes. In September 2000 the first ever Ministerial Meeting of ministers of development co-operation and foreign affairs and other senior officials from donor and programme countries, convened in New York, USA, endorsed UNDP's shift to a results-based orientation.

In accordance with the second phase of the MYFF, covering 2004–07, UNDP was to focus on the following five practice areas: democratic governance; poverty reduction; energy and the environment; crisis prevention and recovery; and combating HIV/AIDS. Other important 'cross-cutting' themes, to be incorporated throughout the programme areas, included gender equality, information and communication technologies, and human rights.

From the mid-1990s UNDP also assumed a more active and integrative role within the UN system-wide development framework. UNDP Resident Representatives—usually also serving as UN Resident Co-ordinators, with responsibility for managing inter-agency co-operation on sustainable human development initiatives at country level—were to play a focal role in implementing this approach. In order to promote its co-ordinating function UNDP allocated increased resources to training and skill-sharing programmes. In 1997 the UNDP Administrator was appointed to chair the UN Development Group (UNDG), which was established as part of a series of structural reform measures initiated by the UN Secretary-General, with the aim of strengthening collaboration between all UN funds, programmes and bodies concerned with development. The UNDG promotes coherent policy at country level through the system of UN Resident Co-ordinators (see above), the Common Country Assessment mechanism (CCA, a country-based process for evaluating national development situations), and the UN Development Assistance Framework (UNDAF, the foundation for planning and co-ordinating development operations at country level, based on the CCA). Within the framework of the Administrator's Business Plans for 2000–03 a new Bureau for Resources and Strategic Partnerships was established to build and strengthen working partnerships with other UN bodies, donor and programme countries, international financial institutions and development banks, civil society organizations and the private sector. The Bureau was also to serve UNDP's regional bureaux and country offices through the exchange of information and promotion of partnership strategies.

In March 1996 the UN Secretary-General inaugurated the UN System-wide Special Initiative on Africa, which was envisaged as a collaborative effort between the principal UN bodies and major regional organizations to secure a set of development objectives for Africa. The cost of the initiative was estimated at US $25,000m. over a 10-year period. UNDP's mandated involvement was in the areas of conflict prevention, strengthening democracy and enhancing public management in African countries. The other priorities of the Initiative were to achieve improvements in basic education, health and hygiene, food and water security and the expansion of South-South co-operation. In 1993 a framework to promote a development partnership between African countries and the international community was initiated at the Tokyo International Conference on African Development (TICAD). A second conference was convened in 1998 and a third in September 2003. In the interim periods the process is pursued through follow-up meetings, regional forums, trade conferences and seminars. In October 2002 the UN General Assembly recognized the New Partnership for Africa's Development (NEPAD) as the framework for the international community's support of development in Africa. UNDP supported the establishment and operation of a voluntary NEPAD initiative providing for countries to evaluate standards of governance in other participating states, the so-called African Peer Review Mechanism, and manages a trust to support the mechanism.

MILLENNIUM DEVELOPMENT GOALS

UNDP, through its leadership of the UNDG and management of the Resident Co-ordinator system, has a co-ordinating function as the focus of UN system-wide efforts to achieve the so-called Millennium Development Goals (MDGs), pledged by 189 governments attending a summit meeting of the UN General Assembly in September 2000. The objectives were to establish a defined agenda to reduce poverty and improve the quality of lives of millions of people and to serve as a framework for measuring development. There are eight MDGs, as follows, for which one or more specific targets have been identified:

i) to eradicate extreme poverty and hunger, with the aim of reducing by 50% the number of people with an income of less than US $1 a day and those suffering from hunger by 2015;

ii) to achieve universal primary education by 2015;

iii) to promote gender equality and empower women, in particular to eliminate gender disparities in primary and secondary education by 2005 and at all levels by 2015;

iv) to reduce child mortality, with a target reduction of two-thirds in the mortality rate among children under five by 2015;

v) to improve maternal health, and specifically to reduce by 75% the numbers of women dying in childbirth;

vi) to combat HIV/AIDS, malaria and other diseases;

vii) to ensure environmental sustainability, including targets to integrate the principles of sustainable development into country policies and programmes, to reduce by 50% the number of people without access to safe drinking water by 2015, to achieve significant improvement in the lives of at least 100m. slum dwellers by 2020;

viii) to develop a global partnership for development, including efforts to deal with international debt, to address the needs of least developed countries and landlocked and small island developing states, to develop decent and productive youth employment, to provide access to affordable, essential drugs in developing countries, and to make available the benefits of new technologies.

UNDP plays a leading role in efforts to integrate the MDGs into all aspects of UN activities at country level and to ensure the MDGs are incorporated into national development strategies. The Programme supports reporting by countries, as well as regions and sub-regions, on progress towards achievement of the goals, and on specific social, economic and environmental indicators, through the formulation of MDG reports. These form the basis of a global report, issued annually by the UN Secretary-General since mid-2002. UNDP provides administrative and technical support to the Millennium Project, an independent advisory body established by the UN Secretary-General in 2002 to develop a practical action plan to achieve the MDGs. Financial support of the Project is channelled through a Millennium Trust Fund, administered by UNDP. In January 2005 the Millennium Project presented its report, based on extensive research conducted by teams of experts, which included recommendations for the international system to support country level development efforts and identified a series of Quick Wins to bring conclusive benefit to millions of people in the short-term. UNDP also works to raise awareness of the MDGs and to support advocacy efforts at all levels, for example through regional publicity campaigns, target-specific publications and support for the Millennium Campaign to generate support for the goals in developing and developed countries.

In January 2002 the Executive Board approved a Regional Co-operation Framework for Africa, following an extensive process of consultation involving representatives of government, the private sector, civil society and academic institutions. The Framework, covering the period 2002–06 identified the following as priority areas for support: strengthening democracy and participatory governance; making globalization work for Africa; conflict prevention, peace-building and disaster management; and reducing the threat and impact of HIV/AIDS on Africa. In January 2004 UNDP launched *Africa 2015*, a campaign, led by well-known personalities, aimed at the continent-wide promotion of all the MDGs, with a special focus on combating poverty and HIV/AIDS.

DEMOCRATIC GOVERNANCE

UNDP supports national efforts to ensure efficient and accountable governance, improve the quality of democratic processes, and to build effective relations between the state, the private sector and civil society, which are essential to achieving sustainable development. As in other practice areas, UNDP assistance includes policy advice and technical support, capacity-building of institutions and individuals, advocacy and public information and communication, the promotion and brokering of dialogue, and knowledge networking and sharing of good practices. In March 2002 a UNDP Governance Centre was inaugurated in Oslo, Norway, to enhance the role of UNDP in support of democratic governance and to assist countries to implement democratic reforms in order to achieve the MDGs.

UNDP works to strengthen parliaments and other legislative bodies as institutions of democratic participation. It assists with constitutional reviews and reform, training of parliamentary staff, and capacity-building of political parties and civil organizations as part of this objective. UNDP undertakes missions to help prepare for and ensure the conduct of free and fair elections. Increasingly, UNDP is also focused on building the long-term capacity of electoral institutions and practices within a country, for example voter registration, election observation, the establishment of electoral commissions, and voter and civic education projects. Similarly,

UNDP aims to ensure an efficient, independent and fair judicial system is available to all, in particular the poor and disadvantaged.

Within its justice sector programme UNDP undertakes a variety of projects to improve access to justice and to promote judicial independence, legal reform and understanding of the legal system. UNDP also works to promote access to information, the integration of human rights issues into activities concerned with sustainable human development, as well as support for the international human rights system.

Since 1997 UNDP has been mandated to assist developing countries to fight corruption and improve accountability, transparency and integrity (ATI). It has worked to establish national and international partnerships in support of its anti-corruption efforts and used its role as a broker of knowledge and experience to uphold ATI principles at all levels of public financial management and governance. UNDP publishes case studies of its anti-corruption efforts and assists governments to conduct self-assessments of their public financial management systems.

Since 1997 UNDP's Regional Bureau for Africa supports the Africa Governance Forum, which has been convened regularly to consider aspects of governance and development.

Within the democratic governance practice area UNDP supports more than 300 projects at international, country and city levels designed to improve conditions for the urban poor, in particular through improvement in urban governance. The Local Initiative Facility for Urban Environment (LIFE) undertakes small-scale projects in low-income communities, in collaboration with local authorities, the private sector and community-based groups, and promotes a participatory approach to local governance. UNDP also works closely with the UN Capital Development Fund to implement projects in support of decentralized governance, which it has recognized as a key element to achieving sustainable development goals.

UNDP aims to ensure that, rather than creating an ever-widening 'digital divide', ongoing rapid advancements in information technology are harnessed by poorer countries to accelerate progress in achieving sustainable human development. UNDP advises governments on technology policy, promotes digital entrepreneurship in programme countries and works with private-sector partners to provide reliable and affordable communications networks. The Bureau for Development Policy operates the Information and Communication Technologies for Development Programme, which aims to promote sustainable human development through increased utilization of information and communications technologies globally. The Programme aims to establish technology access centres in developing countries. A Sustainable Development Networking Programme focuses on expanding internet connectivity in poorer countries through building national capacities and supporting local internet sites. UNDP has used mobile internet units to train people even in isolated rural areas. In 1999 UNDP, in collaboration with an international communications company, Cisco Systems, and other partners, launched NetAid, an internet-based forum (accessible at www.netaid.org) for mobilizing and co-ordinating fundraising and other activities aimed at alleviating poverty and promoting sustainable human development in the developing world. With Cisco Systems and other partners, UNDP has worked to establish academies of information technology to support training and capacity-building in developing countries. UNDP and the World Bank jointly host the secretariat of the Digital Opportunity Task Force, a partnership between industrialized and developing countries, business and non-governmental organizations that was established in 2000. UNDP is a partner in the Global Digital Technology Initiative, launched in 2002 to strengthen the role of information and communications technologies in achieving the development goals of developing countries. In January 2004 UNDP and Microsoft Corporation announced an agreement to develop jointly information and communication technology (ICT) projects aimed at assisting developing countries to achieve the MDGs.

UNDP's Africa regional bureau co-ordinates the Internet Initiative for Africa—IIA, which aims to provide member countries with access to information and expertise; to facilitate policy-making at national level; to assist with the establishment of national information infrastructures; to encourage the involvement of African experts in the development of internet infrastructures, policies, regulations and services; and, through the utilization of ICT, to promote regional development.

POVERTY REDUCTION

UNDP's activities to facilitate poverty eradication include support for capacity-building programmes and initiatives to generate sustainable livelihoods, for example by improving access to credit, land and technologies, and the promotion of strategies to improve education and health provision for the poorest elements of populations (with a focus on women and girls). UNDP aims to help governments to reassess their development priorities and to design initiatives for sustainable human development. In 1996, following the World Summit for Social Development, which was held in Copenhagen, Denmark, in March 1995, UNDP launched the Poverty Strategies Initiative (PSI) to strengthen national capacities to assess and monitor the extent of poverty and to combat the problem. All PSI projects were to involve representatives of governments, the private sector, social organizations and research institutions in policy debate and formulation. Following the introduction, in 1999, by the World Bank and IMF of Poverty Reduction Strategy Papers (PRSPs), UNDP has tended to direct its efforts to helping governments draft these documents, and, since 2001, has focused on linking the papers to efforts to achieve and monitoring progress towards the MDGs. In early 2004 UNDP inaugurated the International Poverty Centre, in Brasília, Brazil, which aimed to foster the capacity of countries to formulate and implement poverty reduction strategies and to encourage South-South co-operation in all relevant areas of research and decision-making. In particular, the Centre aimed to assist countries to meet Millennium goals and targets through the research and implementation of pro-poor growth policies and social protection and human development strategies, and the monitoring of poverty and inequality.

UNDP country offices support the formulation of national human development reports (NHDRs), which aim to facilitate activities such as policy-making, the allocation of resources and monitoring progress towards poverty eradication and sustainable development. In addition, the preparation of Advisory Notes and Country Co-operation Frameworks by UNDP officials helps to highlight country-specific aspects of poverty eradication and national strategic priorities. In January 1998 the Executive Board adopted eight guiding principles relating to sustainable human development that were to be implemented by all country offices, in order to ensure a focus to UNDP activities. Since 1990 UNDP has published an annual *Human Development Report*, incorporating a Human Development Index, which ranks countries in terms of human development, using three key indicators: life expectancy, adult literacy and basic income required for a decent standard of living. In 1997 a Human Poverty Index and a Gender-related Development Index, which assesses gender equality on the basis of life expectancy, education and income, were introduced into the Report for the first time. Also in 1997 a UNDP scheme to support private-sector and community-based initiatives to generate employment opportunities, MicroStart, became operational.

UNDP is committed to ensuring that the process of economic and financial globalization, including national and global trade, debt and capital flow policies, incorporates human development concerns. It has been actively concerned to ensure that the Doha Development Round of World Trade Organization (WTO) negotiations achieves an expansion of trade opportunities and economic growth to less developed countries. With the UN Conference on Trade and Development (UNCTAD), UNDP manages a Global Programme on Globalization, Liberalization and Sustainable Human Development, which aims to support greater integration of developing countries into the global economy. UNDP manages a Trust Fund for the Integrated Framework for trade-related technical assistance to least-developed countries, which was inaugurated in 1997 by UNDP, the IMF, the International Trade Centre, UNCTAD, the World Bank and the WTO, and is the lead agency for its capacity development component.

In 1996 UNDP initiated a process of collaboration between city authorities world-wide to promote implementation of the commitments made at the 1995 Copenhagen summit for social development and to help to combat aspects of poverty and other urban problems, such as poor housing, transport, the management of waste disposal, water supply and sanitation. The so-called World Alliance of Cities Against Poverty was formally launched in October 1997, in the context of the International Decade for the Eradication of Poverty. The first Forum of the Alliance was convened in October 1998, in Lyon, France; it has subsequently been held every two years.

UNDP sponsors the International Day for the Eradication of Poverty, held annually on 17 October.

ENERGY AND THE ENVIRONMENT

UNDP plays a role in developing the agenda for international co-operation on environmental and energy issues, focusing on the relationship between energy policies, environmental protection, poverty and development. UNDP promotes the development of national capacities and other strategies that support sustainable development practices, for example through the formulation and implementation of Poverty Reduction Strategies and National Strategies for Sustainable Development.

UNDP recognizes that desertification and land degradation is a major cause of rural poverty and promotes sustainable land management, drought preparedness and reform of land tenure as means of addressing the problem. It also aims to reduce poverty caused by land degradation through implementation of environmental conventions at a national and international level. In 2002 UNDP inaugurated an Integrated Drylands Development Programme which aimed to ensure that the needs of people living in drylands are met and considered at a local and national level. The Drylands Development

Centre implements the programme in 19 African, Arab and West Asian countries. UNDP is also concerned with sustainable management of forestries, fisheries and agriculture. Its Biodiversity Global Programme assists developing countries and communities to integrate issues relating to sustainable practices and biodiversity into national and global practices. Since 1992 UNDP has administered a Small Grants Programme, funded by the GEF, to support community-based initiatives concerned with biodiversity conservation, prevention of land degradation and the elimination of persistent organic pollutants. The Equator Initiative was inaugurated in 2002 as a partnership between UNDP, representatives of governments, civil society and businesses, with the aim of reducing poverty in communities along the equatorial belt by fostering local partnerships, harnessing local knowledge and promoting conservation and sustainable practices.

Another priority area of UNDP's Energy and Environment Practice is to promote clean energy technologies (through the Clean Development Mechanism) and to extend access to sustainable energy services, including the introduction of renewable alternatives to conventional fuels, as well as access to investment financing for sustainable energy. In December 2005 UNDP launched an MDG Carbon Facility, which aimed to channel increased carbon financing to projects that contribute directly to achieving MDGs in developing countries. UNDP supports other efforts to promote international co-operation in the management of chemicals. It was actively involved in the development of a Strategic Approach to International Chemicals Management which was adopted by representatives of 100 governments at an international conference convened in Dubai, UAE, in February 2006.

UNDP works to ensure the effective governance of freshwater and aquatic resources, and promotes co-operation in transboundary water management. It works closely with other agencies to promote safe sanitation, ocean and coastal management, and community water supplies. In 1996 UNDP, with the World Bank and the Swedish International Development Agency, established a Global Water Partnership to promote and implement water resources management. UNDP, with the Global Environment Facility (GEF), supports an extensive range of projects which incorporate development and ecological requirements in the sustainable management of international waters. These include the Global Mercury Project, The Yellow Sea Large Marine Ecosystem project, the Dnipro Basin Environment Programme, and projects in the Gulf of Guinea, Lake Tanganyika, and the Red Sea and Gulf of Aden.

CRISIS PREVENTION AND RECOVERY

UNDP collaborates with other UN agencies in countries in crisis and with special circumstances to promote relief and development efforts, in order to secure the foundations for sustainable human development and thereby increase national capabilities to prevent or pre-empt future crises. In particular, UNDP is concerned to achieve reconciliation, reintegration and reconstruction in affected countries, as well as to support emergency interventions and management and delivery of programme aid. It aims to facilitate the transition from relief to longer-term recovery and rehabilitation. Special development initiatives include the demobilization of former combatants and destruction of illicit small armaments, rehabilitation of communities for the sustainable reintegration of returning populations and the restoration and strengthening of democratic institutions. UNDP is seeking to incorporate conflict prevention into its development strategies. UNDP has established a mine action unit within its Bureau for Crisis Prevention and Recovery in order to strengthen national and local de-mining capabilities including surveying, mapping and clearance of anti-personnel landmines. UNDP also works closely with UNICEF to raise mine awareness and implement risk reduction education programmes, and manages global partnership projects concerned with training, legislation and the socio-economic impact of anti-personnel devices.

UNDP is the focal point within the UN system for strengthening national capacities for natural disaster reduction (prevention, preparedness and mitigation relating to natural, environmental and technological hazards). UNDP's Bureau of Crisis Prevention and Recovery, in conjunction with the Office for the Co-ordination of Humanitarian Affairs and the secretariat of the International Strategy for Disaster Reduction, oversees the system-wide Capacity for Disaster Reduction Initiative (CADRI). CADRI was inaugurated in 2007, superseding the former United Nations Disaster Management Training Programme. In February 2004 UNDP introduced a Disaster Risk Index that enabled vulnerability and risk to be measured and compared between countries and demonstrated the correspondence between human development and death rates following natural disasters. UNDP was actively involved in preparations for the second World Conference on Disaster Reduction, which was held in Kobe, Japan, in January 2005. During 2005 the Inter-Agency Standing Committee, concerned with co-ordinating the international response to humanitarian disasters, developed a concept of providing assistance through a 'cluster' approach, comprising nine core areas of activity. UNDP was designated the lead agency for the Early Reconstruction and Recovery cluster, linking the immediate needs following a disaster with medium- and long-term recovery efforts.

Special development initiatives undertaken by UNDP in Africa include the demobilization and reintegration of soldiers in Angola and Mali; environmental rehabilitation to resettle displaced populations in the Horn of Africa; and government capacity-building for programme planning and monitoring in Rwanda. UNDP manages a Small Arms Reduction Programme for the Great Lakes Region and supports a plan of action, agreed in November 2003 by representatives of governments in that region, that aims to strengthen anti-small arms legislation and its implementation. Also in 2003 UNDP initiated an 'Arms for Development' scheme in Sierra Leone to help eliminate weapons and rehabilitate community infrastructure. In 2006 UNDP published small arms survey evaluations on the Central African Republic, Republic of the Congo, Kenya, Niger and Sierra Leone.

HIV/AIDS

UNDP regards the HIV/AIDS pandemic as a major challenge to development, and advocates for making HIV/AIDS a focus of national planning; supports decentralized action against HIV/AIDS at community level; helps to strengthen national capacities at all levels to combat the disease; and aims to link support for prevention activities, education and treatment with broader development planning and responses. UNDP places a particular focus on combating the spread of HIV/AIDS through the promotion of women's rights. UNDP is a co-sponsor, jointly with WHO, the World Bank, UNICEF, UNESCO, UNODC, ILO, UNFPA, WFP and UNHCR, of the Joint UN Programme on HIV/AIDS (UNAIDS), which became operational on 1 January 1996. UNAIDS co-ordinates UNDP's HIV and Development Programme.

UNDP administers a global programme concerned with intellectual property and access to HIV/AIDS drugs, to promote wider and cheaper access to antiretroviral drugs. In December 2005 the World Trade Organization agreed to amend the agreement on Trade-Related Aspects of Intellectual Property Rights (TRIPS) to allow countries without a pharmaceutical manufacturing capability to import generic copies of patented medicines.

Finance

UNDP and its various funds and programmes are financed by the voluntary contributions of members of the United Nations and the Programme's participating agencies, as well as through cost-sharing by recipient governments and third-party donors. In 2004–05 total voluntary contributions were projected at US $3,500m., of which a projected $1,700m. constituted regular (core) resources and $1,807m. third-party co-financing and thematic trust fund income. Cost-sharing by programme country governments was projected at $2,100m., bringing total resources (both donor and local) to a projected $5,600m.

Publications

Annual Report of the Administrator.

Choices (quarterly).

Human Development Report (annually).

Poverty Report (annually).

Results-Oriented Annual Report.

Associated Funds and Programmes

UNDP is the central funding, planning and co-ordinating body for technical co-operation within the UN system. A number of associated funds and programmes, financed separately by means of voluntary contributions, provide specific services through the UNDP network. UNDP manages a trust fund to promote economic and technical co-operation among developing countries.

CAPACITY 2015

UNDP initiated Capacity 2015 at the World Summit for Sustainable Development, which was held in August–September 2002. Capacity 2015 aims to support developing countries in expanding their capabilities to meet the Millennium Development Goals pledged by governments at a summit meeting of the UN General Assembly in September 2000.

GLOBAL ENVIRONMENT FACILITY (GEF)

The GEF, which is managed jointly by UNDP, the World Bank (which hosts its secretariat) and UNEP, began operations in 1991 and was restructured in 1994. Its aim is to support projects concerning climate change, the conservation of biological diversity, the protection of international waters, reducing the depletion of the ozone layer in the atmosphere, and (since October 2002) arresting land degradation and addressing the issue of persistent organic pollutants. The GEF acts as the financial mechanism for the Convention on Biological Diversity and the UN Framework Convention on Climate Change. UNDP is responsible for capacity-building, targeted research, pre-investment activities and technical assistance. UNDP also administers the Small Grants Programme of the GEF, which supports community-based activities by local non-governmental organizations, and the Country Dialogue Workshop Programme, which promotes dialogue on national priorities with regard to the GEF. In August 2006 some 32 donor countries pledged US $3,130m. for the fourth periodic replenishment of GEF funds (GEF-4), covering the period 2007–10. During 1991–2006 the GEF allocated $6,200m. in grants and raised $20,000m. in co-financing from other sources in support of more than 1,800 projects.

Chair. and CEO: MONIQUE BARBUT (France).

MONTREAL PROTOCOL

Through its Montreal Protocol Unit UNDP collaborates with public and private partners in developing countries to assist them in eliminating the use of ozone-depleting substances (ODS), in accordance with the Montreal Protocol to the Vienna Convention for the Protection of the Ozone Layer, through the design, monitoring and evaluation of ODS phase-out projects and programmes. In particular, UNDP provides technical assistance and training, national capacity-building and demonstration projects and technology transfer investment projects. By December 2005 the Executive Committee of the Montreal Protocol had approved grants for projects and activities that had resulted in in the elimination of about 190,661 metric tons of ODS production.

UNDP DRYLANDS DEVELOPMENT CENTRE (DDC)

The Centre, based in Nairobi, Kenya, was established in February 2002, superseding the former UN Office to Combat Desertification and Drought (UNSO). (UNSO had been established following the conclusion, in October 1994, of the UN Convention to Combat Desertification in Those Countries Experiencing Serious Drought and/or Desertification, Particularly in Africa; in turn, UNSO had replaced the former UN Sudano-Sahelian Office.) The DDC was to focus on the following areas: ensuring that national development planning takes account of the needs of dryland communities, particularly in poverty reduction strategies; helping countries to cope with the effects of climate variability, especially drought, and to prepare for future climate change; and addressing local issues affecting the utilization of resources.

Director: PHILIP DOBIE (United Kingdom).

UNITED NATIONS CAPITAL DEVELOPMENT FUND (UNCDF)

The Fund was established in 1966 and became fully operational in 1974. It invests in poor communities in least-developed countries through local governance projects and microfinance operations, with the aim of increasing such communities' access to essential local infrastructure and services and thereby improving their productive capacities and self-reliance. UNDCF encourages participation by local people and local governments in the planning, implementation and monitoring of projects. The Fund aims to promote the interests of women in community projects and to enhance their earning capacities. A Special Unit for Microfinance (SUM), established in 1997 as a joint UNDP/UNCDF operation, was fully integrated into UNCDF in 1999. UNDCF/SUM helps to develop financial services for poor communities and supports UNDP's MicroStart initiative. UNCDF was a co-sponsor of the International Year of Microcredit in 2005 and hosts the UN high-level Advisors Group on Inclusive Financial Sectors. In 2006 UNCDF supported local development programmes and funds in 23 countries. Programme expenditure in that year amounted to US $25.2m.

Executive Secretary: RICHARD WEINGARTEN (USA).

UNITED NATIONS DEVELOPMENT FUND FOR WOMEN (UNIFEM)

UNIFEM is the UN's lead agency in addressing the issues relating to women in development and promoting the rights of women worldwide. The Fund provides direct financial and technical support to enable low-income women in developing countries to increase earnings, gain access to labour-saving technologies and otherwise improve the quality of their lives. It also funds activities that include women in decision-making related to mainstream development projects. UNIFEM's Trust Fund in Support of Actions to Eliminate Violence Against Women (established in 1996) awarded grants in excess of US $13.0m. in support of more than 230 initiatives in around 100 countries during 1996–March 2007. UNIFEM has supported the preparation of national reports in 30 countries and used the priorities identified in these reports and in other regional initiatives to formulate a Women's Development Agenda for the 21st century. Through these efforts, UNIFEM played an active role in the preparation for the UN Fourth World Conference on Women, which was held in Beijing, People's Republic of China, in September 1995. UNIFEM participated at a special session of the General Assembly convened in June 2000 to review the conference, entitled Women 2000: Gender Equality, Development and Peace for the 21st Century (Beijing + 5). In March 2001 UNIFEM, in collaboration with International Alert, launched a Millennium Peace Prize for Women. UNIFEM maintains that the empowerment of women is a key to combating the HIV/AIDS pandemic, in view of the fact that women and adolescent girls are often culturally, biologically and economically more vulnerable to infection and more likely to bear responsibility for caring for the sick. In March 2002 UNIFEM launched a three-year programme aimed at making the gender and human rights dimensions of the pandemic central to policy-making in 10 countries. A new online resource (www.genderandaids.org) on the gender dimensions of HIV/AIDS was launched in February 2003. UNIFEM was a co-founder of WomenWatch (accessible online at www.un.org/womenwatch), a UN system-wide resource for the advancement of gender equality. Following the massive earthquake and tsunamis that struck parts of the Indian Ocean in late December 2004, UNIFEM undertook to promote the needs and rights of women and girls in all emergency relief and reconstruction efforts, in particular in Indonesia, Sri Lanka and Somalia, and supported capacity-building of grass-roots organizations. Programme expenditure in 2005 totalled $55.8m.

Director: (vacant); Headquarters: 304 East 45th St, 15th Floor, New York, NY 10017, USA; tel. (212) 906-6400; fax (212) 906-6705; e-mail unifem@undp.org; internet www.unifem.org.

UNITED NATIONS VOLUNTEERS (UNV)

The United Nations Volunteers is an important source of middle-level skills for the UN development system supplied at modest cost, particularly in the least-developed countries. Volunteers expand the scope of UNDP project activities by supplementing the work of international and host-country experts and by extending the influence of projects to local community levels. UNV also supports technical co-operation within and among the developing countries by encouraging volunteers from the countries themselves and by forming regional exchange teams comprising such volunteers. UNV is involved in areas such as peace-building, elections, human rights, humanitarian relief and community-based environmental programmes, in addition to development activities.

The UN International Short-term Advisory (UNISTAR) Programme, which is the private-sector development arm of UNV, has increasingly focused its attention on countries in the process of economic transition. Since 1994 UNV has administered UNDP's Transfer of Knowledge Through Expatriate Nationals (TOKTEN) programme, which was initiated in 1977 to enable specialists and professionals from developing countries to contribute to development efforts in their countries of origin through short-term technical assignments.

At the end of December 2006 5,204 UNVs were serving in 134 countries. At that time the total number of people who had served under the initiative amounted to more than 30,000 in over 140 countries.

In December 2006 some 55% of all UNVs were serving in Africa, with the largest UNV programmes being undertaken in the Democratic Republic of the Congo and Liberia.

Executive Co-ordinator: AD DE RAAD (Netherlands); Headquarters: POB 260111, 53153 Bonn, Germany; tel. (228) 8152000; fax (228) 8152001; e-mail information@unvolunteers.org; internet www.unv.org.

United Nations Environment Programme—UNEP

Address: POB 30552, Nairobi, Kenya.

Telephone: (20) 621234; **fax:** (20) 624489; **e-mail:** cpiinfo@unep.org; **internet:** www.unep.org.

The United Nations Environment Programme was established in 1972 by the UN General Assembly, following recommendations of the 1972 UN Conference on the Human Environment, in Stockholm, Sweden, to encourage international co-operation in matters relating to the human environment.

Organization

(September 2007)

GOVERNING COUNCIL

The main functions of the Governing Council, which meets every two years, are to promote international co-operation in the field of the environment and to provide general policy guidance for the direction and co-ordination of environmental programmes within the UN system. It comprises representatives of 58 states, elected by the UN General Assembly, for four-year terms, on a regional basis. The Council is assisted in its work by a Committee of Permanent Representatives.

HIGH-LEVEL COMMITTEE OF MINISTERS AND OFFICIALS IN CHARGE OF THE ENVIRONMENT

The Committee was established by the Governing Council in 1997, with a mandate to consider the international environmental agenda and to make recommendations to the Council on reform and policy issues. In addition, the Committee, comprising 36 elected members, was to provide guidance and advice to the Executive Director, to enhance UNEP's collaboration and co-operation with other multilateral bodies and to help to mobilize financial resources for UNEP.

SECRETARIAT

Offices and divisions at UNEP headquarters include the Office of the Executive Director; the Secretariat for Governing Bodies: Offices for Evaluation and Oversight, Programme Co-ordination and Management, and Resource Mobilization; and divisions of communications and public information, early warning and assessment, policy development and law, policy implementation, technology and industry and economics, regional co-operation and representation, environmental conventions, and Global Environment Facility co-ordination.

Executive Director: ACHIM STEINER (Germany).

REGIONAL OFFICES

Africa: POB 30552, Nairobi, Kenya; tel. (20) 624292; fax (20) 623928; e-mail roainfo@unep.org; internet www.unep.org/roa.

UNEP Liaison Office in Addis Ababa: ECA New Bldg, 4th Floor, No. 4NC4–4N13, POB 3001, Addis Ababa, Ethiopia; tel. (1) 443431; fax (1) 521633; e-mail unepoffice@uneca.org.

OTHER OFFICES

Convention on International Trade in Endangered Species of Wild Fauna and Flora (CITES): 15 chemin des Anémones, 1219 Châtelaine, Geneva, Switzerland; tel. 229178139; fax 227973417; e-mail info@cites.org; internet www.cites.org; Sec.-Gen. WILLEM WOUTER WIJNSTEKERS (Netherlands).

Global Programme of Action for the Protection of the Marine Environment from Land-based Activities: POB 16227, 2500 BE The Hague, Netherlands; tel. (70) 3114460; fax (70) 3456648; e-mail gpa@unep.nl; internet www.gpa.unep.org; Co-ordinator Dr VEERLE VANDEWEERD.

Secretariat of the Basel Convention: CP 356, 13–15 chemin des Anémones, 1219 Châtelaine, Geneva, Switzerland; tel. 229178218; fax 227973454; e-mail sbc@unep.ch; internet www.basel.int; Exec. Sec. KATHERINA KUMMER PEIRY.

Secretariat of the Multilateral Fund for the Implementation of the Montreal Protocol: 1800 McGill College Ave, 27th Floor, Montréal, QC, Canada H3A 3J6; tel. (514) 282-1122; fax (514) 282-0068; e-mail secretariat@unmfs.org; internet www.multilateralfund.org; Chief Officer MARIA NOLAN.

Secretariat of the UN Framework Convention on Climate Change: Haus Carstanjen, Martin-Luther-King-Str. 8, 53175 Bonn, Germany; tel. (228) 815-1000; fax (228) 815-1999; e-mail secretariat@unfccc.int; internet www.unfccc.int; Exec. Sec. YVO DE BOER (Netherlands).

UNEP/CMS (Convention on the Conservation of Migratory Species of Wild Animals) Secretariat: Hermann-Ehlers-Str. 10, 53113 Bonn, Germany; tel. (228) 8152402; fax (228) 8152449; e-mail secretariat@cms.int; internet www.cms.int; Exec. Sec. ROBERT HEPWORTH.

UNEP Chemicals: International Environment House, 11–13 chemin des Anémones, 1219 Châtelaine, Geneva, Switzerland; tel. 229178192; fax 227973460; e-mail chemicals@unep.ch; internet www.chem.unep.ch; Dir Dr MAGED YOUNES.

UNEP Division of Technology, Industry and Economics: Tour Mirabeau, 39–43, Quai André Citroën, 75739 Paris Cédex 15, France; tel. 1-44-37-14-41; fax 1-44-37-14-74; e-mail unep.tie@unep.fr; internet www.unep.fr; Dir SILVIE LEMMET (France).

UNEP International Environmental Technology Centre (IETC): 2–110 Ryokuchi koen, Tsurumi-ku, Osaka 538-0036, Japan; tel. (6) 6915-4581; fax (6) 6915-0304; e-mail ietc@unep.or.jp; internet www.unep.or.jp; Exec. Dir PER MENZONY BAKKEN (Norway).

UNEP Ozone Secretariat: POB 30552, Nairobi, Kenya; tel. (20) 762-3850; fax (20) 762-4691; e-mail ozoneinfo@unep.org; internet ozone.unep.org; Exec. Sec. MARCO GONZÁLEZ (Costa Rica).

UNEP-SCBD (Convention on Biological Diversity—Secretariat): 413 St Jacques St, Office 800, Montréal, QC, Canada H2Y 1N9; tel. (514) 288-2220; fax (514) 288-6588; e-mail secretariat@cbd.int; internet www.cbd.int; Exec. Sec. AHMED DJOGHLAF (Algeria).

UNEP Secretariat for the UN Scientific Committee on the Effects of Atomic Radiation: Vienna International Centre, Wagramerstrasse 5, POB 500, 1400 Vienna, Austria; tel. (1) 26060-4330; fax (1) 26060-5902; e-mail malcolm.crick@unscear.org; internet www.unscear.org; Sec. Dr MALCOLM CRICK.

Activities

UNEP serves as a focal point for environmental action within the UN system. It aims to maintain a constant watch on the changing state of the environment; to analyse the trends; to assess the problems using a wide range of data and techniques; and to promote projects leading to environmentally sound development. It plays a catalytic and co-ordinating role within and beyond the UN system. Many UNEP projects are implemented in co-operation with other UN agencies, particularly UNDP, the World Bank group, FAO, UNESCO and WHO. About 45 intergovernmental organizations outside the UN system and 60 international non-governmental organizations have official observer status on UNEP's Governing Council, and, through the Environment Liaison Centre in Nairobi, UNEP is linked to more than 6,000 non-governmental bodies concerned with the environment. UNEP also sponsors international conferences, programmes, plans and agreements regarding all aspects of the environment.

In February 1997 the Governing Council, at its 19th session, adopted a ministerial declaration (the Nairobi Declaration) on UNEP's future role and mandate, which recognized the organization as the principal UN body working in the field of the environment and as the leading global environmental authority, setting and overseeing the international environmental agenda. In June a special session of the UN General Assembly, referred to as 'Rio + 5', was convened to review the state of the environment and progress achieved in implementing the objectives of the UN Conference on Environment and Development (UNCED), held in Rio de Janeiro, Brazil, in June 1992. The meeting adopted a Programme for Further Implementation of Agenda 21 (a programme of activities to promote sustainable development, adopted by UNCED) in order to intensify efforts in areas such as energy, freshwater resources and technology transfer. The meeting confirmed UNEP's essential role in advancing the Programme and as a global authority promoting a coherent legal and political approach to the environmental challenges of sustainable development. An extensive process of restructuring and realignment of functions was subsequently initiated by UNEP, and a new organizational structure reflecting the decisions of the Nairobi Declaration was implemented during 1999. UNEP played a leading role in preparing for the World Summit on Sustainable Development (WSSD), held in August–September 2002 in Johannesburg, South Africa, to assess strategies for strengthening the implementation of Agenda 21. Governments participating in the conference adopted the Johannesburg Declaration and WSSD Plan of Implementation, in which they strongly reaffirmed commitment to the principles underlying Agenda 21 and also pledged support to all internationally-agreed development goals, including the UN Millennium Development Goals adopted by governments attending a summit meeting of the UN General Assembly in September 2000. Participating governments made concrete commitments to attaining several specific objectives in the areas of water, energy, health, agriculture and fisheries, and biodiversity. These included a reduction by one-half in the proportion of people world-wide lacking access to clean water or good sanitation by 2015, the restocking of depleted fisheries by 2015, a reduction in the ongoing loss in biodiversity by 2010, and the production and utilization of chemicals without causing harm to human beings and the environment by 2020. Participants determined to increase usage of renewable energy sources and to develop integrated water resources management and water efficiency plans. A large number of partnerships between governments, private-sector interests and civil society groups were announced at the conference.

In May 2000 UNEP sponsored the first annual Global Ministerial Environment Forum (GMEF), held in Malmö, Sweden, and attended by environment ministers and other government delegates from more than 130 countries. Participants reviewed policy issues in the field of the environment and addressed issues such as the impact on the environment of population growth, the depletion of earth's natural resources, climate change and the need for fresh water supplies. The Forum issued the Malmö Declaration, which identified the effective implementation of international agreements on environmental matters at national level as the most pressing challenge for policy-makers. The Declaration emphasized the importance of mobilizing domestic and international resources and urged increased co-operation from civil society and the private sector in achieving sustainable development. The second GMEF, held in Nairobi in February 2001, addressed means of strengthening international environmental governance, establishing an Open-Ended Intergovernmental Group of Ministers or Their Representatives (IGM) to prepare a report on possible reforms. GMEF-6, held in February 2006 in Dubai, United Arab Emirates, considered energy and the environment and chemicals management.

ENVIRONMENTAL ASSESSMENT AND EARLY WARNING

The Nairobi Declaration resolved that the strengthening of UNEP's information, monitoring and assessment capabilities was a crucial element of the organization's restructuring, in order to help establish priorities for international, national and regional action, and to ensure the efficient and accurate dissemination of emerging environmental trends and emergencies.

In 1995 UNEP launched the Global Environment Outlook (GEO) process of environmental assessment. UNEP is assisted in its analysis of the state of the global environment by an extensive network of collaborating centres. The *GEO Year Book* is published annually. The following regional and national *GEO* reports have been produced in recent years: *Africa Environment Outlook* (2002), *Brazil Environment Outlook* (2002), *Caucasus Environment Outlook* (2002), *North America's Environment* (2002), *Latin America and the Caribbean Environment Outlook* (2003), *Andean Environment Outlook* (2003), *Pacific Environment Outlook* (2005), *Caribbean Environment Outlook* (2005), and *Atlantic and Indian Oceans Environment Outlook* (2005). UNEP is leading a major Global International Waters Assessment (GIWA) to consider all aspects of the world's water-related issues, in particular problems of shared transboundary waters, and of future sustainable management of water resources. UNEP is also a sponsoring agency of the Joint Group of Experts on the Scientific Aspects of Marine Environmental Pollution and contributes to the preparation of reports on the state of the marine environment and on the impact of land-based activities on that environment. In November 1995 UNEP published a Global Biodiversity Assessment, which was the first comprehensive study of biological resources throughout the world. The UNEP—World Conservation Monitoring Centre (UNEP—WCMC), established in June 2000, provides biodiversity-related assessment. UNEP is a partner in the International Coral Reef Action Network—ICRAN, which was established in 2000 to manage and protect coral reefs world-wide. In June 2001 UNEP launched the Millennium Ecosystems Assessment, which was completed in March 2005. Other major assessments undertaken included GIWA (see above); the Assessment of Impact and Adaptation to Climate Change; the Solar and Wind Energy Resource Assessment; the Regionally-Based Assessment of Persistent Toxic Substances; the Land Degradation Assessment in Drylands; and the Global Methodology for Mapping Human Impacts on the Biosphere (GLOBIO) project. In July 2007 UNEP launched the 2010 Biodiversity Indicator Partnership (2010BIP), which aimed to monitor conservation efforts to protect global biological diversity.

UNEP's environmental information network includes the Global Resource Information Database (GRID), which converts collected data into information usable by decision-makers. The UNEP-INFOTERRA programme facilitates the exchange of environmental information through an extensive network of national 'focal points'. By July 2007 177 countries were participating in the network. Through UNEP-INFOTERRA UNEP promotes public access to environmental information, as well as participation in environmental concerns. UNEP aims to establish in every developing region an Environment and Natural Resource Information Network (ENRIN) in order to make available technical advice and manage environmental information and data for improved decision-making and action-planning in countries most in need of assistance. UNEP aims to integrate its information resources in order to improve access to information and to promote its international exchange. This has been pursued through UNEPnet, an internet-based interactive environmental information- and data-sharing facility.

UNEP's information, monitoring and assessment structures also serve to enhance early-warning capabilities and to provide accurate information during an environmental emergency.

POLICY DEVELOPMENT AND LAW

UNEP aims to promote the development of policy tools and guidelines in order to achieve the sustainable management of the world environment. At a national level it assists governments to develop and implement appropriate environmental instruments and aims to co-ordinate policy initiatives. Training workshops in various aspects of environmental law and its applications are conducted. UNEP supports the development of new legal, economic and other policy instruments to improve the effectiveness of existing environmental agreements.

UNEP was instrumental in the drafting of a Convention on Biological Diversity (CBD) to preserve the immense variety of plant and animal species, in particular those threatened with extinction. The Convention entered into force at the end of 1993; by July 2007 189 states parties and the European Community were parties to the CBD. The CBD's Cartagena Protocol on Biosafety (so called as it had been addressed at an extraordinary session of parties to the CBD convened in Cartagena, Colombia, in February 1999) was adopted at a meeting of parties to the CBD held in Montréal, Canada, in January 2000, and entered into force in September 2003; by June 2007 the Protocol had been ratified by 140 states parties and the European Community. The Protocol regulates the transboundary movement and use of living modified organisms resulting from biotechnology in order to reduce any potential adverse effects on biodiversity and human health. It establishes an Advanced Informed Agreement procedure to govern the import of such organisms. In January 2002 UNEP launched a major project aimed at supporting developing countries with assessing the potential health and environmental risks and benefits of genetically modified (GM) crops, in preparation for the Protocol's entry into force. In February the parties to the CBD and other partners convened a conference, in Montréal, to address ways in which the traditional knowledge and practices of local communities could be preserved and used to conserve highly threatened species and ecosystems. The sixth conference of parties to the CBD, held in April 2002, adopted detailed voluntary guide-lines concerning access to genetic resources and sharing the benefits attained from such resources with the countries and local communities where they originate; a global work programme on forests; and a set of guiding principles for combating alien invasive species. UNEP supports co-operation for biodiversity assessment and management in selected developing regions and for the development of strategies for the conservation and sustainable exploitation of individual threatened species (e.g. the Global Tiger Action Plan). It also provides assistance for the preparation of individual country studies and strategies to strengthen national biodiversity management and research. UNEP administers the Convention on International Trade in Endangered Species of Wild Flora and Fauna (CITES), which entered into force in 1975.

In May 2001 UNEP launched the Great Apes Survival Project (GRASP), which supports, in 23 countries in Africa and South-East Asia, the conservation of gorillas, chimpanzees, orang-utans and bonobos. GRASP's first intergovernmental meeting, held in Kinshasa, Democratic Republic of the Congo in September 2005, was attended by representatives of governments of great ape habitat states, donor and other interested states, international organizations, NGOs, and private-sector and academic interests. The meeting adopted a Global Strategy for the Survival of Great Apes, and the Kinshasa Declaration pledged commitment and action towards achieving this goal.

In October 1994 87 countries, meeting under UN auspices, signed a Convention to Combat Desertification (see UNDP Drylands Development Centre), which aimed to provide a legal framework to counter the degradation of drylands. An estimated 75% of all drylands have suffered some land degradation, affecting approximately 1,000m. people in 110 countries. UNEP continues to support the implementation of the Convention, as part of its efforts to protect land resources. UNEP also aims to improve the assessment of dryland degradation and desertification in co-operation with governments and other international bodies, as well as identifying the causes of degradation and measures to overcome these.

UNEP is the lead UN agency for promoting environmentally sustainable water management. It regards the unsustainable use of water as the most urgent environmental and sustainable development issue, and estimates that two-thirds of the world's population will suffer chronic water shortages by 2025, owing to rising demand for drinking water as a result of growing populations, decreasing quality of water because of pollution, and increasing requirements of industries and agriculture. In 2000 UNEP adopted a new water policy and strategy, comprising assessment, management and co-ordination components. The Global International Waters Assessment (see above) is the primary framework for the assessment component. The management component includes the Global Programme of Action (GPA) for the Protection of the Marine Environment from Land-based Activities (adopted in November 1995), and UNEP's freshwater programme and regional seas programme. The GPA for the Protection of the Marine Environment for Land-based Activities focuses on the effects of activities such as pollution on freshwater resources, marine biodiversity and the coastal ecosystems of small-island developing states. UNEP aims to develop a similar global instrument to ensure the integrated management of freshwater resources. It promotes international co-operation in the management of river basins and coastal areas and for the development of tools and guide-lines to achieve the sustainable management of freshwater and coastal resources. UNEP provides scientific, technical and administrative support to facilitate the implementation and co-ordination of 14 regional seas conventions and 13 regional plans of action, and is developing a strategy to strengthen collaboration in their implementation. The new water policy and strategy emphasizes the need for improved co-ordination of existing activities. UNEP aims to play an enhanced role within relevant co-ordination mechanisms, such as the UN open-ended informal consultation process on oceans and the law of the sea.

In 1996 UNEP, in collaboration with FAO, began to work towards promoting and formulating a legally binding international convention on prior informed consent (PIC) for hazardous chemicals and pesticides in international trade, extending a voluntary PIC procedure of information exchange undertaken by more than 100 governments since 1991. The Convention was adopted at a conference held in Rotterdam, Netherlands, in September 1998, and entered into force in February 2004. It aims to reduce risks to human health and the environment by restricting the production, export and use of hazardous substances and enhancing information exchange procedures.

In conjunction with UN-Habitat, UNDP, the World Bank and other organizations and institutions, UNEP promotes environmental concerns in urban planning and management through the Sustainable Cities Programme, as well as regional workshops concerned with urban pollution and the impact of transportation systems. In 1994 UNEP inaugurated an International Environmental Technology Centre (IETC), with offices in Osaka and Shiga, Japan, in order to strengthen the capabilities of developing countries and countries with economies in transition to promote environmentally sound management of cities and freshwater reservoirs through technology co-operation and partnerships.

UNEP has played a key role in global efforts to combat risks to the ozone layer, resultant climatic changes and atmospheric pollution. UNEP worked in collaboration with the World Meteorological Organization to formulate the UN Framework Convention on Climate Change (UNFCCC), with the aim of reducing the emission of gases that have a warming effect on the atmosphere, and has remained an active participant in the ongoing process to review and enforce the implementation of the Convention and of its Kyoto Protocol. UNEP was the lead agency in formulating the 1987 Montreal Protocol to the Vienna Convention for the Protection of the Ozone Layer (1985), which provided for a 50% reduction in the production of chlorofluorocarbons (CFCs) by 2000. An amendment to the Protocol was adopted in 1990, which required complete cessation of the production of CFCs by 2000 in industrialized countries and by 2010 in developing countries. The Copenhagen Amendment, adopted in 1992, stipulated the phasing out of production of hydrochlorofluorocarbons (HCFCs) by 2030 in developed countries and by 2040 in developing nations. In 1997 the ninth Conference of the Parties (COP) to the Vienna Convention adopted a further amendment which aimed to introduce a licensing system for all controlled substances. The eleventh COP, meeting in Beijing, People's Republic of China, in November–December 1999, adopted the Beijing Amendment, which imposed tighter controls on the import and export of HCFCs, and on the production and consumption of bromochloromethane (Halon-1011, an industrial solvent and fire extinguisher). The Beijing Amendment entered into force in December 2001. A Multilateral Fund for the Implementation of the Montreal Protocol was established in June 1990 to promote the use of suitable technologies and the transfer of technologies to developing countries. UNEP, UNDP, the World Bank and UNIDO are the sponsors of the Fund, which by March 2007 had approved financing for about 5,500 projects and activities in 144 developing countries at a cost of around US $2,000m. Commitments of $400.4m. were made to the sixth replenishment of the Fund, covering the three-year period 2006–08. (The total budget for 2006–08 was $470.0m., the remainder deriving from the following sources: $59.6m. to be carried over from the 2003–05 triennium and $10m. to be provided from interest accruing.)

POLICY IMPLEMENTATION

UNEP's Division of Environmental Policy Implementation incorporates two main functions: technical co-operation and response to environmental emergencies.

With the UN Office for the Co-ordination of Humanitarian Assistance (OCHA), UNEP has established a joint Environment Unit to mobilize and co-ordinate international assistance and expertise for countries facing environmental emergencies and natural disasters. In mid-1999 UNEP and UN-Habitat jointly established a Balkan Task Force (subsequently renamed UNEP Balkans Unit) to assess the environmental impact of NATO's aerial offensive against the then Federal Republic of Yugoslavia. In November 2000 the Unit led a field assessment to evaluate reports of environmental contamination by debris from NATO ammunition containing depleted uranium. A final report, issued by UNEP in March 2001, concluded that there was no evidence of widespread contamination of the ground surface by depleted uranium and that the radiological and toxicological risk to the local population was negligible. It stated, however, that considerable scientific uncertainties remained, for example as to the safety of groundwater and the longer-term behaviour of depleted uranium in the environment, and recommended precautionary action. In December 2001 UNEP established a Post-conflict Assessment Unit, which replaced, and extended the scope of, the Balkans Unit. In 2007 the Post-conflict Assessment Unit was engaged in Afghanistan, Iraq, Lebanon, Liberia, the Palestinian territories, Somalia and Sudan.

UNEP, together with UNDP and the World Bank, is an implementing agency of the Global Environment Facility (GEF), which was established in 1991 as a mechanism for international co-operation in projects concerned with biological diversity, climate change, international waters and depletion of the ozone layer. UNEP services the Scientific and Technical Advisory Panel, which provides expert advice on GEF programmes and operational strategies. In July 2004 UNEP announced a new three-year initiative to strengthen the legal framework to protect the environment of the Western Indian Ocean. Eight countries—Comoros, Kenya, Madagascar, Mauritius, Mozambique, the Seychelles, South Africa and Tanzania—were to participate in the project, which was to be financed by the GEF and the Government of Norway.

TECHNOLOGY, INDUSTRY AND ECONOMICS

The use of inappropriate industrial technologies and the widespread adoption of unsustainable production and consumption patterns have been identified as being inefficient in the use of renewable resources and wasteful, in particular in the use of energy and water. UNEP aims to encourage governments and the private sector to develop and adopt policies and practices that are cleaner and safer, make efficient use of natural resources, incorporate environmental costs, ensure the environmentally sound management of chemicals, and reduce pollution and risks to human health and the environment. In collaboration with other organizations and agencies UNEP works to define and formulate international guide-lines and agreements to address these issues. UNEP also promotes the transfer of appropriate technologies and organizes conferences and training workshops to provide sustainable production practices. Relevant information is disseminated through the International Cleaner Production Information Clearing House. UNEP, together with UNIDO, has established 27 National Cleaner Production Centres to promote a preventive approach to industrial pollution control. In October 1998 UNEP adopted an International Declaration on Cleaner Production, with a commitment to implement cleaner and more sustainable production methods and to monitor results; the Declaration had 529 signatories at January 2005, including representatives of 54 national governments. In 1997 UNEP and the Coalition for Environmentally Responsible Economies initiated the Global Reporting Initiative, which, with participation by corporations, business associations and other organizations and stakeholders, develops guide-lines for voluntary reporting by companies on their economic, environmental and social performance. In April 2002 UNEP launched the 'Life-Cycle Initiative', which aims to assist governments, businesses and other consumers with adopting environmentally sound policies and practice, in view of the upward trend in global consumption patterns.

UNEP provides institutional servicing to the Basel Convention on the Control of Transboundary Movements of Hazardous Wastes and their Disposal, which was adopted in 1989 with the aim of preventing the disposal of wastes from industrialized countries in countries that have no processing facilities. In March 1994 the second meeting of parties to the Convention determined to ban the exportation of hazardous wastes between industrialized and developing countries. The third meeting of parties to the Convention, held in 1995, proposed that the ban should be incorporated into the Convention as an amendment. The resulting so-called Ban Amendment (prohibiting exports of hazardous wastes for final disposal and recycling from states and/or parties also belonging to OECD and, or, the European Union, and from Liechtenstein, to any other state party to the Convention) required ratification by three-quarters of the 62 signatory states present at the time of adoption before it could enter into effect; by July 2007 the Ban Amendment had been ratified by 63 parties. In 1998 the technical working group of the Convention agreed a new procedure for clarifying the classification and characterization of specific hazardous wastes. The fifth full meeting of parties to the Convention, held in December 1999, adopted the Basel Declaration outlining an agenda for the period 2000–10, with a particular focus on minimizing the production of hazardous wastes. At July 2007 the number of parties to the Convention totalled 170. In December 1999 132 states adopted a Protocol to the Convention to address issues relating to liability and compensation for damages from waste exports. The governments also agreed to establish a multilateral fund to finance immediate clean-up operations following any environmental accident.

The UNEP Chemicals office was established to promote the sound management of hazardous substances, central to which has been the International Register of Potentially Toxic Chemicals (IRPTC). UNEP aims to facilitate access to data on chemicals and hazardous wastes, in order to assess and control health and environmental risks, by using the IRPTC as a clearing house facility of relevant information and by publishing information and technical reports on the impact of the use of chemicals.

A Pollutant Release and Transfer Register (PRTR), for collecting and disseminating data on toxic emissions, is under development in South Africa.

UNEP's OzonAction Programme works to promote information exchange, training and technological awareness. Its objective is to strengthen the capacity of governments and industry in developing countries to undertake measures towards the cost-effective phasing-out of ozone-depleting substances. UNEP also encourages the development of alternative and renewable sources of energy. To achieve this, UNEP is supporting the establishment of a network of centres to research and exchange information of environmentally sound energy technology resources.

REGIONAL CO-OPERATION AND REPRESENTATION

UNEP maintains six regional offices. These work to initiate and promote UNEP objectives and to ensure that all programme formulation and delivery meets the specific needs of countries and regions. They also provide a focal point for building national, sub-regional and regional partnership and enhancing local participation in UNEP initiatives. Following UNEP's reorganization a co-ordination office was established at headquarters to promote regional policy integration, to co-ordinate programme planning, and to provide necessary services to the regional offices.

UNEP provides administrative support to several regional conventions, for example the Lusaka Agreement on Co-operative Enforcement Operations Directed at Illegal Trade in Wild Flora and Fauna, which entered into force in December 1996 having been concluded under UNEP auspices in order to strengthen the implementation of the CBD and CITES in Eastern and Central Africa. UNEP also organizes conferences, workshops and seminars at national and regional levels, and may extend advisory services or technical assistance to individual governments.

CONVENTIONS

UNEP aims to develop and promote international environmental legislation in order to pursue an integrated response to global environmental issues, to enhance collaboration among existing convention secetariats, and to co-ordinate support to implement the work programmes of international instruments.

UNEP has been an active participant in the formulation of several major conventions (see above). The Division of Environmental Conventions is mandated to assist the Division of Policy Development and Law in the formulation of new agreements or protocols to existing conventions. Following the successful adoption of the Rotterdam Convention in September 1998, UNEP played a leading role in formulating a multilateral agreement to reduce and ultimately eliminate the manufacture and use of Persistent Organic Pollutants (POPs), which are considered to be a major global environmental hazard. The agreement on POPs, concluded in December 2000 at a conference sponsored by UNEP in Johannesburg, South Africa, was adopted by 127 countries in May 2001 and entered into force in May 2004.

UNEP has been designated to provide secretariat functions to a number of global and regional environmental conventions (see above for list of offices).

COMMUNICATIONS AND PUBLIC INFORMATION

UNEP's public education campaigns and outreach programmes promote community involvement in environmental issues. Further communication of environmental concerns is undertaken through the media, an information centre service and special promotional events, including World Environment Day, photography competitions, and the awarding of the Sasakawa Prize (to recognize distinguished service to the environment by individuals and groups) and of the Global 500 Award for Environmental Achievement. In 1996 UNEP initiated a Global Environment Citizenship Programme to promote acknowledgment of the environmental responsibilities of all sectors of society.

Finance

UNEP derives its finances from the regular budget of the United Nations and from voluntary contributions to the Environment Fund. A budget of US $144m. was proposed for the two-year period 2006–07, of which $122m. was for programme activities, $5.8m. for programme support, $10.2m. for management and administration, and $6m. for fund programme reserves.

Publications

Annual Report.
APELL Newsletter (2 a year).
Cleaner Production Newsletter (2 a year).
Climate Change Bulletin (quarterly).
Connect (UNESCO-UNEP newsletter on environmental degradation, quarterly).
Earth Views (quarterly).
Environment Forum (quarterly).
Environmental Law Bulletin (2 a year).
Financial Services Initiative (2 a year).
GEF News (quarterly).
GEO Year Book (annually).
Global Water Review.
GPA Newsletter.
IETC Insight (3 a year).
Industry and Environment Review (quarterly).
Leave it to Us (children's magazine, 2 a year).
Managing Hazardous Waste (2 a year).
Our Planet (quarterly).
OzonAction Newsletter (quarterly).
Tierramerica (weekly).
Tourism Focus (2 a year).
UNEP Chemicals Newsletter (2 a year).
UNEP Update (monthly).
World Atlas of Biodiversity.
World Atlas of Coral Reefs.
World Atlas of Desertification.

Studies, reports (including *Atlantic and Indian Oceans Environment Outlook 2005*), legal texts, technical guide-lines, etc.

United Nations High Commissioner for Refugees—UNHCR

Address: CP 2500, 1211 Geneva 2 dépôt, Switzerland.

Telephone: 227398111; **fax:** 227397312; **e-mail:** unhcr@unhcr.org; **internet:** www.unhcr.org.

The Office of the High Commissioner was established in 1951 to provide international protection for refugees and to seek durable solutions to their problems. In 1981 UNHCR was awarded the Nobel Peace Prize.

Organization

(September 2007)

HIGH COMMISSIONER

The High Commissioner is elected by the United Nations General Assembly on the nomination of the Secretary-General, and is responsible to the General Assembly and to the UN Economic and Social Council (ECOSOC).

High Commissioner: António Manuel de Oliveira Guterres (Portugal).

Deputy High Commissioner: L. Craig Johnstone (USA).

EXECUTIVE COMMITTEE

The Executive Committee of the High Commissioner's Programme (ExCom), established by ECOSOC, gives the High Commissioner policy directives in respect of material assistance programmes and advice in the field of international protection. In addition, it oversees UNHCR's general policies and use of funds. ExCom, which comprises representatives of 66 states, both members and non-members of the UN, meets once a year.

ADMINISTRATION

Headquarters include the Executive Office, comprising the offices of the High Commissioner, the Deputy High Commissioner and the Assistant High Commissioner. The Inspector General, the Director of the UNHCR liaison office in New York, and the Director of the Department of International Protection report directly to the High Commissioner. The other principal administrative units are the Division of Financial and Supply Management, the Division of Human Resources Management, the Division of External Relations, the Division of Information Systems and Telecommunications, the Division of International Protection Services, and the Department of Operations, which is responsible for the five regional bureaux covering Africa; Asia and the Pacific; Europe; the Americas and the Caribbean; and Central Asia, South-West Asia, North Africa and the Middle East; and also includes the Division of Operational Services and the Emergency and Security Service. At July 2006 there were 263 UNHCR offices in 116 countries world-wide. At that time UNHCR employed 6,540 people (including short-term staff), of whom more than 80% were working in the field. In 2006 a Structural and Management Change Process was initiated, with the aim of reviewing and improving UNHCR's processes and structures.

OFFICES IN AFRICA

Regional Office for Central Africa: BP 7248, Kinshasa, Democratic Republic of the Congo; e-mail codki@unhcr.ch.

Regional Office for West Africa: BP 3125, Dakar, Senegal; e-mail senda@unhcr.ch.

Regional Office for Southern Africa: BP 12506, Pretoria 0001, South Africa; e-mail rsapr@unhcr.ch.

Activities

The competence of the High Commissioner extends to any person who, owing to well-founded fear of being persecuted for reasons of race, religion, nationality or political opinion, is outside the country of his or her nationality and is unable or, owing to such fear or for reasons other than personal convenience, remains unwilling to accept the protection of that country; or who, not having a nationality and being outside the country of his or her former habitual residence, is unable or, owing to such fear or for reasons other than personal convenience, is unwilling to return to it. This competence may be extended, by resolutions of the UN General Assembly and decisions of ExCom, to cover certain other 'persons of concern', in addition to refugees meeting these criteria. Refugees who are assisted by other UN agencies, or who have the same rights or obligations as nationals of their country of residence, are outside the mandate of UNHCR.

In recent years there has been a significant shift in UNHCR's focus of activities. Increasingly UNHCR has been called upon to support people who have been displaced within their own country (i.e. with similar needs to those of refugees but who have not crossed an international border) or those threatened with displacement as a result of armed conflict. In addition, greater support has been given to refugees who have returned to their country of origin, to assist their reintegration, and UNHCR is working to enable local communities to support the returnees, frequently through the implementation of Quick Impact Projects (QIPs). In 2004 UNHCR led the formulation of a UN system-wide Strategic Plan for internally displaced persons (IDPs).

UNHCR has been increasingly concerned with the problem of statelessness, where people have no legal nationality, and promotes new accessions to the 1954 Convention Relating to the Status of Stateless Persons and the 1964 Convention on the Reduction of Statelessness.

At December 2005 the total population of concern to UNHCR, based on provisional figures, amounted to 20.8m., compared with 19.2m. in the previous year. At the end of 2005 the refugee population world-wide totalled 8.4m. UNHCR was also concerned with some 1.1m. recently returned refugees, 6.6m. IDPs, 2.4m. stateless persons, 773,492 asylum-seekers, 519,430 returned IDPs, and 960,366 others.

World Refugee Day, sponsored by UNHCR, is held annually on 20 June.

INTERNATIONAL PROTECTION

As laid down in the Statute of the Office, UNHCR's primary function is to extend international protection to refugees and its second function is to seek durable solutions to their problems. In the exercise of its mandate UNHCR seeks to ensure that refugees and asylum-seekers are protected against *refoulement* (forcible return), that they receive asylum, and that they are treated according to internationally recognized standards. UNHCR pursues these objectives by a variety of means that include promoting the conclusion and ratification by states of international conventions for the protection of refugees. UNHCR promotes the adoption of liberal practices of asylum by states, so that refugees and asylum-seekers are granted admission, at least on a temporary basis.

The most comprehensive instrument concerning refugees that has been elaborated at the international level is the 1951 United Nations Convention relating to the Status of Refugees. This Convention, the scope of which was extended by a Protocol adopted in 1967, defines the rights and duties of refugees and contains provisions dealing with a variety of matters which affect the day-to-day lives of refugees. The application of the Convention and its Protocol is supervised by UNHCR. Important provisions for the treatment of refugees are also contained in a number of instruments adopted at the regional level. These include the 1969 Convention Governing the Specific Aspects of Refugee Problems adopted by the Organization of African Unity (now the African Union—AU) member states in 1969, the European Agreement on the Abolition of Visas for Refugees, and the 1969 American Convention on Human Rights.

UNHCR has actively encouraged states to accede to the 1951 United Nations Refugee Convention and the 1967 Protocol: 147 states had acceded to either or both of these basic refugee instruments by December 2006. An increasing number of states have also adopted domestic legislation and/or administrative measures to implement the international instruments, particularly in the field of procedures for the determination of refugee status. UNHCR has sought to address the specific needs of refugee women and children, and has also attempted to deal with the problem of military attacks on refugee camps, by adopting and encouraging the acceptance of a set of principles to ensure the safety of refugees. In recent years it has formulated a strategy designed to address the fundamental causes of refugee flows. In 2001, in response to widespread concern about perceived high numbers of asylum-seekers and large-scale international economic migration and human trafficking, UNHCR initiated a series of Global Consultations on International Protection with the signatories to the 1951 Convention and 1967 Protocol, and other interested parties, with a view to strengthening both the application and scope of international refugee legislation. A consultation of 156 Governments, convened in Geneva, in December 2001, reaffirmed commitment to the central role played by the Convention and Protocol. The final consultation, held in May 2002, focused on durable solutions and the protection of refugee women and children.

Subsequently, based on the findings of the Global Consultations process, UNHCR developed an Agenda on Protection with six main objectives: strengthening the implementation of the 1951 Convention and 1967 Protocol; the protection of refugees within broader migration movements; more equitable sharing of burdens and responsibilities and building of capacities to receive and protect refugees; addressing more effectively security-related concerns; increasing efforts to find durable solutions; and meeting the protection needs of refugee women and children. The Agenda was endorsed by the Executive Council in October 2002. In September of that year the High Commissioner for Refugees launched the *Convention Plus* initiative, which aimed to address contemporary global asylum issues by developing, on the basis of the Agenda on Protection, international agreements and measures to supplement the 1951 Convention and 1967 Protocol.

In the mid-2000s UNHCR widened its scope from its mandate to protect and assist people fleeing persecution and violence in response to the enormous impact of two devastating natural disasters: the 2004 Indian Ocean Tsunami and the 2005 South Asian earthquake.

In June 2004 UNHCR became the 10th co-sponsor of UNAIDS.

ASSISTANCE ACTIVITIES

The first phase of an assistance operation uses UNHCR's capacity of emergency response. This enables UNHCR to address the immediate needs of refugees at short notice, for example, by employing specially trained emergency teams and maintaining stockpiles of basic equipment, medical aid and materials. A significant proportion of UNHCR expenditure is allocated to the next phase of an operation, providing 'care and maintenance' in stable refugee circumstances. This assistance can take various forms, including the provision of food, shelter, medical care and essential supplies. Also covered in many instances are basic services, including education and counselling.

As far as possible, assistance is geared towards the identification and implementation of durable solutions to refugee problems—this being the second statutory responsibility of UNHCR. Such solutions generally take one of three forms: voluntary repatriation, local integration or resettlement in another country. Where voluntary repatriation, increasingly the preferred solution, is feasible, the Office assists refugees to overcome obstacles preventing their return to their country of origin. This may be done through negotiations with governments involved, or by providing funds either for the physical movement of refugees or for the rehabilitation of returnees once back in their own country. In 2005 UNHCR was supporting the implementation of the Guidance Note on Durable Solutions for Displaced Persons, adopted in 2004 by the UN Development Group.

When voluntary repatriation is not an option, efforts are made to assist refugees to integrate locally and to become self-supporting in their countries of asylum. This may be done either by granting loans to refugees, or by assisting them, through vocational training or in other ways, to learn a skill and to establish themselves in gainful occupations. One major form of assistance to help refugees re-establish themselves outside camps is the provision of housing. In cases where resettlement through emigration is the only viable solution to a refugee problem, UNHCR negotiates with governments in an endeavour to obtain suitable resettlement opportunities, to encourage liberalization of admission criteria and to draw up special immigration schemes. During 2005 an estimated 30,500 refugees were resettled under UNHCR auspices.

In the early 1990s UNHCR aimed to consolidate efforts to integrate certain priorities into its programme planning and implementation, as a standard discipline in all phases of assistance. The considerations include awareness of specific problems confronting refugee women, the needs of refugee children, the environmental impact of refugee programmes and long-term development objectives. In an effort to improve the effectiveness of its programmes, UNHCR has initiated a process of delegating authority, as well as responsibility for operational budgets, to its regional and field representatives, increasing flexibility and accountability. A Policy Devolopment and Evaluation Service reviews systematically UNHCR's operational effectiveness.

All UNHCR personnel are required to sign, and all interns, contracted staff and staff from partner organizations are required to acknowledge, a Code of Conduct, to which is appended the UN Secretary-General's bulletin on special measures for protection from sexual exploitation and sexual abuse (issued in October 2003). The post of Senior Adviser to the High Commissioner on Gender Issues, within the Executive Office, was established in 2004.

INDIAN OCEAN TSUNAMI

Following a massive earthquake in the Indian Ocean in late December 2004, which caused a series of tidal waves, or tsunamis, that devastated coastal regions in 14 countries in South and South-East Asia and East Africa, UNHCR requested emergency funding totalling US $77m. in support of a 12-month relief operation to provide shelter, non-food relief supplies and logistical support for survivors in Aceh, Indonesia (close to the epicentre of the earthquake), Sri Lanka and Somalia. This was part of a pan-UN inter-agency appeal for $1,100m.

SUB-SAHARAN AFRICA

UNHCR has provided assistance to refugee and internally displaced populations in many parts of the continent where civil conflict, violations of human rights, drought, famine or environmental degradation have forced people to flee their home regions. The majority of African refugees and returnees are located in countries that are themselves suffering major economic problems and are thus unable to provide the basic requirements of the uprooted people. Furthermore, UNHCR has often failed to receive adequate international financial support to implement effective relief programmes. In March 2004 a UNHCR-sponsored Dialogue on Voluntary Repatriation and Sustainable Reintegration in Africa endorsed the creation of an international working group—comprising African governments, UN agencies, the AU and other partners—to support the return and sustainable reintegration of refugees in several African countries, including Angola, Burundi, the Democratic Republic of the Congo (DRC), Eritrea, Liberia, Rwanda, Sierra Leone, Somalia and Sudan. At 31 December 2005 there were an estimated 4.9m. people of concern to UNHCR in sub-Saharan Africa.

The Horn of Africa, afflicted by famine, separatist violence and ethnic conflict, has experienced large-scale population movements in recent years. Following the overthrow of the regime of former Somali president Siad Barre in January 1991 hundreds of thousands of Somalis fled to neighbouring countries. In 1992 UNHCR initiated a repatriation programme for the massive Somali and Ethiopian refugee populations in Kenya, which included assistance with reconstruction projects and the provision of food to returnees and displaced persons. However, continuing instability in many areas of Somalia impeded the completion of the repatriation process to that country and resulted in further population displacement. Repatriations accelerated in the early 2000s owing to advances in the peace process. During 1992–mid-2006 more than 1m. Somali refugees returned to their country, of whom about 485,000 received UNHCR assistance. However, many areas of the country have remained unstable, drought-affected and lacking in basic services. The Office, with other partners, has implemented community-based QIPs, aimed at facilitating long-term self-reliance by improving local education and health provision, water supply and productive capacity. It was hoped that the inauguration of a new transitional Somali parliament in August 2004 might lead to improved stability and an eventual increase in voluntary returns. However, the humanitarian situation in Somalia deteriorated during 2005–06, owing to severe drought in the region. At that time UNHCR, in collaboration with the Somali authorities, was preparing a Comprehensive Plan of Action for Somalia; it was envisaged that this would benefit some 400,000 Somali refugees, 350,000 returnees to Somalia, and 400,000 IDPs, as well as local communities receiving returnees and IDPs. At the end of 2005 there remained an estimated total Somali refugee population of 394,760, of whom 150,459 were in Kenya and 78,582 in Yemen. During February–mid-April 2007 nearly 100,000 people were reported to have fled Mogadishu, the Somali capital, owing to intense fighting between government forces and local militia; at mid-April the high level of insecurity in Mogadishu was preventing UNHCR personnel from accessing basic supplies warehoused there for distribution to the displaced civilian population. By late 1997 UNHCR estimated that some 600,000 Ethiopians had repatriated from neighbouring countries, either by spontaneous or organized movements. The voluntary repatriation operation of Ethiopian refugees from Sudan (which commenced in 1993) was concluded in mid-1998. With effect from 1 March 2000 UNHCR withdrew the automatic refugee status of Ethiopians who left their country before 1991. Transportation and rehabilitation assistance were provided for 9,321 of these, who wished to repatriate. At 31 December 2005 there remained an estimated total Ethiopian refugee population of 65,293; some 14,862 Ethiopians remained in Kenya and 14,633 were in Sudan. At that time Ethiopia itself was hosting a total of 100,817 refugees (of whom the majority were Sudanese), while Kenya was sheltering 251,271 (mainly Somalis).

From 1992 some 500,000 Eritreans took refuge in Sudan as a result of separatist conflicts; however, by 1995 an estimated 125,000 had returned spontaneously, in particular following Eritrea's accession to independence in May 1993. A UNHCR repatriation programme to assist the remaining refugees, which had been delayed for various political, security and funding considerations, was initiated in November 1994. Its implementation, however, was hindered by a shortfall in donor funding and by differences between the Eritrean and Sudanese Governments, and Sudan continued to host substantial numbers of Eritrean refugees. Renewed conflict between Eritrea and Ethiopia, which commenced in 1998, had, by mid-1999, resulted in the displacement of some 350,000 Eritreans and 300,000 Ethiopians. In mid-2000, following an escalation of the conflict in May, UNHCR reported that some 95,000 Eritreans had sought refuge in Sudan, while smaller numbers had fled to Djibouti and Yemen.

Following the conclusion of a cease-fire agreement between Eritrea and Ethiopia in June, UNHCR initiated an operation to repatriate the most recent wave of Eritrean refugees from Sudan, and also inaugurated a scheme to repatriate 147,000 long-term refugees. UNHCR and other agencies collaborated to rehabilitate areas of Eritrea that were receiving returnees. During 2001 UNHCR withdrew assistance to Eritrean IDPs, whose numbers had declined from a peak of 300,000 to about 45,000 by May. At the end of 2002 UNHCR terminated the refugee status of Eritreans who fled their country since 1993. During mid-2000–end-2003 UNHCR assisted 54,000 voluntary repatriations of Eritrean refugees from Sudan. Thereafter UNHCR aimed to support the repatriation of a further 35,000 Eritrean refugees and to close 16 of the 18 camps for Eritreans in Sudan, maintaining the two remaining camps to shelter Eritreans with continuing eligibility for international protection. The initial deadline of end-2004 for achieving this was not met owing to inadequate funding. At 31 December 2005 the total number of Eritreans still sheltering in Sudan was estimated at 116,746, of whom 75,152 were receiving UNHCR assistance.

At 31 December 2005 an estimated 693,267 Sudanese were exiled as refugees, mainly in Chad, Uganda, Ethiopia, Kenya, the DRC and the Central African Republic (CAR), owing to a history of civil unrest in southern Sudan and the emergence in early 2003 of a new conflict zone in the western Sudanese province of Darfur (see below). At end-2005 some 564,585 Sudanese refugees were receiving assistance from UNHCR. The Ugandan Government, hosting an estimated 212,857 Sudanese refugees at that time (168,747 UNHCR-assisted), has provided new resettlement sites and, jointly with UNHCR and other partners, has developed a Self-Reliance Strategy, which envisages achieving self-sufficiency for the long-term refugee population through integrating services for refugees into existing local structures. In view of the conclusion of a comprehensive peace agreement between the Sudanese Government and rebels in January 2005 UNHCR, in collaboration with other humanitarian agencies, planned to support the future voluntary repatriation and reintegration of some 380,000 refugees to southern Sudan from neighbouring countries. During 2005, however, only 131 (of an envisaged 64,000) Sudanese refugees repatriated with assistance from UNHCR. In February 2006 UNHCR and Sudan signed tripartite agreements with Ethiopia, the DRC and the Central African Republic to provide a legal framework for the repatriation of Sudanese refugees remaining in those countries.

From April 2003 more than 200,000 refugees from Sudan's western Darfur region sought shelter across the Sudan-Chad border, having fled an alleged campaign of killing, rapes and destruction of property conducted by pro-government militias against the indigenous population. In addition, an estimated 2m. people became displaced within Darfur. The Office has organized airlifts of basic household items to the camps, has aimed to improve and expand refugees' access to sanitation, healthcare and education, to manage supplementary and therapeutic feeding facilities in order to combat widespread malnutrition, to provide psychosocial support to traumatized refugees, and to promote training and livelihood programmes. The operation has been hampered by severe water shortages resulting from the arid environment of the encampment areas, necessitating costly UNHCR deliveries of stored water, and by intense insecurity. A significant deterioration during 2006 in the security situation in the eastern areas of Chad bordering Darfur (where resources were already stretched to the limit), as well as in Darfur itself, led to further population displacement in the region, including the displacement of 50,000 Chadians. By early 2007 some 20,000 Chadians had fled into Darfur. At January 2007 Chad was still hosting more than 230,000 refugees from Darfur, accommodated in 12 UNHCR camps. UNHCR established a presence within western Darfur in June 2004, and was operating from six offices there in 2007. UNHCR teams have undertaken efforts to train Sudanese managers of camps in Darfur in the areas of protection and human rights. During 2004–05 UNHCR established 24 women's centres in Darfur, which were to provide support to survivors of sexual violence; established 11 centres for IDP youths there; and rehabilitated 24 schools. In January 2007 UNHCR launched a US $19.7m. supplementary appeal to fund protection activities and relief assistance the 700,000 IDPs in western Darfur and some 20,000 Chadian refugees.

Following an outbreak of civil conflict in the CAR in early 2003, resulting in a *coup d'état* in March, some 41,000 CAR refugees fled to southern Chad. Continuing insecurity in northern CAR resulted in further population displacement and influxes of refugees into Chad in 2005–early 2007, by which time 46,000 CAR refugees were accommodated by UNHCR in four camps in Chad, and there were an estimated 212,000 IDPs inside the CAR.

Significant population displacements have occurred in West Africa in recent years, particularly since the outbreak in 1989 of enduring violent conflict in Liberia. Rebel insurgencies, fuelled by the illegal trade in 'conflict diamonds' and a proliferation of small arms, subsequently spread to Sierra Leone, Guinea and, latterly, Côte d'Ivoire (see below). During 1992 and the first half of 1993 refugees fleeing unrest in Senegal and Togo, as well as Liberia, increased the regional refugee population substantially. In accordance with a Liberian peace agreement, signed in July 1993, UNHCR was responsible for the repatriation of Liberian refugees who had fled to Guinea, Côte d'Ivoire and Sierra Leone. UNHCR also began to provide emergency relief to the displaced population within the country. Persisting political insecurity prevented any solution to the refugee problem, and in mid-1996 UNHCR suspended its preparatory activities for a large-scale repatriation and reintegration operation of Liberian refugees, owing to an escalation in hostilities. In early 1997 the prospect of a peaceful settlement in Liberia prompted a spontaneous movement of refugees returning home, and in April UNHCR initiated an organized repatriation of Liberian refugees from Ghana. The establishment of a democratically elected Liberian government in August and the consolidation of the peace settlement were expected to accelerate the return of refugees and other displaced persons. However, the process was hindered by logistical difficulties, the persisting volatility particularly of some border regions, and alleged atrocities perpetrated by Liberian troops. During 1998 and 1999 an estimated 15,000 Liberians fled to Guinea from insecurity in the Lofa area of northern Liberia; meanwhile, UNHCR was forced to suspend its operations in Lofa. By the end of 2000 nearly 400,000 Liberians were reported to have repatriated, more than one-third with UNHCR assistance. UNHCR organized QIPs to facilitate the reintegration of the returnees. Mounting insecurity in southern Guinea from September 2000 (see below) accelerated the return of Liberian refugees from camps there. However, during 2001 some 80,000 Liberians were displaced from their homes, and refugee camps for Sierra Leoneans were disrupted, owing to an escalation of violence particularly in the Lofa and Gbarpolu areas. In mid-2003 a further 147,000 Liberian refugees fled to neighbouring countries following an escalation in hostilities. However, owing to progress subsequently achieved in the Liberian peace process (including, in August 2003, the deployment of an ECOWAS peace-keeping force—ECOMIL—to the country, the exile of President Charles Taylor, and the conclusion of a peace agreement by the parties to the conflict; the deployment in October of a UN peace-keeping force, replacing ECOMIL; the peaceful staging of legislative and presidential elections in, respectively, October and November 2005; and the arrest and detention of Taylor in March 2006), mass voluntary spontaneous returns by Liberian refugees were reported in 2004–06. In February 2006 UNHCR altered its policy from 'facilitating' voluntary returns by Liberian refugees to 'actively promoting' such returns. At 31 December 2005 there remained an estimated 231,114 Liberian refugees (188,089 UNHCR-assisted), of whom 73,078 were in Guinea (54,810 UNHCR-assisted). At that time there were 237,822 Liberian IDPs of concern to UNHCR.

Further large-scale population displacement in West Africa followed an escalation of violence in Sierra Leone in early 1995. By December 1996 there were nearly 370,000 Sierra Leonean refugees in Liberia and Guinea, while a further 654,600 internally displaced Sierra Leoneans were of concern to UNHCR. The repatriation of Sierra Leonean refugees from Liberia was initiated in February 1997. However, the programme was suspended in May, owing to renewed political violence, which forced UNHCR staff to evacuate the country, and the seizure of power by military forces. Thousands of people fled to other parts of the country, as well as to neighbouring countries to escape the hostilities. Following the intervention of the ECOMOG multinational force (authorized by ECOWAS) and the conclusion of a peace agreement in October, residents of the Sierra Leone capital, Freetown, who had been displaced by the conflict, began to return. In February 1998 ECOMOG troops took control of Freetown from the rebel military forces, and in the following month the elected President, Ahmed Tejan Kabbah, was reinstated as Head of State. None the less, large numbers of Sierra Leoneans continued to cross the borders into neighbouring countries, owing to ongoing violence in the northern and eastern regions of the country and severe food shortages. In early 1999 anti-government forces again advanced on Freetown, prompting heavy fighting with ECOMOG troops and the displacement of thousands more civilians. In February a reported 200,000 people fled the town of Kenema in south-eastern Sierra Leone following attacks by rebel militia. In May a cease-fire agreement was concluded between the Government and opposition forces, and a formal peace accord was signed in early July, under which the rebels were to be disarmed and demobilized; however, the agreement broke down in May 2000. The resumption of hostilities delayed a planned repatriation operation and displaced an estimated 50,000 people from their homes. A new cease-fire agreement was signed by the Sierra Leone Government and the principal rebel group in early November. Meanwhile, persistent insecurity in northeastern and some border areas of Sierra Leone prompted further movements of Sierra Leonean refugees to Guinea during 2000. From September, however, unrest in southern Guinea (see below) caused some Sierra Leonean refugees who had been sheltering in camps there to repatriate. In 2001 UNHCR, while assisting, with the International Organization for Migration, returns by sea from the Guinean capital Conakry to Freetown, organized radio broadcasts to southern Guinea warning Sierra Leoneans against attempting to escape the unrest there by returning over the land border into volatile northeastern and other border areas of Sierra Leone. The successful staging of legislative and presidential elections in May 2003 and the consolidation of the peace process accelerated refugee returns. UNHCR terminated voluntary repatriation operations for Sierra Leonean refugees at 31 July 2004, by which time the Office had assisted about 180,000 of a total 280,000 returns since 2000. Thereafter, refugee status was to be determined on an individual basis for those who had not yet returned. At the end of 2005 UNHCR and partners terminated a four-year programme of reintegration assistance, mainly in the form of community development projects, aimed at providing a stable and self-supporting environment for returnees to Sierra Leone.

In August 2000 the security situation in southern border areas of Guinea deteriorated owing to increasing insurgencies by rebels from Liberia and Sierra Leone, which displaced a large number of Guineans from their homes and also endangered an estimated 460,000 mainly Liberian and Sierra Leonean refugees (see above) accommodated in Guinean camps. In mid-September UNHCR and other aid organizations withdrew their international personnel and suspended food distribution in these areas following the murder by armed rebels of a member of UNHCR staff. Insecurity, hunger and mounting hostility from elements of the local population subsequently led significant numbers of refugees to flee the unprotected camps. Many sought to reach northern Guinea, while some returned spontaneously to their countries of origin. Following an escalation in fighting between Guinean government forces and insurgent rebels in early December refugee movements intensified; however, it was reported that an estimated 180,000 refugees and 70,000 IDPs remained stranded without humanitarian assistance in the southwestern Bec de Perroquet area. Later in December UNHCR dispatched emergency teams to assist with the relocation of refugees who had escaped the conflict zone. In February 2001 the High Commissioner negotiated with the parties to the conflict for the establishment of a humanitarian 'lifeline' to enable the delivery of assistance to and possible evacuation of the refugees and IDPs trapped at Bec de Perroquet: conveys of food aid began to reach the area at the end of that month. Meanwhile, UNHCR opened five new refugee settlements in central Guinea and, supported by the Guinean authorities, dispatched search teams into Bec de Perroquet in an attempt to find and evacuate refugees still stranded there. UNHCR withdrew from Bec de Perroquet at the end of May. During 2001 a total of 63,662 mainly Sierra Leonean refugees were relocated.

UNHCR provided assistance to 120,000 people displaced by the extreme insecurity that developed in Côte d'Ivoire from September 2002. About 25,000 Côte d'Ivoire refugees fled to southern Liberia, and others sought shelter in Ghana, Guinea and Mali. In addition, during November–January 2003 an estimated 40,000 Liberian refugees in Côte d'Ivoire repatriated, in both spontaneous and partly UNHCR-assisted movements, having suffered harassment since the onset of the conflict. UNHCR initiated a number of QIPs aimed at rehabilitating the infrastructure of communities that were to receive returned Côte d'Ivoire refugees. At 31 December 2005 there remained 38,039 IDPs in Côte d'Ivoire.

UNHCR's activities in assisting refugees in West Africa have included a focus on the prevention of sexual and gender-based violence in refugee camps—a regional action plan to combat such violence was initiated in 2002—and collaboration with other agencies to ensure continuity between initial humanitarian assistance and long-term development support.

Since 1993 the Great Lakes region of central Africa has experienced massive population displacement, causing immense operational challenges and demands on the resources of international humanitarian and relief agencies. In October of that year a military coup in Burundi prompted some 580,000 people to flee into Rwanda and Tanzania, although many had returned by early 1994. By May 1994, however, an estimated 860,000 people from Burundi and Rwanda had fled to neighbouring states (following a resurgence of ethnic violence in both countries), including 250,000 mainly Rwandan Tutsi refugees who entered Tanzania over a 24-hour period in late April in the most rapid mass exodus ever witnessed by UNHCR. In May UNHCR began an immediate operation to airlift emergency supplies to the refugees. For the first time in an emergency operation UNHCR organized support to be rendered in the form of eight defined 'service packages', for example, to provide domestic fuel, road servicing and security or sanitation facilities. Despite overcrowding in camps and a high incidence of cholera and dysentery (particularly in camps in eastern Zaire, where many thousands of Rwandan Hutus had sought refuge following the establishment of a new Government in July) large numbers of refugees refused to accept UNHCR-assisted repatriation, owing to fears of reprisal ethnic killings. In September reports of mass ethnic violence in Rwanda, which were disputed by some UN agencies, continued to disrupt UNHCR's policy of repatriation and to prompt returnees to cross the border back into Zaire. Security in the refugee camps, which was undermined by the presence of military and political elements of the former Rwandan regime, remained an outstanding concern for UNHCR. A resurgence of violence in Burundi, in February 1995, provoked further mass population movements. However, in March the Tanzanian authorities, reportedly frustrated at the lack of international assistance for the refugees and the environmental degradation resulting from the camps, closed Tanzania's border with Burundi, thus preventing the admission into the country of some 100,000 Rwandan Hutu refugees who were fleeing camps in Burundi. While persisting disturbances in Rwanda disrupted UNHCR's repatriation programme, in April Rwandan government troops employed intimidation tactics to force some 90,000 internally displaced Hutus to leave a heavily populated camp in the south-west of the country; other small camps were closed. In August the Zairean Government initiated a short-lived programme of forcible repatriation of the estimated 1m. Rwandan and 70,000 Burundian Hutu refugees remaining in the country, which prompted as many as 100,000 refugees to flee the camps into the surrounding countryside. In September Rwanda agreed to strengthen its reception facilities and to provide greater security and protection for returnees, in collaboration with UNHCR, in order to prepare for any large-scale repatriation. UNHCR, meanwhile, expanded its information campaign, to promote the return of refugees, and enhanced its facilities at official border entry points. In December UNHCR negotiated an agreement between the Rwandan and Tanzanian authorities concerning the repatriation of the estimated 500,000 Rwandans remaining in camps in Tanzania. UNHCR agreed to establish a separate camp in north-west Tanzania in order to accommodate elements of the refugee population that might disrupt the repatriation programme. The repatriation of Rwandan refugees from all host countries was affected by reports of reprisals against Hutu returnees by the Tutsi-dominated Government in Rwanda. In February 1996 the Zairean Government renewed its efforts to accelerate the repatriation process, owing to concerns that the camps were becoming permanent settlements and that they were being used to train and rearm a Hutu militia. In July the Burundian Government forcibly repatriated 15,000 Rwandan refugees, having announced the closure of all remaining refugee camps. The repatriation programme was condemned by UNHCR and was suspended by the country's new military authorities, but only after many more thousands of refugees had been obliged to return to Rwanda and up to 30,000 had fled to Tanzania.

In October 1996 an escalation of hostilities between Zairean government forces, accused by Rwanda of arming the Hutu *Interahamwe* militia, and Zairean (Banyamulenge) Tutsis, who had been the focus of increasingly violent assaults, resulted in an extreme humanitarian crisis. Some 250,000 refugees fled 12 camps in the east of the country, including 90,000 Burundians who returned home. An estimated 500,000 refugees regrouped in Muganga camp, west of Goma, with insufficient relief assistance, following the temporary evacuation of international aid workers. UNHCR appealed to all Rwandan Hutu refugees to return home, and issued assurances of the presence of human rights observers in Rwanda to enhance their security. In November, with the apparent withdrawal of *Interahamwe* forces and the advance of the Tutsi-dominated Alliance des forces démocratiques pour la libération du Congo-Zaïre (AFDL), an estimated 600,000 refugees unexpectedly returned to Rwanda; however, concern remained on the part of the international community for the substantial number of Rwandan Hutu refugees at large in eastern Zaire. Further mass movement of Rwandan refugee populations occurred in December, owing to the threat of forcible repatriation by the Tanzanian Government, which had announced its intention of closing all camps by the end of the year. UNHCR initiated a repatriation programme; however, 200,000 refugees, unwilling to return to Rwanda, fled their camps. The majority of the refugees were later identified by the Tanzanian national army and escorted to the Rwandan border. By the end of December some 483,000 refugees had returned to Rwanda from Tanzania.

In February 1997 violence in Zaire intensified, which prompted some 56,000 Zaireans to flee into Tanzania and disrupted the distribution of essential humanitarian supplies to refugees remaining in Zaire. An estimated 170,000 refugees abandoned their temporary encampment at Tingi-Tingi, fearing attacks by the advancing AFDL forces. About 75,000 reassembled at Ubundu, south of Kisangani, while the fate of the other refugees remained uncertain. In March and April continued reports of attacks on refugee camps by AFDL forces and local Zaireans, resulted in large numbers of people fleeing into the surrounding countryside, with the consequent deaths of many of the most vulnerable members of the refugee population from disease and starvation. At the end of April the leader of the AFDL, Laurent-Désiré Kabila, ordered the repatriation of all Rwandan Hutu refugees by the UN within 60 days. Emergency air and land operations to evacuate some 185,000 refugees who had regrouped into temporary settlements were initiated a few days later. The repatriation process, however, was hindered by administrative and logistical difficulties and lack of co-operation on the part of the AFDL forces. By June an estimated 215,000 Rwandans were still missing or dispersed throughout the former Zaire (renamed the Democratic Republic of the Congo—DRC—by the AFDL in May). In the following months relations between the Kabila Government and UNHCR deteriorated as a result of several incidences of forcible repatriations of refugees to Rwanda and reports that the authorities were hindering a UN investigation into alleged abuses of human rights, committed against the Rwandan Hutu refugees by AFDL forces. In August an agreement was concluded to provide for the voluntary repatriation of some 75,000 refugees from the DRC remaining in Tanzania, under UNHCR supervision. However, the conflict that erupted in the DRC in August 1998 (see below) led to further large population movements. The repatriation of the estimated 260,000 Burundians remaining in Tanzania was also impeded, from early 1998, by an escalation of violence, which destabilized areas of return for both refugees and IDPs. In December 1997 a tripartite agreement was signed to provide for the organized repatriation of the remaining former Zairean refugees in Rwanda, with both Governments agreeing to observe strict conditions of security for the refugees on both sides of the border.

During the late 1990s UNHCR resolved to work, in co-operation with UNDP and WFP, to rehabilitate areas previously inhabitated by refugees in central African countries of asylum and undertook to repair roads, bridges and other essential transport infrastructure, improve water and sanitation facilities, and strengthen the education sector. However, the political stability of the region remained extremely uncertain, and, from August 1998, DRC government forces and rebels became involved in a civil war in which the militaries of several regional governments were also implicated. From late 1998 substantial numbers of DRC nationals fled to neighbouring countries (mainly Tanzania and Zambia) or were displaced within the DRC. Meanwhile, the DRC, in turn, was hosting a significant refugee population. Although a cease-fire agreement was signed by all parties to the conflict in July 1999, this did not begin to be implemented until early 2001, when Kabila was assassinated and succeeded as President by his son, Maj.-Gen. Joseph Kabila. Following the DRC Government's adoption of peace agreements, in July and August 2002, with, respectively, the Rwandan and Ugandan Governments, nearly all Rwandan and Ugandan forces were withdrawn before the end of that year. Meanwhile, troop withdrawals were also initiated by Angola, Burundi, Namibia and Zimbabwe. In view of the conclusion, in December, of a peace agreement providing for the staging of elections in the DRC after a transition period of 24 months, UNHCR planned for eventual mass refugee returns. The Office, in co-operation with UNDP, the UN Mission in the DRC (MONUC) and the World Bank, was to assist efforts to demobilize, disarm and repatriate former combatants. Insecurity continued to prevail, however, during 2003–06, in north-eastern areas of the DRC, resulting in continuing population displacements. In September 2005 UNHCR and the DRC and Tanzanian Governments signed a tripartite agreement on facilitating returns of DRC refugees from Tanzania. It was envisaged that further returns would be prompted by the holding of legislative and a first stage of presidential elections in the DRC in July 2006, although the security situation subsequently remained uncertain and reintegration efforts were also restricted by insufficient funding. In 2005 UNHCR provided assistance to 20,359 refugees from north-eastern DRC sheltering in Burundi and assisted about 67,000 refugee returns to Burundi (where legislative and presidential elections were successfully staged mid-year). A tripartite agreement on assistance was concluded by the Burundian and Tanzanian Governments and UNHCR in August 2003. UNHCR concluded similar accords during that year with the Rwandan Government and other states hosting Rwandan refugees, paving the way for significant voluntary refugee returns to Rwanda during 2004–06. The major populations of concern to UNHCR in the Great Lakes region at 31 December 2005 were, provisionally, as follows: 204,341 refugees and 39,050 returned refugees in the DRC; 68,248 returned refugees in Burundi; 45,206 refugees in Rwanda; and a refugee population of 548,824 in Tanzania, the largest concentration of refugees on the continent, though reduced from 602,088 at end-2004. UNHCR has provided education, environmental protection and healthcare programmes at camps in Tanzania, with a focus on the empowerment of women, eliminating gender-based violence and controlling the spread of HIV/AIDS. UNHCR also provides support to those refugees permitted by the Tanzanian Government to resettle permanently in that country. The security of international aid personnel in the Great Lakes region has been of concern and UNHCR assists the Tanzanian authorities with ensuring that camps retain a humanitarian, civilian ethos and exclude infiltrators without entitlement to humanitarian protection.

UNHCR is a leading participant in two main HIV/AIDS initiatives in the Great Lakes region, both of which should benefit refugees, returnees, IDPs and host communities: the Great Lakes Initiative on HIV/AIDS and the Congo-Oubangui-Chari Initiative.

In mid-1997 an estimated 40,000 refugees from the Republic of the Congo fled to the DRC, following a short-lived outbreak of civil conflict. In December a memorandum of understanding was signed by representatives of the two Governments and of UNHCR, providing for their immediate repatriation. From late 1998 the resumption of conflict in the Republic of the Congo disrupted UNHCR humanitarian efforts in that country and caused significant numbers of Congolese to seek refuge in the DRC and Gabon, and the internal displacement of as many as 500,000 people. Following the agreement of a cease-fire in December the majority of IDPs returned home. More than 60,000 Congolese refugees had repatriated by the end of 2000. A tripartite accord on the voluntary repatriation of Congolese refugees from Gabon was concluded by UNHCR and the Congolese and Gabon Governments during 2001. The Office was continuing to assist with their repatriation and reintegration in 2004–06, following the conclusion of a peace accord between the Congolese Government and rebels in March 2003. At December 2005 Congolese refugees remaining in Gabon numbered 7,298 (all of whom were being assisted by UNHCR), and some 5,243 Congolese refugees remained in the DRC (only 832 UNHCR-assisted). During 2000 more than 80,000 refugees from the DRC sought protection in the Republic of the Congo. At the end of 2005 that country was still hosting some 56,380 refugees from the DRC.

In 1994 continuing civil conflict in Angola caused some 370,000 people to leave their home areas. Prior to the signing of a peace settlement in November, UNHCR provided assistance to 112,000 internally displaced Angolans and returnees, although military activities, which hindered accessibility, undermined the effectiveness of the assistance programme. In mid-1995, following a consolidation of the peace process in Angola, UNHCR appealed for US $44m. to support the voluntary repatriation of some 300,000 Angolan refugees through a two-and-a-half-year operation. By June 1996 implementation of the repatriation programme was delayed, reportedly owing to poor accommodation and other facilities for returnees, limited progress in confining and disarming opposition troops and the continued hazard of land-mines throughout the country. During 1997 an estimated 53,000 Angolans voluntarily returned from the DRC and Zambia, bringing the total returnees to some 130,000 since mid-1995. In November 1997 UNHCR resolved to implement an operation to provide for the repatriation and reintegration of the remaining Angolan refugees by June 1999. UNHCR allocated $15.7m. to support the repatriation process and other activities in Angola, including strengthening the country's road infrastructure, monitoring areas of return, the implementation of reintegration projects and promoting links with other development programmes. In May 1998, however, the security situation in Angola deteriorated, and at the end of June UNHCR declared a temporary suspension of the repatriation operation. The renewed violence also resulted in further population displacement, with refugee movements into the DRC continuing during 1998–2001. In July 2000 UNHCR expanded its operations in Angola to support IDPs by providing emergency humanitarian assistance and helping IDP communities and local administrations with the provision of basic services, demining and the rehabilitation of local infrastructures. Following the signing of the Luanda Peace Agreement in April 2002 between the Angolan Government and rebels of the União National para a Independência Total de Angola, UNHCR made preparations for the voluntary repatriation of a projected 400,000 Angolan refugees sheltering elsewhere in southern Africa. It was estimated that in all more than 4.3m. Angolans were displaced from their homes during the 1980s and 1990s, and by the end of 2005 a total of nearly 4.4m. IDPs, refugees and demobilized fighters had reportedly returned home. By the end of 2004 the Office had rehabilitated the nine main repatriation corridors into Angola. UNHCR has assisted the Angolan Government with the development of a Sustainable Reintegration Initiative for returned refugees. At 31 December 2005 UNHCR was providing assistance to some 53,771 Angolan returned refugees. Meanwhile, an estimated 215,777 Angolans were still sheltering in neighbouring countries at that time, including 106,772 in the DRC and 75,468 in Zambia. HIV/AIDS- and mine-awareness training have been made available by UNHCR at refugee reception centres.

CO-OPERATION WITH OTHER ORGANIZATIONS

UNHCR works closely with other UN agencies, intergovernmental organizations and non-governmental organizations (NGOs) to increase the scope and effectiveness of its operations. Within the UN system UNHCR co-operates, principally, with the World Food Programme in the distribution of food aid, UNICEF and the World Health Organization in the provision of family welfare and child immunization programmes, OCHA in the delivery of emergency humanitarian relief, UNDP in development-related activities and the preparation of guide-lines for the continuum of emergency assistance to development programmes, and the Office of the UN High Commissioner for Human Rights. UNHCR also has close working relationships with the International Committee of the Red Cross and the International Organization for Migration. In 2005 UNHCR worked with 578 NGOs as 'implementing partners', enabling UNHCR to broaden the use of its resources while maintaining a co-ordinating role in the provision of assistance.

TRAINING

UNHCR organizes training programmes and workshops to enhance the capabilities of field workers and non-UNHCR staff, in the following areas: the identification and registration of refugees; people-orientated planning; resettlement procedures and policies; emergency response and management; security awareness; stress management; and the dissemination of information through the electronic media.

Finance

The United Nations' regular budget finances a proportion of UNHCR's administrative expenditure. The majority of UNHCR's programme expenditure (about 98%) is funded by voluntary contributions, mainly from governments. The Private Sector and Public Affairs Service aims to increase funding from non-governmental donor sources, for example by developing partnerships with foundations and corporations. Following approval of the Unified Annual Programme Budget any subsequently identified requirements are managed in the form of Supplementary Programmes, financed by separate appeals. The total Unified Annual Programme Budget for 2007 was projected at US $1,043m.

Publications

Refugees (quarterly, in English, French, German, Italian, Japanese and Spanish).

Refugee Resettlement: An International Handbook to Guide Reception and Integration.

Refugee Survey Quarterly.

Refworld (annually).

Sexual and Gender-based Violence Against Refugees, Returnees and Displaced Persons: Guide-lines for Prevention and Response.

The State of the World's Refugees (every 2 years).

UNHCR Handbook for Emergencies.

Press releases, reports.

Statistics

PERSONS OF CONCERN TO UNHCR IN AFRICA SOUTH OF THE SAHARA*

('000 persons, at 31 December 2005, provisional figures)

Host Country	Refugees	Asylum-seekers	Returnees	Others of concern†
Burundi	20.7	19.9	68.2	11.5
Chad	275.4	0.1	1.4	—
Democratic Republic of the Congo	204.3	0.1	39.1	—
Ethiopia	100.8	0.2	0.1	—
Kenya	251.3	16.5	—	—
Liberia	10.2	0.0	70.3	498.6
Somalia	0.5	0.1	12.0	400.0
South Africa	29.7	140.1	—	—
Sudan	147.3	4.4	18.5	878.1
Tanzania	548.8	0.3	—	—
Uganda	257.3	1.8	0.0	—
Zambia	155.7	0.1	—	—

* Figures are provided mostly by governments, based on their own records and methods of estimations. Countries with fewer than 100,000 persons of concern to UNHCR are not listed.

† Mainly internally displaced persons (IDPs) or recently-returned IDPs.

United Nations Peace-keeping

Address: Department of Peace-keeping Operations, Room S-3727-B, United Nations, New York, NY 10017, USA.

Telephone: (212) 963-8077; **fax:** (212) 963-9222; **internet:** www.un.org/Depts/dpko/.

United Nations peace-keeping operations have been conceived as instruments of conflict control. The UN has used these operations in various conflicts, with the consent of the parties involved, to maintain international peace and security, without prejudice to the positions or claims of parties, in order to facilitate the search for political settlements through peaceful means such as mediation and the good offices of the UN Secretary-General. Each operation is established with a specific mandate, which requires periodic review by the UN Security Council. United Nations peace-keeping operations fall into two categories: peace-keeping forces and observer missions.

Peace-keeping forces are composed of contingents of military and civilian personnel, made available by member states. These forces assist in preventing the recurrence of fighting, restoring and maintaining peace, and promoting a return to normal conditions. To this end, peace-keeping forces are authorized as necessary to undertake negotiations, persuasion, observation and fact-finding. They conduct patrols and interpose physically between the opposing parties. Peace-keeping forces are permitted to use their weapons only in self-defence.

Military observer missions are composed of officers (usually unarmed), who are made available, on the Secretary-General's request, by member states. A mission's function is to observe and report to the Secretary-General (who, in turn, informs the Security Council) on the maintenance of a cease-fire, to investigate violations and to do what it can to improve the situation. Peace-keeping forces and observer missions must at all times maintain complete impartiality and avoid any action that might affect the claims or positions of the parties.

The UN's peace-keeping forces and observer missions are financed in most cases by assessed contributions from member states of the organization. In recent years a significant expansion in the UN's peace-keeping activities has been accompanied by a perpetual financial crisis within the organization, as a result of the increased financial burden and some member states' delaying payment. At 31 December 2006 outstanding assessed contributions to the peace-keeping budget amounted to some US $1,900m.

In 2007 the Department of Peace-keeping Operations was directly supporting three political and peace-building missions (in addition to those maintained by the Department of Political Affairs): the UN Assistance Mission in Afghanistan (established in March 2002), the UN Integrated Office in Sierra Leone (established in January 2006 as a successor to the UN peace-keeping operation in that country), and the UN Integrated Office in Burundi (established in January 2007, again succeeding a UN peace-keeping operation).

In 1988 the United Nations Peace-keeping Forces were awarded the Nobel Peace Prize.

UNITED NATIONS MISSION IN ETHIOPIA AND ERITREA—UNMEE

Address: Asmara, Eritrea; Addis Ababa, Ethiopia.

Acting Special Representative of the UN Secretary-General and Head of Mission: Azouz Ennifar (Tunisia).

Force Commander: Maj.-Gen. Mohammad Tasir Masadeh (Jordan).

In July 2000 the Security Council authorized the establishment of UNMEE to facilitate compliance with and verify a cease-fire agreement that had been signed by the Governments of Eritrea and Ethiopia in mid-June (having been mediated by the Organization of African Unity—OAU, now African Union—AU), with a view to settling a long-standing border conflict between the two countries. In September the Security Council authorized the deployment of up to 4,200 military personnel to the operation, which was given an initial six-month mandate. The Security Council emphasized that UNMEE's mandate would be terminated on completion of the process to delimit and demarcate the Eritrea–Ethiopia border. In December the Eritrean and Ethiopian authorities concluded a full peace accord, providing for the establishment of a Boundary Commission mandated to delimit the border on the basis of relevant colonial treaties and international law. The eventual decision of the Commission was to be accepted by both parties as 'final and binding'. In February 2001 the Military Co-ordination Commission (which had been established jointly by the UN and the OAU in accordance with the cease-fire accord to address military and technical aspects of the peace process, and had met for the first time in December 2000) agreed a timetable to enable Eritrean and Ethiopian forces, monitored by UNMEE, to redeploy in order to establish a 25km temporary security zone (TSZ) in the border area; the security zone was declared operational in April 2001. UNMEE was subsequently to continue to monitor both forces, to co-ordinate and provide technical assistance for de-mining activities in the vacated and adjacent areas, and to co-ordinate local humanitarian and human rights activities by UN and other agencies. From mid-2001 UNMEE repeatedly protested against alleged restrictions placed on its freedom of movement by the Eritrean authorities in areas adjoining the TSZ, as these impeded the mission's capability to monitor the redeployment of that country's forces. In January 2002 the Security Council urged that UNMEE be allowed full freedom of movement and requested that the Eritrean Government disclose details of an alleged continuing military and police presence within the TSZ. In mid-April the Boundary Commission published its decision on the delimitation of the two countries' common border. The Secretary-General urged Eritrea and Ethiopia to implement the decision without delay. UNMEE was to monitor the next phase of the peace process, involving the border's physical demarcation. During late April and early May the Ethiopian Government temporarily closed the Ethiopian border to UNMEE personnel, claiming that UNMEE had not consulted sufficiently with it regarding the mission's logistical support for, and the transfer of personnel to, the Boundary Commission's field office; that the Commission had not established its field presence on the Ethiopian side of the border; and that UNMEE had inappropriately permitted journalists to visit a border village. In August the Security Council adjusted the mission's mandate to support the implementation of decisions adopted by the Boundary Commission. During 2002–03 UNMEE personnel undertook various humanitarian projects including the provision of medical assistance, rebuilding and extending water supplies, constructing shelters for the internally displaced population, and rehabilitating roads. In July 2002 two outreach centres were opened in the Ethiopian and Eritrean capitals (respectively, Addis Ababa and Asmara) to provide information to the public about the peace process. In 2003 and early 2004 the Secretary-General noted that the movements of UNMEE personnel were being restricted by both the Eritrean and Ethiopian authorities. In January 2004 the Secretary-General appointed a new Special Envoy on Ethiopia and Eritrea, Lloyd Axworthy, who was mandated to consult with the Eritrean and Ethiopian authorities with a view to accelerating the implementation of the December 2000 peace accord. Axworthy held consultations with the Ethiopian authorities in February 2004; the Eritrean leadership, however, refused to receive him. In May the Security Council urged both sides to co-operate more fully with UNMEE and expressed concern at ongoing restrictions on the movement of UN troops. In 2004 UNMEE undertook awareness and training programmes in aspects of de-mining, HIV/AIDS and human rights. Little political progress was achieved during the year; in November, however, the Ethiopian Government presented a new five-point peace plan, which was welcomed by the UN Secretary-General.

In July 2005 the UN Security Council expressed concern at the continued lack of progress in implementing the decision of the Boundary Commission, as well as new restrictions on UNMEE police officers in the Eritrean capital, Asmara, and the suspension of direct flights between the capitals of the two countries. The Council also reiterated concern at worsening food security in both countries. Nonetheless, UNMEE reported that the military situation in the border area remained stable and that ongoing de-mining activities were benefiting the local population and encouraging the return of displaced persons. In September the Security Council again urged Ethiopia to accept the decision of the Boundary Commission, both governments to implement the decision fully and without delay, and Eritrea to remove all existing restrictions on UN movements. In October, however, the Eritrean Government imposed a ban on helicopter flights by UNMEE in its airspace. UNMEE subsequently suspended its mine clearance activities, owing to safety concerns, and evacuated personnel from 18 remote observation posts in the TSZ. In late November the Security Council passed a resolution demanding a reversal of Eritrea's constraints on UNMEE operations, Ethiopia's acceptance of the Boundary Commission decision, and a return to troop deployment levels in the TSZ to those of December 2004, owing to a concern at a build-up of troops on both sides. The resolution provided for the possible imposition of punitive measures if the conditions were not met. A few days later, at a meeting chaired by UNMEE's Force Commander, representatives of both sides agreed not to escalate further tensions in the border region. In December 2005 the UN condemned a request by the Eritrean authorities that all UNMEE personnel from Canada, Russia, the USA and European countries leave the country within 10 days. The UN Secretary-General immediately dispatched two senior officials to the region to review the situation and defuse the escalating political crisis. In mid-December the Security Council reiterated its immediate condemnation of Eritrea's decision and approved the temporary relocation of some 87 military and civilian staff from that country to Ethiopia. At the end of December UNMEE reported that Ethiopian troops had begun to retreat from the border, but expressed concerns at ongoing heightened tensions in the zone.

In October 2006 the UN Security Council expressed concern at the large-scale movement of Eritrean troops within the TSZ and urged their immediate withdrawal. In November the Boundary Commission granted both parties a further 12 months to complete the boundary demarcation process. In January 2007 the UN Secretary-General reported that non-co-operation by Eritrea with his acting Special Representative and continuing obstructions imposed upon UNMEE's movements were severely restricting the operations of the mission and that Ethiopia's continuing refusal to implement the decision of the Boundary Commission was contributing to continued stalemate. The humanitarian situation in the region remained of considerable concern. In March UNMEE expressed concern at further restrictions imposed on its cease-fire monitoring role by the Eritrean authorities and criticised the ordered expulsion of the manager of the mission's Mine Action Co-ordination Centre. In May the UN Security Council urged both countries to refrain from violence, given the increasing tension in the region, violations of the TSZ and lack of progress in resolving the dispute.

At 30 June 2007 UNMEE comprised 1,465 troops and 219 military observers; at 31 May it was supported by 357 international and local civilian personnel and 61 UN Volunteers. The General Assembly appropriation to cover the cost of the mission for the period 1 July 2007–30 June 2008 amounted to US $118.99m., to be financed by a Special Account.

UNITED NATIONS MISSION IN LIBERIA—UNMIL

Address: Monrovia, Liberia.

Special Representative of the UN Secretary-General and Head of Mission: Alan Doss (United Kingdom).

Force Commander: Lt-Gen. Chikadibia Obiakor (Nigeria).

UNMIL was authorized by the UN Security Council in September 2003 to support the implementation of the cease-fire accord agreed in June and the Comprehensive Peace Agreement concluded in August by the parties to the conflict in Liberia. UNMIL was mandated to assist with the development of an action plan for the disarmament, demobilization, reintegration and, where appropriate, repatriation of all armed groups and to undertake a programme of voluntary disarmament; to protect civilians and UN personnel, equipment and facilities; to support humanitarian and human rights activities; to support the implementation of national security reforms; and, in co-operation with ECOWAS and other partners, to assist the National Transitional Government (inaugurated in mid-October) with the training of a national police force and the restructuring of the military. Troops were also to assist with the rehabilitation of damaged physical infrastructure, in particular the road network. On 1 October UNMIL assumed authority from an ECOWAS-led multinational force in Liberia (the ECOWAS Mission in Liberia—ECOMIL) which had been endorsed by the Security Council in August; ECOMIL's 3,600 troops were reassigned to UNMIL, which had an authorized maximum strength of 15,000 military personnel. In 2004 UNMIL's civil affairs component assessed the functional capacities of public administration structures, including government ministries, in order to assist the National Transitional Government in re-establishing authority throughout Liberia. UNMIL was to support the National Transitional Government in preparing the country for national elections, which were expected to be held in October 2005. In December 2003 the programme for disarmament, demobilization, rehabilitation and reintegration (DDRR) officially commenced when the first cantonment site was opened. However, the process was disrupted by an unexpectedly large influx of former combatants and a few days later the process was temporarily suspended. In mid-January 2004 an agreement was concluded by all parties on necessary prerequisites to proceeding with the programme, including the launch of an information campaign, which was to be co-ordinated and organized by UNMIL, and the construction of new reception centres and cantonment sites. The DDRR process resumed, under UNMIL command, in mid-April. A training programme for the country's new police service was inaugurated in July and the first UN-trained police officers were deployed at the end of the year. By July 2007 some 3,500 officers had graduated from the UN training programme. In August 2004 UNMIL launched a further vocational training scheme for some 640 former combatants to learn building skills. By the end of October, when the disarmament phase of the DDRR programme was officially terminated, more than 96,000 former combatants, including 10,000 child soldiers, had handed over their weapons. Some 7,200 commenced formal education. At the same time, however, UNMIL troops were deployed throughout the country to restore order, after an outbreak of sectarian hostilities prompted widespread looting and destruction of property and businesses. In early December the Special Representative of the UN Secretary-General hosted a meeting of the heads of all West African peace-keeping and political missions, in order to initiate a more integrated approach to achieving stability and peace throughout the region.

During 2005 UNMIL continued to work to integrate ex-combatants into society through vocational training schemes, and to support community rehabilitation efforts, in particular through the funding of Quick Impact Projects. By August an estimated 78,000 former combatants had participated in rehabilitation and reintegration schemes, funded bilaterally and by a Trust Fund administered by the UN Development Programme. A programme to enrol 20,000 disarmed combatants in formal education was initiated in November. UNMIL provided technical assistance to the National Elections Commission, which, in April, initiated a process of voter registration in preparation for presidential and legislative elections. UNMIL was also concerned with maintaining a peaceful and secure environment for the electoral campaigns and polling days and undertook a large-scale civic education campaign in support of the democratic election process. In October UNMIL, with the Transitional Government, established a Joint National Security Operations Centre. The elections were held, as scheduled, in October, with a second-round presidential poll in November. The new president and administration were inaugurated in January 2006. UNMIL determined to strengthen its focus on the rule of law, economic recovery and good governance. It also pledged to support the government in efforts to remove UN sanctions against sales of rough diamonds and to become a member of the Kimberley Process Certification Scheme by providing air support for surveillance and mapping activities in mining areas. Throughout 2006 and 2007 UNMIL personnel undertook projects to rehabilitate and construct roads and bridges, police stations, courtrooms and educational facilities. The mission also initiated, with the support of other UN agencies, a scheme to create employment throughout the country. In March 2007 UNMIL initiated a Sports for Peace programme to promote national reconciliation. In late April the UN Security Council removed the embargo against sales of diamonds from Liberia, and in the following month UNMIL transferred control of the regional diamond certification office to the national authorities. In August the UN Secretary-General recognized the efforts of the new government in consolidating peace and promoting economic recovery in the country and recommended a gradual reduction in the number of UN troops.

In September 2005 the UN Security Council authorized a temporary increase in the mission's military strength in order to compensate for the dispatch of 250 troops, with effect from 1 January 2006, to provide protection at the Special Court in Sierra Leone, following the termination of the UN mission in that country.

At 30 June 2007 UNMIL comprised 13,939 troops, 1,176 police and 212 military observers; at 31 May it was supported by 524 international personnel, 931 local civilian staff and 257 UN Volunteers. The General Assembly appropriation to the Special Account for UNMIL amounted to US $721.72m. for the period 1 July 2007–30 June 2008.

UNITED NATIONS MISSION IN SUDAN—UNMIS

Address: Khartoum, Sudan.

Acting Special Representative of the UN Secretary-General and Head of Mission: TAYE-BROOK ZERIHOUN (Ethiopia).

Force Commander: Lt-Gen. JASBIR SINGH LIDDER (India).

In June 2004 the Security Council agreed to establish an Advance Team in Sudan, as a special political mission, in order to support efforts towards achieving a peaceful settlement of the conflict in that country. The Council also expressed concern at the situation of an estimated 2m. people in Darfur, western Sudan, who had been displaced by civil conflict and suffered extensive attacks by militia groups. In July the newly-appointed Special Representative of the UN Secretary-General, Jan Pronk, visited Darfur under the auspices of a Joint Implementation Mechanism, established earlier in that month by the UN and Sudanese Government to work towards alleviating the humanitarian crisis. At the end of that month the Security Council resolved to impose an arms embargo against rebel groups in Darfur, and endorsed efforts of the African Union (AU) in mediating a political solution. In mid-November the Security Council met in special session in Nairobi, Kenya, to assess the situation in Sudan and to address the problems in Darfur. The Council witnessed the signing of a Memorandum of Understanding between the Sudanese Government and Sudan People's Liberation Movement/Army (SPLM/A) to end the conflict in southern Sudan, and pledged to support any lasting settlement. In January 2005 both sides signed a Comprehensive Peace Agreement. The UN Mission in Sudan was formally established under Resolution 1590, which was adopted by the Security Council in March. Its mandate was to support implementation of the Comprehensive Peace Agreement, for example by monitoring the cease-fire arrangements and investigating any violations, assisting in the establishment of a disarmament, demobilization and reintegration programme, supporting a restructuring of the police service, and implementing a public information campaign in support of the peace process. In addition, the mission was to facilitate and co-ordinate the voluntary return of refugees and internally displaced persons, to provide de-mining assistance and technical advice, and to contribute to international efforts to protect and promote human rights in Sudan. UNMIS was to work closely with the AU's Mission in Sudan (AMIS) to foster peace and reinforce stability in Darfur.

In May 2005 the UNMIS Force Commander chaired the first meeting of a Cease-fire Joint Military Committee (CJMC), comprising representatives of the Sudanese Government, the SPLM/A and the UN. In accordance with the Comprehensive Peace Agreement the Committee was to monitor troop locations and strength, the stocks of weapons and ammunition and co-ordinate the clearance of anti-personnel mines, as well as undertake other military tasks assigned under the Agreement. In May and early June UNMIS reported repeated outbreaks of violence, mainly in southern Darfur. The Special Representative of the UN Secretary-General urged an immediate end to hostilities between rebel factions. In July a preliminary agreement was signed by the Government and rebel movements to end the conflict in Darfur. Later in that month a Government of National Unity was inaugurated. A new Interim National Assembly was inaugurated at the end of August. In September the first Area Joint Military Committee meetings were held—in Kadugli and Juba—as subsidiary bodies of the CJMC to oversee the cease-fire process at area sector level. In that month UNMIS expressed its concern for the future of the cease-fire in Darfur and UN humanitarian activities in the region given an escalation of violence. At the end of September an Interim Legislative Council of Southern Sudan was inaugurated, comprising representatives of all political and military factions. Nonetheless, security remained a major concern of UNMIS. In November UNMIS arbitrated a meeting between the leaders of two conflicting groups in Abyei, southern Sudan, in order to build confidence and initiate a reconciliation between the sides. During the second half of 2005 UNMIS personnel assisted in the rehabilitation of infrastructure in southern Sudan, including the construction of two bridges and the reopening of the Juba–Yei road. Its Human Rights Unit organized technical workshops on harmonizing Sudanese law with international humanitarian standards and on the role of parliamentarians in upholding human rights. Other UNMIS activities included training for HIV/AIDS education and measures to strengthen the country's police force. In August 2007 UNMIS officials held the first of regular consultations with the Government of Southern Sudan, agreed in June, on implementation of the January 2005 Comprehensive Peace Agreement.

In August 2006 the UN Security Council expanded the mandate of UNMIS to provide for its deployment to Darfur, in order to enforce a cease-fire and support the implementation of the Darfur Peace Agreement (DPA), which had been signed in early May by the Sudanese Government and the SPLM/A. Under its expanded mandate UNMIS was to monitor and verify the implementation by the parties to the cease-fire agreement and DPA; to observe and monitor the movements of armed groups and deployment of government forces by ground and aerial means; to investigate violations of the agreements; to monitor transborder activities of armed groups along the Sudanese borders with Chad and the Central African Republic; and to promote human rights, civilian protection and monitoring activities, including particular attention to the needs of women and children. The Council also authorized that the mission should be strengthened by up to 17,300 military personnel, up to 3,300 civilian police personnel, and up to 16 police units. Furthermore, the Council requested the Secretary-General to devise jointly with the AU, in consultation with the parties to the DPA, a plan and schedule for a transition from AMIS to a sole UN operation in Darfur. The Sudanese Government, however, initially rejected the concept of an expanded UN peace-keeping mission, on the grounds that it would compromise national sovereignty. In late December the UN, AU and Sudanese Government established a tripartite mechanism which was to facilitate the implementation of a UN-formulated three-phase approach, endorsed by the AU Peace and Security Council in November, that would culminate in a hybrid AU/UN mission in Darfur. In January 2007 UNMIS provided AMIS with supplies and extra personnel under the first ('light support') phase. In April the Sudanese Government endorsed the proposed second ('heavy') phase, which was to involve the delivery of force enablers, police units, civilian personnel and mission support items. In June the Sudanese Government agreed to support unconditionally the deployment of a hybrid AU/UN mission, following a meeting with a delegation from the UN Security Council. The mission, to be known as UNAMID, was authorized by the Security Council in July, with a force strength of up to 26,000 troops and police officers, supported by 5,000 international and local civilian staff. It was scheduled to have its management, command and control structures in place by October and assume command of AMIS at the end of the year. A joint AU/UN envoy, Rodolphe Adada, was named as head of the new mission. From early 2007 UNMIS undertook to engage the non-signatories of the DPA in the political process in Darfur. In June the AU and UN special representatives for Darfur defined a political 'road map' to lead eventually to full negotiations in support of a peaceful settlement. A joint meeting, hosted by both organizations in July, generated international support for the AU/UN peace process. In August the AU and UN special envoys chaired the first 'pre-negotiation' discussions with those rebel groups in Darfur not party to the DPA. An agreement was concluded to co-operate in efforts to secure a settlement for the region. Throughout the first half of 2007 UNMIS reported outbreaks of violence between government troops, rebels forces and local militias, causing further population displacement and disruption to humanitarian activities.

At 30 June 2007 UNMIS comprised 8,824 troops, 591 military observers and 693 police officers; at 31 May it was supported by 973 international and 2,487 local staff and 143 UN Volunteers. The General Assembly appropriation to cover the cost of the mission for the period 1 July 2007–30 June 2008 amounted to US $887.33m.

UNITED NATIONS MISSION IN THE DEMOCRATIC REPUBLIC OF THE CONGO—MONUC

Address: Kinshasa, Democratic Republic of the Congo.

Liaison offices are situated in Bujumbura (Burundi); Addis Ababa (Ethiopia); Windhoek (Namibia); Kigali (Rwanda); Kampala (Uganda); Lusaka (Zambia); and Harare (Zimbabwe).

Special Representative of the UN Secretary-General and Chief of Mission: William Lacy Swing (USA).

Force Commander: Lt-Gen. Babacar Gaye (Senegal).

Police Commissioner: Daniel Cure (France).

In August 1999 the UN Security Council authorized the deployment of up to 90 military liaison personnel to support implementation of a cease-fire agreement for the Democratic Republic of the Congo (DRC) which had been signed in Lusaka, Zambia, in July, by the heads of state of the DRC, Angola, Namibia, Rwanda, Uganda and Zimbabwe. The Council approved the establishment of MONUC in late November. The mission was mandated, in co-operation with a Joint Military Commission comprising representatives of the parties to the conflict, to oversee the implementation of the agreement, including monitoring the cease-fire and the disengagement of forces; to facilitate the delivery of humanitarian assistance; and to develop a mine action plan and undertake emergency de-mining activities. In February 2000 the Security Council authorized the expansion of the mission to comprise up to 5,537 military personnel, including up to 500 military observers who were to be dispatched to the DRC to monitor and verify the cease-fire and disengagement of forces. In April a sub-plan on military disengagement and redeployment was agreed in Kampala, Uganda, by the parties to the conflict and, in December, a revised sub-plan was adopted in Harare, Zimbabwe. However, by early 2001 the Lusaka cease-fire accord and Kampala and Harare sub-plans remained to be implemented and only a small contingent of MONUC observers had been deployed in the DRC. In mid-February the Security Council demanded that the parties to the conflict commence the phased disengagement and redeployment of their forces by mid-March and stipulated that plans for the full withdrawal of foreign troops and the disarmament, demobilization and resettlement of militia must be prepared and adopted by mid-May. The resolution raised the maximum number of military observers to 550, to be stationed around four regional headquarters; the deployment of up to 1,900 armed security personnel to protect these bases was also authorized. River boat units were to be deployed to assist with the transportation of observers and supplies and to reinforce the mission's presence; it was hoped that commercial activity along river routes would thus also be supported. Small contingents of MONUC troops were deployed in the DRC from March, including, in the following month, to the strategic rebel-occupied north-eastern town of Kisangani. In June the Security Council approved a revised concept of operations for MONUC, entailing the establishment of a civilian police element, enhancing the mission's presence in Kisangani and strengthening its logistic support capabilities. In October 2002 the UN Secretary-General reported that 90 teams of military observers were stationed at 50 sites in the DRC. Preparations were under way for the implementation of the mission's third phase of operations (authorized at the end of 2001), which was to entail the deployment of a full peace-keeping force to oversee the complete withdrawal of foreign troops from DRC territory and the disarmament, demobilization and reintegration of rebel forces. In December 2002 the UN Security Council authorized the expansion of the mission to co-ordinate this process.

In July 2001 MONUC launched a Quick Impact Projects programme, which focuses on the areas of education; health; environment; agriculture; public infrastructure rehabilitation; income generating activities; and support for vulnerable groups.

Some progress towards the implementation of the Lusaka cease-fire accord was achieved at the Inter-Congolese Dialogue held in Sun City, South Africa, from February–April 2002, when a bilateral power-sharing agreement was concluded between the DRC Government and Mouvement de libération du Congo—MLC rebels supported by the Ugandan Government. In mid-May a failed mutiny attempt by dissident rebels in Kisangani led to an outbreak of violence that resulted in at least 50 civilian fatalities. MONUC conducted patrols of the city and provided protection to a number of individuals who considered their lives to be at risk. Subsequently the Rwandan-backed Rassemblement congolais pour la démocratie (RCD)-Goma rebels controlling Kisangani accused the Special Representative of the Secretary-General of displaying a pro-Government bias and announced that he and several mission personnel were 'banned' from the area occupied by the grouping. A resolution of the Security Council in early June demanded that the RCD-Goma rebels cease their obstruction of the mission's activities in Kisangani immediately.

Following the adoption in July and August 2002, respectively, of the so-called Pretoria agreement between the DRC and Rwandan Governments, and Luanda agreement between the DRC and Ugandan Governments, nearly all Rwandan and Ugandan forces were withdrawn before the end of that year. Meanwhile, troop withdrawals, under MONUC observation, were also initiated by Angola, Burundi, Namibia and Zimbabwe. In December the Security Council adopted a resolution expanding the mission's authorized military strength to 8,700, to consist mainly of two intervention forces, which were to be deployed gradually. During that month the All-Inclusive Agreement on the Transition in the DRC, providing for the eventual staging of elections in the DRC, was signed by the participants in the Inter-Congolese Dialogue, in Pretoria, South Africa.

In response to continuing armed conflict and human rights violations in Bunia, north-eastern DRC, resulting in the deaths of more than 400 civilians in May 2003, a UN-backed temporary Interim Emergency Multinational Force (IEMF) was deployed to stabilize the situation there from June. In July the Security Council adopted a resolution increasing MONUC's authorized strength to 10,800 troops and extending the mission's mandate. The resolution authorized MONUC to take necessary measures to protect civilians and humanitarian workers under imminent threat of physical violence and to protect UN personnel and facilities, and imposed an arms embargo against all DRC and foreign armed groups in the east of the country. MONUC supported the IEMF during mid-2003, prior to resuming full responsibility for maintaining security in Bunia and thus replacing the Force in mid-September. At the end of June a DRC Transitional Government was established, in accordance with the December 2002 All-Inclusive Agreement on the Transition in the DRC. MONUC retained a presence in the capital, Kinshasa, to provide security for the new administration. An electoral assistance unit was created within the mission to support the preparations for the national elections scheduled under the Agreement to take place within two years. In July 2003 the Security Council adopted a resolution imposing an arms embargo on rebel groups and foreign troops operating in the Kivu and Ituri regions of eastern DRC and mandating MONUC to monitor the flow of arms there.

In May 2004 MONUC attempted to negotiate a cease-fire after fighting occurred in Bukavu, eastern DRC, between troops of the transitional government and forces loyal to two dissident military leaders. At the start of June, however, the dissident forces seized control of Bukavu, in order, it was claimed, to prevent further alleged killings of the minority Congolese Tutsi (Banyamulenge) population. Many properties, including UN warehouses, were looted. In other areas of the country there were violent protests against MONUC for failing to intervene in the situation. A few days later the dissident troops withdrew. In mid-June a MONUC team of human rights investigators determined that there was no evidence of any atrocities having been perpetrated against the Banyamulenge. In July thousands more people living in the eastern Lake Kivu district were displaced as a result of further clashes between government and dissident troops. In August a Burundian Hutu rebel group, the National Liberation Forces (FNL), claimed responsibility for the deaths of more than 160 Banyamulenge at a UN refugee camp in Gatumba, Burundi, close to the DRC border. The UN Security Council met in emergency session following the incident, amid concern at the escalation of tensions in the region. MONUC and UN forces in Burundi determined to reinforce security along the border. A Joint Verification Commission was established, in September, by the DRC and Rwandan authorities to address border security issues and to improve bilateral relations, for which MONUC was to serve as its secretariat. In October the Security Council agreed to expand MONUC to some 16,700 troops (although less than the force strength recommended by the UN Secretary-General) in order to reinforce its operational capabilities and avert further deterioration in the stability of the country. The Council also identified new responsibilities for the mission, including the protection of civilians 'under immediate threat of violence', inspection of air cargo in eastern regions to ensure that the ban on arms trading is upheld, and reporting on the presence of foreign troops and relevant troop movements, as well as tasks in support of the consolidation of the Transitional Government. In November MONUC undertook a joint operation with the Congolese army to protect the eastern Walungu area from rebel troops and deployed an additional brigade to North Kivu to provide additional security in the region. At the same time it established a new operations centre to monitor the disarmament of combatants and the retreat of foreign forces. Efforts to stabilize those parts of the country, however, were undermined from late November by reports from the Rwandan Government that it was prepared to attack former rebels living in the DRC who were perceived to be an ongoing threat to Rwandan security. The Security Council urged all states to refrain from any action that affected regional security or contravened international law, and, specifically, demanded the withdrawal of any Rwandan forces from the DRC and the disarmament of any rebel militia. An escalation of inter-factional hostilities in North Kivu province prompted an estimated 30,000 to leave their homes. MONUC troops established a temporary buffer zone in the worst affected areas in order to facilitate the delivery of humanitarian aid. In late February 2005 nine MONUC peace-keeping soldiers were killed during a patrol of a suspected militia camp in the Ituri district. With effect from early April MONUC declared Ituri an 'Arms Free District', prohibiting the possession of weapons.

In July 2005 MONUC initiated a series of operations in South Kivu province to pursue members of the Forces démocratiques pour la liberation du Rwanda (FDLR), who had reportedly been attacking the local civilian population, and to reinforce security in the eastern region of the country. In October MONUC provided military support for a new government operation to dislodge Rwandan Hutu rebels and to restore security, and in November deployed additional troops close to the border with Uganda to deter ongoing attacks in that region. In December the UN Security Council imposed a deadline of 15 January 2006 for foreign combatants in the DRC to disarm. In early January eight MONUC soldiers were killed by suspected Ugandan rebels in Garamba Park, close to the Sudanese border. At that time an estimated 20,000 civilians fled into western Uganda owing to an escalation in hostilities between the national army and rebel troops and several thousand others were also displaced. In February MONUC supported the army in a new operation against Hutu rebels in Ituri district; this was suspended in March, however, to allow for further training and preparation of the Congolese troops. In late May a MONUC soldier was killed by rebel forces in Ituri and five MONUC soldiers were taken hostage; they were released in July. Ongoing fighting in north-eastern provinces between government troops and rebel militias caused several thousand people to leave their homes. Provisional disarmament, demobilization and reintegration agreements were concluded with three Ituri rebel groups during 2006.

In mid-2005, following the adoption in May of a new draft constitution by the transitional National Assembly, MONUC's electoral assistance unit worked with the DRC Independent Electoral Commission to provide voter registration centres, train registration personnel and initiate the voter registration process in advance of a national referendum on the draft constitution that was initially scheduled to be held in November. Voter registration in Kinshasa was concluded at the end of July, and in early September the UN Security Council authorized US $103m. to provide additional logistical support to the nationwide registration process. The Council also approved a temporary increase in the strength of the mission by 841, including additional police personnel and five formed police units each of 125 officers. A temporary expansion in the military strength of the mission, by 300 troops, was approved in October. MONUC provided extensive technical and logistical assistance during the constitutional referendum, which was conducted, peacefully, in December. In 2006 an extensive electoral support operation was undertaken by the mission to prepare for presidential and legislative elections. In March the UN Secretary-General, Kofi Annan, visited the country to promote the democratic process. In April the UN Security Council authorized a temporary redeployment of an infantry battalion and some 50 military observers from the UN mission in Burundi to strengthen MONUC's security and monitoring capabilities in advance of the elections. MONUC reported the voting, conducted in July, to have been successful and largely peaceful; in August, however, there were violent clashes between supporters of the two leading presidential candidates. MONUC undertook to negotiate between both candidates and promoted confidence-building measures, including investigating allegations of electoral violations. A new National Assembly was inaugurated in September. In October MONUC initiated joint patrols, with European and national security forces, in the capital, Kinshasa, to uncover illegally-held firearms prior to the second round of the presidential election scheduled to be held at the end of that month. MONUC condemned violent demonstrations that followed the provisional release of results. The new President, Joseph Kabila, was inaugurated in December. In early 2007 MONUC appealed for an end to the violence that had erupted in the western Bas-Congo province following the release of local election results, and immediately deployed a multi-disciplinary team to enforce order and investigate the unrest in which an estimated 134 people had died. MONUC troops continued to patrol areas in eastern DRC to maintain stability, and undertook negotiations with a local militia leader to surrender and disarm his troops. In March MONUC condemned intense fighting that had occurred in the capital, Kinshasa, between government troops and forces loyal to the defeated former Vice-President, Jean-Pierre Bemba. MONUC aimed to assist civilians affected by the violence and determined to conduct an inquiry into the events. In June MONUC increased its patrols in North and South Kivu Provinces in order to strengthen security against the continuing military activity of armed groups. In August MONUC dispatched some 200 additional troops to Katale, in North Kivu, to help to control an escalation in hostilities.

MONUC works closely with the Multi-Country Demobilization and Reintegration Programme, administered by the World Bank, and with UNDP, the lead agency for reintegration in the DRC. In August 2007 a further 3,500 members of three armed militia groups in Ituri, eastern DRC, complied with a deadline to join the disarmament programme.

At 30 June 2007 MONUC comprised 16,619 troops, 729 military observers and 1,036 police officers; it is assisted by 933 international staff, 2,042 local civilian personnel and 606 UN Volunteers. The budget for the mission amounted to US $1,166.72 for the period 1 July 2007–30 June 2008, funded from a Special Account comprising assessed contributions from UN member states.

UNITED NATIONS OPERATION IN CÔTE D'IVOIRE—UNOCI

Address: Abidjan, Côte d'Ivoire.

Officer-in-Charge: Abou Moussa.

Force Commander: Maj.-Gen. Fernand Marcel Amoussou (Benin).

UNOCI was authorized by the UN Security Council in February 2004 and began operations in early April. It was mandated to observe and monitor the implementation of the Linas-Marcoussis Agreement, signed by the parties to the conflict in Côte d'Ivoire in January 2003, and hitherto supported by the UN Mission in Côte d'Ivoire (MINUCI), forces of the Economic Community of West African States—ECOWAS and French peace-keeping troops. UNOCI was authorized also to assist with the disarmament, demobilization and reintegration of rebel groups, to protect civilians and UN personnel, institutions and equipment, and to support ongoing humanitarian and human rights activities. With a contingent of the French *'Licorne'* peace-keeping force, UNOCI was to monitor a so-called Zone of Confidence separating the two areas of the country under government and rebel control. In July all parties, attending a meeting of West African heads of state that had been convened by the UN Secretary-General and the President of Ghana, endorsed the Accra III Agreement identifying means of implementing the Linas-Marcoussis Accord. UNOCI was to participate in a tripartite monitoring group, together with ECOWAS and the African Union, to oversee progress in implementing the agreement. In mid-August UNOCI launched a radio station, in accordance with its mandate, to assist the process of national reunification and in the following month established some secure transit routes between the areas under government and rebel control in order to facilitate travel and enable family reunions. None the less, by October UNOCI officials expressed concern at ongoing violations of human rights and a deterioration in security, as well as a lack of progress in implementing provisions of the peace accords.

In early November 2004 government troops violated the cease-fire and the Zone of Confidence by launching attacks against rebel Forces Nouvelles in the north of the country. An emergency session of the UN Security Council, convened following an escalation of the hostilities and a fatal air strike on a French peace-keeping unit, urged both sides to refrain from further violence. Security further deteriorated in the south of the country when French troops destroyed the government air force prompting rioting in the capital, Abidjan, and violence directed towards foreign nationals. UNOCI assisted with the evacuation of foreign workers and their families and provided secure refuge for other personnel. In mid-November the Security Council imposed an immediate embargo on the sale or supply of armaments to Côte d'Ivoire and demanded a cessation of hostilities and of the use of media broadcasts to incite hatred and violence against foreigners. UNOCI was to monitor the terms of the resolution and to broadcast its own messages of support for the peace process. By the end of that month reports indicated that the security situation had improved and that some of the estimated 19,000 who fled the country to Liberia had started to return. In addition, conditions in the northern city of Bouaké were improving as water and electricity supplies were restored. In December UNOCI funded three Quick Impact Projects, in order to highlight the humanitarian aspect of the mission, and commenced joint patrols with government forces to uphold security in Abidjan.

In February 2005 the UN Security Council demanded that all parties co-operate with UNOCI in compiling a comprehensive list of armaments under their control as preparation for implementing a programme of disarmament, demobilization and reintegration. In March UNOCI increased its presence in western regions of the country owing to an increase in reported violent incidents. In the following month UNOCI troops were deployed to the border regions with Liberia and Ghana in order to support implementation of the UN-imposed arms embargo. UNOCI troops also monitored the withdrawal of heavy weaponry by both Government forces and the Forces Nouvelles. In June UN representatives condemned the massacre of almost 60 civilians in Duékoué, in the west of the country, and urged that an inquiry be held into the incident. UNOCI reinforcements were sent to restore stability in the area and undertook joint patrols with local forces. Later in that month the UN Security Council authorized an increase in UNOCI's military and civilian police components, as well as the redeployment of troops from other missions in the region in order to restore security in the country. In July UN troops, investigating reports of violent attacks by rebel groups, were prevented from entering two towns north of Abidjan. UNOCI later complained at further reported obstruction of human rights and civilian police teams. In spite of persisting concerns regarding the political and human rights situation in the country, UNOCI continued to provide logistical and technical assistance to the independent national electoral commission in preparations for elections, scheduled to be held in October; however, these were later postponed. A transitional government of national unity was formed in late December. In early 2006 UN property and personnel were subjected to hostile attacks during a period of unrest by groups protesting against a report of an International Working Group, co-chaired by the Special Representative of the UN Secretary-General, that had recommended the dissolution of the national assembly (the mandate of which had already expired). Several hundred humanitarian personnel were evacuated from the country. In the following month the Security Council imposed 12-month sanctions and travel bans against three leaders deemed to be responsible for directing the disturbances. In January the Council agreed to review UNOCI's authorized strength, but did not authorize a recommendation of the Secretary-General to expand the mission by an additional 3,400 troops and 475 police officers. At the end of February UNOCI initiated a large-scale operation to provide security for school examinations, to be held in the north of the country for the first time in three years. In June the Security Council authorized an increase in the mission's force strength by 1,025 military personnel and 475 police officers needed to strengthen security throughout the country and undertake disarmament operations. In October UNOCI conducted joint border patrols with UN forces in Liberia to monitor movements of combatants and weapons. In January 2007 the Security Council formally enlarged UNOCI's mandate to co-ordinate with UNMIL to monitor the arms embargo and to conduct a voluntary repatriation and resettlement programme for foreign ex-combatants. The Council's resolution also defined UNOCI's mandate as being to monitor the cessation of hostilities and movements of armed groups; to assist programmes for the disarmament, demobilization and reintegration of all combatants; to disarm and dismantle militias; to support population identification and voter registration programmes; to assist the reform of the security sector and other activities to uphold law and order; to support humanitarian assistance and the promotion of human rights; and to provide technical support for the conduct of free and fair elections no later than 31 October. A new political agreement to work towards national reconciliation was signed by leaders of the opposing parties in Ouagadougou, Burkina Faso, in March. According to the agreement the Zone of Confidence was to be dismantled and replaced by a UN-monitored 'green line'. UNOCI organized a series of meetings to ensure the support of traditional leaders for the peace process. The process of disarmament was officially launched on 30 July. In June UNOCI condemned a rocket attack on a plane carrying the country's Prime Minister and endorsed any international inquiry into the incident.

At 30 June 2007 UNOCI had an operational strength of 7,846 troops, 192 military observers and 1,145 police officers; it was supported by 408 international and 548 local civilian personnel and 249 UN Volunteers. The General Assembly appropriated US $493.70m. to finance the mission during the period 1 July 2007–30 June 2008.

United Nations Peace-building

Address: Department of Political Affairs, United Nations, New York, NY 10017, USA.

Telephone: (212) 963-1234; **fax:** (212) 963-4879; **internet:** www.un.org/Depts/dpa/.

The Department of Political Affairs provides support and guidance to UN peace-building operations and political missions working in the field to prevent and resolve conflicts or to promote enduring peace in post-conflict societies. The UN Assistance Mission in Afghanistan, UN Integrated Office in Sierra Leone and UN Integrated Office in Burundi are directed by the Department of Peace-keeping Operations.

The World Summit of UN heads of state held in September 2005 approved recommendations made by the UN Secretary-General in his March 2005 report entitled 'In Larger Freedom: Towards Development, Security and Human Rights for All' for the creation of an intergovernmental advisory Peace-building Commission. In December the UN Security Council and General Assembly authorized the establishment of the Commission; it was inaugurated, as a special subsidiary body of both the Council and Assembly, in June 2006. A multi-year standing peace-building fund, financed by voluntary contributions from member states and mandated to support post-conflict peace-building activities, was established in October 2006. The creation of a Peace-building Support Office within the UN Secretariat is also envisaged.

OFFICE OF THE SPECIAL REPRESENTATIVE OF THE UN SECRETARY-GENERAL FOR WEST AFRICA—UNOWA

Address: BP 23851 Dakar-Ponty, 5 ave Carde, Immeuble Caisse de sécurité sociale, Dakar, Senegal.

Telephone: (221) 849-07-29; **fax:** (221) 842-50-95; **internet:** www.un.org/unowa.

Special Representative of the UN Secretary-General: AHMEDOU OULD-ABDALLAH (Mauritania).

UNOWA was established with an initial, three-year mandate, from January 2002, to elaborate an integrated approach by the United Nations to the prevention and management of conflict in West Africa; and to promote peace, security and development in the sub-region. (UNOWA's mandate was renewed for a further three years from January 2005.) In pursuit of these objectives the Special Representative of the Secretary-General (SRSG) meets regularly with the leaders of UN regional and political offices in West Africa. In 2005 ongoing UNOWA projects included an initiative to address cross-border challenges, such as mercenaries, child-soldiers and small arms proliferation. UNOWA was also involved in monitoring the crisis in Côte d'Ivoire. UNOWA takes part in a joint work programme with the Economic Community of West African States (ECOWAS), whose projects embrace security-sector reform—identified as a key priority for the sub-region—small arms, transborder co-operation, etc. A trilateral partnership between UNOWA, the European Union and ECOWAS has also been established. UNOWA is involved too in the development of a regional harmonized approach to disarmament, demobilization and reintegration in West Africa. UNOWA has launched an initiative to address economic, political, security and humanitarian problems that confront in particular the populations of certain border areas in West Africa. Integrated, multi-agency strategies are to be developed in respect of four border clusters: Guinea/Côte d'Ivoire/Liberia/Sierra Leone (Guinea Forestière); Mali/Burkina Faso/Côte d'Ivoire/Ghana; Mauritania/Mali/Niger; and Senegal/The Gambia/Guinea-Bissau. UNOWA conducts regional good offices missions. One of its major concerns is to help minimize instability arising from elections or the transfer of power. The SRSG serves additionally as chairman of the Cameroon-Nigeria Mixed Commission, which has met regularly since December 2002.

At June 2007 UNOWA comprised seven international civilian and nine local civilian personnel.

UNITED NATIONS INTEGRATED OFFICE IN BURUNDI—BINUB

Address: Bujumbura, Burundi.

Executive Representative of the Secretary-General: YOUSSEF MAHMOUD (Tunisia).

The United Nations Integrated Office in Burundi (Bureau Intégré des Nations Unies au Burundi—BINUB) was established on 1 January 2007, replacing the United Nations Operation in Burundi, which was terminated in December 2006. BINUB is mandated to support the Burundi Government in its efforts to achieve long-term peace and security, with a particular focus on strengthening the conflict-prevention capacities of national institutions and civil society; supporting public institutions with strengthening good governance and accountability; promoting freedom of the press; consolidating the rule of law; supporting the Dar-es-Salaam Comprehensive Cease-fire Agreement concluded in September 2006; supporting the development of a national plan for reform of the security sector; supporting the completion of the ongoing national programme for the demobilization and reintegration of former combatants; supporting efforts to combat the proliferation of small arms; promoting human rights; assisting with the establishment of transitional justice mechanisms, including a truth and reconciliation commission; strengthening the partnership and co-ordination between the Government and international donors; and ensuring effective co-ordination among UN agencies in Burundi.

At June 2007 BINUB comprised 77 international civilian and 164 local civilian personnel, as well as four military observers, 11 police and 58 UN volunteers. A budget of US $33.1m. was approved for the Office in 2007.

UNITED NATIONS INTEGRATED OFFICE IN SIERRA LEONE—UNIOSIL

Address: Freetown, Sierra Leone.

Executive Representative of the Secretary-General and Head of Office: VICTOR DA SILVA ÂNGELO (Portugal).

The United Nations Integrated Office in Sierra Leone (UNIOSIL) was established on 1 January 2006 in accordance with UN Security Council Resolution 1620 (31 August 2005). UNIOSIL is the successor mission to the large UN peace-keeping operation in Sierra Leone, UNAMSIL, whose mandate was completed in December 2005. The key elements of UNIOSIL's mandate, as set out, with an initial term of one year, in Resolution 1620, are that it should assist the government of Sierra Leone: to build the capacity of national institutions to tackle the root causes of the country's conflict, supply basic services and hasten progress towards attainment of the Millennium Developments Goals through poverty reduction and sustainable economic growth; to develop a national action plan for human rights and establishing the national human rights commission; to build the capacity of the National Electoral Commission to conduct, free, fair and credible legislative elections in 2007; to enhance good governance; to strengthen the rule of law; to strengthen the Sierra Leonean security sector; and to promote a culture of peace, dialogue and participation in critical national issues. UNIOSIL is further mandated to liaise with the Sierra Leonean security sector and other partners; to co-ordinate with UN missions and offices and regional organizations in West Africa in tackling cross-border challenges; and to co-ordinate with the Special Court for Sierra Leone. The head of UNIOSIL, the Executive Representative of the Secretary-General, also serves as the Resident Representative of the UN Development Programme and as the UN Resident and Humanitarian Co-ordinator. UNIOSIL comprises five sections that focus respectively on the key areas of its mandate: good governance and peace consolidation; human rights and the rule of law; civilian police and military assistance; development; and public information.

At June 2007 UNIOSIL comprised 73 international civilian and 193 local civilian personnel. There were, in addition, 15 military observers, 27 police and 40 UN volunteers.

UNITED NATIONS PEACE-BUILDING OFFICE IN THE CENTRAL AFRICAN REPUBLIC—BONUCA

Address: POB 4661, Grand Central Station, New York, NY 10163-4661, USA.

Telephone: (212) 963-9718; **fax:** (212) 963-0794.

Special Representative of the UN Secretary-General and Head of Office: Gen. LAMINE CISSÉ (Senegal).

The United Nations Peace-building Office in the Central African Republic (BONUCA) was established in February 2000 following the withdrawal of the UN Peace-keeping Mission in the Central African Republic (MINURCA). BONUCA has contributed good offices and other assistance to the restoration of constitutional order in the Central African Republic following elections in 2005. BONUCA's work has focused on, *inter alia*, electoral assistance, military reform, human rights, training civilian police and the disarmament, demobilization and reintegration of former combatants.

At June 2007 BONUCA comprised 26 international civilian and 50 local civilian personnel. There were in addition five military advisers, six police and two UN volunteers.

UNITED NATIONS PEACE-BUILDING SUPPORT OFFICE IN GUINEA-BISSAU—UNOGBIS

Address: UN Bldg, CP 179, Rua Rui Djassi, Bissau, Guinea-Bissau.

Special Representative of the UN Secretary-General and Head of Office: SHOLA OMOREGIE (Nigeria).

Established to assist Guinea-Bissau in its peace-building efforts, including the electoral process, the United Nations Peace-building Support Office in Guinea-Bissau (UNOGBIS) first became operational in June 1999. Unlike other UN peace-building missions, UNOGBIS was not preceded by a UN peace-keeping mission. The intensification of persistent political violence and uncertainty in 2004 led the UN Security Council to assume authority for the mandate in that year. UN Security Council Resolution 1580 (2004) extended and revised the mandate of UNOGBIS. Since 2003 the work of UNOGBIS has focused on transition to civilian rule in the aftermath of a military coup that took place in that year. UNOGBIS is mandated by the Security Council to promote national reconciliation, respect for human rights and the rule of law; support national capacity for conflict prevention; encourage reform of the security sector and stable civil-military relations; encourage government efforts to suppress trafficking in small arms; and to collaborate with a 'comprehensive peace-building strategy' to strengthen state institutions and mobilize international resources.

At June 2007 UNOGBIS comprised 11 international civilian and 10 local civilian personnel, two military advisers, one police adviser, and one UN volunteer.

UNITED NATIONS POLITICAL OFFICE FOR SOMALIA—UNPOS

Address: Nairobi, Kenya.

Special Representative of the UN Secretary-General and Head of Office: FRANÇOIS LONSENY FALL (Guinea).

The United Nations Political Office for Somalia (UNPOS) was established in Nairobi, Kenya, in 1995 with the objective of assisting the Secretary-General to advance peace and reconciliation in the country by utilizing its contacts with Somali leaders and civic organizations. UNPOS provides good offices, co-ordinates international political support and financial assistance to peace and reconciliation initiatives and monitors and reports on developments in the country. In 2002–04 UNPOS supported the Somali National Reconciliation Conference that was organized in Nairobi under the auspices of the Inter-governmental Authority on Development, and worked with international partners to facilitate agreement among Somali leaders on a transitional administration. By early 2005 the Conference had established a broad-based Transitional Federal Government which was able to relocate to Somalia from its temporary base in Kenya. During 2005, in response to progress in the reconciliation process, UNPOS prepared to expand its personnel and activities. Endorsing this expansion, the UN Security Council authorized UNPOS to promote reconciliation through dialogue between Somali parties; to assist efforts to address the 'Somaliland' issue; to co-ordinate the support of Somalia's neighbours and other international partners for the country's peace process; and to assume a leading political role in peace-building initiatives.

At June 2007 UNPOS comprised 17 international civilian and 10 local civilian personnel.

World Food Programme—WFP

Address: Via Cesare Giulio Viola 68, Parco dei Medici, 00148 Rome, Italy.

Telephone: (06) 65131; **fax:** (06) 6513-2840; **e-mail:** wfpinfo@wfp.org; **internet:** www.wfp.org.

WFP, the principal food aid organization of the United Nations, became operational in 1963. It aims to alleviate acute hunger by providing emergency relief following natural or man-made humanitarian disasters, and supplies food aid to people in developing countries to eradicate chronic undernourishment, to support social development and to promote self-reliant communities.

Organization

(September 2007)

EXECUTIVE BOARD

The governing body of WFP is the Executive Board, comprising 36 members, 18 of whom are elected by the UN Economic and Social Council (ECOSOC) and 18 by the Council of the Food and Agriculture Organization (FAO). The Board meets four times each year at WFP headquarters.

SECRETARIAT

WFP's Executive Director is appointed jointly by the UN Secretary-General and the Director-General of FAO and is responsible for the management and administration of the Programme. In 2006 there were 10,587 staff members, of whom nearly 92% were working in the field. WFP administers some 87 country offices, in order to provide operational, financial and management support at a more local level, and maintains six regional bureaux, located in Bangkok, Thailand (for Asia), Cairo, Egypt (for the Middle East, Central Asia and Eastern Europe), Panama City, Panama (for Latin America and the Caribbean), Johannesburg, South Africa (for Southern Africa), Kampala, Uganda (for Central and Eastern Africa), and Dakar, Senegal (for West Africa).

Executive Director: JOSETTE SHEERAN (USA).

Activities

WFP is the only multilateral organization with a mandate to use food aid as a resource. It is the second largest source of assistance in the UN, after the World Bank group, in terms of actual transfers of resources, and the largest source of grant aid in the UN system. WFP handles more than one-third of the world's food aid. WFP is also the largest contributor to South–South trade within the UN system, through the purchase of food and services from developing countries. WFP's mission is to provide food aid to save lives in refugee and other emergency situations, to improve the nutrition and quality of life of vulnerable groups and to help to develop assets and promote the self-reliance of poor families and communities. WFP aims to focus its efforts on the world's poorest countries and to provide at least 90% of its total assistance to those designated as 'low-income food-deficit'. At the World Food Summit, held in November 1996, WFP endorsed the commitment to reduce by 50% the number of undernourished people, no later than 2015. During 2006 WFP food assistance benefited some 87.8m. people (including 58.8m. children) in 78 countries, of whom 24.3m. received aid through development projects, 16.4m. through emergency operations, and 47.0m. through Protracted Relief and Recovery Operations. Total food deliveries in 2006 amounted to 4.0m. metric tons. WFP rations comprise basic food items (cereals, oil and pulses), and, where possible, additional complementary items (such as meat or fish, vegetables, fruit, fortified cereal blends, sugar and condiments).

WFP aims to address the causes of chronic malnourishment, which it identifies as poverty and lack of opportunity. It emphasizes the role played by women in combating hunger, and endeavours to address the specific nutritional needs of women, to increase their access to food and development resources, and to promote girls' education. It also focuses resources on supporting the food security of households and communities affected by HIV/AIDS and on promoting food security as a means of mitigating extreme poverty and vulnerability and thereby combating the spread and impact of HIV/AIDS. In February 2003 WFP and the Joint UN Programme on HIV/AIDS (UNAIDS) concluded an agreement to address jointly the relationship between HIV/AIDS, regional food shortages and chronic hunger, with a particular focus on Africa, South-East Asia and the Caribbean. In October of that year WFP became a co-sponsor of UNAIDS. WFP urges the development of new food aid strategies as a means of redressing global inequalities and thereby combating the threat of conflict and international terrorism.

WFP food donations must meet internationally-agreed standards applicable to trade in food products. In May 2003 WFP's Executive Board approved a new policy on donations of genetically modified (GM) foods and other foods derived from biotechnology, determining that the Programme would continue to accept donations of GM/biotech food and that, when distributing it, relevant national standards would be respected.

Since the 1990s WFP has developed a range of mechanisms to enhance its preparedness for emergency situations (such as conflict, drought and other natural disasters) and to improve its capacity for responding effectively to crises as they arise. A new programme of emergency response training was inaugurated in 2000, while security concerns for personnel was incorporated as a new element into all general planning and training activities. Through its Vulnerability Analysis and Mapping (VAM) project, WFP aims to identify potentially vulnerable groups by providing information on food security and the capacity of different groups for coping with shortages, and to enhance emergency contingency-planning and long-term assistance objectives. In 2007 VAM field units were operational in more than 50 countries. WFP also co-operates with other UN agencies including UNICEF (the largest partner in 2006), FAO, IFAD, WHO and UNHCR. Since 2003 WFP has been mandated to provide aviation transport services to the wider humanitarian community. The key elements of WFP's emergency response capacity are its strategic stores of food and logistics equipment, stand-by arrangements to enable the rapid deployment of personnel, communications and other essential equipment, and the Augmented Logistics Intervention Team for Emergencies (ALITE), which undertakes capacity assessments and contingency-planning. During 2000 WFP led efforts, undertaken with other UN humanitarian agencies, for the design and application of local UN Joint Logistics Centre facilities, which aimed to co-ordinate resources in an emergency situation. In 2001 a UN Humanitarian Response Depot was opened in Brindisi, Italy, under the direction of WFP experts, for the storage of essential rapid response equipment. In that year the Programme published a set of guide-lines on contingency planning.

Through its development activities, WFP aims to alleviate poverty in developing countries by promoting self-reliant families and communities. Food is supplied, for example, as an incentive in development self-help schemes and as part-wages in labour-intensive projects of many kinds. In all its projects WFP aims to assist the most vulnerable groups and to ensure that beneficiaries have an adequate and balanced diet. Activities supported by the Programme include the settlement and resettlement of groups and communities; land reclamation and improvement; irrigation; the development of forestry and dairy farming; road construction; training of hospital staff; community development; and human resources development such as feeding expectant or nursing mothers and school children, and support for education, training and health programmes. No individual country is permitted to receive more than 10% of the Programme's available development resources. During 2001 WFP initiated a new Global School Feeding Campaign to strengthen international co-operation to expand educational opportunities for poor children and to improve the quality of the teaching environment. In 2003 WFP launched a *19-Cents-a-day* campaign to encourage donors to support its school feeding activities (19 US cents being the estimated cost of one school lunch). During 2006 school feeding projects benefited 20.2m. children.

Following a comprehensive evaluation of its activities, WFP is increasingly focused on linking its relief and development activities to provide a continuum between short-term relief and longer-term rehabilitation and development. In order to achieve this objective, WFP aims to integrate elements that strengthen disaster mitigation into development projects, including soil conservation, reafforestation, irrigation infrastructure, and transport construction and rehabilitation; and to promote capacity-building elements within relief operations, e.g. training, income-generating activities and environmental protection measures. In 1999 WFP adopted a new Food Aid and Development policy, which aims to use food assistance both to cover immediate requirements and to create conditions conducive to enhancing the long-term food security of vulnerable populations. During that year WFP began implementing Protracted Relief and Recovery Operations (PRROs), where the emphasis is on fostering stability, rehabilitation and long-term development for victims of natural disasters, displaced persons and refugees. PRROs are introduced no later than 18 months after the initial emergency operation and last no more than three years. When undertaken in collaboration with UNHCR and other international agencies, WFP has responsibility for mobilizing basic food commodities and for related transport, handling and storage costs. Some 18 new PRROs were approved in 2006.

In 2006 the main regional focus of WFP relief activities was sub-Saharan Africa, which received 62% of global food aid deliveries. Operational expenditure in the region amounted to US $1,761.9m. (66% of total operational expenditure in that year), including $635.8m. for emergency relief operations, $882.1m. for PRROs, and $112.4m. for agricultural, rural and human resource development projects. In 2007 WFP was undertaking operations to feed some 54m. people suffering severe food insecurity in five regions of sub-Saharan Africa.

A US $621m. PRRO was being implemented during 2005–07 in Lesotho, Malawi, Mozambique, Swaziland and Zambia, following on from emergency feeding activities initiated in those countries and Zimbabwe in 2001. The ongoing humanitarian crisis in that sub-region has been attributed to the combined effects of drought, flooding and often weak government capacity to deliver basic social services, aggravated by the effects of the regional epidemic of HIV/AIDS. (It is estimated that one-half of all HIV/AIDS sufferers in southern Africa are employed in farming.) In view of the effects on crop production of flooding in south-eastern Africa in February 2007, followed by a devastating drought, WFP warned in August that nearly 5m. people there might require food assistance by early 2008, including some 4m. in Zimbabwe, which was suffering a severe economic crisis. A PRRO was being implemented in Angola during April 2006–March 2009 to provide food assistance for education in conflict-affected communities. In mid-2004 WFP appealed for $200m. to assist an estimated 2m. people were in urgent need of food aid in Darfur, western Sudan, owing to ongoing ethnic conflict, and a further $30m. to distribute food to an estimated 192,500 people from Darfur who had fled to camps in Chad. During 2005 WFP expanded its presence in Darfur to cover more than 400 sites (compared with 167 sites at the end of 2004) and initiated a school-feeding project in the region. From May 2006, owing to insufficient funding for the operation in Darfur, WFP significantly reduced food supplies there, lowering the daily ration from 2,100 kilocalories (considered an adequate daily requirement) to 1,050 kilocalories. A total of 400 metric tons of food aid were distributed by the Fund in Sudan in that year. A one-year emergency operation in Sudan for 2007 aimed to provide 682,136 metric tons of food aid to 5.5m. beneficiaries (mainly women and children) at a cost of $685.4m. Since late 2004 WFP has been supporting malnourished people in Niger affected by the devastation caused to cereal production by both severe drought and locust infestation; nearly 3m. people from Niger received food assistance from WFP and its partners in 2005, with required funding for the operation estimated in August at $57.6m. Food distribution was continuing in 2007. Drought-affected communities in the Horn of Africa were a particular focus of WFP activities in sub-Saharan Africa in that year. A PRRO to provide food assistance to vulnerable groups and refugees in Djibouti was being undertaken during the period April 2007–March 2009. A two-year PRRO was being implemented during 2007–08 to provide food assistance to Eritrean, Somali and Sudanese refugees in Ethiopia, alongside a PRRO to enable the protection and promotion of livelihoods in Ethiopia, covering 2005–07. A five-year country programme for Ethiopia, covering 2007–11, was to support 2.2m. beneficiaries. A PRRO to provide food assistance to Somali and Sudanese refugees in Kenya was to be implemented during the period October 2007–September 2009, and a PRRO to provide food aid for relief and the protection of livelihoods in Somalia was being implemented during the two-year period August 2006–July 2008. A PRRO to assist refugees encamped in north-western Tanzania was being undertaken during 2007–08.

Following a massive earthquake in the Indian Ocean in December 2004, which caused a series of tidal waves, or tsunamis, that devastated coastal regions in 14 countries in South and South-East Asia and East Africa, initial WFP emergency operations were funded from the Immediate Response Account (see below). In January 2005 WFP requested emergency funding of US $256m., of which $185m. was to support an initial six-month programme to provide food aid to 2m. people affected by the natural disaster, mainly in Sri Lanka, the Maldives and Indonesia, and $72m. was for three Special Operations, concerned with logistics augmentation, air support and the establishment of a UN Joint Logistics Centre for Inter-Agency Co-ordination, of which WFP was the lead agency. In Indonesia (close to the epicentre of the earthquake) WFP established new field offices and an Emergency Operations Centre in the capital, Jakarta. From mid-2005 WFP focused its activities, increasingly, on recovery and rebuilding communities.

Finance

The Programme is funded by voluntary contributions from donor countries, intergovernmental bodies such as the European Commission, and the private sector. Contributions are made in the form of commodities, finance and services (particularly shipping). Commitments to the International Emergency Food Reserve (IEFR), from which WFP provides the majority of its food supplies, and to the Immediate Response Account of the IEFR (IRA), are also made on a voluntary basis by donors. WFP's operational expenditures in 2006 amounted to some US $2,665m. Contributions by donors in that year totalled $2,705m.

Publications

Annual Report.
Food and Nutrition Handbook.
School Feeding Handbook.
World Hunger Series.

Food and Agriculture Organization of the United Nations—FAO

Address: Viale delle Terme di Caracalla, 00100 Rome, Italy.
Telephone: (06) 5705-1; **fax:** (06) 5705-3152; **e-mail:** fao-hq@fao.org; **internet:** www.fao.org.

FAO, the first specialized agency of the UN to be founded after the Second World War, aims to alleviate malnutrition and hunger, and serves as a co-ordinating agency for development programmes in the whole range of food and agriculture, including forestry and fisheries. It helps developing countries to promote educational and training facilities and to create appropriate institutions.

Organization

(September 2007)

CONFERENCE

The governing body is the FAO Conference of member nations. It meets every two years, formulates policy, determines the Organization's programme and budget on a biennial basis, and elects new members. It also elects the Director-General of the Secretariat and the Independent Chairman of the Council. Every other year FAO also holds conferences in each of its five regions (Africa, Asia and the Pacific, Europe, Latin America and the Caribbean, and the Near East).

COUNCIL

The FAO Council is composed of representatives of 49 member nations, elected by the Conference for staggered three-year terms. It is the interim governing body of FAO between sessions of the Conference. The most important standing Committees of the Council are: the Finance and Programme Committees, the Committee on Commodity Problems, the Committee on Fisheries, the Committee on Agriculture and the Committee on Forestry.

SECRETARIAT

The number of FAO staff in 2006 was around 3,700, of whom 1,500 were professional staff and 2,200 general service staff. About one-half of the Organization's staff were based at headquarters. Work is supervised by the following Departments: Administration and Finance; General Affairs and Information; Economic and Social Policy; Agriculture; Forestry; Fisheries; Sustainable Development; and Technical Co-operation.

Director-General: JACQUES DIOUF (Senegal).

REGIONAL OFFICES

Africa: POB 1628, Accra, Ghana; tel. (21) 675000; fax (21) 668427; e-mail fao-raf@fao.org; internet www.fao.org/world/regional/raf; Regional Rep. OLOCHE ANEBI EDACHE.

Sub-regional Office for Southern and Eastern Africa: POB 3730, Harare, Zimbabwe; tel. (4) 791407; fax (4) 703497; e-mail fao-safr-registry@fao.org; internet www.fao.org/world/subregional/safr; Subregional Rep. VICTORIA SEKITOLEKO.

JOINT DIVISION AND LIAISON OFFICE

Joint FAO/IAEA Division of Nuclear Techniques in Food and Agriculture: Wagramerstrasse 5, 1400 Vienna, Austria; tel. (1) 2600-0; fax (1) 2600-7; Dir QU LIANG.

United Nations: Suite DC1-1125, 1 United Nations Plaza, New York, NY 10017, USA; tel. (212) 963-6036; fax (212) 963-5425; e-mail fao-lony@field.fao.org; Dir FLORENCE CHENOWETH.

Activities

FAO aims to raise levels of nutrition and standards of living by improving the production and distribution of food and other commodities derived from farms, fisheries and forests. FAO's ultimate objective is the achievement of world food security, 'Food for All'. The organization provides technical information, advice and assistance by disseminating information; acting as a neutral forum for discussion of food and agricultural issues; advising governments on policy and planning; and developing capacity directly in the field.

In November 1996 FAO hosted the World Food Summit, which was held in Rome and was attended by heads of state and senior government representatives of 186 countries. Participants approved the Rome Declaration on World Food Security and the World Food Summit Plan of Action, with the aim of halving the number of people afflicted by undernutrition, at that time estimated to total 828m. world-wide, by no later than 2015. A review conference to assess progress in achieving the goals of the summit, entitled World Food Summit: Five Years Later, held in June 2002, reaffirmed commitment to this objective, which is also incorporated into the UN Millennium Development Goal (MDG) of eradicating extreme poverty and hunger. During that month FAO announced the formulation of a global 'Anti-Hunger Programme', which aimed to promote investment in the agricultural sector and rural development, with a particular focus on small farmers, and to enhance food access for those most in need, for example through the provision of school meals, schemes to feed pregnant and nursing mothers and food-for-work programmes. FAO hosts the UN System Network on Rural Development and Food Security, comprising some 20 UN bodies, which was established in 1997 as an interagency mechanism to follow-up the World Food Summits.

In November 1999 the FAO Conference approved a long-term Strategic Framework for the period 2000–15, which emphasized national and international co-operation in pursuing the goals of the 1996 World Food Summit. The Framework promoted interdisciplinarity and partnership, and defined three main global objectives: constant access by all people to sufficient nutritionally adequate and safe food to ensure that levels of undernourishment were reduced by 50% by 2015 (see above); the continued contribution of sustainable agriculture and rural development to economic and social progress and well-being; and the conservation, improvement and sustainable use of natural resources. It identified five corporate strategies (each supported by several strategic objectives), covering the following areas: reducing food insecurity and rural poverty; ensuring enabling policy and regulatory frameworks for food, agriculture, fisheries and forestry; creating sustainable increases in the supply and availability of agricultural, fisheries and forestry products; conserving and enhancing sustainable use of the natural resource base; and generating knowledge. In November 2001 the FAO Conference adopted a medium-term plan covering 2002–07, based on the Strategic Framework. In November 2004 the FAO Council adopted a set of voluntary Right to Food Guide-lines that aimed to 'support the progressive realization of the right to adequate food in the context of national food security' by providing practical guidance to countries in support of their efforts to achieve the 1996 World Food Summit commitment and UN MDG relating to hunger reduction.

FAO organizes an annual series of fund-raising events, 'TeleFood', some of which are broadcast on television and the internet, in order to raise public awareness of the problems of hunger and malnutrition. Since its inception in 1997 public donations to TeleFood have reached almost US $19m., financing 2,137 'grass-roots' projects in 127 countries. The projects have provided tools, seeds and other essential supplies directly to small-scale farmers, and have been especially aimed at helping women.

In 1999 FAO signed a memorandum of understanding with UNAIDS on strengthening co-operation. In December 2001 FAO, IFAD and WFP determined to strengthen inter-agency collaboration in developing strategies to combat the threat posed by the HIV/AIDS epidemic to food security, nutrition and rural livelihoods. During that month experts from those organizations and UNAIDS held a technical consultation on means of mitigating the impact of HIV/AIDS on agriculture and rural communities in affected areas.

The Technical Co-operation Department has responsibility for FAO's operational activities, including policy development assistance to member countries; investment support; and the management of activities associated with the development and implementation of country, sub-regional and regional programmes. The Department manages the technical co-operation programme (TCP, which funds 13% of FAO's field programme expenditures), and mobilizes resources.

AGRICULTURE

FAO's most important area of activity is crop production, accounting annually for about one-quarter of total field programme expenditure. FAO assists developing countries in increasing agricultural production, by means of a number of methods, including improved seeds and fertilizer use, soil conservation and reforestation, better water resource management techniques, upgrading storage facilities, and improvements in processing and marketing. FAO places special emphasis on the cultivation of under-exploited traditional food crops, such as cassava, sweet potato and plantains.

In 1985 the FAO Conference approved an International Code of Conduct on the Distribution and Use of Pesticides, and in 1989 the Conference adopted an additional clause concerning 'Prior Informed Consent' (PIC), whereby international shipments of newly banned or restricted pesticides should not proceed without the agreement of importing countries. Under the clause, FAO aims to inform governments about the hazards of toxic chemicals and to urge them to take proper measures to curb trade in highly toxic agrochemicals while keeping the pesticides industry informed of control actions. In 1996 FAO, in collaboration with UNEP, publicized a new initiative which aimed to increase awareness of, and to promote international action on, obsolete and hazardous stocks of pesticides remaining throughout the world (estimated in 2001 to total some 500,000 metric tons). In September 1998 a new legally-binding treaty on trade in hazardous chemicals and pesticides was adopted at an international conference held in Rotterdam, Netherlands. The so-called Rotterdam Convention required that hazardous chemicals and pesticides banned or severely restricted in at least two countries should not be exported unless explicitly agreed by the importing country. It also identified certain pesticide formulations as too dangerous to be used by farmers in developing countries, and incorporated an obligation that countries halt national production of those hazardous compounds. The treaty entered into force in February 2004. FAO was co-operating with UNEP to provide an interim secretariat for the Convention. In July 1999 a conference on the Rotterdam Convention, held in Rome, established an Interim Chemical Review Committee with responsibility for recommending the inclusion of chemicals or pesticide formulations in the PIC procedure. As part of its continued efforts to reduce the environmental risks posed by over-reliance on pesticides, FAO has extended to other regions its Integrated Pest Management (IPM) programme in Asia and the Pacific on the use of safer and more effective methods of pest control, such as biological control methods and natural predators (including spiders and wasps), to avert pests. In February 2001 FAO warned that some 30% of pesticides sold in developing countries did not meet internationally accepted quality standards. A revised International Code of Conduct on the Distribution and Use of Pesticides, adopted in November 2002, aimed to reduce the inappropriate distribution and use of pesticides and other toxic compounds, particularly in developing countries.

FAO's Joint Division with the International Atomic Energy Agency (IAEA) tests controlled-release formulas of pesticides and herbicides that gradually free their substances and can limit the amount of agrochemicals needed to protect crops. The Joint FAO/IAEA Division is engaged in exploring biotechnologies and in developing non-toxic fertilizers (especially those that are locally available) and improved strains of food crops (especially from indigenous varieties). In the area of animal production and health, the Joint Division has developed progesterone-measuring and disease diagnostic kits, of which thousands have been delivered to developing countries. FAO's plant nutrition activities aim to promote nutrient management, such as the Integrated Plant Nutritions Systems (IPNS), which are based on the recycling of nutrients through crop production and the efficient use of mineral fertilizers.

The conservation and sustainable use of plant and animal genetic resources are promoted by FAO's Global System for Plant Genetic Resources, which includes five databases, and the Global Strategy on the Management of Farm Animal Genetic Resources. An FAO programme supports the establishment of gene banks, designed to maintain the world's biological diversity by preserving animal and plant species threatened with extinction. FAO, jointly with UNEP, has published a document listing the current state of global livestock genetic diversity. In June 1996 representatives of more than 150 governments convened in Leipzig, Germany, at a meeting organized by FAO (and hosted by the German Government) to consider the use and conservation of plant genetic resources as an essential means of enhancing food security. The meeting adopted a Global Plan of Action, which included measures to strengthen the development of plant varieties and to promote the use and availability of local varieties and locally adapted crops to farmers, in particular following a natural disaster, war or civil conflict. In November 2001 the FAO Conference adopted the International Treaty on Plant Genetic Resources for Food and Agriculture, which was to provide a framework to ensure access to plant genetic resources and to related knowledge, technologies and funding. The Treaty entered into force on 29 June 2004, having received the required number of ratifications (40) by signatory states. The first meeting of the Treaty's Governing Body was convened in June 2006.

In June 2004 FAO published guide-lines for assessing possible risks posed to plants by living modified organisms (LMOs), a subset of genetically modified—GM—organisms, containing a new combination of genetic material derived from the use of biotechnology.

The Emergency Prevention System for Transboundary Animal and Plant Pests and Diseases (EMPRES) was established in 1994 to strengthen FAO's activities in the prevention, early warning, control and, where possible, eradication of pests and highly contagious livestock diseases (which the system categorizes as epidemic diseases of strategic importance, such as rinderpest or foot-and-mouth; diseases requiring tactical attention at international or regional level, e.g. Rift Valley fever; and emerging diseases, e.g. bovine spongiform encephalopathy—BSE). EMPRES has a desert locust component, and has published guide-lines on all aspects of desert locust monitoring. FAO has assumed responsibility for technical leadership and co-ordination of the Global Rinderpest Eradication Programme (GREP), which has the objective of eliminating the disease by 2010. Following technical consultations in late 1998, an Intensified GREP was launched. In November 1997 FAO initiated a Programme Against African Trypanosomiasis, which aimed to counter the disease affecting cattle in almost one-third of Africa. EMPRES promotes Good Emergency Management Practices (GEMP) in animal health. The system is guided by the annual meeting of the EMPRES Expert Consultation. In May 2004 FAO and the World Organisation for Animal Health (OIE) signed an agreement in which they clarified their respective areas of competence and paved the way for improved co-operation, in response to an increase in contageous transboundary animal diseases (such as foot-and-mouth disease and avian influenza, see below). The two bodies agreed to establish a global framework on the control of transboundary animal diseases, entailing improved international collaboration and circulation of information. FAO advises countries on good agricultural practices, disease control and eradication methods and co-operates with the OIE in building national surveillance and early warning systems.

In September 2004 FAO and the World Health Organization declared an ongoing epidemic in certain east Asian countries of the H5N1 strain of highly pathogenic avian influenza (HPAI) to be a 'crisis of global importance': the disease was spreading rapidly through bird populations and was also transmitting to human populations through contact with diseased birds (mainly poultry). In that month FAO published *Recommendations for the Prevention, Control and Eradication of Highly Pathogenic Avian Influenza in Asia*. In May 2005 FAO, with WHO and the OIE, launched a global strategy for the progressive control of the disease. A conference on Avian Influenza and Human Pandemic Influenza that was jointly organized by FAO, WHO and OIE and the World Bank in November 2005 issued a plan of action identifying a number of responses, including: supporting the development of integrated national plans for H5N1 containment and human pandemic influenza preparedness and response; assisting countries with the aggressive control of H5N1 and with establishing a more detailed understanding of the role of wild birds in virus transmission; nominating rapid response teams of experts to support epidemiological field investigations; expanding national and regional capacity in surveillance, diagnosis, and alert and response systems; expanding the network of influenza laboratories; establishing multi-country networks for the control or prevention of animal transboundary diseases; expanding the global antiviral stockpile; strengthening veterinary infrastructures; and mapping a global strategy and work plan for co-ordinating antiviral and influenza vaccine research and development. An International Pledging Conference on Avian and Human Influenza, convened in mid-January 2006 in Beijing, the People's Republic of China (PRC), and co-sponsored by the World Bank, European Commission and PRC Government, in co-operation with FAO, WHO and OIE, requested a minimum of US $1,200m. in funding towards combating the spread of the virus.

In June 2006 FAO and the OIE convened a scientific conference on the spread of H5N1 that was attended by more than 300 experts from over 100 countries. The conference noted that the virus has been spread by the migration of infected wild birds and through trade (both legal and illegal) in poultry, and advocated as a basis for H5N1 management early detection of the disease in wild birds, improved biosecurity and hygiene in the poultry trade, rapid response to disease outbreaks, and the establishment of a global tracking and monitoring facility involving participation by all relevant organizations, as well as by scientific centres, farmers' groupings, bird-watchers and hunters, and wildlife and wild bird habitat conservation bodies. The conference also urged investment in telemetry/satellite technology to improve tracking capabilities. By October H5N1 cases in poultry were endemic in parts of Asia, and recent outbreaks in poultry had been reported in some European and Middle Eastern countries, and in some countries in West, Central and Northeast Africa. During January 2004–June 2006 FAO sent 392 missions to support anti-H5N1 planning and activities worldwide.

In October 2006 FAO inaugurated a new Crisis Management Centre (CMC) to co-ordinate the Organization's response to outbreaks of H5N1 and other major emergencies related to animal or food health.

FAO's organic agriculture programme provides technical assistance and policy advice on the production, certification and trade of organic produce. In July 2001 the FAO/WHO Codex Alimentarius Commission adopted guide-lines on organic livestock production, covering organic breeding methods, the elimination of growth hormones and certain chemicals in veterinary medicines, and the use of good quality organic feed with no meat or bone meal content.

FAO provided technical assistance to the New Partnership for Africa's Development (NEPAD) in the preparation of its Comprehensive African Agriculture Development Programme, which was adopted at a meeting held under FAO auspices in June 2002.

ENVIRONMENT

At the UN Conference on Environment and Development (UNCED), held in Rio de Janeiro, Brazil, in June 1992, FAO participated in several working parties and supported the adoption of Agenda 21, a programme of activities to promote sustainable development. FAO is responsible for the chapters of Agenda 21 concerning water resources, forests, fragile mountain ecosystems and sustainable agriculture and rural development. FAO was designated by the UN General Assembly as the lead agency for co-ordinating the International Year of Mountains (2002), which aimed to raise awareness of mountain ecosystems and to promote the conservation and sustainable development of mountainous regions.

FISHERIES

FAO's Fisheries Department consists of a multi-disciplinary body of experts who are involved in every aspect of fisheries development from coastal surveys, conservation management and use of aquatic genetic resources, improvement of production, processing and storage, to the compilation and analysis of statistics, development of computer databases, improvement of fishing gear, institution-building and training. In March 1995 a ministerial meeting of fisheries adopted the Rome Consensus on World Fisheries, which identified a need for immediate action to eliminate overfishing and to rebuild and enhance depleting fish stocks. In November the FAO Conference adopted a Code of Conduct for Responsible Fishing, which incorporated many global fisheries and aquaculture issues (including fisheries resource conservation and development, fish catches, seafood and fish processing, commercialization, trade and research) to promote the sustainable development of the sector. In February 1999 the FAO Committee on Fisheries adopted new international measures, within the framework of the Code of Conduct, in order to reduce over-exploitation of the world's fish resources, as well as plans of action for the conservation and management of sharks and the reduction in the incidental catch of seabirds in longline fisheries. The voluntary measures were endorsed at a ministerial meeting, held in March and attended by representatives of some 126 countries, which issued a declaration to promote the implementation of the Code of Conduct and to achieve sustainable management of fisheries and aquaculture. In March 2001 FAO adopted an international plan of action to address the continuing problem of so-called illegal, unreported and unregulated fishing (IUU). In that year FAO estimated that about one-half of major marine fish stocks were fully exploited, one-quarter under-exploited, at least 15% over-exploited, and 10% depleted or recovering from depletion. IUU was estimated to account for up to 30% of total catches in certain fisheries. In October FAO and the Icelandic Government jointly organized the Reykjavik Conference on Responsible Fisheries in the Marine Ecosystem, which adopted a declaration on pursuing responsible and sustainable fishing activities in the context of ecosystem-based fisheries management (EBFM). EBFM involves determining the boundaries of individual marine ecosystems, and maintaining or rebuilding the habitats and biodiversity of each of these so that all species will be supported at levels of maximum production. In March 2005 FAO's Committee of Fisheries adopted voluntary guide-lines for the so-called eco-labelling and certification of fish and fish products, i.e. based on information regarding capture management and the sustainable use of resources. FAO promotes aquaculture (which contributes almost one-third of annual global fish landings) as a valuable source of animal protein and income-generating activity for rural communities. In February 2000 FAO and the Network of Aquaculture Centres in Asia and the Pacific (NACA) jointly convened a Conference on Aquaculture in the Third Millennium, which was held in Bangkok, Thailand, and attended by participants representing more than 200 governmental and non-governmental organizations. The Conference debated global trends in aquaculture and future policy measures to ensure the sustainable development of the sector. It adopted the Bangkok Declaration and Strategy for Aquaculture Beyond 2000.

FORESTRY

FAO focuses on the contribution of forestry to food security, on effective and responsible forest management and on maintaining a balance between the economic, ecological and social benefits of forest resources. The Organization has helped to develop national forestry programmes and to promote the sustainable development of all types of forest. FAO administers the global Forests, Trees and People Programme, which promotes the sustainable management of tree and forest resources, based on local knowledge and management practices, in order to improve the livelihoods of rural people in developing countries. FAO's Strategic Plan for Forestry was approved in March 1999; its main objectives were to maintain the environmental diversity of forests, to realize the economic potential of forests and trees within a sustainable framework, and to expand access to information on forestry.

In sub-Saharan Africa FAO's Forests, Trees and People Programme is implemented in collaboration with organizations and institutions in Benin, Burkina Faso, Cameroon, Ethiopia, Kenya, Mali, Niger, Senegal, Tanzania and Uganda.

NUTRITION

The International Conference on Nutrition, sponsored by FAO and WHO, took place in Rome in December 1992. It approved a World Declaration on Nutrition and a Plan of Action, aimed at promoting efforts to combat malnutrition as a development priority. Since the conference, more than 100 countries have formulated national plans of action for nutrition, many of which were based on existing development plans such as comprehensive food security initiatives, national poverty alleviation programmes and action plans to attain the targets set by the World Summit for Children in September 1990. In October 1996 FAO, WHO and other partners jointly organized the first World Congress on Calcium and Vitamin D in Human Life, held in Rome. In January 2001 a joint team of FAO and WHO experts issued a report concerning the allergenicity of foods derived from biotechnology (i.e. genetically modified—GM—foods). In July the Codex Alimentarius Commission agreed the first global principles for assessing the safety of GM foods, and approved a series of maximum levels of environmental contaminants in food. FAO and WHO jointly convened a Global Forum of Food Safety Regulators in Marrakesh, Morocco, in January 2002. In April the two organizations announced a joint review of their food standards operations, including the activities of the Codex Alimentarius Commission. In July 2004 the Codex Alimentarius Commission adopted a definition of product tracing, increasingly regarded as an important component of national and international food regulatory systems. In October FAO and WHO jointly launched the International Food Safety Authorities Network (INFOSAN), which aimed to promote the exchange of food safety information and to advance co-operation among food safety authorities.

PROCESSING AND MARKETING

An estimated 20% of all food harvested is lost before it can be consumed, and in some developing countries the proportion is much higher. FAO helps reduce immediate post-harvest losses, with the introduction of improved processing methods and storage systems. It also advises on the distribution and marketing of agricultural produce and on the selection and preparation of foods for optimum nutrition. Many of these activities form part of wider rural development projects. Many developing countries rely on agricultural products as their main source of foreign earnings, but the terms under which they are traded are usually more favourable to the industrialized countries. FAO continues to favour the elimination of export subsidies and related discriminatory practices, such as protectionist measures that hamper international trade in agricultural commodities. FAO has organized regional workshops and national projects in order to help member states to implement World Trade Organization regulations, in particular with regard to agricultural policy, intellectual property rights, sanitary and phytosanitary measures, technical barriers to trade and the international standards of the Codex Alimentarius. FAO evaluates new market trends and helps to develop improved plant and animal quarantine procedures. In November 1997 the FAO Conference adopted new guide-lines on surveillance and on export certification systems in order to harmonize plant quarantine standards. FAO participates in PhAction, a forum of 12 agencies that was established in 1999 to promote post-harvest research and the development of effective post-harvest services and infrastructure.

FOOD SECURITY

FAO's policy on food security aims to encourage the production of adequate food supplies, to maximize stability in the flow of supplies, and to ensure access on the part of those who need them. In 1994 FAO initiated the Special Programme for Food Security (SPFS), designed to assist low-income countries with a food deficit to increase food production and productivity as rapidly as possible, primarily through the widespread adoption by farmers of improved production technologies, with emphasis on areas of high potential. FAO was actively involved in the formulation of the Plan of Action on food security that was adopted at the World Food Summit in November 1996, and was to be responsible for monitoring and promoting its implementation. In March 1999 FAO signed agreements with IFAD and WFP that aimed to increase co-operation within the framework of the SPFS. In October 2006 FAO estimated that 852m. people world-wide were experiencing food insecurity. A budget of US $10.5m. was allocated to the SPFS for the two-year period 2004–05. In 2007 the SPFS was operational in 102 countries, of which 82 were categorized as 'low-income food-deficit'. The Programme promotes South-South co-operation to improve food security and the exchange of knowledge and experience. By April 2007 38 bilateral co-operation agreements were in force, for example, between Egypt and Cameroon, and Viet Nam and Benin.

FAO's Global Information and Early Warning System (GIEWS), which become operational in 1975, maintains a database on and monitors the crop and food outlook at global, regional, national and sub-national levels in order to detect emerging food supply difficulties and disasters and to ensure rapid intervention in countries experiencing food supply shortages. It publishes regular reports on the weather conditions and crop prospects in sub-Saharan Africa and in the Sahel region, issues special alerts which describe the situation in countries or sub-regions experiencing food difficulties, and recommends an appropriate international response. FAO's annual publication *State of Food Insecurity in the World* is based on data compiled by the Organization's Food Insecurity and Vulnerability Information and Mapping Systems programme.

In 2007 GIEWS produced special reports on the situation in Ethiopia (February), Swaziland (May), Zimbabwe (June), and Lesotho (July).

An Inter-Agency Task Force on the UN Response to Long-Term Food Security, Agricultural Development and Related Aspects in the Horn of Africa, appointed by the UN Secretary-General in April 2000, is chaired by the Director-General of FAO.

FAO INVESTMENT CENTRE

The Investment Centre was established in 1964 to help countries to prepare viable investment projects that will attract external financing. The Centre focuses its evaluation of projects on two fundamental concerns: the promotion of sustainable activities for land management, forestry development and environmental protection, and the alleviation of rural poverty. Each year the Centre supports around 140 projects in about 100 developing countries.

EMERGENCY RELIEF

FAO works to rehabilitate agricultural production following natural and man-made disasters by providing emergency seed, tools, and technical and other assistance. Jointly with the United Nations, FAO is responsible for WFP, which provides emergency food supplies and food aid in support of development projects. FAO's Division for Emergency Operations and Rehabilitation was responsible for preparing the emergency agricultural relief component of the 2007 UN inter-agency appeals for 13 countries and regions.

In January 2005, following a massive earthquake in the Indian Ocean in December 2004, which caused a series of tidal waves, or tsunamis, that devastated coastal regions in 14 countries in South and South-East Asia and East Africa, FAO requested emergency funding of US $26m. to support an initial six-month rehabilitation operation to restore the livelihoods of fishermen and farmers affected by the natural disaster. FAO subsequently became the lead UN agency for the rehabilitation of agricultural, fisheries and forestry sectors of tsunami-affected countries.

In May 2005 FAO appealed for US $4m. in funds to combat food insecurity in Niger, following damage to crops and pastures inflicted in 2004 by an acute infestation of locusts. FAO renewed the appeal in August owing to a poor international response to its original request combined with a severe deterioration in the food situation in Niger.

INFORMATION

FAO collects, analyses, interprets and disseminates information through various media, including an extensive internet site. It issues regular statistical reports, commodity studies, and technical manuals in local languages (see list of publications below). Other materials produced by the FAO include information booklets, reference papers, reports of meetings, training manuals and audio-visuals.

FAO's internet-based interactive World Agricultural Information Centre (WAICENT) offers access to agricultural publications, technical documentation, codes of conduct, data, statistics and multimedia resources. FAO compiles and co-ordinates an extensive range of international databases on agriculture, fisheries, forestry, food and statistics, the most important of these being AGRIS (the International Information System for the Agricultural Sciences and Technology) and CARIS (the Current Agricultural Research Information System). Statistical databases include the GLOBEFISH databank and electronic library, FISHDAB (the Fisheries Statistical Database), FORIS (Forest Resources Information System), and GIS (the Geographic Information System). In addition, FAOSTAT provides access to updated figures in 10 agriculture-related topics. The AGORA (Access to Global Online Research in Agriculture) initiative, launched in 2003 by FAO and other partners, aims to provide free or low-cost access to more than 400 scientific journals in agriculture, nutrition and related fields for researchers from developing countries.

In June 2000 FAO organized a high-level Consultation on Agricultural Information Management (COAIM), which aimed to increase access to and use of agricultural information by policy-makers and others. The second COAIM was held in September 2002 and the third meeting was convened in June 2007.

World Food Day, commemorating the foundation of FAO, is held annually on 16 October.

FAO Councils and Commissions

(based at the Rome headquarters, unless otherwise indicated)

African Commission on Agricultural Statistics: c/o FAO Regional Office for Africa, POB 1628, Accra, Ghana; f. 1961 to advise member countries on the development and standardization of food and agricultural statistics; 37 member states.

African Forestry and Wildlife Commission: f. 1959 to advise on the formulation of forest policy and to review and co-ordinate its implementation on a regional level; to exchange information and advise on technical problems; 42 member states.

Commission for Controlling the Desert Locust in North-West Africa: f. 1971 to promote research on control of the desert locust in NW Africa.

FAO/WHO Codex Alimentarius Commission: internet www.codexalimentarius.net; f. 1962 to make proposals for the co-ordination of all international food standards work and to publish a code of international food standards; established Intergovernmental Task Force on Foods Derived from Biotechnology in 1999; Trust Fund to support participation by least-developed countries was inaugurated in 2003; 165 member states.

Indian Ocean Fishery Commission: f. 1967 to promote national programmes, research and development activities, and to examine management problems; 41 member states.

South West Indian Ocean Fisheries Commission: f. 2005 to promote the sustainable development and utilization of coastal fishery resources of East Africa and island states in that sub-region; 14 member states.

Finance

FAO's Regular Programme, which is financed by contributions from member governments, covers the cost of FAO's Secretariat, its Technical Co-operation Programme (TCP) and part of the cost of several special action programmes. The proposed budget for the two-year period 2006–07 totalled US $765.7m. Much of FAO's technical assistance programme is funded from extra-budgetary sources, predominantly by trust funds that come mainly from donor countries and international financing institutions. The single largest contributor is the United Nations Development Programme (UNDP).

Publications

Animal Health Yearbook.
Commodity Review and Outlook (annually).
Environment and Energy Bulletin.
Ethical Issues in Food and Agriculture.
Fertilizer Yearbook.
Food Crops and Shortages (6 a year).
Food Outlook (5 a year).
Food Safety and Quality Update (monthly; electronic bulletin).
Forest Resources Assessment.
Plant Protection Bulletin (quarterly).
Production Yearbook.
Quarterly Bulletin of Statistics.
The State of Food and Agriculture (annually).
The State of Food Insecurity in the World (annually).
The State of World Fisheries and Aquaculture (every two years).
The State of the World's Forests (every 2 years).
Trade Yearbook.
Unasylva (quarterly).
Yearbook of Fishery Statistics.
Yearbook of Forest Products.
World Animal Review (quarterly).
World Watch List for Domestic Animal Diversity.
Commodity reviews; studies, manuals.

International Bank for Reconstruction and Development—IBRD (World Bank)

Address: 1818 H St, NW, Washington, DC 20433, USA.

Telephone: (202) 473-1000; **fax:** (202) 477-6391; **e-mail:** pic@worldbank.org; **internet:** www.worldbank.org.

The IBRD was established in December 1945. Initially it was concerned with post-war reconstruction in Europe; since then its aim has been to assist the economic development of member nations by making loans where private capital is not available on reasonable terms to finance productive investments. Loans are made either directly to governments, or to private enterprises with the guarantee of their governments. The World Bank, as it is commonly known, comprises the IBRD and the International Development Association (IDA). The affiliated group of institutions, comprising the IBRD, the IDA, the International Finance Corporation (IFC), the Multilateral Investment Guarantee Agency (MIGA) and the International Centre for Settlement of Investment Disputes (ICSID, see below), is now referred to as the World Bank Group.

Organization

(September 2007)

Officers and staff of the IBRD serve concurrently as officers and staff in the IDA. The World Bank has offices in New York, Brussels, Paris (for Europe), Frankfurt, London, Geneva and Tokyo, as well as in more than 100 countries of operation. Country Directors are located in some 30 country offices.

BOARD OF GOVERNORS

The Board of Governors consists of one Governor appointed by each member nation. Typically, a Governor is the country's finance minister, central bank governor, or a minister or an official of comparable rank. The Board normally meets once a year.

EXECUTIVE DIRECTORS

The general operations of the Bank are conducted by a Board of 24 Executive Directors. Five Directors are appointed by the five members having the largest number of shares of capital stock, and the rest are elected by the Governors representing the other members. The President of the Bank is Chairman of the Board.

PRINCIPAL OFFICERS

The principal officers of the Bank are the President of the Bank, two Managing Directors, three Senior Vice-Presidents and 24 Vice-Presidents.

President and Chairman of Executive Directors: ROBERT B. ZOELLICK (USA).

Vice-President, Africa: OBIAGELI EZEKWESLILI (Nigeria).

Activities

FINANCIAL OPERATIONS

IBRD capital is derived from members' subscriptions to capital shares, the calculation of which is based on their quotas in the IMF. At 30 June 2006 the total subscribed capital of the IBRD was US $189,718m., of which the paid-in portion was $11,483m. (6.1%); the remainder is subject to call if required. Most of the IBRD's lendable funds come from its borrowing, on commercial terms, in world capital markets, and also from its retained earnings and the flow of repayments on its loans. IBRD loans carry a variable interest rate, rather than a rate fixed at the time of borrowing.

IBRD loans usually have a 'grace period' of five years and are repayable over 15 years or fewer. Loans are made to governments, or must be guaranteed by the government concerned, and are normally made for projects likely to offer a commercially viable rate of return. In 1980 the World Bank introduced structural adjustment lending, which (instead of financing specific projects) supports programmes and changes necessary to modify the structure of an economy so that it can restore or maintain its growth and viability in its balance-of-payments over the medium-term.

The IBRD and IDA together made 279 new lending and investment commitments totalling US $23,641.2m. during the year ending 30 June 2006, compared with 278 (amounting to $22,307.0m.) in the previous year. During 2005/06 the IBRD alone approved commitments totalling $14,135.0m. (compared with $13,610.8m. in the previous year). Disbursements by the IBRD in the year ending 30 June 2006 amounted to $11,833m.

IBRD operations are supported by medium- and long-term borrowings in international capital markets. During the year ending 30 June 2006 the IBRD's net income amounted to –US $2,389m.

The World Bank's primary objectives are the achievement of sustainable economic growth and the reduction of poverty in developing countries. In the context of stimulating economic growth the Bank promotes both private-sector development and human resource development and has attempted to respond to the growing demands by developing countries for assistance in these areas. In March 1997 the Board of Executive Directors endorsed a 'Strategic Compact' to increase the effectiveness of the Bank in achieving its central objective of poverty reduction. The reforms included greater decentralization of decision-making, and investment in front-line operations, enhancing the administration of loans, and improving access to information and co-ordination of Bank activities through a knowledge management system comprising four thematic networks: the Human Development Network; the Environmentally and Socially Sustainable Development Network; the Finance, Private Sector and Infrastructure Development Network; and the Poverty Reduction and Economic Management Network. In 2000/01 the Bank adopted a new Strategic Framework which emphasized two essential approaches for Bank support: strengthening the investment climate and prospects for sustainable development in a country, and supporting investment in the poor. In September 2001 the Bank announced that it was to join the UN as a full partner in implementing the so-called Millennium Development Goals (MDGs), and was to make them central to its development agenda. The objectives, which were approved by governments attending a special session of the UN General Assembly in September 2000, represented a new international consensus to achieve determined poverty reduction targets. The Bank was closely involved in preparations for the International Conference on Financing for Development, which was held in Monterrey, Mexico, in March 2002. The meeting adopted the Monterrey Consensus, which outlined measures to support national development efforts and to achieve the MDGs. During 2002/03 the Bank, with the IMF, undertook to develop a monitoring framework to review progress in the MDG agenda. The first *Global Monitoring Report* was issued by the Bank and IMF in April 2004. Other efforts to support a greater emphasis on development results were also undertaken by the Bank during 2003/04 as part of a new strategic action plan, and the Bank has continued closely to monitor its contribution to poverty reduction objectives.

The Bank's efforts to reduce poverty include the compilation of country-specific assessments and the formulation of country assistance strategies (CASs) to review and guide the Bank's country programmes. Since August 1998 the Bank has published CASs, with the approval of the government concerned. A new results-based CAS initiative was piloted in 2003/04. In 1998/99 the Bank's Executive Directors endorsed a Comprehensive Development Framework (CDF) to effect a new approach to development assistance based on partnerships and country responsibility, with an emphasis on the interdependence of the social, structural, human, governmental, economic and environmental elements of development. The Framework, which aimed to enhance the overall effectiveness of development assistance, was formulated after a series of consultative meetings organized by the Bank and attended by representatives of governments, donor agencies, financial institutions, non-governmental organizations, the private sector and academics.

In December 1999 the Bank introduced a new approach to implement the principles of the CDF, as part of its strategy to enhance the debt relief scheme for heavily indebted poor countries (HIPCs, see below). Applicant countries were requested to formulate, in consultation with external partners and other stakeholders, a results-oriented national strategy to reduce poverty, to be presented in the form of a Poverty Reduction Strategy Paper (PRSP). In cases where there might be some delay in issuing a full PRSP, it was permissible for a country to submit a less detailed 'interim' PRSP (I-PRSP) in order to secure the preliminary qualification for debt relief. The approach also requires the publication of annual progress reports. In 2000/01 the Bank introduced a new Poverty Reduction Support Credit to help low-income countries to implement the policy and institutional reforms outlined in their PRSP. The first credits were approved for Uganda and Viet Nam in May and June respectively. Increasingly, PRSPs have been considered by the international community to be the appropriate country-level framework to assess progress towards achieving the MDGs. A joint review of the poverty reduction strategy approach was undertaken by the Bank and IMF in 2004/05.

The Bank's poverty reduction strategy for Africa, where an estimated 45% of the population are affected by poverty, involves projects that aim to alleviate the adverse effects of structural adjustment programmes; that assist governments to assess and monitor poverty; and that increase food security. During 1996/97 the Bank established a Capacity Building Technical Group within the African regional offices to enhance the Bank's effectiveness in working with local partners in the development of human and institutional capacities. Additionally, the Bank established a Poverty Sector Board, within a new Poverty Reduction and Economic Management (PREM) network, to direct the implementation of the Bank's poverty reduction strategy. In March 1996 a new programme to co-ordinate development efforts in Africa was announced by the UN Secretary-General. The World Bank was to facilitate the mobilization of the estimated US $25,000m. required to achieve the objectives of the UN System-wide Special Initiative on Africa over a 10-year period. In addition, the Bank was to provide technical assistance to enable countries to devise economic plans (in particular following a period of civil conflict), agricultural development programmes and a common strategy for African countries to strengthen the management capacities of the public sector. In 1987 the Bank established a Special Programme of Assistance for sub-Saharan Africa (SPA, renamed the Strategic Partnership with Africa in 1997), which aimed to increase concessional lending to heavily-indebted and impoverished African countries, mainly by the co-ordination of international aid contributions and to co-financing mechanisms. Only IDA member countries implementing a policy adjustment programme, with a debt-service ration of more than 30%, were to be eligible for SPA funds. The sixth three-year cycle of the SPA covering the period 2003–05, placed greater emphasis on increased assistance, in particular for countries implementing poverty reduction strategies, and principles consistent with the New Partnership for Africa's Development (NEPAD) initiative. There was also greater direct participation by African countries. The seventh phase (2006–08) was launched in January 2006; priorities included greater focus on achieving MDGs and growth strategies of PRSPs, streamlining conditions for assistance, and addressing challenges created by the imposition of conditions related to political developments. In September 2005 the Bank's Board of Directors approved an African Action Plan to identify specific development objectives for the region, based on results-orientated, country-specific projects. The Plan, which was updated in March 2007, defined the following themes as areas for action: strengthening the private sector; increasing the economic empowerment of women; building skills for competitiveness in the global economy; raising agricultural productivity; improving access to and reliability of clean energy; expanding and upgrading road networks and transit corridors; increasing access to safe water and sanitation; and strengthening national health systems to combat malaria and HIV/AIDS.

In 1991 the African Capacity Building Foundation was established by the World Bank, the African Development Bank and UNDP, with the aim of encouraging indigenous research and managerial capabilities, by supporting or creating institutions for training, research and analysis. From 1999 the Bank has supported the Partnership for Capacity Building in Africa (PACT), for which it committed US $150m. over a five-year period. It also supports various schemes under the Knowledge Partnerships for Africa initiative. The Bank, with IDA and IFC, supports the Chad Cameroon Petroleum Development and Pipeline Project, which was approved in June 2000 to develop Chad's oil fields and undertake construction of a 1,070km connecting pipeline to Cameroon's Atlantic coast. In addition, the Bank supports the Nile Basin Initiative which aims to promote co-operation among basin states of the Nile to achieve sustainable socio-economic development through the equitable use of its water resources. Other regional initiatives supported by the Bank include Early Childhood Development in Africa and the Sub-Saharan Africa Transport Policy Programme. It also focuses on efforts to prevent conflict and assist post-conflict recovery, for example the Multi-Country Demobilization and Reintegration Programme in the Greater Great Lakes Region. In March 2006 the Bank inaugurated an Africa Catalytic Growth Fund to foster investment in infrastructure and support ongoing government programmes to achieve the MDGs.

In September 1996 the World Bank/IMF Development Committee endorsed a joint initiative to assist HIPCs to reduce their debt burden to a sustainable level, in order to make more resources available for poverty reduction and economic growth. A new Trust Fund was established by the World Bank in November to finance the initiative. The Fund, consisting of an initial allocation of US $500m. from the IBRD surplus and other contributions from multilateral creditors, was to be administered by IDA. Of the 41 HIPCs identified by the Bank, 33 were in sub-Saharan Africa. In April 1997 the World Bank and the IMF announced that Uganda was to be the first beneficiary of the initiative, enabling the Ugandan Government to reduce its external debt by some 20%, or an estimated $338m. In early 1999 the World Bank and IMF initiated a comprehensive review of the HIPC initiative. By April meetings of the Group of Seven industrialized nations (G-7) and of the governing bodies of the Bank and IMF indicated a consensus that the scheme needed to be amended and strengthened, in order to allow more countries to benefit from the initiative, to accelerate the process by which a country may qualify for assistance, and to enhance the effectiveness of debt relief. In June the G-7 and Russia (known as the G-8), meeting in Cologne, Germany, agreed to increase contributions to the HIPC Trust Fund and to cancel substantial amounts of outstanding debt, and proposed more flexible terms for eligibility. In September the Bank and IMF reached an agreement on an enhanced HIPC scheme. During the initial phase of the process to ensure suitability for debt relief, each applicant country should formulate a PRSP, and should demonstrate prudent financial management in the implementation of the strategy for at least one year, with support from the IDA and IMF. At the pivotal 'decision point' of the process, having thus developed and successfully applied the poverty reduction strategy, applicant countries still deemed to have an unsustainable level of debt were to qualify for interim debt relief from the IMF and IDA, as well as relief on highly concessional terms from other official bilateral creditors and multilateral institutions. During the ensuing 'interim period' countries were required successfully to implement further economic and social development reforms, as a final demonstration of suitability for securing full debt relief at the 'completion point' of the scheme. Data produced at the decision point was to form the base for calculating the final debt relief (in contrast to the original initiative, which based its calculations on projections of a country's debt stock at the completion point). In the majority of cases a sustainable level of debt was targeted at 150% of the net present value (NPV) of the debt in relation to total annual exports (compared with 200%–250% under the original initiative). Other countries with a lower debt-to-export ratio were to be eligible for assistance under the scheme, providing that their export earnings were at least 30% of GDP (lowered from 40% under the original initiative) and government revenue at least 15% of GDP (reduced from 20%). In March 2005 the Bank and the IMF implemented a new Debt Sustainability Framework in Low-income Countries to provide guidance on lending to low-income countries and to improve monitoring and prevention of the accumulation of unsustainable debt. In June finance ministers of the G-8 proposed providing additional resources to achieve the full cancellation of debts owed by eligible HIPCs to assist those countries to meet their MDG targets. Countries that had reached their completion point were to qualify for immediate assistance. In July the heads of state and government of G-8 countries requested the Bank to ensure the effective delivery of the additional funds and to provide a framework for performance measurement. In September the Bank's Development Committee and the International Monetary and Financial Committee of the IMF endorsed the proposal, subsequently referred to as the Multilateral Debt Relief Initiative (MDRI). The Committees agreed to protect the financial capability of IDA, as one of the institutions (with the IMF and African Development Bank) which was to meet the additional cancellation commitments, and to develop a monitoring programme. By mid-2007 22 countries (Benin, Bolivia, Burkina Faso, Cameroon, Ethiopia, Ghana, Guyana, Honduras, Madagascar, Malawi, Mali, Mauritania, Mozambique, Nicaragua, Niger, Rwanda, São Tomé and Príncipe, Senegal, Sierra Leone, Tanzania, Uganda and Zambia) had reached completion point under the enhanced HIPC initiative, while a further nine countries had reached their decision point. At that time total assistance committed under the HIPC initiative amounted to some $41,900m. in end-2005 NPV terms, or $62,200m. in total estimated nominal debt service relief.

The Bank has been active in supporting countries in the region to deal with the immense challenges of the HIV/AIDS epidemic, for example through the formulation of national AIDS programmes. A multisectoral campaign team for Africa (ACTafrica) has been established to support the Bank's HIV/AIDS strategy. In September 2000 a new Multi-Country HIV/AIDS Programme for Africa (MAP) was launched, in collaboration with UNAIDS and other major donor agencies and non-governmental organizations. Some US $500m. was allocated for the first phase of the initiative and was used to support projects in seven countries. In February 2002 the Bank approved an additional $500m. for a second phase of MAP, which was envisaged to assist HIV/AIDS schemes in a further 12 countries, as well as regional activities. In June 2004 the Bank approved a Treatment Acceleration Programme, with funds of $60m., to support activities in Burkina Faso, Ghana, Mozambique. In November 2001 the Bank appointed its first Global HIV/AIDS Adviser. In November 2004 the Bank launched an AIDS Media Center to improve access to information regarding HIV/AIDS, in particular to journalists in developing countries.

In addition to providing financial services, the Bank also undertakes analytical and advisory services, and supports learning and capacity-building, in particular through the World Bank Institute (see below), the Staff Exchange Programme and knowledge-sharing initiatives. The Bank has supported efforts, such as the Global Development Gateway, to disseminate information on development issues and programmes, and, since 1988, has organized the Annual Bank Conference on Development Economics (ABCDE) to provide a forum for the exchange and discussion of development-related ideas and research. In September 1995 the Bank initiated the Information for Development Programme (InfoDev) with the aim of fostering partnerships between governments, multilateral institutions and private-sector experts in order to promote reform and investment in developing countries through improved access to information technology.

TECHNICAL ASSISTANCE

The provision of technical assistance to member countries has become a major component of World Bank activities. The economic and sector work (ESW) undertaken by the Bank is the vehicle for considerable technical assistance and often forms the basis of CASs and other strategic or advisory reports. In addition, project loans and credits may include funds earmarked specifically for feasibility studies, resource surveys, management or planning advice, and training. The Economic Development Institute has become one of the most important of the Bank's activities in technical assistance. It provides training in national economic management and project analysis for government officials at the middle and upper levels of responsibility. It also runs overseas courses aiming to build up local training capability, and administers a graduate scholarship programme.

The Bank serves as an executing agency for projects financed by the UN Development Programme (UNDP). It also administers projects financed by various trust funds.

Technical assistance (usually reimbursable) is also extended to countries that do not need Bank financial support, e.g. for training and transfer of technology. The Bank encourages the use of local consultants to assist with projects and stimulate institutional capability.

The Project Preparation Facility (PPF) was established in 1975 to provide cash advances to prepare projects that may be financed by the Bank. In 1992 the Bank established an Institutional Development Fund (IDF), which became operational on 1 July; the purpose of the Fund was to provide rapid, small-scale financial assistance, to a maximum value of US $500,000, for capacity-building proposals. In 2002 the IDF was reoriented to focus on good governance, in particular financial accountability and system reforms.

In March 1996 a new programme to co-ordinate development efforts in Africa was announced by the UN Secretary-General. The World Bank was to facilitate the mobilization of the estimated US $25,000m. required to achieve the objectives of the Special Initiative over a 10-year period. In addition, the Bank was to provide technical assistance to enable countries to devise economic plans (in particular following a period of civil conflict), agricultural development programmes and a common strategy for African countries to strengthen the management capacities of the public sector.

ECONOMIC RESEARCH AND STUDIES

In the 1990s the World Bank's research, conducted by its own research staff, was increasingly concerned with providing information to reinforce the Bank's expanding advisory role to developing countries and to improve policy in the Bank's borrowing countries. The principal areas of current research focus on issues such as maintaining sustainable growth while protecting the environment and the poorest sectors of society, encouraging the development of the private sector, and reducing and decentralizing government activities.

The Bank chairs the Consultative Group on International Agricultural Research (CGIAR), which was founded in 1971 to raise financial support for international agricultural research work for improving crops and animal production in developing countries; it supports 15 research centres.

CO-OPERATION WITH OTHER ORGANIZATIONS

The World Bank co-operates with other international partners with the aim of improving the impact of development efforts. It collaborates with the IMF in implementing the HIPC scheme and the two agencies work closely to achieve a common approach to development initiatives. The Bank has established strong working relationships with many other UN bodies, in particular through a mutual commitment to poverty reduction objectives. In May 2000 the Bank signed a joint statement of co-operation with the OECD. The Bank holds regular consultations with other multilateral development banks and with the European Union with respect to development issues. The Bank-NGO Committee provides an annual forum for discussion with non-governmental organizations (NGOs). Strengthening co-operation with external partners was a fundamental element of the Comprehensive Development Framework, which was adopted in 1998/99 (see above). In 2001/02 a Partnership Approval and Tracking System was implemented to provide information on the Bank's regional and global partnerships.

In 1997 a Partnerships Group was established to strengthen the Bank's work with development institutions, representatives of civil society and the private sector. The Group established a new Development Grant Facility, which became operational in October, to support partnership initiatives and to co-ordinate all of the Bank's grant-making activities. Also in 1997 the Bank, in partnership with the IMF, UNCTAD, UNDP, the World Trade Organization (WTO) and International Trade Commission, established an Integrated Framework for Trade-related Assistance to Least Developed Countries, at the request of the WTO, to assist those countries to integrate into the global trading system and improve basic trading capabilities.

In June 1995 the World Bank joined other international donors (including regional development banks, other UN bodies, Canada, France, the Netherlands and the USA) in establishing a Consultative Group to Assist the Poorest (CGAP), which was to channel funds to the most needy through grass-roots agencies. An initial credit of approximately US $200m. was committed by the donors. The Bank manages the CGAP Secretariat, which is responsible for the administration of external funding and for the evaluation and approval of project financing. The CGAP provides technical assistance, training and strategic advice to microfinance institutions and other relevant bodies. As an implementing agency of the Global Environment Facility (GEF) the Bank assists countries to prepare and supervise GEF projects relating to biological diversity, climate change and other environmental protection measures. It is an example of a partnership in action which addresses a global agenda, complementing Bank country assistance activities. A new international partnership, the African Stockpiles Programme, was initiated in June 2004 with the aim of disposing of an estimated 50,000 metric tons of obsolete pesticides throughout the region. The Bank was to manage the Programme's Multi-Donor Trust Fund and to host the unit acting as a secretariat for the Programme's Steering Committee. Ethiopia, Mali, Morocco, Niger, South Africa, Tanzania and Tunisia were to be the first participants in the project, which was anticipated to last for 12–15 years at a cost of US $250m. In 2004/05 two multi-donor trust funds were established, with total committed funds of $508m., to support reconstruction and development needs in Sudan. In the following financial year a multi-donor trust fund was established to finance a study into the feasibility of transferring water from the Red Sea to the Dead Sea. Other funds administered by the Bank include the Global Program to Eradicate Poliomyelitis, launched during the financial year 2002/03, the Least Developed Countries Fund for Climate Change, established in September 2002, an Education for All Fast-Track Initiative Catalytic Trust Fund, established in 2003/04, and a Carbon Finance Assistance Trust Fund, established in 2004/05.

The Bank has worked with FAO, WHO and the World Organisation of Animal Health (OIE) to develop strategies to monitor, contain and eradicate the spread of highly pathogenic avian influenza. In September 2005 the Bank organized a meeting of leading experts on the issue and in November it co-sponsored, with FAO, WHO and the OIE, an international partners conference, focusing on control of the disease and preparedness planning for any future related influenza pandemic in humans. In January 2006 the Bank's Board of Directors approved the establishment of a funding programme, with resources of up to US $500m., to assist countries to combat the disease. Later in that month the Bank co-sponsored, with the European Commission and the People's Republic of China, an International Ministerial Pledging Conference on Avian and Human Pandemic Influenza, convened in Beijing. Participants pledged some $1,900m. to fund disease control and pandemic preparedness activities at global, regional and country levels.

The Bank conducts co-financing and aid co-ordination projects with official aid agencies, export credit institutions, and commercial banks to leverage additional concessional funds for recipient countries. During the year ending 30 June 2006 141 Bank projects leveraged US $4,900m. in co-financing, of which $1,300m. was from the Inter-American Development Bank.

EVALUATION

The Operations Evaluation Department is an independent unit within the World Bank. It conducts Country Assistance Evaluations to assess the development effectiveness of a Bank country programme, and studies and publishes the results of projects after a loan has been fully disbursed, so as to identify problems and possible improvements in future activities. In addition, the department reviews the Bank's global programmes and produces the *Annual Review of Development Effectiveness*. In 1996 a Quality Assurance Group was established to monitor the effectiveness of the Bank's operations and performance.

In September 1993 the Bank established an independent Inspection Panel, consistent with the Bank's objective of improving project implementation and accountability. The Panel, which became operational in September 1994, was to conduct independent investigations and report on complaints from local people concerning the design, appraisal and implementation of development projects supported by the Bank. By mid-2006 the Panel had received 40 formal requests for inspection and had recommended investigations in 20 of those cases.

During 2005/06 the Inspection Panel received four new requests for inspections, relating to a land management project in Honduras, the West African gas pipeline project in Nigeria, mine closure and social protection in Romania, and a transitional support for economic recovery credit and an emergency economic and social reunification project in the Democratic Republic of the Congo.

IBRD INSTITUTIONS

World Bank Institute (WBI): founded in March 1999 by merger of the Bank's Learning and Leadership Centre, previously responsible for internal staff training, and the Economic Development Institute (EDI), which had been established in 1955 to train government officials concerned with development programmes and policies. The new Institute aimed to emphasize the Bank's priority areas through the provision of training courses and seminars relating to poverty, crisis response, good governance and anti-corruption strategies. From 2004 the Institute was to place greater emphasis on individual country needs and on long-term institutional capacity-building. During 2005/06 WBI activities reached some 100,000 participants world-wide. The Institute has continued to support a Global Knowledge Partnership, which was established in 1997 to promote alliances between governments, companies, other agencies and organizations committed to applying information and communication technologies for development purposes. Under the EDI a World Links for Development programme was also initiated to connect schools in developing countries with partner establishments in industrialized nations via the internet. In 1999 the WBI expanded its programmes through distance learning, a Global Development Network, and use of new technologies. A new initiative, Global Development Learning Network (GDLN), aimed to expand access to information and learning opportunities through the internet, videoconferences and organized exchanges. In 2006 there were more than 100 GDLN centres, or affiliates. At that time formal partnership arrangements were in place between WBI and almost 200 learning centres and public, private and non-governmental organizations; a further 250 informal partnerships were also in place; Vice-Pres. FRANNIE LÉAUTIER (Tanzania/France); publs *Annual Report*, *Development Outreach* (quarterly), other books, working papers, case studies.

International Centre for Settlement of Investment Disputes (ICSID): founded in 1966 under the Convention of the Settlement of Investment Disputes between States and Nationals of Other States. The Convention was designed to encourage the growth of private foreign investment for economic development, by creating the possibility, always subject to the consent of both parties, for a Contracting State and a foreign investor who is a national of another Contracting State to settle any legal dispute that might arise out of such an investment by conciliation and/or arbitration before an impartial, international forum. The governing body of the Centre is its Administrative Council, composed of one representative of each Contracting State, all of whom have equal voting power. The President of the World Bank is (*ex officio*) the non-voting Chairman of the Administrative Council. By December 2006 143 countries had signed and ratified the Convention to become ICSID Contracting States. At January of that year the Centre had concluded 99 cases, while 101 were pending; Sec.-Gen. ANA PALACIO (Spain).

Publications

Abstracts of Current Studies: The World Bank Research Program (annually).

African Development Indicators (annually).

Annual Report on Operations Evaluation.

Annual Report on Portfolio Performance.

Annual Review of Development Effectiveness.

Doing Business (annually).

EDI Annual Report.

Global Commodity Markets (quarterly).

Global Development Finance (annually, also on CD-Rom and online).

Global Economic Prospects (annually).

ICSID Annual Report.

ICSID Review—Foreign Investment Law Journal (2 a year).

Joint BIS-IMF-OECD-World Bank Statistics on External Debt (quarterly, also available online).

New Products and Outreach (EDI, annually).

News from ICSID (2 a year).

Poverty Reduction and the World Bank (annually).

Poverty Reduction Strategies Newsletter (quarterly).

Research News (quarterly).

Staff Working Papers.

World Bank Annual Report.

World Bank Atlas (annually).

World Bank Economic Review (3 a year).

The World Bank and the Environment (annually).

World Bank Research Observer

World Development Indicators (annually, also on CD-Rom and online).

World Development Report (annually, also on CD-Rom).

International Development Association—IDA

Address: 1818 H Street, NW, Washington, DC 20433, USA.

Telephone: (202) 473-1000; **fax:** (202) 477-6391; **internet:** www.worldbank.org/ida.

The International Development Association began operations in November 1960. Affiliated to the IBRD, IDA advances capital to the poorer developing member countries on more flexible terms than those offered by the IBRD.

Organization

(September 2007)

Officers and staff of the IBRD serve concurrently as officers and staff of IDA.

President and Chairman of Executive Directors: ROBERT B. ZOELLICK (USA).

Activities

IDA assistance is aimed at the poorer developing countries (i.e. those with an annual GNP per capita of less than US $1,025 were to qualify for assistance in 2006/07) in order to support their poverty reduction strategies. Under IDA lending conditions, credits can be extended to countries whose balance of payments could not sustain the burden of repayment required for IBRD loans. Terms are more favourable than those provided by the IBRD; credits are for a period of 35 or 40 years, with a 'grace period' of 10 years, and carry no interest charges. At mid-2007 82 countries were eligible for IDA assistance, including several small-island economies with a GNP per head greater than $1,025, but which would otherwise have little or no access to Bank funds, and 16 so-called 'blend borrowers' which are entitled to borrow from both the IDA and IBRD.

IDA's total development resources, consisting of members' subscriptions and supplementary resources (additional subscriptions and contributions), are replenished periodically by contributions from the more affluent member countries. An agreement to provide a substantial replenishment of funds, amounting to some US $34,000m. for the period 1 July 2005–30 June 2008, was concluded in February 2005. New contributions pledged by 40 donor countries amounted to $20,700m. of the total replenishment. The agreement incorporated a renewed focus on stimulating economic growth in support of the Millennium Development Goals, with a strengthened monitoring and results-assessment agenda based on poverty reduction objectives. The replenishment programme also placed greater emphasis on the use of grants to address the needs of the poorest countries, in particular those most vulnerable to debt. Negotiations on the 15th replenishment of IDA funds (IDA15) commenced in March 2007, in Paris, France. Participants selected the following 'special themes' for further discussion: the role of IDA in global aid architecture; the effectiveness of IDA assistance at country level; and IDA's role in fragile states. A second round of IDA15 negotiations was held in Maputo, Mozambique, in June.

During the year ending 30 June 2006 new IDA commitments amounted to US $9,506m. for 167 projects in 66 countries, compared with $8,696m. in the previous year. Of total IDA assistance during 2005/06 $4,746.6m. (50%) was for Africa and $2,566.2m. (27%) for South Asia. An increasing proportion of IDA lending, accounting for some 19% of total financing in 2005/06, is in the form of grants for the poorest or most vulnerable countries.

IDA administers a Trust Fund, which was established in November 1996 as part of a World Bank/IMF initiative to assist heavily indebted poor countries (HIPCs). In September 2005 the World Bank's Development Committee and the International Monetary and Financial Committee of the IMF endorsed a proposal of the Group of Eight (G-8) industrialized countries to cancel the remaining multilateral debt owed by HIPCs that had reached their completion point under the scheme (see IBRD). In December IDA convened a meeting of donor countries to discuss funding to uphold its financial capability upon its contribution to the so-called Multilateral Debt Relief Initiative (MDRI). The scheme was approved by the Board of Executive Directors in March 2006 and entered into effect on 1 July. By July 2007 22 countries had reached completion point, of which 18 were in sub-Saharan Africa. At the start of that year total debt relief provided by IDA since the HIPC initiative commenced was estimated to be US $53,600m., including $36,400m. committed under the MDRI.

Publication

Annual Report.

Statistics

IDA CREDITS APPROVED IN SUB-SAHARAN AFRICA, 1 JULY 2005–30 JUNE 2006
(US $ million)

Country	Purpose	Amount
Benin	Malaria control programme	31.0
	Second decentralized city management adaptable programme credit	35.0
Burkina Faso	Sixth poverty reduction support development policy credit	60.0
	Agricultural diversification and market development	66.0
	Post-primary education investment	22.9
	Health sector and HIV/AIDS investment	47.7
Burundi	Public works and employment creation	30.6
Cameroon	Debt relief	31.5
	Forest and environmental management	25.0
Cape Verde	Second poverty reduction support credit	10.0
Congo, Democratic Republic	Economic recovery	90.0
	Emergency multi-sector rehabilitation and reconstruction	125.0
	Health sector rehabilitation	150.0
Djibouti	School access and improvement	10.0
	Power access and diversification	7.0
Ethiopia	Rural capacity-building	54.0
	Financial sector capacity-building	15.0
	Expansion of access to electricity in rural areas	133.4
	Road sector development (phase II)	87.3
	Provision of basic services	215.0
The Gambia	Third education adaptable programme grant	8.0
Ghana	Fourth poverty reduction support development policy credit	40.0
	Micro, small and medium-sized enterprises	45.0
	Economic management capacity-building	25.0
	Multi-sectoral HIV/AIDS specific investment credit	20.0
	Third poverty reduction support credit	125.0
Guinea	Electricity sector efficiency improvements	7.2
	Village communities support	7.0
Guinea-Bissau	Multi-sector infrastructure rehabilitation	15.0
Kenya	Institutional reform and capacity-building	25.0
Lesotho	Health sector reform	6.5
Liberia	Emergency infrastructure recovery grant	30.0
Madagascar	Second poverty reduction support credit	80.0
	Integrated growth poles specific investment credit	129.8
	Second STI/HIV/AIDS prevention specific investment credit	30.0
Malawi	Infrastructure services sector investment and maintenance	40.0
	Irrigation, rural livelihoods and agricultural development grant	40.0
	Emergency recovery grant	30.0
Mali	Economic policy and public finance management	25.0
	Rural community development	60.0
	Agricultural competitiveness and diversification	46.4
Mauritania	Health and nutrition support	10.0
Mozambique	Market-led smallholder development in the Zambezi Valley	20.0
	Technical and vocational education and training	30.0
	Transfrontier conservation areas and tourism development	20.0
	Financial sector technical assistance	10.5
	Second poverty reduction support credit	120.0
Niger	Rural and social sector policy reform	50.0
	Institutional strengthening and health sector support credit	35.0
Nigeria	Avian influenza control and human pandemic preparedness and response	50.0
	Second national urban water sector reform credit	200.0
	National energy development	172.0
Rwanda	Urban infrastructure and city management	20.0
	Second poverty reduction support grant	55.0
Senegal	Agricultural services and producer organizations	20.0
	Participatory local development	50.1
	Second poverty reduction support credit	30.0
	Agricultural markets and agribusiness development	35.0
Sierra Leone	Infrastructure development	44.0
Tanzania	Agricultural sector development	90.0
	Financial sector support	15.0
	Local government support	98.0
	Tax modernization project	12.0
	Accountability, transparency and integrity specific investment credit	40.0
	Fourth poverty reduction support credit	200.0
	Private sector competitiveness specific investment credit	95.0
	Third poverty reduction support credit	150.0
	Marine and coastal environment management	51.0

Country—*continued*	Purpose	Amount
Uganda	Public service performance enhancement	70.0
	Millennium Science Initiative	30.0
	Fifth poverty reduction support credit/grant	22.5/112.5
Zambia	Agricultural development support sector investment grant	37.2
	Public service management programme	30.0
	Malaria booster specific investment credit	20.0
Regional	West Africa power pool facility	60.0
	OMVS Felou Hydroelectricity scheme	75.0
	Senegal river basin multi-purpose water resources development adaptable programme credit/grant	91.9/18.0
	West and Central Africa air transport safety and security technical assistance credit/grant	12.1/21.5
	East Africa trade and transport facilitation credit/grant/partial risk guarantee	134.0/15.0/60.0

Source: *World Bank Annual Report 2006*.

International Finance Corporation—IFC

Address: 2121 Pennsylvania Ave, NW, Washington, DC 20433, USA.

Telephone: (202) 473-3800; **fax:** (202) 974-4384; **e-mail:** information@ifc.org; **internet:** www.ifc.org.

IFC was founded in 1956 as a member of the World Bank Group to stimulate economic growth in developing countries by financing private-sector investments, mobilizing capital in international financial markets, and providing technical assistance and advice to governments and businesses.

Organization

(September 2007)

IFC is a separate legal entity in the World Bank Group. Executive Directors of the World Bank also serve as Directors of IFC. The President of the World Bank is *ex officio* Chairman of the IFC Board of Directors, which has appointed him President of IFC. Subject to his overall supervision, the day-to-day operations of IFC are conducted by its staff under the direction of the Executive Vice-President.

PRINCIPAL OFFICERS

President: Robert B. Zoellick (USA).

Executive Vice-President: Lars Thunell (Sweden).

Director, Sub-Saharan Africa Department: T. Tanoh.

OFFICES IN AFRICA SOUTH OF THE SAHARA

Cameroon: 96 Flatters St, Suite 305, POB 4616, Douala; tel. 3428033; fax 3428014; Country Man. Oumar Seydi.

Côte d'Ivoire: angle rues Booker Washington/Jacques Aka, BP 1850, Abidjan 01; tel. 22-40-04-00; fax 22-44-44-83.

Ghana: Ghana House No.1, Central Link St, South Legon, POB CT2638 Accra; tel. (21) 513152; fax (21) 519068; e-mail ifcaccra@ifc.org; Country Man. Imoni Akpofure.

Kenya: PO Box 30577, Hillpark Bldg, Upper Hill Rd, Nairobi; tel. (20) 3226340; fax (20) 3226383; Regional Man. Jean-Philippe Prosper.

Madagascar: rue Andriamifidy, Anosy, Antananarivo 101; tel. (20) 2326000; fax (20) 2326003; Country Man. Henri Rabarijohn.

Mozambique: 1224 Avda Kenneth Kaunda, Maputo; tel. 21482366; fax 21496247; Country Man. Babatunde Onitiri.

Nigeria: Maersk House, Plot 121 Louis Solomon Close, off Ahmadu Bellow Way, Victoria Island, Lagos; tel. (1) 262-6455; fax (1) 262-6465; Country Man. Solomon Quaynor.

Senegal: Trilenium Bldg, 6 bd Franklin Roosevelt, rue Kleber, BP 3296, Dakar; tel. 849-50-49; fax 849-50-44; Country Man. Aida Der Hovanessian.

South Africa: 14 Fricker Rd, Illovo, Johannesburg; tel. (11) 731-3000; fax (11) 268-0074; Dir Andrew Alli.

Activities

IFC aims to promote economic development in developing member countries by assisting the growth of private enterprise and effective capital markets. It finances private sector projects, through loans, the purchase of equity, quasi-equity products, and risk management services, and assists governments to create conditions that stimulate the flow of domestic and foreign private savings and investment. IFC may provide finance for a project that is partly state-owned, provided that there is participation by the private sector and that the project is operated on a commercial basis. IFC also mobilizes additional resources from other financial institutions, in particular through syndicated loans, thus providing access to international capital markets. IFC provides a range of advisory services to help to improve the investment climate in developing countries and offers technical assistance to private enterprises and governments.

To be eligible for financing, projects must be profitable for investors, as well as financially and economically viable; must benefit the economy of the country concerned; and must comply with IFC's environmental and social guide-lines. IFC aims to promote best corporate governance and management methods and sustainable business practices, and encourages partnerships between governments, non-governmental organizations and community groups. In 2001/02 IFC developed a Sustainability Framework to help to assess the longer-term economic, environmental and social impact of projects. The first Sustainability Review was published in mid-2002. In 2002/03 IFC assisted 10 international banks to draft a voluntary set of guide-lines (the Equator Principles), based on IFC's environmental, social and safeguard monitoring policies, to be applied to their global project finance activities. A revised set of Equator Principles was released in July 2006. (By May 2007 51 financial institutions had signed up to the Equator Principles.)

IFC's authorized capital is US $2,450m. At 30 June 2006 paid-in capital was $2,364m. The World Bank was originally the principal source of borrowed funds, but IFC also borrows from private capital markets. IFC's net income amounted to $1,278m. in 2005/06, compared with $2,015m. in the previous year.

In the year ending 30 June 2006 project financing approved by IFC amounted to US $8,275m. for 284 projects in 66 countries (compared with $6,449m. for 236 projects in the previous year). Of the total approved in 2005/06 $6,703m. was for IFC's own account, while $1,572m. was in the form of loan syndications and underwriting of securities issues and investment funds by more than 100 participant banks and institutional investors. Generally, IFC limits its financing to less than 25% of the total cost of a project, but may take up to a 35% stake in a venture (although never as a majority shareholder). Disbursements for IFC's account amounted to $4,428m. in 2005/06 (compared with $3,456m. in the previous year).

The largest proportion of investment commitments in 2005/06 was allocated to Latin America and the Caribbean (31.8%). Europe and Central Asia received 28.1%, East Asia and the Pacific 14.8%, South Asia 8.5%, sub-Saharan Africa 8.5%, the Middle East and North Africa 8.1% and global projects 0.2%. In that year about one-third of total financing committed (33.2%) was for financial services. Other commitments included utilities (9.6%) and oil, gas and mining (8.1%).

In 2005/06 IFC approved total financing of US $700m. for 38 projects in sub-Saharan Africa (compared with $445m. for 30 projects in the previous financial year). In March 2005 IFC established the Private Enterprise Partnership for Africa, which, during that year, initiated five new long-term technical assistance programmes. IFC has developed a strategic approach to promoting private investment in Africa, with an emphasis on facilitating the development of small and medium-sized enterprises (SMEs), providing technical assistance with the early development of larger-scale projects, identifying and developing new investment opportunities, and improving access to finance. IFC also focuses on investment in countries emerging from conflict, including an extensive effort to identify areas for private sector investment in the Democratic Republic of the Congo.

In April 1989 IFC (with UNDP and the African Development Bank—ADB) initiated the African Management Services Company (AMSCo): its aim is to help find qualified senior executives from around the world to work with African companies, assist in the training of local managers, and provide supporting services. At mid-2006, through the assistance of AMSCo, 180 managers had contracts with 91 African companies in 20 countries, while more than 9,000 people had been trained. IFC's Africa Enterprise Fund (AEF), which began operations in 1988, provides financial assistance to SMEs, typically in the tourism, agribusiness and small-scale manufacturing sectors. Most projects cost less than US $5m., with IFC financing in the range of $100,000 to $1.5m. The Enterprise Support Services for Africa (ESSA) was initiated by IFC in 1995 to provide post-investment operational advice, including the development and strengthening of management information systems and technical capacity, to SMEs in the sub-Saharan region. ESSA commenced operations, on a pilot basis, in Ghana, in March 1996. In 1998/99 ESSA was expanded to be available throughout sub-Saharan Africa as part of the APDF. In the same year IFC approved the establishment of an African Infrastructure Fund, which commenced work evaluating investment in 1999/2000. In November 2004 IFC announced the establishment of a Global Trade Finance Programme, with funding of some $500m., which aimed to support SME importers and exporters in emerging markets, to facilitate South-South trade in goods and services, and to extend technical assistance and training to local financial institutions.

IFC's Private Sector Advisory Services (PSAS), jointly managed with the World Bank, advises governments and private enterprises on policy, transaction implementation and foreign direct investment. The Foreign Investment Advisory Service (FIAS), also jointly operated and financed with the World Bank, provides advice on promoting foreign investment and strengthening the country's investment framework at the request of governments. More than 80 FIAS projects were completed in 2005/06. Under the Technical Assistance Trust Funds Program (TATF), established in 1988, IFC manages resources contributed by various governments and agencies to provide finance for feasibility studies, project identification studies and other types of technical assistance relating to project preparation. During 2005/06 some US $13.6m. in funding for 78 new TATF projects was approved. In 2004 a Grassroots Business Initiative was established, with external donor funding, to support businesses that provide economic opportunities for disadvantaged communities in Africa, Latin America, and South and Southeast Asia.

Private Enterprise Partnership for Africa (PEP-Africa)

PEP-Africa was formally launched by IFC in April 2005, as a successor to the Africa Project Development Facility, which had been operational since 1986. The new facility aimed to enhance its effectiveness in supporting and developing local business capacity. It was to support a new SME Entrepreneurship Development Initiative and to help to develop a network of SME Solution Centers. In addition, PEP-Africa aimed to provide technical assistance to regional member states, in particular on issues relating to the investment.

Headquarters: 14 Fricker Rd, Illovo, Johannesburg, South Africa; tel. (11) 371-3000; fax (11) 325-0582; Dir BERNARD CHIDZERO (Zimbabwe).

Publications

Annual Report.

Emerging Stock Markets Factbook (annually).

Impact (quarterly).

Lessons of Experience (series).

Results on the Ground (series).

Review of Small Businesses (annually).

Sustainability Report (annually).

Discussion papers and technical documents.

Multilateral Investment Guarantee Agency—MIGA

Address: 1818 H Street, NW, Washington, DC 20433, USA.

Telephone: (202) 473-6163; **fax:** (202) 522-2630; **internet:** www.miga.org.

MIGA was founded in 1988 as an affiliate of the World Bank. Its mandate is to encourage the flow of foreign direct investment to, and among, developing member countries, through the provision of political risk insurance and investment marketing services to foreign investors and host governments, respectively.

Organization

(September 2007)

MIGA is legally and financially separate from the World Bank. It is supervised by a Council of Governors (comprising one Governor and one Alternate of each member country) and an elected Board of Directors (of no less than 12 members).

President: ROBERT B. ZOELLICK (USA).

Executive Vice-President: YUKIKO OMURA (Japan).

Activities

The convention establishing MIGA took effect in April 1988. Authorized capital was US $1,082m. In April 1998 the Board of Directors approved an increase in MIGA's capital base. A grant of $150m. was transferred from the IBRD as part of the package, while the capital increase (totalling $700m. callable capital and $150m. paid-in capital) was approved by MIGA's Council of Governors in April 1999. A three-year subscription period then commenced, covering the period April 1999–March 2002 (later extended to March 2003). At 30 June 2006 108 countries had subscribed $745.2m. of the new capital increase. At that time total subscriptions to the capital stock amounted to $1,882.3m., of which $358.9m. was paid-in.

MIGA guarantees eligible investments against losses resulting from non-commercial risks, under four main categories:

(i) transfer risk resulting from host government restrictions on currency conversion and transfer;

(ii) risk of loss resulting from legislative or administrative actions of the host government;

(iii) repudiation by the host government of contracts with investors in cases in which the investor has no access to a competent forum;

(iv) the risk of armed conflict and civil unrest.

Before guaranteeing any investment, MIGA must ensure that it is commercially viable, contributes to the development process and is not harmful to the environment. During the fiscal year 1998/99 MIGA and IFC appointed the first Compliance Advisor and Ombudsman to consider the concerns of local communities directly affected by MIGA- or IFC-sponsored projects. In February 1999 the Board of Directors approved an increase in the amount of political risk insurance available for each project, from US $75m. to $200m.

During the year ending 30 June 2006 MIGA issued 66 investment insurance contracts for 41 projects with a value of US $1,300m., compared with 62 contracts valued at $1,226m. in the previous financial year. Since 1988 the total investment guarantees issued amounted to some $16,000m., through 839 contracts in support of 527 projects.

MIGA works with local insurers, export credit agencies, development finance institutions and other organizations to promote insurance in a country, to ensure a level of consistency among insurers and to support capacity-building within the insurance industry.

MIGA also offers technical assistance and investment marketing services to help to promote foreign investment in developing countries and in transitional economies, and to disseminate information on investment opportunities. In October 1995 MIGA established a new network on investment opportunities, which connected investment promotion agencies (IPAs) throughout the world on an electronic information network. The so-called IPA*net* aimed to encourage further investments among developing countries, to provide access to comprehensive information on investment laws and conditions and to strengthen links between governmental, business and financial associations and investors. A new version of IPA*net* was launched in 1997 (and can be accessed at www.ipanet.net). In June 1998 MIGA initiated a new internet-based facility, 'PrivatizationLink', to provide information on investment opportunities resulting from the privatization of industries in developing economies. In October 2000 a specialized facility within the service was established to facilitate investment in Russia (russia.privatizationlink.com). During 2000/01 an office was established in Paris, France, to promote and co-ordinate European investment in developing countries, in particular in Africa and Eastern Europe. In March 2002 MIGA opened a regional office, based in Johannesburg, South Africa. In September a new regional office was inaugurated in Singapore, in order to facilitate foreign investment in Asia.

In April 2002 MIGA launched a new service, 'FDIXchange', to provide potential investors, advisors and financial institutions with up-to-date market analysis and information on foreign direct investment opportunities in emerging economies (accessible at www.fdixchange.com). An FDIXchange Investor Information Development Programme was launched in January 2003. In January 2004 a new FDI Promotion Centre became available on the internet (www.fdipromotion.com) to facilitate information exchange and knowledge-sharing among investment promotion professionals, in particular in developing countries. (A Serbian language version was launched in June 2005.) During 2003/04 MIGA established a new fund, the Invest-in-Development Facility, to enhance the role of foreign investment in attaining the Millennium Development Goals. In July 2004 an Afghanistan Investment Guarantee Facility, to be administered by MIGA, became operational to provide political risk guarantees for foreign investors in that country. In 2005/06 MIGA supported for the first time a project aimed at selling carbon credits gained by reducing greenhouse gas emissions; it provided US $2m. in guarantee coverage to the El Salvador-based initiative.

Publications

Annual Report.

Other guides, brochures and regional briefs.

International Fund for Agricultural Development—IFAD

Address: Via del Serafico 107, 00142 Rome, Italy.

Telephone: (06) 54591; **fax:** (06) 5043463; **e-mail:** ifad@ifad.org; **internet:** www.ifad.org.

IFAD was established in 1977, following a decision by the 1974 UN World Food Conference, with a mandate to combat hunger and eradicate poverty on a sustainable basis in the low-income, food-deficit regions of the world. Funding operations began in January 1978.

Organization

(September 2007)

GOVERNING COUNCIL

Each member state is represented in the Governing Council (the Fund's highest authority) by a Governor and an Alternate. Sessions are held annually with special sessions as required. The Governing Council elects the President of the Fund (who also chairs the Executive Board) by a two-thirds majority for a four-year term. The President is eligible for re-election.

EXECUTIVE BOARD

Consists of 18 members and 18 alternates, elected by the Governing Council, who serve for three years. The Executive Board is responsible for the conduct and general operation of IFAD and approves loans and grants for projects; it holds three regular sessions each year. An independent Office of Evaluation reports directly to the Board.

The governance structure of the Fund is based on the classification of members. Membership of the Executive Board is distributed as follows: eight List A countries (i.e. industrialized donor countries), four List B (petroleum-exporting developing donor countries), and six List C (recipient developing countries), divided equally among the three Sub-List C categories (i.e. for Africa, Europe, Asia and the Pacific, and Latin America and the Caribbean).

President and Chairman of Executive Board: LENNART BÅGE (Sweden).

Vice-President: CYRIL ENWEZE (Nigeria).

Activities

IFAD provides financing primarily for projects designed to improve food production systems in developing member states and to strengthen related policies, services and institutions. In allocating resources IFAD is guided by: the need to increase food production in the poorest food-deficit countries; the potential for increasing food production in other developing countries; and the importance of improving the nutrition, health and education of the poorest people in developing countries, i.e. small-scale farmers, artisanal fishermen, nomadic pastoralists, indigenous populations, rural women, and the rural landless. All projects emphasize the participation of beneficiaries in development initiatives, both at the local and national level. Issues relating to gender and household food security are incorporated into all aspects of its activities. IFAD is committed to achieving the so-called Millennium Development Goals (MDGs), pledged by governments attending a special session of the UN General Assembly in September 2000, and, in particular, the objective to reduce by 50% the proportion of people living in extreme poverty by 2015. In 2001 the Fund introduced new measures to improve monitoring and impact evaluation, in particular to assess its contribution to achieving the MDGs.

In December 2006 the Executive Board adopted IFAD's Strategic Framework for 2007–10, in which it reiterated its commitment to enabling the rural poor to achieve household food security and to overcome their poverty. Accordingly, the Fund's efforts were to focus on ensuring that poor rural populations have improved and sustainable access to, and sufficiently developed skills to take advantage of: natural resources; better agricultural technologies and production services; a broad range of financial services; transparent competitive agricultural input and produce markets; opportunities for rural off-farm employment and enterprise development; and local and national policy and programming processes. Within this Framework the Fund has also formulated regional strategies for rural poverty reduction, based on a series of regional poverty assessments. In 2003 a new Policy Division was established under the External Affairs Department to co-ordinate policy work at the corporate level. A Policy Forum was launched in 2004, comprising IFAD senior management and staff.

IFAD is a leading repository in the world of knowledge, resources and expertise in the field of rural hunger and poverty alleviation. In 2001 it renewed its commitment to becoming a global knowledge institution for rural poverty-related issues. Through its technical assistance grants, IFAD aims to promote research and capacity-building in the agricultural sector, as well as the development of technologies to increase production and alleviate rural poverty. In recent years IFAD has been increasingly involved in promoting the use of communication technology to facilitate the exchange of information and experience among rural communities, specialized institutions and organizations, and IFAD-sponsored projects. Within the strategic context of knowledge management, IFAD has supported initiatives to support regional electronic networks, such as ENRAP (see below) in Asia and the Pacific and FIDAMERICA in Latin America and the Caribbean, as well as to develop other lines of communication between organizations, local agents and the rural poor.

IFAD is empowered to make both grants and loans. Grants are limited to 7.5% of the resources committed in any one financial year. Loans are available on highly concessionary, intermediate and ordinary terms. Highly concessionary loans carry no interest but have an annual service charge of 0.75% and a repayment period of 40 years, including a 10-year grace period. Intermediate term loans are subject to a variable interest charge, equivalent to 50% of the interest rate charged on World Bank loans, and are repaid over 20 years. Ordinary loans carry a variable interest charge equal to that charged by the World Bank, and are repaid over 15–18 years. In 2006 highly concessionary loans represented some 79% of total lending in that year. In order to increase the impact of its lending resources on food production, the Fund seeks as much as possible to attract other external donors and beneficiary governments as co-financiers of its projects. In 2006 external cofinancing accounted for some 12% of all project funding, while domestic contributions, i.e. from recipient governments and other local sources, accounted for 31%.

IFAD's development projects usually include a number of components, such as infrastructure (e.g. improvement of water supplies, small-scale irrigation and road construction); input supply (e.g. improved seeds, fertilizers and pesticides); institutional support (e.g. research, training and extension services); and producer incentives (e.g. pricing and marketing improvements). IFAD also attempts to enable the landless to acquire income-generating assets: by increasing the provision of credit for the rural poor, it seeks to free them from dependence on the capital market and to generate productive activities.

In addition to its regular efforts to identify projects and programmes, IFAD organizes special programming missions to certain selected countries to undertake a comprehensive review of the constraints affecting the rural poor, and to help countries to design strategies for the removal of these constraints. In general, projects based on the recommendations of these missions tend to focus on institutional improvements at the national and local level to direct inputs and services to small farmers and the landless rural poor. Monitoring and evaluation missions are also sent to check the progress of projects and to assess the impact of poverty reduction efforts.

The Fund supports projects that are concerned with environmental conservation, in an effort to alleviate poverty that results from the deterioration of natural resources. In addition, it extends environmental assessment grants to review the environmental consequences of projects under preparation. In October 1997 IFAD was appointed to administer the Global Mechanism of the Convention to Combat Desertification in those Countries Experiencing Drought and Desertification, particularly in Africa, which entered into force in December 1996. The Mechanism was envisaged as a means of mobilizing and channelling resources for implementation of the Convention. A series of collaborative institutional arrangements were to be concluded between IFAD, UNDP and the World Bank in order to facilitate the effective functioning of the Mechanism. In May 2001 the Global Environmental Facility approved IFAD as an executing agency.

During 2006 IFAD approved lending for seven projects in the Western and Central African region and five in Eastern and Southern Africa, involving loans amounting to US $89.6m. (or 17.2% of total lending in that year) and $93.9m. (18.1%) respectively.

In February 1998 IFAD inaugurated a new Trust Fund to complement the multilateral debt initiative for heavily indebted poor countries (HIPCs). The Fund was intended to assist IFAD's poorest members deemed to be eligible under the initiative to channel resources from debt repayments to communities in need. In February 2000 the Governing Council approved full participation by IFAD in the enhanced HIPC debt initiative agreed by the World Bank and IMF in September 1999.

During 1998 the Executive Board endorsed a policy framework for the Fund's provision of assistance in post-conflict situations, with the aim of achieving a continuum from emergency relief to a secure basis from which to pursue sustainable development. In July 2001 IFAD and UNAIDS signed a memorandum of understanding on developing a co-operation agreement. A meeting of technical experts from IFAD, FAO, WFP and UNAIDS, held in December, addressed means of mitigating the impact of HIV/AIDS on food security and rural livelihoods in affected regions. In January 2005 IFAD announced that it aimed to mobilize some US $100m. to assist countries affected by the devastating tsunami that had struck coastal regions in the Indian Ocean in late December 2004. Following the disaster IFAD also participated in needs assessments in Indonesia, Sri Lanka and the Maldives, which were to provide the basis for longer-term resource allocation and mobilization.

During the late 1990s IFAD established several partnerships within the agribusiness sector, with a view to improving performance at project level, broadening access to capital markets, and encouraging the advancement of new technologies. Since 1996 it has chaired the Support Group of the Global Forum on Agricultural Research (GFAR), which facilitates dialogue between research centres and institutions, farmers' organizations, non-governmental bodies, the private sector and donors. In October 2001 IFAD became a co-sponsor of the Consultative Group on International Agricultural Research (CGIAR). In 2006 IFAD reviewed the work of the International Alliance against Hunger, which was established in 2004 to enhance co-ordination among international agencies and non-governmental organizations concerned with agriculture and rural development, and national alliances against hunger.

Finance

In accordance with the Articles of Agreement establishing IFAD, the Governing Council periodically undertakes a review of the adequacy of resources available to the Fund and may request members to make additional contributions. The seventh replenishment of IFAD funds, covering the period 2007–09, amounted to US $720m. The provisional budget for administrative expenses for 2006 amounted to $61m., while some $4.8m. was allocated in that year to the Fund's Office of Evaluation.

Publications

Annual Report.
IFAD Update (2 a year).
Rural Poverty Report 2001.
Staff Working Papers (series).

Statistics

PROJECTS IN AFRICA SOUTH OF THE SAHARA APPROVED IN 2006

Country	Purpose	Loan amount (SDRm.*)
Burkina Faso	Agricultural commodity chain support project	9.4
Congo, Republic	Rural development project in Niari, Bouenza and Lékoumou departments	5.9
Eritrea	Post-crisis rural recovery and development	8.3
The Gambia	Rural finance project	4.2
Madagascar	Supporting development in Menabe and Melaky regions	9.1
Mali	Kidal integrated rural development programme	7.7
Mozambique	Agricultural support programme	13.9
Niger	Agricultural and rural rehabilitation and development initiative	10.4
Nigeria	Rural finance institutions-building programme	18.5
Senegal	Agricultural services and producer organizations project—phase II	4.1
Tanzania	Rural micro, small and medium enterprise support	13.0
Uganda	District livelihoods support	18.6
Zambia	Smallholder livestock investment project	7.0

* The value of the SDR—Special Drawing Right—at 31 December 2006 was US $1.50440.

International Monetary Fund—IMF

Address: 700 19th St, NW, Washington, DC 20431, USA.

Telephone: (202) 623-7000; **fax:** (202) 623-4661; **e-mail:** publicaffairs@imf.org; **internet:** www.imf.org.

The IMF was established at the same time as the World Bank in December 1945, to promote international monetary co-operation, to facilitate the expansion and balanced growth of international trade and to promote stability in foreign exchange.

Organization

(September 2007)

Managing Director: RODRIGO DE RATO Y FIGAREDO (Spain) (until Oct. 2007).

First Deputy Managing Director: JOHN LIPSKY (USA).

Deputy Managing Directors: TAKATOSHI KATO (Japan), MURILO PORTUGAL.

Director, African Department: ABDOULAYE BIO TCHANÉ (Benin).

BOARD OF GOVERNORS

The highest authority of the Fund is exercised by the Board of Governors, on which each member country is represented by a Governor and an Alternate Governor. The Board normally meets annually. The voting power of each country is related to its quota in the Fund. An International Monetary and Financial Committee (IMFC, formerly the Interim Committee) advises and reports to the Board on matters relating to the management and adaptation of the international monetary and financial system, sudden disturbances that might threaten the system and proposals to amend the Articles of Agreement.

BOARD OF EXECUTIVE DIRECTORS

The 24-member Board of Executive Directors is responsible for the day-to-day operations of the Fund. The USA, the United Kingdom, Germany, France and Japan each appoint one Executive Director. There is also one Executive Director from the People's Republic of China, Russia and Saudi Arabia, while the remainder are elected by groups of the remaining countries.

The voting rights of Liberia and Zimbabwe were suspended on 5 March 2003 and 6 June 2003, respectively.

REGIONAL REPRESENTATION

Special information and liaison offices are also located in Tokyo, Japan (for Asia and the Pacific), in New York, USA (for the United Nations) and in Europe (in Paris, France; Geneva, Switzerland; and Belgium, Brussels).

Activities

The purposes of the IMF, as defined in the Articles of Agreement, are:

(i) To promote international monetary co-operation through a permanent institution which provides the machinery for consultation and collaboration on monetary problems;

(ii) To facilitate the expansion and balanced growth of international trade, and to contribute thereby to the promotion and maintenance of high levels of employment and real income and to the development of members' productive resources;

(iii) To promote exchange stability, to maintain orderly exchange arrangements among members, and to avoid competitive exchange depreciation;

(iv) To assist in the establishment of a multilateral system of payments in respect of current transactions between members and in the elimination of foreign exchange restrictions which hamper the growth of trade;

(v) To give confidence to members by making the general resources of the Fund temporarily available to them, under adequate safeguards, thus providing them with the opportunity to correct maladjustments in their balance of payments, without resorting to measures destructive of national or international prosperity;

(vi) In accordance with the above, to shorten the duration of and lessen the degree of disequilibrium in the international balances of payments of members.

In joining the Fund, each country agrees to co-operate with the above objectives. In accordance with its objective of facilitating the expansion of international trade, the IMF encourages its members to accept the obligations of Article VIII, Sections two, three and four, of the Articles of Agreement. Members that accept Article VIII undertake to refrain from imposing restrictions on the making of payments and transfers for current international transactions and from engaging in discriminatory currency arrangements or multiple currency practices without IMF approval. By May 2006 165 members had accepted Article VIII status.

The financial crises of the late 1990s, notably in several Asian countries, Brazil and Russia, contributed to widespread discussions concerning the strengthening of the international monetary system. In April 1998 the Executive Board identified the following fundamental aspects of the debate: reinforcing international and domestic financial systems; strengthening IMF surveillance; promoting greater availability and transparency of information regarding member countries' economic data and policies; emphasizing the central role of the IMF in crisis management; and establishing effective procedures to involve the private sector in forestalling or resolving financial crises. During 1999/2000 the Fund implemented several measures in connection with its ongoing efforts to appraise and reinforce the global financial architecture, including, in March 2000, the adoption by the Executive Board of a strengthened framework to safeguard the use of IMF resources. During 2000 the Fund established the IMF Center, in Washington, DC, which aimed to promote awareness and understanding of its activities. In September the Fund's new Managing Director announced his intention to focus and streamline the principles of conditionality (which links Fund financing with the implementation of specific economic policies by the recipient countries) as part of the wider reform of the international financial system. A comprehensive review was undertaken, during which the issue was considered by public forums and representatives of civil society. New guide-lines on conditionality, which, *inter alia*, aimed to promote national ownership of policy reforms and to introduce specific criteria for the implementation of conditions given different states' circumstances, were approved by the Executive Board in September 2002. In 2000/01 the Fund established an International Capital Markets Department to improve its understanding of financial markets and a separate Consultative Group on capital markets to serve as a forum for regular dialogue between the Fund and representatives of the private sector.

In 2002 a position of Director for Special Operations was created to enhance the Fund's ability to respond to critical situations affecting member countries. In February the newly appointed Director immediately assumed leadership of the staff team working with the authorities in Argentina to help that country to overcome its extreme economic and social difficulties. Detailed consideration ensued of means of orderly resolution of financial crises. In April 2003 the Board of Directors determined that the Fund promote more actively the use of Collective Action Clauses in international bond contracts, as a voluntary measure to facilitate debt restructuring should the need arise.

SURVEILLANCE

Under its Articles of Agreement, the Fund is mandated to oversee the effective functioning of the international monetary system. Accordingly, the Fund aims to exercise firm surveillance over the exchange rate policies of member states and to assess whether a country's economic situation and policies are consistent with the objectives of sustainable development and domestic and external stability. The Fund's main tools of surveillance are regular, bilateral consultations with member countries conducted in accordance with Article IV of the Articles of Agreement, which cover fiscal and monetary policies, balance-of-payments and external debt developments, as well as policies that affect the economic performance of a country, such as the labour market, social and environmental issues and good governance, and aspects of the country's capital accounts, and finance and banking sectors. In April 1997, in an effort to improve the value of surveillance by means of increased transparency, the Executive Board agreed to the voluntary issue of Press Information Notices (PINs) following each member's Article IV consultation with the Board, to those member countries wishing to make public the Fund's views. Other background papers providing information on and analysis of economic developments in individual countries continued to be made available. The Executive Board monitors global economic developments and discusses policy implications from a multilateral perspective, based partly on World Economic Outlook reports and Global Financial Stability Reports. In addition, the IMF studies the regional implications of global developments and policies pursued under regional fiscal arrangements.

The rapid decline in the value of the Mexican peso in late 1994 and the financial crisis in Asia, which became apparent in mid-1997, focused attention on the importance of IMF surveillance of the economies and financial policies of member states and prompted the Fund to enhance the effectiveness of its surveillance and to encourage the full and timely provision of data by member countries in order to maintain fiscal transparency. In April 1996 the IMF established the Special Data Dissemination Standard (SDDS), which was intended to improve access to reliable economic statistical information for member countries that have, or are seeking, access to international capital markets. In March 1999 the IMF undertook to strengthen the Standard by the introduction of a new reserves data template. By April 2007 64 countries had subscribed to the Standard. In December 1997 the Executive Board approved a new General Data Dissemination System (GDDS), to encourage all member countries to improve the production and dissemination of core economic data. The operational phase of the GDDS commenced in May 2000. By August 2007 89 countries were participating in the GDDS. The Fund maintains a Dissemination Standards Bulletin Board (accessible at dsbb.imf.org), which aims to ensure that information on SDDS subscribing countries is widely available.

In April 1998 the then Interim Committee adopted a voluntary Code of Good Practices on Fiscal Transparency: Declaration of Principles, which aimed to increase the quality and promptness of official reports on economic indicators, and in September 1999 it adopted a Code of Good Practices on Transparency in Monetary and Financial Policies: Declaration of Principles. The IMF and World Bank jointly established a Financial Sector Assessment Programme (FSAP) in May 1999, initially as a pilot project, which aimed to promote greater global financial security through the preparation of confidential detailed evaluations of the financial sectors of individual countries. It remained under regular review by the Boards of Governors of the Fund and World Bank. During 2005/06 16 FSAP assessments were completed, of which four were updated assessments. As part of the FSAP Fund staff may conclude a Financial System Stability Assessment (FSSA), addressing issues relating to macroeconomic stability and the strength of a country's financial system. A separate component of the FSAP are Reports on the Observance of Standards and Codes (ROSCs), which are compiled after an assessment of a country's implementation and observance of internationally recognized financial standards. By 31 July 2007 516 ROSCs had been published for 133 economies.

In March 2000 the IMF Executive Board adopted a strengthened framework to safeguard the use of IMF resources. All member countries making use of Fund resources were to be required to publish annual central bank statements audited in accordance with internationally accepted standards. It was also agreed that any instance of intentional misreporting of information by a member country should be publicized. In the following month the Executive Board approved the establishment of an Independent Evaluation Office (IEO) to conduct objective evaluations of IMF policy and operations. The Office commenced activities in July 2001. In 2005/06 the Office completed evaluations on the Financial Sector Assessment Programme, multilateral surveillance, and the IMF's role in Jordan (1989–2004).

In April 2001 the Executive Board agreed on measures to enhance international efforts to counter money-laundering, in particular through the Fund's ongoing financial supervision activities and its programme of assessment of offshore financial centres (OFCs). In November the IMFC, in response to the terrorist attacks against targets in the USA, which had occurred in September, resolved, *inter alia*, to strengthen the Fund's focus on surveillance, and, in particular, to extend measures to counter money-laundering to include the funds of terrorist organizations. It determined to accelerate efforts to assess offshore centres and to provide technical support to enable poorer countries to meet international financial standards. In March 2004 the Board of Directors resolved that an anti-money laundering and countering the financing of terrorism (AML/CFT) component be introduced into regular OFC and FSAP assessments conducted by the Fund and the World Bank, following a pilot programme undertaken from November 2002 with the World Bank, the Financial Action Task Force and other regional supervisory bodies. The first phase of the OFC assessment programme was concluded in February 2005, at which time 41 of 44 contacted jurisdictions had been assessed and the reports published.

QUOTAS

MEMBERSHIP AND QUOTAS IN AFRICA SOUTH OF THE SAHARA
(million SDR*)

Country	August 2007
Angola	286.3
Benin	61.9
Botswana	63.0
Burkina Faso	60.2
Burundi	77.0
Cameroon	185.7
Cape Verde	9.6
Central African Republic	55.7
Chad	56.0
Comoros	8.9
Congo, Democratic Republic	533.0
Congo, Republic	84.6
Côte d'Ivoire	325.2
Djibouti	15.9
Equatorial Guinea	32.6
Eritrea	15.9
Ethiopia	133.7
Gabon	154.3
The Gambia	31.1
Ghana	369.0
Guinea	107.1
Guinea-Bissau	14.2
Kenya	271.4
Lesotho	34.9
Liberia	71.3
Madagascar	122.2
Malawi	69.4
Mali	93.3
Mauritania	64.4
Mauritius	101.6
Mozambique	113.6
Namibia	136.5
Niger	65.8
Nigeria	1,753.2
Rwanda	80.1
São Tomé and Príncipe	7.4
Senegal	161.8
Seychelles	8.8
Sierra Leone	103.7
Somalia	44.2
South Africa	1,868.5
Sudan	169.7
Swaziland	50.7
Tanzania	198.9
Togo	73.4
Uganda	180.5
Zambia	489.1
Zimbabwe	353.4

* The Special Drawing Right (SDR) was introduced in 1970 as a substitute for gold in international payments, and was intended eventually to become the principal reserve asset in the international monetary system. Its value (which was US $1.53327 at 28 August 2007, and averaged $1.50440 in 2006) is based on the currencies of the five largest exporting countries. Each member is assigned a quota related to its national income, monetary reserves, trade balance and other economic indicators; the quota approximately determines a member's voting power and the amount of foreign exchange it may purchase from the Fund. A member's subscription is equal to its quota. Quotas are reviewed at intervals of not more than five years, to take into account the state of the world economy and members' different rates of development. In January 1998 the Board of Governors approved an increase of some 45% of total IMF resources, bringing the total value of quotas to approximately SDR 212,000m. By January 1999 member states having at least 85% of total quotas (as at December 1997) had consented to the new subscriptions enabling the increase to enter into effect. The Twelfth General Review was concluded at the end of January 2003 without an increase in quotas. At August 2007 total quotas in the Fund amounted to SDR 217,314.8m.

RESOURCES

Members' subscriptions form the basic resource of the IMF. They are supplemented by borrowing. Under the General Arrangements to Borrow (GAB), established in 1962, the 'Group of Ten' industrialized nations (G-10—Belgium, Canada, France, Germany, Italy, Japan, the Netherlands, Sweden, the United Kingdom and the USA) and Switzerland (which became a member of the IMF in May 1992 but which had been a full participant in the GAB from April 1984) undertake to lend the Fund as much as SDR 17,000m. in their own currencies to assist in fulfilling the balance-of-payments requirements of any member of the group, or in response to requests to the Fund from countries with balance-of-payments problems that could threaten the stability of the international monetary system. In 1983 the Fund entered into an agreement with Saudi Arabia, in association with the GAB, making available SDR 1,500m., and other borrowing arrangements were completed in 1984 with the Bank for International Settlements, the Saudi Arabian Monetary Agency, Belgium and Japan, making available a further SDR 6,000m. In 1986 another borrowing arrangement with Japan made available SDR 3,000m. In May 1996 GAB participants concluded an agreement in principle to expand the resources available for borrowing to SDR 34,000m., by securing the support of 25 countries with the financial capacity to support the international monetary system. The so-called New Arrangements to Borrow (NAB) was approved by the Executive Board in January 1997. It was to enter into force, for an initial five-year period, as soon as the five largest potential creditors participating in NAB had approved the initiative and the total credit arrangement of participants endorsing the scheme had reached at least SDR 28,900m. While the GAB credit arrangement was to remain in effect, the NAB was expected to be the first facility to be activated in the event of the Fund's requiring supplementary resources. In July 1998 the GAB was activated for the first time in more than 20 years in order to provide funds of up to US $6,300m. in support of an IMF emergency assistance package for Russia (the first time the GAB had been used for a non-participant). The NAB became effective in November, and was used for the first time as part of an extensive programme of support for Brazil, which was adopted by the IMF in early December. (In March 1999, however, the activation was cancelled.) In November 2002 NAB participants agreed to renew the arrangement for a further five-year period from November 2003, and approved Chile's Central Bank as the 26th participant.

DRAWING ARRANGEMENTS

Exchange transactions within the Fund take the form of members' purchases (i.e. drawings) from the Fund of the currencies of other members for the equivalent amounts of their own currencies. Fund resources are available to eligible members on an essentially short-term and revolving basis to provide members with temporary assistance to contribute to the solution of their payments problems. Before making a purchase, a member must show that its balance of payments or reserve position makes the purchase necessary. Apart from this requirement, reserve tranche purchases (i.e. purchases that do not bring the Fund's holdings of the member's currency to a level above its quota) are permitted unconditionally.

With further purchases, however, the Fund's policy of 'conditionality' means that a member requesting assistance must agree to adjust its economic policies, as stipulated by the IMF. All requests other than for use of the reserve tranche are examined by the Executive Board to determine whether the proposed use would be consistent with the Fund's policies, and a member must discuss its proposed adjustment programme (including fiscal, monetary, exchange and trade policies) with IMF staff. Purchases outside the reserve tranche are made in four credit tranches, each equivalent to 25% of the member's quota; a member must reverse the transaction by repurchasing its own currency (with SDRs or currencies specified by the Fund) within a specified time. A credit tranche purchase is usually made under a 'Stand-by Arrangement' with the Fund, or under the Extended Fund Facility. A Stand-by Arrangement is normally of one or two years' duration, and the amount is made available in instalments, subject to the member's observance of 'performance criteria'; repurchases must be made within three-and-a-quarter to five years. An Extended Arrangement is normally of three years' duration, and the member must submit detailed economic programmes and progress reports for each year; repurchases must be made within four-and-a-half to 10 years. A member whose payments imbalance is large in relation to its quota may make use of temporary facilities established by the Fund using borrowed resources, namely the 'enlarged access policy' established in 1981, which helps to finance Stand-by and Extended Arrangements for such a member, up to a limit of between 90% and 110% of the member's quota annually. Repurchases are made within three-and-a-half to seven years. In October 1994 the Executive Board approved a temporary increase in members' access to IMF resources, on the basis of a recommendation by the then Interim Committee. The annual access limit under IMF regular tranche drawings, Stand-by Arrangements and Extended Fund Facility credits was increased from 68% to 100% of a member's quota, with the cumulative access limit remaining at 300% of quota. The arrangements were extended, on a temporary basis, in November 1997.

In addition, special-purpose arrangements have been introduced, all of which are subject to the member's co-operation with the Fund to find an appropriate solution to its difficulties. The Compensatory Financing Facility (CCF) provides compensation to members whose export earnings are reduced as a result of circumstances beyond their control, or which are affected by excess costs of cereal imports. In December 1997 the Executive Board established a new Supplemental Reserve Facility (SRF) to provide short-term assistance to members experiencing exceptional balance-of-payments difficulties resulting from a sudden loss of market confidence. In April 2004 the Board approved a new financing policy, the Trade Integration Mechanism, to assist countries experiencing short-term balance-of-payments shortfalls as a result of trade liberalization by other countries.

In October 1995 the Interim Committee of the Board of Governors endorsed recent decisions of the Executive Board to strengthen IMF financial support to members requiring exceptional assistance. An Emergency Financing Mechanism was established to enable the IMF to respond swiftly to potential or actual financial crises, while additional funds were made available for short-term currency stabilization. (The Mechanism was activated for the first time in July 1997, in response to a request by the Philippines Government to reinforce the country's international reserves, and was subsequently used during that year to assist Thailand, Indonesia and the Republic of Korea, and, in July 1998, Russia.) Emergency assistance was also to be available to countries in a post-conflict situation, extending the existing arrangements for countries having been affected by natural disasters, to facilitate the rehabilitation of their economies and to improve their eligibility for further IMF concessionary arrangements. Assistance, typically, was to be limited to 25% of a member's quota, although up to 50% would be permitted in certain circumstances. In May 2001 the Executive Board decided to provide a subsidized loan rate for post-conflict emergency assistance for PRGF-eligible countries and an account was established to administer contributions from bilateral donors. In January 2005 the Executive Board decided to extend the subsidized rate for natural disasters. During 2005/06 two countries made purchases under the emergency post-conflict assistance facility: Haiti (SDR 10.2m.) and Central African Republic (SDR 7.0m.).

In November 1999 the Fund's existing facility to provide balance-of-payments assistance on concessionary terms to low-income member countries, the Enhanced Structural Adjustment Facility, was reformulated as the Poverty Reduction and Growth Facility, with greater emphasis on poverty reduction and sustainable development as key elements of growth-orientated economic strategies. Assistance under the PRGF (for which 77 countries were deemed eligible) was to be carefully matched to specific national requirements. Prior to drawing on the facility each recipient country was, in collaboration with representatives of civil society, non-governmental organizations and bilateral and multilateral institutions, to develop a national poverty reduction strategy, which was to be presented in a Poverty Reduction Strategy Paper (PRSP). PRGF loans carry an interest rate of 0.5% per year and are repayable over 10 years, with a five-and-a-half-year grace period; each eligible country is normally permitted to borrow up to 140% of its quota (in exceptional circumstances the maximum access can be raised to 185%). A PRGF Trust replaced the former ESAF Trust. In January 2006 a new Exogenous Shocks Facility was inaugurated to provide concessional assistance on the same terms as those of the PRGF for countries not eligible for funding under the PRGF.

During 2005/06 the IMF approved regular funding commitments for new arrangements amounting to SDR 8,370.9m. for five new Stand-by Arrangements, an Extended Arrangement and one augmentation of an existing Stand-by Arrangement, compared with a total of SDR 1,327m. in the previous year. Seven new PRGF arrangements, and an augmentation of an existing arrangement, were approved in 2005/06 amounting to SDR 127.7m. During 2005/06 members' purchases from the general resources account amounted to SDR 2,559m., compared with SDR 1,608m. in the previous year. Outstanding IMF credit at 30 April 2006 totalled SDR 23,144m., compared with SDR 56,576m. in the previous year.

During 2005/06 new PRGF arrangements were approved for Benin (SDR 6.2m.), Cameroon (SDR 18.6m.), Malawi (SDR 38.2m.), and São Tomé and Príncipe (SDR 3.0m.) An augmentation of an existing arrangement was approved for Niger, amounting to SDR 19.7m.

The PRGF supports, through long-maturity loans and grants, IMF participation in an initiative to provide exceptional assistance to heavily indebted poor countries (HIPCs), in order to help them to achieve a sustainable level of debt management. The initiative was formally approved at the September 1996 meeting of the Interim Committee, having received the support of the 'Paris Club' of official creditors, which agreed to increase the relief on official debt from 67% to 80%. In all 41 HIPCs were identified, of which 33 were in sub-Saharan Africa. Resources for the HIPC initiative are channelled through the PRGF Trust. In early 1999 the IMF and World Bank initiated a comprehensive review of the HIPC scheme, in order to consider modifications of the initiative and to strengthen the link between debt relief and poverty reduction. A consensus emerged among the financial institutions and leading industrialized nations to enhance the scheme, in order to make it available to more countries, and to accelerate the process of providing debt relief. In September the IMF Board of Governors expressed its commitment to undertaking an off-market transaction of a percentage of the Fund's gold reserves (i.e. a sale, at market prices, to central banks of member countries with repayment obligations to the Fund, which were then to be made in gold), as part of the funding arrangements of the enhanced HIPC scheme; this was undertaken during the period December 1999–April 2000. Under the enhanced initiative it was agreed that countries seeking debt relief should first formulate, and successfully implement for at least one year, a national poverty reduction strategy (see above). In May 2000 Uganda became the first country to qualify for full debt relief under the enhanced scheme. At 30 April 2005 the Fund had committed an estimated SDR 1,825.5m. to the initiative. In September the IMF and World Bank endorsed a proposal of the Group of Eight (G-8) nations to achieve the cancellation by the IMF, IDA and African Development Bank of 100% of debt claims on countries that had reached completion point under the HIPC initiative, in order to help them to achieve their Millennium Development Goals. The debt cancellation was to be undertaken within the framework of a Multilateral Debt Relief Initiative (MDRI). The IMF's Executive Board determined, additionally, to extend MDRI debt relief to all countries with an annual per capita of GDP $380, to be financed by IMF's own resources. Other financing was to be made from existing bilateral contributions to the PRGF Trust Subsidy Account. In December the Executive Board gave final approval to the first group of countries assessed as eligible for 100% debt relief under the MDRI, including 17 of the 18 countries that had reached completion point at that time (i.e. Benin, Bolivia, Burkina Faso, Ethiopia, Ghana, Guyana, Honduras, Madagascar, Mali, Mozambique, Nicaragua, Niger, Rwanda, Senegal, Tanzania, Uganda and Zambia, excluding Mauritania) as well as Cambodia and Tajikistan. The initiative became effective in January 2006 once the final consent of the 43 contributors to the PRGF Trust Subsidy Account had been received. By the end of May 2007 a further five countries (Cameroon, Malawi, Mauritania, São Tomé and Príncipe and Sierra Leone) had qualified for and received MDRI relief. At that time the IMF had committed some SDR 2,692m. under the HIPC and MDRI schemes.

TECHNICAL ASSISTANCE

Technical assistance is provided by special missions or resident representatives who advise members on every aspect of economic management, while more specialized assistance is provided by the IMF's various departments. In 2000/01 the IMFC determined that technical assistance should be central to the IMF's work in crisis prevention and management, in capacity-building for low-income countries, and in restoring macroeconomic stability in countries following a financial crisis. Technical assistance activities subsequently underwent a process of review and reorganization to align them more closely with IMF policy priorities and other initiatives, for example the Financial Stability Assessment Programme. During 2005/06 the largest area of technical assistance involvement was sub-Saharan Africa.

The majority of technical assistance is provided by the Departments of Monetary and Exchange Affairs, of Fiscal Affairs and of Statistics, and by the IMF Institute. The Institute, founded in 1964, trains officials from member countries in financial analysis and policy, balance-of-payments methodology and public finance; it also gives assistance to national and regional training centres. During 2005/06 some 4,600 people participated in courses administered by the Institute. The IMF Institute also co-operates with other established regional training centres and institutes in order to refine its delivery of technical assistance and training services. The IMF is a co-sponsor, with UNDP and the Japan administered account, of the Joint Vienna Institute, which was opened in the Austrian capital in October 1992 and which trains officials from former centrally-planned economies in various aspects of economic management and public administration. In May 1998 an IMF—Singapore Regional Training Institute (an affiliate of the IMF Institute) was inaugurated, in collaboration with the Singaporean Government, in order to provide training for officials from the Asia-Pacific region. In January 1999 the IMF, in co-operation with the African Development Bank and the World Bank, announced the establishment of a Joint Africa Institute, in Abidjan, Côte d'Ivoire, which was to offer training to officials from African countries. Also in 1999 a joint Regional Training Programme, administered with the Arab Monetary Fund, was established in the United Arab Emirates. During 2000/01 the Institute established a new training programme with government officials in the People's Republic of China and agreed to establish a regional training centre for Latin America in Brazil.

Since 1993 the IMF has delivered some technical assistance, aimed at strengthening local capacity in economic and financial management through regional centres. The first, established in that year, was a Pacific Financial Technical Assistance Center, located in Fiji. A Caribbean Regional Technical Assistance Centre (CARTAC), located in Barbados, began operations in November 2001. In October 2002 an East African Regional Technical Assistance Centre (East AFRITAC), based in Dar es Salaam, Tanzania, was inaugurated and a second AFRITAC was opened in Bamako, Mali, in May 2003, to cover the West African region. In October 2004 a new technical assistance centre for the Middle East (METAC) was inaugurated, based in Beirut, Lebanon. In September 2002 the IMF signed a memorandum of understanding with the African Capacity Building Foundation to strengthen collaboration, in particular within the context of a new IMF Africa Capacity-Building Initiative.

Publications

Annual Report.

Balance of Payments Statistics Yearbook (also on CD-ROM).

Direction of Trade Statistics (quarterly and annually, also on CD-ROM).

Emerging Markets Financing (quarterly).

Finance and Development (quarterly).

Financial Statements of the IMF (quarterly).

Global Financial Stability Report (2 a year).

Global Monitoring Report (annually, with the World Bank).

Government Finance Statistics Yearbook (also on CD-ROM).

IMF Commodity Prices (monthly).

IMF in Focus (annually).

IMF Research Bulletin (quarterly).

IMF Survey (2 a month).

International Financial Statistics (monthly and annually, also on CD-ROM).

Joint BIS-IMF-OECD-World Bank Statistics on External Debt (quarterly).

Quarterly Report on the Assessments of Standards and Codes.

Staff Papers (quarterly).

World Economic Outlook (2 a year).

Other country reports, economic and financial surveys, occasional papers, pamphlets, books.

United Nations Educational, Scientific and Cultural Organization—UNESCO

Address: 7 place de Fontenoy, 75352 Paris 07 SP, France.

Telephone: 1-45-68-10-00; **fax:** 1-45-67-16-90; **e-mail:** bpi@unesco.org; **internet:** www.unesco.org.

UNESCO was established in 1946 'for the purpose of advancing, through the educational, scientific and cultural relations of the peoples of the world, the objectives of international peace and the common welfare of mankind'.

Organization

(September 2007)

GENERAL CONFERENCE

The supreme governing body of the Organization, the Conference meets in ordinary session once in two years and is composed of representatives of the member states.

EXECUTIVE BOARD

The Board, comprising 58 members, prepares the programme to be submitted to the Conference and supervises its execution; it meets twice or sometimes three times a year.

SECRETARIAT

Director-General: KOÏCHIRO MATSUURA (Japan).

CO-OPERATING BODIES

In accordance with UNESCO's constitution, national Commissions have been set up in most member states. These help to integrate work within the member states and the work of UNESCO.

PRINCIPAL REGIONAL OFFICES

Regional Bureau for Education in Africa: BP 3311, Dakar, Senegal; tel. 849-23-23; fax 823-83-23; e-mail dakar@unesco.org; internet www.dakar.unesco.org; Dir LALLA AÏCHA BEN BARKA.

Regional Bureau for Science in Africa: POB 305920, Nairobi, Kenya; tel. (20) 7621-234; fax (20) 7622-750; e-mail nairobi@unesco.org; internet www.unesco-nairobi.org/; f. 1965 to execute UNESCO's regional science programme, and to assist in the planning and execution of national programmes; Dir JOSEPH M. G. MASSAQUOI.

UNESCO International Institute for Capacity Building in Africa (UNESCO–IICBA): ECA Compound, Africa Ave, POB 2305, Addis Ababa, Ethiopia; tel. (11) 5445284; fax (11) 514936; e-mail info@unesco-iicba.org; internet www.unesco-iicba.org; f. 1999 to promote capacity building in the following areas: teacher education, curriculum development; educational policy, planning and management, and distance education; Dir JOSEPH NJIMBIDT NGU (Cameroon).

Activities

In November 2001 the General Conference approved a medium-term strategy to guide UNESCO during the period 2002–07. The Conference adopted a new unifying theme for the organization: 'UNESCO contributing to peace and human development in an era of globalization through education, the sciences, culture and communication'. UNESCO's central mission as defined under the strategy was to contribute to peace and human development in the globalized world through its programme domains (Education; Natural Sciences; Social and Human Sciences; Culture; and Communication and Information), incorporating the following three principal dimensions: developing universal principles and norms to meet emerging challenges and protect the 'common public good'; promoting pluralism and diversity; and promoting empowerment and participation in the emerging knowledge society through equitable access, capacity-building and knowledge-sharing. Programme activities were to be focused particularly on supporting disadvantaged and excluded groups or geographic regions. The organization aimed to decentralize its operations in order to ensure more country-driven programming. The UN General Assembly designated UNESCO as the lead agency for co-ordinating the International Decade for a Culture of Peace and Non-Violence for the Children of the World (2001–10), with a focus on education, and the UN Literacy Decade (2003–12). In the implementation of all its activities UNESCO aims to contribute to achieving the UN Millennium Development Goal (MDG) of halving levels of extreme poverty by 2015, as well as other MDGs concerned with education and sustainable development (see below).

Since the 1990s Africa has been a priority focus of UNESCO's activities. In November 2001 UNESCO organized an international seminar entitled *Forward-looking approaches and innovative strategies to promote the development of Africa in the 21st century,* which aimed to review UNESCO's strategy on Africa in the light of the recently launched New Partnership on Africa's Development (see under African Union).

EDUCATION

Since its establishment UNESCO has devoted itself to promoting education in accordance with principles based on democracy and respect for human rights. The Associated Schools Project (ASPnet—comprising some 7,900 institutions in 176 countries in July 2007) has, since 1953, promoted the principles of peace, human rights, democracy and international co-operation through education.

In March 1990 UNESCO, with other UN agencies, sponsored the World Conference on Education for All. 'Education for All' was subsequently adopted as a guiding principle of UNESCO's contribution to development. In April 2000 several UN agencies, including UNESCO and UNICEF, and other partners sponsored the World Education Forum, held in Dakar, Senegal, to assess international progress in achieving the goal of 'Education for All' and to adopt a strategy for further action (the 'Dakar Framework'), with the aim of ensuring universal basic education by 2015. The Forum launched the Global Initiative for Education for All (EFA). The Dakar Framework emphasized the role of improved access to education in the reduction of poverty and in diminishing inequalities within and between societies. UNESCO was appointed as the lead agency in the implementation of the Framework. UNESCO's role in pursuing the goals of the Dakar Forum was to focus on co-ordination, advocacy, mobilization of resources, and information-sharing at international, regional and national levels. It was to oversee national policy reforms, with a particular focus on the integration of 'Education for All' objectives into national education plans. The main priority of UNESCO's draft work programme on education for 2006–07 was 'Basic Education for All', with a focus on two key areas: leading the EFA initiative; and improving country-level interventions, with a focus on the following three new core components: the Literacy Initiative for Empowerment (LIFE), the Global Initiative on HIV/AIDS and Education (GIHAE), and the Teacher Training Initiative for sub-Saharan Africa. UNESCO advocates 'Literacy for All' as a key component of 'Education for All', regarding literacy as essential to basic education and to social and human development. In December 2001 the UN General Assembly appointed UNESCO to be the co-ordinating agency of the UN Literacy Decade (2003–12), which aimed to formulate an international plan of action to raise literacy standards throughout the world. UNESCO's LIFE programme component aims to achieve a 50% improvement in levels of adult literacy by 2015. The April 2000 World Education Forum recognized the global HIV/AIDS pandemic to be a significant challenge to the attainment of 'Education for All'. UNESCO, as a co-sponsor of UNAIDS, takes an active role in promoting formal and non-formal preventive health education. Through the GIHAE programme component UNESCO aims to develop comprehensive responses to HIV/AIDS rooted in the education sector, with a particular focus on vulnerable children and young people. The Teacher Training Initiative in sub-Saharan Africa focuses on aims to address the shortage of teachers in that region owing to HIV/AIDS, armed conflict and other causes. UNESCO also supports the UN Girls' Education Initiative, established following the Dakar Forum.

In December 1993 the heads of government of nine highly-populated developing countries (Bangladesh, Brazil, the People's Republic of China, Egypt, India, Indonesia, Mexico, Nigeria and Pakistan), meeting in New Delhi, India, agreed to co-operate, with the objective of achieving comprehensive primary education for all children and of expanding further learning opportunities for children and adults. By September 1999 all of the so-called 'E-9' (or Education-9) countries had officially signed the 'Delhi Declaration' issued by the meeting. UNESCO is working towards the UN MDGs of eliminating gender disparity in primary and secondary education by 2005 and attaining universal primary education in all countries by 2015.

Within the UN system UNESCO is responsible for providing technical assistance and educational services in the context of emergency situations. This includes providing education to refugees and displaced persons, as well as assistance for the rehabilitation of national education systems.

UNESCO is concerned with improving the quality, relevance and efficiency of higher education. It assists member states in reforming their national systems, organizes high-level conferences for Ministers of Education and other decision-makers, and disseminates research papers. A World Conference on Higher Education was convened in October 1998 in Paris, France. The Conference adopted a World Declaration on Higher Education for the 21st Century, incorporating proposals to reform higher education, with emphasis on access to education, and educating for individual development and active participation in society. The Conference also approved a framework for Priority Action for Change and Development of Higher Education, which comprised guide-lines for governments and institutions to meet the objectives of greater accessibility, as well as improved standards and relevancy of higher education.

NATURAL SCIENCES

In November 1999 the General Conference endorsed a Declaration on Science and the Use of Scientific Knowledge and an agenda for action, which had been adopted at the World Conference on Science, held in June–July 1999, in Budapest, Hungary. UNESCO was to co-ordinate the follow-up to the conference and, in conjunction with the International Council for Science, to promote initiatives in international scientific partnership. The principal priority area of UNESCO's draft work programme on Natural Sciences for 2006–07 was Water and associated eco-systems. The two main components are Education for water management, led by the UNESCO Institute for Water Education (inaugurated in Delft, the Netherlands in 2003); and Promotion of sound decision-making for the sustainable use of fresh water. UNESCO hosts the secretariat of the World Water Assessment Programme (WWAP), which prepares the periodic *World Water Development Report* (first issued in March 2003). UNESCO was a joint co-ordinator of the International Year of Freshwater (2003), which aimed to raise global awareness of the importance of improving the protection and management of freshwater resources. Other programme priorities are: Oceans; Capacity-building in the basic and engineering sciences, formulation of science policies, and the promotion of a culture of maintenance; and Promoting the application of science, engineering and appropriate technologies for sustainable development, natural resource use and management, disaster-preparedness and alleviation, and renewable sources of energy.

The Johannesburg Plan of Implementation, adopted by the World Summit on Sustainable Development, held in August–September 2002, reaffirmed the essential role of science (including mathematics, engineering and technology) as a foundation for achieving the MDGs of eradicating extreme poverty and ensuring environmental sustainability: in view of this, the Natural Sciences programme provides key support to the UN Decade of Education for Sustainable Development (2005–14), for which UNESCO was designated as the lead agency. The Decade aims to promote learning and awareness in support of environmental protection, economical development and social and cultural development.

UNESCO aims to improve the level of university teaching of the basic sciences through training courses, establishing national and regional networks and centres of excellence, and fostering co-operative research. In carrying out its mission, UNESCO relies on partnerships with non-governmental organizations and the world scientific communities. With the International Council of Scientific Unions and the Third World Academy of Sciences, UNESCO operates a short-term fellowship programme in the basic sciences and an exchange programme of visiting lecturers. In September 1996 UNESCO initiated a 10-year World Solar Programme, which aimed to promote the application of solar energy and to increase research, development and public awareness of all forms of ecologically sustainable energy use.

UNESCO's Man and the Biosphere Programme supports a world-wide network of biosphere reserves (comprising 507 sites in 102 countries in October 2006), which aim to promote environmental conservation and research, education and training in biodiversity and problems of land use (including the fertility of tropical soils and the cultivation of sacred sites). In October 2002 UNESCO announced that the 138 biospheres in mountainous areas would play a leading role in a new Global Change Monitoring Programme aimed at assessing the impact of global climate changes. Following the signing of the Convention to Combat Desertification in October 1994, UNESCO initiated an International Programme for Arid Land Crops, based on a network of existing institutions, to assist implementation of the Convention.

UNESCO was designated as the lead agency for the New Partnership for Africa's Development (NEPAD) Science and Technology Cluster and the NEPAD Action Plan for the Environment.

SOCIAL AND HUMAN SCIENCES

UNESCO is mandated to contribute to the world-wide development of the social and human sciences and philosophy, which it regards as of great importance in policy-making and maintaining ethical vigilance. The structure of UNESCO's Social and Human Sciences programme takes into account both an ethical and standard-setting dimension, and research, policy-making, action in the field and future-oriented activities. The principal priority area of UNESCO's draft work programme on Social and Human Sciences for 2006–07 was Ethics of science and technology, with a particular emphasis on bioethics. Other priorities include Promotion of human rights and the fight against all forms of discrimination, racism, xenophobia and related intolerance; Foresight, philosophy, human sciences, democracy and the enhancement of human security; and Management of social transformations. The priority Ethics of science and technology element aims to promote intergovernmental discussion and co-operation; to conduct explorative studies on possible UNESCO action on environmental ethics and developing a code of conduct for scientists; enhance public awareness; make available teaching expertise and create regional networks of experts; to promote the development of international and national databases on ethical issues; identify ethical issues related to emerging technologies; to follow up relevant declarations, including the Universal Declaration on the Human Genome and Human Rights (see below); and to support the Global Ethics Observatory, an online world-wide database of information on applied bioethics and other applied science- and technology-related areas (including environmental ethics) that was launched in December 2005 by the International Bioethics Committee (IBC—a group of 36 specialists who meet under UNESCO auspices).

UNESCO aims to promote and protect human rights and acts as an interdisciplinary, multicultural and pluralistic forum for reflection on issues relating to the ethical dimension of scientific advances, for example in biogenetics, new technology, and medicine. In May 1997 the IBC approved a draft version of a Universal Declaration on the Human Genome and Human Rights, in an attempt to provide ethical guide-lines for developments in human genetics. The Declaration, which identified some 100,000 hereditary genes as 'common heritage', was adopted by the UNESCO General Conference in November and committed states to promoting the dissemination of relevant scientific knowledge and co-operating in genome research. In October 2003 the General Conference adopted an International Declaration on Human Genetic Data, establishing standards for scientists working in that field. UNESCO hosts the secretariat of the 18-member World Commission on the Ethics of Scientific Knowledge and Technology (COMEST), which aims to serve as a forum for the exchange of information and ideas and to promote dialogue between scientific communities, decision-makers and the public. COMEST met for the first time in April 1999 in Oslo, Norway. Its second meeting, which took place in December 2001 in Berlin, Germany, focused on the ethics of energy, fresh water and outer space. The third meeting of COMEST, held in Rio de Janeiro, Brazil, in December 2003, inaugurated a new regional-focused approach. An extraordinary meeting of COMEST was held in May 2004, and the fourth regular session was convened in Bangkok, Thailand, in March 2005. The Organization promotes the improvement of human security through better management of the environment and social change. In 1994 UNESCO initiated an international social science research programme, the Management of Social Transformations (MOST), to promote capacity-building in social planning at all levels of decision-making. UNESCO sponsors several research fellowships in the social sciences. In other activities UNESCO promotes the rehabilitation of underprivileged urban areas, the research of socio-cultural factors affecting demographic change, and the study of family issues.

UNESCO aims to assist the building and consolidation of peaceful and democratic societies. An international network of institutions and centres involved in research on conflict resolution is being established to support the promotion of peace. Other training, workshop and research activities have been undertaken in countries that have suffered conflict. An International Youth Clearing House and Information Service (INFOYOUTH) aims to increase and consolidate the information available on the situation of young people in society, and to heighten awareness of their needs, aspirations and potential among public and private decision-makers. UNESCO also focuses on the educational and cultural dimensions of physical education and sport and their capacity to preserve and improve health. Fundamental to UNESCO's mission is the rejection of all forms of discrimination. It disseminates scientific information aimed at combating racial prejudice, works to improve the status of women and their access to education, and promotes equality between men and women.

CULTURE

In undertaking efforts to preserve the world's cultural and natural heritage UNESCO has attempted to emphasize the link between culture and development. In November 2001 the General Conference adopted the UNESCO Universal Declaration on Cultural Diversity, which affirmed the importance of intercultural dialogue in establishing a climate of peace. The principal priority element of UNESCO's draft work programme on Culture for 2006–07 was Promoting cultural diversity, with a special emphasis on the tangible and intangible heritage. Other priorities are cultural policies as well as intercultural and interfaith dialogue and understanding; and cultural industries and artistic expressions. In January 2002 UNESCO inaugurated a six-year initiative, the Global Alliance on Cultural Diversity, to promote partnerships between governments, non-governmental bodies and the private sector with a view to supporting cultural diversity through the strengthening of cultural industries and the prevention of cultural piracy. In October 2005 the General Conference approved a draft International Convention on the Protection of the Diversity of Cultural Expressions.

UNESCO's World Heritage Programme, inaugurated in 1978, aims to protect historic sites and natural landmarks of outstanding universal significance, in accordance with the 1972 UNESCO Convention Concerning the Protection of the World Cultural and Natural Heritage, by providing financial aid for restoration, technical assistance, training and management planning. At July 2007 the 'World Heritage List' comprised 851 sites in 84 countries, of which 660 had cultural significance, 166 were natural landmarks, and 25 were of 'mixed' importance.In addition to numerous nature reserves and national parks, examples in Africa include: the rock-hewn churches at Lalibela (Ethiopia); forts, castles and Ashanti traditional buildings in Ghana; Lamu Old Town (Kenya); the Royal Hill of Ambohimanga (Madagascar); the old town of Djenné and the Bandiagara cliffs of the Dogon people (Mali); four old trading towns in Mauritania; the Sukur Cultural Landscape (Nigeria); Robben Island and the Mapungubwe Cultural Landscape (South Africa); the pyramids at Gebel Barkal and other archaeological sites in the Napatan region (Sudan); the tombs of the Buganda kings at Kasubi (Uganda); the stone town of Zanzibar (Tanzania); and Great Zimbabwe National Monument. UNESCO also maintains a list of World Heritage in Danger; at July 2007 this numbered 30 sites including the royal palaces of Abomey in Benin and the ruins of Kilwa Kisiwani and Songo Mnara ports in Tanzania.

The formulation of a Declaration against the Intentional Destruction of Cultural Heritage was authorized by the General Conference in November 2001. In addition, the November General Conference adopted the Convention on the Protection of the Underwater Cultural Heritage, covering the protection from commercial exploitation of shipwrecks, submerged historical sites, etc., situated in the territorial waters of signatory states. By July 2007 the Convention had been ratified by 14 states (requiring 20 ratifications to enter into force). UNESCO also administers the 1954 Hague Convention on the Protection of Cultural Property in the Event of Armed Conflict and the 1970 Convention on the Means of Prohibiting and Preventing the Illicit Import, Export and Transfer of Ownership of Cultural Property. In 1992 a World Heritage Centre was established to enable rapid mobilization of international technical assistance for the preservation of cultural sites. Through the World Heritage Information Network (WHIN), a world-wide network of more than 800 information providers, UNESCO promotes global awareness and information exchange.

UNESCO supports efforts for the collection and safeguarding of humanity's non-material 'intangible' heritage, including oral traditions, music, dance and medicine. In May 2001, November 2003 and November 2005 UNESCO awarded the title of 'Masterpieces of the Oral and Intangible Heritage of Humanity' to a total of 90 cultural spaces (i.e. physical or temporal spaces hosting recurrent cultural events) and popular forms of expression deemed to be of outstanding value. UNESCO produced two print editions of an *Atlas of the World's Languages in Danger of Disappearing*, in 1996 and 2001, and in May 2005 launched an online version of the *Atlas*, which estimates that, of some 6,000 languages spoken world-wide, about one-half are endangered, including about 800 of the approximately 1,400 minority African languages. In October 2003 the UNESCO General Conference adopted a Convention for the Safeguarding of Intangible Cultural Heritage, which provided for the establishment of an intergovernmental committee and for participating states to formulate national inventories of intangible heritage.

UNESCO encourages the translation and publication of literary works, publishes albums of art, and produces records, audiovisual programmes and travelling art exhibitions. It supports the development of book publishing and distribution, including the free flow of books and educational material across borders, and the training of editors and managers in publishing. UNESCO is active in preparing and encouraging the enforcement of international legislation on copyright.

In December 1992 UNESCO established the World Commission on Culture and Development, to strengthen links between culture and development and to prepare a report on the issue. The first World Conference on Culture and Development was held in June 1999, in Havana, Cuba. The Global Alliance for Cultural Diversity, established in 2001, aims to strengthen cultural industries, such as music, cinema, and publishing, in developing countries.

COMMUNICATION AND INFORMATION

UNESCO regards information, communication and knowledge as being at the core of human progress and well-being. The Organization advocates the concept of knowledge societies, based on the principles of freedom of expression, universal access to information and knowledge, promotion of cultural diversity, and equal access to quality education. It promotes the free flow and broad diffusion of information, knowledge, data and best practices, through the development of communications infrastructures, the elimination of impediments to freedom of expression, the promotion of the right to information, and through efforts to harness informatics for development purposes and strengthen member states' capacities in this field. UNESCO recognizes that the so-called global 'digital divide', in addition to other developmental differences between countries, generates exclusion and marginalization, and that increased participation in the democratic process can be attained through strengthening national communication and information capacities. UNESCO's Information for All Programme (IFAP), introduced in 2001, is the principal policy-guiding framework for the Communication and Information sector. UNESCO aims to promote the formulation of integrated information and communication strategies in its member states on the basis of the Declaration of Principles and Plan of Action adopted by the World Summit on the Information Society (WSIS), which was held in two phases, the first convened in Geneva, Switzerland, in December 2003, and the second in Tunis, Tunisia, in November 2005. The principal priority element of UNESCO's draft work programme on Communication and Information for 2006–07 was Empowering people through access to information and knowledge with special emphasis on freedom of expression. This element targets, in particular, women and youth, primarily in Africa, the least-developed countries, conflict and post-conflict areas, and in countries in transition. Other priority elements are: Promoting communication development; and Advancing the use of ICTs for education, science and culture. Activities include developing effective 'infostructures', such as libraries and archives; strengthening low-cost community media and information access points, for example through the establishment of Community Multimedia Centres (CMCs) in marginalized and poor communities; training librarians, archivists and other information providers; enhancing the capacities of public service broadcasting institutions; supporting the development of independent and pluralistic media, including through the provision of advisory services on media legislation, particularly in developing member states; and improving teaching and learning processes through ICTs and developing innovative ICT-based solutions for education, such as the ICT-Enhanced Learning (ICTEL) initiative. UNESCO promotes the upholding of human rights in the use of cyberspace. UNESCO's Memory of the World project, established in 1992, aims to preserve in digital form, and thereby to promote wide access to, the world's documentary heritage. By July 2007 158 inscriptions had been included on the project's register.

UNESCO is the co-ordinating agency for 'World Press Freedom Day', which is held annually on 3 May. The theme for 2007 was 'Press freedom, safety of journalists and impunity'.

In regions affected by conflict UNESCO supports efforts to establish and maintain an independent media service. This strategy is largely implemented through the International Programme for the Development of Communication (IPDC). IPDC provides support to communication and media development projects in the developing world, including the establishment of news agencies and newspapers and training editorial and technical staff. Since its establishment in 1982, IPDC has financed some 1,000 projects in 135 countries; some 122 new projects were approved by the Programme in 2005.

The first International Congress on Ethical, Legal and Societal Aspects of Digital Information ('INFOethics') was held in Monte Carlo, Monaco, in March 1997. At the second INFOethics Congress, held in October 1998, experts discussed issues concerning privacy, confidentiality and security in the electronic transfer of information. In November 2000 a third INFOethics conference was held, on the theme of the 'Right to universal access to information in the 21st century'. UNESCO maintains an Observatory on the Information Society, which provides up-to-date information on the development of new ICTs, analyses major trends, and aims to raise awareness of related ethical, legal and societal issues.

Finance

UNESCO's activities are funded through a regular budget provided by contributions from member states and extrabudgetary funds from other sources, particularly UNDP, the World Bank, regional banks and other bilateral Funds-in-Trust arrangements. UNESCO co-operates with many other UN agencies and international non-governmental organizations.

UNESCO's proposed Regular Programme budget for the two years 2006–07 was US $635m. Extrabudgetary funds for 2006–07 were estimated at $395m.

Publications

(mostly in English, French and Spanish editions; Arabic, Chinese and Russian versions are also available in many cases)

Atlas of the World's Languages in Danger of Disappearing (internet-based).

Copyright Bulletin (quarterly).

Encyclopedia of Life Support Systems (internet-based).

International Review of Education (quarterly).

International Social Science Journal (quarterly).

Museum International (quarterly).

Nature and Resources (quarterly).

The New Courier (quarterly).

Prospects (quarterly review on education).

UNESCO Sources (monthly).

UNESCO Statistical Yearbook.

World Communication Report.

World Educational Report (every 2 years).

World Heritage Review (quarterly).

World Information Report.

World Science Report (every 2 years).

Books, databases, video and radio documentaries, statistics, scientific maps and atlases.

World Health Organization—WHO

Address: Ave Appia 20, 1211 Geneva 27, Switzerland.

Telephone: 227912111; **fax:** 227913111; **e-mail:** info@who.int; **internet:** www.who.int.

WHO, established in 1948, is the lead agency within the UN system concerned with the protection and improvement of public health.

Organization

(September 2007)

WORLD HEALTH ASSEMBLY

The Assembly meets in Geneva, once a year. It is responsible for policy making and the biennial programme and budget; appoints the Director-General; admits new members; and reviews budget contributions.

EXECUTIVE BOARD

The Board is composed of 32 health experts designated by, but not representing, their governments; they serve for three years, and the World Health Assembly elects 10–12 member states each year to the Board. It meets at least twice a year to review the Director-General's programme, which it forwards to the Assembly with any recommendations that seem necessary. It advises on questions referred to it by the Assembly and is responsible for putting into effect the decisions and policies of the Assembly. It is also empowered to take emergency measures in case of epidemics or disasters.

Chairman: Dr FERNANDO ANTEZANA ARANÍBAR (Colombia).

SECRETARIAT

Director-General: Dr MARGARET CHAN (People's Republic of China).

Assistant Directors-General: DENIS AITKEN (United Kingdom) (Adviser to the Director-General), ALA ALWAN (Iraq) (Health Action in Crises), ANDREY V. PIROGOV (Russia) (Executive Director of the WHO Office at the UN), NAMITA PRADHAM (India) (General Management), DENIS AITKIN (United Kingdom) (Representative of the Director-General for Partnerships and UN Reform), HIROKI NAKATANI (Japan) (HIV/AIDS, TB and Malaria), Dr DAVID L. HEYMANN (USA) (Communicable Diseases), TIMOTHY G. EVANS (Canada) (Information, Evidence and Research), CATHERINE LE GALÈS-CAMUS (France) (Non-Communicable Diseases and Mental Health), Dr ANDERS NORDSTRÖM (Sweden) (Health Systems and Services), HOWARD ZUCKER (USA) (Health Technology and Pharmaceuticals), SUZANNE WEBER-MOSDORF (Germany) (Sustainable Development and Healthy Environments), DAISY MAFUBELU (Family & Community Health).

PRINCIPAL OFFICES

Each of WHO's six geographical regions has its own organization, consisting of a regional committee representing relevant member states and associate members, and a regional office staffed by experts in various fields of health.

WHO Centre for Health Development: I. H. D. Centre Bldg, 9th Floor, 5–1, 1-chome, Wakinohama-Kaigandori, Chuo-ku, Kobe, Japan; tel. (78) 230-3178; fax (78) 230-3178; e-mail wkc@who.or.jp; internet www.who.or.jp; f. 1995 to address health development issues; Dir Dr SOICHIRO IWAO.

WHO Lyon Office for National Epidemic Preparedness and Response: 58 ave Debourg, 69007 Lyon, France; tel. 4-72-71-64-70; fax 4-72-71-64-71; supports global capacity-building for detection of and response to epidemics of infectious diseases; provides bridging role between WHO headquarters, the regional offices and ongoing activities in the field; Dir Dr GUÉNAËL RODIER.

WHO Mediterranean Centre for Vulnerability Reduction (WMC): rue du Lac Windermere, BP 40, 1053 Les Berges du Lac, Tunisia; tel. (71) 964-681; fax (71) 764-4558; e-mail info@wmc.who.int; internet wmc.who.int; f. 1997; advocates globally for appropriate health policies; trains health professionals; supports capacity-building for community action at grassroots level; works closely with WHO's regional offices; Dir Dr ELIL RENGANATHAN.

Activities

WHO's objective is stated in its constitution as 'the attainment by all peoples of the highest possible level of health'. 'Health' is defined as 'a state of complete physical, mental and social well-being and not merely the absence of disease and infirmity'.

WHO has developed a series of international classifications, including the *International Statistical Classification of Disease and Related Health Problems (ICD)*, providing an etiological framework of health conditions, and currently in its 10th edition; and the complementary *International Classification of Functioning, Disability and Health (ICF)*, which describes how people live with their conditions.

WHO acts as the central authority directing international health work, and establishes relations with professional groups and government health authorities on that basis.

It provides, on request from member states, technical and policy assistance in support of programmes to promote health, prevent and control health problems, control or eradicate disease, train health workers best suited to local needs and strengthen national health systems. Aid is provided in emergencies and natural disasters.

A global programme of collaborative research and exchange of scientific information is carried out in co-operation with about 1,200 national institutions. Particular stress is laid on the widespread communicable diseases of the tropics, and the countries directly concerned are assisted in developing their research capabilities.

It keeps diseases and other health problems under constant surveillance, promotes the exchange of prompt and accurate information and of notification of outbreaks of diseases, and administers the International Health Regulations. It sets standards for the quality control of drugs, vaccines and other substances affecting health. It formulates health regulations for international travel.

It collects and disseminates health data and carries out statistical analyses and comparative studies in such diseases as cancer, heart disease and mental illness.

It receives reports on drugs observed to have shown adverse reactions in any country, and transmits the information to other member states.

It promotes improved environmental conditions, including housing, sanitation and working conditions. All available information on effects on human health of the pollutants in the environment is critically reviewed and published.

Co-operation among scientists and professional groups is encouraged. The organization negotiates and sustains national and global partnerships. It may propose international conventions and agreements, and develops and promotes international norms and standards. The organization promotes the development and testing of new technologies, tools and guide-lines. It assists in developing an informed public opinion on matters of health.

WHO's first global strategy for pursuing 'Health for all' was adopted in May 1981 by the 34th World Health Assembly. The objective of 'Health for all' was identified as the attainment by all citizens of the world of a level of health that would permit them to lead a socially and economically productive life, requiring fair distribution of available resources, universal access to essential health care, and the promotion of preventive health care. In May 1998 the 51st World Health Assembly renewed the initiative, adopting a global strategy in support of 'Health for all in the 21st century', to be effected through regional and national health policies. The new approach was to build on the primary health care approach of the initial strategy, but was to strengthen the emphasis on quality of life, equity in health and access to health services. The following have been identified as minimum requirements of 'Health for all':

Safe water in the home or within 15 minutes' walking distance, and adequate sanitary facilities in the home or immediate vicinity;

Immunization against diphtheria, pertussis (whooping cough), tetanus, poliomyelitis, measles and tuberculosis;

Local health care, including availability of essential drugs, within one hour's travel;

Trained personnel to attend childbirth, and to care for pregnant mothers and children up to at least one year old.

In the implementation of all its activities WHO aims to contribute to achieving by 2015 the UN Millennium Development Goals (MDGs) that were agreed by the September 2000 UN Millennium Summit. WHO has particular responsibility for the MDGs of: reducing child mortality, with a target reduction of two-thirds in the mortality rate among children under five; improving maternal health, with a specific goal of reducing by 75% the numbers of women dying in childbirth; and combating HIV/AIDS, malaria and other diseases. In addition, it directly supports the following Millennium 'targets': halving the proportion of people suffering from malnutrition; halving the proportion of people without sustainable access to safe drinking water and basic sanitation; and providing access, in co-operation with pharmaceutical companies, to affordable, essential drugs in developing countries. Furthermore, WHO reports on 17 health-related MDG indicators; co-ordinates, jointly with the World Bank, the High-Level Forum on the Health MDGs, comprising government ministers, senior officials from developing countries, and representatives of bilateral and multilateral agencies, foundations, regional organizations and global partnerships; and undertakes technical and normative work in support of national and regional efforts to reach the MDGs.

The Eleventh General Programme of Work, for the period 2006–15, defined a policy framework for pursuing the principal objectives of building healthy populations and combating ill health. The Programme took into account: increasing understanding of the social, economic, political and cultural factors involved in achieving better health and the role played by better health in poverty reduction; the increasing complexity of health systems; the importance of safeguarding health as a component of humanitarian action; and the need for greater co-ordination among development organizations. It incorporated four interrelated strategic directions: lessening excess mortality, morbidity and disability, especially in poor and marginalized populations; promoting healthy lifestyles and reducing risk factors to human health arising from environmental, economic, social and behavioural causes; developing equitable and financially fair health systems; and establishing an enabling policy and an institutional environment for the health sector and promoting an effective health dimension to social, economic, environmental and development policy. WHO is the sponsoring agency for the Health Workforce Decade (2006–15).

Strengthening national health services has been one of WHO's primary tasks in Africa south of the Sahara. Integrated health systems are being developed to provide services related to medical care, rehabilitation, family health, communicable disease control, environmental health, health education, and health statistics. By providing educators and fellowships and by organizing training courses, support is given to national programmes aimed at preparing health workers best suited to local needs and resources. Specialists and advisory services are provided to assist in planning the health sector, which in most African countries forms an integral part of the overall plan for socio-economic development.

COMMUNICABLE DISEASES

WHO identifies infectious and parasitic communicable diseases as a major obstacle to social and economic progress, particularly in developing countries, where, in addition to disabilities and loss of productivity and household earnings, they cause nearly one-half of all deaths. Emerging and re-emerging diseases, those likely to cause epidemics, increasing incidence of zoonoses (diseases or infections passed from vertebrate animals to humans by means of parasites, viruses, bacteria or unconventional agents), attributable to factors such as environmental changes and changes in farming practices, outbreaks of unknown etiology, and the undermining of some drug therapies by the spread of antimicrobial resistance are main areas of concern. In recent years WHO has noted the global spread of communicable diseases through international travel, voluntary human migration and involuntary population displacement.

WHO's Communicable Diseases group works to reduce the impact of infectious diseases world-wide through surveillance and response; prevention, control and eradication strategies; and research and product development. The group seeks to identify new technologies and tools, and to foster national development through strengthening health services and the better use of existing tools. It aims to strengthen global monitoring of important communicable disease problems. The group advocates a functional approach to disease control. It aims to create consensus and consolidate partnerships around targeted diseases and collaborates with other groups at all stages to provide an integrated response. In 2000 WHO and several partner institutions in epidemic surveillance established a Global Outbreak Alert and Response Network (GOARN). Through the Network WHO aims to maintain constant vigilance regarding outbreaks of disease and to link world-wide expertise to provide an immediate response capability. In March 2005 GOARN responded to an outbreak of Marburg haemorrhagic fever in Angola, which, by July, had killed more than 300 people. From March 2003 WHO, through the Network, was co-ordinating the international investigation into the global spread of Severe Acute Respiratory Syndrome (SARS), a previously unknown atypical pneumonia. From the end of that year WHO was monitoring the spread through several Asian countries of the virus H5N1 (a rapidly mutating strain of zoonotic highly pathogenic avian influenza—HPAI) that was transmitting to human populations through contact with diseased birds, mainly poultry. It was feared that H5N1 would mutate into a form transmissable from human to human. In February 2005 WHO issued guide-lines for the global surveillance of the spread of H5N1 infection in human and animal populations. WHO urged all countries to develop influenza pandemic preparedness plans and to stockpile antiviral drugs, and in May, in co-operation with the UN Food and Agriculture Organization (FAO) and the World Organisation for Animal Health (OIE), it launched a Global Strategy for the Progressive Control of Highly Pathogenic Avian Influenza. A conference on Avian Influenza and Human Pandemic Influenza that was jointly organized by WHO, FAO, OIE and the World Bank in November 2005 issued a plan of action identifying a number of responses, including: supporting the development of integrated national plans for H5N1 containment and human pandemic influenza preparedness and response; assisting countries with the aggressive control of H5N1 and with establishing a more detailed understanding of the role of wild birds in virus transmission; nominating rapid response teams of experts to support epidemiological field investigations; expanding national and regional capacity in surveillance, diagnosis, and alert and response systems; expanding the network of influenza laboratories; establishing multi-country networks for the control or prevention of animal trans-boundary diseases; expanding the global antiviral stockpile; strengthening veterinary infrastructures; and mapping a global strategy and work plan for co-ordinating antiviral and influenza vaccine research and development. An International Pledging Conference on Avian and Human Influenza, convened in January 2006 in Beijing, People's Republic of China (PRC), and co-sponsored by the World Bank, European Commission and PRC Government, in co-operation with WHO, FAO and OIE, requested a minimum of US $1,200m. in funding towards combating the spread of the virus. By July 2007 a total of 318 human cases of H5N1 had been laboratory-confirmed, in Azerbaijan, Cambodia, PRC, Djibouti, Egypt, Indonesia, Iraq, Laos, Nigeria, Thailand, Turkey and Viet Nam, resulting in 192 deaths. Cases in poultry had become endemic in parts of Asia, and recent outbreaks in poultry had been reported in some European and Middle Eastern countries, and in some countries in West, Central and Northeast Africa.

One of WHO's major achievements was the eradication of smallpox. Following a massive international campaign of vaccination and surveillance (begun in 1958 and intensified in 1967), the last case was detected in 1977 and the eradication of the disease was declared in 1980. In May 1996 the World Health Assembly resolved that, pending a final endorsement, all remaining stocks of the smallpox virus were to be destroyed on 30 June 1999, although 500,000 doses of smallpox vaccine were to remain, along with a supply of the smallpox vaccine seed virus, in order to ensure that a further supply of the vaccine could be made available if required. In May 1999, however, the Assembly authorized a temporary retention of stocks of the virus until 2002. In late 2001, in response to fears that illegally-held virus stocks could be used in acts of biological terrorism (see below), WHO reassembled a team of technical experts on smallpox. In January 2002 the Executive Board determined that stocks of the virus should continue to be retained, to enable research into more effective treatments and vaccines.

In 1988 the World Health Assembly launched the Global Polio Eradication Initiative (GPEI), which aimed, initially, to eradicate poliomyelitis by the end of 2000; this target was subsequently advanced to 2005, and most recently to 2008 (see below). National Immunization Days (NIDs, facilitated in conflict zones by the negotiation of so-called 'days of tranquility') have been employed in combating the disease, alongside the strengthening of routine immunization services. Vitamin A has also been administered during NIDS in order to reduce nutritional deficiencies in children and thereby boost their immunity. Since the inauguration of the GPEI WHO has declared the following regions 'polio-free': the Americas (1994); Western Pacific (2000); and Europe (2002). In August 1996 WHO, UNICEF and Rotary International, together with other national and international partners, initiated a campaign to 'Kick Polio out of Africa', with the aim of immunizing more than 100m. children in 46 countries against the disease over a three-year period. In January 2004 the ministers of health of six countries then regarded as 'polio-endemic' (Afghanistan, Egypt, India, Niger, Nigeria and Pakistan), and global partners, meeting under the auspices of WHO and UNICEF, adopted the Geneva Declaration on the Eradication of Poliomyelitis, in which they made a commitment to accelerate the drive towards eradication of the disease, by improving the scope of vaccination programmes. Significant progress in eradication of the virus was reported in Asia during that year. In sub-Saharan Africa, however, an outbreak originating in northern Nigeria in mid-2003—caused by a temporary cessation of vaccination activities in response to local opposition to the vaccination programme—had spread, by mid-2004, to 10 previously polio-free countries. These included Côte d'Ivoire and Sudan, where ongoing civil unrest and population displacements impeded control efforts. During 2004–05 some 23 African governments, including those of the affected West and Central African countries, organized, with support from the African Union, a number of co-ordinated mass vaccination drives, which resulted in the vaccination of about 100m. children. By mid-2005 this localized epidemic was declared over; it was estimated that nearly 200 children in the region had been paralyzed by the disease since mid-2003. In January 2004 the GPEI adopted a strategic plan for the eradication of polio covering the period 2004–08, which entailed the following key objectives: securing the world-wide interruption of poliovirus transmission (from 2004); achieving certification of global polio eradication (during 2006–08);

developing guide-lines for the Global Oral Polio Vaccine Cessation Phase (2006–08); and mainstreaming the GPEI (from 2009). In May 2005 the World Health Assembly reaffirmed the goal of eradicating polio, urged sustained financial and political support towards this, and received for consideration a framework document on the formulation of a post-certification immunization policy for polio. The number of confirmed polio cases world-wide stood at 1,831 during the period January 2005–January 2006. (In 1988 35,000 cases had been confirmed in 125 countries, with the actual number of cases estimated at around 350,000.) At January 2007 Afghanistan, India, Nigeria and Pakistan were still designated as 'polio-endemic'.

WHO's Onchocerciasis Control Programme in West Africa (OCP), active during 1974–2002, succeeded in eliminating transmission in 10 countries in the region, excepting Sierra Leone, of onchocerciasis ('river blindness', spread by blackflies, and previously a major public health problem and impediment to socio-economic development in West Africa). It was estimated that under the OCP some 18m. people were protected from the disease, 600,000 cases of blindness prevented, and 25m. ha of land were rendered safe for cultivation and settlement. The former headquarters of the OCP, based in Ouagadougou, Burkina Faso, were to be transformed into a Multi-disease Surveillance Centre. In January 1996 a new initiative, the African Programme for Onchocerciasis Control (APOC), covering 19 countries outside West Africa, became operational, with funding co-ordinated by the World Bank and with WHO as the executing agency.

WHO is committed to the elimination of leprosy (the reduction of the prevalence of leprosy to less than one case per 10,000 population). The use of a highly effective combination of three drugs (known as multi-drug therapy—MDT) resulted in a reduction in the number of leprosy cases world-wide from 10m.–12m. in 1988 to 286,063 in January 2005. The number of countries having more than one case of leprosy per 10,000 had declined to nine by that time, compared with 122 in 1985. The country with the highest number of active leprosy cases at January 2005 was India (148,910), while Brazil had the second highest number of cases (30,693). The country with the highest prevalence of leprosy cases was Madagascar, with 2.5 cases per 10,000 population. The Global Alliance for the Elimination of Leprosy, launched in November 1999 by WHO, in collaboration with governments of affected countries and several private partners, including a major pharmaceutical company, aims to support the eradication of the disease through the provision until end-2010 of free MDT treatment. In June 2005 WHO adopted a Strategic Plan for Further Reducing the Leprosy Burden and Sustaining Leprosy Control Activities, covering the period 2006–10 and following on from a previous strategic plan for 2000–05. In 1998 WHO launched the Global Buruli Ulcer Initiative, which aimed to co-ordinate control of and research into Buruli ulcer, another mycobacterial disease. In July of that year the Director-General of WHO and representatives of more than 20 countries, meeting in Yamoussoukro, Côte d'Ivoire, signed a declaration on the control of Buruli ulcer. In May 2004 the World Health Assembly adopted a resolution urging improved research into, and detection and treatment of, Buruli ulcer.

The Special Programme for Research and Training in Tropical Diseases, established in 1975 and sponsored jointly by WHO, UNDP and the World Bank, as well as by contributions from donor countries, involves a world-wide network of some 5,000 scientists working on the development and application of vaccines, new drugs, diagnostic kits and preventive measures, and an applied field research on practical community issues affecting the target diseases.

The objective of providing immunization for all children by 1990 was adopted by the World Health Assembly in 1977. Six diseases (measles, whooping cough, tetanus, poliomyelitis, tuberculosis and diphtheria) became the target of the Expanded Programme on Immunization (EPI), in which WHO, UNICEF and many other organizations collaborated. As a result of massive international and national efforts, the global immunization coverage increased from 20% in the early 1980s to the targeted rate of 80% by the end of 1990. In 1992 the Assembly resolved to reach a new target of 90% immunization coverage with the six EPI vaccines; to introduce hepatitis B as a seventh vaccine; and to introduce the yellow fever vaccine in areas where it occurs endemically.

In June 2000 WHO released a report entitled 'Overcoming Antimicrobial Resistance', in which it warned that the misuse of antibiotics could render some common infectious illnesses unresponsive to treatment. At that time WHO issued guide-lines which aimed to mitigate the risks associated with the use of antimicrobials in livestock reared for human consumption.

HIV/AIDS, TB AND MALARIA

Combating the human immunodeficiency virus/acquired immunodeficiency syndrome (HIV/AIDS), tuberculosis (TB) and malaria are organization-wide priorities and, as such, are supported not only by their own areas of work but also by activities undertaken in other areas. In July 2000 a meeting of the Group of Seven industrialized nations and Russia (G-8), convened in Genoa, Italy, announced the formation of a new Global Fund to Fight AIDS, TB and Malaria (as previously proposed by the UN Secretary-General and recommended by the World Health Assembly) (see below).

The HIV/AIDS epidemic represents a major threat to human well-being and socio-economic progress. Some 95% of those known to be infected with HIV/AIDS live in developing countries, and AIDS-related illnesses are the leading cause of death in sub-Saharan Africa. It is estimated that more than 25m. people world-wide died of AIDS during 1981–2005. WHO supports governments in developing effective health-sector responses to the HIV/AIDS epidemic through enhancing their planning and managerial capabilities, implementation capacity, and health systems resources. The Joint UN Programme on HIV/AIDS (UNAIDS) became operational on 1 January 1996, sponsored by WHO and other UN agencies; the UNAIDS secretariat is based at WHO headquarters. Sufferers of HIV/AIDS in developing countries have often failed to receive advanced antiretroviral (ARV) treatments that are widely available in industrialized countries, owing to their high cost. (It was estimated in 2005 that only 15% of HIV/AIDS patients were receiving the optimum treatment.) In May 2000 the World Health Assembly adopted a resolution urging WHO member states to improve access to the prevention and treatment of HIV-related illnesses and to increase the availability and affordability of drugs. A WHO-UNAIDS HIV Vaccine Initiative was launched in that year. In June 2001 governments participating in a special session of the UN General Assembly on HIV/AIDS adopted a Declaration of Commitment on HIV/AIDS. WHO, with UNAIDS, UNICEF, UNFPA, the World Bank, and major pharmaceutical companies, participates in the 'Accelerating Access' initiative, which aims to expand access to care, support and ARVs for people with HIV/AIDS. In March 2002, under its 'Access to Quality HIV/AIDS Drugs and Diagnostics' programme, WHO published a comprehensive list of HIV-related medicines deemed to meet standards recommended by the Organization. In April WHO issued the first treatment guide-lines for HIV/AIDS cases in poor communities, and endorsed the inclusion of HIV/AIDS drugs in its *Model List of Essential Medicines* (see below) in order to encourage their wider availability. The secretariat of the International HIV Treatment Access Coalition, founded in December of that year by governments, non-governmental organizations, donors and others to facilitate access to ARVs for people in low- and middle-income countries, is based at WHO headquarters. In 2006 WHO, UNAIDS and partner organizations negotiated a framework approach aimed at achieving universal access to HIV/AIDS prevention, treatment, care and support by 2010. The resulting document was entitled the '2007–10 Strategic Framework for UNAIDS support to countries' efforts to move towards universal access'. WHO supports the following *Three Ones* principles, endorsed in April 2004 by a high-level meeting organized by UNAIDS, the United Kingdom and the USA, with the aim of strengthening national responses to the HIV/AIDS pandemic: for every country there should be one agreed national HIV/AIDS action framework; one national AIDS co-ordinating authority; and one agreed monitoring and evaluation system.

At December 2006 an estimated 24.7m. people in sub-Saharan Africa were estimated to have HIV/AIDS. In 2005 an estimated 5.8m. people were living with HIV/AIDS in South Africa, more people than in any other country world-wide, while in Botswana, Lesotho, Swaziland and Zimbabwe the prevalence rates in pregnant women attending antenatal clinics indicated national adult prevalence rates in excess of 30%.

In 1995 WHO established a Global Tuberculosis Programme to address the challenges of the TB epidemic, which had been declared a global emergency by the Organization in 1993. According to WHO estimates, one-third of the world's population carries the TB bacillus, generating around 9m. active cases and killing around 2m. people each year. The largest concentration of TB cases is in South-East Asia. TB is the principal cause of death for people infected with the HIV virus and an estimated one-third of people living with HIV/AIDS globally are co-infected with TB. WHO provides technical support to all member countries, with special attention given to those with high TB prevalence, to establish effective national tuberculosis control programmes. WHO's strategy for TB control includes the use of the expanded DOTS (direct observation treatment, short-course) regime, involving the following five tenets: sustained political commitment to increase human and financial resources and to make TB control in endemic countries a nation-wide activity and an integral part of the national health system; access to quality-assured TB sputum microscopy; standardized short-course chemotherapy for all cases of TB under proper case-management conditions; uninterrupted supply of quality-assured drugs; and maintaining a recording and reporting system to enable outcome assessment. Simultaneously, WHO is encouraging research with the aim of further advancing DOTS, developing new tools for prevention, diagnosis and treatment, and containing new threats (such as the HIV/TB co-epidemic). Inadequate control of DOTS in some areas, leading to partial and inconsistent treatments, has resulted in the development of drug-resistant and, often, incurable strains of TB. The incidence of so-called Multidrug Resistant TB (MDR-TB) strains, that are unresponsive to at least two of the four most commonly used anti-TB drugs, has risen in recent years, and WHO estimates that, annually, 300,000 new MDR-TB cases are arising world-wide, of which about four-fifths are 'super strains', resistant to at least three of the main anti-TB drugs. WHO has developed DOTS-Plus, a specialized strategy for controlling the spread of MDR-TB in areas of high prevalence. In September 2006 WHO expressed strong concern at the emergence of strains of Extensive Drug Resistant TB (XDR-TB) that are virtually untreatable with most existing anti-TB drugs. XDR-TB is believed to be most prevalent in Eastern Europe and Asia.

The 'Stop TB' partnership, launched by WHO in 1999, in partnership with the World Bank, the US Government and a coalition of non-governmental organizations, co-ordinates the Global Plan to Stop TB, which represents a 'roadmap' for TB control. The current phase of the plan, covering the period 2006–15, aims to facilitate the achievement of the MDG of halting and beginning to reverse by 2015 the incidence of TB by means of access to quality diagnosis and treatment for all; to supply ARVs to 3m. TB patients co-infected with HIV; to treat nearly 1m. people for MDR-TB; to develop a new anti-TB drug by 2010 and a new vaccine by 2015; and to develop rapid and inexpensive diagnostic tests at the point of care. The Global TB Drug Facility, launched by 'Stop TB' in 2001, aims to increase access to high-quality anti-TB drugs for sufferers in developing countries.

In 2004 WHO reported that the People's Republic of China, Ecuador, Estonia, Israel, Kazakhstan, Latvia, Lithuania, parts of the Russian Federation, South Africa and Uzbekistan had the highest rates of MDR-TB infection in the world.

In October 1998 WHO, jointly with UNICEF, the World Bank and UNDP, formally launched the Roll Back Malaria (RBM) programme. The disease acutely affects at least 350m.–500m. people, and kills an estimated 1m. people, every year. Some 90% of all malaria cases occur in sub-Saharan Africa. It is estimated that the disease directly causes 18% of all child deaths in that region. The global RBM Partnership, linking governments, development agencies, and other parties, aims to mobilize resources and support for controlling malaria. The RBM Partnership Global Strategic Plan for the period 2005–15, adopted in November 2005, lists steps required to intensify malaria control interventions with a view to attaining targets set by the Partnership for 2010 and 2015 (the former targets include: ensuring the protection of 80% of people at risk from malaria and the diagnosis and treatment within one day of 80% of malaria patients, and reducing the global malaria burden by one-half compared with 2000 levels; and the latter: achieving a 75% reduction in malaria morbidity and mortality over levels at 2005). WHO recommends a number of guide-lines for malaria control, focusing on the need for prompt, effective antimalarial treatment, and the issue of drug resistance; vector control, including the use of insecticide-treated bednets; malaria in pregnancy; malaria epidemics; and monitoring and evaluation activities. WHO, with several private- and public-sector partners, supports the development of more effective anti-malaria drugs and vaccines through the 'Medicines for Malaria' venture.

Global Fund to Fight AIDS, TB and Malaria: 6–8 chemin Blandonnet, 1214 Vernier-Geneva, Switzerland; tel. 227911700; fax 227911701; e-mail info@theglobalfund.org; internet www.theglobalfund.org; f. 2000 as a partnership between governments, civil society, private-sector interests, UN bodies (including WHO, UNAIDS, the IBRD and UNDP), and other agencies to raise resources for combating AIDS, TB and malaria; the Fund supports but does not implement assistance programmes; US $3,700m. was pledged by international donors at a conference convened in Sept. 2005 to replenish the Fund during 2006–07; by January 2007 the Fund had approved $7,000m. (of which $3,300m. had been disbursed) in respect of nearly 450 grants supporting prevention and treatment programmes in 136 countries; by that time the cumulative allocation of grant funding by region was as follows: Africa (56%), East Asia and the Pacific (14%), the Middle East and North Africa and South Asia (11%), Latin America and the Caribbean (10%), and Eastern Europe and Central Asia (8%); while the distribution by health sector was: HIV/AIDS (58%), malaria (24%), TB (17%) and strengthening of health systems (1%); Exec. Dir Dr Michel Kazatchkine.

Joint UN Programme on HIV/AIDS (UNAIDS): 20 ave Appia, 1211 Geneva 27, Switzerland; tel. 227913666; fax 227914187; e-mail unaids@unaids.org; internet www.unaids.org; established in 1996 to lead, strengthen and support an expanded response to the global HIV/AIDS pandemic; activities focus on prevention, care and support, reducing vulnerability to infection, and alleviating the socioeconomic and human effects of HIV/AIDS; launched the Global Coalition on Women and AIDS in Feb. 2004; in June 2005 adopted a policy position paper for intensifying HIV prevention; co-sponsors: WHO, UNICEF, UNDP, UNFPA, UNODC, ILO, UNESCO, the World Bank, WFP, UNHCR; Exec. Dir Peter Piot (Belgium).

NON-COMMUNICABLE DISEASES AND MENTAL HEALTH

The Non-communicable Diseases and Mental Health group comprises departments for the surveillance, prevention and management of uninfectious diseases, such as those arising from an unhealthy diet, and departments for health promotion, disability, injury prevention and rehabilitation, mental health and substance abuse. Surveillance, prevention and management of non-communicable diseases, tobacco, and mental health are organization-wide priorities.

Addressing the social and environmental determinants of health is a main priority of WHO. Tobacco use, unhealthy diet and physical inactivity are regarded as common, preventable risk factors for the four most prominent non-communicable diseases: cardiovascular diseases, cancer, chronic respiratory disease and diabetes. WHO aims to monitor the global epidemiological situation of non-communicable diseases, to co-ordinate multinational research activities concerned with prevention and care, and to analyse determining factors such as gender and poverty. In 1998 the organization adopted a resolution on measures to be taken to combat non-communicable diseases; their prevalence was anticipated to increase, particularly in developing countries, owing to rising life expectancy and changes in lifestyles. For example, between 1995 and 2025 the number of adults affected by diabetes world-wide was projected to increase from 135m. to 300m. In 2001 chronic diseases reportedly accounted for about 59% of the estimated 56.5m. total deaths globally and for 46% of the global burden of disease. In February 1999 WHO initiated a new programme, 'Vision 2020: the Right to Sight', which aimed to eliminate avoidable blindness (estimated to be as much as 80% of all cases) by 2020. Blindness was otherwise predicted to increase by as much as twofold, owing to the increased longevity of the global population. In May 2004 the World Health Assembly endorsed a Global Strategy on Diet, Physical Activity and Health; it was estimated at that time that more than 1,000m. adults world-wide were overweight, and that, of these, some 300,000 were clinically obese. WHO has studied obesity-related issues in co-operation with the International Association for the Study of Obesity (IASO). The International Task Force on Obesity, affiliated to the IASO, aims to encourage the development of new policies for managing obesity. WHO and FAO jointly commissioned an expert report on the relationship of diet, nutrition and physical activity to chronic diseases, which was published in March 2003.

WHO's programmes for diabetes mellitus, chronic rheumatic diseases and asthma assist with the development of national initiatives, based upon goals and targets for the improvement of early detection, care and reduction of long-term complications. WHO's cardiovascular diseases programme aims to prevent and control the major cardiovascular diseases, which are responsible for more than 14m. deaths each year. It is estimated that one-third of these deaths could have been prevented with existing scientific knowledge. The programme on cancer control is concerned with the prevention of cancer, improving its detection and cure, and ensuring care of all cancer patients in need. In May 2004 the World Health Assembly adopted a resolution on cancer prevention and control, recognizing an increase in global cancer cases, particularly in developing countries, and stressing that many cases and related deaths could be prevented. The resolution included a number of recommendations for the improvement of national cancer control programmes. WHO is a co-sponsor of the Global Day Against Pain, which was held for the first time in 2004 and was to take place thereafter annually on 11 October. The Global Day highlights the need for improved pain management and palliative care for sufferers of diseases such as cancer and AIDS, with a particular focus on patients living in low-income countries with minimal access to opioid analgesics, and urges recognition of access to pain relief as a basic human right.

The WHO Human Genetics Programme manages genetic approaches for the prevention and control of common hereditary diseases and of those with a genetic predisposition representing a major health importance. The Programme also concentrates on the further development of genetic approaches suitable for incorporation into health care systems, as well as developing a network of international collaborating programmes.

WHO works to assess the impact of injuries, violence and sensory impairments on health, and formulates guide-lines and protocols for the prevention and management of mental problems. The health promotion division promotes decentralized and community-based health programmes and is concerned with developing new approaches to population ageing and encouraging healthy life-styles and self-care. It also seeks to relieve the negative impact of social changes such as urbanization, migration and changes in family structure upon health. WHO advocates a multi-sectoral approach—involving public health, legal and educational systems—to the prevention of injuries, which represent 16% of the global burden of disease. It aims to support governments in developing suitable strategies to prevent and mitigate the consequences of violence, unintentional injury and disability. Several health promotion projects have been undertaken, in collaboration between WHO regional and country offices and other relevant organizations, including: the Global School Health Initiative, to bridge the sectors of health and education and to promote the health of school-age children; the Global Strategy for Occupational Health, to promote the health of the working population and the control of occupational health risks; Community-based Rehabilitation, aimed at providing a more enabling environment for people with disabilities; and a communication strategy to provide training and support for health communications personnel and initiatives. In 2000 WHO, UNESCO, the World Bank and UNICEF adopted the joint Focusing Resources for Effective School Health (FRESH Start) approach to promoting life skills among adolescents.

In July 1997 the fourth International Conference on Health Promotion (ICHP) was held in Jakarta, Indonesia, where a declaration on 'Health Promotion into the 21st Century' was agreed. The fifth ICHP was convened in June 2000, in Mexico City, Mexico.

Mental health problems, which include unipolar and bipolar affective disorders, psychosis, epilepsy, dementia, Parkinson's disease, multiple sclerosis, drug and alcohol dependency, and neuropsychiatric disorders such as post-traumatic stress disorder, obsessive compulsive disorder and panic disorder, have been identified by WHO as significant global health problems. Although, overall, physical health has improved, mental, behavioural and social health problems are increasing, owing to extended life expectancy and improved child mortality rates, and factors such as war and poverty. WHO aims to address mental problems by increasing awareness of mental health issues and promoting improved mental health services and primary care.

The Substance Abuse department is concerned with problems of alcohol, drugs and other substance abuse. Within its Programme on Substance Abuse (PSA), which was established in 1990 in response to the global increase in substance abuse, WHO provides technical support to assist countries in formulating policies with regard to the prevention and reduction of the health and social effects of psychoactive substance abuse. PSA's sphere of activity includes epidemiological surveillance and risk assessment, advocacy and the dissemination of information, strengthening national and regional prevention and health promotion techniques and strategies, the development of cost-effective treatment and rehabilitation approaches, and also encompasses regulatory activities as required under the international drugs-control treaties in force.

The Tobacco or Health Programme aims to reduce the use of tobacco, by educating tobacco-users and preventing young people from adopting the habit. In 1996 WHO published its first report on the tobacco situation world-wide. According to WHO, about one-third of the world's population aged over 15 years smoke tobacco, which causes approximately 3.5m. deaths each year (through lung cancer, heart disease, chronic bronchitis and other effects). In 1998 the 'Tobacco Free Initiative', a major global anti-smoking campaign, was established. In May 1999 the World Health Assembly endorsed the formulation of a Framework Convention on Tobacco Control (FCTC) to help to combat the increase in tobacco use (although a number of tobacco growers expressed concerns about the effect of the convention on their livelihoods). The FCTC entered into force in February 2005. The greatest increase in tobacco use is forecast to occur in developing countries.

FAMILY AND COMMUNITY HEALTH

WHO's Family and Community Health group addresses the following areas of work: child and adolescent health, research and programme development in reproductive health, making pregnancy safer and men and women's health. Making pregnancy safer is an organization-wide priority. The group's aim is to improve access to sustainable health care for all by strengthening health systems and fostering individual, family and community development. Activities include newborn care; child health, including promoting and protecting the health and development of the child through such approaches as promotion of breast-feeding and use of the mother-baby package, as well as care of the sick child, including diarrhoeal and acute respiratory disease control, and support to women and children in difficult circumstances; the promotion of safe motherhood and maternal health; adolescent health, including the promotion and development of young people and the prevention of specific health problems; women, health and development, including addressing issues of gender, sexual violence, and harmful traditional practices; and human reproduction, including research related to contraceptive technologies and effective methods. In addition, WHO aims to provide technical leadership and co-ordination on reproductive health and to support countries in their efforts to ensure that people: experience healthy sexual development and maturation; have the capacity for healthy, equitable and responsible relationships; can achieve their reproductive intentions safely and healthily; avoid illnesses, diseases and injury related to sexuality and reproduction; and receive appropriate counselling, care and rehabilitation for diseases and conditions related to sexuality and reproduction.

In September 1997 WHO, in collaboration with UNICEF, formally launched a programme advocating the Integrated Management of Childhood Illness (IMCI), following successful regional trials in more than 20 developing countries during 1996–97. IMCI recognizes that pneumonia, diarrhoea, measles, malaria and malnutrition cause some 70% of the approximately 11m. childhood deaths each year, and recommends screening sick children for all five conditions, to obtain a more accurate diagnosis than may be achieved from the results of a single assessment. WHO's Division of Diarrhoeal and Acute Respiratory Disease Control encourages national programmes aimed at reducing childhood deaths as a result of diarrhoea, particularly through the use of oral rehydration therapy and preventive measures. The Division is also seeking to reduce deaths from pneumonia in infants through the use of a simple case-management strategy involving the recognition of danger signs and treatment with an appropriate antibiotic.

SUSTAINABLE DEVELOPMENT AND HEALTHY ENVIRONMENTS

The Sustainable Development and Healthy Environments group focuses on the following areas of work: health in sustainable development; nutrition; health and environment; food safety; and emergency preparedness and response. Food safety is an organization-wide priority.

WHO promotes recognition of good health status as one of the most important assets of the poor. The Sustainable Development and Healthy Environment group seeks to monitor the advantages and disadvantages for health, nutrition, environment and development arising from the process of globalization (i.e. increased global flows of capital, goods and services, people, and knowledge); to integrate the issue of health into poverty reduction programmes; and to promote human rights and equality. Adequate and safe food and nutrition is a priority programme area. WHO collaborates with FAO, the World Food Programme, UNICEF and other UN agencies in pursuing its objectives relating to nutrition and food safety. An estimated 780m. people world-wide cannot meet basic needs for energy and protein, more than 2,000m. people lack essential vitamins and minerals, and 170m. children are estimated to be malnourished. In December 1992 WHO and FAO hosted an international conference on nutrition, at which a World Declaration and Plan of Action on Nutrition was adopted to make the fight against malnutrition a development priority. Following the conference, WHO promoted the elaboration and implementation of national plans of action on nutrition. WHO aims to support the enhancement of member states' capabilities in dealing with their nutrition situations, and addressing scientific issues related to preventing, managing and monitoring protein-energy malnutrition; micronutrient malnutrition, including iodine deficiency disorders, vitamin A deficiency, and nutritional anaemia; and diet-related conditions and non-communicable diseases such as obesity (increasingly affecting children, adolescents and adults, mainly in industrialized countries), cancer and heart disease. In 1990 the World Health Assembly resolved to eliminate iodine deficiency (believed to cause mental retardation); a strategy of universal salt iodization was launched in 1993. In collaboration with other international agencies, WHO is implementing a comprehensive strategy for promoting appropriate infant, young child and maternal nutrition, and for dealing effectively with nutritional emergencies in large populations. Areas of emphasis include promoting healthcare practices that enhance successful breast-feeding; appropriate complementary feeding; refining the use and interpretation of body measurements for assessing nutritional status; relevant information, education and training; and action to give effect to the International Code of Marketing of Breast-milk Substitutes. The food safety programme aims to protect human health against risks associated with biological and chemical contaminants and additives in food. With FAO, WHO establishes food standards (through the work of the Codex Alimentarius Commission and its subsidiary committees) and evaluates food additives, pesticide residues and other contaminants and their implications for health. The programme provides expert advice on such issues as food-borne pathogens (e.g. listeria), production methods (e.g. aquaculture) and food biotechnology (e.g. genetic modification). In July 2001 the Codex Alimentarius Commission adopted the first global principles for assessing the safety of genetically modified (GM) foods. In March 2002 an intergovernmental task force established by the Commission finalized 'principles for the risk analysis of foods derived from biotechnology', which were to provide a framework for assessing the safety of GM foods and plants. In the following month WHO and FAO announced a joint review of their food standards operations. In February 2003 the FAO/WHO Project and Fund for Enhanced Participation in Codex was launched to support the participation of poorer countries in the Commission's activities.

WHO's programme area on environment and health undertakes a wide range of initiatives to tackle the increasing threats to health and well-being from a changing environment, especially in relation to air pollution, water quality, sanitation, protection against radiation, management of hazardous waste, chemical safety and housing hygiene. Some 1,100m. people world-wide have no access to clean drinking water, while a further 2,400m. people are denied suitable sanitation systems. WHO helped launch the Water Supply and Sanitation Council in 1990 and regularly updates its *Guidelines for Drinking Water Quality*. In rural areas the emphasis continues to be on the provision and maintenance of safe and sufficient water supplies and adequate sanitation, the health aspects of rural housing, vector control in water resource management, and the safe use of agrochemicals. In urban areas assistance is provided to identify local environmental health priorities and to improve municipal governments' ability to deal with environmental conditions and health problems in an integrated manner; promotion of the 'Healthy City' approach is a major component of the programme. Other programme activities include environmental health information development and management, human resources development, environmental health planning methods, research and work on problems relating to global environment change, such as UV-radiation. A report considering the implications of climate change on human health, prepared jointly by WHO, WMO and UNEP, was published in July 1996. The WHO Global Strategy for Health and Environment, developed in response to the WHO Commission on Health and Environment which reported to the UN Conference on Environment and Development in June 1992, provides the framework for programme activities. In December 2001 WHO published a report on the relationship between macroeconomics and health.

In sub-Saharan Africa, where conditions are considered to be the worst in the world, WHO estimated that, at early 1996, more than half of all people in the region were lacking safe drinking water, and some 70% were living without adequate sanitation, contributing to the problems of endemic malnutrition and diarrhoeal diseases. In October 1998 representatives of 46 African governments convened in Harare, Zimbabwe, to review implementation of the African 2000 initiative on water supply and sanitation, which was adopted in 1993 to strengthen local capacities for the development of safe and effective water supply and sanitation facilities.

Through its International EMF Project WHO is compiling a comprehensive assessment of the potential adverse effects on human health deriving from exposure to electromagnetic fields (EMF). In June 2004 WHO organized a workshop on childhood sensitivity to EMF.

WHO's work in the promotion of chemical safety is undertaken in collaboration with ILO and UNEP through the International Programme on Chemical Safety (IPCS), the Central Unit for which is located in WHO. The Programme provides internationally evaluated scientific information on chemicals, promotes the use of such information in national programmes, assists member states in establishment of their own chemical safety measures and programmes, and helps them strengthen their capabilities in chemical emergency preparedness and response and in chemical risk reduction. In 1995 an Inter-organization Programme for the Social Management of Chemicals was established by UNEP, ILO, FAO, WHO, UNIDO and OECD, in order to strengthen international co-operation in the field of chemical safety. In 1998 WHO led an international assessment of the health risk from bendocine disruptors (chemicals which disrupt hormonal activities).

Since the major terrorist attacks perpetrated against targets in the USA in September 2001, WHO has focused renewed attention on the potential malevolent use of bacteria (such as bacillus anthracis, which causes anthrax), viruses (for example, the variola virus, causing smallpox) or toxins, or of chemical agents, in acts of biological or chemical terrorism. In September 2001 WHO issued draft guidelines entitled 'Health Aspects of Biological and Chemical Weapons'.

Within the UN system, WHO's Department of Emergency and Humanitarian Action co-ordinates the international response to emergencies and natural disasters in the health field, in close co-operation with other agencies and within the framework set out by the UN's Office for the Co-ordination of Humanitarian Affairs. In this context, WHO provides expert advice on epidemiological surveillance, control of communicable diseases, public health information and health emergency training. Its emergency preparedness activities include co-ordination, policy-making and planning, awareness-building, technical advice, training, publication of standards and guide-lines, and research. Its emergency relief activities include organizational support, the provision of emergency drugs and supplies and conducting technical emergency assessment missions. The Division's objective is to strengthen the national capacity of member states to reduce the adverse health consequences of disasters. In responding to emergency situations, WHO always tries to develop projects and activities that will assist the national authorities concerned in rebuilding or strengthening their own capacity to handle the impact of such situations. Under the UN's Consolidated Inter-agency Appeal Process (CAP) for 2007, launched in November 2006, WHO appealed for US $204.1m. to fund emergency activities in 13 countries and regions.

In January 2005, following a massive earthquake in the Indian Ocean in December 2004, which caused a series of tidal waves, or tsunamis, that devastated coastal regions in 14 countries in South and South-East Asia and East Africa, WHO requested emergency funding of US $67.1m. to support an initial six-month relief operation. Priorities included the establishment of a local disease surveillance and early warning system; co-ordination of humanitarian health assistance at international and national level; guidance on critical public health matters (such as disease outbreak response, water quality and sanitation, and mental health and pre-existing disease management); ensuring equitable access to essential health care; and ensuring the prompt provision of medical supplies.

HEALTH TECHNOLOGY AND PHARMACEUTICALS

WHO's Health Technology and Pharmaceuticals group, made up of the departments of essential drugs and other medicines, vaccines and other biologicals, and blood safety and clinical technology, covers the following areas of work: essential medicines—access, quality and rational use; immunization and vaccine development; and world-wide co-operation on blood safety and clinical technology. Blood safety and clinical technology are an organization-wide priority.

In January 1999 the Executive Board adopted a resolution on WHO's Revised Drug Strategy which placed emphasis on the inequalities of access to pharmaceuticals, and also covered specific aspects of drugs policy, quality assurance, drug promotion, drug donation, independent drug information and rational drug use. Plans of action involving co-operation with member states and other international organizations were to be developed to monitor and analyse the pharmaceutical and public health implications of international agreements, including trade agreements. In April 2001 experts from WHO and the World Trade Organization participated in a workshop to address ways of lowering the cost of medicines in less developed countries. In the following month the World Health Assembly adopted a resolution urging member states to promote equitable access to essential drugs, noting that this was denied to about one-third of the world's population. WHO participates with other partners in the 'Accelerating Access' initiative, which aims to expand access to antiretroviral drugs for people with HIV/AIDS (see above).

WHO reports that 2m. children die each year of diseases for which common vaccines exist. In September 1991 the Children's Vaccine Initiative (CVI) was launched, jointly sponsored by the Rockefeller Foundation, UNDP, UNICEF, the World Bank and WHO, to facilitate the development and provision of children's vaccines. The CVI has as its ultimate goal the development of a single oral immunization shortly after birth that will protect against all major childhood diseases. An International Vaccine Institute was established in Seoul, Republic of Korea, as part of the CVI, to provide scientific and technical services for the production of vaccines for developing countries. In September 1996 WHO, jointly with UNICEF, published a comprehensive survey, entitled *State of the World's Vaccines and Immunization*. In 1999 WHO, UNICEF, the World Bank and a number of public- and private-sector partners formed the Global Alliance for Vaccines and Immunization (GAVI), which aimed to expand the provision of existing vaccines and to accelerate the development and introduction of new vaccines and technologies, with the ultimate goal of protecting children of all nations and from all socio-economic backgrounds against vaccine-preventable diseases.

WHO supports states in ensuring access to safe blood, blood products, transfusions, injections, and healthcare technologies.

INFORMATION, EVIDENCE AND RESEARCH

The Information, Evidence and Research group addresses the following areas of work: evidence for health policy; health information management and dissemination; and research policy and promotion and organization of health systems. Through the generation and dissemination of evidence the Information, Evidence and Research group aims to assist policy-makers assess health needs, choose intervention strategies, design policy and monitor performance, and thereby improve the performance of national health systems. The group also supports international and national dialogue on health policy.

WHO co-ordinates the Health InterNetwork Access to Research Initiative (HINARI), which was launched in July 2001 to enable relevant authorities in developing countries to access more than 2,000 biomedical journals through the internet at no or greatly reduced cost, in order to improve the world-wide circulation of scientific information; some 28 medical publishers participate in the initiative.

Finance

WHO's regular budget is provided by assessment of member states and associate members. An additional fund for specific projects is provided by voluntary contributions from members and other sources, including UNDP and UNFPA.

A regular budget of US $915.3m. was proposed for 2006–07, of which some 22.2%, or $203.6m., was provisionally allocated to Africa.

Publications

Bulletin of the World Health Organization (monthly).

Eastern Mediterranean Health Journal (annually).

International Classification of Functioning, Disability and Health—ICF.

International Statistical Classification of Disease and Related Health Problems.

Model List of Essential Medicines (every two years).

Pan-American Journal of Public Health (annually).

3 By 5 Progress Report.

Toxicological Evaluation of Certain Veterinary Drug Residues in Food (annually).

Weekly Epidemiological Record (in English and French, paper and electronic versions available).

WHO Drug Information (quarterly).

WHO Global Atlas of Traditional, Complementary and Alternative Medicine.

WHO Model Formulary.

World Health Report (annually, in English, French and Spanish).

World Malaria Report (with UNICEF).

Zoonoses and Communicable Diseases Common to Man and Animals.

Technical report series; catalogues of specific scientific, technical and medical fields available.

Other UN Organizations Active in the Region

INTERNATIONAL CRIMINAL TRIBUNAL FOR RWANDA—ICTR

Address: Registry: Arusha International Conference Centre, POB 6016, Arusha, Tanzania.

Telephone: (212) 963-2850; **fax:** (212) 963-2848; **e-mail:** ictr-press@un.org; **internet:** www.ictr.org.

In November 1994 the Security Council adopted Resolution 955, establishing an International Criminal Tribunal for Rwanda (ICTR) to prosecute persons responsible for genocide and other serious violations of humanitarian law that had been committed in Rwanda and by Rwandans in neighbouring states. Its temporal jurisdiction was limited to the period 1 January to 31 December 1994. The Tribunal consists of 11 permanent judges, of whom nine sit in four trial chambers (based in Arusha, Tanzania) and two sit in the seven-member appeals chamber that is shared with the ICTY and based at The Hague. In August 2002 the UN Security Council endorsed a proposal by the ICTR President to elect a pool of 18 *ad litem* judges to the Tribunal with a view to accelerating its activities and bringing them to a conclusion by 2008–10. In October 2003 the Security Council increased the number of *ad litem* judges who may serve on the Tribunal at any one time from four to nine. A high security detention facility had been built within the compound of the prison in Arusha. The first plenary session of the Tribunal was held in The Hague in June 1995; formal proceedings at its permanent headquarters in Arusha were initiated in November. The first trial of persons charged by the Tribunal commenced in January 1997, and sentences were imposed in July. In September 1998 the former Rwandan Prime Minister, Jean Kambanda, and a former mayor of Taba, Jean-Paul Akayesu, both Hutu extremists, were found guilty of genocide and crimes against humanity; Kambanda subsequently became the first person ever to be sentenced under the 1948 Convention on the Prevention and Punishment of the Crime of Genocide. In October 2000 the Tribunal rejected an appeal by Kambanda. In November 1999 the Rwandan Government temporarily suspended co-operation with the Tribunal in protest at a decision of the appeals chamber to release an indicted former government official owing to procedural delays. (The appeals chamber subsequently reversed this decision.) In 2001 two ICTR investigators employed on defence teams were arrested and charged with genocide, having been found to be working at the Tribunal under assumed identities. Relations between the Rwandan Government and the ICTR deteriorated again in 2002, with the then Chief Prosecutor accusing the Rwandan authorities of failing to facilitate the travel of witnesses to the Tribunal and withholding access to documentary materials, and counter accusations by the Rwandan Government that the Tribunal's progress was too slow, that further suspected perpetrators of genocide had been inadvertantly employed by the Tribunal and that Rwandan witnesses attending the Tribunal had not received sufficient protection. Reporting to the UN Security Council in July, the then Chief Prosecutor alleged that the Rwandan non-co-operation ensued from her recent decision to indict former members of the Tutsi-dominated Rwanda Patriotic Army for human rights violations committed against Hutus in 1994. In September 2003 the trial of Théoneste Bagosora, a former military commander accused of masterminding the genocide, commenced, after considerable procedural delays. In January 2004 a former minister of culture and education, Jean de Dieu Kamuhanda, was found guilty on two counts of genocide and extermination as a crime against humanity. In the following month Samuel Imanishimwe, a former military commander, was convicted on seven counts of genocide, crimes against humanity and serious violations of the Geneva Conventions. Two others were acquitted of similar charges. In early May 2004 Yussufu Munyakazi, accused of directing mass killings by the Interahamwe militia in Cyangugu and Kibuye Provinces, was arrested in the Democratic Republic of the Congo. By July 2007 the Tribunal had delivered judgments against 33 accused, of whom five were acquitted. A further 28 people were on trial at that time, while nine indictees were awaiting trial. Some 18 of those accused remained at large.

Both the ICTY and ICTR are supported by teams of investigators and human rights experts working in the field to collect forensic and other evidence in order to uphold indictments. Evidence of mass graves resulting from large-scale unlawful killings has been uncovered in both regions.

President of the ICTR: Erik Møse (Norway).

ICTR Prosecutor: Hassan Bubacar Jallow (The Gambia).

ICTR Registrar: Adama Dieng (Senegal).

SPECIAL COURT FOR SIERRA LEONE

Address: Jomo Kenyatta Rd, New England, Freetown, Sierra Leone.

Telephone: (22) 297000; **fax:** (22) 297001; **e-mail:** scsl-mail@un.org; **internet:** www.sc-sl.org.

The Court was established in January 2002 by agreement of the United Nations and the government of Sierra Leone, pursuant to a Security Council resolution of August 2000 to establish an independent Special Court to prosecute those 'bearing the greatest responsibility for committing violations against humanitarian law' since 20 November 1996. Trial proceedings commenced in June 2004. By March 2007 a total of 13 people had been indicted by the Special Court, although two indictments were withdrawn in December 2003 following the deaths of two of the accused. In April 2006 the Special Court for Sierra Leone and the International Criminal Court concluded a memorandum of understanding in accordance with which the Special Court was to use the courtroom and detention facilities of the International Criminal Court for the planned trial of Charles Taylor, the former president of Liberia, on charges of crimes against humanity. Taylor, who had been arrested in Nigeria and transferred to the Special Court in March, was transferred to the Criminal Court's detention centre in The Hague in June. Taylor's trial commenced in June 2007. Shortly afterwards it was adjourned until January 2008.

President of the Court: George Gelaga King (Sierra Leone).

Chief Prosecutor: Stephen Rapp (USA).

OFFICE FOR THE CO-ORDINATION OF HUMANITARIAN AFFAIRS—OCHA

Address: United Nations Plaza, New York, NY 10017, USA.

Telephone: (212) 963-1234; **fax:** (212) 963-1312; **e-mail:** ochany@un.org; **internet:** ochaonline.un.org.

The Office was established in January 1998 as part of the UN Secretariat, with a mandate to co-ordinate international humanitarian assistance and to provide policy and other advice on humanitarian issues. It administers the Humanitarian Early Warning System, as well as Integrated Regional Information Networks (IRIN) to monitor the situation in different countries and a Disaster

Response System. A complementary service, Reliefweb, which was launched in 1996, monitors crises and publishes information on the internet.

Under-Secretary-General for Humanitarian Affairs and Emergency Relief Co-ordinator: JOHN HOLMES (United Kingdom).

UNITED NATIONS OFFICE ON DRUGS AND CRIME—UNODC

Address: Vienna International Centre, POB 500, 1400 Vienna, Austria.

Telephone: (1) 26060-0; **fax:** (1) 26060-5866; **e-mail:** unodc@unodc.org; **internet:** www.unodc.org.

The Office was established in November 1997 (as the UN Office of Drug Control and Crime Prevention) to strengthen the UN's integrated approach to issues relating to drug control, crime prevention and international terrorism. It comprises two principal components: the United Nations Drug Programme and the Crime Programme.

Executive Director: ANTONIO MARIA COSTA (Italy).

OFFICE OF THE UNITED NATIONS HIGH COMMISSIONER FOR HUMAN RIGHTS—OHCHR

Address: Palais Wilson, 52 rue de Paquis, 1201 Geneva, Switzerland.

Telephone: (22) 9179290; **fax:** (22) 9179022; **e-mail:** infodesk@ohchr.org; **internet:** www.ohchr.org.

The Office is a body of the UN Secretariat and is the focal point for UN human-rights activities. Since September 1997 it has incorporated the Centre for Human Rights. The High Commissioner is the UN official with principal responsibility for UN human rights activities.

High Commissioner: LOUISE ARBOUR (Canada).

UNITED NATIONS HUMAN SETTLEMENTS PROGRAMME—UN-HABITAT

Address: POB 30030, Nairobi, Kenya.

Telephone: (20) 621234; **fax:** (20) 624266; **e-mail:** infohabitat@unhabitat.org; **internet:** www.unhabitat.org.

UN-Habitat was established, as the United Nations Centre for Human Settlements, in October 1978 to service the intergovernmental Commission on Human Settlements. It became a full UN programme on 1 January 2002, serving as the focus for human settlements activities in the UN system.

Executive Director: ANNA KAJUMULO TIBAIJUKA (Tanzania).

UNITED NATIONS CONFERENCE ON TRADE AND DEVELOPMENT—UNCTAD

Address: Palais des Nations, 1211 Geneva 10, Switzerland.

Telephone: (22) 9171234; **fax:** (22) 9070043; **e-mail:** info@unctad.org; **internet:** www.unctad.org.

UNCTAD was established in 1964. It is the principal organ of the UN General Assembly concerned with trade and development, and is the focal point within the UN system for integrated activities relating to trade, finance, technology, investment and sustainable development. It aims to maximize the trade and development opportunities of developing countries, in particular least-developed countries, and to assist them to adapt to the increasing globalization and liberalization of the world economy. UNCTAD undertakes consensus-building activities, research and policy analysis and technical co-operation.

Secretary-General: Dr SUPACHAI PANITCHPAKDI (Thailand).

UNITED NATIONS POPULATION FUND—UNFPA

Address: 220 East 42nd St, New York, NY 10017, USA.

Telephone: (212) 297-5020; **fax:** (212) 297-4911; **internet:** www.unfpa.org.

Created in 1967 as the Trust Fund for Population Activities, the UN Fund for Population Activities (UNFPA) was established as a Fund of the UN General Assembly in 1972 and was made a subsidiary organ of the UN General Assembly in 1979, with the UNDP Governing Council (now the Executive Board) designated as its governing body. In 1987 UNFPA's name was changed to the United Nations Population Fund (retaining the same acronym).

Executive Director: THORAYA A. OBAID (Saudi Arabia).

UN Specialized Agencies

INTERNATIONAL CIVIL AVIATION ORGANIZATION—ICAO

Address: 999 University St, Montréal, QC H3C 5H7, Canada.

Telephone: (514) 954-8219; **fax:** (514) 954-6077; **e-mail:** icaohq@icao.org; **internet:** www.icao.int.

ICAO was founded in 1947, on the basis of the Convention on International Civil Aviation, signed in Chicago, in 1944, to develop the techniques of international air navigation and to help in the planning and improvement of international air transport.

Secretary-General: TAÏEB CHÉRIF (Algeria).

INTERNATIONAL LABOUR ORGANIZATION—ILO

Address: 4 route des Morillons, 1211 Geneva 22, Switzerland.

Telephone: (22) 7996111; **fax:** (22) 7988685; **e-mail:** ilo@ilo.org; **internet:** www.ilo.org.

ILO was founded in 1919 to work for social justice as a basis for lasting peace. It carries out this mandate by promoting decent living standards, satisfactory conditions of work and pay and adequate employment opportunities. Methods of action include the creation of international labour standards; the provision of technical co-operation services; and training, education, research and publishing activities to advance ILO objectives.

Director-General: JUAN O. SOMAVÍA (Chile).

Regional Office for Africa: BP 3960, Abidjan 01, Côte d'Ivoire; tel. 20-32-27-16; fax 22-21-28-80; e-mail abidjan@ilo.org.

INTERNATIONAL MARITIME ORGANIZATION—IMO

Address: 4 Albert Embankment, London, SE1 7SR, United Kingdom.

Telephone: (20) 7735-7611; **fax:** (20) 7587-3210; **e-mail:** info@imo.org; **internet:** www.imo.org.

The Inter-Governmental Maritime Consultative Organization (IMCO) began operations in 1959, as a specialized agency of the UN to facilitate co-operation among governments on technical matters affecting international shipping. Its main aims are to improve the safety of international shipping, and to prevent pollution caused by ships. IMCO became IMO in 1982.

Secretary-General: EFTHIMIOS MITROPOULOS (Greece).

INTERNATIONAL TELECOMMUNICATION UNION—ITU

Address: Place des Nations, 1211 Geneva 20, Switzerland.

Telephone: (22) 7305111; **fax:** (22) 7337256; **e-mail:** itumail@itu.int; **internet:** www.itu.int.

Founded in 1865, ITU became a specialized agency of the UN in 1947. It acts to encourage world co-operation for the improvement and use of telecommunications, to promote technical development, to harmonize national policies in the field, and to promote the extension of telecommunications throughout the world.

Secretary-General: HAMADOUN TOURÉ (Mali).

UNITED NATIONS INDUSTRIAL DEVELOPMENT ORGANIZATION—UNIDO

Address: Vienna International Centre, POB 300, 1400 Vienna, Austria.

Telephone: (1) 260260; **fax:** (1) 2692669; **e-mail:** unido@unido.org; **internet:** www.unido.org.

UNIDO began operations in 1967 and became a specialized agency in 1985. Its objectives are to promote sustainable and socially equitable industrial development in developing countries and in countries with economies in transition. It aims to assist such countries to integrate fully into global economic system by mobilizing knowledge, skills, information and technology to promote productive employment, competitive economies and sound environment.

Director-General: KANDEH YUMKELLA (Sierra Leone).

UNIVERSAL POSTAL UNION—UPU

Address: Weltpoststr., 3000 Bern 15, Switzerland.

Telephone: (31) 3503111; **fax:** (31) 3503110; **e-mail:** info@upu.int; **internet:** www.upu.int.

The General Postal Union was founded by the Treaty of Berne (1874), beginning operations in July 1875. Three years later its name was changed to the Universal Postal Union. In 1948 UPU became a specialized agency of the UN. It aims to develop and unify the international postal service, to study problems and to provide training.

Director-General: EDOUARD DAYAN (France).

WORLD INTELLECTUAL PROPERTY ORGANIZATION—WIPO

Address: 34 chemin des Colombettes, 1211 Geneva 20, Switzerland.

Telephone: (22) 3389111; **fax:** (22) 7335428; **e-mail:** wipo.mail@wipo.int; **internet:** www.wipo.int.

WIPO was established in 1970. It became a specialized agency of the UN in 1974 concerned with the protection of intellectual property (e.g. industrial and technical patents and literary copyrights) throughout the world. WIPO formulates and administers treaties embodying international norms and standards of intellectual property, establishes model laws, and facilitates applications for the protection of inventions, trademarks etc. WIPO provides legal and technical assistance to developing countries and countries with economies in transition and advises countries on obligations under the World Trade Organization's agreement on Trade-Related Aspects of Intellectual Property Rights (TRIPS).

Director-General: Dr KAMIL IDRIS (Sudan).

WORLD METEOROLOGICAL ORGANIZATION—WMO

Address: 7 bis, ave de la Paix, 1211 Geneva 2, Switzerland.

Telephone: (22) 7308111; **fax:** (22) 7308181; **e-mail:** wmo@wmo.int; **internet:** www.wmo.int.

WMO was established in 1950 and was recognized as a Specialized Agency of the UN in 1951, aiming to improve the exchange of information in the fields of meteorology, climatology, operational hydrology and related fields, as well as their applications. WMO jointly implements, with UNEP, the UN Framework Convention on Climate Change.

Secretary-General: MICHEL JARRAUD (France).

WORLD TOURISM ORGANIZATION—UNWTO

Address: Capitán Haya 42, 28020 Madrid, Spain.

Telephone: (91) 5678100; **fax:** (91) 5713733; **e-mail:** omt@world-tourism.org; **internet:** www.world-tourism.org.

The World Tourism Organization was established in 1975 and was recognized as a Specialized Agency of the UN in December 2003. It works to promote and develop sustainable tourism, in particular in support of socio-economic growth in developing countries.

Secretary-General: FRANCESCO FRANGIALLI (France).

AFRICAN DEVELOPMENT BANK—ADB

Address: Headquarters: rue Joseph Anoma, 01 BP 1387, Abidjan 01, Côte d'Ivoire.

Telephone: 20-20-44-44; **fax:** 20-20-49-59; **e-mail:** afdb@afdb.org; **internet:** www.afdb.org.

Address: Temporary relocation agency: 15 ave du Ghana, angle des rues Pierre de Coubertin et Hedi Nouira, BP 323, 1002 Tunis Belvédère, Tunisia.

Telephone: (71) 333-511; **fax:** (71) 351-933.

Established in 1964, the Bank began operations in July 1966, with the aim of financing economic and social development in African countries. The Bank's headquarters are based in Abidjan, Côte d'Ivoire. From February 2003, however, in view of ongoing insecurity in Côte d'Ivoire, the Bank's operations were relocated on a temporary basis to Tunis, Tunisia (see above).

AFRICAN MEMBERS

Algeria	Equatorial Guinea	Namibia
Angola	Eritrea	Niger
Benin	Ethiopia	Nigeria
Botswana	Gabon	Rwanda
Burkina Faso	The Gambia	São Tomé and Príncipe
Burundi	Ghana	Senegal
Cameroon	Guinea	Seychelles
Cape Verde	Guinea-Bissau	Sierra Leone
Central African Republic	Kenya	Somalia
Chad	Lesotho	South Africa
Comoros	Liberia	Sudan
Congo, Democratic Republic	Libya	Swaziland
Congo, Republic	Madagascar	Tanzania
Côte d'Ivoire	Malawi	Togo
Djibouti	Mali	Tunisia
Egypt	Mauritania	Uganda
	Mauritius	Zambia
	Morocco	Zimbabwe
	Mozambique	

There are also 24 non-African members.

Organization

(September 2007)

BOARD OF GOVERNORS

The highest policy-making body of the Bank. Each member country nominates one Governor, usually its Minister of Finance and Economic Affairs, and an alternate Governor or the Governor of its Central Bank. The Board meets once a year. It elects the Board of Directors and the President.

BOARD OF DIRECTORS

The Board consists of 18 members (of whom six are non-African), elected by the Board of Governors for a term of three years, renewable once; it is responsible for the general operations of the Bank. The Board meets on a weekly basis.

OFFICERS

The President is responsible for the organization and the day-to-day operations of the Bank under guidance of the Board of Directors. The President is elected for a five-year term and serves as the Chairman of the Board of Directors. A new organizational structure became effective in July 2006, according to which the President oversees the following senior management: Chief Economist; Vice-Presidents of Finance, Corporate Services, Country and Regional Programmes and Policy, Sector Operations, and Infrastructure, Private Sector and Regional Integration; Auditor General; General Counsel; Secretary-General; and Ombudsman.

Executive President and Chairman of Board of Directors: DONALD KABERUKA (Rwanda).

Secretary-General: MODIBO TOURÉ (Mali).

FINANCIAL STRUCTURE

The ADB Group of development financing institutions comprises the African Development Fund (ADF) and the Nigeria Trust Fund (NTF), which provide concessionary loans, and the African Development Bank itself. The group uses a unit of account (UA), which, at December 2005, was valued at US $1.42927.

The capital stock of the Bank was at first exclusively open for subscription by African countries, with each member's subscription consisting of an equal number of paid-up and callable shares. In 1978, however, the Governors agreed to open the capital stock of the Bank to subscription by non-regional states on the basis of nine principles aimed at maintaining the African character of the institution. The decision was finally ratified in May 1982, and the participation of non-regional countries became effective on 30 December. It was agreed that African members should still hold two-thirds of the share capital, that all loan operations should be restricted to African members, and that the Bank's President should always be an African national. In May 1998 the Board of Governors approved an increase in capital of 35%, and resolved that the non-African members' share of the capital be increased from 33.3% to 40%. In 2005 the ADB's authorized capital was US $31,258.13m. At the end of 2005 subscribed capital was $30,923.77m. (of which the paid-up portion was $3,243.10m.).

Activities

At the end of 2005 total loan and grant approvals by the ADB Group since the beginning of its operations amounted to US $55,162.5m. Of that amount agriculture received the largest proportion of assistance (18.1%), while transport received 16.5%, multi-sector activities 15.2%, and finance 13.3%. In 2005 the Group approved 102 loans and grants amounting to $3,278.2m., compared with $4,327.8m. for 124 loans and grants in the previous year.

In 2002 the Bank's Board of Directors approved a Strategic Plan for 2003–07 incorporating four fundamental principles for Bank activities: country ownership; greater selectivity; participatory approaches; and enhanced co-operation with development partners. Bank operations were to continue to emphasis the central objectives of promoting sustainable economic growth and achieving poverty reduction. In March 2004 a Rural Water Supply and Sanitation Initiative was approved to accelerate access in member countries to sustainable safe water and basic sanitation, in order to meet the requirements of several internationally-agreed Millennium Development Goals (MDGs). In October 2006 the Bank established a High Level Panel of eminent personalities to advise on the Bank's future strategic vision.

Since 1996 the Bank has collaborated closely with international partners, in particular the World Bank, in efforts to address the problems of heavily indebted poor countries—HIPCs (see IBRD). Of the 41 countries identified as potentially eligible for assistance under the scheme 33 were in sub-Saharan Africa. Following the introduction of an enhanced framework for the initiative, the Bank has been actively involved in the preparation of Poverty Reduction Strategy Papers, that provide national frameworks for poverty reduction programmes. At the end of 2005 the Bank Group had approved US $4,680m. in HIPC debt relief. In September 2006 the Board of Governors of the ADF endorsed a new Multilateral Debt Relief Initiative which provided for 100% cancellation of eligible debts from the ADF, IMF and the International Development Association. The Initiative aimed to secure additional resources for countries to help them attain their MDGs. ADF's participation was anticipated to provide some $8,540m. in debt relief for 33 African countries.

The Bank contributed funds for the establishment, in 1986, of the Africa Project Development Facility, which assists the private sector in Africa by providing advisory services and finance for entrepreneurs: it was managed by the International Finance Corporation (IFC), until replaced by the Private Enterprise Partnership for Africa in April 2005. In 1989 the Bank, in co-ordination with IFC and UNDP, created the African Management Services Company (AMSCo) which provides management support and training to private companies in Africa. The Bank is one of three multilateral donors, with the World Bank and UNDP, supporting the African Capacity Building Foundation, which was established in 1991 to strengthen and develop institutional and human capacity in support of sustainable development activities. The Bank was to host the secretariat of a new Africa Investment Consortium, which was inaugurated in October 2005 by several major African institutions and donor countries to accelerate efforts to develop the region's infrastructure. The first ADB Economic Conference was held in Tunis, Tunisia, in November 2006.

The Bank also provides technical assistance to regional member countries in the form of experts' services, pre-investment feasibility studies, and staff training; much of this assistance is financed through bilateral aid funds contributed by non-African member states. The Bank's African Development Institute provides training for officials of regional member countries in order to enhance the management of Bank-financed projects and, more broadly, to strengthen national capacities for promoting sustainable development. In 1990 the ADB established the African Business Round Table (ABR), which is composed of the chief executives of Africa's leading corporations. The ABR aims to strengthen Africa's private sector, promote intra-African trade and investment, and attract foreign investment to Africa. The ABR is chaired by the Bank's Executive President. At its fourth annual meeting, held in Arusha, Tanzania, in March 1994, the ABR resolved to establish an African Investment Bank, in co-operation with the ADB, which was to provide financial services to African companies. In November 1999 a Joint Africa Institute, which had been established by the Bank, the World Bank and the IMF, was formally inaugurated in Abidjan, Côte d'Ivoire. The Institute aimed to enhance training opportunities in economic policy and management and to strengthen capacity-building in the region.

In 1990 a Memorandum of Understanding (MOU) for the Reinforcement of Co-operation between the Organization of African Unity, now African Union, the UN Economic Commission for Africa and the ADB was signed by the three organizations. A joint secretariat supports co-operation activities between the organizations. In 1999 a Co-operation Agreement was formally concluded between the Bank and the Common Market for Eastern and Southern Africa (COMESA). In March 2000 the Bank signed an MOU on its strategic partnership with the World Bank. Other MOUs were signed during that year with the United Nations Industrial Development Organization, the World Food Programme, and the Arab Maghreb Union. The Bank is actively involved in the New Partnership for Africa's Development (NEPAD), established in 2001 to promote sustainable development and eradicate poverty throughout the region.

AFRICAN DEVELOPMENT BANK (ADB)

The Bank makes loans at a variable rate of interest, which is adjusted twice a year, plus a commitment fee of 0.75%. Loan approvals amounted to US $1,241.7m. for 34 loans in 2005, compared with $2,359.9m. for 23 loans in the previous year. Since October 1997 new fixed and floating rate loans have also been made available.

AFRICAN DEVELOPMENT FUND (ADF)

The Fund commenced operations in 1974. It grants interest-free loans to low-income African countries for projects with repayment over 50 years (including a 10-year grace period) and with a service charge of 0.75% per annum. Grants for project feasibility studies are made to the poorest countries.

Negotiations for a seventh replenishment of the Fund's resources commenced in May 1993. However, in May 1994, donor countries withheld any new funds owing to dissatisfaction with the Bank's governance. In May 1996, following the implementation of various institutional reforms to strengthen the Bank's financial management and decision-making capabilities and to reduce its administrative costs, an agreement was concluded on the seventh replenishment of the ADF. Donor countries pledged some US $2,690m. for the period 1996–98. An additional allocation of $420m. was endorsed at a special donors' meeting held in Osaka, Japan, in June. The ADF aimed to offer concessional assistance to 42 African countries over the period 1996–98. The seventh replenishment provided for the establishment of an ADF Microfinance Initiative (AMINA), initially for a two-year period, to support small-scale capacity-building projects. In January 1999 negotiations on the eighth replenishment of the Fund were concluded with an agreement to provide additional resources amounting to $3,437m. The replenishment was approved by the Board of Governors in May, and came into effect in December. In September 2002 donor countries pledged resources of around $3,500m. for the ninth replenishment of the Fund, covering the period 2002–04. The so-called ADF-X was concluded in December 2004, with an agreement to replenish the Fund by some $5,400m. It was agreed that poverty reduction and the promotion of sustainable growth were to remain the principal objectives of the Fund for the period 2005–07. The first round of ADF-XI discussions was held in March 2007.

In 2005 65 ADF loans and grants were approved amounting to US $2,032.0m.

NIGERIA TRUST FUND (NTF)

The Agreement establishing the Nigeria Trust Fund was signed in February 1976 by the Bank and the Government of Nigeria. The Fund is administered by the Bank and its loans are granted for up to 25 years, including grace periods of up to five years, and carry 0.75% commission charges and 4% interest charges. The loans are intended to provide financing for projects in co-operation with other lending institutions. The Fund also aims to promote the private sector and trade between African countries by providing information on African and international financial institutions able to finance African trade.

Three loans were approved during 2005 amounting to US $4.6m.

ASSOCIATED INSTITUTIONS

The Bank actively participated in the establishment of five associated institutions:

African Reinsurance Corporation (Africa-Re): Africa Re House, Plot 1679, Karimu Kotun St, Victoria Island, PMB 12765, Lagos, Nigeria; tel. (1) 2626660; fax (1) 2663282; e-mail info@africa-re.com; internet www.africa-re.com; f. 1977; started operations in 1978; its purpose is to foster the development of the insurance and reinsurance industry in Africa and to promote the growth of national and regional underwriting capacities; auth. cap. US $100m., of which the Bank holds 10%; there are 12 directors, one appointed by the Bank; mems: 41 countries, the ADB, and some 110 insurance and reinsurance cos; Man. Dir BAKARY KAMARA; publ. *The African Reinsurer*(annually).

African Export-Import Bank (Afreximbank): POB 404 Gezira, Cairo 11568; World Trade Centre Bldg, 1191 Corniche el-Nil, Cairo 11221, Egypt; tel. (2) 5780282; fax (2) 5780277; e-mail mail@afreximbank.com; internet www.afreximbank.com; f. 1993; aims to increase the volume of African exports and to expand intra-African trade by financing exporters and importers directly and indirectly through trade finance institutions, such as commercial banks; in Nov. 2001, under the auspices of Afreximbank, a Memorandum of General Principles was signed by African bankers for the establishment of an African Bankers Forum; auth. cap. US $750m.; paid-up cap. $149.4(Dec. 2005; Pres. JEAN-LOUIS EKRA; publ. *Annual Report*.

Association of African Development Finance Institutions (AADFI): Immeuble AIAFD, blvd Latrille, rue J61, Cocody Deux Plateaux, Abidjan 04, Côte d'Ivoire; tel. 22-52-33-89; fax 22-52-25-84; e-mail adfi@aviso.ci; internet www.aadfi.org; f. 1975; aims to promote co-operation among financial institutions in the region in matters relating to economic and social development, research, project design, financing and the exchange of information; mems: 92 in 43 African and non-African countries; Chair. Sir REMI OMOTOSO (Nigeria); Sec.-Gen. JOSEPH AMIHERE; publs *Annual Report*, *AADFI Information Bulletin* (quarterly), *Finance and Development in Africa* (2 a year).

Shelter-Afrique (Société pour l'habitat et le logement territorial en Afrique): Longonot Rd, POB 41479, Nairobi, Kenya; tel. (20) 2722305; fax (20) 2722024; e-mail info@shelterafrique.org; internet www.shelterafrique.org; f. 1982 to finance housing in mem. countries; auth. share cap. is US $300m., held by 41 African countries, the ADB, Africa-Re and CDC Group plc (formerly the Commonwealth Development Corpn); Man. Dir P. M'BAYE.

Société Internationale Financière pour les Investissements et le Développement en Afrique (SIFIDA): c/o BNP Paribas (Suisse) SA, Case Postale, 1211 Geneva 11, Switzerland; tel. 582122905; fax 582122920; internet www.sifida.com; f. 1970 by 120 financial and industrial institutions, including the ADB and the IFC; following its purchase by BNP/Paribas in 1996 the company was in the process of being liquidated. SIFIDA remains active in the field of structured finance in emerging (primarily African) markets and also provides financial advisory services, notably in the context of project finance, privatization and medium-term structured finance; Man. Dir JACQUES LOEHR.

Publications

Annual Report.

ADB Business Bulletin (10 a year).

ADB Statistical Pocketbook.

ADB Today (every 2 months).

African Development Report (annually).

African Development Review.

African Economic Outlook (annually, with OECD).

African Statistical Journal (2 a year).

Annual Procurement Report.

Basic Information (annually).

Economic Research Papers.

OPEV Sharing (quarterly newsletter).

Quarterly Operational Summary.

Summaries of operations in each member country and various background documents.

Statistics

SUMMARY OF BANK GROUP ACTIVITIES
(US $ million)

	2004	2005	Cumulative total*
ADB loans			
Number	23	34	991
Amount approved	2,359.86	1,241.65	31,519.18
Disbursements	978.76	850.92	20,185.84
ADF loans and grants			
Number	99	65	2,045
Amount approved	1,953.55	2,032.02	23,236.52
Disbursements	1,056.82	987.72	12,892.32
NTF loans			
Number	2	3	75
Amount approved	14.37	4.56	406.76
Disbursements	7.47	4.85	260.05
Group total			
Number	124	102	3,111
Amount approved	4,327.78	3,278.23	55,162.45
Disbursements	2,043.05	1,843.48	33,338.21

* Since the initial operations of the three institutions (1967 for ADB, 1974 for ADF and 1976 for NTF).

GROUP LOAN AND GRANT APPROVALS BY COUNTRY
(millions of UA)

Country	2004	2005	Cumulative total*
Algeria	—	—	1,889.1
Angola	—	17.5	339.4
Benin	21.2	59.5	489.8
Botswana	34.3	—	362.0
Burkina Faso	39.6	56.8	580.2
Burundi	20.2	12.3	308.8
Cameroon	12.1	25.6	775.9
Cape Verde	3.5	—	166.3
Central African Republic	—	—	139.4
Chad	2.4	37.5	394.7
Comoros	—	—	64.7
Congo, Democratic Republic	55.2	87.5	1,207.6
Congo, Republic	7.0	—	286.0
Côte d'Ivoire	—	—	1,143.5
Djibouti	5.3	0.3	114.2
Egypt	—	284.3	2,013.8
Equatorial Guinea	—	—	67.2
Eritrea	18.6	—	78.8
Ethiopia	62.0	43.6	1,463.1
Gabon	76.3	15.4	688.8
Gambia	5.0	5.5	220.6
Ghana	12.8	86.0	954.6
Guinea	—	22.7	563.2
Guinea Bissau	—	1.4	179.1
Kenya	51.3	41.5	724.2
Lesotho	0.8	—	300.6
Liberia	—	—	154.0
Libya	—	—	—
Madagascar	45.2	57.3	577.6
Malawi	12.0	15.4	606.0
Mali	33.9	49.9	634.5
Mauritania	7.0	0.3	351.5
Mauritius	—	7.7	279.3
Morocco	369.3	175.7	3,891.1
Mozambique	30.0	9.5	915.1
Namibia	59.1	—	167.8
Niger	3.0	40.7	342.4
Nigeria	1.7	108.3	2,306.4
Rwanda	51.9	—	411.2
São Tomé and Príncipe	—	—	99.6
Senegal	9.6	83.2	669.5
Seychelles	—	0.3	89.8
Sierra Leone	3.6	39.7	279.2
Somalia	—	0.3	151.1
South Africa	117.1	—	511.0
Sudan	—	—	350.9
Swaziland	—	0.4	294.6
Tanzania	114.7	—	924.7
Togo	—	—	185.2
Tunisia	140.2	181.7	3,501.8
Uganda	74.2	88.5	944.4
Zambia	13.7	0.4	658.0
Zimbabwe	—	0.4	726.9
Multinational	219.2	85.8	1,151.9
Total	1,733.1	1,742.9	36,691.2

* Since the initial operation of the three institutions (1967 for ADB, 1974 for ADF and 1976 for NTF).

Source: *Annual Report 2005*.

AFRICAN UNION—AU

Address: POB 3243, Addis Ababa, Ethiopia.

Telephone: (11) 5517700; **fax:** (11) 5517844; **e-mail:** webmaster@africa-union.org; **internet:** www.africa-union.org.

In May 2001 the Constitutive Act of the African Union entered into force. In July 2002 the African Union (AU) became fully operational, replacing the Organization of African Unity (OAU), which had been founded in 1963. The AU aims to support unity, solidarity and peace among African states; to promote and defend African common positions on issues of shared interest; to encourage human rights, democratic principles and good governance; to advance the development of member states by encouraging research and by working to eradicate preventable diseases; and to promote sustainable development and political and socio-economic integration, including co-ordinating and harmonizing policy between the continent's various 'regional economic communities' (see below).

MEMBERS*

lgeria
Angola
Benin
Botswana
Burkina Faso
Burundi
Cameroon
Cape Verde
Central African Republic
Chad
Comoros
Congo, Democratic Republic
Congo, Republic
Côte d'Ivoire
Dijbouti
Egypt
Equatorial Guinea
Eritrea
Ethiopia
Gabon
The Gambia
Ghana
Guinea
Guinea-Bissau
Kenya
Lesotho
Liberia
Libya
Madagascar
Malawi
Mali
Mauritania†
Mauritius
Mozambique
Namibia
Niger
Nigeria
Rwanda
São Tomé and Príncipe
Senegal
Seychelles
Sierra Leone
Somalia
South Africa
Sudan
Swaziland
Tanazania
Togo
Tunisia
Uganda
Zambia
Zimbabwe

* The Sahrawi Arab Democratic Republic (SADR–Western Sahara) was admitted to the OAU in February 1982, following recognition by more than one-half of the member states, but its membership was disputed by Morocco and other states which claimed that a two-thirds' majority was needed to admit a state whose existence was in question. Morocco withdrew from the OAU with effect from November 1985, and has not applied to join the AU. The SADR ratified the Constitutive Act in December 2000 and is a full member of the AU.

† In August 2005, following the overthrow of its elected Government in a military *coup d'état*, Mauritania's participation in the activities of the AU was suspended.

Note: The Constitutive Act stipulates that member states in which Governments accede to power by unconstitutional means are liable to suspension from participating in the Union's activities and to the imposition of sanctions by the Union.

Organization

(September 2007)

ASSEMBLY

The Assembly, comprising member countries' heads of state and government, is the supreme organ of the Union and meets at least once a year (with alternate sessions held in Addis Ababa, Ethiopia) to determine and monitor the Union's priorities and common policies and to adopt its annual work programme. Resolutions are passed by a two-thirds' majority, procedural matters by a simple majority. Extraordinary sessions may be convened at the request of a member state and on approval by a two-thirds' majority. A chairperson is elected at each meeting from among the members, to hold office for one year. The Assembly ensures compliance by member states with decisions of the Union, adopts the biennial budget, appoints judges of the African Court of Human and Peoples' Rights, and hears and settles disputes between member states. The first regular Assembly meeting was held in Durban, South Africa, in July 2002. A first extraordinary summit meeting of the Assembly was convened in Addis Ababa in February 2003. The ninth ordinary session of the Assembly was convened in Addis Ababa in June–July 2007.

Chairperson: (2007/08) JOHN KUFUOR (Pres. of Ghana).

EXECUTIVE COUNCIL

Consists of ministers of foreign affairs and others and meets at least twice a year (in February and July), with provision for extraordinary sessions. The Council's Chairperson is the minister of foreign affairs (or another competent authority) of the country that has provided the Chairperson of the Assembly. Prepares meetings of, and is responsible to, the Assembly. Determines the issues to be submitted to the Assembly for decision, co-ordinates and harmonizes the policies, activities and initiatives of the Union in areas of common interest to member states, and monitors the implementation of policies and decisions of the Assembly.

PERMANENT REPRESENTATIVES COMMITTEE

The Committee, which comprises Ambassadors accredited to the AU and meets at least once a month. It is responsible to the Executive Council, which it advises, and whose meetings, including matters for the agenda and draft decisions, it prepares.

COMMISSION

The Commission is the permanent secretariat of the organization. It comprises a Chairperson (elected for a four-year term of office by the Assembly), Deputy Chairperson and eight Commissioners (responsible for: peace and security; political affairs; infrastructure and energy; social affairs; human resources, science and technology; trade and industry; rural economy and agriculture; and economic affairs) who are elected on the basis of equal geographical distribution. Members of the Commission serve a term of four years and may stand for re-election for one further term of office. Further support staff assist the smooth functioning of the Commission. The Commission represents the Union under the guidance of, and as mandated by, the Assembly and the Executive Council, and reports to the Executive Council. It deals with administrative issues, implements the decisions of the Union, and acts as the custodian of the Constitutive Act and Protocols, and other agreements. Its work covers the following domains: control of pandemics; disaster management; international crime and terrorism; environmental management; negotiations relating to external trade; negotiations relating to external debt; population, migration, refugees and displaced persons; food security; socio-economic integration; and all other areas where a common position has been established by Union member states. It has responsibility for the co-ordination of AU activities and meetings.

Chairperson: ALPHA OUMAR KONARÉ (Mali).

SPECIALIZED TECHNICAL COMMITTEES

There are specialized committees for monetary and financial affairs; rural economy and agricultural matters; trade, customs and immigration matters; industry, science and technology, energy, natural resources and environment; transport, communications and tourism; health, labour and social affairs; and education, culture and human resources. These have responsibility for implementing the Union's programmes and projects.

PAN-AFRICAN PARLIAMENT

The Pan-African Parliament, inaugurated in March 2004, comprises five deputies (including at least one woman) from each AU member state, presided over by an elected President assisted by four Vice-Presidents. The President and Vice-Presidents must equitably represent the central, northern, eastern, southern and western African states. The Parliament convenes at least twice a year; an extraordinary session may be called by a two-thirds' majority of the members. The Parliament currently has only advisory and consultative powers. Its eventual evolution into an institution with full legislative authority is planned. In July 2004 it was announced that South Africa would host the permanent seat of the Parliament. The Parliament's second session was convened in September at temporary headquarters in Midrand.

President: Dr GERTRUDE MONGELA (Tanzania).

PEACE AND SECURITY COUNCIL

The Protocol to the Constitutive Act of the African Union Relating to the Peace and Security Council of the African Union entered into force on 26 December 2003; the 15-member Council was formally inaugurated on 25 May 2004. It acts as a decision-making body for the prevention, management and resolution of conflicts.

ECONOMIC, SOCIAL AND CULTURAL COUNCIL

The Economic, Social and Cultural Council (ECOSOCC), inaugurated in March 2005, is to have an advisory function and to comprise representatives of civic, professional and cultural bodies at national, regional and diaspora levels. Its main organs are to be: an elected General Assembly; Standing Committee; Credential Committee; and Sectoral Cluster Communities. It is envisaged that the Council will strengthen the partnership between member governments and African civil society. Following ECOSOCC's inauguration a consultation process was launched for the eventual organization of elections to the planned General Assembly. Prior to the activation of the Assembly an interim elected Standing Committee was to hold office for a two-year period. The Sectoral Cluster Communities were to be established to formulate opinions and influence AU decision-making in the following 10 areas: peace and security; political affairs; infrastructure and energy; social affairs and health; human resources, science and technology; trade and industry; rural economy and agriculture; economic affairs; women and gender; and cross-cutting programmes.

PROPOSED INSTITUTIONS

In April 2007 three financial institutions, for managing the financing of programmes and projects, remained to be established: an African Central Bank, an African Monetary Fund, and an African Investment Bank.

Activities

From the 1950s various attempts were made to establish an inter-African organization. In November 1958 Ghana and Guinea (later joined by Mali) drafted a Charter that was to form the basis of a Union of African States. In January 1961 a conference was held at Casablanca, Morocco, attended by the heads of state of Ghana, Guinea, Mali, Morocco, and representatives of Libya and of the provisional government of the Algerian Republic (GPRA). Tunisia, Nigeria, Liberia and Togo declined the invitation to attend. An African Charter was adopted and it was decided to institute an African Military Command and an African Common Market. Between October 1960 and March 1961 three conferences were held by French-speaking African countries: at Abidjan, Côte d'Ivoire; Brazzaville, Republic of the Congo (ex-French); and Yaoundé, Cameroon. None of the 12 countries that attended these meetings had been present at the Casablanca Conference. These conferences led to the signing, in September 1961, at Tananarive, Madagascar, of a charter establishing the Union africaine et malgache, later the Organisation commune africaine et mauricienne (OCAM). In May 1961 a conference was held at Monrovia, Liberia, attended by the heads of state or representatives of 19 countries: Cameroon, Central African Republic, Chad, Congo Republic (ex-French), Côte d'Ivoire, Dahomey, Ethiopia, Gabon, Liberia, Madagascar, Mauritania, Niger, Nigeria, Senegal, Sierra Leone, Somalia, Togo, Tunisia and Upper Volta. Meeting again (with the exception of Tunisia and with the addition of the ex-Belgian Congo Republic) in January 1962 at Lagos, Nigeria, they established a permanent secretariat and a standing committee of finance ministers, and accepted a draft charter for an Organization of Inter-African and Malagasy States.

It was the Conference of Addis Ababa, convened in 1963, which finally brought together African states despite the regional, political and linguistic differences that divided them. The foreign ministers of 32 African states attended the Preparatory Meeting held in mid-May: Algeria, Burundi, Cameroon, Central African Republic, Chad, Congo (Brazzaville—now Republic of the Congo), Congo (Léopoldville—now Democratic Republic of the Congo), Côte d'Ivoire, Dahomey (now Benin), Ethiopia, Gabon, Ghana, Guinea, Liberia, Libya, Madagascar, Mali, Mauritania, Morocco, Niger, Nigeria, Rwanda, Senegal, Sierra Leone, Somalia, Sudan, Tanganyika (now Tanzania), Togo, Tunisia, Uganda, the United Arab Republic (Egypt) and Upper Volta (now Burkina Faso). The topics discussed by the meeting were: (i) the creation of an Organization of African States; (ii) co-operation among African states in the following fields: economic and social; education, culture and science; collective defence; (iii) decolonization; (iv) apartheid and racial discrimination; (v) the effects of economic grouping on the economic development of Africa; (vi) disarmament; (vii) the creation of a Permanent Conciliation Commission; and (viii) Africa and the United Nations. The Heads of State Conference that opened on 23 May 1963 drew up the Charter of the Organization of African Unity, which was then signed by the heads of 30 states on 25 May. The Charter was essentially functional and reflected a compromise between the concept of a loose association of states favoured by the Monrovia Group and the federal idea supported by the Casablanca Group, in particular by Ghana.

In May 1994 the Abuja Treaty Establishing the African Economic Community (AEC, signed in June 1991) entered into force. The formation of the Community was expected to be a gradual process, to be completed by 2028. An extraordinary summit meeting, convened in September 1999, in Sirte, Libya, at the request of the Libyan leader Col al-Qaddafi, determined to establish an African Union, based on the principles and objectives of the OAU and AEC, but furthering African co-operation, development and integration. Heads of state declared their commitment to accelerating the establishment of regional institutions, including a pan-African parliament, a court of human and peoples' rights and a central bank, as well as the implementation of economic and monetary union, as provided for by the Abuja Treaty Establishing the AEC. In July 2000 at the annual OAU summit meeting, held at Lomé, Togo, 27 heads of state and government signed the draft Constitutive Act of the African Union, which was to enter into force one month after ratification by two-thirds of member states' legislatures; this was achieved on 26 May 2001. The Union was inaugurated, replacing the OAU, on 9 July 2002, at a summit meeting of heads of state and government held in Durban, South Africa, after a transitional period of one year had elapsed since the endorsement of the Act in July 2001. During the transitional year, pending the transfer of all assets and liabilities to the Union, the OAU Charter remained in effect. A review of all OAU treaties was implemented, and those deemed relevant were retained by the AU. The four key organs of the AU were launched in July 2002. Morocco is the only African country that is not a member of the AU. The AU aims to strengthen and advance the process of African political and socio-economic integration initiated by the OAU. The Union operates on the basis of both the Constitutive Act and the Abuja Treaty. It is envisaged that the process of implementing the Abuja Treaty will be accelerated.

The AU has the following areas of interest: peace and security; political affairs; infrastructure and energy; social affairs; human resources, science and technology; trade and industry; rural economy and agriculture; and economic affairs. In July 2001 the OAU adopted a New African Initiative, which was subsequently renamed the New Partnership for Africa's Development (NEPAD, see below). NEPAD, which was officially launched in October, represents a long-term strategy for socio-economic recovery in Africa and aims to promote the strengthening of democracy and economic management in the region. The heads of state of Algeria, Egypt, Nigeria, Senegal and South Africa played leading roles in its preparation and management. In June 2002 NEPAD heads of state and government adopted a Declaration on Democracy, Political, Economic and Corporate Governance and announced the development of an African Peer Review Mechanism (APRM—whose secretariat was to be hosted by the UN Economic Commission for Africa). Meeting during that month the Group of Seven industrialized nations and Russia (the G-8) welcomed the formation of NEPAD and adopted an Africa Action Plan in support of the initiative. NEPAD is ultimately answerable to the AU Assembly. The inaugural summit of the Assembly, held in Durban, South Africa, in July 2002, issued a Declaration on the Implementation of NEPAD, which urged all member states to adopt the Declaration on Democracy, Political, Economic and Corporate Governance and to participate in the peer-review process. By November 2006 25 nations had agreed to participate in the APRM. In that year Ghana, Kenya and Rwanda were examined under the review process. During 2006 NEPAD continued to focus on the following sectoral priorities: infrastructure (covering information and communication technologies, energy, transport, water and sanitation), human resources development, agriculture, culture, science and technology, mobilizing resources, market access and the environment. It was implementing action plans concerned with capacity-building, the environment, and infrastructure. The summit meeting of the AU Assembly convened in Maputo, Mozambique in July 2003 determined that NEPAD should be integrated into AU structures and processes.

In March 2005 the UN Secretary-General issued a report on the functioning of the United Nations which included a clause urging donor nations to focus particularly on the need for a 10-year plan for capacity-building within the AU.

PEACE AND SECURITY

The Protocol to the Constitutive Act of the African Union Relating to the Establishment of the Peace and Security Council, adopted by the inaugural AU summit of heads of state and government in July 2002, entered into force in December 2003, superseding the 1993 Cairo Declaration on the OAU Mechanism for Conflict Prevention, Management and Resolution. The Protocol provides for the inauguration of an AU collective security and early warning mechanism, comprising a 15-country Peace and Security Council, operational at the levels of heads of state and government, ministers of foreign affairs, and permanent representatives, to be supported by a five-member advisory Panel of the Wise, a Continental Early Warning System, an African Standby Force and a Peace Fund (superseding the OAU Peace Fund, which was established in June 1993 and had received contributions of US $42m. by March 2002). In March 2004 the Executive Council elected 15 member states to serve on the inaugural Peace and Security Council. Gabon, Ethiopia, Algeria, South Africa and Nigeria (representing, respectively, the central, eastern, northern, southern and western regions of the continent) were to serve terms of three years on the Council. Ten other countries (Cameroon,

Republic of the Congo, Kenya, Sudan, Libya, Lesotho, Mozambique, Ghana, Senegal and Togo) were elected for two-year periods of service. The activities of the Peace and Security Council were to include the promotion of peace, security and stability; early warning and preventive diplomacy; peace-making mediation; peace support operations and intervention; peace-building activities and post-conflict reconstruction; and humanitarian action and disaster management. The Council was to implement the common defence policy of the Union, and to ensure the implementation of the 1999 OAU Convention on the Prevention and Combating of Terrorism (which provided for the exchange of information to help counter terrorism and for signatory states to refrain from granting asylum to terrorists). Member states were to set aside standby troop contingents for the planned African Standby Force, which was to be mandated to undertake observation, monitoring and other peace-support missions; to deploy in member states as required to prevent the resurgence or escalation of violence; to intervene in member states as required to restore stability; to conduct post-conflict disarmament and demobilization and other peace-building activities; and to provide emergency humanitarian assistance. The Council was to harmonize and co-ordinate the activities of other regional security mechanisms. An extraordinary AU summit meeting, convened in Sirte, Libya, in February 2004, adopted a declaration approving the establishment of the multinational African Standby Force, which was to comprise five regional brigades and to be fully operational by 2010. A Policy Framework Document on the establishment of the African Standby Force and the Military Staff Committee, adopted in May 2003 by the third meeting of the African chiefs of defence staff, was approved by the third regular summit of AU heads of state, held in July 2004.

The extraordinary OAU summit meeting convened in Sirte, Libya, in September 1999 determined to hold a regular ministerial Conference on Security, Stability, Development and Co-operation in Africa (CSSDCA): the first CSSDCA took place in Abuja, Nigeria, in May 2000. The CSSDCA process provides a forum for the development of policies aimed at advancing the common values of the AU and AEC in the areas of peace, security and co-operation. In December 2000 OAU heads of state and government adopted the Bamako Declaration, concerned with arresting the circulation of small arms on the continent.

In June 2003 a meeting of the G-8 and NEPAD adopted a Joint Africa/G-8 Plan to enhance African capabilities to undertake Peace Support Operations. Within the framework of the Plan, a consultation between the AU, the NEPAD Secretariat, the G-8, the African regional economic communities, as well as the European Union (EU) and UN and other partners, was convened in Addis Ababa in April 2005. In September 2002 and October 2004 the AU organized high-level intergovernmental meetings on preventing and combating terrorism in Africa. An AU Special Representative on Protection of Civilians in Armed Conflict Situations in Africa was appointed in September 2004.

In recent years the OAU/AU has been involved in peace-making and peace-building activities in several African countries and regions. Military observer missions were deployed in Rwanda (1991–93), Burundi (1993–96), the Comoros (1998–2002), the Democratic Republic of the Congo (from 1999), Eritrea and Ethiopia (from 2000) and Sudan (from 2004—see below). In February 2002 the OAU mediated talks between President Didier Ratsiraka of Madagascar and the official opposition leader Marc Ravalomanana, who established a rival Madagascan government during that month, having also claimed victory at the presidential election held in that country in December 2001. In March 2002 the OAU held talks with each of the disputing sides in the Madagascan political crisis, facilitating the conclusion in mid-April of the so-called Dakar Agreement, providing for the formation of an interim government of national unity, pending the staging of a new presidential election. However, in the following month Ravalomanana was declared President by a Madagascan constitutional court. In view of significant opposition to this decision, the OAU determined not to recognize the Ravalomanana administration and, in June, suspended Madagascar from its meetings. In July the newly inaugurated AU upheld this decision, suspending the country from AU meetings pending the staging of free and fair elections leading to the establishment of a legitimate and democratic government. In July 2003, however, following new parliamentary elections, held in December 2002 (resulting in a majority of seats for supporters of Ravalomanana), Madagascar's suspension was formally revoked. An extraordinary summit meeting of the Assembly, held in February 2003, urged support for a peace accord concluded in January by parties to the conflict that had erupted in Côte d'Ivoire in September 2002. In March 2003 the AU unequivocally condemned the military *coup d'état* that had taken place in Central African Republic, and subsequently banned that country's leaders from participating at the July Assembly meeting convened in Maputo. In April the AU authorized the establishment of a 3,500-member African Mission in Burundi (AMIB) to oversee the implementation of cease-fire accords in that country, support the disarmament and demobilization of former combatants, and ensure favourable conditions for the deployment of a future UN peace-keeping presence. In June 2004 AMIB was terminated and its troops 'rehatted' as participants in the newly-authorized UN Operation in Burundi (ONUB). In May 2003 the AU, UNDP and UN Office for Project Services agreed a US $6.4m. project entitled 'Support for the Implementation of the Peace and Security Agenda of the African Union'.

The July 2003 Maputo Assembly determined to establish a post-conflict reconstruction ministerial committee on Sudan. The first meeting of the committee, convened in March 2004, resolved to dispatch an AU team of experts to southern Sudan to compile a preliminary assessment of that region's post-conflict requirements; this was undertaken in late June. In early April, meeting in N'Djamena, Chad, the Sudan Government and other Sudanese parties signed, under AU auspices, a Humanitarian Cease-fire Agreement providing for the establishment of an AU-led Cease-fire Commission and for the deployment of an AU military observer mission (the AU Mission in the Sudan—AMIS) to the western Sudanese region of Darfur, where widespread violent unrest (including reportedly systematic attacks on the indigenous civilian population by pro-government militias), resulting in a grave humanitarian crisis, had prevailed since early 2003. Following the adoption in late May 2004 of an accord on the modalities for the implementation of the Humanitarian Cease-fire Agreement (also providing for the future deployment of an armed protection force as an additional component of AMIS, as requested by a recent meeting of the Peace and Security Council), the Cease-fire Commission was inaugurated at the end of that month and, at the beginning of June, the Commission's headquarters were opened in El-Fasher, Sudan; some 60 AMIS military observers were dispatched to the headquarters during that month. In early July the AU Assembly agree to increase the strength of AMIS to 80 observers. From mid-2004 the AU mediated negotiations between the parties to the conflict in Darfur on the achievement of a comprehensive peace agreement. AMIS's military component, agreed in May 2004, initially comprising 310 troops from Nigeria and Rwanda and mandated to monitor the cease-fire and protect the Mission, began to be deployed in mid-August. In October the Peace and Security Council decided to expand AMIS into a full peace-keeping operation, eventually to comprise 3,300 troops, police and civilian support staff. The mission's mandate was enhanced to include promoting increased compliance by all parties with the cease-fire agreement and helping with the process of confidence-building; responsibility for monitoring compliance with any subsequent agreements; assisting IDP and refugee returns; and contributing to the improvement of the security situation throughout Darfur. In April 2005 the Peace and Security Council authorized the further enhancement of AMIS to comprise, by the end of September, some 6,171 military personnel, including up to 1,560 civilian police personnel. A pledging conference for the mission, convened in April, resulted in commitments from AU partners and some member states totalling US $291.6m.; the promised funding included $77.4m. from the EU and $50m. from the USA. In March 2006 the Peace and Security Council agreed, in principle, to support the transformation of AMIS into a UN operation. In late March Arab League heads of state agreed to provide funding for the AU force to remain operational and voted to support Sudanese opposition to the deployment of non-African peace-keeping troops. In late April, following talks in Abuja, Nigeria, AU mediators submitted a proposed peace agreement to representatives of the Sudanese Government and rebel groups; the so-called Darfur Peace Agreement (DPA) was signed on 5 May by the Sudanese Government and the main rebel grouping (the Sudan Liberation Movement).

In August 2006 the UN Security Council expanded the mandate of UNMIS to provide for its deployment to Darfur, in order to enforce a cease-fire and support the implementation of DPA. The Council also requested the UN Secretary-General to devise jointly with the AU, in consultation with the parties to the DPA, a plan and schedule for a transition from AMIS to a sole UN operation in Darfur. The Sudanese Government, however, initially rejected the concept of an expanded UN peace-keeping mission, on the grounds that it would compromise national sovereignty. Eventually, in late December, the UN, AU and Sudanese Government established a tripartite mechanism which was to facilitate the implementation of a UN-formulated three-phase approach, endorsed by the AU Peace and Security Council in November, that would culminate in a hybrid AU/UN mission in Darfur. In January 2007 UNMIS provided AMIS with supplies and extra personnel under the first ('light') phase of the approach; the second ('heavy') phase, finalized in that month, was to involve the delivery of force enablers, police units, civilian personnel and mission support items. UNMIS has continued to make efforts to engage the non-signatories of the DPA in the political process in Darfur. In June the Sudanese Government agreed to support unconditionally the deployment of a UN/AU Hybrid Mission in Darfur (UNAMID); UNAMID was authorized by the UN Security Council in the following month, with a mandated force ceiling of up to 26,000 troops and police officers, supported by 5,000 international and local civilian staff. UNAMID's management, command and control structures were scheduled to be in place by October, and the mission was to assume command of AMIS at the end of the year. A joint AU/UN envoy, Rodolphe Adada, was appointed as head of the new mission. In June the AU and UN special representatives for Darfur defined a political 'road map' to lead eventually to full negotiations in support of a peaceful settlement to the sub-regional conflict. In August the first AU/UN-chaired 'pre-negotiation' discussions with those rebel groups in Darfur that were not party to the DPA approved an agreement on co-operation in attempting to secure a settlement.

Meeting in January 2006 the Peace and Security Council accepted in principle the future deployment of an AU Peace Support Mission in Somalia, with a mandate to support that member country's transitional federal institutions; meanwhile, it was envisaged that an IGAD peace support mission (IGASOM, approved by IGAD in January 2005 and endorsed by that month's AU summit) would be stationed in Somalia. In mid-March 2006 the IGAD Assembly reiterated its support for the deployment of IGASOM, and urged the UN Security Council to grant an exemption to the UN arms embargo applied to Somalia in order to facilitate the regional peace support initiative. At a consultative meeting on the removal of the arms embargo, convened in mid-April, in Nairobi, Kenya, representatives of the Somali transitional federal authorities presented for consideration by the AU and IGAD a draft national security and stabilization plan. It was agreed that a detailed mission plan should be formulated to underpin the proposed AU/IGAD peace missions. In January 2007 the Peace and Security Council authorized the deployment of the AU Mission in Somalia (AMISOM), in place of the proposed IGASOM. AMISOM was to be deployed for an initial period of six months, with a mandate to contribute to the political stabilization of Somalia. It was envisaged that AMISOM would evolve into a UN operation focusing on the post-conflict restoration of Somalia. In the following month the UN Security Council endorsed AMISOM and proposed that it should eventually be superseded by such a UN operation. AMISOM became operational in May.

In January 2005 the African Union Non-Aggression and Common Defence Pact was adopted to promote co-operation in developing a common defence policy and to encourage member states to foster an attitude of non-aggression. The Pact establishes measures aimed at preventing inter-and intra-state conflicts and arriving at peaceful resolutions to conflicts. It also sets out a framework defining, *inter alia,* the terms 'aggression' and 'intervention' and determining those situations in which intervention may be considered an acceptable course of action. As such, the Pact stipulates that an act, or threat, of aggression against an individual member state is to be considered an act, or threat, of aggression against all members states.

The AU strongly condemned the unconstitutional transfer of power effected in Togo in early February 2005, describing it as a *coup d'état*, and suspended that country's participation in activities of the Union pending the restoration of constitutional rule; this was achieved at the end of that month. Following a *coup d'état* in Mauritania in early August that country's active membership of the Union was suspended. However, the overthrow of the regime of Col Maaouiya Ould Sid'Ahmed Taya was reported to have widespread domestic support. In mid-August a delegation from the AU met members of the Military Council for Justice and Democracy, subsequently announcing the willingness of the Union to co-operate with the new leadership of Mauritania, although the country was to remain suspended from the organization pending democratic elections, in accordance with the Constitutive Act of the AU.

The EU assists the AU financially in the areas of peace and security (including €25m. funding granted in December 2003 towards AMIB, and support to AMIS, see above); institutional development; governance; and regional economic integration and trade. In June 2004 the European Commission activated for the first time its newly-established Africa Peace Facility, which provided €12m. in support of the AU's humanitarian and peace-monitoring efforts in Darfur. In February 2007 the EU and the AU began a period of consultation on a joint EU-Africa Strategy, the first to develop a long-term vision of the future partnership between the two parties. The strategy was to be adopted by the EU-Africa Summit scheduled to be held in Lisbon later that year.

INFRASTRUCTURE, ENERGY AND THE ENVIRONMENT

Meeting in Lomé, Togo, in July 2001, OAU heads of state and government authorized the establishment of an African Energy Commission (AFREC), which was to increase co-operation in energy matters between Africa and other regions.

In 1964 the OAU adopted a Declaration on the Denuclearization of Africa, and in April 1996 it adopted the African Nuclear Weapons Free Zone Treaty (also known as the 'Pelindaba Treaty'), which identifies Africa as a nuclear weapons-free zone and promotes co-operation in the peaceful uses of nuclear energy.

In 1968 OAU member states adopted the African Convention on the Conservation of Nature and Natural Resources. The Bamako Convention on the Ban of the Import into Africa and the Control of Transboundary Movement and Management of Hazardous Wastes within Africa was adopted by OAU member states in 1991 and entered into force in April 1998.

In February 2007 the first Conference of African Ministers responsible for Maritime Transport was convened to discuss maritime transport policy in the region. A draft declaration was submitted at the Conference, held in Abuja, Nigeria, outlining the AU's vision for a common maritime transport policy aimed at 'linking Africa' and detailing programmes for co-operation on maritime safety and security and the development of an integrated transport infrastructure. The subsequently adopted Abuja Maritime Transport Declaration formally provided for an annual meeting of maritime transport ministers, to be hosted by each region in turn in a rotational basis.

POLITICAL AND SOCIAL AFFAIRS

The African Charter on Human and People's Rights, which was adopted by the OAU in 1981 and entered into force in October 1986, provided for the establishment of an 11-member African Commission on Human and People's Rights, based in Banjul, The Gambia. A Protocol to the Charter, establishing an African Court of People's and Human Rights, was adopted by the OAU Assembly of Heads of State in June 1998 and entered into force in January 2004. A further Protocol, relating to the Rights of Women, was adopted by the July 2003 Maputo Assembly. The African Charter on the Rights and Welfare of the Child was opened for signature in July 1990 and entered into force in November 1999. A Protocol to the Abuja Treaty Establishing the AEC relating to the Pan-African Parliament, adopted by the OAU in March 2001, entered into force in December 2003. The Parliament was inaugurated in March 2004 and was, initially, to exercise advisory and consultative powers only, although its eventual evolution into an institution with full legislative powers is envisaged. In March 2005 the advisory Economic, Social and Cultural Council was inaugurated.

The July 2002 inaugural summit meeting of AU heads of state and government adopted a Declaration Governing Democratic Elections in Africa, providing guide-lines for the conduct of national elections in member states and outlining the AU's electoral observation and monitoring role. In March an OAU observer team found the Zimbabwean presidential election, held in controversial circumstances during that month, to have been conducted freely and fairly. In April 2003 the AU Commission and the South African Independent Electoral Commission jointly convened an African Conference on Elections, Democracy and Governance, in Pretoria, South Africa. In recent years several large population displacements have occurred in Africa, mainly as a result of violent conflict. In 1969 OAU member states adopted the Convention Governing the Specific Aspects of Refugee Problems in Africa, which entered into force in June 1974 and had been ratified by 45 states at April 2007. The Convention promotes close co-operation with UNHCR. The AU maintains a Special Refugee Contingency Fund to provide relief assistance and to support repatriation activities, education projects, etc., for displaced people in Africa. The AU aims to address pressing health issues affecting member states, including the eradication of endemic parasitic and infectious diseases and improving access to medicines. An African Summit on HIV/AIDS, Tuberculosis and other related Infectious Diseases was convened, under OAU auspices, in March 2001. An AU Scientific, Technical and Research Commission is based in Lagos, Nigeria, and a Centre for Linguistic and Historical Studies by Oral Tradition is based in Niamey, Niger.

The seventh AU summit, convened in Banjul, The Gambia, in July 2006, adopted the African Youth Charter, providing for the implementation of youth policies and strategies across Africa, with the aim of encouraging young African people to participate in the development of the region and to take advantage of increasing opportunities in education and employment. The Charter outlined the basic rights and responsibilities of youths, which were divided into four main categories: youth participation; education and skills development; sustainable livelihoods; and health and wellbeing. The Charter also details the obligations of member state towards young people. In May 2006 the AU convened a Youth Forum, a Youth Experts' meeting and a meeting of the Ministers of Youth of the member states and other interested parties.

TRADE, INDUSTRY AND ECONOMIC CO-OPERATION

In October 1999 a conference on Industrial Partnerships and Investment in Africa was held in Dakar, Senegal, jointly organized by the OAU with UNIDO, the ECA, the African Development Bank and the Alliance for Africa's Industrialization. In June 1997 the first meeting between ministers of the OAU and the EU was convened in New York, USA. In April 2000 the first EU–Africa summit of heads of state and government was held in Cairo, Egypt, under the auspices of the EU and OAU. The summit adopted the Cairo Plan of Action, which addressed areas including economic integration, trade and investment, private-sector development in Africa, human rights and good governance, peace and security, and development issues such as education, health and food security. A second EU–Africa summit meeting, scheduled to be held in April 2003, in Lisbon, Portugal, was postponed, owing to disagreements concerning the participation of President Mugabe of Zimbabwe, against whom the EU had imposed sanctions. More than 200 business representatives participated in an AU Business Summit, convened in July 2002, in Durban, South Africa, alongside the inaugural AU summit of heads of state and government.

The AU aims to reduce obstacles to intra-African trade and to reverse the continuing disproportionate level of trade conducted by many African countries with their former colonial powers. In June 2005 an AU conference of Ministers of Trade was convened in Cairo, Egypt, to discuss issues relating to the development of Trade in Africa, particularly in the context of the World Trade Organization's (WTO) Doha Work Programme. The outcome of the meeting was the adoption of the Cairo Road-Map on the Doha Work Programme, which address several important issues including the import, export and market access of agricultural and non-agricultural commodities, development issues and trade facilitation.

In June 1991 the OAU Assembly of Heads of State signed the Abuja Treaty Establishing the African Economic Community (AEC). The Treaty was to enter into force after ratification by two-thirds of member states. The Community was to be established by 2028, following a gradual six-phase process involving the co-ordination, harmonization and progressive integration of the activities of all existing and future sub-regional economic unions. (There are 14 so-called 'regional economic communities', or RECs, in Africa, including the following major RECs that are regarded as the five pillars, or building blocks, of the AEC: the Common Market for Eastern and Southern Africa—COMESA, the Communauté économique des états de l'Afrique centrale—CEEAC, the Economic Community of West African States—ECOWAS, the Southern African Development Community—SADC, and the Union of the Arab Maghreb. The subsidiary RECs are: the Communauté économique et monétaire de l'Afrique centrale—CEMAC, the Community of Sahel-Saharan States—CEN-SAD, the East African Community—EAC, the Economic Community of the Great Lakes Countries, the Intergovernmental Authority on Development—IGAD, the Indian Ocean Commission—IOC, the Mano River Union, the Southern African Customs Union, and the Union économique et monétaire ouest-africaine—UEMOA.) The Abuja Treaty entered into force on 12 May 1994, having been ratified by the requisite number of OAU member states. The inaugural meeting of the AEC took place in June 1997.

RURAL ECONOMY AND AGRICULTURE

In July 2003 the second Assembly of heads of state and government adopted a Declaration on Agriculture and Food Security in Africa, focusing on the need to revitalize the agricultural sector and to combat hunger on the continent by developing food reserves based on African production. The leaders determined to deploy policies and budgetary resources to remove current constraints on agricultural production, trade and rural development; and to implement the Comprehensive Africa Agriculture Programme (CAADP), which had been developed by NEPAD and FAO in 2002–03. The CAADP focused on increasing investment in the areas of water management, rural infrastructure, programmes to increase productivity, and capacity development for market access; and also on means of addressing emergencies, and the advancement of research and technology. The heads of state and government agreed that, by 2008/09, at least 10% of national budgets should be allocated to agriculture and rural development.

The AU's Programme for the Control of Epizootics (PACE) has co-operated with FAO to combat the further spread of the Highly Pathogenic Avian Influenza (H5N1) virus, outbreaks of which were reported in poultry in several West African countries in 2006–07; joint activities have included establishing a regional network of laboratories and surveillance teams and organizing regional workshops on H5N1 control.

HUMANITARIAN RESPONSE

In December 2005 a ministerial conference on disaster reduction in Africa, organized by the AU Commission, adopted a programme of action for the implementation of the Africa Regional Strategy for Disaster Risk Reduction (2006–10), formulated in the context of the Hyogo Framework of Action for the period 2005–15 that was agreed by 168 countries at the World Conference on Disaster Reduction held in Kobe, Japan in January 2005.

Finance

The AU inherited more than US $50m. in debts owed by member states to the OAU. The programme budget for 2005 totalled $158m., of which $75m. was allocated to peace and security. Some $63m. of the 2005 budget was to be financed by contributions from member states, with the remainder to be derived from international donor support.

Specialized Agencies

African Accounting Council: POB 11223, Kinshasa, Democratic Republic of the Congo; tel. (12) 33567; f. 1979; provides assistance to institutions in member countries on standardization of accounting; promotes education, further training and research in accountancy and related areas of study; publ. *Information and Liaison Bulletin* (every two months).

African Civil Aviation Commission (AFCAC): 15 blvd de la République, BP 2356, Dakar, Senegal; tel. 893-93-73; fax 823-26-61; e-mail cafac@telecomplus.sn; internet www.afcac-cafac.sn; f. 1969 to co-ordinate civil aviation matters in Africa and to co-operate with ICAO and other relevant civil aviation bodies; promotes the development of the civil aviation industry in Africa in accordance with provisions of the 1991 Abuja Treaty; fosters the application of ICAO Standards and Recommended Practices; examines specific problems that might hinder the development and operation of the African civil aviation industry; 46 mem states; promotes co-ordination and better utilization and development of African air transport systems and the standardization of aircraft, flight equipment and training programmes for pilots and mechanics; organizes working groups and seminars, and compiles statistics; Pres. TSHEPO PEEGE (South Africa); Sec. CHARLES MAURICE DIOP.

African Telecommunications Union (ATU): ATU Secretariat, POB 35282 Nairobi, 00200 Kenya; tel. (20) 4453308; fax (20) 4453359; e-mail sg@atu-uat.org; internet www.atu-uat.org; f. 1999 as successor to Pan-African Telecommunications Union (f. 1977); promotes the rapid development of information communications in Africa, with the aim of making Africa an equal participant in the global information society; works towards universal service and access and full inter-country connectivity; promotes development and adoption of appropriate policies and regulatory frameworks; promotes financing of development; encourages co-operation between members and the exchange of information; advocates the harmonization of telecommunications policies; 46 national mems, 16 associate mems comprising fixed and mobile telecoms operators; Sec.-Gen. AKOSSI AKOSSI.

Pan-African Institution of Education for Development (PIED): 29 ave de la Justice, BP 1764, Kinshasa I, Democratic Republic of the Congo; tel. (12) 34527; e-mail baseeduc@hotmail.com; f. 1973, became specialized agency in 1986, present name adopted 2001; undertakes educational research and training, focuses on co-operation and problem-solving, acts as an observatory for education; publs *Bulletin d'Information* (quarterly), *Revue africaine des sciences de l'éducation* (2 a year), *Répertoire africain des institutions de recherche* (annually).

Pan-African News Agency (PANAPRESS): BP 4056, ave Bourjuiba, Dakar, Senegal; tel. 824-13-95; fax 824-13-90; e-mail marketing@panapress.com; internet www.panapress.com; f. 1979 as PanAfrican News Agency, restructured under current name in 1997; regional headquarters in Khartoum, Sudan; Lusaka, Zambia; Kinshasa, Democratic Republic of the Congo; Lagos, Nigeria; Tripoli, Libya; began operations in May 1983, restructured in late 1990s; receives information from national news agencies and circulates news in Arabic, English, French and Portuguese; Dir-Gen. BABACAR FALL; publs *Press Review*, *In-Focus*.

Pan-African Postal Union (PAPU): POB 6026, Arusha, Tanzania; tel. (27) 2508604; fax (27) 2508606; e-mail sg@papu.co.tz; internet www.upap-papu.org; f. 1980 to extend members' co-operation in the improvement of postal services; 43 mem. countries; Sec.-Gen. JILANI BEN HADDADA; publ. *PAPU News*.

Pan-African Railways Union: BP 687, Kinshasa, Democratic Republic of the Congo; tel. (12) 23861; f. 1972 to standardize, expand, co-ordinate and improve members' railway services; the ultimate aim is to link all systems; main organs: Gen. Assembly, Exec. Bd, Gen. Secr., five tech. cttees; mems in 30 African countries.

Supreme Council for Sports in Africa: BP 1363, Yaoundé, Cameroon; tel. and fax 23-95-80; f. 1965; Sec.-Gen. Dr AWOTURE ELEYAE (Nigeria); publs *SCSA News* (6 a year), *African Sports Movement Directory* (annually).

ASSOCIATED PARTNERSHIP

New Partnership for Africa's Development (NEPAD): POB 1234, Halfway House, Midrand, 1685 South Africa; tel. (11) 313-3716; fax (11) 313-3684; e-mail africam@nepad.org; internet www.nepad.org; f. 2001 as a long-term strategy to promote socio-economic development in Africa; adopted Declaration on Democracy, Political,

Economic and Corporate Governance and the African Peer Review Mechanism in June 2002; heads of state implementation cttee comprises representatives of 20 countries (four from each of the AU's five regions: northern, eastern, southern, western and central); steering cttee, comprising Algeria, Egypt, Nigeria, Senegal and South Africa, meets once a month; the UN allocated US $10.8m. in support of NEPAD under its 2006–07 budget; the July 2003 AU Maputo summit decided that NEPAD should be integrated into AU structures and processes; Exec. Head of Secretariat Prof. FIRMINO MUCAVELE (Mozambique).

COMMON MARKET FOR EASTERN AND SOUTHERN AFRICA—COMESA

Address: COMESA Secretariat, Ben Bella Rd, POB 30051, 101101 Lusaka, Zambia.

Telephone: (1) 229725; **fax:** (1) 225107; **e-mail:** comesa@comesa .int; **internet:** www.comesa.int.

The COMESA treaty was signed by member states of the Preferential Trade Area for Eastern and Southern Africa (PTA) in November 1993. COMESA formally succeeded the PTA in December 1994. COMESA aims to promote regional economic and social development.

MEMBERS

Angola	Madagascar
Burundi	Malawi
Comoros	Mauritius
Congo, Democratic Republic	Rwanda
Djibouti	Seychelles
Egypt	Sudan
Eritrea	Swaziland
Ethiopia	Uganda
Kenya	Zambia
Libya	Zimbabwe

Organization

(September 2007)

AUTHORITY

The Authority of the Common Market is the supreme policy organ of COMESA, comprising heads of state or of government of member countries. The inaugural meeting of the Authority took place in Lilongwe, Malawi, in December 1994. The 12th summit meeting was convened in Nairobi, Kenya, in May 2007.

COUNCIL OF MINISTERS

Each member government appoints a minister to participate in the Council. The Council monitors COMESA activities, including supervision of the Secretariat, recommends policy direction and development, and reports to the Authority.

A Committee of Governors of Central Banks advises the Authority and the Council of Ministers on monetary and financial matters.

COURT OF JUSTICE

The inaugural session of the COMESA Court of Justice was held in March 2001. The sub-regional Court is vested with the authority to settle disputes between member states and to adjudicate on matters concerning the interpretation of the COMESA treaty. The Court is composed of seven judges, who serve terms of five years' duration.

President: NZAMBA KITONGA (Kenya).

SECRETARIAT

COMESA's Secretariat comprises the following divisions: Trade, customs and monetary harmonization; Investment promotion and private sector development; Infrastructure development; and Information and networking. The COMESA/SADC task force operates from the secretariats of both organizations.

Secretary-General: J. E. O. (ERASTUS) MWENCHA (Kenya).

Activities

COMESA aims to promote economic and social progress in member states. Since its establishment in 1994 COMESA has pursued efforts to strengthen the process of regional economic integration that was initiated under the PTA, in order to help member states achieve sustainable economic growth. In May 1999 COMESA established a Free-Trade Area (FTA) Committee to facilitate and co-ordinate preparations for the creation of the common market envisaged under the COMESA treaty. An extraordinary summit of COMESA heads of state or government, held in October 2000, inaugurated the FTA, with nine initial members: Djibouti, Egypt, Kenya, Madagascar, Malawi, Mauritius, Sudan, Zambia and Zimbabwe. The final deadline for all states to join was initially 30 April 2002. This was, however, subsequently postponed. Burundi and Rwanda became members of the FTA in January 2004, and Swaziland undertook in April to seek the concurrence of the Southern African Customs Union, of which it is also a member, to allow it to participate in the FTA. Trading practices within the FTA have been fully liberalized, including the elimination of non-tariff barriers, thereby enabling the free internal movement of goods, services and capital. It was envisaged that a regional customs union would be established in May 2005 (immediately prior to the 10th summit meeting of the Authority, whose theme was 'Deepening Regional Integration through COMESA Customs Union'), with a common external tariff (CET) set at 0%, 5%, 15% and 30% for, respectively, capital goods, raw materials, intermediate goods and final goods. This was not achieved, however, and the 10th summit meeting in June decided instead to set a new deadline of December 2008 for its establishment, urging all of those member states that were not participating in the FTA in mid-2005 to proceed to do so in the meantime, in order to enable them to join the eventual customs union. A Protocol establishing the COMESA Fund, aimed at assisting member states address structural imbalances in their economies, came into effect in mid-November 2006. In May 2007 the 12th meeting of heads of state endorsed all technical aspects of the customs union (now with a simplified CET set at 0% for capital goods and raw materials, 10% for intermediate goods and 25% for finished products). COMESA also plans to form an economic community (entailing monetary union and the free movement of people between member states) by 2014. COMESA aims to formulate a common investment procedure to promote domestic, cross-border and direct foreign investment by ensuring the free movement of capital, services and labour. Heads of regional investment agencies, meeting in August 2000, developed a plan of action for the creation of a common investment agency to facilitate the establishment of a COMESA common investment area (CCIA), in accordance with recommendations by the Authority. A draft framework document on the CCIA was submitted for review by member states in December 2004, and was subject to extensive negotiations. The accord to establish the CCIA was adopted at the 12th summit meeting, held in May 2007, and opened for signature. The development of a protocol to the COMESA treaty on the Free Movement of Persons, Labour, Services, the Right of Establishment and Residence was adopted in 2001 at the sixth summit meeting of the Authority, held in Cairo, Egypt.

A clearing house (based in Harare, Zimbabwe) dealing with credit arrangements and balance of payments issues became operational under the PTA in 1984 in order to facilitate intra-regional trade. The role of the clearing house was diminished by the liberalization of foreign exchange markets in the majority of member countries, and it ceased operating in 1996. In the mid-2000s preparations were under way to create a regional payments and settlement system (REPSS). A contract on the implementation of the REPSS—which was to have its headquarters in Lusaka, Zambia—was signed in December 2006. An Automated System of Customs Data (ASYCUDA) has been established to facilitate customs administration in all COMESA member states. Through support for capacity-building activities and the establishment of other specialized institutions (see below) COMESA aims to reinforce its objectives of regional integration. In August 2001 COMESA inaugurated the African Trade Insurance Agency (ATI), based in Nairobi, Kenya. The ATI manages COMESA's Regional Trade Facilitation Project, promoting trade and investment activities throughout the region. The electronic African Commerce Exchange (ACE) was launched by the Authority in 2000.

Co-operation programmes have been implemented by COMESA in the financial, agricultural, transport and communications, industrial, and energy sectors. A regional food security programme aims to ensure continuous adequate food supplies. In 1997 COMESA heads of state advocated that the food sector be supported by the implementation of an irrigation action plan for the region. The organization also supports the establishment of common agricultural standards and phytosanitary regulations throughout the region in order to stimulate trade in food crops. In March 2005 more than 100 standards on quality assurance, covering mainly agricultural products, were adopted. Meeting for the first time in November 2002, COMESA ministers of agriculture determined to formulate a regional policy on genetically modified organisms. At their second meeting, held in October 2004, ministers of agriculture agreed to prioritize agriculture in their development efforts and (in accordance with a Declaration of the African Union) to allocate at least 10% of national budgets to agriculture and rural development by 2008/09. Other organization-wide initiatives include a road customs declaration document, a scheme for third party motor vehicle insurance, a system of regional travellers cheques, and a regional customs bond guarantee scheme. A Trade Information Network co-ordinates information on the production and marketing of goods manufactured and traded in the region. COMESA is implementing the new COMESA Information Network, which aims to develop the utilization by member states of advanced information and communication technologies. A COMESA Telecommunications Company (COMTEL) was registered in May 2000. In January 2003 the Association of Regulators of Information and Communication for Eastern and Southern Africa was launched, under the auspices of COMESA. The first COMESA trade fair was held in Nairobi, Kenya, in May 1999. The first COMESA economic forum was held in Cairo, Egypt, in February 2000. The inaugural COMESA business summit was convened in June 2004 in Kampala, Uganda, concurrently with the ninth annual meeting of the Authority.

In May 1999 the COMESA Authority resolved to establish a Committee on Peace and Security comprising ministers of foreign affairs from member states. It was envisaged that the Committee would convene at least once a year to address matters concerning regional stability. (Instability in certain member states was regarded as a potential threat to the successful implementation of the FTA.) The Committee met for the first time in 2000. It was announced in September 2002 that the COMESA Treaty was to be amended to provide for the establishment of a formal conflict prevention and resolution structure to be governed by member countries' heads of state.

Since COMESA's establishment there have been concerns on the part of member states, as well as other regional non-member countries, in particular South Africa, of adverse rivalry between COMESA and the Southern African Development Community (SADC) and of a duplication of roles. In 1997 Lesotho and Mozambique terminated their membership of COMESA owing to concerns that their continued participation in the organization was incompatible with their SADC membership. Tanzania withdrew from COMESA in September 2000, reportedly also in view of its dual commitment to that organization and to SADC. The summit meeting of COMESA heads of state or government held in May of that year expressed support for an ongoing programme of co-operation by the secretariats of COMESA and SADC aimed at reducing the duplication of roles between the two organizations, and urged further mutual collaboration. A co-ordinating COMESA/SADC task force was established in 2001. It has subsequently been expanded to incorporate the East African Community in discussions to enhance harmonization between the organizations and their programmes of work. COMESA has co-operated with other sub-regional organizations to finalize a common position on co-operation between African ACP countries and the EU under the Cotonou Agreement (concluded in June 2000, see chapter on the European Union). In June 2003 Namibia announced its withdrawal from COMESA. At the 10th summit meeting of the Authority in June 2005 Libya was admitted as a full member of COMESA.

In October 2001 COMESA concluded a Trade and Investment Framework Agreement with the USA. In August 2007 COMESA appointed a Special Representative to the Middle East to establish partnerships with that region and to promote trade opportunities.

COMESA INSTITUTIONS

African Trade Insurance Agency (ATI): POB 10620, 00100-GPO, Nairobi, Kenya; tel. (20) 2719727; fax (20) 2719701; e-mail info@africa-ECA.com; internet www.ati-aca.com; f. 2001; mems: 12 African countries; CEO PETER MICHAEL JONES.

COMESA Bankers Association: Private Bag 271, Kapeni House, 1st Floor, Blantyre, Malawi; tel. and fax (1) 674236; e-mail info@comesabankers.org; internet www.comesabankers.org; f. 1987 as the PTA Association of Commercial Banks; name changed as above in 1994; aims to strengthen co-operation between banks in the region; organizes training activities; conducts studies to harmonize banking laws and operations; initiated a project to combat bank fraud and money laundering in 2000; mems: 55 commercial banking orgs in Burundi, Egypt, Eritrea, Ethiopia, Kenya, Malawi, Rwanda, Sudan, Swaziland; Exec. Sec. ERIC C. CHINKANDA (acting).

COMESA Leather and Leather Products Institute (LLPI): POB 2358, 1110 Addis Ababa, Ethiopia; tel. (1) 431318; fax (1) 431321; e-mail comesa.llpi@telecom.net.et; f. 1990 as the PTA Leather Institute; mems: 16 COMESA mem. states; Dir Dr GEREMEW DEBELE.

COMESA Metallurgical Industries Association (COMESA-MIA): Kampala, Uganda; f. 1999; aims to advance capabilities in the production, processing and marketing of metals and allied engineering products, and to develop co-operation and networking in the sector; Sec. WILLIAM BALU-TABAARO.

Compagnie de réassurance de la Zone d'échanges préférentiels (ZEP-RE) (PTA Reinsurance Co): ZEP-RE Place, Longonot Rd, Upper Hill, POB 42769, 00100 Nairobi, Kenya; tel. (20) 2738221; fax (20) 2738444; e-mail mail@zep-re.com; internet www.zep-re.com; f. 1992 (began operations on 1 January 1993); provides local reinsurance services and training to personnel in the insurance industry; total assets CMD 29.5m; Chair. PETER KENNETH; Man. Dir RAJNI VARIA.

Eastern and Southern African Trade and Development Bank: NSSF Bldg, 22nd/23rd Floor, Bishop's Rd, POB 48596, 00100 Nairobi, Kenya; tel. (20) 2712250; fax (20) 2711510; e-mail official@ptabank.org; internet www.ptabank.co.ke; f. 1983 as PTA Development Bank; aims to mobilize resources and finance COMESA activities to foster regional integration; promotes investment and co-financing within the region; in Jan. 2003 the US dollar replaced the UAPTA (PTA unit of account) as the Bank's reporting currency; shareholders: 15 COMESA mem. states, the People's Republic of China, Somalia, Tanzania and the African Development Bank; cumulative approved investments totalled US $1,965.0m. at 31 Dec. 2005; subscribed cap. $351.4m., paid-up cap. $116.6m. (Dec. 2005); Pres. Dr MICHAEL M. GONDWE; Chair. Bd of Dirs ABII TSIGE.

Finance

COMESA is financed by member states. The organization's activities have been undermined by delays by some countries in paying membership dues.

Publications

Annual Report of the Council of Ministers.
Asycuda Newsletter.
COMESA Journal.
COMESA Trade Directory (annually).
COMESA Trade Information Newsletter (monthly).
e-comesa (monthly newsletter).
Demand/supply surveys, catalogues and reports.

THE COMMONWEALTH

Address: Commonwealth Secretariat, Marlborough House, Pall Mall, London, SW1Y 5HX, United Kingdom.

Telephone: (20) 7747-6500; **fax:** (20) 7930-0827; **e-mail:** info@commonwealth.int; **internet:** www.thecommonwealth.org.

The Commonwealth is a voluntary association of 53 independent states (at September 2007), comprising more than one-quarter of the world's population. It includes the United Kingdom and most of its former dependencies, and former dependencies of Australia and New Zealand (themselves Commonwealth countries). All Commonwealth countries accept Queen Elizabeth II as the symbol of the free association of the independent member nations and as such the Head of the Commonwealth.

MEMBERS IN AFRICA SOUTH OF THE SAHARA

Botswana	Mauritius	Swaziland
Cameroon	Mozambique	Tanzania
The Gambia	Namibia	Uganda
Ghana	Nigeria	Zambia
Kenya	Seychelles	
Lesotho	Sierra Leone	
Malawi	South Africa	

Note: In March 2002 Zimbabwe was suspended from participation in meetings of the Commonwealth. Zimbabwe announced its withdrawal from the Commonwealth in December 2003.

United Kingdom Overseas Territories

British Indian Ocean Territory
St Helena
Ascension
Tristan da Cunha

Organization

(September 2007)

The Commonwealth is not a federation: there is no central government nor are there any rigid contractual obligations such as bind members of the United Nations.

The Commonwealth has no written constitution but its members subscribe to the ideals of the Declaration of Commonwealth Principles unanimously approved by a meeting of heads of government in Singapore in 1971. Members also approved the Gleneagles Agreement concerning apartheid in sport (1977); the Lusaka Declaration on Racism and Racial Prejudice (1979); the Melbourne Declaration on relations between developed and developing countries (1981); the New Delhi Statement on Economic Action (1983); the Goa Declaration on International Security (1983); the Nassau Declaration on World Order (1985); the Commonwealth Accord on Southern Africa (1985); the Vancouver Declaration on World Trade (1987); the Okanagan Statement and Programme of Action on Southern Africa (1987); the Langkawi Declaration on the Environment (1989); the Kuala Lumpur Statement on Southern Africa (1989); the Harare Commonwealth Declaration (1991); the Ottawa Declaration on Women and Structural Adjustment (1991); the Limassol Statement on the Uruguay Round of multilateral trade negotiations (1993); the Millbrook Commonwealth Action Programme on the Harare Declaration (1995); the Edinburgh Commonwealth Economic Declaration (1997); the Fancourt Commonwealth Declaration on Globalization and People-centred Development (1999); the Coolum Declaration on the Commonwealth in the 21st Century: Continuity and Renewal (2002); the Aso Rock Commonwealth Declaration and Statement on Multilateral Trade (2003); and the Malta Commonwealth Declaration on Networking for Development (2005).

MEETINGS OF HEADS OF GOVERNMENT

Commonwealth Heads of Government Meetings (CHOGMs) are private and informal and operate not by voting but by consensus. The emphasis is on consultation and exchange of views for co-operation. A communiqué is issued at the end of every meeting. Meetings are normally held every two years in different capitals in the Commonwealth. The 2005 meeting was held in Malta, in November. The next meeting was scheduled to be held in Kampala, Uganda, in November 2007.

OTHER CONSULTATIONS

Meetings at ministerial and official level are also held regularly. Since 1959 finance ministers have met in a Commonwealth country in the week prior to the annual meetings of the IMF and the World Bank. Meetings on education, legal, women's and youth affairs are held at ministerial level every three years. Ministers of health hold annual meetings, with major meetings every three years, and ministers of agriculture meet every two years. Ministers of finance, trade, labour and employment, industry, science, tourism and the environment also hold periodic meetings.

Senior officials—cabinet secretaries, permanent secretaries to heads of government and others—meet regularly in the year between meetings of heads of government to provide continuity and to exchange views on various developments.

COMMONWEALTH SECRETARIAT

The Secretariat, established by Commonwealth heads of government in 1965, operates as an international organization at the service of all Commonwealth countries. It organizes consultations between governments and runs programmes of co-operation. Meetings of heads of government, ministers and senior officials decide these programmes and provide overall direction. A Board of Governors, on which all eligible member governments are represented, meets annually to review the Secretariat's work and approve its budget. The Board is supported by an Executive Committee which convenes four times a year to monitor implementation of the Secretariat's work programme. The Secretariat is headed by a secretary-general, elected by heads of government.

In 2002 the Secretariat was restructured, with a view to strengthening the effectiveness of the organization to meet the priorities determined by the meeting of heads of government held in Coolum, Australia, in March 2002. Under the reorganization the number of deputy secretaries-general was reduced from three to two. Certain work divisions were amalgamated, while new units or sections, concerned with youth affairs, human rights and good offices, were created to strengthen further activities in those fields. Accordingly, the new divisional structure was as follows: Legal and constitutional affairs; Political affairs; Corporate services; Communications and public affairs; Strategic planning and evaluation; Economic affairs; Governance and institutional development; Social transformation programmes; and Special advisory services. In addition there were units responsible for human rights, youth affairs, and project management and referrals, and an Office of the Secretary-General. In 2004 the youth affairs unit acquired divisional status.

The Secretariat's strategic plan for 2004/05–2007/08 set out two main, long-term objectives for the Commonwealth: to support member countries in preventing or resolving conflicts, to strengthen democracy and the rule of law, and to achieve greater respect for human rights; and to support pro-poor policies for economic growth and sustainable development in member countries. Four programmes were to facilitate the pursuit of the first objective, 'Peace and Democracy': Good Offices for Peace; Democracy and Consensus Building; Rule of Law; and Human Rights. The second objective—'Pro-Poor Growth and Sustainable Development'—was to be achieved through the following nine programmes: International Trade; Investment; Finance and Debt; Public Sector Development; Environmentally Sustainable Development; Small States; Education; Health; and Young People.

Secretary-General: Rt Hon. DONALD (DON) C. MCKINNON (New Zealand).

Deputy Secretaries-General: FLORENCE MUGASHA (Uganda), RANSFORD SMITH (Jamaica).

Activities

INTERNATIONAL AFFAIRS

In October 1991 heads of government, meeting in Harare, Zimbabwe, issued the Harare Commonwealth Declaration, in which they reaffirmed their commitment to the Commonwealth Principles declared in 1971, and stressed the need to promote sustainable development and the alleviation of poverty. The Declaration placed emphasis on the promotion of democracy and respect for human rights and resolved to strengthen the Commonwealth's capacity to assist countries in entrenching democratic practices. In November 1995 Commonwealth heads of government, convened in New Zealand, formulated and adopted the Millbrook Commonwealth Action Programme on the Harare Declaration, to promote adherence by member countries to the fundamental principles of democracy and human rights (as proclaimed in the 1991 Declaration). The Programme incorporated a framework of measures to be pursued in support of democratic processes and institutions, and actions to be taken in response to violations of the Harare Declaration principles, in particular the unlawful removal of a democratically-elected government. A Commonwealth Ministerial Action Group on the

Harare Declaration (CMAG) was to be established to implement this process and to assist the member country involved to comply with the Harare principles. On the basis of this Programme, the leaders suspended Nigeria from the Commonwealth with immediate effect, following the execution by that country's military Government of nine environmental and human rights protesters and a series of other violations of human rights. The meeting determined to expel Nigeria from the Commonwealth if no 'demonstrable progress' had been made towards the establishment of a democratic authority by the time of the next summit meeting. In addition, the Programme formulated measures to promote sustainable development in member countries, which was considered to be an important element in sustaining democracy, and to facilitate consensus-building within the international community.

In December 1995 CMAG convened for its inaugural meeting in London, United Kingdom. The Group, initially comprising the ministers of foreign affairs of Canada, Ghana, Jamaica, Malaysia, New Zealand, South Africa, the United Kingdom and Zimbabwe (with membership to be reconstituted periodically), commenced by considering efforts to restore democratic government in the three Commonwealth countries then under military regimes, i.e. The Gambia, Nigeria and Sierra Leone. At the second meeting of the Group, in April 1996, ministers commended the conduct of presidential and parliamentary elections in Sierra Leone and the announcement by The Gambia's military leaders that there would be a transition to civilian rule. In June a three-member CMAG delegation visited The Gambia to reaffirm Commonwealth support of the transition process in that country and to identify possible areas of further Commonwealth assistance. In August the Gambian authorities issued a decree removing the ban on political activities and parties, although shortly afterwards they prohibited certain parties and candidates involved in political life prior to the military takeover from contesting the elections. CMAG recommended that in such circumstances no Commonwealth observers should be sent to either the presidential or parliamentary elections, which were held in September 1996 and January 1997 respectively. Following the restoration of a civilian Government in early 1997, CMAG requested the Commonwealth Secretary-General to extend technical assistance to The Gambia in order to consolidate the democratic transition process. In April 1996 it was noted that the human rights situation in Nigeria had continued to deteriorate. CMAG, having pursued unsuccessful efforts to initiate dialogue with the Nigerian authorities, outlined a series of punitive and restrictive measures (including visa restrictions on members of the administration, a cessation of sporting contacts and an embargo on the export of armaments) that it would recommend for collective Commonwealth action in order to exert further pressure for reform in Nigeria. Following a meeting of a high-level delegation of the Nigerian Government and CMAG in June, the Group agreed to postpone the implementation of the sanctions, pending progress on the dialogue. (Canada, however, determined, unilaterally, to impose the measures with immediate effect; the United Kingdom did so in accordance with a decision of the European Union to implement limited sanctions against Nigeria.) A proposed CMAG mission to Nigeria was postponed in August, owing to restrictions imposed by the military authorities on access to political detainees and other civilian activists in that country. In September the Group agreed to proceed with the visit (which then took place in November) and to delay further a decision on the implementation of sanction measures. In July 1997 the Group reiterated the Commonwealth Secretary-General's condemnation of a military coup in Sierra Leone in May, and decided that the country's participation in meetings of the Commonwealth should be suspended pending the restoration of a democratic government.

In October 1997 Commonwealth heads of government, meeting in Edinburgh, United Kingdom, endorsed CMAG's recommendation that the imposition of sanctions against Nigeria be held in abeyance pending the scheduled completion of a transition programme towards democracy by October 1998. It was also agreed that CMAG be formally constituted as a permanent organ to investigate abuses of human rights throughout the Commonwealth.

In March 1998 CMAG commended the efforts of the Economic Community of West African States (ECOWAS) in restoring the democratically-elected Government of President Ahmed Tejan Kabbah in Sierra Leone, and agreed to remove all restrictions on Sierra Leone's participation in Commonwealth activities. Later in that month, a representative mission of CMAG visited Sierra Leone to express its support for Kabbah's administration and to consider the country's needs in its process of reconstruction. At the CMAG meeting held in October members agreed that Sierra Leone should no longer be considered under the Group's mandate; however, they urged the Secretary-General to continue to assist that country in the process of national reconciliation and to facilitate negotiations with opposition forces to ensure a lasting cease-fire. A Special Envoy of the Secretary-General was appointed to co-operate with the UN, ECOWAS and the Organization of African Union (OAU, now African Union—AU) in monitoring the implementation of the Sierra Leone peace process, and the Commonwealth has supported the rebuilding of the Sierra Leone police force. In September 2001 CMAG recommended that Sierra Leone be removed from its remit, but that the Secretary-General should continue to monitor developments there.

In April 1998 the Nigerian military leader, Gen. Sani Abacha, announced that a presidential election was to be conducted in August, but indicated that, following an agreement with other political organizations, he was to be the sole candidate. In June, however, Abacha died suddenly. His successor, Gen. Abdulsalam Abubakar, immediately released several prominent political prisoners, and confirmed his intention to abide by the programme for transition to civilian rule. In October CMAG, convened for its 10th formal meeting, acknowledged Abubakar's efforts towards restoring a democratic government and recommended that member states begin to remove sanctions against Nigeria and that it resume participation in certain Commonwealth activities. The Commonwealth Secretary-General subsequently announced a programme of technical assistance to support Nigeria in the planning and conduct of democratic elections. Staff teams from the Commonwealth Secretariat observed local government, and state and governorship elections, held in December and in January 1999, respectively. A Commonwealth Observer Group was also dispatched to Nigeria to monitor preparations and conduct of legislative and presidential elections, held in February. While the Group reported several irregularities in the conduct of the polling, it confirmed that, in general, the conditions had existed for free and fair elections and that the elections were a legitimate basis for the transition of power to a democratic, civilian government. In April CMAG voted to readmit Nigeria to full membership on 29 May, upon the installation of the new civilian administration.

In 1999 the Commonwealth Secretary-General appointed a Special Envoy to broker an agreement in order to end a civil dispute in Honiara, Solomon Islands. An accord was signed in late June, and it was envisaged that the Commonwealth would monitor its implementation. In October a Commonwealth Multinational Police Peace Monitoring Group was stationed in Solomon Islands; this was renamed the Commonwealth Multinational Police Assistance Group in February 2000. Following further internal unrest, however, the Group was disbanded. In June CMAG determined to send a new mission to Solomon Islands in order to facilitate negotiations between the opposing parties, to convey the Commonwealth's concern and to offer assistance. The Commonwealth welcomed the peace accord concluded in Solomon Islands in October, and extended its support to the International Peace Monitoring Team that was established to oversee implementation of the peace accords. CMAG welcomed the conduct of parliamentary elections held in Solomon Islands in December 2001. CMAG removed Solomon Islands from its agenda in December 2003 but was to continue to receive reports from the Secretary-General on future developments.

In mid-October 1999 a special meeting of CMAG was convened to consider the overthrow of the democratically-elected Government in Pakistan in a military coup. The meeting condemned the action as a violation of Commonwealth principles and urged the new authorities to declare a timetable for the return to democratic rule. CMAG also resolved to send a four-member delegation, comprising the ministers of foreign affairs of Barbados, Canada, Ghana and Malaysia, to discuss this future course of action with the military regime. Pakistan was suspended from participation in meetings of the Commonwealth with immediate effect. The suspension, pending the restoration of a democratic government, was endorsed by heads of government, meeting in November, who requested that CMAG keep the situation in Pakistan under review. At the meeting, held in Durban, South Africa, it was agreed that no country would serve for more than two consecutive two-year terms. CMAG was requested to remain actively involved in the post-conflict development and rehabilitation of Sierra Leone and the process of consolidating peace. In addition, it was urged to monitor persistent violations of the Harare Declaration principles in all countries. Heads of government also agreed to establish a new ministerial group on Guyana and to reconvene a ministerial committee on Belize, in order to facilitate dialogue in ongoing territorial disputes with neighbouring countries. The meeting established a 10-member Commonwealth High Level Review Group to evaluate the role and activities of the Commonwealth. In 2000 the Group initiated a programme of consultations to proceed with its mandate and established a working group of experts to consider the Commonwealth's role in supporting information technology capabilities in member countries.

In June 2000, following the overthrow in May of the Fijian Government by a group of armed civilians, and the subsequent illegal detention of members of the elected administration, CMAG suspended Fiji's participation in meetings of the Commonwealth pending the restoration of democratic rule. In September, upon the request of CMAG, the Secretary-General appointed a Special Envoy to support efforts towards political dialogue and a return to democratic rule in Fiji. The Special Envoy undertook his first visit in December. In December 2001, following the staging of democratic legislative elections in August–September, Fiji was readmitted to Commonwealth meetings on the recommendation of CMAG. Fiji was removed from CMAG's agenda in May 2004, although the Group determined to continue to note developments there, as judgments were still pending in the Fiji Supreme Court on unresolved matters concerning the democratic process. In December 2006, following the overthrow of the Fijian Government by a military coup, an extraordinary meeting of CMAG determined that Fiji should once again be suspended from meetings of the Commonwealth, pending the reinstatement of democratic governance.

In March 2001 CMAG resolved to send a ministerial mission to Zimbabwe, in order to relay to the government the Commonwealth's concerns at the ongoing violence and abuses of human rights in that country, as well as to discuss the conduct of parliamentary elections and extend technical assistance. The mission was rejected by the Zimbabwe Government, which queried the basis for CMAG's intervention in the affairs of an elected administration. In September, under the auspices of a group of Commonwealth foreign ministers partly derived from CMAG, the Zimbabwe Government signed the Abuja Agreement, which provided for the cessation of illegal occupations of white-owned farms and the resumption of the rule of law, in return for financial assistance to support the ongoing process of land reform in that country. In January 2002 CMAG expressed strong concern at the continuing violence and political intimidation in Zimbabwe. The summit of Commonwealth heads of government convened in early March (see below) also expressed concern at the situation in Zimbabwe, and, having decided on the principle that CMAG should be permitted to engage with any member Government deemed to be in breach of the organization's core values, mandated a Commonwealth Chairperson's Committee on Zimbabwe to determine appropriate action should an impending presidential election (scheduled to be held during that month) be found not to have been conducted freely and fairly. Following the publication by a Commonwealth observer team of an unfavourable report on the conduct of the election, the Committee decided to suspend Zimbabwe from meetings of the Commonwealth for one year. In March 2003 the Committee concluded that the suspension should remain in force pending consideration by the next summit of heads of government.

In March 2002, meeting in Coolum, near Brisbane, Australia, Commonwealth heads of government adopted the Coolum Declaration on the Commonwealth in the 21st Century: Continuity and Renewal, which reiterated commitment to the organization's principles and values. Leaders at the meeting condemned all forms of terrorism; welcomed the Millennium Development Goals (MDGs) adopted by the UN General Assembly; called on the Secretary-General to constitute a high-level expert group on implementing the objectives of the Fancourt Declaration; pledged continued support for small states; and urged renewed efforts to combat the spread of HIV/AIDS. The meeting adopted a report on the future of the Commonwealth drafted by the High Level Review Group. The document recommended strengthening the Commonwealth's role in conflict prevention and resolution and support of democratic practices; enhancing the good offices role of the Secretary-General; better promoting member states' economic and development needs; strengthening the organization's role in facilitating member states' access to international assistance; and promoting increased access to modern information and communications technologies. The meeting expanded CMAG's mandate to enable the Group to consider action against serious violations of the Commonwealth's core values perpetrated by elected administrations (such as that in Zimbabwe, see above) as well as by military regimes.

A Commonwealth team of observers dispatched to monitor legislative and provincial elections that were held in Pakistan, in October 2002, found them to have been well-organized and conducted in a largely transparent manner. The team made several recommendations on institutional and procedural issues. CMAG subsequently expressed concern over the promulgation of new legislation in Pakistan following the imposition earlier in the year of a number of extra-constitutional measures. CMAG determined that Pakistan should continue to be suspended from meetings of the Commonwealth, pending a review of the role and functioning of its democratic institutions. Pakistan's progress in establishing democratic institutions was welcomed by a meeting of CMAG in May 2003. In November 2002 a Commonwealth Expert Group on Papua New Guinea, established in the previous month to review the electoral process in that country (in view of unsatisfactory legislative elections that were conducted there in July), made several recommendations aimed at enhancing the future management of the electoral process.

In December 2003 the meeting of heads of government, held in Abuja, Nigeria, resolved to maintain the suspension of Pakistan and Zimbabwe from participation in Commonwealth meetings. President Mugabe of Zimbabwe responded by announcing his country's immediate withdrawal from the Commonwealth and alleging a pro-Western bias within the grouping. Support for Zimbabwe's position was declared by a number of members, including South Africa, Mozambique, Namibia and Zambia. A Commonwealth committee, consisting of six heads of government, was established to monitor the situation in Zimbabwe and only when the committee believed sufficient progress had been made towards consolidating democracy and promoting development within Zimbabwe would the Commonwealth be consulted on readmitting the country.

In concluding the 2003 meeting heads of government issued the Aso Rock Commonwealth Declaration, which emphasized their commitment to strengthening development and democracy, and incorporated clear objectives in support of these goals. Priority areas identified included efforts to eradicate poverty and attain the MDGs, to strengthen democratic institutions, empower women, promote the involvement of civil society, combat corruption and recover assets (for which a working group was to be established), facilitate finance for development, address the spread of HIV/AIDS and other diseases, combat the illicit trafficking in human beings, and promote education. The leaders also adopted a separate statement on multilateral trade, in particular in support of the stalled Doha round of World Trade Organization negotiations.

In response to the earthquake and tsunami that devastated coastal areas of several Indian Ocean countries in late December 2004, the Commonwealth Secretary-General appealed for assistance from Commonwealth Governments for the mobilization of emergency humanitarian relief. In early January 2005 the Secretariat dispatched a Disaster Relief Co-ordinator to the Maldives to assess the needs of that country and to co-ordinate ongoing relief and rehabilitation activities, and later in that month the Secretariat sent emergency medical doctors from other member states to the Maldives. In mid-January, meeting during the fifth Summit of the Alliance of Small Island States, in Port Louis, Mauritius, the Secretaries-General of the Commonwealth, the Caribbean Community and Common Market (CARICOM), the Pacific Islands Forum and the Indian Ocean Commission determined to take collective action to strengthen the disaster-preparedness and response capacities of their member countries in the Caribbean, Pacific and Indian Ocean areas.

In February 2005 CMAG expressed serious concern that President Musharraf of Pakistan had failed to relinquish the role of chief of army staff (at meetings held in May and September 2004 CMAG had urged the separation of the military and civilian offices held by the President, deeming this arrangement to be undemocratic). Noting President Musharraf's own undertaking not to continue as chief of army staff beyond 2007, the Group stated its view that the two offices should not be combined in one person beyond the end (in that year) of the current presidential term. CMAG recommended that the Secretary-General should maintain high-level contacts with Pakistan. In September 2005 CMAG urged Pakistan to accelerate its democratic reforms.

Political Affairs Division: assists consultation among member governments on international and Commonwealth matters of common interest. In association with host governments, it organizes the meetings of heads of government and senior officials. The Division services committees and special groups set up by heads of government dealing with political matters. The Secretariat has observer status at the United Nations, and the Division manages a joint office in New York to enable small states, which would otherwise be unable to afford facilities there, to maintain a presence at the United Nations. The Division monitors political developments in the Commonwealth and international progress in such matters as disarmament and the Law of the Sea. It also undertakes research on matters of common interest to member governments, and reports back to them. The Division is involved in diplomatic training and consular co-operation.

In 1990 Commonwealth heads of government mandated the Division to support the promotion of democracy by monitoring the preparations for and conduct of parliamentary, presidential or other elections in member countries at the request of national governments. In 2007 Commonwealth observer groups were dispatched to observe parliamentary elections in Lesotho (in February), Nigeria (April) and Sierra Leone (August) and a referendum in the Maldives (in August).

Under the reorganization of the Secretariat in 2002 a Good Offices Section was established within the Division to strengthen and support the activities of the Secretary-General in addressing political conflict in member states and in assisting countries to adhere to the principles of the Harare Declaration. The Secretary-General's good offices may be directed to preventing or resolving conflict and assisting other international efforts to promote political stability. At August 2007 Special Envoys of the Secretary-General were active in six member countries: Cameroon, The Gambia, Guyana, Kenya, the Maldives and Tonga.

Human Rights Unit: undertakes activities in support of the Commonwealth's commitment to the promotion and protection of fundamental human rights. It develops programmes, publishes human rights materials, co-operates with other organizations working in the field of human rights, in particular within the UN system, advises the Secretary-General, and organizes seminars and meetings of experts. The Unit aims to integrate human rights standards within all divisions of the Secretariat.

LAW

Legal and Constitutional Affairs Division: promotes and facilitates co-operation and the exchange of information among member governments on legal matters and assists in combating financial and organized crime, in particular transborder criminal activities. It administers, jointly with the Commonwealth of Learning, a distance training programme for legislative draftsmen and assists governments to reform national laws to meet the obligations of international conventions. The Division organizes the triennial meeting of ministers, Attorneys General and senior ministry officials concerned with the legal systems in Commonwealth countries. It has also initiated four Commonwealth schemes for co-operation on extradition, the protection of material cultural heritage, mutual assistance in criminal matters and the transfer of convicted offenders within the Commonwealth. It liaises with the Commonwealth Magistrates' and Judges' Association, the Commonwealth Legal Education Association, the Commonwealth Lawyers' Association (with which it helps to prepare the triennial Commonwealth Law Conference for the practising profession), the Commonwealth Association of Legislative Counsel, and with other international non-governmental organizations. The Division provides in-house legal advice for the Secretariat. The *Commonwealth Law Bulletin*, published four times a year, reports on legal developments in and beyond the Commonwealth. The Division promotes the exchange of information regarding national and international efforts to combat serious commercial crime through its other publications, *Commonwealth Legal Assistance News* and *Crimewatch*.

The heads of government meeting held in Coolum, Australia, in March 2002 endorsed a Plan of Action for combating international terrorism. A Commonwealth Committee on Terrorism, convened at ministerial level, was subsequently established to oversee its implementation.

A new expert group on good governance and the elimination of corruption in economic management convened for its first meeting in May 1998. In November 1999 Commonwealth heads of government endorsed a Framework for Principles for Promoting Good Governance and Combating Corruption, which had been drafted by the group. The conference of heads of government that met in Coolum in March 2002 endorsed a Commonwealth Local Government Good Practice Scheme, to be managed by the Commonwealth Local Government Forum (established in 1995).

ECONOMIC CO-OPERATION

In October 1997 Commonwealth heads of government, meeting in Edinburgh, United Kingdom, signed an Economic Declaration that focused on issues relating to global trade, investment and development and committed all member countries to free-market economic principles. The Declaration also incorporated a provision for the establishment of a Trade and Investment Access Facility within the Secretariat in order to assist developing member states in the process of international trade liberalization and promote intra-Commonwealth trade.

In May 1998 the Commonwealth Secretary-General appealed to the Group of Eight industrialized nations (G-8) to accelerate and expand the initiative to ease the debt burden of the most heavily indebted poor countries (HIPCs—see World Bank and IMF). In October Commonwealth finance ministers, convened in Ottawa, Canada, reiterated their appeal to international financial institutions to accelerate the HIPC initiative. The meeting also issued a Commonwealth Statement on the global economic crisis and endorsed proposals to help to counter the difficulties experienced by several countries. These measures included a mechanism to enable countries to suspend payments on all short-term financial obligations at a time of emergency without defaulting, assistance to governments to attract private capital and to manage capital market volatility, and the development of international codes of conduct regarding financial and monetary policies and corporate governance. In March 1999 the Commonwealth Secretariat hosted a joint IMF-World Bank conference to review the HIPC scheme and initiate a process of reform. In November Commonwealth heads of government, meeting in South Africa, declared their support for measures undertaken by the World Bank and IMF to enhance the HIPC initiative. At the end of an informal retreat the leaders adopted the Fancourt Commonwealth Declaration on Globalization and People-Centred Development, which emphasized the need for a more equitable spread of wealth generated by the process of globalization, and expressed a renewed commitment to the elimination of all forms of discrimination, the promotion of people-centred development and capacity-building, and efforts to ensure that developing countries benefit from future multilateral trade liberalization measures. In June 2002 the Commonwealth Secretary-General urged more generous funding of the HIPC initiative. Meetings of ministers of finance from Commonwealth member countries participating in the HIPC initiative are convened twice a year, as the Commonwealth HIPC Ministerial Forum. The Secretariat aims to assist HIPCs and other small economies through its Debt Recording and Management System (DRMS), which was first used in 1985 and updated in 2002. In mid-2005 the People's Republic of China became the 55th country (and the 12th non-Commonwealth member) to sign up to the System. The first Pan Commonwealth CS-DRMS User Group meeting was convened in June 2006, at which time there were 56 user countries. In July 2005 the Commonwealth Secretary-General welcomed an initiative of the G-8 to eliminate the debt of those HIPCs that had reached their completion point in the process, in addition to a commitment substantially to increase aid to Africa.

In February 1998 the Commonwealth Secretariat hosted the first Inter-Governmental Organizations Meeting to promote co-operation between small island states and the formulation of a unified policy approach to international fora. A second meeting was convened in March 2001, where discussions focused on the forthcoming WTO ministerial meeting and OECD's Harmful Tax Competition Initiative. In September 2000 Commonwealth finance ministers, meeting in Malta, reviewed the OECD initiative and agreed that the measures, affecting many member countries with offshore financial centres, should not be imposed on governments. The ministers mandated the involvement of the Commonwealth Secretariat in efforts to resolve the dispute; a joint working group was subsequently established by the Secretariat with the OECD. In April 2002 a meeting on international co-operation in the financial services sector, attended by representatives of international and regional organizations, donors and senior officials from Commonwealth countries, was held under Commonwealth auspices in Saint Lucia. In September 2005 Commonwealth finance ministers, meeting in Barbados, considered new guide-lines for Public Financial Management Reform.

The first meeting of governors of central banks from Commonwealth countries was held in June 2001 in London, United Kingdom.

The Commonwealth Secretariat was to participate in the €20m. 'Hub and Spokes' project, launched in October 2004 by the European Commission, with the Agence Intergouvernementale de la Francophonie, as a capacity-building initiative in the areas of trade policy formulation, mainstreaming trade in poverty reduction strategies, and participation in international trade negotiations for the African, Caribbean and Pacific (ACP) group of countries. The Secretariat was to manage the project in 55 of the 78 ACP member states.

In November 2005 Commonwealth heads of government issued the Malta Declaration on Networking the Commonwealth for Development, expressing their commitment to making available to all the benefits of new technologies and to using information technology networks to enhance the effectiveness of the Commonwealth in supporting development. The meeting endorsed a new Commonwealth Action Programme for the Digital Divide and approved the establishment of a special fund to enable implementation of the programme's objectives. Accordingly a Commonwealth Connects programme was established in August 2006 to develop partnerships and help to strengthen the use of and access to information technology in all Commonwealth countries. The 2005 Heads of Government Meeting also issued the Valletta Statement on Multilateral Trade, emphasizing their concerns that the Doha Round of WTO negotiations proceed steadily, on a development-oriented agenda, to a successful conclusion and reiterating their objectives of achieving a rules-based and equitable international trading system. A separate statement drew attention to the specific needs and challenges of small states and urged continued financial and technical support, in particular for those affected by natural disasters.

Economic Affairs Division: organizes and services the annual meetings of Commonwealth ministers of finance and the ministerial group on small states and assists in servicing the biennial meetings of heads of government and periodic meetings of environment ministers. It engages in research and analysis on economic issues of interest to member governments and organizes seminars and conferences of government officials and experts. The Division actively supports developing Commonwealth countries to participate in the Doha Round of multilateral trade negotiations and is assisting the ACP group of countries to negotiate economic partnership agreements with the European Union. It continues to help developing countries to strengthen their links with international capital markets and foreign investors. The Division also services groups of experts on economic affairs that have been commissioned by governments to report on, among other things, protectionism; obstacles to the North-South negotiating process; reform of the international financial and trading system; the debt crisis; management of technological change; the impact of change on the development process; environmental issues; women and structural adjustment; and youth unemployment. A separate section within the Division addresses the specific needs of small states and provides technical assistance. The work of the section covers a range of issues including trade, vulnerability, environment, politics and economics. A Secretariat Task Force services a Commonwealth Ministerial Group of Small States which was established in 1993 to provide strategic direction in addressing the concerns of small states and to mobilize support for action and assistance within the international community. The

Economic Affairs Division also co-ordinates the Secretariat's environmental work and manages the Iwokrama International Centre for Rainforest Conservation and Development.

The Division played a catalytic role in the establishment of a Commonwealth Equity Fund, initiated in September 1990, to allow developing member countries to improve their access to private institutional investment, and promoted a Caribbean Investment Fund. The Division supported the establishment of a Commonwealth Private Investment Initiative (CPII) to mobilize capital, on a regional basis, for investment in newly-privatized companies and in small and medium-sized businesses in the private sector. The first regional fund under the CPII was launched in July 1996. The Commonwealth Africa Investment Fund (Comafin), was to be managed by the United Kingdom's official development institution, the Commonwealth Development Corporation, to assist businesses in 19 countries in sub-Saharan Africa, with initial resources of US $63.5m. In August 1997 an investment fund for the Pacific Islands was launched, with an initial capital of $15.0m. A successor fund, with financing of some $20m., was launched in October 2005. A $200m. South Asia Regional Fund was established at the heads of government meeting in October 1997. In October 1998 a fund for the Caribbean states was inaugurated, at a meeting of Commonwealth finance ministers. The 2001 summit of Commonwealth heads of government authorized the establishment of a new fund for Africa (Comafin II): this was inaugurated in March 2002, and attracted initial capital in excess of $200m.

SOCIAL WELFARE

Social Transformation Programmes Division: consists of three sections concerned with education, gender and health.

The **Education Section** arranges specialist seminars, workshops and co-operative projects, and commissions studies in areas identified by ministers of education, whose three-yearly meetings it also services. Its present areas of emphasis include improving the quality of and access to basic education; strengthening the culture of science, technology and mathematics education in formal and non-formal areas of education; improving the quality of management in institutions of higher learning and basic education; improving the performance of teachers; strengthening examination assessment systems; and promoting the movement of students between Commonwealth countries. The Section also promotes multi-sectoral strategies to be incorporated in the development of human resources. Emphasis is placed on ensuring a gender balance, the appropriate use of technology, promoting good governance, addressing the problems of scale particular to smaller member countries, and encouraging collaboration between governments, the private sector and other non-governmental organizations.

The **Gender Affairs Section** is responsible for the implementation of the Commonwealth Plan of Action for Gender Equality, covering the period 2005–15, which succeeded the Commonwealth Plan of Action on Gender and Development (adopted in 1995 and updated in 2000). The Plan of Action supports efforts towards achieving the MDGs, and the objectives of gender equality adopted by the 1995 Beijing Declaration and Platform for Action and the follow-up Beijing + 5 review conference held in 2000. Gender equality, poverty eradication, promotion of human rights, and strengthening democracy are recognized as intrinsically inter-related, and the Plan has a particular focus on the advancement of gender mainstreaming in the following areas: democracy, peace and conflict; human rights and law; poverty eradication and economic empowerment; and HIV/AIDS. In February–March 2005 Commonwealth ministers responsible for gender affairs attended the Beijing + 10 review conference.

The **Health Section** organizes ministerial, technical and expert group meetings and workshops, to promote co-operation on health matters, and the exchange of health information and expertise. The Section commissions relevant studies and provides professional and technical advice to member countries and to the Secretariat. It also supports the work of regional health organizations and promotes health for all people in Commonwealth countries.

Youth Affairs: A Youth Affairs unit, reporting directly to a Deputy Secretary-General, was established within the Secretariat in 2002. The unit acquired divisional status in 2004.

The Division administers the **Commonwealth Youth Programme (CYP)**, which was initiated in 1973 to promote the involvement of young people in the economic and social development of their countries. The CYP, funded through separate voluntary contributions from governments, was awarded a budget of £2.5m. for 2005/06. The Programme's activities are centred on four key programmes: Youth Enterprise Development; Youth Networks and Governance; Youth Participation; and Youth Work, Education and Training. Regional centres are located in Zambia (for Africa), India (for Asia), Guyana (for the Caribbean), and Solomon Islands (for the Pacific). The Programme administers a Youth Study Fellowship scheme, a Youth Project Fund, a Youth Exchange Programme (in the Caribbean), and a Youth Service Awards Scheme. It also holds conferences and seminars, carries out research and disseminates information. The Commonwealth Youth Credit Initiative, launched in 1995, provides funds, training and advice to young entrepreneurs. A Plan of Action on Youth Empowerment to the Year 2005 was approved by a Commonwealth ministerial meeting held in Kuala Lumpur, Malaysia, in May 1998. The first Commonwealth Youth and Sports Congress was scheduled to be held in India, in 2009.

In March 2002 Commonwealth heads of government approved the Youth for the Future initiative to encourage and use the skills of young people throughout the Commonwealth. It was to comprise four main components: Youth enterprise development; Youth volunteers; Youth mentors; and Youth leadership awards.

TECHNICAL ASSISTANCE

Commonwealth Fund for Technical Co-operation (CFTC): f. 1971 to facilitate the exchange of skills between member countries and to promote economic and social development; it is administered by the Commonwealth Secretariat and financed by voluntary subscriptions from member governments. The CFTC responds to requests from member governments for technical assistance, such as the provision of experts for short- or medium-term projects, advice on economic or legal matters, in particular in the areas of natural resources management and public-sector reform, and training programmes. The CFTC also administers the Langkawi awards for the study of environmental issues, which is funded by the Canadian Government; the proposed CFTC budget for 2006/07 amounted to £25.6m.

CFTC activities are mainly implemented by the following divisions:

Governance and Institutional Development Division: strengthens good governance in member countries, through advice, training and other expertise in order to build capacity in national public institutions. The Division administers the Commonwealth Service Abroad Programme (CSAP), which is funded by the CFTC. The Programme extends short-term technical assistance through highly qualified volunteers. The main objectives of the scheme are to provide expertise, training and exposure to new technologies and practices, to promote technology transfers and sharing of experiences and knowledge, and to support community workshops and other grassroots activities.

Special Advisory Services Division: advises on economic and legal issues, such as debt and financial management, natural resource development, multilateral trade issues, export marketing, trade facilitation, competitiveness and the development of enterprises.

Finance

The Secretariat's proposed budget for 2006/07 was £13.8m. Member governments meet the cost of the Secretariat through subscriptions on a scale related to income and population.

Publications

Commonwealth Currents (quarterly).

International Development Policies (quarterly).

Report of the Commonwealth Secretary-General (every 2 years).

Numerous reports, studies and papers (catalogue available).

Commonwealth Organizations

(in the United Kingdom, unless otherwise stated)

PRINCIPAL BODIES

Commonwealth Business Council: 18 Pall Mall, London, SW1Y 5LU; tel. (20) 7024-8200; fax (20) 7024-8201; e-mail info@cbcglobal.org; internet www.cbcglobelink.org; f. 1997 by the Commonwealth Heads of Government Meeting to promote co-operation between governments and the private sector in support of trade, investment and development; the Council aims to identify and promote investment opportunities, in particular in Commonwealth developing countries, to support countries and local businesses to work within the context of globalization, to promote capacity-building and the exchange of skills and knowledge (in particular through its Information Communication Technologies for Development programme), and to encourage co-operation among Commonwealth members; promotes good governance; supports the process of multilateral trade negotiations and other liberalization of trade and services; represents the private sector at government level; Dir-Gen. and CEO Dr MOHAN KAUL.

Commonwealth Foundation: Marlborough House, Pall Mall, London, SW1Y 5HY; tel. (20) 7930-3783; fax (20) 7839-8157; e-mail geninfo@commonwealth.int; internet www.commonwealthfoundation.com; f. 1966; intergovernmental body promoting people-to-people interaction, and collaboration within the non-governmental sector of the Commonwealth; supports non-governmental organizations, professional associations and Commonwealth arts and culture; awards an annual Commonwealth Writers' Prize; funds are provided by Commonwealth govts; Chair. Prof. GUIDO DE MARCO (Malta); Dir Dr MARK COLLINS (United Kingdom); publ. *Commonwealth People* (quarterly).

Commonwealth of Learning (COL): 1055 West Hastings St, Suite 1200, Vancouver, BC V6E 2E9, Canada; tel. (604) 775-8200; fax (604) 775-8210; e-mail info@col.org; internet www.col.org; f. 1987 by Commonwealth Heads of Government to promote the devt and sharing of distance education and open learning resources, including materials, expertise and technologies, throughout the Commonwealth and in other countries; implements and assists with national and regional educational programmes; acts as consultant to international agencies and national governments; conducts seminars and studies on specific educational needs; core financing for COL is provided by Commonwealth governments on a voluntary basis; in 2006 heads of government endorsed an annual budget for COL of C $12m; Pres. and CEO Sir JOHN DANIEL (Canada/UK); publs *Connections, EdTech News*.

The following represents a selection of other Commonwealth organizations:

AGRICULTURE AND FORESTRY

Commonwealth Forestry Association: Crib, Dinchope, Craven Arms, Shropshire, SY7 9JJ; tel. (1588) 672868; fax (870) 0116645; e-mail cfa@cfa-international.org; internet www.cfa-international.org; f. 1921; produces, collects and circulates information relating to world forestry and promotes good management, use and conservation of forests and forest lands throughout the world; mems: 1,200; Pres. DAVID BILLS (Australia/UK); publs *International Forestry Review* (quarterly), *Commonwealth Forestry News* (quarterly), *Commonwealth Forestry Handbook* (irregular).

Standing Committee on Commonwealth Forestry: Forestry Commission, 231 Corstorphine Rd, Edinburgh, EH12 7AT; tel. (131) 314-6137; fax (131) 316-4344; e-mail libby.jones@forestry.gsi.gov.uk; f. 1923 to provide continuity between Confs, and to provide a forum for discussion on any forestry matters of common interest to mem. govts which may be brought to the Cttee's notice by any mem. country or organization; 54 mems; 2010 Conference: United Kingdom; Sec. LIBBY JONES; publ. *Newsletter* (quarterly).

COMMONWEALTH STUDIES

Institute of Commonwealth Studies: 28 Russell Sq., London, WC1B 5DS; tel. (20) 7862-8844; fax (20) 7862-8820; e-mail ics@sas.ac.uk; internet commonwealth.sas.ac.uk; f. 1949 to promote advanced study of the Commonwealth; provides a library and meeting place for postgraduate students and academic staff engaged in research in this field; offers postgraduate teaching; Dir Prof. RICHARD CROOK; publs *Annual Report, Collected Seminar Papers, Newsletter, Theses in Progress in Commonwealth Studies*.

COMMUNICATIONS

Commonwealth Telecommunications Organization: 26–28 Hammersmith Grove, London, W6 7BA; tel. (870) 7777697; fax (870) 0345626; e-mail info@cto.int; internet www.cto.int; f. 1967 as an international development partnership between Commonwealth and non-Commonwealth governments, business and civil society organizations; aims to help to bridge the digital divide and to achieve social and economic development by delivering to developing countries knowledge-sharing programmes in the use of information and communication technologies in the specific areas of telecommunications, IT, broadcasting and the internet; CEO Dr EKWOW SPIO-GARBRAH; publs *CTO Update* (quarterly), *Annual Report, Research Reports*.

EDUCATION AND CULTURE

Association of Commonwealth Universities (ACU): Woburn House, 20-24 Tavistock Sq., London, WC1H 9HF; tel. (20) 7380-6700; fax (20) 7387-2655; e-mail info@acu.ac.uk; internet www.acu.ac.uk; f. 1913; promotes international co-operation and understanding; provides assistance with staff and student mobility and development programmes; researches and disseminates information about universities and relevant policy issues; organizes major meetings of Commonwealth universities and their representatives; acts as a liaison office and information centre; administers scholarship and fellowship schemes; operates a policy research unit; mems: c. 500 universities in 36 Commonwealth countries or regions; Sec.-Gen. Dr JOHN ROWETT; publs include *Yearly Review, Commonwealth Universities Yearbook, ACU Bulletin* (quarterly), *Report of the Council of the ACU* (annually), *Who's Who of Executive Heads: Vice-Chancellors, Presidents, Principals and Rectors, International Awards*, student information papers (study abroad series).

Commonwealth Association for Education in Journalism and Communication (CAEJAC): c/o Faculty of Law, University of Western Ontario, London, ON N6A 3K7, Canada; tel. (519) 661-3348; fax (519) 661-3790; e-mail caejc@julian.uwo.ca; f. 1985; aims to foster high standards of journalism and communication education and research in Commonwealth countries and to promote co-operation among institutions and professions; c. 700 mems in 32 Commonwealth countries; Pres. Prof. SYED ARABI IDID (Malaysia); Sec. Prof. ROBERT MARTIN (Canada); publ. *CAEJAC Journal* (annually).

Commonwealth Association of Science, Technology and Mathematics Educators (CASTME): 7 Lion Yard, Tremadoc Rd, London, SW4 7NQ; tel. (20) 7819-3932; fax (20) 7720-5403; e-mail mirkka.juntunen@lect.org.uk; internet www.castme.org; f. 1974; special emphasis is given to the social significance of education in these subjects; organizes an Awards Scheme to promote effective teaching and learning in these subjects, and biennial regional seminars; Hon. Sec. Dr LYN HAINES; publ. *CASTME Journal* (quarterly).

Commonwealth Council for Educational Administration and Management: Department of Education, University of Cyprus, POB 20537, 1678 Lefkosia, Cyprus; tel. 22753739; fax 22377950; e-mail edpetros@ucy.ac.cy; internet www.cceam.org; f. 1970; aims to foster quality in professional development and links among educational administrators; holds nat. and regional confs, as well as visits and seminars; mems: 24 affiliated groups representing 3,000 persons; Pres. Dr PETROS PASHIARDIS; publ. *International Studies in Educational Administration* (2 a year).

Commonwealth Institute: New Zealand House, 80 Haymarket, London, SW1Y 4TQ; tel. (20) 7024-9822; fax (20) 7024-9833; e-mail information@commonwealth-institute.org; internet www.commonwealth.org.uk; f. 1893 as the Imperial Institute; restructured as an independent pan-Commonwealth agency Jan. 2000; governed by a Bd of Trustees elected by the Bd of Governors; Commonwealth High Commissioners to the United Kingdom act as *ex-officio* Governors; the Inst. houses a Commonwealth Resource and Literature Library and a Conference and Events Centre; supplies educational resource materials and training throughout the United Kingdom; provides internet services to the Commonwealth; operates as an arts and conference centre, running a Commonwealth-based cultural programme; a five-year strategic plan, entitled 'Commonwealth 21', was inaugurated in 1998; in 2004 the Institute, in collaboration with Cambridge University, established a Centre of Commonwealth Education; Chair. JUDITH HANRATTY; Chief Exec. DAVID FRENCH; publ. *Annual Review*.

League for the Exchange of Commonwealth Teachers: 7 Lion Yard, Tremadoc Rd, London, SW4 7NQ; tel. (870) 7702636; fax (870) 7702637; e-mail info@lect.org.uk; internet www.lect.org.uk; f. 1901; promotes educational exchanges between teachers throughout the Commonwealth; Dir ANNA TOMLINSON; publ. *Annual Review*.

HEALTH

Commonwealth Medical Trust (COMMAT): BMA House, Tavistock Sq., London, WC1H 9JP; tel. (20) 7272-8492; fax (1689) 890609; e-mail office@commat.org; internet www.commat.org; f. 1962 (as the Commonwealth Medical Association) for the exchange of information; provision of tech. co-operation and advice; formulation and maintenance of a code of ethics; promotes the Right to Health; liaison with WHO and other UN agencies on health issues; meetings of its Council are held every three years; mems: medical asscns in Commonwealth countries; Dir MARIANNE HASLEGRAVE.

Commonwealth Pharmaceutical Association: 1 Lambeth High St, London, SE1 7JN; tel. (20) 7572-2364; fax (20) 7572-2508; e-mail admin@commonwealthpharmacy.org; internet www.commonwealthpharmacy.org; f. 1970 to promote the interests of pharmaceutical sciences and the profession of pharmacy in the Commonwealth; to maintain high professional standards, encourage links between members and the creation of nat. asscns; and to facilitate the dissemination of information; holds confs (every four years) and regional meetings; mems: pharmaceutical asscns from over 40 Commonwealth countries; Pres. Dr GRACE ALLEN YOUNG; publ. *Quarterly Newsletter*.

Commonwealth Society for the Deaf (Sound Seekers): 34 Buckingham Palace Rd, London, SW1W 0RE; tel. (20) 7233-5700; fax (20) 7233-5805; e-mail sound.seekers@btinternet.com; internet www.sound-seekers.org.uk; f. 1959; undertakes initiatives to establish audiology services in developing Commonwealth countries, including mobile clinics to provide outreach services; aims to educate local communities in aural hygiene and the prevention of ear infection and deafness; provides audiological equipment and organizes the training of audiological maintenance technicians; conducts research into the causes and prevention of deafness; Chief Exec. GARY WILLIAMS; publ. *Annual Report*.

Sightsavers International: Grosvenor Hall, Bolnore Rd, Haywards Heath, West Sussex, RH16 4BX; tel. (1444) 446600; fax (1444) 446688; e-mail info@sightsavers.org; internet www.sightsavers.org; f. 1950 to prevent blindness and restore sight in developing countries, and to provide education and community-based training for incurably blind people; operates in collaboration with local partners, with high priority given to training local staff; Chair. Sir JOHN COLES; Chief Exec. Dr CAROLINE HARPER; publ. *Sight Savers News*.

INFORMATION AND THE MEDIA

Commonwealth Broadcasting Association: 17 Fleet St, London, EC4Y 1AA; tel. (20) 7583-5550; fax (20) 7583-5549; e-mail cba@cba.org.uk; internet www.cba.org.uk; f. 1945; gen. confs are held every two years (2008: Bahamas); mems: c. 100 in more than 50 countries; Pres. ABUBAKAR JIJIWA; Sec.-Gen. ELIZABETH SMITH; publs *Commonwealth Broadcaster* (quarterly), *Commonwealth Broadcaster Directory* (annually).

Commonwealth Journalists Association: c/o Canadian Newspaper Association, 890 Yonge St, Suite 200, Toronto, ON M4W 3P4, Canada; tel. (416) 923-3567; fax (416) 923-7206; e-mail bcantley@cna-acj.ca; internet www.cjaweb.com; f. 1978 to promote co-operation between journalists in Commonwealth countries, organize training facilities and confs, and foster understanding among Commonwealth peoples; Exec. Dir BRYAN CANTLEY; publ. *Newsletter* (3 a year).

Commonwealth Press Union (Association of Commonwealth Newspapers, News Agencies and Periodicals): 17 Fleet St, London, EC4Y 1AA; tel. (20) 7583-7733; fax (20) 7583-6868; e-mail lindsay@cpu.org.uk; internet www.cpu.org.uk; f. 1950; promotes the welfare of the Commonwealth press; provides training for journalists and organizes biennial confs; mems: c. 750 newspapers, news agencies, periodicals in 49 Commonwealth countries; Exec. Dir LINDSAY ROSS; publ. *Annual Report*.

LAW

Commonwealth Lawyers' Association: c/o Institute of Commonwealth Studies, 28 Russell Sq., London, WC1B 5DS; tel. (20) 7862-8824; fax (20) 7862-8816; e-mail cla@sas.ac.uk; internet www.commonwealthlawyers.com; f. 1983 (fmrly the Commonwealth Legal Bureau); seeks to maintain and promote the rule of law throughout the Commonwealth, by ensuring that the people of the Commonwealth are served by an independent and efficient legal profession; upholds professional standards and promotes the availability of legal services; organizes the biannual Commonwealth Law Conference; Sec-Gen. CLAIRE MARTIN; publs *The Commonwealth Lawyer*, *Clarion*.

Commonwealth Legal Advisory Service: c/o British Institute of International and Comparative Law, Charles Clore House, 17 Russell Sq., London, WC1B 5DR; tel. (20) 7862-5151; fax (20) 7862-5152; e-mail info@biicl.org; f. 1962; financed by the British Institute and by contributions from Commonwealth govts; provides research facilities for Commonwealth govts and law reform commissions; Chair. Rt Hon. Lord BROWNE-WILKINSON; publ. *New Memoranda* series.

Commonwealth Legal Education Association: c/o Legal and Constitutional Affairs Division, Commonwealth Secretariat, Marlborough House, Pall Mall, London, SW1Y 5HX; tel. (20) 7747-6415; fax (20) 7747-6406; e-mail clea@commonwealth.int; internet www.cleaonline.org; f. 1971 to promote contacts and exchanges and to provide information regarding legal education; Gen. Sec. JOHN HATCHARD; publs *Commonwealth Legal Education Association Newsletter* (3 a year), *Directory of Commonwealth Law Schools* (every 2 years).

Commonwealth Magistrates' and Judges' Association: Uganda House, 58–59 Trafalgar Sq., London, WC2N 5DX; tel. (20) 7976-1007; fax (20) 7976-2394; e-mail info@cmja.org; internet www.cmja.org; f. 1970 to advance the administration of the law by promoting the independence of the judiciary, to further education in law and crime prevention and to disseminate information; confs and study tours; corporate membership for asscns of the judiciary or courts of limited jurisdiction; assoc. membership for individuals; Pres. Rt Hon. Justice Tan Sri Dato' Siti NORMA YAAKOB; Exec. Vice-Pres. Lord Justice HENRY BROOKE; publs *Commonwealth Judicial Journal* (2 a year), *CMJA News*.

PARLIAMENTARY AFFAIRS

Commonwealth Parliamentary Association: Westminster House, Suite 700, 7 Millbank, London, SW1P 3JA; tel. (20) 7799-1460; fax (20) 7222-6073; e-mail hq.sec@cpahq.org; internet www.cpahq.org; f. 1911 to promote understanding and co-operation between Commonwealth parliamentarians; organization: Exec. Cttee of 35 MPs responsible to annual Gen. Assembly; 175 brs in national, state, provincial and territorial parliaments and legislatures throughout the Commonwealth; holds annual Commonwealth Parliamentary Confs and seminars; also regional confs and seminars; Sec.-Gen. Dr WILLIAM F. SHIJA; publ. *The Parliamentarian* (quarterly).

PROFESSIONAL AND INDUSTRIAL RELATIONS

Commonwealth Association of Architects: POB 508, Edgware, Middx, HA8 9XZ; tel. (20) 8951-0550; fax (20) 8951-0550; e-mail info@comarchitect.org; internet comarchitect.org; f. 1964; an asscn of 38 socs of architects in various Commonwealth countries; objectives: to facilitate the reciprocal recognition of professional qualifications; to provide a clearing house for information on architectural practice; and to encourage collaboration. Plenary confs every three years; regional confs are also held; Exec. Dir TONY GODWIN; publs *Handbook, Objectives and Procedures: CAA Schools Visiting Boards*, *Architectural Education in the Commonwealth* (annotated bibliography of research), *CAA Newsnet* (2 a year), a survey and list of schools of architecture.

Commonwealth Association for Public Administration and Management (CAPAM): 1075 Bay St, Suite 402, Toronto, ON M5S 2B1, Canada; tel. (416) 920-3337; fax (416) 920-6574; e-mail capam@capam.org; internet www.capam.org; f. 1994; aims to promote sound management of the public sector in Commonwealth countries and to assist those countries undergoing political or financial reforms; an international awards programme to reward innovation within the public sector was introduced in 1997, and is awarded every 2 years; more than 1,200 individual mems and 80 institutional memberships in some 80 countries; Pres. Hon. JOCELYNE BOURGON (Canada); Exec. Dir GILLIAN MASON (Canada).

SCIENCE AND TECHNOLOGY

Commonwealth Engineers' Council: c/o Institution of Civil Engineers, 1 Great George St, London, SW1P 3AA; tel. (20) 7665-2005; fax (20) 7223-1806; e-mail neil.bailey@ice.org.uk; internet www.ice.org.uk/cec; f. 1946; the Council is a virtual organization that links engineering institutions across the Commonwealth, providing them with an opportunity to exchange views on collaboration and mutual support; mems: 46 institutions in 44 countries; Pres. Prof. TONY RIDLEY; Sec.-Gen. TOM FOULKES.

Commonwealth Geological Surveys Forum: c/o Commonwealth Science Council, CSC Earth Sciences Programme, Marlborough House, Pall Mall, London, SW1Y 5HX; tel. (20) 7839-3411; fax (20) 7839-6174; e-mail comsci@gn.apc.org; f. 1948 to promote collaboration in geological, geochemical, geophysical and remote sensing techniques and the exchange of information; Geological Programme Officer Dr SIYAN MALOMO.

SPORT

Commonwealth Games Federation: 2nd Floor, 138 Piccadilly, London, W1J 7NR; tel. (20) 7491-8801; fax (20) 7409-7803; e-mail info@thecgf.com; internet www.thecgf.com; the Games were first held in 1930 and are now held every four years; participation is limited to competitors representing the mem. countries of the Commonwealth; 2010 games: New Delhi, India, in October; mems: 72 affiliated bodies; Pres. MICHAEL FENNELL; CEO MICHAEL HOOPER.

YOUTH

Commonwealth Youth Exchange Council: 7 Lion Yard, Tremadoc Rd, London, SW4 7NQ; tel. (20) 7498-6151; fax (20) 7622-4365; e-mail mail@cyec.org.uk; internet www.cyec.org.uk; f. 1970; promotes contact between groups of young people of the United Kingdom and other Commonwealth countries by means of educational exchange visits, provides information for organizers and allocates grants; provides host governments with technical assistance for delivery of the Commonwealth Youth Forum, held every two years (2007: Uganda); 222 mem. orgs; Chief Exec. V. S. G. CRAGGS; publs *Contact* (handbook), *Exchange* (newsletter), *Final Communiqués*(of the Commonwealth Youth Forums), *Safety and Welfare* (guide-lines for Commonwealth Youth Exchange groups).

Duke of Edinburgh's Award International Association: Award House, 7–11 St Matthew St, London, SW1P 2JT; tel. (20) 7222-4242; fax (20) 7222-4141; e-mail sect@intaward.org; internet www.intaward.org; f. 1956; offers a programme of leisure activities for young people, comprising Service, Expeditions, Physical Recreation, and Skills; operates in more than 60 countries (not confined to the Commonwealth); International Sec.-Gen. GILLY SHIRAZI; publs *Award World* (2 a year), *Annual Report*, handbooks and guides.

MISCELLANEOUS

Commonwealth Countries League: 7 The Park, London, NW11 7SS; tel. (20) 8451-6711; e-mail info@ccl-int.org.uk; internet www .ccl-int.org.uk; f. 1925 to secure equal opportunities and status between men and women in the Commonwealth, to act as a link between Commonwealth women's orgs, and to promote and finance secondary education of disadvantaged girls of high ability in their own countries, through the CCL Educational Fund; holds meetings with speakers and an annual conf., organizes the annual Commonwealth Fair for fund-raising; individual mems and affiliated socs in the Commonwealth; Sec. STUART HETHERINGTON-BELL; publs *CCL Newsletter* (3 a year), *Annual Report*.

Commonwealth War Graves Commission: 2 Marlow Rd, Maidenhead, Berks, SL6 7DX; tel. (1628) 634221; fax (1628) 771208; internet www.cwgc.org; casualty and cemetery enquiries; e-mail casualty.enq@cwgc.org; f. 1917 (as Imperial War Graves Commission); responsible for the commemoration in perpetuity of the 1.7m. members of the Commonwealth Forces who died during the wars of 1914–18 and 1939–45; provides for the marking and maintenance of war graves and memorials at some 23,000 locations in 150 countries; mems: Australia, Canada, India, New Zealand, South Africa, United Kingdom; Pres. HRH The Duke of KENT; Dir-Gen. RICHARD KELLAWAY.

Council of Commonwealth Societies: c/o Royal Commonwealth Society, 25 Northumberland Ave, London, WC2N 5AP; tel. (20) 7766-9200; fax (20) 7930-9705; e-mail ccs@rcsint.org; internet www .commonwealthday.com; f. 1947; provides a forum for the exchange of information regarding activities of mem. orgs which promote understanding among countries of the Commonwealth; co-ordinates the distribution of the Commonwealth Day message by Queen Elizabeth, organizes the observance of Commonwealth Day and produces educational materials relating to the occasion; mems: 13 unofficial Commonwealth orgs and four official bodies; Chair. Sir PETER MARSHALL; Sec. Sir DAVID THORNE.

Royal Commonwealth Ex-Services League: 48 Pall Mall, London, SW1Y 5JG; tel. (20) 7973-7263; fax (20) 7973-7308; e-mail mgordon-roe@commonwealthveterans.org.uk; internet www .commonwealthveterans.org.uk; links the ex-service orgs in the Commonwealth, assists ex-servicemen of the Crown who are resident abroad; holds triennial confs; 57 mem. orgs in 48 countries; Grand Pres. HRH The Duke of EDINBURGH; publ. *Annual Report*.

Royal Commonwealth Society: 25 Northumberland Ave, London, WC2N 5AP; tel. (20) 7930-6733; fax (20) 7930-9705; e-mail info@ rcsint.org; internet www.rcsint.org; f. 1868; to promote international understanding of the Commonwealth and its people; organizes meetings and seminars on topical issues, and cultural and social events; library housed by Cambridge University Library; more than 10,000 mems; Chair. Baroness PRASHAR; Dir STUART MOLE; publs *Annual Report, Newsletter* (3 a year), conference reports.

Royal Over-Seas League: Over-Seas House, Park Place, St James's St, London, SW1A 1LR; tel. (20) 7408-0214; fax (20) 7499-6738; e-mail info@rosl.org.uk; internet www.rosl.org.uk; f. 1910 to promote friendship and understanding in the Commonwealth; clubhouses in London and Edinburgh; membership is open to all British subjects and Commonwealth citizens; Dir-Gen. ROBERT F. NEWELL; publ. *Overseas* (quarterly).

Victoria League for Commonwealth Friendship: 55 Leinster Sq., London, W2 4PW; tel. (20) 7243-2633; fax (20) 7229-2994; e-mail victorialeaguehq@btconnect.com; internet www.victorialeague.co .uk; f. 1901; aims to further personal friendship among Commonwealth peoples and to provide hospitality for visitors; maintains Student House, providing accommodation for students from Commonwealth countries; has brs elsewhere in the UK and abroad; Chair. JOHN KELLY; Gen. Sec. JOHN M. W. ALLAN; publ. *Annual Report*.

ECONOMIC COMMUNITY OF WEST AFRICAN STATES—ECOWAS

Address: ECOWAS Executive Secretariat, 60 Yakubu Gowon Crescent, PMB 401, Asokoro, Abuja, Nigeria.

Telephone: (9) 3147647; **fax:** (9) 3147646; **e-mail:** info@ecowas.int; **internet:** www.ecowas.int.

The Treaty of Lagos, establishing ECOWAS, was signed in May 1975 by 15 states, with the object of promoting trade, co-operation and self-reliance in West Africa. Outstanding protocols bringing certain key features of the Treaty into effect were ratified in November 1976. Cape Verde joined in 1977. A revised ECOWAS treaty, designed to accelerate economic integration and to increase political co-operation, was signed in July 1993.

MEMBERS

Benin	Ghana	Niger
Burkina Faso	Guinea	Nigeria
Cape Verde	Guinea-Bissau	Senegal
Côte d'Ivoire	Liberia	Sierra Leone
The Gambia	Mali	Togo

Organization

(September 2007)

AUTHORITY OF HEADS OF STATE AND GOVERNMENT

The Authority is the supreme decision-making organ of the Community, with responsibility for its general development and realization of its objectives. The Chairman is elected annually by the Authority from among the member states. The Authority meets at least once a year in ordinary session.

COUNCIL OF MINISTERS

The Council consists of two representatives from each member country; the chairmanship is held by a minister from the same member state as the Chairman of the Authority. The Council meets at least twice a year, and is responsible for the running of the Community.

ECOWAS COMMISSION

The ECOWAS Commission, formerly the Executive Secretariat, was inaugurated in January 2007, following a decision to implement a process of structural reform taken at the January 2006 summit meeting of the Authority. Comprising a President, a Vice-President and seven Commissioners, the Commission is elected for a four-year term, which may be renewed once only.

President: Dr MOHAMED IBN CHAMBAS (Ghana).

SPECIALIZED TECHNICAL COMMISSIONS

There are eight technical commissions, comprising representatives of each member state, which prepare Community projects and programmes in the following areas:

(i) Food and Agriculture;

(ii) Industry, Science and Technology, and Energy;

(iii) Environment and Natural Resources;

(iv) Transport, Communications, and Tourism;

(v) Trade, Customs, Taxation, Statistics, and Money and Payments;

(vi) Political, Judicial and Legal Affairs, Regional Security, and Immigration;

(vii) Human Resources, Information, and Social and Cultural Affairs; and

(viii) Administration and Finance.

ECOWAS PARLIAMENT

The inaugural session of the 120-member ECOWAS Parliament, based in Abuja, Nigeria, was held in November 2000. The January 2006 summit meeting of the Authority determined to restructure the Parliament, in line with a process of wider institutional reform. The number of seats was reduced from 120 to 115 and each member of the Parliament was to be elected for a four-year term (reduced from five years). The second legislature was inaugurated in November 2006. There is a co-ordinating administrative bureau, comprising a speaker and four deputy speakers, and there are also eight standing committees (reduced in number from 13) covering each of the Parliament's areas of activity.

Speaker: MAHAMANE OUSMANE (Niger).

ECOWAS COURT OF JUSTICE

The Court of Justice, established in January 2001, is based in Abuja, Nigeria, and comprises seven judges who serve a five-year renewable term of office. At the January 2006 summit meeting the Authority approved the creation of a Judicial Council, comprising qualified and experienced persons, to contribute to the establishment of community laws. The Authority also approved the inauguration of an appellate division within the Court. The judges will hold (non-renewable) tenure for four years.

President: AMINATA MALLE SANOGO.

Activities

ECOWAS aims to promote co-operation and development in economic, social and cultural activity, particularly in the fields for which specialized technical commissions (see above) are appointed, to raise the standard of living of the people of the member countries, increase and maintain economic stability, improve relations among member countries and contribute to the progress and development of Africa. ECOWAS is committed to abolishing all obstacles to the free movement of people, services and capital, and to promoting: harmonization of agricultural policies; common projects in marketing, research and the agriculturally-based industries; joint development of economic and industrial policies and elimination of disparities in levels of development; and common monetary policies. The ECOWAS treaty provides for compensation for states whose import duties are reduced through trade liberalization and contains a clause permitting safeguard measures in favour of any country affected by economic disturbances through the application of the treaty.

Initial slow progress in achieving many of ECOWAS' aims was attributed to the reluctance of some governments to implement policies at the national level, their failure to provide the agreed financial resources, and the absence of national links with the Secretariat; to the high cost of compensating loss of customs revenue; and to the existence of numerous other intergovernmental organizations in the region (in particular the Union économique et monétaire ouest-africaine—UEMOA, which replaced the francophone Communauté économique de l'Afrique de l'ouest in 1994). In respect of the latter obstacle to progress, however, ECOWAS and UEMOA resolved in February 2000 to create a single monetary zone (see below). In October ECOWAS and the European Union (EU) held their first joint high-level meeting, at which the EU pledged financial support for ECOWAS' economic integration programme, and, in April 2001 it was announced that the IMF had agreed to provide technical assistance for the programme.

A revised treaty for the Community was drawn up by an ECOWAS Committee of Eminent Persons in 1991–92, and was signed at the ECOWAS summit conference that took place in Cotonou, Benin, in July 1993. The treaty, which was to extend economic and political co-operation among member states, designated the achievement of a common market and a single currency as economic objectives, while in the political sphere it envisaged the establishment of an ECOWAS parliament, an economic and social council, and an ECOWAS court of justice to enforce Community decisions. The treaty also formally assigned the Community with the responsibility of preventing and settling regional conflicts. At a summit meeting held in Abuja, Nigeria, in August 1994, ECOWAS heads of state and government signed a protocol agreement for the establishment of a regional parliament. The meeting also adopted a Convention on Extradition of non-political offenders. The new ECOWAS treaty entered into effect in August 1995, having received the required number of ratifications. A draft protocol providing for the creation of a mechanism for the prevention, management and settlement of conflicts, and for the maintenance of peace in the region, was approved by ECOWAS heads of state and government in December 1999. The protocol establishing the ECOWAS Parliament came into effect in March 2000. The inaugural session of the Parliament was held in Abuja, Nigeria, in November, and in January 2001 the seven judges of the ECOWAS Court of Justice were sworn in. In December Mauritania withdrew from ECOWAS.

In May 2002 the ECOWAS Authority met in Yamoussoukro, Côte d'Ivoire, to develop a regional plan of action for the implementation of the New Partnership for Africa's Development (NEPAD).

In February 2005 ECOWAS briefly suspended Togo's membership of the Community and imposed an arms embargo on that country and a travel ban on its leaders, owing to the unconstitutional installation of a new President; the sanctions against Togo were reversed when the illegal appointment was withdrawn at the end of the month. In May, in response to unrest in Togo following the allegedly fraudulent election there of Faure Gnassingbé as President, ECOWAS organized a 'mini-summit' meeting, attended by Gnassingbé himself and the leader of the opposition Union des forces de changement, at the conclusion of which, in a communiqué, the Community urged the establishment of a government of national unity in Togo.

In January 2006 the Authority, meeting in Niamey, Niger, commended the recent establishment of an ECOWAS Project Development and Implementation Unit, aimed at accelerating the implementation of regional infrastructural projects in sectors such as energy, telecommunications and transport. Also at that meeting the Authority approved further amendments to the revised ECOWAS treaty to provide for institutional reform (see above).

Meeting in Abuja, Nigeria, in June 2007, the Authority adopted a long-term ECOWAS Strategic Vision, detailing the proposed establishment by 2020 of a West African region-wide borderless, stateless space and single economic community.

TRADE AND MONETARY UNION

Under the founding ECOWAS treaty elimination of tariffs and other obstructions to trade among member states, and the establishment of a common external tariff, were planned over a transitional period of 15 years, from 1975. At the 1978 Conference of Heads of State and Government it was decided that from May 1979 no member state might increase its customs tariff on goods from another member. This was regarded as the first step towards the abolition of customs duties within the Community. During the first two years import duties on intra-community trade were to be maintained, and then eliminated in phases over the next eight years. Quotas and other restrictions of equivalent effect were to be abolished in the first 10 years. It was envisaged that in the remaining five years all differences between external customs tariffs would be abolished.

In 1980 ECOWAS heads of state and government decided to establish a free-trade area for unprocessed agricultural products and handicrafts from May 1981. Tariffs on industrial products made by specified community enterprises were also to be abolished from that date, but implementation was delayed by difficulties in defining the enterprises. From 1 January 1990 tariffs were eliminated on 25 listed items manufactured in ECOWAS member states. Over the ensuing decade, tariffs on other industrial products were to be eliminated as follows: the 'most-developed' countries of ECOWAS (Côte d'Ivoire, Ghana, Nigeria and Senegal) were to abolish tariffs on 'priority' products within four years and on 'non-priority' products within six years; the second group (Benin, Guinea, Liberia, Sierra Leone and Togo) were to abolish tariffs on 'priority' products within six years, and on 'non-priority' products within eight years; and the 'least-developed' members (Burkina Faso, Cape Verde, The Gambia, Guinea-Bissau, Mali and Niger) were to abolish tariffs on 'priority' products within eight years and on 'non-priority' products within 10 years. By December 2000 only Benin had removed tariffs on all industrial products. During 2007 all 15 ECOWAS member states were participating in the negotiation phase, with the common external tariff due to be finalized by the end of that year.

In 1990 ECOWAS heads of state and government agreed to adopt measures that would create a single monetary zone and remove barriers to trade in goods that originated in the Community. ECOWAS regards monetary union as necessary to encourage investment in the region, since it would greatly facilitate capital transactions with foreign countries. In September 1992 it was announced that, as part of efforts to enhance monetary co-operation and financial harmonization in the region, the West African Clearing House was to be restructured as the West African Monetary Agency (WAMA). As a specialized agency of ECOWAS, WAMA was to be responsible for administering an ECOWAS exchange rate system (EERS) and for establishing the single monetary zone. A credit guarantee scheme and travellers' cheque system were to be established in association with the EERS. The agreement founding WAMA was signed by the Governors of the central banks of ECOWAS member states, meeting in Banjul, The Gambia, in March 1996. In July the Authority agreed to impose a common value-added tax (VAT) on consumer goods, in order to rationalize indirect taxation and to stimulate greater intra-Community trade. In August 1997 ECOWAS heads of state and government appointed an ad hoc monitoring committee to promote and oversee the implementation of trade liberalization measures and the establishment of a single monetary zone. The meeting also authorized the introduction of the regional travellers' cheque scheme. In October 1998 the travellers' cheque scheme was formally inaugurated at a meeting of ECOWAS heads of state. The cheques were to be issued by WAMA in denominations of a West African Unit of Account and convertible into each local currency at the rate of one Special Drawing Right (SDR—see IMF). The cheques entered into circulation on 1 July 1999. In March 1998 senior customs officials of ECOWAS countries agreed to harmonize customs policies and administrations, in order to facilitate intra-Community trade, and to pursue the objective of establishing a common external tariff by 2000. However, this deadline was not met. In December 1999 the ECOWAS Authority determined to pursue a 'Fast Track Approach' to economic integration, involving a two-track implementation of related measures. In April 2000 seven, predominantly anglophone, ECOWAS member states—Cape Verde, The Gambia, Ghana, Guinea, Liberia, Nigeria and Sierra Leone—issued the 'Accra Declaration', in which they agreed to establish a second West African monetary union (the West African Monetary Zone—WAMZ) to co-exist initially alongside UEMOA, which unites eight, mainly francophone, ECOWAS member states. As preconditions for adopting a single currency and common monetary and exchange rate policy, the member states of the second West African monetary union were to attain a number of convergence criteria, including: a satisfactory level of price stability; sustainable budget deficits; a reduction in inflation; and the maintenance of an adequate level of foreign exchange reserves. The two complementary monetary unions were expected to harmonize their economic programmes, with a view to effecting an eventual merger, as outlined in an action plan adopted by ECOWAS and UEMOA in February 2000. The ECOWAS Authority summit held in December in Bamako, Mali, adopted an Agreement Establishing the WAMZ, approved the establishment of a West African Monetary Institute to prepare for the formation of a West African Central Bank, and determined that the harmonization of member countries' tariff structures should be accelerated to facilitate the implementation of the planned customs union. In December 2001 the Authority determined that the currency of the WAMZ (and eventually the ECOWAS-wide currency) would be known as the 'eco' and authorized the establishment during 2002 of an exchange rate mechanism. (This was achieved in April.) Meeting in November 2002 the heads of state and government determined that a forum of ministers of finance from the planned second monetary union should be convened on a regular basis to ensure the effective implementation of fiscal policies. In May 2004 ECOWAS and UEMOA signed a co-operation agreement that provided for the establishment of a Joint Technical Secretariat to enhance the co-ordination of their programmes. Owing to slower-than-anticipated progress in achieving the convergence criteria required for monetary union, the deadline for the inauguration of the WAMZ and launch of the 'eco' was most recently set at 2009.

In January 2006 the Authority approved the implementation of a four-band common external tariff that was to align the WAMZ tariff structure with that of UEMOA, as follows: a 0% tariff would be applied to social goods (for example, educational and medical equipment); 5% would be levied on raw materials and most agricultural inputs; 10% on intermediate goods and rice; and 20% on finished consumer products. At the inaugural meeting of the Joint ECOWAS–UEMOA Management Committee of the ECOWAS Common External Tariff, convened in July 2006, members agreed on a roadmap for implementing the uniform tariff system. The roadmap also outline the legal framework for the introduction of the common external tariff.

In December 1992 ECOWAS ministers agreed on the institutionalization of an ECOWAS trade fair, in order to promote trade liberalization and intra-Community trade. The first trade fair was held in Dakar, Senegal, in 1995; the second was staged in Accra, Ghana, in 1999; and the third fair, at which it was decided that, in future, the event should be biennial, took place in Lomé, Togo, in 2003. A fourth fair was held in Lagos, Nigeria, in October 2005, and the fifth was to take place in Burkina Faso, in March 2008.

TRAVEL, TRANSPORT AND COMMUNICATIONS

In 1979 ECOWAS heads of state signed a Protocol relating to free circulation of the region's citizens and to rights of residence and establishment of commercial enterprises. The first provision (the right of entry without a visa) came into force in 1980. An optional ECOWAS travel certificate, valid for travel within the Community in place of a national passport, was established in July 1985. The second provision of the 1979 Protocol, allowing unlimited rights of residence, was signed in 1986 (although Nigeria indicated that unskilled workers and certain categories of professionals would not be allowed to stay for an indefinite period) and came into force in 1989. The third provision, concerning the right to establish a commercial enterprise in another member state was signed in 1990. In July 1992 the ECOWAS Authority formulated a Minimum Agenda for Action for the implementation of Community agreements regarding the free movement of goods and people, for example the removal of non-tariff barriers, the simplification of customs and transit procedures and a reduction in the number of control posts on international roads. However, implementation of the Minimum Agenda was slow. In April 1997 Gambian and Senegalese finance and trade officials concluded an agreement on measures to facilitate the export of goods via Senegal to neighbouring countries, in accordance with ECOWAS protocols relating to inter-state road transit arrangements. An Inter-state Road Transit Authority has been established. A Brown Card scheme provides recognized third-party liability insurance throughout the region. In October 2001 an ECOWAS passport was reported to be ready for issuance; the ECOWAS travel certificate was to remain in operation, while national passports were to be gradually eliminated over a period of five years. Senegal and Benin were the first two member states to issue the ECOWAS passport, which was approved by the Community's heads of state and government in January 2003.

In February 1996 ECOWAS and several private-sector partners established ECOAir Ltd, based in Abuja, Nigeria, which was to develop a regional airline. A regional shipping company, ECOMARINE, commenced operations in February 2003.

In August 1996 the initial phase of a programme to improve regional telecommunications was reported to have been completed. A second phase of the programme (INTELCOM II), which aimed to modernize and expand the region's telecommunications services, was initiated by ECOWAS heads of state in August 1997. A West African Telecommunications Regulators' Association was established, under the auspices of ECOWAS, in September 2000. A harmonization programme to create a common, liberalized telecommunications market was expected to be completed by 2008. The January 2006 summit meeting of the Authority approved a new Special Fund for Telecommunications to facilitate improvements to cross-border telecommunications connectivity. In May of that year a meeting of ECOWAS ministers of information and telecommunications was convened, during which guide-lines for harmonizing the telecommunications sector were agreed.

A programme for the development of an integrated regional road network was adopted in 1980. Under the programme, two major trans-regional roads were to be completed: the Trans-Coastal Highway, linking Lagos, Nigeria, with Nouackchott, Mauritania (4,767 km); and the Trans-Sahelian Highway, linking Dakar, Senegal, with N'Djamena, Chad (4,633 km). By the end of 2000 about 83% of the trans-coastal route was reportedly complete, and about 87% of the trans-Sahelian route. In 2003 the African Development Bank agreed to finance a study on interconnection of the region's railways.

ECONOMIC AND INDUSTRIAL DEVELOPMENT

In November 1984 ECOWAS heads of state and government approved the establishment of a private regional investment bank, to be known as Ecobank Transnational Inc. The bank, which was based in Lomé, Togo, opened in March 1988. ECOWAS has a 10% share in the bank.

The West African Industrial Forum, sponsored by ECOWAS, is held every two years to promote regional industrial investment. Community ministers of industry are implementing an action plan on the formulation of a West African Industrial Master Plan identifying strategies for stimulating regional economic development and attracting external investment.

In September 1995 Nigeria, Ghana, Togo and Benin resolved to develop a gas pipeline to connect Nigerian gas supplies to the other countries. In August 1999 the participating countries, together with two petroleum companies operating in Nigeria, signed an agreement on the financing and construction of the 600-km West African Gas Pipeline, which was to extend from the Nigerian capital, Lagos, to Takoradi, Togo. It was expected to become operational in 2007. The implementation of a planned energy exchange scheme, known as the West African Power Pool Project (WAPP), is envisaged as a means of efficiently utilizing the region's hydro-electricity and thermal power capabilities by transferring power from surplus producers to countries unable to meet their energy requirements. In May 2003 the Community decided to initiate the first phase of WAPP, which was to be implemented in Benin, Côte d'Ivoire, Ghana, Niger, Nigeria and Togo at an estimated cost of US $335m. In January 2005 the Authority endorsed a revised masterplan for the implementation of WAPP, which was scheduled to be completed by 2020. In July 2005 the World Bank approved a $350m.-facility to support the implementation of WAPP. ECOWAS is also developing an initiative aimed at promoting the use of renewable energy resources.

REGIONAL SECURITY

In 1990 a Standing Mediation Committee was formed to mediate disputes between member states. Member states reaffirmed their commitment to refrain from aggression against one another at a summit conference in 1991. The revised ECOWAS treaty, signed in July 1993, incorporates a separate provision for regional security, requiring member states to work towards the maintenance of peace, stability and security.

In December 1997 an extraordinary meeting of ECOWAS heads of state and government was convened in Lomé, Togo, to consider the future stability and security of the region. It was agreed that a permanent mechanism should be established for conflict prevention and the maintenance of peace. ECOWAS leaders also reaffirmed their commitment to pursuing dialogue to prevent conflicts, co-operating in the early deployment of peace-keeping forces and implementing measures to counter trans-border crime and the illegal trafficking of armaments and drugs. At the meeting ECOWAS leaders acknowledged the role of the ECOWAS Cease-fire Monitoring Group (ECOMOG) in restoring constitutional order in Liberia and expressed their appreciation of the force's current efforts in Sierra Leone (see below). In March 1998 ECOWAS ministers of foreign affairs, meeting in Yamoussoukro, Côte d'Ivoire, resolved that ECOMOG should become the region's permanent peace-keeping force, and upheld the decision of heads of state regarding the establishment of a new body, which should be used to observe, analyse and monitor the security situation in the West African region. Ministers agreed to undertake a redefinition of the command structure within the organization in order to strengthen decision-making and the legal status of the ECOMOG force.

In July 1998 ECOWAS ministers of defence and of security adopted a draft mechanism for conflict management, peace-keeping and security, which provided for ECOWAS intervention in the internal affairs of member states, where a conflict or military uprising threatened the region's security. In October the ECOWAS Authority determined to implement a renewable three-year moratorium on the import, export or manufacture of small armaments in order to enhance the security of the sub-region. In March 1999 the Programme of Co-ordination and Assistance for Security and Development (PCASED) was launched to complement the moratorium. The moratorium was renewed for a further three years in July 2001. (In 2004 ECOWAS announced its intention to transform the moratorium into a convention and PCASED was decommissioned.) The Authority also issued a declaration on the control and prevention of drug abuse, agreeing to allocate US $150,000 to establish an Eco-Drug Fund to finance regional activities in countering substance abuse. In June 2006 the Authority adopted the ECOWAS Convention on Small Arms and Light Weapons, their Ammunitions and other Materials, with the aim of regulating the importation and manufacture of such weapons. The ECOWAS Small Arms Control Programme (ECOSAP) was launched in that month, aimed at improving the capacity of national and regional institutions to reduce the proliferation of small weapons across the region. Based in Bamako, Mali, the Programme replaced PCASED and was expected to run for five years. A three-year work programme was to be implemented to provide technical support to the ECOWAS member states and the newly inaugurated ECOWAS Small Arms Unit. Representatives from ECOWAS member states met in Ouagadougou, Burkina Faso, in September 2007 to draft a new West African strategy for enhanced drug control.

The summit meeting of ECOWAS heads of state and government held in December 1999 in Lomé, Togo, approved a draft protocol to the organization's treaty, providing for the establishment of a Permanent Mechanism for the Prevention, Management and Settlement of Conflicts and the Maintenance of Peace in the Region, as envisaged at their conference in December 1997, and for the creation in connection with the Mechanism of a Mediation and Security Council, to comprise representatives of 10 member states, elected for two-year terms. The Mediation and Security Council was to be supported by an advisory Council of Elders, comprising 32 eminent statesmen from the region; this was inaugurated in July 2001. ECOMOG was to be transformed from an ad hoc cease-fire monitoring group (see below) into a permanent standby force available for immediate deployment to avert emerging conflicts in the region. During 1999 ECOWAS member states established the Intergovernmental Action Group Against Money Laundering in Africa (GIABA), which was mandated to combat drug-trafficking and money laundering throughout the region; a revised regulation for GIABA adopted by the Authority in January 2006 expanded the Group's mandate to cover regional responsibility for combating terrorism. In December 2006 a Technical Committee of Experts on Political Affairs, Peace and Security was established as a subsidiary body of the Mediation and Security Council.

In 2002 ECOWAS, with assistance from the USA, was developing an early warning system for monitoring threats to regional security. In June 2004 the Community approved the establishment of a standby unit of 6,500 troops, including a core rapid reaction component—the ECOWAS Task Force—comprising 1,500 soldiers (deployable within 30 days), a reserve of 1,500 troops, and 3,500 additional troops that could, as necessary, augment the numbers of the Task Force to brigade level (deployable with up to 90 days notice). The ECOWAS Defence and Security Commission approved the operational framework for the standby unit in April 2005.

In October 2006 it was reported that ECOWAS planned to introduce a series of initiatives in each of the member states under the Peace and Development Project (PADEP). The Project intended to foster a 'culture of peace' among the member states of ECOWAS, strengthening social cohesion and promoting economic integration, democracy and good governance.

Peace-keeping Operations

In August 1990 the ECOMOG cease-fire monitoring group was dispatched to Liberia in an attempt to enforce a cease-fire between conflicting factions there, to restore public order, and to establish an interim government, until elections could be held. In November a temporary cease-fire was agreed by the protagonists in Liberia, and an interim president was installed by ECOMOG. Following the signature of a new cease-fire agreement a national conference, organized by ECOWAS in March 1991, established a temporary government, pending elections to be held in early 1992. In June 1991 ECOWAS established a committee (initially comprising representatives of five member states, later expanded to nine) to co-ordinate the peace negotiations. In September, at a meeting in Yamoussoukro, Côte d'Ivoire, held under the aegis of the ECOWAS committee, two of the rival factions in Liberia agreed to encamp their troops in designated areas and to disarm under ECOMOG supervision. During the period preceding the proposed elections, ECOMOG was to occupy Liberian air and sea ports, and create a 'buffer zone' along the country's border with Sierra Leone. By September 1992, however, ECOMOG had been unable either to effect the disarmament of two of the principal military factions, the National Patriotic Front of Liberia (NPFL) and the United Liberation Movement of Liberia for Democracy (ULIMO), or to occupy positions in substantial areas of the country, as a result of resistance on the part of the NPFL. The proposed elections were consequently postponed indefinitely.

In October 1992 ECOMOG began offensive action against NPFL positions, with a campaign of aerial bombardment. In November ECOWAS imposed a land, sea and air blockade on the NPFL's territory, in response to the Front's refusal to comply with the Yamoussoukro accord of October 1991. In April 1993 ECOMOG announced that the disarmament of ULIMO had been completed, amid widespread accusations that ECOMOG had supported ULIMO against the NPFL, and was no longer a neutral force. An ECOWAS-brokered cease-fire agreement was signed in Cotonou, Benin, in July, and took effect on 1 August. In September a UN observer mission (UNOMIL) was established in Liberia to work alongside ECOMOG in monitoring the process of disarming troops, as well as to verify the impartiality of ECOMOG.

In September 1994 leaders of Liberia's main military factions, having negotiated with representatives of ECOWAS, the Organization of African Unity (OAU, now the African Union—AU) and the UN, signed an amendment to the Cotonou accord in Akosombo, Ghana. This provided for a new five-member Council of State, in the context of a cease-fire, as a replacement to the expired interim executive authority, and established a new timetable for democratic elections. In early 1995 negotiations to secure a peace settlement, conducted under ECOWAS auspices, collapsed, owing to disagreement on the composition of the new Council of State. In May, in an attempt to ease the political deadlock, ECOWAS heads of state and of government met leaders of the six main warring factions. Under continuing pressure from the international community, the leaders of the Liberian factions signed a new peace accord, in Abuja, Nigeria, in August. This political development led to renewed efforts on the part of ECOWAS countries to strengthen ECOMOG, and by October Burkina Faso, Nigeria, Ghana and Guinea had pledged troop contributions to increase the force's strength from 7,268 to 12,000. In accordance with the peace agreement, ECOMOG forces, with UNOMIL, were to be deployed throughout Liberia and along its borders to prevent the flow of arms into the country and to monitor the disarmament of the warring parties. In December an attack on ECOMOG troops, by a dissident ULIMO faction (ULIMO–J), disrupted the deployment of the multinational forces and the disarmament process, which was scheduled to commence in mid-January 1996. At least 16 members of the peace-keeping force were killed in the fighting that ensued. Clashes between ECOMOG and the ULIMO–J forces continued in the west of the country in late December 1995 and early January 1996, during which time 130 Nigerian members of ECOMOG were held hostage. In April, following a series of violations of the cease-fire, serious hostilities erupted in the Liberian capital, Monrovia, between government forces and dissident troops. An initial agreement to end the fighting, negotiated under ECOWAS auspices, was unsuccessful; however, it secured the release of several civilians and soldiers who had been taken hostage during the civil disruption. Later in April a further cease-fire agreement was concluded, under the aegis of the US Government, the UN and ECOWAS. In May ministers of foreign affairs of the countries constituting the ECOWAS Committee of Nine advocated that all armed factions be withdrawn from Monrovia and that ECOMOG troops be deployed throughout the capital in order to re-establish the city's 'safe-haven' status. According to the Committee's demands, all property, armaments and equipment seized unlawfully from civilians, ECOMOG and other international organizations during the fighting were to be returned, while efforts to disarm the warring factions and to pursue the restoration of democracy in the country were to be resumed. At the end of May the deployment of ECOMOG troops was initiated. In August a new cease-fire accord was signed by the leaders of the principal factions in Liberia, which envisaged the completion of the disarmament process by the end of January 1997, with elections to be held in May. The disarmament process began in November 1996, and by the end of January 1997 ECOMOG confirmed that 23,000 of the targeted 30,000–35,000 soldiers had been disarmed. The deadline for disarmament was extended by seven days, during which time a further 1,500 soldiers were reported to have been disarmed. However, vigilante attacks by remaining armed faction fighters persisted. The Committee of Nine announced in February that presidential and legislative elections would be held in May, later revising the election schedule to mid-July. ECOMOG was to withdraw from Liberia six months after the election date, until which time it had proposed to offer security for the incoming government and to provide training for a new unified Liberian army. The Committee also agreed, in consultation with the Council of State, to replace the existing Electoral Commission with a new Commission comprising seven members, to reflect all aspects of Liberian society. The Chairman would be selected from among the seven, in consultation with ECOWAS, which along with the UN and the OAU, would act as a 'technical adviser' to the Commission. ECOMOG deployed additional troops, who were joined by other international observers in ensuring that the elections were conducted in the necessary conditions of security. In August, following the inauguration of Charles Taylor (formerly leader of the NPFL) as Liberia's democratically-elected President, ECOWAS heads of state agreed that the ECOMOG force in Liberia was to be reconstituted and would henceforth assist in the process of national reconstruction, including the restructuring of the armed and security forces, and the maintenance of security; it was further envisaged that ECOMOG's mandate (officially due to expire in February 1998) would be extended in agreement with the Liberian Government. A Status of Forces Agreement, which defined ECOMOG's post-conflict responsibilities (i.e. capacity-building and maintenance of security) and imposed conditions on the peace-keeping forces remaining in the country, was signed by the Liberian Government and ECOWAS in June 1998. Relations with the Taylor administration, however, deteriorated, owing to accusations that ECOMOG was providing assistance to opposition groupings. The tense political situation, therefore, and the need for greater resources in Sierra Leone, resulted in ECOMOG transferring its headquarters from Monrovia to Freetown in Sierra Leone. The transfer was reported to have been completed by October, with just two ECOMOG battalions remaining in Liberia. The ECOMOG mission in Liberia was effectively terminated in October 1999 when the final declared stocks of rebel armaments were destroyed. In April 2001 the ECOWAS Authority determined to send a Mediation and Security Council mission to Liberia to monitor compliance with a resolution of the UN Security Council imposing sanctions on the Liberian regime. An ECOWAS military team was sent to Liberia in June 2002 to assess continuing unrest in the country. ECOWAS welcomed a Liberian Leadership Forum that was staged in the following month, in Ouagadougou, Burkina Faso, to address means of achieving peace and reconciliation. In September President Taylor lifted the state of emergency in Liberia. In mid-2003, however, rebel groups began to seize territory in south-eastern areas and to launch a siege on Monrovia. In June a cease-fire brokered by ECOWAS was signed, which provided for a transitional government excluding Taylor. One week later, following the President's announcement that he would stay in power until the expiry of his term of office in January 2004, fighting in the capital resumed, resulting in hundreds of civilian casualties. In July 2003 ECOWAS agreed to send a 3,000-strong force to Liberia; later that month, after considerable international pressure, US President George W. Bush agreed to deploy three US warships to the region to support the Community's troops. In early August troops of the ECOWAS Mission in Liberia (ECOMIL) began to arrive in Monrovia, prompting President Taylor to stand down and to leave the country for exile in Nigeria. At the beginning of October authority was transferred from ECOMIL to a newly-inaugurated UN Mission in Liberia (UNMIL), mandated to support the implementation of the cease-fire accord agreed in June and a Comprehensive Peace Agreement concluded by the parties to the conflict in August. ECOMIL's 3,600 troops were reassigned to UNMIL. ECOWAS was to co-operate with UNMIL and other partners to assist the National Transitional Government (inaugurated in mid-October) with the training of a national police force and the restructuring of the military. Through its mediator for the Liberian peace process, ECOWAS has subsequently played an important role in assisting Liberia prepare for presidential and legislative elections, to be held in October 2005. In September 2004 the ECOWAS Court of Justice indicated its readiness to try former Liberian President Taylor in the event that any Liberian or any other national of the sub-region should file an application on his role in the conflict in Liberia and elsewhere in West Africa. In July 2005 an ECOWAS panel was inaugurated to examine the suitability of prospective members of Liberia's Truth and Reconciliation Commission.

In August 1999 a regional meeting was convened, under ECOWAS auspices, to attempt to defuse escalating tensions between Liberia and Guinea following an incursion into northern Liberia by Guinean rebel forces earlier in that month. In September representatives of eight member countries determined to establish a monitoring body to supervise the border region between Guinea, Liberia and Sierra Leone. Insecurity in the area escalated in the latter part of 2000, particularly in southern Guinea, which was increasingly subjected to insurgencies by Sierra Leonean RUF rebels, combated forcefully by Guinean troops, and prompting massive displacement of and severe hardship for the local population, which included significant numbers of refugees who had fled unrest in Liberia and Sierra Leone. Relations between the three countries deteriorated swiftly, amidst mutual accusations and counter-accusations concerning the provision of external support for dissidents in their respective territories. Allegations that the RUF rebels were supported by the Liberian authorities were the subject of a report issued by an independent UN panel of experts in December. During that month the ECOWAS Authority approved the deployment of a 1,700-strong ECOMOG interposition force to act as a buffer in the Guinea-Liberia-Sierra Leone border region, in order to deter the rebel activity and thereby alleviate the ongoing humanitarian crisis. (In early October the grouping's newly-formed Mediation and Security Council had authorized the deployment of a military observer mission to the area.) Meanwhile, the governments of the three (Mano River Union) countries agreed to disarm rebel groups and to prevent these from entering neighbouring countries from their territories. However, the political crisis subsequently intensified, amid mutual expulsions of diplomatic personnel. In April 2001, by which time the presidents of Guinea and Liberia had still not signed the Status of Force Agreement necessary to enable the deployment of the proposed ECOMOG interposition force, the ECOWAS Authority agreed to postpone the deployment indefinitely. In that month an ECOWAS committee, comprising the presidents of Mali, Nigeria and Togo, was established to mediate a resolution to the crisis. From August ministers of foreign affairs and defence from the three Mano River Union countries held a series of meetings to address the situation. The deployment of the ECOMOG interposition force remained suspended.

In May 1997 the democratically-elected Sierra Leonean leader, President Ahmed Tejan Kabbah, was overthrown by a military coup involving officers of the national army and RUF rebels. Nigerian forces based in Sierra Leone as part of a bilateral defence pact attempted to restore constitutional order. Their numbers were strengthened by the arrival of more than 700 Nigerian soldiers and two naval vessels which had been serving under the ECOMOG mandate in neighbouring Liberia. At the end of June ECOWAS ministers of foreign affairs, convened in Conakry, Guinea, agreed to pursue the objective of restoring a democratic government in Sierra Leone through dialogue and the imposition of economic sanctions. In July a five-member ECOWAS committee, comprising the foreign ministers of Côte d'Ivoire, Ghana, Guinea, Liberia and Nigeria, together with representatives of the OAU, negotiated an agreement with the so-called Armed Forces Revolutionary Council (AFRC) in Sierra Leone to establish an immediate cease-fire and to pursue efforts towards the restoration of constitutional order. In August ECOWAS heads of state reaffirmed the Community's condemnation of the removal of President Kabbah and officially endorsed a series of punitive measures against the AFRC authorities in order to accelerate the restoration of democratic government. The meeting mandated ECOMOG to maintain and monitor the cease-fire and to prevent all goods, excepting essential humanitarian supplies, from entering that country. It was also agreed that the committee on Sierra Leone include Liberia and be convened at the level of heads of state. In October the UN Security Council imposed an embargo on the sale or supply of armaments to Sierra Leone and authorized ECOWAS to ensure implementation of these measures. ECOMOG conducted a number of attacks against commercial and military targets, with the aim of upholding the international sanctions, and clashes occurred between ECOMOG troops and AFRC/RUF soldiers, in particular around the area of Freetown's Lungi international airport which had been seized by ECOMOG. Despite the escalation in hostilities, the ECOWAS Committee of Five pursued negotiations with the military authorities, and at the end of October both sides signed a peace agreement, in Conakry, Guinea, providing for an immediate end to all fighting and the reinstatement of Kabbah's Government by April 1998; all combatants were to be disarmed and demobilized under the supervision of a disarmament committee comprising representatives of ECOMOG, the military authorities and local forces loyal to President Kabbah. In November 1997, however, the peace process was undermined by reports that ECOMOG forces had violated the cease-fire agreement following a series of air raids on Freetown, which ECOMOG claimed to have been in retaliation for attacks by AFRC/RUF-operated anti-aircraft equipment, and a demand by the AFRC authorities that the Nigerian contingent of ECOMOG leave the country. In mid-February 1998, following a series of offensive attacks against forces loyal to the military authorities, ECOMOG assumed control of Freetown and arrested several members of the AFRC/RUC regime. Some 50 AFRC officials were arrested by troops serving under ECOMOG on arrival at James Spriggs Payne Airport in Liberia, prompting protests from the Liberian Government at the Nigerian military intervention. An 11-member supervisory task force, which included the ECOMOG Commander, was established in Sierra Leone to maintain order, pending Kabbah's return from exile. ECOMOG troops subsequently also monitored the removal of the embargo against the use of the airport and port facilities in Freetown. Kabbah returned to Sierra Leone in March and installed a new administration. It was agreed that ECOMOG forces were to remain in the country in order to ensure the full restoration of peace and security, to assist in the restructuring of the armed forces and to help to resolve the problems of the substantial numbers of refugees and internally displaced persons. In early May ECOWAS Chiefs of Staff, meeting in Accra, Ghana, urged member states to provide more troops and logistical support to strengthen the ECOMOG force in Sierra Leone (at that time numbering some 10,000 troops), which was still involved in ongoing clashes with remaining rebel soldiers in eastern regions of the country. The UN established an Observer Mission in Sierra Leone (UNOMSIL) in July, which was to monitor the cease-fire, mainly in areas secured by ECOMOG troops. In October ECOMOG transferred its headquarters to Freetown, in order, partly, to reinforce its presence in the country. In January 1999 rebel soldiers attacked the capital and engaged in heavy fighting with ECOMOG forces, amid reports that the Liberian Government was supporting the rebels. Nigeria dispatched several thousand additional troops to counter the rebel advance and to secure the border with Liberia. In February, however, once ECOMOG had regained control of Freetown, the Nigerian Government expressed its desire to withdraw all of its troops from the peace-keeping force by May, owing to financial restraints. Efforts to negotiate a peace settlement were initiated, with the Chairman of ECOWAS at that time, President Gnassingbé Eyadéma of Togo, actively involved in mediation between the opposing groups, despite persisting reports of fighting between ECOMOG and rebel soldiers in areas east of the capital. A cease-fire agreement was concluded in May, and a political settlement was signed, by Kabbah and the RUF leader, in Lomé, Togo, in July. ECOMOG's mandate in Sierra Leone was adapted to support the consolidation of peace in that country and national reconstruction. In October UNOMSIL was replaced by the UN Mission in Sierra Leone (UNAMSIL), which was to assist with the implementation of the Lomé accord and to assume many of the functions then being performed by ECOMOG, including the provision of security at Lungi international airport and at other key installations, buildings and government institutions in the Freetown area. In consequence the ECOMOG contingent was withdrawn in April 2000. However, following a resurgence of RUF violence in April and May, when as many as 500 members of UNAMSIL (which had not been deployed to full strength) were captured by the rebels, ECOWAS heads of government agreed to reinforce the UN peace-keeping operation with some 3,000 regional troops. A UN Security Council mission to Sierra Leone in September recommended the establishment of a mechanism to co-ordinate the formulation and implementation by the UN, ECOWAS, the Sierra Leone Government and other parties of a unified strategy to resolve the insecurity in Sierra Leone. A new cease-fire accord was agreed by the Sierra Leone Government and the RUF in November, in Abuja, Nigeria, and in January 2002 the process (monitored by UNAMSIL) of disarming, demobilizing and reintegrating former combatants was completed. An ECOWAS observer team was dispatched to monitor legislative and presidential elections that were held in Sierra Leone in May. In April 2001 representatives of the Mediation and Security Council were dispatched to Liberia to monitor, jointly with a UN delegation, the Liberian Government's compliance with a UN Security Council Resolution aimed at ending support for and eradicating RUF activity in that country, and at terminating illicit trading there in Sierra Leonean diamonds.

In July 1998 ECOWAS ministers of defence and of foreign affairs met to consider the political unrest in Guinea-Bissau, following an unsuccessful attempt by rebel soldiers, in June, to overthrow the Government of President João Vieira, and urged both sides to co-operate in negotiating a settlement. An ECOWAS Committee of Seven on Guinea-Bissau (comprising the ministers of foreign affairs of Burkina Faso, Côte d'Ivoire, The Gambia, Ghana, Guinea, Nigeria and Senegal) was established and met for the first time in August. In late August, following mediation by ECOWAS representatives and a contact group of the Comunidade dos Países de Língua Portuguesa (CPLP), which had secured an initial cease-fire, an agreement was signed by the conflicting parties providing for an end to hostilities, the reopening of the international airport to facilitate the provision of humanitarian supplies, and for independent supervision of the cease-fire agreement. ECOWAS subsequently held discussions with the CPLP in order to co-ordinate efforts to secure peace in Guinea-Bissau. In late October ECOWAS heads of state endorsed the deployment of ECOMOG forces in Guinea-Bissau. On 1 November the two sides in the dispute, meeting in Abuja, Nigeria, signed a peace accord under ECOWAS auspices, which reinforced the August cease-fire and incorporated an agreement to establish a government of national unity. ECOMOG forces were to replace all foreign troops, mainly Senegalese, currently in Guinea-Bissau, supervise the security of the border region between those two countries, and enable humanitarian organizations to have free access to those needing assistance. In addition ECOMOG was to be responsible for monitoring the conduct of presidential and legislative elections, scheduled to be held in 1999. In early February President Vieira and the rebel leader Gen. Manè signed a cease-fire accord, under ECOWAS auspices. A new Government of National Unity was established later in that month and an ECOMOG Interposition Force began to be dispatched to Guinea-Bissau. In early May, however, President Vieira was ousted by the rebel forces. Meeting later in that month, in Lomé, Togo, ECOWAS ministers of foreign affairs condemned the overthrow of Vieira. They resolved to withdraw the ECOMOG contingent, at that time numbering 600 troops from Benin, Gabon, Niger and Togo, owing to the political developments and lack of finances. By early June all ECOMOG troops had left Guinea-Bissau. A team of observers was dispatched to Guinea-Bissau to monitor presidential elections held there in July and August 2005.

At the end of September 2002 an extraordinary summit meeting of ECOWAS heads of state and government was convened in Accra, Ghana, to address the violent unrest that had erupted in Côte d'Ivoire during that month, commencing with an attempted *coup d'état* by disloyal elements of the country's armed forces. The summit meeting condemned the attempt to overthrow democratic rule and constitutional order and established a high-level contact group, comprising the heads of state of Ghana, Guinea-Bissau, Mali, Niger, Nigeria and Togo, to prevail upon the rebels to end hostilities, and to negotiate a general framework for the resolution of the crisis. The contact group helped to mediate a cease-fire in the following month; this was to be monitored by an ECOWAS military mission in Côte d'Ivoire (ECOMICI), which was also to be responsible for ensuring safe passage for deliveries of humanitarian assistance. In March 2003, following the conclusion in January by the parties to the conflict of a peace agreement, signed at Marcoussis, France, ECOWAS chiefs of staff endorsed the expansion of ECOMICI from 1,264 to a maximum of 3,411 men, to monitor the implementation of the peace agreement in co-operation with the UN Mission in Côte d'Ivoire (MINUCI), and French forces. In early April 2004 authority was transferred from ECOMICI and MINUCI to the newly-established UN Operation in Côte d'Ivoire (UNOCI). In mid-June ECOWAS heads of state and government convened at a summit to address means of reviving the implementation of the stalled Marcoussis peace accord. A high-level meeting of ECOWAS heads of state and government, other African leaders, the Chairperson of the AU, and the parties to the Côte d'Ivoire conflict, held in Accra in late July, affirmed that a monitoring mechanism, comprising representatives of ECOWAS, the AU, Côte d'Ivoire and the United Nations, should produce regular reports on progress towards peace in Côte d'Ivoire. In October ECOWAS urged the UN to strengthen its peace-keeping mission in Côte d'Ivoire and called for the amendment of the mission's mandate to allow it to use force to prevent armed belligerents from entering the 'zone of confidence' established in the country.

In May 2000 the ECOWAS Authority authorized the initiation of an inquiry into the link between illicit trading in diamonds and ongoing rebel activity in the region, with a particular focus on Liberia and Sierra Leone.

ENVIRONMENTAL PROTECTION

ECOWAS promotes implementation of the UN Convention on Desertification Control and supports programmes initiated at national and sub-regional level within the framework of the treaty. Together with the Permanent Inter-State Committee on Drought Control in the Sahel—CILSS, ECOWAS has been designated as a project leader for implementing the Convention in West Africa. Other environmental initiatives include a regional meteorological project to enhance meteorological activities and applications, and in particular to contribute to food security and natural resource management in the sub-region. ECOWAS pilot schemes have formed the basis of integrated control projects for the control of floating (or invasive aquatic) weeds in five water basins in West Africa, which had hindered the development of the local fishery sectors. In 2005 the African Development Bank granted ECOWAS US $3.1m. to assist in floating weed control. A rural water supply programme aims to ensure adequate water for rural dwellers in order to improve their living standards. The first phase of the project focused on schemes to develop village and pastoral water points in Burkina Faso, Guinea, Mali, Niger and Senegal, with funds from various multilateral donors.

AGRICULTURE AND FISHING

In November 1995 an agro-industrial forum, jointly organized by ECOWAS and the EU, was held in Dakar, Senegal. The forum aimed to facilitate co-operation between companies in the two regions, to develop the agro-industrial sector in West Africa and to promote business opportunities.

In February 2001 ECOWAS ministers of agriculture adopted an action plan for the formulation of a common agricultural policy, as envisaged under the ECOWAS treaty. A draft of the ECOWAS Regional Agricultural Policy (ECOWAP) was endorsed by the January 2005 Authority summit. In January 2006 the Authority approved an action plan for the implementation of ECOWAP. The Policy was aimed at enhancing regional agricultural productivity with a view to guaranteeing food-sufficiency and standards. The Community enforces a transhumance certification scheme for facilitating the monitoring of animal movement and animal health surveillance and protection in the sub-region.

SOCIAL PROGRAMME

Four organizations have been established within ECOWAS by the Executive Secretariat: the Organization of Trade Unions of West Africa, which held its first meeting in 1984; the West African Youth Association; the West African Universities' Association; and the West Africa Women's Association (whose statutes were approved by a meeting of ministers of social affairs in May 1987). Regional sports competitions are held annually. The West African Health Organization (WAHO) was established in 2000 by merger of the West African Health Community and the Organization for Co-ordination and Co-operation in the Struggle against Endemic Diseases. In December 2001 the ECOWAS summit of heads of state and government adopted a plan of action aimed at combating trafficking in human beings and authorized the establishment of an ECOWAS Criminal Intelligence Bureau.

INFORMATION AND MEDIA

In March 1990 ECOWAS ministers of information formulated a policy on the dissemination of information about ECOWAS throughout the region and the appraisal of attitudes of its population towards the Community. The ministers established a new information commission. In November 1991 a conference on press communication and African integration, organized by ECOWAS, recommended the creation of an ECOWAS press card, judicial safeguards to protect journalists, training programmes for journalists and the establishment of a regional documentation centre and data bank. In November 1994 the commission of social and cultural affairs, meeting in Lagos, Nigeria, endorsed a series of measures to promote West African integration. These included special radio, television and newspaper features, sporting events and other competitions or rallies. In December 2000 the Council of Ministers approved a new policy on the dissemination of information about the Community's activities.

SPECIALIZED AGENCIES

ECOWAS Bank for Investment and Development: BP 2704, 128 blvd du 13 janvier, Lomé, Togo; tel. 216864; fax 218684; e-mail bidc@bidc-ebid.org; internet www.bidc-ebid.org; f. 2001, replacing the former ECOWAS Fund for Co-operation, Compensation and Development; comprises two divisions, a Regional Investment Bank and a Regional Development Fund; Pres. CHRISTIAN ADOVELANDE.

West African Monetary Agency (WAMA): 11–13 ECOWAS St, PMB 218, Freetown, Sierra Leone; tel. 224485; fax 223943; e-mail wama@sierratel.sl; f. 1975 as West African Clearing House; administers transactions between its 10 member central banks in order to promote sub-regional trade and monetary co-operation; administers ECOWAS travellers' cheques scheme. Mems: Banque Centrale des Etats de l'Afrique de l'Ouest (serving Benin, Burkina Faso, Côte d'Ivoire, Guinea-Bissau, Mali, Niger, Senegal, Togo) and the central banks of Cape Verde, The Gambia, Ghana, Guinea, Liberia, Mauritania, Nigeria and Sierra Leone; Dir-Gen. ANTOINE M. F. NDIAYE (Senegal); publ. *Annual Report*.

West African Monetary Institute (WAMI): Premier Towers, 8th/9th Floors, Cantonments 75, Accra, Ghana; tel. (21) 676-901; fax (21) 676-903; e-mail info@wami-imao.org; internet www.wami-imao.org; f. by the ECOWAS Authority summit in December 2000 to prepare for the establishment of a West African Central Bank; Dir-Gen. Dr OKO JOSEPH NNANNA.

West African Health Organization (WAHO): BP 153 Bobo-Dioulasso 01, Burkina Faso; tel. and fax (226) 975772; e-mail wahooas@wahooas.org; internet www.waho.ecowas.int; f. 2000 by merger of the West African Health Community (f. 1978) and the Organization for Co-ordination and Co-operation in the Struggle against Endemic Diseases (f. 1960); aims to harmonize member states' health policies and to promote research, training, the sharing of resources and diffusion of information; Dir-Gen. Dr KABBA T. JOINER; publ. *Bulletin Bibliographique* (quarterly).

Finance

ECOWAS is financed by contributions from member states, although there is a poor record of punctual payment of dues, which has hampered the work of the Secretariat. Under the revised treaty, signed in July 1993, ECOWAS was to receive revenue from a community tax, based on the total value of imports from member countries. In July 1996 the summit meeting approved a protocol on a community levy, providing for the imposition of a 0.5% tax on the value of imports from a third country. In August 1997 the Authority of Heads of State and Government determined that the community levy should replace budgetary contributions as the organization's principal source of finance. The protocol came into force in January 2000, having been ratified by nine member states, with the substantive regime entering into effect on 1 January 2003. The January 2006 meeting of the Authority approved a budget of US $121m. for the operations of the Community in that year.

Publications

Annual Report.
Contact.
ECOWAS National Accounts.
ECOWAS News.
ECOWAS Newsletter.
West African Bulletin.

EUROPEAN UNION-ACP PARTNERSHIP

The EU provides emergency humanitarian assistance for developing and other non-EU countries through its European Community Humanitarian Office (ECHO). Allocations by ECHO in 2006 included €40m. to assist vulnerable populations in Sudan in the context of an EU global humanitarian aid plan for 2006, and a further €40 to assist victims of the conflict in Darfur who were encamped at that time in Darfur and neighbouring Chad; and €38m. to support healthcare provision and resettlement activities in the Democratic Republic of the Congo. In June 2004 the European Commission activated for the first time its newly-established Africa Peace Facility, which provided €12m. in support of African Union (AU) humanitarian and peace monitoring activities in Darfur. The Facility was to be replenished by €300m. to cover the three-year period 2008–10. The EU assists the AU financially in the areas of peace and security; institutional development; governance; and regional economic integration and trade.

Organization

PARTIES TO THE COTONOU AGREEMENT

The European Union

Austria, Belgium, Cyprus, Czech Republic, Denmark, Estonia, Finland, France, Germany, Greece, Hungary, Ireland, Italy, Latvia, Lithuania, Luxembourg, Malta, Netherlands, Poland, Portugal, Slovakia, Slovenia, Spain, Sweden, United Kingdom.

African ACP states

Angola, Benin, Botswana, Burkina Faso, Burundi, Cameroon, Cape Verde, Central African Republic, Chad, Comoros, Democratic Republic of the Congo, Republic of the Congo, Côte d'Ivoire, Djibouti, Equatorial Guinea, Eritrea, Ethiopia, Gabon, Gambia, Ghana, Guinea, Guinea-Bissau, Kenya, Lesotho, Liberia, Madagascar, Malawi, Mali, Mauritania, Mauritius, Mozambique, Namibia, Niger, Nigeria, Rwanda, São Tomé and Príncipe, Senegal, Seychelles, Sierra Leone, Somalia, South Africa, Sudan, Swaziland, Tanzania, Togo, Uganda, Zambia, Zimbabwe.

The ACP states also comprise 16 Caribbean states (including Cuba, which is not a signatory to the Cotonou Agreement) and 15 Pacific countries.

ACP-EU INSTITUTIONS

Council of Ministers: one minister from each signatory state; one co-chairman from each of the two groups; meets annually.

Committee of Ambassadors: one ambassador from each signatory state; chairmanship alternates between the two groups; meets at least every six months.

Joint Assembly: EU and ACP are equally represented; attended by parliamentary delegates from each of the ACP countries and an equal number of members of the European Parliament; one co-chairman from each group; meets twice a year.

Secretariat of the ACP–EU Council of Ministers: 175 rue de la Loi, 1048 Brussels, Belgium; tel. (2) 285-61-11; fax (2) 285-74-58.

Centre for the Development of Enterprise (CDE): 52 ave Hermann Debroux, 1160 Brussels, Belgium; tel. (2) 679-18-11; fax (2) 675-19-03; e-mail info@cde.int; internet www.cde.int; f. 1977 to encourage and support the creation, expansion and restructuring of industrial companies (mainly in the fields of manufacturing and agro-industry) in the ACP states by promoting co-operation between ACP and European companies, in the form of financial, technical or commercial partnership, management contracts, licensing of franchise agreements, sub-contracts, etc.; manages the Pro€Invest programme; Dir FERNANDO MATOS ROSA.

Technical Centre for Agricultural and Rural Co-operation: Postbus 380, 6700 AJ Wageningen, Netherlands; tel. (317) 467100; fax (317) 460067; e-mail cta@cta.int; internet www.agricta.int; f. 1983 to provide ACP states with better access to information, research, training and innovations in agricultural development and extension; Dir CARL B. GREENIDGE.

ACP INSTITUTIONS

ACP Secretariat: ACP House, 451 ave Georges Henri, 1200 Brussels, Belgium; tel. (2) 743-06-00; fax (2) 735-55-73; e-mail info@acp.int; internet www.acpsec.org; Sec.-Gen. Sir JOHN KAPUTIN (Papua New Guinea).

There is also an ACP Council of Ministers and an ACP Committee of Ambassadors. On 15 April 2005 27 APC countries signed a charter creating the ACP Consultative Assembly, which formalized the existing inter-parliamentary co-operation between the ACP member states.

Activities

In June 2000, meeting in Cotonou, Benin, heads of state and of government of the EU and African, Caribbean and Pacific (ACP) countries concluded a new 20-year partnership accord between the EU and ACP states. The EU-ACP Partnership Agreement, known as the Cotonou Agreement, entered into force on 1 April 2003 (although many of its provisions had been applicable for a transitional period since August 2000), following ratification by the then 15 EU member states and more than the requisite two-thirds of the ACP countries. Previously, the principal means of co-operation between the Community and developing countries were the Lomé Conventions. The First Lomé Convention (Lomé I), which was concluded at Lomé, Togo, in February 1975 and came into force on 1 April 1976, replaced the Yaoundé Conventions and the Arusha Agreement. Lomé I was designed to provide a new framework of co-operation, taking into account the varying needs of developing ACP countries. The Second Lomé Convention entered into force on 1 January 1981 and the Third Lomé Convention on 1 March 1985 (trade provisions) and 1 May 1986 (aid). The Fourth Lomé Convention, which had a 10-year commitment period, was signed in December 1989: its trade provisions entered into force on 1 March 1990, and the remainder entered into force in September 1991.

The Cotonou Agreement was to cover a 20-year period from 2000 and was subject to revision every five years. A financial protocol was attached to the Agreement which indicated the funds available to the ACP through the European Development Fund (EDF), the main instrument for Community aid for development co-operation in ACP countries. The ninth EDF, covering the initial five-year period from March 2000, provided a total budget of €13,500m., of which €1,300m. was allocated to regional co-operation and €2,200m. was for the new investment facility for the development of the private sector. In addition, uncommitted balances from previous EDFs amounted to a further €2,500m. The new Agreement envisaged a more participatory approach with more effective political co-operation to encourage good governance and democracy, increased flexibility in the provision of aid to reward performance and a new framework for economic and trade co-operation. Its objectives were to alleviate poverty, contribute to sustainable development and integrate the ACP economies into the global economy. Negotiations to revise the Cotonou agreement were initiated in May 2004 and concluded in February 2005. The political dimension of the Agreement was broadly strengthened and a reference to co-operation in counter-terrorism and the prevention of the proliferation of weapons of mass destruction was included.

Under the provisions of the new accord, the EU was to negotiate free-trade arrangements (replacing the previous non-reciprocal trade preferences) with the most developed ACP countries during 2000–08; these would be structured around a system of six regional free-trade zones, and would be designed to ensure full compatibility with World Trade Organization (WTO) provisions. Once in force, the agreements would be subject to revision every five years. The first general stage of negotiations for the Economic Partnership Agreements (EPA), involving discussions with all ACP countries regarding common procedures, began in September 2002. The regional phase of EPA negotiations to establish a new framework for trade and investment commenced in October 2003. Negotiations were scheduled for completion in mid-2007 to allow for ratification by 2008, when the WTO exception for existing arrangements expires. Meanwhile, the least-developed ACP nations were to benefit from an EU initiative to allow free access for most of their products by 2005. The preferential agreements currently in force would be retained initially (phase I), in view of a waiver granted by the WTO; thereafter ACP-EU trade was to be gradually liberalized over a period of 12–15 years (phase II). It was envisaged that Stabex and Sysmin, instruments under the Lomé Conventions designed to stabilize export prices for agricultural and mining commodities, respectively, would be eliminated gradually. However, they were replaced by a system called FLEX, introduced in 2000, to compensate ACP countries for short-term fluctuations in export earnings. In February 2001 the EU agreed to phase out trade barriers on imports of everything but military weapons from the world's 48 least-developed countries, 39 of which were in the ACP group. Duties on sugar, rice, bananas and some other products were to remain until 2009. In May 2001 the EU announced that it would cancel all outstanding debts arising from its trade accords with former colonies of member states.

One major new programme set up on behalf of the ACP countries and financed by the EDF was Pro€Invest, which was launched in 2002, with funding of €110m. over a seven-year period. In October 2003 the Commission proposed to 'budgetize' the EDF, that is to incorporate it into the EU budget (previously the EDF had always been a fund outside the EU budget, to which the EU member states made direct voluntary contributions). The cost-sharing formula for the 25 member states would automatically apply, obviating the need for negotiations about contributions for the 10th EDF. The Commission proposal was endorsed by the European Parliament in April 2004. Despite the fears of ACP countries that the enlargement of the EU could jeopardize funding, the 10th EDF was agreed in December 2005 by the European Council and provided funds of €22,682m. for the period 2008–13.

In June 1995 negotiations opened with a view to concluding a wide-ranging trade and co-operation agreement with South Africa, including the eventual creation of a free-trade area (FTA). The accord was approved by heads of state and of government in March 1999, after agreement was reached to eliminate progressively, over a 12-year period, the use of the terms 'port' and 'sherry' to describe South African fortified wines. The accord provided for the removal of duties from about 99% of South Africa's industrial exports and some 75% of its agricultural products within 10 years, while South Africa was to liberalize its market for some 86% of EU industrial goods (with protection for the motor vehicle and textiles industries), within a 12-year period. The accord also introduced increased development assistance for South Africa after 1999. The long-delayed agreement was finally signed in January 2002, allowing South African wines freer access to the European market. Under the terms of the agreement, South Africa was allowed to export 42m. litres of wine a year duty-free to the EU, in exchange for abandoning the use of names such as 'sherry', 'port', 'ouzo' or 'grappa'. In March 1997 the Commission approved a Special Protocol for South Africa's accession to the Lomé Convention, and in April South Africa attained partial membership. Full membership was withheld, as South Africa was not regarded as, in all respects, a developing country, and was therefore not entitled to aid provisions.

Article 96 of the Cotonou Agreement, which provides for suspension of the Agreement in specific countries in the event of violation of one of its essential elements (respect for human rights, democratic principles and the rule of law) was invoked against Haiti in 2001 and this was extended annually to December 2004. However, relations with Haiti were in the process of normalization from September of that year. A decision was taken to normalize relations with Guinea-Bissau, following positive measures taken by the Government there. Sanctions were applied to Côte d'Ivoire in December 2004. During 2002 the European Council condemned the worsening human rights situation in Zimbabwe, describing the elections held there in 2002 as deeply flawed, and imposed a range of targeted sanctions, including a travel ban on and freezing of the assets of certain members of the leadership, an arms embargo, and the suspension of development aid. In February 2003 it was announced that the second Europe-Africa summit, scheduled to take place in Lisbon, Portugal, in April, had been postponed indefinitely when EU leaders decided that they could not find a way to exclude the Zimbabwean leader, Robert Mugabe. At the same time the EU sanctions against Zimbabwe were renewed for a further year. The number of senior administration officials subject to a travel ban was increased from 79 to 95 in February 2004 as EU sanctions against Zimbabwe were extended for a further year. The EU claimed that the elections held in Zimbabwe in February 2005 were fraudulent and non-democratic, and consequently extended its sanctions for a further year. In January 2006 sanctions were extended for a further year to February 2007. A further extension of sanctions, until February 2008, was announced in February 2007, by which time the number of senior administration officials to whom they applied had been increased to 125. The comprehensive Liberian peace agreement signed in Accra, Ghana, led to the lifting in 2003 of certain restrictions imposed on Liberia in 2002 in order to liberate funds to finance peace-keeping operations and promote the restoration of democracy. Outstanding sanctions against Liberia were lifted in January 2006.

THE FRANC ZONE

Address: Direction des Relations Internationales et Européennes (Service de la Zone Franc), Banque de France, 39 rue Croix-des-Petits-Champs, 75049, Paris Cédex 01, France.

Telephone: 1-42-92-31-46; **fax:** 1-42-92-39-88; **e-mail:** comozof@banque-france.fr; **internet:** www.banque-france.fr/fr/eurosys/zonefr/page2.htm.

MEMBERS*

Benin
Burkina Faso
Cameroon
Central African Republic
Chad
Comoros
Republic of the Congo
Côte d'Ivoire
Equatorial Guinea
French Overseas Territories
Gabon
Guinea-Bissau
Mali
Niger
Senegal
Togo

* Prior to 1 January 2002, when the transition to a single European currency (euro) was finalized (see below), the Franc Zone also included Metropolitan France, the French Overseas Departments (French Guiana, Guadeloupe, Martinique and Réunion), the French Overseas Collectivité Départementale (Mayotte) and the French Overseas Collectivité Territoriale (St Pierre and Miquelon). The French Overseas Territory (French Polynesia) and the French Overseas Countries (New Caledonia and the Wallis and Futuna Islands) have continued to use the franc CFP (franc des Comptoirs français du Pacifique, 'French Pacific franc').

Apart from Guinea and Mauritania (see below), all of the countries that formerly comprised French West and Equatorial Africa are members of the Franc Zone. The former West and Equatorial African territories are still grouped within the two currency areas that existed before independence, each group having its own variant on the CFA, issued by a central bank: the franc de la Communauté Financière d'Afrique ('franc CFA de l'Ouest'), issued by the Banque centrale des états de l'Afrique de l'ouest—BCEAO, and the franc Coopération financière en Afrique centrale ('franc CFA central'), issued by the Banque des états de l'Afrique centrale—BEAC.

The following states withdrew from the Franc Zone during the period 1958–73: Guinea, Tunisia, Morocco, Algeria, Mauritania and Madagascar. Equatorial Guinea, formerly a Spanish territory, joined the Franc Zone in January 1985, and Guinea-Bissau, a former Portuguese territory, joined in May 1997.

The Comoros, formerly a French Overseas Territory, did not join the Franc Zone following its unilateral declaration of independence in 1975. However, the franc CFA was used as the currency of the new state and the Institut d'émission des Comores continued to function as a Franc Zone organization. In 1976 the Comoros formally assumed membership. In July 1981 the Banque centrale des Comores replaced the Institut d'émission des Comores, establishing its own currency, the Comoros franc.

The Franc Zone operates on the basis of agreements concluded between France and each group of member countries, and the Comoros. The currencies in the Franc Zone were formerly linked with the French franc at a fixed rate of exchange. However, following the introduction of the euro (European single currency) in January 1999, within the framework of European economic and monetary union, in which France was a participant, the Franc Zone currencies were effectively linked at fixed parity to the euro (i.e. parity was based on the fixed conversion rate for the French franc and the euro). From 1 January 2002, when European economic and monetary union was finalized and the French franc withdrawn from circulation, the franc CFA, Comoros franc and franc CFP became officially pegged to the euro, at a fixed rate of exchange. (In accordance with Protocol 13 on France, appended to the 1993 Maastricht Treaty on European Union, France was permitted to continue issuing currencies in its Overseas Territories—i.e. the franc CFP—following the completion of European economic and monetary union.) All the convertability arrangements previously concluded between France and the Franc Zone remained in force. Therefore Franc Zone currencies are freely convertible into euros, at the fixed exchange rate, guaranteed by the French Treasury. Each group of member countries, and the Comoros, has its own central issuing bank, with overdraft facilities provided by the French Treasury. (The issuing authority for the French Overseas Territories is the Institut d'émission d'outre-mer, based in Paris.) Monetary reserves are held mainly in the form of euros. The BCEAO and the BEAC are authorized to hold up to 35% of their foreign exchange holdings in currencies other than the euro. Franc Zone ministers of finance normally meet twice a year to review economic and monetary co-operation. The meeting is normally attended by the French Minister of Co-operation and Francophony.

During the late 1980s and early 1990s the economies of the African Franc Zone countries were adversely affected by increasing foreign debt and by a decline in the prices paid for their principal export commodities. The French Government, however, refused to devalue the franc CFA, as recommended by the IMF. In 1990 the Franc Zone governments agreed to develop economic union, with integrated public finances and common commercial legislation. In April 1992, at a meeting of Franc Zone ministers, a treaty on the insurance industry was adopted, providing for the establishment of a regulatory body for the industry, the Conférence Intrafricaine des Marchés d'Assurances (CIMA), and for the creation of a council of Franc Zone ministers responsible for the insurance industry, with its secretariat in Libreville, Gabon. (A code of conduct for members of CIMA entered into force in February 1995.) At the meeting held in April 1992 ministers also agreed that a further council of ministers was to be created with the task of monitoring the social security systems in Franc Zone countries. A programme drawn up by Franc Zone finance ministers concerning the harmonization of commercial legislation in member states through the establishment of l'Organisation pour l'Harmonisation du Droit des Affaires en Afrique (OHADA) was approved by the Franco-African summit in October. A treaty to align corporate and investment regulations was signed by 11 member countries in October 1993.

In August 1993, in view of financial turmoil related to the continuing weakness of the French franc and the abandonment of the European exchange rate mechanism, the BCEAO and the BEAC determined to suspend repurchasing of francs CFA outside the Franc Zone. Effectively this signified the temporary withdrawal of guaranteed convertibility of the franc CFA with the French franc. Devaluations of the franc CFA and the Comoros franc (by 50% and 33.3%, respectively) were implemented in January 1994. Following the devaluation the CFA countries embarked on programmes of economic adjustment, including restrictive fiscal and wage policies and other monetary, structural and social measures, designed to stimulate growth and to ensure eligibility for development assistance from international financial institutions. France established a special development fund of FFr 300m. to alleviate the immediate social consequences of the devaluation, and announced substantial debt cancellations. In April the French Government announced assistance amounting to FFr 10,000m. over three years to Franc Zone countries undertaking structural adjustment programmes. The IMF, which had strongly advocated a devaluation of the franc CFA, and the World Bank approved immediate soft-credit loans, technical assistance and cancellations or rescheduling of debts. In June 1994 heads of state (or representatives) of African Franc Zone countries convened in Libreville, Gabon, to review the effects of the currency realignment. The final communiqué of the meeting urged further international support for the countries' economic development efforts. In April 1995 Franc Zone finance ministers, meeting in Paris, recognized the positive impact of the devaluation on agricultural export sectors, in particular in west African countries. In January 1996 Afristat, a research and training institution based in Bamako, Mali, commenced activities, having been established in accordance with a decision by the Franc Zone member countries and the French Government made in September 1993. Afristat aims to support national statistical organizations in participating states in order to strengthen their economic management capabilities. The IMF and the World Bank have continued to support economic development efforts in the Franc Zone. France provides debt relief to Franc Zone member states eligible under the World Bank's HIPC. In April 2001 the African Franc Zone member states determined jointly to develop anti-money laundering legislation.

In February 2000 UEMOA and ECOWAS adopted an action plan for the creation of a single West African Monetary Zone and consequent replacement of the franc Communauté financière africaine by a single West African currency (see below).

CURRENCIES OF THE FRANC ZONE

1 franc CFA = €0.00152. CFA stands for Communauté financière africaine in the West African area and for Coopération financière en Afrique centrale in the Central African area. Used in the monetary areas of West and Central Africa respectively.

1 Comoros franc = €0.00201. Used in the Comoros, where it replaced the franc CFA in 1981.

1 franc CFP = €0.00839. CFP stands for Comptoirs français du Pacifique. Used in New Caledonia, French Polynesia and the Wallis and Futuna Islands.

WEST AFRICA

Union économique et monétaire ouest-africaine (UEMOA): BP 543, Ouagadougou 01, Burkina Faso; tel. 31-88-73; fax 31-88-72; e-mail commission@uemoa.int; internet www.uemoa.int; f. 1994; promotes regional monetary and economic convergence, and envisages the eventual creation of a sub-regional common market. A preferential tariff scheme, eliminating duties on most local products and reducing by 30% import duties on many Union-produced industrial goods, became operational on 1 July 1996; in addition, from 1 July, a community solidarity tax of 0.5% was imposed on all goods from third countries sold within the Union, in order to strengthen UEMOA's capacity to promote economic integration. (This was increased to 1% in December 1999.) In June 1997 UEMOA heads of state and government agreed to reduce import duties on industrial products originating in the Union by a further 30%. An inter-parliamentary committee, recognized as the predecessor of a UEMOA legislature, was inaugurated in Mali in March 1998. In September Côte d'Ivoire's stock exchange was transformed into the Bourse regionale des valeurs mobilières, a regional stock exchange serving the Union, in order to further economic integration. On 1 January 2000 internal tariffs were eliminated on all local products (including industrial goods) and a joint external tariff system, reportedly in five bands of between 0% and 20%, was imposed on goods deriving from outside the new customs union. Guinea-Bissau was excluded from the arrangement owing to its unstable political situation. The UEMOA member countries also belong to ECOWAS and, in accordance with a decision taken in April 2000, aim to harmonize UEMOA's economic programme with that of a planned second West African monetary union (the West African Monetary Zone—WAMZ), to be established by the remaining—mainly anglophone—ECOWAS member states by 2009. A merger of the two complementary monetary unions, and the replacement of the franc Communauté financière africaine by a new single West African currency, is eventually envisaged. On 29 January 2003 member states adopted a treaty on the establishment of a UEMOA parliament. Mems: Benin, Burkina Faso, Côte d'Ivoire, Guinea-Bissau, Mali, Niger, Senegal and Togo; Pres. SOUMAILA CISSE (Mali)

Union monétaire ouest-africaine (UMOA) (West African Monetary Union): established by Treaty of November 1973, entered into force 1974; in 1990 the UMOA Banking Commission was established, which is responsible for supervising the activities of banks and financial institutions in the region, with the authority to prohibit the operation of a banking institution. UMOA constitutes an integral part of UEMOA.

Banque centrale des états de l'Afrique de l'ouest (BCEAO): ave Abdoulaye Fadiga, BP 3108, Dakar, Senegal; tel. 839-05-00; fax 823-93-35; e-mail webmaster@bceao.int; internet www.bceao.int; f. 1962; central bank of issue for the mems of UEMOA; total assets 5,390,862m. francs CFA (Dec. 2003); mems: Benin, Burkina Faso, Côte d'Ivoire, Guinea-Bissau, Mali, Niger, Senegal and Togo; Gov. DAMO JUSTIN BARO (acting); Sec.-Gen. AMADOU SADICKH DIOP; publs *Annual Report, Notes d'Information et Statistiques* (monthly), *Annuaire des banques, Bilan des banques et établissements financiers* (annually).

Banque ouest-africaine de développement (BOAD): 68 ave de la Libération, BP 1172, Lomé, Togo; tel. 221-42-44; fax 221-52-67; e-mail boadsiege@boad.org; internet www.boad.org; f. 1973 to promote the balanced development of mem. states and the economic integration of West Africa; total assets 673,621m. francs CFA (Dec. 2003); a Guarantee Fund for Private Investment in West Africa, established jtly by BOAD and the European Investment Bank in Dec. 1994, aims to guarantee medium- and long-term credits to private sector businesses in the region; mems: Benin, Burkina Faso, Côte d'Ivoire, Guinea-Bissau, Mali, Niger, Senegal, Togo; Pres. Dr YAYI BONI (Benin); Vice-Pres. ISSA COULIBALY; publs *Rapport Annuel*, *BOAD en Bref* (quarterly).

Bourse Régionale des Valeurs Mobilières (BVRM): 18 ave Joseph Anoma, BP 3802, Abidjan 01, Côte d'Ivoire; tel. 20-32-66-85; fax 20-32-66-84; e-mail brvm@brvm.org; internet www.brvm.org; f. 1998; Pres. COULIBALY TIEMKOKO YADE; Man. JEAN-PAUL GILLET.

CENTRAL AFRICA

Communauté économique et monétaire de l'Afrique centrale (CEMAC): BP 969, Bangui, Central African Republic; tel. and fax 61-21-35; e-mail sgudeac@intnet.cf; f. 1998; formally inaugurated as the successor to the Union douanière et économique de l'Afrique centrale (UDEAC, f. 1966) at a meeting of heads of state held in Malabo, Equatorial Guinea, in June 1999; aims to promote the process of sub-regional integration within the framework of an economic union and a monetary union; CEMAC was also to comprise a parliament and sub-regional tribunal; UDEAC established a common external tariff for imports from other countries and administered a common code for investment policy and a Solidarity Fund to counteract regional disparities of wealth and economic development; mems: Cameroon, Central African Republic, Chad, Republic of the Congo, Equatorial Guinea, Gabon; Sec.-Gen. JEAN NKUETE.

At a summit meeting in December 1981, UDEAC leaders agreed in principle to form an economic community of Central African states (Communauté économique des états de l'Afrique centrale—CEEAC), to include UDEAC members and Burundi, Rwanda, São Tomé and Príncipe and Zaire (now Democratic Republic of the Congo). CEEAC began operations in 1985.

Banque de développement des états de l'Afrique centrale (BDEAC): place du Gouvernement, BP 1177, Brazzaville, Republic of the Congo; tel. 81-18-85; fax 81-18-80; e-mail bdeac@bdeac.org; internet www.bdeac.org; f. 1975; total assets 44,260m. francs CFA (Dec. 2003); shareholders: Cameroon, Central African Republic, Chad, Republic of the Congo, Gabon, Equatorial Guinea, ADB, BEAC, France, Germany and Kuwait; Pres. ANICET GEORGES DOLOGUÉLÉ.

Banque des états de l'Afrique centrale (BEAC): 736 ave Mgr François Xavier Vogt, BP 1917, Yaoundé, Cameroon; tel. 223-40-30; fax 223-33-29; e-mail beac@beac.int; internet www.beac.int; f. 1973 as the central bank of issue of Cameroon, the Central African Republic, Chad, Republic of the Congo, Equatorial Guinea and Gabon; a monetary market, incorporating all national financial institutions of the BEAC countries, came into effect on 1 July 1994; total assets 2,150,301m. francs CFA (Dec. 2003); Gov. JEAN-FÉLIX MAMALEPOT; publs *Rapport annuel*, *Etudes et statistiques* (monthly).

CENTRAL ISSUING BANKS

Banque centrale des Comores: place de France, BP 405, Moroni, Comoros; tel. (73) 1002; fax (73) 0349; e-mail bcc@snpt.km; f. 1981; Gov. AHAMADI ABDOUBASTOI.

Banque centrale des états de l'Afrique de l'ouest: see above.

Banque des états de l'Afrique centrale: see above.

Institut d'émission d'outre-mer (IEOM): 5 rue Roland Barthes, 75598 Paris Cédex 12, France; tel. 1-53-44-41-41; fax 1-43-47-51-34; e-mail contact@iedom-ieom.fr; internet www.ieom.fr; f. 1966; issuing authority for the French Overseas Territories; Dir-Gen. ALAIN VIENNEY; Dir PATRICK BESSE.

FRENCH ECONOMIC AID

France's connection with the African Franc Zone countries involves not only monetary arrangements, but also includes comprehensive French assistance in the forms of budget support, foreign aid, technical assistance and subsidies on commodity exports.

Official French financial aid and technical assistance to developing countries is administered by the following agencies:

Agence française de développement (AFD): 5 rue Roland Barthes, 75598 Paris Cédex 12, France; tel. 1-53-44-31-31; fax 1-44-87-99-39; e-mail com@afd.fr; internet www.afd.fr/; f. 1941; fmrly the Caisse française de développement—CFD; French development bank which lends money to member states and former member states of the Franc Zone and several other states, and executes the financial operations of the FSP (see below). Following the devaluation of the franc CFA in January 1994, the French Government cancelled some FFr 25,000m. in debt arrears owed by member states to the CFD. The CFD established a Special Fund for Development and the Exceptional Facility for Short-term Financing to help alleviate the immediate difficulties resulting from the devaluation. In early 1994 the CFD made available funds totalling 2,420m. francs CFA to assist the establishment of CEMAC (see above). Serves as the secretariat for the Fonds français pour l'environnement mondial (f. 1994). Since 2000 the AFD has been implementing France's support of the World Bank's HIPC initiative; a total of €11.7m. was lent to Franc Zone countries in 2004; Dir-Gen. JEAN-MICHEL SEVERINO.

Fonds de Solidarité Prioritaire (FSP): 20 rue Monsieur, 75007 Paris, France; tel. 1-53-69-37-29; fax 1-53-69-37-55; f. 2000, taking over from the Fonds d'aide et de coopération (f. 1959) the administration of subsidies from the French Government to 54 countries of the Zone de Solidarité prioritaire; FSP is administered by the Ministry of Co-operation and Francophony, which allocates budgetary funds to it.

INTERGOVERNMENTAL AUTHORITY ON DEVELOPMENT—IGAD

Address: BP 2653, Djibouti.

Telephone: 354050; **fax:** 356994; **e-mail:** igad@igad.org; **internet:** www.igad.org.

The Intergovernmental Authority on Development (IGAD), established in 1996 to supersede the Intergovernmental Authority on Drought and Development (IGADD, founded in 1986), aims to co-ordinate the sustainable socio-economic development of member countries, to combat the effects of drought and desertification, and to promote regional food security.

MEMBERS*

Djibouti	Kenya	Sudan
Eritrea*	Somalia	Uganda
Ethiopia		

* Eritrea announced its impending withdrawal from IGAD in April 2007.

Organization

(September 2007)

ASSEMBLY

The Assembly, consisting of heads of state and of government of member states, is the supreme policy-making organ of the Authority. It holds a summit meeting at least once a year. The chairmanship of the Assembly rotates among the member countries on an annual basis.

Chairman: MWAI KIBAKI (Kenya).

COUNCIL OF MINISTERS

The Council of Ministers is composed of the minister of foreign affairs and one other minister from each member state. It meets at least twice a year and approves the work programme and the annual budget of the Secretariat.

COMMITTEE OF AMBASSADORS

The Committee of Ambassadors comprises the ambassadors or plenipotentiaries of member states to Djibouti. It convenes as regularly as required to advise and assist the Executive Secretary concerning the interpretation of policies and guide-lines and the realization of the annual work programme.

SECRETARIAT

The Secretariat, the executive body of IGAD, is headed by the Executive Secretary, who is appointed by the Assembly for a term of four years, renewable once. In addition to the Office of the Executive Secretary, the Secretariat comprises the following three divisions: Agriculture and Environment; Economic Co-operation; and Political and Humanitarian Affairs, each headed by a director.

Executive Secretary: Dr ATTALLA HAMAD BASHIR (Sudan).

Activities

IGADD was established in 1986 by Djibouti, Ethiopia, Kenya, Somalia, Sudan and Uganda, to combat the effects of aridity and desertification arising from the severe drought and famine that has periodically affected the Horn of Africa. Eritrea became a member of IGADD in September 1993, following its proclamation as an independent state. In April 1995, at an extraordinary summit meeting held in Addis Ababa, Ethiopia, heads of state and of government resolved to reorganize and expand the Authority. In March 1996 IGAD was endorsed to supersede IGADD, at a second extraordinary summit meeting of heads of state and of government, held in Nairobi, Kenya. The meeting led to the adoption of an agreement for a new organizational structure and the approval of an extended mandate to co-ordinate and harmonize policy in the areas of economic co-operation and political and humanitarian affairs, in addition to its existing responsibilities for food security and environmental protection.

IGAD aims to achieve regional co-operation and economic integration. To facilitate this IGAD assists the governments of member states to maximize resources and co-ordinates efforts to initiate and implement regional development programmes and projects. In this context, IGAD promotes the harmonization of policies relating to agriculture and natural resources, communications, customs, trade and transport; the implementation of pro-grammes in the fields of social sciences, research, science and technology; and effective participation in the global economy. Meetings between IGAD foreign affairs ministers and the IGAD Joint Partners' Forum, comprising the grouping's donors, are convened periodically to discuss issues such as food security and humanitarian affairs. In October 2001 delegates from IGAD and representatives of government and civil society in member states initiated a process to establish an IGAD-Civil Society Forum; the founding assembly of the Forum was convened in Nairobi, Kenya in July 2003.

In October 2003 the 10th IGAD summit meeting ratified a decision of the eighth summit, held in November 2000, to absorb the Harare, Zimbabwe- and Nairobi-based Drought Monitoring Centre (an initiative of 24 eastern and southern African states inaugurated in 1989 under the auspices of the UNDP and World Meteorological Organization) as a specialized institution of IGAD and to rename it the IGAD Climate Prediction and Applications Centre (ICPAC).

In November 2000 the eighth IGAD summit approved the establishment of an IGAD Inter-parliamentary Union. A draft protocol on the Union, finalized in May 2003, was signed by the participants in the first meeting of regional speakers of parliament in February 2004; the meeting also determined that the headquarters of the Union should be based in Addis Ababa, Ethiopia.

The IGAD Secretariat, in partnership with the World Bank, is developing a mechanism for monitoring the occurrence of HIV/AIDS in member states. In May 2007 it was decided that the project facilitation office for the so-called IGAD Regional HIV and AIDS Programme (IRHAPP) would be located in Kampala, Uganda.

In June 2006 IGAD launched the IGAD Capacity-building Program Against Terrorism (ICPAT), a four-year programme based in Addis Ababa, Ethiopia, which aimed to combat the reach of international terrorism through the enhancement of judicial measures and interdepartmental co-operation, improving border control activities, supporting training and information-sharing, and promoting strategic co-operation.

During 2007 a draft framework for an IGAD Gender Peer Review Mechanism was under consideration; it was envisaged that the Mechanism would be a means of addressing the issue of violence against women in the region as well as other matters relating to women's progress.

FOOD SECURITY AND ENVIRONMENTAL PROTECTION

IGAD seeks to achieve regional food security, the sustainable development of natural resources and environmental protection, and to encourage and assist member states in their efforts to combat the consequences of drought and other natural and man-made disasters. The region suffers from recurrent droughts, which severely impede crop and livestock production. Natural and man-made disasters increase the strain on resources, resulting in annual food deficits. About 80% of the IGAD sub-region is classified as arid or semi-arid, and some 40% of the region is unproductive, owing to severe environmental degradation. Activities to improve food security and preserve natural resources have included: the introduction of remote-sensing services; the development of a Marketing Information System and of a Regional Integrated Information System (RIIS); the establishment of training and credit schemes for fishermen; research into the sustainable production of drought-resistant, high-yielding crop varieties; transboundary livestock disease control and vaccine production; the control of environmental pollution; the promotion of alternative sources of energy in the home; the management of integrated water resources; the promotion of community-based land husbandry; training programmes in grain marketing; and the implementation of the International Convention to Combat Desertification.

ECONOMIC CO-OPERATION

The Economic Co-operation division concentrates on the development of a co-ordinated infrastructure for the region, in particular in the areas of transport and communications, to promote foreign, cross-border and domestic trade and investment opportunities. IGAD seeks to harmonize national transport and trade policy and thereby facilitate the free movement of people, goods and services. The improvements to infrastructure also aim to facilitate more timely interventions in conflicts, disasters and emergencies in the sub-region. Projects under way in the early 2000s included: the construction of missing segments of the Trans-African Highway and the Pan African Telecommunications Network; the removal of barriers to trade and communications; improvements to ports and inland container terminals; and the modernization of railway and telecommunications services. In November 2000 the IGAD Assembly determined to establish an integrated rail network connecting all member countries. In addition, the heads of state and government considered the possibility of drafting legislation to facilitate the expansion of intra-IGAD trade. The development of economic co-operation has been impeded by persisting conflicts in the sub-region (see below). An IGAD Business Forum was to be established in Asmara, Eritrea.

POLITICAL AND HUMANITARIAN AFFAIRS

The field of political and humanitarian affairs focuses on conflict prevention, management and resolution through dialogue. The division's primary aim is to restore peace and stability to member countries affected by conflict, in order that resources may be diverted for development purposes. Efforts have been pursued to strengthen capacity for conflict prevention and to relieve humanitarian crises. The ninth IGAD summit meeting, held in Khartoum in January 2002, adopted a protocol to IGAD's founding agreement establishing a conflict early warning and response mechanism (CEWARN). CEWARN, which was to be based in Addis Ababa, Ethiopia, was to collect and analyse information for the preparation of periodic early warning reports concerning the potential outbreak of violent conflicts in the region. The inaugural meeting of CEWARN was held in June. In February 2006 IGAD convened a ministerial conference on refugees, returnees and internally displaced persons, to consider means of addressing the burden posed by population displacement in member states; at that time it was estimated that 11m. people had been forcibly displaced from their homes in the region.

The Executive Secretary of IGAD participated in the first summit meeting of all East African heads of state and government, convened in April 2005 in Addis Ababa, Ethiopia; the meeting approved a memorandum of understanding on the establishment of the Eastern African Standby Brigade (EASBRIG), which was to form the regional component of the African Union (AU) African Standby Force.

In September 1995 negotiations between the Sudanese Government and opposition leaders were initiated, under the auspices of IGAD, with the aim of resolving the conflict in southern Sudan; these were subsequently reconvened periodically. In March 2001 IGAD's mediation committee on southern Sudan, chaired by President Daniel arap Moi of Kenya, publicized a seven-point plan for a peaceful settlement of the conflict. In early June, at a regional summit on the situation in Sudan convened by IGAD, it was agreed that a permanent negotiating forum comprising representatives of the parties to the conflict would be established at the Authority's secretariat. In mid-July 2002 the Sudanese Government and the main rebel grouping in that country signed, under IGAD auspices, in Machakos, Kenya, a protocol providing for a six-year period of autonomy for southern Sudan to be followed by a referendum on self-determination, and establishing that northern Sudan would be governed in accordance with *Shari'a* law and southern Sudan by a secular judicial system. Peace negotiations subsequently continued under IGAD auspices. A cease-fire agreement was concluded by the parties to the conflict in October, to which an addendum was adopted in February 2003, recommending the deployment of an IGAD verification and monitoring team to oversee compliance with the agreement. In September of that year the parties to the conflict signed an accord on interim security arrangements. During 2003–04 IGAD mediated several further accords that paved the way for the conclusion, in January 2005, of a final, comprehensive peace agreement.

In May–August 2000 a conference aimed at securing peace in Somalia was convened in Arta, Djibouti, under the auspices of IGAD. The conference appointed a transitional Somali legislature, which then elected a transitional national president. The eighth summit of IGAD heads of state and government, held in Khartoum, Sudan, in November, welcomed the conclusion in September of an agreement on reconciliation between the new Somali transitional administration and a prominent opposition alliance, and determined that those member countries that neighboured Somalia (the 'frontline states' of Djibouti, Ethiopia and Kenya) should co-operate in assisting the process of reconstruction and reconciliation in that country. The summit appointed a special envoy to implement IGAD's directives concerning the Somali situation. In January 2002 the ninth IGAD summit meeting determined that a new conference for promoting reconciliation in Somalia (where insecurity continued to prevail) should be convened, under IGAD's auspices. The leaders also issued a statement condemning international terrorism and urged Somalia, in particular, to make a firm commitment to eradicating terrorism. The second Somalia reconciliation conference, initiated in October, in Eldoret, Kenya, under IGAD auspices, issued a Declaration on Cessation of Hostilities, Structures and Principles of the Somalia National Reconciliation Process, as a basis for the pursuit of a peace settlement. In February 2003 the conference was relocated to Nairobi. In July delegates at the ongoing Nairobi conference reached a provisional agreement on the formation of a Somali interim government; however, this was rejected by the president of the transitional government. Progress at the conference stalled further in early October, owing to disagreement between participating groups concerning the adoption of a federal system for the country; later in that month Djibouti withdrew its support from the negotiations, owing to a perceived lack of neutrality on the part of the IGAD technical committee. The Nairobi conference resumed in January 2004 and, later in that month, determined to establish a new parliament; this was inaugurated in August. In January 2005 IGAD heads of state and government authorized the deployment of a Peace Support Mission to Somalia (IGASOM) to assist the transitional federal authorities there, pending the subsequent deployment of an AU peace force; this arrangement was endorsed in the same month by the AU. In mid-March 2006 the IGAD Assembly reiterated its support for the planned deployment of IGASOM, and urged the UN Security Council to grant an exemption to the UN arms embargo applied to Somalia in order to facilitate the regional peace support initiative. At a consultative meeting on the removal of the arms embargo, convened in mid-April, in Nairobi, Kenya, representatives of the Somali transitional federal authorities presented for consideration by IGAD and the AU a draft national security and stabilization plan. It was agreed that a detailed mission plan should be formulated to underpin the proposed IGAD/AU peace missions. In January 2007 the AU Peace and Security Council authorized the deployment of the AU Mission in Somalia (AMISOM) in place of the proposed IGASOM.

Following the violent escalation of a border dispute between Eritrea and Ethiopia in mid-1998 IGAD supported efforts by the Organization of African Unity (now AU) to mediate a cease-fire between the two sides. This was achieved in mid-2000.

Publications

Annual Report.

IGAD News (2 a year).

Proceedings of the Summit of Heads of State and Government; Reports of the Council of Ministers' Meetings.

International Criminal Court

Address: Maanweg 174, 2516 AB The Hague, Netherlands.

Telephone: (70) 515-8097; **fax:** (70) 515-8376; **e-mail:** asp@asp.icc-cpi.int; **internet:** www.icc-cpi.int.

The International Criminal Court (ICC) was established by the Rome Statute of the International Criminal Court, adopted by 120 states participating in a United Nations Diplomatic Conference in July 1998. The Rome Statute (and therefore the temporal jurisdiction of the ICC) entered into force on 1 July 2002, 60 days after ratification by the requisite 60th signatory state in April. The ICC is a permanent, independent body, in relationship with the United Nations, that aims to promote the rule of law and punish the most serious international crimes. The Rome Statute reaffirmed the principles of the UN Charter and stated that the relationship between the Court and the United Nations system should be determined by a framework relationship agreement between the states parties to the Rome Statute and the UN General Assembly: under the so-called negotiated relationship agreement, which entered into force in October 2004, upon signature by the Court's President and the Secretary-General of the United Nations, there was to be mutual exchange of information and documentation to the fullest extent and co-operation and consultation on practical matters, and it was stipulated that the Court might, if deemed appropriate, submit reports on its activities to the UN Secretary-General and propose to the Secretary-General items for consideration by the United Nations.

The Court comprises the Presidency (consisting of a President and first and second Vice-Presidents), Chambers (including a Pre-Trial Division, Trial Division and Appeals Division) with 18 permanent judges, Office of the Prosecutor (comprising the Chief Prosecutor and up to two Deputy Prosecutors), and Registry. The judges must each have a different nationality and equitably represent the major legal systems of the world, a fair geographical distribution, and a fair proportion of men and women. They are elected by the Assembly of States Parties to the Rome Statute from two lists, the first comprising candidates with established competence in criminal law and procedures and the second comprising candidates with established competence in relevant areas of international law, to terms of office of three, six or nine years. The President and Vice-Presidents are elected by an absolute majority of the judges for renewable three-year terms of office. The Chief Prosecutor is elected by an absolute majority of states parties to the Rome Statute to an unrenewable nine-year term of office. The first judges were elected to the Court in February 2003, the first Presidency in March, and the first Chief Prosecutor in April.

The Court has established a Victims Trust Fund to finance compensation, restitution or rehabilitation for victims of crimes (individuals or groups of individuals). The Fund is administered by the Registry and supervised by an independent board of directors.

By 2007 three states party to the Rome Statute had referred cases to the Court: Uganda (in January 2004, relating to the long-term unrest in the north of that country); the Democratic Republic of the Congo (DRC) (in April 2004, relating to alleged war crimes); and the Central African Republic (in January 2005, relating to war crimes and crimes against humanity allegedly committed during the period October 2002–March 2003). In June 2004 the Chief Prosecutor agreed to open an investigation into the situation in the DRC, and in July agreed to consider the case relating to Uganda. In March 2005 the UN Security Council voted to refer to the Court the situation prevailing in Darfur, Sudan, since 1 July 2002, on the basis of the recently-issued report of an International Commission of Inquiry on Darfur; the UN Secretary-General handed the Chief Prosecutor a sealed list of 51 names of people identified in the report as having committed crimes under international law. In October 2005 the Court unsealed warrants for arrest (issued under seal in July) against five commanders of the Ugandan Lord's Resistance Army (LRA), including the LRA leader, Joseph Kony. In March 2006 Thomas Lubanga Dyilo, a DRC militia leader, was arrested by the Congolese authorities and transferred to the Court, thereby becoming the first ICC indictee to be captured; Dyilo was charged with conscripting child soldiers, a sealed warrant for his arrest having been issued in February.

In April 2006 the International Criminal Court and the Special Court for Sierra Leone concluded a memorandum of understanding in accordance with which the Special Court was to use the courtroom and detention facilities of the International Criminal Court for the trial of Charles Taylor, the former president of Liberia, on charges of crimes against humanity. In June Taylor was transferred to the Criminal Court's detention centre in The Hague; his trial commenced in June 2007.

By September 2007 105 states had ratified the Rome Statute.

THE JUDGES
(September 2007)

	Term
President: PHILIPPE KIRSCH (Canada)	6 years
First Vice-President: AKUA KUENYEHIA (Ghana)	3 years
Second Vice President: RENÉ BLATTMANN (Bolivia)	6 years
KARL T. HUDSON PHILLIPS (Trinidad and Tobago)	9 years
CLAUDE JORDA (France)	6 years
GEORGHIOS N. PIKIS (Cyprus)	6 years
ELIZABETH ODIO BENITO(Costa Rica)	9 years
NAVANETHEM PILLAY (South Africa)	6 years
SANG-HYUN SONG (Republic of Korea)	3 years
HANS-PETER KAUL (Germany)	3 years
MAURO POLITI (Italy)	6 years
MAUREEN HARDING CLARK (Ireland)	9 years
ERKKI KOURULA (Finland)	3 years
FATOUMATA DEMBELE DIARRA (Mali)	9 years
ANITA UŠACKA (Latvia)	3 years
Sir ADRIAN FULFORD (United Kingdom)	9 years
SYLVIA DE FIGUEIREDO STEINER (Brazil)	9 years
EKATERINA TRENDAFILOVA (Bulgaria)	9 years

Chief Prosecutor: LUIS MORENO OCAMPO (Argentina).

Registrar: BRUNO CATHALA (France).

Finance

The proposed budget for the International Criminal Court for 2008 amounted to €97.8m.

ISLAMIC DEVELOPMENT BANK

Address: POB 5925, Jeddah 21432, Saudi Arabia.

Telephone: (2) 6361400; **fax:** (2) 6366871; **e-mail:** idbarchives@isdb.org; **internet:** www.isdb.org.

The Bank was established following a conference of Ministers of Finance of member countries of the Organization of the Islamic Conference (OIC), held in Jeddah in December 1973. Its aim is to encourage the economic development and social progress of member countries and of Muslim communities in non-member countries, in accordance with the principles of the Islamic *Shari'a* (sacred law). The Bank formally opened in October 1975. The Bank and its associated entities—the Islamic Research and Training Institute, the Islamic Corporation for the Development of the Private Sector, and the Islamic Corporation for the Insurance of Investment and Export Credit—constitute the Islamic Development Bank Group.

MEMBERS

There are 56 members.

Organization

(September 2007)

BOARD OF GOVERNORS

Each member country is represented by a governor, usually its Minister of Finance, and an alternate. The Board of Governors is the supreme authority of the Bank, and meets annually. The 32nd meeting was convened in Dakar, Senegal, in May 2007.

BOARD OF EXECUTIVE DIRECTORS

The Board consists of 14 members, seven of whom are appointed by the seven largest subscribers to the capital stock of the Bank; the remaining seven are elected by Governors representing the other subscribers. Members of the Board of Executive Directors are elected for three-year terms. The Board is responsible for the direction of the general operations of the Bank.

ADMINISTRATION

In addition to the President of the Bank, there are three Vice-Presidents, responsible for Operations, Trade and Policy, and Corporate Resources and Services.

President of the Bank and Chairman of the Board of Executive Directors: Dr AHMAD MOHAMED ALI (Saudi Arabia).

Vice-President Operations: Dr AMADOU BOUBACAR CISSE (Niger).

Vice-President Trade and Policy: Dr SYED JAAFAR AZNAN (Malaysia).

Vice-President Corporate Resources and Services: (vacant).

FINANCIAL STRUCTURE

The Bank's unit of account is the Islamic Dinar (ID), which is equivalent to the value of one Special Drawing Right (SDR) of the IMF (average value in 2006 SDR 1 = US $1.50440). In May 2006 the Bank's Board of Governors approved an increase in the authorized capital from ID 15,000m. to ID 30,000m. At January 2007 total subscriptions amounted to ID 13,217.68m.

SUBSCRIPTIONS
(million Islamic Dinars, as at 19 January 2007)

Afghanistan	9.93	Maldives	4.96
Albania	9.24	Mali	18.19
Algeria	459.22	Mauritania	9.77
Azerbaijan	9.77	Morocco	91.69
Bahrain	25.88	Mozambique	9.23
Bangladesh	182.16	Niger	24.63
Benin	18.19	Nigeria	4.65
Brunei	24.63	Oman	50.92
Burkina Faso	24.63	Pakistan	459.21
Cameroon	45.85	Palestine	19.55
Chad	9.77	Qatar	97.73
Comoros	2.50	Saudi Arabia	3,685.13
Côte d'Ivoire	4.65	Senegal	45.89
Djibouti	4.96	Sierra Leone	4.96
Egypt	686.84	Somalia	4.96
Gabon	54.58	Sudan	72.77
The Gambia	9.24	Suriname	4.96
Guinea	45.85	Syria	18.49
Guinea-Bissau	4.96	Tajikistan	4.96
Indonesia	406.49	Togo	4.96
Iran	1,293.34	Tunisia	19.55
Iraq	25.91	Turkey	1,165.86
Jordan	73.50	Turkmenistan	4.96
Kazakhstan	19.28	Uganda	187.75
Kuwait	985.88	United Arab Emirates	882.84
Kyrgyzstan	4.96	Uzbekistan	2.50
Lebanon	9.77	Yemen	92.38
Libya	1,478.24		
Malaysia	294.01		

Activities

The Bank adheres to the Islamic principle forbidding usury, and does not grant loans or credits for interest. Instead, its methods of project financing are: provision of interest-free loans, mainly for infrastructural projects which are expected to have a marked impact on long-term socio-economic development; provision of technical assistance (e.g. for feasibility studies); equity participation in industrial and agricultural projects; leasing operations, involving the leasing of equipment such as ships, and instalment sale financing; and profit-sharing operations. Funds not immediately needed for projects are used for foreign trade financing. Under the Import Trade Financing Operations (ITFO) scheme, funds are used for importing commodities for development purposes (i.e. raw materials and intermediate industrial goods, rather than consumer goods), with priority given to the import of goods from other member countries. The Export Financing Scheme (EFS), established as the Longer-term Trade Financing Scheme in 1987/88, aims to provide financing for the export of non-traditional and capital goods. A special programme under the EFS became operational in AH 1419, on the basis of a memorandum of understanding signed between the Bank and the Arab Bank for Economic Development in Africa (BADEA), to finance Arab exports to non-Arab League members of the OAU (now African Union). In AH 1424 the Bank adopted a new group strategic framework, which identified three principal objectives: the promotion of Islamic financial industry and institutions; poverty alleviation; and the promotion of co-operation among member countries. To achieve these objectives, the Bank determined the following as priority areas of activity: human development; agricultural development and food security; infrastructure development; intra-trade among member countries; private sector development; and research and development in Islamic economics, banking and finance.

The Bank's Special Assistance Programme was initiated in AH 1400 to support the economic and social development of Muslim communities in non-member countries, in particular in the education and health sectors. It also aimed to provide emergency aid in times of natural disasters, and to assist Muslim refugees throughout the world. Operations undertaken by the Bank are financed by the Waqf Fund (formerly the Special Assistance Account). By the end of AH 1427 some US $615m. had been approved under the Waqf Fund Special Assistance Programme for 1,129 operations, of which 439 were in member countries and 690 were for Muslim organizations and communities in non-member countries. Other assistance activities include scholarship programmes, technical co-operation projects and the sacrificial meat utilization project. In January 2005 the Bank allocated $500m. to assist the survivors of the Indian Ocean earthquake and tsunami which struck coastal areas in 14 countries in late December 2004. The Bank dispatched missions to provide emergency relief to Indonesia, the Maldives and Sri Lanka, and planned to send further teams to assess the requirements for reconstruction. The Bank approved an assistance programme amounting to $501.6m. following a massive earthquake in north-west Pakistan that occurred in October 2005. The funds aimed to support recovery, rehabilitation and reconstruction efforts. The Bank increasingly has worked to assist post-conflict member countries in rehabilitation and reconstruction. It is a member of the management committee of the Afghanistan Reconstruction Trust Fund, which was established in 2001; during 2003 the Bank approved an operation to assist Afghan refugees. In December 2003 the Bank approved a Programme for Reconstruction of Iraq, with funding of ID 365.5m. ($500m.) to be implemented over a five-year period. In October 2002 the Bank's Board of Governors, meeting in Burkina Faso, adopted the Ouagadougou Declaration on the co-operation between the Bank group and Africa, which identified priority areas for Bank activities, for example education and the private sector. The Bank pledged $2,000m. to finance implementation of the Declaration over the five years 2004–08.

By 19 January 2007 the Bank had approved a total of ID 13,162.4m. for project financing and technical assistance since operations began in 1976, ID 20,254.1m. for foreign trade financing, and ID 484.0m. for special assistance operations, excluding amounts for cancelled operations. During the Islamic year 1427 (31 January 2006 to 19 January 2007) the Bank approved a net total of ID 3,508.3m., for 361 operations.

The Bank approved 40 loans in the Islamic Year 1427, amounting to ID 280.8m. These loans supported projects concerned with the education and health sectors, infrastructural improvements, and agricultural developments. During that year the Bank's total disbursements totalled ID 1,589.1m., bringing the total cumulative disbursements since the Bank began operations to ID 23,613.7m. The Bank approved 62 technical assistance operations during that year in the form of grants and loans, amounting to ID 10.8m.

Import trade financing approved during the Islamic year 1427 amounted to ID 1,435.0m. for 75 operations. By the end of that year cumulative import trade financing amounted to ID 15,950.9m., of which 39% was for imports of crude petroleum, 25% for intermediate industrial goods and 9% for refined petroleum products. During AH 1427 the Bank's export financing scheme was formally dissolved, although continued to fund projects pending the commencement of operations of the International Islamic Trade Finance Corporation (ITFC, see below). At the end of that year total export financing approved under the scheme amounted to ID 1,183.4m. for 217 operations. The Bank also finances other trade financing operations, including the Islamic Corporation for the Development of the Private Sector (see below), the Awqaf Properties Investment Fund and the Treasury Department. In addition, a Trade Co-operation and Promotion Programme supports efforts to enhance trade among OIC member countries. In June 2005 the Board of Governors approved the establishment of the ITFC as an autonomous trade promotion and financing institution within the Bank Group, with an authorized capital of US $3,000m. and subscribed capital of $500m. The inaugural meeting of the ITFC was held in February 2007. In May 2006 the Board of Governors approved a new fund to reduce poverty, in accordance with a proposal of the Organization of the Islamic Conference. It was inaugurated, as the Islamic Solidarity Fund for Development, in May 2007; at that time 28 countries had pledged

$1,600m. to the Fund. It was to commence operations on 1 January 2008.

In AH 1407 (1986–87) the Bank established an Islamic Bank's Portfolio for Investment and Development (IBP) in order to promote the development and diversification of Islamic financial markets and to mobilize the liquidity available to banks and financial institutions. During AH 1427 the IBP approved eight operations amounting to ID 135.8m. The Bank's Unit Investment Fund (UIF) became operational in 1990, with the aim of mobilizing additional resources and providing a profitable channel for investments conforming to *Shari'a*. The initial issue of the UIF was US $100m., which has subsequently been increased to $325m. The Fund finances mainly private-sector industrial projects in middle-income countries and also finances short-term trade operations. In October 1998 the Bank announced the establishment of a new fund to invest in infrastructure projects in member states. The Bank committed $250m. to the fund, which was to comprise $1,000m. equity capital and a $500m. Islamic financing facility. In November 2001 the Bank signed an agreement with Malaysia, Bahrain, Indonesia and Sudan for the establishment of an Islamic financial market. In April 2002 the Bank, jointly with governors of central banks and the Accounting and Auditing Organization for Islamic Financial Institutions, concluded an agreement, under the auspices of the IMF, for the establishment of an Islamic Financial Services Board. The Board, which was to be located in Kuala Lumpur, Malaysia, was intended to elaborate and harmonize standards for best practices in the regulation and supervision of the Islamic financial services industry. In August 2003 the Bank mobilized some $400m. from the international financial markets through the issue of the International Islamic Sukuk bond.

In AH 1404 (1983–84) the Bank established a scholarship programme for Muslim communities in non-member countries to provide opportunities for students to pursue further education or other professional training. The programme also assists nine member countries on an exceptional basis. By the end of the Islamic year 1427 the programme had benefited some 7,450 students, at a cost of ID 46.52m., from 58 countries. The Merit Scholarship Programme, initiated in AH 1412 (1991–92), aims to develop scientific, technological and research capacities in member countries through advanced studies and/or research. A total of 346 scholarships had been awarded, at a cost of ID 10.0m., by the end of AH 1427. In AH 1419 (1998–99) a Scholarship Programme in Science and Technology for IDB Least Developed Member Countries became operational for students in 20 eligible countries. By the end of AH 1427 183 students had been selected under the programme to study in other Bank member countries. of whom 77 had graduated under the Programme.

The Bank's Programme for Technical Co-operation aims to mobilize technical capabilities among member countries and to promote the exchange of expertise, experience and skills through expert missions, training, seminars and workshops. In December 1999 the Board of Executive Directors approved two technical assistance grants to support a programme for the eradication of illiteracy in the Islamic world, and one for self-sufficiency in human vaccine production. The Bank also undertakes the distribution of meat sacrificed by Muslim pilgrims. The Bank was the principal source of funding of the International Center for Biosaline Agriculture, which was established in Dubai, UAE, in September 1999.

BANK GROUP ENTITIES

Islamic Corporation for the Development of the Private Sector: POB 54069, Jeddah 21514, Saudi Arabia; tel. (2) 6441644; fax (2) 6444427; e-mail icd@isdb.org; internet www.icd-idb.org; f. 1999; to identify opportunities in the private sector, provide financial products and services compatible with Islamic law, mobilize additional resources for the private sector in member countries, and encourage the development of Islamic financing and capital markets; auth. cap. ID 675.2m. (of which the Bank's share is 50%, member countries 30% and public financial institutions of member countries 20%), subscribed cap. ID 337.6m. (July 2004); mems: 42 countries, the Bank, and five public financial institutions (a further seven countries have signed the Articles of Agreement and are in the process of ratification); CEO and Gen. Man. Dr ALI A. SULAIMAN.

Islamic Corporation for the Insurance of Investment and Export Credit (ICIEC): POB 15722, Jeddah 21454, Saudi Arabia; tel. (2) 6445666; fax (2) 6379504; e-mail idb.iciec@isdb.org.sa; internet www.iciec.com; f. 1994; aims to promote trade and the flow of investments among member countries of the OIC through the provision of export credit and investment insurance services; auth. cap. ID 100m., subscribed cap. ID 97.24m. (Feb. 2006); mems: 35 member states and the Islamic Development Bank (which contributes 50% of its capital); Gen. Man. Dr ABDEL RAHMAN A. TAHA.

Islamic Research and Training Institute: POB 9201, Jeddah 21413, Saudi Arabia; tel. (2) 6361400; fax (2) 6378927; e-mail maljarhi@isdb.org.sa; internet www.irti.org; f. 1982 to undertake research enabling economic, financial and banking activities to conform to Islamic law, and to provide training for staff involved in development activities in the Bank's member countries; the Institute also organizes seminars and workshops, and holds training courses aimed at furthering the expertise of government and financial officials in Islamic developing countries; Acting Dir BASHIR ALI KHALLAT; publs *Annual Report*, *Islamic Economic Studies* (2 a year), various research studies, monographs, reports.

Publication

Annual Report.

Statistics

OPERATIONS APPROVED, ISLAMIC YEAR 1427
(31 January 2006–19 January 2007)

Type of operation	Number of operations	Total amount (million Islamic Dinars)
Total project financing	181	1,490.0
Project financing	119	1,479.3
Technical assistance	62	10.8
Trade financing operations*	133	2,005.6
Special assistance operations	47	12.6
Total†	361	3,508.3

* Including ITFO, the EFS, the Islamic Bank's Portfolio, the UIF, and the Awqaf Properties Investment Fund.
† Excluding cancelled operations.

DISTRIBUTION OF PROJECT FINANCING AND TECHNICAL ASSISTANCE BY SECTOR, ISLAMIC YEAR 1427
(31 January 2006–19 January 2007)

Sector	Number of operations	Amount (million Islamic Dinars)	%
Agriculture and agro-industry	19	87.2	7.7
Industry and mining	6	145.4	12.9
Transport and communications	19	306.4	27.1
Public utilities	26	328.7	29.1
Social sectors	49	252.5	22.4
Financial services/Other	21	9.3	0.8
Total†	140	1,129.4	100.0

† Excluding cancelled operations.

ORGANIZATION OF THE ISLAMIC CONFERENCE—OIC

Address: Kilo 6, Mecca Rd, POB 178, Jeddah 21411, Saudi Arabia.
Telephone: (2) 690-0001; **fax:** (2) 275-1953; **e-mail:** info@oic-oic.org; **internet:** www.oic-oci.org.

The Organization was formally established in May 1971, when its Secretariat became operational, following a summit meeting of Muslim heads of state at Rabat, Morocco, in September 1969, and the Islamic Foreign Ministers' Conference in Jeddah in March 1970, and in Karachi, Pakistan, in December 1970.

MEMBERS

Afghanistan	Indonesia	Qatar
Albania	Iran	Saudi Arabia
Algeria	Iraq	Senegal
Azerbaijan	Jordan	Sierra Leone
Bahrain	Kazakhstan	Somalia
Bangladesh	Kuwait	Sudan
Benin	Kyrgyzstan	Suriname
Brunei	Lebanon	Syria
Burkina Faso	Libya	Tajikistan
Cameroon	Malaysia	Togo
Chad	The Maldives	Tunisia
Comoros	Mali	Turkey
Côte d'Ivoire	Mauritania	Turkmenistan
Djibouti	Morocco	Uganda
Egypt	Mozambique	United Arab Emirates
Gabon	Niger	Uzbekistan
The Gambia	Nigeria	Yemen
Guinea	Oman	
Guinea-Bissau	Pakistan	
Guyana	Palestine	

Note: Observer status has been granted to Bosnia and Herzegovina, the Central African Republic, Russia, Thailand, the Muslim community of the 'Turkish Republic of Northern Cyprus', the Moro National Liberation Front (MNLF) of the southern Philippines, the United Nations, the African Union, the Non-Aligned Movement, the League of Arab States, the Economic Co-operation Organization, the Union of the Arab Maghreb and the Co-operation Council for the Arab States of the Gulf.

Organization

(September 2007)

SUMMIT CONFERENCES

The supreme body of the Organization is the Conference of Heads of State, which met in 1969 at Rabat, Morocco, in 1974 at Lahore, Pakistan, and in January 1981 at Mecca, Saudi Arabia, when it was decided that ordinary summit conferences would normally be held every three years in future. An extraordinary summit conference was convened in Doha, Qatar, in March 2003, to consider the situation in Iraq. A further extraordinary conference, held in December 2005, in Mecca, Saudi Arabia, determined to restructure the OIC. The 10th ordinary Conference was held in Putrajaya, Malaysia, in October 2003. It was envisaged that the 11th would be hosted by Senegal. The summit conference troika comprises member countries equally representing OIC's African, Arab and Asian membership.

CONFERENCE OF MINISTERS OF FOREIGN AFFAIRS

Conferences take place annually, to consider the means for implementing the general policy of the Organization, although they may also be convened for extraordinary sessions. The ministerial conference troika comprises member countries equally representing OIC's African, Arab and Asian membership.

SECRETARIAT

The executive organ of the Organization, headed by a Secretary-General (who is elected by the Conference of Ministers of Foreign Affairs for a four-year term, renewable only once) and four Assistant Secretaries-General (similarly appointed).

Secretary-General: Prof. Dr EKMELEDDIN IHSANOGLU (Turkey).

At the summit conference in January 1981 it was decided that an International Islamic Court of Justice should be established to adjudicate in disputes between Muslim countries. Experts met in January 1983 to draw up a constitution for the court; however, by 2007 it was not yet in operation.

EXECUTIVE COMMITTEE

The third extraordinary conference of the OIC, convened in Mecca, Saudi Arabia, in December 2005, mandated the establishment of the Executive Committee, comprising the summit conference and ministerial conference troikas, the OIC host country, and the OIC Secretariat, as a mechanism for following-up resolutions of the Conference.

STANDING COMMITTEES

Al-Quds Committee: f. 1975 to implement the resolutions of the Islamic Conference on the status of Jerusalem (Al-Quds); it meets at the level of foreign ministers; maintains the Al-Quds Fund; Chair. King MUHAMMAD VI OF MOROCCO.

Standing Committee for Economic and Commercial Co-operation (COMCEC): f. 1981; Chair. ABDULLAH GÜL (Pres. of Turkey).

Standing Committee for Information and Cultural Affairs (COMIAC): f. 1981; Chair. ABDOULAYE WADE (Pres. of Senegal).

Standing Committee for Scientific and Technological Co-operation (COMSTECH): f. 1981; Chair. Gen. PERVEZ MUSHARRAF (Pres. of Pakistan).

Other committees comprise the Islamic Peace Committee, the Permanent Finance Committee, the Committee of Islamic Solidarity with the Peoples of the Sahel, the Eight-Member Committee on the Situation of Muslims in the Philippines, the Six-Member Committee on Palestine, the Committee on United Nations reform, and the ad hoc Committee on Afghanistan. In addition, there is an Islamic Commission for Economic, Cultural and Social Affairs, and there are OIC contact groups on Bosnia and Herzegovina, Kosovo, Jammu and Kashmir, Sierra Leone, and Somalia. A Commission of Eminent Persons was inaugurated in January 2005.

Activities

The Organization's aims, as proclaimed in the Charter that was adopted in 1972, are:

(i) To promote Islamic solidarity among member states;

(ii) To consolidate co-operation among member states in the economic, social, cultural, scientific and other vital fields, and to arrange consultations among member states belonging to international organizations;

(iii) To endeavour to eliminate racial segregation and discrimination and to eradicate colonialism in all its forms;

(iv) To take necessary measures to support international peace and security founded on justice;

(v) To co-ordinate all efforts for the safeguard of the Holy Places and support of the struggle of the people of Palestine, and help them to regain their rights and liberate their land;

(vi) To strengthen the struggle of all Muslim people with a view to safeguarding their dignity, independence and national rights;

(vii) To create a suitable atmosphere for the promotion of co-operation and understanding among member states and other countries.

The first summit conference of Islamic leaders (representing 24 states) took place in 1969 following the burning of the Al Aqsa Mosque in Jerusalem. At this conference it was decided that Islamic governments should 'consult together with a view to promoting close co-operation and mutual assistance in the economic, scientific, cultural and spiritual fields, inspired by the immortal teachings of Islam'. Thereafter the foreign ministers of the countries concerned met annually, and adopted the Charter of the Organization of the Islamic Conference in 1972.

At the second Islamic summit conference (Lahore, Pakistan, 1974), the Islamic Solidarity Fund was established, together with a committee of representatives which later evolved into the Islamic Commission for Economic, Cultural and Social Affairs. Subsequently, numerous other subsidiary bodies have been set up (see below).

ECONOMIC CO-OPERATION

A general agreement for economic, technical and commercial co-operation came into force in 1981, providing for the establishment of joint investment projects and trade co-ordination. This was followed by an agreement on promotion, protection and guarantee of investments among member states. A plan of action to strengthen economic co-operation was adopted at the third Islamic summit conference in

1981, aiming to promote collective self-reliance and the development of joint ventures in all sectors. In 1994 the 1981 plan of action was revised; the reformulated plan placed greater emphasis on private-sector participation in its implementation. Although several meetings of experts were subsequently held to discuss some of the 10 priority focus areas of the plan, little progress was achieved in implementing it during the 1990s and early 2000s. In October 2003 a meeting of COMCEC endorsed measures aimed at accelerating the implementation of the plan of action.

The fifth summit conference, held in 1987, approved proposals for joint development of modern technology, and for improving scientific and technical skills in the less developed Islamic countries. The first international Islamic trade fair was held in Jeddah, Saudi Arabia, in March 2001.

In 1991 22 OIC member states signed a Framework Agreement on a Trade Preferential System (TPS-OIC) among the OIC Member States; this entered into force in 2003, following the requisite ratification by more than 10 member states, and was envisaged as representing the first step towards the eventual establishment of an Islamic common market. A Trade Negotiating Committee (TNC) was established following the entry into force of the Framework Agreement. The first round of trade negotiations on the establishment of the TPS-OIC, concerning finalizing tariff-reduction modalities and an implementation schedule for the Agreement, was held during April 2004–April 2005. In November 2006, at the launch of the second round of negotiations, ministers adopted a road-map for establishing the TPS-OIC by 1 January 2009. In June 2007 the TNC adopted rules of origin for the TPS-OIC.

CULTURAL CO-OPERATION

The Organization supports education in Muslim communities throughout the world, and was instrumental in the establishment of Islamic universities in Niger and Uganda. It organizes seminars on various aspects of Islam, and encourages dialogue with the other monotheistic religions. Support is given to publications on Islam both in Muslim and Western countries. The OIC organizes meetings at ministerial level to consider aspects of information policy and new technologies.

HUMANITARIAN ASSISTANCE

Assistance is given to Muslim communities affected by wars and natural disasters, in co-operation with UN organizations, particularly UNHCR. The countries of the Sahel region (Burkina Faso, Cape Verde, Chad, The Gambia, Guinea, Guinea-Bissau, Mali, Mauritania, Niger and Senegal) receive particular attention as victims of drought. In July 2005 the OIC launched an emergency appeal to assist people affected by ongoing severe food insecurity in Niger. OIC member states have provided humanitarian assistance to the Muslim population affected by the conflict in Chechnya. In October 2001 the OIC established an Afghan People Assistance Trust Fund. The OIC also administers a Trust Fund to assist the return of refugees and the displaced to Bosnia and Herzegovina, and a Fund for the Reconstruction of Sierra Leone. A resolution on the status of refugees in the Muslim world that was adopted by the 10th OIC summit meeting, held in October 2003, urged all member states to accede to the 1951 UN Convention on the Status of Refugees. In June 2004 the OIC dispatched a mission to assess the situation in Darfur, Sudan. The OIC organized urgent emergency assistance for survivors of the December 2004 Indian Ocean tsunami, and planned to support reconstruction projects in affected countries. In January 2005 the OIC launched an emergency appeal to fund its tsunami-related operations. Following the earthquake that devastated northern parts of Pakistan in early October the OIC extended emergency financial assistance to the Pakistan Government and urged member states to contribute to the ongoing disaster relief operations.

POLITICAL CO-OPERATION

Since its inception the OIC has called for vacation of Arab territories by Israel, recognition of the rights of Palestinians and of the Palestine Liberation Organization (PLO) as their sole legitimate representative, and the restoration of Jerusalem to Arab rule. The 1981 summit conference called for a *jihad* (holy war—though not necessarily in a military sense) 'for the liberation of Jerusalem and the occupied territories'; this was to include an Islamic economic boycott of Israel. In 1982 Islamic ministers of foreign affairs decided to establish Islamic offices for boycotting Israel and for military co-operation with the PLO. The 1984 summit conference agreed to reinstate Egypt (suspended following the peace treaty signed with Israel in 1979) as a member of the OIC, although the resolution was opposed by seven states.

In August 1990 a majority of ministers of foreign affairs condemned Iraq's recent invasion of Kuwait, and demanded the withdrawal of Iraqi forces. In August 1991 the Conference of Ministers of Foreign Affairs obstructed Iraq's attempt to propose a resolution demanding the repeal of economic sanctions against the country. The sixth summit conference, held in Senegal in December, reflected the divisions in the Arab world that resulted from Iraq's invasion of Kuwait and the ensuing war. Twelve heads of state did not attend, reportedly to register protest at the presence of Jordan and the PLO at the conference, both of which had given support to Iraq. Disagreement also arose between the PLO and the majority of other OIC members when a proposal was adopted to cease the OIC's support for the PLO's *jihad* in the Arab territories occupied by Israel, in an attempt to further the Middle East peace negotiations.

In August 1992 the UN General Assembly approved a non-binding resolution, introduced by the OIC, that requested the UN Security Council to take increased action, including the use of force, in order to defend the non-Serbian population of Bosnia and Herzegovina (some 43% of Bosnians being Muslims) from Serbian aggression, and to restore its 'territorial integrity'. The OIC Conference of Ministers of Foreign Affairs, which was held in December, demanded anew that the UN Security Council take all necessary measures against Serbia and Montenegro, including military intervention, in order to protect the Bosnian Muslims.

A report by an OIC fact-finding mission, which in February 1993 visited Azad Kashmir while investigating allegations of repression of the largely Muslim population of the Indian state of Jammu and Kashmir by the Indian armed forces, was presented to the 1993 Conference. The meeting urged member states to take the necessary measures to persuade India to cease the 'massive human rights violations' in Jammu and Kashmir and to allow the Indian Kashmiris to 'exercise their inalienable right to self-determination'. In September 1994 ministers of foreign affairs, meeting in Islamabad, Pakistan, agreed to establish a contact group on Jammu and Kashmir, which was to provide a mechanism for promoting international awareness of the situation in that region and for seeking a peaceful solution to the dispute. In December OIC heads of state approved a resolution condemning reported human rights abuses by Indian security forces in Kashmir.

In July 1994 the OIC Secretary-General visited Afghanistan and proposed the establishment of a preparatory mechanism to promote national reconciliation in that country. In mid-1995 Saudi Arabia, acting as a representative of the OIC, pursued a peace initiative for Afghanistan and issued an invitation for leaders of the different factions to hold negotiations in Jeddah.

A special ministerial meeting on Bosnia and Herzegovina was held in July 1993, at which seven OIC countries committed themselves to making available up to 17,000 troops to serve in the UN Protection Force in the former Yugoslavia (UNPROFOR). The meeting also decided to dispatch immediately a ministerial mission to persuade influential governments to support the OIC's demands for the removal of the arms embargo on Bosnian Muslims and the convening of a restructured international conference to bring about a political solution to the conflict. In December 1994 OIC heads of state, convened in Morocco, proclaimed that the UN arms embargo on Bosnia and Herzegovina could not be applied to the Muslim authorities of that Republic. The Conference also resolved to review economic relations between OIC member states and any country that supported Serbian activities. An aid fund was established, to which member states were requested to contribute between US $500,000 and $5m., in order to provide further humanitarian and economic assistance to Bosnian Muslims. In relation to wider concerns the conference adopted a Code of Conduct for Combating International Terrorism, in an attempt to control Muslim extremist groups. The code commits states to ensuring that militant groups do not use their territory for planning or executing terrorist activity against other states, in addition to states refraining from direct support or participation in acts of terrorism. In a further resolution the OIC supported the decision by Iraq to recognize Kuwait, but advocated that Iraq comply with all UN Security Council decisions.

In July 1995 the OIC contact group on Bosnia and Herzegovina (at that time comprising Egypt, Iran, Malaysia, Morocco, Pakistan, Saudi Arabia, Senegal and Turkey), meeting in Geneva, declared the UN arms embargo against Bosnia and Herzegovina to be 'invalid'. Several Governments subsequently announced their willingness officially to supply weapons and other military assistance to the Bosnian Muslim forces. In September a meeting of all OIC ministers of defence and foreign affairs endorsed the establishment of an 'assistance mobilization group' which was to supply military, economic, legal and other assistance to Bosnia and Herzegovina. In a joint declaration the ministers also demanded the return of all territory seized by Bosnian Serb forces, the continued NATO bombing of Serb military targets, and that the city of Sarajevo be preserved under a Muslim-led Bosnian Government. In November the OIC Secretary-General endorsed the peace accord for the former Yugoslavia, which was concluded, in Dayton, USA, by leaders of all the conflicting factions, and reaffirmed the commitment of Islamic states to participate in efforts to implement the accord. In the following month the OIC Conference of Ministers of Foreign Affairs, convened in Conakry, Guinea, requested the full support of the international community to reconstruct Bosnia and Herzegovina through humanitarian aid as well as economic and technical co-operation. Ministers declared that Palestine and the establishment of fully-autonomous Palestinian control of Jerusalem were issues of central importance for the Muslim world. The Conference urged the removal of all aspects of occupation and the cessation of the construction of Israeli settlements in the occupied territories. In addition, the final statement of the meeting condemned Armenian aggression against Azerbaijan, registered concern at the persisting civil conflict in Afghanistan, demanded the elimination of all weapons of mass destruction and pledged support for Libya (affected by the US trade embargo). Ministers determined that an intergovernmental group of experts should be established in 1996 to address the situation of minority Muslim communities residing in non-OIC states.

In December 1996 OIC ministers of foreign affairs, meeting in Jakarta, Indonesia, urged the international community to apply pressure on Israel in order to ensure its implementation of the terms of the Middle East peace process. The ministers reaffirmed the importance of ensuring that the provisions of the Dayton Peace Agreement for the former Yugoslavia were fully implemented, called for a peaceful settlement of the Kashmir issue, demanded that Iraq fulfil its obligations for the establishment of security, peace and stability in the region and proposed that an international conference on peace and national reconciliation in Somalia be convened. In March 1997, at an extraordinary summit held in Pakistan, OIC heads of state and of government reiterated the organization's objective of increasing international pressure on Israel to ensure the full implementation of the terms of the Middle East peace process. An 'Islamabad Declaration' was also adopted, which pledged to increase co-operation between members of the OIC. In June the OIC condemned the decision by the US House of Representatives to recognize Jerusalem as the Israeli capital. The Secretary-General of the OIC issued a statement rejecting the US decision as counter to the role of the USA as sponsor of the Middle East peace plan.

In early 1998 the OIC appealed for an end to the threat of US-led military action against Iraq arising from a dispute regarding access granted to international weapons inspectors. The crisis was averted by an agreement concluded between the Iraqi authorities and the UN Secretary-General in February. In March OIC ministers of foreign affairs, meeting in Doha, Qatar, requested an end to the international sanctions against Iraq. Additionally, the ministers urged all states to end the process of restoring normal trading and diplomatic relations with Israel pending that country's withdrawal from the occupied territories and acceptance of an independent Palestinian state. In April the OIC, jointly with the UN, sponsored new peace negotiations between the main disputing factions in Afghanistan, which were conducted in Islamabad, Pakistan. In early May, however, the talks collapsed and were postponed indefinitely. In September the Secretaries-General of the OIC and UN agreed to establish a joint mission to counter the deteriorating security situation along the Afghan–Iranian border, following the large-scale deployment of Taliban troops in the region and consequent military manoeuvres by the Iranian authorities. They also reiterated the need to proceed with negotiations to conclude a peaceful settlement in Afghanistan. In December the OIC appealed for a diplomatic solution to the tensions arising from Iraq's withdrawal of co-operation with UN weapons inspectors, and criticized subsequent military airstrikes, led by the USA, as having been conducted without renewed UN authority. An OIC Convention on Combating International Terrorism was adopted in 1998. An OIC committee of experts responsible for formulating a plan of action for safeguarding the rights of Muslim communities and minorities met for the first time in 1998.

In early April 1999 ministers of foreign affairs of the countries comprising OIC's contact group met to consider the crisis in Kosovo. The meeting condemned Serbian atrocities being committed against the local Albanian population and urged the provision of international assistance for the thousands of people displaced by the conflict. The group resolved to establish a committee to co-ordinate relief aid provided by member states. The ministers also expressed their willingness to help to formulate a peaceful settlement and to participate in any subsequent implementation force. In June an OIC Parliamentary Union was inaugurated; its founding conference was convened in Tehran, Iran.

In early March 2000 the OIC mediated contacts between the parties to the conflict in Afghanistan, with a view to reviving peace negotiations. Talks, held under OIC auspices, ensued in May. In November OIC heads of state attended the ninth summit conference, held in Doha, Qatar. In view of the significant deterioration in relations between Israel and the Palestinian (National) Authority (PA) during late 2000, the summit issued a Declaration pledging solidarity with the Palestinian cause and accusing the Israeli authorities of implementing large-scale systematic violations of human rights against Palestinians. The summit also issued the Doha Declaration, which reaffirmed commitment to the OIC Charter and undertook to modernize the organization's organs and mechanisms. Both the elected Government of Afghanistan and the Taliban sent delegations to the Doha conference. The summit determined that Afghanistan's official participation in the OIC, suspended in 1996, should not yet be reinstated. In early 2001 a high-level delegation from the OIC visited Afghanistan in an attempt to prevent further destruction of ancient statues by Taliban supporters.

In May 2001 the OIC convened an emergency meeting, following an escalation of Israeli–Palestinian violence. The meeting resolved to halt all diplomatic and political contacts with the Israeli government, while restrictions remained in force against Palestinian-controlled territories. In June the OIC condemned attacks and ongoing discrimination against the Muslim Community in Myanmar. In the same month the OIC Secretary-General undertook a tour of six African countries—Burkina Faso, The Gambia, Guinea, Mali, Niger and Senegal—to promote co-operation and to consider further OIC support for those states. In August the Secretary-General condemned Israel's seizure of several Palestinian institutions in East Jerusalem and aerial attacks against Palestinian settlements. The OIC initiated high-level diplomatic efforts to convene a meeting of the UN Security Council in order to discuss the situation.

In September 2001 the OIC Secretary-General strongly condemned major terrorist attacks perpetrated against targets in the USA. Soon afterwards the US authorities rejected a proposal by the Taliban regime that an OIC observer mission be deployed to monitor the activities of the Saudi Arabian-born exiled militant Islamist fundamentalist leader Osama bin Laden, who was accused by the US Government of having co-ordinated the attacks from alleged terrorist bases in the Taliban-administered area of Afghanistan. An extraordinary meeting of OIC ministers of foreign affairs, convened in early October, in Doha, Qatar, to consider the implications of the terrorist atrocities, condemned the attacks and declared its support for combating all manifestations of terrorism within the framework of a proposed collective initiative co-ordinated under the auspices of the UN. The meeting, which did not pronounce directly on the recently-initiated US-led military retaliation against targets in Afghanistan, urged that no Arab or Muslim state should be targeted under the pretext of eliminating terrorism. It determined to establish a fund to assist Afghan civilians. In February 2002 the Secretary-General expressed concern at statements of the US administration describing Iran and Iraq (as well as the Democratic People's Republic of Korea) as belonging to an 'axis of evil' involved in international terrorism and the development of weapons of mass destruction. In early April OIC foreign ministers convened an extraordinary session on terrorism, in Kuala Lumpur, Malaysia. The meeting issued the 'Kuala Lumpur Declaration', which reiterated member states' collective resolve to combat terrorism, recalling the organization's 1994 code of conduct and 1998 convention to this effect; condemned attempts to associate terrorist activities with Islamists or any other particular creed, civilization or nationality, and rejected attempts to associate Islamic states or the Palestinian struggle with terrorism; rejected the implementation of international action against any Muslim state on the pretext of combating terrorism; urged the organization of a global conference on international terrorism; and urged an examination of the root causes of international terrorism. In addition, the meeting strongly condemned Israel's ongoing military intervention in areas controlled by the PA. The meeting adopted a plan of action on addressing the issues raised in the declaration. Its implementation was to be co-ordinated by a 13-member committee on international terrorism. Member states were encouraged to sign and ratify the Convention on Combating International Terrorism in order to accelerate its implementation. In June 2002 ministers of foreign affairs, meeting in Khartoum, Sudan, issued a declaration reiterating the OIC call for an international conference to be convened, under UN auspices, in order clearly to define terrorism and to agree on the international procedures and mechanisms for combating terrorism through the UN. The conference also repeated demands for the international community to exert pressure on Israel to withdraw from all Palestinian-controlled territories and for the establishment of an independent Palestinian state. It endorsed the peace plan for the region that had been adopted by the summit meeting of the League of Arab States in March.

In June 2002 the OIC Secretary-General expressed his concern at the escalation of tensions between Pakistan and India regarding Kashmir. He urged both sides to withdraw their troops and to refrain from the use of force. In the following month the OIC pledged its support for Morocco in a territorial dispute with Spain over the small island of Perejil, but called for a negotiated settlement to resolve the issue.

An extraordinary summit conference of Islamic leaders convened in Doha, Qatar, in early March 2003, to consider the ongoing Iraq crisis welcomed the Saddam Hussein regime's acceptance of UN Security Council Resolution 1441 and consequent co-operation with UN weapons inspectors, and emphatically rejected any military strike against Iraq or threat to the security of any other Islamic state. The conference also urged progress towards the elimination of all weapons of mass destruction in the Middle East, including those held by Israel. In May the 30th session of the Conference of Ministers of Foreign Affairs, entitled 'Unity and Dignity', issued the Tehran Declaration, in which it resolved to combat terrorism and to contribute to preserving peace and security in Islamic countries. The

Declaration also pledged its full support for the Palestinian cause and rejected the labelling as 'terrorist' of those Muslim states deemed to be resisting foreign aggression and occupation. The 10th OIC summit meeting, held in October, in Putrajaya, Malaysia, issued the Putrajaya Declaration, in which Islamic leaders resolved to enhance Islamic states' role and influence in international affairs. The leaders adopted a plan of action that entailed: reviewing and strengthening OIC positions on international issues; enhancing dialogue among Muslim thinkers and policy-makers through relevant OIC insitutions; promoting constructive dialogue with other cultures and civilizations; completing an ongoing review of the structure and efficacy of the OIC Secretariat; establishing a working group to address means of enhancing the role of Islamic education; promoting among member states the development of science and technology, discussion of ecological issues, and the role of information communication technology in development; improving mechanisms to assist member states in post-conflict situations; and advancing trade and investment through data-sharing and encouraging access to markets for products from poorer member states.

In mid-May 2004 the OIC Secretary-General urged combat forces in Iraq to respect the inviolability of that country's holy places. Shortly afterwards he condemned the ongoing destruction of Palestinian homes by Israeli forces, and consequent population displacement, particularly in Rafah, Gaza. He urged international organizations to condemn Israel's actions and appealed to the UN Security Council to intervene promptly in the situation and to compel Israel to respect international law. In June the Secretary-General welcomed progress achieved by a round of expert-level talks on nuclear confidence-building measures conducted during that month by India and Pakistan. An observer mission dispatched by the OIC to monitor presidential elections held in the Palestinian territories in early January 2005, at the request of the PA, was rejected by Israel. Later in that month the inaugural meeting of an OIC Commission of Eminent Persons was convened in Putrajaya, Malaysia. The Commission was mandated to finalize recommendations in the following areas: the preparation of a strategy and plan of action enabling the Islamic community to meet the challenges of the 21st century; the preparation of a comprehensive plan for promoting enlightened moderation, both within Islamic societies and universally; and the preparation of proposals for the future reform and restructuring of the OIC system. In December 2005 the third extraordinary OIC summit, convened in Mecca, Saudi Arabia, adopted a 'Ten-Year Programme of Action to Meet the Challenges Facing the Umma in the 21st Century', a related Mecca Declaration and a report by the Commission of Eminent Persons. The summit determined to restructure the OIC, and mandated the establishment of an Executive Committee, comprising the summit conference and ministerial conference troikas (equally reflecting the African, Arab and Asian member states), the OIC host country, and the OIC Secretariat, as a mechanism for following-up Conference resolutions.

In January 2006 the OIC strongly condemned the publication in a Norwegian newspaper of a series of caricatures of the Prophet Muhammad that had originally appeared in a Danish publication in September 2005 and had caused considerable offence to Islamists. In August 2006 the OIC convened a meeting of humanitarian bodies in Istanbul, Turkey, to address means of collecting donations for and delivering assistance to victims of the ongoing crises in Lebanon and the Palestinian territories. Shortly afterwards a meeting of the newly-formed Executive Committee, held in Kuala Lumpur, Malaysia, agreed to form a Contact Group for Lebanon, to be co-ordinated by Malaysia. In October a meeting of Iraqi Islamic scholars from all denominations issued the Makkah Declaration on the Iraqi situation, in which they urged unity between different Islamic factions in that country. The first OIC Conference on Women was held in the following month, on the theme 'the role of women in the development of OIC member states'.

Finance

The OIC's activities are financed by mandatory contributions from member states.

Subsidiary Organs

Islamic Centre for the Development of Trade: Complexe Commercial des Habous, ave des FAR, BP 13545, Casablanca, Morocco; tel. (2) 314974; fax (2) 310110; e-mail icdt@icdt.org; internet www.icdt.org; f. 1983 to encourage regular commercial contacts, harmonize policies and promote investments among OIC mems; Dir-Gen. ALLAL RACHDI; publs *Tijaris: International and Inter-Islamic Trade Magazine* (bi-monthly), *Inter-Islamic Trade Report* (annually).

Islamic Jurisprudence (Fiqh) Academy: POB 13917, Jeddah, Saudi Arabia; tel. (2) 667-1664; fax (2) 667-0873; internet www.fiqhacademy.org.sa; f. 1982; Sec.-Gen. Sheikh MOHAMED HABIB IBN AL-KHODHA.

Islamic Solidarity Fund: c/o OIC Secretariat, POB 178, Jeddah 21411, Saudi Arabia; tel. (2) 680-0800; fax (2) 687-3568; f. 1974 to meet the needs of Islamic communities by providing emergency aid and the finance to build mosques, Islamic centres, hospitals, schools and universities; Chair. Sheikh NASIR ABDULLAH BIN HAMDAN; Exec. Dir ABDULLAH HERSI.

Islamic University in Uganda: POB 2555, Mbale, Uganda; tel. (45) 33502; fax (45) 34452; e-mail iuiu@info.com.co.ug; internet www.iuiu-mbale.com; f. 1988 to meet the educational needs of Muslim populations in English-speaking African countries; second campus in Kampala; mainly financed by OIC; Rector Dr AHMAD KAWESA SENGENDO.

Islamic University of Niger: BP 11507, Niamey, Niger; tel. 723903; fax 733796; f. 1984; provides courses of study in *Shari'a* (Islamic law) and Arabic language and literature; also offers courses in pedagogy and teacher training; receives grants from Islamic Solidarity Fund and contributions from OIC member states; Rector Prof. ABDELALI OUDHRIRI.

Islamic University of Technology (IUT): Board Bazar, Gazipur 1704, Dhaka, Bangladesh; tel. (2) 980-0960; fax (2) 980-0970; e-mail vc@iut-dhaka.edu; internet www.iutoic-dhaka.edu; f. 1981 as the Islamic Centre for Technical and Vocational Training and Resources, named changed to Islamic Institute of Technology in 1994, current name adopted in June 2001; aims to develop human resources in OIC mem. states, with special reference to engineering, technology, tech. and vocational education and research; 135 staff and 646 students; library of 26,500 vols; Vice-Chancellor Prof. Dr M. FAZLI ILAHI; publs *News Bulletin* (annually), *Journal of Engineering and Technology* (2 a year), annual calendar and announcement for admission, reports, human resources development series.

Research Centre for Islamic History, Art and Culture (IRCICA): POB 24, Beşiktaş 80692, İstanbul, Turkey; tel. (212) 2591742; fax (212) 2584365; e-mail ircica@superonline.com; internet www.ircica.org; f. 1980; library of 60,000 vols; Dir-Gen. Prof. Dr EKMELEDDİN IHSANOĞLU; publs *Newsletter* (3 a year), monographical studies.

Statistical, Economic and Social Research and Training Centre for the Islamic Countries: Attar Sok 4, GOP 06700, Ankara, Turkey; tel. (312) 4686172; fax (312) 4673458; e-mail oicankara@sesrtcic.org; internet www.sesrtcic.org; f. 1978; Dir-Gen. ERDINÇ ERDÜN; publs *Journal of Economic Co-operation among Islamic Countries* (quarterly), *InfoReport* (quarterly), *Statistical Yearbook* (annually).

Specialized Institutions

International Islamic News Agency (IINA): King Khalid Palace, Madinah Rd, POB 5054, Jeddah 21422, Saudi Arabia; tel. (2) 665-8561; fax (2) 665-9358; e-mail iina@islamicnews.org.sa; internet www.islamicnews.org.sa; f. 1972; distributes news and reports daily on events in the Islamic world, in Arabic, English and French; Dir-Gen. ABDULWAHAB KASHIF.

Islamic Educational, Scientific and Cultural Organization (ISESCO): BP 2275 Rabat 10104, Morocco; tel. (37) 772433; fax (37) 772058; e-mail cid@isesco.org.ma; internet www.isesco.org.ma; f. 1982; Dir-Gen. Dr ABDULAZIZ BIN OTHMAN ALTWAIJRI; publs *ISESCO Newsletter* (quarterly), *Islam Today* (2 a year), *ISESCO Triennial*.

Islamic States Broadcasting Organization (ISBO): POB 6351, Jeddah 21442, Saudi Arabia; tel. (2) 672-1121; fax (2) 672-2600; e-mail isbo@isbo.org; internet www.isbo.org; f. 1975; Sec.-Gen. HUSSEIN AL-ASKARY.

Affiliated Institutions

International Association of Islamic Banks (IAIB): King Abdulaziz St, Queen's Bldg, 23rd Floor, Al-Balad Dist, POB 9707, Jeddah 21423, Saudi Arabia; tel. (2) 651-6900; fax (2) 651-6552; f. 1977 to link financial institutions operating on Islamic banking principles; activities include training and research; mems: 192 banks and other financial institutions in 34 countries; Sec.-Gen. SAMIR A. SHAIKH.

Islamic Chamber of Commerce and Industry: POB 3831, Clifton, Karachi 75600, Pakistan; tel. (21) 5874756; fax (21) 5870765; e-mail icci@icci-oic.org; internet icci-oic.org; f. 1979 to promote trade and industry among member states; comprises nat. chambers or feds of chambers of commerce and industry; Sec.-Gen. AQEEL AHMAD AL-JASSEM.

Islamic Committee for the International Crescent: POB 17434, Benghazi, Libya; tel. (61) 95823; fax (61) 95829; f. 1979 to attempt to alleviate the suffering caused by natural disasters and war; Sec.-Gen. Dr AHMAD ABDALLAH CHERIF.

Islamic Solidarity Sports Federation: POB 5844, Riyadh 11442, Saudi Arabia; tel. and fax (1) 482-2145; f. 1981; Sec.-Gen. Dr MOHAMMAD SALEH GAZDAR.

Organization of Islamic Capitals and Cities (OICC): POB 13621, Jeddah 21414, Saudi Arabia; tel. (2) 698-1953; fax (2) 698-1053; e-mail webmaster@oicc.org; internet www.oicc.org; f. 1980 to preserve the identity and heritage of Islamic capitals and cities; aims to advance sustainable development in Islamic capitals and cities; to develop comprehensive urban norms, systems and plans with a view to promoting optimum cultural, environmental, urban, economic and social conditions therein; and to support co-operation between member cities; comprises 145 capitals and cities as active members, eight observer members and 15 associate members, in Asia, Africa, Europe and South America; Sec.-Gen. OMAR ABDULLAH KADI.

Organization of the Islamic Shipowners' Association: POB 14900, Jeddah 21434, Saudi Arabia; tel. (2) 663-7882; fax (2) 660-4920; e-mail oisa@sbm.net.sa; f. 1981 to promote co-operation among maritime cos in Islamic countries; in 1998 mems approved the establishment of a new commercial venture, the Bakkah Shipping Company, to enhance sea transport in the region; Sec.-Gen. Dr ABDULLATIF A. SULTAN.

World Federation of Arab-Islamic Schools: POB 3446, Jeddah, Saudi Arabia; tel. (2) 670-0019; fax (2) 671-0823; f. 1976; supports Arab-Islamic schools world-wide and encourages co-operation between the institutions; promotes the dissemination of the Arabic language and Islamic culture; supports the training of personnel.

SOUTHERN AFRICAN DEVELOPMENT COMMUNITY—SADC

Address: SADC House, Government Enclave, Private Bag 0095, Gaborone, Botswana.

Telephone: 3951863; **fax:** 3972848; **e-mail:** registry@sadc.int; **internet:** www.sadc.int.

The first Southern African Development Co-ordination Conference (SADCC) was held at Arusha, Tanzania, in July 1979, to harmonize development plans and to reduce the region's economic dependence on South Africa. In August 1992 the 10 member countries of the SADCC signed a treaty establishing the Southern African Development Community (SADC), which replaced SADCC. The treaty places binding obligations on member countries, with the aim of promoting economic integration towards a fully developed common market. A tribunal was to be established to arbitrate in the case of disputes between member states arising from the treaty. By September 1993 all of the member states had ratified the treaty; it came into effect in early October. A protocol on the establishment of the long-envisaged SADC tribunal was adopted in 2000. The Protocol on Politics, Defence and Security Co-operation, regulating the structure, operations and functions of the Organ on Politics, Defence and Security, established in June 1996 (see under Regional Security), entered into force in March 2004. A troika system, comprising the current, incoming and outgoing SADC chairmanship, operates at the level of the Summit, Council of Ministers and Standing Committee of Officials, and co-ordinates the Organ on Politics, Defence and Security. Other member states may be co-opted into the troika as required. A system of SADC national committees, comprising representatives of government, civil society and the private sector, oversees the implementation of regional programmes at country level and helps to formulate new regional strategies. In recent years SADC institutions have been undergoing a process of intensive restructuring.

MEMBERS

Angola	Malawi	South Africa
Botswana	Mauritius	Swaziland
Congo, Democratic Republic	Mozambique	Tanzania
Lesotho	Namibia	Zambia
Madagascar	Seychelles*	Zimbabwe

* Seychelles, which withdrew from SADC in July 2004, was readmitted to the organization in August 2007.

Organization

(September 2007)

SUMMIT MEETING

The meeting is held at least once a year and is attended by heads of state and government or their representatives. It is the supreme policy-making organ of SADC and is responsible for the appointment of the Executive Secretary. A report on the restructuring of SADC, adopted by an extraordinary summit held in Windhoek, Namibia, in March 2001, recommended that biannual summit meetings should be convened. The most recent summit meeting of heads of state and government was held in Lusaka, Zambia, in August 2007.

COUNCIL OF MINISTERS

Representatives of SADC member countries at ministerial level meet at least once a year.

INTEGRATED COMMITTEE OF MINISTERS

The Integrated Committee of Ministers (ICM), comprising at least two ministers from each member state and responsible to the Council of Ministers, oversees the four priority areas of integration (trade, industry, finance and investment; infrastructure and services; food, agriculture and natural resources; and social and human development and special programmes) and monitors the Directorates that administer these; facilitates the co-ordination and harmonization of cross-sectoral activities; and provides policy guidance to the Secretariat. The ICM also supervises the implementation of the Regional Indicative Strategic Development Plan (RISDP—see below).

STANDING COMMITTEE OF OFFICIALS

The Committee, comprising senior officials, usually from the ministry responsible for economic planning or finance, acts as the technical advisory body to the Council. It meets at least once a year. Members of the Committee also act as a national contact point for matters relating to SADC.

SECRETARIAT

Executive Secretary: TOMÁS AUGUSTO SALOMÃO (Mozambique).

The extraordinary summit held in March 2001 determined that the mandate and resources of the Secretariat should be strengthened. A Department of Strategic Planning, Gender and Development and Policy Harmonization was established, comprising permanently-staffed Directorates covering the four priority areas of integration (see above).

Activities

In July 1979 the first Southern African Development Co-ordination Conference was attended by delegations from Angola, Botswana, Mozambique, Tanzania and Zambia, with representatives from donor governments and international agencies. In April 1980 a regional economic summit conference was held in Lusaka, Zambia, and the Lusaka Declaration, a statement of strategy entitled 'Southern Africa: Towards Economic Liberation', was approved. The members aimed to reduce their dependence on South Africa for rail and air links and port facilities, imports of raw materials and manufactured goods, and the supply of electric power. In 1985, however, an SADCC report noted that since 1980 the region had become still more dependent on South Africa for its trade outlets, and the 1986 summit meeting, although it recommended the adoption of economic sanctions against South Africa, failed to establish a timetable for doing so.

In January 1992 a meeting of the SADCC Council of Ministers approved proposals to transform the organization (by then expanded to include Lesotho, Malawi, Namibia and Swaziland) into a fully integrated economic community, and in August the treaty establishing SADC was signed. An SADC Programme of Action (SPA) was to combine the strategies and objectives of the organization's sectoral programmes. South Africa became a member of SADC in August 1994, thus strengthening the objective of regional co-operation and economic integration. Mauritius became a member in August 1995. In September 1997 SADC heads of state agreed to admit the Democratic Republic of the Congo (DRC) and Seychelles as members of the Community; Seychelles withdrew in July 2004. In August 2005 Madagascar was admitted as a member by SADC heads of state.

A possible merger between SADC and the Preferential Trade Area for Eastern and Southern African States (PTA), which consisted of all the members of SADC apart from Botswana and had similar aims of enhancing economic co-operation, was rejected by SADC's Executive Secretary in January 1993. He denied that the two organizations were duplicating each other's work, as had been suggested. However, concerns of regional rivalry with the PTA's successor, the Common Market for Eastern and Southern Africa (COMESA), persisted. In August 1996 an SADC–COMESA ministerial meeting advocated the continued separate functioning of the two organizations. A programme of co-operation between the secretariats of SADC and COMESA, aimed at reducing all duplication of roles between the two organizations, is under way. A co-ordinating SADC/COMESA task force was established in 2001.

In September 1994 the first conference of ministers of foreign affairs of SADC and the European Union (EU) was held in Berlin, Germany. The two sides agreed to establish working groups to promote closer trade, political, regional and economic co-operation. In particular, a declaration issued from the meeting specified joint objectives, including a reduction of exports of weapons to southern Africa and of the arms trade within the region, promotion of investment in the region's manufacturing sector and support for democracy at all levels. A consultative meeting between representatives of SADC and the EU was held in February 1995, in Lilongwe, Malawi, at which both groupings resolved to strengthen security in the southern African region. A second SADC–EU ministerial conference, held in Namibia in October 1996, endorsed a Regional Indicative Programme (RIP) to enhance co-operation between the two organizations over the next five years. The third ministerial conference took place in Vienna, Austria, in November 1998. In September 1999 SADC signed a co-operation agreement with the US Government, which incorporated measures to promote US investment in the region, and commitments to support HIV/AIDS assessment and prevention programmes and to assist member states to develop environmental protection capabilities. The fourth SADC–EU ministerial conference, convened in Gaborone, Botswana, in November 2000, adopted a joint declaration on the control of small arms and light weapons in the SADC region. The meeting also emphasized that the termination of illicit trading in diamonds would be a major contributory factor in resolving the ongoing conflicts in Angola and the DRC (see below). The fifth SADC–EU ministerial conference was held in Maputo, Mozambique, in November 2002. In October 2004 an EU–SADC ministerial 'double troika' meeting took place in The Hague, Netherlands, to mark 10 years of dialogue between the two organizations. At the meeting both SADC and the EU reaffirmed their commitment to reinforcing co-operation with regard to peace and security in Africa. It was agreed to pursue the revitalization within the SADC region of training for peace-keeping, possibly with the support of the RIP and the European Programme for Reconstruction and Development in South Africa.

In July 1996 the SADC Parliamentary Forum was inaugurated, with the aim of promoting democracy, human rights and good governance throughout the region. Membership of the Forum, which is headquartered in Windhoek, Namibia, is open to national parliaments of all SADC countries, and offers fair representation for women. Representatives serve for a period of five years. The Forum receives funds from member parliaments, governments and charitable and international organizations. In September 1997 SADC heads of state endorsed the establishment of the Forum as an autonomous institution. The Forum frequently deploys missions to monitor parliamentary and presidential elections in the region. A regional women's parliamentary caucus was inaugurated in April 2002.

The August 2004 summit meeting of heads of state and government, held in Grand Baie, Mauritius, adopted a new Protocol on Principles and Guide-lines Governing Democratic Elections, which advocated: full participation by citizens in the political process; freedom of association; political tolerance; elections at regular intervals; equal access to the state media for all political parties; equal opportunity to exercise the right to vote and be voted for; independence of the judiciary; impartiality of the electoral institutions; the right to voter education; the respect of election results proclaimed to be free and fair by a competent national electoral authority; and the right to challenge election results as provided for in the law.

At the summit meeting of heads of state and government held in Maseru, Lesotho, in August 2006 a new Protocol on Finance and Investment was adopted. Amendments to SADC protocols on the Tribunal, trade, immunities and privileges, transport, communications and meteorology, energy and mining, combating illicit drugs and education and training were also approved at the meeting. The summit emphasized the need to scale up implementation of the SADC's agenda for integration, identifying the RISDP (see below) and the Strategic Indicative Plan for the Organ (SIPO) as the principal instruments for achieving this objective. In pursuit of this aim, the summit established a task force—comprising ministers responsible for finance, investment, economic development, trade and industry—charged with defining the measures necessary for the eradication of poverty and how their implementation might be accelerated.

The extraordinary summit meeting convened in March 2001 adopted a report detailing recommendations on the restructuring of SADC's institutions, with a view to facilitating the effective application of the objectives of the organization's treaty and of the SPA. During 2001–03 the Community's former system comprising 21 sectors was, accordingly, reorganized under four new directorates: trade, industry, finance and investment; infrastructure and services; food, agriculture and natural resources; and social and human development and special programmes. The directorates are administered from the secretariat in Gaborone, in order to ensure greater efficiency (the previous sectoral system had been decentralized). The report adopted in March 2001 outlined a Common Agenda for the organization, which covered the promotion of poverty reduction measures and of sustainable and equitable socio-economic development, promotion of democratic political values and systems, and the consolidation of peace and security. The extraordinary summit meeting also authorized the establishment of an integrated committee of ministers mandated to formulate a five-year Regional Indicative Strategic Development Plan (RISDP), intended as the key policy framework for managing the SADC Common Agenda. A draft of the RISDP, adopted by the SADC Council of Ministers in March 2003, was approved by the summit meeting convened in Dar es Salaam, Tanzania, in August. In April 2006 SADC adopted the Windhoek Declaration on a new relationship between the Community and its international co-operating partners. The declaration provides a framework for co-operation and dialogue between the SADC and international partners, facilitating the implementation of the SADC Common Agenda.

In August 2001 SADC established a task force, comprising representatives of five member countries, to address the ongoing political crisis in Zimbabwe. The Community sent two separate observer teams to monitor the controversial presidential election held in Zimbabwe in March 2002; the SADC Council of Ministers team found the election to have been conducted freely and fairly, while the Parliamentary Forum group was reluctant to endorse the poll. Having evaluated both reports, the Community approved the election. An SADC Council of Ministers group was convened to observe the parliamentary elections held in Zimbabwe in March 2005; however, the Zimbabwean Government refused to invite a delegation from the SADC Parliamentary Forum. The Zimbabwean Government claimed to have enacted electoral legislation in accordance with the provisions of the August 2004 SADC Protocol on Principles and Guide-lines Governing Democratic Elections (see above). An extraordinary summit meeting of SADC heads of state and government, convened in Dar es Salaam, Tanzania, in March 2007, to address the political, economic, and security situation in the region, declared 'solidarity with the government and people of Zimbabwe' and mandated President Thabo Mbeki of South Africa to facilitate dialogue between the Zimbabwean government and opposition. Mbeki reported to the ordinary SADC summit held in August of that year that restoring Zimbabwe's capacity to generate foreign exchange through balance-of-payments support would be of pivotal importance in promoting economic recovery and that the SADC should assist Zimbabwe with addressing the issue of international sanctions.

In the mid-2000s SADC, with other African regional economic communities, was considering a draft protocol on relations between them and the African Union (AU). A high-level meeting concerned with integrating the objectives of the New Partnership for Africa's Development (NEPAD) into SADC's regional programme activities was convened in August 2004. The summit meeting of heads of state and government held in Maseru, Lesotho, in August 2006 determined that an extraordinary session of the SADC Council of Ministers should be convened to develop a common approach towards the issue of Union government. In November of that year, at an EU-SADC ministerial 'double troika' meeting held in Maseru, Lesotho, SADC representatives agreed to the development of institutional support to the member states through the establishment of a Human Rights Commission and a new SADC Electoral Advisory Council (SEAC).

REGIONAL SECURITY

In November 1994 SADC ministers of defence, meeting in Arusha, Tanzania, approved the establishment of a regional rapid-deployment peace-keeping force, which could be used to contain regional conflicts or civil unrest in member states. In April 1997 a training programme was organized in Zimbabwe, which aimed to inform troops from nine SADC countries of UN peace-keeping doctrines, procedures and strategies. A peace-keeping exercise involving 4,000 troops was held in South Africa, in April 1999. A further SADC peace-keeping exercise was conducted in February 2002 in Tanzania, jointly with Tanzanian and Ugandan forces. An SADC Mine Action Committee has been established to monitor and co-ordinate the process of removing anti-personnel land devices from countries in the region. The summit meeting of heads of state and government held in August 2007 authorized the establishment of an SADC

Standby Brigade (SADCBRIG), with the aim of ensuring collective regional security and stability.

In June 1996 SADC heads of state and government, meeting in Gaborone, Botswana, inaugurated an Organ on Politics, Defence and Security, which was expected to enhance co-ordination of national policies and activities in these areas. The objectives of the body were, *inter alia*, to safeguard the people and development of the region against instability arising from civil disorder, inter-state conflict and external aggression; to undertake conflict prevention, management and resolution activities, by mediating in inter-state and intra-state disputes and conflicts, pre-empting conflicts through an early-warning system and using diplomacy and peace-keeping to achieve sustainable peace; to promote the development of a common foreign policy, in areas of mutual interest, and the evolution of common political institutions; to develop close co-operation between the police and security services of the region; and to encourage the observance of universal human rights, as provided for in the charters of the UN and the Organization of African Unity (OAU—now AU). There were, however, disagreements within SADC regarding its future status, either as an integrated part of the Community (favoured by South Africa) or as a more autonomous body (supported by Zimbabwe).

In August 1998 the Zimbabwean Government convened a meeting of the heads of state of seven SADC member states to discuss the escalation of civil conflict in the DRC and the threat to regional security, with Rwanda and Uganda reportedly having sent troops to assist anti-government forces. Later in that month ministers of defence and defence officials of several SADC countries declared their support for an initiative of the Zimbabwean Government to send military assistance to the forces loyal to President Kabila in the DRC. South Africa, which did not attend the meeting, rejected any military intervention under SADC auspices and insisted that the organization would pursue a diplomatic initiative. Zimbabwe, Angola and Namibia proceeded to send troops and logistical support to counter rebel Congolese forces. The Presidents of those countries failed to attend an emergency meeting of heads of state, convened by President Mandela of South Africa, which called for an immediate cease-fire and presented a 10-point-peace plan. A further emergency meeting, held in early September and attended by all SADC leaders, agreed to pursue negotiations for a peaceful settlement of the conflict. Some unity within the grouping was restored by Mandela's endorsement of the objective of supporting Kabila as the legitimate leader in the DRC. Furthermore, at the annual SADC summit meeting, held in Mauritius, it was agreed that discussion of the report on the security Organ, scheduled to have been presented to the conference, would be deferred to a specially convened summit meeting (although no date was agreed). Talks attended by Angola, the DRC, Namibia, Rwanda, Uganda, Zambia and Zimbabwe, conducted in mid-September, in Victoria Falls, agreed in principle on a cease-fire in the DRC but failed to conclude a detailed peace accord. Fighting continued to escalate, and in October Zimbabwe, Angola and Namibia resolved to send reinforcements to counter the advancing rebel forces. Meanwhile, in September representatives of SADC attempted to mediate between government and opposition parties in Lesotho amidst a deteriorating security situation in that country. At the end of the month, following an attempt by the Lesotho military to seize power, South Africa, together with Botswana, sent troops into Lesotho to restore civil order. The operation, which was declared to have been conducted under SADC auspices, prompted widespread criticism owing to the troops' involvement in heavy fighting with opposition forces. A committee was established by SADC to secure a cease-fire in Lesotho. Also at the end of September SADC chiefs of staff agreed that the Community would assist the Angolan Government to eliminate the UNITA movement, owing to its adverse impact on the region's security. In October an SADC ministerial team, comprising representatives of South Africa, Botswana, Mozambique and Zimbabwe, negotiated an accord between the opposing sides in Lesotho providing for the conduct of democratic elections. The withdrawal of foreign troops from Lesotho was initiated at the end of April 1999, and was reported to have been completed by mid-May.

During the first half of 1999 Zambia's President Chiluba pursued efforts, under SADC auspices, to negotiate a political solution to the conflict in the DRC. Troops from the region, in particular from Angola and Zimbabwe, remained actively involved in the struggle to uphold Kabila's administration. SADC ministers of defence and of foreign affairs convened in Lusaka, in June, in order to secure a cease-fire agreement. An accord was finally signed in July between Kabila, leaders of the rebel forces and foreign allies of both sides. All foreign troops were to be withdrawn within nine months according to a schedule to be drawn up by the UN, OAU and a Joint Military Commission. However, the disengagement and redeployment of troops from front-line positions did not commence until February 2001. SADC welcomed peace accords signed by the DRC Govenment with Ugandan-backed rebels and with the Rwandan Government, respectively in July and August 2002. In August 2001 SADC heads of state resolved to support the continuing imposition of sanctions by the UN Security Council against the UNITA rebels in Angola; it was agreed to promote the international certification system for illicit trade in rough diamonds (believed to finance UNITA's activities), to install mobile radar systems that would detect illegal cross-border flights in the region, and to establish a body to compile information and to devise a strategy for terminating the supply of petroleum products to UNITA. SADC welcomed the cease-fire that was signed by the Angolan Government and UNITA in April 2002; all UN sanctions against UNITA were withdrawn by December.

In June 2004 SADC sent a fact-finding mission to the DRC to investigate continuing armed military activities, particularly in eastern areas. An SADC Parliamentary Forum observer mission monitored the legislative and first stage of presidential elections that were held in the DRC in July 2006.

In August 2000 proposals were announced (strongly supported by South Africa, see above) to develop the Organ for Politics, Defence and Security as a substructure of SADC, with subdivisions for defence and international diplomacy, to be chaired by a member country's head of state, working within a troika system; these were approved at the extraordinary summit held in March 2001. A Protocol on Politics, Defence and Security Co-operation, regulating the structure, operations and functions of the Organ, was adopted and opened for signature in August and entered into force in March 2004. The protocol was to be implemented by an Inter-state Politics and Diplomacy Committee.

The March 2001 extraordinary SADC summit adopted a Declaration on Small Arms, promoting the curtailment of the proliferation of and illicit trafficking in light weapons in the region. A Protocol on the Control of Firearms, Ammunition and Other Related Materials was adopted in August of that year. In July SADC ministers of defence approved a draft regional defence pact, providing for a mechanism to prevent conflict involving member countries and for member countries to unite against outside aggression. In January 2002 an extraordinary summit of SADC heads of state, held in Blantyre, Malawi, adopted a Declaration against Terrorism.

TRADE, INDUSTRY AND INVESTMENT

Under the treaty establishing SADC, efforts were to be undertaken to achieve regional economic integration. The Directorate of Trade, Industry, Finance and Investment aims to facilitate such integration, and poverty eradication, through the creation of an enabling investment and trade environment in SADC countries. Objectives include the establishment of a single regional market; the progressive removal of barriers to the movement of goods, services and people; and the promotion of cross-border investment. SADC supports programmes for industrial research and development and standardization and quality assurance, and aims to mobilize industrial investment resources and to co-ordinate economic policies and the development of the financial sector. In August 1996, at a summit meeting held in Lesotho, SADC member states signed the Protocol on Trade, providing for the establishment of a regional free-trade area, through the gradual elimination of tariff barriers (with an eight-year implementation schedule envisaged at that time). (Angola and the DRC are not signatories to the Protocol.) In October 1999 representatives of the private sector in SADC member states established the Association of SADC Chambers of Commerce, based in Mauritius. The Protocol on Trade entered into force in January 2000, and an Amendment Protocol on Trade came into force in August, incorporating renegotiated technical details on the gradual elimination of tariffs, rules of origin, customs co-operation, special industry arrangements and dispute settlement procedures. The implementation phase of the Protocol on Trade commenced in September. In accordance with a revised schedule, all intra-SADC trade tariffs were to be removed by 2012, with about 85% to be withdrawn by 1 January 2008. According to the schedule, reaffirmed at the EU–SADC ministerial meeting in 2006, a customs union was to be implemented by 2010, a common market by 2015, monetary union by 2016, and a single currency was to be introduced by 2018. Annual meetings are convened to review the work of expert teams in the areas of standards, quality, assurance, accreditation and metrology. At an SADC Extraordinary Summit convened in October 2006 it was determined that a roadmap was to be developed to facilitate the process of establishing a customs union.

The mining sector contributes about 10% of the SADC region's annual GDP. The principal objective of SADC's programme of action on mining is to stimulate increased local and foreign investment in the sector, through the assimilation and dissemination of data, prospecting activities, and participation in promotional fora. In December 1994 SADC held a mining forum, jointly with the EU, in Lusaka, Zambia, with the aim of demonstrating to potential investors and promoters the possibilities of mining exploration in the region. A second mining investment forum was held in Lusaka in December 1998; and a third ('Mines 2000'), also in Lusaka, in October 2000. Subsequently a Mines 2000 follow-up programme has been implemented. Other objectives of the mining sector are the improvement of industry training, increasing the contribution of small-scale mining, reducing the illicit trade in gemstones and gold, increasing co-operation in mineral exploration and processing, and minimizing the adverse impact of mining operations on the environment. In February 2000 a Protocol on Mining entered into force, providing for the harmonization of policies and programmes relating to the development and exploitation of mineral resources in the region. SADC supports the Kimberley Process Certification Scheme aimed at preventing illicit trade in illegally mined rough diamonds. (The illicit trade in so-called 'conflict diamonds' and other minerals is believed to have motivated and financed many incidences of rebel activity in the continent, for example in Angola and the DRC.)

In July 1998 a Banking Association was officially constituted by representatives of SADC member states. The Association was to establish international banking standards and regional payments systems, organize training and harmonize banking legislation in the region. In April 1999 governors of SADC central banks determined to strengthen and harmonize banking procedures and technology in order to facilitate the financial integration of the region. Efforts to harmonize stock exchanges in the region were also initiated in 1999.

The summit meeting of heads of state and government held in Maseru, Lesotho, in August 2006 adopted a new Protocol on Finance and Investment. The document, regarded as constituting the main framework for economic integration in southern Africa, outlined, *inter alia*, how the region intends to proceed towards monetary union by 2010 and was intended to complement the ongoing implementation of the SADC Protocol on Trade and targets contained in the RISDP.

INFRASTRUCTURE AND SERVICES

The Directorate of Infrastructure and Services focuses on transport, communications and meteorology, energy, tourism and water. At SADC's inception transport was regarded as the most important area to be developed, on the grounds that, as the Lusaka Declaration noted, without the establishment of an adequate regional transport and communications system, other areas of co-operation become impractical. Priority was to be given to the improvement of road and railway services into Mozambique, so that the land-locked countries of the region could transport their goods through Mozambican ports instead of South African ones. The Southern African Transport and Communications Commission (SATCC) was established, in Maputo, Mozambique, in order to undertake SADC's activities in this sector. During 1995 the SATCC undertook a study of regional transport and communications to provide a comprehensive framework and strategy for future courses of action. A task force was also established to identify measures to simplify procedures at border crossings throughout southern Africa. In 1996 the SATCC Road Network Management and Financing Task Force was established. An SADC Transport Investment Forum was convened in Windhoek, Namibia, in April 2001. In March the Association of Southern African National Road Agencies (ASANRA) was established to foster the development of an integrated regional transportation system. Eleven railways in the region form the Interconnected Regional Rail Network (IRRN), comprising nearly 34,000 km of route track.

SADC development projects have aimed to address missing links and over-stretched sections of the regional network, as well as to improve efficiency, operational co-ordination and human resource development, such as management training projects. Other objectives have been to ensure the compatibility of technical systems within the region and to promote the harmonization of regulations relating to intra-regional traffic and trade. In 1997 Namibia announced plans, supported by SADC, to establish a rail link with Angola in order to form a trade route similar to that created in Mozambique, on the western side of southern Africa. In March 1998 the final stage of the trans-Kalahari highway, linking ports on the east and west coasts of southern Africa, was officially opened. In July 1999 a 317-km rail link between Bulawayo, Zimbabwe, and the border town of Beitbridge, administered by SADC as its first build-operate-transfer project, was opened. SADC promotes greater co-operation in the civil aviation sector, in order to improve efficiency and to reverse a steady decline in the region's airline industries. Within the telecommunications sector efforts have been made to increase the capacity of direct exchange lines and international subscriber dialling (ISD) services. In January 1997 the Southern African Telecommunications Regional Authority (SATRA), a regulatory authority, was established.

The SADC's road network, whose length totals more than 1m. km, constitutes the regions's principal mode of transport for both freight and passengers and is thus vital to the economy. Unsurfaced, low-volume roads account for a substantial proportion of the network and many of these are being upgraded to a sealed standard as part of a wider strategy that focuses on the alleviation of poverty and the pursuit of economic growth and development. In 2003 the SADC adopted a guide-line on the best regional and international practice in all matters concerning low-volume sealed roads.

SADC policy guide-lines on 'making information and communications technology a priority in turning SADC into an information-based economy' were adopted in November 2001. Policy guide-lines and model regulations on tariffs for telecommunications services have also been adopted. An SADC Expedited Mail Service operates in the postal services sector. The SATCC's Technical Unit oversees the region's meteorological services and issues a regular *Drought Watch for Southern Africa* bulletin, a monthly *Drought Overview* bulletin, and forewarnings of impending natural disasters. SADC is developing a regional strategy aimed at improving the early warning capabilities of national meteorological services.

Areas of activity in the energy sector include: joint petroleum exploration, training programmes for the petroleum sector and studies for strategic fuel storage facilities; promotion of the use of coal; development of hydroelectric power and the co-ordination of SADC generation and transmission capacities; new and renewable sources of energy, including pilot projects in solar energy; assessment of the environmental and socio-economic impact of wood-fuel scarcity and relevant education programmes; and energy conservation. In July 1995 SADC energy ministers approved the establishment of the Southern African Power Pool, whereby all member states were to be linked into a single electricity grid. (Several grids are already integrated and others are being rehabilitated.) At the same time, ministers endorsed a protocol to promote greater co-operation in energy development within SADC, providing for the establishment of an Energy Commission, responsible for 'demand-side' management, pricing, ensuring private-sector involvement and competition, training and research, collecting information, etc.; the protocol entered into force in September 1998. SADC implements a Petroleum Exploration Programme. In September 1997 heads of state endorsed an Energy Action Plan to proceed with the implementation of co-operative policies and strategies in four key areas of energy: trade, information exchange, training and organizational capacity-building, and investment and financing. A technical unit of the Energy Commission was to be responsible for implementation of the Action Plan. Two major regional energy supply projects were under development in the mid-2000s: utilities from Angola, Botswana, the DRC, Namibia and South Africa were participating in the Western Power Corridor project, approved in October 2002, and a feasibility study was initiated in 2003 for a planned Zambia–Tanzania Inter-connector Project.

The tourism sector operates within the context of national and regional socio-economic development objectives. It comprises four components: tourism product development; tourism marketing and research; tourism services; and human resources development and training. SADC has promoted tourism for the region at trade fairs in Europe, and has initiated a project to provide a range of promotional material and a regional tourism directory. In 1993 the Council approved the implementation of a project to design a standard grading classification system for tourist accommodation in the region, which had been completed with the assistance of the World Tourism Organization. In September 1997 the legal charter for the establishment of a new Regional Tourism Organization for Southern Africa (RETOSA), to be administered jointly by SADC officials and private-sector operators, was signed by ministers of tourism. RETOSA assists member states to formulate tourism promotion policies and strategies. During 1999 a feasibility study on the development of the Upper Zambezi basin as a site for eco-tourism was initiated. Consultations are under way on the development of a common visa (UNIVISA) system to promote tourism in the region. By February 2007 several countries, including Mozambique, South Africa and Swaziland, had abolished visa requirements for citizens of other SADC member states. Preparations for the introduction of the UNIVISA were being undertaken across the region; it was anticipated that the common visa would be in place by 2008, in advance of the 2010 FIFA World Cup, to be hosted by South Africa.

SADC aims to promote equitable distribution and effective management of water resources. A Protocol on Shared Watercourse Systems entered into force in April 1998, and a Revised Protocol on Shared Watercourses came into force in September 2003. A regional strategic action plan for integrated water resources development and management in the SADC region was launched in 1999.

FOOD, AGRICULTURE AND NATURAL RESOURCES

The Directorate of Food, Agriculture and Natural Resources aims to develop, co-ordinate and harmonize policies and programmes on agriculture and natural resources with a focus on sustainability. The Directorate covers the following sectors: agricultural research and training; inland fisheries; forestry; wildlife; marine fisheries and resources; food security; livestock production and animal disease control; and environment and land management. According to SADC figures, agriculture contributes one-third of the region's GNP, accounts for about one-quarter of total earnings of foreign exchange and employs some 80% of the labour force. The principal objectives in this field are regional food security, agricultural development and natural resource development.

The Southern African Centre for Co-operation in Agricultural Research (SACCAR), was established in Gaborone, Botswana, in 1985. It aims to strengthen national agricultural research systems, in order to improve management, increase productivity, promote the development and transfer of technology to assist local farmers, and improve training. Examples of activity include: a sorghum and millet improvement programme; a land and water management research programme; a root crop research network; agroforestry research, implemented in Malawi, Tanzania, Zambia and Zimbabwe; and a grain legume improvement programme, comprising separate research units for groundnuts, beans and cowpeas. SADC's Plant Genetic Resources Centre, based near Lusaka, Zambia, aims to collect, conserve and utilize indigenous and exotic plant genetic resources and to develop appropriate management practices. In 2003 an SADC fact-finding mission on genetically modified organisms (GMOs) visited Belgium and the USA and made a number of recommendations for consideration by a newly-established advisory committee on biosafety and biotechnology based at the SADC Secretariat; the recommendations were endorsed by senior officials of ministries of agriculture in June. SADC member states were to develop national legislation on GMOs by the end of 2004.

SADC aims to promote inland and marine fisheries as an important, sustainable source of animal protein. Marine fisheries are also considered to be a potential source of income of foreign exchange. In May 1993 the first formal meeting of SADC ministers of marine fisheries convened in Namibia, and it was agreed to hold annual meetings. Meeting in May 2002 marine fisheries ministers expressed concern about alleged ongoing illegal, unregulated and unreported (IUU) fisheries activities in regional waters. The development of fresh water fisheries is focused on aquaculture projects, and their integration into rural community activities. The SADC Fisheries Protocol entered into force in September 2003. Environment and land management activities have an emphasis on sustainability as an essential quality of development. SADC aims to protect and improve the health, environment and livelihoods of people living in the southern African region; to preserve the natural heritage and biodiversity of the region; and to support regional economic development on a sustainable basis. There is also a focus on capacity-building, training, regional co-operation and the exchange of information in all areas related to the environment and land management. SADC operates an Environmental Exchange Network and implements a Land Degradation and Desertification Control Programme. Projects on the conservation and sustainable development of forestry and wildlife are under implementation. An SADC Protocol on Forestry was signed in October 2002, and in November 2003 the Protocol on Wildlife Conservation and Law Enforcement entered into force.

Under the food security programme, the Regional Early Warning Unit aims to anticipate and prevent food shortages through the provision of information relating to the food security situation in member states. As a result of frequent drought crises, SADC member states have agreed to inform the food security sector of their food and non-food requirements on a regular basis, in order to assess the needs of the region as a whole. A Regional Food Reserve Facility is to be developed. A programme on irrigation development and water management aims to reduce regional dependency on rain-fed agricultural production, while a programme on the promotion of agricultural trade and food safety aims to increase intra-regional and inter-regional trade with a view to improving agriculture growth and rural incomes. An SADC extraordinary summit on agriculture and food security, held in May 2004 in Dar es Salaam, Tanzania, considered strategies for accelerating development in the agricultural sector and thereby securing food security and reducing poverty in the region.

The sector for livestock production and animal disease control has aimed to improve breeding methods in the region through the Management of Farm Animal Genetic Research Programme. It also seeks to control diseases such as contagious bovine pleuropneumonia, foot-and-mouth disease and African swine fever through diagnosis, monitoring and vaccination programmes. An *Animal Health Mortality Bulletin* is published, as is a monthly *Animal Disease Situation Bulletin*, which alerts member states to outbreaks of disease in the region. An SADC regional foot-and-mouth disease policy was being formulated in the mid-2000s.

SOCIAL AND HUMAN DEVELOPMENT AND SPECIAL PROGRAMMES

SADC helps to supply the region's requirements in skilled manpower by providing training in the following categories: high-level managerial personnel; agricultural managers; high- and medium-level technicians; artisans; and instructors. The Technical Committee on Accreditation and Certification aims to harmonize and strengthen the education and training systems in SADC through initiatives such as the standardization of curricula and examinations. Human resources development activities focus on determining active labour market information systems and institutions in the region, improving education policy analysis and formulation, and addressing issues of teaching and learning materials in the region. SADC administers an Intra-regional Skills Development Programme. SADC has initiated a programme of distance education to enable greater access to education, and operates a scholarship and training awards programme. In September 1997 heads of state, meeting in Blantyre, Malawi, endorsed the establishment of a Gender Department within the Secretariat to promote the advancement and education of women. A Declaration on Gender and Development was adopted. At the same time representatives of all member countries (except Angola) signed a Protocol on Education and Training, which was to provide a legal framework for co-operation in this sector; this entered into force in July 2000. In 2001 a gender audit study of aspects of the SADC SPA was finalized. An SADC regional human development report for 2000 was published in 2001 by UNDP and the Southern African Regional Institute for Policy Studies. An SADC Protocol on Combating Illicit Drugs entered into force in March 1999. In October 2000 an SADC Epidemiological Network on Drug Use was established to enable the systematic collection of narcotics-related data. SADC operates a regional drugs control programme, funded by the EU. In February 2007 a task force was mandated to investigate measures for improving employment conditions in member countries. The development of an SADC Protocol on Gender Equality was under consideration in 2007.

In August 1999 an SADC Protocol on Health was adopted. SADC has adopted a strategic framework (currently covering the period 2004–07) and programme of action for tackling HIV/AIDS, which are endemic in the region. In December 1999 a multisectoral sub-committee on HIV/AIDS was established. In August 2000 SADC adopted a set of guide-lines to underpin any future negotiations with major pharmaceutical companies on improving access to and reducing the cost of drugs to combat HIV/AIDS. In July 2003 an SADC special summit on HIV/AIDS, convened in Maseru, Lesotho, and attended by representatives of the World Bank, UNAIDS and WHO, issued the Maseru Declaration on HIV/AIDS, identifying priority areas for action, including prevention, access to testing and treatment, and social mobilization. The implementation of the strategic framework and Maseru Declaration were to be co-ordinated through an SADC Business Plan on HIV/AIDS, which was under development in 2004. The Plan was to focus on harmonizing regional guidelines on mother-to-child transmission and anti-retroviral therapy; and to address issues relating to access to affordable essential drugs, including bulk procurement and regional production. An SADC Protocol on Sexually Transmitted Infections Treatment was expected to be adopted by the end of 2007 and a regional policy on Orphans and Vulnerable Children has been under development. SADC is implementing a Southern African Tuberculosis Control Initiative (SATCI); the office of SATCI TB/HIV Co-ordinator was inaugurated in February 2001. In May 2000 an SADC Malaria Task Force was established.

SADC seeks to promote employment and harmonize legislation concerning labour and social protection. Activities include: the implementation of International Labour Standards, the improvement of health and safety standards in the workplace, combating child labour and the establishment of a statistical database for employment and labour issues.

Following the ratification of the treaty establishing the Community, regional socio-cultural development was to be emphasized as part of the process of greater integration. The SADC Press Trust was established, in Harare, Zimbabwe, to disseminate information about SADC and to articulate the concerns and priorities of the region. Public education initiatives have commenced to encourage the involvement of people in the process of regional integration and development, as well as to promote democratic and human rights' values. In 1994 the SADC Festival on Arts and Culture project was initiated. Interdisciplinary and monodisciplinary festivals are alternated on a two-yearly basis. The following monodisciplinary festivals are planned: theatre (in 2008) and visual arts (2012). An SADC Cultural Fund was established in 1996. A draft SADC protocol on piracy and protection of copyright and neighbouring rights has been prepared.

Finance

SADC's administrative budget for 2007/08 amounted to US $18.9m., to be financed mainly by contributions from member states.

Publications

Quarterly Food Security Bulletin.

SACCAR Newsletter (quarterly).

SADC Annual Report.

SADC Energy Bulletin.

SADC Today (six a year).

SATCC Bulletin (quarterly).

SKILLS.

SPLASH.

OTHER REGIONAL ORGANIZATIONS

Agriculture, Food, Forestry and Fisheries

(for organizations concerned with agricultural commodities, see Commodities)

African Feed Resources Network (AFRINET): c/o ASARECA, POB 765, Entebbe, Uganda; tel. (41) 320212; fax (41) 321126; e-mail asareca@imul.com; f. 1991 by merger of two African livestock fodder and one animal nutrition research networks; aims to co-ordinate research in all aspects of animal feeding and to strengthen national programmes to develop solutions for inadequate livestock food supplies and poor quality feeds; mems: in 34 countries; publ. *AFRNET Newsletter* (quarterly).

African Timber Organization (ATO): BP 1077, Libreville, Gabon; tel. 732928; fax 734030; e-mail oab-gabon@internetgabon.com; f. 1976 to enable members to study and co-ordinate ways of ensuring the optimum utilization and conservation of their forests; mems: 13 African countries; publs *ATO Information Bulletin* (quarterly), *International Magazine of African Timber* (2 a year).

Association for the Advancement of Agricultural Science in Africa (AAASA): POB 30087, Addis Ababa, Ethiopia; tel. (1) 44-3536; f. 1968 to promote the development and application of agricultural sciences and the exchange of ideas; to encourage Africans to enter training; holds several seminars each year in different African countries; mems: individual agricultural scientists, research institutes in 63 countries; Sec.-Gen. Prof. M. EL-FOULQ (acting); publs *Journal* (2 a year), *Newsletter* (quarterly).

CAB International (CABI): Nosworthy Way, Wallingford, Oxon, OX10 8DE, United Kingdom; tel. (1491) 832111; fax (1491) 833508; e-mail corporate@cabi.org; internet www.cabi.org; f. 1929 as the Imperial Agricultural Bureaux (later Commonwealth Agricultural Bureaux), current name adopted in 1985; aims to improve human welfare world-wide through the generation, dissemination and application of scientific knowledge in support of sustainable development; places particular emphasis on sustainable agriculture, forestry, human health and the management of natural resources, with priority given to the needs of developing countries; compiles and publishes extensive information (in a variety of print and electronic forms) on aspects of agriculture, forestry, veterinary medicine, the environment and natural resources, and Third World rural development; maintains regional centres in the People's Republic of China, India, Kenya, Malaysia, Pakistan, Switzerland, Trinidad and Tobago, and the United Kingdom; mems: 45 countries and territories; Chair. Dr JOHN REGAZZI.

CABI Bioscience: Bakeham Lane, Egham, Surrey, TW20 9TY, United Kingdom; tel. (1491) 829080; fax (1491) 829100; e-mail bioscience.egham@cabi.org; internet www.cabi-bioscience.org; f. 1998 by integration of the following four CABI scientific institutions: International Institute of Biological Control; International Institute of Entomology; International Institute of Parasitology; International Mycological Institute; undertakes research, consultancy, training, capacity-building and institutional development measures in sustainable pest management, biosystematics and molecular biology, ecological applications and environmental and industrial microbiology; maintains centres in Kenya, Malaysia, Pakistan, Switzerland, Trinidad and Tobago, and the United Kingdom; Dir Dr JOAN KELLEY.

Desert Locust Control Organization for Eastern Africa (DLCOEA): POB 4255, Addis Ababa, Ethiopia; tel. (1) 461477; fax (1) 460296; e-mail dlc@ethionet.et; internet www.dlcoea.org.et; f. 1962 to promote effective control of desert locust in the region and to conduct research into the locust's environment and behaviour; also assists member states in the monitoring, forecasting and extermination of other migratory pests; mems: Djibouti, Eritrea, Ethiopia, Kenya, Somalia, Sudan, Tanzania, Uganda; Dir PETER O. ODIYO; Co-ordinator J. M. GATIMU; publs *Desert Locust Situation Reports* (monthly), *Annual Report*, technical reports.

Indian Ocean Tuna Commission (IOTC): POB 1011, Victoria, Mahé, Seychelles; tel. 225494; fax 224364; e-mail iotc.secretary@iotc.org; internet www.iotc.org; f. 1996 as a regional fisheries organization with a mandate for the conservation and management of tuna and tuna-like species in the Indian Ocean; mems: Australia, People's Republic of China, the Comoros, European Union, Eritrea, France, Guinea, India, Iran, Japan, Kenya, Republic of Korea, Madagascar, Malaysia, Mauritius, Oman, Pakistan, Philippines, Seychelles, Sudan, Sri Lanka, Thailand, United Kingdom, Vanuatu; co-operating parties: Indonesia, South Africa; Exec. Sec. ALEJANDRO ANGANUZZI (Mauritius).

International Crops Research Institute for the Semi-Arid Tropics (ICRISAT) Sahelian Centre: BP 12404, Niamey, Niger; tel. 72-25-29; fax 73-43-29; e-mail icrisatsc@cgiar.org; internet www.icrisat.org; headquarters in India; f. 1972 to promote the genetic improvement of crops and for research on the management of resources in the world's semi-arid tropics, with the aim of reducing poverty and protecting the environment; research at the Sahelian Centre focuses on the improvement of pearl millet, the generation of improved resource management technologies (in collaboration with national programmes) and socio-economic studies related to input markets; the Sahelian Centre hosts the Sahelian Programme of the ILRI, the West and Central African Millet Research Network, and the Initiative on Desert Margins of the Consultative Group on International Agricultural Research; Dir Dr SAIDOU KOALA (Niger).

International Food Policy Research Institute (IFPRI): 2033 K St, N.W. Washington, DC 20006, USA; tel. (202) 862-5600; fax (202) 467-4439; e-mail ifpri@cgiar.org; internet www.ifpri.org; f. 1975; co-operates with academic and other institutions in further research; develops policies for cutting hunger and malnutrition; committed to increasing public awareness of food policies; Chair. Dr ROSS GARNAUT (Australia); Dir Gen. JOACHIM VON BRAUN (Germany)

International Service for National Agricultural Research (ISNAR): IFPRI, ISNAR Division, ILRI, POB 5689, Addis Ababa, Ethiopia; tel. (11) 646-3215; fax (11) 646-2927; e-mail ifpri-addisababa@cgiar.org; fmrly based in The Hague, Netherlands, the ISNAR Program relocated to Addis Ababa in 2004, under the governance of IFPRI; Dir Dr WILBERFORCE KISAMBA-MUGERWA.

International Institute of Tropical Agriculture (IITA): Oyo Rd, PMB 5320, Ibadan, Oyo State, Nigeria; tel. (2) 2412626; fax (2) 2412221; e-mail iita@cgiar.org; internet www.iita.org; f. 1967; principal financing arranged by the Consultative Group on International Agricultural Research—CGIAR, co-sponsored by the FAO, the IBRD and the UNDP; research programmes comprise crop management, improvement of crops and plant protection and health; conducts a training programme for researchers in tropical agriculture; maintains a library of 75,000 vols and a database; administers six agro-ecological research stations; Dir-Gen. Dr PETER HARTMAN (USA); publs *Annual Report*, *IITA Research* (quarterly), technical bulletins, research reports.

International Livestock Research Institute (ILRI): POB 30709, Nairobi 00100, Kenya; tel. (20) 4223000; fax (20) 4223001; e-mail ilri-kenya@cgiar.org; internet www.cgiar.org/ilri; f. 1995 to supersede the International Laboratory for Research on Animal Diseases and the International Livestock Centre for Africa; conducts laboratory and field research on animal health and other livestock issues; carries out training programmes for scientists and technicians; maintains a specialized science library; Dir Dr CARLOS SERÉ; publs *Annual Report*, *Livestock Research for Development* (newsletter, 2 a year).

International Red Locust Control Organization for Central and Southern Africa (IRLCO-CSA): POB 240252, Ndola, Zambia; tel. (2) 651251; fax (2) 650117; e-mail locust@zamnet.zm; internet www.irlcocsa.com; f. 1971 to control locusts in eastern, central and southern Africa; also assists in the control of African army-worm and quelea-quelea; mems: six countries; Dir MOSES M. OKHOBA; publs *Annual Report*, *Quarterly Report*, *Monthly Report*, scientific reports.

International Scientific Council for Trypanosomiasis Research and Control: c/o AU Interafrican Bureau for Animal Resources, POB 30786, Nairobi, Kenya; tel. (20) 338544; fax (20) 332046; e-mail parcibar@africaonline.co.ke; f. 1949 to review the work on tsetse and trypanosomiasis problems carried out by organizations and workers concerned in laboratories and in the field; to stimulate further research and discussion and to promote co-ordination between research workers and organizations in the different countries in Africa, and to provide a regular opportunity for the discussion of particular problems and for the exposition of new experiments and discoveries; Sec. Dr SOLOMON H. MARIAM.

World Organisation of Animal Health: 12 rue de Prony, 75017 Paris, France; tel. 1-44-15-18-88; fax 1-42-67-09-87; e-mail oie@oie.int; internet www.oie.int; f. 1924 as Office International des Epizooties (OIE); objectives include promoting international transparency of animal diseases; collecting, analysing and disseminating scientific veterinary information; providing expertise and promoting international co-operation in the control of animal diseases; promoting veterinary services; providing new scientific guide-lines on animal production, food safety and animal welfare; launched in May 2005, jointly with FAO and WHO, a Global Strategy for the Progressive Control of Highly Pathogenic Avian Influenza (H5N1), and, in partnership with other organizations, has convened conferences on avian influenza; experts in a network of 156 collaborating centres and reference laboratories; 167 mems; Dir-Gen. BERNARD VALLAT; publs *Disease Information* (weekly), *World Animal Health* (annually), *Scientific and Technical Review* (3 a year), other manuals, codes etc.

Arts and Culture

Afro-Asian Writers' Association: 'Al Ahram', Al Gala's St, Cairo, Egypt; tel. (2) 5747011; fax (2) 5747023; f. 1958; mems: writers' orgs in 51 countries; Sec.-Gen. LOTFI EL-KHOLY; publs *Lotus Magazine of Afro-Asian Writings* (quarterly in English, French and Arabic), *Afro-Asian Literature Series* (in English, French and Arabic).

Organization of World Heritage Cities: 15 rue Saint-Nicolas, Québec, QC G1K 1M8, Canada; tel. (418) 692-0000; fax (418) 692-5558; e-mail secretariat@ovpm.org; internet www.ovpm.org; f. 1993 to assist cities inscribed on the UNESCO World Heritage List to implement the Convention concerning the Protection of the World Cultural and Natural Heritage (1972); promotes co-operation between city authorities, in particular in the management and sustainable development of historic sites; holds an annual General Assembly, comprising the mayors of member cities; mems: 218 cities world-wide; Sec.-Gen. DENIS RICARD; publ. *OWHC Newsletter* (2 a year, in English, French and Spanish).

Pan-African Writers' Association (PAWA): PAWA House, Roman Ridge, POB C456, Cantonments, Accra, Ghana; tel. (21) 773-062; fax (21) 773-042; e-mail pawa@ghana.com; f. 1989 to link African creative writers, defend the rights of authors and promote awareness of literature; mems: 52 national writers' associations on the continent; Sec.-Gen. ATUKWEI OKAI (Ghana).

Commodities

African Groundnut Council (AGC): Trade Fair Complex, Badagry Expressway Km 15, POB 3025, Marina, Lagos, Nigeria; tel. (1) 8970605; e-mail info@afgroundnutcouncil.org; internet www.afgroundnutcouncil.org; f. 1964 to advise producing countries on marketing policies; mems: Gambia, Mali, Niger, Nigeria, Senegal, Sudan; Exec. Sec. ELHADJ MOUR MAMADOU SAMB (Senegal); publ. *Groundnut Review*.

African Oil Palm Development Association (AFOPDA): 15 BP 341, Abidjan 15, Côte d'Ivoire; tel. 21-25-15-18; fax 20-21-97-06; f. 1985; seeks to increase production of, and investment in, palm oil; mems: Benin, Cameroon, Democratic Republic of the Congo, Côte d'Ivoire, Ghana, Guinea, Nigeria, Togo; Exec. Sec. BAUDELAIRE HOUNSINOU SOUROU.

African Petroleum Producers' Association (APPA): POB 1097, Brazzaville, Republic of the Congo; tel. 665-38-57; fax 669-99-38; e-mail appa@africanpetroleumproducers.org; f. 1987 by African petroleum-producing countries to reinforce co-operation among regional producers and to stabilize prices; council of ministers responsible for the hydrocarbons sector meets twice a year; holds annual Congress and Exhibition: Cotonou, Benin (June 2007); mems: Algeria, Angola, Benin, Cameroon, Democratic Republic of the Congo, Republic of the Congo, Côte d'Ivoire, Egypt, Equatorial Guinea, Gabon, Libya, Nigeria; Exec. Sec. MAXIME OBIANG-NZE; publ. *APPA Bulletin* (2 a year).

Cocoa Producers' Alliance (CPA): National Assembly Complex, Tafawa Balewa Sq., POB 1718, Lagos, Nigeria; tel. (1) 2635574; fax (1) 2635684; e-mail info@copal-cpa.com; internet www.copal-cpa.org; f. 1962 to exchange technical and scientific information, to discuss problems of mutual concern to producers, to ensure adequate supplies at remunerative prices and to promote consumption; mems: Brazil, Cameroon, Côte d'Ivoire, Dominican Republic, Gabon, Ghana, Malaysia, Nigeria, São Tomé and Príncipe, Togo; Sec.-Gen. HOPE SONA EBAI.

Common Fund for Commodities: POB 74658, 1070 BR, Amsterdam, Netherlands; tel. (20) 5754949; fax (20) 6760231; e-mail managing.director@common-fund.org; internet www.common-fund.org; f. 1989 as the result of an UNCTAD negotiation conference; finances commodity development measures including research, marketing, productivity improvements and vertical diversification, with the aim of increasing the long-term competitiveness of particular commodities; paid-in capital US $165m; mems: 106 countries and the AU, EC and COMESA; Man. Dir (also Chief Exec.) ALI MCHUMO.

East Africa Tea Trade Association: Tea Trade Centre, Nyerere Ave, Mombasa, Kenya; tel. (41) 2228460; fax (41) 2225823; e-mail info@eatta.com; internet www.eatta.com; f. 1957; brings together producers, brokers, buyers and packers; Chair. LERIONKA TIAMPATI.

Inter-African Coffee Organization (IACO) (Organisation internationale du café—OIAC): BP V210, Abidjan, Côte d'Ivoire; tel. 20-21-61-31; fax 20-21-62-12; e-mail oiac-iaco@aviso.ci; f. 1960 to adopt a common policy on the marketing and consumption of coffee; aims to foster greater collaboration in research technology transfer through the African Coffee Research Network (ACRN); seeks to improve the quality of coffee exports, and implement poverty reduction programmes focusing on value added product (VAP) and the manufacturing of green coffee; mems: 25 coffee-producing countries in Africa; Chair. AMADOU SOUMAHORO (Côte d'Ivoire); Sec.-Gen. JOSEFA LEONEL CORREIA SACKO (Angola).

International Cocoa Organization (ICCO): Commonwealth House, 1–19 New Oxford St, London, WC1A 1NU, United Kingdom; tel. (20) 7400-5050; fax (20) 7421-5500; e-mail info@icco.org; internet www.icco.org; f. 1973 under the first International Cocoa Agreement, 1972; the ICCO supervises the implementation of the agreements, and provides member governments with up-to-date information on the world cocoa economy; the sixth International Cocoa Agreement (2001) entered into force in October 2003; mems: 22 exporting countries and 30 importing countries; and the European Union; Exec. Dir Dr JAN VINGERHOETS (Netherlands); publs *Quarterly Bulletin of Cocoa Statistics*, *Annual Report*, *World Cocoa Directory*, *Cocoa Newsletter*, studies on the world cocoa economy.

International Coffee Organization (ICO): 22 Berners St, London, W1T 3DD, United Kingdom; tel. (20) 7612-0600; fax (20) 7612-0630; e-mail info@ico.org; internet www.ico.org; f. 1963 under the International Coffee Agreement, 1962, which was renegotiated in 1968, 1976, 1983, 1994 (extended in 1999) and 2001; aims to improve international co-operation and provide a forum for intergovernmental consultations on coffee matters; to facilitate international trade in coffee by the collection, analysis and dissemination of statistics; to act as a centre for the collection, exchange and publication of coffee information; to promote studies in the field of coffee; and to encourage an increase in coffee consumption; mems: 45 exporting and 32 importing countries; Chair. of Council MAURO OREFICE (Italy); Exec. Dir NÉSTOR OSORIO (Colombia).

International Grains Council (IGC): 1 Canada Sq., Canary Wharf, London, E14 5AE, United Kingdom; tel. (20) 7513-1122; fax (20) 7513-0630; e-mail igc@igc.org.uk; internet www.igc.org.uk; f. 1949 as International Wheat Council, present name adopted in 1995; responsible for the administration of the International Grains Agreement, 1995, comprising the Grains Trade Convention (GTC) and the Food Aid Convention (FAC, under which donors pledge specified minimum annual amounts of food aid for developing countries in the form of grain and other eligible products); aims to further international co-operation in all aspects of trade in grains, to promote international trade in grains, and to achieve a free flow of this trade, particularly in developing member countries; seeks to contribute to the stability of the international grain market; acts as a forum for consultations between members; provides comprehensive information on the international grain market; mems: 25 countries and the EU; Exec. Dir ETSUO KITAHARA; publs *World Grain Statistics* (annually), *Wheat and Coarse Grain Shipments* (annually), *Report for the Fiscal Year* (annually), *Grain Market Report* (monthly), *IGC Grain Market Indicators* (weekly).

International Sugar Organization: 1 Canada Sq., Canary Wharf, London, E14 5AA, United Kingdom; tel. (20) 7513-1144; fax (20) 7513-1146; e-mail exdir@isosugar.org; internet www.isosugar.org; administers the International Sugar Agreement (1992), with the objectives of stimulating co-operation, facilitating trade and encouraging demand; aims to improve conditions in the sugar market through debate, analysis and studies; serves as a forum for discussion; holds annual seminars and workshops; sponsors projects from developing countries; mems: 74 countries producing some 83% of total world sugar; Exec. Dir Dr PETER BARON; publs *Sugar Year Book*, *Monthly Statistical Bulletin*, *Market Report and Press Summary*, *Quarterly Market Outlook*, seminar proceedings.

International Tea Committee Ltd (ITC): 1 Carlton House Terrace, London, SW1Y 5DB, United Kingdom; tel. (20) 7839-5090; fax (20) 7839-5052; e-mail inteacom@globalnet.co.uk; internet www.inttea.com; f. 1933 to administer the International Tea Agreement; now serves as a statistical and information centre; in 1979 membership was extended to include consuming countries; producer mems: national tea boards or asscns in Bangladesh, People's Republic of China, India, Indonesia, Kenya, Malawi, Sri Lanka; consumer mems: United Kingdom Tea Asscn, Tea Asscn of the USA Inc., Irish Tea Trade Asscn, Netherland Coffee Roasters and Tea Packers' Asscn, and the Tea Asscn of Canada; assoc. mems: Netherlands and UK ministries of agriculture, and national tea boards/asscns in eight producing countries; Chief Exec. MANUJA PEIRIS; publs *Annual Bulletin of Statistics*, *Monthly Statistical Summary*.

International Tea Promotion Association (ITPA): c/o Tea Board of Kenya, POB 20064, City Sq., 00200 Nairobi, Kenya; tel. (20) 572421; fax (20) 562120; e-mail teaboardk@kenyaweb.com; internet www.teaboard.or.ke; f. 1979; mems: eight countries; Chair. NICHOLAS NGANGA; publ. *International Tea Journal* (2 a year).

International Tobacco Growers' Association (ITGA): Av. Gen. Humberto Delgado 30-A, 6001-081 Castelo Branco, Portugal; tel. (272) 325901; fax (272) 325906; e-mail itga@tobaccoleaf.org; internet www.tobaccoleaf.org; f. 1984 to provide a forum for the exchange of views and information of interest to tobacco producers; mems: 20 countries producing over 80% of the world's internationally traded tobacco; Chief Exec. ANTÓNIO ABRUNHOSA (Portugal); publs *Tobacco Courier* (quarterly), *Tobacco Briefing*.

International Tropical Timber Organization (ITTO): International Organizations Center, 5th Floor, Pacifico-Yokohama, 1-1-1, Minato-Mirai, Nishi-ku, Yokohama 220-0012, Japan; tel. (45) 223-1110; fax (45) 223-1111; e-mail itto@itto.or.jp; internet www.itto.or.jp; f. 1985 under the International Tropical Timber Agreement (1983); a new treaty, ITTA 1994, came into force in 1997; provides a forum for consultation and co-operation between countries that produce and consume tropical timber, and is dedicated to the sustainable development and conservation of tropical forests; facilitates progress towards 'Objective 2000', which aims to move as rapidly as possible towards achieving exports of tropical timber and timber products from sustainably managed resources; encourages, through policy and project work, forest management, conservation and restoration, the further processing of tropical timber in producing countries, and the gathering and analysis of market intelligence and economic information; mems: 33 producing and 26 consuming countries and the EU; Exec. Dir EMMANUEL ZE MEKA (Cameroon) (from Nov. 2007); publs *Annual Review and Assessment of the World Timber Situation*, *Tropical Timber Market Information Service* (every 2 weeks), *Tropical Forest Update* (quarterly).

Organization of the Petroleum Exporting Countries (OPEC): 1020 Vienna, Obere Donaustrasse 93, Austria; tel. (1) 211-12-279; fax (1) 214-98-27; internet www.opec.org; f. 1960 to unify and co-ordinate members' petroleum policies and to safeguard their interests generally; holds regular conferences of member countries to set reference prices and production levels; conducts research in energy studies, economics and finance; provides data services and news services covering petroleum and energy issues; mems: Algeria, Indonesia, Iran, Iraq, Kuwait, Libya, Nigeria, Qatar, Saudi Arabia, United Arab Emirates, Venezuela; Sec.-Gen. ABDULLA SALEM EL-BADRI (Libya); publs *Annual Report*, *Annual Statistical Bulletin*, *OPEC Bulletin* (monthly), *OPEC Review* (quarterly), *Monthly Oil Market Report*.

OPEC Fund for International Development: Postfach 995, 1010 Vienna, Austria; tel. (1) 515-64-0; fax (1) 513-92-38; e-mail info@opecfund.org; internet www.opecfund.org; f. 1976 by mem. countries of OPEC, to provide financial co-operation and assistance for developing countries; in 2004 commitments amounted to US $528.6m; Dir-Gen. SULEIMAN J. AL-HERBISH (Saudi Arabia); publs *Annual Report*, *OPEC Fund Newsletter* (3 a year).

West Africa Rice Development Association (WARDA): 01 BP 2031, Cotonou, Benin; tel. 21-35-01-88; fax 21-35-05-56; e-mail warda@cgiar.org; internet www.cgiar.org/warda; f. 1971 as a mem. of the network of agricultural research centres supported by the Consultative Group on International Agricultural Research (CGIAR); aims to contribute to food security and poverty eradication in poor rural and urban populations, particularly in West and Central Africa, through research, partnerships, capacity strengthening and policy support on rice-based systems; promotes sustainable agricultural development based on environmentally-sound management of natural resources; maintains research stations in Côte d'Ivoire, Nigeria and Senegal; provides training and consulting services; mems: 17 west African countries; Dir-Gen. Dr PAPA ABDOULAYE SECK (Senegal); publs *Program Report* (annually), *Participatory Varietal Selection* (annually), *Rice Interspecific Hybridization Project Research Highlights* (annually), *Biennial WARDA/National Experts Committee Meeting Reports*, *Inland Valley Newsletter*, *ROCARIZ Newsletter*, training series, proceedings, leaflets.

Development and Economic Co-operation

African Capacity Building Foundation (ACBF): Intermarket Life Towers, 7th and 15th Floors, cnr Jason Moyo Ave/Sam Nujoma St, POB 1562, Harare, Zimbabwe; tel. (4) 790398; fax (4) 702915; e-mail root@acbf-pact.org; internet www.acbf-pact.org; f. 1991 by the World Bank, UNDP, the African Development Bank, African and non-African governments; assists African countries to strengthen and build local capacity in economic policy analysis and development management. Implementing agency for the Partnership for Capacity Building in Africa (PACT, established in 1999); Exec. Sec. Dr SOUMANA SAKO.

African Training and Research Centre in Administration for Development (Centre Africain de Formation et de Recherche Administratives pour le Développement—CAFRAD): blvd Pavillon International, BP 310, Tangier, 90001 Morocco; tel. (61) 306269; fax (39) 325785; e-mail cafrad@cafrad.org; internet www.cafrad.org; f. 1964 by agreement between Morocco and UNESCO; undertakes research into administrative problems in Africa and documents results; provides a consultation service for governments and organizations; holds workshops to train senior civil servants; prepares the Biennial Pan-African Conference of Ministers of the Civil Service; mems: 37 African countries; Chair. MOHAMED BOUSSAID; Dir-Gen. Dr SIMON MAMOSI LELO; publs *African Administrative Studies* (2 a year), *Research Studies*, *Newsletter* (internet), *Collection: Etudes et Documents, Répertoires des Consultants et des institutions de formation en Afrique*.

Afro-Asian Rural Development Organization (AARDO): No. 2, State Guest Houses Complex, Chanakyapuri, New Delhi 110 021, India; tel. (11) 24100475; fax (11) 24672045; e-mail aardohq@nde.vsnl.net.in; internet www.aardo.org; f. 1962 to act as a catalyst for the co-operative restructuring of rural life in Africa and Asia and to explore opportunities for the co-ordination of efforts to promote rural welfare and to eradicate hunger, thirst, disease, illiteracy and poverty; carries out collaborative research on development issues; organizes training; encourages the exchange of information; holds international conferences and seminars; awards 100 individual training fellowships at nine institutes in Egypt, India, Japan, the Republic of Korea, Malaysia and Taiwan; mems: 13 African countries, 14 Asian countries, one African associate; Sec.-Gen. ABDALLA YAHIA ADAM (Sudan); publs *Afro-Asian Journal of Rural Development* (2 a year), *Annual Report*, *AARDO Newsletter* (2 a year).

Arab Bank for Economic Development in Africa (Banque arabe pour le développement économique en Afrique—BADEA): Sayed Abdar-Rahman el-Mahdi St, POB 2640, Khartoum 11111, Sudan; tel. (1) 83773646; fax (1) 83770600; e-mail badea@badea.org; internet www.badea.org; f. 1973 by Arab League; provides loans and grants to sub-Saharan African countries to finance development projects; paid-up cap. US $2,200m. (Dec. 2006); during 2006 the Bank approved loans and grants totalling $163.8m., and tech. assistance for feasibility studies and institutional support amounting to $6.3m; by the end of 2005 total financial operations approved since funding activities began in 1975 totalled $2,960.3m; Chair. AHMED ABDALLAH EL-AKEIL (Saudi Arabia); Dir-Gen. ABDELAZIZ KHELEF (Algeria); publs *Annual Report*, *Co-operation for Development* (quarterly), Studies on Afro-Arab co-operation.

Centre on Integrated Rural Development for Africa (CIRDAfrica): POB 6115, Arusha, Tanzania; tel. (57) 2576; fax (57) 8532; f. 1979 (operational 1982) to promote integrated rural development through a network of nat. institutions; to improve the production, income and living conditions of small-scale farmers and other rural groups; to provide tech. support; and to foster the exchange of ideas and experience; financed by mem. states and donor agencies; mems: 17 African countries; Dir Dr ABDELMONEIM M. ELSHEIKH; publ. *CIRDAfrica Rural Tribune* (2 a year).

Club du Sahel et de l'Afrique de l'Ouest (Sahel and West Africa Club): c/o OECD, 2 rue André Pascal, 75775 Paris, France; tel. 1-45-24-89-87; fax 1-45-24-90-31; e-mail sahel.contact@oecd.org; internet www.oecd.org/sah; f. 1977 as Club du Sahel, current name and structure adopted in April 2001; an informal discussion forum for exchange of ideas and experience between OECD donor agencies and African recipients; aims to create, promote and facilitate links between the countries of OECD and West Africa, and between the private and public sectors in order to improve the efficiency of development aid; the secretariat's work programme for 2001–03 focused on the following components: regional prospective study process; local development and decentralization; and partnerships.

Communauté économique des états de l'Afrique centrale (CEEAC) (Economic Community of Central African States): BP 2112, Libreville, Gabon; tel. 73-35-48; internet www.ceeac.org; f. 1983, operational 1 January 1985; aims to promote co-operation between member states by abolishing trade restrictions, establishing a common external customs tariff, linking commercial banks, and setting up a development fund, over a period of 12 years; works to combat drug abuse and to promote regional security; mems: 10 African countries; Sec.-Gen. LOUIS-SYLVAIN GOMA.

Community of Sahel-Saharan States (Communauté des états Sahelo-Sahariens—CEN-SAD): POB 4041, Aljazeera Sq., Tripoli, Libya; tel. (21) 333-2347; fax (21) 444-0076; e-mail censad_sg@yahoo

.com; internet www.cen-sad.org; f. 1998; fmrly known as COMESSA; aims to strengthen co-operation between signatory states in order to promote their economic, social and cultural integration and to facilitate conflict resolution and poverty alleviation; partnership agreements concluded with many orgs, including the AU, the UN and ECOWAS; mems: Benin, Burkina Faso, Central African Republic, Chad, Côte d'Ivoire, Djibouti, Egypt, Eritrea, The Gambia, Ghana, Guinea-Bissau, Liberia, Libya, Mali, Morocco, Niger, Nigeria, Senegal, Sierra Leone, Somalia, Sudan, Togo, Tunisia; Sec.-Gen. Dr MOHAMMED AL-MADANI AL-AZHARI (Libya).

Conseil de l'Entente (Entente Council): 01 BP 3734, angle ave Verdier/rue de Tessières, Abidjan 01, Côte d'Ivoire; tel. 20-33-28-35; fax 20-33-11-49; e-mail fegece@conseil-entente.org; f. 1959 to promote economic development in the region; the Council's Mutual Aid and Loan Guarantee Fund (Fonds d' entraide et de garantie des emprunts) finances development projects, including agricultural projects, support for small and medium-sized enterprises, vocational training centres, research into new sources of energy and building of hotels to encourage tourism. A Convention of Assistance and Co-operation was signed in Feb. 1996. Holds annual summit; mems: Benin, Burkina Faso, Côte d'Ivoire, Niger, Togo; Sec.-Gen. OUSMANE TAMIMOU; publ. *Rapport d'activité* (annually).

Communauté économique du bétail et de la viande (CEBV) du Conseil de l'Entente (Livestock and Meat Economic Community of the Entente Council): 01 BP 638 Ouagadougou, Burkina Faso; tel. 21-30-62-67; fax 21-30-62-68; e-mail cebv@cenatrin.bf; internet www.cenatrin.bf/cebv; f. 1970 to promote the production, processing and marketing of livestock and meat; negotiates between members and with third countries on technical and financial co-operation and co-ordinated legislation; attempts to co-ordinate measures to combat drought and cattle diseases; mems: states belonging to the Conseil de l'Entente; Exec. Sec. Dr ELIE LADIKPO (Togo).

East African Community (EAC): AICC Bldg, Kilimanjaro Wing, 5th Floor, POB 1096, Arusha, Tanzania; tel. (27) 2504253; fax (27) 2504255; e-mail eac@eachq.org; internet www.eac.int; f. 2001, following the adoption of a treaty on political and economic integration (signed in November 1999) by the heads of state of Kenya, Tanzania and Uganda, replacing the Permanent Tripartite Commission for East African Co-operation (f. 1993) and reviving the former East African Community (f. 1967; dissolved 1977); initial areas for co-operation were to be trade and industry, security, immigration, transport and communications, and promotion of investment; further objectives were the elimination of trade barriers and ensuring the free movement of people and capital within the grouping; a customs union came into effect on 1 Jan. 2005; f. a Court of Justice and a Legislative Assembly have been established; in April 2006 heads of state agreed that negotiations on a common market would commence in July and were to be concluded by Dec. 2008; Rwanda and Burundi formally became members of the Community on 1 July 2007; Sec.-Gen. JUMA VOLTER MWAPACHU (Tanzania).

Economic Community of the Great Lakes Countries (Communauté économique des pays des Grands Lacs—CEPGL): POB 58, Gisenyi, Rwanda; tel. 61309; fax 61319; f. 1976 main organs: annual Conference of Heads of State, Council of Ministers of Foreign Affairs, Permanent Executive Secretariat, Consultative Commission, Security Commission, three Specialized Technical Commissions; there are four specialized agencies: a development bank, the Banque de Développement des Etats des Grands Lacs (BDEGL) at Goma, Democratic Republic of the Congo; an energy centre at Bujumbura, Burundi; the Institute of Agronomic and Zootechnical Research, Gitega, Burundi; and a regional electricity company (SINELAC) at Bukavu, Democratic Republic of the Congo; mems: Burundi, the Democratic Republic of the Congo, Rwanda; publs *Grands Lacs* (quarterly review), *Journal* (annually).

Gambia River Basin Development Organization (Organisation pour la mise en valeur du fleuve Gambie—OMVG): BP 2353, 13 passage Leblanc, Dakar, Senegal; tel. 822-31-59; fax 822-59-26; e-mail omvg@omvg.sn; f. 1978 by Senegal and The Gambia; Guinea joined in 1981 and Guinea-Bissau in 1983. A masterplan for the integrated development of the Kayanga/Geba and Koliba/Corubal river basins has been developed, encompassing a projected natural resources management project; a hydraulic development plan for the Gambia river was formulated during 1996–98; a pre-feasibility study on connecting the national electric grids of the four member states has been completed, and a feasibility study for the construction of the proposed Sambangalou hydroelectric dam, was undertaken in the early 2000s; maintains documentation centre; Exec. Sec. JUSTINO VIEIRA.

Indian Ocean Commission (IOC) (Commission de l'Océan Indien—COI): Q4, Ave Sir Guy Forget, BP 7, Quatre Bornes, Mauritius; tel. 425-9564; fax 425-2709; e-mail coi7@intnet.mu; internet www.coi-info.org; f. 1982 to promote regional co-operation, particularly in economic development; projects include tuna-fishing development, protection and management of environmental resources and strengthening of meteorological services; tariff reduction is also envisaged; organizes an annual regional trade fair; mems: Comoros, France (representing the French Overseas Department of Réunion), Madagascar, Mauritius, Seychelles; Sec.-Gen. MONIQUE ANDREAS-ESOAVELOMANDROSO; publ. *La Lettre de l'Océan Indien*.

Indian Ocean Rim Association for Regional Co-operation (IOR–ARC): Sorèze House, Wilson Ave, Vacoas, Mauritius; tel. 698-3979; fax 698-5390; e-mail iorarchq@intnet.mu; the first intergovernmental meeting of countries in the region to promote an Indian Ocean Rim initiative was convened in March 1995; charter to establish the Asscn was signed at a ministerial meeting in March 1997; aims to promote the sustained growth and balanced devt of the region and of its mem. states and to create common ground for regional economic co-operation, *inter alia* through trade, investment, infrastructure, tourism, and science and technology; seventh meeting of Council of Ministers held in Tehran, Iran, March 2007; mems: Australia, Bangladesh, India, Indonesia, Iran, Kenya, Madagascar, Malaysia, Mauritius, Mozambique, Oman, Singapore, South Africa, Sri Lanka, Tanzania, Thailand, United Arab Emirates and Yemen. Dialogue Partner countries: People's Republic of China, Egypt, France, Japan, United Kingdom. Observer: Indian Ocean Tourism Org; Chair. LAKSHMAN KADIRGAMAR (Sri Lanka); Exec. Dir TUAN ZAROOK A. SAMSUDEEN (Sri Lanka).

Lake Chad Basin Commission (LCBC): BP 727, N'Djamena, Chad; tel. 52-41-45; fax 52-41-37; e-mail lcbc@intnet.td; f. 1964 to encourage co-operation in developing the Lake Chad region and to promote the settlement of regional disputes; work programmes emphasize the regulation of the utilization of water and other natural resources in the basin; the co-ordination of natural resources development projects and research; holds annual summit of heads of state; mems: Cameroon, Central African Republic, Chad, Niger, Nigeria; Exec. Sec. MUHAMMAD SANI ADAMU; publ. *Bibliographie générale de la cblt* (2 a year).

Liptako-Gourma Integrated Development Authority (LGA): POB 619, ave M. Thevenond, Ouagadougou, Burkina Faso; tel. (3) 30-61-48; f. 1972; scope of activities includes water infrastructure, telecommunications and construction of roads and railways; in 1986 undertook study on development of water resources in the basin of the Niger river (for hydroelectricity and irrigation); mems: Burkina Faso, Mali, Niger; Dir-Gen. GISANGA DEMBÉLÉ (Mali).

Mano River Union: Private Mail Bag 133, Delco House, Lightfoot Boston St, Freetown, Sierra Leone; tel. (22) 226883; f. 1973 to establish a customs and economic union between member states to accelerate development via integration; a common external tariff was instituted in 1977. Intra-union free trade was officially introduced in May 1981, as the first stage in progress towards a customs union. A non-aggression treaty was signed by heads of state in 1986. The Union was inactive for three years until mid-1994, owing to regional conflict and disagreements regarding funding. In January 1995 a Mano River Centre for Peace and Development was established, which was to be temporarily based in London. The Centre aims to provide a permanent mechanism for conflict prevention and resolution, and monitoring of human rights violations, and to promote sustainable peace and development. A new security structure was approved in 2000. In Aug. 2001 ministers of foreign affairs, security, internal affairs, and justice, meeting as the Joint Security Committee, resolved to deploy joint border security and confidence-building units, and to work to re-establish the free movement of people and goods; mems: Guinea, Liberia, Sierra Leone; Dir Dr ABDOULAYE DIALLO.

Niger Basin Authority (Autorité du Bassin du Niger): BP 729, Niamey, Niger; tel. 723102; fax 724208; e-mail abnsec@intnet.ne; internet www.abn.ne; f. 1964 (as River Niger Commission; name changed 1980) to harmonize national programmes concerned with the River Niger Basin and to execute an integrated development plan; compiles statistics; regulates navigation; runs projects on hydrological forecasting, environmental control; infrastructure and agro-pastoral development; mems: Benin, Burkina Faso, Cameroon, Chad, Côte d'Ivoire, Guinea, Mali, Niger, Nigeria; Exec. Sec. MOHAMMED BELLO TUGA (Nigeria); publ. *NBA-INFO* (quarterly).

Nile Basin Initiative: POB 192, Entebbe, Uganda; tel. (41) 321329; fax (41) 320971; e-mail nbisec@nilebasin.org; internet www.nilebasin.org; f. 1999; aims to achieve sustainable socio-economic development through the equitable use and benefits of the Nile Basin water resources and to create an enabling environment for the implementation of programmes with a shared vision. Highest authority is the Nile Basin Council of Ministers (Nile-COM); other activities undertaken by a Nile Basin Technical Advisory Committee (Nile-TAC); mems: Burundi, Democratic Republic of the Congo, Egypt, Eritrea, Ethiopia, Kenya, Rwanda, Sudan, Tanzania, Uganda; Exec. Dir PATRICK KAHANGIRE.

Organization for the Development of the Senegal River (Organisation pour la mise en valeur du fleuve Sénégal—OMVS): c/o Haut-Commissariat, 46 rue Carnot, BP 3152, Dakar, Senegal; tel.

823-45-30; fax 822-01-63; e-mail omvsphc@sentoo.sn; internet www.omvs.org; f. 1972 to promote the use of the Senegal river for hydroelectricity, irrigation and navigation; the Djama dam in Senegal provides a barrage to prevent salt water from moving upstream, and the Manantali dam in Mali is intended to provide a reservoir for irrigation of about 375,000 ha of land and for production of hydroelectricity and provision of year-round navigation for ocean-going vessels. In 1997 two companies were formed to manage the dams: Société de gestion de l'énergie de Manantali (SOGEM) and Société de gestion et d'exploitation du barrage de Djama (SOGED); mems: Mali, Mauritania, Senegal; Guinea has observer status; Pres. ABOUBACARY COULIBALY (Mali).

Organization for the Management and Development of the Kagera River Basin (Organisation pour l'aménagement et le développement du bassin de la rivière Kagera—OBK): BP 297, Kigali, Rwanda; tel. (7) 84665; fax (7) 82172; f. 1978; envisages joint development and management of resources, including the construction of an 80-MW hydroelectric dam at Rusumo Falls, on the Rwanda-Tanzania border, a 2,000-km railway network between the four member countries, road construction (914 km), and a telecommunications network between member states; mems: Burundi, Rwanda, Tanzania, Uganda; Exec. Sec. JEAN-BOSCO BALINDA.

Pan-African Institute for Development (PAID): BP 4056, Douala, Cameroon; tel. and fax 342-80-30; e-mail ipd.sg@camnet.cm; f. 1964; gives training to people from African countries involved with development at grassroots, intermediate and senior levels; emphasis is given to: development management and financing; agriculture and rural development; issues of gender and development; promotion of small and medium-sized enterprises; training policies and systems; environment, health and community development; research, support and consultancy services; and specialized training. There are four regional institutes: Central Africa (Douala, Cameroon), Sahel (Ouagadougou, Burkina Faso), West Africa (Buéa, Cameroon), Eastern and Southern Africa (Kabwe, Zambia) and a European office in Geneva; Pres. of the Governing Council Dr MBUKI V. MWAMUFIYA; publs *Newsletter* (2 a year), *Annual Progress Report*, *PAID Report* (quarterly).

Partners in Population and Development: IPH Bldg, 2nd Floor, Mohakhali, Dhaka 1212, Bangladesh; tel. (2) 988-1882; fax (2) 882-9387; e-mail partners@ppdsec.org; internet www.south-south-ppd.org; f. 1994; aims to implement the decisions of the International Conference on Population and Development, held in Cairo, Egypt in 1994, in order to expand and improve South-South collaboration in the fields of family planning and reproductive health; administers a Visionary Leadership Programme, a Global Leadership Programme, and other training and technical advisory services; mems: 21 developing countries; Exec. Dir SANGEET HARRY JOOSEERY.

Permanent Interstate Committee on Drought Control in the Sahel (Comité permanent inter états de lutte contre la sécheresse au Sahel—CILSS): POB 7049, Ouagadougou 03, Burkina Faso; tel. 50-37-41-25; fax 50-37-41-32; e-mail cilss@cilss.bf; internet www.cilssnet.org; f. 1973; works in co-operation with UNDP Drylands Development Centre; aims to combat the effects of chronic drought in the Sahel region, by improving irrigation and food production, halting deforestation and creating food reserves; initiated a series of projects to improve food security and to counter poverty, entitled Sahel 21; the heads of state of all members had signed a convention for the establishment of a Fondation pour le Développement Durable du Sahel; maintains Institut du Sahel at Bamako (Mali) and centre at Niamey (Niger); mems: Burkina Faso, Cape Verde, Chad, The Gambia, Guinea-Bissau, Mali, Mauritania, Niger, Senegal; Pres. AMADOU TOUMANI TOURÉ (Mali); Exec. Sec. MUSA S. MBENGA (The Gambia); publ. *Reflets Sahéliens* (quarterly).

United Nations African Institute for Economic Development and Planning (IDEP) (Institut africain de développement économique et de planification): rue du 18 Juin, BP 3186, Dakar, Senegal; tel. 823-10-20; fax 822-29-64; e-mail unidep@unidep.org; internet www.unidep,org; f. 1963 by UN ECA to train economic development planners, conduct research and provide advisory services; has library of books, journals and documents; mems: 53 mem. states; Dir DIÉRY SECK.

World Economic Forum: 91–93 route de la Capite, 1223 Cologny/Geneva, Switzerland; tel. 228691212; fax 227862744; e-mail contact@weforum.org; internet www.weforum.org; f. 1971; the Forum comprises commercial interests gathered on a non-partisan basis, under the stewardship of the Swiss Government, with the aim of improving society through economic development; convenes an annual meeting in Davos, Switzerland; organizes the following programmes: Technology Pioneers; Women Leaders; and Young Global Leaders; and aims to mobilize the resources of the global business community in the implementation of the following initiatives: the Global Health Initiative; the Disaster Relief Network; the West-Islamic World Dialogue; and the G-20/International Monetary Reform Project; the Forum is governed by a guiding Foundation Board; an advisory International Business Council; and an administrative Managing Board; regular mems: representatives of 1,000 leading commercial companies world-wide; selected mem. companies taking a leading role in the movement's activities are known as 'partners'.

Economics and Finance

African Centre for Monetary Studies (ACMS): 15 blvd Franklin Roosevelt, BP 4128, Dakar, Senegal; tel. 821-93-80; fax 822-73-43; e-mail caem@syfed.refer.sn; began operations 1978; aims to promote better understanding of banking and monetary matters; studies monetary problems of African countries and the effect on them of international monetary developments; seeks to enable African countries to co-ordinate strategies in international monetary affairs; established as an organ of the Association of African Central Banks (AACB) following a decision by the OAU Heads of State and Government; mems: all mems of the AACB; Chair. Dr PAUL A. OGWUMA (Nigeria); Dir MAMADOU SIDIBE.

African Insurance Organization (AIO): 30 ave de Gaulle, BP 5860, Douala, Cameroon; tel. 342-47-58; fax 343-20-08; e-mail info@africaninsurance.net; internet www.africaninsurance.net; f. 1972 to promote the expansion of the insurance and reinsurance industry in Africa, and to increase regional co-operation; holds annual conference, periodic seminars and workshops, and arranges meetings for reinsurers, brokers, consultant and regulators in Africa; has established African insurance 'pools' for aviation, petroleum and fire risks, and created asscns of African insurance educators, supervisory authorities and insurance brokers and consultants; Pres. NANA AGYEI DUKU (Ghana); Sec.-Gen. ROLAND RASAMOELY (Cameroon) (acting); publ. *African Insurance Annual Review*.

Association of African Central Banks (AACB): 15 blvd Franklin Roosevelt, BP 4128, Dakar, Senegal; tel. 821-93-80; fax 822-73-43; f. 1968 to promote contacts in the monetary and financial sphere, in order to increase co-operation and trade among member states; aims to strengthen monetary and financial stability on the African continent; mems: 40 African central banks representing 47 states; Chair. FARHAT O. BENGDARA (Libya).

Association of African Tax Administrators (AATA): POB 13255, Yaoundé, Cameroon; tel. 22-41-57; fax 23-18-55; f. 1980 to promote co-operation in the field of taxation policy, legislation and administration among African countries; mems: 20 states; Exec. Sec. OWONA PASCAL-BAYLON.

East African Development Bank: 4 Nile Ave, POB 7128, Kampala, Uganda; tel. (41) 230021; fax (41) 259763; e-mail dg@eadb.org; internet www.eadb.org; f. 1967 by the former East African Community to promote development within Kenya, Tanzania and Uganda, which each hold 24.07% of the equity capital; the remaining equity is held by the African Development Bank and other institutional investors; Chair. Dr EZRA SURUMA; Dir-Gen. GODFREY TUMUSIIME.

Financial Action Task Force (FATF) (Groupe d'action financière—GAFI): 2 rue André-Pascal, 75775 Paris Cédex 16, France; tel. 1-45-24-79-45; fax 1-44-30-61-37; e-mail contact@fatf-gafi.org; internet www.fatf-gafi.org; f. 1989, on the recommendation of the Group of Seven industrialized nations (G-7), to develop and promote policies to combat money laundering and the financing of terrorism; formulated a set of recommendations (40+9) for countries world-wide to implement; established partnerships with regional task forces in the Caribbean, Asia-Pacific, Central Asia, Europe, East and South Africa, the Middle East and North Africa and South America; mems: 34 state jurisdictions, the European Commission, and the Co-operation Council for the Arab States of the Gulf; observer: India, Republic of Korea; Pres. JAMES SASSOON (UK); Exec. Sec. ALAIN DAMAIS; publs *Annual Report*, *e-Bulletin*.

Fonds Africain de Garantie et de Co-opération Economique (FAGACE) (African Guarantee and Economic Co-operation Fund): 01 BP 2045 RP, Cotonou, Benin; tel. 30-03-76; fax 30-02-84; e-mail fagace@intnet.bj; internet www.fagace.org; commenced operations in 1981; guarantees loans for development projects, provides loans and grants for specific operations and supports national and regional enterprises; mems: nine African countries; Dir-Gen. LIBASSE SAMB.

West African Bankers' Association: 11-13 Ecowas St, PMBag 1012, Freetown, Sierra Leone; tel. (22) 226752; fax (22) 229024; e-mail secgwaba@hotmail.com; f. 1981; aims to strengthen links between banks in West Africa, to enable exchange of information, and to contribute to regional economic development; holds annual general assembly; mems: 135 commercial banks in 14 countries; Sec.-Gen. PHILIP A. LATILO; publ. *West African Banking Almanac*.

Education

Association for the Development of Education in Africa: c/o International Institute for Educational Planning, 7-9 rue Eugène Delacroix, 75116 Paris, France; tel. 1-45-03-77-57; fax 1-45-03-39-65; e-mail adea@iiep.unesco.org; internet www.adeanet.org/; f. 1988 as Donors to African Education, adopted present name in 1995; aims to enhance collaboration in the support of African education; promotes policy dialogue and undertakes research, advocacy and capacity-building in areas of education in sub-Saharan Africa through programmes and working groups comprising representatives of donor countries and African ministries of education; Exec. Sec. MAMADOU NDOYE.

Association of African Universities (AAU) (Association des universités africaines): POB 5744, Accra-North, Ghana; tel. (21) 774495; fax (21) 774821; e-mail info@aau.org; internet www.aau.org; f. 1967 to promote exchanges, contact and co-operation among African university institutions and to collect and disseminate information on research and higher education in Africa; mems: 113 mems in 30 countries; Sec.-Gen. Prof. AKILAGPA SAWYERR (Ghana); publs *AAU Newsletter* (3 a year), *Directory of African Universities* (every 2 years).

International Association for the Development of Documentation, Libraries and Archives in Africa: Villa 2547 Dieuppeul II, BP 375, Dakar, Senegal; tel. 824-09-54; f. 1957 to organize and develop documentation and archives in all African countries; mems: national asscns, institutions and individuals in 48 countries; Sec.-Gen. ZACHEUS SUNDAY ALI (Nigeria).

International Congress of African Studies: c/o International African Institute, Thornhaugh St, London, WC1H 0XG, United Kingdom; tel. (20) 7898-4420; fax (20) 7898-4419; e-mail iai@soas.ac.uk; f. 1962 to encourage co-operation and research in African studies; Congress convened approx. every five years; publ. *Proceedings*.

Pan-African Association for Literacy and Adult Education: c/o ANAFA, BP 10358, Dakar, Senegal; tel. 825-48-50; fax 824-44-13; e-mail anafa@metissacana.sn; f. 2000 to succeed African Asscn for Literacy and Adult Education (f. 1984); Co-ordinator Dr LAMINE KANE.

The West African Examinations Council (WAEC) (Conseil des examens de l'Afrique orientale): POB GP125, Accra, Ghana; tel. (21) 248967; fax (21) 222905; e-mail waechqrs@africaonline.com.gh; internet www.waecheadquartersgh.org; f. 1952; administers prescribed examinations in mem. countries; aims to harmonize examinations procedures and standards. Offices in each mem. country and in London, the United Kingdom; mems: The Gambia, Ghana, Liberia, Nigeria, Sierra Leone; Chair. Prof. JEROME S. DJANGMAH; Registrar MATTHEW P. NDURE.

Environmental Conservation

Consortium for Oceanographic Research and Education (CORE): 1201 New York Ave, NW, Suite 420, Washington, DC 20005, USA; tel. (202) 332-0063; fax (202) 332-9751; e-mail coml@coreocean.org; internet www.comlsecretariat.org; f. 1999 to launch and host the International Steering Committee and Secretariat for the Census of Marine Life, a 10-year initiative to assess the diversity, distribution and abundance of marine life being implemented by a network of researchers from more than 70 countries; aims to promote, support and advance the science of oceanography; Pres. RICHARD WEST.

IUCN—The World Conservation Union: 28 rue Mauverney, 1196 Gland, Switzerland; tel. 229990000; fax 229990002; e-mail webmaster@iucn.org; internet www.iucn.org; f. 1948, as the International Union for Conservation of Nature and Natural Resources; supports partnerships and practical field activities to promote the conservation of natural resources, to secure the conservation of biological diversity as an essential foundation for the future; to ensure wise use of the earth's natural resources in an equitable and sustainable way; and to guide the development of human communities towards ways of life in enduring harmony with other components of the biosphere, developing programmes to protect and sustain the most important and threatened species and eco-systems and assisting governments to devise and carry out national conservation strategies; maintains a conservation library and documentation centre and units for monitoring traffic in wildlife; mems: more than 1,000 states, government agencies, non-governmental organizations and affiliates in some 140 countries; Pres. MOHAMMED VALLI MOOSA (South Africa); Dir-Gen. JULIA MARTON-LEFÈVRE (USA); publs *World Conservation Strategy*, *Caring for the Earth*, *Red List of Threatened Plants*, *Red List of Threatened Species*, *United Nations List of National Parks and Protected Areas*, *World Conservation* (quarterly), *IUCN Today*.

Wetlands International: POB 471, 6700 AL Wageningen, Netherlands; tel. (317) 478854; fax (317) 478850; e-mail post@wetlands.org; internet www.wetlands.org; f. 1995 by merger of several regional wetlands organizations; aims to protect and restore wetlands, their resources and biodiversity through research, information exchange and conservation activities; promotes implementation of the 1971 Ramsar Convention on Wetlands; Chair. STEW MORRISON; CEO JANE MADGWICK.

WWF International: ave du Mont-Blanc 27, 1196 Gland, Switzerland; tel. 223649111; fax 223648836; e-mail info@wwfint.org; internet www.panda.org; f. 1961 (as World Wildlife Fund), name changed to World Wide Fund for Nature in 1986, current nomenclature adopted 2001; aims to stop the degradation of natural environments, conserve bio-diversity, ensure the sustainable use of renewable resources, and promote the reduction of both pollution and wasteful consumption; addresses six priority issues: forests, freshwater, marine, species, climate change, and toxics; has identified, and focuses its activities in, 200 'ecoregions' (the 'Global 200'), believed to contain the best part of the world's remaining biological diversity; actively supports and operates conservation programmes in more than 90 countries; mems: 54 offices, five associate orgs, c. 5m. individual mems world-wide; Pres. Chief EMEKA ANYAOKU (Nigeria); Dir-Gen. JAMES P. LEAPE; publs *Annual Report*, *Living Planet Report*.

Government and Politics

Accord de Non-agression et d'Assistance en Matière de Défence (ANAD) (Non-Aggression and Defence Aid Agreement): 08 BP 2065, Abidjan 08, Côte d'Ivoire; tel. 20-21-88-33; fax 20-33-86-13; e-mail colpape@aviso.ci; f. 1977 to serve as a framework for sub-regional co-operation in conflict prevention and resolution; adopted a draft protocol for the establishment of a regional peace-keeping force and a fund to promote peace and security in April 1999; mems: Benin, Burkina Faso, Côte d'Ivoire, Mali, Mauritania, Niger, Senegal, Togo.

African Association for Public Administration and Management (AAPAM): Britak Centre, Ragati and Mara Rds, POB 48677, 00100 GPO, Nairobi, Kenya; tel. (20) 2730555; fax (20) 2731153; e-mail aapam@aapam.org; internet www.aapam.org; f. 1971 to promote good practices, excellence and professionalism in public administration through training, seminars, research, publications; convenes regular conferences to share learning experiences among members, and an annual Roundtable Conference; funded by membership contributions, government and donor grants; mems: 500 individual, 50 corporate; Pres. JOHN MITALA (Uganda); Sec.-Gen. Dr YOLAMA R. BARONGO (Uganda); publs *Newsletter* (quarterly), *Annual Seminar Report*, *Newsletter* (quarterly), *African Journal of Public Administration and Management* (2 a year), studies.

Afro-Asian Peoples' Solidarity Organization (AAPSO): 89 Abdel Aziz Al-Saoud St, POB 11559-61 Manial El-Roda, Cairo, Egypt; tel. (2) 3636081; fax (2) 3637361; e-mail aapso@idsc.net.eg; internet www.aapso.fg2o.org; f. 1958; acts among and for the peoples of Africa and Asia in their struggle for genuine independence, sovereignty, socio-economic development, peace and disarmament; mems: national committees and affiliated organizations in 66 countries and territories, assoc. mems in 15 European countries; Sec.-Gen. NOURI ABDEL RAZZAK HUSSEIN (Iraq); publs *Solidarity Bulletin* (monthly), *Socio-Economic Development* (3 a year).

Comunidade dos Países de Língua Portuguesa (CPLP) (Community of Portuguese-Speaking Countries): rua S. Caetano 32, 1200-829 Lisbon, Portugal; tel. (21) 392-8560; fax (21) 392-8588; e-mail comunicacao@cplp.org; internet www.cplp.org; f. 1996; aims to produce close political, economic, diplomatic and cultural links between Portuguese-speaking countries and to strengthen the influence of the Lusophone commonwealth within the international community; dispatched an observer mission to oversee presidential elections held in Timor-Leste in May 2007; mems: Angola, Brazil, Cape Verde, Guinea-Bissau, Mozambique, Portugal, São Tomé and Príncipe, Timor-Leste; Exec. Sec. LUÍS DE MATOS DE MONTEIRO DA FONSECA (Cape Verde).

Gulf of Guinea Commission (Commission du Golfe de Guinée—CGG): f. 2001 to promote co-operation among mem; countries and the peaceful and sustainable development of natural resources in the sub-region; mems: Angola, Cameroon, the Repub. of the Congo, Equatorial Guinea, Gabon, Nigeria, São Tomé and Príncipe.

International Conference on the Great Lakes Region, Secretariat: Bujumbura, Burundi; f. 2006 following the signing of the Security, Stability and Development Pact for the Great Lakes Region at the second summit meeting of the International Conference on the Great Lakes Region, held in December, in Nairobi, Kenya; the UN Security Council proposed the organization of a Great Lakes Conference to initiate a process that would bring together regional leaders to pursue agreement on a set of principles and to articulate programmes of action to help end the cycle of regional conflict and establish durable peace, stability, security, democracy and development in the whole region; the first summit meeting of the Conference was convened in Dar es Salaam, Tanzania, in November 2004; mems: Angola, Burundi, the Central African Republic, the Democratic Republic of the Congo, the Republic of the Congo, Kenya, Rwanda, Sudan, Tanzania, Uganda, Zambia; Exec. Sec. LIBERATA MULAMALA.

International Institute for Democracy and Electoral Assistance (IDEA): Strömsborg, S-103 34 Stockholm, Sweden; tel. (8) 698-3700; fax (8) 20-2422; e-mail info@idea.int; internet www.idea.int; f. 1995; aims to promote sustainable democracy in new and established democracies; provides world-wide electoral assistance and focuses on broader democratic issues in Africa, the Caucasus and Latin America; 23 mem. states; Sec.-Gen. VIDAR HELGESEN (Norway).

Organisation Internationale de la Francophonie (La Francophonie): 28 rue de Bourgogne, 75007 Paris, France; tel. 1-44-11-12-50; fax 1-44-11-12-76; e-mail oif@francophonie.org; internet www.francophonie.org; f. 1970 as l'Agence de coopération culturelle et technique; promotes co-operation among French-speaking countries in the areas of education, culture, peace and democracy, and technology; implements decisions of the Sommet francophone; technical and financial assistance has been given to projects in every member country, mainly to aid rural people; mems: 55 states and govts; 13 countries with observer status; Sec. Gen. ABDOU DIOUF (Senegal); publ. *Journal de l'Agence de la Francophonie* (quarterly).

Union of African Parliaments: BP V314, Abidjan, Côte d'Ivoire; tel. 20-30-39-70; fax 20-30-44-05; e-mail upa@africaonline.co.ci; internet www.uafparl.org; f. 1976; holds annual conf; mems: 40 parliaments; Sec.-Gen. ABDELGADIR ABDALLA.

Industrial and Professional Relations

International Trade Union Confederation-African Regional Organization (ICFTU-AFRO): Kenya Re Towers, 4th Floor, Upper Hill, off Ragati Rd POB 67273, Nairobi, Kenya; tel. (20) 244336; fax (20) 215072; e-mail info@icftuafro.org; internet www.icftuafro.org; f. 1957; mems: 13m. workers in 44 countries; Gen. Sec. ANDREW KAILEMBO (Tanzania).

Organisation of African Trade Union Unity (OATUU): POB M386, Accra, Ghana; tel. (21) 508855; fax (21) 508851; e-mail oatuu@ighmail.com; f. 1973 as a single continental trade union org., independent of international trade union organizations; has affiliates from all African trade unions. Congress, the supreme policy-making body, is composed of four delegates per country from affiliated national trade union centres, and meets at least every four years; the General Council, composed of one representative from each affiliated trade union, meets annually to implement Congress decisions and to approve the annual budget; mems: trade union movements in 53 independent African countries; Sec.-Gen. Gen. HASSAN A. SUNMONU (Nigeria); publ. *The African Worker*.

Pan-African Employers' Confederation (PEC): c/o Mauritius Employers' Federation, Cerné House, 13 La Chaussée, Port Louis, Mauritius; tel. 212-1599; fax 212-6725; e-mail info@mef-online.org; f. 1986 to link African employers' organizations and represent them at the AU, UN and ILO; mems: representation in 39 countries on the continent; Sec.-Gen. AZAD JEETUN (Mauritius).

Law

African Bar Association: 29/31 Obafemi Awolowo Way, Ikeja, Lagos, Nigeria (temporary address); tel. (1) 4936907; fax (1) 7752202; f. 1972; aims to uphold the rule of law, maintain the independence of the judiciary, and improve legal services; Pres. PETER ALA ADJETY (Ghana); Sec.-Gen. FEMI FELANA (Nigeria).

African Society of International and Comparative Law (ASICL): 402 Holloway Rd, London, N7 6PZ, United Kingdom; tel. (20) 7609-3800; fax (20) 7609-5400; e-mail asicl@compuserve.com; f. 1986; promotes public education on law and civil liberties; aims to provide a legal aid and advice system in each African country, and to facilitate the exchange of information on civil liberties in Africa; Pres. MOHAMED BEDJAOUI; Sec. EMILE YAKPO (Ghana); publs *Newsletter* (every 2 months), *African Journal of International and Comparative Law* (quarterly).

Asian-African Legal Consultative Organization (AALCO): E-66, Vasant Marg, Vasant Vihar, New Delhi 110057, India; tel. (11) 26152251; fax (11) 26152041; e-mail mail@aalco.org; internet www.aalco.org; f. 1956 to consider legal problems referred to it by member countries and to serve as a forum for Afro-Asian co-operation in international law, including international trade law, and economic relations; provides background material for conferences, prepares standard/model contract forms suited to the needs of the region; promotes arbitration as a means of settling international commercial disputes; trains officers of member states; has permanent UN observer status; mems: 47 countries; Pres. CHOI YOUNG-JIN (Republic of Korea); Sec.-Gen. Dr WAFIK ZAHER KAMIL (Egypt).

Inter-African Union of Lawyers (IAUL) (Union interafricaine des avocats): BP14409, Libreville, Gabon; tel. 76-41-44; fax 74-54-01; f. 1980; holds congress every three years; Pres. ABDELAZIZ BENZAKOUR (Morocco); Sec.-Gen. FRANÇOIS XAVIER AGONDJO-OKAWE (Gabon); publ. *L'avocat africain* (2 a year).

Medicine and Health

Organisation panafricaine de lutte contre le SIDA (OPALS): 15/21 rue de L'Ecole de Médecine, 75006 Paris, France; tel. 1-43-26-72-28; fax 1-43-29-70-93; e-mail opals@croix-rouge.fr; f. 1988; disseminates information relating to the treatment and prevention of AIDS; provides training of medical personnel; promotes co-operation between African medical centres and specialized centres in the USA and Europe; Pres. Prof. MARC GENTILINI; publ. *OPALS Liaison*.

Organization for Co-ordination in the Struggle against Endemic Diseases in Central Africa (Organisation de coordination pour la lutte contre les endémies en Afrique Centrale—OCEAC): BP 288, Yaoundé, Cameroon; tel. 23-22-32; fax 23-00-61; e-mail oceac@camnet.cm; internet www.cm.refer.org/site_oceac; f. 1965 to standardize methods of controlling endemic diseases, to co-ordinate national action, and to negotiate programmes of assistance and training on a regional scale; mems: Cameroon, Central African Republic, Chad, Republic of the Congo, Equatorial Guinea, Gabon; Sec.-Gen. Dr AUGUSTE BILONGO-MANÉNÉ; publ. *Bulletin de Liaison et de Documentation* (quarterly).

Posts and Telecommunications

Regional African Satellite Communications System (RASCOM): c/o International Telecommunication Union, place des Nations, 1211 Geneva 20, Switzerland; tel. 227305111; fax 227337256; f. 1992 to launch Africa's first satellite into space; mems: 42 countries.

Press, Radio and Television

African Union of Broadcasting (AUB): 101 rue Carnot, BP 3237, Dakar, Senegal; tel. 821-16-25; fax 822-51-13; e-mail urtnadkr@sentoo.sn; f. 1962 as Union of National Radio and Television Organizations of Africa (URTNA), new org. f. Nov. 2006; co-ordinates radio and television services, including monitoring and frequency allocation, the exchange of information and coverage of national and international events among African countries; mems: 48 organizations and six associate members; CEO a.i. LAWRENCE ATIASE.

Southern African Broadcasting Association (SABA): Postnet Suite 210, P/Bag X9, Melville 2109, Johannesburg, South Africa; tel. (11) 7144918; fax (11) 7144868; e-mail sabahq@sabc.co.za; internet www.saba.co.za; f. 1993; promotes quality public broadcasting; facilitates training of broadcasters at all levels; co-ordinates broadcasting activities in the SADC region; organizes radio news exchange service; produces television and radio programmes; mems: corpns in more than 20 countries; Sec.-Gen. JOHN J. MUSUKUMA.

West African Journalists' Association (Union des Journalists de l'Afrique de l'Ouest—UJAO): 17 blvd de la République, Dakar, Senegal; tel. 842-01-41; fax 842-02-69; e-mail wajaujao@yahoo.fr; internet www.ujaowaja.org; f. 1986; defends journalists and the freedom of the press, and promotes links between journalists' asscns; mems: journalists' asscns in 16 countries; Sec. ALPHA ABDALLAH SALL (Senegal).

Religion

All Africa Conference of Churches (AACC): Waiyaki Way, POB 14205, 00800 Westlands, Nairobi, Kenya; tel. (20) 4441483; fax (20) 4443241; e-mail secretariat@aacc-ceta.org; internet www.aacc-ceta.org; f. 1963; an organ of co-operation and continuing fellowship among Protestant, Orthodox and independent churches and

Christian Councils in Africa; 2008 Assembly: Maputu, Mozambique; mems: 169 churches and affiliated Christian councils in 39 African countries; Pres. The Right Rev. Dr NYANSAKO-NI-NKU (Cameroon); Gen. Sec. Rev. Dr MVUME DANDALA (South Africa); publs *ACIS/APS Bulletin*, *Tam Tam*.

Science

Association for the Taxonomic Study of the Flora of Tropical Africa: National Botanic Garden of Belgium, Domein van Bouchout, 1860 Meise, Belgium; tel. (2) 260-09-28; fax (2) 260-08-45; e-mail rammeloo@br.fgov.be; f. 1950 to facilitate co-operation and liaison between botanists engaged in the study of the flora of tropical Africa south of the Sahara including Madagascar; maintains a library; mems: c. 800 botanists in 63 countries; Sec.-Gen. Prof. J. RAMMELOO; publs *AETFAT Bulletin* (annually), *Proceedings*.

International Council for Science (ICSU): 51 blvd de Montmorency, 75016 Paris, France; tel. 1-45-25-03-29; fax 1-42-88-94-31; e-mail secretariat@icsu.org; internet www.icsu.org; f. 1919 as International Research Council; present name adopted 1931; new statutes adopted 1996; to co-ordinate international co-operation in theoretical and applied sciences and to promote national scientific research through the intermediary of affiliated national organizations; General Assembly of representatives of national and scientific members meets every three years to formulate policy. The following committees have been established: Cttee on Science for Food Security, Scientific Cttee on Antarctic Research, Scientific Cttee on Oceanic Research, Cttee on Space Research, Scientific Cttee on Water Research, Scientific Cttee on Solar-Terrestrial Physics, Cttee on Science and Technology in Developing Countries, Cttee on Data for Science and Technology, Programme on Capacity Building in Science, Scientific Cttee on Problems of the Environment, Steering Cttee on Genetics and Biotechnology and Scientific Cttee on International Geosphere-Biosphere Programme. The following services and Inter-Union Committees and Commissions have been established: Federation of Astronomical and Geophysical Data Analysis Services, Inter-Union Commission on Frequency Allocations for Radio Astronomy and Space Science, Inter-Union Commission on Radio Meteorology, Inter-Union Commission on Spectroscopy, Inter-Union Commission on Lithosphere; national mems: academies or research councils in 98 countries; Scientific mems and assocs: 105 nat. scientific bodies and 29 int. scientific unions; Pres. GOVERDHAN MEHTA; Exec. Sec. THOMAS ROSSWALL; publs *ICSU Yearbook*, *Science International* (quarterly), *Annual Report*.

Pan-African Union of Science and Technology: POB 2339, Brazzaville, Republic of the Congo; tel. 832265; fax 832185; f. 1987 to promote the use of science and technology in furthering the development of Africa; organizes triennial congress; Pres. Prof. EDWARD AYENSU; Sec.-Gen. Prof. LÉVY MAKANY.

Scientific, Technical and Research Commission (STRC): Nigerian Ports Authority Bldg, PMB 2359, Marina, Lagos, Nigeria; tel. (1) 2633430; fax (1) 2636093; e-mail oaustrcl@hyperia.com; f. 1965 to succeed the Commission for Technical Co-operation in Africa (f. 1954); implements priority programmes of the African Union relating to science and technology for development; supervises the Inter-African Bureau for Animal Resources (Nairobi, Kenya), the Inter-African Bureau for Soils (Lagos, Nigeria) and the Inter-African Phytosanitary Commission (Yaoundé, Cameroon) and several joint research projects; provides training in agricultural man., and conducts pest control programmes; services various inter-African committees of experts, including the Scientific Council for Africa; publishes and distributes specialized scientific books and documents of original value to Africa; organizes training courses, seminars, symposia, workshops and technical meetings; Exec. Dir KOLAWOLE O. ADENIJI.

Southern and Eastern African Mineral Centre (SEAMIC): POB 9573, Dar es Salaam, Tanzania; tel. (22) 2650347; fax (22) 2650319; e-mail seamic@seamic.org; internet www.seamic.org; f. 1977 to promote socio-economic and environmentally responsible mineral sector development in the region; sponsored by mem. states; provides advisory and consultancy services in exploration geology, geophysics, geochemistry, mining and mineral processing; archives and processes geoinformation data; organizes training courses; operates specialized laboratory services; mems: Angola, Comoros, Ethiopia, Kenya, Mozambique, Tanzania, Uganda; Dir-Gen. KETEMA TADESSE; publ. *Seamic Newsletter* (2 a year).

United Nations University Institute for Natural Resources in Africa (UNU/INRA): ISSER Bldg Complex, Nasia Rd, University of Ghana, Legon; Private Mail Bag, Kotoka International Airport, Accra, Ghana; tel. (21) 500396; fax (21) 500792; e-mail unuinra@inra.unu.edu.gh; internet www.unu.edu/inra; f. 1986 as a research and training centre of the United Nations University (Tokyo, Japan); operational since 1990; aims at human resource development and institutional capacity building through co-ordination with African universities and research institutes in advanced research, training and dissemination of knowledge and information on the conservation and management of Africa's natural resources and their rational utilization for sustainable devt; Dir. Prof. Dr KARL HARMSEN; INRA has a mineral resources unit (MRU) at the University of Zambia in Lusaka; MRU Co-ordinator Dr GLASSWELL NKONDE.

Social Sciences

African Centre for Applied Research and Training in Social Development (ACARTSOD): Africa Centre, Wahda Quarter, Zawia Rd, POB 80606, Tripoli, Libya; tel. (21) 4835103; fax (21) 4835066; e-mail fituri_acartsod@hotmail.com; f. 1977 under the jt auspices of the ECA and OAU (now AU) to promote and co-ordinate applied research and training in social devt, and to assist in formulating nat. development strategies; Head Dr AHMED SAID FITURI.

African Social and Environmental Studies Programme: Box 4477, Nairobi, Kenya; tel. (20) 747960; fax (20) 747960; f. 1968; develops and disseminates educational material on social and environmental studies in eastern and southern Africa; mems: 18 African countries; Chair. Prof. WILLIAM SENTEZA-KAJUBI; Exec. Dir Prof. PETER MUYANDA MUTEBI; publs *African Social and Environmental Studies Forum* (2 a year), teaching guides.

Afro-Asian Housing Organization (AAHO): POB 5623, 28 Ramses Ave, Cairo, Egypt; f. 1965 to promote co-operation between African and Asian countries in housing, reconstruction, physical planning and related matters; mems: 18 countries; Sec.-Gen. HASSAN M. HASSAN (Egypt).

Council for the Development of Social Science Research in Africa (CODESRIA): Ave Cheikh, Anta Diop x Canal IV, BP 3304, CP 18524, Dakar, Senegal; tel. 824-03-74; fax 824-57-95; e-mail codesria@codesria.sn; internet www.codesria.org; f. 1973; promotes research, organizes conferences, working groups and information services; mems: research institutes and university faculties and researchers in African countries; Exec. Sec. ADEBAYO OLUKOSHI; publs *Africa Development* (quarterly), *CODESRIA Bulletin* (quarterly), *Index of African Social Science Periodical Articles* (annually), *African Journal of International Affairs* (2 a year), *African Sociological Review* (2 a year), *Afrika Zameni* (annually), *Identity, Culture and Politics* (2 a year), *Afro Arab Selections for Social Sciences* (annually), directories of research.

International African Institute (IAI): School of Oriental and African Studies, Thornhaugh St, Russell Sq., London, WC1H 0XG, United Kingdom; tel. (20) 7898-4420; fax (20) 7898-4419; e-mail iai@soas.ac.uk; internet www.iaionthe.net; f. 1926 to promote the study of African peoples, their languages, cultures and social life in their traditional and modern settings; organizes an international seminar programme bringing together scholars from Africa and elsewhere; links scholars in order to facilitate research projects, especially in the social sciences; Chair. Prof. V. Y. MUDIMBE; Hon. Dir Prof. PHILIP BURNHAM; publs *Africa* (quarterly), *Africa Bibliography* (annually).

International Peace Academy (IPA): 777 United Nations Plaza, New York, NY 10017-3521, USA; tel. (212) 687-4300; fax (212) 983-8246; e-mail ipa@ipacademy.org; internet www.ipacademy.org; f. 1970 to promote the prevention and settlement of armed conflicts between and within states through policy research and development; educates government officials in the procedures needed for conflict resolution, peace-keeping, mediation and negotiation, through international training seminars and publications; off-the-record meetings are also conducted to gain complete understanding of a specific conflict; Chair. RITA E. HAUSER; Pres. TERJE ROD-LARSEN.

Southern African Research and Documentation Centre (SARDC): POB 5690, Harare, Zimbabwe; tel. (4) 738695; fax (4) 738693; e-mail sardc@sardc.net; f. 1987; aims to enhance and disseminate information on political, economic, cultural and social developments in southern Africa; Exec. Dir PHYLLIS JOHNSON.

Third World Forum: 39 Dokki St, POB 43, Orman Giza, Cairo, Egypt; tel. (2) 7488092; fax (2) 7480668; e-mail 20sabry2@gega.net; internet www.egypt2020.org; f. 1973 to link social scientists and others from the developing countries, to discuss alternative development policies and encourage research; currently undertaking Egypt 2020 research project; maintains regional offices in Egypt, Mexico, Senegal and Sri Lanka; mems: individuals in more than 50 countries; Chair. ISMAIL-SABRI ABDALLA.

Social Welfare and Human Rights

African Commission on Human and Peoples' Rights: 48 Kairaba Ave, POB 673, Banjul, The Gambia; tel. 4392962; fax 4390764;

e-mail achpr@achpr.org; internet www.achpr.org; f. 1987; mandated to monitor compliance with the African Charter on Human and People's Rights (ratified in 1986); investigates claims of human rights abuses perpetrated by govts that have ratified the Charter (claims may be brought by other African govts, the victims themselves, or by a third party); meets twice a year for 15 days in March and Oct; mems: 11; Sec. Dr MARY MABOREKE.

Global Commission on International Migration (GCIM): rue Richard-Wagner 1, 1202 Geneva, Switzerland; tel. 227484850; fax 227484851; internet www.gcim.org; f. 2003 to place international migration issues on the global agenda, to analyse migration policy, to examine links with other fields, and to present recommendations for consideration by the UN Secretary-General, governments and other parties; Commission ceased operations on 31 Dec. 2005; publ.*Migration in an Interconnected World: New Directions for Action*.

Global Migration Group: f. 2003, as the Geneva Migration Group; renamed as above in 2006; mems: ILO, IOM, UNCTAD, UNDP, United Nations Department of Economic and Social Affairs (UNDESA), UNFPA, OHCHR, UNHCR, UNODC, and the World Bank; holds regular meetings to discuss issues relating to int. migration, chaired by mem. orgs on a six-month rotational basis.

International Federation of Red Cross and Red Crescent Societies: 17 Chemin des Crêts, Petit-Saconnex, CP 372, 1211 Geneva 19, Switzerland; tel. 227304222; fax 227330395; e-mail secretariat@ifrc.org; internet www.ifrc.org; f. 1919 to prevent and alleviate human suffering and to promote humanitarian activities by national Red Cross and Red Crescent societies; conducts relief operations for refugees and victims of disasters, co-ordinates relief supplies and assists in disaster prevention; Pres. JUAN MANUEL SUÁREZ DEL TORO RIVERO (Spain); Sec.-Gen. MARKKU NISKALA (Finland); publs *Annual Report*, *Red Cross Red Crescent* (quarterly), *Weekly News*, *World Disasters Report*, *Emergency Appeal*.

International Organization for Migration (IOM): 17 route des Morillons, CP 71, 1211 Geneva 19, Switzerland; tel. 227179111; fax 227986150; e-mail info@iom.int; internet www.iom.int; f. 1951 as Intergovernmental Committee for Migration; name changed in 1989; a non-political and humanitarian organization, activities include the handling of orderly, planned migration to meet the needs of emigration and immigration countries and the processing and movement of refugees, displaced persons etc. in need of international migration services; mems: 118 states; observer status is held by 20 states and more than 60 intergovernmental and non-governmental organizations; Dir-Gen. BRUNSON MCKINLEY (USA); publs include *International Migration* (quarterly), *Migration* (quarterly, in English, French and Spanish), *World Migration Report* (every 2 years, in English).

Médecins sans frontières (MSF): rue de Lausanne 78, CP 116, 1211 Geneva 21, Switzerland; tel. 228498400; fax 228498404; internet www.msf.org; f. 1971; independent medical humanitarian org. composed of physicians and other members of the medical profession; aims to provide medical assistance to victims of war and natural disasters; operates longer-term programmes of nutrition, immunization, sanitation, public health, and rehabilitation of hospitals and dispensaries; awarded the Nobel peace prize in 1999; mems: national sections in 21 countries in Europe, Asia and North America; Pres. Dr ROWAN GILLIES; publ. *Activity Report* (annually).

World Social Forum (WSF): Support Office: Rua General Jardim 660, 7th Floor, São Paulo, Brazil 01223-010; e-mail forumsocialmundial.org.br; internet www.forumsocialmundial.org; f. 2001 as an annual global meeting of civil society bodies; the first WSF was held in Porto Alegre, Brazil, in Jan. 2001; a Charter of Principles was adopted in June 2002; the WSF is a permanent global process which aims to pursue alternatives to neo-liberal policies and commercial globalization; its objectives include the development and promotion of democratic international systems and institutions serving social justice, equality and the sovereignty of peoples, based on respect for the universal human rights of citizens of all nations and for the environment; the sixth (2006) Forum was polycentric, held in Bamako (Mali), Caracas (Venezuela), and Karachi (Pakistan), and the seventh (2007) Forum was convened in Nairobi, Kenya; an International Council, comprising 129 civil society organizations and commissions, guides the Forum and considers general political questions and methodology; the Support Office in São Paulo, Brazil, provides administrative assistance to the Forum process, to the International Council and to the specific organizing committees for each annual event; mems: civil society organizations and movements world-wide.

Sport and Recreations

African Football Confederation (Confédération africaine de football—CFA): 3 Abdel Khalek Sarwat St, El Hay El Motamayez, POB 23, 6th October City, Egypt; tel. (2) 8371000; fax (2) 8370006; e-mail info@cafonline.com; internet www.cafonline.com; f. 1957; promotes football in Africa; organizes inter-club competitions and Cup of Nations; General Assembly held every two years; mems: national asscns in 52 countries; Sec.-Gen. MUSTAPHA FAHMY; publ. *CAF News* (quarterly).

International Federation of Association Football (Fédération internationale de football association—FIFA): FIFA-Str. 20, POB 8044, Zürich, Switzerland; tel. 432227777; fax 432227878; e-mail media@fifa.org; internet www.fifa.com; f. 1904 to promote the game of association football and foster friendly relations among players and national asscns; to control football and uphold the laws of the game as laid down by the International Football Association Board; to prevent discrimination of any kind between players; and to provide arbitration in disputes between national asscns; organizes World Cup competition every four years; mems: 204 national asscns, six continental confederations; Pres. JOSEPH S. BLATTER (Switzerland); Gen. Sec. URS LINSI; publs *FIFA News* (monthly), *FIFA Magazine* (every 2 months) (both in English, French, German and Spanish), *FIFA Directory* (annually), *Laws of the Game* (annually), *Competitions' Regulations* and *Technical Reports* (before and after FIFA competitions).

Supreme Council for Sport in Africa (SCSA): POB 1363, Yaoundé, Cameroon; tel. 223-95-80; fax 223-45-12; e-mail scsa_yaounde@yahoo.com; f. 1966; co-ordinating authority and forum for the development and promotion of sports in Africa; mems: sports ministers from 53 countries; Sec.-Gen. SONSTONE YAMFWA KASHIBA; publ. *Newsletter* (monthly).

Technology

African Organization of Cartography and Remote Sensing: 5 Route de Bedjarah, BP 102, Hussein Dey, Algiers, Algeria; tel. (2) 77-79-34; fax (2) 77-79-34; e-mail oact@wissal.dz; f. 1988 by amalgamation of African Association of Cartography and African Council for Remote Sensing; aims to encourage the development of cartography and of remote sensing by satellites; organizes conferences and other meetings, promotes establishment of training institutions; maintains four regional training centres (in Burkina Faso, Kenya, Nigeria and Tunisia); mems: national cartographic institutions of 24 African countries; Sec.-Gen. UNIS MUFTAH.

African Regional Centre for Technology: Imm. Fahd, 17th Floor, blvd Djilly Mbaye, BP 2435, Dakar, Senegal; tel. 823-77-12; fax 823-77-13; e-mail arct@sonatel.senet.net; f. 1977 to encourage the development of indigenous technology and to improve the terms of access to imported technology; assists the establishment of national centres; mems: govts of 31 countries; Exec. Dir Dr OUSMANE KANE; publs *African Technodevelopment*, *Alert Africa*.

Regional Centre for Mapping of Resources for Development (RCMRD): POB 632, 00618 Ruaraka, Nairobi, Kenya; tel. (20) 8560227; fax (20) 8561673; e-mail rcmrd@rcmrd.org; internet www.rcmrd.org; f. 1975; present name adopted 1997; provides services for the professional techniques of map-making and the application of satellite and remote sensing data in resource analysis and development planning; undertakes research and provides advisory services to African governments; mems: 15 signatory and 10 non-signatory governments; Dir-Gen. Dr WILBER K. OTTICHILO.

Regional Centre for Training in Aerospace Surveys (RECTAS) (Centre Regional de Formations aux Techniques des leves aerospatiaux): PMB 5545, Ile-Ife, Nigeria; tel. (803) 384-0581; e-mail info@rectas.org; internet www.rectas.org; f. 1972; provides training, research and advisory services in aerospace surveys and geoinformatics; administered by the ECA; mems: eight governments; Exec. Dir Dr OLAJIDE KUFONIYI.

Tourism

Southern African Regional Tourism Council: POB 564 Blantyre, Malawi; tel. 624888; fax 634339; f. 1973 for the devt and marketing of tourism in southern African countries; mems: public and private representatives in 22 countries world-wide.

Trade and Industry

African Regional Industrial Property Organization (ARIPO): POB 4228, Harare, Zimbabwe; tel. (4) 7948404; fax (4) 704025; e-mail info@aripo.wipo.net; internet www.aripo.wipo.net; f. 1976 to grant patents, register industrial designs and marks and to promote devt and harmonization of laws concerning industrial property; mems:

Botswana, The Gambia, Ghana, Kenya, Lesotho, Malawi, Mozambique, Sierra Leone, Somalia, Sudan, Swaziland, Tanzania, Uganda, Zambia and Zimbabwe; Dir-Gen. MZONDI H. CHIRAMBO.

African Regional Organization for Standardization: POB 57363-00200, Nairobi, Kenya; tel. (20) 224561; fax (20) 218792; e-mail arso@bidii.com; internet www.arso-oran.org; f. 1977 to promote standardization, quality control, certification and metrology in the African region, to formulate regional standards, and to co-ordinate participation in international standardization activities; mems: 28 states; Sec.-Gen. DAMIAN UDENNA AGBANELO; publs *ARSO Bulletin* (2 a year), *ARSO Catalogue of Regional Standards* (annually), *ARSO Annual Report*.

African Water Association (Association Africaine de l'Eau): 05 BP 1910, Abidjan 05, Côte d'Ivoire; tel. 21-24-14-43; fax 21-24-26-29; e-mail susher.uade@aviso.ci; f. 1980; facilitates co-operation between public and private bodies concerned with water supply and sewage management in Africa; promotes the study of economic, technical and scientific matters relating to the industry; congress held every two years (2008: Cotonou, Benin); mems: 70 water and sanitation utilities in 40 countries; Sec.-Gen. SYLVAIN USHER.

Association of African Trade Promotion Organizations (AATPO): blvd Muhammad V, Pavillion International, BP 23, 90 000 Tangier, Morocco; tel. (3) 943730; fax (3) 9325275; e-mail aoapc@oaoapc.org; internet www.aoapc.org; f. 1975 under the auspices of the OAU (now AU) and the ECA to foster regular contact between African states in trade matters and to assist in the harmonization of their commercial policies, in order to promote intra-African trade; conducts research and training; organizes meetings and trade information missions; mems: 26 states; Sec.-Gen. Prof. ADEYINKA W. ORIMALADE; publs *FLASH: African Trade* (monthly), *Directory of African Consultants and Experts in Trade Promotion*, *Directory of Trade Information Contacts in Africa*, *Directory of Trade Information Sources in Africa*, *Directory of State Trading Organizations*, *Directory of Importers and Exporters of Food Products in Africa*, *Basic Information on Africa*, studies.

Federation of African Chambers of Commerce: c/o ECA, POB 3001, Addis Ababa, Ethiopia; tel. (1) 517200; fax (1) 514416; f. 1983; Dir Dr B. W. MUTHAUKA.

Southern African Customs Union: c/o Dept of Trade and Industry, Private Bag X84, Pretoria, South Africa; tel. (12) 3109393; fax (12) 3220298; f. 1969; provides common pool of customs, excise and sales duties, according to the relative volume of trade and production in each country; goods are traded within the union free of duty and quotas, subject to certain protective measures for less developed mems; the South African rand is legal tender in Lesotho and Swaziland; the Customs Union Commission meets annually in each of the mems' capital cities in turn; mems: Botswana, Lesotho, Namibia, South Africa, Swaziland.

Union of Producers, Conveyors and Distributors of Electric Power in Africa (UPDEA): 01 BP 1345, Abidjan 01, Côte d'Ivoire; tel. 20-32-64-33; fax 20-33-12-10; e-mail updea.org@aviso.ci; f. 1970 to study tech. matters and to promote efficient devt of enterprises in this sector; operates training school in Côte d'Ivoire; mems: 31 public service operators in 27 countries; Sec.-Gen. ANTOINE KOUASSI; publs *AFRIQUELEC* (periodical), technical papers.

Transport

African Airlines Association: POB 20116, Nairobi 00200, Kenya; tel. (20) 604855; fax (20) 601173; e-mail afraa@afraa.org; internet www.afraa.org; f. 1968 to give African air companies expert advice in technical, financial, juridical and market matters; to improve air transport in Africa through inter-carrier co-operation; and to develop manpower resources; mems: 34 national carriers; Sec.-Gen. CHRISTIAN E. FOLLY-KOSSI; publs *Newsletter*, reports.

Agency for the Safety of Air Navigation in Africa and Madagascar (ASECNA) (Agence pour la Sécurité de la Navigation Aérienne en Afrique et Madagascar): 32–38 ave Jean Jaurès, BP 3144, Dakar, Senegal; tel. 849-66-00; fax 823-46-54; e-mail contact@asecna.aero; internet www.asecna.aero; f. 1959; organizes air-traffic communications in mem. states; co-ordinates meteorological forecasts; provides training for air-traffic controllers, meteorologists and airport fire-fighters; ASECNA is under the authority of a cttee comprising Ministers of Civil Aviation of mem. states; mems: Benin, Burkina Faso, Cameroon, Central African Repub., Chad, Repub. of the Congo, Côte d'Ivoire, Equatorial Guinea, France, Gabon, Madagascar, Mali, Mauritania, Niger, Senegal, Togo; Dir-Gen. YOUSSOUF MAHAMAT.

Youth and Students

Pan-African Youth Movement (Mouvement pan-africain de la jeunesse): 19 rue Debbih Chérif, BP 72, Didouch Mourad, 16000 Algiers, Algeria; tel. and fax (2) 71-64-71; f. 1962; aims to encourage the participation of African youth in socio-economic and political development and democratization; organizes conferences and seminars, youth exchanges and youth festivals; mems: youth groups in 52 African countries and liberation movements; publ. *MPJ News* (quarterly).

WFUNA Youth: c/o WFUNA, 1 United Nations Plaza, Room DC1-1177, New York, NY 10017, USA; tel. (212) 963-5610; fax (212) 963-0447; e-mail coordinating.committee@qmail.com; internet www.wfuna-youth.org; f. 1948 by the World Federation of United Nations Associations (WFUNA) as the International Youth and Student Movement for the United Nations (ISMUN), independent since 1949; an international non-governmental organization of students and young people dedicated especially to supporting the principles embodied in the United Nations Charter and Universal Declaration of Human Rights; encourages constructive action in building economic, social and cultural equality and in working for national independence, social justice and human rights on a world-wide scale; maintains regional offices in Austria, France, Ghana, Panama and the USA; mems: asscns in over 100 mem. states of the UN.

MAJOR COMMODITIES OF AFRICA

Note: For each of the commodities in this section, there is a statistical table relating to recent levels of production. Each production table shows estimates of output for the world and for Africa (including North Africa, a region not covered by this volume). In addition, the table lists the main African producing countries and, for comparison, the leading producers from outside the continent.

ALUMINIUM AND BAUXITE

Aluminium is the most abundant metallic element in the earth's crust, comprising about 8% of the total. However, it is much less widely used than steel, despite having about the same strength and only half the weight. Aluminium has important applications as a metal because of its lightness, ease of fabrication and other desirable properties. Other products of alumina (aluminium oxide trihydrate, into which bauxite, the commonest aluminium ore, is refined) are materials in refractories, abrasives, glass manufacture, other ceramic products, catalysts and absorbers. Alumina hydrates are used for the production of aluminium chemicals, as fire retardants in carpet-backing, and as industrial fillers in plastics and related products.

The major markets for aluminium are in transportation, building and construction, electrical machinery and equipment, consumer durables, and the packaging industry, which in 2000 accounted for more than 20% of all aluminium use. Although the production of aluminium is energy-intensive, its light weight results in a net saving, particularly in the transportation industry. About one-quarter of aluminium output is consumed in the manufacture of transport equipment, particularly road motor vehicles and components, where the metal is increasingly being used as a substitute for steel. In the early 1990s steel substitution accounted for about 16% of world aluminium consumption, and it has been forecast that aluminium demand by the motor vehicle industry alone could more than double, to exceed 5.7m. metric tons in 2010, compared with around 2.4m. tons in 1990. Aluminium is of great value to the aerospace industry for its weight-saving characteristics and its low cost relative to alternative materials. Aluminium-lithium alloys command considerable potential for use in this sector, although the traditional dominance of aluminium in the aerospace sector has been challenged since the 1990s by 'composites' such as carbon-epoxy, a fusion of carbon fibres and hardened resins, the lightness and durability of which can exceed that of many aluminium alloys.

Until recently, world markets for finished and semi-finished aluminium products were dominated by six Western producers—Alcan (Canada), Alcoa, Reynolds, Kaiser (all USA), Pechiney (France) and algroup (Switzerland). Proposals for a merger between Alcan, algroup and Pechiney, and between Alcoa and Reynolds, were announced in August 1999. However, the proposed terms of the Pechiney-Alcan-algroup merger encountered opposition from the European Commission, on the grounds that the combined grouping could restrict market competition and adversely affect the interests of consumers. The tripartite merger plan was abandoned in April 2000, although Alcan and algroup were permitted to merge in October. In 2003, having agreed to meet conditions imposed by the European Commission and the US Department of Justice in respect of safeguarding free competition, Alcan was permitted to purchase Pechiney. One of the most significant of the conditions imposed in respect of Alcan's purchase of Pechiney was a requirement that it divest some of its rolled aluminium products assets. In late 2004, as a consequence of this divestment, a new rolled aluminium products group, Novelis, was emerging. In the USA Alcoa Inc. and Reynolds Metals Co merged in mid-2000. In 2002, after the purchase of Germany's VAW, Norway's Norsk Hydro became the world's third largest integrated aluminium concern. Prior to the mergers detailed above the level of dominance of the six major Western producers had been reduced by a significant geographical shift in the location of alumina and aluminium production to countries where cheap power is available, such as Australia, Brazil, Norway, Canada and Venezuela. The Gulf states of Bahrain and Dubai (United Arab Emirates), with the advantage of low energy costs, also produce primary aluminium. Since the mid-1990s Russia has also become a significant force in the world aluminium market (see below), and in 2000 the country's principal producers, together with a number of plants located in the Commonwealth of Independent States, merged to form the Russian Aluminium Co, whose facilities in 2005 were the source of 75% of Russian and 10% of global primary aluminium output. Sual is Russia's other major producer.

Bauxite is the principal aluminium ore, but nepheline syenite, kaolin, shale, anorthosite and alunite are all potential alternative sources of alumina, although not currently economic to process. Of all bauxite mined, approximately 85% is converted to alumina (Al_2O_3) for the production of aluminium metal. Developing countries, in which at least 70% of known bauxite reserves are located, supply some 50% of the ore required. The industry is structured in three stages: bauxite mining, alumina refining and smelting. While the high degree of 'vertical integration' (i.e. the control of successive stages of production) in the industry means that a significant proportion of trade in bauxite and alumina is in the form of intra-company transfers, and the increasing tendency to site alumina refineries near to bauxite deposits has resulted in a shrinking bauxite trade, there is a growing free market in alumina, serving the needs of the increasing number of independent (i.e. non-integrated) smelters.

The alumina is separated from the ore by the Bayer process. After mining, bauxite is fed direct to process direct if mine-run material is adequate (as in Jamaica) or is otherwise crushed and beneficiated. Where the 'as-mined' ore presents handling problems, or weight reduction is desirable, it may be dried prior to shipment.

At the alumina plant the ore is slurried with spent-liquor direct, if the soft Caribbean type is used, or, in the case of other types, it is ball-milled to reduce it to a size that will facilitate the extraction of the alumina. The bauxite slurry is then digested with caustic soda to extract the alumina from the ore while leaving the impurities as an insoluble residue. The digest conditions depend on the aluminium minerals in the ore and the impurities. The liquor, with the dissolved alumina, is then separated from the insoluble impurities by combinations of sedimentation, decantation and filtration, and the residue is washed to minimize the soda losses. The clarified liquor is concentrated and the alumina precipitated by seeding with hydrate. The precipitated alumina is then filtered, washed and calcined to produce alumina. The ratio of bauxite to alumina is approximately 1.95:1.

The smelting of the aluminium is generally by electrolysis in molten cryolite. Because of the high consumption of electricity by this process, alumina is usually smelted in areas where low-cost electricity is available. However, most of the electricity now used in primary smelting in the Western world is generated by hydroelectricity—a renewable energy source.

The recycling of aluminium is economically (as well as environmentally) desirable, as the process uses only 5% of the electricity required to produce a similar quantity of primary aluminium. Aluminium that has been recycled from scrap currently accounts for almost 30% of the total annual world output of primary aluminium. With the added impetus of environmental concerns, considerable growth occurred world-wide in the recycling of used beverage cans (UBC) during the 1990s. In the middle of that decade, according to aluminium industry estimates, the recycling rate of UBC amounted to at least 55% world-wide. In the USA in 2003 a UBC recycling rate of 50% was reported, while in Brazil in 2005, according to the Associação Brasileira do Aluminío and the Associação Brasileira dos Fabricantes de Latas de Alta Reciclabilidade, 93% of all aluminium cans sold were recycled—a rate equivalent to 136,080 metric tons of metal, or 10,100m. individual cans. More than 160,000 Brazilians were reported to depend on collecting aluminium cans for their livelihoods, selling UBC at more than 6,000 deposit points country-wide.

In 2006, according to the International Aluminium Institute (IAI), world output of primary aluminium totalled an estimated 23.9m. metric tons, of which African producers (Cameroon, Egypt, Ghana, Mozambique, Nigeria and South Africa) accounted for about 1.9m. tons. The USA normally accounts for more than one-quarter of total aluminium consumption (excluding communist and former communist countries). The USA was for long the world's principal producing country, but in 2001 US output of primary aluminium was surpassed by that of Russia and of the People's Republic of China. In 2002, 2003, 2004 and, it was estimated, in 2005 Canadian production, in addition to that of Russia and China, exceeded that of the USA. In 2004 production of primary aluminium by China was estimated to have been substantially more than double that of the USA.

In 2005, according to the US Geological Survey (USGS), Guinea possessed about 30% of the world's known bauxite reserves. The country is the world's leading exporter of bauxite. Formerly ranking second in the world after Australia in terms of ore production, Guinea has recently been overtaken by Brazil and China. Exports of aluminium ore and concentrate dominate the Guinean economy. In 2003 exports of bauxite, valued at US $289.8m., contributed 40% of

Guinea's total revenue from foreign sales, while exports of alumina, valued at $147.6m., contributed a further 20%. In 2004, according to the USGS, bauxite remained Guinea's principal source of foreign exchange. The country refines some of its high-grade bauxite ore domestically and exports some alumina to Cameroon for refining at that country's Edéa smelter. Alumina Co of Guinea, which operates in Lowland Guinea, is a joint venture between Rusal (85%) and the Government. In early 2004 Rusal was reported to be proceeding with plans to expand the company's alumina refinery at Friguia, with the aim of doubling its annual production capacity to 1.4m. metric tons. The cost of the envisaged expansion has been estimated at $350m. In May Alcan and Alcoa signed a memorandum of understanding for the joint construction of an alumina refinery at Kamsar, in Lowland Guinea, with an annual production capacity of 1.5m. tons. The refinery was expected to commence production in 2008. Compagnie des Bauxites de Kindia (CBK), which mines bauxite in Lowland Guinea, is wholly owned by Rusal. In 2004 CBK exported all of its mined output to Ukraine for refining. In October Global Alumina Products Corpn was reported to have signed an agreement with the Government to construct an alumina refinery at Sangaredi, with an annual production capacity of 2.8m. tons. The refinery is expected to produce alumina from 2008. Cameroon has extensive bauxite deposits, estimated at some 1,200m. tons, but these await commercial exploitation. Compagnie Camérounaise de l'Aluminium, in which Alcan Inc. of Canada and the Government have equal shares, produces primary aluminium at Edéa. In 2005 Alcan was reported to have signed a letter of intent in which it undertook to raise the annual capacity of its smelter at Edéa from 90,000 tons to 260,000 tons, and to build a new hydroelectric power plant. The project, the cost of which has been estimated at $900m., is due to be completed by 2010. Malawi's reserves of bauxite, located at Mulanje and estimated at 29m. metric tons in the mid-1990s, remained unexploited as of 2004. Ghana's bauxite reserves have been estimated at 780m. tons. Although the country lacks an alumina refinery, imported alumina has been processed by a smelter at Tema, with an annual production capacity of 200,000 tons. The smelter was operated by the Volta Aluminium Co (Valco), which was 90%-owned by Kaiser Aluminum and Chemical Corpn, a subsidiary, in turn, of Kaiser Aluminum Corpn of the USA. In 2003 Kaiser closed the Tema facility, whose operations had been hampered by inadequate power allocations—a consequence of severe drought—for several years. In 2004 the Government acquired Kaiser's stake in Valco with a view to developing an integrated aluminium industry to supply the Tema smelter with raw materials. In 2002 Ghana produced 117,000 tons of primary aluminium, compared with 144,000 tons in 2001 and 137,000 tons in 2000. However, following the closure, output was just 16,000 tons in 2004 and 13,000 in 2005. The smelting plant at Tema harbour was due to recommence ouput in 2006. Sierra Leone has estimated bauxite reserves of more than 100m. tons. Exploitation of the Mokanji deposits, in the Southern province, began in 1964, but was interrupted from early 1995 by guerrilla insurgency. In 2004 Sierra Minerals Ltd received government approval to resume operations at the Mokanji bauxite mine near Moyamba. Operations at the mine were expected to commence in 2005. South Africa produces primary aluminium from imported alumina. In 2005 BHP Billiton operated the country's two smelters at Richards Bay, producing a total of 851,000 tons of metal, compared with 863,000 tons in 2004 and 738,000 tons in 2003. Alcan announced in 2004 that it would conduct a feasibility study on the construction of a smelter at Coega, Eastern Cape Province, with an envisaged annual capacity of 660,000 tons. A major aluminium smelter project (Mozal) in Mozambique was formally inaugurated in 1998, although the country is not a significant producer of bauxite. The Mozal smelter, located near Maputo and owned by a consortium including the Australian-British mining group BHP Billiton, represents the largest single investment project in Mozambique, with an estimated cost of about $1,300m. The first aluminium was cast at the smelter in 2000. Using alumina from Australia, the smelter increased its output to 266,000 tons in 2001, compared with 54,000 tons in 2000. In 2002 Mozambique's production increased to 273,000 tons. Output rose substantially, to 407,000 tons, in 2003, following the completion of an expansion project at the Mozal smelter which raised its annual production capacity to 506,000 tons. In 2004 production was estimated to have risen again, to 549,000 tons. There was a more modest increase, to 555,000 tons, in 2005. Mozambique is now Africa's second largest producer of aluminium, after South Africa, and exports its output to Europe. In 2004 exports of aluminium, valued at $915m., contributed 61% of the country's total export revenue. In 2004 Alcoa sold to the Nigerian Government its 10% share in the smelter at Ikot Abasi operated by the Aluminium Smelter Co of Nigeria.

Production of Bauxite
(crude ore, '000 metric tons)

	2004	2005*
World total (excl. USA)	160,000	169,000
Africa	15,505	15,744
Leading African producers		
Ghana	498	734†
Guinea*‡	15,000	15,000
Leading non-African producers		
Australia	56,593	59,959
Brazil	19,700	19,800†
China, People's Repub.*	15,000	18,000
India	11,285	11,957
Jamaica‡	13,296	14,118
Kazakhstan	4,706	4,800
Russia*	6,000	6,400
Suriname	4,052	4,584
Venezuela	5,842	5,900

* Estimated production.
† Preliminary.
‡ Dried equivalent of crude ore.

Source: US Geological Survey.

International efforts were undertaken from the early 1990s to address a problem of over-supply that affected world markets for aluminium. The problem of over-supply was exacerbated by a rapid rise, beginning in 1991, of exports by the USSR and its successor states, which had begun to accumulate substantial stocks of aluminium as a consequence of the collapse of the Soviet arms industry. By late 1995 these efforts, which involved, *inter alia*, reductions in output by major Western producers, had, in combination with a strong revival in world demand, created market conditions in which exports of aluminium from Russia were viewed as essential to the maintenance of Western supplies. Demand in 1998, however, was adversely affected by the economic crisis in East Asia, and consumption of aluminium in established market economy countries (EMEC) rose by only 0.1%: the lowest growth in aluminium demand since 1982. However, consumption in the EMEC area increased by an estimated 3.9% in 1999, with demand for aluminium rising strongly in the USA and in much of Asia. Compared with 1998, growth in consumption was, however, reduced in Europe and Latin America. World-wide, the fastest growing sector of aluminium demand in 1999 was the transport industry (the largest market for the metal), with consumption rising by about 9%.

In 2000, according to USGS data, production of primary aluminium grew by 3.4%. At the end of the year, according to the IAI, total world inventories (comprising unwrought aluminium, unprocessed scrap, metal in process and finished, semi-fabricated metal) had declined slightly, compared with the previous year. Stocks of primary aluminium held by the London Metal Exchange (LME), meanwhile, had fallen heavily. Demand from the USA and Asia was characterized by the USGS as weak during 2000, especially during the second half of the year, while European demand remained firm. In 2001 IAI data indicated a slight fall in total world inventories of aluminium, while, conversely, those of primary aluminium held by the LME rose substantially. Production of primary aluminium in 2001 was slightly lower than in 2000. In 2002, however, output rose by about 3.2%. In that year, according to analysis by Alcan, consumption of primary aluminium in the West rose by more than 3.5%, to almost 20m. metric tons. IAI data indicated a decline in total aluminium stocks of about 2.6% in 2002. In 2003, when prices fell to their lowest ever level in real (i.e. constant US dollar) terms, it was evident that reductions in costs had enabled larger, integrated producers to safeguard the viability of their enterprises. (Older and, generally, smaller producers, meanwhile, had been forced into closure.) Analysts cited as evidence of this plans to create substantial new primary metal capacity world-wide up to 2010. According to IAI data, production of primary metal increased by 3.5% in 2003, while stocks held world-wide increased by 1.1%. In 2004 IAI data indicated a substantial increase, of 7%, in global stocks of aluminium, while output of primary metal increased by 3%. The IAI recorded an increase in global production of aluminium of 3.9% in 2005, while inventories of the metal increased by less than 1%. World aluminium production increased at a lower rate, of 1.7%, in 2006, according to IAI data, while inventories of the metal decreased by 7.7% in that year.

With alumina in short supply, prices of aluminium rose during the opening weeks of 2000, and in early February the London quotation reached US $1,743.5 (£1,079) per metric ton: its highest level for more than two years. However, the LME's stocks of the metal also increased, reaching 868,625 tons later that month. The London price of aluminium declined to $1,413 (£891) per ton in April, but recovered to $1,599 (£1,070) in July. Throughout this period there was a steady decrease in LME holdings, which were reduced to less than 700,000 tons in April, under 600,000 tons in May and below 500,000 tons in July. At the end of July aluminium stocks were 461,975 tons: only 53% of the level reached in February; and by the end of August they had fallen to 399,925 tons. In September prices continued to rise, reaching $1,644 per ton on 13 September, even though stocks fell steadily throughout the month, which they ended at 361,050 tons. Thereafter, in October and November, the London quotation for aluminium was somewhat weaker, falling to respective 'lows' in those months of $1,446 and $1,443. Stocks declined simultaneously, standing at 331,250 tons on 31 October, and 320,725 tons on 30 November. Prices strengthened in December, reaching a 'high' for that month of $1,632.5 per ton. The firmer quotation was accompanied by the beginning of a sustained rise in stocks of aluminium held by the LME. Having fallen to 298,925 tons on 18 December, stocks ended the month slightly higher, at 321,850 tons, than at the end of the previous month.

At the end of January 2001 the London quotation rose to US $1,737 per metric ton, thus approaching the highest level recorded in 2000. By the end of January stocks had recovered to 394,075 tons. By the end of February LME holdings stood at 483,200 tons, and the London price had declined to $1,553 per ton. In both March and April, on a month-on-month basis, stocks fell, while prices were generally weaker, the London quotation reaching $1,540 on 27 April. May 2001 marked the beginning of a very substantial accumulation of stocks. Although the London quotation rose as high as $1,586 on 4 May, prices fell precipitously in June–November, reaching a low of $1,243 on 7 November, but recovering to $1,430 at the end of that month. The sustained decline was attributed to slow economic growth world-wide, which had caused the market to be over-supplied, aggravated by the events in the USA on 11 September. For the whole of 2001 the LME average monthly 'spot' price for high-grade aluminium was 65.5 US cents per pound.

On 28 March 2002 LME stocks rose to 1,029,400 metric tons. The London quotation weakened in both April and May, falling to US $1,318 per metric ton on 23 May. In early June the price recovered to $1,398, but had fallen to $1,364.5 per ton by the end of the month, when stocks of aluminium held by the LME totalled more than 1.2m. tons. By the end of July the price of aluminium traded on the LME had fallen to $1,310 per ton, by which time stocks held by the Exchange had risen to 1,291,000 tons. On 14 August the London quotation fell to $1,279 per ton, but had recovered to $1,293.5 per ton by the end of the month. On 13 August, meanwhile, stocks rose to 1,300,125 tons, and were to remain above 1,290,000 until the first day of October, when they fell to 1,288,200. On 11 September the London quotation recovered to $1,340.5, but subsequently weakened, ending the month at $1,280.5 per ton. At the end of the first week of October the price of aluminium fell to $1,275.5 per ton, but had risen to $1,337.5 by 31 October. From early November the London quotation began to recover somewhat, reaching $1,370.5 per ton on 4 November and ending the month at $1,378 per ton. This upward movement continued into December: on 13 December the London quotation was just short of $1,400 per ton. Stocks declined further in the final month of 2002, falling to 1,238,000 tons on 12 December and ending the year at 1,241,350 tons. The price of aluminium, meanwhile, declined to $1,344.5 per ton on 31 December.

On 22 January 2003 the London quotation for primary aluminium closed at more than US $1,400 per metric ton for the first time since 22 March 2002, and the price had risen further, to $1,247 per ton, by the end of the month. By the end of January 2003 stocks held by the LME had fallen to 1,199,550 tons and continued to fall thereafter until about the middle of February. With the exception of 19 February, the London quotation closed at more than $1,400 per ton on each day of that month. The price weakened during March, however, at the same time as stocks were rising. On 31 March the London quotation closed at $1,350 per ton, while stocks were recorded at 1,252,775 tons. The London price continued to fall until around mid-April, subsequently strengthening to finish the month at $1,356.5 per ton. From around mid-May this stronger trend became more pronounced, the London quotation closing at more than $1,400 per ton on each day of the month after 12 May. By the end of May stocks of the metal held by the LME had declined to 1,130,625 tons. On 16 June stocks fell to 1,115,150 tons. Prices remained stable throughout June, at the end of which the London quotation was $1,389 per ton.

On 14 July 2003 the London quotation for primary aluminium closed at US $1,463 per metric ton. Prices were thereafter generally weaker until towards the end of the month. On 28 July the closing price for the metal was $1,484.5 per ton. On 1 August the London quotation closed at $1,505 per ton, the first time a closing price in excess of $1,500 per ton had been recorded since May 2001. On 29 August, the last trading day of that month, the London price closed at $1,432 per ton, having fallen as low as $1,427.5 in the interim. On 11 September the price declined to $1,378 per ton, but it had recovered by the end of the month to $1,407.5 per ton. Generally, from October until the end of 2003, the London price strengthened, reaching $1,552 per ton on 5 December and ending the year at $1,592.5 per ton. During the second half of 2003 stocks of aluminium held by the LME rose steadily. At the end of July they totalled 1,304,450 tons; by the end of December they had increased to 1,423,275 tons.

On 2 January 2004 the London quotation for primary aluminium closed at US $1,600 per metric ton, the first time the quotation had reached that level since February 2001. On 30 January a closing price of $1,636.5 per ton was recorded. The London quotation strengthened further in February, closing at $1,754 per ton on 18 February, but thereafter declined somewhat to end the month at $1,702 per ton. The London price remained above $1,625 per ton throughout March, ending the month at $1,688.5 per ton. Sharp increases occurred from early April, and on 16 April a closing price greater than $1,800 per ton ($1,802) was recorded. Prices in April rose to their highest levels for more than eight years. By 10 May, however, the quotation had fallen to $1,575 per ton. On 2 June a closing price of $1,703.5 was recorded, rising to $1,721 per ton on 21 June. Stocks of aluminium held by the LME rose as high as 1,453,125 tons in January. From February until the end of June, however, they declined steadily. At the end of February they totalled 1,393,675 tons, but had fallen to 940,200 tons by the end of June. For the whole of 2004 the average quotation for primary aluminium traded on the LME was $1,717 per ton, 19.9% higher than the average price recorded in 2003. The higher price in 2004 was attributed to a substantial increase in global demand for aluminium, in particular from China, that had outstripped, and led to a heavy fall in, world inventories—the global market was in deficit for the first time since 2000. Growth in demand world-wide from the aerospace and automotive sectors was especially strong in 2004. Aluminium also benefited, in the early part of the year, from even sharper increases in the prices of those metals, such as copper and steel, for which it can be substituted. At the end of 2004 stocks of aluminium held by the LME, at 692,775 tons, were more than 50% lower than at the end of 2003.

In 2005 the average price of aluminium traded on the LME, at US $ 1,898 per metric ton, was 10.6% higher than in 2004. During the year aluminium traded within a range of $1,675–$2,289 per ton. Stocks of metal held by the Exchange declined steadily during the first half of 2005, from 654,025 tons at the end of January to 535,525 tons at 30 June. By December 2005, however, inventories had recovered to 643,700 tons.

During the first six months of 2006 the average price of aluminium traded on the LME continued to rise, reaching US $2,361 per metric ton in January and $2,861 per ton in May, before falling to $2,477 in June. In January–June 2006 aluminium traded within a range of $2,267–$3,275 per ton. Generally, stocks held by the LME rose in the first half of 2006, reaching 710,075 tons at the end of January and 779,100 tons at the end of March. At the end of June inventories totalled 760,900 tons. At mid-2006 analysts noted that the price of aluminium had been declining since the second week of May, when a peak of $3,275 per ton had been reached. Strong demand for the metal was reflected in IAI data that indicated declines in producers' inventories, while other market observers pointed to steady growth in consumption in January–April. The recent surge in the price of aluminium was attributed to the renewed interest of investment funds in the metal, in combination with restructuring in the European and US aluminium sectors. For the whole of 2006 the average price of aluminium traded on the LME reached US $2,567 per metric ton (an increase of 35.2% on the previous year). LME stocks fell to some 698,425 tons at the end of December, but proceeded to rise incrementally in the first half of 2007, reaching 839,200 tons in July, by which time the average price had risen to $2,733 per ton. Overall, prices fluctuated between January and July 2007, trading within a range of $2,626–$2,953 per ton.

The International Aluminium Institute (IAI), based in London, United Kingdom, is a global forum of producers of aluminium dedicated to the development and wider use of the metal. In 2007 the IAI had 26 member companies, representing every part of the world, including Russia and China, and responsible for about 80% of global primary aluminium production and a significant proportion of the world's secondary output.

CASSAVA (Manioc, Tapioca, Yuca) (*Manihot esculenta*)

Cassava is a perennial woody shrub, up to 5 m in height, which is cultivated mainly for its enlarged starch-rich roots, although the young shoots and leaves of the plant are also edible. The plant can be harvested at any time from seven months to three years after planting. A native of South and Central America, cassava is now one of the most important food plants in all parts of the tropics (except at the highest altitudes), having a wide range of adaptation for rainfall (500 mm–8,000 mm per year). Cassava is also well adapted to low-fertility soils, and grows where other crops will not. It is produced mainly on marginal agricultural land, with virtually no input of fertilizers, fungicides or insecticides.

The varieties of the plant fall into two broad groups, bitter and sweet cassava, formerly classed as two separate species, *M. utilissima* and *M. dulcis* or *aipi*. The roots of the sweet variety are usually boiled and then eaten. The roots of the bitter variety are either soaked, pounded and fermented to make a paste (such as 'fufu' in West Africa), or given an additional roasting to produce 'gari'. They can also be made into flour and starch, or dried and pelletized as animal feed.

The cassava plant contains two toxic substances, linamarin and lotaustralin, in its edible roots and leaves, which release the poison hydrocyanic acid, or cyanide, when plant tissues are damaged. Sweet varieties of cassava produce as little as 20 mg of acid per kg of fresh roots, whereas bitter varieties may produce more than 1,000 mg per kg. Although traditional methods of food preparation are effective in reducing cyanogenic content to harmless levels, if roots of bitter varieties are under-processed and the diet lacks protein and iodine (as occurs during famines and wars), cyanide poisoning can cause fatalities. Despite the disadvantages of the two toxins, some farmers prefer to cultivate the bitter varieties, possibly because the cyanide helps to protect the plant from potential pests, and possibly because the texture of certain food products made from bitter varieties is preferred to that of sweet cassavas.

Cassava, which was introduced to Africa from South America in the 16th century, is the most productive source of carbohydrates and produces more calories per unit of land than any cereal crop. Although the nutrient content of the roots consists almost entirely of starch, the leaves are high in vitamins, minerals and protein and, processed as meal or eaten as a fresh vegetable ('saka saka'), provide a useful source of nutrition in many parts of Africa, especially in the Democratic Republic of the Congo (DRC), the Congo basin, Sierra Leone, Malawi, Mozambique, Niger, Tanzania and Uganda. A plot of cassava may be left unattended in the ground for two years after maturity without deterioration of the roots. As the plant is also resistant to prolonged drought it is valued as a famine reserve. The roots are highly perishable after harvest, however, and if not consumed immediately must be processed (into flour, starch, pellets, etc.).

While the area under cassava has expanded considerably in recent years, there is increasing concern that the rapid expansion of cassava root planting may threaten the fertility of the soil and subsequently other crops. Under cropping systems where no fertilizer is used, cassava is the last crop in the succession because of its particular adaptability to infertile soils and its high nutrient use-efficiency in yield terms (although there is now evidence to suggest that cassava yields increase with the use of fertilizer). Soil fertility is not threatened by cassava itself, but rather by cultivation systems which dispense with fertilizers.

Production of Cassava
('000 metric tons)

	2005	2006
World total*	211,256	222,430
Africa*	118,406	118,125
Leading African producers		
Angola	8,606	8,810
Benin	2,861	2,524*
Cameroon	2,139	2,100*
Congo, Dem. Repub.	14,974	14,974*
Congo, Repub.*	900	1,000
Côte d'Ivoire	2,198	2,200*
Ghana	9,567	9,638
Guinea	1,017	1,069*
Kenya	348	841
Madagascar	2,144	2,359
Mozambique*	11,458	11,458
Nigeria	41,565	45,721*
Tanzania*	7,000	6,500
Uganda	5,576	4,926
Zambia	900	950
Leading non-African producers		
Brazil	25,872	26,713
India*	5,855	7,620
Indonesia	19,321	19,928
Thailand	16,938	22,584

* FAO estimate(s).

As a staple source of carbohydrates in the tropics, cassava is an essential part of the diet of about 300m. people. In 2005 it was harvested from 12.3m. ha in sub-Saharan Africa, and it may provide more than one-half of the caloric requirements of about 200m. people in the continent. The area in Africa from which cassava was harvested in 2005 amounted to about 66% of the area harvested world-wide in that year, and Africa's output accounted for more than 50% of world production. Most of the African crop is produced by subsistence farmers and is traded domestically: only a small quantity enters world trade. The expansion of production in the mid-1980s and 1990s was driven by demand for food consumption. Attempts undertaken in a number of African countries to increase the use of cassava as a feedstuff have met with only limited success, owing to cassava chips and pellets' uncompetitiveness relative to imported feedstuffs.

From the early 1970s African cassava production was seriously undermined by mealybug infestation. Indigenous to South America, the mealybug (*Phenacoccus manihoti*) encountered few natural enemies in Africa, and by about 1992 had infested almost all African cassava-growing areas. In 1981 the parasitic wasp *Epidinocarsis lopezi* was introduced into Nigeria from Paraguay to attack the mealybug, and by 1990 it was successfully established in 25 African countries. The introduction of natural enemies, such as *E. lopezi*, has brought about a 95% reduction in mealybug damage to cassava crops. The green spider mite (*Mononychellus tanajoa*), another threat to cassava cultivation, has also been successfully combated by the introduction of a natural enemy, the phytoseiid mite (*Typhlodromalus aripo*), which by 1997 had established a presence over 400,000 sq km in West Africa and in 1999 was reported to have reduced the presence of the green spider mite by up to 70% in some regions. Overall, there was reported to have been a 50% reduction in green spider mite damage to cassava crops owing to the introduction of natural predators. Other threats include the variegated grasshopper, *Zonocerus variegatus*, and African cassava leaf mosaic disease, which, like the green spider mite, deprives the plant of chlorophyll and causes low yields. Pest and diseases, in combination with poor husbandry, have in the past led to substantial yield losses in African cassava crops. To combat these losses, in addition to the measures described above, new varieties of cassava, developed for resistance to pests and diseases under the aegis of the International Institute of Tropical Agriculture, have been introduced throughout Africa's cassava belt. One such new variety, reported to be resistant to cassava leaf mosaic disease, was introduced in Uganda in 1997, with the aim of restoring production in the 60,000 ha that were being lost annually to this blight. In addition, the development of high-yielding varieties (HYV) was being successfully conducted in Nigeria during the late 1990s. The cultivation of a new HYV, also possessing resistance to pest damage, was reported to be proceeding successfully in Ghana in 1998.

In recent years there has been interest in the utilization of cassava as an industrial raw material as well as a food crop. Cassava has the potential to become a basic energy source for ethyl alcohol (ethanol), a substitute for petroleum. 'Alcogas' (a blend of cassava alcohol and petrol) can be mixed with petrol to provide motor fuel, while the high-protein residue from its production can be used for animal feed. The possibility of utilizing cassava leaves and stems (which represent about 50% of the plant and are normally discarded) as cattle-feed concentrates has also been receiving scientific attention.

In 2000 the average price of hard cassava pellets (f.o.b. Bangkok, Thailand) was US $55 per metric ton. In 2001 an average price of $59 per ton was recorded and in 2002 the average price rose to $66 per ton. Further increases, to, respectively, $71.9 per ton and $78 per ton, were recorded in 2003 and 2004. An average price of $111 per ton was recorded in 2005, followed by an average of $109 in 2006. The recent substantial increase in price was attributed to high transport costs associated with higher fuel prices. In 1999 the average international price of cassava (tapioca) starch (f.o.b. Bangkok) was $181 per ton, the lowest price since 1993. This price declined further throughout 2000, to an average of $157.4 per ton. In 2001 an average price of $173.8 per ton was recorded, and in 2002 the average price increased to $184.6 per ton. After falling to $172.7 per ton in 2003, the average international price of cassava starch recovered to $188.2 per ton in 2004. A very substantial increase, of more than 22%, to $230 per ton, was recorded in the Bangkok price of cassava starch in 2005, but the price decreased slightly in 2006, to $221.7 per ton.

CHROMIUM

Chromium, a metal historically used as an alloying element, is a hard, lustrous metal, the name of which derives from the Greek kroma (colour). It is only obtained from chromite (the name applied both to the metal-bearing mineral and to the ore containing that mineral—the terms chromite ore, chromium ore and chrome ore are used interchangeably). About 91% of total demand for chromite is from the metallurgical industry, some 5% from the chemical industry and about 4% from the refractory and foundry industries. For the metallurgical industry, most chromite ore is smelted in an electric arc furnace to produce ferrochromium. Within this industry the major use of chromium remains as an alloying element—it is essential to the composition of stainless steel, which is valued for its toughness and resistance to most forms of corrosion. Chromium chemicals are also used for wood preservation, dyeing and tanning. Chrome plating is a popular way of enhancing the appearance of motor vehicles, kitchen appliances, etc. Chromite is also used as a refractory mineral.

World reserves of chromite ore were estimated by the US Geological Survey (USGS) to total about 810m. metric tons in 2004. In that year some 12% of known reserves were estimated to be in South

Africa, and about 36% in Kazakhstan. South Africa generally accounts for more than 45% of world chromite ore supplies, and is also the world's dominant ferrochromium producer, accounting for about 47% of estimated world output in 2004. In that year Zimbabwe accounted for 2.9% of estimated world ferrochromium production. South African charge-grade, high-carbon ferrochromium (which has a chromium content of 52%–55%) has been replacing the more expensive high- and low-carbon ferrochromiums (which have a chromium content of 60%–70%) since the development, during 1965–75, of the Argon Oxygen Decarbonizing Process. South Africa's ferrochromium sector has also benefited from its access to inexpensive supplies of electrical power, and from low labour costs.

Production of Chromium Ore
('000 metric tons, gross weight)

	2004	2005
World total*	17,700	19,300
Africa	8,449	8,485†
African producers		
Madagascar	77	141
South Africa	7,677	7,503†
Sudan	26	22
Zimbabwe	668	820
Leading non-African producers		
Albania	54	66
Brazil	593	677
China, People's Repub.*	200	200
Finland	580	598*
India	2,949	3,255
Iran	139	224
Kazakhstan	3,267	3,579
Russia	320	772
Turkey	506	859

* Estimated production.
† Preliminary.

Source: US Geological Survey.

Strong demand for ferrochromium in the late 1980s, together with conditions of under-supply, generated an expansion of capacity both in South Africa and Zimbabwe. However, the potentially damaging effects of international boycotts and trade bans, and of civil disturbances, on South Africa's ferrochrome industry led, in the 1980s, to the development of new production capacity, generally close to ore deposits, in Brazil, Finland, Greece, India, Sweden and Turkey. After 1993, the implementation of political change in South Africa acted to consolidate its pre-eminence in international ferrochromium markets. In the early 2000s ferrochromium plants have increasingly been developed in the country's Bushveld Complex, while ferrochromium producers have sought to make greater use of chromite ore generated as a by-product of platinum mining. South African production of chromite ore totalled some 7,490 metric tons in 2005 (or 39% of world production), while its production of ferrochromium amounted to about 2,810 tons (41% of world production). Exports of chromite amounted to US $69.5m., while exports of ferrochromium amounted to $1,560m. in the same year. South Africa exports less than one-tenth of the chromium ore it produces, while, according to the USGS, exports of ferrochromium ore more than doubled in 1994–2004. In 2004 the sector was reported to be confronted by a number of challenges, including issues of energy and transportation in connection with the ferrochromium export industry. In 2004 there was also, reportedly, increasing concern over the environmental impact of chromium ore mining. Companies involved in chromite ore mining and ferrochromium metal production in 2004 included ASA Metals (Pty) Ltd, which was owned by East Asia Metal Investment (People's Republic of China, 60%) and Limpopo Development and Enterprises; Assmang Ltd and its subsidiary, Ferroalloys Ltd; South African Chrome and Alloys Ltd; Hernic (Pty) Ltd; Xstrata; and Samancar Chrome, which was owned by BHP Billiton (60%) and Anglo American plc (40%). In 2004 International Ferrometals Ltd reportedly planned to construct a chromite mine and a ferrochromium plant near Hartbeesport Dam in North West Province. Tata Iron and Steel Co Ltd of India planned to build a ferrochromim plant at Richards Bay. In December 2004 Xstrata and Merafe began work on a new ferrochromium smelter, Project Lion, projected to have a capacity of 360,000 tons per year upon completion. Zimbabwe's ferrochromium industry has been beset in recent years by problems arising from the currency exchange rate, by inadequate power supplies and by deficiencies in rail transportation. In 2004 Anglo American was reported to be planning to sell Zimbabwe Alloys, which produced high-carbon ferrochromium at its Gweru and Kwekwe smelters.

Prices of ferrochromium in early 1999 were between 32 and 37 US cents per lb: their lowest level since 1993. Over-supply of stainless steel in world markets generated supply surpluses of ferrochromium during most of 1999, although late in the year an improvement in price levels indicated a return to a balance of supply and demand; this recovery was sustained in 2000, the average price for that year being 41 cents per lb. In 2003 the USGS reported that chromite ore production capacity was in balance with average consumption. In 2004, according to South African industry sources, world demand for ferrochromium rose to some 5.5m. metric tons, compared with about 5.2m. tons in 2003. Growth in demand in 2004 was a consequence of continued growth in global, in particular Chinese, output of stainless steel, which accounts for some 80% of ferrochromium consumption world-wide. The average price received for ferrochromium in 2004, again according to South African industry sources, was 68 cents per lb, compared with 46 cents per lb in 2003. During 2004 prices for ferrochromium rose to their highest levels for 10 years. In 2005, according to the USGS, the price of ferrochromium rose to unprecedentedly high levels owing to higher production costs and the strength of the South African rand, in combination with increased demand and restricted availability of stainless steel scrap. The price of high-carbon ferrochromium peaked at 60 cents per lb in 2005, based on Platts Metals Week reported prices, an increase from the previous year's peak price of 72 cents per lb. In 2004 the price of low-carbon ferrochromium reached a high point of $1.17 per lb, but it only reached $1.10 per lb in 2005. The decrease in the price of ferrochromium was attributed to low world production of stainless steel, resulting in less demand for the chromium product, and to the strengthening of South Africa's currency.

COBALT

Cobalt is usually mined as a by-product of another metal; in the case of African cobalt, this is principally copper, although cobalt is also produced from nickel-copper-cobalt ores in Botswana and Zimbabwe and from platinum ores in South Africa. It is rarely mined as the primary product of an ore, and is found in very weak concentration, generally 0.1%–0.5%. The ore must be crushed and ground after mining, and subjected to a flotation process to obtain the concentrate. In the mid-1990s it was predicted that a new method of extraction, known as pressure acid leaching, would substantially increase the rate of recovery of cobalt as a by-product when laterite nickel ore is treated. In the early 2000s, however, this process was still not widely applied.

About 35% of all cobalt produced is used in metallic form as superalloys (in gas turbine aircraft engines, for example), hardfacing and stellite. Approximately 34% is applied to chemical uses in such industries as glass manufacture, paints and inks, rechargeable batteries and, increasingly, as catalysts in the processing of oil and petroleum feed stocks and synthetic materials. A further 10% is used in the manufacture of ceramics, 11% in magnetic alloys and 10% in the fabrication of hard metals. The USA is the world's principal consumer of cobalt.

In 2005 the Democratic Republic of the Congo (DRC) possessed almost one-half of the world's identified cobalt reserves. These reserves, associated with the country's copper deposits, also have the highest grade of the metal, with up to six metric tons of cobalt produced with every 100 tons of copper. In 2005 production of mined cobalt by the DRC totalled an estimated 22,000 metric tons, compared with 20,500 tons in 2004 and 14,500 tons in 2003. Production of refined cobalt in 2005, however, was estimated to have declined to the historically low level of 600 tons, from 735 tons in 2004, 1,200 tons in 2003 and 3,000 tons in 2002. The mining, marketing and export of cobalt from the DRC has been conducted by a state monopoly, La Générale des Carrières et des Mines (Gécamines). From 1990 the country's cobalt output was seriously disrupted by economic dislocation, caused by internal unrest, and by thefts of cobalt. Projects by Gécamines to exploit new deposits and rehabilitate existing mines in partnership with Canadian, South African and other interests were initiated in the late 1990s, but made slow progress as a consequence of continued political instability. In 2004, however, in response to the return of relative stability in the main mining areas of Katanga province, the active reassessment by foreign investors of a number of existing joint ventures with Gécamines, together with proposals for new cobalt projects, appeared to be proceeding apace. Among the companies, domestic and foreign, that were actively or speculatively involved in the DRC's cobalt sector in 2005 were Kababankola Mining Co, L'Entreprise Générale Malta Forrest SPRL, Costamin Resources (a joint venture between Congo Stars Mining Co and a private Canadian firm), Adastra Minerals Inc. (formerly American Mineral Fields Inc.), Casmin SPRL (a joint venture between Central African Mining and Exploration Co PLC and Entreprises Swanepoel), KGHM Polska Miedź, Tenke Mining Corpn and Phelps Dodge Exploration Corpn. The high price of cobalt in 2004, together with strong demand for the metal in the People's Republic of China, reportedly led to a substantial rise in artisanal mining and export (usually unprocessed, without Government approval) of cobalt-rich ores containing heterogenite. Exports of cobalt contributed 13.7% of the DRC's export revenue in 2004, compared with 7.6% in 2003 and 6.5% in 2002.

Production of Cobalt Ore
(cobalt content, metric tons)

	2004	2005*
World total*	57,100	57,900
Africa	32,842*	33,550
African producers		
Botswana	223	200
Congo, Dem. Repub.*	20,500	22,000
Morocco	1,600*	1,600
South Africa*	460	400
Zambia*	10,000	9,300
Zimbabwe	59	250
Leading non-African producers		
Australia*	6,700	6,000
Brazil*	1,236	1,200
Canada	5,060	5,533
Cuba	3,554	3,600
New Caledonia*	1,400	1,200
Russia*	4,700	5,000

* Estimated production.

Source: US Geological Survey.

Since the early 1980s Zambia has promoted the expansion of its cobalt production in an attempt to offset declines in copper output. In 2005 Zambia was the world's largest producer of cobalt, with estimated output of 9,300 metric tons (down from 10,000 tons in the previous year). In 2004 the Government was reported to have awarded a joint venture formed by Equinox Resources Ltd of Australia (51%) and Phelps Dodge Corpn of the USA (49%) a 25-year licence for cobalt, copper, gold and silver operations. Other companies involved in the mining and refining of cobalt in Zambia in 2004 included Mopani Copper Mines PLC, which was owned by Glencore International AG (73.1%), First Quantum Minerals Ltd (16.9%) and ZCCM Investments Holdings PLC (10%); Chambishi Metals PLC, owned by J&W Holdings AG (90%) and ZCCM Investments Holdings PLC (10%); and Metorex. In Morocco cobalt-arsenic deposits are mined and cobalt concentrates produced at Bou Azzer by Compagnie de Tifnout Tiranimine (CTT). In 2005 output of cobalt ore amounted to an estimated 1,600 tons. In 2004, according to the US Geological Survey (USGS), cobalt was being produced as a by-product at six South African platinum-group metal mines and one nickel mine. In addition, two South African mining companies were producing refined cobalt as a by-product of domestic platinum mining and refining. South African production of cobalt ore totalled an estimated 400 tons in 2005, compared with an estimated 460 tons in 2004. In 1992 the Ugandan Government initiated a project to extract cobalt from stockpiles of cobaltiferous concentrate at the Kilembe copper-cobalt mine, in south-western Uganda. An extraction plant was subsequently operated at Kilembe by Kasese Cobalt Co Ltd (KCCL), a joint venture between state-owned Kilembe Mines Ltd and Canada's Banff Resources Ltd. In 2002 MFC Bancorp Ltd acquired control of Banff's Ugandan cobalt interests. Late in that year operations at the Kilembe plant were suspended owing to the low world price of cobalt. Activity resumed in late 2003, when MFC Bancorp announced the forward sale of one-half of cobalt output from its Kasese refinery in 2004. In 2004 MFC Bancorp was reported to have distributed its cobalt assets, including its stake in KCCL, into Blue Earth Refineries Inc. of Hong Kong. Uganda Gold Mining Ltd was reported in 2004 to have agreed to undertake a feasibility study on the resumption of operations at the Kilembe copper-cobalt mine, where mining ceased in 1977. In 2005, according to data cited by the USGS, Uganda exported cobalt with a value of some US $15.6m., representing about 2% of total export revenue. In 2005 production of cobalt ore by Botswana totalled an estimated 200 tons, compared with 223 tons in 2004. In recent years Botswana has exported cobalt to Norway and Zimbabwe for refining. Since 2003 LionOre International Ltd of Botswana has been studying the feasibility of establishing a domestic processing plant. Zimbabwe produced an estimated 250 tons of cobalt ore in 2005; this represented a significant increase from 2004, when just 59 tons was produced. In 2004 Canada's Dynatec Corpn (53%) and the USA's Phelps Dodge Corpn were reported to be conducting a joint venture to develop Madagascar's Ambatovy nickel and cobalt deposits. Nickel-cobalt deposits were first identified in north-western Tanzania in the early 1990s and have since been the object of detailed exploration. Cobalt reserves, estimated initially at about 20,000 tons, remained unexploited as of 2005, as did reserves identified in Côte d'Ivoire.

Traditional cobalt-mining may eventually be complemented, and perhaps superseded, by the wide-scale retrieval of manganese nodules from the world's seabeds. It is estimated that the cobalt content of each nodule is about 0.25%, although nodules recovered from the Pacific Ocean in 1983 had a cobalt content of 2.5%. Ferromanganese crusts, containing extractable cobalt, have been identified at relatively shallow depths within the USA's exclusive economic zones, which extend 370 km (200 nautical miles) into US coastal waters. Research into the potential exploitation of cobalt-bearing nodules continued throughout the 1990s and early 2000s. Some of the most valuable were considered to be those in the Pacific Ocean around the Cook Islands, where estimates of the cobalt resource were placed as high as 32m. metric tons. Nodules off Namibia were thought to have a lesser, but still significant, cobalt content. However, the full exploitation of seabed resources such as these is thought likely to remain impracticable for many years to come.

The Cobalt Development Institute (CDI), an association of producers, users and traders of cobalt, was founded in 1982, and in 2007 comprised 44 members from 18 countries.

Since 1999 WMC Resources Ltd of Australia has offered cobalt for sale via the internet through its Cobalt Open Sales System (COSS). (In August 2005 BHP Billiton Ltd acquired full ownership of WMC Resources.) COSS brings a degree of transparency to the market for cobalt and the price of contracts concluded via COSS are generally accepted as an important indicator of the prevailing price situation for cobalt world-wide. (COSS is not necessarily the most significant indicator, however: during some periods of 2005, for example, contracts concluded by Norilsk Nickel of Russia for sales of cobalt to North American destinations were regarded as the key determinant of the prevailing price situation for the metal.) In late July 2006 cobalt was sold via COSS (for August delivery) at a price of US $15.10 per lb. Contracts for subsequent sales of cobalt (Falconbridge 1 inch x 1 inch cut electrolytic cathodes, 99.8% grade) in August were concluded at a price of $15.40 per lb. The price of cobalt (for European and North American destinations) sold via COSS in January–March 2006 had ranged between $12.50 per lb (February) and $15.15 per lb (March). In April–June the price ranged between $15.20 per lb (May) and $15.90 per lb (April). While demand (in particular Chinese demand) for cobalt remained strong during 2005, driven by strong growth in chemicals and superalloys, prices declined steadily as a consequence of a rise in supplies, falling to around $13 per lb in mid-2005, compared with about $19 per lb at the beginning of the year. In 2004, according to data cited by the USGS, the US 'spot' price for cobalt cathode (minimum 99.8% cobalt) fell from $27–$29 per lb in mid-January to $15.25–$15.75 per lb in late November. By the end of the year, however, the price had recovered to $18.75–$19.50 per lb. The average US 'spot' price in that year was $23.93 per lb, more than double the average price recorded in 2003. According to sources cited by the USGS, the annual average of weekly prices for cobalt from Zambia (minimum 99.6% cobalt) was $23.27 per lb in 2004, while the annual average of weekly prices for Russian cobalt (minimum 99.3% cobalt) was $22.86 per lb. According to the USGS, prices of cobalt traded via COSS in 2004 ranged between $15.75 per lb and $29.50 per lb. In 2005 the annual average 'spot' price for cobalt cathode was $15.96 per lb, showing a 33% decrease from 2004, according to the USGS. The price for Zambian cobalt was slightly lower, at $15.06 per lb, while Russian cobalt traded at an average annual of weekly prices of $14.62. According to the USGS, BHP Billiton reported prices for 99.8% cobalt between $12.10 and $19.25 per lb.

COCOA (*Theobroma cacao*)

This tree, up to 14 m tall, originated in the tropical forests of Central and South America. The first known cocoa plantations were in southern Mexico around AD 600. Cocoa first came to Europe in the 16th century. The Spanish and Portuguese introduced cocoa into Africa—on the islands of Fernando Póo (now Bioko), in Equatorial Guinea, and São Tomé and Príncipe—at the beginning of the 19th century. At the end of the century the tree was established on the African mainland, first in Ghana and then in other West African countries.

Cocoa is now widely grown in the tropics, usually at altitudes less than 300 m above sea-level, where it needs a fairly high rainfall and good soil. The cocoa tree has a much shallower tap root than, for example, the coffee bush, making cocoa more vulnerable to dry weather. Cocoa trees can take up to four years from planting before producing sufficient fruit for harvesting. They may live to 80 years or more, although the fully productive period is usually about 20 years. The tree is highly vulnerable to pests and diseases, and it is also very sensitive to climatic changes. Its fruit is a large pod, about 15–25 cm in length, which at maturity is yellow in some varieties and red in others. The ripe pods are cut from the tree, where they grow directly out of the trunk and branches. When opened, cocoa pods disclose a mass of seeds (beans) surrounded by white mucilage. After harvesting, the beans and mucilage are scooped out and fermented. Fermentation lasts several days, allowing the flavour to develop. The mature fermented beans, dull red in colour, are then dried, ready to be bagged as raw cocoa which may be further processed or exported.

Cultivated cocoa trees may be broadly divided into three groups. All West African cocoas belong to the Amazonian Forastero group, which now accounts for more than 80% of world cocoa production. It includes the Amelonado variety, suitable for chocolate manufacturing, grown in Ghana, Côte d'Ivoire and Nigeria. Criollo cocoa is not widely grown and is used only for luxury confectionery. The third group is Trinitario, which comprises about 15% of world output and is cultivated mainly in Central America and the northern regions of South America.

Cocoa processing takes place mainly in importing countries, although processing capacity was established in West Africa during the 1960s and processed products now account for a significant part of the value of its cocoa exports. The processes include shelling, roasting and grinding the beans. Almost half of each bean after shelling consists of a fat called cocoa butter. In the manufacture of cocoa powder for use as a beverage, this fat is largely removed. Cocoa is a mildly stimulating drink, because of its caffeine content, and, unlike coffee and tea, is highly nutritious.

The most important use of cocoa is in the manufacture of chocolate, of which it is the main ingredient. About 90% of all cocoa produced is used in chocolate-making, for which extra cocoa butter is added, as well as other substances such as sugar and, in the case of milk chocolate, milk. Proposals initially announced in 1993 (and subsequently amended in 1997) by the consumer countries of the European Union (EU), permitting chocolate manufacturers in member states to add as much as 5% vegetable fats to cocoa solids and cocoa fats in the manufacture of chocolate products, were perceived by producers as potentially damaging to the world cocoa trade. In 1998 it was estimated that the implementation of this plan could reduce world demand for cocoa beans by 130,000–200,000 metric tons annually. In July 1999, despite protests from Belgium, which—with France, Germany, Greece, Italy, Luxembourg, the Netherlands and Spain—prohibited the manufacture or import of chocolate containing non-cocoa-butter vegetable fats, the European Commission cleared the way to the abolition of this restriction throughout the EU countries. The new regulations took effect in May 2000. Producers identified another, potentially more damaging threat, when, in March 2007, the US Chocolate Manufacturers Association, following a similar request at the end of 2006 from the Grocery Manufacturers of America, began to lobby the US Food and Drug Administration (FDA) to change the legal definition of chocolate, in order to allow them to substitute at will vegetable fats and oils for cocoa butter in products labelled as chocolate. In response, the FDA initiated a public consultation. Meanwhile, an EU study that evaluated the new regulations, published in June 2006, found that the rate of growth of net cocoa imports had increased to 3.5% by 2005, despite a saturated market for chocolate products. The study attributed this growth mainly to an increase in consumer demand for products with a high cocoa content. According to a report published by the International Cocoa Organization (ICCO) in June 2007, changes in consumption behaviour had had a significant impact on demand for cocoa beans in terms of both quality and quantity. Between 1996/97 and 2004/05 world cocoa consumption expanded by 571,000 tons. Most of the increase resulted from higher consumption in Europe (where it rose by 21%), where consumers were increasingly inclined to purchase organic, fair-trade and high cocoa-content products. In particular, the growing demand for products with a high cocoa content was influenced by research findings on the beneficial health properties of cocoa, and led in turn to increased demand for cocoa beans of superior quality—which command higher prices. Concerns about food safety and environmental issues drove the increased demand for organic chocolate, the share of which in global production was, however, still estimated in 2005 at less than 0.5% of output world-wide.

A combination of growing consumer concerns about poverty in less developed countries and a more organized fair-trade movement has established steady growth in sales of fair-trade products since the early 1990s. Sales of cocoa labelled 'fair-trade' increased from 700 metric tons in 1996 to 5,657 tons in 2005, equivalent to annual growth of 23%, although at the end of that period the share of fair-trade cocoa was still estimated to represent less than 0.2% of global production. In 2005 83% of sales of fair-trade cocoa world-wide were distributed among only six countries: the United Kingdom (40%), Germany and France (13% each), Austria, Italy and Switzerland (6% each).

Cocoa is the most valuable agricultural export commodity in West Africa. Recorded world exports (excluding re-exports) of cocoa beans totalled 2,969,853 metric tons in 2005, of which sub-Saharan African countries accounted for 70%—2,057,575 tons. The world's leading exporters of cocoa beans in 2005 were Côte d'Ivoire (996,126 tons), Ghana (540,012 tons), Indonesia (367,427 tons), Nigeria (269,672 tons), Cameroon (163,702 tons) and Ecuador (78,348 tons).

The principal importers of cocoa are developed countries with market economies, which accounted for about 80% of cocoa imports from developing countries in 2005. Recorded world imports of cocoa beans in 2005 totalled 3,099,692 metric tons. The principal importing countries in that year were the Netherlands (with 650,521 tons, representing about 20%% of the total), the USA (576,169 tons) and Germany (258,918 tons).

Production of Cocoa Beans
('000 metric tons)

	2005	2006
World total	3,807	3,850
Sub-Saharan Africa	2,607	2,713
Leading African producers		
Cameroon*	178	165
Côte d'Ivoire	1,286	1,400†
Ghana*	599	599
Nigeria	441	441†
Leading non-African producers		
Brazil	235	199
Colombia	37	37
Dominican Repub.†	31	31
Ecuador	94	94
Indonesia	610	610†
Malaysia	28	30
Mexico	36†	38
Papua New Guinea†	42	42

* Unofficial figures.
† FAO estimate(s).

Côte d'Ivoire, the region's dominant producer, is also the world's principal cocoa grower, accounting for about 36% of global output in 2006 and for about one-third of international cocoa exports in 2005. Côte d'Ivoire is also the leading grinding country among cocoa-producing countries and the third most important grinding country in the world after the Netherlands and the USA, accounting for 10% of global cocoa-bean grinding. In 2005 an estimated 32% of the country's export revenue was derived from cocoa and cocoa preparations. Government measures implemented in August 1999 to liberalize the country's cocoa sector included the abolition of the state cocoa board, with the consequent removal of guaranteed prices. In November, however, the impact on Ivorian cocoa growers of sharply lower world cocoa prices (see below) prompted the Government to reintroduce a minimum price mechanism and buffer stock arrangements. In 2001 prices paid to farmers reached record high levels. Cocoa is traditionally Ghana's most important cash crop, occupying more than one-half of all the country's cultivated land. In the mid-1960s Ghana accounted for more than one-third of world production.From the mid-1970s to the mid-1990s, however, Ghana's cocoa production underwent a sharp decline. This contraction of the country's cocoa industry has been attributed to neglect and to the official policy of maintaining prices payable to producers at uneconomic levels. The decline was exacerbated by the smuggling of cocoa to neighbouring countries, where higher prices were obtainable. The spread of plant diseases, particularly black pod and swollen shoot, have also inhibited recovery. Ghana endeavoured to revive cocoa production through programmes of replanting and the introduction of disease-resistant varieties, together with pest control, and improved facilities for transport and storage. From July 1993 the Ghana Cocoa Board (COCOBOD) was deprived of its monopoly. Nevertheless, in 1998 the Government restated its intention to resist pressure from the IMF and the World Bank to liberalize the external marketing of cocoa, which was still carried out exclusively by the Government and, in 2001, began to license private cocoa-exporting companies. From the mid-1990s the recovery of Ghana's cocoa sector commenced, assisted to some extent, from 2002, by political instability in Côte d'Ivoire. The 2004 cocoa harvest, of 736,911 tons, was the largest ever recorded in Ghana. Although in 2005 cocoa output declined by 18%, to an estimated 599,000 tons, it remained exceptionally high. In that year the share of Ghana's cocoa accounted for 15% of global production and for 18% of foreign sales world-wide. Although it was overtaken in 1992 cocoa by gold as Ghana's main export commodity, cocoa regained its pre-eminence in 2003–05. In 2005 sales of cocoa beans and cocoa products accounted for 40% of Ghana's export revenue. Among the smaller African producers, cocoa exports are a significant component of the economies of Cameroon—where they contributed about 10% of total export revenue in 2004, Equatorial Guinea, São Tomé and Príncipe—where they contributed more than 90% of total export revenue in 2005—and Togo. Although cocoa remains Nigeria's main export crop, its significance to the economy has been eclipsed by petroleum.

World prices for cocoa are highly sensitive to changes in supply and demand, making its market position volatile. Negotiations to secure international agreement on stabilizing the cocoa industry began in 1956. Full-scale cocoa conferences, under UN auspices, were held in

1963, 1966 and 1967, but all proved abortive. A major difficulty was the failure to agree on a fixed minimum price. In 1972 the fourth UN Cocoa Conference took place in Geneva and resulted in the first International Cocoa Agreement (ICCA), adopted by 52 countries, although the USA, the world's principal cocoa importer at that time, did not participate. The ICCA took formal effect in October 1973. It operated for three quota years and provided for an export quota system for producing countries, a fixed price range for cocoa beans and a buffer stock to support the agreed prices. In accordance with the ICCA, the ICCO, based in London, was established in 1973. In November 2005 the membership of the 2001 ICCA (see below) comprised 40 countries (13 exporting members, 27 importing members), representing about 80% of world cocoa production and some 60% of world cocoa consumption. The European Union is also an intergovernmental party to the 2001 Agreement. In January 2007, with the accession to the EU of Romania and Bulgaria, the membership rose to 42. However, the USA, a leading importer of cocoa, is not a member. Nor is Indonesia, whose production and exports of cocoa have expanded rapidly in recent years. The governing body of the ICCO is the International Cocoa Council (ICC), established to supervise implementation of the ICCA. It is planned to relocate the ICCO to Abidjan, Côte d'Ivoire.

A second ICCA operated during 1979–81. It was followed by an extended agreement, which was in force in 1981–87. A fourth ICCA took effect in 1987. During the period of these ICCAs the effective operation of cocoa price stabilization mechanisms was frequently impeded by a number of factors, principally by crop and stock surpluses, which continued to overshadow the cocoa market in the early 1990s. In addition, the achievement of ICCA objectives was affected by the divergent views of producers and consumers, led by Côte d'Ivoire, on one side, and by the USA, on the other, as to appropriate minimum price levels. Disagreements also developed regarding the allocation of members' export quotas and the conduct of price support measures by means of the buffer stock (which ceased to operate during 1983–88), and subsequently over the disposal of unspent buffer stock funds. The effectiveness of financial operations under the fourth ICCA was severely curtailed by the accumulation of arrears of individual members' levy payments, notably by Côte d'Ivoire and Brazil. The fourth ICCA was extended for a two-year period from October 1990, although the suspension of the economic clauses relating to price-support operations rendered the agreement ineffective in terms of exerting any influence over cocoa market prices.

Preliminary discussions on a fifth ICCA, again held under UN auspices, ended without agreement in May 1992, when consumer members, while agreeing to extend the fourth ICCA for a further year (until October 1993), refused to accept producers' proposals for the creation of an export quota system as a means of stabilizing prices, on the grounds that such arrangements would not impose sufficient limits on total production to restore equilibrium between demand and supply. Additionally, no agreement was reached on the disposition of cocoa buffer stocks, then totalling 240,000 metric tons. In March 1993 ICCO delegates abandoned efforts to formulate arrangements whereby prices would be stabilized by means of a stock-withholding scheme. At a further negotiating conference in July, however, terms were finally agreed for a new ICCA, to take effect from October, subject to its ratification by at least five exporting countries (accounting for at least 80% of total world exports) and by importing countries (representing at least 60% of total imports). Unlike previous commodity agreements sponsored by the UN, the fifth ICCA aimed to achieve stable prices by regulating supplies and promoting consumption, rather than through the operation of buffer stocks and export quotas.

The fifth ICCA, operating until September 1998, entered into effect in February 1994. Under the new agreement, buffer stocks totalling 233,000 metric tons that had accrued from the previous ICCA were to be released on the market at the rate of 51,000 tons annually over a maximum period of four-and-a-half years, beginning in the 1993/94 crop season. At a meeting of the ICCO, held in October 1994, it was agreed that, following the completion of the stocks reduction programme, the extent of stocks held should be limited to the equivalent of three months' consumption. ICCO members also assented to a voluntary reduction in output of 75,000 tons annually, beginning in 1993/94 and terminating in 1998/99. Further measures to achieve a closer balance of production and consumption, under which the level of cocoa stocks would be maintained at 34% of world grindings during the 1996/97 crop year, were introduced by the ICCO in September 1996. The ICCA was subsequently extended until September 2001. In April 2000 the ICCO agreed to implement measures to remedy low levels of world prices (see below), which were to centre on the elimination of sub-grade cocoa in world trade: these cocoas were viewed by the ICCO as partly responsible for the downward trend in prices. In mid-July Côte d'Ivoire, Ghana, Nigeria and Cameroon disclosed that they had agreed to destroy a minimum of 250,000 tons of cocoa at the beginning of the 2000/01 crop season, with a view to assisting prices to recover and to 'improving the quality of cocoa' entering world markets.

A sixth ICCA was negotiated, under the auspices of the UN, in February 2001. Like its predecessor, the sixth ICCA aimed to achieve stable prices through the regulation of supplies and the promotion of consumption. The Agreement took provisional effect on 1 October 2003. In December, in accordance with its provisions, the ICC established a Consultative Board on the World Cocoa Economy, a private-sector board with a mandate to 'contribute to the development of a sustainable cocoa economy; identify threats to supply and demand and propose action to meet the challenges; facilitate the exchange of information on production, consumption and stocks; and advise on other cocoa-related matters within the scope of the Agreement'. In November 2005, on its ratification by the Dominican Republic, the sixth ICCA entered definitively into force (this was the first time that an ICCA had ever entered definitively into forc.). The Agreement was to remain open to new signatories until 2010.

International prices for cocoa have generally been very low in recent years. In 1998 the average of the ICCO's daily prices (based on selected quotations from the London and New York markets) was US $1,676 per metric ton, its highest level since 1982, but in 1999 it slumped to $1,140 (a fall of 32.0%). In 2000 the average of the ICCO's daily prices again declined steeply, falling well below that recorded in 1992—$1,099.5 per ton—to only $888 per ton, a reduction of some 22%. Prices recovered somewhat in 2001, but, even so, the ICCO's daily quotation averaged only $1,089 per ton in that year, the second lowest average price recorded since 1972. In 2002, however, the average price rebounded by almost 63%, compared with the previous year, to reach $1,778 per ton. In 2003 the ICCO's average daily price fell slightly, by 1.3%, to $1,755 per ton. A more substantial decline, of 11.8%, was recorded in 2004, when the ICCO's daily quotation averaged $1,548 per ton. In 2005 the average quotation fell marginally, by 0.6%, compared with the previous year, to $1,538 per ton. The ICCO's average daily price rose by 3.5% in 2006, to $1,592, and increased more substantially in the first six months of 2007, when it averaged $1,906 per ton. In 1999 the highest monthly average was $1,455 per ton in January, and the lowest was $919 in December. In 2000 the average ICCO quotation ranged between $942 per ton in June, and $801 per ton in November, the lowest monthly average since March 1973. The corresponding average prices for 2001 were $1,337 per ton, recorded in December of that year, and $967 per ton, recorded in January. In 2002 the average monthly ICCO quotation ranged between $2,205 per ton, recorded in October, and $1,384 per ton in January of that year. In 2003 the highest monthly average price, $2,239 per ton, was recorded in February, and the lowest, $1,482 per ton, in October. The ICCO average quotation ranged between $1,408 per ton (June) and $1,729 per ton (August) in 2004. In 2005 prices ranged between $1,434 per ton (November) and $1,748 per ton (March). In 2006 the highest monthly average quotation, $1,681 per ton, was recorded in July, and the lowest, $1,526, in October.

In 2005/06, according to the ICCO, following lower output in each of the two preceding cocoa years, production of cocoa beans worldwide rose by 6.2%, to 3.5m. metric tons (a total that was close to the 2003/04 season's record level). Most of the increase was attributed to higher purchases and arrivals in Côte d'Ivoire and Ghana. In the 2005/06 cocoa season, according to the ICCO, consumption of cocoa world-wide, as indicated by the level of grindings, grew by 4%, to 3.5m. tons, compared with increases of 3% in 2004/05 and 5% in 2003/04. According to ICCO data, Côte d'Ivoire and Malaysia were the principal cocoa processors among the cocoa-producing countries. The Netherlands and the USA were the principal importing processors. The share of the Americas decreased slightly compared with the previous year, from 26% to 25%. The most substantial increases in grindings were registered in Germany (where cocoa processing grew by 29% compared with the previous year), in the United Kingdom (8%) and in Brazil (7%). At the end of the 2005/06 cocoa year world stocks of cocoa beans had increased to 1.8m. metric tons, compared with 1.7m. tons in the previous year. The corresponding stocks-to-grindings ratio amounted to 50.8% in 2005/06, compared with 50.5% at the end of 2004/05. Average daily prices recorded for 2005/06 were 4.7% higher than in 2004/05, but displayed a similar high level of volatility. Declines in prices at the beginning of the cocoa year were due to high production in Côte d'Ivoire and Ghana, while the subsequent price recovery resulted largely from speculation that was fuelled by both anticipated strong European demand and by the depreciation of the US dollar, as well as by continued unrest in Côte d'Ivoire. The subsequent sustained increase in the price of cocoa beans in the first half of 2007—which reached its highest level since 2003—has been attributed mainly to an uncertain outlook for the cocoa market and to the ICCO's forecast of a large production deficit in 2006/07.

The Cocoa Producers' Alliance (COPAL), with headquarters in Lagos, Nigeria, had 10 members in 2007, including Cameroon, Côte d'Ivoire, Gabon, Ghana, Nigeria, São Tomé and Príncipe, and Togo. COPAL was formed in 1962 with the aim of preventing excessive price fluctuations by regulating the supply of cocoa. Members of COPAL currently account for about three -quarters of world cocoa production, with its seven African members providing some 69%. COPAL has acted in concert with successive ICCAs.

The principal centres for cocoa-trading in the industrialized countries are the London Cocoa Terminal Market, in the United Kingdom, and the New York Coffee, Sugar and Cocoa Exchange, in the USA.

COFFEE (*Coffea*)

This is an evergreen shrub or small tree, generally 5 m–10 m in height, indigenous to Asia and tropical Africa. Wild trees grow to 10 m, but cultivated shrubs are usually pruned to a maximum of 3 m. The dried seeds (beans) are roasted, ground and brewed in hot water to provide one of the most popular of the world's non-alcoholic beverages. Coffee is drunk in every country in the world, and its consumers comprise an estimated one-third of the world's population. Although it has little nutrient value, coffee acts as a mild stimulant, owing to the presence of caffeine, an alkaloid also present in tea and cocoa.

There are about 40 species of *Coffea*, most of which grow wild in the eastern hemisphere. The species of economic importance are *C. arabica* (native to Ethiopia), which in the early 2000s accounted for about 60%–65% of world production, and *C. canephora* (the source of robusta coffee), which accounted for almost all of the remainder. Arabica coffee is more aromatic, but robusta, as the name implies, is a stronger plant. Coffee grows in the tropical belt, between 20°N and 20°S, and from sea-level to as high as 2,000 m above. The optimum growing conditions are found at 1,250 m–1,500 m above sea-level, with an average temperature of around 17°C and an average annual rainfall of 1,000 mm–1,750 mm. Trees begin bearing fruit three to five years after planting, depending upon the variety, and give their maximum yield (up to 5 kg of fruit per year) from the sixth to the 15th year. Few remain profitable beyond 30 years.

Arabica coffee trees are grown mostly in the American tropics and supply the largest quantity and the best quality of coffee beans. In Africa and Asia arabica coffee is vulnerable in lowland areas to a serious leaf disease, and consequently cultivation has been concentrated on highland areas. Some highland arabicas, such as those grown in Kenya, have a high reputation for quality.

The robusta coffee tree, grown mainly in East and West Africa, and in the Far East, has larger leaves than arabica but the beans are generally smaller and of lower quality and price. However, robusta coffee has a higher yield than arabica as the trees are more resistant to disease. Robusta is also more suitable for the production of soluble ('instant') coffee. About 60% of African coffee is of the robusta variety. Soluble coffee accounts for more than one-fifth of world coffee consumption.

Each coffee berry, green at first but red when ripe, usually contains two beans (white in arabica, light brown in robusta) which are the commercial product of the plant. To produce the best quality arabica beans—known in the trade as 'mild' coffee—the berries are opened by a pulping machine and the beans fermented briefly in water before being dried and hulled into green coffee. Much of the crop is exported in green form. Robusta beans are generally prepared by dry-hulling. Roasting and grinding are usually undertaken in the importing countries, for economic reasons and because roasted beans rapidly lose their freshness when exposed to air.

Apart from beans, coffee produces a few minor by-products. When the coffee beans have been removed from the fruit, what remains is a wet mass of pulp and, at a later stage, the dry material of the 'hull' or fibrous sleeve that protects the beans. Coffee pulp is used as cattle feed, the fermented pulp makes a good fertilizer, and coffee bean oil is an ingredient in soaps, paints and polishes.

More than one-half of the world's coffee is produced on smallholdings of less than 5 ha. In most producing countries, and especially in Africa, coffee is almost entirely an export crop, with little domestic consumption. Green coffee accounts for some 96% of all the coffee that is exported, with soluble and roasted coffee comprising the balance. Tariffs on green/raw coffee are usually low or non-existent, but those applied to soluble coffee may be as high as 30%. The USA is the largest single importer, although its volume of coffee purchases was overtaken in 1975 by the combined imports of the (then) nine countries of the European Community (EC, now the European Union—EU).

After petroleum, coffee is the major raw material in world trade, and the single most valuable agricultural export of the tropics. Latin America (with 63% of estimated world output in 2006/07) is the leading coffee-growing region. Africa, which formerly ranked second, was overtaken in 1992/93 by Asian producers. In 2006/07 African producers accounted for 11.9% of the estimated world coffee crop, compared with 23.1% for Asian countries. (The above shares have been calculated on the basis of data released by the International Coffee Organization (ICO). Non-members of the ICO accounted for 0.9% of the world coffee crop in 2006/07.)

Production of Green Coffee Beans
('000 bags, each of 60 kg, coffee years, ICO members only)

	2005/06	2006/07
World total	110,348	121,601
Sub-Saharan Africa	13,730	14,549
Leading African producers		
Burundi	103	350*
Cameroon	849	750
Congo, Dem. Repub.	335	400
Côte d'Ivoire	2,369	2,482
Ethiopia	4,527	5,000
Kenya	685	817
Madagascar	559	587*
Tanzania	721	750
Togo	140	140
Uganda	2,159	2,350
Leading non-African producers		
Brazil	32,944	42,512*
Colombia	12,329	12,200
Costa Rica	1,778	1,795
Ecuador	1,138	1,172*
El Salvador	1,502	1,242
Guatemala	3,676	3,817
Honduras	3,204	2,700
India	4,617	4,750
Indonesia	8,659	6,973*
Mexico	4,000	4,200
Nicaragua	1,718	1,275
Papua New Guinea	1,268	781*
Peru	2,419	4,250*
Thailand	999	975
Viet Nam	13,499	15,500

* Estimate.

Source: International Coffee Organization.

In every year during 1970–90, except in 1974 and 1984, Côte d'Ivoire was Africa's leading coffee producer, and coffee was the country's leading cash crop. Since 1980 cocoa has overtaken coffee as its most important export crop—in 2005, according to FAO estimates, exports of coffee accounted for 2.3% of the country's total export revenue. In the early 1990s more than three-quarters of the coffee trees in Côte d'Ivoire had passed their most productive age. A programme of extensive replanting begun in the mid-1990s raised the total area under coffee cultivation substantially. In 2005 the area planted with coffee was officially estimated by the US Department of Agriculture (USDA) at 1.5m. ha, while the area harvested was estimated at 750,000 ha. However, more than 60% of Côte d'Ivoire's coffee trees were reported in 2005 to be over 30 years old. Higher prices for coffee contributed to a very substantial increase in Ivorian production from 1995. Production of green coffee totalled some 142,000 metric tons in 2006/06, and was estimated to have increased in 2006/07 to about 150,000 tons, despite the continued insecurity in the west of the country, which affected the maintenance of coffee plantations.

The African countries that have traditionally been most dependent on coffee as a source of foreign exchange are Burundi and Uganda. In 2002 coffee sales accounted for three-quarters of Burundi's total export revenue. The proportion declined to 43% in 2003. By 2005 it had recovered to 71%, and in 2006 the proportion reached 67%. According to FAO, in Uganda coffee provided about 18% of export earnings in 2006. Ethiopia has emerged as the major regional producer, accounting in 2006/07 for about 31% of total African output of coffee. Despite high domestic consumption and widespread smuggling, coffee accounted for 61.6% of Ethiopia's total export earnings in 1991, and for 70.7% in 1997/98. More recently, however, the contribution of coffee to total export earnings has declined, representing only about 39% in 2002, 35% in 2003 and some 36% in 2004. The coffee sector in Rwanda, which contributed more than 60% of export revenue in 1991, was severely affected by civil war, and in 1994 the bulk of the crop was lost. Rwanda's coffee output in 1997 was the smallest since 1974, and it declined still further in 1998. Output recovered in each crop year in 2000/01–2002/03, but fell again in 2003/04. In 2004/05 Rwanda's production was estimated to have risen by more than 70%, to some 27,000 metric tons. It declined in 2005/06, however, by one-third, to only about 18,000 tons, and by a further 8%, to 16,500 tons, in 2006/07. Until 2000, when it was overtaken by tea, coffee was Rwanda's major cash crop. In 1999 coffee still contributed about 56% of Rwanda's total export earnings, but in 2003 its share had declined to about 21%. In 2004 the proportion of the country's total export earnings derived from coffee increased slightly, to about 23%, partly as a consequence of efforts aimed at improving the quality of Rwandan coffee and at product promotion.

Among other African countries where coffee is an important export are Cameroon (where exports of coffee accounted for 2.4% of total export revenue in 2005), the Central African Republic, Kenya (3.9% of total revenue from exports, including re-exports, in 2005) and Tanzania (5.5% of estimated total export revenue in 2005). Angola was formerly the world's leading exporter of robusta coffee, but production during the period 1975–95 was severely disrupted by civil conflict. In 1995 the resumption of production in three provinces produced a crop of 2,300 tons, while plans proceeded during the late 1990s for the transfer to private ownership of the country's major plantations. In 1997 the Government commenced the transfer of the state-controlled marketing monopoly to the private sector, and began to prepare for the sale of all state-owned coffee-producing companies. However, the full rehabilitation of Angola's coffee industry depends on an enduring political and military settlement, and is expected to span many years. In the late 1990s plans were announced for the initial rehabilitation of 50,000 ha of coffee estates over a five-year period to 2002, with the aim of achieving an annual coffee output of 60,000 tons. However, according to FAO, the area harvested in 2006 was still about 40% smaller than that harvested in 1997. Production in the 2005/06 crop year remained far below that target. Angolan output fell in each crop year in 2002/03–2004/05, but increased by 66%, to about 1,500 tons, in 2005/06, and by a further 40% in 2006/07, to an estimated 2,100 tons.

Effective international attempts to stabilize coffee prices began in 1954, when a number of producing countries made a short-term agreement to fix export quotas. After three such agreements, a five-year International Coffee Agreement (ICA), covering both producers and consumers, and introducing a quota system, was signed in 1962. This led to the establishment in 1963 of the International Coffee Organization (ICO), with its headquarters in London. In June 2007 the International Coffee Council, the highest authority of the ICO, comprised 77 members (i.e. participants in the 2001 ICA—45 exporting countries and 32 importing countries; the USA withdrew from the ICO in 1993 and did not rejoin until 2005). Successive ICAs took effect in 1968, 1976, 1983, 1994 and 2001 (see below), but the system of export quotas to stabilize prices was abandoned in July 1989. During each ICA up to and including that implemented in 1994, contention arose over the allocation of members' export quotas, the operation of price support mechanisms, and, most importantly, illicit sales by some members of surplus stocks to non-members of the ICO (notably to the USSR and to countries in Eastern Europe and the Middle East). These 'leaks' of low-price coffee, often at less than one-half of the official ICA rate, also found their way to consumer members of the ICO through free ports, depressing the general market price and making it more difficult for exporters to fulfil their quotas.

The issue of coffee export quotas became further complicated in the 1980s as consumers in the main importing market, the USA, and, to a lesser extent, in the EC came to prefer the milder arabica coffees grown in Central America at the expense of the robustas exported by Brazil and the main African producers. Disagreements over a new system of quota allocations, taking account of coffee by variety, had the effect of undermining efforts in 1989 to preserve the economic provisions of the ICA pending the negotiation of a new agreement. The ensuing deadlock between consumers and producers, as well as among the producers themselves, led in July to the collapse of the quota system and the suspension of the economic provisions of the ICA. The administrative clauses of the agreement, however, continued to operate and were subsequently extended until October 1993, pending an eventual settlement of the quota issue and the entry into force of a successor ICA.

With the abandonment of the ICA quotas, coffee prices fell sharply in world markets, and were further depressed by a substantial accumulation of coffee stocks held by consumers. The response by some Latin American producers was to seek to revive prices by imposing temporary suspensions of exports; this strategy, however, merely increased losses of coffee revenue. By early 1992 there had been general agreement among the ICO exporting members that the export quota mechanism should be revived. However, disagreements persisted over the allocation of quotas, and in April 1993 it was announced that efforts to achieve a new ICA with economic provisions had collapsed. In the following month Brazil and Colombia, the two largest coffee producers at that time, were joined by some Central American producers in a scheme to limit their coffee production and exports in the 1993/94 coffee year. Although world consumption of coffee exceeded the level of shipments, prices were severely depressed by surpluses of coffee stocks totalling 62m. bags (each of 60 kg), with an additional 21m. bags held in reserve by consumer countries. Prices, in real terms, stood at historic 'lows'.

In September 1993 the Latin American producers announced the formation of an Association of Coffee Producing Countries (ACPC) to implement an export-withholding, or coffee-retention, plan. The Inter-African Coffee Organization (IACO, see below), whose membership includes Côte d'Ivoire, Kenya and Uganda, agreed to join the Latin American producers in a new plan to withhold 20% of output whenever market prices fell below an agreed limit. With the participation of Asian producers, a 28-member ACPC was formally established. Angola and Zaire (now the Democratic Republic of the Congo) were subsequently admitted to membership. With headquarters in London, United Kingdom, its signatory member countries numbered 28 in 2001, 14 of which were ratified. Production by the 14 ratified members in 1999/2000 accounted for 61.4% of coffee output world-wide.

The ACPC coffee-retention plan came into operation in October 1993 and gradually generated improved prices; by April 1994 market quotations for all grades and origins of coffee had achieved their highest levels since 1989. In June and July 1994 coffee prices escalated sharply, following reports that as much as 50% of the 1995/96 Brazilian crop had been damaged by frosts. In July 1994 both Brazil and Colombia announced a temporary suspension of coffee exports. The onset of drought following the Brazilian frosts further affected prospects for its 1994/95 harvest, and ensured the maintenance of a firm tone in world coffee prices during the remainder of 1994.

The intervention of speculative activity in the coffee 'futures' market during early 1995 led to a series of price falls, despite expectations that coffee consumption in 1995/96, at a forecast 93.4m. bags, would exceed production by about 1m. bags. In an attempt to restore prices, the ACPC announced in March 1995 that it was to modify the price ranges of the export-withholding scheme. In May the Brazilian authorities, holding coffee stocks of about 14.7m. bags, introduced new arrangements under which these stocks would be released for export only when the 20-day moving average of the ICO arabica coffee indicator rose to about US $1.90 per lb. Prices, however, continued to decline, and in July Brazil joined Colombia, Costa Rica, El Salvador and Honduras in imposing a reduction of 16% in coffee exports for a one-year period. Later in the same month the ACPC collectively agreed to limit coffee shipments to 60.4m. bags from July 1995 to June 1996. This withholding measure provided for a decrease of about 6m. bags in international coffee exports during this period. In July 1997 the ACPC announced that the export-withholding programme was to be replaced by arrangements for the restriction of exports of green coffee. Total exports for 1997/98 were to be limited to 52.75m. bags. Following the withdrawal, in September 1998, of Ecuador from the export-restriction scheme (and subsequently from the ACPC) and the accession of India to membership in September 1999, there were 14 ratified member countries participating in the withholding arrangements. The continuing decline in world coffee prices (see below) prompted the ACPC to announce in February 2000 that it was considering the implementation of a further scheme involving the withholding of export supplies. In the following month the members indicated their intention to withdraw supplies of low-grade beans (representing about 10% of annual world exports), and they announced in May arrangements under which 20% of world exports would be withheld until the ICO 15-day composite price reached 95 US cents per lb (at that time the composite price stood at 69 cents per lb). Retained stocks would only be released when the same indicator price reached 105 cents per lb. Five non-member countries, Guatemala, Honduras, Mexico, Nicaragua and Viet Nam, also signed a so-called London Agreement pledging to support the retention plan. Implementation of the plan, which had a duration of up to two years, was initiated by Brazil in June, with Colombia following in September. In December 2000 the ACPC identified a delay in the full implementation of the retention plan as one of the factors that had caused the average ICO composite indicator price in November to fall to its lowest level since April 1993, and the ICO robusta indicator price to its lowest level since August 1969. In May 2001 the ACPC reported that exchange prices continued to trade at historic lows. Their failure to recover, despite the implementation of the retention plan, was partly attributed to the hedging of a proportion of the 7m. bags of green coffee retained by that time. On the physical market, meanwhile, crop problems and the implementation of the retention plan had significantly increased differentials for good quality coffees, in particular those of Central America. In April 2001 the ICO daily composite indicator price averaged 47.13 cents per lb (compared with an average of 64.24 cents per lb for the whole of 2000, the lowest annual average since 1973), the lowest monthly average since September 1992. In October 2001 the ACPC announced that it would dissolve itself in January 2002. The Association's relevance had been increasingly compromised by the failure of some of its members to comply with the retention plan in operation at that time, and by some members' inability to pay operating contributions to the group owing to the depressed state of the world market for coffee. It was subsequently announced that the ACPC's members would consider establishing a successor organization should market conditions improve.

In June 1993 the members of the ICO agreed to a further extension of the ICA, to September 1994. However, the influence of the ICO, from which the USA withdrew in October 1993, was increasingly perceived as having been eclipsed by the ACPC. In 1994 the ICO agreed provisions for a new ICA, again with primarily consultative and administrative functions, to operate for a five-year period, until September 1999. In November of that year it was agreed to extend this limited ICA until September 2001. A successor ICA took effect, provisionally, in October 2001, and definitively in May 2005. By May 2007 the new ICA had been endorsed by 77 members of the International Coffee Council (45 exporting members and 32 importing members). Among the principal objectives of the ICA of 2001 were the promotion of international co-operation with regard to coffee, and the provision of a forum for consultations, both intergovernmental and with the private sector, with the aim of achieving a reasonable balance between world supply and demand in order to guarantee adequate supplies of coffee at fair prices for consumers, and markets for coffee at remunerative prices for producers.

In February 1995 five African Producers (Burundi, Kenya, Rwanda, Tanzania and Uganda) agreed to participate in coffee price guarantee contract arrangements sponsored by the Eastern and Southern Africa Trade and Development Bank under the auspices of the Common Market for Eastern and Southern Africa (COMESA). This plan sought to promote producer-price guarantees in place of stock-retention schemes. The contract guarantee arrangements would indemnify producers against reductions below an agreed contract price.

In January 2000 the 'spot' price of coffee (for immediate delivery) in London rose strongly towards the end of the month, increasing from US $1,401.5 (£848) per metric ton to $1,727.5 (£1,067) within a week. However, prices of coffee 'futures' continued to be much lower: at the end of January the quotation for March delivery was $1,073.5 per ton. In February prices of robusta coffee 'futures' were below $1,000 per ton for the first time for nearly seven years. In March the 'spot' quotation eased from $993 (£628) per ton to $944 (£593). Prices continued to weaken in April, with the quotation for short-term delivery falling to less than $900 per ton. The 'spot' price in May declined to $891.5 (£602) per ton but recovered to $941 (£639). Another downward movement ensued, and by early July the London 'spot' quotation stood at only $807 (£532) per ton. Prices briefly recovered later that month, owing to concerns about the possible danger of frost damage to coffee crops in Brazil. The 'spot' quotation rose to $886.5 (£585) per ton, while prices of coffee 'futures' advanced to more than $1,000. However, the fear of frost was allayed, and on the next trading day the 'spot' price of coffee in London slumped to $795 (£525) per ton—its lowest level, in terms of US currency, since September 1992.

The weakness in the market was partly attributed to the abundance of supplies, particularly from Viet Nam, which has substantially increased its production and export of coffee in recent years. By mid-2000 Viet Nam had overtaken Indonesia to become the world's leading supplier of robusta coffee and was rivalling Colombia as the second largest coffee-producing country. Viet Nam and Mexico were the most significant producers outside the ACPC, but their representatives supported the Association's plan for a coffee retention scheme to limit exports and thus attempt to raise international prices. The plan was also endorsed by the Organisation africaine et malgache du café (OAMCAF), a grouping of nine African coffee-producing countries based in Paris, France.

In the first week of September 2000 the 'spot' market quotation rallied to US $829 (£577) per metric ton, remaining at this level until 21 September, when another downward movement occurred. Towards the end of the month the 'spot' quotation declined to $776 (£530) per ton. At the beginning of November 2000 the London 'spot' quotation stood at only $709 (£490) per ton and it was to decline steadily throughout the month, reaching $612 (£432) on 30 November. High consumer stocks and uncertainty regarding the size of the Brazilian crop were cited as factors responsible for the substantial decline in November, when the average ICO robusta indicator price fell to its lowest level since August 1969.

In early January 2001 the 'spot' quotation on the London market rallied, rising as high as US $677 (£451) per metric ton. This recovery, which was attributed to concern about the lack of availability of new-crop Central American coffees and reports that producers in some countries were refusing to sell coffee for such low prices, was sustained, broadly, until March, when the downward trend resumed. On 23 March the London 'spot' quotation declined to only $570 (£399) per ton. On 17 April the London price of robusta coffee 'futures' for July delivery declined to a life-of-contract low of $560 per ton, the lowest second-month contract price ever recorded. By May 2001 the collapse in the price of coffee had been described as the deepest crisis in a global commodity market since the 1930s, with prices at their lowest level ever in real terms. The crisis was regarded, fundamentally, as the result of an ongoing increase in world production at twice the rate of growth in consumption, this over-supply having led to an overwhelming accumulation of stocks. During May the London 'spot' quotation fell from $584 (£407) per ton to $539 (£378) per ton.

In June 2001 producers in Colombia, Mexico and Central America were reported to have agreed to destroy more than 1m. bags of low-grade coffee in a further attempt to boost prices. The ACPC hoped that this voluntary initiative would eventually be adopted by all of its members. By this time the ACPC's retention plan was widely regarded as having failed, with only Brazil, Colombia, Costa Rica and Viet Nam having fully implemented it.

In early July 2001 the price of the robusta coffee contract for September delivery fell below $540 per metric ton, marking a record 30-year 'low'. At about the same time the ICO recorded its lowest composite price ever, at 43.80 US cents per lb. Despite a recovery beginning in October, the average composite price recorded by the ICO for 2001 was 45.60 cents per lb, 29% lower than the average composite price (64.25 cents per lb) recorded in 2000. In 2001 coffee prices were at their lowest level since 1973 in nominal terms, and at a record low level in real terms. The decline in the price of robusta coffees was especially marked in 2001, the ICO recording an average composite price of only 27.54 cents per lb, compared with 41.41 cents per lb in 2000, and 67.53 cents per lb in 1999. In 1996–98 the ICO composite price for robusta varieties had averaged 81.11 cents per lb. In 2002 the ICO recorded an average composite price for robustas of 30.02 cents per lb—9% higher than the average price recorded in 2001. The average composite price for all coffees recorded in 2002 was 47.74 cents per lb. In 2003 the average composite price rose by 8.7%, to 51.91 cents per lb. In 2004 the average composite price increased for a third successive year, rising to 62.15 cents per lb, 19.7 higher than in 2003. The average composite price for robustas declined by 2.6% in 2004, compared with 2003, while all of the average prices recorded for arabicas increased.

In 2005 the average composite price recorded by the ICO, at 89.36 US cents per lb, was 43.8% higher than in 2004. In 2005 the average price recorded for robustas increased by 40.5% while all of the average prices recorded for arabicas likewise increased by substantial margins. During the first six months of 2006 the ICO recorded an average composite price for all coffees of 93.60 cents per lb, 4.7% higher than the average composite price recorded for the whole of 2005. In the first half of 2005 the average composite price ranged between 86.04 cents per lb (June) and 101.20 cents per lb (January). In its review of the 2004/05 crop year the ICO noted that the crisis in the coffee economy of exporting countries had abated somewhat. In the 2004/05 crop year the average ICO composite indicator price increased by 47.65% compared with the previous crop year. This strengthening of prices was more marked for robustas than for arabicas. The ICO noted that the differential between Other Mild arabicas and robustas rose from 37.14 cents per lb in the 2003/04 crop year to 67.15 cents per lb in 2004/05.

In 2006 the average composite price recorded by the ICO rose by 7% compared with 2005, to 95.75 cents per lb. However, this increase was derived almost exclusively from a 34% rise in the average price of robustas; average prices recorded for arabica varieties increased only marginally (by less than 1% for both Colombian and Other Milds and by 1.6% for Brazilian Naturals). In the first six months of 2007 the average price for robustas rose by a further 17%, while the average composite price remained firm. According to the ICO, the upward trend in the average price of robustas was due to the low availability of supplies of robustas of average quality used in blends, which were in increasing demand.

The IACO was formed in 1960, with its headquarters in Abidjan, Côte d'Ivoire. In 2003 the IACO represented 25 producer countries, all of which, except Benin and Liberia, were also members of the ICO. The aim of the IACO is to study common problems and to encourage the harmonization of production.

COPPER

The ores containing copper are mainly copper sulphide or copper oxide. They are mined both underground and by open-cast or surface mining. After break-up of the ore body by explosives, the lumps of ore are crushed, ground and mixed with reagents and water in the case of sulphide ores, and then subjected to a flotation process by which copper-rich minerals are extracted. The resulting concentrate, which contains about 30% copper, is then dried, smelted and cast into anode copper, which is further refined to about 99.98% purity by electrolysis (chemical decomposition by electrical action). The cathodes are then cast into convenient shapes for working or are sold as such. Oxide ores, less important than sulphides, are treated in ways rather similar to the solvent extraction process described below.

Two alternative processes of copper extraction, both now in operation in Zambia, have been developed in recent years. The first of these techniques, and as yet of minor importance in the industry, is known as 'Torco' (treatment of refractory copper ores) and is used for extracting copper from silicate ores that were previously not treatable.

The second, and relatively low-cost, technique is the solvent extraction process. This is suited to the treatment of very low-grade oxidized ores and is currently being used on both new ores and waste dumps that have accumulated over previous years from conventional copper working. The copper in the ore or waste material is dissolved in acid, and the copper-bearing leach solution is then mixed with a special organic-containing chemical reagent that selectively extracts the copper. After allowing the two layers to separate, the layer containing the copper is separated from the acid leach solution. The copper is extracted from the concentrated leach solution by means of electrolysis to produce refined cathodes.

Copper is ductile, resists corrosion and is an excellent conductor of heat and electricity. Its industrial uses are mainly in the electrical industry (about 60% of copper is made into wire for use in power cables, telecommunications, domestic and industrial wiring) and the building, engineering and chemical industries. Bronzes and brasses are typical copper alloys used for both industrial and decorative purposes. There are, however, substitutes for copper in almost all of its industrial uses, and in recent years aluminium has presented a challenge in the electrical and transport industries.

Proven world reserves of copper were estimated by the US Geological Survey at 480m. metric tons in 2005. In that year 4% of the world's total reserves were located in Zambia, where copper production is the mainstay of the economy, and copper sales formerly accounted for some 85% of export earnings. In the late 1990s, however, owing to the low price of copper on the world market, the contribution of the metal to export revenues declined substantially. In 2002 sales of refined copper (unwrought) were estimated to have accounted for only about 50% of total export earnings. Zambia's leading copper producers in 2004 were Konkola Copper Mines PLC (KCM) and Mopani Copper Mines PLC (MCM), a consortium comprising Glencore International AG of Switzerland (73.1%), First Quantum Minerals Ltd of Canada (16.9%) and Zambia Consolidated Copper Mines Investment Holdings PLC (ZCCM-IH—10%). KCM was reported to have been reprivatized in 2004, when Vedanta Resources PLC bought a 51% share in the company. Zambia Copper Investments Ltd (ZCI) maintained a 28.4%-share in KCM, ZCCM-IH one of 20.6% and the Government a so-called 'golden share', which allowed it to ensure that the company acted in the country's best interests. It was reported in early 2007 that KCM was planning to increase its copper production capacity to 400,000–450,000 tons per year by 2010, from existing annual capacity of 200,000 tons. The principal generator of the expansion was to be the US $400m. Konkola Deep project, seeking to access the rich ore body beneath existing production. Among the rehabilitation and expansion projects conducted by MCM in 2004 was one to replace an outdated electric arc furnace at the company's Mufulira smelter with an ISASMELT furnace. Other companies active in Zambia's copper sector in 2004 included Luanshya Mines PLC, a subsidiary of Switzerland's J&W Investment Group, South Africa's Metorex and NFC Africa Mining PLC, a subsidiary of China Nonferrous Metal Industry Foreign Engineering and Construction Co Ltd. Lumwana Joint Venture, an undertaking of Australia's Equinox Resources Ltd (51%) and Phelps Dodge Corpn of the USA (49%), was awarded a 25-year large-scale licence to explore for metals, including copper. Equinox, which reportedly sought 100% ownership of the joint venture, intended to develop the Lumwana Copper Project in north-western Zambia in 2005 and to commence output there in 2006. China Nonferrous Metal Mining Co Ltd was in early 2007 in the process of building, at a cost of $200m., a new smelter to process copper from the Chambishi minie, with a capacity of 150,000 tons per year. In the first 10 months of 2006 copper production in Zambia reached 421,000 tons, from 360,000 tons in the same period a year earlier. Before being overtaken by Canada in 1983, Zambia ranked second only to Chile among the world's copper exporters. Zambian copper exports are virtually all in refined but unwrought form. About 43% of its sales were to European Union (EU) countries in the late 1990s. Production of refined copper in Zambia entered a gradual decline in the mid-1980s; dwindling ore grades, high extraction costs, transport problems, shortages of foreign exchange, equipment and skilled labour, lack of maintenance and labour unrest combined to make the copper industry seem an unstable basis for the Zambian economy. However, following the country's change of government in 1991, a number of remedial measures, including the restructuring of ZCCM, were carried out.

Even before the civil conflict, which began in 1993 and was renewed in 1998, led to the suspension of much of the country's normal mining activity—in 1999 La Générale des Carrières et des Mines (Gécamines), the state-owned minerals enterprise, was reported to be operating at only 5%–10% of its production capacity—the copper industry in what is now the Democratic Republic of the Congo (DRC—formerly Zaire) had become increasingly vulnerable to competition from other producers, such as Chile, which have established new open-cast, low-cost mines. The DRC had placed greater emphasis on efforts to increase refined production capacity, and in the late 1980s about one-half of the country's copper exports were in the form of refined copper leach cathodes and blister copper. About 70% of copper exports by the DRC have traditionally been to EU countries. In 2004 Anvil Mining NL of Australia, one of the numerous foreign mining ventures involved in the production and processing of copper in the DRC, was reported to have signed a joint venture with Gécamines and Emiko SPRL to participate in the Mutoshi copper-cobalt project, located near Kolwezi in the south of the country. Anvil anticipated annual output of some 25,000 metric tons of copper from the venture from late 2005. Gécamines was reported to be operating under crisis conditions in 2002–03, and to have put forward a 'minimum survival plan' for 2004 requiring investment of US $27.5m. in order to restore annual copper output to 25,000 tons. The enterprise's five-year investment plan envisaged a requirement of $248m. in order to raise output of copper, in addition to that of other metals, to 100,000 tons. Ageing equipment, inadequate investments, shortages of spare parts and fuel were among the problems that continued to impede the company's rehabilitation efforts in 2004, when the country's mined output of copper was estimated to have totalled about 73,300 tons. No copper metal was smelted or refined in the DRC in that year. Mined utput totalled an estimated 92,000 tons in 2005. Exports of copper contributed 3.3% of the DRC's total export revenue in 2004, compared with 1.4% in 2003 and 4.7% in 2002.

South Africa is the continent's other main producer, although since the 1980s copper output has been affected by declining grades of ore, leading to mine closures and a reduction in the level of operations to about 75% of capacity. In 2005, according to provisional data, mine production of copper totalled 103,907 metric tons. The value of South Africa's copper exports in 2005 was US $103m. Namibia derived more than 10% of its total export revenue from copper in the late 1980s, although by 1997 this proportion had declined to less than 4%. Mining operations there were conducted at four mines by a South African-owned enterprise, Tsumeb Corpn Ltd (TCL), prior to its liquidation in 1999, when TCL's mineral rights reverted to the Namibian Government. Some of TCL's former operations were taken over, from 2000, by a new company, Ongopolo Mining and Processing Ltd, a partnership between former managers of TCL and the National Union of Namibian Workers (NUNW). They included copper mines at Kombat, Khusib Springs (replaced in 2003 by a new mine at Tsumeb West) and Otjihase, and smelting at the refurbished former Tsumeb facility. In Botswana copper and nickel are mined at Selebi-Phikwe, and high-grade copper ore deposits have also been identified in the Ghanzi area. Selebi-Phikwe is expected to remain productive until about 2011. In 2005 exports of copper-nickel matte contributed 10.5% of Botswana's total export revenue. The Sanyati copper mine in Zimbabwe, with estimated ore reserves of 5.5m. tons, entered production in 1995. Targeted output was 5,000 tons annually during the mine's expected life of eight to 10 years.

Production of Copper Ore
(copper content, '000 metric tons)

	2004	2005*
World total*	14,700	15,100
Africa*	541	529
Leading African producers		
Congo, Dem. Repub.*	73	92
South Africa	121	104
Zambia	344	330
Leading non-African producers		
Australia	796	876
Canada	566	567
Chile	3,776	3,736
China, People's Repub.*	742	740
Indonesia	840	1,065
Mexico	334	350
Peru	869	844
Poland	531	523
Russia*	675	700
USA	576	586

* Estimates.

Source: US Geological Survey.

The major copper-importing countries are the member states of the EU, Japan and the USA. At the close of the 1980s demand for copper was not being satisfied in full by current production levels, which were being affected by industrial and political unrest in some of the non-African producing countries, notably Chile, with the consequence that levels of copper stocks were declining. Production surpluses, reflecting the lower levels of industrial activity in the main importing countries, occurred in the early 1990s, but were followed by supply deficits, exacerbated by low levels of copper stocks. In 2005, according to provisional figures from the International Copper Study Group (ICSG), world-wide usage of refined copper declined by 1.3% from its 2004 level, falling to 16,510,000 metric tons, while production, including secondary output (recovery from scrap), increased by 3.9%, to 16,446,000 tons. There was consequently a copper deficit for the year of 64,000 tons, compared with a deficit of 902,000 tons in 2004. Identified stocks of refined copper throughout the world fell by 69,000 tons in 2005, to total 851,000 tons at the end of the year. Provisional data from the ICSG indicated that world-wide usage of refined copper during January–April 2006 reached 5,544,000 tons, a decline of about 2% compared with the corresponding period of 2005. Over the same period, total production (primary and secondary) was 5,621,000 tons: 5.9% higher than in January–April 2005. As a result, there was a surplus of 77,000 tons in world copper supplies for the first four months of 2006. Identified stocks of refined copper also declined, and at the end of April they stood at 826,000 tons. In the first five months of 2007copper usage continued to exceed production, showing a deficit of 300,000 tons, due mainly to high levels of usage in the People's Republic of China (37% higher than in the same period of the previous year). Overall, usage increased by 8.7% in the first five months of 2007, compared with that in the same period a year earlier. Production, however, increased by 6% in the first five months of 2007, compared with that in the same period of 2006. Most major producers (including Chile, China, Japan, India and Russia) increased their production, the exception being the USA, where output decreased by 2.3%.

There is no international agreement between producers and consumers governing the stabilization of supplies and prices. Although most of the world's supply of primary and secondary copper is traded directly between producers and consumers, prices quoted on the London Metal Exchange (LME) and the New York Commodity Exchange (COMEX) provide the principal price-setting mechanism for world copper trading.

On 21 January 2000 the LME's stocks of copper exceeded 800,000 metric tons for the first time. Nevertheless, on the same day, the London price of the metal rose to US $1,893.5 (£1,147) per ton: its highest level for more than two years. The accumulation of stocks continued, and in early March the LME's holdings reached a record 842,975 tons. The copper price was reduced to $1,619 (£1,021) per ton in April, but recovered to $1,859 (£1,228) in July. Throughout this period the LME's stocks of copper steadily declined, falling to less than 700,000 tons in April, under 600,000 tons in June and below 500,000 tons in July. At the end of July copper stocks were 487,750 tons: less than 58% of the level reached in March. By the end of August the LME's holdings had fallen further, to 449,050 tons, while the price of copper had continued to recover, reaching $1,900.0 per ton on 31 August. On 13 September the price rose above $2,000 per ton, and closed, on the following day, at $2,009.0 per ton. The LME's holdings of copper fell steadily throughout September, and on 2 October stood at 399,300 tons. On 3 October the London price of the metal closed at $1,919.0 per ton. During the remainder of October the cash price for copper weakened somewhat, falling to $1,810.0 per ton on 27 October, and closing on the final day of the month at $1,839.0 per ton. During November the LME's holdings of copper and the London quotation declined in tandem, the cash price for the metal closing at a 'low' of $1,759.0 per ton on 23 November, but recovering to $1,820.5 per ton on 28 November. On the final day of the month the LME's stocks of copper stood at 349,300 tons. By the end of December there had been little change in either the London cash price or the level of stocks held by the LME. The London quotation for the metal closed at a 'high' of $1,903.5 per ton on 11 December, but had fallen back to $1,808.5 per ton on the final trading day of 2000, by which time the LME's copper holdings had risen slightly, to 357,225 tons.

During January 2001 the London quotation for copper moved within a range of $1,720.5 per metric ton, recorded on 3 January, and $1,837.0 per ton, the closing price on 23 January. Stocks of the metal, meanwhile, rose as high as 370,225 tons on 10 January, but had declined to 349,825 tons by the end of the month. The LME's holdings of the metal declined steadily during February, and stood at 327,900 tons on the final day of the month. At the same time, the price of the metal weakened, falling to $1,736.0 per ton on 26 February. On 6 March, when the LME's holdings of copper declined to 322,775 tons, the London quotation for the metal rose to $1,822.5 per ton. From 7 March, however, stocks recovered steadily, reaching 400,325 tons on 30 March, while the price of copper fell to $1,664.5 per ton on 29 March. By 29 June the price of the metal had fallen to $1,550.5 per ton, while the LME's stocks of copper had recovered to 464,550 tons. The price of copper fell steadily during July, closing at $1,465.0 per ton on 25 July. The LME's holdings of the metal increased rapidly during July, reaching 654,325 tons on 25 July, and 673,225 tons on 10 August, before declining during the remainder of the month, to 662,825 tons on 30 August. The London quotation for copper closed at a 'low' for the month of $1,426.0 per ton on 14 August, but had recovered to $1,507.0 per ton on the final trading day of the month. During September, however, the price declined sharply, descending to $1,403.0 per ton on 20 September, as stocks continued to rise, reaching 707,100 tons on 24 September. By the end of October the London price of copper stood at only $1,360 per ton, and closed at only $1,319.0 per ton on 7 November. The price of copper 'futures' was boosted in late October by the announcement by US producer Phelps Dodge of its intention to reduce output of the metal by some 220,000 tons per year, in an attempt to stem losses incurred as a result of the price of the metal falling below the price of production. Stocks rose as high as 780,225 tons on 30 November, and, on the final trading day of 2001, stood at 799,225 tons, by which time the London price of copper had recovered to $1,462.0 per ton.

During the second week of January 2002 the London quotation for high-grade copper recovered to US $1,543 per metric ton, and remained above $1,500 per ton for most of the remainder of the month. The LME's holdings of copper continued to rise during January, reaching 857,675 tons by the end of the month. On 1 February the price of copper rose as high as $1,588 per ton and two weeks later closed at $1,609.5 per ton, the first time it had surpassed $1,600 per ton since June 2001. For the remainder of February the price of copper remained comfortably above $1,500 per ton, reaching $1,610.5 per ton at the end of the first week of March. By mid-February stocks of copper had risen as high as 882,425 tons, and on 27 February rose above 900,000 tons. On 19 March the London quotation for copper closed at $1,650.5 per ton, but from the second week of April the price began to weaken, falling as low as $1,551 on 15 April. Stocks rose during March and continued to rise during April, reaching 973,550 tons by the end of the month. During the final week of April, nevertheless, the London quotation for copper was either above or a little less than $1,600 per ton. During May the quotation ranged between $1,562 (7 May) and $1,645 per ton, the higher price recorded on the penultimate day of the month. The rate of increase in the LME's holdings of copper slackened slightly during May, but stocks remained substantially above 900,000 tons for the whole of the month. Throughout June the price of copper remained above $1,600 per ton, closing at $1,689.5 on 6 June, falling to $1,614.5 on 25 June and ending the month at $1,654 per ton. By 21 June the LME's stocks of copper stood at 898,375 tons.

On 15 July 2002 the London price of copper fell to US $1,606 per metric ton, declining to $1,597 per ton on 18 July and to $1,491 per ton on 24 July. Stocks of copper fell to 874,075 tons on 16 July, but by the end of the month were once again approaching 900,000 tons. For almost the whole of August the London quotation remained below $1,500 per ton, ending the month at $1,500 per ton exactly. Stocks reached 896,675 tons on 21 August and ended the month at 896,425 tons. By the end of September the London quotation had fallen to only $1,434.5 per ton. Stocks fell somewhat during the first three weeks of September, declining to 870,375 tons by the end of the month. On 18 October the price of copper rose above $1,500 per ton and remained above that level for the rest of the month, closing at $1,536 per ton on 31 October. Stocks continued to decline throughout October, falling to 860,000 tons on 15 October. The LME's holdings of copper were stable during most of November, ending the month at 862,550 tons. On 20 November the London price of copper closed at $1,600.5 per ton, rising further, to $1,626.5 per ton, on 29 November. During December the quotation ranged between $1,536 per ton, recorded on the final day of 2002, and $1,649.5, recorded on 2 December. Stocks were little changed at the end of the year, compared with one month previously, totalling 855,625 tons.

The London quotation for high-grade copper rose substantially during January 2003, reaching US $1,713.5 per metric ton on the final day of that month, by which time the LME's holdings of copper had declined to 833,225 tons. During February the price of copper ranged between $1,627.5 (19 February) and $1,728 (3 and 27 February). Stocks had fallen to 825,650 tons by the end of February and fell a little further during March, ending that month at 812,950 tons. By the end of March the London quotation for copper had weakened to $1,587.5 per ton. The price of copper rose above $1,600 per ton again on 15 April, ending the month at $1,604 per ton. On 10 April the LME's holdings of copper fell below 800,000 tons and stood at 768,075 tons by the end of the month. By late May the London quotation was once again approaching $1,700 per ton, and on 2 June closed at $1,705. A sudden increase in the LME's copper stocks in early May subsequently gave way to a decline, and by the end of the month holdings totalled 740,600 tons. On 11 June stocks fell below 700,000 tons and had descended to 665,650 tons by the end of the month. For the whole of June the London price of copper ranged between $1,657.5 (26 June) and $1,711.5 (3 June).

During the second half of July 2003, generally, the London quotation for high-grade copper increased, closing at US $1,781 per metric ton on the final trading day of that month. On 1 August the London cash price rose to $1,824.5 per ton, but thereafter, during the remainder of the month, declined somewhat. In September the price of copper ranged between $1,815 per ton (24 September) and $1,759 per ton (1 September). During October the London quotation rose consistently, ending the month at $2,057 per ton, and remaining above $2,000 per ton until 20 November, when it declined to $1,996 per ton. On the final trading day of November a price of $2,073.5 was recorded. During December the price continued to rise, reaching $2,321 per ton on the final trading day of 2003. Stocks of copper held by the LME declined steadily in the second half of 2003, from 612,425 tons at the end of July to 430,525 at the end of the year.

For most of January and February 2004 the London quotation for high-grade copper remained above US $2,400 per metric ton, and on 25 February it rose above $3,000 per ton (to $3,001) for the first time in the 2000s. The London price remained above $3,000 per ton during most of March, declining marginally in April, when it ranged between $3,170 per ton (19 April) and $2,929.5 per ton (13 April). For the whole of May the London quotation remained below $3,000 per ton. In June the London quotation ranged between $2,878 per ton (2 June) and $2,554 per ton (15 June). During the first half of 2004 stocks of copper held by the LME declined steadily, from slightly less than 400,000 on 16 January to 101,475 tons on 30 June. For the whole of 2004 the average price of copper traded on the London exchange was $2,868 per ton, more than 60% higher than the average price recorded in 2003. Stocks of copper held by the LME declined steadily and substantially during the second half of the year, to total 48,875 tons at 31 December. Demand for copper, both for physical metal and as an investment asset, increased markedly in 2004. In the physical sphere, as with other base metals in 2004, strong demand from the China was a key market factor.

In 2005, the average price of copper traded on the LME was US $3,684 per metric ton, an increase of 28.5% compared with 2004. In the final quarter of 2005, the average price of copper was $4,297 per ton. During the year copper traded within a range of $3,072–$4,650 per ton. Stocks of the metal held by the LME rose to 61,000 tons at the end of April, but declined to less than 30,000 tons by the end of June, their lowest level for more than 30 years. During the second half of 2005, however, stocks recovered steadily, rising to 79,950 tons at the end of September and to 92,225 tons at the end of the year. Analysts noted that, unusually, the sustained growth in the price of copper in 2005 had not been accompanied by correspondingly strong growth in global demand, despite the continued rise in Chinese consumption.

At mid-2006 analysts noted that the copper market remained under the influence of the fundamental factors that had propelled prices upwards in the first half of the year. Supply reportedly continued to be affected by disruption. Demand, meanwhile, remained strong, as reflected in ICSG data which indicated a fall in the copper surplus in the first quarter of 2006. Global consumption of copper rose only marginally in the first quarter of 2006, compared with the corresponding period of 2005. The ICSG attributed this marginal growth to a reported fall in Chinese consumption. However, other analysts were more sanguine in their assessment of the underlying conditions affecting demand for copper at mid-2006. It was noted, for instance, that consumption in the main Chinese consuming sectors, including the automotive and power-generation sectors, continued to display strong year-on-year growth. According to ICSG data, production of copper world-wide increased by 4.8% in January–March 2006, compared with the corresponding period of 2005. An increase of 20% was recorded in China, while Indian output grew by 43%. In Chile there was an apparent increase of 2% in copper production in the first quarter of 2006.The average price of copper in 2006 traded on the LME was US $6,731 per metric ton, an increase of 82.7% compared with 2005. Industrial action at mines in Chile, Peru and Mexico had forced temporary closures during 2006, and escalating demad at a time of stagnating production (ICSG data suggested that global ouput had expanded by just 0.6%) had placed upward pressure on international prices. In the final quarter of 2006 the average price of copper was $7,087 per ton. During the year copper traded within a range of $4,537–$8,788 per ton. Stocks recovered steadily in the second half of 2006, rising to 116,875 tons at the end of September and to 190,575 tons at the end of the year.

The average price of copper traded on the LME rose steadily in the first five months of 2007: it was trading at US $5,670 per metric ton in January, $6,452 per ton in March and $7,682 per ton in May. The average price fell in June, to $7,476 per ton, before recovering to $7,974 in July. During the first half of the year copper traded within a price range of $5,226–$8,225 per ton. Inventories of copper held by the LME decreased in the first quarter, reaching 216,000 tons at the end of January and 181,075 tons at the end of March. In the second quarter stocks continued to decline, falling to 103,475 tons at the end of July. Analysts expected the price to continue to rise, reflecting the impact of renewed strikes in Chile and Mexico.

The ICSG, initially comprising 18 producing and importing countries, was formed in 1992 to compile and publish statistical information and to provide an intergovernmental forum on copper. In 2007 ICSG members and observers totalled 22 countries, plus the EU, accounting for more than 80% of world trade in copper. The ICSG, which is based in Lisbon, Portugal, does not participate in trade or exercise any form of intervention in the market.

COTTON (*Gossypium*)

This is the name given to the hairs which grow on the epidermis of the seed of the plant genus *Gossypium*. The initial development of the cotton fibres takes place within a closed pod, called a boll, which, after a period of growth lasting about 50 days (depending upon climatic conditions), opens to reveal the familiar white tufts of cotton hair. After the seed cotton has been picked, the cotton fibre, or lint, has to be separated from the seeds by means of a mechanical process known as ginning. Depending upon the variety and growing conditions, it takes about three metric tons of seed cotton to produce one ton of raw cotton fibre. After ginning, a fuzz of very short cotton hairs remains on the seed. These are called linters, and may be removed and used in the manufacture of paper, cellulose-based chemicals, explosives, etc.

About one-half of all cotton produced world-wide is used in the manufacture of clothing, about one-third is used for household textiles, and the remainder for numerous industrial products (tarpaulins, rubber reinforcement, abrasive backings, filters, high-quality papers, etc.).

The official cotton 'season' (for trade purposes) runs from 1 August to 31 July of the following year. Quantities are measured in both metric tons and bales; for statistical purposes, one bale of cotton is 226.8 kg (500 lb) gross or 217.7 kg (480 lb) net.

Production of Cotton Lint
('000 metric tons, excluding linters)

	2005	2006
World total*	24,809	24,484
Africa*	1,971	1,772
Leading African producers		
Benin	122†	78*
Burkina Faso	250†	290*
Cameroon*	100	58
Chad	76†	86*
Côte d'Ivoire	139	114†
Egypt†	263	277
Mali	250†	160*
Nigeria*	140	152
Sudan	106	106*
Tanzania†	126	99
Zimbabwe†	75	72
Leading non-African producers		
China, People's Repub.*	5,714	6,730
India	3,332	3,564
Pakistan	2,214	2,187
Turkey	864	900
USA	5,201	4,498
Uzbekistan	1,250	1,171

* FAO estimate(s).
† Unofficial figure(s).

The price of a particular type of cotton depends upon its availability relative to demand and upon characteristics related to yarn quality and suitability for processing. These include fibre length, fineness, cleanliness, strength and colour. The most important of these is length. Generally speaking, the length of the fibre determines the quality of the yarn produced from it, with the longer fibres being preferred for the finer, stronger and more expensive yarns.

Cotton is the world's leading textile fibre. However, with the increased use of synthetics, cotton's share in the world's total consumption of fibre declined from 48% in 1988 to only 39% in 1998. About one-third of the decline in its market share was attributed to increases in the real cost of cotton relative to prices of competing fibres, and the remaining two-thirds to other factors, for example greater use of chemical fibre filament yarn (yarn that is not spun but is extruded in a continuous string) in domestic textiles such as carpeting. The break-up of the Council for Mutual Economic Assistance (the trade grouping of the former communist bloc) in 1990, and of the USSR in 1991, led to substantial reductions in cotton consumption in those countries and also contributed to cotton's declining share of the world fibre market. Officially enforced limits on the use of cotton in the People's Republic of China (which generally accounted for about 25%–30% of cotton consumption world-wide) also had an impact on the international market. According to a study conducted by FAO and the International Cotton Advisory Committee (ICAC), there was some recovery in the position of cotton in 1998–2002. Consumption of cotton world-wide rose by 3% in 2002, the fourth consecutive year of expansion. In 1998–2002, according to the same source, global cotton consumption increased by 2m. metric tons, totalling 20.6m. tons in the latter year. The increase in demand in 1998–2002 was a consequence of the low price of cotton relative to other fibres. Among other factors, the higher price of petroleum prevented synthetic fibres from matching the low price of cotton as they had done earlier in the 1990s. In 1998–2002, none the less, the share of cotton in the world fibre market continued to decline owing to faster growth in the use of synthetic fibres. Demand for non-cotton fibres increased by 6% in 2002, and the market share of cotton, which had recovered slightly, to 40.5%, in 2001, totalled only 39.7% in 2002.

The area devoted to cotton cultivation totalled 31m.–36m. ha between the 1950s and the early 1990s, accounting for about 4% of the world cropped area. During the mid-1980s, however, world cotton consumption failed to keep pace with the growth in production, and the resultant surpluses led to a fall in prices, which had serious consequences for the many African countries that rely on cotton sales for a major portion of their export earnings. In the mid-1990s, despite improvements in world price levels, cotton cultivation came under pressure from food crop needs, and world-wide harvested areas under cotton declined from more than 35m. ha in 1995/96 to 33m. ha in 1996/97. According to the US Department of Agriculture

(USDA), the area under cotton world-wide totalled about 35.8m. ha in 2004/05; it was forecast to decline to about 34m. ha in 2005/06, and, again, to some 35m. ha, in 2006/07.

In 2006/07, according to provisional data compiled by the USDA, the leading exporters of cotton were the USA, Uzbekistan, India, Australia and Brazil. The countries of francophone West Africa are also, generally, significant exporters of cotton. In 2006/07, according to provisional USDA data, exports by Mali and Burkina Faso accounted for 6.1% of total world exports of cotton. Burkina Faso and Mali were, respectively, the sixth and eighth largest exporters of cotton in the world in that year. In 2006/07 the main cotton-importing countries were China, Turkey, Bangladesh, Indonesia and Pakistan. China, although one of the major producing countries, was the largest importer of cotton in 1994/95–1996/97, accounting for more than 10% of the world trade in cotton. Chinese imports declined dramatically in 1998/99–2001/02, but rose to some 681,000 metric tons in 2002/03. According to USDA data, China's purchases of cotton increased again, to some 1.9m. tons, in 2003/04, thus accounting for more than one-quarter of all imports world-wide and establishing the country as by far the world's biggest importer. In 2004/05 Chinese imports were estimated to have fallen to about 1.4m. tons, representing about 19% of all cotton imported globally. In 2005/06 USDA estimated that China's imports of cotton almost trebled, compared with the previous year, rising to some 4.1m. tons and thus representing about 43% of world imports of cotton. In 2006/07 USDA estimated that China's imports totalled 2.8m. tons, representing a lower proportion of world cotton imports (34%). Chinese cotton consumption has risen sharply in recent years as a consequence of the rapid expansion of the country's textile industry, in particular its export-orientated sectors. According to FAO, Chinese textiles exports to the USA increased by more than 50% in 2002 compared with the previous year. USDA projected that global cotton output would decline by 3% in 2007/08, mainly reflecting a 20% fall in US production (to its lowest level since 2002/03). However, record consumption was expected to offset lower world production in 2007/08, resulting in a reduction in international cotton stocks. While the US share in global production was projected to fall from a five-year average of 19% to 15% in 2007/08, that of China was expected to grow to 28% in that period.

Cotton is a major source of income and employment for many developing countries, both as a primary product and, increasingly, through sales of yarn, fabrics and finished goods. Cotton is the principal commercial crop, in terms of foreign exchange earnings, in Benin, Burkina Faso, the Central African Republic, Chad, Egypt, Mali, Mozambique and Togo, is second in importance in Sudan, and in 2003/04 was fourth in importance in Tanzania. It was formerly the second most important commercial crop in Senegal, but a very substantial decline in that country's exports of cotton in 1999 and 2000 relegated it to a lower rank. In the early 2000s more than 90% of cotton entering the world market from sub-Saharan Africa came from the francophone countries of the CFA franc zone, in which the total area under cotton cultivation was about 2.3m. ha.

For many years Sudan was the largest cotton producer in sub-Saharan Africa. However, from the 1970s the industry was adversely affected by domestic difficulties resulting from climatic factors, an inflexible, government-dictated marketing policy and crop infestation by whitefly. The area under cotton cultivation in Sudan declined from 360,000 ha in the mid-1980s to 136,000 ha in the 1998/99 crop season. In the interim, in the late 1980s, cotton production, classification and marketing had been reorganized, and in 1990 special foreign exchange incentives had been offered to producers. However, it was not until the early 2000s that improved levels of output seemed likely to be sustained. According to USDA, the area sown to cotton in Sudan in 2005/06 totalled an estimated 170,000 ha, compared with 210,000 ha in 2004/05. The area under cotton was forecast to rise to 180,000 ha in 2006/07. It was hoped that the decision of the Sudanese authorities, in the 2000/01 season, to abolish export taxes on cotton would improve the outlook for the sector and for Sudanese textiles in general. In 2002 overseas sales of cotton represented about 3.4% of the total value of Sudan's exports.

Although co-operation in cotton affairs has a long history, there have been no international agreements governing the cotton trade. Proposals in recent years to link producers and consumers in price-stabilization arrangements have been opposed by the USA (the world's largest cotton exporter), and by Japan and the European Union (EU). The ICAC, an intergovernmental body, established in 1939, with its headquarters in Washington, DC, publishes statistical and economic information and provides a forum for consultation and discussion among its 41 members.

Liverpool, United Kingdom, is the historic centre of cotton-trading activity, and international cotton prices are still collected by organizations located in Liverpool. However, almost no US cotton has been imported through Liverpool in recent years. Consumption in the textile industry in the United Kingdom has fallen to only about 2,000 tons in recent years, according to ICAC data, most of which comes from Africa, Greece, Spain and Central Asia. The price for Memphis cotton, from the USA, quoted in international markets is c.i.f. North European ports, of which Bremen, Germany, is the most important.

The average price for Memphis Territory cotton in North Europe (compiled on the basis of daily prices) declined by 18% in 1999/2000, compared with the previous cotton year, to US $1,328 per metric ton, but recovered somewhat, to $1,371 per ton, in 2000/2001. In 2001/02, however, the average Memphis quotation slumped to only $994 per ton, a decline of more than 27% compared with the previous (cotton) year. According to FAO, and based on calendar years, the weighted average of official weekly prices for cotton that comprise the Cotlook 'A' index was $1,394 per ton in 2003, but declined to $1,365 per ton in 2004. In 2005 the weighted average of official weekly cotton prices fell to $1,220 per ton. In the first half of 2006 the average weekly Cotlook 'A' index ranged between $1,202 per ton (May) and $1,334 per ton.

The principal Liverpool index of cotton import prices in North Europe is based on an average of the cheapest five quotations from a selection of styles of medium-staple fibre. In 1999 the index recorded an average offering price of 53.1 US cents per lb: its lowest annual level since 1986. On a monthly basis, the average price in December 1999 was only 45.0 cents per lb. The decline in prices was attributed to the plentiful availability of cotton, with high levels of production resulting in large stocks (more than 9m. metric tons world-wide in recent years). In 2000 the index recorded an average offering price of 59.0 cents per lb. Slow growth in production and strengthened demand for cotton were the main reasons cited for the recovery in prices. In 2001, however, the decline in prices resumed and in that year the index recorded an average offering price of only 48.1 cents per lb. This declined further in 2002, to only 46.1 cents per lb. In 2003 the index recorded an average offering price of 63.2 cents per lb, but this declined slightly, to 61.9 cents per lb, in 2004. The annual average price of cotton was 55 cents per lb in 2005, and 58 cents per lb in 2006. As of May 2007 the price had contracted to 55 cents per lb.

In March 2003 the World Trade Organization (WTO) established a panel to rule on a claim by Brazil that subsidies and other measures enjoyed by US producers, users and exporters of cotton had harmed its interests. The US Cotton Farm Program had reportedly been represented by Brazil and by some other countries as inconsistent with the USA's obligations in respect of the WTO, and as the most important factor in the fall in world cotton prices from the mid-1990s—to the point at which, in 2001/2002, the Cotlook 'A' index was at its lowest level for 30 years. Some analysts, however, contended that the decline in the world price of cotton could not be attributed solely or even mainly to the subsidization of US (and EU and Chinese) output, but that it was instead the consequence of a combination of structural changes, such as competition from synthetics, affecting the production and consumption of cotton; the appreciation of the US dollar, which had depressed nominal prices of cotton; the extent of China's net trade in cotton; and a number of unusual factors that affected world cotton output in 2001/02. Brazil was the sole initiator of a legal process at the WTO, but, as noted above, it was not the only critic of the subsidization of cotton production in the USA and elsewhere. A number of West and Central African countries have argued that they ought to be compensated, within the framework of the international regulation of trade, for financial losses incurred as a result of the subsidization of US, EU and Chinese cotton production. The cost of producing cotton in West and Central Africa is among the lowest in the world, and African producers would be able to compete strongly with their US, EU and Chinese counterparts were it not for subsidies, which, they have argued, aggravated the fall in the world price of cotton detailed above. In a review of studies of the effects of subsidization on the world market for cotton, FAO stated in the early 2000s that current levels of EU output of cotton could be imported at one-third of the cost of production, and that in some years in the USA the cost of subsidies to cotton producers was greater than the total value of world exports of cotton at prevailing prices. In September 2004 the WTO panel that investigated the US–Brazil dispute ruled overwhelmingly in Brazil's favour. In March 2005, following an appeal by the USA, the panel's ruling was upheld in respect of all critical points of the dispute. As a consequence, the USA would be obliged to bring the subsidies found to be at fault into compliance with its WTO obligations.

DIAMONDS

Diamonds are a crystalline form of carbon, and are the hardest naturally occurring substance. They are of two categories: gem qualities (among the most prized gemstones used in jewellery), which are superior in terms of colour or quality; and industrial quality, about one-half of the total by weight, which are used for high-precision machining or crushed into an abrasive powder called boart. The primary source of diamonds is a rock known as kimberlite, occurring in volcanic pipes which may vary in area from a few to more than 100 ha and volcanic fissures which are considerably smaller. Among the indicator minerals for kimberlite are chrome diopside, pyrope garnet, ilmenite and zircon. Few kimberlites contain diamonds, and in ore which does, the ratio of diamond to waste is about one part per 20m. There are four methods of diamond mining, of which open-cast mining is the commonest; diamonds are also recovered by underground, alluvial and, increasingly, offshore mining.

The diamond is separated from its ore by careful crushing and gravity concentration, which maximizes the diamond's high specific gravity in a process called dense media separation.

The size of diamonds and other precious stones is measured in carats. One metric carat is equal to 0.2 gram, so one ounce avoirdupois equals 141.75 carats.

Africa is the major producing region for natural diamonds, although Australia joined the ranks of the major producers in 1983, and the Argyle open-cast diamond mine, in Western Australia, has become the world's largest producing mine and main source of industrial diamonds. Output is predominantly of industrial-grade diamonds, with some lower-quality gem diamonds and a few pink diamonds. In 1998 Australian diamond output represented almost one-third of world production by volume. In 2001, however, this proportion fell to a little more than 20%, reflecting a sharp decline in output at Argyle, which has been undergoing enlargement to enable access to deeper ores. In 2005 Australia accounted for about 22% of world-wide diamond production.

In terms of value, Botswana ranks as the world's largest producer of diamonds, which are the country's principal source of export earnings, normally accounting for about three-quarters of export receipts and for as much as 50% of government revenues. In 2002, according to the US Geological Survey (USGS), output from Botswana's Orapa mine—where national diamond production began in 1971—reached full capacity following the completion, in 2000, of a major expansion programme. The Orapa mine was expected to remain in production for a further 26 years at an annual rate of 12m.–13m. carats. Output from Orapa was supplemented by that of the new (2002) Damtshaa mine, which has a life-of-mine expectancy of 32 years at an annual rate of 700,000 carats; of the Jwaneng mine (36 years at an annual rate of 11m.–12m. carats); and that of the Letlhakane mine (13 years at an annual rate of 1m. carats). All diamond-mining operations in Botswana are currently conducted by the Debswana Diamond Co (Proprietary) Ltd, which is owned equally by the Botswana Government and De Beers Centenary AG. Debswana will reportedly be able to maintain diamond output at its 2002 level for a further 25–30 years.Among the many companies exploring for diamonds in Botswana in 2005 were DiamonEx Ltd of Australia and Boteti Exploration (Proprietary) Ltd, a joint venture formed by De Beers (51%) and African Diamonds PLC.

About 98% of Namibian diamonds are of gem quality, although recovery costs are high. In 1990 diamond mining commenced at Auchas, and a second mine, at Elizabeth Bay, began operations in 1991. The expectation that mining at the Oranjemund open-cast mine would cease to be economic during the early 2000s stimulated the exploitation of Namibia's extensive deposits of offshore diamonds, which in the late 1990s were estimated at up to 1,500m. carats. Until 1993, when the Government of Namibia granted marine exploration concessions to a new, privately financed venture, the Namibian Minerals Corpn (NAMCO), Consolidated Diamond Mining (CDM), a subsidiary of the De Beers group, held exclusive rights to diamond exploration and mining in Namibia. NAMCO's concession rights initially covered three offshore areas totalling almost 2,000 sq km, containing an estimated 80m. carats of gem-quality diamonds. Commercial recoveries began in late 1995. In 1999 NAMCO acquired a majority stake in Ocean Diamond Mining Holdings Ltd, thereby becoming Namibia's second largest producer of diamonds after Namdeb (see below). In 2003, as part of the liquidation of the assets of NAMCO, which had been forced to cease operations owing to financial problems, the Leviev Group of Israel, via a subsidiary, LL Mining, established a new company, Sakawe Mining Corpn (Samicor), to which it subsequently transferred mining and exploration licences acquired as a result of the purchase of NAMCO and Island Diamonds. In 1994 the Namibian Government and De Beers established the Namdeb Diamond Corpn (Proprietary) Ltd, to which CDM's diamond operations were transferred. Namdeb, owned 50% by De Beers and 50% by the Government, was Namibia's leading producer, accounting for 97% of the country's diamond production in 2005. In 2003 Namdeb initiated a programme to expand, at a cost of some US $50m., its operations at Elizabeth Bay, where it is hoped to extend mine-expectancy by 10 years. In 2005, for the first time, Namdeb's offshore (marine) recoveries exceeded onshore output due to the exhaustion of economic ore at three production sites. In 2001 Diamond Fields International Ltd (DFI) of Canada was granted a 15-year mining licence by the government, and initiated the Sea Diamonds Project in its offshore concession areas as a joint venture with South Africa's Trans Hex Group. In 2002, however, Trans Hex withdrew from the project. In early 2004 DFI was forced to suspend operations for six months pending the renovation of a mining vessel. The government has also granted diamond exploration concessions to other international mining enterprises, including Afri-Can Marine Minerals Corpn of Canada, Mount Burgess Mining NL of Australia, Sonnberg Diamonds (Proprietary) Ltd (a subsidiary of Namibia Resources PLC of the United Kingdom) and Storm Diamond Mining (Proprietary) Ltd (a subsidiary of Australia's Reefton Mining NL). In 2005 Namibia's diamond output declined slightly, owing to reduction of 21% in Namdeb's onshore production and the six-month suspension of offshore exploitation by Diamond Fields. In 2005, according to the Bank of Namibia, the diamond sector accounted for 41% of Namibia's total export earnings and contributed 10% of the country's gross domestic product.

Production of Uncut Diamonds
(gem and industrial stones, million metric carats)

	2004	2005
Leading African producers		
Angola	6.1	6.2
Botswana	31.1	31.9
Central African Repub.	0.3	0.4
Congo, Dem. Repub.	30.9	30.3
Ghana	0.9	1.0
Guinea	0.5	0.5
Namibia	2.0	1.9
Sierra Leone	0.5	0.6
South Africa	14.3	15.2
Producers in other areas		
Australia	43.3	40.0
Canada	12.6	12.3
China, People's Rep.	1.0	1.0
Russia	35.6	38.0
South America	1.4	1.4
Other	0.2	0.3
World total	181.2	183.0

Source: US Geological Survey.

The Mwadui diamond pipe in Tanzania is one of the world's largest producing pipes, covering an area of 146 ha. Tanzania's diamond output was 838,000 carats in 1971, but production later declined, owing to deterioration in diamond grades, technical engineering problems and difficulties in maintaining the mines. By the late 1980s exports from Mwadui had effectively ceased. New prospecting agreements were signed in 1993 by the Government and the De Beers subsidiary that managed operations at Mwadui, and also with Canadian interests, which obtained mining leases and exploration licences covering almost 9,000 sq km. Following extensive rehabilitation, mining at Mwadui recommenced in August 1995, and exports resumed on a small scale in December. In 1999 and 2000 the refining of tailings brought about a substantial increase in production at the Williamson Mine, Tanzania's only diamond mine at that time, where gem-quality stones have accounted for more than 80% of total production in recent years. In 2002 a new processing plant that was constructed in order to increase the mine's ore (tailings only) treatment capacity commenced operations. In 2005 production at the Williamson Mine, which is operated by De Beers, decreased to 190,384 carats, compared with 285,778 carats in 2004. This 34% fall in production was accompanied by a decline in the grade of ore, from 8.4 carats per 100 metric tons in 2004 to 5.6 carats per 100 tons in 2005. In 2005 the DeBeers Group commissioned a feasibility study on a new plant, expected to be completed by December 2008, with the aim of increasing ore treatment and production capacity. All of the diamonds produced at the Williamson Mine in 2005, which represented about 87% of total national output in that year, were exported to the United Kingdom. El Hillal Minerals Ltd of Tanzania commenced operations at a new mine at Mwadui in 2004, with the aim of achieving annual output of 18,000–24,000 carats. In 2005 the company produced 12,875 carats of diamond at a value of US $2.87m. Tan Range Exploration Corpn discovered 11 kimberlites in 2005, including at the Igunga project south of the Williamson Mine and at the Nzega project south-east of the Buzwagi gold deposit. In total, Tanzania exported diamonds with a value of $19.7m. in 2005, a fall of 41% compared with 2004.

More than 90% of South Africa's diamond production derives from the operations of De Beers Consolidated Mines Ltd. In 2005 the company's output totalled 15.2m. carats—96% of South Africa's total output. The locations of South African diamond production include Kimberley, Finsch (west of Kimberley), Namaqualand (north of Port Nolloth), the Cullinan Mine (east of Pretoria), and the Venetia Mine (north of Potgietersrus). The Venetia Mine, discovered in 1980 and opened in 1992, is by far the country's largest producing diamond mine, accounting for a little more than 54% of South African output in 2005. Small-scale marine mining is conducted off Northern Province and Namaqualand.

Angola's diamond output, which totalled 2.4m. carats in 1974, subsequently fell sharply, as a consequence of the civil war. Official diamond production began to revive after 1990, rising from 1m. carats in 1993 to 3.8m. carats in 1996, before declining to 3.3m. carats in 1997 and to about 3.0m. carats in 1998, reflecting continued internal political strife. Production recovered substantially thereafter, and totalled more than 5m. carats in 2001, when diamonds contributed 10.4% of the country's total export earnings. In 2002 output totalled 5m. carats, while exports of diamonds accounted for 7.7% of Angola's export earnings. In 2003, when output remained static, diamonds contributed 8.3% of the country's total export earnings. Production rose to 6m. carats in 2004, but accounted for a reduced share—5%—of export revenue, reflecting the growing importance of petroleum in the country's economy. In 2005 Angola's diamond output increased to 7m. carats, and accounted for 4.5% of export earnings. Angola is known to possess rich diamondiferous deposits, occurring both in kimberlite and alluvial formations, among which particular interest has in recent years been focused on the Catoca kimberlite, 30 km west of Saurimo, in north-eastern Angola. Covering an area of more than 660 ha, its potential reserves have been estimated at 190m. carats. In 2004 Sociedade Mineira de Catoca Ltda (SMC), a joint venture of state-owned Empresa Nacional de Diamantes de Angola (Endiama, formerly Angola's national mining organization), Russia's Almazy Rossii-Sakha Co (Alrosa), Odebrecht Mining Services Inc. of Brazil and the Leviev Group of Israel, was the country's largest diamond producer, with output from its Catoca kimberlite pipe reportedly amounting to about 3.6m. carats. SMC reported in 2004 that it had invested more than US $50m. with the aim of raising the annual production capacity of its Catoca operation to some 4.8m. carats of diamond. A Canadian exploration company, Energem Resources Inc. (formerly Diamond-Works), commenced commercial production in July 1997 from two alluvial projects located at Luo and at Yetwene, in Lunda Norte Province. However, owing to a combination of security and financial problems, both of these projects were placed on a 'care and maintenance basis' (i.e. suspended) in late 1999 and remained so as of December 2005. In 2002 South Africa's TransHex Group Ltd entered into a partnership with Endiama, Micol and Som Vererang to exploit two alluvial diamond concessions at Fucuama and Luarica. Luarica Mine, which began operating in 2003, produced 96,000 carats of diamond in 2005, while Fucauma Mine became operational in 2005, producing a total of 83,000 carats during that year. In 2005 the Government authorized the formation by SouthernEra Diamonds Inc. of Canada, in joint venture with Minex Lda, Endiama (37%), and SARL Comica of Camafuca Sociedade Mineira Lda. The new company was to develop kimberlite deposits associated with the Camafuca-Camazambo kimberlite pipes in Lunda Norte province. The deposits were estimated to contain about 23m. carats of diamond. Production also began at Rio Llapi Garimpo alluvial mine, a joint venture between Angola Resources Pty Ltd (a subsidiary of New Millennium Resources Ltd), Endiama and Mombo Lda. Also in 2005 De Beers and Endiama signed a diamond-prospecting agreement whereby De Beers was to explore for kimberlites in Lunda Norte, with Endiama owning a 51% share in the new joint venture. A number of other foreign companies were either engaged in, or negotiating terms with the Government for, diamond production (including the reactivation of operations suspended some years previously owing to security considerations) or exploration in 2005. Reforms of Angola's diamond sector introduced by the Government in 2004 included an undertaking to recapitalize Endiama and to allow its independent participation, via a subsidiary, in diamond mining; and a proposed licensing system for artisanal diamond miners. The restructuring also included the establishment of Sodiam (see below) as the sole authority to market diamonds in the country and the inauguration, in 2005, of the country's first cutting and polishing factory, the Angola Polishing Diamond SA.

The increasing role of the world diamond trade in the financing of guerrilla insurgencies in Africa, with particular reference to Angola, Sierra Leone and the Democratic Republic of the Congo (DRC), prompted the UN Security Council in June 1998 to adopt Resolution 1173, requiring that international markets ensure that illicitly exported diamonds from these areas did not enter world trade. These 'conflict diamonds' were defined as diamonds that had been either mined or stolen by rebels in opposition to the legitimate government of a country. According to estimates by De Beers, about 3.7% of world diamond production in 1999, with a value of US $255m., could be attributed to areas (principally in Angola and Sierra Leone) under guerrilla control.

Although considerable technical difficulties exist in the identification of diamonds originating in conflict areas, De Beers, as the principal conduit for African diamond sales, implemented a range of measures to comply with the UN sanction. The company, which had in the mid-1980s discontinued purchases from Sierra Leone and Liberia (into which a large proportion of Sierra Leone's diamond output was smuggled), announced in October 1999 that it had suspended all diamond purchases in Angola, and that no diamonds of Angolan origin would be purchased by any of its offices world-wide. In order to eliminate risks that illicit Angolan diamonds might be mixed with officially marketed diamonds, De Beers subsequently suspended all purchases of diamonds originating in West and Central Africa, other than those produced in its own mines, and announced that it was restricting 'outside' purchases to diamonds of Russian and Canadian origin. In March 2000 the company introduced documentation guaranteeing customers that none of its marketed diamonds emanated from conflict areas of Africa. In early 2000 a complete restructuring of the Angolan industry was initiated with the creation of a new state diamond company, Sociedade de Comercialização de Diamantes (Sodiam). The role of Endiama was reduced to that of a prospecting company, retaining its joint ventures with foreign producers. All marketing was transferred to the newly created Angolan Selling Corpn (Ascorp), in which Sodiam held a 51% interest. All existing marketing licences were terminated and operators were given 30 days to sign agreements with Ascorp. It was also announced that prospecting licences were to be reduced in size to an estimated 3,000 sq km. Pressure on the Angolan diamond industry was intensified following the publication, in March 2000, of a report by the UN sanctions committee 'naming and shaming' the presidents of Togo and Burkina Faso, as well as Belgian, Bulgarian and Ukrainian officials, who were all accused of involvement in the illicit diamond trade and of providing military assistance to the União Nacional para a Independência Total de Angola (UNITA). As a result, the Diamond High Council in Antwerp, Belgium, entered into an origin-verification agreement with the Angolan Government. Moreover, De Beers announced a complete restructuring of its own operations (see below). These measures created considerable uncertainty among those foreign companies active in diamond prospecting in Angola. However, several new diamond fields were explored in 2000, and official production increased—although unofficial production remained at a very high level and smuggling was reported also to have risen. In December 2002, following the death of the leader of UNITA, Jonas Savimbi, the UN Security Council voted to end the sanctions it had applied to UNITA's diamond mining and selling operations; none the less, it was widely recognized that UNITA continued to dispose of large quantities of 'conflict diamonds'.

Despite the efforts to stem the trade in 'conflict diamonds' described above, outlets for smuggled stones continued to operate, principally in Antwerp, Mumbai (Bombay), India, and Tel-Aviv, Israel, while illicit output from guerrilla-controlled regions of Angola was marketed under false certification provided mainly by outlets in Côte d'Ivoire, Guinea and Liberia. In May 2000 southern African producing countries initiated the 'Kimberley Process' with the objective of ending the commercialization of 'conflict diamonds'. Endorsed in December by the UN General Assembly, and subsequently expanded to involve, as of August 2007, 47 participants, including the European Union, the 'Kimberley Process' has established the Kimberley Process Certification Scheme that has since 1 January 2003 imposed strict standards on all of its participants in respect of trade in rough diamonds. In July 2000 representatives of the World Federation of Diamond Bourses and the International Diamond Manufacturers Association resolved to implement a certification system that would allow rough diamonds to be monitored direct from mines to trading centres. The proposed licensing regulations would require that all rough diamonds be shipped in sealed parcels which had been individually certified by authorities in exporting countries. At the same time, the World Diamond Council (WDC) was established in order to implement and monitor the certification system. In October 2002 the WDC adopted a resolution in favour of the implementation of a system of warranties that would endorse each transaction of rough diamonds in trading centres world-wide. The WDC scheme was designed to complement the international certification scheme then under development by the 'Kimberley Process'. Both the UN Security Council (in 2003) and the UN General Assembly (in 2004) have adopted resolutions supporting the 'Kimberley Process'. In 2007, according to the WDC, 99.8% of rough diamonds were certified under the Kimberley Process Certification Scheme. In recent years, however, both the UN and some NGOs have documented anomalies within the Kimberley Process, involving in particular Côte d'Ivoire, Ghana and the USA.

In Sierra Leone the diamond industry was long beset by the problems of internal instability and widespread illicit digging and smuggling. Legal exports of diamonds declined steadily after 1970, when 2m. carats of mainly gem-quality diamonds were exported. These sales had dwindled to negligible proportions by the mid-1990s, and they were officially suspended in mid-2000. In 2000 Sierra Leone introduced a UN-approved diamond certification scheme. From 2002 the rehabilitation of the sector began to gather pace. In mid-2003 the UN permitted sanctions applied to trade in diamonds from Sierra Leone to expire. Regulation of the sector has subsequently focused sharply on the activities of artisanal and small-scale miners. All miners and exporters of, and dealers in, diamonds are now required to obtain a licence from the national Director of Mines. In 2004, according to the USGS, the Gold and Diamond Department of the National Revenue Authority assumed responsibility for implementing Sierra Leone's adherence to and compliance with the measures of the Kimberley Process Certification Scheme governing international trade in diamonds. Measures have also been introduced to regulate the access of small-scale and artisanal miners to Chieftancy lands. In 2004, according to the USGS, the US Agency for International Development collaborated with the United Kingdom's Department for International Development, De Beers, Global Witness and the Rapaport Group of New York in the funding of the Integrated

Diamond Management and Policy (IDMP) programme and the Peace Diamond Alliance (PDA). Established in 2002, the PDA seeks to address problems in Sierra Leone's artisanal diamond sector, in particular in the fields of labour rights, the environmental impact of mining and the implementation of the Kimberley Process. In 2005 about 2,400 mining licences had been issued. Since the introduction of the diamond certification scheme in 2000 there has been a substantial increase in Sierra Leone's exports of diamonds, 90% of which were estimated to originate from the production of artisanal miners. In 2005 the value of the country's foreign sales of diamonds, at US $142.2m., represented 90% of total export revenue. At the end of 2005 most diamond production derived from alluvial deposits, and only Koidu Holdings SA (a joint venture between Energen Resources Inc., Magma Diamond Resources Ltd and the Swiss-based Beny Steinmetz), which commenced operations in 2003, was engaged in kimberlite mining. However, several mining consortia were involved in exploration, among them Sierra Leone Diamond Co Ltd and Australia's BHP Billington. The diamond sector in neighbouring Liberia has been beset by problems similar to those encountered by Angola. Liberia's diamond exports averaged about 200,000 carats per year in the mid-1980s, although much of this total was attributable to stones smuggled from adjoining countries and attracted to Liberia by its currency link with the US dollar. In 2001 the UN imposed an embargo on Liberian diamond exports, in order to prevent funds from such sales from being used to finance the conflict in Sierra Leone. The embargo was renewed in 2005 on the grounds that a contract between the National Transitional Government and West Africa Mining Corpn lacked transparency, and that the country had failed to implement the Kimberley Process Certification System. After assuming the presidency of Liberia in January 2006, Ellen Johnson-Sirleaf was reported to have persuaded the UN Security Council to 'move towards' ending the sanctions applied to the country's diamond exports. Althoughthe embargo on Liberia's diamonds was extended in December, in April 2007 the UN Security Council, noting the country's progress towards satisfying the minimum requirements of the Kimberley Process—in particular in respect of internal controls and a diamond valuation scheme—decided to terminate the sanctions. However, in order to determine whether further action was required, Liberia's progress toward becoming 'Kimberley-compliant' was to be reviewed on a quarterly basis.

About 90% of diamond output in the DRC, which is mainly derived from alluvial mining operations in Eastern Kasai, consists of industrial diamonds, of which the DRC (then Zaire) was the world's principal producer until it was overtaken by Australia in 1986. During 1993–96 the DRC's combined output of industrial and gem diamonds exceeded that of Botswana; as much as 50% of its production of gem- or near-gem-quality stones, however, was smuggled out of the country. The Société Minière de Bakwanga (MIBA), which holds the DRC diamond monopoly, cancelled its marketing agreement with De Beers in mid-1997. In 2000 the DRC Government established a joint venture between a state-private enterprise, COMIEX-Congo and Operation Sovereign Legitimacy (COSLEG), owned by the Zimbabwean Defence Forces, to exploit MIBA's Senga-Senga river diamond concession. The involvement of COSLEG apparently represented a repayment for the military support given, since 1998, by the Government of Zimbabwe to the DRC in its counter-insurgency operations. According to UN experts, however, COSLEG lacked both the capital and the technical expertise to administer the concession, which was subsequently reported to have been transferred to a British-Omani company, Oryx Natural Resources. In July 2000 the DRC Government sold International Diamond Industries (IDI) of Israel the right to become the sole purchaser of all uncut diamonds from state-owned mines, in an effort more effectively to monitor the origins of national diamond output. In 2001, however, the Government cancelled IDI's monopoly in favour of an open-bidding and free-market sales and export system that was intended to combat the smuggling that had occurred under the monopoly system. In 2004, according to the USGS, MIBA's output of diamonds, at some 7.3m. carats, represented slightly less than one-quarter of national production, while artisanal producers accounted for most of the remainder. Artisanal production is reported to have been boosted since 2003 by the establishment of a transitional coalition Government in the DRC and by the implementation of the Kimberley Process. Artisanal diamond production was estimated at 22m. carats in 2005, out of total production of some 30.3m. carats. In 2005 the privately owned Congolese company Midamines SPRL commenced diamond production from alluvial deposits in Bandundu and Kasai Occidental provinces. Resources at these deposits were estimated to contain at least 7.2m. carats of diamond. MIBA planned to raise its output of diamonds to 8.5m. carats in 2006 and to 10m. carats in 2008. In 2004 the value of the DRC's foreign sales of diamonds, at US $828m., represented 46% of its total export revenue. Other companies were involved in the exploration of concessions, including a joint venture of Australian Gravity Diamonds Ltd and BHP Billiton Ltd, and SouthernEra Diamonds Inc. of Canada. In July 2004 the Republic of the Congo was removed from the list of participants in the Kimberley Process after a review mission found that the country was unable to account for the origin of a large quantity of the rough diamonds that it exported.

In the Central African Republic (CAR) diamonds are found in alluvial deposits, mainly in the north of the country, and are recovered, for the most part, in small-scale operations. In the past there has been widespread evasion of export duties: it was estimated that during the 1990s upwards of 60% of total diamond production was being smuggled out of the country. The CAR was subsequently adjudged to have met the minimum requirements for participation in the Kimberley Process Certification Scheme. In 2004 official exports of diamonds of 349,451 carats were valued at about US $52m. Foreign sales of uncut diamonds contributed almost 60% of the republic's total export revenue in 2004. In recent years the Government has sought to organize artisanal producers into mining co-operatives in order to improve their access to financial resources and increase their productivity. The Government has also established an exchange in Bangui that allows small-scale producers to sell diamonds direct to international buyers, with the aim of reducing smuggling. Small-scale mining for diamonds is carried out in Côte d'Ivoire, where illicit production is also widespread. The diamond sector in Ghana, which has been in decline since the 1960s, was estimated in 2003 still to contain proven reserves of 15m. carats and probable and possible reserves of some 35m. carats. Artisanal producers, who sell the diamonds they produce to the country's Precious Minerals Marketing Corpn, reportedly accounted for about two-thirds of total output in 2003. The only large-scale commercial operation was undertaken by government-owned Ghana Consolidated Diamonds Ltd, whose share in the country's production continued to decline in 2005. Ghana has been a participant in the Kimberley Process since October 2003. Lesotho, where there has been a considerable increase in exploratory activity in recent years, produced 37,000 carats of diamonds in 2005, compared with 14,000 carats in 2004. In Zimbabwe, Murowa Diamond Private Ltd commenced diamond production on a small scale in 2004 at the country's only commercial mine. In 2005 production totalled some 252,000 carats. Geological assessments of kimberlite pipes located in Mauritania have revealed the presence of diamonds. In 1999 the first licence to prospect for diamonds in Mozambique was granted.

In 1930 the major diamond producers formed The Diamond Corpn to act as the single channel through which most of the world's rough diamond production would be sold. To stabilize the market, the corporation put surplus output into reserve, to be sold at a time when conditions were favourable. The corporation was one of a group of companies, based in London, United Kingdom, which constituted the Central Selling Organisation (CSO). Until mid-2000, when De Beers announced the abandonment of its monopoly of world diamond supply (see below), the CSO, acting on behalf of producers, handled about 65% of world production. The majority of diamonds produced in Africa, although not those of Ghana and Guinea, were marketed through the CSO, which had about 160 direct clients. The CSO marketed the rough diamond production of De Beers Consolidated Mines Ltd. A reorganization of De Beers' interests, undertaken in 1990, placed the CSO, together with the group's diamond stocks and other non-South African-based interests, under the control of a new Swiss-domiciled corporation, De Beers Centenary AG.

In 1990 De Beers Centenary entered into an arrangement with Glavalmazzoloto (the diamond monopoly operated by the former USSR), whereby 95% of rough gem diamonds destined for export were to be purchased and marketed by the CSO, affording Russia a quota of 26% of all CSO sales on the world market. This agreement, which was to operate until December 1995, was continued by the successor Russian diamond corporation, Rosalmazzoloto, and subsequently by Almazy Rossii-Sakha (Alrosa). In 1992 De Beers negotiated an agreement with the Republic of Sakha (Yakutiya), which occupies a large part of Siberia and accounts for approximately 98% of Russian diamond output, to market the proportion of its diamond production not procured by the central diamond authority. In January 1993 the functions of this authority were transferred to an independent body, Diamonds of Russia-Sakha. The 1990 agreement, which expired in December 1995, was extended until March 1996, when a new framework was eventually formulated for the sale of Russian diamonds. Under the revised arrangements, which were to operate for a three-year period, Alrosa obtained the right to market approximately 14% of its exports to buyers outside the CSO. The agreement aimed to achieve a substantial reduction in the volume of diamonds circumventing the CSO marketing network, while assisting Russia in its proposed establishment of a domestic diamond-cutting industry.

In August 1996, however, it was reported that further meetings were to take place between Alrosa and the CSO to discuss continuing increases in sales of Russian diamonds to purchasers outside the CSO. Meanwhile, the Argyle mine in Australia (see above), whose sales accounted for about 6% of the CSO's annual intake, announced in June that it was to terminate its marketing agreement with the CSO with effect from 1 July. For the remainder of 1996 the CSO continued to purchase Russian diamonds under the terms of the agreement that had expired in December 1995, while pursuing negotiations with Alrosa. However, the slow progress in finalizing new arrangements, together with the continuing 'leakage' of Russian diamonds onto the open market, prompted De Beers to inform the Russian Government that it was to cease purchasing diamonds under the existing arrangements with effect from the end of December 1996. Efforts to formulate new marketing arrangements remained unresolved until October 1997, when a new agreement was signed under which the CSO was to market Russian diamonds valued at a minimum of US $550m. annually, with provision for further sales up to a maximum of $1,200m. These arrangements were to operate for a one-year period. In November 1998 a new agreement, operating until 31 December 2001, was finalized, awarding the CSO the right to market Russian diamonds with a minimum value of $550m. annually. However, in July 2000, following the announcement by De Beers that it was to cease exercising control over diamond supplies entering the world markets (see below), Alrosa, which supplied about 26% of diamonds sold through the CSO, indicated that it intended to review the provisions of the 1998 agreement, with a view to obtaining enhanced financial terms. A new five-year trade agreement concluded between Alrosa and De Beers in December 2001 provided for annual sales to De Beers with a value of $800m., subject to the approval of European competition authorities. In the interim, De Beers and Alrosa were to trade on a 'willing-buyer, willing-seller' basis. In January 2003 the European Commission informed De Beers and Alrosa of its preliminary view that the five-year agreement restricted competition in the rough diamond market to an appreciable extent by eliminating competition (with De Beers) from Alrosa, and that De Beers had abused its dominant position in that market. At the same time, the Commission informed De Beers that it had decided to close proceedings with regard to the company's so-called Supplier of Choice distribution system (i.e. the system, focused on adding value to the diamonds already under De Beer's dominion, through marketing and branding initiatives, that the company had proposed as a replacement for its traditional monopolistic approach that had been based on the control of supply). In January 2005 De Beers and Alrosa presented to the European Commission a proposal to modify the terms of their trade agreement: under the proposed revised terms, Alrosa would sell to De Beers diamonds with a value of $700m. in 2005; and the value of Alrosa's sales would fall by $75m. in each subsequent year in 2006–09, and to $275m. from 2010. In February 2006 the European Commission was reported to have accepted a unilateral commitment, made by De Beers in January, to modify the terms of its joint proposal with Alrosa by ceasing purchases (direct and indirect) of Alrosa's diamonds from 2009. In July 2006 Alrosa appealed to the European Court of First Instance against the Commission's acceptance of De Beers' proposal, which effectively cancelled Alrosa's sales contract with De Beers. (Alrosa accused De Beers of reneging on their joint proposal, which was 'market-tested' by the Commission in mid-2005.) In July 2007 the Court of First Instance ruled in favour of Alrosa, annulling the Commission's acceptance of De Beers' proposals on the grounds that the complete prohibition of all commercial relations between the two parties was disproportionate.

Rough diamonds, of which there are currently more than 5,000 categories, were sold by the CSO in mixed packages 10 times each year at regular sales, known as 'sights', in London, Johannesburg and Lucerne, Switzerland. Gems accounted for about 20% of total sales by weight, but, it was estimated, more than 90% by value. After being sold by the CSO, gem diamonds were sent to be cut and polished in preparation for jewellery manufacture. The leading cutting centres are in Antwerp, Mumbai, New York and Tel-Aviv, which in 1993 opened an exchange for 'raw', or uncut, diamonds, with the intention of lessening the dependence of Israeli cutters on allocations from the CSO and purchases from the small, independent diamond exchange in Antwerp. The principal markets for diamond jewellery are the USA and Japan (which together account for about 60% of world consumption).

In July 2000 De Beers announced that it was to relinquish its monopoly control of world diamond sales, and would henceforth concentrate on strategies to stimulate international demand. This decision was widely ascribed to the strains imposed on the CSO by the entry into world markets of increasing quantities of diamonds mined in Australia, North America and Russia. In addition, the substantial stockpiles of diamonds maintained by De Beers required high levels of capital investment, from which no returns accrued to De Beers' shareholders. The Diamond Trading Company (DTC) replaced the CSO as the marketing organization of the De Beers group. In 2007 the DTC handled about 50% of world production.

The CSO provided a guaranteed market to producers and, since 1930, had successfully followed a policy of stockpiling diamonds during times of recession in order to stabilize prices (which were never reduced). At the end of 2000 the value of the stockpile stood at US $3,065m., a decrease of $924m. in 12 months. At the end of 2001 De Beers recorded the value of its diamond stocks and other net assets as $2,065m. In 2002 the value of the stockpile was reportedly reduced by almost $1,000m., and at the end of that year De Beers recorded the value of its diamond stocks and other assets as $2,355m. The value of De Beers' diamond stocks and other assets stood at $1,745m. at the end of 2003, the value of the diamond component having reportedly been reduced by some $700m. in that year. At the end of 2004 diamond stocks and other assets were valued at $1,856m. De Beers had reportedly disposed of the remainder of its 'historical' diamond stockpile in the first half of that year.

As there are so many varieties of diamond, changes to prices (quoted in US dollars) effected by the CSO and its successor, the DTC, represent averages only. There are wide discrepancies in price, depending on such factors as rarity, colour and quality. The sales turnover of US $3,417m. recorded in 1992 by the CSO represented a six-year 'low'. Sales volume advanced strongly, however, in 1993, to $4,366m., an increase of 27.8%. This recovery was partly attributable to reductions in producers' quotas during 1993. Sales turnover declined marginally, to about $4,250m., in 1994, owing in part to an increase of stocks in diamond-cutting centres, and despite Russian sales outside the CSO network. A rise of 6.6% in sales turnover in 1995, to $4,531m., reflected a strong level of demand for quality gem stones, particularly in the USA and Japan. Sales turnover in 1996 advanced by almost 7%, to a record $4,834m., despite the termination of marketing arrangements with the Argyle diamond mine and the impact of direct sales by Russia. In 1997, however, unfavourable economic conditions in East and South-East Asia were responsible for a fall of 4% in sales turnover, to $4,640m. CSO sales in 1998, at $3,350m., stood at their lowest level since 1987, reflecting the weakness of demand from Japan and East Asia, which traditionally account for about 40% of world diamond sales. However, sales turnover achieved a strong recovery in 1999, advancing by 57% on the 1998 total to a record $5,240m., reflecting the onset of an economic recovery in Japan and East Asia and the continuation of strong demand in the USA, which in that year overtook Japan as the principal market for gem diamonds, accounting for almost one-half of world diamond jewellery sales. In 2000 De Beers' sales turnover rose by 8%, to a new record level of $5,670m., compared with 1999. In 2001, however, sales by the DTC totalled only $4,450m., a decline of 21.5% compared with 2000. The decline was attributed to slow growth in the global economy, especially in the USA. The DTC's sales increased by 15.7%, to $5,150m., in 2002, and by a further 7%, to $5,518m., in 2003. The DTC reported strong demand for rough diamonds from cutting centres in 2003, fuelled by strong retail demand for diamond jewellery, especially in the third and final quarters of the year. In 2004, at $5,695m., the value of sales of diamonds by the DTC was 3% higher than in 2003. Growth was attributed to improving economic conditions in the major diamond-consuming countries, in particular in the USA, which accounted for more than one-half of all sales of diamond jewellery world-wide in 2004. The value of sales rose by almost 15% in 2005, to $6,539m. In 2006, a decline of some 6%, to $6.150m., was registered in the value of sales. The decline in 2006 was attributed to the reduced availability of Russian diamonds, and the impact on pipeline demand of a lack of liquidity, margin pressure and higher financing costs in the wholesale market for rough diamonds.

Synthetic diamonds for industrial use have been produced since the mid-1950s by a number of companies, including De Beers, using a method that simulates the intense heat present in the geological formation of diamonds. These stones, which are always very small, account for about 90% of all industrial diamond use, and have a wide variety of industrial applications. The USA, which is the main user of industrial diamonds, is also the leading producer of synthetic diamonds.

GOLD

Gold minerals commonly occur in quartz and are also found in alluvial deposits and in rich thin underground veins. In South Africa gold occurs in sheets of low-grade ore (reefs) which may be at great depths below ground level. Gold is associated with silver, which is its commonest by-product. Uranium oxide is another valuable by-product, particularly in the case of South Africa. Depending upon its associations, gold is separated by cyaniding, or else is concentrated and smelted.

Gold, silver and platinum are customarily measured in troy weight. A troy pound (now obsolete) contains 12 ounces, each of 480 grains. One troy oz is equal to 31.1 grams (1 kg = 32.15 troy oz), compared with the avoirdupois oz of 28.3 grams.

In modern times the principal function of gold has been as bullion in reserve for bank notes issued. Since the early 1970s, however, the USA has actively sought to 'demonetize' gold and so make it simply another commodity. This objective was later adopted by the IMF, which has attempted to end the position that gold occupied for many years in the international monetary system (see below).

Gold was discovered near Johannesburg, South Africa, in 1884, and its exploitation formed the basis of the country's subsequent economic prosperity. For many years, South Africa has been the world's leading gold producer, accounting in 2006 for 11.8% of world output, and for 55% of that mined in Africa. Since the mid-1980s, however, the South African gold industry has been adversely affected by the rising costs of extracting generally declining grades of ore from ageing and increasingly marginal (low-return) mines. Additionally, the level of world gold prices has not been sufficiently high to stimulate the active exploration and development of new mines. The share of gold in South Africa's export revenue has accordingly declined in recent years, and in 1989, for the first time, the commercial profitability of South African gold production was exceeded by profits from mining activities other than gold. In 1996 South Africa's gold production fell to less than 500 metric tons for the first time since 1956. Output continued to fall in 1997 and 1998, although the gold-mining industry substantially reduced its costs. Production declined further in 1999, to its lowest level for 45 years, and again, by 4.7%, in 2000. In 2001, at just under 394 tons, South Africa's output of gold was 8.1% lower than in the previous year. Production recovered, albeit slightly, by 0.4%, in 2002, to about 395 tons. In 2003, however, output declined again, by almost 5%, to 375.8 tons. In 2004 South Africa's output of gold, at 342.7 tons, was 8.8% lower than in 2003. The fall in production in 2004 was attributed, among other things, to shaft closures and suspensions. In 2005, for the first time since 1925, South Africa produced less than 300 tons of gold: at 296.3 tons, output was 13.5% lower than in 2004. The fall in year-on-year production in 2005—46 tons—was reportedly the heaviest single-year loss in terms of tonnage since 1995. Analysts attributed the decline in output in 2005 to the closure, suspension or scaling down of operations at several shafts in order to safeguard reserves pending the eventual return of economic conditions under which it would be possible to exploit them profitably; and to check losses. In 2006 gold production fell for the fourth consecutive year, declining by 7%, to 291.8 tons. The restriction of activity at several shafts for security reasons was partly blamed for the decrease.

Although South Africa remains the world's principal gold producer, the relative decline of its position in world gold markets has been accompanied by substantial increases in output as new capacity has been brought into production in Australia, Brazil, Canada, Indonesia, Papua New Guinea and the USA. Following the dissolution of the USSR in 1991, the successor republics, notably Russia (which accounted for about two-thirds of Soviet output) and Uzbekistan (which contains what is reputedly the world's largest open-cast gold mine), have assumed an increasingly significant role in international gold trading, particularly following the abolition in 1997 of Russia's state monopoly on gold purchases. However, the rate of advance of the gold-mining sector has been inhibited by a number of adverse short-term factors (which have included unpaid debts, shortages of mining equipment, transport difficulties and sharp rises in the cost of electric power). During the late 1990s, however, there was an increase in foreign financial participation in the development of gold deposits in Russia, as well as in Uzbekistan, Kazakhstan, Kyrgyzstan and Armenia. The People's Republic of China, with more than 1,200 operating gold mines in 2005, has consistently increased its output of gold since 1999, when a 1.5% decline in production was believed to represent the first reverse in the country's annual output for about 20 years. In 2000 Chinese output increased by 5.8%, to about 172 metric tons. Production increased by almost 12%, to some 193 tons, in 2001, and by a further 4.7%, to about 202 tons, in 2002. In 2003 Chinese output rose by 1.8%, to some 206 tons. Chinese gold production continued to rise in 2004, increasing by 5.7%, to some 217 tons, and in 2005, by another 3.1%, to 230 tons. In 2006 China's output grew considerably, by 8%, to total 247 tons.

Ghana, formerly a significant African producer of gold, had begun, from 1990, to reverse a long period of decline. Output doubled during 1990–92, and increased in 1993 and 1994 as a result of the continuing rehabilitation of the country's gold industry. Following a minor setback in 1996, the country's gold output advanced each year during 1997–99. In 2000, however, production declined by 5.6%, mainly as a result of technical problems. Further declines in output, of, respectively, 2.8% and 2%, occurred in 2001 and 2002. In 2003 Ghanaian output declined by a further 2%, and in 2004 it fell heavily, by 16.1%, to only 57.8 metric tons, its lowest level since 1997. About 40% of this fifth consecutive decline was attributed to reduced output resulting from technical problems at AngloGold Ashanti's Obuasi and Bibiani operations. The closure of the country's Bonte mine was an additional factor. In 2005 Ghana's production of gold recovered to 62.8 tons., and increase of 8.7%. According to analysts, an increase in output at the Tarkwa open pit, a joint venture operated by Gold Fields and IAMGOLD, made a substantial contribution to the rise in production in 2005. Informal and small-scale producers were also reported to have raised output in response to higher gold prices in 2005. Ghanaian output continued to increase, rising by 12% to reach a four-year high of 70.2 tons in 2006. This substantial increase was largely attributed to the exploitation of two new mines—Red Back's Chicano, which became operational in October 2005, and Newmont's Ahafo, which began processing ore in July 2006. In 2004 some 10 gold mines, open pits or other exploited deposits constituted Ghana's production base. The Obuasi mine, with more than 60 tons of proven and probable reserves, is one of the world's largest. Golden Star Resources Ltd was reported to have commissioned the Wassa mine in late 2004. Reserves at Wassa were assessed at some 19 tons, containing approximately 2.5 tons of gold. In 2004 revenue from foreign sales of gold was estimated to have contributed about 95% of all export revenue generated by Ghana's mining sector. Exports of gold accounted for about 36% of Ghana's foreign revenue in 2003. The proportion decreased to 7% in 2004, but rose significantly again in 2006, reflecting both a 13.2% increase in export volume and to a 26% rise in the world price of gold.

Gold was overtaken in 1980 by tobacco as Zimbabwe's major source of foreign exchange. There, in recent years, the gold-mining industry has contracted substantially as a result of closures and rationalizations. In 2004, after four consecutive years of decline, output increased by almost 18%, to 24.3 metric tons. In 2005, however, production fell to its lowest level—19 tons—for 15 years. Zimbabwe's gold sector was reported to have suffered in particular from insufficient capital, inadequate infrastructure and supply shortages in 2005. The same adverse conditions prevailed in 2006, when production fell by a further 14%, to 16.8 tons. Gold production in Mali increased substantially during 1997–2002, reflecting the exploitation of deposits at Sadiola Hill, with a projected capacity of 11 tons per year. Output rose by almost 20% in 2000, following the commissioning of two new mines during 1999, and by almost 47% in 2001. In 2002 production rose by almost 25%, but this was followed by a decline of some 15% in 2003. In 2004 Mali's output fell by a further 16.1%, to 39.6 tons. Reduced production in 2004 was attributed to the exploitation of lower ore grades at the Morila mine. In 2005, however, output recovered by almost 16%, to 45.9 tons. Gold production rose again, by 17%, to a substantial 54 tons. Analysts attributed the increase mainly to the contribution of two newly commissioned mines. In 2004 gold was Mali's most important source of export revenue, accounting for almost 56% of the country's total export earnings; it continued to account for an absolute majority of Mali's export revenue in 2005 and 2006. Output in Guinea rose by almost 65% in 1998 with the entry into production of the Siguiri mine, operated by Ashanti Goldfields. The Siguiri mine accounted for more than one-half of Guinea's total output of gold in 1999. Output by Guinea increased consistently in 1999–2002, but declined by 3.4% in 2003. In 2004 Guinea's production of gold fell by a further 20.2%, to 13.4 tons. In 2005, however, there was a substantial recovery, of about 10%, in output, to 14.8 tons, which improvement was consolidated in 2006 by a further increase in production (of 9%), to 16.1 tons. Tanzania's first large-scale gold mine commenced operations in November 1998. Production began in June 2000 at another Tanzanian mine, the Geita project, which is the largest producer of gold in East Africa; and, in 2001, at Bulyanhulu. In 2002 a fourth large-scale, modern mine commenced production. Tanzania recorded an increase of almost 87% in its output in 2000, and in 2001 production almost doubled. Further increases in output, of 14.2% and 15.5% respectively, were recorded in 2002 and 2003. In 2004 Tanzania's output rose by a further 7.4%, to 47.9 tons, and the country thus displaced Mali as Africa's third largest producer of gold. Tanzania retained this status in 2005, with production of 48.9 tons. In 2006, however, when its output fell to 44.2 tons, Tanzania was again overtaken by Mali.

Production of Gold Ore
(metric tons, gold content)

	2005	2006
World total	2,550.5	2,471.1
Africa	546.8	530.0
Leading African producers		
Ghana	62.5	70.2
Guinea	14.8	16.1
Mali	46.1	54.0
South Africa	315.1	291.8
Tanzania	48.9	44.2
Zimbabwe	19.5	16.8
Leading non-African producers		
Australia	263.0	244.5
Brazil	45.2	49.7
Canada	119.5	104.5
China, People's Repub.	229.8	247.2
Indonesia	166.4	114.1
Papua New Guinea	69.2	60.4
Peru	207.8	203.3
Russia	175.4	172.8
USA	262.3	251.8
Uzbekistan	79.3	78.5

Source: Gold Fields Mineral Services Ltd.

World supply of gold, after allowing for central bank transactions and not including scrap, totalled 3,586 metric tons in 1997, including net official sales of 326 tons. In 1998, despite a rise in gold output, world supply, other than scrap, declined to 3,034 tons (including net official sales of 363 tons). However, supply from old gold scrap (mostly jewellery) reached 1,105 tons, an increase of more than 75% on the 1997 total. In 1999 the world supply of gold totalled 3,585 tons, an increase of 551 tons on the previous year. Supply from old gold scrap fell by 490 tons, to 615 tons. East Asian supply from scrap declined from 663 tons in 1998 to 152 tons in 1999. The main sources of scrap in 1999 were India (82 tons) and Saudi Arabia and Yemen (63 tons). In 2000 the world supply of gold fell by 144 tons, to 3,401 tons, including net official sales of 479 tons. Supply from old gold scrap in that year, at 616 tons, was at almost exactly the same level as in the previous year. In 2001 the world supply of gold declined again, by 220 tons, to 3,181 tons, including net official sales of 520 tons. An increase of slightly less than 100 tons, to 713 tons, was recorded in the supply from old gold scrap in that year. The world supply of gold declined for a third consecutive year in 2002, to total 3,159 tons, a fall of 22 tons compared with the previous year. Supply from old gold scrap rose to 841 tons in 2002. In 2003, however, the world supply of gold totalled 3,237 tons, an increase of 78 tons compared with 2002. A further increase in the supply from old gold scrap, to 944 tons, was recorded in 2003. The declining trend in the world supply of gold resumed in 2004, when it fell by 242 tons to total 2,995 tons, including net official sales of 469 tons. Supply from old gold scrap declined to 849 tons in 2004. A slight increase in the world supply of gold, to 3,225 tons, including net official sales of 674 tons, was recorded in 2005. In that year supply from old gold scrap amounted to 886 tons, of which India was the source of 94 tons and Saudi Arabia and Yemen the source of about 82 tons. In 2006 the world supply of gold fell again, by 429 tons, to 2,796 tons. A fall of 346 tons in official sales of gold was the main factor behind the decline. In that year, however, scrap supply increased by 25% and contributed 28% of global supply.

World demand for gold, including the former Eastern bloc countries, which totalled 4,017 metric tons in 2000, declined to 3,894 tons in 2001, but rose slightly, to 4,000 tons, in 2002. In 2003 world demand for gold totalled 4,181 tons, but it declined in 2004 to 3,844 tons. In 2005 an increase of 267 tons was recorded in world demand for gold, which rose to 4,111 tons. World demand declined, by 209 tons, to 3,906 tons in 2006. Requirements for jewellery fabrication, which accounted for 3,204 tons (80%) in 2000, declined to 3,008 tons (77.2%) in 2001, and to only 2,660 tons (66.5%) in 2002, its lowest level since 1994. In 2003 a further decline in requirements for jewellery fabrication, to 2,482 tons (59.4%), was recorded. In 2004, however, gold requirements for jewellery fabrication increased somewhat, to 2,613 tons—68% of total demand. In 2005 jewellery fabrication accounted for 2,707 tons, or about 66%, of total world demand for gold. Gold demand for jewellery fabrication declined to 2,280 tons in 2006, while the share of jewellery fabrication in world demand fell to its lowest level for 10 years, 58%. Gold requirements for use in the electronics sector rose by 9%, to some 304 tons, in 2006. Of total gold fabrication in 2006 (2,918 tons), the principal consuming countries were India (21.5%), China (9.2%), (Turkey (8.2%), Italy (7.8%), and the USA (7.3%).

The fabrication of official coins is another important use of gold bullion, although the demand for these coins has declined since the mid-1980s. South African 'krugerrand' coins, containing exactly 1 troy oz of pure (24-carat) gold, were first issued in 1970 and held about 70% of the world market for gold bullion coins until 1985, when international sales virtually ceased, owing to the prohibition of krugerrand imports (during 1986–90) by Japan, the European Community and the USA. A number of other countries, notably Australia, Canada, Austria, Japan and the USA, entered the gold coin market and subsequently benefited from the krugerrand embargo. However, the popularity of these bullion coins in general has been declining in recent years. Following exceptional interest in 1995 in an Austrian gold coin issue, together with the minting of a US Olympic commemorative coin, underpinning a demand increase of 27.3%, the official coin sector in 1996 relapsed to its lowest level of fabrication since 1973. Production of the 'eagle' bullion coin by the US Government led to a substantial revival in 1997, when coin fabrication demand rose internationally by 50.4%. The maintenance of investment interest in official coins in 1998 raised demand by 24.4%. However, demand for US and Canadian issues of coins commemorating the forthcoming millennium failed to make a significant impact on this sector in 1999, when fabrication demand advanced by only 5.1%. In 2000 international coin fabrication demand fell steeply, by 50%, as the result of a collapse in US demand for that purpose. Demand for coin fabrication recovered in 2001 by about 7%, and again in 2002, when it rose by about 17.3%. In 2003, for the third consecutive year, coin fabrication demand increased, by 9.9%. There was a further rise, of 7.2%, in coin fabrication demand in 2004. In 2005 it declined slightly, by 2.6%, but it rose again, by some 16%, in 2006. This substantial increase was attributed mainly to the successful launch of a 'buffalo coin' in the USA.

As a portable real asset which is easily convertible into cash, gold is widely esteemed as a store of value. Another distinguishing feature of gold is that new production in any one year is very small in relation to existing stocks. Much of the world's gold is in private bullion stocks, held for investment purposes, or is hoarded as a 'hedge' against inflation. Private investment stocks of gold throughout the world are estimated at 15,000–20,000 metric tons, much of it held in East Asia and India.

During the 19th century gold was increasingly adopted as a monetary standard, with prices set by governments. In 1919 the Bank of England allowed some South African gold to be traded in London, United Kingdom, 'at the best price obtainable'. The market was suspended in 1925–31, when sterling returned to a limited form of the gold standard, and again between 1939–54. In 1934 the official price of gold was fixed at US $35 per troy oz, and, by international agreement, all transactions in gold had to take place within narrow margins around that price. In 1960 the official gold price came under pressure from market demand. As a result, an international gold 'pool' was established in 1961 at the initiative of the USA. This 'pool' was originally a consortium of leading central banks with the object of restraining the London price of gold in case of excessive demand. It later widened into an arrangement by which eight central banks agreed that all purchases and sales of gold should be handled by the Bank of England. However, growing private demand for gold continued to exert pressure on the official price, and the gold 'pool' was ended in 1968, in favour of a two-tier price system. Central banks continued to operate the official price of $35 per troy oz, but private markets were permitted to deal freely in gold. However, the free-market price did not rise significantly above the official price.

In August 1971 the USA announced that it would cease dealing freely in gold to maintain exchange rates for the dollar within previously agreed margins. This 'floating' of the dollar against other major currencies continued until December, when it was agreed to raise the official gold price to $38 per oz. Gold prices on the free market rose to $70 per oz in August 1972. In February 1973 the US dollar was devalued by a further 10%, the official gold price rising to $42.22 per oz. Thereafter the free-market price rose even higher, reaching $127 per oz in June 1973. In November it was announced that the two-tier system would be terminated, and from 1974 governments were permitted to value their official gold stocks at market prices.

In 1969 the IMF introduced a new unit for international monetary dealings, the special drawing right (SDR), with a value of US $1.00, and the first allocation of SDRs was made on 1 January 1971. The SDR was linked to gold at an exchange rate of SDR 35 per troy oz. When the US dollar was devalued in December 1971 the SDR retained its gold value and a new parity with the US dollar was established. A further adjustment was made following the second dollar devaluation, in February 1973, and in July 1974 the direct link between the SDR and the US dollar was ended and the SDR was valued in terms of a weighted 'basket' of national currencies. At the same time the official gold price of SDR 35 per troy oz was retained as the IMF's basis for valuing official reserves.

In 1976 the membership of the IMF agreed on proposals for far-reaching changes in the international monetary system. These reforms, which were implemented on a gradual basis during 1977–81, included a reduction in the role of gold in the international system and the abolition of the official price of gold. A principal objective of the IMF plan was achieved in April 1978, when central banks were able to buy and sell gold at market prices. The physical quantity of reserve gold held by the IMF and member countries' central banks as national reserves has subsequently fallen (see below). The USA still maintains the largest national stock of gold, although the volume of its reserves has been substantially reduced in recent years. At the end of 1949 US gold reserves were 701.8m. oz, but since the beginning of the 1980s the level has been in the range of 261.4m.–264.6m. oz. At the end of 2006 the total gold reserves held by members of the IMF, excluding international financial organizations and countries not reporting, amounted to 976.57m. oz (30,375 metric tons), of which the USA had 29.7%.

In June 1996 the Group of Seven (G-7) major industrialized countries considered proposals by the United Kingdom and the USA whereby the IMF would release for sale between US $5,000m.–$6,000m. of its $40,000m. gold reserves to finance debt relief for the world's poorest countries, principally in Africa. The plan, which was opposed by Germany, on the grounds that it could prompt demands for similar gold sales by its central bank, remained the subject of discussion within the IMF during 1997. In the spring of 1999 the G-7 endorsed a revised proposal whereby the IMF would sell about 10% of its holdings of gold to provide debt relief for 36 of the world's poorest countries. Under the plan, the proceeds of the IMF disposals would be invested and the resulting revenue used to amortize IMF loans to the designated countries. However, in response to concerns that these disposals by the IMF and central banks would depress world gold prices further (see below) and seriously affect gold-producing countries, the IMF announced in September that the operation was to be restricted at the time to 'off-market' sales. to members having repayment obligations. Between December 1999 and April 2000 13m. oz of gold were 'sold' to Brazil and Mexico at prevailing market prices, and the profit on the sales was placed in special accounts designated for debt relief. Brazil and Mexico then immediately returned the same gold to the IMF, at the same price that they had paid for it, in order to settle debt repayments falling due.

During 1996 substantial amounts of gold bullion, jointly exceeding 500 metric tons, were sold by the central banks of Belgium and the Netherlands, and the Swiss National Bank announced its intention to allocate part of its gold reserves to fund a new humanitarian foundation. In July 1997 the Reserve Bank of Australia announced that it had disposed of more than two-thirds of its bullion holdings (reducing its reserves from 247 tons to 80 tons) over the previous six months. In October a Swiss government advisory group recommended the sale of more than one-half of Switzerland's gold reserves, and in December the Government of Argentina disclosed that it had sold the bulk of its gold reserves during a seven-month period earlier in the year. During 1997 loans to the market of official stocks of gold were carried out by the central banks of Germany, the Netherlands and Switzerland, and in March 1998 Belgium's central bank disposed of one-half of its gold reserves. In April 1999 the Government of Switzerland implemented constitutional changes that removed the requirement for gold to support the national currency. In May the British Government announced that it intended to reduce its gold reserves by 415 tons, to 300 tons, over several years, including the offering for sale of 125 tons in the year to March 2000. The initial disposal, of 25 tons, followed in July 1999, and the second auction of British gold reserves, again offering 25 tons, took place in September. In response to concerns that the official sector's unco-ordinated gold sales were depressing gold prices, later that month the European Central Bank (ECB), in a joint statement with the central banks of Switzerland and 13 members of the European Union (Sweden, the United Kingdom and the 11 in the eurozone), announced a five-year moratorium on new sales of gold held in official reserves. Total gold reserves held by the 15 signatory banks totalled 16,336 metric tons, accounting for around 48% of global gold reserves. The agreement—referred to as the Central Bank Gold Agreement (CBGA) and also known as the Washington Agreement on gold—allowed impending sales that had already been decided to proceed, although total sales were not to exceed 400 tons per year over the five-year period. The announcement also stated that gold would remain an important element of global monetary reserves. The European agreement was generally welcomed for removing uncertainty from the gold market, although the permitted rate of sales (400 tons per year) was more than 100% greater than the average net sales by the signatory countries in 1989–98. In March 2004 the renewal of the CBGA was announced, to cover the five-year period from September 2004 to September 2009, without the United Kingdom, but with Greece as a new signatory. The second CBGA ended the moratorium on sales not already decided, and annual sales quotas were raised to 500 tons, in order to take into account the consolidation of the price of gold that had occurred. In 2006 gold reserves held by the CBGA signatories amounted to 12,754 tons, and constituted 42% of global official sectors' holdings.

The unit of dealing in international gold markets is the 'good delivery' gold bar, weighing about 400 oz (12.5 kg). The principal centres for gold trading are London, Hong Kong and Zürich, Switzerland. The dominant markets for gold 'futures' (buying and selling for future delivery) are the New York Commodity Exchange (COMEX) and the Tokyo Commodity Exchange (TOCOM).

Gold Prices on the London Bullion Market
(afternoon 'fixes', US $ per troy oz)

	Average	Highest	Lowest
1995	384.05		
2000	279.11		
2004	409.7	454.2 (2 Dec.)	375.0 (10 May)
2005	444.4	536.5 (12 Dec.)	411.1 (8 Feb.)
2006	603.8	725.0 (12 May)	524.7 (5 Jan.)

A small group of dealers meet twice on each working day (morning and afternoon) to 'fix' the price of gold in the London Bullion Market, and the table above is based on the second of these daily 'fixes'. During any trading day, however, prices may fluctuate above or below these levels. In the early months of 1999 the London price of gold remained generally within the range of US $280–$295 per oz, but from May, when the proposal for official British gold sales was announced (see above), the market moved steadily downward. The first of a planned series of gold auctions by the Bank of England took place in early July, when 804,000 oz (25 metric tons) were sold at $261.2 (£166.3) per oz. Two weeks later, the London price of gold slumped to $252.8 (£161.1) per oz: its lowest level, in terms of US currency, since May 1979. By the end of July 1999, as the dollar weakened, the sterling equivalent of the US currency price had fallen to only £157.8 per oz. The gold market remained depressed in August, when the London price was again below $253 per oz. In September the sterling equivalent of the dollar price was reduced to £157.0 per oz. Later that month the second Bank of England auction took place, with 804,000 oz (25 tons) of gold sold for $255.75 per oz. However, by the end of September, following the announcement by European central banks that they would restrict sales of gold (see above), the metal's price had risen to more than $300 per oz, and in early October the London quotation reached $330 (almost £200): its highest level for about two years. However, the surge in prices was short-lived. In late November the third sale of official British gold reserves realized $293.5 per oz for the 25 tons on offer. In early December, following the Dutch central bank's announcement of plans to sell gold (see above), the London price of the metal eased to $276.1 (£170.5) per oz. The gold price ended a year of extreme fluctuations at $290.8 (£180.4) per oz, 1.1% higher than its level at the end of 1998. For 1999 as a whole, however, the average London gold price was only $278.6 per oz—5.3% below the 1998 average and the lowest annual level, in nominal terms, since 1978. In real terms (i.e. taking inflation into account), the average price of gold in 1999, measured in US dollars, was the lowest since 1972. Despite the closure of several loss-making mines, global production of gold increased in 1999, although more slowly than in 1998. However, as in other recent years, a major influence on the bullion market in 1999 was the activity of central banks, both through actual sales and lending of gold and through reports of planned disposals.

Gold prices remained relatively stable during the opening weeks of 2000, and in late January the Bank of England sold another 25-metric ton offering at US $289.5 per oz. However, in early February, following the announcement by a leading Canadian gold-mining group that it was suspending 'hedging' operations (forward selling of borrowed gold to protect against falling prices), the London price reached $316.6 (£198.2) per oz. The Bank of England's fifth auction of 25 tons of gold, held in March, realized $285.25 per oz, but later that month the London price of the metal declined to $275.9 (£173.1) per oz. At the next sale of British gold reserves, in May, the 25 tons on offer were sold for $275.25 per oz. Later that month the London price of gold stood at $270.5 (£183.3) per oz. In July the Bank of England auctioned a further 25 tons of gold, which sold for $279.75 per oz. At the subsequent auction, held in September, the 25 tons offered by the Bank of England realized an allotment price of $270.60 per oz, compared with the morning 'fix' on the day of the sale of $272 per oz. At the time of the auction the strength of the US dollar was reported to be exerting strong downward pressure on the price of gold. For 2000 overall the average London price of gold was $279.1 (£187.04) per oz. Gold traded within a range of $263.8 per oz and $312.7 per oz in 2000, equivalent to 17.5%, compared with 26.1% in 1999.

In early February 2001 the London price of gold fell below US $260 per oz. The decline was attributed to the deceleration of the US economy, and to a marked increase in forward selling of gold by mining companies. In March the final 25-metric ton sale of gold by the Bank of England achieved an allotment price of $266 per oz, slightly lower than the morning 'fix' ($267.45 per oz) on the day of the sale. The lowest 'fix' of the year, $256.0 per oz, occurred on 2 April. By late April the price of gold had established itself in a range of $250–$270 per oz. On 20 May the price of gold rose by 7%, its biggest daily increase for almost two years, closing at $290 per oz, compared with the afternoon 'fix' of $291.25 per oz. Rumours that the Bank of China was converting reserves hitherto held in US dollars into gold, and concern about the possibility of the re-emergence of inflation in the USA, were reportedly among the reasons for the sudden increase. By mid-May, however, the London price had declined considerably. The auction at that time by the Bank of England of a 20-ton lot of gold realized a price of $268 per oz. The London price had recovered to $274.55 per oz by late June, and it remained at about that level in late August. On 12 September a further 20 tons of gold was auctioned by the Bank of England, achieving a price of $280 per oz, compared with the afternoon 'fix' of the previous day of $287 per oz. In the aftermath of the suicide attacks against the mainland USA on 11 September, the London price of gold rose as high as $294.30. The highest 'fix' of the year, $293.3 per oz, was recorded on 17 September. By mid-October, however, the role of gold as a secure 'haven' for funds in a period of global political and economic uncertainty appeared to have diminished substantially, the London quotation having fallen to $281.85 per oz on 11 October. For 2001 overall the London price of gold averaged $271.0 per oz; this was the lowest average price, even in nominal terms, since 1978, and 3% lower than the average price in 2000.

In 2002 the lowest afternoon 'fix' of the year, US $277.8 (£192.6) per oz, occurred in the first week of January, while the highest, $349.3 (£218.1) per oz, was recorded in the final week of December. The average price of gold in 2002, at $309.7 (£206.1) per oz, was 14% higher than the average price recorded in 2001. While this was, in percentage terms, the greatest year-on-year increase since 1987, and the greatest increase within a single year since 1979, commentators noted that, in real terms, the average price of gold in 2002 was at its lowest level since 1972. Price volatility (i.e. the percentage of the annual average price represented by the range between the highest and lowest prices recorded during the year) was 23.1% in 2002. The continued reduction of 'hedging' activity by producers, increased resort to gold by investors, and a more sanguine assessment of market conditions were among the factors cited by observers as responsible for the rally that occurred in 2002, in spite of a substantial decline in demand for gold for fabrication purposes.

In 2003 the lowest afternoon 'fix' of the year, US $319.9 (£205.8) per oz, was recorded at the end of the first week of April, while the highest, $416.3 (£240) per oz, occurred on 30 December. In 2003 the average price of gold, at $363.3 (£222.2) per oz, was 17.3% higher than the average price recorded in 2002. The year-on-year increase thus overtook that recorded in 2002 as the highest since 1987. The intra-year increase recorded in 2003, 21.1%, was the second highest since 1979. Price volatility was 16.5% in 2003, the second highest such measurement recorded since 1990. Commentators noted, however, that this relatively high level of volatility applied only to the dollar-denominated price. In 2003 the trading range of gold in terms of, for example, the euro was less than two-thirds of that of the range in terms of the US dollar. Indeed, observers noted that the rally in the price of gold that occurred in 2003 was to a large extent confined to the dollar-denominated price: in terms of other currencies the price of gold rose to a lesser degree, and in some cases it declined. Investment interest, driven in the first half of the year by uncertainty arising from the war in Iraq, was identified as the most important factor behind the rise in the price of gold in 2003. The increased interest of so-called 'hedge' and commodity trading funds in gold was sufficient to outweigh less positive fundamental factors, such as an increase in supplies of gold from all sources, in particular official sector sales, which rose by 11% to reach their highest level since 1992; a 4% decline in fabrication demand, compared with 2002; and a fall in demand from the jewellery sector to its lowest level since 1991.

In 2004 the average London price of gold, at US $409.2 per oz, was almost 13% higher than the average recorded in 2003. During the year gold traded within a range of $375 per oz—the lowest 'fix' of the year, recorded in May—and $454 per oz, the highest 'fix', recorded in December, which represented a 16-year 'high' in nominal terms and was the highest price since 1996 in real terms. Analysts noted that, as in 2003, the rally in the price of gold was far more emphatic in terms of the US dollar than in those of other currencies, expressed in some of which—the South African rand, for example—the price of gold declined in 2004. The rise in the price in terms of the US dollar was attributed to continued high investor interest in the metal, substantial reductions in the supply of gold and a robust performance by the gold fabrication sector. Compared with the sharp intra-year rises in the price of gold that occurred in 2002 and 2003, the increase, of 4.9%, recorded in 2004 was more modest. Price volatility, at 14.3%, was also low compared with the two previous years.

The average London price of gold, at US $444.4 per oz, was 8.6% higher in 2005 than the average recorded in 2004. In nominal terms, the 2005 average was at its highest level since 1987, while in real terms the average was the highest recorded for nine years. During 2005 the London p.m. gold 'fix' ranged between $411.1 per oz (February) and $536.5 per oz (December). The highest 'fix' represented a 24-year high in nominal terms, although in real terms the price was matched more recently in 1993. Price volatility in 2005 was 13.3%. Analysts noted that there was a marked increase in price volatility in the second half of 2005 compared with the first. (Volatility was measured at 10%–11% in the first three quarters of 2005, but rose to 20% in the final quarter.) In terms of the US dollar, there was an intra-year gain of 20% in the London price of gold in 2005. In contrast to the apparent trend since 2002, increases in average prices expressed in terms of other currencies were roughly comparable with those which occurred in US dollar terms, and analysts noted that their intra-year gains were, generally, significantly stronger. In terms of the South African rand, the average price of gold rose by 8% in 2005, while in terms of the Australian dollar it increased by 5%. According to analysts, strong demand from the jewellery fabrication sector, reflecting robust Asian economic growth, was the key fundamental factor that supported gold prices in the first half of 2005. However, prices were reportedly checked in the first half of the year by a surge in net official sector sales, in particular by adherents to the CBGA. Markets for gold were characterized by a sudden alteration in the final quarter of 2005. Fabrication demand, notably from India and Turkey, declined abruptly from September, in response to a clear rally in the price of gold from the middle of that month, which analysts interpreted as a response to the rising price of oil. Higher energy prices, in turn, generated concern over inflation, eroding the prospects of the US economy and triggering a surge of over-the-counter investment in gold.

In 2006 the average London price of gold, expressed in US dollars, increased dramatically, by 35.8%, to US $603.8 per oz. In nominal terms the average price was at its highest level since the $614.5 registered in 1980, while in real terms it was the highest price recorded since 1989. During 2005 the London p.m. gold 'fix' ranged between $524.75 (January) per oz and $725.0 per oz (May). The highest 'fix' represented a 26-year record in nominal terms and a 18-year 'high' in real terms. Price volatility, at 24%, was also exceptional, reaching its highest level for 26 years and almost double that recorded for 2005. The intra-year gain, however, was more modest, and, at 19.2%, just below the 2005 intra-year rise. Analysts noted that comparable increases in the price of gold were registered in other currencies. None the less, the rise in the average price was significantly higher when expressed in terms of the South African rand and the Japanese yen, in which average year-on-year increases of, respectively, 43% and 45% were recorded. Intra-year increases in prices were also more accented when expressed in terms of the rand (32%) and the yen (16%), while the intra-year rise expressed in euros—5%—was considerably lower. According to analysts, strong investment demand combined with reduced above-ground supply—derived mainly from diminishing official sales—underpinned the sharp increase in the first five months of the year. Analysts also noted that the decline in the value of the US dollar had contributed to a change in the attitude of official financial institutions towards gold in recent years. For the first time since the mid-1990s countries outside the CBGA group emerged as net buyers of the metal, while the ECB announced that the sales quota for the second CBGA was unlikely to be reached. The fall in June in the price of gold was largely fuelled by speculative selling in response to concerns about the sustainability of prices, while rumours concerning undeclared sales contributed to depress the price of gold in September–October. Russia's announcement, in September, that it planned to raise its gold reserves, and the Chinese central bank's comments on the need to diversify its reserves, contributed to the recovery in the price of gold in the final quarter of the year.

The World Gold Council (WGC), founded in 1987, is an international association of gold-producing companies which aims to promote gold as a financial asset and to increase demand for the metal. The WGC, based in London, had 23 corporate members in 2007.

GROUNDNUT, PEANUT, MONKEY NUT, EARTH NUT

(*Arachis hypogaea*)

This is not a true nut, although the underground pod, which contains the kernels, forms a more or less dry shell at maturity. The plant is a low-growing annual herb introduced from South America, and resembles the indigenous African Bambarra groundnut, which it now outnumbers.

Each groundnut pod contains between two and four kernels, enclosed in a reddish skin. The kernels are highly nutritious because of their high content both of protein (about 30%) and oil (40%–50%). In tropical countries the crop is grown partly for domestic consumption and partly for export. Whole nuts of selected large dessert types, with the skin removed, are eaten raw or roasted. Peanut butter is made by removing the skin and germ and grinding the roasted nuts. The most important commercial use of groundnuts is the extraction of oil. Groundnut oil is used as a cooking and salad oil, as an ingredient in margarine, and, in the case of lower-quality oil, in soap manufacture. The oil is faced with strong competition from soybean, cottonseed and sunflower oils—all produced in the USA. In 2004 groundnut oil was the fourth most important of soft edible oils in terms of production. In 2003 its position in terms of world exports of food oils was ninth.

Production of Groundnuts
(in shell; '000 metric tons)

	2005	2006
World total*	51,300	47,760
Africa*	8,895	8,958
Leading African producers		
Burkina Faso	221	221*
Chad	450†	450*
Congo, Dem. Repub.	368	369
Côte d'Ivoire†	82	85
Egypt	200	180*
Gambia	107†	100*
Ghana	420	520*
Guinea	275	294
Malawi†	92	145
Mali	280	172
Mozambique†	100	104
Niger	139	139
Nigeria	3,478	3,825*
Senegal	703	460*
South Africa	64	74
Sudan	520	540†
Uganda	159	154
Zimbabwe*	160	160

—continued	2005	2006
Leading non-African producers		
Argentina	593	496
China, People's Repub.*	14,399	14,722
India	7,990	4,980
Indonesia	14,670	14,700
Myanmar†	910	910
USA	2,187	1,479
Viet Nam	489	465

* FAO estimate(s).

† Unofficial figure(s).

An oilcake, used in animal feeding, is manufactured from the groundnut residue left after oil extraction. However, trade in this groundnut meal is limited by health laws in some countries, as groundnuts can be contaminated by a mould which generates toxic and carcinogenic metabolites, the most common and most dangerous of which is aflatoxin B_1. The European Community (EC, now the European Union—EU) has banned imports for use as animal feed of oilcake and meal which contain more than 0.03 mg of aflatoxin per kg. The meal can be treated with ammonia, which both eliminates the aflatoxin and enriches the cake. Groundnut shells, which are usually incinerated or simply discarded as waste, can be converted into a low-cost organic fertilizer, which has been produced since the early 1970s.

In recent years more than 90% of the world's groundnut output has come from developing countries. Groundnuts are the most important of Africa's oil seeds and form the chief export crop of Senegal and The Gambia. In 2005, however, exports of groundnut products contributed just 1.3% of The Gambia's total revenue from exports (including re-exports). This poor performance was partially due to a reduced crop in that year, but was compounded by disruption to the processing of the groundnuts caused by transport difficulties, and also by changes in licensing requirements which left one company as the sole operator. In 2004 groundnuts had contributed 13.3% of total revenue from exports. Except when affected by drought, Sudan and South Africa are also important suppliers, and in 2002 South Africa accounted for 10.5% of groundnut exports world-wide. Niger and Mali, formerly significant exporters, have ceased to feature in the international groundnut trade to any great extent, largely as a consequence of the Sahel drought. However, measures to revive the groundnut export sector in Mali were proceeding in the late 1990s, by which time subsistence output had recovered strongly. In 2002 Mali was reported to have exported groundnuts for the first time in more than 10 years. Efforts to establish commercial production in Uganda had, by 2005, enjoyed negligible success, although cultivation was well established at subsistence level. Groundnut harvests in southern Africa, notably in Mozambique, South Africa and Zimbabwe, were also affected by drought during the second half of the 1980s. Subsistence-level production recovered strongly in Zimbabwe in the late 1990s, but Zimbabwe's trade in groundnuts remained minimal in the early 2000s.

African groundnut exports have been declining since the late 1970s, and most African countries grow the nut as a subsistence, particularly storage, crop. Senegal's groundnut production suffered from persistent drought, and also from marketing problems, in the early 1980s; however, subsequent output was substantially aided by government incentives to producers. These measures included the establishment of a groundnut price guarantee fund, which also had the unwelcome effect of attracting smuggled groundnut supplies from the neighbouring state of The Gambia. Output increased dramatically in 1999, to more than 1m. metric tons, compared with about 580,000 tons in 1998, and remained at that level in 2000. In 2001 production declined slightly, to about 887,000 tons, and in 2002 it slumped to only some 261,000 tons. Output recovered somewhat in 2003, to total about 441,000 tons, and, strongly, in 2004, to some 603,000 tons. Production of about 703,000 tons was achieved in 2005, but output again declined, to an estimated 460,000 tons, in 2006.

In recent years prices for groundnut oil have generally been more volatile than those for groundnuts. The average import price of groundnut oil at the port of Rotterdam, in the Netherlands, declined from US $787.7 per metric ton in 1999 to $713.7 per ton, in 2000, and to $680.3 per ton in 2001. In 2002 the average price rose slightly, to $687.1 per ton. From late 2002 the average import price of groundnut oil at Rotterdam rose precipitously, averaging $718 per ton, $771 per ton and $845 per ton, respectively, in the final three months of the year. In March 2003 an average price of $1,195 per ton was recorded, and in July this rose further, to $1,397 per ton. For the whole of 2003 an average price of $1,243.2 per ton was recorded. One factor behind these sharp increases was anticipation of sharply reduced production of groundnuts in 2002/03 as a consequence of weather-related damage to crops in Argentina, India, Senegal and the USA. Additionally, from the final quarter of 2003 the price of groundnut oil was supported by higher demand for, and lower supply of, soybeans world-wide. In 2004 the average import price of groundnut oil at Rotterdam eased somewhat, to $1,161 per ton. In 2005 an average price of $1,060.4 was recorded. During the first six months of 2006 the average import price eased considerably, ranging between $898 per ton (June) and $930 per ton (January). Meanwhile, in 2000 the average import price of groundnuts at Rotterdam rose slightly, from $835.7 per ton in 1999 to $838 per ton. The import price declined slightly in 2001, to $835 per ton, and again, more substantially, to $750.6 per ton, in 2002. From late 2002 the import price at Rotterdam rose steeply, averaging $943 per ton in November. In March 2003 an average price of $1,000 per ton was recorded and the monthly average remained at, or very close to, that level until July, when it fell slightly, to $984 per ton. For the whole of 2003 an average price of $975.7 per ton was recorded. In 2004 the average import price at Rotterdam, at $1,161 per ton, was slightly lower than in the previous year. In 2005 a more substantial decline in the average import price, to $1,060 per ton, was registered. The price continued to decline in 2006, with an annual average of $970 per ton. As of July 2007 the price had recovered significantly, to $1,342 per ton.

The African Groundnut Council, founded in 1964 with headquarters in Lagos, Nigeria, advises its member producing countries (The Gambia, Mali, Niger, Nigeria, Senegal and Sudan) on marketing policies and, for this purpose, has a sales promotion office in Geneva, Switzerland. Western Europe, particularly France, has traditionally been the principal market for African groundnuts.

IRON ORE

The main economic iron ore minerals are magnetite and haematite, which are used almost exclusively to produce pig-iron and direct-reduced iron (DRI). These comprise the principal raw materials for the production of crude steel. Most iron ore is processed after mining to improve its chemical and physical characteristics and is often agglomerated by pelletizing or sintering. The transformation of the ore into pig-iron is achieved through reduction by coke in blast furnaces; the proportion of ore to pig-iron yielded is usually about 1.5 or 1.6:1. Pig-iron is used to make cast iron and wrought iron products, but most of it is converted into steel by removing most of the carbon content. In the mid-1990s processing technology was being developed in the use of high-grade ore to produce DRI, which, unlike the iron used for traditional blast furnace operations, requires no melting or refining. Particular grades of steel (e.g. stainless) are made by the addition of ferro-alloys such as chromium, nickel and manganese.

Iron is, after aluminium, the second most abundant metallic element in the earth's crust, and its ore volume production is far greater than that of any other metal. Some ores contain 70% iron, while a grade of only 25% is commercially exploitable in certain areas. As the basic feedstock for the production of steel, iron ore is a major raw material in the world economy and in international trade. Because mining the ore usually involves substantial long-term investment, about 60% of trade is conducted under long-term contracts, and the mine investments are financed with some financial participation from consumers.

Iron ore is widely distributed throughout Africa, with several countries having substantial reserves of high-grade deposits (60%–68% iron). One of the world's largest unexploited iron ore deposits (an estimated 850m. metric tons, with a metal content of 64.5%) has been located at Belinga, in north-east Gabon. In 2004 representatives of China Metallurgical Equipment Importation and Exportation Co were reportedly studying transport infrastructure requirements for iron ore production at Belinga. Côte d'Ivoire's as yet unexploited resources of iron ore were estimated at 3,000m. tons (40% iron) in 2003. In 2004 Miferso, a project development venture operated by the Senegalese Government, was reported to have agreed the terms for the development by Kumba Resources Ltd (South Africa) of a prefeasibility study for Senegal's Falémé iron ore project. It was anticipated that the project, whose preliminary capital cost was estimated at US $950m., would include a mine with annual capacity of 12m. tons and rail and marine transport infrastructure. Iron ore reserves in Guinea include deposits totalling an estimated 1,000m. tons at Simandou, one of the world's few remaining unexploited iron ore resources. Rio Tinto was reported to be seeking the rights for its development in 2004, with a view to completing a prefeasibility study before 2007.

The continent's leading producer of iron ore is South Africa. In 2004 Kumba Resources Ltd, in which Anglo American PLC of the United Kingdom has a majority share, was upgrading rail infrastructure between its Sishen iron ore mine in Northern Cape Province and Saldanha Bay Port in Western Cape Province. Kumba Resources reportedly aimed in 2004 to initiate the process of expanding annual production capacity at the Sishen mine from 28m. metric tons to 38m. tons. South African iron ore exports, particularly to Japan, have been an important source of foreign revenue since the late 1980s, despite declining world demand for steel. In 2005 Kumba Resources approved the Sishen Expansion Project, which was projected to increase annual output at the mine to 38,000 tons per year by 2009. Meanwhile, also in 2005 Saldhana Bay Port's export capacity was increased to 32,000 tons per year after operation of a second ship loader began.

Production of Iron Ore
(iron content, '000 metric tons)

	2004	2005*
World total	750,981	828,996
Africa	34,268	34,505
Leading African producers		
Algeria	780*	790
Egypt	1,200*	1,300
Mauritania	7,200	7,200
South Africa	24,800*	24,900
Leading non-African producers		
Australia	145,287	162,527
Brazil	174,300	185,000
Canada†	18,016	18,980‡
China, People's Repub.*	105,000	138,000
India	77,200	90,000
Russia	56,200*	56,100
Ukraine	36,000*	37,700
USA	34,460	34,202

* Estimated production.
† Including the metal content of by-product ore.
‡ Preliminary figure.

Source: US Geological Survey.

Among the African producers, the country most dependent on the mineral as a source of foreign exchange is Mauritania, which derived 64.5% of its total export earnings from shipments of iron ore, valued at some US $389.4m., in 2005. In 2004 Belgium, France, Germany and Italy were the main destinations for Mauritania's foreign sales of iron ore. The Société Nationale Industrielle et Minière (SNIM), which has sole responsibility for iron ore production and beneficiation, operated a mining centre at the northern town of Zouérate, three open-pit iron ore mines (at Guelb El Rhein, Kedia d'Idjill and M'Haoudat) and transport infrastructure including a 700-km railway linking the mining centre with port facilities at Nouadhi.

The exploitation of iron ore deposits in Nigeria, unofficially estimated in 1999 to exceed 3,000m. metric tons, commenced in 1986, but output has been at negligible levels since the late 1990s. In 1980 deposits estimated at 20m. tons of ore (50% iron) were identified in the west of Zambia, but these remained unexploited more than 20 years later. In 2000 Tanzania's National Development Corpn was attempting to attract investment in the development of ore reserves estimated at 45m. tons (52% iron) at Liganga. Tanzania's other iron ore resources reportedly include deposits in the Uluguru Mountains, estimated at 8m. tons (40% iron).

Iron ore mining in Angola was beset by civil conflict and abandoned in 1975. Angola holds considerable ore production stockpiles, but the resumption of export trade in the ore depends on the eventual rehabilitation of the 520-km rail link between mines at Cassinga and the coast. The Marampa mine in Sierra Leone has been inactive since the mid-1980s, although plans exist for the eventual resumption of operations to extract its ore deposits, which have an iron content of 69%. In 2004 Liberia was reported to have agreed terms for the transport of abandoned stockpiles of iron ore totalling 800,000 metric tons to China. Additional quantities of abandoned Liberian ore were reportedly available for purchase. Also in 2004, the Liberian Government was reportedly involved in talks with a venture seeking to reopen Liberia's Yekepa iron ore mine, which had ceased operations in 1992. Cline Mining Corpn of Canada reportedly acquired the Bekipsa iron ore deposit in Madagascar in 2004. The multinational conglomerate Mittal Steel signed an agreement with the Liberian Government in 2005 in order to access the 1,000m. metric tons of iron ore reserves in western Liberia. Infrastructure for the project was expected to cost about US $900m.

In 2003, according to data from the International Iron and Steel Institute (IISI), world exports of iron ore totalled about 586m. metric tons, compared with some 531m. tons in 2002. Australia and Brazil were by far the two dominant exporting countries in 2003, jointly accounting for more than 63% of global iron ore shipments. India and Canada, which jointly accounted for a further 14% of world iron ore exports in 2003, were also significant exporters. There has been tremendous growth in imports of iron ore by the People's Republic of China in recent years. In 2003, as the destination for shipments totalling some 148m. tons—compared with about 70m. tons in 1999—China was the world's leading importer, followed by Japan (132m. tons), the Republic of Korea (41m. tons) and Germany (34m. tons). In 2003 imports of iron ore world-wide totalled about 583m. tons, compared with some 531m. tons in 2002. World reference prices are decided annually at a series of meetings between producers and purchasers (the steel industry accounts for about 95% of all iron ore consumption). The USA and the republics of the former USSR, although major steel producers, rely on domestic ore production and take little part in the price negotiations. It is generally accepted that, because of its diversity in form and quality, iron ore is ill-suited to price stabilization through an international buffer stock arrangement.

Increased prices for iron ore products in recent years have been attributed to growth in demand for steel arising from China's rapid ongoing industrialization. The price of Rio Tinto PLC's Hamersley and BHP Billiton Ltd's Mount Newman fine ores for the 2004 fiscal year (April 2004–March 2005) on the Japanese market was 35.99 US cents per 1% iron per long ton unit, an increase of 17% compared with 2003. The price for lump ore was agreed at 45.93 cents per 1% iron per long ton unit, also an increase of 17% compared with the previous year. Price increases for ore shipped to European destinations were of the same order. In January 2005 Companhia Vale do Rio Doce (CVRD) and Arcelor were reported to have agreed to the largest increase in the price of iron ore fines (for the forthcoming contract year) since the early 1980s. F.o.b. prices in 2005 were to rise by 71.5% compared with the previous year. In June 2006 CVRD announced that iron ore price negotiations with Chinese steel-makers had concluded in agreement that the prices of iron ore fines, lumps and pellet feed (Carajás and Southern System) should increase by 19% relative to contracted prices for 2005. In June 2006, BHP Billiton was reported to have reached agreement with a number of Chinese steel-makers on iron ore prices for the 2006 contract year, whereby prices across the range of lump and iron ore fines products were to rise by 19% relative to the previous contract year. The world indicator price of hot rolled coil steel increased from $247 per ton in December 2001 to $648 per ton in December 2004. According to the IMF, the average price of Brazilian ores (Carajás fines, 67.55% Fe content, contract price to Europe—f.o.b. Ponta da Madeira, CVRD, Rio de Janeiro) in 2004 was 38 US cents per dmt unit, compared with 32 cents per dmt unit in 2003 and 29 cents in 2002. According to the US Geological Survey, the price of Carajás fines reached 65 cents per 1% iron per ton in 2005, a 71.5% increase on the previous year on a cents per dmt unit basis.

The Association of Iron Ore Exporting Countries (Association des pays exportateurs de minerai de fer—APEF) was established in 1975 to promote close co-operation among members, to safeguard their interests as iron ore exporters, to ensure the orderly growth of international trade in iron ore and to secure 'fair and remunerative' returns from its exploitation, processing and marketing. In 1995 APEF, which also collects and disseminates information on iron ore from its secretariat in Geneva, Switzerland, had nine members, including Algeria, Liberia, Mauritania and Sierra Leone. The UN Conference on Trade and Development (UNCTAD) compiles statistics on iron ore production and trade, and in recent years has sought to establish a permanent international forum for discussion of the industry's problems.

MAIZE (Indian Corn, Mealies) (*Zea mays*)

Maize is one of the world's three principal cereal crops, with wheat and rice. Originally from America, maize has been dispersed to many parts of the world. The principal varieties are dent maize (which has large, soft, flat grains) and flint maize (which has round, hard grains). Dent maize is the predominant type world-wide, but flint maize is widely grown in southern Africa. Maize may be white or yellow (there is little nutritional difference), but the former is preferred for human consumption in Africa. Maize is an annual crop, planted from seed, and matures within three to five months. It requires a warm climate and ample water supplies during the growing season. Genetically modified varieties of maize, with improved resistance to pests, are now being cultivated, particularly in the USA and also in Argentina and the People's Republic of China. However, further development of genetically modified maize may be slowed by consumer resistance in importing countries and doubts about its environmental impact.

Maize is an important foodstuff in regions such as sub-Saharan Africa and the tropical zones of Latin America, where the climate precludes the extensive cultivation of other cereals. It is, however, inferior in nutritive value to wheat, being especially deficient in lysine, and tends to be replaced by wheat in diets when the opportunity arises. In many African countries the grain is ground into a meal, mixed with water, and boiled to produce a gruel or porridge. In other areas it is made into (unleavened) corn bread or breakfast cereals. Maize is also the source of an oil used in cooking.

Production of Maize
('000 metric tons)

	2005	2006
World total*	712,878	695,288
Africa*	50,424	46,419
Leading African producers		
Benin	865	672*
Cameroon	1,023	850†
Congo, Dem. Repub.	1,155	1,155
Côte d'Ivoire	640	600
Egypt	7,085	6,838
Ethiopia	3,912	4,030
Ghana	1,171	1,189*
Kenya	2,906	3,247
Malawi	1,253†	1,600*
Mozambique	1,403†	1,300*
Nigeria	5,957	6,404*
South Africa	11,716	6,935
Tanzania	3,288	3,373
Uganda	1,170	1,258
Zambia	866	865*
Zimbabwe†	900†	900*
Leading non-African producers		
Argentina	20,483	14,446
Brazil	35,113	42,632
Canada	9,461	9,268
China, People's Repub.*	139,502	145,625
France	14,688	12,902
India	14,172	14,710
Indonesia	12,524	11,611
Italy	10,428	9,671
Mexico	18,012	21,765
Romania	10,388	8,985
USA	282,311	267,598

* FAO estimate(s).
† Unofficial figure(s).

The high starch content of maize makes it highly suitable as a compound feed ingredient, especially for pigs and poultry. Animal feeding is the main use of maize in the USA, Europe and Japan, and large amounts are also used for feed in developing countries in Far East Asia, Latin America and, to some extent, in North Africa. Maize has a variety of industrial uses, including the preparation of ethyl alcohol (ethanol), which may be added to petrol to produce a blended motor fuel. Maize is also a source of dextrose and fructose, which can be used as artificial sweeteners, many times sweeter than sugar. The amounts of maize used for these purposes depend, critically, on its price to the users relative to that of petroleum, sugar and other potential raw materials. Maize cobs, previously discarded as a waste product, may be used as feedstock to produce various chemicals (e.g. acetic acid and formic acid).

In recent years world production of maize has averaged about 645m. metric tons annually. The USA is by far the largest producer, with annual harvests of, on average, about 260m. tons in recent years. In years of drought or excessive heat, however, US output can fall sharply: in 1995, for example, the US maize crop totalled only about 188m. tons. The People's Republic of China, whose output has been expanding rapidly, is now the world's second largest producer. Its annual harvest has averaged about 120m. tons in recent years. The expansion of the biofuels sector was expected to result in a substantial increase global production of maize in the short-to-medium term.

Apart from Egypt, most maize in Africa is grown south of the Sahara. The sub-Saharan region's production has averaged about 27m. tons annually in recent years, varying according to patterns of rainfall. Maize is not grown under irrigation in most of sub-Saharan Africa, as scarce water supplies are reserved instead for export crops with a higher value. Yields are therefore low. In many countries in the region commercial farming is hindered by the lack of foreign exchange to buy essential equipment, as well as fuels and fertilizers. In addition, transport difficulties make marketing expensive and uncertain. In much of Africa maize is a subsistence crop.

The region's main producer is South Africa, which grows both white corn (for human consumption) and yellow corn (for animal feed). It was formerly an exporter of both types (except in years of severe drought), but market deregulation in 1997 altered the economic basis of commercial maize production. In the absence of government support, domestic maize is not competitive with imported maize in the feed mills of the coastal regions, with the result that sowings, particularly of yellow corn, have fallen. White corn production usually exceeds local food requirements, the surplus being exported to neighbouring food-deficit countries. South African production totalled some 11.4m. metric tons in 2000, but declined to only about 8m. tons in 2001. Output in 2002 increased to about 10m. tons, but declined slightly, to about 9.7m. tons, in 2003. Production totalled a little less than 10m. tons in 2004 and increased to about 12m. tons in 2005. However, output totalled just 7m. in 2006. Zimbabwe's maize crop, like that of South Africa, is vulnerable to drought. After good harvests the country exports maize, but recent crops have fallen short of rapidly increasing domestic needs and imports have been necessary to sustain supplies. In Kenya, the influx of large numbers of refugees has added to domestic food requirements, and imports of maize are now required in most seasons. In Nigeria production, which has averaged about 4.8m. tons annually in recent years, totalled an estimated 6.4m. tons. The potential for output growth has been hindered by marketing difficulties and shortages of essential agricultural inputs. Fertilizer supplies have improved since its procurement and distribution were privatized, but prices remain too high for many farmers to use it. Newly introduced maize varieties have improved yields. In the past, an important end-use of maize in Nigeria was for the brewing of beer, but since a ban on imports of barley and barley malt was lifted in 1998, breweries have used less maize.

One of the most notable differences between maize production in developed and developing countries is in yields. In the USA, the continual development of new hybrids and the availability of adequate fertilizer and water supplies have resulted in a substantial increase in yields, interrupted only by the occasional years of drought. Yields exceed 8 metric tons per ha in good years, and in 2007/08, according to the US Department of Agriculture, they were expected to exceed 10 tons per ha. South Africa usually achieves yields of more than 2.5 tons per ha. Yields of at least 2 tons per ha were formerly the norm in Zimbabwe, although they have declined to below 1 ton per ha in recent years. In much of West and Central Africa, however, yields of 1 ton per ha are normal. Although hybrid forms of maize suited to African conditions are being developed, their adoption is hindered in many countries by low producer prices, inefficient marketing arrangements, and, above all, the inability of producers to obtain regular supplies of fertilizers at economic prices.

World trade in maize totalled about 85m. metric tons in 2006/07, compared with some 83m. tons in 2005/06, and around 76m. tons in 2004/05. In the mid-1990s growth in trade was curtailed by adverse economic conditions in eastern Asia, which caused a decline in the region's meat consumption and, consequently, in its demand for animal feed. Improved economic conditions in eastern Asia, together with growing requirements from Latin America and North Africa, subsequently restored that demand.

The pre-eminent maize exporter is the USA, which, with exports of some 53m. metric tons, accounted for about 63% of total world exports in 2006/07. US sales reached more than 60m. tons in 1995/96, but have subsequently declined as a result of increased competition from Argentina, China and a number of countries in Central and Eastern Europe. US exports in 2000–04 averaged about 47m. tons annually. Argentina's exports fell to only around 3m. tons per year in the late 1980s, but grew rapidly in the 1990s. In 2006/07 they amounted to 14.3m. tons, compared with some 10.4m. tons in 2003/04. China was a major maize exporter in the early 1990s, and its sales increased again at the end of the decade as faltering domestic requirements could not absorb a succession of big crops. To reduce the burden of stocks, the Government subsidized its export sales, which reached 6.6m. tons in 1996/97 before falling to 4.7m. tons in the following season. In 1998/99 Chinese exports declined again, to 4.3m. tons, but more than doubled in the following year when they totalled 10.5m. tons, their highest level since 1992/93. After falling again, to some 6m. tons in 2000/01, in 2001/02 Chinese exports rose to 11.7m. tons. China's foreign sales of maize were estimated to have reached a new record level of more than 16m. tons in 2002/03, but subsequently fell heavily: foreign sales amounted to 3.7m. tons, in 2005/06. South Africa was a significant exporter in the 1980s, when annual sales, mostly of white maize, sometimes exceeded 3m. tons. Owing to smaller crop levels, exports in the second half of the 1990s averaged only about 1.3m. tons per year. In 2000–04 South African exports averaged about 644,000 tons annually.

The world's principal maize importer is Japan, which in every year in 1990–2002, except 1994, purchased more than 16m. metric tons in spite of the progressive opening of the Japanese market to imports of meat. Japanese imports of maize totalled about 16m. tons in 2006/07. Feed users in the Republic of Korea are willing to substitute other grains for maize, particularly feed wheat, when prices are attractive, and maize imports are therefore variable, averaging about 8.7m. tons annually in recent years. In 2006/07 imports of maize by the Republic of Korea totalled some 9.2m. tons. The Republic of China (Taiwan) regularly imports about 5.5m. tons of maize annually, but imports by other countries in the region, particularly Indonesia, Malaysia and the Philippines, have fluctuated considerably in recent years as a result of economic instability. In the 1980s the USSR was a major market, but the livestock industries in the successor republics of the USSR declined very sharply during the 1990s, greatly reducing feed needs. From a total of 18m. tons in 1989/90, these imports declined to 4m. tons in 1993/94 and have subsequently fallen to negligible levels.

Maize imports by sub-Saharan Africa vary from around 1m. metric tons annually in years of good crops to far higher amounts after droughts. In 1992/93, for example, these imports exceeded 8m. tons, most of which entered through South African ports, either for that country's own use or for onward transport overland to neighbouring countries.

Massive levels of carry-over stocks of maize were accumulated in the USA during the mid-1980s, reaching a high point of 124m. metric tons at the end of August 1987. Government support programmes were successful in discouraging surplus production, but several poor harvests also contributed to the depletion of these stocks, which were reduced to only 11m. tons at the close of the 1995/96 marketing year. A succession of good crops in the late 1990s, together with increased competition from Argentina and China, led to a substantial rebuilding of US maize stocks, despite steadily rising domestic requirements for feeds, associated with the strong economy. Carry-over stocks were estimated at 53.6m. tons at the end of the 2004/05 marketing year, but decreased in 2006/07 to just 28.9m. tons.

Export prices of maize are mainly influenced by the level of supplies in the USA, and the intensity of competition between the exporting countries. Record quotations were achieved in April 1996, when the price of US No. 2 Yellow Corn (f.o.b. Gulf ports) reached US $210 per metric ton. The quotation subsequently declined, however. In each of the five years in 2000–04 an increase in the quotation was recorded, the average price rising to $88.4 per ton in 2000, $89.6 per ton in 2001, $99.2 per ton in 2002, $105.2 per ton in 2003 and $111.7 in 2004. In 2005, however, the average export price declined to $98.5 per ton. The price rose substantially in 2006, to $122.1 per ton, not least reflecting the impact of increasing demand for ethanol. During the first eight months of 2007 the average monthly price of US No. 2 Yellow Corn (f.o.b. Gulf ports) ranged between $166.2 per ton (January) and $150.9 (August).

MANGANESE

This metal is obtained from various ores containing such minerals as hausmannite, manganite and pyrolusite. The ore is usually washed or hand-sorted and then smelted to make ferromanganese (80% manganese), in which form it is chiefly used to alloy into steel, manganese steel being particularly hard and tough. Almost 95% of manganese produced is thus used in the manufacture of steel, which, on average, consumes about 6 kg of manganese per metric ton. Electrolytic manganese is used to make stainless steel and in the aluminium industry. Minor uses of manganese as oxides are in dry-cell batteries, paints and varnishes, and in ceramics and glass-making.

In 2006 world reserves of manganese were estimated by the US Geological Survey (USGS) at 440m. metric tons, of which about one-third was located in Ukraine. Gabon, Africa's second major producer, had estimated reserves of 20m. tons. About 77% of the world's reserve base of manganese, estimated at 5,200m. tons in 2006, is in South Africa. Until overtaken by Gabon in 1990, South Africa was, during the late 1980s, the world's leading exporter of manganese ore, disposing of almost three-fifths of its mine output through foreign sales. Where possible, South Africa's policy has been to maximize export revenues by shipping as much as possible in processed ferro-alloy form. Export volumes of ferromanganese generally reflect world trends in steel production. The expansion by Gabon of its manganese exports was stimulated by the opening, in 1988, of a new mineral port at Owendo. In 2000 a conglomeration plant, with annual capacity for 600,000 tons of sintered manganese ore, commenced operations at Gabon's Moanda manganese mine. The mine is expected to increase production to 3,500 tons after a planned €30m. expansion project. In future it is planned to produce ferromanganese in Gabon; at present, however, electricity production is not adequate to achieve this. Companhia Vale do Rio Doce (CVRD) of Brazil, via its subsidiary Compagnie Minière Trois Rivières, reportedly planned to invest US $5m. in exploration for manganese in the Franceville and Okondjá regions of Gabon in 2004. At the end of 2005 CVRD began operating a 'pilot' plant in Francevilleto test feasibility. The company announced it would invest $33m. if the study proved positive. Exports of manganese contributed 7.1% of Gabon's total export revenue in 2004.

Ghana, Africa's third most important producer, has benefited from government measures to revive manganese operations, assisted by loan finance from the World Bank. In 2003 Ghana's annual manganese export capacity was assessed at 1.5m. metric tons. Ghana Manganese Company Ltd planned to raise export capacity to more than 1.6m. tons in 2004. The People's Republic of China constitutes a major market for Ghanaian manganese. Burkina Faso has deposits of manganese ore sufficient to establish it as a minor regional producer. These reserves, located at Tambao, 400 km north-west of Ouagadougou, and estimated at 19m. tons, contain an average ore content of 50% manganese. A joint venture between the Government and Canadian interests to develop these resources was formed in 1995, but this was reportedly suspended in the late 1990s. The development of the project had been impeded by the high cost of overland transport relative to the value of raw manganese ore. In 1994 manganese production resumed in Namibia after a lapse of almost 30 years. The Ofjosondu mine, 160 km north-east of Windhoek, was reactivated for production of medium-grade ore having a relatively low phosphorus content. Its initial annual output was projected at about 100,000 tons. Operations were suspended in 1998, owing to financial difficulties, but resumed in 2001. The Democratic Republic of the Congo, once a significant source of manganese exports, has mined only on a sporadic basis since 1980.

Production of Manganese Ore
(manganese content, '000 metric tons)

	2004	2005
World total*	9,630	10,500
Africa†*	3,520	4,003
African producers		
Gabon	1,090	1,290
Ghana	525	613
South Africa	1,905	2,100
Leading non-African producers		
Australia	1,327	1,450
Brazil	1,346	1,529
China, People's Repub.*	1,100	1,100
India*	630	640
Ukraine*	810	770

* Estimates.

† Figures are the sum of output in the listed countries. Small quantities of manganese ore are also produced in Egypt, Morocco and Namibia.

Source: US Geological Survey.

Extensive accumulations of manganese in marine environments have been identified. The characteristic occurrences are as nodules on deep ocean floors and as crusts on seamounts at shallower depths. Both forms are oxidic and are often termed 'ferromanganese' because they generally contain iron and manganese. The main commercial interest in both types of deposit derives from the copper, nickel and cobalt contents also present, which represent large resources of these metals. Attention was focused initially on nodules, of which the Pacific Ocean encompasses the areas with the densest coverage and highest concentration of potentially economic metals. However, the exploitation of nodules has, to date, been impeded by legal, technical and economic factors.

In 2005, according to estimates by the USGS, the average price of metallurgical-grade ore containing 48% manganese was about US $4.39 per metric ton unit. The price of manganese in ore in 2005 was 43.9 US cents per lb, compared with 28.9 cents per lb in 2004. In 2004 the international benchmark price for metallurgical-grade ore increased by 16% compared with the previous year. On an f.o.b. basis per metric ton unit for delivery during the annual contract year, the agreed price (contracted between BHP Billiton Ltd and major Japanese consumers) was $2.46 for ore from the Groote Eylandt mine in Australia. The rise in manganese ore prices was mainly due to higher demand for manganese ferroalloys from the steel industry, in combination with restricted supply and higher transportation costs. Prices of ferromanganese alloys reached record levels in 2004. The benchmark international price for manganese that was negotiated for the 2005 contract year was reportedly a record 63% higher than that which took effect on 1 April 2004. On an f.o.b. basis per metric ton unit for delivery during the annual contract year in 2005, the agreed price (contracted between BHP Billiton Ltd and major Japanese consumers) was $3.99 for ore from the Groote Eylandt mine.

As the above implies, Japanese industrial consumers exert the strongest influence on the international benchmark price of manganese through the annual contracts that they conclude with its producers. Settlements between other consumers are generally based on the South Africa/Japan and Australia/Japan models.

MILLET AND SORGHUM

Millet and sorghum are often grouped together in economic analyses of world cereals, not because of any affinity between the two grains—in fact they are quite dissimilar—but because in many developing countries both are subsistence crops which are little traded. Figures for the production of the individual grains should be treated only as broad estimates in most cases. Data cover only crops harvested for grain.

Data on millet relate mainly to the following: cat-tail millet (*Pennisetum glaucum* or *typhoides*), also known as bulrush millet, pearl millet or, in India and Pakistan, as 'bajra'; finger millet (*Eleusine coracana*), known in India as 'ragi'; common or bread millet (*Panicum miliaceum*), also called 'proso'; foxtail millet (*Setaria italica*), or Italian millet; and barnyard millet (*Echinochloa crus-galli*), also often called Japanese millet.

Production of Millet and Sorghum
('000 metric tons; M = Millet; S = Sorghum)

	2005	2006
World total: M*	30,589	31,783
World total: S*	59,214	56,526
Africa: M*	16,368	17,789
Africa: S*	24,694	26,155
Leading African producers		
Burkina Faso: M	1,196	1,199*
Burkina Faso: S	1,553	1,554
Chad: M	578	590*
Chad: S	583	694*
Egypt: S	853	890
Ethiopia: M	397	500
Ethiopia: S	2,200	2,313
Mali: M	1,158	1,060*
Mali: S	629	730*
Niger: M	2,652	3,200†
Niger: S	944	800†
Nigeria: M	7,168	7,705*
Nigeria: S	9,178	9,866
Senegal: M	609	494
South Africa: S	260	96
Sudan: M†	745	792
Sudan: S†	4,275	5,203
Tanzania: M	155†	185*
Tanzania: S	890†	750*
Uganda: M	672	687
Uganda: S	449	440
Leading non-African producers		
Argentina: S	2,894	2,328
Australia: S	2,011	996
China, People's Repub.: M*	1,789	1,820
China, People's Repub.: S*	2,558	2,490
India: M	10,500	10,100
India: S	7,244	7,240
Mexico: S	5,524	5,487
USA: S	9,981	7,050

* FAO estimate(s).
† Unofficial figure(s).

Sorghum statistics refer mainly to the several varieties of *Sorghum vulgare*, known by various names such as great millet, Guinea corn, kafir or kafircorn (*caffrorum*), milo (in the USA and Argentina), feterita, durra, jowar, sorgo or maicillo. Other species included in the table are Sudan grass (*S. sudanense*) and Columbus grass or sorgo negro (*S. almum*). The use of grain sorghum hybrids has resulted in a considerable increase in yields in recent years.

Millet and sorghum are cultivated particularly in semi-arid areas where there is too little rainfall to sustain maize and the temperature is too high for wheat. These two cereals constitute the staple diet of people over large areas of Africa, India, the People's Republic of China and parts of the former USSR. They are usually consumed as porridge or unleavened bread. Both grains have good nutritive value, but are less palatable than wheat, and tend to be replaced by the latter when circumstances permit. In many African countries sorghum is used to make beer. Sorghum is also produced and used in certain countries in the western hemisphere (particularly Argentina, Mexico and the USA), where it is used mainly as an animal feed, although the high tannin content of some varieties lowers their value as a feed grain.

World production of sorghum has averaged about 58m. metric tons annually in recent years, and Africa has generally accounted for about one-third of the total. The region's major producers are Nigeria, Sudan, Ethiopia and Burkina Faso. Annual world millet production has averaged about 29m. tons in recent years. Sub-Saharan Africa is one of the main producing regions, accounting, on average, for about 48% of the world millet crop in recent years.

Millet and sorghum are grown largely for human consumption, but are gradually being replaced by wheat and rice, as those cereals become more widely available. Only low-grade sorghum is used for animal feed in Africa, but some is used for starch when maize is in short supply. Apart from food and animal feed requirements, sorghum is used in a number of countries in Asia and Africa for the production of beers and other alcoholic liquors.

World trade in sorghum ranges between 6m.–10m. metric tons per year, but has in recent years been closer to the lower end of this range, reflecting the small volume of exportable supplies. The principal exporters are the USA (which in recent years has, on average, accounted for more than 80% of total world exports and holds the greater part of world sorghum stocks), Argentina and Australia. China, South Africa, Sudan and Thailand are occasional exporters. Japan is one of the principal sorghum markets, although its imports have declined in recent years. Mexico's annual sorghum purchases have averaged more than 4m. tons in recent years, but are more likely to vary, as they depend upon the size of the domestic crop and on the relative prices of sorghum and maize. Annual imports of sorghum by sub-Saharan Africa have averaged more than 225,000 tons in recent years. In 2005 Africa's imports of sorghum rose to 575,600 tons, their highest level since 1992. Export prices for sorghum normally closely follow those of maize, although sorghum is generally slightly cheaper. The price of US No. 2 Yellow Sorghum (f.o.b. US Gulf Ports) reached US $200 per ton in May 1996, but has since been in decline. In 1999 it averaged $89 per ton, about $3 per ton less than the average export price of maize (f.o.b. US Gulf ports) for that year. In 2000 the average price of sorghum was about $90 per ton, while the average export price of maize in that year was $88 per ton. In 2001 the average price of sorghum rose by more than 7.5% compared with the previous year, to $97 per ton, while the average price of maize rose to $90 per ton. An average price of $105 per ton was recorded for sorghum in 2002, while the average price of maize was about $99 per ton. In 2003 the average price of sorghum was $109 per ton, compared with an average price for maize of $105 per ton. In March 2004 the average price of sorghum rose as high as $130.5 per ton, but it declined steadily thereafter until the end of the year, averaging, like maize, about $112 per ton for the whole of 2004. In 2005 an average price of $101 per ton was recorded for sorghum, while that of maize was $99 per ton. The average price of sorghum recovered to $130 per ton in 2006, while the price of maize increased significantly, to $122 per ton. During the first eight months of 2007 the average price of sorghum ranged between $175 per ton (January) and $170 per ton (August). Sorghum traded at a slight premium to maize, the average export price of which ranged between $166 and $150 in the same period.

Very little millet enters international trade, and no reliable export price series can be established.

OIL PALM (*Elaeis guineensis*)

This tree is native to West Africa, and grows wild in tropical forests along the coast of that region. The entire fruit is of use commercially; palm oil is made from its pulp, and palm kernel oil from the seed. Palm oil is a versatile product and, because of its very low acid content (4%–5%), it is almost all used in food. It is used in margarine and other edible fats; as a 'shortener' for pastry and biscuits; as an ingredient in ice cream and chocolate; and in the manufacture of soaps and detergents. Palm kernel oil, which is similar to coconut oil, is also used for making soaps and fats. The sap from the stems of the tree can be used to make palm wine, an intoxicating beverage.

Palm oil can be produced virtually through the year once the palms have reached oil-bearing age, which takes about five years. The palms continue to bear oil for 30 years or more and the yield far exceeds that of any other oil plant, with one ha of oil palms producing as much oil as six ha of groundnuts or 10–12 ha of soybeans. However, it is an intensive crop, needing considerable investment and skilled labour.

During the 1980s palm oil accounted for more than 15% of world production of vegetable oils (second only to soybean oil), owing mainly to a substantial expansion in Malaysian output. Assisted by high levels of demand from Pakistan and the People's Republic of China, palm oil considerably increased its share of world markets for vegetable oils in the early 1990s. In the early 2000s palm oil exports continued substantially to exceed those of soybean oil in international trade: in 2004 more than twice the quantity of palm oil than of soybean oil was exported world-wide.

The increase in output of palm oil has posed a particular challenge to the soybean industry in the USA, which has since the mid-1970s greatly reduced its imports of palm oil. In 1988, in response to health reports that both palm and coconut oils tended to raise levels of cholesterol (a substance believed to promote arteriosclerosis in the body), several leading US food processors announced that they were to discontinue the use of these oils. The scientific validity of these reports has, however, been vigorously challenged by palm oil producers.

In Africa a large proportion of oil palms still grow in wild groves, and the bulk of oil production is for local consumption. In export terms, Africa has since 1980 accounted for less than 3% of world trade in palm oil, and in 2004 African exports comprised less than 1% of the world market. Nigeria was the world's leading producer of palm oil until overtaken by Malaysia in 1971. The loss of Nigeria's market dominance was, in part, a result of civil war and the authorities' neglect to replace old, unproductive trees. Since the early 1980s, however, measures have been taken to revive palm oil output and to enhance the efficiency and capacity of associated mills and refineries. Foreign investment has been encouraged, as has the transfer of inefficiently managed state-owned plantations to private sector ownership. A ban by the Nigerian Government on palm oil imports, in force since 1986, was partially relaxed in 1990, as domestic output (of which an estimated 70% came from smallholder producers) was able to satisfy only two-thirds of a forecast annual demand of 900,000 metric tons. Nigeria's reliance on imports subsequently increased, and increases in domestic production now tend to be used for import substitution rather than to boost exports.

Production of Palm Kernels
('000 metric tons)

	2005	2006
World total*	9,908	10,642
Africa*	1,663	1,685
Leading African producers		
Cameroon†	71	75
Congo, Dem. Repub.†	46	47
Côte d'Ivoire†	77	74
Ghana	39†	40*
Guinea	53†	53*
Nigeria*	1,230	1,250
Sierra Leone*	24*	23†
Leading non-African producers		
Brazil*	121	122
Colombia	158	178†
Indonesia†	3,380	3,860
Malaysia†	3,964	4,125
Thailand†	158	191

* FAO estimate(s).
† Unofficial figure(s).

Production of Palm Oil
('000 metric tons)

	2005	2006
World total*	34,326	37,296
Africa*	2,214	2,359
Leading African producers		
Angola†	53	54
Cameroon†	154	160
Congo, Dem. Repub.	175†	175*
Côte d'Ivoire	320	330
Ghana	117†	121*
Guinea	50†	53*
Nigeria	1,170	1,287*
Sierra Leone*	39	36
Leading non-African producers		
Colombia	673	711†
Indonesia†	14,070	15,900
Malaysia	14,962	15,880†
Thailand	685†	685*

* FAO estimate(s).
† Unofficial figure(s).

In Benin, where the oil palm has traditionally been a staple crop of the national economy, oil palm plantations and natural palm groves cover some 450,000 ha. In 1997 exports of palm and palm-kernel oil contributed 0.8% of Benin's total export earnings. Côte d'Ivoire is now usually Africa's principal palm oil exporter—in 2004 its exports were overtaken by those of Ghana—but it no longer attains the rank of fourth largest exporter in the world (behind Malaysia—by far the largest, accounting, on average, for about 50%–60% of all palm oil trade in recent years—Indonesia and Singapore) as it did throughout most of the 1990s. More than one-half of Côte d'Ivoire's palms were planted in 1965–70 and have passed their peak of productivity. Management and financial difficulties during the 1990s, as well as declining world prices for palm oil, led to the scaling-down of a replanting programme. However, following the revival in prices during 1997 and 1998, when Côte d'Ivoire had recourse to imports from Malaysia in order to satisfy domestic demand, plans were announced in 1999 to increase production capacity to 600,000 metric tons annually by 2010. In 2003 Côte d'Ivoire ranked as the world's ninth largest producer-exporter of palm oil. The palm oil sector in Cameroon has similarly experienced delays in the implementation of replanting. The state-owned palm oil company SOCAPALM was transferred to private-sector ownership (90%) in 1999 and renamed PALMCAM/SOGEPAR. Other African producers, notably Liberia and Ghana, lack sufficient refinery capacity to process their palm oil output. Tanzania has received proposals for the construction by Malaysian producers of a palm oil refinery to process its crude palm oil, with initial output forecast at 30,000 tons of edible oils annually. In 1999 a palm oil extraction mill, financed by the Netherlands, commenced production in south-east Tanzania. Uganda, which has potential to develop a palm oil sector, has received international aid to promote its establishment.

Internationally, palm oil is faced with sustained competition from the other major edible lauric oils—soybean, rapeseed and sunflower oils—and these markets are subject to a complex and changing interaction of production, stocks and trade. In the longer term, prospects for palm oil exporters (particularly the higher-cost producers in sub-Saharan Africa) do not appear favourable. Technological advances in oil palm cultivation, particularly in the introduction of laboratory-produced higher-yielding varieties (HYV), may also militate against the smaller-scale producer, as, for economic and technical reasons, many HYV can be produced only on large estates, exposing smallholder cultivators to increasingly intense price pressure.

In 2000 the average import price (c.i.f. North West Europe) of palm oil declined by almost 29%, compared with the previous year, to US $310.3 per metric ton. A further decline in the average European import price, of 7.9%, to $285.7 per ton, occurred in 2001. In 2002, however, the average price increased by 37%, to $390.3 per ton. Prices continued to rise in 2003, when an average price of $443.3 per ton (13.6% higher than the average price in 2002) was recorded; and in 2004, when the Rotterdam import price averaged $471.3 per ton, an increase of 6.3% compared with 2003. In 2005 the European import price averaged $422.1 per ton, a decline of 10.4% compared with the previous year. In mid-2005 palm oil, in particular, was reported to have benefited from increased consumption world-wide of oils and fats, to the point that its utilization was close to that of soybean oil, traditionally the leading vegetable oil. A sustained increase in incomes in, especially, China, as well as in India and South-East Asia, has been cited as an important factor behind the increase in global demand for vegetable oils and fats in recent years. Those commodities have also benefited from a price advantage relative to fossil oils, and have increasingly been utilized for the production of fuels as well as for food purposes. Prices of oils and fats were reported to have weakened at the beginning of the 2005/06 season, reflecting the pressure of record soybean and palm oil output in 2004/05. They subsequently recovered, according to FAO, owing to a surge in the utilization of oils and fats world-wide, in combination with a pronounced slowdown in the growth of output of palm oil, among other factors. In 2005/06 the average price of palm oil was $478 per ton. During the first seven months of 2007 the European import price of palm oil increased substantially, ranging from between $599 per ton (January) and $811 per ton (July).

PETROLEUM

Crude oils, from which petroleum fuel is derived, consist essentially of a wide range of hydrocarbon molecules which are separated by distillation in the refining process. Refined oil is treated in different ways to make the different varieties of fuel. More than four-fifths of total world oil supplies are used as fuel for the production of energy in the form of power or heating.

Petroleum, together with its associated mineral fuel, natural gas, is extracted both from onshore and offshore wells in many areas of the world. The dominant producing region is the Middle East, whose proven reserves in December 2006 accounted for 61.5% of known world deposits of crude petroleum and natural gas liquids. The Middle East accounted for 31.2% of world output in 2006. Africa contained 15,500m. metric tons of proven reserves (9.4% of the world total) at the end of 2006, and accounted for about 12% of world production in that year.

From storage tanks at the oilfield wellhead, crude petroleum is conveyed, frequently by pumping for long distances through large pipelines, to coastal depots where it is either treated in a refinery or delivered into bulk storage tanks for subsequent shipment for refining overseas. In addition to pipeline transportation of crude petroleum and refined products, natural (petroleum) gas is, in some areas, also transported through networks of pipelines. Crude petroleum varies considerably in colour and viscosity, and these variations are a determinant both of price and of end-use after refining.

In the refining process, crude petroleum is heated until vaporized. The vapours are then separately condensed, according to their molecular properties, passed through airless steel tubes and pumped into the lower section of a high cylindrical tower, as a hot mixture of vapours and liquid. The heavy unvaporized liquid flows out at the base of the tower as a 'residue' from which is obtained heavy fuel and bitumen. The vapours passing upwards then undergo a series of condensation processes that produce 'distillates', which form the basis of the various petroleum products.

The most important of these products is fuel oil, composed of heavy distillates and residues, which is used to produce heating and power for industrial purposes. Products in the kerosene group have a wide number of applications, ranging from heating fuels to the powering of aviation gas turbine engines. Gasoline (petrol) products fuel internal combustion engines (used mainly in road motor vehicles), and naphtha, a gasoline distillate, is a commercial solvent that can also be processed as a feedstock. Propane and butane, the main liquefied petroleum gases, have a wide range of industrial applications and are also used for domestic heating and cooking.

Petroleum is the leading raw material in international trade. World-wide demand for this commodity totalled 83.7m. barrels per day (b/d) in 2006. The world's 'published proven' reserves of petroleum and natural gas liquids at 31 December 2006 were estimated to total 164,500m. metric tons, equivalent to about 1,208,200m. barrels (1 metric ton is equivalent to approximately 7.3 barrels, each of 42 US gallons or 34.97 imperial gallons, i.e. 159 litres).

Nigeria's first petroleum discovery was made in the Niger Delta region in 1956, and exports began in 1958. Production and exports increased steadily until output was disrupted by the outbreak of civil war in 1967. After the end of hostilities, in 1970, Nigeria's petroleum production greatly increased and it became the country's major industry. Since Libya restricted output in 1973, Nigeria has been Africa's leading petroleum-producing country. Being of low sulphur content and high quality, Nigerian petroleum is much in demand on the European market. Nigeria's proven reserves were estimated to be 4,900m. metric tons at 31 December 2006. A member of the Organization of the Petroleum Exporting Countries (OPEC, see below), Nigeria accounted for about 7.3% of total OPEC production of 1,632.7m. tons in 2006. The state petroleum enterprise, the Nigerian National Petroleum Corpn (NNPC), operates refinery facilities at Port Harcourt (I and II), Kaduna and Warri. In 2007, according to the Energy Information Administration (EIA) of the US Department of Energy, Nigeria's 'nameplate' annual refinery capacity amounted to about 22m. tons, but had been reduced, in practice, through sabotage (see below), poor management, etc., to only some 11m. tons—insufficient to meet domestic requirements. Nigeria is consequently dependent on imports of petroleum products. In 2007, according to the EIA, government licensing of the construction of a number of independent refineries was ongoing. Oanda, a petroleum marketing company, was reportedly assessing the viability of constructing, in two phases, a new refinery at Lagos, with total annual capacity of about 9m. tons. The Government was seeking, furthermore, to privatize NNPC's existing refineries, and had engaged in negotiations to this end with Chinese, Indian and Libyan investors. In early 2007 Mittal Steel reportedly expressed an interest in acquiring a majority share in the Port Harcourt Refinery Company. Most of Nigeria's exports of crude petroleum are destined for the US and Western European markets, although foreign sales to Asia and Latin America are of increasing significance. In 2006, of crude exports totalling some 2.2m. b/d (about 110m. tons), 42% was destined for the USA, 13% for India, 6% each for Brazil and France, 5% for Spain, 4% for Italy, and 3% each for Canada, Côte d'Ivoire and South Africa. In 2003 exports of crude petroleum provided about 96% of Nigeria's total export earnings. In 2005, according to the US Geological Survey, exports of crude petroleum, valued provisionally at US $46,800m., accounted for almost 98% of the country's exports by value.

Equitable distribution of Nigeria's 'oil wealth' has been negligible and in spite of the country's status, in 2005, as the world's ninth largest exporter of petroleum, more than two-thirds of the population were reported to live in poverty. (In 2006 Nigeria ranked as the world's eighth largest exporter of crude petroleum.) The operations of multinational oil companies—notably Royal Dutch/Shell—in the Niger Delta have increasingly become the focus of local politically- and environmentally-motivated opposition. This is frequently expressed in acts of sabotage carried out against pipelines and other oil infrastructure and in the kidnapping of expatriate oil workers in the Delta. The Movement for the Emancipation of the Niger Delta is prominent among groups that have claimed responsibility for kidnappings and acts of sabotage in recent years. In early 2007, according to the EIA, some 587,000 b/d of oil was estimated to be 'shut in' as a result of the capture by opposition groups of Delta oil facilities and related security issues.

Angola, which joined OPEC as its 12th member in January 2007, made its first petroleum discovery in 1955 near Luanda. However, Cabinda province has a major offshore deposit, in production since 1968, which now forms the basis of the country's oil industry. Output from Cabinda was briefly disrupted by the country's civil war, but has proceeded uninterruptedly since 1977 and has risen steadily since 1982. Since the late 1980s production of crude petroleum has risen more than fourfold. According to the EIA, output will increase further in 2007–12, as a number of deep-water offshore projects are brought into operation. The World Bank, however, has forecast that Angolan production will peak in 2011 and thereafter decline. In 2005 Angola obtained 94.7% of its foreign earnings from exports by the petroleum sector, which accounted for about 52% of the country's gross domestic product and 80% of government revenue. Angola's proven oil reserves were assessed at 1,200m. metric tons at 31 December 2006. Domestic consumption of crude petroleum has been forecast to increase in coming years, but is at present sufficiently low to allow most of the country's output to be exported. The main destinations for Angola's crude exports are the USA, of which it was the eighth largest crude supplier in 2005, and the People's Republic of China. European and Latin American countries also purchase Angolan crude. Plans exist to augment the annual capacity of Angola's sole refinery, at Luanda, which stood at 2m. tons in 2007. The national oil company, Sociedade Nacional de Combustíveis de Angola, plans to constuct a new refinery at the coastal city of Lobito. China's Sinopec has reportedly undertaken to finance the refinery, whose cost has been estimated at $3,500m. It is anticipated that the new refinery, with planned daily capacity of 200,000 barrels, will be operational by 2009.

Production of Crude Petroleum

(estimates, '000 metric tons, including natural gas liquids and oil from shale)

	2005	2006
World total	3,896,800	3,914,100
Africa	467,200	473,700
Leading African producers		
Algeria	86,500	86,200
Angola	60,700	69,400
Cameroon	3,000	3,200
Congo, Repub.	12,700	13,500
Egypt	33,900	33,000
Gabon	11,700	11,600
Libya	82,100	85,600
Nigeria	125,400	119,200
Leading non-African producers		
Canada	144,900	151,300
China, People's Repub.	180,800	183,700
Iran	207,300	209,800
Iraq	90,000	98,100
Kuwait	130,100	133,200
Mexico	187,100	183,100
Norway	138,200	128,700
Russia	470,000	480,500
Saudi Arabia	526,800	514,600
United Arab Emirates	129,000	138,300
United Kingdom	84,700	76,600
USA	313,300	311,800
Venezuela	151,000	145,100

Source: BP, *Statistical Review of World Energy 2007*.

The Republic of the Congo, with proven recoverable reserves estimated at 300m. metric tons in December 2006, commenced onshore petroleum production in 1957. Subsequent expansion, however, has been in operations off shore, where major new deposits, discovered in 1992, began to augment the country's petroleum output from 1996. Further significant offshore discoveries have been made since 1998. Output declined steadily in 2000–03 as a result of maturing oilfields and delays in bringing new projects into operation, but increased in each year in 2004–06 and was expected to continue to do so as the potential of new discoveries was realized and investment increased. In 2006, with output of 13.5m. tons, the Congo ranked as the fifth largest producer in sub-Saharan Africa, after Nigeria, Angola, Sudan and Equatorial Guinea. In early 2007, according to the EIA, Total accounted for nearly one-half of the Congo's production of crude and Italy's ENI for a little more one-fifth. Smaller producers at that time included Perenco, the Congorep consortium and Likoula SA. In 2005 a proposal by Total to develop the Congo's offshore Moho-Bilondo field was approved by the Government. Output from the field was scheduled to commence in 2008. Chevron, together with a number of partners, was reportedly engaged in early 2007 in the development of resources uncovered by the Lianzi-1 exploration well—located within the Zone of Common Interest established by Angola and the Congo in 2003—where a signficicant discovery was made in 2004. In 2006 the Congo's exports totalled some 12m. tons. Most foreign sales were to Asian destinations, with China accounting for about one-half. In 2003 exports of petroleum and petroleum products accounted for about 80% of total export revenue. In addition to domestic output, a petroleum refinery at Pointe-Noire, with an annual capacity of 10.5m. tons in 2007, processes some Angolan production. In neighbouring Gabon, whose recoverable reserves were estimated at 300m. tons in 2006, the exploitation of petroleum deposits began in 1956, and, as in the Congo, increased as offshore fields were brought into production. In 2004 sales of petroleum and petroleum products provided about 82% of estimated total export revenue. A member of OPEC until its withdrawal from the organization in December 1996, Gabon's output accounted for only 1.4% of OPEC's total output in that year.

Cameroon, which is virtually self-sufficient in oil and petroleum products, derived about 35% of its export income from this source in 2004. However, new exploration and development projects were not actively pursued during the 1990s, and the country's proven reserves were estimated at about 55m. metric tons in 2005. Some 85% of the Chad–Cameroon petroleum pipeline (see below) is located in Cameroon, and the country's derives additional petroleum revenue from Chadian exports. The Democratic Republic of the Congo (DRC) entered offshore petroleum production in 1975, operating from oilfields near the Atlantic coast and at the mouth of the Congo River. These deposits became depleted at the end of the 1980s (estimates of its proven reserves fell from 13.2m. tons in 1989 to 7.6m. tons in 1990). The level of these reserves was substantially replenished during 1991, however, raising estimates to 25.6m. tons for each of the subsequent seven years. Although the DRC has an annual refinery capacity of 850,000 tons, its exceptionally heavy-grade petroleum cannot be processed locally and the country therefore cannot consume its own output.

Côte d'Ivoire, with estimated proven reserves of 13.7m. metric tons in 2007, and Benin, whose proven reserves were estimated at 1.1m. tons in 1998, are among the other smaller sub-Saharan offshore producers. These were joined in 1991 by Equatorial Guinea, where the offshore Zafiro oilfield, discovered north-west of Bioko by ExxonMobil and Ocean Energy, commenced production in late 1996. Subsequent output advanced very rapidly, reaching some 9m. tons in 2001 and contributing greatly to the country's economic growth. In 2002 the government created a national oil company, GEPetrol, primarily in order to manage its stakes in a number of production-sharing agreements with foreign interests. In 2006 production totalled an estimated 17.7m. tons. The Ceiba and Alba fields also contain significant reserves. In 2002 exports of petroleum contributed about 95% of Equatorial Guinea's total export earnings. The value of the country's exports of petroleum amounted to US $7,000m. in 2005, compared with some $4,500m. in the previous year. The value of sales to the USA in 2005 totalled $1,500m., compared with $981m. in 2004. Deposits of an estimated 52m.–58m. tons of petroleum have been identified off the coast of Senegal, but the development of these reserves (which are overwhelmingly of heavy oil) is not economically feasible at present.

At 1 January 2007 the proven petroleum reserves of Chad were assessed at 100m. tons. Production in 2006 was estimated to have amounted to 8m. tons. The exploitation of reserves in the Doba Basin region in south-western Chad commenced in mid-2003. Output from four operational fields (as of 2006) there is conveyed by a 1,060-km pipeline (construction of which was completed in 2004), through Cameroon, to the Atlantic coast. A fifth field was scheduled to enter operation in early 2007. In order to obtain funding to secure a stake in the Chad–Cameroon Pipeline Development Project (CCPDP), Chad became the first country to conclude a loan agreement with the World Bank with terms governing the way in which oil revenues should be spent. Some 80% was to be targeted at such sectors as health, education and rural development, and environmental protection projects were also to benefit. The remaining 20% was to be distributed for government expenditure and as a supplement payable to the country's Doba region. In early 2006 a dispute with the World Bank arose after the Government voted to allocate more than 20% of its oil revenue to the general budget. In response, the World Bank suspended loans to Chad and froze its oil revenue account. The dispute was resolved in mid-2006, when the Government agreed that it would allocate 70% of its oil revenues to development projects. It was agreed that the remaining 30% should be available for government expenditure. The Government of Chad has declared the goals of assuming control of as much as 60% of the country's oil industry and, possibly, of assuming membership of the ExxonMobil-led consortium that controls the CCPDP. The Société des Hydrocarbures du Tchad, the national oil company, was created in 2006 in order to pursue these objectives.

In 1998 Sudan, a relatively minor producer with estimated proven reserves of some 360m. tons in that year, finalized an agreement with four foreign companies to construct a 1,600-km pipeline to convey output from western Sudan to a terminal at Bachair, south of Port Sudan. The pipeline, with the capacity to carry 450,000 b/d, was inaugurated in mid-1999, and output has since risen rapidly to total 19.6m. tons in 2006. In 2003 exports of crude petroleum and petroleum products contributed about 78% of Sudan's total export earnings. Sudan's proven reserves were estimated at about 900m. tons at the end of 2006, but are likely to rise in future as the signature, in January 2005, of a comprehensive peace agreement to end the country's civil war was expected to facilitate the exploration of many areas of potential reserves in southern Sudan. The manner in which both the production of and exploration for petroleum in Sudan have hitherto been conducted has allegedly involved the Government in human rights abuses, including the forced evacuation of populations living in the vicinity of oilfields. In 2007 Sudan was reportedly considering whether to apply for membership of OPEC.

South Africa's proven reserves of petroleum were estimated at about 2m. metric tons at the beginning of 2007. Among other sub-Saharan African countries where petroleum reserves are known or believed to exist, but which do not yet produce, are Guinea, Mozambique, Swaziland, Eritrea, São Tomé and Príncipe, and Tanzania. Exploration has also taken place, or is under way, in Ethiopia, Namibia, Kenya, Madagascar and Zimbabwe.

International petroleum prices are strongly influenced by OPEC, founded in 1960 to co-ordinate the production and marketing policies of those countries whose main source of export earnings is petroleum. In 2007 OPEC had 12 members. Nigeria joined OPEC in 1971; however, Gabon, which became a full member in 1975, terminated its membership with effect from January 1997 (see above). The other African members are Algeria, Angola and Libya.

The (then) four African members of OPEC (Algeria, Gabon, Libya and Nigeria) formed the African Petroleum Producers' Association (APPA) in 1987. Angola, Benin, Cameroon, the DRC, the Congo, Côte d'Ivoire, Egypt and Equatorial Guinea subsequently joined the association, in which Tunisia has observer status. Apart from promoting co-operation among regional producers, the APPA, which is based in Brazzaville, Congo, co-operates with OPEC in stabilizing oil prices.

International prices for crude petroleum rose steadily during the opening weeks of 2000, with OPEC restrictions continuing to operate and stocks declining in industrial countries. In early March the London price for North Sea petroleum exceeded US $31.5 per barrel, but later in the month nine OPEC members agreed to restore production quotas to pre-March 1999 levels from 1 April 2000, representing a combined increase of about 1.7m. b/d. The London petroleum price fell in April to less than $22 per barrel, but the rise in OPEC production was insufficient to increase significantly the stocks held by major consuming countries. In June the price of North Sea petroleum rose to about $31.5 per barrel again, but later that month OPEC ministers agreed to a further rise in quotas (totalling about 700,000 b/d) from 1 July. By the end of July the North Sea petroleum price was below $27 per barrel, but in mid-August it rose to more than $32 for the first time since 1990 (when prices had surged in response to the Iraqi invasion of Kuwait). In New York in the same month, meanwhile, the September contract for light crude traded at a new record level of $33 per barrel at one point. The surge in oil prices in August was attributed to continued fears regarding supply levels in coming months, especially in view of data showing US inventories to be at their lowest level for 24 years, and of indications by both Saudi Arabia and Venezuela that OPEC would not act to raise production before September. Deliberate attempts to raise the price of the expiring London September contract were an additional factor.

In early September 2000 the London price of North Sea petroleum for October delivery climbed to a new 10-year high of US $34.55, reflecting the view that any production increase that OPEC might decide to implement would be insufficient to prevent tight supplies later in the year. In New York, meanwhile, the price of light crude for October delivery rose beyond the $35 per barrel mark. This latest bout of price volatility reflected the imminence of an OPEC meeting, at which Saudi Arabia was expected to seek an agreement to raise the Organization's production by at least 700,000 b/d in order to stabilize the market. In the event, OPEC decided to increase production by 800,000 b/d, with effect from 1 October, causing prices in both London and New York to ease. This relaxation was short-lived, however. Just over a week after OPEC's decision was announced the price of the New York October contract for light crude closed at $36.88 per barrel, in response to concerns over tension in the Persian (Arabian) Gulf area between Iraq and Kuwait. The same contract had at one point risen above $37 per barrel, its highest level for 10 years. These latest increases prompted OPEC representatives to deliver assurances that production would be raised further in order to curb price levels regarded as economically damaging in the USA and other consumer countries. Towards the end of September the London price of North Sea petroleum for November delivery fell below $30 per barrel for the first time in a month, in response to the decision of the USA to release petroleum from its strategic reserve in order to depress prices.

In the first week of October 2000, however, the price of the November contract for both North Sea petroleum traded in London and New York light crude had stabilized at around US $30 per barrel, anxiety over political tension in the Middle East preventing the more marked decline that had been anticipated. This factor exerted stronger upward pressure during the following week, when the London price of North Sea petroleum for November delivery rose above $35 per barrel for the first time since 1990. In early November 2000 crude oil continued to trade at more than $30 per barrel in both London and New York, despite the announcement by OPEC of a further increase in production, this time of 500,000 b/d, and a lessening of political tension in the Middle East. Prices were volatile throughout November, with the price of both London and New York contracts for January delivery remaining in excess of $30 per barrel at the end of the month.

During the first week of December 2000 the price of the January 'futures' contract in both London and New York declined substantially, in response, mainly, to an unresolved dispute between the UN and Iraq over the pricing of Iraqi oil. On 8 December the closing London price of North Sea petroleum for January delivery was US $26.56 per barrel, while the equivalent New York price for light crude was $28.44. Trading during the second week of December was characterized by further declines, the London price of North Sea petroleum for January delivery falling below $25 per barrel at one point. Analysts noted that prices had fallen by some 20% since mid-November, and OPEC representatives indicated that the Organization might decide to cut production in January 2001 if prices fell below its preferred trading range of $22–$28 per barrel. At $23.51 per barrel on 14 December, the price of the OPEC 'basket' of crudes was at its lowest level since May. During the third week of December the price of the OPEC 'basket' of crudes declined further, to $21.64 per barrel. Overall, during December, the price of crudes traded in both London and New York declined by some $10 per barrel, and remained subject to pressure at the end of the month.

Continued expectations that OPEC would decide to reduce production later in the month caused 'futures' prices to strengthen in the first week of January 2001. The London price of North Sea petroleum for February delivery closed at US $25.18 on 5 January, while the corresponding price for light crude traded in New York was $27.95. Prices remained firm in the second week of January, again in anticipation of a decision by OPEC to reduce production. Paradoxically, prices fell immediately after OPEC's decision to reduce production by 1.5m. b/d was announced on 17 January. However, it was widely recognized that the reduction had been factored into markets by that time.

Oil prices rose significantly at the beginning of February 2001, although the gains were attributed mainly to speculative purchases rather than to any fundamental changes in market conditions. On 2 February the London price of North Sea petroleum for March delivery closed at US $29.19 per barrel, while the corresponding price for light crude traded in New York was $31.19. On 8 February prices rose to their highest levels for two months, the London price for North Sea petroleum for March delivery exceeding $30 per barrel at one point. The upward movement came in response to a forecast, issued by the US Energy Information Administration (EIA), that the spot price for West Texas Intermediate (WTI—the US 'marker' crude) would average close to $30 per barrel throughout 2001. For the remainder of the month prices in both London and New York remained largely without direction.

During the early part of March 2001 oil prices in both London and New York drifted downwards while it remained unclear whether OPEC would decide to implement a further cut in production, and what the effect of such a reduction might be. On 9 March the London price of North Sea petroleum for April delivery was US $26.33 per barrel, while the corresponding price for light crude traded in New York was $28.01 per barrel. By late March prices in both London and New York had declined further, the London price of North Sea petroleum for May delivery closing near to $24.82 per barrel on 30 March, while the corresponding price for New York light crude was $26.35.

During the first week of April 2001 crude oil prices on both sides of the Atlantic strengthened in response to fears of a gasoline shortage in the USA later in the year. On 6 April the London price of North Sea petroleum for May delivery was US $25.17 per barrel, while New York light crude for delivery in May closed at $27.06. Strong demand for crude oil by US gasoline refiners was the strongest influence on markets throughout April as gasoline 'futures' rose markedly. Towards the end of April the price of the New York contract for gasoline for May delivery rose to the equivalent of $1.115 per gallon, higher than the previous record price recorded in August 1990.

Fears of a shortage of gasoline supplies in the USA remained the key influence on oil markets in early May 2001, with 'futures' prices rising in response to successive record prices for gasoline 'futures'. On 4 May the London price of North Sea petroleum for June delivery was US $28.19 per barrel, while that of the corresponding contract for light crude traded in New York closed at $28.36. Prices were prevented from rising further during the week ending 4 May by the report of an unexpected increase in US inventories of crude oil. A further check came in the following week, when the International Energy Agency (IEA) reduced its forecast of world growth in demand for crude oil by 300,000 b/d to 1.02m. b/d. On 18 May, however, demand for crude oil by gasoline refiners raised the price of New York crude for June delivery to its highest level for three months, while the price of the July contract rose above $30 per barrel. On 5 June, at an extraordinary conference held in Vienna, Austria, OPEC voted to defer a possible adjustment of its production level for one month, noting that stocks of both crude oil and products were at a satisfactory level, the market in balance and that the year-to-date average of the OPEC reference 'basket' of crudes had been $24.8 per barrel (i.e. within the trading range of $22–$28 per barrel targeted by the Organization). OPEC nevertheless decided to hold a further extraordinary conference in early July in order to take account of future developments. At that meeting OPEC oil ministers once again opted to maintain production at the prevailing level, emphasizing that they would continue to monitor the market and take further measures, if deemed necessary, to maintain prices within the Organization's preferred trading range. The conference appealed to other oil exporters to continue to collaborate with OPEC in order to minimize price volatility and safeguard stability. Towards the end of the month, as prices declined steadily towards (and briefly below) $23 per barrel, the then Secretary-General of OPEC, Dr Ali Rodríguez Araque, indicated that he was consulting OPEC ministers regarding the possibility of holding a further extraordinary conference early in August—ahead of the next ordinary OPEC meeting scheduled for September. Two days later, on 25 July, OPEC agreed to reduce production by a further 1m. b/d, to 23.2m. b/d, with effect from 1 September; the Organization reiterated that it was retaining the option to convene an extraordinary meeting if the market warranted it (this latest reduction, which had been agreed without a full meeting of OPEC, had been ratified by oil ministers by telephone). The Organization again expressed confidence that its action in reducing output would be matched by non-OPEC producing/exporting countries, and recognized in particular Mexico's support for its efforts. While there was general agreement that the production cut would reduce inventories, the consensus remained that demand would also decline in view of the prevailing world economic outlook.

A decline of 1.1% in US inventories of crude oil, reported by the American Petroleum Institute (API) in late July 2001, apparently indicated that US demand was resisting, for the time being, a deceleration in economic growth, and was cited as the main reason for a recovery in the price of Brent blend North Sea petroleum, to US $24.97 per barrel, on 1 August. A further decline of the same order, reported on 7 August, raised the price of Brent to $27.94 per barrel, and that of the OPEC 'basket' of crudes to $24.99 per barrel. Throughout most of the remainder of August declining US inventories of both crude and refined products appeared to suggest a strength of demand that belied pessimistic assessments of US (and global) economic prospects in the near term, combining with anticipation of the reduction of OPEC production by 1m. b/d from 1 September, to support the price of the Brent reference blend and the OPEC 'basket' of crudes.

Immediately following the suicide attacks on mainland USA on 11 September 2001, as the price of Brent blend North Sea petroleum rose above US $30 per barrel, OPEC's Secretary-General was swift to emphasize the Organization's commitment to 'strengthening market stability and ensuring that sufficient supplies are available to satisfy market needs', by utilizing its spare capacity, if necessary. However, there was virtual unanimity among commentators, following the attacks, that their effect would be to worsen the prospects of the global economy, if not plunge it into recession, causing a considerable decline in demand for oil. By mid-October 2001 the price of the OPEC 'basket' of crudes had remained below $22 per barrel, the minimum price the Organization's market management strategy was designed to sustain, since late September, and it was clear that, at the risk of adding to recessionary pressures, OPEC would have to implement a further cut in production if it was to bring the price back into its preferred trading range. In late October Venezuela, Iran, Saudi Arabia, the United Arab Emirates (UAE) and non-OPEC Oman all declared themselves in favour of a further cut in production. However, diplomacy undertaken by President Hugo Chávez Frías of Venezuela and Saudi Arabia's Minister of Petroleum and Mineral Resources, Ali ibn Ibrahim an-Nuaimi, had apparently made no progress in achieving its objective of persuading key non-OPEC producers Mexico, Norway and Russia to support the Organization's management strategy.

In the first week of November 2001 the price of Brent blend North Sea petroleum fell to fractionally above US $19 per barrel, while that of OPEC's 'basket' of crudes declined to $17.56 per barrel. In Vienna, on 14 November, an extraordinary meeting of the OPEC conference observed that 'as a result of the global economic slowdown and the aftermath of the tragic events of 11 September 2001, in order to achieve a balance in the oil market, it will be necessary to reduce the supply from all oil producers by a further 2m. b/d, bringing the total reduction in oil supply to 5.5m. b/d from the levels of January 2001, including the 3.5m. b/d reduction already effected by OPEC this year. In this connection, and reiterating its call on other oil exporters to co-operate so as to minimize price volatility and ensure market stability, the Conference decided to reduce an additional volume of 1.5m. b/d, effective 1 January 2002, subject to a firm commitment from non-OPEC oil producers to cut their production by a volume of 500,000 b/d simultaneously'. The meeting acknowledged the positive response of Mexico and Oman to OPEC's efforts to balance the market. However, it was widely recognized that the success of a collaboration of the kind envisaged depended on the co-operation of Russia. Prior to the extraordinary conference held in November, Russia had indicated that it would be willing to reduce its production, estimated at more than 7m. b/d, by no more than 30,000 b/d, far less than would be necessary for OPEC's strategy to be effective. It was not until early December that Russia's Prime Minister announced the country's commitment to reducing its exports of crude by up to 150,000 b/d, and it was uncertain, in any case, whether a reduction of that magnitude could be enforced, owing to the Russian Government's lack of control over Russia's oil industry.

On 18 December 2001 the price of the OPEC 'basket' of crudes fell to US $16.62 per barrel. Thereafter, in December, however, the price recovered, in response to commitments by major non-OPEC producers to collaborate with the Organization by reducing either output or exports. On 28 December, at a consultative meeting of the OPEC conference, convened in Cairo, Egypt, OPEC confirmed its decision to implement a reduction of 1.5m. b/d in its overall production from 1 January 2002, having received assurances that Angola, Mexico, Norway, Oman and Russia would reduce their output, or, in the case of Russia, exports, of crude petroleum by a total of 462,500 b/d. BP's *Statistical Review of World Energy 2002* noted that, for the whole of 2001, the price of Brent blend North Sea petroleum had averaged $24.77 per barrel. The average price of the reference blend was substantially less than $20 per barrel in October–December 2001, however. In 2001, for the first time since 1993, consumption of oil world-wide declined, albeit marginally.

In January 2002 the decline in the price of the OPEC 'basket' of crudes was halted for the first time since the terrorist attacks in September 2001. According to the Organization's own data, the 'basket' price rose by 4.6% in January 2002, compared with December 2001, but was 24% lower when considered on a year-on-year basis. The price of Brent blend North Sea petroleum, meanwhile, averaged US $19.48 per barrel in January. Reviewing the state of the market in January 2002, OPEC noted that it was still too early to assess the effectiveness of the reduction in output and exports that had begun on 1 January. The recovery in the average price of the OPEC 'basket' had been uneven throughout the month. Low demand, as indicated by data published by the EIA and the API, recording rises in US crude inventories, and either rises or lower-than-expected declines in inventories of distillate products, combined, in the second week of January with uncertainty regarding Russia's commitment to reducing its exports by 150,000 b/d (as it had pledged to do) to exert pressure on prices. During the third week of January, however, prices were supported, according to OPEC, by the strength of product prices, and by the USA's decision to add 22m. barrels of crude to its Strategic Petroleum Reserve. Among other factors, apparently good adherence by OPEC members to the revised quotas announced in December 2001 helped to sustain the upward trend in the final week of January 2002.

In February 2002 the average price of the OPEC 'basket' of crudes rose for the second consecutive month, recording an increase of 3.1% compared with January. As OPEC noted in its review of crude price movements in February, however, the average price of the 'basket' was 25.7% lower when considered on a year-on-year basis. The price of the OPEC 'basket' rose steadily during the first two weeks of February, supported, among other factors, by reports of an explosion at oil-gathering facilities in Kuwait that was initially expected to remove some 600,000 b/d from the market; and by increased political tension between the USA and Iraq. In the third week of February the OPEC 'basket' price fluctuated, but, overall, was weaker compared with the previous week. Continued doubts over Russia's commitment to reducing its exports was one factor that exerted downward pressure on prices. In the final week of the month prices strengthened considerably as a result of the interplay between reportedly higher product inventories, renewed political tension between the West and Iraq, and a dispute between the Venezuelan government and employees of Petróleos de Venezuela.

In early March 2002 a meeting took place between a delegation of senior OPEC representatives and Russian government and energy officials. OPEC's objective at the meeting was to persuade Russia to continue to limit its exports of crude to 150,000 b/d during the second quarter of 2002. OPEC regarded the continued limitation of Russian exports as imperative if market stability was to be maintained at a time of seasonally weak markets for oil. Russia's initial commitment to reduce its exports, however, applied only to the first quarter of 2002, with any continuation of the restriction subject to a review of market conditions. Norway had, by this time, already agreed to continue to restrict its production of crude to 150,000 b/d during April–June 2002. Moreover, it was clear in March that the measures undertaken to stabilize the market since the beginning of the year had been successful. The price of the OPEC 'basket' of crudes rose by 20% in March, compared with the previous month, although it was 5% lower when considered on a year-on-year basis. As OPEC noted in its review of markets for crude in March, prices rose consistently throughout the month. Evidence of economic recovery in the USA was a positive factor in early March—data published by the API indicated declining US inventories of gasoline and distillate products—as was the apparent likelihood of Russia agreeing to carry over into the second quarter the restriction applied to its exports of crude. In the second week of March an intensification of the conflict between Israel and the Palestinians, and OPEC's announcement that it would maintain production at the prevailing level until the end of June at least, were additional factors that supported prices. In the third week of March prices rose above US $25 per barrel, owing, according to OPEC, to technical factors that were subsequently cancelled out by profit-taking. The upward movement continued towards the end of March, when positive inventory data combined with optimism about the sustainability of economic recovery in the USA to support prices.

From late March 2002 the escalating conflict between Israel and the Palestinians was cited as a key factor supporting crude prices. On 1 April, for the first time since 11 September 2001, the price of the OPEC 'basket' of crudes rose above US $25 per barrel. On 8 April Iraq added to the increased political tension in the Middle East by suspending its exports of crude for a period of 30 days in response to attacks by Israeli armed forces against Palestinian targets in the West Bank. Although Iraq's action was of little real consequence for crude markets, since other producers could easily compensate for the loss of its exports if necessary, it came at a time when a number of countries, including Iraq itself, Iran and Libya, had expressed their support for an embargo to be placed on the supply of oil by OPEC, in support of the Palestinian struggle against Israeli occupation. It was generally acknowledged in April that prices were inflated by a so-called 'war premium' of some $4–$6 per barrel, without which they would decline towards the lower end of OPEC's preferred trading range. Political upheaval in Venezuela also lent a degree of volatility to prices in mid-April, when the brief removal of President Chávez from power caused them to decline sharply. Following Chávez's reinstatement as President, the key market influence for the remainder of the month was the perception, supported by a reported decline in US inventories of crude, that demand for oil was growing in response to improved economic conditions in the USA.

A combination of apparently stronger US demand and tighter supplies was regarded as the most significant determinant of the direction of markets for crude in early May 2002. On 7 May the API announced that US inventories of crude had declined by some 4.5m. barrels in the week to 3 May, and on the day of the announcement the price of Brent blend North Sea petroleum reached US $27.14 per barrel, an increase of more than $1 per barrel compared with the previous week. Among other factors contributing to the tightening of supplies at this time was OPEC's apparent decision not to compensate for the 30-day suspension of Iraqi exports. In the second week of May prices declined somewhat in response to data published by the US Department of Energy that indicated an increase in US inventories of crude. Towards the end of the month prices weakened again, in response to the publication of data that appeared to cast doubt on the strength of the US economic recovery.

Prices remained under pressure at the beginning of June 2002, owing to the publication of data indicating a further, unexpected increase in US inventories of crude and of distillate products in late May. Iraqi exports had also risen substantially in late May and early June. Most commentators appeared to agree with OPEC, representatives of whose members referred to a balanced market for crude in statements released early in the month, and indicated that OPEC would not alter its production quotas at its forthcoming extraordinary ministerial conference. In its assessment of the oil market in June, the IEA noted that geopolitical factors (i.e. violence in the Middle East) were now perceived as less of a risk to supplies of crude and predicted that prices would continue to weaken. US inventories of crude and gasoline were reported to have declined slightly in the first week of June. Crude stocks fell again during the second week of June, but this decline was balanced by substantial increases in inventories of gasoline and distillate products, indicating the ongoing weakness of economic recovery in the USA. At an extraordinary ministerial conference, held in Vienna on 26 June, OPEC, as expected, agreed to maintain production at the prevailing level until the end of September 2002. The Organization noted that its 'reduction measures during 2001 and 2002, supported by similar measures from some non-OPEC producers over the first half of the year, had restored relative market balance'. At the same time, OPEC observed that 'the relative strength in current market prices is partially a reflection of the prevailing political situation rather than solely the consequence of market fundamentals', and undertook to continue carefully to monitor market conditions and to take further action, if necessary, to maintain market stability.

The price of OPEC's 'basket' of crudes eased in the final week of July and the first week of August 2002, but rose to about US $26 per barrel in the second week of August owing to increased political tension in the Middle East. The threat of US military action against Iraq continued to support prices during the remainder of August and the first two weeks of September. Prior to the OPEC ministerial conference held in Osaka, Japan, on 19 September, Iraq's expressed willingness to allow the return of UN weapons inspectors caused prices to weaken, but they were subsequently supported by the Organization's decision to maintain production at the prevailing level until 12 December 2002, when the conference would meet again to review the market. The average price of the OPEC 'basket' of crudes in September, at $27.38 per barrel, was the third highest recorded for that month since 1984. At one point during the final week of the month the closing price of the 'basket', at $28.11 per barrel, exceeded the upper limit of the Organization's targeted trading range for the first time since November 2000. The average 'spot' quotation for Brent increased by $1.6 to $28.28 per barrel. WTI for immediate delivery, meanwhile, traded at an average price of $29.52 per barrel, compared with $28.41 per barrel in August. In its review of the markets for crude petroleum in September, OPEC noted that the price of the 'basket' had averaged $23.48 per barrel during the first nine months of the year: $1.23 per barrel lower than the average price recorded during the corresponding period of 2001. In the final week of September 2002 the front-month (October) WTI 'futures' contract traded on the New York Mercantile Exchange (NYMEX) rose to its highest level for 19 months, closing above $30 per barrel at one point, having displayed considerable volatility during the month in accordance with the perceived likelihood of US military action against Iraq. In October 2002 the average 'spot' quotation for the crudes comprising OPEC's reference 'basket' declined slightly, by US $0.06, to $27.32 per barrel, for the first time since July. The average weekly price of the 'basket' reached its highest level, $28.24 per barrel, in the first week of the month, but declined quite steeply, by $1 per barrel and $1.45 per barrel, in, respectively, the third and final weeks. The average 'spot' quotation for Brent declined by $0.59 to $27.69 per barrel, while that of WTI fell by $0.52 to $29.0 per barrel. Accordingly, during the first 10 months of 2002 the cumulative average price of the OPEC reference 'basket' was $23.91 per barrel, $0.02 below the average price recorded during the corresponding period of 2001. In its monthly review, OPEC again identified political developments pertaining to the Middle East, in particular a statement by US President George W. Bush early in the month which appeared to lessen the likelihood of US military action against Iraq, as a key influence—at the expense of fundamental factors, such as a sharp and greater-than-anticipated increase in both OPEC and non-OPEC supplies—on markets for crude petroleum. The price of 'futures' contracts for crude petroleum responded similarly to the perceived reduction in political tension, in combination with a reported increase in OPEC production and rising US stocks. On NYMEX the front-month WTI 'futures' contract declined from $30.83 per barrel (1 October) to only $27.22 per barrel (31 October).

In November 2002 the average price of the OPEC reference 'basket' declined steeply, by more than US $3, to $24.29 per barrel. In the same month, nevertheless, the year-to-date average price of the 'basket' rose above the corresponding price for 2001 for the first time, reaching $23.94 per barrel. The price of the 'basket' was at its weakest in the second week of the month. During the second half of November quotations recovered to the extent that the average price of the 'basket' re-entered OPEC's targeted price range, by a narrow margin, in the final week of the month. In its monthly assessment of markets for crude oil, OPEC attributed the steep decline in prices in the first half of November to the dissipation of the so-called 'political/war premium' after the UN Security Council's approval, and Iraq's subsequent unconditional acceptance of, Resolution 1441. Their recovery, in the second half of the month, was attributed to the perception that OPEC would take action to curb over-production, and to colder weather conditions in northern America and northern Asia. The average 'spot' quotation for Brent fell by $3.7 to $23.99 per barrel in November, while that of WTI fell by $2.69 to $26.31 per barrel. The front-month NYMEX WTI 'futures' contract, meanwhile, fell to a 'low' of $25.16 per barrel on 13 November, subsequently recovering by some $2 per barrel before the end of the month.

During December 2002 the average price of the OPEC reference 'basket' of crudes rose by more than US $4 to $28.39 per barrel, its highest level for two years. Average 'spot' quotations rose consistently during the month, in particular during the third and final weeks. By the end of the month the average price exceeded $30 per barrel, one of the highest levels ever recorded in December. The average 'spot' quotation for Brent rose by $4.84 to $28.83 per barrel, while that of WTI increased by $3.35 to $29.66 per barrel. In its monthly review of markets for crude petroleum, in addition to the continued threat of military conflict in Iraq, OPEC identified declining crude oil inventories (especially in the USA) and a sharp fall in Venezuelan production and exports as a consequence of strike action as the principal market influences. Before an extraordinary meeting of the OPEC conference took place in Vienna on 12 December, there was speculation that the Organization would seek to reassert its credibility by increasing its formal quotas (or overall 'ceiling') while, at the same time, making clear its intent to bring actual production into line with the new (raised) production level in order to restore discipline. In its assessment of market conditions prior to the extraordinary conference, the IEA concluded that an increase of some 1.5m. b/d in OPEC production that had occurred over the previous three months had probably been necessary in order to avert astronomical prices and to prevent a perilous depletion of industrial stocks at a time of geopolitical tension and as winter approached. In the event, as some commentators had predicted, the decision was taken at the conference to raise the production 'ceiling' for member states (excluding Iraq) from 21.7m. b/d to 23m. b/d, with effect from 1 January 2003, and to take steps to ensure that *de facto* production was reduced to within the new 'ceiling'. In its *Statistical Review of World Energy 2003*, BP noted that, as a result of production restraint and various unforeseen disruptions, OPEC's output had fallen by some 1.8m. b/d, or 6.4%, in the course of 2002. Oil demand in 2002 had been exceptionally weak for a third consecutive year, with consumption growing by only 290,000 b/d.

At US $30.34 per barrel, the average price of the OPEC reference 'basket' in January 2003 was the highest recorded for that month since 1983. Declines in the average 'spot' quotation during the first two weeks of the month were offset by an increase in the third week and a further increase, followed by a correction, in the final week. By the end of January the average price of the 'basket' had been above $28 per barrel—the upper limit of OPEC's targeted trading range—for more than 33 consecutive days. The average 'spot' quotation for Brent increased by $2.48, to $31.31 per barrel, while that of WTI rose by $3.42 to $33.08 per barrel. The continued rise in the price of crude petroleum was attributed by OPEC to the combination of preparations for military action against Iraq in the Middle East, ongoing strike action by Venezuelan oil workers and a consequent steep decline in US inventories of crude petroleum, and cold weather conditions in the northern hemisphere. In response to these key market characteristics, at an extraordinary meeting of the OPEC conference convened in Vienna on 12 January, the Organization agreed to raise its production 'ceiling' by 1.5m. b/d to 24.5m. b/d, with effect from 1 February 2003. Production under the new 'ceiling' was to be distributed as follows (former production level in parentheses): Algeria 782,000 b/d (735,000); Indonesia 1,270,000 b/d (1,192,000); Iran 3,597,000 b/d (3,377,000); Kuwait 1,966,000 b/d (1,845,000); Libya 1,312,000 b/d (1,232,000); Nigeria 2,018,000 b/d (1,894,000); Qatar 635,000 b/d (596,000); Saudi Arabia 7,963,000 b/d (7,476,000); UAE 2,138,000 b/d (2,007,000); Venezuela 2,819,000 b/d (2,647,000).

During February 2003 the average price of the OPEC reference 'basket' rose by a further US $1.20 per barrel, to $31.45: the third highest average price recorded in February since 1982 and $12.65 per barrel higher than in February 2002. 'Spot' quotations rose on a weekly basis throughout the month. The average 'spot' quotation for Brent increased by $1.24 to $32.54 per barrel, while that for WTI rose by $2.55 to $35.63 per barrel. As in the previous month, prices were boosted by the continued likelihood of war in Iraq and by very low inventories of crude petroleum and products in the USA. In its overview of market conditions in February, the IEA noted that, 'The issues of high oil prices, stocks and spare capacity have assumed a greater urgency in advance of a potential military invasion of Iraq'. Despite an increase in production of some 2m. b/d in February (of which OPEC had contributed 1.5m. b/d), producers had been unable to restrain prices and their options for further action were now limited by the consequent significant reduction in surplus production capacity.

Markets for crude petroleum were subject to a correction in March 2003. As the US-led military operation against the regime of Saddam Hussain in Iraq commenced, the so-called 'war premium' which had been a key characteristic of markets for many months, evaporated. During March the average price of the OPEC reference 'basket' fell to US $29.78 per barrel, $1.76 per barrel lower than in February. Even so, this was the highest average price recorded in March for 20 years, and the cumulative average price for the first quarter of 2003 was, at more than $30 per barrel, the highest ever recorded. The average 'spot' quotation for Brent fell by $1.56 to $30.98 per barrel, while that of WTI declined by $1.75 to $33.88 per barrel. The correction to prices occurred in spite of ongoing or recent disruptions to supplies from Iraq, Venezuela and Nigeria, and apparently reflected consumers' confidence that measures taken by producers (such as the strategic locating of crude in major consuming areas) to offset these disruptions would be effective. At a meeting of the OPEC ministerial conference held in Vienna on 11 March it was agreed to maintain the Organization's production at its existing level, which was deemed adequate, in view of the restoration of Venezuelan production to normal levels, to meet demand.

The price of crude petroleum declined even more sharply in April 2003, the average price of the OPEC reference 'basket' falling by almost 15%, compared with the previous month, to US $25.34 per barrel. However, as OPEC noted in its monthly market review, despite the steep, consecutive monthly declines in March and April, the average price remained solidly within the Organization's targeted trading range and, indeed, the cumulative average price for the first four months of 2003 exceeded that of the corresponding period of 2002 by some $7.79 per barrel, almost 37%. In April the greatest decline occurred in the final week of the month, when the 'basket' lost some 7% of its value, the average price having fluctuated during the preceding three weeks. The average 'spot' quotation of Brent declined by $5.91 to $25.07 per barrel, while that of WTI fell by $5.48 to $28.40 per barrel. OPEC noted that the US-led military campaign in Iraq remained the key influence on markets for crude, with prices weakening as the likelihood of protracted hostilities diminished. Other factors that exerted downward pressure on markets for crude during the second half of April were the gradual return of Nigerian light-sweet crude to the market and the collapse of European refiners' margins. At a consultative meeting of the OPEC conference held in Vienna on 24 April, it was decided to reduce the Organization's actual production by 2m. b/d and to set a new 'ceiling' for output at 25.4m. b/d, effective from 1 June 2003. Quotas within the new 'ceiling' were as follows (b/d): Algeria 811,000; Indonesia 1,317,000; Iran 3,729,000; Kuwait 2,038,000; Libya 1,360,000; Nigeria 2,092,000; Qatar 658,000; Saudi Arabia 8,256,000; UAE 2,217,000; Venezuela 2,923,000.

In May 2003 the average price of OPEC's reference 'basket' of crude oils rose by US $0.26 to $25.60 per barrel. In its monthly review of markets for crude, the Organization noted that the cumulative average for 2003, at $28.37 per barrel, was almost 30% higher than the average for the corresponding period of 2002. The value of the 'basket' increased consistently throughout the month, in particular in the second week when it rose by 6.4%. The average 'spot' quotation of Brent increased by $0.72 to $25.79 per barrel, while that of WTI declined by $0.17 to $28.23 per barrel. OPEC noted the declining influence of events in Iraq and the re-establishment of fundamental factors as the key market drivers. The most important of these was the low level of US stocks of crude, reformulated gasoline and distillates.

On 11 June 2003, at an extraordinary meeting of the OPEC conference convened in Doha, Qatar, it was agreed to maintain production at the prevailing level of 25.4m. b/d, with strict compliance. The conference noted that, while markets had been stable since OPEC had reduced its actual production to 25.4m. b/d and remained well supplied, prices had recently displayed an upward trend as a consequence of the slower-than-anticipated recovery in Iraqi output and unusually low inventory levels. The average price of the OPEC reference 'basket' did, in fact, rise substantially in June: by 4.5%, to US $26.74 per barrel. At the end of June the cumulative average price of the 'basket' stood at $28.11 per barrel, 27% higher than the average recorded for the first half of 2002. The greatest increase in the value of OPEC crudes occurred in the second week of the month, when the price of the 'basket' rose by 2.5%. This, together with smaller increases in the first and final weeks of June, was sufficient to compensate for a 5% decline in the price that occurred in the third week of the month. The average price of Brent rose by $1.65 to $27.44 per barrel, while that of WTI increased by $2.48 to $30.71 per barrel. Prices were supported in June by a further decline in US stocks of crude petroleum, especially in the early part of the month. OPEC's decision, on 11 June, to maintain production at the prevailing level had been anticipated to a large extent and its influence on prices was regarded as relatively insignificant. Unanticipated delays in the recovery of Iraqi production were another factor that supported prices in June.

In July 2003 the average price of the OPEC reference 'basket' was US $27.43 per barrel, 2.5% higher than the average price recorded in June. During the first seven months of 2003, accordingly, the cumulative average price of the 'basket' was $27.99 per barrel, some 24% higher than the average price recorded in the corresponding period of 2002 and just below the upper limit of OPEC's targeted trading range. In August the price of the 'basket' increased further, averaging $28.63 per barrel. The cumulative average price for the first eight months of 2003, at $28.07 per barrel, was, accordingly, 22% higher than that recorded in the corresponding period of 2002.

At a meeting of the OPEC conference held in Vienna on 24 September 2003, and attended by an Iraqi delegation headed by Iraq's newly appointed Minister of Oil, Ibrahim Bahr al-Ulum, the decision was taken to reduce the Organization's production ceiling to 24.5m. b/d, with effect from 1 November. This decision was made in the light of OPEC's assessment of markets for crude as well supplied, and its observation that 'only normal, seasonal growth in demand [was] expected for the fourth quarter ...'. As a result of continued increases in non-OPEC output and an ongoing recovery in Iraqi supplies, stocks were reported to be rapidly approaching normal seasonal levels. Furthermore, the supply/demand balance in the final quarter of 2003 and first quarter of 2004 indicated a 'contra-seasonal stock build-up' which, it was feared, could destabilize markets. OPEC's decision aimed to avert that threat, and the Organization appealed to non-OPEC producers to support it by likewise restraining increases in output.

In September 2003 the average price of the OPEC reference 'basket' of crude oils declined sharply, by US $2.31, to $26.32 per barrel. In the same month the average 'spot' quotation of Brent fell by $2.46, to $27.32 per barrel, while that of WTI declined by as much as $3.05, to $27.32 per barrel. The decline in the average price of the OPEC 'basket' was most marked in the first two weeks of the month, when it averaged, respectively, $27.61 per barrel and $26.42 per barrel. By 25 September the cumulative decline for the month amounted to more than 12%, but in the final week of September an increase of $1.45 per barrel was recorded. In its review of market developments in September, OPEC noted that the price of crude petroleum had hitherto drawn support from firm speculative US gasoline prices. From the beginning of the month, however, these had declined to a surprising extent, thus removing that support. At mid-September prices were regarded as 'steady', the major fundamental influence being concern over the level of US and EU heating oil stocks. The Organization defended its decision to reduce the production ceiling to 24.5m. b/d—which had taken speculators by surprise—as a 'reasoned response to market fundamentals and as a proactive effort . . .to accommodate the return of Iraqi production'.

In October 2003 the average price of the OPEC 'basket' increased by US $2.22 per barrel, to $28.54. Taking this increase into account, the cumulative average price of the OPEC 'basket' in 2003 stood at $27.91 and was thus approaching the upper limit—$28 per barrel—of OPEC's targeted trading range. The average 'spot' quotation of Brent, meanwhile, rose by $2.53 per barrel, to $29.85, and that of WTI by $1.88, to $30.43 per barrel. Analysts attributed the surge in prices in October to the continued psychological effect of the Organization's unexpected decision in September to reduce production. Another factor in the first three weeks of October was the perception that US stocks of heating oil and distillates, though rising, would be inadequate to meet demand during the long, severe winter that was forecast. In the final week, however, prices fell in response to more realistic formulations of the supply/demand equation likely to pertain in coming months.

The average price of the OPEC 'basket' declined marginally, by US $0.09, to $28.45 per barrel, in November 2003. The average 'spot' quotation for Brent declined by $1.17 per barrel, to $28.68, while that of WTI rose by $0.51, to $30.94 per barrel. Quotations, which had been relatively weak in the second half of October, strengthened during most of November, before weakening again at the end of the month. The most influential fundamental factor remained continued concern regarding the level of US stocks of heating oil as the winter approached. In mid-November speculation was identified as the factor behind surges in the prices of WTI and Brent. In its review of market developments in November, OPEC noted that the speculative rally was fuelled by 'fears of inadequate crude oil and product inventories in the USA and Europe, preliminary figures showing OPEC-10 [i.e. all OPEC members except Iraq] was implementing the September 24 Agreement calling for production cuts, and the dramatic increase in speculators' long positions at the NYMEX, which indicates that the market expects prices to rise in the future'. The speculative rally ended at the close of the month with profit-taking by market participants and reduction of exposure in advance of a forthcoming extraordinary meeting of OPEC.

On 4 December 2003, at the extraordinary conference held in Vienna, OPEC decided to maintain production at its current level until further notice. During the month the average price of the OPEC 'basket' of crude oils rose by US $0.99 per barrel, to $29.44, its highest level since March. At the same time, the average quotation of Brent rose by $1.14, to $29.82 per barrel, and that of WTI by $1.21, to $32.15. In its review of market developments in December, OPEC noted that the cumulative average 'spot' quotation of its reference 'basket' in 2003 was, at $28.10, the highest nominal annual average since 1984. During December 2003 prices were initially supported by very strong Asian, in particular Chinese, demand for petroleum products, by declines in US commercial inventories of crude and by indications that economic recovery was well established in the USA. As the month progressed these factors were reinforced by cold weather conditions. BP noted, in its *Statistical Review of World Energy 2004*, that oil prices in 2003 had been at their highest level in nominal terms (i.e. without taking inflation into account) for 20 years. Consumption world-wide had also risen strongly, by 2.1%. Despite interruptions to the output of Iraq and Venezuela, OPEC production had increased substantially in 2003, by some 1.9m. b/d.

In January 2004 the average price of the OPEC reference 'basket' of crudes rose by US $0.89 per barrel, to $30.33. The average 'spot' quotation of Brent rose by $1.51, to $31.33, in that month, while the average quotation of WTI increased by as much as $2.18, to $34.33. The surge in the price of WTI was attributed to a combination of very low US inventories of crude oil, which in mid-January reportedly fell below the minimum operational level that had been established in 1998, and very cold weather in eastern areas of the USA early in the month. In spite of the substantial discount in the price of North Sea and West African crudes relative to WTI, deliveries of these crudes to US markets were restricted throughout most of January 2004 by very high freight rates.

On 10 February 2004, at an extraordinary conference held in Algiers, Algeria, OPEC decided to reduce its production 'ceiling' from 24.5m. b/d to 23.5m. b/d, with effect from 1 April 2004. This decision was taken in response to projections of a 'significant supply surplus in the seasonally low demand second quarter [of 2004]', in order to avert downward pressure on prices. Production under the new 'ceiling' was to be distributed as follows (b/d, former production level in parentheses): Algeria 750,000 (782,000); Indonesia 1,218,000 (1,270,000); Iran 3,450,000 (3,597,000); Kuwait 1,886,000 (1,966,000); Libya 1,258,000 (1,312,000); Nigeria 1,936,000 (2,018,000); Qatar 609,000 (635,000); Saudi Arabia 7,638,000 (7,963,000); UAE 2,051,000 (2,138,000); Venezuela 2,704,000 (2,819,000). During February the average price of the OPEC 'basket' of crudes declined by US $0.77, to $29.56 per barrel. The average 'spot' quotation of Brent declined by $0.68 per barrel, to $30.65, in February, while that of WTI rose by $0.29, to $34.62 per barrel. In its review of market developments in February, OPEC indicated the increasing importance as an influence on markets for crude of the US market for gasoline, which faced a potential supply shortage owing to a combination of steady and rising demand, the inability of Asia-Pacific refiners to supply it, and low domestic (US) inventories.

In March 2004 the average price of the OPEC reference 'basket' increased by US $2.49, to $32.05 per barrel. It was the first time that an average price in excess of $32 per barrel had been recorded since October 1990. The average 'spot' quotation of Brent rose by $3.05, to $33.70 per barrel in March 2004, while that of WTI increased by $1.97, to $36.59 per barrel. According to OPEC, the US gasoline market remained the key influence on markets for crude, while strong global demand for crude petroleum and economic growth were other important factors. At a conference held in Vienna on 31 March OPEC confirmed that it would adjust its production 'ceiling' to 23.5m. b/d from the beginning of April, in accordance with the decision announced in February. In the view of the Organization, prevailing high prices for crude petroleum did not reflect supply/demand fundamental factors, but rather were 'predominantly a consequence of long positions of market speculators in the futures markets coupled with a tightening in the US gasoline market in some regions, and exacerbated by uncertainties arising from prevailing geopolitical concerns ...'.

The average price of the OPEC reference 'basket' in April 2004, at US $32.35 per barrel, was the second highest ever recorded—the highest was (at that time) $34.32, registered in October 1990. The average 'spot' quotation of Brent fell by $0.47 in April, to $33.23 per barrel, while that of WTI rose by $0.21, to $36.80. OPEC indicated that the cumulative average price of its reference 'basket' up to 30 April 2004 was $31.13 per barrel, compared with $29.02 per barrel for the corresponding period of 2003. The continued strength of markets for crude was attributed to, among other things, low US inventories of gasoline, in particular RFG, stocks of which were reportedly some 32% lower at 30 April 2004 than at 30 April 2003, and some 41% lower than the five-year average, according to the EIA. Continued strong US demand for gasoline was likely to face further pressure, as it rose during the summer months, from new specifications, introduced from January 2004, banning the use of methyl-tertiary-butane ether for the production of RFG in the states of California, Connecticut and New York. OPEC also identified very strong demand on the part of the People's Republic of China for gasoline and its consequent reduced availability for export as an additional factor supporting gasoline markets. In addition to these fundamental factors, greater concern over unrest in petroleum-producing countries had reportedly led to increased speculative activity on crude markets, pushing prices further upward.

In May 2004 the average price of the OPEC 'basket' of crudes, at US $36.27, was the highest ever recorded. At the same time the average 'spot' quotation of Brent rose by $4.48 per barrel to $37.71, while that of WTI increased by $3.31 per barrel to $40.11. At the end of May the cumulative average price of the OPEC reference 'basket' had reached $32.11 per barrel, an increase in excess of 13% compared with the corresponding period of 2003. OPEC indicated that prices had continued to be propelled upwards by 'tight gasoline markets, especially in the USA, where new and more stringent specifications have created operational bottlenecks'. Gasoline consumption was reported to have been some 4.5% higher in 2004 than in 2003, and it was noted that the increase in demand had occurred before the onset of the US 'driving season'. OPEC also acknowledged the influence on speculative activity of fears of a disruption to supplies. Increasingly, in view of 'understated world oil demand for the present year, which has been revised up as much as 1m. b/d according to many market analysts', markets had begun to question whether supplies would be sufficient to meet seasonal demand in the final part of the year, which was perceived as likely to approach total world production capacity. Nevertheless, OPEC concluded that 'the market is well supplied with crude and the current high oil prices are rooted in exuberant speculations by the futures market on perceptions of possible supply disruptions'.

In early June 2004, following attacks by militant Islamists, who were suspected of having links with the al-Qa'ida (Base) organization, on foreign workers in the Saudi Arabian city of al-Khobar, an important centre for the Saudi oil industry, the price of crude petroleum traded in the USA rose to the record level of US $42.45 per barrel, while that of Brent approached $40 per barrel. On 3 June, at an extraordinary conference held in Beirut, Lebanon, OPEC decided to raise its production 'ceiling' to 25.5m. b/d with effect from 1 July, and to 26m. b/d with effect from 1 August. The Organization noted that prices had continued to escalate, in spite of its efforts to ensure that markets were well supplied, as a result of continued growth in demand in the USA and China, geopolitical tensions, problems in respect of refining and distribution in some consuming regions and more stringent product specifications. Production under the new 'ceiling' was to be distributed as follows from 1 July (b/d): Algeria 814,000; Indonesia 1,322,000; Iran 3,744,000; Kuwait 2,046,000; Libya 1,365,000; Nigeria 2,101,000; Qatar 661,000; Saudi Arabia 8,288,000; UAE 2,225,000; Venezuela 2,934,000. From 1 August the distribution of OPEC production was to be: Algeria 830,000; Indonesia 1,347,000; Iran 3,817,000; Kuwait 2,087,000; Libya 1,392,000; Nigeria 2,142,000; Qatar 674,000; Saudi Arabia 8,450,000; UAE 2,269,000; Venezuela 2,992,000.

In the immediate aftermath of OPEC's announcement of its new production 'ceilings' the price of both US-traded crudes and of Brent declined. However, some analysts expressed doubts over whether OPEC's action was sufficient to exercise a sustained calming effect on markets, noting that most of its members were already producing at close to capacity, in some cases in breach of prevailing quotas. The new 'ceilings' would thus, in the view of those observers, simply legitimize over-production. Representatives of some OPEC member states, meanwhile, conceded that the new production limits would not necessarily bring prices back within the Organization's preferred trading range, but would counter any perception of shortages.

In July 2004 the average price of the OPEC reference 'basket' rose to a new record level of US $36.29 per barrel—in June it had declined slightly in comparison with May, to $34.61 per barrel, none the less the highest average price recorded in the month of June for 22 years. In July the average price of Brent increased by $3.21 per barrel to $38.33, while that of WTI rose by $2.51 per barrel to $40.69. The cumulative average price of the OPEC reference basket for January–July 2004 rose accordingly to $33.45 per barrel, some 18% higher than the average price recorded in the corresponding period of 2003. In its assessment of markets for crude in July, OPEC attempted to clarify the market's perception of tightness in supplies, indicating that while there had been a scarcity of light, sweet crudes, 'it is also true that sour crudes are inundating the market ...'. OPEC also noted that the global refining system was operating at close to full capacity and concluded its assessment by indicating that, apparently, 'the market has entered a new reality, one where tightness in upstream spare capacity due to lack of capacity expansion and surprisingly robust oil demand growth promises to set the scene for a new market dynamic'.

In a statement issued in early August 2004, OPEC noted that production by its members (excluding Iraq) had continued to increase in order to meet greater-than-expected growth in demand. Output was estimated to have been substantially greater than 29m. b/d in July 2004, and it was forecast that total OPEC production, including that of Iraq, would approach 30m. b/d in August. With reference to possible future market-stabilization measures, the Organization indicated that it retained spare production capacity of some 1m. b/d–1.5m. b/d, which would permit an immediate further increase in output, and that OPEC members intended to raise production capacity by some 1m. b/d in late 2004 and during 2005. Oil continued to trade at record levels in August 2004: the average price of the OPEC reference 'basket' of crude oils was, for the first time since the Organization adopted the reference price system, in excess of US $40 per barrel, having risen by 11% compared with the previous month. In the same month the average 'spot' quotation of Brent rose by 11.8%, to $42.87 per barrel, and that of WTI by 10%, to $44.77 per barrel. The cumulative average price of the OPEC 'basket' in January–August 2004 was 21% higher than in the corresponding period in 2003.

As oil prices reached record levels in the third week of August 2004, some analysts warned of a future energy crisis—in which oil prices would continue to rise, perhaps above US $65 per barrel—that might give rise to economic recession world-wide. It was noted at this time that some traders did not appear to view the current 'spike' in prices as a cyclical high: since May 2003 futures prices for oil, for delivery in two years' time, had risen by almost as much as those of oil for immediate or imminent delivery. Factors cited as responsible for the record prices recorded in August 2004 included the perceived insecurity of supplies from important producing countries such as Iraq, Saudi Arabia, Russia and Venezuela, and the economic boom that was occurring in China. Prices, according to some observers, were likely to remain at unprecedented levels until they had triggered a recession which would bring growth in demand for oil back into line with existing capacity for production, refining and distribution.

In the view of OPEC, the dramatic increases in the price of crudes that took place in August 2004 were attributable to a combination of both fundamental and non-fundamental factors. The estimated extent of the total increase in demand for oil world-wide in 2004 continued to be revised upwards, and was assessed in August at some 2.5m. b/d, to be followed by a further increase in 2005 of some 1.7m. b/d. The forecast increase in demand from China for the whole of 2004, at more than 0.8m. b/d, was already characterized by OPEC as 'spectacular' and had the potential to rise further before the end of the year. There were indications, according to OPEC, that growth in demand in the second quarter of 2004, at some 3.80m. b/d (4.95% higher than in the corresponding three-month period of 2003), had been higher than at any time since 1985. With regard to supply, intermittent interruptions to Iraqi output had delayed and continued to delay the return of that country's production to 2.8m. b/d. Other factors that had combined to strengthen the prices of crude oil and petroleum products in August included the maintenance of stocks at comparatively low levels and fears of increased unrest in Iraq and in the Middle East generally. These concerns had, according to OPEC, been exacerbated by speculative activity on futures markets for crude oil: with regard to fundamental factors, OPEC concluded that supply was more than sufficient to meet the increases in demand forecast to occur during the remainder of 2004 and in early 2005.

In late August and early September 2004 the price of the OPEC reference 'basket' of crudes eased somewhat, as concerns regarding supplies (in particular those from Venezuela and Iraq) subsided. As September progressed, however, adequate supplies and OPEC's express commitment to raising its production 'ceiling' to 27m. b/d from 1 November 2004 (see below) were insufficient to calm continued fears of disruption to Russian supplies (arising from the so-called Yukos affair—from late 2003 senior officials of Russia's prominent petroleum company, Yukos, and its subsidiaries were accused of tax evasion and fraud, resulting in the company being dismantled by the Russian authorities in late 2004), and these, in combination with the actual disruption of production and refining in the Gulf of Mexico by hurricane weather conditions, propelled the average price of the 'basket' to a new record level of US $40.36 per barrel for the whole of September, 0.2% higher than the average price recorded in August. Average quotations for Brent and WTI rose, respectively, by 1.3%, to $43.43 per barrel, and by 2.7%, to $45.98 per barrel. Compared with January–September 2003, the cumulative average price of the OPEC 'basket' in the first nine months of 2004 was almost 25% higher, at $34.98 per barrel.

In mid-September 2004, at a meeting of the OPEC conference in Vienna, it was agreed to increase the production 'ceiling' for the Organization (excluding Iraq) by 1m. b/d, to 27m. b/d, effective from 1 November 2004, with the aim of reducing the high prices recently recorded to 'a more sustainable level'. Commenting on market conditions at the time of the conference, OPEC summarized the factors responsible for recent price increases as: the rise in demand that had occurred earlier in the year, especially in North America, China and other Asian countries—preliminary figures published by OPEC in September 2004 indicated that demand for oil world-wide had increased by 1.8m. b/d, or 2.3%, in the first quarter of 2004, and by 4m. b/d, more than 5%, in the second quarter; geopolitical considerations; doubts over the adequacy of existing spare capacity to meet possible supply disruptions; speculative investment activity; and constraints within the downstream industry.

In October 2004 the average price of the OPEC reference 'basket' of crude oils rose by 12.4%, compared with the previous month, to US $45.37 per barrel, its highest ever level. During the third week of the month, moreover, the highest ever weekly price, $46.04 per barrel, was recorded. The average 'spot' quotation of Brent increased by 14.5% in October, to $49.74 per barrel, while that of WTI rose by 16%, to $53.32 per barrel. (During the second and third weeks of October the price of WTI rose to successive record levels of $55.08 per barrel and $56.42 per barrel, boosted by, among other factors, low US stocks of heating oil and industrial action in Norway.) In Europe record prices for Brent were recorded owing to concerns that there would be shortages of winter fuels. Hurricane weather conditions on the US Gulf coast and concern that supplies from Nigeria would be restricted were identified as the main factors driving prices upwards in the early part of the month. In the third week of October fears that winter fuels would be in short supply combined with industrial action in Nigeria to support prices.

As concerns over possible shortages of winter fuels, especially in the USA, subsided in response to mild weather conditions world-wide and the accumulation of stocks of middle distillates, and crude production by OPEC members reached record levels, the average price of the OPEC reference 'basket' of crudes in November 2004 was, at US $38.96 per barrel, some 14% lower than in October. At the same time, the average 'spot' quotations of Brent and WTI declined, respectively, by some 14%, to $42.80 per barrel, and by 9.6%, to $48.22 per barrel. The average price of the OPEC reference 'basket' in November was the lowest recorded since July 2003, and the fall in the price in November 2004, compared with October, was the steepest month-on-month decline ever recorded. In January–November 2004 the cumulative average price of the OPEC reference 'basket', at $36.07 per barrel, was 29% higher than in the first 11 months of 2003. Heavy selling of crude oil 'futures' contracts by speculative investors, in order to realize profits, was reported to have occurred in November 2004, as the level of OPEC production, in combination with slower growth in demand, allowed stocks to accumulate in advance of winter in the northern hemisphere.

The ready availability of Middle Eastern crudes remained an important influence on the market in December 2004. At an extraordinary meeting held in Cairo on 10 December, the OPEC conference observed that its recent initiative to raise supplies had caused 'current crude oil prices [to] reflect convergence towards market fundamentals'. The conference agreed to maintain OPEC's production 'ceiling' and individual production levels unchanged, but reported that member countries 'which have responded to the market need for additional supply over the course of this year by producing above their allocations, have agreed to collectively reduce the over-production by 1m. b/d from their current actual output, effective 1 January 2005'. At the beginning of December adequate Middle Eastern supplies had applied downward pressure to prices. As the month progressed, other depressive factors, including a resumption of Nigerian output and forecast mild winter weather conditions, prevailed over factors, such as concerns about the security of Middle Eastern oil infrastructure and the decision of the OPEC conference to maintain its production 'ceiling' unchanged, that tended to strengthen prices: overall in December the average price of the OPEC reference 'basket' of crude oils declined by 8.4%, compared with November, to US $35.70 per barrel. At the same time, the average 'spot' quotation of Brent declined by 7.9%, to $39.43 per barrel, while that of WTI fell by 10.6%, to $43.12 per barrel. The average price of the OPEC reference 'basket' for the whole of 2004, at $36.05, was 28% higher than in 2003, in spite of the consecutive monthly declines recorded in November and December 2004. According to data published by OPEC at the end of the year, demand for oil world-wide in 2004 averaged 81.99m. b/d.

At the beginning of 2005, assessing the prospects for oil in the next 12 months, some analysts noted that since mid-2003 economic growth, in particular in North America, China and other emerging Asian economies, such as India, had caused the price of oil and other commodities to increase sharply. If the world economy were to conform to typical, cyclical patterns, however, it was anticipated that growth would decline overall by about 20% in 2005, curbing demand for oil. It was noted, too, that during the course of 2004 there had been a substantial rise in the supply of oil world-wide, from both OPEC members and other countries. The perceived vulnerability of supplies to, *inter alia*, developments in the Yukos affair in Russia and hurricane weather conditions in the Gulf of Mexico, in combination with the insecurity of Iraq's oil infrastructure, social and political instability in Nigeria and Mexico, and the continued, gradual decline in North Sea output, had applied upward pressure to prices; and these were the factors to which OPEC was attempting to respond by raising its members' output, to the point that actual production, at 29.1m. b/d, was at its highest level for 25 years. Globally, in 2004, supply grew by about 1m. b/d more than demand, thus meeting demand and allowing the recovery of commercial stocks and strategic reserves.

In January 2005 the average price of the OPEC reference 'basket' of crude oils, at US $40.24 per barrel, was 12.7% higher than in December 2004. At the same time, the average 'spot' quotation of Brent increased by 11.6%, to $44.01 per barrel, and that of WTI by 8.2%, to $44.39 per barrel. The average price of the OPEC reference 'basket' in January 2005 was 33% higher than in the corresponding month of 2004. Among the factors that were cited as having contributed to the increase in prices at the beginning of 2005 were cold weather conditions in the northern hemisphere, instability in Iraq, expectations of industrial action in Venezuela and declines in US stocks of crude. At an extraordinary meeting of the OPEC conference held in Vienna on 30 January, OPEC noted that supplies of oil world-wide exceeded demand, and that commercial stocks had been replenished to above their five-year average levels. An element of volatility remained in the market, however, owing to concerns over interruption of supply and the predicted persistence of strong demand. With reference to forecasts indicating that markets would remain in balance during the first quarter of 2005, OPEC agreed to maintain output of crude at its prevailing level. The conference noted, furthermore, that prices had remained outside of the Organization's preferred trading range of $22–$28 per barrel for more than one year, owing to changes in the market that had made the range 'unrealistic'. The decision was taken therefore to suspend the price range 'pending completion of further studies on the subject'.

OPEC's decision to suspend the preferred trading range of US $22–$28 per barrel was interpreted by some analysts as a further sign that the recent unprecedentedly high price of oil should be viewed as the result of a fundamental change that was occurring in the supply/demand equation rather than as a temporary phenomenon. It was argued that spare production capacity in the oil industry world-wide had been almost exhausted. (This argument had been used earlier to explain the apparently disproportionate effect of perceived threats to supplies from Norway and Nigeria on the price of oil in October 2004: analysts had suggested that oil producers in general and OPEC member countries in particular had neglected to expand and upgrade their production capacity to enable it to accommodate rapid rises in global demand for oil. OPEC's production capacity was estimated by some observers to have risen to close to its upper limit, where other members would be unable to compensate for, for example, disruption to Nigerian output.) It was reported at the end of 2004 that production was declining in some 70% of the world's largest oil-producing countries, and that in 2004 only Russia and the Gulf states had been able to raise output. In July 2004 Saudi Arabian officials had announced that they regarded the price of oil at that time—about $35 per barrel—as fair, suggesting that, like other members of OPEC, Saudi Arabia no longer favoured the trading range of $22–$28 per barrel. Some analysts regarded this as a tacit acknowledgement by Saudi Arabia of its inability to increase production from its ageing oilfields to any great extent beyond current levels, and thus as a step closer towards so-called 'peak' production and, in turn, the end of 'cheap' oil. Other observers, however, remained confident that the issue of spare capacity would decline in significance. As in the past, high prices for oil would encourage new exploration initiatives and world oil production would continue to rise for the indefinite future.

In February 2005 the average price of the OPEC reference 'basket' of crude oils, at US $41.68 per barrel, was 3.6% higher than the average price recorded in the previous month. The average 'spot' quotation of Brent increased by almost 2% in February, to $44.87 per barrel, while that of WTI rose by 2.3%, to $47.69 per barrel. During the first two weeks of February prices generally declined in response to factors such as the predicted warmer weather conditions. Gains occurred in the latter part of the month, in response to industry concerns over a possible reduction of OPEC output, colder weather conditions, increased demand for winter fuels and a decline in the value of the US dollar.

At US $49.07 per barrel, 17.7% higher than in February 2005, the average price of the OPEC reference 'basket' of crude oils in March was the highest ever recorded. During March the average 'spot' quotations of Brent and WTI rose, respectively, by 17.2%, to $52.60 per barrel, and by 13.4%, to $54.09 per barrel. Projected high demand was a key determinant of market movements in the early part of March, in combination with continued cold weather conditions. Fears that demand would exceed supply propelled prices to a level close to $50 per barrel in the second week of March. In the second half of the month prices rose above $50 per barrel in response, among other things, to a substantial decline in US stocks of gasoline, distillates and heating oil. Towards the end of March the price of the OPEC 'basket' of crudes rose to a record high level of $50.72 per barrel after an accident at a US refinery prompted fears of a shortage of refined products. The price declined in the final days of the month, however. On 16 March, meeting in Esfahan, Iran, the OPEC conference agreed to increase the Organization's production 'ceiling' to 27.5m. b/d, with immediate effect. Moreover, the conference authorized OPEC's President to announce a further increase of 500,000 b/d in the 'ceiling' before the next meeting of the conference, should 'oil prices remain at current levels or continue to rise further'. In its assessment of market conditions prior to this decision, OPEC noted that world crude oil prices had begun to rise again even though all indicators pointed to a market that was fundamentally well supplied. In explanation, OPEC's concluding statement referred to late cold weather conditions in the northern hemisphere, the anticipated continued strength of demand, speculative activity in oil futures markets, geopolitical tensions and downstream bottlenecks. Another factor cited by analysts in explanation of the so-called spring 'spike' in oil prices was the continued decline in the value of the US dollar in relation to the euro.

In April 2005 the average price of the OPEC reference 'basket' of crude oils increased by 1.1%—the lowest monthly increase for four months—to US $49.63 per barrel. The average 'spot' quotation of both Brent and WTI also declined in April, by 1.4%, to $51.87 per barrel, and by 1.8%, to $53.09 per barrel, respectively. Early in the month prices rose in response to a report by the investment bank Goldman Sachs in which the possibility that oil prices might double from their current levels was discussed. Indeed, in the first week of April the average price of OPEC 'basket' crudes, at $52.07 per barrel, was the highest ever recorded. In the second week of April, however, continued increases in US stocks of crude, high OPEC output and a revised, lower forecast of world demand for oil in 2005 by the IEA combined to bring down prices. During the third week of April markets for oil lacked clear direction, responding to developments in the Yukos affair by rising, for instance, and declining in response to the ready availability of OPEC crudes.

In May 2005 the average price of the OPEC reference 'basket' of crude oils fell by more than 5%, to US $46.96 per barrel. At the same time, the average 'spot' quotation of Brent declined by 5.7%, compared with the previous month, to $48.90 per barrel, while that of WTI declined by 5.3%, to $50.25 per barrel. During the first three weeks of May OPEC's reference price fell steadily in response to such factors as the ready availability of OPEC crudes and, in particular, the high level of US crude inventories. In the final week of the month, however, prices were supported by fears that supplies of refined products would be disrupted in advance of the US driving season. May marked the first time for six months when an average price lower than that of the preceding month had been recorded.

At an extraordinary meeting of the OPEC conference held in Vienna on 15 June 2005, the Organization took the decision to raise its production 'ceiling' by 500,000 b/d, with effect from 1 July. Commenting on prevailing market conditions, OPEC noted that although markets were well supplied, world crude prices had remained high and volatile owing to concerns over a lack of effective global oil refining capacity. Refiners' difficulties in meeting strong growth in demand for distillates, moreover, were being exacerbated by geopolitical developments and speculative investment activity on futures markets. OPEC's decision to raise the production 'ceiling' was taken in the light of this analysis and in response to anticipated continued strong growth in demand for crude oil in 2005 and renewed price increases. The conference also authorized its President, after having consulted with heads of delegations, to announce an additional increase of 500,000 b/d in the production 'ceiling' if crude prices remained at their current levels or continued to rise. Separately, the conference announced its decision to change the composition of the OPEC reference 'basket' from 16 June 2005. The new 'basket' would comprise the main export crudes (Saharan Blend—Algeria; Minas—Indonesia; Iran Heavy—Iran; Basra Light—Iraq; Kuwait Export—Kuwait; Es Sider—Libya; Bonny Light—Nigeria; Qatar Marine—Qatar; Arabian Light—Saudi Arabia; Murban—UAE; BCF 17—Venezuela) of all OPEC member states and would be weighted according to production and exports to the principal markets. The new 'basket' would also better reflect the average quality of member countries' crudes.

In June 2005 the average price of the OPEC reference 'basket' of crudes (calculated on the basis of both the old and the new components of the 'basket'—see above) rose by 11%, to US $52.04 per barrel. The average price of the 'basket' as composed until 16 June increased by 12%, to $52.72 per barrel, while that of its newly defined counterpart rose by 13%, to $52.92 per barrel. In June the average 'spot' quotation of Brent increased by 11.9%, to $54.73 per barrel, while that of WTI rose by 12.6%, to $56.60 per barrel. Concern over possible shortages of refined products was identified as the key determinant of price movements in June. Assessing the prospects for world petroleum markets in 2006 in mid-2005, OPEC noted that growth in demand in 2005 was estimated at, on average, 1.6m. b/d. Forecasts of growth in non-OPEC supplies had been reduced owing, chiefly, to a fall in Russian output. OPEC production, meanwhile, was estimated to have averaged 30m. b/d in the first half of 2005, an increase of 1m. b/d compared with the first half of 2004, and this had led to counter-seasonal growth in inventories in the first quarter and the first two months of the second quarter of 2005. Record price levels had thus been recorded in spite of abundant supplies of crude and increased stocks.

In July 2005 the average price of the OPEC reference 'basket' increased by 2%, to US $53.13 per barrel. At the same time, the average quotation of Brent for immediate delivery rose by 5%, to $54.47 per barrel, while that of WTI strengthened by 3.6%, to $58.66 per barrel. Oil prices were reported to have been boosted in the early part of the month by stormy weather conditions in the Gulf of Mexico that had revived fears of possible shortages of crude and petroleum products. Having eased somewhat, oil prices were subsequently driven upwards once again by a recurrence of adverse weather in the Gulf of Mexico, although they were checked on this occasion by reported accumulations of stocks of distillate fuels. In the third week of July the average price of the OPEC reference 'basket' declined in response to lower Chinese consumption of oil, and to forecasts of slower growth in demand for oil. In the final week of the month prices were supported by concern that supplies would be disrupted by adverse weather conditions and by problems at US refineries.

In August 2005 the average price of the OPEC reference 'basket' rose by US $4.69, equivalent to almost 9%, compared with the previous month, to $57.82 per barrel. The average 'spot' quotation of Brent blend increased by $6.59 in August, to $64.06 per barrel, while that of WTI rose by $6.3, to $64.96 per barrel. During the course of the month prices were propelled to record levels owing to concern that 'refinery outages' would be aggravated by hurricane weather conditions. In its review of the markets for oil in July, OPEC had identified 'refinery outages' as a key factor behind the recent price volatility of oil and urged 'rapid and sizeable investment in the refining sector, particularly in conversion capacity, which has persistently lagged market requirements . . .'. (Some analysts concurred in the view that the prevailing high price of oil was due to lack of refinery capacity rather than to any shortage of crude. Others, however, interpreted shortages of refining capacity as a sign that global output of light sweet crudes had peaked, and emphasized the lack of refining facilities for processing heavier crudes.) Strike action in Ecuador was another factor behind the volatile market conditions in August. In late August the price of US light crude rose to more than $70 per barrel in response to damage to US production and refining facilities caused by hurricane weather conditions in the Gulf of Mexico. It was reported that 'Hurricane Katrina' had caused the closure of up to 90% of US oil production facilities in the Gulf of Mexico and fears were expressed that the damage would be long-lasting. Upward pressure on prices was subsequently checked by the decision, announced on 31 August, of the US Administration to release stocks from the US SPR; and by the announcement by the IEA on 2 September that its signatory countries would begin to release a total of 60m. barrels from American, Asian and European strategic stocks at a daily rate of 2m. barrels.

In September 2005 the average price of the OPEC reference 'basket' increased marginally, by US $0.06 per barrel, to $57.88 per barrel. The average 'spot' quotation of Brent declined by $1.31, to $62.75 per barrel, while that of WTI rose slightly, by $0.32, to $65.28 per barrel. In the first week of the month upward movement was checked by the release of US and IEA strategic stocks. In the second week of September downward pressure was reinforced by the IEA's prediction that global demand for oil in 2005 would be lower than previously forecast and by speculative sales on 'futures' markets. Prices subsequently strengthened in response to fears of damage to oil production and refining facilities in the Gulf of Mexico by 'Hurricane Rita', but eased again, albeit marginally, towards the end of the month as, among other factors, speculators took profits on 'futures' markets. At the OPEC ministerial conference held on 19–20 September in Vienna, in response to the continued rise in crude prices, the Organization undertook, if necessary, to make available to the market the spare capacity of some 2m. b/d held by OPEC members for a period of three months from 1 October 2005. At the same time, the Organization emphasized (as it had already done on previous occasions) that 'the continuing shortage of appropriate refining capacity remains one of the main reasons behind recent oil price increases and price volatility', urging industry and consumer governments to take urgent action to address the issue of refining shortages and expand refinery capacity.

OPEC's decision in September 2005 to make its spare capacity available to the market was interpreted by some analysts as of little significance to the supply/demand equation. Rather, they viewed it as part of an attempt to rebuff criticism of the Organization and to allay fears concerning the impact of the high price of oil on global economic growth in the wake of 'Hurricane Katrina' in August. Early in September the Organisation for Economic Co-operation and Development (OECD) had warned of the possible effect of high energy prices on economic growth, in particular in the euro zone. In mid-September the British Chancellor of the Exchequer, Gordon Brown, had announced a 'concerted international plan' to address volatility in global markets for oil that had urged OPEC to increase its ouput 'because this is, at root, a problem of demand outstripping supply . . .'. Brown had also urged OPEC to become more transparent since 'lack of transparency about the world's reserves and plans for their development undermine stability and cause speculation'. Finally, the British Chancellor had called for additional new investment in production and refining capacity world-wide. The response of OPEC's acting Secretary-General, Dr Adnan Shibab-Eldin, to Brown's assertions was to state his view that global demand for oil was not, in fact, outstripping supply. OPEC's decision at the ministerial conference held on 19–20 September reportedly reflected its willingness to help ease prices, while its decision not to raise its official production limit was stated to reflect its unwillingness to jeopardize its markets by creating an oil surplus. On 21 September the IMF warned that global investment in oil production and refining capacity would not be sufficient to prevent oil prices from rising over the next five years.

In October 2005 the average price of the OPEC reference 'basket' fell by US $3.25, equivalent to 5.6%, to $54.63 per barrel. The average 'spot' quotation of Brent declined by $4, to $58.75 per barrel, while that of WTI fell by $2.61, to $62.67 per barrel. In the first week of the month prices of OPEC crudes were reportedly depressed by a wider divergence in the price of sweet/sour grades and by the US Administration's stated intention to resort to the SPR for supplies of crude and heating oil, should this be required. In the second week prices strengthened initially, in response, among other things, to growing Asian demand for winter fuels and to a lower assessment by the IEA of OPEC supply in 2005, while growth in demand world-wide was expected to continue well into 2006; but were subsequently depressed by such factors as ample supply of OPEC crudes and weaker US demand for gasoline. In mid-October prices strengthened in response to fears that US production and refining facilities in the Gulf of Mexico would suffer further damage from an imminent hurricane, but began to weaken once it appeared that 'Hurricane Wilma' would strike the US coast elsewhere. Six US refineries reportedly remained closed as a consequence of Hurricanes Katrina and Rita at this time. The downward trend persisted throughout the remainder of the month, reinforced, *inter alia*, by reportedly substantial growth in US crude inventories, which had benefited from the release of IEA strategic stocks from early September. The price of the OPEC reference 'basket' remained under pressure in the final week of October, abundant supplies being the predominant market influence.

Further declines in the price of the OPEC reference 'basket' occurred in November 2005, the price of its components averaging US $51.29 per barrel, a decline of $3.34, equivalent to more than 6%, compared with the previous month. At the same time, the average 'spot' price of Brent declined by $3.34, to $55.41 per barrel, while that of WTI fell by $4.25, to $58.42 per barrel. Growth in crude oil inventories was among the factors that caused prices to ease marginally in the first two weeks of the month. Prices also came under pressure as a result of a lower estimate of global demand for oil by the IEA, in combination with ongoing and projected increases in OPEC's production capacity. In the third week of the month profit-taking on 'futures' markets added further downward pressure to prices, but declines were checked by a fall in US crude inventories and forecasts of colder weather conditions in the northern hemisphere. In the final week of November, for the first time in nine weeks, prices strengthened overall as concerns over colder weather conditions intensified. In the final days of the month, however, the prices of some crudes declined sharply in response to unusually warm winter weather conditions in some northern areas of the USA. On 30 November OECD published reduced estimates of economic growth in the principal industrialized regions world-wide, citing the high price of oil as the main cause of the revision.

Reviewing (towards the end of the year) markets for oil in 2005, OPEC noted that, in the light of current data, its initial forecast for oil demand had been over-optimisitic. Actual data for the first three-quarters of 2005 and projections for the final quarter now indicated that demand for oil would increase by 1.2m. b/d, equivalent to 1.5%, in 2005, rather than by 1.7m. b/d, or 2%, as initially predicted. Lower-than-anticipated growth in apparent Chinese demand for oil, a consequence of a greater-than-expected rise in China's power-generation capacity in 2005, was a key factor cited by OPEC in explanation of its downward revision. Growth in apparent US demand was also reported to have been less than initially expected, in part owing to disruptions to supply caused by hurricane weather conditions. In view of prevailing optimism regarding the prospects for the world economy in 2006, OPEC revised upwards its forecast of growth in demand for oil world-wide to 1.6m. b/d, equivalent to 1.9%. At an extraordinary meeting of the OPEC ministerial conference held in Kuwait City on 12 December, OPEC assessed the ceiling of 28m. b/d adopted in June 2005 as adequate to maintain market equilibrium in the first quarter of 2006, but determined to hold a further extraordinary meeting at the end of January 2006 in order to decide upon the appropriate level of production for the second and third quarters of the year. The conference once again urged consumers and industry to take action to reduce 'refinery bottlenecks', which it described as the main determinant of price in the prevailing market conditions of abundant supply. Late in the month inaugural OPEC 'Energy Dialogues' were held with China and Russia in order to establish frameworks for co-operation and the ongoing exchange of views between the parties.

In December 2005 the average price of the OPEC reference 'basket' increased by US $1.36, equivalent to 2.6%, to $52.65 per barrel. The average 'spot' quotation of Brent, meanwhile, rose by $1.61, to $57.02 per barrel and that of WTI by $0.94, to $59.36 per barrel. During the whole of 2005 the price of the OPEC 'basket' averaged $50.46 per barrel, an increase of 40% compared with 2004. In early December 2005 forecasts of warmer weather in the northern hemisphere were among the factors that caused the composite price to decline marginally, but during the second week of the month the price rose by more than 5%, partly in response to concerns over the adequacy of supplies of heating fuels. (In the USA, where extreme cold weather struck north-eastern regions in early December, prices of heating oil were reported to be close to record levels.) The price of OPEC crudes rose further in the third week of the month as cold weather persisted and the IEA revised upwards its forecast of demand for oil world-wide in 2006, but upward pressure was relieved by profit-taking on 'futures' markets. In the final week of December 2005 the price of the OPEC reference 'basket' declined by more than 4% in response, according to OPEC, to the publication of 'bearish data' in the USA and forecasts of warmer weather. Prices had begun to rise again before the end of the year, however, as Nigerian supplies were disrupted and Japanese demand for sweet crudes increased after heavy snowfall caused the closure of some of the country's nuclear facilities.

The price of the OPEC reference 'basket' rose substantially in January 2006, to US $58.47 per barrel. Substantial increases also occurred in the average 'spot' quotations of both Brent, which rose to $63.05 per barrel, and WTI, which rose to $65.39 per barrel. During the first week of January the price of the OPEC reference 'basket' rose by more than 7% in response to disruption of the supply of Russian natural gas to European markets. Tension in the Middle East—in particular concerns over the health of the Israeli Prime Minister, ongoing instability in Iraq and, most seriously, an escalating international dispute concerning Iran's nuclear programme, and its possible consequences in view of Iran's position as the world's fourth largest exporter of crude petroleum—in combination with disruption to Nigerian supplies reportedly kept prices firm in the second week of the month. Concerns over tension in the Middle East remained a key concern in the third week of January, although prices were checked at the same time by, among other things, forecasts of warmer weather in the northern hemisphere. Geopolitical issues, combined in the final week of the month with a reduction in Russian supplies as a consequence of cold weather conditions and continued disruption of supplies from Nigeria, where insurgent attacks on the country's oil infrastructure were ongoing, maintained the upward pressure on prices, although increases were restrained by OPEC members' assurances that production would be maintained at an adequate level and by low seasonal demand from US refineries. At an extraordinary meeting of the OPEC conference held in Vienna on 31 January it was decided to maintain OPEC's output at 28m. b/d, as part of the effort to restrain prices.

Compared with the previous month, the average price of the OPEC reference 'basket' in February 2006, at US $56.62 per barrel, declined by 3%, or $1.85. Declines were also registered in the average 'spot' quotation of Brent, which fell by $2.93, to $60.12 per barrel, and in that of WTI, which fell by $3.9, to $61.49 per barrel. In the first week of February OPEC's decision, taken at the extraordinary ministerial conference in Vienna, to maintain its output unchanged, caused prices generally to ease, although tension in the Middle East, in particular Iran's announcement that it would no longer allow unscheduled inspections of its nuclear facilities, caused prices to rise sharply on 6 February. Other factors that contributed to a further, more substantial decline in the price of the OPEC reference 'basket' in the second week of February were reportedly abundant Middle Eastern supplies and a substantial increase in US stocks of gasoline. The downward trend was reinforced in the third week of the month, when the price of the OPEC reference 'basket' fell to its lowest level of the year to date, by, among other things, an IEA report that indicated that growth in supplies world-wide was increasing at a faster rate than incremental demand in 2006. The price of the reference 'basket' subsequently recovered somewhat, in response, partly, to the disruption of supplies from Nigeria where, on 17–18 February, members of the so-called Movement for the Emancipation of the Niger Delta had attacked production facilities and kidnapped oil workers, causing a fall of some 15% in the country's exports of petroleum. Other factors responsible for the recovery in prices in late February were ongoing tension in the Middle East, growing demand for light sweet crudes and an attempt by militants to disrupt activity at Saudi Arabia's Abqaiq oil-processing facility, the largest of its kind in the world.

In March 2006 the average price of the OPEC reference 'basket' rose by US $1.24—more than 2%—to $57.86 per barrel. At the same time, the price of Brent increased by $1.96, to $62.08 per barrel, and that of WTI by $1.33, to $62.82 per barrel. Prices strengthened in the first week of the month in response to fears of disruption to some Middle Eastern and West African supplies. Fears that supplies of refined products would be depleted as a result of the seasonal maintenance of refineries were another factor that, according to OPEC, lent strength to prices in the first few days of March. OPEC's decision, taken at the ministerial conference held in Vienna on 8 March, to maintain output at 28m. b/d, in combination with an increase in US inventories of crude, subsequently checked upward movement temporarily, but prices quickly began to rise again under the influence of concerns over the adequacy of gasoline supplies as US maintenance schedules proceeded. OPEC's decision not to reduce production was taken explicitly in the light of geopolitical threats to supplies—threats that were underlined on 20 March when militants were reported to have carried out an attack on a pipeline in Nigeria, further boosting prices. (Analysts cited the security situation in Iraq and the ongoing international dispute over Iran's nuclear programme as the other key geopolitical factors supporting the price of oil at this time. Although Iran had stated early in the month that it had no intention to use the price of oil as a 'weapon' in the dispute over its nuclear programme, it had none the less warned that if action, in the form of economic sanctions, were taken against it, the price of oil would automatically be affected. Around mid-March a US-led military operation against 'a suspected insurgent operating area' in Iraq caused a sharp increase in the price of oil traded on the New York Stock Exchange.) In the fourth week of the month prices weakened in response to the perceived abundance of crude supplies world-wide and anticipated lower growth in world demand for oil. Prices rose substantially in the final week of the month in response to conflict in southern Iraq, as a result of which Iraqi exports were forecast to be unavailable for up to three months; and to a heavy fall in US inventories of gasoline.

Assessing markets for oil at the ministerial conference held in Vienna on 8 March 2006 (at which it was decided to maintain the Organization's output unchanged at 28m. b/d), OPEC noted that despite indications that markets were well supplied and the high level of inventories in OECD countries, prices remained volatile as a result of geopolitical tensions which, it was feared, might in future disrupt supplies, and of 'downstream bottlenecks'. These factors were reflected in increased speculative activity on 'futures' markets and the continued 'pattern of disconnect and commercial stock levels, that has become apparent since 2004'.

At US $64.44 per barrel, $6.57 or 11.35% higher than in March, the average price of the OPEC reference 'basket' in April 2006 was the highest ever recorded. At the same time, the average 'spot' quotation of Brent increased by $8.27 compared with the previous month, to $70.35 per barrel, and that of WTI by $6.64, to $69.46 per barrel. The price of both Brent and US light, sweet crudes rose to record levels in April. Geopolitical issues, in particular an escalation of the international dispute over Iran's nuclear programme, continued to exert the strongest influence on markets for OPEC crudes. On 18 April, speaking after Iranian President Mahmoud Ahmadinejad had stated that Iran would robustly defend itself against any aggression, US President Bush refused to exclude the use of force in order to preempt Iran's possible development of nuclear weapons. Other inflationary influences were the publication, on 19 April, of data that indicated a greater-than-expected decline in US inventories of gasoline. Prices moved upwards consistently during the first three weeks of the month, but stabilized during the final week in response to the interplay of profit-taking on 'futures' markets and strong Chinese demand for crude. Another factor that exerted a calming influence on the market in late April was a speech (on 25 April) by President Bush in which he undertook to: boost supplies to US markets at the expense of increasing the US SPR; encourage the use of motor vehicles with relatively low fuel consumption; and order an investigation into the high price of gasoline. However, analysts expressed fears late in the month that tension between the USA and certain factions in Iraq would inevitably cause further increases in the price of oil.

In May 2006, as in April, the average price of the OPEC reference 'basket' was the highest ever recorded, rising to US $65.11, an increase of more than 1%. The average price of Brent, meanwhile, declined fractionally, to $69.83 per barrel, while that of WTI increased by some 2%, to $70.89 per barrel. The key determinants of price movements during the early part of May were, on the one hand, continued geopolitical tension and conditions—especially in the USA—of abundant supply. During the first three weeks of the month, markets remained volatile, but prices generally moved downwards, in response, notably, to fears that the level to which they had risen had begun to cause demand to weaken. In the third week of May, the average price of the OPEC crudes was $63.72 per barrel, its lowest average for six weeks. In the final week of May, however, geopolitical tensions came to the fore once again, reinforced, according to OPEC, by concern over the approaching hurricane season in the Gulf of Mexico. Strong US demand (as indicated by growth in US gross domestic product) was an additional factor that supported prices in the final week of the month.

At an extraordinary ministerial conference held in Caracas, Venezuela, on 1 June 2006, OPEC decided to maintain output of crude by its members at the prevailing level. The decision proceeded from the Organization's assessment of markets for oil as 'oversupplied' and its identification as the key influence on markets characterized by high prices and volatility of 'the lack of effective global oil refining capacity, in the short and medium term, coupled with anxiety about the ability of oil producers to meet anticipated future oil demand'.

In June 2006 the average price of the OPEC 'basket', at US $64.69 per barrel, was fractionally lower than in May. Geopolitical tensions having eased somewhat in the first week of the month, in the second week the average price declined by almost 3% in response to data indicating that OPEC stocks of crude were at their highest level for 20 years, and to fears that demand was under threat from higher interest rates and inflation. In the final week of the month prices strengthened in response to renewed fears regarding the adequacy of gasoline supplies in the summer months, forecast strong Chinese demand and the disruption of some US refining operations.

The average price of OPEC 'basket' crudes rose substantially, by more than 6% compared with the previous month, to US $68.92 per barrel in July 2006. At the same time, the average price of North Sea Brent crude increased by more than 7%, to $73.66 per barrel, while that of WTI rose by nearly 5%, to $74.33. The average prices of the component crudes of the OPEC reference 'basket' ranged between $58.72 (BCF-17) and $75.49 (Bonny Light) per barrel in July. Among the key influences on petroleum prices in July were increased seasonal demand and, especially, conflict in the Middle East, both between the Israeli armed forces and Palestinian fighters in the Gaza Strip and the West Bank and between Israeli forces and the militant Shi'a organization Hezbollah in Lebanon. On 14 July the average price of OPEC crudes rose to $71.71 per barrel, a record high, prompting the Organization to issue a statement in which it reaffirmed its commitment to market stability and emphasized, once again, that markets for oil continued, fundamentally, to be characterized by excess of supply. Later in the month prices were supported by factors including damage to Russia's Druzhba pipeline and, indirectly, the effect of very high seasonal demand for electricity on natural gas prices.

The closure of a pipeline (operated by BP) at Prudhoe Bay, Alaska, USA, led OPEC on 10 August 2006 to issue another statement in which it sought to calm the volatility of oil markets by re-emphasizing the adequacy of crude supplies *vis-à-vis* demand. Already, during the first week of August, the average price of OPEC reference crudes had risen to more than US $70 per barrel in response to the continued effects of conflict in the Middle East and the damage to Russia's Druzhba facility. Further inflationary pressure, in the form of adverse weather conditions in the Gulf of Mexico and anxiety, in the light of newly released data, about the adequacy of US crude inventories, propelled the average price of the OPEC reference 'basket' to a new record level of $72.67 per barrel. In the second half of August, generally, prices eased as political tension in the Middle East subsided somewhat and a perception of the adequacy of crude supplies overrode previous concerns. For the whole of August an average price of $68.81 per barrel was recorded for OPEC crudes, representing a slight decline, of only about 0.1%, compared with the previous month. During August the average price of Brent fell (by less than 1%) to $73.11 per barrel, while that of WTI declined by $1.32 per barrel, or 1.8%, to $73.01. The average price of the crudes comprising OPEC's reference basket ranged between $60.29 (BCF-17) and $75.42 (Minas).

During the first week of September 2006 the average price of OPEC reference crudes eased further, to US $63.14 per barrel, as political tension in the Middle East continued to subside and the availability of supplies from both the Gulf of Mexico and Nigeria improved. This downward trend became more pronounced in the second week of the month, in response to, among other factors, OPEC's decision, taken at a ministerial conference held in Vienna on 11 September, to leave its production 'ceiling' unchanged. In the third week of August the average price of OPEC reference crudes declined further, by some 4%, to $57.16 per barrel, as markets remained confident of the adequacy of OPEC supplies and Asian refiners' demand for oil was reduced. An average price of $56.35 per barrel was recorded for OPEC crudes in the final week of September. Overall, the average price of the OPEC reference 'basket' fell substantially, by more than $10 per barrel, equivalent to 14%, compared with the previous month, in September. At the same time, the average price of Brent registered a decline of more than $11 per barrel, to $61.71, while that of WTI fell by more than 12%, to $64 per barrel. The average price of OPEC reference crudes ranged between $50.96 (BCF-17) and $65.01 (Murban) in September.

During October 2006 the average price of the OPEC reference 'basket' declined by a further 7.4% (US $4.37) per barrel, compared with the previous month, to $54.97—its lowest level of the year to date. At the same time, the average price of Brent crude declined by 6.3%, to $57.80 per barrel, while that of WTI fell by more than 8%, to $58.82 per barrel. The average price of the crudes comprising the OPEC reference 'basket' ranged between $46.99 (BCF-17) and $61.04 (Murban) per barrel in October. The ready availability of crude oil was the key influence on markets throughout the month. At a consultative meeting of the OPEC conference convened in Doha, Qatar, on 19–20 October, delegates observed with concern that markets were characterized by excess of supply (citing in particular the above-average level of OECD crude oil inventories as evidence of this) and had been destabilized as a consequence. The consultative meeting decided to address this by reducing OPEC output by some 1.2m. b/d, to 26.3m. b/d, from 1 November 2006. Individual members' quotas were to be cut as follows: Algeria 59,000 b/d; Indonesia 39,000 b/d; Iran 176,000 b/d; Kuwait 100,000 b/d; Libya 72,000 b/d; Nigeria 100,000 b/d; Qatar 35,000 b/d; Saudi Arabia 380,000 b/d; UAE 101,000 b/d; Venezuela 138,000 b/d. The reduction was to be reviewed at an extraordinary meeting of the OPEC conference scheduled to be held in Nigeria in mid-December.

At the extraordinary meeting of the OPEC conference that was duly convened in mid-December 2006, it was observed 'with satisfaction' that the decision to reduce member states' output from 1 November had achieved a better balance between supply and demand, although an element of volatility remained, 'reflecting the continuing supply overhang in the market'. In November the average price of the OPEC crudes comprising the reference 'basket' rose slightly, by less than US $0.5, to $55.42 per barrel. During November an increase of $1.12, to $58.92 per barrel, was registered in the average price of North Sea Brent, while the average price of WTI rose marginally, by $0.12, to $58.94 per barrel. The average price of OPEC crudes ranged between $46.86 (BCF-17) and $60.94 per barrel (Murban) in November. In spite of the reduction in OPEC output from 1 November, it was not until the final week of the month that there was decisive upward movement in prices, markets having been influenced by such depressive factors as, in particular, ample OECD crude inventories, during the first three weeks of the month. Having noted at the extraordinary meeting held in December that markets continued to be characterized by residual volatility, it was agreed that an additional reduction in OPEC members' output, of 500,000 b/d, should be implemented from 1 February 2007 in order to maintain market equilibrium.

During the first week of December 2006 the average price of the OPEC reference 'basket' continued to strengthen, in response to anticipated normal winter demand and to the perceived likelihood of an additional reduction in OPEC output. At US $59.06 per barrel, the average price of OPEC reference crudes recorded in the the first week of the month was the highest since mid-September. However, the average price retreated in the second week of the month by approximately the same amount as it had risen in the first, owing to the effect on demand of forecasts of warmer winter weather in the northern hemisphere. A lack of clear direction in the third week of December was succeeded, as the end of 2006 approached, by a decline in the average price of more than 2.5%, to $56.50 per barrel, in response to mild weather in the western hemisphere and the perceived adequacy of supplies. For the whole of December, none the less, the average price of the OPEC reference 'basket' increased by $2.53, equivalent to 4.6%, to $57.95 per barrel. The average price of Brent, meanwhile, rose by some 5.8%, to $62.33 per barrel, in December, while that of WTI increased by about 5.1%, to $61.96 per barrel. Average prices recorded in December for OPEC reference crudes ranged between $48.56 (BCF-17) and $64.28 (Bonny Light) per barrel. In an assessment of the principal trends and developments that had characterized markets for oil in 2006, conducted towards the end of the year, OPEC noted that prices had risen emphatically, although in real terms they had remained far below the prices recorded in 1980. Price volatility had been another salient feature in 2006, a sharp correction having occurred since, broadly, the summer. Looking ahead to 2007, the Organization expressed its uncertainty regarding the prospects for market stability, noting that prices were judged more likely to decline than to rise, not least owing to forecasts of weak economic growth, if not recession, in the USA in 2007 and its consequences for economic growth world-wide.

During the first week of 2007 the average price of OPEC reference crudes declined by more than 5%, to US $53.99 per barrel, as a consequence of warm winter weather. Unseasonably high temperatures, especially in the USA, and, accordingly, low demand for winter fuels, combined in the second week of January to exert further downward pressure on markets for crude, the average price of the OPEC reference 'basket' falling by more than 8%, to $50.27 per barrel. This pressure was checked somewhat in the third week of the month as colder weather returned, but, even so, the average weekly price, at $48.45 per barrel, was the lowest recorded since May 2005. In the final week of January cold weather combined with the US Administration's decision to replenish the SPR with some 100,000 b/d of crude caused the average price of OPEC reference crudes to strengthen to $50.42 per barrel. For the whole of January 2007 the average price of the OPEC reference 'basket' fell by more than 12%, to $50.73 per barrel, the lowest monthly average recorded since May 2005. The average price of North Sea Brent, meanwhile, declined by almost 14%, to $53.68 per barrel, while that of WTI fell by more than 12%, to $54.40 per barrel. During January the average price of OPEC reference crudes ranged between $42.68 (BCF-17) and $56.42 per barrel (Murban). At the extraordinary meeting of the OPEC conference held in mid-December 2006 its was decided to admit Angola as the Organization's 12th member, with effect from 1 January 2007, from which time, accordingly, Angola's Cabinda crude was to be included in calculations of OPEC production, although it was not immediately to be included as a constituent of the OPEC reference 'basket'.

In February 2007 the supplementary reduction (from 1 February) in OPEC output agreed upon in December 2006, continued cold weather in the USA, an increase in political tension in the Middle East and an upward adjustment to forecast world demand for oil were the predominant influences on markets for crude petroleum, overriding OPEC member states' assurances of steady supply, lower demand for winter fuels as mild weather returned and an abrupt reversal in Chinese equity values to raise the average price of the OPEC reference 'basket' by more than 7%, to US $54.45 per barrel. During February the average price of Brent rose by almost 7%, to $57.43 per barrel, while that of WTI increased by 8.8%, to $59.21 per barrel. The average price of crudes included in the OPEC reference 'basket' ranged between $48.04 (BCF-17) and $59.58 (Murban and Bonny Light) per barrel in February.

During the first week of March 2007 a marginal increase, of 0.6%, to US $57.85 per barrel, was recorded in the average price of the OPEC reference 'basket'. A possible increase in demand for crude, owing to the recent lower prices, was among the factors to which stronger prices were attributed at the beginning of March. As the month progressed, factors such as improved weather conditions and concern about the prospects for economic growth world-wide came to the fore, causing the average price of OPEC reference crudes to decline by more than 1%, to $57.12 per barrel. Having risen marginally in the third week, in the final week of March the average price of OPEC reference crudes increased by 7.5%, to $61.58 per barrel, influenced in particular by political tension in the Middle East and lower US inventories of summer fuels. For the whole of March, at $58.47 per barrel, an increase of 7.4% compared with February, the average price recorded for the OPEC reference' basket' was the highest for six months. During March the average price of Brent rose by some $4.7, to $62.15 per barrel, while that of WTI increased by about $1.4, to $60.63 per barrel. Average prices recorded for OPEC reference 'basket' crudes ranged between $50.27 (BCF-17) and $64.59 (Bonny Light) per barrel. At a meeting of the OPEC conference held in Vienna on 15 March, ministers decided to leave the Organization's output unchanged at its current level, noting that markets remained well supplied and that commercial oil inventories of crude oil in OECD countries were 'healthy'. The conference noted, none the less, that markets for oil were likely to continue to be characterized by volatility.

Concern about the adequacy of summer fuel supplies was the dominant market influence in the first week of April 2007, causing the average price of the OPEC reference 'basket' to rise by 3.4%, to US $63.73 per barrel, the highest weekly average recorded since August 2006. In the second week of the month, at $63.59 per barrel, the average price was little changed compared with the previous week. A decline of 1.7% in the average price in the third week of April was cancelled in the final week of the month, when the average price of OPEC reference crudes increased by 1.7% in response to concern about possible shortages of some grades of West African crude and falls in US gasoline inventories. For the whole of April the average price of the OPEC reference 'basket' increased by 8.4%, to $63.39 per barrel, the third consecutive monthly increase, which raised the 'basket' price by one-quarter compared with that recorded in January. During April an average price of $67.51 per barrel was recorded for North Sea Brent, while the average price of WTI rose by some $3.2, to $63.85 per barrel. The average price of OPEC reference crudes ranged between $54.93 (BCF-17) and $70.01 (Bonny Light) per barrel in April.

During May 2007, albeit less clearly defined, the upward trend in the price of OPEC crudes continued: an average price of US $64.36 per barrel was recorded, an increase of $0.97, or 1.5%, compared with the previous month. Increases in US inventories of crude exerted a depressive influence on prices during the first half of May, although declines were checked by concern regarding disruption to West African supplies and the adequacy of summer fuel supplies. In the third week of May the average price of the OPEC reference 'basket' rose by 3.7%, to $64.55 per barrel, as concern about disruption to supplies from Nigeria was reinforced by technical problems at some US refineries. In the final week of the month the average price of the reference 'basket' increased by a further 3% in response to industrial action planned in Nigeria and a rise in political tension in the Middle East. During May the average price of Brent, meanwhile, declined slightly, compared with the previous month, to $67.38 per barrel, while that of WTI fell by 0.6%, to $63.46 per barrel. The average price of reference 'basket' crudes ranged between $56.06 (BCF-17) and $70.13 (Saharan Blend) per barrel in May.

A further increase, of 2.41%, to US $66.77 per barrel, was recorded in the average price of OPEC crudes in June 2007. Concern about whether US gasoline supplies would be sufficient to meet demand during the driving season exerted a key influence on markets for crude in the first week of the month, as did concern about the possible effect of 'Cyclone Gonu' on production in Oman and on transportation of oil from Middle Eastern locations. In the second week of the month, despite continued concern about US gasoline supplies, the average price of the OPEC reference 'basket' eased marginally, but it was driven upward again in the third week of June, to $67.74 per barrel, the highest weekly average of the year to date, by enduring concern about US gasoline supplies and the possible effects of industrial action planned in Brazil and Nigeria, among other factors. In the final week of the month the average price of the reference 'basket' eased somewhat, to $67.49 per barrel. The average price of Brent rose by more than 6% in June, compared with the previous month, to $71.55 per barrel, while that of WTI likewise rose by more than 6%, to $67.44 per barrel. The average price of OPEC reference 'basket' crudes ranged between $60.69 (BCF-17) and $74.45 (Bonny Light) per barrel in June. A further increase in the price of the 'basket', to $70.86, its highest level for 10 months, was recorded in the first two weeks of July.

In mid-June 2007 OPEC's Secretary-General, Abdalla Salem el-Bardi, issued a statement addressing the issue of oil market fundamentals. Noting that world-wide inventories of crude were 'healthy', especially in Europe, where they had reach an historically high level to total more than 66m. barrels above the five-year average; and that non-OPEC production was expected to rise in the second half of 2007, el-Badri assessed supply as adequate to meet global demand in the immediate future, and to cope with possible upward revisions to demand during the second half of the year.

In July 2007 the average price of the OPEC reference 'basket' increased by almost US $5 per barrel, compared with the previous month, to reach a record high of $71.75 per barrel. The price of North Sea Brent, meanwhile, rose by $5.46, to $77.01 per barrel, while a gain of more than $6.50, to $73.98 per barrel, was registered in the price of WTI. The average prices of OPEC reference crudes ranged between $65.79 per barrel (BCF-17) and $79.21 (Bonny Light) in July. Previously existing concerns about the adequacy of gasoline supplies to meet US demand were reportedly exacerbated in early July by restricted Nigerian output of gasoline-rich crude, and these exerted a key influence on markets throughout the month. Other factors that combined to support prices were a fall in US crude inventories and indications of strong economic growth in both the USA and China. During the first two weeks of August, however, prices declined in response to less sanguine assessments of the prospects for the US economy. The decline was stemmed by fears of possible damage to Texan oil facilities as a result of hurricane weather conditions in the third week of the month.

PLATINUM

Platinum is one of a group of six related metals known as the platinum-group metals (PGM), which also includes palladium, rhodium, ruthenium, iridium and osmium. In nature, platinum is usually associated with the sulphides of iron, copper and nickel. Depending on the relative concentration of the PGM and copper and nickel in the deposit, platinum is either the major product or a by-product of base metal production. PGM are highly resistant to corrosion, and do not oxidize in air. They are also extremely malleable and have a high melting point, giving them a wide range of industrial uses.

Although widely employed in the petroleum-refining and petrochemical sectors, the principal industrial use for platinum is in catalytic converters in motor vehicles (which reduce pollution from exhaust emissions), now usually accounting for more than one-third of total platinum consumption by Europe (including Eastern Europe), Japan, North America and other Western countries (an estimated 51.1%, or 3,847,000 troy oz, allowing for 840,000 oz in recovery from scrapped autocatalysts, in 2005). The USA, Canada, Japan, Australia, the Republic of China (Taiwan), the Republic of Korea, the European Union (EU) and certain Latin American countries have implemented legislation to neutralize vehicle exhaust gases, and this necessitates the fitting of catalytic converters, using platinum, rhodium and palladium, to vehicles. In 1989 the Council of (Environment) Ministers of the European Community (subsequently the EU) decided to oblige vehicle manufacturers within the Community to fit three-way catalytic converters as compulsory features in passenger cars with an engine capacity of less than 1,400 cc, effective for all new models from mid-1992 and for all new cars from January 1993. It was predicted that the new measures would reduce emissions of exhaust gases by 60%–70%. The Commission of the European Community subsequently extended similar anti-pollution requirements to larger cars, and to heavy trucks, with effect from 1995. The resultant increase in demand for automotive emission control catalysts (autocatalysts) generated a rising trend in the consumption of platinum, rhodium and palladium during the 1990s. In 1996 the EU announced proposals, implemented in 1998, for stricter limits on emissions, which took effect in 2000. Further restrictions on levels of emissions have since been gradually introduced and others will take effect before 2008. In the USA regulations to reduce emissions of exhaust gases by 50%–70% have required full compliance by vehicle manufacturers since 2001. The increasing use of palladium-rich catalysts, principally by US and European motor vehicle manufacturers, was reflected in a strong advance in autocatalyst demand for palladium in 1999, to 5,574,000 oz (allowing for 183,000 oz in recovery from scrapped autocatalysts). In 2000 demand from this sector increased by 7.7%, to 6,005,000 oz (allowing for 230,000 oz in recovery from scrapped autocatalysts). In 2001, however, autocatalyst demand for palladium fell by 11.3%, to total 5,325,000 oz (allowing for 280,000 oz in recovery from scrapped autocatalysts). The decline in 2001 was attributed to the utilization of stocks in favour of new purchases, and to the high price of the metal, relative to other PGM, which led some manufacturers to substitute platinum or rhodium in autocatalysts. In 2002 another decline, of 591,000, or 11%, to 4,734,000 oz (allowing for 350,000 oz in recovery from scrapped autocatalysts), occurred in autocatalyst demand for palladium. This decline was attributed to the increased utilization of palladium inventories held by (mainly) US vehicle manufacturers. In 2003 autocatalyst demand for palladium fell again, by 7.4% to 4,382,000 oz (allowing for 415,000 oz in recovery from scrapped autocatalysts). Autocatalyst demand for palladium continued to decline in 2004, when it totalled an estimated 4,137,000 oz (allowing for 494,000 oz in recovery from scrapped autocatalysts), a fall of 5.5% compared with 2003. At an estimated 4,135,000 oz in 2005 (allowing for 636,000 oz in recovery from scrapped autocatalysts), autocatalyst demand for palladium was stable, at almost exactly the same level as in the previous year. Autocatalyst demand increased to 4,456,000 oz in 2006 (allowing for 764,000 oz in recovery from scrapped autocatalysts), an increase of 7.8% on the previous year.

Alloyed platinum is very heavy and hard. Platinum's white colour makes it popular for jewellery, which accounts for the other principal source of consumption (22.0%, or 1,700,000 oz, in 2006). Japan is the world's main consumer of platinum, and its jewellery industry absorbed 1m. oz in 2000. In 2001 Japanese demand for platinum for jewellery fell by 24%, to 760,000 oz, and by a further 17% in 2002, to 631,000 oz. A downward trend became firmly established in 2003, when Japanese demand for platinum for jewellery fell by 12%, to 555,000 oz. In 2004 there was a further decline, of 9%, to 505,000 oz. Japanese demand for platinum for jewellery fell by 8%, to 465,000 oz, in 2005. In 2006 the decline continued, with Japanese demand for platinum jewellery falling by 7%, to 432,000 oz. Industrial and other miscellaneous applications account for the balance of platinum consumption; these uses include platinum for minting coins and small bars purchased as an investment, petroleum refining, production of nitric acid, glass manufacture, electrical applications and dentistry. Demand by industrial consumers, particularly in the motor vehicle industry and in jewellery fabrication, raised international demand for platinum to 6,461,000 oz in 2000, to 7,018,000 oz in 2001, and to 7,520,000 oz in 2002. In 2003 total demand rose again, to 7,630,000 oz, but in 2004 it fell fractionally, to 7,615,000 oz. There was a further decline, of less than 1%, in 2005, when international demand for platinum was estimated at 7,579,000 oz. Supplies entering the market in 2005 increased to an estimated 6,639,000 oz, from 6,393,000 oz in 2004. Growth in supply in 2005 was propelled by a continued increase in South African mined output of the metal. Demand recovered marginally in 2006, increasing by 1.8%, to 7,715,000 oz.

World production of PGM is dominated by South Africa, which normally accounts for about three-quarters of supplies of platinum and more than one-third of supplies of palladium to the international market. Russia has accounted for approximately 45%–50% of the world's palladium supplies in recent years. In 2005 official data relating to Russian PGM were declassified. Russian platinum production in that year was reported to have totalled an estimated 960,000m. oz, while output of palladium amounted to 3,133,000 oz. In 2006 production of platinum in Russia totalled 961,000 oz, while palladium production also increased slightly, to 3,164,000 oz.

In 1991 South African technical assistance was made available to the USSR (and subsequently to Russia) for the development of its platinum industry. Russian PGM are produced mainly as by-products of coal and nickel mining (see below) in the far north of Siberia. Following the break-up of the USSR in 1991, these operations were adversely affected by deterioration in plant and equipment, as the result of a lack of funds for essential maintenance. Production began to stabilize, however, in 1994, although it was estimated that in 1995 and 1996 about 1m. oz of marketed shipments were supplied from Russian government platinum stocks. No supplies of PGM were exported by Russia during the first six months of 1997, and shipments were again interrupted during the first three months of 1998, owing to delays in authorization by the Russian Government, for which the central bank acts as marketing agent. In 1999, owing to a change in Russian legislation which prevented exports by Norilsk Nickel, the country's principal producer of PGM, most, if not all, of the 860,000 oz of platinum sold by Russia were believed to have come from central government stocks. Palladium exports were not affected by this legislation, which was amended in 2000, allowing Russian exports of platinum to resume. In 2001, however, Russian exports of platinum fell to 811,000 oz, compared with 872,000 oz in 2000. Russian sales of platinum increased slightly, to 816,000 oz in 2002, and again, to about 834,000 oz, in 2003. In 2004 Russian exports of platinum rose to 840,000 oz. Russia's foreign sales of platinum were estimated to have totalled 960,000 oz in 2005 and 961,000 oz in 2006. Meanwhile, Russian exports of palladium declined by about 2.6% in 2001, as a consequence of Norilsk Nickel's decision, in August, to suspend 'spot' sales of the metal in view of weak world demand for it and, accordingly, falling prices. In 2002 Russian sales of palladium recovered to about 2.7m. oz (an increase of about 1% compared with 2001), even though, owing to Norilsk Nickel's continued suspension of 'spot' sales, palladium was sold by contract only in 2002 and no sales of palladium from Russian government inventories were made in 2002. In 2003, however, Russia sold 2.7m. oz of palladium, an increase of 3% compared with the previous year. In 2004 Russian exports of palladium rose to about 2.8m. oz, an increase of some 4% compared with 2003. Russia's foreign sales were estimated to have totalled 3.1m. oz in 2005, an increase of 10.3% compared with 2004. Russian foreign sales of palladium increased again in 2006, to around 3.2m. oz., representing an increase of 1%. In 1998 Russia's exports of PGM (unwrought, unworked, or semi-manufactured) accounted for 2.8% of the country's total export earnings. Control of Norilsk Nickel was transferred in 1995 to a bank, in preparation for full privatization. Subsequently, however, the enterprise encountered severe financial problems and underwent further restructuring in 1998. In April 1999 Norilsk Nickel announced plans to invest US $3,500m. during the period to 2010 in mine and infrastructural development.

Canada is the third largest producer, its platinum being a by-product of its nickel production. Minor producers include Austria, Colombia, Finland and the USA. In 1999 it was reported that significant deposits of PGM had been identified in Mongolia. Zimbabwe, the only other African platinum producer, has significant deposits of PGM. There are two mines for PGM: the Mimosa mine, which is operated as a joint venture between Aquarius Platinum and Impala Platinum of South Africa; and the Ngezi mine, which is operated by Zimplats. In 2004 draft legislation governing the mining sector recommended that indigenous ownerhip should rise to 20% within two years, to 25% within seven years and to 30% within 10 years of the legislation's enactment. Plans to expand operations at Zimbabwe's PGM mines have reportedly been suspended pending full clarification of the Government's intentions for the mining sector. In 2006 Zimbabwe's output of platinum increased by around 4%, compared with the previous year, to total almost 167,000 oz. In percentage terms, a similar increase was recorded in the production of palladium, which amounted to 135,000 oz. Elsewhere in Africa, there are known or probable deposits of platinum in Ethiopia, Kenya and Sierra Leone.

Whereas PGM are produced in Canada and Russia as by-products of copper and/or nickel mining, PGM in South Africa are produced as the primary products, with nickel and copper as by-products. Another fundamental difference between the platinum deposits in South Africa and those in Russia and Canada is the ratio of platinum to palladium. In South Africa the percentage of platinum contained in PGM has, to date, exceeded that of palladium, although the ratio is expected to favour palladium in new mines that were brought into production from the early 1990s (see below). In Russia, Canada and the USA there is a higher proportion of palladium than platinum.

South African production capacity was substantially increased in 1993, following the completion of a number of expansion projects which had been under development since the mid-1980s. However, the level of world platinum prices, together with rises in production costs, led to the subsequent postponement or cancellation of several of these projects and to the closure of unprofitable operations. From the mid-1990s, none the less, improved productivity in the platinum industry, together with the prospect of increasing demand for PGM and continued uncertainty regarding Russian exports, encouraged South African producers to undertake a number of new expansion programmes. South Africa's platinum sales declined from 3,898,000 oz in 1999 to 3,765,000 oz in 2000, but recovered strongly, to 4,167,000 oz, in 2001. There was further growth in 2002, with sales rising to 4,441,000 oz, and, more emphatically, in 2003, when sales increased by 7%, to 4,756,000 oz. In 2004 output rose by 4.3% to 4,961,000 oz. There was a further, modest increase in South Africa's foreign sales of platinum in 2005, when they were estimated to have totalled 5,084,000 oz. In 2006 sales increased by 7.1%, to 5,445,000 oz. With greater productive capacity and the prospect of a sustained high level of prices during the early 2000s, it has been forecast that the value of South Africa's PGM output could eventually exceed that of its gold. In 2004 South Africa's exports of PGM (unwrought, unworked, or semi-manufactured) contributed 11.5% of the country's total export earnings.

Prices for Platinum

(London Platinum and Palladium Market, morning and afternoon 'fixes', US $ per troy oz)

	Average	Highest	Lowest
1990	471.7		
1995	424.2		
2004	845.5	936.0 (April)	767.0 (May)
2005	896.6	1,012.0 (Dec.)	844.0 (Jan.)
2006	1,142.6	1,264.9 (May)	1,029.0 (Jan.)

A surge in the early weeks of 2000 took the London price of platinum to US $573 (£357) per oz in February. The price eased in April to $470 (£297) per oz, following the resumption of Russian exports of platinum, but it rose in June to $579 (£386)—its highest level since 1989. The platinum price reached $582 (£389) per oz at the end of July 2000. On 2 August a shortage of Russian supplies raised the London quotation for platinum to $612 (£377) per oz, its highest level since December 1988. However, this rally was short-lived, with the quotation falling to $564 (£374) per oz on 7 August and remaining at around $570 (£382) per oz for most of the remainder of the month. On 30 August, however, strong demand brought about a recovery in the price to $598 (£411) per oz.

In early September 2000 the London quotation for platinum rose back to its previous 'high' of US $612 (£419) per oz on several trading days. From mid-September, however, the price began to decline, owing, apparently, to concerns about the possible impact of rising fuel prices on global economic growth. Prices subsequently stabilized in October, generally trading within the range of $575–$585 (£392–£399) per oz.

The London price of platinum rose to US $600 (£414) per oz on 3 November 2000, remaining close to this level until around the middle of the month. The rally appeared to be due to reports that Gokhran of Russia did not intend to export any PGM in 2001. In late November the London quotation once again rose above $600 per oz, reaching $605 (£426) on 30 November owing to fund buying in the USA. The London quotation rose higher still in early December, attaining a new 'high' for the year of $623 (£428) per oz on 4 December. Once again the rise was attributed to concerns about a possible shortage of Russian PGM supplies in 2001. On 13 December the London quotation achieved a new peak for the year of $625 (£430) per oz, its highest level for 13 years. The London quotation remained above $600 per oz for the rest of the month, trading for the year closing at $611 (£409) per oz on 29 December.

In January 2001 the London price of platinum attained its highest level for 14 years, rising to US $645 (£437) per oz in the middle of the month. The abrupt increase came about as a result of physical buying, prompted by rumours that Russia's PGM export quotas would not be fixed until February, and of the sharp rise in the London price of palladium (see below). By the end of January, however, the price had declined to $604 (£413) per oz as a result of profit-taking by market participants. By 13 February the London price had fallen to $592 (£407) per oz, partly as a consequence of a fall in the value of palladium. By the end of February, however, firm physical demand had caused the price of platinum to recover to $610 (£423) per oz. In early March the price of palladium continued to decline, and that of platinum followed in its wake, falling to only $576 (£399) per oz on 5 March. On 30 March renewed selling by investment funds prompted a further decline, the London price of platinum falling as low as $563 (£396) per oz. A weakening in the London price of platinum to $555 (£390) per oz on 2 April was succeeded by a recovery lasting two weeks, during which the quotation for the metal attained $630 (£439) per oz. By the end of the month, however, the price had slipped back to $594 (£415) per oz. Twice during May the price was driven back to $622 (£436) per oz, but both rallies were of short duration and at the end of the month platinum traded at $607 (£427) per oz. By 13 June the price had fallen to $574 (£410) per oz, and, thereafter, declined further, in response to the deceleration of the US economy and a forecast recession of Japanese demand, reaching $558 (£397) per oz at the end of June.

On 18 July 2001, having traded in a range of US $550–$560 (£389–£396) per oz since the beginning of the month, the London price of platinum plunged abruptly, to $520 per oz, as a consequence of the liquidation of 'long' positions on the Japanese futures market, and the closure, in response, of corresponding positions on the New York 'futures' market. By the end of the month, owing to further sales, the value of the metal had fallen to only $476 (£334) per oz. On 9 August the continued closure of 'long' positions by Japanese investors, combined with weak physical demand, depressed the London price of platinum to its lowest level, $433 (£301) per oz, for more than 18 months. Further sales on the Japanese 'futures' market caused the price to decline to only $422 (£294) per oz on 16 August. Delayed Russian exports, the result of reforms to domestic legislation, raised the London price of platinum above $460 (£322) per oz on 25 August, but, by the end of the month, concerns about Russian shipments had subsided and the London price fell to $446 (£307) per oz. The suicide attacks against US targets in New York and Washington, DC, on 11 September had little immediate effect on the price of platinum. By 20 September the price of the metal had risen to $495 (£338) per oz, but on 25 September, in response to predictions of slower US economic growth, among other factors, the London quotation sank to $447 (£316) per oz. On 2 October the price of the metal fell to its lowest level, $406 (£280) per oz, for the whole of 2001 in response to the decline of prices on the Japanese 'futures' market by their maximum permitted daily limit. On 15 October 'short covering' on the Japanese 'futures' market, in response to a substantial increase in one-month loco Zürich lease rates, brought about a recovery, to $462 (£318) per oz. By the end of October, however, the London 'fix' had fallen to $425 (£292) per oz. During November London platinum traded within a range of $416–$443 (£290–£309) per oz. By 10 December, however, more positive assessments of economic prospects for 2002 had lifted the price of platinum to $470 (£326) per oz. The price of the metal remained above $450 per oz for the remainder of the month, ending the year at $477 (£327) per oz as concerns about Russian export quotas in 2002 surfaced.

For most of January 2002 the London price of platinum ranged between US $470 and $480 per oz, but it declined sharply at the very end of the month as a result of the liquidation of 'long' positions held on 'futures' markets, particuarly by Japanese investors. In early February the lowest 'fix' of the year, $449 per oz, was recorded, but by the beginning of the second week of that month the price had recovered to $474 per oz. By the end of February the London price had risen to $493 per oz. By 11 March, in response to increasingly optimistic perceptions of US economic prospects, the London price of platinum had risen to $526 per oz, and for the remainder of the month traded within a range of $510–$520 per oz. In early April strong physical demand for the metal, together with the liquidation of 'short' positions held on 'futures' markets, propelled the London price of platinum to $537 per oz. The absence of supplies of platinum from Russia had begun to be felt as a strong market influence in March, and remained so until around mid-April, by which time the London price had risen as high as $543 per oz. A renewal of Russian 'spot' sales, however, subsequently restrained the London price from rising above $560 per oz. By the end of the month the London price had fallen to $536 per oz. After falling to $519 per oz in early May, the London price was subsequently supported by strong demand for the metal, which traded within a range of $537–$548 per oz in the latter part of the month. At the end of the first week of June the London price of platinum reached $564 per oz, remaining above $560 per oz for the remainder of the month.

From late June 2002, partly in response to revelations of corporate fraud on a huge scale in the USA, the price of platinum began to decline, falling to US $520 per oz in the first week of July. Fundamentally, however, the London price of the metal was supported by strong demand. In August the price rallied, reaching $558 per oz by the end of the second week of the month. 'Short-covering' in the palladium market was cited as responsible for a further, abrupt increase in the London price of platinum in the final week of August. Sales of the metal in early September, in response to less favourable US economic data, caused the London price of platinum to fall to $540 per oz, but it was subsequently buoyed by strong physical demand and speculative purchases. Having risen as high as $574 per oz in September, in early October the price of platinum fell to $557 per oz in the face of plentiful supplies. 'Short-covering' of positions held on 'futures' markets by Japanese investors subsequently lifted the London 'spot' price above $590 per oz. In early November platinum generally traded within a range of $580–$590 per oz. On 14 November 'short-covering' by London dealers propelled the London morning 'fix' of platinum above $600 per oz for the first time since May 2001. Thereafter, the market remained strong until the end of the year, the London price rallying, in response to a rally in the price of gold, to $607 per oz, its highest level of the year, on 17 December. At the end of 2002 the London price of platinum was $598 per oz.

The London price of platinum rose steeply in 2003. Having reached US $700 per oz in February, supported by positive fundamental factors, in March–April the price fell in response to declining investor interest amid global political uncertainty resulting from the outbreak of war in Iraq. In April the lowest price of the year, $603 per oz, first registered in January, was repeated, but it did not subsequently descend any further for the remainder of the year. From July prices moved upwards, driven initially by Japanese investor interest, rising above $700 per oz in late August. There was a renewed surge in the London price from October, in response to fears that South African supplies would be disrupted, in combination with strong investor activity and a resurgence in Chinese purchases for jewellery. The highest price of the year, $840 per oz, was recorded in December. The average price for platinum in 2003, at $691.2 per oz, was some 28% higher than that recorded in 2002. Intra-year growth of 34% was recorded in 2003. For the whole of the year platinum traded at a premium of $618 per oz (317%) to palladium.

In mid-January 2004 the London price of platinum, which had begun the year at around US $815 per oz, climbed steeply, to $868 per oz, in response to purchases by Chinese jewellery manufacturers and renewed buying interest by institutional investors on 'futures' markets in New York and Tokyo. At the end of February the London 'fix' rose as high as $877 per oz, in response, again, to investors' purchases of platinum 'futures', in particular on the Tokyo market. On 1 March the London price of platinum reached $900 per oz as investors reportedly supplemented their 'long' positions on 'futures' markets, and it remained at close to that level for most of March and April. On 19 April the price of platinum was 'fixed' at $937 per oz, its highest level for 24 years. On 29 April, however, the price was 'fixed' at only $783 per oz, following a rapid decline that had been triggered by investors' liquidation of 'long' positions held on 'futures' markets. Having fallen further in the interim, the price subsequently rallied in late May, reaching $845 per oz on 27 May. After falling as low as $774 per oz in mid-June, in July the London price of platinum moved above $800 per oz once again, in response, among other factors, to renewed buying interest on the part of institutional investors. This rally continued in August, when the London price peaked at $885 per oz. After declining in the early part of September, the rally was renewed in the second half of that month as a result of disruptions to mine output of platinum in South Africa. In October the London price of platinum was more volatile, ranging between $821.5–$863 per oz. The value of the US dollar relative to other currencies, price trends in other commodities and higher demand for platinum from Chinese buyers were identified as important market influences in October. In November investors reportedly began to rebuild 'long' positions on 'futures' markets, boosting the London price of platinum to more than $871 per oz on 12 November. The price subsequently declined, however, in response, *inter alia*, to profit-taking by institutional investors. Having risen as high as $884 per oz on 2 December, the price of platinum declined sharply, to $822 per oz, on 8 December as the value of the US dollar rose, triggering liquidation of 'long' positions on 'futures' markets. At the end of the year the London price of platinum was $861 per oz. In 2004 the average price of platinum, at $845.8 per oz, was 22% higher than that recorded in 2003. In terms of US dollars, there was intra-year growth of 5.6% in the price of platinum in 2004. In terms of the Japanese yen, however, there was little change, and in terms of euros the price of platinum declined in 2004, emphasizing the significance of the decline in the value of the US dollar to the price of platinum during the year.

In 2005, on the London market for platinum, the lowest 'fix' of the year, US $844 per oz, was recorded on the first trading day of the year, 4 January. In February the price rose as high as $880, driven upwards by firm demand from the physical market. Having fallen back in the interim, in mid-March, in response to strong prices for gold and silver, the price of platinum rose briefly above $880 per oz, fuelled by speculative demand. Thereafter, until the end of May, platinum traded within a range of $850–$880 per oz, apparently in a close relationship with prices for gold and energy. In mid-May a sharp correction occurred, with prices approaching the 'low' for the year that had been recorded in January. Losses were short-lived, however, the abrupt decline prompting strong investment interest in the metal. During the second half of 2005 the London price of platinum rallied emphatically. In June the price rose as high as $900 per oz in response to the strength of the price of gold and the weakness of the US dollar, but the rally was not sustained. From early August, the rally in the price of platinum became firmly established, however, driven initially by such factors as uncertainty in South Africa's mining sector and then, subsequently, from late August, by hurricane weather conditions in the Gulf of Mexico and their effect on energy prices. In September a price of $930 per oz was attained, although it fell back to $915 in October. Later in October the highest price for platinum for 25 years—more than $940 per oz—was recorded and in November speculative interest propelled the price to almost $1,000 per oz. In December the price of platinum rose above $1,000 per oz for the first time in 25 years. Profit-taking, among other factors, reduced the price to $964 per oz at the end of the year. In 2005, at $896.6 per oz, the average price of platinum, was 6% higher than the average price recorded in 2004. In terms of US dollars, there was intra-year growth of 14.2% in the price of platinum in 2005.

Platinum again performed strongly in 2006. It began the year trading at US $1,029.0 per oz, and reached its highest point of the year—$1,264.9 per oz—by May. The price decreased in the following month, to $1,188.6 per oz, before recovering to $1,234.0 per oz by the end of August. The price fluctuated in the last four months of 2006, ending the year at $1,121.5 per oz. The annual average price for 2006 was $1,142.6 per oz.

A strong upward trend in the price of palladium that had been established in late 1999 was maintained during the opening weeks of 2000, and in February the London quotation reached US $785 (£491) per oz. In April the price of palladium eased to $554 (£350) per oz, but at the end of July it reached a new record of $822 (£549) per oz. As in the case of platinum, the main influence on market sentiment was the delay in Russian shipments. On 2 August the London quotation for palladium attained a new record level of $855 (£574) per oz. This level was not sustained, however, and by the end of August the London quotation for palladium had fallen to $716 (£492) per oz. Heavy industrial demand caused the price to rally again in early September, but once again the rally was not sustained, the London quotation for palladium declining to $711 (£490) per oz on 28 September. From the end of October 2000 the London quotation for palladium rose sharply once again, reaching $794 (£548) per oz on 3 November in response to concerns about the level of Russian PGM supplies in 2001. The Russian supply situation brought about further substantial increases in the London quotation in December. On 12 December the price rose to $940 (£649) per oz, a fifth consecutive all-time high. On 27 December palladium attained a new all-time record price of $972 (£652) per oz, before declining to $954 (£638) per oz at the final 'fix' of the year.

On 8 January 2001 the London price of palladium rose above US $1,000 per oz for the first time ever. As in December 2000, the Russian supply situation was the key to the successive all-time record prices recorded in January 2001. On 26 January the London price of palladium reached a zenith of $1,094 (£741) per oz. Between 8 and 11 February, however, the value of the metal declined to $975 (£671) per oz as concerns about supplies from Russia were allayed. From 21 February 'spot' sales of palladium in London commenced that would cause the value of the metal to decline relentlessly until October. Already, by the end of February, the London price had fallen to $839 (£590) per oz, and on 5 March it fell to $750 (£519) per oz, its lowest level for four months. Rising physical sales depressed the London 'fix' for palladium to less than $700 per oz on 4 April, and on 12 April the London quotation declined to $650 (£453) per oz. These falls were succeeded by a period of volatility during which the London 'spot' price rose above $700 per oz and the London 'fix' recovered to as high a level as $765 (£533) per oz at one point. This rally was short-lived, however, and by the end of the month the London price had fallen back to $682 (£477) per oz. A further weakening occurred during the first two weeks of May. On 14 May the London 'fix' was $630 (£442) per oz. Thereafter, for the remainder of the month, palladium traded in a range of $640–$660 per oz. Weak demand had depressed the price of the metal further, to below $600 per oz, by late June.

On 13 July 2001 the price of palladium declined to US $559 (£390) per oz. Thereafter the market was characterized by an abundance of supplies from a variety of sources, which, combined with an absence of demand, caused the London price of palladium to fall to $543 on 16 July, thus trading at a discount to platinum for the first time since May 2000, and to less than $500 per oz on 20 July. On 31 July the London price fell as low as $438 (£307) per oz, but subsequently recovered to $457 per oz. On 7 August a further sharp fall in the price of palladium, to $438 (£305) per oz, occurred in response to a substantial reduction in the value of platinum. From 24 September palladium was depressed further by a decline in the price of platinum, the London quotation for the former falling to only $400 (£273) per oz on 26 September. In spite of this loss of value, demand remained weak and on 28 September the London price of palladium fell to $360 per oz. On 2 October the London quotation declined to $315 (£217) per oz, its lowest level for 24 months, in response to heavy selling of physical metal. However, the new 'low' spurred industrial buyers to enter the market and palladium traded in a range of $340–$360 per oz until 17 October when the value of the metal began, once again, to decline in line with that of platinum, falling to $317 per oz on 22 October. During November, amid subdued market activity, palladium generally traded at around $330 (£230) per oz. By 10 December industrial purchases, combined with an absence of Russian 'spot' sales, had raised the London quotation to $423 (£294) per oz. Thereafter, for the remainder of December, palladium traded at close to $400 per oz, rising to $440 (£302) per oz at the final 'fix' of the year in response to speculation that Russian PGM export quotas for 2002 would be delayed.

The highest palladium 'fix' of 2002, US $440 per oz, occurred as early as 2 January. Later in the month, after it appeared that Ford Motor Co of the USA would purchase little palladium during the course of the year and would possibly sell surplus metal, the London price declined to $413 per oz. By the end of January the price of palladium had fallen to only $370 per oz. After rallying from around mid-February, the London price subsequently traded within a range of $370–$380 per oz during the remainder of that month. Heavy sales depressed the London price of palladium still further, to $360 per oz, in early March, but by the end of the month it had recovered to $386 per oz. Confirmation of Ford Motor Co's apparent decision to sell metal from its PGM stocks reduced the London price of palladium to $362 per oz by the beginning of the second week of April, however. In early May palladium generally traded within a range of $349–$357 per oz, but it had fallen by the end of the month to only $348 per oz. By late June the London price had fallen further, to around $320 per oz.

For much of July and August 2002 the London price of palladium remained at around US $320 per oz. On 27 August, however, 'short-covering' by Japanese investors raised the London afternoon 'fix' to $342 per oz. Before the end of the month the London price appeared to have stabilized at about $365 per oz, but it declined to only $330 per oz on 30 August. In early September the London price of palladium returned to about $320 per oz, and it had fallen to only $315 per oz by the end of the month. During October the London price of palladium generally ranged between $310–$320 per oz. In early November, in response to over-supply and weak demand, the price of palladium declined sharply, to less than $290 per oz, and before the end of the month it had fallen as low as $261 per oz. In December, as Russian supplies of palladium increased substantially, the London price of palladium fell below $250 per oz for the first time since March 1998. On 23 December the lowest 'fix' of the year, $222 per oz, was recorded. At the end of 2002 the London price of palladium was $233 per oz. The metal thus traded at a discount of $365 per oz to platinum.

In 2003 the average London price of palladium declined by 41% compared with that recorded in 2002, to US $200.52 per oz. Within the year a decline in the price of 18% occurred. The price was strongest in January, when the 'high' for the year of $269 per oz was recorded. In March–April 2003, however, the London price of palladium declined steeply in response to political uncertainty engendered by the outbreak of war in Iraq, among other factors. The 'low' for the year of $148 per oz, recorded in late April, reportedly represented a decline of 44% in the value of the metal within three months. The London price revived somewhat in May, partly in response to reports that the US General Motors Corpn intended to increase its use of palladium in vehicle manufacture. However, gains were limited in mid-2003 by high US vehicle inventories. From August the London price was supported by speculative and investment activity, and in September a 'fix' of $232 per oz was recorded. However, this recovery was not sustained for long beyond mid-September. In the final quarter of the year the London price of palladium moved within a range of $184–$214 per oz, when speculative activity was identified as the principal market determinant, in combination, at the end of the year, with increased supplies of physical metal.

During January 2004 the London price of palladium rose from US $194 per oz at the beginning of the month to $242 per oz on 22 January, propelled by investment fund purchases. During February the price climbed as high as $246 per oz. Investment fund purchases, together with increased demand for physical metal from Chinese jewellery manufacturers, had raised the London price of palladium to $333 per oz by 13 April. However, profit-taking reduced it to only $240 per oz towards the end of April. In May, generally, the price declined further as investors liquidated 'long' positions held on 'futures' markets. By 15 June, in response to a decline in the price of platinum, the London price of palladium had fallen as low as $215.5 per oz. A slight recovery occurred in mid-July as the price of both platinum and gold rallied, but the price of palladium had fallen to $216 per oz by the end of July. Having moved little in either direction in August, in early September the London price of palladium was reduced to $204.5 per oz. Investment fund purchases supported the price subsequently in September, however. On 8 October the price rose to its highest level, $234 per oz, for four months, but thereafter eased. During most of November palladium was traded in London within a range of $210–$220 per oz. In November and December speculative interest in the metal, which was reported to have sustained the price since the beginning of the year, evaporated. Sales by investors were supplemented, too, by a substantial increase in Russian sales of palladium to Switzerland in November and December. By 16 December the London price had fallen to less than $180 per oz. At the end of 2004 palladium traded at $184 per oz, exactly $10 per oz lower than at the beginning of the year.

In 2005, initially, palladium traded at US $180 per oz on the London market, falling below this level in early February, but subsequently recovering to trade at $180–$190 per oz in late February. Prices were driven upwards in anticipation of the release by Russia of data related to government stocks of palladium, but eased to below $200 per oz when it became clear that no such data would be made available. Throughout most of May–September palladium traded between $180–$190 per oz. Analysts have speculated that supplies may have been supplemented during this period by sales from above-ground inventories, since consumer demand for palladium was robust during the first three-quarters of 2005 and normal producer sales were generally in line with it. From late September, possibly in response to the abatement of sales from above-ground stocks, the price of palladium rose steadily, reaching $227 per oz in October, $258 per oz in November and the 'high' of the year, $297 per oz, in early December. Before the end of the year, however, the price declined in response to sales of gold and platinum, falling to $253 per oz at the close of 2005. The average price of palladium declined by 12.7% in 2005, compared with 2004. Within the year, however, a gain of 40% was recorded.

As with platinum, positive investor sentiment was an important factor in palladium's strong performance in 2006. Palladium began the year trading at US $273.7 per oz, and reached its high for the year of $369.4 per oz in May. The price, while fluctuating, remained above $310 per oz for the remainder of 2006. The price of palladium at the end of December was $326.1 per oz.

RICE (*Oryza*)

Rice is an annual grass belonging to the same family as (and having many similar characteristics to) small grains such as wheat, oats, rye and barley. It is principally the semi-aquatic nature of rice that distinguishes it from other grain species, and this is an important factor in determining its place of origin. In Africa and Asia unmilled rice is referred to as 'paddy', although 'rough' rice is the common appellation in the West. After removal of the outer husk, it is called 'brown' rice. After the grain is milled to varying degrees to remove the bran layers, it is called 'milled' rice. Since rice loses 30%–40% of its weight in the milling process, most rice is traded in the milled form to save shipping expenses.

There are two cultivated species of rice, *Oryza sativa* and *O. glaberrima*. Originating in tropical Asia, *O. sativa* is widely grown in tropical and semi-tropical areas, while the cultivation of *O. glaberrima* is limited to the high rainfall zone of West Africa. In Africa rice is grown mainly as a subsistence crop, principally by smallholder farmers of whom a disproportionate number are women. Methods of cultivation differ from region to region and yields tend to be low by world standards. Rice is a staple food in several African countries, including Côte d'Ivoire, The Gambia, Guinea, Guinea-Bissau, Liberia, Madagascar, Senegal and Sierra Leone. In West African countries generally rice is a staple food of 40% of the population. As a consequence of population growth and increased dietary preference for rice, African demand for consumption has increased rapidly in recent years, outstripping supply, and now amounts in total to more than 10m. metric tons (milled rice) annually. In 1998 sub-Saharan African demand was some 4m. tons (milled rice) greater than supply.

Production of Paddy Rice
('000 metric tons)

	2005	2006
World total*	631,509	634,576
Africa*	20,118	21,118
Leading African producers		
Côte d'Ivoire	704	700*
Egypt	6,125	6,500*
Guinea	1,272	1,340
Madagascar	3,400	3,485
Mali	946	1,019
Nigeria	3,567	3,924*
Tanzania	957	784
Leading non-African producers		
Bangladesh	39,796	43,729
China, People's Repub.*	181,999	184,070
India	137,620	136,510
Indonesia	53,985	54,400†
Myanmar	25,364	25,200†
Thailand	30,292	29,269
Viet Nam	35,791	35,827

* FAO estimate(s).
† Unofficial figure.

World rice production is dominated by the Asian region (which produces more than 90% of the world's total). African rice production increased steadily from the 1970s, as a consequence of expanded cultivation and improved yields, to total more than 17m. metric tons at the end of the 1990s. Nevertheless, African output has only accounted for about 3%—or less—of total world output in recent years. As the bulk of rice production is consumed mainly in the producing countries, international trade until very recently usually accounted for only 3%–5% of world output. In the early 2000s, however, the quantity of rice traded has been equivalent to as much as 7% of the total produced world-wide. The market is subject to great volatility and fluctuating prices. Less than 1% of the African rice crop enters international trade, and more than 90% of African rice exports have traditionally been supplied by Egypt. Africa has, especially in recent years, been a substantial net importer of rice, although the volume growth in imports has been held in check by the impact of higher world rice prices on the depleted foreign exchange reserves of many African importing countries. The major African importers include Côte d'Ivoire, Nigeria, Guinea, Sierra Leone, Senegal and Madagascar, the last ranking as the world's largest consumer of rice in per caput terms. Despite the completion in 1995 of the rehabilitation of its main rice-growing areas, Madagascar has yet to achieve its goal of self-sufficiency in rice. In 2006 Madagascar harvested rice from a little more than 1.3m. ha. Nigeria, the largest producer in the sub-Saharan region, had about 2.8m. ha under rice in 2006, and Côte d'Ivoire 370,000 ha. In 2006, according to FAO, rice was harvested from 8.5m. ha in sub-Saharan Africa.

Because most of the varieties of rice cultivated in Africa originated in Asia and are relatively new to the region, suitable high-yielding varieties (HYV) have only recently begun to be propagated. The development of HYV is among the activities of the 17-member Africa Rice Center (WARDA), formed by the producing countries in 1971 as the West Africa Rice Development Association. From the beginning of 2005 WARDA transferred its operations to Cotonou, Benin, from its headquarters in Bouaké, Côte d'Ivoire, owing to ongoing political instability in the latter country. WARDA maintains research centres in Nigeria and Senegal, from which it conducts scientific research on crop improvement and provides technical assistance, with the aim of advancing the region towards eventual self-sufficiency in rice production. Since 2000 several New Rice for Africa (NERICA) cultivation projects have been initiated. The NERICA varieties have been developed by WARDA, and it is hoped that their adaptation to West African growing conditions will increase their yields by at least 25%, compared with conventional rice crops.

Africa imports large quantities of rice from Thailand and the USA, two of the world's four major exporters—Viet Nam and India are the others. In 2005, according to FAO, rising demand for imports from Africa (and Asia) was among the factors that drove international trade in rice to a record level of 29.4m. metric tons. There was a contraction in world rice trade in 2006, to 28.5m. tons, according to FAO estimates. Weaker demand from Africa, where there had been good crops in 2005, was one of the factors contributing to this decline. Nigeria was reported to have banned imports of milled rice from the beginning of 2006. Purchases by Côte d'Ivoire, Senegal and South Africa were all forecast to decline. It was anticipated that African countries would import some 9.2m. tons of rice in 2006 (from 8.2m. tons in 2005), these purchases representing almost one-third of the world total. FAO forecast that world trade in rice would total 30.2m. tons.

The world's leading exporter of rice in recent years has been Thailand. The average export price of Thai milled white rice ('Thai 100% B second grade', f.o.b. Bangkok) in 2000 was US 206.7 per metric ton, but in 2001 the price fell to only $177.4 per ton. The decline, part of a marked downward trend, was partly attributable to the plentiful supply of rice, with abundant stocks available, particularly in China and India. While world output of rice advanced in 1999/2000, the volume of trade declined, as many major importing countries, assisted by favourable weather, increased production. In 2002 the average export price of Thai milled white rice recovered to $196.9 per ton, and in 2003 an average price of $200.9 per ton was recorded. In 2004 the average price strengthened again, to $244.5 per ton, and in 2005 it rose by almost 19%, to $290.5 per ton. In 2006 it increased by 7.1%, to $311.2 per ton. Factors that boosted the price of rice from late 2004 included a strengthening of the Thai currency, the baht, relative to the US dollar, and reduced availability of rice for foreign sales. In January–August 2007 the average export price of Thai milled white rice ranged between $318.3 per ton (January) and $335.8 per ton (August).

SISAL (*Agave sisalana*)

Sisal, which is not indigenous to Africa, was introduced to Tanganyika (now mainland Tanzania) from Mexico at the end of the 19th century. The leaf tissue of this plant yields hard, flexible fibres which are suitable for making rope and twine, cord matting, padding and upholstery. In 2005 sisal accounted for about 80% of world production of sisal, henequen and similar hard fibres. Traditionally, about three-quarters of sisal consumption has been for agricultural twine. World output of sisal and other hard fibres has generally declined in recent years, owing to competition from nylons and petroleum-based synthetics (in particular, polypropylene harvest twine, which is stronger than sisal and less labour-intensive to produce), although the intensity of the competition and the success of hard fibres depend on fluctuations in the price of petroleum.

Production of Sisal
('000 metric tons)

	2005	2006
World total*	385	428
Africa*	75	76
Leading African producers		
Kenya	25	25*
Madagascar	17	17*
Tanzania	27	28
Leading non-African producers		
Brazil	207	248
China*	18	20
Mexico	27	27

* FAO estimate(s).

In 1970 Tanzania, whose sisal is generally regarded as being of the best quality, was overtaken as the world's leading producer by Brazil. The nationalization of more than one-half of Tanzania's sisal estates in 1976, together with low prices, inefficient management and lack of equipment and spare parts, contributed to the decline of the Tanzanian crop. From the 1980s, however, the Government sought to revive the industry by returning some state-owned estates to private or co-operative ownership, and in 1998 it completed the transfer of its sisal estates and factories to a consortium of European and Tanzanian entrepreneurs from the private sector. Tanzania's annual exports of sisal and henequen fibres and manufactures have stabilized at about 14,000–15,000 metric tons in recent years. However, prospects remain overshadowed by the longer-term outlook for sisal. According to FAO, annual world demand for sisal (and henequen) declined from some 800,000 tons in the early 1970s to only slightly more than 300,000 tons in the mid-1990s. Over the same period consumption of sisal in the manufacture of agricultural twine fell from 230,000 tons to only 130,000 tons. World imports of raw sisal fibre were reported to have totalled 86,500 tons in 2005, compared with 101,700 tons in 2004 and some 98,600 tons in 2003. Imports of sisal manufactures world-wide in 2005 reportedly amounted to 79,900 tons, compared with 103,300 tons in 2004 and 103,500 tons in 2003. The decline of the sisal sector in Tanzania spurred the development of production in Kenya to the extent that the country was able to compete strongly with both Brazil and Tanzania, even though, having no processing industry, it has never exported sisal products. However, Kenyan production peaked, at some 87,000 tons, as long ago as 1974, and totalled only an estimated 25,000 tons in 2006. Kenya's annual exports of sisal and henequen have, on average, totalled about 20,000 tons in recent years. The contribution of exports of sisal to Kenya's total export earnings is less than 1%, however.

Although sisal producers operate a quota system, in an attempt to improve the pricing structure of the crop, the average price of sisal was in general decline between the early 1980s and the early 1990s, as relatively stable prices for petroleum allowed polypropylene to regain its competitiveness.

The average import price of ungraded East African sisal (c.i.f. European ports) was US $635 per metric ton, rising to $699 per ton in 2001. In 2002, however, it declined to $650 per ton. The average price rose in each year in 2003–05, to, respectively, $674 per ton, $874 per ton and $901 per ton. During the first half of 2006 the average import price of ungraded East African sisal increased further, to $913 per ton. According to FAO, the import price of East African 3L grade sisal (c.i.f. European ports) averaged $843 per ton in 2001, but declined to $775 per ton in 2002. In 2003 the average price was $786 per ton, and in 2004 an average price of $968 per ton was recorded. In 2005 the average price increased to $1,001 per ton. During the first six months of 2006 the average import price of East African 3L sisal was $1,013 per ton. In 2001 the average import price of Brazilian No. 3 grade sisal (c.i.f. European ports) was $449 per ton. In 2002 the average import price of Brazilian sisal fell to $404 per ton. In 2003 an average price of $505 per ton was recorded, and in 2004 a further increase, to $593 per ton, occurred. A very substantial increase in the average price, to $763 per ton, was recorded in 2005. In the first half of 2006 the average import price of Brazilian No. 3 grade sisal continued to rise, averaging $779 per ton. At the end of 2005, as in 2003 and 2004, global markets for sisal remained characterized by strong demand. Imports of raw fibre by the People's Republic of China had risen markedly, from less than 2,000 tons in 1999 to more than 30,000 tons in 2003, although Brazil was reported by FAO to have been the principal beneficiary of growth in this sector. Strong demand for African fibre for non-traditional uses was reported by the same source to have exerted a key influence on the price of the commodity since the beginning of 2003. As of December 2005 prices for sisal were at their highest level (in nominal terms) since 1974, although in real terms they remained below the levels of the 1970s and 1980s.

In 2005, according to FAO, imports of raw sisal fibres by China accounted for about 34% of global imports totalling 86,500 metric tons, compared with only about 9% in 2001. Chinese imports in 2005 thus exceeded those by the member states of the European Union, which together accounted for about 27% of the total imported world-wide. In 2005 the USA was the major market for sisal manufactures, accounting for about 46% of world imports totalling 79,800 tons.

SUGAR

Sugar is a sweet crystalline substance, which may be derived from the juices of various plants. Chemically, the basis of sugar is sucrose, one of a group of soluble carbohydrates which are important sources of energy in the human diet. It can be obtained from trees, including the maple and certain palms, but virtually all manufactured sugar comes from two plants, sugar beet (*Beta vulgaris*), and sugar cane, a giant perennial grass of the genus *Saccharum*.

Sugar cane, found in tropical areas, grows to a height of up to 5 m. The plant is native to Polynesia, but its distribution is now widespread. It is not necessary to plant cane every season as, if the root of the plant is left in the ground, it will grow again in the following year. This practice, known as 'ratooning', may be continued for as long as three years, when yields begin to decline. Cane is ready for cutting 12–24 months after planting, depending on local conditions. Much of the world's sugar cane is still cut by hand, but rising costs are hastening the changeover to mechanical harvesting. The cane is cut as close as possible to the ground, and the top leaves, which may be used as cattle fodder, are removed.

After cutting, the cane is loaded by hand or by machine into trucks or trailers and towed directly to a factory for processing. Sugar cane deteriorates rapidly after it has been cut and should be processed as soon as possible. At the factory the cane passes first through shredding knives or crushing rollers, which break up the hard rind and expose the inner fibre, and then to squeezing rollers, where the crushed cane is subjected to high pressure and sprayed with water. The resulting juice is heated and lime is added for clarification and the removal of impurities. The clean juice is then concentrated in evaporators. This thickened juice is next boiled in steam-heated vacuum pans until a mixture or 'massecuite' of sugar crystals and 'mother syrup' is produced. The massecuite is then spun in centrifugal machines to separate the sugar crystals (raw cane sugar) from the residual syrup (cane molasses).

The production of beet sugar follows the same process, except that the juice is extracted by osmotic diffusion. Its manufacture produces white sugar crystals which do not require further refining. In most producing countries it is consumed domestically, although the European Union (EU), which generally accounts for about 13% of total world sugar production, is a net exporter of white refined sugar. Beet sugar usually accounts for more than one-third of world production. Production data for sugar cane and sugar beet generally cover all crops harvested, except crops grown explicitly for feed. The third table covers the production of raw sugar by the centrifugal process. In 2004 global output of non-centrifugal sugar (i.e. produced from sugar cane which has not undergone centrifugation) was estimated at about 11.5m. metric tons. The main producer of non-centrifugal sugar is India, with output of 7.3m. tons in 2004.

Most of the world's output of raw cane sugar is sent to refineries outside the country of origin, unless the sugar is for local consumption. Cuba, Thailand, Brazil and India are among the few producers of cane that export part of their output as refined sugar. The refining process further purifies the sugar crystals and eventually results in finished products of various grades, such as granulated, icing or castor sugar. The ratio of refined to raw sugar is usually about 0.9:1.

As well as providing sugar, quantities of cane are grown in some countries for seed, feed, fresh consumption, the manufacture of alcohol and other uses. Molasses may be used as cattle feed or fermented to produce alcoholic beverages for human consumption, such as rum, a distilled spirit manufactured in Caribbean countries. Sugar cane juice may be used to produce ethyl alcohol (ethanol). This chemical can be utilized, either exclusively or mixed with petroleum derivatives, as a fuel for motor vehicles. The steep rise in the price of petroleum after 1973 made the large-scale conversion of sugar cane into ethanol economically attractive (particularly to developing nations), especially as sugar, unlike petroleum, is a renewable source of energy. Several countries developed ethanol production by this means in order to reduce petroleum imports and to support cane growers. Ethanol-based fuel, which generates fewer harmful exhaust hydrocarbons than petroleum-based fuel, may be known as 'gasohol', 'alcogas', 'green petrol' or, as in Brazil, simply as 'alcohol'. Brazil was the pioneer in this field, establishing the largest ethanol-based fuel production programme—'PROALCOOL'—in the world. Public subsidies and tax concessions encouraged farmers to plant more sugar cane, investors to construct more distilleries and designers to blueprint cars fuelled exclusively by ethanol. At the same time, the Government created an extensive distribution network to transport ethanol-based fuel to filling stations, where its price was maintained low through subsidization. By the mid-1980s almost every new car sold in Brazil was fuelled exclusively by ethanol. In the 1990s, however, a shortage of ethanol, in conjunction with lower world petroleum prices and the Government's withdrawal of ethanol subsidies resulted in a sharp fall in Brazil's output of these vehicles. Since mid-2005, however, the popularity of ethanol-fuelled motor vehicles has begun to rise again. A programme is under way in Brazil which aims to establish ethanol as a global export commodity, in the world trade of which Brazil currently accounts for more than 50%. US imports of ethanol were expected to rise substantially in 2006 as domestic refineries phased out the use of the gasoline additive methyl tertiary butyl ether (MTBE). According to FAO, the prospects for the use of ethanol as a fuel world-wide have been boosted by the historically high levels to which petroleum prices have risen in 2005 and 2006. Global output of ethanol (including ethanol derived from crops other than sugar, such as maize) increased by 53% in 2000–05, from 30,000m. litres to 46,000m. litres. It has been forecast that ethanol production will reach 54,000m. litres—equivalent to 1% of world petroleum consumption—in 2010. In Africa ethanol has been blended with gasoline for use in fuel for motor vehicles in Kenya, Malawi and Zimbabwe, but Zimbabwe is the only one of those countries to have legally required it to be used.

Production of Sugar Cane
('000 metric tons)

	2005	2006
World total*	1,295,501	1,387,777
Africa*	93,013	91,697
Leading African producers		
Congo, Dem. Repub.	1,522	1,522*
Egypt	16,317	16,317*
Ethiopia*	2,450	2,600
Kenya	4,801	4,933
Madagascar	2,446	2,691
Malawi*	2,100	2,400
Mauritius	4,984	4,749
Réunion*	2,000	2,000
South Africa	21,265	20,275
Sudan	7,186	7,186*
Swaziland	5,200	5,000
Uganda	2,150†	1,950*
Zambia*	1,800	2,700
Zimbabwe	3,290†	3,600*
Leading non-African producers		
Australia	37,822	38,169
Brazil	422,957	455,291
China, People's Repub.*	87,513	100,684
Cuba	11,600	11,060
India	237,088	281,170
Mexico	45,195	50,597
Pakistan	47,244	44,666
Thailand	49,586	47,658

* FAO estimate(s).
† Unofficial figure.

Production of Sugar Beets
('000 metric tons)

	2005	2006
World total*	251,872	256,328
Africa*	6,734	5,682
Leading African producers		
Egypt	3,430	3,430*
Morocco	3,302	2,252
Leading non-African producers		
France	31,150	29,879
Germany	25,285	20,647
Turkey	15,181	14,452
Ukraine	15,468	22,421
USA	25,087	28,880

* FAO estimate(s).

After the milling of sugar, the cane has dry fibrous remnants known as bagasse, which is usually burned as fuel in sugar mills. Bagasse can also be pulped and used for making fibreboard, particle board and most grades of paper. As the costs of imported wood pulp have risen, cane-growing regions have turned increasingly to the manufacture of paper from bagasse. A paper mill based on this process has been established in South Africa. Mauritius has successfully used bagasse to meet its sugar industry's electricity requirements, achieving a surplus that has been fed into the national grid to account for as much as 16% of total electricity demand. Another by-product, cachaza, has been utilized as an animal feed.

In recent years sugar has encountered increased competition from other sweeteners, including maize-based products, such as isoglucose (a form of high-fructose corn syrup, or HFCS), and chemical additives, such as saccharine, aspartame and xylitol. Aspartame (APM) was the most widely used high-intensity artificial sweetener in the early 1990s, although its market dominance was under challenge from sucralose, which is about 600 times as sweet as sugar (compared with 200–300 times for other intense sweeteners) and is more resistant to chemical deterioration than APM. From the late 1980s research was conducted in the USA to formulate means of synthesizing thaumatin, a substance derived from the fruit of the West African katemfe plant, *Thaumatococcus daniellii*, which is about 2,500 times as sweet as sugar. As of 2005, the use of thaumatin had been approved in the EU, Israel, Japan and—as a flavouring agent—the USA. In 1998 the US Government approved the domestic marketing of sucralose, the only artificial sweetener made from sugar. Sucralose was stated to avoid many of the taste problems associated with other artificial sweeteners.

South Africa is the principal producer and exporter of sugar in sub-Saharan Africa. In the mid-1990s South Africa ranked as the world's seventh largest sugar exporter. With regard to the domestic market, however, the South African sugar industry has encountered increased competition from neighbouring countries, most notably Swaziland, as a result of free trade agreements in the context of the Southern African Customs Union (SACU) and the Southern African Development Community. The South African industry's share of the SACU market was reported in 2005 to have declined from 95% to less than 80% in recent years. According to the US Department of Agriculture (USDA), the 2003/04 sugar season in South Africa was disastrous, as a result of a heavy fall in cane output and lower foreign and domestic sales. Cane growers' income was reported to have fallen by 33%. No significant improvement in these conditions occurred in the 2004/05 season, when the crop was the smallest since 1995/96 owing to low rainfall. In 2005/06 and 2006/07 rainfall patterns were reported to have returned to normal.

Sugar is the staple product in the economies of Mauritius and Réunion, although output is vulnerable to climatic conditions, as both islands are subject to cyclones. In Mauritius, where it was estimated that more than 75% (72,750 ha) of cultivated land was devoted to sugar production in the late 1990s, sugar sales accounted for about 24% of the island's revenue from exports (excluding re-exports) in 2005. In Réunion 59.1% of the island's 63,050 ha of cultivable land was planted with sugar cane in 1998, and sales of sugar provided 50.4% of export income in 2005. The expansion of sugar output, however, has been impeded in recent years by unfavourable weather, and by the pressure on agricultural land use from the increasing demands of road construction and housing.

Mozambique's sugar industry, formerly the country's primary source of foreign exchange, has begun to surmount the effects of many years of disruption and neglect. The resolution of internal civil conflict has made possible the rehabilitation both of cane-growing and of the country's six sugar complexes. Production of raw sugar has almost doubled since the peace agreement, rising from 234,000 metric tons in 1994 to 400,000 tons in 2000, and remaining at that level in 2001–03. In 1999 the government of Mozambique was reported to be seeking annual export quotas to the US and EU sugar markets. However, considerable foreign aid and investment is still needed to complete the revitalization of this sector. In 2004 sugar was Malawi's third most important export commodity (after tobacco and tea), providing 4.2% of revenue from foreign sales (including re-exports). Tanzania sought to develop its sugar sector during the 1990s, with the aim of reducing reliance on imports from Malawi and Zambia. Output of sugar cane was estimated by FAO at 2.8m. tons in 2006. In 2003 the country produced about 163,000 tons of sugar. Although local demand, at about 415,000 tons annually, outstrips production, Tanzania exports about 10,000 tons of sugar each year to the EU. In 2000 the government banned the import of sugar into all but the country's three largest ports, in an attempt to suppress the widespread smuggling of cheaper foreign sugar into Tanzania.

In Sudan one of the world's largest single sugar projects was inaugurated in 1981 at Kenana, on the eastern bank of the White Nile, south of Khartoum. The Kenana Sugar Co (in which the governments of Sudan, Kuwait and Saudi Arabia are the major shareholders), comprising an estate and processing facilities, has been instrumental in the elimination of the drain on reserves of foreign exchange of sugar, which was, until the mid-1980s, Sudan's costliest import item after petroleum. However, the subsequent imposition by the Sudanese authorities of a regional quota distribution system led to supply shortages and high prices, and during the 1990s the renewal of Sudan's sugar sector was further impeded by drought, inadequate investment and technical and management problems. In 1999 plans were announced for the construction of a second growing and refining facility in the White Nile region, north of the Kenana site, at a cost of some US $400m. The Arab Fund for Economic and Social Development was reported to have granted a loan of US $71m. towards the funding of the White Nile Sugar Project in late 2004. Sudanese sugar exports fluctuate widely. In 1998 total exports of sugar from all sources (raw equivalent) exceeded 200,000 tons. In subsequent years, however, Sudan has exported far smaller quantities—some 43,640 tons in 2005. In 2000–04 Sudanese annual production of centrifugal sugar averaged about 750,000 tons. Sugar cane grows wild throughout Nigeria, but domestic production has not been developed and the country's sugar industry depends on imports, mainly from Brazil, Guatemala and the EU. In 2005 one sugar refinery was reported to be in operation in Nigeria. The Government's aim is to achieve 70% self-sufficiency in refined sugar production by 2010. Since the 1990s the country has consistently been a significant importer of raw sugar. In 2004/05 imports of raw sugar totalled 850,000 tons, while those of refined sugar amounted to some 300,000 tons.

The first International Sugar Agreement (ISA) was negotiated in 1958, and its economic provisions operated until 1961. A second ISA did not come into operation until 1969. It included quota arrangements and associated provisions for regulating the price of sugar traded on the open market, and established the International Sugar Organization (ISO) to administer the agreement. However, the USA and the six original members of the European Community (EC, now EU) did not participate in the ISA, and, following its expiry in 1974, it was replaced by a purely administrative interim agreement, which remained operational until the finalization of a third ISA, which took effect in 1978. The new agreement's implementation was supervised by an International Sugar Council (ISC), which was empowered to establish price ranges for sugar-trading and to operate a system of quotas and special sugar stocks. Owing to the reluctance of the USA and EC countries (which were not a party to the agreement) to accept export controls, the ISO ultimately lost most of its power to regulate the market, and since 1984 the activities of the organization have been restricted to recording statistics and providing a forum for discussion between producers and consumers. Subsequent ISAs, without effective regulatory powers, have been in operation since 1985.

Production of Centrifugal Sugar
(raw value, '000 metric tons)

	2003	2004*
World total	149,819	146,383
Africa	9,670	9,681
Leading African producers		
Egypt†	1,419	1,543
Ethiopia	323†	296‡
Kenya	448	513†
Malawi	260	283‡
Mauritius	537	540‡
Morocco†	552	575
Réunion†	227	222
South Africa	2,412†	2,247‡
Sudan†	820	837
Swaziland	616†	616‡
Zambia	230†	230‡
Zimbabwe†	580	540
Leading non-African producers		
Australia	5,461	5,022
Brazil†	26,400	28,150
China†	10,943	11,391
Cuba	2,205	2,530†
France†	4,340	4,613
Germany†	4,120	4,456
India	22,140	15,450
Mexico†	5,442	5,540
Thailand†	7,670	7,460
USA	8,118	7,100‡

* Provisional figures.
† Unofficial figure(s).
‡ FAO estimate.

Special arrangements for exports of African sugar were incorporated into the successive Lomé Conventions that were in operation from 1975 between the EU and a group of African, Caribbean and Pacific (ACP) countries, whereby a special Protocol on sugar, forming part of each Convention, required the EU to import specified quantities of raw sugar annually from ACP countries. In June 1998, however, the EU indicated its intention to phase out preferential sugar prices paid to ACP countries within three years. Under the terms of the Cotonou Agreement, a successor convention to the fourth Lomé Convention covering the period 2000–2020, the Protocol on sugar was to be maintained initially, but would become subject to review within the framework of negotiations for new trading arrangements.

In tandem with world output of cane and beet sugars, stock levels (of centrifugal sugar) are an important factor in determining the prices at which sugar is traded internationally. These stocks, which were at relatively low levels in the late 1980s, increased significantly in the 1990s, although not, according to USDA data, in each successive trading year (September–August). In the early 1990s rises in stocks were due partly to the disruptive effects of the Gulf War on demand in the Middle East (normally a major sugar-consuming area), and were also a result of considerably increased production in Mexico and the Far East. Another factor was the increased area under sugar cane and beet in the EU and in Australia. In 2003/04, according to data released by USDA, when world sugar production totalled about 142m. metric tons and consumption some 140m. tons, stocks of sugar held world-wide totalled about 38m. tons. In 2004/05, when the output of sugar world-wide totalled about 141m. tons and consumption rose to about 142m. tons, stocks declined, to some 34m. tons. In 2005/06, when world production of sugar amounted to about 145m. tons and world consumption to some 144m. tons, world sugar stocks fell for a third consecutive year, to about 31m. tons. USDA estimated that world production of sugar was 161m. tons in 2006/07, with global consumption estimated at 149m. tons. Exports were projected to reach 49m. tons in 2006/07, while global stocks were forecast at 39m. tons. USDA forecast sugar production at 163m. tons for 2007/08, with consumption at 149m. tons; exports were projected to reach 50.8m. tons, and stocks 45.0m. tons

The world market for sugar has been described as one of the most distorted of all commodity markets, and reference has frequently been made to the sugar regime of the EU to explain how this distortion has arisen. EU sugar producers have been protected, through the Union's Common Agricultural Policy, by means of import duties, production quotas and export subsidies. First, international competition has been excluded from EU markets by the application of very high duties on imported sugar. Second, the EU has guaranteed member states' producers high production quotas for which it has paid prices substantially in excess of the prevailing world price of sugar, leading to over-production. Third, export subsidies have then been paid to allow surplus EU sugar to be sold on world markets at prices that are lower than the cost of production—a practice known as 'dumping'. As a consequence, the EU has become the world's largest exporter of refined sugar. The disposal of large quantities of sugar in this way has depressed the world price of sugar, on which smaller producers world-wide, who have, for the most part, no access to government subsidies, depend. As sugar is traded on commodity markets, its price fluctuates constantly. It has been calculated that in 1980–2000, in real terms, the world price of sugar declined by 76%, and this situation has been largely attributed to the increase in supply caused by regimes like that of the EU while demand, owing to such factors as the greater popularity of sugar substitutes, has been falling. In mid-2005 the European Commission announced proposals radically to reform the EU's sugar regime. In April the WTO, in response to a complaint by Brazil, Australia and Thailand, had ruled that some of the EU's subsidized exports of sugar originating in ACP countries were illegal. ACP sugar producers, however, have criticized the EU's intention to remove the trade preferences their sugars enjoy (see above) as part of the reform of the sugar regime. A significant contraction in EU sugar production was expected to result from the reform of the regime, which was to be implemented from July 2006. Reforms included a substantial reduction in support granted to domestic (EU) sugar producers—the EU's intervention price was to be reduced by 36% over four years—and quota adjustments.

In 2001 world sugar prices rose in response to, among other factors, reduced output in Cuba as a consequence of hurricane damage to crops there and reduced sugar beet production in the EU. For the whole of the year the ISA daily price averaged 8.64 US cents per lb. In 2002, however, the average ISA daily price declined to only 6.9 cents per lb. The decline in 2002 was particularly pronounced in the early part of the year as it became clear that there would be a substantial increase in Brazil's output of sugar cane and, consequently, in that country's export potential. The ISA recorded a marginally higher average daily price, of 7.10 cents per lb, in 2003. In 2004, again, a marginally higher daily price, of 7.16 cents per lb, was recorded. On a monthly basis, however, the ISA daily price rose markedly in the final quarter of 2004, averaging 8.41 cents per lb in October, 8.14 cents per lb in November and 8.26 cents per lb in December. In February 2005 the average ISA daily price rose to 9.12 cents per lb, and in November an average daily price of 11.38 cents per lb was recorded. For the whole of 2005 the average ISA daily price was 9.90 cents per lb. The average price in 2006 was 14.8 cents per lb. In the first six months of 2007, however, FAO data estimated a significant fall in prices, ranging between 11.0 cents per lb (in January) and 9.33 cents per lb (in June). The average price of the No. 5 sugar contract (refined sugar, f.o.b. Europe, for immediate delivery) traded on the London International Financial Futures Exchange (LIFFE) was 11.29 cents per lb in 2001. Successive declines in the average price, to, respectively, 10.35 cents per lb and 9.74 cents per lb, were recorded in 2002 and 2003. In 2004, however, the average price recovered to 10.87 cents per lb. In 2005 a substantial increase in the average contract price, to 13.19 US cents per lb, was recorded. This upward trend continued in the first four months of 2006, the price of the contract averaging 16.92 cents per lb in January, 19.99 cents per lb in February, 20.45 cents per lb in March and 21.35 cents per lb in April.

The Group of Latin American and Caribbean Sugar Exporting Countries (GEPLACEA) complements the activities of the ISO (whose 71 members, on the basis of data for 2002, accounted for 83% of world sugar production, 65% of world sugar consumption, 92% of world sugar exports and 36% of world sugar imports) as a forum for co-operation and research. The USA withdrew from the ISO in 1992, following a disagreement over the formulation of members' financial contributions. The USA had previously provided about 9% of the ISO's annual budget.

TEA (*Camellia sinensis*)

Tea is a beverage made by infusing in boiling water the dried young leaves and unopened leaf-buds of the tea plant, an evergreen shrub or small tree. Black and green tea are the most common finished products. The former accounts for the bulk of the world's supply, and is associated with machine manufacture and, generally, the plantation system, which guarantees an adequate supply of leaf to the factory. The latter, produced mainly in the People's Republic of China and Japan, is grown mostly on smallholdings, and much of it is consumed locally. There are two main varieties of tea, the China and the Assam, although hybrids may be obtained, such as Darjeeling. In this survey, wherever possible, data on production and trade relate to made tea, i.e. dry, manufactured tea. Where figures have been reported in terms of green (unmanufactured) leaf, appropriate allowances have been made to convert the reported amounts to the approximate equivalent weight of made tea.

Total recorded tea exports by producing countries achieved successive records in each of the years 1983–90. World exports (excluding transactions between former Soviet republics) declined in 1991 and 1992, but increased by 13.7% in 1993. However, the total fell by 10.3% in 1994. Export volume increased again in 1995 and 1996, rising further, to 1,203,785 metric tons, in 1997. World tea exports reached a new record of 1,304,896 tons in 1998, but eased to 1,261,399 tons in 1999. In 2000 export volume attained a new record level of 1,328,909 tons, but this figure was surpassed in 2001, when exports rose to 1,392,163 tons. In 2002 world tea exports attained a record level for the third consecutive year, rising to 1,439,873 tons. In 2003, however, world tea exports fell by 2.9%, to 1,397,921 tons. Tea exports world-wide rose substantially, by 10%, to a new record level of 1,537,133 tons in 2004, and continued to rise in 2005, to 1,556,260tons. In 2006 world exports of tea totalled an estimated 1,578,558 tons, another all-time high. Global production of tea reached an unprecedented level in 1998, with record crops in all of the major producing countries (India, China, Kenya and Sri Lanka). In 1999, however, world output declined (from 3,026,340 tons in 1998) to 2,944,961 tons, although China and Sri Lanka again reported record crops. In 2000 production fell slightly, to 2,939,779 tons, even though record output was once again achieved by China and Sri Lanka. In 2001 world production of tea surpassed 3m. tons for a second time. Record crops in China and Kenya contributed to an increase in global output of 4.2%, to 3,064,483 tons. In 2002 production rose again, albeit by a small margin, to 3,085,355 tons. Once again China and Sri Lanka achieved record output in 2002. In 2003 world production of tea increased by about 3.8%, to 3,201,809 tons, China having achieved record output once more. World production of tea reached a record level, of 3,314,953 tons, for a fourth consecutive year in 2004, China, Kenya and India having recorded their highest output ever in that year. The advance in world tea output continued in both 2005, when global production rose by 3.6%, to an estimated 3,435,650 tons, and 2006, when it increased by a further 2.6%, to reach another record level, of 3,523,476 tons. In 2005 all four of the world's major tea producers recorded their highest production ever, while China overtook India as the world's largest producer. In 2006 China and India's joint tea output contributed one-half of global production. (China's production represented 29% of world output, while that of India accounted for 21%.)

India (the world's largest consumer) and Sri Lanka have traditionally been the two leading tea exporters, with approximately equal sales. The quantity which they jointly supplied remained fairly stable in 1977–96 (350,000–425,000 metric tons per year), but advanced to some 458,000 tons in 1997). Their joint export sales rose to 472,947 tons in 1998, but declined to 452,044 tons in 1999. In 2000 Indian and Sri Lankan joint export sales increased to 484,486 tons, but declined to 467,360 in 2001. In 2002 exports by India and Sri Lanka amounted to 484,072 tons. Joint Indian and Sri Lankan export sales fell to only 460,844 tons in 2003, but recovered to 484,512 tons in 2004. In 2005 foreign sales of tea by India and Sri Lanka increased only marginally, by 0.5%. In 2006 their combined foreign sales exceeded 500,000 tons for the first time, having increased by 6.5%, to an estimated 518,691 tons. During the 1960s these two countries together exported more than two-thirds of all the tea sold by producing countries, but their joint foreign sales gradually declined; during the 1970s they came to constitute less than one-half of world exports, and in 2006 the proportion was estimated at about one-third. From 1990 until 1995, when it was displaced by Kenya (see below), Sri Lanka ranked as the main exporting country. Exports by Sri Lanka again took primacy in 1997, when Kenya's tea sales declined sharply. Sri Lanka remained the principal tea exporter in 1998, despite a strong revival in Kenyan exports, and again in 1999, although tea sales by both countries declined in the latter year. By 2003 Sri Lanka had apparently re-established itself as the world's leading exporter of tea, its foreign sales having exceeded those of Kenya by, on average, a fairly substantial margin in each year in 2000–03. In 2004–05, however, Kenya again overtook Sri Lanka as the main tea exporting country. In 2004 Kenya's shipments rose sharply, by about 24%, to some 333,802 tons, compared with 2003, and in 2005 the country's foreign sales rose by a further 1.6%, to an estimated 339,134 tons. Kenya's exports in 2005 were equivalent to almost 70% of the combined foreign sales of India and Sri Lanka. In 2006 Sri Lanka regained the rank of principal exporting country, Kenyan sales having declined by 8%. Exports from China (whose sales include a large proportion of green tea) have exceeded those of India in every year since 1996. Exports of tea by African producers accounted for about one-quarter of world trade during the early 1990s, and the proportion rose to about 30% at the end of that decade—a record shipment of 389,499 was achieved in 1998. Although in 2000 the share of African teas in the world tea trade declined to 26.5%, with shipments falling to 351,673 tons, in 2001 foreign sales of African teas recovered strongly to total 403,545 tons, equivalent to 28.8% of world trade in tea. In 2002 African exports of tea rose to 418,462 tons, representing 29% of world tea sales. In 2003 the proportion of exports from Africa rose again, to account for 29.8% of world tea trade, despite a slight decline in export volume. In 2004, a record shipment of 481,511 tons was achieved, which accounted for 31.3% of the world total. Foreign sales of tea by African countries declined slightly in 2005, to 476,782 tons, representing 30.6% of the world total. In 2006 tea shipments from Africa were estimated to have fallen further, to 453,443 tons, and constituted 28.7% of global tea sales.

Production of Made Tea
('000 metric tons)

	2005	2006
World total*	3,435.6	3,523.5
Africa*	493.3	482.4
Leading African producers		
Kenya	328.6	310.6
Malawi	37.9	45.0
Rwanda	16.4	17.0
South Africa	2.2	2.8
Tanzania	30.4	31.3
Uganda	37.7	36.7
Zimbabwe	14.9	15.7
Leading non-African producers		
China, People's Repub.[1]	934.9	1,020.0*
India*[2]	928.0	955.9
Indonesia[3]	165.8	139.8*
Japan*[4]	100.0	99.5
Sri Lanka	317.2	310.8
Turkey*	135.0	142.0

* Provisional.

[1] Mainly green tea (about 691,020 tons in 2005).

[2] Including a small quantity of green tea (about 6,000 tons in 2005).

[3] Including green tea (about 40,800 tons in 2005).

[4] Almost all green tea (about 99,300 tons in 2005).

Source: International Tea Committee, *Supplement to Annual Bulletin of Statistics 2006*.

Prior to its set-back in 1997, Kenya was one of the fastest growing exporters, ranking fourth in the world during 1975–92, third in 1993, and second in 1994, when its tea exports exceeded those of China. Kenya was the principal world exporter of tea in 1995 and 1996. Conditions of severe drought during the first seven months of 1997 reduced Kenya's position to fourth in terms of world exports in that year, but the expansion of the country's tea sales was resumed in 1998, when Kenya ranked second, after Sri Lanka, with exports of 263,402 metric tons, accounting for 68% of African tea exports and more than 20% of all tea traded internationally. Kenya retained the second position in terms of world exports in 1999, although the volume of its sales fell by 8.2%. In 2000, however, Kenya was reduced to the rank of third, after Sri Lanka and China, when its tea sales declined by 10.2%, to 216,990 tons. In 2001 Kenyan exports of tea recovered strongly, by almost 19%, to 258,118 tons, and were surpassed only by those of Sri Lanka. In 2002 Kenya again ranked as the world's second largest exporter of tea, after Sri Lanka, with foreign sales totalling 272,459 tons, an increase of 5.6% compared with 2001. Kenya remained the world's second largest exporter of tea in 2003, with foreign sales of 269,268 tons, a fall of 1.2% compared with the previous year. In 2004 Kenya was the world's largest exporter of tea by a considerable margin, its foreign sales having risen by almost 24%, compared with 2003, to 333,802 tons. Kenya retained the rank of leading exporter in both 2005 and 2006, with foreign sales of 339,134 tons and 313,721 tons respectively. In recent years the conservation of tea supplies by India, in order to satisfy rising domestic consumption, has enabled Kenya to replace India as the United Kingdom's principal supplier. In 1999 Kenya provided 50% of British tea imports, but the proportion declined in 2000 to only about 35%. In 2001–04 Kenya supplied between 43%–46% of all tea imported into the United Kingdom. The proportion increased to 48% in 2005. Kenya's tea sales provided 17% of its total export receipts in 2004, making tea the country's most valuable export crop. In 2005 about 141,315 ha in Kenya were planted with tea, an increase of 7% compared with 2004.

Malawi, with about 19,000 ha under tea in 2005, is Africa's second largest producer and exporter of tea. Its exports in 2006 totalled an estimated 42,500 metric tons, accounting for 9.4% of all African exports. In 2005 exports of tea accounted for 9.4% of Malawi's total export earnings. Tea was thus the country's second most valuable export crop after tobacco in that year. Prior to the Amin regime and the nationalization of tea plantations in 1972, neighbouring Uganda was second only to Kenya among African producers. Uganda's tea exports were negligible by the early 1980s, but, following agreements between tea companies and the subsequent Ugandan governments, exports were resumed. There has been a sustained recovery since 1990, when sales of tea totalled only 4,760 tons. In 1994 Uganda's exports of tea reached their highest annual total since 1977. Exports in subsequent years have advanced strongly, reaching 31,073 tons in 2002 and 34,069 tons in 2003. In 2004, however, there was a reversal when Uganda's foreign sales totalled only 29,686 tons. Uganda's foreign sales of tea recovered to 33,071 tons in 2005, but were estimated to have declined slightly, to 32,699 tons, in 2006. In 2005 exports of tea contributed 4% of the country's total export earnings. Uganda has established itself, since the late 1990s, as the leading East African producer of tea. During the 1980s Tanzania's exports of tea ranged between 10,000 tons and 15,000 tons annually. These sales advanced significantly during the 1990s, moving from 20,511 tons in 1995 to 22,218 tons in 1998 and 22,462 tons in 2000. In 2006 Tanzania's exports of tea amounted to 24,132 tons, compared with 22,498 tons in 2005. Foreign sales of tea contributed 1.7% of Tanzania's estimated total revenue from exports in 2005. Zimbabwe was Africa's sixth largest exporter of tea in 1997–2006. Tea shipments from Zimbabwe increased in each consecutive year in 1998–2002, reaching 17,634 tons in the latter year, but fell to a decade-low in 2005—8,451 tons. In 2006 foreign sales of tea recovered by 34% to totaled 11,384 tons. Historically, however, tea is not a significant cash crop in Zimbabwe—in 2000 it accounted for only about 1% of the country's total export earnings. Tea has traditionally made a significant contribution to the export earnings of Burundi and Rwanda, whose foreign sales were estimated at 5,903 tons and 12,859 tons, respectively, in 2006. In that year exports of tea were estimated to have accounted for 17% of Burundi's total export earnings. Since 1997 Rwanda's tea industry has recovered from the disruption caused by civil unrest during 1993–96. In 2003 exports of tea accounted for 23.6% of the country's total export earnings.

For many years the United Kingdom was the largest single importer of tea. However, the country's annual consumption of tea per person, which amounted to 4.55 kg in 1958, has declined in recent years, averaging 2.46 kg in 1994–96 and 1995–97, before recovering marginally, to 2.51 kg, in 1996–98. In 1997–99, however, consumption fell back to 2.44 kg, and again, in 1998–2000, to 2.33 kg. In 1999–2001 an average of 2.27 kg per caput of tea was consumed in the United Kingdom. Average consumption per head in the United Kingdom declined again in 2000–02, to 2.26 kg; and once more, to 2.24 kg, in 2001–03. In 2002–04 annual average British consumption of tea per head fell again, to 2.20 kg, and it continued to decline in 2003–05, to an estimated 2.12 kg. A similar trend has been observed in other developed countries, although it is not so clear in the Republic of Ireland, the world's largest per caput consumer of tea, where annual consumption per person advanced from 3.17 kg in 1994–96 to 3.23 kg in 1995–97, before evidencing a slight decline, to 2.95 kg, in 1996–98. Irish annual consumption per person declined again, to 2.78 kg, in 1997–99, and to 2.69 kg in 1998–2000. In 1999–2001, however, average Irish consumption per head rose to 2.71 kg, and in 2000–02 a further increase, to 2.75 kg, was recorded. Annual consumption per person of tea in the Republic of Ireland rose sharply in 2001–03, to 2.96 kg, and it remained at that level in 2002–04. Annual comsumption per person declined again in 2003–05, however. At 2.79 kg, none the less, it remained above the levels recorded in 1996–2002. From the late 1980s consumption and imports expanded significantly in the developing countries (notably Middle Eastern countries) and, particularly, in the USSR, which in 1989 overtook the United Kingdom as the world's principal tea importer. However, internal factors, following the break-up of the USSR in 1991, caused a sharp decline in tea imports by its successor republics; as a result, the United Kingdom regained its position as the leading tea importer in 1992. In 1993 the former Soviet republics (whose own tea production had fallen sharply) once more displaced the United Kingdom as the major importer, but in 1994 the United Kingdom was again the principal importing country. Since 1995, however, imports by the former USSR have exceeded those of the United Kingdom by a substantial and, generally, increasing margin. In 2006 the former USSR imported an estimated 236,900 metric tons of tea, accounting for 15.2% of the world market, followed by the United Kingdom, with an estimated 128,159 tons (9.2%), Pakistan (127,000 tons, or 8.6%) and the USA (108,997 tons, or 7.4%). Other major importers of tea in 2006 were—in order of importance—Egypt, Iraq, Dubai (United Arab Emirates), Morocco and Japan.

Much of the tea traded internationally is sold by auction, principally in the exporting countries. Until declining volumes brought about their termination in June 1998 (Kenya having withdrawn in 1997, and a number of other exporters, including Malawi and Tanzania, having established their own auctions), the weekly London auctions had formed the centre of the international tea trade. At the London auctions, five categories of tea were offered for sale: 'low medium' (based on a medium Malawi tea), 'medium' (based on a medium Assam and Kenyan tea), 'good medium' (representing an above-average East African tea), 'good' (referring to teas of above-average standard) and (from April 1994) 'best available'. At the end of June 1998, with the prospect of a record Kenyan crop, the quotation for 'medium' tea at the final London auction was £980 per ton. Based on country of origin, the highest priced tea at London auctions during 1989–94 was that from Rwanda, which realized an average of £1,613 per ton in the latter year. The quantity of tea sold at these auctions declined from 43,658 tons in 1990 to 11,208 tons in 1997.

The main tea auctions in Africa are the weekly sales at Mombasa, Kenya. In contrast to London, volumes traded at the Mombasa auctions moved generally upward during the 1990s, and Mombasa is now one of the world's major centres for the international tea trade. The tea sold at Mombasa is mainly from Kenya, but smaller amounts from Tanzania, Uganda and other African producers are also traded. Total annual sales at the Mombasa auctions increased from 173,757 metric tons in 1995 to 189,800 tons in 1996. Owing to Kenya's drought, the total declined in 1997 to 166,618 tons. In 1998, however, volume rose to a record 243,566 tons (including 212,620 tons from Kenya). The volume of tea traded at Mombasa in 1999 declined to 210,786 tons, but increased in 2000 to 221,601 tons. In 2001 tea traded at Mombasa totalled 276,220 tons, including 216,946 tons of Kenyan tea. In 2002 there was a decline in the volume of tea traded, which totalled 270,635 tons in that year, including 211,791 tons of Kenyan tea. In 2003 a record volume of tea, totalling 285,843 tons (including 217,062 tons of Kenyan tea), was traded at Mombasa. A record volume of trade was achieved in both 2004 and 2005. In the latter year the quantity of tea traded in Mombasa totalled 306,833 tons—88% of which was Kenyan. Meanwhile, average prices per ton in Mombasa rose from $1,420 in 1996 to $2,000 in 1997. They eased to $1,890 per ton in 1998, and to $1,780 in 1999. In 2000 prices of teas traded at Mombasa averaged $2,020 per ton, but they declined sharply in 2001, to only $1,530 per ton, and fell further in 2002, to $1,490 per ton. The average price of teas traded at Mombasa recovered somewhat, to $1,550 per ton, in 2005, but fell again in 2006, to $1,470 per ton. During the first six months of 2006 the average price of teas traded in Mombasa ranged between $1,677 per ton (January) and $2,124 per ton (June).

An International Tea Agreement (ITA), signed in 1933 by the governments of India, Ceylon (now Sri Lanka) and the Netherlands East Indies (now Indonesia), established the International Tea Committee (ITC), based in London, as an administrative body. Although ITA operations ceased after 1955, the ITC has continued to function as a statistical and information centre. In 2007 there were seven producer/exporter members (the tea boards or associations of Kenya, Malawi, India, Indonesia, Bangladesh and Sri Lanka, and the tea sub-chamber of the Chinese Chamber of Commerce), five consumer members, 13 associate members and 13 corporate members.

In 1969 the FAO Consultative Committee on Tea (renamed as the Intergovernmental Group on Tea in 1970) was formed, and an exporters' group, meeting under this committee's auspices, set voluntary export quotas in an attempt to avert an overall long-term decline in the real price of tea. These succeeded in raising prices for two consecutive years, but subsequently collapsed as (mainly) African countries—Kenya in particular—opposed efforts to restrict their rapidly increasing production. The regulation of tea prices is in any case complicated by the perishability of the commodity, which impedes the effective operation of a buffer stock. India, while opposed to the revival of a formal ITA to regulate supplies and prices, has advocated greater co-operation between producers to regulate the market.

TOBACCO (*Nicotiana tabacum*)

Tobacco originated in South America and was used in rituals and ceremonials or as a medicine; it was smoked and chewed for centuries before its introduction into Europe in the 16th century. The generic name *Nicotiana* denotes the presence of the alkaloid nicotine in its leaves. The most important species in commercial tobacco cultivation is *N. tabacum*. Another species, *N. rustica*, is widely grown, but on a smaller scale, to yield cured leaf for snuff or simple cigarettes and cigars.

Production of Tobacco Leaves
(farm sales weight, '000 metric tons)

	2004	2005
World total	6,443	6,564
Africa	324	320
Leading African producers		
Côte d'Ivoire	10*	10†
Kenya	20†	20
Malawi	70†	70
Morocco	6*	7†
South Africa	32	24
Tanzania	24*	25†
Zimbabwe	62*	65†
Leading non-African producers		
Brazil	921	879
China, People's Repub.	2,410	2,686*
Greece	127	124
India	598*	598†
Indonesia	141*	141†
Italy	103*	110†
Turkey	157	141
USA	399	290

* Unofficial figure.
† FAO estimate.

Commercially grown tobacco (from *N. tabacum*) can be divided into four major types—flue-cured, air-cured (including burley, cigar, light and dark), fire-cured and sun-cured (including oriental)—depending on the procedures used to dry or 'cure' the leaves. Each system imparts specific chemical and smoking characteristics to the cured leaf, although these may also be affected by other factors, such as the type of soil on which the crop is grown, the type and quantity of fertilizer applied to the crop, the cultivar used, the spacing of the crop in the field and the number of leaves left at topping (the removal of the terminal growing point). Each type is used, separately or in combination, in specific products (e.g. flue-cured in Virginia cigarettes). All types are grown in Africa.

As in other major producing areas, local research organizations in Africa have developed new cultivars with specific desirable chemical characteristics, disease-resistance properties and improved yields. The principal tobacco research centres are in Zimbabwe, Malawi and South Africa. In recent years, efforts have been made to develop low-cost sources of tobacco in Tanzania and, more recently, in Swaziland and Mozambique.

In Malawi, South Africa and, to a lesser extent, in Zambia and Tanzania, tobacco is grown mainly as a direct-labour crop on large farms, some capable of producing as much as 250 metric tons of cured leaf per year. In other parts of Africa, however, tobacco is a smallholders' crop, with each farmer cultivating, on average, 1 or 2 ha of tobacco as well as essential food crops and, usually, other cash crops. Emphasis has been placed on improving yields by the selection of cultivars, by the increased use of fertilizers, by the reduction of crop loss (through the use of crop chemicals) and by reducing hand-labour requirements through the mechanization of land-preparation and the use of crop chemicals. Where small farmers are responsible for producing the crop, harvesting remains a manual operation, as the area under tobacco and their limited financial means preclude the adoption of mechanical harvesting devices.

The principal type of tobacco commercially cultivated in Africa is flue-cured, of which Malawi and Zimbabwe are the dominant regional producers. The tobacco sector formerly normally accounted for about 47% of Zimbabwe's total agricultural earnings and as recently as 2001 provided 38% of the country's total export revenue. The Zimbabwean tobacco crop, of which 98% has traditionally been exported, is highly regarded for its quality and flavour, and its marketability has been assisted by its relatively low tar content. Nevertheless, depressed conditions in international tobacco markets in the early 1990s encouraged some Zimbabwean growers to switch to cotton cultivation. During the 1990s Zimbabwe officially encouraged small-scale producers of burley and flue-cured tobaccos. In 1999, however, Zimbabwean tobacco plantings declined by about 8%, reflecting an accumulation in world levels of stocks held by manufacturers. Subsequently the country's tobacco sector has been overshadowed by a controversial programme of land reform pursued by the Government. In 2004 the Zimbabwe tobacco sector was reported to have lost, in the four years since 2000, 50% of the growth it had achieved in 1990–2000. Output was reported by FAO to have reached an all-time low of 55,000 metric tons in 2005/06, compared with about 202,000 tons in 1999/2000, in spite of an increase in the number of tobacco farmers to 12,700 in 2004, compared with 8,531 in 2000 and 1,493 in 1990. (According to the US Department of Agriculture (USDA), the number of farmers engaged in tobacco production in 2005 exceeded 30,000.) The area planted to tobacco more than halved in 1999/2000–2005/06, falling from 76,000 ha to an estimated 27,000 ha, while the average annual per hectare yield was reported to have fallen from 2,600 kg in, approximately, 1990–2000 to 1,500 kg in 2004. The increase in the number of farmers reflects an officially encouraged transfer away from the large-scale, estate-based cultivation of tobacco to a smallholder-based sector. As a consequence of land reform, many former estate cultivators of tobacco are reported to have relocated to countries such as Zambia and Mozambique and to have resumed large-scale tobacco cultivation there. Additional factors in the decline in production have been the under-utilization of irrigation and curing capacity, and farmers' loss of access to finance despite the extension of contract cultivation (a system under which buyers supply production inputs—seeds, fertilizers, etc.) to 60% of the tobacco crop in 2006. In 2006 tobacco sales accounted for only 12.9% of the country's contracted export revenues. Zimbabwe reportedly accounted for about 2.7% of global exports of tobacco in 2006, compared with some 20% in the late 1990s. Althought slight increases were recorded both in the area planted—30,000 ha—and in output—63,000 tons—in the 2006/07 crop year, FAO forecast that the tobacco sector would continue to decline. USDA estimated that small-scale production would have an adverse effect on quality, with about 50% of the 2005 crop expected to comprise low-grade tobacco leaf. The Zimbabwe Tobacco Industry Marketing Board reported an average auction price for tobacco of $2,010 per ton in 2004, compared with $2,160 per ton in 2003. In April 2005 Zimbabwean tobacco farmers were reported to have refused to sell tobacco at auction owing to the low price—45 US cents per kg—offered. In April 2004 the price offered to growers had reportedly been US $3 per kg. In 2005, according to industry sources, an average auction price of $1.61 per kg was recorded. The average price was expected to rise to $2 per kg in 2006. However, farmers reportedly remained dissatisfied with payments made in Zimbabwe dollars, with some seeking payment in foreign currency. In April 2006 a bonus scheme was introduced to encourage early deliveries to auctions by tobacco growers. This bonus was in addition to a 65% subsidy known as the Tobacco Performance, Research and Development Facility. The two programmes together constitute a 95% subsidization of tobacco prices.

In the mid-1990s Malawi obtained up to 70% of its export revenue from tobacco, exporting more than 98% of the mainly flue-cured, fire-cured and burley varieties that it produced. Thereafter, output, especially of burley tobacco, of which Malawi formerly supplied about one-fifth of world output, declined. From the early 2000s, however, Malawi was reported to have benefited indirectly from the problems faced by the tobacco sector in Zimbabwe, and to have attracted increased investment from multinational tobacco companies. In 2004 Malawi's production of flue-cured tobacco was reported to have almost doubled, while an increase of some 19% in output of burley tobacco was also achieved. In 2004 exports of tobacco accounted for 42.4% of Malawi's total earnings from exports (including re-exports). Small-scale tobacco growers in Malawi, backed by the Government and some independent sources, have claimed that the national auction system employed for tobacco has been manipulated by international buyers who, by establishing what amounts to a cartel, have artificially depressed tobacco prices to their own advantage. According to Malawi's Tobacco Control Commission, Burley tobacco auctioned in Malawi in 2006 achieved an average price of US $0.91 per kg, compared with $0.99 per kg in 2005 and $1.09 per kg in 2004. The recorded prices achieved thus fell below those recommended by the Government in April 2006—$1.1 per kg for low-grade tobacco and $1.7 per kg for top-grade tobacco. It has been claimed that the auction price offered to small-scale tobacco producers in Malawi is insufficient to meet their production costs—it reportedly costs a Malawian grower $1.00 on average to produce one kilo of leaf. According to Malawi's Tobacco Control Commission, low auction prices result from a lack of competition among buyers that proceeds from a calculated decision not to compete in order buy tobacco cheaply. Large-scale growers, meanwhile, deal directly with buyers, growing their crops under contract and receiving a price ($1.06 per kg in 2006) that is fixed in advance of the selling season. Low prices were also attributed to over-supply of tobacco in that year. In 2007 tobacco output fell by some 11%, to 141,000, compared with 158,000 tons in 2006. At the opening of the 2007 auction season in April considerably higher prices, of $1.60–$1.70 per kg, were recorded.

Tanzania contributes a small but significant quantity of flue-cured tobacco to the world market, and in 2004 exports of tobacco contributed 4.5% of the country's total export earnings. Tobacco production in Nigeria is fairly static, and its flue-cured crop is entirely reserved for local consumption. Kenya has greatly increased its output of flue-cured leaf since commencing tobacco exports in 1984, and tobacco cultivation has recently been increasing in importance in Uganda, as part of a government programme to offset declining earnings from coffee. Exports of tobacco contributed about 4% of Uganda's total export earnings in 2005. There are also small exports of flue-cured tobacco from Sierra Leone, to whose total export earnings foreign sales of unmanufactured tobacco and tobacco refuse contributed 2.2% in 1995. Nigeria, Malawi and South Africa account for the African crop of sun- and air-cured types of tobacco. Modest quantities of oriental tobacco are cultivated in Malawi and South Africa.

About one-quarter of world tobacco production is traded internationally. Until 1993, when it was overtaken by Brazil, the USA was the world's principal tobacco-exporting country. According to the USDA, the average value of US exports of unmanufactured tobacco was US $6,450 per metric ton in 2005. The country's total earnings from such exports were $1,058m. in 2005. Since 1993 Brazil has consolidated its position as the world's leading exporter of tobacco, largely at the expense of the USA and Zimbabwe. Brazil's share of global exports (in terms of volume) increased from 13% in 1993 to about one-quarter in 2005. Tobacco exports contributed 1.2% of Brazil's total export revenue in 2005. Flue-cured Virginia and Burley account for by far the majority of Brazilian output—respectively 79% and 16% in 2005. In that year in southern Brazil flue-cured Virginia and Burley were sown on 88% of all land cultivated with tobacco. North-east Brazil, meanwhile, specializes in the production of cigar and cigarettes leaves. As a consequence of increased international demand for flue-cured Virginia, the area cultivated with tobacco in southern Brazil increased by 26% in 2003–05, while it declined by 12% in the north-east.

The International Tobacco Growers' Association (ITGA), with headquarters in Portugal, was formed in 1984 by growers' groups in Argentina, Brazil, Canada, Malawi, the USA and Zimbabwe. The ITGA's member countries numbered 20 in 2007, accounting for more than 80% of the world's internationally traded tobacco. African members of the ITGA in 2006 comprised Kenya, Malawi, South Africa, Tanzania, Uganda, Zambia and Zimbabwe. The ITGA provides a forum for the exchange of information among tobacco producers, conducts research and publishes studies on tobacco issues.

URANIUM

Uranium occurs in a variety of ores, often in association with other minerals such as gold, phosphate and copper, and may be mined by open-cast, underground or *in situ* leach methods, depending on the circumstances. The concentration of uranium that is needed to form an economic mineral deposit varies widely, depending upon its geological setting and physical location. Average ore grades at operating uranium mines vary from 0.03% U to as high as 15% U, but are most frequently less than 1% U. South Africa produces uranium concentrates as a by-product of gold mining and copper mining, and possesses uranium conversion and enrichment facilities. Both copper mining and the exploitation of phosphates by wet (phosphoric acid-yielding) processes offer a more widespread potential for by-product uranium production.

Uranium is principally used as a fuel in nuclear reactors for the production of electricity. There were 439 commercial nuclear reactors operating in 30 countries world-wide in August 2007, generating 16% of the world's electricity, and more than 30 others were under construction. Enriched uranium is used as fuel in most nuclear power stations and in the manufacture of nuclear weapons. With regard to the latter, however, the abandonment of East–West confrontation and the conclusion of a series of nuclear disarmament treaties between the USA and Russia (and other former Soviet republics) has led to the ongoing release from military stockpiles of substantial quantities of uranium for civil energy programmes. In 2006, according to data cited by the World Nuclear Association (WNA), the world's known recoverable resources of uranium (defined as reasonably assured resources plus estimated additional resources, recoverable up to a cost of US $80 per kg) totalled about 4.7m. metric tons.

Because of uranium's strategic military value, there was intense prospecting activity in the 1940s and 1950s, but the market was later depressed as government purchasing programmes ceased. Uranium demand fell in the late 1960s and early 1970s, until industrialized countries responded to the 1973–74 petroleum crisis by intensifying their civil nuclear power programmes. Anticipated strong demand for rapidly expanding nuclear power further improved the uranium market until the early 1980s, when lower than expected growth in electricity consumption forced nuclear power programmes to be restricted, leaving both producers and consumers with high levels of accumulated stocks requiring liquidation. A number of mining operations were also scaled down or closed. The market was further depressed in the aftermath of the accident in 1986 at the Chornobyl (Chernobyl) nuclear plant in Ukraine (then part of the USSR). Following nine consecutive years of reduced output, uranium production achieved modest advances in each year during 1995–97. In 1998, however, world production declined by 5.5%, to 33,728 metric tons, which represented only about 53% of annual nuclear reactor requirements, necessitating recourse to inventories to meet a significant portion of world demand. Output declined once more, to 31,065 tons, in 1999, but increased in 2000, to 35,186 tons, and again in 2001, when it amounted to 36,366 tons. In 2002 output of uranium world-wide declined slightly, by about 0.9%, to 36,027 tons. It fell again, by 1.1%, to 35,622 tons, in 2003, but in 2004 rose substantially, by 13.0%, to 40,251 tons. There was a more modest increase, of 3.6%, to 41,702 tons, in world production of uranium in 2005. Production declined by 4.9% in 2006, to 39,655 tons. Production from world uranium mines is generally sufficient to meet about 60% of annual requirements for power generation. Since 1999, according to the WNA, the dilution of 30 tons of highly enriched military uranium has displaced some 10,600 tons of mined uranium oxide (about 15% of world reactor requirements) annually.

Production of Uranium
(uranium content of ores, metric tons)

	2005	2006
World total*	41,702	39,655
Africa	6,914	7,045
African producers		
Namibia	3,147	3,077
Niger	3,093	3,434
South Africa	674	534
Leading non-African producers		
Australia	9,519	7,593
Canada	11,628	9,862
Kazakhstan	4,357	5,279
Russia*	3,431	3,400
USA	1,039	1,692
Uzbekistan	2,300	2,270

* Estimates.

Source: World Nuclear Association.

Canada accounted for about 25% of world uranium production in 2006, and is expected to remain the leading producer in the immediate future. South Africa has Africa's largest known recoverable resources (estimated at some 341,000 metric tons), followed by Namibia (about 282,000 tons). The ore reserves of Niger amount to 225,000 tons. Uranium production has been an important component of the South African mining industry since uranium extraction began in 1951, with output reaching a record 6,146 tons in 1980. South Africa's production has subsequently declined sharply, and has been overtaken by that of both Namibia and Niger. In 2005 Namibia ranked as the world's fifth largest producer. Deliveries of ore from the world's largest open-pit uranium mine, at Rössing in Namibia, began in 1976. Output exceeded its planned level in 1980, but subsequently declined, owing to a reduction in demand and increased competition from low-cost producers. During the second half of the 1990s production had stabilized at, on average, about 2,500 tons annually. In 2003 output was 2,036 tons, but it rose very substantially, by 49%, in 2004, to 3,038 tons. In 2004 the Rössing mine, the source of all of Namibia's uranium output, was the world's fourth largest uranium mine in production, contributing 7.5% of total world supplies of uranium oxide. In 2006, following two years of growth, Namibia's output of uranium slowed to 3,077 tons. Exports of ores and concentrates of uranium and thorium contributed 3.6% of Namibia's total revenue from exports in 2003. Meanwhile, it was announced in early 2007 that West Australian Metals had discovered new deposits at its Marenica project.

Uranium exploration in Niger started in the 1950s, around the Aïr mountains near Agadez, with production commencing at the Arlit mine in 1971. Niger's other main uranium mine, where operations commenced in 1978, is at Akouta. France purchases most of Niger's uranium production, with the remainder taken by German, Japanese and Spanish customers. Like Namibia, Niger was compelled in the early 1990s to restructure and streamline its uranium operations, and output has subsequently risen. In 2006 production increased to 3,434 metric tons, compared with 3,093 tons in 2005. In 2003, according to data cited by the US Geological Survey, exports of uranium ore, valued at US $113m., contributed 32% of Niger's total export earnings. New concessions have been awarded to Canadian and Chinese interests since 2006, with the first discoveries being announced in 2007. The Nigerien Government's target at this time was to increase its annual uranium production to 10,500 tons within a few years. Gabon, which commenced uranium production in 1958, possesses six identified deposits containing sufficient reserves to support 30 years' output at production rates achieved during the mid-1990s. However, the depressed level of uranium prices in the late 1990s, with little prospect of recovery in the short term, prompted French interests, exploiting the deposits in conjunction with the Government of Gabon, to terminate uranium-mining operations there from early 1999, leaving Namibia, Niger and South Africa as the only regional producers. Reclamation work at Gabon's Mounana uranium mine was reported to have been completed in 2004.

Uranium has also been found in Algeria, Botswana, the Central African Republic, Chad, the Democratic Republic of the Congo, Egypt, Guinea, Madagascar, Mali, Mauritania, Morocco, Nigeria, Somalia, Tanzania, Togo and Zambia. In all of these countries, however, deposits remain unexploited.

The market for uranium is small, comprising only about 100 buyers world-wide, according to industry sources. Marginal trading, to which 'spot' prices for uranium apply, accounts for only a small proportion of the total quantity of the metal traded, but 'spot' prices nevertheless provide a reference price for long-term contracts concluded between miners and utilities. According to the WNA, very high prices for uranium in the 1970s were succeeded by very low prices in the early 1990s, to the extent that 'spot' prices fell below the cost of production in most mines. In 1996 'spot' prices reportedly recovered to the extent that most mines were able to produce at a profit. That recovery, however, was succeeded by a further decline which lasted until late 2003. By late 2004 the price of uranium had risen to more than US $20 per lb, compared with about $10 per lb in early 2003. In early 2005 'spot' prices rose further, to about $25 per lb, and in mid-2005 prices of about $29 per lb were reported. According to industry sources, the price rises that have occurred since late 2003 have been due to the weakness of the US dollar relative to the currencies of the major uranium-producing countries; disruptions to the uranium supply chain; lower commercial inventories; Russia's withdrawal from the market for uranium concentrates; and rising demand.

The WNA, which succeeded the Uranium Institute in 2001, is a global industrial organization that seeks to promote the peaceful use of nuclear power world-wide as a sustainable source of energy. The WNA concerns itself with all stages of the nuclear fuel cycle, including the mining of uranium, its enrichment, the manufacture of nuclear plants and the safe disposal of spent fuel.

WHEAT (*Triticum*)

The most common species of wheat (*T. vulgare*) includes hard, semi-hard and soft varieties which have different milling characteristics but which, in general, are suitable for bread-making. Another species, *T. durum*, is grown mainly in semi-arid areas, including North Africa and the Mediterranean. This wheat is very hard and is suitable for the manufacture of semolina. In North Africa, in addition to being used for making local bread, semolina is the basic ingredient of pasta and couscous. A third species, spelt (*T. spelta*), is also included in production figures for wheat. It is grown in very small quantities in parts of Europe and is used mainly as animal feed.

Although a most adaptable crop, wheat does not thrive in hot and humid climates. Africa's wheat production is mainly concentrated in a narrow strip along the Mediterranean coast from Morocco to Tunisia, in the Nile valley, and in parts of South Africa. Zimbabwe, Kenya, Ethiopia and Sudan also grow limited quantities, but very little is grown in West Africa. In contrast with some developing countries of Asia, the potential of improved wheat varieties has yet to be realized in much of Africa, especially south of the Sahara. One reason is the undeveloped state of the transport systems in many countries in the region, which hinders both the distribution of production inputs (e.g. seeds and fertilizers) and the marketing of farmers' surplus produce. Until recently, many governments have also been unwilling to pay sufficiently attractive producer prices to encourage farmers to grow wheat for marketing.

Wheat production in sub-Saharan Africa (excluding South Africa) has averaged about 2.7m. metric tons annually in recent years. It is principally grown in the south and east of the region, often at high altitudes where conditions are less humid. South Africa is the main regional producer, with annual output averaging about 2.1m. tons. Ethiopia is the second largest regional producer, with average annual output of some 1.5m. tons in recent years. While improved fertilizer inputs stimulated production in the late 1990s, the size of Ethiopia's crop is constrained by insecurity of land tenure and lack of good seed supplies. In some other wheat-producing countries (e.g. Tanzania and Zimbabwe) the crop is grown mainly on large commercial farms, and, with the benefit of irrigation, usually yields well. Efforts to produce wheat in tropical countries such as the Democratic Republic of the Congo (DRC) and Nigeria have shown mixed results. In the case of the DRC, production has declined since the mid-1990s, although this is at least partially attributable to the prevalence of civil unrest rather than purely agricultural considerations. In Nigeria output of wheat increased two-fold during 1990–99, albeit from the low level of a reported 50,000 tons. It has since declined sharply, however, totalling 62,000 tons in 2004 and 66,000 tons in 2005; output in 2006 was 71,000 tons.

Wheat production is highly variable from year to year. Part of the variation is due to weather conditions, particularly rainfall, in the main producing regions, but national producer-support policies are also a major influence. During the 1990s several major wheat-producing countries, including leading exporters, pursued policies of market deregulation and began to dismantle support arrangements for the production of particular crops. This has encouraged farmers more readily to switch between crops according to their expectation of relative market returns. After 1996, for example, when wheat was in short supply on world markets, output was stimulated in many growing areas, and a record 613m. metric tons was harvested in 1997. Unfavourable weather conditions in a number of countries reduced output to about 594m. tons in 1998, but, owing to low growth in consumption, exporting countries' stocks remained high, and farmers' returns fell. This discouraged plantings for the 1999 season, when production totalled only about 588m. tons. Production declined further in 2000, to some 586m. tons, but increased to about 590m. tons in 2001. In 2002 wheat production world-wide fell sharply, to only about 575m. tons, partly as a result of substantial declines in Australian and North American output. A further sharp decline occurred in 2003, when estimated output totalled only about 561m. tons. In 2004 wheat production recovered to a new record level of 633m. tons. In 2005 output totalled an estimated 629m. tons, although output contracted to 605m. tons in 2006. This decline in production was attributed to lower output in the USA, Russia and Ukraine, where crops had been affected by adverse weather conditions, in particular drought. Crops were also expected to decline in Canada, India, Pakistan and Romania, outweighing production gains in Argentina, China, North Africa and the EU. International trade in wheat in 2006/07 was estimated at the high level that had characterized the two previous seasons. While imports by North African countries were expected to slow somewhat as a consequence of higher output, higher import requirements were thought to be likely in Ethiopia and Nigeria. In Ethiopia imports would possibly double, compared with the previous season, owing to lower output. In Nigeria, the second largest African importer of wheat after Egypt, expansion of the country's milling capacity was expected to propel imports to an all-time high of more than 4m. tons. FAO forecast a 5.2% increase in global production in 2007/08, bringing output to some 630m. tons. Larger wheat crops anticipated in Europe, North America and Asia were cited by FAO as contributing factors to this increase. In August 2007, however, the International Grains Council (IGC) reduced its own production forecast by about 7m. tons, to 607m. tons, citing the impact of wet weather conditions in Northern Europe, poor output in Ukraine, and drought conditions in both Argentina and Australia.

On average, 72% of world wheat production is used for human food, and 15%–20% for animal feed. Feed use is variable, depending on the amount of sub-standard wheat produced each season, and also on the relationship between wheat prices and those of feed grains, especially maize. Of approximately 415m. metric tons of wheat consumed annually as food, developing countries account for about 70%. North Africa is an important wheat consuming region, but in sub-Saharan Africa consumption is mostly restricted to the larger towns and cities. Wheat use in the region amounts to some 12m. tons a year (2% of the world total).

Wheat is the principal cereal in international trade. Amounts exported in recent years have ranged between 110m.–120m. metric tons annually, including wheat flour, durum wheat and semolina, feed wheat, and wheat of bread-making quality (some of which, however, was used to make other food products, such as noodles). The main exporters are the USA (whose share declined from about 30% of the total in the first half of the 1990s to about 27% in 2004), the European Union (EU), Canada, Australia and Argentina. In 2001/02 and 2002/03 the EU was not only a major exporter of wheat, but also the world's biggest importer of the cereal. EU imports fell very sharply in 2003/04, however, owing to the introduction of a system of import quotas designed to curb purchases of cheap Ukrainian and Russian wheat. Developed countries were formerly the main markets for wheat, but the role of developing countries as importers has been steadily increasing and they now regularly account for approximately two-thirds of world imports. Africa's imports have recently averaged more than 20m. tons per year. Most of this is accounted for by North Africa, where Egypt and Algeria are regularly among the world's largest wheat importing countries. Imports by sub-Saharan Africa (excluding South Africa) have averaged more than 8m. tons annually in recent years. Most countries in the region import at least small amounts (often including wheat or flour supplied as food aid), but the only markets whose imports have averaged more than 500,000 tons in recent years are Ethiopia, Kenya, Nigeria, South Africa and Sudan.

Production of Wheat
('000 metric tons)

	2005	2006
World total*	628,698	605,257
Africa*	20,911	25,109
Leading African producers		
Algeria	2,415	2,688
Egypt	8,141	8,308
Ethiopia	2,307	2,779
Kenya	369	358
Morocco	3,043	6,300†
South Africa	1,905	2,105
Sudan†	415	642
Tunisia	1,627	1,251
Zimbabwe	140†	140*
Leading non-African producers		
Argentina	12,574	14,000
Australia	25,090	9,819
Canada	26,775	27,277
China, People's Repub.*	97,449	104,470
France	36,886	35,367
Germany	23,693	22,428
India	68,637	69,350
Pakistan	21,612	21,277
Russia	47,698	45,006
Turkey	21,500	20,010
Ukraine	18,699	14,000
United Kingdom	14,863	14,735
USA	58,740	57,298

* FAO estimate.
† Unofficial figure(s).

The export price (f.o.b. Gulf ports) of US No. 2 Hard Winter, one of the most widely traded wheat varieties, averaged US $119 per metric ton in 2000, rising to $130 per ton in 2001. An average price of $151 per ton was recorded in 2002. In 2003 the average price declined marginally, to $150 per ton. In 2004 an increase of about 7.3%, to $161 per ton, was recorded in the export price of wheat, but in 2005 the average price fell to $158 per ton. In 2006 the average price had increased to $200 per ton. During the first eight months of 2007 the average monthly export price of US No. 2 Hard Winter wheat rose considerably, trading between $209 per ton (January) and $273 per ton (August). Global stocks by the end of August were reported to be at their lowest level for 25 years. The World Food Programme expressed concern at this time regarding the impact of low stock levels of wheat and other vital commodities on its ability to distribute food aid, notably citing increased demand for biofuels, and the assignment of agricultural land to associated production, as a contributory factor.

Since 1949 nearly all world trade in wheat has been conducted under the auspices of successive international agreements, administered by the International Wheat Council (IWC) in London. The early agreements involved regulatory price controls and supply and purchase obligations, but such provisions became inoperable in more competitive market conditions, and were abandoned in 1972. The IWC subsequently concentrated on providing detailed market assessments to its members and encouraging them to confer on matters of mutual concern. A new Grains Trade Convention, which entered into force in July 1995, allows for improvements in the provision of information on all grains to members of the IGC (the successor to the IWC), and enhances opportunities for consultations. In mid-2007 the IGC had eight individual exporting members, together with the member states of the EU, and 17 importing members. African members, all of which are importers, comprised Algeria, Côte d'Ivoire, Egypt, Kenya, Morocco, South Africa and Tunisia.

Since 1967 a series of Food Aid Conventions (FACs), linked to the successive Wheat and Grains Trade Conventions, have ensured continuity of supplies of food aid in the form of cereals to needy countries. Under the latest FAC, negotiated in 1999, the 22 donor countries (including the member states of the EU) have pledged to supply a minimum of some 5m. metric tons of food aid annually to developing countries, priority being given to least developed countries and other low-income food-importing countries. Aid is to be provided mostly in the form of cereals, and all aid given to least developed countries is to be in the form of grants. The FAC seeks to improve the effectiveness, and increase the impact, of food aid by improved monitoring and consultative procedures. During the late 1990s donors' cereal shipments under the FAC, 1995, averaged about 5m. tons per year, nearly one-third of which was sent to sub-Saharan Africa. Ethiopia, Rwanda, Angola and Mozambique were regularly among the main beneficiaries of the FAC. In mid-2004 FAC members undertook a renegotiation of the 1999 FAC in order 'to strengthen its capacity to meet identified needs when food aid is the appropriate response'. However, it was decided that this renegotiation should await the conclusion of discussions on trade-related food aid issues in agriculture negotiations at the World Trade Organization. In the mean time, it was agreed to extend the FAC, 1999, for two years from July 2005; a further one-year extension was agreed in mid-2007.

ACKNOWLEDGEMENTS

We gratefully acknowledge the assistance of the following organizations in the preparation of this section: Centro Internacional de Agricultura Tropical; De Beers; Food and Agricultural Organization of the United Nations (FAO); Gold Fields Mineral Services Ltd; International Cocoa Organization; International Coffee Organization; International Copper Study Group; International Cotton Advisory Committee; International Monetary Fund; International Aluminium Institute; International Rice Research Institute; International Tea Committee; International Tobacco Growers' Association; Johnson Matthey PLC; US Department of Agriculture; US Department of Energy; US Geological Survey, US Department of the Interior; World Nuclear Association. Unless otherwise indicated, FAO is the source for all agricultural production tables.

CALENDARS AND WEIGHTS AND MEASURES

The Islamic Calendar

The Islamic era dates from 16 July 622, which was the beginning of the Arab year in which the *Hijra* ('flight' or migration) of the prophet Muhammad (the founder of Islam), from Mecca to Medina (in modern Saudi Arabia), took place. The Islamic or *Hijri* Calendar is lunar, each year having 354 or 355 days, the extra day being intercalated 11 times every 30 years. Accordingly, the beginning of the *Hijri* year occurs earlier in the Gregorian Calendar by a few days each year. Dates are reckoned in terms of the *anno Hegirae* (AH) or year of the Hegira (*Hijra*). The Islamic year AH 1428 began on 20 January 2007.

The year is divided into the following months:

1. Muharram	30 days	7. Rajab	30 days
2. Safar	29 days	8. Shaaban	29 days
3. Rabia I	30 days	9. Ramadan	30 days
4. Rabia II	29 days	10. Shawwal	29 days
5. Jumada I	30 days	11. Dhu'l-Qa'da	30 days
6. Jumada II	29 days	12. Dhu'l-Hijja	29 or 30 days

The *Hijri* Calendar is used for religious purposes throughout the Islamic world.

PRINCIPAL ISLAMIC FESTIVALS

New Year: 1st Muharram. The first 10 days of the year are regarded as holy, especially the 10th.

Ashoura: 10th Muharram. Celebrates the first meeting of Adam and Eve after leaving Paradise, also the ending of the Flood and the death of Hussain, grandson of the prophet Muhammad. The feast is celebrated with fairs and processions.

Mouloud (Birth of Muhammad): 12th Rabia I.

Leilat al-Meiraj (Ascension of Muhammad): 27th Rajab.

Ramadan (Month of Fasting).

Id al-Fitr or Id al-Saghir or Küçük Bayram (The Small Feast): Three days beginning 1st Shawwal. This celebration follows the constraint of the Ramadan fast.

Id al-Adha or Id al-Kabir or Büyük Bayram (The Great Feast, Feast of the Sacrifice): Four days beginning on 10th Dhu'l-Hijja. The principal Islamic festival, commemorating Abraham's sacrifice and coinciding with the pilgrimage to Mecca. Celebrated by the sacrifice of a sheep, by feasting and by donations to the poor.

Islamic Year	1427	1428	1429
New Year	31 Jan. 2006	20 Jan. 2007	10 Jan. 2008
Ashoura	9 Feb. 2006	29 Jan. 2007	19 Jan. 2008
Mouloud	10 April 2006	31 March 2007	20 March 2008
Leilat al-Meiraj	21 Aug. 2006	10 Aug. 2007	30 July 2008
Ramadan begins	24 Sept. 2006	13 Sept. 2007	1 Sept. 2008
Id al-Fitr	23 Oct. 2006	13 Oct. 2007	1 Oct. 2008
Id al-Adha	31 Dec. 2006	20 Dec. 2007	8 Dec. 2008

Note: Local determinations may vary by one day from those given here.

The Ethiopian Calendar

The Ethiopian Calendar is solar, and is the traditional calendar of the Ethiopian Church. New Year (1st Maskarem) usually occurs on 11 September Gregorian. The Ethiopian year 2000 began on 12 September 2007.

The year is divided into 13 months, of which 12 have 30 days each. The 13th and last month (Paguemen) has five or six days, the extra day occurring in leap years. The months are as follows:

1. Maskarem	5. Tir	10. Sene
2. Tikimit	6. Yekatit	11. Hamle
3. Hidar	7. Megabit	12. Nahasse
4. Tahsas	8. Maiza	13. Paguemen
	9. Ginbat	

The Ethiopian Calendar is used for most purposes, religious and secular, in Ethiopia.

Weights and Measures

Principal weights and units of measurement in common use as alternatives to the imperial and metric systems.

WEIGHT

Unit	Country	Metric equivalent	Imperial equivalent
Frasula	Ethiopia	17 kg	37.38 lb
Frazila	Tanzania (Zanzibar)	15.87 kg	35 lb
Kantar	Sudan	44.928 kg	99.05 lb
Nater	Ethiopia	450 grams	1 lb
Pound (Dutch)	South Africa	494 grams	1.09 lb
Wakiah	Tanzania (Zanzibar)	280 grams	9.88 oz
Wokiet	Ethiopia	28 grams	1 oz

LENGTH

Unit	Country	Metric equivalent	Imperial equivalent
Busa	Sudan	2.54 cm	1 in
Cubito	Somalia	55.88 cm	22 in
Foot (Cape)	South Africa	31.5 cm	12.4 in
Foot (French)	Mauritius	32.5 cm	12.8 in
Gemad	Ethiopia	100 m	328 ft
Kadam or Qadam	Sudan	30.48 cm	12 in
Kan	Ethiopia	25 km	15.5 miles
Kend	Ethiopia	40 cm–60 cm	20 in
Pouce	Mauritius	2.54 cm	1 in
Senzer	Ethiopia	20 cm	8 in

CAPACITY

Unit	Country	Metric equivalent	Imperial equivalent
Ardabb or Ardeb	Sudan	198.024 litres	45.36 gallons
Bali	South Africa	46 litres	10.119 gallons
Corde	Mauritius	3.584 cu m	128 cu ft
Gantang	South Africa	9.2 litres	2.024 gallons
Kadah	Sudan	2.063 litres	3.63 pints
Keila	Sudan	16.502 litres	3.63 gallons
Kubaya	Ethiopia	0.3 litres	0.5 pints
Kuna	Ethiopia	5 litres	1.1 gallons
Mud or Muid	South Africa	109.1 litres	24 gallons
Ratel	Sudan	0.568 litres	1 pint
Tanika	Ethiopia	20 litres	5.28 gallons

AREA

Unit	Country	Metric equivalent	Imperial equivalent
Are	Mauritius	0.01 ha	0.0247 acre
Darat or Dural	Somalia	8,000 sq m	1.98 acres
Feddan	Sudan	4,201 sq m	1.038 acres
Gasha	Ethiopia	40 ha	99 acres
Morgen	South Africa	0.857 ha	2.117 acres

RESEARCH INSTITUTES

ASSOCIATIONS AND INSTITUTIONS STUDYING AFRICA

ARGENTINA

Facultad de Filosofía y Letras, Sección Interdisciplinaria de Estudios de Asia y Africa: Universidad de Buenos Aires, Moreno 350, 1002 Buenos Aires; tel. and fax (11) 4345-8196; e-mail africayasia@yahoo.com.ar; f. 1982; research and lectures; Dir Prof. MARISA PINEAU; publs include *Temas de Africa y Asia* (2 a year).

Nigeria House: Galerías Boston, Florida 142, Local 3, 1337 Buenos Aires; tel. (11) 4326-5543; fax (11) 4827-3887; f. 1965; library specializing in Nigerian material and general information on Africa; Dir EMILIA MARÍA SANNAZZARI.

AUSTRALIA

Australian Institute of International Affairs: 32 Thesiger Court, Deakin, ACT 2600; tel. (2) 6282-2133; fax (2) 6285-2334; e-mail ceo@aiia.asn.au; internet www.aiia.asn.au; f. 1933; 1,800 mems; brs in all States; Pres. NEAL BLEWETT; Exec. Dir CHARLES HAMILTON STUART; publs include *Australian Journal of International Affairs* (4 a year).

Indian Ocean Centre for Peace Studies: University of Western Australia, Nedlands, WA 6009; tel. (8) 9380-2278; fax (8) 9380-1060; f. 1991; Contact Dr SAMINA YASMEEN; publ. *Indian Ocean Review* (quarterly).

AUSTRIA

Afro-Asiatisches Institut in Wien (Afro-Asian Institute in Vienna): 1090 Vienna, Türkenstr. 3; tel. (1) 310-51-45-210; fax (1) 310-51-45-312; e-mail office@aai-wien.at; internet www.aai-wien.at; f. 1959; cultural and other exchanges between Austria and African and Asian countries; assistance to students from Africa and Asia; economic and social research; lectures, seminars; Rector KONSTANTIN SPIEGELFELD; Gen. Sec. GERHARD LANG.

Österreichische Forschungsstiftung für Entwicklungshilfe (ÖFSE) (Austrian Foundation for Development Research): 1090 Vienna, Berggasse 7; tel. (1) 317-40-10; fax (1) 317-40-15; e-mail office@oefse.at; internet www.oefse.at; f. 1967; documentation and information on devt aid and developing countries, particularly in relation to Austria; library of 35,000 vols and 250 periodicals; publs include *Ausgewählte neue Literatur zur Entwicklungspolitik* (2 a year), *Österreichische Entwicklungspolitik* (annually).

Österreichische Gesellschaft für Aussenpolitik und Internationale Beziehungen (Austrian Association for Foreign Policy and International Relations): 1010 Vienna, Hofburg/Schweizerhof/Brunnenstiege; tel. (1) 535-46-27; fax (1) 532-26-05; e-mail oega@start.at; internet start.at/oega; f. 1958; lectures, discussions; c. 400 mems; Pres. Dr WOLFGANG SCHALLENBERG; publ. *Österreichisches Jahrbuch für Internationale Politik* (annually).

Österreichisches Institut für Entwicklungshilfe und Technische Zusammenarbeit mit den Entwicklungsländern (Austrian Institute for Development Aid and Technical Co-operation with the Developing Countries): 1010 Vienna, Wipplingerstr. 35; tel. (1) 426-504; f. 1963; projects for management training; Pres Dr HANS INGLER, ERICH HOFSTETTER.

BELGIUM

Académie Royale des Sciences d'Outre-Mer/Koninklijke Academie voor Overzeese Wetenschappen: rue Defacqz 1, Boîte 3, 1000 Brussels; tel. (2) 538-02-11; fax (2) 539-23-53; e-mail kaowarsom@skynet.be; internet www.kaowarsom.be; f. 1928; the promotion of scientific knowledge of overseas areas, especially those with special devt problems; 116 mems, 73 assoc. mems, 95 correspondence mems; Perm. Sec. Prof. DANIELLE SWINNE.

Afrika Instituut/Institut africain (ASDOC/CEDAF): c/o Africa Museum, Leuvensesteenweg 13, 3080 Tervuren; tel. (2) 769-57-41; fax (2) 769-57-46; e-mail esimons@africamuseum.be; internet cedaf-asdoc.africamuseum.be; f. 1970; research and documentation on African social and economic problems, with special reference to Burundi, Rwanda and the Dem. Repub. of the Congo; Dir G. DE VILLERS; publ. *Cahiers Africains-Afrika Studies* (6 a year).

Bibliothèque africaine: 19 rue des Petites Carmes, 1000 Brussels; tel. (2) 501-80-98; fax (2) 501-37-36; e-mail biblio@dipobel.fed.be; f. 1885; library of 225,000 vols; large collections in the fields of African history, ethnography, economics, politics; Dir MICHEL ERKENS.

Centre international des langues, littératures et traditions d'Afrique au service du développement (CILTADE): ave des Clos 30, 1348 Louvain-la-Neuve; tel. (32) 45-06-65; fax (32) 45-56-85; e-mail nzuji@acla.ucl.ac.be; Dir Dr CLÉMENTINE MADIYA FAÏK-NZUJI.

Institut voor Ontwikkelingsbeleid en beheer—Institute of Development Policy and Management: University of Antwerp, Venusstraat, 20000 Antwerp; tel. (3) 220-49-98; fax (3) 220-44-81; e-mail dev@ua.ac.be; internet www.ua.ac.be/dev; conducts postgraduate study courses; library and documentation centre; Pres. Prof. Dr F. REYNTJENS; publs research reports and papers.

Fondation pour favoriser les recherches scientifiques en Afrique: 1 rue Defacqz, BP 5, 1050 Brussels; tel. (2) 269-39-05; f. 1969 to conduct scientific research in Africa with special reference to environmental management and conservation; Dir Dr A. G. ROBYNS; publs *Exploration des Parcs nationaux*, *Etudes du Continent africain*.

Institut d'études du développement: Université catholique de Louvain, Dépt des sciences de la population et du développement, 1 place Montesquieu, 1348 Louvain-La-Neuve; tel. (32) 47-40-41; fax (32) 47-29-52; e-mail vandenbossche@dvlp.ucl.ac.be; internet www.sped.ucl.ac.be; f. 1961; Pres. J.-M. WAUTELET.

Institut royal des relations internationales: 13 rue de la Charité, 1210 Brussels; tel. (2) 223-41-14; fax (2) 223-41-16; e-mail irri.kiib@euronet.be; f. 1947; research in international relations, economics, law and politics; archives and library of 16,500 vols and 600 periodicals; Dir-Gen. ÉMILE MASSA; publs include *Studia Diplomatica* (bimonthly).

Koninklijk Museum voor Midden-Afrika/Musée royal de l'Afrique centrale: Leuvensesteenweg 13, 3080 Tervuren; tel. (2) 686-02-73; fax (2) 686-02-76; e-mail edwine.simons@africamuseum.be; internet www.africamuseum.be; f. 1897; collections of prehistory, ethnography, nature arts and crafts; geology, mineralogy, palaeontology; zoology (entomology, ornithology, mammals, reptiles, etc.); history; economics; library of 90,000 vols and 4,500 periodicals; Dir GUIDO GRYSEELS; publs include *Annales du Musée royal de l'Afrique centrale*.

Société belge d'études géographiques (Belgian Society for Geographical Studies): de Croylaan 42, 3001 Heverlee (Leuven); tel. (16) 32-24-45; fax (16) 32-29-80; f. 1931; centralizes and co-ordinates geographical research in Belgium; 395 mems; Pres. Y. VERHASSELT; Sec. H. VAN DER HAEGEN; publ. *Bulletin* (2 a year).

BRAZIL

Centro de Estudos Africanos (African Studies Centre): University of São Paulo, CP 26097, 05513-970 São Paulo, SP; tel. (11) 3032-9416; e-mail cea@usp.br; internet www.fflch.usp.br/cea; f. 1969; co-ordinating unit for all depts with African interests; specialist studies in sociology, international relations and literature concerning Africa; library; Dir Prof. CARLOS SERRANO; publ. *África* (annually).

Centro de Estudos Afro-Asiáticos (CEAA) (Afro-Asian Studies Centre): Praça Pio X 7, 9°, 20040-020, Rio de Janeiro, RJ; tel. (21) 2516-7157; fax (21) 2518-2798; e-mail beluce@candidomendes.br; internet www.candidomendes.br/ceaa/equipe.htm; f. 1973; instruction and seminars; library; Dir CANDIDO MENDES; publ. *Estudos Afro-Asiáticos*.

Centro de Estudos Afro-Orientais (CEAO) (Afro-Oriental Studies Centre): Praça XV de Novembro 17, Terreiro de Jesús, 40025-010 Salvador-BA; tel. (71) 322-6742; fax (71) 322-8070; e-mail ceao@ufba.br; internet www.ceao.ufba.br; f. 1959; African and Afro-Oriental Studies; library; Dir Prof. JOCÉLIO TELES DOS SANTOS; publ. *Afro-Ásia* (irregular).

Centro de Estudos e Pesquisas de Cultura Yorubana (Yoruba Culture Study and Research Centre): CP 40099, CEP 20272, Rio de Janeiro, RJ; tel. (21) 2293-0649; instruction in Yoruba language and religion; Dir Prof. FERNANDES PORTUGAL; publs include occasional papers.

Núcleo de Estudos Afro-Asiáticos (Afro-Asian Studies Unit): State University of Londrina, CP 6001, CEP 86051-970 Londrina, PR; tel. (43) 371-4599; fax (43) 371-4679; f. 1985; seminars and lectures; Dir Prof. EDUARDO JUDAS BARROS; publ. *Africa Asia* (annually).

CANADA

Canadian Association of African Studies (CAAS): CCASLS SB-115, Concordia University, 1455 de Maisonneuve Oueste, Montréal, QC H3G 1M8; tel. (514) 848-2280; fax (514) 848-4514; e-mail caas@concordia.ca; internet caas.concordia.ca; f. 1970; Sec. ANNAMARIA

PICCIONI; publs *CAAS Journal* (English and French—3 a year), *CAAS Newsletter* (online; English and French—irregular).

Canadian Council for International Co-operation: 1 Nicholas St, Suite 300, Ottawa, ON K1N 7B7; tel. (613) 241-7007; fax (613) 241-5302; e-mail info@ccic.ca; internet www.ccic.ca; f. 1968; information and training centre for international devt and forum for voluntary agencies; 100 mems; Pres. JO HINCHLIFFE; CEO GERRY BARR; publs include *Au Courant* (2 a year).

Canadian Institute of International Affairs: 205 Richmond St West, Suite 302, Toronto, ON M5V 1V3; tel. (416) 977-9000; fax (416) 977-7521; e-mail mailbox@ciia.org; internet www.ciia.org; f. 1928; research in international relations; library of 8,000 vols; Chair. JOHN MACNAUGHTON; Pres. and CEO DOUGLAS GOLD; publs include *International Journal* (quarterly), *Behind the Headlines* (quarterly).

Centre for African Studies: Dalhousie University, Dept of International Development Studies, Henry Hicks Administration Bldg, Halifax, NS B3H 4H6; tel. (902) 494-3814; fax (902) 494-2105; e-mail parpart@dal.ca; f. 1975; Dir Dr JANE L. PARPART; publs include *Dalhousie African Studies* series, *Dalhousie African Working Papers* series, *Briefing Papers on the African Crisis*.

Centre for Developing-Area Studies: McGill University, 3715 rue Peel, Montréal, QC H3A 1X1; tel. (514) 398-3507; fax (514) 398-8432; e-mail pubcdas@mcgill.ca; internet www.mcgill.ca/cdas; Dir Dr ROSALIND BOYD; publs include *Labour, Capital and Society* (English and French—2 a year), discussion papers.

International Development Research Centre: POB 8500, Ottawa, ON K1G 3H9; tel. (613) 236-6163; fax (613) 238-7230; e-mail info@idrc.ca; internet www.idrc.ca; f. 1970 by the Govt to support research projects designed to meet the basic needs of developing countries and to address problems associated with poverty; regional offices in Kenya, Senegal, Egypt, Singapore, Uruguay and India; Pres. MAUREEN O'NEIL; publs include *Reports Magazine* (French, Spanish and English—weekly).

PEOPLE'S REPUBLIC OF CHINA

Centre for International Studies: 22 Xianmen Dajie, POB 7411, Beijing; tel. (10) 63097083; fax (10) 63095802; f. 1982; conducts research on international relations and problems; organizes academic exchanges; Dir-Gen. ZHANG YIJUN.

China Institute of Contemporary International Relations: 2A Wanshousi, Haidian, Beijing 100081; tel. (10) 8418640; fax (10) 8418641; f. 1980; research on international devt and peace issues; Pres. SHEN QURONG; publ. *Contemporary International Relations* (monthly).

Institute of African Studies: Xiangtan University, Xiangtan, Hunan; tel. 24812; f. 1978.

Institute of West Asian and African Studies: Chinese Academy of Social Sciences, 3 Zhangzhizhong Rd, Beijing 100007; tel. (10) 64039171; fax (10) 64035718; e-mail iwaas@public.fhnet.cn.net; f. 1961; 40 full-time research fellows; library of 40,000 vols; Dir-Gen. YANG GUANG; publ. *West Asia and Africa* (Chinese, with summary in English—6 a year).

CZECH REPUBLIC

Ústav mezinárodních vztahů (Institute of International Relations): Nerudova 3, 118 50 Prague 1; tel. 251108111; fax 251108222; e-mail umv@iir.cz; internet www.iir.cz; f. 1957; Dir Dr Ing. PETR DRULÁK; publs include *Mezinárodní politika/International Politics* (in Czech—monthly), *Mezinárodní vztahy/International Relations* (in Czech—quarterly), *Perspectives—The Central European Review of International Affairs* (in English—2 a year).

DENMARK

Center for Udviklingsforskning (Centre for Development Research): Gammel Kongevej 5, 1610 Copenhagen V; tel. 33-85-46-00; fax 33-25-81-10; e-mail cdr@cdr.dk; internet www.cdr.dk; f. 1969 to promote and undertake research in the economic, social and political problems of developing countries; library of 60,000 vols; Dir Dr POUL ENGBERG-PEDERSEN; publs include *Den Ny Verden* (quarterly), *CDR Library Papers* (irregular), *CDR Policy Papers* (in English—irregular), *CDR Working Papers* (in English—irregular), *Researching Development* (in English—quarterly), *Aid Policy and Practice* (in English—irregular).

FRANCE

Académie des sciences d'outre-mer: 15 rue Lapérouse, 75116 Paris; tel. 1-47-20-87-93; fax 1-47-20-89-72; e-mail bibliotheque@academiedoutremer.fr; internet www.academiedoutremer.fr; f. 1922; 275 mems, of which 200 mems are attached to sections on geography, politics and administration, law, economics and sociology, science and medicine, education; library of 70,000 vols and 2,500 periodicals; Perm. Sec. GILBERT MANGIN; publs include *Mondes et Cultures* (quarterly).

Centre d'étude d'Afrique noire: 11 allée Ausone, Domaine universitaire, 33607 Pessac; tel. 5-56-84-42-82; fax 5-56-84-43-24; e-mail info@cean.sciencespobordeaux.fr; internet www.cean.sciencespobordeaux.fr; Dir RENÉ OTAYEK.

Centre d'études juridiques et politiques du monde africain (CEJPMA): Université de Paris I, 9 rue Mahler, 75181 Paris Cedex 04; tel. 1-44-78-33-25; fax 1-44-78-33-39; e-mail politique.africaine@univ-paris1.fr; internet www.politique-africaine.com; Dir RICHARD BANÉGAS.

Centre d'études et de recherches sur le développement international (CERDI): Université d'Auvergne, 65 blvd François Mitterrand, 63000 Clermont-Ferrand; tel. 4-73-17-74-00; fax 4-73-17-74-28; e-mail cerdi@u-clermont1.fr; internet www.cerdi.org; f. 1976; Dir PATRICK PLANE.

Centre de recherches africaines: 9 rue Malher, 75181 Paris Cedex 04; tel. 1-44-78-33-40; fax 1-44-78-33-33; e-mail cra@univ-paris1.fr; an institute of the University of Paris I; Dir JEAN BOULEGUE.

Institut français des relations internationales (Ifri): 27 rue de la Procession, 75740 Paris Cedex 15; tel. 1-40-61-60-00; fax 1-40-61-60-60; e-mail accueil@ifri.org; internet www.ifri.org; f. 1979; international politics and economy, security issues, regional studies; library of 32,000 vols and 250 periodicals; Pres. Prof. THIERRY DE MONTBRIAL; Exec. Dir PIERRE LEPETIT; publs *Politique étrangère* (quarterly), *Ramses* (annually), *Notes de l'Ifri*, *Cahiers et conférences de l'Ifri*, *Travaux et recherches de l'Ifri*, *Publications du CFE à l'Ifri*, *Cahiers du Centre asie Ifri*.

Institut de recherche pour le développement (IRD): 213 rue La Fayette, 75480 Paris Cedex 10; tel. 1-48-03-77-77; fax 1-48-03-08-29; e-mail dic@paris.ird.fr; internet www.ird.fr; f. 1943, reorg. 1982 and 1998; self-financing; centres, missions and rep. offices in Benin, Bolivia, Brazil, Burkina Faso, Cameroon, Côte d'Ivoire, Chile, Ecuador, Egypt, French Guiana, Guinea, Indonesia, Kenya, Madagascar, Mali, Mexico, New Caledonia, Niger, Peru, Senegal, South Africa, Thailand, Tunisia and Viet Nam; Pres. JEAN-FRANÇOIS GIRARD; Dir-Gen. SERGE CALABRE.

Musée de l'Homme: Palais de Chaillot, 17 place du Trocadéro, 75116 Paris; tel. 1-44-05-72-72; e-mail liongau@mnhn.fr; internet www.mnhn.fr; f. 1878; library of 250,000 vols (c. 30,000 on Africa), 5,000 periodicals and c. 300,000 photographic images; ethnography, physical anthropology, prehistory; also a research and education centre; Dirs Profs ZEEV GOURARIER (Musée de l'Homme), FRANÇOIS SÉMAH (Prehistory), SERGE BAHUCHET (Mankind and Society).

Société des africanistes (CSSF): Musée de l'Homme, Palais de Chaillot, 17 place du Trocadéro, 75116 Paris; tel. 1-47-27-72-55; e-mail africanistes@wanadoo.fr; f. 1931; 350 mems; Pres. Dr JEAN-LOUIS BOPPE; publ. *Journal des Africanistes* (2 a year).

Société française d'historie d'outre-mer: 15 rue Catulienne, 93200 Saint-Denis; tel. 6-07-30-04-22; fax 1-45-85-62-05; e-mail sfhom@noos.fr; f. 1913; 500 mems; Pres. HÉLÈNE D'ALMEIDA-TOPOR; Sec.-Gen. JOSETTE RIVALLAIS; publ. *Revue française d'histoire d'outre-mer* (2 a year).

GERMANY

Deutsche Gesellschaft für Auswärtige Politik eV (German Council on Foreign Relations): Rauchstr. 17/18, 10787 Berlin; tel. (30) 254231; fax (30) 254216; e-mail info@dgap.org; internet www.dgap.org; f. 1955; promotes research on problems of international politics; library of 65,500 vols; 1,600 mems; Pres. HANS-DIETRICH GENSCHER; Exec. Vice-Pres. LEOPOLD BILL VON BREDOW; Dir Research Inst. Prof. Dr EBERHARD SANDSCHNEIDER; publs *Internationale Politik* (monthly), *Internationale Politik: Transatlantic Edition* (quarterly), *Die Internationale Politik* (annually).

GIGA Institute of African Affairs: Neuer Jungfernstieg 21, 20354 Hamburg; tel. (40) 42825523; fax (40) 42825511; e-mail iaa@giga-hamburg.de; internet www.giga-hamburg.de/iaa; f. 1963; research, documentation, information; library of 47,000 vols and 350 periodicals; Dir Dr ANDREAS MEHLER; publs include *Afrika Spectrum*, *GIGA Focus Afrika*, *GIGA Working Paper Series*.

IFO—Institut für Wirtschaftsforschung (Institute for Economic Research): Poschingerstr. 5, 81679 Munich; tel. (89) 92240; fax (89) 9224-1462; e-mail ifo@ifo.de; internet www.ifo.de; f. 1949; library of 80,000 vols; Pres. Prof. Dr HANS-WERNER SINN; publs include *Afrika-Studien*, *IFO-Studien zur Entwicklungsforschung*, *Forschungsberichte der Abteilung Entwicklungsländer*.

Informationsstelle Südliches Afrika eV (Information Centre on Southern Africa): Königswintererstr. 116, 53227 Bonn; tel. (228) 464369; fax (228) 468177; e-mail issa@comlink.org; internet www.issa-bonn.org; f. 1971; research, documentation, and information on southern Africa; publs include *Afrika Süd* (6 a year).

Institut für Afrikanistik: Leipzig University, Beethovenstr. 15, 04107 Leipzig; tel. (341) 9737030; fax (341) 9737048; e-mail mgrosze@rz.uni-leipzig.de; internet www.uni-leipzig.de/afrika; Dir Prof. Dr ADAM JONES.

HUNGARY

Magyar Tudományos Akadémia Világgazdasági Kutató Intézete (Institute for World Economics of the Hungarian Academy of Sciences): 1014 Budapest, Országház u. 30; tel. (1) 224-6700; fax (1) 224-6765; e-mail vki@vki.hu; internet www.vki.hu; f. 1965; library of 103,000 vols; Man. Dir EVA NAGY.

INDIA

African Studies Association of India: School of International Studies, Jawaharlal Nehru University, New Mehrauli Rd, New Delhi 110 067; tel. (11) 26704607; fax (11) 26704607; e-mail office@asadelhi.com; internet www.asadelhi.com; to foster and promote the study, knowledge and understanding of African affairs in India and Indian affairs in Africa through research and studies; Pres. Prof. RAJEN G. HARSHE; Chair. SHRI SHASHANK.

Centre for African Studies: University of Mumbai, Vidyanagari Kalina Campus, Santacruz (East), Mumbai 400 098; tel. (22) 26526091, ext. 329; fax (22) 26526893; internet www.mu.ac.in; f. 1971; Dir Dr APARAJITA BISWAS; publ. *African Currents* (2 a year).

Centre for Development Studies: Prasanth Nagar Rd, Ulloor, Thiruvananthapuram 695 011; tel. (471) 2448881; fax (471) 2447137; e-mail cdsedp@vsnl.com; f. 1971; instruction and research in disciplines relevant to economic devt; library of 125,000 vols; Dir Dr CHANDAN MUKHERJEE.

Centre for West Asian and African Studies: School of International Studies, Jawaharlal Nehru University, New Mehrauli Rd, New Delhi 110 067; tel. (11) 26107676; fax (11) 26165886; Chair. Dr AJAY K. DUBEY.

Department of African Studies: University of Delhi, Delhi 110 007; tel. and fax (11) 27666673; e-mail isaas@vsnl.com; f. 1955; Head of Dept JAGDISH PRASAD SHARMA; publs include *Indian Journal of African Studies*, *Documentation on Africa*.

Indian Centre for Africa: Indian Council for Cultural Relations, Azad Bhavan, Indraprastha Estate, New Delhi 110 002; tel. (11) 23319226; fax (11) 3712639; f. 1987; publ. *Africa Quarterly*.

Indian Council of World Affairs: Sapru House, Barakhamba Rd, New Delhi 110 001; tel. (11) 23317246; f. 1943; independent institution for the study of Indian and international issues; library of 127,000 vols, 490 periodicals, 2.5m. press clippings, also UN documents and microfiches; 2,480 mems; Pres. HARCHARAN SINGH JOSH; publs include *Foreign Affairs Reports* (monthly), *India Quarterly*.

Indian Society for Afro-Asian Studies: 297 Saraswati Kunj, Indraprastha Ext., Mother Dairy Rd, New Delhi 110 092; tel. (11) 22722801; fax (11) 22725024; e-mail isaas@vsnl.com; f. 1980; conducts research and holds seminars and confs; Pres. LALIT BHASIN; Gen. Sec. Dr DHARAMPAL; publs include *Indian Review of African Affairs* (6 a year).

IRAN

Institute for Political and International Studies: Shaheed Bahonar Ave, Shaheed Aghaii Ave, POB 19395-1793, Tajrish, Tehran; tel. (21) 2571010; fax (21) 2710964; e-mail IPIS@www.dci.co.ir; f. 1983; research and information on international relations, foreign policy, economics, culture and law; library of 22,000 vols; publs include *Iranian Journal of International Affairs* (quarterly).

ISRAEL

Harry S. Truman Research Institute for the Advancement of Peace: The Hebrew University of Jerusalem, Mt Scopus, Jerusalem 91905; tel. 25882300; fax 25828076; e-mail mstruman@mscc.huji.ac.il; internet truman.huji.ac.il; f. 1965; conducts a broad range of research relating to non-Western and developing countries; Dir Prof. AMNON COHEN; Exec. Dir Dr EDY KAUFMAN.

International Institute—Histadrut: Bet Berl 44905, Kfar Saba; tel. 9987382; f. 1958 to train leadership for trade unions, co-operatives, community orgs, women's and youth groups, etc. in developing countries; library of 35,000 vols; Chair. HAIM RAMON; Dir and Prin. Dr YEHUDAH PAZ.

Moshe Dayan Center for Middle Eastern and African Studies, Shiloah Institute: Tel Aviv University, Ramat-Aviv, Tel-Aviv 69978; tel. 36409646; fax 36415802; e-mail dayancen@ccsg.tau.ac.il; internet www.dayan.org; f. 1959; Dir Prof. ASHER SUSSER; publs include *Current Contents of Periodicals on the Middle East* (6 a year), *Middle East Contemporary Survey* (annually), *The Moshe Dayan Center Bulletin* (2 a year).

ITALY

The Bologna Center, Paul H. Nitze School of Advanced International Studies, The Johns Hopkins University: Via Belmeloro 11, 40126 Bologna; tel. (051) 2917811; fax (051) 228505; e-mail registrar@jhubc.it; internet www.jhubc.it; f. 1955; graduate studies in international affairs; Dir MARISA R. LINO; publs include occasional papers series.

Istituto Italiano per l'Africa e l'Oriente (IsIAO): Via Ulisse Aldrovandi 16, 00197 Rome; tel. (06) 3218551; fax (06) 3225348; e-mail info@isiao.it; internet www.isiao.it; f. 1906; Chair. Prof. GHERARDO GNOLI; Dir-Gen. GIANCARLO GARGARUTI; publ. *Africa* (quarterly).

Istituto per gli Studi di Politica Internazionale (ISPI): Palazzo Clerici, Via Clerici 5, 20121 Milan; tel. (02) 8633131; fax (02) 8692055; f. 1933 for the promotion of the study of international relations; conducts research, documentation and training; Pres. Ambassador BORIS BIANCHERI; Man. Dir Dr GIOVANNI ROGGERO FOSSATI; publs include *Relazioni Internazionali* (6 a year).

JAPAN

Ajia Keizai Kenkyusho (IDE—JETRO) (Institute of Developing Economies, Japan External Trade Organization): 3-2-2, Wakaba, Mihama-ku, Chiba-shi, Chiba 261-8545; tel. (4) 3299-9500; fax (4) 3299-9724; internet www.ide.go.jp; f. 1960; library of 557,000 vols; Chair. OSAMU WATANABE; Pres. MASAHISA FUJITA; publs *Ajia Keizai* (Japanese, monthly), *The Developing Economies* (English, quarterly), *Africa Report* (Japanese, biannually).

Nihon Afurika Gakkai (Japan Association for African Studies): c/o Dogura and Co Ltd, 1-8, Nishihanaikecho, Koyama, Kita-ku, Kyoto 603; tel. (75) 451-4844; fax (75) 441-0436; promotes multi-disciplinary African studies; Pres. H. ODA; publs *Afurika Kenkyu / Journal of African Studies* (2 a year), *Kaiho* (annually).

Nihon Kokusai Mondai Kenkyusho (Japan Institute of International Affairs): 11F Kasumigaseki Bldg, 3-2-5, Kasumigaseki, Chiyoda-ku, Tokyo 100-6011; tel. (3) 3503-7261; fax (3) 3595-1755; e-mail info@jiia.or.jp; internet www.jiia.or.jp; f. 1959; Chair. GAISHI HIRAIWA; Pres. HISASHI OWADA; publs include *Kokusai Mondai* (International Affairs, monthly), *Japan Review of International Affairs* (quarterly).

Research Institute for the Study of Languages and Cultures of Asia and Africa: Tokyo University of Foreign Studies, 3-11-1, Asahi-cho, Fuchu, Tokyo 183-8534; tel. (42) 330-5601; fax (42) 330-5610; e-mail editcom@aa.tufs.ac.jp; internet www.aa.tufs.ac.jp; f. 1964; library of c. 91,000 vols; Dir Prof. KOJI MIYAZAKI; publs *Newsletter* (3 a year), *Journal of Asian and African Studies* (2 a year).

MEXICO

Asociación Latinoamericana de Estudios de Asia y Africa (Latin American Asscn for Asian and African Studies): El Colegio de México, Camino al Ajusco 20, Pedregal de Santa Teresa, CP 10740, 1000 Alvaro Obregón, México DF; tel. (55) 5449-3000; fax (55) 5645-0464; e-mail aladaa@colmex.mx; internet www.colmex.mx/ver_text/informacion_academica/centros/ceaa/aladaa/aladaa.html; f. 1976; promotes African and Asian studies in Latin America; 450 mems; Sec.-Gen. Prof. MICHIKO TANAKA; publs newsletters and proceedings.

Centro de Estudios de Asia y Africa (CEAA) (Centre for Asian and African Studies): El Colegio de México, Camino al Ajusco 20, Pedregal de Santa Teresa, CP 10740, 01000 Alvaro Obrégon, México DF; tel. (55) 5449-3025; fax (55) 5645-0464; internet www.colmex.mx/centros/ceaa; f. 1964; postgraduate studies and research; library; Dir Prof. JUAN JOSÉ RAMÍREZ BONILLA; publs include *Estudios de Asia y Africa* (3 a year).

THE NETHERLANDS

Afrika-Studiecentrum (African Studies Centre): Wassenaarseweg 52, 2333 AK, Leiden; POB 9555, 2300 RB, Leiden; tel. (71) 5273372; fax (71) 5273344; e-mail asc@ascleiden.nl; internet asc.ascleiden.nl; f. 1948 to carry out research on sub-Saharan Africa in the social sciences, and to disseminate information on African affairs; library of 55,000 vols and 450 periodicals; Chair. E. M. A. SCHMITZ; Dir Prof. Dr L. J. DE HAAN; publs include *African Dynamics* (2 a year), *Afrika-Studiecentrum Series* (2–3 titles a year) and *African Studies Abstracts Online* (quarterly).

Institute of Social Studies (ISS): POB 29776, 2502 LT, The Hague; tel. (70) 4260419; fax (70) 4260799; e-mail promotions@iss.nl; internet www.iss.nl; f. 1952; postgraduate instruction, research and consultancy in devt studies; Rector Prof. L. DE LA RIVE BOX; publs *Development and Change* (quarterly), *Development Issues*, working papers.

Netherlands-African Business Council: Bezuidenhoutseweg 181, 2594 AH, The Hague; tel. (70) 3836070; fax (70) 3814296; e-mail info@nabc.nl; internet www.nabc.nl; f. 1946; trade and investment promotion for sub-Saharan Africa; Chair. J. W. B. NOLST TRENITÉ; Gen. Man. J. J. B. DERKSEN.

Netherlands Institute for Southern Africa (NiZA): Prins Hendrikkade 33, POB 10707, 1001 ES, Amsterdam; tel. (20) 5206210; fax (20) 5206249; e-mail niza@niza.nl; internet www.niza.nl; f. 1997; promotes democracy in southern Africa; publs *Zuidelijk Afrika*, *NiZA Informatie* (quarterly), *Niza Cahiers* and reports of seminars and conferences.

NORWAY

Norsk Utenrikspolitisk Institutt (Norwegian Institute of International Affairs): Grønlandsleiret 25, POB 8159 Dep, 0033 Oslo; tel. 22056500; fax 22177015; e-mail info@nupi.no; internet www.nupi.no/; f. 1959; information and research in international relations; Pres. PAUL CHAFFEY; Dir SVERRE LODGAARD; publs include Hvor Hender Det (weekly), *Internasjonal Politikk* (quarterly), Nordisk Østforum (quarterly), *Forum for Development Studies* (2 a year), *NUPI Notat* and *NUPI Rapport* (research reports).

PAKISTAN

Pakistan Institute of International Affairs: Aiwan-e-Sadar Rd, POB 1447, Karachi 74200; tel. (21) 5682891; fax (21) 5686069; f. 1947 to study international affairs and to promote the study of international politics, economics and law; over 600 mems; library of c. 28,000 vols; Chair. FATEHYAB ALI KHAN; publs include *Pakistan Horizon* (quarterly).

POLAND

Departament Studiów i Planowania (MSZ) (Dept of Studies and Planning, Ministry of Foreign Affairs): 00-950 Warsaw, ul. Warecka 1A; tel. (22) 8263021; fax (22) 8263026; f. 1947; library of 125,000 vols; Dir Dr HENRYK SZLAJFER; publs include *Sprawy Międzynarodowe* (quarterly, in Polish and English), *Zbiór Dokumentów* (quarterly, in Polish, French, English and German), occasional papers (in English).

Institute of Oriental Studies, Department of African Languages and Cultures, University of Warsaw: 00-927 Warsaw, Krakowskie Przedmieście 26/28; tel. (22) 5520517; fax (22) 8263683; e-mail afrykanistyka.orient@uw.edu.pl; f. 1950; postgraduate studies and research in linguistics, literature, history, sociology and ethnology; Head of Dept Prof. Dr STANISŁAW PIŁASZEWICZ; publ. *Studies of the Department of African Languages and Cultures*.

Instytut Krajów Rozwijających się (Institute of Developing Countries): 00-324 Warsaw, Karowa 20; tel. and fax (22) 8268547; e-mail ikr@mercury.ci.uw.edu.pl; internet www.ikr.uw.edu.pl; undergraduate and postgraduate studies; interdisciplinary research on developing countries; Dir Prof. JAN J. MILEWSKI; publs include *Africana Bulletin* (annually, in French and English), *Afryka, Azja, Ameryka Łacińska* (annually, with summaries in French and English).

PORTUGAL

Centro de Estudos Africanos (African Studies Centre): Faculty of Letters, University of Lisbon, Cidade Universitária, 1600-214 Lisbon; tel. (21) 7920000; fax (21) 7960063; e-mail ceafrica@fl.ul.pt; internet www.fl.ul.pt/unidades/centros/ceafrica; literary studies and documentation centre; Dir Prof. ISABEL CASTRO HENRIQUES.

Centro de Estudos Africanos (African Studies Centre): Instituto Superior de Ciências do Trabalho e da Empresa (ISCTE), Av. das Forças Armadas, Ed. ISCTE 1649-026 Lisbon; tel. (21) 7903067; fax (21) 7955361; e-mail cea@iscte.pt; internet cea.iscte.pt; f. 1990; research and post-graduate courses in African Studies; Dir Prof. JOSÉ FIALHO FELICIANO; publ. *Cadernos de Estudos Africanos*.

Centro de Estudos Africanos (African Studies Centre): University of Porto, Via Panorâmica s/n, 4150-564 Porto; tel. and fax (22) 6077141; e-mail ceaup@letras.up.pt; internet www.africanos.eu/ceaup; f. 1997; research and post-graduate courses in African Studies; Dir Prof. ELVIRA CUNHA DE AZEVEDO MEA; publ. *Africana Studia*.

Centro de Estudos Sobre África e do Desenvolvimento (Centre of African and Development Studies): Instituto Superior de Economia e Gestão, Rua Miguel Lupi 20, 1200 Lisbon; tel. (21) 3925983; fax (21) 3976271; e-mail cesa@iseg.ult.pt; internet pascal.iseg.utl.pt/~cesa; f. 1982; conducts research and holds seminars; Dir Prof. JOCHEN OPPENHEIMER; publs occasional papers.

Centro de Intervenção para o Desenvolvimento Amílcar Cabral (CIDAC) (Amílcar Cabral Information and Documentation Centre): Rua Pinheiro Chagas, 77-2° esq., 1069-069 Lisbon; tel. (21) 3172860; fax (21) 3172870; e-mail cidac@cidac.pt; internet www.cidac.pt; Pres. LUISA TEOTÓNIO PEREIRA.

Instituto de Investigação Científica Tropical (IICT) (Institute for Tropical Scientific Research): Rua da Junqueira 86, 1300-344 Lisbon; tel. (21) 3616340; fax (21) 3631460; e-mail iict@iict.pt; internet www2.iict.pt; f. 1883; comprises departments of social sciences and natural sciences, colonial archives and a documentation centre, dealing mainly with lusophone African countries; Pres. JORGE BRAGA DE MACEDO; publs include monographs, serials and maps.

Instituto de Estudos Estratégicos e Internacionais (IEEI): Largo de S Sebastião, 8 Paço do Lumiar, 1600-762 Lisbon; tel. (21) 0306700; fax (21) 7593983; e-mail ieei@ieei.pt; internet www.ieet.pt; f. 1980; Dir ÁLVARO DE VASCONCELOS; publs include *O Mundo em Português* and *Estratégia, Cadernos do Lumiar*.

RUSSIA

Council of Afro-Asian Studies: Afro-Aziatskiye Obshchestvo, Istoria i Sovremnost, Institut Vostokovedeniya, Institut Afriki, Rossiyskaya Akad. Nauk, 123001 Moscow, 30/1 Spiridonovka; tel. (495) 2026650; e-mail info@inafr.ru; internet www.inafr.ru; Chair. A. M. VASSILIEV; publ. *Vostok (Oriens)* (6 a year).

Institute of World Economy and International Relations (IMEMO): 117997 Moscow, ul. Profsoyuznaya 23; tel. (495) 1204332; fax (495) 1206575; e-mail simonia@imemo.ru; f. 1956; Dir SIMONIA NODARI; publs include *Otnosheniya* (monthly).

Moscow State Institute of International Relations (MGIMO): 117454 Moscow, Vernadskogo pr. 76; tel. (495) 4349158; fax (495) 4349066; internet www.mgimo.ru; f. 1944; library of 718,000 vols; Rector ANATOLII V. TURKUNOV; publ. *Moscow Journal of International Law*.

Moscow State University Institute of Asian and African Studies: 103009 Moscow, Mokhovaja 11; tel. (495) 2036476; fax (495) 2033647; e-mail office@iaas.msu.ru; internet www.iaas.msu.ru.

SAUDI ARABIA

King Faisal Centre for Research and Islamic Studies: POB 5149, Riyadh 11543; tel. (1) 4652255; internet www.kff.com; f. 1983; advances research and studies into Islamic civilization; provides grants for research and organizes symposia, lectures and confs on Islamic matters; library of over 30,000 vols and periodicals; Dir-Gen. Dr ZEID AL-HUSAIN; publ. *Newsletter*.

SENEGAL

Council for the Development of Social Science Research in Africa (CODESRIA): ave Cheikh Anta Diop, angle Canal IV, BP 3304, Dakar; tel. 825-98-22; fax 824-12-89; e-mail codesria@codesria.sn; internet www.codesria.org; f. 1973; pan-African org., focusing on the social sciences; Exec. Sec. ADEBAYO OLUKOSHI; publs include *Africa Development* (quarterly), *African Sociological Review* (biannually), *African Journal of International Affairs* (biannually) and *CODESRIA Bulletin* (quarterly).

SOUTH AFRICA

Africa Institute of South Africa: Nipilar House, cnr Hamilton and Vermeulen Sts, Arcadia, Pretoria 0083; tel. (12) 3286970; fax (12) 3238153; e-mail ai@ai.org.za; internet www.ai.org.za; f. 1960; undertakes research and collects and disseminates information on all aspects of continental Africa and its offshore islands, with particular focus on politics, economics and devt issues; library of about 66,500 vols and periodicals; Dir Dr EDDY MALOKA; publs include *Africa Insight* (quarterly).

Centre for African Studies: University of Cape Town, Faculty of Humanities, Private Bag, Rondebosch 7701; tel. (21) 6502308; fax (21) 6861505; e-mail africas@humanities.uct.ac.za; internet www.africanstudies.uct.ac.za; f. 1976; incorporates the Harry Oppenheimer Inst. for African Studies; promotes comparative study of Africa and research; offers multi-disciplinary courses at postgraduate level; Dir Prof. BRENDA COOPER; publs include *Social Dynamics* (2 a year).

Institute for Advanced Social Research: University of the Witwatersrand, 1 Jan Smuts Ave, Private Bag 3, Wits 2050, Johannesburg; tel. (11) 7162414; fax (11) 7168030; f. 1973; Dir Prof. CHARLES VAN ONSELEN.

Institute for the Study of Man in Africa (ISMA): Rm 2B17, University of the Witwatersrand Medical School, York Rd, Parktown, Johannesburg 2193; tel. (11) 7172203; fax (11) 6434318; e-mail 055JSK@chiron.wits.ac.za; internet www.wits.ac.za/isma; f. 1960 to perpetuate the work of the late Prof. Raymond A. Dart on the study of man in Africa, past and present; serves as a centre of anthropological and related field work; publs include the Raymond Dart series and occasional papers.

National Research Foundation: Meiring Naudé Rd, Brummeria, POB 2600, Pretoria; tel. (12) 4814000; fax (12) 3491179; e-mail info@nrf.ac.za; internet www.nrf.ac.za; f. 1999; govt agency, responsible for supporting and promoting research; CEO Dr KHOTSO MOKHELE; Chair. Prof. DAYA REDDY.

South African Institute of Race Relations: POB 31044, Braamfontein 2017; tel. (11) 4033600; fax (11) 4033671; e-mail sairr@milkyway.co.za; f. 1929; research, education, publishing; library;

4,313 mems, 600 affiliated bodies; Pres. Prof. THEMBA SONO; Dir J. KANE-BERMAN; publs include *Fast Facts* (monthly), *Frontiers of Freedom* (quarterly), *South Africa Survey* (annually).

SPAIN

Cátedra UNESCO de Estudios Afroiberoamericanos: Departamento de Fundamentos de Economía, Facultad de Ciencias Económicas, Universidad de Alcalá 28801 Alcalá de Henares; tel. (91) 8855233; fax (91) 8854239; e-mail luis.beltran@uah.es; f. 1994; promotes and co-ordinates co-operation with African universities and research centres; organizes seminars, lectures, exhibitions and courses, as well as publishing books and promoting scholarly exchanges, on African influences in Iberian America; Dir Dr LUIS BELTRÁN.

Centro de Información y Documentación Africanas (CIDAF): Gaztambide 31, 28015 Madrid; tel. (1) 915441818; fax (1) 915497789; e-mail cidaf@planalfa.es; internet www3.planalfa.es/cidaf; f. 1979; seminars and lectures; specialized library of 16,000 vols and periodicals; Dir ODILO COUGIL; Chief Librarian RAFAEL SÁNCHEZ SANZ; publs include *Noticias de Africa* (monthly), *Cuadernos del CIDAF*.

Colegio Mayor Universitario Nuestra Señora de Africa: Avda Ramiro de Maeztu s/n, Ciudad Universitaria, 28040 Madrid; tel. (1) 5540104; fax (1) 5540401; e-mail cmunsa@telcom.es; f. 1964; attached inst. of the Complutense Univ. of Madrid and the Spanish Ministry of Foreign Affairs; linguistic studies and cultural activities; Dir BASILIO RODRÍGUEZ CAÑADA.

Mundo Negro: Arturo Soria 101, 28043 Madrid; tel. (1) 4158000; fax (1) 5192550; e-mail mundonegro@combonianos.com; internet www .combonianos.com; f. 1960; holds lectures; library and museum; Dir Fr FRANCISCO CARRERA AUGUSTO; publ. *Mundo Negro* (monthly).

SWEDEN

Institutet för Internationell Ekonomi (Institute for International Economic Studies): 106 91 Stockholm; tel. (8) 162000; fax (8) 161443; e-mail postmaster@iies.su.se; internet www.iies.su.se; attached to Stockholm Univ.; f. 1962; Dir Prof. TORSTEN PERSSON.

Nordiska Afrikainstitutet (The Nordic Africa Institute): POB 1703, 751 47 Uppsala; tel. (18) 562200; fax (18) 562290; e-mail nai@nai.uu.se; internet www.nai.uu.se; f. 1962; documentation, information and research centre for contemporary African affairs, publication work, lectures and seminars; library of 60,000 vols and 6,000 periodicals; Dir LENNART WOHLGEMUTH; publs include *Current African Issues*, *News from the Nordic Africa Institute*, seminar proceedings, research reports, discussion papers, annual report.

Utrikespolitiska Institutet (Swedish Institute of International Affairs): Lilla Nygatan 23, POB 1253, 111 82 Stockholm; tel. (8) 234060; fax (8) 201049; e-mail siia@ui.se; internet www.ui.se; f. 1938; promotes studies of international affairs; library of c. 20,000 vols and 400 periodicals; Pres. Ambassador LEIF LEIFLAND; Dir ANDERS MELLBOURN; publs include *Världspolitikens Dagsfrågor*, *Världens Fakta*, *Internationella Studier*, *Länder i fickformat*, *Yearbook*, conference papers, research reports (in English).

SWITZERLAND

Institut universitaire d'études du développement (IUED): 20 rue Rothschild, CP 136, 1211 Geneva 21; tel. (22) 9084365; fax (22) 9086273; e-mail Nathalie.Tanner@iued.unige.ch; internet www .iued.unige.ch; f. 1961; a centre of higher education and research into devt problems of Africa, Latin America, Asia and Eastern Europe; conducts courses, seminars and practical work; Dir MICHEL CARTON; publs include *Annuaire suisse de politique de développement*, *Itinéraires*.

Institut universitaire de hautes études internationales: 132 rue de Lausanne, BP 36, 1211 Geneva 21; tel. (22) 9085700; fax (22) 9085710; internet heiwww.unige.ch; f. 1927; a research and teaching institution studying international judicial, historical, political and economic questions; Dir PETER TSCHOPP.

UNITED KINGDOM

African Studies Association of the United Kingdom: School of Oriental and African Studies, Thornhaugh St, Russell Sq., London, WC1H 0XG; tel. (20) 7898-4390; e-mail asa@soas.ac.uk; internet www.asauk.net; f. 1963 to advance academic studies relating to Africa by providing facilities for the interchange of information and ideas; holds inter-disciplinary confs and symposia; 575 mems; Pres. Prof. GRAHAM FURNISS; Hon. Sec. Dr INSA NOLTE.

African Studies Centre: Free School Lane, Cambridge, CB2 3RQ; tel. and fax (1223) 334396; e-mail african-studies@lists.cam.ac.uk; internet www.african.cam.ac.uk; attached inst. of the Univ. of Cambridge; Dir Dr ATO QUAYSON.

Bradford Centre for International Development (BCID): University of Bradford, Bradford, West Yorkshire, BD7 1DP; tel. (1274) 233980; fax (1274) 235280; e-mail bcid@bradford.ac.uk; internet www.brad.ac.uk/acad/bcid; f. 1969; undergraduate economics and postgraduate devt degrees, professional training, research and consultancy in economic and social policy; an attached inst. of the Univ. of Bradford; Head of Centre PATRICK RYAN; publs include research papers.

Centre for the Study of African Economies: Dept of Economics, University of Oxford, Manor Rd Bldg, Manor Rd, Oxford, OX1 3UQ; tel. (1865) 271084; fax (1865) 281447; e-mail csae.enquiries@ economics.oxford.ac.uk; internet www.csae.ox.ac.uk; Dir Prof. P. COLLIER; publ. *Journal of African Economies* (quarterly).

Centre of African Studies: University of London, School of Oriental and African Studies, Thornhaugh Street, Russell Sq., London, WC1H 0XG; tel. (20) 7898-4370; fax (20) 7898-4369; e-mail cas@soas.ac.uk; internet www.cas.ed.ac.uk; f. 1965; co-ordinates interdisciplinary study, research and discussion on Africa; Chair. Prof. CHRISTOPHER CRAMER.

Centre of African Studies: University of Edinburgh, 21 George Sq., Edinburgh, EH8 9LD, Scotland; tel. (131) 650-3878; fax (131) 650-6535; e-mail africanstudies@ed.ac.uk; internet www.ed.ac.uk/ centas; f. 1962; postgraduate studies; Dir Prof. PAUL NUGENT; publs include occasional paper series and annual conference proceedings.

Centre of West African Studies: The University of Birmingham, School of Historical Studies, Edgbaston, Birmingham, B15 2TT; tel. (121) 4145128; fax (121) 4143228; e-mail CWAS@bham.ac.uk; internet www.bham.ac.uk/WestAfricanStudies/index.htm; Dir Dr LYNNE BRYDON.

Institute of Commonwealth Studies (ICS): 28 Russell Sq., London, WC1B 5DS; tel. (20) 7862-8844; fax (20) 7862-8820; e-mail ics@sas.ac.uk; internet www.sas.ac.uk/ commonwealthstudies/index.htm; f. 1949; conducts postgraduate research in social sciences and recent history relating to the Commonwealth; library of 180,000 vols and archive of 140 collections, including party-political and trade-union material; Dir Prof. RICHARD CROOK.

Institute of Development Studies: University of Sussex, Brighton, East Sussex, BN1 9RE; tel. (1273) 606261; fax (1273) 621202; e-mail ids@ids.ac.uk; internet www.ids.ac.uk; f. 1966; research, training, postgraduate teaching, advisory work, information services; Dir Prof. LAWRENCE HADDAD; publs *IDS Bulletin* (quarterly).

International African Institute (IAI): School of Oriental and African Studies, Thornhaugh St, Russell Sq., London, WC1H 0XG; tel. (20) 7898-4420; fax (20) 7898-4419; e-mail iai@soas.ac.uk; internet www.iaionthe.net; f. 1926 to promote the study of African peoples, their languages, cultures and social life in their traditional and modern settings; holds seminars and conducts projects; Chair. Prof. V. Y. MUDIMBE; publs include *Africa* (quarterly), *Africa Bibliography* (annually), monograph and reprint series.

Leeds University Centre for African Studies: University of Leeds, Leeds, West Yorkshire, LS2 9JT; tel. (113) 3435069; e-mail african-studies@leeds.ac.uk; internet www.leeds.ac.uk/lucas; a liaison unit for all depts with African interests; organizes public seminars and conferences; publ. *Leeds African Studies Bulletin* (annually).

Overseas Development Institute (ODI): 111 Westminster Bridge Rd, London, SE1 7JD; tel. (20) 7922-0300; fax (20) 7922-0399; e-mail publications@odi.org.uk; internet www.odi.org.uk; f. 1960 as a research centre and forum for the discussion of devt issues and problems; publishes its research findings in books and working papers; Chair. Baroness JAY; Dir SIMON MAXWELL; publs include *Development Policy Review* (quarterly), *Disasters* (quarterly).

Progressio: Unit 3, Canonbury Yard, 190 A New North Rd, London, N1 7BJ; tel. (20) 7354-0883; fax (20) 7359-0017; e-mail enquiries@ progressio.org.uk; internet www.progressio.org.uk; f. 1940; fmrly the Catholic Institute for International Relations (CIIR); information and analysis of socio-economic, political, church and human rights issues in the developing countries; Exec. Dir CHRISTINE ALLEN; publs include specialized studies on southern Africa and EU development policy.

Royal African Society: School of Oriental and African Studies, Thornhaugh St, Russell Sq., London, WC1H 0XG; tel. (20) 7898-4390; e-mail ras@soas.ac.uk; internet www.royalafricansociety.org; f. 1901; 1,000 mems; Chair. Lord HOLME OF CHELTENHAM; Exec. Dir RICHARD DOWDEN; Sec. M. L. ALLAN; publ. *African Affairs* (quarterly).

Royal Institute of International Affairs: Chatham House, 10 St James's Sq., London, SW1Y 4LE; tel. (20) 7957-5700; fax (20) 7957-5710; e-mail contact@riia.org; internet www.riia.org; f. 1920; independent body, which aims to promote the study and understanding of international affairs; over 300 corporate mems; library of 160,000 vols and 650 periodicals; Chair. Dr DEANNE JULIUS; Dir Dr VICTOR

BULMER-THOMAS; publs include *International Affairs* (5 a year), *The World Today* (monthly).

School of Development Studies: University of East Anglia, Norwich, NR4 7TJ; tel. (1603) 592807; fax (1603) 451999; e-mail dev.general@uea.ac.uk; internet www.uea.ac.uk/dev; Dean Prof. MICHAEL STOCKING.

School of Oriental and African Studies: Thornhaugh St, Russell Sq., London, WC1H 0XG; tel. (20) 7637-2388; fax (20) 7436-3844; e-mail study@soas.ac.uk; internet www.soas.ac.uk; f. 1916; a school of the Univ. of London; Dir Prof. COLIN BUNDY; Academic Registrar TERRY HARVEY; 220 teachers, incl. 44 professors; 3,220 students; publs *The Bulletin*, *Calendar*, *Annual Report*, *Journal of African Law*.

School of Oriental and African Studies Library: Thornhaugh St, Russell Sq., London, WC1H 0XG; tel. (20) 7898-4163; fax (20) 7898-4159; e-mail libenquiry@soas.ac.uk; internet www.soas.ac.uk/library/; f. 1916; 1.2m. vols and pamphlets; 4,500 current periodicals, 50,000 maps, 6,300 microforms, 2,800 MSS and private papers collections, extensive missionary archives, all covering Asian and African languages, literatures, philosophy, religions, history, law, cultural anthropology, art and archaeology, social sciences, geography and music; Librarian ANNE POULSON.

UNITED STATES OF AMERICA

Africa Action: 110 Maryland Ave, NE, Suite 508, Washington, DC 20002-5616; tel. (202) 546-7961; fax (202) 546-1545; e-mail africaaction@igc.org; internet www.africaaction.org; f. 2001 by merger of the Africa Fund, the Africa Policy Information Center and the American Committee on Africa; supports political, economic and social justice in Africa and, through the provision of information and analysis, aims to encourage positive US and international policies on African issues; Pres. Rev. Dr WYATT TEE WALKER; Exec. Dir SALIH BOOKER.

Africa-America Institute: 420 Lexington Ave, Suite 1706, New York, NY 10170; tel. (212) 949-5666; fax (212) 682-6174; e-mail aainy@aaionline.org; internet www.aaionline.org; f. 1953; organizes training programmes and offers devt assistance; maintains reps in 21 African countries; also sponsors confs and seminars; Pres. MORA MCLEAN; COO KOFI BOATENG.

Africa Center for Strategic Studies: National Defense University, 300 5th Ave, Building 62, Fort McNair, Washington, DC 20319-5066; tel. (202) 685-7300; fax (202) 685-3210; e-mail hejlikk@ndu.edu; internet www.africacenter.org; supports the devet of US strategic policy towards Africa by providing academic programs, fostering awareness of and dialogue on US strategic priorities and African security issues; Dir. PETER R. CHAVEAS.

African and Afro-American Studies Center: University of Texas, Jester Center A232A, Austin, TX 78705; tel. (512) 471-1784; fax (512) 471-1798; e-mail caaas@uts.cc.utexas.edu; internet www.utexas/edu/depts/caaas; f. 1969; Dir Prof. SHEILA S. WALKER; publs working papers and reprint series (irregular).

African Development Foundation: 1400 I St, NW, 10th Floor, Washington, DC 20005-2248; tel. (202) 673-3916; fax (202) 673-3810; e-mail info@adf.gov; internet www.adf.gov; f. 1984; an independent agency of the US Federal Govt focused on community-based devt; pursues strategic objectives in small- and micro-enterprise devt, trade and investment for African small businesses and HIV/AIDS prevention and mitigation; Pres. NATHANIEL FIELDS; publs include online news sources *ADF e-news* (monthly) and *The ADF Approach* (quarterly).

African Studies Association of the US: c/o African Studies Assen, Rutgers, The State University, 132 George St, New Brunswick, NJ 08901-1400; tel. (732) 932-8173; fax (732) 932-3394; e-mail members@rci.rutgers.edu; internet www.africanstudies.org; f. 1957; 2,700 mems; collects information on Africa; Pres. SANDRA BARNES; Exec. Dir Dr CAROL L. MARTIN; publs *African Studies Review*, *African Issues*, *ASA News*, *History in Africa*.

African Studies Center: Boston University, 270 Bay State Rd, Boston, MA 02215; tel. (617) 353-3673; fax (617) 353-4975; e-mail buasc@acs.bu.edu; internet www.bu.edu.AFR; f. 1953; research and teaching on archaeology, African languages, anthropology, economics, history, geography and political science of Africa; library of 125,000 vols and document titles, 1,000 periodicals and an extensive collection of non-current newspapers and periodicals; Dir Dr JAMES A. PRITCHETT; publs include *International Journal of African Historical Studies* (3 a year), working papers, discussion papers.

African Studies Center: Center for International Programs, Michigan State University, East Lansing, MI 48824; tel. (517) 353-1700; fax (517) 336-1209; e-mail africa@msu.edu; internet www.africa.msu.edu; f. 1960; Dir Dr DAVID WILEY; offers instruction in 30 African languages; library of over 200,000 vols; online resources include database of 11,000 films and videos on Africa; publs include *African Rural and Urban Studies* (3 a year), *Northeast African Studies* (3 a year).

African Studies Program: Ohio University, Yamada Intl House, Athens, OH 45701; tel. (740) 593-1834; fax (740) 593-1837; e-mail african.studies@ohio.edu; internet www.ohiou.edu/african; African politics, education, economics, geography, community health, anthropology, languages, literature, philosophy and history; related institutes Institute for the African Child; Dir Prof. STEPHEN HOWARD.

African Studies Program: Princeton University, 228 Bendheim Hall, Princeton, NJ 08544; tel. (609) 258-9400; f. 1961; Dir DANIEL RUBENSTEIN.

African Studies Program: University of Wisconsin-Madison, 205 Ingraham Hall, 1155 Observatory Drive, Madison, WI 53706; tel. (608) 262-2380; fax (608) 265-5851; e-mail asp@africa.wisc.edu; internet africa.wisc.edu; study courses; library of over 220,000 vols; Chair. Prof. MICHAEL SCHATZBERG; publs include *News and Notes* (biannually), *African Economic History* (annually), *Ghana Studies* (annually), *Mande Studies* (annually), occasional papers and African texts and grammars.

African Studies and Research Program: Dept of African Studies, Howard University, Washington, DC 20059; tel. (202) 238-2328; fax (202) 238-2326; e-mail rcummings@howard.edu; f. 1959; Chair. Dr ROBERT J. CUMMINGS; publs include monographs and occasional papers.

Africare: 440 R St, NW, Washington, DC 20001; tel. (202) 462-3614; fax (202) 387-1034; e-mail africare@africare.org; internet www.africare.org; f. 1971; supports programmes in agriculture, water resource devt, environmental man., health and emergency aid, as well as private-sector devt; Pres. JULIUS E. COLES; publs include *Newsletter* (2 a year).

Association of African Studies Programs: Dept of African and African-American Studies, 236 Grange Bldg, Penn State University, University Park, PA 16802; tel. (814) 863-4243; internet aaas.la.psu.edu; mems represent more than 40 centres of African studies at US colleges and univs; publ. *Newsletter* (2 a year).

Brookings Institution: 1775 Massachusetts Ave, NW, Washington, DC 20036-2188; tel. (202) 797-6000; fax (202) 797-6004; e-mail brookinfo@brook.edu; internet www.brookings.edu; f. 1916; research, education, and publishing in economics, govt and foreign policy; organizes confs and seminars; library of c. 75,000 vols and 700 periodicals; Pres. STROBE TALBOTT; publs include *The Brookings Review* (quarterly), *Brookings Papers on Economic Activity* (2 a year), *Brookings Trade Forum* (2 a year).

Center for African Studies: Stanford University, Encina Hall West, Room 210, Stanford, CA 94305-6045; tel. (650) 723-0295; fax (650) 723-3010; e-mail africanstudies@stanford.edu; internet africanstudies.stanford.edu; f. 1963; African languages, society, culture, foreign policy and social and behavioural sciences; holds research confs; offers jt degree in African studies for students enrolled in professional schools; Dir Prof. RICHARD ROBERTS; Assoc. Dir KIM RAPP.

Center for African Studies: 427 Grinter Hall, University of Florida, Gainesville, FL 32611; tel. (352) 392-2183; fax (352) 392-2435; e-mail villalon@africa.ufl.edu; internet web.africa.ufl.edu; encourages research projects and sponsors lectures, exhbns and confs; library of 50,000 vols, 500 periodical titles, 40,000 maps; Dir LEONARDO VILLALON; publ. *African Studies Quarterly*.

Center for African Studies: University of Illinois at Urbana-Champaign, 210 International Studies Bldg, 910 South Fifth St, Champaign, IL 61820; tel. (217) 333-6335; e-mail african@uiuc.edu; internet wsi.cso.uiuc.edu/CAS.

Center for International Studies: Massachusetts Institute of Technology, Bldg E38, Room 235, Cambridge, MA 02139; tel. (617) 253-8093; fax (617) 253-9330; internet web.mit.edu/cis; f. 1951; Dir RICHARD J. SAMUELS.

Council on Foreign Relations, Inc: 58 East 68th St, New York, NY 10021; tel. (212) 434-9400; fax (212) 434-9800; e-mail communications@cfr.org; internet www.cfr.org; f. 1921; 3,010 mems; library of 10,000 vols, 221 periodicals and databases; Pres. RICHARD N. HAASS; publs include *Foreign Affairs* (bimonthly).

Human Rights Watch/Africa: 350 Fifth Ave, 34th Floor, New York, NY 10118-3299; tel. (212) 290-4700; fax (212) 736-1300; e-mail hrwnyc@hrw.org; internet www.humanrightswatch.org; Chair. JONATHAN FANTON.

Institute of African Affairs: Duquesne University, 600 Forbes Ave, Pittsburgh, PA 15282; tel. (412) 434-6000; fax (412) 434-5146; f. 1957; research into uncommon languages of sub-Saharan Africa; library of 9,000 vols; Dir Rev. JOSEPH L. VARGA; publ. *African Reprint Series*.

Institute of African Studies: Columbia University School of International and Public Affairs, 420 West 118th St, New York, NY 10027; tel. (212) 854-4633; fax (212) 854-4639; e-mail mm1124@

columbia.edu; internet www.columbia.edu.cu/sipa/REGIONAL/IAS/index.html; Dir MAHMOOD MAMDANI.

Institute of World Affairs (IWA): 1321 Pennsylvania Ave, SE, Washington, DC 20003-2027; tel. (860) 544-4141; fax (860) 544-5115; e-mail info@iwa.org; internet www.iwa.org; f. 1924; conducts seminars on international issues; Pres. HRACH GREGORIAN; publ. *IWA International* (irregular).

James S. Coleman African Studies Center: University of California, Los Angeles, CA 90095-1310; tel. (310) 825-3686; fax (310) 206-2250; e-mail africa@international.ucla.edu; internet www.international.ucla.edu/africa; f. 1959; centre for co-ordination of and research on Africa in the social sciences, the arts, humanities, the sciences and public health; and for multi-disciplinary graduate training in African studies; Dir ALLEN ROBERTS; publs include *African Arts* (quarterly), *African Studies Center Newsletter* (2 a year), *UFAHAMU* (quarterly).

Library of International Relations: Chicago-Kent College of Law, Illinois Institute of Technology, 565 West Adams St, Chicago, IL 60661-3691; tel. (312) 906-5600; fax (312) 906-5679; internet www.infoctr.edu; f. 1932; financed by voluntary contributions; stimulates interest and research in international problems; conducts seminars and offers special services to businesses and academic institutions; library of 520,000 items; Pres. HOKEN SEKI; Dir MICKIE A. VOGES; publ. *Newsletter* (5 a year).

Princeton Institute for International and Regional Studies: Bendheim Hall, Princeton University, Princeton, NJ 08544-1022; tel. (609) 258-4851; fax (609) 258-3988; e-mail pzimmer@princeton.edu; internet www.princeton.edu/~piirs; f. 2003; Dir MIGUEL A. CENTENO; publ. *World Politics* (quarterly).

Program of African and Asian Languages: Northwestern University, 4–400 Kresge Hall, 1880 Campus Drive, Evanston, IL 60208-2209; tel. (847) 491-5288; fax (847) 467-1097; e-mail r.susan@northwestern.edu; internet www.cas.northwestern.edu/paal; f. 1973; Dir RICHARD M. LEPINE.

Program of African Studies: Northwestern University, 620 Library Place, Evanston, IL 60208-4110; tel. (847) 491-7323; fax (847) 491-3739; e-mail african-studies@northwestern.edu; internet www.northwestern.edu/african-studies; f. 1948; supported by various private and govt grants for research in Africa and the USA, as well as by university; awards undergraduate minor and graduate certificate of African studies to students enrolled at Northwestern University; sponsors fellowship awards for African students pursuing doctoral studies at Northwestern University; also sponsors brief residencies for students and practitioners of the African humanities; Dir Prof. RICHARD JOSEPH; publs include *PAS Newsletter*, *PAS Working Paper* series, conference proceedings.

School of Advanced International Studies: Johns Hopkins University, 1740 Massachusetts Ave, NW, Washington, DC 20036-1983; tel. (202) 663-5676; fax (202) 663-5683; e-mail africanstudies@jhu.edu; internet www.sais-jhu.edu; Dean JESSICA EINHORN; Dir of African Studies PETER LEWIS; publs *SAIS Studies on Africa*, *SAIS African Library*.

TransAfrica Forum: 1426 21st St, NW, Second Floor, Washington, DC 20036; tel. (202) 223-1960; fax (202) 223-1966; e-mail info@transafricaforum.org; internet www.transafricaforum.org; f. 1981; Pres. BILL FLETCHER, Jr.

Woodrow Wilson School of Public and International Affairs (African Studies Program): Bendheim Hall, Princeton University, Princeton, NJ 08540; tel. (609) 258-5633; fax (609) 258-5974; e-mail herbst@princeton.edu; Program Dir Prof. JEFFREY HERBST.

VATICAN CITY

Pontificio Instituto di Studi Arabi e d'Islamistica: Viale di Trastevere 89, 00153 Rome; tel. (06) 58392611; fax (06) 5882595; e-mail info@pisai.org; internet www.pisai.org; f. 1949; library of 30,000 vols; Dir P. JUSTO LACUNZA BALDA; publs include *Encounter* (monthly), *Islamochristiana* (annually), *Etudes arabes* (annually).

SELECT BIBLIOGRAPHY (BOOKS)

See also bibliographies at end of relevant chapters in Part Two.

Abbink, Jon, and Hesseling, Gerti. *Election Observation and Democratization in Africa*. London, Palgrave Macmillan, 1999.

Adamoleku, Ladipo (Ed.). *Public Administration in Africa*. Boulder, CO, Westview Press, 1999.

Adams, W. M. *The Physical Geography of Africa*. Oxford, Oxford University Press, 1999.

Addison, Tony (Ed.). *From Conflict to Recovery in Africa*. Oxford, Oxford University Press, 2003.

Adebajo, Adekeye, and Rashid, Ismail (Eds). *West Africa's Security Challenges: Building Peace in a Troubled Region*. Boulder, CO, Lynne Rienner, 2004.

Adedeji, Adebayo. *South Africa and Africa: Within or Apart?* London, Zed Publishing/African Centre for Strategic Studies and Development, 1996.

Adepoju, Aderanti (Ed.). *Family, Population and Development in Africa*. London, Zed Publishing, 1997.

Adu Boahen, A. *African Perspectives on Colonialism*. Baltimore, MD, Johns Hopkins University Press, 1992.

Adu Boahen, A. (Ed.). *UNESCO General History of Africa*. Berkeley, CA, University of California Press, 1993.

African Centre for Monetary Studies. *Debt Conversion Schemes in Africa*. Oxford, James Currey Publishers, 1992.

Agyeman, Opoku. *Africa's Persistent Vulnerable Link: Global Politics*. New York, NY, New York University Press, 2001.

Ajayi, J. F. A., and Crowder, M. *History of West Africa*. Cambridge, Cambridge University Press.

Ake, Claude. *Democracy and Development in Africa*. Washington, Brookings, 1996.

Akeya Agnango, George (Ed.). *Issues and Trends in Contemporary African Politics*. New York, NY, Peter Lang, 2003.

Akyuz, Yilma, and Gore, Charles. *African Development in a Comparative Perspective*. Oxford, James Currey Publishers, 2000.

Ali, Taisier M., and Matthews, Robert O. *Civil Wars in Africa: Roots and Resolution*. Montréal, QC, McGill-Queen's University Press, 1999.

Appiah, Kwame Anthony. *In My Father's House: A Statement of African Ideology*. Oxford, Oxford University Press, 1992.

Arnold, Guy. *A Guide to African Political and Economic Development*. London, Frank Cass, 2001.

Africa: A Modern History. Southend-on-Sea, Atlantic, 2006.

Aryeetey, Ernest, and Nissanke, Machiko. *Financial Integration and Development: Liberalization and Reform in Sub-Saharan Africa*. London, Routledge, 1998.

Asante, M. K. *The History of Africa: The Quest for Eternal Harmony*. London, Routledge, 2007.

Asante, S. K. *Regionism and Africa's Development*. London, Palgrave Macmillan, 1997.

Asiwaju, Anthony I., and de Leeuw, M. E. J. A. (Eds). *Border Region Development in Africa: Focus on Eastern and Southern Sub-Regions*. Nagoya, United Nations Centre for Regional Development, 1998.

Assensoh, A. B., and Alex-Assensoh, Yvette M. *African History and Politics*. London, Palgrave Macmillan, 2003.

Austen, Ralph. *African Economic History*. Cambridge, Cambridge University Press, 1987.

Ayittey, George B. N. *Africa in Chaos*. London, Palgrave Macmillan, 1998.

Africa Unchained. New York, NY, Palgrave Macmillan, 2005.

Bach, Daniel. *State and Society in Francophone Africa since Independence*. London, Palgrave Macmillan, 1995.

Regionalisation in Africa. Oxford, James Currey Publishers, 1999.

Bakut, Bakut Tswah, and Dutt, Sagarika. *Africa at the Millennium*. London, Palgrave Macmillan, 2000.

Banham, Martin (Ed.). *Southern Africa*. Oxford, James Currey Publishers, 2004.

Bardhan, Pranab. *International Trade, Growth and Development*. Malden, MA, Blackwell Publishing, 2002.

Barratt Brown, Michael. *Africa's Choices after Thirty Years of the World Bank*. Boulder, CO, Westview Press, 1997.

Bart, François, and Lenoble-Bart, Annie. *Afrique des réseaux et mondialisation*. Paris, Editions Karthala, 2003.

Basu, Anupam *et al*. *Foreign Direct Investment in Africa: Some Case Studies*. Washington, DC, IMF Publications, 2002.

Bates, R. *Essays on the Political Economy of Rural Africa*. Berkely, CA, University of California Press, 1987.

Bayart, Jean-François. *The State in Africa: The Politics of the Belly*. London, Longman, 1993.

Bayart, Jean-François *et al*. *The Criminalisation of the State in Africa*. Bloomington, IN, Indiana University Press, 1999.

Beauchamp, Claude. *Démocratie, Culture et Développement en Afrique noire*. Paris, L'Harmattan, 1997.

Beinart, William, and McGregor, Jo Ann (Eds). *Social History and African Environments*. Athens, OH, Ohio University Press, 2003.

Belshaw, D., and Livingstone, I. *Renewing Development in Sub-Saharan Africa*. London, Routledge, 2001.

Ben Hammouda, Hakim. *Afrique: Pour un nouveau contrat de développement*. Paris, L'Harmattan, 2000.

Ben Hammouda, Hakim, and Kasse, Moustapha. *L'avenir de la zone franc*. Paris, Editions Karthala, 2001.

Berger, Iris, and White, E. Frances. *Women in Sub-Saharan Africa: Restoring Women to History*. Bloomington, IN, Indiana University Press, 1999.

Berkeley, Bill. *The Graves are Not Yet Full: race, tribe and power in the heart of Africa*. Oxford, Basic Books, 2003.

Bernault, Florence. *Démocraties ambigues en Afrique Centrale: Congo-Brazzaville, Gabon 1940–65*. Paris, Editions Karthala, 1996.

Berry, Sara. *No Condition is Permament: The Social Dynamics of Agrarian Change in Sub-Saharan Africa*. Madison, University of Wisconsin Press, 1993.

Berthélemy, Jean-Claude. *Will There Be New Emerging Market Economies in Africa by the Year 2020?* Washington, DC, IMF Publications, 2002.

Bhalla, Surjit S. *Imagine There's No Country: Poverty, Inequality and Growth in the Era of Globalization*. Washington, DC, Institute for International Economics, 2002.

Birmingham, David. *The Decolonization of Africa*. Athens, OH, Ohio University Press, 1996.

Birmingham, David, and Martin, Phyllis. *History of Central Africa: The Contemporary Years since 1960*. London, Longman, 1998.

Bond, George. *Aids in Africa and the Caribbean*. Boulder, CO, Westview Press, 2002.

Contested Terrains and Constructed Categories: Contemporary Africa in Focus. Boulder, CO, Westview Press, 1997.

Boulden, Jane. *Dealing with Conflict in Africa*. London, Palgrave Macmillan, 2004.

Bratton, Michael, and Van de Walle, Nicholas. *Democratic Experiments in Africa: Regime Transitions in Comparative Perspective*. Cambridge, Cambridge University Press, 1997.

Brauer, Jurgen, and Hartley, Keith. *The Economics of Regional Security*. London, Routledge, 2000.

Bridges, Roy. *Imperialism, Decolonization and Africa*. London, Palgrave Macmillan, 1999.

Broch-Due, Vigdis. *Violence and Belonging*. London, Routledge, 2004.

Brownbridge, Martin, and Harvey, Charles. *Banking in Africa*. Oxford, James Currey Publishers, 1998.

Brune, Stefan, *et al*. *Africa and Europe: Relations of Two Continents in Transition*. Hamburg, LIT Verlag, 1994.

Calamitsis, E. A. *Adjustment and Growth in Sub-Saharan Africa*. Washington, DC, IMF Publications, 2000.

Cambridge University Press. *Cambridge History of Africa*. Cambridge, Cambridge University Press.

Chabal, Patrick. *Africa Works: Disorder as Political Instrument*. Oxford, James Currey Publishers, 1999.

Chabal, Patrick, *et al*. *A History of Postcolonial Lusophone Africa*. London, Hurst and Company, 2002.

Chabal, Patrick, and Deloz, Jean-Pascal. *L'Afrique est partie!* Paris, Economica, 1999.

Chazan, Naomi, *et al*. *Politics and Society in Contemporary Africa*. Boulder, CO, Lynne Rienner Publishers, 1999.

Choucane-Verdier, Audrey. *Libéralisation financière et croissance économique: le cas de l'Afrique subsaharienne*. Paris, L'Harmattan, 2001.

Chrétien, Jean-Pierre. *The Great Lakes of Africa: 2,000 years of history*. New York, NY, Zone, 2003.

Christopher, A. J. *Atlas of Changing Africa*. London, Routledge, 2000.

Clapham, Christopher. *Africa and the International System: The Politics of State Survival*. Cambridge, Cambridge University Press, 1996.

Clapp, Jennifer. *Adjustment and Agriculture in Africa*. London, Palgrave Macmillan, 1997.

Clarke, John F. *Political Reform in Francophone Africa*. Boulder, CO, Westview Press, 1996.

Clarke, P. *West Africans at War*. Ethnographica.

Cleaver, Kevin M., and Graeme Donovan, W. *Agriculture, pauvreté et réforme des politiques en Afrique Sub-saharienne*. Guinea, Editions Ganndal, 2000.

Club du Sahel. *Preparing for the Future—A Vision of West Africa in the Year 2020*. Paris, OECD, 1999.

Cohen, Abner. *Custom and Politics in Urban Africa*. London, Frank Cass, 2003.

Coleman, James S. *Nationalism and Development in Africa: Selected Essays*. Berkeley, CA, University of California Press, 1994.

Collins, R. *Historical Problems of Imperial Africa*. Princeton, NJ, Markus Wiener, 1998.

Constantin, François, and Coulon, Christian. *Réligion et transition démocratique en Afrique*. Paris, Editions Karthala, 1997.

Cooper, Frederick. *Africa Since 1940: The Past of the Present*. Cambridge, Cambridge University Press, 2002.

Decolonization and African Society. Cambridge, Cambridge University Press, 1996.

Coquery-Vidrovitch, Catherine. *African Women: A Modern History*. Boulder, CO, Westview Press,1997.

Africa: Endurance and Change South of the Sahara. Berkeley, CA, University of California Press, 1998.

Cowan, Michael, and Laakso, Liisa. *Multiparty Elections in Africa*. Oxford, James Currey Publishers, 2002.

Cruise O'Brien, Donal, *et al* (Eds). *Contemporary West African States*. Cambridge, Cambridge University Press, 1990.

Curtin, P., *et al*. *African History*. London, Longman,1995.

D'Almeida Topor, Helene, Coquery-Vidrovitch, Catherine, and Georg, Odile (Eds). *Les jeunes en Afrique*. Paris, L'Harmattan, 1992.

Daumont, Roland, *et al*. *Banking in Sub-Saharan Africa: What went wrong?* Washington, DC, IMF Institute, 2004.

Davids, Yul, *et al*. *Measuring Democracy and Human Rights in Southern Africa*. Uppsala, Nordic Africa Institute, 2002.

Davidson, Basil. *Africa in History: Themes and Outlines*. London, Simon and Schuster, 1995.

African Civilization Revisited. Trenton, NJ, Africa World Press, 1993.

The Black Man's Burden: Africa and the Curse of the Nation-State. Oxford, James Currey Publishers, 1992.

Let Freedom Come. Boston, MA, Little, Brown & Co.

Modern Africa. London, Longman, 1989.

De Waal, Alex. *Famine Crimes: Politics and the Disaster Relief Industry in Africa*. Oxford, James Currey Publishers, 1997.

Debrun, Xavier, Masson, Paul R. and Pattillo, Catherine A. *Monetary Union in West Africa: Who Might Gain, Who Might Lose, and Why?* Washington, DC, IMF Publication Services, 2003.

Decalo, Samuel. *Coups and military rule in Africa: Motivations and Constraints*. Newhaven, Yale University Press, CT, 1990.

Deng, Francis M., and Lyons, Terrence. *Africa Reckoning: A Quest for Good Governance*. Washington, DC, Brookings Institution Press, 1998.

Dessart, Michael A. *Capacity Building, Governance and Economic Reform in Africa*. Washington, DC, IMF Publication Services, 2002.

Diamond, Larry, Linz, Juan J., and Lipset, Seymour M. (Eds). *Democracy in Developing Countries: Africa*. Boulder, CO, Lynne Rienner Publishers, 1988.

Diamond, Larry, and Plattner, Marc F. (Eds). *Nationalism, Ethnic Conflict and Democracy*. Baltimore, MD, Johns Hopkins University Press, 1997.

Diawara, Manthia. *In Search of Africa*. Cambridge, MA, Harvard University Press, 1998.

Dibie, Robert (Ed.). *Non-governmental Organizations and Sustainable Development in sub-Saharan Africa*. Lanham, MD, Lexington Books, 2007.

Diop, Momar-Coumba, and Diouf, Mamadou. *Les Figures du politique en Afrique: Des pouvoirs hérités aux pouvoirs élus*. Paris, Editions Karthala, 1999.

Diouf, Makhtar. *L'Afrique dans la mondialisation*. Paris, L'Harmattan, 2002.

Doo Kinge, Michel. *Quelle démocratie en Afrique?* Senegal, Nouvelles Editions Africaines de Senegal, 1999.

Dussey, Robert. *L'Afrique face au sida*. Côte d'Ivoire, Editions Bognini.

Ehui, Félix T. *L'Afrique noire: de la superpuissance au sous-développement*. Côte d'Ivoire, Nouvelles Editions Ivoiriennes, 2002.

Elbadawi, Ibrahim, and Ndula, Benno. *Economic Development in SubSaharan Africa. Proceedings of the Eleventh World Congress of the International Economic Association, Tunis*. London, Palgrave Macmillan, 2001.

Ellis, Stephen. *Africa Now*. Oxford, James Currey Publishers, 1996.

Engelhard, Philippe. *L'Afrique: Plaidoyer pour une nouvelle économie*. Senegal, Enda tiers-monde.

Englebert, Pierre. *State Legitimacy and Development in Africa*. Boulder, CO, Lynne Rienner Publishers, 2000.

Europa Publications. *A Political Chronology of Africa*. London, Europa Publications, 2001.

Eyene-Mba, J. *Afrique sur le chemin de la croissance et de l'évolution*. Paris, L'Harmattan, 2003.

Fage, John (updated by Tordoff, William). *A History of Africa*. London, Frank Cass, 2001.

Falola, Toyin. *Nationalism and African Intellectuals*. Rochester, NY, University of Rochester Press, 2001.

Forest People's Programme. *From Principles to Practice*. 2003.

French, Howard W. *A Continent for the Taking: The Tragedy and Hope of Africa*. New York, NY, Alfred A. Knopf, 2004.

Freund, Bill. *The Making of Contemporary Africa*. London, Palgrave Macmillan, 1998.

Fuller, Bruce. *Government Confronts Culture: The Struggle for Local Democracy in Southern Africa*. London, Garland Science, 1999.

Funke, Norbert. *The New Partnership for Africa's Development (NEPAD): Opportunities and Challenges*. Washington, DC, IMF Institute, 2003.

Futurs africains. *Afrique 2025*. Paris, Editions Karthala, 2003.

Gebissa, Ezekiel. *Leaf of Allah: Khat and Agricultural Transformation*. Oxford, James Currey Publishers, 2005.

Geda, Alemayehu. *Finance and Trade in Africa*. London, Palgrave Macmillan, 2002.

Ghaia, Dharam. *Renewing Social and Economic Progress in Africa*. London, Palgrave Macmillan, 2000.

Gikandi, Simon. *Encyclopaedia of African Literature*. London, Routledge, 2003.

Gooneratne, Wilbert, and Mbilinyi, Marjorie (Eds). *Reviving Local Self-reliance: People's Responses to the Economic Crisis in Eastern and Southern Africa*. Nagoya, United Nations Centre for Regional Development, 1992.

Gordon, April A., and Donald L. (Eds). *Understanding Contemporary Africa*. Boulder, CO, Lynne Rienner Publishers, 2001.

Grosh, Barbara, and Mukandala, Rwekaza. *State-Owned Enterprises in Africa*. Boulder, CO, Lynne Rienner Publishers, 1993.

Gulliver, P. H. (Ed.). *Tradition and Transition in East Africa*. London, Routledge, 2004.

Gunning, Jan Willem, and Oostendorp, Remco. *Industrial Change in Africa*. London, Palgrave Macmillan, 2001.

Guyer, Jane. *Money Matters: Instability, Values and Social Payments in the Modern History of West African Communities*. Portsmouth, NH, Heinemann, 1995.

Gyimah-Boadi, E. *Democratic Reform in Africa: The Quality of Progress*. Boulder, CO, Lynne Rienner Publishers, 2004.

Harbeson, John W. *Africa in World Politics: The African State System in Flux*. Boulder, CO, Westview Press, 1999.

Harbeson, John W., Rothchild, Donald and Chazan, Naomi (Eds). *Civil Society and the State in Africa*. Boulder, CO, Lynne Rienner Publishers, 1994.

Hargreaves, J. D. *Decolonization in Africa*. London, Longman, 2003.

Harrison, Graham. *Issues in the Contemporary Politics of Sub-Saharan Africa*. London, Palgrave Macmillan, 2002.

The World Bank and Africa. London, Frank Cass, 2004.

Hastings, Adrian. *The Construction of Nationhood: Ethnicity, Religion and Nationalism.* Cambridge, Cambridge University Press, 1997.

Havinden, Michael, and Meredith, David. *Colonialism and Development: Britain and its Tropical Colonies.* London, Routledge, 1993.

Herbst, Jeffrey. *States and Power in Africa: Comparative Lessons in Authority and Control.* Princeton, NJ, Princeton University Press, 2000.

Herbst, Jeffrey, and Mills, Greg. *The Future of Africa: A New Order in Sight?* Oxford, Oxford University Press, 2003.

Hiscox, Michael J. *International Trade and Political Conflict: Commerce, Coalitions and Mobility.* Princeton, NJ, Princeton University Press, 2002.

Hope, Christopher. *Brothers under the Skin: Travels in Tyranny.* London, Macmillan, 2003.

Hope, Kempe Ronald and Chikulo, Bornwell C. *Corruption and Development in Africa.* London, Palgrave Macmillan, 1999.

Hopkins, A. G. *An Economic History of West Africa.* Cambridge, Cambridge University Press.

Houngnikpo, Mathurin C. *L'Illusion démocratique en Afrique.* Paris, L'Harmattan, 2004.

Huband, Mark. *The Skull beneath the Skin: Africa and the Cold War.* Boulder, CO, Westview Press, 2002.

Hugon, Philippe. *La zone franc à l'heure de l'Euro.* Paris, Editions Karthala, 1999.

Hyden, Goran, and Bratton, Michael (Eds). *Governance and Politics in Africa.* Boulder, CO, Lynne Rienner Publishers, 1992.

Iliffe, John. *Africans: The History of a Continent.* Cambridge, Cambridge University Press, 1995.

Institute of African Studies. *African Perspectives: Selected Works.* Pretoria, Centre for Development Analysis, 1993.

Jackson, Robert, and Rosberg, Carl. *Personal Rule in Black Africa.* Berkeley, CA, University of California Press, 1982.

Jackson, Terence. *Management and Change in Africa.* London, Frank Cass, 2004.

Joseph, Richard (Ed.). *State, Conflict and Democracy in Africa.* Boulder, CO, Lynne Rienner Publishers, 1992.

Kabbaj, Omar. *The Challenge of African Development.* Oxford, Oxford University Press, 2003.

Kamate, Eli. *Quel développement pour l'Afrique?* Mali, Editions Jamana, 1997.

Kayizzi-Mugerwa, Steve. *The African Economy.* London, Frank Cass, 1998.

Kayizzi-Mugerwa, Steve, *et al. Towards a New Partnership with Africa.* Uppsala, Nordic Africa Institute, 2000.

Keller, E. J., and Rothchild, D. *Africa in the New International Order: Rethinking State Sovereignty and Regional Security.* Boulder, CO, Lynne Rienner Publishers, 1996.

Kidanu, Aklilu, and Kumssa, Asfaw (Eds). *Social Development in Africa.* Nairobi, United Nations Centre for Regional Development Africa Office, 2001.

Kingma, Kees. *Demobilization in Sub-Saharan Africa.* London, Palgrave Macmillan, 2000.

Kiros, Teodros (Ed.). *Explorations in African Political Thought.* London, Frank Cass, 2001.

Koser, Khalid (Ed.). *New African Diasporas.* London, Routledge, 2003.

Kouvouama, Abel. *Modernité africaine: Les figures du politique et du religieux.* Congo, Editions Paari, 2002.

Kumssa, Asfaw, and Khan, Haider A. (Eds). *Transnational Economies and Regional Economic Development Strategies: Lessons from Five Low-income Developing Countries.* Nagoya, United Nations Centre for Regional Development, 1996.

Lawrence, Peter, and Thirtle, Colin. *Africa and Asia in Comparative Economic Perspective.* London, Palgrave Macmillan, 2001.

Le Vine, Victor T. *Politics in Francophone Africa.* Boulder, CO, Lynne Rienner Publishers, 2004.

Lebeau, Yann, Niane, Boubacar, Piriou, Anne, and de Saint Marie, Monique. *Etat et acteurs émergents en Afrique.* Paris, Editions Karthala, 2003.

Leonard, David K., and Straus, Scott. *Africa's Stalled Development: International Causes and Cures.* Boulder, CO, Lynne Rienner Publishers, 2003.

Lewis, Peter. *Africa: Dilemmas of Development and Change.* Boulder, CO, Westview Press, 1998.

Lumumba-Kasongo, Tukumbi. *The Dynamics of Political and Economic Relations between Africa and the Foreign Powers: A Study in International Relations.* Westernport, CT, Praeger, 1998.

Political Re-Mapping of Africa: Transnational Ideology and Redefinition of Africa in World Politics. Lanham, MD, University Press of America, 1993.

The Rise of Multipartyism and Democracy in the Context of Contemporary Global Change: the Case of Africa. Westernport, CT, Praeger, 1998.

Lundahl, Mats (Ed.). *From Crisis to Growth in Africa.* London, Frank Cass, 2001.

Lynn, Martin. *Commerce and Economic Change in West Africa.* Cambridge, Cambridge University Press, 1997.

Mahadevan, V. *Contemporary African Politics and Development: A Comprehensive Bibliography, 1981–1990.* Boulder, CO, Lynne Rienner Publishers, 1995.

Mailafia, Obed O. *Europe and Economic Reform in Africa.* London, Frank Cass, 1997.

Magyar, Karl P., and Conteh-Morgan, Earl. *Peacekeeping in Africa.* London, Palgrave Macmillan, 1998.

Makhan, Vijay. *Economic Recovery in Africa.* London, Palgrave Macmillan, 2002.

Mamdami, Mahmood, and Wamba dia Wamba, Ernest. *African Studies in Social Movements and Democracy.* Dakar, CODESRIA, 1995.

Manning, Patrick. *Francophone Sub-Saharan Africa 1880–1995.* Cambridge, Cambridge University Press, 1999.

Martin, Denis-Constant. *Nouveaux langages du politique en Afrique orientale.* Paris, Editions Karthala, 1998.

Masson, Paul, *et al. Monetary Union in West Africa (ECOWAS).* Washington, DC, IMF Publications, 2001.

Maupeu, Hervé (Ed.). *L'Afrique Orientale: Annuaire 2003.* Paris, L'Harmattan, 2004.

Mazrui, Ali, and Mazrui, Alamin M. *The Power of Babel: Language and Governance in the African Experience.* Oxford, James Currey, 1998.

Mazumdar, Dipak, and Mazaher, Ata. *The African Manufacturing Firm.* London, Routledge, 2003.

McAleese, Dermot, *et al. Africa and the European Community after 1992.* Washington, DC, Economic Development Institute of the World Bank, 1993.

McDonald, David (Ed.). *On Borders: Perspectives on Internal Migration in Southern Africa.* New York, NY, St Martin's Press, 2000.

McEvedy, Colin. *The Penguin Atlas of African History.* London, Penguin Books, 1987.

McIntyre, W. David. *British Decolonization, 1946–1997.* London, Palgrave Macmillan, 1998.

Medard, Jean-François (Ed.). *Etats d'Afrique Noire: Formation, mécanismes et crises.* Paris, Editions Karthala, 1994.

Melber, Henning, *et al. The New Partnership for African Development (NEPAD): African Perspectives.* Uppsala, Nordic Africa Institute, 2002.

Mengistae, Taye, and Pattillo, Catherine A. *Export Orientation and Productivity in Sub-Saharan Africa.* Washington, DC, IMF Publications, 1989.

Meredith, Martin. *The Fate of Africa.* New York, NY, PublicAffairs, 2005.

Merlin, Pierre. *L'Afrique peut gagner.* Paris, Editions Karthala, 2001.

Middleton, John. *Encyclopaedia of Africa South of the Sahara.* New York, NY, Scribners, 1997.

Mikell, Gwendolyn (Ed.). *African Feminism: The Politics of Survival in Sub-Saharan Africa.* Philadelphia, PA, University of Pennsylvania Press, 1997.

Monga, Celestin. *The Anthropology of Anger: Civil Society and Democracy in Africa.* Boulder, CO, Lynne Rienner Publishers, 1996.

Mortimore, Michael. *Adapting to Drought: Farmers, Famines, and Desertification in West Africa.* Cambridge, Cambridge University Press, 1990.

Moser, Gary G., *et al. Economic Growth and Poverty Reduction in Africa.* Washington, DC, IMF Publications, 2001.

Mouandjo Lewis, Pierre. *Crise et croissance en Afrique.* Paris, L'Harmattan, 2002.

Muchie, Mammo (Ed.). *The Making of the African Nation: Pan-Africanism and the African Renaissance.* London, Adonis and Abbey, 2005.

Nohlen, Dieter, *et al* (Eds). *Elections in Africa: A Data Handbook.* Oxford, Oxford University Press, 1999.

Nordic Africa Institute. *Regionalism and Regional Integration in Africa.* Uppsala, Nordic Africa Institute, 2001.

Nugent, Paul. *Africa Since Independence.* London, Palgrave Macmillan, 2004.

Obudho, R. A. *Small Urban Centres in Africa: A Bibliographical Survey.* Nagoya, United Nations Centre for Regional Development, 1995.

OECD. *African Economic Outlook 2002/2003.* Paris, OECD.

Aid Activities in Africa 2002. Paris, OECD, 2004.

Privatisation in Sub-Saharan Africa: Where Do We Stand? Paris, OECD, 2004.

Regional Integration in Africa. Paris, OECD, 2002.

Towards a Better Regional Approach to Development in West Africa: Conclusions of the Special Event of Sahel and West Africa Club. Paris, OECD, 2002.

OECD Development Centre. *Conflict and Growth in Africa.* Paris, OECD, 1999.

Emerging Africa. Paris, OECD, 2002.

Reform and Growth in Africa. Paris, OECD, 2000.

Ohaegbelum, F. Ugboaja. *U.S. Policy in Postcolonial Africa: Four Case Studies in Conflict Resolution.* New York, NY, Peter Lang, 2004.

Oliver, Rowland. *The African Experience.* London, Weidenfeld & Nicolson, 1991.

Oliver, Rowland, and Fage, J. D. *A Short History of Africa.* London, Penguin Books, 1988.

Olowu, Dele, and Sako, Soumana (Eds). *Better Governance and Public Policy.* Bloomsfield, CT, Kumarian Press, 2003.

Olukoshi, Adebayo. *The Politics of Opposition in Contemporary Africa.* Uppsala, Nordic Africa Institute, 1998.

Olukoshi, Adebayo, and Liisa Laakso (Eds). *Challenges to the Nation-State in Africa.* Uppsala, Nordic Africa Institute, 1996.

Onwuka, Ralph I., and Shaw, Timothy M. *Africa in World Politics.* London, Palgrave Macmillan, 1989.

Oyejide, Ademola, Ndulu, Benno, and Greenaway, David. *Regional Integration and Trade Liberalization in Subsaharan Africa.* London, Palgrave Macmillan, 1999.

Pakenham, T. *The Scramble for Africa.* London, 1991.

Pathe Gueye, Semou. *Du bon usage de la démocratie en Afrique.* Dakar, Nouvelles Editions Africaines du Sénégal (NEAS), 2003.

Paulson, Jo Ann. *African Economies in Transition.* London, Palgrave Macmillan, 1999.

Prendergast, J. *Frontline Diplomacy: Humanitarian Aid and Conflict in Africa.* Boulder, CO, Lynne Rienner Publishers, 1996.

Quantin, Patrick (Ed.). *Voter en Afrique: comparaisons et differenciations.* Paris, L'Harmattan, 2004.

Reader, John. *Africa: A Biography of the Continent.* London, Penguin Books, 1998.

Reno, William. *Warlord Politics and African States.* Boulder, CO, Lynne Rienner Publishers, 1999.

Reynolds, Andrew. *Electoral Systems and Democratization in Southern Africa.* Oxford, Oxford University Press, 1999.

Riddell, Roger C. *Foreign Aid Reconsidered.* Oxford, James Currey, 1987.

Rimmer, Douglas. *Africa Thirty Years On.* Oxford, James Currey, 1991.

Roberts, A. (Ed.). *The Colonial Moment in Africa: Essays on the Movement of Minds and Materials.* Cambridge, Cambridge University Press, 1990.

Rotberg, Robert I. (Ed.). *Battling Terrorism in the Horn of Africa.* Washington, DC, Brookings Institution Press and the World Peace Foundation, 2005.

Roy, Jean-Louis. *Une nouvelle Afrique.* Mali, Le Figuier, 1999.

Ruben N'Dongo, Manuel. *L'Afrique sud-saharienne du XXème siecle.* Paris, L'Harmattan, 1997.

Sachs, Jeffrey. *The End of Poverty.* London, Allen Lane, 2005.

Salih, M. A. Mohammed (Ed.). *African Political Parties: Evolution, Institutionalisation and Governance.* Sterling, VA, Pluto Press, 2003.

Sall, Alioune (Ed.). *Africa 2025: What possible futures for sub-Saharan Africa?* Pretoria, Unisa Press, 2003.

Saxena, Suresh Chandra. *Politics in Africa.* Delhi, Kalinga Publications, 1993.

Schraeder, Peter. *African Politics and Society: A Mosaic in Transformation.* Boston, MA, Wadsworth, 2003.

Schwab, Peter. *Africa: A Continent Self Destructs.* London, Palgrave Macmillan, 2003.

Scoones, Martin, and Wolmer, William. *Pathways of Change in Africa.* Oxford, James Currey, 2002.

Seck, Cheikh Serim. *Afrique: Le spectre de l'échec.* Paris, L'Harmattan, 2001.

Sherwood, Marika, and Adi, Hakim. *Pan-African History.* London, Frank Cass, 2003.

Shillington, Kevin. *Encyclopedia of African History.* London, Frank Cass, 2004.

Shorter, Aylward. *East African Societies.* London, Frank Cass, 2004.

Sindayigaya, Jean-Marie. *Mondialisation: Le nouvel esclavage de l'Afrique.* Paris, L'Harmattan, 2000.

Skard, Torild. *Continent of Mothers, Continent of Hope: Understanding and Promoting Development in Africa Today.* London, Zed Books, 2003.

Smith, Anthony D. *State and nation in the Third World: the Western state and African nationalism.* Brighton, Wheatsheaf Books, 1983.

Sorensen, John. *Disaster and Development in the Horn of Africa.* London, Palgrave Macmillan, 1995.

Stock, Robert. *Africa South of the Sahara.* London, Frank Cass, 1995.

Subramanian, Arvind. *Africa's Trade Revisited.* Washington, DC, IMF Publications, 2001.

Suttner, Raymond (Ed.) *Africa in the New Millennium.* Uppsala, Nordic Africa Institute.

Taylor, Ian, and Williams, Paul (Eds). *Africa in International Politics.* London, Routledge, 2004.

Thomas, Caroline, and Wilkin, Peter (Eds). *Globalization, Human Security and the African Experience.* Boulder, CO, Lynne Rienner Publishers, 1999.

Thomson, Alex. *An Introduction to African Politics.* London, Routledge, 2004.

Tiyambe Zeleza, Paul, and Eyoh, Dickson (Eds). *Encyclopaedia of Twentieth-Century African History.* London, Routledge, 2003.

Tordoff, William. *Government and Politics in Africa.* Basingstoke, Macmillan, 1997.

Totte, Marc, Dahou, Tarik, and Billaz, René. *La décentralisation en Afrique de l'Ouest.* Paris, Editions Karthala, 2003.

Tranfo, Luigi. *Africa: La transizione tra sfruttamento e indifferenza.* Bologna, EMI, 1995.

Twaddle, Michael. *The Making of Modern Africa: 1787 to the Present.* Oxford, Oxford University Press, 2004.

United Nations Centre for Regional Development. *Regional Development Policy Analysis: Issues in Food Security, Resource Management and Democratic Empowerment in Eastern and Southern Africa.* Nagoya, UNCRD, 1996.

Van de Walle, Nicholas. *African Economies and the Politics of Permanent Crisis, 1979–1999.* Cambridge, Cambridge University Press, 2001.

Villalon, Leonardo, and Huxtable, Philip (Eds). *The African State at a Critical Juncture: Between Disintegration and Reconfiguration.* Boulder, CO, Lynne Rienner Publishers, 1998.

White, Luise. *Speaking with Vampires: Rumor and History in Colonial Africa.* Berkeley, CA, University of California Press, 2000.

White, Owen. *Children of the French Empire.* Oxford, Oxford University Press, 1999.

Widner, Jennifer (Ed.). *Economic Change and Political Liberalization in Sub-Saharan Africa.* Baltimore, MD, Johns Hopkins University Press, 1994.

Wills, A. J. *An Introduction to the History of Central Africa.* Oxford, Oxford University Press, 1985.

Wiseman, John A. (Ed.). *Democracy and Political Change in Sub-Saharan Africa.* London, Frank Cass, 1995.

Wohlgemuth, Lennart, *et al. Institution Building and Leadership in Africa.* Uppsala, Nordic Africa Institute, 1998.

World Bank. *African Development Indicators 2004.* Washington, DC, World Bank, 2004.

Can Africa Claim the 21st Century? Washington, DC, World Bank, 2000.

Will the Euro Create a Bonanza for Africa? Washington, DC, World Bank, 1999.

World Economic Forum. *The Africa Competitiveness Report 2000–2001.* Oxford, Oxford University Press, 2000.

Yalae, Papa. *The Road to a New Africa: An Essay to the African People.* New York, NY, Random House Ventures, 2003.

Young, Crawford. *The African Colonial State in Comparative Perspective.* New Haven, CT, Yale University Press, 1994.

Young, Tom (Ed.). *Readings in African Politics.* Bloomington, IN, Indiana University Press, 2003.

Zartman, William, *et al. Europe and Africa: The New Phase.* Boulder, CO, Lynne Rienner Publishers, 1992.

Zell, Hans M. (Ed.). *The African Studies Companion: A Guide to Information Resources.* Glais Bheinn, Hans Zell Publishing Consultants, 2003.

Zossou, Gaston. *Au nom de l'Afrique.* Paris, L'Harmattan, 2000.

SELECT BIBLIOGRAPHY (PERIODICALS)

The ACP-EU Courier: Commission of the European Communities, 200 rue de la Loi, 1049 Brussels, Belgium; tel. f; tel. (2) 299-30-12; fax (2) 299-30-02; e-mail development@cec.eu.net; internet europa.eu .int/comm/development/publicat/courier/index_en.htm; affairs of the African, Caribbean and Pacific countries and the European Union; English and French edns; 6 a year.

Actividade Económica de Angola: Fundo de Comercialização, CP 1338, Luanda, Angola; tel. (2) 330420; f. 1935; Dir MARIO ALBERTO ADAUTA DE SOUSA; quarterly.

AFRE (African Trade Review): Germán Pérez Carrasco 63, 28027 Madrid, Spain; tel. (91) 3672403; fax (91) 4087837; e-mail ofice@ editorialofice.com; Editor ARSENIO PARDO RODRÍGUEZ; monthly.

Africa: Istituto Italiano per l'Africa e l'Oriente, Via Ulisse Aldrovandi 16, 00197 Rome, Italy; tel. (06) 32855214; fax (06) 3225348; e-mail bacchetti@isiao.it; internet www.isiao.it; f. 1946; Dir Prof. GIAN LUIGI ROSSI; in English, French and Italian; quarterly.

Africa: Edinburgh University Press, 22 George Sq., Edinburgh, EH8 9LF, Scotland; tel. (131) 650-4220; fax (131) 662-0053; e-mail journals@eup.ed.ac.uk; internet www.eup.ed.ac.uk; Editor Prof. MURRAY LAST; quarterly; also annual bibliography.

Africa Analysis: Suite 2F, Diamond House, 36–38 Hatton Garden, London, EC1N 8EB, England; tel. (20) 7404-4321; fax (20) 7404-4351; e-mail aa@africaanalysis.com; internet www.africaanalysis.com; f. 1986; Editor AHMED RAJAB; fortnightly.

Africa Confidential: 73 Farringdon Rd, London, EC1M 3JQ, England; tel. (20) 7831-3511; fax (20) 7831-6778; internet www .africa-confidential.com; f. 1960; political news and analysis; Editor PATRICK SMITH; fortnightly.

Africa Contemporary Record: Africana Publishing Co, Holmes & Meier Publishers, Inc, POB 943, Teaneck, NJ 07666, USA; tel. (201) 833-2270; fax (201) 833-2272; e-mail info@holmesandmeier.com; annual documents, country surveys, special essays, indices; Publr MIRIAM HOLMES.

Africa Development: Council for the Development of Social Science Research in Africa (CODESRIA), BP 3304, Dakar, Senegal; tel. 259822; fax 241289; e-mail CODESRIA@telecomplus.sn; internet www.sas.upenn.edu/African_Studies/codesria/codes_Menu.html; f. 1976; in French and English; Editor TADE AKIN AINA; quarterly.

Africa Energy Intelligence: 142 rue Montmartre, 75002 Paris, France; tel. 1-44-88-26-10; fax 1-44-88-26-15; e-mail info@ africaintelligence.com; internet www.africaintelligence.com; f. 1983; French and English edns; Editor-in-Chief PHILIPPE VASSET; fortnightly.

Africa Health: Vine House, Fair Green, Reach, Cambridge, CB5 0JD, England; tel. (1638) 743633; fax (1638) 743998; e-mail info@fsg.co .uk; internet www.fsg.co.uk; f. 1978; Editor BRYAN PEARSON; 6 a year.

Africa Insight: Africa Institute, POB 630, Pretoria 0001, South Africa; tel. (12) 3286970; fax (12) 3238153; e-mail beth@ia.org.za; internet www.ai.org.za; f. 1971; Editor ELIZABETH LE ROUX; quarterly.

Africa International: 242 blvd Voltaire, 75011 Paris, France; tel. 1-44-93-85-95; fax 1-44-93-74-68; e-mail 101445.2367@compuserve .com; internet www.focusintl.com/pilypily.htm; f. 1958; political, economic and social devt in francophone Africa; Editor MARIE-ROGER BILOA; monthly.

Africa and Middle East Textiles: Alain Charles Publishing Ltd, 27 Wilfred St, London, SW1E 6PR, England; tel. (20) 7834-7676; fax (20) 7973-0076; e-mail post@alaincharles.com; internet www .alaincharles.com; in English and French; Editor ZSA TEBBIT; 5 a year.

Africa Mining Intelligence: 142 rue Montmartre, 75002 Paris, France; tel. 1-44-88-26-10; fax 1-44-88-26-15; e-mail info@ africaintelligence.com; internet www.africaintelligence.com; f. 1983; global mining information on exploration, contracts, legislation, corporate strategy and project funding, etc; French and English edns; Editor-in-Chief GAE'LLE ARENSON; fortnightly.

Africa Quarterly: Indian Council for Cultural Relations, Azad Bhavan, Indraprastha Estate, New Delhi 110 002, India; tel. (11) 23319309; fax (11) 23318647; Editor Dr T. G. RAMAMURTHI.

Africa Renewal / Afrique Renouveau: Rm DC1-550, United Nations, New York, NY 10017, USA; tel. (212) 963-6833; fax (212) 963-4556; e-mail africarenewal@un.org; internet www.un.org/ecosocdev/ geninfo/afrec; Man. Editor ERNEST HARSCH; in English and French; quarterly.

Africa Research Bulletin: Blackwell Publishing Ltd, 9600 Garsington Rd, Oxford, OX4 2DQ, England; tel. (1865) 776868; fax (1865) 714591; e-mail info@africa-research-bulletin.com; internet www .africa-research-bulletin.com; f. 1964; separate bulletins on political and economic topics; Editor PITA ADAMS; monthly.

Africa Review: CEB Ltd, 2 Market St, Saffron Walden, Essex, CB10 1HZ, England; tel. (1799) 521150; fax (1799) 524805; e-mail enquiries@worldinformation.com; internet www.worldinformation .com; f. 1977; Gen. Editor TONY AXON; annually.

Africa Today: Indiana University Press, 601 North Morton St, Bloomington, IN 47404, USA; tel. (812) 855-9449; fax (812) 855-8507; e-mail journals@indiana.edu/URL; internet www.iupjournals .org; Editors GRACIA CLARK, MARIA GROSZ-NGATÉ, JOHN HANSON, RUTH STONE.

African Administrative Studies: Centre africain de formation et de recherche administratives pour le développement (CAFRAD), BP 310, Tangier, 90001 Morocco; fax (3) 9325785; e-mail cafrad@cafrad .org; internet www.cafrad.org; 2 a year.

African Affairs: Royal African Society, School of African and Oriental Studies, Thornhaugh St, Russell Sq., London, WC1H 0XB, England; tel. (20) 7898-4390; e-mail ras@soas.ac.uk; internet www .royalafricansociety.org; f. 1901; social sciences and history; Editors Dr TIM KELSALL, Dr STEPHEN ELLIS; quarterly.

African Arts: James S. Coleman African Studies Center, 10363 Bunche Hill, Box 951310, University of California, Los Angeles, CA 90095-1310, USA; tel. (310) 825-1218; fax (310) 206-2250; e-mail afriartsedit@international.ucla.edu; internet www .mitpressjournals.org/loi/afar; Editors MARLA BERNS, ALLEN ROBERTS, MARY NOOTER ROBERTS, DORAN ROSS; quarterly.

African Book Publishing Record: K. G. Saur Verlag GmbH, Ortlerstr. 8, 81373 München, Germany; tel. (89) 769020; fax (89) 76902150; e-mail info@saur.de; internet www.saur.de; f. 1975; bibliographic listings, book reviews, articles and information on book trade activities in Africa; Editor CECILE LOMER; quarterly.

African Business: 7 Coldbath Sq., London, EC1R 4LQ, England; tel. (20) 7713-7711; fax (20) 7713-7970; e-mail icpubs@africasia.com; internet www.africasia.com; f. 1966; economics, business, commerce and finance; Editor ANVER VERSI; monthly.

African Environment: BP 3370, Dakar, Senegal; tel. 22-42-29; f. 1975; environmental issues; English and French edns; quarterly.

African Farming and Food Processing: Alain Charles Publishing Ltd, 27 Wilfred St, London, SW1E 6PR, England; tel. (20) 7834-7676; fax (20) 7973-0076; e-mail post@alaincharles.com; internet www .alaincharles.com; Editor JONQUIL L. PHELAN; 6 a year.

African Journal of Health Sciences: African Forum for Health Sciences, POB 54840, Nairobi, Kenya; tel. (20) 272251; fax (20) 720030; e-mail kemrilib@nairobi.minicom.net; internet www .kemri.org; f. 1994; Editor Dr DAVY KOECH; quarterly.

African Journal of International Affairs & Development: POB 30678, Ibadan, Nigeria; tel. (2) 8101963; fax (2) 8104165; e-mail eduserve@ skannet.com.ng; internet www.inasp.org.uk/ajol/journals/ajiad; Editor JIDE OWOEYE; 2 a year.

African Publishing Review: Immeuble Roume, 7e étage, blvd Roume, BP 3429, Abidjan 01, Cote d'Ivoire; tel. 20-21-18-01; fax 20-21-18-03; e-mail apnetes@yahoo.com; internet www.africanpublishers.org; English and French edns; Editors SARAH GUMBIE (English), ALICE MOUKO-MINKALA (French); 6 a year.

African Recorder: A-126 Niti Bagh, POB 595, New Delhi 110 049, India; tel. (11) 26565405; f. 1962; news digest; Editor A. K. B. MENON; fortnightly.

African Review: Dept of Political Science and Public Administration, University of Dar es Salaam, POB 35042, Dar es Salaam, Tanzania; tel. (22) 2410130; fax (22) 2410395; e-mail politics@ucc.ac.tz; internet www.udsm.ac.tz; f. 1971; Editor Prof. DAUDI MUKANGARA; 2 a year.

African Review of Business and Technology: Alain Charles Publishing Ltd, 27 Wilfred St, London, SW1E 6PR, England; tel. (20) 7834-7676; fax (20) 7973-0076; e-mail post@alaincharles.com; internet www.alaincharles.com; Editor JONQUIL L. PHELAN; 11 a year.

African Security Review: Institute for Security Studies, POB 1787, Brooklyn Sq. 0075, South Africa; tel. (12) 3469500; fax (12) 4600997;

e-mail iss@iss.co.za; internet www.iss.co.za; African security and defence issues; Editor ANDRÉ SNYDERS; 4 a year.

African Studies: Carfax Publishing Ltd, POB 25, Abingdon, Oxfordshire, OX14 3UE, England; tel. (1235) 401000; fax (1235) 401550; internet www.tandf.co.uk/journals; f. 1921; social and cultural studies of southern Africa; Editor Dr CLIVE GLASER; 2 a year.

African Studies Review: African Studies Association, Rutgers-The State University, Douglass Campus, 132 George St, New Brunswick, NJ 08901-1400, USA; tel. (732) 932-8173; e-mail asapub@rci.rutgers.edu; internet www.africanstudies.org; Editors RALPH FAULKINGHAM, MITZI GOHEEN; 3 a year.

Africana Bulletin: Institute of Developing Countries, Faculty of Geography and Regional Studies, University of Warsaw, Krakowskie Przedmieście 30, 00-927 Warsaw 64, Poland; tel. (22) 5520638; fax (22) 5521521; e-mail africana@uw.edu.pl; f. 1964; articles in English and French; Editor Dr BOGDAN STEFAŃSKI; annual.

Africana Marburgensia: Philipps-Universität Marburg, Fachgebiet Religionsgeschichte, Fachbereich 05, Am Plan 3, 35032 Marburg, Germany; tel. (6421) 283930; e-mail relgesch@mailer.uni-marburgide; f. 1968; religion, law, economics; in English, French and German; Editors CHRISTOPH ELSAS, REINER MAHLKE, HANS H. MÜNKNER; 2 a year.

Africanus: Unisa Press, Periodicals, POB 392, Unisa 0003, South Africa; tel. (12) 429-2953; fax (12) 429-3449; e-mail delpoa@unisa.ac.za; internet www.unisa.ac.za/dept/press; f. 1972; devt issues; 2 a year.

Afrika: Afrika-Verlag, Raiffeisenstr. 24, 85276 Pfaffenhofen, Germany; tel. 8441-8690; fax 8441-76582; f. 1960; edns in German and French; Editors INGA KRUGMAN-RANDOLF, URSULA BELL; 6 a year.

Afrika Spectrum: Institut für Afrika-Kunde, Neuer Jungfernstieg 21, 20354 Hamburg, Germany; tel. (40) 42825523; fax (40) 42825511; e-mail iak@giga-hamburg.de; internet www.giga-hamburg.de/iak; articles in German, English and French; Editor Dr DIRK KOHNERT; 3 a year.

Afrika Süd: Informationsstelle Südliches Afrika eV, Königswinterer-str. 116, 53227 Bonn, Germany; tel. (228) 464369; fax (228) 468177; e-mail issa@comlink.org; internet www.issa-bonn.org; politics, economics, social and military affairs of southern Africa and German relations with the area; 6 a year.

Afrika und Übersee, Sprachen-Kulturen: c/o Dietrich Reimer Verlag, Neue Grünstr. 10179 Berlin, Germany; tel. (30) 2790760; fax (30) 27907611; e-mail vertrieb-kunstverlage@reimer-verlag.de; f. 1910; African linguistics and cultures; in German, English and French; Editors E. DAMMANN, L. GERHARDT, H. MEYER-BAHLBURG, L. M. REH, S. UHLIG, J. ZWERNEMANN; 2 a year.

Afrique Agriculture: BP 90146, 57004 Metz, Cedex 1, France; tel. 3-87-69-18-18; fax 3-87-69-18-14; f. 1975; monthly.

Afrique-Asie: 3 rue de Metz, 75010 Paris, France; tel. 1-40-22-06-72; fax 1-45-23-28-02; e-mail africasi@wanadoo.fr; internet www.afrique-asie.com; monthly.

Afrique Contemporaine: Editions de Boeck, Fond Jean-Pâques 4, 1348 Laivan-la-Neuve, Belgium; e-mail afrique-contemporaire@ofd.fr; f. 1962; political, economic and sociological studies; Editors-in-Chief FRANÇOIS GAULME, JEAN-BERNARD VÉRON, THOMAS MELONIO; quarterly.

Afrique Entreprise: IC Publications, 10 rue Vineuse, 75784 Paris Cedex 16, France; tel. 1-44-30-81-00; fax 1-44-30-81-11; e-mail rosenwal@wanadoo.fr; internet www.rosenwald.com; 22 a year.

Afrique Expansion: 17 rue d'Uzes, 75002 Paris, France; tel. 1-40-13-30-30; fax 1-40-41-94-95; building and construction; Editor MICHEL LEVRON.

Afrique Médicale: BP 1826, Dakar, Senegal; tel. (221) 234880; fax (221) 225630; f. 1960; f. 1960; medical review; Editor Prof. PAUL CORREA; 11 a year.

Afryka, Azja, Ameryka Łacińska: Institute of Developing Countries, Faculty of Geography and Regional Studies, Warsaw University, 00-927 Warsaw, Krakowskie Przedmieście 30, Poland; tel. (2) 5520624; f. 1974; in Polish, with English summary; Editor Prof. FLORIAN PLIT; annually.

Annales Aequatoria: Centre Aequatoria, Maison MSC, BP 779, 3ème rue, Limete, Kinshasa 1, Democratic Republic of the Congo; e-mail vinck.aequatoria@belgacom.net; internet ger-www.uia.ac.be/aequatoria; f. 1980; central African culture, languages and history; Editor HONORÉ VINCK; annually.

El Arbol del Centro: Centro Cultural Español de Malabo, Carretera del Aeropuerto, Malabo, Equatorial Guinea; tel. (09) 2186; fax (09) 3275; e-mail ccem@wanadoo.gq; f. 2005; Equato-Guinean social and cultural review; Spanish; Editor GLORIA NISTAL; quarterly.

BBC Focus on Africa Magazine: Bush House, Strand, London, WC2B 4PH, England; tel. (20) 7240-3456; fax (20) 7557-1258; e-mail focus.magazine@bbc.co.uk; internet www.bbc.co.uk/worldservice/africa/features/focus_magazine; 4 a year.

Botswana Notes and Records: The Botswana Society, POB 71, Gaborone, Botswana; tel. 3919673; fax 3919745; e-mail botsoc@info.bw; internet www.botsoc.org.bw; f. 1969; Editor LENE BAY; annually.

Bulletin of the School of Oriental and African Studies: School of Oriental and African Studies, Thornhaugh St, Russell Sq., London, WC1H 0XG, England; tel. (20) 7898-4064; fax (20) 7898-4849; e-mail bulletin@soas.ac.uk; internet uk.cambridge.org/journals/bso; f. 1917; Chair. of Editorial Bd G. R. HAWTING; 3 a year.

Business in Africa: The Club Suite, 100 Piccadilly, POB 2602, London, W1A 3NY, England; tel. (20) 7495-7969; fax (20) 7495-7966; e-mail enquiries@businessinafrica.co.uk; internet www.businessinafrica.net; Editor DIANNA GAMES; monthly.

Business Monitor International: Mermaid House, 2 Puddle Dock, London, EC4V 3DS, England; tel. (20) 7248-0468; fax (20) 7248-0467; e-mail emartins@businessmonitor.com; internet www.businessinmonitor.com; f. 1984; political and economic brief with macroeconomic forecasts covering sub-Saharan Africa; Editors LIZ MARTINS, JAMES LORD; weekly, monthly and quarterly publs.

Cahiers d'Etudes Africaines: Ecole des hautes études en sciences sociales, 131 blvd St-Michel, 75005 Paris, France; tel. 1-40-46-70-80; fax 1-44-07-08-89; e-mail cahiers-afr@chess.fr; f. 1960; Editor J.-L. AMSELLE; in French and English; quarterly.

Canadian Journal of African Studies: c/o Roger Prendeau, Man. Editor, Innis College, University of Toronto, 2 Sussex Ave, Toronto, ON M55 1J5, Canada; in French and English; Editors Dr D. D. CORDELL, Dr M. A. KLEIN; 3 a year.

Communications Africa: Alain Charles Publishing Ltd, 27 Wilfred St, London, SW1E 6PR, England; tel. (20) 7834-7676; fax (20) 7973-0076; e-mail post@alaincharles.com; internet www.alaincharles.com; f. 1991; telecommunications, broadcasting and information technology; in French and English; Editor ANDREW CROFT; 6 a year.

Development Policy Review: Overseas Development Institute, Portland House, Stag Place, London, SW1 5DP, England; tel. (20) 7922-0300; fax (20) 7922-0399; e-mail p.gee@odi.org.uk; internet www.odi.org.uk; f. 1982; Editor DAVID BOOTH; quarterly.

Development and Socio-Economic Progress: Afro-Asian People's Solidarity Organization, 89 Abdel Aziz al-Saoud St, Manial El-Roda, Cairo, Egypt; tel. (2) 845495; English, Arabic and French edns; Editor-in-Chief NOURI ABDEL RAZZAK; quarterly.

Development Southern Africa: Routledge, Taylor & Francis, 4 Park Sq., Milton Park, Abingdon, Oxfordshire, OX14 4RN, England; tel. (20) 7017-6000; fax (20) 7017-6336; e-mail enquiry@tandf.co.uk; internet www.tandf.co.uk/journals; debates among devt specialists, policy decision makers, scholars and students in the wider professional fraternity and especially in southern Africa; Editor CAROLINE KIHATO; 5 a year.

East Africa Journal: POB 3209, Dar es Salaam, Tanzania; tel. 724711; internet www.home.vic.com/syost/africa/journal; f. 1964; Editor B. A. OGOT; monthly.

East African Studies: Makerere Institute of Social Research, Makerere University, POB 16022, Kampala, Uganda; irregular.

Economia de Moçambique: Companhia Editoria de Moçambique, CP 81, Beira, Mozambique; Editor ANTONIA DE ALMEIDA.

Economic Bulletin of Ghana: Economic Society of Ghana, POB 22, Legon, Accra, Ghana; tel. (1) 775381; Editor J. C. DEGRAFT-JOHNSON; quarterly.

English Studies in Africa: c/o Dept of English, University of the Witwatersrand, 1 Jan Smuts Ave, PO Wits, 2050 Johannesburg, South Africa; tel. (11) 7174106; fax (11) 4037309; e-mail vhouliston@languages.wits.ac.za; internet www.wits.ac.za; f. 1959; journal of the humanities; Editor Prof. V. H. HOULISTON; biannually.

Ethiopian Review: POB 98499, Atlanta, GA 30539, USA; tel. (404) 325-8411; e-mail EthRev@aol.com; internet www.ethiopic.com/ethrev.htm; Editor ELIAS KIFLE; monthly.

Heritage of Zimbabwe: History Society of Zimbabwe, POB 8268, Causeway, Zimbabwe; tel. (4) 39175; f. 1956; history of Zimbabwe and adjoining territories; Editor MICHAEL J. KIMBERLEY; annually.

Horn of Africa Bulletin: Life and Peace Institute, POB 1520, SE-75145 Uppsala, Sweden; tel. (18) 169500; fax (18) 693059; e-mail mats.lundstrom@life-peace.org; internet www.life-peace.org; Editor MATS LUNDSTRÖM; bimonthly.

Indian Ocean Newsletter: 142 rue Montmartre, 75002 Paris, France; tel. 1-44-88-26-10; fax 1-44-88-26-15; e-mail info@africaintelligence.com; internet www.africaintelligence.com; f. 1981; articles on politics, power-brokers, business networks, regional diplomacy and business intelligence in the Horn of Africa, East Africa, southern Africa and the islands of the Indian Ocean; French and English edns; Editor-in-Chief FRANCIS SOLER; fortnightly.

International African Bibliography: KG Saur, Windsor Court, East Grinstead House, East Grinstead, West Sussex, RH19 1XA, England; tel. (1342) 326972; fax (1342) 336192; e-mail customerservices@

bowker-saur.co.uk; internet www.bowker-saur.co.uk; bibliographic listings; quarterly.

International Journal of African Historical Studies: African Studies Center, Boston University, 270 Bay State Rd, Boston, MA 02215, USA; tel. (617) 353-7306; fax (617) 353-4975; e-mail ascpub@bu.edu; internet www.bu.edu/africa/publications/index.html; f. 1968; Editor JEAN HAY; 3 a year.

Jeune Afrique L'Intelligent: Groupe Jeune Afrique, 57 bis, rue d'Auteuil, 75016 Paris, France; tel. 1-44-30-19-60; fax 1-44-30-19-30; e-mail mailbox@jeuneafrique.com; internet www.lintelligent.com; f. 1960; Editor-in-Chief BÉCHIR BEN YAHMED; weekly.

Journal of African Economies: Oxford University Press, Great Clarendon St, Oxford, OX2 6DP, England; tel. (1865) 267907; fax (1865) 267485; e-mail jnl.info@oup.co.uk; internet jae.oupjournals.org; f. 1992; Editor MARCEL FAFCHAMPS; quarterly.

Journal of African History: School of Oriental and African Studies, Thornhaugh St, Russell Sq., London, WC1H 0XG, England; tel. (20) 7637-2388; fax (20) 7436-3844; e-mail louisbrennerLB2@soas.ac.uk; f. 1960; Editor LOUIS BRENNER; 3 a year.

Journal des Africanistes: Société des Africanistes, Musée de l'Homme, Palais de Chaillot, 17 place du Trocadéro, 75116 Paris, France; tel. 1-47-27-72-55; e-mail africanistes@wanadoo.fr; f. 1931; some articles in English; 2 a year.

Journal of Asian and African Studies: Dept of Sociology, Vari Hall 2106, York University, 4700 Keele St, Downsview, ON M3J 1P3, Canada; tel. (416) 441-6343; Editor SHIVU ISHWARAN.

Journal of Contemporary African Studies: Routledge, Taylor & Francis, 4 Park Sq., Milton Park, Abingdon, Oxfordshire, OX14 4RN, England; tel. (20) 7017-6000; fax (20) 7017-6336; e-mail enquiry@tandf.co.uk; internet www.tandf.co.uk/journals; economics, political science, international affairs, military strategy, modern history, law, sociology, education, industrial relations, urban studies, demography, social anthropology, literature, devt studies and related fields; Man. Editor ROGER SOUTHALL; 3 a year.

The Journal of Development Studies: Routledge, Taylor & Francis, 4 Park Sq., Milton Park, Abingdon, Oxfordshire, OX14 4RN, England; tel. (20) 7017-6000; fax (20) 7017-6336; e-mail info@frankcass.com; internet www.tandf.co.uk/journals; f. 1964; Editors JOHN HARISS, HOWARD WHITE, CHRIS MILNER; 8 a year.

Journal of Eastern African Studies: Routledge, Taylor & Francis, 4 Park Sq., Milton Park, Abingdon, Oxfordshire, OX14 4RN, England; tel. (20) 7017-6000; fax (20) 7017-6336; e-mail jeas@sant.ox.ac.uk; internet www.tandf.co.uk/journals; f. 2007; Editors Prof. DAVID ANDERSON, Dr HASAN ARERO, Dr JOYCE NYAIRO, Prof. PAUL TIYAMBE ZELEZA; 3 a year.

Journal of Ethiopian Studies: Institute of Ethiopian Studies, Addis Ababa University, POB 1176, Addis Ababa, Ethiopia; tel. (1) 119469; fax (1) 552688; e-mail IES.AAU@telecom.net.et; f. 1963; social and cultural anthropology, literature, history, linguistics; Man. Editor BIRHANU TEFERRA; 2 a year.

The Journal of Imperial and Commonwealth History: Routledge, Taylor & Francis, 4 Park Sq., Milton Park, Abingdon, Oxford-shire, OX14 4RN, England; tel. (20) 7017-6000; fax (20) 7017-6336; e-mail enquiry@tandf.co.uk; internet www.tandf.co.uk/journals; f. 1972; Editors A. J. STOCKWELL, PETER BURROUGHS; 3 a year.

Journal of Modern African Studies: Cambridge University Press, The Edinburgh Bldg, Shaftesbury Rd, Cambridge, CB2 2RU, England; tel. (1223) 312393; fax (1223) 315052; e-mail information@cup.cam.ac.uk; internet www.cup.cam.ac.uk; politics and economics; Editor Prof. CHRISTOPHER CLAPHAM; quarterly.

The Journal of Peasant Studies: Routledge, Taylor & Francis, 4 Park Sq., Milton Park, Abingdon, Oxfordshire, OX14 4RN, England; tel. (20) 7017-6000; fax (20) 7017-6336; e-mail info@frankcass.com; internet www.frankcass.com; f. 1973; Editor TOM BRASS; quarterly.

Journal of Religion in Africa: The Mirfield Centre, Stocksbank Rd, Mirfield, West Yorkshire, WF14 0BW, England; tel. (1924) 481914; e-mail jraedit@aol.com; internet www.mirfield.org.uk/jra; f. 1967; Exec. Editor BRAD WEISS; quarterly.

Journal of Southern African Studies: Old School, Swine, Hull, HU11 4JE, England; tel. (1482) 811227; fax (1482) 815857; e-mail jsas@stoneman.karoo.co.uk; internet www.tandf.co.uk/journals; f. 1974; Co-ordinating Editor COLIN STONEMAN; quarterly.

Journal of the Third World Spectrum: POB 44843, Washington, DC 20026-4843, USA; tel. (202) 806-7649; e-mail fshams@fac.howard.edu; internet www.founders.howard.edu/spectrum.htm; f. 1989; Editor Prof. FERAIDOON SHAMS; 2 a year.

La Lettre d'Afrique Expansion: 17 rue d'Uzès, 75002 Paris, France; tel. 1-40-13-33-81; fax 1-40-41-94-95; f. 1984; business affairs; Editor HASSAN ZIADY; weekly.

La Lettre du Continent: 142 rue Montmartre, 75002 Paris, France; tel. 1-44-88-26-10; fax 1-44-88-26-15; e-mail info@africaintelligence.fr; internet www.africaintelligence.fr; f. 1985; political power and business networks in francophone Africa; Editor ANTOINE GLASER; fortnightly.

Marchés Tropicaux et Mediterranéens: 11 rue du Faubourg Poissonière, 75009 Paris, France; tel. 1-43-18-87-00; fax 1-43-18-87-02; e-mail moreux@wanadoo.fr; internet www.marches-tropicaux.com; f. 1945; current affairs, mainly economics; Editor SERGE MARPAUD; weekly.

New African: 7 Coldbath Sq., London, EC1R 4LQ, England; tel. (20) 7713-7711; fax (20) 7713-7970; e-mail icpubs@africasia.com; internet www.africasia.com; f. 1966; politics and general interest; Editor BAFFOUR ANKOMAH; monthly.

Newslink Africa: 15 Kensington High St, London, W8 5NP, England; tel. (20) 7376-1996; fax (20) 7938-4168; e-mail info@adlinkinternational.co.uk; internet www.adlinkint-newslinkafri.com; business and devt issues; Editor SHAMLAL PURI; weekly.

Nigrizia-Il Mensile dell'Africa e del Mondo Nero: Vicolo Pozzo 1, 37129 Verona, Italy; tel. (45) 8092390; fax (45) 8092391; e-mail redazione@nigrizia.it; internet www.nigrizia.it; f. 1883; Dir CARMINE CURCI; monthly.

Nouveaux Cahiers de l'IUED: 20 rue Rothschild, CP 136, 1211 Geneva 21, Switzerland; tel. (22) 9084365; fax (22) 9086273; e-mail Nathalie.Tanner@iued.unige.ch; internet www.iued.unige.ch; 2 a year.

Odu: A Journal of West African Studies, New Series (1969–): Obafemi Awolowo University Press, Periodicals Dept, Ile-Ife, Nigeria; tel. (36) 230284; Editor BIADUN ADEDIREN; 2 a year.

Optima: POB 61587, Marshalltown 2107, South Africa; tel. (11) 638-5189; fax (11) 638-2557; e-mail edhlaudhla@angloamerican.co.za; internet www.angloamerican.co.uk; f. 1951; political, economic, social, cultural and scientific aspects of South and southern African devt; Editor NORMAN BARBER; 2 a year.

Politikon: South African Journal of Political Studies: Routledge, Taylor & Francis, 4 Park Sq., Milton Park, Abingdon, Oxfordshire, OX14 4RN, England; tel. (20) 6017-6000; fax (20) 6017-6636; internet www.tandf.co.uk/journals; f. 1974; primarily South African politics; Editor Dr STEPHEN LOUW; 2 a year.

Politique Africaine: Editions Karthala, 22–24 blvd Arago, 75013 Paris, France; tel. 1-43-31-15-59; fax 1-45-35-27-05; e-mail karthala@wanadoo.fr; internet www.karthala.com; f. 1981; political science and international relations; Editor-in-Chief RICHARD BANÉGAS; quarterly.

Red Cross, Red Crescent: BP 372, 1211 Geneva 19, Switzerland; tel. (22) 7304222; fax (22) 7530395; e-mail rcrc@ifrc.org; English, French and Spanish edns; Editors JEAN MILLIGAN, JEAN-FRANÇOIS BERGER; quarterly.

Research in African Literatures: Indiana University Press, 601 North Morton St, Bloomington, IN 47404, USA; tel. (812) 855-9449; fax (812) 855-8507; e-mail journals@indiana.edu/URL; internet www.iupjournals.org; Editor JOHN CONTEH-MORGAN; quarterly.

Research Review: Institute of African Studies, POB 73, University of Ghana, Legon, Ghana; tel. (21) 502397; fax (21) 513389; e-mail iaspubs@ug.edu.gh; internet www.ug.edu.gh; f. 1965; Editor M. E. KROPP DAKUBU; 2 a year.

Review of African Political Economy: Routledge, Taylor & Francis, 4 Park Sq., Milton Park, Abingdon, Oxfordshire, OX14 4RN, England; tel. (20) 6017-6000; fax (20) 6017-6636; e-mail editor@roape.org; internet www.roape.org; f. 1974; Editors JAN BURGESS, RAY BUSH; quarterly.

Revue Diplomatique de l'Ocean Indien: rue H. Rabesahala, BP 46, Antsakaviro, 101 Antananarivo, Madagascar; tel. 22536; fax 34534; f. 1982; Editor GEORGES RANAIVASOA; quarterly.

Revue Française d'Etudes Politiques Africaines: Société Africaine d'Edition, BP 1877, Dakar, Senegal; f. 1966; political; Editors PIERRE BIARNÈS, PHILIPPE DECRAENE; monthly.

Revue Tiers Monde: Institut d'Etude du Développement Economique et Social, 45 bis ave de la Belle Gabrielle, 94736 Nogent sur Marne Cédex, France; tel. 1-43-94-72-26; fax 1-43-94-72-44; e-mail tiermond@univ-paris1.fr; internet iedes.univ-paris1.fr/dossierRevueTiersMonde/PublicationsTM.htm; f. 1960; devt issues; Editor-in-Chief BLANDINE GRAVELIN; quarterly.

Serving in Mission Together: SIM International Communication, 1838 Gold Hill Rd, Fort Mill, SC 29708, USA; tel. (803) 802-7300; fax (803) 548-0885; e-mail editor@sim.org; internet www.sim.org; f. 1958; edns also publ. in Australia, NZ, South Africa, Republic of Korea, Singapore, Switzerland, United Kingdom and USA; French, German, Italian, Korean and Mandarin edns; Editorial Dir CAROL WILSON; quarterly.

South Africa Survey: South African Institute of Race Relations, POB 31044, Braamfontein 2017, South Africa; tel. (11) 403-3600; fax (11)

403-3671; internet www.sairr.org.za/publications/survey.htm; Dir J. S. KANE-BERMAN; annually.

Southern Africa Monitor: 179 Queen Victoria St, London, EC4V 4DU, England; tel. (20) 7248-0468; fax (20) 7248-0467; e-mail marketing@businessmonitor.com; internet www.businessmonitor.com/southernafrica.html; f. 1996; business; Editors PAUL GAMBLE, NICK BROUGHTON; monthly.

Southern Africa Monthly Regional Bulletin (MRB): 920 M St, SE, Washington, DC 20003, USA; tel. (202) 546-0676; fax (202) 543-7957; e-mail southscan@allafrica.com; internet www.southscan.net; f. 1992; political, security and economic issues within the Southern African Development Community; Publr DAVID COETZEE.

Southern Africa Report: POB 261579, Excom 2023, South Africa; tel. (11) 646-8790; fax (11) 646-2596; e-mail rlouw@sn.apc.org; internet www.sareport.co.za; f. 1983; current affairs and financial newsletter; Publr and Editor RAYMOND LOUW; 50 a year.

Southscan: 112 4th St, NE, Washington, DC 20002, USA; tel. (202) 543-9050; fax (202) 543-7957; e-mail southscan@allafrica.com; internet www.southscan.net; f. 1986; political and economic affairs in South Africa and the other countries of the Southern African Development Community; Publr DAVID COETZEE; fortnightly.

Sudan Democratic Gazette: POB 2295, London, W14 0ND, England; tel. (20) 7602-4401; fax (20) 7602-0106; e-mail malwal@sudemgaz.demon.co.uk; f. 1990; Publr and Editor BONA MALWAL.

Sudanow: POB 2651, 7 Gamhouria Ave, Khartoum, Sudan; tel. (11) 77915; f. 1976.

Third World Quarterly: Dept of Geography, Royal Holloway College, Egham, Surrey, TW20 0EX, England; fax (20) 8947-1243; e-mail sqadir@globalnet.co.uk; internet www.tandf.co.uk/journals; Editor SHAHID QADIR.

Uganda Confidential: POB 9948, Kampala, Uganda; fax (41) 245580; Editors GERALD MWAITA, JOHN KATEEBA; weekly.

Vostok (Oriens): Afro-Aziatskiye Obtchestva, Istoria i Sovremenost, Institut Vostokovedeniya, Institut Afriki, Rossiyskaya Akad. Nauk, Moscow 107031, 12 Rozhdestvenka St, Russia; tel. (495) 9255146; e-mail ctrrus@relcom.ru; f. 1955; text in Russian, summaries in English; Editor-in-Chief Dr V. V. NAUMKIN; 6 a year.

West Africa: Allenby House, 1A Temple Rd, London, NW2 6PJ, England; tel. (20) 8450-4848; fax (20) 8450-8885; e-mail wa@westafricamagazine.com; internet www.westafricamagazine.com; f. 1917; Editor DESMOND DAVIES; weekly.

West African Journal of Archaeology: c/o Dept of Archaeology, University of Ibadan, Ibadan, Nigeria; f. 1971; annually.

INDEX OF REGIONAL ORGANIZATIONS

(Main reference only)

A

B

C

U

V

W

Z

The
Europa World of Learning Online

'The World of Learning Online **is a welcome addition to academic reference.'**
- *Reference Reviews*

www.worldoflearning.com

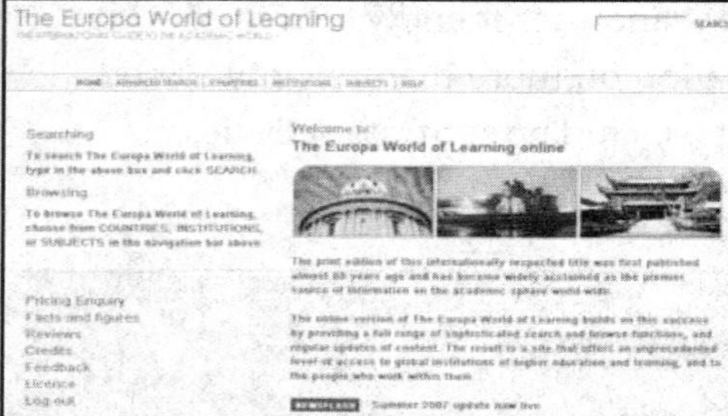

Instant access to educational contacts around the globe

- Librarians
- Professors
- Deans
- Curators
- Chancellors
- University presidents
- Rectors

Locate academic institutions of every type, worldwide

- Universities and Colleges
- Schools of Art, Music and Architecture
- Learned Societies
- Research Institutes
- Libraries and Archives
- Museums and Art Galleries

Additional features of The Europa World of Learning online

- Multi-user product
- Fully searchable
- Updated throughout the year

Free 30 day trials available
For further information e-mail: **reference.online@tandf.co.uk**

160°
120°
80°
40°
0°
ARCTIC OCEAN
Beaufort Sea
Baffin Bay
GREENLAND (DENMARK)
JAN MAYEN (NORWAY)
Davis Strait
Denmark Strait
ICELAND
Reykjavík
Norwegian Sea
FAROE ISLANDS (DENMARK)
Arctic Circle
ALASKA (USA)
Gulf of Alaska
Hudson Bay
CANADA
UNITED KINGDOM
North Sea
ISLE OF MAN (UK)
NORTHERN IRELAND
GREAT BRITAIN
IRELAND
Dublin
London
Amsterdam
BELGIUM
CHANNEL ISLANDS (UK)
Paris
FRANCE
ANDORRA
Ottawa
SAINT PIERRE AND MIQUELON (FRANCE)
UNITED STATES OF AMERICA
Washington DC
PORTUGAL
SPAIN
Madrid
Lisbon
GIBRALTAR (UK)
MELILLA (SP)
CEUTA (SP)
Rabat
MOROCCO
NORTH ATLANTIC OCEAN
BERMUDA (UNITED KINGDOM)
Gulf of Mexico
BAHAMAS
Tropic of Cancer
HAWAII (USA)
MEXICO
Havana
CUBA
TURKS AND CAICOS ISLANDS (UK)
DOMINICAN REPUBLIC
PUERTO RICO (USA)
BRITISH VIRGIN ISLANDS (UK)
US VIRGIN ISLANDS (USA)
SAINT CHRISTOPHER AND NEVIS
ANTIGUA AND BARBUDA
GUADELOUPE (FRANCE)
MARTINIQUE (FRANCE)
BARBADOS
SAINT VINCENT AND THE GRENADINES
CAYMAN ISLANDS (UK)
JAMAICA
Kingston
HAITI
Port-au-Prince
Santo Domingo
ANGUILLA (UK)
MONTSERRAT (UK)
DOMINICA
SAINT LUCIA
NETHERLANDS ANTILLES (NL)
ARUBA (NL)
GRENADA
TRINIDAD AND TOBAGO
Mexico City
GUATEMALA
BELIZE
Belmopan
HONDURAS
Tegucigalpa
Guatemala City
San Salvador
EL SALVADOR
NICARAGUA
Managua
COSTA RICA
San José
PANAMA
Panamá
Caracas
VENEZUELA
Georgetown
GUYANA
SURINAME
Paramaribo
FRENCH GUIANA (FRANCE)
Bogotá
COLOMBIA
Quito
ECUADOR
WESTERN SAHARA
MAURITANIA
Nouakchott
MALI
CAPE VERDE
Praia
SENEGAL
Dakar
GAMBIA
Banjul
Bamako
BURKINA FASO
Ouagadougou
GUINEA-BISSAU
GUINEA
Conakry
Freetown
SIERRA LEONE
Monrovia
LIBERIA
CÔTE D'IVOIRE
Yamoussoukro
Abidjan
GHANA
Accra
TOGO
BENIN
EQUATORIAL GUINEA
SÃO TOMÉ AND PRÍNCIPE
São Tomé
PERU
Lima
BRAZIL
Brasília
PACIFIC OCEAN
ASCENSION (UNITED KINGDOM)
SOUTH ATLANTIC OCEAN
SAINT HELENA (UNITED KINGDOM)
FRENCH POLYNESIA (FRANCE)
COOK ISLANDS (NEW ZEALAND)
Tropic of Capricorn
La Paz
BOLIVIA
Sucre
PARAGUAY
Asunción
CHILE
PITCAIRN ISLANDS (UNITED KINGDOM)
Santiago
Buenos Aires
URUGUAY
Montevideo
ARGENTINA
TRISTAN DA CUNHA (UNITED KINGDOM)
FALKLAND ISLANDS (UNITED KINGDOM)
SOUTH GEORGIA AND THE SOUTH SANDWICH ISLANDS (UNITED KINGDOM)
Africa South of the Sahara
Central and South-Eastern Europe
Eastern Europe, Russia and Central Asia
The Far East and Australasia
The Middle East and North Africa
South America, Central America and the Caribbean
South Asia
The USA and Canada
Western Europe
Antarctic Circle
www.europaworld.com